BARRON'S

PROFILES OF AMERICAN Colleges

32ND EDITION 2016

Compiled and Edited by
the College Division of
Barron's Educational Series

Opinions and details expressed in articles and profiles in this publication are those of the individual writers and the schools, and do not necessarily reflect those of the publisher.

All inquiries should be addressed to:
Barron's Educational Series, Inc.
250 Wireless Boulevard
Hauppauge, New York 11788
www.barronseduc.com

ISBN-13: 978-1-4380-0650-5
5660 6972 7/15
International Standard Serial No. 1065-5026

PRINTED IN THE UNITED STATES OF AMERICA
9 8 7 6 5 4 3 2 1

10%
POST-CONSUMER WASTE
Paper contains a minimum of 10% post-consumer waste (PCW). Paper used in this book was derived from certified, sustainable forestlands.

CONTENTS

PREFACE

Barron's *Profiles of American Colleges* is the most all-encompassing, easy-to-use guide available. All four-year institutions that offer bachelor's degrees are described if they are fully accredited or are recognized candidates for accreditation. The comprehensive, concise capsule and detailed essay on each school give an easy-to-absorb, complete picture of the colleges that interest the reader. The attractive graphic design provides added readability.

The capsule of each profile lists important information for quick reference: address and phone and fax numbers; enrollment; calendar; fall application deadline; size and salary level of the faculty; percentage of faculty members who hold doctorates; student/faculty ratio; tuition and fees; room-and-board costs; the number of students who applied to the freshman class, were accepted, and enrolled; the median SAT* and/or ACT scores; and finally, the College Admissions Selector Rating for the school. The information in the essay portion of each profile ranges from available housing and the financial aid climate to admissions requirements and the success of graduates. There are twenty-one categories of information under eight main headings: Student Life, Faculty/Classrooms, Programs of Study, Activities, Services, Requirements, Admissions, and Financial Aid. The Admissions section also gives contact information and Internet addresses.

As a purchaser of the 32nd edition of *Profiles of American Colleges*, you are eligible for a free six-month subscription to our *Profiles of American Colleges* on-line edition. The web site will simplify your college search and ease your college application process. To access, go to BarronsPAC.com and register today!

A Word of Thanks

To all the admissions officers, institutional research staff at the colleges, to participating high school advisers, to the students, parents, and other supporters of Barron's *Profiles of American Colleges*, over the last thirty editions, we offer our sincere thanks and appreciation.

Our appreciation to the editorial staff, including Bruce Morris, Lena Perfetto, and David Rodman; production department, including Navi Persaud, Chris Ciaschini, and graphic artist Lou Vasquez. Thanks and appreciation to Greg Hammond of Reliable Internet Solutions for database management and technical support.

CONTRIBUTORS

Steven R. Antonoff, Ph.D.
Educational Consultant
Antonoff Associates, Inc.
Denver, Colorado

Barbara J. Aronson
Career Center Coordinator
Miramonte High School
Orinda, California

Marguerite J. Dennis
Former Vice President for
Enrollment and International
Programs
Suffolk University
Boston, Massachusetts

Benjamin W. Griffith
Former Dean
University of West Georgia
Carrolton, Georgia

Sheldon Halpern
Former Dean
Enrollment Management
Caldwell College
Caldwell, New Jersey

Anthony F. Capraro, III, Ph.D.
President, Teach Inc.
College Counseling
Ocoee, Florida

James Wagner
Center for Academic Support
and Advisement Center
Associate Professor of Education
Liberty University

*SAT is a registered trademark owned by the College Entrance Examination Board. No endorsement of this product is implied or given.

AN EXPLANATION OF THE BOOK

You have been thinking about going to college within the coming years, and have decided that it's time to get serious and take the necessary steps that will lead to your ultimate college decisions, right?

But how do you take these steps? How much will your college education cost? How can you and your parents afford it? What about the entrance exams? What kinds of scores are you going to need to be considered? How do you decide what to major in? Which colleges offer the skills and career preparation that you're going to need? Even if you get past these hurdles, what if you decide which colleges you want to attend, apply to them, and then get turned down? Is there anything you can do to prevent *that* from happening?

So where do you begin? In addition to hundreds of two-year schools, there are more than 1,650 accredited four-year colleges in the United States, and your options are almost unlimited. Barron's *Profiles of American Colleges* can help by pointing you in the right direction, and guiding you through the coming months of preparation and decision making.

Within the pages of this directory, you will find articles that will assist you in evaluating your own needs and interests, selecting the colleges you want to apply to, filling out the application, writing the essay, going through the interview process, finding the money, and surviving your freshman year.

The Index of College Majors lists which colleges offer the field that you're interested in. The section also offers advice on deciding your major, career opportunities and the skills you are going to need for the occupation you choose. More than 700 majors are listed, along with the in-state costs and the Admissions Selector Rating in easy-to-read columns.

Advice for international students is included, as well as a list of schools' in-state costs from least to most expensive. The Colleges at a Glance geographic chart provides students quick information about the schools on a state-by-state basis.

The College Admissions Selector Ratings give applicants an idea of the competition they will encounter when applying to a particular school. For your convenience, a key to abbreviations is also included, as well as an explanation of the actual college entries.

The heart of the book, of course, is the detailed descriptions of the colleges, including a special section of religious schools, for those students wishing to pursue a career in the clergy and related fields. The college Profiles are arranged in alphabetical order by state. Each chapter opens with a map that pinpoints the geographic location of the colleges mentioned. Barron's *Profiles of American Colleges* covers the United States; and describes colleges in Puerto Rico, universities in Canada and abroad (along with advice for international students) as well as state and private systems of higher education, for a total of approximately 1700 Profile entries.

This updated and revised edition of *Profiles of American Colleges* will prove to be a valuable resource as you embark on a tremendous learning and growth time of your life—your college education.

KEY TO ABBREVIATIONS

DEGREES

A.A.—Associate of Arts
A.A.S.—Associate of Applied Science
A.B. or B.A.—Bachelor of Arts
A.B.J.—Bachelor of Arts in Journalism
A.S.—Associate of Science

B.A.—Bachelor of Arts
B.A.A.—Bachelor of Applied Arts
B.A.A.S. or B.Applied A.S.—Bachelor of Applied Arts and Sciences
B.Ac. or B.Acc.—Bachelor of Accountancy
B.A.C.—Bachelor of Science in Air Commerce
B.A.C.V.I.—Bachelor of Arts in Computer and Video Imaging
B.A.E. or B.A.Ed.—Bachelor of Arts in Education
B.A.G.E.—Bachelor of Arts in General Education
B.Agri.—Bachelor of Agriculture
B.A.G.S.—Bachelor of Arts in General Studies
B.A.J.S.—Bachelor of Arts in Judaic Studies
B.A.M.—Bachelor of Arts in Music
B.Applied Sc.—Bachelor of Applied Science
B.A.R.—Bachelor of Religion
B.Arch.—Bachelor of Architecture
B.Arch.Hist.—Bachelor of Architectural History
B.Arch.Tech.—Bachelor of Architectural Technology
B.Ar.Sc.—Baccalaurium Artium et Scientiae (honors college degree) (Bachelor of Arts & Sciences)
B.Art.Ed.—Bachelor of Art Education
B.A.S.—Bachelor of Applied Science
B.A.S.—Bachelor of Arts and Sciences
B.A.Sec.Ed.—Bachelor of Arts in Secondary Ed.
B.A.S.W.—Bachelor of Arts in Social Work
B.A.T.—Bachelor of Arts in Teaching
B.B. or B.Bus.—Bachelor of Business
B.B.A.—Bachelor of Business Administration
B.B.E.—Bachelor of Business Education
B.C. or B.Com. or B.Comm.—Bachelor of Commerce
B.C.A.—Bachelor of Creative Arts
B.C.E.—Bachelor of Civil Engineering
B.C.E.—Bachelor of Computer Engineering
B.Ch. or B.Chem.—Bachelor of Chemistry
B.Ch.E.—Bachelor of Chemical Engineering
B.C.J.—Bachelor of Criminal Justice
B.C.M.—Bachelor of Christian Ministries
B.Church Mus.—Bachelor of Church Music
B.C.S.—Bachelor of College Studies
B.E.—Bachelor of English
B.E. or B.Ed.—Bachelor of Education
B.E.—Bachelor of Engineering
B.E.D.—Bachelor of Environmental Design
B.E.E.—Bachelor of Electrical Engineering
B.En. or B.Eng.—Bachelor of Engineering
B.E.S. or B.Eng.Sc.—Bachelor of Engineering Science
B.E.T.—Bachelor of Engineering Technology
B.F.A.—Bachelor of Fine Arts
B.G.S.—Bachelor of General Studies
B.G.S.—Bachelor of Geological Sciences
B.H.E.—Bachelor of Health Education
B.H.P.E.—Bachelor of Health and Physical Education
B.H.S.—Bachelor of Health Science
B.I.D.—Bachelor of Industrial Design
B.I.M.—Bachelor of Industrial Management
B.Ind.Tech.—Bachelor of Industrial Technology
B.Int.Arch.—Bachelor of Interior Architecture
B.Int.Design—Bachelor of Interior Design
B.I.S.—Bachelor of Industrial Safety
B.I.S.—Bachelor of Interdisciplinary Studies
B.J.—Bachelor of Journalism
B.J.S.—Bachelor of Judaic Studies
B.L.A. or B.Lib.Arts—Bachelor of Liberal Arts
B.L.A. or B.Land.Arch.—Bachelor in Landscape Architecture
B.L.I.—Bachelor of Literary Interpretation
B.L.S.—Bachelor of Liberal Studies
B.M. or B.Mus. or Mus.Bac.—Bachelor of Music
B.M.E.—Bachelor of Mechanical Engineering
B.M.E. or B.M.Ed. or B.Mus.Ed.—Bachelor of Music Education

B.Med.Lab.Sc.—Bachelor of Medical Laboratory Science
B.Min—Bachelor of Ministry
B.M.P. or B.Mu.—Bachelor of Music in Performance
B.Mus.A.—Bachelor of Applied Music
B.M.T.—Bachelor of Music Therapy
B.O.T.—Bachelor of Occupational Therapy
B.P.A.—Bachelor of Public Administration
B.P.E.—Bachelor of Physical Education
B.Perf.Arts—Bachelor of Performing Arts
B.Ph.—Bachelor of Philosophy
B.Pharm.—Bachelor of Pharmacy
B.Phys.Hlth.Ed.—Bachelor of Physical Health Education
B.P.S.—Bachelor of Professional Studies
B.P.T.—Bachelor of Physical Therapy
B.R.E.—Bachelor of Religious Education
B.R.T.—Bachelor of Respiratory Therapy
B.S. or B.Sc. or S.B.—Bachelor of Science
B.S.A. or B.S.Ag. or B.S.Agr.—Bachelor of Science in Agriculture
B.Sacred Mus.—Bachelor of Sacred Music
B.Sacred Theol.—Bachelor of Sacred Theology
B.S.A.E.—Bachelor of Science in Agricultural Engineering
B.S.A.E. or B.S.Art Ed.—Bachelor of Science in Art Education
B.S.Ag.E.—Bachelor of Science in Agricultural Engineering
B.S.A.S.—Bachelor of Science in Administrative Sciences
B.S.A.T.—Bachelor of Science in Athletic Training
B.S.B.—Bachelor of Science (Business)
B.S.B.A. or B.S.Bus. Adm.—Bachelor of Science in Business Administration
B.S.Bus.—Bachelor of Science in Business
B.S.Bus.Ed.—Bachelor of Science in Business Education
B.S.C.—Bachelor of Science in Commerce
B.S.C.E. or B.S.C.I.E.—Bachelor of Science in Civil Engineering
B.S.C.E.T—B.S. in Computer Engineering Technology
B.S.Ch. or B.S.Chem. or B.S. in Ch.—Bachelor of Science in Chemistry
B.S.C.H.—Bachelor of Science in Community Health
B.S.Ch.E.—Bachelor of Science in Chemical Engineering
B.S.C.I.S.—Bachelor of Science in Computer Information Sciences
B.S.C.J.—Bachelor of Science in Criminal Justice
B.S.C.L.S.—Bachelor of Science in Clinical Laboratory Science
B.S.Comp.Eng.—Bachelor of Science in Computer Engineering
B.S.Comp.Sci. or B.S.C.S.—Bachelor of Science in Computer Science
B.S.Comp.Soft—Bachelor of Science in Computer Software
B.S.Comp.Tech.—Bachelor of Science in Computer Technology
B.Sc.(P.T.)—Bachelor of Science in Physical Therapy
B.S.C.S.T.—Bachelor of Science in Computer Science Technology
B.S.D.H.—Bachelor of Science in Dental Hygiene
B.S.Die—Bachelor of Science in Dietetics
B.S.E. or B.S.Ed. or B.S.Educ.—Bachelor of Science in Education
B.S.E. or B.S in E. or B.S. in Eng.—Bachelor of Science in Engineering
B.S.E.E.—Bachelor of Science in Electrical Engineering
B.S.E.E.T.—Bachelor of Science in Electrical Engineering Technology
B.S.E.H.—Bachelor of Science in Environmental Health
B.S.Elect.T.—Bachelor of Science in Electronics Technology
B.S.El.Ed. or B.S. in Elem. Ed.—Bachelor of Science in Elementary Education
B.S.E.P.H.—Bachelor of Science in Environmental and Public Health
B.S.E.S.—Bachelor of Science in Engineering Science
B.S.E.S.—Bachelor of Science in Environmental Studies
B.S.E.T.—Bachelor of Science in Engineering Technology
B.S.F.—Bachelor of Science in Forestry
B.S.F.R.—Bachelor of Science in Forestry Resources
B.S.F.W.—Bachelor of Science in Fisheries and Wildlife
B.S.G.—Bachelor of Science in Geology
B.S.G.—Bachelor of Science in Gerontology
B.S.G.E.—Bachelor of Science in Geological Engineering

B.S.G.S.—Bachelor of Science in General Studies
B.S.H.C.A.—Bachelor of Science in Health Care Administration
B.S.H.E.—Bachelor of Science in Home Economics
B.S.H.F.—Bachelor of Science in Health Fitness
B.S.H.M.S.—Bachelor of Science in Health Management Systems
B.S.H.S.—Bachelor of Science in Health Sciences
B.S.H.S.—Bachelor of Science in Human Services
B.S.I.A.—Bachelor of Science in Industrial Arts
B.S.I.E.—Bachelor of Science in Industrial Engineering
B.S.I.M.—Bachelor of Science in Industrial Management
B.S. in Biomed.Eng.—Bachelor of Science in Biomedical Engineering
B.S. in C.D.—Bachelor of Science in Communication Disorders
B.S.Ind.Ed.—Bachelor of Science in Industrial Education
B.S.Ind.Tech.—Bachelor of Science in Industrial Technology
B.S. in Sec.Ed.—Bachelor of Science in Secondary Education
B.S.I.S.—Bachelor of Science in Interdisciplinary Studies
B.S.I.T.—Bachelor of Science in Industrial Technology
B.S.J.—Bachelor of Science in Journalism
B.S.L.E.—Bachelor of Science in Law Enforcement
B.S.M.—Bachelor of Science in Management
B.S.M.—Bachelor of Science in Music
B.S.M.E.—Bachelor of Science in Mechanical Engineering
B.S.Med.Tech. or **B.S.M.T.**—Bachelor of Science in Medical Technology
B.S.Met.E.—Bachelor of Science in Metallurgical Engineering
B.S.M.R.A.—Bachelor of Science in Medical Records Administration
B.S.M.T.—Bachelor of Science in Medical Technology
B.S.M.T.—Bachelor of Science in Music Therapy
B.S.Mt.E.—Bachelor of Science in Materials Engineering
B.S.Mus.Ed.—Bachelor of Science in Music Education
B.S.N.—Bachelor of Science in Nursing
B.S.Nuc.T.—Bachelor of Science in Nuclear Technology
B.S.O.A.—Bachelor of Science in Office Administration
B.S.O.E.—Bachelor of Science in Occupational Education
B.S.O.T.—Bachelor of Science in Occupational Therapy
B.S.P. or **B.S.Pharm**—Bachelor of Science in Pharmacy
B.S.P.A.—Bachelor of Science in Public Administration
B.S.Pcs.—Bachelor of Science in Physics
B.S.P.E.—Bachelor of Science in Physical Education
B.S.P.T.—Bachelor of Science in Physical Therapy
B.S.Rad.Tech.—Bachelor of Science in Radiation Technology
B.S.R.C.—Bachelor of Science in Respiratory Care
B.S.R.S.—Bachelor of Science in Radiological Science
B.S.R.T.T.—Bachelor of Science in Radiation Therapy Technology
B.S.S.—Bachelor of Science in Surveying
B.S.S.—Bachelor of Special Studies
B.S.S.A.—Bachelor of Science in Systems Analysis
B.S.Soc. Work or **B.S.S.W.**—Bachelor of Science in Social Work
B.S.Sp.—Bachelor of Science in Speech
B.S.S.T.—Bachelor of Science in Surveying and Topography
B.S.T. or **B.S.Tech.**—Bachelor of Science in Technology
B.S.S.W.E.—Bachelor of Science in Software Engineering
B.S.V.T.E.—Bachelor of Science in Vocational Technical Education
B.S.W.—Bachelor of Social Work
B.T. or **B.Tech.**—Bachelor of Technology
B.Th.—Bachelor of Theology
B.T.S.—Bachelor of Technical Studies
B.U.S.—Bachelor of Urban Studies
B.V.M.—Bachelor of Veterinarian Medicine
B.Voc.Arts or **B.V.A.**—Bachelor of Vocational Arts
B.V.E.D. or **B.Voc.Ed.**—Bachelor of Vocational Education

D.D.S.—Doctor of Dental Surgery

Ed.D.—Doctor of Education
Ed.S.—Education Specialist

J.D.—Doctor of Jurisprudence

LL.B.—Bachelor of Laws

M.A.—Master of Arts
M.A.Ed.—Master of Arts in Education
M.A.T.—Master of Arts in Teaching
M.B.A.—Master of Business Administration
M.D.—Doctor of Medicine
M.F.A.—Master of Fine Arts
M.P.A.—Master of Public Administration
M.S.—Master of Science
Mus.B. or **Mus.Bac.**—Bachelor of Music

Ph.D.—Doctor of Philosophy

R.N.—Registered Nurse

S.B. or **B.S.** or **B.Sc.**—Bachelor of Science

OTHER ABBREVIATIONS

AAAHC—Accreditation Association for Ambulatory Health Care
AABC—Accrediting Association of Bible Colleges
AABI—Aviation Accreditation Board International
AACN—American Association of Colleges of Nursing
AACSB—American Assembly of Collegiate Schools of Business
AACT—American Association of Community Theatre
AACT—Advanced Application Certification Testing
AACTE—American Association of Colleges for Teacher Education
AAFCS—American Association of Family and Consumer Sciences
AAHE—American Association for Health Education
AAHE—American Association for Higher Education
AAHEP—Accreditation of Allied Health Programs
AAHPERD—American Alliance for Health, Physical Education, Recreation, and Dance
AAHPERD—American Association of Health, Physical Education, Recreation, and Dance
AALE—American Academy for Liberal Education
AALS—Association of American Law Schools
AAM—American Academy of Microbiology
AAMA—American Association for Medical Assistants
AAMA—American Alternative Medical Association
AAMC—Association of American Medical Colleges
AAMFT—American Association for Marriage and Family Therapy
AANA—American Association of Nurse Anesthetists
AAPAR—American Association for Physical Activity and Recreation
AATA—American Art Therapy Association, Inc.
AAVLD—American Association of Veterinary Laboratory Diagnosticians
ABA—American Bar Association
ABAI—American Board of Allergy & Immunology
ABE—Association of Building Engineers Association of Building Engineers
ABET—Accreditation Board for Engineering and Technology
ABFSE—American Board of Funeral Service Education
ABHE—Association for Biblical Higher Education
ABHES—Accrediting Bureau of Health Education Schools
ACA—American Chiropractic Association
ACAE—Accreditation Commission for Audiology Education
ACBSP—Accreditation Council for Business Schools and Programs
ACCE—American Council for Construction Education
ACCGC—Accrediting Council for Collegiate Graphic Communications
ACCME—Accreditation Council for Continuing Medical Education
ACCNE—American Catholic Church of New England
ACE HSA—Accrediting Commission on Education for Health Services Administration
ACEI—Association for Cultural Economics International
ACEJ—American Council on Education for Journalism

ACE JMC—American Council on Education in Journalism and Mass Communication

ACF—American Culinary Federation

ACFEF— American Culinary Federation's Education Foundation, Inc. Accrediting Commission

ACGME—Accreditation Council for Graduate Medical Education

ACICS—Accrediting Council for Independent Colleges and Schools

ACNM—American College of Nuclear Medicine

ACNM—American College of Nurse-Midwives

ACOT—American College of Technology

ACOT—Advanced Communications-Computer Officer Training

ACOTE—Accreditation Council for Occupational Therapy Education

ACPE—Association for Clinical Pastoral Education, Inc.

ACPE—Accreditation Council on Pharmaceutical Education

ACPHA—Accreditation Commission for Programs in Hospitality Administration

ACS—American Chemical Society

ACSCU—Accrediting Commission for Senior Colleges and Universities

ACSI—Association of Christian Schools International

ACT—American College Testing Program

ACTFL—American Council on the Teaching of Foreign Languages

ACU—Association of Commonwealth Universities

ADA—American Dietetic Association

ADA—American Dental Association

ADDA—American Design Drafting Association

AEE—Association for Experiential Education

AFIT—Accelerated Flight & Instrument Training

AFSA—Application for Federal Student Aid

AHEA—American Home Economics Association

AHIMA—American Health Information Management Association

AICE—Advanced International Certificate of Education

AIChe—American Institute of Chemical Engineers

ALA—American Library Association

ALIGU—American Language Institute of Georgetown University

AMA—American Medical Association

AMA- CAHEA—American Medical Association Committee on Allied Health Education and Accreditation

AMTA – American Music Therapy Association

AMTA—American Massage Therapy Association

AOA—American Osteopathic Association

AOA—American Optometric Association

AOBFP—American Osteopathic Board of Family Physicians

AOSA—American Optometric Student Association

AOSA—American Overseas Schools Archive

AOTA—American Occupational Therapy Association

AP—Advanced Placement

APA—American Podiatry Association

APA—American Psychological Association

APET—Asset Placement Evaluation Test

APIEL—Advance Placement International English Language Exam

APMA—American Podiatric Medical Association

APTA—American Physical Therapy Association

ARC-PA—Accreditation Review Commission on Education for the Physician Assistant, Inc.

ARC-PA—Accreditation Review Commission on Education for the Physician Assistant, Inc.

ASABE—American Society of Agricultural and Biological Engineers

ASC—Accredited Standards Committee

ASCP—Association of Collegiate Schools of Planning

ASCP—American Society of Concierge Physicians

ASCP—American Society of Cardiovascular Professionals

ASCP—American Society of Clinical Psychopharmacology

ASCP—American Society of Clinical Pathologists

ASHA—American Social Health Association

ASHA—American School Health Association

ASHA—American Speech-Language-Hearing Association

ASLH—American Society for Legal History

ASHA—American School Health Association

ASLA—American Society of Landscape Architects

ASLHA (ASHA)—American Speech-Language-Hearing Association

ASPT—American Society of Plant Taxonomists

ATEP—Athletic Training Education Program

ATMAE—Association of Technology, Management, and Applied Engineering

ATME—Association of Theatre Movement Educators

ATMNE—Association of Teachers of Mathematics in New England

ATS—Association of Theological Schools in the U.S. and Canada

ATSUSC—Association of Theological Schools in the United States and Canada

AUCC—Association of Universities and Colleges of Canada

AUPHA—Association of University Programs of Health Administration

AVMA—American Veterinary Medical Association

AWI—Agency for Workforce Innovation

BENHA—Board of Examiners of Nursing Home Administrators

BEOG—Basic Educational Opportunity Grant (now Pell Grant)

CAA—Council on Aviation Accreditation

CAADE—California Association for Alcohol/Drug Educators

CAAHEP—Commission on Accreditation of Allied Health Education Programs

CAAP—College Achievement Admission Program

CAAT—Center for Alternatives to Animal Testing

CAATE—Commission on Accreditation of Athletic Training Education

CACREP—Council for Accreditation of Counseling and Related Educational Programs

CADE—Commission on Accreditation for Dietetics Education

CAHEA—See AMA-CAHEA

CAHIIM—Commission on Accreditation for Health Informatics and Information Management Education

CAHME—Commission on Accreditation of Healthcare Management Education

CANAEP—Council on Accreditation of Nurse Anesthesia Educational Programs

CAPTE—Commission on Accreditation in Physical Therapy Education

CARC—Canadian Agri-Food Research Council

CARF—Commission on Accreditation of Rehabilitation Facilities

CAS—Certificate of Advanced Study

CCE—Council on Chiropractic Education

CCIE—California Colleges for International Education

CCNE—Commission on Collegiate Nursing Education

CCTC—California Commission on Teacher Credentialing

CDN—Canadian/Canada

CEA—Canadian Education Association

CEA—Colorado Education Association

CEC—Commission on Education and Communication

CEC—Community Education Council

CED—Council for Education of the Deaf

CEEB—College Entrance Examination Board

CELT—Comprehensive English Language Test

CEPH—Council on Education for Public Health

CHEA—Council for Higher Education Accreditation

CIDA—Council for Interior Design Accreditation

CLAST—College Level Academic Skills Test

CLEP—College-Level Examination Program

CNNE—Commission on Collegiate Nursing Education

CoA—Committee on Accreditation

CoA-NA—Council on Accreditation of Nurse Anesthesia Educational Programs

COA—Commission on Opticianry Accreditation

COAMFTE—Commission on Accreditation for Marriage and Family Therapy Education
CoARC—Committee on Accreditation for Respiratory Care
COAPRT—Council on Accreditation of Parks, Recreation, Tourism, and Related Professions
COC—Certificate of Completion
COCA—Comprehensive Outcomes of Cognitive Assessment
CODA—Commission on Dental Accreditation
COE—Council on Occupational Education
COLA—Commission on Office Laboratory Accreditation
COPRA—Commission on Peer Review and Accreditation
CORE—Central Operation of Resources for Educators
CORE—Council On Rehabilitation Education
CORE—Consortium for Oceanographic Research and Education
CORE—Center for Organ Recovery and Education
CPME—Council on Podiatric Medical Education
CRDA—Candidates Reply Date Agreement
CRE—Council on Rehabilitation Education
CSAB—Computing Science Accreditation Board
CSAC—Consensus Standards Advisory Committee (of NQF)
CSHSE—Council for Standards in Human Service Education
CSLE—Center for the Study of Law and Economics
CSS—College Scholarship Service
CSS/Profile—College Scholarship Service Financial Aid Profile
CSWE—Council on Social Work Education Office of Social Work Accreditation
CVTEA—Committee on Veterinary Technician Education and Activities
CWS—College Work-Study

DECA—Discovering the Educational Consequences of Advanced Technical Education (DECA), a National Science Foundation funded research grant
DECM—Department of Education of the Commonwealth of MA

EAC—Engineering Accreditation Commission
EESL—Examination of English as a Second Language
EHAC—National Environmental Health Science and Protection Accreditation Council
ELPT—English Language Proficiency Test (SAT subject)
ELS/ALA—English Language Services/American Language Academy
EMH—Educable Mentally Handicapped
EOP—Equal Opportunity Program
EPH—Epidemiology and Public Health
EPSB—Education Professional Standards Board
ESL—English as a Second Language
ETS—Educational Testing Service

FAFSA—Free Application for Federal Student Aid
FEF—Foundry Educational Foundation
FET—Full-time equivalent
FFS—Family Financial Statement
FIDER—Foundation for Interior Design Education Research
FISL—Federally Insured Student Loan
FTE—Full-Time Equivalent

GED—General Educational Development (high school equivalency examination)
GPA—Grade Point Average
GPSC—Georgia Professional Student Commission
GPSC—Graduate and Professional Student Council
GRE—Graduate Record Examination
GSLP—Guaranteed Student Loan Program
G-STEP—Georgia State Test for English Proficiency

HEPAC—Higher Education Program Alumni Council
HEOP—Higher Equal Opportunity Program
HLC—Higher Learning Commission
HPER—Health, Physical Education, and Recreation

IACBE—International Assembly for Collegiate Business Education

IAME—International Association for Management Education
IB—International Baccalaureate
IELTS—International English Language Testing System

JRC-AT—Joint Review Committee on Educational Programs in Athletic Training
JRCE—Joint Review Committee on Education
JRCDMS—Joint Review Committee on Education in Diagnostic Medical Sonography
JRCERT—Joint Review Committee on Education in Radiologic Technology
JRCNMT—Joint Review Committee on Educational Programs in Nuclear Medicine Technology

LAAB—Landscape Architectural Accreditation Board
LCME—Liaison Committee on Medical Education

MACTE—Montessori Accreditation Council for Teacher Education
MAPS—Multiple Assessment Program/Services
MBHE—Massachusetts Board of Higher Education
MDOE—Michigan Department of Education
MELAB—Michigan English Language Assessment Battery
MSACS—Middle States Association of Colleges and Schools
MSCHE (MSACHE)—Middle States Commission on Higher Education
MUSIC—Multi User System for Interactive Computing

NAAB—National Architectural Accrediting Board
NAACLS—National Accrediting Agency for Clinical Laboratory Sciences
NAALS—National Assessment of Adult Literacy Survey
NACEP—Nurse Aide Competency Evaluation Program
NAEYC—National Association for the Education of Young Children
NAIT—National Association of Industrial Technology
NAMT—National Association for Music Therapy
NAPNES—National Association for Practical Nurse Education and Service
NASAD—National Association of Schools of Art and Design
NASD—National Association of Schools of Dance
NASDTEC—National Association of State Development Teacher Education
NASSM—North American Society for Sport Management
NASM—National Association of Schools of Music
NASO—National Adult School Organization
NASP—National Association of School Psychologists
NASPAA—National Association of Schools of Public Affairs and Administration
NASPE—National Association of Sport and Physical Education
NAST—National Association of Schools of Theatre
NATA—National Athletic Trainers' Association
NCA—North Central Association of Colleges and Schools, Higher Learning Commission
NCAA—National Collegiate Athletic Association
NCACE—National Council for Accreditation of Coaching Education
NCACS—North Central Association of Colleges and Schools
NCA-HLC—North Central Association of Colleges and Schools, The Higher Learning Commission
NCATE—National Council for Accreditation of Teacher Education
NCCAA—National Christian College Athletic Association
NCDPI—North Carolina Department of Public Instruction
NCIDQ—National Council for Interior Design Qualification
NCOPE—National Commission on Orthotic and Prosthetic Education
NCTE—National Council of Teachers of English
NCTM—National Council of Teachers of Mathematics
NDEA—National Defense Education Act
NEASC-CIHE—New England Association of Schools and Colleges, Commission on Institutions of Higher Education

NEASC-CTCI—New England Association of Schools and Colleges, Commission on Technical and Career Institutions
NEHA—National Environmental Health Association
NEHSPAC—National Environmental Health Science and Protection Council
NLN—National League for Nursing
NLNAC—National League for Nursing Accrediting Commission, Inc.
NMPED—New Mexico Public Education Department
NMSA—National Middle School Association
NRPA—National Recreation and Park Association
NSTA—National Science Teachers Association
NWCCU—Northwest Commission on Colleges and Universities
NYSED—New York State Education Department

OAKE—Organization of American Kodály Educators
OBN—Ohio Board of Nursing
ODE—Ohio Department of Education
ODPS—Ohio Department of Public Safety

PAB—Planning Accreditation Board
PAIR—PHEAA Aid Information Request
PCS—Parents' Confidential Statement
PDE—Pennsylvania Department of Education
PEP—Proficiency Examination Program
PHEAA—Pennsylvania Higher Education Assistance Agency
PSAT/NMSQT—Preliminary Scholastic Aptitude Test/National Merit Scholarship Qualifying Test

ROTC—Reserve Officers Training Corps
RSE—Regents Scholarship Examination (New York State)

SAAC—Student Aid Application for California
SACU—Service for Admission to College and University (Canada)

SACS—Southern Association of Colleges and Schools, Commission on Colleges
SAF—Society of American Foresters
SAM—Single Application Method
SAR—Student Aid Report
SAT—Scholastic Assessment Testing (*formerly ATP–Admissions Testing Program*)
SATE—Security Awareness Training & Education
SBEC—State Board for Educator Certification (Texas)
SCAT—Scholastic College Aptitude Test
SCS—Students' Confidential Statement
SDBN—South Dakota Board of Nursing
SEOG—Supplementary Educational Opportunity Grant
SOA—Society of Actuaries

TAC—Technology Accreditation Commission
TAP—Tuition Assistance Program (New York State)
TDD/TTY—Telecommunications Device for the Deaf/TeleTYpewriter
TEA—Texas Education Agency
TEAC—Teacher Education Accreditation Council
TOEFL—Test of English as a Foreign Language
TRACS—Transnational Association of Christian Colleges and Schools, Accreditation Commission

UAP—Undergraduate Assessment Program
UMC—United Methodist Church
UP—Undergraduate Program (area tests)

VFAF—Virginia Financial Assistance Form

WASC-ACCJC—Western Association of Schools and Colleges, Accrediting Commission for Community and Junior Colleges
WASC-ACSCU—Western Association of Schools and Colleges, Accrediting Commission for Senior Colleges and Universities
WPCT—Washington Pre-College Test

PART I

AN INTRODUCTION

TO COLLEGE

You'll soon be on your way to college—but how much thought have you given it so far? Have you started thinking about the career that's in your future?

- Which college will help you make the most of your natural abilities and interests, and get you ready for life?
- Which courses should you take?

This section will help you find answers to these questions. It will also give you advice on:

- how to apply to schools
- how to increase your chances of acceptance
- how to finance your education

And just as important, this introductory section will give you valuable tips on how to get through that critical freshman year.

It's not just about statistics like median SAT scores, the endowment, the number of majors or student-professor ratios; a college should feel right to you, from the structure of the classrooms to the food that's served in the dining halls.

Arielle Shipper, Connecticut College, Class of 2010

You have in your hands a book that will give you answers to your questions about the qualities and features of more than 1650 colleges. But before you start reading the descriptions and getting the answers, you need to know what questions to ask about finding the college that is right for you. Although you need to ask questions about "getting in" i.e., exploring colleges in terms of ease of admission for you, most of your questions should focus on the more significant issue of "fitting in." Fitting in means finding a college where you will be comfortable; where you are compatible with your peers, and where the overall atmosphere encourages your growth as a student and as a person.

This article is designed to help you assess some values and attitudes that will help you determine where you will fit in. It will enable you to ask the right questions. Not all colleges are for everyone; careful thinking about your interests, ideals, and values will lead you to find the college that is right *for you*. Colleges are not "good" or "bad" in a generic sense; they are either good or bad matches for you.

The two assessments that follow will be helpful in thinking about yourself as a future college student; they should help you make the right college choice.

THE COLLEGE PLANNING VALUES ASSESSMENT

Students have different reasons for going to college. Eleven reasons or values are found to be most important to students as they think about college. Knowing about your values is the important first step in identifying the colleges where you will fit in and be happy.

To complete the assessment, read through the list of ten values—A through K. Think about the outcomes you hope college will produce for you. Each student will rank them differently; hence, there are no "right" answers. Whereas several, or even most, of these values may be significant for you in one way or another, the goal is to decide which three are the most important. After you read each of the values, go back and circle the THREE most important ones on the basis of the following question:

What do you want college to do for you?
—— A. To provide me with a place to learn and study.
—— B. To provide me with opportunities to interact with teachers inside and outside the classroom.
—— C. To provide me with lots of fun experiences.
—— D. To prepare me to make a lot of money.
—— E. To provide me with recognition for accomplishments.
—— F. To get politically involved and/or to use much of my college years to help those who are disadvantaged.
—— G. To help me prepare for a career.
—— H. To enable me to be more independent.
—— I. To provide opportunities for me to grow religiously or spiritually.
—— J. To provide me with a variety of new experiences.
—— K. To enable me to receive a degree from a prestigious school.
What do your college planning values say about you?

If **A** was among the top three priorities on your list, you will want to explore the academic character of the colleges you are considering. Although all colleges are, by definition, intellectual centers, some put more priority on challenging students and pushing them to their limits. Reading about the academic features of the colleges you are considering will be important. (In the college Profiles, pay attention to the *special* section to learn about these features.) Your high ranking of this value says that you will be able to take advantage of intellectual opportunities at college. You may want to select a college where your SAT scores are similar to or slightly above the ranges of other admitted students—at those colleges you will be able to shine academically. You may desire to take an active part in classroom discussions and will want a college where the student faculty ratio is low.

If **B** was among your top three priorities, you feel challenged and stimulated by academics and classroom learning. You will want to find a college where your mind will be stretched. You will want to choose a college where you can explore a range of new academic subjects. A liberal arts and sciences college may give you an enriching breadth of academic offerings. You will want to look for a college where academic clubs are popular and where you have a good chance of knowing professors and sharing ideas with them. Access to faculty is important to you and you will want to look at the student faculty ratio in colleges you consider. Also note the ratio of undergraduate students to graduate students. Primarily undergraduate institutions will be the colleges that may best be able to meet your needs, because you will be the focus of teachers' attention. Teachers at such colleges place their priority on teaching and are not distracted by the needs of graduate students or by pressure to balance teaching and student time with research and writing.

If **C** was circled, you derive satisfaction from social opportunities. You will want a college where the academic demands will not diminish your ability to socialize. You likely will want a good balance between the social and academic sides of campus life. You will want to explore the percentage of students who get involved in intramural sports, clubs, or fraternities and sororities. (This information is listed in each college profile.) Look at your college choices on the basis of school spirit and sporting events offered. The profiles list popular campus events—see if they sound exciting to you. Also look at the percentage of students who stay on campus over the weekend. You will also want a college where it is easy to make friends. Both small and larger colleges would be appropriate for you. Although a larger college would expose you to more students and a larger quantity of potential friends, studies show that students at smaller colleges become more involved in activities and build deep friendships more quickly. Look for supportiveness and camaraderie in the student body.

If **D** is circled, you will want to consider earning potential, advancement opportunities, and the future market for the careers you consider. You will want to consider this value in your career planning. Remember, however, that there is no sure road to riches! You not only must pick a career direction carefully, but must choose a college where the potential for academic success—good grades—is high. The name of a particular college is less important than good grades or contributions to campus life when securing a good job or being admitted to graduate school. Even if you find that a particular career has tremendous earning potential, those earnings may come to only those who are most successful in the profession. Look at average salaries, but also consider your interests, values, and personality before making your final career choice. Be sure to take advantage of hands-on learning opportunities. Perhaps, for example, there are internships that meet your needs. Also, finding good, career-focused summer jobs can be helpful.

If **E** is high on your list, you take pleasure in being known for your success in an area of interest. For instance, you might feel good about being recognized or known in school as a good student, a top athlete, or a leader in a club. No doubt this type of recognition contributes to your confidence. You might look for colleges where you will be able to acquire or continue to receive this recognition. Often, recognition is easier to achieve at smaller colleges where you would not be competing against large numbers of students hoping to achieve the same recognition. You will also want to choose colleges where it is easy to get involved and where the activities offered are appealing to you. You may want to consider the benefits of being a "big fish in a small pond."

If **F** is important, that value will no doubt guide your vocational or avocational pursuits. You may find yourself choosing a career in which this value can be fulfilled, or you may seek opportunities on a college campus where you can be of service to others. You will want to choose a college where community service is valued. Look at the *activities* section and note whether community service-related involvements are available. Colleges vary a great deal in terms of political awareness. At some colleges, students are attuned to national and international events, often express feelings about current issues and policies, and in general, show interest in political affairs. Students at other colleges show little or no interest in these matters and find other ways to interact with peers.

If **G** was circled, you may know what career you want to pursue or you may be concerned but uncertain about your career decision. If you have tentatively selected a career, you will want to choose a college where you can take courses leading to the attainment of a degree in your chosen field. Explore the *programs of study* section in the profiles to determine whether a college you are considering offers the course work you desire. You will want to make a note of the most popular majors and the strongest majors as they are listed. If you don't yet know what career would suit you, remember, that for most careers, a broad, solid liberal arts foundation is considered good preparation. You will want to look at opportunities for internships and take advantage of the career planning and placement office at your chosen college. Finding a career that will be fulfilling is one of the most important choices you will make in your life. Your selection of a college will be your first step toward achieving your career goal.

If **H** is circled, it suggests that personal autonomy is important to you. College is, in general, a time for independence, and students are often anxious to make their own decisions without parental involvement. If you feel you can handle lots of independence, you will want to look for colleges where there is some freedom in choosing courses and where students are given responsibility for their own lives. Colleges vary in terms of these factors. Note particularly the *required* section under *programs of study*, which tells you the courses that must be fulfilled by all students. Be certain that you will not be stifled by too many rules and regulations. You may also want to look for colleges where the personal development of students receives high priority. A priority on independence also suggests that you will be comfortable being away from home and on your own.

If **I** is one of your top three choices, you will want to look first at the religious affiliation of each of your college options. There are two ways to consider religious life on college campuses. First is the question of how religion affects the day-to-day life of the college. For example, are biblical references made in class? Are religious convocations mandatory? Second is the question of whether there is a religious heritage at the college. Many hundreds of colleges have historical relationships with a religious denomination, but this tie does not affect the rules or the general life of the students. (For example, the college may have a certain number of religion classes required to graduate, but these classes are typically broad-based and not doctrinal.) You may want a college that has a relationship with your particular religious group. Or you may desire a large number of students who belong to the same denomination as you do. The profiles will also give you the percentage of students who are members of the major religious denominations. As you explore colleges, you will also want to see if the college has a commitment to the values and ideals held by you or your family.

If **J** is appealing, you like newness and will likely be stimulated by new experiences and new activities. You are in for a treat at most colleges. New experiences are the "stuff" of which college life is made. You may see college-going as an adventure and will want to pick colleges where you can meet your need for stimulation and excitement. Because you value newness, you should not hesitate to attend college in a different part of the country or to experience an environment or a climate that is quite different from your high school. You will also want to look for evidence of diversity in the student body. As you read the descriptions, look for colleges with lots of new opportunities for growth and for personal expansion.

If **K** is appealing, be cautious. Students who are overly concerned about this value might find college planning traumatic, and even painful, because of the admission selectivity of "name brand" colleges. Even though it is perfectly acceptable for students to be attuned to the overall excellence of a college, academic quality and prestige are not the same thing. Some colleges are well-known because of, say, a fine football team or because of academic excellence in a subject like psychology or physics. Although it is appropriate to look for a strong faculty and a highly regarded college, you want a college that will give you the greatest chance of academic success. It is success in college, not just academic reputation or prestige, that will lead to admission into graduate school or a broad selection of jobs.

Now that you've read about your top three values, answer the following question on a separate sheet of paper: In your own words, what do your top three values say about what you are looking for in a college? Then, share that information with your college adviser as he or she assists you in finding colleges that are right for you.

SELF-KNOWLEDGE QUESTIONNAIRE

The following seven items—A–G—will help you in thinking about yourself as a college student and the ease with which you will likely proceed through the college selection process. Read each statement and determine whether it is true or not true of you. After each question, you will see numbers ranging from 1 to 5. Circle 1 if the statement is very true of you. Circle 5 if the statement is not true of you. Use 2, 3, or 4 to reflect varying levels of preference. Be realistic and honest.

A. My academic abilities for college (such as reading, writing, and note taking) are good.
Very true of me   1   2   3   4   5   Not true of me

Academic abilities such as reading speed and comprehension, writing, note taking, calculating, speaking, and listening are important for college students. You will be called upon to use such skills in your college classes. If you are confident about your academic skills, you can approach picking a college with the ease of knowing that you will be able to master the academic rigors of college life. If you circled 3, 4, or 5 you will want to work on these skills in your remaining days in high school. You will want to choose colleges where you can work to strengthen these skills. Some colleges provide a learning skills center in which you are able to get help if you are having difficulty writing a paper or understanding the content of a class. If you are less than confident, you might look to colleges where you will not be intimidated by the skills of the other students.

B. My study skills and time management are good.
Very true of me   1   2   3   4   5   Not true of me

Study skills and time management are two of the most important qualities for an efficient and productive college student. Successful college students are average or above in organizing themselves for studying, scheduling, and using study time productively, and differentiating important content of a lecture or a book from supplementary information. In addition, they complete assignments on time and don't get flustered if they have several papers or a couple of tests due on the same day. If you circled 3, 4, or 5, it is important to work on improving these skills during your remaining high school days. You might consider the following:

- Seek help from your parents, a teacher, a counselor, or a learning specialist in becoming more organized.
- Try keeping a calendar. Anticipate each step necessary in preparing for every test and every paper.
- Be responsible for your own appointments.
- Check to see if a study skills course is offered at a local community college or university. Or consider reading a book on study skills.

C. I am motivated to succeed in college.

Very true of me   1   2   3   4   5   Not true of me

Motivation is definitely the most important skill you bring to college. Those students who want to succeed do succeed! Studies show that it is motivation, not your SAT scores, that determines academic success in college. And motivation means knowing not only that you want to go to college, but that you also want to be a student. Some students want to go to college for the fun aspects, but forget that college is primarily an academic experience. So if you circled 1 or 2, great, you're off to a good start. If you circled 3, 4, or 5, it may be an appropriate time to consider your wants and needs in a college. What sort of college would help motivate you? Would a college with a balance between academics and social life be appealing? Would you be more motivated if you were near a large and interesting city? Would nice weather be a distraction rather than an energizer? Is a trade or technical school best for you? Have you considered taking some time off between high school and college? Considering such questions is important, and the time to do that exploration is now.

D. I am a good decision maker.

Very true of me   1   2   3   4   5   Not true of me

Decisions, decisions, decisions. The college selection process is full of decisions! What colleges will I initially consider? To which colleges will I apply for admission? What college will I eventually attend? You will be facing these decisions in the upcoming months. If you circled 1 or 2, you are on your way. If you circled 3, 4, or 5, think about an important decision you made recently. Why didn't it go well? If you can analyze your decision-making weakness in that situation, it may help to avoid any potential pitfalls in your college decision-making. The following suggestions will help you improve your ability to make the right college choice:

- Clearly articulate what you're looking for in a college. Write down those features that will make a college right for you.
- Involve lots of people and resources in your search for a college. Your parents, counselors, and friends can help you.
- List and compare pros and cons of alternative colleges. Every college has both.
- Evaluate each college on the basis of the criteria you set for yourself.

Remember, you're looking for a college where you will get in *and* fit in.

E. I'm a good information gatherer; for example, I am usually able to find books, articles, and so on to help me do a research paper for, say, a history class.

Very true of me   1   2   3   4   5   Not true of me

Finding a college requires you to be a good researcher. There is so much information about colleges to sort through and analyze. If you feel you can do good research, fine, you're on your way. If you circled 3, 4, or 5, the following ideas may be helpful:

- Start with this book and look for colleges that are consistent with what you want. Remember that your primary concern is where you will fit in. Use your college-going values and your responses in this questionnaire to guide your thinking about colleges that will match you.
- Work closely with your college counselor, and seek impressions from students and others with reliable and up-to-date

information about colleges of interest. You will make a better decision with credible and extensive input.

- Look for differences in features that are important to you. Is ease of making friends important to you? What about balance between academics and social life? Do you want teachers to know you?

F. I feel I adapt to new situations easily.

Very true of me   1   2   3   4   5   Not true of me

Everyone goes through changes in life. Some move through transition periods with great ease, others find them more difficult. You may have experienced the changes that come after a change of schools (even from middle school to high school), the illness or death of a relative, or the divorce of your parents. If you circled 1 or 2, you are not likely to be intimidated by a college in another part of the country or a college very different from your high school. If you circled 3, 4, or 5, you may want to carefully look at colleges that are a bit closer to home or colleges where the same values, perceptions, and attitudes exist as were true in your high school. Almost everyone has fear and apprehension about leaving for college. But if that fear is significant, you will want to choose a college where you will feel comfortable. Visits to college campuses may be particularly significant in feeling good about potential choices.

G. It is easy for me to meet people and establish friendships.

Very true of me   1   2   3   4   5   Not true of me

Identifying and nurturing friendships is an important skill for college adjustment. If you circled 3, 4, or 5, you will want to look carefully at colleges where there are few cliques, where there is an atmosphere of sharing, and where students report that it is relatively easy to integrate into the campus environment. Your choice of a college is a quest for a good social fit. Your thorough review of the profiles and even visits to college campuses will be helpful in assuring your ability to fit in and be comfortable.

FINAL THOUGHTS

If you took time to carefully consider the issues raised in both the Values Assessment and the Self-Knowledge Questionnaire, you should have gained new insights and perspectives about yourself. You will want to share these results with your parents and with your guidance counselor. Elicit their help in getting more insight as to how they see you as a prospective college student. Finally, two suggestions:

- As you research colleges, consider what you have learned about yourself. You want a college that is a good match with your values and interests.
- Spend time on your college search. It will take many hours of organized planning and investigation. But the time spent will result in a better choice and a greater likelihood that you will spend four productive and exciting years in college.

Good luck. There are lots of colleges out there that want you. Let your knowledge of yourself and your objective analysis of potential college options guide you to college environments where you will be able to shine. Success in college is in your hands. Make the most of the opportunity.

Steven R. Antonoff, Ph.D., Certified Educational Planner
Educational Consultant
Antonoff Associates, Inc.
Denver, Colorado

FINDING THE RIGHT COLLEGE

*Location is a key factor in looking at colleges. Those seeking adventures
should look toward city schools where there are endless possibilities,
and those looking for a quiet atmosphere should look for schools in rural locations.*

Bryan Cosca, Boston University College of Engineering, Class of 2014

Start your college search positively. Start with the knowledge that there are many schools out there that want you. Start with the idea that there are many good college choices for every student. Too often these days, articles on college admission make students and their parents apprehensive. You can have choices. You can get financial aid. You can have a happy, successful college career.

When you begin to think about college, you are embarking on a major research project. You have many choices available to you in order to get the best possible education for which you are qualified. This article is intended to help you think of some of the important variables in your college search.

Let us help make the book work for you!

THE CURRENT ADMISSION SCENE

Today there are approximately 1,650 four-year colleges and universities accredited. Most existing institutions have grown larger, and many have expanded their programs, offering master's and doctoral degrees as well as bachelor's.

Total graduate and undergraduate students has also grown, from under 4 million in 1960 to more than 16 million today. Almost 40 percent are part-time students, including many working adults. Part-time enrollments are mostly concentrated in the two-year colleges, which enroll about a third of all students.

What does this all mean to you? There is good news and bad news. The good news is that most of the colleges you will read about in this book are colleges you can get into! In other words, the vast majority of colleges in the U.S. admit more than 70 percent of those who apply. Many hundreds admit all of those who apply. So, on one level, you shouldn't worry that you won't be able to get a college education. The bad news is for the student with extremely high grades who seeks admission to the 50 or so most competitive colleges in the country. These "brand name" colleges have many times more candidates than they admit. Even incredibly qualified students are sometimes denied admission.

The key to good college planning is, as mentioned above, research. Find out about what makes one college different from another. Find out what students say about their experiences. Rely on many sources of information—many people, many books, many web sites, and so on. There are lots of people and materials available to help you. This book is one of them. Let the information be your guide. But also let your instincts and your sense of what's best for you play a part. The higher education opportunities in the U.S. are unlimited. The opportunity to let education help pave the way to achieving your dreams is a worthy goal of your college search.

MAKING A SHORT LIST

You have probably already started a list of colleges you know about from friends or relatives who have attended them, from recommendations by counselors or teachers, or by their academic or social reputations. This list will grow as you read the Profiles, receive college mailings, and attend college fairs. If you are interested in preparing for a very specific career, such as engineering, agriculture, nursing, or architecture, you should add only institutions that offer that program. If you want to study business, teacher education, or the arts and sciences, almost every college can provide a suitable major. Either way, your list will soon include dozens of institutions. Most students apply to between four and seven colleges. To narrow your list, you should keep the following process in mind:

- As you explore, be attuned to the admission requirements. You will want to have colleges on your list that span the admission selectivity continuum—from "reach" colleges (those where your grades, test scores, etc., suggest less chance of admission) to "safety" schools (those where your credentials are a bit better than the average student admitted), eliminating colleges at which you clearly would not qualify for admission.
- You also will want to keep an eye on cost. You want to consider colleges that are generally in line with your family's ability to finance your education. Be very cautious as you do this. Literally millions of dollars are available each year for students. There is both "need-based" aid (aid based on your family's ability to pay) and "merit-based" aid (aid based on such things as grades, test scores, and leadership ability).
- Screen the list according to your preferences, such as size, academic competitiveness, religious focus, and location.
- Make quality judgments, using published information and campus visits, to decide which colleges can give you the best quality and value.

The following sections are organized around the factors most important in researching a college. Discussion of admission competitiveness and cost comes first. After that, a wide range of factors important to consider as you evaluate colleges is examined. These include size, housing, the faculty, academic programs, internships, accreditation, libraries and computer technology, and religious/racial considerations. The final two sections are a discussion of campus visits and, finally, a checklist of 25 important questions to ask about each of the colleges you are exploring.

In the end, you must allow yourself to be a good decision maker. You will have to make some quality judgments. It is not as difficult as you may think. You have to be willing to read the information in this book and the literature that the schools make available, to visit a few campuses, and to ask plenty of questions. Usually you can ask questions of the admissions office by regular mail, e-mail, or in person during a campus visit. Because colleges sincerely are interested in helping you make the right choice, they generally will welcome your questions and answer them politely and honestly. In addition, your high school counselor is a key person who can offer advice and guidance. Finally, there are many resources available, in printed form and on the web, to help you.

SELECTION FACTORS

Admissions Competitiveness

The first question most students ask about a college is, "How hard is it to get in?" It should certainly not be the last question. Admissions competitiveness is not the only, or even the most important, measurement of institutional quality. It makes sense to avoid wasting time, money, and useless disappointment applying to institutions for which you clearly are not qualified. Nevertheless, there are many colleges for which you are qualified, and you can make a good choice from among them. The most prestigious institutions are rarely affected by market conditions. Most of the better known private and public colleges and universities have raised their admission standards in recent years. But there remain hundreds of fine public and private colleges, with good local reputations, that will welcome your application.

Use the College Admissions Selector to compare your qualifications to the admissions competitiveness of the institutions of your list. Make sure you read the descriptions of standards very carefully. Even if you meet the stated qualifications for *Most Competitive* or *Highly Competitive* institutions, you cannot assume that you will be offered admission. These colleges receive applications from many more students than they can enroll and reject far more than they accept. When considering colleges rated *Very Competitive* or *Competitive*, remember that the median test scores identify the middle of the most recent freshman class; half of the admitted students had scores lower than the median, and half were above. Students of average ability are admissible to most of the colleges and universities rated as *Competitive* and to virtually all of those rated as *Less Competitive*.

Cost

The basic cost of the most expensive colleges and universities can exceed $40,000 a year. This is widely publicized and very frightening, especially to your parents. But you don't have to spend that much for a good education. Private colleges charge an average of nearly $30,000 a year for tuition and room and board. Public institutions generally cost an average of $14,000 a year for in-state residents. Because many states have been cutting budgets in recent years, tuition at public institutions is now rising faster than at private ones. If you can commute to school from home, you can save about $6000 to $7000 in room and board, but should add the cost of transportation. The least expensive option is to attend a local community college for two years, at about $1500 a year, and then transfer to a four-year institution to complete your bachelor's degree. Depending on what you may qualify for in financial aid, and what your family is willing to sacrifice, you may have more choices than you think.

Size

Only one-fifth of American colleges and universities have enrollments of 5000 or more, but they account for more than half the ten million plus students who are pursuing bachelor's degrees. The rest are spread out among more than 1000 smaller schools. There are advantages and disadvantages that go with size.

At a college of 5000 or fewer students, you will get to know the campus quickly. You will not have to compete with many other students when registering for courses or for use of the library or other facilities. You can get to know your professors personally and become familiar with most of your fellow students. On the other hand, the school may not have as many majors and it may have less emphasis on spectator sports. Students at small schools are not able to be as "anonymous" as those at larger schools.

As colleges and universities enroll more students, they offer more courses and activities. Within a large campus community, you can probably find others who share your special interests and form a circle of good friends. But you may also find the facilities more crowded, classes closed out, and competition very stiff for athletic teams or musical groups.

Many of the largest institutions are universities offering medical, law, or other doctoral programs as well as bachelor's and master's degrees. Many colleges that do not offer these programs call themselves universities; and a few universities, Dartmouth among them, continue to call themselves colleges. Don't go by the name, but by the academic program. Universities emphasize research. University faculty need specialized laboratory equipment, computers, library material, and technical assistance for their research. Colleges tend to emphasize teaching.

Because research is very expensive, universities usually charge higher tuition than colleges, even to their undergraduate students. In effect, undergraduates at universities subsidize the high cost of graduate programs. Freshmen and sophomores usually receive some instruction from graduate student assistants and fellows, who are paid to be apprentice faculty members.

Of course, many larger private universities, and many public ones, have fine reputations. They have larger and more up-to-date libraries, laboratories, computers, and other special resources than colleges. They attract students from many states and countries and provide a rich social and cultural environment.

Housing

Deciding whether you will stay in a residence hall or at home is more than a matter of finances or how close to the college you live. You should be aware that students who live on campus, especially during the freshman year, are more likely to pass their courses and graduate than students who commute from home. Campus residents spend more time with faculty members, have more opportunity to use the library and laboratories, and are linked to other students who help one another with their studies. Residence hall life usually helps students mature faster as they participate in social and organizational activities.

If you commute to school, you can get maximum benefits from your college experience by spending time on campus between and after classes. If you need a part-time job, get employment in the college library, offices, or dining halls. Use the library to do homework in an environment that may be less distracting than home. If possible, have some dinners on campus, to make friends with other students and participate in evening social and cultural events. Get involved in campus activities, participating in athletics, working on the newspaper, attending a meeting, or rehearsing a play.

You will have a choice of food plans. Most meal plans include a certain number of meals per week. Other plans allow you to prepay a fixed dollar amount and purchase food by the item rather than by the meal. Choose a meal plan that fits your own eating habits. Most colleges today offer a tremendous variety of food and are accommodating to most diets and preferences.

Many students live off campus after their freshman or sophomore year, either by choice or because the school does not have room for them on campus. Schools try to provide listings of available off-campus rooms and apartments that meet good standards for safety and cleanliness. Many colleges also offer health care and food services to students who live off campus.

It is usually more expensive to live in an apartment than in a residence hall, especially if you plan to prepare your own meals. But that option is appealing to some students, particularly those in their junior or senior years.

The Faculty

The most important resources of any college or university are its professors. Admissions brochures usually point out the strengths of the faculty, but provide little detail. You should direct your questions about the faculty and other academic matters to the specific department or to the office that coordinates academic advising. Recruiting brochures also emphasize faculty research, because the prestige of professors depends largely on the books and articles they have published. Good researchers may or may not make good teachers. Ask how often the best researchers teach undergraduate courses, and whether they instruct small as well as large classes. For example, a Nobel prize chemist may lecture to 500 students at a time but never show up in the laboratories where graduate assistants actually teach individual students.

Also ask about class size, because this determines the amount of individual attention students get from professors. Student/faculty ratios, which usually range from 10 to 20 students per professor, don't really tell you much. Every school offers a mixture of large and small classes. Ask admission officers for the average size of a freshman class. You will want to look for such factors as those that follow:

- Science and technology courses should enroll only 25 to 30 students in each laboratory session, but may combine a number of laboratory classes for large weekly lectures.
- Skill development courses such as speech, foreign language, English composition, and fine and performing arts should have classes of 25 or fewer. Mathematics and computer science require considerable graded homework, and classes should be no larger than 35.

- Most other courses in humanities, social sciences, and professional areas are taught by classroom lectures and discussion. Classes should average 35 to 45 in introductory courses such as general psychology or American government. They should be smaller in advanced or specialized courses, such as Shakespeare or tax accounting.
- Many introductory courses, especially at universities, are taught in lecture classes of 100 or more. This is acceptable, if those courses also include small weekly discussion groups for individual instruction. Sometimes these discussion groups are taught by graduate student assistants rather than regular professors. Although graduate assistants lack teaching experience, they are very often highly capable. You should ask whether the teaching done by graduate assistants is closely supervised by regular faculty members.

Academic Programs

Even colleges and universities that boast fine and well qualified faculties can be short of professors in certain programs. Some schools depend on instruction by part-time faculty members or fill in with available teachers from other specializations. Many international students are enrolled in technical doctoral programs, so you may find yourself being taught mathematics or engineering by a teaching assistant who is not a native English speaker. If you are interested in these subjects, check to see whether full-time faculty members teach the majority of the courses.

Other programs may have sufficient faculty but too few student majors. Majors such as physics and philosophy, for example, often have many students in required introductory courses, but few taking the major. Because of small enrollments, these departments may not be able to offer their advanced and specialized courses on a regular basis.

Academic departments give strength to the program by bringing together faculty members who share a common area of study and make sure their students get the classes they need. Some programs, usually called interdisciplinary, are taught by groups of faculty members from several departments. These programs generally have the word *studies* in their titles; for example, Middle-Eastern Studies, Communication Studies, Women's Studies, or Ethnic Studies. If you are enrolled in one of these programs, be sure to ask about the student advising. (Sometimes, advising suffers if faculty members are primarily loyal to their own department.)

Internships

Internships are available at many colleges. They provide an opportunity to experience work in your major and learn from experienced people in your field. Many students have received job offers after participating in an internship program during the school year or during summer vacation. These internships can make a big difference as you enter the job market.

Accreditation

General standards of academic quality are established by associations of colleges and universities through a process called voluntary accreditation. The criteria include: standards for admission of students; faculty qualifications; content of courses; grading standards; professional success of alumni; adequacy of libraries, laboratories, computers, and other support facilities; administrative systems and policy decision making; and financial support.

Six regional associations (New England, Middle States, Southern, North Central, Northwest, and Western) evaluate and accredit colleges as total institutions. Bible colleges have their own accrediting association. Other organizations evaluate and accredit specific programs, primarily in technical fields, like engineering and architecture; or those that require licensing, such as teaching and health care.

Libraries and Computer Technology

Most people judge libraries by the size of the collection, the bigger the better. Collection size is important, but only in relation to the variety and level of programs offered. A small liberal arts college can support its baccalaureate programs with a collection of 200,000 to 400,000 volumes. A university with many professional schools and doctoral programs may require over 2 million. Many books and journals are available through various methods of information technology, computer storage, and the Internet.

The main stacks should be open to students, with the possible exception of rare books, bound journals, and other special items. Open stacks encourage browsing and save students from waiting on line while a library assistant fetches a few books at a time. Instead, assistants constantly should be picking up unused materials from reading desks or carts and putting them back on the shelves.

Good circulation policies encourage students to check materials out for short periods and to return them promptly. One week or less loans are appropriate for books regularly used in courses, and four week loans should be the maximum for other materials. A recall system should be available to get back borrowed material when it is needed. Journals, reference material, or books placed on reserve for assigned reading should be used within the library while it is open, and circulated overnight only at closing time.

Using a computer is integral to university study. Some institutions require students to have personal computers. Colleges often offer the best price for new computers. You may want to check out the options on campus before you purchase a computer elsewhere. Many residence hall rooms are wired for computers and direct connections are linked to the main campus system. More and more campuses have wireless capability.

Religious/Ethnic Considerations

For some students, the religious life of the campus is important as college choices are reviewed. Religious life can vary from being pervasive to being absent. Most colleges are independent of religious influence. Some are historically affiliated with a religious group, yet religious matters are not part of student life. Other schools exist, in part, to educate students in the doctrine and the practices of their own religious perspective. Information you find on these pages will give you answers to some of your initial questions about religious life at particular schools.

If connecting with and learning from members of your racial/ethnic heritage is important, you will find many colleges and universities from which to choose. Again, this guide provides information about the diversity of the campus and the composition of students who are white, African-American, Hispanic, Asian-American, Latino, and so forth.

GETTING THE MOST FROM YOUR CAMPUS VISIT

It is best not to eliminate any options without at least visiting a few campuses of different types to judge their feeling and style first hand.

To learn everything important about a college, you need more than the standard presentation and tour given to visiting students and parents. Plan your visit for a weekday during the school term. This will let you see how classes are taught and how students live. It also is the best time to meet faculty and staff members. If the college does not schedule group presentations or tours at the time you want, call the office of admissions to arrange for an individual tour and interview. (This is more likely at a small college.) At the same time, ask the admissions office to make appointments with people you want to meet.

To find out about a specific academic program, ask to meet the department chairperson or a professor. If you are interested in athletics, religion, or music, arrange to meet with the coach, the chaplain, or the conductor of the orchestra. Your parents will also want to talk to a financial aid counselor about scholarships, grants, and loans. The office of academic affairs can help with your questions about courses or the faculty. The office of student affairs is in charge of residence halls, health services, and extracurricular activities. Each of these areas has a dean or vice president and a number of assistants, so you should be able to get your questions answered even if you go in without an appointment.

Take advantage of a group presentation and tour if one is scheduled on the day of your visit. Much of what you learn may be familiar, but other students and parents will ask about some of the same things you want to know. Student tour guides are also good sources of information. They love to talk about their own courses, professors, and campus experiences.

Finally, explore the campus on your own. Check the condition of the buildings and the grounds. If they appear well maintained, the college probably has good overall management. If they look run down, the college may have financial problems that also make it scrimp on the book budget or laboratory supplies. Visit a service office, such as the registrar, career planning, or academic advising. Observe whether they treat students courteously and seem genuinely interested in helping them. Look at bulletin boards for signs of campus activities.

And, perhaps most importantly, talk to some of the students who are already enrolled at the college. They will usually speak frankly about weekend activities, whether they find it easy to talk to professors out of class, and how much drinking or drug abuse there is on campus. Most importantly, meeting other students will help you discover how friendly the campus is and whether the college will suit you socially and intellectually.

More than buildings and courses of study, a college is a community of people. Only during a campus visit can you experience the human environment in which you will live and work during four critical years.

25 CRITICAL QUESTIONS

The following questions form a checklist to evaluate each college or university you are considering. Use the profiles, material from the colleges, and your own inquiries and observations to get the answers.

1. Do I have a reasonable chance of being admitted?
2. Can my family manage the costs?
3. Is the overall size of the school right for my personality?
4. Is the location right? (Consider such specifics as region, distance from a major city, distance from home, and weather.)
5. Are class sizes right for my learning style and my need for involvement in class?
6. Will I be comfortable with the setting of the campus?
7. Are the housing and food services suitable?
8. Does the college offer the program I want to study? (Or, often more importantly, does the college offer people and classes that will help me decide what I want to study?)
9. Will the college push me academically, but not shove me?
10. Do the best professors teach undergraduate courses?
11. Can I change majors easily, if I need to?
12. Do students say the majority of classes are taught by fun, stimulating, interesting professors?
13. Is the library collection adequate and accessible?
14. Are computer facilities readily available and are campus networking opportunities up-to-date?
15. Is the connection to the Internet adequate?
16. Are there resources for career development?
17. Do the people in the financial aid, housing, and other service offices seem attentive and genuinely interested in helping students?
18. Are there opportunities for me to use my abilities on campus—for example, a musical or acting.
19. Does the campus seem well maintained and managed?
20. Will the college meet my religious and/or ethnic needs?

And, finally, the five most critical questions:
21. Is there a good chance I will be academically successful there?
22. Will I be happy as a student there?
23. Do I seem compatible with the student population? Do they seem to enjoy what I enjoy?
24. Does the student life seem in sync with my personality and my goals? Is the student life what I'm looking for in a college?
25. Does the college "feel" right for me?

Steven R. Antonoff
Sheldon Halpern
Barbara Aronson

Take your entrance exams seriously. When the opportunity of a lifetime presents itself, you'd better be ready for everything life has to offer, or live with regrets forever.

2Lt Jocelyn Booker, United States Air Force Academy, Class of 2010

COLLEGE ENTRANCE EXAMINATIONS

By providing you with exactly the same information about each of the colleges in which you are interested, the book you are now reading, *Profiles of American Colleges*, will help you narrow down the list of colleges to which you will apply. Of course, your final decision will be influenced by many other factors, many of which are far more important: actual visits to the colleges; virtual visits on the Internet; viewings of videotapes; advice from guidance counselors, parents, teachers, and friends.

In much the same way, by providing college admissions officers with the same information about thousands of applicants, the results of college entrance exams can help them narrow down the list of students they are considering accepting. The results of these exams help admissions officers compare students with widely differing backgrounds. Students from different high schools in different states who earn the same grade in their biology classes, B+ say, have used different textbooks, have performed different labs, have taken different tests, and in general often exhibit great disparity in their level of mastery of the subject; indeed, even within the same school, a grade of B+ from one teacher might not represent the same level of accomplishment as a B+ from another teacher. However, a grade of 650 on the Biology SAT Subject Test, or a 4 on the Biology AP test means the same thing whether it was earned by a student from a rural community in Idaho, an inner-city school in New York, or a private prep school in Massachusetts. Because students all across the country take the same standardized test on the same day, colleges can give greater credence to the results of those tests than they can to the results of final exams from different schools.

KINDS OF COLLEGE ENTRANCE EXAMINATIONS

Although some students who go from high school to two-year community colleges do not take any college entrance tests, most do, and virtually all students who are applying to four-year colleges will take some of the following exams:

- PSAT/NMSQT or the Preliminary SAT/National Merit Scholarship Qualifying Test.
- SAT Reasoning Test.
- SAT Subject Tests.
- Advanced Placement (AP) Examinations.
- The ACT Assessment.

The PSAT/NMSQT

The PSAT/NMSQT measures verbal and mathematical reasoning necessary for success in college. It is a standardized test taken by students in high schools throughout the country in October of their junior year. The test consists of five sections: two 25-minute critical reading sections, two 25-minute math sections, and one 30-minute writing section.

This Preliminary SAT is also the qualifying test for the scholarship competition conducted by the National Merit Scholarship Corporation, an independent, nonprofit organization supported by grants from over 600 corporations, private foundations, colleges, and universities. All students whose scores are in the top 5% of students taking the exam that year receive National Merit Letters of Commendation. In addition, students whose scores are in the top 1% of those taking the exam that year become National Merit Semifinalists. Those who advance to finalist standing by meeting additional requirements compete for one-time National Merit $2000 Scholarships and renewable four-year Merit Scholarships, which may be worth as much as $2000 a year or more for four years.

In addition, this test is used by the National Achievement Scholarship Program for outstanding African-American students. Top-scoring African-American students in each of the regional selection units established for the competition continue in the competition for nonrenewable National Achievement $2000 Scholarships and for four-year Achievement Scholarships sponsored by more than 175 organizations.

Test-Taking Strategies for the PSAT/NMSQT

1. Know what to expect. Each critical reading section has sentence completion questions and reading comprehension questions. A few of the reading questions are based on short passages (often a single paragraph), whereas most are based on longer passages (typically four to seven paragraphs). The first math section has 20 multiple-choice questions; the second math section has 8 quantitative comparison questions and 10 questions for which no choices are provided and whose answers must be entered in a special grid. Calculators may be used on any question in the math sections. The writing skills section, which does *not* have an essay, has three types of multiple-choice questions that test your knowledge of standard written English (grammar and usage).

2. On average, wild guessing has no effect on your score. Educated guessing, on the other hand, can improve your score dramatically. On all multiple-choice questions, try to eliminate as many obviously incorrect answer choices as possible, and then guess from among the choices still remaining.

3. Expect easy questions at the beginning of each set of the same question type. Within each set (except for the reading comprehension questions), the questions progress from easy to difficult. In other words, the first sentence completion questions in a set will be easier than the last sentence completion questions in that set; the first grid-in questions will be easier than the last ones.

4. Take advantage of the easy questions to boost your score. Remember: each question is worth the same number of points. Whether it is easy or difficult, whether it takes you ten seconds or two minutes to answer, you get the same number of points for each question you answer correctly. Your job is to answer as many questions as you can without rushing so fast that you make careless errors. Take enough time to get those easy questions right!

You should be aware that there are eight primary changes coming to the PSAT/SAT. These begin with the PSAT offered in October 2015. The first SAT with the new changes is scheduled for March 2016. These changes affect the class of 2017 and beyond.

For detailed information on these changes, please refer to the SAT web sites below:

www.collegeboard.org/delivering-opportunity/sat/redesign

www.collegeboard.org/delivering-opportunity/sat

The SAT

The SAT is a reasoning test consisting of three parts—critical reading, mathematical reasoning, and writing. It is designed to measure your ability to do college work. Part of the test deals with verbal skills with an emphasis on critical reading, including a double passage with different points of view. The critical reading sections measure the extent of your vocabulary, your ability to interpret and create ideas, and your ability to reason logically and draw conclusions correctly. The mathematics part measures your ability to reason with numbers and mathematical concepts. It tests your ability to handle general number concepts rather than specific achievement in mathematics. Calculators are permitted on each math section.

The writing part consists of a short essay and multiple-choice questions that test your knowledge of standard written English (grammar and usage).

The SAT is given on seven Saturdays during the year—once each in January, March, May, June, October, November, and December. Applicants may request, for religious reasons, to take the test on the Sunday following the regularly scheduled date.

You can register online at *www.collegeboard.org* or by mail by using the registration form available at your school.

On each part of the SAT—critical reading, math, and writing—you will receive a scaled score between 200 and 800. On each part the national mean is approximately 500.

Test-Taking Strategies for the SAT

1. Pace yourself properly. It is much better to slow down and avoid careless errors than it is to speed up in an effort to answer all the questions. You can earn an above-average score (over 1000) by correctly answering fewer than half of the questions on the test and omitting the rest. Even scores of 1300 can be achieved by omitting more than 20% of the questions.

2. Read carefully. Make sure you are answering the question asked, not a similar one you once encountered. Underline key words (e.g., NOT and EXCEPT) to make sure you do not answer the opposite of the question asked.

3. Learn the directions for each type of question before taking the test. During the test, do not waste even one second reading the directions or looking at the sample questions.

4. Always answer the easy questions first (the ones at the beginning of each section). Do not panic if you can't answer a question. Do not spend too much time on any one question. If you are truly stuck, make an educated guess if possible (see below), and move on. Remember that each question is worth the same one point, and the next few questions may be much easier for you.

5. On average, wild guessing does not affect your score—it is unlikely to help, but it is equally unlikely to hurt you. The choice is yours. However, educated guessing—when you can eliminate one or more of the answer choices—can significantly increase your score! In particular, don't omit critical reading questions if you have read the passage; you can always eliminate some of the choices. Most math questions contain at least one or two choices that are absurd (for example, negative choices when you know that the answer must be positive); eliminate them and guess.

SAT Subject Tests

These tests are one-hour multiple-choice question tests. You may take one, two, or three tests on any one test date. Some colleges do not require SAT Subject Tests. Of those that do, some colleges require specific subject tests, whereas others allow applicants to choose the ones they wish to present

with the admission application. Those colleges that do require these tests may use them to determine acceptance or placement in college courses. The tests in foreign language are used not only for placement but also for possible exemption from a foreign language requirement. If the college of your choice does not require these tests but you would like to demonstrate proficiency in a particular field, take the test anyway and have your scores sent. Tests are given in literature, history, mathematics, sciences, and several foreign languages.

Advanced Placement (AP) Examinations

The College Board also conducts Advanced Placement tests, given to high school students who have completed advanced or honors courses and wish to get college credit. Many secondary schools offer college-level courses in calculus, statistics, art, psychology, European history, American history, Latin, Spanish, French, German, biology, chemistry, and physics. As a result of scores obtained on these tests, colleges grant credit or use the results for placement in advanced college courses.

The ACT Assessment

The registration form for the ACT includes a detailed questionnaire that takes about one hour to complete. As a result of the answers to those questions about your high school courses, personal interests, and career plans, plus the scores on your ACT, an ACT Assessment Student Report is produced. This is made available to you, your high school, and to any college or scholarship source that you request. Decisions regarding college acceptance and award of scholarships are the result. This information is kept confidential and is released only according to your written instructions. To obtain an ACT application form, logon to www.actstudent.org, and click on online registration. When you visit the website you will find answers to other questions you may have as well.

The ACT measures knowledge, understanding, and skills acquired in the educational process. The test is made up of four distinct sections: English, mathematics, reading, and science reasoning.

In addition, you may register to take an optional fifth section: a 30-minute writing test. Some colleges require their applicants to take the writing test, but most do not. Check with the colleges to which you will be applying to know whether you need to take the writing part of the ACT.

On the ACT, you should answer all questions, because your score is based on the number of questions you answer correctly. There is no penalty for wrong answers. For each of the four tests the total number of correct responses yields a raw score. A table is used to convert the raw scores to *scaled scores*. The highest possible scaled score for each test is 36. The average of the four scaled scores yields the *composite score*.

The ACT English Test is a 75-question, 45-minute test that measures punctuation, grammar, usage, and sentence structure. The test consists of five passages, each accompanied by multiple-choice test items.

Test-Taking Strategies for the ACT English Test

1. Pace yourself. You have 45 minutes to complete 75 questions.

2. Read the sentences immediately before and after the one containing an underlined portion.

The ACT Mathematics Test has 60 questions to answer in 60 minutes. The test emphasizes quantitative reasoning rather than memorized formulas. Five content areas are included in the mathematics test. About 14 questions deal with pre-algebra topics, such as operations with whole numbers, decimals, fractions, and integers and about 10 questions deal with elementary algebra. Usually 18 questions are based on intermediate algebra and coordinate geometry. About 14 questions are based on plane geometry and usually four items are based on right triangle trigonometry and basic trigonometric identities.

Test-Taking Strategies for the ACT Mathematics Test

1. Spend an average of one minute on each question, less on the easy questions, more on the difficult ones.
2. Be sure to answer each question even if you have to guess.
3. Make sure your answers are reasonable.

The ACT Reading Test is a 40-question, 35-minute test that measures reading comprehension. Three scores are reported for this test: a total score, a subscore based on the 20 items in the social studies and natural sciences sections, and a subscore on the 20 items in the prose fiction and humanities   sections.

Test-Taking Strategies for the ACT Reading Test

1. Read each passage carefully. Underline important ideas in the passage.
2. Pace yourself. You have 40 questions to answer in 35 minutes.
3. Refer to the passage and in particular to your underlined sections when answering the questions.

The ACT Science Reasoning Test presents seven sets of scientific information in three different formats: data representations (graphs, tables, and other schematic forms); research summaries (description of experiments); and conflicting viewpoints. The 40 questions are to be answered in 35 minutes. The content of the test is drawn from biology, chemistry, physics, geology, astronomy, and meteorology. Background knowledge at the level of a high school general science course is all that is needed to answer these questions. The test emphasizes scientific reasoning skills rather than recall of scientific content, skill in mathematics, or reading ability.

Test-Taking Strategies for the ACT Science Reasoning Test

1. Read the scientific material before you begin answering a question. Read tables and text carefully, underlining important ideas.
2. Look for flaws in the experiments and devise ways of improving the experiments.
3. When you are asked to compare viewpoints, make notes in the margin of the printed material summarizing each viewpoint.

Beginning in the fall of 2015, students who take the ACT will also receive new readiness scores and indicators, which are designed to show performance and preparedness in areas important for success after high school. The addition of these new scores and indicators will provide students, parents, and educators with a more detailed insight to better plan for future success.

For more information on these changes, please refer to the web site, *act.org*

A FINAL WORD

Don't take any examination without preparation, even though you will find descriptions of these tests that say they test skills developed over years of study both in and out of school. Don't walk in cold, even though you believe that you meet all the qualities colleges are looking for.

Although the College Board suggests no special preparation, it does distribute to applicants the booklet, "Taking the SAT Reasoning Test." It also makes available other publications containing former test questions along with advice on how to cope with the questions. Evidently, all candidates need some form of preparation.

The American College Testing Program furnishes the booklet, "Preparing for the ACT Assessment." This gives specific information about the test, test questions, and strategies for taking each of the four parts. It also describes what to expect on the test day and gives practice with typical questions.

Barron's Educational Series publishes books to help you prepare for these tests. They are available at all bookstores and in many libraries. You should be sure to use them before taking any of these tests.

Although no high school student takes all of the college-entrance exams described above, virtually all students planning to attend a four-year college take at least one of them—the SAT or ACT. Prepare conscientiously for each exam that you take and you will provide the colleges to which you are applying with valuable information about your abilities. Good luck!

Ira K. Wolf
President
PowerPrep, Inc.

Don't be afraid to be yourself in every aspect of the applications process. No admissions officer wants to see the proverbial "perfect" application; rather, they're looking for individuals with unique stories, interests and voices that will contribute to the college community.

Arielle Shipper, Connecticut College, Class of 2010

The college admission process—getting in—begins the minute you start making your first choices in course selection and in cocurricular activities in junior high school, middle school, and high school. These initial and ongoing decisions are crucial to your future well-being. They lay the groundwork for the curriculum you will follow throughout your high school career: they are not easily reversed. These are the decisions that will allow you to market yourself to the colleges of your choice.

STUDENTS TAKE NOTE!

There is a myth prevalent among college-bound students throughout the country that the best way to gain entrance to the selective colleges is to be well rounded. This term usually refers to students who have earned good grades in high school (B+ or better) and participated in a wide range of cocurricular activities.

However, most admission officers at the selective colleges prefer applications from candidates they term angular—students who have demonstrated solid academic achievement in and out of school *and* who have developed one or two particularly strong cocurricular skills, interests, and activities. These angular students are very different in character from the well-rounded students who are very good at everything, yet excel at little, if anything.

William Fitzsimmons, Dean of Admission at Harvard, says that Harvard is looking for a well-rounded class, which means Harvard is most interested in admitting angular students—students who have excelled at something. He cautions, though, that "...It is a mistake to denigrate or underestimate that persuasive power of high grades, rank, triple 800s on the SAT, 36 on the ACT, and equally impressive SAT Subject Test scores. The selective colleges take many of these academically high profile applicants. But the numbers game alone often won't get you in! It would be fairly simple for Harvard to enroll an entire freshman class with a superior academic profile and little depth of quality in areas that make up the personality of the class. We just would not do that!"

Dean Fitzsimmons is saying that the majority of the successful applicants to selective colleges must have some major commitment(s) combined with excellent academic qualities. A strong impact results from quality involvements rather than a proliferation of joinings and transient interests. Essentially, the angular applicant is a committed individual, while the well-rounded candidate is merely involved.

STUDENTS AND PARENTS TAKE AN EARLY, ACTIVE ROLE

Students and parents must make time to ensure an early, active role in the college admissions process. Each year, starting in the seventh grade, students and parents should take the time to sit down with the student's guidance counselor and talk meaningfully about the following:
- selection and level of courses, projecting through the senior year of high school;
- cocurricular activities available, such as drama, music, athletics, academic clubs, community activities, student government, and other special interest groups; and
- summer study, work, or recreation.

Why is this important to getting in? As sure as taxes and death, there is going to come a time in your senior year when you, the college-bound student, will be asked to choose colleges, complete the college application, write your college essay(s), and have an interview—either on the college campus, or in your hometown.

You must create the personal marketing, which will take place during the application process in your senior year, long before your senior year starts. By the time you reach that long-awaited dream of being a senior, you and you alone have created the person you must market to the colleges of your choice. You must understand that the person you have created is the only person you have to market. There is no Madison Avenue glitz involved in this marketing process! You don't create a pseudo marketing campaign that shows you jumping off a bridge with a bungee cord tied to your sneakers. Admission counselors can tell the difference between a real marketing effort and a pseudo marketing campaign.

THE APPLICATION FORM

Each college on-line application form differs from college to college, with the exception of those colleges that use the common application. When you start to work, be sure to note all deadlines, follow all directions, be complete, be neat, fill out the geographical data with accurate facts, and type it all (unless you print exceptionally well). Always review the entire application before you start to fill it out, and complete the entire application before you start the next one. Remember the application is *you* to the admissions committee member reading it. Even though "a book should not be judged by its cover," appearances do influence opinions.

It is best to work through a rough draft of the application before you actually work on the application copy to be submitted. Remember to make a copy of all parts of the finished application in the event that your submission gets lost and a replacement must be sent.

You are responsible for giving the Secondary School Report, found in each application, directly to your high school guidance counselor. Your counselor is responsible for sending official copies of grades, rank in class (if any), the school's profile, and a written recommendation regarding you. It also is your responsibility to call or fill out the appropriate forms for either the SAT and/or SAT Subject Tests or the ACT, to send the appropriate test information directly to each college to which you have applied, even if your scores are on your high school transcript. Your college file will not be considered complete, and will not be sent to the admission committee for a decision, without these official scores. Additionally, many colleges want recommendations from one or two teachers. Choose wisely and allow each teacher plenty of time. Request letters from teachers who know you best. If English is your interest, be sure to choose an English teacher. If you are fluent in Spanish and have future interest in Spanish at college, ask the Spanish teacher. Remember, though you have many interests and have participated in many activities—you are developing an admissions package as part of your marketing of yourself. Emphasize your strengths and show how they are integrated into your activities and achievements.

Cocurricular activities usually are athletic or nonathletic. If you have won athletic awards, note them. If you have had the starring role in the spring musical for the last two years, say so. If you are an editor on the school newspaper, specify this. Admissions people view your activities with special interest. They realize how very time consuming these activities can be and how they sometimes bring very few accolades. List these activities in the order of importance to you. If you do not believe that the application allows you the opportunity to show your depth of commitment to one or two cocurricular areas, you may add an addendum. Use the KISS (Keep It Short and Simple) method. This is an addendum, not an essay, letter, or dissertation. Be honest!

Some applications have mini essays. When space is provided, be sure you are concise, clear, and grammatically correct. Here, less is more. Your ability to organize your thoughts and present them concisely is being tested. You will receive your chance to impress each college with your prose in the long essay segment of the application. Some colleges have as many as four long essays, whereas some require none. In addition to the short and long essay questions, some colleges ask the student for a graded paper signed by the teacher.

Some colleges encourage you to support your application with additional materials. If you are given this option, consider what will strengthen your application: musical tapes, art and/or photography portfolios, published writings, an exceptional graded term paper, all the additional opportunities for the college to get to know you better and for you to increase your image as an angular candidate. Such additions help the admissions committee to get a better handle on who you are in relation to other applicants. Be sure your presentation is clear and as professional as possible. These additions are not going to be evaluated by the admissions committee. Your material will be directed to the appropriate department for evaluation and an evaluative note will be sent back to the admissions committee. It is this note that will become part of your admissions package, the same way an athletic coach evaluates potential student/athletes.

Proofread all parts of the application. Be sure you, the student, place your signature where it is required. If you are not sending your application on-line, then place everything, including the registration fee check, in a large manila envelope and give it to your college guidance counselor. After adding the completed Secondary School Report to the application, your guidance counselor will mail it. Your job is now finished and the waiting begins!

E-Mail, On-line Services through the College or the Internet

Applying online directly to the college(s) of your choice and communicating by e-mail has made the college application process less time consuming and easier than ever before. Certainly ecologically correct, by producing as close to a paperless process as possible, this method is still in cyberspace. Be sure you know what you are doing when you use any of these methods. It is seriously suggested that you take the time to call the college shortly after sending this type of application, to ensure that your application is on file. If you have an addendum or two, you may want to speak to an admission clerk to make sure each addendum has reached the office of admission in the format you desired. If it were my application and I chose any of these methods, I'd still send my musical tape, the slides for my art portfolio, and such, by certified or registered mail. Clarity is so important to the professionals who will be evaluating these addenda for your college admission process!

The Common Application

Almost all colleges in the United States have agreed that students may apply to their colleges by completing one common application. Some of the colleges using the common application also have their own application. Students applying to a college that allows an applicant a choice of using either the college's own application or the common application, obviously face a choice. The use of the common application substantially reduces the time spent composing different essay answers and neatly typing separate application forms. If you are one of those who must make a choice between the common application and the application of the college, you should understand that each college using the common application (either as its only application or as an alternative application) has the right to ask for a supplement. If you choose the common application, be very sure to read the pages surrounding the common application carefully. Each college has a paragraph in which they discuss their deadlines, requirements for admission, and specify if they require supplemental information. The supplemental information can range from an additional essay or two, to additional information about your cocurricular activities.

All the colleges participating in the common application have each member of their admission staff sign a statement that they will NOT discriminate in the admissions process among students who submit the common application versus students who submit the college's application. However, there are counselors who believe that when there is a choice, the applicant has a better chance of conveying information by using the college's application; there is a vast difference in format between the two applications, even if the college requires a supplement. Check with your guidance counselor if you are unsure regarding your choice of format. To access the common application online, go to:

www.commonapp.org

College Web Sites

Most colleges today have their own web site. Here you will find a wealth of information. Some colleges have even put their viewbook, course curriculum guide, a campus tour, as well as their application, on their site. Visit each college's web page—the addresses are in the Admissions Contact section of the college Profiles in this book. You'll be a much better informed consumer.

THE INTERVIEW

The interview is a contrived situation that few people enjoy, of which many people misunderstand the value, and about which everyone is apprehensive. However, no information from a college catalog, no friend's friend, no high school guidance counselor's comments, and no parental remembrances from bygone days can surpass the value of your college campus visit and interview. This first hand opportunity to assess your future alma mater will confirm or contradict other impressions and help you make a sound college acceptance.

Many colleges will recommend or request a personal interview. It is best to travel to the campus to meet with a member of the admissions staff if you can; however, if you can't, many colleges will arrange to have one of their representatives, usually an alumnus, interview you in your hometown.

Even though the thought of an interview might give you enough butterflies to lift you to the top of your high school's flagpole, here are some tips that might make it a little easier.

1. **Go prepared.** Read the college's catalog and this book's Profile ahead of time so you won't ask "How many books are in your library?" or "How many students do you have?" Ask intelligent questions that introduce a topic of conversation that you want the interviewer to know about you. The key is to distinguish yourself in a positive way from thousands of other applicants. Forge the final steps in the marketing process you have been building since your first choices in the college admission process back in junior high school. The interview is your chance to enhance those decisions.

2. **Nervousness** is absolutely and entirely normal. The best way to handle it is to admit it, out loud, to the interviewer. Richard Shaw, Dean of Undergraduate Admissions and Financial Aid at Stanford University, sometimes relates this true story to his apprehensive applicants. One extremely agitated young applicant sat opposite him for her interview with her legs crossed, wearing loafers on her feet. She swung her top leg back and forth to some inaudible rhythm. The loafer on her top foot flew off her foot, hit him in the

head, ricocheted to the desk lamp and broke it. She looked at him in terror, but when their glances met, they both dissolved in laughter. The moral of the story—the person on the other side of the desk is also a human being and wants to put you at ease. So admit to your anxiety, and don't swing your foot if you're wearing loafers! (And by the way, she was admitted.)

3. **Be yourself.** Nobody's perfect, and everyone knows nobody's perfect, so admit to a flaw or two before the interviewer goes hunting for them. The truly impressive candidate will convey a thorough knowledge of self.

4. **Interview the interviewer.** Don't passively sit there and allow the interviewer to ask all the questions and direct the conversation. Participate in this responsibility by assuming an active role. A thoughtful questioner will accomplish three important tasks in a successful interview:

demonstrate interest, initiative, and maturity for taking partial responsibility for the content of the conversation; **guide the conversation** to areas where he/she feels most secure and accomplished; and **obtain answers.** Use your genuine feelings to react to the answers you hear. If you are delighted to learn of a certain program or activity, show it. If you are curious, ask more questions. If you are disappointed by something you learn, try to find a path to a positive answer. Then consider yourself lucky that you discovered this particular inadequacy in time.

5. **Parents** do belong in your college decision process as your advisers! Often it is they who spend the megabucks for your next four years. They can provide psychological support and a stabilizing influence for sensible, rational decisions. However, they do NOT belong in your interview session. In essence, the sage senior will find constructive ways to include parents in the decision-making process as catalysts, without letting them take over (as many are apt to do) the interview process. You may want your parents to meet and speak briefly to your interviewer prior to your interview and that is fine, but parents may not accompany you into the interview session! Arrange with your parents to meet somewhere out of the interview building after your interview is over. You do not want the interviewer inviting your parents back to the interview room. As intelligent as parents may be, they do not perceive the answers to questions the same way you do. The worst scenario I can imagine is the interviewer asking your parents some of the same questions that were asked you, and that is highly likely. Parents just answer questions differently than teenagers. At best, the scenario creates a long, long ride home, and when you get home you can't punish your parents by taking the car keys away from them, or grounding them for a week. At worst, the scenario has caused a blight in your admissions file. This is your time! Keep it that way!

6. **Practice makes perfect.** Begin your interviews at colleges that are low on your list of preferred choices, and leave your first-choice colleges until last. If you are shy, you will have a chance to practice vocalizing what your usually silent inner voice tells you. Others will have the opportunity to commit their inevitable first blunders where they won't count as much.

7. **Departing impressions.** There is a remarkable tendency for the student to base final college preferences on the quality of the interview only, or on the personal reaction to the interviewer as the personification of the entire institution. Do not do yourself the disservice of letting it influence an otherwise rational selection, one based on institutional programs, students, services, and environment. After the last good-bye and thank you has been smiled, and you exhale deeply on your way out the door, go ahead and congratulate yourself. If you used the interview properly, you will know whether or not you wish to attend that college and why.

8. **Send a thank-you note** to your interviewer. A short and simple handwritten or typed note will do—and if you forgot to mention something important about yourself at the interview, here's your chance.

WRITING THE COLLEGE ESSAY

Do the colleges read the essays you write on their applications? You bet your diploma they do. Here is your chance to strut your stuff, stand up, be counted, and stylize your way into the hearts of the decision makers.

Write it, edit it, review it. Rewrite it. Try to show why you are unique and how the college will benefit having you in its student body. This is not a routine homework assignment, but a college level essay that will be carefully examined for spelling, grammar, content, and style of a high school senior. As strenuous an effort as it may be, completing the essay gives the admissions committee a chance to know the real you, a three-dimensional human being with passions, preferences, strengths, weaknesses, imagination, energy, and ambition. Your ability to market yourself will help the deans and directors of admission remember your application from among the sea of thousands that flood their offices each year.

First, maximize your strengths—use your essays to say what you want to say. The answer to a specific question on the college's part still provides an opening for you to furnish background information about yourself, your interests, ambitions, and insights. For example, the essay that asks you to name your favorite book and the reason for your selection could be answered with the title of a Dr. Seuss book because you are considering a career as an elementary school teacher. If you are interested in business, read about a famous businessman you admire and then discuss your interest in business.

Whatever the essay questions are, autobiographical or otherwise, select the person or issue that puts you in the position to discuss the subject in which you are the most well versed. In essence, all of your essay responses are autobiographical in the sense that they will illustrate something important about yourself, your values, and the kind of person you are (or hope to become). If personal values are important to you, and they should be, then here is your opportunity to stress their importance.

Because many colleges will ask for more than one essay, make sure that the *sum* of the essays in any one college application covers your best points. Do not repeat your answers, even if the questions sound alike. Cover the most important academic and cocurricular activities (most important meaning the one in which you excelled and/or in which you spent the most quality time).

If you are fortunate to have a cooperative English teacher, you might request a critique of your first draft, but be sure to allow enough time for a careful evaluation and your revision.

Write the essays yourself—no substitutes or stand-ins. College admission professionals can discern mature adult prose from student prose.

PARTING WORDS

You may wish to ask yourself the following questions to help you decide which is your Paradise College. Most of this information is in the individual college Profiles in this book.

1. **Caliber of School Programs**   Is the college known for its English department or chemistry department? What are its strengths?

2. **Selectivity of Admissions**   Is the college Most Competitive, Highly Competitive, Very Competitive, Competitive, Less Competitive or Noncompetitive? Check the Selector Ratings.

3. **Chances of Admission**   Be realistic. What are your chances of getting in? How far can you reach? Listen when you are given advice!

4. **Location of the School**   Is the school near home, one hour away, 300 miles away, or across the United States?

5. **Rural, Suburban, Urban Campus**   Is the school in the city or in a rural area?

6. **Size of the School**   Can you spend four years at a small liberal arts college of 800 undergraduates? Do you need the larger atmosphere of a university? Do not equate size with social life!

7. **State College vs. Private College**   Is the college a large state university with most of the student population from the state where it's located? Is it one of the public "Ivies"? Will you be a minority in the state school?

8. **Geographical Diversity**   Is the college a regional one attracting students from the same state or region? Or is it a college, regardless of its size, which attracts students from all over the United States, or the world at large?

9. **Cost of College**   What is the tuition? What are the living costs? What travel costs are there from home to campus? Are there hidden costs?

10. **Financial Aid**   With a great percentage of undergraduates at many private colleges on financial aid of some type, where do you fit? What monies are available for the students at the schools of your choice? Is the college need blind in its admission program?

11. **Living Conditions**   Is housing on campus guaranteed for all four years? Are the dorms coed? Are there single-sex dorms? Are alternatives in housing available?

12. **Socialization**   Is it a grind school—all work, work, work? Is it fraternity- and sorority-oriented? What are the on-campus facilities for socialization?

13. **Safety on Campus**   Are the dorms secure and locked? What's the safety system on the campus?

14. **Core Curriculum—Distribution Credits**   Does the college require (for graduation) a specific number of credits in different academic disciplines? For example, does the student have to take six credits in philosophy before graduating? Is a self-designed curriculum possible?

15. **Sophomore Standing**   Does the college accept AP credits? Does it offer advanced standing for an AP course, or just a credit toward graduation?

16. **Junior Year Abroad**   Are there opportunities to study in Italy, Japan, or Australia, for example, while you are an undergraduate?

17. **Internships**   Are there opportunities for hands-on experience while in college? Which departments have formal internship opportunities?

18. **Graduate School After College**   What percentage of its graduates go on to graduate school immediately upon graduation, or within five years? What is the record of those who successfully get into the law, medical, or business school of their choice?

19. **Placement After Graduation**   Is there an office for job placement after college? Is there an alumni network that helps in job placement?

20. **Weekend College**   Do the students remain on campus on weekends, or is it a suitcase college?

21. **Minorities**   What percentage of the students are minorities? Reflect on the racial, ethnic, and religious minority roles in the college you are considering. How would you feel being Jewish at a Roman Catholic college for example—or Catholic at a Jewish college?

22. **Sports Facilities**   Is there a swimming pool? Are there horse stables? Is there an ice hockey rink on campus?

23. **Library Facilities**   How many books are in the library? Is it computerized? Is the campus library tied into a larger network?

24. **Athletic Programs**   Is the ice hockey team a varsity sport? Does the lacrosse team play Division I or III? Is basketball strong? Do they have a women's squash team?

25. **Honors Programs**   Are honors programs available? What are they? Who is eligible?

26. **Student Body**   Are the students politically active? Are they professional in orientation?

27. **Faculty**   Are all classes taught by full professors? Or are TAs (teaching assistants) the norm?

28. **Computer Labs**   Are computers required of incoming freshmen? What are the facilities on campus? Can you have your own PC in your room?

29. **Campus Visits**   If possible, make a visit to the campus. Spend some time talking to students for a feel of the campus.

30. **Special Talents**   Recognize your special talents and discover where they fit best. Often, a special talent becomes a scale-tipper in the admissions process.

31. **Special Family Circumstances**   Talk with your parents about their expectations. Discuss your needs as well as their thoughts.

32. **Legacy**   Does your family have a history at a specific school? Are you interested in continuing the tradition?

33. **Note Well—Final List**   Be sure the final list is a realistic one. It should include "reaches," "targets," and "safeties." No matter which one admits you—it must fit!

Finding and applying to the best colleges for you is not supposed to be easy, but it can be fun. Parents, guidance counselors, and teachers are there to help you, so don't struggle alone. Keep your sense of humor and a smile on your face as you go about researching, exploring, and discovering your ideal college.

Last but not least is The Parent Credo: The right college is the one where your child will fit in scholastically and socially. Be realistic in your aspirations and support the child's choice!

Anthony F. Capraro, III, Ph.D.
President, Teach Inc.
College Counseling
Ocoee, Florida

Sometimes getting more aid is a matter of simply applying for it.
Raymond A. Lutzky, Rensselaer Polytechnic Institute, Class of 2002

Postsecondary education is a major American industry. A greater proportion of students pursue postsecondary education in the United States than in any other industrialized country. Annually, more than 13 million students study at over 8000 institutions of higher learning. The diversity of our system of higher education is admired by educators and students throughout the world. There is no reason to believe that this system will change in the future. However, college costs and the resources available to parents and students to meet those costs have changed.

Unfortunately, many high school students and their parents believe either that there is no financial aid available or that they will not qualify for any type of financial assistance from any source. Neither assumption is correct. College costs have increased and will continue to increase. Federal allocations, for some financial aid programs, have decreased. But this decline has been met with generous increases in financial aid from state and school sources.

American students and their parents should realize that they must assume the primary role in planning to meet their future college costs and that the family financial planning process must begin much earlier than has been the case.

COLLEGE COSTS

- Nearly all parents believe college costs are too expensive.
- Currently, the average cost of education, including tuition and fees for one year at a public college would have been about $23,000 and for a private college and university, the cost could have exceeded $45,000.
- While college costs will increase each year, it is important to remember that currently a majority of all college students attend schools with tuition costs below $5,000.

STUDENT FINANCIAL AID

- In 2015, the total amount of financial aid available from federal, state, and institutional sources to postsecondary students is approximately $170 billion.
- A majority of all students enrolled in higher education receive some type of financial assistance.
- Federal student aid remains the largest source of funding.
- Not long ago the majority of federal financial assistance was grants. Today, a greater amount of financial aid is from loan money.

TIMETABLE FOR APPLYING FOR FINANCIAL AID

Sophomore Year of High School

Most families wait until a child has been accepted into a college or university to begin planning on how the family will meet those college costs. However, a family's college financial planning should begin much earlier.

Students, as early as the sophomore year of high school, should begin a systematic search for colleges that offer courses of study that are of interest. There are many computer programs that can be helpful in this process. These programs can match a student's interest with colleges fitting the profile. Considering that half of all students who enter college either drop out or transfer to another school, this type of early selection analysis can be invaluable.

After selecting certain schools for further consideration, you should write to the school and request a viewbook, catalog, and financial aid brochure. After receiving this information, you and your family should compare the schools. Your comparison should include academic considerations as well as financial. Don't rule out a school because you think you can't afford it. Remember the financial aid programs at that school may be more generous than at a lower-priced school. If possible, visit the college and speak with both an admission and financial aid counselor. If it is not possible to visit all the schools, call the schools and obtain answers to your questions about admission, financial aid, and placement after graduation.

Junior Year of High School

The comparative analysis of colleges and universities that you began in your sophomore year should continue in your junior year. By the completion of your junior year, you and your parents should have some idea of what it will cost to attend and the financial aid policies of each of the schools you are considering.

Some colleges and universities offer prospective applicants an early estimate of their financial aid award. This estimate is based upon information supplied by the family and can provide assistance in planning a family's budget. Remember that for most families, financial aid from federal, state, and school sources will probably not meet the total cost of attendance.

Families should remember that college costs can be met over the course of the academic year. It is not necessary to have all of the money needed to attend school available at the beginning of the academic year. Student and family savings, as well as student employment throughout the year, can be used to meet college costs.

Senior Year of High School

January

By January of your senior year of high school you should know which colleges and universities you want to receive your financial aid application forms. Be certain that you have completed not only the federal financial aid application form, but also any necessary state or school forms. Read carefully all of the instructions. Application methods and deadline dates may differ from one college to another. Submit an application clean of erasures or notations in the margins, and sign all of the application forms.

February

You will receive a report from the service agency you selected containing information on your family's expected contribution and your eligibility for financial aid. You and your parents should discuss the results of the financial aid application with regard to family contribution, educational costs, and how those costs can be met.

March

Beginning in March, most colleges begin to make financial aid decisions. If your application is complete, your chances of receiving an award letter early are greater than if additional information is required.

The financial aid award letter you receive from your school serves as your official document indicating the amount of financial aid you will receive for the year. You must sign and return a copy of the award letter to your school if you agree to accept their offer of financial aid.

If your family's financial circumstances change and you need additional funding, you should make an appointment to speak with your school's financial aid director or counselor. College financial aid personnel are permitted to exercise professional judgment and make adjustments to a student's financial need. Your letter of appeal should state explicitly how much money you need and why you need it.

TIPS ON APPLYING FOR FINANCIAL AID

1. Families can no longer wait until a child is accepted into college before deciding how they will finance that education. Earlier college financial planning is necessary.

2. Families should assume a much more active role in locating the resources necessary to fund future college costs.

3. Families should assume that college costs will continue to increase.

4. Families should assume that in the future the federal government will not substantially increase financial aid allocations.

5. Families should obtain information on a wide range of colleges including the many excellent low-cost schools.

6. Families should seek information about all of the funding sources available at each school they are considering.

7. Families should seek the advice and expertise of financial experts for college financing strategies. College financial planning should specify the amount of money a family should invest or save each month in order to meet future college bills.

8. Families should investigate all of the legitimate ways of reducing their income and assets before filing for financial aid.

9. Families should know how financial aid is awarded and the financial aid policies and programs of each school they are considering.

10. Families should realize that although the job of financing a college education rests primarily with them, they probably will not be able to save the entire cost of their child's college education. They probably will be eligible to receive some type of financial aid from some source and they will have to borrow a portion of their child's college education costs.

11. Families should be advised that the federal government frequently changes the rules and regulations governing financial aid eligibility. Check with your high school guidance counselor or college financial aid administrator for the latest program qualifications.

12. Part-time employment during the school year and full-time employment during the summer should be a part of every family's financing plan.

13. Families should investigate all colleges and universities that offer three-year graduation options.

14. Not every student can afford to live on campus. Commuting to college is one way to reduce college costs

15. It is important to find out a school's policy on awarding financial aid on the basis of need and merit.

16. Check with the financial aid office on the availability of loan forgiveness programs.

17. Find out if the aid awarded in the first year will be awarded in subsequent years if the family income does not change.

18. Find out the statistics on graduating seniors: how many were employed or accepted to graduate schools at the time of graduation.

19. Plan for the future. What was the average debt of graduating students in each of the schools you applied to?

20. Going to college should be a family decision. All family members should be aware of the financial implications of attendance, not just for the first year, but for all four years.

Marguerite J. Dennis
Former Vice President for Enrollment
and International Programs
Suffolk University
Boston, Massachusetts

SURVIVING THE FRESHMAN YEAR

Explore the campus and make yourself aware of all it has to offer. Most colleges have what seems like an endless supply of resources for its students. By taking advantage of these resources sooner, rather than later, they will prepare you for the years to come.

Shannon Scott, James Madison University, Class of 2013

COLLEGE: IT'S DIFFERENT

In college you are likely to hear fellow students say, "I don't know what that prof *wants*, and she won't *tell* me." "I wrote about three papers in high school, and now they want one every week." Though these students may be exaggerating a bit, college *is* different, both in the quality and the amount of work expected. Sometimes in high school the basic concepts of a course are reduced to a set of facts on a study sheet, handed to students to be reviewed and learned for a test.

In college, it is the concepts and ideas that are most important. These can only be grasped through a real understanding of the facts as they interrelate and form larger patterns. Writing papers and answering essay questions on tests can demonstrate a genuine understanding of the concepts, and this is why they are so important to college instructors. Learning to deal with ideas in this way can be a long-term asset, developing your independence, intellectual interests, and self-awareness.

Don't be discouraged; you are not alone. Most of your fellow students are having equally difficult times adjusting to a new learning method. Persist, and you will improve, leading to a lifetime habit of critical thinking and problem solving that can benefit you in many important ways.

College is also different outside of classes. Now that you have the freedom to choose how to spend time and what types of relationships to make, you have a bewildering number of possibilities.

In high school, you competed against the entire population, and you did well enough to get accepted into college. But now the population has changed, and you are competing against the very best high school students, many of whom may have better academic profiles than you. Because of this reality, you need to be at your best from day one. Here are some tips to help you.

MAKING A GOOD IMPRESSION

Here you are, plopped down in a strange place, feeling a bit like Dorothy transported to Oz. Your first goal is to make a good impression, showing your best self to those who will be important in your life for the next four years and even longer.

Impressing Faculty Members Favorably

Faculty members come in all ranks, from the graduate assistant, who teaches part-time while pursuing a degree, to a lofty full professor, who teaches primarily graduate students. Though different in rank and seniority, they respond to their students in roughly the same ways. They are, after all, people, with families and relationships much like your own. To have a good working relationship with them, try the following suggestions:

- **Make up your own mind about your instructors.** Listening to other students talk about teachers can be confusing. If you listen long enough, you will hear arguments for and against each of them. Don't allow hearsay to affect your own personal opinion.
- **Get to know your instructors firsthand.** Set up a meeting, during regular office hours. Don't try to settle important issues in the few moments before and after class.
- **Approach a discussion of grades carefully.** If you honestly believe that you have been graded too low, schedule a conference. Do not attack your instructor's integrity or judgment. Instead, say that you had expected your work

to result in a better grade and would like to know ways to improve. Be serious about overcoming faults.
- **Don't make excuses.** Instructors have heard them all and can rarely be fooled. Accept responsibility for your mistakes, and learn from them.
- **Pay attention in class.** Conversing and daydreaming can insult your instructor and inhibit the learning process.
- **Arrive ahead of time for class.** You will be more relaxed, and you can use these moments to review notes or talk with classmates. You also demonstrate to your instructor a commitment to the class.
- **Participate in class discussions.** Ask questions and give answers to the instructor's questions. Nothing pleases an instructor more than an intelligent question that proves you are interested and prepared.
- **Learn from criticism.** It is an instructor's job to correct your errors in thinking. Don't take in-class criticism personally.

Impressing Fellow Students Favorably

Relationships with other students can be complex, but there are some basic suggestions that may make life easier in the residence halls and classrooms:

- **Don't get into the habit of bragging.** Frequent references to your wealth, your outstanding friends, your social status, or your family's successes are offensive to others.
- **Don't pry.** When your fellow students share their feelings and problems, listen carefully and avoid any tendency to intrude or ask embarrassing questions.
- **Don't borrow.** Borrowing a book, a basketball, or a few bucks may seem like a small thing to you, but some people who have trouble saying no may resent your request.
- **Divide chores.** Do your part; agree on a fair division of work in a lab project or a household task.
- **Support others.** Respect your friends' study time and the "Do not disturb" signs on their doors. Helping them to reach their goals will help you as well.
- **Allow others to be upset.** Sometimes, turning someone's anger into a joke, minimizing their difficulties, or belittling their frustration is your worst response. Support them by letting them release their emotions.
- **Don't preach.** Share your opinions when asked for, but don't try to reform the world around you.
- **Tell the truth.** Your reputation is your most important asset. When you make an agreement, keep it.

MANAGING YOUR TIME

Everyone, no matter how prominent or how insignificant, has 168 hours a week to spend. In this one asset we are all equal. There are students on every college campus, however, who seem to accomplish all their goals and still find time for play and socializing. There are others who seem to be alternating between frantic dashes and dull idleness, accomplishing very little. To the first group, college is a happy, fulfilling experience; to the latter, it is maddeningly frustrating. The first group has gained control of time, the second is controlled by that elusive and precious commodity.

- **Know where your time goes.** Unfortunately, we cannot store up time as we do money, to be used when the need is greatest. We use it as it comes, and it is amazing how it sometimes comes slowly (as in the last five minutes of a Friday afternoon class) or quickly (as in the last hour before a final exam). The first step in controlling time is to determine exactly how you use it. For a while, at least, you should carefully record how much time you spend in class, going to and from class, studying, sleeping, eating, listening to music, watching television, and running errands. You need to know what happens to your 168 hours. Only then can you make sensible decisions about managing them.

- **Make a weekly schedule.** You can schedule your routine for the week, using the time plan forms available at most college bookstores or by making your own forms.

- **First schedule the inflexible blocks of time.** Your class periods, transportation time, sleeping, and eating will form relatively routine patterns throughout the week. Trying to shave minutes off these important activities is often a mistake.

- **Plan your study time.** It is preferable, though not always possible, to set your study hours at the same time every weekday. Try to make your study time *prime time*, when your body and mind are ready for a peak performance.

- **Plan time for fun.** No one should plan to spend four years of college as a working robot. Fun and recreation are important, but they can be enjoyed in short periods just as well as long. For example, jogging with friends for 30 minutes can clear the mind, tone up the muscles, and give you those all-important social contacts. Parties and group activities can be scheduled for weekends.

- **Be reasonable in your time allotments.** As you progress through your freshman year, you will learn more precisely how much time is required to write a paper or complete a book report. Until then, schedule some extra minutes for these tasks. You are being unfair to yourself by planning one hour for a job that requires two.

- **Allow flexibility.** The unexpected is to be expected. There will be interruptions to your routine and errands that must be run at certain times. Allow for these unforeseen circumstances.

LISTENING AND NOTE-TAKING IN CLASS

Listening

If you're interested in really improving your chances for success in college, you'll want to evaluate your listening skills to see if there are changes that you need to make. You'll also want to become familiar with note-taking strategies that can help you get more out of a lecture or PowerPoint presentation.

There is a difference between hearing and listening. Hearing just means that your ears are doing what they're designed to do; they're picking up sound waves. Listening requires that you pay attention and process information for later retrieval.

Here are some helpful tips for active listening.

1. Check the syllabus so that you'll be ready to discuss the topic for the day. Also, be sure to see if there's an assignment due in class so that you won't be caught off guard.

2. Reading the assignment before going to class really increases the chance of you being able to understand what is being presented. (Reading before class lays the foundation for the material that is given in class.)

3. Regular attendance at class is important, whether a professor requires it or not. Make class attendance a top priority and attend all classes.

4. Prepare mentally to pay attention to gain as much information as you can.

5. Sit in the "T-zone," or what is referred to in the military as "front and center."

6. Watch your posture. Don't slouch, but sit up straight and focus on what is being said or shown.

7. Do your best to stay healthy. Exercise, good nutrition, and adequate rest can all contribute to your being an active listener in class.

Being a more active listener can definitely lead to greater academic success.

Distractions can be a major problem in class, so here are some tips that may help you win the battle over distractions:

1. Don't sit with a friend.

2. Take careful notes. Taking notes helps you stay focused and can help all types of learners gain more information from a lecture.

3. Drinking water during class may help keep you from getting tired.

4. Avoid distractions during class such as the Internet, e-mail, or cell phones.

5. If you find yourself distracted by hunger, eat something before class or bring a "quiet" snack.

6. Plan ahead so that you arrive on time.

Note-taking

Effective note-taking will provide more material that will help you prepare adequately for tests and quizzes.

Tips for Effective Note-taking:

If you plan on handwriting your notes, consider the following:

1. Using a three ring binder with dividers for each subject is an effective way to take notes. Handouts don't get misplaced. They can easily be punched and added to notes taken in class. Notes can be removed and grouped together when studied.

2. Record the information from PowerPoints, drawings, charts, etc. when copies are not provided for the class.

3. Consider talking to professors and having them assess your note-taking in their classes.

The amount of material that you record should reflect the emphasis that was placed on the subject during the lecture.

You may want to take notes on your computer, but there are some things to consider:

1. The use of a computer in class is receiving mixed reviews from professors. Some welcome technology as a learning aid, while others reject it because it is a distraction.

2. If you want to take notes on your computer, you need to ask each professor.

3. Determine what note-taking or word processing software you're going to use. You may be able to use note-taking software, such as Notes PP or Microsoft OneNote. Most note-taking software allows you to easily format and customize your notes. If you choose word processing software, make sure you don't waste too much time formatting during the lecture. This could lead to missing valuable information given by your professor.

4. Power up your lap top prior to class. If possible, sit by a power outlet. This will ensure that your computer won't go dead during the middle of a lecture. Turn the brightness of your monitor down, so as not to draw attention to yourself. Make sure you have the mute function turned on.

5. Avoid distractions, such as instant messaging, e-mail, and the Internet.

6. Use the keyboard or a computer pen tablet. Keyboards allow you to type data, while you'll be able to draw and write notes with the help of a computer pen tablet. You may choose to stick with the keyboard method if you type faster than you write. For certain classes, such as engineering and science, you may find that the computer pen tablet provides you with greater note-taking flexibility.

You should be aware that some recent research indicates that taking notes on a computer is less effective than on paper, so choose wisely.

Note-taking Systems

There are several styles of taking notes:

Outline. This works best when the professor presents material in a very structured format. It's easy when main points and subpoints are clearly identified during a presentation. Outlining increases retention and memory recall, because you are determining how points relate to one another as you record them.

Block Style. This is very similar to outlines, but without the Roman numerals and letters. Main ideas are written flush with the left margin. Subpoints and bullets are indented to indicate their relationship to the main points.

Paragraphs. This works well when a main theme is presented with ideas and examples supporting it.

Visual (or Concept) Maps. They are made up of lines and circles. They help you to be able to see how each part fits together to form the whole picture. These maps work great for visual learners.

STUDYING EFFECTIVELY

Your most important activity in college is studying. Efficient study skills separate the inept student (who may spend just as many hours studying as an "A" student) from the excellent student, who thinks while studying and who uses common sense strategies to discover the important core of courses. The following suggested game plan for good study has worked in the past; it can work for you.

- **Make a commitment.** It is universally recommended that you spend two hours studying for every hour in class. At the beginning of your college career, be determined to do just that. It doesn't get easy until you make up your mind to do it.

- **Do the tough jobs first.** If certain courses are boring or particularly difficult, study them first. Don't read the interesting, enjoyable materials first, saving the toughies for the last sleepy twinges of your weary brain.

- **Study in short sessions.** Three two-hour sessions, separated from each other by a different activity, are much better than a long six-hour session.

- **Use your bits of time.** Use those minutes when you're waiting for a bus, a return call, laundry to wash, or a friend to arrive. Some of the best students I know carry 3 × 5 cards filled with definitions, formulas, or equations and learn during brief waiting periods. Most chief executives form the habit early of using bits of time wisely.

Digesting a Textbook

1. **Preview chapters.** Before you read a chapter in your textbook, preview it. Quickly examine the introductory paragraphs, headings, tables, illustrations, and other features of the chapter. The purpose is to discover the major topics. Then you can read with increased comprehension because you know where the author is leading.

2. **Underline the important points as you read.** Underlining should never be overdone; it can leave your textbook almost completely marked and less legible to read. Only the major ideas and concepts should be highlighted.

3. **Seven categories of information are commonly found in textbooks.** Be particularly alert when you see the following; get your marking pen ready.
   Definitions of terms.
   Types or *categories* of items.
   Methods of accomplishing certain tasks.
   Sequences of events or stages in a process.
   Reasons or *causes*.
   Results or *effects*.
   Contrasts or *comparisons* between items.

4. **Repeat information you need to learn.** When the object is to learn information, nothing is so effective as reciting the material, either silently or aloud.

5. **Don't read all material the same way.** Decide what you need to learn from the material and read accordingly. You read a work of fiction to learn the characters and the narrative; a poem, to learn an idea, an emotion, or a theme: a work of history, to learn the interrelationships of events. Do not read every sentence with the same speed and concentration; learn when to skim rapidly along. Remember, your study time is limited and the trick is to discriminate between the most important and the least important. No one can learn *everything* equally well.

6. **The five-minute golden secret.** As soon as possible after class is over—preferably at your desk in the classroom—skim through the chapter that has just been covered, marking the points primarily discussed. Copy what was written on the board. Now you know what the professor thinks is important!

TAKING TESTS SKILLFULLY

Try to predict the test questions. At some college libraries, copies of old examinations are made available to students. If you can legally find out your professor's previous test methods do so.

Ask your professor to describe the format of the upcoming test: multiple-choice? true-false? essay questions? problems? Adjust your study to the format described.

Listen for clues in the professor's lecture. Sometimes the questions posed in class have a way of reappearing on tests. If a statement is repeated several times or recurs in a subsequent lecture, note it as important.

As you review for the test, devise questions based on the material, and answer them. If you are part of a study group, have members ask questions of the others.

Common Sense Tactics

Arrive on the scene early; relax by breathing deeply. If the instructor gives instructions while distributing the test, listen very carefully.

- **Scan the whole test first.** Notice the point value for each section and budget your time accordingly.

- **Read the directions carefully** and then reread them. Don't lose points because you misread the directions.

- **Answer the short, easy questions first.** A bit of early success stimulates the mind and builds your confidence.

- **Leave space between answers.** You may think of a brilliant comment to add later.

- **Your first instinct is often the best** in answering true-false and multiple-choice questions. Look for qualifiers such as *never, all, often,* or *seldom* in true-false statements. Usually a qualifier that is absolute (*never, all,* or *none*) will indicate a false statement. Work fast on short-answer questions: they seldom count many points.

- **Open-book tests are no picnic.** Don't think that less study is required for an open-book test. They are often the most difficult of all examinations. If the material is unfamiliar, you won't have time to locate it and learn it during the test period.

Important Essay Strategies

- **Read the question carefully** and find out exactly what is asked for. If you are asked to contrast the French Revolution with the American Revolution and you spend your time describing each, without any contrasting references, your grade will be lowered.

- **Know the definitions of key words** used in essay questions:
    analyze: discuss the component parts.
    compare: examine for similarities.
    criticize: give a judgment or evaluation.
    define: state precise meaning of terms.
    describe: give a detailed picture of qualities and characteristics.
    discuss: give the pros and cons; debate them, and come to a conclusion.
    enumerate: briefly mention a number of ideas, things, or events.
    evaluate: give an opinion, with supporting evidence.
    illustrate: give examples (illustrations) relating to a general statement.
    interpret: usually means to state in other words, to explain, make clear.
    outline: another way of asking for brief listings of principal ideas or characteristics. Normally the sentence or topic outline format is not required.
    prove: give evidence and facts to support the premise stated in the test.
    summarize: give an abbreviated account, with your conclusions.

- **Write a short outline** before you begin your essay. This organizes your thinking, making you less likely to leave out major topics.

- **Get to the point immediately.** Don't get bogged down in a lengthy introduction.

- **Read your essay over** before you hand it in. Words can be left out or misspelled. Remember that essay answers are graded somewhat subjectively, and papers that are correctly and neatly written make a better impression.

- **Learn from your test paper** when it is returned. Students who look at a test grade and discard the paper are throwing away a valuable tool. Analyze your mistakes honestly; look for clues for improvement in the professor's comments.

WRITING A TERM PAPER

Doing convincing library research and writing a term paper with correct footnotes and bibliography is a complicated procedure. Most first-year English composition courses include this process. Good students will work hard to master this skill because they know that research papers are integral parts of undergraduate and graduate courses.

Many students make the mistake of waiting until near the deadline to begin a term paper. At the busy end of the term, with final exams approaching, they embark on the uncertain time span of research and writing. Begin your term paper early, when the library staff is unhurried and ready to help and when you are under less pressure. It will pay dividends.

REGULATING YOUR RELATIONSHIPS

Find your special friends who believe in your definition of success. In a fast-paced environment like college, it is important to spend most of your time with people who share your ideas toward learning, where you can be yourself, without defensiveness. To find your kind of friends, first ask yourself: What is success? Is it a secure position and a comfortable home? A life of serving others? A position of power with a commodious executive suite? A challenging job that allows you to be creative? When you have answered honestly, you will have a set of long-range personal goals, and you can begin looking for kindred souls to walk with you on the road to success.

There will be, of course, some persons around you who are determined not to succeed, who for some reason program their lives for failure. Many college freshmen never receive a college degree; some may start college with no intention of passing courses. Their goal is to spend one hectic term as a party animal. If you intend to succeed at college, spending time among this type will be a considerable handicap. Consider making friends who will be around longer than the first year.

If possible, steer clear of highly emotional relationships during your first year of college. You don't have time for a broken heart, and relationships that begin with a rush often end that way.

MAINTAINING YOUR HEALTH

Poor health can threaten your success in the first year of college as nothing else can. No matter how busy you are, you must not forget your body and its needs: proper food, sufficient sleep, and healthy exercise. Many students, faced with the stress of college life, find themselves overmunching junk foods and gaining weight. Guard against this. Drugs and alcohol threaten the health and the success of many college students.

A FINAL WORD

So there it is. If you have read this far, you probably have a serious interest in succeeding in your first year of college. You probably have also realized that these suggestions, even if they sound a bit preachy, are practical and workable. They are based on many years of observing college students.

Benjamin W. Griffith
Former Dean,
University of West Georgia
Carrollton, Georgia

PART II

COLLEGE FACTS

AND FINANCES

Now that you've read through Part I, you'll need specific information on the colleges that best match your needs and aptitudes. Here's where you'll find essential information in a nutshell.

Facts and figures on all schools are listed in chart form to help you make quick and easy comparisons. Thumbnail data include:

- campus environment
- degrees offered
- composition of the student body
- enrollment figures
- test scores of entering freshmen
- fall application deadlines

You'll also see at a glance how much it's going to cost you for tuition, room-and-board, and related expenses. In-state costs are broken down on a state-by-state basis, each range starting with colleges that don't charge tuition and going up the scale to the most expensive schools.

COLLEGES AT A GLANCE

The charts on these pages present some of the basic data that initially concerns many students. All of the four-year accredited schools in the United States are listed here alphabetically by state. The type of college environment (from urban to rural) is given, followed by degrees offered and whether the institution is public or private. Information about whether the student body is coed or primarily men or women, and whether fraternities or sororities are on campus follows. The undergraduate enrollment for the fall of 2014 is given as well as the median test scores for freshmen who took the ACT or the SAT. Finally, the fall admissions deadline is shown. "Open" usually indicates that admission applications will be accepted until a few weeks before classes begin.

TEST SCORES

Column key
- STUDENTS: C-Coed M-Men W-Women PM-Primarily Men PW-Primarily Women
- FRATERNITIES AND SORORITIES: F-Fraternities S-Sororities F,S-Both No-Neither
- CONTROL: Pri-Private, Pub-Public
- DEGREES AWARDED: A-Associate B-Bachelor M-Master D-Doctorate
- ENVIRONMENT: U-Urban R-Rural SU-Suburban SM-Small Town

Name of School	Town	Env	Degrees	Control	Frat/Sor	Students	Undergrad Enroll. Fall 2014	ACT Median	ACT <21	ACT 21-23	ACT 24-26	ACT 27-28	ACT >28	SAT CR Median	CR <500	CR 500-599	CR 600-700	CR >700	SAT Math Median	Math <500	Math 500-599	Math 600-700	Math >700	SAT Writ Median	Writ <500	Writ 500-599	Writ 600-700	Writ >700	App. Deadline

Alabama

Name of School	Town	Env	Degrees	Control	Frat/Sor	Students	Enroll.	ACT Med	<21	21-23	24-26	27-28	>28	CR Med	<500	500-599	600-700	>700	Math Med	<500	500-599	600-700	>700	Writ Med	<500	500-599	600-700	>700	Deadline
Alabama Agricultural and Mechanical University	Normal	SU	A,M,D	Pub	F,S	C	4,415	17	60					434	79	16	4	1	430	79	14	6	1						7/15
Alabama State University	Montgomery	SM	B,M,D	Pub	F,S	C	4,802																						7/30
Amridge University	Montgomery	U	A,B,M,D	Pri	No	C	322																						Open
Auburn University	Auburn	SM	B,M,D	Pub	F,S	C	20,629	26	2	18	27	15	37	570	13	51	28	8	590	10	45	35	8	560	17	50	26	7 2/1
Auburn University at Montgomery	Montgomery	SU	B,M,D	Pub	F,S	C	4,377	27	47	23	18	6	3	570	54	35	8	3	470	60	32	8		470	63	25		12 8/1
Birmingham-Southern College	Birmingham	U	B	Pri	F,S	C	1,305	26	4	23	27	19	25	570	18	44	32	6	580	12	44	32	11	570	16	45	28	12 2/1
Concordia College - Alabama	Selma	SM	A,B	Pri	No	C	600																						2/1
Faulkner University	Montgomery	U	A,B,M,D	Pri	F,S	C	2,670	20	55	24	15	3	3	490	62	34	2	2	490	57	36	7	2	470	66			2 2/1
Huntingdon College	Montgomery	U	B	Pri	F,S	C	1,160	22	33	38	17	9	3	480	55	36	3	3	480	58	27	15	3					Open
Jacksonville State University	Jacksonville	SU	B,M	Pub	F,S	C	7,895		60				8		17	16	50	17			50				33	17	33	50	Open
Judson College	Marion	SM	A,B	Pri	No	PW	347																						Open
Miles College	Birmingham	U	B	Pri	No	C	1,634																						Open
Oakwood University	Huntsville	SU	B	Pri	No	C	2,000	25	9	19	32	15	25	560	18	47	29	6	560	21	47	26	6	550	23	45	45	5 7/1
Samford University	Birmingham	SU	B,M,D	Pri	F,S	C	3,051	24	14	32	26	15	13	550	35	39	20	6	530	27	48	25			17			7/15
Spring Hill College	Mobile	SU	B,M	Pri	F,S	C	1,274																						7/15
Stillman College	Tuscaloosa	SU	B	Pri	F,S	C	1,580																						Open
Talladega College	Talladega	SM	B	Pri	F,S	C	740							500	67	27	4		480	64	26	8		501				Open
Troy University	Troy	R	A,B,M	Pub	F,S	C	21,900	21	17	61	15	6	1																6/1
Tuskegee University	Tuskegee	SU	B,M,D	Pri	F,S	C	2,598	24	13	29	25	14	20	587	67	24	9		598	64	33	3	17					3/1
University of Alabama at Birmingham	Birmingham	SU	B,M,D	Pub	F,S	C	26,234	27	11	10	26	16	36		17	37	32	14		12	41	31						6/1
University of Alabama at Tuscaloosa	Tuscaloosa	SU	B,M,D	Pub	F,S	C	5,618	27	24					514	67				513	64	33			530	38	39		8/1
University of Alabama in Huntsville	Huntsville	SU	A,B,M	Pub	No	C	1,466	22	23																				8/1
University of Mobile	Mobile	SU	B,M	Pri	F,S	C	2,665	23	23																				Open
University of Montevallo	Montevallo	SM	B,M	Pub	F,S	C								560	21	39	33	7	560		42	30	6	530		39		Open
University of North Alabama	Florence	U	B,M,D	Pub	F,S	C	6,161	23	33	26	23	9		523	36	45	17	2	520	36	45	17	2	503	47	39	12	Open
University of South Alabama	Mobile	SU	A,B,M	Pub	F,S	C	11,315							565	29	41	18	12	520	44	26	24	6	534	33	50	11	Open
University of West Alabama	Livingston	SM	A,B,M	Pub	F,S	C	1,873																						Open

Alaska

Name of School	Town	Env	Degrees	Control	Frat/Sor	Students	Enroll.	ACT Med	<21	21-23	24-26	27-28	>28	CR Med	<500	500-599	600-700	>700	Math Med	<500	500-599	600-700	>700	Writ Med	<500	500-599	600-700	>700	Deadline
Alaska Pacific University	Anchorage	SU	A,B,M	Pri	No	C	545																						Open
University of Alaska Anchorage	Anchorage	SM	A,B,M	Pub	No	C	10,825																						Open
University of Alaska Fairbanks	Fairbanks	SM	A,B,M,D	Pub	No	C	7,563	24	23	26	24	15	12	560	21	39	33	7	560	21	42	30	6	530	38	39	22	6/15
University of Alaska Southeast	Juneau	SU	A,B,M	Pub	No	C	2,095																						Open

Arizona

Name of School	Town	Env	Degrees	Control	Frat/Sor	Students	Enroll.	ACT Med	<21	21-23	24-26	27-28	>28	CR Med	<500	500-599	600-700	>700	Math Med	<500	500-599	600-700	>700	Writ Med	<500	500-599	600-700	>700	Deadline
American Indian College	Phoenix	SM	A,B	Pri	No	C	130																						Open
Arizona State University, at the Downtown Phoenix Campus	Phoenix	U	B,M,D	Pub	F,S	No	9,150	23	20	31	23	12	13	540	31	46	20	4	540	29	49	21	2					Open
Arizona State University, at the Polytechnic Campus	Mesa	SU	B,M,D	Pub	F,S	No	3,750	25	16	26	23	16	19	550	26	43	25	7	570	19	39	33	9		29	44	12	2/1
Arizona State University, at the Tempe Campus	Tempe	SU	B,M,D	Pub	F,S	No	39,968	23	13	29	29	16	21	560	23	42	28	7	580	16	40	34	10					2/1
Arizona State University, at the West Campus	Phoenix	SU	B,M,D	Pub	F,S	No	3,256	23	22	31	22	15	10	540	30	44	23	3	540	29	40	27						2/1
Embry-Riddle Aeronautical University - Prescott Campus	Prescott	R	B,M	Pri	F,S	No	1,813	26	6	19	27	16	32	570	19	42	31	2	600	13	35	43	9	530				2 7/1
Grand Canyon University	Phoenix	SU	B,M,D	Pri	No	C	27,680	23	30	27	26	10	7	523	36	45	17	2	520	36	45	17	2	503	47	39	12	Open
Northern Arizona University	Flagstaff	SM	B,M,D	Pub	F,S	No	23,705	23	8	42		33	17	565	29	41	18	12	520	44	26	24	6	534	33	50	11	Open
Prescott College	Prescott	SM	A,B,M	Pri	No	C	545																						8/15
University of Arizona	Tucson	U	B,M,D	Pub	F,S	No	32,987																						8/15

Arkansas

Name of School	Town	Env	Degrees	Control	Frat/Sor	Students	Enroll.	ACT Med	<21	21-23	24-26	27-28	>28	CR Med	<500	500-599	600-700	>700	Math Med	<500	500-599	600-700	>700	Writ Med	<500	500-599	600-700	>700	Deadline
Arkansas Baptist College	Little Rock	SM	A,B	Pri	F,S	C	400	24	20	30	26	13	11	470	68	29	3		510	38	41	21		440	82	18		6 8/15
Arkansas State University	State University	SM	A,B,M,D	Pub	F,S	C	9,857	21	44	22	20	9	6	495	50	40	10		490	58	33	8						8/17
Arkansas Tech University	Russellville	SM	A,B,M	Pub	F,S	C	11,099	25	16	21	20	14	23	540	26	41	24		530	27	39	28	6					Open
Harding University	Searcy	SM	B,M,D	Pri	F,S	C	4,492	25	21	21	19	16	24	500	58	42	9		536	42	42							6/1
Henderson State University	Arkadelphia	SM	B,M	Pub	F,S	C	3,199	21	45	23	23	4	4	595	15	37	34	13	594	12	34	45	9	545	31	41	28	Open
Hendrix College	Conway	SU	B	Pri	No	C	1,348	26	2	13	23	17	45	577	18	39	33	7	563	17	47	33	4	498	59	24	17	Open
John Brown University	Siloam Springs	SM	A,B,M	Pri	No	C	1,781	26	1	29	26	26	17	518	41	41	18	7	563	17	53	18						5/1
Lyon College	Batesville	SM	B	Pri	F,S	C	713	25	10	33	24	13	20	531	33	48	18	3	555	29	47	22						8/1
Ouachita Baptist University	Arkadelphia	SM	A,B	Pri	F,S	C	1,501												540	28	47							Open

The following table lists colleges with their city, campus setting, degrees offered, control (Pri = Private, Pub = Public), housing, total enrollment, cost category, and application deadline.

College	City	Setting	Degrees	Control	Housing	Enrollment	Deadline
Philander Smith College	Little Rock	U	B	Pri	F,S	732	7/15
Southern Arkansas University	Magnolia	SM	A,B,M	Pub	F,S	3,130	Open
University of Arkansas at Fayetteville	Fayetteville	U	A,B,M,D	Pub	F,S	21,009	8/1
University of Arkansas at Little Rock	Little Rock	SM	A,B,M,D	Pub	F,S	3,363	Open
University of Arkansas at Monticello	Monticello	SM	A,B,M	Pub	F,S	3,115	Open
University of Arkansas at Pine Bluff	Pine Bluff	SM	A,B,M	Pub	F,S	9,842	Open
University of Central Arkansas	Conway	SM	A,B,M,D	Pri	No	660	4/1
University of the Ozarks	Clarksville	SM	B	Pri	No	550	Open
Williams Baptist College	Walnut Ridge	R	A,B	Pri			Open

California

College	City	Setting	Degrees	Control	Housing	Enrollment	Deadline
American Jewish University - College of Arts and Sciences	Los Angeles	SU	B,M	Pri	No	110	5/31
Art Center College of Design	Pasadena	SM	B,M	Pri	No	1,565	Open
Ashford University	San Diego	SM	A,B,M	Pri	No	45,348	Open
Azusa Pacific University	Azusa	SM	B,M,D	Pri	No	6,160	5/1
Biola University	La Mirada	SU	B,M,D	Pri	F,S	4,337	Open
California Baptist University	Riverside	SU	B,M,D	Pri	No	6,435	Open
California College of the Arts	San Francisco	SM	B,M	Pri	F,S	1,464	1/3
California Institute of Technology	Pasadena	SU	B,M,D	Pri	No	997	Open
California Institute of the Arts	Valencia	SU	B,M,D	Pri	F,S	895	1/5
California Lutheran University	Thousand Oaks	SU	B,M,D	Pri	No	2,808	1/15
California Maritime Academy	Vallejo	SU	B	Pub	F,S	868	1/15
California Polytechnic State University	San Luis Obispo	SU	B,M	Pub	F,S	22,395	11/30
California State Polytechnic University, Pomona	Pomona	SM	B,M,D	Pub	F,S	5,370	11/1
California State University, Bakersfield	Bakersfield	SM	B,M	Pub	F,S	16,255	Open
California State University, Chico	Chico	SM	B,M	Pub	F,S	12,617	11/30
California State University, Dominguez Hills	Carson	SM	B,M	Pub	F,S	11,853	11/30
California State University, East Bay	Hayward	U	B,M,D	Pub	F,S	19,704	11/30
California State University, Fresno	Fresno	U	B,M,D	Pub	F,S	33,086	11/30
California State University, Fullerton	Fullerton	SM	B,M,D	Pub	F,S	31,523	11/30
California State University, Long Beach	Long Beach	U	B,M	Pub	F,S	19,574	11/30
California State University, Los Angeles	Los Angeles	SU	B,M	Pub	F,S	6,234	6/15
California State University, Monterey Bay	Seaside	SU	B,M,D	Pub	F,S	35,206	3/15
California State University, Northridge	Northridge	SU	B,M	Pub	F,S	24,701	3/15
California State University, Sacramento	Sacramento	SU	B,M,D	Pub	F,S	14,732	11/30
California State University, San Bernardino	San Bernardino	SU	B,M,D	Pub	F,S	9,482	Open
California State University, San Marcos	San Marcos	SU	B,M	Pub	F,S	6,620	11/30
California State University, Stanislaus	Turlock	SU	B,M,D	Pub	F,S	6,281	11/30
Chapman University	Orange	SU	B,M,D	Pri	No	1,301	1/15
Claremont McKenna College	Claremont	SU	B,M	Pri	No	288	1/1
Cogswell Polytechnical College	Sunnyvale	SU	A,B,D	Pri	No	1,738	Open
Concordia University Irvine	Irvine	SU	B,M	Pri	F,S	1,625	Open
Dominican University of California	San Rafael	SU	B,M,D	Pri	No	2,439	Open
Fresno Pacific University	Fresno	U	A,B,M	Pri	No	645	Open
Golden Gate University	San Francisco	U	B	Pri	W	807	Open
Harvey Mudd College	Claremont	SU	B	Pri	No	640	1/1
Holy Names University	Oakland	U	A,B,M	Pri	No	6,830	1/1
Hope International University	Fullerton	SU	A,B,M	Pri	F,S	620	Open
Humboldt State University	Arcata	SM	A,B,D	Pub	No	1,680	Open
Humphreys College	Stockton	SU	B,M	Pri	No	514	Open
La Sierra University	Riverside	SU	A,B,M	Pri	No	6,184	Open
Laguna College of Art and Design	Laguna Beach	SM	B,M	Pri	No	713	1/15
Loyola Marymount University	Los Angeles	SU	B,M,D	Pri	F,S	985	1/15
Menlo College	Atherton	SU	B	Pri	No	2,288	Open
Mills College	Oakland	U	A,B,M,D	Pri	No	5,920	2/15
Mount St. Mary's College - Chalon Campus	Los Angeles	U	A,B	Pri	S	375	Open
National University	La Jolla	U	A,B,M,D	Pri	No	1,147	Open
NewSchool of Architecture & Design	San Diego	SU	B,M,D	Pri	No	2,117	26
Notre Dame de Namur University	Belmont	U	B,M	Pri	F,S	1,158	1/10
Occidental College	Los Angeles	SU	B,M	Pri	No	1,375	2
Otis College of Art and Design	Los Angeles	R	A,B,M	Pri	No	3,488	Open
Pacific Union College	Angwin	SU	B,M,D	Pri	F,S	1,099	Open
Pepperdine University	Malibu	SU	B	Pri	No	2,568	18
Pitzer College	Claremont	SU	B	Pri	No	1,612	1/5
Point Loma Nazarene University	San Diego	SU	B,M,D	Pri	F,S	3,035	1/1
Pomona College	Claremont	SU	A,B	Pri	No	752	3/1
Saint Mary's College of California	Moraga	SU	B,M	Pri	No	28,362	2/1
San Diego Christian College	El Cajon	SU	B,M,D	Pub	F,S	467	Open
San Diego State University	San Diego	U	A,B	Pri	No		11/30
San Francisco Art Institute	San Francisco	U	B,M	Pri	No		2/1

TEST SCORES — COLLEGES AT A GLANCE

Legend:
- ENVIRONMENT: U-Urban, R-Rural, SU-Suburban, SM-Small Town
- DEGREES AWARDED: A-Associate, B-Bachelor, M-Master, D-Doctorate
- CONTROL: Pri-Private, Pub-Public
- FRATERNITIES AND SORORITIES: F-Fraternities, S-Sororities, F,S-Both, No-Neither
- STUDENTS: C-Coed, M-Men, W-Women, PM-Primarily Men, PW-Primarily Women

Name of School	Town	Env.	Degrees	Control	Frat/Sor	Students	Undergrad Enroll. Fall 2014	ACT Median	SAT Crit. Reading Median	SAT Math Median	SAT Writing Median	Application Deadline
San Francisco Conservatory of Music	San Francisco	U	B,M	Pri	No	C	171					12/1
San Francisco State University	San Francisco	U	B,M,D	Pub	F,S	C	26,664		490	505	490	11/30
San Jose State University	San Jose	U	B,M,D	Pub	F,S	C			490	520	490	11/30
Scripps College	Claremont	SU	B	Pri	No	W	972			500	538	1/2
Simpson University	Redding	SU	A,B,M	Pri	No	C	1,019		500	495		Open
Sonoma State University	Rohnert Park	SU	B,M	Pub	F,S	C	8,351		490	536	630	11/30
Stanford University	Stanford	SU	B,M,D	Pri	F,S	C	7,089		552	610	670	1/3
The Masters College	Santa Clarita	SU	B	Pri	No	C	1,098		660	700	550	3/2
Thomas Aquinas College	Santa Paula	R	B	Pri	No	C	378		660			Open
University of California at Berkeley	Berkeley	U	B,M,D	Pub	F,S	C	35,646		540	610	660	11/30
University of California at Davis	Davis	SU	B,M,D	Pub	F,S	C	27,728		640	680	580	11/30
University of California at Irvine	Irvine	SU	B,M,D	Pub	F,S	C	22,216		540	540	630	11/30
University of California at Los Angeles	Los Angeles	SU	B,M,D	Pub	F,S	C	26,162		610	640	550	11/30
University of California at Riverside	Riverside	SU	B,M,D	Pub	F,S	C	18,612		550	560	510	11/30
University of California at San Diego	La Jolla	SU	B,M,D	Pub	F,S	C	20,475		510	520	610	11/30
University of California at Santa Barbara	Santa Barbara	SU	B,M,D	Pub	F,S	C	19,362		600	620	570	11/30
University of California at Santa Cruz	Santa Cruz	SM	B,M,D	Pub	F,S	C	15,695		560	570	570	11/30
University of La Verne	La Verne	SU	A,B,M,D	Pri	F,S	C	2,682		570	605		2/1
University of Redlands	Redlands	SU	B,M	Pri	F,S	C	2,375		526	532		2/1
University of San Diego	San Diego	SU	B,M,D	Pri	F,S	C	5,741		480	500	460	12/15
University of San Francisco	San Francisco	U	B,M,D	Pri	F,S	C	6,845		660	670	670	1/15
University of Southern California	Los Angeles	U	B,M,D	Pri	F,S	C	18,316		480	490		1/10
University of the Pacific	Stockton	SU	B,M,D	Pri	F,S	C	2,041		570	580		2/15
Vanguard University of Southern California	Costa Mesa	SU	A,B,M	Pri	No	C	1,340		570	600		3/2
Westmont College	Santa Barbara	SU	B	Pri	F,S	C	1,368		540	540	580	2/1
Whittier College	Whittier	SU	B,M	Pri	F,S	C	1,310		610	610	550	2/1
Woodbury University	Burbank	SU	B,M	Pri	F,S	C			531	533	510	Open

Colorado

Name of School	Town	Env.	Degrees	Control	Frat/Sor	Students	Undergrad Enroll. Fall 2014	ACT Median	SAT Crit. Reading Median	SAT Math Median	SAT Writing Median	Application Deadline
Adams State University	Alamosa	SM	A,B,M	Pub	No	C	2,742		509	516	516	8/1
Colorado Christian University	Lakewood	SU	A,B,M	Pri	No	C	1,475		456	448	472	8/1
Colorado College	Colorado Springs	U	B,M	Pri	F,S	C	2,050		500	510	500	1/15
Colorado Mesa University	Grand Junction	SM	A,B,M,D	Pub	No	C	9,414					Open
Colorado School of Mines	Golden	SM	B,M,D	Pub	F,S	C	3,320			580		Open
Colorado State University-Fort Collins	Fort Collins	SU	B,M,D	Pub	F,S	C	22,506					2/1
Colorado State University-Pueblo	Pueblo	U	B,M	Pub	No	C	36,207					Open
Colorado Technical University	Colorado Springs	SM	A,B,M,D	Pri	No	C	1,200					8/1
Fort Lewis College	Durango	SM	A,B	Pub	No	C	4,028					Open
Johnson & Wales University/Denver Campus	Denver	SU	A,B	Pri	S	C	21,975					Open
Metropolitan State University of Denver	Denver	U	B	Pub	No	C	386					1/15
Naropa University	Boulder	SU	B,M,D	Pri	No	C	1,520					Open
Regis University	Denver	U	B,M	Pri	F,S	C	670					Open
Rocky Mountain College of Art and Design	Denver	SU	B,M	Pri	No	C	4,470					Open
United States Air Force Academy	Colorado Springs	SM	B,M,D	Pub	No	C	25,461		570	600	580	1/15
University of Colorado at Colorado Springs	Colorado Springs	SU	B,M,D	Pub	F,S	C	13,103		540	540		2/1
University of Colorado Boulder	Boulder	U	B,M,D	Pub	F,S	C	5,517		610	610		7/22
University of Denver	Denver	U	B,M,D	Pri	F,S	C	10,231		531	533		1/15
University of Northern Colorado	Greeley	SU	B,M,D	Pub	F,S	C	2,338		509	516		8/1
Western State Colorado University	Gunnison	R	B,M	Pub	No	C						6/1

Connecticut

Name of School	Town	Env.	Degrees	Control	Frat/Sor	Students	Undergrad Enroll. Fall 2014	ACT Median	SAT Crit. Reading Median	SAT Math Median	SAT Writing Median	Application Deadline
Albertus Magnus College	New Haven	SU	A,B,M	Pri	No	C	1,605		456	448	472	Open
Central Connecticut State University	New Britain	SU	B,M,D	Pub	F,S	C	9,871		500	510	500	Open
Charter Oak State College	New Britain	SU	A,B	Pub	No	C	1,929					Open
Connecticut College	New London	SU	B,M	Pri	No	C	1,926	29	670	650	690	1/1
Eastern Connecticut State University	Willimantic	SM	A,B,M	Pub	No	C	5,179		510	510	520	5/1
Fairfield University	Fairfield	SU	B,M,D	Pri	No	C	3,982		580	600	600	1/15
Goodwin College	East Hartford	U	A,B	Pri	No	C	3,388					Open

College	City	Type	Degrees	Control	Transfer	Housing	Enrollment	Deadline
Mitchell College	New London	SU	A,B	Pri	No	C	858	Open
Post University	Waterbury	U	A,B	Pri	No	C	1,275	Open
Quinnipiac University	Hamden	SU	B,M,D	Pri	F,S	C	6,553	2/1
Sacred Heart University	Fairfield	SU	A,B,M,D	Pri	F,S	C	4,997	2/1
Southern Connecticut State University	New Haven	U	B,M	Pub	F,S	C	8,525	4/1
Trinity College	Hartford	U	B,M	Pri	F	C	2,308	1/1
United States Coast Guard Academy	New London	SU	B	Pub	F	C	896	10/1
University of Bridgeport	Bridgeport	SM	A,B,M,D	Pri	F,S	C	2,503	2/1
University of Connecticut	Storrs	R	A,B,M,D	Pub	F,S	C	18,032	4/1
University of Hartford	West Hartford	SU	A,B,M,D	Pri	F,S	C	5,284	4/1
University of New Haven	West Haven	SU	A,B,M,D	Pri	F,S	C	5,048	Open
University of Saint Joseph	West Hartford	SU	B,M,D	Pri	No	PW	1,060	Open
Wesleyan University	Middletown	SU	B,M,D	Pri	F,S	C	2,928	Open
Western Connecticut State University	Danbury	SU	A,B,M	Pub	F,S	C	5,583	1/1
Yale University	New Haven	U	B,M,D	Pri	F,S	C	5,405	12/31

Delaware

College	City	Type	Degrees	Control	Transfer	Housing	Enrollment	Deadline
Delaware State University	Dover	SU	B,M	Pub	F,S	C	3,050	12/31
Goldey-Beacom College	Wilmington	SU	A,B,M	Pri	No	C	625	Open
University of Delaware	Newark	SM	A,B,M,D	Pub	F,S	C	16,868	1/15
Wesley College	Dover	SM	A,B,M	Pri	F,S	C	1,603	Open
Wilmington University	New Castle	U	A,B,M,D	Pri	No	C	8,809	Open

District of Columbia

College	City	Type	Degrees	Control	Transfer	Housing	Enrollment	Deadline
American University	Washington	SU	A,B,M,D	Pri	F,S	C	7,706	1/15
Corcoran College of Art and Design	Washington	SU	A,B,M	Pri	No	C	420	Open
Gallaudet University	Washington	U	B,M,D	Pri	F,S	C	1,077	Open
George Washington University	Washington	U	A,B,M,D	Pri	F,S	C	10,443	Open
Georgetown University	Washington	SU	B,M,D	Pri	F,S	C	7,552	1/10
Howard University	Washington	SU	B,M,D	Pri	No	C	7,013	Open
The Catholic University of America	Washington	SU	B,M,D	Pri	F,S	C	3,799	2/15
Trinity Washington University	Washington	U	A,B,M	Pri	F,S	W	1,391	Open
University of the District of Columbia	Washington	SU	A,B,M,D	Pub	No	C	5,110	Open

Florida

College	City	Type	Degrees	Control	Transfer	Housing	Enrollment	Deadline
Adventist University of Health Sciences	Orlando	U	A,B,M	Pri	No	C	2,576	7/1
Barry University	Miami Shores	SU	B,M,D	Pri	No	C	5,150	Open
Beacon College	Leesburg	SM	A,B	Pri	F,S	C	140	Open
Bethune-Cookman University	Daytona Beach	SM	B,M	Pri	F,S	C	3,527	7/30
Carlos Albizu University	Miami	SM	B,M,D	Pri	No	C	431	Open
Clearwater Christian College	Clearwater	R	A,B,M	Pri	No	C	590	Open
Eckerd College	St. Petersburg	SU	B	Pri	No	C	1,893	4/1
Edward Waters College	Jacksonville	SU	B	Pri	F,S	C	1,400	Open
Embry-Riddle Aeronautical University - Daytona Beach	Daytona Beach	SU	A,B,M,D	Pri	F,S	C	4,679	4/1
Embry-Riddle Aeronautical University - Worldwide	Daytona Beach	SU	A,B,M,D	Pri	No	C	10,412	7/1
Flagler College	St. Augustine	SM	A,B	Pri	No	C	2,774	3/1
Florida Agricultural and Mechanical University	Tallahassee	SU	B,M,D	Pub	F,S	C	10,053	5/15
Florida Atlantic University	Boca Raton	SU	A,B,M,D	Pub	F,S	C	24,823	5/1
Florida Gulf Coast University	Fort Myers	SU	A,B,M,D	Pub	F,S	C	12,861	5/1
Florida Institute of Technology	Melbourne	SU	B,M,D	Pri	F,S	C	2,978	Open
Florida International University	Miami	SU	A,B,M,D	Pub	F,S	C	37,468	Open
Florida Memorial University	Miami	U	B	Pri	F,S	C		2/15
Florida Southern College	Lakeland	SU	B,M,D	Pri	F,S	C	2,172	Open
Florida State University	Tallahassee	SU	B,M,D	Pub	F,S	C	32,528	3/1
Hodges University	Naples	SU	A,B,M,D	Pri	No	C	1,515	Open
Jacksonville University	Jacksonville	SU	B,M	Pri	F,S	C	3,040	1/25
Johnson & Wales University/North Miami Campus	North Miami	SU	A,B	Pub	No	C	1,657	Open
Lynn University	Boca Raton	SU	A,B,M,D	Pri	F,S	C	801	Open
New College of Florida	Sarasota	SU	B	Pub	No	C	497	Open
Northwood University	West Palm Beach	SU	A,B,M	Pri	No	C	4,699	Open
Nova Southeastern University	Fort Lauderdale	U	B	Pri	F,S	C	3,021	Open
Palm Beach Atlantic University	West Palm Beach	SU	A,B,M,D	Pri	No	C	1,263	2/15
Ringling College of Art and Design	Sarasota	U	B	Pri	No	C	1,884	Open
Rollins College	Winter Park	R	A,B,M	Pri	F,S	C	2,290	2/15
Saint Leo University	Saint Leo	SU	A,B,M,D	Pri	F,S	C	2,448	Open
Southeastern University	Lakeland	SU	A,B,M	Pri	No	C	1,145	Open
St. Thomas University	Miami	SU	A,B,M,D	Pri	F,S	C	1,145	Open
Stetson University	Deland	SM	B,M,D	Pri	F,S	C	2,841	7

NAME OF SCHOOL	TOWN	ENVIRONMENT	DEGREES AWARDED	CONTROL	FRATERNITIES AND SORORITIES	STUDENTS	UNDERGRAD ENROLLMENT FALL 2014	ACT Median	ACT Below 21	ACT 21-23	ACT 24-26	ACT 27-28	ACT Above 28	SAT CR Median	SAT CR Below 500	SAT CR 500-599	SAT CR 600-700	SAT CR Above 700	SAT Math Median	SAT Math Below 500	SAT Math 500-599	SAT Math 600-700	SAT Math Above 700	SAT Writing Median	SAT Writing Below 500	SAT Writing 500-599	SAT Writing 600-700	SAT Writing Above 700	APP DEADLINE
University of Central Florida	Orlando	SU	A,B,M,D	Pub	F,S	C	52,532	26	2	19	38	20	21	591	8	45	40	6	596	6	44	42	8	564	16	52	28		5/1
University of Florida	Gainesville	SU	A,B,M,D	Pub	F,S	C	33,720	28	2	6	17	24	54	629	8	28	53	16	637	2	23	53	22	625	3	23	53	51	11/1
University of Miami	Coral Gables	SU	A,B,M,D	Pri	F,S	C	11,380	30	1		46		74	640	4	21	49	26	680	2	12	48	38	640	3	23	50	50	1/1
University of North Florida	Jacksonville	SU	A,B,M,D	Pub	F,S	C	14,121	26		17	18	18	18	601	2	36	55	7	615	3	44	49	4	510	10	51	36	36	Open
University of South Florida/St. Petersburg	St. Petersburg	SU	A,B,M,D	Pub	No	C	4,006	23	15	36	30	13	6	530		32	13		530	24					37				3/15
University of South Florida/Tampa	Tampa	U	A,B,M,D	Pub	F,S	C	34,985	24	8	56	32	2	2	525	32	54	10	1	540	49	55	19	1	520	37	49	13	13	3/15
University of Tampa	Tampa	U	A,B,M	Pri	F,S	C	6,499		20						44	44					41	9	6		60	34	5	5	Open
University of West Florida	Pensacola	SU	A,B,M,D	Pub	No	C	10,332		70						68	29				63	32	4	54						6/30
Warner University	Lake Wales	R	A,B,M	Pri	No	C	1,090																						Open
Webber International University	Babson Park	SM	A,B,M	Pri	No	C	655																						8/1
Georgia																														
Agnes Scott College	Decatur	U	B	Pri	No	W	913	26	16	19	26	16	23	590	17	38	33	12	570	19	40	27	14	570	16	40	36	36	3/1
Albany State University	Albany	U	A,B,M	Pub	F,S	C	3,025	21	45	31	13	7	4	519	39	47	13	1	494	55	37	7	1	489	56	37	7	7	6/1
Armstrong State University	Savannah	SU	A,B	Pub	No	C	6,346	26	1	22	30	7	28	590	8	46	38	1	580	7	52	36	4	550	18	51	27	27	7/1
Art Institute of Atlanta	Atlanta	SU	B,M	Pri	No	C	2,720	26	42	32	16	7	2		39	46	14			59	31	10			65	29	6	6	Open
Berry College	Mount Berry	SU	B,M	Pri	S	C	2,141	23	1	32	87	11	2	590	8	12	38	1	580	7	29	9	1	550		18			2/1
Brenau University – Women's College	Gainesville	R	A,B	Pri	No	W	867		82		5	1			65	12	2			65	12	2			65	29			Open
Brewton-Parker College	Mt. Vernon	SU	B	Pri	No	C	629	18						430	86				420	86									Open
Clark Atlanta University	Atlanta	SU	B,M,D	Pri	F,S	C	2,567		59	25	12	3	1	508	48	38	13		496	54	36	9	1	490	57	34	8	8	Open
Clayton State University	Morrow	SU	A,B,M	Pub	F,S	C	5,230		7	18	25	21	28	610	10	38	35	17	570	17	45	32	6	590	19	35	37	37	5/1
Columbus State University	Columbus	SU	A,B,M	Pub	F,S	C	7,069	26			2		66	660	19	10	47	33	700	10	36	54		690	1	10	44	44	1/15
Covenant College	Lookout Mountain	R	A,B	Pri	No	C	1,066	31							47														1/15
Emory University	Atlanta	SM	A,B,M,D	Pri	F,S	C	7,836		8		40	16	7	570	11	53	33	3	560	13	55	29	2	550	18	54	26	26	4/1
Fort Valley State University	Fort Valley	U	A,B,M,D	Pub	F,S	C	3,421	24	1	4			86	670		9	53	37	730		4	29	67	680	1	9	48	48	4/1
Georgia College and State University	Milledgeville	SM	B,M,D	Pub	F,S	C	5,927	24		58	26	8	7	550	12	63	22	2	550	13	63	22		520	33	52			1/10
Georgia Institute of Technology	Atlanta	U	B,M,D	Pub	F,S	C	14,682	32	1	20	12	8	3	670	56	34	9		480	58	36	9		470	66	29			1/10
Georgia Regents University	Augusta	SM	A,B,M,D	Pub	No	C	5,224	23	61	52	26	11	7	550	35	60	17		530	37	43	16		510	39	47			5/1
Georgia Southern University	Statesboro	SM	B,M,D	Pub	F,S	C	18,004	23	22	37	21	3	3	540	18	60	20	1	510	26	56	17	1	490	39	47	13	13	7/21
Georgia Southwestern State University	Americus	U	B,M	Pub	F,S	C	2,527	20	35	19	19	1	1	520	39	39	20	2	590	7	44	44	1	560	58	46	29	29	3/1
Georgia State University	Atlanta	U	B,M,D	Pub	F,S	C	24,762	24	22	29	25	2	13	500	49	47	15	6	590	48	37	35		480	58	31	19	19	5/8
Kennesaw State University	Kennesaw	SU	B,M,D	Pub	F,S	C	23,592	23	35	30	19	8	4	580	9	35	36	1	500	7	52	14		560	24	31	38	38	Open
LaGrange College	LaGrange	SM	B,M	Pri	F,S	C	880	21	26	29	21	6	19	570	49	48	35	6	550	48	52	37		480	96	46	29		4/1
Mercer University	Macon	SU	A,B,M,D	Pri	F,S	C	2,538	26	24	26	25	14	4	580	51	49	10		550	20	27	14		550	58				6/1
Morehouse College	Atlanta	U	B,M	Pri	F,S	M	2,106	21	12	30	30	1		500	94				488	92		8				4			2/15
Oglethorpe University	Atlanta	SU	B,M	Pri	F,S	C	1,095	24	95	25	7	1	4	570	59	51	36	6	550	64	27			550	96				2/15
Paine College	Augusta	U	B	Pri	F	C	924	21	48	16	2			489	94				488	64									7/1
Piedmont College	Demorest	R	B,M	Pri	No	C	1,286	21		25	26	18		540	29	43	23	5	520	38	41	18	2	530	39	40	18	18	Open
Reinhardt College	Waleska	SM	A,B	Pri	No	C	1,120	24	25	23	15	9			29	32	11	1		52	34	13			65	26			Open
Savannah College of Art and Design	Savannah	U	B,M	Pri	No	C	9,695	20	51	23	9	9	4	540	56	32	23		490	52	41	18	2	460	65	26			7/15
Savannah State University	Savannah	U	A,B,M	Pub	F,S	C	4,413	20	17	29	25			475	32	20	11		590	9	45	13		520	39	46			Open
Shorter University	Rome	SU	A,B,M	Pri	No	C	1,642	24	29	12		7	1	550	20	52	24	4		45	39				39				Open
South University	Savannah	U	A,B,M,D	Pri	No	C	5,402	23																					7/1
Southern Polytechnic State University	Marietta	U	A,B,M,D	Pub	F,S	C	2,318	24	69	18	9	3	1	505	44	36	20		500	49	41	9		505	44	36			2/1
Spelman College	Atlanta	U	B	Pri	S	W	874	23																					8/1
Thomas University	Thomasville	R	A,B	Pri	No	C	700	19																					Open
Toccoa Falls College	Toccoa Falls	SM	A,B,M,D	Pri	No	C	874																						1/15
University of Georgia	Athens	SM	B,M,D	Pub	F,S	C	26,882	26	20	24	32	14	5	470	64	31	26		460	70	26	4		450	72	25	18	18	1/15
University of North Georgia	Dahlonega	SM	A,B,M	Pub	No	C	4,005	21	21	28	11	1	7	503	51	35	30		492	58	35	7		482	59	35			6/1
University of West Georgia	Carrollton	R	B,M,D	Pub	F,S	C	10,249	20	47	30	14	5			57	40	8			52	38	9			63		9	9	7/1
Valdosta State University	Valdosta	SU	A,B	Pub	F,S	C	10,568	21	25	27	10			530	34	46		3	560	24	47	25	4	520	36	49	14	14	2/1
Wesleyan College	Macon	SU	B,M	Pri	No	W	592	23	32	26																			
Hawaii																														
Brigham Young University/Hawaii	Laie	R	B	Pri	No	C	2,397	23	26	22	24	16	12	470	65	31	6		465	63	31	6		470	63	32			2/15
Chaminade University of Honolulu	Honolulu	U	A,B,M	Pri	No	C	1,307	20	60	28	11	1		480	57	35	9		490	52	38	9							Open
Hawaii Pacific University	Honolulu	U	A,B,M	Pri	No	C	6,168	21	47	30	14	5															3	3	Open
University of Hawaii at Hilo	Hilo	SM	B,M	Pub	No	C	2,850	21	25	27	24	5	5	530	34	46	25		560	24	47	25		520	36	49			Open
University of Hawaii at Manoa	Honolulu	SM	B,M,D	Pub	F,S	C	14,402	23	25	32	26	10	7		46		18			24	47	25	2				14	14	5/1

Legend: ENVIRONMENT — U-Urban, R-Rural, SU-Suburban, SM-Small Town. DEGREES AWARDED — A-Associate, B-Bachelor, M-Master, D-Doctorate. CONTROL — Pri-Private, Pub-Public. FRATERNITIES AND SORORITIES — F-Fraternities, S-Sororities, F,S-Both, No-Neither. STUDENTS — C-Coed, M-Men, W-Women, PM-Primarily Men, PW-Primarily Women.

Idaho

Institution	City	Type	Degrees	Control	Housing	Calendar	Enrollment	App. Deadline
Boise State University	Boise	U	A,B,M,D	Pub	F,S	C	19,026	5/15
Idaho State University	Pocatello	U	A,B,M,D	Pub	F,S	C	11,764	8/1
Lewis-Clark State College	Lewiston	U	A,B	Pub	No	C	3,495	Open
Northwest Nazarene University	Nampa	SM	B,M,D	Pri	No	C	1,322	8/15
The College of Idaho	Caldwell	SM	B,M	Pri	F,S	C	1,042	7/15
University of Idaho	Moscow	SM	B,M,D	Pub	F,S	C	9,456	8/1

Illinois

Institution	City	Degrees	Control	Housing	Calendar	Enrollment	App. Deadline
Augustana College	Rock Island	B	Pri	F,S	C	2,541	Open
Aurora University	Aurora	B,M,D	Pri	F,S	C	3,246	6/20
Benedictine University	Lisle	A,B,M,D	Pri	No	C	2,940	Open
Blackburn College	Carlinville	B	Pri	F,S	C	549	7/31
Bradley University	Peoria	B,M,D	Pri	F,S	C	5,061	Open
Chicago State University	Chicago	B,M,D	Pub	No	C	4,618	7/15
Columbia College Chicago	Chicago	B,M	Pri	No	C	11,858	7/15
Concordia University, River Forest	River Forest	B,M,D	Pri	No	C	1,032	Open
DePaul University	Chicago	B,M,D	Pri	No	C	16,153	2/1
Dominican University	River Forest	B,M,D	Pri	F,S	C	2,069	Open
Eastern Illinois University	Charleston	B,M	Pub	F,S	C	7,640	Open
Elmhurst College	Elmhurst	B,M	Pri	F,S	C	2,853	Open
Eureka College	Eureka	B	Pri	No	C	550	8/1
Greenville College	Greenville	B,M	Pri	F,S	C	1,382	8/1
Illinois College	Jacksonville	B	Pri	No	C	970	Open
Illinois Institute of Technology	Chicago	B,M,D	Pri	F,S	C	2,801	Open
Illinois State University	Normal	B,M,D	Pub	F,S	C	18,155	4/1
Illinois Wesleyan University	Bloomington	B	Pri	No	C	2,009	3/1
Judson University	Elgin	B,M	Pri	F,S	C	1,195	Open
Kendall College	Chicago	A,B	Pri	F,S	C	2,545	Open
Knox College	Galesburg	B	Pri	No	C	1,399	2/1
Lake Forest College	Lake Forest	B,M	Pri	F,S	C	1,607	2/15
Lewis University	Romeoville	A,B,M	Pri	F,S	C	3,230	Open
Loyola University Chicago	Chicago	B,M,D	Pri	F,S	C	10,322	4/1
MacMurray College	Jacksonville	A,B	Pri	F,S	C	701	Open
McKendree University	Lebanon	B,M	Pri	F,S	C	2,194	Open
Millikin University	Decatur	B,M	Pri	No	C	2,112	Open
Monmouth College	Monmouth	B	Pri	F,S	C	1,300	Open
National Louis University	Chicago	B,M,D	Pri	No	PW	2,084	Open
North Central College	Naperville	B,M	Pri	F,S	C	2,755	4/1
North Park University	Chicago	B,M	Pri	F,S	C	2,224	7/1
Northeastern Illinois University	Chicago	B,M,D	Pub	No	C	8,412	8/1
Northern Illinois University	DeKalb	B,M,D	Pub	F,S	C	18,727	1/1
Northwestern University	Evanston	B,M,D	Pri	F,S	C	8,688	1/1
Olivet Nazarene University	Bourbonnais	B,M	Pri	F,S	C	3,187	5/1
Principia College	Elsah	B	Pri	F,S	C	491	5/1
Quincy University	Quincy	A,B,M	Pri	No	C	1,241	Open
Rockford College	Rockford	B,M,D	Pri	F,S	C	869	Open
Roosevelt University	Chicago	B,M	Pub	No	C	4,300	Open
Saint Xavier University	Chicago	B,M	Pub	F,S	C	3,070	Open
School of the Art Institute of Chicago	Chicago	B	Pri	No	C	3,393	5/1
Shimer College	Chicago	A,B,M,D	Pri	No	C	77	5/1
Southern Illinois University Carbondale	Carbondale	B,M,D	Pub	F,S	C	13,461	5/1
Southern Illinois University Edwardsville	Edwardsville	B	Pub	F,S	C	11,341	8/15
Trinity Christian College	Palos Heights	A,B	Pri	No	C	1,450	8/15
Trinity College of Nursing and Health Sciences	Rock Island	B,M,D	Pri	F,S	C		Open
Trinity International University	Deerfield	B,M,D	Pri	F,S	C	1,265	Open
University of Chicago	Chicago	B,M,D	Pri	F,S	C	5,681	1/1
University of Illinois at Chicago	Chicago	B,M	Pub	F,S	C	16,707	1/1
University of Illinois at Urbana-Champaign	Urbana	B,M,D	Pub	F,S	C	32,695	12/1
University of St. Francis	Joliet	B	Pri	S	C	1,381	8/1
VanderCook College of Music	Chicago	B,M	Pub	F,S	C	90	8/1
Western Illinois University	Macomb	B,M,D	Pub	F,S	C	9,645	5/15
Wheaton College	Wheaton	B,M,D	Pri	No	C	2,432	1/10

Indiana

Institution	City	Type	Degrees	Control	Housing	Calendar	Enrollment	App. Deadline
Anderson University	Anderson	SU	A,B,M,D	Pri	No	C	1,976	Open
Ball State University	Muncie	SU	A,B,M,D	Pub	F,S	C	16,652	5/1
Bethel College	Mishawaka	SU	A,B,M	Pri	No	C	1,801	Open

Column key (read from the header):

- **ENVIRONMENT:** U-Urban R-Rural SU-Suburban SM-Small Town
- **DEGREES AWARDED:** A-Associate B-Bachelor M-Master D-Doctorate
- **CONTROL:** Pri-Private, Pub-Public
- **FRATERNITIES AND SORORITIES:** F-Fraternities S-Sororities F,S-Both No-Neither
- **STUDENTS:** C-Coed M-Men W-Women PM-Primarily Men PW-Primarily Women

Name of School	Town	Env.	Degrees	Control	Frat/Sor	Students	Undergrad Enroll. Fall 2014	ACT Med	ACT <21	ACT 21-23	ACT 24-26	ACT 27-28	ACT >28	SAT CR Med	CR <500	CR 500-599	CR 600-700	CR >700	SAT Math Med	M <500	M 500-599	M 600-700	M >700	SAT Writ Med	W <500	W 500-599	W 600-700	W >700	App. Deadline
Butler University	Indianapolis	SU	A,B,M	Pri	F,S	C	4,311	28	4	8	27	20	41	580	9	47	37	7	600	10	38	43	9	570		16	47	33	Open
Calumet College of St. Joseph	Whiting	SM	A,B,M	Pri	No	C	1,200	27			27			580	14	40	35	10	600	8	36	41	14	580	13		42	37	Open
DePauw University	Greencastle	SM	B	Pri	F,S	C	2,336	27	1	7	34	27	35	650	2	17	55	24	620	6	31	55		620	5	5	34	47	3/1
Earlham College	Richmond	SM	B,M	Pri	No	C	993	17	12	33	16	11	41	500	46	42	11		510	41	43	15		480	55		36		2/15
Franklin College	Franklin	SM	B	Pri	F,S	C	1,075	22																					Open
Goshen College	Goshen	SM	B,M	Pri	No	C	879																						Open
Grace College and Seminary	Winona Lake	SM	A,B,M	Pri	No	C	870	25		27	29	13	24	530	26	49	22	3	530	21	50	27	2	500	31		53	13	Open
Hanover College	Hanover	SM	B	Pri	F,S	R	1,145	24	7	42	44	30	8	509	43	42	12	3	503	49	36	12	3	486	56		42	10	3/1
Huntington University	Huntington	SM	A,B,M	Pri	No	C	1,053	20	53	27	16		2	447	69	27			468	59	32	8		430	81			1	Open
Indiana Institute of Technology	Fort Wayne	U	A,B,M,D	Pri	No	C	5,697	25		27	29	13		575	17	46	30	4	600	9	39	38	14	565	18		47		Open
Indiana State University	Terre Haute	U	A,B,M,D	Pub	F,S	C	8,565							460	66	25	7	1	470	64	30	6	1	440	76		21		6/1
Indiana University Bloomington	Bloomington	SM	B,M,D	Pub	F,S	C	36,419	27		27	44	30		465	68	24	5		470	64	31	5		445	76		20	3	Open
Indiana University East	Richmond	SM	A,B,M	Pub	No	C	4,004							450	72	21			455	71	25	4		440	72		17		7/1
Indiana University Kokomo	Kokomo	SM	A,B,M	Pub	No	C	5,661							480	61	32	6		480	62	31	7		450	72		24	4	Open
Indiana University Northwest	Gary	SU	A,B,M	Pub	No	C	7,293							480	59	35	6		470	62	33	5		460	73		22	5	8/17
Indiana University South Bend	South Bend	SU	A,B,M	Pub	No	C	5,989		39					480	53	35	10	2	498	55	35	10	1	477	63		29	6	8/1
Indiana University Southeast	New Albany	SU	A,B,M	Pub	F	C	12,674			27	17	5	13	495	51	36	12	1	505	47	36	12	2	480	59		31	9	1/1
Indiana University-Purdue University Fort Wayne	Fort Wayne	U	A,B,M	Pub	No	C	22,525			38	47			525	33	45	19	3	535	32	44	19	2	515	43		40		Open
Indiana University-Purdue University Indianapolis	Indianapolis	U	A,B,M,D	Pub	No	C	14,859		5				10																2/1
Indiana Wesleyan University	Marion	SM	A,B	Pri	No	C	1,217	22	32	28	20	11	9	500	48	39	12		510	39	47	12	1	460	64		29	6	1/8
Manchester University	North Manchester	SM	A,B,M	Pri	No	C	2,150	20																					Open
Marian University	Indianapolis	U	B,M	Pri	No	C	615																						Open
Oakland City University	Oakland City	SM	A,B,M	Pri	No	C	2,100																						Open
Purdue University/Calumet	Hammond	U	A,B,M	Pub	F,S	C	8,405		8	16	23	13	41	570	16	44	32	9	640	7	27	37	28	570	16		43	33	1/8
Purdue University/West Lafayette	West Lafayette	SM	B,M,D	Pub	F,S	C	29,255	27	43	31	19	17	61	610	2	40	43	14	670		13	55	32	590	11		42	39	3/1
Rose-Hulman Institute of Technology	Terre Haute	SM	B,M	Pri	F,S	C	2,280		60	16	16	5	10	505	47	43	10		505	47	36	16		450	75			5	Open
Saint Joseph's College	Rensselaer	SM	A,B,M	Pri	No	C	1,142		12	20	5		15	460	66	30	2		440	68	32			550	23		49	4	6/2
Saint Mary-of-the-Woods College	St Mary of the Woods	R	A,B,M	Pri	No	PW	748		16	20	18	20	20	560	23	28	22	6	540	24	46	22	6	545	30		41	6	2/15
Saint Mary's College	Notre Dame	SU	B	Pri	No	W	1,479		12	16	24	27	31	560	23	37	37	3	570	28	33	35		530		33	42	9	4/12
Taylor University	Upland	R	A,B,M	Pri	No	C	2,104				25	30		510	46	41	11	1	546	24	43	25	4	530		33		6	3/8
Trine University	Angola	SM	A,B,M	Pri	F,S	C	1,655			16	18	13	7	560	20	37	23	7	560	28	45	21		700	2		9		8/1
University of Evansville	Evansville	U	A,B,M,D	Pri	F,S	C	2,420		10	20	25	33	28	560	20	48	30	2	560	18	41	16	6	530		33	42		3/8
University of Indianapolis	Indianapolis	SM	A,B,M,D	Pri	No	C	4,205		26	26				510	46	37	13	1		41	4	27						9		52/1
University of Notre Dame	Notre Dame	SU	B,M,D	Pri	No	C	8,477	33					90	710	1		33	58	720		4	27	69	700		2			1/1
University of Saint Francis	Fort Wayne	SM	A,B,M	Pri	No	C	1,850	22	41	30	19	7	3	499	51	39	10	1	503	49	38	12	4	476	63		30	6	8/15
University of Southern Indiana	Evansville	SU	A,B,M,D	Pub	F,S	C	8,414	26	8	19	29	16	28	551	24	50	25	1	558	22	45	29	1	534	34		44	19	1/8
Valparaiso University	Valparaiso	SM	A,B,M,D	Pri	F,S	C	3,260	25	14	23	31	27	16	550	24	47	25	4	570	18	41	35	6	510	39		39	20	2/2
Wabash College	Crawfordsville	SM	B	Pri	F	M	926				39																		2/12/1
Iowa																														
Allen College	Waterloo	SU	A,B,M,D	Pri	No	PW	379	21	40	28	20	9	3																2/1
Briar Cliff University	Sioux City	SU	A,B,M	Pri	No	C	1,079	22	31	29	26	7	7																Open
Buena Vista University	Storm Lake	SM	B,M	Pri	No	C	861	22	24	26	24	11	17																3/1
Central College	Pella	SM	B	Pri	No	C	1,308	24	24	23	27	15	10	473	75	25			506	37	63			530	32		38	27	Open
Clarke College	Dubuque	SU	A,B,M,D	Pri	No	C	949	23	25	23	27	17	8	570	13	41	34	5	570	12	46	32	10	580	18		42	33	3/1
Coe College	Cedar Rapids	U	B	Pri	No	C	1,435	25	12	17	29	17	23	610	47	33	35	19	570	19	37	34	10		43		40	17	7/1
Cornell College	Mount Vernon	SM	B	Pri	No	C	1,122	25	15	25	36	20	32		14	29	30	3	570	10	45	30	3						8/1
Dordt College	Sioux Center	R	A,B,M	Pri	No	C	1,430	25	15	16	36	26	15		42	31	36	13		22	36							19	8/1
Drake University	Des Moines	U	B,M,D	Pri	F,S	C	3,364	27	27	57	16		26								20					96			8/1
Graceland University	Lamoni	R	A,B,M	Pri	No	C	2,045	21			18				96	4				80	20				96				4/1
Grand View University	Des Moines	U	B,M	Pri	No	C	2,094		48		27		3		1	17				1	13				1		4		4/1
Grinnell College	Grinnell	SM	B	Pri	No	C	1,721		21		18	3	5				46	49				36						4/1
Iowa State University	Ames	U	B,M,D	Pub	F,S	C	21,985				22	34	16	520	38	31	22	11	560	20	37	32	9	520	42		32	17	Open
Iowa Wesleyan College	Mount Pleasant	SM	A,B	Pri	No	S	875																						Open
Loras College	Dubuque	SU	B,M,D	Pri	No	C	1,535	23	26	30	34	19																	Open
Luther College	Decorah	SM	B	Pri	No	C	2,385	26		19	25																		9
Maharishi University of Management	Fairfield	SM	B,M,D	Pri	No	C	220																						6/15
Mercy College of Health Sciences	Des Moines	U	A,B	Pri	No	C	846																						Open
Morningside College	Sioux City	SU	B,M	Pri	No	C	1,321	23	26	30	25	10	9																Open

College	City
Mount Mercy University	Cedar Rapids
Northwestern College of Iowa	Orange City
Simpson College	Indianola
St. Ambrose University	Davenport
University of Dubuque	Dubuque
University of Iowa	Iowa City
University of Northern Iowa	Cedar Falls
Upper Iowa University	Fayette
Wartburg College	Waverly
William Penn University	Oskaloosa

Kansas

College	City
Baker University	Baldwin City
Benedictine College	Atchison
Bethany College	Lindsborg
Bethel College	North Newton
Emporia State University	Emporia
Fort Hays State University	Hays
Friends University	Wichita
Kansas State University	Manhattan
Kansas Wesleyan University	Salina
McPherson College	McPherson
MidAmerica Nazarene University	Olathe
Newman University	Wichita
Ottawa University	Ottawa
Pittsburg State University	Pittsburg
Southwestern College	Winfield
Sterling College	Sterling
Tabor College	Hillsboro
University of Kansas	Lawrence
University of Saint Mary	Leavenworth
Washburn University	Topeka
Wichita State University	Wichita

Kentucky

College	City
Alice Lloyd College	Pippa Passes
Asbury University	Wilmore
Bellarmine University	Louisville
Berea College	Berea
Brescia University	Owensboro
Campbellsville University	Campbellsville
Centre College	Danville
Eastern Kentucky University	Richmond
Georgetown College	Georgetown
Kentucky Christian University	Grayson
Kentucky State University	Frankfort
Kentucky Wesleyan College	Owensboro
Lindsey Wilson College	Columbia
Midway College	Midway
Morehead State University	Morehead
Murray State University	Murray
Northern Kentucky University	Highland Heights
Spalding University	Louisville
Thomas More College	Crestview Hills
Transylvania University	Lexington
Union College	Barbourville
University of Kentucky	Lexington
University of Louisville	Louisville
University of Pikeville	Pikeville
University of the Cumberlands	Williamsburg
Western Kentucky University	Bowling Green

Louisiana

College	City
Centenary College of Louisiana	Shreveport
Dillard University	New Orleans
Grambling State University	Grambling
Louisiana College	Pineville
Louisiana State University	Baton Rouge

TEST SCORES

Key:
- **ENVIRONMENT:** U-Urban R-Rural SU-Suburban SM-Small Town
- **DEGREES AWARDED:** A-Associate B-Bachelor M-Master D-Doctorate
- **CONTROL:** Pri-Private, Pub-Public
- **FRATERNITIES AND SORORITIES:** F-Fraternities S-Sororities F,S-Both No-Neither
- **STUDENTS:** C-Coed M-Men W-Women PM-Primarily Men PW-Primarily Women

Name of School	Town	Env	Degrees	Control	Frat/Sor	Students	Undergrad Enroll. Fall 2014	ACT Median	ACT <21	ACT 21-23	ACT 24-26	ACT 27-28	ACT >28	SAT CR Median	SAT CR <500	SAT CR 500-599	SAT CR 600-700	SAT CR >700	SAT Math Median	SAT Math <500	SAT Math 500-599	SAT Math 600-700	SAT Math >700	SAT Writing Median	SAT Writing <500	SAT Writing 500-599	SAT Writing 600-700	SAT Writing >700	Appl. Deadline
Louisiana State University in Shreveport	Shreveport	U	B,M	Pub	F,S	C	3,655	22	22	30	24		5	500	40		60		530	17	83								4/15
Louisiana Tech University	Ruston	SM	A,B,M,D	Pub	F,S	C	10,800	24	24						4	42					50					44				4/15
Loyola University New Orleans	New Orleans	U	B,M,D	Pri	F,S	C	3,200			36	17	5	5				43	4	490	7		39			7				Open
McNeese State University	Lake Charles	SU	A,B,M	Pub	F,S	C	7,501	20	20	47	15	3	5		68				500	51	40	7							Open
Nicholls State University	Thibodaux	SM	A,B,M	Pub	F,S	C	6,201	21	21	42	17	3	4	480	28		3			40									Open
Northwestern State University of Louisiana	Natchitoches	SM	A,B,M	Pub	No	C	7,836	21	21		7	7									34								7/6
Our Lady of Holy Cross College	New Orleans	U	A,B,M	Pri	No	No	1,314																						7/20
Southeastern Louisiana University	Hammond	SM	A,B,M,D	Pub	F,S	C	13,744	21	21	35	18	6	4	480	81	16	3			77	19	3			2				7/15
Southern University and A&M College	Baton Rouge	U	A,B,M	Pub	No	No	6,491	19	19	76	2	1																	7/15
Southern University at New Orleans	New Orleans	SU	A,B,M,D	Pub	No	No	3,165		31										660				30	680					7/1
Tulane University	New Orleans	U	B,M,D	Pri	F,S	C	8,353					7	83	660	2	15	53	30	660		11	58	30	680	2		58	38	7/1
University of Louisiana at Lafayette	Lafayette	U	A,B,M,D	Pub	F,S	C	14,560	22	22	34	22	6	7	500	45	32	20	4	540	37	37	22	5	540	35	40	22		Open
University of Louisiana at Monroe	Monroe	U	A,B,M,D	Pub	F,S	C	7,276	22	22	37	6	6	1	550	35	30	22	4	550	34	32	29	4	470	63	31	6		Open
University of New Orleans	New Orleans	U	A,B,M,D	Pub	F,S	C	8,653	22	22	35	29	1		480	55	35	9		480	57	32	11							Open
Xavier University of Louisiana	New Orleans	U	B,M,D	Pri	F,S	C	2,750	22	22	14										59	34	6	1		64	33			7/1

Maine

Name of School	Town	Env	Degrees	Control	Frat/Sor	Students	Undergrad Enroll. Fall 2014	ACT Median	ACT <21	ACT 21-23	ACT 24-26	ACT 27-28	ACT >28	SAT CR Median	SAT CR <500	SAT CR 500-599	SAT CR 600-700	SAT CR >700	SAT Math Median	SAT Math <500	SAT Math 500-599	SAT Math 600-700	SAT Math >700	SAT Writing Median	SAT Writing <500	SAT Writing 500-599	SAT Writing 600-700	SAT Writing >700	Appl. Deadline
Bates College	Lewiston	SM	B	Pri	No	C	1,773							680	4	9	63	33	680	1	7	60	32	680		9	48	43	1/1
Bowdoin College	Brunswick	SM	B	Pri	No	C	1,805					14	83	720	3	3	27	70	720	1	1	32	67	720		3	29	68	1/1
Colby College	Waterville	SM	B	Pri	No	C	1,820					6	94	660	2	15	51	31	680	1	12	49	39	670	1	14	48	36	1/1
College of the Atlantic	Bar Harbor	SU	A,B,M,D	Pri	No	C	356					16	74	640	2	23	54	21	610	12	42	53		610	7	33	58		2/15
Husson University	Bangor	SU	A,B,M,D	Pri	No	C	2,704			53	30	20	50	476	58	38	4		478	34		6		469	64	33	4		8/15
Maine College of Art	Portland	U	B	Pub	No	F	370					2	2																Open
Maine Maritime Academy	Castine	SM	A,B	Pri	F	No	935																						5/1
Saint Joseph's College of Maine	Standish	R	A,B	Pri	No	C	1,339			50	10	17	13	445	70	26	3	1	453	66	27	7		435	77	19	4		Open
Thomas College	Waterville	SM	A,B,M	Pri	No	C	554			20	24			530	32	44	21		540	28	44	24	4	510	41	42	16		Open
Unity College	Unity	R	B	Pri	No	C	930		50	27		7	7	490	49	36	14	1	490	51	36	13	2	490	53	35	12		2/15
University of Maine	Orono	SM	B,M,D	Pub	F,S	C	9,339			64	9	6	16	460	72	25	2		460	77	21	2		450	73	23	4		6/15
University of Maine at Augusta	Augusta	SM	A,B	Pub	No	C	4,990			43	29	3	5																Open
University of Maine at Farmington	Farmington	SM	B,M	Pub	No	C	1,773																						Open
University of Maine at Fort Kent	Fort Kent	R	B	Pub	No	C	1,209													53	19	2			77				Open
University of Maine at Machias	Machias	R	A,B	Pub	No	C	1,187							531	32	49	17		540	25	53	19	2						Open
University of Maine at Presque Isle	Presque Isle	R	A,B	Pub	No	C	1,536							500	47	39	12		500	50	40	9	2	490	51	37	11		2/15
University of New England	Biddeford	SU	B,M,D	Pri	No	C	2,217			22	19	6																	2/15
University of Southern Maine	Gorham	U	A,B,M,D	Pub	F,S	C	7,618			45	15	3	5																

Maryland

Name of School	Town	Env	Degrees	Control	Frat/Sor	Students	Undergrad Enroll. Fall 2014	ACT Median	ACT <21	ACT 21-23	ACT 24-26	ACT 27-28	ACT >28	SAT CR Median	SAT CR <500	SAT CR 500-599	SAT CR 600-700	SAT CR >700	SAT Math Median	SAT Math <500	SAT Math 500-599	SAT Math 600-700	SAT Math >700	SAT Writing Median	SAT Writing <500	SAT Writing 500-599	SAT Writing 600-700	SAT Writing >700	Appl. Deadline
Bowie State University	Bowie	SU	B,M,D	Pub	F,S	C	4,311							410	77	21			400	82	16	2		390					4/1
Capitol College	Laurel	R	A,B,M	Pri	No	C	300																						Open
Coppin State University	Baltimore	U	B,M	Pub	F,S	C	3,242																						6/15
Frostburg State University	Frostburg	SM	B,M,D	Pub	F,S	C	4,704		20	13	30	17	29	488	59	33	8	1	492	58	34	8	1	469	66	27	6	1	Open
Goucher College	Baltimore	SU	B,M	Pri	No	C	1,471		26	30	12	18	4	590	23	41	34	6	570	23	41	30	6	560	21	42	28	9	1/15
Hood College	Frederick	SU	B,M,D	Pri	No	C	1,359		36	2	13	11	74	520	41	41	16	2	515	45	38	15	2	500	47	39	13	1	Open
Johns Hopkins University	Baltimore	U	B,M,D	Pri	F,S	C	4,591		31				19	680	1	11	51	37	710	7	7	39	53	680		13	51	35	6/15
Loyola University Maryland	Baltimore	SU	B,M,D	Pri	No	C	4,084		27					591	4	51	39	6	599	40		48							1/1
Maryland Institute College of Art	Baltimore	U	B,M	Pri	No	C	1,680			1			51				72		545	6	69	26							1/15
McDaniel College	Westminster	SM	B,M	Pri	F,S	C	1,255		24	48		5	4	545		22	72	6	545	1			6						2/15
Morgan State University	Baltimore	SU	B,M,D	Pub	F,S	C	6,591		22		18					45			530	34	50	14	3	510	42	43	13		2/15
Mount Saint Mary's University	Emmitsburg	R	B,M	Pri	F,S	C	1,810		34	39	35	13		520	34	59	33	3	530		55		3						Open
Notre Dame of Maryland University	Baltimore	SU	B,M,D	Pri	No	C	1,620		22	35				578	5			4	578	3	8	35	3	572	7	62	29		2/15
Salisbury University	Salisbury	SU	B,M	Pub	F,S	C	7,997	PW	24																				Open
Sojourner-Douglass College	Baltimore	U	B	Pri	No	No	250		27	19	12	46	42	640	6	10	40	42	570	29			48	580	18	42	34		2/15
St. John's College-Annapolis	Annapolis	U	B,M	Pri	No	C	463				29	17	24	590	12	2	37	10	580	14	43	38	10		51	40	8		Open
St. Mary's College of Maryland	St. Marys City	SM	B,M	Pub	No	C	1,771		26					590	49	42	8		580	47	40	8							2/15
Stevenson University	Stevenson	SU	B,M	Pri	No	S	3,808																						Open
Towson University	Towson	SU	B,M,D	Pub	F,S	C	16,230							661	5	32	44	19	679	1	19	51	23				34	29	1/31
United States Naval Academy	Annapolis	SU	B	Pub	No	C	4,511								6	23	49	22		3	15	42	40			42	8		1/20
University of Maryland - College Park	College Park	SU	B,M,D	Pub	F,S	C	27,056																						1/20
University of Maryland/Baltimore County	Baltimore	SU	B,M,D	Pub	F,S	C	9,470																						

College	City	Level	Degrees	Control	Housing	Student Body	Enrollment
University of Maryland/Eastern Shore	Princess Anne	R	B,M,D	Pub	F,S	C	3,335
University of Maryland/University College	Adelphi	U	B,M,D	Pub	No	C	28,119
Washington Adventist University	Takoma Park	SU	A,B,M	Pri	F,S	C	995
Washington College	Chestertown	SM	B,M	Pri	F,S	C	1,454

Massachusetts

College	City	Level	Degrees	Control	Housing	Student Body	Enrollment
American International College	Springfield	U	A,B,M,D	Pri	F,S	C	1,729
Amherst College	Amherst	SM	B	Pri	No	C	1,785
Anna Maria College	Paxton	R	A,B,M	Pri	No	C	930
Assumption College	Worcester	SU	B,M	Pri	No	C	1,996
Atlantic Union College	South Lancaster	SM	A,B,M	Pri	No	C	450
Babson College	Babson Park	SU	B,M	Pri	No	C	1,800
Bard College at Simon's Rock	Great Barrington	SU	A,B	Pri	F,S	C	329
Bay Path College	Longmeadow	SM	A,B,M	Pri	No	W	1,360
Becker College	Worcester	U	A,B	Pri	No	C	1,826
Benjamin Franklin Institute of Technology	Boston	U	A,B	Pri	No	C	564
Bentley University	Waltham	SU	B,M,D	Pri	F,S	C	4,264
Berklee College of Music	Boston	U	B,M	Pri	No	C	4,090
Boston Architectural College	Boston	U	B,M	Pri	No	C	407
Boston College	Chestnut Hill	SU	B,M,D	Pri	No	C	9,154
Boston Conservatory	Boston	U	B,M	Pri	F,S	C	512
Boston University	Boston	U	B,M,D	Pri	F,S	C	18,017
Brandeis University	Waltham	SU	B,M,D	Pri	No	C	3,729
Bridgewater State University	Bridgewater	SU	B,M	Pub	F,S	C	9,684
Cambridge College	Cambridge	U	B,M,D	Pri	No	C	1,048
Clark University	Worcester	U	B,M,D	Pri	No	C	2,380
College of Art and Design at Lesley University	Boston	U	B	Pri	No	C	1,267
College of the Holy Cross	Worcester	SU	B	Pri	No	C	2,937
Curry College	Milton	SU	B,M	Pri	No	C	2,900
Eastern Nazarene College	Quincy	SU	A,B,M	Pri	No	C	640
Elms College	Chicopee	SU	A,B,M	Pri	No	C	640
Emerson College	Boston	U	B,M	Pri	F,S	C	3,765
Emmanuel College	Boston	U	B,M	Pri	No	C	2,176
Endicott College	Beverly	SU	B,M	Pri	F,S	C	2,955
Fitchburg State University	Fitchburg	SU	B,M,D	Pub	No	C	4,217
Framingham State University	Framingham	SU	B,M	Pub	F	C	4,609
Franklin W. Olin College of Engineering	Needham	SU	B	Pri	No	C	370
Gordon College	Wenham	SU	B	Pri	No	C	1,736
Hampshire College	Amherst	R	B	Pri	No	C	1,491
Harvard College/Harvard University	Cambridge	U	B,M,D	Pri	No	C	6,670
Hellenic College/Holy Cross Greek Orthodox School of Theology	Brookline	SU	B,M	Pri	No	C	91
Lasell College	Newton	U	B,M	Pri	No	C	1,743
Lesley University	Cambridge	U	A,B,M,D	Pri	F,S	C	1,598
Massachusetts College of Liberal Arts	North Adams	R	B,M	Pub	F	C	1,554
Massachusetts College of Pharmacy and Health Sciences	Boston	U	B,M,D	Pri	No	C	2,883
Massachusetts Institute of Technology	Cambridge	U	B,M	Pub	No	C	4,503
Massachusetts Maritime Academy	Buzzards Bay	SU	B,M	Pub	No	C	975
Merrimack College	North Andover	SU	A,B,M	Pri	No	C	2,319
Montserrat College of Art	Beverly	U	B	Pri	F,S	C	305
Mount Holyoke College	South Hadley	SM	B	Pri	No	W	2,189
Mount Ida College	Newton	U	A,B	Pri	No	C	1,130
New England Conservatory of Music	Boston	U	B,M,D	Pri	No	C	436
Newbury College	Brookline	SU	A,B	Pri	No	C	873
Nichols College	Dudley	R	A,B,M	Pri	No	C	1,332
Northeastern University	Boston	U	B,M,D	Pri	No	C	17,107
Pine Manor College	Chestnut Hill	SM	A,B	Pri	F,S	W	458
Regis College	Weston	SU	A,B,M,D	Pri	No	C	1,149
Salem State University	Salem	SM	B,M	Pub	No	C	7,298
Simmons College	Boston	U	B,M,D	Pri	No	W	1,709
Smith College	Northampton	SM	B,M	Pri	No	W	2,563
Springfield College	Springfield	SU	B,M,D	Pri	No	C	2,200
Stonehill College	Easton	SU	B	Pri	F,S	C	2,582
Suffolk University	Boston	U	A,B,M,D	Pri	No	C	5,496
Tufts University	Medford	SM	B,M,D	Pri	No	C	5,232
University of Massachusetts Amherst	Amherst	U	B,M,D	Pub	F,S	C	22,252
University of Massachusetts Boston	Boston	U	B,M,D	Pub	No	C	12,108
University of Massachusetts Dartmouth	North Dartmouth	SU	B,M,D	Pub	No	C	7,437
University of Massachusetts Lowell	Lowell	SU	B,M,D	Pub	F,S	C	10,548
Wellesley College	Wellesley	SU	B	Pri	No	W	2,172
Wentworth Institute of Technology	Boston	U	A,B	Pri	No	C	3,728

NAME OF SCHOOL	TOWN	ENVIRONMENT	DEGREES AWARDED	CONTROL	FRATERNITIES AND SORORITIES	STUDENTS	UNDERGRADUATE ENROLLMENT FALL 2014	ACT Median	ACT Below 21	ACT 21-23	ACT 24-26	ACT 27-28	ACT Above 28	SAT CR Median	SAT CR Below 500	SAT CR 500-599	SAT CR 600-700	SAT CR Above 700	SAT Math Median	SAT Math Below 500	SAT Math 500-599	SAT Math 600-700	SAT Math Above 700	SAT Writing Median	SAT Writing Below 500	SAT Writing 500-599	SAT Writing 600-700	SAT Writing Above 700	Application Deadline
Western New England University	Springfield	SU	A,B,M	Pri	No	C	2,732	24	15	27	37	12	9	520	38	46	15		550	25	49	24	2						Open
Westfield State University	Westfield	SU	B,M	Pub	No	C	5,607	24	50	28				500	46	46		1	510	37	50	12	2						3/1
Wheaton College	Norton	SM	B	Pri	No	C	1,622	29		11	27	19	54	625	6	26	50	17	620	6	26	52	16						1/15
Wheelock College	Boston	U	A,B,M	Pri	No	C	680	33	56					740		5	26	69	720		5	30	65	740		6	3	24	3/1
Williams College	Williamstown	SM	B,M	Pri	No	C	2,045	30		2	12	21	65	620	8	30	44	19	700	44	9	43	48	620			31	48	1/1
Worcester Polytechnic Institute	Worcester	SU	B,M,D	Pri	F,S	C	4,235	30		27	22	13	5	490	52	39	8		500		45	10	1						2/1
Worcester State University	Worcester	U	B,M	Pub	No	C	5,563	22	33	27	33																		5/1
Michigan																													
Adrian College	Adrian	SM	A,B,M	Pri	F,S	C	1,606	22	38	34	16	11	6	480	55	36	45	18	500	41	52	7	6	496	6	56	39		Open
Albion College	Albion	SM	B	Pri	F,S	C	1,396	24	21	29	25	17	17	540	24	21	58	22	540	12	70	12							Open
Alma College	Alma	SM	B	Pri	F,S	C	1,964	23	22	25	27	16	10	518	39	34	39		546	56	33	11							Open
Andrews University	Berrien Springs	R	A,B,M,D	Pri	No	C	1,789	23	34	27	22	11	7																Open
Aquinas College	Grand Rapids	SU	A,B,M	Pri	No	C	4,400	26	10	30	24	14			19	36	26	13	600	13	34	40	13						Open
Baker College of Flint	Flint	U	A,B	Pri	No	C	3,894																						8/15
Calvin College	Grand Rapids	SU	B,M	Pri	No	C	3,901	26		19	24	17	30	590	36	36	21	6	550	28	43	29	6	496	43	43	7	11	8/1
College for Creative Studies	Detroit	U	B	Pri	No	C	521	22	36	20	27	11	6	575	36	21	31	22	550	28	43	17		560	20	20	23	29	21
Concordia University, Ann Arbor	Ann Arbor	SU	A,B,M	Pri	No	C	2,152	22	27	30	19	16	8	544	31	34	31	3	529	34	46	17	3	504		37	23	6	8/15
Cornerstone University and Grand Rapids Theological Seminary	Grand Rapids	SU	A,B,M	Pri	No	C	8,882	22	22	29	19		6						509	35	37	17							Open
Davenport University	Grand Rapids	SU	B,M,D	Pri	F,S	C	18,208	21	36	26	26	7	6	483	40	33	17			2				486	37	37	8		2/8
Eastern Michigan University	Ypsilanti	SU	B,M,D	Pub	F,S	C	13,357	24	27	31	19	12	10	560	35	66			540	34	66			500	34	34			8/30
Ferris State University	Big Rapids	SM	A,B,M	Pub	F,S	C	194	26	22	18	28	18	61	680	3	17	43	37	620	3	27	47	23	650	3		50	33	8/1
Grace Bible College	Grand Rapids	SU	A,B	Pri	No	C	21,231	27	21	19	31	17	29	590	14	37	39	9	590	12	39	39	9	606	11	3	33	39	7/23
Grand Valley State University	Allendale	SM	B,M,D	Pub	F,S	C	1,472	24	28	27	27	18	40	600	13	40	35	27	632	6	34	39	27						2/15
Hillsdale College	Hillsdale	SM	B,M,D	Pri	F,S	C	3,432	19	8	10	20	17	8	600	17	47	37	18	630	6	25	51							1/15
Hope College	Holland	SM	B	Pri	No	C	1,461	21	3	12	29	21	23																Open
Kalamazoo College	Kalamazoo	SU	B	Pri	No	C	2,178	24	35	29	40	26	20	540	25	47	58	10	600	17	27	50	6	520	38	38	44	15	Open
Kettering University	Flint	SM	B,M	Pub	F,S	C	2,521	26	24	24	21	9	6	20	20	20	60		580	20	40	20	20	560	20	20	60		Open
Lake Superior State University	Sault Sainte Marie	SU	A,B,M	Pub	F,S	C	2,797	25	27	25	25	11	23	630	20	48													8/15
Lawrence Technological University	Southfield	SU	A,B,M,D	Pri	F,S	C	3,368	23	27	27	29																		Open
Madonna University	Livonia	U	A,B,M	Pri	No	C	788	17	26	28	17	5	16	600	40	30	30	15	650	11	27	40	24	595	37	37	43	15	20
Marygrove College	Detroit	SU	B,M,D	Pri	F,S	C	37,625	26	26	14	30	28	34			30	36	37		1	28	49	22		20	30	30	43	4/7/25
Michigan State University	East Lansing	SU	B,M,D	Pub	F,S	C	5,658	26	5	24	22	22	6					3	650	1	28	49				64	29	7	7/1
Michigan Technological University	Houghton	U	A,B,M,D	Pub	F,S	C	7,841	27	22	27	19	19	3	600	76		17			55	34	10							8/1
Northern Michigan University	Marquette	SM	A,B,M	Pub	F,S	C	1,819	22	48	26	16	5																	8/1
Northwood University	Midland	SM	A,B,M	Pri	F,S	C	16,190	22	19	40	25	15	5																8/1
Oakland University	Rochester	SU	B,M	Pub	F,S	C	1,052	19	20	21	40	7	5																8/30
Olivet College	Olivet	SM	A,B,M	Pri	F,S	C	908	20	50	24	20	5																	Open
Rochester College	Rochester Hills	SU	A,B,M	Pri	No	C	8,797	20	45	25	25																		8/1
Saginaw Valley State University	University Center	SM	A,B,M	Pub	F,S	C	2,402	19																					Open
Siena Heights University	Adrian	SM	A,B,M	Pri	No	C	1,555	21	21																				Open
Spring Arbor University	Spring Arbor	U	A,B,M	Pri	No	C	3,400	30		2	4	31	50	640	3	3	23	51	690	2	10	23	49	660	3	3	17	46	2/1
University of Detroit Mercy	Detroit	U	B,M,D	Pri	F,S	C	27,366	21	45	13	29	13	12				23	1			1	39	1				1	2/1
University of Michigan/Ann Arbor	Ann Arbor	SU	B,M,D	Pub	F,S	C	7,328	28	25	29	16	28	7	610	30	10	40	20	595	55	30	20	20	580	20	20	50	20	8/20
University of Michigan/Dearborn	Dearborn	SU	B,M,D	Pub	F,S	C	7,143	23	23	24	21	11	7																8/1
University of Michigan/Flint	Flint	U	A,B,M,D	Pub	F,S	C	18,347	22	25	23	28	8	7																Open
Wayne State University	Detroit	U	B,M,D	Pub	F,S	C	18,889	22	22	31	24	20	13																11/1
Minnesota																													
Augsburg College	Minneapolis	U	B,M,D	Pri	No	C	3,124	22		38	23	8	4	505	50	25	21	8	565	21	33	38	4						5/1
Bemidji State University	Bemidji	SM	A,B,M	Pub	F,S	C	4,744	25	17	27	26	14	21	590	20	31	30	19	580	20	39	28	14					32	Open
Bethel University	St. Paul	SU	A,B,M,D	Pri	No	C	3,421			3	4	10	84			6	37	58	1	5	36	58					7	26	1/15
Carleton College	Northfield	SM	B	Pri	No	C	2,050			3	19	16	26	20	20	53	24		41	28	13	6		30	30	40	40	Open
College of Saint Benedict	St. Joseph	R	B	Pri	No	W	2,059	24	10	22	29	17	13	67	67	23	13		480	67	41	13	8	470	60	60	40	26	Open
College of Saint Scholastica	Duluth	SM	A,B,M,D	Pri	No	C	2,859	22	13	29	22	16	3	570	23	33	33	35	550	33	29	23	10		31	31	40	23	8/1
Concordia College - Moorhead	Moorhead	SM	B	Pri	No	C	2,531	23	18	25	21	16	3		23	23											37		Open
Concordia University Saint Paul	St. Paul	SU	A,B,M,D	Pri	No	C	2,420	21	47	25	18	7	2																10
Gustavus Adolphus College	St. Peter	SM	B	Pri	F,S	C	2,455	27	2	13	31	20	34																11/1

The following table continues the *Colleges at a Glance* listing. The rotated numeric columns (application deadlines, test-score medians, admissions and cost figures) are too densely overlaid to transcribe reliably cell-by-cell; the clearly legible identifying columns are reproduced below.

College	City	Category	Degrees	Control	Enrollment
Hamline University	St. Paul	U	B,M,D	Pri	2,242
Macalester College	St. Paul	U	B	Pri	2,073
Metropolitan State University	St. Paul	U	B,M,D	Pub	6,974
Minneapolis College of Art and Design	Minneapolis	U	B,M	Pri	740
Minnesota State University, Mankato	Mankato	R	A,B,M,D	Pub	13,388
Minnesota State University, Moorhead	Moorhead	SU	A,B,M,D	Pub	7,012
North Central University	Minneapolis	U	A,B	Pri	1,366
Northwestern College	St. Paul	SU	A,B	Pri	1,865
Saint John's University	Collegeville	R	B,M	Pri	1,789
Saint Mary's University of Minnesota	Winona	SM	B,M,D	Pri	1,904
Southwest Minnesota State University	Marshall	R	A,B,M	Pub	2,710
St. Catherine University	St. Paul	SM	A,B,M,D	Pri	3,559
St. Cloud State University	St. Cloud	SU	A,B,M,D	Pub	14,525
St. Olaf College	Northfield	SM	B	Pri	3,034
University of Minnesota Crookston	Crookston	SM	B	Pub	2,764
University of Minnesota/Duluth	Duluth	U	B,M,D	Pub	9,918
University of Minnesota/Morris	Morris	SM	B	Pub	1,850
University of Minnesota/Twin Cities	Minneapolis/St. Paul	U	B,M,D	Pub	34,351
University of Saint Thomas	St. Paul	U	B,M,D	Pri	6,350
Winona State University	Winona	U	A,B,M,D	Pub	8,109

Mississippi

College	City	Category	Degrees	Control	Enrollment
Alcorn State University	Alcorn State	R	A,B,M	Pub	3,010
Belhaven University	Jackson	U	A,B,M	Pri	2,576
Blue Mountain College	Blue Mountain	SM	B,M	Pri	520
Delta State University	Cleveland	R	B,M,D	Pub	2,756
Jackson State University	Jackson	U	B,M,D	Pub	6,902
Millsaps College	Jackson	SU	B,M	Pri	744
Mississippi College	Clinton	SU	B,M,D	Pri	5,000
Mississippi State University	Mississippi State	SM	B,M,D	Pub	16,390
Mississippi University for Women	Columbus	SM	A,B,M,D	Pub	3,200
Mississippi Valley State University	Itta Bena	SM	B,M	Pub	2,748
Rust College	Holly Springs	SU	A,B	Pri	1,015
Tougaloo College	Tougaloo	SU	A,B	Pri	940
University of Mississippi	University	U	B,M,D	Pub	18,101
University of Southern Mississippi	Hattiesburg	SU	B,M,D	Pub	13,658
William Carey University	Hattiesburg	SM	B,M	Pub	1,850

Missouri

College	City	Category	Degrees	Control	Enrollment
Avila University	Kansas City	SU	B,M	Pri	1,135
Central Methodist University	Fayette	SM	A,B,M	Pri	1,173
College of the Ozarks	Point Lookout	SM	B	Pri	1,455
Columbia College	Columbia	U	A,B,M	Pub	874
Cox College	Springfield	U	A,B	Pub	600
Culver-Stockton College	Canton	SM	B,M	Pri	830
Drury University	Springfield	U	B,M	Pri	1,454
Evangel University	Springfield	SU	B,M	Pri	1,879
Fontbonne University	St. Louis	SM	A,B,M	Pri	2,085
Harris-Stowe State University	St. Louis	U	B	Pub	1,106
Hannibal-LaGrange University	Hannibal	U	A,B	Pri	1,280
Kansas City Art Institute	Kansas City	SM	B	Pri	660
Lincoln University	Jefferson City	SU	A,B,M	Pub	2,977
Lindenwood University	St. Charles	SU	B,M,D	Pub	5,905
Maryville University of Saint Louis	St. Louis	SU	A,B,M,D	Pub	2,818
Missouri Baptist University	St. Louis	SU	A,B,M	Pri	4,091
Missouri Southern State University	Joplin	U	B,M,D	Pub	5,561
Missouri State University	Springfield	SM	B,M,D	Pub	16,177
Missouri University of Science and Technology	Rolla	SM	B,M,D	Pub	1,430
Missouri Valley College	Marshall	SU	A,B	Pri	5,250
Missouri Western State University	St. Joseph	SU	B,M	Pub	1,674
Northwest Missouri State University	Maryville	SU	B,M	Pub	330
Park University	Parkville	SU	A,B	Pub	2,325
Research College of Nursing	Kansas City	SU	B,M,D	Pri	8,564
Rockhurst University	Kansas City	U	A,B	Pri	10,698
Saint Louis University	St. Louis	U	B,M,D	Pri	3,009
Southeast Missouri State University	Cape Girardeau	SM	A,B,M,D	Pub	679
Southwest Baptist University	Bolivar	SM	B,M	Pri	5,910
Stephens College	Columbia	U	B,M	Pri	
Truman State University	Kirksville	SM	B,M	Pub	

TEST SCORES

NAME OF SCHOOL	TOWN	ENVIRONMENT	DEGREES AWARDED	CONTROL	FRATERNITIES AND SORORITIES	STUDENTS	UNDERGRAD ENROLLMENT FALL 2014	ACT Median	ACT Below 21	ACT 21-23	ACT 24-26	ACT 27-28	ACT Above 28	SAT CR Median	SAT CR Below 500	SAT CR 500-599	SAT CR 600-700	SAT CR Above 700	SAT Math Median	SAT Math Below 500	SAT Math 500-599	SAT Math 600-700	SAT Math Above 700	SAT Writing Median	SAT Writing Below 500	SAT Writing 500-599	SAT Writing 600-700	SAT Writing Above 700	APPLICATION DEADLINE Month/Day
University of Central Missouri	Warrensburg	SM	A,B,M	Pub	F,S	C	9,739	22	40	29	16	6	4	550	36		37	27	570	24	34	25	17	540	19	43		19	Open
University of Missouri/Columbia	Columbia	SU	B,M,D	Pub	F,S	C	26,996	24	6	23	23	11	23						612	33				510	46	27		27	5/1
University of Missouri-Kansas City	Kansas City	U	B,M,D	Pub	F,S	C	10,247	24	22	25	24	11	18													1		21	Open
University of Missouri-St. Louis	St. Louis	U	B,M,D	Pub	F,S	C	13,887	24	17	28	28	13	14									89							1/15
Washington University in St. Louis	St. Louis	SU	A,B,M,D	Pri	F,S	C	7,401		25	27	22	11	99									78							8/1
Webster University	St. Louis	SU	B,M	Pri	No	S	2,928	24	17	28	22	11	15	560	24	30	30	7	510	21		34	7	530		43	34		Open
Westminster College	Fulton	SM	B	Pri	F,S	C	944	26	26	22	22	17	18			39	39	2		44	44	2			36	30	2		8/15
William Jewell College	Liberty	SM	B	Pri	F,S	C	1,030	26	9	22	22	18	26											26					Open
William Woods University	Fulton	SM	A,B,M	Pri	F,S	C	1,069	23	37	20	20	9	12												45		18		Open
Montana																													
Carroll College	Helena	SM	A,B	Pri	No	C	1,550	24	21	23	23	13	19	550	27	39	27	6	560	24	39	29	6	540		43	21		Open
Montana State University	Bozeman	SM	B,M,D	Pub	F,S	C	11,579	21	51	27	13	8	1	470	64	34	2		480	59	31	10			31				Open
Montana State University-Billings	Billings	U	A,B,M	Pub	No	C	4,465	24	14	31	31	12	12	545	25	44	26	4	610	11	31	46	13	530	38	36		24	Open
Montana State University-Northern	Havre	SM	A,B,M	Pub	No	C	1,440	23	32	26	22	8	11	511	43	38	16	2	504	40	48	12	1	478	62	26		11	Open
Montana Tech of The University of Montana	Butte	SM	A,B,M	Pub	No	C	2,757	23			13																		Open
Rocky Mountain College	Billings	SU	A,B,M	Pri	No	C	903	23	62	23		3		550	26	44	25	5	542	26	50	20	3	530	35	45		18	3/1
University of Great Falls	Great Falls	U	A,B,M,D	Pub	No	C	840	20						460	68	20	10	2	470	63	29	8							7/1
University of Montana	Missoula	U	A,B,M,D	Pub	F,S	C	11,692	23																					
University of Montana-Western	Dillon	SM	A,B	Pub	No	C	1,255	20																					
Nebraska																													
Bellevue University	Bellevue	SU	B,M	Pri	No	C	3,775																						Open
Chadron State College	Chadron	SM	B,M	Pri	No	C	2,375																						Open
Clarkson College	Omaha	U	A,B,M,D	Pri	No	C	770						6																Open
College of Saint Mary	Omaha	SM	A,B,M,D	Pri	No	PW	770	23	26	23	10	10	32	580	17	40	39	4	610	8	35	41	16	580	13	44		33	Open
Concordia University Nebraska	Seward	SM	B	Pri	No	PW	1,085	27	4	35	29	20	6																2/15
Creighton University	Omaha	U	A,B,M,D	Pri	F,S	C	4,065	27	24	15	25	10	10																8/1
Doane College	Crete	SM	B	Pri	F,S	C	1,067	23	37	35	20		3																Open
Hastings College	Hastings	R	B,M	Pri	F,S	C	1,104	24		23		18	3																3/1
Midland University	Fremont	SU	A,B,M,D	Pri	F,S	C	1,200		45	28	28	3	17		34	29	16			31	32	13							5/1
Nebraska Methodist College of Nursing and Allied Health	Omaha	SU	B,M	Pub	No	S	747	25	10	27					42					42		5							Open
Nebraska Wesleyan University	Lincoln	SU	B,M	Pri	F,S	No	1,903	22	14	26	26	14	25	570	24	34	29	13	590	19	31	32	18						5/1
Peru State College	Peru	R	B,M	Pub	No	C	1,485	23	30	23	22	9	10		37	42	16			11	42		5						8/1
Union College	Lincoln	SU	A,B,M	Pub	No	No	813	21	45	21	15	8	6																Open
University of Nebraska - Lincoln	Lincoln	U	B,M,D	Pub	F,S	No	19,979																						Open
University of Nebraska at Kearney	Kearney	SU	B,M,D	Pub	F,S	No	5,502																						5/1
University of Nebraska at Omaha	Omaha	U	B,M,D	Pub	F,S	No	11,525																						8/1
Wayne State College	Wayne	R	B,M	Pub	F,S	No	2,991																						Open
York College	York	SM	A,B,M	Pri	No	C	415																						Open
Nevada																													
Sierra Nevada College	Incline Village	R	B	Pri	No	C	195	23	16	15	14	3		540	50	36	13	1	540	42	38	17	1	520	42	42		14	2/15
University of Nevada, Las Vegas	Las Vegas	U	B,M,D	Pub	F,S	No	22,708	23	22	25	14	10	10	32	45	20		33	45	23									2/1
University of Nevada/Reno	Reno	U	B,M,D	Pub	F,S	No	16,839	23	22	37	25	4		36	28		3	42	45		3								2/1
New Hampshire																													
Colby-Sawyer College	New London	SM	A,B	Pri	No	C	1,375																						2/1
Daniel Webster College	Nashua	SU	A,B,M	Pri	No	C	725	21	9		72		19	480	58	36	6	65	480	54	37	7	67	470	63	32		23	Open
Dartmouth College	Hanover	R	B,M,D	Pri	F,S	C	4,147							1	8	26			7				1	8	5		5	1/1
Franklin Pierce University	Rindge	R	A,B,M,D	Pri	No	C	1,687																						Open
Granite State College	Concord	SM	A,B	Pub	No	C	1,518	21	40	40	20	4	1	440	56	35	8	1	430	56	36	7	1	440	56	37		6	4/1
Keene State College	Keene	SM	A,B,M	Pub	F,S	C	4,667	20	59	20	14	5	2	469	62	31	7	3	484	68	29	3	3	478	78	15		7	Open
New England College	Henniker	R	A,B,M,D	Pri	F,S	C	1,635	20	40	20				62	31	7		57	34	8			65	30		5	4/1
Plymouth State University	Plymouth	SM	A,B,M	Pub	F,S	C	4,064	20	59	20	14	4	1	479	62	31	7	484	57	34	7				478	65	30		4/1
Rivier University	Nashua	SU	A,B,M	Pri	No	C	1,630	25	6	37	37	22	12	560	10	57	29	4	570	11	51	36	2	570	11	51		34	Open
Saint Anselm College	Manchester	SU	B	Pri	No	C	1,923																						2/1

College	City		Degrees	Control			Enrollment
Southern New Hampshire University	Manchester	SU	A,B,M,D	Pri	F,S	C	1,995
Thomas More College of Liberal Arts	Merrimack	SM	B	Pri	No	C	96
University of New Hampshire	Durham	SM	A,B,M,D		F,S	C	12,840
New Jersey							
Berkeley College/New Jersey	Woodland Park	SU	A,B	Pri	No		3,052
Bloomfield College	Bloomfield	SU	B,M	Pri	F,S		1,999
Caldwell College	Caldwell	SU	B,M,D	Pri	F,S		1,705
Centenary College	Hackettstown	SU	A,B,M	Pri	F,S		1,993
College of New Jersey	Ewing	SU	B,M	Pub	F,S	PW	6,653
College of Saint Elizabeth	Morristown	SU	B,M,D	Pri	No		987
Drew University/College of Liberal Arts	Madison	SU	B,M,D	Pri	F,S	C	1,417
Fairleigh Dickinson University/College at Florham	Madison	SU	B,M	Pri	F,S	No	2,480
Fairleigh Dickinson University/Metropolitan Campus	Teaneck	SU	A,B,M,D	Pri	No	C	6,044
Felician College	Lodi	SU	A,B,M,D	Pri	No	C	1,621
Georgian Court University	Lakewood	SU	B,M	Pri	F,S	C	1,621
Kean University	Union	SU	B,M,D	Pub	F,S	C	11,987
Monmouth University	West Long Branch	SU	B,M,D	Pri	F,S	C	4,634
Montclair State University	Montclair	SU	B,M,D	Pub	F,S	C	14,432
New Jersey City University	Jersey City	U	B,M,D	Pub	F,S	C	6,229
New Jersey Institute of Technology	Newark	U	B,M,D	Pub	No	C	7,111
Princeton University	Princeton	SM	B,M,D	Pri	F,S	C	5,244
Ramapo College of New Jersey	Mahwah	SU	B,M	Pub	F,S	C	6,790
Richard Stockton College of New Jersey	Pomona	SU	B,M	Pub	F,S	C	4,549
Rider University	Lawrenceville	SU	A,B,M	Pri	F,S	C	12,022
Rowan University	Glassboro	SU	B,M,D	Pub	No	C	4,857
Rutgers, The State University of New Jersey/Camden Campus	Camden	U	A,B,M	Pub	No	C	34,544
Rutgers, The State University of New Jersey/New Brunswick	Piscataway	U	B,M,D	Pub	F,S	C	7,408
Rutgers, The State University of New Jersey/Newark Campus	Newark	U	A,B,M,D	Pub	No	C	2,317
Saint Peter's University	Jersey City	SU	A,B,M,D	Pri	F,S	C	5,148
Seton Hall University	South Orange	SU	B,M,D	Pri	F,S	C	2,234
Stevens Institute of Technology	Hoboken	U	B,M,D	Pri	F,S	C	19,596
Thomas Edison State College	Trenton	SU	A,B,M	Pub	No	C	355
Westminster Choir College	Princeton	SU	B,M	Pri	No	C	10,089
William Paterson University of New Jersey	Wayne	SU	B,M,D	Pub	No	C	
New Mexico							
Eastern New Mexico University	Portales	SM	A,B,M	Pub	F,S	C	4,572
New Mexico Highlands University	Las Vegas	SM	A,B,M	Pub	No	C	2,275
New Mexico Institute of Mining and Technology	Socorro	SM	B,M,D	Pub	F,S	C	1,525
New Mexico State University	Las Cruces	SM	A,B,M,D	Pub	No	C	12,784
Santa Fe University of Art and Design	Santa Fe	U	B	Pri	F,S	C	544
St. John's College, Santa Fe	Santa Fe	U	B,M	Pri	No	W	349
University of New Mexico	Albuquerque	U	A,B,M,D	Pub	F,S	C	20,852
Western New Mexico University	Hobbs	SM	A,B,M	Pub	No	C	425
	Silver City						660
New York							
Adelphi University	Garden City	SU	A,B,M,D	Pri	F,S	C	5,040
Albany College of Pharmacy and Health Sciences	Albany	U	B,M,D	Pri	F,S	C	1,076
Alfred State/SUNY College of Technology	Alfred	R	A,B	Pub	F,S	C	3,600
Alfred University	Alfred	R	B,M,D	Pri	No	C	1,960
Bard College	Annandale-on-Hudson	SM	A,B,M,D	Pri	No	C	2,059
Barnard College/Columbia University	New York	U	A,B	Pri	No	C	2,355
Berkeley College of New York City	New York	U	A,B	Pri	No	C	2,622
Berkeley College/Westchester Campus	White Plains	SU	B,M,D	Pri	No	C	640
Binghamton University/The State University of New York	Binghamton	SU	A,B	Pub	F,S	C	13,412
Boricua College	New York	U	B,M	Pri	No	C	1,170
Buffalo State College / State University of New York	Buffalo	U	B,M	Pub	F,S	C	9,822
Canisius College	Buffalo	U	B,M	Pri	F,S	C	3,084
Cazenovia College	Cazenovia	SM	A,B	Pri	No	C	1,105
City University of New York/Baruch College	New York	U	B,M	Pub	F,S	C	14,857
City University of New York/Brooklyn College	Brooklyn	U	B,M	Pub	F,S	C	13,099
City University of New York/City College	New York	U	B,M,D	Pub	No	C	
Clarkson University	Potsdam	R	B,M,D	Pri	F,S	C	3,247
Colgate University	Hamilton	R	B,M	Pri	F,S	C	2,825
College of Mount Saint Vincent	Riverdale	U	B,M	Pri	No	C	1,595
College of Staten Island/The City of New Yok	Staten Island	U	A,B,M,D	Pub	No	C	13,398

TEST SCORES

Legend:
- **STUDENTS:** C-Coed, M-Men, W-Women, PM-Primarily Men, PW-Primarily Women
- **FRATERNITIES AND SORORITIES:** F-Fraternities, S-Sororities, F,S-Both, No-Neither
- **CONTROL:** Pri-Private, Pub-Public
- **DEGREES AWARDED:** A-Associate, B-Bachelor, M-Master, D-Doctorate
- **ENVIRONMENT:** U-Urban, R-Rural, SU-Suburban, SM-Small Town

The following reproduces the columns that are legibly readable on this dense table (name, town, environment, degrees awarded, control, fraternities/sororities, students, undergraduate enrollment Fall 2014, median SAT scores where reported, and application deadline). The test-score distribution sub-columns (Below 500, 500-599, 600-700, Above 700, ACT bands) are present on the page but are omitted here where they could not be read reliably.

Name of School	Town	Env.	Degrees	Control	Frat./Sor.	Students	Undergrad Enroll. 2014	SAT CR Median	SAT Math Median	SAT Writing Median	Application Deadline
Columbia University/City of New York	New York	U	B,M,D	Pri	F,S	C	6,084	740	750	750	1/1
Columbia University/School of General Studies	New York	U	B	Pri	F,S	C	1,763				6/1
Concordia College – New York	Bronxville	SU	A,B,M	Pri	F,S	C	887	460	460	448	3/15
Cooper Union for the Advancement of Science and Art	New York	U	B,M	Pri	F	C	868	650	730		1/1
Cornell University	Ithaca	R	B,M,D	Pri	F,S	C	14,453				1/2
Daemen College	Amherst	SU	B,M,D	Pri	F,S	C	1,685	451	451	448	Open
Dominican College	Orangeburg	SU	A,B,M,D	Pri	No	C	1,677				Open
Dowling College	Oakdale	SU	B,M,D	Pri	No	C	3,435				Open
D'Youville College	Buffalo	U	B,M,D	Pri	No	C	1,866		530		12/1
Eastman School of Music	Rochester	U	B,M,D	Pri	F,S	C	505				12/1
Elmira College	Elmira	SU	A,B,M	Pri	F,S	C	1,408	520	530	510	1/6
Eugene Lang College/The New School for Liberal Arts	New York	U	B	Pri	No	C	1,457	540	530		Open
Excelsior College	Albany	SU	A,B,M	Pri	No	C	37,219				Open
Farmingdale State College	Farmingdale	SU	A,B	Pub	No	C	8,394	480	500	470	Open
Fashion Institute of Technology/State University of New York	New York	U	A,B,M,D	Pub	No	C	10,710	450	430	430	1/1
Five Towns College	Dix Hills	SU	B,M,D	Pri	No	C	749				Open
Fordham University	Bronx	U	B,M,D	Pri	F,S	C	8,633	620	620	630	1/1
Hamilton College	Clinton	R	B	Pri	F,S	C	1,884	700	700	700	1/1
Hartwick College	Oneonta	SM	B	Pri	F,S	C	1,540	555	550	545	Open
Hilbert College	Hamburg	SM	A,B,M	Pri	No	C	1,019				Open
Hobart and William Smith Colleges	Geneva	SM	B,M	Pri	F	C	2,421	560	570		2/1
Hofstra University	Hempstead	SU	B,M,D	Pri	F,S	C	6,904	569	569	610	Open
Houghton College	Houghton	R	A,B,M	Pri	No	C	1,081	574	548	547	Open
Hunter College	New York	U	B,M	Pub	F,S	C	16,638	500	598		2/15
Iona College	New Rochelle	SU	B,M	Pri	F,S	C	3,462	460	500		2/15
Ithaca College	Ithaca	SM	B,M,D	Pri	F,S	C	6,124	620	600	590	2/1
John Jay College of Criminal Justice/The City University of New York	New York	U	B,M,D	Pub	F,S	C	13,305	460	480		Open
Juilliard School	New York	U	B,M,D	Pri	No	C	495				12/1
Keuka College	Keuka Park	R	B,M	Pri	No	C	1,829				Open
Le Moyne College	Syracuse	SU	B,M	Pri	No	C	2,849	520	530		2/1
Lehman College/The City University of New York	Bronx	U	B,M	Pub	No	C	9,577	470	490	460	2/1
LIM College	New York	SM	A,B,M	Pri	No	C	1,357	483	474		Open
List College	New York	U	B	Pri	No	C	210				Open
LIU Brooklyn	Brooklyn	U	A,B,M,D	Pri	F,S	C	4,871	440	475	450	Open
LIU Post	Brookville	SU	A,B,M,D	Pri	F,S	C	7,117	490	500	490	Open
Manhattan College	Riverdale	U	B,M	Pri	F,S	C	3,351	526	535	528	2/1
Manhattan School of Music	New York	U	B,M,D	Pri	No	C	430				3/1
Manhattanville College	Purchase	SU	B,M	Pri	No	C	1,798				2/1
Mannes College New School for Music	New York	U	B,M	Pri	No	C	210				Open
Marist College	Poughkeepsie	SU	A,B,M	Pri	F,S	C	4,875	510	550	510	2/1
Maritime College/State University of New York	Throgs Neck	SU	B,M	Pub	No	C	1,575				12/1
Marymount Manhattan College	New York	U	A,B	Pri	No	C	1,945	460	460		2/15
Medaille College	Buffalo	U	A,B,M,D	Pri	No	C	1,843	380	380	380	Open
Megar Evers College/The City University of New York	Brooklyn	U	A,B	Pub	No	C	7,081				Open
Mercy College	Dobbs Ferry	SU	A,B,M	Pri	No	C	7,939				Open
Metropolitan College of New York	New York	U	B,M	Pri	No	C	676				Open
Molloy College	Rockville Centre	SU	A,B,M,D	Pri	No	C	3,336	520	530	510	Open
Monroe College	Bronx	U	A,B,M	Pri	No	C	5,480				Open
Mount Saint Mary College	Newburgh	SU	B,M,D	Pri	No	C	2,123	497	508	493	8/15
Nazareth College of Rochester	Rochester	SU	A,B,M,D	Pri	No	C	2,034	540	540	520	2/1
New York City College of Technology/The City University of New York	Brooklyn	U	A,B	Pub	No	C	16,207				2/1
New York Institute of Technology	Old Westbury	SU	A,B,M,D	Pri	No	C	4,456				1/1
New York University	New York	U	A,B,M,D	Pri	F,S	C	22,615	670	680	680	1/1
Niagara University	Niagara University	SU	A,B,M,D	Pri	F,S	C	3,176	510	530	500	Open
Nyack College	Nyack	SU	B,M	Pri	No	C	1,705				8/15
Oswego / State University of New York	Oswego	SM	B,M	Pub	F,S	C	7,628	540	560	510	1/15
Pace University	New York	U	B,M,D	Pri	F,S	C	8,694	550	554		2/15
Parsons The New School for Design	New York	U	A,B,M	Pri	No	C	4,260				1/1
Polytechnic Institute of New York University	Brooklyn	U	B,M,D	Pri	F,S	C	2,071	600	680	600	1/1
Pratt Institute	Brooklyn	U	B,M	Pri	F,S	C	3,158	581	598	589	1/5
Queens College/The City University of New York	Flushing	U	B,M	Pub	F,S	C	15,351	540	574		1/5

Institution	City	Cat	Degrees	Control	Aid	Coed	Enrollment
Rensselaer Polytechnic Institute	Troy	SU	B,M,D	Pri	F,S	C	5,452
Roberts Wesleyan College	Rochester	SU	A,B,M	Pri	No	C	1,336
Rochester Institute of Technology	Rochester	SU	A,B,M,D	Pri	F,S	C	14,224
Russell Sage College	Troy	U	B,M	Pri	No	W	823
Sarah Lawrence College	Bronxville	U	B,M	Pri	No	C	1,330
School of Visual Arts	New York	U	B,M	Pri	No	C	3,335
Siena College	Loudonville	SM	B,M	Pri	No	C	3,161
Skidmore College	Saratoga Springs	SM	B,M	Pri	No	C	2,684
St. Bonaventure University	St. Bonaventure	SM	B,M	Pri	No	C	1,771
St. Francis College	Brooklyn	U	A,B,M	Pri	No	C	2,764
St. John Fisher College	Rochester	SU	B,M	Pri	No	C	2,857
St. John's University	Queens	SU	A,B,M,D	Pri	F,S	C	15,765
St. Joseph's College, New York/Brooklyn Campus	Brooklyn	SU	B,M	Pri	F,S	C	1,115
St. Joseph's College, New York/Suffolk Campus	Patchogue	SU	B,M	Pri	F,S	C	3,023
St. Lawrence University	Canton	SM	B,M	Pri	F,S	C	2,361
St. Thomas Aquinas College	Sparkill	SU	A,B,M	Pri	No	C	2,120
State University of New York / College of Environmental Science and Forestry	Syracuse	U	A,B,M,D	Pub	F,S	C	2,177
State University of New York at Purchase	Purchase	SU	B,M	Pub	No	C	3,830
State University of New York Polytechnic Institute	Utica	SU	B,M	Pub	No	C	2,034
State University of New York/Empire State College	Saratoga Springs	SU	A,B,M	Pub	No	C	10,851
Stony Brook University / State University of New York	Stony Brook	SM	B,M,D	Pub	F,S	C	16,480
SUNY College at Geneseo	Geneseo	SM	B,M	Pub	F,S	C	5,497
SUNY College at Old Westbury	Old Westbury	SM	B,M	Pub	F,S	C	4,158
SUNY Cortland/The State University of New York	Cortland	SM	B,M	Pub	F,S	C	4,943
SUNY Fredonia/The State University of New York at Fredonia	Fredonia	SM	B,M	Pub	F,S	C	6,130
SUNY New Paltz	New Paltz	SM	B,M	Pub	F,S	C	5,863
SUNY Oneonta / State University of New York	Oneonta	SU	B,M	Pub	F,S	C	5,659
SUNY Plattsburgh / State University of New York	Plattsburgh	SU	B,M	Pub	F,S	C	15,224
Syracuse University	Syracuse	U	A,B,M,D	Pri	No	C	1,025
The College of New Rochelle	New Rochelle	U	B,M	Pri	F,S	PW	2,891
The College of Saint Rose	Albany	U	B,M	Pri	No	C	3,681
The State University of New York at Potsdam	Potsdam	R	B,M	Pub	F,S	C	2,532
The State University of New York College of Agriculture and Tech at Cobleskill	Cobleskill	R	A,B	Pub	No	C	7,040
The State University of New York/College at Brockport	Brockport	SM	A,B,M	Pub	F,S	C	11,259
Touro College	New York	SM	B	Pri	No	C	2,242
Union College	Schenectady	SU	B,M	Pub	F,S	C	987
United States Merchant Marine Academy	Kings Point	SU	B	Pub	No	C	4,175
United States Military Academy	West Point	SM	B	Pub	F,S	C	12,542
University at Albany / SUNY	Albany	SU	B,M,D	Pri	F,S	C	19,505
University at Buffalo / The State University of New York	Buffalo	SU	B,M,D	Pri	F,S	C	6,266
University of Rochester	Rochester	SU	B,M,D	Pri	No	C	2,931
Utica College	Utica	SU	B,M,D	Pri	No	C	2,418
Vassar College	Poughkeepsie	SU	B,M	Pri	No	C	1,799
Vaughn College of Aeronautics and Technology	Flushing	SU	A,B,M	Pri	F,S	C	1,818
Wagner College	Staten Island	SU	B,M	Pri	No	C	85
Webb Institute	Glen Cove	SU	B	Pri	No	C	560
Wells College	Aurora	SM	B	Pri	No	C	2,869
Yeshiva University	New York	SU	A,B	Pri	No	C	8,350
York College / The City University of New York	Jamaica	U	B,M	Pub	No	C	

North Carolina

Institution	City	Cat	Degrees	Control	Aid	Coed	Enrollment
Appalachian State University	Boone	SM	B,M,D	Pub	F,S	C	15,712
Barton College	Wilson	SU	B	Pri	F,S	C	1,150
Belmont Abbey College	Belmont	SU	B	Pri	S	C	1,706
Bennett College for Women	Greensboro	U	B	Pri	No	W	766
Cabarrus College of Health Sciences	Concord	SU	A,B	Pri	No	C	355
Campbell University	Buies Creek	SU	A,B,M,D	Pri	F,S	C	4,500
Catawba College	Salisbury	R	B	Pri	F,S	C	1,309
Davidson College	Davidson	SM	B	Pri	F,S	C	1,770
Duke University	Durham	SU	B,M,D	Pri	F,S	C	6,270
East Carolina University	Greenville	U	B,M,D	Pub	F,S	C	21,298
Elizabeth City State University	Elizabeth City	SM	B,M	Pub	F,S	C	3,395
Elon University	Elon	U	B,M,D	Pub	F,S	W	5,782
Fayetteville State University	Fayetteville	SM	B,M,D	Pri	No	C	5,287
Gardner-Webb University	Boiling Springs	SM	A,B,M,D	Pri	F,S	C	2,572
Greensboro College	Greensboro	SU	B	Pri	F,S	C	1,066
Guilford College	Greensboro	SU	B,M,D	Pub	No	C	2,137
High Point University	High Point	SU	B	Pri	F,S	C	3,964
Johnson & Wales University/Charlotte Campus	Charlotte	U	A,B	Pri	No	C	

NAME OF SCHOOL	TOWN	ENVIRONMENT	DEGREES AWARDED	CONTROL	FRATERNITIES AND SORORITIES	STUDENTS	UNDERGRADUATE ENROLLMENT FALL 2014	ACT Median	ACT Below 21	ACT 21-23	ACT 24-26	ACT 27-28	ACT Above 28	SAT CR Median	SAT CR Below 500	SAT CR 500-599	SAT CR 600-700	SAT CR Above 700	SAT Math Median	SAT Math Below 500	SAT Math 500-599	SAT Math 600-700	SAT Math Above 700	SAT Writing Median	SAT Writing Below 500	SAT Writing 500-599	SAT Writing 600-700	SAT Writing Above 700	APPLICATION DEADLINE
Johnson C. Smith University	Charlotte	U	B,M	Pri	F,S	C	1,375	17	92					400	87	11	2		410	89	11	1							Open
Lees-McRae College	Banner Elk	R	B	Pri	No	C	940	21	74	7	1	2	1	480	59	34	6		500	53	35	12							Open
Lenoir-Rhyne College	Hickory	SU	B,M	Pri	F,S	C	1,564	15	15	6	17				57	33	10		500	46	39	14							Open
Livingstone College	Salisbury	SM	A,B	Pri	F,S	C	1,250																						6
Mars Hill University	Mars Hill	R	B		F,S	W	1,967	21	47	24	21	5	6	519	41	42	16	1	520	39	43	17	1	466	60	33	6		2/15
Meredith College	Raleigh	SU	B,M	Pri	No	C	2,280	21	50	30	10	6	4	484	59	34	6	1	510	45	40	14	1	445	81	17	1		Open
Methodist University	Fayetteville	SM	A,B,M	Pri	F,S	C	735	18	44					475	20	73	7	1	466	16	76	7		440	13				Open
Montreat College	Montreat	SU	B	Pri	No	C	9,203			49				450	76	21			460	71	26	3							Open
North Carolina Agricultural and Technical State University	Greensboro	U	A,B,M,D	Pub	F,S	C	5,300	26			6			590	7	47	28	8	630	3	27	54	16	570	13	52	30		11/1
North Carolina Central University	Durham	U	A,B,M,D	Pub	F,S	C	24,833																						Open
North Carolina State University	Raleigh	SU	B,M	Pub	F,S	C	1,756	20	55	32	5			460	63	31	6		500	49	40	11		450	71	26	2		8/25
North Carolina Wesleyan College	Rocky Mount	R	B,M	Pri	No	C	955	24	22	26	13			520	41	44	11		520	39	43	17		510	45	37	15		Open
Pfeiffer University	Misenheimer	SU		Pri	F,S	C	1,703	28																					Open
Queens University of Charlotte	Charlotte	SU	B	Pri	F,S	C	1,360						10	590	7									570					7/30
Saint Augustine's University	Raleigh	SU	B,M	Pri	F,S	C	871	19	70	21	6	2		460	67	27	4	2	480	66	29	5		500	54	36	9	1	Open
Salem College	Winston-Salem	U	A,B,M	Pri	No	PW	2,572							510	44	42	12		520	40	46	12		430	83	16	1		3/1
Shaw University	Raleigh	U	B,M,D	Pub	F,S	C	460			6	2			460	72	24	4		460	70	27	3							Open
St. Andrews University	Laurinburg	SM	B,M	Pub	No	C	15,023	19	22	39	17	18		600	7	41	42	7	590	5	46	42	11	570	15	47	31		2/15
The University of North Carolina at Greensboro	Greensboro	U	A,B	Pub	F,S	C	5,504	25	5	6	18	58	24	640	2	21	52	24	660	17	16	50	32	640		23	48	25	1/10
The University of North Carolina at Pembroke	Pembroke	SM	B,M	Pri	F,S	C	3,116	23	1	17	10	16	1	530	26	57	16	1	560	17	57	12	4	520	35	52	12		7/1
University of Mount Olive	Asheville	SU	B,M,D	Pub	F,S	C	3,693	23	17	43	30	14	8	592	6	56	35	3	605	4	50	42		561	16	56	26		2/1
University of North Carolina at Asheville	Chapel Hill	SU	B,M,D	Pub	F,S	C	18,350	26	10	30			50	650	3	19	49	29	675	2	13	49	36						2/1
University of North Carolina at Chapel Hill	Charlotte	SU	B,M,D	Pub	F,S	C	22,216	29	4	21	32	22	22	580	15	39	35	11	540	32	46	20	2	486	60	32	7		1/15
University of North Carolina at Charlotte	Wilmington	SU	B,M,D	Pub	F,S	C	11,770	26	8	16	16	8		515	43	43	13		526	36	47	16							2/1
University of North Carolina at Wilmington	Winston-Salem	SU	B,M,D	Pub	No	C	781	26	21	38	6	6		440	72	24	3		440	73	24	3		490	53	37	9		3/1
University of North Carolina School of the Arts	Winston-Salem	SU	B,M,D	Pub	No	C	4,812	29	34	18	34			500	49	39	11		520	37	42	21	1	420	79	7	1		Open
Wake Forest University	Asheville	R	B,M	Pri	F,S	C	7,979	26	64	64	10								440	78	12								1
Warren Wilson College	Cullowhee	SU	B,M,D	Pub	No	C	824	18																					1/15
Western Carolina University	Raleigh	U	R	Pri	F,S	S	791	22																					3/1
William Peace University	Wingate	SM	B,M,D	Pri	F,S	C	1,773																						Open
Wingate University	Winston-Salem	SU	B,M	Pub	F,S	C	5,458																						Open

North Dakota

NAME OF SCHOOL	TOWN	ENVIRONMENT	DEGREES AWARDED	CONTROL	FRATERNITIES	STUDENTS	ENROLLMENT	ACT Median	ACT Below 21	ACT 21-23	ACT 24-26	ACT 27-28	ACT Above 28	SAT CR Median					SAT Math Median				SAT Math Above 700	SAT Writing Median					DEADLINE
Dickinson State University	Dickinson	R	A,B	Pub	No	C	1,474	19	68	20	7		2																8/1
Mayville State University	Mayville	R	A,B	Pub	No	C	1,036																						Open
Minot State University	Minot	SM	B,M	Pub	No	C	3,298	24																					Open
North Dakota State University	Fargo	U	B,M,D	Pri	F,S	C	12,124	24		24	27	8	53	498	32	55	33	15	495	22	34	22	2	41		30	25		4
University of Jamestown	Jamestown	SM	B,M	Pri	No	C	938	22	32	32	8	4								57	28	11							Open
University of Mary	Bismarck	SU	B,M,D	Pri	F,S	C	2,060	22	27	33	10	5																	8/15
University of North Dakota	Grand Forks	U	B,M,D	Pub	F,S	C	11,537	23	18	27	27	11																	7/1
Valley City State University	Valley City	SM	B,M	Pub	No	C	1,211	20	58	24	12	4	2	444	90		10		460	56	27	17							Open

Ohio

NAME OF SCHOOL	TOWN	ENVIRONMENT	DEGREES AWARDED	CONTROL	FRATERNITIES	STUDENTS	ENROLLMENT	ACT Median	ACT Below 21	ACT 21-23	ACT 24-26	ACT 27-28	ACT Above 28	SAT CR Median					SAT Math Median				SAT Math Above 700	SAT Writing Median					DEADLINE
Art Academy of Cincinnati	Cincinnati	U	A,B,M	Pri	No	C	138	21	43	36	14	7		550	33	50	6	11	460	68	26	6		500	47				6/30
Ashland University	Ashland	SM	A,B,M,D	Pri	F,S	C	2,785	23	30	28	25	6	6	540	28	48	19	5	540	27	47	23	3	530	33	46	18	3	Open
Baldwin Wallace University	Berea	SU	B,M	Pri	F,S	C	3,362	23	37	22	23	11	6	495	44	40	12	5	510	48	36	12	4		46	12	8	3	Open
Bluffton University	Bluffton	SM	B,M	Pri	No	C	997	22	31	22	20	8	8	520	39	39	18	3	520	48	43	8		490	34	40	16	3	5/31
Bowling Green State University	Bowling Green	SM	B,M,D	Pub	F,S	C	14,099	22	31	29	25	12	15	537	32	44	19	5	548	35	38	19	3	537	43	40	16	1	7/15
Capital University	Columbus	SU	B,M,D	Pri	F,S	C	2,742	24	19	25	29	10	8	537	1		53	35	710	7		37	56	670	1	17	47	35	7/15
Case Western Reserve University	Cleveland	SM	B,M,D	Pri	F,S	C	4,911	31		1	8	12	81	670	11	41	53	11	590	11	7	37	11	570	16	46	31		1/15
Cedarville University	Cedarville	R	B,M	Pri	No	C	3,307	26	6	20	27	10	27	590	11	41	37		590	11	39	39		570	16	46	31		1/15
Central State University	Wilberforce	R	A,B,M	Pub	F,S	C	1,335																						Open
Chancellor University	Cleveland	U	B	Pri	No	C	1,105																						Open
Cleveland Institute of Art	Cleveland	U	B	Pri	No	C	559	23	22	28	17		12	550	27	40	28	5	520	41	32	22		500	44	32	22		2/1
Cleveland Institute of Music	Cleveland	U	B,M,D	Pri	No	C	240	33	7	20	10	7	5	510	42	34	21	7	520	42	36	17							3/1
College of Mount Saint Joseph	Cincinnati	SU	A,B,M,D	Pri	F,S	C	12,194	22	40	29	22	6	5	475	62	30	9	1	468	61	30	9							3/1
College of Wooster	Wooster	SU	B	Pri	F,S	C	1,820																						3/1

The dense tabular data on this page lists Ohio and Oklahoma colleges with numerous numeric columns (application deadlines, test scores, and percentage figures). The most reliably legible columns are reproduced below.

Institution	City	Control	Enrollment
Columbus College of Art and Design	Columbus	Pri	1,333
Defiance College	Defiance	Pri	957
Denison University	Granville	Pri	2,336
Franciscan University of Steubenville	Steubenville	Pri	2,040
Franklin University	Columbus	Pri	7,055
Heidelberg University	Tiffin	Pri	1,110
Hiram College	Hiram	Pri	1,380
John Carroll University	University Heights	Pri	3,125
Kent State University	Kent	Pub	23,328
Kenyon College	Gambier	Pri	1,662
Lake Erie College	Painesville	Pri	848
Lourdes University	Sylvania	Pri	2,118
Malone University	Canton	Pri	1,588
Marietta College	Marietta	Pri	1,487
Miami University	Oxford	Pub	15,071
Mount Vernon Nazarene University	Mount Vernon	Pri	1,756
Muskingum University	New Concord	Pri	1,741
Notre Dame College	South Euclid	Pri	1,363
Oberlin College	Oberlin	Pri	2,961
Ohio Dominican University	Columbus	Pri	2,005
Ohio Northern University	Ada	Pri	2,305
Ohio State University at Lima	Lima	Pub	1,041
Ohio State University at Mansfield	Mansfield	Pub	1,155
Ohio State University at Marion	Marion	Pub	1,192
Ohio State University at Newark	Newark	Pub	2,384
Ohio University	Athens	Pub	23,524
Ohio Wesleyan University	Delaware	Pri	1,821
Otterbein College	Westerville	Pri	2,715
Shawnee State University	Portsmouth	Pub	4,114
The Ohio State University-Columbus Campus	Columbus	Pub	44,741
Tiffin University	Tiffin	Pri	1,129
Union Institute & University	Cincinnati	Pri	3,764
University of Akron	Akron	Pub	19,810
University of Cincinnati	Cincinnati	Pub	24,407
University of Dayton	Dayton	Pri	8,554
University of Findlay	Findlay	Pri	4,004
University of Mount Union	Alliance	Pri	2,175
University of Rio Grande	Rio Grande	Pri	1,855
University of Toledo	Toledo	Pub	16,877
Urbana University	Urbana	Pri	1,457
Ursuline College	Pepper Pike	Pri	953
Walsh University	North Canton	Pri	2,385
Wilberforce University	Wilberforce	Pri	800
Wilmington College	Wilmington	Pri	1,395
Wittenberg University	Springfield	Pri	1,948
Wright State University	Dayton	Pub	12,682
Xavier University	Cincinnati	Pri	4,633
Youngstown State University	Youngstown	Pub	11,348

Oklahoma

Institution	City	Control	Enrollment
Cameron University	Lawton	Pub	5,056
East Central University	Ada	Pub	3,757
Langston University	Langston	Pub	4,020
Northeastern State University	Tahlequah	Pub	8,659
Northwestern Oklahoma State University	Alva	Pub	1,809
Oklahoma Baptist University	Shawnee	Pri	2,019
Oklahoma Christian University	Oklahoma City	Pri	1,973
Oklahoma City University	Oklahoma City	Pri	1,781
Oklahoma Panhandle State University	Goodwell	Pub	1,387
Oklahoma State University	Stillwater	Pub	20,130
Oklahoma Wesleyan University	Bartlesville	Pri	1,059
Oral Roberts University	Tulsa	Pri	2,782
Southeastern Oklahoma State University	Durant	Pub	3,615
Southern Nazarene University	Bethany	Pri	1,653
Southwestern Oklahoma State University	Weatherford	Pub	4,577
St. Gregory's University	Shawnee	Pri	770
The University of Oklahoma	Norman	Pub	21,011
University of Central Oklahoma	Edmond	Pub	15,367
University of Science and Arts of Oklahoma	Chickasha	Pub	983
University of Tulsa	Tulsa	Pri	3,473

Key to columns:

- **ENVIRONMENT:** U-Urban, R-Rural, SU-Suburban, SM-Small Town
- **DEGREES AWARDED:** A-Associate, B-Bachelor, M-Master, D-Doctorate
- **CONTROL:** Pri-Private, Pub-Public
- **FRATERNITIES AND SORORITIES:** F-Fraternities, S-Sororities, F,S-Both, No-Neither
- **STUDENTS:** C-Coed, M-Men, W-Women, PM-Primarily Men, PW-Primarily Women

Oregon

Name of School	Town	Environment	Degrees Awarded	Control	Frat/Sor	Students	Undergrad Enrollment (Fall 2014)	Application Deadline (Month/Day)
Art Institute of Portland	Portland	U	A,B	Pri	No	C	1,327	Open
Concordia University	Portland	U	A,B,M,D	Pri	No	C	1,598	Open
Corban University	Salem	SU	B,M,D	Pri	No	C	933	8/1
Eastern Oregon University	La Grande	R	B,M,D	Pub	No	C	3,050	Open
George Fox University	Newberg	SM	B,M,D	Pri	No	C	2,443	2/1
Lewis & Clark College	Portland	SU	B,M	Pri	F,S	C	2,179	1/15
Linfield College-McMinnville Campus	McMinnville	SM	B,M	Pri	F,S	C	1,683	2/15
Marylhurst University	Marylhurst	SU	B,M	Pri	No	C	817	Open
Northwest Christian University	Eugene	U	A,B,M	Pri	No	C	400	6/1
Oregon Institute of Technology	Klamath Falls	SM	A,B,M	Pub	F,S	C	3,070	9/1
Oregon State University	Corvallis	SM	B,M,D	Pub	F,S	C	23,903	8/15
Pacific Northwest College of Art	Portland	U	B,M,D	Pri	No	C	446	2/15
Pacific University	Forest Grove	SM	B,M,D	Pri	F,S	C	1,730	Open
Portland State University	Portland	U	B,M,D	Pub	No	C	23,170	1/15
Reed College	Portland	SM	B,M	Pri	No	C	1,395	1/15
Southern Oregon University	Ashland	SU	B,M	Pub	F,S	C	5,414	Open
University of Oregon	Eugene	SU	B,M,D	Pub	F,S	C	20,559	1/15
University of Portland	Portland	SU	B,M,D	Pri	No	C	2,572	2/1
Warner Pacific College	Portland	U	A,B	Pri	No	C	1,550	Open
Western Oregon University	Monmouth	R	A,B,M	Pub	No	C	4,875	Open
Willamette University	Salem	U	B,M,D	Pri	F,S	C	3,058	2/1

Pennsylvania

Name of School	Town	Environment	Degrees Awarded	Control	Frat/Sor	Students	Undergrad Enrollment (Fall 2014)	Application Deadline (Month/Day)
Albright College	Reading	SU	B,M	Pri	No	C	1,751	Open
Allegheny College	Meadville	SU	B	Pri	F,S	C	2,023	2/15
Alvernia University	Reading	SU	A,B,M,D	Pri	No	C	2,371	Open
Arcadia University	Glenside	SU	B,M,D	Pri	No	C	1,957	Open
Bloomsburg University of Pennsylvania	Bloomsburg	SM	A,B,M,D	Pub	F,S	C	8,605	Open
Bryn Athyn College	Bryn Athyn	SU	A,B	Pri	No	C	267	1/15
Bryn Mawr College	Bryn Mawr	SU	B,M,D	Pri	No	W	1,308	1/15
Bucknell University	Lewisburg	SM	B,M	Pri	F,S	C	3,565	1/15
Cabrini College	Radnor	SU	B,M	Pri	No	C	1,312	Open
Cairn University	Langhorne	SU	A,B,M	Pri	No	C	817	Open
California University of Pennsylvania	California	SU	A,B,M,D	Pub	F,S	C	5,970	Open
Carlow University	Pittsburgh	U	B,M,D	Pri	No	PW	1,818	7/1
Carnegie Mellon University	Pittsburgh	SU	B,M,D	Pri	F,S	C	5,951	1/1
Cedar Crest College	Allentown	SU	B,M	Pri	No	W	1,286	Open
Chatham University	Pittsburgh	U	B,M,D	Pri	No	C	932	Open
Chestnut Hill College	Philadelphia	SU	A,B,M,D	Pri	No	C	1,481	Open
Cheyney University of Pennsylvania	Cheyney	SU	A,B,M	Pub	F,S	C	1,224	5/30
Clarion University of Pennsylvania	Clarion	SM	A,B,M	Pub	F,S	C		Open
Curtis Institute of Music	Philadelphia	U	B,M	Pri	No	C	130	Open
De Sales University	Center Valley	SU	B,M,D	Pri	No	C	2,381	3/1
Delaware Valley College	Doylestown	SU	A,B,M	Pri	No	C	2,000	Open
Dickinson College	Carlisle	SU	B,M	Pri	F,S	C	2,352	1/1
Drexel University	Philadelphia	U	A,B,M,D	Pri	F,S	C	16,896	Open
Duquesne University	Pittsburgh	U	B,M,D	Pri	F,S	C	5,995	7/1
East Stroudsburg University of Pennsylvania	East Stroudsburg	SM	B,M	Pub	No	C	6,186	4/1
Eastern University	St. Davids	SU	A,B,M,D	Pri	No	C	2,701	1/4
Edinboro University of Pennsylvania	Edinboro	SU	A,B,M	Pub	F,S	C	5,595	Open
Elizabethtown College	Elizabethtown	SM	B,M	Pri	No	C	1,788	Open
Elizabethtown College School of Continuing and Professional Studies	Elizabethtown	SM	A,B,M	Pri	No	C	346	Open
Franklin and Marshall College	Lancaster	SU	B	Pri	F,S	C	2,209	1/15
Gannon University	Erie	U	A,B,M,D	Pri	No	C	3,205	Open
Geneva College	Beaver Falls	SM	A,B,M	Pri	No	C	1,395	Open
Gettysburg College	Gettysburg	SM	B	Pri	F,S	C	2,451	1/15
Grove City College	Grove City	SM	B	Pri	F,S	C	2,509	2/1
Gwynedd-Mercy College	Gwynedd Valley	SU	A,B,M	Pri	No	C	2,196	2/1

College	City	Setting	Degrees	Control	Housing	Enrollment	Deadline
Haverford College	Haverford	SU	B	Pri	No	1,194	1/15
Holy Family University	Philadelphia	SU	A,B,M,D	Pri	No	2,139	Open
Immaculata	Immaculata	SU	A,B,M,D	Pri	F,S	2,883	3/1
Indiana University of Pennsylvania	Indiana	SM	A,B,M,D	Pub	No	12,130	Open
Juniata College	Huntingdon	R	A,B	Pri	No	1,615	6/15
Keystone College	La Plume	U	A,B,M	Pri	No	1,995	6/15
King's College	Wilkes Barre	SM	A,B,M	Pri	No	8,815	Open
Kutztown University of Pennsylvania	Kutztown	SU	A,B,M	Pub	F,S	1,305	Open
La Roche College	Pittsburgh	SU	A,B	Pri	No	4,409	Open
La Salle University	Philadelphia	SU	A,B,M,D	Pri	F,S	2,503	4/1
Lafayette College	Easton	SM	B	Pri	F,S	1,747	1/15
Lebanon Valley College	Annville	SU	A,B,M	Pri	F,S	5,062	Open
Lehigh University	Bethlehem	SU	B,M,D	Pri	F,S	4,521	1/1
Lock Haven University of Pennsylvania	Lock Haven	R	A,B,M	Pub	F,S	1,357	Open
Lycoming College	Williamsport	SM	B	Pri	F,S	2,717	3/1
Mansfield University	Mansfield	SU	A,B,M	Pub	S	2,038	3/1
Marywood University	Scranton	SU	B,M,D	Pri	F,S	3,840	Open
Mercyhurst University	Erie	SU	A,B,M,D	Pri	No	2,789	Open
Messiah College	Mechanicsburg	SM	B,M	Pri	F,S	7,171	Open
Millersville University of Pennsylvania	Millersville	SM	A,B,M	Pub	F,S	2,465	Open
Misericordia University	Dallas	SU	B,M,D	Pri	No	437	Open
Moore College of Art and Design	Philadelphia	U	B	Pri	No	1,770	Open
Moravian College	Bethlehem	SU	B,M	Pri	F,S	1,611	3/1
Mount Aloysius College	Cresson	SU	A,B	Pri	F,S	2,448	3/1
Muhlenberg College	Allentown	SM	A,B,M	Pri	No	2,501	2/15
Neumann University	Aston	SU	A,B	Pri	No	1,962	Open
Peirce College	Philadelphia	SU	A,B	Pri	No	4,015	Open
Penn State Erie/The Behrend College	Erie	SU	B,M	Pub	F,S	4,032	7/1
Penn State University/Altoona	Altoona	SU	A,B,M	Pub	F	5,623	Open
Pennsylvania College of Technology	Williamsport	U	A,B,M,D	Pub	F,S	2,888	Open
Philadelphia University	Philadelphia	SU	A,B	Pri	F,S	3,226	Open
Point Park University	Pittsburgh	U	A,B,M	Pri	F,S	4,574	Open
Robert Morris University	Moon Township	SU	B,M,D	Pri	F,S	524	5/1
Rosemont College	Rosemont	R	B,M	Pri	No	1,772	Open
Saint Francis University	Loretto	SU	B,M	Pri	F,S	5,512	Open
Saint Joseph's University	Philadelphia	SM	A,B,M,D	Pri	No	1,660	2/1
Saint Vincent College	Latrobe	SU	B,M	Pri	F,S	1,572	4/1
Seton Hill University	Greensburg	SM	B,M	Pri	No	6,305	Open
Shippensburg University of Pennsylvania	Shippensburg	SU	B,M,D	Pub	F,S	7,065	Open
Slippery Rock University of Pennsylvania	Slippery Rock	SU	B,M,D	Pub	F,S	2,084	2/15
Susquehanna University	Selinsgrove	SM	B	Pri	No	1,534	Open
Swarthmore College	Swarthmore	SU	A,B,M,D	Pri	F,S	28,243	1/1
Temple University	Philadelphia	SM	B,M	Pub	F,S	1,624	3/1
The Lincoln University	Lincoln University	R	A,B,M,D	Pub	F,S	39,958	Open
The Pennsylvania State University - University Park	University Park	U	A,B	Pub	No	1,074	11/30
Thiel College	Greenville	R	A,B,M,D	Pri	F,S	9,712	11/30
University of Pennsylvania	Philadelphia	SM	A,B	Pri	No	1,499	1/1
University of Pittsburgh at Bradford	Bradford	SU	B	Pub	F,S	1,795	Open
University of Pittsburgh at Greensburg	Greensburg	SU	A,B	Pub	No	2,932	Open
University of Pittsburgh at Johnstown	Johnstown	SU	B,M,D	Pub	F,S	18,615	Open
University of Pittsburgh at Pittsburgh	Pittsburgh	U	B,M,D	Pub	No	4,041	3/1
University of Scranton	Scranton	U	A,B,M,D	Pri	F,S	2,079	Open
University of the Arts	Philadelphia	SU	B,M	Pri	F,S	2,438	Open
Ursinus College	Collegeville	SU	B,M,D	Pri	No	1,681	2/15
Villanova University	Villanova	SM	A,B,M	Pri	F,S	7,118	2/15
Washington and Jefferson College	Washington	SM	B,M	Pri	F,S	1,362	1/15
Waynesburg University	Waynesburg	SU	B,M,D	Pri	F,S	1,528	3/1
West Chester University of Pennsylvania	West Chester	SU	B,M	Pub	No	13,844	Open
Westminster College	New Wilmington	SU	B,M,D	Pri	F,S	1,469	Open
Widener University	Chester	SU	A,B,M,D	Pri	No	3,437	2/15
Wilkes University	Wilkes Barre	SU	B,M,D	Pri	F,S	2,360	Open
Wilson College	Chambersburg	SU	A,B,M	Pri	F,S	607	Open
York College of Pennsylvania	York	SU	A,B,M,D	Pri	F,S	5,008	Open

Puerto Rico

College	City	Setting	Degrees	Control	Housing	Enrollment	Deadline
American University of Puerto Rico	Bayamon	U	A,B	Pri	No	1,211	Open
Caribbean University	Bayamon	U	A,B,M	Pri	No	3,931	Open
Central University of Bayamon	Bayamon	U	A,B,M	Pri	No	2,910	Open
Conservatory of Music of Puerto Rico	San Juan	U	B	Pub	No	255	Open

Legend:
ENVIRONMENT: U-Urban R-Rural SU-Suburban SM-Small Town
DEGREES AWARDED: A-Associate B-Bachelor M-Master D-Doctorate
CONTROL: Pri-Private, Pub-Public
FRATERNITIES AND SORORITIES: F-Fraternities S-Sororities F,S-Both No-Neither
STUDENTS: C-Coed M-Men W-Women PM-Primarily Men PW-Primarily Women

Name of School	Town	Env.	Degrees	Control	Frat./Sor.	Students	Undergrad Enroll. Fall 2014	ACT Median	ACT <21	21-23	24-26	27-28	>28	SAT CR Median	CR <500	CR 500-599	CR 600-700	CR >700	SAT Math Median	M <500	M 500-599	M 600-700	M >700	SAT Writing Median	W <500	W 500-599	W 600-700	W >700	Application Deadline
Escuela de Artes Plasticas de Puerto Rico	San Juan	U	B	Pub	No	C	515																						Open
Inter-American University of Puerto Rico/Aguadilla Campus	Aguadilla	SU	A,B,M	Pri	No	C	4,357																						5/1
Inter-American University of Puerto Rico/Arecibo Campus	Arecibo	SU	A,B,M	Pri	No	C	4,135																						5/1
Inter-American University of Puerto Rico/Barranquitas	Barranquitas	SM	A,B	Pri	No	C	1,720																						5/1
Inter-American University of Puerto Rico/Bayamon University College	Bayamon	U	A,B,M	Pri	No	C	4,942																						5/1
Inter-American University of Puerto Rico/Fajardo Campus	Fajardo	U	A,B,M,D	Pri	No	C	2,171																						8/15
Inter-American University of Puerto Rico/Metropolitan Campus	San Juan	U	A,B,M,D	Pri	No	C	7,100																						8/15
Inter-American University of Puerto Rico/Ponce	Ponce	U	B	Pri	No	C	5,090																						8/15
Pontifical Catholic University of Puerto Rico/San Germán	San Germán	R	A,B,M,D	Pri	F,S	C	8,020																						8/15
Universidad Adventista de las Antillas	Mayaguez	SM	A,B,M	Pri	No	C	760																						Open
Universidad de Puerto Rico/Arecibo	Arecibo	U	A,B,M	Pub	F,S	C	4,146																						11/30
Universidad del Turabo	Gurabo	SU	A,B,M	Pub	No	C																							11/30
Universidad Metropolitana	Rio Piedras	SU	A,B,M	Pri	No	C																							Open
Universidad Politecnica de Puerto Rico	Hato Rey	U	A,B,M	Pri	No	C	3,861																						Open
University of Puerto Rico Recinto de Rio Piedras	San Juan	U	B,M,D	Pub	F,S	C	17,860																						Open
University of Puerto Rico/Bayamon	Bayamon	SU	A,B	Pub	No	C	5,327																						Open
University of Puerto Rico/Cayey	Cayey	SU	A,B	Pub	No	C	3,659																						Open
University of Puerto Rico/Humacao	Humacao	SU	A,B	Pub	S	C	4,542																						11/14
University of Puerto Rico/Mayaguez	Mayaguez	SU	A,B,M,D	Pub	F,S	C	11,095																						11/14
University of the Sacred Heart	Santurce	U	A,B,M	Pri	No	C	4,565																						11/14

Rhode Island

Name of School	Town	Env.	Degrees	Control	Frat./Sor.	Students	Undergrad Enroll. Fall 2014	ACT Median	ACT <21	21-23	24-26	27-28	>28	SAT CR Median	CR <500	CR 500-599	CR 600-700	CR >700	SAT Math Median	M <500	M 500-599	M 600-700	M >700	SAT Writing Median	W <500	W 500-599	W 600-700	W >700	Application Deadline
Brown University	Providence	U	B,M,D	Pri	F,S	C	6,264	31		3	10	12	74	730		6	28	66	730		5	28	67	730			5	27	1/1
Bryant University	Smithfield	SU	B,M	Pri	F,S	C	3,287	25	3	23	45	16	13	550	18	59	20	3	585	8	48	20	3	545		22	53	23	2/1
Johnson & Wales University/Providence Campus	Providence	U	A,B,M,D	Pri	F,S	C																							Open
Providence College	Providence	SU	A,B,M,D	Pri	No	C	4,176	25						560					580					580					1/15
Rhode Island College	Providence	U	B,M,D	Pub		C	7,271	18						460					460					450					3/15
Rhode Island School of Design	Providence	U	B,M	Pri	No	C	2,014	27						627					639					632					2/1
Roger Williams University	Bristol	SM	B,M	Pri	No	C	4,610	24						545					548					555					2/1
Salve Regina University	Newport	SU	B,M,D	Pri	No	C	2,121	24						550					548					548					2/1
University of Rhode Island	Kingston	SU	B,M,D	Pub	F,S	C	13,589	24						540					560					530					2/1

South Carolina

Name of School	Town	Env.	Degrees	Control	Frat./Sor.	Students	Undergrad Enroll. Fall 2014	ACT Median	ACT <21	21-23	24-26	27-28	>28	SAT CR Median	CR <500	CR 500-599	CR 600-700	CR >700	SAT Math Median	M <500	M 500-599	M 600-700	M >700	SAT Writing Median	W <500	W 500-599	W 600-700	W >700	Application Deadline
Allen University	Columbia	SM	A,B	Pri	F,S	C	350																						Open
Benedict College	Columbia	U	B	Pri	F,S	C	2,641																						Open
Charleston Southern University	Charleston	SU	B,M	Pri	No	C	2,490							436					440					450					Open
Citadel, The	Charleston	U	B,M	Pub	No	C	2,735	23						538					549					540					Open
Claflin University	Orangeburg	SU	B,M	Pri	F,S	C	1,883																						5/1
Clemson University	Clemson	SM	B,M,D	Pub	F,S	C	15,836	27						600					630										2/1
Coastal Carolina University	Conway	SU	B,M	Pub	F,S	C	9,364	21						490					500					490					6/1
Coker College	Hartsville	SM	B,M	Pri	No	C	1,178							460					480										Open
College of Charleston	Charleston	U	B,M	Pub	F,S	C	10,440	25						560					570					555					4/1
Columbia College	Columbia	U	B,M	Pri	No	W	1,239							500					500										8/1
Converse College	Spartanburg	SU	B,M	Pri	No	W	690							530					520										8/1
Erskine College	Due West	R	B	Pri	No	C	553							531					543										Open
Francis Marion University	Florence	R	B,M	Pub	F,S	C	3,714							476					476					446					8/15
Furman University	Greenville	SU	B,M	Pri	F,S	C	2,798	27						610					620					610					1/15
Lander University	Greenwood	SM	B,M	Pub	F,S	C	2,363							470					500										Open
Limestone College	Gaffney	SM	A,B,M	Pri	No	C	1,188							500					510										Open
Morris College	Sumter	SU	B	Pri	F	C	780																						4/30
Newberry College	Newberry	SM	B	Pri	F,S	C	795							550					550					540					Open
Presbyterian College	Clinton	SM	B,D	Pri	F,S	C	1,123							550					550										2/1
South Carolina State University	Orangeburg	SM	B,M,D	Pub	F,S	C	4,050							490					490					480					7/31
Southern Wesleyan University	Central	SM	A,B,M	Pri	No	C	1,677							480					480					460					Open
University of South Carolina Aiken	Aiken	SU	B,M	Pub	F,S	C	3,229																						Open
University of South Carolina at Columbia	Columbia	U	A,B,M,D	Pub	F,S	C	23,363							590					610					450					12/1
University of South Carolina Upstate	Spartanburg	U	B,M	Pub	F,S	C	5,334							470					470										Open
Voorhees College	Denmark	SM	B	Pri	No	C	533																						Open

College	City	Setting	Degrees	Control	Housing	Enroll.
Winthrop University	Rock Hill	SM	B,M	Pub	F,S	
Wofford College	Spartanburg	U	B	Pri	F,S	
South Dakota						
Augustana College	Sioux Falls	U	B,M	Pri	No	
Black Hills State University	Spearfish	SM	A,B,M	Pub	F,S	
Dakota State University	Madison	R	A,B,M,D	Pub	No	
Dakota Wesleyan University	Mitchell	SM	A,B,M	Pri	No	
Mount Marty College	Yankton	SM	A,B,M	Pri	No	
Northern State University - Aberdeen	Aberdeen	U	A,B,M	Pub	No	
Oglala Lakota University	Kyle	R	B	Pub	No	
Presentation College	Aberdeen	SM	A,B	Pri	F,S	
Sinte Gleska University	Rosebud	R	A,B,M	Pub	No	
South Dakota School of Mines and Technology	Rapid City	SU	A,B,M,D	Pub	F,S	
South Dakota State University	Brookings	SM	A,B,M,D	Pub	F,S	
University of Sioux Falls	Sioux Falls	SU	A,B	Pri	F,S	
University of South Dakota	Vermillion	SM	A,B,M,D	Pub	F,S	
Tennessee						
Aquinas College	Nashville	U	A,B,M	Pri	No	417
Austin Peay State University	Clarksville	U	A,B,M	Pub	F,S	9,550
Belmont University	Nashville	U	B,M,D	Pri	F,S	5,837
Bethel University	McKenzie	SM	B,M	Pri	F,S	2,232
Bryan College	Dayton	SM	B,M	Pri	No	1,011
Carson-Newman University	Jefferson City	SM	A,B,M	Pri	F,S	1,646
Christian Brothers University	Memphis	SM	B,M	Pri	F,S	1,351
Cumberland University	Lebanon	SM	A,B,M,D	Pri	F,S	623
East Tennessee State University	Johnson City	U	A,B,M	Pub	F,S	9,580
Fisk University	Nashville	SM	B,M	Pri	F,S	868
Freed-Hardeman University	Henderson	SM	A,B,M	Pri	F,S	1,479
King University	Bristol	SM	B,M	Pri	F,S	1,963
Lane College	Jackson	SM	B	Pri	F,S	965
Lee University	Cleveland	SU	B,M	Pri	F,S	4,016
LeMoyne-Owen College	Memphis	U	B	Pri	No	785
Lincoln Memorial University	Harrogate	R	A,B,M,D	Pri	F,S	1,654
Lipscomb University	Nashville	SU	B,M,D	Pri	F,S	2,883
Maryville College	Maryville	SU	B	Pri	F,S	1,176
Memphis College of Art	Memphis	U	B,M	Pri	No	377
Middle Tennessee State University	Murfreesboro	SU	B,M,D	Pub	No	22,299
Milligan College	Milligan College	U	B,M	Pri	F,S	903
Rhodes College	Memphis	SU	B	Pri	F,S	2,031
Sewanee: The University of the South	Sewanee	SM	B,M	Pri	No	1,631
Southern Adventist University	Collegedale	SM	B,M,D	Pri	F,S	2,477
Tennessee State University	Nashville	U	B,M,D	Pub	No	6,919
Tennessee Technological University	Cookeville	SM	A,B,M,D	Pub	F,S	8,060
Tennessee Wesleyan College	Athens	SM	B,M	Pri	F,S	1,070
The University of Memphis	Memphis	U	B,M,D	Pub	No	17,647
The University of Tennessee at Chattanooga	Chattanooga	U	A,B,M,D	Pub	No	10,297
Trevecca Nazarene University	Nashville	SM	B,M,D	Pri	F,S	1,677
Tusculum College	Greeneville	SM	B,M	Pri	F,S	2,446
Union University	Jackson	SU	A,B,M,D	Pri	F,S	2,829
University of Tennessee at Knoxville	Knoxville	U	B,M,D	Pub	F,S	21,033
University of Tennessee at Martin	Martin	R	B,M	Pub	F,S	6,677
Vanderbilt University	Nashville	U	B,M,D	Pri	F,S	6,851
Texas						
Abilene Christian University	Abilene	SM	A,B,M,D	Pri	F,S	3,727
Angelo State University	San Angelo	U	B,M,D	Pub	F,S	5,546
Austin College	Sherman	R	B,M	Pri	F,S	1,288
Baylor University	Waco	SM	B,M,D	Pri	F,S	13,859
Concordia University Texas	Austin	U	A,B,M	Pri	No	1,030
Dallas Baptist University	Dallas	SU	B,M,D	Pri	F,S	3,457
East Texas Baptist University	Marshall	SM	B,M	Pri	F,S	1,232
Hardin-Simmons University	Abilene	U	B,M,D	Pri	F,S	2,030
Houston Baptist University	Houston	SM	B,M,D	Pri	F,S	2,447
Howard Payne University	Brownwood	U	B,M	Pri	F,S	1,371
Huston-Tillotson University	Austin	R	A,B	Pri	F,S	844
Jarvis Christian College	Hawkins	U	B	Pri	F,S	735

TEST SCORES

NAME OF SCHOOL	TOWN	ENVIRONMENT	DEGREES AWARDED	CONTROL	FRATERNITIES AND SORORITIES	STUDENTS	UNDERGRADUATE ENROLLMENT FALL 2014	ACT Median	ACT Below 21	ACT 21-23	ACT 24-26	ACT 27-28	ACT Above 28	SAT CR Median	SAT CR Below 500	SAT CR 500-599	SAT CR 600-700	SAT CR Above 700	SAT Math Median	SAT Math Below 500	SAT Math 500-599	SAT Math 600-700	SAT Math Above 700	SAT Writing Median	SAT Writing Below 500	SAT Writing 500-599	SAT Writing 600-700	SAT Writing Above 700	APPLICATION DEADLINE Month/Day
Lamar University	Beaumont	U	A,B,M,D	Pub	F,S	C	8,430	26	41				8	576	21	35	32		591	13	40	35	12	555	25	39		30	8/1
LeTourneau University	Longview	SM	A,B,M	Pri	No	C	2,250	22	53	24	21		7	502	47	35	16		510	49	29	19	2	473	61	31		8	8/1
Lubbock Christian University	Lubbock	U	B	Pri	F,S	C	1,439	20	52	19	16		5	460	61	28	10		500	49	38	13							Open
McMurry University	Abilene	U	A,B,M	Pri	F,S	C	1,509	21	41	28	14	5			34	34	12		500	48	38	13	1	490	55	38	7		8/13
Midwestern State University	Wichita Falls	U	A,B,M	Pub	F,S	C	5,348	21	66	23	6		2	490	53	25			500	54	32	14		490	73	23	5		8/7
Northwood University	Cedar Hill	SU	A,B,M	Pri	No	C	514	19	68						68														8/1
Our Lady of the Lake University	San Antonio	U	B,M,D	Pri	F,S	C	1,792	17	57	36		4		410	85	13	1		420	82	16	2		417		9			Open
Paul Quinn College	Dallas	U	B	Pri	F,S	C	193	30	3				79	650		9	37	53	670		26	65		640	3	38	37		Open
Prairie View A&M University	Prairie View	SM	B,M,D	Pub	F,S	C	6,757	22	25	42	21	6		510	43	12			530	31	51	17	1	490	52	9			6/1
Rice University	Houston	U	B,M,D	Pri	F,S	C	3,102			1	2	1	6		46	30	12	1		40	33	9	1		68	26		51	5/1
Saint Mary's University	San Antonio	SU	B,M,D	Pri	F,S	C	2,391		25	12		1			55	34	8			41	48	10	1		3	21	6	51	1
Sam Houston State University	Huntsville	SM	B,M,D	Pub	F,S	C	14,995						64	650				32	600	8	53	43	15	640		26	42	26	8/1
Schreiner University	Kerrville	R	A,B,M	Pri	F,S	C	1,065	30	30	1	21		1	650	3	19	55			2	13	34		640	3				1/15
Southern Methodist University	Dallas	U	B,M,D	Pri	F,S	C	6,391																						1/15
Southern Adventist University	Keene	R	A,B,M	Pri	No	C	875																1						25
Southwestern University	Georgetown	SU	B,M,D	Pri	F,S	C	1,535	26	20	28	16	7		590	16	39	35	10	580	7	44	37	9	550	26	47	25	9	2/1
St. Edward's University	Austin	SU	B	Pri	F,S	C	4,003	24	10	32	14			560	15	29	31	2	550	9	57	19	2	460	67	28	5	1	2/1
Stephen F. Austin State University	Nacogdoches	SM	B,M,D	Pub	F,S	C	11,269	20	52	26	4		1	470	62	29	8		490	55	35	10			94	6	4		5/1
Sul Ross State University	Alpine	R	A,B,M	Pub	No	C	1,310								91	8	1			87	12					27			8/1
Tarleton State University	Stephenville	SM	B,M,D	Pub	F,S	C	9,585	20	47	32	16	7		470	60	31	8		500	2	41	10	1	460	68	6		5	2/15
Texas A&M University	College Station	SU	B,M,D	Pub	F,S	C	47,094	26	7	10	22	11	9	570	17	39	35	50	600	8	34	43	15	550	26	42	26		8/6
Texas A&M University at Commerce	Commerce	SM	B,M,D	Pub	F,S	C	5,185	23	20	30			7		30		14		540	30	55	14	1						Open
Texas A&M University at Galveston	Galveston	SM	B,M,D	Pub	F,S	C	1,565	22	10	40	40		2	520	50	37	12	1		19	45	16	1	470	61	33	5	1	Open
Texas A&M University at Kingsville	Kingsville	SU	B,M,D	Pub	F,S	C	5,580	22	52						62				490	55	35	10	2	400	92				2/15
Texas Christian University	Fort Worth	SU	B,M,D	Pri	F,S	C	8,647	21	47	28		7		500	60	30	9		520	87	12	27		490	94	54	6	1	6/1
Texas Lutheran University	Seguin	SM	B,M	Pri	F,S	C	1,306	21	7	21	20		2	400	91	31	8		420	37	41	5		510	68		27	2	8/15
Texas Southern University	Houston	U	B,M,D	Pub	F,S	C	7,021	17	44	37	23	9		500	45	44	2	1	520	49	51	1	1	460	60	33	18	3	5/1
Texas State University	San Marcos	SU	B,M,D	Pub	F,S	C	32,215	22	25	37	11				82	10	19		560	42	49	27	1						5/1
Texas Tech University	Lubbock	U	B,M,D	Pub	F,S	C	23,021	21	17	12	15		2	490	56	38	6		500	53	42	5	2	607			33		Open
Texas Wesleyan University	Fort Worth	SU	B,M	Pri	F,S	C	1,917	21	21	36					38									595	13	60			7/15
Texas Woman's University	Denton	U	B,M,D	Pub	F,S	PW	9,441	29	29	23	20		55	631	3	29	48	19	639	1	25	53	22	607	8	32	48		11
Trinity University	San Antonio	U	B,M,D	Pri	F,S	C	2,293	27	4	29	14		31	615	7	36	39	18	595	12	44	29	15	595	13	40	30		3/1
University of Dallas	Irving	U	B,M	Pri	No	C	1,404	27	12	33	15		12	554	22	49	25	4	588	66	31	38	8						17
University of Houston	Houston	U	B,M,D	Pub	F,S	C	32,915	18	49	47	39		2	520	82		4	7	470	44	31	16	1	430	80	16	3	2	8/1
University of Houston-Downtown	Houston	U	B,M	Pub	F,S	C	13,662	24	24	48	13		4	430	38	47	12		470	66	25	9		475	58	31	9	1	8/1
University of Mary Hardin-Baylor	Belton	SM	B,M	Pri	No	C	3,103		4	50			7	520	29	31	23		525	31	45	17	6	520	80	42		1	8/1
University of North Texas	Denton	SU	B,M,D	Pub	F,S	C	28,283	23	21	31	25	13		540	29	44	20	6	550	23	43	25	6	530	58	32	13	6	2/1
University of St. Thomas - Houston	Houston	U	B,M,D	Pri	No	C	1,645	23	12	30	30		22	530	27	26	7		560	12	43	20	7	530	33	42	13	4	4/1
University of Texas - Pan American	Edinburg	U	B,M,D	Pub	F,S	C	18,200	19	64	24	9		1	460	66	26	1		490	53	35	11	2	450	71	23	5	2	1/8
University of Texas at Arlington	Arlington	U	B,M,D	Pub	F,S	C	19,604		10	26	18		30	610	9	33	22		650	3	22	46	16	590	14	38	34		6/1
University of Texas at Austin	Austin	U	B,M,D	Pub	F,S	C	39,955		3	23	17		47																2/1
University of Texas at Dallas	Richardson	SU	B,M,D	Pub	F,S	C	14,300	28	10	29	21	7	5	500	49	36	13		530	35	45	18	2	460	67	27	5	2	14
University of Texas at El Paso	El Paso	SU	B,M,D	Pub	F,S	C	15,806		28	29	24	5		470	61	32	6		490	53	37	9	1	430	79	18	3	1	7/1
University of Texas at San Antonio	San Antonio	U	B,M,D	Pub	F,S	C	24,342	22	38	56	23		2	450	69	27	3		470	59	32	8							7/1
University of the Incarnate Word	San Antonio	SU	B,M,D	Pri	F,S	C	6,496	20	57	15	15		2																1
Wayland Baptist University	Plainview	SM	A,B,M	Pri	F,S	C	3,980	20	49	28																			Open
West Texas A&M University	Canyon	SM	A,B,M	Pub	F,S	C	6,908	21																					Open
Wiley College	Marshall	SM	B	Pri	No	C	741																						Open

Utah

Brigham Young University	Provo	SU	B,M,D	Pri	No	C	27,767		2	6	25	20	47		6	28	43			4	24	50	23		10	37	41	22	12
Southern Utah University	Cedar City	SM	A,B,M	Pub	F,S	C	6,953	5	19	20	13		22	39	43	16		585	44	42	11	3		50	36	12	3	2/5
The University of Utah	Salt Lake City	U	B,M,D	Pub	F,S	C	23,907	25	23	24	11		23	570	23	38	30	9		19	36	34		550	28	41	27	11	4
Utah State University	Logan	SM	A,B,M,D	Pub	F,S	C	24,271	24	15	26	17		16	560	25	41	30	4	560	25	41	30	4						4/1
Westminster College	Salt Lake City	U	B,M	Pri	No	C	2,233																						Open

Vermont

| Bennington College | Bennington | SM | B,M | Pri | No | C | 688 | 29 | 5 | 23 | 23 | | 50 | 690 | 13 | 46 | 41 | | 610 | 2 | 38 | 48 | 13 | 660 | 2 | 21 | 51 | | 27 |
| Burlington College | Burlington | U | A,B,M | Pri | No | C | 219 | | | | | | | | | | | | | | | | | | | | | | 1/3, 8 |

College	City	Setting	Degrees	Control	Aid	Type	Enrollment
Vermont							
Castleton State College	Castleton	R	A,B,M	Pub	No	C	1,985
Champlain College	Burlington	U	A,B,M	Pri	S	C	2,226
College of St Joseph	Rutland	SM	A,B,M	Pri	No	C	176
Goddard College	Plainfield	R	B,M	Pri	No	C	209
Green Mountain College	Poultney	SM	B,M	Pri	No	C	573
Johnson State College	Johnson	SM	A,B,M	Pub	No	C	1,540
Lyndon State College	Lyndonville	SM	B,M	Pub	No	C	1,430
Marlboro College	Marlboro	SM	B,M	Pri	No	C	336
Middlebury College	Middlebury	SM	B,M,D	Pri	No	C	2,526
Norwich University	Northfield	SU	B,M	Pri	No	C	1,903
Saint Michael's College	Colchester	SU	B,M	Pri	No	C	2,123
Southern Vermont College	Bennington	SM	A,B	Pri	No	C	532
Sterling College	Craftsbury Common	R	B	Pri	No	C	105
University of Vermont	Burlington	SU	B,M,D	Pub	F,S	C	10,912
Vermont Technical College	Randolph Center	R	A,B	Pub	No	C	1,356
Virginia							
Averett University	Danville	SM	A,B,M	Pri	S	C	840
Bluefield College	Bluefield	SM	B	Pri	F,S	C	776
Bridgewater College	Bridgewater	SM	B	Pri	No	C	1,785
Christendom College	Front Royal	R	A,B,M	Pri	No	C	433
Christopher Newport University	Newport News	SU	B,M	Pub	F,S	C	5,096
College of William & Mary	Williamsburg	SM	B,M,D	Pub	No	C	6,299
Eastern Mennonite University	Harrisonburg	SM	A,B,M	Pri	F,S	C	983
Emory and Henry College	Emory	R	B	Pri	F,S	C	1,211
Ferrum College	Ferrum	R	B	Pri	F,S	C	1,240
George Mason University	Fairfax	SU	B,M,D	Pub	F	C	19,702
Hampden-Sydney College	Hampden-Sydney	R	B	Pri	No	M	1,070
Hampton University	Hampton	U	A,B,M,D	Pri	F,S	C	3,851
Hollins University	Roanoke	SU	B,M	Pri	No	W	610
James Madison University	Harrisonburg	SU	B,M,D	Pub	No	C	18,107
Liberty University	Lynchburg	SU	A,B,M,D	Pri	F,S	C	6,330
Longwood University	Farmville	SM	B,M	Pub	F,S	C	4,497
Lynchburg College	Lynchburg	SM	B,M,D	Pri	No	C	2,178
Mary Baldwin College	Staunton	SM	B,M,D	Pri	No	W	1,414
Marymount University	Arlington	SU	A,B,M,D	Pri	F,S	C	2,363
Norfolk State University	Norfolk	U	A,B,M,D	Pub	No	C	5,337
Old Dominion University	Norfolk	U	B,M,D	Pub	F,S	C	20,115
Radford University	Radford	SM	B,M,D	Pub	F,S	C	8,885
Randolph College	Lynchburg	SU	B	Pri	No	C	658
Randolph-Macon College	Ashland	SU	B	Pri	F,S	C	1,394
Roanoke College	Salem	SM	B	Pri	F,S	C	2,054
Saint Paul's College	Lawrenceville	SM	B	Pri	No	C	690
Shenandoah University	Winchester	SM	B,M,D	Pri	F,S	C	1,892
The University of Virginia's College at Wise	Wise	SM	B	Pub	No	C	1,892
University of Mary Washington	Fredericksburg	SU	B,M	Pub	F,S	C	4,515
University of Virginia	Charlottesville	SU	B,M,D	Pub	No	C	16,483
Virginia Commonwealth University	Richmond	SU	B,M,D	Pub	F,S	C	23,962
Virginia Military Institute	Lexington	SM	B,M	Pub	No	C	1,378
Virginia Polytechnic Institute and State University	Blacksburg	SU	B,M,D	Pub	F,S	C	30,855
Virginia State University	Petersburg	SU	B,M,D	Pub	F,S	C	3,600
Virginia Union University	Richmond	U	B,M,D	Pri	F,S	C	1,260
Virginia Wesleyan College	Norfolk	SM	B	Pri	F,S	C	1,671
Washington and Lee University	Lexington	SM	B,M,D	Pri	No	C	1,838
Washington							
Central Washington University	Ellensburg	R	B,M	Pub	No	C	8,587
City University of Seattle	Seattle	U	A,B,M,D	Pri	No	C	1,190
Cornish College of the Arts	Seattle	U	B	Pri	No	C	710
Eastern Washington University	Cheney	SM	B,M	Pub	F,S	C	12,411
Gonzaga University	Spokane	SM	B,M,D	Pri	No	C	4,837
Heritage University	Toppenish	R	A,B,M	Pri	No	C	876
Northwest University	Kirkland	SU	A,B,M	Pri	No	C	1,057
Pacific Lutheran University	Tacoma	SU	B,M,D	Pri	No	C	2,959
Saint Martin's University	Lacey	SU	B,M	Pri	No	C	1,415
Seattle Pacific University	Seattle	U	B,M,D	Pri	No	C	3,395
Seattle University	Seattle	U	B,M,D	Pri	No	C	4,511
The Evergreen State College	Olympia	SM	B,M	Pub	F,S	C	4,282
University of Puget Sound	Tacoma	U	B,M,D	Pri	F,S	C	2,551

TEST SCORES

Legend:
- **STUDENTS:** C-Coed M-Men W-Women PM-Primarily Men PW-Primarily Women
- **FRATERNITIES AND SORORITIES:** F-Fraternities S-Sororities F,S-Both No-Neither
- **CONTROL:** Pri-Private Pub-Public
- **DEGREES AWARDED:** A-Associate B-Bachelor M-Master D-Doctorate
- **ENVIRONMENT:** U-Urban R-Rural SU-Suburban SM-Small Town

Name of School	Town	Env	Degrees	Control	Frat/Sor	Students	Undergrad Enroll Fall 2014	ACT Above 28	ACT 27-28	ACT 24-26	ACT 21-23	ACT Below 21	ACT Median	SAT CR Above 700	SAT CR 600-700	SAT CR 500-599	SAT CR Below 500	SAT CR Median	SAT M Above 700	SAT M 600-700	SAT M 500-599	SAT M Below 500	SAT M Median	SAT W Above 700	SAT W 600-700	SAT W 500-599	SAT W Below 500	SAT W Median	App Deadline
University of Washington	Seattle	U	B,M,D	Pub	F,S	C	28,570	28	20	27	16	9	25	12	36	36	16	550	16	44	32	9	550		34	42	17		1/15
Walla Walla University	College Place	SM	A,B,M	Pri	F,S	C	1,563		11	24	26	26	30	5	15	38	46	550	17	42	39		550	11	36	48		530	Open
Washington State University	Pullman	SM	B,M,D	Pub	F,S	C	23,604	10	15	28	26	13	26	2	27	43	25		26	47	18	4	550	21	45	32		660	1/31
Western Washington University	Bellingham	SM	B	Pub	No	C	13,925	18	15	28	26	13		10	32	43	4	486	5	18	45	18	600	46	20	20		590	3/1
Whitman College	Walla Walla	SU	B,M	Pri	No	C	1,498	70	16	10	1			32	32			670	33	35		13		32	42	20			1/15
Whitworth University	Spokane	SU	B,M	Pri	No	C	2,370											600	9				600						3/1

West Virginia

Name of School	Town	Env	Degrees	Control	Frat/Sor	Students	Undergrad Enroll Fall 2014	ACT Above 28	ACT 27-28	ACT 24-26	ACT 21-23	ACT Below 21	ACT Median	SAT CR Above 700	SAT CR 600-700	SAT CR 500-599	SAT CR Below 500	SAT CR Median	SAT M Above 700	SAT M 600-700	SAT M 500-599	SAT M Below 500	SAT M Median	SAT W Above 700	SAT W 600-700	SAT W 500-599	SAT W Below 500	SAT W Median	App Deadline
Alderson Broaddus University	Philippi	SM	A,B,M	Pri	F,S	C	1,052	2	3	18	29	47	21	5	38	57		470	7	32	61		470	2	29	69		470	8/1
Bethany College	Bethany	R	B,M	Pri	F,S	C	917	1	7	13	27	51	20	6	20	29	65	460	6	25	69		450	1	18	81		440	Open
Bluefield State College	Bluefield	SM	A,B	Pub	F,S	C	2,063	1		8	17	73	18	2	43	55	57		10	33	57		482		23	68			Open
Concord University	Athens	SM	A,B,M	Pub	No	C	2,652						21		32	58	58	486	7	34	58		482						1
Davis & Elkins College	Elkins	SM	A,B	Pri	F,S	C	874		2	12	24	61			24														Open
Fairmont State University	Fairmont	SM	A,B,M	Pub	F,S	C	4,362	2	3	9	25	75	21	2	29	69	65	468	2	33	65		484						Open
Glenville State College	Glenville	R	A,B	Pri	F,S	C	1,719	1	7	8	29	51	20	4	20	75	77	428	4	19	77		438						Open
Marshall University	Huntington	SU	A,B,M,D	Pub	F,S	C	9,762						23	1				500					480						Open
Ohio Valley University	Vienna	R	A,B	Pri	No	C	659	2	3	9	25	51	21		11	41	47		11	30	58								Open
Salem International University	Salem	SM	B,M	Pri	F,S	C	568	1	7	18	29	44	21		7	31	61	470	14	35	51		490						Open
Shepherd University	Shepherdstown	SM	A,B,M,D	Pub	F,S	C	3,776	3	6	17	33	46	21					470					480						Open
University of Charleston	Charleston	SM	A,B,M	Pri	F,S	C	1,549	2	6	15	33	46			11	41	47	512	2	43	39		490						Open
West Liberty University	Institute	SU	A,B	Pub	F,S	C	2,266	4	6	16	20	54	19		11	41	47	512		43	39		533	3	36	54		490	8/1
West Virginia State University	Institute	SM	A,B,M	Pub	F,S	C	3,449	6	6	23	19	24	24		13	42	45	520	13	41	46		500	9	36	54			8/1
West Virginia University	Morgantown	SU	B,M,D	Pub	F,S	C	22,563				32	18	23					520					500						Open
West Virginia University Institute of Technology	Montgomery	SM	B,M	Pub	F,S	C	2,400						23																8/1
West Virginia Wesleyan College	Buckhannon	SM	B,M	Pri	F,S	C	1,327						23																8/1
Wheeling Jesuit University	Wheeling	SU	B,M,D	Pri	No	C	1,180						22																1

Wisconsin

Name of School	Town	Env	Degrees	Control	Frat/Sor	Students	Undergrad Enroll Fall 2014	ACT Above 28	ACT 27-28	ACT 24-26	ACT 21-23	ACT Below 21	ACT Median	SAT CR Above 700	SAT CR 600-700	SAT CR 500-599	SAT CR Below 500	SAT CR Median	SAT M Above 700	SAT M 600-700	SAT M 500-599	SAT M Below 500	SAT M Median	SAT W Above 700	SAT W 600-700	SAT W 500-599	SAT W Below 500	SAT W Median	App Deadline
Alverno College	Milwaukee	U	A,B,M	Pri	No	W	1,723	2	3	15	21	65	20			24	53		2		36	36							Open
Beloit College	Beloit	SM	A,B,M	Pri	F,S	C	1,303	30	47	12	22	2	27	35	48	51		630	24	48	6		620	38	31	6			1/15
Cardinal Stritch University	Milwaukee	SU	A,B,M,D	Pri	No	C	3,130		13	29	31	17	24																Open
Carroll University	Waukesha	SU	B,M	Pri	F,S	C	3,015																						Open
Carthage College	Kenosha	SU	B,M	Pri	F,S	C	2,265		7	22	31	38	22																8/1
Concordia University Wisconsin	Mequon	SU	A,B,M,D	Pri	No	C	4,419	3	20	15	6		22	1	21	51		580	30	26	2		600		6			580	8/25
Edgewood College	Madison	R	B,M	Pri	No	C	2,206	5	4	12	18	61	22		34	34	7	580	8	48	10		600	35	13				8/25
Lakeland College	Sheboygan	SM	B	Pri	F,S	C	840		23	11	11	1			19	53	17	570	11	58	8		630		47				1/15
Lawrence University	Appleton	SM	B	Pri	F,S	C	1,496	20	28	28	20	27	20																12/1
Marian University	Fond du Lac	SM	B,M,D	Pri	No	C	1,598	4	10	29	29	29	27																12/1
Marquette University	Milwaukee	U	B,M,D	Pri	F,S	C	8,410	34	23	28	11	7	27	9	35	53		570	15	58	19		630		13				12/1
Milwaukee Institute of Art and Design	Milwaukee	U	B	Pri	No	C	628																						Open
Milwaukee School of Engineering	Milwaukee	U	B,M,D	Pri	F,S	C	2,378	20	35	29	13	3	27	20	19	17		570	11	58	8		630	35	13				Open
Mount Mary University	Milwaukee	U	B,M,D	Pri	No	PW	860																						Open
Northland College	Ashland	SM	B	Pri	F,S	C	739	10	14	28	29	27	24	3	19	35	53	500	23	38	36		528						8/1
Ripon College	Ripon	SM	A,B,M	Pri	F,S	C	1,065	15	17	28	23	24	24	9	35	53	53	500	23	38	36		528	3			5		Open
Silver Lake College	Manitowoc	SU	B,M	Pri	No	C	1,540																						Open
St. Norbert College	De Pere	SU	A,B,M	Pri	F,S	C	2,112	11	28	28	28	11	23	18	59		23	530	6	35	29		520			525		525	Open
University of Wisconsin/Whitewater	Whitewater	SU	A,B,M,D	Pub	F,S	C	10,687		11	32	35	27	1050																Open
University of Wisconsin/Eau Claire	Eau Claire	U	A,B,M,D	Pub	F,S	C	10,164	6	7	25	36	7	24	18	59	23	23	550	18	35	29		546					513	1/1
University of Wisconsin/Green Bay	Green Bay	SU	A,B,M	Pub	No	C	6,668		7	36	37	27	23		32	29	29			43	29	1	546		24		5		Open
University of Wisconsin/La Crosse	La Crosse	SU	A,B,M,D	Pub	F,S	C	9,755	5	36	22		6	25		32	39	7	550	14	40	1		680		5			640	Open
University of Wisconsin/Madison	Madison	U	B,M,D	Pub	F,S	C	31,126	46	25	22	6		28	14	40	39	7	600	45	40	14		680	52		5		640	2/1
University of Wisconsin/Oshkosh	Oshkosh	SU	A,B,M	Pub	F,S	C	9,800		11	24	32		23																2/1
University of Wisconsin/Parkside	Kenosha	SU	A,B,M	Pub	F,S	C	6,640	9		24	37	21	23		21	55	23	546		23	32		536		46			528	8/1
University of Wisconsin/Platteville	Platteville	SU	A,B,M	Pub	F,S	C	8,047		8	23	37	27	23		14	55	23	546	9	23	41	32	536	23	32	46		528	Open
University of Wisconsin/River Falls	River Falls	SM	A,B,M	Pub	F,S	C	6,390	5		24	37	22	23																Open
University of Wisconsin/Stevens Point	Stevens Point	SU	A,B,M	Pub	F,S	C	9,118	5	8	23	37	27	23					546					536					528	Open
University of Wisconsin/Stout	Menomonie	R	B,M,D	Pub	No	C	8,254	3	11	31	59	7	22																Open
University of Wisconsin/Superior	Superior	U	A,B,M	Pub	No	C	2,455	2	6	19	31	42	22																8/1
University of Wisconsin-Milwaukee	Milwaukee	U	B,M,D	Pub	F,S	C	23,004	5	9	19	29	41	22																7/1

Institution	City																								
Viterbo University	La Crosse	Open											5	8	29	34	24	23	2,105	C	No	Pri	A,B,M	SU
Wisconsin Lutheran College	Milwaukee	Open																	740	C	No	Pri	B	SU
Wyoming																								
University of Wyoming	Laramie	8/10	7	23	38	32	542	4	22	40	35	530	17	14	27	27	15	24	9,910	C	F,S		B,M,D	SM

The breakdown of in-state tuition, room, and board costs for the 2014-2015 academic year is arranged from least expensive to most expensive. Within each range are lists of schools that don't charge for tuition or room and board, and those that do. Listings that say (no R & B) means complete information was not provided by the school at press time. For any late additions, please refer to the school profile on our website, *barronspac.com*.

Colleges Where There Are No Fees for Tuition, Room/Board

College of the Ozarks, MO
United States Air Force Academy, CO
United States Coast Guard Academy, CT
United States Merchant Marine Academy, NY
United States Military Academy, NY
United States Naval Academy, MD

Less Than $2000

Colleges with Tuition, Room, and Board

Conservatory of Music of Puerto Rico, PR
University of Puerto Rico/Bayamon , PR
University of Puerto Rico/Cayey, PR
University of Puerto Rico/Humacao, PR
University of Puerto Rico/Mayaguez, PR

$2000-$3999

Colleges with Tuition, Room, and Board

Bluefield State College, WV
Central University of Bayamon, PR
Escuela de Artes Plasticas de Puerto Rico, PR
Inter-American University of Puerto Rico/Arecibo Campus, PR
Inter-American University of Puerto Rico/Barranquitas, PR
Langston University, OK
McNeese State University, LA
Oglala Lakota College, SD
Sinte Gleska University, SD
Southern University at New Orleans, LA
Universidad Metropolitana, PR

$4000-$5999

Colleges with Tuition, Room, and Board

Alice Lloyd College, KY
American University of Puerto Rico, PR
Bellevue University, NE
Chicago State University, IL
City University of New York/Brooklyn College, NY
Excelsior College, NY
Inter-American University of Puerto Rico/Aguadilla Campus, PR
Inter-American University of Puerto Rico/Bayamon University College, PR
Inter-American University of Puerto Rico/Fajardo Campus, PR
Inter-American University of Puerto Rico/Metropolitan Campus, PR
Inter-American University of Puerto Rico/Ponce, PR
Lehman College/The City University of New York, NY
Louisiana State University in Shreveport, LA
Megar Evers College/The City University of New York, NY
Metropolitan State University, MN
Metropolitan State University of Denver, CO
New York College of Technology/The City University of New York, NY
Thomas Edison State College, NJ
Universidad del Turabo, PR
University of Puerto Rico Recinto de Rio Piedras, PR
University of the Sacred Heart, PR
York College/The City University of New York, NY

$6000-$7999

Citadel, The, SC

Colleges with Tuition, Room, and Board

Amridge University, AL
Baker College of Flint, MI
Berea College, KY
Chadron State College, NE
Granite State College, NH
Indiana University East, IN
Indiana University Kokomo, IN
Indiana University Northwest, IN
Inter-American University of Puerto Rico/San Germán, PR
John Jay College of Criminal Justice/The City University of New York, NY
Kennesaw State University, GA
Lamar University, TX
Lewis-Clark State College, ID
Mississippi University for Women, MS
Nicholls State University, LA
North Dakota State University, ND
Northwestern Oklahoma State University, OK
Ohio State University at Lima, OH
Pontifical Catholic University of Puerto Rico, PR
South Carolina State University, SC
Southeastern Oklahoma State University, OK
State University of New York/Empire State College, NY
Texas A&M University at Kingsville, TX
Universidad Adventista de las Antillas, PR
Universidad de Puerto/Arecibo, PR
University of Louisiana at Lafayette, LA
University of Maine at Augusta, ME
University of Maryland/University College, MD
University of North Carolina School of the Arts, NC
University of the District of Columbia, DC

$8000-$9999

Colleges with Tuition, Room, and Board

Albany State University, GA
Alcorn State University, MS
Boricua College, NY
California State University, Bakersfield, CA
Central State University, OH
Charter Oak State College, CT
East Tennessee State University, TN
Elizabethtown College School of Continuing and Professional Studies, PA
Middle Tennessee State University, TN
Midwestern State University, TX
Mississippi Valley State University, MS
North Carolina Central University, NC
Northeastern State University, OK
Oklahoma Panhandle State University, OK
Oregon Institute of Technology, OR
Our Lady of Holy Cross College, LA
Peru State College, NE
Sojourner-Douglass College, MD
Southern University and A&M College, LA
Southwestern Oklahoma State University, OK
Tennessee State University, TN
Union Institute & University, OH
University of Michigan/Dearborn, MI
University of Missouri-St. Louis, MO
University of Montana-Western, MT
University of New Orleans, LA
University of North Alabama, AL

University of North Georgia, GA
University of Rio Grande, OH
University of Texas at El Paso, TX
University of Wisconsin/La Crosse, WI
University of Wisconsin/River Falls, WI
West Liberty University, WV
West Virginia State University, WV
Western New Mexico University, NM
Wiley College, TX
Wilmington University, DE
Winston-Salem State University, NC

$10,000-$11,999

Colleges with Tuition, Room, and Board

Alabama Agricultural and Mechanical University, AL
Ashford University, CA
Brigham Young University/Hawaii, HI
Cabarrus College of Health Sciences, NC
Cameron University, OK
Caribbean University, PR
Central Washington University, WA
Chancellor University, OH
Colorado Technical University, CO
Dickinson State University, ND
East Central University, OK
Eastern Kentucky University, KY
Eastern New Mexico University, NM
Eastern Oregon University, OR
Elizabeth City State University, NC
Fayetteville State University, NC
Fort Hays State University, KS
Fort Valley State University, GA
Glenville State College, WV
Kentucky State University, KY
Lane College, TN
Louisiana Tech University, LA
Martin University, IN
Mayville State University, ND
Miles College, AL
Minot State University, ND
Morehead State University, KY
New Mexico Highlands University, NM
Norfolk State University, VA
Northeastern Illinois University, IL
Penn State University/Altoona, PA
Rust College, MS
Slippery Rock University of Pennsylvania, PA
St. Cloud State University, MN
Tennessee Technological University, TN
Texas A&M University at Commerce, TX
Texas A&M University at Corpus Christi, TX
Texas A&M University at Galveston, TX
The University of Virginia's College at Wise, VA
Thomas University, GA
Troy University, AL
University of Alaska Southeast, AK
University of Maine at Machias, ME
University of Science and Arts of Oklahoma, OK
University of Texas - Pan American, TX
University of Texas at Arlington, TX
University of Wisconsin/Oshkosh, WI
University of Wisconsin/Parkside, WI
Valdosta State University, GA
Virginia State University, VA
Wayne State College, NE
Weber State University, UT
Western Kentucky University, KY

$12,000-$13,999

Colleges with Tuition, Room, and Board

Adams State University, CO
Appalachian State University, NC
Arkansas Tech University, AR

Bemidji State University, MN
Black Hills State University, SD
Bloomsburg University of Pennsylvania, PA
Boise State University, ID
Brigham Young University, UT
California State University, San Bernardino, CA
Cambridge College, MA
Carlos Albizu University, FL
Clayton State University, GA
Columbus State University, GA
Concord University, WV
Dakota State University, SD
Delta State University, MS
Emporia State University, KS
Fairmont State University, WV
Georgia Southwestern State University, GA
Grambling State University, LA
Hodges University, FL
Howard University, DC
Idaho State University, ID
Jackson State University, MS
Jacksonville State University, AL
LeMoyne-Owen College, TN
Lincoln University, MO
Minnesota State University, Moorhead, MN
Missouri Southern State University, MO
Missouri State University, MO
Missouri Western State University, MO
Montana State University-Billings, MT
Montana State University-Northern, MT
New Mexico Institute of Mining and Technology, NM
North Carolina Agricultural and Technical State University, NC
Ohio State University at Mansfield, OH
Peirce College, PA
Pittsburg State University, KS
Salem State University, MA
Savannah State University, GA
Southeastern Louisiana University, LA
Southern Polytechnic State University, GA
Southern Utah University, UT
Sul Ross State University, TX
Tarleton State University, TX
Texas Woman's University, TX
The Evergreen State College, WA
The University of North Carolina at Greensboro, NC
The University of North Carolina at Pembroke, NC
University of Arkansas at Monticello, AR
University of Arkansas at Pine Bluff, AR
University of California at Davis, CA
University of Central Arkansas, AR
University of Central Oklahoma, OK
University of Louisiana at Monroe, LA
University of Nebraska at Omaha, NE
University of North Carolina at Asheville, NC
University of North Carolina at Wilmington, NC
University of South Alabama, AL
University of South Florida/St. Petersburg, FL
University of South Florida/Tampa, FL
University of Southern Mississippi, MS
University of Tennessee at Martin, TN
University of Wisconsin Whitewater, WI
Utah State University, UT
Valley City State University, ND
Washburn University, KS
West Texas A&M University, TX
Western Carolina University, NC
William Carey University, MS

$14,000-$15,999

Colleges with Tuition, Room, and Board

Alabama State University, AL

Angelo State University, TX
Arkansas Baptist College, AR
Arkansas State University, AR
Armstrong State University, GA
Auburn University at Montgomery, AL
Austin Peay State University, TN
Blue Mountain College, MS
Buffalo State College/State University of New York, NY
California Maritime Academy, CA
California State University, San Marcos, CA
California University of Pennsylvania, PA
Calumet College of St. Joseph, IN
City University of Seattle, WA
Concordia College-Alabama, AL
Cox College, MO
East Carolina University, NC
Edinboro University of Pennsylvania, PA
Embry-Riddle Aeronautical University-Worldwide, FL
Florida Agricultural and Mechanical University, FL
Florida Gulf Coast University, FL
Fort Lewis College, CO
Frostburg State University, MD
George Mason University, VA
Georgia State University, GA
Harris-Stowe State University, MO
Henderson State University, AR
Hunter College, NY
Indiana University South Bend, IN
Indiana University-Purdue University Fort Wayne, IN
Kansas State University, KS
Louisiana College, LA
Lyndon State College, VT
Marshall University, WV
Massachusetts Maritime Academy, MA
Mercy College of Health Sciences, IA
Minnesota State University, Mankato, MN
Mississippi State University, MS
Montana State University, MT
Montana Tech of The University of Montana, MT
Morgan State University, MD
Murray State University, KY
National University, CA
New College of Florida, FL
New Mexico State University, NM
Northern State University - Aberdeen, SD
Northwestern State University of Louisiana, LA
Oklahoma State University, OK
Ottawa University, KS
Prairie View A&M University, TX
Presentation College, SD
Purdue University/Calumet, IN
Saint Augustine's University, NC
Shaw University, NC
Shepherd University, WV
South Dakota School of Mines and Technology, SD
South Dakota State University, SD
Southeast Missouri State University, MO
Southern Arkansas University, AR
Southwest Minnesota State University, MN
Stephen F. Austin State University, TX
SUNY New Paltz, NY
Texas Tech University, TX
The Lincoln University, PA
The University of Memphis, TN
Tougaloo College, MS
Truman State University, MO
University of Alaska Fairbanks, AK
University of Central Florida, FL
University of Central Missouri, MO
University of Colorado at Colorado Springs, CO
University of Florida, FL
University of Houston-Downtown, TX
University of Idaho, ID
University of Maine at Fort Kent, ME
University of Maine at Presque Isle, ME
University of Maryland/Eastern Shore, MD
University of Montana, MT
University of Nebraska at Kearney, NE
University of New Mexico, NM
University of North Carolina at Charlotte, NC
University of North Dakota, ND
University of North Florida, FL
University of North Texas, TX
University of Northern Iowa, IA

University of South Dakota, SD
University of Southern Indiana, IN
University of the Southwest, NM
University of Washington, WA
University of West Alabama, AL
University of West Florida, FL
University of West Georgia, GA
University of Wisconsin/Eau Claire, WI
University of Wisconsin/Platteville, WI
University of Wisconsin/Stevens Point, WI
University of Wisconsin/Stout, WI
University of Wisconsin/Superior, WI
University of Wyoming, WY
Vermont Technical College, VT
Virginia Polytechnic Institute and State University, VA
Webb Institute, NY
West Virginia University Institute of Technology, WV
Western Oregon University, OR
Wichita State University, KS
Wilberforce University, OH

$16,000-$17,999

Colleges with Tuition, Room, and Board

Adventist University of Health Sciences, FL
Allen University, SC
Ball State University, IN
Bluefield College, VA
California State University, Dominguez Hills, CA
California State University, East Bay, CA
California State University, Fresno, CA
California State University, Long Beach, CA
California State University, Los Angeles, CA
California State University, Sacramento, CA
Clarion University of Pennsylvania, PA
Clarkson College, NE
College of Staten Island/The City of New York, NY
Colorado Mesa University, CO
Colorado State University-Pueblo, CO
Coppin State University, MD
Delaware State University, DE
Florida Atlantic University, FL
Florida International University, FL
Florida State University, FL
Francis Marion University, SC
Georgia Southern University, GA
Goddard College, VT
Golden Gate University, CA
Grand Valley State University, MI
Heritage University, WA
Howard Payne University, TX
Humphreys College, CA
Indiana State University, IN
Indiana University Southeast, IN
Indiana University-Purdue University Indianapolis, IN
Iowa State University, IA
Johnson State College, VT
Kentucky Christian University, KY
Kutztown University of Pennsylvania, PA
Livingstone College, NC
Maritime College/State University of New York, NY
Metropolitan College of New York, NY
Morris College, SC
National Louis University, IL
North Carolina State University, NC
Northwest Missouri State University, MO
Ohio State University at Marion, OH
Ohio State University at Newark, OH
Ohio Valley University, WV
Park University, MO
Penn State Erie/The Behrend College, PA
Queens College/The City University of New York, NY
Radford University, VA
Rhode Island College, RI
Saginaw Valley State University, MI
Saint Paul's College, VA
Sam Houston State University, TX
Shawnee State University, OH
Southern Illinois University Edwardsville, IL
Southern Oregon University, OR
St. Gregory's University, OK

State University of New York at Purchase, NY
SUNY College at Old Westbury, NY
SUNY Oneonta / State University of New York, NY
Talladega College, AL
Texas State University, TX
The University of Tennessee at Chattanooga, TN
The University of Utah, UT
Towson University, MD
University of Alabama at Tuscaloosa, AL
University of Alabama in Huntsville, AL
University of Alaska Anchorage, AK
University of Arkansas at Little Rock, AR
University of Colorado Denver , CO
University of Iowa, IA
University of Kansas, KS
University of Louisville, KY
University of Mary, ND
University of Michigan-Flint, MI
University of Minnesota Crookston, MN
University of Minnesota/Morris, MN
University of Mississippi, MS
University of Montevallo, AL
University of Nevada, Las Vegas, NV
University of Nevada/Reno, NV
University of Pittsburgh at Greensburg, PA
University of South Carolina Aiken, SC
University of Southern Maine, ME
Virginia Military Institute, VA
West Chester University of Pennsylvania, PA
West Virginia University, WV
Western State Colorado University, CO
Winona State University, MN
Wright State University, OH
Youngstown State University, OH

$18,000-$19,999

Colleges with Tuition, Room, and Board

Alfred State/SUNY College of Technology, NY
American Indian College, AZ
Arizona State University, at the West Campus, AZ
Berkeley College of New York City, NY
Bethel University, TN
Boston Architectural College, MA
Bowling Green State University, OH
Bridgewater State University, MA
California Polytechnic State University, CA
California State University, Stanislaus, CA
Central Connecticut State University, CT
Clemson University, SC
Coastal Carolina University, SC
Colorado School of Mines, CO
East Stroudsburg University of Pennsylvania, PA
Eastern Michigan University, MI
Eastern Washington University, WA
Edward Waters College, FL
Eureka College, IL
Farmingdale State College, NY
Fashion Institute of Technology/State University of New York, NY
Fisk University, TN
Fitchburg State University, MA
Framingham State University, MA
Freed-Hardeman University, TN
Georgia College and State University, GA
Goodwin College, CT
Humboldt State University, CA
Huston-Tillotson University, TX
Indiana University Bloomington, IN
James Madison University, VA
Jarvis Christian College, TX
Kent State University, OH
Lake Superior State University, MI
Lee University, TN
Liberty University, VA
Lincoln Memorial University, TN
Lock Haven University of Pennsylvania, PA
Louisiana State University, LA
Mansfield University, PA
Massachusetts College of Liberal Arts, MA
Missouri University of Science and Technology, MO
Northern Arizona University, AZ
Northern Illinois University, IL

Northern Michigan University, MI
Northwest University, WA
Oakland University, MI
Old Dominion University, VA
Olivet College, MI
Paine College, GA
Philander Smith College, AR
Portland State University, OR
Rochester College, MI
Salisbury University, MD
San Francisco State University, CA
San Jose State University, CA
Southern Connecticut State University, CT
State University of New York/College of Environmental Science and Forestry, NY
State University of New York Polytechnic Institute, NY
Stillman College, AL
SUNY College at Geneseo, NY
SUNY Cortland/The State University of New York, NY
SUNY Fredonia/The State University of New York at Fredonia, NY
SUNY Plattsburgh/State University of New York, NY
Texas A&M University, TX
Texas Southern University, TX
The Ohio State University-Columbus Campus, OH
The State University of New York at Potsdam, NY
The State University of New York College of Agriculture and Tech at Cobleskill, NY
The State University of New York/College at Brockport, NY
The University of Oklahoma, OK
Universidad Politecnica de Puerto Rico, PR
University at Albany/SUNY, NY
University of Alabama at Birmingham, AL
University of Arkansas at Fayetteville, AR
University of Hawaii at Manoa, HI
University of Houston, TX
University of Kentucky, KY
University of Maine, ME
University of Maine at Farmington, ME
University of Mary Washington, VA
University of Maryland/Baltimore County, MD
University of Massachusetts Lowell, MA
University of Minnesota/Duluth, MN
University of Missouri/Columbia, MO
University of Missouri-Kansas City, MO
University of Nebraska-Lincoln, NE
University of North Carolina at Chapel Hill, NC
University of Northern Colorado, CO
University of South Carolina at Columbia, SC
University of South Carolina Upstate, SC
University of Texas at San Antonio, TX
University of Toledo, OH
University of Wisconsin/Green Bay, WI
University of Wisconsin/Madison, WI
University of Wisconsin-Milwaukee, WI
Victory University, TN
Virginia Union University, VA
Voorhees College, SC
Warner University, FL
Wayland Baptist University, TX
Western Connecticut State University, CT
Western Michigan University, MI
Western Washington University, WA
Westfield State University, MA
Worcester State University, MA
York College, NE

$20,000-$21,999

Colleges with Tuition, Room, and Board

Arizona State University, at the Polytechnic Campus, AZ
Arizona State University, at the Tempe Campus, AZ
Benedict College, SC
Bennett College for Women, NC
Binghamton University/The State University of New York, NY
Blackburn College, IL

California State Polytechnic University, Pomona, CA
California State University, Chico, CA
Capitol College, MD
Castleton State College, VT
Central Michigan University, MI
Cheney University of Pennsylvania, PA
Christopher Newport University, VA
City University of New York/Baruch College, NY
City University of New York/City College, NY
Cleveland State University, OH
Colorado State University-Fort Collins, CO
Cornish College of the Arts, WA
Cumberland University, TN
Curtis Institute of Music, PA
Davenport University, MI
Dillard University, LA
Eastern Connecticut State University, CT
Eastern Illinois University, IL
Ferris State University, MI
Florida Memorial University, FL
Franklin University, OH
Georgia Institute of Technology, GA
Grace Bible College, MI
Indiana University of Pennsylvania, PA
Lindenwood University, MO
List College, NY
Longwood University, VA
MacMurray College, IL
Maine Maritime Academy, ME
Marylhurst University, OR
Midway College, KY
Millersville University of Pennsylvania, PA
Mississippi College, MS
Monroe College, NY
New Jersey City University, NJ
Northern Kentucky University, KY
Ohio University, OH
Oklahoma Wesleyan University, OK
Oregon State University, OR
Oswego/State University of New York, NY
Purdue University/West Lafayette, IN
Richard Stockton College of New Jersey, NJ
Rockhurst University, MO
Salem International University, WV
San Diego State University, CA
Shippensburg University of Pennsylvania, PA
Sonoma State University, CA
Southern Illinois University Carbondale, IL
Stony Brook University/State University of New York, NY
Tennessee Wesleyan College, TN
University at Buffalo/The State University of New York, NY
University of Akron, OH
University of Arizona, AZ
University of California at San Diego, CA
University of Cincinnati, OH
University of Georgia, GA
University of Maryland-College Park, MD
University of Mount Olive, NC
University of Oregon, OR
University of Pittsburgh at Bradford, PA
University of Pittsburgh at Johnstown, PA
University of Tennessee at Knoxville, TN
University of Texas at Dallas, TX
Virginia Commonwealth University, VA
Washington State University, WA
Western Illinois University, IL
William Paterson University of New Jersey, NJ
Williams Baptist College, AR
Winthrop University, SC

$22,000–$23,999

Colleges with Tuition, Room, and Board

Arizona State University, at the Downtown Phoenix Campus, AZ
Art Institute of Portland, OR
Auburn University, AL
Bethune-Cookman University, FL
Bowie State University, MD
Charleston Southern University, SC
Claflin University, SC

Clearwater Christian College, FL
College of Charleston, SC
Concordia University Texas, TX
Dakota Wesleyan University, SD
Elms College, MA
Evangel University, MO
Harding University, AR
Hardin-Simmons University, TX
Illinois State University, IL
Kean University, NJ
Keene State College, NH
Lakeland College, WI
Lander University, SC
Lewis University, IL
Mars Hill University, NC
Massachusetts College of Art and Design, MA
Michigan State University, MI
Michigan Technological University, MI
Missouri Valley College, MO
Montclair State University, NJ
Nebraska Methodist College of Nursing and Allied Health, NE
Our Lady of the Lake University, TX
Plymouth State University, NH
Rocky Mountain College of Art and Design, CO
Roosevelt University, IL
Silver Lake College, WI
Southwestern Adventist University, TX
St. Joseph's College, New York/Brooklyn Campus, NY
St. Joseph's College, New York/Suffolk Campus, NY
Toccoa Falls College, GA
Union College, NE
University of California at Berkeley, CA
University of Colorado Boulder, CO
University of Delaware, DE
University of Hawaii at Hilo, HI
University of Massachusetts Boston, MA
University of Massachusetts Dartmouth, MA
University of Michigan/Ann Arbor, MI
University of Minnesota/Twin Cities, MN
University of Sioux Falls, SD
University of Virginia, VA
Wayne State University, MI
Wisconsin Lutheran College, WI

$24,000–$25,999

Colleges with Tuition, Room, and Board

Art Academy of Cincinnati, OH
Art Institute of Atlanta, GA
Ashland University, OH
Atlantic Union College, MA
Bryan College, TN
California State University, Fullerton, CA
Cardinal Stritch University, WI
College of New Jersey, NJ
Daniel Webster College, NH
Dowling College, NY
Faulkner University, AL
Flagler College, FL
Gallaudet University, DC
Grand Canyon University, AZ
Grove City College, PA
Hannibal-LaGrange University, MO
Husson University, ME
Illinois College, IL
Johnson C. Smith University, NC
Judson University, IL
Madonna University, MI
McMurry University, TX
Miami University, OH
NewSchool of Architecture & Design, CA
Northwestern College, MN
Northwood University, TX
Oakland City University, IN
Oakwood University, AL
Oklahoma Christian University, OK
Paul Quinn College, TX
Ramapo College of New Jersey, NJ
Reinhardt College, GA
Rowan University, NJ
Rutgers, The State University of New Jersey/Camden Campus, NJ
Rutgers, The State University of New Jersey/New Brunswick, NJ
Southern Nazarene University, OK
Southern Wesleyan University, SC
Southwest Baptist University, MO
Spelman College, GA

Springfield College, MA
St. Mary's College of Maryland, MD
Temple University, PA
Tusculum College, TN
University of California at Irvine, CA
University of California at Los Angeles, CA
University of Connecticut, CT
University of Illinois at Chicago, IL
University of Jamestown, ND
University of Massachusetts Amherst, MA
University of Pikeville, KY
University of Rhode Island, RI
Warner Pacific College, OR
Washington Adventist University, MD
Wesleyan College, GA
William Woods University, MO
Xavier University of Louisiana, LA

$26,000–$29,999

Colleges with Tuition, Room, and Board

Alderson Broaddus University, WV
Allen College, IA
Andrews University, MI
Aquinas College, TN
Avila University, MO
Barton College, NC
Belhaven University, MS
Benedictine College, KS
Benjamin Franklin Institute of Technology, MA
Berkeley College/New Jersey, NJ
Berkeley College/Westchester Campus, NY
Brenau University - Women's College, GA
Brescia University, KY
Briar Cliff University, IA
Bryn Athyn College , PA
California State University, Monterey Bay, CA
California State University, Northridge, CA
Campbellsville University, KY
Carroll College, MT
Carson-Newman University, TN
Central Methodist University, MO
College of William & Mary, VA
Colorado Christian University, CO
Columbia College, SC
Concordia University Nebraska, NE
Concordia University Saint Paul, MN
Concordia University Wisconsin, WI
Concordia University, Ann Arbor, MI
Concordia University, River Forest, IL
Delaware Valley College, PA
D'Youville College, NY
Ferrum College, VA
Franciscan University of Steubenville, OH
Friends University, KS
Geneva College, PA
Georgia Regents University, GA
Goldey-Beacom College, DE
Grace College and Seminary, IN
Graceland University, IA
Greensboro College, NC
Greenville College, IL
Hampton University, VA
Hastings College, NE
Hilbert College, NY
Johnson & Wales University/Charlotte Campus, NC
Johnson & Wales University/Denver Campus, CO
Johnson & Wales University/North Miami Campus, FL
Johnson & Wales University/Providence Campus, RI
Judson College, AL
Kentucky Wesleyan College, KY
Keystone College, PA
Laguna College of Art and Design, CA
Lourdes University, OH
Lubbock Christian University, TX
Maine College of Art, ME
Marygrove College, MI
McKendree University, IL
McPherson College, KS
MidAmerica Nazarene University, KS
Milligan College, TN
Mount Aloysius College, PA
Mount Marty College, SD
Mount Vernon Nazarene University, OH

Nebraska Wesleyan University, NE
New Jersey Institute of Technology, NJ
Newberry College, SC
North Carolina Wesleyan College, NC
North Central University, MN
Northland College, WI
Northwest Christian University, OR
Northwood University, MI
Norwich University, VT
Notre Dame of Maryland University, MD
Oklahoma Baptist University, OK
Olivet Nazarene University, IL
Pacific Union College, CA
Pennsylvania College of Technology, PA
Salem College, NC
Simpson University, CA
Southeastern University, FL
Southern Adventist University, TN
Southwestern College, KS
Spring Arbor University, MI
Sterling College, KS
Sterling College, VT
Tabor College, KS
The College of Saint Rose, NY
The Pennsylvania State University-University Park , PA
Thomas More College of Liberal Arts, NH
Touro College, NY
Trinity Christian College, IL
Tuskegee University, AL
Union College, KY
Union University, TN
University of California at Riverside, CA
University of California at Santa Barbara, CA
University of California at Santa Cruz, CA
University of Great Falls, MT
University of Illinois at Urbana-Champaign, IL
University of Mobile, AL
University of New Hampshire, NH
University of Pittsburgh at Pittsburgh, PA
University of Saint Francis, IN
University of Saint Mary, KS
University of the Cumberlands, KY
University of Vermont, VT
VanderCook College of Music, IL
Virginia Wesleyan College, VA
Walla Walla University, WA
Wentworth Institute of Technology, MA
West Virginia Wesleyan College, WV
William Penn University, IA
Wilmington College, OH
York College of Pennsylvania, PA

$30,000 and over

Colleges with Tuition, Room, and Board

Abilene Christian University, TX
Adelphi University, NY
Adrian College, MI
Agnes Scott College, GA
Alaska Pacific University, AK
Albany College of Pharmacy and Health Sciences, NY
Albertus Magnus College, CT
Albion College, MI
Albright College, PA
Alfred University, NY
Allegheny College, PA
Alma College, MI
Alvernia University, PA
Alverno College, WI
American International College, MA
American Jewish University - College of Arts and Sciences, CA
American University, DC
Amherst College, MA
Anderson University, IN
Anna Maria College, MA
Aquinas College, MI
Arcadia University, PA
Art Center College of Design, CA
Asbury University, KY
Assumption College, MA
Augsburg College, MN
Augustana College, IL
Augustana College, SD
Aurora University, IL
Austin College, TX
Averett University, VA
Azusa Pacific University, CA

Babson College, MA
Baker University, KS
Baldwin Wallace University, OH
Bard College, NY
Bard College at Simon's Rock, MA
Barnard College/Columbia University, NY
Barry University, FL
Bates College, ME
Bay Path College, MA
Baylor University, TX
Beacon College, FL
Becker College, MA
Bellarmine University, KY
Belmont Abbey College, NC
Belmont University, TN
Beloit College, WI
Benedictine University, IL
Bennington College, VT
Bentley University, MA
Berklee College of Music, MA
Berry College, GA
Bethany College, KS
Bethany College, WV
Bethel College, IN
Bethel College, KS
Bethel University, MN
Biola University, CA
Birmingham-Southern College, AL
Bloomfield College, NJ
Bluffton University, OH
Boston College, MA
Boston Conservatory, MA
Boston University, MA
Bowdoin College, ME
Bradley University, IL
Brandeis University, MA
Brewton-Parker College, GA
Bridgewater College, VA
Brown University, RI
Bryant University, RI
Bryn Mawr College, PA
Bucknell University, PA
Buena Vista University, IA
Burlington College, VT
Butler University, IN
Cabrini College, PA
Cairn University, PA
Caldwell College, NJ
California Baptist University, CA
California College of the Arts, CA
California Institute of Technology, CA
California Institute of the Arts, CA
California Lutheran University, CA
Calvin College, MI
Campbell University, NC
Canisius College, NY
Capital University, OH
Carleton College, MN
Carlow University, PA
Carnegie Mellon University, PA
Carroll University, WI
Carthage College, WI
Case Western Reserve University, OH
Catawba College, NC
Cazenovia College, NY
Cedar Crest College, PA
Cedarville University, OH
Centenary College, NJ
Centenary College of Louisiana, LA
Central College, IA
Centre College, KY
Chaminade University of Honolulu, HI
Champlain College, VT
Chapman University, CA
Chatham University, PA
Chestnut Hill College, PA
Christendom College, VA
Christian Brothers University, TN
Claremont McKenna College, CA
Clark Atlanta University, GA
Clark University, MA
Clarke University, IA
Clarkson University, NY
Cleveland Institute of Art, OH
Cleveland Institute of Music, OH
Coe College, IA
Cogswell Polytechnical College, CA
Coker College, SC
Colby College, ME
Colby-Sawyer College, NH
Colgate University, NY
College for Creative Studies, MI
College of Art and Design at Lesley University, MA
College of Mount Saint Joseph, OH
College of Mount Saint Vincent, NY
College of Saint Benedict , MN
College of Saint Elizabeth, NJ

College of Saint Mary, NE
College of Saint Scholastica, MN
College of St Joseph, VT
College of the Atlantic, ME
College of the Holy Cross, MA
College of Wooster, OH
Colorado College, CO
Columbia College, MO
Columbia College Chicago, IL
Columbia University/City of New York, NY
Columbia University/School of General Studies, NY
Columbus College of Art and Design, OH
Concordia College - Moorhead, MN
Concordia College - New York, NY
Concordia University , OR
Concordia University Irvine, CA
Connecticut College, CT
Converse College, SC
Cooper Union for the Advancement of Science and Art, NY
Corban University, OR
Corcoran College of Art and Design, DC
Cornell College, IA
Cornell University, NY
Cornerstone University and Grand Rapids Theological Seminary, MI
Covenant College, GA
Creighton University, NE
Culver-Stockton College, MO
Curry College, MA
Daemen College, NY
Dallas Baptist University, TX
Dartmouth College, NH
Davidson College, NC
Davis & Elkins College, WV
De Sales University, PA
Defiance College, OH
Denison University, OH
DePaul University, IL
DePauw University, IN
Dickinson College, PA
Doane College, NE
Dominican College, NY
Dominican University, IL
Dominican University of California, CA
Dordt College, IA
Drake University, IA
Drew University/College of Liberal Arts, NJ
Drexel University, PA
Drury University, MO
Duke University, NC
Duquesne University, PA
Earlham College, IN
East Texas Baptist University, TX
Eastern Mennonite University, VA
Eastern Nazarene College, MA
Eastern University, PA
Eastman School of Music, NY
Eckerd College, FL
Edgewood College, WI
Elizabethtown College, PA
Elmhurst College, IL
Elmira College, NY
Elon University, NC
Embry-Riddle Aeronautical University - Daytona Beach, FL
Embry-Riddle Aeronautical University - Prescott Campus, AZ
Emerson College, MA
Emmanuel College, MA
Emory and Henry College, VA
Emory University, GA
Endicott College, MA
Erskine College, SC
Eugene Lang College/The New School for Liberal Arts, NY
Fairfield University, CT
Fairleigh Dickinson University/College at Florham, NJ
Fairleigh Dickinson University/Metropolitan Campus, NJ
Felician College, NJ
Five Towns College, NY
Florida Institute of Technology, FL
Florida Southern College, FL
Fontbonne University, MO
Fordham University, NY
Franklin and Marshall College, PA
Franklin College, IN
Franklin Pierce University, NH
Franklin W. Olin College of Engineering, MA
Fresno Pacific University, CA
Furman University, SC
Gannon University, PA

Gardner-Webb University, NC
George Fox University, OR
George Washington University, DC
Georgetown College, KY
Georgetown University, DC
Georgian Court University, NJ
Gettysburg College, PA
Gonzaga University, WA
Gordon College, MA
Goshen College, IN
Goucher College, MD
Grand View University, IA
Green Mountain College, VT
Grinnell College, IA
Guilford College, NC
Gustavus Adolphus College, MN
Gwynedd-Mercy College, PA
Hamilton College, NY
Hamline University, MN
Hampden-Sydney College, VA
Hampshire College, MA
Hanover College, IN
Hartwick College, NY
Harvard College/Harvard University, MA
Harvey Mudd College, CA
Haverford College, PA
Hawaii Pacific University, HI
Heidelberg University, OH
Hellenic College/Holy Cross Greek Orthodox School of Theology, MA
Hendrix College, AR
High Point University, NC
Hillsdale College, MI
Hiram College, OH
Hobart and William Smith Colleges, NY
Hofstra University, NY
Hollins University, VA
Holy Family University, PA
Holy Names University, CA
Hood College, MD
Hope College, MI
Hope International University, CA
Houghton College, NY
Houston Baptist University, TX
Huntingdon College, AL
Huntington University, IN
Illinois Institute of Technology, IL
Indiana Institute of Technology, IN
Indiana Wesleyan University, IN
Iona College, NY
Iowa Wesleyan College, IA
Ithaca College, NY
Jacksonville University, FL
John Brown University, AR
John Carroll University, OH
Johns Hopkins University, MD
Juilliard School, NY
Juniata College, PA
Kalamazoo College, MI
Kansas City Art Institute, MO
Kansas Wesleyan University, KS
Kendall College, IL
Kenyon College, OH
Kettering University, MI
Keuka College, NY
King University, TN
King's College, PA
Knox College, IL
La Roche College, PA
La Salle University, PA
La Sierra University, CA
Lafayette College, PA
LaGrange College, GA
Lake Erie College, OH
Lake Forest College, IL
Lasell College, MA
Lawrence Technological University, MI
Lawrence University, WI
Le Moyne College, NY
Lebanon Valley College, PA
Lees-McRae College, NC
Lehigh University, PA
Lenoir-Rhyne College, NC
Lesley University, MA
LeTourneau University, TX
Lewis & Clark College, OR
LIM College, NY
Limestone College, SC
Lindsey Wilson College, KY
Linfield College-McMinnville Campus, OR
Lipscomb University, TN
LIU Brooklyn, NY
LIU Post, NY
Loras College, IA
Loyola Marymount University, CA
Loyola University Chicago, IL

Loyola University Maryland, MD
Loyola University New Orleans, LA
Luther College, IA
Lycoming College, PA
Lynchburg College, VA
Lynn University, FL
Lyon College, AR
Macalester College, MN
Maharishi University of Management, IA
Malone University, OH
Manchester University, IN
Manhattan College, NY
Manhattan School of Music, NY
Manhattanville College, NY
Mannes College New School for Music, NY
Marian University, IN
Marian University, WI
Marietta College, OH
Marist College, NY
Marlboro College, VT
Marquette University, WI
Mary Baldwin College, VA
Maryland Institute College of Art, MD
Marymount Manhattan College, NY
Marymount University, VA
Maryville College, TN
Maryville University of Saint Louis, MO
Marywood University, PA
Massachusetts College of Pharmacy and Health Sciences, MA
Massachusetts Institute of Technology, MA
McDaniel College, MD
Medaille College, NY
Memphis College of Art, TN
Menlo College, CA
Mercer University, GA
Mercy College, NY
Mercyhurst University, PA
Meredith College, NC
Merrimack College, MA
Messiah College, PA
Methodist University, NC
Middlebury College, VT
Midland University, NE
Millikin University, IL
Mills College, CA
Millsaps College, MS
Milwaukee Institute of Art and Design, WI
Milwaukee School of Engineering, WI
Minneapolis College of Art and Design, MN
Misericordia University, PA
Missouri Baptist University, MO
Mitchell College, CT
Molloy College, NY
Monmouth College, IL
Monmouth University, NJ
Montreat College, NC
Montserrat College of Art, MA
Moore College of Art and Design, PA
Moravian College, PA
Morehouse College, GA
Morningside College, IA
Mount Holyoke College, MA
Mount Ida College, MA
Mount Mary University, WI
Mount Mercy University, IA
Mount Saint Mary College, NY
Mount Saint Mary's University, MD
Mount St. Mary's College - Chalon Campus, CA
Muhlenberg College, PA
Muskingum University, OH
Naropa University, CO
Nazareth College of Rochester, NY
Neumann University, PA
New England College, NH
New England Conservatory of Music, MA
New York Institute of Technology, NY
New York University, NY
Newbury College, MA
Newman University, KS
Niagara University, NY
Nichols College, MA
North Central College, IL
North Park University, IL
Northeastern University, MA
Northwest Nazarene University, ID
Northwestern College of Iowa, IA
Northwestern University, IL
Northwood University, FL
Notre Dame College, OH
Notre Dame de Namur University, CA
Nova Southeastern University, FL
Nyack College, NY

Oberlin College, OH
Occidental College, CA
Oglethorpe University, GA
Ohio Dominican University, OH
Ohio Northern University, OH
Ohio Wesleyan University, OH
Oklahoma City University, OK
Oral Roberts University, OK
Otis College of Art and Design, CA
Otterbein College, OH
Ouachita Baptist University, AR
Pace University, NY
Pacific Lutheran University, WA
Pacific Northwest College of Art, OR
Pacific University, OR
Palm Beach Atlantic University, FL
Parsons The New School for Design, NY
Pepperdine University, CA
Pfeiffer University, NC
Philadelphia University, PA
Piedmont College, GA
Pine Manor College, MA
Pitzer College, CA
Point Loma Nazarene University, CA
Point Park University, PA
Polytechnic Institute of New York University, NY
Pomona College, CA
Post University, CT
Pratt Institute, NY
Presbyterian College, SC
Prescott College, AZ
Princeton University, NJ
Principia College, IL
Providence College, RI
Queens University of Charlotte, NC
Quincy University, IL
Quinnipiac University, CT
Randolph College, VA
Randolph-Macon College, VA
Reed College, OR
Regis College, MA
Regis University, CO
Rensselaer Polytechnic Institute, NY
Research College of Nursing, MO
Rhode Island School of Design, RI
Rhodes College, TN
Rice University, TX
Rider University, NJ
Ringling College of Art and Design, FL
Ripon College, WI
Rivier University, NH
Roanoke College, VA
Robert Morris University, PA
Roberts Wesleyan College, NY
Rochester Institute of Technology, NY
Rockford College, IL
Rocky Mountain College, MT
Roger Williams University, RI
Rollins College, FL
Rose-Hulman Institute of Technology, IN
Rosemont College, PA
Russell Sage College, NY
Rutgers, The State University of New Jersey/Newark Campus, NJ
Sacred Heart University, CT
Saint Anselm College, NH
Saint Francis University, PA
Saint John's University, MN

Saint Joseph's College, IN
Saint Joseph's College of Maine, ME
Saint Joseph's University, PA
Saint Leo University, FL
Saint Louis University, MO
Saint Martin's University, WA
Saint Mary-of-the-Woods College, IN
Saint Mary's College, IN
Saint Mary's College of California, CA
Saint Mary's University , TX
Saint Mary's University of Minnesota, MN
Saint Michael's College, VT
Saint Peter's University, NJ
Saint Vincent College, PA
Saint Xavier University, IL
Salve Regina University, RI
Samford University, AL
San Diego Christian College, CA
San Francisco Art Institute, CA
San Francisco Conservatory of Music, CA
Santa Fe University of Art and Design, NM
Sarah Lawrence College, NY
Savannah College of Art and Design, GA
School of the Art Institute of Chicago, IL
School of Visual Arts, NY
Schreiner University, TX
Scripps College, CA
Seattle Pacific University, WA
Seattle University, WA
Seton Hall University, NJ
Seton Hill University, PA
Sewanee: The University of the South, TN
Shenandoah University, VA
Shimer College, IL
Shorter University, GA
Siena College, NY
Siena Heights University, MI
Sierra Nevada College, NV
Simmons College, MA
Simpson College, IA
Skidmore College, NY
Smith College, MA
South University, GA
Southern Methodist University, TX
Southern New Hampshire University, NH
Southern Vermont College, VT
Southwestern University, TX
Spalding University, KY
Spring Hill College, AL
St. Ambrose University, IA
St. Andrews University, NC
St. Bonaventure University, NY
St. Catherine University, MN
St. Edward's University, TX
St. Francis College, NY
St. John Fisher College, NY
St. John's College, Santa Fe, NM
St. John's College-Annapolis, MD
St. John's University, NY
St. Lawrence University, NY
St. Norbert College, WI
St. Olaf College, MN
St. Thomas Aquinas College, NY
St. Thomas University, FL

Stanford University, CA
Stephens College, MO
Stetson University, FL
Stevens Institute of Technology, NJ
Stevenson University, MD
Stonehill College, MA
Suffolk University, MA
Susquehanna University, PA
Swarthmore College, PA
Syracuse University, NY
Taylor University, IN
Texas Christian University, TX
Texas Lutheran University, TX
Texas Wesleyan University, TX
The Catholic University of America, DC
The College of Idaho, ID
The College of New Rochelle, NY
The Masters College, CA
Thiel College, PA
Thomas Aquinas College, CA
Thomas College, ME
Thomas More College, KY
Tiffin University, OH
Transylvania University, KY
Trevecca Nazarene University, TN
Trine University, IN
Trinity College, CT
Trinity College of Nursing and Health Sciences, IL
Trinity International University, IL
Trinity University, TX
Trinity Washington University, DC
Tufts University, MA
Tulane University, LA
Union College, NY
Unity College, ME
University of Bridgeport, CT
University of Charleston, WV
University of Chicago, IL
University of Dallas, TX
University of Dayton, OH
University of Denver, CO
University of Detroit Mercy, MI
University of Dubuque, IA
University of Evansville, IN
University of Findlay, OH
University of Hartford, CT
University of Indianapolis, IN
University of La Verne, CA
University of Mary Hardin-Baylor, TX
University of Miami, FL
University of Mount Union , OH
University of New England, ME
University of New Haven, CT
University of Notre Dame, IN
University of Pennsylvania, PA
University of Portland, OR
University of Puget Sound, WA
University of Redlands, CA
University of Richmond, VA
University of Rochester, NY
University of Saint Joseph , CT
University of Saint Thomas, MN
University of San Diego, CA
University of San Francisco, CA
University of Scranton, PA
University of Southern California, CA
University of St. Francis, IL
University of St. Thomas - Houston, TX
University of Tampa, FL

University of Texas at Austin, TX
University of the Arts, PA
University of the Incarnate Word, TX
University of the Ozarks, AR
University of the Pacific, CA
University of the Sciences , PA
University of Tulsa, OK
Upper Iowa University, IA
Urbana University, OH
Ursinus College, PA
Ursuline College, OH
Utica College, NY
Valparaiso University, IN
Vanderbilt University, TN
Vanguard University of Southern California, CA
Vassar College, NY
Vaughn College of Aeronautics and Technology, NY
Villanova University, PA
Virginia Intermont College, VA
Viterbo University, WI
Wabash College, IN
Wagner College, NY
Wake Forest University, NC
Walsh University, OH
Warren Wilson College, NC
Wartburg College, IA
Washington and Jefferson College, PA
Washington and Lee University, VA
Washington College, MD
Washington University in St. Louis, MO
Waynesburg University, PA
Webber International University, FL
Webster University, MO
Wellesley College, MA
Wells College, NY
Wesley College, DE
Wesleyan University, CT
Western New England University, MA
Westminster Choir College, NJ
Westminster College, MO
Westminster College, PA
Westminster College, UT
Westmont College, CA
Wheaton College, IL
Wheaton College, MA
Wheeling Jesuit University, WV
Wheelock College, MA
Whitman College, WA
Whittier College, CA
Whitworth University, WA
Widener University, PA
Wilkes University, PA
Willamette University, OR
William Jewell College, MO
William Peace University, NC
Williams College, MA
Wilson College, PA
Wingate University, NC
Wittenberg University, OH
Wofford College, SC
Woodbury University, CA
Worcester Polytechnic Institute, MA
Xavier University, OH
Yale University, CT
Yeshiva University, NY

PART III

INDEX OF

COLLEGE MAJORS

By now, you either have a clear idea about what your college major will be, or you are worrying about it. This section presents an overview of academic majors as well as information about some of the careers for which each major prepares you.

Majors are listed alphabetically in chart form. This lets you compare the various schools that offer the majors that interest you. You'll also be able to compare each school's Selector Rating and in-state costs.

After you've found a representative sampling of the schools that offer majors in the fields you may want to pursue, go on to the college Profiles that make up this book's main section.

What Is a College Major? A major is a field of study in which a student chooses an academic specialty to receive a college degree. A major consists of a concentration of specialized subject matter in a field of study. Most majors occupy about one-quarter to two-thirds of courses in that subject. Most college and university students must complete a required number of courses in their major to earn a Bachelor of Arts (B.A.) or a Bachelor of Science (B.S.) degree. The other twenty-five to fifty percent of courses are occupied by "general education" requirements for graduation, or electives that enhance and broaden a student's academic knowledge. Students' choice of major should be made carefully considering their interests and special talents.

What Is a College Minor? A minor in a field of study usually consists of a number of courses in a field of study other than the major. However, the required units of study are fewer than those required of the major. Many colleges today do not require a formal minor for graduation. The practical reason for a minor is to supplement and strengthen a major. For example, a computer science major may require specified courses in mathematics that, when totaled up, meet the definition of a minor, or perhaps a dual major.

Majors and Careers. Choosing a field of study is one of the most important decisions a student will make in the process of choosing a college major leading to an associate or bachelor's degree. A major with a structured course of study not only provides for intellectual growth, self-improvement, general knowledge, and a search for truth and understanding, but often provides the required technical training to enter and become successful in the world of work. Personal enlightenment is a noble goal, but most students no longer can afford the monetary expenses and the time to pursue courses that do not lead to a major that ties into career goals. Information on majors and careers is presented here to help students to make wise educational and career decisions. Informed educational and career decisions should include interests, academic abilities, and work values.

WHAT ARE SOME DIFFERENT APPROACHES TO CHOOSING A COLLEGE MAJOR?

JOB TRAINING: A student may want to go to college for one main reason: to acquire specific job skills to qualify for direct job entry. Job training course work is usually work-related and technical and it is evident that the skills learned in class can be directly applied to an occupation. For example, students who want to work as engineers in one of the many engineering specialties should pursue a two-year program course work as engineering technicians, or a four- to five-year engineering curriculum to become professional engineers.

Technical preparation: Technical preparation students generally enroll in associate degree programs that provide them with advanced skills through studies and experiences in applied academics, skills, and advanced technology. These students join the workforce after grade 14 or continue their formal preparation by working toward a baccalaureate degree in applied technology. Technical majors can be planned in agriculture, arts and communications, business, engineering and mechanics, health, human service, and natural science.

A general approach: Students may want to pursue a more general major that may not directly tie in to job entry, but will improve their general knowledge and prepare them as generalists with intellectual and problem-solving skills rather than technical training. This kind of major is often referred to as liberal arts, humanities, or general studies. Liberal arts majors can be planned in Social and Behavioral Sciences, The Arts, Communications, Humanities, and Ethnic Studies. A liberal arts major, leading to a baccalaureate degree, may not guarantee direct entry into an occupation associated with the major.

Special talent approach: Students may want to select a major because of a special talent and a strong interest in a certain field of study. Students with a strong interest in writing, drama, music, art, or an academic subject should select a major that helps to further the talent. College life will be more enjoyable if students select majors that will provide personal satisfaction. Designing a career plan that will allow a lifestyle compatible with the special talent will also provide personal satisfaction.

Double major approach: Students often decide to choose two majors in preparation for a career. A double major may be necessary in preparing for occupations in the science field where it is essential to be well-grounded in both the physical and biological sciences.

Independent approach: Students may have highly divergent interests that cut across two or more fields of study. Many colleges allow students to design a major to satisfy their goals. For example, students may have artistic talents and scientific interests. They might combine the two interests and design a scientific illustration major that meets faculty approval.

CONNECTING COLLEGE MAJOR PLANNING AND CAREER PLANNING

All students from the ninth grade through postsecondary school should be following a program of study that will prepare them for specific careers—studies that blend appropriate academics with appropriate skills and knowledge in a particular career area. All students in postsecondary studies should be preparing for life and work after completing their studies. This assertion eliminates a justification for a "general plan" of studies that in theory "leads anywhere," but in fact "leads nowhere." Students should either be in a postsecondary associate, technical, or baccalaureate educational plan that leads to a satisfying career.

The next section presents relevant educational and career information on 14 fields of study from which students may choose a major based on career plans. Each of the 14 fields of study has specific information on majors and careers that students should consider carefully when choosing a college major. Information about employment, growth, and earnings is taken from the Department of Labor figures for 2012, with growth projected to 2022.

1. AGRICULTURAL SCIENCES

Agriculture is a broad and diverse field of study that trains scientists for many rewarding and satisfying careers. These play an important part in maintaining the nation's food supply through ensuring agricultural productivity and the safety of the food supply. Agricultural scientists engage in research, development, and production of farm crops and animals, food sciences, plant sciences, and soil sciences. Others manage marketing or production operations in companies that produce food products or agricultural chemicals, supplies, and machinery. Other agricultural scientists are consultants to business firms, private clients, or governmental agencies.

Interests: Agricultural research, development, and production of farm crops and animals, and development of ways to improve their quantity and quality

Popular majors in this field of study: Agribusiness, Agricultural Education, Agronomy, Animal Science, Entomology, Farm and Ranch Management, Fisheries and Wildlife, Food Sciences, Forestry, Horticultural Science, and Soil Sciences

Employment information/outlook: More than 2,024,179 people worked in related occupations in this field of study in 2012. The 2012-2022 employment growth is expected to be 9%.

In May 2012, median annual wages of food scientists and technologists were $58,070; soil and plant scientists, $58,740; and animal scientists, $61,680. Incomes of farmers and ranchers vary greatly from year to year, because prices of farm products fluctuate with weather conditions and other factors that influence the quantity and quality of farm output and the demand for those products. In addition to farm business income, farmers often receive government subsidies or other payments that supplement their incomes and reduce some of the risk of farming. Many farmers—primarily operators of small farms—have recently been relying more and more on off-farm sources of income. Full-time, salaried agricultural managers had median weekly earnings of $1,332.80 in 2012. Farm income can vary substantially depending on a number of factors, including the type of crop or livestock being raised, price fluctuations for various agricultural products, and weather conditions that affect yield. In some cases, government subsidies may supplement a farmer's income. For a growing number of farmers and ranchers, particularly those working on farms for residential and lifestyle reasons, crop or livestock production is not their major occupation or source of income.

Agribusiness

Agribusiness majors will learn the business aspect of farms, firms, and industries that supply and service the farmer and other farm-related businesses. They will study merchandising, advertising, finance, marketing, and international trade.

Interests: Taking initiative, leadership, decision making, problem solving, analyzing data, global interdependence, working with people

Skills and abilities: Planning, organizing, making business decisions, leadership, teamwork, creative and critical thinking, working with people, written and verbal skills, adapting to change

Occupations related to this major: Agricultural Crop Farm Managers, Farm Products Purchasing Agents and Buyers, Farm and Ranch Managers, Fish Hatchery Managers, Farmers and Ranchers, Agricultural Statisticians, and Farm and Home Management advisers.

Agricultural Education

Agricultural Education majors will study those basic courses in agriculture that will prepare them to teach agricultural science in high schools, community colleges, or universities. They will also complete general preparation for a service-type career in agriculture, such as extension services. They will learn to supervise youth and adult groups and to direct programs in both agricultural and human resources.

Interests: Working with people, working with plants, working with animals

Skills and abilities: Communication, science (especially natural sciences and chemistry)

Occupations related to this major: Farm and Home Management Advisers, Park Naturalists, Farmers and Ranchers, Agricultural Science Teachers, and 4-H and Agricultural Extension Agents

Agronomy

Agronomy majors will learn about three basic natural elements—crops, soils, and climates—and their interdependence in producing food, feed, fiber, and fuel. Agronomists study theory and practices for improving crop production while conserving natural resources and maintaining environmental quality.

Interests: Nature and the outdoors, environmental quality (soil, water, and air), conservation of natural resources, biological and physical sciences, problem solving, plant growth and experimentation, weather, climate, geologic formations

Skills and qualities: Oral and written communication skills, group dynamics, leadership, organizational (interpersonal) skills, analytic reasoning, creative thinking

Occupations related to this major: Agricultural Climatologists, Agrochemical Technologists, Environmental Technicians, Food and Drug Inspectors, Farm or Ranch Managers, Plant Breeders, Agricultural Technicians, Soil and Water Conservationists, and Greenhouse Managers

Animal Science

Animal Science majors will learn how to manage livestock and poultry. They will study the role of animals in the economy, how animal products influence eating habits and are part of the global food supply, and how animals help serve people's recreation needs. They will carry out investigations and experiments in the areas of breeding, feeding, management, and disease control in farm and domestic animals.

Interests: Working with plants, working with animals, working with people

Skills and abilities: Speaking and writing effectively

Occupations related to this major: Animal Scientists, Soil and Plant Scientists, Park Naturalists, Biologists, Farm and Ranch Managers, and Soil Conservationists

Entomology

Entomology majors will study the biology, ecology, classification, distribution, physiology, economic importance, and management of insects and their relation to plant and animal life. They will learn to identify species of insects and allied forms, such as mites and spiders. They will study methods of controlling and eliminating agri-cultural, structural, and forest pests by developing new and improved pesticides and cultural and biological methods, including using natural enemies of pests. They will also study insect distribution and habitat, and methods to prevent importation and spread of injurious species.

Interests: Science, techniques of scientific research, the environment, the health and well-being of people

Skills and abilities: Curiosity, rational thinking, objective thinking, performing laboratory tasks carefully

Occupations related to this major: Entomologists, Environmental Scientists, Soil and Plant Scientists, Biologists, Clinical Laboratory Technologists, and Pest Control Workers

Farm and Ranch Management

Farm and Ranch Management majors will learn to guide and assist farmers and ranchers in maximizing the financial returns to their land by managing the day-to-day activities. Duties and responsibilities may vary widely. For example, the owner of a very large livestock farm may employ a farm manager to oversee a single activity, such as feeding livestock. When managing a small crop farm, on the other hand, a farm manager may assume responsibility for all functions, from selecting the crop to participating in planting and harvesting.

Interests: Directing and coordinating worker activities, decision making, problem solving, nature and the outdoors, conservation of natural resources, biological and physical science

Skills and abilities: Speaking, motivating people, creative and critical thinking, oral and written expression and comprehension, organizational skills, leadership

Occupations related to this major: Agricultural Crop Farm Managers, Farm and Ranch Managers, Foresters, Dairy Farm Managers, Poultry Farm Managers, and Farm and Home Management Advisers

Fisheries and Wildlife

Fisheries and Wildlife majors will learn about fish eggs, larvae, fish parasites, and diseases. They will learn to operate fish culture facilities, tag and mark fish, detect problems of water pollution, analyze, identify, collect, control, and preserve populations of fur and game animals.

Interests: Nature and the outdoors, science, research

Skills and abilities: Solving problems, communicating effectively, working with others

Occupations related to this major: Fish Culturists, Fish Hatchery Managers, Environmental Scientists, Zoo Workers, Fisheries and Wildlife Biologists, and Park Naturalists

Food Sciences

Food Science majors will learn to use biological, physical, and social sciences to transform raw materials into safe, nutritious, and economical foods. They will learn to apply scientific and engineering principles in research, development, and food production technology. They will also work to improve methods of processing, preserving, packaging, distributing, and preparing food.

Interests: Biological and physical science, public well-being, teamwork, observing details, solving complex problems

Skills and abilities: Good laboratory technique, oral and written expression and comprehension, mathematical reasoning

Occupations related to this major: Food Scientists, Food Science Technicians, Food Chemists, Food Plant Managers, Food Microbiologists, and Biological and Agricultural Technologists

Forestry

Forestry majors will learn to manage, protect, and develop forest lands and other resources for economic and recreational purposes; plan and supervise the cutting and harvesting of timber; carry out forestation and reforestation activities and manage parks and camps.

Interests: Nature and the outdoors, working with people, planning activities, investigative research, solving problems

Skills and abilities: Communicating effectively, working with quantitative and qualitative problems, presenting ideas to others

Occupations related to this major: Foresters, Soil Conservationists, Environmental Scientists, Biologists, Range Managers, Nursery and Greenhouse Managers, Agricultural Engineers, and Forest and Conservation Technicians

Horticultural Science

Horticultural Science majors will study problems of plant production, processing, and disease resistance. They will also study soil and climate to learn the conditions in which different types of plants thrive. They will be concerned with orchards, garden plants, flowers, ornamental plants, and nursery stock.

Interests: Science, working with plants, business, working with people, solving problems, improving the environment

Skills and abilities: Biological and physical sciences, written and oral communication, organization, creativity, quantitative thinking, computer competency, working with people

Occupations related to this major: Horticulturists, Foresters, Conservation Scientists, Landscape Architects, Plant Scientists, Farmers, and Farm Managers

Soil Sciences

Soil Science majors will study the physical, chemical, and geological characteristics and behaviors of soils. They will learn how to investigate soil both in the field and in the lab, and to classify soils in terms of their capability in producing crops, grasses, and trees. They also will learn how to make land appraisals.

Interests: Nature and the outdoors, conservation of natural resources, the environment, science

Skills and abilities: Quantitative reasoning, keen observation of natural phenomena, oral and written communication, applying scientific knowledge to complex systems

Occupations related to this major: Plant Scientists, Conservation Scientists, Botanists, Biochemists, Park Naturalists, and Farm and Range Managers

2. ARCHITECTURE AND DESIGN

Architects learn to plan, design, and supervise the construction of buildings, houses, factories, skyscrapers, schools, and other structures. They learn to make them attractive, usable, energy efficient, and economical. Architects must qualify for a state license after graduation. Most architects work for architectural firms. Others work directly for builders, real estate developers, or large construction projects, as well as governmental agencies responsible for housing and community planning, such as the Department of Defense, Interior, and Housing and Urban Development. Students interested in the field of architecture will do well in such courses as architectural theory design, computer graphics, computer science, general engineering urban planning, mathematics, physics, and economics.

Interests: Architects have an interest in planning, designing, and supervising the construction of buildings, houses, factories, skyscrapers, schools, and other structures.

Popular majors in this field of study: Architectural Engineering, Architecture, City and Regional Planning, Construction Science, Interior Design, Landscape Architecture, Marine Architecture, and Surveying

Employment information/outlook: More than 2,474,500 people worked in related occupations in this field of study in 2012. The 2012-2022 employment growth is expected to be 7.3%.

Median annual wages of wage-and-salary architects were $73,900 in May 2012. Those just starting their internships can expect to earn considerably less. Earnings of partners in established architectural firms may fluctuate because of changing business conditions. Some architects may have difficulty establishing their own practices and may go through a period when their expenses are greater than their incomes, requiring substantial financial resources. Many firms pay tuition and fees toward continuing education requirements for their employees. Median annual wages of urban and regional planners were $65,230 in May 2012. Earnings also vary by the worker's education and experience, type of work, complexity of the construction project, and geographic location. Wages of construction workers often are affected when poor weather prevents them from working. Traditionally, winter is the slack period for construction activity, especially in colder parts of the country, but there is a trend toward more year-round construction, even in colder areas. Construction trades are dependent on one another to complete specific parts of a project—especially on large projects—so work delays affecting one trade can delay or stop the work of another trade.

Architectural Engineering

Architectural Engineering majors will learn how different materials interact. They also will learn to calculate loads and stress and study the strength, durability, and safety-factor of materials. They will use artistic, applied physics, and material science skills in the design of buildings.

Interests: Mathematics, physical science, building things, applying mathematics and science to practical use, design, computers

Skills and abilities: Oral and written expression and comprehension, speech clarity, logical thinking, interpersonal skills, teamwork

Occupations related to this major: Architects, Civil Engineers, Marine Architects, Materials Engineers, and Architectural Drafters

Architecture

Architecture majors learn to plan, design, and supervise the construction of buildings, houses, factories, skyscrapers, schools, and other structures. They learn to make them attractive, usable, energy efficient, and economical. They must qualify for a license after graduation. They work in design studios that develop skills and foster creative expression. Architecture students also study the history of the building environment (rooms, buildings, landscapes, cities), the technology required to create it, and related graphic communication.

Interests: The formation of the physical environment; the history of buildings, cities, and landscapes; applied creative expression

Skills and abilities: Communicating by sketching and drafting; solving spatial problems; sensitivity to visual forms, proportions, and colors

Occupations related to this major: Architects, Naval Architects, Landscape Architects, Civil Engineers, Industrial Designers, Interior Designers, and Drafters

City and Regional Planning

City and Regional Planning majors learn to deal with land use and environmental issues created by population movements. They learn how to draw plans for new city environments including streets, sewers, water, and electricity. They also learn to zone areas for residential, commercial, or industrial use. Students commit themselves, through planning, to the future, and to social and environmental improvement.

Interests: Solving problems, working with people, helping groups, communities, and organizations improve people's lives

Skills and abilities: Working with numbers, listening, interpreting and communicating what was observed or heard

Occupations related to this major: Urban and Regional Planners, Architects, Landscape Architects, City Managers, Civil Engineers, and Environmental Engineers

Construction Science

Construction Science majors learn about all areas of construction technology. These areas include contracting, remodeling, cabinet making, building inspection, carpentry, and estimating the costs of building projects.

Interests: Starting and completing projects; leading people and making decisions; risk taking; activities that include practical, hands-on problems and solutions

Skills and abilities: Listening to and understanding information; reading and understanding information; managing one's own time and the time of others; communicating information and ideas in writing

Occupations related to this major: Architects, Property and Real Estate Managers, Real Estate Appraisers, Construction and Building Inspectors, and Industrial Engineers

Interior Design

Interior Design majors learn to arrange the interiors of buildings to fit the functional and aesthetic needs of their owners. They will design everything from lighting and furniture to home decorating accessories. Interior design majors study all aspects of the building environment: scale, proportion, arrangement, light, acoustics, temperature, textures, colors, and materials. They learn how to develop surroundings that are satisfying, creative, and appropriate to human needs.

Interests: Architecture, design (interior, industrial, graphic), building construction, interaction of colors, nature of materials, and textures

Skills and abilities: Design, organization, working with people, drawing, communicating ideas

Occupations related to this major: Interior Designers, Fashion, Furniture, Textile, and Floral Designers, Exhibition Designers, Architects, and Landscape Architects

Landscape Architecture

Landscape Architecture majors learn skills and techniques for planning, designing, and managing the land. They learn about weather, drainage, botany, and construction. They are frequently involved in mapping and consultation. They creatively apply information and principles drawn from both the arts and the sciences to reshape and conserve landscapes.

Interests: Visual arts, ecology, nature, environmental issues

Skills and abilities: Drawing and graphic expression, problem solving, written communication

Occupations related to this major: Landscape Architects, Architects, Surveyors, Civil Engineers, Urban and Regional Planners, Botanists, and Park Naturalists

Marine Architecture

Marine Architecture majors learn to design and oversee construction and repair of marine craft and floating structures, such as ships, barges, tugs, dredges, submarines, torpedoes, floats, and buoys. May confer with marine engineers.

Interests: Design techniques, engineering science and technology, building materials, construction and repair of structures

Skills and abilities: Problem solving, listening and understanding information and ideas, creativity, communicating information and ideas in writing, fluency of ideas

Occupations related to this major: Marine Architects, Aerospace Engineers, Civil Engineers, Materials Engineers, Engineering Technicians, and Drafters

Surveying

Surveying majors learn to make exact measurements and determine property boundaries. They learn to provide data relevant to the shape, contour, gravitation, location, elevation, or dimension of land, or land features on or near the earth's surface, for engineering, mapping, mining, land evaluation, construction, and other purposes.

Interests: Shapes and elevations of geomorphic and topographic features, geography, and methods for describing the features of land, sea, and air masses

Skills and abilities: Communicating effectively in writing; using mathematics to solve problems; understanding written information; using scientific methods to solve problems; motivating, developing, and directing people as they work

Occupations related to this major: Surveyors, Cartographers, Urban Planners, Civil Drafters, Agricultural Engineers, and Landscape Architects

3. THE ARTS

The Arts is a field of study that includes a wider range of subjects than found in other areas of concentration. If students major in one of the arts, they will learn to design products, articles, and materials; they will develop talents as actors; they will study the theory and practice of film production; they will develop talents to draw, paint, or design interpretations of objects, people, and nature, or they will develop talents dealing with the art of sound that express ideas and emotions either by song, dance, or by instrumental musical instruments. This field, in contrast to a liberal arts education, is often thought of as professional training. A major in this field gives information, methods, procedures, and techniques needed in a career. A professional program in this field will offer students good training to make a contribution in the world of art.

Interests: Developing talents to draw, paint, or design interpretations of objects, people, and nature; or developing the art of sound that expresses ideas and emotions either by speech, song, dance, or musical instruments.

Popular majors in this field of study: Art Education, Art History, Arts Management, Dance, Dramatic Arts, Film Arts, Fine Arts, Graphic Design, Music Business Management, Music Education, Music Performance, Music Therapy, Photography, Religious Music, and Studio Art

Employment information/outlook: More than 2,570,900 people worked in related occupations in this field of study in 2012. The 2012-2022 employment growth is expected to be 7.0%.

In May 2012, median annual wages of salaried art directors were $80,880; advertising, public relations and related services, $115,750; salaried craft artists, $44,380; multimedia artists and animators were $61,370; motion picture and video industries, $71,350; advertising and related services, $46,290. The hourly wages of actors were $20.26; hourly wages for performing arts companies were $15.87; and motion picture and video industry occupations

came in at $34.31. The median annual wages in May 2012 for producers and directors were $71,350; radio and television broadcasting, $37,090; graphic designers, $44,150. Hourly wages of wage-and-salary musicians and singers were $23.50; performing arts companies, $18.33; and religious organizations, $14.69. The median annual wages for salaried music directors and composers were $47,350 in May 2012. Self-employed artist wages vary considerably. Most artists, including actors, musicians, and singers, were not available because of the variation in the number of hours they work, and the lack of guaranteed employment. The more successful performers may belong to one of the talent unions, such as SAG/AFTRA, American Guild of Musical Artists, or The American Federation of Musicians, which negotiates minimum contracts.

Art Education

Art Education majors learn to develop their artistic talents and gain the knowledge and skills needed to teach art at various education levels. They will explore the value of art both to the individual and to various cultures throughout history.

Interests: Visual arts, creating art, teaching

Skills and abilities: Working with others, solving problems creatively, manipulating materials creatively, responding to other people's art with sensitivity

Occupations related to this major: Art Teachers, Curriculum Specialists, Art Administrators, Manual Arts Therapists, Craft Demonstrators, Curators, Archivists, and Museum Research Workers

Art History

Art History majors study works of art—how they came about and what they mean. They will examine works of art as they appear now and also consider appearance and function in their original contexts. Through their visual analysis and extensive reading and writing, students explore the traditions of appearance and technique that guided the creation of art in different cultures.

Interests: Visual arts, past civilizations, the connections between different aspects of a civilization, artists, art technique

Skills and abilities: Observing carefully, information gathering, reading critically, written expression and comprehension

Occupations related to this major: High School Teachers, College Teachers, Curators, Archivists, Conservators, Museum Directors, and Museum Technicians

Arts Management

Arts Management majors learn to organize and manage art organizations and facilities. They receive instruction in business and financial management and labor relations, event promotion and management, public relations and arts advocacy, and arts law. They will learn to analyze and address the issues concerning the health of theaters, dance companies, museums, and other arts organizations.

Interests: Visual and performance arts, leadership, working with people

Skills and abilities: Oral and written communication, organizational ability, creative thinking, critical thinking

Occupations related to this major: Theater Managers, Symphony Orchestra Managers, Dance Company Managers, Curators, and Museum Technicians and Conservators

Dance

Dance majors learn to interpret an idea or a story through physical expression or rhythm and/or sound. Dance forms vary from ballet and modern interpretative dance to tap and chorus lines. Dance is a demanding discipline. Students learn to develop their bodies as articulate instruments for dance expression: to understand contributions that dance has made to the arts, and to create their own dances.

Interests: Dance, other arts, the physicality of movement

Skills and abilities: Sense of rhythm and musicality, physical stamina, dynamic strength, speed of limb movement, gross body coordination

Occupations related to this major: Dance Teachers, Actors and Performers, Choreographers, Dance Researchers, and Dance Therapists

Dramatic Arts

Dramatic Arts majors learn how to play a part to entertain, inform, or instruct an audience. They learn to be involved in interpreting plays or scripts, selecting plays or scripts, or planning and supervising performances. They gain breadth of knowledge about past and present culture, art, literature, politics, psychology, and philosophy.

Interests: Self-expression, communication of ideas and feelings, literature and language, art and music, human personality and motivation

Skills and abilities: Speech clarity, memorization, originality, oral and written expression and comprehension, emotional openness

Occupations related to this major: Actors, Directors, Designers, Playwrights, Stage Managers, Talent Directors, and Teachers

Film Arts

Film Arts majors study the theory and practice of film production and the techniques used in this medium of communication. They learn to do creative work, as well as learn the rapidly changing technology. They study cinema history, screenwriting, and the aesthetic and technical aspects of cinema production, including directing, cinematography, and editing. They also examine the economic, technical, social, cultural, and ideological aspects of film as a medium for communication and personal expression.

Interests: Film literature, psychology, theater, music, art history, biography, current events

Skills and abilities: Creativity, ability to express oneself verbally and visually, self-discipline, understanding of human psychology, organization, attention to detail, flexibility, working with people

Occupations related to this major: Directors—Stage, Motion Pictures, Television and Radio, Cinematographers, Technical Directors, Programming and Script Editors, Production Assistants

Fine Arts

Fine Arts majors learn to draw or design their interpretations of objects, people, and nature, using a wide variety of materials from watercolors and oils to stone and metal. They learn to create art to satisfy their own need for self-expression. They learn about the creation of art historically, in contemporary society, and through their own efforts in studio classes. They may display their work in museums, art galleries, corporate collections, and private homes.

Interests: Making things with the hands, other cultures, history, paintings, sculpture, film, self-expression

Skills and abilities: Oral and written expression and comprehension, fluency of ideas, originality, visual color discrimination, manual and finger dexterity

Occupations related to this major: Fine Artists, Graphic Artists, Sculptors, Painters, Illustrators, and Cartoonists and Animators

Graphic Design

Graphic Design majors study the principles of design to learn how to create attractive and effective advertisements, flyers, brochures, logos, magazines, or books. They learn how to create images through the use of silkscreen, computers, and printing presses. Students learn to communicate information visually using words and images. They also study how people perceive and interpret information.

Interests: Visual arts, creativity, critical thinking, working with people

Skills and abilities: Drawing, photography, originality, fluency of ideas, oral expression, visual color discrimination

Occupations related to this major: Graphic Designers, Painters, Illustrators, Cartoonists, Animators, Fashion Designers, and Interior Designers

Music Business Management

Music Business Management majors learn to organize and manage music operations, facilities, and personnel. They receive instruction in business and financial management, personnel management and labor relations, event promotion, and music products merchandising. They study the functional area of business as well as music performance, history, and theory.

Interests: Music, leadership, organizing people, business, solving problems, negotiating

Skills and abilities: Oral expression and comprehension, written expression and comprehension, leadership, organization, creative thinking

Occupations related to this major: Music Facilities Managers, Recording Studio Managers, Artists' Representatives, Orchestra Managers, Music Directors, and Concert Booking Agents

Music Education

Music Education majors learn to become music teachers in public and private schools. They learn the basics of music and the fundamentals of teaching to share music with people of all ages and abilities.

Interests: Listening to music, performing, working with young people, leadership

Skills and abilities: Musical ability, a sense of rhythm and pitch, oral and written expression and comprehension, speech clarity, discriminating listening

Occupations related to this major: Music Teachers, Music Therapists, Choir Directors, Conductors, Composers, Arrangers, and Music Librarians

Music Performance

Music Performance majors learn to develop a high level of performance skill and musical understanding. They reach a high level of technical proficiency and musical sensitivity as music performance majors. They become well-rounded musicians through the study of core music theory and history courses.

Interests: Communicating through music performance, the theoretical and historical aspects of musical structure and style, the relation of music to society

Skills and abilities: Natural aptitude for music, technical skill, strong background in piano

Occupations related to this major: Musicians, Singers, Music Directors, Music Composers, Music Teachers, and Positions with Orchestras and Ensembles

Music Therapy

Music Therapy majors learn to design music experiences and activities to the treatment of individuals and groups in all age categories who have psychological, emotional, physical, social, intellectual, or medical disorders.

Interests: Music, the arts, behavioral and life sciences, helping others

Skills and abilities: Competency in music performance and theory, oral and written expression and comprehension, working with people

Occupations related to this major: Music Therapists, Occupational Therapists, Physical Therapists, Musicians, Singers, and Music Directors

Photography

Photography majors learn the use of camera and film to portray people, places, and events. They become involved in everything from creating motion pictures and video/television to still, portrait, aerial, and commercial photography. They learn both the artistic and technical aspects of photography and a broad understanding of the social, political, and interpersonal aspects of society.

Interests: Expressing oneself in a visual medium, creating images from ideas, helping people see and understand subjects to which they might not otherwise have access

Skills and abilities: Visualization, far vision, fluency of ideas, arm-hand steadiness, control precision, color discrimination

Occupations related to this major: Commercial Photographers, Portrait Photographers, Graphic Designers, Photojournalists, Photo Editors, and Technical and Science Photographers

Religious Music

Religious Music majors develop their skills and interests as musicians and learn to use music in religious celebrations while focusing on the role and history of music in worship. They study the history, theory, composition, and performance of music for religious or sacred purposes.

Interests: Music, music history, the fine arts, the place of music in religious celebrations, matters of faith, working with people

Skills and abilities: Ability to listen carefully, hearing sensitivity, auditory attention, oral expression and comprehension, working with people

Occupations related to this major: Music Directors, Music Teachers, Music Conductors, Organists, Cantors, Musicians, and Singers

Studio Art

Studio Art majors learn to create works of art by exploring a variety of techniques and materials. They learn to focus on learning to master new media, discovering unique solutions to visual problems, exploring fresh ways to create satisfying images, and evaluating what is worth doing.

Interests: Visual arts, manipulating materials, observing visual phenomena in nature and works of art, communicating and experimenting with forms, colors, images, and symbols

Skills and abilities: Working independently, creativity, problem solving, oral and written expression and comprehension

Occupations related to this major: Fine Artists, Commercial Artists, Graphic Designers, Art Teachers, Exhibit Designers, and Set Designers

4. BIOLOGICAL AND LIFE SCIENCES

Biological and Life Sciences majors are concerned with the world of living things—people and microbes, wild and domestic animals, plants and insects, birds and fish. Some biological scientists conduct research. Still others apply biological knowledge to the solution of practical problems, such as the development of new drugs and vaccines or new strains of plants. Biological scientists, who may also be called life scientists, study the structure of living organisms, their life processes, and evolutionary development. They may be classified into groups characterized by the type of organism with which they work or the specific activity they perform. Examples of these groups are botanists who study plants, microbiologists who work with microorganisms, and zoologists who work with animals.

Interests: The world of living things—people and microbes, wild and domestic animals, plants and insects, birds and fish—or the evolutionary development of living organisms.

Popular majors in this field of study: Biochemistry, Biology, Biophysics, Biotechnology, Botany, Marine/Aquatic Biology, Microbiology, Molecular and Cell Biology, Science Education, Wildlife Management, and Zoology

Employment information/outlook: More than 103,100 people worked in related occupations in this field of study in 2012. The 2012-2022 employment growth is expected to be 13%.

In May 2012, median annual wages of biochemists and biophysicists were $81,480; microbiologists, $66,260. Median annual wages of zoologists and wildlife biologists were $57,710 in May 2012.

Biochemistry

Biochemistry majors learn how chemical substances enter into or are created in living things; how drugs, foods, hormones, serums, and other substances can influence organisms. They perform tests to identify, classify, and analyze various chemical reactions. They learn to use the physical and biological sciences to explore the nature of living organisms. They study the structure and behavior of complex molecules and how they interact to form cells, tissues, and entire organisms. They also gain a fundamental grasp of metabolism, energy flow, and the regulation of various life processes.

Interests: Nature, problem solving, investigative research

Skills and abilities: Using information from many areas of science, inductive and deductive reasoning, handling and interpreting data, written expression and comprehension

Occupations related to this major: Microbiologists, Biologists, Toxicologists, Plant Pathologists, Physiologists, Cytologists, and Food Scientists

Biology

Biology majors learn about the structure of living organisms, their life processes and evolutionary development, and the relation between these organisms and their environment. They may specialize in research centering on plants, animals, or human organisms. They study animals, plants, and microorganisms that constitute the living world at the levels of molecule, cell, organism, and population.

Interests: Quality of life, investigative laboratory work, fieldwork

Skills and abilities: Problem solving, deductive and inductive reasoning, information gathering, written expression and comprehension

Occupations related to this major: Biologists, Biochemists, Botanists, Microbiologists, Geneticists, and Zoologists

Biophysics

Biophysics majors learn to apply the laws of physics to biological systems. They study vision, hearing, nerve action, blood flow, and even the behavior of DNA. They also study the effects of radiation and radioactivity on biological systems, and the use of ultrasound scanners to construct images of body interiors. They use biology, physics, chemistry, and mathematics to explore the properties of biological molecules and groups of molecules. They study the inner workings of biological systems with precision to learn how proteins fold, how genes are switched on and off, how organisms respond to light, how cells move, and how the nervous system works.

Interests: Natural history, investigative problem solving

Skills and abilities: Curiosity, deductive and inductive reasoning, written expression and comprehension, information ordering, manual dexterity

Occupations related to this major: Biophysicists, Biologists, Botanists, Geneticists, Microbiologists, and Soil Scientists

Biotechnology

Biotechnology is an interdisciplinary field of study involving the molecular life sciences and engineering fields of study. Students learn techniques for using living matter to develop new products and services in agriculture (plant growth hormones, food additives), health care (vaccines, improved drugs and vitamins), the environment (detoxification of chemicals), and other areas.

Interests: Science, treating and preventing disease, investigative research, and problem solving

Skills and abilities: Creative thinking, oral and written expression and comprehension, deductive and inductive reasoning, problem sensitivity

Occupations related to this major: Biological Technologists, Agricultural Technologists, Environmental Scientists, Food Scientists, Animal Scientists, Botanists, and Microbiologists

Botany

Botany majors focus on all aspects of plant life including taxonomy, genetics, physiology, and plant anatomy. They learn about the economic value of plants in their application to agronomy, forestry, horticulture, and pharmacology. Students study all aspects of plant biology to become familiar with the cellular and molecular functioning of life.

Interests: Nature, investigative problem solving, analytic reasoning

Skills and abilities: Deductive and inductive reasoning, information ordering, written expression and comprehension

Occupations related to this major: Botanists, Agricultural Scientists, Soil Scientists, Ecologists, Microbiologists, Physiologists

Marine/Aquatic Biology

Marine/Aquatic Biology majors learn to research and study marine organisms and their environments. They receive instruction in freshwater and saltwater organisms, physiological and anatomical marine adaptations, ocean and freshwater ecologies, marine microbiology, marine mammalogy, ichthyology, marine botany, and biochemical products of marine life used by humans. They learn about the diversity of life in the ocean, how ocean species relate to each other as food and prey, and how different species depend on and use the physical and chemical structures of the ocean.

Interests: Life in the ocean, how organisms use the sea as a habitat

Skills and abilities: Quantitative thinking, deductive and inductive reasoning, information ordering, written expression and comprehension

Occupations related to this major: Marine Biologists, Aquatic Biologists, Biochemists, Botanists, Agricultural Scientists, and Zoologists

Microbiology

Microbiology majors concentrate on microorganisms, bacteria, yeasts, fungi, protozoa, and one-celled algae. They learn about the application of these organisms in the production of food products, antibiotics, and industrial chemicals. They learn to use the basic knowledge acquired from other biological sciences, chemistry/biochemistry, and physics to study microscopic organisms such as bacteria, yeasts, molds, viruses, rickettsia, and protozoa.

Interests: Biological sciences, health and medicine, ecology, food production, investigative research

Skills and abilities: Working with detail, analytic thinking, deductive and inductive reasoning, information ordering

Occupations related to this major: Microbiologists, Botanists, Medical Scientists, Zoologists, Physiologists, and Geneticists

Molecular and Cell Biology

Molecular and Cell Biology majors study the nature of biological phenomena at the molecular level through the study of DNA proteins and other macromolecules relating to genetic information and cell function. They study what cells are, how they are put together, what makes them work, what makes them differ from each other, how they associate and interact, what goes wrong in disease states, and how they can intervene beneficially in these processes. They study how molecular biology underlies many aspects of genetic engineering, protein engineering, and other new approaches to improving upon nature.

Interests: Organisms and their development, how things work, the molecular basis of plant, animal, and human disease, disease prevention

Skills and abilities: Investigative research, laboratory skills, information gathering, deductive and inductive reasoning, oral and written expression and comprehension

Occupations related to this major: Molecular Biologists, Medical Doctors, Toxicologists, Botanists, Plant Pathologists, and Biologists

Science Education

Science Education majors prepare to teach science in grades 7 through 12. Students typically major in one science and take additional course work in two other sciences. They learn techniques for teaching science.

Interests: Working with young people, helping others, the learning process, solving practical problems, understanding complex processes, learning how things work

Skills and abilities: Oral and written expression and comprehension, speech clarity, fluency of ideas, deductive reasoning, working with numbers

Occupations related to this major: Biological Technicians, Health Specialties Teachers, Elementary School Teachers, Dietitians, Nutritionists, Pharmacists, Psychiatrists, Veterinarians, and Medical and Clinical Laboratory Technologists

Wildlife Management

Wildlife Management majors receive a solid background in basic biology. They study natural resources and wildlife management. They study conservation of animal populations and their habitats, paying special attention to species that are hunted regularly and species that are threatened or endangered. They learn to analyze characteristics of animals to identify and classify them; to conduct experimental studies with live animals in controlled or natural surroundings; to study animals in their natural habitats; and to study characteristics of animals such as origin, interrelationships, classification, life histories and diseases, development, genetics, and distribution.

Interests: Nature, conservation of natural resources, hunting, bird-watching

Skills and abilities: Using scientific rules and methods to solve problems, mathematics, deductive and inductive reasoning, problem sensitivity

Occupations related to this major: Wildlife Biologists, Environmental Scientists, Park Naturalists, and Research Wildlife Biologists

Zoology

Zoology majors study the identification, description, and classification of animals. They study life histories, habits, diseases, life processes, and distribution of animal species within the environment. They study living organisms in the animal kingdom, exploring their form and function, chemistry and structure, growth, reproduction, maintenance, and interactions with each other and their world. They study the transmission of characteristics from one generation to the next (genetics and evolution).

Interests: Natural history, wildlife, the outdoors, bird-watching, how things work, living things, fossils, working with animals

Skills and abilities: Deductive and inductive reasoning, synthesizing information, gathering and analyzing information, working with numbers

Occupations related to this major: Zoologists, Ecologists, Agricultural Scientists, Physiologists, Cytologists, Microbiologists, and Botanists

5. BUSINESS AND MANAGEMENT

Business and Management majors are found in every industry. Business executives, administrators, managers, and support staff are found in every organization. They direct and coordinate operations and activities of an organization. Business majors must be comfortable with numbers and the manipulation of data, enjoy working with a computer, and have good communication skills, both written and oral. Business majors deal with large amounts of information to make production, personnel, financial, and marketing decisions.

Interests: Business managers and support workers have an interest in directing and coordinating operations and activities of a business or organization; an interest in making production, personnel, financial, and market decisions of a business.

Popular majors in this field of study: Accounting, Business Administration, Business Education, Finance, Human Resource Management, Insurance and Risk Management, International Business Management, Labor Relations Management, Management, Management Information Systems, Management Science, Marketing, and Real Estate

Employment information/outlook: More than 10,228,200 people worked in related occupations in this field of study in 2012. The 2012-2022 employment growth is expected to be 13.8%.

In May 2012, median annual wages of wage and salary accountants and auditors were $63,550. Median annual wages, excluding annual bonuses and stock options, of wage and salary financial managers were $109,740. Annual salary rates for human resources workers vary according to occupation, level of experience, training, location, and firm size. Median annual wages in May 2012 were $80,220 for advertising and promotions managers, $134,250 for marketing managers, $129,870 for sales managers, and $108,260 for public relations managers. Median annual wages of salaried property, real estate, and community association managers were $52,610 in May 2012.

Accounting

Accounting majors learn to keep track of expenditures, income, profit and loss, prepare financial reports, and calculate taxes. They may specialize in auditing, taxes, or consulting. Many accountants seek Certified Public Accountant (CPA) certification after graduation. Students will learn to apply this knowledge in all areas of business, government, and nonprofit enterprises.

Interests: Working with numbers, competition, economics, computers, mathematics, entrepreneurship, social and political activism, moral and ethical responsibility

Skills and abilities: Mathematical reasoning, written and oral expression and comprehension, working with people, leadership

Occupations related to this major: Accountants, Auditors, Loan Officers, Loan Counselors, Credit Analysts, Tax Preparers, Budget Analysts, and Marketing Managers

Business Administration

Business Administration majors learn about a variety of managerial opportunities in finance, accounting, marketing, information management, operations and production, general management, retailing, and consulting. They learn the fundamental principles, concepts, and applications of accounting, finance, and management.

Interests: Leadership, organizing people, taking initiative, starting and running a business, working with numbers, solving problems, competing, taking risks, working with people

Skills and abilities: Oral and written expression and comprehension, speech clarity, inductive reasoning, creative and critical thinking

Occupations related to this major: Private Sector Executives, Administrative Services Managers, Human Resources Specialists, Production Managers, Labor Relations Specialists, and Financial Analysts

Business Education

Business Education majors learn to teach vocational business programs at various education levels. They develop instructional methods and training techniques including curriculum design principles, learning theory, group and individual teaching techniques, design of individual development plans, and test design principles.

Interests: Teaching young people, helping people develop their academic interests in business, and helping people develop career plans

Skills and abilities: Working with young people, speech clarity, oral and written expression and comprehension, teaching, learning, understanding human behavior

Occupations related to this major: Business Education Teacher, Education Administrators, Training and Development Managers, and Educational Program Directors

Finance

Finance majors study financial and accounting information, economic models, and analytic techniques that can be applied to financing problems. They learn to determine prices of assets such as stocks, bonds, and businesses, and to manage assets to maximize their economic value.

Interests: Business, the stock market, the economy, budgets

Skills and abilities: Logical thinking, organizational skills, oral and written expression and comprehension, problem sensitivity, mathematical reasoning, working with people, solving problems with computers

Occupations related to this major: Financial Managers, Financial Planners, Treasurers, Controllers, Chief Financial Officers, and Loan Officers and Counselors

Human Resource Management

Human Resource Management majors learn to deal with many personnel activities, including hiring competent workers and dismissing workers when necessary, keeping records, classifying jobs, evaluating and properly placing workers, analyzing and assisting in morale and discipline problems, and promoting and rewarding employees. They learn to deal with issues that affect men and women at work.

Interests: Solving problems, working with numbers, working with people of different ages and backgrounds, leadership

Skills and abilities: Logical and critical thinking, speech clarity, oral and written expression and comprehension, analyzing numerical data, teamwork

Occupations related to this major: Human Resource Specialists, Training and Development Managers, Labor Relations Managers, Employee Assistance Specialists, Employee Benefits Managers, and Career Planning and Placement Counselors

Insurance and Risk Management

Insurance and Risk Management majors learn to analyze and solve problems involving loss of personal and corporate assets. They study programs, integrate knowledge from finance, quantitative analysis, and management, and include study of the legal, social, and institutional environment in which losses may occur.

Interests: Working with numbers, solving problems, competing, leadership, taking initiative

Skills and abilities: Oral and written expression and comprehension, fluency of ideas, problem sensitivity, deductive and inductive reasoning, creative and critical thinking

Occupations related to this major: Insurance Adjusters, Insurance Appraisers, Risk Managers, Insurance Brokers, Insurance Sales Representatives, and Insurance Underwriters

International Business Management

International Business Management majors learn to determine and formulate policies, and provide the overall direction of international companies or private and public sector organizations with international business activities. They learn to conduct management guidelines set up by a board of directors or similar governing body. They learn basic business management techniques and practices and how business is conducted in other countries and between different countries.

Interests: Business operations, other cultures, different people and environments

Skills and abilities: Learning languages, organizing and managing people, oral and written expression and comprehension, deductive and inductive reasoning, fluency of ideas

Occupations related to this major: International Business Managers, International Purchasing Agents and Buyers, International Marketing Managers, International Advertising and Promotions Managers, Compliance Officers and Inspectors, and Investment Bankers

Labor Relations Management

Labor Relations Management majors learn to deal with various aspects of employer-employee relations. They learn to deal with wage and salary negotiations, benefits and welfare, affirmative action, grievances, abuses and demands, labor laws, union organization, and collective bargaining. Particular attention is given to government policies, labor unions, and human resources management.

Interests: The employment relationship, human behavior, problem solving

Skills and abilities: Working with people, oral and written expression and comprehension, problem sensitivity, inductive reasoning

Occupations related to this major: Labor Relations Managers, Human Resource Managers, Training and Development Managers, Employee Assistance Specialists, Employee Benefits Managers, and Union Organizers

Management

Management majors study courses designed for the generalist who wants a broad business background. They take courses in business areas, such as accounting, marketing, finance, and business law, and courses that prepare them to function as managers in any organization.

Interests: Working with people, listening, persuading, leading, starting new systems

Skills and abilities: Thinking analytically, problem sensitivity, oral and written expression and comprehension, speech clarity

Occupations related to this major: General and Operations Managers, Marketing Managers, Public Relations Managers, Corporate Communications Specialists, Human Resource Specialists, and Human Resources Recruiters

Management Information Systems

Management Information Systems majors unite studies in computer science and business knowledge. They learn to act as intermediaries between persons with information needs and the computer programmers who provide the solutions to the problems.

Interests: Computer languages, computer programming, problem solving, logic, taking initiative, organizing groups

Skills and abilities: Oral and written expression and comprehension, deductive and inductive reasoning, information ordering, fluency of ideas, creativity

Occupations related to this major: Management Information Systems Managers, Systems Analysts, Computer Support Specialists, Database Administrators, and Computer Programmers

Management Science

Management Science majors learn to plan, organize, direct, and control the functions and processes of a business firm or organization. They learn about management theory, human resources, management and behavior, accounting and other quantitative methods, purchasing and logistics organization and production, marketing and business decision making. They learn to use mathematics, computers, and statistical and economic analysis to solve managerial and business problems.

Interests: Mathematics, solving business and management problems, computer languages, computer programming

Skills and abilities: Quantitative thinking, computer programming, creativity, oral and written expression and comprehension, speech clarity

Occupations related to this major: Employee Training Specialists, Administrative Service Managers, Purchasing Managers, Association Managers, and Property Managers

Marketing

Marketing majors learn to increase sales of products or services by analyzing and compiling data, and researching and influencing the purchasing power of the public through inventory procedures. They study trend forecasting, product development, management, wholesale selling, and operations. They learn how to display and to buy and sell items through showrooms, department stores, and specialty shops. They learn to make decisions about product design and quality, pricing, advertising, selling, and distribution.

Interests: Running a business, economic issues, social issues, working on new products, problem solving, analyzing data, understanding how people buy, use, and sell products and services

Skills and abilities: Oral and written expression and comprehension, speech clarity, originality, fluency of ideas, mathematical reasoning, persuasion

Occupations related to this major: Marketing Managers, Sales Managers, Public Relations Representatives, Advertising and Promotions Managers, Market Research Analysts, and Advertising Account Executives

Real Estate

Real Estate majors learn to show real estate properties to clients, evaluate and list properties for sale, and advise and arrange financing. They study property management and insurance. They act as independent agents, brokers, or appraisers. They gain an understanding of and proficiency in the business and social principles that affect how real property—buildings and land—is developed, operated, and traded.

Interests: Business, people and social conditions, the economy, public affairs

Skills and abilities: Oral and written expression and comprehension, mathematical reasoning, working independently, critical and analytic thinking

Occupations related to this major: Property Managers, Real Estate Sales Agents, Real Estate Financial Analysts, Real Estate Brokers, Loan Processors, and Real Estate Appraisers

6. COMMUNICATIONS

Communications is the giving or exchanging of information. It is a way to share facts, experiences, or emotions with others. A message can be conveyed through a wide variety of means. These can include writing, speaking, drawing, or using face, hand, and body movements. People receive messages through each of the five senses: taste, touch, sight, smell, and hearing. Communications studies involve the understanding of the role of mass communication in society; broadcast satellites, cable television transmitters, computer networks, and other mass media technology provide a global communication system. The field of communications includes training for those occupations necessary for the system to work efficiently.

Interests: The ways and means of exchanging information; an interest in broadcast satellites, television transmitters, computer networks, and other mass media technology.

Popular majors in this field of study: Advertising, Communications, Creative Writing, Journalism, Public Relations, Radio/Television Broadcasting, and Speech

Employment information/outlook: More than 1,531,000 people worked in related occupations in this field of study in 2012. The 2012-2022 employment growth is expected to be 10.8%.

In 2012, nonsupervisory workers in advertising and public relations services earned an average of $747 a week—significantly higher than the $608 a week for all nonsupervisory workers in private industry.

Median annual wages for salaried writers and authors were $51,510 in May 2012. Median annual wages were $76,790 for those working in advertising, public relations, and related services and $51,510 for those working for newspaper, periodical, book and directory publishers. In May 2012, median annual wages for salaried editors were $53,880; those working for newspaper, periodical, book, and directory publishers were $52,000. Freelance writers earn income from their articles, books, and less commonly, television and movie scripts. While most work on an individual project basis for multiple publishers, many support themselves with income derived from other sources. Unless gotten from another job, freelancers generally have to provide for their own health insurance and pension. Weekly earnings of nonsupervisory workers in broadcasting averaged $852 in 2012, higher than the average of $608 for all private industry. Earnings of broadcast personnel typically are highest in large metropolitan areas.

Advertising

Advertising majors learn to plan and prepare advertisements for newspapers, magazines, radio, television, billboards, and brochures. They may specialize in writing copy, layout, or research. They use creative talents to market a product to prospective clients. They learn how advertising campaigns are produced, how advertising is coordinated with marketing, and how advertising strategies develop from research. They learn to write advertising copy for broadcasting and print, and to select media for advertising campaigns.

Interests: Writing, art and design, analysis, knowing something about lots of things, investigative research

Skills and abilities: Oral and written expression and comprehension, originality, fluency of ideas, analytic reasoning, public speaking, art and design

Occupations related to this major: Advertising and Promotions Managers, Advertising Agency Account Executives, Marketing Managers, Sales Managers, Fund-raising Directors, and Advertising Research Specialists

Communications

Communications majors study the role of mass communication in society. They study the nature, function, content, values, and effects of communication on public policy and opinion. They study the nature of language and how it is communicated. They study the history of political and religious oratory; explore the sociology of interpersonal relations, group dynamics, and messages; examine ways of thinking about human symbol systems (semiotics); and examine the ethics of communication.

Interests: Politics, presentations, advertising, television, film, analyzing oral and electronic messages

Skills and abilities: Oral and written expression and comprehension, critical listening, logical analysis, leadership

Occupations related to this major: Communications Managers, Public Relations Specialists, Television Producers and Directors, Press Secretaries, Reporters, and Speech Writers

Creative Writing

Creative Writing majors study the processes and techniques of original composition in various literary forms, such as short stories, novels, biographies, articles, plays, and scripts. They receive instruction in technical and editorial skills, criticism, and the marketing of finished manuscripts.

Interests: Reading, fiction and nonfiction prose, writing, factual information, English language, critical thinking, computers

Skills and abilities: Written and oral expression and comprehension, information ordering, deductive and inductive reasoning, fluency of ideas

Occupations related to this major: Radio and Television Announcers, Broadcast News Analysts, Reporters and Correspondents, Editors, Technical Writers, and Poets and Lyricists

Journalism

Journalism majors learn to write, edit, manage, and produce newspapers and magazines. They learn to interview people, review records, observe events, and conduct journalistic research. They study the liberal arts and sciences to acquire the depth and breadth of knowledge they need to understand the world better and communicate information about it to others. They learn special skills needed by reporters, editors, broadcasters, and photojournalists.

Interests: Human psychology and behavior, reading widely, photography, world events

Skills and abilities: Writing, oral and written expression and comprehension, speech clarity, learning quickly about a wide range of topics

Occupations related to this major: Reporters and Correspondents, Magazine Writers and Editors, Columnists, Critics, Commentators, Creative Writers, Radio and Television Reporters, and Photojournalists

Public Relations

Public Relations majors learn how to manage an organization's or an individual's communication and relationship with others. They develop skills to build trust between an organization and the public. They learn how to write news articles and press releases, give speeches, and create audiovisual presentations designed to build trust. They learn technical and managerial skills, such as writing and producing printed and visual materials, and study strategic planning and problem solving.

Interests: Solving problems, mediating between opposing groups, writing, public speaking, giving advice

Skills and abilities: Communicating clearly, oral and written expression and comprehension, speech clarity, fluency of ideas, creative and critical thinking

Occupations related to this major: Public Relations Specialists, Publicity Writers, Advertising and Promotions Managers, Corporate Video Producers, Staff Writers and Editors, Special Events Planners, and Reporters and Correspondents

Radio/Television Broadcasting

Radio/Television Broadcasting majors learn about the planning, preparation, and production of radio and television programs. They may specialize in announcing, programming, engineering, or sales. They study the relationship between the mass media and society and develop skills in such specialties as reporting, performance, production, sales, and management

Interests: Writing, speaking, editing words, pictures, or sound; operating a camera; sound recording

Skills and abilities: Interviewing people, oral and written expression and comprehension, speech clarity, persuasion, operating technical equipment

Occupations related to this major: Broadcast News Analysts, Reporters and Correspondents, Radio/Television Announcers, Radio/Television Producers, Station Managers, Radio/Television Writers

Speech

Speech majors learn about the human communication process. They learn the principles and practical application of speech communication, and the skills and techniques essential for effective interpersonal communication. They learn to develop listening skills.

Interests: Public speaking, human behavior

Skills and abilities: Working with people, oral and written expression and comprehension, speech clarity

Occupations related to this major: Speech Teachers, Speech Writers, Public Relations Specialists, Journalists, Writers, Editors, and Radio and Television Reporters

7. COMPUTER AND INFORMATION SCIENCES

Computer and Information Sciences field of study prepares students for a wide variety of occupations in most sectors of the economy. This field of study prepares a wide range of professionals who design computers and the software that runs them. Information technology occupations are comprised of computer-related occupations engaged in either managing, storing, transmitting, or generating the information organizations use to make decisions, as well as installing and repairing computer hardware and software used to perform such tasks. Computer science is distinguished by a high level of theoretical expertise and innovation applied to complex problems, as well as the creation or application of new technology. Computer scientists and technicians can be theorists, researchers, or inventors. They may work at an academic institution on theory, hardware, or language design. Others work in industry to apply theory, develop specialized languages, or design programming tools and knowledge-based systems.

Interests: Designing computers and the software that runs them; managing, storing, transmitting, or generating and repairing computer hardware and software used to perform such tasks

Popular majors in this field of study: Computer Software Engineering, Computer Science, Information Sciences and Systems, Computer Programming, Mathematics, Mathematics Education, and Statistics

Employment information/outlook: More than 1,549,700 people worked in related occupations in this field of study in 2012. The 2012-2022 employment growth is expected to be 16.8%.

In May 2012, median annual wages of wage-and-salary computer applications software engineers were $85,430; computer systems software engineers, $92,430; mathematicians, $95,150; and statisticians, $72,610.

Computer Software Engineering

Computer Software Engineering majors study applied mathematical and scientific principles to the design, development, and operational evaluation of computer hardware and software systems and related equipment and facilities. They learn to develop, create, and test applications software and/or operating systems level software. They learn to analyze specific problems in computer applications.

Interests: Computers and electronics, computer programming, problem solving, engineering technology, design

Skills and abilities: Using mathematics to solve problems, computer programming, critical thinking, oral and written expression and comprehension, speech clarity, problem sensitivity

Occupations related to this major: Computer Support Specialists, Mathematical Technicians, Computer Science Teachers, and Numerical Tool and Process Control Programmers

Computer Science

Computer Science majors learn to design new computers, computer languages, and related devices, and research new ways to use computers effectively. They become involved in aspects of artificial intelligence, from pattern recognition to problem solving. They learn how computers work and how to program computers to perform tasks and provide services. They study the physical hardware components of computer systems and software procedures for making computers work.

Interests: Mathematics, electronics, investigative research

Skills and abilities: Oral and written expression and comprehension, mathematical reasoning, problem solving, abstract reasoning, working with people

Occupations related to this major: Computer Scientists, Computer Engineers, Computer Science Teachers, Computer Programmers, Software and Hardware Developers

Information Sciences and Systems

Information Sciences and Systems majors receive broad exposure to computer and programming concepts. They learn to bring people and computers together to solve problems in businesses and other organizations. They learn to plan, direct, and coordinate activities in such fields as electronic data processing, information systems, systems analysis, and computer programming.

Interests: Solving problems, working with details, taking initiative, working with numbers, organizing information, working with people

Skills and abilities: Oral and written expression and comprehension, mathematical reasoning, deductive reasoning, critical and logical thinking, working with changing technology

Occupations related to this major: Computer Programmers, Information Systems Designers, Information Systems Analysts, Computer Security Specialists, Database Administrators

Computer Programming

Computer Programming majors learn to write step-by-step instructions in several computer languages and create video games and software packages. They learn how to write software to handle specific jobs. They learn to convert project specifications and statements of problems and procedures to detailed logical flowcharts for coding into computer language. They learn to develop and write computer programs to store, locate, and retrieve specific documents, data, and information. They learn how to maintain software that controls the operations of entire computer systems.

Interests: Mathematics, electronics, using computers, investigative research, problem solving

Skills and abilities: Programming, critical thinking, active listening, oral and written expression and comprehension, mathematical reasoning, fluency of ideas, problem sensitivity

Occupations related to this major: Computer Programmers, Computer and Information Systems Managers, Computer Support Specialists, Computer Systems Analysts, Numerical Tool and Process Control Programmers, and Computer Science Teachers

Mathematics

Mathematics majors learn to solve both theoretical and practical problems that can be explained in mathematical terms. They study all aspects of algebra, geometry, advanced mathematics, and computer languages. They develop the abilities to explore, conjecture, and reason logically as well as the ability to use various mathematical methods effectively to solve problems.

Interests: Problem solving, working with numbers, games requiring analytic reasoning, investigative research

Skills and abilities: Oral and written comprehension, number facility, mathematical reasoning, deductive reasoning, analytic skills

Occupations related to this major: Mathematicians, Statisticians, Mathematics Teachers, and Financial Analysts

Mathematics Education

Mathematics Education majors learn to teach mathematics at the high school or middle school level. They learn techniques to help students develop skills and knowledge in the field of mathematics; they also take professional education courses.

Interests: Problem solving, analytic reasoning, working with young students, working with computers, leadership, organizing people

Skills and abilities: Oral and written expression and comprehension, speech clarity, organizational skills, creativity, using computers

Occupations related to this major: Middle School Teachers, High School Teachers, Insurance Underwriters, Business Training Specialists, and Education Administrators

Statistics

Statistics majors learn the science of dealing with data. They learn to design efficient data collection systems and to analyze and interpret information derived from the data. They learn to use mathematical theory or apply statistical theory and methods to collect, organize, interpret, and summarize numerical data to provide usable information. They may specialize in fields such as biostatistics, agricultural statistics, business statistics, economic statistics, or other fields.

Interests: Mathematics, working with numbers, problem solving, quantitative problems

Skills and abilities: Mathematical reasoning, computer operations, critical thinking, deductive and inductive reasoning, written expression

Occupations related to this major: Statisticians, Actuaries, Mathematicians, Operations Research Analysts, and Cost Estimators

8. EDUCATION

Education is a people-oriented field of study providing teachers, librarians, and school counselors involved in helping others to learn, acquire information, or gain insight into it. There are many levels on which one can teach. These include preschool and day care facilities, elementary schools, secondary schools, colleges and universities, as well as public and private vocational education institutions, dance, music, and art studios, and many other places. Librarianship and counseling are smaller fields than teaching. Archivists and curators are more involved with things than people. They may also help people learn and gain information, but they do not usually work as closely with people as do teachers, librarians, and counselors. All of these professions usually require a bachelor's degree, although some require a master's or doctoral degree.

Interest: Helping others learn, acquire information; teaching, counseling, or librarianship

Popular majors in this field of study: Early Childhood Education, Elementary School Education, Library Science, Middle School Education, Parks and Recreation Management, Physical Education, Secondary School Education, Special Education, Technology Education, and Vocational and Educational Counseling

Employment information/outlook: More than 6,758,700 people worked in related occupations in this field of study in 2012. The 2012-2022 employment growth is expected to be 15%.

In May 2012, median annual wages of preschool teachers was $27,130; kindergarten, elementary, middle, and secondary school teachers ranged from $53,090 to $57,810 in that same period. In 2012, the majority of all elementary, middle, and secondary school teachers belonged to unions—mainly the American Federation of Teachers and the National Education Association—that bargain with school systems over salaries, hours, and other terms and conditions of employment. Median annual wages in May 2012 of special education teachers who worked primarily in preschools, kindergartens, and elementary schools was $55,060; middle school special education teachers, $87,760; and special education teachers who worked primarily in secondary schools, $51,260. Median annual wages of vocational education teachers in elementary and secondary schools in May 2012 were $56,270.

Early Childhood Education

Early Childhood Education majors learn to teach preschool students through art, music, play, poetry, and stories to prepare for learning language, science, numbers, and social studies. They learn to design programs to develop students' mental capacities, learning abilities, and emotional health. They learn a variety of appropriate teaching methods and strategies.

Interests: Childhood development, working with children, communicating with children and their parents

Skills and abilities: Oral expression and comprehension, speech clarity, problem sensitivity, time sharing, creativity, music or artistic ability

Occupations related to this major: Preschool Teachers, Kindergarten Teachers, Elementary School Teachers, Early Childhood Education Program Directors, Child Care Administrators, and Family Service Coordinators

Elementary School Education

Elementary School Education majors learn to teach young students (kindergarten through grade 6) basic academic, social, and manipulative skills. They learn to instill good study and work habits and an appreciation for learning. They learn to prepare lesson plans, tests, records, and reports, and to conduct conferences with parents. They learn a variety of methods for understanding how and why children develop socially and intellectually, and get professional experience that includes research in teaching and learning.

Interests: Communication, creativity, problem solving, flexibility, ability to organize, energy, enthusiasm

Skills and abilities: Oral and written expression and comprehension, speech clarity, problem sensitivity

Occupations related to this major: Elementary School Teachers, Kindergarten Teachers, Middle School Teachers, Secondary School Teachers, Special Education Teachers, and School Counselors

Library Science

Library Science majors learn the science of acquiring and organizing collections of books, pamphlets, manuscripts, clippings, and reports, and assisting readers in their use. They learn how to analyze reader needs, prepare bibliographies, and organize films, tapes, and maps.

Interests: Reading, multimedia communication, working with people, computers

Skills and abilities: Reading comprehension, active listening, oral and written expression and comprehension, speech clarity, fluency of ideas, information ordering

Occupations related to this major: Librarians, Computer and Information Systems Managers, Elementary School Teachers, Secondary School Teachers, and School Administrators

Middle School Education

Middle School Education majors learn to develop a wide array of instructional skills, which include multimedia approaches, classroom management, advisory ability, effective communication, and alternatives to teacher-centered instruction. They learn to build on and extend basic academic skills developed in elementary school students, and introduce them to the world of more abstract thinking and knowledge that they will encounter in high school.

Interests: Helping or providing service to others, communicating with young people, teaching young people, working with ideas

Skills and abilities: Instructing others, active listening, social perceptiveness, oral and written expression and comprehension, speech clarity, problem sensitivity

Occupations related to this major: Middle School Teachers, High School Teachers, Vocational Education Teachers, School Counselors, and Librarians

Parks and Recreation Management

Parks and Recreation Management majors study how individuals and communities pursue leisure and recreation. They explore what recreation is, investigate what motivates people's recreational choices, and develop skills to manage a variety of leisure and recreation enterprises and organizations.

Interests: Working with people; scientific, historic, and natural features of parks, forests, and other attractions

Skills and abilities: Helping others, leadership, solving problems, oral and written expression, speech clarity, problem sensitivity

Occupations related to this major: Community Recreation Planners/Directors, Social Directors, Park Naturalists, Forest Rangers, Amusement and Recreation Establishment Managers, and Camp Directors

Physical Education

Physical Education majors learn to teach and supervise individual and team sports. They learn to demonstrate sports techniques, analyze physical capabilities and needs of students, and administer corrective exercises and physical conditioning. They learn to provide students with activities to maximize physical fitness.

Interests: Physical activity, sports, working with people, health-related issues, biological science

Skills and abilities: Physical stamina, leadership, oral expression, speech clarity, multilimb coordination

Occupations related to this major: Physical Education Teachers, Sports Coaches, Physical Training Instructors, Aerobic Dance Instructors, Athletic Trainers, Fitness Directors, and Athletic Administrators

Secondary School Education

Secondary School Education majors learn to teach one or more high school subjects using various teaching methods. They learn to develop and plan teaching materials and assignments. They learn to construct tests to evaluate learning. They gain depth of knowledge in the subject they intend to teach and develop teaching skills in subject matters such as science, mathematics, social studies, English, music, art, business, physical education, or other subjects.

Interests: Serving others, teaching young people and helping them develop their academic interests and career choices

Skills and abilities: Working with people, teaching, learning, understanding human behavior, oral and written expression and comprehension, speech clarity

Occupations related to this major: Secondary School Teachers, Middle School Teachers, Special Education Teachers, Vocational Education Teachers, and Vocational and Educational School Counselors

Special Education

Special Education majors prepare for a career working with disabled children and adults in a variety of settings. They learn to coordinate the services available to people with disabilities, and provide appropriate educational experiences for people with varying disabilities, including deafness, blindness, aphasia, and mobility impairments.

Interests: Helping others, working with people

Skills and abilities: Accepting differences in people, communicating effectively, teaching, oral and written expression and comprehension, speech clarity, problem sensitivity

Occupations related to this major: Special Education Teachers; Teachers of the Emotionally and Mentally Impaired; Teachers of the Physically, Visually, and Hearing Impaired; Rehabilitation Counselors

Technology Education

Technology Education majors are trained to teach the design, operation, and impact of technological systems to students. They learn technical skills to be used in advanced communication, applied higher mathematics, and science. This major prepares students to teach technical pathway programs found in middle schools, high schools, and colleges. Technical majors can be planned in agriculture, arts, communication, business, engineering, information science, mechanics, and other fields.

Interests: Helping people, design, technological systems, network technology, graphics and multimedia, system designs, programming, teaching

Skills and abilities: Working with people, oral and written expression and comprehension, analyzing and describing technological systems

Occupations related to this major: Agriculture Teachers, Art Teachers, Computer Science Teachers, Business Teachers, Engineering Technology Teachers, and Science Teachers

Vocational and Educational Counseling

Vocational and Educational Counseling majors learn to counsel individuals and provide group educational and vocational guidance services. They learn to promote and enhance student learning through three broad and interrelated areas of student development: academic development, career development, and personal/social development.

Interests: Working with, communicating with, and teaching people; providing service to others

Skills and abilities: Speaking, active listening, oral and written expression and comprehension, problem sensitivity, speech clarity, fluency of ideas

Occupations related to this major: Educational and Vocational School Counselors, Child, Family, and School Social Workers, Health Educators, and Probation Officers

9. ENGINEERING

Engineering field of study involves planning and designing various things. Engineers design machines, processes, systems, and structures. They apply physical laws and mathematical theories and principles to solve practical technical problems. Engineers work in research, development, design, manufacturing and construction, operations, management, technical sales, teaching, and consulting services.

Interests: Designing machines, processes, systems and structures; research, development, design, manufacturing and construction, operations, management, and technical consulting services

Popular majors in this field of study: Aerospace/Aeronautical Engineering, Agricultural Engineering, Chemical Engineering, Civil Engineering, Computer Engineering, Electrical Engineering, Industrial Engineering, Materials Engineering, Mechanical Engineering, and Petroleum Engineering

Employment information/outlook: More than 1,166,700 people worked in related occupations in this field of study in 2012. The 2012-2022 employment growth is expected to be 9.7%.

Earnings for engineers vary significantly by specialty, industry, and education. Variation in median earnings and in the earnings distributions for engineers in a number of specialties is especially significant. Median annual wages of aerospace engineers in May 2012 was $103,720; agricultural engineers, $74,000; chemical engineers, $94,350; civil engineers, $79,340; computer engineers, $100,920; electrical engineers, $89,630; industrial engineers, $78,860; materials engineers, $85,150; mechanical engineers, $80,580; and petroleum engineers, $130,280.

Aerospace/Aeronautical Engineering

Aerospace/Aeronautical Engineering majors learn to perform a variety of engineering work in designing, constructing, and testing aircraft, missiles, and spacecraft. They learn to conduct basic and applied research to evaluate adaptability of materials and equipment to aircraft design and manufacture. They learn to make improvements in testing equipment and techniques.

Interests: Model aircraft and rocketry, astronomy, piloting, space exploration, computers, problem solving, working with people

Skills and abilities: Leadership, computer technology, physical science, oral and written expression and comprehension, mathematical reasoning, deductive and inductive reasoning

Occupations related to this major: Aerospace/Aeronautical Engineers, Electronics Engineers, Nuclear Engineers, Ceramic Engineers, Chemical Engineers, and Civil Engineers

Agricultural Engineering

Agricultural Engineering majors learn to apply knowledge of engineering technology and biological science to agricultural problems concerned with power and machinery, electrification, structures, soil and water conservation, and processing of agricultural products.

Interests: Solving problems, improving the quality of life, computers, leadership

Skills and abilities: Problem solving, oral and written expression and comprehension, computer operation, deductive and inductive reasoning, number facility

Occupations related to this major: Soil Conservationists, Landscape Architects, Geoscientists, Foresters, Chemical Engineers, Industrial Engineers, and Mechanical Engineers

Chemical Engineering

Chemical Engineering majors learn to turn chemicals into products through research and development. They learn to devise economical and efficient production processes. They learn to work in a number of fields, such as cosmetics, fertilizers, paints, dyes, pesticides, oil refining, and pollution prevention.

Interests: Science, chemistry, mathematics

Skills and abilities: Applying knowledge of science and mathematics to real-world problems, written expression and comprehension, mathematical reasoning, originality, deductive reasoning

Occupations related to this major: Chemical Engineers, Nuclear Engineers, Civil Engineers, Petroleum Engineers, Agricultural Engineers, and Electrical Engineers

Civil Engineering

Civil Engineering majors learn to solve technical problems involved in providing buildings, bridges, airports, transportation systems, foundations, coastal facilities, environmental control systems, and water supply and purification systems. They become involved in the conception, planning, design, construction, operation, and maintenance of these important public facilities. Studies will include soil mechanics, hydraulics, and structural engineering.

Interests: Mathematics, physical sciences, computers, building things, public service, applying mathematics and science to practical uses

Skills and abilities: Mathematics, physical sciences, logical thinking, interpersonal skills, oral and written expression and comprehension, inductive and deductive reasoning

Occupations related to this major: Civil Engineers, Civil Engineering Technicians, Architectural Engineers, Nuclear Engineers, Electrical Engineers, and Industrial Engineers

Computer Engineering

Computer Engineering majors learn to design and develop computer and computer-related systems. These systems include software systems, hardware systems, and combined hardware/software systems. Students take courses in basic sciences, mathematics, and engineering science and design.

Interests: Mathematics, science, computing, investigative research

Skills and abilities: Mathematics, computer operations, oral and written expression and comprehension, inductive and deductive reasoning

Occupations related to this major: Computer Hardware Engineers, Computer Software Engineers, Electronics Engineers, and Computer Service Technicians

Electrical Engineering

Electrical Engineering majors learn to design, develop, test, or supervise the manufacturing and installation of electrical equipment components or systems for commercial, industrial, military, or scientific use. They learn to design and manufacture a broad array of electrical and electronic devices and systems to meet society's needs.

Interests: Computer languages, computer programming, electronic equipment

Skills and abilities: Mathematics, physical science, oral and written expression and comprehension, deductive reasoning

Occupations related to this major: Electrical Engineers, Electronics Engineers, Mechanical Engineers, Electricians, Nuclear Engineers, and Production Engineers

Industrial Engineering

Industrial Engineering majors learn to plan, design, and implement complex systems for industry that take into account the availability, capabilities, and needs of people, machines, and materials. They learn to plan the layout of factories for efficiency, and engage in time, motion, and incentive studies. They learn about safety studies, cost, and quality control measures, and long-range planning goals.

Interests: Problem solving, leadership

Skills and abilities: Working with people, critical thinking, written and oral expression and comprehension, fluency of ideas, mathematical reasoning

Occupations related to this major: Aerospace Engineers, Materials Engineers, Petroleum Engineers, Industrial Engineers, Mechanical Engineers, and Engineering Technicians

Materials Engineering

Materials Engineering majors learn to evaluate properties of materials used to manufacture products that must meet specialized design and performance criteria. They learn to develop machinery and processes to manufacture materials, such as polymers, plastics, and alloys.

Interests: Nature and the physical sciences, problem solving, computer operations, working with ideas

Skills and abilities: Creative and critical thinking, problem sensitivity, oral and written expression and comprehension, deductive and inductive reasoning

Occupations related to this major: Materials Engineers, Marine Architects, Mechanical Engineers, Electrical Drafters, and Electrical Engineering Technicians

Mechanical Engineering

Mechanical Engineering majors learn to plan and design tools, engines, machines, and other mechanically functioning equipment. They learn to oversee installation, operation, maintenance, and repair of such equipment as centralized heat, gas, water, and steam systems. They learn to create and build machines, devices, and systems that perform useful services.

Interests: Mechanical devices, computers, cars, solving problems, mathematics, physical science

Skills and abilities: Mathematics, critical thinking, complex problem solving, mathematical reasoning, deductive and inductive reasoning, oral and written comprehension

Occupations related to this major: Mechanical Engineers, Marine Architects, Materials Engineers, Petroleum Engineers, Engineering Technicians, and Mechanical Drafters

Petroleum Engineering

Petroleum Engineering majors learn about exploring and drilling for fossil fuel, both on land and under the sea, and how to maximize the recovery of oil and gas through engineering processes. They learn methods of searching for new sources of energy, for example, geothermal energy. They learn to devise methods to improve oil and gas well production and determine the need for new or modified tool designs.

Interests: Solving problems, working with others, using computers, outdoor activities

Skills and abilities: Mathematics, physics, oral and written expression and comprehension, inductive and deductive reasoning, problem sensitivity, fluency of ideas

Occupations related to this major: Petroleum Engineers, Aerospace Engineers, Marine Engineers, Materials Engineers, Mining and Geological Engineers, and Geologists

10. FAMILY AND CONSUMER SCIENCES

Family and Consumer Sciences majors concentrate on issues concerning feeding, clothing, and caring for children, managing resources, and providing housing for individuals and families. Family and Consumer Science majors provide information, gained through research, about families and individuals as consumers and decision makers. These majors provide information about child care, elder care, food, clothing, housing, finance, and other issues of resource management.

Interests: Issues concerning feeding, clothing, and caring for children, managing resources, and providing housing for individuals and families; an interest in families as consumers and decision makers.

Popular majors in this field of study: Day Care Administration, Family and Consumer Education, Fashion Merchandising, Food Science and Nutrition, Hotel and Motel Management, Housing and Human Development, Individual and Family Development, Leisure Studies, Textile Sciences, and Tourism

Employment information/outlook: More than 1,011,500 people worked in related occupations in this field of study in 2012. The 2012-2022 employment growth is expected to be 7.8%.

Pay depends on the educational attainment of the worker and the type of establishment. Although the pay generally is very low, more education usually means higher earnings. Median hourly wages of child care workers were $9.38 in May 2012. Hourly earnings of nonsupervisory workers in clothing, accessory, and general merchandise stores in 2012 were well below the average for all workers in private industry. This reality reflects both the high proportion of part-time and less experienced workers in these stores and the fact that even experienced workers receive relatively low pay compared with the pay of experienced workers in many other industries. Median annual wages of dietitians and nutritionists were $55,240 in May 2012. For that same period, lodging managers were $46,810; lodging managers in traveler accommodations, $53,780. Salaries of lodging managers vary greatly according to their responsibilities, location, and the segment of the hotel industry in which they work.

Day Care Administration

Day Care Administration majors learn to manage programs that provide education or social services to young children and their families. They gain knowledge of child development and develop skills in teaching young children, in supervising staff, and in business management.

Interests: Leadership, management, supervising people, administering programs, working with children

Skills and abilities: Organizational and managerial skills, program development, oral and written expression and comprehension, speech clarity

Occupations related to this major: Day Care Director, Preschool Director, Head Start Directors, Early Childhood Education Program Directors, and Child Care Workers

Family and Consumer Education

Family and Consumer Education majors learn to use community resources to meet the needs of the individual and the family in the management of time, energy, and money. They learn about parenting skills, communication skills, relationship skills, wellness, foods and nutrition, consumerism, clothing selection, and job skills. They prepare to become family and consumer teachers for preschool through adult education in subjects related to the family. They study various aspects of family life including human development, nutrition, and decision making, in addition to teaching strategies.

Interests: Family life, using current technology, working with people

Skills and abilities: Critical and analytical thinking, oral and written expression and comprehension, speech clarity

Occupations related to this major: Family and Consumer Science Teachers, Consumer Advocates, Education Consultants, Extension Agents, Financial Planners, Housing Administrators

Fashion Merchandising

Fashion Merchandising majors study how to manufacture fashions for consumers and effectively sell those fashions.

Interests: Current trends in apparel, arts, furnishings, travel and leisure, food business trends, fabrics, fashion and fashion designers

Skills and abilities: Motivating people, leadership, organizational ability, originality, fluency of ideas, color discrimination, oral comprehension

Occupations related to this major: Retail Buyers, Manufacturers' Representatives, Product Designer-Pattern Makers, and Fashion Designers

Food Science and Nutrition

Food Science and Nutrition majors study the nature of foods, the causes of their deterioration, and the principles of food processing. They will learn about the selection, preservation, processing, packaging, distribution, and use of safe, nutritious, and wholesome food.

Interests: Social, health, economic, and political issues involved in food production and availability; chemical reactions and what happens to food when it enters the human body; solving problems

Skills and abilities: Organizational abilities, critical thinking, oral and written expression and comprehension, speech clarity, mathematical reasoning

Occupations related to this major: Dietitians, Nutritionists, Nutrition Educators, and Food Scientists and Technicians

Hotel and Motel Management

Hotel Management majors learn the operation of a hotel. They learn the principles of managing lodging facilities efficiently and profitably. They learn about personnel management, services, supplies, business aspects, decision making, accounting, and public relations. They are introduced to the principles of managing these key components of the hospitality industry.

Interests: Working with people, problem solving, attention to detail, leadership

Skills and abilities: Organization ability, creativity, oral and written expression and comprehension, speech clarity, speech recognition

Occupations related to this major: Lodging Managers, Food Service Managers, Retail Store Managers, and Office Managers

Housing and Human Development

Housing and Human Development majors learn to analyze the use of investment in housing and its impact on families, the community, and the larger economy and society.

Interests: Working with people, serving others, real estate, home automation, the family, marketing, management, interior design, environmental design, finance

Skills and abilities: Computer skills, analytical skills, oral and written expression and comprehension, problem sensitivity

Occupations related to this major: Real Estate Managers, Property Managers, Consumer Affairs Specialists, Extension Agents, and Financial/Mortgage Specialists

Individual and Family Development

Individual and Family Development majors study interpersonal relationships and human development from infancy to old age. They study theories of development with an emphasis on techniques to improve quality of life for individuals and families.

Interests: Helping others, family and individual well-being, prevention and elimination of problems facing people in their daily lives

Skills and abilities: Working with people, critical thinking, oral and written expression and comprehension, curiosity about interpersonal and family dynamics, speech clarity

Occupations related to this major: Child Life Specialists, Day Care Teachers, Recreation Activities Directors, Drug and Alcohol Rehabilitation Counselors, and Crisis Center Directors

Leisure Studies

Leisure Studies majors learn to design, manage, and deliver leisure services to a variety of people in diverse settings. They learn about the impact of leisure services upon individual satisfaction and the quality of life.

Interests: Helping people, leadership, organizing individual and group activities

Skills and abilities: Working with people, oral and written expression and comprehension, speech clarity, problem sensitivity, fluency of ideas, memorization

Occupations related to this major: Amusement and Recreation Establishment Managers, Recreation Workers, Tour Guides and Escorts, Social and Community Service Managers, and Meeting and Convention Planners

Textile Sciences

Textile Sciences majors learn how to design fabrics for garments, upholstery, rugs, and other products. They study print, woven, and embroidery styles, and learn how to buy and sell certain fabrics and trims. They learn how to analyze fabric performance in the marketplace.

Interests: Fashion design, garment fashion, art, history of textiles, textile technology, design principles

Skills and abilities: Originality, visualization, visual color discrimination, fluency of ideas, oral expression and comprehension

Occupations related to this major: Textile Designers, Fashion Designers, Quality Control Analysts, Sales Representatives, and Wardrobe Planners

Tourism

Tourism majors study how to manage travel-related enterprises and conventions and tour services. They learn about travel agency management, travel industry operations and procedures, tourism marketing and promotion strategies, and travel industry law.

Interests: Travel, tourism planning, human resource management, travel industry operations, marketing

Skills and abilities: Oral and written expression and comprehension, mathematical reasoning, speech clarity, fluency of ideas

Occupations related to this major: Travel Agents, Travel Guides, Tour Guides and Escorts, Reservation and Transportation Ticket Agents, and Amusement and Recreation Establishment Managers

11. HEALTH SCIENCE

The **Health Science** field of study trains workers in a vast array of occupations. Occupational titles vary, and the training necessary to fill these occupations requires lengthy postgraduate education. Health practitioners diagnose, treat, and prevent illness and disease. While all health practitioners practice the art of healing, they differ in methods of treatment and areas of specialization. Training for this profession is more rigorous than training for most other professional occupations, but practice also offers unusual rewards. Incomes of health practitioners generally are higher than those of other professional workers with similar years of education. Furthermore, most health practitioners derive considerable satisfaction from knowing that their work contributes directly to the well-being of others. Workers in the industry must have the ability and perseverance to complete the years of study required. They should be emotionally stable, able to make decisions in emergencies, and have a strong desire to help the sick and injured. Sincerity and an ability to gain the confidence of patients are important qualities.

Interests: Diagnosing, treating, and preventing illness and disease; an interest in the well-being of others and a desire to help the sick and injured

Popular majors in this field of study: Athletic Training, Clinical Laboratory Science, Dental Hygiene, Health Services Management, Medical Record Administration, Nuclear Medical Technology, Nursing, Occupational Therapy, Pharmacy, and Physical Therapy

Employment information/outlook: More than 2,775,600 people worked in related occupations in this field of study in 2012. The 2012-2022 employment growth is expected to be 27%.

Most athletic trainers work in full-time positions, and typically receive benefits. The salary of an athletic trainer depends on experience and job responsibilities, and varies by job setting. In May 2012, median annual wages for athletic trainers were $42,690; medical and clinical laboratory technologists, $47,820; and dental hygienists, $70,210; Earnings vary by geographic location, employment setting, and years of experience. Dental hygienists may be paid on an hourly, daily, salary, or commission basis. Median annual wages of wage and salary medical and health services managers were $88,580; medical records and health information technicians, $34,160. The median annual wage in May 2012 of nuclear medicine technologists was $70,180; registered nurses, $65,470; occupational therapists, $75,400; salary pharmacists, $116,670; physical therapists, $79,860; and speech-language pathologists, $69,870.

Athletic Training

Athletic Training majors learn to prevent, recognize, refer, and treat injuries and illnesses sustained by athletes. They learn about the administration of athletic training programs in public and private schools, colleges, universities, and with professional teams. They study exercise sciences and the medical aspects of sport. Together with clinical experience, this prepares students for national certification in the field.

Interests: Sports, helping others, health and medicine, physical fitness and exercise, anatomy, nutrition, first aid

Skills and abilities: Manual skills, science, problem solving, interpersonal communication, integrity, oral expression, speech clarity, physical strength

Occupations related to this major: Athletic Trainers, Sports Medicine Clinic Administrators, Exercise Physiologists, Physical and Corrective Therapists, and Occupational Therapists

Clinical Laboratory Science

Clinical Laboratory Science majors learn to perform medical tests to determine the presence and cause of disease. They study sophisticated instrumentation used to perform a variety of laboratory procedures. They study blood and other body fluids that aid in the diagnosis of disease and the maintenance of health.

Interests: Solving problems, working with complex machinery, computer science, laboratory work, helping others, medicine, biological science

Skills and abilities: Computer skills, analytic skills, oral and written expression and comprehension, arm-hand steadiness, visual color discrimination

Occupations related to this major: Laboratory Technologists and Technicians, Research Analysts, Coroners, Clinical Scientists, Environmental Health Officers, and Toxicologists

Dental Hygiene

Dental Hygiene majors learn to work under the supervision of a dentist to clean and polish teeth, massage gums, apply fluoride to prevent decay, and provide dental health education. They obtain the knowledge and clinical skills needed to provide preventive oral health care. They learn skills as an assistant to a dentist performing a number of duties.

Interests: Working with people, helping individuals maintain their health, science

Skills and abilities: Critical thinking, oral expression, arm-hand steadiness, manual dexterity, near vision

Occupations related to this major: Dental Hygienists, Dental Assistants, Dentists, and Medical Assistants

Health Services Management

Health Services Management majors prepare for entry-level positions managing a wide variety of health care organizations such as hospitals, nursing homes, insurance companies, and public agen-

cies. They learn to direct the many activities of health care organizations and coordinate administrative duties with medical services. They learn about space needs, staffing, and supplies. They learn to supervise personnel, prepare budgets, and direct the policies of the organization.

Interests: Working with people, taking initiative, solving problems, working with data

Skills and abilities: Oral and written expression and comprehension, speech clarity, organizational skills, interpersonal skills, critical thinking

Occupations related to this major: Medical and Health Services Managers, Public Health Directors, Educational Program Directors, Nursing Directors, Social Welfare Administrators, and Health Insurance Underwriters

Medical Record Administration

Medical Record Administration majors learn to supervise and manage the preparation, storage, and use of medical records and related information systems. They study the legal and technical aspects of medical records, and the design and management of secure data systems. They learn to merge the study of business and medicine. Students prepare to direct medical record departments in varied health care settings by exploring the health care environment, health care organizations, clinical information systems, medical record department operations, and health care reimbursement systems.

Interests: Leadership, working with people, designing and implementing systems, problem solving, working with detail

Skills and abilities: Writing and speaking effectively, working in a changing environment, oral and written expression and comprehension, near vision, mathematical reasoning

Occupations related to this major: Medical Records Administrators and Directors, Quality Assurance Coordinators, Health Care Administrators, Medical Records Educators, and Research Coordinators

Nuclear Medicine Technology

Nuclear Medicine Technology majors learn how to administer radionuclides to patients and to monitor the characteristics and functions of tissues or organs in which they localize. They learn to operate the cameras that detect the radionuclides and maintain patient records. They learn to prepare and administer radioactive drugs to patients, operate radiation detection equipment, and perform the calculations or computer analysis needed to complete the patient's examination.

Interests: Biological sciences, new technologies, helping others, working in a medical setting, working with people

Skills and abilities: Biological and physical science, working with others, oral and written expression and comprehension, problem sensitivity

Occupations related to this major: Nuclear Medicine Technologists, Radiation Therapists, Radiologic Technologists, Electroneurodiagnostic Technologists, and Medical and Clinical Laboratory Technologists

Nursing

Nursing majors learn to administer nursing care to ill or injured persons. They learn to administer medication and treatments prescribed by medical doctors, observe and record symptoms and behaviors of patients, and promote good health. They learn how to rehabilitate, counsel, and educate patients, and how to work as part of a health care team in many settings. They study humanities, natural sciences, and nursing theory to serve individuals, families, groups, and communities.

Interests: Provide intimate helping services to people, ethical care, chemistry, physics, anatomy, biology

Skills and abilities: Clear thinking, oral and written expression and comprehension, problem sensitivity, speech clarity

Occupations related to this major: Registered Nurses, Doctors of Medicine, Nursing Instructors, Physical Therapists, Medical Assistants, Chiropractors, and Podiatrists

Occupational Therapy

Occupational Therapy majors learn to determine the educational, recreational, and vocational activities needed to hasten a patient's recovery from physical, psychological, social, or developmental problems. They learn to instruct patients in the use of artificial limbs or to regain the use of muscles. They learn to help patients function independently so that they may work, play, take care of themselves, and relate to others in a productive and satisfying manner.

Interests: Solving problems, anatomy, working with people, medicine, health, rehabilitation

Skills and abilities: Logical thinking, working with others, oral and written expression and comprehension, deductive reasoning

Occupations related to this major: Occupational Therapists, Respiratory Therapists, Physical Therapists, Speech-Language Pathologists and Audiologists, Recreational Therapists, and Exercise Physiologists

Pharmacy

Pharmacy majors study the science of drugs, including their chemical and physical properties and composition. They learn to understand the effects of drugs, to test those drugs for purity and strength. They learn to provide drug products and drug information in all areas of patient care. They learn to monitor drug therapy to ensure that the treatment is appropriate, safe, therapeutically effective, and cost-effective.

Interests: Chemistry, biology, mathematics, solving problems, helping others

Skills and abilities: Patience, tact, adapting to change, working carefully, oral and written expression and comprehension, information ordering, mathematical reasoning

Occupations related to this major: Pharmacists, Pharmacy Technicians, Physician Assistants, Opticians, Licensed Practical Nurses, and Dietitians and Nutritionists

Physical Therapy

Physical Therapy majors learn to assist and help persons with injuries, muscle, nerve, and joint problems, burns, and bone diseases. They learn to use exercise, massage, and heat and light to assist in healing. They prepare to take state licensure examinations in this field and qualify for service in the prevention of disabilities and the rehabilitation of the disabled. They learn to test, evaluate, and plan a treatment program for patients who are physically incapacitated as the result of accidents or disease, and for healthy individuals who wish to prevent injuries in work or recreational settings.

Interests: Biological and physical sciences, exercise and fitness, people, analytic reasoning

Skills and abilities: Interpersonal communication, problem solving, visual spatial perception, emotional sensitivity, oral and written expression, speech clarity, problem sensitivity, manual dexterity

Occupations related to this major: Physical Therapists, Occupational Therapists, Respiratory Therapists, Manual Arts Therapists, Corrective Therapists, and Speech-Language Pathologists and Audiologists

Speech Pathology/Audiology

Speech Pathology majors learn to treat people with speech, language, voice, hearing, and communication disorders. These disorders may be the result of hearing loss, brain injury or deterioration, cerebral palsy, stroke, cleft palate, mental retardation, or emotional problems. They receive training in the identification and treatment of human communication disorders. They learn about the normal processes of speech and language development, why problems may occur, and what can be done to minimize their impact.

Interests: Working with children, working with adults, identifying and solving behavioral problems, applying technology to human needs

Skills and abilities: Oral and written expression and comprehension, speech clarity, creativity, working cooperatively in groups

Occupations related to this major: Speech-Language Pathologists and Audiologists, Recreation Therapists, Corrective Therapists, Exercise Physiologists, Occupational Therapists, and Respiratory Therapists

12. HUMANITIES

Humanities students explore thought and expression through aesthetic, historical, philosophical, social, political, psychological, and symbolic contexts. Humanities studies serve as a liberal and broad training for professional careers. Students will enjoy courses in English, literature, history, classics, culture studies, history of art and music, philosophy, foreign language, social and natural sciences. Graduates with a bachelor's degree may qualify for management trainee positions in corporations, banks, and federal and state governmental agencies. Many students use humanities as an undergraduate degree for the teaching or law professions. Other students may become writers or communications specialists in humanistic endeavors.

Interests: Exploring thoughts and expressions through aesthetic, historical, philosophical, social, political, psychological and symbolic contests; literature, history, foreign language, social and natural sciences

Popular majors in this field of study: American Literature, Anthropology, Classics, Comparative Literature, English, English Education, Foreign Language, History, Linguistics, Philosophy, Religion, and Sociology

Employment information/outlook: More than 972,100 people worked in related occupations in this field of study in 2012. The 2012-2022 employment growth is expected to be 11%.

In May 2012, median annual wages for anthropologists and archaeologists were $57,420; historians, $52,480; sociologists, $74,960. Wages of anthropologists and archaeologists, geographers, and historians vary. The same applies to English and Foreign Language specialists and people in the clergy.

American Literature

American Literature majors study the historical development of the culture in which they live. They study the literature and literary development of the United States from the Colonial Era to the present. They learn about the forces—intellectual, economic, geographic, and social—that have shaped their own character. They study periods and genres, authors, literary criticism, and regional and oral traditions.

Interests: Sensitivity to language, the power of ideas, exploring the development of different regional and ethnic traditions that make up American culture

Skills and abilities: Assessing conflicting points of view, oral and written expression and comprehension, speech clarity

Occupations related to this major: English Teachers, Creative Writers, Art, Drama, and Music Teachers, Reporters and Correspondents, and Publicity Writers

Anthropology

Anthropology majors learn to make comparative studies of the distribution, origin, and evolution of man, cultures that man has created, and their social and physical characteristics. Studies include ancient as well as modern man.

Interests: Writing, archeology, sociology, social sciences, investigative research

Skills and abilities: Writing, science, critical thinking, oral and written expression and comprehension, inductive reasoning, fluency of ideas

Occupations related to this major: Anthropologists, Archeologists, Historians, Sociologists, Linguistic Scientists, and Genealogists

Classics

Classics majors immerse themselves in two cultures fundamental to the West—the cultures of ancient Greece and ancient Rome. Students explore the literature, history, art, philosophy, and architecture of those civilizations. Connecting with the past creates a sense of belonging to humanity and participating in human achievement and evokes reflections on the present. Students will explore their poetry, prose, and drama, and consider the relation of literature to other arts and to other fields of study.

Interests: Language, literature, exploring the past, acquiring a broad liberal education

Skills and abilities: Oral and written expression and comprehension, information ordering, skills of analysis and criticism

Occupations related to this major: Classicists, Anthropologists, Art History Teachers, English Teachers, Foreign Language Teachers, and Literature Teachers

Comparative Literature

Comparative Literature majors study the literature of different countries, cultures, and languages. They explore their poetry, prose, and drama, and consider the relation of literature to other arts and to other fields of study.

Interests: Literature, foreign languages, differences between cultures as expressed in their languages and works of art

Skills and abilities: Reading critically, speaking, active listening, oral and written expression and comprehension, speech recognition, information ordering

Occupations related to this major: English Teachers, Foreign Language Teachers, Postsecondary Teachers, Journalists, Lawyers, Reporters and Correspondents, and Writers

English

English majors study the linguistic and literary richness of the English language as well as some of the cultural history of the English-speaking world. They concentrate on specific areas such as creative writing, comparative or American literature, or semantics. They study important works of literature—drama, prose, and poetry—focusing on the point of view, organization, and language of the works. They develop critical and analytical reading skills, and practice language use and composition.

Interests: Reading, talking, writing about literature; music, theater, and film

Skills and abilities: Speaking, writing, oral and written expression and comprehension, speech clarity

Occupations related to this major: English Teachers, Teachers, Journalists, Publishers, Radio and Television Broadcasters, and Social Workers

English Education

English Education majors learn to teach students about English grammar and linguistics. They learn to instruct students in different types of literature such as poetry, short stories, plays, and novels. They learn how to teach students to research and prepare research papers. They learn how to teach public speaking, drama, and English as a second language

Interests: Nature and history of languages, reading, literature, journalism, creative writing, linguistic development of children and teenagers

Skills and abilities: Speaking, working with students, art, guiding discussions

Occupations related to this major: Elementary School Teachers, Secondary School Teachers, Postsecondary School Teachers, Linguistic Scientists, and Speech-Language Pathologists and Audiologists

Foreign Language

Foreign Language majors study foreign languages (French, German, Italian, Japanese, Russian, Spanish, etc.). They study the language, literature, and culture of the country where the language is spoken.

Interests: Literature, history, culture of a language

Skills and abilities: Fluency in speaking and writing, learning languages, oral and written expression and comprehension, speech clarity

Occupations related to this major: Foreign Language Teachers, Translators, Journalists, Foreign Travel Consultants, Diplomats, and Linguists

History

History majors study the social, economic, and political developments of societies. They learn to analyze historical happenings and, as reporters, writers, or teachers, report on their significance. Students expand their knowledge and understanding of the past. Working with written, oral, visual, and art factual evidence they examine the causes, contexts, and chronologies of historical events, thus cultivating a sense of continuity and change in human experiences.

Interests: Curiosity about when, where, and why historical happenings occurred; what it was like to have lived in different times and places

Skills and abilities: Reading carefully, writing clearly, speaking articulately, thinking analytically, oral and written expression and comprehension, expressing ideas with clarity and precision

Occupations related to this major: Historians, Archeologists, Anthropologists, Genealogists, Curators, Archivists, and Teachers

Linguistics

Linguistics majors study the common properties of the world's languages. They study the structure and development of a specific language or language group. They trace the origin and evolution of words through comparative analysis of ancient parent languages and modern language groups. They study word and structural characteristics, such as phonetics and phonology, morphology, syntax, and semantics.

Interests: Language, foreign languages, how people talk and express themselves

Skills and abilities: Learning foreign languages, problem solving, oral and written expression and comprehension, speech recognition

Occupations related to this major: Linguistic Scientists, English as a Second Language Teachers, English Teachers, Foreign Language Teachers, Interpreters, Translators, Public Relations Specialists, and Speech Pathologists

Philosophy

Philosophy majors learn the process of developing a philosophy. They gain insight into how the great minds of the past and present have attempted to answer the most serious questions of the universe. They participate in a tradition of thought as old as civilized life and as new as artificial intelligence and medical ethics. They examine issues of morality, reality, and knowledge. Philosophy is a foundation for teaching, religion, wisdom, and logical thinking.

Interests: Solitary meditation, argument with family and friends, reading, asking the "why" question, seeing the connections between different things

Skills and abilities: Writing, debating, thinking logically, mathematics, oral and written expression and comprehension, speech recognition, information ordering

Occupations related to this major: Philologists, Political Scientists, Anthropologists, Psychologists, Sociologists, and Historians

Religion

Religion majors study and compare the major world religions, as well as many of the lesser-known religions. They study the various branches, sects, and denominations of particular religions. They learn how religion plays an integral part in all societies. They learn to use a range of approaches when examining religion—historical, textual, psychological, philosophical, sociological, and anthropological.

Interests: Different cultures and societies, world religions, human problems and mysteries, such as birth, growth, love, death, grief

Skills and abilities: Reading carefully and critically, foreign languages, oral and written expression and comprehension, problem sensitivity, speech clarity

Occupations related to this major: Clergy, Directors of Religious Activities and Education, Therapists and Counselors, Psychologists, Social Workers, and Teachers

Sociology

Sociology majors study the origin, development, organization, and functions of human society. They trace the origin and growth of human organizations and the behavior and interaction within social groups. They analyze the influence of group activities on individual and group behavior.

Interests: Anthropology, geography, criminology, psychology, investigative research, politics

Skills and abilities: Reading critically, critical thinking, solving problems, oral and written expression and comprehension, deductive reasoning

Occupations related to this major: Sociologists, Anthropologists, Political Scientists, Counseling Psychologists, Historians, and Linguistic Scientists

13. PHYSICAL SCIENCES

Physical Sciences majors in this field of study investigate the structure and composition of the Earth and the universe. Everything in our physical environment, whether naturally occurring or of human design, is composed of chemicals. Chemists search for, and put to practical use, new knowledge about chemicals. Geological scientists play an important role in preserving and cleaning up the environment. Meteorologists forecast the weather. Physicists design and perform experiments with lasers, cyclotrons, telescopes, mass spectrometers, and other equipment. Physical science technicians use the principles and theories of science and mathematics to solve problems in research and development and to help invent and improve products and processes.

Interests: The structure and composition of the Earth and the universe; an interest in our physical environment, whether naturally occurring or of human design

Popular majors in this field of study: Astronomy, Atmospheric Sciences, Chemistry, Environmental Sciences, Geology, Geophysics, and Physics

Employment information/outlook: More than 978,300 people worked in related occupations in this field of study in 2012. The 2012-2022 employment growth is expected to be 10%.

In May 2012, median wages for physicists and astronomers were $106,360; chemists were $73,060; and environmental scientists, $63,570.

Astronomy

Astronomy majors study the sizes, shapes, motions, and all other physical properties of the sun, moon, stars, and planets. They may use knowledge of astronomy in space exploration and the development of space technology. Students seek to understand the entire universe—its constituent parts, such as the stars and planets, and the physical and mathematical laws that govern them.

Interests: Nature, the night sky, the expanding universe, physical science, astronomical science

Skills and abilities: Mathematics, science, computers, inductive and deductive reasoning, written comprehension

Occupations related to this major: Astronomers, Geophysicists, Physicists, Geologists, Chemists, and Atmospheric and Space Scientists

Atmospheric Sciences

Atmospheric Sciences majors learn to investigate atmospheric phenomena and interpret meteorological data gathered by surface and air stations, satellites, and radar to prepare reports and weather forecasts for public and other uses. They study the basic principles of atmospheric physics and dynamics and are concerned with understanding and forecasting weather.

Interests: Weather, environment, climate, science, mathematics, computer science, geography, serving the public

Skills and abilities: Analytic reasoning, mechanical reasoning, problem solving, oral and written expression and comprehension, speech clarity, inductive reasoning

Occupations related to this major: Atmospheric Scientists, Space Scientists, Climatologists, Geophysicists, Astronomers, and Meteorologists

Chemistry

Chemistry majors study the sciences of physical substances, atoms, molecules, elements, and compounds. They learn to perform chemical tests, develop new chemical products, and monitor the purity of air, food, and drugs. Because it is an experimental science, students learn to design and perform the experiments that allow a better understanding of the physical world.

Interests: Investigative research, problem solving, curiosity about how things work

Skills and abilities: Analytic and mathematical skills, oral and written expression and comprehension, deductive reasoning, mathematical reasoning

Occupations related to this major: Chemists, Chemical Engineers, Chemical Engineering Technicians, Agricultural Scientists, Biological Scientists, and Physicists

Environmental Sciences

Environmental Sciences majors study the biological and physical aspects of the environment. They learn about the conservation and/or improvement of natural resources, such as air, soil, water, land, fish, and wildlife, as well as methods of controlling environmental pollution. They conduct research or perform investigation for the purpose of identifying, abating, or eliminating sources of pollutants or hazards that affect either the environment or the health of the population.

Interests: Investigative research, solving problems, working with ideas

Skills and abilities: Working with others, oral and written expression and comprehension, problem sensitivity, mathematical reasoning, inductive reasoning

Occupations related to this major: Environmental Scientists, Materials Scientists, Geographers, Geologists, Atmospheric Scientists, and Space Scientists

Geology

Geology majors study the Earth's structure, composition, and history. They examine rocks, minerals, and fossils. They record data, prepare maps, conduct surveys, and advise suitability of sites. They develop skills that are useful for basic research and applied problem solving.

Interests: The outdoors, remote places, problem solving, collecting minerals or fossils

Skills and abilities: Reasoning ability, critical thinking, mathematics, oral and written expression and comprehension, number facility, inductive reasoning

Occupations related to this major: Geologists, Physicists, Geophysicists, Materials Scientists, Geological Data Technicians, and Geographers

Geophysics

Geophysics majors study aspects of the earth, including the atmosphere and hydrosphere. They investigate and measure seismic, gravitational, electrical, thermal, and magnetic forces affecting the Earth, and utilize principles of physics, mathematics, and chemistry. They study the Earth and its atmosphere by physical measurements. Students learn to use mathematics and physics, along with electrical engineering, computer science, geology, and other earth sciences to analyze measurements taken at the surface to infer properties and processes deep within the Earth's complex interior.

Interests: The outdoors, travel, taking measurements, computer languages, graphics, computer programming

Skills and abilities: Natural curiosity, mathematics, physical science, computers, oral and written comprehension, mathematical reasoning, deductive reasoning

Occupations related to this major: Geophysicists, Geologists, Astronomers, Physicists, Atmospheric Scientists, Space Scientists, and Chemists

Physics

Physics majors learn to explore and identify the basic principles of the structure and behavior of matter, the generation and transfer of energy, and the interaction of matter and energy. They learn to use these principles in theoretical areas such as the origin of the universe, or in practical areas to develop advanced materials, electronic devices, or medical equipment.

Interests: Investigative research, mathematics, problem solving, improving the quality of life

Skills and abilities: Computational skills, reasoning logically, solving problems, oral and written expression and comprehension, mathematical reasoning

Occupations related to this major: Physicists, Astronomers, Geologists, Atmospheric Scientists, Space Scientists, Geophysicists, and Environmental Scientists

14. SOCIAL AND BEHAVIORAL SCIENCES

Social and Behavioral Sciences majors learn about the social needs of people. Clinical psychologists help the mentally or emotionally disturbed adjust to life through behavior modification programs and other techniques. Social workers address the needs of individuals, families, groups, and communities. Their work may involve everything from helping an elderly person adjust to life in a nursing home, to organizing fund-raising for community social welfare activities. Other social scientists conduct basic and applied research in the social sciences. They use established methods to assemble a body of fact and theory that contributes to human knowledge. Social scientists investigate all aspects of human society—from anthropologists studying the origins of the human race, or historians studying an ancient civilization—to political scientists analyzing the results of presidential elections.

Interests: Social and emotional needs of people; an interest in all aspects of society—from the origins of the human race, or an ancient civilization, to political results of presidential elections

Popular majors in this field of study: Criminal Justice Studies, Economics, Geography, Gerontology, Political Sciences, Psychology, Public Administration, Social Studies Education, and Social Work

Employment information/outlook: More than 4,153,700 people worked in related occupations in this field of study in 2012. The 2012-2022 employment growth is expected to be 19%.

In May 2012, median annual wages of probation officers and correctional treatment specialists were $38,970; economists, $91,860; salary clinical, counseling, and school psychologists, $69,280; social and human service assistants, $28,850; political scientists, $102,000; sociologists, $74,960; child, family, and school social workers, $44,200. Public administration positions vary by occupation, size of the state or locality, and region of the country.

Criminal Justice Studies

Criminal Justice Studies majors learn about the dimensions and causes of crime and delinquency; the structure of the American criminal justice system; the operation of criminal courts; and the techniques and theories of law enforcement.

Interests: Serving others, court procedures, criminal law, private security, criminal justice

Skills and abilities: Working with others, making decisions, oral and written expression and comprehension, inductive reasoning, speech clarity, problem sensitivity

Occupations related to this major: Criminal Investigators, United States Marshals, Police Detectives, Sheriffs and Deputy Sheriffs, Correction Officers and Jailers, and Child Support and Missing Persons Investigators

Economics

Economics majors learn to plan, design, and conduct research into activities devoted to satisfying human wants. They learn to analyze the relationship between supply and demand. They study the problems of inflation, unemployment, tariffs, taxation, and foreign trade. They learn to analyze such issues as inflation, unemployment, monopoly, and economic growth. They study theory, policy, and trends and explore ways to deal with the economic problems of society and the individual.

Interests: Current issues such as taxes, poverty, health, inflation, the environment, human behavior

Skills and abilities: Solving problems, oral and written expression and comprehension, mathematical reasoning, logical reasoning

Occupations related to this major: Economists, Market Research Analysts, Urban and Regional Planners, Financial Managers, Financial Analysts, and Underwriters

Geography

Geography majors study the activities of people. Students study where people live, why they are located there, and how they earn a living. Students study the physical characteristics of the Earth, such as landforms, vegetation, climate, locale, and mineral and water resources. They study how people relate to and are shaped by their environment. They gain a broad perspective on the world's environments and its peoples while gaining a strong background in the physical and social sciences.

Interests: Analyzing and solving social and environmental problems, doing social and physical scientific research, the relationship between people and their environment

Skills and abilities: Oral and written expression and comprehension, spatial orientation, working individually and in groups, information gathering, working with computers

Occupations related to this major: Geographers, Geophysicists, Geologists, Atmospheric and Space Scientists, Environmental Scientists, and Materials Scientists

Gerontology

Gerontology majors learn about aging and older persons. They study physical, emotional, and intellectual changes in the elderly, cultural aspects of aging, and governmental policies and programs for the aging.

Interests: Helping people, human development, older people, family relations, improving the quality of life

Skills and abilities: Oral and written expression and comprehension, listening, objectivity, deductive reasoning, determining needs and interests, organizing and managing projects

Occupations related to this major: Gerontologists, Geriatric Nurses, Nursing Home Administrators, Social Welfare Administrators, and Occupational and Physical Therapists

Political Sciences

Political Sciences majors study government and the nature of politics. They analyze the operations of different forms of government, and attempt to find theoretical and practical solutions to political problems. Students learn about the origins, historical development, and social functions of government. They study how electoral, legislative, judicial, and administrative structures and processes vary from one country and one age to another; how and why govern-

ments change, fail, and engage in wars. They study the behavior of public officials and other citizens involved in politics.

Interests: Public policy issues such as health care and environmental protection; politicians and public figures, justice, good and bad government, law, criminal justice, the legal system

Skills and abilities: Reading critically, thinking analytically, oral and written expression and comprehension, understanding graphic material

Occupations related to this major: Political Scientists, Legislators, Sociologists, Historians, Anthropologists, and Political Science Teachers

Psychology

Psychology majors learn to collect and interpret scientific data relating to human behavior to understand people and explain their actions. They learn to interview patients, give diagnostic tests, and offer therapy to help people make behavioral adjustments. Students study human and animal behavior and explore the processes involved in normal and abnormal thoughts, feelings, and actions. They increase their understanding of behavior while learning psychological facts, methods, principles, and generalizations about individuals and groups.

Interests: Working with people, scientific method, human and animal behavior

Skills and abilities: Critical thinking, oral and written expression and comprehension, inductive reasoning

Occupations related to this major: Developmental Psychologists, Experimental Psychologists, Educational Psychologists, Social Psychologists, Clinical Psychologists, and Counseling Psychologists

Public Administration

Public Administration majors may study in five areas of specialization: personnel, management, public relations, finance, and planning. They learn to establish government policy, and develop laws, rules and regulations. These studies will prepare students to find positions managing public agencies. Students deal with the operations of all forms and levels of government. Students learn about the many skills and challenges associated with implementing public policy in government and in nonprofit organizations.

Interests: Public and community service, organizing people, leadership, working with people from different backgrounds

Skills and abilities: Leadership, organizational ability, problem solving, oral and written expression and comprehension, inductive reasoning

Occupations related to this major: Government Service Executives, City Managers, Management Analysts, Government Affairs Specialists, and Legislators

Social Studies Education

Social Studies Education majors learn to teach courses pertaining to human society and its characteristic elements. They learn to teach subjects such as psychology, economics, history, political science, and sociology. They learn to teach students in middle school and high school courses in history, citizenship, and other social sciences.

Interests: Serving people, working with people, history, social sciences

Skills and abilities: Speaking, organizing working with people, oral and written expression and comprehension, speech clarity

Occupations related to this major: Middle School Teachers, High School Teachers, Postsecondary School Teachers, Historians, Sociologists, and Psychologists

Social Work

Social Work majors study many types of social issues and needs. They learn to aid families with physical, mental, or social problems, such as poverty, unemployment, illness, broken homes, various disabilities, antisocial behavior, and inadequate housing. Students acquire the knowledge and skills to assist individuals, families, groups, and communities in preventing and alleviating the problems of a modern, rapidly changing society. They learn to help others and to modify harmful social conditions, promote social and economic well being, and increase opportunities for all people to live with dignity and freedom.

Interests: Helping those in need, particularly children, the poor, minorities, the aged, the disabled, and women, enabling others to develop unique, positive responses and solutions to their problems

Skills and abilities: Objectivity, ability to listen, analytic ability, oral and written expression and comprehension, problem sensitivity

Occupations related to this major: Social Workers, Medical and Psychiatric Social Workers, Community Organization Social Workers, Residential Counselors, Probation and Correctional Treatment Specialists, and Human Services Workers

LOCATING OCCUPATIONAL INFORMATION RELATED TO YOUR MAJOR

Students may find occupations in a Field of Study in which they have a work interest. They may wish to conduct research to find specific information about an occupation. Good sources for occupational information are public libraries, high school and college career resource centers, One-Stop Career Centers, America's InfoNet (*www.acinet.org*) and O*Net (*www.online.onetcenter.org*), the occupational information Network.

Recommended books for occupations and college entry research:

Occupational Outlook Handbook, 2012–2022 Edition,
U.S. Bureau of Labor Statistics, Postal Square Building
2 Massachusetts Avenue, NE, Washington, DC 20212-0001
www.bls.gov

A Guide to the College Admission Process,
National Association for College Admissions Counseling,
1050 North Highland Street, Suite 400, Arlington, VA 22201
www.nacacnet.org

College Major Handbook, 3rd Edition, CFKR Career Materials, Inc.
11860 Kemper Road, # 7, Auburn, CA 95603
www.cfkr.com

Federal Student Aid Information Center,
An Office of the U.S. Department of Education, P.O. Box 84
Washington, DC 20044-0084
www.fafsa.ed.gov

CHOOSING A COLLEGE

A student's choice of institution may depend on individual needs and talents. A person's career goals, career plans, and choice of college major are very important criteria in choosing a college. A student's choice may be limited by financial or other considerations. However, if at all possible, students should give high priority to their career plans and choice of a college major when choosing a college that best matches their career plans. Students' choice of their college major may influence their final college choice.

Some majors are rare and specialized. Special attention must be given to those majors that are fairly rare and specialized. Students will be limited in the number of colleges from which to choose. There are more than 1800 four-year colleges in the United States; only 78 offer aerospace engineering; 42 offer landscape architecture; 81 offer astronomy; 24 offer petroleum engineering; 8 offer statistics; 8 offer business statistics; 26 offer oceanography; 59 offer pharmacy; and 115 offer occupational therapy majors. This is a partial listing. A student who chooses a specialized major may find it necessary to travel a distance to find a college offering that major. School career centers and public libraries may carry listings of colleges that offer the major of the student's choice.

The most widely offered baccalaureate-level majors are found in four-year colleges. No college, not even the largest university, offers every major; some offer relatively few. Students will want to attend a college that offers several of the majors they are considering. Students can keep their choice of major open by selecting a university or college that offers a wide range of majors. The most common majors are found in the Art, Business, Computer and Information Science, Education, Engineering, Health, Humanities, and the Social and Behavioral Science fields of study.

MAKING THE FINAL DECISION

Making important decisions and setting long-range goals is never an easy task. Making a decision on what to study in college for four or more years, and how this will fit into students' lifestyles and career goals is very important and very personal. With the soaring costs of education and the increasing complexity of the job market, students cannot afford the luxury of trial and error in preparing for a career that requires college training; entering college without a career or major in mind can add time and expense to the entire journey. Good decision-making calls for awareness of one's needs and the matching of those needs with a wide variety of alternate choices. It is to this end that sufficient information has been explored for making a final decision.

In making a final decision, students must take a broad view of the fourteen Fields of Study. They should look carefully at all career and major options within the fourteen fields. Students should not limit themselves to a career or major that has been recommended to them by family or friends. The final decision should be the student's, along with the responsibility to reach their goals. In the final analysis, students will have to look at themselves. As Plato once said, "Know thyself, and to thine own self be true."

- **Assess work interests.** Identify work-related interests. Discover the type of work activities and occupations that match work interests. Identify and learn about the most relevant broad interest areas. Use interest results to explore the world of work.
- **Assess work values.** Pinpoint what is important in a job. Identify occupations that provide satisfaction based on the similarity among work values, conditions of work, and the characteristics of an occupation.
- **Assess work abilities.** Identify user ability strength, parts of work that the user likes to do, parts of work that the user finds important, and training needs of the user.

The more students know about their interests, work values, abilities, and career goals, the better their decisions will be. In the final analysis, good decision-making by students is based on knowing oneself and being flexible enough to sense whether they are on the right track, and to alter decisions when they are not in their best interest. No matter what major is chosen, students must keep in ming that intellectual flexibility is the skill that enables them to work productively when the knowledge they have mastered is challenged or replaced by new ideas.

We wish all students well in their college studies and in the career path that they have chosen.

Robert Kauk and Francis Ferry

Portions of the *College Major Handbook* and *Choosing a Major* have been adapted with the authors' permission. © CFKR Career Materials, *www.cfkr.com*

Occupational information was gathered from O*Net, U.S. Department of Labor.

INDEX OF COLLEGE MAJORS

This section of *Profiles of American Colleges* will help you quickly determine which schools offer the major in which you are interested, the in-state tuition, room and board costs, and the Selector Rating. The colleges are listed alphabetically and the first column indicates the state where each is located. These data reflect the 2014-2015 academic year. You will be able to compare schools offering those majors that interest you the most and see what their in-state costs and Selector Ratings are, before reading the Profiles in the main section of the book (see page 249 for Selector Rating details). You may also discover some new schools or majors that interset you.

School	ST	$IS	SR

(BIOLOGICAL) PRE-HEALTH STUDIES

School	ST	$IS	SR
Bethel College	IN	31,560	C
Elmhurst College	IL	43,336	C
John Carroll Univ	OH	46,300	C+
Oswego / SUNY	NY	20,009	VC
Shippensburg Univ of Pennsylvania	PA	20,934	C
Univ of Arkansas at Little Rock	AR	17,609	LC
Urbana Univ	OH	30,820	C

(EDUCATION) CHILDHOOD EDUCATION

School	ST	$IS	SR
Aquinas College	MI	33,060	C
Bethel College	IN	31,560	C
Bloomfield College	NJ	37,850	LC
Campbell Univ	NC	37,570	VC
Canisius Univ	NY	44,900	C
CUNY/Brooklyn College	NY	5,884	C
Dordt College	IA	34,160	C+
Hofstra Univ	NY	51,810	VC+
Houghton College	NY	36,808	C+
Iona College	NY	44,028	C
Kennesaw State Univ	GA		C
Marshall Univ	WV	14,820	C
Mass College of Liberal Arts	MA	18,613	C
Missouri Southern State Univ	MO	12,061	C
Mount Aloysius College	PA	29,976	C
New York Univ	NY	61,470	MC
Niagara Univ	NY	41,010	C
Nyack College	NY	33,250	C
Oswego / SUNY	NY	20,009	VC
Point Park Univ	PA	36,390	C
Taylor Univ	IN	37,821	VC+
The Univ of N Car at Pembroke	NC	13,388	LC
Univ of Arkansas at Fayetteville	AR	18,352	C+
Univ of Nebr - Lincoln	NE	18,031	VC
Univ of Texas at San Antonio	TX	18,372	C
Wright State Univ	OH	16,983	C
Youngstown State Univ	OH	16,732	C

(SOCIAL SCIENCE) GLOBAL STUDIES

School	ST	$IS	SR
Aquinas College	MI	33,060	C
Arizona State Univ, at the West Campus	AZ	19,251	C
Bryant Univ	RI	49,179	VC
Carroll Univ	WI	38,100	C
Colby College	ME	57,510	MC
Hofstra Univ	NY	51,810	VC+
Lehigh Univ	PA	56,770	MC
Missouri State Univ	MO	13,996	C+
New York Univ	NY	61,470	MC
St. Mary's Univ of Minn	MN	38,280	C
Samford Univ	AL	39,040	C
Tulane Univ	LA	60,861	MC
Univ of Calif at Irvine	CA	25,961	VC
Univ of Central Florida	FL	15,668	VC+
Univ of Nebr - Lincoln	NE	18,031	VC
Univ of New Haven	CT	48,940	C
Warren Wilson College	NC	40,132	VC
Wilson College	PA	35,080	C
Winona State Univ	MN	16,640	C

ACCOUNTING

School	ST	$IS	SR
Abilene Christian Univ	TX	38,400	C+
Adams State Univ	CO	13,358	LC
Adelphi Univ	NY	44,670	VC
Adrian College	MI	42,400	C
Alabama A&M Univ	AL	10,084	C
Alabama State Univ	AL	14,142	NC
Albany State Univ	GA	8,500	C
Albertus Magnus College	CT	37,382	LC
Albion College	MI	46,010	C
Albright College	PA	46,660	C
Alcorn State Univ	MS	9,500	C
Alderson Broaddus Univ	WV	28,656	C
Alfred Univ	NY	41,770	C
Alma College	MI	44,075	C
Alvernia Univ	PA	39,250	LC
Alverno College	WI	31,434	LC

School	ST	$IS	SR
American International College	MA	36,100	LC
Anderson Univ	IN	36,100	C
Andrews Univ	MI	28,030	C+
Angelo State Univ	TX	15,049	NC
Appalachian State Univ	NC	12,919	VC
Aquinas College	MI	33,060	C
Arcadia Univ	PA	33,570	C+
Arizona State Univ, at the Tempe Campus	AZ	20,137	C+
Arizona State Univ, at the West Campus	AZ	19,251	C
Arkansas Baptist College	AR	15,750	NC
Arkansas State Univ	AR	15,470	C
Arkansas Tech Univ	AR	13,982	LC
Asbury Univ	KY	32,038	VC
Ashford Univ	CA	10,480	C
Ashland Univ	OH	25,000	C
Assumption College	MA	47,122	C+
Atlantic Union College	MA	24,600	C
Auburn Univ	AL	22,378	VC+
Auburn Univ at Montgomery	AL	14,470	LC
Augsburg College	MN	35,142	C
Augustana College	IL	43,398	VC
Augustana College	SD	36,500	VC
Aurora Univ	IL	33,228	C
Avila Univ	MO	26,900	C
Azusa Pacific Univ	CA	42,086	C
Baker College of Flint	MI	7,800	NC
Baker Univ	KS	33,350	C+
Baldwin Wallace Univ	OH	38,318	C
Ball State Univ	IN	17,850	C
Barry Univ	FL	38,190	C
Barton College	NC	27,660	LC
Baylor Univ	TX	50,329	HC
Belhaven Univ	MS	27,170	C
Bellarmine Univ	KY	42,950	VC
Bellevue Univ	NE	4,600	NC
Belmont Abbey College	NC	37,716	C
Belmont Univ	TN	39,190	VC+
Bemidji State Univ	MN	13,500	VC
Benedict College	SC	20,454	NC
Benedictine College	KS	29,180	VC
Benedictine Univ	IL	37,820	C
Bennett College for Women	NC	21,970	LC
Bentley Univ	MA	56,454	HC+
Berkeley College of New York City	NY	18,300	LC
Berkeley College/New Jersey	NJ	27,300	LC
Berkeley College/Westchester Campus	NY	28,500	LC
Berry College	GA	39,254	VC
Bethany College	KS	30,605	NC
Bethany College	WV	35,282	LC
Bethel College	IN	31,560	C
Bethel Univ	MN	34,940	VC
Bethune-Cookman Univ	FL	22,958	C
Binghamton Univ/The SUNY	NY	21,648	HC+
Biola Univ	CA	40,320	C+
Birmingham-Southern College	AL	44,168	VC+
Black Hills State Univ	SD	13,947	C
Blackburn College	IL	21,350	C
Bloomfield College	NJ	37,850	LC
Bloomsburg Univ of Pennsylvania	PA	13,598	C
Bluefield State College	WV	3,140	LC
Bluffton Univ	OH	38,948	C
Boise State Univ	ID	13,469	LC
Boston College	MA	60,622	MC
Bowling Green State Univ	OH	18,970	C
Bradley Univ	IL	31,874	VC
Brenau Univ - Women's College	GA	26,650	LC
Brescia Univ	KY	26,140	VC+
Brewton-Parker College	GA	33,388	C
Briar Cliff Univ	IA	29,514	C
Bridgewater State Univ	MA	18,752	C
Brigham Young Univ	UT	12,100	HC
Brigham Young Univ/Hawaii	HI	10,686	VC
Bryant Univ	RI	49,179	VC
Bucknell Univ	PA	60,140	MC
Buena Vista Univ	IA	39,188	C
Butler Univ	IN	47,572	VC+
Cabrini College	PA	40,859	LC
Cairn Univ	PA	33,270	C
Caldwell College	NJ	35,602	NC
Calif Baptist Univ	CA	38,792	C
Calif Lutheran Univ	CA	49,540	C+
Cal State, East Bay	CA	16,549	C

School	ST	$IS	SR
Cal State, Fresno	CA	17,405	C
Cal State, Long Beach	CA	17,502	C+
Cal State, Northridge	CA	28,690	LC
Cal State, Sacramento	CA	16,200	C
Cal State, San Bernardino	CA	12,000	C
Calif Univ of Pennsylvania	PA	14,217	C
Calumet College of St. Joseph	IN	15,000	C
Calvin College	MI	39,120	VC
Cameron Univ	OK	10,004	LC
Campbell Univ	NC	37,570	VC
Campbellsville Univ	KY	27,720	C
Canisius College	NY	44,900	C
Capital Univ	OH	41,050	VC
Cardinal Stritch Univ	WI	24,054	C
Caribbean Univ	PR	10,375	
Carlow Univ	PA	30,272	C
Carroll College	MT	28,000	C
Carroll Univ	WI	38,100	C
Carson-Newman Univ	TN	29,058	C+
Carthage College	WI	33,000	C
Case Western Reserve Univ	OH	56,534	MC
Catawba College	NC	37,240	LC
Cedar Crest College	PA	43,240	C
Cedarville Univ	OH	32,860	VC
Centenary College	NJ	38,618	C
Central College	IA	42,104	C+
Central Conn State Univ	CT	19,749	C
Central Methodist Univ	MO	28,240	VC
Central State Univ	OH	9,010	C
Central Univ of Bayamon	PR	3,350	
Central Washington Univ	WA	11,730	C
Chaminade Univ of Honolulu	HI	31,664	LC
Champlain College	VT	46,650	VC+
Chancellor Univ	OH	11,000	C
Chapman Univ	CA	58,347	VC+
Chatham Univ	PA	43,797	C
Chestnut Hill College	PA	42,110	LC
Cheyney Univ of Pennsylvania	PA	20,372	LC
Chicago State Univ	IL	5,482	C
Christian Brothers Univ	TN	31,670	HC
Christopher Newport Univ	VA	21,960	VC
CUNY/Baruch College	NY		HC
CUNY/Brooklyn College	NY	5,884	C+
City Univ of Seattle	WA	14,880	NC
Claremont McKenna College	CA	62,215	MC
Clarion Univ of Pennsylvania	PA	17,370	LC
Clark Atlanta Univ	GA	30,006	LC
Clarke Univ	IA	37,600	C
Clarkson Univ	NY	57,330	HC
Clayton State Univ	GA	12,000	LC
Clearwater Christian College	FL	23,720	C
Clemson Univ	SC	19,136	HC
Cleveland State Univ	OH	21,776	C
Coastal Carolina Univ	SC	18,580	C
Coe College	IA	45,550	VC
Colby-Sawyer College	NH	50,790	C
College of Charleston	SC	22,145	VC
College of Mount St. Joseph	OH	33,880	C
College of New Jersey	NJ	25,376	VC
College of St. Benedict	MN	49,359	VC
College of St. Scholastica	MN	41,440	C
College of St Joseph	VT	30,600	LC
College of Staten Island/The City of New Yok	NY	16,778	NC
College of the Holy Cross	MA	58,042	MC
College of the Ozarks	MO		VC
College of William & Mary	VA	28,000	MC
Colo Christian Univ	CO	27,500	VC
Colo Mesa Univ	CO	17,690	LC
Colo State Univ-Pueblo	CO	16,183	C
Columbia College	MO	24,578	C
Columbia College	SC	27,882	C
Columbus State Univ	GA	13,176	C
Concord Univ	WV	13,102	C
Concordia College - Moorhead	MN	39,974	VC
Concordia College - New York	NY	39,035	LC
Concordia Univ Nebr	NE	26,000	VC
Concordia Univ St. Paul	MN	28,250	C
Concordia Univ Texas	TX	23,640	C
Concordia Univ Wisc	WI	28,980	C
Concordia Univ, River Forest	IL	26,300	C
Converse College	SC	37,130	C
Coppin State Univ	MD	16,227	VC
Corban Univ	OR	37,380	C+
Cornerstone Univ and Grand Rapids Theological Seminary	MI	33,338	C

School	ST	$IS	SR
Creighton Univ	NE	45,356	VC
Culver-Stockton College	MO	30,900	C
Cumberland Univ	TN	21,220	C
Daemen College	NY	34,770	C
Dakota Wesleyan Univ	SD	23,000	C
Dallas Baptist Univ	TX	30,580	VC
Davenport Univ	MI	21,002	C
Davis & Elkins College	WV	33,742	C
De Sales Univ	PA	43,970	C
Defiance College	OH	30,645	C
Delaware State Univ	DE	16,722	LC
Delaware Valley College	PA	29,944	C
Delta State Univ	MS	12,292	LC
DePaul Univ	IL	47,623	VC
Dickinson State Univ	ND	11,900	VC
Dillard Univ	LA	20,940	VC
Doane College	NE	35,230	C
Dominican College	NY	31,270	LC
Dominican Univ	IL	37,628	C
Dordt College	IA	34,160	C+
Dowling College	NY	25,000	LC
Drake Univ	IA	41,516	VC+
Drexel Univ	PA	61,418	VC+
Drury Univ	MO	31,909	VC
Duquesne Univ	PA	43,720	VC
D'Youville College	NY	29,850	C
East Carolina Univ	NC	14,169	C
East Central Univ	OK	10,223	LC
East Tenn State Univ	TN	9,000	C
Eastern Conn State Univ	CT	20,584	C
Eastern Illinois Univ	IL	20,466	C
Eastern Kentucky Univ	KY	11,161	C
Eastern Mennonite Univ	VA	40,660	C
Eastern Mich Univ	MI	18,604	C
Eastern Nazarene College	MA	30,000	C
Eastern New Mexico Univ	NM	10,682	C
Eastern Oregon Univ	OR	10,400	C
Eastern Univ	PA	37,704	C
Eastern Washington Univ	WA		C
Edgewood College	WI	33,294	C
Edward Waters College	FL	19,607	LC
Elizabeth City State Univ	NC	11,638	C
Elizabethtown College	PA	49,740	VC
Elizabethtown College School of Continuing and Professional Studies	PA		VC
Elmhurst College	IL	43,336	C
Elmira College	NY	49,950	C+
Elms College	MA	33,900	VC
Elon Univ	NC	41,914	VC+
Emmanuel College	MA	47,985	VC
Emory Univ	GA	56,368	MC
Emporia State Univ	KS	12,897	C
Endicott College	MA	43,228	VC+
Eureka College	IL	19,280	C
Evangel Univ	MO	23,090	C
Excelsior College	NY	5,580	SP
Fairfield Univ	CT	56,960	VC
Fairleigh Dickinson Univ/College at Florham	NJ	42,142	C
Fairleigh Dickinson Univ/Metropolitan Campus	NJ	40,254	C
Fairmont State Univ	WV	12,098	LC
Faulkner Univ	AL	25,720	LC
Fayetteville State Univ	NC	10,816	C
Felician College	NJ	41,640	LC
Ferris State Univ	MI	20,047	C
Ferrum College	VA	27,740	LC
Fitchburg State Univ	MA	18,173	C
Flagler College	FL	25,180	C
Florida A&M Univ	FL	14,935	LC
Florida Atlantic Univ	FL	17,339	C
Florida Gulf Coast Univ	FL		C
Florida Inst of Technology	FL	48,290	VC
Florida International Univ	FL	17,747	C+
Florida Memorial Univ	FL	20,888	LC
Florida Southern College	FL	40,150	C+
Florida State Univ	FL	16,715	VC
Fontbonne Univ	MO	31,384	C
Fordham Univ	NY	61,588	HC+
Fort Hays State Univ	KS	11,354	C
Fort Lewis College	CO	15,513	C
Fort Valley State Univ	GA	11,200	VC
Framingham State Univ	MA	18,854	C
Francis Marion Univ	SC	16,464	LC
Franciscan Univ of Steubenville	OH	27,320	VC
Franklin College	IN	36,585	C
Franklin Pierce Univ	NH	41,598	C
Franklin Univ	OH	20,985	SP

ST = STATE $IS = IN-STATE COSTS   SR = SELECTOR RATING

School	ST	$IS	SR
Freed-Hardeman Univ	TN	19,697	VC
Fresno Pacific Univ	CA	32,136	C
Friends Univ	KS	29,100	C
Frostburg State Univ	MD	15,264	LC
Furman Univ	SC	54,006	HC
Gallaudet Univ	DC	25,380	SP
Gannon Univ	PA	39,608	C
Gardner-Webb Univ	NC	34,375	C+
Geneva College	PA	27,280	C
George Fox Univ	OR	40,750	C+
George Mason Univ	VA	15,724	VC
George Washington Univ	DC	57,108	MC
Georgetown College	KY	41,440	C+
Georgetown Univ	DC	52,910	MC
Georgia College and State Univ	GA	18,900	C+
Georgia Regents Univ	GA		
Georgia Southern Univ	GA	16,942	C
Georgia Southwestern State Univ	GA	13,246	C
Georgia State Univ	GA	15,582	VC
Georgian Court Univ	NJ	41,594	LC
Glenville State College	WV	11,348	NC
Golden Gate Univ	CA	17,000	C
Goldey-Beacom College	DE	27,943	C
Gonzaga Univ	WA	46,441	HC
Gordon College	MA	44,320	C
Goshen College	IN	35,900	VC
Grace College and Seminary	IN	28,800	VC
Graceland Univ	IA	28,020	C
Grambling State Univ	LA	13,384	LC
Grand Canyon Univ	AZ	24,540	VC
Grand Valley State Univ	MI	17,998	C
Grand View Univ	IA	31,050	C
Greensboro College	NC	28,740	LC
Greenville College	IL	27,012	C
Grove City College	PA	24,022	VC
Guilford College	NC	42,800	C
Gustavus Adolphus College	MN	48,170	HC
Gwynedd-Mercy College	PA	33,560	C
Hamline Univ	MN	45,678	VC
Hampton Univ	VA	28,528	C
Hannibal-LaGrange Univ	MO	24,490	C
Harding Univ	AR	23,556	C
Hardin-Simmons Univ	TX	23,560	C+
Harris-Stowe State Univ	MO	14,360	NC
Hartwick College	NY	51,270	C
Hastings College	NE	27,782	C+
Hawaii Pacific Univ	HI	34,360	VC
Heidelberg Univ	OH	34,100	C
Henderson State Univ	AR	14,584	C
Hendrix College	AR	50,202	VC+
Heritage Univ	WA	17,664	NC
High Point Univ	NC	39,800	C
Hilbert College	NY	28,550	C
Hillsdale College	MI	32,866	MC
Hiram College	OH	37,300	VC
Hodges Univ	FL	12,000	LC
Hofstra Univ	NY	51,810	VC+
Holy Family Univ	PA	40,030	LC
Hood College	MD	45,730	C
Hope College	MI	38,650	VC
Houghton College	NY	36,808	C+
Houston Baptist Univ	TX	36,450	C
Howard Payne Univ	TX	17,115	C
Howard Univ	DC	13,646	C
Humphreys College	CA	17,000	NC
Hunter Univ	NY	14,429	VC
Huntingdon College	AL	33,100	C
Huntington Univ	IN	32,220	C+
Husson Univ	ME	24,194	LC
Idaho State Univ	ID	12,307	C
Illinois College	IL	25,770	VC
Illinois State Univ	IL	23,110	VC
Illinois Wesleyan Univ	IL	48,452	HC
Immaculata Univ	PA	43,000	C
Indiana Inst of Technology	IN	34,240	LC
Indiana State Univ	IN	16,000	C
Indiana Univ Bloomington	IN	19,801	VC
Indiana Univ Kokomo	IN	6,811	C
Indiana Univ Northwest	IN	6,854	LC
Indiana Univ of Pennsylvania	PA	20,846	LC
Indiana Univ-Purdue Univ Fort Wayne	IN	15,521	C
Indiana Univ-Purdue Univ Indianapolis	IN	17,611	C
Indiana Wesleyan Univ	IN	31,815	VC
Inter-American Univ of PR/ Aguadilla Campus	PR	5,578	
Inter-American Univ of PR/ Arecibo Campus	PR	3,350	
Inter-American Univ of PR/ Barranquitas	PR	3,350	
Inter-American Univ of PR/ Bayamon Univ College	PR	4,428	
Inter-American Univ of PR/ Fajardo Campus	PR	4,200	
Inter-American Univ of PR/ Metropolitan Campus	PR	4,320	
Inter-American Univ of PR/ Ponce	PR		
Inter-American Univ of PR/ San Germán	PR	6,720	
Iona College	NY	44,028	C
Iowa State Univ	IA	16,403	C
Iowa Wesleyan College	IA	30,850	LC

School	ST	$IS	SR
Ithaca College	NY	53,864	HC
Jackson State Univ	MS	13,512	LC
Jacksonville State Univ	AL	12,480	LC
Jacksonville Univ	FL	37,780	C
James Madison Univ	VA	18,049	VC
John Brown Univ	AR	32,056	VC+
John Carroll Univ	OH	46,300	C+
Johnson & Wales Univ/ Charlotte Campus	NC	29,576	C
Johnson & Wales Univ/ Denver Campus	CO	29,576	C
Johnson & Wales Univ/North Miami Campus	FL		C
Johnson & Wales Univ/ Providence Campus	RI	29,576	C
Judson Univ	IL	25,130	C
Juniata College	PA	49,340	VC
Kansas State Univ	KS	15,497	VC
Kansas Wesleyan Univ	KS	32,000	C
Kean Univ	NJ	23,444	C
Kennesaw State Univ	GA		C
Kent State Univ	OH	19,920	C
Kentucky Wesleyan College	KY	27,440	C
Keuka College	NY	30,300	C
Keystone College	PA	28,680	LC
King Univ	TN	33,140	C
King's College	PA	43,502	C
Kutztown Univ of Pennsylvania	PA	16,909	LC
La Roche College	PA	35,824	LC
La Salle Univ	PA	50,270	C
La Sierra Univ	CA	35,694	VC
LaGrange College	GA	37,670	C
Lake Erie College	OH	37,266	C
Lake Superior State Univ	MI	18,121	C
Lakeland College	WI	22,990	C
Lamar Univ	TX	6,820	LC
Langston Univ	OK	3,000	C
Lasell College	MA	43,750	LC
Le Moyne College	NY	43,470	C
Lebanon Valley College	PA	38,570	C
Lee Univ	TN	18,690	C+
Lehigh Univ	PA	56,770	MC
Lehman College/The CUNY	NY	5,778	LC
LeMoyne-Owen College	TN	13,100	C
Lenoir-Rhyne College	NC	35,984	C
LeTourneau Univ	TX	36,210	VC
Lewis Univ	IL	23,050	C
Liberty Univ	VA	19,101	C
Limestone College	SC	30,800	C
Lincoln Memorial Univ	TN	18,144	C
Lincoln Univ	MO	12,904	NC
Lindenwood Univ	MO	20,750	C
Lindsey Wilson College	KY	31,220	C
Linfield College-McMinnville Campus	OR	47,676	C
Lipscomb Univ	TN	37,490	VC
LIU Brooklyn	NY	47,182	LC
LIU Post	NY	47,660	C
Louisiana State Univ	LA	18,677	C+
Louisiana State Univ in Shreveport	LA	5,606	C
Louisiana Tech Univ	LA	11,302	C
Lourdes Univ	OH	26,055	LC
Loyola Marymount Univ	CA	54,649	VC+
Loyola Univ Chicago	IL	51,646	VC+
Loyola Univ Maryland	MD	56,880	VC+
Loyola Univ New Orleans	LA	46,581	VC
Lubbock Christian Univ	TX	26,308	C
Luther College	IA	45,720	C+
Lycoming College	PA	45,379	C
Lynchburg College	VA	42,645	C
Lyndon State College	VT	14,233	C
Lyon College	AR	32,090	C+
MacMurray College	IL	20,755	C
Madonna Univ	MI	24,540	VC
Malone Univ	OH	35,364	C
Manchester Univ	IN	35,070	C
Manhattan College	NY	49,588	C+
Manhattanville College	NY	50,740	VC
Marian Univ	IN	38,540	C
Marian Univ	WI	32,420	LC
Marietta College	OH	42,135	C+
Marist College	NY	35,500	C
Marquette Univ	WI	46,930	VC+
Mars Hill College	NC	22,950	LC
Marshall Univ	WV	14,820	C
Martin Univ	IN	11,000	SP
Marymount Manhattan College	NY	40,118	VC
Maryville Univ of St. Louis	MO	35,856	VC
Marywood Univ	PA	45,595	C
Mass College of Liberal Arts	MA	18,613	C
McKendree Univ	IL	29,920	C+
McMurry Univ	TX	25,962	LC
McNeese State Univ	LA	2,649	C
Megar Evers College/The CUNY	NY	4,920	NC
Menlo College	CA	49,002	C
Mercer Univ	GA	44,201	VC
Mercy College	NY	30,456	C
Mercyhurst Univ	PA	40,700	C
Meredith College	NC	31,420	C
Merrimack College	MA	44,215	C
Messiah College	PA	40,690	C+
Methodist Univ	NC	37,185	C

School	ST	$IS	SR
Metropolitan State Univ	MN	5,923	
Metropolitan State Univ of Denver	CO	4,835	LC
Miami Univ	OH	24,191	VC
Mich State Univ	MI	22,450	VC
Mich Tech Univ	MI	23,556	HC
MidAmerica Nazarene Univ	KS	28,000	C
Middle Tenn State Univ	TN	8,650	C
Midland Univ	NE	34,000	C
Midwestern State Univ	TX	9,722	C
Miles College	AL	11,164	NC
Millersville Univ of Pennsylvania	PA	21,648	C
Milligan College	TN	27,510	C
Millikin Univ	IL	38,940	C
Millsaps College	MS	43,888	VC+
Minn State Univ, Mankato	MN	15,616	C
Minn State Univ, Moorhead	MN	13,392	VC
Minot State Univ	ND	10,915	C
Misericordia Univ	PA	41,060	C
Miss College	MS	21,998	C
Miss State Univ	MS	14,750	C
Miss Univ for Women	MS	7,400	C
Miss Valley State Univ	MS	9,706	LC
Missouri Baptist Univ	MO	31,830	C
Missouri Southern State Univ	MO	12,061	C
Missouri State Univ	MO	13,996	C+
Missouri Valley College	MO	22,200	C
Missouri Western State Univ	MO	12,260	NC
Molloy College	NY	40,440	C
Monmouth College	IL	40,850	C
Monmouth Univ	NJ	44,108	C
Monroe College	NY	20,240	C
Montclair State Univ	NJ	22,614	C
Moravian College	PA	36,381	VC
Morehead State Univ	KY	10,900	C
Morgan State Univ	MD	14,500	C
Mount Aloysius College	PA	29,976	C
Mount Marty College	SD	29,638	C
Mount Mary Univ	WI	33,590	LC
Mount Mercy Univ	IA	35,320	C
Mount St. Mary College	NY	41,138	C
Mount St. Mary's Univ	MD	47,996	C
Mount Vernon Nazarene Univ	OH	29,590	C
Muhlenberg College	PA	52,837	HC
Murray State Univ	KY	15,304	C
Muskingum Univ	OH	30,502	C
National Univ	CA	14,730	SP
Nazareth College of Rochester	NY	43,028	C+
Nebr Wesleyan Univ	NE	29,774	C+
Neumann Univ	PA	31,078	C
New Jersey City Univ	NJ	21,456	LC
New Mexico Highlands Univ	NM	11,904	NC
New Mexico State Univ	NM	14,050	C
New York Univ	NY	61,470	MC
Newbury College	MA	43,280	LC
Newman Univ	KS	30,380	C+
Niagara Univ	NY	41,010	C
Nichols State Univ	LA	7,095	C
Nichols College	MA	37,240	LC
Norfolk State Univ	VA	10,531	LC
N Car Agricultural and Technical State Univ	NC	13,365	LC
N Car Central Univ	NC	9,000	C
N Car State Univ	NC	16,202	HC
N Car Wesleyan College	NC	29,440	C
North Central College	IL	38,343	VC
N Dak State Univ	ND		C
North Park Univ	IL	30,130	C
Northeastern Illinois Univ	IL	10,318	LC
Northeastern State Univ	OK	8,615	VC
Northeastern Univ	MA	55,296	MC
Northern Arizona Univ	AZ	19,010	C
Northern Illinois Univ	IL	19,768	C
Northern Kentucky Univ	KY	21,134	C
Northern Mich Univ	MI	18,278	C
Northern State Univ - Aberdeen	SD	14,505	C
Northwest Christian Univ	OR	27,399	C
Northwest Missouri State Univ	MO	17,347	C
Northwest Nazarene Univ	ID	34,000	C
Northwestern College	MN	24,000	C
Northwestern College of Iowa	IA	36,240	VC
Northwestern Okla State Univ	OK	7,275	NC
Northwestern State Univ of Louisiana	LA	14,368	C
Northwood Univ	FL	33,192	LC
Northwood Univ	MI	26,331	LC
Northwood Univ	TX	25,296	LC
Norwich Univ	VT	28,212	C
Notre Dame College	OH	34,942	NC
Notre Dame de Namur Univ	CA	44,236	LC
Notre Dame of Maryland Univ	MD	27,700	C
Nova Southeastern Univ	FL	37,280	VC
Nyack College	NY	33,250	C
Oakland City Univ	IN	24,500	NC
Oakland Univ	MI	19,391	C
Oakwood Univ	AL	25,529	NC
Oglethorpe Univ	GA	44,200	C+
Ohio Dominican Univ	OH	38,380	C+
Ohio Northern Univ	OH	42,075	VC
Ohio Univ	OH	21,080	C

School	ST	$IS	SR
Ohio Valley Univ	WV	17,752	C
Ohio Wesleyan Univ	OH	49,460	C+
Okla Baptist Univ	OK	28,202	C
Okla Christian Univ	OK	25,870	VC
Okla City Univ	OK	40,476	VC
Okla Panhandle State Univ	OK	8,996	C
Okla State Univ	OK	14,310	VC
Okla Wesleyan Univ	OK	21,300	C
Old Dominion Univ	VA	19,483	LC
Olivet College	MI	19,984	LC
Olivet Nazarene Univ	IL	29,990	C
Oral Roberts Univ	OK	31,734	C
Oregon State Univ	OR	20,273	VC
Oswego / SUNY	NY	20,009	VC
Ottawa Univ	KS	15,000	VC
Otterbein College	OH	32,214	C
Ouachita Baptist Univ	AR	30,220	VC
Our Lady of Holy Cross College	LA	8,090	C
Our Lady of the Lake Univ	TX	22,430	LC
Pace Univ	NY	53,367	C
Park Univ	MO	17,525	C
Paul Quinn College	TX	25,350	LC
Peirce College	PA	12,760	NC
Penn State Erie/The Behrend College	PA	16,256	C
Pennsylvania College of Technology	PA	26,286	NC
Pepperdine Univ	CA	55,372	HC+
Peru State College	NE	8,600	NC
Pfeiffer Univ	NC	33,700	LC
Philadelphia Univ	PA	44,160	C
Pittsburg State Univ	KS	12,032	C
Plymouth State Univ	NH	23,148	LC
Point Loma Nazarene Univ	CA	41,006	C+
Point Park Univ	PA	36,390	C
Pontifical Catholic Univ of PR	PR	7,310	
Portland State Univ	OR	18,672	C
Post Univ	CT	35,750	C
Prairie View A&M Univ	TX	15,205	LC
Providence College	RI	57,383	VC
Purdue Univ/Calumet	IN	14,336	C
Purdue Univ/West Lafayette	IN	20,024	HC
Queens College/The CUNY	NY	17,107	VC
Queens Univ of Charlotte	NC	39,543	C+
Quincy Univ	IL	34,980	LC
Quinnipiac Univ	CT	55,160	VC
Radford Univ	VA	17,766	C
Ramapo College of New Jersey	NJ	24,938	C
Randolph-Macon College	VA	49,869	C+
Regis Univ	CO	41,318	C
Rhode Island College	RI	17,694	LC
Richard Stockton College of New Jersey	NJ	20,000	C
Rider Univ	NJ	45,720	C
Robert Morris Univ	PA	37,864	C
Roberts Wesleyan College	NY	38,306	C+
Rochester College	MI	18,320	LC
Rochester Inst of Technology	NY	42,450	VC
Rockford College	IL	31,000	C
Rocky Mountain College	MT	32,242	C
Roger Williams Univ	RI	46,296	VC
Roosevelt Univ	IL	22,605	VC
Rosemont College	PA	42,350	C
Rowan Univ	NJ	24,022	VC+
Rutgers, The State Univ of New Jersey/Camden Campus	NJ	25,121	C
Rutgers, The State Univ of New Jersey/New Brunswick	NJ	25,562	VC
Rutgers, The State Univ of New Jersey/Newark Campus	NJ	258,806	C
Sacred Heart Univ	CT	49,264	VC
Saginaw Valley State Univ	MI	17,369	C
St. Anselm College	NH	49,376	VC
St. Augustine's Univ	NC	14,000	C
St. Francis Univ	PA	30,029	LC
St. John's Univ	MN	47,984	C
St. Joseph's College	IN	36,500	C
St. Joseph's Univ	PA	55,006	VC
St. Leo Univ	FL	30,340	C
St. Martin's Univ	WA	41,678	C
St. Mary-of-the-Woods College	IN	37,722	LC
St. Mary's College	IN	45,160	C+
St. Mary's College of Calif	CA	53,550	C
St. Mary's Univ	TX	33,854	C
St. Mary's Univ of Minn	MN	38,280	C
St. Michael's College	VT	49,975	VC
St. Peter's Univ	NJ	44,240	C
St. Vincent College	PA	40,244	C
St. Xavier Univ	IL	32,840	C
Salem College	NC	29,326	VC
Salem State Univ	MA	13,161	LC
Salisbury Univ	MD	19,180	VC
Salve Regina Univ	RI	48,550	VC
Sam Houston State Univ	TX	17,082	C
Samford Univ	AL	37,060	C
San Diego State Univ	CA	21,611	C+
San Francisco State Univ	CA	18,514	C
San Jose State Univ	CA	19,133	C
Savannah State Univ	GA	13,156	C
Schreiner Univ	TX	32,734	LC

ST = STATE $IS = IN-STATE COSTS   SR = SELECTOR RATING

School	ST	$IS	SR
Seattle Pacific Univ	WA	41,559	VC+
Seattle Univ	WA	49,035	VC+
Seton Hall Univ	NJ	45,902	C
Seton Hill Univ	PA	35,172	C
Shaw Univ	NC	15,488	C
Shepherd Univ	WV	15,875	C
Shippensburg Univ of Pennsylvania	PA	20,934	C
Shorter Univ	GA	30,650	LC
Siena College	NY	43,863	VC
Siena Heights Univ	MI	32,040	C
Silver Lake College	WI	22,600	LC
Simpson College	IA	36,086	C+
Simpson Univ	CA	28,900	C
Slippery Rock Univ of Pennsylvania	PA	10,360	C
S Car State Univ	SC	6,700	LC
Southeast Missouri State Univ	MO	15,370	LC
Southeastern Louisiana Univ	LA	13,325	C
Southeastern Okla State Univ	OK	7,966	LC
Southeastern Univ	FL	27,201	C
Southern Adventist Univ	TN	26,190	C
Southern Arkansas Univ	AR	14,316	C
Southern Conn State Univ	CT	18,033	LC
Southern Illinois Univ Carbondale	IL	21,942	C
Southern Illinois Univ Edwardsville	IL	17,532	C
Southern Methodist Univ	TX	60,585	MC
Southern Nazarene Univ	OK	24,354	C
Southern New Hampshire Univ	NH	38,100	C
Southern Oregon Univ	OR	17,874	C
Southern Polytechnic State Univ	GA	13,958	C
Southern Univ and A&M College	LA	9,761	LC
Southern Univ at New Orleans	LA	2,963	NC
Southwest Baptist Univ	MO	24,710	C
Southwest Minn State Univ	MN	14,000	C
Southwestern College	KS	29,270	C
Southwestern Okla State Univ	OK	9,160	C
Southwestern Univ	TX	45,660	VC
Spalding Univ	KY	32,287	LC
Spring Arbor Univ	MI	26,740	C
Spring Hill College	AL	44,164	VC
St. Ambrose Univ	IA	30,845	C
St. Bonaventure Univ	NY	41,575	C
St. Catherine Univ	MN	37,782	C+
St. Cloud State Univ	MN	10,600	C
St. Edward's Univ	TX	47,784	C
St. Francis College	NY	34,200	C
St. John Fisher College	NY	40,768	C+
St. John's Univ	NY	55,070	C+
St. Joseph's College, New York/Brooklyn Campus	NY	22,630	C
St. Joseph's College, New York/Suffolk Campus	NY	22,630	C
St. Norbert College	WI	41,478	VC
St. Thomas Aquinas College	NY	40,230	C
St. Thomas Univ	FL	32,310	LC
SUNY Polytechnic Inst	NY	19,690	C
SUNY/Empire State College	NY	6,315	SP
Stephen F. Austin State Univ	TX	14,668	C
Stephens College	MO	38,042	VC
Stetson Univ	FL	51,516	VC
Stevenson Univ	MD	41,470	C
Stonehill College	MA	46,780	HC
Suffolk Univ	MA	47,298	C
Sul Ross State Univ	TX	13,410	LC
SUNY College at Geneseo	NY	18,670	HC
SUNY College at Old Westbury	NY	16,324	C
SUNY Fredonia/The SUNY at Fredonia	NY	19,840	VC
SUNY New Paltz	NY	14,348	C
SUNY Oneonta / SUNY	NY	16,919	C+
SUNY Plattsburgh / SUNY	NY	18,083	C
Susquehanna Univ	PA	51,150	C
Syracuse Univ	NY	56,346	VC
Tabor College	KS	29,010	C
Talladega College	AL	17,996	C
Tarleton State Univ	TX	13,489	LC
Taylor Univ	IN	37,821	VC+
Temple Univ	PA	24,392	VC
Tenn State Univ	TN	9,048	C
Tenn Tech Univ	TN	11,310	C
Tenn Wesleyan College	TN	21,250	C
Texas A&M Univ	TX	19,207	VC
Texas A&M Univ at Commerce	TX	10,496	C
Texas A&M Univ at Corpus Christi	TX	11,544	LC
Texas A&M Univ at Kingsville	TX	7,500	LC
Texas Christian Univ	TX	49,980	HC
Texas Lutheran Univ	TX	36,040	C
Texas Southern Univ	TX	18,212	LC
Texas State Univ	TX	17,128	C
Texas Wesleyan Univ	TX	31,382	C
Texas Woman's Univ	TX	13,633	LC
The Catholic Univ of America	DC	52,852	VC
The College of Idaho	ID	31,277	C+
The College of St. Rose	NY	26,750	C

School	ST	$IS	SR
The Lincoln Univ	PA	15,154	LC
Ohio State Univ-Columbus Campus	OH	19,887	HC+
The Pennsylvania State Univ - Univ Park	PA	28,022	VC+
The SUNY/College at Brockport	NY	19,002	C
The Univ of Memphis	TN	15,094	C
The Univ of N Car at Greensboro	NC	12,848	C
The Univ of N Car at Pembroke	NC	13,388	LC
The Univ of Okla	OK	18,621	VC
The Univ of Utah	UT	16,463	VC
The Univ of Virginia's College at Wise	VA	11,076	C
Thiel College	PA	38,728	LC
Thomas College	ME	33,560	LC
Thomas Edison State College	NJ	5,700	SP
Thomas More College	KY	34,760	C
Tiffin Univ	OH	30,273	LC
Touro College	NY	27,959	VC
Towson Univ	MD	16,000	VC
Transylvania Univ	KY	42,660	VC+
Trevecca Nazarene Univ	TN	31,186	C
Trine Univ	IN	39,400	HC+
Trinity Christian College	IL	28,869	C
Trinity International Univ	IL	31,070	VC
Troy Univ	AL	10,650	C
Truman State Univ	MO	15,541	HC
Tulane Univ	LA	60,861	MC
Tuskegee Univ	AL	26,750	C
Union College	KY	29,955	C
Union College	NE	23,270	C
Union Univ	TN	28,260	VC
Universidad de Puerto/Arecibo	PR	7,227	
Universidad del Turabo	PR	4,110	
Universidad Metropolitana	PR	3,500	
Univ at Albany / SUNY	NY	18,674	VC
Univ of Akron	OH	20,436	C
Univ of Alabama at Birmingham	AL	18,484	C+
Univ of Alabama at Tuscaloosa	AL	17,164	C+
Univ of Alabama in Huntsville	AL	17,591	VC+
Univ of Alaska Anchorage	AK	16,673	NC
Univ of Alaska Fairbanks	AK	15,130	C
Univ of Alaska Southeast	AK	11,493	C
Univ of Arizona	AZ	20,657	C
Univ of Arkansas at Fayetteville	AR	18,352	C+
Univ of Arkansas at Little Rock	AR	17,609	LC
Univ of Arkansas at Monticello	AR	12,076	NC
Univ of Arkansas at Pine Bluff	AR	13,378	C
Univ of Bridgeport	CT	39,030	LC
Univ of Calif at Santa Barbara	CA	27,551	HC
Univ of Central Arkansas	AR	13,667	VC
Univ of Central Florida	FL	15,668	VC+
Univ of Central Missouri	MO	14,605	C
Univ of Central Okla	OK	12,293	C
Univ of Charleston	WV	32,300	C
Univ of Cincinnati	OH	21,506	VC
Univ of Colo Boulder	CO	22,605	VC+
Univ of Conn	CT	24,706	HC
Univ of Dayton	OH	49,070	VC
Univ of Delaware	DE	23,612	VC
Univ of Denver	CO	51,787	VC+
Univ of Detroit Mercy	MI	30,450	VC
Univ of Dubuque	IA	30,200	C
Univ of Evansville	IN	42,656	VC+
Univ of Findlay	OH	31,916	C
Univ of Florida	FL	15,943	HC
Univ of Georgia	GA	20,082	VC
Univ of Great Falls	MT	27,970	C
Univ of Hartford	CT	42,674	C
Univ of Hawaii at Manoa	HI	19,379	C
Univ of Houston	TX	19,796	VC
Univ of Houston-Downtown	TX	15,170	LC
Univ of Idaho	ID	14,558	C
Univ of Illinois at Chicago	IL	24,505	VC
Univ of Illinois at Urbana-Champaign	IL	26,450	HC
Univ of Indianapolis	IN	31,740	LC
Univ of Iowa	IA	17,693	VC
Univ of Jamestown	ND	24,738	C
Univ of Kansas	KS	17,603	C+
Univ of Kentucky	KY	19,868	C
Univ of La Verne	CA	47,010	C
Univ of Louisiana at Lafayette	LA	6,130	C
Univ of Louisiana at Monroe	LA	12,998	C
Univ of Louisville	KY	17,946	C
Univ of Maine	ME	19,902	C+
Univ of Maine at Augusta	ME	6,855	C
Univ of Maine at Machias	ME	10,523	C
Univ of Maine at Presque Isle	ME	15,011	LC
Univ of Mary	ND	16,714	C
Univ of Mary Hardin-Baylor	TX	31,950	C+
Univ of Maryland - College Park	MD	20,060	HC
Univ of Maryland/Eastern Shore	MD	14,000	VC

School	ST	$IS	SR
Univ of Maryland/Univ College	MD	6,168	SP
Univ of Mass Amherst	MA	24,215	VC+
Univ of Mass Dartmouth	MA	22,223	C
Univ of Miami	FL	57,034	MC
Univ of Mich/Dearborn	MI	9,885	VC
Univ of Mich-Flint	MI	17,547	C+
Univ of Minn Crookston	MN	17,834	C
Univ of Minn/Duluth	MN	19,806	C
Univ of Minn/Twin Cities	MN		HC
Univ of Missouri/Columbia	MO	18,201	MC
Univ of Missouri-Kansas City	MO	19,603	C
Univ of Missouri-St. Louis	MO		VC
Univ of Mobile	AL	28,935	VC
Univ of Montana	MT	14,105	C
Univ of Montevallo	AL	17,060	C
Univ of Mount Olive	NC	18,426	C
Univ of Mount Union	OH	35,130	C
Univ of Nebr - Lincoln	NE	18,031	VC
Univ of Nebr at Kearney	NE	14,855	LC
Univ of Nebr at Omaha	NE	12,700	C
Univ of Nevada, Las Vegas	NV	17,303	C
Univ of Nevada/Reno	NV	17,507	C
Univ of New Haven	CT	48,940	C
Univ of New Orleans	LA	9,224	C
Univ of North Alabama	AL	9,960	C
Univ of N Car at Asheville	NC	13,500	VC
Univ of N Car at Charlotte	NC	15,547	C
Univ of N Car at Wilmington	NC	13,572	VC
Univ of N Dak	ND	14,551	C
Univ of North Florida	FL	15,870	VC
Univ of North Georgia	GA	8,500	C
Univ of North Texas	TX	15,628	C
Univ of Northern Iowa	IA	15,795	C
Univ of Notre Dame	IN	57,117	MC
Univ of Oregon	OR	21,360	C+
Univ of Pennsylvania	PA	61,132	MC
Univ of Pittsburgh at Bradford	PA	21,802	C
Univ of Pittsburgh at Greensburg	PA	17,640	C
Univ of Pittsburgh at Johnstown	PA	20,862	LC
Univ of Pittsburgh at Pittsburgh	PA	28,572	HC+
Univ of Portland	OR	49,964	VC
Univ of PR Recinto de Rio Piedras	PR	5,750	
Univ of PR/Bayamon	PR	1,600	
Univ of PR/Cayey	PR	1,504	
Univ of PR/Humacao	PR	1,877	
Univ of PR/Mayaguez	PR	1,250	
Univ of Redlands	CA	40,500	VC
Univ of Rio Grande	OH	8,750	NC
Univ of St. Francis	IN	29,810	C
Univ of St. Joseph	CT	45,630	C
Univ of St. Mary	KS	28,400	C+
Univ of San Diego	CA	54,818	HC+
Univ of San Francisco	CA	54,770	VC
Univ of Scranton	PA	51,940	VC
Univ of Sioux Falls	SD	22,990	C
Univ of South Alabama	AL	13,510	C
Univ of S Car at Columbia	SC	19,725	VC+
Univ of S Car Upstate	SC	18,200	LC
Univ of S Dak	SD	15,111	C
Univ of South Florida/St. Petersburg	FL	12,769	C
Univ of South Florida/Tampa	FL	13,000	C
Univ of Southern Calif	CA	56,903	MC
Univ of Southern Indiana	IN	14,885	C
Univ of Southern Maine	ME	16,576	C
Univ of Southern Miss	MS	13,170	C
Univ of St. Francis	IL	37,560	C
Univ of St. Thomas - Houston	TX	37,690	C
Univ of Tampa	FL	35,160	VC
Univ of Tenn at Knoxville	TN	20,364	VC+
Univ of Tenn at Martin	TN	13,734	C
Univ of Texas - Pan American	TX	11,125	LC
Univ of Texas at Arlington	TX	10,908	LC
Univ of Texas at Austin	TX	44,074	HC
Univ of Texas at Dallas	TX	21,348	HC+
Univ of Texas at El Paso	TX	8,764	NC
Univ of Texas at San Antonio	TX	18,372	C
Univ of the Cumberlands	KY	27,500	C
Univ of the District of Columbia	DC	7,244	LC
Univ of the Ozarks	AR	31,440	C
Univ of the Sacred Heart	PR	5,590	
Univ of the Southwest	NM	15,000	C
Univ of Toledo	OH	18,464	C
Univ of Tulsa	OK	46,331	MC
Univ of Washington	WA	14,722	VC
Univ of West Alabama	AL	14,274	C
Univ of West Florida	FL	14,656	C
Univ of West Georgia	GA	15,488	LC
Univ of Wisc Whitewater	WI	13,314	C
Univ of Wisc/Eau Claire	WI	15,730	VC
Univ of Wisc/Green Bay	WI	19,074	C
Univ of Wisc/La Crosse	WI	9,304	VC
Univ of Wisc/Madison	WI	18,757	HC+
Univ of Wisc/Oshkosh	WI	10,426	LC
Univ of Wisc/Platteville	WI	14,564	C
Univ of Wisc/River Falls	WI	9,722	LC
Univ of Wisc/Stevens Point	WI	14,043	C

School	ST	$IS	SR
Univ of Wisc/Superior	WI	14,314	C
Univ of Wisc-Milwaukee	WI	18,436	C
Univ of Wyoming	WY	14,401	C+
Upper Iowa Univ	IA	30,426	NC
Ursuline College	OH	33,198	LC
Utah State Univ	UT	12,044	C
Utica College	NY	45,670	C
Valparaiso Univ	IN	44,940	VC+
Vanguard Univ of Southern Calif	CA	35,833	VC
Villanova Univ	PA	58,394	MC
Virginia Commonwealth Univ	VA	21,716	C
Virginia Polytechnic Inst and State Univ	VA	14,629	HC
Virginia State Univ	VA	11,318	C+
Virginia Union Univ	VA	18,432	C
Viterbo Univ	WI	30,070	C
Voorhees College	SC	18,126	C
Wagner College	NY	48,600	C+
Wake Forest Univ	NC	58,838	MC
Walsh Univ	OH	35,100	C
Warner Univ	FL	18,000	C
Wartburg College	IA	41,055	VC
Washburn Univ	KS	12,579	C
Washington Adventist Univ	MD	25,859	LC
Washington and Jefferson College	PA	51,948	VC
Washington and Lee Univ	VA	52,812	MC
Washington State Univ	WA	20,461	C
Washington Univ in St. Louis	MO	69,844	MC
Wayland Baptist Univ	TX	18,912	LC
Wayne State Univ	MI	22,063	C
Waynesburg Univ	PA	30,150	C
Webber International Univ	FL	30,147	C
Webster Univ	MO	35,100	C+
Wesley College	DE	31,115	C
West Chester Univ of Pennsylvania	PA	17,186	C
West Liberty Univ	WV	9,142	LC
West Texas A&M Univ	TX	13,478	LC
West Virginia State Univ	WV	8,378	NC
West Virginia Univ	WV	16,542	C+
West Virginia Univ Inst of Technology	WV	14,094	NC
West Virginia Wesleyan College	WV	26,880	C
Western Carolina Univ	NC	13,965	C
Western Conn State Univ	CT	18,327	LC
Western Illinois Univ	IL	20,732	C
Western Kentucky Univ	KY	11,000	LC
Western Mich Univ	MI	19,628	C
Western New England Univ	MA	46,154	C
Western New Mexico Univ	NM	8,500	LC
Western State Colo Univ	CO	16,924	C
Western Washington Univ	WA	18,519	VC
Westminster College	MO	31,720	VC
Westminster College	PA	31,290	C+
Westminster College	UT	37,708	C+
Wheeling Jesuit Univ	WV	33,500	C
Whitworth Univ	WA	47,734	VC
Wichita State Univ	KS	14,607	C+
Widener Univ	PA	52,418	C
Wilberforce Univ	OH	15,100	LC
Wilkes Univ	PA	44,070	C
William Jewell College	MO	31,000	VC+
William Paterson Univ of New Jersey	NJ	21,694	C
William Penn Univ	IA	26,000	C
William Woods Univ	MO	24,260	C
Wilmington College	OH	29,784	C
Wilmington Univ	DE	8,112	NC
Wilson College	PA	35,080	C
Wingate Univ	NC	34,990	C
Winona State Univ	MN	16,640	C
Winston-Salem State Univ	NC	9,418	LC
Wofford College	SC	45,795	VC
Woodbury Univ	CA	34,500	LC
Wright State Univ	OH	16,983	C
Xavier Univ	OH	44,980	VC
Xavier Univ of Louisiana	LA	25,300	C
Yeshiva Univ	NY	47,250	VC+
York College	NE	19,475	C
York College / The CUNY	NY	5,496	VC
York College of Pennsylvania	PA	26,590	C
Youngstown State Univ	OH	16,732	C

ACCOUNTING (FINANCE)

School	ST	$IS	SR
Murray State Univ	KY	15,304	C
Univ of Miss	MS	16,704	C+

ACCOUNTING (FINANCIAL PLANNING)

School	ST	$IS	SR
Murray State Univ	KY	15,304	C

ACCOUNTING (INFORMATION SYSTEMS)

School	ST	$IS	SR
Murray State Univ	KY	15,304	C

ACCOUNTING/CPA

School	ST	$IS	SR
Albion College	MI	46,010	C

School	ST	$IS	SR
Alma College	MI	44,075	C
Bloomfield College	NJ	37,850	LC
Calvin College	MI	39,120	VC
Campbell Univ	NC	37,570	VC
Hope College	MI	38,650	VC
New York Inst of Technology	NY	45,010	VC
Niagara Univ	NY	41,010	C
SUNY Fredonia/The SUNY at Fredonia	NY	19,840	VC
Thomas Edison State College	NJ	5,700	SP
Univ of Georgia	GA	20,082	VC
Univ of Tulsa	OK	46,331	MC

ACTING

School	ST	$IS	SR
Baldwin Wallace Univ	OH	38,318	C
Baylor Univ	TX	50,329	HC
Chapman Univ	CA	58,347	VC+
Elon Univ	NC	41,914	VC+
Faulkner Univ	AL	25,720	LC
Howard Univ	DC	13,646	C
Lipscomb Univ	TN	37,490	VC
Millikin Univ	IL	38,940	C
Oberlin College	OH	61,788	MC
Ohio Univ	OH	21,080	C
Okla City Univ	OK	40,476	VC
Old Dominion Univ	VA	19,483	LC
Pace Univ	NY	53,367	C
Shenandoah Univ	VA	39,916	C
St. Edward's Univ	TX	47,784	VC
SUNY Fredonia/The SUNY at Fredonia	NY	19,840	VC
Syracuse Univ	NY	56,346	VC
The Pennsylvania State Univ - Univ Park	PA	28,022	VC+
Webster Univ	MO	35,100	C+

ACTUARIAL MATHEMATICS

School	ST	$IS	SR
Albion College	MI	46,010	C
Asbury Univ	KY	32,038	VC
Binghamton Univ/The SUNY	NY	21,648	HC+
Bryant Univ	RI	49,179	VC
Lycoming College	PA	45,379	C
Univ of Conn	CT	24,706	HC
Univ of Pittsburgh at Pittsburgh	PA	28,572	HC+
Univ of Texas at San Antonio	TX	18,372	C
Wilson College	PA	35,080	C
Youngstown State Univ	OH	16,732	C

ACTUARIAL SCIENCE

School	ST	$IS	SR
Appalachian State Univ	NC	12,919	VC
Arizona State Univ, at the Tempe Campus	AZ	20,137	C+
Auburn Univ	AL	22,378	VC+
Aurora Univ	IL	33,228	C
Ball State Univ	IN	17,850	C
Bellarmine Univ	KY	42,950	VC
Bentley Univ	MA	56,454	HC+
Bradley Univ	IL	31,874	VC
Brigham Young Univ	UT	12,100	VC
Bryant Univ	RI	49,179	VC
Butler Univ	IN	47,572	VC+
Carroll Univ	WI	38,100	C
Central College	IA	42,104	C+
Central Washington Univ	WA	11,730	C
CUNY/Baruch College	NY		HC
Dordt College	IA	34,160	C+
Drake Univ	IA	41,516	VC+
Eastern Mich Univ	MI	18,604	C
Elizabethtown College	PA	49,740	VC
Ferris State Univ	MI	20,047	C
Florida A&M Univ	FL	14,935	LC
Florida State Univ	FL	16,715	VC
Georgia State Univ	GA	15,582	VC
High Point Univ	NC	39,800	C
Indiana Univ Northwest	IN	6,854	LC
Indiana Univ South Bend	IN	15,501	C
Indiana Univ-Purdue Univ Fort Wayne	IN	15,521	C
Indiana Univ-Purdue Univ Indianapolis	IN	17,611	C
Le Moyne College	NY	43,470	C
Lebanon Valley College	PA	38,570	C
Maryville Univ of St. Louis	MO	35,856	VC
Millersville Univ of Pennsylvania	PA	21,648	C
Millikin Univ	IL	38,940	C
Milwaukee School of Engineering	WI	39,948	VC+
Mount Mercy Univ	IA	35,320	C
New York Univ	NY	61,470	MC
North Central College	IL	38,343	VC
N Dak State Univ	ND		C
Northwestern College of Iowa	IA	36,240	VC
Ohio Univ	OH	21,080	C
Olivet Nazarene Univ	IL	29,990	VC
Pittsburg State Univ	KS	12,032	C
Purdue Univ/West Lafayette	IN	20,024	HC
Queens College/The CUNY	NY	17,107	VC
Rider Univ	NJ	45,720	C
Robert Morris Univ	PA	37,864	C
Roosevelt Univ	IL	22,605	VC
St. Joseph's Univ	PA	55,006	VC

School	ST	$IS	SR
St. Mary's Univ of Minn	MN	38,280	C
Seton Hill Univ	PA	35,172	C
Siena College	NY	43,863	VC
Simpson College	IA	36,086	C+
Southeast Missouri State Univ	MO	15,370	LC
Southern Illinois Univ Edwardsville	IL	17,532	C
St. John's Univ	NY	55,070	C+
Temple Univ	PA	24,392	VC
Ohio State Univ-Columbus Campus	OH	19,887	HC+
Thiel College	PA	38,728	LC
Univ at Albany / SUNY	NY	18,674	VC
Univ of Calif at Santa Barbara	CA	27,551	HC
Univ of Central Missouri	MO	14,605	C
Univ of Central Okla	OK	12,293	C
Univ of Illinois at Urbana-Champaign	IL	26,450	HC
Univ of Iowa	IA	17,693	VC
Univ of Maine at Farmington	ME	18,187	LC
Univ of Minn/Duluth	MN	19,806	C
Univ of Minn/Twin Cities	MN		HC
Univ of Nebr - Lincoln	NE	18,031	VC
Univ of Pennsylvania	PA	61,132	MC
Univ of Texas at Dallas	TX	21,348	HC+
Univ of Texas at San Antonio	TX	18,372	C
Univ of Wisc/Madison	WI	18,757	HC+
Univ of Wisc-Milwaukee	WI	18,436	C
Valparaiso Univ	IN	44,940	VC+
West Chester Univ of Pennsylvania	PA	17,186	C
Worcester Polytechnic Inst	MA	55,860	MC
Xavier Univ	OH	44,980	VC

ADDICTION STUDIES

School	ST	$IS	SR
Bethany College	KS	30,605	NC
Brescia Univ	KY	26,140	VC+
Elizabethtown College School of Continuing and Professional Studies	PA		VC
Goddard College	VT	16,418	VC
Graceland Univ	IA	28,020	C
Grand Canyon Univ	AZ	24,540	VC
Indiana Wesleyan Univ	IN	31,815	VC
Kansas Wesleyan Univ	KS	32,000	C
Keene State College	NH	23,232	LC
Metropolitan State Univ	MN	5,923	
Minot State Univ	ND	10,915	C
Missouri Valley College	MO	22,200	C
Northwestern State Univ of Louisiana	LA	14,368	C
Okla City Univ	OK	40,476	VC
Prescott College	AZ	33,284	C
Rhode Island College	RI	17,694	LC
Southern Univ at New Orleans	LA	2,963	NC
Texas Tech Univ	TX	14,243	C
Univ of Central Okla	OK	12,293	C
Univ of Cincinnati	OH	21,506	VC
Univ of Detroit Mercy	MI	30,450	VC
Univ of Mary	ND	16,714	C
Univ of S Dak	SD	15,111	C
Viterbo Univ	WI	30,070	C

ADMINISTRATION OF JUSTICE

School	ST	$IS	SR
Campbell Univ	NC	37,570	VC
Catawba College	NC	37,240	LC
Howard Univ	DC	13,646	C
Texas Southern Univ	TX	18,212	LC
Univ of Hawaii at Hilo	HI	23,066	C
Univ of Louisville	KY	17,946	C
Univ of Pittsburgh at Pittsburgh	PA	28,572	HC+

ADVERTISING

School	ST	$IS	SR
Abilene Christian Univ	TX	38,400	C+
Adams State Univ	CO	13,358	LC
American International College	MA	36,100	LC
Appalachian State Univ	NC	12,919	VC
Art Center College of Design	CA	34,044	SP
Art Inst of Atlanta	GA	24,000	SP
Art Inst of Portland	OR	23,040	SP
Barry Univ	FL	38,190	C
Bethany College	WV	35,282	LC
Biola Univ	CA	40,320	C+
Brigham Young Univ	UT	12,100	VC
Butler Univ	IN	47,572	VC+
Cal State, East Bay	CA	16,549	C
Cal State, Fullerton	CA	25,188	C
Campbell Univ	NC	37,570	VC
Central State Univ	OH	18,190	C
Champlain College	VT	46,650	VC+
CUNY/Baruch College	NY		HC
Clarke Univ	IA	37,600	C
College for Creative Studies	MI	45,340	C
College of St. Scholastica	MN	41,440	C
Columbia College Chicago	IL	30,940	LC
Columbus College of Art and Design	OH	37,732	SP

School	ST	$IS	SR
Cornerstone Univ and Grand Rapids Theological Seminary	MI	33,338	C
Davenport Univ	MI	21,002	LC
Dordt College	IA	34,160	C+
Drake Univ	IA	41,516	VC+
Drury Univ	MO	31,909	VC
Duquesne Univ	PA	43,720	VC
East Central Univ	OK	10,223	LC
Eastern Mich Univ	MI	18,604	C
Eastern Nazarene College	MA	30,000	C
Emerson College	MA	52,446	HC+
Fashion Inst of Technology/SUNY	NY	18,362	SP
Ferris State Univ	MI	20,047	C
Florida Southern College	FL	40,150	C+
Florida State Univ	FL	16,715	VC
Fontbonne Univ	MO	31,384	C
Gannon Univ	PA	39,608	C
Grand Valley State Univ	MI	17,998	C
Harding Univ	AR	23,556	C
Hawaii Pacific Univ	HI	34,360	C
Howard Univ	DC	13,646	C
Iowa State Univ	IA	16,403	C
Johnson & Wales Univ/Providence Campus	RI	29,576	C
Kent State Univ	OH	19,920	C
Lamar Univ	TX	6,820	LC
Lasell College	MA	43,750	LC
Le Moyne College	NY	43,470	C
Loyola Univ Chicago	IL	51,646	VC+
Lynn Univ	FL	43,500	LC
Marietta College	OH	42,135	C+
Marquette Univ	WI	46,930	VC+
Marshall Univ	WV	14,820	C
Marywood Univ	PA	45,595	C
Mercyhurst Univ	PA	40,700	C
Metropolitan State Univ	MN	5,923	
Mich State Univ	MI	22,450	VC
Midland Univ	NE	34,000	C
Minneapolis College of Art and Design	MN	36,700	SP
Morningside College	IA	35,430	C
Murray State Univ	KY	15,304	C
New York Inst of Technology	NY	45,010	VC
North Park Univ	IL	30,130	C
Northeastern State Univ	OK	8,615	VC
Northwest Missouri State Univ	MO	17,347	C
Northwood Univ	FL	33,192	LC
Northwood Univ	MI	26,331	LC
Ohio Univ	OH	21,080	C
Okla Christian Univ	OK	25,870	VC
Okla City Univ	OK	40,476	VC
Otis College of Art and Design	CA	35,404	SP
Pace Univ	NY	53,367	C
Parsons The New School for Design	NY	56,610	SP
Pepperdine Univ	CA	55,372	HC+
Pittsburg State Univ	KS	12,032	C
Point Park Univ	PA	36,390	C
Portland State Univ	OR	18,672	C
Purdue Univ/West Lafayette	IN	20,024	HC
Quinnipiac Univ	CT	55,160	VC
Rider Univ	NJ	45,720	C
Ringling College of Art and Design	FL	46,130	SP
Roosevelt Univ	IL	22,605	VC
Rowan Univ	NJ	24,022	VC+
Salem State Univ	MA	13,161	LC
San Jose State Univ	CA	19,133	LC
Savannah College of Art and Design	GA	48,005	SP
School of Visual Arts	NY	36,500	VC
Southeast Missouri State Univ	MO	15,370	LC
Southern Methodist Univ	TX	60,585	MC
Southern New Hampshire Univ	NH	38,100	C
Spring Arbor Univ	MI	26,740	C
St. Cloud State Univ	MN	10,600	C
St. John's Univ	NY	55,070	C+
Suffolk Univ	MA	47,298	C
Syracuse Univ	NY	56,346	VC
Temple Univ	PA	24,392	VC
Texas A&M Univ at Commerce	TX	10,496	C
Texas State Univ	TX	17,128	C
Texas Tech Univ	TX	14,243	C
Texas Wesleyan Univ	TX	31,382	C
The Pennsylvania State Univ - Univ Park	PA	28,022	VC+
The Univ of Okla	OK	18,621	VC
Union Univ	TN	28,260	VC
Univ of Alabama at Tuscaloosa	AL	17,164	C+
Univ of Arkansas at Fayetteville	AR	18,352	C+
Univ of Arkansas at Little Rock	AR	17,609	LC
Univ of Central Florida	FL	15,668	VC+
Univ of Central Okla	OK	12,293	C
Univ of Colo Boulder	CO	22,605	VC+
Univ of Florida	FL	15,943	HC
Univ of Georgia	GA	20,082	VC
Univ of Idaho	ID	14,558	C

School	ST	$IS	SR
Univ of Illinois at Urbana-Champaign	IL	26,450	HC
Univ of Kentucky	KY	19,868	C
Univ of Louisiana at Lafayette	LA	6,130	C
Univ of Miami	FL	57,034	MC
Univ of Missouri/Columbia	MO	18,201	MC
Univ of Nebr - Lincoln	NE	18,031	VC
Univ of Nebr at Kearney	NE	14,855	LC
Univ of New Haven	CT	48,940	C
Univ of Oregon	OR	21,360	C+
Univ of San Francisco	CA	54,770	VC
Univ of S Car at Columbia	SC	19,725	VC+
Univ of Southern Indiana	IN	14,885	C
Univ of Southern Miss	MS	13,170	C
Univ of Tampa	FL	35,160	VC
Univ of Tenn at Knoxville	TN	20,364	VC+
Univ of Texas at Austin	TX	44,074	HC
Univ of the Sacred Heart	PR	5,590	
Washington State Univ	WA	20,461	C
Washington Univ in St. Louis	MO	69,844	MC
Waynesburg Univ	PA	30,150	C
Webster Univ	MO	35,100	C+
Wesleyan College	GA	24,000	C
West Virginia Univ	WV	16,542	C+
Western Kentucky Univ	KY	11,000	LC
Western Mich Univ	MI	19,628	C
Western New England Univ	MA	46,154	C+
Wilmington College	OH	29,784	C
Xavier Univ	OH	44,980	VC
Youngstown State Univ	OH	16,732	C

AERONAUTICAL ENGINEERING

School	ST	$IS	SR
Auburn Univ	AL	22,378	VC+
Calif Polytechnic State Univ	CA	19,847	HC
Case Western Reserve Univ	OH	56,534	MC
Clarkson Univ	NY	57,330	HC
Daniel Webster College	NH	25,380	C
Embry-Riddle Aeronautical Univ - Daytona Beach	FL	40,884	C+
Florida Inst of Technology	FL	48,290	VC
Georgia Inst of Technology	GA	21,828	MC
Illinois Inst of Technology	IL	38,512	HC+
Iowa State Univ	IA	16,403	C
Mass Inst of Technology	MA	58,240	MC
Missouri Univ of Science and Technology	MO	18,655	VC+
N Car State Univ	NC	16,202	HC
Princeton Univ	NJ	53,795	MC
Purdue Univ/West Lafayette	IN	20,024	HC
Rensselaer Polytechnic Inst	NY	61,529	MC
St. Louis Univ	MO	48,346	HC
San Jose State Univ	CA	19,133	LC
Stanford Univ	CA	58,388	MC
Texas A&M Univ	TX	19,207	VC
Ohio State Univ-Columbus Campus	OH	19,887	HC+
The Univ of Okla	OK	18,621	VC
Tuskegee Univ	AL	26,750	C
United States Air Force Academy	CO		MC
United States Naval Academy	MD		MC
Univ of Arizona	AZ	20,657	C
Univ of Calif at Davis	CA		HC
Univ of Calif at Irvine	CA	25,961	VC
Univ of Calif at Los Angeles	CA	25,686	MC
Univ of Central Florida	FL	15,668	VC+
Univ of Cincinnati	OH	21,506	VC
Univ of Colo Boulder	CO	22,605	VC+
Univ of Florida	FL	15,943	HC
Univ of Illinois at Urbana-Champaign	IL	26,450	HC
Univ of Kansas	KS	17,603	C+
Univ of Mich/Ann Arbor	MI	22,102	MC
Univ of Notre Dame	IN	57,117	MC
Univ of Southern Calif	CA	56,903	MC
Univ of Washington	WA	14,722	VC
West Virginia Univ	WV	16,542	C+
Wichita State Univ	KS	14,607	C+
Worcester Polytechnic Inst	MA	55,860	MC

AERONAUTICAL SCIENCE

School	ST	$IS	SR
Bridgewater State Univ	MA	18,752	C
Dowling College	NY	25,000	LC
Embry-Riddle Aeronautical Univ - Daytona Beach	FL	40,884	C+
Embry-Riddle Aeronautical Univ - Prescott Campus	AZ	40,444	VC+
Embry-Riddle Aeronautical Univ - Worldwide	FL	15,512	C
Farmingdale State College	NY	19,673	C
Florida Inst of Technology	FL	48,290	VC
Inter-American Univ of PR/ Bayamon Univ College	PR	4,428	
Kent State Univ	OH	19,920	C
LeTourneau Univ	TX	36,210	VC
Rocky Mountain College	MT	32,242	C
Univ of Maryland/Eastern Shore	MD	14,000	C
Wilmington Univ	DE	8,112	NC

AERONAUTICAL TECHNOLOGY

School	ST	$IS	SR
Andrews Univ	MI	28,030	C+

ST = STATE $IS = IN-STATE COSTS   SR = SELECTOR RATING

School	ST	$IS	SR
Arizona State Univ, at the Polytechnic Campus	AZ	20,531	C+
Central Washington Univ	WA	11,730	C
Dowling College	NY	25,000	LC
Indiana State Univ	IN	16,000	C
Inter-American Univ of PR/ Bayamon Univ College	PR	4,428	
Kansas State Univ	KS	15,497	VC
Kent State Univ	OH	19,920	C
LeTourneau Univ	TX	36,210	VC
Purdue Univ/West Lafayette	IN	20,024	HC
St. Louis Univ	MO	48,346	HC
Tenn State Univ	TN	9,048	C
Univ of Alaska Anchorage	AK	16,673	NC

AEROSPACE ENGINEERING

School	ST	$IS	SR
Arizona State Univ, at the Tempe Campus	AZ	20,137	C+
Cal State, Long Beach	CA	17,502	C
Embry-Riddle Aeronautical Univ - Prescott Campus	AZ	40,444	VC+
New Mexico State Univ	NM	14,050	C
San Diego State Univ	CA	21,611	C+
Syracuse Univ	NY	56,346	VC
The Pennsylvania State Univ - Univ Park	PA	28,022	VC+
Univ of Maryland - College Park	MD	20,060	HC
Western Mich Univ	MI	19,628	C

AEROSPACE STUDIES

School	ST	$IS	SR
Embry-Riddle Aeronautical Univ - Daytona Beach	FL	40,884	C+
Mass Inst of Technology	MA	58,240	MC
Miss State Univ	MS	14,750	C
New Mexico State Univ	NM	14,050	C
Okla State Univ	OK	14,310	VC
Rochester Inst of Technology	NY	42,450	VC
St. Louis Univ	MO	48,346	MC
United States Air Force Academy	CO		MC
Univ at Buffalo / The SUNY	NY	20,283	VC
Univ of Alabama at Tuscaloosa	AL	17,164	C+
Univ of Alaska Anchorage	AK	16,673	NC
Univ of Calif at Los Angeles	CA	25,686	MC
Univ of Calif at San Diego	CA	21,000	VC
Univ of Central Florida	FL	15,668	VC+
Univ of Miami	FL	57,034	MC
Univ of Mich/Ann Arbor	MI	22,102	MC
Univ of Minn/Twin Cities	MN		HC
Univ of Southern Calif	CA	56,903	MC
Univ of Tenn at Knoxville	TN	20,364	VC+
Univ of Texas at Austin	TX	44,074	HC
Univ of Virginia	VA	23,050	MC
Virginia Polytechnic Inst and State Univ	VA	14,629	HC
West Virginia Univ	WV	16,542	C+

AFRICAN AMERICAN STUDIES

School	ST	$IS	SR
Amherst College	MA	58,744	MC
Arizona State Univ, at the Tempe Campus	AZ	20,137	C+
Bard College at Simon's Rock	MA	61,749	HC+
Bates College	ME	60,720	MC
Berea College	KY	7,192	C
Brandeis Univ	MA		MC
Brown Univ	RI	59,428	MC
Cabrini College	PA	40,859	LC
Cal State, Fresno	CA	17,405	C+
Cal State, Fullerton	CA	25,188	C
Cal State, Los Angeles	CA	17,186	C
Cal State, Northridge	CA	28,690	LC
Carleton College	MN	60,102	MC
Chicago State Univ	IL	5,482	C
Claflin Univ	SC	22,368	LC
Coe College	IA	45,550	VC
Colby College	ME	57,510	MC
College of Charleston	SC	22,145	VC
College of Staten Island/The City of New Yok	NY	16,778	NC
College of Wooster	OH	52,600	VC
Columbia Univ/City of New York	NY	61,116	MC
Columbia Univ/School of General Studies	NY	58,231	MC
Dartmouth College	NH	57,996	MC
Denison Univ	OH	54,670	HC+
DePauw Univ	IN	48,950	VC+
Duke Univ	NC	50,250	MC
Earlham College	IN	51,470	HC
East Carolina Univ	NC	14,169	C
Eastern Mich Univ	MI	18,604	C
Emory Univ	GA	56,368	MC
Fordham Univ	NY	61,588	HC+
Georgia State Univ	GA	15,582	VC
Guilford College	NC	42,800	C
Hampshire College	MA	58,320	MC
Harvard College/Harvard Univ	MA	49,000	MC
Howard Univ	DC	13,646	C
Hunter College	NY	14,429	VC
Indiana State Univ	IN	16,000	C
Indiana Univ Bloomington	IN	19,801	VC
Indiana Univ Northwest	IN	6,854	LC
Lehman College/The CUNY	NY	5,778	LC
Loyola Marymount Univ	CA	54,649	VC+
Loyola Univ Chicago	IL	51,646	VC+
Luther College	IA	45,720	C+
Martin Univ	IN	11,000	SP
Metropolitan State Univ of Denver	CO	4,835	LC
Miami Univ	OH	24,191	VC
Middlebury College	VT	59,160	MC
Morehouse College	GA	39,412	C
Morgan State Univ	MD	14,500	VC
New York Univ	NY	61,470	MC
Northeastern Univ	MA	55,296	MC
Northwestern Univ	IL	61,640	MC
Oakland Univ	MI	19,391	C
Oberlin College	OH	61,788	MC
Ohio Univ	OH	21,080	C
Ohio Wesleyan Univ	OH	49,460	C+
Old Dominion Univ	VA	19,483	LC
Pitzer College	CA	54,988	MC
Purdue Univ/West Lafayette	IN	20,024	HC
Rhode Island College	RI	17,694	LC
Roosevelt Univ	IL	22,605	VC
Rutgers, The State Univ of New Jersey/Camden Campus	NJ	25,121	C
Rutgers, The State Univ of New Jersey/New Brunswick	NJ	25,562	VC
Rutgers, The State Univ of New Jersey/Newark Campus	NJ	258,806	C
St. Augustine's Univ	NC	14,000	C
St. Louis Univ	MO	48,346	HC
St. Peter's Univ	NJ	44,240	C
San Diego State Univ	CA	21,611	C+
Scripps College	CA	61,940	MC
Seton Hall Univ	NJ	45,902	C
Simmons College	MA	49,966	VC
Smith College	MA	59,674	MC
Sonoma State Univ	CA	20,541	C
Southern Methodist Univ	TX	60,585	MC
Stanford Univ	CA	58,388	MC
Suffolk Univ	MA	47,298	C
SUNY College at Geneseo	NY	18,670	HC
SUNY Cortland/The SUNY	NY	19,759	C+
SUNY New Paltz	NY	14,348	C
Syracuse Univ	NY	56,346	VC
Temple Univ	PA	24,392	VC
Ohio State Univ-Columbus Campus	OH	19,887	HC+
The Pennsylvania State Univ - Univ Park	PA	28,022	VC+
The SUNY/College at Brockport	NY	19,002	C
The Univ of Memphis	TN	15,094	C
The Univ of N Car at Greensboro	NC	12,848	C
The Univ of Okla	OK	18,621	VC
Univ at Albany / SUNY	NY	18,674	VC
Univ at Buffalo / The SUNY	NY	20,283	VC
Univ of Alabama at Birmingham	AL	18,484	C+
Univ of Arkansas at Fayetteville	AR	18,352	C+
Univ of Calif at Berkeley	CA	23,322	MC
Univ of Calif at Irvine	CA	25,961	VC
Univ of Calif at Los Angeles	CA	25,686	MC
Univ of Calif at Riverside	CA	27,204	C+
Univ of Calif at Santa Barbara	CA	27,551	HC
Univ of Central Arkansas	AR	13,667	VC
Univ of Chicago	IL	55,416	MC
Univ of Cincinnati	OH	21,506	VC
Univ of Georgia	GA	20,082	VC
Univ of Illinois at Chicago	IL	24,505	VC
Univ of Iowa	IA	17,693	VC
Univ of Kansas	KS	17,603	C+
Univ of Maryland - College Park	MD	20,060	HC
Univ of Maryland/Baltimore County	MD	18,000	VC
Univ of Mass Amherst	MA	24,215	VC+
Univ of Mass Boston	MA	23,066	VC
Univ of Mich/Ann Arbor	MI	22,102	MC
Univ of Mich/Dearborn	MI	9,885	VC
Univ of Minn/Twin Cities	MN		HC
Univ of Miss	MS	16,704	C
Univ of Nebr at Omaha	NE	12,700	C
Univ of N Car at Chapel Hill	NC	18,928	MC
Univ of Northern Colo	CO	18,446	C
Univ of Pennsylvania	PA	61,132	MC
Univ of Rochester	NY	60,668	MC
Univ of S Car at Columbia	SC	19,725	VC+
Univ of South Florida/Tampa	FL	13,000	C
Univ of Southern Calif	CA	56,903	MC
Univ of Virginia	VA	23,050	MC
Univ of Washington	WA	14,722	VC
Univ of Wisc/Madison	WI	18,757	HC+
Univ of Wisc-Milwaukee	WI	18,436	C
Vanderbilt Univ	TN	58,220	MC
Virginia Commonwealth Univ	VA	21,716	C
Washington Univ in St. Louis	MO	69,844	MC
Wellesley College	MA	59,038	MC
Wesleyan Univ	CT	61,198	MC
Western Illinois Univ	IL	20,732	C
Wheaton College	MA	54,934	HC+
William Paterson Univ of New Jersey	NJ	21,694	C
Wofford College	SC	45,795	VC
Wright State Univ	OH	16,983	C
Yale Univ	CT	55,300	MC
York College / The CUNY	NY	5,496	VC

AFRICAN LANGUAGES

School	ST	$IS	SR
Cal State, Northridge	CA	28,690	LC
Duke Univ	NC	50,250	MC
Univ of Wisc/Madison	WI	18,757	HC+

AFRICAN STUDIES

School	ST	$IS	SR
Agnes Scott College	GA	45,323	C+
Bard College	NY	61,940	HC
Berea College	KY	7,192	C
Bowling Green State Univ	OH	18,970	C
Brown Univ	RI	59,428	MC
Cal State, Dominguez Hills	CA	17,090	LC
Cal State, Long Beach	CA	17,502	C+
Carleton College	MN	60,102	MC
Claflin Univ	SC	22,368	LC
Claremont McKenna College	CA	62,215	MC
Colgate Univ	NY	58,135	MC
Conn College	CT	54,970	MC
DePaul Univ	IL	47,623	VC
Dickinson College	PA	57,662	HC+
Drew Univ/College of Liberal Arts	NJ	57,516	C
Duke Univ	NC	50,250	MC
Eastern Mich Univ	MI	18,604	C
Emory Univ	GA	56,368	MC
Fordham Univ	NY	61,588	HC+
Franklin and Marshall College	PA	60,799	MC
Hamilton College	NY	55,620	MC
Hampshire College	MA	58,320	MC
Hobart and William Smith Colleges	NY	60,034	HC+
Hofstra Univ	NY	51,810	VC+
Howard Univ	DC	13,646	C
Johns Hopkins Univ	MD	47,492	MC
Kennesaw State Univ	GA		C
Kent State Univ	OH	19,920	C
Lafayette College	PA	59,155	HC+
Lehigh Univ	PA	56,770	MC
Linfield College-McMinnville Campus	OR	47,676	C
Loyola Univ Chicago	IL	51,646	VC+
Mercer Univ	GA	44,201	VC
New York Univ	NY	61,470	MC
North Park Univ	IL	30,130	C
Old Dominion Univ	VA	19,483	LC
Queens College/The CUNY	NY	17,107	VC
Ramapo College of New Jersey	NJ	24,938	C
Rowan Univ	NJ	24,022	VC+
San Francisco State Univ	CA	18,514	C
Savannah State Univ	GA	13,156	C
Shaw Univ	NC	15,488	C
Smith College	MA	59,674	MC
St. Lawrence Univ	NY	59,972	VC
Stony Brook Univ / SUNY	NY	20,078	HC+
SUNY Oneonta / SUNY	NY	16,919	C+
Tenn State Univ	TN	9,048	C
The Pennsylvania State Univ - Univ Park	PA	28,022	VC+
The SUNY/College at Brockport	NY	19,002	C
Tufts Univ	MA	58,780	MC
Tulane Univ	LA	60,861	MC
Univ of Arizona	AZ	20,657	C
Univ of Arkansas at Fayetteville	AR	18,352	C+
Univ of Calif at Davis	CA		HC
Univ of Calif at Los Angeles	CA	25,686	MC
Univ of Kansas	KS	17,603	C+
Univ of Mich/Ann Arbor	MI	22,102	MC
Univ of Minn/Twin Cities	MN		HC
Univ of Notre Dame	IN	57,117	MC
Univ of Pennsylvania	PA	61,132	MC
Vassar College	NY	61,140	MC
Washington Univ in St. Louis	MO	69,844	MC
Wayne State Univ	MI	22,063	C
Western Mich Univ	MI	19,628	C
Wheaton College	MA	54,934	HC+
Yale Univ	CT	55,300	MC
Youngstown State Univ	OH	16,732	C

AFRICANA STUDIES

School	ST	$IS	SR
Binghamton Univ/The SUNY	NY	21,648	HC+
Bowdoin College	ME	59,568	MC
College of William & Mary	VA	28,000	MC
Cornell Univ	NY	60,964	MC
Davidson College	NC	58,146	MC
Eastern Illinois Univ	IL	20,466	C
Hobart and William Smith Colleges	NY	60,034	HC+
Indiana Univ-Purdue Univ Indianapolis	IN	17,611	C
Knox College	IL	44,865	VC+
Mount Holyoke College	MA	55,146	MC
New York Univ	NY	61,470	MC
Oberlin College	OH	61,788	MC
Pomona College	CA	57,680	MC
Southern Illinois Univ Carbondale	IL	21,942	C
Univ of Miami	FL	57,034	MC
Univ of New Mexico	NM	15,300	C
Univ of N Car at Charlotte	NC	15,547	C
Univ of Pittsburgh at Pittsburgh	PA	28,572	VC+

AGR AGRONOMY

School	ST	$IS	SR
College of the Ozarks	MO		VC
Murray State Univ	KY	15,304	C

AGRI HORTIULTURE

School	ST	$IS	SR
College of the Ozarks	MO		VC
Murray State Univ	KY	15,304	C

AGRICULTURAL BUSINESS MANAGEMENT

School	ST	$IS	SR
Abilene Christian Univ	TX	38,400	C+
Adams State Univ	CO	13,358	LC
Alabama A&M Univ	AL	10,084	C
Alcorn State Univ	MS	9,500	C
Angelo State Univ	TX	15,049	NC
Appalachian State Univ	NC	12,919	VC
Arizona State Univ, at the Polytechnic Campus	AZ	20,531	C+
Arkansas State Univ	AR	15,470	C
Arkansas Tech Univ	AR	13,982	LC
Auburn Univ	AL	22,378	VC+
Brigham Young Univ	UT	12,100	HC
Calif Polytechnic State Univ	CA	19,847	HC
Calif State Polytechnic Univ, Pomona	CA	20,156	C
Cal State, Chico	CA	20,158	C
Cal State, Fresno	CA	17,405	C
College of the Ozarks	MO		VC
Colo State Univ-Fort Collins	CO	20,385	VC
Delaware State Univ	DE	16,722	LC
Dickinson State Univ	ND	11,900	NC
Dordt College	IA	34,160	C+
Eastern New Mexico Univ	NM	10,682	C
Eastern Oregon Univ	OR	10,400	C
Florida Southern College	FL	40,150	C+
Fort Hays State Univ	KS	11,354	C
Hardin-Simmons Univ	TX	23,560	C+
Illinois State Univ	IL	23,110	VC
Iowa State Univ	IA	16,403	C
Kansas State Univ	KS	15,497	VC
Kent State Univ	OH	19,920	C
Lincoln Univ	MO	12,904	NC
Louisiana State Univ	LA	18,677	C+
Louisiana Tech Univ	LA	11,302	C
Middle Tenn State Univ	TN	8,650	C
Miss State Univ	MS	14,750	C
Montana State Univ	MT	14,068	C
Morningside College	IA	35,430	C
Murray State Univ	KY	15,304	C
New Mexico State Univ	NM	14,050	C
Nicholls State Univ	LA	7,095	C
N Car Agricultural and Technical State Univ	NC	13,365	LC
N Car State Univ	NC	16,202	HC
N Dak State Univ	ND		C
Northwest Missouri State Univ	MO	17,347	C
Northwestern College of Iowa	IA	36,240	VC
Northwestern Okla State Univ	OK	7,275	NC
Okla Panhandle State Univ	OK	8,996	C
Okla State Univ	OK	14,310	VC
Oregon State Univ	OR	20,273	VC
Prairie View A&M Univ	TX	15,205	LC
Purdue Univ/West Lafayette	IN	20,024	HC
San Diego State Univ	CA	21,611	C+
S Car State Univ	SC	6,700	C
S Dak State Univ	SD	14,296	C
Southeast Missouri State Univ	MO	15,370	LC
Southern Arkansas Univ	AR	14,316	C
Southwest Minn State Univ	MN	14,000	C
Stephen F. Austin State Univ	TX	14,668	C
Sul Ross State Univ	TX	13,410	LC
Tarleton State Univ	TX	13,489	LC
Texas A&M Univ	TX	19,207	C
Texas A&M Univ at Kingsville	TX	7,500	LC
Texas State Univ	TX	17,128	C
Texas Tech Univ	TX	14,243	C
Ohio State Univ-Columbus Campus	OH	19,887	HC+
The Pennsylvania State Univ - Univ Park	PA	28,022	VC+
The SUNY College of Agriculture and Tech at Cobleskill	NY	19,749	C
Truman State Univ	MO	15,541	HC
Univ of Arizona	AZ	20,657	C

School	ST	$IS	SR
Univ of Arkansas at Fayetteville	AR	18,352	C+
Univ of Calif at Davis	CA		HC
Univ of Central Missouri	MO	14,605	C
Univ of Delaware	DE	23,612	C
Univ of Florida	FL	15,943	HC
Univ of Idaho	ID	14,558	C
Univ of Illinois at Urbana-Champaign	IL	26,450	HC
Univ of Louisiana at Monroe	LA	12,998	C
Univ of Maryland - College Park	MD	20,060	HC
Univ of Minn Crookston	MN	17,834	C
Univ of Minn/Twin Cities	MN		HC
Univ of Missouri/Columbia	MO	18,201	MC
Univ of Nebr - Lincoln	NE	18,031	C
Univ of Tenn at Martin	TN	13,734	C
Univ of Wisc/Madison	WI	18,757	HC+
Univ of Wisc/Platteville	WI	14,564	C
Univ of Wisc/River Falls	WI	9,722	LC
Univ of Wyoming	WY	14,401	C+
Urbana Univ	OH	30,820	C
Utah State Univ	UT	12,044	C
Washington State Univ	WA	20,461	C
West Texas A&M Univ	TX	13,478	C
Wilmington College	OH	29,784	C

AGRICULTURAL COMMUNICATIONS

School	ST	$IS	SR
Auburn Univ	AL	22,378	VC+
Calif Polytechnic State Univ	CA	19,847	HC
Cal State, Fresno	CA	17,405	C
Kansas State Univ	KS	15,497	C
N Dak State Univ	ND		C
Okla State Univ	OK	14,310	VC
Purdue Univ/West Lafayette	IN	20,024	HC
S Dak State Univ	SD	14,296	C
Texas A&M Univ	TX	19,207	VC
Texas Tech Univ	TX	14,243	C
Univ of Arkansas at Fayetteville	AR	18,352	C+
Univ of Georgia	GA	20,082	VC
Univ of Idaho	ID	14,558	C
Univ of Illinois at Urbana-Champaign	IL	26,450	HC
Univ of Nebr - Lincoln	NE	18,031	VC
Univ of Wisc/Madison	WI	18,757	HC+
Univ of Wyoming	WY	14,401	C+
Washington State Univ	WA	20,461	C

AGRICULTURAL ECONOMICS

School	ST	$IS	SR
Alabama A&M Univ	AL	10,084	C
Alcorn State Univ	MS	9,500	C
Auburn Univ	AL	22,378	VC+
Colo State Univ-Fort Collins	CO	20,385	VC
Eastern Oregon Univ	OR	10,400	C
Fort Valley State Univ	GA	11,200	VC
Kansas State Univ	KS	15,497	VC
Langston Univ	OK	3,000	C
Miss State Univ	MS	14,750	C
New Mexico State Univ	NM	14,050	C
N Car Agricultural and Technical State Univ	NC	13,365	LC
N Car State Univ	NC	16,202	HC
N Dak State Univ	ND		C
Northwest Missouri State Univ	MO	17,347	C
Okla State Univ	OK	14,310	VC
Oregon State Univ	OR	20,273	VC
Prairie View A&M Univ	TX	15,205	LC
Purdue Univ/West Lafayette	IN	20,024	HC
S Dak State Univ	SD	14,296	C
Southern Illinois Univ Carbondale	IL	21,942	C
Southern Univ and A&M College	LA	9,761	LC
Tarleton State Univ	TX	13,489	LC
Tenn Tech Univ	TN	11,310	C
Texas A&M Univ	TX	19,207	VC
Texas A&M Univ at Commerce	TX	10,496	C
Texas Tech Univ	TX	14,243	C
Ohio State Univ-Columbus Campus	OH	19,887	HC+
Tuskegee Univ	AL	26,750	C
Univ of Arizona	AZ	20,657	C
Univ of Arkansas at Fayetteville	AR	18,352	C+
Univ of Calif at Davis	CA		HC
Univ of Conn	CT	24,706	HC
Univ of Delaware	DE	23,612	VC
Univ of Georgia	GA	20,082	VC
Univ of Idaho	ID	14,558	C
Univ of Illinois at Urbana-Champaign	IL	26,450	HC
Univ of Kentucky	KY	19,868	C
Univ of Maryland - College Park	MD	20,060	HC
Univ of Mass Amherst	MA	24,215	VC+
Univ of Minn/Twin Cities	MN		HC
Univ of Missouri/Columbia	MO	18,201	MC
Univ of Nebr - Lincoln	NE	18,031	VC
Univ of Tenn at Knoxville	TN	20,364	VC+
Univ of Wisc/Madison	WI	18,757	HC+
Utah State Univ	UT	12,044	C
Virginia Polytechnic Inst and State Univ	VA	14,629	HC
Washington State Univ	WA	20,461	C
West Texas A&M Univ	TX	13,478	C

AGRICULTURAL EDUCATION

School	ST	$IS	SR
Alabama A&M Univ	AL	10,084	C
Arkansas Tech Univ	AR	13,982	LC
Calif Polytechnic State Univ	CA	19,847	HC
Cal State, Fresno	CA	17,405	C
Clemson Univ	SC	19,136	HC
College of the Ozarks	MO		VC
Colo State Univ-Fort Collins	CO	20,385	VC
Delaware State Univ	DE	16,722	C
Dordt College	IA	34,160	C+
Eastern New Mexico Univ	NM	10,682	C
Fort Valley State Univ	GA	11,200	VC
Iowa State Univ	IA	16,403	C
Kansas State Univ	KS	15,497	VC
Louisiana State Univ	LA	18,677	C+
Mich State Univ	MI	22,450	VC
Miss State Univ	MS	14,750	C
Missouri State Univ	MO	13,996	C+
Montana State Univ	MT	14,068	C
Morehead State Univ	KY	10,900	C
Murray State Univ	KY	15,304	C
New Mexico State Univ	NM	14,050	C
N Car Agricultural and Technical State Univ	NC	13,365	LC
N Car State Univ	NC	16,202	HC
N Dak State Univ	ND		C
Northwest Missouri State Univ	MO	17,347	C
Okla Panhandle State Univ	OK	8,996	C
Okla State Univ	OK	14,310	VC
Oswego / SUNY	NY	20,009	VC
Prescott College	AZ	33,284	C
Purdue Univ/West Lafayette	IN	20,024	HC
S Dak State Univ	SD	14,296	C
Southern Arkansas Univ	AR	14,316	C
Southern Univ and A&M College	LA	9,761	LC
Stephen F. Austin State Univ	TX	14,668	C
Tarleton State Univ	TX	13,489	LC
Tenn Tech Univ	TN	11,310	C
Texas A&M Univ	TX	19,207	VC
Texas A&M Univ at Commerce	TX	10,496	C
Texas A&M Univ at Kingsville	TX	7,500	LC
Ohio State Univ-Columbus Campus	OH	19,887	HC+
The Pennsylvania State Univ - Univ Park	PA	28,022	VC+
Univ of Arizona	AZ	20,657	C
Univ of Arkansas at Fayetteville	AR	18,352	C+
Univ of Arkansas at Pine Bluff	AR	13,378	C
Univ of Central Missouri	MO	14,605	C
Univ of Conn	CT	24,706	VC
Univ of Florida	FL	15,943	HC
Univ of Georgia	GA	20,082	VC
Univ of Idaho	ID	14,558	C
Univ of Illinois at Urbana-Champaign	IL	26,450	HC
Univ of Kentucky	KY	19,868	C
Univ of Louisiana at Lafayette	LA	6,130	C
Univ of Maryland/Eastern Shore	MD	14,000	C
Univ of Minn/Twin Cities	MN		HC
Univ of Nebr - Lincoln	NE	18,031	VC
Univ of Wisc/Platteville	WI	14,564	C
Univ of Wisc/River Falls	WI	9,722	C
Univ of Wyoming	WY	14,401	C+
Utah State Univ	UT	12,044	C
Virginia Polytechnic Inst and State Univ	VA	14,629	HC
Washington State Univ	WA	20,461	C
Western Illinois Univ	IL	20,732	C
Wilmington College	OH	29,784	C

AGRICULTURAL ENGINEERING

School	ST	$IS	SR
Auburn Univ	AL	22,378	VC+
Clemson Univ	SC	19,136	HC
Iowa State Univ	IA	16,403	C
Kansas State Univ	KS	15,497	VC
N Car State Univ	NC	16,202	HC
N Dak State Univ	ND		C
Oregon State Univ	OR	20,273	VC
Purdue Univ/West Lafayette	IN	20,024	HC
S Dak State Univ	SD	14,296	C
Texas A&M Univ	TX	19,207	VC
The Pennsylvania State Univ - Univ Park	PA	28,022	VC+
Univ of Arizona	AZ	20,657	C
Univ of Calif at Davis	CA		HC
Univ of Florida	FL	15,943	HC
Univ of Georgia	GA	20,082	VC
Univ of Idaho	ID	14,558	C
Univ of Illinois at Urbana-Champaign	IL	26,450	HC
Univ of Nebr - Lincoln	NE	18,031	VC

AGRICULTURAL ENGINEERING TECHNOLOGY

School	ST	$IS	SR
Fort Valley State Univ	GA	11,200	VC
Kansas State Univ	KS	15,497	VC
Miss State Univ	MS	14,750	C
Montana State Univ	MT	14,068	C
Murray State Univ	KY	15,304	C
N Dak State Univ	ND		C
S Dak State Univ	SD	14,296	C
Univ of Central Missouri	MO	14,605	C
Univ of Minn Crookston	MN	17,834	C

AGRICULTURAL MECHANICS

School	ST	$IS	SR
Calif Polytechnic State Univ	CA	19,847	HC
Montana State Univ-Northern	MT	12,500	NC
Murray State Univ	KY	15,304	C
N Dak State Univ	ND		C
Northwest Missouri State Univ	MO	17,347	C
Stephen F. Austin State Univ	TX	14,668	C
Tarleton State Univ	TX	13,489	LC
The SUNY College of Agriculture and Tech at Cobleskill	NY	19,749	LC
Univ of Idaho	ID	14,558	C
Univ of Illinois at Urbana-Champaign	IL	26,450	HC
Univ of Nebr - Lincoln	NE	18,031	VC
Washington State Univ	WA	20,461	C

AGRICULTURAL SCIENCES

School	ST	$IS	SR
Calif Polytechnic State Univ	CA	19,847	HC
College of the Ozarks	MO		VC
Cornell Univ	NY	60,964	MC
Morningside College	IA	35,430	C
Murray State Univ	KY	15,304	C
The Pennsylvania State Univ - Univ Park	PA	28,022	VC+
Univ of Idaho	ID	14,558	C
Univ of Nevada/Reno	NV	17,507	C

AGRICULTURE

School	ST	$IS	SR
Andrews Univ	MI	28,030	C+
Arkansas State Univ	AR	15,470	C
Auburn Univ	AL	22,378	VC+
Austin Peay State Univ	TN	15,274	C
Berea College	KY	7,192	C
Calif State Polytechnic Univ, Pomona	CA	20,156	C
Cal State, Chico	CA	20,158	C
Cal State, Stanislaus	CA	18,582	C
Cameron Univ	OK	10,004	VC
Clemson Univ	SC	19,136	HC
College of the Ozarks	MO		VC
Dordt College	IA	34,160	C+
Eastern Kentucky Univ	KY	11,161	C
Eastern New Mexico Univ	NM	10,682	C
Ferrum College	VA	27,740	LC
Florida Southern College	FL	40,150	C+
Fort Hays State Univ	KS	11,354	C
Green Mountain College	VT	45,228	LC
Hampshire College	MA	58,320	MC
Hardin-Simmons Univ	TX	23,560	C+
Illinois State Univ	IL	23,110	VC
Iowa State Univ	IA	16,403	C
Lincoln Univ	MO	12,904	NC
Lubbock Christian Univ	TX	26,308	C
McNeese State Univ	LA	2,649	C
Mich State Univ	MI	22,450	VC
Miss State Univ	MS	14,750	C
Missouri State Univ	MO	13,996	C+
Morehead State Univ	KY	10,900	C
New Mexico State Univ	NM	14,050	C
N Car State Univ	NC	16,202	HC
N Dak State Univ	ND		C
Northwest Missouri State Univ	MO	17,347	C
Northwestern Okla State Univ	OK	7,275	NC
Oregon State Univ	OR	20,273	VC
Prescott College	AZ	33,284	C
Purdue Univ/West Lafayette	IN	20,024	HC
Rutgers, The State Univ of New Jersey/New Brunswick	NJ	25,562	VC
Sam Houston State Univ	TX	17,082	C
S Dak State Univ	SD	14,296	C
Southern Arkansas Univ	AR	14,316	C
Southern Illinois Univ Carbondale	IL	21,942	C
Southern Univ and A&M College	LA	9,761	LC
Stephen F. Austin State Univ	TX	14,668	C
Sterling College	VT	26,160	C
Tarleton State Univ	TX	13,489	LC
Tenn State Univ	TN	9,048	C
Tenn Tech Univ	TN	11,310	C
Texas A&M Univ at Commerce	TX	10,496	C
Texas State Univ	TX	17,128	C
The Pennsylvania State Univ - Univ Park	PA	28,022	VC+
Truman State Univ	MO	15,541	HC
Unity College	ME	34,054	C
Univ of Arkansas at Monticello	AR	12,076	NC
Univ of Arkansas at Pine Bluff	AR	13,378	C
Univ of Conn	CT	24,706	HC
Univ of Delaware	DE	23,612	VC
Univ of Hawaii at Hilo	HI	23,066	C
Univ of Idaho	ID	14,558	C
Univ of Kentucky	KY	19,868	C
Univ of Maine	ME	19,902	C+
Univ of Maryland - College Park	MD	20,060	HC
Univ of Maryland/Eastern Shore	MD	14,000	VC
Univ of Missouri/Columbia	MO	18,201	MC
Univ of Nebr - Lincoln	NE	18,031	VC
Univ of Tenn at Knoxville	TN	20,364	VC+
Univ of Tenn at Martin	TN	13,734	C
Univ of Vermont	VT	27,006	VC+
Virginia State Univ	VA	11,318	C+
Washington State Univ	WA	20,461	C
West Texas A&M Univ	TX	13,478	C
West Virginia Univ	WV	16,542	C+
Western Illinois Univ	IL	20,732	C
Western Kentucky Univ	KY	11,000	LC
Xavier Univ	OH	44,980	VC

AGRONOMY

School	ST	$IS	SR
Alabama A&M Univ	AL	10,084	C
Auburn Univ	AL	22,378	VC+
Calif Polytechnic State Univ	CA	19,847	HC
College of the Ozarks	MO		VC
Delaware Valley College	PA	29,944	C
Iowa State Univ	IA	16,403	C
Kansas State Univ	KS	15,497	VC
Miss State Univ	MS	14,750	C
New Mexico State Univ	NM	14,050	C
N Car State Univ	NC	16,202	HC
Northwest Missouri State Univ	MO	17,347	C
Okla Panhandle State Univ	OK	8,996	C
Oregon State Univ	OR	20,273	VC
Prairie View A&M Univ	TX	15,205	LC
Purdue Univ/West Lafayette	IN	20,024	HC
S Dak State Univ	SD	14,296	C
Tarleton State Univ	TX	13,489	LC
Texas A&M Univ	TX	19,207	VC
Texas Tech Univ	TX	14,243	C
Truman State Univ	MO	15,541	HC
Univ of Conn	CT	24,706	HC
Univ of Florida	FL	15,943	HC
Univ of Illinois at Urbana-Champaign	IL	26,450	HC
Univ of Minn Crookston	MN	17,834	C
Univ of Nebr - Lincoln	NE	18,031	C
Univ of Wisc/Madison	WI	18,757	HC+
Univ of Wisc/River Falls	WI	9,722	LC
Washington State Univ	WA	20,461	C
West Virginia Univ	WV	16,542	C+
Wilmington College	OH	29,784	C

AIR TRAFFIC CONTROL

School	ST	$IS	SR
Daniel Webster College	NH	25,380	C
Embry-Riddle Aeronautical Univ - Daytona Beach	FL	40,884	C+
Florida Memorial Univ	FL	20,888	LC
Kent State Univ	OH	19,920	C
Purdue Univ/West Lafayette	IN	20,024	HC
Thomas Edison State College	NJ	5,700	SP
Univ of Alaska Anchorage	AK	16,673	NC
Univ of N Dak	ND	14,551	C
Vaughn College of Aeronautics and Technology	NY	31,360	C

AIR TRAFFIC MANAGEMENT

School	ST	$IS	SR
Arizona State Univ, at the Polytechnic Campus	AZ	20,531	C+
Embry-Riddle Aeronautical Univ - Prescott Campus	AZ	40,444	VC+

AIRCRAFT MECHANICS

School	ST	$IS	SR
Andrews Univ	MI	28,030	C+
Embry-Riddle Aeronautical Univ - Worldwide	FL	15,512	C
Idaho State Univ	ID	12,307	C
Lewis Univ	IL	23,050	C
Pennsylvania College of Technology	PA	26,286	NC
Vaughn College of Aeronautics and Technology	NY	31,360	C
Western Mich Univ	MI	19,628	C

ST = STATE $IS = IN-STATE COSTS   SR = SELECTOR RATING

AIRLINE PILOTING AND NAVIGATION

School	ST	$IS	SR
Averett Univ	VA	37,750	LC
Baylor Univ	TX	50,329	HC
Daniel Webster College	NH	25,380	C
Eastern Kentucky Univ	KY	11,161	C
Eastern Mich Univ	MI	18,604	C
Embry-Riddle Aeronautical Univ - Daytona Beach	FL	40,884	C+
Indiana State Univ	IN	16,000	C
Kansas State Univ	KS	15,497	C
Lewis Univ	IL	23,050	C
Louisiana Tech Univ	LA	11,302	C
Metropolitan State Univ of Denver	CO	4,835	LC
Ohio Univ	OH	21,080	C
Pacific Union College	CA	28,150	VC
Purdue Univ/West Lafayette	IN	20,024	HC
St. Louis Univ	MO	48,346	HC
Univ of Alaska Anchorage	AK	16,673	NC
Univ of Illinois at Urbana-Champaign	IL	26,450	HC
Univ of Minn Crookston	MN	17,834	C
Vaughn College of Aeronautics and Technology	NY	31,360	C
Western Mich Univ	MI	19,628	C

ALLIED HEALTH

School	ST	$IS	SR
Adams State Univ	CO	13,358	LC
Albany State Univ	GA	8,500	C
Andrews Univ	MI	28,030	C+
Bloomfield College	NJ	37,850	LC
Cedarville Univ	OH	32,860	VC
Clayton State Univ	GA	12,000	C
College of the Ozarks	MO		VC
East Tenn State Univ	TN	9,000	C
Eastern Mich Univ	MI	18,604	C
Fairleigh Dickinson Univ/College at Florham	NJ	42,142	C
Fairleigh Dickinson Univ/Metropolitan Campus	NJ	40,254	C
Felician College	NJ	41,640	LC
Ferris State Univ	MI	20,047	C
George Fox Univ	OR	40,750	C+
Hendrix College	AR	50,202	VC+
Hofstra Univ	NY	51,810	VC+
Howard Univ	DC	13,646	C
Ithaca College	NY	53,864	HC
Johnson State College	VT	16,721	C
Kent State Univ	OH	19,920	C
Madonna Univ	MI	24,540	C
Mars Hill Univ	NC	22,950	LC
Marshall Univ	WV	14,820	C
Mass College of Liberal Arts	MA	18,613	C
Merrimack College	MA	44,215	C
Millersville Univ of Pennsylvania	PA	21,648	C
Millikin Univ	IL	38,940	C
Minn State Univ, Mankato	MN	15,616	C
Montclair State Univ	NJ	22,614	C
Mount Aloysius College	PA	29,976	C
National Univ	CA	14,730	SP
Nebr Methodist College of Nursing and Allied Health	NE	22,690	SP
Northwestern State Univ of Louisiana	LA	14,368	C
Oakland Univ	MI	19,391	C
Oakwood Univ	AL	25,529	NC
Ramapo College of New Jersey	NJ	24,938	C
Rochester Inst of Technology	NY	42,450	VC
Roosevelt Univ	IL	22,605	VC
Rutgers, The State Univ of New Jersey/New Brunswick	NJ	25,562	C
Rutgers, The State Univ of New Jersey/Newark Campus	NJ	258,806	C
St. Louis Univ	MO	48,346	HC
Tuskegee Univ	AL	26,750	C
Univ of Central Okla	OK	12,293	C
Univ of Fl	FL	15,943	HC
Univ of Illinois at Chicago	IL	24,505	VC
Univ of St. Francis	IL	37,560	C
Univ of Texas at El Paso	TX	8,764	NC
Washington Univ in St. Louis	MO	69,844	MC
West Texas A&M Univ	TX	13,478	C
Youngstown State Univ	OH	16,732	C

AMERICAN INDIAN STUDIES

School	ST	$IS	SR
Arizona State Univ, at the Tempe Campus	AZ	20,137	C+
Fort Lewis College	CO	15,513	C
Minn State Univ, Mankato	MN	15,616	C
San Diego State Univ	CA	21,611	C+
Sonoma State Univ	CA	20,541	C
Southern Oregon Univ	OR	17,874	C
The Univ of N Car at Pembroke	NC	13,388	LC
Univ of Arizona	AZ	20,657	C
Univ of Calif at Los Angeles	CA	25,686	MC
Univ of Minn/Twin Cities	MN		HC
Univ of N Dak	ND	14,551	C
Univ of Science and Arts of Okla	OK	10,560	VC
Univ of S Dak	SD	15,111	C
Univ of Wisc/Eau Claire	WI	15,730	VC
Univ of Wisc/Green Bay	WI	19,074	C
Univ of Wyoming	WY	14,401	C+

AMERICAN LITERATURE

School	ST	$IS	SR
American Univ	DC	56,015	HC+
Bennington College	VT	56,990	HC+
Biola Univ	CA	40,320	C+
Brown Univ	RI	59,428	MC
Calvin College	MI	39,120	VC
Eastern Mich Univ	MI	18,604	C
Florida State Univ	FL	16,715	VC
Hofstra Univ	NY	51,810	VC
New York Univ	NY	61,470	MC
Southern Illinois Univ Edwardsville	IL	17,532	C
Univ of Calif at Los Angeles	CA	25,686	MC
Washington Univ in St. Louis	MO	69,844	MC
Wheeling Jesuit Univ	WV	33,500	C

AMERICAN SIGN LANGUAGE

School	ST	$IS	SR
Augustana College	SD	36,500	VC
Bethel College	IN	31,560	C
Biola Univ	CA	40,320	C+
Bloomsburg Univ of Pennsylvania	PA	13,598	C
Framingham State Univ	MA	18,854	C
Gallaudet Univ	DC	25,380	SP
Gardner-Webb Univ	NC	34,375	C+
Goshen College	IN	35,900	VC
Indiana Univ-Purdue Univ Indianapolis	IN	17,611	C
Kent State Univ	OH	19,920	C
Keuka College	NY	30,300	C
Maryville College	TN	33,150	C
Mount Aloysius College	PA	29,976	C
Northeastern Univ	MA	55,296	MC
Northwest Missouri State Univ	MO	17,347	C
St. Catherine Univ	MN	37,782	C+
Univ of Arkansas at Little Rock	AR	17,609	LC
Univ of Houston	TX	19,796	VC
Univ of Louisville	KY	17,946	C
Univ of New Mexico	NM	15,300	C
Univ of North Florida	FL	15,870	VC
Univ of Northern Colo	CO	18,446	C
Univ of Rochester	NY	60,668	MC
Western Oregon Univ	OR	15,021	C
Wright State Univ	OH	16,983	C

AMERICAN STUDIES

School	ST	$IS	SR
Albright College	PA	46,660	C
American Univ	DC	56,015	HC+
Amherst College	MA	58,744	MC
Arizona State Univ, at the West Campus	AZ	19,251	C
Ashland Univ	OH	25,000	C
Augustana College	SD	36,500	VC
Austin College	TX	45,875	VC
Bard College	NY	61,940	HC
Bard College at Simon's Rock	MA	61,749	HC+
Barnard College/Columbia Univ	NY	61,960	MC
Bates College	ME	60,720	MC
Baylor Univ	TX	50,329	HC
Bennington College	VT	56,990	HC+
Boston Univ	MA	60,694	MC
Bowling Green State Univ	OH	18,970	C
Brandeis Univ	MA		MC
Brigham Young Univ	UT	12,100	HC
Brown Univ	RI	59,428	MC
Bryant Univ	RI	49,179	VC
Cabrini College	PA	40,859	LC
Cal State, Fullerton	CA	25,188	C
Cal State, Long Beach	CA	17,502	C
Cal State, San Bernardino	CA	12,000	C
Carleton College	MN	60,102	MC
Case Western Reserve Univ	OH	56,534	MC
Cedarville Univ	OH	32,860	VC
Christopher Newport Univ	VA	21,960	VC
CUNY/Brooklyn College	NY	5,884	C+
CUNY/City College	NY	20,319	VC+
Claflin Univ	SC	22,368	LC
Claremont McKenna College	CA	62,215	MC
Clarkson Univ	NY	57,330	HC
Coe College	IA	45,550	VC
Colby College	ME	57,510	MC
College of St. Elizabeth	NJ	43,839	LC
College of Staten Island/The City of New York	NY	16,778	NC
College of William & Mary	VA	28,000	MC
Columbia College	MO	24,578	C
Columbia Univ/City of New York	NY	61,116	MC
Conn College	CT	54,970	MC
Cornell Univ	NY	60,964	MC
Creighton Univ	NE	45,356	VC
Cumberland Univ	TN	21,220	C
DePaul Univ	IL	47,623	VC
Dickinson College	PA	57,662	HC+
Dominican Univ	IL	37,628	C
Drury Univ	MO	31,909	VC
Eckerd College	FL	43,902	C
Elmhurst College	IL	43,336	C
Elmira College	NY	49,950	C+
Elms College	MA	23,900	VC
Emmanuel College	MA	47,985	VC
Emory Univ	GA	56,368	MC
Erskine College	SC	37,360	C
Fairfield Univ	CT	56,960	VC
Florida State Univ	FL	16,715	VC
Fordham Univ	NY	61,588	HC+
Franklin and Marshall College	PA	60,799	MC
Franklin Pierce Univ	NH	41,598	C
George Washington Univ	DC	57,108	MC
Georgetown College	KY	41,440	C+
Georgetown Univ	DC	52,910	MC
Goucher College	MD	52,040	VC+
Hamilton College	NY	55,620	MC
Hampshire College	MA	58,320	MC
Harding Univ	AR	23,556	C
Harvard College/Harvard Univ	MA	49,000	MC
Hendrix College	AR	50,202	VC+
Hillsdale College	MI	32,866	MC
Hobart and William Smith Colleges	NY	60,034	HC+
Hofstra Univ	NY	51,810	VC+
Illinois College	IL	25,770	VC
Illinois Wesleyan Univ	IL	48,452	HC
Indiana Univ Bloomington	IN	19,801	VC
Keene State College	NH	23,232	LC
Kent State Univ	OH	19,920	C
Kenyon College	OH	58,890	MC
Knox College	IL	44,865	VC+
Lafayette College	PA	59,155	HC+
Lake Forest College	IL	50,652	VC
Lebanon Valley College	PA	38,570	C
Lehman College/The CUNY	NY	5,778	C+
Lenoir-Rhyne College	NC	35,984	C
Lindsey Wilson College	KY	31,220	C
Lipscomb Univ	TN	37,490	VC
LIU Post	NY	47,660	C
Lycoming College	PA	45,379	C
Macalester College	MN	57,691	MC
Manhattanville College	NY	50,740	VC
Marist College	NY	35,500	C
Mary Baldwin College	VA	38,245	C
Meredith College	NC	31,420	C
Miami Univ	OH	24,191	VC
Mich State Univ	MI	22,450	VC
Middlebury College	VT	59,160	MC
Mills College	CA	54,119	VC
Miss College	MS	21,998	C
Montreat College	NC	31,298	C
Mount St. Mary's College - Chalon Campus	CA	43,897	VC+
Muhlenberg College	PA	52,837	HC
Muskingum Univ	OH	30,502	C
Nazareth College of Rochester	NY	43,028	C+
New York Univ	NY	61,470	MC
Northwestern Univ	IL	61,640	MC
Oberlin College	OH	61,788	MC
Occidental College	CA	60,972	MC
Oglethorpe Univ	GA	44,200	C+
Okla State Univ	OK	14,310	VC
Oregon State Univ	OR	20,273	VC
Oswego / SUNY	NY	20,009	VC
Pace Univ	NY	53,367	C
Pitzer College	CA	54,988	MC
Pomona College	CA	57,680	MC
Providence College	RI	57,383	VC
Queens College/The CUNY	NY	17,107	VC
Ramapo College of New Jersey	NJ	24,938	C
Reed College	OR	57,780	MC
Rider Univ	NJ	45,720	C
Roger Williams Univ	RI	46,296	VC
Roosevelt Univ	IL	22,605	VC
Rowan Univ	NJ	24,022	VC+
Rutgers, The State Univ of New Jersey/New Brunswick	NJ	25,562	C
Rutgers, The State Univ of New Jersey/Newark Campus	NJ	258,806	C
St. Louis Univ	MO	48,346	HC
St. Michael's College	VT	49,975	VC
St. Peter's College	NJ	44,240	C
Salem College	NC	29,326	VC
Salve Regina Univ	RI	48,550	VC
San Diego State Univ	CA	21,611	C+
San Francisco State Univ	CA	18,514	C
Scripps College	CA	61,940	MC
Sewanee: The Univ of the South	TN	47,700	HC+
Siena College	NY	43,863	VC
Skidmore College	NY	59,942	HC
Smith College	MA	59,674	MC
Southern Nazarene Univ	OK	24,354	C
St. John Fisher College	NY	40,708	C+
St. Olaf College	MN	51,200	HC+
Stanford Univ	CA	58,388	MC
Stetson Univ	FL	51,516	VC
Stonehill College	MA	46,780	HC
Stony Brook Univ / SUNY	NY	20,078	HC+
Suffolk Univ	MA	47,298	C
SUNY College at Geneseo	NY	18,670	HC
SUNY College at Old Westbury	NY	16,324	C
SUNY Fredonia/The SUNY at Fredonia	NY	19,840	VC
Temple Univ	PA	24,392	VC
Texas State Univ	TX	17,128	C
The College of St. Rose	NY	26,750	C
Trinity College	CT		HC+
Tufts Univ	MA	58,780	MC
Tulane Univ	LA	60,861	MC
Union College	NY	60,240	MC
Univ at Buffalo / The SUNY	NY	20,283	VC
Univ of Alabama at Tuscaloosa	AL	17,164	C+
Univ of Arkansas at Fayetteville	AR	18,352	C+
Univ of Calif at Berkeley	CA	23,322	MC
Univ of Calif at Davis	CA		HC
Univ of Calif at Santa Cruz	CA	27,807	C+
Univ of Dayton	OH	49,070	VC
Univ of Florida	FL	15,943	HC
Univ of Hawaii at Manoa	HI	19,379	C
Univ of Idaho	ID	14,558	C
Univ of Iowa	IA	17,693	VC
Univ of Kansas	KS	17,603	C+
Univ of Mary Washington	VA	19,484	VC
Univ of Maryland - College Park	MD	20,060	HC
Univ of Maryland/Baltimore County	MD	18,000	VC
Univ of Mass Boston	MA	23,066	VC
Univ of Mass Lowell	MA	19,316	C
Univ of Miami	FL	57,034	MC
Univ of Mich/Ann Arbor	MI	22,102	MC
Univ of Mich/Dearborn	MI	9,885	VC
Univ of Minn/Twin Cities	MN		HC
Univ of Mount Union	OH	35,130	C
Univ of New Mexico	NM	15,300	C
Univ of N Car at Chapel Hill	NC	18,928	MC
Univ of Notre Dame	IN	57,117	MC
Univ of Pennsylvania	PA	61,132	MC
Univ of Pittsburgh at Greensburg	PA	17,640	C
Univ of Pittsburgh at Johnstown	PA	20,862	LC
Univ of Rio Grande	OH	8,750	NC
Univ of Rochester	NY	60,668	MC
Univ of St. Francis	IN	29,810	C
Univ of South Florida/Tampa	FL	13,000	C
Univ of Southern Calif	CA	56,903	MC
Univ of Texas at Austin	TX	44,074	HC
Univ of Texas at Dallas	TX	21,348	HC+
Univ of Texas at San Antonio	TX	18,372	C
Univ of Wisc/Stevens Point	WI	14,043	C
Univ of Wyoming	WY	14,401	C
Upper Iowa Univ	IA	30,426	NC
Ursinus College	PA	57,580	VC
Utah State Univ	UT	12,044	C
Valparaiso Univ	IN	44,940	VC+
Vanderbilt Univ	TN	58,220	MC
Vassar College	NY	61,140	MC
Virginia Wesleyan College	VA	28,433	LC
Warner Pacific College	OR	25,550	C
Washington College	MD	52,602	VC
Washington Univ in St. Louis	MO	69,844	MC
Webster Univ	MO	35,100	C+
Wellesley College	MA	59,038	MC
Wells College	NY	49,400	VC
Wesley College	DE	31,115	LC
Wesleyan College	GA	24,000	C
Wesleyan Univ	CT	61,198	MC
West Chester Univ of Pennsylvania	PA	17,186	C
Western Conn State Univ	CT	18,327	LC
Western Washington Univ	WA	18,519	VC
Wheaton College	MA	54,934	HC+
Whitworth Univ	WA	47,734	VC
Willamette Univ	OR	56,450	VC+
Williams College	MA	61,070	MC
Wittenberg Univ	OH	47,962	C+
Yale Univ	CT	55,300	MC
Youngstown State Univ	OH	16,732	C

ANATOMY

School	ST	$IS	SR
Andrews Univ	MI	28,030	C+
Duke Univ	NC	50,250	MC
Howard Univ	DC	13,646	C
Marshall Univ	WV	14,820	C

ANIMAL FEED SCIENCE

School	ST	$IS	SR
Kansas State Univ	KS	15,497	VC

ANIMAL SCIENCE

School	ST	$IS	SR
Abilene Christian Univ	TX	38,400	C+
Alabama A&M Univ	AL	10,084	C
Andrews Univ	MI	28,030	C
Angelo State Univ	TX	15,049	NC
Arkansas State Univ	AR	15,470	C
Auburn Univ	AL	22,378	VC+

ST = STATE $IS = IN-STATE COSTS SR = SELECTOR RATING

School	ST	$IS	SR
Becker College	MA	41,420	C
Berry College	GA	39,254	VC
Bucknell Univ	PA	60,140	MC
Calif Polytechnic State Univ	CA	19,847	HC
Calif State Polytechnic Univ, Pomona	CA	20,156	C
Cal State, Chico	CA	20,158	C
Cal State, Fresno	CA	17,405	C
Clemson Univ	SC	19,136	HC
College of the Ozarks	MO		VC
Colo State Univ-Fort Collins	CO	20,385	VC
Cornell Univ	NY	60,964	MC
Delaware Valley College	PA	29,944	C
Dordt College	IA	34,160	C+
Eastern New Mexico Univ	NM	10,682	C
Florida A&M Univ	FL	14,935	LC
Fort Valley State Univ	GA	11,200	VC
Hampshire College	MA	58,320	MC
Hardin-Simmons Univ	TX	23,560	C+
Indiana Univ Bloomington	IN	19,801	VC
Iowa State Univ	IA	16,403	C
Kansas State Univ	KS	15,497	VC
Langston Univ	OK	3,000	C
Louisiana State Univ	LA	18,677	C+
Louisiana Tech Univ	LA	11,302	C
Lubbock Christian Univ	TX	26,308	C
Mich State Univ	MI	22,450	VC
Middle Tenn State Univ	TN	8,650	C
Millersville Univ of Pennsylvania	PA	21,648	C
Miss State Univ	MS	14,750	C
Missouri State Univ	MO	13,996	C+
Montana State Univ	MT	14,068	C
New Mexico State Univ	NM	14,050	C
N Car Agricultural and Technical State Univ	NC	13,365	LC
N Car State Univ	NC	16,202	HC
N Dak State Univ	ND		C
Northwest Missouri State Univ	MO	17,347	C
Okla Panhandle State Univ	OK	8,996	C
Okla State Univ	OK	14,310	VC
Oregon State Univ	OR	20,273	VC
Prairie View A&M Univ	TX	15,205	LC
Purdue Univ/West Lafayette	IN	20,024	HC
Rutgers, The State Univ of New Jersey/New Brunswick	NJ	25,562	VC
Sam Houston State Univ	TX	17,082	C
S Dak State Univ	SD	14,296	C
Southern Illinois Univ Carbondale	IL	21,942	C
Southwestern Univ	TX	45,660	VC
SUNY / College of Environmental Science and Forestry	NY	18,351	VC
Stephen F. Austin State Univ	TX	14,668	C
Sul Ross State Univ	TX	13,410	LC
Tarleton State Univ	TX	13,489	LC
Tenn Tech Univ	TN	11,310	C
Texas A&M Univ	TX	19,207	VC
Texas A&M Univ at Commerce	TX	10,496	C
Texas A&M Univ at Kingsville	TX	7,500	LC
Texas State Univ	TX	17,128	C
Texas Tech Univ	TX	14,243	C
Ohio State Univ-Columbus Campus	OH	19,887	HC+
The Pennsylvania State Univ - Univ Park	PA	28,022	VC+
The SUNY College of Agriculture and Tech at Cobleskill	NY	19,749	VC
Truman State Univ	MO	15,541	HC
Tuskegee Univ	AL	26,750	C
Unity College	ME	34,054	C
Univ of Arizona	AZ	20,657	C
Univ of Arkansas at Fayetteville	AR	18,352	C+
Univ of Calif at Davis	CA		HC
Univ of Calif at San Diego	CA	21,000	VC
Univ of Conn	CT	24,706	HC
Univ of Delaware	DE	23,612	VC
Univ of Florida	FL	15,943	HC
Univ of Georgia	GA	20,082	VC
Univ of Hawaii at Manoa	HI	19,379	VC
Univ of Idaho	ID	14,558	C
Univ of Illinois at Urbana-Champaign	IL	26,450	HC
Univ of Kentucky	KY	19,868	C
Univ of Maine	ME	19,902	C+
Univ of Maryland - College Park	MD	20,060	HC
Univ of Mass Amherst	MA	24,215	VC+
Univ of Minn Crookston	MN	17,834	C
Univ of Minn/Twin Cities	MN		HC
Univ of Missouri/Columbia	MO	18,201	MC
Univ of Montana-Western	MT	9,753	LC
Univ of Nebr - Lincoln	NE	18,031	VC
Univ of New England	ME	46,750	C
Univ of New Hampshire	NH	26,912	C
Univ of PR/Mayaguez	PR	1,250	
Univ of Tenn at Knoxville	TN	20,364	VC+
Univ of Tenn at Martin	TN	13,734	C
Univ of Vermont	VT	27,006	VC+
Univ of Wisc/Madison	WI	18,757	HC+
Univ of Wisc/Platteville	WI	14,564	C
Univ of Wisc/River Falls	WI	9,722	LC
Univ of Wyoming	WY	14,401	C+
Utah State Univ	UT	12,044	C
Virginia Polytechnic Inst and State Univ	VA	14,629	HC
Washington State Univ	WA	20,461	C
West Texas A&M Univ	TX	13,478	C
West Virginia Univ	WV	16,542	C+
Western Illinois Univ	IL	20,732	C
Wilmington College	OH	29,784	C
Wilson College	PA	35,080	C

ANIMAL SCIENCE & TECHNOLOGY

School	ST	$IS	SR
Univ of Rhode Island	RI	24,002	C

ANIMATION

School	ST	$IS	SR
Art Inst of Atlanta	GA	24,000	SP
Art Inst of Portland	OR	23,040	SP
Bennington College	VT	56,990	HC+
Bloomfield College	NJ	37,850	LC
Brigham Young Univ	UT	12,100	HC
Calif College of the Arts	CA	48,334	SP
Calif Inst of the Arts	CA	51,902	SP
Cleveland Inst of Art	OH	48,685	VC
Cogswell Polytechnical College	CA	30,531	C
College for Creative Studies	MI	45,340	C
Columbus College of Art and Design	OH	37,732	SP
Daemen College	NY	34,770	C
DePaul Univ	IL	47,623	VC
Drexel Univ	PA	61,418	VC+
Eastern Mich Univ	MI	18,604	C
Fairleigh Dickinson Univ/College at Florham	NJ	42,142	C
Huntington Univ	IN	32,220	C+
Kansas City Art Inst	MO	44,308	SP
Laguna College of Art and Design	CA	27,300	SP
Lawrence Tech Univ	MI	37,630	VC
Loyola Marymount Univ	CA	54,649	VC+
Maryland Inst College of Art	MD	39,500	SP
Memphis College of Art	TN	33,550	SP
Minneapolis College of Art and Design	MN	36,700	SP
Moore College of Art and Design	PA	50,135	SP
Moore College of Art and Design	PA	50,135	SP
New Mexico State Univ	NM	14,050	C
New York Univ	NY	61,470	MC
NewSchool of Architecture & Design	CA	24,900	SP
Northwestern College	MN	24,000	C
Rochester Inst of Technology	NY	42,450	VC
Rocky Mountain College of Art and Design	CO	22,470	SP
Santa Fe Univ of Art and Design	NM	39,666	SP
Savannah College of Art and Design	GA	48,005	SP
School of Visual Arts	NY	36,500	VC
Southern Adventist Univ	TN	26,190	C
SUNY Fredonia/The SUNY at Fredonia	NY	19,840	VC
The Univ of Utah	UT	16,463	VC
Univ of Denver	CO	51,787	VC+
Univ of Idaho	ID	14,558	C
Webster Univ	MO	35,100	C+
Woodbury Univ	CA	34,500	LC

ANTHROPOLOGY

School	ST	$IS	SR
Adelphi Univ	NY	44,670	VC
Agnes Scott College	GA	45,323	C+
Albion College	MI	46,010	C
Alma College	MI	44,075	C
American Univ	DC	56,015	HC+
Amherst College	MA	58,744	MC
Andrews Univ	MI	28,030	C+
Appalachian State Univ	NC	12,919	VC
Arizona State Univ, at the Tempe Campus	AZ	20,137	C+
Ashford Univ	CA	10,480	C
Auburn Univ	AL	22,378	VC+
Augustana College	IL	43,398	VC
Augustana College	SD	36,500	VC
Ball State Univ	IN	17,850	C
Bard College	NY	61,940	HC
Barnard College/Columbia Univ	NY	39,000	MC
Bates College	ME	60,720	MC
Baylor Univ	TX	50,329	HC
Beloit College	WI	49,970	HC
Bennington College	VT	56,990	HC+
Berry College	GA	39,254	VC
Binghamton Univ/The SUNY	NY	21,648	HC+
Biola Univ	CA	40,320	C+
Bloomsburg Univ of Pennsylvania	PA	13,598	C
Boise State Univ	ID	13,469	LC
Boston Univ	MA	60,694	MC
Bowdoin College	ME	59,568	MC
Brandeis Univ	MA		MC
Bridgewater State Univ	MA	18,752	C
Brigham Young Univ	UT	12,100	HC
Brown Univ	RI	59,428	MC
Bryn Mawr College	PA	59,890	MC
Bucknell Univ	PA	60,140	MC
Buffalo State College / SUNY	NY	15,733	C+
Butler Univ	IN	47,572	VC+
Calif Baptist Univ	CA	38,792	C
Calif Polytechnic State Univ	CA	19,847	HC
Calif State Polytechnic Univ, Pomona	CA	20,156	C
Cal State, Bakersfield	CA	8,000	C
Cal State, Chico	CA	20,158	C
Cal State, Dominguez Hills	CA	17,090	LC
Cal State, East Bay	CA	16,549	C
Cal State, Fresno	CA	17,405	C
Cal State, Fullerton	CA	25,188	C
Cal State, Long Beach	CA	17,502	C+
Cal State, Los Angeles	CA	17,186	LC
Cal State, Northridge	CA	28,690	LC
Cal State, Sacramento	CA	16,200	C
Cal State, San Bernardino	CA	12,000	C
Cal State, Stanislaus	CA	18,582	C
Canisius College	NY	44,900	C
Carleton College	MN	60,102	MC
Case Western Reserve Univ	OH	56,534	MC
Central College	IA	42,104	C+
Central Conn State Univ	CT	19,749	C
Central Washington Univ	WA	11,730	C
Centre College	KY	35,000	HC+
CUNY/Brooklyn College	NY	5,884	C+
CUNY/City College	NY	20,319	HC+
Clarion Univ of Pennsylvania	PA	17,370	LC
Cleveland State Univ	OH	21,776	C
Colby College	ME	57,510	MC
College of Charleston	SC	22,145	VC
College of the Holy Cross	MA	58,042	MC
College of William & Mary	VA	28,000	MC
College of Wooster	OH	52,600	VC
Colo College	CO	57,162	MC
Colo State Univ-Fort Collins	CO	20,385	VC
Columbia Univ/City of New York	NY	61,116	MC
Columbia Univ/School of General Studies	NY	58,231	MC
Conn College	CT	54,970	MC
Cornell Univ	NY	60,964	MC
Creighton Univ	NE	45,356	VC
Dartmouth College	NH	57,996	MC
Davidson College	NC	58,146	MC
Denison Univ	OH	54,670	HC+
DePaul Univ	IL	47,623	VC
DePauw Univ	IN	48,950	VC+
Dickinson College	PA	57,662	HC+
Drew Univ/College of Liberal Arts	NJ	57,516	C
Drexel Univ	PA	61,418	VC+
Duke Univ	NC	50,250	MC
Earlham College	IN	51,470	HC
East Carolina Univ	NC	14,169	C
Eastern Kentucky Univ	KY	11,161	C
Eastern Mich Univ	MI	18,604	C
Eastern New Mexico Univ	NM	10,682	C
Eastern Oregon Univ	OR	10,400	C
Eastern Washington Univ	WA		C
Eckerd College	FL	43,902	C
Edinboro Univ of Pennsylvania	PA	15,940	LC
Elmira College	NY	49,950	C+
Elon Univ	NC	41,914	VC+
Emory Univ	GA	56,368	MC
Eugene Lang College/The New School for Liberal Arts	NY	55,650	C
Fairfield Univ	CT	56,960	VC
Florida Atlantic Univ	FL	17,339	C
Florida Gulf Coast Univ	FL		C
Florida State Univ	FL	16,715	VC
Fordham Univ	NY	61,588	HC+
Fort Lewis College	CO	15,513	C
Franciscan Univ of Steubenville	OH	27,320	VC
Franklin and Marshall College	PA	60,799	MC
Franklin Pierce Univ	NH	41,598	C
George Mason Univ	VA	15,724	VC
George Washington Univ	DC	57,108	MC
Georgetown Univ	DC	52,910	MC
Georgia Regents Univ	GA		C
Georgia Southern Univ	GA	16,942	C
Georgia State Univ	GA	15,582	VC
Gettysburg College	PA	58,820	HC
Goucher College	MD	52,040	VC+
Grand Valley State Univ	MI	17,998	C+
Grinnell College	IA	53,654	HC
Guilford College	NC	42,800	C
Gustavus Adolphus College	MN	48,170	HC
Hamilton College	NY	55,620	MC
Hamline Univ	MN	45,678	VC
Hampshire College	MA	58,320	MC
Hanover College	IN	43,073	C+
Hartwick College	NY	51,270	C
Harvard College/Harvard Univ	MA	49,000	MC
Haverford College	PA	61,564	MC
Hawaii Pacific Univ	HI	34,360	C
Heidelberg Univ	OH	34,100	C
Hendrix College	AR	50,202	VC+
Hobart and William Smith Colleges	NY	60,034	HC+
Hofstra Univ	NY	51,810	VC+
Howard Univ	DC	13,646	C
Humboldt State Univ	CA	18,400	C
Hunter College	NY	14,429	VC
Idaho State Univ	ID	12,307	C
Illinois State Univ	IL	23,110	VC
Illinois Wesleyan Univ	IL	48,452	HC
Indiana State Univ	IN	16,000	C
Indiana Univ Bloomington	IN	19,801	VC
Indiana Univ Northwest	IN	6,854	LC
Indiana Univ of Pennsylvania	PA	20,846	LC
Indiana Univ South Bend	IN	15,501	C
Indiana Univ-Purdue Univ Fort Wayne	IN	15,521	C
Indiana Univ-Purdue Univ Indianapolis	IN	17,611	C
Iowa State Univ	IA	16,403	C
Ithaca College	NY	53,864	HC
James Madison Univ	VA	18,049	VC
Johns Hopkins Univ	MD	47,492	MC
Johnson State College	VT	16,721	C
Judson Univ	IL	25,130	C
Juniata College	PA	49,340	VC
Kalamazoo College	MI	49,740	HC
Kansas State Univ	KS	15,497	VC
Keene State College	NH	23,232	LC
Kennesaw State Univ	GA		C
Kent State Univ	OH	19,920	C
Kenyon College	OH	58,890	MC
Knox College	IL	46,845	VC+
Kutztown Univ of Pennsylvania	PA	16,909	LC
Lafayette College	PA	59,155	HC+
Lake Forest College	IL	50,652	VC
Lawrence Univ	WI	46,371	HC
Le Moyne College	NY	43,470	C
Lee Univ	TN	18,690	C+
Lehigh Univ	PA	56,770	MC
Lehman College/The CUNY	NY	5,778	LC
Lewis & Clark College	OR	54,382	MC
Linfield College-McMinnville Campus	OR	47,676	C
LIU Brooklyn	NY	47,182	LC
Longwood Univ	VA	20,924	C
Louisiana State Univ	LA	18,677	C+
Loyola Univ Chicago	IL	51,646	VC+
Loyola Univ New Orleans	LA	46,581	VC
Luther College	IA	45,720	C+
Lycoming College	PA	45,379	C
Macalester College	MN	57,691	MC
Mansfield Univ	PA	19,468	LC
Marlboro College	VT	35,980	VC
Marquette Univ	WI	46,930	VC+
Mary Baldwin College	VA	38,245	C
Mass Inst of Technology	MA	58,240	MC
Mercer Univ	GA	44,201	VC
Mercyhurst Univ	PA	40,700	C
Metropolitan State Univ of Denver	CO	4,835	LC
Miami Univ	OH	24,191	VC
Mich State Univ	MI	22,450	VC
Mich Tech Univ	MI	23,556	HC
Middle Tenn State Univ	TN	8,650	C
Middlebury College	VT	59,160	MC
Millersville Univ of Pennsylvania	PA	21,648	C
Mills College	CA	54,119	VC
Millsaps College	MS	43,888	VC+
Minn State Univ, Mankato	MN	15,616	C
Minn State Univ, Moorhead	MN	13,392	VC
Miss State Univ	MS	14,750	C
Missouri State Univ	MO	13,996	C+
Missouri Valley College	MO	22,200	C
Monmouth College	IL	40,850	C
Monmouth Univ	NJ	44,108	C
Montana State Univ	MT	14,068	C
Montclair State Univ	NJ	22,614	C
Mount Holyoke College	MA	55,146	MC
Muhlenberg College	PA	52,837	HC
National Louis Univ	IL	16,915	LC
Nazareth College of Rochester	NY	43,028	C+
New College of Florida	FL	14,504	MC
New Mexico Highlands Univ	NM	11,904	NC
New Mexico State Univ	NM	14,050	C
New York Univ	NY	61,470	MC
North Central College	IL	38,343	VC
N Dak State Univ	ND		C
North Park Univ	IL	30,130	C
Northeastern Illinois Univ	IL	10,318	LC
Northeastern Univ	MA	55,296	MC
Northern Arizona Univ	AZ	19,010	C
Northern Illinois Univ	IL	19,768	C
Northern Kentucky Univ	KY	21,134	C
Northwestern Univ	IL	61,640	MC
Nova Southeastern Univ	FL	37,280	VC
Oakland Univ	MI	19,391	C
Oberlin College	OH	61,788	MC
Ohio Univ	OH	21,080	C
Ohio Wesleyan Univ	OH	49,460	C+
Olivet College	MI	19,984	LC
Oregon State Univ	OR	20,273	VC

ST = STATE $IS = IN-STATE COSTS   SR = SELECTOR RATING

School	ST	$IS	SR
Oswego / SUNY	NY	20,009	VC
Pacific Lutheran Univ	WA	46,760	C+
Pitzer College	CA	54,988	MC
Plymouth State Univ	NH	23,148	LC
Pomona College	CA	57,680	MC
Portland State Univ	OR	18,672	C
Prescott College	AZ	33,284	C
Princeton Univ	NJ	53,795	MC
Purdue Univ/West Lafayette	IN	20,024	HC
Queens College/The CUNY	NY	17,107	VC
Radford Univ	VA	17,766	LC
Reed College	OR	57,780	MC
Rhode Island College	RI	17,694	LC
Rhodes College	TN	51,900	HC+
Rice Univ	TX	43,288	MC
Richard Stockton College of New Jersey	NJ	20,000	VC
Ripon College	WI	36,959	C+
Rockford College	IL	31,000	C
Roger Williams Univ	RI	46,296	VC
Rollins College	FL	52,370	HC
Rutgers, The State Univ of New Jersey/New Brunswick	NJ	25,562	VC
Rutgers, The State Univ of New Jersey/Newark Campus	NJ	258,806	C
St. Louis Univ	MO	48,346	HC
St. Mary's College of Calif	CA	53,550	C
St. Michael's College	VT	49,975	VC
St. Vincent College	PA	40,244	C
San Diego State Univ	CA	21,611	C+
San Francisco State Univ	CA	18,514	C
San Jose State Univ	CA	19,133	LC
Sarah Lawrence College	NY	48,000	HC
Scripps College	CA	61,940	MC
Seattle Univ	WA	49,035	VC+
Seton Hall Univ	NJ	45,902	C
Sewanee: The Univ of the South	TN	47,700	HC+
Skidmore College	NY	59,942	HC
Slippery Rock Univ of Pennsylvania	PA	10,360	C
Smith College	MA	59,674	MC
Sonoma State Univ	CA	20,541	C
Southern Illinois Univ Carbondale	IL	21,942	C
Southern Illinois Univ Edwardsville	IL	17,532	C
Southern Methodist Univ	TX	60,585	MC
Southern Oregon Univ	OR	17,874	C
Southwestern Univ	TX	45,660	VC
Spelman College	GA	24,650	C
St. Cloud State Univ	MN	10,600	C
St. John Fisher College	NY	40,708	C+
St. John's Univ	NY	55,070	C+
St. Lawrence Univ	NY	59,972	VC
St. Mary's College of Maryland	MD	25,754	VC
Stanford Univ	CA	58,388	MC
SUNY at Purchase	NY	16,951	C
Stony Brook Univ / SUNY	NY	20,078	HC+
SUNY College at Geneseo	NY	18,670	HC
SUNY Cortland/The SUNY	NY	19,759	C+
SUNY New Paltz	NY	14,348	C
SUNY Oneonta / SUNY	NY	16,919	C+
SUNY Plattsburgh / SUNY	NY	18,083	C
Susquehanna Univ	PA	51,150	C
Swarthmore College	PA	57,870	MC
Syracuse Univ	NY	56,346	VC
Temple Univ	PA	24,392	VC
Texas A&M Univ	TX	19,207	VC
Texas A&M Univ at Commerce	TX	10,496	C
Texas A&M Univ at Kingsville	TX	7,500	LC
Texas Christian Univ	TX	49,980	HC
Texas State Univ	TX	17,128	C
Texas Tech Univ	TX	14,243	C
The Catholic Univ of America	DC	52,852	VC
The College of Idaho	ID	31,277	C+
The Lincoln Univ	PA	15,154	LC
Ohio State Univ-Columbus Campus	OH	19,887	HC+
The Pennsylvania State Univ - Univ Park	PA	28,022	VC+
The SUNY at Potsdam	NY	18,473	C
The SUNY/College at Brockport	NY	19,002	C
The Univ of Memphis	TN	15,094	C
The Univ of N Car at Greensboro	NC	12,848	C
The Univ of Okla	OK	18,621	VC
The Univ of Utah	UT	16,463	VC
Thomas Edison State College	NJ	5,700	SP
Towson Univ	MD	16,000	VC
Transylvania Univ	KY	42,660	VC+
Trinity College	CT		HC+
Trinity Univ	TX	48,150	HC+
Truman State Univ	MO	15,541	HC
Tufts Univ	MA	58,780	MC
Tulane Univ	LA	60,861	MC
Union College	NY	60,240	MC
Univ at Albany / SUNY	NY	18,674	VC
Univ at Buffalo / The SUNY	NY	20,283	VC
Univ of Akron	OH	20,436	C
Univ of Alabama at Birmingham	AL	18,484	C+
Univ of Alabama at Tuscaloosa	AL	17,164	C+
Univ of Alaska Anchorage	AK	16,673	NC
Univ of Alaska Fairbanks	AK	15,130	C
Univ of Arizona	AZ	20,657	C
Univ of Arkansas at Fayetteville	AR	18,352	C+
Univ of Calif at Berkeley	CA	23,322	MC
Univ of Calif at Davis	CA		HC
Univ of Calif at Irvine	CA	25,961	VC
Univ of Calif at Los Angeles	CA	25,686	MC
Univ of Calif at Riverside	CA	27,204	C+
Univ of Calif at San Diego	CA	21,000	VC
Univ of Calif at Santa Barbara	CA	27,551	HC
Univ of Calif at Santa Cruz	CA	27,807	C+
Univ of Central Florida	FL	15,668	VC+
Univ of Chicago	IL	55,416	MC
Univ of Cincinnati	OH	21,506	VC
Univ of Colo at Colo Springs	CO	15,000	VC
Univ of Colo Boulder	CO	22,605	VC+
Univ of Colo Denver	CO	17,904	V
Univ of Conn	CT	24,706	HC
Univ of Delaware	DE	23,612	VC
Univ of Denver	CO	51,787	VC+
Univ of Florida	FL	15,943	HC
Univ of Georgia	GA	20,082	VC
Univ of Hawaii at Hilo	HI	23,066	C
Univ of Hawaii at Manoa	HI	19,379	C
Univ of Houston	TX	19,796	VC
Univ of Idaho	ID	14,558	C
Univ of Illinois at Chicago	IL	24,505	VC
Univ of Illinois at Urbana-Champaign	IL	26,450	HC
Univ of Indianapolis	IN	31,740	LC
Univ of Iowa	IA	17,693	VC
Univ of Kansas	KS	17,603	C+
Univ of Kentucky	KY	19,868	C
Univ of La Verne	CA	47,010	C
Univ of Louisiana at Lafayette	LA	6,130	C
Univ of Louisville	KY	17,946	C
Univ of Maine	ME	19,902	VC
Univ of Maine at Farmington	ME	18,187	LC
Univ of Mary Washington	VA	19,484	VC
Univ of Maryland - College Park	MD	20,060	HC
Univ of Maryland/Baltimore County	MD	18,000	VC
Univ of Mass Amherst	MA	24,215	VC+
Univ of Mass Boston	MA	23,066	VC
Univ of Mass Dartmouth	MA	22,223	C
Univ of Miami	FL	57,034	MC
Univ of Mich/Ann Arbor	MI	22,102	MC
Univ of Mich/Dearborn	MI	9,885	VC
Univ of Mich-Flint	MI	17,547	C+
Univ of Minn/Duluth	MN	19,806	C
Univ of Minn/Morris	MN	17,150	VC
Univ of Minn/Twin Cities	MN		HC
Univ of Miss	MS	16,704	C+
Univ of Missouri/Columbia	MO	18,201	MC
Univ of Missouri-St. Louis	MO		VC
Univ of Montana	MT	14,105	C
Univ of Montana-Western	MT	9,753	C
Univ of Nebr - Lincoln	NE	18,031	VC
Univ of Nevada, Las Vegas	NV	17,303	C
Univ of Nevada/Reno	NV	17,507	C
Univ of New Hampshire	NH	26,912	C
Univ of New Mexico	NM	15,300	C
Univ of New Orleans	LA	9,224	C
Univ of N Car at Asheville	NC	13,500	VC
Univ of N Car at Chapel Hill	NC	18,928	MC
Univ of N Car at Charlotte	NC	15,547	C
Univ of N Car at Wilmington	NC	13,572	VC
Univ of N Dak	ND	14,551	C
Univ of North Florida	FL	15,870	VC
Univ of North Texas	TX	15,628	C
Univ of Northern Colo	CO	18,446	C
Univ of Northern Iowa	IA	15,795	C
Univ of Notre Dame	IN	57,117	MC
Univ of Oregon	OR	21,360	C+
Univ of Pennsylvania	PA	61,132	MC
Univ of Pittsburgh at Greensburg	PA	17,640	C
Univ of Pittsburgh at Pittsburgh	PA	28,572	HC+
Univ of PR Recinto de Rio Piedras	PR	5,750	
Univ of Redlands	CA	40,500	VC
Univ of Rochester	NY	60,668	MC
Univ of San Diego	CA	54,818	HC+
Univ of South Alabama	AL	13,510	C
Univ of S Car at Columbia	SC	19,725	VC+
Univ of S Dak	SD	15,111	C
Univ of South Florida/St. Petersburg	FL	12,769	C
Univ of South Florida/Tampa	FL	13,000	C
Univ of Southern Calif	CA	56,903	MC
Univ of Southern Indiana	IN	14,885	C
Univ of Southern Maine	ME	16,576	C
Univ of Southern Miss	MS	13,170	C
Univ of Tenn at Knoxville	TN	20,364	VC+
Univ of Texas - Pan American	TX	11,125	LC
Univ of Texas at Arlington	TX	10,908	LC
Univ of Texas at Austin	TX	44,074	HC
Univ of Texas at El Paso	TX	8,764	NC
Univ of Texas at San Antonio	TX	18,372	C
Univ of Toledo	OH	18,464	C
Univ of Tulsa	OK	46,331	MC
Univ of Vermont	VT	27,006	VC+
Univ of Virginia	VA	23,050	MC
Univ of Washington	WA	14,722	VC
Univ of West Georgia	GA	15,488	LC
Univ of Wisc/Madison	WI	18,757	HC+
Univ of Wisc/Oshkosh	WI	10,426	LC
Univ of Wisc-Milwaukee	WI	18,436	C
Univ of Wyoming	WY	14,401	C+
Ursinus College	PA	57,580	VC
Vanderbilt Univ	TN	58,220	MC
Vanguard Univ of Southern Calif	CA	35,833	VC
Vassar College	NY	61,140	MC
Virginia Commonwealth Univ	VA	21,716	C
Wagner College	NY	48,600	C+
Wake Forest Univ	NC	58,838	MC
Warren Wilson College	NC	40,132	VC
Washburn Univ	KS	12,579	C
Washington and Lee Univ	VA	52,812	MC
Washington College	MD	52,602	VC
Washington State Univ	WA	20,461	C
Washington Univ in St. Louis	MO	69,844	MC
Wayne State Univ	MI	22,063	C
Wellesley College	MA	59,038	MC
Wells College	NY	49,400	VC
Wesleyan Univ	CT	61,198	MC
West Chester Univ of Pennsylvania	PA	17,186	C
West Virginia Univ	WV	16,542	C+
Western Carolina Univ	NC	13,965	C
Western Conn State Univ	CT	18,327	LC
Western Illinois Univ	IL	20,732	C
Western Kentucky Univ	KY	11,000	LC
Western Mich Univ	MI	19,628	C
Western Oregon Univ	OR	15,021	C
Western State Colo Univ	CO	16,924	C
Western Washington Univ	WA	18,519	VC
Westminster College	MO	31,720	VC
Wheaton College	IL	40,720	MC
Wheaton College	MA	54,934	HC+
Whitman College	WA	55,988	MC
Wichita State Univ	KS	14,607	C+
Widener Univ	PA	52,418	C
Willamette Univ	OR	56,450	VC+
William Paterson Univ of New Jersey	NJ	21,694	C
Williams College	MA	61,070	MC
Wright State Univ	OH	16,983	C
Yale Univ	CT	55,300	MC
York College / The CUNY	NY	5,496	VC
Youngstown State Univ	OH	16,732	C

APPAREL AND ACCESSORIES MARKETING

School	ST	$IS	SR
Auburn Univ	AL	22,378	VC+
Baylor Univ	TX	50,329	HC
Calif State Polytechnic Univ, Pomona	CA	20,156	C
Cheyney Univ of Pennsylvania	PA	20,372	LC
Colo State Univ-Fort Collins	CO	20,385	VC
Dominican Univ	IL	37,628	C
Eastern Mich Univ	MI	18,604	C
Fashion Inst of Technology/SUNY	NY	18,362	SP
Fontbonne Univ	MO	31,384	C
Indiana Univ Bloomington	IN	19,801	VC
Kansas State Univ	KS	15,497	VC
Kentucky State Univ	KY	11,000	LC
S Dak State Univ	SD	14,296	C
The Univ of N Car at Greensboro	NC	12,848	C
Univ of Arkansas at Fayetteville	AR	18,352	C+
Univ of Nebr - Lincoln	NE	18,031	VC
Virginia Polytechnic Inst and State Univ	VA	14,629	HC
Youngstown State Univ	OH	16,732	C

APPAREL AND TEXTILES

School	ST	$IS	SR
Baylor Univ	TX	50,329	HC
Missouri State Univ	MO	13,996	C+
Northwest Missouri State Univ	MO	17,347	C
Southern Polytechnic State Univ	GA	13,958	C
Univ of Nebr - Lincoln	NE	18,031	VC

APPAREL DESIGN

School	ST	$IS	SR
Appalachian State Univ	NC	12,919	VC
Art Inst of Portland	OR	23,040	SP
Auburn Univ	AL	22,378	VC+
Baylor Univ	TX	50,329	HC
Bowling Green State Univ	OH	18,970	C
Colo State Univ-Fort Collins	CO	20,385	VC
Dominican Univ	IL	37,628	C
Florida State Univ	FL	16,715	VC

School	ST	$IS	SR
Kansas State Univ	KS	15,497	VC
Kent State Univ	OH	19,920	C
N Dak State Univ	ND		C
Oregon State Univ	OR	20,273	VC
Purdue Univ/West Lafayette	IN	20,024	HC
Rhode Island School of Design	RI	57,234	MC
San Francisco State Univ	CA	18,514	C
Texas Tech Univ	TX	14,243	C
Univ of Delaware	DE	23,612	VC
Univ of Hawaii at Manoa	HI	19,379	C
Univ of Idaho	ID	14,558	C
Univ of Minn/Twin Cities	MN		HC
Univ of Nebr - Lincoln	NE	18,031	VC
Univ of Wisc/Stout	WI	15,459	C
Western Washington Univ	WA	18,519	VC

APPLIED ART

School	ST	$IS	SR
Centenary College	NJ	38,618	C
Daemen College	NY	34,770	C
Edinboro Univ of Pennsylvania	PA	15,940	LC
Georgian Court Univ	NJ	41,594	LC
Goddard College	VT	16,418	VC
Marshall Univ	WV	14,820	C
Memphis College of Art	TN	33,550	SP
Oral Roberts Univ	OK	31,734	C
Oregon State Univ	OR	20,273	VC
Point Park Univ	PA	36,390	C
Roberts Wesleyan College	NY	38,306	C+
Rochester Inst of Technology	NY	42,450	VC
Santa Fe Univ of Art and Design	NM	39,666	SP
Tabor College	KS	29,010	C
Texas State Univ	TX	17,128	C
Univ of Idaho	ID	14,558	C
Univ of Maine at Presque Isle	ME	15,011	LC
Univ of North Texas	TX	15,628	C
West Texas A&M Univ	TX	13,478	C

APPLIED AVIATION

School	ST	$IS	SR
Calif Baptist Univ	CA	38,792	C
Eastern Mich Univ	MI	18,604	C
Univ of Minn Crookston	MN	17,834	C

APPLIED CHEMISTRY

School	ST	$IS	SR
Bethany College	WV	35,282	LC
Bridgewater College	VA	41,450	C

APPLIED COMMUNICATION

School	ST	$IS	SR
Ohio Univ	OH	21,080	C

APPLIED ECONOMICS / MANAGEMENT

School	ST	$IS	SR
Bethany College	WV	35,282	LC
Bryant Univ	RI	49,179	VC
Cornell Univ	NY	60,964	MC
Farmingdale State College	NY	19,673	C
Ithaca College	NY	53,864	HC

APPLIED GEOSCIENCE

School	ST	$IS	SR
Texas Christian Univ	TX	49,980	HC

APPLIED MANAGEMENT

School	ST	$IS	SR
Missouri Baptist Univ	MO	31,830	C
Ohio Univ	OH	21,080	C
Univ of New Hampshire	NH	26,912	C

APPLIED MATHEMATICS

School	ST	$IS	SR
American Univ	DC	56,015	HC+
Andrews Univ	MI	28,030	C+
Arizona State Univ, at the Tempe Campus	AZ	20,137	C+
Arizona State Univ, at the West Campus	AZ	19,251	C
Asbury Univ	KY	32,038	VC
Auburn Univ	AL	22,378	VC+
Baylor Univ	TX	50,329	HC
Belmont Univ	TN	39,190	VC+
Berea College	KY	7,192	C
Bethany College	WV	35,282	LC
Biola Univ	CA	40,320	C+
Brown Univ	RI	59,428	MC
Bryant Univ	RI	49,179	VC
Bucknell Univ	PA	60,140	MC
Calif Inst of Technology	CA	54,045	MC
Cal State, Fullerton	CA	25,188	C
Cal State, Long Beach	CA	17,502	C+
Case Western Reserve Univ	OH	56,534	MC
Christopher Newport Univ	VA	21,960	VC
Clarkson Univ	NY	57,330	HC
Colby College	ME	57,510	MC
Colo State Univ-Fort Collins	CO	20,385	VC
Columbia Univ/City of New York	NY	61,116	MC
Columbia Univ/School of General Studies	NY	58,231	MC

School	ST	$IS	SR
DePaul Univ	IL	47,623	VC
Dowling College	NY	25,000	LC
East Central Univ	OK	10,223	LC
Eastern Mich Univ	MI	18,604	C
Elizabethtown College	PA	49,740	VC
Elon Univ	NC	41,914	VC+
Endicott College	MA	43,228	VC+
Farmingdale State College	NY	19,673	C
Ferris State Univ	MI	20,047	C
Fitchburg State Univ	MA	18,173	C
Florida Inst of Technology	FL	48,290	VC
Florida State Univ	FL	16,715	VC
Franklin College	IN	36,585	C
Geneva College	PA	27,280	C
George Washington Univ	DC	57,108	MC
Georgia Inst of Technology	GA	21,828	MC
Hampden-Sydney College	VA	51,758	C
Harvard College/Harvard Univ	MA	49,000	MC
Hawaii Pacific Univ	HI	34,360	C
Hofstra Univ	NY	51,810	VC+
Illinois Inst of Technology	IL	38,512	HC+
Indiana Univ South Bend	IN	15,501	C
Iona College	NY	44,028	C
Johns Hopkins Univ	MD	47,492	MC
Johnson C. Smith Univ	NC	25,336	LC
Kent State Univ	OH	19,920	C
Kentucky State Univ	KY	11,000	LC
Kettering Univ	MI	31,456	NC
Lasell College	MA	43,750	LC
Le Moyne College	NY	43,470	C
Lehigh Univ	PA	56,770	MC
Lipscomb Univ	TN	37,490	VC
LIU Post	NY	47,660	C
Marshall Univ	WV	14,820	C
Mary Baldwin College	VA	38,245	C
Metropolitan State Univ	MN	5,923	
Millersville Univ of Pennsylvania	PA	21,648	C
Millsaps College	MS	43,888	VC+
Missouri Univ of Science and Technology	MO	18,655	VC+
Montclair State Univ	NJ	22,614	C
Murray State Univ	KY	15,304	C
New College of Florida	FL	14,504	MC
New Jersey Inst of Technology	NJ	26,490	C+
New York College of Technology/The CUNY	NY	5,769	NC
North Central College	IL	38,343	VC
Northwestern Univ	IL	61,640	MC
Oberlin College	OH	61,788	MC
Ohio Univ	OH	21,080	C
Oswego / SUNY	NY	20,009	VC
Pacific Union College	CA	28,150	VC
Piedmont College	GA	30,136	C
Purdue Univ/West Lafayette	IN	20,024	HC
Rice Univ	TX	43,288	MC
Robert Morris Univ	PA	37,864	C
Rochester Inst of Technology	NY	42,450	VC
Rutgers, The State Univ of New Jersey/Newark Campus	NJ	258,806	C
Saginaw Valley State Univ	MI	17,369	C
St. Augustine's Univ	NC	14,000	C
San Diego State Univ	CA	21,611	C+
San Francisco State Univ	CA	18,514	C
San Jose State Univ	CA	19,133	LC
Seattle Univ	WA	49,035	VC+
Southern Illinois Univ Edwardsville	IL	17,532	C
SUNY Polytechnic Inst	NY	19,690	C
Stevenson Univ	MD	41,470	C
Stony Brook Univ / SUNY	NY	20,078	HC+
SUNY Fredonia/The SUNY at Fredonia	NY	19,840	VC
Syracuse Univ	NY	56,346	VC
Temple Univ	PA	24,392	VC
The Univ of Tenn at Chattanooga	TN	16,883	C
The Univ of Utah	UT	16,463	VC
Tufts Univ	MA	58,780	MC
Univ at Albany / SUNY	NY	18,674	VC
Univ of Akron	OH	20,436	C
Univ of Arizona	AZ	20,657	C
Univ of Arkansas at Little Rock	AR	17,609	LC
Univ of Arkansas at Pine Bluff	AR	13,378	C
Univ of Calif at Berkeley	CA	23,322	MC
Univ of Calif at Los Angeles	CA	25,686	MC
Univ of Calif at San Diego	CA	21,000	VC
Univ of Central Arkansas	AR	13,667	VC
Univ of Central Okla	OK	12,293	C
Univ of Chicago	IL	55,416	MC
Univ of Colo Boulder	CO	22,605	VC+
Univ of Houston-Downtown	TX	15,170	LC
Univ of Idaho	ID	14,558	C
Univ of Mass Lowell	MA	19,316	C
Univ of Miami	FL	57,034	MC
Univ of Montana-Western	MT	9,753	LC
Univ of New Hampshire	NH	26,912	C
Univ of New Haven	CT	48,940	C
Univ of N Car at Chapel Hill	NC	18,928	MC
Univ of North Florida	FL	15,870	VC
Univ of Pittsburgh at Bradford	PA	21,802	C
Univ of Pittsburgh at Greensburg	PA	17,640	C
Univ of Pittsburgh at Pittsburgh	PA	28,572	HC+
Univ of PR Recinto de Rio Piedras	PR	5,750	
Univ of Rochester	NY	60,668	MC
Univ of S Car Aiken	SC	16,712	C
Univ of Southern Calif	CA	56,903	MC
Univ of St. Thomas - Houston	TX	37,690	C
Univ of Texas at El Paso	TX	8,764	NC
Univ of the Pacific	CA	52,146	VC
Univ of Tulsa	OK	46,331	MC
Univ of Wisc/Madison	WI	18,757	HC+
Univ of Wisc/Stout	WI	15,459	C
Univ of Wisc-Milwaukee	WI	18,436	C
Washington State Univ	WA	20,461	C
Washington Univ in St. Louis	MO	69,844	MC
West Virginia State Univ	WV	8,378	NC
Western Mich Univ	MI	19,628	C
Western Washington Univ	WA	18,519	VC
Wheaton College	IL	40,720	MC
Wofford College	SC	45,795	VC
Wright State Univ	OH	16,983	C
Yale Univ	CT	55,300	MC
Youngstown State Univ	OH	16,732	C

APPLIED METEOROLOGY

School	ST	$IS	SR
Embry-Riddle Aeronautical Univ - Prescott Campus	AZ	40,444	VC+

APPLIED MUSIC

School	ST	$IS	SR
Baldwin Wallace Univ	OH	38,318	C
Baylor Univ	TX	50,329	HC
Concordia College - New York	NY	39,035	LC
Cornerstone Univ and Grand Rapids Theological Seminary	MI	33,338	C
Dallas Baptist Univ	TX	30,580	VC
Eastern Mich Univ	MI	18,604	C
Geneva College	PA	27,280	C
Indiana Wesleyan Univ	IN	31,815	VC
Inter-American Univ of PR/Fajardo Campus	PR	4,200	
Inter-American Univ of PR/Ponce	PR		
Judson College	AL	26,794	C
Kansas State Univ	KS	15,497	VC
Lenoir-Rhyne College	NC	35,984	C
Mannes College New School for Music	NY	44,500	SP
Meredith College	NC	31,420	C
Miss College	MS	21,998	C
Nebr Wesleyan Univ	NE	29,774	C+
New England Conservatory of Music	MA	52,550	SP
Newberry College	SC	26,850	LC
Ouachita Baptist Univ	AR	30,220	VC
Roberts Wesleyan College	NY	38,306	C+
Seton Hall Univ	NJ	45,902	C
Trinity Christian College	IL	28,869	C
Univ of Delaware	DE	23,612	VC
Univ of Houston	TX	19,796	VC
Univ of Idaho	ID	14,558	C
Univ of Illinois at Chicago	IL	24,505	VC
Univ of Nevada/Reno	NV	17,507	C
Univ of Texas at Austin	TX	44,074	HC
Wartburg College	IA	41,055	VC
Youngstown State Univ	OH	16,732	C

APPLIED NUTRITION

School	ST	$IS	SR
Ohio Univ	OH	21,080	C

APPLIED PHYSICS

School	ST	$IS	SR
Angelo State Univ	TX	15,049	NC
Armstrong State Univ	GA	15,532	C
Beloit College	WI	49,970	HC
Bethel Univ	MN	34,940	VC
Bridgewater College	VA	41,450	C
Cal State, San Bernardino	CA	12,000	C
Cal State, Stanislaus	CA	18,582	C
Carroll Univ	WI	38,100	C
Christopher Newport Univ	VA	21,960	VC
Columbia Univ/City of New York	NY	61,116	MC
Creighton Univ	NE	45,356	VC
East Carolina Univ	NC	14,169	C
Georgia Inst of Technology	GA	21,828	MC
Hofstra Univ	NY	51,810	VC+
Houghton College	NY	36,808	C+
Kettering Univ	MI	31,456	NC
Linfield College-McMinnville Campus	OR	47,676	C
Marietta College	OH	42,135	C+
Mich Tech Univ	MI	23,556	HC
Murray State Univ	KY	15,304	C
New Jersey Inst of Technology	NJ	26,490	C+
Northeastern Univ	MA	55,296	MC
Ohio Univ	OH	21,080	C
Pacific Lutheran Univ	WA	46,760	C+
Piedmont College	GA	30,136	C
Providence College	RI	57,383	VC
Purdue Univ/West Lafayette	IN	20,024	HC
Rensselaer Polytechnic Inst	NY	61,529	MC
Rutgers, The State Univ of New Jersey/Newark Campus	NJ	258,806	C
Shippensburg Univ of Pennsylvania	PA	20,934	C
SUNY College at Geneseo	NY	18,670	HC
Tufts Univ	MA	58,780	MC
Univ of Alaska Fairbanks	AK	15,130	C
Univ of Calif at San Diego	CA	21,000	VC
Univ of Iowa	IA	17,693	VC
Univ of Minn/Duluth	MN	19,806	C
Univ of Nevada, Las Vegas	NV	17,303	C
Univ of Notre Dame	IN	57,117	MC
Western Washington Univ	WA	18,519	VC
Wheeling Jesuit Univ	WV	33,500	C
Whitworth Univ	WA	47,734	VC
Xavier Univ	OH	44,980	VC
Yale Univ	CT	55,300	MC

APPLIED PHYSICS (PRE-MBA)

School	ST	$IS	SR
Murray State Univ	KY	15,304	C

APPLIED PSYCHOLOGY

School	ST	$IS	SR
Belmont Abbey College	NC	37,716	C
Biola Univ	CA	40,320	C+
Boston College	MA	60,622	MC
Bryant Univ	RI	49,179	VC
Cedarville Univ	OH	32,860	VC
Christian Brothers Univ	TN	31,670	NC
College of St. Mary	NE	35,184	C
Coppin State Univ	MD	16,227	VC
Farmingdale State College	NY	19,673	C
Franklin Univ	OH	20,985	SP
Ithaca College	NY	53,864	HC
Loyola Univ Chicago	IL	41,960	VC+
Mayville State Univ	ND	11,401	NC
New York Univ	NY	61,470	MC
Pace Univ	NY	53,367	C
Russell Sage College	NY	39,370	C
The SUNY College of Agriculture and Tech at Cobleskill	NY	19,749	LC
Univ of Illinois at Chicago	IL	24,505	VC
Univ of Mich-Flint	MI	17,547	C+
Univ of North Texas	TX	15,628	C
Univ of Pittsburgh at Pittsburgh	PA	28,572	HC+
Univ of St. Mary	KS	28,400	C+
Wright State Univ	OH	16,983	C

APPLIED SCIENCE

School	ST	$IS	SR
Alcorn State Univ	MS	9,500	C
Arizona State Univ, at the Downtown Phoenix Campus	AZ	22,101	C
Arizona State Univ, at the Polytechnic Campus	AZ	20,531	C+
Arizona State Univ, at the West Campus	AZ	19,251	C
Black Hills State Univ	SD	13,947	C
Concordia College - Moorhead	MN	39,974	VC
Florida Gulf Coast Univ	FL		C
Granite State College	NH	6,195	NC
Indiana Univ East	IN	6,783	C
Indiana Univ Kokomo	IN	6,811	LC
Indiana Univ Northwest	IN	6,854	C
Indiana Univ South Bend	IN	15,501	C
Indiana Univ Southeast	IN	16,035	C
Lehigh Univ	PA	56,770	MC
Madonna Univ	MI	24,540	VC
Messiah College	PA	40,690	C+
Missouri Southern State Univ	MO	12,061	C
Northern Arizona Univ	AZ	19,010	C
Saginaw Valley State Univ	MI	17,369	C
Southern Polytechnic State Univ	GA	13,958	C
Southwest Minn State Univ	MN	14,000	C
Southwestern Univ	TX	45,660	VC
Texas Lutheran Univ	TX	36,040	C
Univ of Arizona	AZ	20,657	C
Univ of Arkansas at Monticello	AR	12,076	NC
Univ of Central Florida	FL	15,668	VC+
Univ of Maine at Augusta	ME	6,855	C
Univ of Mich-Flint	MI	17,547	C+
Univ of Montana	MT	14,105	C
Univ of N Car at Chapel Hill	NC	18,928	MC
Univ of Pennsylvania	PA	61,132	MC
Univ of Wisc/Stout	WI	15,459	C
Wheeling Jesuit Univ	WV	33,500	C
Winona State Univ	MN	16,640	C

APPLIED SOCIAL SCIENCE

School	ST	$IS	SR
Bryant Univ	RI	49,179	VC
East Carolina Univ	NC	14,169	C
Univ of Wisc/Stout	WI	15,459	C

APPLIED SPEECH COMMUNICATION

School	ST	$IS	SR
Ferris State Univ	MI	20,047	C

AQUACULTURE & FISHERY TECHNOLOGY

School	ST	$IS	SR
Univ of Rhode Island	RI	24,002	C

ARABIC

School	ST	$IS	SR
American Univ	DC	56,015	HC+
Bard College	NY	61,940	HC
Binghamton Univ/The SUNY	NY	21,648	HC+
Dartmouth College	NH	57,996	MC
DePaul Univ	IL	47,623	VC
Georgetown Univ	DC	52,910	MC
Middlebury College	VT	59,160	MC
New York Univ	NY	61,470	MC
Ohio State Univ-Columbus Campus	OH	19,887	HC+
The Univ of Okla	OK	18,621	VC
The Univ of Utah	UT	16,463	VC
Thomas Edison State College	NJ	5,700	SP
Tufts Univ	MA	58,780	VC
United States Naval Academy	MD		MC
Univ of Calif at Los Angeles	CA	25,686	MC
Univ of Cincinnati	OH	21,506	VC
Univ of Georgia	GA	20,082	VC
Univ of Iowa	IA	17,693	VC
Univ of Maryland - College Park	MD	20,060	HC
Univ of Mich/Ann Arbor	MI	22,102	MC
Univ of Miss	MS	16,704	C+
Univ of Notre Dame	IN	57,117	MC
Univ of Texas at Austin	TX	44,074	HC
Washington Univ in St. Louis	MO	69,844	MC
Williams College	MA	61,070	MC

ARCHEOLOGY

School	ST	$IS	SR
Biola Univ	CA	40,320	C+
Boston Univ	MA	60,694	MC
Brigham Young Univ	UT	12,100	HC
Brown Univ	RI	59,428	MC
Bryn Mawr College	PA	59,890	MC
College of Charleston	SC	22,145	VC
College of Wooster	OH	52,600	MC
Columbia Univ/City of New York	NY	61,116	MC
Columbia Univ/School of General Studies	NY	58,231	MC
Cornell College	IA	44,930	VC
Cornell Univ	NY	60,964	MC
Dickinson College	PA	57,662	HC+
George Washington Univ	DC	57,108	MC
Hamilton College	NY	55,620	MC
Haverford College	PA	61,564	MC
Hood College	MD	45,730	C
Hunter College	NY	14,429	VC
Kent State Univ	OH	19,920	C
Lycoming College	PA	45,379	C
Mass Inst of Technology	MA	58,240	MC
Mercyhurst Univ	PA	40,700	C
Millersville Univ of Pennsylvania	PA	21,648	C
Murray State Univ	KY	15,304	C
Oberlin College	OH	61,788	MC
Prescott College	AZ	33,284	C
Princeton Univ	NJ	53,795	MC
Randolph-Macon College	VA	49,869	C+
Stanford Univ	CA	58,388	MC
Texas A&M Univ at Galveston	TX	11,258	C
The Pennsylvania State Univ - Univ Park	PA	28,022	VC+
The SUNY at Potsdam	NY	18,473	C
Tufts Univ	MA	58,780	MC
Univ of Cincinnati	OH	21,506	VC
Univ of Evansville	IN	42,656	VC+
Univ of Indianapolis	IN	31,740	LC
Univ of Kansas	KS	17,603	C+
Univ of Mich/Ann Arbor	MI	22,102	MC
Univ of Missouri/Columbia	MO	18,201	MC
Univ of N Car at Chapel Hill	NC	18,928	MC
Univ of Rochester	NY	60,668	MC
Univ of Texas at Austin	TX	44,074	HC
Univ of Tulsa	OK	46,331	MC
Univ of Wisc/La Crosse	WI	9,304	C
Washington and Lee Univ	VA	52,812	MC
Washington Univ in St. Louis	MO	69,844	MC
Wellesley College	MA	59,038	MC
Wesleyan Univ	CT	61,198	MC
Wheaton College	IL	40,720	MC
Yale Univ	CT	55,300	MC

School	ST	$IS	SR

ARCHITECTURAL ENGINEERING

School	ST	$IS	SR
Calif Polytechnic State Univ	CA	19,847	HC
Dordt College	IA	34,160	C+
Drexel Univ	PA	61,418	VC+
Illinois Inst of Technology	IL	38,512	HC+
Kansas State Univ	KS	15,497	VC
Lawrence Tech Univ	MI	37,630	VC
Milwaukee School of Engineering	WI	39,948	VC+
Missouri Univ of Science and Technology	MO	18,655	VC+
N Car Agricultural and Technical State Univ	NC	13,365	LC
Northern Kentucky Univ	KY	21,134	C
Okla State Univ	OK	14,310	VC
Parsons The New School for Design	NY	56,610	SP
Princeton Univ	NJ	53,795	MC
Rice Univ	TX	43,288	MC
Stanford Univ	CA	58,388	MC
Tenn State Univ	TN	9,048	C
The Pennsylvania State Univ - Univ Park	PA	28,022	VC+
The Univ of Okla	OK	18,621	VC
Univ of Cincinnati	OH	21,506	VC
Univ of Colo Boulder	CO	22,605	VC+
Univ of Hartford	CT	42,674	C
Univ of Illinois at Urbana-Champaign	IL	26,450	HC
Univ of Kansas	KS	17,603	VC
Univ of Miami	FL	57,034	MC
Univ of Nebr - Lincoln	NE	18,031	VC
Univ of Nevada, Las Vegas	NV	17,303	C
Univ of Texas at Austin	TX	44,074	HC
Univ of Wyoming	WY	14,401	C+
Vermont Technical College	VT	15,751	C
Worcester Polytechnic Inst	MA	55,860	MC

ARCHITECTURAL HISTORY

School	ST	$IS	SR
Brown Univ	RI	59,428	MC
DePaul Univ	IL	47,623	VC
Miami Univ	OH	24,191	VC
Middlebury College	VT	59,160	MC
Savannah College of Art and Design	GA	48,005	SP
Syracuse Univ	NY	56,346	VC
Univ of Kansas	KS	17,603	C+
Univ of Virginia	VA	23,050	MC

ARCHITECTURAL STUDIES

School	ST	$IS	SR
Amherst College	MA	58,744	MC
Arizona State Univ, at the Tempe Campus	AZ	20,137	C+
Boston Univ	MA	60,694	MC
Bowling Green State Univ	OH	18,970	C
Hobart and William Smith Colleges	NY	60,034	HC+
Ithaca College	NY	53,864	HC
Kent State Univ	OH	19,920	C
Lawrence Tech Univ	MI	37,630	VC
New York Univ	NY	61,470	MC
Southern Illinois Univ Carbondale	IL	21,942	C
The Univ of Utah	UT	16,463	VC
Univ of Arkansas at Fayetteville	AR	18,352	C+
Univ of Illinois at Chicago	IL	24,505	VC
Univ of Nebr - Lincoln	NE	18,031	VC
Univ of Pittsburgh at Pittsburgh	PA	28,572	HC+
Univ of San Diego	CA	54,818	HC+

ARCHITECTURAL TECHNOLOGY

School	ST	$IS	SR
Alfred State/SUNY College of Technology	NY	18,034	C
Brown Univ	RI	59,428	MC
Fairmont State Univ	WV	12,098	LC
Farmingdale State College	NY	19,673	VC
Fitchburg State Univ	MA	18,173	C
Murray State Univ	KY	15,304	C
New York College of Technology/The CUNY	NY	5,769	NC
New York Inst of Technology	NY	45,010	VC
Pennsylvania College of Technology	PA	26,286	NC
Univ of Cincinnati	OH	21,506	VC
Univ of Southern Miss	MS	13,170	C
Washington Univ in St. Louis	MO	69,844	MC

ARCHITECTURE

School	ST	$IS	SR
Andrews Univ	MI	28,030	C+
Appalachian State Univ	NC	12,919	VC
Auburn Univ	AL	22,378	VC+
Ball State Univ	IN	17,850	C
Barnard College/Columbia Univ	NY	39,000	MC
Bennington College	VT	56,990	HC+
Boston Architectural College	MA	18,622	SP
Brown Univ	RI	59,428	MC
Calif Baptist Univ	CA	38,792	C
Calif College of the Arts	CA	48,334	SP
Calif Polytechnic State Univ	CA	19,847	HC
Calif State Polytechnic Univ, Pomona	CA	20,156	C
Case Western Reserve Univ	OH	56,534	MC
College of the Holy Cross	MA	58,042	MC
Columbia Univ/City of New York	NY	61,116	MC
Columbia Univ/School of General Studies	NY	58,231	MC
Conn College	CT	54,970	MC
Cooper Union for the Advancement of Science and Art	NY	55,600	MC
Cornell Univ	NY	60,964	MC
Drexel Univ	PA	61,418	VC+
Drury Univ	MO	31,909	VC
Florida Atlantic Univ	FL	17,339	C
Florida International Univ	FL	17,747	C+
Georgia Inst of Technology	GA	21,828	MC
Hampshire College	MA	58,320	MC
Hampton Univ	VA	28,528	C
Hobart and William Smith Colleges	NY	60,034	HC+
Howard Univ	DC	13,646	C
Illinois Inst of Technology	IL	38,512	HC+
Iowa State Univ	IA	16,403	C
Kansas State Univ	KS	15,497	VC
Keene State College	NH	23,232	LC
Kent State Univ	OH	19,920	C
Lawrence Tech Univ	MI	37,630	VC
Lehigh Univ	PA	56,770	MC
Louisiana State Univ	LA	18,677	C+
Louisiana Tech Univ	LA	11,302	C
Marywood Univ	PA	45,595	C
Mass Inst of Technology	MA	58,240	MC
Miami Univ	OH	24,191	VC
Miss State Univ	MS	14,750	C
Mount Holyoke College	MA	55,146	MC
New Jersey Inst of Technology	NJ	26,490	C+
New York Inst of Technology	NY	45,010	VC
NewSchool of Architecture & Design	CA	24,900	SP
N Car State Univ	NC	16,202	HC
N Dak State Univ	ND		C
Northeastern Univ	MA	55,296	MC
Northern Mich Univ	MI	18,278	C
Norwich Univ	VT	28,212	C
Okla State Univ	OK	14,310	VC
Otis College of Art and Design	CA	35,404	SP
Philadelphia Univ	PA	44,160	C
Portland State Univ	OR	18,672	C
Prairie View A&M Univ	TX	15,205	LC
Pratt Inst	NY	55,956	SP
Princeton Univ	NJ	53,795	MC
Rensselaer Polytechnic Inst	NY	61,529	MC
Rhode Island School of Design	RI	57,234	MC
Rice Univ	TX	43,288	MC
Roger Williams Univ	RI	46,296	VC
Savannah College of Art and Design	GA	48,005	SP
Smith College	MA	59,674	MC
S Dak State Univ	SD	14,296	C
Southern Illinois Univ Carbondale	IL	21,942	C
Southern Polytechnic State Univ	GA	13,958	C
Southern Univ and A&M College	LA	9,761	LC
Syracuse Univ	NY	56,346	VC
Temple Univ	PA	24,392	VC
Texas Tech Univ	TX	14,243	C
The Catholic Univ of America	DC	52,852	VC
Ohio State Univ-Columbus Campus	OH	19,887	HC+
The Pennsylvania State Univ - Univ Park	PA	28,022	VC+
The Univ of Memphis	TN	15,094	C
The Univ of Okla	OK	18,621	VC
The Univ of Utah	UT	16,463	VC
Tufts Univ	MA	58,780	MC
Tulane Univ	LA	60,861	MC
Tuskegee Univ	AL	26,750	C
Univ at Buffalo / The SUNY	NY	20,283	VC
Univ of Arizona	AZ	20,657	C
Univ of Arkansas at Fayetteville	AR	18,352	C+
Univ of Calif at Berkeley	CA	23,322	MC
Univ of Calif at Los Angeles	CA	25,686	MC
Univ of Central Florida	FL	15,668	VC+
Univ of Colo Denver	CO	17,904	C
Univ of Detroit Mercy	MI	30,450	VC
Univ of Florida	FL	15,943	HC
Univ of Houston	TX	19,796	VC
Univ of Idaho	ID	14,558	C
Univ of Illinois at Chicago	IL	24,505	VC
Univ of Illinois at Urbana-Champaign	IL	26,450	HC
Univ of Kansas	KS	17,603	C+
Univ of Maine at Augusta	ME	6,855	C
Univ of Maryland - College Park	MD	20,060	HC
Univ of Mass Amherst	MA	24,215	VC+
Univ of Miami	FL	57,034	MC
Univ of Mich/Ann Arbor	MI	22,102	MC
Univ of Minn/Twin Cities	MN		HC
Univ of Nebr - Lincoln	NE	18,031	VC
Univ of New Mexico	NM	15,300	C
Univ of N Car at Charlotte	NC	15,547	C
Univ of Notre Dame	IN	57,117	MC
Univ of Oregon	OR	21,360	C+
Univ of Pennsylvania	PA	61,132	MC
Univ of San Francisco	CA	54,770	VC
Univ of Southern Calif	CA	56,903	MC
Univ of Tenn at Knoxville	TN	20,364	VC+
Univ of Texas at Arlington	TX	10,908	LC
Univ of Texas at Austin	TX	44,074	HC
Univ of Texas at San Antonio	TX	18,372	C
Univ of the District of Columbia	DC	7,244	C
Univ of Virginia	VA	23,050	MC
Univ of Wisc-Milwaukee	WI	18,436	C
Virginia Polytechnic Inst and State Univ	VA	14,629	HC
Washington State Univ	WA	20,461	C
Washington Univ in St. Louis	MO	69,844	MC
Wellesley College	MA	59,038	MC
Wentworth Inst of Technology	MA	29,800	C
Woodbury Univ	CA	34,500	LC
Yale Univ	CT	55,300	MC

ARCHITECTURE & SUSTAINABILITY

School	ST	$IS	SR
Ferris State Univ	MI	20,047	C

AREA STUDIES

School	ST	$IS	SR
American Univ	DC	56,015	HC+
Appalachian State Univ	NC	12,919	VC
Bard College	NY	61,940	HC
Baylor Univ	TX	50,329	HC
Calvin College	MI	39,120	VC
CUNY/City College	NY	20,319	HC+
College of Wooster	OH	52,600	VC
Columbia Univ/City of New York	NY	61,116	MC
Duke Univ	NC	50,250	MC
Eastern Mich Univ	MI	18,604	C
Huntington Univ	IN	33,220	C+
Ithaca College	NY	53,864	HC
Lake Forest College	IL	50,652	VC
Mercer Univ	GA	44,201	VC
New York Univ	NY	61,470	MC
Prescott College	AZ	33,284	C
Rutgers, The State Univ of New Jersey/Newark Campus	NJ	258,806	C
Stanford Univ	CA	58,388	MC
The Univ of Okla	OK	18,621	VC
Univ of Alaska Fairbanks	AK	15,130	C
Univ of Miss	MS	16,704	C+
Univ of Vermont	VT	27,006	VC+
Univ of Virginia	VA	23,050	MC
Washington Univ in St. Louis	MO	69,844	MC
Webster Univ	MO	35,100	C+

ART

School	ST	$IS	SR
Abilene Christian Univ	TX	38,400	C
Adams State Univ	CO	13,358	LC
Alabama A&M Univ	AL	10,084	C
Alabama State Univ	AL	14,142	NC
Albany State Univ	GA	8,500	C
Albion College	MI	46,010	C
Albright College	PA	46,660	C
Allegheny College	PA	50,980	HC
Alma College	MI	44,075	C
Alverno College	WI	31,434	LC
American Univ	DC	56,015	HC+
Andrews Univ	MI	28,030	C+
Angelo State Univ	TX	15,049	NC
Anna Maria College	MA	34,600	C
Appalachian State Univ	NC	12,919	VC
Aquinas College	MI	33,060	C
Arizona State Univ, at the Tempe Campus	AZ	20,137	C+
Arkansas State Univ	AR	15,470	C
Arkansas Tech Univ	AR	13,982	LC
Armstrong State Univ	GA	15,532	C
Asbury Univ	KY	32,038	VC
Ashland Univ	OH	25,000	C
Atlantic Union College	MA	24,600	C
Auburn Univ	AL	22,378	VC+
Augustana College	IL	43,398	VC
Augustana College	SD	36,500	VC
Aurora Univ	IL	33,228	C
Austin College	TX	45,875	HC
Austin Peay State Univ	TN	15,274	C
Averett Univ	VA	37,750	C
Avila Univ	MO	26,900	C
Ball State Univ	IN	17,850	C
Barry Univ	FL	38,190	C
Baylor Univ	TX	50,329	HC
Belhaven Univ	MS	27,170	C
Beloit College	WI	49,970	HC
Benedictine College	KS	29,180	VC
Bennington College	VT	56,990	HC+
Berea College	KY	7,192	C
Berry College	GA	39,254	VC
Bethany College	KS	30,605	NC
Bethel College	IN	31,560	C
Bethel College	KS	32,160	C
Bethel Univ	MN	34,940	VC
Binghamton Univ/The SUNY	NY	21,648	HC+
Biola Univ	CA	40,320	C+
Black Hills State Univ	SD	13,947	C
Blackburn College	IL	21,350	C
Bluffton Univ	OH	38,948	C
Boise State Univ	ID	13,469	LC
Bowling Green State Univ	OH	18,970	C
Brescia Univ	KY	26,140	VC+
Briar Cliff Univ	IA	29,514	C
Bridgewater College	VA	41,450	C
Bridgewater State Univ	MA	18,752	C
Brigham Young Univ	UT	12,100	HC
Brigham Young Univ/Hawaii	HI	10,686	VC
Brown Univ	RI	59,428	MC
Bucknell Univ	PA	60,140	MC
Buena Vista Univ	IA	39,188	C
Buffalo State College / SUNY	NY	15,733	C+
Butler Univ	IN	47,572	VC+
Caldwell College	NJ	35,602	NC
Calif College of the Arts	CA	48,334	SP
Calif Lutheran Univ	CA	49,540	C+
Calif State Polytechnic Univ, Pomona	CA	20,156	C
Cal State, Bakersfield	CA	8,000	C
Cal State, Chico	CA	20,158	C
Cal State, Dominguez Hills	CA	17,090	LC
Cal State, East Bay	CA	16,549	C
Cal State, Fresno	CA	17,405	C
Cal State, Fullerton	CA	25,188	C
Cal State, Long Beach	CA	17,502	C+
Cal State, Northridge	CA	28,690	NC
Cal State, San Bernardino	CA	12,000	C
Cal State, Stanislaus	CA	18,582	C
Calif Univ of Pennsylvania	PA	14,217	C
Calvin College	MI	39,120	VC
Cameron Univ	OK	10,004	LC
Campbell Univ	NC	37,570	VC
Campbellsville Univ	KY	27,720	C
Capital Univ	OH	41,050	VC
Cardinal Stritch Univ	WI	24,054	C
Carlow Univ	PA	30,272	C
Carroll Univ	WI	38,100	C
Carthage College	WI	33,000	C
Castleton State College	VT	20,186	C
Cedar Crest College	PA	43,240	C
Centenary College of Louisiana	LA	45,650	C+
Central College	IA	42,104	C+
Central Conn State Univ	CT	19,749	C
Central Washington Univ	WA	11,730	C
Chadron State College	NE	7,400	NC
Chapman Univ	CA	58,347	VC+
Chestnut Hill College	PA	42,110	LC
Chicago State Univ	IL	5,482	C
CUNY/Brooklyn College	NY	5,884	C+
CUNY/City College	NY	20,319	HC+
Claflin Univ	SC	22,368	LC
Clarion Univ of Pennsylvania	PA	17,370	LC
Clark Atlanta Univ	GA	30,006	LC
Clarke Univ	IA	37,600	C
Cleveland State Univ	OH	21,776	C
Coe College	IA	45,550	VC
Coker College	SC	32,256	LC
Colby-Sawyer College	NH	50,790	C
College of Mount St. Joseph	OH	33,880	C
College of New Jersey	NJ	25,376	HC
College of St. Benedict	MN	49,359	VC
College of St. Elizabeth	NJ	43,839	LC
College of St. Mary	NE	35,184	C
College of Staten Island/The City of New Yok	NY	16,778	NC
College of the Ozarks	MO		VC
College of William & Mary	VA	28,000	MC
Colo Christian Univ	CO	27,500	VC
Colo Mesa Univ	CO	17,690	LC
Colo State Univ-Fort Collins	CO	20,385	VC
Colo State Univ-Pueblo	CO	16,183	C
Columbia College	MO	24,578	C
Columbia College Chicago	IL	30,940	LC
Columbus State Univ	GA	13,176	C
Concordia College - Moorhead	MN	39,974	VC
Concordia Univ Irvine	CA	35,390	VC
Concordia Univ St. Paul	MN	28,250	C
Concordia Univ Wisc	WI	28,980	C
Concordia Univ, Ann Arbor	MI	27,220	VC
Concordia Univ, River Forest	IL	26,300	C
Conn College	CT	54,970	MC
Covenant College	GA	38,990	VC+
Creighton Univ	NE	45,356	VC
Culver-Stockton College	MO	30,900	C
Daemen College	NY	34,770	C
Dakota Wesleyan Univ	SD	23,000	C
Dallas Baptist Univ	TX	30,580	VC
Davidson College	NC	58,146	MC
Davis & Elkins College	WV	33,742	C
Defiance College	OH	30,645	C
Delta State Univ	MS	12,292	LC
DePaul Univ	IL	47,623	VC

School	ST	$IS	SR
Dillard Univ	LA	20,940	VC
Doane College	NE	35,230	C
Dominican Univ of Calif	CA	51,250	C
Dordt Univ	IA	34,160	C+
Drew Univ/College of Liberal Arts	NJ	57,516	C
Earlham College	IN	51,470	HC
East Carolina Univ	NC	14,169	C
East Central Univ	OK	10,223	VC
East Stroudsburg Univ of Pennsylvania	PA	18,868	LC
East Tenn State Univ	TN	9,000	C
Eastern Illinois Univ	IL	20,466	C
Eastern Kentucky Univ	KY	11,161	C
Eastern Mennonite Univ	VA	40,660	C
Eastern Mich Univ	MI	18,604	C
Eastern New Mexico Univ	NM	10,682	C
Eastern Oregon Univ	OR	10,400	C
Eastern Washington Univ	WA		C
Edgewood College	WI	33,294	C
Edinboro Univ of Pennsylvania	PA	15,940	LC
Elizabeth City State Univ	NC	11,638	C
Elmhurst College	IL	43,336	C
Elmira College	NY	49,950	C+
Elon Univ	NC	41,914	VC+
Emory and Henry College	VA	387,460	C
Emory Univ	GA	56,368	MC
Emporia State Univ	KS	12,897	C
Erskine College	SC	37,360	C
Evangel Univ	MO	23,090	C
Felician College	NJ	41,640	LC
Ferrum College	VA	27,740	LC
Florida Atlantic Univ	FL	17,339	C
Florida Gulf Coast Univ	FL		C
Florida International Univ	FL	17,747	C+
Fontbonne Univ	MO	31,384	C
Fort Hays State Univ	KS	11,354	C
Fort Lewis College	CO	15,513	C
Franklin College	IN	36,585	C
Freed-Hardeman Univ	TN	19,697	VC
Friends Univ	KS	29,100	C
Furman Univ	SC	54,006	HC
Gardner-Webb Univ	NC	34,375	C+
George Fox Univ	OR	40,750	C+
Georgetown College	KY	41,440	C+
Georgetown Univ	DC	52,910	MC
Georgia College and State Univ	GA	18,900	C+
Georgia Regents Univ	GA		C
Georgia Southern Univ	GA	16,942	C
Georgia Southwestern State Univ	GA	13,246	C
Georgia State Univ	GA	15,582	VC
Georgian Court Univ	NJ	41,594	LC
Goddard College	VT	16,418	VC
Gonzaga Univ	WA	46,441	HC
Gordon College	MA	44,320	VC
Goshen College	IN	35,900	VC
Goucher College	MD	52,040	VC+
Grace College and Seminary	IN	28,800	VC
Grand Valley State Univ	MI	17,998	C+
Green Mountain College	VT	45,228	LC
Greensboro College	NC	28,740	LC
Greenville College	IL	27,012	C
Grinnell College	IA	53,654	HC
Guilford College	NC	42,800	C
Hamilton College	NY	55,620	MC
Hamline Univ	MN	45,678	VC
Hampton Univ	VA	28,528	C
Hannibal-LaGrange Univ	MO	24,490	C
Hanover College	IN	43,073	C+
Harding Univ	AR	23,556	C
Hardin-Simmons Univ	TX	34,521	C+
Hartwick College	NY	51,270	C
Hendrix College	AR	50,202	VC+
Heritage Univ	WA	17,664	NC
High Point Univ	NC	39,800	C
Hillsdale College	MI	32,866	MC
Hiram College	OH	37,300	VC
Holy Family Univ	PA	40,030	LC
Hood College	MD	45,730	C
Hope College	MI	38,650	VC
Houghton College	NY	36,808	C+
Houston Baptist Univ	TX	36,450	C
Howard Payne Univ	TX	17,115	C
Humboldt State Univ	CA	18,400	C
Huntingdon College	AL	33,100	C
Huntington Univ	IN	32,220	C+
Idaho State Univ	ID	12,307	C
Illinois State Univ	IL	23,110	VC
Illinois Wesleyan Univ	IL	48,452	HC
Indiana Univ of Pennsylvania	PA	20,846	LC
Indiana Wesleyan Univ	IN	31,815	VC
Ithaca College	NY	53,864	HC
Jackson State Univ	MS	13,512	LC
James Madison Univ	VA	18,049	VC
Johnson State College	VT	16,721	C
Judson College	AL	26,794	C
Kalamazoo College	MI	49,740	HC
Kansas State Univ	KS	15,497	VC
Keene State College	NH	23,232	LC
Kennesaw State Univ	GA		C
Kentucky State Univ	KY	11,000	LC
Kentucky Wesleyan College	KY	27,440	C
Kenyon College	OH	58,890	MC
La Sierra Univ	CA	35,694	VC
Lafayette College	PA	59,155	HC+
LaGrange College	GA	37,670	C
Lake Forest College	IL	50,652	VC
Lakeland College	WI	22,990	C
Lebanon Valley College	PA	38,570	C
Lees-McRae College	NC	33,944	C
Lehigh Univ	PA	56,770	MC
LeMoyne-Owen College	TN	13,100	C
Lindsey Wilson College	KY	31,220	C
Linfield College-McMinnville Campus	OR	47,676	C
Lipscomb Univ	TN	37,490	VC
LIU Post	NY	47,660	C
Longwood Univ	VA	20,924	C
Lourdes Univ	OH	26,055	LC
Luther College	IA	45,720	C+
Lycoming College	PA	45,379	C
Lynchburg College	VA	42,645	C
Lyon College	AR	32,090	C+
Macalester College	MN	57,691	MC
MacMurray College	IL	20,755	C
Madonna Univ	MI	24,540	VC
Malone Univ	OH	35,364	C
Manchester Univ	IN	35,070	C
Marian Univ	WI	32,420	LC
Marshall Univ	WV	14,820	C
Mary Baldwin College	VA	38,245	C
Marygrove College	MI	28,926	C
Marylhurst Univ	OR	20,295	NC
Marymount Univ	VA	39,480	C
Maryville College	TN	33,150	C+
Mass College of Liberal Arts	MA	18,613	C
McKendree Univ	IL	29,920	C+
McMurry Univ	TX	25,962	LC
McNeese State Univ	LA	2,649	C
McPherson College	KS	28,138	C
Mercer Univ	GA	44,201	VC
Meredith College	NC	31,420	C
Methodist Univ	NC	37,185	C
Metropolitan State Univ of Denver	CO	4,835	LC
Miami Univ	OH	24,191	VC
Millersville Univ of Pennsylvania	PA	21,648	C
Millikin Univ	IL	38,940	C
Minn State Univ, Mankato	MN	15,616	C
Minot State Univ	ND	10,915	C
Miss College	MS	21,998	C
Miss State Univ	MS	14,750	C
Miss Valley State Univ	MS	9,706	LC
Missouri Southern State Univ	MO	12,061	C
Missouri State Univ	MO	13,996	C+
Missouri Valley College	MO	22,200	C
Molloy College	NY	40,440	C
Monmouth College	IL	40,850	C
Monmouth Univ	NJ	44,108	C
Montana State Univ	MT	14,068	C
Montana State Univ-Billings	MT	12,425	LC
Montclair State Univ	NJ	22,614	C
Morehouse College	GA	39,412	C
Morningside College	IA	35,430	C
Mount Mercy Univ	IA	35,320	C
Mount St. Mary's College - Chalon Campus	CA	43,897	VC+
Mount Vernon Nazarene Univ	OH	29,590	C
Muhlenberg College	PA	52,837	HC
Muskingum Univ	OH	30,502	C
Nazareth College of Rochester	NY	43,028	C+
Nebr Wesleyan Univ	NE	29,774	C
New College of Florida	FL	14,504	MC
New Mexico Highlands Univ	NM	11,904	NC
New Mexico State Univ	NM	14,050	C
Newberry College	SC	26,850	LC
Newman Univ	KS	30,380	C+
Nicholls State Univ	LA	7,095	C
N Car Central Univ	NC	9,000	LC
North Central College	IL	38,343	VC
N Dak State Univ	ND		C
Northeastern Illinois Univ	IL	10,318	LC
Northeastern Univ	MA	55,296	MC
Northern Illinois Univ	IL	19,768	C
Northwest Missouri State Univ	MO	17,347	C
Northwest Nazarene Univ	ID	34,000	C
Northwestern Univ	IL	61,640	MC
Notre Dame College	OH	34,942	VC
Notre Dame de Namur Univ	CA	44,236	LC
Oberlin College	OH	61,788	MC
Oglethorpe Univ	GA	44,200	C
Ohio Dominican Univ	OH	38,380	C+
Ohio Univ	OH	21,080	C
Okla Christian Univ	OK	25,870	VC
Okla City Univ	OK	40,476	VC
Okla State Univ	OK	14,310	VC
Olivet Nazarene Univ	IL	29,990	C
Oregon State Univ	OR	20,273	VC
Oswego / SUNY	NY	20,009	VC
Ottawa Univ	KS	15,000	VC
Otterbein College	OH	32,214	C
Ouachita Baptist Univ	AR	30,220	VC
Our Lady of the Lake Univ	TX	22,430	LC
Pace Univ	NY	53,367	C
Pacific Lutheran Univ	WA	46,760	C+
Palm Beach Atlantic Univ	FL	34,874	C+
Pepperdine Univ	CA	55,372	HC+
Pfeiffer Univ	NC	33,700	LC
Piedmont College	GA	30,136	C
Pine Manor College	MA	32,659	LC
Pittsburg State Univ	KS	12,032	C
Pitzer College	CA	54,988	MC
Plymouth State Univ	NH	23,148	LC
Prairie View A&M Univ	TX	15,205	LC
Presbyterian College	SC	42,678	C+
Prescott College	AZ	33,284	C
Queens College/The CUNY	NY	17,107	VC
Queens Univ of Charlotte	NC	39,543	C+
Radford Univ	VA	17,766	LC
Ramapo College of New Jersey	NJ	24,938	C
Randolph College	VA	45,660	VC
Reed College	OR	57,780	MC
Rhodes College	TN	51,900	HC+
Ringling College of Art and Design	FL	46,130	SP
Ripon College	WI	36,959	C+
Roanoke College	VA	49,976	C
Roberts Wesleyan College	NY	38,306	C
Rockford College	IL	31,000	C
Rocky Mountain College	MT	32,242	C
Rowan Univ	NJ	24,022	VC
Rutgers, The State Univ of New Jersey/Camden Campus	NJ	25,121	C
Rutgers, The State Univ of New Jersey/New Brunswick	NJ	25,562	VC
Rutgers, The State Univ of New Jersey/Newark Campus	NJ	258,806	C
Saginaw Valley State Univ	MI	17,369	C
St. John's Univ	MN	47,984	C
St. Joseph's College	IN	36,500	C
St. Joseph's Univ	PA	45,006	VC
St. Mary-of-the-Woods College	IN	37,722	LC
St. Mary's College	IN	45,160	C+
St. Mary's College of Calif	CA	53,550	C
St. Mary's Univ of Minn	MN	38,280	C
St. Vincent College	PA	40,244	C
Salisbury Univ	MD	19,180	VC
Sam Houston State Univ	TX	17,082	C
Samford Univ	AL	37,060	C+
San Diego State Univ	CA	21,611	C+
San Francisco State Univ	CA	18,514	C
Savannah College of Art and Design	GA	48,005	SP
Schreiner Univ	TX	32,734	LC
Seattle Pacific Univ	WA	41,559	VC+
Shepherd Univ	WV	15,875	C
Shippensburg Univ of Pennsylvania	PA	20,934	C
Shorter Univ	GA	30,650	LC
Simpson College	IA	36,086	C+
Sinte Gleska Univ	SD	2,300	NC
Skidmore College	NY	59,942	HC
Sonoma State Univ	CA	20,541	C
S Dak State Univ	SD	14,296	C
Southeast Missouri State Univ	MO	15,370	LC
Southeastern Louisiana Univ	LA	13,325	C
Southeastern Okla State Univ	OK	7,966	LC
Southern Adventist Univ	TN	26,190	C
Southern Arkansas Univ	AR	14,316	C
Southern Illinois Univ Carbondale	IL	21,942	C
Southern Illinois Univ Edwardsville	IL	17,532	C
Southern Oregon Univ	OR	17,874	C
Southwest Baptist Univ	MO	24,710	C
Southwest Minn State Univ	MN	14,000	C
Southwestern Univ	TX	45,660	VC
Spelman College	GA	24,650	C
Spring Arbor Univ	MI	26,740	C
St. Catherine Univ	MN	37,782	C+
St. Edward's Univ	TX	47,784	C
St. Lawrence Univ	NY	59,972	VC
St. Mary's College of Maryland	MD	25,754	VC
St. Norbert College	WI	41,478	VC
Stanford Univ	CA	58,388	MC
Stephen F. Austin State Univ	TX	14,668	C
Sterling College	KS	27,216	C
Stevenson Univ	MD	41,470	C
Stillman College	AL	19,470	C
SUNY Cortland/The SUNY	NY	19,759	C+
SUNY Oneonta / SUNY	NY	16,919	VC
SUNY Plattsburgh / SUNY	NY	18,083	C
Swarthmore College	PA	57,870	MC
Syracuse Univ	NY	56,346	VC
Tarleton State Univ	TX	13,489	LC
Taylor Univ	IN	37,821	VC+
Temple Univ	PA	24,392	VC
Tenn State Univ	TN	9,048	C
Texas A&M Univ at Corpus Christi	TX	11,544	LC
Texas Lutheran Univ	TX	36,040	C
Texas Southern Univ	TX	18,212	LC
Texas State Univ	TX	17,128	C
Texas Wesleyan Univ	TX	31,382	C
Texas Woman's Univ	TX	13,633	LC
The Catholic Univ of America	DC	52,852	VC
The College of Idaho	ID	31,277	C+
Ohio State Univ-Columbus Campus	OH	19,887	HC+
The SUNY at Potsdam	NY	18,473	C
The Univ of Memphis	TN	15,094	C
The Univ of N Car at Greensboro	NC	12,848	C
The Univ of N Car at Pembroke	NC	13,388	LC
The Univ of Okla	OK	18,621	VC
The Univ of Tenn at Chattanooga	TN	16,883	C
The Univ of Utah	UT	16,463	VC
The Univ of Virginia's College at Wise	VA	11,076	C
Thiel College	PA	38,728	LC
Thomas Edison State College	NJ	5,700	SP
Thomas More College	KY	34,760	C
Tougaloo College	MS	15,275	NC
Towson Univ	MD	16,000	C
Transylvania Univ	KY	42,660	VC+
Trinity Christian College	IL	28,869	C
Trinity Univ	TX	48,150	HC+
Troy Univ	AL	10,650	C
Truman State Univ	MO	15,541	HC
Union Univ	TN	28,260	VC
Unity College	ME	34,054	C
Univ at Buffalo / The SUNY	NY	20,283	VC
Univ of Akron	OH	20,436	C
Univ of Alabama at Birmingham	AL	18,484	C+
Univ of Alabama in Huntsville	AL	17,591	VC+
Univ of Alaska Anchorage	AK	16,673	NC
Univ of Alaska Fairbanks	AK	15,130	C
Univ of Alaska Southeast	AK	11,493	C
Univ of Arizona	AZ	20,657	C
Univ of Arkansas at Fayetteville	AR	18,352	C+
Univ of Arkansas at Little Rock	AR	17,609	LC
Univ of Arkansas at Monticello	AR	12,076	NC
Univ of Arkansas at Pine Bluff	AR	13,378	C
Univ of Calif at Berkeley	CA	23,322	MC
Univ of Calif at Los Angeles	CA	25,686	MC
Univ of Calif at Riverside	CA	27,204	C+
Univ of Calif at Santa Barbara	CA	27,551	HC
Univ of Calif at Santa Cruz	CA	27,807	C+
Univ of Central Florida	FL	15,668	VC+
Univ of Central Okla	OK	12,293	C
Univ of Charleston	WV	32,300	C
Univ of Conn	CT	24,706	HC
Univ of Dayton	OH	49,070	VC
Univ of Delaware	DE	23,612	VC
Univ of Denver	CO	51,787	VC+
Univ of Evansville	IN	42,656	VC+
Univ of Florida	FL	15,943	HC
Univ of Georgia	GA	20,082	VC
Univ of Great Falls	MT	27,970	C
Univ of Hawaii at Hilo	HI	23,066	C
Univ of Hawaii at Manoa	HI	19,379	C
Univ of Houston	TX	19,796	VC
Univ of Idaho	ID	14,558	C
Univ of Indianapolis	IN	31,740	LC
Univ of Iowa	IA	17,693	VC
Univ of Kansas	KS	17,603	C+
Univ of La Verne	CA	47,010	C
Univ of Louisiana at Monroe	LA	12,998	C
Univ of Louisville	KY	17,946	C
Univ of Maine at Augusta	ME	6,855	C
Univ of Maine at Farmington	ME	18,187	LC
Univ of Maine at Presque Isle	ME	15,011	LC
Univ of Mary Hardin-Baylor	TX	31,950	C+
Univ of Mass Boston	MA	23,066	VC
Univ of Miami	FL	57,034	MC
Univ of Mich/Ann Arbor	MI	22,102	MC
Univ of Mich-Flint	MI	17,547	C
Univ of Minn/Duluth	MN	19,806	C
Univ of Minn/Twin Cities	MN		HC
Univ of Miss	MS	16,704	C
Univ of Missouri/Columbia	MO	18,201	MC
Univ of Mobile	AL	28,935	VC
Univ of Montana-Western	MT	9,753	LC
Univ of Montevallo	AL	17,060	C
Univ of Mount Olive	NC	18,426	C
Univ of Mount Union	OH	35,130	C
Univ of Nebr - Lincoln	NE	18,031	VC
Univ of Nebr at Omaha	NE	12,700	C
Univ of Nevada/Reno	NV	17,507	C
Univ of New Haven	CT	48,940	C
Univ of New Mexico	NM	15,300	C
Univ of New Orleans	LA	9,224	C
Univ of North Alabama	AL	9,960	C
Univ of N Car at Asheville	NC	13,500	VC
Univ of N Car at Charlotte	NC	15,547	C
Univ of N Car at Wilmington	NC	13,572	VC
Univ of North Florida	FL	15,870	VC
Univ of North Georgia	GA	8,500	C
Univ of North Texas	TX	15,628	C
Univ of Northern Colo	CO	18,545	C
Univ of Oregon	OR	21,360	C+
Univ of Pikeville	KY	25,500	NC
Univ of Puget Sound	WA	54,608	HC

ST = STATE $IS = IN-STATE COSTS   SR = SELECTOR RATING

School	ST	$IS	SR
Univ of Redlands	CA	40,500	VC
Univ of Rio Grande	OH	8,750	NC
Univ of St. Mary	KS	28,400	C+
Univ of Science and Arts of Okla	OK	10,560	VC
Univ of S Dak	SD	15,111	C
Univ of Southern Indiana	IN	14,885	C
Univ of Tampa	FL	35,160	VC
Univ of Tenn at Knoxville	TN	20,364	VC+
Univ of Texas - Pan American	TX	11,125	LC
Univ of Texas at El Paso	TX	8,764	NC
Univ of Texas at San Antonio	TX	18,372	C
Univ of the Cumberlands	KY	27,500	C
Univ of the Incarnate Word	TX	37,316	VC
Univ of the Ozarks	AR	31,440	C
Univ of the Pacific	CA	52,146	VC
Univ of Tulsa	OK	46,331	MC
Univ of Vermont	VT	27,006	VC+
Univ of Virginia	VA	23,050	MC
Univ of West Georgia	GA	15,488	LC
Univ of Wisc/Eau Claire	WI	15,730	VC
Univ of Wisc/Green Bay	WI	19,074	C
Univ of Wisc/La Crosse	WI	9,304	VC
Univ of Wisc/Madison	WI	18,757	HC+
Univ of Wisc/Oshkosh	WI	10,426	LC
Univ of Wisc/Platteville	WI	14,564	C
Univ of Wisc/River Falls	WI	9,722	C
Univ of Wisc/Stevens Point	WI	14,043	C
Univ of Wisc/Stout	WI	15,459	C
Univ of Wisc/Superior	WI	14,314	C
Univ of Wisc-Milwaukee	WI	18,436	LC
Univ of Wyoming	WY	14,401	C+
Upper Iowa Univ	IA	30,426	NC
Ursinus College	PA	57,580	VC
Ursuline College	OH	33,198	LC
Valley City State Univ	ND	12,286	LC
Valparaiso Univ	IN	44,940	VC+
Vanderbilt Univ	TN	58,220	MC
Vassar College	NY	61,140	MC
Virginia Polytechnic Inst and State Univ	VA	14,629	HC
Virginia Wesleyan College	VA	28,433	LC
Viterbo Univ	WI	30,070	C
Wabash College	IN	43,680	C+
Wake Forest Univ	NC	58,838	MC
Walla Walla Univ	WA	26,256	NC
Warren Wilson College	NC	40,132	VC
Wartburg College	IA	41,055	VC
Washburn Univ	KS	12,579	C
Washington and Jefferson College	PA	51,948	VC
Washington College	MD	52,602	VC
Wayland Baptist Univ	TX	18,912	LC
Wayne State College	NE	11,764	NC
Wayne State Univ	MI	22,063	C
Waynesburg Univ	PA	30,150	C
Webster Univ	MO	35,100	C+
West Chester Univ of Pennsylvania	PA	17,186	C
West Texas A&M Univ	TX	13,478	C
West Virginia Univ	WV	16,542	C+
Western Carolina Univ	NC	13,965	C
Western Conn State Univ	CT	18,327	LC
Western Illinois Univ	IL	20,732	C
Western Mich Univ	MI	19,628	C
Western Oregon Univ	OR	15,021	C
Western State Colo Univ	CO	16,924	C
Western Washington Univ	WA	18,519	VC
Westfield State Univ	MA	18,297	C
Westminster College	PA	31,290	C+
Westminster College	UT	37,708	C+
Westmont College	CA	41,500	HC
Wheaton College	IL	40,720	MC
Whittier College	CA	43,416	VC
Whitworth Univ	WA	47,734	VC
Wichita State Univ	KS	14,607	C+
Widener Univ	PA	52,418	C
William Carey Univ	MS	13,500	LC
William Jewell College	MO	31,000	VC+
William Woods Univ	MO	24,260	C
Williams Baptist College	AR	20,070	C
Williams College	MA	61,070	MC
Wilmington College	OH	29,784	C
Winston-Salem State Univ	NC	9,418	LC
Winthrop Univ	SC	21,120	C
Wisc Lutheran College	WI	23,510	VC
Wright State Univ	OH	16,983	C
Xavier Univ	OH	44,980	VC
Yale Univ	CT	55,300	MC
Youngstown State Univ	OH	16,732	C

ART AND DESIGN

School	ST	$IS	SR
Bryant Univ	RI	49,179	VC
Calif Polytechnic State Univ	CA	19,847	HC
Calvin College	MI	39,120	VC
Missouri Southern State Univ	MO	12,061	C
Univ of San Diego	CA	54,818	HC+
Univ of St. Francis	IL	37,560	C

ART EDUCATION

School	ST	$IS	SR
Abilene Christian Univ	TX	38,400	C+
Adams State Univ	CO	13,358	LC
Adelphi Univ	NY	44,670	VC
Alabama A&M Univ	AL	10,084	C
Alabama State Univ	AL	14,142	NC
Alfred Univ	NY	41,770	C
Alverno College	WI	31,434	LC
Anderson Univ	IN	36,100	C
Andrews Univ	MI	28,030	C+
Appalachian State Univ	NC	12,919	VC
Aquinas College	MI	33,060	C
Arcadia Univ	PA	33,570	C+
Arizona State Univ, at the Tempe Campus	AZ	20,137	C+
Arkansas Tech Univ	AR	13,982	LC
Armstrong State Univ	GA	15,532	C
Asbury Univ	KY	32,038	VC
Ashland Univ	OH	25,000	C
Augustana College	IL	43,398	VC
Averett Univ	VA	37,750	LC
Azusa Pacific Univ	CA	42,086	C
Baker Univ	KS	33,350	C+
Baldwin Wallace Univ	OH	38,318	C
Barton College	NC	27,660	LC
Baylor Univ	TX	50,329	HC
Beloit College	WI	49,970	VC
Bemidji State Univ	MN	13,500	VC
Berry College	GA	39,254	VC
Bethany College	KS	30,605	NC
Bethany College	WV	35,282	LC
Bethel College	IN	31,560	C
Birmingham-Southern College	AL	44,168	VC+
Blackburn College	IL	21,350	C
Boise State Univ	ID	13,469	LC
Boston Univ	MA	60,694	MC
Bowling Green State Univ	OH	18,970	C
Bradley Univ	IL	31,874	VC
Brenau Univ - Women's College	GA	26,650	LC
Brescia Univ	KY	26,140	VC+
Bridgewater State Univ	MA	18,752	C
Brigham Young Univ	UT	12,100	HC
Brigham Young Univ/Hawaii	HI	10,686	VC
Buena Vista Univ	IA	39,188	C
Buffalo State College / SUNY	NY	15,733	C+
Cal State, Chico	CA	20,158	C
Calvin College	MI	39,120	VC
Capital Univ	OH	41,050	VC
Carlow Univ	PA	30,272	C
Carroll Univ	WI	38,100	C
Carson-Newman Univ	TN	29,058	C+
Case Western Reserve Univ	OH	56,534	MC
Central Conn State Univ	CT	19,749	C
Central State Univ	OH	9,010	C
Central Washington Univ	WA	11,730	C
Chicago State Univ	IL	5,482	C
CUNY/Brooklyn College	NY	5,884	C+
CUNY/City College	NY	20,319	HC+
Claflin Univ	SC	22,368	LC
Clarke Univ	IA	37,600	C
Coker College	SC	32,256	LC
Colby-Sawyer College	NH	50,790	C
College for Creative Studies	MI	45,340	C
College of Mount St. Joseph	OH	33,880	C
College of New Jersey	NJ	25,376	HC
College of the Ozarks	MO	0	VC
Colo State Univ-Fort Collins	CO	20,385	VC
Columbus State Univ	GA	13,176	C
Concord Univ	WV	13,102	C
Concordia College - Moorhead	MN	39,974	VC
Concordia College - New York	NY	39,035	LC
Concordia Univ St. Paul	MN	28,250	C
Converse College	SC	37,130	C
Corcoran College of Art and Design	DC	36,500	SP
Cornell College	IA	44,930	VC
Culver-Stockton College	MO	30,900	C
Daemen College	NY	34,770	C
Defiance College	OH	30,645	C
Delaware State Univ	DE	16,722	LC
DePaul Univ	IL	47,623	VC
Dickinson State Univ	ND	11,900	NC
Dordt College	IA	34,160	LC
Dowling College	NY	25,000	LC
East Carolina Univ	NC	14,169	C
East Central Univ	OK	10,223	LC
Eastern Kentucky Univ	KY	11,161	C
Eastern Mich Univ	MI	18,604	C
Eastern Washington Univ	WA		C
Edinboro Univ of Pennsylvania	PA	15,940	LC
Elizabethtown College	PA	49,740	VC
Elmhurst College	IL	43,336	C
Elmira College	NY	49,950	C+
Emporia State Univ	KS	12,897	C
Escuela de Artes Plasticas de PR		2,660	
Fairmont State Univ	WV	12,098	LC
Fisk Univ	TN	19,830	C
Flagler College	FL	25,180	C
Florida A&M Univ	FL	14,935	LC
Florida International Univ	FL	17,747	C+
Florida Southern College	FL	40,150	LC
Florida State Univ	FL	16,715	VC
Fort Hays State Univ	KS	11,354	C
Francis Marion Univ	SC	16,464	LC
Freed-Hardeman Univ	TN	19,697	VC
Friends Univ	KS	29,100	C
Georgia State Univ	GA	15,582	VC
Goddard College	VT	16,418	VC
Goshen College	IN	35,900	VC
Grace College and Seminary	IN	28,800	VC
Grand Valley State Univ	MI	17,998	C+
Grand View Univ	IA	31,050	C
Green Mountain College	VT	45,228	LC
Greensboro College	NC	28,740	LC
Gustavus Adolphus College	MN	48,170	HC
Hardin-Simmons Univ	TX	23,560	C+
Hastings College	NE	27,782	C+
Henderson State Univ	AR	14,584	C
Heritage Univ	WA	17,664	NC
Hofstra Univ	NY	51,810	VC+
Hope College	MI	38,650	VC
Houghton College	NY	36,808	C+
Houston Baptist Univ	TX	36,450	C
Howard Univ	DC	13,646	C
Hunter College	NY	14,429	VC
Huntington Univ	IN	32,220	C+
Indiana State Univ	IN	16,000	C
Indiana Univ Bloomington	IN	19,801	VC
Indiana Univ of Pennsylvania	PA	20,846	LC
Indiana Univ South Bend	IN	15,501	C
Indiana Univ-Purdue Univ Fort Wayne	IN	15,521	C
Indiana Univ-Purdue Univ Indianapolis	IN	17,611	C
Indiana Wesleyan Univ	IN	31,815	VC
Inter-American Univ of PR/San Germán	PR	6,720	
Iowa Wesleyan College	IA	30,850	LC
Ithaca College	NY	53,864	HC
Jacksonville Univ	FL	37,780	C
Johnson State College	VT	16,721	C
Kansas State Univ	KS	15,497	VC
Kansas Wesleyan Univ	KS	32,000	C
Kennesaw State Univ	GA		C
Kent State Univ	OH	19,920	C
Kentucky State Univ	KY	11,000	C
Kentucky Wesleyan College	KY	27,440	C
Keystone College	PA	26,308	C
Kutztown Univ of Pennsylvania	PA	16,909	LC
Lamar Univ	TX	6,820	LC
Lehman College/The CUNY	NY	5,778	LC
Lincoln Univ	MO	12,904	NC
Lindsey Wilson College	KY	31,220	C
Lipscomb Univ	TN	37,490	VC
LIU Brooklyn	NY	47,182	LC
LIU Post	NY	47,660	C
Longwood Univ	VA	20,924	C
Louisiana College	LA	15,746	C
Louisiana Tech Univ	LA	11,302	C
Lubbock Christian Univ	TX	26,308	C
Madonna Univ	MI	24,540	VC
Manchester Univ	IN	35,070	C
Mansfield Univ	PA	19,468	LC
Marian Univ	WI	32,420	LC
Mars Hill Univ	NC	22,950	LC
Marymount Univ	VA	39,480	C
Maryville Univ of St. Louis	MO	35,856	VC
Marywood Univ	PA	45,595	C
McKendree Univ	IL	29,920	C+
McMurry Univ	TX	25,962	LC
Mercyhurst Univ	PA	40,700	C
Messiah College	PA	40,690	C+
Methodist Univ	NC	37,185	C
Miami Univ	OH	24,191	VC
Mich State Univ	MI	22,450	VC
Middle Tenn State Univ	TN	8,650	C
Midland Univ	NE	34,000	C
Millersville Univ of Pennsylvania	PA	21,648	C
Millikin Univ	IL	38,940	VC
Minn State Univ, Mankato	MN	15,616	C
Minn State Univ, Moorhead	MN	13,392	VC
Miss College	MS	21,998	C
Miss Univ for Women	MS	7,400	C
Missouri Western State Univ	MO	12,260	NC
Monmouth Univ	NJ	44,108	C
Montana State Univ-Billings	MT	14,225	LC
Montclair State Univ	NJ	22,614	C
Montserrat College of Art	MA	31,000	C
Moore College of Art and Design	PA	50,135	SP
Moravian College	PA	36,381	VC
Morningside College	IA	35,430	C
Mount Mary Univ	WI	33,590	LC
Mount Vernon Nazarene Univ	OH	29,590	C
Murray State Univ	KY	15,304	C
Nazareth College of Rochester	NY	43,028	C+
New Jersey City Univ	NJ	21,456	LC
New York Univ	NY	61,470	MC
N Car Agricultural and Technical State Univ	NC	13,365	LC
North Central College	IL	38,343	VC
Northeastern State Univ	OK	8,615	VC
Northern Illinois Univ	IL	19,768	C
Northern Mich Univ	MI	18,278	C
Northern State Univ - Aberdeen	SD	14,505	C
Northwest Missouri State Univ	MO	17,347	C
Northwest Nazarene Univ	ID	34,000	C
Northwestern College	IA	24,000	C
Northwestern College of Iowa	IA	36,240	VC
Notre Dame of Maryland Univ	MD	27,700	VC
Nova Southeastern Univ	FL	37,280	VC
Oakland City Univ	IN	24,500	NC
Ohio Wesleyan Univ	OH	49,460	C+
Okla Baptist Univ	OK	28,202	C
Old Dominion Univ	VA	19,483	LC
Olivet Nazarene Univ	IL	29,990	C
Oral Roberts Univ	OK	31,734	C
Ouachita Baptist Univ	AR	30,220	VC
Our Lady of the Lake Univ	TX	22,430	LC
Palm Beach Atlantic Univ	FL	34,874	C+
Peru State College	NE	8,600	NC
Piedmont College	GA	30,136	C
Pittsburg State Univ	KS	12,032	C
Plymouth State Univ	NH	23,148	LC
Point Loma Nazarene Univ	CA	41,006	C+
Pontifical Catholic Univ of PR	PR	7,310	
Pratt Inst	NY	55,956	SP
Prescott College	AZ	33,284	C
Purdue Univ/West Lafayette	IN	20,024	HC
Queens College/The CUNY	NY	17,107	VC
Rhode Island College	RI	17,694	LC
Rivier Univ	NH	35,000	VC
Rocky Mountain College	MT	32,242	C
Rocky Mountain College of Art and Design	CO	22,470	SP
Rosemont College	PA	42,350	C
Rowan Univ	NJ	24,022	VC+
Saginaw Valley State Univ	MI	17,369	C
St. Joseph's Univ	PA	55,006	VC
St. Mary-of-the-Woods College	IN	37,722	LC
St. Michael's College	VT	49,975	VC
St. Vincent College	PA	40,244	C
St. Xavier Univ	IL	32,840	C
Salem State Univ	MA	13,161	LC
School of the Art Inst of Chicago	IL	56,230	SP
Seton Hill Univ	PA	35,172	C
Shepherd Univ	WV	15,875	C
Shippensburg Univ of Pennsylvania	PA	20,934	C
Siena Heights Univ	MI	32,040	C
Silver Lake College	WI	22,600	LC
S Car State Univ	SC	6,700	LC
S Dak State Univ	SD	14,296	C
Southeast Missouri State Univ	MO	15,370	LC
Southeastern Okla State Univ	OK	7,966	LC
Southern Arkansas Univ	AR	14,316	C
Southern Conn State Univ	CT	18,033	LC
Southern Illinois Univ Edwardsville	IL	17,532	C
Southern Univ and A&M College	LA	9,761	LC
Southern Univ at New Orleans	LA	2,963	NC
Southwest Baptist Univ	MO	24,710	C
Southwest Minn State Univ	MN	14,000	C
Southwestern Okla State Univ	OK	9,160	C
Spelman College	GA	24,650	C
St. Ambrose Univ	IA	30,845	C
St. Catherine Univ	MN	37,782	C+
St. Cloud State Univ	MN	10,600	C
St. Edward's Univ	TX	47,784	C
St. Thomas Aquinas College	NY	40,230	C
Sul Ross State Univ	TX	13,410	LC
SUNY New Paltz	NY	14,348	C
Syracuse Univ	NY	56,346	VC
Tarleton State Univ	TX	13,489	LC
Taylor Univ	IN	37,821	VC+
Temple Univ	PA	24,392	VC
Tenn Tech Univ	TN	11,310	C
Texas Christian Univ	TX	49,980	HC
The Catholic Univ of America	DC	52,852	VC
The College of New Rochelle	NY	33,600	VC
The College of St. Rose	NY	26,750	C
Ohio State Univ-Columbus Campus	OH	19,887	HC+
The Pennsylvania State Univ - Univ Park	PA	28,022	VC+
The Univ of N Car at Greensboro	NC	12,848	C
The Univ of Tenn at Chattanooga	TN	16,883	C
The Univ of Utah	UT	16,463	VC
Thomas More College	KY	34,760	C
Towson Univ	MD	16,000	VC
Trinity Christian College	IL	28,869	C
Troy Univ	AL	10,650	C
Union College	NE	23,270	C
Univ of Akron	OH	20,436	C
Univ of Arizona	AZ	20,657	C
Univ of Arkansas at Pine Bluff	AR	13,378	C
Univ of Central Arkansas	AR	13,667	VC
Univ of Central Florida	FL	15,668	VC+
Univ of Central Missouri	MO	14,605	C
Univ of Central Okla	OK	12,293	C

ST = STATE $IS = IN-STATE COSTS SR = SELECTOR RATING

School	ST	$IS	SR
Univ of Cincinnati	OH	21,506	VC
Univ of Dallas	TX	45,500	VC+
Univ of Dayton	OH	49,070	VC
Univ of Evansville	IN	42,656	VC+
Univ of Findlay	OH	31,916	C
Univ of Florida	FL	15,943	HC
Univ of Georgia	GA	20,082	VC
Univ of Idaho	ID	14,558	C
Univ of Illinois at Chicago	IL	24,505	VC
Univ of Illinois at Urbana-Champaign	IL	26,450	MC
Univ of Indianapolis	IN	31,740	LC
Univ of Iowa	IA	17,693	VC
Univ of Kansas	KS	17,603	C+
Univ of Kentucky	KY	19,868	C
Univ of Louisiana at Lafayette	LA	6,130	C
Univ of Louisville	KY	17,946	C
Univ of Maine	ME	19,902	C+
Univ of Maine at Presque Isle	ME	15,011	LC
Univ of Mary Hardin-Baylor	TX	31,950	C+
Univ of Maryland - College Park	MD	20,060	HC
Univ of Maryland/Eastern Shore	MD	14,000	VC
Univ of Mass Dartmouth	MA	22,223	C
Univ of Minn/Duluth	MN	19,806	C
Univ of Minn/Twin Cities	MN		HC
Univ of Missouri/Columbia	MO	18,201	MC
Univ of Montana-Western	MT	9,753	C
Univ of Montevallo	AL	17,060	C
Univ of Nebr at Kearney	NE	14,855	LC
Univ of New England	ME	46,750	C
Univ of New Mexico	NM	15,300	C
Univ of North Alabama	AL	9,960	C
Univ of North Florida	FL	15,870	VC
Univ of North Georgia	GA	8,500	C
Univ of Northern Iowa	IA	15,795	C
Univ of Rio Grande	OH	8,750	NC
Univ of St. Francis	IN	29,810	C
Univ of Sioux Falls	SD	22,990	C
Univ of S Car at Columbia	SC	19,725	VC+
Univ of S Car Upstate	SC	18,200	LC
Univ of S Dak	SD	15,111	C
Univ of South Florida/Tampa	FL	13,000	C
Univ of Southern Indiana	IN	14,885	C
Univ of Southern Miss	MS	13,170	C
Univ of St. Francis	IL	37,560	C
Univ of the Cumberlands	KY	27,500	C
Univ of the Incarnate Word	TX	37,316	C
Univ of Toledo	OH	18,464	C
Univ of Vermont	VT	27,006	VC+
Univ of West Florida	FL	14,656	C
Univ of Wisc Whitewater	WI	13,314	C
Univ of Wisc/Green Bay	WI	19,074	C
Univ of Wisc/Madison	WI	18,757	HC+
Univ of Wisc/Oshkosh	WI	10,426	LC
Univ of Wisc/Platteville	WI	14,564	C
Univ of Wisc/River Falls	WI	9,722	LC
Univ of Wisc/Stout	WI	15,459	C
Univ of Wisc/Superior	WI	14,314	C
Univ of Wisc-Milwaukee	WI	18,436	C
Utah State Univ	UT	12,044	C
Valparaiso Univ	IN	44,940	VC+
Virginia Commonwealth Univ	VA	21,716	C
Virginia Union Univ	VA	18,432	C
Virginia Wesleyan College	VA	28,433	LC
Viterbo Univ	WI	30,070	C
Wartburg College	IA	41,055	VC
Washburn Univ	KS	12,579	C
Washington and Jefferson College	PA	51,948	VC
Washington Univ in St. Louis	MO	69,844	MC
Wayne State Univ	MI	22,063	C
Webster Univ	MO	35,100	C+
West Liberty Univ	WV	9,142	LC
West Texas A&M Univ	TX	13,478	C
West Virginia State Univ	WV	8,378	NC
West Virginia Wesleyan College	WV	26,880	C
Western Carolina Univ	NC	13,965	C
Western Illinois Univ	IL	20,732	C
Western Kentucky Univ	KY	11,000	LC
Western Mich Univ	MI	19,628	C
Western New Mexico Univ	NM	8,500	LC
Western State Colo Univ	CO	16,924	C
Western Washington Univ	WA	18,519	VC
Westmont College	CA	41,500	HC
Wichita State Univ	KS	14,607	C+
Winona State Univ	MN	16,640	C
Wright State Univ	OH	16,983	C
Xavier Univ of Louisiana	LA	25,300	C
Youngstown State Univ	OH	16,732	C

ART HISTORY

School	ST	$IS	SR
Amherst College	MA	58,744	MC
Aquinas College	MI	33,060	C
Arizona State Univ, at the Tempe Campus	AZ	20,137	C+
Assumption College	MA	47,122	C+
Austin College	TX	45,875	HC
Baldwin Wallace Univ	OH	38,318	C
Baylor Univ	TX	50,329	HC
Belmont Univ	TN	39,190	VC+
Beloit College	WI	49,970	HC

School	ST	$IS	SR
Binghamton Univ/The SUNY	NY	21,648	HC+
Bowdoin College	ME	59,568	MC
Bowling Green State Univ	OH	18,970	C
Cal State, Fullerton	CA	25,188	C
Cal State, Long Beach	CA	17,502	C+
Calvin College	MI	39,120	VC
Canisius College	NY	44,900	C
Colby College	ME	57,510	MC
College of Charleston	SC	22,145	VC
College of Mount St. Joseph	OH	33,880	C
College of William & Mary	VA	28,000	MC
Cornell Univ	NY	60,964	MC
Creighton Univ	NE	45,356	VC
DePaul Univ	IL	47,623	VC
Dickinson College	PA	57,662	HC+
Dominican Univ	IL	37,628	C
Dordt College	IA	34,160	C+
Elon Univ	NC	41,914	VC+
Fairfield Univ	CT	56,960	VC
Flagler College	FL	25,180	C
Fordham Univ	NY	61,588	HC+
Franklin College	IN	36,585	C
Georgetown Univ	DC	52,910	MC
Goucher College	MD	52,040	VC+
Hamline Univ	MN	45,678	VC
Hobart and William Smith Colleges	NY	60,034	HC+
Indiana Univ-Purdue Univ Indianapolis	IN	17,611	C
Ithaca College	NY	53,864	VC
John Carroll Univ	OH	46,300	C+
Kennesaw State Univ	GA		C
Kenyon College	OH	58,890	MC
Loyola Univ Chicago	IL	51,646	VC+
Mills College	CA	54,119	VC
Missouri State Univ	MO	13,996	C+
Moore College of Art and Design	PA	50,135	SP
Murray State Univ	KY	15,304	C
Nazareth College of Rochester	NY	43,028	C+
New York Univ	NY	61,470	MC
Niagara Univ	NY	41,010	C
North Central College	IL	38,343	VC
Northeastern Illinois Univ	IL	10,318	LC
Oberlin College	OH	61,788	MC
Occidental College	CA	60,972	MC
Ohio Univ	OH	21,080	C
Pace Univ	NY	53,367	C
Plymouth State Univ	NH	23,148	LC
Providence College	RI	57,383	VC
St. Louis Univ	MO	48,346	HC
San Jose State Univ	CA	19,133	LC
Seattle Univ	WA	49,035	VC+
Seton Hall Univ	NJ	45,902	C
Sewanee: The Univ of the South	TN	47,700	HC+
Southern Oregon Univ	OR	17,874	C
Southwestern Univ	TX	45,660	VC
St. Bonaventure Univ	NY	41,575	C
Stetson Univ	FL	51,516	VC
Syracuse Univ	NY	56,346	VC
Texas Christian Univ	TX	49,980	HC
The Catholic Univ of America	DC	52,852	VC
The Pennsylvania State Univ - Univ Park	PA	28,022	VC+
The SUNY at Potsdam	NY	18,473	C
The Univ of Utah	UT	16,463	VC
Transylvania Univ	KY	42,660	VC+
Trinity Univ	TX	48,150	HC+
Univ of Arizona	AZ	20,657	C
Univ of Calif at Irvine	CA	25,961	VC
Univ of Calif at Riverside	CA	27,204	C+
Univ of Central Okla	OK	12,293	C
Univ of Cincinnati	OH	21,506	VC
Univ of Colo Boulder	CO	22,605	VC+
Univ of Denver	CO	51,787	VC+
Univ of Evansville	IN	42,656	VC+
Univ of Georgia	GA	20,082	VC
Univ of Illinois at Chicago	IL	24,505	VC
Univ of Louisville	KY	17,946	C
Univ of Maine	ME	19,902	C+
Univ of Miami	FL	57,034	MC
Univ of Nebr - Lincoln	NE	18,031	VC
Univ of Nevada/Reno	NV	17,507	C
Univ of New Hampshire	NH	26,912	C
Univ of New Mexico	NM	15,300	C
Univ of San Diego	CA	54,818	HC+
Univ of Tenn at Knoxville	TN	20,364	VC+
Univ of Tulsa	OK	46,331	MC
Univ of Wisc/Superior	WI	14,314	C
Vassar College	NY	61,140	MC
Wake Forest Univ	NC	58,838	MC
Webster Univ	MO	35,100	C+
Western Mich Univ	MI	19,628	C
Whitman College	WA	55,988	MC
Wofford College	SC	45,795	VC
Wright State Univ	OH	16,983	C
Yale Univ	CT	55,300	MC
Youngstown State Univ	OH	16,732	C

ART HISTORY AND APPRECIATION

School	ST	$IS	SR
Adams State Univ	CO	13,358	LC

School	ST	$IS	SR
Adelphi Univ	NY	44,670	VC
Agnes Scott College	GA	45,323	C+
Albion College	MI	46,010	C
Alfred Univ	NY	41,770	C
Allegheny College	PA	50,980	HC
American Univ	DC	56,015	HC+
Aquinas College	MI	33,060	C
Arcadia Univ	PA	33,570	C+
Art Academy of Cincinnati	OH	25,940	SP
Augsburg College	MN	35,142	C
Augustana College	IL	43,398	VC
Baker Univ	KS	33,350	C+
Bard College	NY	61,940	HC
Bard College at Simon's Rock	MA	61,749	HC+
Barnard College/Columbia Univ	NY	39,000	MC
Baylor Univ	TX	50,329	HC
Berry College	GA	39,254	VC
Birmingham-Southern College	AL	44,168	VC+
Bloomsburg Univ of Pennsylvania	PA	13,598	C
Boston College	MA	60,622	MC
Boston Univ	MA	60,694	MC
Bradley Univ	IL	31,874	VC
Brandeis Univ	MA		MC
Bridgewater State Univ	MA	18,752	C
Brigham Young Univ	UT	12,100	HC
Brown Univ	RI	59,428	MC
Bryn Mawr College	PA	59,890	MC
Bucknell Univ	PA	60,140	MC
Buffalo State College / SUNY	NY	15,733	C+
Cal State, San Bernardino	CA	12,000	C
Cal State, Stanislaus	CA	18,582	C
Calvin College	MI	39,120	VC
Carleton College	MN	60,102	MC
Carlow Univ	PA	30,272	C
Case Western Reserve Univ	OH	56,534	MC
Centre College	KY	35,000	HC+
Chapman Univ	CA	58,347	VC+
Chatham Univ	PA	43,797	C
CUNY/Brooklyn College	NY	5,884	C+
Clark Univ	MA	47,020	HC+
Clarke Univ	IA	37,600	C
Coe College	IA	45,550	VC
Colgate Univ	NY	58,135	MC
College of New Jersey	NJ	25,376	HC
College of the Holy Cross	MA	58,042	MC
Colo College	CO	57,162	MC
Colo State Univ-Fort Collins	CO	20,385	VC
Columbia Univ/City of New York	NY	61,116	MC
Columbia Univ/School of General Studies	NY	58,231	MC
Conn College	CT	54,970	MC
Cornell College	IA	44,930	VC
Dartmouth College	NH	57,996	MC
Denison Univ	OH	54,670	HC+
DePauw Univ	IN	48,950	VC+
Dominican Univ of Calif	CA	51,250	C
Drake Univ	IA	41,516	VC+
Drew Univ/College of Liberal Arts	NJ	57,516	C
Drury Univ	MO	31,909	VC
Duke Univ	NC	50,250	MC
Duquesne Univ	PA	43,720	VC
East Carolina Univ	NC	14,169	C
Eastern Mich Univ	MI	18,604	C
Eastern Washington Univ	WA		C
Edinboro Univ of Pennsylvania	PA	15,940	LC
Elizabethtown College	PA	49,740	VC
Emory Univ	GA	56,368	MC
Ferris State Univ	MI	20,047	C
Florida International Univ	FL	17,747	C+
Florida Southern College	FL	40,150	C+
Florida State Univ	FL	16,715	VC
Framingham State Univ	MA	18,854	C
Franklin and Marshall College	PA	60,799	MC
Gallaudet Univ	DC	25,380	SP
George Mason Univ	VA	15,724	VC
George Washington Univ	DC	57,108	MC
Georgia State Univ	GA	15,582	VC
Gettysburg College	PA	58,820	HC
Grand Valley State Univ	MI	17,998	C
Hamilton College	NY	55,620	MC
Hampshire College	MA	58,320	MC
Hanover College	IN	43,073	C+
Hartwick College	NY	51,270	C
Harvard College/Harvard Univ	MA	49,000	MC
Haverford College	PA	61,564	MC
Hofstra Univ	NY	51,810	VC+
Hollins Univ	VA	43,295	VC
Hope College	MI	38,650	VC
Howard Univ	DC	13,646	C
Indiana State Univ	IN	16,000	C
Ithaca College	NY	53,864	VC
Jacksonville Univ	FL	37,780	C
James Madison Univ	VA	18,049	VC
John Carroll Univ	OH	46,300	C+
Johns Hopkins Univ	MD	47,492	MC
Juniata College	PA	49,340	VC
Kalamazoo College	MI	49,740	HC
Kansas City Art Inst	MO	44,308	SP

School	ST	$IS	SR
Kean Univ	NJ	23,444	C
Kent State Univ	OH	19,920	C
Knox College	IL	44,865	VC+
Lawrence Univ	WI	46,371	HC
Lehigh Univ	PA	56,770	MC
Lewis & Clark College	OR	54,382	MC
Lindenwood Univ	MO	20,750	C
LIU Post	NY	47,660	C
Lourdes Univ	OH	26,055	LC
Loyola Marymount Univ	CA	54,649	VC+
Lycoming College	PA	45,379	C
Manhattanville College	NY	50,740	VC
Mansfield Univ	PA	19,468	LC
Marian Univ	IN	38,540	C
Mars Hill Univ	NC	22,950	LC
Mary Baldwin College	VA	38,245	C
Maryland Inst College of Art	MD	39,500	SP
Maryville College	TN	33,150	C+
McDaniel College	MD	47,450	VC
Messiah College	PA	40,690	C+
Miami Univ	OH	24,191	VC
Mich State Univ	MI	22,450	VC
Millsaps College	MS	43,888	VC+
Monmouth Univ	NJ	44,108	C
Montclair State Univ	NJ	22,614	C
Moravian College	PA	36,381	VC
Mount Holyoke College	MA	55,146	MC
New College of Florida	FL	14,504	MC
New England College	NH	45,930	LC
New York Univ	NY	61,470	MC
Northern Illinois Univ	IL	19,768	C
Northwestern Univ	IL	61,640	MC
Notre Dame of Maryland Univ	MD	27,700	VC
Oakland Univ	MI	19,391	C
Oglethorpe Univ	GA	44,200	C
Old Dominion Univ	VA	19,483	LC
Pace Univ	NY	53,367	C
Pepperdine Univ	CA	55,372	HC+
Pomona College	CA	57,680	MC
Portland State Univ	OR	18,672	C
Pratt Inst	NY	55,956	SP
Presbyterian College	SC	42,678	C+
Purdue Univ/West Lafayette	IN	20,024	HC
Queens College/The CUNY	NY	17,107	VC
Randolph-Macon College	VA	49,869	C+
Rhode Island College	RI	17,694	LC
Rice Univ	TX	43,288	MC
Ripon College	WI	36,959	C+
Roanoke College	VA	49,976	C
Rockford College	IL	31,000	C
Roger Williams Univ	RI	46,296	VC
Rollins College	FL	52,370	VC
Roosevelt Univ	IL	22,605	VC
Rutgers, The State Univ of New Jersey/Camden Campus	NJ	25,121	C
Rutgers, The State Univ of New Jersey/New Brunswick	NJ	25,562	VC
St. Peter's Univ	NJ	44,240	C
St. Vincent College	PA	40,244	C
Salem College	NC	29,326	VC
Salve Regina Univ	RI	48,550	VC
San Francisco Art Inst	CA	55,762	SP
Sarah Lawrence College	NY	48,000	HC
Savannah College of Art and Design	GA	48,005	SP
School of the Art Inst of Chicago	IL	56,230	SP
Scripps College	CA	61,940	MC
Seton Hill Univ	PA	35,172	C
Siena Heights Univ	MI	32,040	C
Skidmore College	NY	59,942	HC
Smith College	MA	59,674	MC
Southern Conn State Univ	CT	18,033	LC
Southern Illinois Univ Edwardsville	IL	17,532	C
Southern Methodist Univ	TX	60,585	MC
St. Lawrence Univ	NY	59,972	VC
St. Mary's College of Maryland	MD	25,754	VC
St. Olaf College	MN	51,200	HC+
Stanford Univ	CA	58,388	MC
SUNY at Purchase	NY	16,951	C
Stonehill College	MA	46,780	MC
Stony Brook Univ / SUNY	NY	20,078	HC+
Suffolk Univ	MA	47,298	C
SUNY College at Geneseo	NY	18,670	HC
SUNY New Paltz	NY	14,348	C
Susquehanna Univ	PA	51,150	C
Swarthmore College	PA	57,870	MC
Syracuse Univ	NY	56,346	VC
Temple Univ	PA	24,392	VC
Texas State Univ	TX	17,128	C
Texas Tech Univ	TX	14,243	C
The Catholic Univ of America	DC	52,852	VC
The College of New Rochelle	NY	33,600	VC
The Univ of Memphis	TN	15,094	C
The Univ of Okla	OK	18,621	VC
The Univ of Utah	UT	16,463	VC
Trinity College	CT		HC+
Troy Univ	AL	10,650	C
Truman State Univ	MO	15,541	HC
Tufts Univ	MA	58,780	MC
Tulane Univ	LA	60,861	MC

ST = STATE $IS = IN-STATE COSTS   SR = SELECTOR RATING

School	ST	$IS	SR
Univ at Albany / SUNY	NY	18,674	VC
Univ at Buffalo / The SUNY	NY	20,283	VC
Univ of Alabama at Tuscaloosa	AL	17,164	C+
Univ of Arkansas at Little Rock	AR	17,609	LC
Univ of Calif at Berkeley	CA	23,322	MC
Univ of Calif at Davis	CA		HC
Univ of Calif at Los Angeles	CA	25,686	MC
Univ of Calif at Riverside	CA	27,204	C+
Univ of Calif at San Diego	CA	21,000	VC
Univ of Calif at Santa Barbara	CA	27,551	HC
Univ of Calif at Santa Cruz	CA	27,807	C+
Univ of Chicago	IL	55,416	MC
Univ of Colo Boulder	CO	22,605	VC+
Univ of Conn	CT	24,706	HC
Univ of Dallas	TX	45,500	VC+
Univ of Dayton	OH	49,070	VC
Univ of Delaware	DE	23,612	VC
Univ of Denver	CO	51,787	VC+
Univ of Florida	FL	15,943	HC+
Univ of Georgia	GA	20,082	VC
Univ of Hartford	CT	42,674	C
Univ of Illinois at Chicago	IL	24,505	VC
Univ of Illinois at Urbana-Champaign	IL	26,450	HC
Univ of Iowa	IA	17,693	VC
Univ of Kansas	KS	17,603	C+
Univ of Kentucky	KY	19,868	VC
Univ of La Verne	CA	47,010	C
Univ of Louisville	KY	17,946	C
Univ of Mary Washington	VA	19,484	VC
Univ of Maryland - College Park	MD	20,060	HC
Univ of Mass Amherst	MA	24,215	VC+
Univ of Mass Dartmouth	MA	22,223	C
Univ of Mich/Ann Arbor	MI	22,102	MC
Univ of Mich/Dearborn	MI	9,885	VC
Univ of Minn/Duluth	MN	19,806	C
Univ of Minn/Morris	MN	17,150	VC
Univ of Minn/Twin Cities	MN		HC
Univ of Miss	MS	16,704	C+
Univ of Missouri/Columbia	MO	18,201	MC
Univ of Missouri-Kansas City	MO	19,603	C
Univ of Missouri-St. Louis	MO		VC
Univ of Nebr - Lincoln	NE	18,031	VC
Univ of Nebr at Omaha	NE	12,700	C
Univ of Nevada, Las Vegas	NV	17,303	C
Univ of New Orleans	LA	9,224	C
Univ of N Car at Chapel Hill	NC	18,928	MC
Univ of N Car at Charlotte	NC	15,547	C
Univ of N Car at Wilmington	NC	13,572	VC
Univ of North Texas	TX	15,628	C
Univ of Northern Iowa	IA	15,795	C
Univ of Notre Dame	IN	57,117	MC
Univ of Oregon	OR	21,360	C+
Univ of Pennsylvania	PA	61,132	MC
Univ of Rochester	NY	60,668	MC
Univ of St. Joseph	CT	45,630	C
Univ of San Francisco	CA	54,770	VC
Univ of S Car at Columbia	SC	19,725	VC+
Univ of Southern Calif	CA	56,903	MC
Univ of Texas at Arlington	TX	10,908	LC
Univ of Texas at Austin	TX	44,074	HC
Univ of Texas at San Antonio	TX	18,372	C
Univ of Toledo	OH	18,464	C
Univ of Vermont	VT	27,006	VC+
Univ of Washington	WA.	14,722	VC
Univ of Wisc Whitewater	WI	13,314	C
Univ of Wisc/Madison	WI	18,757	HC+
Univ of Wisc-Milwaukee	WI	18,436	C
Villanova Univ	PA	58,394	MC
Virginia Commonwealth Univ	VA	21,716	C
Washburn Univ	KS	12,579	C
Washington and Lee Univ	VA	52,812	MC
Washington Univ in St. Louis	MO	69,844	MC
Wayne State Univ	MI	22,063	C
Webster Univ	MO	35,100	C+
Wellesley College	MA	59,038	MC
Wesleyan College	GA	24,000	C
Wesleyan Univ	CT	61,198	MC
Wheaton College	MA	54,934	VC+
Wichita State Univ	KS	14,607	C
Willamette Univ	OR	56,450	VC+
William Paterson Univ of New Jersey	NJ	21,694	C
Williams College	MA	61,070	MC
Winthrop Univ	SC	21,120	C
Wright State Univ	OH	16,983	C
York College / The CUNY	NY	5,496	VC
Youngstown State Univ	OH	16,732	C

ART THERAPY

School	ST	$IS	SR
Albertus Magnus College	CT	37,382	LC
Alverno College	WI	31,434	LC
Andrews Univ	MI	28,030	C+
Anna Maria College	MA	34,600	C
Arcadia Univ	PA	33,570	C+
Bethany College	KS	30,605	NC
Bethel College	IN	31,560	C
Capital Univ	OH	41,050	VC
Carlow Univ	PA	30,272	C
Converse College	SC	37,130	C

School	ST	$IS	SR
DePaul Univ	IL	47,623	VC
Edgewood College	WI	33,294	C
Emmanuel College	MA	47,985	VC
Endicott College	MA	43,228	VC+
Lipscomb Univ	TN	37,490	VC
LIU Post	NY	47,660	C
Marygrove College	MI	28,926	C
Marywood Univ	PA	45,595	C
Mercyhurst Univ	PA	40,700	C
Millikin Univ	IL	38,940	C
Mount Mary Univ	WI	33,590	LC
New York Univ	NY	61,470	MC
Prescott College	AZ	33,284	C
Russell Sage College	NY	39,370	C
Seton Hill Univ	PA	35,172	C
Springfield College	MA	25,000	C
The College of New Rochelle	NY	33,600	VC
Univ of Central Okla	OK	12,293	C
Univ of Indianapolis	IN	31,740	LC
Univ of Montana-Western	MT	9,753	LC
Univ of Wisc/Superior	WI	14,314	C

ART/ART STUDIES

School	ST	$IS	SR
Arizona State Univ, at the Tempe Campus	AZ	20,137	C+
Bard College at Simon's Rock	MA	61,749	HC+
Black Hills State Univ	SD	13,947	C
Calvin College	MI	39,120	VC
St. Joseph's Univ	PA	55,006	VC
The Pennsylvania State Univ - Univ Park	PA	28,022	VC+
Univ of Denver	CO	51,787	VC+
Univ of Hawaii at Hilo	HI	23,066	C
Univ of Illinois at Chicago	IL	24,505	VC

ART/VISUAL CULTURE

School	ST	$IS	SR
Bates College	ME	60,720	MC
Bryant Univ	RI	49,179	VC
Calvin College	MI	39,120	VC
Missouri Southern State Univ	MO	12,061	C
Oberlin College	OH	61,788	MC

ARTS ADMINISTRATION/ MANAGEMENT

School	ST	$IS	SR
Adrian College	MI	42,400	C
Appalachian State Univ	NC	12,919	VC
Aquinas College	MI	33,060	C
Belhaven Univ	MS	27,170	C
Bellarmine Univ	KY	42,950	VC
Benedictine Univ	IL	37,820	C
Bennett College for Women	NC	21,970	LC
Bethany College	KS	30,605	NC
Blackburn College	IL	21,350	C
Brenau Univ - Women's College	GA	26,650	LC
Buena Vista Univ	IA	39,188	C
Butler Univ	IN	47,572	VC+
Chatham Univ	PA	43,797	C
College of Charleston	SC	22,145	VC
Concordia College - New York	NY	39,035	LC
Culver-Stockton College	MO	30,900	C
Daemen College	NY	34,770	C
Drury Univ	MO	31,909	VC
Eastern Mich Univ	MI	18,604	C
Elmhurst College	IL	43,336	C
Elon Univ	NC	41,914	VC+
Franklin Pierce Univ	NH	41,598	C
Indiana Univ Bloomington	IN	19,801	VC
LIU Post	NY	47,660	C
Mary Baldwin College	VA	38,245	C
Marywood Univ	PA	45,595	C
Mass College of Liberal Arts	MA	18,613	C
Messiah College	PA	40,690	C+
New York Univ	NY	61,470	MC
Nichols College	MA	37,240	LC
Piedmont College	GA	30,136	C
Point Park Univ	PA	36,390	C
Prescott College	AZ	33,284	C
Randolph-Macon College	VA	49,869	C+
St. Vincent College	PA	40,244	C
Salem College	NC	29,326	VC
Seton Hill Univ	PA	35,172	C
Simmons College	MA	49,966	VC
Spring Hill College	AL	44,164	VC
SUNY Fredonia/The SUNY at Fredonia	NY	19,840	VC
Tiffin Univ	OH	30,273	LC
Univ of Findlay	OH	31,916	C
Univ of Kentucky	KY	19,868	VC
Univ of Mich/Dearborn	MI	9,885	VC
Univ of Montana-Western	MT	9,753	LC
Univ of North Georgia	GA	8,500	C
Univ of San Francisco	CA	54,770	VC
Univ of Tulsa	OK	46,331	MC
Univ of Wisc/Green Bay	WI	19,074	C
Univ of Wisc/Stevens Point	WI	14,043	C
Upper Iowa Univ	IA	30,426	NC
Viterbo Univ	WI	30,070	C
Wagner College	NY	48,600	C+
Wartburg College	IA	41,055	VC
Waynesburg Univ	PA	30,150	C

School	ST	$IS	SR
Westminster College	UT	37,708	C+
Wright State Univ	OH	16,983	C

ASIAN STUDIES

School	ST	$IS	SR
Amherst College	MA	58,744	MC
Bates College	ME	60,720	MC
Boston Univ	MA	60,694	MC
Bowdoin College	ME	59,568	MC
Cal State, Chico	CA	20,158	C
Calvin College	MI	39,120	VC
Cornell Univ	NY	60,964	MC
Indiana Univ Bloomington	IN	19,801	VC
Indiana Univ of Pennsylvania	PA	20,846	LC
Kenyon College	OH	58,890	MC
McDaniel College	MD	47,450	VC
Nazareth College of Rochester	NY	43,028	C+
New York Univ	NY	61,470	MC
Occidental College	CA	60,972	MC
Pace Univ	NY	53,367	C
St. Joseph's Univ	PA	55,006	VC
Seattle Univ	WA	49,035	VC+
The Pennsylvania State Univ - Univ Park	PA	28,022	VC+
Univ of Arkansas at Fayetteville	AR	18,352	C+
Univ of Colo Boulder	CO	22,605	VC+
Univ of Mass Boston	MA	23,066	VC
Vanderbilt Univ	TN	58,220	MC

ASIAN/AMERICAN STUDIES

School	ST	$IS	SR
Arizona State Univ, at the Tempe Campus	AZ	20,137	C+
Binghamton Univ/The SUNY	NY	21,648	HC+
Brigham Young Univ	UT	12,100	HC
Cal State, Fullerton	CA	25,188	C
Cal State, Northridge	CA	28,690	LC
Columbia Univ/City of New York	NY	61,116	MC
Emory Univ	GA	56,368	MC
Indiana Univ Bloomington	IN	19,801	VC
New York Univ	NY	61,470	MC
Ohio Univ	OH	21,080	C
Pitzer College	CA	54,988	MC
Pomona College	CA	57,680	MC
Purdue Univ/West Lafayette	IN	20,024	HC
San Francisco State Univ	CA	18,514	C
Scripps College	CA	61,940	MC
St. Olaf College	MN	51,200	HC+
Stanford Univ	CA	58,388	MC
Stony Brook Univ / SUNY	NY	20,078	HC+
Univ of Calif at Berkeley	CA	23,322	MC
Univ of Calif at Irvine	CA	25,961	VC
Univ of Calif at Los Angeles	CA	25,686	MC
Univ of Calif at Santa Barbara	CA	27,551	HC
Univ of Denver	CO	51,787	VC+
Univ of Northern Colo	CO	18,446	C
Univ of Southern Calif	CA	56,903	MC
Univ of Washington	WA	14,722	VC
Univ of Wisc-Milwaukee	WI	18,436	C

ASIAN/ORIENTAL STUDIES

School	ST	$IS	SR
Arizona State Univ, at the Tempe Campus	AZ	20,137	C+
Augustana College	IL	43,398	VC
Bard College	NY	61,940	HC
Bard College at Simon's Rock	MA	61,749	HC+
Baylor Univ	TX	50,329	HC
Belmont Univ	TN	39,190	VC+
Berea College	KY	7,192	C
Birmingham-Southern College	AL	44,168	VC+
Bowling Green State Univ	OH	18,970	C
Brigham Young Univ	UT	12,100	HC
Cal State, Long Beach	CA	17,502	C+
Calvin College	MI	39,120	VC
Carleton College	MN	60,102	MC
Case Western Reserve Univ	OH	56,534	MC
Central Washington Univ	WA	11,730	C
CUNY/City College	NY	20,319	HC+
Claremont McKenna College	CA	62,215	MC
Clark Univ	MA	47,020	HC+
Coe College	IA	45,550	VC
Colgate Univ	NY	58,135	MC
College of St. Benedict	MN	49,359	VC
College of the Holy Cross	MA	58,042	MC
Colo College	CO	57,162	MC
Dartmouth College	NH	57,996	MC
Duke Univ	NC	50,250	MC
Eastern Mich Univ	MI	18,604	C
Emory Univ	GA	56,368	MC
Florida International Univ	FL	17,747	C+
Florida State Univ	FL	16,715	VC
Furman Univ	SC	54,006	HC
Hamilton College	NY	55,620	MC
Hampshire College	MA	58,320	MC
Harvard College/Harvard Univ	MA	49,000	MC
Hobart and William Smith Colleges	NY	60,034	HC+
John Carroll Univ	OH	46,300	C+
Kean Univ	NJ	23,444	VC

School	ST	$IS	SR
Knox College	IL	44,865	VC+
Lafayette College	PA	59,155	HC+
Lake Forest College	IL	50,652	VC
Lehigh Univ	PA	56,770	MC
Loyola Marymount Univ	CA	54,649	VC+
Macalester College	MN	57,691	MC
Manhattanville College	NY	50,740	VC
Marietta College	OH	42,135	C+
Mary Baldwin College	VA	38,245	C
Mount Holyoke College	MA	55,146	MC
New York Univ	NY	61,470	MC
Northeastern Univ	MA	55,296	MC
Old Dominion Univ	VA	19,483	LC
Pacific Lutheran Univ	WA	46,760	C+
Pitzer College	CA	54,988	MC
Pomona College	CA	57,680	MC
Purdue Univ/West Lafayette	IN	20,024	HC
Randolph-Macon College	VA	49,869	C+
Rice Univ	TX	43,288	MC
Rollins College	FL	52,370	HC
Rutgers, The State Univ of New Jersey/New Brunswick	NJ	25,562	VC
St. John's Univ	MN	47,984	C
San Diego State Univ	CA	21,611	C+
Sarah Lawrence College	NY	48,000	HC
Scripps College	CA	61,940	MC
Seton Hall Univ	NJ	45,902	C
Sewanee: The Univ of the South	TN	47,700	HC+
Skidmore College	NY	59,942	HC
St. John's Univ	NY	55,070	VC
St. Lawrence Univ	NY	59,972	VC
St. Mary's College of Maryland	MD	25,754	VC
SUNY New Paltz	NY	14,348	C
Swarthmore College	PA	57,870	MC
Temple Univ	PA	24,392	VC
Texas State Univ	TX	17,128	C
The Univ of Utah	UT	16,463	VC
Tufts Univ	MA	58,780	MC
Tulane Univ	LA	60,861	MC
Union College	NY	60,240	MC
Univ at Albany / SUNY	NY	18,674	VC
Univ at Buffalo / The SUNY	NY	20,283	VC
Univ of Calif at Berkeley	CA	23,322	MC
Univ of Calif at Los Angeles	CA	25,686	MC
Univ of Calif at Riverside	CA	27,204	C+
Univ of Calif at Santa Barbara	CA	27,551	HC
Univ of Cincinnati	OH	21,506	VC
Univ of Colo Boulder	CO	22,605	VC+
Univ of Florida	FL	15,943	HC+
Univ of Hawaii at Manoa	HI	19,379	C
Univ of Iowa	IA	17,693	VC
Univ of Maryland/Univ College	MD	6,168	SP
Univ of Mich/Ann Arbor	MI	22,102	MC
Univ of Minn/Twin Cities	MN		HC
Univ of New Mexico	NM	15,300	C
Univ of N Car at Chapel Hill	NC	18,928	MC
Univ of Oregon	OR	21,360	C+
Univ of Pennsylvania	PA	61,132	MC
Univ of Puget Sound	WA	54,608	HC
Univ of Redlands	CA	40,500	VC
Univ of Texas at Austin	TX	44,074	HC
Univ of Vermont	VT	27,006	VC+
Univ of Washington	WA	14,722	VC
Univ of Wisc/Madison	WI	18,757	HC+
Vassar College	NY	61,140	MC
Washington State Univ	WA	20,461	C
Washington Univ in St. Louis	MO	69,844	MC
Wayne State Univ	MI	22,063	C
Wellesley College	MA	59,038	MC
Wheaton College	MA	54,934	VC+
Whitman College	WA	55,988	MC
Willamette Univ	OR	56,450	VC+
Williams College	MA	61,070	MC

ASTRONOMY

School	ST	$IS	SR
Amherst College	MA	58,744	MC
Barnard College/Columbia Univ	NY	39,000	MC
Benedictine College	KS	29,180	VC
Bennington College	VT	56,990	HC+
Boston Univ	MA	60,694	MC
Brigham Young Univ	UT	12,100	HC
Bryn Mawr College	PA	59,890	MC
Case Western Reserve Univ	OH	56,534	MC
Colgate Univ	NY	58,135	MC
College of Charleston	SC	22,145	VC
Columbia Univ/City of New York	NY	61,116	MC
Columbia Univ/School of General Studies	NY	58,231	MC
Cornell Univ	NY	60,964	MC
Eastern Mich Univ	MI	18,604	C
Embry-Riddle Aeronautical Univ - Prescott Campus	AZ	40,444	VC+
Florida Inst of Technology	FL	48,290	VC
Franklin and Marshall College	PA	60,799	MC
George Mason Univ	VA	15,724	VC
Harvard College/Harvard Univ	MA	49,000	MC
Haverford College	PA	61,564	MC

School	ST	$IS	SR
Indiana Univ Bloomington	IN	19,801	VC
Lehigh Univ	PA	56,770	MC
Lycoming College	PA	45,379	C
Montclair State Univ	NJ	22,614	C
Mount Holyoke College	MA	55,146	MC
New Mexico State Univ	NM	14,050	C
Northern Arizona Univ	AZ	19,010	C
Northwestern Univ	IL	61,640	MC
Oberlin College	OH	61,788	MC
San Diego State Univ	CA	21,611	C+
San Francisco State Univ	CA	18,514	C
Smith College	MA	59,674	MC
Stony Brook Univ / SUNY	NY	20,078	HC+
Swarthmore College	PA	57,870	MC
Ohio State Univ-Columbus Campus	OH	19,887	HC+
The Pennsylvania State Univ - Univ Park	PA	28,022	VC+
The Univ of Okla	OK	18,621	VC
Union College	NY	60,240	MC
Univ of Arizona	AZ	20,657	C
Univ of Colo Boulder	CO	22,605	VC+
Univ of Delaware	DE	23,612	VC
Univ of Florida	FL	15,943	HC
Univ of Hawaii at Hilo	HI	23,066	C
Univ of Illinois at Urbana-Champaign	IL	26,450	HC
Univ of Iowa	IA	17,693	VC
Univ of Kansas	KS	17,603	C+
Univ of Maryland - College Park	MD	20,060	HC
Univ of Mass Amherst	MA	24,215	VC+
Univ of Mich/Ann Arbor	MI	22,102	MC
Univ of Mount Union	OH	35,130	C
Univ of Nebr - Lincoln	NE	18,031	VC
Univ of Pittsburgh at Pittsburgh	PA	28,572	HC+
Univ of Rochester	NY	60,668	MC
Univ of Southern Calif	CA	56,903	MC
Univ of Texas at Austin	TX	44,074	HC
Univ of Virginia	VA	23,050	VC
Univ of Washington	WA	14,722	VC
Univ of Wisc/Madison	WI	18,757	HC+
Valparaiso Univ	IN	44,940	VC+
Vassar College	NY	61,140	MC
Villanova Univ	PA	58,394	MC
Wayne State Univ	MI	22,063	C
Wellesley College	MA	59,038	MC
Wesleyan Univ	CT	61,198	MC
Whitman College	WA	55,988	MC
Williams College	MA	61,070	MC
Wilmington College	OH	29,784	VC
Yale Univ	CT	55,300	MC

ASTRONOMY AND PHYSICS

School	ST	$IS	SR
Boston Univ	MA	60,694	MC
Oberlin College	OH	61,788	MC
Texas Christian Univ	TX	49,980	HC
Univ of Georgia	GA	20,082	VC
Univ of Mass Dartmouth	MA	22,223	C
Univ of Wyoming	WY	14,401	C+
Youngstown State Univ	OH	16,732	C

ASTROPHYSICS

School	ST	$IS	SR
Agnes Scott College	GA	45,323	C
Boston Univ	MA	60,694	MC
Calif Inst of Technology	CA	54,045	MC
Cal State, Northridge	CA	28,690	LC
Colgate Univ	NY	58,135	MC
College of Charleston	SC	22,145	VC
Columbia Univ/City of New York	NY	61,116	MC
Dartmouth College	NH	57,996	MC
Florida Inst of Technology	FL	48,290	VC
Franklin and Marshall College	PA	60,799	MC
Haverford College	PA	61,564	MC
Indiana Univ Bloomington	IN	19,801	VC
Lehigh Univ	PA	56,770	MC
Lycoming College	PA	45,379	C
Mich State Univ	MI	22,450	VC+
Ohio Univ	OH	21,080	C
Princeton Univ	NJ	53,795	MC
Rutgers, The State Univ of New Jersey/New Brunswick	NJ	25,562	VC
San Francisco State Univ	CA	18,514	C
Swarthmore College	PA	57,870	MC
Ohio State Univ-Columbus Campus	OH	19,887	HC+
The Univ of Okla	OK	18,621	VC
Tufts Univ	MA	58,780	MC
Univ of Calif at Berkeley	CA	23,322	HC
Univ of Calif at Los Angeles	CA	25,686	MC
Univ of Cincinnati	OH	21,506	VC
Univ of Mich/Ann Arbor	MI	22,102	MC
Univ of Minn/Twin Cities	MN		HC
Univ of New Mexico	NM	15,300	C
Villanova Univ	PA	58,394	MC
Wellesley College	MA	59,038	MC
Williams College	MA	61,070	MC

ATHLETIC TRAINING

School	ST	$IS	SR
Adams State Univ	CO	13,358	LC
Albion College	MI	46,010	C
Alderson Broaddus Univ	WV	28,656	C
Alfred Univ	NY	41,770	C
Alma College	MI	44,075	C
Alvernia Univ	PA	39,250	LC
Angelo State Univ	TX	15,049	NC
Appalachian State Univ	NC	12,919	VC
Aquinas College	MI	33,060	C
Arkansas State Univ	AR	15,470	C
Ashland Univ	OH	25,000	C
Augustana College	SD	36,500	VC
Aurora Univ	IL	33,228	C
Averett Univ	VA	37,750	C
Baldwin Wallace Univ	OH	38,318	C
Barton College	NC	27,660	LC
Baylor Univ	TX	50,329	NC
Belhaven Univ	MS	27,170	C
Benedictine College	KS	29,180	VC
Bethany College	KS	30,605	NC
Bethel College	KS	32,160	C
Bethel Univ	MN	34,940	VC
Boston Univ	MA	60,694	MC
Bowling Green State Univ	OH	18,970	C
Bridgewater College	VA	41,450	C
Bridgewater State Univ	MA	18,752	C
Cal State, Fullerton	CA	25,188	C
Calif Univ of Pennsylvania	PA	14,217	C
Campbell Univ	NC	37,570	VC
Campbellsville Univ	KY	27,720	C
Canisius College	NY	44,900	C
Capital Univ	OH	41,050	VC
Carroll Univ	WI	38,100	C
Castleton State College	VT	20,186	C
Catawba College	NC	37,240	LC
Cedarville Univ	OH	32,860	VC
Central College	IA	42,104	C+
Central Conn State Univ	CT	19,749	C
Central Methodist Univ	MO	28,240	VC
Chapman Univ	CA	58,347	VC+
Clarion Univ of Pennsylvania	PA	17,370	LC
Clarke Univ	IA	37,600	C
Coe College	IA	45,550	VC
Colby-Sawyer College	NH	50,790	C
College of Charleston	SC	22,145	VC
College of Mount St. Joseph	OH	33,880	C
Concordia Univ Wisc	WI	28,980	C
Culver-Stockton College	MO	30,900	C
Dakota Wesleyan Univ	SD	23,000	C
Defiance College	OH	30,645	C
Delta State Univ	MS	12,292	LC
Dominican College	NY	31,270	LC
Dordt College	IA	34,160	C+
Duquesne Univ	PA	43,720	VC
East Carolina Univ	NC	14,169	C
East Central Univ	OK	10,223	LC
East Texas Baptist Univ	TX	31,577	LC
Eastern Illinois Univ	IL	20,466	C
Eastern Mich Univ	MI	18,604	C
Eastern Nazarene College	MA	30,000	C
Eastern Univ	PA	37,704	C
Emporia State Univ	KS	12,897	C
Endicott College	MA	43,228	VC+
Erskine College	SC	37,360	C
Eureka College	IL	19,280	C
Florida Gulf Coast Univ	FL		C
Florida Southern College	FL	40,150	C+
Florida State Univ	FL	16,715	VC
Fort Lewis College	CO	15,513	C
Franklin College	IN	36,585	C
Gardner-Webb Univ	NC	34,375	C
George Fox Univ	OR	40,750	C+
George Mason Univ	VA	15,724	VC
Georgetown College	KY	41,440	C+
Georgia College and State Univ	GA	18,900	C+
Georgia Southern Univ	GA	16,942	C
Graceland Univ	IA	28,020	C
Grand Canyon Univ	AZ	24,540	VC
Grand Valley State Univ	MI	17,998	C+
Greensboro College	NC	28,740	LC
Hamline Univ	MN	45,678	VC
Harding Univ	AR	23,556	C
Hardin-Simmons Univ	TX	23,560	C+
Heidelberg Univ	OH	34,100	C
Henderson State Univ	AR	14,584	C
High Point Univ	NC	39,800	C
Hofstra Univ	NY	51,810	VC+
Hope College	MI	38,650	VC
Howard Payne Univ	TX	17,115	C
Indiana Univ Bloomington	IN	19,801	VC
Indiana Univ of Pennsylvania	PA	20,846	LC
Indiana Wesleyan Univ	IN	31,815	VC
Ithaca College	NY	53,864	HC
James Madison Univ	VA	18,049	VC
Johnson State College	VT	16,721	C
Kansas State Univ	KS	15,497	VC
Kean Univ	NJ	23,444	C
Keene State College	NH	23,232	LC
Kent State Univ	OH	19,920	C
King Univ	TN	33,140	C
Lake Superior State Univ	MI	18,121	C
Lasell College	MA	43,750	LC
Lee Univ	TN	18,690	C+
Lees-McRae College	NC	33,944	C
Lenoir-Rhyne College	NC	35,984	C
Lewis Univ	IL	23,050	C
Liberty Univ	VA	19,101	C
Limestone College	SC	30,800	C
Lincoln Memorial Univ	TN	18,144	C
Lindenwood Univ	MO	20,750	C
Linfield College-McMinnville Campus	OR	47,676	C
LIU Brooklyn	NY	47,182	LC
Longwood Univ	VA	20,924	C
Loras College	IA	37,432	VC
Louisiana College	LA	15,746	C
Louisiana State Univ	LA	18,677	C+
Loyola Marymount Univ	CA	54,649	VC+
Lubbock Christian Univ	TX	26,308	C
Luther College	IA	45,720	C+
Lynchburg College	VA	42,645	C
Marietta College	OH	42,135	C
Marist College	NY	35,500	C
Marquette Univ	WI	46,930	VC+
Mars Hill Univ	NC	22,950	LC
Marshall Univ	WV	14,820	C
Marywood Univ	PA	45,595	C
Mass College of Liberal Arts	MA	18,613	C
McKendree Univ	IL	29,920	C+
McMurry Univ	TX	25,962	C
McNeese State Univ	LA	2,649	C
Mercyhurst Univ	PA	40,700	C
Messiah College	PA	40,690	C+
Methodist Univ	NC	37,185	C
Miami Univ	OH	24,191	VC
MidAmerica Nazarene Univ	KS	28,000	C
Middle Tenn State Univ	TN	8,650	C
Millikin Univ	IL	38,940	C
Minn State Univ, Moorhead	MN	13,392	VC
Missouri State Univ	MO	13,996	C+
Montclair State Univ	NJ	22,614	C
Mount Marty College	SD	29,638	C
Murray State Univ	KY	15,304	C
Nebr Wesleyan Univ	NE	29,774	C+
Neumann Univ	PA	31,078	LC
New Mexico State Univ	NM	14,050	C
North Central College	IL	38,343	VC
N Dak State Univ	ND		C
North Park Univ	IL	30,130	C
Northern Kentucky Univ	KY	21,134	C
Northwestern College of Iowa	IA	36,240	VC
Ohio Northern Univ	OH	42,075	VC
Ohio Univ	OH	21,080	C
Okla State Univ	OK	14,310	VC
Olivet College	MI	19,984	C
Olivet Nazarene Univ	IL	29,990	C
Otterbein College	OH	32,214	C
Palm Beach Atlantic Univ	FL	34,874	C+
Park Univ	MO	17,525	C
Piedmont College	GA	30,136	C
Plymouth State Univ	NH	23,148	LC
Point Loma Nazarene Univ	CA	41,006	C+
Purdue Univ/West Lafayette	IN	20,024	HC
Quinnipiac Univ	CT	55,160	VC
Radford Univ	VA	17,766	LC
Roanoke College	VA	49,976	C
Rocky Mountain College	MT	32,242	C
Rowan Univ	NJ	24,022	VC+
Sacred Heart Univ	CT	49,264	VC
Saginaw Valley State Univ	MI	17,369	C
St. Joseph's College	IN	36,500	C
Salem International Univ	WV	21,090	LC
Salisbury Univ	MD	19,180	VC
Samford Univ	AL	37,060	C
San Diego State Univ	CA	21,611	C+
Shaw Univ	NC	15,488	C
Shawnee State Univ	OH	16,916	C
Simpson College	IA	36,086	C+
S Dak State Univ	SD	14,296	C
Southeast Missouri State Univ	MO	15,370	C
Southeastern Louisiana Univ	LA	13,325	C
Southern Illinois Univ Carbondale	IL	21,942	C
Southern Nazarene Univ	OK	24,354	C
Southwest Baptist Univ	MO	24,710	C
Southwestern College	KS	29,270	C
Southwestern Okla State Univ	OK	9,160	C
St. Edward's Univ	TX	47,784	C
Sterling College	KS	27,216	C
Stony Brook Univ / SUNY	NY	20,078	HC+
SUNY Cortland/The SUNY	NY	19,759	C+
Tabor College	KS	29,010	C
Temple Univ	PA	24,392	VC
Texas Christian Univ	TX	49,980	HC
Texas Lutheran Univ	TX	36,040	C
Texas State Univ	TX	17,128	C
Texas Wesleyan Univ	TX	31,382	C
Ohio State Univ-Columbus Campus	OH	19,887	HC+
The Pennsylvania State Univ - Univ Park	PA	28,022	VC+
The Univ of N Car at Pembroke	NC	13,388	LC
The Univ of Utah	UT	16,463	VC
Towson Univ	MD	16,000	VC
Trinity International Univ	IL	31,070	VC
Troy Univ	AL	10,650	C
Truman State Univ	MO	15,541	HC
Tusculum College	TN	24,295	C
Union College	KY	29,955	C
Univ of Akron	OH	20,436	C
Univ of Alabama at Tuscaloosa	AL	17,164	C+
Univ of Central Arkansas	AR	13,667	VC
Univ of Central Florida	FL	15,668	VC+
Univ of Central Okla	OK	12,293	C
Univ of Charleston	WV	32,300	C
Univ of Cincinnati	OH	21,506	VC
Univ of Conn	CT	24,706	HC
Univ of Delaware	DE	23,612	VC
Univ of Evansville	IN	42,656	VC+
Univ of Georgia	GA	20,082	VC
Univ of Idaho	ID	14,558	C
Univ of Illinois at Urbana-Champaign	IL	26,450	HC
Univ of Indianapolis	IN	31,740	LC
Univ of Iowa	IA	17,693	VC
Univ of Kansas	KS	17,603	C+
Univ of La Verne	CA	47,010	C
Univ of Maine	ME	19,902	C+
Univ of Maine at Presque Isle	ME	15,011	LC
Univ of Mary	ND	16,714	C
Univ of Miami	FL	57,034	MC
Univ of Mich/Ann Arbor	MI	22,102	MC
Univ of Minn/Duluth	MN	19,806	C
Univ of Mobile	AL	28,935	VC
Univ of Montana	MT	14,105	C
Univ of Montana-Western	MT	9,753	LC
Univ of Mount Union	OH	35,130	C
Univ of Nebr - Lincoln	NE	18,031	VC
Univ of New England	ME	46,750	C
Univ of New Hampshire	NH	26,912	C
Univ of New Mexico	NM	15,300	C
Univ of N Car at Charlotte	NC	15,547	C
Univ of N Car at Wilmington	NC	13,572	VC
Univ of N Dak	ND	14,551	C
Univ of North Florida	FL	15,870	VC
Univ of Northern Colo	CO	18,446	C
Univ of Northern Iowa	IA	15,795	C
Univ of Pittsburgh at Bradford	PA	21,802	C
Univ of Pittsburgh at Pittsburgh	PA	28,572	HC+
Univ of San Francisco	CA	54,770	VC
Univ of Tampa	FL	35,160	VC
Univ of the Incarnate Word	TX	37,316	C
Univ of Tulsa	OK	46,331	MC
Univ of Vermont	VT	27,006	VC+
Univ of West Alabama	AL	14,274	C
Univ of Wisc/Eau Claire	WI	15,730	VC
Univ of Wisc/La Crosse	WI	9,304	VC
Univ of Wisc/Madison	WI	18,757	HC+
Univ of Wisc/Stevens Point	WI	14,043	C
Univ of Wisc-Milwaukee	WI	18,436	C
Upper Iowa Univ	IA	30,426	NC
Vanguard Univ of Southern Calif	CA	35,833	VC
Virginia State Univ	VA	11,318	C+
Washburn Univ	KS	12,579	C
Washington State Univ	WA	20,461	C
Waynesburg Univ	PA	30,150	C
West Chester Univ of Pennsylvania	PA	17,186	C
West Texas A&M Univ	TX	13,478	C
West Virginia Univ	WV	16,542	C+
Western Mich Univ	MI	19,628	C
Westfield State Univ	MA	18,297	C
Wheeling Jesuit Univ	WV	33,500	C
Whitworth Univ	WA	47,734	VC
William Woods Univ	MO	24,260	C
Wilmington College	OH	29,784	C
Wingate Univ	NC	34,990	C
Winona State Univ	MN	16,640	C
Winthrop Univ	SC	21,120	C
Wright State Univ	OH	16,983	C
Xavier Univ	OH	44,980	VC

ATMOSPHERIC SCIENCE

School	ST	$IS	SR
Cornell Univ	NY	60,964	MC

ATMOSPHERIC SCIENCES AND METEOROLOGY

School	ST	$IS	SR
CUNY/City College	NY	20,319	HC+
East Carolina Univ	NC	14,169	C
Embry-Riddle Aeronautical Univ - Daytona Beach	FL	40,884	C+
Embry-Riddle Aeronautical Univ - Prescott Campus	AZ	40,444	VC+
Florida Inst of Technology	FL	48,290	VC
Florida State Univ	FL	16,715	VC
Howard Univ	DC	13,646	C
Iowa State Univ	IA	16,403	C
Jackson State Univ	MS	13,512	LC
Lewis Univ	IL	23,050	C
Lyndon State College	VT	14,233	C
Maritime College/SUNY	NY	16,020	C
Metropolitan State Univ of Denver	CO	4,835	LC
Millersville Univ of Pennsylvania	PA	21,648	C
N Car State Univ	NC	16,202	HC
Northern Illinois Univ	IL	19,768	C
Northland College	WI	26,680	C
Ohio Univ	OH	21,080	C
Oswego / SUNY	NY	20,009	VC

ST = STATE   **$IS** = IN-STATE COSTS   **SR** = SELECTOR RATING

School	ST	$IS	SR
Plymouth State Univ	NH	23,148	LC
Purdue Univ/West Lafayette	IN	20,024	HC
Rutgers, The State Univ of New Jersey/New Brunswick	NJ	25,562	VC
St. Louis Univ	MO	48,346	HC
San Francisco State Univ	CA	18,514	C
St. Cloud State Univ	MN	10,600	C
Stony Brook Univ / SUNY	NY	20,078	HC+
SUNY Oneonta / SUNY	NY	16,919	C+
Texas A&M Univ	TX	19,207	VC
Ohio State Univ-Columbus Campus	OH	19,887	HC+
The Pennsylvania State Univ - Univ Park	PA	28,022	VC+
The SUNY/College at Brockport	NY	19,002	C
The Univ of Okla	OK	18,621	VC
The Univ of Utah	UT	16,463	VC
United States Air Force Academy	CO		MC
Univ at Albany / SUNY	NY	18,674	VC
Univ of Arizona	AZ	20,657	C
Univ of Calif at Davis	CA		HC
Univ of Calif at Los Angeles	CA	25,686	MC
Univ of Hawaii at Manoa	HI	19,379	C
Univ of Kansas	KS	17,603	C+
Univ of Louisiana at Monroe	LA	12,998	C
Univ of Louisville	KY	17,946	C
Univ of Maryland - College Park	MD	20,060	HC
Univ of Miami	FL	57,034	MC
Univ of Mich/Ann Arbor	MI	22,102	MC
Univ of Missouri/Columbia	MO	18,201	HC
Univ of Nebr - Lincoln	NE	18,031	VC
Univ of N Car at Asheville	NC	13,500	VC
Univ of N Car at Charlotte	NC	15,547	C
Univ of N Dak	ND	14,551	C
Univ of South Alabama	AL	13,510	C
Univ of Washington	WA	14,722	VC
Univ of Wisc/Madison	WI	18,757	HC+
Univ of Wisc-Milwaukee	WI	18,436	C
Valparaiso Univ	IN	44,940	VC+
Western Conn State Univ	CT	18,327	LC

AUDIO TECHNOLOGY

School	ST	$IS	SR
American Univ	DC	56,015	HC+
Belmont Univ	TN	39,190	VC+
Brigham Young Univ	UT	12,100	HC
Cogswell Polytechnical College	CA	30,531	C
Columbia College Chicago	IL	30,940	LC
Cornerstone Univ and Grand Rapids Theological Seminary	MI	33,338	C
Five Towns College	NY	34,550	C
Hofstra Univ	NY	51,810	VC+
Ithaca College	NY	53,864	HC
Lawrence Tech Univ	MI	37,630	VC
Lebanon Valley College	PA	38,570	C
Mich Tech Univ	MI	23,556	HC
Ohio Univ	OH	21,080	C
Purdue Univ/West Lafayette	IN	20,024	HC
Savannah College of Art and Design	GA	48,005	SP
School of the Art Inst of Chicago	IL	56,230	SP
SUNY Fredonia/The SUNY at Fredonia	NY	19,840	VC
Texas State Univ	TX	17,128	C
Univ of Hartford	CT	42,674	C
Univ of Mich/Ann Arbor	MI	22,102	MC
Univ of New Haven	CT	48,940	C
Univ of Rochester	NY	60,668	MC
Webster Univ	MO	35,100	C+

AUTOMOTIVE TECHNOLOGY

School	ST	$IS	SR
Benjamin Franklin Inst of Technology	MA	27,190	SP
Colo State Univ-Pueblo	CO	16,183	C
Farmingdale State College	NY	19,673	C
Ferris State Univ	MI	20,047	C
Idaho State Univ	ID	12,307	C
Minn State Univ, Mankato	MN	15,616	C
Montana State Univ-Northern	MT	12,500	NC
Pennsylvania College of Technology	PA	26,286	NC
Pittsburg State Univ	KS	12,032	C
Southern Illinois Univ Carbondale	IL	21,942	C
Thomas Edison State College	NJ	5,700	SP
Univ of Akron	OH	20,436	C
Univ of Central Missouri	MO	14,605	C
Walla Walla Univ	WA	26,256	NC

AVIAN SCIENCES

School	ST	$IS	SR
Bowling Green State Univ	OH	18,970	C
Eastern New Mexico Univ	NM	10,682	C
Southern Illinois Univ Carbondale	IL	21,942	C
Ohio State Univ-Columbus Campus	OH	19,887	HC+
Univ of Calif at Davis	CA		HC

AVIATION ADMINISTRATION/MANAGEMENT

School	ST	$IS	SR
Andrews Univ	MI	28,030	C+
Auburn Univ	AL	22,378	VC+
Averett Univ	VA	37,750	LC
Baker College of Flint	MI	7,800	NC
Calif Baptist Univ	CA	38,792	C
Central Washington Univ	WA	11,730	C
Daniel Webster College	NH	25,380	C
Delta State Univ	MS	12,292	LC
Dowling College	NY	25,000	LC
Eastern Mich Univ	MI	18,604	C
Farmingdale State College	NY	19,673	C
Florida Inst of Technology	FL	48,290	VC
Florida Memorial Univ	FL	20,888	LC
Geneva College	PA	27,280	C
Henderson State Univ	AR	14,584	C
Inter-American Univ of PR/ Bayamon Univ College	PR	4,428	
Jacksonville Univ	FL	37,780	C
Lewis Univ	IL	23,050	C
Louisiana Tech Univ	LA	11,302	C
Lynn Univ	FL	43,500	LC
Marywood Univ	PA	45,595	C
Metropolitan State Univ of Denver	CO	4,835	LC
Minn State Univ, Mankato	MN	15,616	C
Ohio Univ	OH	21,080	C
Park Univ	MO	17,525	C
Purdue Univ/West Lafayette	IN	20,024	HC
Quincy Univ	IL	34,980	LC
Rocky Mountain College	MT	32,242	C
St. Louis Univ	MO	48,346	HC
Salem International Univ	WV	21,090	LC
San Diego Christian College	CA	31,012	C
S Dak State Univ	SD	14,296	C
Southeastern Okla State Univ	OK	7,966	LC
Southern Illinois Univ Carbondale	IL	21,942	C
Southern Nazarene Univ	OK	24,354	C
St. Cloud State Univ	MN	10,600	C
Texas Southern Univ	TX	18,212	LC
The Univ of Okla	OK	18,621	VC
Univ of Alaska Anchorage	AK	16,673	NC
Univ of Dubuque	IA	30,200	C
Univ of Illinois at Urbana-Champaign	IL	26,450	HC
Univ of Louisiana at Monroe	LA	12,998	C
Univ of Nebr at Kearney	NE	14,855	LC
Univ of Nebr at Omaha	NE	12,700	C
Univ of North Texas	TX	15,628	C
Univ of the District of Columbia	DC	7,244	C
Vaughn College of Aeronautics and Technology	NY	31,360	C
Western Mich Univ	MI	19,628	C
Westminster College	UT	37,708	C+
Wilmington Univ	DE	8,112	NC

AVIATION BUSINESS ADMINISTRATION

School	ST	$IS	SR
Embry-Riddle Aeronautical Univ - Prescott Campus	AZ	40,444	VC+

AVIATION COMPUTER TECHNOLOGY

School	ST	$IS	SR
Andrews Univ	MI	28,030	C+
Florida Inst of Technology	FL	48,290	VC
Florida Memorial Univ	FL	20,888	LC
Inter-American Univ of PR/ Bayamon Univ College	PR	4,428	
Metropolitan State Univ of Denver	CO	4,835	LC
Purdue Univ/West Lafayette	IN	20,024	HC
Southern Illinois Univ Carbondale	IL	21,942	C
Univ of Central Missouri	MO	14,605	C
Walla Walla Univ	WA	26,256	NC
Westminster College	UT	37,708	C+

AVIATION FLIGHT TECHNOLOGY

School	ST	$IS	SR
Calif Baptist Univ	CA	38,792	C
Thomas Edison State College	NJ	5,700	SP

AVIATION MAINTENANCE MANAGEMENT

School	ST	$IS	SR
Central Washington Univ	WA	11,730	C
Embry-Riddle Aeronautical Univ - Daytona Beach	FL	40,884	C+
S Dak State Univ	SD	14,296	C
Univ of N Dak	ND	14,551	C

AVIATION MAINTENANCE TECHNOLOGY

School	ST	$IS	SR
Thomas Edison State College	NJ	5,700	SP
Univ of Alaska Anchorage	AK	16,673	NC

BACTERIOLOGY

School	ST	$IS	SR
Univ of Calif at Davis	CA		HC
Wilmington College	OH	29,784	C

BAKERY SCIENCE

School	ST	$IS	SR
Kansas State Univ	KS	15,497	VC

BALLET

School	ST	$IS	SR
Belhaven Univ	MS	27,170	C
Friends Univ	KS	29,100	C
Indiana Univ Bloomington	IN	19,801	VC
Texas Christian Univ	TX	49,980	HC
The Univ of Utah	UT	16,463	C
Univ of N Car School of the Arts	NC	7,401	SP
Webster Univ	MO	35,100	C+

BALLET MODERN DANCE

School	ST	$IS	SR
Texas Christian Univ	TX	49,980	HC

BANKING AND FINANCE

School	ST	$IS	SR
Adams State Univ	CO	13,358	LC
Adelphi Univ	NY	44,670	VC
Alabama A&M Univ	AL	10,084	C
Alabama State Univ	AL	14,142	NC
Alfred State/SUNY College of Technology	NY	18,034	C
Anderson Univ	IN	36,100	C
Andrews Univ	MI	28,030	C+
Angelo State Univ	TX	15,049	NC
Appalachian State Univ	NC	12,919	VC
Arcadia Univ	PA	33,570	C+
Arizona State Univ, at the Tempe Campus	AZ	20,137	C+
Arkansas State Univ	AR	15,470	C
Ashland Univ	OH	25,000	C
Auburn Univ	AL	22,378	VC+
Auburn Univ at Montgomery	AL	14,470	LC
Avila Univ	MO	26,900	C
Ball State Univ	IN	17,850	C
Baylor Univ	TX	50,329	HC
Bellarmine Univ	KY	42,950	VC
Benedictine Univ	IL	37,820	C
Bethel Univ	MN	34,940	VC
Boston College	MA	60,622	MC
Bradley Univ	IL	31,874	VC
Brescia Univ	KY	26,140	VC+
Bryant Univ	RI	49,179	VC
Buena Vista Univ	IA	39,188	C
Butler Univ	IN	47,572	VC+
Cal State, Long Beach	CA	17,502	C+
Cal State, Northridge	CA	28,690	LC
Cal State, Sacramento	CA	16,200	C
Cal State, San Bernardino	CA	12,000	C
Campbell Univ	NC	37,570	VC
Canisius College	NY	44,900	C
Caribbean Univ	PR	10,375	
Central State Univ	OH	9,010	C
Central Washington Univ	WA	11,730	C
Chicago State Univ	IL	5,482	C
Clarion Univ of Pennsylvania	PA	17,370	LC
Clemson Univ	SC	19,136	NC
Coastal Carolina Univ	SC	18,580	C
College of William & Mary	VA	28,000	MC
Colo State Univ-Fort Collins	CO	20,385	VC
Columbia College	MO	24,578	C
Columbus State Univ	GA	13,176	C
Concord Univ	WV	13,102	C
Concordia Univ St. Paul	MN	28,250	C
Concordia Univ Wisc	WI	28,980	C
Creighton Univ	NE	45,356	VC
Dallas Baptist Univ	TX	30,580	VC
Davenport Univ	MI	21,002	LC
Defiance College	OH	30,645	C
DePaul Univ	IL	47,623	VC
Dominican College	NY	31,270	LC
Dordt College	IA	34,160	C+
Dowling College	NY	25,000	LC
Drake Univ	IA	41,516	VC+
Drury Univ	MO	31,909	VC
Duquesne Univ	PA	43,720	VC
East Carolina Univ	NC	14,169	C
East Central Univ	OK	10,223	LC
Eastern Kentucky Univ	KY	11,161	C
Eastern Mich Univ	MI	18,604	C
Eastern Washington Univ	WA		C
Emory Univ	GA	56,368	MC
Excelsior College	NY	5,580	SP
Fairleigh Dickinson Univ/ College at Florham	NJ	42,142	C
Fairmont State Univ	WV	12,098	LC
Fayetteville State Univ	NC	10,816	C
Ferris State Univ	MI	20,047	C
Florida A&M Univ	FL	14,935	LC
Florida Atlantic Univ	FL	17,339	C
Florida Gulf Coast Univ	FL		C
Florida International Univ	FL	17,747	C+
Florida State Univ	FL	16,715	VC
Fort Hays State Univ	KS	11,354	C
Francis Marion Univ	SC	16,464	LC
Franklin Pierce Univ	NH	41,598	C
Franklin Univ	OH	20,985	SP
Freed-Hardeman Univ	TN	19,697	C
Friends Univ	KS	29,100	C
Gannon Univ	PA	39,608	C
George Mason Univ	VA	15,724	VC
George Washington Univ	DC	57,108	MC
Georgetown College	KY	41,440	C+
Georgetown Univ	DC	52,910	MC
Georgia Regents Univ	GA		C
Georgia State Univ	GA	15,582	VC
Golden Gate Univ	CA	17,000	C
Goldey-Beacom College	DE	27,493	C
Gordon College	MA	44,320	C
Grand Valley State Univ	MI	17,998	C+
Gwynedd-Mercy College	PA	33,560	C
Hampton Univ	VA	28,528	C
Harding Univ	AR	23,556	C
Hardin-Simmons Univ	TX	23,560	C+
Hawaii Pacific Univ	HI	34,360	C
Hofstra Univ	NY	51,810	VC+
Houston Baptist Univ	TX	36,450	C
Howard Univ	DC	13,646	C
Husson Univ	ME	24,194	LC
Idaho State Univ	ID	12,307	C
Immaculata Univ	PA	43,000	C
Indiana State Univ	IN	16,000	C
Indiana Univ-Purdue Univ Fort Wayne	IN	15,521	C
Indiana Wesleyan Univ	IN	31,815	VC
Inter-American Univ of PR/ Bayamon Univ College	PR	4,428	
Inter-American Univ of PR/ Fajardo Campus	PR	4,200	
Inter-American Univ of PR/ Metropolitan Campus	PR	4,320	
Inter-American Univ of PR/ Ponce	PR		
Inter-American Univ of PR/ San Germán	PR	6,720	
Iowa State Univ	IA	16,403	C
Jacksonville State Univ	AL	12,480	LC
Jacksonville Univ	FL	37,780	C
James Madison Univ	VA	18,049	VC
John Carroll Univ	OH	46,300	C+
Johnson & Wales Univ/ Denver Campus	CO	29,576	C
Juniata College	PA	49,340	VC
Kansas State Univ	KS	15,497	VC
Kent State Univ	OH	19,920	C
King's College	PA	43,502	C
Kutztown Univ of Pennsylvania	PA	16,909	LC
La Roche College	PA	35,824	LC
La Salle Univ	PA	50,270	C
La Sierra Univ	CA	35,694	VC
Lake Superior State Univ	MI	18,121	C
Lasell College	MA	43,750	LC
Le Moyne College	NY	43,470	C
Lewis Univ	IL	23,050	C
Lindenwood Univ	MO	20,750	C
Linfield College-McMinnville Campus	OR	47,676	C
Loras College	IA	37,432	VC
Louisiana State Univ	LA	18,677	C+
Louisiana State Univ in Shreveport	LA	5,606	C
Louisiana Tech Univ	LA	11,302	C
Loyola Univ New Orleans	LA	46,581	VC
Lubbock Christian Univ	TX	26,308	C
Manchester Univ	IN	35,070	C
Manhattan College	NY	49,588	C+
Manhattanville College	NY	50,740	VC
Marian Univ	IN	38,540	C
Marietta College	OH	42,135	C+
Marshall Univ	WV	14,820	C
Marywood Univ	PA	45,595	C
McKendree Univ	IL	29,920	C+
McMurry Univ	TX	25,962	LC
Mercy College	NY	30,456	C
Mercyhurst Univ	PA	40,700	C
Metropolitan State Univ	MN	5,923	
Metropolitan State Univ of Denver	CO	4,835	LC
Miami Univ	OH	24,191	VC
Mich State Univ	MI	22,450	VC
Middle Tenn State Univ	TN	8,650	C
Midwestern State Univ	TX	9,722	C
Minn State Univ, Mankato	MN	15,616	C
Minn State Univ, Moorhead	MN	13,392	VC
Minot State Univ	ND	10,915	C
Miss State Univ	MS	14,750	C
Monmouth Univ	NJ	44,108	C
Montclair State Univ	NJ	22,614	C
Morehead State Univ	KY	10,900	C
Muhlenberg College	PA	52,837	HC
National Univ	CA	14,730	SP
New Mexico Highlands Univ	NM	11,904	NC
New York Univ	NY	61,470	MC
Nicholls State Univ	LA	7,095	C
Norfolk State Univ	VA	10,531	LC
North Park Univ	IL	30,130	C
Northeastern Illinois Univ	IL	10,318	LC
Northeastern State Univ	OK	8,615	VC
Northern Illinois Univ	IL	19,768	C

ST = STATE $IS = IN-STATE COSTS   SR = SELECTOR RATING

School	ST	$IS	SR
Northern Mich Univ	MI	18,278	C
Northern State Univ - Aberdeen	SD	14,505	C
Northwest Missouri State Univ	MO	17,347	C
Northwestern College	MN	24,000	C
Northwood Univ	MI	26,331	C
Notre Dame of Maryland Univ	MD	27,700	VC
Oakland Univ	MI	19,391	C
Ohio Dominican Univ	OH	38,380	C+
Ohio Univ	OH	21,080	C
Okla Baptist Univ	OK	28,202	C
Okla Christian Univ	OK	25,870	VC
Okla City Univ	OK	40,476	VC
Okla State Univ	OK	14,310	VC
Oral Roberts Univ	OK	31,734	C
Pace Univ	NY	53,367	C
Palm Beach Atlantic Univ	FL	34,874	C+
Penn State Erie/The Behrend College	PA	16,256	C
Philadelphia Univ	PA	44,160	C
Pittsburg State Univ	KS	12,032	C
Pontifical Catholic Univ of PR	PR	7,310	
Post Univ	CT	35,750	C
Prairie View A&M Univ	TX	15,205	LC
Purdue Univ/Calumet	IN	14,336	C
Purdue Univ/West Lafayette	IN	20,024	HC
Queens College/The CUNY	NY	17,107	VC
Quincy Univ	IL	34,980	LC
Quinnipiac Univ	CT	55,160	VC
Radford Univ	VA	17,766	LC
Rhode Island College	RI	17,694	C
Richard Stockton College of New Jersey	NJ	20,000	VC
Rider Univ	NJ	45,720	C
Robert Morris Univ	PA	37,864	C
Rochester Inst of Technology	NY	42,450	VC
Roger Williams Univ	RI	46,296	VC
Roosevelt Univ	IL	22,605	VC
Rutgers, The State Univ of New Jersey/Camden Campus	NJ	25,121	C
Rutgers, The State Univ of New Jersey/New Brunswick	NJ	25,562	VC
Rutgers, The State Univ of New Jersey/Newark Campus	NJ	258,806	C
Sacred Heart Univ	CT	49,264	VC
Saginaw Valley State Univ	MI	17,369	C
St. Anselm College	NH	49,376	VC
St. Mary's Univ	TX	33,854	C
St. Vincent College	PA	40,244	C
St. Xavier Univ	IL	32,840	C
Salem State Univ	MA	13,161	LC
Salisbury Univ	MD	19,180	VC
Sam Houston State Univ	TX	17,082	C
San Francisco State Univ	CA	18,514	C
San Jose State Univ	CA	19,133	LC
Shippensburg Univ of Pennsylvania	PA	20,934	C
Siena College	NY	43,863	VC
Southeastern Univ	FL	27,201	C
Southern Adventist Univ	TN	26,190	C
Southern Conn State Univ	CT	18,033	LC
Southern Illinois Univ Carbondale	IL	21,942	C
Southern Nazarene Univ	OK	24,354	C
Southern Univ and A&M College	LA	9,761	LC
Southwestern Okla State Univ	OK	9,160	C
St. Bonaventure Univ	NY	41,575	C
St. Cloud State Univ	MN	10,600	C
St. Edward's Univ	TX	47,784	C
St. Thomas Aquinas College	NY	40,230	C
St. Thomas Univ	FL	32,310	C
SUNY Polytechnic Inst	NY	19,690	C
Stephen F. Austin State Univ	TX	14,668	C
Stetson Univ	FL	51,516	VC
Stonehill College	MA	46,780	HC
Suffolk Univ	MA	47,298	C
SUNY College at Old Westbury	NY	16,324	C
SUNY New Paltz	NY	14,348	C
Talladega Univ	AL	17,996	C
Tarleton State Univ	TX	13,489	LC
Taylor Univ	IN	37,821	VC+
Temple Univ	PA	24,392	VC
Tenn Tech Univ	TN	11,310	C
Tenn Wesleyan College	TN	21,250	C
Texas A&M Univ	TX	19,207	VC
Texas A&M Univ at Commerce	TX	10,496	C
Texas A&M Univ at Corpus Christi	TX	11,544	LC
Texas A&M Univ at Kingsville	TX	7,500	LC
Texas Southern Univ	TX	18,212	LC
Texas State Univ	TX	17,128	C
Texas Tech Univ	TX	14,243	C
The Catholic Univ of America	DC	52,852	VC
Ohio State Univ-Columbus Campus	OH	19,887	HC+
The Univ of Memphis	TN	15,094	C

School	ST	$IS	SR
The Univ of N Car at Greensboro	NC	12,848	C
Tiffin Univ	OH	30,273	LC
Touro College	NY	27,959	VC
Trine Univ	IN	39,400	HC+
Troy Univ	AL	10,650	C
Tulane Univ	LA	60,861	MC
Tuskegee Univ	AL	26,750	C
Union College	NE	23,270	C
Union Univ	TN	28,260	VC
Universidad de Puerto/ Arecibo	PR	7,227	
Univ of Akron	OH	20,436	C
Univ of Alabama at Birmingham	AL	18,484	C+
Univ of Alabama in Huntsville	AL	17,591	VC+
Univ of Alaska Anchorage	AK	16,673	NC
Univ of Arkansas at Fayetteville	AR	18,352	C+
Univ of Arkansas at Little Rock	AR	17,609	LC
Univ of Bridgeport	CT	39,030	LC
Univ of Central Arkansas	AR	13,667	VC
Univ of Central Florida	FL	15,668	VC+
Univ of Central Okla	OK	12,293	C
Univ of Cincinnati	OH	21,506	VC
Univ of Conn	CT	24,706	HC
Univ of Dayton	OH	49,070	VC
Univ of Delaware	DE	23,612	VC
Univ of Denver	CO	51,787	VC+
Univ of Findlay	OH	31,916	C
Univ of Florida	FL	15,943	HC
Univ of Hartford	CT	42,674	C
Univ of Hawaii at Manoa	HI	19,379	C
Univ of Houston-Downtown	TX	15,170	LC
Univ of Illinois at Chicago	IL	24,505	VC
Univ of Illinois at Urbana-Champaign	IL	26,450	VC
Univ of Indianapolis	IN	31,740	LC
Univ of Iowa	IA	17,693	VC
Univ of Kentucky	KY	19,868	C
Univ of Louisiana at Lafayette	LA	6,130	C
Univ of Louisville	KY	17,946	C
Univ of Mass Amherst	MA	24,215	VC+
Univ of Mich-Flint	MI	17,547	C+
Univ of Miss	MS	16,704	C+
Univ of Missouri/Columbia	MO	18,201	MC
Univ of Montana	MT	14,105	C
Univ of Montevallo	AL	17,060	C
Univ of Nebr - Lincoln	NE	18,031	VC
Univ of Nebr at Kearney	NE	14,855	LC
Univ of Nebr at Omaha	NE	12,700	C
Univ of Nevada, Las Vegas	NV	17,303	C
Univ of New Haven	CT	48,940	C
Univ of New Orleans	LA	9,224	C
Univ of North Alabama	AL	9,960	C
Univ of N Car at Charlotte	NC	15,547	C
Univ of N Car at Wilmington	NC	13,572	VC
Univ of N Dak	ND	14,551	C
Univ of North Florida	FL	15,870	VC
Univ of North Georgia	GA	8,500	C
Univ of North Texas	TX	15,628	C
Univ of Northern Iowa	IA	15,795	C
Univ of Notre Dame	IN	57,117	MC
Univ of Pittsburgh at Johnstown	PA	20,862	LC
Univ of Pittsburgh at Pittsburgh	PA	28,572	HC+
Univ of Portland	OR	49,964	VC
Univ of PR Recinto de Rio Piedras	PR	5,750	
Univ of PR/Bayamon	PR	1,600	
Univ of PR/Mayaguez	PR	1,250	
Univ of San Francisco	CA	54,770	VC
Univ of Scranton	PA	51,940	VC
Univ of South Alabama	AL	13,510	C
Univ of S Car at Columbia	SC	19,725	VC+
Univ of S Dak	SD	15,111	C
Univ of South Florida/Tampa	FL	13,000	C
Univ of Southern Miss	MS	13,170	C
Univ of St. Francis	IL	37,560	C
Univ of St. Thomas - Houston	TX	37,690	C
Univ of Tampa	FL	35,160	VC
Univ of Texas - Pan American	TX	11,125	LC
Univ of Texas at Arlington	TX	10,908	LC
Univ of Texas at Austin	TX	44,074	HC
Univ of Texas at Dallas	TX	21,348	HC+
Univ of Texas at El Paso	TX	8,764	NC
Univ of the District of Columbia	DC	7,244	LC
Univ of Toledo	OH	18,464	C
Univ of Tulsa	OK	46,331	MC
Univ of Washington	WA	14,722	VC
Univ of West Florida	FL	14,656	C
Univ of Wisc Whitewater	WI	13,314	C
Univ of Wisc/Eau Claire	WI	15,730	VC
Univ of Wisc/La Crosse	WI	9,304	C
Univ of Wisc/Madison	WI	18,757	HC+
Univ of Wisc/Oshkosh	WI	10,426	LC
Upper Iowa Univ	IA	30,426	NC
Utah State Univ	UT	12,044	C
Valparaiso Univ	IN	44,940	VC+
Villanova Univ	PA	58,394	MC

School	ST	$IS	SR
Virginia Polytechnic Inst and State Univ	VA	14,629	HC
Virginia Union Univ	VA	18,432	C
Wake Forest Univ	NC	58,838	MC
Warner Univ	FL	18,000	C
Wartburg College	IA	41,055	VC
Washburn Univ	KS	12,579	C
Washington Univ in St. Louis	MO	69,844	MC
Wayne State Univ	MI	22,063	C
Webber International Univ	FL	30,147	C
West Chester Univ of Pennsylvania	PA	17,186	C
West Liberty Univ	WV	9,142	LC
West Texas A&M Univ	TX	13,478	C
West Virginia State Univ	WV	8,378	NC
West Virginia Univ	WV	16,542	C+
Western Carolina Univ	NC	13,965	C
Western Conn State Univ	CT	18,327	LC
Western Kentucky Univ	KY	11,000	LC
Western Mich Univ	MI	19,628	C
Westminster College	PA	31,290	C+
Westminster College	UT	37,708	C+
Wichita State Univ	KS	14,607	C+
Wilberforce Univ	OH	15,100	LC
William Paterson Univ of New Jersey	NJ	21,694	C
Wilmington Univ	DE	8,112	NC
Winona State Univ	MN	16,640	C
Wofford College	SC	45,795	VC
Wright State Univ	OH	16,983	C
Xavier Univ	OH	44,980	VC
York College of Pennsylvania	PA	26,590	C
Youngstown State Univ	OH	16,732	C

BEHAVIORAL SCIENCE

School	ST	$IS	SR
Alvernia Univ	PA	39,250	LC
Andrews Univ	MI	28,030	C+
Ashford Univ	CA	10,480	C
Calif Baptist Univ	CA	38,792	C
Cal State, Dominguez Hills	CA	17,090	LC
Cal State, Monterey Bay	CA	26,871	C
Capital Univ	OH	41,050	VC
Chaminade Univ of Honolulu	HI	31,664	LC
College of St. Scholastica	MN	41,440	C
Concordia College - New York	NY	39,035	LC
Concordia Univ Irvine	CA	35,390	VC
Concordia Univ Nebr	NE	26,000	VC
Concordia Univ Texas	TX	23,640	C
Dakota Wesleyan Univ	SD	23,000	C
Duquesne Univ	PA	43,720	VC
Elizabethtown College School of Continuing and Professional Studies	PA		VC
Erskine College	SC	37,360	C
Fontbonne Univ	MO	31,384	C
George Fox Univ	OR	40,750	C+
Grand Valley State Univ	MI	17,998	C+
Granite State College	NH	6,195	NC
Johnson State College	VT	16,721	C
Lakeland College	WI	22,990	C
Lehigh Univ	PA	56,770	MC
Mercy College	NY	30,456	C
Metropolitan State Univ of Denver	CO	4,835	LC
Missouri Baptist Univ	MO	31,830	C
Mount Aloysius College	PA	29,976	C
Mount Marty College	SD	29,638	C
Mount Mary Univ	WI	33,590	LC
National Univ	CA	14,730	SP
New York Inst of Technology	NY	45,010	VC
North Central Univ	MN	26,400	C
Northwest Univ	WA	18,854	C
Nova Southeastern Univ	FL	37,280	VC
Oglethorpe Univ	GA	44,200	C+
Okla City Univ	OK	40,476	VC
Okla Wesleyan Univ	OK	21,300	C
Our Lady of Holy Cross College	LA	8,090	C
Our Lady of the Lake Univ	TX	22,430	LC
Point Park Univ	PA	36,390	C
Purdue Univ/West Lafayette	IN	20,024	HC
Rochester College	MI	18,320	LC
Savannah State Univ	GA	13,156	C
Southern Adventist Univ	TN	26,190	C
Sterling College	KS	27,216	C
Tenn Wesleyan College	TN	21,250	C
The Univ of Utah	UT	16,463	VC
Trevecca Nazarene Univ	TN	31,186	C
United States Air Force Academy	CO		MC
United States Military Academy	NY		MC
Univ of Calif at Davis	CA		HC
Univ of Kansas	KS	17,603	C+
Univ of La Verne	CA	47,010	C
Univ of Maine at Fort Kent	ME	15,195	LC
Univ of Maine at Machias	ME	10,523	C
Univ of Mary	ND	16,714	C
Univ of Mich/Ann Arbor	MI	22,102	MC
Univ of Mich/Dearborn	MI	9,885	VC
Univ of New Haven	CT	48,940	C
Univ of Rio Grande	OH	8,750	NC
Univ of San Diego	CA	54,818	HC+
Univ of Wisc-Milwaukee	WI	18,436	C

School	ST	$IS	SR
Western Mich Univ	MI	19,628	C
Western Washington Univ	WA	18,519	VC
Widener Univ	PA	52,418	C
Wilmington Univ	DE	8,112	NC
York College of Pennsylvania	PA	26,590	C

BIBLICAL LANGUAGES

School	ST	$IS	SR
Asbury Univ	KY	32,038	C
Baylor Univ	TX	50,329	HC
Belmont Univ	TN	39,190	VC+
Concordia Univ Irvine	CA	35,390	VC
Concordia Univ Wisc	WI	28,980	C
Concordia Univ, Ann Arbor	MI	27,220	VC
Faulkner Univ	AL	25,720	LC
Harding Univ	AR	23,556	C
Houston Baptist Univ	TX	36,450	C
Lipscomb Univ	TN	37,490	VC
Luther College	IA	45,720	C+
North Central Univ	MN	26,400	C
Ouachita Baptist Univ	AR	30,220	VC
Union Univ	TN	28,260	VC
Walla Walla Univ	WA	26,256	NC

BIBLICAL STUDIES

School	ST	$IS	SR
Abilene Christian Univ	TX	38,400	C+
Amridge Univ	AL	6,870	LC
Asbury Univ	KY	32,038	C
Azusa Pacific Univ	CA	42,086	C
Belhaven Univ	MS	27,170	C
Belmont Univ	TN	39,190	VC+
Bethel College	IN	31,560	C
Bethel Univ	MN	34,940	VC
Biola Univ	CA	40,320	C+
Blue Mountain College	MS	15,634	LC
Bluffton Univ	OH	38,948	C
Cairn Univ	PA	33,270	C
Campbellsville Univ	KY	27,720	C
Canisius College	NY	44,900	C
Cedarville Univ	OH	32,860	VC
Clearwater Christian College	FL	23,720	C
College of the Ozarks	MO		VC
Colo Christian Univ	CO	27,500	VC
Corban Univ	OR	37,380	C+
Cornerstone Univ and Grand Rapids Theological Seminary	MI	33,338	C
Covenant College	GA	38,990	VC+
Dallas Baptist Univ	TX	30,580	VC
East Texas Baptist Univ	TX	31,577	LC
Eastern Mennonite Univ	VA	40,660	C
Eastern Univ	PA	37,704	C
Evangel Univ	MO	23,090	C
Faulkner Univ	AL	25,720	LC
Freed-Hardeman Univ	TN	19,697	VC
Geneva College	PA	27,280	C
George Fox Univ	OR	40,750	C+
Gordon College	MA	44,320	VC
Goshen College	IN	35,900	VC
Grace Bible College	MI	20,770	C
Grace College and Seminary	IN	28,800	VC
Grove City College	PA	24,022	VC
Hannibal-LaGrange Univ	MO	24,490	C
Harding Univ	AR	23,556	C
Hardin-Simmons Univ	TX	23,560	C+
Hope International Univ	CA	34,650	C
Houghton College	NY	36,808	C+
Huntington Univ	IN	33,220	C+
Indiana Wesleyan Univ	IN	31,815	VC
John Brown Univ	AR	32,056	VC+
Kentucky Christian Univ	KY	17,622	LC
King Univ	TN	33,140	C
Lee Univ	TN	18,690	C+
LeTourneau Univ	TX	36,210	VC
Lipscomb Univ	TN	37,490	VC
List College	NY	21,600	
Lubbock Christian Univ	TX	26,308	C
Malone Univ	OH	35,364	C
Messiah College	PA	40,690	C+
Milligan College	TN	27,510	C
Montreat College	NC	31,298	C
Mount Vernon Nazarene Univ	OH	29,590	C
North Park Univ	IL	30,130	C
Northwest Nazarene Univ	ID	34,000	C
Northwest Univ	WA	18,854	C
Northwestern College	MN	24,000	C
Nyack College	NY	33,250	C
Ohio Valley Univ	WV	17,752	C
Okla Christian Univ	OK	25,870	VC
Olivet Nazarene Univ	IL	29,990	C
Oral Roberts Univ	OK	31,734	C
Ouachita Baptist Univ	AR	30,220	VC
Palm Beach Atlantic Univ	FL	34,874	C+
Point Loma Nazarene Univ	CA	41,006	C+
Roberts Wesleyan College	NY	38,306	C+
Rochester College	MI	18,320	LC
San Diego Christian College	CA	31,012	C
Simpson Univ	CA	28,900	C
Southeastern Univ	FL	27,201	C
Southwest Baptist Univ	MO	24,710	C
Spring Arbor Univ	MI	26,740	C
Tabor College	KS	29,010	C
Taylor Univ	IN	37,821	VC+

School	ST	$IS	SR
The Masters College	CA	38,160	C+
Toccoa Falls College	GA	23,210	LC
Trinity Bible College	ND		
Trinity Christian College	IL	28,869	C
Trinity International Univ	IL	31,070	VC
Union Univ	TN	28,260	VC
Univ of Evansville	IN	42,656	VC+
Univ of Mary Hardin-Baylor	TX	31,950	C+
Univ of Mich/Ann Arbor	MI	22,102	MC
Vanguard Univ of Southern Calif	CA	35,833	VC
Warner Univ	FL	18,000	C
Waynesburg Univ	PA	30,150	C
Wheaton College	IL	40,720	MC
York College	NE	19,475	C

BILINGUAL EARLY CHILDHOOD EDUCATION

School	ST	$IS	SR
Texas Christian Univ	TX	49,980	HC

BILINGUAL/BICULTURAL EDUCATION

School	ST	$IS	SR
Aurora Univ	IL	33,228	C
Boston Univ	MA	60,694	MC
Cal State, San Bernardino	CA	12,000	C
Chicago State Univ	IL	5,482	C
CUNY/Brooklyn College	NY	5,884	C+
CUNY/City College	NY	20,319	HC+
Eastern Mich Univ	MI	18,604	C
Elms College	MA	23,900	VC
Loyola Univ Chicago	IL	51,646	VC+
Mount Mary Univ	WI	33,590	LC
New Mexico State Univ	NM	14,050	C
New York Univ	NY	61,470	MC
Northeastern Illinois Univ	IL	10,318	LC
St. Thomas Aquinas College	NY	40,230	C
SUNY College at Old Westbury	NY	16,324	C
Univ of Central Okla	OK	12,293	C
Univ of Findlay	OH	31,916	C
Univ of Minn/Twin Cities	MN		HC
Washington State Univ	WA	20,461	C
Western Illinois Univ	IL	20,732	C

BIOCHEMISTRY

School	ST	$IS	SR
Abilene Christian Univ	TX	38,400	C+
Adams State Univ	CO	13,358	LC
Adelphi Univ	NY	44,670	VC
Agnes Scott College	GA	45,323	C+
Albion College	MI	46,010	C
Albright College	PA	46,660	C
Allegheny College	PA	50,980	HC
Alma College	MI	44,075	C
Alvernia Univ	PA	39,250	LC
American International College	MA	36,100	C
American Univ	DC	56,015	HC+
Amherst College	MA	58,744	MC
Andrews Univ	MI	28,030	C+
Angelo State Univ	TX	15,049	NC
Arizona State Univ, at the Tempe Campus	AZ	20,137	C+
Armstrong State Univ	GA	15,532	C
Asbury Univ	KY	32,038	VC
Auburn Univ	AL	22,378	VC+
Augustana College	IL	43,398	VC
Augustana College	SD	36,500	VC
Austin College	TX	45,875	VC
Azusa Pacific Univ	CA	42,086	C
Barnard College/Columbia Univ	NY	39,000	MC
Bates College	ME	60,720	MC
Baylor Univ	TX	50,329	HC
Bellarmine Univ	KY	42,950	VC
Belmont Univ	TN	39,190	VC+
Beloit College	WI	49,970	HC
Benedictine College	KS	29,180	VC
Benedictine Univ	IL	37,820	C
Berry College	GA	39,254	VC
Bethany College	WV	35,282	LC
Bethel Univ	MN	34,940	VC
Binghamton Univ/The SUNY	NY	21,648	HC+
Biola Univ	CA	40,320	C+
Blackburn College	IL	21,350	C
Bloomfield College	NJ	37,850	LC
Boston College	MA	60,622	MC
Boston Univ	MA	60,694	MC
Bowdoin College	ME	59,568	MC
Bradley Univ	IL	31,874	VC
Brandeis Univ	MA		MC
Brescia Univ	KY	26,140	VC+
Brigham Young Univ	UT	12,100	HC
Brown Univ	RI	59,428	MC
Bucknell Univ	PA	60,140	MC
Calif Baptist Univ	CA	38,792	C
Calif Lutheran Univ	CA	49,540	C+
Calif Polytechnic State Univ	CA	19,847	HC
Cal State, Chico	CA	20,158	C
Cal State, Dominguez Hills	CA	15,450	C
Cal State, Fullerton	CA	25,188	C
Cal State, Long Beach	CA	17,502	C+
Cal State, Los Angeles	CA	17,186	LC
Cal State, Northridge	CA	28,690	LC
Cal State, San Bernardino	CA	12,000	C
Cal State, San Marcos	CA	14,576	LC
Calvin College	MI	39,120	VC
Campbell Univ	NC	37,570	VC
Canisius College	NY	44,900	C
Capital Univ	OH	41,050	VC
Carroll Univ	WI	38,100	C
Case Western Reserve Univ	OH	56,534	MC
Cedar Crest College	PA	43,240	C
Centenary College of Louisiana	LA	45,650	C+
Central College	IA	42,104	C+
Central Conn State Univ	CT	19,749	C
Centre Univ	KY	35,000	HC+
Chaminade Univ of Honolulu	HI	31,664	LC
Chapman Univ	CA	58,347	VC+
Charleston Southern Univ	SC	22,420	C
Chatham Univ	PA	43,797	C
Chestnut Hill College	PA	42,110	LC
Chicago State Univ	IL	5,482	C
Christian Brothers Univ	TN	31,670	HC
Christopher Newport Univ	VA	21,960	VC
Claflin Univ	SC	22,368	LC
Claremont McKenna College	CA	62,215	MC
Clark Univ	MA	47,020	HC+
Clarke Univ	IA	37,600	C
Clemson Univ	SC	19,136	HC
Coastal Carolina Univ	SC	18,580	C
Coe College	IA	45,550	VC
Colby College	ME	57,510	MC
Colgate Univ	NY	58,135	MC
College of Charleston	SC	22,145	VC
College of Mount St. Joseph	OH	33,880	C
College of Mount St. Vincent	NY	41,040	MC
College of St. Benedict	MN	49,359	VC
College of St. Elizabeth	NJ	43,839	LC
College of St. Scholastica	MN	41,440	C
College of Staten Island/The City of New Yok	NY	16,778	NC
College of Wooster	OH	52,600	VC
Colo College	CO	57,162	MC
Colo State Univ-Fort Collins	CO	20,385	VC
Colo State Univ-Pueblo	CO	16,183	C
Columbia Univ/City of New York	NY	61,116	MC
Conn College	CT	54,970	MC
Cornell College	IA	44,930	VC
Creighton Univ	NE	45,356	VC
Culver-Stockton College	MO	30,900	C
Curry College	MA	48,925	LC
Daemen College	NY	34,770	C
Dartmouth College	NH	57,996	MC
De Sales Univ	PA	43,970	C
Denison Univ	OH	54,670	HC+
DePauw Univ	IN	48,950	VC+
Dickinson College	PA	57,662	HC+
Doane College	NE	35,230	C
Dominican Univ	IL	37,628	C
Drew Univ/College of Liberal Arts	NJ	57,516	C
Duquesne Univ	PA	43,720	VC
Earlham College	IN	51,470	HC
East Carolina Univ	NC	14,169	C
East Stroudsburg Univ of Pennsylvania	PA	18,868	LC
Eastern Conn State Univ	CT	20,584	C
Eastern Mennonite Univ	VA	40,660	C
Eastern Mich Univ	MI	18,604	C
Eastern New Mexico Univ	NM	10,682	C
Eastern Univ	PA	37,704	C
Eastern Washington Univ	WA		C
Eckerd College	FL	43,902	C
Elizabethtown College	PA	49,740	VC
Elmira College	NY	49,950	C+
Elon Univ	NC	41,914	VC+
Emmanuel College	MA	47,985	VC
Emporia State Univ	KS	12,897	C
Fairfield Univ	CT	56,960	VC
Fairleigh Dickinson Univ/College at Florham	NJ	42,142	C
Fairleigh Dickinson Univ/Metropolitan Campus	NJ	40,254	C
Faulkner Univ	AL	25,720	LC
Ferris State Univ	MI	20,047	C
Florida Inst of Technology	FL	48,290	VC
Florida Southern College	FL	40,150	C+
Florida State Univ	FL	16,715	VC
Fort Lewis College	CO	15,513	C
Franklin and Marshall College	PA	60,799	MC
Freed-Hardeman Univ	TN	19,697	VC
Georgetown College	KY	41,440	C+
Georgetown Univ	DC	52,910	MC
Georgia Inst of Technology	GA	21,828	MC
Georgian Court Univ	NJ	41,594	LC
Gettysburg College	PA	58,820	HC
Gonzaga Univ	WA	46,441	HC
Goshen College	IN	35,900	VC
Goucher College	MD	52,040	VC+
Grand View Univ	IA	31,050	C
Grinnell College	IA	53,654	HC
Grove City College	PA	24,022	VC
Gustavus Adolphus College	MN	48,170	HC
Hamilton College	NY	55,620	MC
Hamline Univ	MN	45,678	VC
Hanover College	IN	43,073	C+
Harding Univ	AR	23,556	C
Hardin-Simmons Univ	TX	23,560	C+
Hartwick College	NY	51,270	C
Harvard College/Harvard Univ	MA	49,000	MC
Hawaii Pacific Univ	HI	34,360	C
Heidelberg Univ	OH	34,100	C
Hendrix Univ	AR	50,202	VC+
High Point Univ	NC	39,800	C
Hillsdale College	MI	32,866	MC
Hiram College	OH	37,300	VC
Hobart and William Smith Colleges	NY	60,034	HC+
Hofstra Univ	NY	51,810	VC+
Holy Family Univ	PA	40,030	LC
Hood College	MD	45,730	C
Hope College	MI	38,650	VC
Houghton College	NY	36,808	C+
Howard Univ	DC	13,646	C
Huntingdon College	AL	33,100	C
Idaho State Univ	ID	12,307	C
Illinois College	IL	25,770	VC
Illinois Inst of Technology	IL	38,512	HC+
Illinois State Univ	IL	23,110	VC
Immaculata Univ	PA	43,000	C
Indiana Univ Bloomington	IN	19,801	VC
Indiana Univ East	IN	6,783	C
Indiana Univ Kokomo	IN	6,811	LC
Indiana Univ of Pennsylvania	PA	20,846	LC
Indiana Univ South Bend	IN	15,501	C
Indiana Univ Southeast	IN	16,035	C
Indiana Univ-Purdue Univ Fort Wayne	IN	15,521	C
Iona College	NY	44,028	C
Iowa State Univ	IA	16,403	VC
Ithaca College	NY	53,864	HC
John Brown Univ	AR	32,056	VC+
John Carroll Univ	OH	46,300	C
Juniata College	PA	49,340	VC
Kansas State Univ	KS	15,497	VC
Kennesaw State Univ	GA		C
Kent State Univ	OH	19,920	C
Kenyon College	OH	58,890	MC
Kettering Univ	MI	31,456	HC
Keuka College	NY	30,300	C
King Univ	TN	33,140	C
Knox College	IL	44,865	VC+
Kutztown Univ of Pennsylvania	PA	16,909	LC
La Salle Univ	PA	50,270	C
La Sierra Univ	CA	35,694	VC
Lafayette College	PA	59,155	HC+
LaGrange College	GA	37,670	C
Lawrence Tech Univ	MI	37,630	VC
Lawrence Univ	WI	46,371	HC
Le Moyne College	NY	43,470	C
Lebanon Valley College	PA	38,570	C
Lee Univ	TN	18,690	C+
Lehigh Univ	PA	56,770	MC
Lewis & Clark College	OR	54,382	MC
Lewis Univ	IL	23,050	C
Linfield College-McMinnville Campus	OR	47,676	C
Lipscomb Univ	TN	37,490	VC
LIU Brooklyn	NY	47,182	LC
Loras College	IA	37,432	VC
Louisiana State Univ	LA	18,677	C+
Louisiana State Univ in Shreveport	LA	5,606	C
Loyola Marymount Univ	CA	54,649	VC+
Loyola Univ Chicago	IL	51,646	VC+
Lubbock Christian Univ	TX	26,308	C
Madonna Univ	MI	24,540	VC
Manchester Univ	IN	35,070	C
Manhattan College	NY	49,588	C+
Manhattanville College	NY	50,740	VC
Mansfield Univ	PA	19,468	LC
Marietta College	OH	42,135	C+
Marlboro College	VT	35,980	VC
Marquette Univ	WI	46,930	VC+
Marshall Univ	WV	14,820	C
Marymount Univ	VA	39,480	C
Maryville College	TN	33,150	C+
Maryville Univ of St. Louis	MO	35,856	VC
McMurry Univ	TX	25,962	LC
Mercer Univ	GA	44,201	VC
Mercyhurst Univ	PA	40,700	C
Merrimack College	MA	44,215	C
Messiah College	PA	40,690	C+
Miami Univ	OH	24,191	VC
Mich State Univ	MI	22,450	VC
Mich Tech Univ	MI	23,556	VC
Middlebury College	VT	59,160	MC
Millersville Univ of Pennsylvania	PA	21,648	C
Millikin Univ	IL	38,940	C
Mills College	CA	54,119	VC
Millsaps College	MS	43,888	VC+
Minn State Univ, Mankato	MN	15,616	C
Misericordia Univ	PA	41,060	C
Miss College	MS	21,998	C
Miss State Univ	MS	14,750	C
Missouri Baptist Univ	MO	31,830	C
Missouri Southern State Univ	MO	12,061	C
Monmouth College	IL	40,850	C
Montclair State Univ	NJ	22,614	C
Moravian College	PA	36,381	VC
Mount Holyoke College	MA	55,146	MC
Mount St. Mary's Univ	MD	47,996	C
Mount St. Mary's College - Chalon Campus	CA	43,897	VC+
Muhlenberg College	PA	52,837	HC
Nazareth College of Rochester	NY	43,028	C+
Nebr Wesleyan Univ	NE	29,774	C+
New College of Florida	FL	14,504	MC
New Mexico State Univ	NM	14,050	C
New York Univ	NY	61,470	MC
Newman Univ	KS	30,380	C+
Niagara Univ	NY	41,010	C
N Car State Univ	NC	16,202	NC
North Central College	IL	38,343	VC
N Dak State Univ	ND		C
Northeastern Univ	MA	55,296	MC
Northern Mich Univ	MI	18,278	C
Northwest Nazarene Univ	ID	34,000	C
Northwestern College	MN	24,000	C
Norwich Univ	VT	28,212	C
Notre Dame de Namur Univ	CA	44,236	LC
Oakland Univ	MI	19,391	C
Oakwood Univ	AL	25,529	NC
Oberlin College	OH	61,788	MC
Occidental College	CA	60,972	MC
Ohio Northern Univ	OH	42,075	VC
Ohio Univ	OH	21,080	C
Ohio Valley Univ	WV	17,752	C
Ohio Wesleyan Univ	OH	49,460	C+
Okla Christian Univ	OK	25,870	VC
Okla City Univ	OK	40,476	VC
Okla State Univ	OK	14,310	VC
Old Dominion Univ	VA	19,483	C
Olivet College	MI	19,984	LC
Oregon State Univ	OR	20,273	VC
Oswego / SUNY	NY	20,009	VC
Otterbein College	OH	32,214	C
Philadelphia Univ	PA	44,160	C
Pittsburg State Univ	KS	12,032	C
Pitzer College	CA	54,988	MC
Point Loma Nazarene Univ	CA	41,006	C+
Portland State Univ	OR	18,672	C
Presbyterian College	SC	42,678	C+
Providence College	RI	57,383	VC
Purdue Univ/West Lafayette	IN	20,024	HC
Queens Univ of Charlotte	NC	39,543	C+
Quinnipiac Univ	CT	55,160	VC
Ramapo College of New Jersey	NJ	24,938	C
Reed College	OR	57,780	MC
Regis College	MA	47,565	LC
Regis Univ	CO	41,318	C
Rensselaer Polytechnic Inst	NY	61,529	MC
Rhodes College	TN	51,900	HC+
Richard Stockton College of New Jersey	NJ	20,000	VC
Rider Univ	NJ	45,720	C
Ripon College	WI	36,959	C+
Roanoke College	VA	49,976	C
Roberts Wesleyan College	NY	38,306	C+
Rochester Inst of Technology	NY	42,450	VC
Rockford College	IL	31,000	C
Rockhurst Univ	MO	20,625	C
Roger Williams Univ	RI	46,296	VC
Rollins College	FL	52,370	HC
Rose-Hulman Inst of Technology	IN	53,340	MC
Rosemont College	PA	42,350	C
Rowan Univ	NJ	24,022	VC+
Russell Sage College	NY	39,370	C
Rutgers, The State Univ of New Jersey/Camden Campus	NJ	25,121	C
Rutgers, The State Univ of New Jersey/New Brunswick	NJ	25,562	VC
Saginaw Valley State Univ	MI	17,369	C
St. Anselm College	NH	49,376	VC
St. John's Univ	MN	47,984	C
St. Joseph's Univ	PA	55,006	VC
St. Louis Univ	MO	48,346	HC
St. Mary's Univ	TX	33,854	C
St. Mary's Univ of Minn	MN	38,280	C
St. Michael's College	VT	49,975	VC
St. Peter's Univ	NJ	44,240	C
St. Vincent College	PA	40,244	C
Samford Univ	AL	37,060	C+
San Francisco State Univ	CA	18,514	C
San Jose State Univ	CA	19,133	LC
Schreiner Univ	TX	32,734	LC
Seattle Pacific Univ	WA	41,559	VC+
Seattle Univ	WA	49,035	VC+
Seton Hall Univ	NJ	45,902	C
Seton Hill Univ	PA	35,172	C
Sewanee: The Univ of the South	TN	47,700	HC+
Siena College	NY	43,863	VC
Simmons College	MA	49,966	VC
Simpson College	IA	36,086	C+
Skidmore College	NY	59,942	HC
Smith College	MA	59,674	MC
Sonoma State Univ	CA	20,541	C
S Dak State Univ	SD	14,296	C
Southern Conn State Univ	CT	18,033	LC

ST = STATE $IS = IN-STATE COSTS   SR = SELECTOR RATING

School	ST	$IS	SR
Southern Illinois Univ Edwardsville	IL	17,532	C
Southern Methodist Univ	TX	60,585	MC
Southern Nazarene Univ	OK	24,354	C
Southwestern College	KS	29,270	C
Southwestern Univ	TX	45,660	VC
Spelman College	GA	24,650	C
Spring Arbor Univ	MI	26,740	C
Spring Hill College	AL	44,164	VC
Springfield College	MA	25,000	C
St. Bonaventure Univ	NY	41,575	C
St. Catherine Univ	MN	37,782	C+
St. Edward's Univ	TX	47,784	C
St. Lawrence Univ	NY	59,972	VC
St. Mary's College of Maryland	MD	25,754	VC
Stetson Univ	FL	51,516	VC
Stevens Inst of Technology	NJ	50,130	HC
Stonehill College	MA	46,780	HC
Stony Brook Univ / SUNY	NY	20,078	HC+
Suffolk Univ	MA	47,298	C
SUNY College at Geneseo	NY	18,670	HC
SUNY College at Old Westbury	NY	16,324	C
SUNY Fredonia/The SUNY at Fredonia	NY	19,840	VC
SUNY Plattsburgh / SUNY	NY	18,083	C
Susquehanna Univ	PA	51,150	C
Swarthmore College	PA	57,870	MC
Syracuse Univ	NY	56,346	VC
Temple Univ	PA	24,392	VC
Tenn Tech Univ	TN	11,310	C
Texas A&M Univ	TX	19,207	VC
Texas Christian Univ	TX	49,980	VC
Texas Lutheran Univ	TX	36,040	C
Texas State Univ	TX	17,128	C
Texas Tech Univ	TX	14,243	C
Texas Wesleyan Univ	TX	31,382	C
The Catholic Univ of America	DC	52,852	VC
The College of St. Rose	NY	26,750	C
Ohio State Univ-Columbus Campus	OH	19,887	HC+
The Pennsylvania State Univ - Univ Park	PA	28,022	VC+
The SUNY at Potsdam	NY	18,473	C
The SUNY/College at Brockport	NY	19,002	C
The Univ of N Car at Greensboro	NC	12,848	C
The Univ of Okla	OK	18,621	VC
Transylvania Univ	KY	42,660	VC+
Trinity College	CT		HC+
Trinity Univ	TX	48,150	HC+
Trinity Washington Univ	DC	30,250	C
Tufts Univ	MA	58,780	MC
Tulane Univ	LA	60,861	MC
Union College	NY	60,240	MC
Univ at Albany / SUNY	NY	18,674	VC
Univ at Buffalo / The SUNY	NY	20,283	VC
Univ of Arizona	AZ	20,657	C
Univ of Calif at Davis	CA		HC
Univ of Calif at Irvine	CA	25,961	VC
Univ of Calif at Los Angeles	CA	25,686	MC
Univ of Calif at Riverside	CA	27,204	C+
Univ of Calif at San Diego	CA	21,000	VC
Univ of Calif at Santa Barbara	CA	27,551	HC
Univ of Calif at Santa Cruz	CA	27,807	C+
Univ of Chicago	IL	55,416	MC
Univ of Cincinnati	OH	21,506	VC
Univ of Colo Boulder	CO	22,605	VC
Univ of Dallas	TX	45,500	VC+
Univ of Dayton	OH	49,070	VC
Univ of Delaware	DE	23,612	VC
Univ of Denver	CO	51,787	VC+
Univ of Detroit Mercy	MI	30,450	VC
Univ of Evansville	IN	42,656	VC+
Univ of Georgia	GA	20,082	VC
Univ of Idaho	ID	14,558	C
Univ of Illinois at Chicago	IL	24,505	VC
Univ of Iowa	IA	17,693	VC
Univ of Jamestown	ND	24,738	C
Univ of Kansas	KS	17,603	C+
Univ of Maine	ME	19,902	C+
Univ of Maryland - College Park	MD	20,060	VC
Univ of Maryland/Baltimore County	MD	18,000	VC
Univ of Mass Amherst	MA	24,215	VC+
Univ of Mass Boston	MA	23,066	VC
Univ of Mass Dartmouth	MA	22,223	C
Univ of Miami	FL	57,034	MC
Univ of Mich/Ann Arbor	MI	22,102	MC
Univ of Mich/Dearborn	MI	9,885	VC
Univ of Minn/Duluth	MN	19,806	C
Univ of Minn/Twin Cities	MN		HC
Univ of Missouri/Columbia	MO	18,201	MC
Univ of Missouri-St. Louis	MO		VC
Univ of Montana	MT	14,105	VC
Univ of Mount Union	OH	35,130	C
Univ of Nebr - Lincoln	NE	18,031	VC
Univ of Nevada/Reno	NV	17,507	C
Univ of New England	ME	46,750	C
Univ of New Hampshire	NH	26,912	C
Univ of New Haven	CT	48,940	C

School	ST	$IS	SR
Univ of New Mexico	NM	15,300	C
Univ of N Car at Wilmington	NC	13,572	VC
Univ of North Texas	TX	15,628	C
Univ of Northern Iowa	IA	15,795	C
Univ of Notre Dame	IN	57,117	MC
Univ of Oregon	OR	21,360	C+
Univ of Pennsylvania	PA	61,132	MC
Univ of PR/Mayaguez	PR	1,250	
Univ of Puget Sound	WA	54,608	HC
Univ of Redlands	CA	40,500	VC
Univ of Rochester	NY	60,668	MC
Univ of St. Joseph	CT	45,630	C
Univ of San Diego	CA	54,818	HC+
Univ of Scranton	PA	51,940	VC
Univ of St. Thomas - Houston	TX	37,690	C
Oberlin College	OH	35,160	VC
Univ of Tampa	FL	35,160	VC
Univ of Texas at Arlington	TX	10,908	LC
Univ of Texas at Austin	TX	44,074	HC
Univ of Texas at Dallas	TX	21,348	HC+
Univ of Texas at San Antonio	TX	18,372	C
Univ of the Pacific	CA	52,146	VC
Univ of the Sciences	PA	48,320	VC+
Univ of Tulsa	OK	46,331	MC
Southern Vermont	VT	27,006	VC+
Univ of Vermont	VT	27,006	VC+
Univ of Washington	WA	14,722	VC
Univ of Wisc/Eau Claire	WI	15,730	VC
Univ of Wisc/Madison	WI	18,757	HC+
Univ of Wisc/Stevens Point	WI	14,043	C
Univ of Wisc-Milwaukee	WI	18,436	C
Ursinus College	PA	57,580	VC
Utah State Univ	UT	12,044	C
Utica College	NY	45,670	C
Valparaiso Univ	IN	44,940	VC
Vanguard Univ of Southern Calif	CA	35,833	VC
Vassar College	NY	61,140	MC
Villanova Univ	PA	58,394	MC
Virginia Polytechnic Inst and State Univ	VA	14,629	HC
Viterbo Univ	WI	30,070	C
Wabash College	IN	46,850	C+
Walla Walla Univ	WA	26,256	NC
Walsh Univ	OH	35,100	C
Wartburg College	IA	41,055	VC
Washburn Univ	KS	12,579	C
Washington Adventist Univ	MD	25,859	LC
Washington and Jefferson College	PA	51,948	VC
Washington and Lee Univ	VA	52,812	MC
Washington State Univ	WA	20,461	C
Washington Univ in St. Louis	MO	69,844	MC
Wayne State Univ	MI	22,063	C
Wellesley College	MA	59,038	MC
Wells College	NY	49,400	VC
West Chester Univ of Pennsylvania	PA	17,186	C
Western Kentucky Univ	KY	11,000	LC
Western Mich Univ	MI	19,628	C
Western Washington Univ	WA	18,519	VC
Westminster College	MO	31,720	VC
Wheaton College	MA	54,934	HC+
Whitman College	WA	55,988	MC+
Whittier College	CA	43,416	VC
Widener Univ	PA	52,418	C
Wilkes Univ	PA	44,070	C
William Jewell College	MO	31,000	VC+
Wilmington College	OH	29,784	C
Wilson College	PA	35,080	C
Worcester Polytechnic Inst	MA	55,860	HC
Xavier Univ of Louisiana	LA	25,300	C
Yale Univ	CT	55,300	MC

BIOENGINEERING

School	ST	$IS	SR
Binghamton Univ/The SUNY	NY	21,648	HC+
Calif Baptist Univ	CA	38,792	C
Colo State Univ-Fort Collins	CO	20,385	VC
Cornell Univ	NY	60,964	MC
Dordt Univ	IA	34,160	C+
Endicott College	MA	43,228	VC+
Fairfield Univ	CT	56,960	VC
Florida State Univ	FL	16,715	VC
Indiana Univ-Purdue Univ Indianapolis	IN	17,611	C
Lehigh Univ	PA	56,770	MC
Louisiana State Univ	LA	18,677	C+
Marquette Univ	WI	46,930	VC+
Mass Inst of Technology	MA	58,240	MC
Miami Univ	OH	24,191	VC
Miss State Univ	MS	14,750	C
Ohio Univ	OH	21,080	C
Okla State Univ	OK	14,310	VC
Oral Roberts Univ	OK	31,734	C
Oregon State Univ	OR	20,273	VC
Purdue Univ/West Lafayette	IN	20,024	HC
Rice Univ	TX	43,288	MC
Stanford Univ	CA	58,388	MC
Syracuse Univ	NY	56,346	VC
Texas A&M Univ	TX	19,207	VC
The Univ of Utah	UT	16,463	VC
Union College	NY	60,240	MC
Univ of Arkansas at Fayetteville	AR	18,352	C+
Univ of Calif at Berkeley	CA	23,322	MC
Univ of Calif at Davis	CA		HC

School	ST	$IS	SR
Univ of Calif at Los Angeles	CA	25,686	MC
Univ of Calif at Riverside	CA	27,204	C+
Univ of Calif at San Diego	CA	21,000	VC
Univ of Cincinnati	OH	21,506	VC
Univ of Colo Boulder	CO	22,605	VC+
Univ of Colo Denver	CO	17,904	C
Univ of Delaware	DE	23,612	VC
Univ of Denver	CO	51,787	VC+
Univ of Hawaii at Manoa	HI	19,379	C
Univ of Idaho	ID	14,558	C
Univ of Illinois at Chicago	IL	24,505	VC
Univ of Illinois at Urbana-Champaign	IL		HC
Univ of Louisville	KY	17,946	C
Univ of Maine	ME	19,902	C+
Univ of Maryland - College Park	MD	20,060	HC
Univ of Mass Dartmouth	MA	22,223	C
Univ of Mich/Dearborn	MI	9,885	VC
Univ of Minn/Twin Cities	MN		HC
Univ of Nebr - Lincoln	NE	18,031	VC
Univ of New Hampshire	NH	26,912	C
Univ of Pennsylvania	PA	61,132	MC
Univ of Pittsburgh at Pittsburgh	PA	28,572	HC+
Univ of Toledo	OH	18,464	C
Univ of Wisc/Madison	WI	18,757	HC+
Vanderbilt Univ	TN	58,220	MC
Virginia Commonwealth Univ	VA	21,716	C
Walla Walla Univ	WA	26,256	NC
Washington State Univ	WA	20,461	C
Washington Univ in St. Louis	MO	69,844	MC
Western New England Univ	MA	46,154	C+

BIOINFORMATICS

School	ST	$IS	SR
Baylor Univ	TX	50,329	HC
Brigham Young Univ	UT	12,100	HC
Canisius College	NY	44,900	C
Claflin Univ	SC	22,368	LC
Clarke Univ	IA	37,600	C
Gannon Univ	PA	39,608	C
Inter-American Univ of PR/ Bayamon Univ College	PR	4,428	
Loyola Univ Chicago	IL	51,646	VC+
Mich State Univ	MI	22,450	VC
Mich Tech Univ	MI	23,556	HC
Missouri Southern State Univ	MO	12,061	C
New York College of Technology/The CUNY	NY	5,769	NC
Niagara Univ	NY	41,010	C
Ramapo College of New Jersey	NJ	24,938	C
Rochester Inst of Technology	NY	42,450	VC
Rockhurst Univ	MO	20,625	C
Rowan Univ	NJ	24,022	VC+
St. Vincent College	PA	40,244	C
St. Bonaventure Univ	NY	41,575	C
St. Edward's Univ	TX	47,784	C
Stevens Inst of Technology	NJ	50,130	HC
The College of St. Rose	NY	26,750	C
Univ at Buffalo / The SUNY	NY	20,283	VC
Univ of Arkansas at Little Rock	AR	17,609	LC
Univ of Calif at Irvine	CA	25,961	VC
Univ of Calif at San Diego	CA	21,000	VC
Univ of Calif at Santa Cruz	CA	27,807	C+
Univ of Denver	CO	51,787	VC+
Univ of Georgia	GA	20,082	VC
Univ of Maryland/Baltimore County	MD	18,000	VC
Univ of Missouri-Kansas City	MO	19,603	C
Univ of Nebr at Omaha	NE	12,700	C
Univ of Northern Iowa	IA	15,795	C
Univ of Pittsburgh at Pittsburgh	PA	28,572	HC+
Univ of St. Thomas - Houston	TX	37,690	C
Univ of the Sciences	PA	48,320	VC+
Virginia Commonwealth Univ	VA	21,716	C
Walsh Univ	OH	35,100	C
Washington Univ in St. Louis	MO	69,844	MC
Wheaton College	MA	54,934	HC+

BIOLOGICAL SCIENCES

School	ST	$IS	SR
Univ of Rhode Island	RI	24,002	C

BIOLOGY

School	ST	$IS	SR
Aurora Univ	IL	33,228	C
Black Hills State Univ	SD	13,947	C
Bloomfield College	NJ	37,850	LC
Bowling Green State Univ	OH	18,970	C
Bryant Univ	RI	49,179	VC
Cabrini College	PA	40,859	LC
Calvin College	MI	39,120	VC
Campbell Univ	NC	37,570	VC
College of William & Mary	VA	28,000	MC
Dallas Baptist Univ	TX	30,580	VC
Drexel Univ	PA	61,418	VC+
Elon Univ	NC	41,914	VC+
Ferris State Univ	MI	20,047	C
Franklin College	IN	36,585	C

School	ST	$IS	SR
Indiana Univ Bloomington	IN	19,801	VC
Indiana Univ East	IN	6,783	C
Indiana Univ Kokomo	IN	6,811	LC
Indiana Univ Northwest	IN	6,854	LC
Indiana Univ Southeast	IN	16,035	C
Indiana Univ-Purdue Univ Indianapolis	IN	17,611	C
Montreat College	NC	31,298	C
New York Rist of Technology	NY	45,010	VC
Niagara Univ	NY	41,010	C
Northwest Missouri State Univ	MO	17,347	C
Northwestern State Univ of Louisiana	LA	14,368	C
Nova Southeastern Univ	FL	37,280	VC
Nyack College	NY	33,250	C
Oberlin College	OH	61,788	MC
Ohio Valley Univ	WV	17,752	C
Okla Christian Univ	OK	25,870	C
Okla City Univ	OK	40,476	VC
Roberts Wesleyan College	NY	38,306	C+
Rocky Mountain College	MT	32,242	C
St. Louis Univ	MO	48,346	VC
Southeast Missouri State Univ	MO	15,370	LC
Southern Oregon Univ	OR	17,874	C
Taylor Univ	IN	37,821	VC+
Thomas Edison State College	NJ	5,700	SP
Trevecca Nazarene Univ	TN	31,186	C
Univ of Denver	CO	51,787	VC+
Univ of Georgia	GA	20,082	VC
Univ of Louisiana at Monroe	LA	12,998	C
Univ of Miami	FL	57,034	MC
Univ of Mich/Dearborn	MI	9,885	VC
Univ of Tulsa	OK	46,331	MC
Univ of Wisc/Superior	WI	14,314	C
Univ of Wyoming	WY	14,401	C+
Warren Wilson College	NC	40,132	VC
Wayne State Univ	MI	22,063	C
Western Illinois Univ	IL	20,732	C
Whitman College	WA	55,988	MC
Wilson College	PA	35,080	C

BIOLOGY (PRE-PHYSICIAN ASSISTANT)

School	ST	$IS	SR
Murray State Univ	KY	15,304	C

BIOLOGY AND SOCIETY

School	ST	$IS	SR
Arizona State Univ, at the Tempe Campus	AZ	20,137	C+
Cornell Univ	NY	60,964	MC

BIOLOGY ECOLOGY AND FIELD BIOLOGY

School	ST	$IS	SR
Beloit College	WI	49,970	HC
College of the Ozarks	MO		VC
Franklin College	IN	36,585	C

BIOLOGY/ADOLESCENCE EDUCATION

School	ST	$IS	SR
Arizona State Univ, at the Polytechnic Campus	AZ	20,531	C+
Bethany College	WV	35,282	LC
Biola Univ	CA	40,320	C+
Black Hills State Univ	SD	13,947	C
College of the Ozarks	MO		VC
Duquesne Univ	PA	43,720	VC
Elizabethtown College	PA	49,740	VC
Faulkner Univ	AL	25,720	LC
Ferris State Univ	MI	20,047	C
Gannon Univ	PA	39,608	C
Hope College	MI	38,650	VC
Houghton College	NY	36,808	C+
Huntingdon College	AL	33,100	C
Indiana Univ Bloomington	IN	19,801	VC
Indiana Univ Northwest	IN	6,854	LC
Indiana Univ South Bend	IN	15,501	C
Indiana Univ-Purdue Univ Indianapolis	IN	17,611	C
Lipscomb Univ	TN	37,490	VC
LIU Post	NY	47,660	C
Messiah College	PA	40,690	C+
Millikin Univ	IL	38,940	C
Missouri Southern State Univ	MO	12,061	C
Murray State Univ	KY	15,304	C
Nazareth College of Rochester	NY	43,028	C+
Niagara Univ	NY	41,010	C
Northern Kentucky Univ	KY	21,134	C
Old Dominion Univ	VA	19,483	LC
Oswego / SUNY	NY	20,009	VC
Pace Univ	NY	53,367	C
Roberts Wesleyan College	NY	38,306	C+
Seattle Univ	WA	49,035	VC+
St. John's Univ	NY	55,070	C+
SUNY Fredonia/The SUNY at Fredonia	NY	19,840	VC
SUNY Plattsburgh / SUNY	NY	18,083	C
Syracuse Univ	NY	56,346	VC
Temple Univ	PA	24,392	VC
The College of St. Rose	NY	26,750	C
Univ of Mary Hardin-Baylor	TX	31,950	C+

ST = STATE $IS = IN-STATE COSTS SR = SELECTOR RATING

BIOLOGY/BIOLOGICAL SCIENCE

School	ST	$IS	SR
Abilene Christian Univ	TX	38,400	C+
Adams State Univ	CO	13,358	LC
Adelphi Univ	NY	44,670	VC
Adrian College	MI	42,400	C
Agnes Scott College	GA	45,323	C+
Alabama A&M Univ	AL	10,084	C
Alabama State Univ	AL	14,142	NC
Albany State Univ	GA	8,500	C
Albertus Magnus College	CT	37,382	LC
Albion College	MI	46,010	C
Albright College	PA	46,660	C
Alcorn State Univ	MS	9,500	C
Alderson Broaddus Univ	WV	28,656	C
Alfred Univ	NY	41,770	C
Alice Lloyd College	KY	4,900	LC
Allegheny College	PA	50,980	HC
Allen Univ	SC	16,124	NC
Alma College	MI	44,075	C
Alvernia Univ	PA	39,250	LC
Alverno College	WI	31,434	LC
American International College	MA	36,100	LC
American Univ	DC	56,015	HC+
Amherst College	MA	58,744	MC
Anderson Univ	IN	36,100	C
Andrews Univ	MI	28,030	C+
Angelo State Univ	TX	15,049	NC
Appalachian State Univ	NC	12,919	VC
Aquinas College	MI	33,060	C
Arcadia Univ	PA	33,570	C+
Arizona State Univ, at the Tempe Campus	AZ	20,137	C+
Arkansas State Univ	AR	15,470	C
Arkansas Tech Univ	AR	13,982	LC
Armstrong State Univ	GA	15,532	C
Asbury Univ	KY	32,038	VC
Ashford Univ	CA	10,480	C
Ashland Univ	OH	25,000	C
Assumption College	MA	47,122	C+
Atlantic Union College	MA	24,600	C
Auburn Univ	AL	22,378	VC+
Auburn Univ at Montgomery	AL	14,470	LC
Augsburg College	MN	35,142	C
Augustana College	IL	43,398	VC
Augustana College	SD	36,500	VC
Aurora Univ	IL	33,228	C
Austin College	TX	45,875	HC
Austin Peay State Univ	TN	15,274	C
Averett Univ	VA	37,750	LC
Avila Univ	MO	26,900	C
Azusa Pacific Univ	CA	42,086	C
Baker Univ	KS	33,350	C+
Baldwin Wallace Univ	OH	38,318	C
Ball State Univ	IN	17,850	C
Bard College	NY	61,940	HC
Bard College at Simon's Rock	MA	61,749	HC+
Barnard College/Columbia Univ	NY	39,000	MC
Barry Univ	FL	38,190	C
Barton College	NC	27,660	LC
Bates College	ME	60,720	MC
Bay Path College	MA	34,565	C
Baylor Univ	TX	50,329	HC
Becker College	MA	41,420	C
Belhaven Univ	MS	27,170	C
Bellarmine Univ	KY	42,950	VC
Belmont Abbey College	NC	37,716	C
Belmont Univ	TN	39,190	VC+
Beloit College	WI	49,970	HC
Bemidji State Univ	MN	13,500	VC
Benedict College	SC	20,454	NC
Benedictine College	KS	29,180	VC
Benedictine Univ	IL	37,820	C
Bennett College for Women	NC	21,970	LC
Bennington College	VT	56,990	HC+
Berea College	KY	7,192	C
Berry College	GA	39,254	VC
Bethany College	KS	30,605	NC
Bethany College	WV	35,282	LC
Bethel College	IN	31,560	C
Bethel College	KS	32,160	C
Bethel Univ	MN	34,940	VC
Bethel Univ	TN	19,186	C
Bethune-Cookman Univ	FL	22,958	C
Binghamton Univ/The SUNY	NY	21,648	HC+
Biola Univ	CA	40,320	C+
Birmingham-Southern College	AL	44,168	VC+
Black Hills State Univ	SD	13,947	C
Blackburn College	IL	21,350	C
Bloomfield College	NJ	37,850	LC
Bloomsburg Univ of Pennsylvania	PA	13,598	C
Blue Mountain College	MS	15,634	LC
Bluefield College	VA	17,230	C+
Bluefield State College	WV	3,140	LC
Bluffton Univ	OH	38,948	C
Boise State Univ	ID	13,469	LC
Boston College	MA	60,622	MC
Boston Univ	MA	60,694	MC
Bowdoin College	ME	59,568	MC
Bowie State Univ	MD	23,990	LC
Bradley Univ	IL	31,874	VC
Brandeis Univ	MA		MC
Brenau Univ - Women's College	GA	26,650	LC
Brescia Univ	KY	26,140	VC+
Brewton-Parker College	GA	33,388	C
Briar Cliff Univ	IA	29,514	C
Bridgewater College	VA	41,450	C
Bridgewater State Univ	MA	18,752	C
Brigham Young Univ	UT	12,100	HC
Brigham Young Univ/Hawaii	HI	10,686	VC
Brown Univ	RI	59,428	MC
Bryan College	TN	24,194	C
Bryant Univ	RI	49,179	VC
Bryn Athyn College	PA	27,984	C
Bryn Mawr College	PA	59,890	MC
Bucknell Univ	PA	60,140	MC
Buena Vista Univ	IA	39,188	C
Buffalo State College / SUNY	NY	15,733	C+
Butler Univ	IN	47,572	VC+
Caldwell College	NJ	35,602	NC
Calif Baptist Univ	CA	38,792	C
Calif Inst of Technology	CA	54,045	MC
Calif Lutheran Univ	CA	49,540	C+
Calif Polytechnic State Univ	CA	19,847	HC
Calif State Polytechnic Univ, Pomona	CA	20,156	C
Cal State, Bakersfield	CA	8,000	C
Cal State, Chico	CA	20,158	C
Cal State, Dominguez Hills	CA	17,090	LC
Cal State, East Bay	CA	16,549	C
Cal State, Fresno	CA	17,405	C
Cal State, Fullerton	CA	25,188	C
Cal State, Long Beach	CA	17,502	C+
Cal State, Los Angeles	CA	17,186	LC
Cal State, Monterey Bay	CA	26,871	LC
Cal State, Northridge	CA	28,690	LC
Cal State, Sacramento	CA	16,200	C
Cal State, San Bernardino	CA	12,000	C
Cal State, San Marcos	CA	14,576	LC
Cal State, Stanislaus	CA	18,582	C
Calif Univ of Pennsylvania	PA	14,217	C
Calvin College	MI	39,120	VC
Cameron Univ	OK	10,004	LC
Campbell Univ	NC	37,570	VC
Campbellsville Univ	KY	27,720	C
Canisius College	NY	44,900	C
Capital Univ	OH	41,050	VC
Cardinal Stritch Univ	WI	24,054	C
Caribbean Univ	PR	10,375	
Carleton College	MN	60,102	MC
Carlow Univ	PA	30,272	C
Carnegie Mellon Univ	PA	51,260	MC
Carroll College	MT	28,000	C
Carroll Univ	WI	38,100	C
Carson-Newman Univ	TN	29,058	C+
Carthage College	WI	33,000	C
Case Western Reserve Univ	OH	56,534	MC
Castleton State College	VT	20,186	C
Catawba College	NC	37,240	LC
Cedar Crest College	PA	43,240	C
Cedarville Univ	OH	32,860	VC
Centenary College	NJ	38,618	C
Centenary College of Louisiana	LA	45,650	C+
Central College	IA	42,104	C+
Central Conn State Univ	CT	19,749	C
Central Methodist Univ	MO	28,240	VC
Central State Univ	OH	9,010	C
Central Univ of Bayamon	PR	3,350	
Central Washington Univ	WA	11,730	C
Centre College	KY	35,000	HC+
Chadron State College	NE	7,400	NC
Chaminade Univ of Honolulu	HI	31,664	LC
Chapman Univ	CA	58,347	VC+
Charleston Southern Univ	SC	22,420	C
Chatham Univ	PA	43,797	C
Chestnut Hill College	PA	42,110	LC
Cheyney Univ of Pennsylvania	PA	20,372	LC
Chicago State Univ	IL	5,482	C
Christian Brothers Univ	TN	31,670	HC
Christopher Newport Univ	VA	21,960	VC
Citadel, The	SC		C
CUNY/Brooklyn College	NY	5,884	C+
CUNY/City College	NY	20,319	HC+
Claflin Univ	SC	22,368	LC
Claremont McKenna College	CA	62,215	MC
Clarion Univ of Pennsylvania	PA	17,370	LC
Clark Atlanta Univ	GA	30,006	LC
Clark Univ	MA	47,020	HC+
Clarke Univ	IA	37,600	C
Clarkson Univ	NY	57,330	HC
Clearwater Christian College	FL	23,720	C
Clemson Univ	SC	19,136	HC
Cleveland State Univ	OH	21,776	C
Coastal Carolina Univ	SC	18,580	C
Coe College	IA	45,550	VC
Coker College	SC	32,256	LC
Colby College	ME	57,510	MC
Colby-Sawyer College	NH	50,790	C
Colgate Univ	NY	58,135	MC
College of Charleston	SC	22,145	VC
College of Mount St. Joseph	OH	33,880	C
College of Mount St. Vincent	NY	41,040	MC
College of New Jersey	NJ	25,376	NC
College of St. Benedict	MN	49,359	VC
College of St. Elizabeth	NJ	43,839	LC
College of St. Mary	NE	35,184	C
College of St. Scholastica	MN	41,440	C
College of Staten Island/The City of New Yok	NY	16,778	NC
College of the Holy Cross	MA	58,042	MC
College of the Ozarks	MO		VC
College of Wooster	OH	52,600	VC
Colo Christian Univ	CO	27,500	VC
Colo College	CO	57,162	MC
Colo Mesa Univ	CO	17,690	LC
Colo State Univ-Fort Collins	CO	20,385	VC
Colo State Univ-Pueblo	CO	16,183	C
Columbia College	MO	24,578	C
Columbia College	SC	27,882	C
Columbia Univ/City of New York	NY	61,116	MC
Columbia Univ/School of General Studies	NY	58,231	MC
Columbus State Univ	GA	13,176	C
Concord Univ	WV	13,102	C
Concordia College - Moorhead	MN	39,974	VC
Concordia College - New York	NY	39,035	LC
Concordia Univ	OR	35,000	C
Concordia Univ Irvine	CA	35,390	VC
Concordia Univ Nebr	NE	26,000	VC
Concordia Univ St. Paul	MN	28,250	C
Concordia Univ Wisc	WI	28,980	C
Concordia Univ, Ann Arbor	MI	27,220	VC
Concordia Univ, River Forest	IL	26,300	C
Conn College	CT	54,970	MC
Converse College	SC	37,130	C
Coppin State Univ	MD	16,227	VC
Cornell College	IA	44,930	VC
Cornell Univ	NY	60,964	MC
Cornerstone Univ and Grand Rapids Theological Seminary	MI	33,338	C
Covenant College	GA	38,990	VC+
Creighton Univ	NE	45,356	VC
Culver-Stockton College	MO	30,900	C
Cumberland Univ	TN	21,220	C
Curry College	MA	48,925	LC
Daemen College	NY	34,770	C
Dakota State Univ	SD	13,811	C
Dakota Wesleyan Univ	SD	23,000	C
Dallas Baptist Univ	TX	30,580	VC
Dartmouth College	NH	57,996	MC
Davidson College	NC	58,146	MC
Davis & Elkins College	WV	33,742	C
De Sales Univ	PA	43,970	C
Defiance College	OH	30,645	C
Delaware State Univ	DE	16,722	LC
Delaware Valley College	PA	29,944	C
Delta State Univ	MS	12,292	LC
Denison Univ	OH	54,670	HC+
DePaul Univ	IL	47,623	VC
DePauw Univ	IN	48,950	VC+
Dickinson College	PA	57,662	HC+
Dickinson State Univ	ND	11,900	NC
Dillard Univ	LA	20,940	VC
Doane College	NE	35,230	C
Dominican College	NY	31,270	LC
Dominican Univ	IL	37,628	C
Dominican Univ of Calif	CA	51,250	C
Dordt College	IA	34,160	C+
Dowling College	NY	25,000	C
Drake Univ	IA	41,516	VC+
Drew Univ/College of Liberal Arts	NJ	57,516	C
Drexel Univ	PA	61,418	VC+
Drury Univ	MO	31,909	VC
Duke Univ	NC	50,250	MC
Duquesne Univ	PA	43,720	VC
D'Youville College	NY	29,850	C
Earlham College	IN	51,470	HC
East Carolina Univ	NC	14,169	C
East Central Univ	OK	10,223	LC
East Stroudsburg Univ of Pennsylvania	PA	18,868	LC
East Tenn State Univ	TN	9,000	C
East Texas Baptist Univ	TX	31,577	LC
Eastern Conn State Univ	CT	20,584	C
Eastern Illinois Univ	IL	20,466	C
Eastern Kentucky Univ	KY	11,161	C
Eastern Mennonite Univ	VA	40,660	C
Eastern Mich Univ	MI	18,604	C
Eastern Nazarene College	MA	30,000	C
Eastern New Mexico Univ	NM	10,682	C
Eastern Oregon Univ	OR	10,400	C
Eastern Univ	PA	37,704	C
Eastern Washington Univ	WA		C
Eckerd College	FL	43,902	C
Edgewood College	WI	33,294	C
Edinboro Univ of Pennsylvania	PA	15,940	LC
Edward Waters College	FL	19,607	LC
Elizabeth City State Univ	NC	11,638	C
Elizabethtown College	PA	49,740	C
Elmhurst College	IL	43,336	C
Elmira College	NY	49,950	C+
Elms College	MA	23,900	LC
Emmanuel College	MA	47,985	VC
Emory and Henry College	VA	387,460	C
Emory Univ	GA	56,368	MC
Emporia State Univ	KS	12,897	C
Erskine College	SC	37,360	C
Eureka College	IL	19,280	C
Evangel Univ	MO	23,090	C
Excelsior College	NY	5,580	SP
Fairfield Univ	CT	56,960	VC
Fairleigh Dickinson Univ/ College at Florham	NJ	42,142	C
Fairleigh Dickinson Univ/ Metropolitan Campus	NJ	40,254	C
Fairmont State Univ	WV	12,098	LC
Farmingdale State College	NY	19,673	C
Faulkner Univ	AL	25,720	LC
Fayetteville State Univ	NC	10,816	C
Felician College	NJ	41,640	LC
Ferris State Univ	MI	20,047	C
Ferrum College	VA	27,740	LC
Fisk Univ	TN	19,830	C
Fitchburg State Univ	MA	18,173	C
Florida A&M Univ	FL	14,935	LC
Florida Atlantic Univ	FL	17,339	C
Florida Gulf Coast Univ	FL		C
Florida Inst of Technology	FL	48,290	VC
Florida International Univ	FL	17,747	C+
Florida Memorial Univ	FL	20,888	LC
Florida Southern College	FL	40,150	C+
Florida State Univ	FL	16,715	VC
Fontbonne Univ	MO	31,384	C
Fordham Univ	NY	61,588	HC+
Fort Hays State Univ	KS	11,354	C
Fort Lewis College	CO	15,513	C
Fort Valley State Univ	GA	11,200	VC
Framingham State Univ	MA	18,854	C
Francis Marion Univ	SC	16,464	LC
Franciscan Univ of Steubenville	OH	27,320	VC
Franklin and Marshall College	PA	60,799	MC
Franklin College	IN	36,585	C
Franklin Pierce Univ	NH	41,598	C
Freed-Hardeman Univ	TN	19,697	VC
Fresno Pacific Univ	CA	32,136	C
Friends Univ	KS	29,100	C
Frostburg State Univ	MD	15,264	LC
Furman Univ	SC	54,006	HC
Gallaudet Univ	DC	25,380	SP
Gannon Univ	PA	39,608	C
Gardner-Webb Univ	NC	34,375	C+
Geneva College	PA	27,280	C
George Fox Univ	OR	40,750	C+
George Mason Univ	VA	15,724	VC
George Washington Univ	DC	57,108	MC
Georgetown College	KY	41,440	C+
Georgetown Univ	DC	52,910	MC
Georgia College and State Univ	GA	18,900	C+
Georgia Inst of Technology	GA	21,828	MC
Georgia Regents Univ	GA		C
Georgia Southern Univ	GA	16,942	C
Georgia Southwestern State Univ	GA	13,246	C
Georgia State Univ	GA	15,582	VC
Georgian Court Univ	NJ	41,594	LC
Gettysburg College	PA	58,820	HC
Glenville State College	WV	11,348	NC
Gonzaga Univ	WA	46,441	HC
Gordon College	MA	44,320	VC
Goshen College	IN	35,900	VC
Goucher College	MD	52,040	VC+
Grace College and Seminary	IN	28,800	VC
Graceland Univ	IA	28,020	C
Grambling State Univ	LA	13,384	LC
Grand Canyon Univ	AZ	24,540	VC
Grand Valley State Univ	MI	17,998	C+
Grand View Univ	IA	31,050	C
Green Mountain College	VT	45,228	LC
Greensboro College	NC	28,740	LC
Greenville College	IL	27,012	C
Grinnell College	IA	53,654	MC
Grove City College	PA	24,022	VC
Guilford College	NC	42,800	C
Gustavus Adolphus College	MN	48,170	HC
Gwynedd-Mercy College	PA	33,560	C
Hamilton College	NY	55,620	MC
Hamline Univ	MN	45,678	VC
Hampden-Sydney College	VA	51,758	C
Hampshire College	MA	58,320	MC
Hampton Univ	VA	28,528	C
Hannibal-LaGrange Univ	MO	24,490	C
Hanover College	IN	43,073	C+
Harding Univ	AR	23,556	C
Hardin-Simmons Univ	TX	23,560	C
Harris-Stowe State Univ	MO	14,360	NC
Hartwick College	NY	51,270	C
Harvard College/Harvard Univ	MA	49,000	MC
Harvey Mudd College	CA	64,527	MC
Hastings College	NE	27,782	C+
Haverford College	PA	61,564	MC
Hawaii Pacific Univ	HI	34,360	C
Heidelberg Univ	OH	34,100	C
Henderson State Univ	AR	14,584	C
Hendrix College	AR	50,202	VC+
High Point Univ	NC	39,800	C
Hillsdale College	MI	32,866	MC

ST = STATE $IS = IN-STATE COSTS   SR = SELECTOR RATING

School	ST	$IS	SR
Hiram College	OH	37,300	VC
Hobart and William Smith Colleges	NY	60,034	HC+
Hofstra Univ	NY	51,810	VC+
Hollins Univ	VA	43,295	VC
Holy Family Univ	PA	40,030	LC
Holy Names Univ	CA	40,310	NC
Hood College	MD	45,730	C
Hope College	MI	38,650	VC
Houghton College	NY	36,808	C+
Houston Baptist Univ	TX	36,450	C
Howard Payne Univ	TX	17,115	C
Howard Univ	DC	13,646	C
Humboldt State Univ	CA	18,400	C
Hunter College	NY	14,429	VC
Huntingdon College	AL	33,100	C
Huntington Univ	IN	32,220	C+
Husson Univ	ME	24,194	LC
Huston-Tillotson Univ	TX	18,124	C+
Idaho State Univ	ID	12,307	C
Illinois College	IL	25,770	VC
Illinois Inst of Technology	IL	38,512	HC+
Illinois State Univ	IL	23,110	VC
Illinois Wesleyan Univ	IL	48,452	HC
Immaculata Univ	PA	43,000	C
Indiana State Univ	IN	16,000	C
Indiana Univ Kokomo	IN	6,811	LC
Indiana Univ of Pennsylvania	PA	20,846	LC
Indiana Univ South Bend	IN	15,501	C
Indiana Univ-Purdue Univ Fort Wayne	IN	15,521	C
Indiana Wesleyan Univ	IN	31,815	VC
Inter-American Univ of PR/ Aguadilla Campus	PR	5,578	
Inter-American Univ of PR/ Arecibo Campus	PR	3,350	
Inter-American Univ of PR/ Bayamon Univ College	PR	4,428	
Inter-American Univ of PR/ Fajardo Campus	PR	4,200	
Inter-American Univ of PR/ Metropolitan Campus	PR	4,320	
Inter-American Univ of PR/ Ponce	PR		
Inter-American Univ of PR/ San Germán	PR	6,720	
Iona College	NY	44,028	C
Iowa State Univ	IA	16,403	C
Iowa Wesleyan College	IA	30,850	LC
Ithaca College	NY	53,864	HC
Jackson State Univ	MS	13,512	LC
Jacksonville State Univ	AL	12,480	LC
Jacksonville Univ	FL	37,780	C
James Madison Univ	VA	18,049	VC
Jarvis Christian College	TX	19,552	NC
John Brown Univ	AR	32,056	VC+
John Carroll Univ	OH	46,300	C+
Johns Hopkins Univ	MD	47,492	MC
Johnson C. Smith Univ	NC	25,336	LC
Johnson State College	VT	16,721	C
Judson College	AL	26,794	C
Judson Univ	IL	25,130	C
Juniata College	PA	49,340	VC
Kalamazoo College	MI	49,740	HC
Kansas State Univ	KS	15,497	VC
Kansas Wesleyan Univ	KS	32,000	C
Kean Univ	NJ	23,444	C
Keene State College	NH	23,232	LC
Kennesaw State Univ	GA		C
Kent State Univ	OH	19,920	C
Kentucky State Univ	KY	11,000	LC
Kentucky Wesleyan College	KY	27,440	C
Kenyon College	OH	58,890	MC
Keuka College	NY	30,300	C
Keystone College	PA	28,680	LC
King Univ	TN	33,140	C
King's College	PA	43,502	C
Knox College	IL	44,865	VC+
Kutztown Univ of Pennsylvania	PA	16,909	LC
La Roche College	PA	35,824	LC
La Salle Univ	PA	50,270	C
La Sierra Univ	CA	35,694	VC
Lafayette College	PA	59,155	HC+
LaGrange College	GA	37,670	C
Lake Erie College	OH	37,266	C
Lake Forest College	IL	50,652	VC
Lake Superior State Univ	MI	18,121	C
Lakeland College	WI	22,990	C
Lamar Univ	TX	6,820	LC
Lander Univ	SC	22,514	C+
Lane College	TN	11,212	C
Langston Univ	OK	3,000	C
Lawrence Univ	WI	46,371	HC
Le Moyne College	NY	43,470	C
Lebanon Valley College	PA	38,570	C
Lee Univ	TN	18,690	C+
Lees-McRae College	NC	35,984	C
Lehigh Univ	PA	56,770	HC
Lehman College/The CUNY	NY	5,778	LC
LeMoyne-Owen College	TN	13,100	C
Lenoir-Rhyne College	NC	35,984	C
LeTourneau Univ	TX	36,210	VC
Lewis & Clark College	OR	54,382	MC
Lewis Univ	IL	23,050	C
Lewis-Clark State College	ID	6,990	C
Liberty Univ	VA	19,101	C
Limestone College	SC	30,800	C
Lincoln Memorial Univ	TN	18,144	C
Lincoln Univ	MO	12,904	NC
Lindenwood Univ	MO	20,750	C
Lindsey Wilson College	KY	31,220	C
Linfield College-McMinnville Campus	OR	47,676	C
Lipscomb Univ	TN	37,490	VC
LIU Brooklyn	NY	47,182	LC
LIU Post	NY	47,660	C
Livingstone College	NC	17,815	LC
Lock Haven Univ of Pennsylvania	PA	18,028	LC
Longwood Univ	VA	20,924	C
Loras College	IA	37,432	VC
Louisiana College	LA	15,746	C
Louisiana State Univ	LA	18,677	C+
Louisiana State Univ in Shreveport	LA	5,606	C
Louisiana Tech Univ	LA	11,302	C
Lourdes Univ	OH	26,055	LC
Loyola Marymount Univ	CA	54,649	VC+
Loyola Univ Chicago	IL	51,646	VC+
Loyola Univ Maryland	MD	56,880	VC+
Loyola Univ New Orleans	LA	46,581	VC
Lubbock Christian Univ	TX	26,308	C
Luther College	IA	45,720	C+
Lycoming College	PA	45,379	C
Lynchburg College	VA	42,645	C
Lynn Univ	FL	43,500	LC
Lyon College	AR	32,090	C+
Macalester College	MN	57,691	MC
MacMurray College	IL	20,755	C
Madonna Univ	MI	24,540	VC
Malone Univ	OH	35,364	C
Manchester Univ	IN	35,070	C
Manhattan College	NY	49,588	C+
Manhattanville College	NY	50,740	VC
Mansfield Univ	PA	19,468	LC
Marian Univ	IN	38,540	C
Marian Univ	WI	32,420	C
Marietta College	OH	42,135	C+
Marist College	NY	35,500	C
Marlboro College	VT	35,980	VC
Marquette Univ	WI	46,930	VC+
Mars Hill Univ	NC	22,950	LC
Marshall Univ	WV	14,820	C
Martin Univ	IN	11,000	SP
Mary Baldwin College	VA	38,245	C
Marygrove College	MI	28,926	C
Marymount Manhattan College	NY	40,118	VC
Marymount Univ	VA	39,480	C
Maryville College	TN	33,150	C+
Maryville Univ of St. Louis	MO	35,856	VC
Marywood Univ	PA	45,595	C
Mass College of Liberal Arts	MA	18,613	C
Mass Inst of Technology	MA	58,240	MC
Mayville State Univ	ND	11,401	NC
McDaniel College	MD	47,450	VC
McKendree Univ	IL	29,920	C+
McMurry Univ	TX	25,962	C
McNeese State Univ	LA	2,649	C
McPherson College	KS	28,138	C
Medaille College	NY	35,112	C
Megar Evers College/The CUNY	NY	4,920	NC
Mercer Univ	GA	44,201	VC
Mercy College	NY	30,456	C
Mercyhurst Univ	PA	40,700	C
Meredith College	NC	31,420	C
Merrimack College	MA	44,215	C
Messiah College	PA	40,690	C+
Methodist Univ	NC	37,185	C
Metropolitan State Univ	MN	5,923	
Metropolitan State Univ of Denver	CO	4,835	LC
Mich State Univ	MI	22,450	VC
Mich Tech Univ	MI	23,556	HC
MidAmerica Nazarene Univ	KS	28,000	C
Middle Tenn State Univ	TN	8,650	C
Middlebury College	VT	59,160	MC
Midland Univ	NE	34,000	C
Midway College	KY	20,150	LC
Midwestern State Univ	TX	9,722	C
Miles College	AL	11,164	NC
Millersville Univ of Pennsylvania	PA	21,648	C
Milligan College	TN	27,510	C
Millikin Univ	IL	38,940	C
Mills College	CA	54,119	VC
Millsaps College	MS	43,888	VC+
Minn State Univ, Mankato	MN	15,616	C
Minn State Univ, Moorhead	MN	13,392	VC
Minot State Univ	ND	10,915	C
Misericordia Univ	PA	41,060	C
Miss College	MS	21,998	C
Miss State Univ	MS	14,750	C
Miss Univ for Women	MS	7,400	C
Miss Valley State Univ	MS	9,706	LC
Missouri Baptist Univ	MO	31,830	C
Missouri State Univ	MO	13,996	C+
Missouri Univ of Science and Technology	MO	18,655	VC+
Missouri Valley College	MO	22,200	C
Missouri Western State Univ	MO	12,260	NC
Molloy College	NY	40,440	C
Monmouth College	IL	40,850	C
Monmouth Univ	NJ	44,108	C
Montana State Univ	MT	14,068	C
Montana State Univ-Billings	MT	12,425	LC
Montana State Univ-Northern	MT	12,500	NC
Montana Tech of The Univ of Montana	MT	14,650	VC
Montclair State Univ	NJ	22,614	C
Moravian College	PA	36,381	VC
Morehead State Univ	KY	10,900	C
Morehouse College	GA	39,412	C
Morgan State Univ	MD	14,500	C
Morningside College	IA	35,430	C
Morris College	SC	16,310	LC
Mount Aloysius College	PA	29,976	C
Mount Holyoke College	MA	55,146	MC
Mount Marty College	SD	29,638	C
Mount Mary Univ	WI	33,590	LC
Mount Mercy Univ	IA	35,320	C
Mount St. Mary College	NY	41,138	C
Mount St. Mary's Univ	MD	47,996	C
Mount St. Mary's College - Chalon Campus	CA	43,897	VC+
Mount Vernon Nazarene Univ	OH	29,590	C
Muhlenberg College	PA	52,837	HC
Murray State Univ	KY	15,304	C
Muskingum Univ	OH	30,502	C
National Louis Univ	IL	16,915	LC
Nazareth College of Rochester	NY	43,028	C+
Nebr Wesleyan Univ	NE	29,774	C+
Neumann Univ	PA	31,078	LC
New College of Florida	FL	14,504	MC
New England College	NH	45,930	LC
New Jersey City Univ	NJ	21,456	LC
New Jersey Inst of Technology	NJ	26,490	C
New Mexico Highlands Univ	NM	11,904	NC
New Mexico Inst of Mining and Technology	NM	13,592	VC
New Mexico State Univ	NM	14,050	C
New York Univ	NY	61,470	MC
Newberry College	SC	26,850	LC
Newman Univ	KS	30,380	C+
Niagara Univ	NY	41,010	C
Nicholls State Univ	LA	7,095	C
Norfolk State Univ	VA	10,531	LC
N Agricultural and Technical State Univ	NC	13,365	LC
N Car Central Univ	NC	9,000	C
N Car State Univ	NC	16,202	HC
N Car Wesleyan College	NC	29,440	C
North Central College	IL	38,343	VC
N Dak State Univ	ND		C
North Park Univ	IL	30,130	C
Northeastern Illinois Univ	IL	10,318	LC
Northeastern State Univ	OK	8,615	VC
Northeastern Univ	MA	55,296	MC
Northern Arizona Univ	AZ	19,010	C
Northern Illinois Univ	IL	19,768	C
Northern Kentucky Univ	KY	21,134	C
Northern Mich Univ	MI	18,278	C
Northern State Univ - Aberdeen	SD	14,505	C
Northland College	WI	26,680	C
Northwest Missouri State Univ	MO	17,347	C
Northwest Nazarene Univ	ID	34,000	C
Northwestern College	MN	24,000	C
Northwestern College of Iowa	IA	36,240	VC
Northwestern Okla State Univ	OK	7,275	NC
Northwestern State Univ of Louisiana	LA	14,368	C
Northwestern Univ	IL	61,640	MC
Norwich Univ	VT	28,212	C
Notre Dame College	OH	34,942	VC
Notre Dame de Namur Univ	CA	44,236	LC
Notre Dame of Maryland Univ	MD	27,700	VC
Oakland City Univ	IN	24,500	NC
Oakland Univ	MI	19,391	C
Oakwood Univ	AL	25,529	NC
Oberlin College	OH	61,788	MC
Occidental College	CA	60,972	MC
Oglethorpe Univ	GA	44,200	C+
Ohio Dominican Univ	OH	38,380	C+
Ohio Northern Univ	OH	42,075	C
Ohio State Univ at Lima	OH	7,140	C
Ohio Univ	OH	21,080	C
Ohio Wesleyan Univ	OH	49,460	C+
Okla Baptist Univ	OK	28,202	C
Okla Christian Univ	OK	25,870	VC
Okla Panhandle State Univ	OK	8,996	C
Okla State Univ	OK	14,310	VC
Okla Wesleyan Univ	OK	21,300	C
Old Dominion Univ	VA	19,483	LC
Olivet College	MI	19,984	C
Olivet Nazarene Univ	IL	29,990	C
Oral Roberts Univ	OK	31,734	C
Oregon State Univ	OR	20,273	VC
Oswego / SUNY	NY	20,009	VC
Ottawa Univ	KS	15,000	VC
Ouachita Baptist Univ	AR	30,220	VC
Our Lady of Holy Cross College	LA	8,090	C
Our Lady of the Lake Univ	TX	22,430	LC
Pace Univ	NY	53,367	C
Pacific Lutheran Univ	WA	46,760	C+
Pacific Union College	CA	28,150	VC
Pacific Univ	OR	49,626	C+
Paine College	GA	19,826	LC
Palm Beach Atlantic Univ	FL	34,874	C+
Park Univ	MO	17,525	C
Penn State Erie/The Behrend College	PA	16,256	C
Penn State Univ/Altoona	PA	11,464	C
Pepperdine Univ	CA	55,372	HC+
Peru State College	NE	8,600	NC
Pfeiffer Univ	NC	33,700	C
Philadelphia Univ	PA	44,160	C
Philander Smith College	AR	19,760	LC
Piedmont College	GA	30,136	C
Pine Manor College	MA	32,659	LC
Pittsburg State Univ	KS	12,032	C
Pitzer College	CA	54,988	MC
Plymouth State Univ	NH	23,148	LC
Point Loma Nazarene Univ	CA	41,006	C+
Point Park Univ	PA	36,390	C
Pomona College	CA	57,680	MC
Pontifical Catholic Univ of PR	PR	7,310	
Portland State Univ	OR	18,672	C
Prairie View A&M Univ	TX	15,205	LC
Presbyterian College	SC	42,678	C+
Prescott College	AZ	33,284	C
Presentation College	SD	14,800	LC
Principia College	IL	35,140	C+
Providence College	RI	57,383	VC
Purdue Univ/Calumet	IN	14,336	C
Purdue Univ/West Lafayette	IN	20,024	NC
Queens College/The CUNY	NY	17,107	VC
Queens Univ of Charlotte	NC	39,543	C+
Quincy Univ	IL	34,980	LC
Quinnipiac Univ	CT	55,160	VC
Radford Univ	VA	17,766	LC
Ramapo College of New Jersey	NJ	24,938	C
Randolph College	VA	45,660	VC
Randolph-Macon College	VA	49,869	C+
Reed College	OR	57,780	MC
Regis College	MA	47,565	C
Regis Univ	CO	41,318	C
Reinhardt College	GA	25,000	C
Rensselaer Polytechnic Inst	NY	61,529	MC
Rhode Island College	RI	17,694	LC
Rhodes College	TN	51,900	HC+
Rice Univ	TX	43,288	MC
Richard Stockton College of New Jersey	NJ	20,000	VC
Rider Univ	NJ	45,720	C
Ripon College	WI	36,959	C+
Rivier Univ	NH	35,000	C
Roanoke College	VA	49,976	C
Robert Morris Univ	PA	37,864	C
Roberts Wesleyan College	NY	38,306	C+
Rochester Inst of Technology	NY	42,450	VC
Rockford College	IL	31,000	C
Rockhurst Univ	MO	20,625	C
Roger Williams Univ	RI	46,296	VC
Rollins College	FL	52,370	HC
Roosevelt Univ	IL	22,605	VC
Rose-Hulman Inst of Technology	IN	53,340	MC
Rosemont College	PA	42,350	C
Rowan Univ	NJ	24,022	VC+
Russell Sage College	NY	39,370	C
Rust College	MS	10,600	C
Rutgers, The State Univ of New Jersey/Camden Campus	NJ	25,121	C
Rutgers, The State Univ of New Jersey/New Brunswick	NJ	25,562	VC
Rutgers, The State Univ of New Jersey/Newark Campus	NJ	258,806	C
Sacred Heart Univ	CT	49,264	VC
Saginaw Valley State Univ	MI	17,369	C
St. Anselm College	NH	49,376	VC
St. Augustine's Univ	NC	14,000	C
St. Francis Univ	PA	30,029	LC
St. John's Univ	MN	47,984	C
St. Joseph's College	IN	36,500	C
St. Joseph's College of Maine	ME	31,580	C
St. Joseph's Univ	PA	55,006	VC
St. Leo Univ	FL	30,340	C
St. Louis Univ	MO	48,346	VC
St. Martin's Univ	WA	41,678	C
St. Mary-of-the-Woods College	IN	37,722	C
St. Mary's College	IN	45,160	C+
St. Mary's College of Calif	CA	53,550	C
St. Mary's College	TX	33,854	C
St. Mary's Univ of Minn	MN	38,280	C
St. Michael's College	VT	49,975	VC
St. Paul's College	VA	16,030	NC
St. Peter's Univ	NJ	44,240	C
St. Vincent College	PA	40,244	C
St. Xavier Univ	IL	32,840	C

ST = STATE $IS = IN-STATE COSTS   SR = SELECTOR RATING

School	ST	$IS	SR
Salem College	NC	29,326	VC
Salem International Univ	WV	21,090	LC
Salem State Univ	MA	13,161	LC
Salisbury Univ	MD	19,180	VC
Salve Regina Univ	RI	48,550	VC
Sam Houston State Univ	TX	17,082	C
Samford Univ	AL	37,060	C+
San Diego Christian College	CA	31,012	C
San Diego State Univ	CA	21,611	C+
San Francisco State Univ	CA	18,514	C
San Jose State Univ	CA	19,133	LC
Sarah Lawrence College	NY	48,000	HC
Savannah State Univ	GA	13,156	C
Schreiner Univ	TX	32,734	LC
Scripps College	CA	61,940	MC
Seattle Pacific Univ	WA	41,559	VC+
Seattle Univ	WA	49,035	VC+
Seton Hall Univ	NJ	45,902	C
Seton Hill Univ	PA	35,172	C
Sewanee: The Univ of the South	TN	47,700	HC+
Shaw Univ	NC	15,488	C
Shawnee State Univ	OH	16,916	C
Shenandoah Univ	VA	39,916	C
Shepherd Univ	WV	15,875	C
Shippensburg Univ of Pennsylvania	PA	20,934	C
Shorter Univ	GA	30,650	LC
Siena College	NY	43,863	VC
Siena Heights Univ	MI	32,040	C
Silver Lake College	WI	22,600	C
Simmons College	MA	49,966	VC
Simpson College	IA	36,086	C+
Simpson Univ	CA	28,900	C
Skidmore College	NY	59,942	HC
Slippery Rock Univ of Pennsylvania	PA	10,360	C
Smith College	MA	59,674	MC
Sonoma State Univ	CA	20,541	C
S Car State Univ	SC	6,700	LC
S Dak State Univ	SD	14,296	C
Southeastern Louisiana Univ	LA	13,325	C
Southeastern Okla State Univ	OK	7,966	LC
Southeastern Univ	FL	27,201	C
Southern Adventist Univ	TN	26,190	C
Southern Arkansas Univ	AR	14,316	C
Southern Conn State Univ	CT	18,033	LC
Southern Illinois Univ Carbondale	IL	21,942	C
Southern Illinois Univ Edwardsville	IL	17,532	C
Southern Methodist Univ	TX	60,585	MC
Southern Nazarene Univ	OK	24,354	C
Southern Oregon Univ	OR	17,874	C
Southern Polytechnic State Univ	GA	13,958	C
Southern Univ and A&M College	LA	9,761	LC
Southern Univ at New Orleans	LA	2,963	NC
Southern Wesleyan Univ	SC	25,600	C
Southwest Baptist Univ	MO	24,710	C
Southwest Minn State Univ	MN	14,000	C
Southwestern Adventist Univ	TX	23,026	LC
Southwestern College	KS	29,270	C
Southwestern Okla State Univ	OK	9,160	C
Southwestern Univ	TX	45,660	VC
Spalding Univ	KY	32,287	LC
Spelman College	GA	24,650	C
Spring Arbor Univ	MI	26,740	C
Spring Hill College	AL	44,164	VC
Springfield College	MA	25,000	C
St. Ambrose Univ	IA	30,845	C
St. Andrews Univ	NC	32,050	LC
St. Bonaventure Univ	NY	41,575	C
St. Catherine Univ	MN	37,782	C+
St. Cloud State Univ	MN	10,600	C
St. Edward's Univ	TX	47,784	C
St. Francis College	NY	34,200	C
St. John Fisher College	NY	40,708	C+
St. John's Univ	NY	55,070	C+
St. Joseph's College, New York/Brooklyn Campus	NY	22,630	C
St. Joseph's College, New York/Suffolk Campus	NY	22,630	C
St. Lawrence Univ	NY	59,972	VC
St. Mary's College of Maryland	MD	25,754	VC
St. Norbert College	WI	41,478	VC
St. Olaf College	MN	51,200	HC+
St. Thomas Univ	FL	32,310	C
Stanford Univ	CA	58,388	MC
SUNY / College of Environmental Science and Forestry	NY	18,351	VC
SUNY at Purchase	NY	16,951	C
Stephen F. Austin State Univ	TX	14,668	C
Stephens College	MO	38,042	VC
Sterling College	KS	27,216	C
Stetson Univ	FL	51,516	VC
Stevenson Univ	MD	41,470	C
Stillman College	AL	19,470	C
Stonehill College	MA	46,780	NC
Stony Brook Univ / SUNY	NY	20,078	HC+
Suffolk Univ	MA	47,298	C
Sul Ross State Univ	TX	13,410	LC
SUNY College at Geneseo	NY	18,670	HC
SUNY College at Old Westbury	NY	16,324	C
SUNY Cortland/The SUNY	NY	19,759	C+
SUNY Fredonia/The SUNY at Fredonia	NY	19,840	VC
SUNY New Paltz	NY	14,348	C
SUNY Oneonta / SUNY	NY	16,919	C+
SUNY Plattsburgh / SUNY	NY	18,083	C
Susquehanna Univ	PA	51,150	C
Swarthmore College	PA	57,870	MC
Syracuse Univ	NY	56,346	VC
Tabor College	KS	29,010	C
Talladega College	AL	17,996	C
Tarleton State Univ	TX	13,489	LC
Taylor Univ	IN	37,821	VC+
Temple Univ	PA	24,392	VC
Tenn State Univ	TN	9,048	C
Tenn Tech Univ	TN	11,310	C
Tenn Wesleyan College	TN	21,250	C
Texas A&M Univ	TX	19,207	VC
Texas A&M Univ at Commerce	TX	10,496	C
Texas A&M Univ at Corpus Christi	TX	11,544	LC
Texas A&M Univ at Galveston	TX	11,258	C
Texas A&M Univ at Kingsville	TX	7,500	LC
Texas Christian Univ	TX	49,980	HC
Texas Lutheran Univ	TX	36,040	C
Texas Southern Univ	TX	18,212	LC
Texas State Univ	TX	17,128	C
Texas Tech Univ	TX	14,243	C
Texas Wesleyan Univ	TX	31,382	C
Texas Woman's Univ	TX	13,633	LC
The Catholic Univ of America	DC	52,852	VC
The College of Idaho	ID	31,277	C+
The College of New Rochelle	NY	33,600	VC
The College of St. Rose	NY	26,750	C
The Lincoln Univ	PA	15,154	LC
The Masters College	CA	38,160	C+
Ohio State Univ-Columbus Campus	OH	19,887	HC+
The Pennsylvania State Univ - Univ Park	PA	28,022	VC+
The SUNY at Potsdam	NY	18,473	C
The SUNY/College at Brockport	NY	19,002	C
The Univ of Memphis	TN	15,094	C
The Univ of N Car at Greensboro	NC	12,848	C
The Univ of N Car at Pembroke	NC	13,388	LC
The Univ of Tenn at Chattanooga	TN	16,883	C
The Univ of Utah	UT	16,463	VC
The Univ of Virginia's College at Wise	VA	11,076	C
Thiel College	PA	38,728	LC
Thomas More College	KY	34,760	C
Thomas Univ	GA	11,520	NC
Toccoa Falls College	GA	23,210	LC
Tougaloo College	MS	15,275	NC
Touro College	NY	27,959	VC
Towson Univ	MD	16,000	VC
Transylvania Univ	KY	42,660	VC+
Trevecca Nazarene Univ	TN	31,186	C
Trine Univ	IN	39,400	HC+
Trinity Christian College	IL	28,869	C
Trinity College	CT		HC+
Trinity International Univ	IL	31,070	VC
Trinity Univ	TX	48,150	HC+
Trinity Washington Univ	DC	30,250	C+
Troy Univ	AL	10,650	C
Truman State Univ	MO	15,541	HC
Tufts Univ	MA	58,780	MC
Tusculum College	TN	24,295	C
Tuskegee Univ	AL	26,750	C
Union College	KY	29,955	C
Union College	NE	23,270	C
Union College	NY	60,240	MC
Union Univ	TN	28,260	C
United States Air Force Academy	CO		MC
Unity College	ME	34,054	C
Universidad Adventista de las Antillas	PR	7,360	
Universidad del Turabo	PR	4,110	
Univ at Albany / SUNY	NY	18,674	VC
Univ at Buffalo / The SUNY	NY	20,283	VC
Univ of Akron	OH	20,436	C
Univ of Alabama at Birmingham	AL	18,484	C+
Univ of Alabama at Tuscaloosa	AL	17,164	C
Univ of Alabama in Huntsville	AL	17,591	VC+
Univ of Alaska Anchorage	AK	16,673	NC
Univ of Alaska Fairbanks	AK	15,130	C
Univ of Alaska Southeast	AK	11,493	C
Univ of Arizona	AZ	20,657	C
Univ of Arkansas at Fayetteville	AR	18,352	C
Univ of Arkansas at Little Rock	AR	17,609	LC
Univ of Arkansas at Monticello	AR	12,076	NC
Univ of Arkansas at Pine Bluff	AR	13,378	C
Univ of Bridgeport	CT	39,030	LC
Univ of Calif at Berkeley	CA	23,322	MC
Univ of Calif at Davis	CA		HC
Univ of Calif at Irvine	CA	25,961	VC
Univ of Calif at Los Angeles	CA	25,686	MC
Univ of Calif at Riverside	CA	27,204	C+
Univ of Calif at San Diego	CA	21,000	VC
Univ of Calif at Santa Barbara	CA	27,551	HC
Univ of Calif at Santa Cruz	CA	27,807	C+
Univ of Central Arkansas	AR	13,667	VC
Univ of Central Florida	FL	15,668	VC+
Univ of Central Missouri	MO	14,605	C
Univ of Central Okla	OK	12,293	C
Univ of Charleston	WV	14,600	C
Univ of Chicago	IL	55,416	MC
Univ of Cincinnati	OH	21,506	VC
Univ of Colo at Colo Springs	CO	15,000	VC
Univ of Colo Denver	CO	17,904	C
Univ of Conn	CT	24,706	HC
Univ of Dallas	TX	45,500	VC+
Univ of Dayton	OH	49,070	VC
Univ of Delaware	DE	23,612	VC
Univ of Denver	CO	51,787	VC+
Univ of Detroit Mercy	MI	30,450	VC
Univ of Dubuque	IA	30,200	C
Univ of Evansville	IN	42,656	VC+
Univ of Findlay	OH	31,916	C
Univ of Georgia	GA	20,082	VC
Univ of Great Falls	MT	27,970	C
Univ of Hartford	CT	42,674	C
Univ of Hawaii at Hilo	HI	23,066	C
Univ of Hawaii at Manoa	HI	19,379	C
Univ of Houston	TX	19,796	VC
Univ of Houston-Downtown	TX	15,170	LC
Univ of Idaho	ID	14,558	C
Univ of Illinois at Chicago	IL	24,505	VC
Univ of Illinois at Urbana-Champaign	IL	26,450	HC
Univ of Indianapolis	IN	31,740	LC
Univ of Iowa	IA	17,693	VC
Univ of Jamestown	ND	24,738	C
Univ of Kansas	KS	17,603	C+
Univ of Kentucky	KY	19,868	C
Univ of La Verne	CA	47,010	C
Univ of Louisiana at Monroe	LA	12,998	C
Univ of Louisville	KY	17,946	C
Univ of Maine	ME	19,902	C+
Univ of Maine at Augusta	ME	6,855	C
Univ of Maine at Farmington	ME	18,187	LC
Univ of Maine at Fort Kent	ME	15,195	LC
Univ of Maine at Machias	ME	10,523	C
Univ of Maine at Presque Isle	ME	15,011	LC
Univ of Mary	ND	16,714	C
Univ of Mary Hardin-Baylor	TX	31,950	C+
Univ of Mary Washington	VA	19,484	VC
Univ of Maryland - College Park	MD	20,060	HC
Univ of Maryland/Baltimore County	MD	18,000	C
Univ of Maryland/Eastern Shore	MD	14,000	C
Univ of Mass Amherst	MA	24,215	VC+
Univ of Mass Boston	MA	23,066	VC
Univ of Mass Dartmouth	MA	22,223	C
Univ of Mass Lowell	MA	19,316	C
Univ of Mich/Ann Arbor	MI	22,120	MC
Univ of Mich/Dearborn	MI	9,885	VC
Univ of Mich-Flint	MI	17,547	C+
Univ of Minn Crookston	MN	17,834	C
Univ of Minn/Duluth	MN	19,806	C
Univ of Minn/Morris	MN	17,150	VC
Univ of Minn/Twin Cities	MN		HC
Univ of Miss	MS	16,704	C
Univ of Missouri/Columbia	MO	18,201	MC
Univ of Missouri-Kansas City	MO	19,603	C
Univ of Missouri-St. Louis	MO		VC
Univ of Mobile	AL	28,935	VC
Univ of Montana	MT	14,105	C
Univ of Montevallo	AL	17,060	VC
Univ of Mount Olive	NC	18,426	C
Univ of Mount Union	OH	35,130	C
Univ of Nebr - Lincoln	NE	18,031	VC
Univ of Nebr at Kearney	NE	14,855	LC
Univ of Nebr at Omaha	NE	12,700	C
Univ of Nevada, Las Vegas	NV	17,303	C
Univ of Nevada/Reno	NV	17,507	C
Univ of New England	ME	46,750	VC
Univ of New Hampshire	NH	26,912	C
Univ of New Haven	CT	48,940	VC
Univ of New Mexico	NM	15,300	C
Univ of New Orleans	LA	9,224	C
Univ of North Alabama	AL	9,960	C
Univ of N Car at Asheville	NC	13,500	VC
Univ of N Car at Chapel Hill	NC	18,928	MC
Univ of N Car at Charlotte	NC	15,547	C
Univ of N Car at Wilmington	NC	13,572	VC
Univ of N Dak	ND	14,551	C
Univ of North Florida	FL	15,905	VC
Univ of North Georgia	GA	8,500	C
Univ of North Texas	TX	15,628	C
Univ of Northern Colo	CO	18,446	C
Univ of Northern Iowa	IA	15,795	C
Univ of Notre Dame	IN	57,117	MC
Univ of Oregon	OR	21,360	C+
Univ of Pennsylvania	PA	61,132	MC
Univ of Pikeville	KY	25,500	NC
Univ of Pittsburgh at Bradford	PA	21,802	C
Univ of Pittsburgh at Greensburg	PA	17,640	C
Univ of Pittsburgh at Johnstown	PA	20,862	LC
Univ of Pittsburgh at Pittsburgh	PA	28,572	HC+
Univ of Portland	OR	49,964	VC
Univ of PR Recinto de Rio Piedras	PR	5,750	
Univ of PR/Cayey	PR	1,504	
Univ of PR/Humacao	PR	1,877	
Univ of PR/Mayaguez	PR	1,520	
Univ of Puget Sound	WA	54,608	HC
Univ of Redlands	CA	40,500	VC
Univ of Rio Grande	OH	8,750	NC
Univ of Rochester	NY	60,668	MC
Univ of St. Francis	IN	29,810	C
Univ of St. Joseph	CT	45,630	C
Univ of St. Mary	KS	28,400	C+
Univ of San Diego	CA	54,818	HC+
Univ of San Francisco	CA	54,770	VC
Univ of Science and Arts of Okla	OK	10,560	VC
Univ of Scranton	PA	51,940	VC
Univ of Sioux Falls	SD	22,990	C
Univ of South Alabama	AL	13,510	C
Univ of S Car Aiken	SC	16,712	C
Univ of S Car at Columbia	SC	19,725	VC+
Univ of S Car Upstate	SC	18,200	LC
Univ of S Dak	SD	15,111	C
Univ of South Florida/St. Petersburg	FL	12,769	C
Univ of South Florida/Tampa	FL	13,000	C
Univ of Southern Calif	CA	56,903	MC
Univ of Southern Indiana	IN	14,885	C
Univ of Southern Maine	ME	16,576	C
Univ of Southern Miss	MS	13,170	C
Univ of St. Francis	IL	37,560	C
Univ of St. Thomas - Houston	TX	37,690	C
Univ of Tampa	FL	35,160	VC
Univ of Tenn at Knoxville	TN	20,364	VC+
Univ of Tenn at Martin	TN	13,734	C
Univ of Texas - Pan American	TX	11,125	LC
Univ of Texas at Arlington	TX	10,908	LC
Univ of Texas at Austin	TX	44,074	HC
Univ of Texas at Dallas	TX	21,348	HC+
Univ of Texas at El Paso	TX	8,764	NC
Univ of Texas at San Antonio	TX	18,372	C
Univ of the Cumberlands	KY	27,500	C
Univ of the District of Columbia	DC	7,244	LC
Univ of the Incarnate Word	TX	37,316	LC
Univ of the Ozarks	AR	31,440	C
Univ of the Pacific	CA	52,146	VC
Univ of the Sacred Heart	PR	5,590	
Univ of the Sciences	PA	48,320	VC+
Univ of the Southwest	NM	15,000	C
Univ of Toledo	OH	18,464	C
Univ of Tulsa	OK	46,331	MC
Univ of Vermont	VT	27,006	VC+
Univ of Virginia	VA	23,050	MC
Univ of Washington	WA	14,722	VC
Univ of West Alabama	AL	14,274	C
Univ of West Florida	FL	14,656	VC
Univ of West Georgia	GA	15,488	LC
Univ of Wisc Whitewater	WI	13,314	C
Univ of Wisc/Eau Claire	WI	15,730	VC
Univ of Wisc/Green Bay	WI	19,074	C
Univ of Wisc/La Crosse	WI	9,304	VC
Univ of Wisc/Madison	WI	18,757	HC+
Univ of Wisc/Oshkosh	WI	10,426	LC
Univ of Wisc/Parkside	WI	10,181	LC
Univ of Wisc/Platteville	WI	14,564	C
Univ of Wisc/River Falls	WI	9,722	LC
Univ of Wisc/Stevens Point	WI	14,043	C
Univ of Wisc/Superior	WI	14,314	C
Univ of Wisc-Milwaukee	WI	18,436	C
Upper Iowa Univ	IA	30,426	NC
Ursinus College	PA	57,580	VC
Ursuline College	OH	33,198	LC
Utah State Univ	UT	12,044	C
Utica College	NY	45,670	C
Valley City State Univ	ND	12,286	LC
Valparaiso Univ	IN	44,940	VC+
Vanderbilt Univ	TN	58,220	MC
Vanguard Univ of Southern Calif	CA	35,833	VC
Vassar College	NY	61,140	MC
Villanova Univ	PA	58,394	MC
Virginia Commonwealth Univ	VA	21,716	C
Virginia Military Inst	VA	16,156	C
Virginia Polytechnic Inst and State Univ	VA	14,629	HC
Virginia State Univ	VA	11,318	C+
Virginia Union Univ	VA	18,432	C
Virginia Wesleyan College	VA	28,433	LC

ST = STATE $IS = IN-STATE COSTS   SR = SELECTOR RATING

School	ST	$IS	SR
Viterbo Univ	WI	30,070	C
Voorhees College	SC	18,126	C
Wabash College	IN	46,850	C+
Wagner College	NY	48,600	C
Wake Forest Univ	NC	58,838	MC
Walla Walla Univ	WA	26,256	NC
Walsh Univ	OH	35,100	C
Warner Pacific College	OR	25,550	C
Warner Univ	FL	18,000	C
Warren Wilson College	NC	40,132	VC
Wartburg College	IA	41,055	VC
Washburn Univ	KS	12,579	C
Washington Adventist Univ	MD	25,859	LC
Washington and Jefferson College	PA	51,948	VC
Washington and Lee Univ	VA	52,812	MC
Washington College	MD	52,602	VC
Washington State Univ	WA	20,461	C
Washington Univ in St. Louis	MO	69,844	MC
Wayland Baptist Univ	TX	18,912	LC
Wayne State College	NE	11,764	NC
Wayne State Univ	MI	22,063	C
Waynesburg Univ	PA	30,150	C
Webster Univ	MO	35,100	C+
Wellesley College	MA	59,038	MC
Wells College	NY	49,400	VC
Wesley College	DE	31,115	LC
Wesleyan College	GA	24,000	C
Wesleyan Univ	CT	61,198	MC
West Chester Univ of Pennsylvania	PA	17,186	C
West Liberty Univ	WV	9,142	LC
West Texas A&M Univ	TX	13,478	C
West Virginia State Univ	WV	8,378	NC
West Virginia Univ	WV	16,542	C+
West Virginia Univ Inst of Technology	WV	14,094	NC
West Virginia Wesleyan College	WV	26,880	C
Western Carolina Univ	NC	13,965	C
Western Conn State Univ	CT	18,327	LC
Western Kentucky Univ	KY	11,000	C
Western Mich Univ	MI	19,628	C
Western New England Univ	MA	46,154	C+
Western New Mexico Univ	NM	8,500	LC
Western Oregon Univ	OR	15,021	C
Western State Colo Univ	CO	16,924	C
Western Washington Univ	WA	18,519	VC
Westfield State Univ	MA	18,297	C
Westminster College	MO	31,720	VC
Westminster College	PA	31,290	C
Westminster College	UT	37,708	C+
Westmont College	CA	41,500	HC
Wheaton College	IL	40,720	MC
Wheaton College	MA	54,934	HC+
Wheeling Jesuit Univ	WV	33,500	C
Whittier College	CA	43,416	C
Whitworth Univ	WA	47,734	VC
Wichita State Univ	KS	14,607	C+
Widener Univ	PA	52,418	C
Wilberforce Univ	OH	15,100	LC
Wiley College	TX		LC
Wilkes Univ	PA	44,070	C
Willamette Univ	OR	56,450	VC+
William Carey Univ	MS	13,500	LC
William Jewell College	MO	31,000	VC+
William Paterson Univ of New Jersey	NJ	21,694	C
William Peace Univ	NC	32,900	LC
William Penn Univ	IA	26,000	C
William Woods Univ	MO	24,260	C
Williams Baptist College	AR	20,070	C
Williams College	MA	61,070	MC
Wilmington College	OH	29,784	C
Wilson College	PA	35,080	C
Wingate Univ	NC	34,990	C
Winona State Univ	MN	16,640	C
Winston-Salem State Univ	NC	9,418	LC
Winthrop Univ	SC	21,120	C
Wisc Lutheran College	WI	23,510	VC
Wittenberg Univ	OH	47,962	C+
Wofford College	SC	45,795	VC
Worcester State Univ	MA	19,812	C
Wright State Univ	OH	16,983	C
Xavier Univ	OH	44,980	VC
Xavier Univ of Louisiana	LA	25,300	C
Yale Univ	CT	55,300	MC
Yeshiva Univ	NY	47,250	VC+
York College	NE	19,475	C
York College / The CUNY	NY	5,496	VC
York College of Pennsylvania	PA	26,590	C
Youngstown State Univ	OH	16,732	C

BIOMATHEMATICS

School	ST	$IS	SR
Emmanuel College	MA	47,985	VC
Florida Inst of Technology	FL	48,290	VC
Rutgers, The State Univ of New Jersey/New Brunswick	NJ	25,562	VC
Univ of Montana-Western	MT	9,753	LC
Univ of Scranton	PA	51,940	VC
Washington Univ in St. Louis	MO	69,844	MC

BIOMEDICAL ART

School	ST	$IS	SR
Cleveland Inst of Art	OH	48,685	SP

BIOMEDICAL ELECTRONICS

School	ST	$IS	SR
Thomas Edison State College	NJ	5,700	SP

BIOMEDICAL ENGINEERING

School	ST	$IS	SR
Arizona State Univ, at the Tempe Campus	AZ	20,137	C+
Binghamton Univ/The SUNY	NY	21,648	HC+
Boston Univ	MA	60,694	MC
Bucknell Univ	PA	60,140	MC
Butler Univ	IN	47,572	VC+
Calif Polytechnic State Univ	CA	19,847	HC
Case Western Reserve Univ	OH	56,534	MC
CUNY/City College	NY	20,319	HC+
College of New Jersey	NJ	25,376	C
Colo State Univ-Fort Collins	CO	20,385	VC
Columbia Univ/City of New York	NY	61,116	MC
Drexel Univ	PA	61,418	VC+
Duke Univ	NC	50,250	MC
Duquesne Univ	PA	43,720	VC
Elon Univ	NC	41,914	VC+
Florida Inst of Technology	FL	48,290	VC
Florida International Univ	FL	17,747	C+
Florida State Univ	FL	16,715	VC
Gannon Univ	PA	39,608	C
Georgia Inst of Technology	GA	21,828	MC
Harding Univ	AR	23,556	C
Hofstra Univ	NY	51,810	VC+
Indiana Inst of Technology	IN	34,240	LC
Indiana Univ-Purdue Univ Indianapolis	IN	17,611	C
Johns Hopkins Univ	MD	47,492	MC
Lawrence Tech Univ	MI	37,630	VC
Louisiana Tech Univ	LA	11,302	C
Marquette Univ	WI	46,930	VC+
Mass Inst of Technology	MA	58,240	MC
Mich Tech Univ	MI	23,556	HC
Milwaukee School of Engineering	WI	39,948	VC+
New Jersey Inst of Technology	NJ	26,490	C+
New York Univ	NY	61,470	MC
N Dak State Univ	ND		C
Northwestern Univ	IL	61,640	MC
Purdue Univ/West Lafayette	IN	20,024	HC
Rensselaer Polytechnic Inst	NY	61,529	MC
Rochester Inst of Technology	NY	42,450	VC
Rose-Hulman Inst of Technology	IN	53,340	MC
Rowan Univ	NJ	24,022	VC+
Rutgers, The State Univ of New Jersey/New Brunswick	NJ	25,562	VC
St. Louis Univ	MO	48,346	HC
San Jose State Univ	CA	19,133	LC
Stevens Inst of Technology	NJ	50,130	HC
Stony Brook Univ / SUNY	NY	20,078	HC+
Texas A&M Univ	TX	19,207	VC
The Catholic Univ of America	DC	52,852	VC
Ohio State Univ-Columbus Campus	OH	19,887	HC+
The Pennsylvania State Univ - Univ Park	PA	28,022	VC+
The Univ of Memphis	TN	15,094	C
The Univ of Utah	UT	16,463	VC
Tufts Univ	MA	58,780	MC
Tulane Univ	LA	60,861	MC
Tuskegee Univ	AL	26,750	C
Univ at Buffalo / The SUNY	NY	20,283	VC
Univ of Akron	OH	20,436	C
Univ of Alabama at Birmingham	AL	18,484	C+
Univ of Arizona	AZ	20,657	C
Univ of Calif at Irvine	CA	25,961	VC
Univ of Calif at Los Angeles	CA	25,686	MC
Univ of Central Okla	OK	12,293	C
Univ of Cincinnati	OH	21,506	VC
Univ of Conn	CT	24,706	HC
Univ of Hartford	CT	42,674	C
Univ of Houston	TX	19,796	VC
Univ of Idaho	ID	14,558	C
Univ of Iowa	IA	17,693	VC
Univ of Miami	FL	57,034	MC
Univ of Mich/Ann Arbor	MI	22,102	MC
Univ of Missouri/Columbia	MO	18,201	VC
Univ of Rochester	NY	60,668	MC
Univ of S Car at Columbia	SC	19,725	VC+
Univ of Southern Calif	CA	56,903	MC
Univ of Tenn at Knoxville	TN	20,364	VC+
Univ of Texas at Austin	TX	44,074	HC
Univ of Texas at Dallas	TX	21,348	HC+
Univ of Texas at San Antonio	TX	18,372	C
Univ of Virginia	VA	23,050	MC
Univ of Wisc/Madison	WI	18,757	HC+
Vanderbilt Univ	TN	58,220	MC
Virginia Commonwealth Univ	VA	21,716	C
Washington State Univ	WA	20,461	C
Washington Univ in St. Louis	MO	69,844	MC
Wayne State Univ	MI	22,063	C
Wentworth Inst of Technology	MA	29,800	C
Western New England Univ	MA	46,154	C+
Widener Univ	PA	52,418	C
Worcester Polytechnic Inst	MA	55,860	MC
Wright State Univ	OH	16,983	C
Yale Univ	CT	55,300	MC

BIOMEDICAL EQUIPMENT TECHNOLOGY

School	ST	$IS	SR
Andrews Univ	MI	28,030	C+
Roberts Wesleyan College	NY	38,306	C+

BIOMEDICAL SCIENCE

School	ST	$IS	SR
Adventist Univ of Health Sciences	FL	16,344	NC
Albany College of Pharmacy and Health Sciences	NY	40,331	SP
Andrews Univ	MI	28,030	C+
Arizona State Univ, at the Tempe Campus	AZ	20,137	C+
Auburn Univ	AL	22,378	VC+
Averett Univ	VA	37,750	LC
Boston Univ	MA	60,694	MC
Brown Univ	RI	59,428	MC
Cal State, Northridge	CA	28,690	LC
Christian Brothers Univ	TN	31,670	RC
CUNY/City College	NY	20,319	HC+
Colo State Univ-Fort Collins	CO	20,385	VC
Grand Valley State Univ	MI	17,998	C+
Heritage Univ	WA	17,664	NC
Hiram College	OH	37,300	VC
LIU Post	NY	47,660	C
Lynchburg College	VA	42,645	C
Marquette Univ	WI	46,930	VC+
McMurry Univ	TX	25,962	LC
Murray State Univ	KY	15,304	C
Northern Arizona Univ	AZ	19,010	C
Okla City Univ	OK	40,476	VC
Oral Roberts Univ	OK	31,734	C
Quinnipiac Univ	CT	55,160	VC
Rutgers, The State Univ of New Jersey/New Brunswick	NJ	25,562	VC
St. Peter's Univ	NJ	44,240	C
Southern Oregon Univ	OR	17,874	C
Texas A&M Univ	TX	19,207	VC
Ohio State Univ-Columbus Campus	OH	19,887	HC+
The Pennsylvania State Univ - Univ Park	PA	28,022	VC+
Univ at Buffalo / The SUNY	NY	20,283	VC
Univ of Alabama at Birmingham	AL	18,484	C+
Univ of Calif at Riverside	CA	27,204	C+
Univ of Central Florida	FL	15,668	VC+
Univ of Georgia	GA	20,082	VC
Univ of Illinois at Urbana-Champaign	IL	26,450	HC
Univ of New England	ME	46,750	C
Univ of New Hampshire	NH	26,912	C
Univ of St. Mary	KS	28,400	C
Univ of South Alabama	AL	13,510	C
Univ of Vermont	VT	27,006	VC+
Washington State Univ	WA	20,461	C
Western Mich Univ	MI	19,628	C

BIOMETRICS AND BIOSTATISTICS

School	ST	$IS	SR
Cornell Univ	NY	60,964	MC
La Sierra Univ	CA	35,694	VC
Simmons College	MA	49,966	VC
Univ of Arizona	AZ	20,657	C
Univ of N Car at Chapel Hill	NC	18,928	MC

BIOPHYSICS

School	ST	$IS	SR
Amherst College	MA	58,744	MC
Andrews Univ	MI	28,030	C+
Arizona State Univ, at the Tempe Campus	AZ	20,137	C+
Bellarmine Univ	KY	42,950	VC
Brandeis Univ	MA		MC
Brigham Young Univ	UT	12,100	HC
Brown Univ	RI	59,428	MC
Cal State, Fresno	CA	17,405	C
Centenary College of Louisiana	LA	45,650	C+
Claremont McKenna College	CA	62,215	MC
Columbia Univ/City of New York	NY	61,116	MC
Elon Univ	NC	41,914	VC+
Harvard College/Harvard Univ	MA	49,000	MC
Illinois Inst of Technology	IL	38,512	HC+
Iowa State Univ	IA	16,403	C
Johns Hopkins Univ	MD	47,492	MC
La Sierra Univ	CA	35,694	VC
Lipscomb Univ	TN	37,490	VC
Loyola Univ Chicago	IL	51,646	VC+
Pacific Union College	CA	28,150	VC
Rensselaer Polytechnic Inst	NY	61,529	MC
St. Mary's Univ of Minn	MN	38,280	C
Southern Nazarene Univ	OK	24,354	C
Southwestern Okla State Univ	OK	9,160	LC
St. Bonaventure Univ	NY	41,575	C
St. Lawrence Univ	NY	59,972	VC
SUNY College at Geneseo	NY	18,670	HC

BIOPSYCHOLOGY

School	ST	$IS	SR
Barnard College/Columbia Univ	NY	39,000	MC
Birmingham-Southern College	AL	44,168	VC+
Grand Valley State Univ	MI	17,998	C+
Messiah College	PA	40,690	C+
Mills College	CA	54,119	VC
Monmouth College	IL	40,850	C
Nebr Wesleyan Univ	NE	29,774	C+
Oglethorpe Univ	GA	44,200	C
Pace Univ	NY	53,367	C
Philadelphia Univ	PA	44,160	C
Rider Univ	NJ	45,720	C
Simmons College	MA	49,966	VC
Spring Hill College	AL	44,164	VC
The Lincoln Univ	PA	15,154	LC
Tufts Univ	MA	58,780	MC
Univ of Calif at Santa Barbara	CA	27,551	VC
Viterbo Univ	WI	30,070	C
Washington Univ in St. Louis	MO	69,844	MC
York College	NE	19,475	C

BIORESOURCE ENGINEERING

School	ST	$IS	SR
Calif Polytechnic State Univ	CA	19,847	HC
Rutgers, The State Univ of New Jersey/New Brunswick	NJ	25,562	VC

BIOTECHNOLOGY

School	ST	$IS	SR
Alma College	MI	44,075	C
Arkansas State Univ	AR	15,470	C
Assumption College	MA	47,122	C+
Brigham Young Univ	UT	12,100	HC
Calif State Polytechnic Univ, Pomona	CA	20,156	C
Cal State, San Marcos	CA	14,576	LC
Calvin College	MI	39,120	VC
Claflin Univ	SC	22,368	LC
Colo State Univ-Pueblo	CO	16,183	C
Elizabethtown College	PA	49,740	VC
Endicott College	MA	43,228	VC+
Ferris State Univ	MI	20,047	C
Fitchburg State Univ	MA	18,173	C
Florida Gulf Coast Univ	FL		C
Grand View Univ	IA	31,050	C
Indiana Univ Bloomington	IN	19,801	VC
Indiana Univ East	IN	6,783	C
Indiana Univ-Purdue Univ Indianapolis	IN	17,611	C
Inter-American Univ of PR/ Bayamon Univ College	PR	4,428	
James Madison Univ	VA	18,049	VC
Kennesaw State Univ	GA		C
Kent State Univ	OH	19,920	C
Lawrence Tech Univ	MI	37,630	VC
Marshall Univ	WV	14,820	C
Marywood Univ	PA	45,595	C
Mich State Univ	MI	22,450	VC
Millersville Univ of Pennsylvania	PA	21,648	C
Minn State Univ, Mankato	MN	15,616	C
Missouri Baptist Univ	MO	31,830	C
Montana State Univ	MT	14,068	C
Mount Aloysius College	PA	29,976	C
New York Inst of Technology	NY	45,010	VC
N Dak State Univ	ND		C
Ohio Univ	OH	21,080	C
Oregon State Univ	OR	20,273	VC
Plymouth State Univ	NH	23,148	LC
Point Park Univ	PA	36,390	C
Purdue Univ/Calumet	IN	14,336	C
Quinnipiac Univ	CT	55,160	VC
Roberts Wesleyan College	NY	38,306	C+
Rochester Inst of Technology	NY	42,450	VC
Rutgers, The State Univ of New Jersey/New Brunswick	NJ	25,562	VC
S Dak State Univ	SD	14,296	C
Southeastern Okla State Univ	OK	7,966	LC

School	ST	$IS	SR
Springfield College	MA	25,000	C
SUNY / College of Environmental Science and Forestry	NY	18,351	VC
Stevenson Univ	MD	41,470	C
Suffolk Univ	MA	47,298	C
Syracuse Univ	NY	56,346	VC
The Catholic Univ of America	DC	52,852	VC
The Pennsylvania State Univ - Univ Park	PA	28,022	VC
The SUNY College of Agriculture and Tech at Cobleskill	NY	19,749	LC
The Univ of N Car at Pembroke	NC	13,388	C
Tufts Univ	MA	58,780	MC
Univ at Buffalo / The SUNY	NY	20,283	VC
Univ of Calif at San Diego	CA	21,000	C
Univ of Central Florida	FL	15,668	VC+
Univ of Delaware	DE	23,612	VC
Univ of Georgia	GA	20,082	VC
Univ of Houston-Downtown	TX	15,170	LC
Univ of Illinois at Urbana-Champaign	IL	26,450	HC
Univ of Maryland/Univ College	MD	6,168	SP
Univ of Mass Dartmouth	MA	22,223	C
Univ of Missouri-Kansas City	MO	19,603	C
Univ of Missouri-St. Louis	MO		VC
Univ of Nebr at Omaha	NE	12,700	C
Univ of Nevada/Reno	NV	17,507	C
Univ of New Haven	CT	48,940	VC
Univ of Northern Iowa	IA	15,795	C
Univ of PR/Mayaguez	PR	1,250	
Univ of Wisc/River Falls	WI	9,722	LC
Ursuline College	OH	33,198	LC
West Texas A&M Univ	TX	13,478	C
William Paterson Univ of New Jersey	NJ	21,694	C
William Penn Univ	IA	26,000	C
Worcester Polytechnic Inst	MA	55,860	MC
Worcester State Univ	MA	19,812	C
York College / The CUNY	NY	5,496	VC

BOTANY

School	ST	$IS	SR
Andrews Univ	MI	28,030	C+
Auburn Univ	AL	22,378	VC+
Bennington College	VT	56,990	HC+
Brigham Young Univ	UT	12,100	C
Cal State, Long Beach	CA	17,502	C+
Colo State Univ-Fort Collins	CO	20,385	VC
Conn College	CT	54,970	MC
Delaware State Univ	DE	16,722	LC
Eastern Washington Univ	WA		C
Hampshire College	MA	58,320	MC
Humboldt State Univ	CA	18,400	C
Idaho State Univ	ID	12,307	C
Kent State Univ	OH	19,920	C
Marlboro College	VT	35,980	VC
Mars Hill Univ	NC	22,950	LC
Miami Univ	OH	24,191	VC
Mich State Univ	MI	22,450	VC
Millersville Univ of Pennsylvania	PA	21,648	C
N Car State Univ	NC	16,202	HC
N Dak State Univ	ND		C
Northern Mich Univ	MI	18,278	C
Northwest Missouri State Univ	MO	17,347	C
Ohio Univ	OH	21,080	C
Ohio Wesleyan Univ	OH	49,460	C+
Okla State Univ	OK	14,310	VC
Oregon State Univ	OR	20,273	VC
Rutgers, The State Univ of New Jersey/New Brunswick	NJ	25,562	VC
Rutgers, The State Univ of New Jersey/Newark Campus	NJ	258,806	VC
San Diego State Univ	CA	21,611	C+
San Francisco State Univ	CA	18,514	C
San Jose State Univ	CA	19,133	LC
Southern Illinois Univ Carbondale	IL	21,942	C
SUNY / College of Environmental Science and Forestry	NY	18,351	VC
Texas A&M Univ	TX	19,207	VC
Texas A&M Univ at Commerce	TX	10,496	C
The Univ of Okla	OK	18,621	VC
Univ of Calif at Davis	CA		HC
Univ of Calif at Irvine	CA	25,961	VC
Univ of Florida	FL	15,943	HC
Univ of Great Falls	MT	27,970	C
Univ of Hawaii at Manoa	HI	19,379	C
Univ of Idaho	ID	14,558	VC
Univ of Illinois at Urbana-Champaign	IL	26,450	HC
Univ of Kentucky	KY	19,868	C
Univ of Maine	ME	19,902	C+
Univ of Mich/Ann Arbor	MI	22,102	MC
Univ of Minn/Twin Cities	MN		HC
Univ of Montana	MT	14,105	C
Univ of Vermont	VT	27,006	VC+
Univ of Washington	WA	14,722	VC

School	ST	$IS	SR
Univ of Wisc/Madison	WI	18,757	HC+
Univ of Wyoming	WY	14,401	C+
Western New Mexico Univ	NM	8,500	LC

BROADCASTING

School	ST	$IS	SR
Alabama State Univ	AL	14,142	NC
Ashland Univ	OH	25,000	C
Baldwin Wallace Univ	OH	38,318	C
Barry Univ	FL	38,190	C
Baylor Univ	TX	50,329	HC
Belhaven Univ	MS	27,170	C
Bemidji State Univ	MN	13,500	VC
Biola Univ	CA	40,320	C+
Bloomfield College	NJ	37,850	LC
Bluffton Univ	OH	38,948	C
Buffalo State College / SUNY	NY	15,733	C+
Cedarville Univ	OH	32,860	VC
Central Methodist Univ	MO	28,240	VC
Central State Univ	OH	9,010	C
Central Washington Univ	WA	11,730	C
Champlain College	VT	46,650	VC+
Chapman Univ	CA	58,347	VC+
Chicago State Univ	IL	5,482	C
CUNY/Brooklyn College	NY	5,884	C
Colo State Univ-Pueblo	CO	16,183	C
Concord Univ	WV	13,102	C
Dordt College	IA	34,160	C
Drake Univ	IA	41,516	VC+
Eastern Kentucky Univ	KY	11,161	C
Eastern Nazarene College	MA	30,000	C
Eastern Washington Univ	WA		C
Elon Univ	NC	41,914	VC+
Emerson College	MA	52,446	HC+
Evangel Univ	MO	23,090	C
Florida Southern College	FL	40,150	C
Florida State Univ	FL	16,715	VC
Freed-Hardeman Univ	TN	19,697	VC
Geneva College	PA	27,280	C
George Washington Univ	DC	57,108	MC
Gonzaga Univ	WA	46,441	HC
Goshen College	IN	35,900	VC
Grand Valley State Univ	MI	17,998	C+
Grand View Univ	IA	31,050	C
Harding Univ	AR	23,556	C
Hardin-Simmons Univ	TX	23,560	C+
Hastings College	NE	27,782	C+
Howard Univ	DC	13,646	C
Huntington Univ	IN	32,220	C
Ithaca College	NY	53,864	HC
John Brown Univ	AR	32,056	VC+
Lewis Univ	IL	23,050	C
Lincoln Memorial Univ	TN	18,144	C
LIU Post	NY	47,660	C
Loras College	IA	37,432	VC
Madonna Univ	MI	24,540	VC
Malone Univ	OH	35,364	C
Manhattan College	NY	49,588	C+
Mansfield Univ	PA	19,468	LC
Marietta College	OH	42,135	C+
Marquette Univ	WI	46,930	VC+
Marshall Univ	WV	14,820	C
Marywood Univ	PA	45,595	C
Mercy College	NY	30,456	C
Mercyhurst Univ	PA	40,700	C
Millersville Univ of Pennsylvania	PA	21,648	C
Minn State Univ, Moorhead	MN	13,392	VC
Minot State Univ	ND	10,915	C
Montclair State Univ	NJ	22,614	C
Mount Vernon Nazarene Univ	OH	29,590	C
North Central College	IL	38,343	VC
Northern Michigan Univ	MI	18,278	C
Northwest Missouri State Univ	MO	17,347	C
Northwestern College	MN	24,000	C
Northwestern Okla State Univ	OK	7,275	NC
Ohio Northern Univ	OH	42,075	VC
Ohio Univ	OH	21,080	C
Okla Baptist Univ	OK	28,202	C
Okla Christian Univ	OK	25,870	VC
Okla City Univ	OK	40,476	VC
Okla State Univ	OK	14,310	VC
Oral Roberts Univ	OK	31,734	C
Oswego / SUNY	NY	20,009	VC
Otterbein Univ	OH	32,214	C
Pittsburg State Univ	KS	12,032	C
Point Loma Nazarene Univ	CA	41,006	C+
Point Park Univ	PA	36,390	C
Prairie View A&M Univ	TX	15,205	LC
Purdue Univ/Calumet	IN	14,336	C
Purdue Univ/West Lafayette	IN	20,024	HC
Roosevelt Univ	IL	22,605	VC
Rowan Univ	NJ	24,022	VC+
San Francisco State Univ	CA	18,514	C
San Jose State Univ	CA	19,133	LC
Savannah College of Art and Design	GA	48,005	SP
Seton Hall Univ	NJ	45,902	C
Shaw Univ	NC	15,488	C
Sojourner-Douglass College	MD	9,160	LC
Southeastern Univ	FL	27,201	C
Southern Adventist Univ	TN	26,190	C
Southern Arkansas Univ	AR	14,316	C

School	ST	$IS	SR
Southern Illinois Univ Carbondale	IL	21,942	C
Southern Methodist Univ	TX	60,585	MC
Southwestern Adventist Univ	TX	23,026	LC
Spring Arbor Univ	MI	26,740	C
St. Cloud State Univ	MN	10,600	C
Stephen F. Austin State Univ	TX	14,668	C
Suffolk Univ	MA	47,298	C
Syracuse Univ	NY	56,346	VC
Temple Univ	PA	24,392	VC
Texas A&M Univ at Commerce	TX	10,496	C
Texas State Univ	TX	17,128	C
Texas Tech Univ	TX	14,243	C
Texas Wesleyan Univ	TX	31,382	C
The Lincoln Univ	PA	15,154	LC
The Univ of Okla	OK	18,621	VC
Troy Univ	AL	10,650	C
Union Univ	TN	28,260	VC
Univ of Central Florida	FL	15,668	VC+
Univ of Central Missouri	MO	14,605	C
Univ of Central Okla	OK	12,293	C
Univ of Cincinnati	OH	21,506	VC
Univ of Colo Boulder	CO	22,605	VC+
Univ of Findlay	OH	31,916	C
Univ of Georgia	GA	20,082	VC
Univ of Idaho	ID	14,558	VC
Univ of Illinois at Urbana-Champaign	IL	26,450	HC
Univ of Indianapolis	IN	21,740	LC
Univ of La Verne	CA	47,010	C
Univ of Louisiana at Lafayette	LA	6,130	C
Univ of Missouri/Columbia	MO	18,201	MC
Univ of Nebr - Lincoln	NE	18,031	VC
Univ of Nebr at Kearney	NE	14,855	LC
Univ of Nebr at Omaha	NE	12,700	C
Univ of North Texas	TX	15,628	C
Univ of Northern Iowa	IA	15,795	C
Univ of S Car at Columbia	SC	19,725	VC+
Univ of Southern Calif	CA	56,903	MC
Univ of Southern Indiana	IN	14,885	C
Univ of Texas at Arlington	TX	10,908	C
Vanguard Univ of Southern Calif	CA	35,833	VC
Wartburg College	IA	41,055	VC
Washington State Univ	WA	20,461	C
Waynesburg Univ	PA	30,150	C
West Texas A&M Univ	TX	13,478	C
West Virginia Univ	WV	16,542	C+
Western Illinois Univ	IL	20,732	C
Western Kentucky Univ	KY	10,000	LC
Westminster College	PA	31,290	C+
Winona State Univ	MN	16,640	C
York College of Pennsylvania	PA	26,590	C
Youngstown State Univ	OH	16,732	C

BUSINESS (DUAL MAJOR PROGRAM)

School	ST	$IS	SR
Bentley Univ	MA	56,454	HC+
CUNY/Brooklyn College	NY	5,884	C+
John Carroll Univ	OH	46,300	C+
Mercy College	NY	30,456	C
Southern Oregon Univ	OR	17,874	C
Univ of Pittsburgh at Pittsburgh	PA	28,572	HC+
Univ of Tulsa	OK	46,331	MC

BUSINESS ADMINISTRATION - INTERNATIONAL

School	ST	$IS	SR
Aquinas College	MI	33,060	C
Arizona State Univ, at the Polytechnic Campus	AZ	20,531	C+
Arizona State Univ, at the Tempe Campus	AZ	20,137	C+
Arizona State Univ, at the West Campus	AZ	19,251	C
Bloomfield College	NJ	37,850	LC
Campbell Univ	NC	37,570	VC
College of the Ozarks	MO		VC
Franklin College	IN	36,585	C
Millersville Univ of Pennsylvania	PA	21,648	C
Monmouth Univ	NJ	44,108	C
Okla Christian Univ	OK	25,870	VC
Trevecca Nazarene Univ	TN	31,186	C
Univ of Nevada/Reno	NV	17,507	C

BUSINESS ADMINISTRATION AND MANAGEMENT

School	ST	$IS	SR
Adams State Univ	CO	13,358	LC
Adelphi Univ	NY	44,670	VC
Adrian College	MI	42,400	C
Agnes Scott College	GA	45,323	C+
Alabama A&M Univ	AL	10,044	C
Alabama State Univ	AL	14,142	NC
Alaska Pacific Univ	AK	43,592	VC
Albertus Magnus College	CT	37,382	C
Albion College	MI	46,010	C
Albright College	PA	46,660	C+
Alcorn State Univ	MS	9,500	C
Alderson Broaddus Univ	WV	28,656	VC
Alfred Univ	NY	41,770	C

School	ST	$IS	SR
Alice Lloyd College	KY	4,900	LC
Allen Univ	SC	16,124	NC
Alma College	MI	44,075	C
Alvernia Univ	PA	39,250	LC
Alverno College	WI	31,434	LC
American International College	MA	36,100	LC
American Jewish Univ - College of A&S	CA	32,600	C
American Univ	DC	56,015	HC+
Amridge Univ	AL	6,870	LC
Anderson Univ	IN	36,100	C
Andrews Univ	MI	28,030	C+
Angelo State Univ	TX	15,049	NC
Anna Maria College	MA	34,600	C
Aquinas College	MI	33,060	C
Aquinas College	TN	29,250	VC+
Arcadia Univ	PA	33,570	C
Arizona State Univ, at the Polytechnic Campus	AZ	20,531	C+
Arizona State Univ, at the Tempe Campus	AZ	20,137	C+
Arizona State Univ, at the West Campus	AZ	19,251	C
Arkansas Baptist College	AR	15,750	NC
Arkansas State Univ	AR	15,470	C
Asbury Univ	KY	32,038	VC
Ashford Univ	CA	10,480	C
Ashland Univ	OH	25,000	C
Assumption College	MA	47,122	C+
Atlantic Union College	MA	24,600	C
Auburn Univ	AL	22,378	VC+
Auburn Univ at Montgomery	AL	14,470	LC
Augsburg College	MN	35,142	C
Augustana College	IL	43,398	VC
Augustana College	SD	36,500	VC
Aurora Univ	IL	33,228	C
Austin College	TX	45,875	HC
Austin Peay State Univ	TN	15,274	C
Averett Univ	VA	37,750	C
Avila Univ	MO	26,900	C
Azusa Pacific Univ	CA	42,086	C
Babson College	MA	51,940	HC
Baker College of Flint	MI	7,800	NC
Baker Univ	KS	33,350	C+
Baldwin Wallace Univ	OH	38,318	C
Ball State Univ	IN	17,850	C
Barton College	NC	27,660	LC
Bay Path College	MA	34,565	C
Baylor Univ	TX	50,329	HC
Becker College	MA	41,420	C
Belhaven Univ	MS	27,170	C
Bellarmine Univ	KY	42,950	VC
Bellevue Univ	NE	4,600	NC
Belmont Abbey College	NC	37,716	C
Belmont Univ	TN	39,190	VC+
Beloit College	WI	49,970	HC
Bemidji State Univ	MN	13,500	VC
Benedict College	SC	20,454	NC
Benedictine College	KS	29,180	VC
Benedictine Univ	IL	37,820	C
Bennett College for Women	NC	21,970	LC
Bentley Univ	MA	56,454	HC+
Berea College	KY	7,192	C
Berkeley College of New York City	NY	18,300	LC
Berkeley College/New Jersey	NJ	27,300	LC
Berkeley College/Westchester Campus	NY	28,500	LC
Berry College	GA	39,254	VC
Bethany College	KS	30,605	NC
Bethany College	WV	35,282	LC
Bethel College	IN	31,560	C
Bethel College	KS	32,160	C
Bethel Univ	MN	34,940	VC
Bethel Univ	TN	19,186	C
Bethune-Cookman Univ	FL	22,958	C
Binghamton Univ/The SUNY	NY	21,648	HC+
Biola Univ	CA	40,320	C+
Birmingham-Southern College	AL	44,168	VC+
Black Hills State Univ	SD	13,947	C
Blackburn College	IL	21,350	C
Bloomfield College	NJ	37,850	LC
Bloomsburg Univ of Pennsylvania	PA	13,598	C
Blue Mountain College	MS	15,634	LC
Bluefield College	VA	17,230	C+
Bluefield State College	WV	3,140	LC
Bluffton Univ	OH	38,948	C
Boise State Univ	ID	13,469	LC
Boricua College	NY	8,600	C
Boston College	MA	60,622	HC
Boston Univ	MA	60,694	MC
Bowie State Univ	MD	23,990	LC
Bowling Green State Univ	OH	18,970	C
Bradley Univ	IL	31,874	VC
Brandeis Univ	MA		MC
Brenau Univ - Women's College	GA	26,650	C
Brescia Univ	KY	26,140	VC+
Brewton-Parker College	GA	33,388	C
Briar Cliff Univ	IA	29,514	C
Bridgewater College	VA	41,450	C
Brigham Young Univ	UT	12,100	HC
Bryan College	TN	24,194	C

ST = STATE $IS = IN-STATE COSTS SR = SELECTOR RATING

School	ST	$IS	SR
Bryant Univ	RI	49,179	VC
Bucknell Univ	PA	60,140	MC
Buena Vista Univ	IA	39,188	C
Buffalo State College / SUNY	NY	15,733	C+
Cabrini College	PA	40,859	LC
Cairn Univ	PA	33,270	C
Caldwell College	NJ	35,602	NC
Calif Baptist Univ	CA	38,792	C
Calif Inst of Technology	CA	54,045	MC
Calif Lutheran Univ	CA	49,540	C+
Calif Maritime Academy	CA	15,496	LC
Calif Polytechnic State Univ	CA	19,847	HC
Calif State Polytechnic Univ, Pomona	CA	20,156	C
Cal State, Bakersfield	CA	8,000	C
Cal State, Chico	CA	20,158	C
Cal State, Dominguez Hills	CA	17,090	LC
Cal State, East Bay	CA	16,549	C
Cal State, Fresno	CA	17,405	C
Cal State, Fullerton	CA	25,188	C
Cal State, Long Beach	CA	17,502	C+
Cal State, Los Angeles	CA	17,186	LC
Cal State, Monterey Bay	CA	26,871	LC
Cal State, Northridge	CA	28,690	LC
Cal State, Sacramento	CA	16,200	C
Cal State, San Bernardino	CA	12,000	C
Cal State, San Marcos	CA	14,576	LC
Cal State, Stanislaus	CA	18,582	C
Calif Univ of Pennsylvania	PA	14,217	C
Calumet College of St. Joseph	IN	15,000	C
Calvin College	MI	39,120	VC
Cameron Univ	OK	10,004	LC
Campbell Univ	NC	37,570	C
Campbellsville Univ	KY	27,720	C
Canisius College	NY	44,900	C
Capital Univ	OH	41,050	VC
Cardinal Stritch Univ	WI	24,054	C
Caribbean Univ	PR	10,375	
Carlos Albizu Univ	FL	12,053	LC
Carlow Univ	PA	30,272	C
Carnegie Mellon Univ	PA	51,260	MC
Carroll College	MT	28,000	C
Carroll Univ	WI	38,100	C
Carson-Newman Univ	TN	29,058	C+
Carthage College	WI	33,000	C
Case Western Reserve Univ	OH	56,534	MC
Castleton State College	VT	20,186	C
Catawba College	NC	37,240	LC
Cazenovia College	NY	43,464	C
Cedar Crest College	PA	43,240	C
Cedarville Univ	OH	32,860	VC
Centenary College	NJ	38,618	C
Centenary College of Louisiana	LA	45,650	C+
Central College	IA	42,104	C+
Central Conn State Univ	CT	19,749	C
Central Methodist Univ	MO	28,240	VC
Central State Univ	OH	9,010	C
Central Univ of Bayamon	PR	3,350	
Central Washington Univ	WA	11,730	C
Chadron State College	NE	7,400	NC
Chaminade Univ of Honolulu	HI	31,664	LC
Champlain College	VT	46,650	VC+
Chancellor Univ	OH	11,000	C
Chapman Univ	CA	58,347	VC+
Charleston Southern Univ	SC	22,420	C
Chatham Univ	PA	43,797	C
Chestnut Hill College	PA	42,110	LC
Cheyney Univ of Pennsylvania	PA	20,372	LC
Chicago State Univ	IL	5,482	C
Christian Brothers Univ	TN	31,670	HC
Christopher Newport Univ	VA	21,960	VC
Citadel, The	SC		C
CUNY/Brooklyn College	NY	5,884	C+
CUNY/City College	NY	20,319	HC+
City Univ of Seattle	WA	14,880	NC
Claflin Univ	SC	22,368	C
Clarion Univ of Pennsylvania	PA	17,370	LC
Clark Atlanta Univ	GA	30,006	LC
Clark Univ	MA	47,020	HC+
Clarke Univ	IA	37,600	C
Clarkson College	NE	16,300	C
Clarkson Univ	NY	57,330	HC
Clayton State Univ	GA	12,000	LC
Clearwater Christian College	FL	23,720	C
Clemson Univ	SC	19,136	HC
Coastal Carolina Univ	SC	18,580	C
Coe College	IA	45,550	VC
Coker College	SC	32,256	C
Colby-Sawyer College	NH	50,790	C
College of Charleston	SC	22,145	VC
College of Mount St. Joseph	OH	33,880	C
College of Mount St. Vincent	NY	41,040	MC
College of New Jersey	NJ	25,376	MC
College of St. Elizabeth	NJ	43,839	LC
College of St. Scholastica	MN	41,440	C
College of St Joseph	VT	30,600	LC
College of Staten Island/The City of New Yok	NY	16,778	NC
College of the Ozarks	MO		VC
College of William & Mary	VA	28,000	MC
Colo Christian Univ	CO	27,500	C
Colo Mesa Univ	CO	17,690	LC
Colo State Univ-Fort Collins	CO	20,385	VC
Colo State Univ-Pueblo	CO	16,183	C
Colo Technical Univ	CO	10,500	LC
Columbia College	MO	24,578	C
Columbia College	SC	27,882	C
Columbus State Univ	GA	13,176	C
Concord Univ	WV	13,102	C
Concordia College - Alabama	AL	15,720	NC
Concordia College - Moorhead	MN	39,974	VC
Concordia College - New York	NY	39,035	LC
Concordia Univ	OR	35,000	C
Concordia Univ Irvine	CA	35,390	C
Concordia Univ Nebr	NE	26,000	VC
Concordia Univ St. Paul	MN	28,250	C
Concordia Univ Texas	TX	23,640	C
Concordia Univ Wisc	WI	28,980	C
Concordia Univ, Ann Arbor	MI	27,220	VC
Concordia Univ, River Forest	IL	26,300	C
Converse College	SC	37,130	C
Coppin State Univ	MD	16,227	LC
Corban Univ	OR	37,380	C+
Cornerstone Univ and Grand Rapids Theological Seminary	MI	33,338	C
Covenant College	GA	38,990	VC+
Creighton Univ	NE	45,356	VC
Culver-Stockton College	MO	30,900	C
Cumberland Univ	TN	21,220	C
Curry College	MA	48,925	LC
Daemen College	NY	34,770	C
Dakota State Univ	SD	13,811	C
Dakota Wesleyan Univ	SD	23,000	C
Dallas Baptist Univ	TX	30,580	VC
Daniel Webster College	NH	25,380	C
Davenport Univ	MI	21,002	LC
Davis & Elkins College	WV	33,742	C
De Sales Univ	PA	43,970	C
Defiance College	OH	30,645	C
Delaware State Univ	DE	16,722	LC
Delaware Valley College	PA	29,944	C
Delta State Univ	MS	12,292	LC
DePaul Univ	IL	47,623	VC
Dickinson State Univ	ND	11,900	NC
Dillard Univ	LA	20,940	VC
Doane College	NE	35,230	C
Dominican College	NY	31,270	LC
Dominican Univ	IL	37,628	C
Dominican Univ of Calif	CA	51,250	C
Dordt College	IA	34,160	C
Dowling College	NY	25,000	LC
Drake Univ	IA	41,516	VC+
Drexel Univ	PA	61,418	VC+
Drury Univ	MO	31,909	VC
Duquesne Univ	PA	43,720	VC
D'Youville College	NY	29,850	C
Earlham College	IN	51,470	HC
East Carolina Univ	NC	14,169	C
East Central Univ	OK	10,223	LC
East Stroudsburg Univ of Pennsylvania	PA	18,868	LC
East Texas Baptist Univ	TX	31,577	LC
Eastern Conn State Univ	CT	20,584	C
Eastern Illinois Univ	IL	20,466	C
Eastern Kentucky Univ	KY	11,161	C
Eastern Mennonite Univ	VA	40,660	C
Eastern Mich Univ	MI	18,604	C
Eastern Nazarene College	MA	30,000	C
Eastern New Mexico Univ	NM	10,682	C
Eastern Oregon Univ	OR	10,400	C
Eastern Univ	PA	37,704	C
Eastern Washington Univ	WA		C
Eckerd College	FL	43,902	C
Edgewood College	WI	33,294	C
Edinboro Univ of Pennsylvania	PA	15,940	LC
Edward Waters College	FL	19,607	LC
Elizabeth City State Univ	NC	11,638	C
Elizabethtown College	PA	49,740	VC
Elizabethtown College School of Continuing and Professional Studies	PA		VC
Elmhurst College	IL	43,336	C
Elmira College	NY	49,950	C+
Elms College	MA	23,900	VC
Elon Univ	NC	41,914	VC+
Embry-Riddle Aeronautical Univ - Daytona Beach	FL	40,884	C+
Embry-Riddle Aeronautical Univ - Worldwide	FL	15,512	C
Emmanuel College	MA	47,985	VC
Emory and Henry College	VA	387,460	C
Emory Univ	GA	56,368	MC
Emporia State Univ	KS	12,897	C
Endicott College	MA	43,228	VC+
Erskine College	SC	37,360	C
Eureka College	IL	19,280	C
Excelsior College	NY	5,580	SP
Fairleigh Dickinson Univ/ College at Florham	NJ	42,142	C
Fairleigh Dickinson Univ/ Metropolitan Campus	NJ	40,254	C
Fairmont State Univ	WV	12,098	LC
Farmingdale State College	NY	19,673	C
Faulkner Univ	AL	25,720	LC
Fayetteville State Univ	NC	10,816	C
Felician College	NJ	41,640	LC
Ferris State Univ	MI	20,047	C
Ferrum College	VA	27,740	LC
Fisk Univ	TN	19,830	C
Fitchburg State Univ	MA	18,173	C
Flagler College	FL	25,180	C
Florida A&M Univ	FL	14,935	LC
Florida Atlantic Univ	FL	17,339	C
Florida Inst of Technology	FL	48,290	VC
Florida International Univ	FL	17,747	C+
Florida Memorial Univ	FL	20,888	LC
Florida Southern College	FL	40,150	C+
Florida State Univ	FL	16,715	MC
Fontbonne Univ	MO	31,384	C
Fordham Univ	NY	61,588	HC+
Fort Hays State Univ	KS	11,354	C
Fort Lewis College	CO	15,513	C
Fort Valley State Univ	GA	11,200	VC
Framingham State Univ	MA	18,854	C
Francis Marion Univ	SC	16,464	LC
Franciscan Univ of Steubenville	OH	27,320	VC
Franklin and Marshall College	PA	60,799	MC
Franklin College	IN	36,585	C
Franklin Pierce Univ	NH	41,598	C
Franklin Univ	OH	20,985	SP
Freed-Hardeman Univ	TN	19,697	VC
Fresno Pacific Univ	CA	32,136	C
Friends Univ	KS	29,100	C
Frostburg State Univ	MD	15,264	LC
Furman Univ	SC	54,006	HC
Gallaudet Univ	DC	25,380	SP
Gannon Univ	PA	39,608	C
Gardner-Webb Univ	NC	34,375	C+
Geneva College	PA	27,280	C
George Fox Univ	OR	40,750	C+
George Mason Univ	VA	15,724	VC
George Washington Univ	DC	57,108	MC
Georgetown College	KY	41,440	C+
Georgetown Univ	DC	52,910	MC
Georgia College and State Univ	GA	18,900	C+
Georgia Inst of Technology	GA	21,828	MC
Georgia Regents Univ	GA		C
Georgia Southwestern State Univ	GA	13,246	C
Georgia State Univ	GA	15,582	VC
Georgian Court Univ	NJ	41,594	LC
Gettysburg College	PA	58,820	HC
Glenville State College	WV	11,348	NC
Goldey-Beacom College	DE	27,493	C
Gonzaga Univ	WA	46,441	HC
Goodwin College	CT	19,400	LC
Gordon College	MA	44,320	VC
Goshen College	IN	35,900	VC
Goucher College	MD	52,040	VC+
Grace Bible College	MI	20,770	C
Grace College and Seminary	IN	28,800	VC
Graceland Univ	IA	28,020	C
Grambling State Univ	LA	13,384	C
Grand Canyon Univ	AZ	24,540	VC
Grand Valley State Univ	MI	17,998	C+
Grand View Univ	IA	31,050	C
Green Mountain College	VT	45,228	LC
Greensboro College	NC	28,740	C
Greenville College	IL	27,012	C
Grove City College	PA	24,022	VC
Guilford College	NC	42,800	C
Gustavus Adolphus College	MN	48,170	HC
Gwynedd-Mercy College	PA	33,560	C
Hamline Univ	MN	45,678	VC
Hampton Univ	VA	28,528	C
Hannibal-LaGrange Univ	MO	24,490	C
Harding Univ	AR	23,556	C
Hardin-Simmons Univ	TX	23,560	C+
Harris-Stowe State Univ	MO	14,360	NC
Hartwick College	NY	51,270	C
Hastings College	NE	27,782	C+
Hawaii Pacific Univ	HI	34,360	C
Heidelberg Univ	OH	34,100	C
Hellenic College/Holy Cross Greek Orthodox School of Theology	MA	33,190	C
Henderson State Univ	AR	14,584	C
Heritage Univ	WA	17,664	NC
High Point Univ	NC	39,800	C
Hilbert College	NY	28,550	C
Hodges Univ	FL	12,000	VC
Hofstra Univ	NY	51,810	VC+
Hollins Univ	VA	43,295	VC
Holy Cross College	IN	34,030	LC
Holy Family Univ	PA	40,030	LC
Holy Names Univ	CA	40,310	NC
Hood College	MD	45,730	C
Hope College	MI	38,650	VC
Hope International Univ	CA	34,650	C
Houghton College	NY	36,808	C+
Houston Baptist Univ	TX	36,450	C
Howard Payne Univ	TX	17,115	C
Howard Univ	DC	13,646	C
Humboldt State Univ	CA	18,400	C
Humphreys College	CA	17,000	NC
Huntingdon College	AL	33,100	C
Huntington Univ	IN	32,220	C+
Husson Univ	ME	24,194	LC
Huston-Tillotson Univ	TX	18,124	C+
Idaho State Univ	ID	12,307	C
Illinois College	IL	25,770	VC
Illinois State Univ	IL	23,110	VC
Illinois Wesleyan Univ	IL	48,452	VC
Immaculata Univ	PA	43,000	C
Indiana Inst of Technology	IN	34,240	LC
Indiana State Univ	IN	16,000	C
Indiana Univ Bloomington	IN	19,801	VC
Indiana Univ East	IN	6,783	C
Indiana Univ Kokomo	IN	6,811	LC
Indiana Univ Northwest	IN	6,854	LC
Indiana Univ of Pennsylvania	PA	20,846	LC
Indiana Univ South Bend	IN	15,501	C
Indiana Univ Southeast	IN	16,035	C
Indiana Univ-Purdue Univ Fort Wayne	IN	15,521	C
Indiana Univ-Purdue Univ Indianapolis	IN	17,611	C
Indiana Wesleyan Univ	IN	31,815	VC
Inter-American Univ of PR/ Aguadilla Campus	PR	5,578	
Inter-American Univ of PR/ Arecibo Campus	PR	3,350	
Inter-American Univ of PR/ Barranquitas	PR	3,350	
Inter-American Univ of PR/ Bayamon Univ College	PR	4,428	
Inter-American Univ of PR/ Fajardo Campus	PR	4,200	
Inter-American Univ of PR/ Metropolitan Campus	PR	4,320	
Inter-American Univ of PR/ Ponce	PR		
Inter-American Univ of PR/ San Germán	PR	6,720	
Iona College	NY	44,028	C
Iowa State Univ	IA	16,403	C
Iowa Wesleyan College	IA	30,850	LC
Ithaca College	NY	53,864	HC
Jackson State Univ	MS	13,512	LC
Jacksonville Univ	FL	37,780	C
James Madison Univ	VA	18,049	VC
Jarvis Christian College	TX	19,552	NC
John Brown Univ	AR	32,056	VC+
John Carroll Univ	OH	46,300	C+
Johnson & Wales Univ/ Charlotte Campus	NC	29,576	C
Johnson & Wales Univ/North Miami Campus	FL		C
Johnson & Wales Univ/ Providence Campus	RI	29,576	C
Johnson C. Smith Univ	NC	25,336	LC
Johnson State College	VT	16,721	C
Judson College	AL	26,794	C
Judson Univ	IL	25,130	C
Juniata College	PA	49,340	VC
Kansas State Univ	KS	15,497	VC
Keene State College	NH	23,232	C
Kendall College	IL	32,610	NC
Kennesaw State Univ	GA		C
Kent State Univ	OH	19,920	C
Kentucky Christian Univ	KY	17,622	C
Kentucky State Univ	KY	11,000	C
Kentucky Wesleyan College	KY	27,440	C
Keuka College	NY	30,300	C
Keystone College	PA	28,680	C
King Univ	TN	33,140	C
King's College	PA	43,502	C
Kutztown Univ of Pennsylvania	PA	16,909	LC
La Roche College	PA	35,824	LC
La Salle Univ	PA	50,270	C
La Sierra Univ	CA	35,694	VC
LaGrange College	GA	37,670	C
Lake Erie College	OH	37,266	C
Lake Superior State Univ	MI	18,121	C
Lakeland College	WI	22,990	C
Lamar Univ	TX	6,820	LC
Lander Univ	SC	22,514	C+
Lane College	TN	11,212	C
Langston Univ	OK	3,000	C
Lasell College	MA	43,750	LC
Lawrence Tech Univ	MI	37,630	VC
Le Moyne College	NY	43,470	C
Lebanon Valley College	PA	38,570	C
Lee Univ	TN	18,690	C+
Lees-McRae College	NC	33,944	C
Lehman College/The CUNY	NY	5,778	LC
LeMoyne-Owen College	TN	13,100	C
Lenoir-Rhyne College	NC	35,984	C
LeTourneau Univ	TX	36,210	VC
Lewis Univ	IL	23,050	C
Lewis-Clark State College	ID	6,990	C
Liberty Univ	VA	19,101	C
LIM College	NY	41,575	LC
Limestone College	SC	30,800	C
Lincoln Memorial Univ	TN	18,144	C
Lincoln Univ	MO	12,904	NC
Lindenwood Univ	MO	20,750	C
Lindsey Wilson College	KY	31,220	C
Linfield College-McMinnville Campus	OR	47,676	C
Lipscomb Univ	TN	37,490	VC
LIU Brooklyn	NY	47,182	LC
LIU Post	NY	47,660	C
Livingstone College	NC	17,815	C

ST = STATE   **$IS** = IN-STATE COSTS   **SR** = SELECTOR RATING

School	ST	$IS	SR
Lock Haven Univ of Pennsylvania	PA	18,028	LC
Longwood Univ	VA	20,924	C
Loras College	IA	37,432	VC
Louisiana College	LA	15,746	C
Louisiana State Univ	LA	18,677	C+
Louisiana State Univ in Shreveport	LA	5,606	C
Louisiana Tech Univ	LA	11,302	C
Lourdes Univ	OH	26,055	LC
Loyola Marymount Univ	CA	54,649	VC+
Loyola Univ Chicago	IL	51,646	VC+
Loyola Univ Maryland	MD	56,880	VC+
Loyola Univ New Orleans	LA	46,581	VC
Lubbock Christian Univ	TX	26,308	C
Lycoming College	PA	45,379	C
Lynchburg College	VA	42,645	C
Lyndon State College	VT	14,233	C
Lyon College	AR	32,090	C+
MacMurray College	IL	20,755	C
Madonna Univ	MI	24,540	VC
Malone Univ	OH	35,364	C
Manchester Univ	IN	35,070	C
Manhattanville College	NY	50,740	VC
Mansfield Univ	PA	19,468	LC
Marian Univ	IN	38,540	C
Marian Univ	WI	32,420	LC
Marietta College	OH	42,135	C+
Marist College	NY	35,500	C
Maritime College/SUNY	NY	16,020	C
Marquette Univ	WI	46,930	VC+
Mars Hill Univ	NC	22,950	LC
Martin Univ	IN	11,000	SP
Mary Baldwin College	VA	38,245	C
Marygrove College	MI	28,926	C
Marylhurst Univ	OR	20,295	NC
Marymount Manhattan College	NY	40,118	VC
Marymount Univ	VA	39,480	C
Maryville College	TN	33,150	C+
Maryville Univ of St. Louis	MO	35,856	VC
Marywood Univ	PA	45,595	C
Mass College of Liberal Arts	MA	18,613	C
Mayville State Univ	ND	11,401	NC
McDaniel College	MD	47,450	VC
McKendree Univ	IL	29,920	C+
McMurry Univ	TX	25,962	LC
McNeese State Univ	LA	2,649	C
McPherson College	KS	28,138	C
Medaille College	NY	35,112	C
Megar Evers College/The CUNY	NY	4,920	NC
Mercer Univ	GA	44,201	VC
Mercy College	NY	30,456	C
Mercyhurst Univ	PA	40,700	C
Meredith College	NC	31,420	C
Merrimack College	MA	44,215	C
Messiah College	PA	40,690	C+
Methodist Univ	NC	37,185	C
Metropolitan College of New York	NY	16,720	VC
Metropolitan State Univ	MN	5,923	
Mich State Univ	MI	22,450	VC
MidAmerica Nazarene Univ	KS	28,000	C
Middle Tenn State Univ	TN	8,650	C
Midland Univ	NE	34,000	C
Midway College	KY	20,150	LC
Midwestern State Univ	TX	9,722	C
Miles College	AL	11,164	NC
Millersville Univ of Pennsylvania	PA	21,648	C
Milligan College	TN	27,510	C
Millikin Univ	IL	38,940	C
Millsaps College	MS	43,888	VC+
Milwaukee School of Engineering	WI	39,948	VC+
Minn State Univ, Mankato	MN	15,616	C
Minn State Univ, Moorhead	MN	13,392	VC
Misericordia Univ	PA	41,060	C
Miss College	MS	21,998	C
Miss State Univ	MS	14,750	C
Miss Univ for Women	MS	7,400	C
Miss Valley State Univ	MS	9,706	LC
Missouri Baptist Univ	MO	31,830	C
Missouri Southern State Univ	MO	12,061	C
Missouri State Univ	MO	13,996	C+
Missouri Univ of Science and Technology	MO	18,655	VC+
Missouri Valley College	MO	22,200	C
Missouri Western State Univ	MO	12,260	NC
Mitchell College	CT	40,983	C
Molloy College	NY	40,440	C
Monmouth College	IL	40,850	C
Monmouth Univ	NJ	44,108	C
Monroe College	NY	20,240	C
Montana State Univ	MT	14,068	C
Montana State Univ-Billings	MT	12,425	LC
Montclair State Univ	NJ	22,614	C
Montreat College	NC	31,298	C
Moravian College	PA	36,381	VC
Morehouse College	GA	39,412	C
Morgan State Univ	MD	14,500	VC
Morningside College	IA	35,430	C
Morris College	SC	16,310	LC
Mount Aloysius College	PA	29,976	C
Mount Ida College	MA	30,115	LC
Mount Marty College	SD	29,638	C
Mount Mary Univ	WI	33,590	LC
Mount Mercy Univ	IA	35,320	C
Mount St. Mary College	NY	41,138	C
Mount St. Mary's Univ	MD	47,996	C
Mount St. Mary's College - Chalon Campus	CA	43,897	VC+
Mount Vernon Nazarene Univ	OH	29,590	C
Muhlenberg College	PA	52,837	HC
Murray State Univ	KY	15,304	C
Muskingum Univ	OH	30,502	C
National Louis Univ	IL	16,915	LC
Nazareth College of Rochester	NY	43,028	C
Nebr Wesleyan Univ	NE	29,774	C+
Neumann Univ	PA	31,078	LC
New England College	NH	45,930	LC
New Jersey City Univ	NJ	21,456	LC
New Mexico Highlands Univ	NM	11,904	NC
New Mexico Inst of Mining and Technology	NM	13,592	VC
New Mexico State Univ	NM	14,050	C
New York Inst of Technology	NY	45,010	VC
New York Univ	NY	61,470	MC
Newberry College	SC	26,850	LC
Newbury College	MA	43,280	LC
Newman Univ	KS	30,380	C+
Niagara Univ	NY	41,010	C
Nicholls State Univ	LA	7,095	C
Nichols College	MA	37,240	LC
N Car Agricultural and Technical State Univ	NC	13,365	LC
N Car Central Univ	NC	9,000	C
N Car State Univ	NC	16,202	HC
N Car Wesleyan College	NC	29,440	C
North Central College	IL	38,343	VC
N Dak State Univ	ND		C
North Park Univ	IL	30,130	C
Northeastern Illinois Univ	IL	10,318	LC
Northeastern State Univ	OK	8,615	VC
Northeastern Univ	MA	55,296	MC
Northern Arizona Univ	AZ	19,010	C
Northern Illinois Univ	IL	19,768	C
Northern Kentucky Univ	KY	21,134	C
Northern Mich Univ	MI	18,278	C
Northern State Univ - Aberdeen	SD	14,505	C
Northland College	WI	26,680	C
Northwest Christian Univ	OR	27,399	C
Northwest Missouri State Univ	MO	17,347	C
Northwest Nazarene Univ	ID	34,000	C
Northwest Univ	WA	18,854	C
Northwestern College	MN	24,000	C
Northwestern College of Iowa	IA	36,240	VC
Northwestern Okla State Univ	OK	7,275	NC
Northwestern State Univ of Louisiana	LA	14,368	C
Northwood Univ	FL	33,192	LC
Northwood Univ	MI	26,331	LC
Norwich Univ	VT	28,212	C
Notre Dame de Namur Univ	CA	44,236	LC
Notre Dame of Maryland Univ	MD	27,700	VC
Nova Southeastern Univ	FL	37,280	VC
Nyack College	NY	33,250	C
Oakland City Univ	IN	24,500	NC
Oakland Univ	MI	19,391	C
Oakwood Univ	AL	25,529	NC
Oglala Lakota College	SD	2,000	NC
Oglethorpe Univ	GA	44,200	C+
Ohio Dominican Univ	OH	38,380	C+
Ohio Northern Univ	OH	42,075	VC
Ohio State Univ at Lima	OH	7,140	C
Ohio State Univ at Mansfield	OH	13,160	C
Ohio State Univ at Marion	OH	16,990	MC
Ohio State Univ at Newark	OH	17,510	C
Ohio Univ	OH	21,080	C
Ohio Valley Univ	WV	17,752	C
Okla Baptist Univ	OK	28,202	C
Okla Christian Univ	OK	25,870	VC
Okla City Univ	OK	40,476	VC
Okla Panhandle State Univ	OK	8,996	C
Okla State Univ	OK	14,310	VC
Okla Wesleyan Univ	OK	21,300	C
Old Dominion Univ	VA	19,483	LC
Olivet College	MI	19,984	LC
Olivet Nazarene Univ	IL	29,990	C
Oral Roberts Univ	OK	31,734	C
Oregon State Univ	OR	20,273	VC
Oswego / SUNY	NY	20,009	VC
Ottawa Univ	KS	15,000	VC
Otterbein Univ	OH	32,214	C
Ouachita Baptist Univ	AR	30,220	VC
Our Lady of Holy Cross College	LA	8,090	C
Our Lady of the Lake Univ	TX	22,430	LC
Pace Univ	NY	53,367	C
Pacific Lutheran Univ	WA	46,760	C+
Pacific Union College	CA	28,150	VC
Pacific Univ	OR	49,626	C+
Paine College	GA	19,826	LC
Palm Beach Atlantic Univ	FL	34,874	C+
Park Univ	MO	17,525	C
Paul Quinn College	TX	25,350	LC
Peirce College	PA	12,760	NC
Penn State Erie/The Behrend College	PA	16,256	C
Penn State Univ/Altoona	PA	11,464	C
Pennsylvania College of Technology	PA	26,286	NC
Pepperdine Univ	CA	55,372	HC+
Peru State College	NE	8,600	NC
Pfeiffer Univ	NC	33,700	LC
Philander Smith College	AR	19,760	LC
Piedmont College	GA	30,136	C
Pine Manor College	MA	32,659	LC
Pittsburg State Univ	KS	12,032	C
Plymouth State Univ	NH	23,148	LC
Point Loma Nazarene Univ	CA	41,006	C+
Point Park Univ	PA	36,390	C
Polytechnic Inst of New York Univ	NY	53,064	HC+
Pontifical Catholic Univ of PR	PR	7,310	
Portland State Univ	OR	18,672	C
Post Univ	CT	35,750	C
Prairie View A&M Univ	TX	15,205	LC
Presbyterian College	SC	42,678	C+
Presentation College	SD	14,800	LC
Principia College	IL	35,140	C+
Providence College	RI	57,383	VC
Queens College/The CUNY	NY	17,107	VC
Queens Univ of Charlotte	NC	39,543	C+
Quincy Univ	IL	34,980	LC
Quinnipiac Univ	CT	55,160	VC
Radford Univ	VA	17,766	LC
Ramapo College of New Jersey	NJ	24,938	C
Randolph College	VA	45,660	VC
Regis Univ	CO	41,318	C
Reinhardt College	GA	25,000	C
Rhode Island College	RI	17,694	LC
Rhodes College	TN	51,900	HC+
Richard Stockton College of New Jersey	NJ	20,000	VC
Rider Univ	NJ	45,720	C
Ripon College	WI	36,959	C+
Rivier Univ	NH	35,000	VC
Roanoke College	VA	49,976	C
Robert Morris Univ	PA	37,864	C
Roberts Wesleyan College	NY	38,306	C+
Rochester Inst of Technology	NY	42,450	VC
Rockford College	IL	31,000	C
Rockhurst Univ	MO	20,625	C
Rocky Mountain College	MT	32,242	C
Roger Williams Univ	RI	46,296	VC
Roosevelt Univ	IL	22,605	VC
Rosemont College	PA	42,350	C
Rowan Univ	NJ	24,022	VC+
Rust College	MS	10,600	C
Rutgers, The State Univ of New Jersey/New Brunswick	NJ	25,562	VC
Rutgers, The State Univ of New Jersey/Newark Campus	NJ	258,806	C
Sacred Heart Univ	CT	49,264	VC
Saginaw Valley State Univ	MI	17,369	C
St. Anselm College	NH	49,376	VC
St. Augustine's Univ	NC	14,000	C
St. Joseph's Univ	IN	36,500	C
St. Joseph's College of Maine	ME	31,580	C
St. Joseph's Univ	PA	55,006	VC
St. Leo Univ	FL	30,340	C
St. Louis Univ	MO	48,346	HC
St. Martin's Univ	WA	41,678	C
St. Mary-of-the-Woods College	IN	37,722	C
St. Mary's College	IN	45,160	C+
St. Mary's College of Calif	CA	53,550	C
St. Mary's Univ	TX	33,854	C
St. Mary's Univ of Minn	MN	38,280	C
St. Michael's College	VT	49,975	VC
St. Paul's College	VA	16,030	NC
St. Peter's Univ	NJ	44,240	C
St. Vincent College	PA	40,244	C
St. Xavier Univ	IL	32,840	C
Salem College	NC	29,326	VC
Salem International Univ	WV	21,090	LC
Salem State Univ	MA	13,161	VC
Salisbury Univ	MD	19,180	VC
Salve Regina Univ	RI	48,550	VC
Sam Houston State Univ	TX	17,082	C
San Diego Christian College	CA	31,012	C
San Diego State Univ	CA	21,611	C+
San Francisco State Univ	CA	18,514	C
San Jose State Univ	CA	19,133	LC
Savannah State Univ	GA	13,156	C
Schreiner Univ	TX	32,734	LC
Seattle Pacific Univ	WA	41,559	VC+
Seattle Univ	WA	49,035	VC
Seton Hall Univ	NJ	45,902	C
Seton Hill Univ	PA	35,172	C
Shaw Univ	NC	15,488	C
Shawnee State Univ	OH	16,916	C
Shenandoah Univ	VA	39,916	C
Shepherd Univ	WV	15,875	C
Shippensburg Univ of Pennsylvania	PA	20,934	C
Shorter Univ	GA	30,650	LC
Siena College	NY	43,863	VC
Siena Heights Univ	MI	32,040	C
Sierra Nevada College	NV	32,700	VC
Silver Lake College	WI	22,600	LC
Simmons College	MA	49,966	VC
Simpson College	IA	36,086	C+
Simpson Univ	CA	28,900	C
Skidmore College	NY	59,942	HC
Slippery Rock Univ of Pennsylvania	PA	10,360	C
Sojourner-Douglass College	MD	9,160	LC
Sonoma State Univ	CA	20,541	C
S Car State Univ	SC	6,700	LC
South Univ	GA	36,070	LC
Southeast Missouri State Univ	MO	15,370	LC
Southeastern Louisiana Univ	LA	13,325	C
Southeastern Okla State Univ	OK	7,966	LC
Southeastern Univ	FL	27,201	C
Southern Adventist Univ	TN	26,190	C
Southern Arkansas Univ	AR	14,316	C
Southern Conn State Univ	CT	18,033	LC
Southern Illinois Univ Carbondale	IL	21,942	C
Southern Illinois Univ Edwardsville	IL	17,532	C
Southern Methodist Univ	TX	60,585	MC
Southern Nazarene Univ	OK	24,354	C
Southern New Hampshire Univ	NH	38,100	C
Southern Oregon Univ	OR	17,874	C
Southern Polytechnic State Univ	GA	13,958	C
Southern Univ and A&M College	LA	9,761	LC
Southern Univ at New Orleans	LA	2,963	NC
Southern Vermont College	VT	30,740	LC
Southern Wesleyan Univ	SC	25,600	C
Southwest Baptist Univ	MO	24,710	C
Southwest Minn State Univ	MN	14,000	C
Southwestern Adventist Univ	TX	23,026	LC
Southwestern College	KS	29,270	C
Southwestern Okla State Univ	OK	9,160	C
Southwestern Univ	TX	45,660	VC
Spalding Univ	KY	32,287	LC
Spring Arbor Univ	MI	26,740	C
Spring Hill College	AL	44,164	VC
Springfield College	MA	25,000	C
St. Ambrose Univ	IA	30,845	C
St. Andrews Univ	NC	32,050	LC
St. Catherine Univ	MN	37,782	C+
St. Cloud State Univ	MN	10,600	C
St. Edward's Univ	TX	47,784	C
St. Francis College	NY	34,200	C
St. John Fisher College	NY	40,708	C+
St. John's Univ	NY	55,070	C+
St. Joseph's College, New York/Brooklyn Campus	NY	22,630	C
St. Joseph's College, New York/Suffolk Campus	NY	22,630	C
St. Norbert College	WI	41,478	VC
St. Thomas Aquinas College	NY	40,230	C
St. Thomas Univ	FL	32,130	LC
SUNY Polytechnic Inst	NY	19,690	C
SUNY/Empire State College	NY	6,315	SP
Stephen F. Austin State Univ	TX	14,668	C
Stephens College	MO	38,042	VC
Sterling College	KS	27,216	C
Stetson Univ	FL	51,516	VC
Stevens Inst of Technology	NJ	50,130	HC
Stevenson Univ	MD	41,470	C
Stillman College	AL	19,470	C
Stonehill College	MA	46,780	HC
Stony Brook Univ / SUNY	NY	20,078	HC+
Sul Ross State Univ	TX	13,410	LC
SUNY College at Geneseo	NY	18,670	HC
SUNY College at Old Westbury	NY	16,324	C
SUNY Fredonia/The SUNY at Fredonia	NY	19,840	VC
SUNY New Paltz	NY	14,348	C
SUNY Plattsburgh / SUNY	NY	18,083	C
Susquehanna Univ	PA	51,150	C
Tabor College	KS	29,010	C
Talladega College	AL	17,996	C
Tarleton State Univ	TX	13,489	LC
Taylor Univ	IN	37,821	VC+
Temple Univ	PA	24,392	VC
Tenn State Univ	TN	9,048	C
Tenn Tech Univ	TN	11,310	C
Tenn Wesleyan College	TN	21,250	C
Texas A&M Univ at Commerce	TX	10,496	C
Texas A&M Univ at Corpus Christi	TX	11,544	LC
Texas A&M Univ at Kingsville	TX	7,500	LC
Texas Lutheran Univ	TX	36,040	C
Texas Southern Univ	TX	18,212	LC
Texas State Univ	TX	17,128	C
Texas Tech Univ	TX	14,243	C
Texas Wesleyan Univ	TX	31,382	C
Texas Woman's Univ	TX	13,633	LC
The Catholic Univ of America	DC	52,852	VC
The College of Idaho	ID	31,277	C+
The College of New Rochelle	NY	33,600	VC

ST = STATE   **$IS** = IN-STATE COSTS   **SR** = SELECTOR RATING

School	ST	$IS	SR
The College of St. Rose	NY	26,750	C
The Masters College	CA	38,160	C+
Ohio State Univ-Columbus Campus	OH	19,887	HC+
The Pennsylvania State Univ - Univ Park	PA	28,022	VC+
The SUNY at Potsdam	NY	18,473	C
The SUNY College of Agriculture and Tech at Cobleskill	NY	19,749	LC
The SUNY/College at Brockport	NY	19,002	C
The Univ of N Car at Greensboro	NC	12,848	C
The Univ of N Car at Pembroke	NC	13,388	LC
The Univ of Okla	OK	18,621	VC
The Univ of Tenn at Chattanooga	TN	16,883	C
The Univ of Utah	UT	16,463	VC
The Univ of Virginia's College at Wise	VA	11,076	C
Thiel College	PA	38,728	LC
Thomas College	ME	33,560	LC
Thomas More College	KY	34,760	C
Thomas Univ	GA	11,520	NC
Tiffin Univ	OH	30,273	LC
Toccoa Falls College	GA	23,210	LC
Touro College	NY	27,959	VC
Towson Univ	MD	16,000	VC
Transylvania Univ	KY	42,660	VC+
Trevecca Nazarene Univ	TN	31,186	C
Trine Univ	IN	39,400	HC+
Trinity Christian College	IL	28,869	C
Trinity International Univ	IL	31,070	VC
Trinity Univ	TX	48,150	HC+
Trinity Washington Univ	DC	30,250	C
Troy Univ	AL	10,650	C
Truman State Univ	MO	15,541	HC
Tulane Univ	LA	60,861	MC
Tuskegee Univ	AL	26,750	C
Union College	KY	29,955	C
Union College	NE	23,270	C
Union Inst & Univ	OH	8,912	SP
Union Univ	TN	28,260	VC
Universidad Adventista de las Antillas	PR	7,360	
Universidad de Puerto/Arecibo	PR	7,227	
Universidad del Turabo	PR	4,110	
Universidad Metropolitana	PR	3,500	
Universidad Politecnica de PR	PR	19,252	
Univ at Albany / SUNY	NY	18,674	VC
Univ at Buffalo / The SUNY	NY	20,283	VC
Univ of Akron	OH	20,436	C
Univ of Alabama in Huntsville	AL	17,591	VC+
Univ of Alaska Anchorage	AK	16,673	NC
Univ of Alaska Fairbanks	AK	15,130	C
Univ of Alaska Southeast	AK	11,493	C
Univ of Arizona	AZ	20,657	C
Univ of Arkansas at Fayetteville	AR	18,352	C+
Univ of Arkansas at Little Rock	AR	17,609	LC
Univ of Arkansas at Monticello	AR	12,076	NC
Univ of Arkansas at Pine Bluff	AR	13,378	C
Univ of Bridgeport	CT	39,030	LC
Univ of Calif at Berkeley	CA	33,322	MC
Univ of Calif at Irvine	CA	25,961	VC
Univ of Calif at Riverside	CA	27,204	VC
Univ of Central Arkansas	AR	13,667	VC
Univ of Central Florida	FL	15,668	VC+
Univ of Central Missouri	MO	14,605	C
Univ of Central Okla	OK	12,293	C
Univ of Charleston	WV	32,300	C
Univ of Cincinnati	OH	21,506	VC
Univ of Colo at Colo Springs	CO	15,000	C
Univ of Colo Boulder	CO	22,605	VC+
Univ of Colo Denver	CO	17,904	C
Univ of Conn	CT	24,706	HC
Univ of Dallas	TX	30,450	VC+
Univ of Dayton	OH	49,070	VC
Univ of Delaware	DE	23,612	VC
Univ of Denver	CO	51,787	VC+
Univ of Detroit Mercy	MI	30,450	VC
Univ of Dubuque	IA	30,200	C
Univ of Evansville	IN	42,656	VC+
Univ of Findlay	OH	31,916	C
Univ of Florida	FL	15,943	HC
Univ of Georgia	GA	20,082	VC
Univ of Great Falls	MT	27,970	C
Univ of Hartford	CT	42,674	C
Univ of Hawaii at Hilo	HI	23,066	C
Univ of Hawaii at Manoa	HI	19,379	VC
Univ of Houston-Downtown	TX	15,170	LC
Univ of Idaho	ID	14,558	C
Univ of Illinois at Chicago	IL	24,505	VC
Univ of Indianapolis	IN	31,740	C
Univ of Iowa	IA	17,693	VC
Univ of Jamestown	ND	24,738	C
Univ of Kansas	KS	17,603	C+
Univ of La Verne	CA	47,010	C
Univ of Louisiana at Lafayette	LA	6,130	C
Univ of Louisiana at Monroe	LA	12,998	C
Univ of Louisville	KY	17,946	C
Univ of Maine	ME	19,902	C+
Univ of Maine at Augusta	ME	6,855	C
Univ of Maine at Farmington	ME	18,187	LC
Univ of Maine at Fort Kent	ME	15,195	LC
Univ of Maine at Machias	ME	10,523	C
Univ of Maine at Presque Isle	ME	15,011	LC
Univ of Mary	ND	16,714	C
Univ of Mary Hardin-Baylor	TX	31,950	C+
Univ of Mary Washington	VA	19,484	VC
Univ of Maryland - College Park	MD	20,060	HC
Univ of Maryland/Eastern Shore	MD	14,000	VC
Univ of Maryland/Univ College	MD	6,168	SP
Univ of Mass Amherst	MA	24,215	VC+
Univ of Mass Dartmouth	MA	22,223	C
Univ of Mass Lowell	MA	19,316	C
Univ of Mich/Ann Arbor	MI	22,102	MC
Univ of Mich/Dearborn	MI	9,885	VC
Univ of Mich-Flint	MI	17,547	C+
Univ of Minn Crookston	MN	17,834	C
Univ of Minn/Duluth	MN	19,806	C
Univ of Minn/Twin Cities	MN		HC
Univ of Miss	MS	16,704	C+
Univ of Missouri/Columbia	MO	18,201	MC
Univ of Missouri-Kansas City	MO	19,603	C
Univ of Missouri-St. Louis	MO		VC
Univ of Mobile	AL	28,935	VC
Univ of Montana	MT	14,105	C
Univ of Montevallo	AL	17,060	C
Univ of Mount Olive	NC	18,426	C
Univ of Mount Union	OH	35,130	C
Univ of Nebr - Lincoln	NE	18,031	VC
Univ of Nebr at Kearney	NE	14,855	LC
Univ of New England	ME	46,750	C
Univ of New Hampshire	NH	26,912	C
Univ of New Haven	CT	48,940	VC
Univ of New Mexico	NM	15,300	C
Univ of New Orleans	LA	9,224	C
Univ of N Car at Asheville	NC	13,500	VC
Univ of N Car at Chapel Hill	NC	18,928	MC
Univ of N Car at Charlotte	NC	15,547	C
Univ of N Car at Wilmington	NC	13,572	VC
Univ of North Florida	FL	15,870	VC
Univ of North Georgia	GA	8,500	C
Univ of North Texas	TX	15,628	C
Univ of Northern Colo	CO	18,446	C
Univ of Oregon	OR	21,360	C+
Univ of Pennsylvania	PA	61,132	MC
Univ of Pikeville	KY	25,500	NC
Univ of Pittsburgh at Bradford	PA	21,802	C
Univ of Pittsburgh at Johnstown	PA	20,862	LC
Univ of Pittsburgh at Pittsburgh	PA	28,572	HC+
Univ of PR Recinto de Rio Piedras	PR	5,750	
Univ of PR/Bayamon	PR	1,600	
Univ of PR/Cayey	PR	1,504	
Univ of PR/Humacao	PR	1,877	
Univ of PR/Mayaguez	PR	1,250	
Univ of Puget Sound	WA	54,608	HC
Univ of Redlands	CA	40,500	VC
Univ of Rio Grande	OH	8,750	NC
Univ of Rochester	NY	60,668	MC
Univ of St. Francis	IN	29,810	C
Univ of St. Mary	KS	28,400	C+
Univ of San Diego	CA	54,818	HC+
Univ of San Francisco	CA	54,770	VC
Univ of Science and Arts of Okla	OK	10,560	VC
Univ of Scranton	PA	51,940	VC
Univ of Sioux Falls	SD	22,990	C
Univ of South Alabama	AL	13,510	C
Univ of S Car at Aiken	SC	16,712	C
Univ of S Car at Columbia	SC	19,725	VC+
Univ of S Car Upstate	SC	18,200	LC
Univ of South Florida/St. Petersburg	FL	12,769	C
Univ of South Florida/Tampa	FL	13,000	C
Univ of Southern Calif	CA	56,903	MC
Univ of Southern Indiana	IN	14,885	C
Univ of Southern Maine	ME	16,576	C
Univ of Southern Miss	MS	13,170	C
Univ of St. Francis	IL	37,560	C
Univ of St. Thomas - Houston	TX	37,690	C
Univ of Tampa	FL	35,160	VC
Univ of Tenn at Martin	TN	13,734	C
Univ of Texas at Arlington	TX	10,908	LC
Univ of Texas at Austin	TX	44,074	HC
Univ of Texas at Dallas	TX	21,348	HC+
Univ of Texas at San Antonio	TX	18,372	C
Univ of the Cumberlands	KY	27,500	C
Univ of the District of Columbia	DC	7,244	LC
Univ of the Incarnate Word	TX	37,316	LC
Univ of the Ozarks	AR	31,440	C
Univ of the Pacific	CA	52,146	VC
Univ of the Sacred Heart	PR	5,590	
Univ of the Southwest	NM	15,000	C
Univ of Toledo	OH	18,464	C
Univ of Tulsa	OK	46,331	MC
Univ of Vermont	VT	27,006	VC+
Univ of Virginia	VA	23,050	MC
Univ of Washington	WA	14,722	VC
Univ of West Alabama	AL	14,274	C
Univ of West Florida	FL	14,656	C
Univ of West Georgia	GA	15,488	LC
Univ of Wisc Whitewater	WI	13,314	C
Univ of Wisc/Eau Claire	WI	15,730	VC
Univ of Wisc/Green Bay	WI	19,074	C
Univ of Wisc/La Crosse	WI	9,304	VC
Univ of Wisc/Oshkosh	WI	10,426	C
Univ of Wisc/Parkside	WI	10,181	C
Univ of Wisc/Platteville	WI	14,564	C
Univ of Wisc/River Falls	WI	9,722	C
Univ of Wisc/Stevens Point	WI	14,043	C
Univ of Wisc/Stout	WI	15,459	C
Univ of Wisc/Superior	WI	14,314	C
Univ of Wisc-Milwaukee	WI	18,436	C
Univ of Wyoming	WY	14,401	C+
Upper Iowa Univ	IA	30,426	NC
Urbana Univ	OH	30,820	C
Ursuline College	OH	33,198	LC
Utah State Univ	UT	12,044	C
Utica College	NY	45,670	C
Valley City State Univ	ND	12,286	C
Valparaiso Univ	IN	44,940	VC+
Vanguard Univ of Southern Calif	CA	35,833	VC
Vaughn College of Aeronautics and Technology	NY	31,360	C
Villanova Univ	PA	58,394	MC
Virginia Commonwealth Univ	VA	21,716	C
Virginia State Univ	VA	11,318	C+
Virginia Union Univ	VA	18,432	C
Virginia Wesleyan College	VA	28,433	LC
Voorhees College	SC	18,126	C
Wagner College	NY	48,600	C+
Wake Forest Univ	NC	58,838	MC
Walla Walla Univ	WA	26,256	NC
Walsh Univ	OH	35,100	C
Warner Pacific College	OR	25,550	C
Warner Univ	FL	18,000	C
Wartburg College	IA	41,055	VC
Washburn Univ	KS	12,579	C
Washington Adventist Univ	MD	25,859	LC
Washington and Jefferson College	PA	51,948	VC
Washington and Lee Univ	VA	52,812	MC
Washington College	MD	52,602	VC
Washington State Univ	WA	20,461	C
Washington Univ in St. Louis	MO	69,844	MC
Wayland Baptist Univ	TX	18,912	LC
Wayne State College	NE	11,764	NC
Wayne State Univ	MI	22,063	C
Webber International Univ	FL	30,147	C
Webster Univ	MO	35,100	C+
Wells College	NY	49,400	VC
Wesley College	DE	31,115	LC
Wesleyan College	GA	24,000	C
West Chester Univ of Pennsylvania	PA	17,186	C
West Liberty Univ	WV	9,142	LC
West Texas A&M Univ	TX	13,478	C
West Virginia State Univ	WV	8,378	NC
West Virginia Univ	WV	16,542	C+
West Virginia Univ Inst of Technology	WV	14,094	NC
West Virginia Wesleyan College	WV	26,880	C
Western Conn State Univ	CT	18,327	LC
Western Illinois Univ	IL	20,732	C
Western Mich Univ	MI	19,628	C
Western New England Univ	MA	46,154	C+
Western New Mexico Univ	NM	8,500	C
Western Oregon Univ	OR	15,021	C
Western State Colo Univ	CO	16,924	C
Western Washington Univ	WA	18,519	VC
Westfield State Univ	MA	18,297	C
Westminster College	MO	31,720	VC
Westminster College	PA	31,290	C+
Westminster College	UT	37,708	C+
Wheeling Jesuit Univ	WV	33,500	C
Whittier College	CA	43,416	C
Whitworth Univ	WA	47,734	VC
Wichita State Univ	KS	14,607	C+
Widener Univ	PA	52,418	C
Wilberforce Univ	OH	15,100	LC
Wiley College	TX		LC
Wilkes Univ	PA	44,070	C
William Carey Univ	MS	13,500	LC
William Jewell College	MO	31,000	VC+
William Paterson Univ of New Jersey	NJ	21,694	C
William Peace Univ	NC	32,900	LC
William Penn Univ	IA	26,000	C
William Woods Univ	MO	24,260	C
Williams Baptist College	AR	20,070	C
Wilmington College	OH	29,784	C
Wilmington Univ	DE	8,112	NC
Wingate Univ	NC	34,990	C
Winona State Univ	MN	16,640	C
Winston-Salem State Univ	NC	9,418	LC
Winthrop Univ	SC	21,120	C

School	ST	$IS	SR
Wittenberg Univ	OH	47,962	C+
Woodbury Univ	CA	34,500	LC
Worcester Polytechnic Inst	MA	55,860	MC
Worcester State Univ	MA	19,812	C
Xavier Univ	OH	44,980	VC
Xavier Univ of Louisiana	LA	25,300	C
Yeshiva Univ	NY	47,250	VC+
York College	NE	19,475	C
York College / The CUNY	NY	5,496	C
York College of Pennsylvania	PA	26,590	C
Youngstown State Univ	OH	16,732	C

BUSINESS ADMINISTRATION MARKETING

School	ST	$IS	SR
Aquinas College	MI	33,060	C
Arizona State Univ, at the Tempe Campus	AZ	20,137	C+
Bentley Univ	MA	56,454	HC+
Black Hills State Univ	SD	13,947	C
Bloomfield College	NJ	37,850	LC
Campbell Univ	NC	37,570	VC
College of the Ozarks	MO		VC
Franklin College	IN	36,585	C
Hood College	MD	45,730	C
Millersville Univ of Pennsylvania	PA	21,648	C
Monmouth Univ	NJ	44,108	C
Niagara Univ	NY	41,010	C
Okla Christian Univ	OK	25,870	VC
Taylor Univ	IN	37,821	VC+
The Pennsylvania State Univ - Univ Park	PA	28,022	VC+
Univ of Maine	ME	19,902	C+
Urbana Univ	OH	30,820	C
Western Illinois Univ	IL	20,732	C

BUSINESS ADMINISTRATION W/ LEGAL STUDIES

School	ST	$IS	SR
Ferris State Univ	MI	20,047	C

BUSINESS ADMINISTRATION, MGMT, OPERATIONS

School	ST	$IS	SR
Black Hills State Univ	SD	13,947	C
Campbell Univ	NC	37,570	VC
College of the Ozarks	MO		VC
Concordia College - New York	NY	39,035	LC
Excelsior College	NY	5,580	SP
Fairfield Univ	CT	56,960	VC
Franklin College	IN	36,585	C
Indiana Univ Bloomington	IN	19,801	VC
Northwest Nazarene Univ	ID	34,000	C
Okla Christian Univ	OK	25,870	VC
Univ of Georgia	GA	20,082	VC

BUSINESS ADMINISTRATION/ AVIATION

School	ST	$IS	SR
Ferris State Univ	MI	20,047	C

BUSINESS AND TECHNOLOGY

School	ST	$IS	SR
Arizona State Univ, at the Polytechnic Campus	AZ	20,531	C+

BUSINESS COMMUNICATIONS

School	ST	$IS	SR
Aquinas College	MI	33,060	C
Arizona State Univ, at the Polytechnic Campus	AZ	20,531	C+
Arizona State Univ, at the Tempe Campus	AZ	20,137	C+
Arizona State Univ, at the West Campus	AZ	19,251	C
Augustana College	SD	36,500	VC
Bentley Univ	MA	56,454	HC+
Biola Univ	CA	40,320	C+
Bryant Univ	RI	49,179	VC
Calvin College	MI	39,120	VC
Canisius College	NY	44,900	C
Carlow Univ	PA	30,272	C
Chestnut Hill College	PA	42,110	LC
Duquesne Univ	PA	43,720	VC
George Fox Univ	OR	40,750	C+
Ithaca College	NY	53,864	HC
Murray State Univ	KY	15,304	C
Nichols College	MA	37,240	LC
Olivet Nazarene Univ	IL	29,990	C
Point Loma Nazarene Univ	CA	41,006	C+
Rockhurst Univ	MO	20,625	C
St. Leo Univ	FL	30,340	C
Southeast Missouri State Univ	MO	15,370	LC
Southwestern College	KS	29,270	C
Stevenson Univ	MD	41,470	C
Univ of Akron	OH	20,436	C
Univ of Indianapolis	IN	31,740	LC
Univ of Mary	ND	16,714	C
Univ of Nebr at Omaha	NE	12,700	C
Univ of Southern Indiana	IN	14,885	C
Walsh Univ	OH	35,100	C
Webber International Univ	FL	30,147	C
Westminster College	MO	31,720	VC

ST = STATE $IS = IN-STATE COSTS   SR = SELECTOR RATING

BUSINESS DATA PROCESSING

School	ST	$IS	SR
Bryant Univ	RI	49,179	VC
Cal State, Fresno	CA	17,405	C
Eastern Mich Univ	MI	18,604	C
Ferris State Univ	MI	20,047	C
Idaho State Univ	ID	12,307	C
Mount Vernon Nazarene Univ	OH	29,590	C

BUSINESS ECONOMICS

School	ST	$IS	SR
Adams State Univ	CO	13,358	LC
Alabama State Univ	AL	14,142	NC
American International College	MA	36,100	LC
Andrews Univ	MI	28,030	C+
Aquinas College	MI	33,060	C
Arkansas State Univ	AR	15,470	C
Ashford Univ	CA	10,480	C
Ashland Univ	OH	25,000	C
Auburn Univ	AL	22,378	VC+
Auburn Univ at Montgomery	AL	14,470	C
Ball State Univ	IN	17,850	C
Baylor Univ	TX	50,329	HC
Beloit College	WI	49,970	HC
Benedictine Univ	IL	37,820	C
Bentley Univ	MA	56,454	HC+
Bethany College	KS	30,605	NC
Bethel College	IN	31,560	C
Biola Univ	CA	40,320	C+
Bloomfield College	NJ	37,850	LC
Bloomsburg Univ of Pennsylvania	PA	13,598	C
Boston College	MA	60,622	MC
Brescia Univ	KY	26,140	VC+
Bryant Univ	RI	49,179	VC
Buena Vista Univ	IA	39,188	C
Cal State, Fullerton	CA	25,188	C
Cal State, Long Beach	CA	17,502	C+
Cal State, San Bernardino	CA	12,000	C
Campbell Univ	NC	37,570	VC
Campbellsville Univ	KY	27,720	C
Canisius College	NY	44,900	C
Carnegie Mellon Univ	PA	51,260	MC
Carson-Newman Univ	TN	29,058	C+
Centenary College of Louisiana	LA	45,650	C+
Central Washington Univ	WA	11,730	C
Clarion Univ of Pennsylvania	PA	17,370	LC
Cleveland State Univ	OH	21,776	C
College of the Ozarks	MO		VC
College of Wooster	OH	52,600	VC
Cornell College	IA	44,930	VC
DePaul Univ	IL	47,623	VC
Dominican College	NY	31,270	LC
Dordt College	IA	34,160	C+
Drexel Univ	PA	61,418	VC+
Duquesne Univ	PA	43,720	VC
Eastern Mich Univ	MI	18,604	C
Elizabethtown College	PA	49,740	VC
Elmira College	NY	49,950	C+
Emory Univ	GA	56,368	MC
Eureka College	IL	19,280	C
Fairleigh Dickinson Univ/Metropolitan Campus	NJ	40,254	C
Fairmont State Univ	WV	12,098	LC
Fayetteville State Univ	NC	10,816	LC
Florida A&M Univ	FL	14,935	LC
Florida Atlantic Univ	FL	17,339	C
Fordham Univ	NY	61,588	HC+
Fort Lewis College	CO	15,513	C
Francis Marion Univ	SC	16,464	LC
Friends Univ	KS	29,100	C
George Washington Univ	DC	57,108	MC
Georgetown College	KY	41,440	C+
Georgia State Univ	GA	15,582	VC
Gonzaga Univ	WA	46,441	HC
Grambling State Univ	LA	13,384	C
Grand Valley State Univ	MI	17,998	C+
Grove City College	PA	24,022	VC
Gustavus Adolphus College	MN	48,170	HC
Hampden-Sydney College	VA	51,758	C
Hawaii Pacific Univ	HI	34,360	C
Heidelberg Univ	OH	34,100	C
Hendrix College	AR	50,202	VC+
Hofstra Univ	NY	51,810	VC+
Humboldt State Univ	CA	18,400	C
Indiana Univ-Purdue Univ Fort Wayne	IN	15,521	C
Inter-American Univ of PR/Bayamon Univ College	PR	4,428	
James Madison Univ	VA	18,049	VC
Johnson C. Smith Univ	NC	25,336	LC
Kalamazoo College	MI	49,740	HC
Kansas Wesleyan Univ	KS	32,000	C
Kentucky Wesleyan College	KY	27,440	C
King Univ	TN	33,140	C
Kutztown Univ of Pennsylvania	PA	16,909	LC
Lafayette College	PA	59,155	HC+
Lake Forest College	IL	50,652	VC
Lakeland College	WI	22,990	C
Lamar Univ	TX	6,820	LC
Lehigh Univ	PA	56,770	MC
Limestone College	SC	30,800	C
Louisiana Tech Univ	LA	11,302	C
Loyola Univ Chicago	IL	51,646	VC+
Manhattan College	NY	49,588	C+
Mansfield Univ	PA	19,468	LC
Marquette Univ	WI	46,930	VC+
Marshall Univ	WV	14,820	C
Merrimack College	MA	44,215	C
Miami Univ	OH	24,191	VC
Midland Univ	NE	34,000	C
Midwestern State Univ	TX	9,722	C
Mills College	CA	54,119	VC
Monmouth Univ	NJ	44,108	C
Montclair State Univ	NJ	22,614	C
Moravian College	PA	36,381	VC
Morehead State Univ	KY	10,900	C
Mount Aloysius College	PA	29,976	C
New Mexico State Univ	NM	14,050	C
New York Univ	NY	61,470	MC
Niagara Univ	NY	41,010	C
N Car State Univ	NC	16,202	HC
Northern Arizona Univ	AZ	19,010	C
Northern State Univ - Aberdeen	SD	14,505	C
Northland College	WI	26,680	C
Northwest Missouri State Univ	MO	17,347	C
Northwestern College of Iowa	IA	36,240	VC
Northwood Univ	MI	26,331	LC
Norwich Univ	VT	28,212	C
Notre Dame College	OH	34,942	VC
Oakland Univ	MI	19,391	C
Ohio Northern Univ	OH	42,075	VC
Ohio Univ	OH	21,080	C
Ohio Wesleyan Univ	OH	49,460	C+
Pace Univ	NY	53,367	C
Park Univ	MO	17,525	C
Penn State Erie/The Behrend College	PA	16,256	C
Pittsburg State Univ	KS	12,032	C
Pontifical Catholic Univ of PR	PR	7,310	
Presbyterian College	SC	42,678	C+
Providence College	RI	57,383	VC
Purdue Univ/Calumet	IN	14,336	C
Randolph-Macon College	VA	49,869	C+
Regis Univ	CO	41,318	C
Rider Univ	NJ	45,720	C
Rockhurst Univ	MO	20,625	C
Sacred Heart Univ	CT	49,264	VC
Saginaw Valley State Univ	MI	17,369	C
Seattle Univ	WA	49,035	VC+
Seton Hall Univ	NJ	45,902	C
Seton Hill Univ	PA	35,172	C
Skidmore College	NY	59,942	HC
S Car State Univ	SC	6,700	LC
Southeast Missouri State Univ	MO	15,370	LC
Southern Conn State Univ	CT	18,033	LC
Southern Illinois Univ Carbondale	IL	21,942	C
Southern Illinois Univ Edwardsville	IL	17,532	C
Southern Univ and A&M College	LA	9,761	LC
St. Ambrose Univ	IA	30,845	C
St. Cloud State Univ	MN	10,600	C
St. John's Univ	NY	55,070	C+
Stetson Univ	FL	51,516	VC
SUNY Fredonia/The SUNY at Fredonia	NY	19,840	VC
SUNY Oneonta / SUNY	NY	16,919	C+
Tenn State Univ	TN	9,048	C
Texas A&M Univ at Kingsville	TX	7,500	LC
Texas State Univ	TX	17,128	C
Texas Tech Univ	TX	14,243	C
Texas Wesleyan Univ	TX	31,382	C
The SUNY at Potsdam	NY	18,473	C
The Univ of Memphis	TN	15,094	C
The Univ of N Car at Greensboro	NC	12,848	C
The Univ of Okla	OK	18,621	VC
Thomas College	ME	33,560	LC
Trinity Washington Univ	DC	30,250	C+
Troy Univ	AL	10,650	C
Tuskegee Univ	AL	26,750	C
Univ of Arizona	AZ	20,657	C
Univ of Arkansas at Fayetteville	AR	18,352	C+
Univ of Calif at Irvine	CA	25,961	VC
Univ of Calif at Los Angeles	CA	25,686	MC
Univ of Calif at Riverside	CA	27,204	C+
Univ of Calif at Santa Cruz	CA	27,807	C+
Univ of Central Arkansas	AR	13,667	VC
Univ of Central Florida	FL	15,668	VC+
Univ of Dayton	OH	49,070	VC
Univ of Denver	CO	51,787	VC+
Univ of Findlay	OH	31,916	C
Univ of Idaho	ID	14,558	C
Univ of Illinois at Chicago	IL	24,505	VC
Univ of Indianapolis	IN	31,740	LC
Univ of Iowa	IA	17,693	VC
Univ of Kentucky	KY	19,868	C
Univ of La Verne	CA	47,010	C
Univ of Louisville	KY	17,946	C
Univ of Maine	ME	19,902	C+
Univ of Maine at Farmington	ME	18,187	LC
Univ of Miss	MS	16,704	C+
Univ of Missouri/Columbia	MO	18,201	MC
Univ of Nebr - Lincoln	NE	18,031	VC
Univ of Nebr at Kearney	NE	14,855	LC
Univ of North Alabama	AL	9,960	C
Univ of N Car at Charlotte	NC	15,547	C
Univ of N Car at Wilmington	NC	13,572	VC
Univ of N Dak	ND	14,551	C
Univ of North Florida	FL	15,870	VC
Univ of North Georgia	GA	8,500	C
Univ of Pittsburgh at Johnstown	PA	20,862	LC
Univ of PR Recinto de Rio Piedras	PR	5,750	
Univ of PR/Mayaguez	PR	1,250	
Univ of Rio Grande	OH	8,750	NC
Univ of San Diego	CA	54,818	HC+
Univ of Scranton	PA	51,940	VC
Univ of Sioux Falls	SD	22,990	C
Univ of South Alabama	AL	13,510	C
Univ of S Car at Columbia	SC	19,725	VC+
Univ of South Florida/Tampa	FL	13,000	C
Univ of Southern Miss	MS	13,170	C
Univ of Tampa	FL	35,160	VC
Univ of Tenn at Martin	TN	13,734	C
Univ of Texas at Arlington	TX	10,908	LC
Univ of Texas at El Paso	TX	8,764	NC
Univ of Washington	WA	14,722	VC
Univ of West Florida	FL	14,656	C
Univ of West Georgia	GA	15,488	LC
Univ of Wisc Whitewater	WI	13,314	C
Univ of Wyoming	WY	14,401	C+
Ursinus College	PA	57,580	VC
Utah State Univ	UT	12,044	C
Utica College	NY	45,670	C
Villanova Univ	PA	58,394	MC
Virginia Military Inst	VA	16,156	C
Virginia Polytechnic Inst and State Univ	VA	14,629	HC
Washburn Univ	KS	12,579	C
Washington State Univ	WA	20,461	C
Washington Univ in St. Louis	MO	69,844	MC
West Liberty Univ	WV	9,142	LC
West Texas A&M Univ	TX	13,478	C
Western Kentucky Univ	KY	11,000	LC
Western Mich Univ	MI	19,628	C
Westmont College	CA	41,500	HC
Wheaton College	IL	40,720	MC
Widener Univ	PA	52,418	C
Wilberforce Univ	OH	15,100	LC
William Jewell College	MO	31,000	VC+
Wilson College	PA	35,080	C
Winona State Univ	MN	16,640	C
Wisc Lutheran College	WI	23,510	VC
Wofford College	SC	45,795	VC
Wright State Univ	OH	16,983	C
Xavier Univ	OH	44,980	VC
Xavier Univ of Louisiana	LA	25,300	C
Youngstown State Univ	OH	16,732	C

BUSINESS EDUCATION

School	ST	$IS	SR
Adams State Univ	CO	13,358	LC
Alabama State Univ	AL	14,142	NC
Alfred Univ	NY	41,770	C
Appalachian State Univ	NC	12,919	VC
Arizona State Univ, at the Polytechnic Campus	AZ	20,531	C+
Arizona State Univ, at the West Campus	AZ	19,251	C
Arkansas State Univ	AR	15,470	C
Arkansas Tech Univ	AR	13,982	LC
Auburn Univ	AL	22,378	VC+
Avila Univ	MO	26,900	C
Ball State Univ	IN	17,850	C
Baylor Univ	TX	50,329	HC
Bethany College	KS	30,605	NC
Bethel Univ	MN	34,940	VC
Bethune-Cookman Univ	FL	22,958	C
Black Hills State Univ	SD	13,947	C
Bloomsburg Univ of Pennsylvania	PA	13,598	C
Bowling Green State Univ	OH	18,970	C
Brigham Young Univ/Hawaii	HI	10,686	VC
Bryant Univ	RI	49,179	VC
Buena Vista Univ	IA	39,188	C
Buffalo State College / SUNY	NY	15,733	C+
Cal State, Northridge	CA	28,690	LC
Cal State, Sacramento	CA	16,200	C
Canisius College	NY	44,900	C
Caribbean Univ	PR	10,375	
Central Washington Univ	WA	11,730	C
Chicago State Univ	IL	5,482	C
Clark Atlanta Univ	GA	30,006	LC
College of the Ozarks	MO		VC
Concord Univ	WV	13,102	C
Concordia College - Moorhead	MN	39,974	VC
Concordia Univ Nebr	NE	26,000	VC
Corban Univ	OR	37,380	C+
Dakota State Univ	SD	13,811	C
Delaware State Univ	DE	16,722	LC
Dickinson State Univ	ND	11,900	NC
Doane Univ	NE	35,230	C
Dordt College	IA	34,160	C+
East Carolina Univ	NC	14,169	C
East Central Univ	OK	10,223	LC
Eastern Kentucky Univ	KY	11,161	C
Eastern Mich Univ	MI	18,604	C
Eastern New Mexico Univ	NM	10,682	C
Elizabeth City State Univ	NC	11,638	C
Emporia State Univ	KS	12,897	C
Evangel Univ	MO	23,090	C
Fairmont State Univ	WV	12,098	LC
Fayetteville State Univ	NC	10,816	LC
Ferris State Univ	MI	20,047	C
Florida A&M Univ	FL	14,935	LC
Framingham State Univ	MA	18,854	C
Friends Univ	KS	29,100	C
Glenville State College	WV	11,348	NC
Goshen College	IN	35,900	VC
Grace College and Seminary	IN	28,800	VC
Gustavus Adolphus College	MN	48,170	HC
Gwynedd-Mercy College	PA	33,560	C
Hardin-Simmons Univ	TX	23,560	C+
Hastings College	NE	27,782	C+
Henderson State Univ	AR	14,584	C
Hofstra Univ	NY	51,810	VC+
Humboldt State Univ	CA	18,400	C
Illinois State Univ	IL	23,110	VC
Indiana State Univ	IN	16,000	C
Jackson State Univ	MS	13,512	LC
Lakeland College	WI	22,990	C
Langston Univ	OK	3,000	C
Lee Univ	TN	18,690	C+
Lehman College/The CUNY	NY	5,778	LC
LeTourneau Univ	TX	36,210	VC
Lincoln Memorial Univ	TN	18,144	C
Lincoln Univ	MO	12,904	NC
Lindenwood Univ	MO	20,750	C
Louisiana College	LA	15,746	C
McKendree Univ	IL	29,920	C+
McMurry Univ	TX	25,962	LC
Mercyhurst Univ	PA	40,700	C
MidAmerica Nazarene Univ	KS	28,000	C
Middle Tenn State Univ	TN	8,650	C
Midland Univ	NE	34,000	C
Minot State Univ	ND	10,915	C
Miss College	MS	21,998	C
Miss State Univ	MS	14,750	C
Missouri Baptist Univ	MO	31,830	C
Missouri Southern State Univ	MO	12,061	C
Missouri State Univ	MO	13,996	C+
Montana State Univ-Northern	MT	12,500	NC
Montclair State Univ	NJ	22,614	C
Morehead State Univ	KY	10,900	C
Mount Vernon Nazarene Univ	OH	29,590	C
Nazareth College of Rochester	NY	43,028	C+
Niagara Univ	NY	41,010	C
Nicholls State Univ	LA	7,095	C
Norfolk State Univ	VA	10,531	LC
N Car Agricultural and Technical State Univ	NC	13,365	C
Northern Kentucky Univ	KY	21,134	C
Northern Mich Univ	MI	18,278	C
Northern State Univ - Aberdeen	SD	14,505	C
Northwest Missouri State Univ	MO	17,347	C
Northwestern College of Iowa	IA	36,240	VC
Northwestern Okla State Univ	OK	7,275	NC
Oakland City Univ	IN	24,500	C
Oakwood Univ	AL	25,529	NC
Oglala Lakota College	SD	2,000	NC
Ohio Univ	OH	21,080	C
Okla Panhandle State Univ	OK	8,996	C
Okla Wesleyan Univ	OK	21,300	C
Oral Roberts Univ	OK	31,734	C
Oswego / SUNY	NY	20,009	VC
Ouachita Baptist Univ	AR	30,220	VC
Philander Smith College	AR	19,760	LC
Pontifical Catholic Univ of PR	PR	7,310	
Rider Univ	NJ	45,720	C
Robert Morris Univ	PA	37,864	C
Rust College	MS	10,600	C
Sacred Heart Univ	CT	49,264	VC
St. Augustine's Univ	NC	14,000	C
St. Mary's Univ	TX	33,854	C
St. Paul's College	VA	16,030	NC
St. Vincent College	PA	40,244	C
Salem State Univ	MA	13,161	LC
Shippensburg Univ of Pennsylvania	PA	20,934	C
S Car State Univ	SC	6,700	LC
Southeastern Okla State Univ	OK	7,966	LC
Southern Arkansas Univ	AR	14,316	C
Southern New Hampshire Univ	NH	38,100	C
Southern Univ at New Orleans	LA	2,963	NC
Southwestern Adventist Univ	TX	23,026	LC
Suffolk Univ	MA	47,298	C
SUNY Oneonta / SUNY	NY	16,919	C+
Tabor College	KS	29,010	C
Tarleton State Univ	TX	13,489	C
Texas A&M Univ at Commerce	TX	10,496	C

ST = STATE   **$IS** = IN-STATE COSTS   **SR** = SELECTOR RATING

School	ST	$IS	SR
Thomas College	ME	33,560	LC
Thomas More College	KY	34,760	C
Trevecca Nazarene Univ	TN	31,186	C
Union College	NE	23,270	C
Univ of Arkansas at Fayetteville	AR	18,352	C+
Univ of Arkansas at Pine Bluff	AR	13,378	C
Univ of Central Florida	FL	15,668	VC+
Univ of Central Missouri	MO	14,605	C
Univ of Cincinnati	OH	21,506	VC
Univ of Idaho	ID	14,558	C
Univ of Indianapolis	IN	31,740	LC
Univ of Kentucky	KY	19,868	C
Univ of Louisville	KY	17,946	C
Univ of Maine at Machias	ME	10,523	C
Univ of Maryland/Eastern Shore	MD	14,000	C
Univ of Minn/Twin Cities	MN		HC
Univ of Montana-Western	MT	9,753	LC
Univ of Nebr - Lincoln	NE	18,031	VC
Univ of Nebr at Kearney	NE	14,855	LC
Univ of North Alabama	AL	9,960	C
Univ of N Dak	ND	14,551	C
Univ of Northern Iowa	IA	15,795	C
Univ of Pittsburgh at Bradford	PA	21,802	C
Univ of Rio Grande	OH	8,750	NC
Univ of St. Francis	IN	29,810	C
Univ of South Florida/Tampa	FL	13,000	C
Univ of Southern Indiana	IN	14,885	C
Univ of Southern Miss	MS	13,170	C
Univ of St. Thomas - Houston	TX	37,690	C
Univ of the Ozarks	AR	31,440	C
Univ of Toledo	OH	18,464	C
Univ of West Georgia	GA	15,488	LC
Univ of Wisc Whitewater	WI	13,314	C
Utah State Univ	UT	12,044	C
Valley City State Univ	ND	12,286	LC
Vermont Technical College	VT	15,751	C
Virginia Polytechnic Inst and State Univ	VA	14,629	HC
Virginia State Univ	VA	11,318	C+
Virginia Union Univ	VA	18,432	C
Viterbo Univ	WI	30,070	C
Walla Walla Univ	WA	26,256	NC
Warner Univ	FL	18,000	C
Wayland Baptist Univ	TX	18,912	LC
West Texas A&M Univ	TX	13,478	C
Western Kentucky Univ	KY	11,000	LC
Western Mich Univ	MI	19,628	C
Western New Mexico Univ	NM	8,500	LC
Wiley College	TX		LC
Winona State Univ	MN	16,640	C
Wright State Univ	OH	16,983	C

BUSINESS INFORMATION SYSTEMS

School	ST	$IS	SR
Arizona State Univ, at the Tempe Campus	AZ	20,137	C+
Ashford Univ	CA	10,480	C
Bentley Univ	MA	56,454	HC+
Biola Univ	CA	40,320	C+
Bloomfield College	NJ	37,850	LC
Bryant Univ	RI	49,179	VC
CUNY/Brooklyn College	NY	5,884	C+
Faulkner Univ	AL	25,720	LC
Illinois State Univ	IL	23,110	VC
Lehigh Univ	PA	56,770	MC
Northern Kentucky Univ	KY	21,134	C
Texas Christian Univ	TX	49,980	HC
Univ of Arkansas at Fayetteville	AR	18,352	C+
Univ of Illinois at Chicago	IL	24,505	VC
Univ of Pittsburgh at Pittsburgh	PA	28,572	HC+

BUSINESS INSTITUTIONS

School	ST	$IS	SR
Univ of Rhode Island	RI	24,002	C

BUSINESS INTELLIGENCE AND ANALYTICS

School	ST	$IS	SR
Bryant Univ	RI	49,179	VC
College of St. Mary	NE	35,184	C
Creighton Univ	NE	45,356	VC
Murray State Univ	KY	15,304	C
Old Dominion Univ	VA	19,483	LC
St. Mary's Univ of Minn	MN	38,280	C
Valparaiso Univ	IN	44,940	VC+

BUSINESS LAW

School	ST	$IS	SR
Adams State Univ	CO	13,358	LC
Arizona State Univ, at the Tempe Campus	AZ	20,137	C+
Bryant Univ	RI	49,179	VC
Cal State, Fresno	CA	17,405	C
Hofstra Univ	NY	51,810	VC+
Lamar Univ	TX	6,820	LC
New York Univ	NY	61,470	MC
Ohio Univ	OH	21,080	C

School	ST	$IS	SR
Peirce College	PA	12,760	NC
Roger Williams Univ	RI	46,296	VC
Warner Univ	FL	18,000	C
Washington State Univ	WA	20,461	C
Western Carolina Univ	NC	13,965	C

BUSINESS LEADERSHIP

School	ST	$IS	SR
Ashford Univ	CA	10,480	C

BUSINESS STATISTICS

School	ST	$IS	SR
Arizona State Univ, at the Tempe Campus	AZ	20,137	C+
Arizona State Univ, at the West Campus	AZ	19,251	C
Baylor Univ	TX	50,329	HC
Bryant Univ	RI	49,179	VC
Univ of Denver	CO	51,787	VC+
Univ of PR Recinto de Rio Piedras	PR	5,750	
Univ of Texas at San Antonio	TX	18,372	C
Washington State Univ	WA	20,461	C

BUSINESS SYSTEMS ANALYSIS

School	ST	$IS	SR
Arizona State Univ, at the Tempe Campus	AZ	20,137	C+
Baylor Univ	TX	50,329	HC
Bentley Univ	MA	56,454	HC+
Bryant Univ	RI	49,179	VC
CUNY/Brooklyn College	NY	5,884	C+
Clarkson Univ	NY	57,330	HC
Eastern Mich Univ	MI	18,604	C
Elizabethtown College	PA	49,740	VC
Husson Univ	ME	24,194	LC
Johnson State College	VT	16,721	C
Louisiana Tech Univ	LA	11,302	C
Montana Tech of The Univ of Montana	MT	14,650	VC
Oregon State Univ	OR	20,273	VC
Rochester Inst of Technology	NY	42,450	VC
Stevenson Univ	MD	41,470	C
Texas A&M Univ	TX	19,207	VC
Univ of Findlay	OH	31,916	C
Univ of N Car at Wilmington	NC	13,572	VC
Univ of Tenn at Knoxville	TN	20,364	VC+

CANADIAN STUDIES

School	ST	$IS	SR
Duke Univ	NC	50,250	MC
St. Lawrence Univ	NY	59,972	VC
SUNY Plattsburgh / SUNY	NY	18,083	C
Univ of Washington	WA	14,722	VC
Western Washington Univ	WA	18,519	VC

CARDIAC SONOGRAPHY

School	ST	$IS	SR
St. Mary's Univ of Minn	MN	38,280	C
Thomas Edison State College	NJ	5,700	SP

CAREER, TECHNICAL EDUCATION & TRAINING

School	ST	$IS	SR
Temple Univ	PA	24,392	VC
Univ of Arkansas at Fayetteville	AR	18,352	C+
Univ of Wisc/Stout	WI	15,459	C
Wright State Univ	OH	16,983	C

CARIBBEAN STUDIES

School	ST	$IS	SR
Binghamton Univ/The SUNY	NY	21,648	HC+
Burlington College	VT	32,510	SP
CUNY/Brooklyn College	NY	5,884	C+
Emory Univ	GA	56,368	MC
Florida State Univ	FL	16,715	VC
Gettysburg College	PA	58,820	HC
Hofstra Univ	NY	51,810	VC+
Pitzer College	CA	54,988	MC
Union College	NY	60,240	MC
Univ at Albany / SUNY	NY	18,674	VC
Univ of Mich/Ann Arbor	MI	22,102	MC

CARTOGRAPHY

School	ST	$IS	SR
East Central Univ	OK	10,223	LC
Salem State Univ	MA	13,161	LC
Texas State Univ	TX	17,128	C
Univ of Wisc/Madison	WI	18,757	HC+

CELL & MOLECULAR BIOLOGY

School	ST	$IS	SR
Univ of Rhode Island	RI	24,002	C

CELL BIOLOGY

School	ST	$IS	SR
Adams State Univ	CO	13,358	LC
Auburn Univ	AL	22,378	VC+
Beloit College	WI	49,970	HC
Bethel College	IN	31,560	C
Binghamton Univ/The SUNY	NY	21,648	HC+
Bucknell Univ	PA	60,140	MC
Cal State, Long Beach	CA	17,502	C+
Canisius College	NY	44,900	C

School	ST	$IS	SR
Dallas Baptist Univ	TX	30,580	VC
Florida State Univ	FL	16,715	VC
Georgia State Univ	GA		C
Grand Valley State Univ	MI	17,998	C+
Hope College	MI	38,650	VC
Huntingdon College	AL	33,100	C
John Carroll Univ	OH	46,300	C+
Johns Hopkins Univ	MD	47,492	MC
Johnson State College	VT	16,721	C
LIU Post	NY	47,660	C
Marshall Univ	WV	14,820	C
Missouri State Univ	MO	13,996	C+
Montana State Univ	MT	14,068	C
New York Univ	NY	61,470	MC
Ohio Univ	OH	21,080	C
Okla City Univ	OK	40,476	VC
Okla State Univ	OK	14,310	VC
Pittsburg State Univ	KS	12,032	C
Purdue Univ/West Lafayette	IN	20,024	HC
Rutgers, The State Univ of New Jersey/New Brunswick	NJ	25,562	VC
San Francisco State Univ	CA	18,514	C
Seattle Univ	WA	49,035	VC+
Texas Tech Univ	TX	14,243	C
Tulane Univ	LA	60,861	MC
Univ of Arizona	AZ	20,657	C
Univ of Calif at Irvine	CA	25,961	VC
Univ of Calif at Los Angeles	CA	25,686	MC
Univ of Calif at Riverside	CA	27,204	C
Univ of Calif at Santa Barbara	CA	27,551	HC
Univ of Calif at Santa Cruz	CA	27,807	C+
Univ of Illinois at Urbana-Champaign	IL	26,450	HC
Univ of Mich/Ann Arbor	MI	22,102	MC
Univ of Minn/Duluth	MN	19,806	C
Univ of Minn/Twin Cities	MN		HC
Univ of Montana-Western	MT	9,753	LC
Univ of Puget Sound	WA	54,608	HC
Univ of Rochester	NY	60,668	MC
Washington and Jefferson College	PA	51,948	VC
Washington State Univ	WA	20,461	C
West Chester Univ of Pennsylvania	PA	17,186	C
Western Washington Univ	WA	18,519	VC

CELTIC STUDIES

School	ST	$IS	SR
Bard College	NY	61,940	HC
Univ of Calif at Berkeley	CA	23,322	MC

CERAMIC ART AND DESIGN

School	ST	$IS	SR
Adams State Univ	CO	13,358	LC
Alfred Univ	NY	41,770	C
Andrews Univ	MI	28,030	C+
Aquinas College	MI	33,060	C
Arizona State Univ, at the Tempe Campus	AZ	20,137	C+
Bard College at Simon's Rock	MA	61,749	HC+
Bennington College	VT	56,990	HC+
Calif College of the Arts	CA	48,334	SP
Cal State, San Bernardino	CA	12,000	C
Cleveland Inst of Art	OH	48,685	SP
College for Creative Studies	MI	45,340	C
Columbia College	MO	24,578	C
Hofstra Univ	NY	51,810	VC+
Howard Univ	DC	13,646	C
Indiana Univ-Purdue Univ Indianapolis	IN	17,611	C
Indiana Wesleyan Univ	IN	31,815	VC
Kansas City Art Inst	MO	44,308	SP
Kent State Univ	OH	19,920	C
Kutztown Univ of Pennsylvania	PA	16,909	LC
Marshall Univ	WV	14,820	C
Maryland Inst College of Art	MD	39,500	SP
Marywood Univ	PA	45,595	C
Ohio Northern Univ	OH	42,075	VC
Ohio Univ	OH	21,080	C
Pittsburg State Univ	KS	12,032	C
Rhode Island School of Design	RI	57,234	MC
Rochester Inst of Technology	NY	42,450	VC
School of the Art Inst of Chicago	IL	56,230	SP
Syracuse Univ	NY	56,346	VC
Temple Univ	PA	24,392	VC
The Catholic Univ of America	DC	52,852	VC
Univ of Dallas	TX	45,500	VC+
Univ of Hartford	CT	42,674	C
Univ of Iowa	IA	17,693	VC
Univ of Kansas	KS	17,603	C+
Univ of Mass Dartmouth	MA	22,223	C
Univ of Miami	FL	57,034	MC
Univ of Mich/Ann Arbor	MI	22,102	MC
Univ of Oregon	OR	21,360	C+
Washington Univ in St. Louis	MO	69,844	MC
Webster Univ	MO	35,100	C+
Western Washington Univ	WA	18,519	VC

CERAMIC ENGINEERING

School	ST	$IS	SR
Alfred Univ	NY	41,770	C

School	ST	$IS	SR
Clemson Univ	SC	19,136	HC
Missouri Univ of Science and Technology	MO	18,655	VC+
Rutgers, The State Univ of New Jersey/New Brunswick	NJ	25,562	VC
Univ of Illinois at Urbana-Champaign	IL	26,450	HC
Univ of Washington	WA	14,722	VC

CERAMIC SCIENCE

School	ST	$IS	SR
Maine College of Art	ME	28,812	SP

CHEMICAL ENGINEERING

School	ST	$IS	SR
Arizona State Univ, at the Tempe Campus	AZ	20,137	C+
Auburn Univ	AL	22,378	VC+
Bethel College	IN	31,560	C
Brigham Young Univ	UT	12,100	HC
Bucknell Univ	PA	60,140	MC
Calif Baptist Univ	CA	38,792	C
Calif Inst of Technology	CA	54,045	MC
Calif State Polytechnic Univ, Pomona	CA	20,156	C
Cal State, Long Beach	CA	17,502	C+
Calvin College	MI	39,120	VC
Carnegie Mellon Univ	PA	51,260	MC
Case Western Reserve Univ	OH	56,534	MC
Christian Brothers Univ	TN	31,670	C
CUNY/City College	NY	20,319	HC+
Clarkson Univ	NY	57,330	HC
Clemson Univ	SC	19,136	HC
Cleveland State Univ	OH	21,776	C
Colo School of Mines	CO	18,000	HC
Colo State Univ-Fort Collins	CO	20,385	VC
Columbia Univ/City of New York	NY	61,116	MC
Cooper Union for the Advancement of Science and Art	NY	55,600	MC
Cornell Univ	NY	60,964	MC
Delaware State Univ	DE	16,722	LC
Dordt College	IA	34,160	C+
Drexel Univ	PA	61,418	VC+
Elon Univ	NC	41,914	VC+
Florida A&M Univ	FL	14,935	LC
Florida Inst of Technology	FL	48,290	VC
Florida State Univ	FL	16,715	VC
Gannon Univ	PA	39,608	C
Geneva College	PA	27,280	C
Georgia Inst of Technology	GA	21,828	MC
Hampton Univ	VA	28,528	C
Howard Univ	DC	13,646	C
Illinois Inst of Technology	IL	38,512	HC+
Iowa State Univ	IA	16,403	C
Johns Hopkins Univ	MD	47,492	MC
Kansas State Univ	KS	15,497	VC
Lafayette College	PA	59,155	HC+
Lamar Univ	TX	6,820	LC
Lehigh Univ	PA	56,770	MC
Louisiana State Univ	LA	18,677	C+
Louisiana Tech Univ	LA	11,302	C
Manhattan College	NY	49,588	C+
Mass Inst of Technology	MA	58,240	MC
Miami Univ	OH	24,191	VC
Mich State Univ	MI	22,450	VC
Mich Tech Univ	MI	23,556	VC
Miss State Univ	MS	14,750	C
Missouri Univ of Science and Technology	MO	18,655	VC+
Montana State Univ	MT	14,068	C
New Jersey Inst of Technology	NJ	26,490	C+
New Mexico Inst of Mining and Technology	NM	13,592	VC
New Mexico State Univ	NM	14,050	C
New York Univ	NY	61,470	MC
N Car Agricultural and Technical State Univ	NC	13,365	LC
N Car State Univ	NC	16,202	HC
Northeastern Univ	MA	55,296	MC
Northwestern Univ	IL	61,640	MC
Ohio Univ	OH	21,080	C
Okla State Univ	OK	14,310	VC
Oregon State Univ	OR	20,273	VC
Polytechnic Inst of New York Univ	NY	53,064	HC+
Prairie View A&M Univ	TX	15,205	LC
Princeton Univ	NJ	53,795	MC
Purdue Univ/West Lafayette	IN	20,024	HC
Rensselaer Polytechnic Inst	NY	61,529	MC
Rice Univ	TX	43,288	MC
Rochester Inst of Technology	NY	42,450	VC
Rose-Hulman Inst of Technology	IN	53,340	MC
Rowan Univ	NJ	24,022	VC+
Rutgers, The State Univ of New Jersey/New Brunswick	NJ	25,562	VC
San Jose State Univ	CA	19,133	LC
S Dak School of Mines and Technology	SD	15,260	VC
Stanford Univ	CA	58,388	MC
SUNY / College of Environmental Science and Forestry	NY	18,351	VC
Stevens Inst of Technology	NJ	50,130	HC

School	ST	$IS	SR
Stony Brook Univ / SUNY	NY	20,078	HC+
Syracuse Univ	NY	56,346	VC
Tenn Tech Univ	TN	11,310	C
Texas A&M Univ	TX	19,207	VC
Texas A&M Univ at Kingsville	TX	7,500	LC
Texas Tech Univ	TX	14,243	C
Ohio State Univ-Columbus Campus	OH	19,887	HC+
The Pennsylvania State Univ - Univ Park	PA	28,022	VC+
The Univ of Okla	OK	18,621	VC
The Univ of Tenn at Chattanooga	TN	16,883	C
The Univ of Utah	UT	16,463	VC
Trine Univ	IN	39,400	HC+
Tufts Univ	MA	58,780	MC
Tulane Univ	LA	60,861	MC
Tuskegee Univ	AL	26,750	C
Universidad Politecnica de PR	PR	19,252	
Univ at Buffalo / The SUNY	NY	20,283	VC
Univ of Akron	OH	20,436	C
Univ of Alabama at Tuscaloosa	AL	17,164	C+
Univ of Alabama in Huntsville	AL	17,591	VC+
Univ of Arizona	AZ	20,657	C
Univ of Arkansas at Fayetteville	AR	18,352	C+
Univ of Calif at Berkeley	CA	23,322	MC
Univ of Calif at Davis	CA		HC
Univ of Calif at Irvine	CA	25,961	VC
Univ of Calif at Los Angeles	CA	25,686	MC
Univ of Calif at Riverside	CA	27,204	C+
Univ of Calif at San Diego	CA	21,000	VC
Univ of Calif at Santa Barbara	CA	27,551	VC
Univ of Cincinnati	OH	21,506	VC
Univ of Colo Boulder	CO	22,605	VC+
Univ of Conn	CT	24,706	HC
Univ of Dayton	OH	49,070	VC
Univ of Delaware	DE	23,612	VC
Univ of Florida	FL	15,943	HC
Univ of Houston	TX	19,796	VC
Univ of Idaho	ID	14,558	C
Univ of Illinois at Chicago	IL	24,505	VC
Univ of Illinois at Urbana-Champaign	IL	26,450	HC
Univ of Iowa	IA	17,693	VC
Univ of Kansas	KS	17,603	C+
Univ of Kentucky	KY	19,868	C
Univ of Louisiana at Lafayette	LA	6,130	C
Univ of Louisville	KY	17,946	C
Univ of Maine	ME	19,902	C+
Univ of Maryland - College Park	MD	20,060	HC
Univ of Maryland/Baltimore County	MD	18,000	C
Univ of Mass Amherst	MA	24,215	VC+
Univ of Mass Lowell	MA	19,316	C
Univ of Mich/Ann Arbor	MI	22,102	MC
Univ of Minn/Duluth	MN	19,806	C
Univ of Minn/Twin Cities	MN		HC
Univ of Miss	MS	16,704	C+
Univ of Missouri/Columbia	MO	18,201	MC
Univ of Nebr - Lincoln	NE	18,031	VC
Univ of Nevada/Reno	NV	17,507	C
Univ of New Hampshire	NH	26,912	C
Univ of New Haven	CT	48,940	C
Univ of New Mexico	NM	15,300	C
Univ of N Dak	ND	14,551	C
Univ of Notre Dame	IN	57,117	MC
Univ of Pennsylvania	PA	61,132	MC
Univ of Pittsburgh at Pittsburgh	PA	28,572	HC+
Univ of PR/Mayaguez	PR	1,250	
Univ of Rochester	NY	60,668	MC
Univ of South Alabama	AL	13,510	C
Univ of S Car at Columbia	SC	19,725	VC+
Univ of South Florida/Tampa	FL	13,000	C
Univ of Southern Calif	CA	56,903	MC
Univ of Tenn at Knoxville	TN	20,364	VC+
Univ of Texas at Austin	TX	44,074	HC
Univ of Toledo	OH	18,464	C
Univ of Tulsa	OK	46,331	MC
Univ of Virginia	VA	23,050	MC
Univ of Washington	WA	14,722	VC
Univ of Wisc/Madison	WI	18,757	HC+
Univ of Wyoming	WY	14,401	C+
Vanderbilt Univ	TN	58,220	MC
Villanova Univ	PA	58,394	MC
Virginia Commonwealth Univ	VA	21,716	C
Virginia Polytechnic Inst and State Univ	VA	14,629	HC
Washington and Lee Univ	VA	52,812	MC
Washington State Univ	WA	20,461	C
Washington Univ in St. Louis	MO	69,844	MC
Wayne State Univ	MI	22,063	C
West Virginia Univ	WV	16,542	C+
West Virginia Univ Inst of Technology	WV	14,094	NC
Western Mich Univ	MI	19,628	C
Widener Univ	PA	52,418	C
Worcester Polytechnic Inst	MA	55,860	MC
Yale Univ	CT	55,300	MC
Youngstown State Univ	OH	16,732	C

CHEMICAL ENGINEERING TECHNOLOGY

School	ST	$IS	SR
Purdue Univ/West Lafayette	IN	20,024	HC
Universidad de Puerto/Arecibo	PR	7,227	
Univ of Hartford	CT	42,674	C

CHEMICAL PHYSICS

School	ST	$IS	SR
Adams State Univ	CO	13,358	LC
Augustana College	SD	36,500	VC
Bowdoin College	ME	59,568	MC
Brown Univ	RI	59,428	MC
Centre College	KY	35,000	HC+
Hamilton College	NY	55,620	MC
Hendrix College	AR	50,202	VC+
Maryville College	TN	33,150	C+
Mich State Univ	MI	22,450	VC
Reed College	OR	57,780	MC
Saginaw Valley State Univ	MI	17,369	C
San Diego State Univ	CA	21,611	C+
Swarthmore College	PA	57,870	MC
The Catholic Univ of America	DC	52,852	VC
Tufts Univ	MA	58,780	MC

CHEMICAL TECHNOLOGY

School	ST	$IS	SR
Florida State Univ	FL	16,715	VC
Inter-American Univ of PR/Arecibo Campus	PR	3,350	
Inter-American Univ of PR/Bayamon Univ College	PR	4,428	
Inter-American Univ of PR/Fajardo Campus	PR	4,200	
Inter-American Univ of PR/Ponce	PR		
Midwestern State Univ	TX	9,722	C
Univ of Cincinnati	OH	21,506	VC

CHEMISTRY

School	ST	$IS	SR
Abilene Christian Univ	TX	38,400	C+
Adams State Univ	CO	13,358	LC
Adelphi Univ	NY	44,670	VC
Adrian College	MI	42,400	C
Agnes Scott College	GA	45,323	C+
Alabama A&M Univ	AL	10,084	C
Alabama State Univ	AL	14,142	NC
Albany College of Pharmacy and Health Sciences	NY	40,331	SP
Albany State Univ	GA	8,500	C
Albion College	MI	46,010	C
Albright College	PA	46,660	C
Alcorn State Univ	MS	9,500	C
Alderson Broaddus Univ	WV	28,656	C
Alfred Univ	NY	41,770	C
Allegheny College	PA	50,980	VC
Alma College	MI	44,075	C
Alvernia Univ	PA	39,250	LC
Alverno College	WI	31,434	LC
American International College	MA	36,100	LC
American Univ	DC	56,015	HC+
Amherst College	MA	58,744	MC
Anderson Univ	IN	36,100	C
Andrews Univ	MI	28,030	C+
Angelo State Univ	TX	15,049	NC
Appalachian State Univ	NC	12,919	VC
Aquinas College	MI	33,060	C
Arcadia Univ	PA	33,570	C+
Arizona State Univ, at the Tempe Campus	AZ	20,137	C+
Arkansas State Univ	AR	15,470	C
Arkansas Tech Univ	AR	13,982	LC
Armstrong State Univ	GA	15,532	C
Asbury Univ	KY	32,038	VC
Ashland Univ	OH	25,000	C
Assumption College	MA	47,122	C+
Auburn Univ	AL	22,378	VC+
Auburn Univ at Montgomery	AL	14,470	LC
Augsburg College	MN	35,142	C
Augustana College	IL	43,398	VC
Augustana College	SD	36,500	VC
Austin College	TX	45,875	HC
Austin Peay State Univ	TN	15,274	C
Avila Univ	MO	26,900	C
Azusa Pacific Univ	CA	42,086	C
Baker Univ	KS	33,350	C+
Baldwin Wallace Univ	OH	38,318	C
Ball State Univ	IN	17,850	C
Bard College	NY	61,940	HC
Bard College at Simon's Rock	MA	61,749	HC+
Barnard College/Columbia Univ	NY	39,000	MC
Barry Univ	FL	38,190	C
Barton College	NC	27,660	LC
Bates College	ME	60,720	MC
Baylor Univ	TX	50,329	HC
Belhaven Univ	MS	27,170	C
Bellarmine Univ	KY	42,950	VC
Belmont Univ	TN	39,190	VC+
Beloit College	WI	49,970	HC
Bemidji State Univ	MN	13,500	VC
Benedict College	SC	20,454	NC
Benedictine College	KS	29,180	VC
Benedictine Univ	IL	37,820	C
Bennett College for Women	NC	21,970	LC
Bennington College	VT	56,990	HC+
Berea College	KY	7,192	C
Berry College	GA	39,254	VC
Bethany College	KS	30,605	NC
Bethany College	WV	35,282	LC
Bethel College	IN	31,560	C
Bethel College	KS	32,160	C
Bethel Univ	MN	34,940	VC
Bethel Univ	TN	19,186	C
Bethune-Cookman Univ	FL	22,958	C
Binghamton Univ/The SUNY	NY	21,648	HC+
Biola Univ	CA	40,320	C+
Birmingham-Southern College	AL	44,168	VC+
Black Hills State Univ	SD	13,947	LC
Blackburn College	IL	21,350	C
Bloomfield College	NJ	37,850	LC
Bloomsburg Univ of Pennsylvania	PA	13,598	C
Bluefield College	VA	17,230	C+
Bluffton Univ	OH	38,948	C
Boise State Univ	ID	13,469	LC
Boston College	MA	60,622	MC
Boston Univ	MA	60,694	MC
Bowdoin College	ME	59,568	MC
Bowling Green State Univ	OH	18,970	C
Bradley Univ	IL	31,874	VC
Brandeis Univ	MA		MC
Brescia Univ	KY	26,140	VC+
Briar Cliff Univ	IA	29,514	C
Bridgewater College	VA	41,450	C
Bridgewater State Univ	MA	18,752	C
Brigham Young Univ	UT	12,100	HC
Brown Univ	RI	59,428	MC
Bryn Mawr College	PA	59,890	MC
Bucknell Univ	PA	60,140	MC
Buena Vista Univ	IA	39,188	C
Buffalo State College / SUNY	NY	15,733	C+
Butler Univ	IN	47,572	VC+
Cabrini College	PA	40,859	LC
Caldwell College	NJ	35,602	NC
Calif Baptist Univ	CA	38,792	C
Calif Inst of Technology	CA	54,045	MC
Calif Lutheran Univ	CA	49,540	C+
Calif Polytechnic State Univ	CA	19,847	HC
Calif State Polytechnic Univ, Pomona	CA	20,156	C
Cal State, Bakersfield	CA	8,000	C
Cal State, Chico	CA	20,158	C
Cal State, Dominguez Hills	CA	17,090	LC
Cal State, East Bay	CA	16,549	C
Cal State, Fresno	CA	17,405	C
Cal State, Fullerton	CA	25,188	C
Cal State, Long Beach	CA	17,502	C+
Cal State, Los Angeles	CA	17,186	LC
Cal State, Northridge	CA	28,690	VC
Cal State, Sacramento	CA	16,200	C
Cal State, San Bernardino	CA	12,000	C
Cal State, San Marcos	CA	14,576	LC
Cal State, Stanislaus	CA	18,582	C
Calif Univ of Pennsylvania	PA	14,217	C
Calvin College	MI	39,120	VC
Cameron Univ	OK	10,004	LC
Campbell Univ	NC	37,570	VC
Campbellsville Univ	KY	27,720	C
Canisius College	NY	44,900	C
Capital Univ	OH	41,050	VC
Cardinal Stritch Univ	WI	24,054	C
Carleton College	MN	60,102	MC
Carlow Univ	PA	30,272	C
Carnegie Mellon Univ	PA	51,260	MC
Carroll College	MT	28,000	C
Carroll Univ	WI	38,100	C
Carthage College	WI	33,000	C
Case Western Reserve Univ	OH	56,534	MC
Castleton State College	VT	20,186	C
Catawba College	NC	37,240	C
Cedar Crest College	PA	43,240	C
Cedarville Univ	OH	32,860	VC
Centenary College of Louisiana	LA	45,650	C
Central College	IA	42,104	C
Central Conn State Univ	CT	19,749	C
Central Methodist Univ	MO	28,240	VC
Central State Univ	OH	9,010	C
Central Univ of Bayamon	PR	3,350	
Central Washington Univ	WA	11,730	C
Centre College	KY	35,000	HC+
Chadron State College	NE	7,400	NC
Chapman Univ	CA	58,347	VC+
Charleston Southern Univ	SC	22,420	C
Chatham Univ	PA	43,797	C
Chestnut Hill College	PA	42,110	C
Cheyney Univ of Pennsylvania	PA	20,372	LC
Chicago State Univ	IL	5,482	C
Christian Brothers Univ	TN	31,670	VC
Christopher Newport Univ	VA	21,960	VC
Citadel, The	SC		C
CUNY/Brooklyn College	NY	5,884	C+
CUNY/City College	NY	20,319	HC+
Claflin Univ	SC	22,368	LC
Claremont McKenna College	CA	62,215	MC
Clarion Univ of Pennsylvania	PA	17,370	LC
Clark Atlanta Univ	GA	30,006	C
Clark Univ	MA	47,020	HC+
Clarke Univ	IA	37,600	C
Clarkson Univ	NY	57,330	HC
Clemson Univ	SC	19,136	HC
Cleveland State Univ	OH	21,776	C
Coastal Carolina Univ	SC	18,580	C
Coe College	IA	45,550	VC
Coker College	SC	32,256	LC
Colby College	ME	57,510	MC
Colgate Univ	NY	58,135	MC
College of Charleston	SC	22,145	VC
College of Mount St. Joseph	OH	33,880	C
College of Mount St. Vincent	NY	41,040	MC
College of New Jersey	NJ	25,376	HC
College of St. Benedict	MN	49,359	VC
College of St. Elizabeth	NJ	43,839	LC
College of St. Mary	NE	35,184	C
College of St. Scholastica	MN	41,440	C
College of Staten Island/The City of New York	NY	16,778	NC
College of the Holy Cross	MA	58,042	MC
College of the Ozarks	MO		VC
College of William & Mary	VA	28,000	MC
College of Wooster	OH	52,600	VC
Colo College	CO	57,162	MC
Colo School of Mines	CO	18,000	HC
Colo State Univ-Fort Collins	CO	20,385	VC
Colo State Univ-Pueblo	CO	16,183	C
Columbia College	MO	24,578	C
Columbia College	SC	27,882	C
Columbia Univ/City of New York	NY	61,116	MC
Columbia Univ/School of General Studies	NY	58,231	MC
Columbus State Univ	GA	13,176	C
Concord Univ	WV	13,102	C
Concordia College - Moorhead	MN	39,974	VC
Concordia Univ	OR	35,000	C
Concordia Univ Irvine	CA	35,390	VC
Concordia Univ Nebr	NE	26,000	VC
Concordia Univ, Ann Arbor	MI	27,220	VC
Concordia Univ, River Forest	IL	26,300	C
Conn College	CT	54,970	MC
Converse College	SC	37,130	C
Coppin State Univ	MD	16,227	VC
Cornell College	IA	44,930	VC
Cornerstone Univ and Grand Rapids Theological Seminary	MI	33,338	C
Covenant College	GA	38,990	VC+
Creighton Univ	NE	45,356	VC
Dartmouth College	NH	57,996	MC
Davidson College	NC	58,146	MC
Davis & Elkins College	WV	33,742	C
De Sales Univ	PA	43,970	C
Delaware State Univ	DE	16,722	LC
Delaware Valley College	PA	29,944	C
Delta State Univ	MS	12,292	LC
Denison Univ	OH	54,670	HC+
DePaul Univ	IL	47,623	VC
DePauw Univ	IN	48,950	VC+
Dickinson College	PA	57,662	HC+
Dickinson State Univ	ND	11,900	VC
Dillard Univ	LA	20,940	VC
Doane College	NE	35,230	C
Dominican Univ	IL	37,628	C
Dordt College	IA	34,160	C+
Drake Univ	IA	41,516	VC
Drew Univ/College of Liberal Arts	NJ	57,516	C
Drexel Univ	PA	61,418	VC+
Drury Univ	MO	31,909	VC
Duke Univ	NC	50,250	MC
Duquesne Univ	PA	43,720	VC
Earlham College	IN	51,470	HC
East Carolina Univ	NC	14,169	C
East Central Univ	OK	10,223	LC
East Stroudsburg Univ of Pennsylvania	PA	18,868	LC
East Tenn State Univ	TN	9,000	C
East Texas Baptist Univ	TX	31,577	C
Eastern Illinois Univ	IL	20,466	C
Eastern Kentucky Univ	KY	11,161	C
Eastern Mennonite Univ	VA	40,660	C
Eastern Mich Univ	MI	18,604	C
Eastern Nazarene College	MA	30,000	C
Eastern New Mexico Univ	NM	10,682	C
Eastern Oregon Univ	OR	10,400	C
Eastern Univ	PA	37,704	C
Eastern Washington Univ	WA		C
Eckerd College	FL	43,902	C
Edgewood College	WI	33,294	C
Edinboro Univ of Pennsylvania	PA	15,940	LC
Elizabeth City State Univ	NC	11,638	C
Elizabethtown College	PA	49,740	VC
Elmhurst College	IL	43,336	C
Elmira College	NY	49,950	C+
Elms College	MA	23,900	VC
Elon Univ	NC	41,914	VC+

ST = STATE $IS = IN-STATE COSTS   SR = SELECTOR RATING

School	ST	$IS	SR
Emmanuel College	MA	47,985	VC
Emory and Henry College	VA	387,460	C
Emory Univ	GA	56,368	MC
Emporia State Univ	KS	12,897	C
Erskine College	SC	37,360	C
Eureka College	IL	19,280	C
Evangel Univ	MO	23,090	C
Excelsior College	NY	5,580	SP
Fairfield Univ	CT	56,960	VC
Fairleigh Dickinson Univ/ College at Florham	NJ	42,142	C
Fairleigh Dickinson Univ/ Metropolitan Campus	NJ	40,254	C
Fairmont State Univ	WV	12,098	LC
Fayetteville State Univ	NC	10,816	C
Ferris State Univ	MI	20,047	C
Ferrum College	VA	27,740	LC
Fisk Univ	TN	19,830	C
Fitchburg State Univ	MA	18,173	C
Florida A&M Univ	FL	14,935	LC
Florida Atlantic Univ	FL	17,339	C
Florida Gulf Coast Univ	FL		C
Florida Inst of Technology	FL	48,290	VC
Florida International Univ	FL	17,747	C+
Florida Memorial Univ	FL	20,888	LC
Florida Southern College	FL	40,150	C+
Florida State Univ	FL	16,715	VC
Fordham Univ	NY	61,588	HC+
Fort Hays State Univ	KS	11,354	C
Fort Lewis College	CO	15,513	C
Fort Valley State Univ	GA	11,200	C
Framingham State Univ	MA	18,854	C
Francis Marion Univ	SC	16,464	LC
Franciscan Univ of Steubenville	OH	27,320	VC
Franklin and Marshall College	PA	60,799	MC
Franklin College	IN	36,585	C
Freed-Hardeman Univ	TN	19,697	VC
Fresno Pacific Univ	CA	32,136	C
Friends Univ	KS	29,100	C
Frostburg State Univ	MD	15,264	LC
Furman Univ	SC	54,006	HC
Gallaudet Univ	DC	25,380	SP
Gannon Univ	PA	39,608	C
Gardner-Webb Univ	NC	34,375	C+
Geneva College	PA	27,280	C
George Fox Univ	OR	40,750	C+
George Mason Univ	VA	15,724	VC
George Washington Univ	DC	57,108	MC
Georgetown College	KY	41,440	C+
Georgetown Univ	DC	52,910	MC
Georgia College and State Univ	GA	18,900	C+
Georgia Inst of Technology	GA	21,828	MC
Georgia Regents Univ	GA		C
Georgia Southern Univ	GA	16,942	C
Georgia Southwestern State Univ	GA	13,246	C
Georgia State Univ	GA	15,582	VC
Georgian Court Univ	NJ	41,594	LC
Gettysburg College	PA	58,820	HC
Glenville State College	WV	11,348	NC
Gonzaga Univ	WA	46,441	HC
Gordon College	MA	44,320	VC
Goshen College	IN	35,900	VC
Goucher College	MD	52,040	VC+
Graceland Univ	IA	28,020	C
Grambling State Univ	LA	13,384	LC
Grand Valley State Univ	MI	17,998	C+
Greensboro College	NC	28,740	LC
Greenville College	IL	27,012	C
Grinnell College	IA	53,654	HC
Grove City College	PA	24,022	VC
Guilford College	NC	42,800	C
Gustavus Adolphus College	MN	48,170	HC
Hamilton College	NY	55,620	MC
Hamline Univ	MN	45,678	VC
Hampden-Sydney College	VA	51,758	C
Hampshire College	MA	58,320	MC
Hampton Univ	VA	28,528	C
Hanover College	IN	43,073	C+
Harding Univ	AR	23,556	C
Hardin-Simmons Univ	TX	23,560	C+
Hartwick College	NY	51,270	C
Harvard College/Harvard Univ	MA	49,000	MC
Harvey Mudd College	CA	64,527	MC
Hastings College	NE	27,782	C+
Haverford College	PA	61,564	MC
Hawaii Pacific Univ	HI	34,360	C
Heidelberg Univ	OH	34,100	C
Henderson State Univ	AR	14,584	C
Hendrix College	AR	50,202	VC+
High Point Univ	NC	39,960	C
Hillsdale College	MI	32,866	MC
Hiram College	OH	37,300	VC
Hobart and William Smith Colleges	NY	60,034	HC+
Hofstra Univ	NY	51,810	VC+
Hollins Univ	VA	43,295	VC
Hood College	MD	45,730	C
Hope College	MI	38,650	VC
Houghton College	NY	36,808	C+
Houston Baptist Univ	TX	36,450	C
Howard Payne Univ	TX	17,115	C
Howard Univ	DC	13,646	C
Humboldt State Univ	CA	18,400	C
Hunter College	NY	14,429	VC
Huntingdon College	AL	33,100	C
Huntington Univ	IN	32,220	C+
Husson Univ	ME	24,194	LC
Huston-Tillotson Univ	TX	18,124	C+
Idaho State Univ	ID	12,307	C
Illinois College	IL	25,770	VC
Illinois Inst of Technology	IL	38,512	HC+
Illinois State Univ	IL	23,110	VC
Illinois Wesleyan Univ	IL	48,452	HC
Indiana State Univ	IN	16,000	C
Indiana Univ Bloomington	IN	19,801	VC
Indiana Univ Kokomo	IN	6,811	LC
Indiana Univ Northwest	IN	6,854	LC
Indiana Univ of Pennsylvania	PA	20,846	LC
Indiana Univ South Bend	IN	15,501	C
Indiana Univ Southeast	IN	16,035	C
Indiana Univ-Purdue Univ Fort Wayne	IN	15,521	C
Indiana Univ-Purdue Univ Indianapolis	IN	17,611	C
Indiana Wesleyan Univ	IN	31,815	VC
Inter-American Univ of PR/ Arecibo Campus	PR	3,350	
Inter-American Univ of PR/ Bayamon Univ College	PR	4,428	
Inter-American Univ of PR/ Fajardo Campus	PR	4,200	
Inter-American Univ of PR/ Metropolitan Campus	PR	4,320	
Inter-American Univ of PR/ Ponce	PR		
Inter-American Univ of PR/ San Germán	PR	6,720	
Iona College	NY	44,028	C
Iowa State Univ	IA	16,403	C
Iowa Wesleyan College	IA	30,850	LC
Ithaca College	NY	53,864	VC
Jackson State Univ	MS	13,512	LC
Jacksonville State Univ	AL	12,480	LC
Jacksonville Univ	FL	37,780	C
James Madison Univ	VA	18,049	VC
Jarvis Christian College	TX	19,552	NC
John Brown Univ	AR	22,056	VC+
John Carroll Univ	OH	46,300	C+
Johns Hopkins Univ	MD	47,492	MC
Johnson C. Smith Univ	NC	25,336	C
Judson College	AL	26,794	C
Judson Univ	IL	25,130	C
Juniata College	PA	49,340	VC
Kalamazoo College	MI	49,740	HC
Kansas State Univ	KS	15,497	VC
Kansas Wesleyan Univ	KS	32,000	C
Kean Univ	NJ	23,444	C
Keene State College	NH	23,232	LC
Kennesaw State Univ	GA		C
Kent State Univ	OH	19,920	C
Kentucky State Univ	KY	11,000	LC
Kentucky Wesleyan College	KY	27,460	C
Kenyon College	OH	58,890	MC
Kettering Univ	MI	31,456	HC
King Univ	TN	33,140	C
King's College	PA	43,502	C
Knox College	IL	44,865	VC+
Kutztown Univ of Pennsylvania	PA	16,909	LC
La Roche College	PA	35,824	LC
La Salle Univ	PA	50,270	C
La Sierra Univ	CA	35,694	VC
Lafayette College	PA	59,155	HC+
LaGrange College	GA	37,670	C
Lake Erie College	OH	37,266	C
Lake Forest College	IL	50,652	VC
Lake Superior State Univ	MI	18,121	C
Lakeland College	WI	22,990	C
Lamar Univ	TX	6,820	LC
Lander Univ	SC	22,514	C+
Lane College	TN	11,212	C
Langston Univ	OK	3,000	C
Lawrence Tech Univ	MI	37,630	VC
Lawrence Univ	WI	46,371	HC
Le Moyne College	NY	43,470	C
Lebanon Valley College	PA	38,570	C
Lee Univ	TN	18,690	C
Lehigh Univ	PA	56,770	MC
Lehman College/The CUNY	NY	5,778	LC
LeMoyne-Owen College	TN	13,100	C
Lenoir-Rhyne College	NC	35,984	C
LeTourneau Univ	TX	36,210	VC
Lewis & Clark College	OR	54,382	MC
Lewis Univ	IL	23,050	C
Lewis-Clark State College	ID	6,990	C
Limestone College	SC	30,800	C
Lincoln Memorial Univ	TN	18,144	C
Lincoln Univ	MO	12,904	NC
Lindenwood Univ	MO	20,750	C
Linfield College-McMinnville Campus	OR	47,676	C
Lipscomb Univ	TN	37,490	VC
LIU Brooklyn	NY	47,182	LC
LIU Post	NY	47,660	C
Lock Haven Univ of Pennsylvania	PA	18,028	LC
Longwood Univ	VA	20,924	C
Loras College	IA	37,432	VC
Louisiana College	LA	15,746	C
Louisiana State Univ	LA	18,677	C+
Louisiana State Univ in Shreveport	LA	5,606	C
Louisiana Tech Univ	LA	11,302	C
Loyola Marymount Univ	CA	54,649	VC+
Loyola Univ Chicago	IL	51,646	VC+
Loyola Univ Maryland	MD	56,880	VC+
Loyola Univ New Orleans	LA	46,581	VC
Lubbock Christian Univ	TX	26,308	C
Luther College	IA	45,720	C
Lycoming College	PA	45,379	C
Lynchburg College	VA	42,645	C
Lyon College	AR	32,090	C+
Macalester College	MN	57,691	MC
MacMurray College	IL	20,755	C
Madonna Univ	MI	24,540	VC
Malone Univ	OH	35,364	C
Manchester Univ	IN	35,070	C
Manhattan College	NY	49,588	C+
Manhattanville College	NY	50,740	VC
Mansfield Univ	PA	19,468	LC
Marian Univ	IN	38,540	C
Marian Univ	WI	32,420	LC
Marietta College	OH	42,135	C+
Marist College	NY	35,500	C
Marlboro College	VT	35,980	VC
Marquette Univ	WI	46,930	VC+
Mars Hill Univ	NC	22,950	LC
Marshall Univ	WV	14,820	C
Martin Univ	IN	11,000	SP
Mary Baldwin College	VA	38,245	C
Marygrove College	MI	28,926	C
Maryville College	TN	33,150	C+
Maryville Univ of St. Louis	MO	35,856	VC
Mass College of Liberal Arts	MA	18,613	C
Mass College of Pharmacy and Health Sciences	MA	36,450	SP
Mass Inst of Technology	MA	58,240	MC
Mayville State Univ	ND	11,401	NC
McDaniel College	MD	47,450	VC
McKendree Univ	IL	29,920	C+
McMurry Univ	TX	25,962	LC
McNeese State Univ	LA	2,649	C
McPherson College	KS	28,118	C
Mercer Univ	GA	44,201	VC
Mercyhurst Univ	PA	40,700	C
Meredith College	NC	31,420	C
Merrimack College	MA	44,215	C
Messiah College	PA	40,690	C+
Methodist Univ	NC	37,185	C
Metropolitan State Univ of Denver	CO	4,835	LC
Miami Univ	OH	24,191	VC
Mich State Univ	MI	22,450	VC
Mich Tech Univ	MI	23,556	HC
MidAmerica Nazarene Univ	KS	28,000	C
Middle Tenn State Univ	TN	8,650	C
Middlebury College	VT	59,160	MC
Midland Univ	NE	34,000	C
Midway Univ	KY	20,150	LC
Midwestern State Univ	TX	9,722	C
Miles College	AL	11,164	NC
Millersville Univ of Pennsylvania	PA	21,648	C
Milligan College	TN	27,510	C
Millikin Univ	IL	38,940	C
Mills College	CA	54,119	VC
Millsaps College	MS	43,888	VC+
Minn State Univ, Mankato	MN	15,616	C
Minn State Univ, Moorhead	MN	13,392	VC
Minot State Univ	ND	10,915	C
Misericordia Univ	PA	41,060	C
Miss College	MS	21,998	C
Miss State Univ	MS	14,750	C
Miss Univ for Women	MS	7,400	C
Miss Valley State Univ	MS	9,706	LC
Missouri Baptist Univ	MO	31,830	C
Missouri Southern State Univ	MO	12,061	C
Missouri State Univ	MO	13,996	C+
Missouri Univ of Science and Technology	MO	18,655	VC+
Missouri Western State Univ	MO	12,260	NC
Monmouth College	IL	40,850	C
Monmouth Univ	NJ	44,108	C
Montana State Univ	MT	14,068	C
Montana State Univ-Billings	MT	12,425	LC
Montana State Univ-Northern	MT	12,500	NC
Montana Tech of The Univ of Montana	MT	14,650	VC
Montclair State Univ	NJ	22,614	C
Moravian College	PA	36,381	VC
Morehead State Univ	KY	10,900	C
Morehouse College	GA	39,412	C
Morgan State Univ	MD	14,500	VC
Morningside College	IA	35,430	C
Mount Holyoke College	MA	55,146	MC
Mount Marty College	SD	29,638	C
Mount Mary Univ	WI	33,590	LC
Mount St. Mary College	NY	41,138	C
Mount St. Mary's Univ	MD	47,996	C
Mount St. Mary's College - Chalon Campus	CA	43,897	VC+
Mount Vernon Nazarene Univ	OH	29,590	C
Muhlenberg College	PA	52,837	HC
Murray State Univ	KY	15,304	C
Muskingum Univ	OH	30,502	C
Nazareth College of Rochester	NY	43,028	C+
Nebr Wesleyan Univ	NE	29,774	C+
New College of Florida	FL	14,504	VC
New Jersey City Univ	NJ	21,456	LC
New Jersey Inst of Technology	NJ	26,490	C+
New Mexico Highlands Univ	NM	11,904	NC
New Mexico Inst of Mining and Technology	NM	13,592	VC
New Mexico State Univ	NM	14,050	C
New York Inst of Technology	NY	45,010	VC
New York Univ	NY	61,470	MC
Newberry College	SC	26,850	LC
Newman Univ	KS	30,380	C+
Niagara Univ	NY	41,010	C
Nicholls State Univ	LA	7,095	C
Norfolk State Univ	VA	10,531	LC
N Car Agricultural and Technical State Univ	NC	13,365	LC
N Car Central Univ	NC	9,000	C
N Car State Univ	NC	16,202	HC
N Car Wesleyan College	NC	29,440	C
North Central College	IL	38,343	VC
N Dak State Univ	ND		C
North Park Univ	IL	30,130	C
Northeastern Illinois Univ	IL	10,318	LC
Northeastern State Univ	OK	8,615	VC
Northeastern Univ	MA	55,296	MC
Northern Arizona Univ	AZ	19,010	C
Northern Illinois Univ	IL	19,768	C
Northern Kentucky Univ	KY	21,134	C
Northern Mich Univ	MI	18,278	C
Northern State Univ - Aberdeen	SD	14,505	C
Northland College	WI	26,680	C
Northwest Missouri State Univ	MO	17,347	C
Northwest Nazarene Univ	ID	34,000	C
Northwestern College of Iowa	IA	36,240	VC
Northwestern Okla State Univ	OK	7,275	NC
Northwestern Univ	IL	61,640	MC
Norwich Univ	VT	28,212	C
Notre Dame College	OH	34,942	VC
Notre Dame of Maryland Univ	MD	27,700	VC
Nova Southeastern Univ	FL	37,280	VC
Oakland Univ	MI	19,391	C
Oakwood Univ	AL	25,529	NC
Oberlin College	OH	61,788	MC
Occidental College	CA	60,972	MC
Oglethorpe Univ	GA	44,200	C
Ohio Dominican Univ	OH	38,380	C+
Ohio Northern Univ	OH	42,075	VC
Ohio Univ	OH	21,080	C
Ohio Wesleyan Univ	OH	49,460	C+
Okla Baptist Univ	OK	28,202	C
Okla Christian Univ	OK	25,870	VC
Okla City Univ	OK	40,476	VC
Okla Panhandle State Univ	OK	8,996	C
Okla State Univ	OK	14,310	VC
Okla Wesleyan Univ	OK	21,300	C
Old Dominion Univ	VA	19,483	LC
Olivet College	MI	19,984	LC
Olivet Nazarene Univ	IL	29,990	C
Oral Roberts Univ	OK	31,734	C
Oregon State Univ	OR	20,273	VC
Oswego / SUNY	NY	20,009	VC
Ottawa Univ	KS	15,000	VC
Otterbein College	OH	32,214	C
Ouachita Baptist Univ	AR	30,220	VC
Our Lady of the Lake Univ	TX	22,430	LC
Pace Univ	NY	53,367	C
Pacific Lutheran Univ	WA	46,760	C+
Pacific Union College	CA	28,150	VC
Pacific Univ	OR	49,626	C+
Paine College	GA	19,826	LC
Palm Beach Atlantic Univ	FL	34,874	C+
Park Univ	MO	17,525	C
Penn State Erie/The Behrend College	PA	16,256	C
Pepperdine Univ	CA	55,372	HC+
Pfeiffer Univ	NC	33,700	LC
Philadelphia Univ	PA	44,160	C
Philander Smith College	AR	19,760	LC
Piedmont College	GA	30,136	C
Pittsburg State Univ	KS	12,032	C
Pitzer College	CA	54,988	MC
Plymouth State Univ	NH	23,148	LC
Point Loma Nazarene Univ	CA	41,006	C+
Polytechnic Inst of New York Univ	NY	53,064	HC+
Pomona College	CA	57,680	MC
Pontifical Catholic Univ of PR	PR	7,310	
Portland State Univ	OR	18,672	C
Prairie View A&M Univ	TX	15,205	LC
Presbyterian College	SC	42,678	C+
Princeton Univ	NJ	53,795	MC
Principia College	IL	35,140	C+
Providence College	RI	57,383	VC

ST = STATE $IS = IN-STATE COSTS   SR = SELECTOR RATING

School	ST	$IS	SR
Purdue Univ/Calumet	IN	14,336	C
Purdue Univ/West Lafayette	IN	20,024	HC
Queens College/The CUNY	NY	17,107	VC
Queens Univ of Charlotte	NC	39,543	C+
Quincy Univ	IL	34,980	LC
Quinnipiac Univ	CT	55,160	VC
Radford Univ	VA	17,766	LC
Ramapo College of New Jersey	NJ	24,938	C
Randolph College	VA	45,660	VC
Randolph-Macon College	VA	49,869	C+
Reed College	OR	57,780	MC
Regis College	MA	47,565	LC
Regis Univ	CO	41,318	C
Rensselaer Polytechnic Inst	NY	61,529	MC
Rhode Island College	RI	17,694	LC
Rhodes College	TN	51,900	HC+
Rice Univ	TX	43,288	MC
Richard Stockton College of New Jersey	NJ	20,000	VC
Rider Univ	NJ	45,720	C
Ripon College	WI	36,959	C+
Roanoke College	VA	49,976	C
Roberts Wesleyan College	NY	38,306	C+
Rochester Inst of Technology	NY	42,450	VC
Rockford College	IL	31,000	C
Rockhurst Univ	MO	20,625	C
Rocky Mountain College	MT	32,242	C
Roger Williams Univ	RI	46,296	VC
Rollins College	FL	52,370	HC
Roosevelt Univ	IL	22,605	VC
Rose-Hulman Inst of Technology	IN	53,340	MC
Rosemont College	PA	42,350	C
Rowan Univ	NJ	24,022	VC+
Russell Sage College	NY	39,370	C
Rust College	MS	10,600	C
Rutgers, The State Univ of New Jersey/Camden Campus	NJ	25,121	C
Rutgers, The State Univ of New Jersey/New Brunswick	NJ	25,562	VC
Rutgers, The State Univ of New Jersey/Newark Campus	NJ	258,806	C
Sacred Heart Univ	CT	49,264	VC
Saginaw Valley State Univ	MI	17,369	C
St. Anselm College	NH	49,376	VC
St. Augustine's Univ	NC	14,000	C
St. Francis Univ	PA	30,029	LC
St. John's Univ	MN	47,984	C
St. Joseph's College	IN	36,500	C
St. Joseph's College of Maine	ME	31,580	C
St. Joseph's Univ	PA	55,006	VC
St. Louis Univ	MO	48,346	VC
St. Martin's Univ	WA	41,678	C
St. Mary's College	IN	45,160	C+
St. Mary's College of Calif	CA	53,550	C
St. Mary's Univ	TX	33,854	C
St. Mary's Univ of Minn	MN	38,280	C
St. Michael's College	VT	49,975	VC
St. Peter's Univ	NJ	44,240	C
St. Vincent College	PA	40,244	C
St. Xavier Univ	IL	32,840	C
Salem College	NC	29,326	VC
Salem State Univ	MA	13,161	LC
Salisbury Univ	MD	19,180	VC
Salve Regina Univ	RI	48,550	VC
Sam Houston State Univ	TX	17,082	C
Samford Univ	AL	37,060	C+
San Diego State Univ	CA	21,611	C+
San Francisco State Univ	CA	18,514	C
San Jose State Univ	CA	19,133	LC
Sarah Lawrence College	NY	48,000	HC
Savannah State Univ	GA	13,156	C
Schreiner Univ	TX	32,734	LC
Scripps College	CA	61,940	MC
Seattle Pacific Univ	WA	41,559	VC+
Seattle Univ	WA	49,035	VC+
Seton Hall Univ	NJ	45,902	C
Seton Hill Univ	PA	35,172	C
Sewanee: The Univ of the South	TN	47,700	VC
Shaw Univ	NC	15,488	C
Shawnee State Univ	OH	16,916	C
Shenandoah Univ	VA	39,916	C
Shepherd Univ	WV	15,875	C
Shippensburg Univ of Pennsylvania	PA	20,934	C
Shorter Univ	GA	30,650	LC
Siena College	NY	43,863	VC
Siena Heights Univ	MI	32,040	C
Simmons College	MA	49,966	VC
Simpson College	IA	36,086	C+
Skidmore College	NY	59,942	HC
Slippery Rock Univ of Pennsylvania	PA	10,360	C
Smith College	MA	59,674	MC
Sonoma State Univ	CA	20,541	C
S Car State Univ	SC	6,700	LC
S Dak School of Mines and Technology	SD	15,260	VC
S Dak State Univ	SD	14,296	C
Southeast Missouri State Univ	MO	15,370	LC
Southeastern Louisiana Univ	LA	13,325	C
Southeastern Okla State Univ	OK	7,966	LC
Southern Adventist Univ	TN	26,190	C
Southern Arkansas Univ	AR	14,316	C
Southern Conn State Univ	CT	18,033	LC
Southern Illinois Univ Carbondale	IL	21,942	C
Southern Illinois Univ Edwardsville	IL	17,532	C
Southern Methodist Univ	TX	60,585	MC
Southern Nazarene Univ	OK	24,354	C
Southern Oregon Univ	OR	17,874	C
Southern Polytechnic State Univ	GA	13,958	C
Southern Univ and A&M College	LA	9,761	LC
Southern Univ at New Orleans	LA	2,963	NC
Southern Wesleyan Univ	SC	25,600	C
Southwest Baptist Univ	MO	24,710	C
Southwest Minn State Univ	MN	14,000	C
Southwestern Adventist Univ	TX	23,026	LC
Southwestern College	KS	29,270	C
Southwestern Okla State Univ	OK	9,160	C
Southwestern Univ	TX	45,660	VC
Spelman College	GA	24,650	C
Spring Arbor Univ	MI	26,740	C
Spring Hill College	AL	44,164	VC
Springfield College	MA	25,000	C
St. Ambrose Univ	IA	30,845	C
St. Bonaventure Univ	NY	41,575	C
St. Catherine Univ	MN	37,782	C+
St. Cloud State Univ	MN	10,600	C
St. Edward's Univ	TX	47,784	C
St. Francis College	NY	34,200	C
St. John Fisher College	NY	40,708	C+
St. John's Univ	NY	55,070	C+
St. Joseph's College, New York/Brooklyn Campus	NY	22,630	C
St. Joseph's College, New York/Suffolk Campus	NY	22,630	C
St. Lawrence Univ	NY	59,972	VC
St. Mary's College of Maryland	MD	25,754	VC
St. Norbert College	WI	41,478	VC
St. Olaf College	MN	51,200	HC+
Stanford Univ	CA	58,388	MC
SUNY / College of Environmental Science and Forestry	NY	18,351	VC
SUNY at Purchase	NY	16,951	C
Stephen F. Austin State Univ	TX	14,668	C
Sterling College	KS	27,216	C
Stetson Univ	FL	51,516	VC
Stevens Inst of Technology	NJ	50,130	HC
Stevenson Univ	MD	41,470	C
Stonehill College	MA	46,780	HC
Stony Brook Univ / SUNY	NY	20,078	HC+
Suffolk Univ	MA	47,298	C
SUNY College at Geneseo	NY	18,670	HC
SUNY College at Old Westbury	NY	16,324	C
SUNY Cortland/The SUNY	NY	19,759	C+
SUNY Fredonia/The SUNY at Fredonia	NY	19,840	VC
SUNY New Paltz	NY	14,348	C
SUNY Oneonta / SUNY	NY	16,919	C+
SUNY Plattsburgh / SUNY	NY	18,083	C
Susquehanna Univ	PA	51,150	C
Swarthmore College	PA	57,870	MC
Syracuse Univ	NY	56,346	VC
Tabor College	KS	29,010	C
Talladega College	AL	17,996	C
Tarleton State Univ	TX	13,489	LC
Taylor Univ	IN	37,821	VC+
Temple Univ	PA	24,392	VC
Tenn State Univ	TN	9,048	C
Tenn Tech Univ	TN	11,310	C
Tenn Wesleyan College	TN	21,250	C
Texas A&M Univ	TX	19,207	VC
Texas A&M Univ at Commerce	TX	10,496	C
Texas A&M Univ at Corpus Christi	TX	11,544	LC
Texas A&M Univ at Kingsville	TX	7,500	LC
Texas Christian Univ	TX	49,980	HC
Texas Lutheran Univ	TX	36,040	C
Texas Southern Univ	TX	18,212	LC
Texas State Univ	TX	17,128	C
Texas Tech Univ	TX	14,243	C
Texas Wesleyan Univ	TX	31,382	C
Texas Woman's Univ	TX	13,633	LC
The Catholic Univ of America	DC	52,852	VC
The College of Idaho	ID	31,277	C+
The College of New Rochelle	NY	33,600	VC
The College of St. Rose	NY	26,750	C
The Lincoln Univ	PA	15,154	LC
Ohio State Univ-Columbus Campus	OH	19,887	HC+
The Pennsylvania State Univ - Univ Park	PA	28,022	VC+
The SUNY at Potsdam	NY	18,473	C
The SUNY/College at Brockport	NY	19,002	C
The Univ of Memphis	TN	15,094	C
The Univ of N Car at Greensboro	NC	12,848	C
The Univ of N Car at Pembroke	NC	13,388	LC
The Univ of Okla	OK	18,621	VC
The Univ of Tenn at Chattanooga	TN	16,883	C
The Univ of Utah	UT	16,463	VC
The Univ of Virginia's College at Wise	VA	11,076	C
Thiel College	PA	38,728	LC
Thomas More College	KY	34,760	C
Tougaloo College	MS	15,275	NC
Touro College	NY	27,959	VC
Towson Univ	MD	16,000	VC
Transylvania Univ	KY	42,660	VC+
Trevecca Nazarene Univ	TN	31,186	C
Trine Univ	IN	39,400	HC+
Trinity Christian College	IL	28,869	C
Trinity College	CT		HC+
Trinity International Univ	IL	31,070	VC
Trinity Univ	TX	48,150	HC+
Trinity Washington Univ	DC	30,250	C+
Troy Univ	AL	10,650	C
Truman State Univ	MO	15,541	HC
Tufts Univ	MA	58,780	MC
Tulane Univ	LA	60,861	MC
Tuskegee Univ	AL	26,750	C
Union College	KY	29,955	C
Union College	NE	23,270	C
Union College	NY	60,240	MC
Union Univ	TN	28,260	VC
United States Air Force Academy	CO		MC
United States Military Academy	NY		MC
United States Naval Academy	MD		MC
Universidad del Turabo	PR	4,110	
Univ at Albany / SUNY	NY	18,674	VC
Univ at Buffalo / The SUNY	NY	20,283	VC
Univ of Akron	OH	20,436	C
Univ of Alabama at Birmingham	AL	18,484	C+
Univ of Alabama at Tuscaloosa	AL	17,164	C+
Univ of Alabama in Huntsville	AL	17,591	VC+
Univ of Alaska Anchorage	AK	16,673	NC
Univ of Alaska Fairbanks	AK	15,130	C
Univ of Arizona	AZ	20,657	C
Univ of Arkansas at Fayetteville	AR	18,352	C
Univ of Arkansas at Little Rock	AR	17,609	LC
Univ of Arkansas at Monticello	AR	12,076	NC
Univ of Arkansas at Pine Bluff	AR	13,378	C
Univ of Calif at Berkeley	CA	23,322	MC
Univ of Calif at Davis	CA		HC
Univ of Calif at Irvine	CA	25,961	VC
Univ of Calif at Los Angeles	CA	25,686	MC
Univ of Calif at Riverside	CA	27,204	C+
Univ of Calif at San Diego	CA	21,000	VC
Univ of Calif at Santa Barbara	CA	27,551	HC
Univ of Calif at Santa Cruz	CA	27,807	C+
Univ of Central Arkansas	AR	13,667	VC
Univ of Central Florida	FL	15,668	VC+
Univ of Central Missouri	MO	14,605	C
Univ of Central Okla	OK	12,293	C
Univ of Charleston	WV	32,300	C
Univ of Chicago	IL	55,416	MC
Univ of Cincinnati	OH	21,506	VC
Univ of Colo at Colo Springs	CO	15,000	VC
Univ of Colo Boulder	CO	22,605	VC+
Univ of Colo Denver	CO	17,904	C
Univ of Conn	CT	24,706	HC
Univ of Dallas	TX	45,500	VC+
Univ of Dayton	OH	49,070	VC
Univ of Delaware	DE	23,612	VC
Univ of Denver	CO	51,787	VC+
Univ of Detroit Mercy	MI	30,450	VC
Univ of Evansville	IN	42,656	VC+
Univ of Findlay	OH	31,916	C
Univ of Florida	FL	15,943	HC
Univ of Georgia	GA	20,082	VC
Univ of Hartford	CT	42,674	C
Univ of Hawaii at Hilo	HI	23,066	C
Univ of Hawaii at Manoa	HI	19,379	C
Univ of Houston	TX	19,796	Vc
Univ of Houston-Downtown	TX	15,170	LC
Univ of Idaho	ID	14,558	C
Univ of Illinois at Chicago	IL	24,505	VC
Univ of Illinois at Urbana-Champaign	IL	26,450	HC
Univ of Indianapolis	IN	31,740	LC
Univ of Iowa	IA	17,693	VC
Univ of Jamestown	ND	24,738	C
Univ of Kansas	KS	17,603	C+
Univ of Kentucky	KY	19,868	C
Univ of La Verne	CA	47,010	C
Univ of Louisiana at Lafayette	LA	6,130	C
Univ of Louisville	KY	17,946	C
Univ of Maine	ME	19,902	C+
Univ of Mary Hardin-Baylor	TX	31,950	C+
Univ of Mary Washington	VA	19,484	VC
Univ of Maryland - College Park	MD	20,060	HC
Univ of Maryland/Baltimore County	MD	18,000	VC
Univ of Maryland/Eastern Shore	MD	14,000	VC
Univ of Mass Amherst	MA	24,215	VC+
Univ of Mass Boston	MA	23,066	VC
Univ of Mass Dartmouth	MA	22,223	C
Univ of Mass Lowell	MA	19,316	C
Univ of Miami	FL	57,034	MC
Univ of Mich/Ann Arbor	MI	22,102	MC
Univ of Mich/Dearborn	MI	9,885	VC
Univ of Mich-Flint	MI	17,547	C+
Univ of Minn/Duluth	MN	19,806	C
Univ of Minn/Morris	MN	17,150	VC
Univ of Minn/Twin Cities	MN		HC
Univ of Miss	MS	16,704	C+
Univ of Missouri/Columbia	MO	18,201	MC
Univ of Missouri-Kansas City	MO	19,603	C
Univ of Missouri-St. Louis	MO		VC
Univ of Montana	MT	14,105	C
Univ of Montevallo	AL	17,060	C
Univ of Mount Union	OH	35,130	C
Univ of Nebr - Lincoln	NE	18,031	VC
Univ of Nebr at Kearney	NE	14,855	LC
Univ of Nebr at Omaha	NE	12,700	C
Univ of Nevada, Las Vegas	NV	17,303	C
Univ of Nevada/Reno	NV	17,507	C
Univ of New England	ME	46,750	C
Univ of New Hampshire	NH	26,912	C
Univ of New Haven	CT	48,940	C
Univ of New Mexico	NM	15,300	C
Univ of New Orleans	LA	9,224	C
Univ of North Alabama	AL	9,960	C
Univ of N Car at Asheville	NC	13,500	VC
Univ of N Car at Chapel Hill	NC	18,928	MC
Univ of N Car at Charlotte	NC	15,547	C
Univ of N Car at Wilmington	NC	13,572	VC
Univ of N Dak	ND	14,551	C
Univ of North Florida	FL	15,870	VC
Univ of North Georgia	GA	8,500	C
Univ of North Texas	TX	15,628	C
Univ of Northern Colo	CO	18,446	C
Univ of Northern Iowa	IA	15,795	C
Univ of Notre Dame	IN	57,117	MC
Univ of Oregon	OR	21,360	C+
Univ of Pennsylvania	PA	61,132	MC
Univ of Pikeville	KY	25,500	NC
Univ of Pittsburgh at Bradford	PA	21,802	C
Univ of Pittsburgh at Johnstown	PA	20,862	LC
Univ of Pittsburgh at Pittsburgh	PA	28,572	HC+
Univ of Portland	OR	49,964	VC
Univ of PR Recinto de Rio Piedras	PR	5,750	
Univ of PR/Cayey	PR	1,504	
Univ of PR/Humacao	PR	1,877	
Univ of PR/Mayaguez	PR	1,250	
Univ of Puget Sound	WA	54,608	HC
Univ of Redlands	CA	40,500	VC
Univ of Rio Grande	OH	8,750	NC
Univ of Rochester	NY	60,668	MC
Univ of St. Francis	IN	29,810	C
Univ of St. Joseph	CT	45,630	C
Univ of St. Mary	KS	28,400	C+
Univ of San Diego	CA	54,818	HC+
Univ of San Francisco	CA	54,770	VC
Univ of Science and Arts of Okla	OK	10,560	VC
Univ of Scranton	PA	51,940	VC
Univ of Sioux Falls	SD	22,990	C
Univ of South Alabama	AL	13,510	C
Univ of S Car Aiken	SC	16,712	C
Univ of S Car at Columbia	SC	19,725	VC+
Univ of S Car Upstate	SC	18,200	C
Univ of S Dak	SD	15,111	C
Univ of South Florida/Tampa	FL	13,000	C
Univ of Southern Calif	CA	56,903	MC
Univ of Southern Indiana	IN	14,885	C
Univ of Southern Maine	ME	16,576	C
Univ of Southern Miss	MS	13,170	C
Univ of St. Thomas - Houston	TX	37,690	C
Univ of Tampa	FL	35,160	VC
Univ of Tenn at Knoxville	TN	20,364	VC+
Univ of Tenn at Martin	TN	13,734	C
Univ of Texas - Pan American	TX	11,125	LC
Univ of Texas at Arlington	TX	10,908	LC
Univ of Texas at Austin	TX	44,074	HC
Univ of Texas at Dallas	TX	21,348	HC+
Univ of Texas at El Paso	TX	8,764	NC
Univ of Texas at San Antonio	TX	18,372	C
Univ of the Cumberlands	KY	27,500	C
Univ of the District of Columbia	DC	7,244	LC
Univ of the Incarnate Word	TX	37,316	C
Univ of the Ozarks	AR	31,440	C
Univ of the Pacific	CA	52,146	VC
Univ of the Sacred Heart	PR	5,590	
Univ of the Sciences	PA	48,320	VC+
Univ of Toledo	OH	18,464	C
Univ of Tulsa	OK	46,331	MC

School	ST	$IS	SR
Univ of Vermont	VT	27,006	VC+
Univ of Virginia	VA	23,050	MC
Univ of West Alabama	AL	14,274	C
Univ of West Florida	FL	14,656	C
Univ of West Georgia	GA	15,488	LC
Univ of Wisc Whitewater	WI	13,314	C
Univ of Wisc/Eau Claire	WI	15,730	VC
Univ of Wisc/Green Bay	WI	19,074	C
Univ of Wisc/La Crosse	WI	9,304	VC
Univ of Wisc/Madison	WI	18,757	HC+
Univ of Wisc/Oshkosh	WI	10,426	LC
Univ of Wisc/Parkside	WI	10,181	LC
Univ of Wisc/Platteville	WI	14,564	C
Univ of Wisc/River Falls	WI	9,722	LC
Univ of Wisc/Stevens Point	WI	14,043	C
Univ of Wisc/Superior	WI	14,314	C
Univ of Wisc-Milwaukee	WI	18,436	C
Univ of Wyoming	WY	14,401	C+
Upper Iowa Univ	IA	30,426	NC
Ursinus College	PA	57,580	VC
Utah State Univ	UT	12,044	C
Utica College	NY	45,670	C
Valley City State Univ	ND	12,286	LC
Valparaiso Univ	IN	44,940	VC+
Vanderbilt Univ	TN	58,220	MC
Vanguard Univ of Southern Calif	CA	35,833	VC
Vassar College	NY	61,140	MC
Villanova Univ	PA	58,394	MC
Virginia Commonwealth Univ	VA	21,716	C
Virginia Military Inst	VA	16,156	C
Virginia Polytechnic Inst and State Univ	VA	14,629	HC
Virginia State Univ	VA	11,318	C+
Virginia Union Univ	VA	18,432	C
Virginia Wesleyan College	VA	28,433	LC
Viterbo Univ	WI	30,070	C
Wabash College	IN	46,850	C+
Wagner College	NY	48,600	C+
Wake Forest Univ	NC	58,838	MC
Walla Walla Univ	WA	26,256	NC
Walsh Univ	OH	35,100	C
Warren Wilson College	NC	40,132	VC
Wartburg College	IA	41,055	VC
Washburn Univ	KS	12,579	C
Washington Adventist Univ	MD	25,859	LC
Washington and Jefferson College	PA	51,948	VC
Washington and Lee Univ	VA	52,812	MC
Washington College	MD	52,602	VC
Washington State Univ	WA	20,461	C
Washington Univ in St. Louis	MO	69,844	MC
Wayland Baptist Univ	TX	18,912	LC
Wayne State College	NE	11,764	NC
Wayne State Univ	MI	22,063	C
Waynesburg Univ	PA	30,150	C
Wellesley College	MA	59,038	MC
Wells College	NY	49,400	VC
Wesleyan College	GA	24,000	C
Wesleyan Univ	CT	61,198	MC
West Chester Univ of Pennsylvania	PA	17,186	C
West Liberty Univ	WV	9,142	LC
West Texas A&M Univ	TX	13,478	C
West Virginia State Univ	WV	8,378	NC
West Virginia Univ	WV	16,542	C+
West Virginia Univ Inst of Technology	WV	14,094	NC
West Virginia Wesleyan College	WV	26,880	C
Western Carolina Univ	NC	13,965	C
Western Conn State Univ	CT	18,327	LC
Western Illinois Univ	IL	20,732	C
Western Kentucky Univ	KY	11,000	LC
Western Mich Univ	MI	19,628	C
Western New England Univ	MA	46,154	C+
Western New Mexico Univ	NM	8,500	LC
Western Oregon Univ	OR	15,021	C
Western State Colo Univ	CO	16,924	C
Western Washington Univ	WA	18,519	VC
Westfield State Univ	MA	18,297	C
Westminster College	MO	31,720	VC
Westminster College	PA	31,290	C+
Westminster College	UT	37,708	C+
Westmont College	CA	41,500	HC
Wheaton College	IL	40,720	NC
Wheaton College	MA	54,934	HC+
Wheeling Jesuit Univ	WV	33,500	C
Whitman College	WA	55,988	MC
Whittier College	CA	43,416	C
Whitworth Univ	WA	47,734	VC
Wichita State Univ	KS	14,607	C
Widener Univ	PA	52,418	C
Wilberforce Univ	OH	15,100	LC
Wiley College	TX		LC
Wilkes Univ	PA	44,070	C
Willamette Univ	OR	56,450	VC+
William Carey Univ	MS	13,500	LC
William Jewell College	MO	31,000	VC+
William Paterson Univ of New Jersey	NJ	21,694	C
Williams College	MA	61,070	MC
Wilmington College	OH	29,784	C
Wilson College	PA	35,080	C
Wingate Univ	NC	34,990	C
Winona State Univ	MN	16,640	C
Winston-Salem State Univ	NC	9,418	LC
Winthrop Univ	SC	21,120	C
Wisc Lutheran College	WI	23,510	VC
Wittenberg Univ	OH	47,962	C+
Wofford College	SC	45,795	VC
Worcester Polytechnic Inst	MA	55,860	MC
Worcester State Univ	MA	19,812	C
Wright State Univ	OH	16,983	C
Xavier Univ	OH	44,980	VC
Xavier Univ of Louisiana	LA	25,300	C
Yale Univ	CT	55,300	MC
Yeshiva Univ	NY	47,250	VC+
York College / The CUNY	NY	5,496	VC
York College of Pennsylvania	PA	26,590	C
Youngstown State Univ	OH	16,732	C

CHEMISTRY (PRE-MBA)

School	ST	$IS	SR
Murray State Univ	KY	15,304	C

CHEMISTRY / CHEMICAL BIOLOGY

School	ST	$IS	SR
Bethany College	WV	35,282	LC
Case Western Reserve Univ	OH	56,534	MC
Cornell Univ	NY	60,964	MC
Indiana Univ Kokomo	IN	6,811	C
Murray State Univ	KY	15,304	C

CHEMISTRY EDUCATION

School	ST	$IS	SR
Arizona State Univ, at the West Campus	AZ	19,251	C
Arkansas State Univ	AR	15,470	C
Bethany College	WV	35,282	LC
Bloomfield College	NJ	37,850	LC
Boston Univ	MA	60,694	MC
Creighton Univ	NE	45,356	VC
Ferris State Univ	MI	20,047	C
Georgia Southern Univ	GA	16,942	C
Hope College	MI	38,650	VC
Monmouth Univ	NJ	44,108	C
Niagara Univ	NY	41,010	C
Oakwood Univ	AL	25,529	NC
Syracuse Univ	NY	56,346	VC

CHEMISTRY/ADOLESCENCE EDUCATION

School	ST	$IS	SR
Arizona State Univ, at the Polytechnic Campus	AZ	20,531	C+
Bethany College	WV	35,282	LC
Black Hills State Univ	SD	13,947	C
College of the Ozarks	MO		VC
Duquesne Univ	PA	43,720	VC
Elizabethtown College	PA	49,740	VC
Houghton College	NY	36,808	C+
Huntingdon College	AL	33,100	C
Indiana Univ Bloomington	IN	19,801	VC
Indiana Univ Northwest	IN	6,854	LC
Indiana Univ South Bend	IN	15,501	C
Indiana Univ-Purdue Univ Indianapolis	IN	17,611	C
Lipscomb Univ	TN	37,490	VC
LIU Post	NY	47,660	C
Messiah College	PA	40,690	C+
Millikin Univ	IL	38,940	C
Minn State Univ, Mankato	MN	15,616	C
Murray State Univ	KY	15,304	C
Nazareth College of Rochester	NY	43,028	C+
Niagara Univ	NY	41,010	C
Northern Kentucky Univ	KY	21,134	C
Old Dominion Univ	VA	19,483	LC
Roberts Wesleyan College	NY	38,306	C+
St. Mary's Univ of Minn	MN	38,280	C
Seattle Univ	WA	49,035	VC+
SUNY Fredonia/The SUNY at Fredonia	NY	19,840	VC
SUNY Plattsburgh / SUNY	NY	18,083	C
Temple Univ	PA	24,392	VC
The College of St. Rose	NY	26,750	C
Trevecca Nazarene Univ	TN	31,186	C
Univ of Mary Hardin-Baylor	TX	31,950	C+
Univ of Nebr - Lincoln	NE	18,031	VC

CHEMISTRY/FORENSIC CHEMISTRY

School	ST	$IS	SR
Univ of Rhode Island	RI	24,002	C

CHILD CARE/CHILD AND FAMILY STUDIES

School	ST	$IS	SR
Albright College	PA	46,660	C
Ashland Univ	OH	25,000	C
Baylor Univ	TX	50,329	HC
Berea College	KY	7,192	C
Cal State, Fresno	CA	17,405	C
Cal State, Fullerton	CA	25,188	C
Cal State, Long Beach	CA	17,502	C+
Cameron Univ	OK	10,004	LC
Chestnut Hill College	PA	42,110	LC
CUNY/Brooklyn College	NY	5,884	C+
College of the Ozarks	MO		VC
Concordia Univ St. Paul	MN	28,250	C
East Carolina Univ	NC	14,169	C
Eastern Kentucky Univ	KY	11,161	C
Eastern Mich Univ	MI	18,604	C
Edgewood College	WI	33,294	C
Eureka College	IL	19,280	C
Florida State Univ	FL	16,715	VC
Fontbonne Univ	MO	31,384	C
Freed-Hardeman Univ	TN	19,697	VC
Gallaudet Univ	DC	25,380	SP
Georgia Southern Univ	GA	16,942	C
Goodwin College	CT	19,400	C
Harding Univ	AR	23,556	C
Indiana State Univ	IN	16,000	C
Indiana Univ of Pennsylvania	PA	20,846	LC
Iowa State Univ	IA	16,403	C
Jackson State Univ	MS	13,512	LC
Kansas State Univ	KS	15,497	VC
La Roche College	PA	35,824	LC
Lasell College	MA	43,750	LC
Louisiana State Univ	LA	18,677	C+
Mayville State Univ	ND	11,401	NC
Messiah College	PA	40,690	C+
Metropolitan College of New York	NY	16,720	VC
Mount Aloysius College	PA	29,976	C
New York Univ	NY	61,470	MC
N Car Central Univ	NC	9,000	C
N Dak State Univ	ND		C
Northern Illinois Univ	IL	19,768	C
Northwest Missouri State Univ	MO	17,347	C
Ohio Univ	OH	21,080	C
Okla Christian Univ	OK	25,870	VC
Okla State Univ	OK	14,310	VC
Park Univ	MO	17,525	C
Plymouth State Univ	NH	23,148	LC
Portland State Univ	OR	18,672	C
Rutgers, The State Univ of New Jersey/Camden Campus	NJ	25,121	C
Seton Hall Univ	PA	35,172	C
St. Bonaventure Univ	NY	41,575	C
SUNY/Empire State College	NY	6,315	SP
SUNY Oneonta / SUNY	NY	16,919	C+
SUNY Plattsburgh / SUNY	NY	18,083	C
Syracuse Univ	NY	56,346	VC
Tenn Tech Univ	TN	11,310	C
Texas A&M Univ at Kingsville	TX	7,500	LC
Texas State Univ	TX	17,128	C
The SUNY College of Agriculture and Tech at Cobleskill	NY	19,749	LC
The Univ of N Car at Greensboro	NC	12,848	C
Univ of Alaska Fairbanks	AK	15,130	C
Univ of Idaho	ID	14,558	C
Univ of Maine	ME	19,902	C+
Univ of Missouri/Columbia	MO	18,201	MC
Univ of Nebr - Lincoln	NE	18,031	VC
Univ of Nevada/Reno	NV	17,507	C
Univ of New Mexico	NM	15,300	C
Univ of N Car at Chapel Hill	NC	18,928	MC
Univ of N Car at Charlotte	NC	15,547	C
Univ of North Texas	TX	15,628	C
Univ of Tenn at Knoxville	TN	20,364	VC+
Univ of Tenn at Martin	TN	13,734	C
Univ of Texas at Austin	TX	44,074	HC
Univ of Texas at San Antonio	TX	18,372	C
Univ of the Incarnate Word	TX	37,316	LC
Univ of Vermont	VT	27,006	VC+
Univ of Wisc/Madison	WI	18,757	HC+
Univ of Wisc/Stout	WI	15,459	C
Utah State Univ	UT	12,044	C
West Virginia Univ	WV	16,542	C+
Western Mich Univ	MI	19,628	C
Wheelock College	MA	33,075	C
Youngstown State Univ	OH	16,732	C

CHILD PSYCHOLOGY/DEVELOPMENT

School	ST	$IS	SR
Alcorn State Univ	MS	9,500	C
Angelo State Univ	TX	15,049	NC
Appalachian State Univ	NC	12,919	VC
Ashford Univ	CA	10,480	C
Bay Path College	MA	34,565	C
Bennington College	VT	56,990	HC+
Bethel Univ	TN	19,186	C
Bluffton Univ	OH	38,948	C
Calif Polytechnic State Univ	CA	19,847	HC
Cal State, Bakersfield	CA	8,000	C
Cal State, Chico	CA	20,158	C
Cal State, Dominguez Hills	CA	17,090	LC
Cal State, Fresno	CA	17,405	C
Cal State, Long Beach	CA	17,502	C+
Cal State, Los Angeles	CA	17,186	LC
Cal State, Northridge	CA	28,690	LC
Cal State, San Bernardino	CA	12,000	C
Cal State, Stanislaus	CA	18,582	C
Colby-Sawyer College	NH	50,790	C
East Tenn State Univ	TN	9,000	C
East Texas Baptist Univ	TX	31,577	LC
Eastern Nazarene College	MA	30,000	C
Florida Gulf Coast Univ	FL		C
Fort Valley State Univ	GA	11,200	VC
Hope International Univ	CA	34,650	C
Howard Univ	DC	13,646	C
Humboldt State Univ	CA	18,400	C
Iowa State Univ	IA	16,403	C
Madonna Univ	MI	24,540	VC
Marygrove College	MI	28,926	C
Meredith College	NC	31,420	C
Metropolitan State Univ	MN	5,923	C
Mich State Univ	MI	22,450	VC
Mills College	CA	54,119	VC
Missouri Baptist Univ	MO	31,830	C
Missouri State Univ	MO	13,996	C+
Mount Ida College	MA	30,115	C
Mount St. Mary's College - Chalon Campus	CA	43,897	VC+
Niagara Univ	NY	41,010	C
N Car Agricultural and Technical State Univ	NC	13,365	LC
N Car Central Univ	NC	9,000	C
Olivet Nazarene Univ	IL	29,990	C
Point Loma Nazarene Univ	CA	41,006	C+
San Diego State Univ	CA	21,611	C+
Siena Heights Univ	MI	32,040	C
Southern New Hampshire Univ	NH	38,100	C
Spelman College	GA	24,650	C
St. Joseph's College, New York/Suffolk Campus	NY	22,630	C
Stephen F. Austin State Univ	TX	14,668	C
Texas Christian Univ	TX	49,980	HC
Texas Tech Univ	TX	14,243	C
Texas Woman's Univ	TX	13,633	LC
Tougaloo College	MS	15,275	NC
Tufts Univ	MA	58,780	MC
Univ of Akron	OH	20,436	C
Univ of Central Okla	OK	12,293	C
Univ of Illinois at Urbana-Champaign	IL	26,450	MC
Univ of La Verne	CA	47,010	C
Univ of Minn/Twin Cities	MN		HC
Univ of N Car at Charlotte	NC	15,547	C
Univ of St. Joseph	CT	45,630	C
Univ of St. Mary	KS	28,400	C+
Univ of Texas at Dallas	TX	21,348	HC+
Univ of Virginia	VA	23,050	MC
Utica College	NY	45,670	C
Vanderbilt Univ	TN	58,220	MC
Western Washington Univ	WA	18,519	VC
Whittier College	CA	43,416	C

CHILDHOOD EDUCATION: 1-6

School	ST	$IS	SR
Bloomfield College	NJ	37,850	LC
Campbell Univ	NC	37,570	VC
CUNY/Brooklyn College	NY	5,884	C+
Concordia Univ St. Paul	MN	28,250	C
Fontbonne Univ	MO	31,384	C
Houghton College	NY	36,808	C+
LIU Brooklyn	NY	47,182	C
Molloy College	NY	40,440	C
New York Univ	NY	61,470	MC
Niagara Univ	NY	41,010	C
St. John's Univ	NY	55,070	C+
St. Joseph's College, New York/Brooklyn Campus	NY	22,630	C
SUNY Fredonia/The SUNY at Fredonia	NY	19,840	VC
SUNY Plattsburgh / SUNY	NY	18,083	C
The College of St. Rose	NY	26,750	C
The Pennsylvania State Univ - Univ Park	PA	28,022	VC+
Univ of Arkansas at Fayetteville	AR	18,352	C+
Univ of Illinois at Chicago	IL	24,505	VC
Univ of Louisiana at Monroe	LA	12,998	C
Vanderbilt Univ	TN	58,220	MC

CHINA ASIA-PACIFIC STUDIES

School	ST	$IS	SR
Cornell Univ	NY	60,964	MC
Hofstra Univ	NY	51,810	VC+

CHINESE

School	ST	$IS	SR
American Univ	DC	56,015	HC+
Bard College	NY	61,940	HC
Bates College	ME	60,720	MC
Beloit College	WI	49,970	VC
Bennington College	VT	56,990	HC+
Boston Univ	MA	60,694	MC
Brigham Young Univ	UT	12,100	VC
Bryant Univ	RI	49,179	VC
Cal State, Long Beach	CA	17,502	C+
Calvin College	MI	39,120	VC
Central Washington Univ	WA	11,730	C
Colgate Univ	NY	58,135	MC
College of the Holy Cross	MA	58,042	MC
College of William & Mary	VA	28,000	MC
Concordia College - Moorhead	MN	39,974	VC
Conn College	CT	54,970	MC
Dartmouth College	NH	57,996	MC
Davidson College	NC	58,146	MC
DePaul Univ	IL	47,623	VC

School	ST	$IS	SR
Drew Univ/College of Liberal Arts	NJ	57,516	C
Emory Univ	GA	56,368	MC
George Washington Univ	DC	57,108	MC
Georgetown Univ	DC	52,910	MC
Grand Valley State Univ	MI	17,998	C+
Grinnell College	IA	53,654	HC
Hamilton College	NY	55,620	MC
Harvard College/Harvard Univ	MA	49,000	MC
Hofstra Univ	NY	51,810	VC+
Hunter College	NY	14,429	VC
Lawrence Univ	WI	46,371	HC
Lehigh Univ	PA	56,770	MC
Macalester College	MN	57,691	MC
Middlebury Univ	VT	59,160	MC
Nazareth College of Rochester	NY	43,028	C+
New College of Florida	FL	14,504	LC
North Central College	IL	38,343	VC
Oakland Univ	MI	19,391	C
Occidental College	CA	60,972	MC
Pomona College	CA	57,680	MC
Portland State Univ	OR	18,672	C
Queens College/The CUNY	NY	17,107	VC
Reed College	OR	57,780	MC
Rutgers, The State Univ of New Jersey/New Brunswick	NJ	25,562	VC
San Francisco State Univ	CA	18,514	C
San Jose State Univ	CA	19,133	LC
Scripps College	CA	61,940	MC
Stanford Univ	CA	58,388	MC
Swarthmore College	PA	57,870	MC
Ohio State Univ-Columbus Campus	OH	19,887	HC+
The Pennsylvania State Univ - Univ Park	PA	28,022	VC+
The Univ of Okla	OK	18,621	VC
The Univ of Utah	UT	16,463	VC
Thomas Edison State College	NJ	5,700	SP
Trinity Univ	TX	48,150	HC+
Tufts Univ	MA	58,780	MC
United States Naval Academy	MD		MC
Univ at Albany / SUNY	NY	18,674	VC
Univ of Calif at Berkeley	CA	23,322	MC
Univ of Calif at Davis	CA		HC
Univ of Calif at Los Angeles	CA	25,686	MC
Univ of Calif at Riverside	CA	27,204	C+
Univ of Calif at San Diego	CA	21,000	VC
Univ of Calif at Santa Barbara	CA	27,551	VC
Univ of Colo Boulder	CO	22,605	VC+
Univ of Georgia	GA	20,082	VC
Univ of Hawaii at Manoa	HI	19,379	VC
Univ of Houston	TX	19,796	VC
Univ of Iowa	IA	17,693	VC
Univ of Maryland - College Park	MD	20,060	HC
Univ of Mass Amherst	MA	24,215	VC+
Univ of Minn/Twin Cities	MN		HC
Univ of Miss	MS	16,704	C+
Univ of N Dak	ND	14,551	C
Univ of Notre Dame	IN	57,117	MC
Univ of Oregon	OR	21,360	VC
Univ of Pittsburgh at Pittsburgh	PA	28,572	VC+
Univ of Puget Sound	WA	54,608	HC
Univ of Vermont	VT	27,006	VC
Univ of Wisc/Madison	WI	18,757	HC+
Vassar College	NY	61,140	MC
Wake Forest Univ	NC	58,838	MC
Washington State Univ	WA	20,461	C
Washington Univ in St. Louis	MO	69,844	MC
Wellesley College	MA	59,038	MC
Whittier College	CA	43,416	C
Wofford College	SC	45,795	VC
Yale Univ	CT	55,300	MC

CHINESE STUDIES

School	ST	$IS	SR
Beloit College	WI	49,970	HC
Binghamton Univ/The SUNY	NY	21,648	HC+
Eugene Lang College/The New School for Liberal Arts	NY	55,650	C
Hofstra Univ	NY	51,810	VC+
Messiah College	PA	40,690	C+
Swarthmore College	PA	57,870	MC
Univ of Calif at Irvine	CA	25,961	VC

CHIROPRACTIC

School	ST	$IS	SR
Colo State Univ-Pueblo	CO	16,183	C
Mount Aloysius College	PA	29,976	C
Northern Mich Univ	MI	18,278	C

CHORAL MUSIC

School	ST	$IS	SR
Baylor Univ	TX	50,329	HC
Campbell Univ	NC	37,570	VC
Concordia Univ St. Paul	MN	28,250	C
Dallas Baptist Univ	TX	30,580	VC
Kent State Univ	OH	19,920	C
Mannes College New School for Music	NY	44,500	SP
Missouri Southern State Univ	MO	12,061	C
Mount Aloysius College	PA	29,976	C

School	ST	$IS	SR
Ohio Univ	OH	21,080	C
Toccoa Falls College	GA	23,210	LC
Univ of Kansas	KS	17,603	C+
Univ of North Texas	TX	15,628	C
Webster Univ	MO	35,100	C+

CHRISTIAN EDUCATION

School	ST	$IS	SR
Anderson Univ	IN	36,100	C
Asbury Univ	KY	32,038	VC
Bethany College	KS	30,605	NC
Biola Univ	CA	40,320	C+
Cedarville Univ	OH	32,860	VC
Columbia Univ	SC	27,882	C
Concordia Univ Irvine	CA	35,390	VC
Concordia Univ Nebr	NE	26,000	VC
Concordia Univ St. Paul	MN	28,250	C
Defiance College	OH	30,645	C
Erskine College	SC	37,360	C
Hannibal-LaGrange Univ	MO	24,490	C
Harding Univ	AR	23,556	C
Houghton College	NY	36,808	C+
Lenoir-Rhyne College	NC	35,984	C
Malone Univ	OH	35,364	C
MidAmerica Nazarene Univ	KS	28,000	C
Muskingum Univ	OH	30,502	C
Northwest Nazarene Univ	ID	34,000	C
Northwestern College of Iowa	IA	36,240	VC
Olivet Nazarene Univ	IL	29,990	C
Pfeiffer Univ	NC	33,700	LC
Southern Nazarene Univ	OK	24,354	C
Spring Arbor Univ	MI	26,740	C
Taylor Univ	IN	37,821	VC+
Westminster College	PA	31,290	C+
Wheaton College	IL	40,720	MC

CHRISTIAN STUDIES

School	ST	$IS	SR
Alderson Broaddus Univ	WV	28,656	C
Aquinas College	MI	33,060	C
Belmont Univ	TN	39,190	VC+
Bethel College	IN	31,560	C
Blue Mountain College	MS	15,634	LC
Bluefield College	VA	17,230	C+
Brewton-Parker College	GA	33,388	C
Bryan College	TN	24,194	C
Calif Baptist Univ	CA	38,792	C
Campbellsville Univ	KY	27,720	C
College of the Ozarks	MO		VC
Cornerstone Univ and Grand Rapids Theological Seminary	MI	33,338	C
Dallas Baptist Univ	TX	30,580	VC
Eastern Nazarene College	MA	30,000	C
Friends Univ	KS	29,100	C
Grand Canyon Univ	AZ	24,540	VC
Hillsdale College	MI	32,866	MC
Houghton College	NY	36,808	C+
Houston Baptist Univ	TX	36,450	C
Howard Payne Univ	TX	17,115	C
Huntingdon College	AL	33,100	C
Lewis Univ	IL	23,050	C
Mercer Univ	GA	44,201	VC
Miss College	MS	21,998	C
Missouri Baptist Univ	MO	31,830	C
Ouachita Baptist Univ	AR	30,220	VC
Point Loma Nazarene Univ	CA	41,006	C+
Roanoke College	VA	49,976	C
Roberts Wesleyan College	NY	38,306	C+
Seattle Pacific Univ	WA	41,559	VC+
Shorter Univ	GA	30,650	LC
Stonehill College	MA	46,780	HC
Taylor Univ	IN	37,821	VC+
Toccoa Falls College	GA	23,210	LC
Trinity International Univ	IL	31,070	VC
Union Univ	TN	28,260	VC
Univ of Mary Hardin-Baylor	TX	31,950	C+
Vanguard Univ of Southern Calif	CA	35,833	VC
Wayland Baptist Univ	TX	18,912	LC

CHURCH MUSIC

School	ST	$IS	SR
Blue Mountain College	MS	15,634	LC
Campbell Univ	NC	37,570	VC
Cedarville Univ	OH	32,860	VC
Concordia Univ St. Paul	MN	28,250	C
Dordt College	IA	34,160	C+
Hope International Univ	CA	34,650	C
Montreat College	NC	31,298	C
Nyack College	NY	33,250	C
Okla City Univ	OK	40,476	VC
Ouachita Baptist Univ	AR	30,220	VC
Samford Univ	AL	37,060	C+
Shenandoah Univ	VA	39,916	C
Texas Christian Univ	TX	49,980	HC
Univ of Mary Hardin-Baylor	TX	31,950	C+
Univ of the Cumberlands	KY	27,500	C

CITY/COMMUNITY/REGIONAL PLANNING

School	ST	$IS	SR
Alabama A&M Univ	AL	10,084	C
Arizona State Univ, at the Tempe Campus	AZ	20,137	C+

School	ST	$IS	SR
Brigham Young Univ	UT	12,100	HC
Calif Polytechnic State Univ	CA	19,847	HC
East Carolina Univ	NC	14,169	C
Eastern Mich Univ	MI	18,604	C
Indiana Univ of Pennsylvania	PA	20,846	LC
Iowa State Univ	IA	16,403	C
Mansfield Univ	PA	19,468	LC
Mich State Univ	MI	22,450	VC
New Mexico State Univ	NM	14,050	C
Plymouth State Univ	NH	23,148	LC
Temple Univ	PA	24,392	VC
Texas State Univ	TX	17,128	C
Ohio State Univ-Columbus Campus	OH	19,887	HC+
Univ of Cincinnati	OH	21,506	VC
Univ of Illinois at Urbana-Champaign	IL	26,450	HC
Univ of New Hampshire	NH	26,912	C
Univ of Virginia	VA	23,050	MC
Univ of Wisc/Green Bay	WI	19,074	C
Western Mich Univ	MI	19,628	C
Westfield State Univ	MA	18,297	C

CIVIL AND ENVIRONMENTAL ENGINEERING

School	ST	$IS	SR
Arizona State Univ, at the Tempe Campus	AZ	20,137	C+
Univ of Nevada/Reno	NV	17,507	C

CIVIL ENGINEERING

School	ST	$IS	SR
Alabama A&M Univ	AL	10,084	C
Arizona State Univ, at the Tempe Campus	AZ	20,137	C+
Auburn Univ	AL	22,378	VC+
Bethel College	IN	31,560	C
Boise State Univ	ID	13,469	LC
Bradley Univ	IL	31,874	VC
Brigham Young Univ	UT	12,100	HC
Bucknell Univ	PA	60,140	MC
Calif Baptist Univ	CA	38,792	C
Calif Polytechnic State Univ	CA	19,847	HC
Calif State Polytechnic Univ, Pomona	CA	20,156	C
Cal State, Chico	CA	20,158	C
Cal State, Fresno	CA	17,405	C
Cal State, Fullerton	CA	25,188	C
Cal State, Long Beach	CA	17,502	C+
Cal State, Los Angeles	CA	17,186	LC
Cal State, Northridge	CA	28,690	LC
Cal State, Sacramento	CA	16,200	C
Calvin College	MI	39,120	VC
Caribbean Univ	PR	10,375	
Carnegie Mellon Univ	PA	51,260	MC
Carroll College	MT	28,000	C
Case Western Reserve Univ	OH	56,534	MC
Central Conn State Univ	CT	19,749	C
Christian Brothers Univ	TN	31,670	MC
Citadel, The	SC		C
CUNY/City College	NY	20,319	HC+
Clarkson Univ	NY	57,330	HC
Clemson Univ	SC	19,136	HC
Cleveland State Univ	OH	21,776	C
College of New Jersey	NJ	25,376	HC
Colo State Univ-Fort Collins	CO	20,385	VC
Columbia Univ/City of New York	NY	61,116	MC
Cooper Union for the Advancement of Science and Art	NY	55,600	MC
Cornell Univ	NY	60,964	MC
Delaware State Univ	DE	16,722	LC
Dordt College	IA	34,160	C+
Drexel Univ	PA	61,418	VC+
Duke Univ	NC	50,250	MC
Embry-Riddle Aeronautical Univ - Daytona Beach	FL	40,884	C+
Florida A&M Univ	FL	14,935	LC
Florida Atlantic Univ	FL	17,339	C
Florida Gulf Coast Univ	FL		C
Florida Inst of Technology	FL	48,290	VC
Florida International Univ	FL	17,747	C+
Florida State Univ	FL	16,715	VC
George Mason Univ	VA	15,724	VC
George Washington Univ	DC	57,108	MC
Georgia Inst of Technology	GA	21,828	MC
Georgia Southern Univ	GA	16,942	C
Gonzaga Univ	WA	46,441	HC
Hofstra Univ	NY	51,810	VC+
Howard Univ	DC	13,646	C
Idaho State Univ	ID	12,307	C
Illinois Inst of Technology	IL	38,512	HC+
Indiana Univ-Purdue Univ Fort Wayne	IN	15,521	C
Iowa State Univ	IA	16,403	C
Jackson State Univ	MS	13,512	LC
Johns Hopkins Univ	MD	47,442	MC
Kansas State Univ	KS	15,497	VC
Lafayette College	PA	59,155	HC+
Lamar Univ	TX	6,820	C
Lawrence Tech Univ	MI	37,630	C
Lehigh Univ	PA	56,770	MC
Lipscomb Univ	TN	37,490	VC
Louisiana State Univ	LA	18,677	C+
Louisiana Tech Univ	LA	11,302	C

School	ST	$IS	SR
Loyola Marymount Univ	CA	54,649	VC+
Manhattan College	NY	49,588	C+
Marquette Univ	WI	46,930	VC+
Marshall Univ	WV	14,820	C
Mass Inst of Technology	MA	58,240	MC
Merrimack College	MA	44,215	C
Mich State Univ	MI	22,450	VC
Mich Tech Univ	MI	23,556	HC
Minn State Univ, Mankato	MN	15,616	C
Miss State Univ	MS	14,750	C
Missouri Univ of Science and Technology	MO	18,655	VC+
Montana State Univ	MT	14,068	C
Morgan State Univ	MD	14,500	C
New Jersey Inst of Technology	NJ	26,490	C+
New Mexico Inst of Mining and Technology	NM	13,592	VC
New Mexico State Univ	NM	14,050	C
New York Univ	NY	61,470	MC
N Car Agricultural and Technical State Univ	NC	13,365	LC
N Car State Univ	NC	16,202	HC
N Dak State Univ	ND		C
Northeastern Univ	MA	55,296	MC
Northern Arizona Univ	AZ	19,010	C
Northwestern Univ	IL	61,640	MC
Norwich Univ	VT	28,212	C
Ohio Northern Univ	OH	42,075	VC
Ohio Univ	OH	21,080	C
Okla State Univ	OK	14,310	VC
Old Dominion Univ	VA	19,483	LC
Oregon Inst of Technology	OR	8,910	C
Oregon State Univ	OR	20,273	VC
Point Park Univ	PA	36,390	C
Polytechnic Inst of New York Univ	NY	53,064	HC+
Portland State Univ	OR	18,672	C
Prairie View A&M Univ	TX	15,205	LC
Princeton Univ	NJ	53,795	MC
Purdue Univ/West Lafayette	IN	20,024	VC
Quinnipiac Univ	CT	55,160	VC
Rensselaer Polytechnic Inst	NY	61,529	MC
Rice Univ	TX	43,288	MC
Rose-Hulman Inst of Technology	IN	53,340	MC
Rowan Univ	NJ	24,022	VC+
Rutgers, The State Univ of New Jersey/New Brunswick	NJ	25,562	VC
St. Louis Univ	MO	48,346	HC
St. Martin's Univ	WA	41,678	C
San Diego State Univ	CA	21,611	C+
San Francisco State Univ	CA	18,514	C
San Jose State Univ	CA	19,133	LC
Savannah State Univ	GA	13,156	C
Seattle Univ	WA	49,035	VC+
S Dak School of Mines and Technology	SD	15,260	VC
S Dak State Univ	SD	14,296	C
Southern Illinois Univ Carbondale	IL	21,942	C
Southern Illinois Univ Edwardsville	IL	17,532	C
Southern Methodist Univ	TX	60,585	MC
Southern Polytechnic State Univ	GA	13,958	C
Southern Univ and A&M College	LA	9,761	LC
Stanford Univ	CA	58,388	MC
Stevens Inst of Technology	NJ	50,130	HC
Syracuse Univ	NY	56,346	VC
Temple Univ	PA	24,392	VC
Tenn State Univ	TN	9,048	C
Tenn Tech Univ	TN	11,310	C
Texas A&M Univ	TX	19,207	VC
Texas A&M Univ at Galveston	TX	11,258	C
Texas A&M Univ at Kingsville	TX	7,500	LC
Texas Tech Univ	TX	14,243	C
The Catholic Univ of America	DC	52,852	VC
Ohio State Univ-Columbus Campus	OH	19,887	HC+
The Pennsylvania State Univ - Univ Park	PA	28,022	VC+
The Univ of Memphis	TN	15,094	C
The Univ of Okla	OK	18,621	VC
The Univ of Tenn at Chattanooga	TN	16,883	C
The Univ of Utah	UT	16,463	VC
Trine Univ	IN	39,400	HC+
Tufts Univ	MA	58,780	MC
United States Air Force Academy	CO		MC
United States Coast Guard Academy	CT	942	HC
United States Military Academy	NY		MC
Universidad Politecnica de PR	PR	19,252	
Univ at Buffalo / The SUNY	NY	20,283	VC
Univ of Akron	OH	20,436	C
Univ of Alabama at Birmingham	AL	18,484	C+
Univ of Alabama at Tuscaloosa	AL	17,164	C+

School	ST	$IS	SR
Univ of Alabama in Huntsville	AL	17,591	VC+
Univ of Alaska Anchorage	AK	16,673	NC
Univ of Alaska Fairbanks	AK	15,130	C
Univ of Arizona	AZ	20,657	C
Univ of Arkansas at Fayetteville	AR	18,352	C+
Univ of Calif at Berkeley	CA	23,322	MC
Univ of Calif at Davis	CA		HC
Univ of Calif at Irvine	CA	25,961	MC
Univ of Calif at Los Angeles	CA	25,686	MC
Univ of Central Florida	FL	15,668	VC+
Univ of Cincinnati	OH	21,506	VC
Univ of Colo Boulder	CO	22,605	VC+
Univ of Colo Denver	CO	17,904	C
Univ of Conn	CT	24,706	HC
Univ of Dayton	OH	49,070	VC
Univ of Delaware	DE	23,612	VC
Univ of Detroit Mercy	MI	30,450	VC
Univ of Evansville	IN	42,656	VC+
Univ of Florida	FL	15,943	HC
Univ of Georgia	GA	20,082	VC
Univ of Hartford	CT	42,674	C
Univ of Hawaii at Manoa	HI	19,379	C
Univ of Houston	TX	19,796	VC
Univ of Idaho	ID	14,558	C
Univ of Illinois at Chicago	IL	24,505	VC
Univ of Illinois at Urbana-Champaign	IL	26,450	HC
Univ of Iowa	IA	17,693	VC
Univ of Kansas	KS	17,603	C
Univ of Kentucky	KY	19,868	C
Univ of Louisiana at Lafayette	LA	6,130	C
Univ of Louisville	KY	17,946	C
Univ of Maine	ME	19,902	C+
Univ of Maryland - College Park	MD	20,060	HC
Univ of Mass Amherst	MA	24,215	VC+
Univ of Mass Dartmouth	MA	22,223	C
Univ of Mass Lowell	MA	19,316	C
Univ of Miami	FL	57,034	MC
Univ of Mich/Ann Arbor	MI	22,102	MC
Univ of Minn/Duluth	MN	19,806	C
Univ of Minn/Twin Cities	MN		HC
Univ of Miss	MS	16,704	C+
Univ of Missouri/Columbia	MO	18,201	MC
Univ of Missouri-Kansas City	MO	19,603	C
Univ of Missouri-St. Louis	MO		VC
Univ of Mount Union	OH	35,130	C
Univ of Nebr - Lincoln	NE	18,031	VC
Univ of Nevada, Las Vegas	NV	17,303	C
Univ of Nevada/Reno	NV	17,507	C
Univ of New Hampshire	NH	26,912	C
Univ of New Haven	CT	48,940	VC
Univ of New Mexico	NM	15,300	C
Univ of New Orleans	LA	9,224	C
Univ of N Car at Charlotte	NC	15,547	C
Univ of North Dak	ND	14,551	C
Univ of North Florida	FL	15,870	VC
Univ of Notre Dame	IN	57,117	MC
Univ of Pennsylvania	PA	61,132	MC
Univ of Pittsburgh at Pittsburgh	PA	28,572	HC+
Univ of Portland	OR	49,964	VC
Univ of PR/Mayaguez	PR	1,250	
Univ of South Alabama	AL	13,510	C
Univ of S Car at Columbia	SC	19,725	VC+
Univ of South Florida/Tampa	FL	13,000	C
Univ of Southern Calif	CA	56,903	MC
Univ of Tenn at Knoxville	TN	20,364	VC+
Univ of Texas - Pan American	TX	11,125	LC
Univ of Texas at Arlington	TX	10,908	LC
Univ of Texas at Austin	TX	44,074	HC
Univ of Texas at El Paso	TX	8,764	NC
Univ of Texas at San Antonio	TX	18,372	C
Univ of the District of Columbia	DC	7,244	LC
Univ of the Pacific	CA	52,146	VC
Univ of Toledo	OH	18,464	C
Univ of Vermont	VT	27,006	VC+
Univ of Virginia	VA	23,050	MC
Univ of Washington	WA	14,722	VC
Univ of Wisc/Madison	WI	18,757	HC+
Univ of Wisc/Platteville	WI	14,564	C
Univ of Wisc-Milwaukee	WI	18,436	C
Univ of Wyoming	WY	14,401	C+
Utah State Univ	UT	12,044	C
Valparaiso Univ	IN	44,940	VC+
Vanderbilt Univ	TN	58,220	MC
Villanova Univ	PA	58,394	MC
Virginia Military Inst	VA	16,156	C
Virginia Polytechnic Inst and State Univ	VA	14,629	HC
Washington State Univ	WA	20,461	C
Washington Univ in St. Louis	MO	69,844	MC
Wayne State Univ	MI	22,063	C
West Virginia Univ	WV	16,542	LC
West Virginia Univ Inst of Technology	WV	14,094	NC
Western Kentucky Univ	KY	11,000	LC
Western Mich Univ	MI	19,628	C
Western New England Univ	MA	46,151	C+
Widener Univ	PA	52,418	C
Worcester Polytechnic Inst	MA	55,860	MC
Youngstown State Univ	OH	16,732	C

CIVIL ENGINEERING TECHNOLOGY

School	ST	$IS	SR
Alabama A&M Univ	AL	10,084	C
Arkansas State Univ	AR	15,470	C
Cal State, Fresno	CA	17,405	C
Central Conn State Univ	CT	19,749	C
Colo State Univ-Pueblo	CO	16,183	C
Fairleigh Dickinson Univ/ Metropolitan Campus	NJ	40,254	C
Fairmont State Univ	WV	12,098	LC
Idaho State Univ	ID	12,307	C
Lincoln Univ	MO	12,904	NC
Metropolitan State Univ of Denver	CO	4,835	C
Montana State Univ-Northern	MT	12,500	NC
Murray State Univ	KY	15,304	C
Old Dominion Univ	VA	19,483	LC
Pennsylvania College of Technology	PA	26,286	NC
Point Park Univ	PA	36,390	C
Rochester Inst of Technology	NY	42,450	VC
S Car State Univ	SC	6,700	LC
Southern Polytechnic State Univ	GA	13,958	C
SUNY Polytechnic Inst	NY	19,690	C
Texas Southern Univ	TX	18,212	LC
Univ of N Car at Charlotte	NC	15,547	C
Univ of Pittsburgh at Johnstown	PA	20,862	LC
Wentworth Inst of Technology	MA	29,800	C
Youngstown State Univ	OH	16,732	C

CLASSICAL AND NEAR EASTERN CIVILIZATION

School	ST	$IS	SR
Calvin College	MI	39,120	VC
Creighton Univ	NE	45,356	VC
Indiana Univ Bloomington	IN	19,801	VC

CLASSICAL LANGUAGES

School	ST	$IS	SR
Agnes Scott College	GA	45,323	C+
Asbury Univ	KY	32,038	VC
Austin College	TX	45,875	VC
Ball State Univ	IN	17,850	C
Bard College	NY	61,940	HC
Beloit College	WI	49,970	HC
Boston Univ	MA	60,694	MC
Brigham Young Univ	UT	12,100	HC
Bryn Mawr College	PA	59,890	MC
Calvin College	MI	39,120	VC
Canisius College	NY	44,900	C
Carroll College	MT	28,000	C
Christopher Newport Univ	VA	21,960	VC
Concordia College - Moorhead	MN	39,974	VC
Creighton Univ	NE	45,356	VC
Dartmouth College	NH	57,996	MC
DePauw Univ	IN	48,950	VC+
Dickinson College	PA	57,662	VC+
Duke Univ	NC	50,250	MC
Duquesne Univ	PA	43,720	VC
Eastern Mich Univ	MI	18,604	C
Fordham Univ	NY	61,588	HC+
Hillsdale College	MI	32,866	MC
Hope College	MI	38,650	VC
John Carroll Univ	OH	46,300	C+
La Salle Univ	PA	50,270	C
Luther College	IA	45,720	C
Marquette Univ	WI	46,930	VC+
Miami Univ	OH	24,191	VC
New York Univ	NY	61,470	MC
St. Louis Univ	MO	48,346	HC
St. Mary's College of Calif	CA	53,550	C
St. Peter's Univ	NJ	44,240	C
Scripps College	CA	61,940	MC
Sewanee: The Univ of the South	TN	47,700	HC+
St. Bonaventure Univ	NY	41,575	C
The Pennsylvania State Univ - Univ Park	PA	28,022	VC+
The Univ of N Car at Greensboro	NC	12,848	C
The Univ of Okla	OK	18,621	VC
Univ of Calif at Berkeley	CA	23,322	MC
Univ of Calif at Riverside	CA	27,204	C+
Univ of Calif at Santa Cruz	CA	27,807	C+
Univ of Georgia	GA	20,082	VC
Univ of Kansas	KS	17,603	C+
Univ of Mass Boston	MA	23,066	VC
Univ of Miami	FL	57,034	MC
Univ of Mich/Ann Arbor	MI	22,102	MC
Univ of Minn/Twin Cities	MN		HC
Univ of Nebr - Lincoln	NE	18,031	VC
Univ of N Dak	ND	14,551	C
Vanderbilt Univ	TN	58,220	MC
Washington Univ in St. Louis	MO	69,844	MC
Wheaton College	IL	40,720	MC
Wright State Univ	OH	16,983	C
Yeshiva Univ	NY	47,250	VC+

CLASSICAL STUDIES

School	ST	$IS	SR
Univ of Rhode Island	RI	24,002	C

CLASSICAL/ANCIENT CIVILIZATION

School	ST	$IS	SR
Agnes Scott College	GA	45,323	C+
Bard College	NY	61,940	HC
Barnard College/Columbia Univ	NY	39,000	MC
Bates College	ME	60,720	MC
Beloit College	WI	49,970	HC
Binghamton Univ/The SUNY	NY	21,648	HC+
Boston College	MA	60,622	MC
Boston Univ	MA	60,694	MC
Bowdoin College	ME	59,568	MC
Brigham Young Univ	UT	12,100	HC
Brown Univ	RI	59,428	MC
Carleton College	MN	60,102	MC
Centre College	KY	35,000	HC+
Christendom College	VA	32,600	VC
Clark Univ	MA	47,020	HC+
Cleveland State Univ	OH	21,776	C
Colby College	ME	57,510	MC
College of William & Mary	VA	28,000	MC
Columbia Univ/City of New York	NY	61,116	MC
Columbia Univ/School of General Studies	NY	58,231	MC
Cornell College	IA	44,930	VC
Dartmouth College	NH	57,996	MC
Denison Univ	OH	54,670	HC+
DePauw Univ	IN	48,950	VC+
Dickinson College	PA	57,662	VC+
Duke Univ	NC	50,250	MC
Duquesne Univ	PA	43,720	VC
Earlham College	IN	51,470	HC
Eckerd College	FL	43,902	C
Emory Univ	GA	56,368	MC
Florida State Univ	FL	16,715	VC
Fordham Univ	NY	61,588	HC+
Gonzaga Univ	WA	46,441	HC
Hawaii Pacific Univ	HI	34,360	C
Hollins Univ	VA	43,295	VC
Howard Univ	DC	13,646	C
Indiana Univ Bloomington	IN	19,801	VC
Kalamazoo College	MI	49,740	HC
Kent State Univ	OH	19,920	C
Lehigh Univ	PA	56,770	MC
Loyola Marymount Univ	CA	54,649	VC+
Loyola Univ Chicago	IL	51,646	VC+
Loyola Univ Maryland	MD	56,880	VC+
Loyola Univ New Orleans	LA	46,581	VC
Mich State Univ	MI	22,450	VC
Mount Holyoke College	MA	55,146	MC
New York Univ	NY	61,470	MC
North Central College	IL	38,343	VC
Ohio Univ	OH	21,080	C
Queens College/The CUNY	NY	17,107	VC
Rhodes College	TN	51,900	HC+
Rice Univ	TX	53,288	MC
Rollins College	FL	52,370	HC
Rutgers, The State Univ of New Jersey/Newark Campus	NJ	258,806	C
St. Peter's Univ	NJ	44,240	C
Scripps College	CA	61,940	MC
Smith College	MA	59,674	MC
St. Olaf College	MN	51,200	HC+
Swarthmore College	PA	57,870	MC
Syracuse Univ	NY	56,346	VC
Trinity College	CT		HC+
Univ of Arkansas at Fayetteville	AR	18,352	C+
Univ of Calif at Berkeley	CA	23,322	MC
Univ of Calif at Davis	CA		HC
Univ of Calif at Irvine	CA	25,961	MC
Univ of Calif at Los Angeles	CA	25,686	MC
Univ of Calif at Riverside	CA	27,204	C+
Univ of Chicago	IL	55,416	MC
Univ of Cincinnati	OH	21,506	VC
Univ of Evansville	IN	42,656	VC+
Univ of Florida	FL	15,943	HC
Univ of Illinois at Chicago	IL	24,505	VC
Univ of Iowa	IA	17,693	VC
Univ of Kansas	KS	17,603	C+
Univ of Maryland/Baltimore County	MD	18,000	VC
Univ of Miami	FL	57,034	MC
Univ of Mich/Ann Arbor	MI	22,102	MC
Univ of Miss	MS	16,704	C+
Univ of Nebr - Lincoln	NE	18,031	VC
Univ of Notre Dame	IN	57,117	MC
Univ of Oregon	OR	21,360	C+
Univ of Southern Calif	CA	56,903	MC
Univ of Texas at Arlington	TX	10,908	LC
Univ of Texas at Austin	TX	44,074	HC
Vassar College	NY	61,140	MC
Wellesley College	MA	59,038	MC
Wesleyan Univ	CT	61,198	MC
Willamette Univ	OR	56,450	VC+
Yale Univ	CT	55,300	MC

CLASSICS

School	ST	$IS	SR
Alabama A&M Univ	AL	10,084	C
Amherst College	MA	58,744	MC
Assumption College	MA	47,122	C+
Augustana College	IL	43,398	VC
Augustana College	SD	36,500	VC
Austin College	TX	45,875	VC
Ball State Univ	IN	17,850	C
Barnard College/Columbia Univ	NY	39,000	MC
Baylor Univ	TX	50,329	VC
Belmont Univ	TN	39,190	VC+
Beloit College	WI	49,970	HC
Binghamton Univ/The SUNY	NY	21,648	HC+
Boston College	MA	60,622	MC
Boston Univ	MA	60,694	MC
Bowdoin College	ME	59,568	MC
Bowling Green State Univ	OH	18,970	C
Brandeis Univ	MA		MC
Brigham Young Univ	UT	12,100	HC
Brown Univ	RI	59,428	MC
Bryn Mawr College	PA	59,890	MC
Bucknell Univ	PA	60,140	MC
Cal State, Long Beach	CA	17,502	C+
Calvin College	MI	39,120	VC
Carleton College	MN	60,102	MC
Case Western Reserve Univ	OH	56,534	MC
CUNY/Brooklyn College	NY	5,884	C+
Claremont McKenna College	CA	62,215	MC
Colby College	ME	57,510	MC
Colgate Univ	NY	58,135	MC
College of Charleston	SC	22,145	VC
College of St. Benedict	MN	49,359	VC
College of the Holy Cross	MA	58,042	MC
Colo College	CO	57,162	MC
Columbia Univ/City of New York	NY	61,116	MC
Columbia Univ/School of General Studies	NY	58,231	MC
Concordia College - Moorhead	MN	39,974	VC
Conn Coll	CT	54,970	MC
Cornell Univ	NY	60,964	MC
Dartmouth College	NH	57,996	MC
Davidson College	NC	58,146	MC
Drew Univ/College of Liberal Arts	NJ	57,516	C
Elmira College	NY	49,950	C+
Emory Univ	GA	56,368	MC
Florida State Univ	FL	16,715	VC
Fordham Univ	NY	61,588	HC+
Franciscan Univ of Steubenville	OH	27,320	VC
Franklin and Marshall College	PA	60,799	MC
Furman Univ	SC	54,006	HC
George Washington Univ	DC	57,108	MC
Georgetown Univ	DC	52,910	MC
Georgia State Univ	GA	15,582	VC
Gettysburg College	PA	58,820	PC
Gonzaga Univ	WA	46,441	HC
Grand Valley State Univ	MI	17,998	C+
Grinnell College	IA	53,654	HC
Gustavus Adolphus College	MN	48,170	HC
Hamilton College	NY	55,620	MC
Hampden-Sydney College	VA	51,758	C
Hanover College	IN	43,073	C
Harvard College/Harvard Univ	MA	49,000	MC
Haverford College	PA	61,564	MC
Hellenic College/Holy Cross Greek Orthodox School of Theology	MA	33,190	C
Hillsdale College	MI	32,866	MC
Hobart and William Smith Colleges	NY	60,034	HC+
Hofstra Univ	NY	51,810	VC+
Hunter College	NY	14,429	VC
Illinois Wesleyan Univ	IL	48,452	VC
John Carroll Univ	OH	46,300	C+
Johns Hopkins Univ	MD	47,492	MC
Kent State Univ	OH	19,920	C
Kenyon College	OH	58,890	MC
Knox College	IL	44,865	VC+
Lawrence Univ	WI	46,371	HC
Lehigh Univ	PA	56,770	MC
Lewis & Clark College	OR	54,382	MC
Loyola Marymount Univ	CA	54,649	VC+
Macalester College	MN	57,691	MC
Marquette Univ	WI	46,930	VC+
Marshall Univ	WV	14,820	C
Miami Univ	OH	24,191	VC
Middlebury College	VT	59,160	MC
Millsaps College	MS	43,888	VC+
Monmouth College	IL	40,850	C
Montclair State Univ	NJ	22,614	C
Moravian College	PA	36,381	VC
Mount Holyoke College	MA	55,146	MC
New College of Florida	FL	14,504	NC
New York Univ	NY	61,470	MC
Northwestern Univ	IL	61,640	MC
Notre Dame of Maryland Univ	MD	27,700	VC
Oberlin College	OH	61,788	MC
Ohio Univ	OH	21,080	C

School	ST	$IS	SR
Pacific Lutheran Univ	WA	46,760	C+
Pitzer College	CA	54,988	MC
Pomona College	CA	57,680	MC
Princeton Univ	NJ	53,795	MC
Purdue Univ/West Lafayette	IN	20,024	HC
Randolph College	VA	45,660	VC
Randolph-Macon College	VA	49,869	C+
Reed College	OR	57,780	MC
Rice Univ	TX	43,288	MC
Rockford College	IL	31,000	C
Rutgers, The State Univ of New Jersey/New Brunswick	NJ	25,562	VC
St. Anselm College	NH	49,376	VC
St. John's Univ	MN	47,984	C
St. Louis Univ	MO	48,346	HC
Samford Univ	AL	37,060	C+
San Diego State Univ	CA	21,611	C+
San Francisco State Univ	CA	18,514	C
Sarah Lawrence College	NY	48,000	HC
Seattle Pacific Univ	WA	41,559	VC+
Seton Hall Univ	NJ	45,902	C
Siena College	NY	43,863	VC
Skidmore College	NY	59,942	MC
Smith College	MA	59,674	MC
Southern Illinois Univ Carbondale	IL	21,942	C
Southwestern Univ	TX	45,660	VC
St. Catherine Univ	MN	37,782	C+
St. Olaf College	MN	51,200	HC+
Stanford Univ	CA	58,388	MC
Swarthmore College	PA	57,870	MC
Syracuse Univ	NY	56,346	VC
Temple Univ	PA	24,392	VC
Texas Tech Univ	TX	14,243	C
The Catholic Univ of America	DC	52,852	VC
The College of New Rochelle	NY	33,600	VC
Ohio State Univ-Columbus Campus	OH	19,887	HC+
The Univ of Okla	OK	18,621	VC
The Univ of Utah	UT	16,463	VC
Transylvania Univ	KY	42,660	VC+
Trinity College	CT		HC+
Trinity Univ	TX	48,150	HC+
Truman State Univ	MO	15,541	HC
Tufts Univ	MA	58,780	MC
Tulane Univ	LA	60,861	MC
Union College	NY	60,240	MC
Univ at Buffalo / The SUNY	NY	20,283	VC
Univ of Akron	OH	20,436	C
Univ of Alabama at Tuscaloosa	AL	17,164	C+
Univ of Arizona	AZ	20,657	C
Univ of Calif at Irvine	CA	25,961	VC
Univ of Calif at Los Angeles	CA	25,686	MC
Univ of Calif at San Diego	CA	21,000	VC
Univ of Calif at Santa Barbara	CA	27,551	VC
Univ of Chicago	IL	55,416	MC
Univ of Colo Boulder	CO	22,605	VC+
Univ of Conn	CT	24,706	HC
Univ of Dallas	TX	45,500	VC+
Univ of Hawaii at Manoa	HI	19,379	C
Univ of Illinois at Urbana-Champaign	IL	26,450	HC
Univ of Iowa	IA	17,693	VC
Univ of Mary Washington	VA	19,484	VC
Univ of Maryland - College Park	MD	20,060	HC
Univ of Mass Amherst	MA	24,215	VC+
Univ of Mass Boston	MA	23,066	VC
Univ of Miami	FL	57,034	MC
Univ of Mich/Ann Arbor	MI	22,102	MC
Univ of Missouri/Columbia	MO	18,201	VC
Univ of Montana	MT	14,105	C
Univ of Nebr - Lincoln	NE	18,031	VC
Univ of New Hampshire	NH	26,912	C
Univ of New Mexico	NM	15,300	C
Univ of N Car at Asheville	NC	13,500	VC
Univ of N Car at Chapel Hill	NC	18,928	MC
Univ of Oregon	OR	21,360	C+
Univ of Pennsylvania	PA	61,132	MC
Univ of Pittsburgh at Pittsburgh	PA	28,572	VC+
Univ of Puget Sound	WA	54,608	HC
Univ of Rochester	NY	60,668	MC
Univ of S Car at Columbia	SC	19,725	VC+
Univ of South Florida/Tampa	FL	13,000	C
Univ of Southern Calif	CA	56,903	MC
Univ of Tenn at Knoxville	TN	20,364	VC+
Univ of Texas at Austin	TX	44,074	VC
Univ of Texas at San Antonio	TX	18,372	C
Univ of Vermont	VT	27,006	VC+
Univ of Virginia	VA	23,050	MC
Univ of Washington	WA	14,722	VC
Univ of Wisc/Madison	WI	18,757	HC+
Univ of Wisc-Milwaukee	WI	18,436	C
Ursinus College	PA	57,580	VC
Valparaiso Univ	IN	44,940	VC+
Vanderbilt Univ	TN	58,220	MC
Villanova Univ	PA	58,394	MC
Virginia Wesleyan College	VA	28,433	LC
Wabash College	IN	46,850	C+
Wake Forest Univ	NC	58,838	MC
Washington and Lee Univ	VA	52,812	MC
Washington Univ in St. Louis	MO	69,844	MC
Wayne State Univ	MI	22,063	C
Wesleyan Univ	CT	61,198	MC
Western Washington Univ	WA	18,519	VC
Wheaton College	MA	54,934	HC+
Whitman College	WA	55,988	MC
Williams College	MA	61,070	MC
Xavier Univ	OH	44,980	VC
Yale Univ	CT	55,300	MC

CLINICAL LABORATORY SCIENCE

School	ST	$IS	SR
Albany College of Pharmacy and Health Sciences	NY	40,331	SP
Arkansas State Univ	AR	15,470	C
Bloomfield College	NJ	37,850	LC
Eastern Illinois Univ	IL	20,466	C
Indiana Univ Southeast	IN	16,035	C
Indiana Univ-Purdue Univ Indianapolis	IN	17,611	C
Monmouth Univ	NJ	44,108	C
St. Louis Univ	MO	48,346	HC
Thomas Edison State College	NJ	5,700	SP
Univ of Evansville	IN	42,656	VC+
Univ of Mary Hardin-Baylor	TX	31,950	C+
Western Illinois Univ	IL	20,732	C

CLINICAL PSYCHOLOGY

School	ST	$IS	SR
American Univ	DC	56,015	HC+
Eastern Nazarene College	MA	30,000	C
Faulkner Univ	AL	25,720	LC
Goddard College	VT	16,418	VC
Kutztown Univ of Pennsylvania	PA	16,909	LC
Marywood Univ	PA	45,595	C
Seattle Pacific Univ	WA	41,559	VC+
The Lincoln Univ	PA	15,154	LC
Univ of Louisiana at Monroe	LA	12,998	C
Univ of New Haven	CT	48,940	C

CLINICAL SCIENCE

School	ST	$IS	SR
Bellarmine Univ	KY	42,950	VC
Benedictine Univ	IL	37,820	C
Bethune-Cookman Univ	FL	22,958	C
Brigham Young Univ	UT	12,100	HC
Cal State, Bakersfield	CA	8,000	C
Cal State, Dominguez Hills	CA	17,090	LC
Campbell Univ	NC	37,570	VC
Canisius College	NY	44,900	C
Carroll College	MT	28,000	C
Carroll Univ	WI	38,100	C
Concordia College - Moorhead	MN	39,974	VC
DePaul Univ	IL	47,623	VC
Fairleigh Dickinson Univ/ College at Florham	NJ	42,142	C
Fairleigh Dickinson Univ/ Metropolitan Campus	NJ	40,254	C
Florida Gulf Coast Univ	FL		C
George Washington Univ	DC	57,108	MC
Georgian Court Univ	NJ	41,594	LC
Grand Valley State Univ	MI	17,998	C+
Gwynedd-Mercy College	PA	33,560	C
Howard Univ	DC	13,646	C
Indiana Univ of Pennsylvania	PA	20,846	LC
Ithaca College	NY	53,864	HC
Lake Superior State Univ	MI	18,121	C
LIU Brooklyn	NY	47,182	LC
LIU Post	NY	47,660	C
Loyola Univ Chicago	IL	51,646	VC+
Marquette Univ	WI	46,930	VC+
Mary Baldwin College	VA	38,245	C
Maryville Univ of St. Louis	MO	35,856	VC
McNeese State Univ	LA	2,649	C
Miami Univ	OH	24,191	VC
Mich State Univ	MI	22,450	VC
Minn State Univ, Mankato	MN	15,616	C
Missouri State Univ	MO	13,996	C+
New Mexico State Univ	NM	14,050	C
N Dak State Univ	ND		C
Northern Illinois Univ	IL	19,768	C
Northern Mich Univ	MI	18,278	C
Purdue Univ/West Lafayette	IN	20,024	HC
Quincy Univ	IL	34,980	LC
Ramapo College of New Jersey	NJ	24,938	C
Rockhurst Univ	MO	20,625	C
Rutgers, The State Univ of New Jersey/Newark Campus	NJ	258,806	C
San Francisco State Univ	CA	18,514	C
S Dak State Univ	SD	14,296	C
St. John's Univ	NY	55,070	C+
Stony Brook Univ / SUNY	NY	20,078	HC+
Texas A&M Univ at Corpus Christi	TX	11,544	LC
Texas State Univ	TX	17,128	C
The College of Idaho	ID	31,277	C+
Truman State Univ	MO	15,541	HC
Univ of Idaho	ID	14,558	C
Univ of Jamestown	ND	24,738	C
Univ of Louisiana at Monroe	LA	12,998	C
Univ of Mass Dartmouth	MA	22,223	C
Univ of Mass Lowell	MA	19,316	C
Univ of Nevada, Las Vegas	NV	17,303	C
Univ of N Car at Chapel Hill	NC	18,928	MC
Univ of N Car at Wilmington	NC	13,572	VC
Univ of N Dak	ND	14,551	C
Univ of St. Mary	KS	28,400	C+
Univ of Tenn at Knoxville	TN	20,364	VC+
Univ of Texas - Pan American	TX	11,125	LC
Univ of Texas at El Paso	TX	8,764	NC
Univ of Wisc/Stevens Point	WI	14,043	C
Virginia Commonwealth Univ	VA	21,716	C
Walsh Univ	OH	35,100	C
Washburn Univ	KS	12,579	C
Wayne State Univ	MI	22,063	C
West Liberty Univ	WV	9,142	LC
Wright State Univ	OH	16,983	C
Youngstown State Univ	OH	16,732	C

CLOTHING AND TEXTILES MANAGEMENT/PRODUCTION/SERVICES

School	ST	$IS	SR
Cheyney Univ of Pennsylvania	PA	20,372	LC
College of the Ozarks	MO		VC
East Carolina Univ	NC	14,169	C
Eastern Mich Univ	MI	18,604	C
Florida State Univ	FL	16,715	VC
Johnson & Wales Univ/ Charlotte Campus	NC	29,576	C
Johnson & Wales Univ/North Miami Campus	FL		C
Johnson & Wales Univ/ Providence Campus	RI	29,576	C
N Car Agricultural and Technical State Univ	NC	13,365	LC
N Car State Univ	NC	16,202	HC
San Francisco State Univ	CA	18,514	C
Southern Illinois Univ Carbondale	IL	21,942	C
Texas Tech Univ	TX	14,243	C
Univ of Alabama at Tuscaloosa	AL	17,164	C+
Univ of Northern Iowa	IA	15,795	C
Washington State Univ	WA	20,461	C
Western Mich Univ	MI	19,628	C

COASTAL MARINE POLICY MANAGEMENT

School	ST	$IS	SR
Univ of Rhode Island	RI	24,002	C

COASTAL MARINE POLICY STANDARDS

School	ST	$IS	SR
Univ of Rhode Island	RI	24,002	C

COGNITIVE SCIENCE

School	ST	$IS	SR
Ashford Univ	CA	10,480	C
Beloit College	WI	49,970	HC
Brown Univ	RI	59,428	MC
Cal State, Stanislaus	CA	18,582	C
Canisius College	NY	44,900	C
Case Western Reserve Univ	OH	56,534	MC
Dartmouth College	NH	57,996	MC
Fitchburg State Univ	MA	18,173	C
George Fox Univ	OR	40,750	C+
Hampshire College	MA	58,320	MC
Indiana Univ Bloomington	IN	19,801	VC
Johns Hopkins Univ	MD	47,492	MC
Lawrence Univ	WI	46,371	HC
Lehigh Univ	PA	56,770	MC
Mass Inst of Technology	MA	58,240	MC
Minn State Univ, Mankato	MN	15,616	C
Northwestern Univ	IL	61,640	MC
Occidental College	CA	60,972	MC
Oswego / SUNY	NY	20,009	VC
Pomona College	CA	57,680	MC
Rice Univ	TX	43,288	MC
Smith College	MA	59,674	MC
Tufts Univ	MA	58,780	MC
Tulane Univ	LA	60,861	MC
Univ at Buffalo / The SUNY	NY	20,283	VC
Univ of Calif at Berkeley	CA	23,322	MC
Univ of Calif at Los Angeles	CA	25,686	MC
Univ of Calif at San Diego	CA	21,000	VC
Univ of Denver	CO	51,787	VC+
Univ of Evansville	IN	42,656	VC+
Univ of Georgia	GA	20,082	VC
Univ of Mich/Ann Arbor	MI	22,102	MC
Univ of Mount Union	OH	35,130	C
Univ of Pennsylvania	PA	61,132	MC
Univ of Rochester	NY	60,668	MC
Univ of Texas at Dallas	TX	21,348	HC+
Univ of Wisc/Stout	WI	15,459	C
Vanderbilt Univ	TN	58,220	MC
Vassar College	NY	58,140	MC
Wellesley College	MA	59,038	MC
Wright State Univ	OH	16,983	C
Yale Univ	CT	55,300	MC

COLLABORATIVE DESIGN

School	ST	$IS	SR
Ferris State Univ	MI	20,047	C

COLLABORATIVE EDUCATION

School	ST	$IS	SR
Birmingham-Southern College	AL	44,168	VC+
Goddard College	VT	16,418	VC
Huntingdon College	AL	33,100	C
Rowan Univ	NJ	24,022	VC+
Troy Univ	AL	10,650	C

COLLABORATIVE PIANO

School	ST	$IS	SR
Shenandoah Univ	VA	39,916	C

COMBINED SCIENCE

School	ST	$IS	SR
Calif Baptist Univ	CA	38,792	C
Indiana Univ Southeast	IN	16,035	C
Texas Christian Univ	TX	49,980	HC
Univ of Montana	MT	14,105	C

COMMERCIAL ART

School	ST	$IS	SR
Ashland Univ	OH	25,000	C
Brenau Univ - Women's College	GA	26,650	LC
Calif Univ of Pennsylvania	PA	14,217	C
Cazenovia College	NY	43,464	C
Fort Valley State Univ	GA	11,200	VC
Graceland Univ	IA	28,020	C
LIU Brooklyn	NY	47,182	LC
LIU Post	NY	47,660	C
Madonna Univ	MI	24,540	VC
Millikin Univ	IL	38,940	C
Oral Roberts Univ	OK	31,734	C
Pittsburg State Univ	KS	12,032	C
Southwest Baptist Univ	MO	24,710	C
St. Norbert College	WI	41,478	VC
St. Thomas Aquinas College	NY	40,230	C
Univ of Central Missouri	MO	14,605	C
Univ of Indianapolis	IN	31,740	C
Univ of North Texas	TX	15,628	C
Univ of S Car Upstate	SC	18,200	LC
Washington Univ in St. Louis	MO	69,844	MC

COMMUNICATION

School	ST	$IS	SR
American Univ	DC	56,015	HC+
Arizona State Univ, at the Downtown Phoenix Campus	AZ	22,101	C
Arizona State Univ, at the Polytechnic Campus	AZ	20,531	C+
Black Hills State Univ	SD	13,947	C
Bowling Green State Univ	OH	18,970	C
Bryant Univ	RI	49,179	VC
Cabrini College	PA	40,859	LC
Cal State, Chico	CA	20,158	C
Chestnut Hill College	PA	42,110	LC
College of the Ozarks	MO		VC
Cornell Univ	NY	60,964	MC
Curry College	MA	48,925	LC
Dallas Baptist Univ	TX	30,580	VC
Dordt College	IA	34,160	C
Fairfield Univ	CT	56,960	VC
Ferris State Univ	MI	20,047	C
Fordham Univ	NY	61,588	HC+
Houghton College	NY	36,808	C+
Indiana Univ Kokomo	IN	6,811	LC
Indiana Univ Northwest	IN	6,854	LC
Indiana Univ Southeast	IN	16,035	C
Ithaca College	NY	53,864	HC
Mansfield Univ	PA	19,468	LC
McNeese State Univ	LA	2,649	C
Millikin Univ	IL	38,940	C
Molloy College	NY	40,440	C
Montreat College	NC	31,298	C
Northwest Nazarene Univ	ID	34,000	C
Old Dominion Univ	VA	19,483	LC
Roberts Wesleyan College	NY	38,306	C+
Southern Oregon Univ	OR	17,874	C
SUNY Fredonia/The SUNY at Fredonia	NY	19,840	VC
Univ of Arkansas at Fayetteville	AR	18,352	C+
Univ of Louisiana at Monroe	LA	12,998	C
Univ of Maine	ME	19,902	C+
Univ of Miami	FL	57,034	MC
Univ of Wyoming	WY	14,401	C+
Viterbo Univ	WI	30,070	C
Western Illinois Univ	IL	20,732	C

COMMUNICATION ARTS - SPEECH

School	ST	$IS	SR
Black Hills State Univ	SD	13,947	C
College of the Ozarks	MO		VC
Indiana Univ Kokomo	IN	6,811	C
Indiana Univ South Bend	IN	15,501	C
The SUNY at Potsdam	NY	18,473	C

COMMUNICATION DESIGN

School	ST	$IS	SR
Bryant Univ	RI	49,179	VC
Cal State, Chico	CA	20,158	C
Dallas Baptist Univ	TX	30,580	VC
Syracuse Univ	NY	56,346	VC
Texas State Univ	TX	17,128	C

COMMUNICATION RHETORIC/ COMMUNICATION

School	ST	$IS	SR
Bryant Univ	RI	49,179	VC
Florida Southern College	FL	40,150	C+
Hobart and William Smith Colleges	NY	60,034	HC+
Huntingdon College	AL	33,100	C
Marshall Univ	WV	14,820	C
Mercer Univ	GA	44,201	VC
Nazareth College of Rochester	NY	43,028	C+
Nyack College	NY	33,250	C
Spalding Univ	KY	32,287	LC
Syracuse Univ	NY	56,346	VC
Univ of Nebr - Lincoln	NE	18,031	VC
Univ of Pittsburgh at Pittsburgh	PA	28,572	HC+
Washington and Jefferson College	PA	51,948	VC
Waynesburg Univ	PA	30,150	C
Xavier Univ	OH	44,980	VC

COMMUNICATION SCIENCE

School	ST	$IS	SR
Abilene Christian Univ	TX	38,400	C+
Bryant Univ	RI	49,179	VC
Elmhurst College	IL	43,336	C
Howard Univ	DC	13,646	C
Idaho State Univ	ID	12,307	C
LIU Brooklyn	NY	47,182	LC
Missouri State Univ	MO	13,996	C+
St. Louis Univ	MO	48,346	HC
The Pennsylvania State Univ - Univ Park	PA	28,022	VC+
Univ of Cincinnati	OH	21,506	VC
Univ of Georgia	GA	20,082	VC
Univ of Miss	MS	16,704	C+
Univ of Oregon	OR	21,360	C+
Univ of Pittsburgh at Pittsburgh	PA	28,572	HC+
Univ of Wisc/Madison	WI	18,757	HC+
Wayne State Univ	MI	22,063	C

COMMUNICATION SCIENCES & DISORDERS

School	ST	$IS	SR
Arkansas State Univ	AR	15,470	C
Armstrong State Univ	GA	15,532	C
Baldwin Wallace Univ	OH	38,318	C
Calif Baptist Univ	CA	38,792	C
Cal State, Chico	CA	20,158	C
Eastern Illinois Univ	IL	20,466	C
Fontbonne Univ	MO	31,384	C
Jackson State Univ	MS	13,512	LC
Marywood Univ	PA	45,595	C
Mercy College	NY	30,456	C
Minn State Univ, Mankato	MN	15,616	C
Nazareth College of Rochester	NY	43,028	C+
Ohio Univ	OH	21,080	C
Southern Illinois Univ Carbondale	IL	21,942	C
SUNY Plattsburgh / SUNY	NY	18,083	C
Syracuse Univ	NY	56,346	VC
Texas State Univ	TX	17,128	C
The College of St. Rose	NY	26,750	C
The Pennsylvania State Univ - Univ Park	PA	28,022	VC+
Univ of Georgia	GA	20,082	VC
Univ of Louisiana at Monroe	LA	12,998	C
Univ of Montana	MT	14,105	C
Univ of Tulsa	OK	46,331	MC
Univ of Wisc/Eau Claire	WI	15,730	C
Wayne State Univ	MI	22,063	C
Western Illinois Univ	IL	20,732	C

COMMUNICATION STUDIES

School	ST	$IS	SR
Albion College	MI	46,010	C
Ashford Univ	CA	10,480	C
Baldwin Wallace Univ	OH	38,318	C
Black Hills State Univ	SD	13,947	C
Bryant Univ	RI	49,179	C
Calif Baptist Univ	CA	38,792	C
Calif Polytechnic State Univ	CA	20,156	C
Cal State, Northridge	CA	28,690	LC
Creighton Univ	NE	45,356	VC
Eastern Illinois Univ	IL	20,466	C
Illinois State Univ	IL	23,110	VC
Indiana Univ Bloomington	IN	19,801	VC
Indiana Univ East	IN	6,783	C
Indiana Univ South Bend	IN	15,501	C
Indiana Univ-Purdue Univ Indianapolis	IN	17,611	C
Kent State Univ	OH	19,920	C
Millersville Univ of Pennsylvania	PA	21,648	C
Minn State Univ, Mankato	MN	15,616	C
Niagara Univ	NY	41,010	C
Nova Southeastern Univ	FL	37,280	VC
San Jose State Univ	CA	19,133	LC
Southeast Missouri State Univ	MO	15,370	LC
SUNY Fredonia/The SUNY at Fredonia	NY	19,840	VC
Syracuse Univ	NY	56,346	VC
Texas State Univ	TX	17,128	C
The Univ of N Car at Pembroke	NC	13,388	LC
Tiffin Univ	OH	30,273	LC
Trevecca Nazarene Univ	TN	31,186	C
Univ of Denver	CO	51,787	VC+
Univ of Georgia	GA	20,082	VC
Univ of Louisiana at Monroe	LA	12,998	C
Univ of Miami	FL	57,034	MC
Winona State Univ	MN	16,640	C

COMMUNICATIONS

School	ST	$IS	SR
Abilene Christian Univ	TX	38,400	C+
Adams State Univ	CO	13,358	LC
Adelphi Univ	NY	44,670	VC
Adrian College	MI	42,400	C
Alabama State Univ	AL	14,142	NC
Albertus Magnus College	CT	37,382	VC
Albright College	PA	46,660	C
Alcorn State Univ	MS	9,500	C
Alderson Broaddus Univ	WV	28,656	C
Alfred Univ	NY	41,770	C
Allegheny College	PA	50,980	HC
Alma College	MI	44,075	C
Alvernia Univ	PA	39,250	LC
Alverno College	WI	31,434	LC
American International College	MA	36,100	LC
American Univ	DC	56,015	HC+
Anderson Univ	IN	36,100	C
Andrews Univ	MI	28,030	C
Angelo State Univ	TX	15,049	NC
Appalachian State Univ	NC	12,919	NC
Aquinas College	MI	33,060	C
Arcadia Univ	PA	33,570	C+
Arizona State Univ, at the Tempe Campus	AZ	20,137	C+
Arizona State Univ, at the West Campus	AZ	19,251	C
Arkansas State Univ	AR	15,470	C
Arkansas Tech Univ	AR	13,982	LC
Asbury Univ	KY	32,038	VC
Ashland Univ	OH	25,000	C
Auburn Univ	AL	22,378	VC+
Auburn Univ at Montgomery	AL	14,470	LC
Augsburg College	MN	35,142	C
Augustana College	IL	43,398	VC
Augustana College	SD	36,500	VC
Aurora Univ	IL	33,228	C
Austin College	TX	45,875	HC
Austin Peay State Univ	TN	15,274	C
Avila Univ	MO	26,900	C
Azusa Pacific Univ	CA	42,086	C
Baker Univ	KS	33,350	C+
Barry Univ	FL	38,190	C
Barton College	NC	27,660	LC
Bay Path College	MA	34,565	C
Baylor Univ	TX	50,329	HC
Becker College	MA	41,420	C
Belhaven Univ	MS	27,170	C
Bellarmine Univ	KY	42,950	VC
Bellevue Univ	NE	4,600	NC
Belmont Univ	TN	39,190	VC+
Bemidji State Univ	MN	13,500	VC
Benedictine Univ	IL	37,820	C
Bennett College for Women	NC	21,970	LC
Berea College	KY	7,192	C
Berry College	GA	39,254	VC
Bethany College	KS	30,605	NC
Bethany College	WV	35,282	LC
Bethel College	IN	31,560	C
Bethel College	KS	32,160	C
Bethel Univ	MN	34,940	VC
Bethune-Cookman Univ	FL	22,958	C
Biola Univ	CA	40,320	C+
Blackburn College	IL	21,350	C
Bloomfield College	NJ	37,850	LC
Bloomsburg Univ of Pennsylvania	PA	13,598	C
Bluefield College	VA	17,230	C+
Bluffton Univ	OH	38,948	C
Boise State Univ	ID	13,469	LC
Boston College	MA	60,622	MC
Boston Univ	MA	60,694	MC
Bradley Univ	IL	31,874	VC
Brenau Univ - Women's College	GA	26,650	LC
Brewton-Parker College	GA	33,388	C
Briar Cliff Univ	IA	29,514	C
Bridgewater College	VA	41,450	C
Brigham Young Univ	UT	12,100	HC
Bryan College	TN	24,194	C
Bryant Univ	RI	49,179	VC
Buena Vista Univ	IA	39,188	C
Buffalo State College / SUNY	NY	15,733	C+
Butler Univ	IN	47,572	VC+
Caldwell College	NJ	35,602	NC
Calif Baptist Univ	CA	38,792	C
Calif Lutheran Univ	CA	49,540	C+
Calif State Polytechnic Univ, Pomona	CA	20,156	C
Cal State, Bakersfield	CA	8,000	C
Cal State, Dominguez Hills	CA	17,090	LC
Cal State, East Bay	CA	16,549	C
Cal State, Fresno	CA	17,405	C
Cal State, Fullerton	CA	25,188	C
Cal State, Long Beach	CA	17,502	C+
Cal State, Sacramento	CA	16,200	C
Cal State, San Bernardino	CA	12,000	C
Cal State, San Marcos	CA	14,576	LC
Cal State, Stanislaus	CA	18,582	C
Calvin College	MI	39,120	VC
Cameron Univ	OK	10,004	LC
Campbell Univ	NC	37,570	VC
Campbellsville Univ	KY	27,720	C
Canisius College	NY	44,900	VC
Capital Univ	OH	41,050	VC
Cardinal Stritch Univ	WI	24,054	C
Carlow Univ	PA	30,272	C
Carnegie Mellon Univ	PA	51,260	MC
Carroll College	MT	28,000	C
Carroll Univ	WI	38,100	C
Carson-Newman Univ	TN	29,058	C+
Castleton State College	VT	20,186	C
Catawba College	NC	37,240	LC
Cazenovia College	NY	43,464	C
Cedar Crest College	PA	43,240	C
Cedarville Univ	OH	32,860	VC
Centenary College	NJ	38,618	C
Centenary College of Louisiana	LA	45,650	C+
Central College	IA	42,104	C+
Central Conn State Univ	CT	19,749	C
Central Methodist Univ	MO	28,240	VC
Central Washington Univ	WA	11,730	C
Chaminade Univ of Honolulu	HI	31,664	LC
Champlain College	VT	46,650	VC+
Chapman Univ	CA	58,347	VC+
Chatham Univ	PA	43,797	C
Cheyney Univ of Pennsylvania	PA	20,372	LC
Christopher Newport Univ	VA	21,960	VC
CUNY/Baruch College	NY		HC
CUNY/Brooklyn College	NY	5,884	C+
CUNY/City College	NY	20,319	HC+
Claflin Univ	SC	22,368	LC
Clarion Univ of Pennsylvania	PA	17,370	LC
Clark Atlanta Univ	GA	30,006	LC
Clark Univ	MA	47,020	HC+
Clarke Univ	IA	37,600	C
Clarkson Univ	NY	57,330	HC
Clearwater Christian College	FL	23,720	C
Clemson Univ	SC	19,136	HC
Cleveland State Univ	OH	21,776	C
Coastal Carolina Univ	SC	18,580	C
Coe College	IA	45,550	VC
Coker College	SC	32,256	LC
Colby-Sawyer College	NH	50,790	C
College of Charleston	SC	22,145	VC
College of Mount St. Joseph	OH	33,880	C
College of Mount St. Vincent	NY	41,040	MC
College of New Jersey	NJ	25,376	NC
College of St. Benedict	MN	49,359	VC
College of St. Elizabeth	NJ	43,839	LC
College of St. Scholastica	MN	41,440	C
College of Staten Island/The City of New Yok	NY	16,778	NC
College of the Ozarks	MO		VC
College of Wooster	OH	52,600	VC
Colo Christian Univ	CO	27,500	VC
Colo Mesa Univ	CO	17,690	LC
Colo State Univ-Fort Collins	CO	20,385	VC
Colo State Univ-Pueblo	CO	16,183	C
Columbia College	MO	24,578	C
Columbia College	SC	27,882	C
Columbus State Univ	GA	13,176	C
Concord Univ	WV	13,102	C
Concordia College - Moorhead	MN	39,974	VC
Concordia Univ Irvine	CA	35,390	VC
Concordia Univ Nebr	NE	26,000	VC
Concordia Univ St. Paul	MN	28,250	C
Concordia Univ Texas	TX	23,640	C
Concordia Univ Wisc	WI	28,980	C
Concordia Univ, Ann Arbor	MI	27,220	VC
Concordia Univ, River Forest	IL	26,300	C
Corban Univ	OR	37,380	C+
Cornerstone Univ and Grand Rapids Theological Seminary	MI	33,338	C
Culver-Stockton College	MO	30,900	C
Dakota Wesleyan Univ	SD	23,000	C
Dallas Baptist Univ	TX	30,580	VC
Davis & Elkins College	WV	33,742	C
De Sales Univ	PA	43,970	C
Defiance College	OH	30,645	C
Delta State Univ	MS	12,292	LC
Denison Univ	OH	54,670	HC+
DePaul Univ	IL	47,623	VC
DePauw Univ	IN	48,950	VC+
Dickinson College	PA	61,588	HC+
Dillard Univ	LA	20,940	VC
Dominican Univ	IL	37,628	C
Dominican Univ of Calif	CA	51,250	C
Dordt College	IA	34,160	C+
Dowling College	NY	25,000	LC
Drake Univ	IA	41,516	VC+
Drexel Univ	PA	61,418	VC+
Drury Univ	MO	31,909	VC
Duquesne Univ	PA	43,720	VC
East Carolina Univ	NC	14,169	C
East Central Univ	OK	10,223	LC
East Stroudsburg Univ of Pennsylvania	PA	18,868	C
East Tenn State Univ	TN	9,000	C
East Texas Baptist Univ	TX	31,577	LC
Eastern Conn State Univ	CT	20,584	C
Eastern Mennonite Univ	VA	40,660	C
Eastern Mich Univ	MI	18,604	C
Eastern Nazarene College	MA	30,000	C
Eastern New Mexico Univ	NM	10,682	C
Eastern Univ	PA	37,704	C
Eastern Washington Univ	WA		C
Eckerd College	FL	43,902	C
Edinboro Univ of Pennsylvania	PA	15,940	LC
Edward Waters College	FL	19,607	LC
Elizabethtown College	PA	49,740	VC
Elizabethtown College School of Continuing and Professional Studies	PA		VC
Elmhurst College	IL	43,336	C
Elon Univ	NC	41,914	VC+
Embry-Riddle Aeronautical Univ - Daytona Beach	FL	40,884	C+
Emerson College	MA	52,446	HC+
Emmanuel College	MA	47,985	VC
Emory and Henry College	VA	387,460	C
Emporia State Univ	KS	12,897	C
Endicott College	MA	43,228	VC+
Eureka College	IL	19,280	C
Evangel Univ	MO	23,090	C
Excelsior College	NY	5,580	SP
Fairleigh Dickinson Univ/ College at Florham	NJ	42,142	C
Fairleigh Dickinson Univ/ Metropolitan Campus	NJ	40,254	C
Fairmont State Univ	WV	12,098	LC
Felician College	NJ	41,640	LC
Ferris State Univ	MI	20,047	C
Fitchburg State Univ	MA	18,173	C
Five Towns College	NY	34,550	C
Flagler College	FL	25,180	C
Florida Atlantic Univ	FL	17,339	C
Florida Gulf Coast Univ	FL		C
Florida Inst of Technology	FL	48,290	VC
Florida Southern College	FL	40,150	C+
Florida State Univ	FL	16,715	VC
Fontbonne Univ	MO	31,384	C
Fordham Univ	NY	61,588	HC+
Fort Hays State Univ	KS	11,354	C
Fort Valley State Univ	GA	11,200	VC
Framingham State Univ	MA	18,854	C
Francis Marion Univ	SC	16,464	LC
Franciscan Univ of Steubenville	OH	27,320	VC
Franklin Pierce Univ	NH	41,598	C
Freed-Hardeman Univ	TN	19,697	VC
Friends Univ	KS	29,100	C
Frostburg State Univ	MD	15,264	LC
Furman Univ	SC	54,006	HC
Gallaudet Univ	DC	25,380	SP
Gannon Univ	PA	39,608	C
Gardner-Webb Univ	NC	34,375	C+
Geneva College	PA	27,280	C
George Fox Univ	OR	40,750	C+
George Mason Univ	VA	15,724	VC
George Washington Univ	DC	57,108	MC
Georgetown College	KY	41,440	C
Georgia Regents Univ	GA		C
Georgia Southern Univ	GA	16,942	C
Gonzaga Univ	WA	46,441	HC
Gordon College	MA	44,320	C
Goshen College	IN	35,900	VC
Goucher College	MD	52,040	VC+
Grace College and Seminary	IN	28,800	VC
Graceland Univ	IA	28,020	C
Grambling State Univ	LA	13,384	LC
Grand Canyon Univ	AZ	24,540	C
Grand Valley State Univ	MI	17,998	C+
Grand View Univ	IA	31,050	C
Green Mountain College	VT	45,228	LC
Greenville College	IL	27,012	C
Grove City College	PA	24,022	VC
Gustavus Adolphus College	MN	48,170	HC
Gwynedd-Mercy College	PA	33,560	C
Hamilton College	NY	55,620	MC
Hamline Univ	MN	45,678	VC
Hampshire College	MA	58,320	MC
Hampton Univ	VA	28,528	C
Hannibal-LaGrange Univ	MO	24,490	C
Hanover College	IN	44,073	C+
Harding Univ	AR	23,556	C
Hardin-Simmons Univ	TX	23,560	C+
Hastings College	NE	27,782	C+
Hawaii Pacific Univ	HI	34,360	C
Heidelberg Univ	OH	34,100	C
Henderson State Univ	AR	14,584	C
High Point Univ	NC	39,800	C
Hiram College	OH	37,300	VC

School	ST	$IS	SR
Hollins Univ	VA	43,295	VC
Holy Family Univ	PA	40,030	LC
Holy Names Univ	CA	40,310	NC
Hood College	MD	45,730	C
Hope College	MI	38,650	VC
Hope International Univ	CA	34,650	C
Houston Baptist Univ	TX	36,450	C
Howard Payne Univ	TX	17,115	C
Howard Univ	DC	13,646	C
Humboldt State Univ	CA	18,400	C
Huntington Univ	IN	32,220	C+
Idaho State Univ	ID	12,307	C
Illinois College	IL	25,770	VC
Indiana Inst of Technology	IN	34,240	LC
Indiana State Univ	IN	16,000	C
Indiana Univ Kokomo	IN	6,811	LC
Indiana Univ South Bend	IN	15,501	C
Indiana Univ-Purdue Univ Fort Wayne	IN	15,521	C
Indiana Wesleyan Univ	IN	31,815	VC
Iona College	NY	44,028	C
Iowa State Univ	IA	16,403	C
Iowa Wesleyan College	IA	30,850	LC
Ithaca College	NY	53,864	HC
Jackson State Univ	MS	13,512	LC
Jacksonville State Univ	AL	12,480	LC
Jacksonville Univ	FL	37,780	C
James Madison Univ	VA	18,049	VC
John Carroll Univ	OH	46,300	C+
Johnson C. Smith Univ	NC	25,336	LC
Judson Univ	IL	25,130	C
Juniata College	PA	49,340	VC
Kansas State Univ	KS	15,497	VC
Kansas Wesleyan Univ	KS	32,000	C
Kean Univ	NJ	23,444	C
Keene State College	NH	23,232	LC
Kennesaw State Univ	GA		C
Kent State Univ	OH	19,920	C
Kentucky Wesleyan College	KY	27,440	C
Keuka College	NY	30,300	C
Keystone College	PA	28,680	LC
King's College	PA	43,502	C
La Roche College	PA	35,824	LC
La Salle Univ	PA	50,270	C
La Sierra Univ	CA	35,694	VC
Lake Erie College	OH	37,266	C
Lake Forest College	IL	50,652	VC
Lake Superior State Univ	MI	18,121	C
Lamar Univ	TX	6,820	LC
Lander Univ	SC	22,514	C+
Lane College	TN	11,212	C
Lasell College	MA	43,750	C
Lawrence Tech Univ	MI	37,630	VC
Le Moyne College	NY	43,470	C
Lee Univ	TN	18,690	C+
Lees-McRae College	NC	33,944	C
Lehman College/The CUNY	NY	5,778	LC
Lenoir-Rhyne College	NC	35,984	C
Lewis & Clark College	OR	54,382	VC
Lewis Univ	IL	23,050	C
Lewis-Clark State College	ID	6,990	C
Liberty Univ	VA	19,101	C
Limestone College	SC	30,800	C
Lincoln Memorial Univ	TN	18,144	C
Lindenwood Univ	MO	20,750	C
Lindsey Wilson College	KY	31,220	C
Linfield College-McMinnville Campus	OR	47,676	C
Lipscomb Univ	TN	37,490	VC
Lock Haven Univ of Pennsylvania	PA	18,028	LC
Longwood Univ	VA	20,924	C
Louisiana College	LA	15,746	C
Louisiana State Univ	LA	18,667	C+
Louisiana State Univ in Shreveport	LA	5,606	C
Loyola Marymount Univ	CA	54,649	VC+
Loyola Univ Chicago	IL	51,646	VC+
Loyola Univ Maryland	MD	56,880	VC+
Loyola Univ New Orleans	LA	46,581	VC
Lubbock Christian Univ	TX	26,308	C
Luther College	IA	45,720	VC
Lycoming College	PA	45,379	C
Lynchburg College	VA	42,645	C
Lyndon State College	VT	14,233	C
Lynn Univ	FL	43,500	LC
Madonna Univ	MI	24,540	VC
Malone Univ	OH	35,364	C
Manchester Univ	IN	35,070	C
Manhattan College	NY	49,588	C+
Manhattanville College	NY	50,740	VC
Marian Univ	IN	38,540	C
Marian Univ	WI	32,420	LC
Marietta College	OH	42,135	C+
Marist College	NY	35,500	C
Marquette Univ	WI	46,930	VC+
Mars Hill Univ	NC	22,950	LC
Marshall Univ	WV	14,820	C
Martin Univ	IN	11,000	SP
Marylhurst Univ	OR	20,295	NC
Marymount Manhattan College	NY	40,118	VC
Marymount Univ	VA	39,480	C
Maryville Univ of St. Louis	MO	35,856	VC
Marywood Univ	PA	45,595	C
Mass College of Liberal Arts	MA	18,613	C
Mayville State Univ	ND	11,401	NC
McDaniel College	MD	47,450	VC
McPherson College	KS	28,138	C
Medaille College	NY	35,112	C
Mercer Univ	GA	44,201	VC
Mercy College	NY	30,456	C
Mercyhurst Univ	PA	40,700	C
Meredith College	NC	31,420	C
Merrimack College	MA	44,215	C
Messiah College	PA	40,690	C+
Methodist Univ	NC	37,185	C
Metropolitan State Univ	MN	5,923	
Metropolitan State Univ of Denver	CO	4,835	LC
Miami Univ	OH	24,191	VC
Mich State Univ	MI	22,450	VC
Mich Tech Univ	MI	23,556	HC
MidAmerica Nazarene Univ	KS	28,000	C
Middle Tenn State Univ	TN	8,650	C
Midland Univ	NE	34,000	C
Midwestern State Univ	TX	9,722	C
Miles College	AL	11,164	NC
Millersville Univ of Pennsylvania	PA	21,648	C
Milligan College	TN	27,510	C
Millsaps College	MS	43,888	VC+
Minn State Univ, Mankato	MN	15,616	C
Minn State Univ, Moorhead	MN	13,392	VC
Minot State Univ	ND	10,915	C
Misericordia Univ	PA	41,060	C
Miss College	MS	21,998	C
Miss State Univ	MS	14,750	C
Miss Univ for Women	MS	7,400	C
Miss Valley State Univ	MS	9,706	LC
Missouri Baptist Univ	MO	31,830	C
Missouri Southern State Univ	MO	12,061	C
Missouri State Univ	MO	13,996	C+
Missouri Valley College	MO	22,200	C
Missouri Western State Univ	MO	12,260	NC
Mitchell College	CT	40,983	C
Monmouth College	IL	40,850	C
Monmouth Univ	NJ	44,108	C
Montana State Univ-Billings	MT	12,425	LC
Montana State Univ-Northern	MT	12,500	NC
Montana Tech of The Univ of Montana	MT	14,650	VC
Montclair State Univ	NJ	22,614	C
Morehead State Univ	KY	10,900	C
Morningside College	IA	35,430	C
Morris College	SC	16,310	LC
Mount Ida College	MA	30,115	LC
Mount Mary Univ	WI	33,590	LC
Mount Mercy Univ	IA	35,320	C
Mount St. Mary's Univ	MD	47,996	C
Mount Vernon Nazarene Univ	OH	29,590	C
Muhlenberg College	PA	52,837	HC
Muskingum Univ	OH	30,502	C
Nebr Wesleyan Univ	NE	29,774	C+
Neumann Univ	PA	31,078	LC
New England College	NH	45,930	LC
New Jersey Inst of Technology	NJ	26,490	C+
New Mexico Highlands Univ	NM	11,904	NC
New Mexico State Univ	NM	14,050	C
New York College of Technology/The CUNY	NY	5,769	NC
New York Inst of Technology	NY	45,010	VC
New York Univ	NY	61,470	MC
Newberry College	SC	26,850	LC
Newbury College	MA	43,280	LC
Newman Univ	KS	30,380	C+
Niagara Univ	NY	41,010	C
Nicholls State Univ	LA	7,095	C
Norfolk State Univ	VA	10,531	LC
N Car Agricultural and Technical State Univ	NC	13,365	LC
N Car State Univ	NC	16,202	HC
North Central College	IL	38,343	VC
North Central Univ	MN	26,400	C
N Dak State Univ	ND		C
North Park Univ	IL	30,130	C
Northeastern Illinois Univ	IL	10,318	LC
Northeastern State Univ	OK	8,615	VC
Northeastern Univ	MA	55,296	MC
Northern Arizona Univ	AZ	19,010	C
Northern Illinois Univ	IL	19,768	C
Northern Kentucky Univ	KY	21,134	C
Northern Mich Univ	MI	18,278	C
Northwest Christian Univ	OR	27,399	C
Northwest Missouri State Univ	MO	17,347	C
Northwest Univ	WA	18,854	C
Northwestern College	MN	24,000	C
Northwestern Okla State Univ	OK	7,275	NC
Northwestern State Univ of Louisiana	LA	14,368	C
Northwestern Univ	IL	61,640	MC
Norwich Univ	VT	28,212	C
Notre Dame College	OH	34,942	VC
Notre Dame de Namur Univ	CA	44,236	LC
Notre Dame of Maryland Univ	MD	27,700	C
Nyack College	NY	33,250	C
Oakland Univ	MI	19,391	C
Oakwood Univ	AL	25,529	NC
Oglethorpe Univ	GA	44,200	C+
Ohio Dominican Univ	OH	38,380	C+
Ohio Northern Univ	OH	42,075	VC
Ohio Univ	OH	21,080	C
Okla Baptist Univ	OK	28,202	C
Okla Christian Univ	OK	25,870	VC
Okla City Univ	OK	40,476	VC
Okla Wesleyan Univ	OK	21,300	C
Olivet College	MI	19,984	LC
Olivet Nazarene Univ	IL	29,990	C
Oral Roberts Univ	OK	31,734	C
Oswego / SUNY	NY	20,009	VC
Ottawa Univ	KS	15,000	VC
Otterbein College	OH	32,214	C
Ouachita Baptist Univ	AR	30,220	VC
Our Lady of the Lake Univ	TX	22,430	LC
Pace Univ	NY	53,367	C
Pacific Lutheran Univ	WA	46,760	C+
Pacific Union College	CA	28,150	VC
Paine College	GA	19,826	LC
Palm Beach Atlantic Univ	FL	34,874	C+
Park Univ	MO	17,525	C
Paul Quinn College	TX	25,350	LC
Penn State Erie/The Behrend College	PA	16,256	C
Penn State Univ/Altoona	PA	11,464	C
Pepperdine Univ	CA	55,372	HC+
Pfeiffer Univ	NC	33,700	LC
Piedmont College	GA	30,136	C
Pine Manor College	MA	32,659	LC
Pittsburg State Univ	KS	12,032	C
Plymouth State Univ	NH	23,148	LC
Point Loma Nazarene Univ	CA	41,006	C+
Point Park Univ	PA	36,390	C
Pontifical Catholic Univ of PR	PR	7,310	
Prairie View A&M Univ	TX	15,205	LC
Pratt Inst	NY	55,956	SP
Prescott College	AZ	33,284	C
Presentation College	SD	14,800	LC
Principia College	IL	35,140	C+
Purdue Univ/Calumet	IN	14,336	C
Purdue Univ/West Lafayette	IN	20,024	HC
Queens Univ of Charlotte	NC	39,543	C+
Quincy Univ	IL	34,980	LC
Quinnipiac Univ	CT	55,160	VC
Radford Univ	VA	17,766	LC
Ramapo College of New Jersey	NJ	24,938	C
Randolph College	VA	45,660	VC
Randolph-Macon College	VA	49,869	C+
Regis College	MA	47,565	LC
Regis Univ	CO	41,318	C
Reinhardt College	GA	25,000	C
Rensselaer Polytechnic Inst	NY	61,529	MC
Rhode Island College	RI	17,694	LC
Richard Stockton College of New Jersey	NJ	20,000	VC
Rider Univ	NJ	45,720	C
Ripon College	WI	36,959	C+
Rivier Univ	NH	35,000	VC
Roanoke College	VA	49,976	C
Robert Morris Univ	PA	37,864	C
Rochester College	MI	18,320	LC
Rochester Inst of Technology	NY	42,450	VC
Rockhurst Univ	MO	20,625	C
Rocky Mountain College	MT	32,242	C
Roger Williams Univ	RI	46,296	VC
Rollins College	FL	52,370	HC
Roosevelt Univ	IL	22,605	VC
Rosemont College	PA	42,350	C
Rowan Univ	NJ	24,022	VC+
Rust College	MS	10,600	C
Rutgers, The State Univ of New Jersey/New Brunswick	NJ	25,562	VC
Sacred Heart Univ	CT	49,264	VC
Saginaw Valley State Univ	MI	17,369	C
St. Augustine's Univ	NC	14,000	C
St. Francis Univ	PA	30,029	LC
St. John's Univ	MN	47,984	C
St. Joseph's College	IN	36,500	C
St. Joseph's College of Maine	ME	31,580	C
St. Joseph's Univ	PA	55,006	VC
St. Louis Univ	MO	48,346	HC
St. Martin's Univ	WA	41,678	C
St. Mary's College	IN	45,160	C+
St. Mary's College of Calif	CA	53,550	C
St. Mary's Univ	TX	33,854	C
St. Peter's Univ	NJ	44,240	C
St. Vincent College	PA	40,244	C
St. Xavier Univ	IL	32,840	C
Salem College	NC	29,326	VC
Salem International Univ	WV	21,090	LC
Salem State Univ	MA	13,161	LC
Salisbury Univ	MD	19,180	VC
Salve Regina Univ	RI	48,550	VC
Samford Univ	AL	37,060	VC
San Diego Christian College	CA	31,012	C
San Diego State Univ	CA	21,611	C+
San Francisco State Univ	CA	18,514	C
Savannah College of Art and Design	GA	48,005	SP
Savannah State Univ	GA	13,156	C
Scripps College	CA	61,940	MC
Seattle Pacific Univ	WA	41,559	VC+
Seattle Univ	WA	49,035	VC+
Seton Hall Univ	NJ	45,902	C
Seton Hill Univ	PA	35,172	C
Shenandoah Univ	VA	39,916	C
Shepherd Univ	WV	15,875	C
Shippensburg Univ of Pennsylvania	PA	20,934	C
Shorter Univ	GA	30,650	LC
Siena Heights Univ	MI	32,040	C
Simmons College	MA	49,966	VC
Simpson College	IA	36,086	C+
Simpson Univ	CA	28,900	C
Slippery Rock Univ of Pennsylvania	PA	10,360	C
Sonoma State Univ	CA	20,541	C
S Dak State Univ	SD	14,296	C
Southeastern Louisiana Univ	LA	13,325	C
Southeastern Okla State Univ	OK	7,966	LC
Southeastern Univ	FL	27,201	C
Southern Adventist Univ	TN	26,190	C
Southern Arkansas Univ	AR	14,316	C
Southern Conn State Univ	CT	18,033	LC
Southern Illinois Univ Edwardsville	IL	17,532	C
Southern Methodist Univ	TX	60,585	MC
Southern Nazarene Univ	OK	24,354	C
Southern New Hampshire Univ	NH	38,100	C
Southern Univ and A&M College	LA	9,761	LC
Southern Vermont College	VT	30,740	LC
Southern Wesleyan Univ	SC	25,600	C
Southwest Baptist Univ	MO	24,710	C
Southwest Minn State Univ	MN	14,000	C
Southwestern Adventist Univ	TX	23,026	LC
Southwestern College	KS	29,270	C
Southwestern Okla State Univ	OK	9,160	C
Southwestern Univ	TX	45,660	VC
Spring Arbor Univ	MI	26,740	C
Spring Hill College	AL	44,164	VC
St. Ambrose Univ	IA	30,845	C
St. Bonaventure Univ	NY	41,575	C
St. Catherine Univ	MN	37,782	C+
St. Cloud State Univ	MN	10,600	C
St. Edward's Univ	TX	47,784	C
St. Francis College	NY	34,200	C
St. John Fisher College	NY	40,708	C+
St. John's Univ	NY	55,070	C+
St. Lawrence Univ	NY	59,972	VC
St. Norbert College	WI	41,478	VC
St. Thomas Aquinas College	NY	40,230	C
St. Thomas Univ	FL	32,310	LC
Stanford Univ	CA	58,388	MC
Stephen F. Austin State Univ	TX	14,668	C
Sterling College	KS	27,216	C
Stetson Univ	FL	51,516	VC
Stonehill College	MA	46,780	HC
Suffolk Univ	MA	47,298	C
Sul Ross State Univ	TX	13,410	C
SUNY College at Geneseo	NY	18,670	HC
SUNY College at Old Westbury	NY	16,324	C
SUNY Cortland/The SUNY	NY	19,759	C+
SUNY Fredonia/The SUNY at Fredonia	NY	19,840	VC
SUNY New Paltz	NY	14,348	C
SUNY Oneonta / SUNY	NY	16,919	C+
SUNY Plattsburgh / SUNY	NY	18,083	C
Susquehanna Univ	PA	51,150	C
Tabor College	KS	29,010	C
Taylor Univ	IN	37,821	VC+
Temple Univ	PA	24,392	VC
Texas A&M Univ at Corpus Christi	TX	11,544	LC
Texas A&M Univ at Kingsville	TX	7,500	LC
Texas Christian Univ	TX	49,980	HC
Texas Lutheran Univ	TX	36,040	C
Texas Southern Univ	TX	18,212	LC
Texas State Univ	TX	17,128	C
Texas Tech Univ	TX	14,243	C
Texas Woman's Univ	TX	13,633	LC
The Catholic Univ of America	DC	52,852	VC
The College of New Rochelle	NY	33,600	VC
The College of St. Rose	NY	26,750	C
The Masters College	CA	38,160	C+
Ohio State Univ-Columbus Campus	OH	19,887	HC+
The SUNY College of Agriculture and Tech at Cobleskill	NY	19,749	LC
The SUNY/College at Brockport	NY	19,002	C
The Univ of Memphis	TN	15,094	C
The Univ of N Car at Greensboro	NC	12,848	C
The Univ of Okla	OK	18,621	VC
The Univ of Tenn at Chattanooga	TN	16,883	C
The Univ of Utah	UT	16,463	VC
The Univ of Virginia's College at Wise	VA	11,076	C
Thiel College	PA	38,728	LC
Thomas College	ME	33,560	LC
Thomas Edison State College	NJ	5,700	SP

ST = STATE   **$IS** = IN-STATE COSTS   **SR** = SELECTOR RATING

School	ST	$IS	SR
Thomas More College	KY	34,760	C
Tiffin Univ	OH	30,273	LC
Toccoa Falls College	GA	23,210	LC
Tougaloo College	MS	15,275	NC
Towson Univ	MD	16,000	VC
Trine Univ	IN	39,400	HC+
Trinity Christian College	IL	28,869	C
Trinity International Univ	IL	31,070	VC
Trinity Univ	TX	48,150	HC+
Trinity Washington Univ	DC	30,250	C+
Troy Univ	AL	10,650	C
Truman State Univ	MO	15,541	HC
Tulane Univ	LA	60,861	MC
Union College	KY	29,955	C
Union College	NE	23,270	C
Union Inst & Univ	OH	8,912	SP
Union Univ	TN	28,260	VC
Univ at Albany / SUNY	NY	18,674	VC
Univ at Buffalo / The SUNY	NY	20,283	VC
Univ of Alabama at Birmingham	AL	18,484	C+
Univ of Alabama at Tuscaloosa	AL	17,164	C+
Univ of Alabama in Huntsville	AL	17,591	VC+
Univ of Alaska Anchorage	AK	16,673	NC
Univ of Alaska Fairbanks	AK	15,130	C
Univ of Alaska Southeast	AK	11,493	C
Univ of Arizona	AZ	20,657	C
Univ of Bridgeport	CT	39,030	LC
Univ of Calif at Berkeley	CA	23,322	MC
Univ of Calif at Davis	CA		HC
Univ of Calif at Los Angeles	CA	25,686	MC
Univ of Calif at San Diego	CA	21,000	MC
Univ of Calif at Santa Barbara	CA	27,551	HC
Univ of Central Arkansas	AR	13,667	VC
Univ of Central Florida	FL	15,668	VC+
Univ of Central Missouri	MO	14,605	C
Univ of Central Okla	OK	12,293	C
Univ of Charleston	WV	32,300	C
Univ of Cincinnati	OH	21,506	VC
Univ of Colo at Colo Springs	CO		
Univ of Colo Boulder	CO	22,605	VC+
Univ of Colo Denver	CO	17,904	C
Univ of Conn	CT	24,706	HC
Univ of Dayton	OH	49,070	VC
Univ of Delaware	DE	23,612	VC
Univ of Detroit Mercy	MI	30,450	VC
Univ of Evansville	IN	42,656	VC+
Univ of Findlay	OH	31,916	C
Univ of Hartford	CT	42,674	C
Univ of Hawaii at Hilo	HI	23,066	C
Univ of Hawaii at Manoa	HI	19,379	C
Univ of Houston	TX	19,796	VC
Univ of Houston-Downtown	TX	15,170	LC
Univ of Illinois at Chicago	IL	24,505	VC
Univ of Illinois at Urbana-Champaign	IL	26,450	HC
Univ of Indianapolis	IN	31,740	LC
Univ of Iowa	IA	17,693	VC
Univ of Jamestown	ND	24,738	C
Univ of Kentucky	KY	19,868	C
Univ of La Verne	CA	47,010	C
Univ of Louisiana at Lafayette	LA	6,130	C
Univ of Louisiana at Monroe	LA	12,998	C
Univ of Louisville	KY	17,646	C
Univ of Maine	ME	19,902	C+
Univ of Mary	ND	16,714	C
Univ of Mary Hardin-Baylor	TX	31,950	C+
Univ of Maryland - College Park	MD	20,060	HC
Univ of Maryland/Baltimore County	MD	18,000	VC
Univ of Maryland/Univ College	MD	6,168	SP
Univ of Mass Amherst	MA	24,215	VC+
Univ of Mass Boston	MA	23,066	VC
Univ of Mich/Ann Arbor	MI	22,102	MC
Univ of Mich/Dearborn	MI	9,885	VC
Univ of Mich-Flint	MI	17,547	C+
Univ of Minn Crookston	MN	17,834	C
Univ of Minn/Duluth	MN	19,806	C
Univ of Missouri/Columbia	MO	18,201	MC
Univ of Missouri-Kansas City	MO	19,603	C
Univ of Missouri-St. Louis	MO		VC
Univ of Mobile	AL	28,935	VC
Univ of Montana	MT	14,105	C
Univ of Montana-Western	MT	9,753	LC
Univ of Montevallo	AL	17,060	C
Univ of Mount Olive	NC	18,426	C
Univ of Mount Union	OH	35,130	C
Univ of Nebr - Lincoln	NE	18,031	VC
Univ of Nebr at Kearney	NE	14,855	LC
Univ of Nebr at Omaha	NE	12,700	C
Univ of Nevada, Las Vegas	NV	17,303	C
Univ of Nevada/Reno	NV	17,507	C
Univ of New England	ME	46,750	C
Univ of New Hampshire	NH	26,912	C
Univ of New Haven	CT	48,940	C
Univ of New Mexico	NM	15,300	C
Univ of New Orleans	LA	9,224	C
Univ of North Alabama	AL	15,300	C
Univ of N Car at Asheville	NC	13,500	VC
Univ of N Car at Chapel Hill	NC	18,928	MC
Univ of N Car at Charlotte	NC	15,547	C
Univ of N Car at Wilmington	NC	13,572	VC
Univ of N Dak	ND	14,551	C
Univ of North Florida	FL	15,870	VC
Univ of North Texas	TX	15,628	C
Univ of Northern Colo	CO	18,446	C
Univ of Northern Iowa	IA	15,795	C
Univ of Oregon	OR	21,360	C+
Univ of Pennsylvania	PA	61,132	MC
Univ of Pikeville	KY	25,500	NC
Univ of Pittsburgh at Bradford	PA	21,802	C
Univ of Pittsburgh at Greensburg	PA	17,640	C
Univ of Pittsburgh at Johnstown	PA	20,862	LC
Univ of Pittsburgh at Pittsburgh	PA	28,572	HC+
Univ of Portland	OR	49,964	VC
Univ of Puget Sound	WA	54,608	HC
Univ of Rio Grande	OH	8,750	C
Univ of St. Francis	IN	29,810	C
Univ of San Diego	CA	54,818	HC+
Univ of San Francisco	CA	54,770	VC
Univ of Science and Arts of Okla	OK	10,560	VC
Univ of Scranton	PA	51,940	VC
Univ of Sioux Falls	SD	22,990	C
Univ of South Alabama	AL	13,510	C
Univ of S Car Aiken	SC	16,712	C
Univ of S Car at Columbia	SC	19,725	VC+
Univ of S Car Upstate	SC	18,200	LC
Univ of South Florida/St. Petersburg	FL	12,769	C
Univ of South Florida/Tampa	FL	13,000	C
Univ of Southern Calif	CA	56,903	MC
Univ of Southern Indiana	IN	14,885	C
Univ of Southern Maine	ME	16,576	C
Univ of Southern Miss	MS	13,170	C
Univ of St. Francis	IL	37,560	C
Univ of St. Thomas - Houston	TX	37,690	C
Univ of Tampa	FL	35,160	VC
Univ of Tenn at Knoxville	TN	20,364	VC+
Univ of Tenn at Martin	TN	13,734	C
Univ of Texas - Pan American	TX	11,125	LC
Univ of Texas at Arlington	TX	10,908	LC
Univ of Texas at El Paso	TX	8,764	NC
Univ of Texas at San Antonio	TX	18,372	C
Univ of the Arts	PA	38,450	SP
Univ of the Cumberlands	KY	27,500	C
Univ of the Incarnate Word	TX	37,316	C
Univ of the Ozarks	AR	31,440	C
Univ of the Pacific	CA	52,146	VC
Univ of the Sacred Heart	PR	5,590	
Univ of Toledo	OH	18,464	C
Univ of Tulsa	OK	46,331	MC
Univ of Vermont	VT	27,006	VC+
Univ of Washington	WA	14,722	VC
Univ of West Florida	FL	14,656	C
Univ of Wisc Whitewater	WI	13,314	C
Univ of Wisc/Eau Claire	WI	15,730	VC
Univ of Wisc/Green Bay	WI	19,074	C
Univ of Wisc/La Crosse	WI	9,304	VC
Univ of Wisc/Madison	WI	18,757	HC+
Univ of Wisc/Parkside	WI	10,181	LC
Univ of Wisc/River Falls	WI	9,722	C
Univ of Wisc/Stevens Point	WI	14,043	C
Univ of Wisc/Stout	WI	15,459	C
Univ of Wisc/Superior	WI	14,314	C
Univ of Wisc-Milwaukee	WI	18,436	C
Upper Iowa Univ	IA	30,426	NC
Urbana Univ	OH	30,820	C
Ursinus College	PA	57,580	VC
Utica College	NY	45,670	C
Valparaiso Univ	IN	44,940	VC+
Vanderbilt Univ	TN	58,220	MC
Vanguard Univ of Southern Calif	CA	35,833	VC
Villanova Univ	PA	58,394	MC
Virginia Commonwealth Univ	VA	21,716	C
Virginia Polytechnic Inst and State Univ	VA	14,629	HC
Virginia Wesleyan College	VA	28,433	LC
Voorhees College	SC	18,126	C
Wake Forest Univ	NC	58,838	MC
Walla Walla Univ	WA	26,256	NC
Walsh Univ	OH	35,100	C
Warner Univ	FL	18,000	C
Wartburg College	IA	41,055	VC
Washburn Univ	KS	12,579	C
Washington Adventist Univ	MD	25,859	LC
Washington State Univ	WA	20,461	C
Washington Univ in St. Louis	MO	69,844	MC
Wayland Baptist Univ	TX	18,912	LC
Wayne State College	NE	11,764	NC
Wayne State Univ	MI	22,063	C
Webster Univ	MO	35,100	C+
Wesleyan College	GA	24,000	C
West Chester Univ of Pennsylvania	PA	17,186	C
West Liberty Univ	WV	9,142	LC
West Virginia State Univ	WV	8,378	NC
West Virginia Univ	WV	16,542	C+
Western Carolina Univ	NC	13,944	C
Western Conn State Univ	CT	18,327	LC
Western Kentucky Univ	KY	11,000	LC
Western Mich Univ	MI	19,628	C
Western New England Univ	MA	46,154	C+
Western State Colo Univ	CO	16,924	C
Western Washington Univ	WA	18,519	VC
Westfield State Univ	MA	18,297	C
Westminster College	PA	31,290	C+
Westminster College	UT	37,708	C+
Westmont College	CA	41,500	HC
Wheaton College	IL	40,720	MC
Wheeling Jesuit Univ	WV	33,500	C
Whitworth Univ	WA	47,734	VC
Wichita State Univ	KS	14,607	C+
Widener Univ	PA	52,418	C
Wilberforce Univ	OH	15,100	LC
Wiley College	TX		LC
Wilkes Univ	PA	44,070	C
William Carey Univ	MS	13,500	VC
William Jewell College	MO	31,000	VC+
William Paterson Univ of New Jersey	NJ	21,694	C
William Peace Univ	NC	32,900	LC
William Penn Univ	IA	26,000	C
William Woods Univ	MO	24,260	C
Wilmington College	OH	29,784	C
Wilson College	PA	35,080	C
Wingate Univ	NC	34,990	C
Winston-Salem State Univ	NC	9,418	LC
Winthrop Univ	SC	21,120	C
Wisc Lutheran College	WI	23,510	VC
Wittenberg Univ	OH	47,962	C+
Woodbury Univ	CA	34,500	LC
Worcester State Univ	MA	19,812	C
Wright State Univ	OH	16,983	C
Xavier Univ of Louisiana	LA	25,300	C
Yeshiva Univ	NY	47,250	VC+
York College	NE	19,475	C
York College of Pennsylvania	PA	26,590	C
Youngstown State Univ	OH	16,732	C

COMMUNICATIONS TECHNOLOGY

School	ST	$IS	SR
Alverno College	WI	31,434	LC
Calif College of the Arts	CA	48,334	SP
Cal State, Monterey Bay	CA	26,871	C
Champlain College	VT	46,650	VC+
Chestnut Hill College	PA	42,110	LC
College of the Ozarks	MO		VC
Dakota State Univ	SD	13,811	C
Eastern Mich Univ	MI	18,604	C
George Mason Univ	VA	15,724	VC
Grand Canyon Univ	AZ	24,540	VC
Indiana Univ of Pennsylvania	PA	20,846	LC
Inter-American Univ of PR/Bayamon Univ College	PR	4,428	
James Madison Univ	VA	18,049	VC
Lebanon Valley College	PA	38,570	C
Lewis Univ	IL	23,050	C
Lubbock Christian Univ	TX	26,308	C
Montana Tech of The Univ of Montana	MT	14,650	VC
Montclair State Univ	NJ	22,614	C
New York Univ	NY	61,470	MC
Northwestern Univ	IL	61,640	MC
Ohio Univ	OH	21,080	C
Rochester Inst of Technology	NY	42,450	VC
Sacred Heart Univ	CT	49,264	VC
Salve Regina Univ	RI	48,550	VC
SUNY Polytechnic Inst	NY	19,690	C
Taylor Univ	IN	37,821	VC+
Univ of New Haven	CT	48,940	C
Univ of S Dak	SD	15,111	C
Wilmington Univ	DE	8,112	NC

COMMUNICATIVE DISORDERS

School	ST	$IS	SR
Univ of Rhode Island	RI	24,002	C

COMMUNITY HEALTH WORK

School	ST	$IS	SR
Ashford Univ	CA	10,480	C
Baylor Univ	TX	50,329	HC
Bethel Univ	MN	34,940	VC
Brown Univ	RI	59,428	MC
Central Washington Univ	WA	11,730	C
Concordia Univ St. Paul	MN	28,250	C
Delaware State Univ	DE	16,722	LC
Florida Gulf Coast Univ	FL		C
Florida State Univ	FL	16,715	VC
George Mason Univ	VA	15,724	VC
Georgia College and State Univ	GA	18,900	C+
Hofstra Univ	NY	51,810	VC+
Howard Univ	DC	13,646	C
Indiana Univ Bloomington	IN	19,801	VC
Ithaca College	NY	53,864	HC
John Brown Univ	AR	32,056	VC+
Johnson C. Smith Univ	NC	25,336	LC
Kent State Univ	OH	19,920	C
Lewis Univ	IL	23,050	C
Liberty Univ	VA	19,101	C
Longwood Univ	VA	20,924	C
Louisiana State Univ in Shreveport	LA	5,606	C
Malone Univ	OH	35,364	C
Minn State Univ, Mankato	MN	15,616	C
Minn State Univ, Moorhead	MN	13,392	VC
Montclair State Univ	NJ	22,614	C
Morris College	SC	16,310	LC
Murray State Univ	KY	15,304	C
New Mexico State Univ	NM	14,050	C
Northern Illinois Univ	IL	19,768	C
Ohio Univ	OH	21,080	C
Prescott College	AZ	33,284	C
Rhode Island College	RI	17,694	LC
Slippery Rock Univ of Pennsylvania	PA	10,360	C
Southern Illinois Univ Edwardsville	IL	17,532	C
SUNY College at Old Westbury	NY	16,324	C
The SUNY at Potsdam	NY	18,473	C
Tufts Univ	MA	58,780	MC
Tulane Univ	LA	60,861	C
Univ of Calif at Davis	CA		HC
Univ of Central Okla	OK	12,293	C
Univ of Illinois at Urbana-Champaign	IL	26,450	HC
Univ of Kansas	KS	17,603	C+
Univ of Maine at Farmington	ME	18,187	LC
Univ of Maryland - College Park	MD	20,060	HC
Univ of Mass Lowell	MA	19,316	C
Univ of Nebr at Omaha	NE	12,700	C
Univ of Scranton	PA	51,940	C
Univ of Wisc/La Crosse	WI	9,304	VC
Univ of Wisc/Superior	WI	14,314	C
Western Mich Univ	MI	19,628	VC
Whitworth Univ	WA	47,734	VC
William Paterson Univ of New Jersey	NJ	21,694	C
Winona State Univ	MN	16,640	C
Wright State Univ	OH	16,983	C
York College / The CUNY	NY	5,496	VC

COMMUNITY PSYCHOLOGY

School	ST	$IS	SR
Mount Aloysius College	PA	29,976	C
Southwestern Okla State Univ	OK	9,160	C
Univ of Mich-Flint	MI	17,547	C+
Univ of New Haven	CT	48,940	C

COMMUNITY SERVICES

School	ST	$IS	SR
Alverno College	WI	31,434	LC
Aquinas College	MI	33,060	C
Bemidji State Univ	MN	13,500	VC
Bryant Univ	RI	49,179	VC
DePaul Univ	IL	47,623	VC
Emory and Henry College	VA	387,460	C
Guilford College	NC	42,800	C
Humphreys College	CA	17,000	C
Martin Univ	IN	11,000	SP
Metropolitan College of New York	NY	16,720	VC
Midland Univ	NE	34,000	C
New Mexico State Univ	NM	14,050	C
Northern State Univ - Aberdeen	SD	14,505	C
Ohio Univ	OH	21,080	C
Portland State Univ	OR	18,672	C
Prescott College	AZ	33,284	C
Providence College	RI	57,383	VC
Queens Univ of Charlotte	NC	39,543	C+
Roger Williams Univ	RI	46,296	VC
St. Martin's Univ	WA	41,678	C
Southern Arkansas Univ	AR	14,316	C
SUNY/Empire State College	NY	6,315	SP
Ohio State Univ-Columbus Campus	OH	19,887	HC+
Univ of Calif at Santa Cruz	CA	27,807	C+
Univ of Mass Boston	MA	23,066	VC
Univ of Toledo	OH	18,464	C
Woodbury Inst of Champlain College	VT	15,150	LC

COMPARATIVE LITERATURE

School	ST	$IS	SR
Barnard College/Columbia Univ	NY	39,000	MC
Beloit College	WI	49,970	HC
Bennington College	VT	56,990	HC+
Binghamton Univ/The SUNY	NY	21,648	HC+
Brandeis Univ	MA		MC
Brigham Young Univ	UT	12,100	HC
Brown Univ	RI	59,428	MC
Bryant Univ	RI	49,179	VC
Bryn Mawr College	PA	59,890	HC
Cal State, Fullerton	CA	25,188	C
Cal State, Long Beach	CA	17,502	C+
Case Western Reserve Univ	OH	56,534	MC
CUNY/Brooklyn College	NY	20,319	VC
CUNY/City College	NY	20,319	VC
Clark Univ	MA	47,020	HC+
College of Wooster	OH	52,600	VC
Colo College	CO	57,162	MC
Columbia Univ/City of New York	NY	61,116	MC

ST = STATE $IS = IN-STATE COSTS   SR = SELECTOR RATING

School	ST	$IS	SR
Columbia Univ/School of General Studies	NY	58,231	MC
Cornell Univ	NY	60,964	MC
Dartmouth College	NH	57,996	MC
Eckerd College	FL	43,902	MC
Emory Univ	GA	56,368	MC
Fordham Univ	NY	61,588	HC+
Georgetown Univ	DC	52,910	MC
Goddard College	VT	16,418	VC
Hamilton College	NY	55,620	MC
Hampshire College	MA	58,320	MC
Haverford College	PA	61,564	MC
Hillsdale College	MI	32,866	MC
Hobart and William Smith Colleges	NY	60,034	HC+
Hofstra Univ	NY	51,810	VC+
Hunter College	NY	14,429	VC
Indiana Univ Bloomington	IN	19,801	VC
Lehman College/The CUNY	NY	5,778	LC
Middlebury College	VT	59,160	MC
Mills College	CA	54,119	VC
New England College	NH	45,930	LC
New York Univ	NY	61,470	MC
Northwestern Univ	IL	61,640	MC
Oberlin College	OH	61,788	MC
Princeton Univ	NJ	53,795	MC
Purdue Univ/West Lafayette	IN	20,024	HC
Queens College/The CUNY	NY	17,107	VC
Rutgers, The State Univ of New Jersey/New Brunswick	NJ	25,562	VC
San Diego State Univ	CA	21,611	C+
San Francisco State Univ	CA	18,514	C
Smith College	MA	59,674	MC
Stanford Univ	CA	58,388	MC
Stony Brook Univ / SUNY	NY	20,078	HC+
SUNY College at Geneseo	NY	18,670	HC
Swarthmore College	PA	57,870	MC
The Pennsylvania State Univ - Univ Park	PA	28,022	VC+
The Univ of Utah	UT	16,463	VC
Trinity College	CT		HC+
Univ of Calif at Berkeley	CA	23,322	MC
Univ of Calif at Davis	CA		HC
Univ of Calif at Irvine	CA	25,961	VC
Univ of Calif at Riverside	CA	27,204	C+
Univ of Calif at Santa Barbara	CA	27,551	HC
Univ of Chicago	IL	55,416	MC
Univ of Cincinnati	OH	21,506	VC
Univ of Delaware	DE	23,612	VC
Univ of Georgia	GA	20,082	VC
Univ of Illinois at Urbana-Champaign	IL	26,450	HC
Univ of Iowa	IA	17,693	VC
Univ of La Verne	CA	47,010	C
Univ of Mass Amherst	MA	24,215	VC+
Univ of Mich/Ann Arbor	MI	22,102	MC
Univ of New Mexico	NM	15,300	C
Univ of N Car at Chapel Hill	NC	18,928	MC
Univ of Oregon	OR	21,360	C+
Univ of Pennsylvania	PA	61,132	MC
Univ of PR Recinto de Rio Piedras	PR	5,750	
Univ of Rochester	NY	60,668	MC
Univ of San Francisco	CA	54,770	VC
Univ of S Car at Columbia	SC	19,725	VC+
Univ of Southern Calif	CA	56,903	MC
Univ of Virginia	VA	23,050	MC
Univ of Washington	WA	14,722	VC
Univ of Wisc/Madison	WI	18,757	HC+
Univ of Wisc-Milwaukee	WI	18,436	VC
Washington Univ in St. Louis	MO	69,844	MC
Wellesley College	MA	59,038	MC
Willamette Univ	OR	56,450	VC+

COMPLEMENTARY/ALTERNATIVE HEALTH

School	ST	$IS	SR
Ashford Univ	CA	10,480	C

COMPOSITION

School	ST	$IS	SR
Indiana Univ Bloomington	IN	19,801	VC
Oberlin College	OH	61,788	MC
Shenandoah Univ	VA	39,916	C
Vanderbilt Univ	TN	58,220	MC

COMPUTATIONAL SCIENCES

School	ST	$IS	SR
Biola Univ	CA	40,320	C+
Brown Univ	RI	59,428	MC
Bryant Univ	RI	49,179	VC
Canisius College	NY	44,900	C
Carroll Univ	WI	38,100	C
Champlain College	VT	46,650	VC+
Creighton Univ	NE	45,356	VC
DePaul Univ	IL	47,623	VC
George Mason Univ	VA	15,724	VC
Hood College	MD	45,730	C
Indiana Univ Bloomington	IN	19,801	VC
Kent State Univ	OH	19,920	C
Kent State Univ	OH	19,920	C
Marquette Univ	WI	46,930	VC+
Mercer Univ	GA	44,201	VC
Mich State Univ	MI	22,450	VC
Mount Aloysius College	PA	29,976	C
New College of Florida	FL	14,504	MC
New York Univ	NY	61,470	MC
Park Univ	MO	17,525	C
Purdue Univ/West Lafayette	IN	20,024	HC
Richard Stockton College of New Jersey	NJ	20,000	VC
Stevens Inst of Technology	NJ	50,130	HC
The SUNY/College at Brockport	NY	19,002	C
Univ at Buffalo / The SUNY	NY	20,283	VC
Univ of Illinois at Urbana-Champaign	IL	26,450	HC

COMPUTER EDUCATION

School	ST	$IS	SR
Appalachian State Univ	NC	12,919	VC
Baylor Univ	TX	50,329	HC
Concordia Univ, River Forest	IL	26,300	C
Dakota State Univ	SD	13,811	C
Duquesne Univ	PA	43,720	VC
Eastern Mich Univ	MI	18,604	C
Eastern Washington Univ	WA		C
Hardin-Simmons Univ	TX	23,560	C+
Indiana Univ-Purdue Univ Fort Wayne	IN	15,521	C
Missouri Southern State Univ	MO	12,061	C
Missouri State Univ	MO	13,996	C+
Northern Mich Univ	MI	18,278	C
Union College	NE	23,270	C
Univ of Illinois at Urbana-Champaign	IL	26,450	HC
Univ of Montana-Western	MT	9,753	LC
Univ of Nebr - Lincoln	NE	18,031	VC
Youngstown State Univ	OH	16,732	C

COMPUTER ENGINEERING

School	ST	$IS	SR
Arizona State Univ, at the Tempe Campus	AZ	20,137	C+
Auburn Univ	AL	22,378	VC+
Baylor Univ	TX	50,329	HC
Bellarmine Univ	KY	42,950	VC
Benedict College	SC	20,454	NC
Bethune-Cookman Univ	FL	22,958	C
Binghamton Univ/The SUNY	NY	21,648	HC+
Boston Univ	MA	60,694	MC
Brigham Young Univ	UT	12,100	HC
Bucknell Univ	PA	60,140	MC
Calif Inst of Technology	CA	54,045	MC
Calif Polytechnic State Univ	CA	19,847	HC
Cal State, Chico	CA	20,158	C
Cal State, Fresno	CA	17,405	C
Cal State, Fullerton	CA	25,188	C
Cal State, Long Beach	CA	17,502	C+
Cal State, Sacramento	CA	16,200	C
Calvin College	MI	39,120	VC
Capitol College	MD	21,250	C
Carnegie Mellon Univ	PA	51,260	MC
Case Western Reserve Univ	OH	56,534	MC
Cedarville Univ	OH	32,860	VC
Christopher Newport Univ	VA	21,960	VC
CUNY/City College	NY	20,319	HC+
Claflin Univ	SC	22,368	LC
Clarkson Univ	NY	57,330	HC
Clemson Univ	SC	19,136	HC
Cogswell Polytechnical College	CA	30,531	C
College of New Jersey	NJ	25,376	HC
Colo State Univ-Fort Collins	CO	20,385	VC
Colo Technical Univ	CO	10,500	LC
Columbia Univ/City of New York	NY	61,116	MC
Dordt College	IA	34,160	C+
Drexel Univ	PA	61,418	VC+
Eastern Mich Univ	MI	18,604	C
Eastern Nazarene College	MA	30,000	C
Elizabethtown College	PA	49,740	VC
Elon Univ	NC	41,914	VC+
Embry-Riddle Aeronautical Univ - Daytona Beach	FL	40,884	C+
Embry-Riddle Aeronautical Univ - Prescott Campus	AZ	40,444	VC+
Fairfield Univ	CT	56,960	VC
Florida Atlantic Univ	FL	17,339	C
Florida Inst of Technology	FL	48,290	VC
Florida International Univ	FL	17,747	C+
Florida State Univ	FL	16,715	VC
George Mason Univ	VA	15,724	VC
George Washington Univ	DC	57,108	MC
Georgia Inst of Technology	GA	21,828	MC
Gonzaga Univ	WA	46,441	HC
Harding Univ	AR	23,556	C
Hofstra Univ	NY	51,810	VC+
Howard Univ	DC	13,646	V
Illinois Inst of Technology	IL	38,512	HC+
Indiana Inst of Technology	IN	34,240	LC
Indiana Univ-Purdue Univ Fort Wayne	IN	15,521	C
Indiana Univ-Purdue Univ Indianapolis	IN	17,611	C
Iowa State Univ	IA	16,403	C
Jackson State Univ	MS	13,512	LC
Johns Hopkins Univ	MD	47,492	MC
Johnson C. Smith Univ	NC	25,336	LC
Kansas State Univ	KS	15,497	VC
Kettering Univ	MI	31,456	HC
Lake Superior State Univ	MI	18,121	C
Lawrence Tech Univ	MI	37,630	VC
Lehigh Univ	PA	56,770	MC
LeTourneau Univ	TX	36,210	VC
Lipscomb Univ	TN	37,490	VC
Louisiana State Univ	LA	18,677	C+
Marquette Univ	WI	46,930	VC+
Miami Univ	OH	24,191	VC
Mich State Univ	MI	22,450	VC
Mich Tech Univ	MI	23,556	HC
Milwaukee School of Engineering	WI	39,948	VC+
Minn State Univ, Mankato	MN	15,616	C
Miss State Univ	MS	14,750	C
Missouri Univ of Science and Technology	MO	18,655	VC
Montana State Univ	MT	14,068	C
Montana Tech of The Univ of Montana	MT	14,650	VC
New Jersey Inst of Technology	NJ	26,490	C+
New York College of Technology/The CUNY	NY	5,769	NC
New York Univ	NY	61,470	MC
N Car State Univ	NC	16,202	HC
N Dak State Univ	ND		C
Northeastern Univ	MA	55,296	MC
Northwestern Univ	IL	61,640	MC
Norwich Univ	VT	28,212	C
Nova Southeastern Univ	FL	37,280	VC
Oakland Univ	MI	19,391	C
Ohio Northern Univ	OH	42,075	VC
Ohio Univ	OH	21,080	C
Okla Christian Univ	OK	25,870	VC
Okla State Univ	OK	14,310	VC
Old Dominion Univ	VA	19,483	LC
Olivet Nazarene Univ	IL	29,990	C
Oral Roberts Univ	OK	31,734	C
Oregon State Univ	OR	20,273	VC
Pacific Lutheran Univ	WA	46,760	C+
Penn State Erie/The Behrend College	PA	16,256	C
Pennsylvania College of Technology	PA	26,286	NC
Polytechnic Inst of New York Univ	NY	53,064	HC+
Portland State Univ	OR	18,672	C
Prairie View A&M Univ	TX	15,205	LC
Purdue Univ/Calumet	IN	14,336	C
Purdue Univ/West Lafayette	IN	20,024	HC
Rensselaer Polytechnic Inst	NY	61,529	MC
Rochester Inst of Technology	NY	42,450	VC
Rose-Hulman Inst of Technology	IN	53,340	MC
St. Louis Univ	MO	48,346	HC
St. Mary's Univ	TX	33,854	C
San Diego State Univ	CA	21,611	C+
San Francisco State Univ	CA	18,514	C
San Jose State Univ	CA	19,133	LC
Seattle Univ	WA	49,035	VC+
Shepherd Univ	WV	15,875	C
Shippensburg Univ of Pennsylvania	PA	20,934	C
S Dak School of Mines and Technology	SD	15,260	VC
Southern Illinois Univ Carbondale	IL	21,942	C
Southern Illinois Univ Edwardsville	IL	17,532	C
Southern Methodist Univ	TX	60,585	MC
Southwestern Okla State Univ	OK	9,160	C
Stevens Inst of Technology	NJ	50,130	HC
Stony Brook Univ / SUNY	NY	20,078	HC+
Suffolk Univ	MA	47,298	C
SUNY New Paltz	NY	14,348	C
Syracuse Univ	NY	56,346	VC
Taylor Univ	IN	37,821	VC+
Texas A&M Univ	TX	19,207	VC
The Catholic Univ of America	DC	52,852	VC
Ohio State Univ-Columbus Campus	OH	19,887	HC+
The Univ of Memphis	TN	15,094	C
The Univ of Okla	OK	18,621	VC
The Univ of Utah	UT	16,463	VC
Trine Univ	IN	39,400	HC+
Tufts Univ	MA	58,780	MC
Union College	NY	60,240	MC
United States Air Force Academy	CO		MC
United States Naval Academy	MD		MC
Universidad Politecnica de PR	PR	19,252	
Univ at Buffalo / The SUNY	NY	20,283	VC
Univ of Akron	OH	20,436	C
Univ of Alabama at Huntsville	AL	17,591	VC+
Univ of Alaska Fairbanks	AK	15,130	C
Univ of Arkansas at Fayetteville	AR	18,352	C+
Univ of Bridgeport	CT	39,030	LC
Univ of Calif at Berkeley	CA	23,322	MC
Univ of Calif at Davis	CA		HC
Univ of Calif at Irvine	CA	25,961	VC
Univ of Calif at Los Angeles	CA	25,686	MC
Univ of Calif at San Diego	CA	21,000	VC
Univ of Calif at Santa Barbara	CA	27,551	HC
Univ of Calif at Santa Cruz	CA	27,807	C+
Univ of Central Florida	FL	15,668	VC+
Univ of Cincinnati	OH	21,506	VC
Univ of Colo Boulder	CO	22,605	VC+
Univ of Conn	CT	24,706	HC
Univ of Dayton	OH	49,070	VC
Univ of Delaware	DE	23,612	VC
Univ of Denver	CO	51,787	VC+
Univ of Evansville	IN	42,656	VC+
Univ of Florida	FL	15,943	HC
Univ of Hartford	CT	42,674	C
Univ of Houston	TX	19,796	VC
Univ of Idaho	ID	14,558	C
Univ of Illinois at Chicago	IL	24,505	VC
Univ of Illinois at Urbana-Champaign	IL	26,450	HC
Univ of Kansas	KS	17,603	C+
Univ of La Verne	CA	47,010	C
Univ of Louisiana at Lafayette	LA	6,130	C
Univ of Louisville	KY	17,946	C
Univ of Maine	ME	19,902	C
Univ of Maryland - College Park	MD	20,060	HC
Univ of Maryland/Baltimore County	MD	18,000	VC
Univ of Mass Amherst	MA	24,215	VC+
Univ of Mass Dartmouth	MA	22,223	C
Univ of Miami	FL	57,034	MC
Univ of Mich/Ann Arbor	MI	22,102	MC
Univ of Mich/Dearborn	MI	9,885	VC
Univ of Minn/Duluth	MN	19,806	C
Univ of Missouri/Columbia	MO	18,201	MC
Univ of Nebr - Lincoln	NE	18,031	VC
Univ of Nevada, Las Vegas	NV	17,303	C
Univ of New Hampshire	NH	26,912	C
Univ of New Haven	CT	48,940	C
Univ of New Mexico	NM	15,300	C
Univ of N Car at Charlotte	NC	15,547	C
Univ of North Texas	TX	15,628	C
Univ of Notre Dame	IN	57,117	MC
Univ of Pennsylvania	PA	61,132	MC
Univ of Pittsburgh at Johnstown	PA	20,862	LC
Univ of Pittsburgh at Pittsburgh	PA	28,572	HC+
Univ of PR/Mayaguez	PR	1,250	
Univ of Scranton	PA	51,940	VC
Univ of South Alabama	AL	13,510	C
Univ of S Car at Columbia	SC	19,725	VC+
Univ of South Florida/Tampa	FL	13,000	C
Univ of Southern Calif	CA	56,903	MC
Univ of Tenn at Knoxville	TN	20,364	VC+
Univ of Texas - Pan American	TX	11,125	LC
Univ of Texas at Arlington	TX	10,908	LC
Univ of Texas at Dallas	TX	21,348	VC+
Univ of Texas at San Antonio	TX	18,372	C
Univ of the Pacific	CA	52,146	VC
Univ of Toledo	OH	18,464	C
Univ of Tulsa	OK	46,331	MC
Univ of Virginia	VA	23,050	MC
Univ of Washington	WA	14,722	VC
Univ of West Florida	FL	14,656	C
Univ of Wisc/Madison	WI	18,757	HC+
Univ of Wisc/Stout	WI	15,459	C
Univ of Wisc-Milwaukee	WI	18,436	C
Univ of Wyoming	WY	14,401	C
Valparaiso Univ	IN	44,940	VC+
Vanderbilt Univ	TN	58,220	MC
Vermont Technical College	VT	15,751	C
Villanova Univ	PA	58,394	MC
Virginia Commonwealth Univ	VA	21,716	C
Virginia Polytechnic Inst and State Univ	VA	14,629	HC
Washington State Univ	WA	20,461	C
Washington Univ in St. Louis	MO	69,844	MC
West Virginia Univ	WV	16,542	C+
Western Mich Univ	MI	19,628	C
Western New England Univ	MA	46,154	C+
Wichita State Univ	KS	14,607	C
Wright State Univ	OH	16,983	C
York College of Pennsylvania	PA	26,590	C

COMPUTER ENGINEERING TECHNOLOGY

School	ST	$IS	SR
Cal State, Fresno	CA	17,405	C
Cal State, Long Beach	CA	17,502	C+
Central Conn State Univ	CT	19,749	C
Farmingdale State College	NY	19,673	C
Howard Univ	DC	13,646	C
Indiana Univ-Purdue Univ Indianapolis	IN	17,611	C
Kent State Univ	OH	19,920	C
Minn State Univ, Mankato	MN	15,616	C
Missouri Southern State Univ	MO	12,061	C
Mount Vernon Nazarene Univ	OH	29,590	C
New York Univ	NY	61,470	MC
Northern Kentucky Univ	KY	21,134	C
Nova Southeastern Univ	FL	37,280	VC
Shawnee State Univ	OH	16,916	C

ST = STATE $IS = IN-STATE COSTS   SR = SELECTOR RATING

School	ST	$IS	SR
Southern Polytechnic State Univ	GA	13,958	C
Syracuse Univ	NY	56,346	VC
Taylor Univ	IN	37,821	VC+
The Pennsylvania State Univ - Univ Park	PA	28,022	VC+
Univ of Cincinnati	OH	21,506	VC
Univ of S Car Upstate	SC	18,200	LC

COMPUTER GAME DESIGN/DEVELOPMENT

School	ST	$IS	SR
Abilene Christian Univ	TX	38,400	C+
Becker College	MA	41,420	C
Bloomfield College	NJ	37,850	LC
Champlain College	VT	46,650	VC+
Dakota State Univ	SD	13,811	C
De Sales Univ	PA	43,970	C
DePaul Univ	IL	47,623	VC
Elmhurst College	IL	43,336	C
Indiana Inst of Technology	IN	34,240	LC
Kent State Univ	OH	19,920	C
Marshall Univ	WV	14,820	C
Okla Christian Univ	OK	25,870	VC
Shawnee State Univ	OH	16,916	C
Southern Polytechnic State Univ	GA	13,958	C
Univ of Calif at Santa Cruz	CA	27,807	C+
Univ of Denver	CO	51,787	VC+
Univ of Miami	FL	57,034	MC

COMPUTER GRAPHICS

School	ST	$IS	SR
Andrews Univ	MI	28,030	C+
Art Inst of Atlanta	GA	24,000	SP
Ashford Univ	CA	10,480	C
Bloomfield College	NJ	37,850	LC
Cal State, Chico	CA	20,158	C
Cogswell Polytechnical College	CA	30,531	C
Columbia College Chicago	IL	30,940	LC
Dakota State Univ	SD	13,811	C
DePaul Univ	IL	47,623	VC
Eastern Mich Univ	MI	18,604	C
Escuela de Artes Plasticas de PR	PR	2,660	
Fashion Inst of Technology/SUNY	NY	18,362	SP
Indiana Univ-Purdue Univ Fort Wayne	IN	15,521	C
Indiana Univ-Purdue Univ Indianapolis	IN	17,611	C
Indiana Wesleyan Univ	IN	31,815	VC
Jacksonville Univ	FL	37,780	C
La Salle Univ	PA	50,270	C
Lawrence Tech Univ	MI	37,630	VC
Lewis Univ	IL	23,050	C
Millikin Univ	IL	38,940	C
Monmouth Univ	NJ	44,108	C
New York Inst of Technology	NY	45,010	VC
Northwest Nazarene Univ	ID	34,000	C
Pennsylvania College of Technology	PA	26,286	NC
Pratt Inst	NY	55,956	SP
Purdue Univ/Calumet	IN	14,336	C
Purdue Univ/West Lafayette	IN	20,024	HC
Ringling College of Art and Design	FL	46,130	SP
Rochester Inst of Technology	NY	42,450	VC
Sacred Heart Univ	CT	49,264	VC
Savannah College of Art and Design	GA	48,005	SP
School of Visual Arts	NY	36,500	VC
Springfield College	MA	25,000	C
Syracuse Univ	NY	56,346	VC
Taylor Univ	IN	37,821	VC+
Univ of Dubuque	IA	30,200	C
Univ of Great Falls	MT	27,970	C
Univ of Mary Hardin-Baylor	TX	31,950	C+
Univ of Miami	FL	57,034	MC
Univ of Tampa	FL	35,160	VC
Worcester Polytechnic Inst	MA	55,860	MC

COMPUTER INFORMATION SYSTEMS

School	ST	$IS	SR
Arizona State Univ, at the Polytechnic Campus	AZ	20,531	C+
Arizona State Univ, at the Tempe Campus	AZ	20,137	C+
Bentley Univ	MA	56,454	HC+
Bloomfield College	NJ	37,850	LC
Bryant Univ	RI	49,179	VC
Cabrini College	PA	40,859	C
Cal State, Chico	CA	20,158	C
Campbell Univ	NC	37,570	VC
College of Charleston	SC	22,145	VC
Faulkner Univ	AL	25,720	LC
Ferris State Univ	MI	20,047	C
Franklin College	IN	36,585	C
Husson Univ	ME	24,194	LC
Indiana Univ Northwest	IN	6,854	LC
Keene State College	NH	23,232	LC
Livingstone College	NC	17,815	LC
Mich Tech Univ	MI	23,556	HC
Missouri Southern State Univ	MO	12,061	C

School	ST	$IS	SR
Molloy College	NY	40,440	C
Murray State Univ	KY	15,304	C
Niagara Univ	NY	41,010	C
Northwest Nazarene Univ	ID	34,000	C
Nova Southeastern Univ	FL	37,280	VC
Point Loma Nazarene Univ	CA	41,006	C+
St. Louis Univ	MO	48,346	HC
Siena Heights Univ	MI	32,040	C
Southeast Missouri State Univ	MO	15,370	LC
Southern Oregon Univ	OR	17,874	VC
SUNY Fredonia/The SUNY at Fredonia	NY	19,840	VC
Texas State Univ	TX	17,128	C
Thomas Edison State College	NJ	5,700	SP
Univ of Louisiana at Monroe	LA	12,998	C
Univ of Miami	FL	57,034	MC
Univ of New Hampshire	NH	26,912	C
Univ of Texas - Pan American	TX	11,125	LC
Western Mich Univ	MI	19,628	C

COMPUTER INFORMATION TECHNOLOGY

School	ST	$IS	SR
Biola Univ	CA	40,320	C+
Bryant Univ	RI	49,179	VC
Campbell Univ	NC	37,570	VC
Champlain College	VT	46,650	VC+
City Univ of Seattle	WA	14,880	NC
Georgia Southwestern State Univ	GA	13,246	C
Grove City College	PA	24,022	VC
Indiana Univ-Purdue Univ Indianapolis	IN	17,611	C
John Jay College of Criminal Justice/The CUNY	NY	6,359	LC
Limestone College	SC	30,800	C
Minn State Univ, Mankato	MN	15,616	C
New York Inst of Technology	NY	45,010	VC
Niagara Univ	NY	41,010	C
Northern Arizona Univ	AZ	19,010	C
Northern Kentucky Univ	KY	21,134	C
Ohio Valley Univ	WV	17,752	C
St. Edward's Univ	TX	47,784	C
St. Joseph's College, New York/Brooklyn Campus	NY	22,630	C
St. Joseph's College, New York/Suffolk Campus	NY	22,630	C
Texas Christian Univ	TX	49,980	HC
Thomas College	ME	33,560	LC
Trevecca Nazarene Univ	TN	31,186	C
Univ of Cincinnati	OH	21,506	VC
Washington and Jefferson College	PA	51,948	VC

COMPUTER MANAGEMENT

School	ST	$IS	SR
Bryant Univ	RI	49,179	VC
Caldwell College	NJ	35,602	NC
Chestnut Hill College	PA	42,110	LC
Colo Christian Univ	CO	27,500	VC
Eastern Mennonite Univ	VA	40,660	C
Emory and Henry College	VA	387,460	C
Johnson & Wales Univ/Providence Campus	RI	29,576	C
Lake Superior State Univ	MI	18,121	C
Mayville State Univ	ND	11,401	NC
Metropolitan State Univ of Denver	CO	4,835	LC
New Jersey Inst of Technology	NJ	26,490	C+
Northwest Missouri State Univ	MO	17,347	C
Northwest Univ	WA	18,854	C
Northwood Univ	MI	26,331	C
Peirce College	PA	12,760	NC
Peru State College	NE	8,600	NC
Rochester College	MI	18,320	LC
Southern Adventist Univ	TN	26,190	C
Southern Illinois Univ Edwardsville	IL	17,532	C
Univ of Great Falls	MT	27,970	C
Univ of Illinois at Urbana-Champaign	IL	26,450	HC
Univ of Mount Olive	NC	18,426	C
Univ of New Haven	CT	48,940	C
Univ of Northern Iowa	IA	15,795	C
Webster Univ	MO	35,100	C+

COMPUTER MATHEMATICS

School	ST	$IS	SR
Arizona State Univ, at the Tempe Campus	AZ	20,137	C+
Bethany College	WV	35,282	LC
Biola Univ	CA	40,320	C+
Bowdoin College	ME	59,568	MC
Calif Inst of Technology	CA	54,045	MC
Florida Southern College	FL	40,150	C+
Ithaca College	NY	53,864	HC
LeTourneau Univ	TX	36,210	VC
Lewis & Clark College	OR	54,382	MC
Marist College	NY	35,500	C
New York Univ	NY	61,470	MC
Oakwood Univ	AL	25,529	NC
Rochester Inst of Technology	NY	42,450	VC
Salem International Univ	WV	21,090	LC

School	ST	$IS	SR
Southern Oregon Univ	OR	17,874	C
Univ of Illinois at Chicago	IL	24,505	VC
Univ of Illinois at Urbana-Champaign	IL	26,450	HC
Univ of New Haven	CT	48,940	C
Univ of S Car Aiken	SC	16,712	C
Wheaton College	MA	54,934	HC+

COMPUTER NETWORKS & SYSTEMS

School	ST	$IS	SR
Arizona State Univ, at the Tempe Campus	AZ	20,137	C+
Bloomfield College	NJ	37,850	LC
Ferris State Univ	MI	20,047	C
Univ of Alaska Anchorage	AK	16,673	NC

COMPUTER PROGRAMMING

School	ST	$IS	SR
Arizona State Univ, at the Tempe Campus	AZ	20,137	C+
Baker College of Flint	MI	7,800	NC
Bloomfield College	NJ	37,850	LC
Calvin College	MI	39,120	VC
Caribbean Univ	PR	10,375	
Carnegie Mellon Univ	PA	51,260	MC
Central Washington Univ	WA	11,730	C
City Univ of Seattle	WA	14,880	NC
Cogswell Polytechnical College	CA	30,531	C
Concord Univ	WV	13,102	C
Concordia Univ, River Forest	IL	26,300	C
Dakota State Univ	SD	13,811	C
DePaul Univ	IL	47,623	VC
Dickinson State Univ	ND	11,900	NC
Dordt College	IA	34,160	C+
Eastern Kentucky Univ	KY	11,161	C
Eastern Mich Univ	MI	18,604	C
Farmingdale State College	NY	19,673	C
Ferris State Univ	MI	20,047	C
Freed-Hardeman Univ	TN	19,697	VC
Goshen College	IN	35,900	VC
Hannibal-LaGrange Univ	MO	24,490	C
Hawaii Pacific Univ	HI	34,360	C
Idaho State Univ	ID	12,307	C
Indiana Univ-Purdue Univ Fort Wayne	IN	15,521	C
Lamar Univ	TX	6,820	C
Le Moyne College	NY	43,470	C
Limestone College	SC	30,800	C
Mayville State Univ	ND	11,401	NC
Midland Univ	NE	34,000	C
Missouri Western State Univ	MO	12,260	NC
Monmouth College	IL	40,850	C
Montana Tech of The Univ of Montana	MT	14,650	VC
Northeastern Univ	MA	55,296	MC
Northern Mich Univ	MI	18,278	C
Pacific Lutheran Univ	WA	46,760	C+
Peirce College	PA	12,760	NC
Pennsylvania College of Technology	PA	26,286	NC
Peru State College	NE	8,600	NC
Pontifical Catholic Univ of PR	PR	7,310	
Purdue Univ/Calumet	IN	14,336	C
Salem State Univ	MA	13,161	LC
Southern Oregon Univ	OR	17,874	C
Southwestern Okla State Univ	OK	9,160	C
St. Thomas Univ	FL	32,310	LC
Stephen F. Austin State Univ	TX	14,668	C
Suffolk Univ	MA	47,298	C
Tarleton State Univ	TX	13,489	LC
Universidad del Turabo	PR	4,110	
Univ of Arkansas at Little Rock	AR	17,609	LC
Univ of Great Falls	MT	27,970	C
Univ of Illinois at Urbana-Champaign	IL	26,450	HC
Univ of Nebr at Kearney	NE	14,855	LC
Univ of New Haven	CT	48,940	C
Univ of St. Francis	IL	37,560	C
Univ of Wisc Whitewater	WI	13,314	C
Univ of Wisc/River Falls	WI	9,722	LC
Washington Univ in St. Louis	MO	69,844	MC
West Virginia Univ Inst of Technology	WV	14,094	NC
Youngstown State Univ	OH	16,732	C

COMPUTER SCIENCE

School	ST	$IS	SR
Abilene Christian Univ	TX	38,400	C+
Adams State Univ	CO	13,358	LC
Adelphi Univ	NY	44,670	VC
Agnes Scott College	GA	45,323	C+
Alabama A&M Univ	AL	10,084	C
Albany State Univ	GA	8,500	C
Albright College	PA	46,660	C
Alcorn State Univ	MS	9,500	C
Alderson Broaddus Univ	WV	28,656	C
Allegheny College	PA	50,980	HC
Alma College	MI	44,075	C
American Univ	DC	56,015	HC+
Amherst College	MA	58,744	MC
Anderson Univ	IN	36,100	C
Andrews Univ	MI	28,030	C+

School	ST	$IS	SR
Angelo State Univ	TX	15,049	NC
Anna Maria College	MA	34,600	C
Appalachian State Univ	NC	12,919	VC
Arcadia Univ	PA	33,570	C+
Arizona State Univ, at the Tempe Campus	AZ	20,137	C+
Arkansas Baptist College	AR	15,750	NC
Arkansas State Univ	AR	15,470	C
Arkansas Tech Univ	AR	13,982	LC
Armstrong State Univ	GA	15,532	C
Ashford Univ	CA	10,480	C
Ashland Univ	OH	25,000	C
Assumption College	MA	47,122	C+
Atlantic Union College	MA	24,600	C
Auburn Univ	AL	22,378	VC+
Augsburg College	MN	35,142	C
Augustana College	IL	43,398	VC
Augustana College	SD	36,500	VC
Aurora Univ	IL	33,228	C
Austin College	TX	45,875	HC
Austin Peay State Univ	TN	15,274	C
Averett Univ	VA	37,750	LC
Avila Univ	MO	26,900	C
Azusa Pacific Univ	CA	42,086	C
Baker Univ	KS	33,350	C+
Baldwin Wallace Univ	OH	38,318	C
Ball State Univ	IN	17,850	C
Bard College	NY	61,940	HC
Bard College at Simon's Rock	MA	61,749	HC+
Barnard College/Columbia Univ	NY	39,000	MC
Barry Univ	FL	38,190	C
Baylor Univ	TX	50,329	HC
Belhaven Univ	MS	27,170	C
Bellarmine Univ	KY	42,950	VC
Belmont Univ	TN	39,190	VC+
Beloit College	WI	49,970	HC
Bemidji State Univ	MN	13,500	VC
Benedict College	SC	20,454	NC
Benedictine College	KS	29,180	VC
Benedictine Univ	IL	37,820	C
Bennett College for Women	NC	21,970	LC
Bennington College	VT	56,990	HC+
Berea College	KY	7,192	C
Bethany College	WV	35,282	LC
Bethel Univ	MN	34,940	VC
Bethune-Cookman Univ	FL	22,958	C
Binghamton Univ/The SUNY	NY	21,648	HC+
Biola Univ	CA	40,320	C+
Birmingham-Southern College	AL	44,168	VC+
Blackburn College	IL	21,350	C
Bloomfield College	NJ	37,850	LC
Bloomsburg Univ of Pennsylvania	PA	13,598	C
Bluefield State College	WV	3,140	LC
Bluffton Univ	OH	38,948	C
Boise State Univ	ID	13,469	LC
Boston College	MA	60,622	MC
Boston Univ	MA	60,694	MC
Bowdoin College	ME	59,568	MC
Bowie State Univ	MD	23,990	LC
Bowling Green State Univ	OH	18,970	C
Bradley Univ	IL	31,874	VC
Brandeis Univ	MA		MC
Brescia Univ	KY	26,140	VC+
Briar Cliff Univ	IA	29,514	C
Bridgewater College	VA	41,450	C
Bridgewater State Univ	MA	18,752	C
Brigham Young Univ	UT	12,100	HC
Brigham Young Univ/Hawaii	HI	10,686	VC
Brown Univ	RI	59,428	MC
Bryan College	TN	24,194	C
Bryn Mawr College	PA	59,890	MC
Bucknell Univ	PA	60,140	MC
Buena Vista Univ	IA	39,188	C
Butler Univ	IN	47,572	VC+
Caldwell College	NJ	35,602	NC
Calif Baptist Univ	CA	38,792	C
Calif Inst of Technology	CA	54,045	MC
Calif Lutheran Univ	CA	49,540	C+
Calif Polytechnic State Univ	CA	19,847	HC
Calif State Polytechnic Univ, Pomona	CA	20,156	C
Cal State, Bakersfield	CA	8,000	C
Cal State, Chico	CA	20,158	C
Cal State, Dominguez Hills	CA	17,090	LC
Cal State, East Bay	CA	16,549	C
Cal State, Fresno	CA	17,405	C
Cal State, Fullerton	CA	25,188	C
Cal State, Long Beach	CA	17,502	C+
Cal State, Los Angeles	CA	17,186	LC
Cal State, Monterey Bay	CA	26,871	LC
Cal State, Northridge	CA	28,690	LC
Cal State, Sacramento	CA	16,200	C
Cal State, San Bernardino	CA	12,000	C
Cal State, San Marcos	CA	14,576	LC
Cal State, Stanislaus	CA	18,582	C
Calvin College	MI	39,120	VC
Cameron Univ	OK	10,004	LC
Campbell Univ	NC	37,570	VC
Campbellsville Univ	KY	27,720	C
Canisius College	NY	44,900	VC
Capital Univ	OH	41,050	VC
Cardinal Stritch Univ	WI	24,054	C
Caribbean Univ	PR	10,375	

ST = STATE　　**$IS** = IN-STATE COSTS　　**SR** = SELECTOR RATING

School	ST	$IS	SR
Carleton College	MN	60,102	MC
Carnegie Mellon Univ	PA	51,260	MC
Carroll College	MT	28,000	C
Carroll Univ	WI	38,100	C
Case Western Reserve Univ	OH	56,534	MC
Castleton State College	VT	20,186	C
Catawba College	NC	37,240	LC
Cedar Crest College	PA	43,240	C
Cedarville Univ	OH	32,860	VC
Central College	IA	42,104	C+
Central Conn State Univ	CT	19,749	C
Central Methodist Univ	MO	28,240	VC
Central State Univ	OH	9,010	C
Central Univ of Bayamon	PR	3,350	
Central Washington Univ	WA	11,730	C
Centre College	KY	35,000	HC+
Chaminade Univ of Honolulu	HI	31,664	LC
Champlain College	VT	46,650	VC
Chapman Univ	CA	58,347	VC+
Charleston Southern Univ	SC	22,420	C
Chestnut Hill College	PA	42,110	C
Cheyney Univ of Pennsylvania	PA	20,372	LC
Chicago State Univ	IL	5,482	C
Christian Brothers Univ	TN	31,670	HC
Christopher Newport Univ	VA	21,960	VC
Citadel, The	SC		C
CUNY/Brooklyn College	NY	5,884	C+
CUNY/City College	NY	20,319	HC+
Claflin Univ	SC	22,368	LC
Clarion Univ of Pennsylvania	PA	17,370	LC
Clark Atlanta Univ	GA	30,006	LC
Clark Univ	MA	47,020	HC+
Clarke Univ	IA	37,600	C
Clarkson Univ	NY	57,330	HC
Clemson Univ	SC	19,136	HC
Cleveland State Univ	OH	21,776	C
Coastal Carolina Univ	SC	18,580	C
Coe College	IA	45,550	VC
Coker College	SC	32,256	LC
Colby College	ME	57,510	MC
Colgate Univ	NY	58,135	MC
College of Charleston	SC	22,145	VC
College of Mount St. Vincent	NY	41,040	MC
College of New Jersey	NJ	25,376	HC
College of St. Benedict	MN	49,359	VC
College of St. Elizabeth	NJ	43,839	LC
College of St. Scholastica	MN	41,440	C
College of Staten Island/The City of New Yok	NY	16,778	NC
College of the Holy Cross	MA	58,042	MC
College of the Ozarks	MO		VC
College of William & Mary	VA	28,000	MC
College of Wooster	OH	52,600	VC
Colo College	CO	57,162	MC
Colo Mesa Univ	CO	17,690	LC
Colo State Univ-Fort Collins	CO	20,385	VC
Colo Technical Univ	CO	10,500	LC
Columbia Univ	NY	24,578	C
Columbia Univ/City of New York	NY	61,116	MC
Columbia Univ/School of General Studies	NY	58,231	MC
Columbus State Univ	GA	13,176	LC
Concord Univ	WV	13,102	C
Concordia Univ Nebr	NE	26,000	VC
Concordia Univ Texas	TX	23,640	C
Concordia Univ, River Forest	IL	26,300	C
Converse College	SC	37,130	C
Coppin State Univ	MD	16,227	VC
Cornell College	IA	44,930	VC
Cornell Univ	NY	60,964	MC
Covenant College	GA	38,990	VC+
Creighton Univ	NE	45,356	VC
Dakota State Univ	SD	13,811	C
Dallas Baptist Univ	TX	30,580	VC
Daniel Webster College	NH	25,380	C
Dartmouth College	NH	57,996	MC
Davis & Elkins College	WV	33,742	C
De Sales Univ	PA	43,970	C
Delaware State Univ	DE	16,722	LC
Delaware Valley College	PA	29,644	C
Denison Univ	OH	54,670	HC+
DePaul Univ	IL	47,623	VC
DePauw Univ	IN	48,950	VC+
Dickinson College	PA	57,662	HC+
Dickinson State Univ	ND	11,900	NC
Dillard Univ	LA	20,940	VC
Doane College	NE	35,230	C
Dominican College	NY	31,270	C
Dominican Univ	IL	37,628	C
Dordt College	IA	34,160	C
Dowling College	NY	25,000	LC
Drake Univ	IA	41,516	VC+
Drew Univ/College of Liberal Arts	NJ	57,516	C
Drexel Univ	PA	61,418	VC+
Drury Univ	MO	31,909	VC
Duke Univ	NC	50,250	MC
Duquesne Univ	PA	43,720	VC
Earlham College	IN	51,470	HC
East Carolina Univ	NC	14,169	C
East Central Univ	OK	10,223	C
East Stroudsburg Univ of Pennsylvania	PA	18,868	LC
East Tenn State Univ	TN	9,000	C
Eastern Conn State Univ	CT	20,584	C
Eastern Illinois Univ	IL	20,466	C
Eastern Kentucky Univ	KY	11,161	C
Eastern Mennonite Univ	VA	40,660	C
Eastern Mich Univ	MI	18,604	C
Eastern Nazarene College	MA	30,000	C
Eastern New Mexico Univ	NM	10,682	C
Eastern Oregon Univ	OR	10,400	C
Eastern Washington Univ	WA		C
Eckerd College	FL	43,902	C
Edinboro Univ of Pennsylvania	PA	15,940	LC
Edward Waters College	FL	19,607	LC
Elizabeth City State Univ	NC	11,638	C
Elizabethtown College	PA	49,740	VC
Elmhurst College	IL	43,336	C
Elms College	MA	23,900	VC
Elon Univ	NC	41,914	VC+
Embry-Riddle Aeronautical Univ - Daytona Beach	FL	40,884	C+
Emory and Henry College	VA	387,460	C
Emory Univ	GA	56,368	MC
Emporia State Univ	KS	12,897	C
Endicott College	MA	43,228	VC+
Eureka College	IL	19,280	C
Evangel Univ	MO	23,090	C
Fairfield Univ	CT	56,960	VC
Fairleigh Dickinson Univ/College at Florham	NJ	42,142	C
Fairleigh Dickinson Univ/Metropolitan Campus	NJ	40,254	C
Fairmont State Univ	WV	12,098	LC
Faulkner Univ	AL	25,720	LC
Fayetteville State Univ	NC	10,816	C
Fisk Univ	TN	19,830	C
Fitchburg State Univ	MA	18,173	C
Florida A&M Univ	FL	14,935	LC
Florida Atlantic Univ	FL	17,339	C
Florida Gulf Coast Univ	FL		C
Florida Inst of Technology	FL	48,290	VC
Florida International Univ	FL	17,747	C+
Florida Memorial Univ	FL	20,888	LC
Florida Southern College	FL	40,150	C+
Florida State Univ	FL	16,715	VC
Fontbonne Univ	MO	31,384	C
Fordham Univ	NY	61,588	HC+
Fort Hays State Univ	KS	11,354	C
Fort Valley State Univ	GA	11,200	VC
Framingham State Univ	MA	18,854	C
Francis Marion Univ	SC	16,464	LC
Franciscan Univ of Steubenville	OH	27,320	VC
Franklin College	IN	36,585	C
Franklin Univ	OH	20,985	SP
Freed-Hardeman Univ	TN	19,697	VC
Friends Univ	KS	29,100	C
Frostburg State Univ	MD	15,264	LC
Furman Univ	SC	54,006	HC
Gallaudet Univ	DC	25,380	SP
Gannon Univ	PA	39,608	C
Gardner-Webb Univ	NC	34,375	C+
Geneva College	PA	27,280	C
George Fox Univ	OR	40,750	C+
George Mason Univ	VA	15,724	VC
George Washington Univ	DC	57,108	MC
Georgetown Univ	DC	52,910	MC
Georgia College and State Univ	GA	18,900	C+
Georgia Inst of Technology	GA	21,828	MC
Georgia Regents Univ	GA		C
Georgia Southern Univ	GA	16,942	C
Georgia Southwestern State Univ	GA	13,246	C
Georgia State Univ	GA	15,582	VC
Gettysburg College	PA	58,820	HC
Gonzaga Univ	WA	46,441	HC
Gordon College	MA	44,320	VC
Goucher College	MD	52,040	VC+
Graceland Univ	IA	28,020	C
Grambling State Univ	LA	13,384	LC
Grand Valley State Univ	MI	17,998	C+
Grand View Univ	IA	31,050	C
Greenville College	IL	27,012	C
Grinnell College	IA	53,654	HC
Grove City College	PA	24,022	VC
Gustavus Adolphus College	MN	48,170	HC
Gwynedd-Mercy College	PA	33,560	C
Hamilton College	NY	55,620	MC
Hampden-Sydney College	VA	51,758	C
Hampshire College	MA	58,320	MC
Hampton Univ	VA	28,528	C
Hanover College	IN	43,073	C+
Harding Univ	AR	23,556	C
Hardin-Simmons Univ	TX	23,560	C+
Hartwick College	NY	51,270	C
Harvard College/Harvard Univ	MA	49,000	MC
Harvey Mudd College	CA	64,527	MC
Hastings College	NE	27,782	C+
Haverford College	PA	61,564	MC
Hawaii Pacific Univ	HI	34,360	C
Heidelberg Univ	OH	34,100	C
Henderson State Univ	AR	14,584	C
Hendrix College	AR	50,202	VC+
Heritage Univ	WA	17,664	NC
High Point Univ	NC	39,800	C
Hiram College	OH	37,300	VC
Hobart and William Smith Colleges	NY	60,034	HC+
Hofstra Univ	NY	51,810	VC+
Holy Names Univ	CA	40,310	NC
Hood College	MD	45,730	C
Hope College	MI	38,650	VC
Houghton College	NY	36,808	C+
Howard Payne Univ	TX	17,115	C
Howard Univ	DC	13,646	C
Hunter College	NY	14,429	VC
Huntington Univ	IN	32,220	C+
Huston-Tillotson Univ	TX	18,124	C
Idaho State Univ	ID	12,307	C
Illinois College	IL	25,770	VC
Illinois Inst of Technology	IL	38,512	HC+
Illinois State Univ	IL	23,110	VC
Illinois Wesleyan Univ	IL	48,452	HC
Indiana Inst of Technology	IN	34,240	LC
Indiana State Univ	IN	16,000	C
Indiana Univ Bloomington	IN	19,801	VC
Indiana Univ Kokomo	IN	6,811	LC
Indiana Univ of Pennsylvania	PA	20,846	LC
Indiana Univ South Bend	IN	15,501	C
Indiana Univ-Purdue Univ Fort Wayne	IN	15,521	C
Indiana Univ-Purdue Univ Indianapolis	IN	17,611	C
Indiana Wesleyan Univ	IN	31,815	VC
Inter-American Univ of PR/Aguadilla Campus	PR	5,578	
Inter-American Univ of PR/Arecibo Campus	PR	3,350	
Inter-American Univ of PR/Bayamon Univ College	PR	4,428	
Inter-American Univ of PR/Fajardo Campus	PR	4,200	
Inter-American Univ of PR/Metropolitan Campus	PR	4,320	
Inter-American Univ of PR/Ponce	PR		
Inter-American Univ of PR/San Germán	PR	6,720	
Iona College	NY	44,028	C
Iowa State Univ	IA	16,403	C
Iowa Wesleyan College	IA	30,850	LC
Ithaca College	NY	53,864	HC
Jackson State Univ	MS	13,512	LC
Jacksonville State Univ	AL	12,480	LC
Jacksonville Univ	FL	37,780	C
James Madison Univ	VA	18,049	VC
John Brown Univ	AR	32,056	VC+
John Carroll Univ	OH	46,300	C+
Johns Hopkins Univ	MD	47,492	MC
Johnson & Wales Univ/Providence Campus	RI	29,576	C
Johnson C. Smith Univ	NC	25,336	LC
Judson Univ	IL	25,130	C
Juniata College	PA	49,340	VC
Kalamazoo College	MI	49,740	HC
Kansas State Univ	KS	15,497	VC
Kansas Wesleyan Univ	KS	32,000	C
Kean Univ	NJ	23,444	C
Keene State College	NH	23,232	LC
Kennesaw State Univ	GA		C
Kent State Univ	OH	19,920	C
Kentucky State Univ	KY	10,608	LC
Kentucky Wesleyan College	KY	27,440	C
Kettering Univ	MI	31,456	HC
King's College	PA	43,502	C
Knox College	IL	44,865	VC+
Kutztown Univ of Pennsylvania	PA	16,909	LC
La Roche College	PA	35,824	LC
La Salle Univ	PA	50,270	C
La Sierra Univ	CA	35,694	VC
Lafayette College	PA	59,155	HC+
LaGrange College	GA	37,670	C
Lake Forest College	IL	50,652	VC
Lake Superior State Univ	MI	18,121	C
Lakeland College	WI	22,990	C
Lamar Univ	TX	6,820	LC
Lander Univ	SC	22,514	C
Lane College	TN	11,212	C
Langston Univ	OK	3,000	C
Lawrence Tech Univ	MI	37,630	VC
Lawrence Univ	WI	46,371	HC
Le Moyne College	NY	43,470	C
Lebanon Valley College	PA	38,570	C
Lehigh Univ	PA	56,770	MC
Lehman College/The CUNY	NY	5,778	LC
LeMoyne-Owen College	TN	13,100	C
Lenoir-Rhyne College	NC	35,984	C
LeTourneau Univ	TX	36,210	VC
Lewis & Clark College	OR	54,382	MC
Lewis Univ	IL	23,050	C
Lewis-Clark State College	ID	6,990	C
Liberty Univ	VA	19,101	VC
Limestone College	SC	30,800	C
Lincoln Univ	MO	12,904	NC
Lindenwood Univ	MO	20,750	C
Linfield College-McMinnville Campus	OR	47,676	C
Lipscomb Univ	TN	37,490	VC
LIU Brooklyn	NY	47,182	LC
LIU Post	NY	47,660	C
Lock Haven Univ of Pennsylvania	PA	18,028	LC
Longwood Univ	VA	20,924	C
Loras College	IA	37,432	VC
Louisiana State Univ	LA	18,677	C+
Louisiana State Univ in Shreveport	LA	5,606	C
Louisiana Tech Univ	LA	11,302	C
Loyola Marymount Univ	CA	54,649	VC+
Loyola Univ Chicago	IL	51,646	VC+
Loyola Univ Maryland	MD	56,880	VC+
Luther College	IA	45,720	C+
Lynchburg College	VA	42,645	C
Macalester College	MN	57,691	MC
MacMurray College	IL	20,755	C
Madonna Univ	MI	24,540	VC
Maharishi Univ of Management	IA	31,000	VC
Malone Univ	OH	35,364	C
Manchester Univ	IN	35,070	C
Manhattan College	NY	49,588	C+
Manhattanville College	NY	50,740	VC
Mansfield Univ	PA	19,468	LC
Marietta College	OH	42,135	C+
Marist College	NY	35,500	C
Marlboro College	VT	35,980	VC
Marquette Univ	WI	46,930	VC+
Mars Hill College	NC	22,950	LC
Marshall Univ	WV	14,820	C
Marygrove College	MI	28,926	C
Marymount Univ	VA	39,480	C
Maryville College	TN	33,150	C+
Mass College of Liberal Arts	MA	18,613	C
Mass Inst of Technology	MA	58,240	MC
McDaniel College	MD	47,450	VC
McKendree Univ	IL	29,920	C
McMurry Univ	TX	25,962	C
McNeese State Univ	LA	2,649	C
Megar Evers College/The CUNY	NY	4,920	NC
Mercer Univ	GA	44,201	VC
Mercy College	NY	30,456	C
Meredith College	NC	31,420	C
Merrimack College	MA	44,215	C
Messiah College	PA	40,690	C+
Methodist Univ	NC	37,185	C
Metropolitan State Univ	MN	5,923	
Metropolitan State Univ of Denver	CO	4,835	LC
Miami Univ	OH	24,191	VC
Mich State Univ	MI	22,450	VC
Mich Tech Univ	MI	23,556	HC
MidAmerica Nazarene Univ	KS	28,000	C
Middle Tenn State Univ	TN	8,650	C
Middlebury College	VT	59,160	MC
Midland Univ	NE	34,000	C
Midwestern State Univ	TX	9,722	C
Miles College	AL	11,164	NC
Millersville Univ of Pennsylvania	PA	21,648	C
Mills College	CA	54,119	VC
Minn State Univ, Moorhead	MN	13,392	VC
Minot State Univ	ND	10,915	C
Misericordia Univ	PA	41,060	C
Miss College	MS	21,998	C
Miss State Univ	MS	14,750	C
Miss Valley State Univ	MS	9,706	LC
Missouri Southern State Univ	MO	12,061	C
Missouri State Univ	MO	13,996	C+
Missouri Univ of Science and Technology	MO	18,655	VC+
Missouri Western State Univ	MO	12,260	NC
Molloy College	NY	40,440	C
Monmouth College	IL	40,850	C
Monmouth Univ	NJ	44,108	C
Montana State Univ	MT	14,068	C
Montana Tech of The Univ of Montana	MT	14,650	VC
Montclair State Univ	NJ	22,614	C
Moravian College	PA	36,381	VC
Morehead State Univ	KY	10,900	C
Morehouse College	GA	39,412	C
Morgan State Univ	MD	14,500	VC
Morningside College	IA	35,430	C
Mount Holyoke College	MA	55,146	MC
Mount Marty College	SD	29,638	C
Mount Mercy Univ	IA	35,320	C
Mount St. Mary's Univ	MD	47,996	C
Mount Vernon Nazarene Univ	OH	29,590	C
Muhlenberg College	PA	52,837	HC
Murray State Univ	KY	15,304	C
Muskingum Univ	OH	30,502	C
National Univ	CA	14,730	SP
Nebr Wesleyan Univ	NE	29,774	C+
Neumann Univ	PA	31,078	LC
New England College	NH	45,930	LC
New Jersey City Univ	NJ	21,456	LC
New Jersey Inst of Technology	NJ	26,490	C+
New Mexico Highlands Univ	NM	11,904	NC
New Mexico Inst of Mining and Technology	NM	13,592	VC
New Mexico State Univ	NM	14,050	C
New York Inst of Technology	NY	45,010	VC
New York Univ	NY	61,470	MC

ST = STATE $IS = IN-STATE COSTS SR = SELECTOR RATING

School	ST	$IS	SR
Newberry College	SC	26,850	LC
Newbury College	MA	43,280	LC
Niagara Univ	NY	41,010	C
Nicholls State Univ	LA	7,095	C
Norfolk State Univ	VA	10,531	LC
N Car Agricultural and Technical State Univ	NC	13,365	LC
N Car Central Univ	NC	9,000	C
N Car State Univ	NC	16,202	LC
North Central College	IL	38,343	VC
N Dak State Univ	ND		C
Northeastern Illinois Univ	IL	10,318	LC
Northeastern State Univ	OK	8,615	VC
Northeastern Univ	MA	55,296	MC
Northern Arizona Univ	AZ	19,010	C
Northern Illinois Univ	IL	19,768	C
Northern Kentucky Univ	KY	21,134	C
Northern Mich Univ	MI	18,278	C
Northwest Christian Univ	OR	27,399	C
Northwest Missouri State Univ	MO	17,347	C
Northwest Nazarene Univ	ID	34,000	C
Northwestern College of Iowa	IA	36,240	VC
Northwestern Okla State Univ	OK	7,275	NC
Northwestern Univ	IL	61,640	MC
Norwich Univ	VT	28,212	C
Notre Dame de Namur Univ	CA	44,236	LC
Notre Dame of Maryland Univ	MD	27,700	C
Nova Southeastern Univ	FL	37,280	VC
Nyack College	NY	33,250	C
Oakland Univ	MI	19,391	C
Oakwood Univ	AL	25,529	NC
Oberlin College	OH	61,788	MC
Ohio Dominican Univ	OH	38,380	C+
Ohio Northern Univ	OH	42,075	VC
Ohio Univ	OH	21,080	C
Ohio Wesleyan Univ	OH	49,460	C+
Okla Baptist Univ	OK	28,202	C
Okla Christian Univ	OK	25,870	VC
Okla State Univ	OK	14,310	VC
Old Dominion Univ	VA	19,483	LC
Olivet College	MI	19,984	LC
Olivet Nazarene Univ	IL	29,990	C
Oral Roberts Univ	OK	31,734	C
Oregon State Univ	OR	20,273	VC
Oswego / SUNY	NY	20,009	VC
Otterbein College	OH	32,214	C
Ouachita Baptist Univ	AR	30,220	VC
Pace Univ	NY	53,367	C
Pacific Lutheran Univ	WA	46,760	C+
Pacific Union College	CA	28,150	VC
Pacific Univ	OR	49,626	C+
Palm Beach Atlantic Univ	FL	34,874	C
Park Univ	MO	17,525	C
Penn State Erie/The Behrend College	PA	16,256	C
Pepperdine Univ	CA	55,372	HC+
Peru State College	NE	8,600	NC
Philander Smith College	AR	19,760	LC
Plymouth State Univ	NH	23,148	LC
Point Loma Nazarene Univ	CA	41,006	C+
Point Park Univ	PA	36,390	C
Polytechnic Inst of New York Univ	NY	53,064	HC+
Pomona College	CA	57,680	MC
Portland State Univ	OR	18,672	C
Prairie View A&M Univ	TX	15,205	LC
Princeton Univ	NJ	53,795	MC
Principia College	IL	35,140	C+
Providence College	RI	57,383	VC
Purdue Univ/Calumet	IN	14,336	C
Purdue Univ/West Lafayette	IN	20,024	HC
Queens College/The CUNY	NY	17,107	VC
Quincy Univ	IL	34,980	C
Quinnipiac Univ	CT	55,160	VC
Radford Univ	VA	17,766	LC
Ramapo College of New Jersey	NJ	24,938	C
Randolph-Macon College	VA	49,869	C+
Regis College	MA	47,565	LC
Regis Univ	CO	41,318	C
Rensselaer Polytechnic Inst	NY	61,529	MC
Rhode Island College	RI	17,694	LC
Rhodes College	TN	51,900	HC+
Rice Univ	TX	43,288	NC
Richard Stockton College of New Jersey	NJ	20,000	VC
Ripon College	WI	36,959	C+
Rivier Univ	NH	35,000	VC
Roanoke College	VA	49,976	C
Rochester Inst of Technology	NY	42,450	VC
Rockford College	IL	31,000	C
Rockhurst Univ	MO	20,625	C
Rocky Mountain College	MT	32,242	C
Roger Williams Univ	RI	46,296	VC
Rollins College	FL	52,370	HC
Roosevelt Univ	IL	22,605	VC
Rose-Hulman Inst of Technology	IN	53,340	MC
Rowan Univ	NJ	24,022	VC+
Rust College	MS	10,600	LC
Rutgers, The State Univ of New Jersey/Camden Campus	NJ	25,121	C
Rutgers, The State Univ of New Jersey/New Brunswick	NJ	25,562	VC
Rutgers, The State Univ of New Jersey/Newark Campus	NJ	258,806	C
Sacred Heart Univ	CT	49,264	VC
Saginaw Valley State Univ	MI	17,369	C
St. Anselm College	NH	49,376	VC
St. Augustine's Univ	NC	14,000	C
St. Francis Univ	PA	30,029	LC
St. John's Univ	MN	47,984	C
St. Joseph's College	IN	36,500	C
St. Joseph's Univ	PA	55,006	VC
St. Martin's Univ	WA	41,678	C
St. Mary-of-the-Woods College	IN	37,722	LC
St. Mary's College of Calif	CA	53,550	C
St. Mary's Univ	TX	33,854	C
St. Mary's Univ of Minn	MN	38,280	C
St. Michael's College	VT	49,975	VC
St. Peter's Univ	NJ	44,240	C
St. Vincent College	PA	40,244	C
St. Xavier Univ	IL	32,840	C
Salisbury Univ	MD	19,180	VC
Sam Houston State Univ	TX	17,082	C
Samford Univ	AL	37,060	C+
San Diego State Univ	CA	21,611	C+
San Francisco State Univ	CA	18,514	C
San Jose State Univ	CA	19,133	LC
Savannah State Univ	GA	13,156	C
Scripps College	CA	61,940	MC
Seattle Pacific Univ	WA	41,559	VC+
Seattle Univ	WA	49,035	VC+
Seton Hall Univ	NJ	45,902	C
Seton Hill Univ	PA	35,172	C
Sewanee: The Univ of the South	TN	47,700	HC+
Shaw Univ	NC	15,488	C
Shepherd Univ	WV	15,875	C
Shippensburg Univ of Pennsylvania	PA	20,934	C
Siena College	NY	43,863	VC
Silver Lake College	WI	22,600	LC
Simmons College	MA	49,966	VC
Simpson College	IA	36,086	C+
Skidmore College	NY	59,942	HC
Slippery Rock Univ of Pennsylvania	PA	10,360	C
Smith College	MA	59,674	MC
Sonoma State Univ	CA	20,541	C
S Car State Univ	SC	6,700	LC
S Dak School of Mines and Technology	SD	15,260	VC
S Dak State Univ	SD	14,296	C
Southeast Missouri State Univ	MO	15,370	LC
Southeastern Louisiana Univ	LA	13,325	C
Southeastern Okla State Univ	OK	7,966	LC
Southern Adventist Univ	TN	26,190	C
Southern Arkansas Univ	AR	14,316	C
Southern Conn State Univ	CT	18,033	LC
Southern Illinois Univ Carbondale	IL	21,942	C
Southern Illinois Univ Edwardsville	IL	17,532	C
Southern Methodist Univ	TX	60,585	MC
Southern Nazarene Univ	OK	24,354	C
Southern New Hampshire Univ	NH	38,100	C
Southern Oregon Univ	OR	17,874	C
Southern Polytechnic State Univ	GA	13,958	C
Southern Univ and A&M College	LA	9,761	LC
Southern Univ at New Orleans	LA	2,963	NC
Southern Wesleyan Univ	SC	25,600	C
Southwest Baptist Univ	MO	24,710	C
Southwest Minn State Univ	MN	14,000	C
Southwestern Adventist Univ	TX	23,026	LC
Southwestern College	KS	29,270	C
Southwestern Okla State Univ	OK	9,160	LC
Spelman College	GA	24,650	C
Spring Arbor Univ	MI	26,740	C
Spring Hill College	AL	44,164	VC
St. Ambrose Univ	IA	30,845	C
St. Bonaventure Univ	NY	41,575	C
St. Cloud State Univ	MN	10,600	C
St. Edward's Univ	TX	47,784	C
St. John Fisher College	NY	40,708	C+
St. John's Univ	NY	55,070	C+
St. Joseph's College, New York/Suffolk Campus	NY	22,630	C
St. Lawrence Univ	NY	59,972	VC
St. Mary's College of Maryland	MD	25,754	VC
St. Norbert College	WI	41,478	VC
St. Olaf College	MN	51,200	HC+
St. Thomas Univ	FL	32,310	LC
Stanford Univ	CA	58,388	MC
SUNY Polytechnic Inst	NY	19,690	C
SUNY/Empire State College	NY	6,315	SP
Stephen F. Austin State Univ	TX	14,668	C
Stetson Univ	FL	51,516	VC
Stevens Inst of Technology	NJ	50,130	HC
Stillman College	AL	19,470	C
Stonehill College	MA	46,780	HC
Stony Brook Univ / SUNY	NY	20,078	HC+
Suffolk Univ	MA	47,298	C
Sul Ross State Univ	TX	13,410	LC
SUNY College at Old Westbury	NY	16,324	C
SUNY Fredonia/The SUNY at Fredonia	NY	19,840	VC
SUNY New Paltz	NY	14,348	C
SUNY Oneonta / SUNY	NY	16,919	C+
SUNY Plattsburgh / SUNY	NY	18,083	C
Susquehanna Univ	PA	51,150	C
Swarthmore College	PA	57,870	MC
Syracuse Univ	NY	56,346	VC
Tabor College	KS	29,010	C
Talladega College	AL	17,996	C
Tarleton State Univ	TX	13,489	LC
Taylor Univ	IN	37,821	VC+
Temple Univ	PA	24,392	VC
Tenn State Univ	TN	9,048	C
Tenn Tech Univ	TN	11,310	C
Texas A&M Univ	TX	19,207	VC
Texas A&M Univ at Commerce	TX	10,496	C
Texas A&M Univ at Corpus Christi	TX	11,544	LC
Texas A&M Univ at Kingsville	TX	7,500	C
Texas Christian Univ	TX	49,980	HC
Texas Lutheran Univ	TX	36,040	C
Texas Southern Univ	TX	18,212	LC
Texas State Univ	TX	17,128	C
Texas Tech Univ	TX	14,243	C
Texas Wesleyan Univ	TX	31,382	C
Texas Woman's Univ	TX	13,633	LC
The Catholic Univ of America	DC	52,852	VC
The College of St. Rose	NY	26,750	C
The Lincoln Univ	PA	15,154	LC
Ohio State Univ-Columbus Campus	OH	19,887	HC+
The Pennsylvania State Univ - Univ Park	PA	28,022	VC+
The SUNY at Potsdam	NY	18,473	C
The SUNY/College at Brockport	NY	19,002	C
The Univ of Memphis	TN	15,094	C
The Univ of N Car at Greensboro	NC	12,848	C
The Univ of N Car at Pembroke	NC	13,388	LC
The Univ of Okla	OK	18,621	VC
The Univ of Tenn at Chattanooga	TN	16,883	C
The Univ of Utah	UT	16,463	VC
Thiel College	PA	38,728	LC
Thomas College	ME	33,560	LC
Thomas More College	KY	34,760	C
Tougaloo College	MS	15,275	NC
Touro College	NY	27,959	VC
Towson Univ	MD	16,000	VC
Transylvania Univ	KY	42,660	VC+
Trine Univ	IN	39,400	HC+
Trinity Christian College	IL	28,869	C
Trinity College	CT		HC+
Trinity Univ	TX	48,150	HC+
Troy Univ	AL	10,650	C
Truman State Univ	MO	15,541	HC
Tufts Univ	MA	58,780	MC
Tusculum College	TN	24,295	C
Tuskegee Univ	AL	26,750	C
Union College	NE	23,270	C
Union College	NY	60,240	MC
Union Inst & Univ	OH	8,912	SP
Union Univ	TN	28,260	VC
United States Air Force Academy	CO		MC
United States Military Academy	NY		MC
United States Naval Academy	MD		MC
Universidad Adventista de las Antillas	PR	7,360	
Universidad de Puerto/Arecibo	PR	7,227	
Universidad Politecnica de PR	PR	19,252	
Univ at Albany / SUNY	NY	18,674	VC
Univ at Buffalo / The SUNY	NY	20,283	VC
Univ of Akron	OH	20,436	C
Univ of Alabama at Birmingham	AL	18,484	C+
Univ of Alabama at Tuscaloosa	AL	17,164	C+
Univ of Alabama in Huntsville	AL	17,591	VC+
Univ of Alaska Anchorage	AK	16,673	NC
Univ of Alaska Fairbanks	AK	15,130	C
Univ of Arizona	AZ	20,657	C
Univ of Arkansas at Fayetteville	AR	18,352	C+
Univ of Arkansas at Little Rock	AR	17,609	LC
Univ of Arkansas at Pine Bluff	AR	13,378	C
Univ of Bridgeport	CT	39,030	LC
Univ of Calif at Berkeley	CA	23,322	MC
Univ of Calif at Davis	CA		HC
Univ of Calif at Irvine	CA	25,961	VC
Univ of Calif at Los Angeles	CA	25,686	MC
Univ of Calif at Riverside	CA	27,204	C+
Univ of Calif at San Diego	CA	21,000	C
Univ of Calif at Santa Barbara	CA	27,551	HC
Univ of Calif at Santa Cruz	CA	27,807	C
Univ of Central Arkansas	AR	13,667	VC
Univ of Central Florida	FL	15,668	VC+
Univ of Central Missouri	MO	14,605	C
Univ of Central Okla	OK	12,293	C
Univ of Chicago	IL	55,416	MC
Univ of Cincinnati	OH	21,506	C
Univ of Colo at Colo Springs	CO	15,000	VC
Univ of Colo Boulder	CO	22,605	VC+
Univ of Colo Denver	CO	17,904	C
Univ of Conn	CT	24,706	HC
Univ of Dallas	TX	45,500	VC+
Univ of Dayton	OH	49,070	VC
Univ of Delaware	DE	23,612	VC
Univ of Denver	CO	51,787	VC+
Univ of Detroit Mercy	MI	30,450	VC
Univ of Dubuque	IA	30,200	C
Univ of Evansville	IN	42,656	VC+
Univ of Findlay	OH	31,916	C
Univ of Florida	FL	15,943	HC
Univ of Georgia	GA	20,082	VC
Univ of Great Falls	MT	27,970	C
Univ of Hartford	CT	42,674	C
Univ of Hawaii at Hilo	HI	23,066	C
Univ of Hawaii at Manoa	HI	19,379	C
Univ of Houston-Downtown	TX	15,170	LC
Univ of Idaho	ID	14,558	C
Univ of Illinois at Chicago	IL	24,505	VC
Univ of Indianapolis	IN	31,740	C
Univ of Iowa	IA	17,693	VC
Univ of Jamestown	ND	24,738	C
Univ of Kansas	KS	17,603	C+
Univ of Kentucky	KY	19,868	C
Univ of La Verne	CA	47,010	C
Univ of Louisiana at Lafayette	LA	6,130	C
Univ of Louisiana at Monroe	LA	12,998	C
Univ of Louisville	KY	17,946	C
Univ of Maine	ME	19,902	C+
Univ of Maine at Farmington	ME	18,187	LC
Univ of Maine at Fort Kent	ME	15,195	LC
Univ of Mary Hardin-Baylor	TX	31,950	C+
Univ of Mary Washington	VA	19,484	VC
Univ of Maryland - College Park	MD	20,060	HC
Univ of Maryland/Baltimore County	MD	18,000	VC
Univ of Maryland/Eastern Shore	MD	14,000	VC
Univ of Maryland/Univ College	MD	6,168	SP
Univ of Mass Amherst	MA	24,215	VC+
Univ of Mass Boston	MA	23,066	VC
Univ of Mass Dartmouth	MA	22,223	C
Univ of Mass Lowell	MA	19,316	C
Univ of Miami	FL	57,034	MC
Univ of Mich/Ann Arbor	MI	22,102	MC
Univ of Mich/Dearborn	MI	9,885	VC
Univ of Mich-Flint	MI	17,547	C+
Univ of Minn/Duluth	MN	19,806	C
Univ of Minn/Morris	MN	17,150	VC
Univ of Minn/Twin Cities	MN		HC
Univ of Miss	MS	16,704	C+
Univ of Missouri/Columbia	MO	18,201	MC
Univ of Missouri-Kansas City	MO	19,603	C
Univ of Missouri-St. Louis	MO		VC
Univ of Montana	MT	14,105	C
Univ of Mount Union	OH	35,130	C
Univ of Nebr - Lincoln	NE	18,031	VC
Univ of Nebr at Kearney	NE	14,855	LC
Univ of Nebr at Omaha	NE	12,700	C
Univ of Nevada, Las Vegas	NV	17,303	C
Univ of Nevada/Reno	NV	17,507	C
Univ of New Hampshire	NH	26,912	C
Univ of New Haven	CT	48,940	C
Univ of New Mexico	NM	15,300	C
Univ of New Orleans	LA	9,224	C
Univ of North Alabama	AL	9,960	C
Univ of N Car at Asheville	NC	13,500	VC
Univ of N Car at Chapel Hill	NC	18,928	MC
Univ of N Car at Charlotte	NC	15,547	C
Univ of N Car at Wilmington	NC	13,572	VC
Univ of N Dak	ND	14,551	C
Univ of North Florida	FL	15,870	VC
Univ of North Georgia	GA	8,500	C
Univ of North Texas	TX	15,628	C
Univ of Northern Iowa	IA	15,795	C
Univ of Notre Dame	IN	57,117	MC
Univ of Oregon	OR	21,360	C+
Univ of Pennsylvania	PA	61,132	MC
Univ of Pikeville	KY	25,500	NC
Univ of Pittsburgh at Johnstown	PA	20,862	LC
Univ of Pittsburgh at Pittsburgh	PA	28,572	HC+
Univ of Portland	OR	49,964	VC
Univ of PR Recinto de Rio Piedras	PR	5,750	
Univ of PR/Bayamon	PR	1,600	
Univ of PR/Mayaguez	PR	1,250	
Univ of Puget Sound	WA	54,608	HC
Univ of Redlands	CA	40,500	VC

ST = STATE $IS = IN-STATE COSTS   SR = SELECTOR RATING

School	ST	$IS	SR
Univ of Rio Grande	OH	8,750	NC
Univ of Rochester	NY	60,668	MC
Univ of San Diego	CA	54,818	HC+
Univ of San Francisco	CA	54,770	VC
Univ of Scranton	PA	51,940	VC
Univ of Sioux Falls	SD	22,990	C
Univ of South Alabama	AL	13,510	C
Univ of S Car at Columbia	SC	19,725	VC+
Univ of S Car Upstate	SC	18,200	LC
Univ of S Dak	SD	15,111	C
Univ of Southern Calif	CA	56,903	MC
Univ of Southern Indiana	IN	14,885	C
Univ of Southern Maine	ME	16,576	C
Univ of Southern Miss	MS	13,170	C
Univ of St. Francis	IL	37,560	C
Univ of St. Thomas - Houston	TX	37,690	C
Univ of Tenn at Knoxville	TN	20,364	VC+
Univ of Tenn at Martin	TN	13,734	C
Univ of Texas - Pan American	TX	11,125	LC
Univ of Texas at Arlington	TX	10,908	LC
Univ of Texas at Austin	TX	44,074	HC
Univ of Texas at Dallas	TX	21,348	HC+
Univ of Texas at El Paso	TX	8,764	NC
Univ of Texas at San Antonio	TX	18,372	C
Univ of the District of Columbia	DC	7,244	LC
Univ of the Pacific	CA	52,146	VC
Univ of the Sacred Heart	PR	5,590	
Univ of the Sciences	PA	48,320	VC+
Univ of Toledo	OH	18,464	C
Univ of Tulsa	OK	46,331	MC
Univ of Vermont	VT	27,006	VC+
Univ of Virginia	VA	23,050	MC
Univ of Washington	WA	14,722	VC
Univ of West Alabama	AL	14,274	C
Univ of West Florida	FL	14,656	C
Univ of West Georgia	GA	15,488	LC
Univ of Wisc/Eau Claire	WI	15,730	VC
Univ of Wisc/Green Bay	WI	19,074	C
Univ of Wisc/La Crosse	WI	9,304	VC
Univ of Wisc/Madison	WI	18,757	HC+
Univ of Wisc/Oshkosh	WI	10,426	C
Univ of Wisc/Parkside	WI	10,181	LC
Univ of Wisc/Platteville	WI	14,564	C
Univ of Wisc/Superior	WI	14,314	C
Univ of Wisc-Milwaukee	WI	18,436	C
Univ of Wyoming	WY	14,401	C+
Ursinus College	PA	57,580	VC
Utah State Univ	UT	12,044	C
Utica College	NY	45,670	C
Valparaiso Univ	IN	44,940	VC+
Vanderbilt Univ	TN	58,220	MC
Vassar College	NY	61,140	MC
Villanova Univ	PA	58,394	MC
Virginia Commonwealth Univ	VA	21,716	C
Virginia Military Inst	VA	16,156	C
Virginia Polytechnic Inst and State Univ	VA	14,629	HC
Virginia Wesleyan College	VA	28,433	LC
Voorhees College	SC	18,126	C
Wagner College	NY	48,600	C+
Wake Forest Univ	NC	58,838	MC
Walla Walla Univ	WA	26,256	NC
Walsh Univ	OH	35,100	C
Wartburg College	IA	41,055	VC
Washburn Univ	KS	12,579	C
Washington Adventist Univ	MD	25,859	LC
Washington and Lee Univ	VA	52,812	MC
Washington College	MD	52,602	VC
Washington State Univ	WA	20,461	C
Washington Univ in St. Louis	MO	69,844	MC
Wayland Baptist Univ	TX	18,912	LC
Wayne State College	NE	11,764	NC
Wayne State Univ	MI	22,063	C
Waynesburg Univ	PA	30,150	C
Webster Univ	MO	35,100	C+
Wellesley College	MA	59,038	MC
Wells College	NY	49,400	VC
Wentworth Inst of Technology	MA	29,800	C
Wesleyan Univ	CT	61,198	MC
West Chester Univ of Pennsylvania	PA	17,186	C
West Texas A&M Univ	TX	13,478	C
West Virginia Univ	WV	16,542	C+
West Virginia Univ Inst of Technology	WV	14,094	NC
West Virginia Wesleyan College	WV	26,880	C
Western Carolina Univ	NC	13,965	C
Western Conn State Univ	CT	18,327	LC
Western Illinois Univ	IL	10,732	C
Western Kentucky Univ	KY	11,000	VC
Western Mich Univ	MI	19,628	C
Western New England Univ	MA	46,154	C+
Western New Mexico Univ	NM	8,500	LC
Western Oregon Univ	OR	15,021	C
Western State Colo Univ	CO	16,924	C
Western Washington Univ	WA	18,519	VC
Westfield State Univ	MA	18,697	C
Westminster College	MO	31,720	VC
Westminster College	PA	31,290	C+
Westminster College	UT	37,708	C+

School	ST	$IS	SR
Westmont College	CA	41,500	HC
Wheaton College	IL	40,720	MC
Wheaton College	MA	54,934	HC+
Wheeling Jesuit Univ	WV	33,500	C
Whitworth Univ	WA	47,734	VC
Wichita State Univ	KS	14,607	C+
Widener Univ	PA	52,418	C
Wilberforce Univ	OH	15,100	LC
Wiley College	TX		LC
Wilkes Univ	PA	44,070	C
Willamette Univ	OR	56,450	VC+
William Paterson Univ of New Jersey	NJ	21,694	C
William Penn Univ	IA	26,000	C
William Woods Univ	MO	24,260	C
Williams Baptist College	AR	20,070	C
Williams College	MA	61,070	MC
Wilmington College	OH	29,784	C
Winona State Univ	MN	16,640	C
Winston-Salem State Univ	NC	9,418	LC
Winthrop Univ	SC	21,120	C
Wittenberg Univ	OH	47,962	C+
Wofford College	SC	45,795	VC
Worcester Polytechnic Inst	MA	55,860	MC
Worcester State Univ	MA	19,812	C
Wright State Univ	OH	16,983	C
Xavier Univ	OH	44,980	VC
Xavier Univ of Louisiana	LA	25,300	C
Yale Univ	CT	55,300	MC
Yeshiva Univ	NY	47,250	VC+
York College of Pennsylvania	PA	26,590	C
Youngstown State Univ	OH	16,732	C

COMPUTER SECURITY AND INFORMATION ASSURANCE

School	ST	$IS	SR
Baldwin Wallace Univ	OH	38,318	C
Bloomfield College	NJ	37,850	LC
Champlain College	VT	46,650	VC+
Charter Oak State College	CT	8,592	
Clarke Univ	IA	37,600	C
Dakota State Univ	SD	13,811	C
DePaul Univ	IL	47,623	VC
Eastern Mich Univ	MI	18,604	C
Felician College	NJ	41,640	LC
Florida Atlantic Univ	FL	17,339	C
Fontbonne Univ	MO	31,384	C
Frostburg State Univ	MD	15,264	LC
Hilbert College	NY	28,550	C
Kennesaw State Univ	GA		C
Kent State Univ	OH	19,920	C
Limestone College	SC	30,800	C
Loyola Univ Chicago	IL	51,646	VC+
Marshall Univ	WV	14,820	C
Marymount Univ	VA	39,480	C
Metropolitan State Univ	MN	5,923	
Minn State Univ, Mankato	MN	15,616	C
Minn State Univ, Moorhead	MN	13,392	VC
Mount Aloysius College	PA	29,976	C
Norwich Univ	VT	28,212	C
Pace Univ	NY	53,367	C
Pennsylvania College of Technology	PA	26,286	NC
Pittsburg State Univ	KS	12,032	C
Roger Williams Univ	RI	46,296	VC
Sacred Heart Univ	CT	49,264	VC
St. John's Univ	NY	55,070	C+
Stevens Inst of Technology	NJ	50,130	HC
Stevenson Univ	MD	41,470	C
Thomas College	ME	33,560	LC
Univ of Akron	OH	20,436	C
Univ of Maryland/Univ College	MD	6,168	SP
Univ of Texas at San Antonio	TX	18,372	C
Utica College	NY	45,670	C
Webber International Univ	FL	30,147	C
Youngstown State Univ	OH	16,732	C

COMPUTER TECHNOLOGY

School	ST	$IS	SR
Alcorn State Univ	MS	9,500	C
Alfred State/SUNY College of Technology	NY	18,034	C
Alverno College	WI	31,434	LC
Andrews Univ	MI	28,030	C+
Appalachian State Univ	NC	12,919	VC
Bellarmine Univ	KY	42,950	VC
Biola Univ	CA	40,320	C+
Bowie State Univ	MD	23,990	LC
Calif State Polytechnic Univ, Pomona	CA	20,156	C
Cal State, Dominguez Hills	CA	17,090	LC
Calif Univ of Pennsylvania	PA	14,217	C
Chestnut Hill College	PA	42,110	LC
Colo State Univ-Fort Collins	CO	20,385	VC
Daniel Webster College	NH	25,380	C
DePaul Univ	IL	47,623	VC
Duquesne Univ	PA	43,720	VC
Eastern Mich Univ	MI	18,604	C
Eastern Washington Univ	WA		C
Excelsior College	NY	5,580	SP
Guilford College	NC	42,800	C
Hodges Univ	FL	12,000	LC
Idaho State Univ	ID	12,307	C
Indiana State Univ	IN	16,000	C

School	ST	$IS	SR
Inter-American Univ of PR/Bayamon Univ College	PR	4,428	
Kent State Univ	OH	19,920	VC
LeTourneau Univ	TX	36,210	VC
Limestone College	SC	30,800	C
Martin Univ	IN	11,000	SP
Methodist Univ	NC	37,185	C
New Jersey Inst of Technology	NJ	26,490	C+
New Mexico State Univ	NM	14,050	C
Norfolk State Univ	VA	10,531	LC
Oregon Inst of Technology	OR	8,910	C
Peirce College	PA	12,760	NC
Purdue Univ/Calumet	IN	14,336	C
Purdue Univ/West Lafayette	IN	20,024	HC
Rochester Inst of Technology	NY	42,450	VC
Rockhurst Univ	MO	20,625	C
Shepherd Univ	WV	15,875	C
Southern Wesleyan Univ	SC	25,600	C
SUNY Polytechnic Inst	NY	19,690	C
The Univ of Memphis	TN	15,094	C
Tulane Univ	LA	60,861	MC
Union College	KY	29,955	C
Univ of Arkansas at Little Rock	AR	17,609	LC
Univ of Dayton	OH	49,070	VC
Univ of Illinois at Urbana-Champaign	IL	26,450	HC
Univ of Maryland/Univ College	MD	6,168	SP
Univ of Minn Crookston	MN	17,834	C
Univ of Northern Iowa	IA	15,795	C
Univ of Rio Grande	OH	8,750	NC
Univ of Southern Miss	MS	13,170	C
Univ of St. Francis	IL	37,560	C
Univ of Wisc/Stevens Point	WI	14,043	C
Valparaiso Univ	IN	44,940	VC+
Wayne State Univ	MI	22,063	C
Wentworth Inst of Technology	MA	29,800	C
Youngstown State Univ	OH	16,732	C

CONDUCTING

School	ST	$IS	SR
Oberlin College	OH	61,788	MC

CONSERVATION AND REGULATION

School	ST	$IS	SR
Arizona State Univ, at the Tempe Campus	AZ	20,137	C+
College of the Ozarks	MO		VC
Florida Inst of Technology	FL	48,290	VC
Kent State Univ	OH	19,920	C
Lipscomb Univ	TN	37,490	VC
Missouri Southern State Univ	MO	12,061	C
Mount Mercy Univ	IA	35,320	C
Muskingum Univ	OH	30,502	C
N Car State Univ	NC	16,202	HC
Northwest Missouri State Univ	MO	17,347	C
Northwestern Okla State Univ	OK	7,275	NC
Southeastern Okla State Univ	OK	7,966	LC
St. Lawrence Univ	NY	59,972	VC
Texas Tech Univ	TX	14,243	C
Unity College	ME	34,054	C
Univ of Arkansas at Pine Bluff	AR	13,378	C
Univ of Calif at Berkeley	CA	23,322	MC
Univ of Central Missouri	MO	14,605	C
Univ of Idaho	ID	14,558	C
Univ of Montana	MT	14,105	C
Univ of Wisc/River Falls	WI	9,722	LC
Upper Iowa Univ	IA	30,426	NC

CONSTRUCTION

School	ST	$IS	SR
Cal State, Northridge	CA	28,690	LC
Thomas Edison State College	NJ	5,700	SP
Univ of Alaska Anchorage	AK	16,673	NC
Univ of Louisiana at Monroe	LA	12,998	C

CONSTRUCTION ENGINEERING

School	ST	$IS	SR
Arizona State Univ, at the Tempe Campus	AZ	20,137	C+
Bradley Univ	IL	31,874	VC
Fairleigh Dickinson Univ/Metropolitan Campus	NJ	40,254	C
Florida Inst of Technology	FL	48,290	VC
Florida International Univ	FL	17,747	C+
Iowa State Univ	IA	16,403	C
Louisiana Tech Univ	LA	11,302	C
Marquette Univ	WI	46,930	VC+
Montana State Univ	MT	14,068	C
National Univ	CA	14,730	SP
N Dak State Univ	ND		C
Purdue Univ/West Lafayette	IN	20,024	HC
Rensselaer Polytechnic Inst	NY	61,529	MC
San Diego State Univ	CA	21,611	C+
Southern Polytechnic State Univ	GA	13,958	C
Texas A&M Univ	TX	19,207	VC
The Catholic Univ of America	DC	52,852	VC

School	ST	$IS	SR
Univ of Arkansas at Little Rock	AR	17,609	LC
Univ of Central Florida	FL	15,668	VC+
Univ of Florida	FL	15,943	HC
Univ of Nebr - Lincoln	NE	18,031	VC
Univ of New Mexico	NM	15,300	C
Univ of North Florida	FL	15,870	VC
Univ of North Texas	TX	15,628	C
Univ of Southern Calif	CA	56,903	MC
Univ of the District of Columbia	DC	7,244	LC
Univ of Washington	WA	14,722	VC
Virginia Polytechnic Inst and State Univ	VA	14,629	HC
Western Mich Univ	MI	19,628	C

CONSTRUCTION MANAGEMENT

School	ST	$IS	SR
Alfred State/SUNY College of Technology	NY	18,034	C
Appalachian State Univ	NC	12,919	VC
Arizona State Univ, at the Tempe Campus	AZ	20,137	C+
Auburn Univ	AL	22,378	VC+
Boise State Univ	ID	13,469	LC
Bowling Green State Univ	OH	18,970	C
Brigham Young Univ	UT	12,100	HC
Calif Baptist Univ	CA	38,792	C
Calif Polytechnic State Univ	CA	19,847	HC
Cal State, Chico	CA	20,158	C
Cal State, Fresno	CA	17,405	C
Central Conn State Univ	CT	19,749	C
Central Washington Univ	WA	11,730	C
Clemson Univ	SC	19,136	HC
Colo State Univ-Fort Collins	CO	20,385	VC
Dordt College	IA	34,160	C+
Drexel Univ	PA	61,418	VC+
East Carolina Univ	NC	14,169	C
Eastern Mich Univ	MI	18,604	C
Ferris State Univ	MI	20,047	C
Florida Inst of Technology	FL	48,290	VC
Georgia Inst of Technology	GA	21,828	MC
Georgia Southern Univ	GA	16,942	C
Illinois State Univ	IL	23,110	VC
John Brown Univ	AR	32,056	VC+
Kansas State Univ	KS	15,497	VC
Lawrence Tech Univ	MI	37,630	VC
Louisiana State Univ	LA	18,677	C+
Mich State Univ	MI	22,450	VC
Mich Tech Univ	MI	23,556	HC
Milwaukee School of Engineering	WI	39,948	VC+
Minn State Univ, Mankato	MN	15,616	C
Minn State Univ, Moorhead	MN	13,392	VC
Missouri State Univ	MO	13,996	C+
National Univ	CA	14,730	SP
New York Inst of Technology	NY	45,010	VC
New York Univ	NY	61,470	MC
NewSchool of Architecture & Design	CA	24,900	SP
N Car State Univ	NC	16,202	HC
N Dak State Univ	ND		C
Northern Arizona Univ	AZ	19,010	C
Northern Kentucky Univ	KY	21,134	C
Northern Mich Univ	MI	18,278	C
Okla State Univ	OK	14,310	VC
Oregon State Univ	OR	20,273	VC
Pennsylvania College of Technology	PA	26,286	NC
Pittsburg State Univ	KS	12,032	C
Polytechnic Inst of New York Univ	NY	53,064	HC+
Pratt Inst	NY	55,956	SP
Purdue Univ/West Lafayette	IN	20,024	HC
Roger Williams Univ	RI	46,296	VC
S Dak State Univ	SD	14,296	C
Southern Illinois Univ Edwardsville	IL	17,532	C
Southern Polytechnic State Univ	GA	13,958	C
SUNY / College of Environmental Science and Forestry	NY	18,351	VC
Temple Univ	PA	24,392	VC
Texas State Univ	TX	17,128	C
Ohio State Univ-Columbus Campus	OH	19,887	HC+
The Univ of Okla	OK	18,621	VC
The Univ of Tenn at Chattanooga	TN	16,883	C
Tuskegee Univ	AL	26,750	C
Univ of Arkansas at Little Rock	AR	17,609	LC
Univ of Central Missouri	MO	14,605	C
Univ of Cincinnati	OH	21,506	VC
Univ of Denver	CO	51,787	VC+
Univ of Houston	TX	19,796	VC
Univ of Louisiana at Monroe	LA	12,998	C
Univ of Nebr - Lincoln	NE	18,031	VC
Univ of Nebr at Kearney	NE	14,855	LC
Univ of Nevada, Las Vegas	NV	17,303	C
Univ of New Mexico	NM	15,300	C
Univ of N Car at Charlotte	NC	15,547	C
Univ of North Florida	FL	15,870	VC
Univ of Northern Iowa	IA	15,795	C
Univ of Texas at San Antonio	TX	18,372	C

ST = STATE $IS = IN-STATE COSTS   SR = SELECTOR RATING

School	ST	$IS	SR
Utica College	NY	45,670	C
Virginia Polytechnic Inst and State Univ	VA	14,629	HC
Washington State Univ	WA	20,461	C
Wayne State Univ	MI	22,063	C
Wentworth Inst of Technology	MA	29,800	C
Western Carolina Univ	NC	13,965	C
Western Illinois Univ	IL	20,732	C
Western Kentucky Univ	KY	11,000	LC

CONSTRUCTION MGMT/ COMMERCIAL/INDUSTRIAL

School	ST	$IS	SR
Ferris State Univ	MI	20,047	C

CONSTRUCTION MGMT/ HIGHWAY/BRIDGE

School	ST	$IS	SR
Ferris State Univ	MI	20,047	C

CONSTRUCTION TECHNOLOGY

School	ST	$IS	SR
Appalachian State Univ	NC	12,919	VC
Black Hills State Univ	SD	13,947	C
Calif State Polytechnic Univ, Pomona	CA	20,156	C
Eastern Kentucky Univ	KY	11,161	C
Farmingdale State College	NY	19,673	C
Fitchburg State Univ	MA	18,173	C
Florida International Univ	FL	17,747	C
Idaho State Univ	ID	12,307	C
Indiana State Univ	IN	16,000	C
Millersville Univ of Pennsylvania	PA	21,648	C
Montana State Univ-Northern	MT	12,500	NC
Murray State Univ	KY	15,304	C
Norfolk State Univ	VA	10,531	LC
Northern Kentucky Univ	KY	21,134	C
Okla State Univ	OK	14,310	VC
Pennsylvania College of Technology	PA	26,286	C
Pittsburg State Univ	KS	12,032	C
Purdue Univ/Calumet	IN	14,336	C
Purdue Univ/West Lafayette	IN	20,024	HC
Texas State Univ	TX	17,128	C
Texas Tech Univ	TX	14,243	C
Univ of Akron	OH	20,436	C
Univ of Arkansas at Little Rock	AR	17,609	LC
Univ of Maine	ME	19,902	C+
Univ of Maryland/Eastern Shore	MD	14,000	C
Univ of Mass Amherst	MA	24,215	VC+
Univ of Southern Miss	MS	13,170	C
Univ of Wisc/Stout	WI	15,459	C
Wentworth Inst of Technology	MA	29,800	C

CONSUMER SERVICES

School	ST	$IS	SR
San Francisco State Univ	CA	18,514	C
S Dak State Univ	SD	14,296	C
Texas Woman's Univ	TX	13,633	LC
The Univ of Utah	UT	16,463	C

CONTEMPORARY CHRISTIAN MUSIC

School	ST	$IS	SR
Greenville College	IL	27,012	C

CORE STUDIES

School	ST	$IS	SR
Shenandoah Univ	VA	39,916	C

CORRECTIONS

School	ST	$IS	SR
Adams State Univ	CO	13,358	LC
College of the Ozarks	MO		VC
Eastern Kentucky Univ	KY	11,161	C
Hardin-Simmons Univ	TX	23,560	C+
Jackson State Univ	MS	13,512	LC
Kent State Univ	OH	19,920	C
Minn State Univ, Mankato	MN	15,616	C
Stephen F. Austin State Univ	TX	14,668	C
Texas State Univ	TX	17,128	C
Tiffin Univ	OH	30,273	LC
Univ of Indianapolis	IN	31,740	LC
Univ of New Haven	CT	48,940	C
Washburn Univ	KS	12,579	C
Western Oregon Univ	OR	15,021	C

COSTUME DESIGN

School	ST	$IS	SR
Shenandoah Univ	VA	39,916	C
Webster Univ	MO	35,100	C+

COUNSELING/PSYCHOLOGY

School	ST	$IS	SR
Adams State Univ	CO	13,358	LC
Biola Univ	CA	40,320	C+
Blackburn College	IL	21,350	C
Cal State, Fresno	CA	17,405	C
Campbell Univ	NC	37,570	VC

School	ST	$IS	SR
City Univ of Seattle	WA	14,880	NC
Corban Univ	OR	37,380	C+
Dallas Baptist Univ	TX	30,580	VC
East Central Univ	OK	10,223	LC
Eastern Mich Univ	MI	18,604	C
Eastern New Mexico Univ	NM	10,682	C
Edinboro Univ of Pennsylvania	PA	15,940	LC
Emmanuel College	MA	47,985	VC
Faulkner Univ	AL	25,720	LC
Florida Gulf Coast Univ	FL		C
Friends Univ	KS	29,100	C
Geneva College	PA	27,280	C
Goddard College	VT	16,418	VC
Grace College and Seminary	IN	28,800	C
Houghton College	NY	36,808	C+
Howard Univ	DC	13,646	C
Huntington Univ	IN	32,220	C+
Husson Univ	ME	24,194	LC
Kentucky Christian Univ	KY	17,622	LC
Kutztown Univ of Pennsylvania	PA	16,909	LC
Martin Univ	IN	11,000	SP
Missouri State Univ	MO	13,996	C
Mount St. Mary's College - Chalon Campus	CA	43,897	VC+
New York Univ	NY	61,470	MC
Newman Univ	KS	30,380	C+
Northwest Univ	WA	18,854	C
Pittsburg State Univ	KS	12,032	C
Prescott College	AZ	33,284	C
Rochester College	MI	18,320	LC
SUNY/Empire State College	NY	6,315	SP
The Univ of N Car at Pembroke	NC	13,388	LC
Toccoa Falls College	GA	23,210	LC
Univ of Arizona	AZ	20,657	C
Univ of Georgia	GA	20,082	VC
Univ of Great Falls	MT	27,970	C
Univ of Idaho	ID	14,558	C
Univ of Louisiana at Monroe	LA	12,998	C
Univ of Missouri/Columbia	MO	18,201	MC
Univ of New Haven	CT	48,940	C
Univ of North Florida	FL	15,870	VC
Univ of St. Francis	IL	37,560	C
Washington Adventist Univ	MD	25,859	LC
Wayne State College	NE	11,764	NC
Williams Baptist College	AR	20,070	C
Xavier Univ	OH	44,980	VC

COURT REPORTING

School	ST	$IS	SR
Humphreys College	CA	17,000	NC

CRAFTS

School	ST	$IS	SR
Indiana Univ-Purdue Univ Fort Wayne	IN	15,521	C
Kent State Univ	OH	19,920	C
Kutztown Univ of Pennsylvania	PA	16,909	C
Rochester Inst of Technology	NY	42,450	VC
Univ of Illinois at Urbana-Champaign	IL	26,450	HC
Virginia Commonwealth Univ	VA	21,716	C

CREATIVE WRITING

School	ST	$IS	SR
Adams State Univ	CO	13,358	LC
Agnes Scott College	GA	45,323	C+
Albion College	MI	46,010	C
Alderson Broaddus Univ	WV	28,656	C
American Univ	DC	56,015	HC+
Andrews Univ	MI	28,030	C+
Arkansas Tech Univ	AR	13,982	LC
Asbury Univ	KY	32,038	VC
Ashland Univ	OH	25,000	C
Baldwin Wallace Univ	OH	38,318	C
Bard College	NY	61,940	HC
Bard College at Simon's Rock	MA	61,749	HC+
Baylor Univ	TX	50,329	HC
Belhaven Univ	MS	27,170	C
Beloit College	WI	49,970	HC
Benedictine Univ	IL	37,820	C
Bennington College	VT	56,990	HC+
Bethany College	WV	35,282	LC
Bethel College	IN	31,560	C
Binghamton Univ/The SUNY	NY	21,648	HC+
Blackburn College	IL	21,350	C
Bloomfield College	NJ	37,850	LC
Bluffton Univ	OH	38,948	C
Bowling Green State Univ	OH	18,970	C
Brandeis Univ	MA		MC
Burlington College	VT	32,510	SP
Calif College of the Arts	CA	48,334	SP
Cal State, Long Beach	CA	17,502	C+
Calvin College	MI	39,120	VC
Canisius College	NY	44,900	C
Capital Univ	OH	41,050	VC
Cardinal Stritch Univ	WI	24,054	C
Carlow Univ	PA	30,272	C
Carroll College	MT	28,000	C
Chapman Univ	CA	58,347	VC+
Chatham Univ	PA	43,797	C
CUNY/Brooklyn College	NY	5,884	C+

School	ST	$IS	SR
Coe College	IA	45,550	VC
Colby College	ME	57,510	MC
Colby-Sawyer College	NH	50,790	C
Colo College	CO	57,162	MC
Colo State Univ-Fort Collins	CO	20,385	VC
Columbia College Chicago	IL	30,940	LC
Concordia Univ St. Paul	MN	28,250	C
Corban Univ	OR	37,380	C+
DePaul Univ	IL	47,623	VC
Dominican Univ of Calif	CA	51,250	C
Eastern Mich Univ	MI	18,604	C
Eastern Washington Univ	WA		C
Eckerd College	FL	43,902	C
Elon Univ	NC	41,914	VC+
Emerson College	MA	52,446	HC+
Emory and Henry College	VA	387,460	C
Emory Univ	GA	56,368	MC
Fairleigh Dickinson Univ/ College at Florham	NJ	42,142	C
Faulkner Univ	AL	25,720	LC
Florida Southern College	FL	40,150	C+
Florida State Univ	FL	16,715	VC
Franklin College	IN	36,585	C
Geneva College	PA	27,280	C
George Fox Univ	OR	40,750	C+
Georgetown College	KY	41,440	C+
Goddard College	VT	16,418	VC
Goshen College	IN	35,900	VC
Grand Valley State Univ	MI	17,998	C+
Green Mountain College	VT	45,228	LC
Hamilton College	NY	55,620	MC
Hamline Univ	MN	45,678	VC
Hampshire College	MA	58,320	MC
Harvard College/Harvard Univ	MA	49,000	MC
Hiram College	OH	37,300	VC
Hofstra Univ	NY	51,810	VC+
Hope College	MI	38,650	VC
Hunter College	NY	14,429	VC
Huntington Univ	IN	32,220	C+
Indiana Wesleyan Univ	IN	31,815	VC
Iowa State Univ	IA	16,403	C
Ithaca College	NY	53,864	VC
Johns Hopkins Univ	MD	47,492	MC
Johnson State College	VT	16,721	C
Kansas City Art Inst	MO	44,308	SP
Knox College	IL	44,865	VC+
La Roche College	PA	35,824	LC
Lakeland College	WI	22,990	C
Le Moyne College	NY	43,470	C
Lesley Univ	MA	46,350	C
Lindenwood Univ	MO	20,750	C
Linfield College-McMinnville Campus	OR	47,676	C
Loras College	IA	37,432	VC
Loyola Univ Maryland	MD	56,880	VC+
Loyola Univ New Orleans	LA	46,581	VC
Lubbock Christian Univ	TX	26,308	C
Malone Univ	OH	35,364	C
Marlboro College	VT	35,980	VC
Marshall Univ	WV	14,820	C
Maryville College	TN	33,150	C+
Mass Inst of Technology	MA	58,240	MC
Mercer Univ	GA	44,201	VC
Methodist Univ	NC	37,185	C
Mills College	CA	54,119	VC
Millsaps College	MS	43,888	VC+
Montclair State Univ	NJ	22,614	C
Murray State Univ	KY	15,304	C
New England College	NH	45,930	LC
New York Univ	NY	61,470	MC
Northland College	WI	26,680	C
Oberlin College	OH	61,788	MC
Ohio Northern Univ	OH	42,075	VC
Ohio Univ	OH	21,080	C
Okla Christian Univ	OK	25,870	VC
Old Dominion Univ	VA	19,483	LC
Oswego / SUNY	NY	20,009	VC
Pacific Univ	OR	49,626	C+
Pepperdine Univ	CA	55,372	HC+
Pfeiffer Univ	NC	33,700	LC
Pittsburg State Univ	KS	12,032	C
Pratt Inst	NY	55,956	SP
Prescott College	AZ	33,284	C
Purdue Univ/West Lafayette	IN	20,024	HC
Queens Univ of Charlotte	NC	39,543	C
Roanoke College	VA	49,976	C
Rocky Mountain College	MT	32,242	C
Roger Williams Univ	RI	46,296	VC
Rosemont College	PA	42,350	C
Rutgers, The State Univ of New Jersey/Newark Campus	NJ	258,806	C
Sacred Heart Univ	CT	49,264	VC
Saginaw Valley State Univ	MI	17,369	C
St. Joseph's College	IN	36,500	C
St. Mary-of-the-Woods College	IN	37,722	LC
St. Mary's College	IN	45,160	C+
San Francisco State Univ	CA	18,514	C
Santa Fe Univ of Art and Design	NM	39,666	SP
Sarah Lawrence College	NY	48,000	HC
School of the Art Inst of Chicago	IL	56,230	SP
Seattle Pacific Univ	WA	41,559	VC+

School	ST	$IS	SR
Seattle Univ	WA	49,035	VC+
Seton Hall Univ	NJ	45,902	C
Seton Hill Univ	PA	35,172	C
Smith College	MA	59,674	MC
Southern Methodist Univ	TX	60,585	MC
Southern New Hampshire Univ	NH	38,100	C
Southern Vermont College	VT	30,740	LC
Southwest Minn State Univ	MN	14,000	C
Spalding Univ	KY	32,287	LC
St. Andrews Univ	NC	32,050	LC
St. Lawrence Univ	NY	59,972	VC
SUNY at Purchase	NY	16,951	C
Stephens College	MO	38,042	VC
Suffolk Univ	MA	47,298	C
The College of Idaho	ID	31,277	C+
The SUNY at Potsdam	NY	18,473	C
Truman State Univ	MO	15,541	HC
Univ of Arizona	AZ	20,657	C
Univ of Calif at Irvine	CA	25,961	VC
Univ of Calif at Riverside	CA	27,204	C
Univ of Central Okla	OK	12,293	C
Univ of Cincinnati	OH	21,506	VC
Univ of Colo Boulder	CO	22,605	VC+
Univ of Evansville	IN	42,656	VC+
Univ of Florida	FL	15,943	HC
Univ of Idaho	ID	14,558	C
Univ of Maine at Farmington	ME	18,187	LC
Univ of Mich/Ann Arbor	MI	22,140	HC
Univ of Missouri/Columbia	MO	18,201	MC
Univ of Montana-Western	MT	9,753	C
Univ of Mount Union	OH	35,130	C
Univ of Nebr at Omaha	NE	12,700	C
Univ of New Haven	CT	48,940	C
Univ of N Car at Wilmington	NC	13,572	VC
Univ of Oregon	OR	21,360	C+
Univ of Pittsburgh at Greensburg	PA	17,640	C
Univ of Pittsburgh at Johnstown	PA	20,862	LC
Univ of Redlands	CA	40,500	VC
Univ of Southern Calif	CA	56,903	MC
Univ of Tampa	FL	35,160	VC
Univ of Texas at Austin	TX	44,074	HC
Univ of Wisc/Green Bay	WI	19,074	C
Valparaiso Univ	IN	44,940	VC+
Warren Wilson College	NC	40,132	VC
Wartburg College	IA	41,055	VC
Washington Univ in St. Louis	MO	69,844	MC
Waynesburg Univ	PA	30,150	C
Webster Univ	MO	35,100	C+
Western Mich Univ	MI	19,628	C
Western New England Univ	MA	46,154	C+
Western Washington Univ	WA	18,519	VC
Wheaton College	MA	54,934	HC+
Wheeling Jesuit Univ	WV	33,500	C
Widener Univ	PA	52,418	C
Wilson College	PA	35,080	C
Wofford College	SC	45,795	VC
Wright State Univ	OH	16,983	C
York College of Pennsylvania	PA	26,590	C

CRIMINAL JUSTICE

School	ST	$IS	SR
Abilene Christian Univ	TX	38,400	C+
Adelphi Univ	NY	44,670	VC
Adrian College	MI	42,400	C
Alabama State Univ	AL	14,142	NC
Albany State Univ	GA	8,500	C
Albright College	PA	46,660	C
Alcorn State Univ	MS	9,500	C
Alfred Univ	NY	41,770	C
Alvernia Univ	PA	39,250	LC
American International College	MA	36,100	C
American Univ	DC	56,015	HC+
Anderson Univ	IN	36,100	C
Angelo State Univ	TX	15,049	NC
Anna Maria College	MA	34,600	C
Appalachian State Univ	NC	12,919	VC
Arcadia Univ	PA	33,570	C+
Arizona State Univ, at the Downtown Phoenix Campus	AZ	22,101	C
Armstrong State Univ	GA	15,532	C
Asbury Univ	KY	32,038	VC
Ashford Univ	CA	10,480	C
Ashland Univ	OH	25,000	C
Auburn Univ at Montgomery	AL	14,470	LC
Aurora Univ	IL	33,228	C
Austin Peay State Univ	TN	15,274	C
Averett Univ	VA	37,750	LC
Baldwin Wallace Univ	OH	38,318	C
Ball State Univ	IN	17,850	C
Barton College	NC	27,660	LC
Bay Path College	MA	34,565	C
Becker College	MA	41,420	C
Bellarmine Univ	KY	42,950	VC
Bellevue Univ	NE	4,600	NC
Belmont Abbey College	NC	37,716	C
Bemidji State Univ	MN	13,500	VC
Benedict College	SC	20,454	NC
Bethany College	KS	30,605	VC
Bethel College	IN	31,560	C
Bethune-Cookman Univ	FL	22,958	C
Blackburn College	IL	21,350	C

School	ST	$IS	SR
Bloomfield College	NJ	37,850	LC
Bloomsburg Univ of Pennsylvania	PA	13,598	C
Blue Mountain College	MS	15,634	LC
Bluefield College	VA	17,230	C+
Bluefield State College	WV	3,140	LC
Bluffton Univ	OH	38,948	C
Boise State Univ	ID	13,469	LC
Boston Univ	MA	60,694	MC
Bowie State Univ	MD	23,990	C
Bowling Green State Univ	OH	18,970	C
Bradley Univ	IL	31,874	VC
Briar Cliff Univ	IA	29,514	C
Bridgewater State Univ	MA	18,752	C
Buena Vista Univ	IA	39,188	C
Buffalo State College / SUNY	NY	15,733	LC
Butler Univ	IN	47,572	VC+
Caldwell College	NJ	35,602	NC
Calif Baptist Univ	CA	38,792	C
Calif Lutheran Univ	CA	49,540	C+
Cal State, Bakersfield	CA	8,000	C
Cal State, Chico	CA	20,158	C
Cal State, Dominguez Hills	CA	17,090	LC
Cal State, East Bay	CA	16,549	C
Cal State, Fullerton	CA	25,188	C
Cal State, Long Beach	CA	17,502	C+
Cal State, Los Angeles	CA	17,186	LC
Cal State, Sacramento	CA	16,200	C
Cal State, San Bernardino	CA	12,000	C
Cal State, Stanislaus	CA	18,582	C
Calif Univ of Pennsylvania	PA	14,217	C
Calumet College of St. Joseph	IN	15,000	C
Cameron Univ	OK	10,004	LC
Campbell Univ	NC	37,570	VC
Campbellsville Univ	KY	27,720	C
Canisius College	NY	44,900	C
Capital Univ	OH	41,050	VC
Caribbean Univ	PR	10,375	
Carroll Univ	WI	38,100	C
Carthage College	WI	33,000	C
Castleton State College	VT	20,186	C
Cedar Crest College	PA	43,240	C
Cedarville Univ	OH	32,860	VC
Centenary College	NJ	38,618	C
Central Methodist Univ	MO	28,240	VC
Central Washington Univ	WA	11,730	C
Chadron State College	NE	7,400	NC
Chaminade Univ of Honolulu	HI	31,664	LC
Champlain College	VT	46,650	VC+
Charleston Southern Univ	SC	22,420	C
Chestnut Hill College	PA	42,110	LC
Cheyney Univ of Pennsylvania	PA	20,372	LC
Chicago State Univ	IL	5,482	LC
Citadel, The	SC		C
City Univ of Seattle	WA	14,880	NC
Claflin Univ	SC	22,368	LC
College of New Jersey	NJ	25,576	HC
College of St Joseph	VT	30,600	LC
College of the Ozarks	MO		VC
Colo Technical Univ	CO	10,500	LC
Columbia College	MO	24,578	C
Columbus State Univ	GA	13,176	C
Concordia Univ St. Paul	MN	28,250	C
Concordia Univ Wisc	WI	28,980	C
Concordia Univ, Ann Arbor	MI	27,220	VC
Coppin State Univ	MD	16,227	VC
Corban Univ	OR	37,380	C+
Culver-Stockton College	MO	30,900	C
Cumberland Univ	TN	21,220	C
Curry College	MA	48,925	LC
Dakota Wesleyan Univ	SD	23,000	C
Dallas Baptist Univ	TX	30,580	VC
De Sales Univ	PA	43,970	C
Defiance College	OH	30,645	C
Delaware Valley College	PA	29,944	C
Delta State Univ	MS	12,292	LC
Dominican College	NY	31,270	LC
Dominican Univ	IL	37,628	C
Dordt College	IA	34,160	C+
Drexel Univ	PA	61,418	VC+
Drury Univ	MO	31,909	VC
East Carolina Univ	NC	14,169	C
East Central Univ	OK	10,223	LC
East Stroudsburg Univ of Pennsylvania	PA	18,868	LC
East Tenn State Univ	TN	9,000	C
East Texas Baptist Univ	TX	31,577	LC
Eastern Mich Univ	MI	18,604	C
Eastern New Mexico Univ	NM	10,682	C
Eastern Washington Univ	WA		C
Edgewood College	WI	33,294	C
Edinboro Univ of Pennsylvania	PA	15,940	LC
Edward Waters College	FL	19,607	LC
Elizabeth City State Univ	NC	11,638	C
Elizabethtown College	PA	49,740	VC
Elizabethtown College School of Continuing and Professional Studies	PA		VC
Elmhurst College	IL	43,336	C
Elmira College	NY	49,950	C+
Emporia State Univ	KS	12,897	C
Endicott College	MA	43,228	VC+
Evangel Univ	MO	23,090	C
Excelsior College	NY	5,580	SP
Fairleigh Dickinson Univ/ Metropolitan Campus	NJ	40,254	C
Fairmont State Univ	WV	12,098	LC
Farmingdale State College	NY	19,673	C
Faulkner Univ	AL	25,720	LC
Fayetteville State Univ	NC	10,816	C
Felician College	NJ	41,640	LC
Ferris State Univ	MI	20,047	C
Ferrum College	VA	27,740	LC
Fitchburg State Univ	MA	18,173	C
Florida A&M Univ	FL	14,935	LC
Florida Atlantic Univ	FL	17,339	C
Florida Gulf Coast Univ	FL		C
Florida International Univ	FL	17,747	C+
Florida Memorial Univ	FL	20,888	LC
Fort Hays State Univ	KS	11,354	C
Fort Valley State Univ	GA	11,200	VC
Franklin Pierce Univ	NH	41,598	C
Freed-Hardeman Univ	TN	19,697	VC
Friends Univ	KS	29,100	C
Frostburg State Univ	MD	15,264	LC
Gannon Univ	PA	39,608	C
George Mason Univ	VA	15,724	VC
George Washington Univ	DC	57,108	MC
Georgia College and State Univ	GA	18,900	C+
Georgia Regents Univ	GA		C
Georgia State Univ	GA	15,582	VC
Georgian Court Univ	NJ	41,594	LC
Glenville State College	WV	11,348	NC
Gonzaga Univ	WA	46,441	HC
Grace College and Seminary	IN	28,800	VC
Graceland Univ	IA	28,020	C
Grambling State Univ	LA	13,384	LC
Grand Valley State Univ	MI	17,998	C+
Grand View Univ	IA	31,050	C
Granite State College	NH	6,195	NC
Greenville College	IL	27,012	C
Guilford College	NC	42,800	C
Gwynedd-Mercy College	PA	33,560	C
Hamline Univ	MN	45,678	VC
Hannibal-LaGrange Univ	MO	24,490	C
Harding Univ	AR	23,556	C
Hardin-Simmons Univ	TX	23,560	C+
Harris-Stowe State Univ	MO	14,360	NC
Hawaii Pacific Univ	HI	34,360	C
Heidelberg Univ	OH	34,100	C
Henderson State Univ	AR	14,584	C
High Point Univ	NC	39,800	C
Hilbert College	NY	28,550	C
Hodges Univ	FL	12,000	LC
Holy Family Univ	PA	40,030	LC
Howard Univ	DC	13,646	C
Huntington Univ	IN	32,220	C+
Husson Univ	ME	24,194	LC
Huston-Tillotson Univ	TX	18,124	C+
Illinois State Univ	IL	23,110	VC
Indiana Inst of Technology	IN	34,240	LC
Indiana Univ Bloomington	IN	19,801	VC
Indiana Univ East	IN	6,783	C
Indiana Univ Kokomo	IN	6,811	C
Indiana Univ Northwest	IN	6,854	C
Indiana Univ South Bend	IN	15,501	C
Indiana Univ Southeast	IN	16,035	C
Indiana Univ-Purdue Univ Fort Wayne	IN	15,521	C
Indiana Univ-Purdue Univ Indianapolis	IN	17,611	C
Indiana Wesleyan Univ	IN	31,815	VC
Inter-American Univ of PR/ Aguadilla Campus	PR	5,578	
Inter-American Univ of PR/ Arecibo Campus	PR	3,350	
Inter-American Univ of PR/ Barranquitas	PR	3,350	
Inter-American Univ of PR/ Fajardo Campus	PR	4,200	
Inter-American Univ of PR/ Metropolitan Campus	PR	4,320	
Inter-American Univ of PR/ Ponce	PR		
Iona College	NY	44,028	C
Iowa Wesleyan College	IA	30,850	LC
Jackson State Univ	MS	13,512	LC
Jacksonville State Univ	AL	12,480	LC
James Madison Univ	VA	18,049	VC
Jarvis Christian College	TX	19,552	NC
John Carroll Univ	OH	46,300	C+
John Jay College of Criminal Justice/ The CUNY	NY	6,359	LC
Johnson & Wales Univ/ Denver Campus	CO	29,576	C
Johnson & Wales Univ/North Miami Campus	FL		C
Johnson & Wales Univ/ Providence Campus	RI	29,576	C
Johnson C. Smith Univ	NC	25,336	LC
Judson College	AL	26,794	C
Kansas Wesleyan Univ	KS	32,000	C
Kean Univ	NJ	23,444	C
Keene State College	NH	23,232	LC
Kennesaw State Univ	GA		C
Kent State Univ	OH	19,920	C
Kentucky State Univ	KY	11,000	LC
Kentucky Wesleyan College	KY	27,440	C
Keuka College	NY	30,300	C
Keystone College	PA	28,680	LC
King's College	PA	43,502	C
Kutztown Univ of Pennsylvania	PA	16,909	LC
La Roche College	PA	35,824	LC
La Salle Univ	PA	50,270	C
Lake Erie College	OH	37,266	C
Lake Superior State Univ	MI	18,121	C
Lakeland College	WI	22,990	C
Lamar Univ	TX	6,820	C
Lane College	TN	11,212	C
Langston Univ	OK	3,600	C
Lasell College	MA	43,750	LC
Lebanon Valley College	PA	38,570	C
Lees-McRae College	NC	33,944	C
LeMoyne-Owen College	TN	13,100	C
Lewis Univ	IL	23,050	C
Lewis-Clark State College	ID	6,990	C
Limestone College	SC	30,800	C
Lincoln Univ	MO	12,904	NC
Lindenwood Univ	MO	20,750	C
Lindsey Wilson College	KY	31,220	C
LIU Post	NY	47,660	C
Livingstone College	NC	17,815	LC
Lock Haven Univ of Pennsylvania	PA	18,028	LC
Longwood Univ	VA	20,924	C
Loras College	IA	37,432	VC
Louisiana College	LA	15,746	C
Lourdes Univ	OH	26,055	LC
Loyola Univ Chicago	IL	51,646	VC+
Loyola Univ New Orleans	LA	46,581	VC
Lubbock Christian Univ	TX	26,308	C
Lycoming College	PA	45,379	C
Lynn Univ	FL	43,500	LC
MacMurray College	IL	20,755	C
Madonna Univ	MI	24,540	VC
Mansfield Univ	PA	19,468	LC
Marian Univ	WI	32,420	C
Marist College	NY	35,500	C
Marshall Univ	WV	14,425	C
Martin Univ	IN	11,000	SP
Mary Baldwin College	VA	38,245	C
Marygrove College	MI	28,926	C
Marymount Univ	VA	39,480	C
Marywood Univ	PA	45,595	C
McKendree Univ	IL	29,920	C+
McNeese State Univ	LA	2,649	C
Medaille College	NY	35,112	C
Mercer Univ	GA	44,201	VC
Mercy College	NY	30,456	C
Mercyhurst Univ	PA	40,700	C
Messiah College	PA	40,690	C+
Methodist Univ	NC	37,185	C
Metropolitan State Univ	MN	5,923	
Metropolitan State Univ of Denver	CO	4,835	LC
Miami Univ	OH	24,191	VC
Mich State Univ	MI	22,450	VC
MidAmerica Nazarene Univ	KS	28,000	C
Middle Tenn State Univ	TN	8,650	C
Midwestern State Univ	TX	9,722	C
Miles College	AL	11,164	NC
Minn State Univ, Mankato	MN	15,616	C
Minn State Univ, Moorhead	MN	13,392	VC
Minot State Univ	ND	10,915	C
Miss College	MS	21,998	C
Miss Valley State Univ	MS	9,706	C
Missouri Baptist Univ	MO	31,830	C
Missouri Southern State Univ	MO	12,061	C
Missouri Valley College	MO	22,200	C
Missouri Western State Univ	MO	12,260	NC
Mitchell College	CT	40,983	C
Molloy College	NY	40,440	C
Monmouth Univ	NJ	44,108	C
Monroe College	NY	20,240	C
Montana State Univ-Billings	MT	12,425	LC
Montclair State Univ	NJ	22,614	C
Moravian College	PA	36,381	VC
Morris College	SC	16,310	LC
Mount Aloysius College	PA	29,976	C
Mount Ida College	MA	30,115	LC
Mount Marty College	SD	29,638	C
Mount Mercy Univ	IA	35,320	C
Mount St. Mary's Univ	MD	47,996	C
Mount Vernon Nazarene Univ	OH	29,590	C
Murray State Univ	KY	15,304	C
Muskingum Univ	OH	30,502	C
National Univ	CA	14,730	SP
Neumann Univ	PA	31,078	LC
New England College	NH	45,930	LC
New Jersey City Univ	NJ	21,456	LC
New Mexico State Univ	NM	14,050	C
New York Inst of Technology	NY	45,010	VC
Newbury College	MA	43,280	LC
Newman Univ	KS	30,380	C+
Niagara Univ	NY	41,010	C
Nichols College	MA	37,240	LC
N Car Central Univ	NC	9,000	C
N Car State Univ	NC	16,202	HC
N Car Wesleyan College	NC	29,440	C
N Dak State Univ	ND		C
North Park Univ	IL	30,130	C
Northeastern State Univ	OK	8,615	VC
Northeastern Univ	MA	55,296	MC
Northern Arizona Univ	AZ	19,010	C
Northern Kentucky Univ	KY	21,134	C
Northern Mich Univ	MI	18,278	C
Northern State Univ - Aberdeen	SD	14,505	C
Northwest Nazarene Univ	ID	34,000	C
Northwestern College	MN	24,000	C
Northwestern College of Iowa	IA	36,240	VC
Northwestern Okla State Univ	OK	7,275	NC
Northwestern State Univ of Louisiana	LA	14,368	C
Norwich Univ	VT	28,212	C
Nova Southeastern Univ	FL	37,280	VC
Nyack College	NY	33,250	C
Ohio Dominican Univ	OH	38,380	C+
Ohio Northern Univ	OH	42,075	VC
Ohio Univ	OH	21,080	C
Ohio Valley Univ	WV	17,752	C
Old Dominion Univ	VA	19,483	LC
Olivet College	MI	19,984	LC
Olivet Nazarene Univ	IL	29,990	C
Oswego / SUNY	NY	20,009	VC
Pace Univ	NY	53,367	C
Park Univ	MO	17,525	C
Penn State Univ/Altoona	PA	11,464	C
Pfeiffer Univ	NC	33,700	LC
Piedmont College	GA	30,136	C
Pittsburg State Univ	KS	12,032	C
Plymouth State Univ	NH	23,148	LC
Point Park Univ	PA	36,390	C
Post Univ	CT	35,750	C
Prairie View A&M Univ	TX	15,205	LC
Purdue Univ/Calumet	IN	14,336	C
Purdue Univ/West Lafayette	IN	20,024	HC
Quincy Univ	IL	34,980	LC
Quinnipiac Univ	CT	55,160	VC
Radford Univ	VA	17,766	C
Rhode Island College	RI	17,694	LC
Richard Stockton College of New Jersey	NJ	20,000	VC
Roanoke College	VA	49,976	C
Roberts Wesleyan College	NY	38,306	C+
Rochester Inst of Technology	NY	42,450	VC
Roger Williams Univ	RI	46,296	VC
Rowan Univ	NJ	24,022	VC+
Russell Sage College	NY	39,370	C
Rutgers, The State Univ of New Jersey/Camden Campus	NJ	25,121	C
Rutgers, The State Univ of New Jersey/New Brunswick	NJ	25,562	VC
Rutgers, The State Univ of New Jersey/Newark Campus	NJ	258,806	C
Sacred Heart Univ	CT	49,264	VC
Saginaw Valley State Univ	MI	17,369	C
St. Anselm College	NH	49,376	VC
St. Augustine's Univ	NC	14,000	C
St. Francis Univ	PA	30,029	LC
St. Joseph's College	IN	36,500	C
St. Joseph's College of Maine	ME	31,580	C
St. Joseph's Univ	PA	55,006	VC
St. Leo Univ	FL	30,340	C
St. Louis Univ	MO	48,346	HC
St. Martin's Univ	WA	41,678	C
St. Mary's Univ	TX	33,854	C
St. Mary's Univ of Minn	MN	38,280	C
St. Peter's Univ	NJ	44,240	C
St. Xavier Univ	IL	32,840	C
Salem International Univ	WV	21,090	LC
Salem State Univ	MA	13,161	LC
Salve Regina Univ	RI	48,550	VC
Sam Houston State Univ	TX	17,082	C
Samford Univ	AL	37,060	C+
San Diego State Univ	CA	21,611	C+
San Francisco State Univ	CA	18,514	C
San Jose State Univ	CA	19,133	LC
Savannah State Univ	GA	13,156	C
Seattle Univ	WA	49,035	VC+
Seton Hall Univ	NJ	45,902	C
Seton Hill Univ	PA	35,172	C
Shaw Univ	NC	15,488	C
Shenandoah Univ	VA	39,916	C
Shippensburg Univ of Pennsylvania	PA	20,934	C
Shorter Univ	GA	30,650	LC
Siena Heights Univ	MI	32,040	C
Simpson College	IA	36,086	C+
Sojourner-Douglass College	MD	9,160	LC
Sonoma State Univ	CA	20,541	C
S Car State Univ	SC	6,700	LC
South Univ	GA	36,070	LC
Southeast Missouri State Univ	MO	15,370	LC
Southeastern Louisiana Univ	LA	13,325	C
Southeastern Okla State Univ	OK	7,966	LC
Southeastern Univ	FL	27,201	C
Southern Illinois Univ Carbondale	IL	21,942	C
Southern Illinois Univ Edwardsville	IL	17,532	C
Southern Oregon Univ	OR	17,874	C
Southern Univ and A&M College	LA	9,761	LC
Southern Univ at New Orleans	LA	2,963	NC

ST = STATE   **$IS** = IN-STATE COSTS   **SR** = SELECTOR RATING

School	ST	$IS	SR
Southern Vermont College	VT	30,740	LC
Southern Wesleyan Univ	SC	25,600	C
Southwest Baptist Univ	MO	24,710	C
Southwestern Okla State Univ	OK	9,160	C
St. Ambrose Univ	IA	30,845	C
St. Cloud State Univ	MN	10,600	C
St. Edward's Univ	TX	47,784	C
St. Francis College	NY	34,200	C
St. John's Univ	NY	55,070	C+
St. Joseph's College, New York/Brooklyn Campus	NY	22,630	C
St. Joseph's College, New York/Suffolk Campus	NY	22,630	C
St. Thomas Aquinas College	NY	40,230	C
St. Thomas Univ	FL	32,310	LC
SUNY/Empire State College	NY	6,315	SP
Stephen F. Austin State Univ	TX	14,668	C
Suffolk Univ	MA	47,298	C
Sul Ross State Univ	TX	13,410	LC
Tarleton State Univ	TX	13,489	LC
Temple Univ	PA	24,392	VC
Tenn State Univ	TN	9,048	C
Texas A&M Univ at Commerce	TX	10,496	C
Texas A&M Univ at Corpus Christi	TX	11,544	LC
Texas Christian Univ	TX	49,980	HC
Texas Southern Univ	TX	18,212	LC
Texas State Univ	TX	17,128	C
Texas Wesleyan Univ	TX	31,382	C
Texas Woman's Univ	TX	13,633	LC
The College of St. Rose	NY	26,750	C
The Lincoln Univ	PA	15,154	LC
Ohio State Univ-Columbus Campus	OH	19,887	HC+
The Pennsylvania State Univ - Univ Park	PA	28,022	VC+
The SUNY at Potsdam	NY	18,473	C
The SUNY/College at Brockport	NY	19,002	C
The Univ of Memphis	TN	15,094	C
The Univ of N Car at Pembroke	NC	13,388	LC
The Univ of Okla	OK	18,621	VC
The Univ of Tenn at Chattanooga	TN	16,883	C
The Univ of Virginia's College at Wise	VA	11,076	C
Thiel College	PA	38,728	LC
Thomas College	ME	33,560	LC
Thomas Edison State College	NJ	5,700	SP
Thomas More College	KY	34,760	C
Thomas Univ	GA	11,520	NC
Tiffin Univ	OH	30,273	LC
Trevecca Nazarene Univ	TN	31,186	C
Trine Univ	IN	39,400	HC+
Trinity Christian College	IL	28,869	C
Trinity Washington Univ	DC	30,250	C
Troy Univ	AL	10,650	C
Truman State Univ	MO	15,541	HC
Union College	KY	29,955	C
Union Inst & Univ	OH	8,912	SP
Univ at Albany / SUNY	NY	18,674	VC
Univ of Akron	OH	20,436	C
Univ of Alabama at Birmingham	AL	18,484	C+
Univ of Alabama at Tuscaloosa	AL	17,164	C+
Univ of Arkansas at Fayetteville	AR	18,352	C+
Univ of Arkansas at Little Rock	AR	17,609	LC
Univ of Arkansas at Monticello	AR	12,076	NC
Univ of Arkansas at Pine Bluff	AR	13,378	C
Univ of Bridgeport	CT	39,030	LC
Univ of Central Florida	FL	15,668	VC+
Univ of Central Missouri	MO	14,605	C
Univ of Central Okla	OK	12,293	C
Univ of Cincinnati	OH	21,506	VC
Univ of Colo Denver	CO	17,904	C
Univ of Dayton	OH	49,070	VC
Univ of Delaware	DE	23,612	VC
Univ of Detroit Mercy	MI	30,450	VC
Univ of Evansville	IN	42,656	VC+
Univ of Findlay	OH	31,916	C
Univ of Georgia	GA	20,082	VC
Univ of Great Falls	MT	27,970	C
Univ of Hartford	CT	42,674	C
Univ of Hawaii at Hilo	HI	23,066	C
Univ of Houston-Downtown	TX	15,170	LC
Univ of Idaho	ID	14,558	C
Univ of Illinois at Chicago	IL	24,505	VC
Univ of Jamestown	ND	24,738	C
Univ of Louisiana at Lafayette	LA	6,130	C
Univ of Louisiana at Monroe	LA	15,195	LC
Univ of Louisville	KY	17,946	C
Univ of Maine at Fort Kent	ME	15,195	LC
Univ of Maine at Presque Isle	ME	15,011	LC
Univ of Mary	ND	16,714	C
Univ of Mary Hardin-Baylor	TX	31,950	C
Univ of Maryland - College Park	MD	20,060	HC

School	ST	$IS	SR
Univ of Maryland/Eastern Shore	MD	14,000	VC
Univ of Maryland/Univ College	MD	6,168	SP
Univ of Mass Boston	MA	23,066	VC
Univ of Mass Dartmouth	MA	22,223	C
Univ of Mass Lowell	MA	19,316	C
Univ of Mich/Dearborn	MI	9,885	VC
Univ of Mich-Flint	MI	17,547	C+
Univ of Minn Crookston	MN	17,834	C
Univ of Miss	MS	16,704	C+
Univ of Missouri-Kansas City	MO	19,603	C
Univ of Missouri-St. Louis	MO		VC
Univ of Montana-Western	MT	9,753	LC
Univ of Mount Olive	NC	18,426	C
Univ of Mount Union	OH	35,130	C
Univ of Nebr at Kearney	NE	14,855	LC
Univ of Nebr at Omaha	NE	12,700	C
Univ of Nevada, Las Vegas	NV	17,303	C
Univ of Nevada/Reno	NV	17,507	C
Univ of New Haven	CT	48,940	C
Univ of North Alabama	AL	9,960	C
Univ of N Car at Charlotte	NC	15,547	C
Univ of N Car at Wilmington	NC	13,572	VC
Univ of N Dak	ND	14,551	C
Univ of North Florida	FL	15,870	VC
Univ of North Georgia	GA	8,500	C
Univ of North Texas	TX	15,628	C
Univ of Northern Colo	CO	18,446	C
Univ of Pikeville	KY	25,500	NC
Univ of Pittsburgh at Bradford	PA	21,802	C
Univ of Pittsburgh at Johnstown	PA	20,862	LC
Univ of Scranton	PA	51,940	VC
Univ of South Alabama	AL	13,510	C
Univ of S Car at Columbia	SC	19,725	VC+
Univ of S Car Upstate	SC	18,200	LC
Univ of S Dak	SD	15,111	C
Univ of Southern Indiana	IN	14,885	C
Univ of Southern Miss	MS	13,170	C
Univ of St. Francis	IL	37,560	C
Univ of Tenn at Martin	TN	13,734	C
Univ of Texas - Pan American	TX	11,125	LC
Univ of Texas at Arlington	TX	10,908	LC
Univ of Texas at El Paso	TX	8,764	NC
Univ of Texas at San Antonio	TX	18,372	C
Univ of the Cumberlands	KY	27,500	C
Univ of the District of Columbia	DC	7,244	C
Univ of the Sacred Heart	PR	5,590	
Univ of the Southwest	NM	15,000	C
Univ of Toledo	OH	18,464	C
Univ of West Florida	FL	14,656	C
Univ of Wisc/Eau Claire	WI	15,730	VC
Univ of Wisc/Oshkosh	WI	10,426	C
Univ of Wisc/Platteville	WI	14,564	C
Univ of Wisc/Superior	WI	14,314	C
Univ of Wisc-Milwaukee	WI	18,436	C
Univ of Wyoming	WY	14,401	C+
Urbana Univ	OH	30,820	C
Utica College	NY	45,670	C
Villanova Univ	PA	58,394	MC
Virginia Commonwealth Univ	VA	21,716	C
Virginia Wesleyan College	VA	28,433	LC
Viterbo Univ	WI	30,070	C
Voorhees College	SC	18,126	C
Walsh Univ	OH	35,100	C
Washburn Univ	KS	12,579	C
Washington State Univ	WA	20,461	C
Wayland Baptist Univ	TX	18,912	LC
Wayne State College	NE	11,764	NC
Wayne State Univ	MI	22,063	C
Waynesburg Univ	PA	30,150	C
West Chester Univ of Pennsylvania	PA	17,186	C
West Liberty Univ	WV	9,142	LC
West Texas A&M Univ	TX	13,478	C
West Virginia State Univ	WV	8,378	NC
Western Carolina Univ	NC	13,965	C
Western Conn State Univ	CT	18,327	LC
Western Illinois Univ	IL	20,732	C
Western Mich Univ	MI	19,628	C
Western New England Univ	MA	46,154	C+
Westfield State Univ	MA	18,297	C
Westminster College	PA	31,290	C+
Westminster College	UT	37,708	C+
Wheeling Jesuit Univ	WV	33,500	C
Wichita State Univ	KS	14,607	C+
Widener Univ	PA	52,418	C
Wilmington College	OH	29,784	C
Wilmington Univ	DE	8,112	NC
Wingate Univ	NC	34,990	C
Winona State Univ	MN	16,640	C
Worcester State Univ	MA	19,812	C
Wright State Univ	OH	16,983	C
Xavier Univ	OH	44,980	VC
York College of Pennsylvania	PA	26,590	C
Youngstown State Univ	OH	16,732	C

CRIMINOLOGY

School	ST	$IS	SR
Adams State Univ	CO	13,358	LC
Alabama A&M Univ	AL	10,084	C

School	ST	$IS	SR
Albertus Magnus College	CT	37,382	LC
Alderson Broaddus Univ	WV	28,656	C
Arkansas State Univ	AR	15,470	C
Assumption College	MA	47,122	C+
Auburn Univ	AL	22,378	VC+
Barry Univ	FL	38,190	C
Cabrini College	PA	40,859	LC
Cal State, Fresno	CA	17,405	C
Cal State, Long Beach	CA	17,502	C+
Cal State, Northridge	CA	28,690	LC
Cal State, San Marcos	CA	14,576	LC
Cazenovia College	NY	43,464	C
Central Conn State Univ	CT	19,749	C
Clarke Univ	IA	37,600	C
Cleveland State Univ	OH	21,776	C
Coker College	SC	32,256	LC
College of Mount St. Joseph	OH	33,880	C
College of the Ozarks	MO		VC
Colo State Univ-Pueblo	CO	16,183	C
Drexel Univ	PA	61,418	VC+
Drury Univ	MO	31,909	VC
Faulkner Univ	AL	25,720	LC
Florida Gulf Coast Univ	FL		C
Florida Southern College	FL	40,150	C+
Florida State Univ	FL	16,715	VC
Framingham State Univ	MA	18,854	C
Hilbert College	NY	28,550	C
Hofstra Univ	NY	51,810	VC+
Indiana Inst of Technology	IN	34,240	C
Indiana State Univ	IN	16,000	C
Indiana Univ of Pennsylvania	PA	20,846	LC
Indiana Univ Southeast	IN	16,035	C
John Carroll Univ	OH	46,300	C+
John Jay College of Criminal Justice/The CUNY	NY	6,359	C
Kent State Univ	OH	19,920	C
Le Moyne College	NY	43,470	C
Longwood Univ	VA	20,924	C
Lycoming College	PA	45,379	C
Lynchburg College	VA	42,645	C
Marquette Univ	WI	46,930	VC+
Maryville Univ of St. Louis	MO	35,856	VC
Millersville Univ of Pennsylvania	PA	21,648	C
Missouri State Univ	MO	13,996	C+
Mount Aloysius College	PA	29,976	C
Niagara Univ	NY	41,010	C
Northern Arizona Univ	AZ	19,010	C
Ohio Univ	OH	21,080	C
Pontifical Catholic Univ of PR	PR	7,310	
St. Mary-of-the-Woods College	IN	37,722	LC
Southern Oregon Univ	OR	17,874	C
St. Ambrose Univ	IA	30,845	C
St. Edward's Univ	TX	47,784	C
St. John Fisher College	NY	40,708	C+
Stonehill College	MA	46,780	HC
SUNY College at Old Westbury	NY	16,324	C
Ohio State Univ-Columbus Campus	OH	19,887	HC+
The Pennsylvania State Univ - Univ Park	PA	28,022	VC+
The Univ of Memphis	TN	15,094	C
Universidad del Turabo	PR	4,110	
Univ of Akron	OH	20,436	C
Univ of Calif at Irvine	CA	25,961	VC
Univ of Denver	CO	51,787	VC+
Univ of Florida	FL	15,943	HC
Univ of Illinois at Chicago	IL	24,505	VC
Univ of La Verne	CA	47,010	C
Univ of Maryland - College Park	MD	20,060	HC
Univ of Miami	FL	57,034	MC
Univ of Minn/Duluth	MN	19,806	C
Univ of New Haven	CT	48,940	C
Univ of New Mexico	NM	15,300	C
Univ of Northern Iowa	IA	15,795	C
Univ of St. Mary	KS	28,400	C+
Univ of South Florida/St. Petersburg	FL	12,769	C
Univ of South Florida/Tampa	FL	13,000	C
Univ of Tampa	FL	35,160	VC
Univ of Texas at Dallas	TX	21,348	NC+
Univ of West Georgia	GA	15,488	LC
Upper Iowa Univ	IA	30,426	NC
Valparaiso Univ	IN	44,940	VC+
Virginia Union Univ	VA	18,432	C
Wilkes Univ	PA	44,070	C
William Penn Univ	IA	26,000	C

CROSSCULTURAL STUDIES

School	ST	$IS	SR
Alfred Univ	NY	41,770	C
Andrews Univ	MI	28,030	C+
Bard College at Simon's Rock	MA	61,749	HC+
Biola Univ	CA	40,320	C+
Chatham Univ	PA	43,797	C
Columbia College Chicago	IL	30,940	LC
Corban Univ	OR	37,380	C+
Goddard College	VT	16,418	VC
Hampshire College	MA	64,320	MC
Hope International Univ	CA	34,650	C
Houghton College	NY	36,808	C+
John Brown Univ	AR	32,056	VC+

School	ST	$IS	SR
Kentucky Christian Univ	KY	17,622	LC
Lee Univ	TN	18,690	C+
Linfield College-McMinnville Campus	OR	47,676	C
National Louis Univ	IL	16,915	LC
Northern Arizona Univ	AZ	19,010	C
Northwestern College	MN	24,000	C
Nyack College	NY	33,250	C
Olivet Nazarene Univ	IL	39,990	C
Palm Beach Atlantic Univ	FL	34,874	C+
Rollins College	FL	52,370	HC
Simpson Univ	CA	28,900	C
Stanford Univ	CA	58,388	MC
Toccoa Falls College	GA	23,210	LC
Towson Univ	MD	16,000	C
Villanova Univ	PA	58,394	MC
Washington State Univ	WA	20,461	C
Whitworth Univ	WA	47,734	VC
Wofford College	SC	45,795	VC

CULINARY ARTS

School	ST	$IS	SR
Art Inst of Atlanta	GA	24,000	SP
Atlantic Union College	MA	24,600	C
College of the Ozarks	MO		VC
Drexel Univ	PA	61,418	VC+
Idaho State Univ	ID	12,307	C
Kendall College	IL	32,610	NC
Kennesaw State Univ	GA		C
Livingstone College	NC	17,815	LC
Miss Univ for Women	MS	7,400	C
Pennsylvania College of Technology	PA	26,286	NC
Southern New Hampshire Univ	NH	38,100	C
The SUNY College of Agriculture and Tech at Cobleskill	NY	19,749	LC
Univ of Alaska Anchorage	AK	16,673	NC
Univ of Nebr - Lincoln	NE	18,031	VC
Univ of New Hampshire	NH	26,912	C

CULTURAL ANTHROPOLOGY

School	ST	$IS	SR
Creighton Univ	NE	45,356	VC
Webster Univ	MO	35,100	C+

CULTURAL STUDIES/CRITICAL THEORY & ANALYSIS

School	ST	$IS	SR
Arizona State Univ, at the West Campus	AZ	19,251	C
Bard College at Simon's Rock	MA	61,749	HC+
Dallas Baptist Univ	TX	30,580	VC
Goddard College	VT	16,418	VC
Indiana Univ Bloomington	IN	19,801	VC
Northwest Nazarene Univ	ID	34,000	C
Occidental College	CA	60,972	MC

CUSTOMER SERVICE

School	ST	$IS	SR
Ohio Univ	OH	21,080	C

CYBER INTELLIGENCE/ SECURITY STUDIES

School	ST	$IS	SR
Auburn Univ at Montgomery	AL	14,470	LC
Champlain College	VT	46,650	VC+
Embry-Riddle Aeronautical Univ - Prescott Campus	AZ	40,444	VC+
Excelsior College	NY	5,580	SP
Montreat College	NC	31,298	C
Southeast Missouri State Univ	MO	15,370	LC
Trine Univ	IN	39,400	HC+

CYTOTECHNOLOGY

School	ST	$IS	SR
Barry Univ	FL	38,190	C
Bloomfield College	NJ	37,850	LC
Edgewood College	WI	33,294	C
Indiana Univ-Purdue Univ Indianapolis	IN	17,611	C
Marian Univ	WI	32,420	C
Marshall Univ	WV	14,820	C
Mass College of Liberal Arts	MA	18,613	C
Northern Mich Univ	MI	18,278	C
Old Dominion Univ	VA	19,483	LC
St. Louis Univ	MO	48,346	HC
St. Mary's Univ of Minn	MN	38,280	C
Stony Brook Univ / SUNY	NY	20,078	HC+
SUNY Plattsburgh / SUNY	NY	18,083	C
The College of St. Rose	NY	26,750	C
Thiel College	PA	38,728	LC
United States Naval Academy	MD		MC
Univ of Conn	CT	24,706	HC
Univ of Kansas	KS	17,603	C+
Univ of Mass Dartmouth	MA	22,223	C
Univ of Miss	MS	16,704	C+
Univ of N Dak	ND	14,551	C
Univ of North Texas	TX	15,628	C
Winona State Univ	MN	16,640	C

DAIRY SCIENCE

School	ST	$IS	SR
Calif Polytechnic State Univ	CA	19,847	HC

School	ST	$IS	SR
Cal State, Fresno	CA	17,405	C
Delaware Valley College	PA	29,944	C
Iowa State Univ	IA	16,403	C
S Dak State Univ	SD	14,296	C
Texas A&M Univ	TX	19,207	C
Univ of Florida	FL	15,943	HC
Univ of Georgia	GA	20,082	VC
Univ of Idaho	ID	14,558	C
Univ of New Hampshire	NH	26,912	C
Univ of Wisc/Madison	WI	18,757	HC+
Utah State Univ	UT	12,044	C
Virginia Polytechnic Inst and State Univ	VA	14,629	HC

DANCE

School	ST	$IS	SR
Adelphi Univ	NY	44,670	C
Agnes Scott College	GA	45,323	C+
Alma College	MI	44,075	C
Amherst College	MA	58,744	MC
Appalachian State Univ	NC	12,919	VC
Arizona State Univ, at the Tempe Campus	AZ	20,137	C+
Ball State Univ	IN	17,850	C
Bard College	NY	61,940	MC
Bard College at Simon's Rock	MA	61,749	HC+
Barnard College/Columbia Univ	NY	39,000	MC
Belhaven Univ	MS	27,170	C
Beloit College	WI	49,970	HC
Bennington College	VT	56,990	HC+
Binghamton Univ/The SUNY	NY	21,648	HC+
Birmingham-Southern College	AL	44,168	VC+
Boston Conservatory	MA	56,380	VC
Bowling Green State Univ	OH	18,970	C
Brenau Univ - Women's College	GA	26,650	LC
Brigham Young Univ	UT	12,100	HC
Butler Univ	IN	47,572	VC+
Calif Inst of the Arts	CA	51,902	SP
Cal State, Fullerton	CA	25,188	C
Cal State, Long Beach	CA	17,502	C+
Cal State, Northridge	CA	28,690	LC
Cal State, San Bernardino	CA	12,000	C
Case Western Reserve Univ	OH	56,534	MC
Cedar Crest College	PA	43,240	C
Centenary College of Louisiana	LA	45,650	C+
Chapman Univ	CA	58,347	VC+
Coker College	SC	32,256	LC
College of Charleston	SC	22,145	VC
Colo College	CO	57,162	MC
Colo State Univ-Fort Collins	CO	20,385	VC
Columbia College	SC	27,882	C
Columbia College Chicago	IL	30,940	LC
Columbia Univ/City of New York	NY	61,116	MC
Columbia Univ/School of General Studies	NY	58,231	MC
Conn College	CT	54,970	MC
Cornish College of the Arts	WA	21,200	SP
Creighton Univ	NE	45,356	VC
De Sales Univ	PA	43,970	C
Denison Univ	OH	54,670	HC+
Dickinson College	PA	57,662	HC+
Dominican Univ of Calif	CA	51,250	C
East Carolina Univ	NC	14,169	C
Eastern Mich Univ	MI	18,604	C
Eastern Univ	PA	37,704	C
Eastern Washington Univ	WA		C
Elon Univ	NC	41,914	VC+
Emory Univ	GA	56,368	MC
Eugene Lang College/The New School for Liberal Arts	NY	55,650	C
Florida Southern College	FL	40,150	C+
Florida State Univ	FL	16,715	VC
Fordham Univ	NY	61,588	HC+
Franklin Pierce Univ	NH	41,598	C
George Mason Univ	VA	15,724	VC
George Washington Univ	DC	55,624	MC
Georgian Court Univ	NJ	41,594	LC
Goucher College	MD	52,040	VC+
Grand Valley State Univ	MI	17,998	C
Gustavus Adolphus College	MN	48,170	HC
Hamilton College	NY	55,620	MC
Hampshire College	MA	58,320	MC
Hobart and William Smith Colleges	NY	60,034	HC+
Hofstra Univ	NY	51,810	VC+
Hollins Univ	VA	43,295	VC
Hope College	MI	38,650	VC
Howard Univ	DC	13,646	C
Hunter College	NY	14,429	VC
Indiana Univ Bloomington	IN	19,801	VC
Jacksonville Univ	FL	37,780	C
James Madison Univ	VA	18,049	VC
Juilliard School	NY	44,460	SP
Kennesaw State Univ	GA		C
Kent State Univ	OH	19,920	C
Kenyon College	OH	58,890	MC
La Roche College	PA	35,824	LC
Lehman College/The CUNY	NY	5,778	LC
Lindenwood Univ	MO	20,750	C
LIU Brooklyn	NY	47,182	LC
LIU Post	NY	47,660	C
Loyola Marymount Univ	CA	54,649	VC+
Loyola Univ Chicago	IL	51,646	VC+
Luther College	IA	45,720	C+
Manhattanville College	NY	50,740	VC
Marlboro College	VT	35,980	VC
Marygrove College	MI	28,926	C
Marymount Manhattan College	NY	40,118	VC
Mercyhurst Univ	PA	40,700	C
Meredith College	NC	31,420	C
Messiah College	PA	40,690	C+
Middlebury College	VT	59,160	MC
Mills College	CA	54,119	VC
Minn State Univ, Mankato	MN	15,616	C
Montclair State Univ	NJ	22,614	C
Mount Holyoke College	MA	55,146	MC
Muhlenberg College	PA	52,837	HC
New Mexico State Univ	NM	14,050	C
New York Univ	NY	61,470	MC
Northeastern Illinois Univ	IL	10,318	LC
Northwestern Univ	IL	61,640	MC
Nova Southeastern Univ	FL	37,280	VC
Oakland Univ	MI	19,391	C
Oberlin College	OH	61,788	MC
Ohio Univ	OH	21,080	C
Okla City Univ	OK	40,476	VC
Old Dominion Univ	VA	19,483	LC
Oral Roberts Univ	OK	31,734	C
Pace Univ	NY	53,367	C
Palm Beach Atlantic Univ	FL	34,874	C+
Pitzer College	CA	54,988	MC
Point Park Univ	PA	36,390	C
Pomona College	CA	57,680	MC
Prescott College	AZ	33,284	C
Queens College/The CUNY	NY	17,107	VC
Radford Univ	VA	17,766	LC
Randolph College	VA	45,660	VC
Rhode Island College	RI	17,694	LC
Richard Stockton College of New Jersey	NJ	20,000	VC
Rider Univ	NJ	45,720	C
Roger Williams Univ	RI	46,296	VC
Rutgers, The State Univ of New Jersey/New Brunswick	NJ	25,562	VC
Sam Houston State Univ	TX	17,082	C
San Diego State Univ	CA	21,611	C+
San Francisco State Univ	CA	18,514	C
San Jose State Univ	CA	19,133	LC
Santa Fe Univ of Art and Design	NM	39,666	SP
Sarah Lawrence College	NY	48,000	HC
Scripps College	CA	61,940	MC
Shenandoah Univ	VA	39,916	C
Skidmore College	NY	59,942	HC
Slippery Rock Univ of Pennsylvania	PA	10,360	C
Smith College	MA	59,674	MC
Southeast Missouri State Univ	MO	15,370	LC
Southern Illinois Univ Edwardsville	IL	17,532	C
Southern Methodist Univ	TX	60,585	MC
St. Olaf College	MN	51,200	HC+
SUNY at Purchase	NY	16,951	C
Stephen F. Austin State Univ	TX	14,668	C
Stephens College	MO	38,042	VC
SUNY Fredonia/The SUNY at Fredonia	NY	19,840	VC
Swarthmore College	PA	57,870	MC
Temple Univ	PA	24,392	VC
Texas State Univ	TX	17,128	C
Texas Tech Univ	TX	14,243	C
Texas Woman's Univ	TX	13,633	LC
Ohio State Univ-Columbus Campus	OH	19,887	HC+
The SUNY at Potsdam	NY	18,473	C
The SUNY/College at Brockport	NY	19,002	C
The Univ of N Car at Greensboro	NC	12,848	C
Towson Univ	MD	16,000	VC
Trinity College	CT		HC+
Tulane Univ	LA	60,861	MC
Univ at Buffalo / The SUNY	NY	20,283	VC
Univ of Akron	OH	20,436	C
Univ of Alabama at Tuscaloosa	AL	17,164	C
Univ of Arizona	AZ	20,657	C
Univ of Arkansas at Little Rock	AR	17,609	LC
Univ of Calif at Berkeley	CA	23,322	MC
Univ of Calif at Irvine	CA	25,961	VC
Univ of Calif at Riverside	CA	27,204	C
Univ of Calif at San Diego	CA	21,000	VC
Univ of Calif at Santa Barbara	CA	27,551	HC
Univ of Central Okla	OK	12,293	C
Univ of Cincinnati	OH	21,506	VC
Univ of Colo Boulder	CO	22,605	VC+
Univ of Florida	FL	15,943	HC
Univ of Georgia	GA	20,082	VC
Univ of Hartford	CT	42,674	C
Univ of Hawaii at Manoa	HI	19,379	C
Univ of Houston	TX	19,796	VC
Univ of Idaho	ID	14,558	C
Univ of Illinois at Urbana-Champaign	IL	26,450	HC
Univ of Iowa	IA	17,693	VC
Univ of Kansas	KS	17,603	C+
Univ of Louisiana at Lafayette	LA	6,130	C
Univ of Maryland - College Park	MD	20,060	HC
Univ of Maryland/Baltimore County	MD	18,000	VC
Univ of Mass Amherst	MA	24,215	VC+
Univ of Mich/Ann Arbor	MI	22,102	MC
Univ of Minn/Twin Cities	MN		HC
Univ of Missouri-Kansas City	MO	19,603	C
Univ of Missouri-St. Louis	MO		VC
Univ of Nebr - Lincoln	NE	18,031	VC
Univ of Nevada, Las Vegas	NV	17,303	C
Univ of New Mexico	NM	15,300	C
Univ of N Car at Charlotte	NC	15,547	C
Univ of N Car School of the Arts	NC	7,401	SP
Univ of North Texas	TX	15,628	C
Univ of Oregon	OR	21,360	C+
Univ of S Car at Columbia	SC	19,725	VC+
Univ of South Florida/Tampa	FL	13,000	C
Univ of Southern Miss	MS	13,170	C
Univ of Texas - Pan American	TX	11,125	LC
Univ of Texas at Austin	TX	44,074	HC
Univ of the Arts	PA	38,450	SP
Univ of Washington	WA	14,722	VC
Univ of Wisc/Madison	WI	18,757	HC+
Univ of Wisc/Stevens Point	WI	14,043	C
Univ of Wisc-Milwaukee	WI	18,436	C
Ursinus College	PA	57,580	VC
Utah State Univ	UT	12,044	C
Virginia Commonwealth Univ	VA	21,716	C
Washington Univ in St. Louis	MO	69,844	MC
Wayne State Univ	MI	22,063	C
Webster Univ	MO	35,100	C+
Wells College	NY	49,400	VC
Wesleyan Univ	CT	61,198	MC
West Chester Univ of Pennsylvania	PA	17,186	C
West Texas A&M Univ	TX	13,478	C
Western Mich Univ	MI	19,628	C
Western Oregon Univ	OR	15,021	C
Western Washington Univ	WA	18,519	VC
Wheaton College	MA	54,934	HC+
Whitman College	WA	55,988	MC
Winthrop Univ	SC	21,120	C
Wright State Univ	OH	16,983	C
Youngstown State Univ	OH	16,732	C

DANCE EDUCATION

School	ST	$IS	SR
Birmingham-Southern College	AL	44,168	VC+
Brenau Univ - Women's College	GA	26,650	LC
Bridgewater State Univ	MA	18,752	C
Brigham Young Univ	UT	12,100	HC
Columbia College	SC	27,882	C
East Carolina Univ	NC	14,169	C
Grand Canyon Univ	AZ	24,540	VC
Hofstra Univ	NY	51,810	VC+
Hope College	MI	38,650	VC
Jacksonville Univ	FL	37,780	C
Marywood Univ	PA	45,595	C
Minn State Univ, Mankato	MN	15,616	C
New York Univ	NY	61,470	MC
Old Dominion Univ	VA	19,483	LC
Point Park Univ	PA	36,390	C
Ohio State Univ-Columbus Campus	OH	19,887	HC+
The Univ of N Car at Greensboro	NC	12,848	C
Towson Univ	MD	16,000	VC
Univ of Central Okla	OK	12,293	C
Univ of the Arts	PA	38,450	SP

DATA PROCESSING

School	ST	$IS	SR
Northwest Missouri State Univ	MO	17,347	C

DENTAL EDUCATION

School	ST	$IS	SR
Indiana Univ South Bend	IN	15,501	C
Thomas Edison State College	NJ	5,700	SP

DENTAL HYGIENE

School	ST	$IS	SR
Allen College	IA	26,110	SP
Clayton State Univ	GA	12,000	LC
Creighton Univ	NE	45,356	VC
East Tenn State Univ	TN	9,000	C
Eastern Washington Univ	WA		C
Farmingdale State College	NY	19,673	C
Ferris State Univ	MI	20,047	C
Georgia Regents Univ	GA		C
Howard Univ	DC	13,646	C
Idaho State Univ	ID	12,307	C
Indiana Univ Northwest	IN	6,854	LC
Indiana Univ South Bend	IN	15,501	C
Indiana Univ-Purdue Univ Indianapolis	IN	17,611	C
Mass College of Pharmacy and Health Sciences	MA	36,450	SP
Metropolitan State Univ	MN	5,923	
Midwestern State Univ	TX	9,722	C
Minn State Univ, Mankato	MN	15,616	C
Missouri Southern State Univ	MO	12,061	C
New York Univ	NY	61,470	MC
Northern Arizona Univ	AZ	19,010	C
Ohio State Univ at Lima	OH	7,140	C
Old Dominion Univ	VA	19,483	LC
Oregon Inst of Technology	OR	8,910	C
Pennsylvania College of Technology	PA	26,286	NC
Rhode Island College	RI	17,694	LC
Southern Illinois Univ Carbondale	IL	21,942	C
Tenn State Univ	TN	9,048	C
Texas Woman's Univ	TX	13,633	LC
Ohio State Univ-Columbus Campus	OH	19,887	HC+
Thomas Edison State College	NJ	5,700	SP
Univ of Alaska Anchorage	AK	16,673	NC
Univ of Bridgeport	CT	39,030	LC
Univ of Detroit Mercy	MI	30,450	VC
Univ of Hawaii at Manoa	HI	19,379	C
Univ of Illinois at Chicago	IL	24,505	VC
Univ of Louisiana at Monroe	LA	12,998	C
Univ of Louisville	KY	17,946	C
Univ of Maine at Augusta	ME	6,855	C
Univ of Mich/Ann Arbor	MI	22,102	MC
Univ of Minn/Twin Cities	MN		HC
Univ of Miss	MS	16,704	C+
Univ of Missouri-Kansas City	MO	19,603	C
Univ of New England	ME	46,750	C
Univ of New Haven	CT	48,940	C
Univ of New Mexico	NM	15,300	C
Univ of N Car at Chapel Hill	NC	18,928	HC
Univ of Pittsburgh at Pittsburgh	PA	28,572	HC+
Univ of S Dak	SD	15,111	C
Univ of Southern Calif	CA	56,903	MC
Univ of Southern Indiana	IN	14,885	C
Univ of Tenn at Knoxville	TN	20,364	VC+
Univ of Washington	WA	14,722	VC
Univ of Wyoming	WY	14,401	C+
Virginia Commonwealth Univ	VA	21,716	C
West Liberty Univ	WV	9,142	LC
West Virginia Univ	WV	16,542	LC
Western Kentucky Univ	KY	11,000	LC
Youngstown State Univ	OH	16,732	C

DENTAL LABORATORY TECHNOLOGY

School	ST	$IS	SR
Minot State Univ	ND	10,915	C
Southern Illinois Univ Carbondale	IL	21,942	C
Southwest Minn State Univ	MN	14,000	C
Univ of Louisiana at Monroe	LA	12,998	C

DESIGN

School	ST	$IS	SR
Adams State Univ	CO	13,358	LC
Adelphi Univ	NY	44,670	C
Andrews Univ	MI	28,030	C+
Arizona State Univ, at the Tempe Campus	AZ	20,137	C+
Art Center College of Design	CA	34,044	SP
Auburn Univ	AL	22,378	VC+
Becker College	MA	41,420	C
Belmont Univ	TN	39,190	VC+
Bennington College	VT	56,990	HC+
Boston Architectural College	MA	18,622	SP
Bowling Green State Univ	OH	18,970	C
Buffalo State College / SUNY	NY	15,733	C+
Cal State, Long Beach	CA	17,502	C+
Carnegie Mellon Univ	PA	51,260	MC
Clemson Univ	SC	19,136	HC
College of Art and Design at Lesley Univ	MA	39,730	SP
Concordia Univ St. Paul	MN	28,250	C
Cornish College of the Arts	WA	21,200	SP
Drexel Univ	PA	61,418	VC+
Drury Univ	MO	31,909	VC
East Carolina Univ	NC	14,169	C
Eastern Mich Univ	MI	18,604	C
Evangel Univ	MO	23,090	C
Fashion Inst of Technology/SUNY	NY	18,362	SP
Grand Valley State Univ	MI	17,998	C+
Harding Univ	AR	23,556	C
Hofstra Univ	NY	51,810	VC+
Howard Univ	DC	13,646	C
Iowa State Univ	IA	16,403	C
John Brown Univ	AR	32,056	VC+
Kansas City Art Inst	MO	44,308	SP
Lamar Univ	TX	6,820	LC
Lees-McRae College	NC	33,944	C
Lehigh Univ	PA	56,770	MC
Memphis College of Art	TN	33,550	SP
Minneapolis College of Art and Design	MN	36,700	SP
Missouri State Univ	MO	13,996	C+

ST = STATE $IS = IN-STATE COSTS   SR = SELECTOR RATING

School	ST	$IS	SR
National Univ	CA	14,730	SP
New York Univ	NY	61,470	MC
N Car State Univ	NC	16,202	HC
Northern Mich Univ	MI	18,278	C
Ohio Univ	OH	21,080	C
Okla Christian Univ	OK	25,870	VC
Okla State Univ	OK	14,310	VC
Olivet College	MI	19,984	LC
Otis College of Art and Design	CA	35,404	SP
Parsons The New School for Design	NY	56,610	SP
Radford Univ	VA	17,766	LC
Rochester Inst of Technology	NY	42,450	VC
Saginaw Valley State Univ	MI	17,369	C
Salem State Univ	MA	13,161	LC
San Francisco State Univ	CA	18,514	C
San Jose State Univ	CA	19,133	LC
Savannah College of Art and Design	GA	48,005	SP
School of the Art Inst of Chicago	IL	56,230	SP
Southern Illinois Univ Carbondale	IL	21,942	C
Texas Tech Univ	TX	14,243	C
The Pennsylvania State Univ - Univ Park	PA	28,022	VC+
The Univ of Utah	UT	16,463	VC
Troy Univ	AL	10,650	C
Tusculum College	TN	24,295	C
Univ of Calif at Davis	CA		HC
Univ of Cincinnati	OH	21,506	VC
Univ of Hartford	CT	42,674	C
Univ of Idaho	ID	14,558	C
Univ of Kansas	KS	17,603	C+
Univ of Mich/Ann Arbor	MI	22,102	MC
Univ of Missouri/Columbia	MO	18,201	MC
Univ of New Haven	CT	48,940	C
Univ of North Texas	TX	15,628	C
Univ of Notre Dame	IN	57,117	MC
Univ of Oregon	OR	21,360	C+
Univ of Pennsylvania	PA	61,132	MC
Univ of San Francisco	CA	54,770	VC
Univ of Southern Miss	MS	13,170	C
Univ of Texas at Austin	TX	44,074	HC
Univ of Wisc/Green Bay	WI	19,074	C
Washington Univ in St. Louis	MO	69,844	MC
Wayne State Univ	MI	22,063	C
Western Kentucky Univ	KY	11,000	LC
Western Washington Univ	WA	18,519	VC
Xavier Univ	OH	44,980	VC
Youngstown State Univ	OH	16,732	C

DESIGN AND ENVIRONMENTAL ANALYSIS

School	ST	$IS	SR
Cornell Univ	NY	60,964	MC

DEVELOPMENT ECONOMICS

School	ST	$IS	SR
Calvin College	MI	39,120	VC
Eastern Mennonite Univ	VA	40,660	C
Taylor Univ	IN	37,821	VC+

DEVELOPMENTAL PSYCHOLOGY

School	ST	$IS	SR
Boston College	MA	60,622	MC
Brown Univ	RI	59,428	MC
Cal State, Stanislaus	CA	18,582	C
Emmanuel College	MA	47,985	VC
Fitchburg State Univ	MA	18,173	C
Metropolitan State Univ	MN	5,923	
New York Univ	NY	61,470	MC
Univ of Kansas	KS	17,603	C+

DEVELOPMENTAL SOCIOLOGY

School	ST	$IS	SR
Cornell Univ	NY	60,964	MC

DIAGNOSTIC MEDICAL SONOGRAPHY

School	ST	$IS	SR
Carroll Univ	WI	38,100	C
Mount Mary Univ	WI	33,590	LC
Nova Southeastern Univ	FL	37,280	VC
Thomas Edison State College	NJ	5,700	SP
Univ of Charleston	WV	32,300	C

DIETETICS

School	ST	$IS	SR
Andrews Univ	MI	28,030	C+
Arkansas State Univ	AR	15,470	C
Ball State Univ	IN	17,850	VC
Baylor Univ	TX	50,329	HC
Bowling Green State Univ	OH	18,970	C
Bradley Univ	IL	31,874	VC
Brigham Young Univ	UT	12,100	HC
Buffalo State College / SUNY	NY	15,733	C+
Cal State, Chico	CA	20,158	C
Cal State, Los Angeles	CA	17,186	LC
College of the Ozarks	MO		VC
Dominican Univ	IL	37,628	C
D'Youville College	NY	29,850	C
East Carolina Univ	NC	14,169	C
Eastern Kentucky Univ	KY	11,161	C

School	ST	$IS	SR
Eastern Mich Univ	MI	18,604	C
Florida International Univ	FL	17,747	C+
Florida State Univ	FL	16,715	VC
Fontbonne Univ	MO	31,384	C
Harding Univ	AR	23,556	C
Idaho State Univ	ID	12,307	C
Immaculata Univ	PA	43,000	C
Indiana State Univ	IN	16,000	C
Iowa State Univ	IA	16,403	C
James Madison Univ	VA	18,049	VC
Kansas State Univ	KS	15,497	VC
Lehman College/The CUNY	NY	5,778	LC
Lipscomb Univ	TN	37,490	VC
Louisiana Tech Univ	LA	11,302	C
Madonna Univ	MI	24,540	VC
Mansfield Univ	PA	19,468	LC
Marshall Univ	WV	14,820	C
Marywood Univ	PA	45,595	C
Messiah College	PA	40,690	C+
Mich State Univ	MI	22,450	VC
Minn State Univ, Mankato	MN	15,616	C
Missouri State Univ	MO	13,996	C+
Montclair State Univ	NJ	22,614	C
Mount Mary Univ	WI	33,590	LC
Nicholls State Univ	LA	7,095	C
N Dak State Univ	ND		C
Northern Illinois Univ	IL	19,768	C
Oakwood Univ	AL	25,529	NC
Olivet Nazarene Univ	IL	29,990	C
Ouachita Baptist Univ	AR	30,220	VC
Point Loma Nazarene Univ	CA	41,006	C+
Prairie View A&M Univ	TX	15,205	LC
Purdue Univ/West Lafayette	IN	20,024	HC
Radford Univ	VA	17,766	LC
Rochester Inst of Technology	NY	42,450	VC
Samford Univ	AL	37,060	C
San Francisco State Univ	CA	18,514	C
Seton Hill Univ	PA	35,172	C
Simmons College	MA	49,966	VC
St. Catherine Univ	MN	37,782	C+
Stephen F. Austin State Univ	TX	14,668	C
SUNY Oneonta / SUNY	NY	16,919	C+
Tarleton State Univ	TX	13,489	LC
Texas Christian Univ	TX	49,980	HC
Texas Southern Univ	TX	18,212	LC
Texas Tech Univ	TX	14,243	C
Texas Woman's Univ	TX	13,633	LC
Thomas Edison State College	NJ	5,700	SP
Tuskegee Univ	AL	26,750	C
Univ of Akron	OH	20,436	C
Univ of Arkansas at Fayetteville	AR	18,352	C+
Univ of Calif at Davis	CA		HC
Univ of Central Arkansas	AR	13,667	VC
Univ of Central Missouri	MO	14,605	C
Univ of Cincinnati	OH	21,506	VC
Univ of Conn	CT	24,706	HC
Univ of Dayton	OH	49,010	VC
Univ of Delaware	DE	23,612	VC
Univ of Georgia	GA	20,082	VC
Univ of Illinois at Chicago	IL	24,505	VC
Univ of Illinois at Urbana-Champaign	IL	26,450	HC
Univ of Louisiana at Lafayette	LA	6,130	C
Univ of Miss	MS	16,704	C+
Univ of Nebr - Lincoln	NE	18,031	VC
Univ of New Haven	CT	48,940	C
Univ of N Dak	ND	14,551	C
Univ of North Florida	FL	15,870	VC
Univ of Northern Colo	CO	18,446	C
Univ of Texas - Pan American	TX	11,125	LC
Univ of Texas at Austin	TX	44,074	HC
Univ of Vermont	VT	27,006	VC+
Univ of Wisc/Green Bay	WI	19,074	C
Univ of Wisc/Stevens Point	WI	14,043	C
Univ of Wisc/Stout	WI	15,459	C
Virginia Polytechnic Inst and State Univ	VA	14,629	HC
Viterbo Univ	WI	30,070	C
Wayne State Univ	MI	22,063	C
West Chester Univ of Pennsylvania	PA	17,186	C
Western Carolina Univ	NC	13,965	C
Western Mich Univ	MI	19,628	C
Youngstown State Univ	OH	16,732	C

DIGITAL ANIMATION & GAME DESIGN

School	ST	$IS	SR
Arizona State Univ, at the Tempe Campus	AZ	20,137	C+
Bloomfield College	NJ	37,850	LC
Ferris State Univ	MI	20,047	C

DIGITAL ARTS/TECHNOLOGY

School	ST	$IS	SR
Arizona State Univ, at the Tempe Campus	AZ	20,137	C+
Art Academy of Cincinnati	OH	25,940	SP
Baldwin Wallace Univ	OH	38,318	C
Bennington College	VT	56,990	HC+
Bethel College	IN	31,560	C
Bowling Green State Univ	OH	18,970	C
Calif Baptist Univ	CA	38,792	C

School	ST	$IS	SR
Calif College of the Arts	CA	48,334	SP
Cal State, Dominguez Hills	CA	17,090	LC
Calvin College	MI	39,120	VC
Chapman Univ	CA	58,347	VC+
Claflin Univ	SC	22,368	LC
Clarkson Univ	NY	57,330	HC
Cogswell Polytechnical College	CA	30,531	C
College for Creative Studies	MI	45,340	C
College of New Jersey	NJ	25,376	HC
Dakota State Univ	SD	13,811	C
DePaul Univ	IL	47,623	VC
Dominican Univ	IL	37,628	C
Drexel Univ	PA	61,418	VC+
Elon Univ	NC	41,914	VC+
Gallaudet Univ	DC	25,380	SP
Grace Bible College	MI	20,770	C
Grand Canyon Univ	AZ	24,540	VC
Greenville College	IL	27,012	C
Hamline Univ	MN	45,678	VC
Huntingdon College	AL	33,100	C
Illinois State Univ	IL	23,110	VC
John Brown Univ	AR	32,056	VC+
Kansas City Art Inst	MO	44,308	SP
Lake Erie College	OH	37,266	C
LIU Post	NY	47,660	C
Lubbock Christian Univ	TX	26,308	C
Marist College	NY	35,500	C
Memphis College of Art	TN	33,550	SP
Mercy College	NY	30,456	C
Messiah College	PA	40,690	C+
Minneapolis College of Art and Design	MN	36,700	SP
Moore College of Art and Design	PA	50,135	SP
Moore College of Art and Design	PA	50,135	SP
New York Univ	NY	61,470	MC
NewSchool of Architecture & Design	CA	24,900	SP
Northeastern Univ	MA	55,296	MC
Ohio Univ	OH	21,080	C
Olivet Nazarene Univ	IL	29,990	C
Otis College of Art and Design	CA	35,404	SP
Parsons The New School for Design	NY	56,610	SP
Philadelphia Univ	PA	44,160	C
Point Park Univ	PA	36,390	C
Quinnipiac Univ	CT	55,160	VC
Ringling College of Art and Design	FL	46,130	SP
Roberts Wesleyan College	NY	38,306	C+
San Francisco Art Inst	CA	55,762	SP
Santa Fe Univ of Art and Design	NM	39,666	SP
Savannah College of Art and Design	GA	48,005	SP
School of the Art Inst of Chicago	IL	56,230	SP
Seattle Univ	WA	49,035	VC+
Southern New Hampshire Univ	NH	38,100	C
Southern Oregon Univ	OR	17,874	C
Southwestern College	KS	29,270	C
Stetson Univ	FL	51,516	VC
Stevens Inst of Technology	NJ	50,130	HC
Tulane Univ	LA	60,861	MC
Univ of Central Florida	FL	15,668	VC+
Univ of Denver	CO	51,787	VC+
Univ of Idaho	ID	14,558	C
Univ of Illinois at Chicago	IL	24,505	VC
Univ of Maryland/Univ College	MD	6,168	SP
Univ of Oregon	OR	21,360	C+
Univ of Pennsylvania	PA	61,132	MC
Univ of Tampa	FL	35,160	VC
Viterbo Univ	WI	30,070	C
Walla Walla Univ	WA	26,256	NC
Washington State Univ	WA	20,461	C
Worcester Polytechnic Inst	MA	55,860	MC
Youngstown State Univ	OH	16,732	C

DIGITAL COMMUNICATIONS

School	ST	$IS	SR
Albright College	PA	46,660	C
Baldwin Wallace Univ	OH	38,318	C
Bennington College	VT	56,990	HC+
Bethany College	WV	35,282	LC
Calvin College	MI	39,120	VC
Canisius College	NY	44,900	C
Endicott College	MA	43,228	VC+
Florida Southern College	FL	40,150	C+
Georgia Inst of Technology	GA	21,828	MC
Georgian Court Univ	NJ	41,594	LC
Hilbert College	NY	28,550	C
Indiana Inst of Technology	IN	34,240	LC
Juniata College	PA	49,340	VC
Kansas City Art Inst	MO	44,308	SP
King Univ	TN	33,140	C
Lycoming College	PA	45,379	C
Marywood Univ	PA	45,595	C
Mass Inst of Technology	MA	58,240	MC
Muskingum Univ	OH	30,502	C
Neumann Univ	PA	31,078	LC
New York Univ	NY	61,470	MC

School	ST	$IS	SR
Ohio Univ	OH	21,080	C
Olivet Nazarene Univ	IL	29,990	C
Queens Univ of Charlotte	NC	39,543	C+
Spring Hill College	AL	44,164	VC
St. Bonaventure Univ	NY	41,575	C
St. Edward's Univ	TX	47,784	C
St. John Fisher College	NY	40,708	C+
Syracuse Univ	NY	56,346	VC
Trevecca Nazarene Univ	TN	31,186	C
Univ of Cincinnati	OH	21,506	VC
Univ of Idaho	ID	14,558	C
Univ of Oregon	OR	21,360	C+
Univ of Rochester	NY	60,668	MC
Valparaiso Univ	IN	44,940	VC+
Vanguard Univ of Southern Calif	CA	35,833	VC
Washington State Univ	WA	20,461	C
Webster Univ	MO	35,100	C+
William Penn Univ	IA	26,000	C

DIGITAL MEDIA

School	ST	$IS	SR
Arizona State Univ, at the Tempe Campus	AZ	20,137	C+
Bethany College	WV	35,282	LC
Bloomfield College	NJ	37,850	LC
Ferris State Univ	MI	20,047	C
Manhattanville College	NY	50,740	VC
Ohio Univ	OH	21,080	C
Youngstown State Univ	OH	16,732	C

DIGITAL MEDIA SOFTWARE ENGINEERING

School	ST	$IS	SR
Arizona State Univ, at the Tempe Campus	AZ	20,137	C+
Ferris State Univ	MI	20,047	C

DRAFTING AND DESIGN

School	ST	$IS	SR
Pennsylvania College of Technology	PA	26,286	NC

DRAFTING AND DESIGN TECHNOLOGY

School	ST	$IS	SR
Alabama A&M Univ	AL	10,084	C
Baker College of Flint	MI	7,800	NC
Montana State Univ-Northern	MT	12,500	NC
Norfolk State Univ	VA	10,531	LC
School of the Art Inst of Chicago	IL	56,230	SP
Texas Southern Univ	TX	18,212	LC
Trine Univ	IN	39,400	HC+
Univ of Central Missouri	MO	14,605	C
Univ of Rio Grande	OH	8,750	NC
Western Mich Univ	MI	19,628	C

DRAMA EDUCATION

School	ST	$IS	SR
Appalachian State Univ	NC	12,919	VC
Augustana College	SD	36,500	VC
Averett Univ	VA	37,750	LC
Baylor Univ	TX	50,329	HC
Bennington College	VT	56,990	HC+
Bradley Univ	IL	31,874	VC
Bridgewater State Univ	MA	18,752	C
Brigham Young Univ	UT	12,100	HC
Columbus State Univ	GA	13,176	C
Culver-Stockton College	MO	30,900	C
East Carolina Univ	NC	14,169	C
East Texas Baptist Univ	TX	31,577	LC
Eastern Mich Univ	MI	18,604	C
Fontbonne Univ	MO	31,384	C
Friends Univ	KS	29,100	C
Greensboro College	NC	28,740	LC
Hardin-Simmons Univ	TX	23,560	C+
Lees-McRae College	NC	33,944	C
Lipscomb Univ	TN	37,490	VC
Mars Hill Univ	NC	22,950	LC
Minot State Univ	ND	10,915	C
Old Dominion Univ	VA	19,483	LC
Oral Roberts Univ	OK	31,734	C
Point Park Univ	PA	36,390	C
Saginaw Valley State Univ	MI	17,369	C
Southwestern College	KS	29,270	C
St. Edward's Univ	TX	47,784	C
The Catholic Univ of America	DC	52,852	VC
The Univ of N Car at Greensboro	NC	12,848	C
Trevecca Nazarene Univ	TN	31,186	C
Univ of Evansville	IN	42,656	VC+
Univ of Indianapolis	IN	31,740	C
Univ of Maryland - College Park	MD	20,060	HC
Univ of Montana-Western	MT	9,753	LC
Univ of Nebr - Lincoln	NE	18,031	VC
Univ of New Mexico	NM	15,300	C
West Texas A&M Univ	TX	13,478	C
York College	NE	19,475	C

ST = STATE $IS = IN-STATE COSTS   SR = SELECTOR RATING

DRAMATIC ARTS

School	ST	$IS	SR
Abilene Christian Univ	TX	38,400	C+
Adams State Univ	CO	13,358	LC
Adelphi Univ	NY	44,670	VC
Adrian College	MI	42,400	C
Agnes Scott College	GA	45,323	C+
Alabama A&M Univ	AL	10,084	C
Alabama State Univ	AL	14,142	NC
Albany State Univ	GA	8,500	C
Albertus Magnus College	CT	37,382	VC
Albright College	PA	46,660	C
Alfred Univ	NY	41,770	C
Allegheny College	PA	50,980	HC
American Univ	DC	56,015	HC+
Anderson Univ	IN	36,100	C
Appalachian State Univ	NC	12,919	VC
Arcadia Univ	PA	33,570	C+
Arizona State Univ, at the Tempe Campus	AZ	20,137	C+
Asbury Univ	KY	32,038	VC
Ashland Univ	OH	25,000	C
Auburn Univ	AL	22,378	VC+
Augsburg College	MN	35,142	C
Augustana College	IL	43,398	VC
Augustana College	SD	36,500	C
Aurora Univ	IL	33,228	C
Averett Univ	VA	37,750	LC
Avila Univ	MO	26,900	C
Baker Univ	KS	33,350	C
Ball State Univ	IN	17,850	C
Bard College	NY	61,940	HC
Bard College at Simon's Rock	MA	61,749	HC+
Barnard College/Columbia Univ	NY	39,000	MC
Barry Univ	FL	38,190	C
Barton College	NC	27,660	LC
Baylor Univ	TX	50,329	HC
Belhaven Univ	MS	27,170	C
Beloit College	WI	49,970	HC
Benedictine College	KS	29,180	VC
Bennington College	VT	56,990	HC+
Berea College	KY	7,192	C
Bethel College	IN	31,560	C
Bethel Univ	MN	34,940	VC
Bethune-Cookman Univ	FL	22,958	C
Binghamton Univ/The SUNY	NY	21,648	HC+
Biola Univ	CA	40,320	C+
Birmingham-Southern College	AL	44,168	VC+
Bloomsburg Univ of Pennsylvania	PA	13,598	C
Boise State Univ	ID	13,469	LC
Boston College	MA	60,622	MC
Boston Univ	MA	60,694	MC
Bradley Univ	IL	31,874	VC
Brenau Univ - Women's College	GA	26,650	LC
Brewton-Parker College	GA	33,388	C
Briar Cliff Univ	IA	29,513	C
Brigham Young Univ	UT	12,100	HC
Bucknell Univ	PA	60,140	MC
Buffalo State College / SUNY	NY	15,733	C+
Butler Univ	IN	47,572	VC+
Calif Baptist Univ	CA	38,792	C
Calif Inst of the Arts	CA	51,902	SP
Calif State Polytechnic Univ, Pomona	CA	20,156	C
Cal State, Bakersfield	CA	8,000	C
Cal State, Dominguez Hills	CA	17,090	LC
Cal State, East Bay	CA	16,549	C
Cal State, Fresno	CA	17,405	C
Cal State, Fullerton	CA	25,188	C
Cal State, Long Beach	CA	17,502	C+
Cal State, Los Angeles	CA	17,186	LC
Cal State, Northridge	CA	28,690	LC
Cal State, Sacramento	CA	16,200	C
Cal State, San Bernardino	CA	12,000	C
Cal State, Stanislaus	CA	18,582	C
Calif Univ of Pennsylvania	PA	14,217	C
Calvin College	MI	39,120	VC
Capital Univ	OH	41,050	VC
Cardinal Stritch Univ	WI	24,054	C
Carnegie Mellon Univ	PA	51,260	MC
Carroll College	MT	28,000	C
Carroll Univ	WI	38,100	C
Case Western Reserve Univ	OH	56,534	MC
Cedar Crest College	PA	43,240	C
Centenary College	NJ	38,618	C
Centenary College of Louisiana	LA	45,650	C+
Central College	IA	42,104	C+
Central Conn State Univ	CT	19,749	C
Central Methodist Univ	MO	28,240	VC
Central Washington Univ	WA	11,730	C
Centre College	KY	35,000	HC+
Chadron State College	NE	7,400	NC
Chapman Univ	CA	58,347	VC+
Charleston Southern Univ	SC	22,420	C
Cheyney Univ of Pennsylvania	PA	20,372	LC
CUNY/City College	NY	20,319	HC+
Clarion Univ of Pennsylvania	PA	17,370	LC
Clark Univ	MA	47,020	HC+
Clarke Univ	IA	37,600	C
Cleveland State Univ	OH	21,776	C
Coastal Carolina Univ	SC	18,580	C
Coker College	SC	32,256	LC
Colgate Univ	NY	58,135	MC
College of Staten Island/The City of New Yok	NY	16,778	NC
College of the Holy Cross	MA	58,042	MC
College of the Ozarks	MO		VC
College of Wooster	OH	52,600	VC
Colo College	CO	57,162	MC
Colo State Univ-Fort Collins	CO	20,385	VC
Columbia College Chicago	IL	30,940	LC
Columbia Univ/City of New York	NY	61,116	MC
Columbia Univ/School of General Studies	NY	58,231	MC
Columbus State Univ	GA	13,176	C
Concordia College - Moorhead	MN	39,974	VC
Concordia Univ Irvine	CA	35,390	VC
Concordia Univ Nebr	NE	26,000	VC
Concordia Univ St. Paul	MN	28,250	C
Concordia Univ, Ann Arbor	MI	27,220	VC
Conn College	CT	54,970	MC
Cornell College	IA	44,930	VC
Cornish College of the Arts	WA	21,200	SP
Covenant College	GA	38,990	VC+
Creighton Univ	NE	45,356	VC
Culver-Stockton College	MO	30,900	C
Dakota Wesleyan Univ	SD	23,000	C
Dartmouth College	NH	57,996	MC
Davidson College	NC	58,146	MC
Davis & Elkins College	WV	33,742	C
De Sales Univ	PA	43,970	C
Denison Univ	OH	54,670	HC+
DePaul Univ	IL	47,623	VC
Doane College	NE	35,230	C
Dominican Univ	IL	37,628	C
Dordt College	IA	34,160	C+
Drake Univ	IA	41,516	VC+
Drury Univ	MO	31,909	VC
Duke Univ	NC	50,250	MC
Duquesne Univ	PA	43,720	VC
Earlham College	IN	51,470	HC
East Carolina Univ	NC	14,169	C
East Central Univ	OK	10,223	LC
East Stroudsburg Univ of Pennsylvania	PA	18,868	LC
Eastern Kentucky Univ	KY	11,161	C
Eastern Mennonite Univ	VA	40,660	C
Eastern Mich Univ	MI	18,604	C
Eastern Nazarene College	MA	30,000	C
Eastern New Mexico Univ	NM	10,682	C
Eastern Oregon Univ	OR	10,400	C
Eastern Washington Univ	WA		C
Eckerd College	FL	43,902	C
Edinboro Univ of Pennsylvania	PA	15,940	LC
Elizabethtown College	PA	49,740	VC
Elmira College	NY	49,950	C+
Elon Univ	NC	41,914	VC+
Emerson College	MA	52,446	HC+
Emory and Henry College	VA	387,460	C
Emory Univ	GA	56,368	MC
Emporia State Univ	KS	12,897	C
Eugene Lang College/The New School for Liberal Arts	NY	55,650	C
Eureka College	IL	19,280	C
Evangel Univ	MO	23,090	C
Fairleigh Dickinson Univ/College at Florham	NJ	42,142	C
Fayetteville State Univ	NC	10,816	C
Ferrum College	VA	27,740	LC
Fisk Univ	TN	19,830	C
Fitchburg State Univ	MA	18,173	C
Five Towns College	NY	34,550	C
Flagler College	FL	25,180	C
Florida A&M Univ	FL	14,935	LC
Florida Atlantic Univ	FL	17,339	C
Florida International Univ	FL	17,747	C+
Florida Southern College	FL	40,150	C+
Florida State Univ	FL	16,575	C
Fontbonne Univ	MO	31,384	C
Fordham Univ	NY	61,588	HC+
Fort Lewis College	CO	15,513	C
Francis Marion Univ	SC	16,464	LC
Franciscan Univ of Steubenville	OH	27,320	VC
Franklin and Marshall College	PA	60,799	MC
Franklin Pierce Univ	NH	41,598	C
Freed-Hardeman Univ	TN	19,697	VC
Frostburg State Univ	MD	15,264	LC
Furman Univ	SC	54,006	HC
Gannon Univ	PA	39,608	C
George Fox Univ	OR	40,750	VC
George Mason Univ	VA	15,724	VC
George Washington Univ	DC	57,108	MC
Georgetown College	KY	41,440	C+
Georgia Southwestern State Univ	GA	13,246	C
Gettysburg College	PA	58,820	HC
Goddard College	VT	16,418	VC
Gonzaga Univ	WA	46,441	HC
Gordon College	MA	44,320	VC
Goshen College	IN	35,900	VC
Graceland Univ	IA	28,020	C
Grand Valley State Univ	MI	17,998	C+
Greensboro College	NC	28,740	LC
Greenville College	IL	27,012	C
Grinnell College	IA	53,654	HC
Guilford College	NC	42,800	C
Gustavus Adolphus College	MN	48,170	VC
Hamilton College	NY	55,620	MC
Hamline Univ	MN	45,678	VC
Hampshire College	MA	58,320	MC
Hampton Univ	VA	28,528	C
Hannibal-LaGrange Univ	MO	24,490	C
Hanover College	IN	43,073	C+
Harding Univ	AR	23,556	C
Hardin-Simmons Univ	TX	23,560	C+
Hartwick College	NY	51,270	C
Hastings College	NE	27,782	C+
Heidelberg Univ	OH	34,100	C
Henderson State Univ	AR	14,584	C
Hendrix College	AR	50,202	VC+
Hiram College	OH	37,300	VC
Hofstra Univ	NY	51,810	VC+
Hollins Univ	VA	43,295	VC
Hope College	MI	38,650	VC
Howard Payne Univ	TX	17,115	C
Howard Univ	DC	13,646	C
Humboldt State Univ	CA	18,400	C
Hunter College	NY	14,429	VC
Huntington Univ	IN	32,220	C+
Idaho State Univ	ID	12,307	C
Illinois College	IL	25,770	VC
Illinois State Univ	IL	23,110	VC
Indiana State Univ	IN	16,000	C
Indiana Univ Bloomington	IN	19,801	VC
Indiana Univ Bloomington	IN	19,801	VC
Indiana Univ-Purdue Univ Fort Wayne	IN	15,521	C
Ithaca College	NY	53,864	HC
Jacksonville State Univ	AL	12,480	LC
Jacksonville Univ	FL	37,780	C
James Madison Univ	VA	18,049	VC
Judson Univ	IL	25,130	C
Juilliard School	NY	44,460	SP
Juniata College	PA	49,340	VC
Kalamazoo College	MI	49,740	HC
Kansas State Univ	KS	15,497	VC
Kansas Wesleyan Univ	KS	32,000	C
Kent State Univ	OH	19,920	C
Kenyon College	OH	58,890	MC
King's College	PA	43,502	C
Knox College	IL	44,865	VC+
Kutztown Univ of Pennsylvania	PA	16,909	LC
Lakeland College	WI	22,990	C
Lamar Univ	TX	6,820	LC
Lander Univ	SC	22,514	C+
Langston Univ	OK	3,000	C
Lawrence Univ	WI	46,371	HC
Le Moyne College	NY	43,470	C
Lee Univ	TN	18,690	C+
Lees-McRae College	NC	33,944	C
Lenoir-Rhyne Univ	NC	35,984	C
Lewis & Clark College	OR	54,382	MC
Lewis Univ	IL	23,050	C
Lindenwood Univ	MO	20,750	C
Linfield College-McMinnville Campus	OR	47,676	C
LIU Post	NY	47,660	C
Louisiana College	LA	15,746	C
Louisiana State Univ	LA	18,677	C+
Loyola Marymount Univ	CA	54,649	VC+
Loyola Univ New Orleans	LA	46,581	VC
Lycoming College	PA	45,379	C
Lynn Univ	FL	43,500	LC
Lyon College	AR	32,090	C+
Macalester College	MN	57,691	MC
MacMurray College	IL	20,755	C
Maharishi Univ of Management	IA	31,000	C
Manhattanville College	NY	50,740	VC
Marietta College	OH	42,135	C+
Marlboro College	VT	35,980	VC
Marquette Univ	WI	46,930	VC+
Mars Hill Univ	NC	22,950	LC
Marymount Manhattan College	NY	40,118	VC
Maryville College	TN	33,150	C
Marywood Univ	PA	45,595	C
McDaniel College	MD	47,450	VC
McKendree Univ	IL	29,920	C+
McMurry Univ	TX	25,962	LC
McPherson College	KS	28,138	C
Mercer Univ	GA	44,201	VC
Meredith College	NC	31,420	C
Messiah College	PA	40,690	C+
Methodist Univ	NC	37,185	C
Metropolitan State Univ	MN	5,923	
Miami Univ	OH	24,191	VC
Mich State Univ	MI	22,450	VC
MidAmerica Nazarene Univ	KS	28,000	C
Middlebury College	VT	59,160	MC
Midwestern State Univ	TX	9,722	C
Millikin Univ	IL	38,940	VC
Minn State Univ, Mankato	MN	15,616	C
Minn State Univ, Moorhead	MN	13,392	VC
Missouri Valley College	MO	22,200	C
Monmouth College	IL	40,850	C
Montana State Univ-Billings	MT	12,425	LC
Montana State Univ-Northern	MT	12,500	NC
Montclair State Univ	NJ	22,614	C
Moravian College	PA	36,381	VC
Morehead State Univ	KY	10,900	C
Morehouse College	GA	39,412	C
Morgan State Univ	MD	14,500	VC
Morningside College	IA	35,430	C
Mount Holyoke College	MA	55,146	MC
Mount Vernon Nazarene Univ	OH	29,590	C
Muhlenberg College	PA	52,837	HC
Muskingum Univ	OH	30,502	C
Nebr Wesleyan Univ	NE	29,774	C+
New England College	NH	45,930	LC
New Mexico State Univ	NM	14,050	C
New York Univ	NY	61,470	MC
Newberry College	SC	26,850	LC
Niagara Univ	NY	41,010	C
N Car Agricultural and Technical State Univ	NC	13,365	LC
N Car Central Univ	NC	9,000	C
N Car Wesleyan College	NC	29,440	C
N Dak State Univ	ND		C
Northeastern Univ	MA	55,296	MC
Northern Illinois Univ	IL	19,768	C
Northern Kentucky Univ	KY	21,134	C
Northern Mich Univ	MI	18,278	C
Northwest Missouri State Univ	MO	17,347	C
Northwestern College	MN	24,000	C
Northwestern College of Iowa	IA	36,240	VC
Northwestern Okla State Univ	OK	7,275	NC
Northwestern State Univ of Louisiana	LA	14,368	C
Northwestern Univ	IL	61,640	MC
Notre Dame de Namur Univ	CA	44,236	LC
Nova Southeastern Univ	FL	37,280	VC
Oakland Univ	MI	19,391	C
Oberlin College	OH	61,788	MC
Ohio Northern Univ	OH	42,075	VC
Ohio Univ	OH	21,080	C
Ohio Wesleyan Univ	OH	49,640	C+
Okla Baptist Univ	OK	28,202	C
Okla State Univ	OK	14,310	VC
Old Dominion Univ	VA	19,483	LC
Olivet Nazarene Univ	IL	29,990	C
Oral Roberts Univ	OK	31,734	C
Oswego / SUNY	NY	20,009	VC
Ottawa Univ	KS	15,000	VC
Otterbein College	OH	32,214	C
Ouachita Baptist Univ	AR	30,220	VC
Our Lady of the Lake Univ	TX	22,430	LC
Pacific Univ	OR	49,626	C+
Park Univ	MO	17,525	C
Pepperdine Univ	CA	55,372	HC+
Piedmont College	GA	30,136	C
Pittsburg State Univ	KS	12,032	C
Pitzer College	CA	54,988	MC
Point Park Univ	PA	36,390	C
Portland State Univ	OR	18,672	C
Prairie View A&M Univ	TX	15,205	LC
Presbyterian College	SC	42,678	C+
Prescott College	AZ	33,284	C
Principia College	IL	35,140	C
Providence College	RI	57,383	VC
Purdue Univ West Lafayette	IN	20,024	HC
Queens College/The CUNY	NY	17,107	VC
Queens Univ of Charlotte	NC	35,543	C+
Quinnipiac Univ	CT	55,160	VC
Ramapo College of New Jersey	NJ	24,938	C
Randolph College	VA	45,660	VC
Randolph-Macon College	VA	49,869	C+
Reed College	OR	57,780	MC
Rhode Island College	RI	17,694	LC
Richard Stockton College of New Jersey	NJ	20,000	C
Rider Univ	NJ	45,720	C
Ripon College	WI	36,959	C+
Rockford College	IL	31,000	C
Roger Williams Univ	RI	46,296	VC
Rollins College	FL	52,370	HC
Roosevelt Univ	IL	22,605	VC
Rowan Univ	NJ	24,022	VC+
Rutgers, The State Univ of New Jersey/Camden Campus	NJ	25,121	C
Rutgers, The State Univ of New Jersey/New Brunswick	NJ	25,562	VC
Rutgers, The State Univ of New Jersey/Newark Campus	NJ	258,806	C
Saginaw Valley State Univ	MI	17,369	C
St. Joseph's College	IN	36,500	C
St. Louis Univ	MO	48,346	HC
St. Michael's College	VT	49,975	VC
Salem State Univ	MA	13,161	LC
Salve Regina Univ	RI	48,550	VC
Sam Houston State Univ	TX	17,082	C
San Francisco State Univ	CA	18,514	C
San Jose State Univ	CA	19,133	LC

School	ST	$IS	SR
Santa Fe Univ of Art and Design	NM	39,666	SP
Sarah Lawrence College	NY	48,000	HC
Schreiner Univ	TX	32,734	LC
Scripps College	CA	61,940	MC
Seton Hill Univ	PA	35,172	C
Shenandoah Univ	VA	39,916	C
Shorter Univ	GA	30,650	LC
Simpson College	IA	36,086	C+
Skidmore College	NY	59,942	HC
Smith College	MA	59,674	MC
S Car State Univ	SC	6,700	LC
S Dak State Univ	SD	14,296	C
Southeastern Okla State Univ	OK	7,966	LC
Southeastern Univ	FL	27,201	C
Southern Conn State Univ	CT	18,033	LC
Southern Illinois Univ Carbondale	IL	21,942	C
Southern Illinois Univ Edwardsville	IL	17,532	C
Southern Methodist Univ	TX	60,585	MC
Southern Oregon Univ	OR	17,874	C
Southern Univ and A&M College	LA	9,761	LC
Southwest Minn State Univ	MN	14,000	C
Southwestern College	KS	29,270	C
Southwestern Univ	TX	45,660	VC
Spelman College	GA	24,650	C
St. Bonaventure Univ	NY	41,575	C
St. Catherine Univ	MN	37,782	C+
St. Cloud State Univ	MN	10,600	C
St. John's Univ	NY	55,070	C+
St. Lawrence Univ	NY	59,972	VC
St. Mary's College of Maryland	MD	25,754	VC
Stanford Univ	CA	58,388	MC
SUNY at Purchase	NY	16,951	VC
Stephen F. Austin State Univ	TX	14,668	C
Stephens College	MO	38,042	VC
Sterling College	KS	27,216	C
Stetson Univ	FL	51,516	VC
Stevenson Univ	MD	41,470	C
Stony Brook Univ / SUNY	NY	20,078	HC+
Suffolk Univ	MA	47,298	C
Sul Ross State Univ	TX	13,410	LC
SUNY Fredonia/The SUNY at Fredonia	NY	19,840	VC
SUNY New Paltz	NY	14,348	C
SUNY Oneonta / SUNY	NY	16,919	C+
Swarthmore College	PA	57,870	MC
Syracuse Univ	NY	56,346	VC
Tarleton State Univ	TX	13,489	LC
Taylor Univ	IN	37,821	VC+
Tenn State Univ	TN	9,048	LC
Texas A&M Univ at Commerce	TX	10,496	C
Texas A&M Univ at Corpus Christi	TX	11,544	LC
Texas A&M Univ at Kingsville	TX	7,500	LC
Texas Lutheran Univ	TX	36,040	C
Texas Southern Univ	TX	18,212	LC
Texas State Univ	TX	17,128	C
Texas Tech Univ	TX	14,243	C
Texas Wesleyan Univ	TX	31,382	C
Texas Woman's Univ	TX	13,633	LC
The Catholic Univ of America	DC	52,852	VC
The Univ of Memphis	TN	15,094	C
The Univ of N Car at Greensboro	NC	12,848	C
The Univ of N Car at Pembroke	NC	13,388	LC
The Univ of Okla	OK	18,621	VC
The Univ of Tenn at Chattanooga	TN	16,883	C
The Univ of Utah	UT	16,463	VC
The Univ of Virginia's College at Wise	VA	11,076	C
Thomas More College	KY	34,760	C
Transylvania Univ	KY	42,660	VC+
Trevecca Nazarene Univ	TN	31,186	C
Trinity College	CT		HC+
Trinity Univ	TX	48,150	HC+
Troy Univ	AL	10,650	C
Truman State Univ	MO	15,541	HC
Tufts Univ	MA	58,780	MC
Tulane Univ	LA	60,861	MC
Union College	KY	29,955	C
Union Univ	TN	28,260	VC
Univ of Alabama at Birmingham	AL	18,484	C+
Univ of Alaska Anchorage	AK	16,673	NC
Univ of Arkansas at Fayetteville	AR	18,352	C+
Univ of Arkansas at Little Rock	AR	17,609	LC
Univ of Calif at Berkeley	CA	23,322	MC
Univ of Calif at Davis	CA		HC
Univ of Calif at Irvine	CA	25,961	VC
Univ of Calif at Los Angeles	CA	25,686	MC
Univ of Calif at Riverside	CA	27,204	C+
Univ of Calif at San Diego	CA	21,000	VC
Univ of Calif at Santa Barbara	CA	27,551	HC
Univ of Calif at Santa Cruz	CA	27,807	C+
Univ of Central Florida	FL	15,668	VC+

School	ST	$IS	SR
Univ of Cincinnati	OH	21,506	VC
Univ of Conn	CT	24,706	HC
Univ of Dallas	TX	45,500	VC+
Univ of Dayton	OH	49,070	VC
Univ of Denver	CO	51,787	VC+
Univ of Detroit Mercy	MI	30,450	VC
Univ of Evansville	IN	42,656	VC+
Univ of Findlay	OH	31,916	C
Univ of Hartford	CT	42,674	C
Univ of Hawaii at Manoa	HI	19,379	C
Univ of Idaho	ID	14,558	C
Univ of Illinois at Chicago	IL	24,505	VC
Univ of Illinois at Urbana-Champaign	IL	26,450	HC
Univ of Indianapolis	IN	31,740	LC
Univ of Iowa	IA	17,693	VC
Univ of Kansas	KS	17,603	C+
Univ of Kentucky	KY	19,868	C
Univ of La Verne	CA	47,010	C
Univ of Louisiana at Lafayette	LA	6,130	C
Univ of Louisville	KY	17,946	C
Univ of Maine	ME	19,902	C+
Univ of Mary Washington	VA	19,484	VC
Univ of Maryland - College Park	MD	20,060	HC
Univ of Maryland/Baltimore County	MD	18,000	VC
Univ of Mass Amherst	MA	24,215	VC+
Univ of Mass Boston	MA	23,066	VC
Univ of Mich/Ann Arbor	MI	22,102	MC
Univ of Mich-Flint	MI	17,547	C+
Univ of Minn/Duluth	MN	19,806	C
Univ of Minn/Morris	MN	17,150	VC
Univ of Missouri/Columbia	MO	18,201	MC
Univ of Missouri-Kansas City	MO	19,603	C
Univ of Missouri-St. Louis	MO		VC
Univ of Montana	MT	14,105	C
Univ of Montana-Western	MT	9,753	LC
Univ of Montevallo	AL	17,060	C
Univ of Mount Union	OH	35,130	C
Univ of Nebr - Lincoln	NE	18,031	VC
Univ of Nebr at Kearney	NE	14,855	LC
Univ of Nebr at Omaha	NE	12,700	C
Univ of Nevada, Las Vegas	NV	17,303	C
Univ of Nevada/Reno	NV	17,507	C
Univ of New Orleans	LA	9,224	C
Univ of North Alabama	AL	9,560	C
Univ of N Car at Asheville	NC	13,906	VC
Univ of N Car at Chapel Hill	NC	18,928	MC
Univ of N Car at Wilmington	NC	13,572	VC
Univ of N Car School of the Arts	NC	7,401	SP
Univ of North Texas	TX	15,628	C
Univ of Northern Iowa	IA	15,795	C
Univ of Oregon	OR	21,360	C+
Univ of Pennsylvania	PA	61,132	MC
Univ of Pittsburgh at Johnstown	PA	20,862	LC
Univ of Portland	OR	49,964	VC
Univ of PR Recinto de Rio Piedras	PR	5,750	
Univ of Puget Sound	WA	54,608	HC
Univ of Redlands	CA	40,500	VC
Univ of St. Mary	KS	28,400	C+
Univ of Science and Arts of Okla	OK	10,560	LC
Univ of South Alabama	AL	13,510	C
Canisius of S Car at Columbia	SC	19,725	VC+
Univ of S Dak	SD	15,111	C
Univ of South Florida/Tampa	FL	13,000	C
Univ of Southern Calif	CA	56,903	MC
Univ of Southern Maine	ME	16,576	C
Univ of Southern Miss	MS	13,170	C
Univ of St. Thomas - Houston	TX	37,690	C
Univ of Tampa	FL	35,160	VC
Univ of Texas - Pan American	TX	11,125	LC
Univ of Texas at Arlington	TX	10,908	LC
Univ of Texas at Austin	TX	44,074	HC
Univ of Texas at El Paso	TX	8,764	NC
Univ of the Cumberlands	KY	27,500	C
Univ of the District of Columbia	DC	7,244	LC
Univ of the Incarnate Word	TX	37,316	LC
Univ of the Ozarks	AR	31,440	C
Univ of the Pacific	CA	52,146	VC
Univ of Toledo	OH	18,464	C
Univ of Vermont	VT	27,006	VC+
Univ of Virginia	VA	23,050	MC
Univ of Washington	WA	14,722	VC
Univ of Wisc Whitewater	WI	13,314	C
Univ of Wisc/Green Bay	WI	19,074	C
Univ of Wisc/La Crosse	WI	9,304	VC
Univ of Wisc/Madison	WI	18,757	HC+
Univ of Wisc/Parkside	WI	10,181	C
Univ of Wisc/Stevens Point	WI	14,043	C
Univ of Wisc/Superior	WI	14,314	C
Univ of Wisc-Milwaukee	WI	18,436	C
Ursinus College	PA	57,580	VC
Utah State Univ	UT	12,044	C
Valparaiso Univ	IN	44,940	VC+
Vanguard Univ of Southern Calif	CA	35,833	VC
Vassar College	NY	61,140	MC

School	ST	$IS	SR
Virginia Commonwealth Univ	VA	21,716	C
Virginia Polytechnic Inst and State Univ	VA	14,629	HC
Virginia Wesleyan College	VA	28,433	LC
Viterbo Univ	WI	30,070	C
Wabash College	IN	46,850	C+
Wagner College	NY	48,600	C+
Wartburg College	IA	41,055	VC
Washburn Univ	KS	12,579	C
Washington and Lee Univ	VA	52,812	MC
Washington College	MD	52,602	VC
Washington Univ in St. Louis	MO	69,844	MC
Wayland Baptist Univ	TX	18,912	LC
Wayne State College	NE	11,764	NC
Wayne State Univ	MI	22,063	C
Webster Univ	MO	35,100	C+
Wellesley College	MA	59,038	MC
Wells College	NY	49,400	VC
Wesleyan College	GA	24,000	C
Wesleyan Univ	CT	61,198	MC
West Chester Univ of Pennsylvania	PA	17,186	C
West Texas A&M Univ	TX	13,478	C
West Virginia Univ	WV	16,542	C+
West Virginia Wesleyan College	WV	26,880	C
Western Carolina Univ	NC	13,965	C
Western Conn State Univ	CT	18,327	LC
Western Kentucky Univ	KY	11,000	LC
Western Mich Univ	MI	19,628	C
Western Oregon Univ	OR	15,021	C
Western State Colo Univ	CO	16,924	C
Western Washington Univ	WA	18,519	VC
Westminster College	PA	31,290	C+
Westminster College	UT	37,708	C+
Westmont College	CA	41,500	VC
Wheaton College	MA	54,934	HC+
Whittier College	CA	43,416	C
Whitworth Univ	WA	47,734	VC
Wilkes Univ	PA	44,070	C
Willamette Univ	OR	56,450	VC+
William Carey Univ	MS	13,500	LC
William Jewell College	MO	31,000	VC+
William Paterson Univ of New Jersey	NJ	21,694	C
William Woods Univ	MO	24,260	C
Williams College	MA	61,070	MC
Wilmington College	OH	29,784	C
Winona State Univ	MN	16,640	C
Wisc Lutheran College	WI	23,510	VC
Wittenberg Univ	OH	47,962	C+
Wofford College	SC	45,795	VC
Wright State Univ	OH	16,983	C
Yale Univ	CT	55,300	MC
York College / The CUNY	NY	5,496	VC
York College of Pennsylvania	PA	26,590	C
Youngstown State Univ	OH	16,732	C

DRAWING

School	ST	$IS	SR
Adams State Univ	CO	13,358	LC
Aquinas College	MI	33,060	VC
Art Academy of Cincinnati	OH	25,940	SP
Bard College at Simon's Rock	MA	61,749	HC+
Bennington College	VT	56,990	HC+
Binghamton Univ/The SUNY	NY	21,648	HC+
Biola Univ	CA	40,320	C+
Calif College of the Arts	CA	48,334	SP
Cleveland Inst of Art	OH	48,685	SP
Ferris State Univ	MI	20,047	C
Indiana Univ-Purdue Univ Fort Wayne	IN	15,521	C
Kent State Univ	OH	19,920	C
Kutztown Univ of Pennsylvania	PA	16,909	LC
Laguna College of Art and Design	CA	27,300	SP
Lewis Univ	IL	23,050	C
Maryland Inst College of Art	MD	39,500	SP
Memphis College of Art	TN	33,550	SP
Milwaukee Inst of Art and Design	WI	31,938	SP
Minneapolis College of Art and Design	MN	36,700	SP
Old Dominion Univ	VA	19,483	LC
Olivet Nazarene Univ	IL	29,990	C
Pacific Northwest College of Art	OR	38,494	C
School of the Art Inst of Chicago	IL	56,230	SP
SUNY Fredonia/The SUNY at Fredonia	NY	19,840	VC
Univ of Hartford	CT	42,674	C
Univ of Iowa	IA	17,693	VC
Univ of Mich/Ann Arbor	MI	22,102	MC
Univ of San Francisco	CA	54,770	VC
Washington Univ in St. Louis	MO	69,844	MC

DRAWING WITH PRINTMAKING FOCUS

School	ST	$IS	SR
Ferris State Univ	MI	20,047	C

School	ST	$IS	SR

DUTCH

School	ST	$IS	SR
Calvin College	MI	39,120	VC
Dordt College	IA	34,160	C+
Univ of Calif at Berkeley	CA	23,322	MC

EARLY CHILDHOOD EDUCATION

School	ST	$IS	SR
Abilene Christian Univ	TX	38,400	C+
Alabama A&M Univ	AL	10,084	C
Alabama State Univ	AL	14,142	NC
Albany State Univ	GA	8,500	C
Alfred Univ	NY	41,770	C
Alma College	MI	44,075	C
American International College	MA	36,100	LC
American Univ	DC	56,015	HC+
Anna Maria College	MA	34,600	C
Aquinas College	MI	33,060	C
Arcadia Univ	PA	33,570	C+
Arizona State Univ, at the Tempe Campus	AZ	20,137	C+
Arkansas State Univ	AR	15,470	C
Arkansas Tech Univ	AR	13,982	LC
Armstrong State Univ	GA	15,532	C
Ashford Univ	CA	10,480	C
Ashland Univ	OH	25,000	C
Atlantic Union College	MA	24,600	C
Auburn Univ	AL	22,378	VC+
Averett Univ	VA	37,550	LC
Baldwin Wallace Univ	OH	38,318	C
Ball State Univ	IN	17,850	C
Barry Univ	FL	38,190	C
Bay Path College	MA	34,565	C
Becker College	MA	41,420	C
Belmont Univ	TN	39,190	VC+
Bemidji State Univ	MN	13,500	VC
Benedict College	SC	20,454	NC
Bennington College	VT	56,990	HC+
Berry College	GA	39,254	VC
Bethel College	IN	31,560	C
Bethel Univ	MN	34,940	VC
Biola Univ	CA	40,320	C
Black Hills State Univ	SD	13,947	C
Bloomfield College	NJ	37,850	LC
Bloomsburg Univ of Pennsylvania	PA	13,598	C
Bluffton Univ	OH	38,948	C
Boston College	MA	60,622	VC
Boston Univ	MA	60,694	VC
Bowie State Univ	MD	23,990	VC
Bowling Green State Univ	OH	18,970	C
Bradley Univ	IL	31,874	VC
Brenau Univ - Women's College	GA	26,650	LC
Brescia Univ	KY	26,140	VC+
Brewton-Parker College	GA	33,388	C
Bridgewater State Univ	MA	18,752	C
Brigham Young Univ	UT	12,100	HC
Bucknell Univ	PA	60,140	HC
Cal State, Sacramento	CA	16,200	C
Calif Univ of Pennsylvania	PA	14,217	C
Calvin College	MI	39,120	VC
Cameron Univ	OK	10,004	LC
Campbell Univ	NC	37,570	VC
Campbellsville Univ	KY	27,720	C
Canisius Univ	NY	44,900	C
Cardinal Stritch Univ	WI	24,054	C
Carlow Univ	PA	30,272	C
Carroll Univ	WI	38,100	C
Carson-Newman Univ	TN	29,058	C+
Cazenovia College	NY	43,464	C
Cedar Crest College	PA	43,240	C
Cedarville Univ	OH	32,860	VC
Central Methodist Univ	MO	28,240	VC
Central Washington Univ	WA	11,730	C
Chadron State College	NE	7,400	NC
Chaminade Univ of Honolulu	HI	31,664	LC
Champlain College	VT	46,650	VC+
Charleston Southern Univ	SC	22,420	C
Chatham Univ	PA	43,797	C
Chestnut Hill College	PA	42,110	C
Cheyney Univ of Pennsylvania	PA	20,372	LC
Chicago State Univ	IL	5,482	C
Christian Brothers Univ	TN	31,670	HC
CUNY/Brooklyn College	NY	5,884	C+
CUNY/City College	NY	20,319	HC+
Claflin Univ	SC	22,368	C
Clarion Univ of Pennsylvania	PA	17,370	LC
Clark Atlanta Univ	GA	30,006	LC
Clemson Univ	SC	19,136	HC
Cleveland State Univ	OH	21,776	C
Coastal Carolina Univ	SC	18,580	C
Coker College	SC	32,256	VC
Colby-Sawyer College	NH	50,790	C
College of Charleston	SC	22,145	VC
College of Mount St. Joseph	OH	33,880	C
College of New Jersey	NJ	25,376	HC
College of St. Mary	NE	35,184	C
College of the Ozarks	MO		VC
Columbia College	SC	27,882	C
Columbia College Chicago	IL	30,940	LC
Columbus State Univ	GA	13,176	C

School	ST	$IS	SR
Concord Univ	WV	13,102	C
Concordia College - Alabama	AL	15,720	NC
Concordia College - New York	NY	39,035	LC
Concordia Univ	OR	35,000	C
Concordia Univ Irvine	CA	35,390	VC
Concordia Univ Nebr	NE	26,000	C
Concordia Univ St. Paul	MN	28,250	C
Concordia Univ Wisc	WI	28,980	C
Concordia Univ, Ann Arbor	MI	27,220	C
Concordia Univ, River Forest	IL	26,300	C
Converse College	SC	37,130	C
Curry College	MA	48,925	LC
Daemen College	NY	34,770	C
De Sales Univ	PA	43,970	C
Defiance College	OH	30,645	C
Delaware State Univ	DE	16,722	LC
DePaul Univ	IL	47,623	VC
Dickinson State Univ	ND	11,900	NC
Dominican Univ	IL	37,628	C
Dordt College	IA	34,160	C+
Duquesne Univ	PA	43,720	VC
East Carolina Univ	NC	14,169	C
East Central Univ	OK	10,223	C
East Stroudsburg Univ of Pennsylvania	PA	18,868	LC
East Texas Baptist Univ	TX	31,577	LC
Eastern Conn State Univ	CT	20,584	C
Eastern Illinois Univ	IL	20,466	C
Eastern Mennonite Univ	VA	40,660	C
Eastern Mich Univ	MI	18,604	C
Eastern New Mexico Univ	NM	10,682	C
Eastern Univ	PA	37,704	C
Edgewood College	WI	33,294	C
Edinboro Univ of Pennsylvania	PA	15,940	LC
Edward Waters College	FL	19,607	LC
Elizabethtown College	PA	49,740	VC
Elmhurst College	IL	43,336	C
Elms College	MA	23,900	VC
Elon Univ	NC	41,914	VC+
Erskine College	SC	37,360	C
Evangel Univ	MO	23,090	C
Fairmont State Univ	WV	12,098	LC
Faulkner Univ	AL	25,720	LC
Fayetteville State Univ	NC	10,816	C
Felician College	NJ	41,640	LC
Ferris State Univ	MI	20,047	C
Fitchburg State Univ	MA	18,173	C
Florida A&M Univ	FL	14,935	LC
Florida Gulf Coast Univ	FL		C
Florida International Univ	FL	17,747	C+
Florida State Univ	FL	16,715	VC
Fontbonne Univ	MO	31,384	C
Fort Valley State Univ	GA	11,200	VC
Framingham State Univ	MA	18,854	C
Francis Marion Univ	SC	16,464	LC
Freed-Hardeman Univ	TN	19,697	VC
Frostburg State Univ	MD	15,264	LC
Gallaudet Univ	DC	25,380	SP
Gannon Univ	PA	39,608	C
Georgia College and State Univ	GA	18,900	C+
Georgia Southern Univ	GA	16,942	C
Georgia Southwestern State Univ	GA	13,246	C
Georgia State Univ	GA	15,582	VC
Glenville State College	WV	11,348	NC
Goddard College	VT	16,418	VC
Gordon College	MA	44,320	VC
Goshen College	IN	35,900	C
Grambling State Univ	LA	13,384	LC
Granite State College	NH	6,195	NC
Greensboro College	NC	28,740	LC
Greenville College	IL	27,012	C
Grove City College	PA	24,022	VC
Hannibal-LaGrange Univ	MO	24,490	C
Harding Univ	AR	23,556	C
Hardin-Simmons Univ	TX	23,560	C+
Harris-Stowe State Univ	MO	14,360	NC
Henderson State Univ	AR	14,584	C
Hendrix College	AR	50,202	VC+
Heritage Univ	WA	17,664	NC
Holy Family Univ	PA	40,030	C
Hood College	MD	45,730	C
Houston Baptist Univ	TX	36,450	C
Howard Univ	DC	13,646	C
Humphreys College	CA	17,000	NC
Hunter College	NY	14,429	VC
Idaho State Univ	ID	12,307	C
Illinois State Univ	IL	23,110	VC
Immaculata Univ	PA	43,000	C
Indiana State Univ	IN	16,000	C
Indiana Univ Bloomington	IN	19,961	VC
Indiana Univ Kokomo	IN	6,811	LC
Indiana Univ of Pennsylvania	PA	20,846	LC
Indiana Univ-Purdue Univ Fort Wayne	IN	15,521	C
Indiana Univ-Purdue Univ Indianapolis	IN	17,611	C
Inter-American Univ of PR/ Aguadilla Campus	PR	5,578	
Inter-American Univ of PR/ Barranquitas	PR	3,350	
Inter-American Univ of PR/ Fajardo Campus	PR	4,200	
Inter-American Univ of PR/ Metropolitan Campus	PR	4,320	
Inter-American Univ of PR/ Ponce	PR		
Inter-American Univ of PR/ San Germán	PR	6,720	
Iona College	NY	44,028	C
Iowa State Univ	IA	16,403	C
Iowa Wesleyan Univ	IA	30,850	LC
Jacksonville State Univ	AL	12,480	LC
John Brown Univ	AR	32,056	VC+
John Carroll Univ	OH	46,300	C+
Judson Univ	IL	25,130	C
Juniata College	PA	49,340	VC
Kansas State Univ	KS	15,497	VC
Kean Univ	NJ	23,444	C
Kendall College	IL	32,610	NC
Kennesaw State Univ	GA		C
Kent State Univ	OH	19,920	C
Kentucky State Univ	KY	11,000	LC
Keystone College	PA	28,680	LC
King's College	PA	43,502	C
Kutztown Univ of Pennsylvania	PA	16,909	LC
LaGrange College	GA	37,670	C
Lake Erie College	OH	37,266	C
Lake Superior State Univ	MI	18,121	C
Lakeland College	WI	22,990	C
Lamar Univ	TX	6,820	LC
Lander Univ	SC	22,514	C+
Lasell College	MA	43,750	LC
Lebanon Valley College	PA	38,570	C
Lehman College/The CUNY	NY	5,778	LC
LeMoyne-Owen College	TN	13,100	C
Lenoir-Rhyne College	NC	35,984	C
Lesley Univ	MA	46,350	C
Limestone College	SC	30,800	C
Lincoln Memorial Univ	TN	18,144	C
Lindenwood Univ	MO	20,750	C
Lipscomb Univ	TN	37,490	VC
LIU Brooklyn	NY	47,182	LC
LIU Post	NY	47,660	C
Livingstone College	NC	17,815	LC
Lock Haven Univ of Pennsylvania	PA	18,028	LC
Loras College	IA	37,432	VC
Louisiana State Univ	LA	18,677	C+
Louisiana Tech Univ	LA	11,302	C
Loyola Univ Chicago	IL	51,646	VC+
Lubbock Christian Univ	TX	26,308	C
Lyndon State College	VT	14,233	C
Lyon College	AR	32,090	C+
Malone Univ	OH	35,364	C
Manhattan College	NY	49,588	C+
Mansfield Univ	PA	19,468	LC
Marian Univ	WI	32,420	C
Marietta College	OH	42,135	C+
Marshall Univ	WV	14,820	C
Martin Univ	IN	11,000	NC
Marygrove College	MI	28,926	C
Maryville Univ of St. Louis	MO	35,856	VC
Marywood Univ	PA	45,595	C
Mayville State Univ	ND	11,401	NC
McNeese State Univ	LA	2,649	C
Medaille College	NY	35,112	C
Mercer Univ	GA	44,201	VC
Mercyhurst Univ	PA	40,700	C
Messiah College	PA	40,690	C+
Metropolitan College of New York	NY	16,720	VC
Metropolitan State Univ	MN	5,923	
Miami Univ	OH	24,191	VC
Middle Tenn State Univ	TN	8,650	C
Midland Univ	NE	34,000	C
Miles College	AL	11,164	NC
Millersville Univ of Pennsylvania	PA	21,648	C
Milligan College	TN	27,510	C
Millikin Univ	IL	38,940	C
Minn State Univ, Mankato	MN	15,616	C
Minn State Univ, Moorhead	MN	13,392	VC
Miss Valley State Univ	MS	9,706	LC
Missouri Baptist Univ	MO	31,830	C
Missouri Southern State Univ	MO	12,061	C
Missouri State Univ	MO	13,996	C+
Missouri Western State Univ	MO	12,260	NC
Mitchell College	CT	40,983	C
Molloy College	NY	40,440	C
Monmouth Univ	NJ	44,108	C
Montana State Univ-Billings	MT	12,425	LC
Montclair State Univ	NJ	22,614	C
Morehouse College	GA	39,412	C
Morris College	SC	16,310	LC
Mount Aloysius College	PA	29,976	C
Mount Ida College	MA	30,115	LC
Mount Mary Univ	WI	33,590	LC
Mount Mercy Univ	IA	35,320	C
Mount Vernon Nazarene Univ	OH	29,590	C
Murray State Univ	KY	15,304	C
Muskingum Univ	OH	30,502	C
Naropa Univ	CO	39,166	SP
National Louis Univ	IL	16,915	LC
Neumann Univ	PA	31,078	LC
New Jersey City Univ	NJ	21,456	LC
New Mexico Highlands Univ	NM	11,904	NC
New Mexico State Univ	NM	14,050	C
New York Univ	NY	61,470	MC
Newberry College	SC	26,850	LC
Newman Univ	KS	30,380	C+
Niagara Univ	NY	41,010	C
Norfolk State Univ	VA	10,531	LC
N Car Agricultural and Technical State Univ	NC	13,365	LC
North Park Univ	IL	30,130	C
Northeastern Illinois Univ	IL	10,318	LC
Northeastern State Univ	OK	8,615	VC
Northern Arizona Univ	AZ	19,010	C
Northern Illinois Univ	IL	19,768	C
Northern Kentucky Univ	KY	21,134	C
Northern State Univ - Aberdeen	SD	14,505	C
Northwest Missouri State Univ	MO	17,347	C
Northwestern College	MN	24,000	C
Northwestern College of Iowa	IA	36,240	VC
Northwestern Okla State Univ	OK	7,275	NC
Northwestern State Univ of Louisiana	LA	14,368	C
Notre Dame College	OH	34,942	VC
Notre Dame of Maryland Univ	MD	27,700	VC
Nyack College	NY	33,250	C
Ohio Dominican Univ	OH	38,380	C+
Ohio Northern Univ	OH	42,075	VC
Ohio Univ	OH	21,080	C
Ohio Wesleyan Univ	OH	49,460	C+
Okla Baptist Univ	OK	28,202	C
Okla Christian Univ	OK	25,870	VC
Okla City Univ	OK	40,476	VC
Olivet Nazarene Univ	IL	29,990	C
Oral Roberts Univ	OK	31,734	C
Ouachita Baptist Univ	AR	30,220	VC
Our Lady of the Lake Univ	TX	22,430	LC
Pacific Union College	CA	28,150	VC
Paine College	GA	19,826	LC
Park Univ	MO	17,525	C
Philander Smith College	AR	19,760	LC
Piedmont College	GA	30,136	C
Pittsburg State Univ	KS	12,032	C
Point Park Univ	PA	36,390	C
Presbyterian College	SC	42,678	C+
Prescott College	AZ	33,284	C
Purdue Univ/Calumet	IN	14,336	C
Purdue Univ/West Lafayette	IN	20,024	HC
Queens College/The CUNY	NY	17,107	VC
Rhode Island College	RI	17,694	LC
Rider Univ	NJ	45,720	C
Ripon College	WI	36,959	C+
Rivier Univ	NH	35,000	VC
Roberts Wesleyan College	NY	38,306	C+
Roosevelt Univ	IL	22,605	VC
Rowan Univ	NJ	24,022	VC+
St. Joseph's Univ	PA	55,006	VC
St. Mary-of-the-Woods College	IN	37,722	LC
St. Vincent College	PA	40,244	C
St. Xavier Univ	IL	32,840	C
Salisbury Univ	MD	19,180	VC
Salve Regina Univ	RI	48,550	VC
Samford Univ	AL	37,060	C+
San Jose State Univ	CA	19,133	LC
Schreiner Univ	TX	32,734	LC
Seton Hill Univ	PA	35,172	C
Shawnee State Univ	OH	16,916	C
Shippensburg Univ of Pennsylvania	PA	20,934	C
Shorter Univ	GA	30,650	LC
Silver Lake College	WI	22,600	LC
Sinte Gleska Univ	SD	2,300	NC
Slippery Rock Univ of Pennsylvania	PA	10,360	C
Smith College	MA	59,674	MC
Sojourner-Douglass College	MD	9,160	LC
S Car State Univ	SC	6,700	LC
S Dak State Univ	SD	14,296	C
Southeast Missouri State Univ	MO	15,370	LC
Southeastern Louisiana Univ	LA	13,325	C
Southeastern Okla State Univ	OK	7,966	LC
Southern Conn State Univ	CT	18,033	LC
Southern Illinois Univ Carbondale	IL	21,942	C
Southern Illinois Univ Edwardsville	IL	17,532	C
Southern Nazarene Univ	OK	24,354	C
Southern New Hampshire Univ	NH	38,100	C
Southern Oregon Univ	OR	17,874	C
Southern Univ and A&M College	LA	9,761	LC
Southern Univ at New Orleans	LA	2,963	NC
Southern Wesleyan Univ	SC	25,600	C
Southwest Baptist Univ	MO	24,710	C
Southwest Minn State Univ	MN	14,000	C
Southwestern College	KS	29,270	C
Spring Hill College	AL	44,164	VC
Springfield College	MA	25,000	C
St. Ambrose Univ	IA	30,845	C
St. Catherine Univ	MN	37,782	C+
St. Cloud State Univ	MN	10,600	C
St. John's Univ	NY	55,070	C+
Stephens College	MO	38,042	VC
Stevenson Univ	MD	41,470	C
SUNY College at Geneseo	NY	18,670	HC
SUNY College at Old Westbury	NY	16,324	C
SUNY Fredonia/The SUNY at Fredonia	NY	19,840	C
SUNY New Paltz	NY	14,348	C
Susquehanna Univ	PA	51,150	C
Syracuse Univ	NY	56,346	VC
Taylor Univ	IN	37,821	VC+
Temple Univ	PA	24,392	VC
Tenn State Univ	TN	9,048	C
Tenn Wesleyan College	TN	21,250	C
Texas A&M Univ at Commerce	TX	10,496	C
Texas Christian Univ	TX	49,980	HC
Texas Tech Univ	TX	14,243	C
The Catholic Univ of America	DC	52,852	VC
The College of St. Rose	NY	26,750	C
The Lincoln Univ	PA	15,154	LC
The Pennsylvania State Univ - Univ Park	PA	28,022	VC+
The SUNY at Potsdam	NY	18,473	C
The Univ of N Car at Greensboro	NC	12,848	C
The Univ of N Car at Pembroke	NC	13,388	LC
The Univ of Okla	OK	18,621	VC
The Univ of Tenn at Chattanooga	TN	16,883	C
Thomas College	ME	33,560	LC
Thomas Univ	GA	11,520	NC
Toccoa Falls College	GA	23,210	LC
Towson Univ	MD	16,000	VC
Trevecca Nazarene Univ	TN	31,186	C
Trinity Washington Univ	DC	30,250	C+
Troy Univ	AL	10,650	C
Tulane Univ	LA	60,861	MC
Tusculum College	TN	24,295	C
Tuskegee Univ	AL	26,750	C
Univ of Akron	OH	20,436	C
Univ of Alabama at Birmingham	AL	18,484	C
Univ of Alabama at Tuscaloosa	AL	17,164	C+
Univ of Arizona	AZ	20,657	C
Univ of Arkansas at Fayetteville	AR	18,352	C+
Univ of Arkansas at Little Rock	AR	17,609	LC
Univ of Arkansas at Monticello	AR	12,076	NC
Univ of Arkansas at Pine Bluff	AR	13,378	C
Univ of Central Arkansas	AR	13,667	VC
Univ of Central Florida	FL	15,668	VC+
Univ of Central Missouri	MO	14,605	C
Univ of Central Okla	OK	12,293	C
Univ of Cincinnati	OH	21,506	VC
Univ of Dayton	OH	49,070	VC
Univ of Delaware	DE	23,612	VC
Univ of Detroit Mercy	MI	30,450	VC
Univ of Georgia	GA	20,082	VC
Univ of Hartford	CT	42,674	C
Univ of Illinois at Chicago	IL	24,505	VC
Univ of Illinois at Urbana-Champaign	IL	26,450	HC
Univ of Kansas	KS	17,603	C+
Univ of Kentucky	KY	19,868	C
Univ of Louisville	KY	17,946	C
Univ of Maine at Farmington	ME	18,187	LC
Univ of Mary	ND	16,714	C
Univ of Mary Hardin-Baylor	TX	31,950	C+
Univ of Maryland - College Park	MD	20,060	HC
Univ of Mass Boston	MA	23,066	VC
Univ of Mich/Dearborn	MI	9,885	VC
Univ of Mich-Flint	MI	17,547	C+
Univ of Minn Crookston	MN	17,834	C
Univ of Minn/Twin Cities	MN		HC
Univ of Missouri/Columbia	MO	18,201	MC
Univ of Missouri-Kansas City	MO	19,603	C
Univ of Missouri-St. Louis	MO		VC
Univ of Mobile	AL	28,935	VC
Univ of Montana-Western	MT	9,753	C
Univ of Mount Union	OH	35,130	C
Univ of Nebr - Lincoln	NE	18,031	VC
Univ of Nebr at Kearney	NE	14,855	LC
Univ of Nevada/Reno	NV	17,507	C
Univ of New Mexico	NM	15,300	C
Univ of New Orleans	LA	9,224	C
Univ of North Alabama	AL	9,960	C
Univ of N Car at Wilmington	NC	13,572	VC
Univ of N Dak	ND	14,551	C
Univ of North Georgia	GA	8,500	C
Univ of Northern Iowa	IA	15,795	C
Univ of PR/Bayamon	PR	1,600	
Univ of Rio Grande	OH	8,750	NC
Univ of Science and Arts of Okla	OK	10,560	C
Univ of Scranton	PA	51,940	VC
Univ of Sioux Falls	SD	22,990	C
Univ of South Alabama	AL	13,510	C
Univ of S Car Aiken	SC	16,712	C

ST = STATE　　　$IS = IN-STATE COSTS　　　SR = SELECTOR RATING

School	ST	$IS	SR
Univ of S Car at Columbia	SC	19,725	VC+
Univ of S Car Upstate	SC	18,200	LC
Univ of Southern Indiana	IN	14,885	C
Univ of Southern Miss	MS	13,170	C
Univ of Texas at San Antonio	TX	18,372	C
Univ of the District of Columbia	DC	7,244	LC
Univ of the Ozarks	AR	31,440	C
Univ of Toledo	OH	18,464	C
Univ of Vermont	VT	27,006	VC+
Univ of West Alabama	AL	14,274	C
Univ of West Florida	FL	14,656	C
Univ of West Georgia	GA	15,488	LC
Univ of Wisc Whitewater	WI	13,314	C
Univ of Wisc/Stevens Point	WI	14,043	C
Univ of Wisc/Stout	WI	15,459	C
Urbana Univ	OH	30,820	C
Ursuline College	OH	33,198	LC
Utah State Univ	UT	12,044	C
Vanderbilt Univ	TN	58,220	MC
Virginia Union Univ	VA	18,432	C
Walsh Univ	OH	35,100	C
Washburn Univ	KS	12,579	C
Washington State Univ	WA	20,461	C
Wayland Baptist Univ	TX	18,912	LC
Waynesburg Univ	PA	30,150	C
Webster Univ	MO	35,100	C+
Wesleyan College	GA	24,000	C
West Chester Univ of Pennsylvania	PA	17,186	C
West Liberty Univ	WV	9,142	LC
West Virginia State Univ	WV	8,378	NC
Western Carolina Univ	NC	13,965	C
Western Kentucky Univ	KY	11,000	LC
Western Mich Univ	MI	19,628	C
Western Washington Univ	WA	18,519	VC
Westfield State Univ	MA	18,297	C
Westminster College	UT	37,708	C+
Wheelock College	MA	33,075	C
Widener Univ	PA	52,418	C
William Woods Univ	MO	24,260	C
Wilmington College	OH	29,784	C
Wilmington Univ	DE	8,112	NC
Wilson College	PA	35,080	C
Winona State Univ	MN	16,640	C
Winthrop Univ	SC	21,120	C
Worcester State Univ	MA	19,812	C
Wright State Univ	OH	16,983	C
Xavier Univ	OH	44,980	VC
Youngstown State Univ	OH	16,732	C

EARLY CHILDHOOD STUDIES

School	ST	$IS	SR
Becker College	MA	41,420	C
Biola Univ	CA	40,320	C+
Bluffton Univ	OH	38,948	C
Boise State Univ	ID	13,469	LC
Calif Baptist Univ	CA	38,792	C
Grace Bible College	MI	20,770	C
Idaho State Univ	ID	12,307	C
Langston Univ	OK	3,000	C
Mayville State Univ	ND	11,401	NC
Metropolitan State Univ	MN	5,923	
Mills College	CA	54,119	VC
Missouri Southern State Univ	MO	12,061	C
Mount Mary Univ	WI	33,590	LC
National Univ	CA	14,730	SP
New York Univ	NY	61,470	MC
Niagara Univ	NY	41,010	C
Northern Illinois Univ	IL	19,768	C
Pittsburg State Univ	KS	12,032	C
Plymouth State Univ	NH	23,148	LC
Point Park Univ	PA	36,390	C
Rochester College	MI	18,320	LC
Samford Univ	AL	37,060	C+
Shippensburg Univ of Pennsylvania	PA	20,934	C
S Dak State Univ	SD	14,296	C
SUNY/Empire State College	NY	6,315	SP
SUNY Fredonia/The SUNY at Fredonia	NY	19,840	VC
Univ of Dayton	OH	49,070	VC
Univ of Minn/Duluth	MN	19,806	C
Univ of Missouri/Columbia	MO	18,201	MC
Univ of Nebr - Lincoln	NE	18,031	VC
Univ of N Dak	ND	14,551	C
Univ of Texas - Pan American	TX	11,125	LC
Wayne State College	NE	11,764	NC
Youngstown State Univ	OH	16,732	C

EARTH SCIENCE

School	ST	$IS	SR
Adams State Univ	CO	13,358	LC
Adrian College	MI	42,400	C
Alaska Pacific Univ	AK	43,592	VC
Albion College	MI	46,010	C
Arizona State Univ, at the Tempe Campus	AZ	20,137	C+
Augustana College	IL	43,398	VC
Baylor Univ	TX	50,329	HC
Bemidji State Univ	MN	13,500	VC
Boston Univ	MA	60,694	MC
Bowdoin College	ME	59,568	MC
Bowling Green State Univ	OH	18,970	C
Bridgewater State Univ	MA	18,752	C
Buffalo State College / SUNY	NY	15,733	C+
Calif Polytechnic State Univ	CA	19,847	HC
Cal State, Long Beach	CA	17,502	C+
Cal State, Monterey Bay	CA	26,871	C
Cal State, Northridge	CA	28,690	LC
Calvin College	MI	39,120	VC
Central Conn State Univ	CT	19,749	C
Central Washington Univ	WA	11,730	C
CUNY/Brooklyn College	NY	5,884	C+
CUNY/City College	NY	20,319	C+
Columbia Univ/City of New York	NY	61,116	MC
Columbus State Univ	GA	13,176	C
Dartmouth College	NH	57,996	MC
DePauw Univ	IN	48,950	VC+
Dickinson College	PA	57,662	HC+
Dickinson State Univ	ND	11,900	NC
East Stroudsburg Univ of Pennsylvania	PA	18,868	LC
Eastern Mich Univ	MI	18,604	C
Edinboro Univ of Pennsylvania	PA	15,940	LC
Emporia State Univ	KS	12,897	C
Fitchburg State Univ	MA	18,173	C
George Mason Univ	VA	15,724	VC
Georgia Inst of Technology	GA	21,828	MC
Grand Valley State Univ	MI	17,998	C+
Indiana Univ Kokomo	IN	6,811	C
Indiana Univ of Pennsylvania	PA	20,846	LC
Indiana Univ-Purdue Univ Fort Wayne	IN	15,521	C
Iowa State Univ	IA	16,403	C
Jackson State Univ	MS	13,512	LC
Johns Hopkins Univ	MD	47,492	MC
Kean Univ	NJ	23,444	C
Keene State College	NH	23,232	LC
Kent State Univ	OH	19,920	C
Lehigh Univ	PA	56,770	MC
Lock Haven Univ of Pennsylvania	PA	18,028	LC
Mass Inst of Technology	MA	58,240	MC
Mercer Univ	GA	44,201	VC
Mercyhurst Univ	PA	40,700	C
Miami Univ	OH	24,191	VC
Mich State Univ	MI	22,450	VC
Millersville Univ of Pennsylvania	PA	21,648	C
Minn State Univ, Mankato	MN	15,616	C
Minn State Univ, Moorhead	MN	13,392	VC
Minot State Univ	ND	10,915	C
Montana State Univ	MT	14,068	C
Morehead State Univ	KY	10,900	C
Murray State Univ	KY	15,304	C
Muskingum Univ	OH	30,502	C
National Univ	CA	14,730	SP
New Mexico Inst of Mining and Technology	NM	13,592	VC
New York Univ	NY	61,470	MC
N Car State Univ	NC	16,202	NC
N Dak State Univ	ND		
Northeastern Illinois Univ	IL	10,318	LC
Northeastern Univ	MA	55,296	MC
Northern Mich Univ	MI	18,278	C
Northland College	WI	26,680	C
Northwest Missouri State Univ	MO	17,347	C
Ohio Univ	OH	21,080	C
Ohio Wesleyan Univ	OH	49,460	C+
Old Dominion Univ	VA	19,483	LC
Oregon State Univ	OR	20,273	VC
Oswego / SUNY	NY	20,009	VC
Point Park Univ	PA	36,390	C
Prescott College	AZ	33,284	C
Purdue Univ/West Lafayette	IN	20,024	HC
Rice Univ	TX	43,288	MC
St. Louis Univ	MO	48,346	HC
St. Mary's Univ	TX	33,854	C
Salem State Univ	MA	13,161	LC
Salisbury Univ	MD	19,180	VC
San Francisco State Univ	CA	18,514	C
Shippensburg Univ of Pennsylvania	PA	20,934	C
Slippery Rock Univ of Pennsylvania	PA	10,360	C
Southern Conn State Univ	CT	18,033	LC
Southern Illinois Univ Edwardsville	IL	17,532	C
St. Cloud State Univ	MN	10,600	C
Stanford Univ	CA	58,388	MC
Stony Brook Univ / SUNY	NY	20,078	HC+
SUNY Fredonia/The SUNY at Fredonia	NY	19,840	VC
SUNY Oneonta / SUNY	NY	16,919	C+
Susquehanna Univ	PA	51,150	C
Syracuse Univ	NY	56,346	VC
Tarleton State Univ	TX	13,489	LC
Texas A&M Univ at Commerce	TX	10,496	C
Texas A&M Univ at Galveston	TX	11,258	C
Ohio State Univ-Columbus Campus	OH	19,887	HC+
The Pennsylvania State Univ - Univ Park	PA	28,022	VC+
The SUNY/College at Brockport	NY	19,002	C
The Univ of Memphis	TN	15,094	C
The Univ of Utah	UT	16,463	VC
Towson Univ	MD	16,000	VC
Tulane Univ	LA	60,861	MC
Univ at Albany / SUNY	NY	18,674	VC
Univ of Alabama in Huntsville	AL	17,591	VC+
Univ of Alaska Fairbanks	AK	15,130	C
Univ of Arkansas at Fayetteville	AR	18,352	C+
Univ of Calif at Berkeley	CA	23,322	MC
Univ of Calif at Irvine	CA	25,961	VC
Univ of Calif at Los Angeles	CA	25,686	MC
Univ of Calif at San Diego	CA	21,000	VC
Univ of Calif at Santa Barbara	CA	27,551	HC
Univ of Calif at Santa Cruz	CA	27,807	C+
Univ of Central Missouri	MO	14,605	C
Univ of Florida	FL	15,943	HC
Univ of Illinois at Chicago	IL	24,505	VC
Univ of Indianapolis	IN	31,740	LC
Univ of Maine	ME	19,902	C+
Univ of Mass Amherst	MA	24,215	VC+
Univ of Mass Boston	MA	23,066	VC
Univ of Mich/Ann Arbor	MI	22,102	MC
Univ of Nevada, Las Vegas	NV	17,303	C
Univ of New Hampshire	NH	26,912	C
Univ of New Mexico	NM	15,300	C
Univ of New Orleans	LA	9,224	C
Univ of N Car at Charlotte	NC	15,547	C
Univ of Northern Colo	CO	18,446	C
Univ of Northern Iowa	IA	15,795	C
Univ of S Dak	SD	15,111	C
Univ of Texas at El Paso	TX	8,764	NC
Univ of Wisc/Green Bay	WI	19,074	C
Univ of Wyoming	WY	14,401	C+
Utah State Univ	UT	12,044	C
Vanderbilt Univ	TN	58,220	MC
Vassar College	NY	61,140	MC
Virginia Wesleyan College	VA	28,433	LC
Washington Univ in St. Louis	MO	69,844	MC
Wesleyan Univ	CT	61,198	MC
West Chester Univ of Pennsylvania	PA	17,186	C
Western Conn State Univ	CT	18,327	LC
Western Mich Univ	MI	19,628	C
Western Oregon Univ	OR	15,021	C
Western Washington Univ	WA	18,519	VC
Wilkes Univ	PA	44,070	C
Winona State Univ	MN	16,640	C

EARTH SCIENCE / ADOLESCENCE EDUCATION

School	ST	$IS	SR
Arizona State Univ, at the Polytechnic Campus	AZ	20,531	C+
Arizona State Univ, at the West Campus	AZ	19,251	C
Elizabethtown College	PA	49,740	VC
Indiana Univ Bloomington	IN	19,801	VC
Indiana Univ-Purdue Univ Indianapolis	IN	17,611	C
LIU Post	NY	47,660	C
Murray State Univ	KY	15,304	C
Old Dominion Univ	VA	19,483	LC
Oswego / SUNY	NY	20,009	VC
Pace Univ	NY	53,367	C
Syracuse Univ	NY	56,346	VC
Temple Univ	PA	24,392	VC
The College of St. Rose	NY	26,750	C
Univ of Nebr - Lincoln	NE	18,031	VC
Winona State Univ	MN	16,640	C

EAST ASIAN LANGUAGES AND LITERATURE

School	ST	$IS	SR
Austin College	TX	45,875	HC
Beloit College	WI	49,970	VC
Indiana Univ Bloomington	IN	19,801	VC
Miami Univ	OH	24,191	VC
Mich State Univ	MI	22,450	VC
Rutgers, The State Univ of New Jersey/New Brunswick	NJ	25,562	VC
Smith College	MA	59,674	MC
Univ of Chicago	IL	55,416	MC
Univ of Florida	FL	15,943	HC
Univ of Illinois at Urbana-Champaign	IL	26,450	HC
Univ of Kansas	KS	17,603	C+
Univ of Puget Sound	WA	54,608	HC
Univ of Southern Calif	CA	56,903	MC
Washington Univ in St. Louis	MO	69,844	MC
Yale Univ	CT	55,300	MC

EAST ASIAN STUDIES

School	ST	$IS	SR
Appalachian State Univ	NC	12,919	VC
Augsburg College	MN	35,142	C
Barnard College/Columbia Univ	NY	39,000	MC
Bates College	ME	60,720	MC
Binghamton Univ/The SUNY	NY	21,648	HC+
Brandeis Univ	MA		MC
Brown Univ	RI	59,428	MC
Bryn Mawr College	PA	59,890	MC
Bucknell Univ	PA	60,140	MC
Colby College	ME	57,510	MC
Columbia Univ/City of New York	NY	61,116	MC
Columbia Univ/School of General Studies	NY	58,231	MC
Conn College	CT	54,970	MC
Davidson College	NC	58,146	MC
Denison Univ	OH	54,670	HC+
DePaul Univ	IL	47,623	VC
DePauw Univ	IN	48,950	VC+
Dickinson College	PA	57,662	HC+
Eckerd College	FL	43,902	C
Emory and Henry College	VA	387,460	C
George Washington Univ	DC	57,108	MC
Hamline Univ	MN	45,678	VC
Haverford College	PA	61,564	MC
Indiana Univ Bloomington	IN	19,801	VC
John Carroll Univ	OH	46,300	C+
Johns Hopkins Univ	MD	47,492	MC
Lawrence Univ	WI	46,371	VC
Lewis & Clark College	OR	54,382	MC
Mary Baldwin College	VA	38,245	C
Middlebury College	VT	59,160	MC
Minn State Univ, Moorhead	MN	13,392	VC
Mount Holyoke College	MA	45,146	MC
New York Univ	NY	61,470	MC
North Central College	IL	38,343	VC
Oakland Univ	MI	39,391	C
Oberlin College	OH	61,788	MC
Occidental College	CA	60,972	MC
Princeton Univ	NJ	53,795	MC
Queens College/The CUNY	NY	17,107	VC
Simmons College	MA	49,966	C
Stanford Univ	CA	58,388	MC
Univ at Albany / SUNY	NY	18,674	VC
Univ of Arizona	AZ	20,657	C
Univ of Calif at Davis	CA		HC
Univ of Calif at Irvine	CA	25,961	VC
Univ of Calif at Los Angeles	CA	25,686	MC
Univ of Delaware	DE	23,612	VC
Univ of Illinois at Urbana-Champaign	IL	26,450	HC
Univ of Minn/Twin Cities	MN		HC
Univ of Rochester	NY	60,668	MC
Univ of Southern Calif	CA	56,903	MC
Ursinus College	PA	57,580	VC
Valparaiso Univ	IN	44,940	VC+
Vanderbilt Univ	TN	58,220	MC
Washington and Lee Univ	VA	52,812	MC
Washington Univ in St. Louis	MO	69,844	MC
Wesleyan Univ	CT	61,198	MC
Western Washington Univ	WA	18,519	VC
Wittenberg Univ	OH	47,962	C+
Yale Univ	CT	55,300	MC

EASTERN EUROPEAN STUDIES

School	ST	$IS	SR
Bowdoin College	ME	59,568	MC
Florida State Univ	FL	16,715	VC
Indiana Univ Bloomington	IN	19,801	VC
Kent State Univ	OH	19,920	C
Oberlin College	OH	61,788	MC
Ohio Univ	OH	21,080	C
Rutgers, The State Univ of New Jersey/Newark Campus	NJ	258,806	C
Univ of Mich/Ann Arbor	MI	22,102	MC
Univ of Texas at Austin	TX	44,074	HC
Washington Univ in St. Louis	MO	69,844	MC
Yale Univ	CT	55,300	MC

ECOLOGY

School	ST	$IS	SR
Adams State Univ	CO	13,358	LC
Angelo State Univ	TX	15,049	NC
Appalachian State Univ	NC	12,919	VC
Bard College at Simon's Rock	MA	61,749	HC+
Beloit College	WI	49,970	VC
Bennington College	VT	56,990	HC+
Boston Univ	MA	60,694	MC
Cal State, Long Beach	CA	17,502	C+
Castleton State College	VT	20,186	C
Colo State Univ-Fort Collins	CO	20,385	VC
Defiance College	OH	30,645	C
Florida Inst of Technology	FL	48,290	VC
Florida State Univ	FL	16,715	VC
Georgia Regents Univ	GA		C
Goshen College	IN	35,900	VC
Hampshire College	MA	58,320	MC
Idaho State Univ	ID	12,307	C
Kutztown Univ of Pennsylvania	PA	16,909	LC
Le Moyne College	NY	43,470	C
Marshall Univ	WV	14,820	C
Mich Tech Univ	MI	23,556	HC
Missouri Southern State Univ	MO	12,061	C
Montana State Univ-Northern	MT	12,500	NC
Morehead State Univ	KY	10,900	C
New Mexico State Univ	NM	14,050	C
Northern Mich Univ	MI	18,278	C
Northwest Missouri State Univ	MO	17,347	C
Northwestern Univ	IL	61,640	MC
Ohio Univ	OH	21,080	C
Oregon State Univ	OR	20,273	VC

ST = STATE $IS = IN-STATE COSTS   SR = SELECTOR RATING

School	ST	$IS	SR
Prescott College	AZ	33,284	C
Princeton Univ	NJ	53,795	MC
Purdue Univ/West Lafayette	IN	20,024	HC
Rutgers, The State Univ of New Jersey/New Brunswick	NJ	25,562	VC
Sacred Heart Univ	CT	49,264	VC
San Diego State Univ	CA	21,611	C+
San Francisco State Univ	CA	18,514	C
S Dak State Univ	SD	14,296	C
Southern Illinois Univ Edwardsville	IL	17,532	C
SUNY / College of Environmental Science and Forestry	NY	18,351	VC
Sterling College	VT	26,160	C
Stony Brook Univ / SUNY	NY	20,078	HC+
SUNY Plattsburgh / SUNY	NY	18,083	C
Susquehanna Univ	PA	51,150	C
Ohio State Univ-Columbus Campus	OH	19,887	HC+
Tulane Univ	LA	60,861	MC
Unity College	ME	34,054	C
Univ of Arizona	AZ	20,657	C
Univ of Calif at Davis	CA		HC
Univ of Calif at Irvine	CA	25,961	VC
Univ of Calif at Los Angeles	CA	25,686	MC
Univ of Calif at San Diego	CA	21,000	VC
Univ of Calif at Santa Barbara	CA	27,551	MC
Univ of Calif at Santa Cruz	CA	27,807	C+
Univ of Colo Boulder	CO	22,605	VC+
Univ of Denver	CO	51,787	VC+
Univ of Georgia	GA	20,082	VC
Univ of Mich/Ann Arbor	MI	22,102	MC
Univ of Mich-Flint	MI	17,547	C+
Univ of Minn/Twin Cities	MN		HC
Univ of Montana	MT	14,105	C
Univ of Pittsburgh at Pittsburgh	PA	28,572	HC+
Univ of Rochester	NY	60,668	MC
Univ of Wyoming	WY	14,401	C+
Vanderbilt Univ	TN	58,220	MC
Washington Univ in St. Louis	MO	69,844	MC
West Chester Univ of Pennsylvania	PA	17,186	C
Western Washington Univ	WA	18,519	VC

ECONOMICS

School	ST	$IS	SR
Adams State Univ	CO	13,358	LC
Adelphi Univ	NY	44,670	VC
Adrian College	MI	42,400	C
Agnes Scott College	GA	45,323	C+
Alabama A&M Univ	AL	10,084	C
Albion College	MI	46,010	C
Albright College	PA	46,660	C
Alcorn State Univ	MS	9,500	C
Allegheny College	PA	50,980	HC
Alma College	MI	44,075	C
American International College	MA	36,100	LC
American Univ	DC	56,015	HC+
Amherst College	MA	58,744	MC
Anderson Univ	IN	36,100	C
Andrews Univ	MI	28,030	C+
Appalachian State Univ	NC	12,919	VC
Aquinas College	MI	33,060	C
Arizona State Univ, at the Tempe Campus	AZ	20,137	C+
Arkansas State Univ	AR	15,470	C
Arkansas Tech Univ	AR	13,982	LC
Armstrong State Univ	GA	15,532	C
Ashland Univ	OH	25,000	C
Assumption College	MA	47,122	C+
Auburn Univ	AL	22,378	VC+
Augsburg College	MN	35,142	C
Augustana College	IL	43,398	VC
Augustana College	SD	36,500	VC
Austin College	TX	45,875	HC
Baker Univ	KS	33,350	C+
Baldwin Wallace Univ	OH	38,318	C
Ball State Univ	IN	17,850	C
Bard College	NY	61,940	HC
Barnard College/Columbia Univ	NY	39,000	MC
Barry Univ	FL	38,190	C
Barton College	NC	27,660	LC
Bates College	ME	60,720	MC
Baylor Univ	TX	50,329	VC
Bellarmine Univ	KY	42,950	VC
Belmont Univ	TN	39,190	VC+
Beloit College	WI	49,970	VC
Bemidji State Univ	MN	13,500	VC
Benedict College	SC	20,454	NC
Benedictine College	KS	29,180	VC
Benedictine Univ	IL	37,820	C
Bentley Univ	MA	56,454	HC+
Berea College	KY	7,192	C
Berry College	GA	39,254	VC
Bethany College	WV	35,282	LC
Bethel College	IN	31,560	C
Bethel Univ	MN	34,940	VC
Binghamton Univ/The SUNY	NY	21,648	HC+
Biola Univ	CA	40,320	C
Birmingham-Southern College	AL	44,168	VC+

School	ST	$IS	SR
Black Hills State Univ	SD	13,947	C
Bloomsburg Univ of Pennsylvania	PA	13,598	C
Bluffton Univ	OH	38,948	C
Boise State Univ	ID	13,469	LC
Boston College	MA	60,622	MC
Boston Univ	MA	60,694	MC
Bowdoin College	ME	59,568	MC
Bowling Green State Univ	OH	18,970	C
Bradley Univ	IL	31,874	VC
Brandeis Univ	MA		MC
Bridgewater College	VA	41,450	C
Bridgewater State Univ	MA	18,752	C
Brigham Young Univ	UT	12,100	HC
Brown Univ	RI	59,428	MC
Bryant Univ	RI	49,179	VC
Bryn Mawr College	PA	59,890	MC
Bucknell Univ	PA	60,140	MC
Buena Vista Univ	IA	39,188	C
Buffalo State College / SUNY	NY	15,733	C+
Butler Univ	IN	47,572	VC+
Cabrini College	PA	40,859	LC
Calif Inst of Technology	CA	54,045	MC
Calif Lutheran Univ	CA	49,540	C+
Calif Polytechnic State Univ	CA	19,847	HC
Calif State Polytechnic Univ, Pomona	CA	20,156	C
Cal State, Bakersfield	CA	8,000	C
Cal State, Chico	CA	20,158	C
Cal State, East Bay	CA	16,549	C
Cal State, Fresno	CA	17,405	C
Cal State, Fullerton	CA	25,188	C
Cal State, Long Beach	CA	17,502	C+
Cal State, Los Angeles	CA	17,186	LC
Cal State, Northridge	CA	28,690	LC
Cal State, Sacramento	CA	16,200	C
Cal State, San Bernardino	CA	12,000	C
Cal State, San Marcos	CA	14,576	LC
Cal State, Stanislaus	CA	18,582	C
Calvin College	MI	39,120	VC
Campbell Univ	NC	37,570	VC
Campbellsville Univ	KY	27,720	C
Capital Univ	OH	41,050	VC
Carleton College	MN	60,102	MC
Carnegie Mellon Univ	PA	51,260	MC
Carroll Univ	WI	38,100	C
Carson-Newman Univ	TN	29,058	C+
Carthage College	WI	33,000	C
Case Western Reserve Univ	OH	56,534	MC
Castleton State College	VT	20,186	C
Catawba College	NC	37,240	LC
Centenary College of Louisiana	LA	45,650	C+
Central College	IA	42,104	C
Central Conn State Univ	CT	19,749	C
Central State Univ	OH	9,010	C
Central Washington Univ	WA	11,730	C
Centre College	KY	35,000	HC+
Chancellor Univ	OH	11,000	C
Chapman Univ	CA	58,347	VC+
Charleston Southern Univ	SC	22,420	C
Chatham Univ	PA	43,797	C
Cheyney Univ of Pennsylvania	PA	20,372	C
Chicago State Univ	IL	5,482	C
Christopher Newport Univ	VA	21,960	VC
CUNY/Baruch College	NY		HC
CUNY/Brooklyn College	NY	5,884	C+
CUNY/City College	NY	20,319	HC+
Claremont McKenna College	CA	62,215	MC
Clarion Univ of Pennsylvania	PA	17,370	LC
Clark Atlanta Univ	GA	30,006	LC
Clark Univ	MA	47,020	HC+
Clemson Univ	SC	19,136	HC
Cleveland State Univ	OH	21,776	C
Coastal Carolina Univ	SC	18,580	C
Coe College	IA	45,550	VC
Colby College	ME	57,510	MC
Colgate Univ	NY	58,135	MC
College of Charleston	SC	22,145	VC
College of Mount St. Vincent	NY	41,040	MC
College of New Jersey	NJ	25,376	HC
College of St. Benedict	MN	49,359	VC
College of St. Elizabeth	NJ	43,839	C
College of St. Scholastica	MN	41,440	C
College of Staten Island/The City of New Yok	NY	16,778	NC
College of the Holy Cross	MA	58,042	MC
College of William & Mary	VA	28,000	MC
College of Wooster	OH	52,600	VC
Colo College	CO	57,162	MC
Colo School of Mines	CO	18,000	HC
Colo State Univ-Fort Collins	CO	20,385	VC
Colo State Univ-Pueblo	CO	16,183	C
Columbia Univ/City of New York	NY	61,116	MC
Columbia Univ/School of General Studies	NY	58,231	MC
Conn College	CT	54,970	MC
Converse College	SC	37,130	C
Cornell College	IA	44,930	VC
Cornell Univ	NY	60,964	MC
Covenant College	GA	38,990	VC+
Creighton Univ	NE	45,356	VC
Dartmouth College	NH	57,996	MC
Davidson College	NC	58,146	MC

School	ST	$IS	SR
Davis & Elkins College	WV	33,742	C
Delaware State Univ	DE	16,722	LC
Denison Univ	OH	54,670	HC+
DePaul Univ	IL	47,623	VC
DePauw Univ	IN	48,950	VC+
Dickinson College	PA	57,662	HC+
Dillard Univ	LA	20,940	VC
Doane College	NE	35,230	C
Dominican Univ	IL	37,628	C
Dordt College	IA	34,160	C+
Dowling College	NY	25,000	LC
Drake Univ	IA	41,516	VC+
Drew Univ/College of Liberal Arts	NJ	57,516	C
Drexel Univ	PA	61,418	VC+
Drury Univ	MO	31,909	VC
Duke Univ	NC	50,250	MC
Duquesne Univ	PA	43,720	VC
Earlham College	IN	51,470	HC
East Carolina Univ	NC	14,169	C
East Stroudsburg Univ of Pennsylvania	PA	18,868	LC
East Tenn State Univ	TN	9,000	C
Eastern Conn State Univ	CT	20,584	C
Eastern Illinois Univ	IL	20,466	C
Eastern Kentucky Univ	KY	11,161	C
Eastern Mennonite Univ	VA	40,660	C
Eastern Mich Univ	MI	18,604	C
Eastern Washington Univ	WA		C
Eckerd College	FL	43,902	C
Edgewood College	WI	33,294	C
Edinboro Univ of Pennsylvania	PA	15,940	LC
Elizabethtown College	PA	49,740	VC
Elmhurst College	IL	43,336	C
Elon Univ	NC	41,914	VC+
Emory and Henry College	VA	387,460	C
Emory Univ	GA	56,368	MC
Emporia State Univ	KS	12,897	C
Eugene Lang College/The New School for Liberal Arts	NY	55,650	C
Excelsior College	NY	5,580	SP
Fairfield Univ	CT	56,960	VC
Fairleigh Dickinson Univ/ College at Florham	NJ	42,142	C
Fairleigh Dickinson Univ/ Metropolitan Campus	NJ	40,254	C
Fayetteville State Univ	NC	10,816	C
Fisk Univ	TN	19,830	C
Fitchburg State Univ	MA	18,173	C
Flagler College	FL	25,180	C
Florida A&M Univ	FL	14,935	LC
Florida Atlantic Univ	FL	17,339	C
Florida Gulf Coast Univ	FL		C
Florida International Univ	FL	17,747	C+
Florida Southern College	FL	40,150	C+
Florida State Univ	FL	16,715	VC
Fordham Univ	NY	61,588	HC+
Fort Hays State Univ	KS	11,354	C
Fort Lewis College	CO	15,513	C
Fort Valley State Univ	GA	11,200	VC
Framingham State Univ	MA	18,854	C
Francis Marion Univ	SC	16,464	LC
Franciscan Univ of Steubenville	OH	27,320	VC
Franklin and Marshall College	PA	60,799	MC
Franklin College	IN	36,585	C
Frostburg State Univ	MD	15,264	LC
Furman Univ	SC	54,006	HC
Gallaudet Univ	DC	25,380	SP
George Fox Univ	OR	40,750	C+
George Mason Univ	VA	15,724	VC
George Washington Univ	DC	57,108	MC
Georgetown College	KY	41,440	C+
Georgetown Univ	DC	52,910	MC
Georgia College and State Univ	GA	18,900	C+
Georgia Inst of Technology	GA	21,828	MC
Georgia Southern Univ	GA	16,942	C
Georgia State Univ	GA	15,582	VC
Gettysburg College	PA	58,820	HC
Goldey-Beacom College	DE	27,493	C
Gonzaga Univ	WA	46,441	HC
Gordon College	MA	44,320	VC
Goshen College	IN	35,900	VC
Goucher College	MD	52,040	VC+
Graceland Univ	IA	28,020	C
Grambling State Univ	LA	13,384	LC
Grand Valley State Univ	MI	17,998	C+
Grinnell College	IA	53,654	HC
Grove City College	PA	24,022	VC
Guilford College	NC	42,800	C
Gustavus Adolphus College	MN	48,170	HC
Hamilton College	NY	55,620	MC
Hamline Univ	MN	45,678	VC
Hampden-Sydney College	VA	51,758	C+
Hampshire College	MA	58,320	MC
Hampton Univ	VA	28,528	C
Hanover College	IN	43,073	C+
Harding Univ	AR	23,556	C
Hardin-Simmons Univ	TX	23,560	C
Hartwick College	NY	51,270	C
Harvard College/Harvard Univ	MA	49,000	MC

School	ST	$IS	SR
Hastings College	NE	27,782	C+
Haverford College	PA	61,564	MC
Hawaii Pacific Univ	HI	34,360	C
Heidelberg Univ	OH	34,100	C
Hendrix College	AR	50,202	VC+
Hillsdale College	MI	32,866	MC
Hiram College	OH	37,300	VC
Hobart and William Smith Colleges	NY	60,034	HC+
Hofstra Univ	NY	51,810	VC+
Hollins Univ	VA	43,295	VC
Hood College	MD	45,730	C
Hope College	MI	38,650	VC
Houston Baptist Univ	TX	36,450	C
Howard Univ	DC	13,646	C
Hunter College	NY	14,429	VC
Huntington Univ	IN	32,220	C+
Idaho State Univ	ID	12,307	C
Illinois College	IL	25,770	VC
Illinois State Univ	IL	23,110	VC
Illinois Wesleyan Univ	IL	48,452	HC
Immaculata Univ	PA	43,000	C
Indiana State Univ	IN	16,000	C
Indiana Univ Bloomington	IN	19,801	VC
Indiana Univ Northwest	IN	6,854	LC
Indiana Univ of Pennsylvania	PA	20,846	LC
Indiana Univ South Bend	IN	15,501	C
Indiana Univ Southeast	IN	16,035	C
Indiana Univ-Purdue Univ Fort Wayne	IN	15,521	C
Indiana Univ-Purdue Univ Indianapolis	IN	17,611	C
Indiana Wesleyan Univ	IN	31,815	VC
Inter-American Univ of PR/ San Germán	PR	6,720	
Iona College	NY	44,028	C
Iowa State Univ	IA	16,403	C
Ithaca College	NY	53,864	HC
Jackson State Univ	MS	13,512	LC
Jacksonville State Univ	AL	12,480	LC
Jacksonville Univ	FL	37,780	C
James Madison Univ	VA	18,049	VC
John Carroll Univ	OH	46,300	C+
John Jay College of Criminal Justice/The CUNY	NY	6,359	LC
Johns Hopkins Univ	MD	47,492	MC
Johnson C. Smith Univ	NC	25,336	LC
Juniata College	PA	49,340	VC
Kalamazoo College	MI	49,740	HC
Kansas State Univ	KS	15,497	VC
Kean Univ	NJ	23,444	C
Keene State College	NH	23,232	LC
Kennesaw State Univ	GA		C
Kent State Univ	OH	19,920	C
Kenyon College	OH	58,890	MC
King Univ	TN	33,140	C
King's College	PA	43,502	C
Knox College	IL	44,865	VC+
La Salle Univ	PA	50,270	C
Lafayette College	PA	59,155	HC+
Lake Forest College	IL	50,652	VC
Lake Superior State Univ	MI	18,121	C
Lakeland College	WI	22,990	C
Lamar Univ	TX	6,820	LC
Langston Univ	OK	3,000	C
Lawrence Univ	WI	46,371	HC
Le Moyne College	NY	43,470	C
Lebanon Valley College	PA	38,570	C
Lehigh Univ	PA	56,770	MC
Lehman College/The CUNY	NY	5,778	LC
Lenoir-Rhyne College	NC	35,984	C
Lewis & Clark College	OR	54,382	MC
Lewis Univ	IL	23,050	C
Limestone College	SC	30,800	C
Linfield College-McMinnville Campus	OR	47,676	C
Lipscomb Univ	TN	37,490	VC
LIU Brooklyn	NY	47,182	LC
LIU Post	NY	47,660	C
Lock Haven Univ of Pennsylvania	PA	18,028	LC
Longwood Univ	VA	20,924	C
Loras College	IA	37,432	VC
Louisiana College	LA	15,746	C
Louisiana State Univ	LA	18,677	C+
Loyola Marymount Univ	CA	54,649	VC+
Loyola Univ Chicago	IL	51,646	VC+
Loyola Univ Maryland	MD	56,880	VC+
Loyola Univ New Orleans	LA	46,581	VC
Lubbock Christian Univ	TX	26,308	C
Luther College	IA	45,720	C
Lycoming College	PA	45,379	C
Lynchburg College	VA	42,645	C
Lyon College	AR	32,090	C+
Macalester College	MN	57,691	MC
Manchester Univ	IN	35,070	C
Manhattan College	NY	49,588	C+
Manhattanville College	NY	50,740	VC
Mansfield Univ	PA	19,468	LC
Marian Univ	IN	38,540	C
Marian Univ	WI	32,420	LC
Marietta College	OH	42,135	C
Marist College	NY	35,500	C
Marlboro College	VT	35,980	VC
Marquette Univ	WI	46,930	VC+
Marshall Univ	WV	14,820	C

ST = STATE   **$IS** = IN-STATE COSTS   **SR** = SELECTOR RATING

School	ST	$IS	SR
Mary Baldwin College	VA	38,245	C
Marymount Univ	VA	39,480	C
Maryville College	TN	33,150	C+
Mass Inst of Technology	MA	58,240	MC
McDaniel College	MD	47,450	VC
McKendree Univ	IL	29,920	C+
Mercer Univ	GA	44,201	VC
Meredith College	NC	31,420	C
Merrimack College	MA	44,215	C
Messiah College	PA	40,690	C+
Methodist Univ	NC	37,185	C
Metropolitan State Univ	MN	5,923	
Metropolitan State Univ of Denver	CO	4,835	LC
Miami Univ	OH	24,191	VC
Mich State Univ	MI	22,450	VC
Mich Tech Univ	MI	23,556	HC
Middle Tenn State Univ	TN	8,650	C
Middlebury College	VT	59,160	MC
Midland Univ	NE	34,000	C
Midwestern State Univ	TX	9,722	C
Millersville Univ of Pennsylvania	PA	21,648	C
Mills College	CA	54,119	VC
Millsaps College	MS	43,888	VC+
Minn State Univ, Mankato	MN	15,616	C
Minn State Univ, Moorhead	MN	13,392	VC
Minot State Univ	ND	10,915	C
Miss State Univ	MS	14,750	C
Missouri Southern State Univ	MO	12,061	C
Missouri State Univ	MO	13,996	C+
Missouri Univ of Science and Technology	MO	18,655	VC+
Missouri Valley College	MO	22,200	C
Missouri Western State Univ	MO	12,260	NC
Monmouth College	IL	40,850	C
Montana State Univ	MT	14,068	C
Montclair State Univ	NJ	22,614	C
Moravian College	PA	36,381	VC
Morehouse College	GA	39,412	C
Morgan State Univ	MD	14,500	VC
Mount Holyoke College	MA	55,146	MC
Mount St. Mary's Univ	MD	47,996	C
Muhlenberg College	PA	52,837	HC
Murray State Univ	KY	15,304	C
Muskingum Univ	OH	30,502	C
Nazareth College of Rochester	NY	43,028	C+
Nebr Wesleyan Univ	NE	29,774	C+
New College of Florida	FL	14,504	NC
New Jersey City Univ	NJ	21,456	LC
New Mexico State Univ	NM	14,050	C
New York Univ	NY	61,470	MC
Niagara Univ	NY	41,010	C
Nichols College	MA	37,240	LC
N Car Agricultural and Technical State Univ	NC	13,365	LC
N Car State Univ	NC	16,202	HC
North Central College	IL	38,343	VC
N Dak State Univ	ND		C
North Park Univ	IL	30,130	C
Northeastern Illinois Univ	IL	10,318	LC
Northeastern Univ	MA	55,296	MC
Northern Illinois Univ	IL	19,768	C
Northern Kentucky Univ	KY	21,134	C
Northern Mich Univ	MI	19,278	C
Northern State Univ - Aberdeen	SD	14,505	C
Northwest Missouri State Univ	MO	17,347	C
Northwestern College of Iowa	IA	36,240	VC
Northwestern Okla State Univ	OK	7,275	NC
Northwestern Univ	IL	61,640	MC
Notre Dame College	OH	34,942	VC
Notre Dame of Maryland Univ	MD	27,700	VC
Oakland Univ	MI	19,391	C
Oberlin College	OH	61,284	C
Occidental College	CA	60,972	MC
Oglethorpe Univ	GA	44,200	C+
Ohio Dominican Univ	OH	38,380	C
Ohio Univ	OH	21,080	C
Ohio Wesleyan Univ	OH	49,460	C+
Okla City Univ	OK	40,476	VC
Okla State Univ	OK	14,310	VC
Old Dominion Univ	VA	19,483	LC
Olivet College	MI	19,984	LC
Olivet Nazarene Univ	IL	29,990	C
Oregon State Univ	OR	20,273	VC
Oswego / SUNY	NY	20,009	VC
Otterbein College	OH	32,214	C
Pace Univ	NY	53,367	C
Pacific Lutheran Univ	WA	46,760	C+
Pacific Univ	OR	49,626	C+
Park Univ	MO	17,525	C
Penn State Erie/The Behrend College	PA	16,256	C
Pepperdine Univ	CA	55,372	HC+
Pitzer College	CA	54,988	MC
Plymouth State Univ	NH	23,148	LC
Point Loma Nazarene Univ	CA	41,006	C+
Pomona College	CA	57,680	MC
Portland State Univ	OR	18,672	C
Prescott College	AZ	33,284	C
Princeton Univ	NJ	53,795	MC
Principia College	IL	35,140	C+
Providence College	RI	57,383	VC
Purdue Univ/West Lafayette	IN	20,024	HC
Queens College/The CUNY	NY	17,107	C
Quinnipiac Univ	CT	55,160	VC
Radford Univ	VA	17,766	LC
Ramapo College of New Jersey	NJ	24,938	C
Randolph College	VA	45,660	VC
Randolph-Macon College	VA	49,869	C+
Reed College	OR	57,780	MC
Regis Univ	CO	41,318	C
Rensselaer Polytechnic Inst	NY	61,529	MC
Rhode Island College	RI	17,694	LC
Rhodes College	TN	51,900	HC+
Rice Univ	TX	43,288	MC
Richard Stockton College of New Jersey	NJ	20,000	VC
Rider Univ	NJ	45,720	C
Ripon College	WI	36,959	C+
Roanoke College	VA	49,976	C
Robert Morris Univ	PA	37,864	C
Rochester Inst of Technology	NY	42,450	VC
Rockford College	IL	31,000	C
Rockhurst Univ	MO	20,625	C
Roger Williams Univ	RI	46,296	VC
Rollins College	FL	52,370	HC
Roosevelt Univ	IL	22,605	VC
Rose-Hulman Inst of Technology	IN	53,340	MC
Rosemont College	PA	42,350	C
Rowan Univ	NJ	24,022	VC+
Rutgers, The State Univ of New Jersey/Camden Campus	NJ	25,121	C
Rutgers, The State Univ of New Jersey/New Brunswick	NJ	25,562	VC
Rutgers, The State Univ of New Jersey/Newark Campus	NJ	258,806	C
Saginaw Valley State Univ	MI	17,369	C
St. Anselm College	NH	49,376	VC
St. Francis Univ	PA	30,029	LC
St. John's Univ	MN	47,984	C
St. Joseph's College	IN	36,500	C
St. Joseph's Univ	PA	55,006	VC
St. Leo Univ	FL	30,340	C
St. Mary's College	IN	45,160	C+
St. Mary's College of Calif	CA	53,550	C
St. Mary's Univ	TX	33,854	C
St. Michael's College	VT	49,975	VC
St. Peter's Univ	NJ	44,240	C
St. Vincent College	PA	40,244	C
Salem College	NC	29,326	VC
Salem State Univ	MA	13,161	LC
Salisbury Univ	MD	19,180	VC
Salve Regina Univ	RI	48,550	VC
Sam Houston State Univ	TX	17,082	C
Samford Univ	AL	37,060	C
San Diego State Univ	CA	21,611	C+
San Francisco State Univ	CA	18,514	C
San Jose State Univ	CA	19,133	LC
Sarah Lawrence College	NY	48,000	HC
Scripps College	CA	61,940	MC
Seattle Pacific Univ	WA	41,559	VC+
Seattle Univ	WA	49,035	VC+
Seton Hall Univ	NJ	45,902	C
Seton Hill Univ	PA	35,172	C
Sewanee: The Univ of the South	TN	47,700	HC+
Shenandoah Univ	VA	39,916	C
Shepherd Univ	WV	15,875	C
Shippensburg Univ of Pennsylvania	PA	20,934	C
Shorter Univ	GA	30,650	LC
Siena College	NY	43,863	VC
Simmons College	MA	49,966	VC
Simpson College	IA	36,086	C+
Skidmore College	NY	59,942	HC
Slippery Rock Univ of Pennsylvania	PA	10,360	C
Smith College	MA	59,674	MC
Sonoma State Univ	CA	20,541	C
S Dak State Univ	SD	14,296	C
Southeast Missouri State Univ	MO	15,370	LC
Southeastern Okla State Univ	OK	7,966	LC
Southern Connecticut State Univ	CT	18,033	LC
Southern Illinois Univ Carbondale	IL	21,942	C
Southern Illinois Univ Edwardsville	IL	17,532	C
Southern Methodist Univ	TX	60,585	MC
Southern Oregon Univ	OR	17,874	C
Southern Univ at New Orleans	LA	2,963	NC
Southwest Baptist Univ	MO	24,710	C
Southwestern Univ	TX	45,660	VC
Spelman College	GA	24,650	C
Spring Hill College	AL	44,164	VC
St. Ambrose Univ	IA	30,845	C
St. Catherine Univ	MN	37,782	C+
St. Cloud State Univ	MN	10,600	C
St. Edward's Univ	TX	47,784	C
St. Francis College	NY	34,200	C
St. John Fisher College	NY	40,708	C+
St. John's Univ	NY	55,070	C+
St. Lawrence Univ	NY	59,972	VC
St. Mary's College of Maryland	MD	25,754	VC
St. Norbert College	WI	41,478	VC
St. Olaf College	MN	51,200	HC+
Stanford Univ	CA	58,388	MC
SUNY at Purchase	NY	16,951	C
SUNY/Empire State College	NY	6,315	SP
Stephen F. Austin State Univ	TX	14,668	C
Stetson Univ	FL	51,516	VC
Stonehill College	MA	46,780	HC
Stony Brook Univ / SUNY	NY	20,078	HC+
Suffolk Univ	MA	47,298	C
SUNY College at Geneseo	NY	18,670	HC
SUNY Cortland/The SUNY	NY	19,759	C+
SUNY Fredonia/The SUNY at Fredonia	NY	19,840	C
SUNY New Paltz	NY	14,348	C
SUNY Oneonta / SUNY	NY	16,919	C+
SUNY Plattsburgh / SUNY	NY	18,083	C
Susquehanna Univ	PA	51,150	C
Swarthmore College	PA	57,870	MC
Syracuse Univ	NY	56,346	VC
Talladega College	AL	17,996	C
Tarleton State Univ	TX	13,489	LC
Taylor Univ	IN	37,821	VC+
Temple Univ	PA	24,392	VC
Tenn Tech Univ	TN	11,310	C
Texas A&M Univ	TX	19,207	VC
Texas A&M Univ at Commerce	TX	10,496	C
Texas Christian Univ	TX	49,980	HC
Texas Lutheran Univ	TX	36,040	C
Texas Southern Univ	TX	18,212	LC
Texas State Univ	TX	17,128	C
Texas Tech Univ	TX	14,243	C
Texas Wesleyan Univ	TX	31,382	C
The Catholic Univ of America	DC	52,852	VC
The College of New Rochelle	NY	33,600	VC
The College of St. Rose	NY	26,750	C
Ohio State Univ-Columbus Campus	OH	19,887	HC+
The Pennsylvania State Univ - Univ Park	PA	28,022	VC+
The SUNY at Potsdam	NY	18,473	C
The Univ of Memphis	TN	15,094	C
The Univ of N Car at Greensboro	NC	12,848	C
The Univ of Okla	OK	18,621	VC
The Univ of Tenn at Chattanooga	TN	16,883	C
The Univ of Utah	UT	16,463	VC
The Univ of Virginia's College at Wise	VA	11,076	C
Thomas Edison State College	NJ	5,700	SP
Thomas More College	KY	34,760	C
Tougaloo College	MS	15,275	NC
Touro College	NY	27,959	VC
Towson Univ	MD	16,000	VC
Transylvania Univ	KY	42,660	VC+
Trinity College	CT		HC+
Trinity Univ	TX	48,150	HC+
Trinity Washington Univ	DC	30,250	C
Truman State Univ	MO	15,541	HC
Tufts Univ	MA	58,780	MC
Tulane Univ	LA	60,861	MC
Tuskegee Univ	AL	26,750	C
Union College	NY	60,240	MC
Union Univ	TN	28,260	VC
United States Air Force Academy	CO		MC
United States Military Academy	NY		MC
United States Naval Academy	MD		MC
Universidad del Turabo	PR	4,110	
Univ at Albany / SUNY	NY	18,674	VC
Univ at Buffalo / The SUNY	NY	20,283	VC
Univ of Akron	OH	20,436	C
Univ of Alabama at Birmingham	AL	18,484	C+
Univ of Alabama at Tuscaloosa	AL	17,164	C+
Univ of Alaska Anchorage	AK	16,673	NC
Univ of Alaska Fairbanks	AK	15,130	C
Univ of Arizona	AZ	20,657	C
Univ of Arkansas at Fayetteville	AR	18,352	C+
Univ of Arkansas at Little Rock	AR	17,609	LC
Univ of Calif at Berkeley	CA	23,322	MC
Univ of Calif at Davis	CA		HC
Univ of Calif at Irvine	CA	25,961	VC
Univ of Calif at Los Angeles	CA	25,686	MC
Univ of Calif at Riverside	CA	27,204	C+
Univ of Calif at San Diego	CA	21,000	C
Univ of Calif at Santa Barbara	CA	27,551	HC
Univ of Calif at Santa Cruz	CA	27,807	C+
Univ of Central Arkansas	AR	13,667	VC
Univ of Central Florida	FL	15,668	VC+
Univ of Central Missouri	MO	14,605	C
Univ of Central Okla	OK	12,293	C
Univ of Chicago	IL	55,416	MC
Univ of Cincinnati	OH	21,506	VC
Univ of Colo at Colo Springs	CO	15,000	VC
Univ of Colo Boulder	CO	22,605	VC+
Univ of Colo Denver	CO	17,904	C
Univ of Conn	CT	24,706	HC
Univ of Dallas	TX	45,500	VC+
Univ of Dayton	OH	49,070	VC
Univ of Delaware	DE	23,612	VC
Univ of Denver	CO	51,787	VC+
Univ of Detroit Mercy	MI	30,450	VC
Univ of Evansville	IN	42,656	VC+
Univ of Findlay	OH	31,916	C
Univ of Florida	FL	15,943	HC
Univ of Georgia	GA	20,082	VC
Univ of Hartford	CT	42,674	C
Univ of Hawaii at Hilo	HI	23,066	C
Univ of Hawaii at Manoa	HI	19,379	C
Univ of Idaho	ID	14,558	C
Univ of Illinois at Chicago	IL	24,505	VC
Univ of Illinois at Urbana-Champaign	IL	26,450	HC
Univ of Indianapolis	IN	31,740	LC
Univ of Iowa	IA	17,693	VC
Univ of Kansas	KS	17,603	C+
Univ of Kentucky	KY	19,868	C
Univ of Louisiana at Lafayette	LA	6,130	C
Univ of Louisiana at Monroe	LA	12,998	C
Univ of Maine	ME	19,902	C+
Univ of Mary Hardin-Baylor	TX	31,950	C+
Univ of Mary Washington	VA	19,484	VC
Univ of Maryland - College Park	MD	20,060	HC
Univ of Maryland/Baltimore County	MD	18,000	VC
Univ of Mass Amherst	MA	24,215	VC+
Univ of Mass Boston	MA	23,066	VC
Univ of Mass Dartmouth	MA	22,223	C
Univ of Mass Lowell	MA	19,316	C
Univ of Miami	FL	57,034	MC
Univ of Mich/Ann Arbor	MI	22,102	MC
Univ of Mich/Dearborn	MI	9,885	VC
Univ of Mich-Flint	MI	17,547	C+
Univ of Minn/Duluth	MN	19,806	C
Univ of Minn/Morris	MN	17,150	VC
Univ of Minn/Twin Cities	MN		HC
Univ of Miss	MS	16,704	C+
Univ of Missouri/Columbia	MO	18,201	MC
Univ of Missouri-Kansas City	MO	19,603	C
Univ of Missouri-St. Louis	MO		VC
Univ of Montana	MT	14,105	C
Univ of Mount Union	OH	35,130	C
Univ of Nebr - Lincoln	NE	18,931	C
Univ of Nebr at Kearney	NE	14,855	LC
Univ of Nebr at Omaha	NE	12,700	C
Univ of Nevada, Las Vegas	NV	17,303	C
Univ of Nevada/Reno	NV	17,507	C
Univ of New Hampshire	NH	26,912	C
Univ of New Haven	CT	48,940	C
Univ of New Mexico	NM	15,300	C
Univ of New Orleans	LA	9,224	C
Univ of N Car at Asheville	NC	13,500	VC
Univ of N Car at Chapel Hill	NC	18,928	MC
Univ of N Car at Charlotte	NC	15,547	C
Univ of N Car at Wilmington	NC	13,572	VC
Univ of N Dak	ND	14,551	C
Univ of North Florida	FL	15,870	VC
Univ of North Texas	TX	15,628	C
Univ of Northern Colo	CO	18,446	C
Univ of Northern Iowa	IA	15,795	C
Univ of Notre Dame	IN	57,117	MC
Univ of Oregon	OR	21,360	C+
Univ of Pennsylvania	PA	61,132	MC
Univ of Pittsburgh at Bradford	PA	21,802	C
Univ of Pittsburgh at Johnstown	PA	20,862	LC
Univ of Pittsburgh at Pittsburgh	PA	28,572	HC+
Univ of Portland	OR	49,964	VC
Univ of PR Recinto de Rio Piedras	PR	5,750	
Univ of PR/Cayey	PR	1,504	
Univ of PR/Mayaguez	PR	1,250	
Univ of Puget Sound	WA	54,608	HC
Univ of Redlands	CA	40,500	VC
Univ of Rio Grande	OH	8,750	NC
Univ of Rochester	NY	60,668	MC
Univ of San Diego	CA	54,818	HC+
Univ of San Francisco	CA	54,770	VC
Univ of Science and Arts of Okla	OK	10,560	VC
Univ of Scranton	PA	51,940	VC
Univ of S Car at Columbia	SC	19,725	VC+
Univ of S Car Upstate	SC	18,200	LC
Univ of S Dak	SD	15,111	C
Univ of South Florida/St. Petersburg	FL	12,769	C
Univ of South Florida/Tampa	FL	13,000	C
Univ of Southern Calif	CA	56,903	MC
Univ of Southern Indiana	IN	14,885	C
Univ of Southern Maine	ME	16,576	C
Univ of Southern Miss	MS	13,170	C
Univ of St. Thomas - Houston	TX	37,690	C
Univ of Tampa	FL	35,160	VC
Univ of Tenn at Knoxville	TN	20,364	VC+
Univ of Tenn at Martin	TN	13,734	C
Univ of Texas - Pan American	TX	11,125	LC

ST = STATE $IS = IN-STATE COSTS   SR = SELECTOR RATING

School	ST	$IS	SR
Univ of Texas at Arlington	TX	10,908	LC
Univ of Texas at Austin	TX	44,074	HC
Univ of Texas at Dallas	TX	21,348	HC+
Univ of Texas at El Paso	TX	8,764	NC
Univ of Texas at San Antonio	TX	18,372	C
Univ of the District of Columbia	DC	7,244	LC
Univ of the Ozarks	AR	31,440	C
Univ of the Pacific	CA	52,146	VC
Univ of Toledo	OH	18,464	LC
Univ of Tulsa	OK	46,331	MC
Univ of Vermont	VT	27,006	VC+
Univ of Virginia	VA	23,050	VC
Univ of Washington	WA	14,722	VC
Univ of West Georgia	GA	15,488	LC
Univ of Wisc Whitewater	WI	13,314	C
Univ of Wisc/Eau Claire	WI	15,730	VC
Univ of Wisc/Green Bay	WI	19,074	C
Univ of Wisc/La Crosse	WI	9,304	VC
Univ of Wisc/Madison	WI	18,757	HC+
Univ of Wisc/Oshkosh	WI	10,426	LC
Univ of Wisc/Parkside	WI	10,181	LC
Univ of Wisc/Platteville	WI	14,564	C
Univ of Wisc/River Falls	WI	9,722	LC
Univ of Wisc/Stevens Point	WI	14,043	C
Univ of Wisc/Superior	WI	14,314	C
Univ of Wisc-Milwaukee	WI	18,436	C
Univ of Wyoming	WY	14,401	C+
Utah State Univ	UT	12,044	C
Utica College	NY	45,670	C
Valparaiso Univ	IN	44,940	VC+
Vanderbilt Univ	TN	58,220	MC
Vassar College	NY	61,140	MC
Villanova Univ	PA	58,394	MC
Virginia Commonwealth Univ	VA	21,716	C
Virginia Polytechnic Inst and State Univ	VA	14,629	HC
Virginia State Univ	VA	11,318	C+
Wabash College	IN	46,850	C+
Wake Forest Univ	NC	58,838	MC
Wartburg College	IA	41,055	VC
Washburn Univ	KS	12,579	LC
Washington and Jefferson College	PA	51,948	VC
Washington and Lee Univ	VA	52,812	MC
Washington College	MD	52,602	VC
Washington State Univ	WA	20,461	C
Washington Univ in St. Louis	MO	69,844	MC
Wayland Baptist Univ	TX	18,912	LC
Wayne State Univ	MI	22,063	C
Webster Univ	MO	35,100	C+
Wellesley College	MA	59,038	MC
Wells College	NY	49,400	VC
Wesleyan College	GA	24,000	C
Wesleyan Univ	CT	61,198	MC
West Chester Univ of Pennsylvania	PA	17,186	C
West Liberty Univ	WV	9,142	LC
West Texas A&M Univ	TX	13,478	C
West Virginia State Univ	WV	8,378	NC
West Virginia Univ	WV	16,542	C+
West Virginia Wesleyan College	WV	26,880	C
Western Conn State Univ	CT	18,327	LC
Western Illinois Univ	IL	20,732	C
Western Kentucky Univ	KY	11,000	LC
Western Mich Univ	MI	19,628	C
Western New England Univ	MA	46,154	C+
Western Oregon Univ	OR	15,021	C
Western State Colo Univ	CO	16,924	C
Western Washington Univ	WA	18,519	VC
Westfield State Univ	MA	18,297	C
Westminster College	MO	31,720	VC
Westminster College	PA	31,290	C+
Westminster College	UT	37,708	C+
Wheaton College	IL	40,720	MC
Wheaton College	MA	54,934	HC+
Whitman College	WA	55,988	MC
Whittier College	CA	43,416	C
Whitworth Univ	WA	47,734	VC
Wichita State Univ	KS	14,607	C+
Widener Univ	PA	52,418	C
Wilberforce Univ	OH	15,100	LC
Willamette Univ	OR	56,450	VC+
William Paterson Univ of New Jersey	NJ	21,694	C
Williams College	MA	61,070	MC
Wilmington College	OH	29,784	C
Wilson College	PA	35,080	C
Winona State Univ	MN	16,640	C
Winston-Salem State Univ	NC	9,418	LC
Winthrop Univ	SC	21,120	C
Wittenberg Univ	OH	47,962	C+
Wofford College	SC	45,795	VC
Worcester Polytechnic Inst	MA	55,860	MC
Worcester State Univ	MA	19,812	C
Wright State Univ	OH	16,983	C
Xavier Univ	OH	44,980	VC
Yale Univ	CT	55,300	MC
Yeshiva Univ	NY	47,250	VC+
York College / The CUNY	NY	5,496	LC
York College of Pennsylvania	PA	26,590	C
Youngstown State Univ	OH	16,732	C

ECONOMICS – STATISTICS

School	ST	$IS	SR
Biola Univ	CA	40,320	C+
Boise State Univ	ID	13,469	LC
Bryant Univ	RI	49,179	VC
Southern Methodist Univ	TX	60,585	MC
Univ of Alabama in Huntsville	AL	17,591	VC+
Univ of Calif at Irvine	CA	25,961	VC
Univ of Pittsburgh at Pittsburgh	PA	28,572	HC+
Univ of West Georgia	GA	15,488	LC

EDUCATION

School	ST	$IS	SR
Adams State Univ	CO	13,358	LC
Albertus Magnus College	CT	37,382	LC
Appalachian State Univ	NC	12,919	VC
Aquinas College	MI	33,060	C
Arizona State Univ, at the Tempe Campus	AZ	20,137	C+
Arizona State Univ, at the West Campus	AZ	19,251	C
Arkansas Tech Univ	AR	13,982	LC
Ashford Univ	CA	10,480	C
Assumption College	MA	47,122	C+
Auburn Univ	AL	22,378	VC+
Averett Univ	VA	37,750	LC
Belmont Abbey College	NC	37,716	C
Beloit College	WI	49,970	HC
Bennington College	VT	56,990	HC+
Berea College	KY	7,192	C
Bethany College	WV	35,282	LC
Bethel College	IN	31,560	C
Bethel Univ	MN	34,940	VC
Bethune-Cookman Univ	FL	22,958	C
Bloomfield College	NJ	37,850	LC
Boise State Univ	ID	13,469	LC
Boston Univ	MA	60,694	MC
Bowling Green State Univ	OH	18,970	C
Brown Univ	RI	59,428	MC
Bryant Univ	RI	49,179	VC
Bryn Athyn College	PA	27,984	C
Bucknell Univ	PA	60,140	MC
Cabrini College	PA	40,859	LC
Cairn Univ	PA	33,270	C
Calif Polytechnic State Univ	CA	19,847	HC
Cal State, Monterey Bay	CA	26,871	C
Calif Univ of Pennsylvania	PA	14,217	C
Calvin College	MI	39,120	VC
Campbell Univ	NC	37,570	C
Canisius College	NY	44,900	C
Carroll Univ	WI	38,100	C
Case Western Reserve Univ	OH	56,534	MC
Castleton State College	VT	20,186	C
Catawba College	NC	37,240	LC
Cedar Crest College	PA	43,240	C
Chapman Univ	CA	58,347	VC+
Chatham Univ	PA	43,797	C
Coker College	SC	32,256	LC
Colgate Univ	NY	58,135	MC
College of St. Elizabeth	NJ	43,839	LC
College of St. Mary	NE	35,184	C
College of St. Scholastica	MN	41,440	C
Colo College	CO	57,162	MC
Colo State Univ-Fort Collins	CO	20,385	VC
Columbia College	MO	24,578	C
Columbia Univ/City of New York	NY	61,116	MC
Concordia College - New York	NY	39,035	LC
Corban Univ	OR	37,380	C+
Cornerstone Univ and Grand Rapids Theological Seminary	MI	33,338	C
Culver-Stockton College	MO	30,900	C
Curry College	MA	48,925	LC
Dallas Baptist Univ	TX	30,580	VC
Denison Univ	OH	54,670	HC+
DePaul Univ	IL	47,623	VC
Dominican Univ	IL	37,628	C
Dordt College	IA	34,160	C
Drexel Univ	PA	61,418	VC+
Duquesne Univ	PA	43,720	VC
East Texas Baptist Univ	TX	31,577	LC
Eastern Mich Univ	MI	18,604	C
Eastern Nazarene College	MA	30,000	C
Eastern Oregon Univ	OR	10,400	C
Elizabethtown College	PA	44,940	VC
Elon Univ	NC	41,914	VC+
Endicott College	MA	43,228	VC+
Eugene Lang College/The New School for Liberal Arts	NY	55,650	C
Eureka College	IL	19,280	C
Felician College	NJ	41,640	LC
Fitchburg State Univ	MA	18,173	C
Florida International Univ	FL	17,747	VC
Fontbonne Univ	MO	31,384	C
Franklin Pierce Univ	NH	41,598	C
Friends Univ	KS	29,100	C
Furman Univ	SC	54,006	HC
Georgian Court Univ	NJ	41,594	LC
Goddard College	VT	16,418	VC
Goucher College	MD	52,040	VC+

School	ST	$IS	SR
Grand Canyon Univ	AZ	24,540	VC
Guilford College	NC	42,800	C
Hamline Univ	MN	45,678	VC
Hampshire College	MA	58,320	MC
Hardin-Simmons Univ	TX	23,560	C+
Harris-Stowe State Univ	MO	14,360	NC
Henderson State Univ	AR	14,584	C
Hiram College	OH	37,300	VC
Hope International Univ	CA	34,650	C
Howard Univ	DC	13,646	C
Huntington Univ	IN	32,220	C+
Huston-Tillotson Univ	TX	18,124	C+
Illinois Wesleyan Univ	IL	48,452	HC
Indiana Univ of Pennsylvania	PA	20,846	LC
Ithaca College	NY	53,864	HC
John Carroll Univ	OH	46,300	C+
Johnson State College	VT	16,721	C
Keene State College	NH	23,232	LC
LaGrange College	GA	37,670	C
Lake Forest College	IL	50,652	VC
Lees-McRae College	NC	33,944	C
Lipscomb Univ	TN	37,490	VC
Loras College	IA	37,432	VC
Lourdes Univ	OH	26,055	LC
Lynchburg College	VA	42,645	C
Macalester College	MN	57,691	MC
Maharishi Univ of Management	IA	31,000	VC
Manhattan College	NY	49,588	C+
Manhattanville College	NY	50,740	VC
Marquette Univ	WI	46,930	VC+
Marshall Univ	WV	14,820	C
Martin Univ	IN	11,000	SP
Mass College of Liberal Arts	MA	18,613	C
Mayville State Univ	ND	11,401	NC
Mercer Univ	GA	44,201	VC
Mich State Univ	MI	22,450	VC
Midway College	KY	20,150	LC
Millikin Univ	IL	38,940	C
Millsaps College	MS	43,888	VC+
Minn State Univ, Mankato	MN	15,616	C
Miss State Univ	MS	14,750	C
Monmouth Univ	NJ	44,108	C
Montana State Univ-Billings	MT	12,425	LC
Morningside College	IA	35,430	C
Mount Aloysius College	PA	29,976	C
Mount St. Mary College	NY	41,138	C
New England College	NH	45,930	LC
New York Univ	NY	61,470	MC
Niagara Univ	NY	41,010	C
N Car State Univ	NC	16,202	HC
Northwest Christian Univ	OR	27,399	C
Northwest Univ	WA	18,854	C
Northwestern Univ	IL	61,640	MC
Nova Southeastern Univ	FL	37,280	VC
Oakwood Univ	AL	25,529	NC
Ohio State Univ at Lima	OH	7,140	C
Ohio State Univ at Marion	OH	16,990	MC
Okla City Univ	OK	40,476	VC
Okla State Univ	OK	14,310	VC
Oregon State Univ	OR	20,273	VC
Pacific Lutheran Univ	WA	46,760	C+
Piedmont College	GA	30,136	C
Pittsburg State Univ	KS	12,032	C
Point Loma Nazarene Univ	CA	41,006	C+
Point Park Univ	PA	36,390	C
Prescott College	AZ	33,284	C
Purdue Univ/West Lafayette	IN	20,024	HC
Quincy Univ	IL	34,980	LC
Randolph College	VA	45,660	VC
Regis Univ	CO	41,318	C
Richard Stockton College of New Jersey	NJ	20,000	VC
Rocky Mountain College	MT	32,242	C
Roger Williams Univ	RI	46,296	VC
Rosemont College	PA	42,350	C
Rowan Univ	NJ	24,022	VC+
Sacred Heart Univ	CT	49,264	VC
St. Anselm College	NH	49,376	VC
St. Louis Univ	MO	48,346	HC
St. Martin's Univ	WA	41,678	C
Salem State Univ	MA	13,161	LC
Salisbury Univ	MD	19,180	VC
San Diego Christian College	CA	31,012	C
Schreiner Univ	TX	32,734	LC
Seattle Pacific Univ	WA	41,559	VC+
Shawnee State Univ	OH	16,916	C
Simmons College	MA	49,966	VC
Smith College	MA	59,674	MC
S Dak State Univ	SD	14,296	C
Southern Nazarene Univ	OK	24,354	C
Southern New Hampshire Univ	NH	38,100	C
Southern Oregon Univ	OR	17,874	C
Southern Polytechnic State Univ	GA	13,958	C
Southwestern Univ	TX	45,660	VC
Spalding Univ	KY	32,287	LC
St. Bonaventure Univ	NY	41,575	C
St. Francis College	NY	34,200	C
St. John's Univ	NY	55,070	C+
St. Joseph's College, New York/Suffolk Campus	NY	22,630	C
SUNY/Empire State College	NY	6,315	SP
Stonehill College	MA	46,780	HC

School	ST	$IS	SR
SUNY Fredonia/The SUNY at Fredonia	NY	19,840	VC
Swarthmore College	PA	57,870	MC
Syracuse Univ	NY	56,346	VC
Taylor Univ	IN	37,821	VC+
Texas A&M Univ at Corpus Christi	TX	11,544	LC
Texas Lutheran Univ	TX	36,040	C
Texas State Univ	TX	17,128	C
Texas Wesleyan Univ	TX	31,382	C
The Catholic Univ of America	DC	52,852	VC
The College of Idaho	ID	31,277	C+
Ohio State Univ-Columbus Campus	OH	19,887	HC+
The Univ of Tenn at Chattanooga	TN	16,883	C
Towson Univ	MD	16,000	VC
Transylvania Univ	KY	42,660	VC+
Trevecca Nazarene Univ	TN	31,186	C
Trinity Christian College	IL	28,869	C
Trinity College	CT		HC+
Trinity Washington Univ	DC	30,250	C+
Tusculum College	TN	24,295	C
Union College	KY	29,955	C
Union Inst & Univ	OH	8,912	SP
Union Univ	TN	28,260	VC
Unity College	ME	34,054	C
Univ of Akron	OH	20,436	C
Univ of Alaska Fairbanks	AK	15,130	C
Univ of Arizona	AZ	20,657	C
Univ of Colo Denver	CO	17,904	C
Univ of Conn	CT	24,706	HC
Univ of Dallas	TX	45,500	VC+
Univ of Delaware	DE	23,612	VC
Univ of Dubuque	IA	30,200	C
Univ of Idaho	ID	14,558	C
Univ of Illinois at Urbana-Champaign	IL	26,450	HC
Univ of La Verne	CA	47,010	C
Univ of Maryland - College Park	MD	20,060	HC
Univ of Mass Amherst	MA	24,215	VC+
Univ of Mich/Dearborn	MI	9,885	VC
Univ of Mich-Flint	MI	17,547	C+
Univ of Missouri/Columbia	MO	18,201	HC
Univ of Missouri-St. Louis	MO		VC
Univ of Montana-Western	MT	9,753	LC
Univ of Nebr - Lincoln	NE	18,031	VC
Univ of New England	ME	46,750	C
Univ of Northern Colo	CO	18,446	C
Univ of Oregon	OR	21,360	C
Univ of PR Recinto de Rio Piedras	PR	5,750	
Univ of South Alabama	AL	13,510	C
Univ of South Florida/St. Petersburg	FL	12,769	C
Univ of South Florida/Tampa	FL	13,000	C
Univ of St. Thomas - Houston	TX	37,690	C
Univ of Tenn at Knoxville	TN	20,364	VC+
Univ of Texas at San Antonio	TX	18,372	C
Univ of the Pacific	CA	52,146	VC
Univ of Tulsa	OK	46,331	MC
Univ of Vermont	VT	27,006	VC+
Univ of Wisc/Green Bay	WI	19,074	C
Univ of Wisc/Parkside	WI	10,181	LC
Univ of Wisc/Platteville	WI	14,564	C
Univ of Wisc/Stevens Point	WI	14,043	C
Univ of Wisc-Milwaukee	WI	18,436	C
Utica College	NY	45,670	C
Vanderbilt Univ	TN	58,220	MC
Vanguard Univ of Southern Calif	CA	35,833	VC
Vassar College	NY	61,140	MC
Wake Forest Univ	NC	58,838	MC
Washburn Univ	KS	12,579	C
Washington and Jefferson College	PA	51,948	VC
Washington State Univ	WA	20,461	C
Washington Univ in St. Louis	MO	69,844	MC
Webster Univ	MO	35,100	C+
Western Mich Univ	MI	19,628	C
Western Oregon Univ	OR	15,021	C
William Peace Univ	NC	32,900	LC
Wilmington College	OH	29,784	C
Wright State Univ	OH	16,983	C
Xavier Univ	OH	44,980	VC
York College	NE	19,475	C
York College of Pennsylvania	PA	26,590	C
Youngstown State Univ	OH	16,732	C

EDUCATION ADMINISTRATION

School	ST	$IS	SR
Ashford Univ	CA	10,480	C
Ashland Univ	OH	25,000	C
Auburn Univ	AL	22,378	VC+
Bryant Univ	RI	49,179	VC
Cairn Univ	PA	33,270	C
Canisius College	NY	44,900	C
Columbia College	MO	24,578	C
DePaul Univ	IL	47,623	VC
Howard Univ	DC	13,646	C
Missouri State Univ	MO	13,996	C+
Salisbury Univ	MD	19,180	VC
San Jose State Univ	CA	19,133	LC

ST = STATE $IS = IN-STATE COSTS   SR = SELECTOR RATING

School	ST	$IS	SR
Southwestern Okla State Univ	OK	9,160	C
Univ of Arkansas at Little Rock	AR	17,609	C
Univ of Georgia	GA	20,082	VC
Univ of Idaho	ID	14,558	C
Univ of Louisiana at Monroe	LA	12,998	C
Univ of Missouri/Columbia	MO	18,201	MC
Univ of Tenn at Martin	TN	13,734	C
Western Washington Univ	WA	18,519	VC

EDUCATION OF THE DEAF AND HEARING IMPAIRED

School	ST	$IS	SR
Barton College	NC	27,660	LC
Boston Univ	MA	60,694	MC
Bowling Green State Univ	OH	18,970	C
Cal State, Northridge	CA	28,690	LC
Canisius College	NY	44,900	C
College of New Jersey	NJ	25,376	HC
Eastern Kentucky Univ	KY	11,161	C
Eastern Mich Univ	MI	18,604	C
Flagler College	FL	25,180	C
Fontbonne Univ	MO	31,384	C
Ithaca College	NY	53,864	HC
MacMurray College	IL	20,755	C
Marywood Univ	PA	45,595	C
Minot State Univ	ND	10,915	C
Pace Univ	NY	53,367	C
Rochester Inst of Technology	NY	42,450	VC
San Jose State Univ	CA	19,133	LC
Southern Univ at New Orleans	LA	2,963	NC
Stephen F. Austin State Univ	TX	14,668	C
The Univ of N Car at Greensboro	NC	12,848	C
Towson Univ	MD	16,000	VC
Univ of Arkansas at Little Rock	AR	17,609	LC
Univ of Montevallo	AL	17,060	C
Univ of Nebr - Lincoln	NE	18,031	VC
Univ of Science and Arts of Okla	OK	10,560	VC
Univ of Tulsa	OK	46,331	MC

EDUCATION OF THE EMOTIONALLY HANDICAPPED

School	ST	$IS	SR
CUNY/City College	NY	20,319	HC+
Concordia Univ St. Paul	MN	28,250	C
East Carolina Univ	NC	14,169	C
Eastern Mich Univ	MI	18,604	C
Florida State Univ	FL	16,715	VC
Manhattan College	NY	49,588	C+
Prescott College	AZ	33,284	C
Univ of South Florida/Tampa	FL	13,000	C
Walsh Univ	OH	35,100	C
Western Mich Univ	MI	19,628	C

EDUCATION OF THE EXCEPTIONAL CHILD

School	ST	$IS	SR
Ashland Univ	OH	25,000	C
Bethel Univ	TN	19,186	C
Bethune-Cookman Univ	FL	22,958	C
Canisius College	NY	44,900	C
Edgewood College	WI	33,294	C
Flagler College	FL	25,180	C
Florida Atlantic Univ	FL	17,339	C
Houghton College	NY	36,808	C+
Jacksonville Univ	FL	37,780	C
Mansfield Univ	PA	19,468	LC
Mayville State Univ	ND	11,401	NC
Minot State Univ	ND	10,915	C
Niagara Univ	NY	41,010	C
Northwest Nazarene Univ	ID	34,000	C
Nova Southeastern Univ	FL	37,280	VC
Prescott College	AZ	33,284	C
St. Augustine's Univ	NC	14,000	C
Southeast Missouri State Univ	MO	15,370	LC
Southeastern Univ	FL	27,201	C
The Univ of Tenn at Chattanooga	TN	16,883	C
Univ of Central Arkansas	AR	13,667	VC
Univ of Central Florida	FL	15,668	VC+
Univ of Great Falls	MT	27,970	C
Univ of Miami	FL	57,034	MC
Univ of Wisc/Stevens Point	WI	14,043	C
Walsh Univ	OH	35,100	C
Warner Univ	FL	18,000	C
Western Kentucky Univ	KY	11,000	LC

EDUCATION OF THE MENTALLY HANDICAPPED

School	ST	$IS	SR
Brescia Univ	KY	26,140	VC+
CUNY/City College	NY	20,319	HC+
East Carolina Univ	NC	14,169	C
Eastern Mich Univ	MI	18,604	C
Florida State Univ	FL	16,715	VC
Kutztown Univ of Pennsylvania	PA	16,909	LC
Minot State Univ	ND	10,915	C
Northern Mich Univ	MI	18,278	C

School	ST	$IS	SR
Northwest Missouri State Univ	MO	17,347	C
Prescott College	AZ	33,284	C
Southeastern Okla State Univ	OK	7,966	LC
Univ of Rio Grande	OH	8,750	NC
Univ of South Florida/Tampa	FL	13,000	C
Urbana Univ	OH	30,820	C
Walsh Univ	OH	35,100	C
Western Mich Univ	MI	19,628	C

EDUCATION OF THE MULTIPLY HANDICAPPED

School	ST	$IS	SR
Aquinas College	MI	33,060	C
Ball State Univ	IN	17,850	C
Bowling Green State Univ	OH	18,970	C
Eastern Mich Univ	MI	18,604	C
Univ of Illinois at Urbana-Champaign	IL	26,450	HC

EDUCATION OF THE PHYSICALLY HANDICAPPED

School	ST	$IS	SR
Aquinas College	MI	33,060	C
Eastern Mich Univ	MI	18,604	C
Kutztown Univ of Pennsylvania	PA	16,909	LC
Walsh Univ	OH	35,100	C

EDUCATION OF THE VISUALLY HANDICAPPED

School	ST	$IS	SR
Eastern Mich Univ	MI	18,604	C
Florida State Univ	FL	16,715	VC
Kutztown Univ of Pennsylvania	PA	16,909	LC
Stephen F. Austin State Univ	TX	14,668	C

EDUCATION SERVICES

School	ST	$IS	SR
Birmingham-Southern College	AL	44,168	VC+
St. Leo Univ	FL	30,340	C
SUNY Cortland/The SUNY	NY	19,759	C+

EDUCATIONAL MEDIA

School	ST	$IS	SR
Eastern Mich Univ	MI	18,604	C

EDUCATIONAL STATISTICS AND RESEARCH

School	ST	$IS	SR
Bryant Univ	RI	49,179	VC
Bucknell Univ	PA	60,140	MC
Emory Univ	GA	56,368	MC
The Pennsylvania State Univ - Univ Park	PA	28,022	VC+

EDUCATIONAL STUDIES

School	ST	$IS	SR
Alma College	MI	44,075	C
Arizona State Univ, at the Polytechnic Campus	AZ	20,531	C+
Arizona State Univ, at the Tempe Campus	AZ	20,137	C+
Ashford Univ	CA	10,480	C
Texas Christian Univ	TX	49,980	HC

ELECTRICAL AND COMPUTER ENGINEERING

School	ST	$IS	SR
Bowling Green State Univ	OH	18,970	C
Calif Baptist Univ	CA	38,792	C
Christopher Newport Univ	VA	21,960	VC
Cornell Univ	NY	60,964	MC
Fairfield Univ	CT	56,960	VC
Franklin W. Olin College of Engineering	MA	59,225	SP
New York Inst of Technology	NY	45,010	VC
New York Univ	NY	61,470	MC
Northern Arizona Univ	AZ	19,010	C
Okla Christian Univ	OK	25,870	VC
Oswego / SUNY	NY	20,009	VC
The Pennsylvania State Univ - Univ Park	PA	28,022	VC+
Univ of Denver	CO	51,787	VC+
Univ of Idaho	ID	14,558	C
Univ of Mass Boston	MA	23,066	VC
Wayne State Univ	MI	22,063	C

ELECTRICAL TECHNOLOGY

School	ST	$IS	SR
Thomas Edison State College	NJ	5,700	SP

ELECTRICAL/ELECTRONICS ENGINEERING

School	ST	$IS	SR
Alabama A&M Univ	AL	10,084	C
Andrews Univ	MI	28,030	C+
Arizona State Univ, at the Tempe Campus	AZ	20,137	C+
Arkansas State Univ	AR	15,470	C
Arkansas Tech Univ	AR	13,982	LC
Auburn Univ	AL	22,378	VC+
Baylor Univ	TX	50,329	HC

School	ST	$IS	SR
Benedict College	SC	20,454	NC
Bethel College	IN	31,560	C
Binghamton Univ/The SUNY	NY	21,648	HC+
Bloomsburg Univ of Pennsylvania	PA	13,598	C
Boise State Univ	ID	13,469	LC
Boston Univ	MA	60,694	MC
Bradley Univ	IL	31,874	VC
Brigham Young Univ	UT	12,100	HC
Bucknell Univ	PA	60,140	MC
Calif Baptist Univ	CA	38,792	C
Calif Inst of Technology	CA	54,045	MC
Calif Polytechnic State Univ	CA	19,847	HC
Calif State Polytechnic Univ, Pomona	CA	20,156	C
Cal State, Chico	CA	20,158	C
Cal State, Fresno	CA	17,405	C
Cal State, Fullerton	CA	25,288	C
Cal State, Long Beach	CA	17,502	C+
Cal State, Los Angeles	CA	17,186	LC
Cal State, Sacramento	CA	16,200	C
Calvin College	MI	39,120	VC
Capitol College	MD	21,250	C
Carnegie Mellon Univ	PA	51,260	MC
Case Western Reserve Univ	OH	56,534	MC
Cedarville Univ	OH	32,860	VC
Central Washington Univ	WA	11,730	C
Christian Brothers Univ	TN	31,670	HC
Citadel, The	SC		C
CUNY/City College	NY	20,319	HC+
Clarkson Univ	NY	57,330	HC
Clemson Univ	SC	19,136	HC
Cleveland State Univ	OH	21,776	C
College of New Jersey	NJ	25,376	HC
Colo State Univ-Fort Collins	CO	20,385	VC
Colo Technical Univ	CO	10,500	LC
Columbia Univ/City of New York	NY	61,116	MC
Cooper Union for the Advancement of Science and Art	NY	55,600	MC
Delaware State Univ	DE	16,722	LC
Dordt College	IA	34,160	C+
Drexel Univ	PA	61,418	VC+
Duke Univ	NC	50,250	MC
Elizabethtown College	PA	49,740	VC
Embry-Riddle Aeronautical Univ - Daytona Beach	FL	40,884	C+
Embry-Riddle Aeronautical Univ - Prescott Campus	AZ	40,444	VC+
Fairleigh Dickinson Univ/ Metropolitan Campus	NJ	40,254	C
Florida A&M Univ	FL	14,935	LC
Florida Atlantic Univ	FL	17,339	C
Florida Inst of Technology	FL	48,290	VC
Florida International Univ	FL	17,747	C+
Florida State Univ	FL	16,715	VC
Gannon Univ	PA	39,608	C
George Mason Univ	VA	15,724	VC
George Washington Univ	DC	57,108	MC
Georgia Inst of Technology	GA	21,828	MC
Georgia Southern Univ	GA	16,942	C
Gonzaga Univ	WA	46,441	HC
Grove City College	PA	24,022	VC
Hampton Univ	VA	28,528	C
Harding Univ	AR	23,556	C
Hofstra Univ	NY	51,810	VC+
Howard Univ	DC	13,646	C
Idaho State Univ	ID	12,307	C
Illinois Inst of Technology	IL	38,512	HC+
Indiana Inst of Technology	IN	34,240	LC
Indiana Univ-Purdue Univ Fort Wayne	IN	15,521	C
Indiana Univ-Purdue Univ Indianapolis	IN	17,611	C
Inter-American Univ of PR/ Bayamon Univ College	PR	4,428	
Iowa State Univ	IA	16,403	C
Jackson State Univ	MS	13,512	LC
Jacksonville Univ	FL	37,780	C
John Brown Univ	AR	32,056	VC+
Johns Hopkins Univ	MD	47,492	MC
Johnson & Wales Univ/North Miami Campus	FL		C
Johnson & Wales Univ/ Providence Campus	RI	29,576	C
Kansas State Univ	KS	15,497	VC
Kettering Univ	MI	31,456	NC
Lafayette College	PA	59,155	HC+
Lake Superior State Univ	MI	18,121	C
Lamar Univ	TX	6,820	LC
Lawrence Tech Univ	MI	37,630	VC
Lehigh Univ	PA	56,770	MC
LeTourneau Univ	TX	36,210	VC
Lipscomb Univ	TN	37,490	VC
Loras College	IA	37,432	VC
Louisiana State Univ	LA	18,677	C+
Loyola Marymount Univ	CA	54,649	VC+
Manhattan College	NY	49,588	C+
Maritime College/SUNY	NY	16,020	C
Marquette Univ	WI	46,930	VC+
Mass Inst of Technology	MA	58,240	MC
Merrimack College	MA	44,215	C
Miami Univ	OH	24,191	VC
Mich State Univ	MI	22,450	VC
Mich Tech Univ	MI	23,556	HC

School	ST	$IS	SR
Milwaukee School of Engineering	WI	39,948	VC+
Minn State Univ, Mankato	MN	15,616	C
Miss State Univ	MS	14,750	C
Missouri Univ of Science and Technology	MO	18,655	VC+
Montana State Univ	MT	14,068	C
Morgan State Univ	MD	14,500	VC
New Jersey Inst of Technology	NJ	26,490	C+
New Mexico Inst of Mining and Technology	NM	13,592	VC
New Mexico State Univ	NM	14,050	C
New York Univ	NY	61,470	MC
N Car Agricultural and Technical State Univ	NC	13,365	LC
N Car State Univ	NC	16,202	HC
N Dak State Univ	ND		C
Northeastern Univ	MA	55,296	MC
Northern Illinois Univ	IL	19,768	C
Northwestern Univ	IL	61,640	MC
Norwich Univ	VT	28,212	C
Oakland Univ	MI	19,391	C
Ohio Northern Univ	OH	42,075	VC
Ohio Univ	OH	21,080	C
Okla Christian Univ	OK	25,870	VC
Okla State Univ	OK	14,310	VC
Old Dominion Univ	VA	19,483	LC
Oral Roberts Univ	OK	31,734	C
Oregon State Univ	OR	20,273	VC
Point Park Univ	PA	36,390	C
Polytechnic Inst of New York Univ	NY	53,064	HC+
Portland State Univ	OR	18,672	C
Prairie View A&M Univ	TX	15,205	LC
Princeton Univ	NJ	53,795	MC
Purdue Univ/Calumet	IN	14,336	C
Purdue Univ/West Lafayette	IN	20,024	HC
Rensselaer Polytechnic Inst	NY	61,529	MC
Rice Univ	TX	43,288	MC
Rochester Inst of Technology	NY	42,450	VC
Rose-Hulman Inst of Technology	IN	53,340	MC
Rutgers, The State Univ of New Jersey/New Brunswick	NJ	25,562	VC
Saginaw Valley State Univ	MI	17,369	C
St. Louis Univ	MO	48,346	HC
St. Mary's Univ	TX	33,854	C
San Diego State Univ	CA	21,611	C+
San Francisco State Univ	CA	18,514	C
San Jose State Univ	CA	19,133	LC
Seattle Pacific Univ	WA	41,559	VC+
Seattle Univ	WA	49,035	VC+
Shippensburg Univ of Pennsylvania	PA	20,934	C
S Dak School of Mines and Technology	SD	15,260	VC
S Dak State Univ	SD	14,296	C
Southern Illinois Univ Carbondale	IL	21,942	C
Southern Illinois Univ Edwardsville	IL	17,532	C
Southern Methodist Univ	TX	60,585	MC
Southern Polytechnic State Univ	GA	13,958	C
Southern Univ and A&M College	LA	9,761	LC
St. Cloud State Univ	MN	10,600	C
Stanford Univ	CA	58,388	MC
SUNY Polytechnic Inst	NY	19,690	C
Stevens Inst of Technology	NJ	50,130	HC
Stony Brook Univ / SUNY	NY	20,078	HC+
Suffolk Univ	MA	47,298	C
SUNY New Paltz	NY	14,348	C
Syracuse Univ	NY	56,346	VC
Temple Univ	PA	24,392	VC
Tenn State Univ	TN	9,048	C
Tenn Tech Univ	TN	11,310	C
Texas A&M Univ	TX	19,207	VC
Texas A&M Univ at Kingsville	TX	7,500	LC
Texas Christian Univ	TX	49,980	HC
Texas State Univ	TX	17,128	C
Texas Tech Univ	TX	14,243	C
The Catholic Univ of America	DC	52,852	VC
Ohio State Univ-Columbus Campus	OH	19,887	HC+
The Univ of Memphis	TN	15,094	C
The Univ of Okla	OK	18,621	VC
The Univ of Tenn at Chattanooga	TN	16,883	C
The Univ of Utah	UT	16,463	VC
Trine Univ	IN	39,400	VC
Tufts Univ	MA	58,780	MC
Tuskegee Univ	AL	26,750	C
Union College	NY	60,240	MC
United States Air Force Academy	CO		MC
United States Coast Guard Academy	CT	942	HC
United States Military Academy	NY		MC
Universidad Politecnica de PR	PR	19,252	
Univ at Buffalo / The SUNY	NY	20,283	VC
Univ of Akron	OH	20,436	C

School	ST	$IS	SR
Univ of Alabama at Birmingham	AL	18,484	C+
Univ of Alabama at Tuscaloosa	AL	17,164	C+
Univ of Alabama in Huntsville	AL	17,591	VC+
Univ of Alaska Anchorage	AK	16,673	NC
Univ of Alaska Fairbanks	AK	15,130	C
Univ of Arizona	AZ	20,657	C
Univ of Arkansas at Fayetteville	AR	18,352	C
Univ of Calif at Berkeley	CA	23,322	MC
Univ of Calif at Davis	CA		HC
Univ of Calif at Irvine	CA	25,961	VC
Univ of Calif at Los Angeles	CA	25,686	MC
Univ of Calif at Riverside	CA	27,204	C+
Univ of Calif at San Diego	CA	21,000	VC
Univ of Calif at Santa Barbara	CA	27,551	HC
Univ of Calif at Santa Cruz	CA	27,807	C+
Univ of Central Florida	FL	15,668	VC+
Univ of Central Missouri	MO	14,605	C
Univ of Central Okla	OK	12,293	C
Univ of Cincinnati	OH	21,506	VC
Univ of Colo at Colo Springs	CO	15,500	VC
Univ of Colo Boulder	CO	22,605	VC+
Univ of Colo Denver	CO	17,904	C
Univ of Conn	CT	24,706	HC
Univ of Dayton	OH	49,070	VC
Univ of Delaware	DE	23,612	VC
Univ of Denver	CO	51,787	VC+
Univ of Detroit Mercy	MI	30,450	VC
Univ of Evansville	IN	42,656	VC+
Univ of Florida	FL	15,943	HC
Univ of Georgia	GA	20,082	VC
Univ of Hartford	CT	42,674	C
Univ of Hawaii at Manoa	HI	19,379	C
Univ of Houston	TX	19,796	VC
Univ of Idaho	ID	14,558	C
Univ of Illinois at Chicago	IL	24,505	VC
Univ of Illinois at Urbana-Champaign	IL	26,450	HC
Univ of Indianapolis	IN	31,740	LC
Univ of Iowa	IA	17,693	VC
Univ of Kansas	KS	17,603	C+
Univ of Kentucky	KY	19,868	C
Univ of Louisiana at Lafayette	LA	6,130	C
Univ of Louisville	KY	17,946	C
Univ of Maine	ME	19,902	C+
Univ of Maryland - College Park	MD	20,060	HC
Univ of Mass Amherst	MA	24,215	VC+
Univ of Mass Dartmouth	MA	22,223	C
Univ of Mass Lowell	MA	19,316	C
Univ of Miami	FL	57,034	MC
Univ of Mich/Ann Arbor	MI	22,102	MC
Univ of Minn/Duluth	MN	19,806	C
Univ of Minn/Twin Cities	MN		HC
Univ of Miss	MS	16,704	C+
Univ of Missouri/Columbia	MO	18,201	MC
Univ of Missouri-Kansas City	MO	19,603	C
Univ of Missouri-St. Louis	MO		VC
Univ of Nebr - Lincoln	NE	18,031	VC
Univ of Nevada, Las Vegas	NV	17,303	C
Univ of Nevada/Reno	NV	17,507	C
Univ of New Hampshire	NH	26,912	C
Univ of New Haven	CT	48,940	C
Univ of New Mexico	NM	15,300	C
Univ of New Orleans	LA	9,224	C
Univ of N Car at Charlotte	NC	15,547	C
Univ of North Dak	ND	14,551	C
Univ of North Florida	FL	15,870	VC
Univ of North Texas	TX	15,628	C
Univ of Notre Dame	IN	57,117	MC
Univ of Pennsylvania	PA	61,132	MC
Univ of Pittsburgh at Pittsburgh	PA	28,572	HC+
Univ of Portland	OR	49,964	VC
Univ of PR/Mayaguez	PR	1,250	
Univ of Rochester	NY	60,668	MC
Univ of San Diego	CA	54,818	HC+
Univ of Scranton	PA	51,940	VC
Univ of South Alabama	AL	13,510	C
Univ of S Car at Columbia	SC	19,725	VC+
Univ of South Florida/Tampa	FL	13,000	C
Univ of Southern Calif	CA	56,903	MC
Univ of Southern Maine	ME	16,576	C
Univ of Tenn at Knoxville	TN	20,364	VC+
Univ of Texas - Pan American	TX	11,125	C
Univ of Texas at Arlington	TX	10,908	LC
Univ of Texas at Austin	TX	44,074	HC
Univ of Texas at Dallas	TX	21,348	HC+
Univ of Texas at El Paso	TX	8,764	VC
Univ of Texas at San Antonio	TX	18,372	C
Univ of the District of Columbia	DC	7,244	LC
Univ of the Pacific	CA	52,146	VC
Univ of Toledo	OH	18,464	C
Univ of Tulsa	OK	46,331	MC
Univ of Vermont	VT	27,006	VC+
Univ of Virginia	VA	23,050	MC
Univ of Washington	WA	14,722	VC
Univ of West Florida	FL	14,656	C
Univ of Wisc/Madison	WI	18,757	HC+
Univ of Wisc/Platteville	WI	14,564	C
Univ of Wisc-Milwaukee	WI	18,436	C
Univ of Wyoming	WY	14,401	C+
Utah State Univ	UT	12,044	C
Valparaiso Univ	IN	44,940	VC+
Vanderbilt Univ	TN	58,220	MC
Villanova Univ	PA	58,394	MC
Virginia Commonwealth Univ	VA	21,716	C
Virginia Military Inst	VA	16,156	C
Virginia Polytechnic Inst and State Univ	VA	14,629	HC
Washington State Univ	WA	20,461	C
Washington Univ in St. Louis	MO	69,844	MC
Wayne State Univ	MI	22,063	C
West Virginia Univ	WV	16,542	C+
West Virginia Univ Inst of Technology	WV	14,094	NC
Western Carolina Univ	NC	13,965	C
Western Kentucky Univ	KY	11,000	LC
Western Mich Univ	MI	19,628	C
Western New England Univ	MA	46,154	C+
Western Washington Univ	WA	18,519	VC
Wichita State Univ	KS	14,607	C+
Widener Univ	PA	52,418	C
Wilkes Univ	PA	44,070	C
Worcester Polytechnic Inst	MA	55,860	MC
Wright State Univ	OH	16,983	C
Yale Univ	CT	55,300	MC
York College of Pennsylvania	PA	26,590	C
Youngstown State Univ	OH	16,732	C

ELECTRICAL/ELECTRONICS ENGINEERING TECHNOLOGY

School	ST	$IS	SR
Alabama A&M Univ	AL	10,084	C
Alfred State/SUNY College of Technology	NY	18,034	C
Appalachian State Univ	NC	12,919	VC
Arizona State Univ, at the Polytechnic Campus	AZ	20,531	C+
Arizona State Univ, at the Tempe Campus	AZ	20,137	C+
Baker College of Flint	MI	7,800	NC
Bowling Green State Univ	OH	18,970	C
Brigham Young Univ	UT	12,100	HC
Buffalo State College / SUNY	NY	15,733	C+
Calif Univ of Pennsylvania	PA	14,217	C
Central Conn State Univ	CT	19,749	C
Cleveland State Univ	OH	21,776	C
Colo State Univ-Pueblo	CO	16,183	C
Colo Technical Univ	CO	10,500	LC
East Carolina Univ	NC	14,169	C
Eastern Mich Univ	MI	18,604	C
Eastern New Mexico Univ	NM	10,682	C
Excelsior College	NY	5,580	SP
Fairleigh Dickinson Univ/ Metropolitan Campus	NJ	40,254	C
Fairmont State Univ	WV	12,098	LC
Farmingdale State College	NY	19,673	C
Ferris State Univ	MI	20,047	C
Fitchburg State Univ	MA	18,173	C
Fort Valley State Univ	GA	11,200	VC
Indiana State Univ	IN	16,000	C
Indiana Univ-Purdue Univ Fort Wayne	IN	15,521	C
Indiana Univ-Purdue Univ Indianapolis	IN	17,611	C
Inter-American Univ of PR/ Aguadilla Campus	PR	5,578	
Inter-American Univ of PR/ Bayamon Univ College	PR	4,428	
Inter-American Univ of PR/ Fajardo Campus	PR	4,200	
Inter-American Univ of PR/ Ponce	PR		
Kansas State Univ	KS	15,497	VC
Kent State Univ	OH	19,920	C
Louisiana Tech Univ	LA	11,302	C
Metropolitan State Univ of Denver	CO	4,835	LC
Mich Tech Univ	MI	23,556	HC
Minn State Univ, Mankato	MN	15,616	C
Montana State Univ-Northern	MT	12,500	NC
Murray State Univ	KY	15,304	C
Norfolk State Univ	VA	10,531	LC
Northern Kentucky Univ	KY	21,134	C
Northern Mich Univ	MI	18,278	C
Northwestern State Univ of Louisiana	LA	14,368	C
Okla State Univ	OK	14,310	VC
Old Dominion Univ	VA	19,483	LC
Oregon Inst of Technology	OR	8,910	C
Pennsylvania College of Technology	PA	26,286	NC
Pittsburg State Univ	KS	12,032	C
Point Park Univ	PA	36,390	C
Purdue Univ/Calumet	IN	14,336	C
Purdue Univ/West Lafayette	IN	20,024	HC
Rochester Inst of Technology	NY	42,450	VC
Roosevelt Univ	IL	22,605	VC
Savannah State Univ	GA	13,156	C
S Car State Univ	SC	6,700	LC
S Dak State Univ	SD	14,296	C
Southern Illinois Univ Carbondale	IL	21,942	C
Southern Polytechnic State Univ	GA	13,958	C
Southwestern Okla State Univ	OK	9,160	C
SUNY Polytechnic Inst	NY	19,690	C
Texas A&M Univ at Galveston	TX	11,258	C
Texas Southern Univ	TX	18,212	LC
Texas Tech Univ	TX	14,243	C
The Pennsylvania State Univ - Univ Park	PA	28,022	VC+
The Univ of Memphis	TN	15,094	C
Thomas Edison State College	NJ	5,700	SP
Tuskegee Univ	AL	26,750	C
United States Naval Academy	MD		MC
Univ of Akron	OH	20,436	C
Univ of Arkansas at Little Rock	AR	17,609	LC
Univ of Central Missouri	MO	14,605	C
Univ of Cincinnati	OH	21,506	VC
Univ of Dallas	TX	45,500	VC+
Univ of Dayton	OH	49,070	VC
Univ of Hartford	CT	42,674	C
Univ of Maine	ME	19,902	C+
Univ of Mich/Dearborn	MI	9,885	VC
Univ of N Car at Charlotte	NC	15,547	C
Univ of North Texas	TX	15,628	C
Univ of Pittsburgh at Johnstown	PA	20,862	LC
Univ of PR/Bayamon	PR	1,600	
Univ of Rio Grande	OH	8,750	NC
Univ of Southern Miss	MS	13,170	C
Univ of Wisc/Green Bay	WI	19,074	C
Vaughn College of Aeronautics and Technology	NY	31,360	C
Virginia Commonwealth Univ	VA	21,716	C
Wayne State Univ	MI	22,063	C
Wentworth Inst of Technology	MA	29,800	C
West Virginia Univ Inst of Technology	WV	14,094	NC
Western Carolina Univ	NC	13,965	C
Western Washington Univ	WA	18,519	VC
Youngstown State Univ	OH	16,732	C

ELECTROMECHANICAL TECHNOLOGY

School	ST	$IS	SR
Idaho State Univ	ID	12,307	C
Penn State Univ/Altoona	PA	11,464	C
Texas A&M Univ at Galveston	TX	11,258	C
Univ of Northern Iowa	IA	15,795	C
Univ of the District of Columbia	DC	7,244	LC
Univ of Toledo	OH	18,464	C
Vermont Technical College	VT	15,751	C
Wayne State Univ	MI	22,063	C
Wentworth Inst of Technology	MA	29,800	C
Western Kentucky Univ	KY	11,000	LC

ELECTRONIC BUSINESS

School	ST	$IS	SR
Davenport Univ	MI	21,002	LC
Florida Inst of Technology	FL	48,290	VC
Kent State Univ	OH	19,920	C
La Sierra Univ	CA	35,694	VC
Limestone College	SC	30,800	C
Old Dominion Univ	VA	19,483	LC
San Francisco State Univ	CA	18,514	C
Southern Univ and A&M College	LA	9,761	LC
Thiel College	PA	38,728	LC
Trevecca Nazarene Univ	TN	31,186	C
Univ of La Verne	CA	47,010	C
Univ of North Texas	TX	15,628	C
Univ of Scranton	PA	51,940	VC
Univ of Southern Indiana	IN	14,885	C
Winthrop Univ	SC	21,120	C

ELEMENTARY EDUCATION

School	ST	$IS	SR
Abilene Christian Univ	TX	38,400	C+
Adams State Univ	CO	13,358	LC
Adrian College	MI	42,400	C
Alabama A&M Univ	AL	10,084	C
Alabama State Univ	AL	14,142	NC
Alaska Pacific Univ	AK	43,592	VC
Albright College	PA	46,660	C
Alcorn State Univ	MS	9,500	C
Alderson Broaddus Univ	WV	28,656	C
Alice Lloyd College	KY	4,900	LC
Alma College	MI	44,075	C
Alvernia Univ	PA	39,250	LC
Alverno College	WI	31,434	LC
American Indian College	AZ	18,142	C
American International College	MA	36,100	LC
American Univ	DC	56,015	HC+
Anderson Univ	IN	36,100	C
Andrews Univ	MI	28,030	C
Anna Maria College	MA	34,600	C
Appalachian State Univ	NC	12,919	VC
Aquinas College	MI	33,060	C
Aquinas College	TN	29,250	VC+
Arcadia Univ	PA	33,570	C+
Arizona State Univ, at the Polytechnic Campus	AZ	20,531	C+
Arizona State Univ, at the Tempe Campus	AZ	20,137	C+
Arizona State Univ, at the West Campus	AZ	19,251	C
Arkansas Baptist College	AR	15,750	NC
Arkansas Tech Univ	AR	13,982	LC
Asbury Univ	KY	32,038	VC
Ashford Univ	CA	10,480	C
Ashland Univ	OH	25,000	C
Atlantic Union College	MA	24,600	C
Auburn Univ	AL	22,378	VC+
Auburn Univ at Montgomery	AL	14,470	C
Augsburg College	MN	35,142	C
Augustana College	IL	43,398	VC
Augustana College	SD	36,500	VC
Aurora Univ	IL	33,228	C
Averett Univ	VA	37,750	LC
Avila Univ	MO	26,900	C
Baker Univ	KS	33,350	C+
Ball State Univ	IN	17,850	C
Barton College	NC	27,660	LC
Bay Path College	MA	34,565	C
Baylor Univ	TX	50,329	HC
Becker College	MA	41,420	C
Belhaven Univ	MS	27,170	C
Bellarmine Univ	KY	42,950	VC
Belmont Abbey College	NC	37,716	C
Belmont Univ	TN	39,190	VC+
Bemidji State Univ	MN	13,500	VC
Benedict College	SC	20,454	NC
Benedictine College	KS	29,180	VC
Benedictine Univ	IL	37,820	C
Bennett College for Women	NC	21,970	LC
Bennington College	VT	56,990	HC+
Berea College	KY	7,192	C
Bethany College	KS	30,605	NC
Bethany College	WV	35,282	LC
Bethel College	IN	31,560	C
Bethel College	KS	32,160	C
Bethel Univ	MN	34,940	VC
Bethune-Cookman Univ	FL	22,958	C
Black Hills State Univ	SD	13,947	C
Blackburn College	IL	21,350	C
Bloomfield College	NJ	37,850	LC
Blue Mountain College	MS	15,634	LC
Bluefield State College	WV	3,140	LC
Boise State Univ	ID	13,469	LC
Boricua College	NY	8,600	C
Boston College	MA	60,622	MC
Boston Univ	MA	60,604	MC
Bowie State Univ	MD	23,990	VC
Bowling Green State Univ	OH	18,970	C
Bradley Univ	IL	31,874	VC
Brescia Univ	KY	26,140	VC+
Briar Cliff Univ	IA	29,514	C
Bridgewater State Univ	MA	18,752	C
Brigham Young Univ	UT	12,100	HC
Brigham Young Univ/Hawaii	HI	10,686	VC
Bryan College	TN	24,194	C
Bucknell Univ	PA	60,140	MC
Buena Vista Univ	IA	39,188	C
Buffalo State College / SUNY	NY	15,733	C+
Butler Univ	IN	47,572	VC+
Cabrini College	PA	40,859	LC
Caldwell College	NJ	35,602	NC
Cal State, Long Beach	CA	17,502	C+
Calif Univ of Pennsylvania	PA	14,217	C
Calumet College of St. Joseph	IN	15,000	C
Calvin College	MI	39,120	VC
Cameron Univ	OK	10,004	LC
Campbell Univ	NC	37,570	VC
Campbellsville Univ	KY	27,720	C
Canisius College	NY	44,900	C
Capital Univ	OH	41,050	VC
Cardinal Stritch Univ	WI	24,054	C
Caribbean Univ	PR	10,375	
Carlos Albizu Univ	FL	12,053	LC
Carlow Univ	PA	30,272	C
Carroll College	MT	28,000	C
Carroll Univ	WI	38,100	C
Carson-Newman Univ	TN	29,058	C+
Carthage College	WI	33,000	C
Catawba College	NC	37,240	LC
Cazenovia College	NY	43,464	C
Cedar Crest College	PA	43,240	C
Cedarville Univ	OH	32,860	VC
Centenary College	NJ	38,618	C
Central College	IA	42,104	C+
Central Conn State Univ	CT	19,749	C
Central Methodist Univ	MO	28,240	VC
Central State Univ	OH	9,010	C
Central Univ of Bayamon	PR	3,350	
Central Washington Univ	WA	11,730	C
Centre College	KY	35,000	HC+
Chadron State College	NE	7,400	NC
Chaminade Univ of Honolulu	HI	31,664	C
Champlain College	VT	46,820	C+
Charleston Southern Univ	SC	22,420	C
Chatham Univ	PA	43,797	C
Chestnut Hill College	PA	42,110	LC
Cheyney Univ of Pennsylvania	PA	20,372	C

ST = STATE $IS = IN-STATE COSTS   SR = SELECTOR RATING

School	ST	$IS	SR
Chicago State Univ	IL	5,482	C
CUNY/Brooklyn College	NY	5,884	C+
CUNY/City College	NY	20,319	HC+
City Univ of Seattle	WA	14,880	NC
Claflin Univ	SC	22,368	LC
Clarion Univ of Pennsylvania	PA	17,370	LC
Clarke Univ	IA	37,600	C
Clearwater Christian College	FL	23,720	C
Clemson Univ	SC	19,136	HC
Cleveland State Univ	OH	21,776	C
Coastal Carolina Univ	SC	18,580	C
Coe College	IA	45,550	VC
Coker College	SC	32,256	LC
College of Charleston	SC	22,145	VC
College of Mount St. Joseph	OH	33,880	C
College of New Jersey	NJ	25,376	HC
College of St. Benedict	MN	49,359	VC
College of St. Elizabeth	NJ	43,839	LC
College of St. Mary	NE	35,184	C
College of St Joseph	VT	30,600	LC
College of the Ozarks	MO		VC
Colo Christian Univ	CO	27,500	VC
Columbia College	MO	24,578	C
Columbia College	SC	27,882	C
Concord Univ	WV	13,102	C
Concordia College - Alabama	AL	15,720	NC
Concordia College - Moorhead	MN	39,974	VC
Concordia College - New York	NY	39,035	LC
Concordia Univ	OR	35,000	C
Concordia Univ Nebr	NE	26,000	VC
Concordia Univ St. Paul	MN	28,250	C
Concordia Univ Texas	TX	23,640	C
Concordia Univ Wisc	WI	28,980	C
Concordia Univ, Ann Arbor	MI	27,220	VC
Concordia Univ, River Forest	IL	26,300	C
Converse College	SC	37,130	C
Coppin State Univ	MD	16,227	VC
Corban Univ	OR	37,380	C+
Cornell College	IA	44,930	VC
Cornerstone Univ and Grand Rapids Theological Seminary	MI	33,338	C
Covenant College	GA	38,990	VC+
Creighton Univ	NE	45,356	VC
Culver-Stockton College	MO	30,900	C
Cumberland Univ	TN	21,220	C
Curry College	MA	48,925	LC
Daemen College	NY	34,770	C
Dakota State Univ	SD	13,811	C
Dakota Wesleyan Univ	SD	23,000	C
Dallas Baptist Univ	TX	30,580	VC
Davis & Elkins College	WV	33,742	C
De Sales Univ	PA	43,970	C
Defiance College	OH	30,645	C
Delaware State Univ	DE	16,722	LC
Delta State Univ	MS	12,292	LC
DePaul Univ	IL	47,623	VC
DePauw Univ	IN	48,950	VC+
Dickinson State Univ	ND	11,900	NC
Doane College	NE	35,230	C
Dominican College	NY	31,270	LC
Dominican Univ	IL	37,628	C
Dordt College	IA	34,160	C+
Dowling College	NY	25,000	LC
Drake Univ	IA	41,516	VC+
Drexel Univ	PA	61,418	VC+
Drury Univ	MO	31,909	VC
East Carolina Univ	NC	14,169	C
East Central Univ	OK	10,223	LC
East Stroudsburg Univ of Pennsylvania	PA	18,868	LC
East Texas Baptist Univ	TX	31,577	LC
Eastern Conn State Univ	CT	20,584	C
Eastern Illinois Univ	IL	20,466	C
Eastern Kentucky Univ	KY	11,161	C
Eastern Mennonite Univ	VA	40,660	C
Eastern Mich Univ	MI	18,604	C
Eastern Nazarene College	MA	30,000	C
Eastern New Mexico Univ	NM	10,682	C
Eastern Washington Univ	WA		C
Edgewood College	WI	33,294	C
Edinboro Univ of Pennsylvania	PA	15,940	LC
Edward Waters College	FL	19,607	LC
Elizabeth City State Univ	NC	11,638	C
Elizabethtown College	PA	49,740	VC
Elmhurst College	IL	43,336	C
Elmira College	NY	49,950	C+
Elms College	MA	23,900	VC
Elon Univ	NC	41,914	VC+
Emmanuel College	MA	47,985	VC
Emporia State Univ	KS	12,897	C
Erskine College	SC	37,360	C
Eureka College	IL	19,280	C
Evangel Univ	MO	23,090	C
Fairmont State Univ	WV	12,098	LC
Faulkner Univ	AL	25,720	LC
Fayetteville State Univ	NC	10,816	C
Felician College	NJ	41,640	LC
Ferris State Univ	MI	20,047	C
Fitchburg State Univ	MA	18,173	C
Five Towns College	NY	34,550	C
Flagler College	FL	25,180	C
Florida A&M Univ	FL	14,935	LC
Florida Atlantic Univ	FL	17,339	C
Florida Gulf Coast Univ	FL		C
Florida International Univ	FL	17,747	C+
Florida Memorial Univ	FL	20,888	LC
Florida Southern College	FL	40,150	C+
Florida State Univ	FL	16,715	VC
Fontbonne Univ	MO	31,384	C
Fort Hays State Univ	KS	11,354	C
Framingham State Univ	MA	18,854	C
Francis Marion Univ	SC	16,464	LC
Franciscan Univ of Steubenville	OH	27,320	VC
Franklin College	IN	36,585	C
Franklin Pierce Univ	NH	41,598	C
Freed-Hardeman Univ	TN	19,697	VC
Friends Univ	KS	29,100	C
Frostburg State Univ	MD	15,264	LC
Furman Univ	SC	54,006	HC
Gallaudet Univ	DC	25,380	SP
Gardner-Webb Univ	NC	34,375	C+
Geneva College	PA	27,280	C
George Fox Univ	OR	40,750	C+
Georgetown College	KY	41,440	C+
Georgia Regents Univ	GA		C
Georgian Court Univ	NJ	41,594	LC
Gettysburg College	PA	58,820	HC
Glenville State College	WV	11,348	NC
Goddard College	VT	16,418	VC
Gordon College	MA	44,320	VC
Goshen College	IN	35,900	VC
Grace Bible College	MI	20,770	C
Grace College and Seminary	IN	28,800	VC
Graceland Univ	IA	28,020	C
Grambling State Univ	LA	13,384	LC
Grand Canyon Univ	AZ	24,540	VC
Grand Valley State Univ	MI	17,998	C+
Grand View Univ	IA	31,050	C
Green Mountain College	VT	45,228	LC
Greensboro College	NC	28,740	LC
Greenville College	IL	27,012	C
Grove City College	PA	24,022	VC
Gustavus Adolphus College	MN	48,170	HC
Gwynedd-Mercy College	PA	33,560	C
Hamline Univ	MN	45,678	VC
Hannibal-LaGrange Univ	MO	24,490	C
Hanover College	IN	43,073	C+
Harding Univ	AR	23,556	C
Hardin-Simmons Univ	TX	23,560	C
Harris-Stowe State Univ	MO	14,360	NC
Hastings College	NE	27,782	C+
Hawaii Pacific Univ	HI	34,360	C
Heidelberg Univ	OH	34,100	C
Hellenic College/Holy Cross Greek Orthodox School of Theology	MA	33,190	C
Heritage Univ	WA	17,664	NC
High Point Univ	NC	39,800	C
Hofstra Univ	NY	51,810	VC+
Holy Family Univ	PA	40,030	LC
Hood College	MD	45,730	C
Hope College	MI	38,650	VC
Houghton College	NY	36,808	C+
Houston Baptist Univ	TX	36,450	C
Howard Payne Univ	TX	17,115	C
Howard Univ	DC	13,646	C
Humboldt State Univ	CA	18,400	C
Hunter College	NY	14,429	VC
Huntingdon College	AL	33,100	C
Huntington Univ	IN	32,220	C+
Husson Univ	ME	24,194	LC
Huston-Tillotson Univ	TX	18,124	C+
Idaho State Univ	ID	12,307	C
Illinois College	IL	25,770	VC
Illinois State Univ	IL	23,110	VC
Immaculata Univ	PA	43,000	C
Indiana Inst of Technology	IN	34,240	LC
Indiana State Univ	IN	16,000	C
Indiana Univ Bloomington	IN	19,801	VC
Indiana Univ East	IN	6,783	C
Indiana Univ Kokomo	IN	6,811	LC
Indiana Univ Northwest	IN	6,854	LC
Indiana Univ South Bend	IN	15,501	C
Indiana Univ Southeast	IN	16,035	C
Indiana Univ-Purdue Univ Fort Wayne	IN	15,521	C
Indiana Univ-Purdue Univ Indianapolis	IN	17,611	C
Indiana Wesleyan Univ	IN	31,815	VC
Inter-American Univ of PR/ Aguadilla Campus	PR	5,578	
Inter-American Univ of PR/ Arecibo Campus	PR	3,350	
Inter-American Univ of PR/ Barranquitas	PR	3,350	
Inter-American Univ of PR/ Fajardo Campus	PR	4,200	
Inter-American Univ of PR/ Metropolitan Campus	PR	4,320	
Inter-American Univ of PR/ Ponce	PR		
Inter-American Univ of PR/ San Germán	PR	6,720	
Iowa State Univ	IA	16,403	C
Iowa Wesleyan College	IA	30,850	LC
Jackson State Univ	MS	13,512	LC
Jacksonville State Univ	AL	12,480	LC
Jacksonville Univ	FL	37,780	C
Jarvis Christian College	TX	19,552	NC
John Brown Univ	AR	32,056	VC+
Johnson State College	VT	16,721	C
Judson College	AL	26,794	C
Judson Univ	IL	25,130	C
Juniata College	PA	49,340	VC
Kansas State Univ	KS	15,497	NC
Kean Univ	NJ	23,444	C
Kentucky Christian Univ	KY	17,622	LC
Kentucky State Univ	KY	11,000	LC
Kentucky Wesleyan College	KY	27,440	C
Keuka College	NY	30,300	C
Keystone College	PA	28,680	LC
King Univ	TN	33,140	C
King's College	PA	43,502	C
Knox College	IL	44,865	VC+
Kutztown Univ of Pennsylvania	PA	16,909	LC
La Roche College	PA	35,824	LC
La Salle Univ	PA	50,270	C
La Sierra Univ	CA	35,694	VC
Lake Superior State Univ	MI	18,121	C
Lakeland College	WI	22,990	C
Lamar Univ	TX	6,820	LC
Lander Univ	SC	22,514	C+
Langston Univ	OK	3,000	C
Lasell College	MA	43,750	LC
Le Moyne College	NY	43,470	C
Lebanon Valley College	PA	38,570	C
Lee Univ	TN	18,690	C+
Lees-McRae College	NC	33,944	C
Lehman College/The CUNY	NY	5,778	LC
Lenoir-Rhyne College	NC	35,984	C
Lesley Univ	MA	46,350	C
LeTourneau Univ	TX	36,210	VC
Lewis Univ	IL	23,050	C
Lewis-Clark State College	ID	6,990	C
Liberty Univ	VA	19,101	C
Limestone College	SC	30,800	C
Lincoln Memorial Univ	TN	18,144	C
Lincoln Univ	MO	12,904	NC
Lindenwood Univ	MO	20,750	C
Lindsey Wilson College	KY	31,220	C
Linfield College-McMinnville Campus	OR	47,676	C
Lipscomb Univ	TN	37,490	VC
LIU Brooklyn	NY	47,182	LC
LIU Post	NY	47,660	C
Livingstone College	NC	17,815	LC
Lock Haven Univ of Pennsylvania	PA	18,028	LC
Longwood Univ	VA	20,924	C
Loras College	IA	37,432	VC
Louisiana College	LA	15,746	C
Louisiana State Univ	LA	18,677	C+
Louisiana State Univ in Shreveport	LA	5,606	C
Louisiana Tech Univ	LA	11,302	C
Loyola Univ Chicago	IL	51,646	VC+
Loyola Univ Maryland	MD	56,880	VC+
Lubbock Christian Univ	TX	26,308	C
Luther College	IA	45,720	C+
Lynchburg College	VA	42,645	C
Lyndon State College	VT	14,233	C
Lynn Univ	FL	43,500	LC
MacMurray College	IL	20,755	C
Manchester Univ	IN	35,070	C
Manhattan College	NY	49,588	C+
Mansfield Univ	PA	19,468	LC
Marian Univ	IN	38,540	C
Marian Univ	WI	32,420	LC
Mars Hill Univ	NC	22,950	LC
Marshall Univ	WV	14,820	C
Marymount Manhattan College	NY	40,118	VC
Maryville Univ	MO	33,150	C+
Maryville Univ of St. Louis	MO	35,856	VC
Marywood Univ	PA	45,595	C
Mayville State Univ	ND	11,401	NC
McKendree Univ	IL	29,920	C+
McMurry Univ	TX	25,962	LC
McNeese State Univ	LA	2,649	C
McPherson College	KS	28,138	C
Medaille College	NY	35,112	C
Megar Evers College/The CUNY	NY	4,920	NC
Mercer Univ	GA	44,201	VC
Mercy College	NY	30,456	C
Mercyhurst Univ	PA	40,700	C
Merrimack College	MA	44,215	C
Messiah College	PA	40,690	C+
Methodist Univ	NC	37,185	C
Miami Univ	OH	24,191	VC
MidAmerica Nazarene Univ	KS	28,000	C
Midland Univ	NE	34,000	C
Miles College	AL	11,164	NC
Millersville Univ of Pennsylvania	PA	21,648	C
Millikin Univ	IL	38,940	C
Minn State Univ, Mankato	MN	15,616	C
Minn State Univ, Moorhead	MN	13,392	VC
Minot State Univ	ND	10,915	C
Misericordia Univ	PA	41,060	C
Miss College	MS	21,998	C
Miss State Univ	MS	14,750	C
Miss Univ for Women	MS	7,400	C
Miss Valley State Univ	MS	9,706	LC
Missouri Baptist Univ	MO	31,830	C
Missouri Southern State Univ	MO	12,061	C
Missouri State Univ	MO	13,996	C+
Missouri Valley College	MO	22,200	C
Missouri Western State Univ	MO	12,260	NC
Monmouth College	IL	40,850	C
Monmouth Univ	NJ	44,108	C
Montana State Univ	MT	14,068	C
Montana State Univ-Billings	MT	12,425	LC
Montana State Univ-Northern	MT	12,500	NC
Montreat College	NC	31,298	C
Moravian College	PA	36,381	VC
Morehead State Univ	KY	10,900	C
Morgan State Univ	MD	14,500	VC
Morningside College	IA	35,430	C
Morris College	SC	16,310	LC
Mount Aloysius College	PA	29,976	C
Mount Marty College	SD	29,638	C
Mount Mercy Univ	IA	35,320	C
Mount St. Mary's Univ	MD	47,996	C
Mount St. Mary's College - Chalon Campus	CA	43,897	VC+
Murray State Univ	KY	15,304	C
Muskingum Univ	OH	30,502	C
National Louis Univ	IL	16,915	LC
Nazareth College of Rochester	NY	43,028	C+
Nebr Wesleyan Univ	NE	29,774	C+
Neumann Univ	PA	31,078	LC
New England College	NH	45,930	LC
New Jersey City Univ	NJ	21,546	LC
New Mexico Highlands Univ	NM	11,904	NC
New Mexico State Univ	NM	14,050	C
New York Univ	NY	61,470	MC
Newberry College	SC	26,850	LC
Newman Univ	KS	30,380	C+
Niagara Univ	NY	41,010	C
Nicholls State Univ	LA	7,095	C
N Car Central Univ	NC	9,000	C
N Car Wesleyan College	NC	29,440	C
North Central College	IL	38,343	VC
North Central Univ	MN	26,400	C
N Dak State Univ	ND		C
North Park Univ	IL	30,130	C
Northeastern Illinois Univ	IL	10,318	LC
Northeastern State Univ	OK	8,615	VC
Northern Arizona Univ	AZ	19,010	C
Northern Illinois Univ	IL	19,768	C
Northern Kentucky Univ	KY	21,134	C
Northern Mich Univ	MI	18,278	C
Northern State Univ - Aberdeen	SD	14,505	C
Northland College	WI	26,680	C
Northwest Christian Univ	OR	27,399	C
Northwest Missouri State Univ	MO	17,347	C
Northwest Nazarene Univ	ID	34,000	C
Northwest Univ	WA	18,854	C
Northwestern College	MN	24,000	C
Northwestern College of Iowa	IA	36,240	VC
Northwestern Okla State Univ	OK	7,275	NC
Northwestern State Univ of Louisiana	LA	14,368	C
Notre Dame College	OH	34,942	VC
Notre Dame of Maryland Univ	MD	27,700	VC
Nova Southeastern Univ	FL	37,280	VC
Nyack College	NY	33,250	C
Oakland City Univ	IN	24,500	NC
Oakland Univ	MI	19,391	C
Oakwood Univ	AL	25,529	NC
Oglala Lakota College	SD	2,000	NC
Ohio State Univ at Mansfield	OH	13,160	C
Ohio State Univ at Marion	OH	16,990	MC
Ohio State Univ at Newark	OH	17,510	C
Ohio Valley Univ	WV	17,752	C
Ohio Wesleyan Univ	OH	49,460	C+
Okla Baptist Univ	OK	28,202	C
Okla Christian Univ	OK	25,870	VC
Okla City Univ	OK	40,476	VC
Okla State Univ	OK	14,310	VC
Okla Wesleyan Univ	OK	21,300	C
Old Dominion Univ	VA	19,483	LC
Olivet College	MI	19,984	LC
Olivet Nazarene Univ	IL	29,990	C
Oral Roberts Univ	OK	31,734	C
Oswego / SUNY	NY	20,009	VC
Ottawa Univ	KS	15,000	VC
Otterbein College	OH	32,214	C
Ouachita Baptist Univ	AR	30,220	VC
Our Lady of Holy Cross College	LA	8,090	C
Pace Univ	NY	53,367	C
Palm Beach Atlantic Univ	FL	34,874	C+
Park Univ	MO	17,525	C
Penn State Univ/Altoona	PA	11,464	C
Pepperdine Univ	CA	55,372	HC+
Peru State College	NE	8,600	NC
Pfeiffer Univ	NC	33,700	LC
Pittsburg State Univ	KS	12,032	C
Point Park Univ	PA	36,390	C
Pontifical Catholic Univ of PR	PR	7,310	

ST = STATE $IS = IN-STATE COSTS   SR = SELECTOR RATING

School	ST	$IS	SR
Univ of Florida	FL	15,943	HC
Univ of Maryland/Univ College	MD	6,168	SP
Univ of North Texas	TX	15,628	C
West Texas A&M Univ	TX	13,478	C
Western Carolina Univ	NC	13,965	C
Western Illinois Univ	IL	20,732	C

ENERGY MANAGEMENT TECHNOLOGY

School	ST	$IS	SR
Creighton Univ	NE	45,356	VC
Fitchburg State Univ	MA	18,173	C
Hunter College	NY	14,429	VC
Idaho State Univ	ID	12,307	C
Illinois State Univ	IL	23,110	VC
Ohio Univ	OH	21,080	C
Texas Tech Univ	TX	14,243	C
Univ of Northern Iowa	IA	15,795	C
Univ of Tulsa	OK	46,331	MC
Univ of Wyoming	WY	14,401	C+

ENERGY SCIENCE

School	ST	$IS	SR
Creighton Univ	NE	45,356	VC
Indiana Univ-Purdue Univ Indianapolis	IN	17,611	C
Syracuse Univ	NY	56,346	VC

ENERGY SYSTEMS TECHNOLOGY

School	ST	$IS	SR
Thomas Edison State College	NJ	5,700	SP
Univ of Illinois at Chicago	IL	24,505	VC
Univ of Wyoming	WY	14,401	C+

ENERGY UTILITY TECHNOLOGY

School	ST	$IS	SR
Thomas Edison State College	NJ	5,700	SP

ENGINEERING

School	ST	$IS	SR
Abilene Christian Univ	TX	38,400	C+
Agnes Scott College	GA	45,323	C+
Alabama State Univ	AL	14,142	NC
Albion College	MI	46,010	C
Andrews Univ	MI	28,030	C+
Arcadia Univ	PA	33,570	C+
Arizona State Univ, at the Polytechnic Campus	AZ	20,531	C+
Arizona State Univ, at the Tempe Campus	AZ	20,137	C+
Arkansas State Univ	AR	15,470	C
Ball State Univ	IN	17,850	C
Baylor Univ	TX	50,329	HC
Benedictine College	KS	29,180	VC
Bethel College	IN	31,560	C
Binghamton Univ/The SUNY	NY	21,648	HC+
Biola Univ	CA	40,320	C+
Boston Univ	MA	60,694	MC
Brown Univ	RI	59,428	MC
Bucknell Univ	PA	60,140	MC
Butler Univ	IN	47,572	VC+
Calif Baptist Univ	CA	38,792	C
Calif State Polytechnic Univ, Pomona	CA	20,156	C
Cal State, East Bay	CA	16,549	C
Cal State, Los Angeles	CA	17,186	LC
Cal State, Northridge	CA	28,690	LC
Calvin College	MI	39,120	VC
Carnegie Mellon Univ	PA	51,260	MC
Case Western Reserve Univ	OH	56,534	MC
Cedarville Univ	OH	32,860	VC
Colo School of Mines	CO	18,000	HC
Colo State Univ-Fort Collins	CO	20,385	VC
Cooper Union for the Advancement of Science and Art	NY	55,600	MC
Dominican Univ	IL	37,628	C
Dordt College	IA	34,160	C+
Drexel Univ	PA	61,418	VC+
East Carolina Univ	NC	14,169	C
Eastern Illinois Univ	IL	20,466	C
Eastern Washington Univ	WA		C
Elizabethtown College	PA	49,740	VC
Elon Univ	NC	41,914	VC+
Embry-Riddle Aeronautical Univ - Daytona Beach	FL	40,884	C+
Florida Atlantic Univ	FL	17,339	C
Franklin W. Olin College of Engineering	MA	59,225	SP
Geneva College	PA	27,280	C
George Washington Univ	DC	57,108	MC
Grand Valley State Univ	MI	17,998	C+
Harvard College/Harvard Univ	MA	49,000	MC
Harvey Mudd College	CA	64,527	MC
Hope College	MI	38,650	VC
Indiana Inst of Technology	IN	34,240	LC
Indiana Univ-Purdue Univ Fort Wayne	IN	15,521	C
Iowa State Univ	IA	16,403	C
James Madison Univ	VA	18,049	VC
John Brown Univ	AR	32,056	VC+
Johns Hopkins Univ	MD	47,492	MC
Johnson C. Smith Univ	NC	25,336	LC

School	ST	$IS	SR
Lafayette College	PA	59,155	HC+
Lake Superior State Univ	MI	18,121	C
Lawrence Tech Univ	MI	37,630	VC
LeTourneau Univ	TX	36,210	VC
Lindenwood Univ	MO	20,750	C
Loyola Univ Maryland	MD	56,880	VC+
Lubbock Christian Univ	TX	26,308	C
Maine Maritime Academy	ME	21,073	C
Manchester Univ	IN	35,070	C
Maritime College/SUNY	NY	16,020	C
Marquette Univ	WI	46,930	VC+
Marshall Univ	WV	14,820	C
Maryville College	TN	33,150	C
Maryville Univ of St. Louis	MO	35,856	VC
Mass Inst of Technology	MA	58,240	MC
McNeese State Univ	LA	2,649	C
Mercer Univ	GA	44,201	VC
Messiah College	PA	40,690	C+
Miami Univ	OH	24,191	VC
Mich State Univ	MI	22,450	VC
Mich Tech Univ	MI	23,556	HC
Milwaukee School of Engineering	WI	39,948	VC+
Montana Tech of The Univ of Montana	MT	14,650	VC
Muskingum Univ	OH	30,502	C
New Mexico Highlands Univ	NM	11,904	NC
New York Univ	NY	61,470	MC
N Car State Univ	NC	16,202	HC
Northwest Nazarene Univ	ID	34,000	C
Northwestern Univ	IL	61,640	MC
Olivet Nazarene Univ	IL	29,990	C
Oral Roberts Univ	OK	31,734	C
Penn State Erie/The Behrend College	PA	16,256	C
Pepperdine Univ	CA	55,372	HC+
Philadelphia Univ	PA	44,160	C
Purdue Univ/Calumet	IN	14,336	C
Quinnipiac Univ	CT	55,160	VC
Rensselaer Polytechnic Inst	NY	61,529	MC
Robert Morris Univ	PA	37,864	C
Rochester Inst of Technology	NY	42,450	VC
Roger Williams Univ	RI	46,296	VC
Rowan Univ	NJ	24,022	VC+
St. Anselm College	NH	49,376	VC
St. Louis Univ	MO	48,346	VC
St. Mary's Univ	TX	33,854	C
St. Vincent College	PA	40,244	C
San Diego State Univ	CA	21,611	C+
San Jose State Univ	CA	19,133	LC
Seattle Pacific Univ	WA	41,559	VC+
Seton Hill Univ	PA	35,172	C
Smith College	MA	59,674	MC
S Dak State Univ	SD	14,296	C
Spelman College	GA	24,650	C
Spring Hill College	AL	44,164	VC
Stanford Univ	CA	58,388	MC
Swarthmore College	PA	57,870	MC
Temple Univ	PA	24,392	VC
Tenn Tech Univ	TN	11,310	C
Texas Christian Univ	TX	49,980	HC
Texas Tech Univ	TX	14,243	C
The Catholic Univ of America	DC	52,852	VC
The Pennsylvania State Univ - Univ Park	PA	28,022	VC+
The Univ of Okla	OK	18,621	VC
The Univ of Tenn at Chattanooga	TN	16,883	C
The Univ of Utah	UT	16,463	VC
Trinity College	CT		HC+
Tufts Univ	MA	58,780	MC
United States Air Force Academy	CO		MC
United States Naval Academy	MD		MC
Univ of Akron	OH	20,436	C
Univ of Alaska Fairbanks	AK	15,130	C
Univ of Arizona	AZ	20,657	C
Univ of Calif at Irvine	CA	25,961	VC
Univ of Calif at San Diego	CA	21,000	VC
Univ of Central Missouri	MO	14,605	C
Univ of Central Okla	OK	12,293	C
Univ of Cincinnati	OH	21,506	VC
Univ of Delaware	DE	23,612	VC
Univ of Detroit Mercy	MI	30,450	VC
Univ of Georgia	GA	20,082	VC
Univ of Hartford	CT	42,674	C
Univ of Idaho	ID	14,558	C
Univ of Illinois at Chicago	IL	24,505	VC
Univ of Illinois at Urbana-Champaign	IL	26,450	HC
Univ of Iowa	IA	17,693	VC
Univ of Louisville	KY	17,946	C
Univ of Maryland - College Park	MD	20,060	VC
Univ of Mass Boston	MA	23,066	VC
Univ of Mich/Ann Arbor	MI	22,102	MC
Univ of Mich/Dearborn	MI	9,885	VC
Univ of Mich-Flint	MI	17,547	C+
Univ of Miss	MS	16,704	C+
Univ of Missouri/Columbia	MO	18,201	MC
Univ of New Haven	CT	48,940	C
Univ of N Car at Asheville	NC	13,500	VC
Univ of Pittsburgh at Bradford	PA	21,802	C
Univ of Portland	OR	49,964	VC

School	ST	$IS	SR
Univ of PR/Mayaguez	PR	1,250	
Univ of South Florida/Tampa	FL	13,000	C
Univ of Southern Indiana	IN	14,885	C
Univ of Tenn at Martin	TN	13,734	C
Univ of Texas at San Antonio	TX	18,372	C
Univ of Toledo	OH	18,464	C
Univ of Vermont	VT	27,006	VC+
Univ of Washington	WA	14,722	VC
Univ of Wisc-Milwaukee	WI	18,436	C
Utah State Univ	UT	12,044	C
Walla Walla Univ	WA	26,256	NC
Washington Univ in St. Louis	MO	69,844	MC
Waynesburg Univ	PA	30,150	C
West Virginia Univ	WV	16,542	C+
Western Illinois Univ	IL	20,732	C
Wheaton College	IL	40,720	MC
Wheeling Jesuit Univ	WV	33,500	C
Widener Univ	PA	52,418	C
Yale Univ	CT	55,300	MC
York College of Pennsylvania	PA	26,590	C
Youngstown State Univ	OH	16,732	C

ENGINEERING AND APPLIED SCIENCE

School	ST	$IS	SR
Benedictine Univ	IL	37,820	C
Bethel Univ	MN	34,940	VC
Calif Inst of Technology	CA	54,045	MC
Cal State, Fullerton	CA	25,188	C
College of New Jersey	NJ	25,376	VC
College of Staten Island/The City of New Yok	NY	16,778	NC
Colo State Univ-Fort Collins	CO	20,385	VC
Dartmouth College	NH	57,996	MC
George Fox Univ	OR	40,750	C+
Hofstra Univ	NY	51,810	VC+
New Jersey Inst of Technology	NJ	26,490	C+
Pacific Lutheran Univ	WA	46,760	C+
Rutgers, The State Univ of New Jersey/New Brunswick	NJ	25,562	VC
Seattle Pacific Univ	WA	41,559	VC+
Stony Brook Univ / SUNY	NY	20,078	HC+
Trinity Univ	TX	48,150	HC+
Tufts Univ	MA	58,780	MC
United States Air Force Academy	CO		MC
Univ of Calif at Berkeley	CA	23,322	MC
Univ of Calif at Riverside	CA	27,204	C+
Univ of Florida	FL	15,943	HC
Univ of Mary	ND	16,714	C
Univ of Rochester	NY	60,668	MC
Univ of Virginia	VA	23,050	MC
Vanderbilt Univ	TN	58,220	MC
Wartburg College	IA	41,055	VC
Wilkes Univ	PA	44,070	C
Yale Univ	CT	55,300	MC

ENGINEERING CHEMISTRY

School	ST	$IS	SR
Ithaca College	NY	53,864	HC
New York Univ	NY	61,470	MC
Oakland Univ	MI	19,391	C
Stony Brook Univ / SUNY	NY	20,078	HC+

ENGINEERING GRAPHICS & DESIGN

School	ST	$IS	SR
Murray State Univ	KY	15,304	C

ENGINEERING MANAGEMENT

School	ST	$IS	SR
Arizona State Univ, at the Tempe Campus	AZ	20,137	C+
Christian Brothers Univ	TN	31,670	HC
Clarkson Univ	NY	57,330	HC
Columbia Univ/City of New York	NY	61,116	MC
Gonzaga Univ	WA	46,441	HC
Illinois Inst of Technology	IL	38,512	HC+
Indiana Univ-Purdue Univ Indianapolis	IN	17,611	C
Kansas State Univ	KS	15,497	VC
Lake Superior State Univ	MI	18,121	C
Miami Univ	OH	24,191	VC
Missouri Univ of Science and Technology	MO	18,655	VC+
New York Inst of Technology	NY	45,010	VC
N Dak State Univ	ND		C
Oral Roberts Univ	OK	31,734	C
Park Univ	MO	17,525	C
Point Park Univ	PA	36,390	C
Purdue Univ/West Lafayette	IN	20,024	VC
Stevens Inst of Technology	NJ	50,130	HC
Texas A&M Univ at Kingsville	TX	7,500	LC
The Univ of Tenn at Chattanooga	TN	16,883	C
Trine Univ	IN	39,400	HC+
United States Military Academy	NY		MC
Univ of Louisville	KY	17,946	C
Univ of N Car at Asheville	NC	13,500	VC
Univ of the Incarnate Word	TX	37,316	LC
Univ of the Pacific	CA	52,146	VC
Univ of Vermont	VT	27,006	VC+

School	ST	$IS	SR
Western Mich Univ	MI	19,628	C
Wilkes Univ	PA	44,070	C
York College of Pennsylvania	PA	26,590	C

ENGINEERING MECHANICS

School	ST	$IS	SR
Columbia Univ/City of New York	NY	61,116	MC
Johns Hopkins Univ	MD	47,492	MC
Lehigh Univ	PA	56,770	MC
Mich State Univ	MI	22,450	VC
Missouri Univ of Science and Technology	MO	18,655	VC+
New York Univ	NY	61,470	MC
United States Air Force Academy	CO		MC
Univ of Arkansas at Little Rock	AR	17,609	LC
Univ of Calif at Riverside	CA	27,204	C+
Univ of Cincinnati	OH	21,506	VC
Univ of Illinois at Urbana-Champaign	IL	26,450	HC
Univ of Wisc/Madison	WI	18,757	HC+
Virginia Polytechnic Inst and State Univ	VA	14,629	HC
Washington Univ in St. Louis	MO	69,844	MC

ENGINEERING PHYSICS

School	ST	$IS	SR
Arkansas Tech Univ	AR	13,982	LC
Augustana College	IL	43,398	VC
Augustana College	SD	36,500	VC
Belmont Univ	TN	39,190	VC+
Bethel College	IN	31,560	C
Bradley Univ	IL	31,874	VC
Case Western Reserve Univ	OH	56,534	MC
Christian Brothers Univ	TN	31,670	HC
Colo State Univ-Fort Collins	CO	20,385	VC
Cornell Univ	NY	60,964	MC
Dartmouth College	NH	57,996	MC
Eastern Mich Univ	MI	18,604	C
Eastern Nazarene College	MA	30,000	C
Edinboro Univ of Pennsylvania	PA	15,940	LC
Elon Univ	NC	41,914	VC+
Embry-Riddle Aeronautical Univ - Daytona Beach	FL	40,884	C+
Fordham Univ	NY	61,588	HC+
Henderson State Univ	AR	14,584	C
Ithaca College	NY	53,864	HC
Jacksonville Univ	FL	37,780	C
John Carroll Univ	OH	46,300	C+
Juniata College	PA	49,340	VC
Kettering Univ	MI	31,456	HC
Lehigh Univ	PA	56,770	MC
Loyola Marymount Univ	CA	54,649	VC+
Miami Univ	OH	24,191	VC
Miss College	MS	21,998	C
Morehouse College	GA	39,412	C
Morgan State Univ	MD	14,500	VC
Murray State Univ	KY	15,304	C
New Mexico State Univ	NM	14,050	C
New York Univ	NY	61,470	MC
N Car Agricultural and Technical State Univ	NC	13,365	LC
Northwest Nazarene Univ	ID	34,000	C
Oakland Univ	MI	19,391	C
Ohio Univ	OH	21,080	C
Oregon State Univ	OR	20,273	VC
Point Loma Nazarene Univ	CA	41,006	C+
Ramapo College of New Jersey	NJ	24,938	C
Randolph College	VA	45,660	VC
Randolph-Macon College	VA	49,869	C+
Rensselaer Polytechnic Inst	NY	61,529	MC
Rose-Hulman Inst of Technology	IN	53,340	MC
St. Louis Univ	MO	48,346	HC
St. Mary's Univ of Minn	MN	38,280	C
S Dak State Univ	SD	14,296	C
Southeast Missouri State Univ	MO	15,370	LC
Southwestern Okla State Univ	OK	9,160	C
St. Ambrose Univ	IA	30,845	C
St. Bonaventure Univ	NY	41,575	C
Stanford Univ	CA	58,388	MC
Stevens Inst of Technology	NJ	50,130	HC
Taylor Univ	IN	37,821	VC+
Texas Tech Univ	TX	14,243	C
Ohio State Univ-Columbus Campus	OH	19,887	HC+
The Univ of Okla	OK	18,621	VC
Tufts Univ	MA	58,780	MC
Tulane Univ	LA	60,861	MC
United States Military Academy	NY		MC
Univ at Buffalo / The SUNY	NY	20,283	VC
Univ of Calif at Berkeley	CA	23,322	MC
Univ of Calif at San Diego	CA	21,000	VC
Univ of Central Okla	OK	12,293	C
Univ of Colo Boulder	CO	22,605	VC+
Univ of Illinois at Chicago	IL	24,505	VC
Univ of Illinois at Urbana-Champaign	IL	26,450	HC
Univ of Kansas	KS	17,603	C+
Univ of Maine	ME	19,902	C+

ST = STATE $IS = IN-STATE COSTS   SR = SELECTOR RATING

School	ST	$IS	SR
Univ of Mass Boston	MA	23,066	VC
Univ of Mich/Ann Arbor	MI	22,102	MC
Univ of Nebr at Omaha	NE	12,700	C
Univ of Nevada/Reno	NV	17,507	C
Univ of North Texas	TX	15,628	C
Univ of Pittsburgh at Pittsburgh	PA	28,572	HC+
Univ of the Pacific	CA	52,146	VC
Univ of Tulsa	OK	46,331	MC
Univ of Wisc/Madison	WI	18,757	HC+
Univ of Wisc/Platteville	WI	14,564	C
Washington and Lee Univ	VA	52,812	MC
West Chester Univ of Pennsylvania	PA	17,186	C
West Virginia Wesleyan College	WV	26,880	C
Westmont College	CA	41,500	HC
Whitworth Univ	WA	47,734	VC
Worcester Polytechnic Inst	MA	55,860	MC
Wright State Univ	OH	16,983	C
Xavier Univ	OH	44,980	VC

ENGINEERING SCIENCE

School	ST	$IS	SR
Calif Polytechnic State Univ	CA	19,847	HC
Morehouse College	GA	39,412	C
The Pennsylvania State Univ - Univ Park	PA	28,022	VC+
Univ of Mary Hardin-Baylor	TX	31,950	C+
Univ of Miami	FL	57,034	MC

ENGINEERING TECHNOLOGY

School	ST	$IS	SR
Appalachian State Univ	NC	12,919	VC
Austin Peay State Univ	TN	15,274	C
Bluefield State College	WV	3,140	LC
Bowling Green State Univ	OH	18,970	C
Calif Maritime Academy	CA	15,496	LC
Calif State Polytechnic Univ, Pomona	CA	20,156	C
Cal State, Long Beach	CA	17,502	C+
Cal State, Sacramento	CA	16,200	C
Calif Univ of Pennsylvania	PA	14,217	C
Capitol College	MD	21,250	C
Central Washington Univ	WA	11,730	C
Colo Mesa Univ	CO	17,690	LC
East Tenn State Univ	TN	9,000	C
Eastern Mich Univ	MI	18,604	C
Eastern Washington Univ	WA		C
Embry-Riddle Aeronautical Univ - Daytona Beach	FL	40,884	C+
Fairmont State Univ	WV	12,098	LC
Ferris State Univ	MI	20,047	C
Florida A&M Univ	FL	14,935	LC
Grambling State Univ	LA	13,384	LC
Indiana Univ-Purdue Univ Fort Wayne	IN	15,521	C
Iowa State Univ	IA	16,403	C
Kansas State Univ	KS	15,497	VC
Lake Superior State Univ	MI	18,121	C
Lawrence Tech Univ	MI	37,630	VC
LeTourneau Univ	TX	36,210	VC
Maine Maritime Academy	ME	21,073	C
McNeese State Univ	LA	2,649	C
Miami Univ	OH	24,191	VC
Middle Tenn State Univ	TN	8,650	C
Midwestern State Univ	TX	9,722	C
Milwaukee School of Engineering	WI	39,948	VC+
Minn State Univ, Mankato	MN	15,616	C
Missouri Western State Univ	MO	12,260	NC
Montana State Univ-Northern	MT	12,500	NC
New Jersey Inst of Technology	NJ	26,490	C+
New Mexico State Univ	NM	14,050	C
Ohio Univ	OH	21,080	C
Old Dominion Univ	VA	19,483	LC
Oregon Inst of Technology	OR	8,910	C
Penn State Erie/The Behrend College	PA	16,256	C
Pennsylvania College of Technology	PA	26,286	NC
Point Park Univ	PA	36,390	C
Prairie View A&M Univ	TX	15,205	LC
Purdue Univ/Calumet	IN	14,336	C
Rochester Inst of Technology	NY	42,450	VC
Saginaw Valley State Univ	MI	17,369	C
Shawnee State Univ	OH	16,916	C
S Car State Univ	SC	6,700	LC
S Dak State Univ	SD	14,296	C
Southeast Missouri State Univ	MO	15,370	LC
Southeastern Louisiana Univ	LA	13,325	C
Southern Illinois Univ Carbondale	IL	21,942	C
Southern Univ and A&M College	LA	9,761	LC
Southwestern Okla State Univ	OK	9,160	C
St. Cloud State Univ	MN	10,600	C
Temple Univ	PA	24,392	VC
Texas A&M Univ	TX	19,207	VC
Texas A&M Univ at Commerce	TX	10,496	C
Texas A&M Univ at Corpus Christi	TX	11,544	LC
Texas Southern Univ	TX	18,212	LC
Texas State Univ	TX	17,128	C
Texas Tech Univ	TX	14,243	C
The Univ of Memphis	TN	15,094	C
Univ of Arkansas at Little Rock	AR	17,609	LC
Univ of Central Missouri	MO	14,605	C
Univ of Cincinnati	OH	21,506	VC
Univ of Dayton	OH	49,070	VC
Univ of Delaware	DE	23,612	VC
Univ of Hartford	CT	42,674	C
Univ of Houston-Downtown	TX	15,170	LC
Univ of Maryland/Eastern Shore	MD	14,000	VC
Univ of Mass Lowell	MA	19,316	C
Univ of N Car at Charlotte	NC	15,547	C
Univ of North Texas	TX	15,628	C
Univ of S Car Upstate	SC	18,200	LC
Univ of Southern Miss	MS	13,170	C
Univ of Toledo	OH	18,464	C
Univ of Wisc/Green Bay	WI	19,074	C
Univ of Wisc/Stout	WI	15,459	C
Virginia State Univ	VA	11,318	C+
West Texas A&M Univ	TX	13,478	C
West Virginia Univ Inst of Technology	WV	14,094	NC
Western Carolina Univ	NC	13,965	C
Western Illinois Univ	IL	20,732	C
Western Washington Univ	WA	18,519	VC

ENGINEERING/ELE EMPHASIS/ENERGY SYS FOCUS

School	ST	$IS	SR
Texas Christian Univ	TX	49,980	HC

ENGINEERING/MECHANICAL EMP/ENERGY SYS FOCUS

School	ST	$IS	SR
Texas Christian Univ	TX	49,980	HC

ENGLISH

School	ST	$IS	SR
Abilene Christian Univ	TX	38,400	C+
Adams State Univ	CO	13,358	LC
Adelphi Univ	NY	44,670	VC
Adrian College	MI	42,400	C
Alabama A&M Univ	AL	10,084	LC
Alabama State Univ	AL	14,142	NC
Albany State Univ	GA	8,500	C
Albertus Magnus College	CT	37,382	LC
Albion College	MI	46,010	C
Albright College	PA	46,660	C
Alcorn State Univ	MS	9,500	C
Alfred Univ	NY	41,770	C
Alice Lloyd College	KY	4,900	LC
Allegheny College	PA	50,980	HC
Allen Univ	SC	16,124	NC
Alma College	MI	44,075	C
Alvernia Univ	PA	39,250	LC
Alverno College	WI	31,434	LC
American International College	MA	36,100	LC
Amherst College	MA	58,744	MC
Anderson Univ	IN	36,100	C
Andrews Univ	MI	28,030	C+
Angelo State Univ	TX	15,049	NC
Anna Maria College	MA	34,600	C
Appalachian State Univ	NC	12,919	VC
Aquinas College	MI	33,060	C
Aquinas College	TN	29,250	VC+
Arcadia Univ	PA	33,570	C+
Arizona State Univ, at the Polytechnic Campus	AZ	20,531	C+
Arizona State Univ, at the Tempe Campus	AZ	20,137	C
Arizona State Univ, at the West Campus	AZ	19,251	C
Arkansas State Univ	AR	15,470	C
Arkansas Tech Univ	AR	13,982	LC
Armstrong State Univ	GA	15,532	C
Asbury Univ	KY	32,038	VC
Ashford Univ	CA	10,480	C
Ashland Univ	OH	25,000	C
Assumption College	MA	47,122	C+
Atlantic Union College	MA	24,600	C
Auburn Univ	AL	22,378	VC+
Auburn Univ at Montgomery	AL	14,470	LC
Augsburg College	MN	35,142	C
Augustana College	IL	43,398	VC
Augustana College	SD	36,500	VC
Aurora Univ	IL	33,228	C
Austin College	TX	45,875	HC
Austin Peay State Univ	TN	15,274	C
Averett Univ	VA	37,750	LC
Avila Univ	MO	26,900	C
Azusa Pacific Univ	CA	42,086	C
Baker Univ	KS	33,350	C+
Baldwin Wallace Univ	OH	38,318	C
Ball State Univ	IN	17,850	C
Barnard College/Columbia Univ	NY	39,000	MC
Barry Univ	FL	38,190	C
Barton College	NC	27,660	LC
Bates College	ME	60,720	MC
Baylor Univ	TX	50,329	HC
Belhaven Univ	MS	27,170	C
Bellarmine Univ	KY	42,950	VC
Bellevue Univ	NE	4,600	NC
Belmont Abbey College	NC	37,716	C
Belmont Univ	TN	39,190	VC+
Beloit College	WI	49,970	HC
Bemidji State Univ	MN	13,500	VC
Benedict College	SC	20,454	NC
Benedictine Univ	KS	29,180	VC
Bennett College for Women	NC	21,970	LC
Bennington College	VT	56,990	HC+
Berea College	KY	7,192	C
Berry College	GA	39,254	VC
Bethany College	KS	30,605	NC
Bethany College	WV	35,282	LC
Bethel College	IN	31,560	C
Bethel College	KS	32,160	C
Bethel Univ	MN	34,940	VC
Bethel Univ	TN	19,186	C
Bethune-Cookman Univ	FL	22,958	C
Binghamton Univ/The SUNY	NY	21,648	HC+
Biola Univ	CA	40,320	C+
Birmingham-Southern College	AL	44,168	VC+
Black Hills State Univ	SD	13,947	C
Bloomfield College	NJ	37,850	LC
Bloomsburg Univ of Pennsylvania	PA	13,598	C
Blue Mountain College	MS	15,634	LC
Bluefield College	VA	17,230	C+
Bluffton Univ	OH	38,948	C
Boise State Univ	ID	13,469	LC
Boston College	MA	60,622	MC
Boston Univ	MA	60,694	MC
Bowdoin College	ME	59,568	MC
Bowie State Univ	MD	23,990	LC
Bowling Green State Univ	OH	18,970	C
Bradley Univ	IL	31,874	VC
Brandeis Univ	MA		MC
Brenau Univ - Women's College	GA	26,650	LC
Brescia Univ	KY	26,140	VC+
Brewton-Parker College	GA	33,388	C
Briar Cliff Univ	IA	29,514	C
Bridgewater College	VA	41,450	C
Bridgewater State Univ	MA	18,752	C
Brigham Young Univ	UT	12,100	HC
Brigham Young Univ/Hawaii	HI	10,686	VC
Brown Univ	RI	59,428	MC
Bryan College	TN	24,194	C
Bryant Univ	RI	49,179	VC
Bryn Athyn College	PA	27,984	C
Bryn Mawr College	PA	59,890	MC
Bucknell Univ	PA	60,140	MC
Buena Vista Univ	IA	39,188	C
Buffalo State College / SUNY	NY	15,733	C+
Butler Univ	IN	47,572	VC+
Cabrini College	PA	40,859	LC
Cairn Univ	PA	33,270	C
Caldwell College	NJ	35,602	NC
Calif Baptist Univ	CA	38,792	C
Calif College of the Arts	CA	48,334	SP
Calif Lutheran Univ	CA	49,540	C
Calif Polytechnic State Univ	CA	19,847	HC
Calif State Polytechnic Univ, Pomona	CA	20,156	C
Cal State, Bakersfield	CA	8,000	C
Cal State, Chico	CA	20,158	C
Cal State, Dominguez Hills	CA	17,090	LC
Cal State, East Bay	CA	16,549	C
Cal State, Fresno	CA	17,405	C
Cal State, Fullerton	CA	25,188	C
Cal State, Long Beach	CA	17,502	C+
Cal State, Los Angeles	CA	17,186	LC
Cal State, Northridge	CA	28,690	C
Cal State, Sacramento	CA	16,200	C
Cal State, San Bernardino	CA	12,000	C
Cal State, Stanislaus	CA	18,582	C
Calif Univ of Pennsylvania	PA	14,217	C
Calumet College of St. Joseph	IN	15,000	C
Calvin College	MI	39,120	VC
Cameron Univ	OK	10,004	LC
Campbell Univ	NC	37,570	VC
Campbellsville Univ	KY	27,720	C
Canisius College	NY	44,900	C
Capital Univ	OH	41,050	VC
Cardinal Stritch Univ	WI	24,054	C
Carleton College	MN	60,102	MC
Carlow Univ	PA	30,272	C
Carnegie Mellon Univ	PA	51,260	MC
Carroll College	MT	28,000	C
Carroll Univ	WI	38,100	C
Carson-Newman Univ	TN	29,058	C+
Carthage College	WI	33,000	C
Case Western Reserve Univ	OH	56,534	MC
Castleton State College	VT	20,186	C
Catawba College	NC	37,240	LC
Cazenovia College	NY	43,464	C
Cedar Crest College	PA	43,240	C
Cedarville Univ	OH	32,860	VC
Centenary College	NJ	38,618	C
Centenary College of Louisiana	LA	45,650	C+
Central College	IA	42,104	C+
Central Conn State Univ	CT	19,749	C
Central Methodist Univ	MO	28,240	VC
Central Univ	OH	9,010	C
Central Washington Univ	WA	11,730	C
Centre College	KY	35,000	HC+
Chadron State College	NE	7,400	NC
Chaminade Univ of Honolulu	HI	31,664	LC
Chapman Univ	CA	58,347	VC+
Charleston Southern Univ	SC	22,420	C
Chatham Univ	PA	43,797	C
Cheyney Univ of Pennsylvania	PA	20,372	LC
Chicago State Univ	IL	5,482	C
Christendom College	VA	32,600	VC
Christian Brothers Univ	TN	31,670	VC
Christopher Newport Univ	VA	21,960	VC
Citadel, The	SC		C
CUNY/Baruch College	NY		HC
CUNY/Brooklyn College	NY	5,884	C+
CUNY/City College	NY	20,319	VC+
Claflin Univ	SC	22,368	LC
Clarion Univ of Pennsylvania	PA	17,370	LC
Clark Atlanta Univ	GA	30,006	C
Clark Univ	MA	47,020	HC+
Clarke Univ	IA	37,600	C
Clearwater Christian College	FL	23,720	C
Clemson Univ	SC	19,136	HC
Cleveland State Univ	OH	21,776	C
Coastal Carolina Univ	SC	18,580	C
Coe College	IA	44,550	VC
Coker College	SC	32,256	LC
Colby College	ME	57,510	MC
Colby-Sawyer College	NH	50,790	C
Colgate Univ	NY	58,135	MC
College of Charleston	SC	22,145	VC
College of Mount St. Joseph	OH	33,880	C
College of Mount St. Vincent	NY	41,040	MC
College of New Jersey	NJ	25,376	NC
College of St. Benedict	MN	49,359	VC
College of St. Elizabeth	NJ	43,839	LC
College of St. Mary	NE	35,184	C
College of St. Scholastica	MN	41,440	C
College of St Joseph	VT	30,600	LC
College of Staten Island/The City of New Yok	NY	16,778	NC
College of the Holy Cross	MA	58,042	MC
College of the Ozarks	MO		VC
College of William & Mary	VA	28,000	MC
College of Wooster	OH	52,600	VC
Colo Christian Univ	CO	27,500	VC
Colo College	CO	57,162	MC
Colo Mesa Univ	CO	17,690	VC
Colo State Univ-Fort Collins	CO	20,385	VC
Colo State Univ-Pueblo	CO	16,183	C
Columbia College	MO	24,578	C
Columbia College	SC	27,882	C
Columbia Univ/City of New York	NY	61,116	MC
Columbus State Univ	GA	13,176	C
Concord Univ	WV	13,102	C
Concordia College - Moorhead	MN	39,974	VC
Concordia College - New York	NY	39,035	LC
Concordia Univ	OR	35,000	C
Concordia Univ Irvine	CA	35,390	VC
Concordia Univ Nebr	NE	26,000	VC
Concordia Univ St. Paul	MN	28,250	C
Concordia Univ Texas	TX	23,640	C
Concordia Univ Wisc	WI	28,980	C
Concordia Univ, Ann Arbor	MI	27,220	VC
Concordia Univ, River Forest	IL	26,300	C
Conn College	CT	54,970	MC
Converse College	SC	37,130	C
Coppin State Univ	MD	16,227	VC
Corban Univ	OR	37,380	C+
Cornell College	IA	44,930	VC
Cornell Univ	NY	60,964	MC
Cornerstone Univ and Grand Rapids Theological Seminary	MI	33,338	C
Covenant College	GA	38,990	VC+
Creighton Univ	NE	45,356	VC
Culver-Stockton College	MO	30,900	C
Cumberland Univ	TN	21,220	C
Curry College	MA	48,925	LC
Daemen College	NY	34,770	C
Dakota State Univ	SD	13,811	C
Dakota Wesleyan Univ	SD	23,000	C
Dallas Baptist Univ	TX	30,580	VC
Dartmouth College	NH	57,996	MC
Davidson College	NC	58,146	MC
Davis & Elkins College	WV	33,742	C
De Sales Univ	PA	43,970	C
Delaware State Univ	DE	16,722	LC
Delaware Valley College	PA	29,944	C
Delta State Univ	MS	12,292	LC
Denison Univ	OH	54,670	VC+
DePaul Univ	IL	47,623	VC
DePauw Univ	IN	48,950	VC+
Dickinson College	PA	57,662	HC+
Dickinson State Univ	ND	11,900	NC
Dillard Univ	LA	20,940	VC
Doane College	NE	35,230	C
Dominican College	NY	31,270	LC
Dominican Univ	IL	36,528	C
Dordt College	IA	34,160	C+
Dowling College	NY	25,000	C
Drake Univ	IA	41,516	VC+

ST = STATE $IS = IN-STATE COSTS   SR = SELECTOR RATING

School	ST	$IS	SR	School	ST	$IS	SR	School	ST	$IS	SR	School	ST	$IS	SR
Drew Univ/College of Liberal Arts	NJ	57,516	C	Grinnell College	IA	53,654	HC	Lamar Univ	TX	6,820	LC	Millsaps College	MS	43,888	VC+
Drury Univ	MO	31,909	VC	Grove City College	PA	24,022	VC	Lander Univ	SC	22,514	C+	Minn State Univ, Mankato	MN	15,616	C
Duke Univ	NC	50,250	MC	Guilford College	NC	42,800	C	Lane College	TN	11,212	C	Minn State Univ, Moorhead	MN	13,392	VC
Duquesne Univ	PA	43,720	VC	Gustavus Adolphus College	MN	48,170	HC	Langston Univ	OK	3,000	C	Minot State Univ	ND	10,915	C
D'Youville College	NY	29,850	C	Gwynedd-Mercy College	PA	33,560	C	Lasell College	MA	43,750	LC	Misericordia Univ	PA	41,060	C
Earlham College	IN	51,470	MC	Hamilton College	NY	55,620	MC	Lawrence Tech Univ	MI	37,630	VC	Miss College	MS	21,998	C
East Carolina Univ	NC	14,169	C	Hamline Univ	MN	45,678	VC	Lawrence Univ	WI	46,371	HC	Miss State Univ	MS	14,750	C
East Central Univ	OK	10,223	LC	Hampden-Sydney College	VA	51,758	C	Le Moyne College	NY	43,470	C	Miss Univ for Women	MS	7,400	C
East Stroudsburg Univ of Pennsylvania	PA	18,868	LC	Hampton Univ	VA	28,528	C	Lebanon Valley College	PA	38,570	C	Miss Valley State Univ	MS	9,706	LC
East Tenn State Univ	TN	9,000	C	Hannibal-LaGrange Univ	MO	24,490	C	Lee Univ	TN	18,690	C+	Missouri Baptist Univ	MO	31,830	C
East Texas Baptist Univ	TX	31,577	LC	Hanover College	IN	43,073	C+	Lees-McRae College	NC	33,944	C	Missouri Southern State Univ	MO	12,061	C
Eastern Conn State Univ	CT	20,584	C	Harding Univ	AR	23,556	C	LeMoyne-Owen College	TN	13,100	C	Missouri State Univ	MO	13,996	C+
Eastern Illinois Univ	IL	20,466	C	Hardin-Simmons Univ	TX	23,560	C+	Lenoir-Rhyne College	NC	35,984	C	Missouri Univ of Science and Technology	MO	18,655	VC+
Eastern Kentucky Univ	KY	11,161	C	Hartwick College	NY	51,270	C	LeTourneau Univ	TX	36,210	VC	Missouri Valley College	MO	22,200	C
Eastern Mennonite Univ	VA	40,660	C	Harvard College/Harvard Univ	MA	49,000	MC	Lewis & Clark College	OR	54,382	MC	Missouri Western State Univ	MO	12,260	NC
Eastern Mich Univ	MI	18,604	C	Hastings College	NE	27,782	C+	Lewis Univ	IL	23,050	C	Molloy College	NY	40,440	C
Eastern Nazarene College	MA	30,000	C	Haverford College	PA	61,564	MC	Lewis-Clark State College	ID	6,990	C	Monmouth College	IL	40,850	C
Eastern New Mexico Univ	NM	10,682	C	Hawaii Pacific Univ	HI	34,360	C	Liberty Univ	VA	19,101	C	Monmouth Univ	NJ	44,108	C
Eastern Oregon Univ	OR	10,400	C	Heidelberg Univ	OH	34,100	C	Limestone College	SC	30,800	C	Montana State Univ	MT	14,068	C
Eastern Univ	PA	37,704	C	Henderson State Univ	AR	14,584	C	Lincoln Memorial Univ	TN	18,144	C	Montana State Univ-Billings	MT	12,425	LC
Eastern Washington Univ	WA		C	Hendrix College	AR	50,202	VC+	Lincoln Univ	MO	12,904	NC	Montana State Univ-Northern	MT	12,500	NC
Edgewood College	WI	33,294	C	Heritage Univ	WA	17,664	NC	Lindenwood Univ	MO	20,750	C	Montclair State Univ	NJ	22,614	C
Edinboro Univ of Pennsylvania	PA	15,940	LC	Hilbert College	NY	28,550	C	Lindsey Wilson College	KY	31,220	C	Montreat College	NC	31,298	C
Edward Waters College	FL	19,607	LC	Hillsdale College	MI	32,866	MC	Linfield College-McMinnville Campus	OR	47,676	C	Moravian College	PA	36,381	VC
Elizabeth City State Univ	NC	11,638	C	Hiram College	OH	37,300	VC	Lipscomb Univ	TN	37,490	VC	Morehead State Univ	KY	10,900	C
Elizabethtown College	PA	49,740	VC	Hobart and William Smith Colleges	NY	60,034	HC+	LIU Brooklyn	NY	47,182	LC	Morehouse College	GA	39,412	C
Elmhurst College	IL	43,336	C	Hollins Univ	VA	43,295	VC	LIU Post	NY	47,660	C	Morgan State Univ	MD	14,500	C
Elms College	MA	23,900	C	Holy Family Univ	PA	40,030	LC	Livingstone College	NC	17,815	LC	Morningside College	IA	35,430	C
Elon Univ	NC	41,914	VC+	Holy Names Univ	CA	40,310	NC	Lock Haven Univ of Pennsylvania	PA	18,028	LC	Morris College	SC	16,310	LC
Emmanuel College	MA	47,985	VC	Hood College	MD	45,730	C	Longwood Univ	VA	20,924	C	Mount Aloysius College	PA	29,976	C
Emory Univ	GA	56,368	MC	Hope College	MI	38,650	VC	Louisiana College	LA	15,746	C	Mount Holyoke College	MA	55,146	MC
Emporia State Univ	KS	12,897	C	Houghton College	NY	36,808	C+	Louisiana State Univ	LA	18,677	C+	Mount Marty College	SD	29,638	C
Endicott College	MA	43,228	VC+	Houston Baptist Univ	TX	36,450	C	Louisiana State Univ in Shreveport	LA	5,606	C	Mount Mary Univ	WI	33,590	LC
Erskine College	SC	37,360	C	Howard Payne Univ	TX	17,115	C	Louisiana Tech Univ	LA	11,302	C	Mount Mercy Univ	IA	35,320	C
Eureka College	IL	19,280	C	Howard Univ	DC	13,646	C	Lourdes Univ	OH	26,055	LC	Mount St. Mary College	NY	41,138	C
Evangel Univ	MO	23,090	C	Humboldt State Univ	CA	18,400	C	Loyola Marymount Univ	CA	54,649	VC+	Mount St. Mary's Univ	MD	47,996	C
Fairfield Univ	CT	56,960	VC	Hunter College	NY	14,429	VC	Loyola Univ Chicago	IL	51,646	VC+	Mount St. Mary's College - Chalon Campus	CA	43,897	VC+
Fairmont State Univ	WV	12,098	LC	Huntingdon College	AL	33,100	C	Loyola Univ Maryland	MD	56,880	VC+	Mount Vernon Nazarene Univ	OH	29,590	C
Faulkner Univ	AL	25,720	LC	Huntington Univ	IN	32,220	C+	Luther College	IA	45,720	C	Muhlenberg College	PA	52,837	HC
Fayetteville State Univ	NC	10,816	C	Husson Univ	ME	24,194	LC	Lycoming College	PA	45,379	C	Muskingum Univ	OH	30,502	C
Felician College	NJ	41,640	LC	Huston-Tillotson Univ	TX	18,124	C+	Lynchburg College	VA	42,645	C	Naropa Univ	CO	39,166	SP
Ferris State Univ	MI	20,047	C	Idaho State Univ	ID	12,307	C	Lyndon State College	VT	14,233	C	National Louis Univ	IL	16,915	LC
Ferrum College	VA	27,740	LC	Illinois College	IL	25,770	VC	Lyon College	AR	32,090	C+	National Univ	CA	14,730	SP
Fisk Univ	TN	19,830	C	Illinois State Univ	IL	23,110	VC	Macalester College	MN	57,691	MC	Nazareth College of Rochester	NY	43,028	C+
Fitchburg State Univ	MA	18,173	C	Illinois Wesleyan Univ	IL	48,452	HC	MacMurray College	IL	20,755	C	Nebr Wesleyan Univ	NE	29,774	C+
Flagler College	FL	25,180	C	Immaculata Univ	PA	43,000	C	Madonna Univ	MI	24,540	VC	Neumann Univ	PA	31,078	LC
Florida A&M Univ	FL	14,935	LC	Indiana State Univ	IN	16,000	C	Malone Univ	OH	35,364	C	New College of Florida	FL	14,504	MC
Florida Atlantic Univ	FL	17,339	C	Indiana Univ Bloomington	IN	19,801	VC	Manchester Univ	IN	35,070	C	New Jersey City Univ	NJ	21,456	LC
Florida Gulf Coast Univ	FL		C	Indiana Univ East	IN	6,783	C	Manhattan College	NY	49,588	C+	New Mexico Highlands Univ	NM	11,904	NC
Florida International Univ	FL	17,747	C	Indiana Univ Kokomo	IN	6,811	C	Manhattanville College	NY	50,740	VC	New Mexico State Univ	NM	14,050	C
Florida Memorial Univ	FL	20,888	LC	Indiana Univ Northwest	IN	6,854	C	Mansfield Univ	PA	19,468	LC	New York Inst of Technology	NY	45,010	VC
Florida Southern College	FL	40,150	C+	Indiana Univ of Pennsylvania	PA	20,846	LC	Marian Univ	IN	38,540	C	New York Univ	NY	61,470	MC
Florida State Univ	FL	16,715	VC	Indiana Univ South Bend	IN	15,501	C	Marian Univ	WI	32,420	LC	Newberry College	SC	26,850	LC
Fontbonne Univ	MO	31,384	C	Indiana Univ Southeast	IN	16,035	C	Marietta College	OH	42,135	C+	Newman Univ	KS	30,380	C+
Fordham Univ	NY	61,588	HC+	Indiana Univ-Purdue Univ Fort Wayne	IN	15,521	C	Marist College	NY	35,500	C	Niagara Univ	NY	41,010	C
Fort Hays State Univ	KS	11,354	C	Indiana Univ-Purdue Univ Indianapolis	IN	17,611	C	Marlboro College	VT	35,980	VC	Nicholls State Univ	LA	7,095	C
Fort Lewis College	CO	15,513	C	Indiana Wesleyan Univ	IN	31,815	VC	Marquette Univ	WI	46,930	VC+	Nichols College	MA	37,240	LC
Fort Valley State Univ	GA	11,200	VC	Inter-American Univ of PR/San Germán	PR	6,720		Mars Hill Univ	NC	22,950	LC	Norfolk State Univ	VA	10,531	LC
Framingham State Univ	MA	18,854	C	Iona College	NY	44,028	C	Marshall Univ	WV	14,820	C	N Car Agricultural and Technical State Univ	NC	13,365	LC
Francis Marion Univ	SC	16,464	LC	Iowa State Univ	IA	16,403	C	Mary Baldwin College	VA	38,245	C	N Car Central Univ	NC	9,000	C
Franciscan Univ of Steubenville	OH	27,320	VC	Iowa Wesleyan College	IA	30,850	LC	Marygrove College	MI	28,926	C	N Car State Univ	NC	16,202	HC
Franklin and Marshall College	PA	60,799	MC	Ithaca College	NY	53,864	HC	Marymount Manhattan College	NY	40,118	VC	N Car Wesleyan College	NC	29,440	C
Franklin College	IN	36,585	C	Jackson State Univ	MS	13,512	LC	Marymount Univ	VA	39,480	C	North Central College	IL	38,343	VC
Franklin Pierce Univ	NH	41,598	C	Jacksonville State Univ	AL	12,480	LC	Maryville College	TN	33,150	C+	N Dak State Univ	ND		C
Freed-Hardeman Univ	TN	19,697	LC	Jacksonville Univ	FL	37,780	C	Maryville Univ of St. Louis	MO	35,856	VC	North Park Univ	IL	30,130	C
Fresno Pacific Univ	CA	32,136	C	James Madison Univ	VA	18,049	VC	Marywood Univ	PA	45,595	C	Northeastern Illinois Univ	IL	10,318	LC
Friends Univ	KS	29,100	C	Jarvis Christian College	TX	19,552	NC	Mass College of Liberal Arts	MA	18,613	C	Northeastern State Univ	OK	8,615	VC
Frostburg State Univ	MD	15,264	LC	John Brown Univ	AR	32,056	VC+	Mayville State Univ	ND	11,401	NC	Northeastern Univ	MA	55,296	MC
Furman Univ	SC	54,006	HC	John Carroll Univ	OH	46,300	C+	McDaniel College	MD	47,450	VC	Northern Arizona Univ	AZ	19,010	C
Gallaudet Univ	DC	25,380	SP	John Jay College of Criminal Justice/The CUNY	NY	6,359	LC	McKendree Univ	IL	29,920	C+	Northern Illinois Univ	IL	19,768	C
Gannon Univ	PA	39,608	C	Johns Hopkins Univ	MD	47,492	MC	McMurry Univ	TX	25,962	LC	Northern Kentucky Univ	KY	21,134	C
Gardner-Webb Univ	NC	34,375	C+	Johnson C. Smith Univ	NC	25,336	LC	McNeese State Univ	LA	2,649	C	Northern Mich Univ	MI	18,278	C
Geneva College	PA	27,280	C	Johnson State College	VT	16,721	C	McPherson College	KS	28,138	C	Northern State Univ - Aberdeen	SD	14,505	C
George Mason Univ	VA	15,724	VC	Judson College	AL	26,794	C	Medaille College	NY	35,112	C	Northland College	WI	26,680	C
George Washington Univ	DC	57,108	MC	Judson Univ	IL	25,130	C	Megar Evers College/The CUNY	NY	4,920	NC	Northwest Missouri State Univ	MO	17,347	C
Georgetown College	KY	41,440	C+	Juniata College	PA	49,340	VC	Mercy College	NY	30,456	C	Northwest Nazarene Univ	ID	34,000	C
Georgetown Univ	DC	52,910	MC	Kalamazoo College	MI	49,740	HC	Mercyhurst Univ	PA	40,700	C	Northwest Univ	WA	18,854	C
Georgia College and State Univ	GA	18,900	C	Kansas State Univ	KS	15,497	VC	Meredith College	NC	31,420	C	Northwestern College	MN	24,000	C
Georgia Regents Univ	GA		C	Kansas Wesleyan Univ	KS	32,000	C	Merrimack College	MA	44,215	C	Northwestern Okla State Univ	OK	7,275	NC
Georgia Southern Univ	GA	16,942	C	Kean Univ	NJ	23,444	C	Messiah College	PA	40,690	C+	Northwestern State Univ of Louisiana	LA	14,368	C
Georgia Southwestern State Univ	GA	13,246	C	Keene State College	NH	23,232	LC	Methodist Univ	NC	37,185	C	Northwestern Univ	IL	61,640	MC
Georgia State Univ	GA	15,582	VC	Kennesaw State Univ	GA		C	Metropolitan State Univ	MN	5,923		Norwich Univ	VT	28,212	C
Georgian Court Univ	NJ	41,594	LC	Kent State Univ	OH	19,920	C	Metropolitan State Univ of Denver	CO	4,835	LC	Notre Dame College	OH	34,942	VC
Gettysburg College	PA	58,820	HC	Kentucky State Univ	KY	11,000	LC	Miami Univ	OH	24,191	VC	Notre Dame de Namur Univ	CA	44,236	LC
Glenville State College	WV	11,348	LC	Kentucky Wesleyan College	KY	27,440	C	Mich State Univ	MI	22,450	VC	Notre Dame of Maryland Univ	MD	27,700	VC
Goddard College	VT	16,418	VC	Kenyon College	OH	58,890	MC	Mich Tech Univ	MI	23,556	HC	Nyack College	NY	33,250	C
Gonzaga Univ	WA	46,441	HC	Keuka College	NY	30,300	C	MidAmerica Nazarene Univ	KS	28,000	C	Oakland City Univ	IN	24,500	NC
Gordon College	MA	44,320	VC	King Univ	TN	33,140	C	Middle Tenn State Univ	TN	8,650	C	Oakland Univ	MI	19,391	C
Goshen College	IN	35,900	C	King's College	PA	43,502	C	Middlebury College	VT	59,160	MC	Oakwood Univ	AL	25,529	NC
Goucher College	MD	52,040	VC+	Kutztown Univ of Pennsylvania	PA	16,909	LC	Midland Univ	NE	34,000	C	Oberlin College	OH	61,788	MC
Grace College and Seminary	IN	28,800	VC					Midway College	KY	20,150	LC	Occidental College	CA	60,972	MC
Graceland Univ	IA	28,020	C					Midwestern State Univ	TX	9,722	C	Oglethorpe Univ	GA	44,200	C+
Grambling State Univ	LA	13,384	LC					Miles College	AL	11,164	NC	Ohio Dominican Univ	OH	38,380	C
Grand Canyon Univ	AZ	24,540	VC					Millersville Univ of Pennsylvania	PA	21,648	C	Ohio Northern Univ	OH	42,075	VC
Grand Valley State Univ	MI	17,998	C+					Milligan College	TN	27,510	C	Ohio State Univ at Lima	OH	7,140	C
Grand View Univ	IA	31,050	C					Millikin Univ	IL	38,940	C	Ohio State Univ at Mansfield	OH	13,160	C
Green Mountain College	VT	45,228	LC					Mills College	CA	54,119	VC				
Greensboro College	NC	28,740	LC												
Greenville College	IL	27,012	C												

ST = STATE   **$IS** = IN-STATE COSTS   **SR** = SELECTOR RATING

School	ST	$IS	SR
Ohio State Univ at Marion	OH	16,990	MC
Ohio State Univ at Newark	OH	17,510	C
Ohio Univ	OH	21,080	C
Ohio Valley Univ	WV	17,752	C
Ohio Wesleyan Univ	OH	49,460	C+
Okla Baptist Univ	OK	28,202	C
Okla Christian Univ	OK	25,870	VC
Okla City Univ	OK	40,476	VC
Okla Panhandle State Univ	OK	8,996	C
Okla State Univ	OK	14,310	VC
Okla Wesleyan Univ	OK	21,300	C
Old Dominion Univ	VA	19,483	LC
Olivet College	MI	19,984	LC
Olivet Nazarene Univ	IL	29,990	C
Oral Roberts Univ	OK	31,734	C
Oregon State Univ	OR	20,273	VC
Oswego / SUNY	NY	20,009	VC
Ottawa Univ	KS	15,000	C
Otterbein College	OH	32,214	C
Ouachita Baptist Univ	AR	8,090	C
Our Lady of Holy Cross College	LA		
Our Lady of the Lake Univ	TX	22,430	LC
Pace Univ	NY	53,367	C
Pacific Lutheran Univ	WA	46,760	C+
Pacific Union College	CA	28,150	VC
Paine College	GA	19,826	LC
Palm Beach Atlantic Univ	FL	34,874	C+
Park Univ	MO	17,525	C
Paul Quinn College	TX	25,350	LC
Penn State Erie/The Behrend College	PA	16,256	C
Penn State Univ/Altoona	PA	11,464	C
Pepperdine Univ	CA	55,372	HC+
Peru State College	NE	8,600	NC
Philander Smith College	AR	19,760	LC
Piedmont College	GA	30,136	C
Pine Manor College	MA	32,659	LC
Pittsburg State Univ	KS	12,032	C
Pitzer College	CA	54,988	MC
Plymouth State Univ	NH	23,148	LC
Point Park Univ	PA	36,390	C
Pomona College	CA	57,680	MC
Pontifical Catholic Univ of PR	PR	7,310	
Portland State Univ	OR	18,672	C
Post Univ	CT	35,750	C
Prairie View A&M Univ	TX	15,205	LC
Presbyterian College	SC	42,678	C+
Prescott College	AZ	33,284	C
Princeton Univ	NJ	53,795	MC
Principia College	IL	35,140	C+
Providence College	RI	57,383	VC
Purdue Univ/Calumet	IN	14,336	C
Purdue Univ/West Lafayette	IN	20,024	HC
Queens College/The CUNY	NY	17,107	VC
Quincy Univ	IL	34,980	LC
Quinnipiac Univ	CT	55,160	VC
Radford Univ	VA	17,766	C
Randolph College	VA	45,660	VC
Randolph-Macon College	VA	49,869	C+
Regis College	MA	47,565	C
Regis Univ	CO	41,318	C
Rhode Island College	RI	17,694	LC
Rhodes College	TN	51,900	HC+
Rice Univ	TX	43,288	MC
Rider Univ	NJ	45,720	C
Ripon College	WI	36,959	C+
Rivier Univ	NH	35,000	VC
Robert Morris Univ	PA	37,864	C
Roberts Wesleyan College	NY	38,306	C+
Rochester College	MI	18,320	C
Rockford College	IL	31,000	C
Rockhurst Univ	MO	20,625	C
Roger Williams Univ	RI	46,296	VC
Rollins College	FL	52,370	HC
Roosevelt Univ	IL	22,605	VC
Rosemont College	PA	42,350	C
Rowan Univ	NJ	24,022	VC+
Russell Sage College	NY	39,370	C
Rust College	MS	10,600	C
Rutgers, The State Univ of New Jersey/Camden Campus	NJ	25,121	C
Rutgers, The State Univ of New Jersey/New Brunswick	NJ	25,562	C
Rutgers, The State Univ of New Jersey/Newark Campus	NJ	258,806	C
Sacred Heart Univ	CT	49,264	VC
Saginaw Valley State Univ	MI	17,369	C
St. Anselm College	NH	49,376	VC
St. Augustine's Univ	NC	14,000	C
St. Francis Univ	PA	30,029	LC
St. John's Univ	MN	47,984	C
St. Joseph's College	IN	36,500	C
St. Joseph's College of Maine	ME	31,580	C
St. Joseph's Univ	PA	55,006	VC
St. Leo Univ	FL	30,340	C
St. Louis Univ	MO	48,346	HC
St. Martin's Univ	WA	41,678	C
St. Mary-of-the-Woods College	IN	37,722	LC
St. Mary's College of Calif	CA	53,550	VC
St. Mary's Univ	TX	33,854	C
St. Michael's College	VT	49,975	VC
St. Paul's College	VA	16,030	NC
St. Peter's Univ	NJ	44,240	C
St. Vincent College	PA	40,244	C
St. Xavier Univ	IL	32,840	C
Salem College	NC	29,326	VC
Salem State Univ	MA	13,161	LC
Salisbury Univ	MD	19,180	VC
Salve Regina Univ	RI	48,550	VC
Sam Houston State Univ	TX	17,082	C
Samford Univ	AL	37,060	C+
San Diego Christian College	CA	31,012	C
San Diego State Univ	CA	21,611	C
San Francisco State Univ	CA	18,514	C
San Jose State Univ	CA	19,133	LC
Sarah Lawrence College	NY	48,000	HC
Savannah State Univ	GA	13,156	C
Schreiner Univ	TX	32,734	LC
Scripps College	CA	61,940	MC
Seattle Pacific Univ	WA	41,559	VC+
Seattle Univ	WA	49,035	VC+
Seton Hall Univ	NJ	45,902	C
Seton Hill Univ	PA	35,172	C
Sewanee: The Univ of the South	TN	47,700	HC+
Shaw Univ	NC	15,488	C
Shawnee State Univ	OH	16,916	C
Shenandoah Univ	VA	39,916	C
Shepherd Univ	WV	15,875	C
Shippensburg Univ of Pennsylvania	PA	20,934	C
Shorter Univ	GA	30,650	LC
Siena College	NY	43,863	VC
Siena Heights Univ	MI	32,040	C
Silver Lake College	WI	22,600	LC
Simmons College	MA	49,966	VC
Simpson College	IA	36,086	C+
Simpson Univ	CA	28,900	C
Skidmore College	NY	59,942	HC
Slippery Rock Univ of Pennsylvania	PA	10,360	C
Smith College	MA	59,674	MC
Sonoma State Univ	CA	20,541	C
S Car State Univ	SC	6,700	LC
S Dak State Univ	SD	14,296	C
Southeast Missouri State Univ	MO	15,370	LC
Southeastern Louisiana Univ	LA	13,325	C
Southeastern Okla State Univ	OK	7,966	LC
Southeastern Univ	FL	27,201	C
Southern Adventist Univ	TN	26,190	C
Southern Arkansas Univ	AR	14,316	C
Southern Conn State Univ	CT	18,033	LC
Southern Illinois Univ Carbondale	IL	21,942	C
Southern Illinois Univ Edwardsville	IL	17,532	C
Southern Methodist Univ	TX	60,585	MC
Southern Nazarene Univ	OK	24,354	C
Southern New Hampshire Univ	NH	38,100	C
Southern Oregon Univ	OR	17,874	C
Southern Univ and A&M College	LA	9,761	LC
Southern Univ at New Orleans	LA	2,963	NC
Southern Vermont College	VT	30,740	LC
Southern Wesleyan Univ	SC	25,600	C
Southwest Baptist Univ	MO	24,710	C
Southwestern Adventist Univ	TX	23,026	LC
Southwestern College	KS	29,270	C
Southwestern Okla State Univ	OK	9,160	C
Southwestern Univ	TX	45,660	VC
Spelman College	GA	24,650	C
Spring Arbor Univ	MI	26,740	C
Spring Hill College	AL	44,164	VC
Springfield College	MA	25,000	C
St. Ambrose Univ	IA	30,845	C
St. Bonaventure Univ	NY	41,575	C
St. Catherine Univ	MN	37,782	C+
St. Cloud State Univ	MN	10,600	C
St. Francis College	NY	34,200	C
St. John Fisher College	NY	40,708	C+
St. John's Univ	NY	55,070	C+
St. Joseph's College, New York/Brooklyn Campus	NY	22,630	C
St. Joseph's College, New York/Suffolk Campus	NY	22,630	C
St. Lawrence Univ	NY	59,972	VC
St. Mary's College of Maryland	MD	25,754	C
St. Norbert College	WI	41,478	VC
St. Olaf College	MN	51,200	HC+
St. Thomas Aquinas College	NY	40,230	C
St. Thomas Univ	FL	32,310	LC
Stanford Univ	CA	58,388	MC
Stephen F. Austin State Univ	TX	14,668	C
Stephens College	MO	38,042	VC
Sterling College	KS	27,216	C
Stetson Univ	FL	51,516	VC
Stillman College	AL	19,470	C
Stonehill College	MA	46,780	HC
Stony Brook Univ / SUNY	NY	20,078	HC+
Suffolk Univ	MA	47,298	C
Sul Ross State Univ	TX	13,410	LC
SUNY College at Geneseo	NY	18,670	HC
SUNY Cortland/The SUNY	NY	19,759	C+
SUNY Fredonia/The SUNY at Fredonia	NY	19,840	VC
SUNY New Paltz	NY	14,348	C
SUNY Oneonta / SUNY	NY	16,919	C+
SUNY Plattsburgh / SUNY	NY	18,083	C
Susquehanna Univ	PA	51,150	C
Syracuse Univ	NY	56,346	VC
Tabor College	KS	29,010	C
Talladega College	AL	17,996	C
Tarleton State Univ	TX	13,489	LC
Taylor Univ	IN	37,821	VC+
Temple Univ	PA	24,392	VC
Tenn State Univ	TN	9,048	C
Tenn Tech Univ	TN	11,310	C
Tenn Wesleyan College	TN	21,250	C
Texas A&M Univ	TX	19,207	VC
Texas A&M Univ at Commerce	TX	10,496	C
Texas A&M Univ at Corpus Christi	TX	11,544	LC
Texas A&M Univ at Kingsville	TX	7,500	LC
Texas Christian Univ	TX	49,980	HC
Texas Lutheran Univ	TX	36,040	C
Texas Southern Univ	TX	18,212	LC
Texas State Univ	TX	17,128	C
Texas Tech Univ	TX	14,243	C
Texas Wesleyan Univ	TX	31,382	C
Texas Woman's Univ	TX	13,633	LC
The Catholic Univ of America	DC	52,852	VC
The College of New Rochelle	NY	33,600	VC
The College of St. Rose	NY	26,750	C
The Masters College	CA	38,160	C+
Ohio State Univ-Columbus Campus	OH	19,887	HC+
The Pennsylvania State Univ - Univ Park	PA	28,022	VC+
The SUNY at Potsdam	NY	18,473	C
The SUNY/College at Brockport	NY	19,002	C
The Univ of Memphis	TN	15,094	C
The Univ of N Car at Greensboro	NC	12,848	C
The Univ of N Car at Pembroke	NC	13,388	LC
The Univ of Okla	OK	18,621	VC
The Univ of Tenn at Chattanooga	TN	16,883	C
The Univ of Utah	UT	16,463	VC
The Univ of Virginia's College at Wise	VA	11,076	C
Thiel College	PA	38,728	LC
Thomas College	ME	33,560	LC
Thomas Edison State College	NJ	5,700	SP
Thomas More College	KY	34,760	C
Thomas Univ	GA	11,520	NC
Tiffin Univ	OH	30,273	LC
Toccoa Falls College	GA	23,210	LC
Tougaloo College	MS	15,275	NC
Touro College	NY	27,959	VC
Towson Univ	MD	16,000	VC
Transylvania Univ	KY	42,660	VC+
Trevecca Nazarene Univ	TN	31,186	C
Trinity Christian College	IL	28,869	C
Trinity College	CT		HC+
Trinity International Univ	IL	31,070	VC
Trinity Univ	TX	48,510	HC+
Trinity Washington Univ	DC	30,250	VC
Troy Univ	AL	10,650	C
Truman State Univ	MO	15,541	NC
Tufts Univ	MA	58,780	MC
Tulane Univ	LA	60,861	MC
Tusculum College	TN	24,295	C
Tuskegee Univ	AL	26,750	C
Union College	KY	29,955	C
Union College	NE	23,270	C
Union College	NY	60,240	MC
Union Univ	TN	28,260	VC
United States Air Force Academy	CO		MC
United States Naval Academy	MD		MC
Unity College	ME	34,054	C
Universidad del Turabo	PR	4,110	
Univ at Albany / SUNY	NY	18,674	VC
Univ at Buffalo / The SUNY	NY	20,283	VC
Univ of Akron	OH	20,436	C
Univ of Alabama at Birmingham	AL	18,484	C+
Univ of Alabama at Tuscaloosa	AL	17,164	C+
Univ of Alabama in Huntsville	AL	17,591	VC+
Univ of Alaska Anchorage	AK	16,673	NC
Univ of Alaska Fairbanks	AK	15,130	C
Univ of Arizona	AZ	20,657	C
Univ of Arkansas at Fayetteville	AR	18,352	C+
Univ of Arkansas at Little Rock	AR	17,609	C
Univ of Arkansas at Monticello	AR	12,076	NC
Univ of Arkansas at Pine Bluff	AR	13,378	C
Univ of Calif at Irvine	CA	25,961	VC
Univ of Calif at Los Angeles	CA	25,686	MC
Univ of Calif at Riverside	CA	27,204	C+
Univ of Calif at Santa Barbara	CA	27,551	VC
Univ of Central Arkansas	AR	13,667	VC
Univ of Central Florida	FL	15,668	VC+
Univ of Central Missouri	MO	14,605	C
Univ of Central Okla	OK	12,293	C
Univ of Chicago	IL	55,416	MC
Univ of Cincinnati	OH	21,506	VC
Univ of Colo at Colo Springs	CO	15,000	VC
Univ of Colo Boulder	CO	22,605	VC+
Univ of Colo Denver	CO	17,904	C
Univ of Conn	CT	24,706	VC
Univ of Dallas	TX	45,500	VC+
Univ of Dayton	OH	49,070	VC
Univ of Delaware	DE	23,612	VC
Univ of Denver	CO	51,787	VC+
Univ of Detroit Mercy	MI	30,450	VC
Univ of Dubuque	IA	30,200	C
Univ of Findlay	OH	31,916	C
Univ of Florida	FL	15,943	HC
Univ of Georgia	GA	20,082	VC
Univ of Great Falls	MT	27,970	C
Univ of Hartford	CT	42,674	C
Univ of Hawaii at Hilo	HI	23,066	C
Univ of Hawaii at Manoa	HI	19,379	C
Univ of Houston	TX	19,796	VC
Univ of Houston-Downtown	TX	15,170	LC
Univ of Idaho	ID	14,558	C
Univ of Illinois at Chicago	IL	24,505	VC
Univ of Illinois at Urbana-Champaign	IL	26,450	HC
Univ of Indianapolis	IN	31,740	LC
Univ of Iowa	IA	17,693	VC
Univ of Jamestown	ND	24,738	C
Univ of Kansas	KS	17,603	C+
Univ of Kentucky	KY	19,868	C
Univ of La Verne	CA	47,010	C
Univ of Louisiana at Lafayette	LA	6,130	C
Univ of Louisiana at Monroe	LA	12,998	C
Univ of Louisville	KY	17,946	C
Univ of Maine	ME	19,902	C+
Univ of Maine at Augusta	ME	6,855	C
Univ of Maine at Farmington	ME	18,187	LC
Univ of Maine at Fort Kent	ME	15,195	LC
Univ of Maine at Machias	ME	10,523	C
Univ of Maine at Presque Isle	ME	15,011	LC
Univ of Mary	ND	16,714	C
Univ of Mary Hardin-Baylor	TX	31,950	C+
Univ of Mary Washington	VA	19,484	VC
Univ of Maryland - College Park	MD	20,060	HC
Univ of Maryland/Baltimore County	MD	18,000	VC
Univ of Maryland/Eastern Shore	MD	14,000	VC
Univ of Maryland/Univ College	MD	6,168	SP
Univ of Mass Amherst	MA	24,215	VC+
Univ of Mass Boston	MA	23,066	VC
Univ of Mass Dartmouth	MA	22,223	C
Univ of Mass Lowell	MA	19,316	C
Univ of Miami	FL	57,034	MC
Univ of Mich/Ann Arbor	MI	22,102	MC
Univ of Mich/Dearborn	MI	9,885	VC
Univ of Mich-Flint	MI	17,547	C+
Univ of Minn/Duluth	MN	19,806	C
Univ of Minn/Morris	MN	17,150	VC
Univ of Minn/Twin Cities	MN		HC
Univ of Miss	MS	16,704	C+
Univ of Missouri/Columbia	MO	18,201	MC
Univ of Missouri-Kansas City	MO	19,603	C
Univ of Missouri-St. Louis	MO		VC
Univ of Mobile	AL	28,935	VC
Univ of Montana	MT	14,105	C
Univ of Montana-Western	MT	9,753	LC
Univ of Montevallo	AL	17,060	C
Univ of Mount Olive	NC	18,426	C
Univ of Mount Union	OH	35,130	C
Univ of Nebr - Lincoln	NE	18,031	VC
Univ of Nebr at Kearney	NE	14,855	LC
Univ of Nebr at Omaha	NE	12,700	C
Univ of Nevada, Las Vegas	NV	17,303	C
Univ of Nevada/Reno	NV	17,507	C
Univ of New England	ME	46,750	C
Univ of New Hampshire	NH	26,912	C
Univ of New Haven	CT	48,940	C
Univ of New Mexico	NM	15,300	C
Univ of New Orleans	LA	9,224	C
Univ of North Alabama	AL	9,960	C
Univ of N Car at Chapel Hill	NC	18,928	MC
Univ of N Car at Charlotte	NC	15,547	C
Univ of N Car at Wilmington	NC	13,572	VC
Univ of N Dak	ND	14,551	C
Univ of North Florida	FL	15,870	VC
Univ of North Georgia	GA	8,500	C
Univ of North Texas	TX	15,628	C
Univ of Northern Colo	CO	18,446	C
Univ of Northern Iowa	IA	15,795	C
Univ of Notre Dame	IN	57,117	MC
Univ of Oregon	OR	21,360	C+
Univ of Pennsylvania	PA	61,132	MC
Univ of Pikeville	KY	25,500	NC

ST = STATE   **$IS** = IN-STATE COSTS   **SR** = SELECTOR RATING

School	ST	$IS	SR
Univ of Pittsburgh at Bradford	PA	21,802	C
Univ of Pittsburgh at Johnstown	PA	20,862	LC
Univ of Portland	OR	49,964	VC
Univ of PR Recinto de Rio Piedras	PR	5,750	
Univ of PR/Cayey	PR	1,504	
Univ of PR/Humacao	PR	1,877	
Univ of PR/Mayaguez	PR	1,250	
Univ of Puget Sound	WA	54,608	HC
Univ of Redlands	CA	40,500	VC
Univ of Rio Grande	OH	8,750	LC
Univ of Rochester	NY	60,668	MC
Univ of St. Francis	IN	29,810	C
Univ of St. Joseph	CT	45,630	C
Univ of St. Mary	KS	28,400	C+
Univ of San Diego	CA	54,818	HC+
Univ of San Francisco	CA	54,770	VC
Univ of Science and Arts of Okla	OK	10,560	LC
Univ of Scranton	PA	51,940	VC
Univ of Sioux Falls	SD	22,990	C
Univ of South Alabama	AL	13,510	C
Univ of S Car Aiken	SC	16,712	C
Univ of S Car at Columbia	SC	19,725	VC+
Univ of S Car Upstate	SC	18,200	LC
Univ of S Dak	SD	15,111	C
Univ of South Florida/St. Petersburg	FL	12,769	C
Univ of Southern Calif	CA	56,903	MC
Univ of Southern Indiana	IN	14,885	C
Univ of Southern Maine	ME	16,576	C
Univ of Southern Miss	MS	13,170	C
Univ of St. Francis	IL	37,560	C
Univ of St. Thomas - Houston	TX	37,690	C
Univ of Tampa	FL	35,160	VC
Univ of Tenn at Knoxville	TN	20,364	VC+
Univ of Tenn at Martin	TN	13,734	C
Univ of Texas - Pan American	TX	11,125	LC
Univ of Texas at Arlington	TX	10,908	LC
Univ of Texas at Austin	TX	44,074	HC
Univ of Texas at El Paso	TX	8,764	LC
Univ of Texas at San Antonio	TX	18,372	C
Univ of the Cumberlands	KY	27,500	C
Univ of the District of Columbia	DC	7,244	LC
Univ of the Incarnate Word	TX	37,316	LC
Univ of the Ozarks	AR	31,440	C
Univ of the Pacific	CA	52,146	VC
Univ of the Southwest	NM	15,000	C
Univ of Toledo	OH	18,464	C
Univ of Tulsa	OK	46,331	MC
Univ of Vermont	VT	27,006	VC+
Univ of Virginia	VA	23,050	MC
Univ of Washington	WA	14,722	VC
Univ of West Alabama	AL	14,274	C
Univ of West Florida	FL	14,656	C
Univ of West Georgia	GA	15,488	LC
Univ of Wisc Whitewater	WI	13,314	C
Univ of Wisc/Eau Claire	WI	15,730	VC
Univ of Wisc/Green Bay	WI	19,074	C
Univ of Wisc/La Crosse	WI	9,304	C
Univ of Wisc/Madison	WI	18,757	HC+
Univ of Wisc/Oshkosh	WI	10,426	LC
Univ of Wisc/Parkside	WI	10,181	LC
Univ of Wisc/Platteville	WI	14,564	C
Univ of Wisc/River Falls	WI	9,722	LC
Univ of Wisc/Stevens Point	WI	14,043	C
Univ of Wisc/Superior	WI	14,314	C
Univ of Wisc-Milwaukee	WI	18,436	C
Univ of Wyoming	WY	14,401	C+
Upper Iowa Univ	IA	30,426	NC
Urbana Univ	OH	30,820	C
Ursinus College	PA	57,580	VC
Ursuline College	OH	33,198	LC
Utah State Univ	UT	12,044	C
Utica College	NY	45,670	C
Valley City State Univ	ND	12,286	LC
Valparaiso Univ	IN	44,940	VC+
Vanderbilt Univ	TN	58,220	MC
Vanguard Univ of Southern Calif	CA	35,833	VC
Vassar College	NY	61,140	MC
Villanova Univ	PA	58,394	MC
Virginia Commonwealth Univ	VA	21,716	C
Virginia Military Inst	VA	16,156	C
Virginia Polytechnic Inst and State Univ	VA	14,629	HC
Virginia Union Univ	VA	18,432	C
Virginia Wesleyan College	VA	28,433	LC
Viterbo Univ	WI	30,070	C
Voorhees College	SC	18,126	C
Wabash College	IN	46,850	C+
Wagner College	NY	48,600	C+
Wake Forest Univ	NC	58,838	MC
Walla Walla Univ	WA	26,256	NC
Walsh Univ	OH	35,100	C
Warner Pacific College	OR	25,550	C
Warner Univ	FL	18,000	C
Warren Wilson College	NC	40,132	VC
Wartburg College	IA	41,055	VC
Washburn Univ	KS	12,579	C

School	ST	$IS	SR
Washington Adventist Univ	MD	25,859	LC
Washington and Jefferson College	PA	51,948	VC
Washington and Lee Univ	VA	52,812	MC
Washington College	MD	52,602	VC
Washington State Univ	WA	20,461	C
Washington Univ in St. Louis	MO	69,844	MC
Wayland Baptist Univ	TX	18,912	LC
Wayne State College	NE	11,764	NC
Wayne State Univ	MI	22,063	C
Waynesburg Univ	PA	30,150	C
Webster Univ	MO	35,100	C+
Wellesley College	MA	59,038	MC
Wells College	NY	49,400	VC
Wesley College	DE	31,115	LC
Wesleyan College	GA	24,000	C
Wesleyan Univ	CT	61,198	MC
West Chester Univ of Pennsylvania	PA	17,186	C
West Liberty Univ	WV	9,142	LC
West Texas A&M Univ	TX	13,478	C
West Virginia State Univ	WV	8,378	NC
West Virginia Univ	WV	16,542	C+
West Virginia Wesleyan College	WV	26,880	C
Western Carolina Univ	NC	13,965	C
Western Conn State Univ	CT	18,327	LC
Western Illinois Univ	IL	20,732	C
Western Kentucky Univ	KY	11,000	LC
Western Mich Univ	MI	19,628	C
Western New England Univ	MA	46,154	C+
Western New Mexico Univ	NM	8,500	LC
Western Oregon Univ	OR	15,021	C
Western State Colo Univ	CO	16,924	C
Western Washington Univ	WA	18,519	VC
Westfield State Univ	MA	18,297	C
Westminster College	MO	31,720	VC
Westminster College	PA	31,290	C+
Westminster College	UT	37,708	C
Westmont College	CA	41,500	HC
Wheaton College	IL	40,720	MC
Wheaton College	MA	54,934	HC+
Wheeling Jesuit Univ	WV	33,500	C
Whitman College	WA	55,988	MC
Whittier College	CA	43,416	C
Whitworth Univ	WA	47,734	VC
Wichita State Univ	KS	14,607	C+
Widener Univ	PA	52,418	C
Wiley College	TX		LC
Wilkes Univ	PA	44,070	C
Willamette Univ	OR	56,450	VC+
William Carey Univ	MS	13,500	LC
William Jewell College	MO	31,000	VC+
William Paterson Univ of New Jersey	NJ	21,694	C
William Peace Univ	NC	32,900	LC
William Penn Univ	IA	26,000	C
William Woods Univ	MO	24,260	C
Williams Baptist College	AR	20,070	C
Williams College	MA	61,070	MC
Wilmington College	OH	29,784	C
Wilson College	PA	35,080	C
Wingate Univ	NC	34,990	C
Winona State Univ	MN	16,640	C
Winston-Salem State Univ	NC	9,418	LC
Winthrop Univ	SC	21,120	C
Wisc Lutheran College	WI	23,510	VC
Wittenberg Univ	OH	47,962	C+
Wofford College	SC	45,795	VC
Worcester State Univ	MA	19,812	C
Wright State Univ	OH	16,983	C
Xavier Univ	OH	44,980	VC
Xavier Univ of Louisiana	LA	25,300	C
Yale Univ	CT	55,300	MC
Yeshiva Univ	NY	47,250	VC+
York College	NE	19,475	C
York College / The CUNY	NY	5,496	VC
York College of Pennsylvania	PA	26,590	C
Youngstown State Univ	OH	16,732	C

ENGLISH AND PROFESSIONAL COMMUNICATION

School	ST	$IS	SR
Black Hills State Univ	SD	13,947	C
Bloomfield College	NJ	37,850	LC
Farmingdale State College	NY	19,673	C
Southern Polytechnic State Univ	GA	13,958	C
Taylor Univ	IN	37,821	VC+
Wheeling Jesuit Univ	WV	33,500	C

ENGLISH AS A SECOND/FOREIGN LANGUAGE

School	ST	$IS	SR
Arizona State Univ, at the Polytechnic Campus	AZ	20,531	C+
Arizona State Univ, at the Tempe Campus	AZ	20,137	C+
Arizona State Univ, at the West Campus	AZ	19,251	C
Bloomfield College	NJ	37,850	LC
Doane College	NE	35,230	C
Dordt College	IA	34,160	C+
Holy Names Univ	CA	40,310	NC
Houghton College	NY	36,808	C+

School	ST	$IS	SR
Huntington Univ	IN	32,220	C+
Indiana Univ-Purdue Univ Indianapolis	IN	17,611	C
La Sierra Univ	CA	35,694	VC
Lenoir-Rhyne College	NC	35,984	C
Liberty Univ	VA	19,101	C
Maryville College	TN	33,150	C
Minn State Univ, Mankato	MN	15,616	C
Northwestern College	MN	24,000	C
Oswego / SUNY	NY	20,009	VC
Salem International Univ	WV	21,090	LC
Salisbury Univ	MD	19,180	VC
Southern New Hampshire Univ	NH	38,100	C
Taylor Univ	IN	37,821	VC+
Union Univ	TN	28,260	VC
Univ of Arizona	AZ	20,657	C
Univ of Central Okla	OK	12,293	C
Univ of Findlay	OH	31,916	C
Univ of Hawaii at Manoa	HI	19,379	C
Univ of Nebr - Lincoln	NE	18,031	VC
Univ of Wisc/Green Bay	WI	19,074	C

ENGLISH EDUCATION

School	ST	$IS	SR
Adams State Univ	CO	13,358	LC
Alabama State Univ	AL	14,142	NC
Albion College	MI	46,010	C
Andrews Univ	MI	28,030	C+
Appalachian State Univ	NC	12,919	VC
Aquinas College	MI	33,060	C
Arizona State Univ, at the Polytechnic Campus	AZ	20,531	C+
Arizona State Univ, at the West Campus	AZ	19,251	C
Arkansas State Univ	AR	15,470	C
Asbury Univ	KY	32,038	VC
Ashford Univ	CA	10,480	C
Ashland Univ	OH	25,000	C
Auburn Univ	AL	22,378	VC+
Averett Univ	VA	37,750	C
Baker Univ	KS	33,350	C+
Baylor Univ	TX	50,329	HC
Bennett College for Women	NC	21,970	LC
Bethany College	KS	30,605	NC
Bethany College	WV	35,282	LC
Bethel College	IN	31,560	C
Bethel Univ	MN	34,940	VC
Bethune-Cookman Univ	FL	22,958	C
Black Hills State Univ	SD	13,947	C
Blackburn College	IL	21,350	C
Bloomfield College	NJ	37,850	LC
Blue Mountain College	MS	15,634	LC
Boise State Univ	ID	13,445	C
Boston Univ	MA	60,694	MC
Brigham Young Univ	UT	12,100	HC
Brigham Young Univ/Hawaii	HI	10,686	VC
Bryant Univ	RI	49,179	VC
Calvin College	MI	39,120	VC
Cameron Univ	OK	10,004	LC
Campbell Univ	NC	37,570	VC
Canisius College	NY	44,900	C
Carthage College	WI	33,000	C
Cedarville Univ	OH	32,860	VC
Central Univ of Bayamon	PR	3,350	
Central Washington Univ	WA	11,730	C
CUNY/Brooklyn College	NY	5,884	C+
CUNY/City College	NY	20,319	HC+
Claflin Univ	SC	22,368	LC
Coker College	SC	32,256	LC
Colby-Sawyer College	NH	50,790	C
College of New Jersey	NJ	25,376	HC
College of the Ozarks	MO		VC
Colo State Univ-Fort Collins	CO	20,385	VC
Concordia Univ St. Paul	MN	28,250	C
Cornerstone Univ and Grand Rapids Theological Seminary	MI	33,338	C
Covenant College	GA	38,990	VC+
Daemen College	NY	34,770	C
Dakota State Univ	SD	13,811	C
Delta State Univ	MS	12,292	LC
Dordt College	IA	34,160	C+
Duquesne Univ	PA	43,720	VC
East Carolina Univ	NC	14,169	C
East Central Univ	OK	10,223	LC
East Texas Baptist Univ	TX	31,577	LC
Eastern Mich Univ	MI	18,604	C
Elizabethtown College	PA	49,740	VC
Emory and Henry College	VA	387,460	C
Faulkner Univ	AL	25,720	LC
Ferris State Univ	MI	20,047	C
Florida Atlantic Univ	FL	17,339	C
Florida State Univ	FL	16,715	VC
Fontbonne Univ	MO	31,384	C
Franklin College	IN	36,585	C
Fresno Pacific Univ	CA	32,136	C
Friends Univ	KS	29,100	C
Gannon Univ	PA	39,608	C
Georgetown College	KY	41,440	C+
Glenville State College	WV	11,348	NC
Goddard College	VT	16,418	VC
Goshen College	IN	35,900	VC
Grace College and Seminary	IN	28,800	VC

School	ST	$IS	SR
Grambling State Univ	LA	13,384	LC
Green Mountain College	VT	45,228	LC
Greensboro College	NC	28,740	LC
Greenville College	IL	27,012	C
Hardin-Simmons Univ	TX	23,560	C+
Hofstra Univ	NY	51,810	VC+
Hood College	MD	45,730	C
Hope College	MI	38,650	VC
Houghton College	NY	36,808	C+
Humboldt State Univ	CA	18,400	C
Huntingdon College	AL	33,100	C
Huntington Univ	IN	32,220	C
Husson Univ	ME	24,194	LC
Indiana Univ Bloomington	IN	19,801	VC
Indiana Univ Northwest	IN	6,854	LC
Indiana Univ South Bend	IN	15,501	C
Indiana Univ Southeast	IN	16,035	C
Indiana Univ-Purdue Univ Fort Wayne	IN	15,521	C
Indiana Univ-Purdue Univ Indianapolis	IN	17,611	C
Indiana Wesleyan Univ	IN	31,815	VC
Ithaca College	NY	53,864	HC
Johnson State College	VT	16,721	C
Judson College	AL	26,794	C
Judson Univ	IL	25,130	C
Juniata College	PA	49,340	VC
Kennesaw State Univ	GA		C
Kentucky Christian Univ	KY	17,622	LC
Kutztown Univ of Pennsylvania	PA	16,909	LC
La Roche College	PA	35,824	LC
Le Moyne College	NY	43,470	C
Lenoir-Rhyne College	NC	35,984	C
Limestone College	SC	30,800	C
Lincoln Univ	MO	12,904	NC
Lipscomb Univ	TN	37,490	VC
LIU Brooklyn	NY	47,182	LC
LIU Post	NY	47,660	C
Louisiana College	LA	15,746	C
Lyndon State College	VT	14,233	C
Mansfield Univ	PA	19,468	LC
Marian Univ	WI	32,420	LC
Marshall Univ	WV	14,820	C
Marymount Univ	VA	39,480	C
Marywood Univ	PA	45,595	C
Mayville State Univ	ND	11,401	NC
McMurry Univ	TX	25,962	LC
Messiah College	PA	40,690	C+
MidAmerica Nazarene Univ	KS	28,000	C
Millersville Univ of Pennsylvania	PA	21,648	C
Millikin Univ	IL	38,940	C
Minn State Univ, Moorhead	MN	13,392	VC
Minot State Univ	ND	10,915	C
Miss Valley State Univ	MS	9,706	LC
Missouri Southern State Univ	MO	12,061	C
Monmouth Univ	NJ	44,108	C
Morningside College	IA	35,430	C
Morris College	SC	16,310	LC
Mount Aloysius College	PA	29,976	C
Mount Mary Univ	WI	33,590	LC
Mount Vernon Nazarene Univ	OH	29,590	C
Murray State Univ	KY	15,304	C
Nazareth College of Rochester	NY	43,028	C+
Nebr Wesleyan Univ	NE	29,774	C+
New York Univ	NY	61,470	MC
Niagara Univ	NY	41,010	C
N Car Agricultural and Technical State Univ	NC	13,365	LC
Northeastern Illinois Univ	IL	10,318	LC
Northern Kentucky Univ	KY	21,134	C
Northwest Missouri State Univ	MO	17,347	C
Northwest Nazarene Univ	ID	34,000	C
Northwestern College	MN	24,000	C
Northwestern Okla State Univ	OK	7,275	NC
Nova Southeastern Univ	FL	37,280	VC
Nyack College	NY	33,250	C
Oakwood Univ	AL	25,529	NC
Ohio Valley Univ	WV	17,752	C
Okla Christian Univ	OK	25,870	C
Okla Wesleyan Univ	OK	21,300	C
Old Dominion Univ	VA	19,483	LC
Olivet Nazarene Univ	IL	29,990	C
Oral Roberts Univ	OK	31,734	C
Oswego / SUNY	NY	20,009	VC
Palm Beach Atlantic Univ	FL	34,874	C+
Pfeiffer Univ	NC	33,700	LC
Piedmont College	GA	30,136	C
Pittsburg State Univ	KS	12,032	C
Providence College	RI	57,383	VC
Purdue Univ/West Lafayette	IN	20,024	HC
Rider Univ	NJ	45,720	C
Rivier Univ	NH	35,000	C
Roberts Wesleyan College	NY	38,306	C+
Rocky Mountain College	MT	32,242	C
Rust College	MS	10,600	C
Sacred Heart Univ	CT	49,264	VC
Saginaw Valley State Univ	MI	17,369	C
St. Augustine's Univ	NC	14,000	C
St. Mary's Univ of Minn	MN	38,280	C
Samford Univ	AL	37,060	C+
Schreiner Univ	TX	32,734	LC

School	ST	$IS	SR
Seton Hill Univ	PA	35,172	C
Shaw Univ	NC	15,488	C
Shepherd Univ	WV	15,875	C
Shippensburg Univ of Pennsylvania	PA	20,934	C
Shorter Univ	GA	30,650	LC
Simpson Univ	CA	28,900	C
Southeast Missouri State Univ	MO	15,370	C
Southeastern Louisiana Univ	LA	13,325	C
Southern Nazarene Univ	OK	24,354	C
Southern New Hampshire Univ	NH	38,100	C
Southern Oregon Univ	OR	17,874	C
Southern Univ and A&M College	LA	9,761	LC
Southern Univ at New Orleans	LA	2,963	NC
Southern Wesleyan Univ	SC	25,600	C
Southwestern Okla State Univ	OK	9,160	C
St. Edward's Univ	TX	47,784	C
St. John Fisher College	NY	40,708	C+
St. John's Univ	NY	55,070	C+
Suffolk Univ	MA	47,298	C
SUNY Fredonia/The SUNY at Fredonia	NY	19,840	VC
SUNY New Paltz	NY	14,348	C
SUNY Oneonta / SUNY	NY	16,919	C+
SUNY Plattsburgh / SUNY	NY	18,083	C
Syracuse Univ	NY	56,346	VC
Taylor Univ	IN	37,821	VC+
Texas Southern Univ	TX	18,212	LC
The Catholic Univ of America	DC	52,852	VC
The College of St. Rose	NY	26,750	C
The Lincoln Univ	PA	15,154	LC
The SUNY at Potsdam	NY	18,473	C
The Univ of N Car at Greensboro	NC	12,848	C
The Univ of Tenn at Chattanooga	TN	16,883	C
The Univ of Utah	UT	16,463	VC
Tiffin Univ	OH	30,273	LC
Tougaloo College	MS	15,255	NC
Trevecca Nazarene Univ	TN	31,186	C
Trine Univ	IN	39,400	HC+
Troy Univ	AL	10,650	C
Union College	NE	23,270	C
Universidad del Turabo	PR	4,110	
Univ of Arkansas at Pine Bluff	AR	13,378	C
Univ of Central Florida	FL	15,668	VC+
Univ of Central Missouri	MO	14,605	C
Univ of Central Okla	OK	12,293	C
Univ of Charleston	WV	32,300	C
Univ of Conn	CT	24,706	HC
Univ of Delaware	DE	23,612	VC
Univ of Evansville	IN	42,656	VC+
Univ of Georgia	GA	20,082	VC
Univ of Illinois at Chicago	IL	24,505	VC
Univ of Illinois at Urbana-Champaign	IL	26,450	HC
Univ of Indianapolis	IN	31,740	LC
Univ of Louisiana at Lafayette	LA	6,130	C
Univ of Louisiana at Monroe	LA	12,998	C
Univ of Mary	ND	16,714	C
Univ of Mary Hardin-Baylor	TX	31,950	C+
Univ of Minn/Twin Cities	MN		HC
Univ of Miss	MS	16,704	C+
Univ of Missouri/Columbia	MO	18,201	MC
Univ of Montana-Western	MT	9,753	LC
Univ of Nebr - Lincoln	NE	18,031	VC
Univ of New Orleans	LA	9,224	C
Univ of N Car at Charlotte	NC	15,547	C
Univ of North Florida	FL	15,870	VC
Univ of Pittsburgh at Bradford	PA	21,802	C
Univ of Pittsburgh at Johnstown	PA	20,862	LC
Univ of Rio Grande	OH	8,750	NC
Univ of St. Francis	IN	29,810	C
Univ of S Car Upstate	SC	18,200	LC
Univ of South Florida/Tampa	FL	13,000	C
Univ of Southern Indiana	IN	14,885	C
Univ of the Cumberlands	KY	27,500	C
Univ of Vermont	VT	27,006	VC+
Univ of Wisc/Green Bay	WI	19,074	C
Univ of Wisc/Superior	WI	14,314	C
Urbana Univ	OH	30,820	C
Valparaiso Univ	IN	44,940	VC+
Viterbo Univ	WI	30,070	C
Warner Univ	FL	18,000	C
Wartburg College	IA	41,055	VC
Washington Adventist Univ	MD	25,859	LC
Washington State Univ	WA	20,461	C
Wayne State Univ	MI	22,063	C
West Chester Univ of Pennsylvania	PA	17,186	C
West Texas A&M Univ	TX	13,478	C
West Virginia Univ	WV	16,542	C+
Western Carolina Univ	NC	13,965	C
Westmont College	CA	41,500	VC
Whitworth Univ	WA	47,734	VC
Wiley College	TX		LC
Wilmington College	OH	29,784	C
Wilson College	PA	35,080	C
Wingate Univ	NC	34,990	C

School	ST	$IS	SR
Xavier Univ of Louisiana	LA	25,300	C
York College	NE	19,475	C
York College of Pennsylvania	PA	26,590	C
Youngstown State Univ	OH	16,732	C

ENGLISH LITERATURE

School	ST	$IS	SR
Agnes Scott College	GA	45,323	C+
Aquinas College	MI	33,060	C
Arizona State Univ, at the Tempe Campus	AZ	20,137	C+
Bard College	NY	61,940	HC
Beloit College	WI	49,970	HC
Bennington College	VT	56,990	HC+
Berry College	GA	39,254	VC
Bethany College	WV	35,282	LC
Bethel Univ	MN	34,940	VC
Binghamton Univ/The SUNY	NY	21,648	HC+
Blackburn College	IL	21,350	C
Boise State Univ	ID	13,469	LC
Bowling Green State Univ	OH	18,970	C
Calvin College	MI	39,120	VC
Chatham Univ	PA	43,797	C
Chestnut Hill College	PA	42,110	LC
Columbia Univ/School of General Studies	NY	58,231	MC
Concordia College - New York	NY	39,035	LC
DePauw Univ	IN	48,950	VC+
Dominican Univ of Calif	CA	51,250	C
Eastern Mich Univ	MI	18,604	C
Edinboro Univ of Pennsylvania	PA	15,940	LC
Elizabethtown College	PA	49,740	VC
Elmira College	NY	49,950	C+
Emmanuel College	MA	47,985	VC
Emory and Henry College	VA	387,460	C
Excelsior College	NY	5,580	SP
Fairleigh Dickinson Univ/ Metropolitan Campus	NJ	40,254	C
Faulkner Univ	AL	25,720	LC
Fontbonne Univ	MO	31,384	C
Fordham Univ	NY	61,588	HC+
Hamilton College	NY	55,620	MC
High Point Univ	NC	39,800	C
Hope International Univ	CA	34,650	C
Houghton College	NY	36,808	C+
Hunter College	NY	14,429	VC
Huntington Univ	IN	32,220	C+
Indiana Univ-Purdue Univ Fort Wayne	IN	15,521	C
Ithaca College	NY	53,864	HC
Keene State College	NH	23,232	LC
Knox College	IL	44,865	VC+
Loras College	IA	37,432	VC
Loyola Univ New Orleans	LA	46,581	VC
Marshall Univ	WV	14,820	C
Marylhurst Univ	OR	20,295	NC
Mass College of Liberal Arts	MA	18,613	C
Mercer Univ	GA	44,201	VC
Millersville Univ of Pennsylvania	PA	21,648	C
Mills College	CA	54,119	VC
Missouri Southern State Univ	MO	12,061	C
Murray State Univ	KY	15,304	C
New England College	NH	45,930	LC
New York Univ	NY	61,470	MC
North Central College	IL	38,343	VC
Northeastern Illinois Univ	IL	10,318	LC
Oral Roberts Univ	OK	31,734	C
Pfeiffer Univ	NC	33,700	LC
Purdue Univ/Calumet	IN	14,336	C
Queens Univ of Charlotte	NC	39,543	C+
Reed College	OR	57,780	MC
Rider Univ	NJ	45,720	C
St. Louis Univ	MO	48,346	HC
St. Mary's College	IN	45,160	C+
Santa Fe Univ of Art and Design	NM	39,666	SP
Southern Illinois Univ Carbondale	IL	21,942	C
Southern New Hampshire Univ	NH	38,100	C
St. Edward's Univ	TX	47,784	C
Stevenson Univ	MD	41,470	C
SUNY Plattsburgh / SUNY	NY	18,083	C
Swarthmore College	PA	57,870	MC
Syracuse Univ	NY	56,346	VC
Taylor Univ	IN	37,821	VC+
The Catholic Univ of America	DC	52,852	VC
The Lincoln Univ	PA	15,154	LC
The Pennsylvania State Univ - Univ Park	PA	28,022	VC+
The SUNY at Potsdam	NY	18,473	C
Union Univ	TN	28,260	VC
Univ of Calif at San Diego	CA	21,000	VC
Univ of Illinois at Chicago	IL	24,505	VC
Univ of Illinois at Urbana-Champaign	IL	26,450	HC
Univ of Maryland - College Park	MD	20,060	HC
Univ of Mass Dartmouth	MA	22,223	C
Univ of Mich/Ann Arbor	MI	22,102	MC
Univ of Missouri/Columbia	MO	18,201	MC
Univ of Montana-Western	MT	9,753	LC

School	ST	$IS	SR
Univ of North Florida	FL	15,870	VC
Univ of Pittsburgh at Greensburg	PA	17,640	C
Univ of Pittsburgh at Pittsburgh	PA	28,572	HC+
Univ of Redlands	CA	40,500	VC
Univ of Rochester	NY	60,668	MC
Univ of South Florida/Tampa	FL	13,000	C
Univ of Southern Calif	CA	56,903	MC
Virginia State Univ	VA	11,318	C+
Warren Wilson College	NC	40,132	VC
Washington Univ in St. Louis	MO	69,844	MC
Wesleyan Univ	CT	61,198	MC
Wheeling Jesuit Univ	WV	33,500	C
Winthrop Univ	SC	21,120	C
York College of Pennsylvania	PA	26,590	C
Youngstown State Univ	OH	16,732	C

ENGLISH WRITING

School	ST	$IS	SR
Aquinas College	MI	33,060	C
Arizona State Univ, at the Tempe Campus	AZ	20,137	C+
Bethel College	IN	31,560	C
Bloomfield College	NJ	37,850	LC
Boise State Univ	ID	13,469	LC
Concordia Univ St. Paul	MN	28,250	C
Cornerstone Univ and Grand Rapids Theological Seminary	MI	33,338	C
Elizabethtown College	PA	49,740	VC
Fontbonne Univ	MO	31,384	C
Fordham Univ	NY	61,588	HC+
Goddard College	VT	16,418	NC
Goshen College	IN	35,900	VC
High Point Univ	NC	39,800	C
Houghton College	NY	36,808	C+
Ithaca College	NY	53,864	HC
Keene State College	NH	23,232	LC
Limestone College	SC	30,800	C
Marylhurst Univ	OR	20,295	NC
Mass College of Liberal Arts	MA	18,613	C
Millersville Univ of Pennsylvania	PA	21,648	C
Mills College	CA	54,119	VC
Missouri Southern State Univ	MO	12,061	C
North Central College	IL	38,343	VC
Okla Christian Univ	OK	25,870	VC
Oswego / SUNY	NY	20,009	VC
Southern Oregon Univ	OR	17,874	C
Spring Hill College	AL	44,164	VC
St. Edward's Univ	TX	47,784	C
SUNY Plattsburgh / SUNY	NY	18,083	C
Taylor Univ	IN	37,821	VC+
The SUNY at Potsdam	NY	18,473	C
Univ of Colo Denver	CO	17,904	C
Univ of Idaho	ID	14,558	C
Univ of Mass Dartmouth	MA	22,223	C
Univ of Pittsburgh at Pittsburgh	PA	28,572	HC+
Valparaiso Univ	IN	44,940	VC+
Warren Wilson College	NC	40,132	VC

ENTOMOLOGY

School	ST	$IS	SR
Cornell Univ	NY	60,964	MC
Iowa State Univ	IA	16,403	C
Mich State Univ	MI	22,450	VC
Okla State Univ	OK	14,310	VC
Purdue Univ/West Lafayette	IN	20,024	HC
SUNY / College of Environmental Science and Forestry	NY	18,351	VC
Texas A&M Univ	TX	19,207	VC
Ohio State Univ-Columbus Campus	OH	19,887	VC+
Univ of Arizona	AZ	20,657	C
Univ of Calif at Davis	CA		HC
Univ of Calif at Riverside	CA	27,204	C+
Univ of Delaware	DE	23,612	VC
Univ of Florida	FL	15,943	VC
Univ of Georgia	GA	20,082	VC
Univ of Illinois at Urbana-Champaign	IL	26,450	HC
Univ of Nebr - Lincoln	NE	18,031	VC
Univ of Wisc/Madison	WI	18,757	HC+
Washington State Univ	WA	20,461	C

ENTREPRENEURIAL STUDIES

School	ST	$IS	SR
American International College	MA	36,100	LC
Ashford Univ	CA	10,480	C
Baldwin Wallace Univ	OH	38,318	C
Ball State Univ	IN	17,850	C
Baylor Univ	TX	50,329	HC
Belmont Univ	TN	39,190	VC+
Binghamton Univ/The SUNY	NY	21,648	HC+
Black Hills State Univ	SD	13,947	C
Bradley Univ	IL	31,874	VC
Brown Univ	RI	59,428	MC
Bryant Univ	RI	49,179	VC
Cal State, Fullerton	CA	25,188	C
Canisius College	NY	44,900	C
Clarke Univ	IA	37,600	C
Clarkson Univ	NY	57,330	HC

School	ST	$IS	SR
Cogswell Polytechnical College	CA	30,531	C
College of William & Mary	VA	28,000	MC
Columbia College	MO	24,578	C
Creighton Univ	NE	45,356	VC
Davenport Univ	MI	21,002	LC
Drexel Univ	PA	61,418	VC+
Duquesne Univ	PA	43,720	VC
Eastern Mich Univ	MI	18,604	C
Eastern Univ	PA	37,704	C
Elon Univ	NC	41,914	VC+
Endicott College	MA	43,228	VC+
Fairleigh Dickinson Univ/ College at Florham	NJ	42,142	C
Fairleigh Dickinson Univ/ Metropolitan Campus	NJ	40,254	C
Florida State Univ	FL	16,715	VC
Gannon Univ	PA	39,608	C
Grand Canyon Univ	AZ	24,540	VC
Grove City College	PA	24,022	VC
Hawaii Pacific Univ	HI	34,360	C
Hofstra Univ	NY	51,810	VC+
Houston Baptist Univ	TX	36,450	C
Huntington Univ	IN	32,220	C
Indiana Univ Bloomington	IN	19,801	VC
Jackson State Univ	MS	13,512	LC
John Carroll Univ	OH	46,300	C+
Johnson & Wales Univ/ Charlotte Campus	NC	29,576	C
Johnson & Wales Univ/ Denver Campus	CO	29,576	C
Johnson & Wales Univ/North Miami Campus	FL		C
Johnson & Wales Univ/ Providence Campus	RI	29,576	C
Kansas State Univ	KS	15,497	VC
Kent State Univ	OH	19,920	C
Kent State Univ	OH	19,920	C
Lake Erie College	OH	37,266	C
Lasell College	MA	43,750	LC
Lipscomb Univ	TN	37,490	VC
LIU Brooklyn	NY	47,182	LC
Loyola Marymount Univ	CA	54,649	VC+
Loyola Univ Chicago	IL	51,646	VC+
Lynn Univ	FL	43,500	LC
Marquette Univ	WI	46,930	VC+
Menlo College	CA	49,002	C
Mercy College	NY	30,456	C
Middle Tenn State Univ	TN	8,650	C
Millikin Univ	IL	38,940	C
Missouri State Univ	MO	13,996	C+
Mount Aloysius College	PA	29,976	C
Murray State Univ	KY	15,304	C
New York Inst of Technology	NY	45,010	VC
Northern Kentucky Univ	KY	21,134	C
Northern Mich Univ	MI	18,278	C
Ohio Univ	OH	21,080	C
Okla State Univ	OK	14,310	VC
Pace Univ	NY	53,367	C
Paul Quinn College	TX	25,350	LC
Peirce College	PA	12,760	NC
Purdue Univ/West Lafayette	IN	20,024	HC
Quinnipiac Univ	CT	55,160	VC
Rowan Univ	NJ	24,022	VC+
St. Joseph's Univ	PA	55,006	VC
St. Mary's Univ of Minn	MN	38,280	C
Samford Univ	AL	37,060	C+
San Francisco State Univ	CA	18,514	C
Seton Hill Univ	PA	35,172	C
Shenandoah Univ	VA	39,916	C
S Dak State Univ	SD	14,296	C
Southern Adventist Univ	TN	26,190	C
Southern Illinois Univ Edwardsville	IL	17,532	C
Southern Vermont College	VT	30,740	LC
St. Edward's Univ	TX	47,784	C
Suffolk Univ	MA	47,298	C
SUNY Plattsburgh / SUNY	NY	18,083	C
Syracuse Univ	NY	56,346	VC
Temple Univ	PA	24,392	VC
Texas Christian Univ	TX	49,980	HC
The Univ of N Car at Greensboro	NC	12,848	C
The Univ of N Car at Pembroke	NC	13,388	LC
The Univ of Utah	UT	16,463	VC
Thomas Edison State College	NJ	5,700	SP
Tulane Univ	LA	60,861	MC
Univ of Alaska Anchorage	AK	16,673	NC
Univ of Arizona	AZ	20,657	C
Univ of Dayton	OH	49,070	VC
Univ of Hartford	CT	42,674	C
Univ of Illinois at Chicago	IL	24,505	VC
Univ of Illinois at Urbana-Champaign	IL	26,450	HC
Univ of Indianapolis	IN	31,740	LC
Univ of Miami	FL	57,034	MC
Univ of Nebr - Lincoln	NE	18,031	VC
Univ of North Texas	TX	15,628	C
Univ of Pennsylvania	PA	61,132	MC
Univ of Portland	OR	49,964	VC
Univ of San Francisco	CA	54,770	VC
Univ of South Florida/St. Petersburg	FL	12,769	C
Univ of St. Francis	IL	37,560	C
Univ of Tampa	FL	35,160	VC

School	ST	$IS	SR
Univ of Vermont	VT	27,006	VC+
Univ of Wisc-Milwaukee	WI	18,436	C
Virginia Polytechnic Inst and State Univ	VA	14,629	HC
Washington State Univ	WA	20,461	C
Washington Univ in St. Louis	MO	69,844	MC
Waynesburg Univ	PA	30,150	C
Western Carolina Univ	NC	13,965	C
Western Mich Univ	MI	19,628	C
Wichita State Univ	KS	14,607	C+
Wilkes Univ	PA	44,070	C
Xavier Univ	OH	44,980	VC+
York College of Pennsylvania	PA	26,590	C

ENVIRONMENT & NATNL RESOURCE ECONOMICS

School	ST	$IS	SR
Arizona State Univ, at the Polytechnic Campus	AZ	20,531	C+
Univ of Rhode Island	RI	24,002	C

ENVIRONMENTAL BIOLOGY

School	ST	$IS	SR
Aquinas College	MI	33,060	C
Averett Univ	VA	37,750	LC
Belmont Univ	TN	39,190	VC+
Beloit College	WI	49,970	HC
Bennington College	VT	56,990	HC+
Bethel Univ	IN	31,560	C
Blackburn College	IL	21,350	C
Boston Univ	MA	60,694	MC
Cal State, Northridge	CA	28,690	VC
Cedar Crest College	PA	43,240	C
Christopher Newport Univ	VA	21,960	VC
Colby College	ME	57,510	MC
Columbia Univ/City of New York	NY	61,116	MC
Faulkner Univ	AL	25,720	LC
Fitchburg State Univ	MA	18,173	C
Georgetown Univ	DC	52,910	MC
Greenville College	IL	27,012	C
Hanover College	IN	43,073	C+
Heidelberg Univ	OH	34,100	C
Houghton College	NY	36,808	C+
Kent State Univ	OH	19,920	C
Lock Haven Univ of Pennsylvania	PA	18,028	LC
Mercer Univ	GA	44,201	VC
Mich State Univ	MI	22,450	VC
Millersville Univ of Pennsylvania	PA	21,648	C
Missouri Univ of Science and Technology	MO	18,655	VC+
Montclair State Univ	NJ	22,614	C
Mount Aloysius College	PA	29,976	C
Norfolk State Univ	VA	10,531	A
Ohio Univ	OH	21,080	C
Pittsburg State Univ	KS	12,032	C
Plymouth State Univ	NH	23,148	LC
Prescott College	AZ	33,284	C
Queens College/The CUNY	NY	17,107	VC
St. Mary's Univ of Minn	MN	38,280	C
Sewanee: The Univ of the South	TN	47,700	HC+
S Dak State Univ	SD	14,296	C
Southeast Missouri State Univ	MO	15,370	C
SUNY / College of Environmental Science and Forestry	NY	18,351	VC
Texas A&M Univ at Galveston	TX	11,258	C
Tulane Univ	LA	60,861	MC
Univ of Calif at Davis	CA		HC
Univ of Dayton	OH	49,070	VC
Univ of La Verne	CA	47,010	C
Univ of Mount Union	OH	35,130	C
Univ of North Alabama	AL	9,960	C
West Chester Univ of Pennsylvania	PA	17,186	C
Wilmington College	OH	29,784	C
Wingate Univ	NC	34,990	C

ENVIRONMENTAL CHEMISTRY

School	ST	$IS	SR
Binghamton Univ/The SUNY	NY	21,648	HC+
Lawrence Tech Univ	MI	37,630	VC
Marshall Univ	WV	14,820	C
Millersville Univ of Pennsylvania	PA	21,648	C
Pittsburg State Univ	KS	12,032	C
Southeast Missouri State Univ	MO	15,370	LC
St. Edward's Univ	TX	47,784	C
Univ of Denver	CO	51,787	VC+
Univ of Georgia	GA	20,082	VC

ENVIRONMENTAL DESIGN

School	ST	$IS	SR
Arizona State Univ, at the Tempe Campus	AZ	20,137	C+
Art Center College of Design	CA	34,044	SP
Ball State Univ	IN	17,850	C
Bethel College	IN	31,560	C
Binghamton Univ/The SUNY	NY	21,648	HC+
Brigham Young Univ	UT	12,100	HC
Green Mountain College	VT	45,228	LC
Hampshire College	MA	58,320	MC

School	ST	$IS	SR
Harvard College/Harvard Univ	MA	49,000	MC
Maryland Inst College of Art	MD	39,500	SP
Marywood Univ	PA	45,595	C
Montana State Univ	MT	14,068	C
N Car State Univ	NC	16,202	HC
N Dak State Univ	ND		C
Olivet Nazarene Univ	IL	29,990	C
Prescott College	AZ	33,284	C
Rutgers, The State Univ of New Jersey/New Brunswick	NJ	25,562	VC
SUNY / College of Environmental Science and Forestry	NY	18,351	VC
Stony Brook Univ / SUNY	NY	20,078	HC+
Syracuse Univ	NY	56,346	VC
Texas A&M Univ	TX	19,207	VC
The Univ of Okla	OK	18,621	VC
Univ at Buffalo / The SUNY	NY	20,283	VC
Univ of Calif at Davis	CA		HC
Univ of Colo Boulder	CO	22,605	VC+
Univ of Houston	TX	19,796	VC
Univ of Mass Amherst	MA	24,215	VC+
Univ of Minn/Twin Cities	MN		HC
Univ of New Mexico	NM	15,300	C
Univ of PR Recinto de Rio Piedras	PR	5,750	

ENVIRONMENTAL EARTH RESOURCES

School	ST	$IS	SR
Binghamton Univ/The SUNY	NY	21,648	HC+

ENVIRONMENTAL EDUCATION

School	ST	$IS	SR
Catawba College	NC	37,240	LC
Goshen College	IN	35,900	VC
Johnson State College	VT	16,721	C
Messiah College	PA	40,690	C+
Prescott College	AZ	33,284	C
Seattle Univ	WA	49,035	VC+
Southern Oregon Univ	OR	17,874	C
SUNY / College of Environmental Science and Forestry	NY	18,351	VC
Ohio State Univ-Columbus Campus	OH	19,887	HC+
Univ of Montana-Western	MT	9,753	C
Univ of Nebr - Lincoln	NE	18,031	VC
Univ of Pittsburgh at Bradford	PA	21,802	C
Virginia Polytechnic Inst and State Univ	VA	14,629	HC
West Virginia Univ	WV	16,542	C+

ENVIRONMENTAL ENGINEERING

School	ST	$IS	SR
Alabama A&M Univ	AL	10,084	C
Bucknell Univ	PA	60,140	MC
Calif Polytechnic State Univ	CA	19,847	HC
CUNY/City College	NY	20,319	VC
Colo State Univ-Fort Collins	CO	20,385	VC
Cornell Univ	NY	60,964	MC
Drexel Univ	PA	61,418	VC+
Elon Univ	NC	41,914	VC+
Florida Gulf Coast Univ	FL		C
Florida International Univ	FL	17,747	C+
Florida State Univ	FL	16,715	VC
Gannon Univ	PA	39,608	C
Georgia Inst of Technology	GA	21,828	MC
Humboldt State Univ	CA	18,400	C
Johns Hopkins Univ	MD	47,492	MC
Lehigh Univ	PA	56,770	MC
Louisiana State Univ	LA	18,677	C+
Manhattan College	NY	49,588	C+
Marquette Univ	WI	46,930	VC+
Mass Inst of Technology	MA	58,240	MC
Mass Maritime Academy	MA	15,340	C
Mich Tech Univ	MI	23,556	HC
Missouri Univ of Science and Technology	MO	18,655	VC+
Montana Tech of The Univ of Montana	MT	14,650	C
New Jersey Inst of Technology	NJ	26,490	C+
New Mexico Inst of Mining and Technology	NM	13,592	VC
New Mexico State Univ	NM	14,050	C
N Car State Univ	NC	16,202	HC
Northern Arizona Univ	AZ	19,010	C
Northwestern Univ	IL	61,640	MC
Ohio Univ	OH	21,080	C
Oregon State Univ	OR	20,273	VC
Rensselaer Polytechnic Inst	NY	61,529	MC
Rice Univ	TX	43,288	MC
San Diego State Univ	CA	21,611	C+
Seattle Univ	WA	49,035	VC+
S Dak School of Mines and Technology	SD	15,260	VC
S Dak State Univ	SD	14,296	C
Southern Methodist Univ	TX	60,585	MC
Stanford Univ	CA	58,388	MC

School	ST	$IS	SR
SUNY / College of Environmental Science and Forestry	NY	18,351	VC
Stevens Inst of Technology	NJ	50,130	HC
Suffolk Univ	MA	47,298	C
Syracuse Univ	NY	56,346	VC
Tenn Tech Univ	TN	11,310	C
Texas Tech Univ	TX	14,243	VC
The Catholic Univ of America	DC	52,852	VC
Ohio State Univ-Columbus Campus	OH	19,887	HC+
The Pennsylvania State Univ - Univ Park	PA	28,022	VC+
The Univ of Okla	OK	18,621	VC
The Univ of Tenn at Chattanooga	TN	16,883	C
Tufts Univ	MA	58,780	MC
United States Air Force Academy	CO		MC
United States Military Academy	NY		MC
Universidad Politecnica de PR	PR	19,252	
Univ at Buffalo / The SUNY	NY	20,283	VC
Univ of Arizona	AZ	20,657	C
Univ of Calif at Berkeley	CA	23,322	MC
Univ of Calif at Irvine	CA	25,961	VC
Univ of Calif at Riverside	CA	27,204	C+
Univ of Calif at San Diego	CA	21,000	VC
Univ of Central Florida	FL	15,668	VC+
Univ of Colo Boulder	CO	22,605	VC+
Univ of Conn	CT	24,706	HC
Univ of Delaware	DE	23,612	VC
Univ of Florida	FL	15,943	HC
Univ of Georgia	GA	20,082	VC
Univ of Idaho	ID	14,558	C
Univ of Miami	FL	57,034	MC
Univ of Mich/Ann Arbor	MI	22,102	MC
Univ of New Hampshire	NH	26,912	C
Univ of Southern Calif	CA	56,903	MC
Univ of Vermont	VT	27,006	VC+
Univ of Wisc/Platteville	WI	14,564	C
Wilkes Univ	PA	44,070	C
Worcester Polytechnic Inst	MA	55,860	MC
Yale Univ	CT	55,300	MC

ENVIRONMENTAL ENGINEERING TECHNOLOGY

School	ST	$IS	SR
East Carolina Univ	NC	14,169	C
Indiana Inst of Technology	IN	34,240	LC
Inter-American Univ of PR/Bayamon Junior College	PR	4,428	
Lake Superior State Univ	MI	18,121	C
Murray State Univ	KY	15,304	C
Rochester Inst of Technology	NY	42,450	VC
Shawnee State Univ	OH	16,916	C
Southwestern Okla State Univ	OK	9,160	C
Texas Southern Univ	TX	18,212	LC
Univ of Wisc/Green Bay	WI	19,074	C

ENVIRONMENTAL GEOLOGY

School	ST	$IS	SR
Allegheny College	PA	50,980	HC
Beloit College	WI	49,970	HC
Binghamton Univ/The SUNY	NY	21,648	HC+
Calvin College	MI	39,120	VC
Hanover College	IN	43,073	C+
Kutztown Univ of Pennsylvania	PA	16,909	LC
Millersville Univ of Pennsylvania	PA	21,648	C
Murray State Univ	KY	15,304	C
Ohio Univ	OH	21,080	C
Oswego / SUNY	NY	20,009	VC
Prescott College	AZ	33,284	C
Queens College/The CUNY	NY	17,107	VC
Southern Methodist Univ	TX	60,585	MC
SUNY New Paltz	NY	14,348	VC
The Univ of Okla	OK	18,621	VC
The Univ of Utah	UT	16,463	VC
Univ of Akron	OH	20,436	C
Univ of Calif at Irvine	CA	25,961	VC
Univ of Dayton	OH	49,070	VC
Univ of Illinois at Chicago	IL	24,505	VC
Univ of Mich/Ann Arbor	MI	22,102	MC
Univ of Pittsburgh at Pittsburgh	PA	28,572	HC+
Univ of Wyoming	WY	14,401	C+

ENVIRONMENTAL HEALTH SCIENCE

School	ST	$IS	SR
Benedict College	SC	20,454	NC
Boise State Univ	ID	13,469	LC
Calif Inst of Technology	CA	54,045	MC
Cal State, Sacramento	CA	16,200	C
Cal State, San Bernardino	CA	12,000	C
Clarkson Univ	NY	57,330	HC
Colo State Univ-Fort Collins	CO	20,385	VC
Colo State Univ-Pueblo	CO	16,183	C
Delaware State Univ	DE	16,722	LC
Drury Univ	MO	31,909	VC
East Carolina Univ	NC	14,169	C
East Central Univ	OK	10,223	LC

School	ST	$IS	SR
East Tenn State Univ	TN	9,000	C
Eastern Kentucky Univ	KY	11,161	C
Illinois State Univ	IL	23,110	VC
Indiana State Univ	IN	16,000	C
Indiana Univ-Purdue Univ Indianapolis	IN	17,611	C
Iowa Wesleyan College	IA	30,850	LC
Kent State Univ	OH	19,920	C
Lake Superior State Univ	MI	18,121	C
Miss Valley State Univ	MS	9,706	C
Missouri Southern State Univ	MO	12,061	C
New Mexico State Univ	NM	14,050	C
New York Univ	NY	61,470	MC
Ohio Univ	OH	21,080	C
Old Dominion Univ	VA	19,483	LC
Point Park Univ	PA	36,390	C
Purdue Univ/West Lafayette	IN	20,024	HC
Salisbury Univ	MD	19,180	VC
San Diego State Univ	CA	21,611	C+
Springfield College	MA	25,000	C
Texas Southern Univ	TX	18,212	LC
Univ of Arizona	AZ	20,657	C
Univ of Arkansas at Little Rock	AR	17,609	LC
Univ of Calif at Davis	CA		HC
Univ of Georgia	GA	20,082	VC
Univ of Mich-Flint	MI	17,547	C+
Univ of N Car at Chapel Hill	NC	18,928	MC
Univ of Southern Maine	ME	16,576	C
Univ of Washington	WA	14,722	VC
Western Carolina Univ	NC	13,965	C
Western Kentucky Univ	KY	11,000	C
Wright State Univ	OH	16,983	C
York College / The CUNY	NY	5,496	VC

ENVIRONMENTAL HORTICULTURE & TURF MGMT

School	ST	$IS	SR
Univ of Rhode Island	RI	24,002	C
Univ of Wisc/Platteville	WI	14,564	C

ENVIRONMENTAL SCIENCE

School	ST	$IS	SR
Abilene Christian Univ	TX	38,400	C+
Adrian College	MI	42,400	C
Alaska Pacific Univ	AK	43,592	VC
Albion College	MI	46,010	C
Albright College	PA	46,660	C
Alderson Broaddus Univ	WV	28,656	C
Allegheny College	PA	50,980	HC
Alverno College	WI	31,434	C
American Univ	DC	56,015	MC+
Andrews Univ	MI	28,030	C+
Anna Maria College	MA	34,600	C
Appalachian State Univ	NC	12,919	VC
Aquinas College	MI	33,060	C
Arcadia Univ	PA	33,570	C+
Arizona State Univ, at the West Campus	AZ	19,251	C
Ashland Univ	OH	25,000	C
Assumption College	MA	47,122	C+
Auburn Univ	AL	22,378	VC+
Averett Univ	VA	37,750	LC
Barnard College/Columbia Univ	NY	39,000	MC
Barton College	NC	27,660	LC
Baylor Univ	TX	50,329	HC
Benedictine Univ	IL	37,820	C
Bennington College	VT	56,990	HC+
Bentley Univ	MA	56,454	HC+
Berry College	GA	39,254	VC
Bethany College	WV	35,282	LC
Bethel College	IN	31,560	C
Bethel Univ	MN	34,940	VC
Binghamton Univ/The SUNY	NY	21,648	HC+
Biola Univ	CA	40,320	C
Boston College	MA	60,622	MC
Bowling Green State Univ	OH	18,970	C
Bradley Univ	IL	31,874	VC
Briar Cliff Univ	IA	29,514	C
Bridgewater College	VA	41,450	C
Brown Univ	RI	59,428	MC
Bryant Univ	RI	49,179	VC
Bucknell Univ	PA	60,140	MC
Buena Vista Univ	IA	39,188	C
Cabrini College	PA	40,859	C
Calif Baptist Univ	CA	38,792	C
Calif Polytechnic State Univ	CA	19,847	HC
Cal State, Chico	CA	20,158	C
Cal State, East Bay	CA	16,549	C
Cal State, Long Beach	CA	17,502	C+
Calif Univ of Pennsylvania	PA	14,217	C
Calvin College	MI	39,120	VC
Canisius College	NY	44,900	C
Capital Univ	OH	41,050	VC
Carroll College	MT	28,000	C
Carroll Univ	WI	38,100	C
Case Western Reserve Univ	OH	56,534	MC
Castleton State College	VT	20,186	C
Catawba College	NC	37,240	LC
Cedarville Univ	OH	32,860	VC
Centenary College of Louisiana	LA	45,650	C+
Central College	IA	42,104	C+

School	ST	$IS	SR
Central Methodist Univ	MO	28,240	VC
Chapman Univ	CA	58,347	VC+
Charleston Southern Univ	SC	22,420	C
Chatham Univ	PA	43,797	C
Chestnut Hill College	PA	42,110	LC
CUNY/City College	NY	20,319	HC+
Claflin Univ	SC	22,368	LC
Claremont McKenna College	CA	62,215	MC
Clarion Univ of Pennsylvania	PA	17,370	LC
Clark Univ	MA	47,020	HC+
Clarkson Univ	NY	57,330	HC
Cleveland State Univ	OH	21,776	C
Coe College	IA	45,550	VC
Colby-Sawyer College	NH	50,790	C
Colgate Univ	NY	58,135	MC
Colo College	CO	57,162	MC
Colo Mesa Univ	CO	17,690	LC
Columbia Univ/City of New York	NY	61,116	MC
Columbia Univ/School of General Studies	NY	58,231	MC
Concordia College - Moorhead	MN	39,974	VC
Concordia College - New York	NY	39,035	LC
Concordia Univ	OR	35,000	C
Concordia Univ Texas	TX	23,640	C
Conn College	CT	54,970	MC
Cornell College	IA	44,930	VC
Creighton Univ	NE	45,356	VC
Curry College	MA	48,925	LC
Dallas Baptist Univ	TX	30,580	VC
Dartmouth College	NH	57,996	MC
Davis & Elkins College	WV	33,742	C
Defiance College	OH	30,645	C
Delaware Valley College	PA	29,944	C
Delta State Univ	MS	12,292	LC
DePaul Univ	IL	47,623	VC
DePauw Univ	IN	48,950	VC+
Dickinson College	PA	57,662	HC+
Doane College	NE	35,230	C
Dominican Univ	IL	37,628	C
Dordt College	IA	34,160	C+
Drake Univ	IA	41,516	VC+
Drexel Univ	PA	61,418	VC+
Drury Univ	MO	31,909	VC
Duke Univ	NC	50,250	MC
Duquesne Univ	PA	43,720	VC
Earlham College	IN	51,470	HC
East Stroudsburg Univ of Pennsylvania	PA	18,868	LC
Eastern Conn State Univ	CT	20,584	C
Eastern Kentucky Univ	KY	11,161	C
Eastern Mennonite Univ	VA	40,660	C
Eastern Nazarene College	MA	30,000	C
Eastern New Mexico Univ	NM	10,682	C
Edinboro Univ of Pennsylvania	PA	15,940	LC
Elizabethtown College	PA	49,740	VC
Elmhurst College	IL	43,336	C
Elmira College	NY	49,950	C+
Elon Univ	NC	41,914	VC+
Emory and Henry College	VA	387,460	C
Endicott College	MA	43,544	C
Ferrum College	VA	27,740	LC
Flagler College	FL	25,180	C
Florida Inst of Technology	FL	48,290	VC
Florida International Univ	FL	17,747	C+
Florida State Univ	FL	16,715	VC
Fordham Univ	NY	61,588	HC+
Framingham State Univ	MA	18,854	C
Franklin and Marshall College	PA	60,799	MC
Franklin Pierce Univ	NH	41,598	C
Fresno Pacific Univ	CA	32,136	C
Friends Univ	KS	29,100	C
Frostburg State Univ	MD	15,264	LC
Furman Univ	SC	54,006	HC
Gannon Univ	PA	39,608	C
George Washington Univ	DC	57,108	MC
Georgetown College	KY	41,440	C
Georgia College and State Univ	GA	18,900	C+
Gettysburg College	PA	58,820	HC
Glenville State College	WV	11,348	NC
Goshen College	IN	35,900	VC
Hampshire College	MA	58,320	MC
Hanover College	IN	43,073	C+
Hardin-Simmons Univ	TX	23,560	C
Hartwick College	NY	51,270	C
Harvard College/Harvard Univ	MA	49,000	MC
Hawaii Pacific Univ	HI	34,360	C
Heritage Univ	WA	17,664	NC
Hiram College	OH	37,300	VC
Hobart and William Smith Colleges	NY	60,034	HC+
Hood College	MD	45,730	C
Houghton College	NY	36,808	C+
Howard Univ	DC	13,646	C
Humboldt State Univ	CA	18,640	VC
Hunter College	NY	14,429	VC
Husson Univ	ME	24,194	LC
Idaho State Univ	ID	12,307	C
Illinois College	IL	25,770	VC
Indiana Univ Bloomington	IN	19,801	VC
Indiana Univ-Purdue Univ Indianapolis	IN	17,611	C
Iona College	NY	44,028	C
Iowa State Univ	IA	16,403	C
Ithaca College	NY	53,864	HC
Jacksonville Univ	FL	37,780	C
John Brown Univ	AR	32,056	VC+
John Carroll Univ	OH	46,300	C+
Johns Hopkins Univ	MD	47,492	MC
Johnson State College	VT	16,721	C
Juniata College	PA	49,340	VC
Keuka College	NY	30,300	C
Keystone College	PA	28,680	LC
Kutztown Univ of Pennsylvania	PA	16,909	LC
La Salle Univ	PA	50,270	C
Lake Forest College	IL	50,652	VC
Lake Superior State Univ	MI	18,121	C
Lander Univ	SC	22,514	C+
Le Moyne College	NY	43,470	C
Lehigh Univ	PA	56,770	MC
Lewis Univ	IL	23,050	C
Lincoln Memorial Univ	TN	18,144	C
Lincoln Univ	MO	12,904	NC
Lipscomb Univ	TN	37,490	VC
Louisiana State Univ	LA	18,677	C+
Louisiana Tech Univ	LA	11,302	C
Lourdes Univ	OH	26,055	LC
Loyola Marymount Univ	CA	54,649	VC+
Loyola Univ Chicago	IL	51,646	VC+
Lynchburg College	VA	42,645	C
Madonna Univ	MI	24,540	VC
Mansfield Univ	PA	19,468	LC
Marian Univ	IN	38,540	C
Marietta College	OH	42,135	C+
Marist College	NY	35,500	C
Maritime College/SUNY	NY	16,020	C
Marshall Univ	WV	14,820	C
Martin Univ	IN	11,000	SP
Marygrove College	MI	28,926	C
Maryville Univ of St. Louis	MO	35,856	VC
Marywood Univ	PA	45,595	C
McDaniel College	MD	47,450	VC
Megar Evers College/The CUNY	NY	4,920	NC
Mercyhurst College	PA	40,700	C
Merrimack College	MA	44,215	C
Messiah College	PA	40,690	C+
Metropolitan State Univ of Denver	CO	4,835	LC
Miami Univ	OH	24,191	VC
Middle Tenn State Univ	TN	8,650	C
Midway College	KY	20,150	LC
Midwestern State Univ	TX	9,722	VC
Miles College	AL	11,164	NC
Mills College	CA	54,119	VC
Minn State Univ, Mankato	MN	15,616	C
Monmouth College	IL	40,850	C
Montana State Univ	MT	14,068	C
Montana State Univ-Billings	MT	12,425	LC
Montana State Univ-Northern	MT	12,500	NC
Montreat College	NC	31,298	C
Mount Aloysius College	PA	29,976	C
Mount Marty College	SD	29,638	C
Mount St. Mary's Univ	MD	47,996	C
Muhlenberg College	PA	52,837	HC
Muskingum Univ	OH	30,502	C
National Univ	CA	14,730	SP
Nazareth College of Rochester	NY	43,028	C+
New England College	NH	45,930	LC
New Jersey Inst of Technology	NJ	26,490	C+
New Mexico Highlands Univ	NM	11,904	NC
New Mexico Inst of Mining and Technology	NM	13,592	VC
New Mexico State Univ	NM	14,050	C
N Car Central Univ	NC	9,000	C
N Car State Univ	NC	16,202	HC
N Car Wesleyan College	NC	29,440	C
North Park Univ	IL	30,130	C
Northeastern Univ	MA	55,296	MC
Northern Arizona Univ	AZ	19,010	C
Northern Kentucky Univ	KY	21,134	C
Northern State Univ - Aberdeen	SD	14,505	C
Northland College	WI	26,680	C
Northwest Univ	WA	18,854	C
Northwestern Univ	IL	61,640	MC
Norwich Univ	VT	28,212	C
Notre Dame College	OH	34,942	VC
Nova Southeastern Univ	FL	37,280	VC
Oakland Univ	MI	19,391	C
Ohio Wesleyan Univ	OH	49,460	C+
Okla State Univ	OK	14,310	VC
Olivet College	MI	19,984	LC
Olivet Nazarene Univ	IL	29,990	C
Oregon Inst of Technology	OR	8,910	C
Oregon State Univ	OR	20,273	VC
Pace Univ	NY	53,367	VC
Pacific Lutheran Univ	WA	46,760	C+
Pfeiffer Univ	NC	33,700	LC
Philadelphia Univ	PA	44,160	C
Piedmont College	GA	30,136	C
Pitzer College	CA	54,988	MC
Point Loma Nazarene Univ	CA	41,006	C+
Point Park Univ	PA	36,390	C
Portland State Univ	OR	18,672	C
Prescott College	AZ	33,284	C
Principia College	IL	35,140	C+
Purdue Univ/West Lafayette	IN	20,024	HC
Queens College/The CUNY	NY	17,107	VC
Queens Univ of Charlotte	NC	39,543	C+
Ramapo College of New Jersey	NJ	24,938	C
Randolph College	VA	45,660	VC
Rhodes College	TN	51,900	HC+
Richard Stockton College of New Jersey	NJ	20,000	VC
Rider Univ	NJ	45,720	C
Ripon College	WI	36,959	C+
Robert Morris Univ	PA	37,864	C
Rochester Inst of Technology	NY	42,450	VC
Rocky Mountain College	MT	32,242	C
Roger Williams Univ	RI	46,296	VC
Rollins College	FL	52,370	HC
Roosevelt Univ	IL	22,605	VC
Rosemont College	PA	42,350	C
Russell Sage College	NY	39,370	C
Rutgers, The State Univ of New Jersey/New Brunswick	NJ	25,562	VC
Rutgers, The State Univ of New Jersey/Newark Campus	NJ	258,806	C
St. Anselm College	NH	49,376	VC
St. Joseph's College of Maine	ME	31,580	C
St. Joseph's Univ	PA	55,006	VC
St. Mary's College of Calif	CA	53,550	C
St. Mary's Univ	TX	33,854	C
St. Paul's College	VA	16,030	NC
St. Vincent College	PA	40,244	C
Salem International Univ	WV	21,090	LC
Sam Houston State Univ	TX	17,082	C
Samford Univ	AL	37,060	C+
San Diego State Univ	CA	21,611	C+
Savannah State Univ	GA	13,156	C
Scripps College	CA	61,940	MC
Seattle Univ	WA	49,035	VC+
Shaw Univ	NC	15,488	C
Shenandoah Univ	VA	39,916	C
Shippensburg Univ of Pennsylvania	PA	20,934	C
Siena College	NY	43,863	VC
Sierra Nevada College	NV	32,700	VC
Simpson College	IA	36,086	C+
Smith College	MA	59,674	MC
Sonoma State Univ	CA	20,541	C
Southeast Missouri State Univ	MO	15,370	LC
Southern Methodist Univ	TX	60,585	MC
Southern Oregon Univ	OR	17,874	C
Southwest Minn State Univ	MN	14,000	C
St. Bonaventure Univ	NY	41,575	C
St. Edward's Univ	TX	47,784	C
St. Lawrence Univ	NY	59,972	VC
St. Norbert College	WI	41,478	VC
SUNY / College of Environmental Science and Forestry	NY	18,351	VC
SUNY at Purchase	NY	16,951	C
Stephen F. Austin State Univ	TX	14,668	C
Stetson Univ	FL	51,516	VC
Stony Brook Univ / SUNY	NY	20,078	HC+
Suffolk Univ	MA	47,298	C
SUNY Cortland/The SUNY	NY	19,759	C+
SUNY Fredonia/The SUNY at Fredonia	NY	19,840	VC
SUNY Oneonta / SUNY	NY	16,919	C+
SUNY Plattsburgh / SUNY	NY	18,083	C
Susquehanna Univ	PA	51,150	C
Taylor Univ	IN	37,821	VC+
Temple Univ	PA	24,392	VC
Texas A&M Univ	TX	19,207	VC
Texas A&M Univ at Corpus Christi	TX	11,544	LC
Texas A&M Univ at Galveston	TX	11,258	C
Texas Christian Univ	TX	49,980	HC
Texas State Univ	TX	17,128	C
The Catholic Univ of America	DC	52,852	VC
The Lincoln Univ	PA	15,154	LC
Ohio State Univ-Columbus Campus	OH	19,887	HC+
The SUNY/College at Brockport	NY	19,002	C
The Univ of N Car at Pembroke	NC	13,388	C
The Univ of Okla	OK	18,621	VC
The Univ of Tenn at Chattanooga	TN	16,883	C
The Univ of Virginia's College at Wise	VA	11,076	C
Thiel College	PA	38,728	LC
Thomas Edison State College	NJ	5,700	SP
Thomas More College	KY	34,760	C
Towson Univ	MD	16,000	VC
Trine Univ	IN	39,400	HC+
Trinity College	CT		HC+
Troy Univ	AL	10,650	C
Tufts Univ	MA	58,780	MC
Tulane Univ	LA	60,861	MC
Tusculum College	TN	24,295	C
Union College	NY	60,240	MC
Unity College	ME	34,054	C
Univ of Alabama at Tuscaloosa	AL	17,164	C+
Univ of Alaska Southeast	AK	11,493	C
Univ of Arizona	AZ	20,657	C
Univ of Arkansas at Fayetteville	AR	18,352	C+
Univ of Calif at Berkeley	CA	23,322	MC
Univ of Calif at Davis	CA		HC
Univ of Calif at Irvine	CA	25,961	VC
Univ of Calif at Los Angeles	CA	25,686	MC
Univ of Calif at Riverside	CA	27,204	C+
Univ of Calif at San Diego	CA	21,000	VC
Univ of Calif at Santa Barbara	CA	27,551	HC
Univ of Central Arkansas	AR	13,667	VC
Univ of Chicago	IL	55,416	MC
Univ of Colo Boulder	CO	22,605	VC+
Univ of Conn	CT	24,706	HC
Univ of Delaware	DE	23,612	VC
Univ of Denver	CO	51,787	VC+
Univ of Dubuque	IA	30,200	C
Univ of Evansville	IN	42,656	VC+
Univ of Findlay	OH	31,916	C
Univ of Hawaii at Hilo	HI	23,066	C
Univ of Hawaii at Manoa	HI	19,379	C
Univ of Houston	TX	19,796	VC
Univ of Idaho	ID	14,558	C
Univ of Indianapolis	IN	31,740	C
Univ of Iowa	IA	17,693	VC
Univ of La Verne	CA	47,010	C
Univ of Maine	ME	19,902	C+
Univ of Maine at Farmington	ME	18,187	LC
Univ of Maine at Fort Kent	ME	15,195	LC
Univ of Maine at Machias	ME	10,523	C
Univ of Maine at Presque Isle	ME	15,011	LC
Univ of Mary Washington	VA	19,484	VC
Univ of Maryland - College Park	MD	20,060	HC
Univ of Maryland/Baltimore County	MD	18,000	VC
Univ of Maryland/Eastern Shore	MD	14,000	C
Univ of Maryland/Univ College	MD	6,168	SP
Univ of Mass Amherst	MA	24,215	VC+
Univ of Mass Lowell	MA	19,316	C
Univ of Miami	FL	57,034	MC
Univ of Mich/Dearborn	MI	9,885	VC
Univ of Minn Crookston	MN	17,834	C
Univ of Minn/Duluth	MN	19,806	C
Univ of Missouri-Kansas City	MO	19,603	C
Univ of Montana-Western	MT	9,753	LC
Univ of Montevallo	AL	17,060	C
Univ of Mount Olive	NC	18,426	C
Univ of Mount Union	OH	35,130	C
Univ of Nebr - Lincoln	NE	18,031	VC
Univ of Nevada, Las Vegas	NV	17,303	C
Univ of Nevada/Reno	NV	17,507	C
Univ of New England	ME	46,750	C
Univ of New Hampshire	NH	26,912	C
Univ of New Haven	CT	48,940	C
Univ of New Mexico	NM	15,300	C
Univ of New Orleans	LA	9,224	C
Univ of N Car at Asheville	NC	13,500	VC
Univ of N Car at Chapel Hill	NC	18,928	MC
Univ of N Car at Wilmington	NC	13,572	VC
Univ of Northern Iowa	IA	15,795	C
Univ of Notre Dame	IN	57,117	MC
Univ of Oregon	OR	21,360	C
Univ of Portland	OR	49,964	VC
Univ of Redlands	CA	40,500	VC
Univ of Rio Grande	OH	8,750	NC
Univ of Rochester	NY	60,668	MC
Univ of St. Francis	IN	29,810	C
Univ of San Francisco	CA	54,770	VC
Univ of Scranton	PA	51,940	VC
Univ of S Car at Columbia	SC	19,725	VC+
Univ of South Florida/St. Petersburg	FL	12,769	C
Univ of South Florida/Tampa	FL	13,000	C
Univ of Southern Calif	CA	56,903	MC
Univ of Southern Indiana	IN	14,885	C
Univ of Southern Maine	ME	16,576	C
Univ of St. Francis	IL	37,560	C
Univ of St. Thomas - Houston	TX	37,690	C
Univ of Tampa	FL	35,160	VC
Univ of Tenn at Knoxville	TN	20,364	VC+
Univ of Texas - Pan American	TX	11,125	LC
Univ of Texas at San Antonio	TX	18,372	C
Univ of the District of Columbia	DC	7,244	LC
Univ of the Incarnate Word	TX	37,316	LC
Univ of the Ozarks	AR	31,440	C
Univ of the Pacific	CA	52,146	VC
Univ of the Sciences	PA	48,320	VC+
Univ of Toledo	OH	18,464	C
Univ of Vermont	VT	27,006	VC+
Univ of Virginia	VA	23,050	MC
Univ of West Alabama	AL	14,274	C
Univ of Wisc/Green Bay	WI	19,074	C
Univ of Wisc/Madison	WI	18,757	HC+
Univ of Wisc-Milwaukee	WI	18,436	C
Ursinus College	PA	57,580	VC

ST = STATE **$IS** = IN-STATE COSTS **SR** = SELECTOR RATING

School	ST	$IS	SR
Utah State Univ	UT	12,044	C
Valparaiso Univ	IN	44,940	VC+
Villanova Univ	PA	58,394	MC
Virginia Polytechnic Inst and State Univ	VA	14,629	HC
Walla Walla Univ	WA	26,256	NC
Walsh Univ	OH	35,100	C
Washington and Lee Univ	VA	52,812	MC
Washington College	MD	52,602	VC
Washington State Univ	WA	20,461	C
Washington Univ in St. Louis	MO	69,844	MC
Wayland Baptist Univ	TX	18,912	LC
Wayne State Univ	MI	22,063	C
Waynesburg Univ	PA	30,150	C
Wentworth Inst of Technology	MA	29,800	C
Wesley College	DE	31,115	LC
Wesleyan College	GA	24,000	C
West Texas A&M Univ	TX	13,478	C
West Virginia Univ	WV	16,542	C+
Western Conn State Univ	CT	18,327	LC
Western Washington Univ	WA	18,519	VC
Westfield State Univ	MA	18,297	C
Westminster College	MO	31,720	VC
Wheaton College	IL	40,720	MC
Wheaton College	MA	54,934	HC+
Whitman College	WA	55,988	MC
Whittier College	CA	43,416	VC
Widener Univ	PA	52,418	C
Willamette Univ	OR	56,450	VC+
William Paterson Univ of New Jersey	NJ	21,694	C
William Penn Univ	IA	26,000	C
Wilson College	PA	35,080	C
Winthrop Univ	SC	21,120	C
Wittenberg Univ	OH	47,962	C+
Wright State Univ	OH	16,983	C
Xavier Univ	OH	44,980	VC

ENVIRONMENTAL STUDIES

School	ST	$IS	SR
Adelphi Univ	NY	44,670	VC
Adrian College	MI	42,400	C
Alaska Pacific Univ	AK	43,592	VC
Albion College	MI	46,010	C
Alfred Univ	NY	41,770	C
Allegheny College	PA	50,980	HC
Alma College	MI	44,075	C
American Univ	DC	56,015	HC+
Amherst College	MA	58,744	MC
Appalachian State Univ	NC	12,919	VC
Aquinas College	MI	33,060	C
Ashford Univ	CA	10,480	C
Bard College	NY	61,940	MC
Bard College at Simon's Rock	MA	61,749	HC+
Bates College	ME	60,720	MC
Beloit College	WI	49,970	HC
Bemidji State Univ	MN	13,500	VC
Bennington College	VT	56,990	HC+
Bethel Univ	MN	34,940	VC
Binghamton Univ/The SUNY	NY	21,648	HC+
Birmingham-Southern College	AL	44,168	VC+
Boise State Univ	ID	13,469	LC
Boston Univ	MA	60,694	MC
Bowdoin College	ME	59,568	MC
Bowling Green State Univ	OH	18,970	C
Brandeis Univ	MA		MC
Brenau Univ - Women's College	GA	26,650	LC
Brigham Young Univ	UT	12,100	HC
Brown Univ	RI	59,428	MC
Calif Lutheran Univ	CA	49,540	C+
Cal State, East Bay	CA	16,549	C
Cal State, San Bernardino	CA	12,000	C
Calvin College	MI	39,120	VC
Canisius College	NY	44,900	C
Carleton College	MN	60,102	MC
Catawba College	NC	37,240	LC
Cazenovia College	NY	43,464	C
Chaminade Univ of Honolulu	HI	31,664	LC
Champlain College	VT	46,650	VC+
Chatham Univ	PA	43,797	C
Christopher Newport Univ	VA	21,960	VC
CUNY/Brooklyn College	NY	15,884	C+
Claremont McKenna College	CA	62,215	MC
Coe College	IA	45,550	VC
Colby College	ME	57,510	MC
Colby-Sawyer College	NH	50,790	C
College of St. Benedict	MN	49,359	VC
College of the Holy Cross	MA	58,042	MC
Columbia College	MO	24,578	C
Concordia College - New York	NY	39,035	LC
Daemen College	NY	34,770	C
Dartmouth College	NH	57,996	HC
Davidson College	NC	58,146	MC
Denison Univ	OH	54,640	HC+
Dickinson College	PA	57,662	HC+
Dominican Univ of Calif	CA	51,250	C
Drew Univ/College of Liberal Arts	NJ	57,516	C
Drexel Univ	PA	61,418	VC+
Drury Univ	MO	31,909	VC
Earlham College	IN	51,470	HC
Eastern Univ	PA	37,704	C

School	ST	$IS	SR
Eckerd College	FL	43,902	C
Elon Univ	NC	41,914	VC+
Emmanuel College	MA	47,985	VC
Emory Univ	GA	56,368	MC
Eugene Lang College/The New School for Liberal Arts	NY	55,650	C
Florida Gulf Coast Univ	FL		C
Florida Inst of Technology	FL	48,290	VC
Florida Southern College	FL	40,150	C
Florida State Univ	FL	16,715	VC
Fort Lewis College	CO	15,513	C
Franklin and Marshall College	PA	60,799	MC
George Mason Univ	VA	15,724	VC
Goddard College	VT	16,418	VC
Gonzaga Univ	WA	46,441	HC
Goodwin College	CT	19,400	LC
Goshen College	IN	35,900	VC
Goucher College	MD	52,040	VC+
Green Mountain College	VT	45,228	LC
Guilford College	NC	42,800	C
Gustavus Adolphus College	MN	48,170	VC
Hamilton College	NY	55,620	MC
Hamline Univ	MN	45,678	VC
Hawaii Pacific Univ	HI	34,360	C
Hendrix College	AR	50,202	VC
Hofstra Univ	NY	51,810	VC+
Hollins Univ	VA	43,295	VC
Illinois Wesleyan Univ	IL	48,452	HC
Indiana Univ Bloomington	IN	19,801	VC
Indiana Univ-Purdue Univ Indianapolis	IN	17,611	C
Ithaca College	NY	53,864	HC
Juniata College	PA	49,340	VC
Keene State College	NH	23,232	LC
King's College	PA	43,502	C
Knox College	IL	44,865	VC+
Lasell College	MA	43,750	C
Lawrence Univ	WI	46,371	HC
Lehigh Univ	PA	56,770	MC
Lenoir-Rhyne College	NC	35,984	C
Lewis & Clark College	OR	54,382	MC
Linfield College-McMinnville Campus	OR	47,676	C
Louisiana State Univ	LA	18,677	C+
Loyola Univ New Orleans	LA	46,581	VC
Luther College	IA	45,720	C+
Lynchburg College	VA	42,645	C
Lynn Univ	FL	43,500	LC
Lyon College	AR	32,090	C+
Macalester College	MN	57,691	MC
Manchester Univ	IN	35,070	C
Manhattanville College	NY	50,740	VC
Marietta College	OH	42,135	C+
Maryville College	TN	33,150	C+
Maryville Univ of St. Louis	MO	35,856	VC
Mass College of Liberal Arts	MA	18,613	C
Mercer Univ	GA	44,201	VC
Meredith College	NC	31,420	C
Mich State Univ	MI	22,450	VC
Middlebury College	VT	59,160	MC
Mills College	CA	54,119	VC
Missouri State Univ	MO	13,996	C+
Mitchell College	CT	40,983	C
Molloy College	NY	40,440	C
Mount Holyoke College	MA	55,146	MC
Naropa Univ	CO	39,166	SP
Neumann Univ	PA	31,078	LC
New College of Florida	FL	14,504	VC
New York Univ	NY	61,470	MC
Niagara Univ	NY	41,010	C
Northeastern Illinois Univ	IL	10,318	LC
Northeastern Univ	MA	55,296	MC
Northern Arizona Univ	AZ	19,010	C
Oberlin College	OH	61,788	MC
Ohio Dominican Univ	OH	38,380	C+
Ohio Northern Univ	OH	42,075	VC
Okla City Univ	OK	40,476	VC
Pace Univ	NY	53,367	C
Penn State Univ/Altoona	PA	11,464	C
Piedmont College	GA	30,136	C
Pittsburg State Univ	KS	12,032	C
Plymouth State Univ	NH	23,148	LC
Point Park Univ	PA	36,390	C
Pomona College	CA	57,680	MC
Prescott College	AZ	33,284	C
Queens College/The CUNY	NY	17,107	VC
Queens Univ of Charlotte	NC	39,543	C+
Ramapo College of New Jersey	NJ	24,938	C
Randolph College	VA	45,660	VC
Randolph-Macon College	VA	49,869	C+
Reed College	OR	57,780	MC
Regis Univ	CO	41,318	C
Rhodes College	TN	51,900	HC+
Roanoke College	VA	49,976	C
Rocky Mountain College	MT	32,242	C
Rowan Univ	NJ	24,022	VC+
St. John's Univ	MN	47,984	C
St. Mary's College of Calif	CA	53,550	C
St. Michael's College	VT	49,975	VC
Salisbury Univ	MD	19,180	VC
San Diego State Univ	CA	21,611	C+
San Francisco State Univ	CA	18,514	C
San Jose State Univ	CA	19,133	LC

School	ST	$IS	SR
Scripps College	CA	61,940	MC
Seattle Univ	WA	49,035	VC+
Seton Hall Univ	NJ	45,902	C
Sewanee: The Univ of the South	TN	47,700	HC+
Shepherd Univ	WV	15,875	C
Simmons College	MA	49,966	VC
Skidmore College	NY	59,942	HC
Southeastern Okla State Univ	OK	7,966	LC
Southern Methodist Univ	TX	60,585	MC
Southern Nazarene Univ	OK	24,354	C
Southern New Hampshire Univ	NH	38,100	C
Southern Oregon Univ	OR	17,874	C
Southwestern Univ	TX	45,660	VC
St. John's Univ	NY	55,070	C+
St. Lawrence Univ	NY	59,972	VC
St. Olaf College	MN	51,200	HC+
SUNY / College of Environmental Science and Forestry	NY	18,351	VC
Stonehill College	MA	46,780	HC
Stony Brook Univ / SUNY	NY	20,078	HC+
Suffolk Univ	MA	47,298	C
SUNY Fredonia/The SUNY at Fredonia	NY	19,840	VC
Taylor Univ	IN	37,821	VC+
Temple Univ	PA	24,392	VC
Tenn Wesleyan College	TN	21,250	C
Texas A&M Univ at Galveston	TX	11,258	C
The College of Idaho	ID	31,277	C+
The College of New Rochelle	NY	33,600	VC
The Pennsylvania State Univ - Univ Park	PA	28,022	VC+
The SUNY at Potsdam	NY	18,473	C
The Univ of Okla	OK	18,621	VC
The Univ of Utah	UT	16,463	VC
Thomas Edison State College	NJ	5,700	SP
Trinity Univ	TX	48,150	HC+
Union College	NY	60,240	MC
Unity College	ME	34,054	C
Univ at Albany / SUNY	NY	18,674	VC
Univ at Buffalo / The SUNY	NY	20,283	VC
Univ of Arizona	AZ	20,657	C
Univ of Calif at Irvine	CA	25,961	VC
Univ of Calif at Los Angeles	CA	25,686	MC
Univ of Calif at San Diego	CA	21,000	MC
Univ of Calif at Santa Cruz	CA	27,807	C+
Univ of Cincinnati	OH	21,506	VC
Univ of Evansville	IN	42,656	VC+
Univ of Hawaii at Hilo	HI	23,066	C
Univ of Illinois at Chicago	IL	24,505	VC
Univ of Kansas	KS	17,603	C+
Univ of Maine at Farmington	ME	18,187	LC
Univ of Maryland/Baltimore County	MD	18,000	VC
Univ of Mich/Ann Arbor	MI	22,102	MC
Univ of Mich/Dearborn	MI	9,885	VC
Univ of Minn/Duluth	MN	19,806	C
Univ of Montana	MT	14,105	C
Univ of Montana-Western	MT	9,753	LC
Univ of Nebr - Lincoln	NE	18,031	VC
Univ of Nebr at Omaha	NE	12,700	C
Univ of New England	ME	46,750	C
Univ of New Hampshire	NH	26,912	C
Univ of N Car at Chapel Hill	NC	18,928	MC
Univ of N Dak	ND	14,551	C
Univ of Oregon	OR	21,360	C+
Univ of Pennsylvania	PA	61,132	MC
Univ of Pittsburgh at Bradford	PA	21,802	C
Univ of Pittsburgh at Johnstown	PA	20,862	LC
Univ of Pittsburgh at Pittsburgh	PA	28,572	HC+
Univ of Redlands	CA	40,500	VC
Univ of Rochester	NY	60,668	MC
Univ of San Diego	CA	54,818	HC+
Univ of Southern Calif	CA	56,903	MC
Univ of St. Thomas - Houston	TX	37,690	C
Univ of Tulsa	OK	46,331	MC
Univ of Vermont	VT	27,006	VC+
Univ of Wisc/Green Bay	WI	19,074	C
Univ of Wisc/Madison	WI	18,757	HC+
Univ of Wyoming	WY	14,401	C+
Vassar College	NY	61,140	MC
Villanova Univ	PA	58,394	MC
Virginia Commonwealth Univ	VA	21,716	C
Virginia Wesleyan College	VA	28,433	LC
Viterbo Univ	WI	30,070	C
Warren Wilson College	NC	40,132	VC
Washington and Jefferson College	PA	51,948	VC
Washington College	MD	52,602	VC
Washington Univ in St. Louis	MO	69,844	MC
Wayland Baptist Univ	TX	18,912	LC
Webster Univ	MO	35,100	C+
Wellesley College	MA	59,038	MC
Wells College	NY	49,400	VC
Wesleyan Univ	CT	61,198	MC
West Chester Univ of Pennsylvania	PA	17,186	C
Western Mich Univ	MI	19,628	C

School	ST	$IS	SR
Western State Colo Univ	CO	16,924	C
Western Washington Univ	WA	18,519	VC
Westminster College	UT	37,708	C+
Wheeling Jesuit Univ	WV	33,500	C
Whitman College	WA	55,988	MC
Wilson College	PA	35,080	C
Winthrop Univ	SC	21,120	C
Wofford College	SC	45,795	VC
Worcester Polytechnic Inst	MA	55,860	MC
Yale Univ	CT	55,300	MC
Youngstown State Univ	OH	16,732	C

EQUESTRIAN STUDIES

School	ST	$IS	SR
Rocky Mountain College	MT	32,242	C

EQUINE SCIENCE

School	ST	$IS	SR
Asbury Univ	KY	32,038	VC
Auburn Univ	AL	22,378	VC+
Averett Univ	VA	37,750	LC
Bethany College	WV	35,282	LC
Centenary College	NJ	38,618	C
Colo State Univ-Fort Collins	CO	20,385	VC
Delaware Valley College	PA	29,944	C
Houghton College	NY	36,808	C
Johnson & Wales Univ/ Providence Campus	RI	29,576	C
Judson College	AL	26,794	C
Lake Erie College	OH	37,266	C
Midway College	KY	20,150	LC
Mount Ida College	MA	30,115	LC
Murray State Univ	KY	15,304	C
N Dak State Univ	ND		C
Okla Panhandle State Univ	OK	8,996	C
Otterbein College	OH	32,214	C
Rocky Mountain College	MT	32,242	C
St. Mary-of-the-Woods College	IN	37,722	LC
Salem International Univ	WV	21,090	LC
Savannah College of Art and Design	GA	48,005	SP
Stephens College	MO	38,042	VC
Truman State Univ	MO	15,541	HC
Univ of Findlay	OH	31,916	C
Univ of Louisville	KY	17,946	C
Univ of Minn Crookston	MN	17,834	C
Univ of Montana-Western	MT	9,753	LC
William Woods Univ	MO	24,260	C
Wilmington College	OH	29,784	C
Wilson College	PA	35,080	C

ESKIMO

School	ST	$IS	SR
Univ of Alaska Fairbanks	AK	15,130	C

ETHICS, POLITICS, AND SOCIAL POLICY

School	ST	$IS	SR
American Jewish Univ - College of A&S	CA	32,600	C
Drake Univ	IA	41,516	VC+
Goddard College	VT	16,418	VC
Millikin Univ	IL	38,940	C
Northwestern Univ	IL	61,640	MC
Pine Manor College	MA	32,659	LC
Prescott College	AZ	33,284	C
Smith College	MA	59,674	MC
Syracuse Univ	NY	56,346	VC
Unity College	ME	34,054	C
Univ of Dayton	OH	49,070	VC
Univ of Mass Boston	MA	23,066	VC
Univ of Northern Colo	CO	18,446	C
Univ of Southern Calif	CA	56,903	MC
Wells College	NY	49,400	VC
Wheeling Jesuit Univ	WV	33,500	C
Yale Univ	CT	55,300	MC

ETHNIC STUDIES

School	ST	$IS	SR
Albion College	MI	46,010	C
Arizona State Univ, at the West Campus	AZ	19,251	C
Bowling Green State Univ	OH	18,970	C
Brown Univ	RI	59,428	MC
Calif Polytechnic State Univ	CA	19,847	HC
Cal State, East Bay	CA	16,549	C
Cal State, Fullerton	CA	25,188	C
Cal State, San Bernardino	CA	12,000	C
Cal State, Stanislaus	CA	18,582	C
CUNY/City College	NY	20,319	HC+
Colo State Univ-Fort Collins	CO	20,385	VC
Cornell College	IA	44,930	VC
Kansas State Univ	KS	15,497	VC
Kent State Univ	OH	19,920	C
Messiah College	PA	40,690	C+
Metropolitan State Univ	MN	5,923	
Mills College	CA	54,119	VC
Minn State Univ, Mankato	MN	15,616	C
New York Univ	NY	61,470	MC
Oregon State Univ	OR	20,273	VC
Sonoma State Univ	CA	20,541	C
St. Catherine Univ	MN	37,782	C+
St. Olaf College	MN	51,200	HC+
SUNY at Purchase	NY	16,951	C

ST = STATE   **$IS = IN-STATE COSTS**   **SR = SELECTOR RATING**

School	ST	$IS	SR
Stony Brook Univ / SUNY	NY	20,078	HC+
The Univ of Utah	UT	16,463	VC
Univ of Calif at Berkeley	CA	23,322	MC
Univ of Calif at Riverside	CA	27,204	C+
Univ of Calif at San Diego	CA	21,000	MC
Univ of Colo Boulder	CO	22,605	VC+
Univ of Colo Denver	CO	17,904	C
Univ of Hawaii at Manoa	HI	19,379	VC
Univ of Illinois at Chicago	IL	24,505	VC
Univ of Nebr - Lincoln	NE	18,031	VC
Univ of North Florida	FL	15,870	VC
Univ of Oregon	OR	21,360	C+
Univ of San Diego	CA	54,818	HC+
Univ of Texas at Austin	TX	44,074	HC
Univ of Vermont	VT	27,006	VC+
Univ of Washington	WA	14,722	VC
Univ of Wisc-Milwaukee	WI	18,436	C
Washington State Univ	WA	20,461	C
Washington Univ in St. Louis	MO	69,844	MC
Westfield State Univ	MA	18,297	C
Whitman College	WA	55,988	MC
Wichita State Univ	KS	14,607	C
Yale Univ	CT	55,300	MC

EUROPEAN STUDIES

School	ST	$IS	SR
Amherst College	MA	58,744	MC
Barnard College/Columbia Univ	NY	39,000	MC
Bates College	ME	60,720	MC
Belmont Univ	TN	39,190	VC+
Bennington College	VT	56,990	HC+
Boston Univ	MA	60,694	MC
Brandeis Univ	MA		MC
Cal State, Fullerton	CA	25,188	C
Canisius College	NY	44,900	C
Emory and Henry College	VA	387,460	C
George Washington Univ	DC	57,108	MC
Georgetown College	KY	41,440	C+
Harvard College/Harvard Univ	MA	49,000	MC
Hillsdale College	MI	32,866	MC
Hobart and William Smith Colleges	NY	60,034	HC+
John Carroll Univ	OH	46,300	C+
Lipscomb Univ	TN	37,490	VC
Loyola Marymount Univ	CA	54,649	VC+
Middlebury College	VT	59,160	MC
Millsaps College	MS	43,888	VC+
New York Univ	NY	61,470	MC
Northwestern Univ	IL	61,640	MC
Ohio Univ	OH	21,080	C
Pitzer College	CA	54,988	MC
St. Joseph's Univ	PA	55,006	VC
San Diego State Univ	CA	21,611	C+
Scripps College	CA	61,940	MC
Seattle Pacific Univ	WA	41,559	VC+
Smith College	MA	59,674	MC
Stony Brook Univ / SUNY	NY	20,078	HC+
Suffolk Univ	MA	47,298	C
Syracuse Univ	NY	56,346	VC
Texas State Univ	TX	17,128	C
Univ of Arkansas at Fayetteville	AR	18,352	C+
Univ of Calif at Irvine	CA	25,961	VC
Univ of Calif at Los Angeles	CA	25,686	MC
Univ of Delaware	DE	23,612	VC
Univ of Kansas	KS	17,603	C+
Univ of Mich/Ann Arbor	MI	22,102	MC
Univ of Minn/Morris	MN	17,150	VC
Univ of Nebr - Lincoln	NE	18,031	VC
Univ of New Hampshire	NH	26,912	C
Univ of New Mexico	NM	15,300	C
Univ of N Car at Chapel Hill	NC	18,928	MC
Univ of S Car at Columbia	SC	19,725	VC+
Univ of Vermont	VT	27,006	VC+
Vanderbilt Univ	TN	58,220	MC
Washington Univ in St. Louis	MO	69,844	MC
Webster Univ	MO	35,100	C
Westmont College	CA	41,500	HC

EVOLUTIONARY BIOLOGY

School	ST	$IS	SR
Angelo State Univ	TX	15,049	NC
Bennington College	VT	56,990	HC+
Binghamton Univ/The SUNY	NY	21,648	HC+
Case Western Reserve Univ	OH	56,534	MC
Florida State Univ	FL	16,715	VC
Marshall Univ	WV	14,820	C
Princeton Univ	NJ	53,795	MC
Rutgers, The State Univ of New Jersey/New Brunswick	NJ	25,562	VC
Ohio State Univ-Columbus Campus	OH	19,887	HC+
Tulane Univ	LA	60,861	MC
Univ of Calif at Santa Barbara	CA	27,551	HC
Univ of Calif at Santa Cruz	CA	27,807	C+
Univ of Colo Boulder	CO	22,605	VC+
Univ of Conn	CT	24,706	VC
Univ of Mich/Ann Arbor	MI	22,102	MC
Univ of Minn/Twin Cities	MN		HC
Yale Univ	CT	55,300	MC

EXERCISE SCIENCE

School	ST	$IS	SR
Abilene Christian Univ	TX	38,400	C+
Adams State Univ	CO	13,358	LC
Adrian College	MI	42,400	C
Albion College	MI	46,010	C
Alma College	MI	44,075	C
Angelo State Univ	TX	15,049	NC
Appalachian State Univ	NC	12,919	VC
Arkansas State Univ	AR	15,470	C
Asbury Univ	KY	32,038	VC
Augustana College	SD	36,500	VC
Baker Univ	KS	33,350	C+
Baldwin Wallace Univ	OH	38,318	C
Barton College	NC	27,660	LC
Becker College	MA	41,420	C
Belhaven Univ	MS	27,170	C
Bellarmine Univ	KY	42,950	VC
Belmont Univ	TN	39,190	VC+
Berry College	GA	39,254	VC
Bethel College	IN	31,560	C
Bethel Univ	MN	34,940	VC
Black Hills State Univ	SD	13,947	C
Bloomsburg Univ of Pennsylvania	PA	13,598	C
Blue Mountain College	MS	15,634	LC
Bluefield College	VA	17,230	C+
Bowling Green State Univ	OH	18,970	C
Bridgewater College	VA	41,450	C
Brigham Young Univ	UT	12,100	HC
Bryan College	TN	24,194	C
Cabrini Univ	PA	40,859	LC
Calif Baptist Univ	CA	38,792	C
Calif Lutheran Univ	CA	49,540	C+
Cal State, Fullerton	CA	25,188	C
Cal State, Northridge	CA	28,690	LC
Cal State, San Bernardino	CA	12,000	C
Calvin College	MI	39,120	VC
Campbell Univ	NC	37,570	VC
Campbellsville Univ	KY	27,720	C
Canisius College	NY	44,900	C
Capital Univ	OH	41,050	VC
Carroll Univ	WI	38,100	C
Castleton State College	VT	20,186	C
Cedarville Univ	OH	32,860	VC
Central College	IA	42,104	C+
Central Washington Univ	WA	11,730	C
Chatham Univ	PA	43,797	C
Cleveland State Univ	OH	21,776	C
Coastal Carolina Univ	SC	18,580	C
Colby-Sawyer College	NH	50,790	C
College of Charleston	SC	22,145	VC
College of New Jersey	NJ	25,376	NC
College of St. Scholastica	MN	41,440	C
Colo State Univ-Fort Collins	CO	20,385	VC
Colo State Univ-Pueblo	CO	16,183	C
Columbus State Univ	GA	13,176	C
Concordia College - Moorhead	MN	39,974	C
Concordia Univ Irvine	CA	35,390	C
Concordia Univ Nebr	NE	26,000	VC
Corban Univ	OR	37,380	C+
Cornerstone Univ and Grand Rapids Theological Seminary	MI	33,338	C
Creighton Univ	NE	45,356	VC
De Sales Univ	PA	43,970	C
Dordt College	IA	34,160	C+
Drury Univ	MO	31,909	VC
D'Youville College	NY	29,850	C
East Carolina Univ	NC	14,169	C
East Central Univ	OK	10,223	LC
Eastern Mich Univ	MI	18,604	C
Eastern Univ	PA	37,704	C
Elmhurst College	IL	43,336	C
Elon Univ	NC	41,914	VC+
Endicott College	MA	43,228	VC+
Fitchburg State Univ	MA	18,173	C
Florida Gulf Coast Univ	FL		C
Florida International Univ	FL	17,747	C+
Florida Southern College	FL	40,150	C+
Fort Lewis College	CO	15,513	C
Franklin College	IN	36,585	C
Frostburg State Univ	MD	15,264	LC
Furman Univ	SC	54,006	HC
Georgetown College	KY	41,440	C+
Georgia College and State Univ	GA	18,900	C+
Georgia Southern Univ	GA	16,942	C
Georgia Southwestern State Univ	GA	13,246	C
Georgia State Univ	GA	15,582	VC
Georgian Court Univ	NJ	41,594	LC
Gonzaga Univ	WA	46,441	HC
Grand Canyon Univ	AZ	24,540	VC
Grand Valley State Univ	MI	17,998	C+
Greensboro College	NC	28,740	LC
Grove City College	PA	24,022	VC
Guilford College	NC	42,800	C
Hamline Univ	MN	45,678	VC
Hannibal-LaGrange Univ	MO	24,490	C
Harding Univ	AR	23,556	C
Hardin-Simmons Univ	TX	23,560	C+
Hendrix College	AR	50,202	VC+
High Point Univ	NC	39,800	C
Hillsdale College	MI	32,866	MC
Hofstra Univ	NY	51,810	VC+
Hope College	MI	38,650	VC
Howard Payne Univ	TX	17,115	C
Huntingdon College	AL	33,100	C
Huntington Univ	IN	32,220	C+
Illinois College	IL	25,770	VC
Illinois State Univ	IL	23,110	VC
Indiana Univ Bloomington	IN	19,801	VC
Indiana Univ-Purdue Univ Indianapolis	IN	17,611	C
Ithaca College	NY	53,864	HC
John Carroll Univ	OH	46,300	C+
Kansas State Univ	KS	15,497	VC
Kennesaw State Univ	GA		C
King's College	PA	43,502	C
La Sierra Univ	CA	35,694	VC
LaGrange College	GA	37,670	C
Lake Superior State Univ	MI	18,121	C
Lander Univ	SC	22,514	C+
Lenoir-Rhyne College	NC	35,984	C
Liberty Univ	VA	19,101	C
Linfield College-McMinnville Campus	OR	47,676	C
Lipscomb Univ	TN	37,490	VC
Loras College	IA	37,432	VC
Louisiana College	LA	15,746	C
Loyola Univ Chicago	IL	51,646	VC+
Lubbock Christian Univ	TX	26,308	C
Lynchburg College	VA	42,645	C
Malone Univ	OH	35,364	C
Marquette Univ	WI	46,930	VC+
Marshall Univ	WV	14,820	C
McMurry Univ	TX	25,962	LC
Mercy College	NY	30,456	C
Meredith College	NC	31,420	C
Messiah College	PA	40,690	C+
Mich Tech Univ	MI	23,556	HC
Milligan College	TN	27,510	C
Minn State Univ, Mankato	MN	15,616	C
Minn State Univ, Moorhead	MN	13,392	VC
Missouri Baptist Univ	MO	31,830	C
Missouri State Univ	MO	13,996	C+
Missouri Valley College	MO	22,200	C
Monmouth College	IL	40,850	C
Montreat College	NC	31,298	C
Mount Vernon Nazarene Univ	OH	29,590	C
Murray State Univ	KY	15,304	C
Nebr Wesleyan Univ	NE	29,774	C+
Norfolk State Univ	VA	10,531	LC
N Car Wesleyan College	NC	29,440	C
North Central College	IL	38,343	VC
North Park Univ	IL	30,130	C
Northern Arizona Univ	AZ	19,010	C
Northern Kentucky Univ	KY	21,134	C
Northwest Christian Univ	OR	27,399	C
Northwestern College	MN	24,000	C
Northwestern State Univ of Louisiana	LA	14,368	C
Nova Southeastern Univ	FL	37,280	VC
Ohio Dominican Univ	OH	38,380	C+
Ohio Univ	OH	21,080	C
Okla City Univ	OK	40,476	VC
Olivet Nazarene Univ	IL	29,990	C
Oregon State Univ	OR	20,273	VC
Palm Beach Atlantic Univ	FL	34,874	VC
Pennsylvania College of Technology	PA	26,286	NC
Pfeiffer Univ	NC	33,700	LC
Point Loma Nazarene Univ	CA	41,006	C+
Purdue Univ/West Lafayette	IN	20,024	HC
Queens College/The CUNY	NY	17,107	VC
Queens Univ of Charlotte	NC	39,543	C+
Quincy Univ	IL	34,980	LC
Rice Univ	TX	43,288	MC
Ripon College	WI	36,959	C+
Roanoke College	VA	49,976	C
Rocky Mountain College	MT	32,242	C
Rutgers, The State Univ of New Jersey/New Brunswick	NJ	25,562	VC
Sacred Heart Univ	CT	49,264	VC
Saginaw Valley State Univ	MI	17,369	C
St. Louis Univ	MO	48,346	HC
Salisbury Univ	MD	19,180	VC
Samford Univ	AL	37,060	C+
San Diego State Univ	CA	21,611	C+
San Francisco State Univ	CA	18,514	C
Schreiner Univ	TX	32,734	LC
Seattle Pacific Univ	WA	41,559	VC+
Seattle Univ	WA	49,035	VC+
Shenandoah Univ	VA	39,916	C
Shippensburg Univ of Pennsylvania	PA	20,934	C
Simmons College	MA	49,996	VC
Simpson College	IA	36,086	C
Skidmore College	NY	59,942	HC
Smith College	MA	59,674	MC
S Dak State Univ	SD	14,296	C
Southern Illinois Univ Edwardsville	IL	17,532	C
Southern Nazarene Univ	OK	24,354	C
Southwestern Adventist Univ	TX	23,026	LC
Southwestern Univ	TX	45,660	VC
Spring Arbor Univ	MI	26,740	C
St. Catherine Univ	MN	37,782	C+
St. Olaf College	MN	51,200	HC+
Sterling College	KS	27,216	C
Taylor Univ	IN	37,821	VC+
Tenn Wesleyan College	TN	21,250	C
Texas State Univ	TX	17,128	C
Texas Tech Univ	TX	14,243	C
Texas Wesleyan Univ	TX	31,382	C
The College of Idaho	ID	31,277	C+
Ohio State Univ-Columbus Campus	OH	19,887	HC+
The SUNY/College at Brockport	NY	19,002	C
The Univ of N Car at Greensboro	NC	12,848	C
The Univ of N Car at Pembroke	NC	13,388	LC
The Univ of Okla	OK	18,621	VC
The Univ of Utah	UT	16,463	VC
Towson Univ	MD	16,000	VC
Transylvania Univ	KY	42,660	VC+
Trevecca Nazarene Univ	TN	31,186	C
Trinity Washington Univ	DC	30,250	C+
Truman State Univ	MO	15,541	HC
Union College	KY	29,955	C
Univ at Buffalo / The SUNY	NY	20,283	VC
Univ of Akron	OH	20,436	C
Univ of Arkansas at Fayetteville	AR	18,352	C+
Univ of Arkansas at Monticello	AR	12,076	NC
Univ of Central Arkansas	AR	13,667	VC
Univ of Central Florida	FL	15,668	VC+
Univ of Central Okla	OK	12,293	C
Univ of Conn	CT	24,706	VC
Univ of Dayton	OH	49,070	VC
Univ of Evansville	IN	42,656	VC
Univ of Florida	FL	15,943	HC
Univ of Georgia	GA	20,082	VC
Univ of Hawaii at Manoa	HI	19,379	VC
Univ of Idaho	ID	14,558	C
Univ of Illinois at Chicago	IL	24,505	VC
Univ of Illinois at Urbana-Champaign	IL	26,450	VC
Univ of Indianapolis	IN	31,740	LC
Univ of Jamestown	ND	24,738	C
Univ of Louisiana at Monroe	LA	12,998	C
Univ of Mary	ND	26,714	C
Univ of Mary Hardin-Baylor	TX	31,950	C+
Univ of Mass Amherst	MA	24,215	VC+
Univ of Mass Boston	MA	23,066	VC
Univ of Mass Lowell	MA	19,316	C
Univ of Miami	FL	57,034	MC
Univ of Mich/Ann Arbor	MI	22,102	MC
Univ of Miss	MS	16,704	C+
Univ of Mount Union	OH	35,130	C
Univ of Nebr - Lincoln	NE	18,031	VC
Univ of Nevada, Las Vegas	NV	17,303	C
Univ of New England	ME	46,750	C
Univ of New Mexico	NM	15,300	C
Univ of N Car at Chapel Hill	NC	18,928	MC
Univ of N Car at Charlotte	NC	15,547	C
Univ of Northern Colo	CO	18,446	C
Univ of Puget Sound	WA	54,608	HC
Univ of St. Francis	IN	29,810	C
Univ of San Francisco	CA	54,770	VC
Univ of Scranton	PA	51,940	VC
Univ of S Car Aiken	SC	16,712	C
Univ of S Car at Columbia	SC	19,725	VC+
Univ of Southern Calif	CA	56,903	MC
Univ of Southern Indiana	IN	14,885	C
Univ of Tampa	FL	35,160	VC
Univ of the Cumberlands	KY	27,500	C
Univ of Tulsa	OK	46,331	MC
Univ of Vermont	VT	27,006	VC+
Univ of Wisc/Green Bay	WI	19,074	C
Univ of Wisc/La Crosse	WI	9,304	VC
Univ of Wisc/Superior	WI	14,314	C
Univ of Wisc-Milwaukee	WI	18,436	C
Urbana Univ	OH	30,820	C
Ursinus College	PA	57,580	VC
Valparaiso Univ	IN	44,940	VC+
Vanguard Univ of Southern Calif	CA	35,833	VC
Wake Forest Univ	NC	58,838	MC
Walsh Univ	OH	35,100	C
Warner Univ	FL	18,000	C
Washington Adventist Univ	MD	25,859	LC
Washington State Univ	WA	20,461	C
Wayne State College	NE	11,764	NC
Wayne State Univ	MI	22,063	C
Waynesburg Univ	PA	30,150	C
Wesley College	DE	31,115	LC
West Chester Univ of Pennsylvania	PA	17,186	C
West Texas A&M Univ	TX	13,478	C
Western Illinois Univ	IL	20,732	C
Western Mich Univ	MI	19,628	C
Westmont College	CA	41,500	HC
Willamette Univ	OR	56,450	VC+
Wilson College	PA	35,080	C
Winona State Univ	MN	16,640	C
Winthrop Univ	SC	21,120	C
Wright State Univ	OH	16,983	C
York College / The CUNY	NY	5,496	VC
Youngstown State Univ	OH	16,732	C

ST = STATE $IS = IN-STATE COSTS   SR = SELECTOR RATING

EXPERIMENTAL PSYCHOLOGY

School	ST	$IS	SR
Blackburn College	IL	21,350	C
Immaculata Univ	PA	43,000	C
Prescott College	AZ	33,284	C
Univ of Louisiana at Monroe	LA	12,998	C
Univ of S Car at Columbia	SC	19,725	VC+

FACILITIES MANAGEMENT

School	ST	$IS	SR
Farmingdale State College	NY	19,673	C
Ferris State Univ	MI	20,047	C

FAMILY AND COMMUNITY SERVICES

School	ST	$IS	SR
Central Washington Univ	WA	11,730	C
East Carolina Univ	NC	14,169	C
John Brown Univ	AR	32,056	VC+
Kansas State Univ	KS	15,497	VC
Mich State Univ	MI	22,450	VC
Montclair State Univ	NJ	22,614	C
Ohio Univ	OH	21,080	C
Point Loma Nazarene Univ	CA	41,006	C+
Prairie View A&M Univ	TX	15,205	LC
Purdue Univ/West Lafayette	IN	20,024	HC
Union Univ	TN	28,260	VC
Univ of Delaware	DE	23,612	VC
Univ of New Haven	CT	48,940	C
Univ of Northern Iowa	IA	15,795	C
Univ of Oregon	OR	21,360	C+

FAMILY STUDIES/SOC SERV/ MARRIAGE FAMILY

School	ST	$IS	SR
College of the Ozarks	MO		VC
Indiana Univ Bloomington	IN	19,801	VC

FAMILY/CONSUMER RESOURCE MANAGEMENT

School	ST	$IS	SR
Cal State, Northridge	CA	28,690	LC
East Central Univ	OK	10,223	VC
Iowa State Univ	IA	16,403	C
Mich State Univ	MI	22,450	VC
Northwest Missouri State Univ	MO	17,347	C
Ohio State Univ at Lima	OH	7,140	C
Ohio Univ	OH	21,080	C
Pittsburg State Univ	KS	12,032	C
Seattle Pacific Univ	WA	41,559	VC+
Seton Hill Univ	PA	35,172	C
S Dak State Univ	SD	14,296	C
Southern Illinois Univ Carbondale	IL	21,942	C
Texas Tech Univ	TX	14,243	C
Ohio State Univ-Columbus Campus	OH	19,887	HC+
Univ of Hawaii at Manoa	HI	19,379	C
Univ of Missouri/Columbia	MO	18,201	MC
West Virginia Univ	WV	16,542	C+

FAMILY/CONSUMER STUDIES

School	ST	$IS	SR
Abilene Christian Univ	TX	38,400	C+
Alabama A&M Univ	AL	10,084	C
Alderson Broaddus Univ	WV	28,656	C
Anderson Univ	IN	36,100	C
Andrews Univ	MI	28,030	C
Appalachian State Univ	NC	12,919	VC
Ashford Univ	CA	10,480	C
Ball State Univ	IN	17,850	C
Baylor Univ	TX	50,329	HC
Bluffton Univ	OH	38,948	C
Bowling Green State Univ	OH	18,970	C
Bradley Univ	IL	31,874	VC
Bridgewater College	VA	41,450	C
Brigham Young Univ	UT	12,100	HC
Cal State, Fresno	CA	17,405	C
Cal State, Long Beach	CA	17,502	C+
Cal State, Northridge	CA	28,690	LC
Central Washington Univ	WA	11,730	C
College of the Ozarks	MO		VC
Colo State Univ-Fort Collins	CO	20,385	VC
Concordia Univ, Ann Arbor	MI	27,220	VC
Cornerstone Univ and Grand Rapids Theological Seminary	MI	33,338	C
Delta State Univ	MS	12,292	LC
East Central Univ	OK	10,223	VC
Eastern Illinois Univ	IL	20,466	C
Fairmont State Univ	WV	12,098	LC
Florida State Univ	FL	16,715	VC
Fontbonne Univ	MO	31,384	C
Framingham State Univ	MA	18,854	C
Freed-Hardeman Univ	TN	19,060	C
Gallaudet Univ	DC	25,380	SP
George Fox Univ	OR	40,750	C+
Hampshire College	MA	58,320	MC
Henderson State Univ	AR	14,584	C
Idaho State Univ	ID	12,307	C
Illinois State Univ	IL	23,110	VC
Indiana Univ of Pennsylvania	PA	20,846	LC
Iowa State Univ	IA	16,403	C
Kansas State Univ	KS	15,497	VC
Lamar Univ	TX	6,820	LC
Liberty Univ	VA	19,101	C
Lipscomb Univ	TN	37,490	VC
Lubbock Christian Univ	TX	26,308	C
Madonna Univ	MI	24,540	VC
Marywood Univ	PA	45,595	C
Mercyhurst Univ	PA	40,700	C
Meredith College	NC	31,420	C
Messiah College	PA	40,690	C+
Miami Univ	OH	24,191	VC
Mich State Univ	MI	22,450	VC
Middle Tenn State Univ	TN	8,650	C
Minn State Univ, Mankato	MN	15,616	C
Miss College	MS	21,998	C
Missouri State Univ	MO	13,996	C+
Mount Vernon Nazarene Univ	OH	29,590	C
New Mexico State Univ	NM	14,050	C
Nicholls State Univ	LA	7,095	C
Northwestern State Univ of Louisiana	LA	14,368	C
Oakwood Univ	AL	25,529	NC
Ohio Univ	OH	21,080	C
Olivet Nazarene Univ	IL	29,990	C
Oregon State Univ	OR	20,273	VC
Oswego / SUNY	NY	20,009	VC
Pittsburg State Univ	KS	12,032	C
Purdue Univ/West Lafayette	IN	20,024	HC
Queens College/The CUNY	NY	17,107	VC
San Francisco State Univ	CA	18,514	C
Seattle Pacific Univ	WA	41,559	VC+
Seton Hill Univ	PA	35,172	C
Shepherd Univ	WV	15,875	C
S Dak State Univ	SD	14,296	C
Southeastern Louisiana Univ	LA	13,325	C
Southern Univ and A&M College	LA	9,761	LC
St. Catherine Univ	MN	37,782	C+
Stephen F. Austin State Univ	TX	14,668	C
Tenn State Univ	TN	9,048	C
Texas State Univ	TX	17,128	C
Texas Tech Univ	TX	14,243	C
Texas Woman's Univ	TX	13,633	LC
Ohio State Univ-Columbus Campus	OH	19,887	HC+
The Univ of Utah	UT	16,463	VC
Towson Univ	MD	16,000	VC
Univ of Akron	OH	20,436	C
Univ of Arizona	AZ	20,657	C
Univ of Arkansas at Pine Bluff	AR	13,378	C
Univ of Central Arkansas	AR	13,667	VC
Univ of Central Okla	OK	12,293	C
Univ of Idaho	ID	14,558	C
Univ of Illinois at Urbana-Champaign	IL	26,450	HC
Univ of Maryland - College Park	MD	20,060	HC
Univ of Montevallo	AL	17,060	C
Univ of Nebr - Lincoln	NE	18,031	VC
Univ of Nebr at Kearney	NE	14,855	LC
Univ of New Hampshire	NH	26,912	C
Univ of New Mexico	NM	15,300	C
Univ of PR Recinto de Rio Piedras	PR	5,750	
Univ of St. Joseph	CT	45,630	C
Univ of Wisc/Madison	WI	18,757	HC+
Univ of Wisc/Stevens Point	WI	14,043	C
Univ of Wisc/Stout	WI	15,459	C
Univ of Wyoming	WY	14,401	C+
Urbana Univ	OH	30,820	C
Walsh Univ	OH	35,100	C
Washington State Univ	WA	20,461	C
Wayne State College	NE	11,764	NC
Western Illinois Univ	IL	20,732	C
Western Mich Univ	MI	19,628	C
Youngstown State Univ	OH	16,732	C

FAMILY/JUVENILE JUSTICE

School	ST	$IS	SR
Georgetown College	KY	41,440	C+
Univ of Akron	OH	20,436	C
Univ of New Haven	CT	48,940	C
William Woods Univ	MO	24,260	C

FASHION DESIGN AND TECHNOLOGY

School	ST	$IS	SR
Baylor Univ	TX	50,329	HC
Bennington College	VT	56,990	HC+
Calif College of the Arts	CA	48,334	SP
Cazenovia College	NY	43,464	C
Centenary College	NJ	38,618	C
Columbus College of Art and Design	OH	37,732	SP
Dominican Univ	IL	37,628	C
Drexel Univ	PA	61,418	VC+
Fashion Inst of Technology/ SUNY	NY	18,362	SP
Florida State Univ	FL	16,715	VC
Framingham State Univ	MA	18,854	C
Howard Univ	DC	13,646	C
Illinois State Univ	IL	23,110	VC
Indiana Univ Bloomington	IN	19,801	VC
Iowa State Univ	IA	16,403	C
Kent State Univ	OH	19,920	C
Lasell College	MA	43,750	LC
Lindenwood Univ	MO	20,750	C
Marist College	NY	35,500	C
Marymount Univ	VA	39,480	C
Missouri State Univ	MO	13,996	C+
Moore College of Art and Design	PA	50,135	SP
Mount Ida College	MA	30,115	LC
Mount Mary Univ	WI	33,590	LC
Otis College of Art and Design	CA	35,404	SP
Parsons The New School for Design	NY	56,610	SP
Philadelphia Univ	PA	44,160	C
Pratt Inst	NY	55,956	SP
Purdue Univ/West Lafayette	IN	20,024	HC
Savannah College of Art and Design	GA	48,005	SP
School of the Art Inst of Chicago	IL	56,230	SP
St. Catherine Univ	MN	37,782	C+
Stephens College	MO	38,042	VC
Stevenson Univ	MD	41,470	C
Syracuse Univ	NY	56,346	VC
Texas Woman's Univ	TX	13,633	LC
Univ of Cincinnati	OH	21,506	VC
Univ of Delaware	DE	23,612	VC
Univ of North Texas	TX	15,628	C
Univ of the Incarnate Word	TX	37,316	LC
Ursuline College	OH	33,198	LC
Virginia Commonwealth Univ	VA	21,716	C
Washington Univ in St. Louis	MO	69,844	MC
Woodbury Univ	CA	34,500	LC

FASHION MERCHANDISING

School	ST	$IS	SR
Albright College	PA	46,660	C
Ashland Univ	OH	25,000	C
Auburn Univ	AL	22,378	VC+
Baylor Univ	TX	50,329	HC
Brenau Univ - Women's College	GA	26,650	LC
Canisius College	NY	44,900	C
Central Washington Univ	WA	11,730	C
Delaware State Univ	DE	16,722	LC
Dominican Univ	IL	37,628	C
Drexel Univ	PA	61,418	VC+
Eastern Mich Univ	MI	18,604	C
Fashion Inst of Technology/ SUNY	NY	18,362	SP
Florida State Univ	FL	16,715	VC
Fontbonne Univ	MO	31,384	C
Framingham State Univ	MA	18,854	C
Harding Univ	AR	23,556	C
Howard Univ	DC	13,646	C
Immaculata Univ	PA	43,000	C
Indiana Inst of Technology	IN	34,240	LC
Indiana Univ of Pennsylvania	PA	20,846	LC
Iowa State Univ	IA	16,403	C
Johnson & Wales Univ/ Providence Campus	RI	29,576	C
Kent State Univ	OH	19,920	C
Lasell College	MA	43,750	LC
LIM College	NY	41,575	LC
Lipscomb Univ	TN	37,490	VC
Lynn Univ	FL	43,500	LC
Marist College	NY	35,500	C
Mars Hill Univ	NC	22,950	LC
Marymount Univ	VA	39,480	C
Mercyhurst Univ	PA	40,700	C
Meredith College	NC	31,420	C
Missouri State Univ	MO	13,996	C+
Mount Ida College	MA	30,115	LC
Mount Mary Univ	WI	33,590	LC
New Mexico State Univ	NM	14,050	C
Newbury College	MA	43,280	LC
Northwood Univ	MI	26,331	LC
Ohio Univ	OH	21,080	C
Old Dominion Univ	VA	19,483	LC
Olivet Nazarene Univ	IL	29,990	C
Philadelphia Univ	PA	44,160	C
Pittsburg State Univ	KS	12,032	C
Purdue Univ/West Lafayette	IN	20,024	HC
Sacred Heart Univ	CT	49,264	VC
Savannah College of Art and Design	GA	48,005	SP
Southern Illinois Univ Carbondale	IL	21,942	C
Southern New Hampshire Univ	NH	38,100	C
St. Catherine Univ	MN	37,782	C+
Stephen F. Austin State Univ	TX	14,668	C
Stephens College	MO	38,042	VC
Stevenson Univ	MD	41,470	C
SUNY Oneonta / SUNY	NY	16,919	C+
Tarleton State Univ	TX	13,489	LC
Texas A&M Univ at Kingsville	TX	7,500	LC
Texas Christian Univ	TX	49,980	HC
Texas State Univ	TX	17,128	C
Texas Woman's Univ	TX	13,633	LC
Ohio State Univ-Columbus Campus	OH	19,887	HC+
Univ of Akron	OH	20,436	C
Univ of Bridgeport	CT	39,030	LC
Univ of Central Okla	OK	12,293	C
Univ of Georgia	GA	20,082	VC
Univ of Louisiana at Lafayette	LA	6,130	C
Univ of Nebr - Lincoln	NE	18,031	VC
Univ of the Incarnate Word	TX	37,316	LC
Ursuline College	OH	33,198	LC
Utah State Univ	UT	12,044	C
West Virginia Univ	WV	16,542	C+
Western Mich Univ	MI	19,628	C
Western Washington Univ	WA	18,519	VC
Woodbury Univ	CA	34,500	LC
Youngstown State Univ	OH	16,732	C

FASHION STUDIES

School	ST	$IS	SR
Ferris State Univ	MI	20,047	C

FEMINIST, GENDER, SEXUALITY STUDIES

School	ST	$IS	SR
Bryant Univ	RI	49,179	VC
Cornell Univ	NY	60,964	MC

FIBER SCIENCE AND APPAREL DESIGN

School	ST	$IS	SR
Cornell Univ	NY	60,964	MC

FIBER/TEXTILES/WEAVING

School	ST	$IS	SR
Adams State Univ	CO	13,358	LC
Fashion Inst of Technology/ SUNY	NY	18,362	SP
Florida State Univ	FL	16,715	VC
Kansas City Art Inst	MO	44,308	SP
Kutztown Univ of Pennsylvania	PA	16,909	LC
Maryland Inst College of Art	MD	39,500	SP
Savannah College of Art and Design	GA	48,005	SP
School of the Art Inst of Chicago	IL	56,230	SP
Temple Univ	PA	24,392	VC
Univ of Kansas	KS	17,603	C+
Univ of Mass Dartmouth	MA	22,223	C
Univ of Mich/Ann Arbor	MI	22,102	MC
Univ of Oregon	OR	21,360	C+

FILM ARTS

School	ST	$IS	SR
American Univ	DC	56,015	HC+
Arizona State Univ, at the Tempe Campus	AZ	20,137	C+
Art Center College of Design	CA	34,044	SP
Bard College	NY	61,940	HC
Barnard College/Columbia Univ	NY	39,000	MC
Bennington College	VT	56,990	HC+
Berklee College of Music	MA	47,100	SP
Binghamton Univ/The SUNY	NY	21,648	HC+
Biola Univ	CA	40,320	C
Boston College	MA	60,622	MC
Boston Univ	MA	60,694	MC
Bowling Green State Univ	OH	18,970	C
Brandeis Univ	MA		MC
Burlington College	VT	32,510	SP
Calif Baptist Univ	CA	38,792	C
Calif College of the Arts	CA	48,334	SP
Cal State, Long Beach	CA	17,502	C+
Cal State, Northridge	CA	28,690	LC
Calvin College	MI	39,120	VC
Champlain College	VT	46,650	VC+
Chapman Univ	CA	58,347	VC+
CUNY/Brooklyn College	NY	5,884	C+
CUNY/City College	NY	20,319	HC+
Claremont McKenna College	CA	62,215	MC
Clark Univ	MA	47,020	HC+
Coe College	IA	45,550	VC
College of Staten Island/The City of New Yok	NY	16,778	NC
Colo College	CO	57,162	MC
Columbia College Chicago	IL	30,940	LC
Columbia Univ/City of New York	NY	61,116	MC
Columbia Univ/School of General Studies	NY	58,231	MC
Columbus College of Art and Design	OH	37,732	SP
Concordia Univ Irvine	CA	35,390	VC
Conn College	CT	54,970	MC
Dartmouth College	NH	57,996	MC
De Sales Univ	PA	43,970	C
Denison Univ	OH	54,670	HC+
Dominican Univ	IL	37,628	C
Drexel Univ	PA	61,418	VC+
Eastern Mich Univ	MI	18,604	C
Elon Univ	NC	41,914	VC+
Emerson College	MA	52,446	HC+
Emory Univ	GA	56,368	MC
Fairleigh Dickinson Univ/ College at Florham	NJ	42,142	C
Florida State Univ	FL	16,715	VC
George Fox Univ	OR	40,750	C+
George Mason Univ	VA	15,724	VC
Georgia State Univ	GA	15,582	VC

ST = STATE $IS = IN-STATE COSTS   SR = SELECTOR RATING

School	ST	$IS	SR
Grand Valley State Univ	MI	17,998	MC
Hampshire College	MA	58,320	MC
Hofstra Univ	NY	51,810	VC+
Hollins Univ	VA	43,295	VC
Howard Univ	DC	13,646	C
Hunter College	NY	14,429	VC
Huntington Univ	IN	32,220	C+
Ithaca College	NY	53,864	HC
Kansas City Art Inst	MO	44,308	SP
Keene State College	NH	23,232	LC
Kenyon College	OH	58,890	MC
Le Moyne College	NY	43,470	C
LIU Post	NY	47,660	C
Lynn Univ	FL	43,500	LC
Memphis College of Art	TN	22,614	C
Middlebury College	VT	59,160	MC
Minneapolis College of Art and Design	MN	36,700	SP
Minn State Univ, Moorhead	MN	13,392	VC
Montclair State Univ	NJ	22,614	C
Mount Holyoke College	MA	55,146	MC
Mount St. Mary's College - Chalon Campus	CA	43,897	VC+
Muhlenberg College	PA	52,837	HC
New Mexico State Univ	NM	14,050	C
New York Univ	NY	61,470	MC
Northeastern Univ	MA	55,296	MC
Oakland Univ	MI	19,391	C
Oberlin College	OH	61,788	MC
Ohio Univ	OH	21,080	C
Okla City Univ	OK	40,476	VC
Old Dominion Univ	VA	19,483	LC
Oral Roberts Univ	OK	31,734	C
Oswego / SUNY	NY	20,009	VC
Pace Univ	NY	53,367	C
Palm Beach Atlantic Univ	FL	34,874	C+
Pepperdine Univ	CA	55,372	HC+
Pitzer College	CA	54,988	MC
Point Park Univ	PA	36,390	C
Pratt Inst	NY	55,956	SP
Purdue Univ/West Lafayette	IN	20,024	HC
Queens College/The CUNY	NY	17,107	VC
Rhode Island College	RI	17,694	LC
Rhode Island School of Design	RI	57,234	MC
Rochester Inst of Technology	NY	42,450	VC
San Francisco Art Inst	CA	55,762	SP
San Francisco State Univ	CA	18,514	C
San Jose State Univ	CA	19,133	LC
Santa Fe Univ of Art and Design	NM	39,666	SP
Sarah Lawrence College	NY	48,000	MC
Savannah College of Art and Design	GA	48,005	SP
School of the Art Inst of Chicago	IL	56,230	SP
School of Visual Arts	NY	36,500	VC
Seattle Univ	WA	49,035	VC+
Smith College	MA	54,874	MC
Southern Adventist Univ	TN	26,190	C
Southern Illinois Univ Carbondale	IL	21,942	C
Southern Methodist Univ	TX	60,585	MC
Spring Arbor Univ	MI	26,740	C
St. Mary's College of Maryland	MD	25,754	VC
Stanford Univ	CA	58,388	MC
SUNY at Purchase	NY	16,951	C
Stephens College	MO	38,042	VC
Stevenson Univ	MD	41,470	C
Stony Brook Univ / SUNY	NY	20,078	HC+
Suffolk Univ	MA	47,298	C
SUNY Cortland/The SUNY	NY	19,759	C+
Swarthmore College	PA	57,870	MC
Syracuse Univ	NY	56,346	VC
Taylor Univ	IN	37,821	VC+
Temple Univ	PA	24,392	VC
The Pennsylvania State Univ - Univ Park	PA	28,022	VC+
The Univ of Okla	OK	18,621	VC
The Univ of Utah	UT	16,463	VC
Tulane Univ	LA	60,861	MC
Univ at Buffalo / The SUNY	NY	20,283	VC
Univ of Alaska Fairbanks	AK	15,130	C
Univ of Arizona	AZ	20,657	C
Univ of Calif at Berkeley	CA	23,322	MC
Univ of Calif at Irvine	CA	25,961	VC
Univ of Calif at Los Angeles	CA	25,686	MC
Univ of Calif at Riverside	CA	27,204	C+
Univ of Calif at Santa Barbara	CA	27,551	HC
Univ of Calif at Santa Cruz	CA	27,807	C+
Univ of Central Florida	FL	15,668	VC+
Univ of Chicago	IL	55,416	MC
Univ of Colo Boulder	CO	22,605	VC+
Univ of Denver	CO	51,787	VC+
Univ of Hartford	CT	42,674	C
Univ of Illinois at Chicago	IL	24,505	VC
Univ of Illinois at Urbana-Champaign	IL	26,450	HC
Univ of Iowa	IA	17,693	VC
Univ of Kansas	KS	17,603	C+
Univ of Maryland - College Park	MD	20,060	HC
Univ of Miami	FL	57,034	MC
Univ of Mich/Ann Arbor	MI	22,102	MC
Univ of Minn/Twin Cities	MN		HC
Univ of Nebr - Lincoln	NE	18,031	VC
Univ of Nevada, Las Vegas	NV	17,303	C
Univ of N Car at Wilmington	NC	13,572	VC
Univ of N Car School of the Arts	NC	7,401	SP
Univ of Notre Dame	IN	57,117	MC
Univ of Oregon	OR	21,360	C+
Univ of Pittsburgh at Pittsburgh	PA	28,572	HC+
Univ of Rochester	NY	60,668	MC
Univ of Southern Calif	CA	56,903	MC
Univ of Tampa	FL	35,160	VC
Univ of Texas at Austin	TX	44,074	MC
Univ of the Arts	PA	38,450	SP
Univ of Toledo	OH	18,464	C
Univ of Tulsa	OK	46,331	MC
Univ of Vermont	VT	27,006	VC+
Univ of Wisc-Milwaukee	WI	18,436	C
Vassar College	NY	61,140	MC
Virginia Commonwealth Univ	VA	21,716	C
Washington Univ in St. Louis	MO	69,844	MC
Wayne State Univ	MI	22,063	C
Webster Univ	MO	35,100	C+
Wellesley College	MA	59,038	MC
Wesleyan Univ	CT	61,198	MC
Wheaton College	MA	54,934	HC+
Whitman College	WA	55,988	MC
Wright State Univ	OH	16,983	C
Yale Univ	CT	55,300	MC

FILM, TELEVISION AND DIGITAL MEDIA

School	ST	$IS	SR
Amherst College	MA	58,744	MC
Asbury Univ	KY	32,038	VC
Baldwin Wallace Univ	OH	38,318	C
Calvin College	MI	39,120	VC
Chapman Univ	CA	58,347	VC+
Chatham Univ	PA	43,797	C
Cleveland State Univ	OH	21,776	C
Dordt College	IA	34,160	C
Fairfield Univ	CT	56,960	VC
Hobart and William Smith Colleges	NY	60,034	HC+
Kansas City Art Inst	MO	44,308	SP
Mercy College	NY	30,456	C
Messiah College	PA	40,690	C+
Morehouse College	GA	39,412	C
Northern Arizona Univ	AZ	19,010	C
Southern Oregon Univ	OR	17,874	C
St. John's Univ	NY	55,070	C+
SUNY Fredonia/The SUNY at Fredonia	NY	19,840	VC
Taylor Univ	IN	37,821	VC+
Texas Christian Univ	TX	49,980	HC
The Univ of Utah	UT	16,463	VC
Univ of Illinois at Chicago	IL	24,505	VC
Univ of Nebr - Lincoln	NE	18,031	VC
Univ of New Mexico	NM	15,300	C
Univ of Pikeville	KY	25,500	NC
Western Mich Univ	MI	19,628	C

FINANCE

School	ST	$IS	SR
Abilene Christian Univ	TX	38,400	C+
Albion College	MI	46,010	C
Alma College	MI	44,075	C
Aquinas College	TN	29,250	VC+
Ashford Univ	CA	10,480	C
Baldwin Wallace Univ	OH	38,318	C
Belmont Univ	TN	39,190	VC+
Bentley Univ	MA	56,454	HC+
Berry College	GA	39,254	VC
Bethany College	KS	30,605	NC
Bethany College	WV	35,282	LC
Binghamton Univ/The SUNY	NY	21,648	HC+
Bloomfield College	NJ	37,850	LC
Boise State Univ	ID	13,469	LC
Bridgewater State Univ	MA	18,752	C
Bryant Univ	RI	49,179	VC
Cabrini College	PA	40,859	LC
Cal State, Fullerton	CA	25,188	C
Cal State, Long Beach	CA	17,502	C+
Canisius College	NY	44,900	C
Case Western Reserve Univ	OH	56,534	MC
Cedarville Univ	OH	32,860	VC
Central Conn State Univ	CT	19,749	C
Champlain College	VT	46,650	VC
Christopher Newport Univ	VA	21,960	VC
Clarkson Univ	NY	57,330	HC
Cleveland State Univ	OH	21,776	C
College of Charleston	SC	22,145	VC
College of St. Scholastica	MN	41,440	C
Columbia College	MO	24,578	C
Creighton Univ	NE	45,356	VC
Culver-Stockton College	MO	30,900	C
Dallas Baptist Univ	TX	30,580	VC
De Sales Univ	PA	43,970	C
DePaul Univ	IL	47,623	VC
Dominican Univ	IL	37,628	C
Eastern Illinois Univ	IL	20,466	C
Elmhurst College	IL	43,336	C
Elon Univ	NC	41,914	VC+
Endicott College	MA	43,228	VC+
Fairfield Univ	CT	56,960	VC
Ferris State Univ	MI	20,047	C
Fordham Univ	NY	61,588	HC+
Framingham State Univ	MA	18,854	C
Georgetown Univ	DC	52,910	MC
Georgia Southern Univ	GA	16,942	C
Gordon College	MA	44,320	VC
Grove City College	PA	24,022	VC
Hawaii Pacific Univ	HI	34,360	C
Hawaii Pacific Univ	HI	34,360	C
Hawaii Pacific Univ	HI	34,360	C
Hillsdale College	MI	32,866	MC
Holy Family Univ	PA	40,030	LC
Illinois State Univ	IL	23,110	VC
Indiana Univ Bloomington	IN	19,801	VC
Indiana Univ of Pennsylvania	PA	20,846	LC
Indiana Univ-Purdue Univ Indianapolis	IN	17,611	C
Iona College	NY	44,028	C
Jackson State Univ	MS	13,512	LC
John Carroll Univ	OH	46,300	C+
Kean Univ	NJ	23,444	C
Kennesaw State Univ	GA		C
Kent State Univ	OH	19,920	C
Lake Erie College	OH	37,266	C
Lake Forest College	IL	50,652	VC
Lehigh Univ	PA	56,770	MC
Limestone College	SC	30,800	C
Lipscomb Univ	TN	37,490	VC
LIU Brooklyn	NY	47,182	LC
Lourdes Univ	OH	26,055	LC
Loyola Univ Chicago	IL	51,646	VC+
Lubbock Christian Univ	TX	26,308	C
Marquette Univ	WI	46,930	VC+
Marshall Univ	WV	14,820	C
Menlo College	CA	49,002	C
Mercer Univ	GA	44,201	VC
Mich Tech Univ	MI	23,556	NC
Millersville Univ of Pennsylvania	PA	21,648	C
Millikin Univ	IL	38,940	C
Minn State Univ, Mankato	MN	15,616	C
Missouri Southern State Univ	MO	12,061	C
Missouri State Univ	MO	13,996	C+
Molloy College	NY	40,440	C
Mount Mercy Univ	IA	35,320	C
Mount Vernon Nazarene Univ	OH	29,590	C
Murray State Univ	KY	15,304	C
Nazareth College of Rochester	NY	43,028	C+
New Mexico State Univ	NM	14,050	C
New York Inst of Technology	NY	45,010	VC
New York Univ	NY	61,470	MC
Niagara Univ	NY	41,010	C
North Central College	IL	38,343	VC
N Dak State Univ	ND		C
Northern Arizona Univ	AZ	19,010	C
Northern Kentucky Univ	KY	21,134	C
Northwood Univ	FL	33,912	LC
Nova Southeastern Univ	FL	37,280	VC
Ohio Univ	OH	21,080	C
Okla Christian Univ	OK	25,870	VC
Old Dominion Univ	VA	19,483	LC
Oswego / SUNY	NY	20,009	VC
Pace Univ	NY	53,367	C
Point Loma Nazarene Univ	CA	41,006	C+
Point Park Univ	PA	36,390	C
Providence College	RI	57,383	VC
Queens Univ of Charlotte	NC	39,543	C+
Quinnipiac Univ	CT	55,160	VC
Rutgers, The State Univ of New Jersey/New Brunswick	NJ	25,562	VC
Rutgers, The State Univ of New Jersey/Newark Campus	NJ	258,806	C
Saginaw Valley State Univ	MI	17,369	C
St. Joseph's Univ	PA	55,006	VC
St. Mary's Univ of Minn	MN	38,280	C
Samford Univ	AL	37,060	C+
San Diego State Univ	CA	21,611	C
Seattle Univ	WA	49,035	VC+
Seton Hall Univ	NJ	45,902	C
Simmons College	MA	49,966	VC
Southeast Missouri State Univ	MO	15,370	LC
Southern Methodist Univ	TX	60,585	MC
St. John's Univ	NY	55,070	C+
SUNY Fredonia/The SUNY at Fredonia	NY	19,840	VC
SUNY Plattsburgh / SUNY	NY	18,083	C
Syracuse Univ	NY	56,346	VC
Taylor Univ	IN	37,821	VC+
Temple Univ	PA	24,392	VC
Texas Christian Univ	TX	49,980	VC
Texas State Univ	TX	17,128	C
The Catholic Univ of America	DC	52,852	VC
The Lincoln Univ	PA	15,154	LC
The Pennsylvania State Univ - Univ Park	PA	28,022	VC+
The SUNY/College at Brockport	NY	19,002	C
The Univ of N Car at Greensboro	NC	12,848	C
The Univ of Okla	OK	18,621	C
The Univ of Utah	UT	16,463	VC
Thomas College	ME	33,560	LC
Thomas Edison State College	NJ	5,700	SP
Tulane Univ	LA	60,861	MC
Univ of Arizona	AZ	20,657	C
Univ of Arkansas at Fayetteville	AR	18,352	C+
Univ of Central Okla	OK	12,293	C
Univ of Charleston	WV	32,300	C
Univ of Cincinnati	OH	21,506	VC
Univ of Colo Boulder	CO	22,605	VC+
Univ of Denver	CO	51,787	VC+
Univ of Evansville	IN	42,656	VC+
Univ of Georgia	GA	20,082	VC
Univ of Illinois at Chicago	IL	24,505	VC
Univ of Kansas	KS	17,603	C+
Univ of Louisiana at Monroe	LA	12,998	C
Univ of Maine	ME	19,902	VC+
Univ of Mary Hardin-Baylor	TX	31,950	C+
Univ of Maryland - College Park	MD	20,060	HC
Univ of Mass Dartmouth	MA	22,223	C
Univ of Miami	FL	57,034	MC
Univ of Miss	MS	16,704	C+
Univ of Missouri-St. Louis	MO		VC
Univ of Nebr - Lincoln	NE	18,031	VC
Univ of Nevada/Reno	NV	17,507	C
Univ of N Car at Charlotte	NC	15,547	C
Univ of North Florida	FL	15,870	VC
Univ of Pittsburgh at Pittsburgh	PA	28,572	HC+
Univ of San Diego	CA	54,818	HC+
Univ of San Francisco	CA	54,770	VC
Univ of South Florida/St. Petersburg	FL	12,769	C
Univ of Southern Indiana	IN	14,885	C
Univ of St. Thomas - Houston	TX	37,690	C
Univ of Tenn at Knoxville	TN	20,364	VC+
Univ of Texas - Pan American	TX	11,125	LC
Univ of Texas at San Antonio	TX	18,372	C
Univ of West Georgia	GA	15,488	LC
Univ of Wisc/Green Bay	WI	19,074	C
Univ of Wisc/Superior	WI	14,314	C
Univ of Wisc-Milwaukee	WI	18,436	C
Univ of Wyoming	WY	14,401	C+
Valparaiso Univ	IN	44,940	VC+
Wabash College	IN	46,850	C+
Waynesburg Univ	PA	30,150	C
Webster Univ	MO	35,100	C+
Western Illinois Univ	IL	20,732	C
Western Mich Univ	MI	19,628	C
Western New England Univ	MA	46,154	C+
Widener Univ	PA	52,418	C
Wingate Univ	NC	34,990	C
Wofford College	SC	45,795	VC

FINANCE (FINANCIAL PLANNING)

School	ST	$IS	SR
Murray State Univ	KY	15,304	C
Southern Methodist Univ	TX	60,585	MC

FINANCIAL INSTITUTIONS MANAGEMENT

School	ST	$IS	SR
Thomas Edison State College	NJ	5,700	SP

FINANCIAL SERVICES

School	ST	$IS	SR
Bryant Univ	RI	49,179	VC
Missouri Southern State Univ	MO	12,061	C
Old Dominion Univ	VA	19,483	LC
San Diego State Univ	CA	21,611	C+

FINE ARTS

School	ST	$IS	SR
Abilene Christian Univ	TX	38,400	C+
Adelphi Univ	NY	44,670	VC
Alabama State Univ	AL	14,142	NC
Albany State Univ	GA	8,500	C
Albertus Magnus College	CT	37,382	LC
Alfred Univ	NY	41,770	C
American Univ	DC	56,015	HC+
Amherst College	MA	58,744	MC
Anderson Univ	IN	36,100	C
Aquinas College	MI	33,060	C
Arcadia Univ	PA	33,570	C+
Arizona State Univ, at the Tempe Campus	AZ	20,137	C+
Art Academy of Cincinnati	OH	25,940	SP
Art Center College of Design	CA	34,044	SP
Ashland Univ	OH	25,000	C
Auburn Univ	AL	22,378	VC+
Auburn Univ at Montgomery	AL	14,470	LC
Bellarmine Univ	KY	42,950	VC
Bellevue Univ	NE	4,600	NC
Bemidji State Univ	MN	13,500	VC
Benedictine Univ	IL	37,820	C
Bennington College	VT	56,990	HC+
Bethany College	WV	35,282	LC
Biola Univ	CA	40,320	C+
Blue Mountain College	MS	15,634	LC
Bluefield College	VA	17,230	C+
Boise State Univ	ID	13,469	LC

School	ST	$IS	SR
Bowie State Univ	MD	23,990	LC
Bowling Green State Univ	OH	18,970	C
Brenau Univ - Women's College	GA	26,650	LC
Bridgewater State Univ	MA	18,752	C
Brigham Young Univ	UT	12,100	HC
Brigham Young Univ/Hawaii	HI	10,686	VC
Bryn Mawr College	PA	59,890	MC
Bucknell Univ	PA	60,140	MC
Buffalo State College / SUNY	NY	15,733	C+
Burlington College	VT	32,510	SP
Caldwell Univ	NJ	35,602	NC
Calif Inst of the Arts	CA	51,902	SP
Cal State, Chico	CA	20,158	C
Cal State, Fullerton	CA	25,188	C
Cal State, Stanislaus	CA	18,582	C
Calvin College	MI	39,120	VC
Campbell Univ	NC	37,570	VC
Canisius College	NY	44,900	C
Cardinal Stritch Univ	WI	24,054	C
Carnegie Mellon Univ	PA	51,260	MC
Carson-Newman Univ	TN	29,058	C+
Carthage College	WI	33,000	C
Cedar Crest College	PA	43,240	C
Central Washington Univ	WA	11,730	C
Centre College	KY	35,000	HC+
Champlain College	VT	46,650	VC+
Charleston Southern Univ	SC	22,420	C
Christopher Newport Univ	VA	21,960	VC
CUNY/City College	NY	20,319	HC+
Clark Univ	MA	47,020	HC+
Clemson Univ	SC	19,136	NC
Coastal Carolina Univ	SC	18,580	C
College for Creative Studies	MI	45,340	C
College of Art and Design at Lesley Univ	MA	39,730	SP
College of Mount St. Joseph	OH	33,880	C
College of New Jersey	NJ	25,376	HC
College of St. Elizabeth	NJ	43,839	LC
College of Wooster	OH	52,600	VC
Colo State Univ-Fort Collins	CO	20,385	VC
Columbia College	MO	24,578	C
Columbus College of Art and Design	OH	37,732	SP
Concordia Univ Nebr	NE	26,000	VC
Converse College	SC	37,130	C
Cooper Union for the Advancement of Science and Art	NY	55,600	MC
Corcoran College of Art and Design	DC	36,500	SP
Cornell College	IA	44,930	VC
Cornell Univ	NY	60,964	MC
Cornerstone Univ and Grand Rapids Theological Seminary	MI	33,338	C
Cornish College of the Arts	WA	21,200	SP
Creighton Univ	NE	45,356	VC
Culver-Stockton College	MO	30,900	C
Cumberland Univ	TN	21,220	C
Daemen College	NY	34,770	C
Dallas Baptist Univ	TX	30,580	VC
Denison Univ	OH	54,670	HC+
DePaul Univ	IL	47,623	VC
Dickinson State Univ	ND	11,900	NC
Dominican Univ	IL	37,628	C
Dordt College	IA	34,160	C+
Dowling College	NY	25,000	LC
Drury Univ	MO	31,909	VC
East Stroudsburg Univ of Pennsylvania	PA	18,868	LC
East Tenn State Univ	TN	9,000	C
Eastern Mich Univ	MI	18,604	C
Edinboro Univ of Pennsylvania	PA	15,940	LC
Elizabethtown College	PA	49,740	VC
Elmira College	NY	49,950	C+
Elms College	MA	23,900	VC
Emory Univ	GA	56,368	MC
Endicott College	MA	43,228	VC+
Eureka College	IL	19,280	C
Fairleigh Dickinson Univ/College at Florham	NJ	42,142	C
Fairleigh Dickinson Univ/Metropolitan Campus	NJ	40,254	C
Felician College	NJ	41,640	LC
Ferris State Univ	MI	20,047	C
Fisk Univ	TN	19,830	C
Flagler College	FL	25,180	C
Florida A&M Univ	FL	14,935	LC
Florida Atlantic Univ	FL	17,339	C
Florida International Univ	FL	17,747	C+
Florida Memorial Univ	FL	20,888	LC
Fontbonne Univ	MO	31,384	C
Fordham Univ	NY	61,588	HC+
Fort Hays State Univ	KS	11,354	C
Franklin and Marshall College	PA	60,799	MC
Franklin Pierce Univ	NH	41,598	C
Freed-Hardeman Univ	TN	19,697	VC
Friends Univ	KS	29,100	C
George Washington Univ	DC	57,108	MC
Georgetown Univ	DC	52,910	MC
Georgia Southwestern State Univ	GA	13,246	C
Georgia State Univ	GA	15,582	VC
Goddard College	VT	16,418	VC
Grand Valley State Univ	MI	17,998	C+
Green Mountain College	VT	45,228	LC
Gustavus Adolphus College	MN	48,170	HC
Hamline Univ	MN	45,678	VC
Hampden-Sydney College	VA	51,758	C
Hampshire College	MA	58,320	MC
Harding Univ	AR	23,556	C
Harvard College/Harvard Univ	MA	49,000	MC
Hastings College	NE	27,782	C+
Haverford College	PA	61,564	MC
High Point Univ	NC	39,800	C
Hobart and William Smith Colleges	NY	60,034	HC+
Hofstra Univ	NY	51,810	VC+
Hope College	MI	38,650	VC
Humboldt State Univ	CA	18,400	C
Hunter College	NY	14,429	VC
Huntington Univ	IN	32,220	C+
Illinois College	IL	25,770	VC
Indiana State Univ	IN	16,000	C
Indiana Univ Bloomington	IN	19,801	VC
Indiana Univ East	IN	6,783	C
Indiana Univ Kokomo	IN	6,811	LC
Indiana Univ Northwest	IN	6,854	LC
Indiana Univ of Pennsylvania	PA	20,846	LC
Indiana Univ South Bend	IN	15,501	C
Indiana Univ Southeast	IN	16,035	C
Indiana Univ-Purdue Univ Fort Wayne	IN	15,521	C
Indiana Univ-Purdue Univ Indianapolis	IN	17,611	C
Inter-American Univ of PR/San Germán	PR	6,720	
Iowa State Univ	IA	16,403	C
Iowa Wesleyan College	IA	30,850	LC
Ithaca College	NY	53,864	HC
James Madison Univ	VA	18,049	VC
Johnson State College	VT	16,721	C
Judson Univ	IL	25,130	C
Kansas City Art Inst	MO	44,308	SP
Kean Univ	NJ	23,444	C
Kentucky State Univ	KY	11,000	LC
Kentucky Wesleyan College	KY	27,440	C
Kutztown Univ of Pennsylvania	PA	16,909	LC
La Salle Univ	PA	50,270	C
La Sierra Univ	CA	35,694	VC
Lake Erie College	OH	37,266	C
Lake Superior State Univ	MI	18,121	C
Lamar Univ	TX	6,820	LC
Lehman College/The CUNY	NY	5,778	C
Lewis & Clark College	OR	54,382	MC
Lincoln Memorial Univ	TN	18,144	C
Lincoln Univ	MO	12,904	NC
LIU Brooklyn	NY	47,182	LC
LIU Post	NY	47,660	C
Lock Haven Univ of Pennsylvania	PA	18,028	LC
Louisiana State Univ in Shreveport	LA	5,606	C
Louisiana Tech Univ	LA	11,302	C
Loyola Univ Chicago	IL	51,646	VC+
Loyola Univ Maryland	MD	56,880	VC+
Loyola Univ New Orleans	LA	46,581	VC
Madonna Univ	MI	24,540	VC
Maharishi Univ of Management	IA	31,000	VC
Marist College	NY	35,500	C
Marlboro College	VT	35,980	VC
Martin Univ	IN	11,000	SP
Maryland Inst College of Art	MD	39,500	SP
Marylhurst Univ	OR	20,295	NC
Marymount Manhattan College	NY	40,118	VC
Mass College of Liberal Arts	MA	18,613	C
McDaniel College	MD	47,450	VC
Memphis College of Art	TN	33,550	SP
Mercy College	NY	30,456	C
Meredith College	NC	31,420	C
Metropolitan State Univ of Denver	CO	4,835	LC
Midland Univ	NE	34,000	C
Midwestern State Univ	TX	9,722	C
Milligan College	TN	27,510	C
Milwaukee Inst of Art and Design	WI	31,938	SP
Minn State Univ, Moorhead	MN	13,392	VC
Miss Univ for Women	MS	7,400	C
Miss Valley State Univ	MS	9,706	LC
Missouri Southern State Univ	MO	12,061	C
Missouri Western State Univ	MO	12,260	NC
Montana State Univ	MT	14,068	C
Montana State Univ-Northern	MT	12,500	NC
Montclair State Univ	NJ	22,614	C
Montserrat College of Art	MA	31,000	C
Moore College of Art and Design	PA	50,135	SP
Morgan State Univ	MD	14,500	VC
Mount Mary Univ	WI	33,590	LC
Mount St. Mary's Univ	MD	47,996	C
National Louis Univ	IL	16,915	LC
Nazareth College of Rochester	NY	43,028	C+
New England College	NH	45,930	LC
New Jersey City Univ	NJ	21,456	LC
New Mexico State Univ	NM	14,050	C
New York Univ	NY	61,470	MC
Norfolk State Univ	VA	10,531	LC
Northeastern State Univ	OK	8,615	VC
Northern Kentucky Univ	KY	21,134	C
Northern Mich Univ	MI	18,278	C
Northern State Univ - Aberdeen	SD	14,505	C
Northland College	WI	26,680	C
Northwest Missouri State Univ	MO	17,347	C
Northwestern State Univ of Louisiana	LA	14,368	C
Northwestern Univ	IL	61,640	MC
Notre Dame de Namur Univ	CA	44,236	LC
Nova Southeastern Univ	FL	37,280	VC
Oakland City Univ	IN	24,500	NC
Oberlin College	OH	61,788	MC
Ohio Northern Univ	OH	42,075	VC
Ohio Wesleyan Univ	OH	49,460	C+
Okla Baptist Univ	OK	28,202	C
Okla Panhandle State Univ	OK	8,996	C
Old Dominion Univ	VA	19,483	LC
Olivet College	MI	19,984	C
Our Lady of the Lake Univ	TX	22,430	LC
Pace Univ	NY	53,367	C
Pacific Lutheran Univ	WA	46,760	C+
Pacific Northwest College of Art	OR	38,494	C
Pacific Union College	CA	28,150	VC
Park Univ	MO	17,525	C
Parsons The New School for Design	NY	56,610	SP
Piedmont College	GA	30,136	C
Pomona College	CA	57,680	MC
Pontifical Catholic Univ of PR	PR	7,310	
Portland State Univ	OR	18,672	C
Pratt Inst	NY	55,956	SP
Prescott College	AZ	33,284	C
Principia College	IL	35,140	C+
Purdue Univ/West Lafayette	IN	20,024	HC
Radford Univ	VA	17,766	LC
Richard Stockton College of New Jersey	NJ	20,000	VC
Rider Univ	NJ	45,720	C
Ringling College of Art and Design	FL	46,130	SP
Rochester Inst of Technology	NY	42,450	VC
Rocky Mountain College of Art and Design	CO	22,470	SP
Rosemont College	PA	42,350	C
Rowan Univ	NJ	24,022	VC+
Saginaw Valley State Univ	MI	17,369	C
St. Anselm College	NH	49,376	VC
St. Augustine's Univ	NC	14,000	C
St. Louis Univ	MO	48,346	HC
St. Mary's College	IN	45,160	C+
St. Michael's College	VT	49,975	VC
St. Peter's Univ	NJ	44,240	C
St. Vincent College	PA	40,244	C
Salem State Univ	MA	13,161	LC
Salisbury Univ	MD	19,180	VC
San Jose State Univ	CA	19,133	LC
Santa Fe Univ of Art and Design	NM	39,666	SP
Sarah Lawrence College	NY	48,000	HC
School of Visual Arts	NY	36,500	VC
Seattle Pacific Univ	WA	41,559	VC+
Seattle Univ	WA	49,035	VC+
Seton Hall Univ	NJ	45,902	C
Seton Hill Univ	PA	35,172	C
Sewanee: The Univ of the South	TN	47,700	HC+
Shawnee State Univ	OH	16,916	C
Siena Heights Univ	MI	32,040	C
Sierra Nevada College	NV	32,700	VC
Silver Lake College	WI	22,600	LC
Slippery Rock Univ of Pennsylvania	PA	10,360	C
Sonoma State Univ	CA	20,541	C
S Car State Univ	SC	6,700	C
Southeastern Okla State Univ	OK	7,966	LC
Southern Adventist Univ	TN	26,190	C
Southern Conn State Univ	CT	18,033	LC
Southern Illinois Univ Carbondale	IL	21,942	C
Southern Oregon Univ	OR	17,874	C
Southern Univ and A&M College	LA	9,761	LC
Southern Univ at New Orleans	LA	2,963	NC
Spelman College	GA	24,650	C
Springfield College	MA	25,000	C
St. Ambrose Univ	IA	30,845	C
St. Catherine Univ	MN	37,782	C+
St. Cloud State Univ	MN	10,600	C
St. John's Univ	NY	55,070	C+
St. Lawrence Univ	NY	59,972	VC
St. Thomas Aquinas College	NY	40,230	C
Stanford Univ	CA	58,388	MC
Stonehill College	MA	46,780	HC
Suffolk Univ	MA	47,298	C
Sul Ross State Univ	TX	13,410	LC
SUNY Fredonia/The SUNY at Fredonia	NY	19,840	VC
SUNY Oneonta / SUNY	NY	16,919	C+
Syracuse Univ	NY	56,346	VC
Tarleton State Univ	TX	13,489	LC
Taylor Univ	IN	37,821	VC+
Tenn Tech Univ	TN	11,310	C
Texas A&M Univ at Commerce	TX	10,496	C
Texas A&M Univ at Kingsville	TX	7,500	LC
Texas Woman's Univ	TX	13,633	LC
Ohio State Univ-Columbus Campus	OH	19,887	HC+
The SUNY at Potsdam	NY	18,473	C
The Univ of N Car at Greensboro	NC	12,848	C
The Univ of Tenn at Chattanooga	TN	16,883	C
The Univ of Utah	UT	16,463	VC
Trinity College	CT		HC+
Truman State Univ	MO	15,541	HC
Tusculum College	TN	24,295	C
Union College	KY	29,955	C
Union College	NY	60,240	MC
Univ at Albany / SUNY	NY	18,674	VC
Univ of Alaska Anchorage	AK	16,673	NC
Univ of Arizona	AZ	20,657	C
Univ of Calif at Davis	CA		HC
Univ of Central Florida	FL	15,668	VC+
Univ of Cincinnati	OH	21,506	VC
Univ of Colo at Colo Springs	CO	15,000	VC
Univ of Colo Boulder	CO	22,605	VC+
Univ of Colo Denver	CO	17,904	C
Univ of Dayton	OH	49,070	VC
Univ of Delaware	DE	23,612	VC
Univ of Great Falls	MT	27,970	C
Univ of Houston-Downtown	TX	15,170	C
Univ of Idaho	ID	14,558	C
Univ of Illinois at Chicago	IL	24,505	VC
Univ of Illinois at Urbana-Champaign	IL	26,450	HC
Univ of Iowa	IA	17,693	VC
Univ of Jamestown	ND	24,738	C
Univ of Kansas	KS	17,603	C+
Univ of Louisiana at Lafayette	LA	6,130	C
Univ of Maine at Machias	ME	10,523	C
Univ of Maryland/Baltimore County	MD	18,000	VC
Univ of Mass Lowell	MA	19,316	C
Univ of Miami	FL	57,034	MC
Univ of Montana	MT	14,105	C
Univ of Mount Olive	NC	18,426	C
Univ of Nebr - Lincoln	NE	18,031	VC
Univ of Nebr at Kearney	NE	14,855	LC
Univ of Nebr at Omaha	NE	12,700	C
Univ of Nevada, Las Vegas	NV	17,303	C
Univ of New Hampshire	NH	26,912	C
Univ of New Haven	CT	48,940	C
Univ of New Orleans	LA	9,224	C
Univ of N Car at Asheville	NC	13,500	VC
Univ of N Car at Charlotte	NC	15,547	C
Univ of North Florida	FL	15,870	VC
Univ of Northern Colo	CO	18,446	C
Univ of Northern Iowa	IA	15,795	C
Univ of Oregon	OR	21,360	C+
Univ of Pennsylvania	PA	61,132	MC
Univ of PR Recinto de Rio Piedras	PR	5,750	
Univ of PR/Mayaguez	PR	1,250	
Univ of Rio Grande	OH	8,750	NC
Univ of St. Francis	IN	29,810	C
Univ of San Francisco	CA	54,770	VC
Univ of Science and Arts of Okla	OK	10,560	VC
Univ of South Alabama	AL	13,510	C
Univ of S Car Aiken	SC	16,712	C
Univ of S Car at Columbia	SC	19,725	VC+
Univ of Southern Calif	CA	56,903	MC
Univ of Southern Maine	ME	16,576	C
Univ of Southern Miss	MS	13,170	C
Univ of Tenn at Martin	TN	13,734	C
Univ of Texas at Dallas	TX	21,348	HC+
Univ of the District of Columbia	DC	7,244	C
Univ of the Southwest	NM	15,000	C
Univ of Toledo	OH	18,464	C
Univ of Wisc/Green Bay	WI	19,074	C
Univ of Wisc/La Crosse	WI	9,304	VC
Univ of Wisc/Oshkosh	WI	10,426	LC
Univ of Wisc/Parkside	WI	10,181	LC
Univ of Wisc/River Falls	WI	9,722	LC
Univ of Wisc/Stevens Point	WI	14,043	C
Univ of Wisc/Stout	WI	15,459	C
Univ of Wisc/Superior	WI	14,314	C
Upper Iowa Univ	IA	30,426	NC
Utah State Univ	UT	12,044	C
Vanderbilt Univ	TN	58,200	MC
Wagner College	NY	48,600	C
Washington College	MD	52,602	VC
Washington State Univ	WA	20,461	C
Washington Univ in St. Louis	MO	69,844	MC
Wayne State Univ	MI	22,063	C
Wells College	NY	49,400	VC
West Liberty Univ	WV	9,142	LC
West Virginia State Univ	WV	8,378	NC

ST = STATE $IS = IN-STATE COSTS   SR = SELECTOR RATING

School	ST	$IS	SR
Western New Mexico Univ	NM	8,500	LC
Western State Colo Univ	CO	16,924	C
Western Washington Univ	WA	18,519	VC
Westminster College	PA	31,290	C+
Westminster College	UT	37,708	C+
Wheaton College	MA	54,934	HC+
Whitman College	WA	55,988	MC
Widener Univ	PA	52,418	C
Wilberforce Univ	OH	15,100	LC
William Paterson Univ of New Jersey	NJ	21,694	C
William Penn Univ	IA	26,000	C
Williams College	MA	61,070	MC
Wilson College	PA	35,080	C
Wingate Univ	NC	34,990	C
Winona State Univ	MN	16,640	C
Winthrop Univ	SC	21,120	C
Wittenberg Univ	OH	47,962	C+
Wright State Univ	OH	16,983	C
Xavier Univ	OH	44,980	VC
Xavier Univ of Louisiana	LA	25,300	C
York College of Pennsylvania	PA	26,590	C

FINE/STUDIO ARTS, GENERAL

School	ST	$IS	SR
Georgetown College	KY	41,440	C+
Kean Univ	NJ	23,444	C
Missouri Southern State Univ	MO	12,061	C
Southern Methodist Univ	TX	60,585	MC
Univ of New Haven	CT	48,940	C

FIRE CONTROL AND SAFETY TECHNOLOGY

School	ST	$IS	SR
Cogswell Polytechnical College	CA	30,531	C
Okla State Univ	OK	14,310	VC
Univ of New Haven	CT	48,940	C
Univ of N Car at Charlotte	NC	15,547	C

FIRE PROTECTION

School	ST	$IS	SR
Cal State, Los Angeles	CA	17,186	LC
Cogswell Polytechnical College	CA	30,531	C
Eastern Kentucky Univ	KY	11,161	C
Park Univ	MO	17,525	C
Southern Illinois Univ Carbondale	IL	21,942	C
Univ of New Haven	CT	48,940	C
Western Illinois Univ	IL	20,732	C
Western Oregon Univ	OR	15,021	C
Worcester Polytechnic Inst	MA	55,860	MC

FIRE PROTECTION ENGINEERING

School	ST	$IS	SR
Univ of Houston-Downtown	TX	15,170	LC
Univ of Maryland - College Park	MD	20,060	HC
Univ of New Haven	CT	48,940	C

FIRE PROTECTION SCIENCE

School	ST	$IS	SR
Thomas Edison State College	NJ	5,700	SP

FIRE SCIENCE

School	ST	$IS	SR
Anna Maria College	MA	34,600	C
Embry-Riddle Aeronautical Univ - Worldwide	FL	15,512	C
John Jay College of Criminal Justice/The CUNY	NY	6,359	LC
Lake Superior State Univ	MI	18,121	C
Madonna Univ	MI	24,540	VC
Providence College	RI	57,383	VC
Univ of Maryland/Univ College	MD	6,168	SP
Univ of New Haven	CT	48,940	C
Univ of the District of Columbia	DC	7,244	LC

FIRE SERVICES ADMINISTRATION

School	ST	$IS	SR
Bowling Green State Univ	OH	18,970	C
Colo State Univ-Fort Collins	CO	20,385	VC
Columbia College	MO	24,578	C
Holy Family Univ	PA	40,030	LC
Idaho State Univ	ID	12,307	C
John Jay College of Criminal Justice/The CUNY	NY	6,359	LC
Park Univ	MO	17,525	C
SUNY/Empire State College	NY	6,315	SP
Univ of New Haven	CT	48,940	C

FISH AND GAME MANAGEMENT

School	ST	$IS	SR
Delaware State Univ	DE	16,722	LC
Frostburg State Univ	MD	15,264	LC
Kansas State Univ	KS	15,497	VC
Lake Superior State Univ	MI	18,121	C
S Dak State Univ	SD	14,296	C
Stephen F. Austin State Univ	TX	14,668	C
Tenn Tech Univ	TN	11,310	C

School	ST	$IS	SR
Texas A&M Univ	TX	19,207	VC
Texas Tech Univ	TX	14,243	C
Univ of Montana-Western	MT	9,753	LC
Univ of Nebr - Lincoln	NE	18,031	VC
Univ of Wyoming	WY	14,401	C+
West Virginia Univ	WV	16,542	C+

FISHING AND FISHERIES

School	ST	$IS	SR
Auburn Univ	AL	22,378	VC+
Colo State Univ-Fort Collins	CO	20,385	VC
Humboldt State Univ	CA	18,400	C
Mansfield Univ	PA	19,468	LC
Mich State Univ	MI	22,450	VC
Miss State Univ	MS	14,750	C
N Car State Univ	NC	16,202	HC
Oregon State Univ	OR	20,273	VC
Purdue Univ/West Lafayette	IN	20,024	HC
SUNY / College of Environmental Science and Forestry	NY	18,351	VC
Texas A&M Univ	TX	19,207	VC
Texas A&M Univ at Galveston	TX	11,258	C
Ohio State Univ-Columbus Campus	OH	19,887	HC+
The SUNY College of Agriculture and Tech at Cobleskill	NY	19,749	LC
Univ of Alaska Fairbanks	AK	15,130	C
Univ of Arkansas at Pine Bluff	AR	13,378	C
Univ of Georgia	GA	20,082	VC
Univ of Idaho	ID	14,558	C
Univ of Minn/Twin Cities	MN		HC
Univ of Missouri/Columbia	MO	18,201	MC
Univ of N Dak	ND	14,551	C
Univ of Vermont	VT	27,006	VC+
Univ of Washington	WA	14,722	VC
Univ of Wisc/Stevens Point	WI	14,043	C
West Virginia Univ	WV	16,542	C+

FLUID AND THERMAL SCIENCE

School	ST	$IS	SR
Case Western Reserve Univ	OH	56,534	MC

FOLKLORE AND MYTHOLOGY

School	ST	$IS	SR
Goddard College	VT	16,418	VC
Harvard College/Harvard Univ	MA	49,000	MC
Indiana Univ Bloomington	IN	19,801	VC
Univ of Oregon	OR	21,360	C+
Univ of Pennsylvania	PA	61,132	MC

FOOD PRODUCTION/ MANAGEMENT/SERVICES

School	ST	$IS	SR
Arizona State Univ, at the Polytechnic Campus	AZ	20,531	C+
Concordia Univ St. Paul	MN	28,250	C
Delaware Valley College	PA	29,944	C
Dominican Univ	IL	37,628	C
Johnson & Wales Univ/ Charlotte Campus	NC	29,576	C
Johnson & Wales Univ/ Denver Campus	CO	29,576	C
Johnson & Wales Univ/North Miami Campus	FL		C
Johnson & Wales Univ/ Providence Campus	RI	29,576	C
Lipscomb Univ	TN	37,490	VC
Metropolitan State Univ	MN	5,923	
Mich State Univ	MI	22,450	VC
Miss Univ for Women	MS	7,400	C
Montclair State Univ	NJ	22,614	C
Mount Marty College	SD	29,638	C
Murray State Univ	KY	15,304	C
Newbury College	MA	43,280	LC
Nicholls State Univ	LA	7,095	C
Purdue Univ/West Lafayette	IN	20,024	HC
Rochester Inst of Technology	NY	42,450	VC
Seton Hill Univ	PA	35,172	C
Simmons College	MA	49,966	VC
S Dak State Univ	SD	14,296	C
Southern Illinois Univ Carbondale	IL	21,942	C
Texas A&M Univ at Kingsville	TX	7,500	LC
Texas Christian Univ	TX	49,980	HC
Texas Tech Univ	TX	14,243	C
Univ of Central Florida	FL	15,668	VC+
Univ of Delaware	DE	23,612	VC
Univ of Georgia	GA	20,082	VC
Univ of Illinois at Urbana-Champaign	IL	26,450	HC
Univ of Nebr - Lincoln	NE	18,031	VC
Univ of Nevada, Las Vegas	NV	17,303	C
Univ of Wisc/Stout	WI	15,459	C
Western Mich Univ	MI	19,628	C

FOOD SCIENCE

School	ST	$IS	SR
Alabama A&M Univ	AL	10,084	C
Ashland Univ	OH	25,000	C
Auburn Univ	AL	22,378	VC+

School	ST	$IS	SR
Bluffton Univ	OH	38,948	C
Brigham Young Univ	UT	12,100	HC
Calif Polytechnic State Univ	CA	19,847	HC
Calif State Polytechnic Univ, Pomona	CA	20,156	C
Cal State, Fresno	CA	17,405	C
Cal State, San Bernardino	CA	12,000	C
Central Washington Univ	WA	11,730	C
Clarke Univ	IA	37,600	C
Clemson Univ	SC	19,136	HC
College of the Ozarks	MO		VC
Colo State Univ-Fort Collins	CO	20,385	VC
Cornell Univ	NY	60,964	MC
Delaware Valley College	PA	29,944	C
Dominican Univ	IL	37,628	C
Florida State Univ	FL	16,715	VC
Framingham State Univ	MA	18,854	C
Immaculata Univ	PA	43,000	C
Indiana State Univ	IN	16,000	C
Iowa State Univ	IA	16,403	C
Kansas State Univ	KS	15,497	VC
Madonna Univ	MI	24,540	VC
Mich State Univ	MI	22,450	VC
Miss State Univ	MS	14,750	C
N Car State Univ	NC	16,202	HC
N Dak State Univ	ND		C
Northwest Missouri State Univ	MO	17,347	C
Okla State Univ	OK	14,310	VC
Oregon State Univ	OR	20,273	VC
Purdue Univ/West Lafayette	IN	20,024	HC
Rutgers, The State Univ of New Jersey/New Brunswick	NJ	25,562	VC
San Jose State Univ	CA	19,133	LC
Seattle Pacific Univ	WA	41,559	VC+
Simmons College	MA	49,966	VC
S Car State Univ	SC	6,700	LC
S Dak State Univ	SD	14,296	C
Southern Illinois Univ Carbondale	IL	21,942	C
Syracuse Univ	NY	56,346	VC
Texas A&M Univ at Kingsville	TX	7,500	LC
Texas Tech Univ	TX	14,243	C
The Pennsylvania State Univ - Univ Park	PA	28,022	VC+
Tuskegee Univ	AL	26,750	C
Univ of Alabama at Tuscaloosa	AL	17,164	C+
Univ of Arkansas at Fayetteville	AR	18,352	C+
Univ of Calif at Davis	CA		HC
Univ of Delaware	DE	23,612	VC
Univ of Florida	FL	15,943	HC
Univ of Georgia	GA	20,082	VC
Univ of Hawaii at Manoa	HI	19,379	C
Univ of Idaho	ID	14,558	C
Univ of Illinois at Urbana-Champaign	IL	26,450	HC
Univ of Kentucky	KY	19,868	C
Univ of Maine	ME	19,902	C+
Univ of Mass Amherst	MA	24,215	VC+
Univ of Minn/Twin Cities	MN		HC
Univ of Missouri/Columbia	MO	18,201	MC
Univ of Nebr - Lincoln	NE	18,031	VC
Univ of Tenn at Knoxville	TN	20,364	VC+
Univ of the District of Columbia	DC	7,244	LC
Univ of Vermont	VT	27,006	VC+
Univ of Washington	WA	14,722	VC
Univ of Wisc/Madison	WI	18,757	HC+
Univ of Wisc/River Falls	WI	9,722	C
Utah State Univ	UT	12,044	C
Virginia Polytechnic Inst and State Univ	VA	14,629	HC
Washington State Univ	WA	20,461	C
Wayne State Univ	MI	22,063	C
Youngstown State Univ	OH	16,732	C

FOOD SERVICES TECHNOLOGY

School	ST	$IS	SR
Brigham Young Univ	UT	12,100	HC
Delaware Valley College	PA	29,944	C
Inter-American Univ of PR/ Bayamon Univ College	PR	4,428	
Johnson & Wales Univ/ Charlotte Campus	NC	29,576	C
Johnson & Wales Univ/North Miami Campus	FL		C
Johnson & Wales Univ/ Providence Campus	RI	29,576	C
Minn State Univ, Mankato	MN	15,616	C
Purdue Univ/West Lafayette	IN	20,024	HC
St. Catherine Univ	MN	37,782	C+
Univ of Central Florida	FL	15,668	VC+
Univ of Wisc/Stout	WI	15,459	C

FOOD TECHNOLOGY FOR COMPANION ANIMALS

School	ST	$IS	SR
Univ of Nebr - Lincoln	NE	18,031	VC

FOREIGN LANGUAGE

School	ST	$IS	SR
Arkansas State Univ	AR	15,470	C
Bowling Green State Univ	OH	18,970	C

School	ST	$IS	SR
Bryant Univ	RI	49,179	VC
Eastern Illinois Univ	IL	20,466	C
Gannon Univ	PA	39,608	C
New Mexico State Univ	NM	14,050	C
Niagara Univ	NY	41,010	C
Northwestern State Univ of Louisiana	LA	14,368	C
Oakwood Univ	AL	25,529	NC
Southern Illinois Univ Carbondale	IL	21,942	C
Southern Oregon Univ	OR	17,874	C
Thomas Edison State College	NJ	5,700	SP
Univ of Alabama at Birmingham	AL	18,484	C+
Univ of Louisiana at Monroe	LA	12,998	C
Univ of Maryland - College Park	MD	20,060	HC
Western Illinois Univ	IL	20,732	C

FOREIGN LANGUAGES EDUCATION

School	ST	$IS	SR
Abilene Christian Univ	TX	38,400	C+
Adams State Univ	CO	13,358	LC
Alabama State Univ	AL	14,142	NC
American International College	MA	36,100	LC
American Univ	DC	56,015	HC+
Anderson Univ	IN	36,100	C
Appalachian State Univ	NC	12,919	VC
Arizona State Univ, at the Tempe Campus	AZ	20,137	C+
Arkansas State Univ	AR	15,470	C
Arkansas Tech Univ	AR	13,982	LC
Asbury Univ	KY	32,038	VC
Ashland Univ	OH	25,000	C
Auburn Univ	AL	22,378	VC+
Baylor Univ	TX	50,329	HC
Bemidji State Univ	MN	13,500	VC
Bennington College	VT	56,990	HC+
Bethel Univ	MN	34,940	VC
Boston Univ	MA	60,694	MC
Bowling Green State Univ	OH	18,970	C
Bryant Univ	RI	49,179	VC
Buffalo State College / SUNY	NY	15,733	C+
Cameron Univ	OK	10,004	LC
Canisius College	NY	44,900	C
Carroll College	MT	28,000	C
Carroll Univ	WI	38,100	C
Carson-Newman Univ	TN	29,058	C+
Carthage College	WI	33,000	C
Cedarville Univ	OH	32,860	VC
Central Washington Univ	WA	11,730	C
CUNY/Brooklyn College	NY	5,884	C+
CUNY/City College	NY	20,319	HC+
Clarion Univ of Pennsylvania	PA	17,370	LC
College of Charleston	SC	22,145	VC
Colo State Univ-Fort Collins	CO	20,385	VC
Columbus State Univ	GA	13,176	C
Concordia College - Moorhead	MN	39,974	VC
Converse College	SC	37,130	C
Cornell College	IA	44,930	VC
Daemen College	NY	34,770	C
Delta State Univ	MS	12,292	LC
DePaul Univ	IL	47,623	VC
DePauw Univ	IN	48,950	VC+
Dordt College	IA	34,160	C+
Duquesne Univ	PA	43,720	VC
East Carolina Univ	NC	14,169	C
East Stroudsburg Univ of Pennsylvania	PA	18,868	LC
East Tenn State Univ	TN	9,000	C
East Texas Baptist Univ	TX	31,577	LC
Eastern Kentucky Univ	KY	11,161	C
Eastern Mich Univ	MI	18,604	C
Eastern Washington Univ	WA		C
Edinboro Univ of Pennsylvania	PA	15,940	LC
Elmira College	NY	49,950	C+
Elms College	MA	23,900	VC
Elon Univ	NC	41,914	VC+
Emporia State Univ	KS	12,897	C
Erskine College	SC	37,360	C
Eugene Lang College/The New School for Liberal Arts	NY	55,650	C
Evangel Univ	MO	23,090	C
Fairmont State Univ	WV	12,098	LC
Florida Atlantic Univ	FL	17,339	C
Florida State Univ	FL	16,715	VC
Friends Univ	KS	29,100	C
Gardner-Webb Univ	NC	34,375	C+
Georgetown College	KY	41,440	C+
Georgia Regents Univ	GA		C
Gettysburg College	PA	58,820	HC
Goshen College	IN	35,900	VC
Grace College and Seminary	IN	28,800	VC
Grand Valley State Univ	MI	17,998	C+
Greensboro College	NC	28,740	LC
Gustavus Adolphus College	MN	48,170	VC
Hamline Univ	MN	45,678	VC
Harding Univ	AR	23,556	C
Hardin-Simmons Univ	TX	23,560	C+
Hastings College	NE	27,782	C+
Heidelberg Univ	OH	34,100	C

ST = STATE $IS = IN-STATE COSTS   SR = SELECTOR RATING

School	ST	$IS	SR
Hofstra Univ	NY	51,810	VC+
Holy Family Univ	PA	40,030	LC
Hood College	MD	45,730	C
Hope College	MI	38,650	VC
Houghton College	NY	36,808	C+
Hunter College	NY	14,429	VC
Illinois College	IL	25,770	VC
Immaculata Univ	PA	43,000	C
Indiana State Univ	IN	16,000	C
Indiana Univ-Purdue Univ Fort Wayne	IN	15,521	C
Ithaca College	NY	53,864	HC
Juniata College	PA	49,340	VC
King's College	PA	43,502	C
Kutztown Univ of Pennsylvania	PA	16,909	LC
La Salle Univ	PA	50,270	C
Lamar Univ	TX	6,820	LC
Le Moyne College	NY	43,470	C
Lehman College/The CUNY	NY	5,778	LC
Lenoir-Rhyne College	NC	35,984	C
Lipscomb Univ	TN	37,490	VC
LIU Post	NY	47,660	C
Lock Haven Univ of Pennsylvania	PA	18,028	LC
Louisiana Tech Univ	LA	11,302	C
Manhattan College	NY	49,588	C+
Mansfield Univ	PA	19,468	LC
Marshall Univ	WV	14,820	C
Marywood Univ	PA	45,595	C
Messiah College	PA	40,690	C+
Miami Univ	OH	24,191	VC
Minn State Univ, Mankato	MN	15,616	C
Minn State Univ, Moorhead	MN	13,392	VC
Minot State Univ	ND	10,915	C
Missouri Western State Univ	MO	12,260	NC
Monmouth Univ	NJ	44,108	C
Murray State Univ	KY	15,304	C
Muskingum Univ	OH	30,502	C
Nazareth College of Rochester	NY	43,028	C+
New York Univ	NY	61,470	MC
Niagara Univ	NY	41,010	C
N Car State Univ	NC	16,202	HC
Northern State Univ - Aberdeen	SD	14,505	C
Northwestern College of Iowa	IA	36,240	VC
Notre Dame of Maryland Univ	MD	27,700	VC
Ohio Wesleyan Univ	OH	49,460	C+
Okla Baptist Univ	OK	28,202	C
Old Dominion Univ	VA	19,483	LC
Oral Roberts Univ	OK	31,734	C
Oswego / SUNY	NY	20,009	VC
Ouachita Baptist Univ	AR	30,220	VC
Prescott College	AZ	33,284	C
Providence College	RI	57,383	VC
Purdue Univ/Calumet	IN	14,336	C
Purdue Univ/West Lafayette	IN	20,024	HC
Radford Univ	VA	17,766	LC
Rhode Island College	RI	17,694	LC
Rider Univ	NJ	45,720	C
Rockhurst Univ	MO	20,625	C
Rosemont College	PA	42,350	C
Rowan Univ	NJ	24,022	VC+
Sacred Heart Univ	CT	49,264	VC
Saginaw Valley State Univ	MI	17,369	C
St. Michael's College	VT	49,975	VC
St. Xavier Univ	IL	32,840	C
Seton Hill Univ	PA	35,172	C
Shippensburg Univ of Pennsylvania	PA	20,934	C
Slippery Rock Univ of Pennsylvania	PA	10,360	C
Southeast Missouri State Univ	MO	15,370	LC
Southern Conn State Univ	CT	18,033	LC
Southern Univ at New Orleans	LA	2,963	NC
Southwest Minn State Univ	MN	14,000	C
St. Cloud State Univ	MN	10,600	C
St. Edward's Univ	TX	47,784	C
St. John Fisher College	NY	40,708	C+
St. John's Univ	NY	55,070	C+
St. Thomas Aquinas College	NY	40,230	C
SUNY College at Old Westbury	NY	16,324	C
SUNY Cortland/The SUNY	NY	19,759	C+
SUNY Fredonia/The SUNY at Fredonia	NY	19,840	VC
SUNY New Paltz	NY	14,348	C
SUNY Oneonta / SUNY	NY	16,919	C+
Taylor Univ	IN	37,821	VC+
Texas Southern Univ	TX	18,212	LC
Texas Wesleyan Univ	TX	31,382	C
The Pennsylvania State Univ - Univ Park	PA	28,022	VC+
The Univ of N Car at Greensboro	NC	12,848	C
The Univ of Okla	OK	18,621	VC
Universidad del Turabo	PR	4,110	
Univ of Central Arkansas	AR	13,667	VC
Univ of Central Florida	FL	15,668	VC+
Univ of Central Missouri	MO	14,605	C
Univ of Central Okla	OK	12,293	C
Univ of Cincinnati	OH	21,506	VC
Univ of Conn	CT	24,706	HC
Univ of Delaware	DE	23,612	VC
Univ of Evansville	IN	42,656	VC+
Univ of Findlay	OH	31,916	C
Univ of Idaho	ID	14,558	C
Univ of Illinois at Urbana-Champaign	IL	26,450	HC
Univ of Indianapolis	IN	31,740	LC
Univ of Iowa	IA	17,693	VC
Univ of Kentucky	KY	19,868	C
Univ of Louisiana at Lafayette	LA	6,130	C
Univ of Louisiana at Monroe	LA	12,998	C
Univ of Louisville	KY	17,946	C
Univ of Mary Hardin-Baylor	TX	31,950	C+
Univ of Mich-Flint	MI	17,547	C+
Univ of Minn/Duluth	MN	19,806	C
Univ of Nebr - Lincoln	NE	18,031	VC
Univ of Nebr at Kearney	NE	14,855	C
Univ of New Orleans	LA	9,224	C
Univ of North Alabama	AL	9,960	C
Univ of N Car at Charlotte	NC	15,547	C
Univ of North Georgia	GA	8,500	C
Univ of Northern Iowa	IA	15,795	C
Univ of PR/Mayaguez	PR	1,250	
Univ of South Florida/Tampa	FL	13,000	C
Univ of Southern Miss	MS	13,170	C
Univ of Toledo	OH	18,464	C
Univ of Vermont	VT	27,006	VC+
Univ of West Georgia	GA	15,488	LC
Univ of Wisc Whitewater	WI	13,314	C
Univ of Wisc/Green Bay	WI	19,074	C
Univ of Wisc/River Falls	WI	9,722	LC
Utah State Univ	UT	12,044	C
Utica College	NY	45,670	C
Valparaiso Univ	IN	44,940	VC+
Virginia Commonwealth Univ	VA	21,716	C
Virginia Polytechnic Inst and State Univ	VA	14,629	HC
Wartburg College	IA	41,055	VC
Washington State Univ	WA	20,461	C
Washington Univ in St. Louis	MO	69,844	MC
Webster Univ	MO	35,100	C
West Texas A&M Univ	TX	13,478	C
West Virginia Univ	WV	16,542	C+
Western Carolina Univ	NC	13,965	C
Western Mich Univ	MI	19,628	C
Western State Colo Univ	CO	16,924	C
Western Washington Univ	WA	18,519	VC
Whitworth Univ	WA	47,734	VC
Wilson College	PA	35,080	C
Winona State Univ	MN	16,640	C
Wittenberg Univ	OH	47,962	C+
Wright State Univ	OH	16,983	C

FORENSIC PSYCHOLOGY

School	ST	$IS	SR
Faulkner Univ	AL	25,720	LC
The College of St. Rose	NY	26,750	C
Univ of Central Okla	OK	12,293	C
Univ of Louisiana at Monroe	LA	12,998	C

FORENSIC SCIENCE

School	ST	$IS	SR
Alvernia Univ	PA	39,250	LC
Arizona State Univ, at the West Campus	AZ	19,251	C
Bethany College	KS	30,605	NC
Bethany College	WV	35,282	LC
Bryant Univ	RI	49,179	VC
Embry-Riddle Aeronautical Univ - Prescott Campus	AZ	40,444	VC+
Hilbert College	NY	28,550	C
Indiana Univ-Purdue Univ Indianapolis	IN	17,611	C
Marymount Univ	VA	39,480	C
Missouri Southern State Univ	MO	12,061	C
Murray State Univ	KY	15,304	C
Okla Christian Univ	OK	25,870	VC
Pace Univ	NY	53,367	C
Point Park Univ	PA	36,390	C
Roberts Wesleyan College	NY	38,306	C
San Jose State Univ	CA	19,133	LC
The College of St. Rose	NY	26,750	C
Univ of Central Florida	FL	15,668	VC+
Univ of Central Okla	OK	12,293	C
Univ of Illinois at Chicago	IL	24,505	VC
Univ of Nebr - Lincoln	NE	18,031	VC
Waynesburg Univ	PA	30,150	C
Western Illinois Univ	IL	20,732	C

FORENSIC STUDIES

School	ST	$IS	SR
Albany State Univ	GA	8,500	C
Arizona State Univ, at the West Campus	AZ	19,251	C
Bay Path College	MA	34,565	C
Baylor Univ	TX	50,329	HC
Becker College	MA	41,420	C
Bryant Univ	RI	49,179	VC
Cal State, Fresno	CA	17,405	C
Carlow Univ	PA	30,272	C
Cedarville Univ	OH	32,860	VC
Chaminade Univ of Honolulu	HI	31,664	LC
Champlain College	VT	46,650	VC+
Chatham Univ	PA	43,797	C
Chestnut Hill College	PA	42,110	LC
Columbia College	MO	24,578	C
Defiance College	OH	30,645	C
Eastern Kentucky Univ	KY	11,161	C
Eastern New Mexico Univ	NM	10,682	C
Edinboro Univ of Pennsylvania	PA	15,940	LC
Emmanuel College	MA	47,985	VC
Florida Gulf Coast Univ	FL		C
Florida Inst of Technology	FL	48,290	VC
Friends Univ	KS	29,100	C
Grand Canyon Univ	AZ	24,540	VC
Guilford College	NC	42,800	C
Hamline Univ	MN	45,678	VC
Heidelberg Univ	OH	34,100	C
Hilbert College	NY	28,550	C
Hofstra Univ	NY	51,810	VC+
Husson Univ	ME	24,194	VC
Inter-American Univ of PR/ Aguadilla Campus	PR	5,578	
Inter-American Univ of PR/ Bayamon Univ College	PR	4,428	
John Jay College of Criminal Justice/The CUNY	NY	6,359	LC
Keystone College	PA	28,680	LC
King Univ	TN	33,140	C
Lake Superior State Univ	MI	18,121	C
LIU Post	NY	47,660	C
Loyola Univ Chicago	IL	51,646	VC+
Loyola Univ New Orleans	LA	46,581	VC
Lynn Univ	FL	43,500	LC
Marshall Univ	WV	14,820	C
Marygrove College	MI	28,926	C
Maryville Univ of St. Louis	MO	35,856	VC
Mercyhurst Univ	PA	40,700	C
Missouri Southern State Univ	MO	12,061	C
Newman Univ	KS	30,380	C+
Northern Kentucky Univ	KY	21,134	C
Ohio Univ	OH	21,080	C
Pace Univ	NY	53,367	C
Russell Sage College	NY	39,370	C
St. Anselm College	NH	49,376	VC
Seattle Univ	WA	49,035	VC+
Seton Hill Univ	PA	35,172	C
Simpson College	IA	36,086	C+
Southern Illinois Univ Edwardsville	IL	17,532	C
Southern Univ at New Orleans	LA	2,963	NC
Southern Wesleyan Univ	SC	25,600	C
St. Ambrose Univ	IA	30,845	C
St. Andrews Univ	NC	32,050	LC
St. Edward's Univ	TX	47,784	C
Syracuse Univ	NY	56,346	VC
The Pennsylvania State Univ - Univ Park	PA	28,022	VC+
Thomas More College	KY	34,760	C
Tiffin Univ	OH	30,273	LC
Trine Univ	IN	39,400	HC+
Univ of Central Florida	FL	15,668	VC+
Univ of Central Okla	OK	12,293	C
Univ of Findlay	OH	31,916	C
Univ of Illinois at Chicago	IL	24,505	VC
Univ of Miss	MS	16,704	C+
Univ of New Haven	CT	48,940	C
Univ of N Dak	ND	14,551	C
Univ of Scranton	PA	51,940	VC
Univ of Tampa	FL	35,160	VC
Univ of Wisc/Platteville	WI	14,564	C
Univ of Wisc-Milwaukee	WI	18,436	C
Virginia Commonwealth Univ	VA	21,716	C
Washburn Univ	KS	12,579	C
West Chester Univ of Pennsylvania	PA	17,186	C
Western Carolina Univ	NC	13,965	C
Western New England Univ	MA	46,154	C+
Youngstown State Univ	OH	16,732	C

FOREST ENGINEERING

School	ST	$IS	SR
Auburn Univ	AL	22,378	VC+
Oregon State Univ	OR	20,273	VC
SUNY / College of Environmental Science and Forestry	NY	18,351	VC
Univ of Maine	ME	19,902	C+
Univ of Washington	WA	14,722	VC

FORESTRY AND RELATED SCIENCES

School	ST	$IS	SR
Alabama A&M Univ	AL	10,084	C
Albion College	MI	46,010	C
Beloit College	WI	49,970	HC
Calif Polytechnic State Univ	CA	19,847	HC
Clemson Univ	SC	19,136	NC
Colo State Univ-Fort Collins	CO	20,385	VC
Eastern Oregon Univ	OR	10,400	C
Elizabethtown College	PA	49,740	VC
Glenville State College	WV	11,348	NC
Humboldt State Univ	CA	18,400	C
Iowa State Univ	IA	16,403	C
Louisiana State Univ	LA	18,677	C+
Louisiana Tech Univ	LA	11,302	C
Mich State Univ	MI	22,450	VC
Mich Tech Univ	MI	23,556	HC
N Car State Univ	NC	16,202	HC
Northern Arizona Univ	AZ	19,010	C
Northwest Missouri State Univ	MO	17,347	C
Oregon State Univ	OR	20,273	VC
Prescott College	AZ	33,284	C
Purdue Univ/West Lafayette	IN	20,024	HC
Sewanee: The Univ of the South	TN	47,700	HC+
S Dak State Univ	SD	14,296	C
Southern Illinois Univ Carbondale	IL	21,942	C
Southern Univ and A&M College	LA	9,761	LC
SUNY / College of Environmental Science and Forestry	NY	18,351	VC
Stephen F. Austin State Univ	TX	14,668	C
Texas A&M Univ	TX	19,207	VC
Ohio State Univ-Columbus Campus	OH	19,887	HC+
The Pennsylvania State Univ - Univ Park	PA	28,022	VC+
Univ of Arkansas at Monticello	AR	12,076	NC
Univ of Calif at Berkeley	CA	23,322	MC
Univ of Florida	FL	15,943	HC
Univ of Georgia	GA	20,082	VC
Univ of Idaho	ID	14,558	C
Univ of Illinois at Urbana-Champaign	IL	26,450	HC
Univ of Kentucky	KY	19,868	C
Univ of Maine	ME	19,902	C+
Univ of Maine at Fort Kent	ME	15,195	C
Univ of Minn/Twin Cities	MN		HC
Univ of Missouri/Columbia	MO	18,201	HC
Univ of Montana	MT	14,105	C
Univ of New Hampshire	NH	26,912	C
Univ of Tenn at Knoxville	TN	20,364	VC+
Univ of Vermont	VT	27,006	VC+
Univ of Wisc/Madison	WI	18,757	HC+
Univ of Wisc/Stevens Point	WI	14,043	C
Utah State Univ	UT	12,044	C
Virginia Polytechnic Inst and State Univ	VA	14,629	HC
West Virginia Univ	WV	16,542	C+
Western New Mexico Univ	NM	8,500	LC

FORESTRY PRODUCTION AND PROCESSING

School	ST	$IS	SR
Auburn Univ	AL	22,378	VC+
Clemson Univ	SC	19,136	HC
Miss State Univ	MS	14,750	C
Oregon State Univ	OR	20,273	VC
Stephen F. Austin State Univ	TX	14,668	C
Univ of Idaho	ID	14,558	C
Univ of Minn/Twin Cities	MN		HC
Univ of Washington	WA	14,722	VC

FRENCH

School	ST	$IS	SR
Adelphi Univ	NY	44,670	VC
Adrian College	MI	42,400	C
Agnes Scott College	GA	45,323	C+
Alabama A&M Univ	AL	10,084	C
Alabama State Univ	AL	14,142	NC
Albany State Univ	GA	8,500	C
Albion College	MI	46,010	C
Albright College	PA	46,660	C
Allegheny College	PA	50,980	HC
Alma College	MI	44,075	C
American Univ	DC	56,015	HC+
Amherst College	MA	58,744	MC
Anderson Univ	IN	36,100	C
Andrews Univ	MI	28,030	C
Angelo State Univ	TX	15,049	NC
Appalachian State Univ	NC	12,919	VC
Aquinas College	MI	33,060	C
Arizona State Univ, at the Tempe Campus	AZ	20,137	C+
Asbury Univ	KY	32,038	VC
Ashland Univ	OH	25,000	C
Assumption College	MA	47,122	C
Auburn Univ	AL	22,378	VC+
Augsburg College	MN	35,142	C
Augustana College	IL	43,398	VC
Augustana College	SD	36,500	VC
Austin College	TX	45,875	HC
Baker Univ	KS	33,350	C+
Baldwin Wallace Univ	OH	38,318	C
Ball State Univ	IN	17,850	C
Bard College	NY	61,940	HC
Barnard College/Columbia Univ	NY	39,000	MC
Barry Univ	FL	38,190	C
Baylor Univ	TX	50,329	HC
Belmont Univ	TN	39,190	VC+
Beloit College	WI	49,970	HC
Benedictine College	KS	29,180	VC
Bennington College	VT	56,990	HC+
Berea College	KY	7,192	C
Berry College	GA	39,254	VC
Bethel Univ	MN	34,940	VC
Binghamton Univ/The SUNY	NY	21,648	HC+
Birmingham-Southern College	AL	44,168	VC+

ST = STATE $IS = IN-STATE COSTS   SR = SELECTOR RATING

School	ST	$IS	SR
Bloomsburg Univ of Pennsylvania	PA	13,598	C
Boise State Univ	ID	13,469	LC
Boston College	MA	60,622	MC
Boston Univ	MA	60,694	MC
Bowdoin College	ME	59,568	MC
Bowling Green State Univ	OH	18,970	C
Bradley Univ	IL	31,874	VC
Brandeis Univ	MA		MC
Bridgewater College	VA	41,450	C
Brigham Young Univ	UT	12,100	HC
Bryant Univ	RI	49,179	VC
Bryn Mawr College	PA	59,890	MC
Bucknell Univ	PA	60,140	MC
Buffalo State College / SUNY	NY	15,733	C+
Butler Univ	IN	47,572	VC+
Cabrini College	PA	40,859	LC
Caldwell College	NJ	35,602	NC
Calif Lutheran Univ	CA	49,540	C+
Cal State, Fresno	CA	17,405	C
Cal State, Fullerton	CA	25,188	C
Cal State, Long Beach	CA	17,502	C+
Cal State, Los Angeles	CA	17,186	LC
Cal State, Northridge	CA	28,690	LC
Cal State, Sacramento	CA	16,200	C
Cal State, San Bernardino	CA	12,000	C
Cal State, Stanislaus	CA	18,582	C
Calif Univ of Pennsylvania	PA	14,217	C
Calvin College	MI	39,120	VC
Campbell Univ	NC	37,570	VC
Canisius College	NY	44,900	C
Capital Univ	OH	41,050	VC
Cardinal Stritch Univ	WI	24,054	C
Carleton College	MN	60,102	MC
Carnegie Mellon Univ	PA	51,260	MC
Carroll College	MT	28,000	C
Carson-Newman Univ	TN	29,058	C+
Carthage College	WI	33,000	C
Case Western Reserve Univ	OH	56,534	MC
Centenary College of Louisiana	LA	45,650	C+
Central College	IA	42,104	C+
Central Conn State Univ	CT	19,749	C
Central Washington Univ	WA	11,730	C
Centre College	KY	35,000	HC+
Chapman Univ	CA	58,347	VC+
Chestnut Hill College	PA	42,110	LC
Christopher Newport Univ	VA	21,960	VC
Citadel, The	SC		C
CUNY/Brooklyn College	NY	5,884	C+
CUNY/City College	NY	20,519	HC+
Claremont McKenna College	CA	62,215	MC
Clarion Univ of Pennsylvania	PA	17,370	LC
Clark Univ	MA	47,020	HC
Clemson Univ	SC	19,136	HC
Cleveland State Univ	OH	21,776	C
Coe College	IA	45,550	VC
Colgate Univ	NY	58,135	MC
College of Mount St. Vincent	NY	41,040	NC
College of St. Benedict	MN	49,359	VC
College of the Holy Cross	MA	58,042	MC
College of William & Mary	VA	28,000	MC
College of Wooster	OH	52,600	VC
Colo State Univ-Fort Collins	CO	20,385	VC
Columbia College	SC	27,882	C
Columbia Univ/City of New York	NY	61,116	MC
Columbia Univ/School of General Studies	NY	58,231	MC
Columbus State Univ	GA	13,176	C
Concordia College - Moorhead	MN	39,974	VC
Conn College	CT	54,970	MC
Converse College	SC	37,130	C
Cornell College	IA	44,930	VC
Cornell Univ	NY	60,964	MC
Covenant College	GA	38,990	VC+
Daemen College	NY	34,770	C
Dartmouth College	NH	57,996	MC
Davidson College	NC	58,146	MC
Delaware State Univ	DE	16,722	C
Denison Univ	OH	54,670	HC+
DePaul Univ	IL	47,623	VC
DePauw Univ	IN	48,950	VC+
Dickinson College	PA	57,662	HC+
Doane College	NE	35,230	C
Dominican Univ	IL	31,909	VC
Drew Univ/College of Liberal Arts	NJ	57,516	C
Drury Univ	MO	31,909	VC
Earlham College	IN	51,470	HC
East Carolina Univ	NC	14,169	C
East Stroudsburg Univ of Pennsylvania	PA	18,868	LC
Eastern Kentucky Univ	KY	11,161	C
Eastern Mennonite Univ	VA	40,660	C
Eastern Mich Univ	MI	18,604	C
Eastern Nazarene College	MA	30,000	C
Eastern Washington Univ	WA		C
Eckerd College	FL	43,902	C
Edgewood College	WI	33,294	VC
Elizabethtown College	PA	49,740	VC
Elmhurst College	IL	43,336	C
Elmira College	NY	49,950	C+
Elon Univ	NC	41,914	VC+
Emory Univ	GA	56,368	MC
Fairfield Univ	CT	56,960	VC
Fairmont State Univ	WV	12,098	LC
Fisk Univ	TN	19,830	C
Florida Atlantic Univ	FL	17,339	C
Florida International Univ	FL	17,747	C+
Florida State Univ	FL	16,715	VC
Fordham Univ	NY	61,588	HC+
Fort Hays State Univ	KS	11,354	C
Franciscan Univ of Steubenville	OH	27,320	VC
Franklin and Marshall College	PA	60,799	MC
Franklin College	IN	36,585	C
Furman Univ	SC	54,006	HC
Gardner-Webb Univ	NC	34,375	C+
George Mason Univ	VA	15,724	VC
George Washington Univ	DC	57,108	MC
Georgetown College	KY	41,440	C+
Georgetown Univ	DC	52,910	MC
Georgia College and State Univ	GA	18,900	C+
Georgia State Univ	GA	15,582	VC
Gettysburg College	PA	58,820	HC
Gonzaga Univ	WA	46,441	HC
Gordon College	MA	44,320	VC
Goucher College	MD	52,040	VC+
Grace College and Seminary	IN	28,800	VC
Grand Valley State Univ	MI	17,998	C+
Greensboro College	NC	28,740	LC
Grinnell College	IA	53,654	HC
Grove City College	PA	24,022	VC
Guilford College	NC	42,800	C
Gustavus Adolphus College	MN	48,170	HC
Hamilton College	NY	55,620	MC
Hamline Univ	MN	45,678	VC
Hampden-Sydney College	VA	51,758	C
Hanover College	IN	43,073	C+
Harding Univ	AR	23,556	C
Hartwick College	NY	51,270	C
Harvard College/Harvard Univ	MA	49,000	MC
Haverford College	PA	61,564	MC
Hendrix College	AR	50,202	VC+
High Point Univ	NC	39,800	C
Hillsdale College	MI	32,866	MC
Hiram College	OH	37,300	VC
Hobart and William Smith Colleges	NY	60,034	HC+
Hofstra Univ	NY	51,810	VC+
Hollins Univ	VA	43,295	VC
Hood College	MD	45,730	C
Hope College	MI	38,650	VC
Houston Baptist Univ	TX	36,450	C
Howard Univ	DC	13,646	C
Humboldt State Univ	CA	18,400	C
Hunter College	NY	14,429	VC
Idaho State Univ	ID	12,307	C
Illinois College	IL	25,770	VC
Illinois State Univ	IL	23,110	VC
Illinois Wesleyan Univ	IL	48,452	HC
Immaculata Univ	PA	43,000	C
Indiana State Univ	IN	16,000	C
Indiana Univ Bloomington	IN	19,801	VC
Indiana Univ Northwest	IN	6,854	LC
Indiana Univ South Bend	IN	15,501	C
Indiana Univ Southeast	IN	16,035	C
Indiana-Purdue Univ Fort Wayne	IN	15,521	C
Indiana-Purdue Univ Indianapolis	IN	17,611	C
Iona College	NY	44,028	C
Iowa State Univ	IA	16,403	VC
Ithaca College	NY	53,864	HC
Jacksonville Univ	FL	37,780	C
John Carroll Univ	OH	46,300	C+
Johns Hopkins Univ	MD	47,492	MC
Johnson C. Smith Univ	NC	25,336	LC
Juniata College	PA	49,340	VC
Kalamazoo College	MI	49,740	HC
Kent State Univ	OH	19,920	C
Kenyon College	OH	58,890	MC
King Univ	TN	33,140	C
King's College	PA	43,502	C
Knox College	IL	44,865	VC+
Kutztown Univ of Pennsylvania	PA	16,909	LC
La Salle Univ	PA	50,270	C
Lafayette College	PA	59,155	HC+
Lake Forest College	IL	50,652	VC
Lamar Univ	TX	6,820	LC
Lane College	TN	11,212	C
Lawrence Univ	WI	46,371	HC
Le Moyne College	NY	43,470	C
Lebanon Valley College	PA	38,570	C
Lee Univ	TN	18,690	C+
Lehigh Univ	PA	56,770	MC
Lehman College/The CUNY	NY	5,778	LC
Lenoir-Rhyne College	NC	35,984	C
Lindenwood Univ	MO	20,750	C
Linfield College-McMinnville Campus	OR	47,676	C
Lipscomb Univ	TN	37,490	VC
LIU Brooklyn	NY	47,182	LC
LIU Post	NY	47,660	C
Lock Haven Univ of Pennsylvania	PA	18,028	LC
Louisiana College	LA	15,746	C
Louisiana State Univ	LA	18,677	C+
Louisiana Tech Univ	LA	11,302	C
Loyola Marymount Univ	CA	54,649	VC+
Loyola Univ Chicago	IL	51,646	VC+
Loyola Univ Maryland	MD	56,880	VC+
Loyola Univ New Orleans	LA	46,581	VC
Luther College	IA	45,720	C+
Lycoming College	PA	45,379	C
Lynchburg College	VA	42,645	C
Macalester College	MN	57,691	MC
Manchester Univ	IN	35,070	C
Manhattan College	NY	49,588	C+
Manhattanville College	NY	50,740	VC
Mansfield Univ	PA	19,468	LC
Marian Univ	IN	38,540	C
Marist College	NY	35,500	C
Marlboro College	VT	35,980	VC
Marquette Univ	WI	46,930	VC+
Marshall Univ	WV	14,820	C
Marywood Univ	PA	45,595	C
McDaniel College	MD	47,450	VC
Mercer Univ	GA	44,201	VC
Meredith College	NC	31,420	C
Messiah College	PA	40,690	C+
Methodist Univ	NC	37,185	C
Miami Univ	OH	24,191	VC
Mich State Univ	MI	22,450	VC
Middle Tenn State Univ	TN	8,650	C
Middlebury College	VT	59,160	MC
Millersville Univ of Pennsylvania	PA	21,648	C
Mills College	CA	54,119	VC
Minn State Univ, Mankato	MN	15,616	C
Minot State Univ	ND	10,915	C
Miss College	MS	21,998	C
Missouri Southern State Univ	MO	12,061	C
Missouri State Univ	MO	13,596	C
Missouri Western State Univ	MO	12,260	NC
Monmouth College	IL	40,850	C
Montana State Univ-Northern	MT	12,500	NC
Montclair State Univ	NJ	22,614	C
Moravian College	PA	36,381	VC
Morehouse College	GA	39,412	C
Mount Holyoke College	MA	55,146	MC
Mount St. Mary's Univ	MD	47,996	C
Mount St. Mary's College - Chalon Campus	CA	43,897	VC+
Muhlenberg College	PA	52,837	HC
Murray State Univ	KY	15,304	C
Muskingum Univ	OH	30,502	C
Nazareth College of Rochester	NY	43,028	C+
Nebr Wesleyan Univ	NE	29,774	C+
New College of Florida	FL	14,504	MC
New York Univ	NY	61,470	MC
Newberry College	SC	26,850	LC
Niagara Univ	NY	41,010	C
Nicholls State Univ	LA	7,095	C
N Car Agricultural and Technical State Univ	NC	13,365	LC
N Car Central Univ	NC	9,000	C
N Car State Univ	NC	16,202	HC
North Central College	IL	38,343	VC
N Dak State Univ	ND		C
North Park Univ	IL	30,130	C
Northeastern Illinois Univ	IL	10,318	LC
Northern Illinois Univ	IL	19,768	C
Northern Kentucky Univ	KY	21,134	C
Northern Mich Univ	MI	18,278	C
Northern State Univ - Aberdeen	SD	14,505	C
Northwestern Univ	IL	61,640	MC
Oakland Univ	MI	19,391	C
Oakwood Univ	AL	25,529	NC
Oberlin College	OH	61,788	MC
Occidental College	CA	60,972	MC
Oglethorpe Univ	GA	44,200	C+
Ohio Northern Univ	OH	42,075	VC
Ohio Univ	OH	21,080	C
Ohio Wesleyan Univ	OH	49,460	C+
Okla Baptist Univ	OK	28,202	C
Okla City Univ	OK	40,476	VC
Okla State Univ	OK	14,310	VC
Old Dominion Univ	VA	19,483	LC
Oral Roberts Univ	OK	31,734	C
Oregon State Univ	OR	20,273	VC
Oswego / SUNY	NY	20,009	VC
Otterbein College	OH	32,214	C
Pacific Lutheran Univ	WA	46,760	C+
Pacific Union College	CA	28,150	VC
Pepperdine Univ	CA	55,372	HC+
Pittsburg State Univ	KS	12,032	C
Pitzer College	CA	54,988	MC
Plymouth State Univ	NH	23,148	C
Pomona College	CA	57,680	MC
Portland State Univ	OR	18,672	C
Presbyterian College	SC	42,678	C+
Princeton Univ	NJ	53,795	MC
Principia College	IL	35,140	C+
Providence College	RI	57,383	VC
Purdue Univ/Calumet	IN	14,336	C
Purdue Univ/West Lafayette	IN	20,024	HC
Queens College/The CUNY	NY	17,107	VC
Queens Univ of Charlotte	NC	39,543	C+
Randolph College	VA	45,660	VC
Randolph-Macon College	VA	49,869	C+
Regis Univ	CO	41,318	C
Rhode Island College	RI	17,694	LC
Rhodes College	TN	51,900	HC+
Rider Univ	NJ	45,720	C
Ripon College	WI	36,959	C+
Roanoke College	VA	49,976	C
Rockford College	IL	31,000	C
Rockhurst Univ	MO	20,625	C
Rollins College	FL	52,370	HC
Roosevelt Univ	IL	22,605	VC
Rosemont College	PA	42,350	C
Rutgers, The State Univ of New Jersey/Camden Campus	NJ	25,121	C
Rutgers, The State Univ of New Jersey/New Brunswick	NJ	25,562	VC
Rutgers, The State Univ of New Jersey/Newark Campus	NJ	258,806	C
Saginaw Valley State Univ	MI	17,369	C
St. Anselm College	NH	49,376	VC
St. Augustine's Univ	NC	14,000	C
St. Francis Univ	PA	30,029	LC
St. John's College	MN	47,984	C
St. Joseph's Univ	PA	55,006	VC
St. Louis Univ	MO	48,346	HC
St. Mary's College	IN	45,160	C+
St. Mary's College of Calif	CA	53,550	C
St. Mary's Univ	TX	33,854	C
St. Michael's College	VT	49,975	VC
St. Vincent College	PA	40,244	C
St. Xavier Univ	IL	32,840	C
Salem College	NC	29,326	VC
Salisbury Univ	MD	19,180	VC
Salve Regina Univ	RI	48,550	VC
Sam Houston State Univ	TX	17,082	C
Samford Univ	AL	37,060	C+
San Diego State Univ	CA	21,611	C+
San Francisco State Univ	CA	18,514	C
San Jose State Univ	CA	19,133	LC
Sarah Lawrence College	NY	48,000	HC
Seattle Pacific Univ	WA	41,559	VC+
Seattle Univ	WA	49,035	VC+
Seton Hall Univ	NJ	45,902	C
Sewanee: The Univ of the South	TN	47,700	HC+
Shippensburg Univ of Pennsylvania	PA	20,934	C
Shorter Univ	GA	30,650	LC
Siena College	NY	43,863	VC
Simmons College	MA	49,966	VC
Simpson College	IA	36,086	C+
Skidmore College	NY	59,942	HC
Slippery Rock Univ of Pennsylvania	PA	10,360	C
Smith College	MA	59,674	MC
Sonoma State Univ	CA	20,541	C
S Car State Univ	SC	6,700	LC
Southern Conn State Univ	CT	18,033	LC
Southern Illinois Univ Carbondale	IL	21,942	C
Southern Illinois Univ Edwardsville	IL	17,532	C
Southern Methodist Univ	TX	60,585	MC
Southern Univ and A&M College	LA	9,761	LC
Southwestern Univ	TX	45,660	VC
Spelman College	GA	24,650	C
St. Ambrose Univ	IA	30,845	C
St. Bonaventure Univ	NY	41,575	C
St. Catherine Univ	MN	37,782	C+
St. Edward's Univ	TX	47,784	C
St. John Fisher College	NY	40,708	C+
St. John's Univ	NY	55,070	C+
St. Lawrence Univ	NY	59,972	VC
St. Norbert College	WI	41,478	VC
St. Olaf College	MN	51,200	HC+
Stanford Univ	CA	58,388	MC
Stephen F. Austin State Univ	TX	14,668	C
Stetson Univ	FL	51,516	VC
Stonehill College	MA	46,780	HC
Suffolk Univ	MA	47,298	C
SUNY College at Geneseo	NY	18,670	HC
SUNY Fredonia/The SUNY at Fredonia	NY	19,840	VC
SUNY New Paltz	NY	14,348	C
SUNY Oneonta / SUNY	NY	16,919	C+
SUNY Plattsburgh / SUNY	NY	18,083	C
Susquehanna Univ	PA	51,150	C
Swarthmore College	PA	57,870	MC
Syracuse Univ	NY	56,346	VC
Temple Univ	PA	24,392	VC
Tenn Tech Univ	TN	11,310	C
Texas A&M Univ	TX	19,207	VC
Texas A&M Univ at Commerce	TX	10,496	C
Texas Christian Univ	TX	49,980	HC
Texas State Univ	TX	17,128	C
Texas Tech Univ	TX	14,243	C
The Catholic Univ of America	DC	52,852	VC
The College of New Rochelle	NY	33,600	C
The Lincoln Univ	PA	15,154	LC
Ohio State Univ-Columbus Campus	OH	19,887	HC+

ST = STATE　　$IS = IN-STATE COSTS　　SR = SELECTOR RATING

School	ST	$IS	SR
The Pennsylvania State Univ - Univ Park	PA	28,022	VC+
The SUNY at Potsdam	NY	18,473	C
The SUNY/College at Brockport	NY	19,002	C
The Univ of N Car at Greensboro	NC	12,848	C
The Univ of Okla	OK	18,621	VC
The Univ of Tenn at Chattanooga	TN	16,883	C
The Univ of Utah	UT	16,463	VC
The Univ of Virginia's College at Wise	VA	11,076	C
Thomas Edison State College	NJ	5,700	SP
Towson Univ	MD	16,000	VC
Transylvania Univ	KY	42,660	VC+
Trinity College	CT		HC+
Trinity Univ	TX	48,150	HC+
Truman State Univ	MO	15,541	HC
Tufts Univ	MA	58,780	MC
Tulane Univ	LA	60,861	MC
Union College	NE	23,270	C
Union Univ	TN	28,260	VC
Univ at Buffalo / The SUNY	NY	20,283	VC
Univ of Akron	OH	20,436	C
Univ of Alabama at Tuscaloosa	AL	17,164	C+
Univ of Alaska Fairbanks	AK	15,130	C
Univ of Arizona	AZ	20,657	C
Univ of Arkansas at Fayetteville	AR	18,352	C+
Univ of Arkansas at Little Rock	AR	17,609	LC
Univ of Calif at Berkeley	CA	23,322	MC
Univ of Calif at Davis	CA		HC
Univ of Calif at Irvine	CA	25,961	VC
Univ of Calif at Los Angeles	CA	25,686	MC
Univ of Calif at Riverside	CA	27,204	C+
Univ of Calif at Santa Barbara	CA	27,551	HC
Univ of Central Arkansas	AR	13,667	VC
Univ of Central Florida	FL	15,668	VC+
Univ of Central Missouri	MO	14,605	C
Univ of Central Okla	OK	12,293	C
Univ of Cincinnati	OH	21,506	VC
Univ of Colo Boulder	CO	22,605	VC+
Univ of Colo Denver	CO	17,904	C
Univ of Conn	CT	24,706	VC
Univ of Dallas	TX	45,500	VC+
Univ of Dayton	OH	49,070	VC
Univ of Denver	CO	51,787	VC+
Univ of Evansville	IN	42,656	VC+
Univ of Florida	FL	15,943	HC
Univ of Georgia	GA	20,082	VC
Univ of Hawaii at Manoa	HI	19,379	C
Univ of Houston	TX	19,796	VC
Univ of Idaho	ID	14,558	C
Univ of Illinois at Chicago	IL	24,505	VC
Univ of Illinois at Urbana-Champaign	IL	26,450	HC
Univ of Indianapolis	IN	31,740	LC
Univ of Iowa	IA	17,693	VC
Univ of Jamestown	ND	24,738	C
Univ of Kansas	KS	17,603	C+
Univ of Kentucky	KY	19,868	C
Univ of La Verne	CA	47,010	C
Univ of Louisiana at Lafayette	LA	6,130	C
Univ of Louisiana at Monroe	LA	12,998	C
Univ of Louisville	KY	17,946	C
Univ of Maine	ME	19,902	C+
Univ of Maine at Fort Kent	ME	15,195	LC
Univ of Mary Washington	VA	19,484	VC
Univ of Maryland - College Park	MD	20,060	HC
Univ of Maryland/Baltimore County	MD	18,000	VC
Univ of Mass Boston	MA	23,066	VC
Univ of Mass Dartmouth	MA	22,223	C
Univ of Miami	FL	57,034	MC
Univ of Mich/Ann Arbor	MI	22,102	MC
Univ of Mich/Dearborn	MI	9,885	VC
Univ of Mich-Flint	MI	17,547	C+
Univ of Minn/Morris	MN	17,150	VC
Univ of Minn/Twin Cities	MN		HC
Univ of Miss	MS	16,704	C+
Univ of Missouri/Columbia	MO	18,201	MC
Univ of Missouri-Kansas City	MO	19,603	C
Univ of Missouri-St. Louis	MO		VC
Univ of Montana	MT	14,105	C
Univ of Montevallo	AL	17,060	VC
Univ of Mount Union	OH	35,130	C
Univ of Nebr - Lincoln	NE	18,031	VC
Univ of Nebr at Kearney	NE	14,855	LC
Univ of Nebr at Omaha	NE	12,700	C
Univ of Nevada, Las Vegas	NV	17,303	C
Univ of Nevada/Reno	NV	17,507	C
Univ of New Hampshire	NH	26,912	C
Univ of New Mexico	NM	15,300	C
Univ of New Orleans	LA	9,224	C
Univ of North Alabama	AL	9,960	C
Univ of N Car at Asheville	NC	13,500	VC
Univ of N Car at Charlotte	NC	15,547	C
Univ of N Car at Wilmington	NC	13,572	VC
Univ of N Dak	ND	14,551	C
Univ of North Georgia	GA	8,500	C
Univ of North Texas	TX	15,628	C
Univ of Northern Colo	CO	18,446	C
Univ of Notre Dame	IN	57,117	MC
Univ of Oregon	OR	21,360	C+
Univ of Pennsylvania	PA	61,132	MC
Univ of Pittsburgh at Pittsburgh	PA	28,572	HC+
Univ of PR/Mayaguez	PR	1,250	
Univ of Puget Sound	WA	54,608	HC
Univ of Redlands	CA	40,500	VC
Univ of Rochester	NY	60,668	MC
Univ of San Diego	CA	54,818	HC+
Univ of San Francisco	CA	54,770	VC
Univ of Scranton	PA	51,940	VC
Univ of S Car at Columbia	SC	19,725	VC+
Univ of South Florida/Tampa	FL	13,000	VC
Univ of Southern Calif	CA	56,903	MC
Univ of Southern Indiana	IN	14,885	C
Univ of Southern Maine	ME	16,576	C
Univ of St. Thomas - Houston	TX	37,690	C
Univ of Tenn at Knoxville	TN	20,364	VC+
Univ of Tenn at Martin	TN	13,734	C
Univ of Texas at Arlington	TX	10,908	LC
Univ of Texas at Austin	TX	44,074	HC
Univ of Texas at El Paso	TX	8,764	NC
Univ of the District of Columbia	DC	7,244	LC
Univ of the Pacific	CA	52,146	VC
Univ of Toledo	OH	18,464	C
Univ of Tulsa	OK	46,331	MC
Univ of Vermont	VT	27,006	VC+
Univ of Virginia	VA	23,050	MC
Univ of Washington	WA	14,722	VC
Univ of Wisc Whitewater	WI	13,314	C
Univ of Wisc/Eau Claire	WI	15,730	VC
Univ of Wisc/Green Bay	WI	19,074	C
Univ of Wisc/La Crosse	WI	9,304	VC
Univ of Wisc/Madison	WI	18,757	HC+
Univ of Wisc/Oshkosh	WI	10,426	LC
Univ of Wisc/Parkside	WI	10,181	LC
Univ of Wisc/Stevens Point	WI	14,043	C
Univ of Wisc-Milwaukee	WI	18,436	C
Univ of Wyoming	WY	14,401	C+
Ursinus College	PA	57,580	VC
Utah State Univ	UT	12,044	C
Valparaiso Univ	IN	44,940	VC+
Vanderbilt Univ	TN	58,220	MC
Vassar College	NY	61,140	MC
Villanova Univ	PA	58,394	MC
Virginia Polytechnic Inst and State Univ	VA	14,629	HC
Virginia Wesleyan College	VA	28,433	LC
Wabash College	IN	46,850	VC
Wake Forest Univ	NC	58,838	MC
Walla Walla Univ	WA	26,256	NC
Walsh Univ	OH	35,100	C
Wartburg College	IA	41,055	VC
Washburn Univ	KS	12,579	C
Washington and Jefferson College	PA	51,948	VC
Washington and Lee Univ	VA	52,812	MC
Washington College	MD	52,602	VC
Washington State Univ	WA	20,461	C
Washington Univ in St. Louis	MO	69,844	MC
Webster Univ	MO	35,100	C+
Wellesley College	MA	59,038	MC
Wells College	NY	49,400	VC
Wesleyan College	GA	24,000	C
West Chester Univ of Pennsylvania	PA	17,186	C
Western Carolina Univ	NC	13,965	C
Western Kentucky Univ	KY	11,000	LC
Western Mich Univ	MI	19,628	C
Western Washington Univ	WA	18,519	VC
Westminster College	MO	31,720	VC
Westminster College	PA	31,290	C+
Westmont College	CA	41,500	VC
Wheaton College	IL	40,720	MC
Wheeling Jesuit Univ	WV	33,500	C
Whitman College	WA	55,988	MC
Whittier College	CA	43,416	C
Whitworth Univ	WA	47,734	VC
Wichita State Univ	KS	14,607	C+
Widener Univ	PA	52,418	C
Willamette Univ	OR	56,450	VC+
William Jewell College	MO	31,000	VC+
Williams College	MA	61,070	MC
Wilson College	PA	35,080	C
Winthrop Univ	SC	21,120	C
Wittenberg Univ	OH	47,962	C+
Wofford College	SC	45,795	VC
Wright State Univ	OH	16,983	C
Xavier Univ	OH	44,980	VC
Xavier Univ of Louisiana	LA	25,300	C
Yale Univ	CT	55,300	MC
Yeshiva Univ	NY	47,250	VC+
York College / The CUNY	NY	5,496	VC
Youngstown State Univ	OH	16,732	C

FRENCH AND FRANCOPHONE STUDIES

School	ST	$IS	SR
Bates College	ME	60,720	MC
Cal State, Long Beach	CA	17,502	C+
Creighton Univ	NE	45,356	VC

School	ST	$IS	SR
Kent State Univ	OH	19,920	C
Linfield College-McMinnville Campus	OR	47,676	C
Rhode Island College	RI	17,694	LC
Univ of Illinois at Chicago	IL	24,505	VC

FRENCH STUDIES

School	ST	$IS	SR
American Univ	DC	56,015	HC+
Appalachian State Univ	NC	12,919	VC
Aquinas College	MI	33,060	C
Bard College	NY	61,940	MC
Bard College at Simon's Rock	MA	61,749	HC+
Boston Univ	MA	60,694	MC
Brown Univ	RI	59,428	MC
Cal State, Chico	CA	20,158	C
Cal State, Fresno	CA	17,405	C
Cal State, Northridge	CA	28,690	C
Case Western Reserve Univ	OH	56,534	MC
Coe College	IA	45,550	VC
Colby College	ME	57,510	MC
College of Charleston	SC	22,145	C
Colo College	CO	57,162	MC
Columbia Univ/School of General Studies	NY	58,231	MC
Dartmouth College	NH	57,996	MC
Duke Univ	NC	50,250	MC
Emory Univ	GA	56,368	MC
Fairleigh Dickinson Univ/College at Florham	NJ	42,142	C
Fordham Univ	NY	61,588	HC+
Keene State College	NH	23,232	LC
Lake Erie College	OH	37,266	C
Lake Superior State Univ	MI	18,121	C
Lewis & Clark College	OR	54,382	MC
Mills College	CA	54,119	C
New College of Florida	FL	14,504	MC
New York Univ	NY	61,470	MC
North Park Univ	IL	30,130	C
Northeastern Illinois Univ	IL	10,318	LC
Oswego / SUNY	NY	20,009	VC
Purdue Univ/West Lafayette	IN	20,024	HC
Reed College	OR	57,780	MC
Rice Univ	TX	43,288	MC
St. Joseph's Univ	PA	55,006	C
St. Louis Univ	MO	48,346	VC
Scripps College	CA	61,940	MC
Sewanee: The Univ of the South	TN	47,700	HC+
Skidmore College	NY	59,942	MC
Smith College	MA	59,674	MC
S Dak State Univ	SD	14,296	C
Stony Brook Univ / SUNY	NY	20,078	HC+
SUNY Plattsburgh / SUNY	NY	18,083	C
The Catholic Univ of America	DC	52,852	VC
Ohio State Univ-Columbus Campus	OH	19,887	HC+
The SUNY at Potsdam	NY	18,473	C
Union College	NY	60,240	MC
Univ of Calif at Los Angeles	CA	25,686	MC
Univ of Calif at San Diego	CA	21,000	VC
Univ of Illinois at Chicago	IL	24,505	VC
Univ of Mass Amherst	MA	24,215	VC+
Univ of New Hampshire	NH	26,912	C
Univ of North Florida	FL	15,870	VC
Univ of Portland	OR	49,964	VC
Univ of S Dak	SD	15,111	C
Univ of Texas - Pan American	TX	11,125	LC
Univ of Wisc/Green Bay	WI	19,074	C
Wartburg College	IA	41,055	VC
Wellesley College	MA	59,038	MC
Wesleyan Univ	CT	61,198	MC
Wheaton College	MA	54,934	HC+
Youngstown State Univ	OH	16,732	C

FUNERAL HOME SERVICES

School	ST	$IS	SR
Gannon Univ	PA	39,608	C
Mount Ida College	MA	30,115	LC
Point Park Univ	PA	36,390	C
Southern Illinois Univ Carbondale	IL	21,942	C
St. John's Univ	NY	55,070	C+
Univ of Central Okla	OK	12,293	C
Wayne State Univ	MI	22,063	C

FURNITURE DESIGN

School	ST	$IS	SR
Calif College of the Arts	CA	48,334	SP
Cal State, Fresno	CA	17,405	C
Ferris State Univ	MI	20,047	C
Indiana Univ-Purdue Univ Indianapolis	IN	17,611	C
Minneapolis College of Art and Design	MN	36,700	SP
N Car State Univ	NC	16,202	HC
Rhode Island School of Design	RI	57,234	MC
Rochester Inst of Technology	NY	42,450	VC
Savannah College of Art and Design	GA	48,005	SP

GAME ART

School	ST	$IS	SR
Champlain College	VT	46,650	VC+

GAME DESIGN AND DEVELOPMENT

School	ST	$IS	SR
Abilene Christian Univ	TX	38,400	C+
Bloomfield College	NJ	37,850	LC
Champlain College	VT	46,650	VC+
Cleveland Inst of Art	OH	48,685	SP
Kent State Univ	OH	19,920	C
Lawrence Tech Univ	MI	37,630	VC
Okla Christian Univ	OK	25,870	C
Rocky Mountain College of Art and Design	CO	22,470	SP
St. Edward's Univ	TX	47,784	C
Univ of Wisc/Stout	WI	15,459	C
William Peace Univ	NC	32,900	LC

GAME PROGRAMMING

School	ST	$IS	SR
Bloomfield College	NJ	37,850	LC
Champlain College	VT	46,650	VC+
Kansas City Art Inst	MO	44,308	SP

GENDER STUDIES

School	ST	$IS	SR
Albion College	MI	46,010	C
American Univ	DC	56,015	HC+
Bard College	NY	61,940	MC
Bard College at Simon's Rock	MA	61,749	HC+
Beloit College	WI	49,970	VC
Bowdoin College	ME	59,568	MC
Brown Univ	RI	59,428	MC
Bryant Univ	RI	49,179	VC
Butler Univ	IN	47,572	VC+
Calif State Polytechnic Univ, Pomona	CA	20,156	C
Cal State, Chico	CA	20,158	C
Coe College	IA	45,550	VC
College of St. Benedict	MN	49,359	VC
College of William & Mary	VA	28,000	MC
Colo College	CO	57,162	MC
Conn College	CT	54,970	MC
Davidson College	NC	58,146	MC
DePauw Univ	IN	48,950	VC+
Dominican Univ	IL	37,628	C
Eastern Mich Univ	MI	18,604	C
Eugene Lang College/The New School for Liberal Arts	NY	55,650	C
Fort Lewis College	CO	15,513	C
Gettysburg College	PA	58,820	VC
Guilford College	NC	42,800	C
Hanover College	IN	43,073	C+
Hollins Univ	VA	43,295	VC
Indiana Univ Bloomington	IN	19,801	VC
John Carroll Univ	OH	46,300	C+
John Jay College of Criminal Justice/The CUNY	NY	6,359	LC
Lawrence Univ	WI	46,371	HC
McNeese State Univ	LA	2,649	C
Mercer Univ	GA	44,201	VC
Mount Holyoke College	MA	55,146	MC
New College of Florida	FL	14,504	MC
New York Univ	NY	61,470	MC
Northeastern Illinois Univ	IL	10,318	LC
Northwestern Univ	IL	61,640	MC
Oberlin College	OH	61,788	MC
Ohio Univ	OH	21,080	C
Prescott College	AZ	33,284	C
St. John's Univ	MN	47,984	C
St. Michael's College	VT	49,975	VC
San Diego State Univ	CA	21,611	C+
Skidmore College	NY	59,942	HC
Sonoma State Univ	CA	20,541	C
Southern Oregon Univ	OR	17,874	C
Stonehill College	MA	46,780	VC
SUNY Plattsburgh / SUNY	NY	18,083	C
Swarthmore College	PA	57,870	MC
The Univ of Utah	UT	16,463	VC
Tulane Univ	LA	60,861	MC
Univ of Arizona	AZ	20,657	C
Univ of Calif at San Diego	CA	21,000	VC
Univ of Chicago	IL	55,416	MC
Univ of Illinois at Chicago	IL	24,505	VC
Univ of Iowa	IA	17,693	VC
Univ of Maryland/Baltimore County	MD	18,000	VC
Univ of Mass Amherst	MA	24,215	VC+
Univ of Miami	FL	57,034	MC
Univ of Pennsylvania	PA	61,132	MC
Univ of Vermont	VT	27,006	VC+
Univ of Wisc/Green Bay	WI	19,074	C
Univ of Wisc/Madison	WI	18,757	HC+
Villanova Univ	PA	58,394	MC
Wesleyan Univ	CT	61,198	MC
Western Mich Univ	MI	19,628	C
Westminster College	UT	37,708	C
Widener Univ	PA	52,418	C
Wofford College	SC	45,795	VC
Xavier Univ	OH	44,980	VC

ST = STATE $IS = IN-STATE COSTS   SR = SELECTOR RATING

School	ST	$IS	SR

GENERAL STUDIES

School	ST	$IS	SR
Aquinas College	MI	33,060	C
Arkansas State Univ	AR	15,470	C
Black Hills State Univ	SD	13,947	C
College of Mount St. Joseph	OH	33,880	C
Eastern Illinois Univ	IL	20,466	C
Fontbonne Univ	MO	31,384	C
Houghton College	NY	36,808	C+
Indiana Univ Bloomington	IN	19,801	VC
Indiana Univ East	IN	6,783	C
Indiana Univ Kokomo	IN	6,811	LC
Indiana Univ Northwest	IN	6,854	LC
Indiana Univ South Bend	IN	15,501	C
Indiana Univ Southeast	IN	16,035	C
Indiana Univ-Purdue Univ Indianapolis	IN	17,611	C
Kent State Univ	OH	19,920	C
Minn State Univ, Mankato	MN	15,616	C
New York Univ	NY	61,470	MC
Nova Southeastern Univ	FL	37,280	VC
Rowan Univ	NJ	24,022	VC+
St. Louis Univ	MO	48,346	HC
Southeast Missouri State Univ	MO	15,370	LC
Texas Christian Univ	TX	49,980	HC
Univ of Central Okla	OK	12,293	C
Univ of Idaho	ID	14,558	C
Univ of Nevada/Reno	NV	17,507	C
Youngstown State Univ	OH	16,732	C

GENETICS

School	ST	$IS	SR
Cal State, Northridge	CA	28,690	LC
Cedar Crest College	PA	43,240	C
Dartmouth College	NH	57,996	MC
Florida State Univ	FL	16,715	VC
Howard Univ	DC	13,646	C
Iowa State Univ	IA	16,403	C
New Mexico State Univ	NM	14,050	C
Ohio Wesleyan Univ	OH	49,460	C+
Purdue Univ/West Lafayette	IN	20,024	HC
Rutgers, The State Univ of New Jersey/New Brunswick	NJ	25,562	VC
Southern Illinois Univ Edwardsville	IL	17,532	C
SUNY Fredonia/The SUNY at Fredonia	NY	19,840	VC
Texas A&M Univ	TX	19,207	VC
Univ of Arizona	AZ	20,657	C
Univ of Calif at Davis	CA		HC
Univ of Calif at Irvine	CA	25,961	VC
Univ of Calif at Riverside	CA	27,204	C+
Univ of Conn	CT	24,706	HC
Univ of Georgia	GA	20,082	VC
Univ of Minn/Twin Cities	MN		HC
Univ of New Hampshire	NH	26,912	C
Univ of Vermont	VT	27,006	VC+
Univ of Wisc/Madison	WI	18,757	HC+
Washington State Univ	WA	20,461	C
Western Kentucky Univ	KY	11,000	LC

GEOCHEMISTRY

School	ST	$IS	SR
Bridgewater State Univ	MA	18,752	C
Calif Inst of Technology	CA	54,045	MC
Columbia Univ/City of New York	NY	61,116	MC
Grand Valley State Univ	MI	17,998	C+
Oswego / SUNY	NY	20,009	VC
SUNY College at Geneseo	NY	18,670	HC
SUNY Cortland/The SUNY	NY	19,759	C+
SUNY Fredonia/The SUNY at Fredonia	NY	19,840	VC
Western Mich Univ	MI	19,628	C

GEODETIC SCIENCE

School	ST	$IS	SR
Univ of Arkansas at Monticello	AR	12,076	NC

GEOENVIRONMENTAL STUDIES

School	ST	$IS	SR
Northeastern Illinois Univ	IL	10,318	LC
Shippensburg Univ of Pennsylvania	PA	20,934	C
The Univ of N Car at Pembroke	NC	13,388	LC
Univ of Illinois at Chicago	IL	24,505	VC
Univ of Notre Dame	IN	57,117	MC

GEOGRAPHY

School	ST	$IS	SR
Adams State Univ	CO	13,358	C
Appalachian State Univ	NC	12,919	VC
Aquinas College	MI	33,060	C
Arizona State Univ, at the Tempe Campus	AZ	20,137	C+
Auburn Univ	AL	22,378	VC+
Augustana College	IL	43,398	C
Ball State Univ	IN	17,850	C
Bard College at Simon's Rock	MA	61,749	HC+
Bellevue Univ	NE	4,600	NC
Bemidji State Univ	MN	13,500	VC
Binghamton Univ/The SUNY	NY	21,648	HC+

School	ST	$IS	SR
Bloomsburg Univ of Pennsylvania	PA	13,598	C
Boston Univ	MA	60,694	MC
Bowling Green State Univ	OH	18,970	C
Bridgewater State Univ	MA	18,752	C
Brigham Young Univ	UT	12,100	HC
Bucknell Univ	PA	60,140	MC
Buffalo State College / SUNY	NY	15,733	C+
Calif State Polytechnic Univ, Pomona	CA	20,156	C
Cal State, Chico	CA	20,158	C
Cal State, Dominguez Hills	CA	17,090	LC
Cal State, East Bay	CA	16,549	C
Cal State, Fresno	CA	17,405	C
Cal State, Fullerton	CA	25,188	C
Cal State, Long Beach	CA	17,502	C+
Cal State, Los Angeles	CA	17,186	LC
Cal State, Northridge	CA	28,690	LC
Cal State, Sacramento	CA	16,200	C
Cal State, San Bernardino	CA	12,000	C
Cal State, Stanislaus	CA	18,582	C
Calif Univ of Pennsylvania	PA	14,217	C
Calvin College	MI	39,120	VC
Carthage College	WI	33,000	C
Central Conn State Univ	CT	19,749	C
Central Washington Univ	WA	11,730	C
Charleston Southern Univ	SC	22,420	C
Cheyney Univ of Pennsylvania	PA	20,372	LC
Chicago State Univ	IL	5,482	C
Clark Univ	MA	47,020	HC+
Colgate Univ	NY	58,135	MC
Concord Univ	WV	13,102	C
Concordia Univ Nebr	NE	26,000	VC
Concordia Univ, River Forest	IL	26,300	C
Dartmouth College	NH	57,996	MC
DePaul Univ	IL	47,623	VC
DePauw Univ	IN	48,950	C
Dickinson State Univ	ND	11,900	NC
East Carolina Univ	NC	14,169	C
East Stroudsburg Univ of Pennsylvania	PA	18,868	LC
East Tenn State Univ	TN	9,000	C
Eastern Illinois Univ	IL	20,466	C
Eastern Kentucky Univ	KY	11,161	C
Eastern Mich Univ	MI	18,604	C
Eastern Washington Univ	WA		C
Edinboro Univ of Pennsylvania	PA	15,940	LC
Elmhurst College	IL	43,336	C
Emory and Henry College	VA	387,460	C
Excelsior College	NY	5,580	SP
Fayetteville State Univ	NC	10,816	C
Fitchburg State Univ	MA	18,173	C
Florida Atlantic Univ	FL	17,339	C
Florida International Univ	FL	17,747	C+
Florida State Univ	FL	16,715	VC
Framingham State Univ	MA	18,854	C
Frostburg State Univ	MD	15,264	LC
George Mason Univ	VA	15,724	VC
George Washington Univ	DC	57,108	MC
Georgia College and State Univ	GA	18,900	C+
Georgia Southern Univ	GA	16,942	C
Georgia State Univ	GA	15,582	VC
Grand Valley State Univ	MI	17,998	C+
Gustavus Adolphus College	MN	48,170	HC
Hampshire College	MA	58,320	MC
Hofstra Univ	NY	51,810	VC+
Howard Univ	DC	13,646	C
Humboldt State Univ	CA	18,400	C
Hunter College	NY	14,429	VC
Illinois State Univ	IL	23,110	VC
Indiana State Univ	IN	16,000	C
Indiana Univ Bloomington	IN	19,801	VC
Indiana Univ of Pennsylvania	PA	20,846	C
Indiana Univ-Purdue Univ Indianapolis	IN	17,611	C
Jacksonville State Univ	AL	12,480	LC
Jacksonville Univ	FL	37,780	C
James Madison Univ	VA	18,049	VC
Kansas State Univ	KS	15,497	VC
Keene State College	NH	23,232	LC
Kennesaw State Univ	GA		C
Kent State Univ	OH	19,920	C
Kutztown Univ of Pennsylvania	PA	16,909	LC
Lehman College/The CUNY	NY	5,778	LC
LIU Post	NY	47,660	C
Lock Haven Univ of Pennsylvania	PA	18,028	LC
Louisiana State Univ	LA	18,677	C+
Louisiana Tech Univ	LA	11,302	C
Macalester College	MN	57,691	MC
Mansfield Univ	PA	19,468	LC
Marshall Univ	WV	14,820	C
Miami Univ	OH	24,191	VC
Mich State Univ	MI	22,450	VC
Middle Tenn State Univ	TN	8,650	C
Middlebury College	VT	59,160	MC
Millersville Univ of Pennsylvania	PA	21,648	C
Minn State Univ, Mankato	MN	15,616	C
Missouri State Univ	MO	13,996	C+
Montclair State Univ	NJ	22,614	C
Morehead State Univ	KY	10,900	C

School	ST	$IS	SR
Mount Holyoke College	MA	55,146	MC
New Jersey City Univ	NJ	21,456	LC
New Mexico State Univ	NM	14,050	C
N Car Central Univ	NC	9,000	C
Northeastern Illinois Univ	IL	10,318	LC
Northeastern State Univ	OK	8,615	VC
Northern Arizona Univ	AZ	19,010	C
Northern Illinois Univ	IL	19,768	C
Northern Kentucky Univ	KY	21,134	C
Northern Mich Univ	MI	18,278	C
Northwest Missouri State Univ	MO	17,347	C
Northwestern State Univ of Louisiana	LA	14,368	C
Northwestern Univ	IL	61,640	MC
Ohio Univ	OH	21,080	C
Ohio Wesleyan Univ	OH	49,460	C+
Okla State Univ	OK	14,310	VC
Old Dominion Univ	VA	19,483	LC
Olivet Nazarene Univ	IL	29,990	C
Park Univ	MO	17,525	C
Pittsburg State Univ	KS	12,032	C
Plymouth State Univ	NH	23,148	LC
Portland State Univ	OR	18,672	C
Prairie View A&M Univ	TX	15,205	LC
Prescott College	AZ	33,284	C
Radford Univ	VA	17,766	LC
Rhode Island College	RI	17,694	LC
Rowan Univ	NJ	24,022	VC+
Rutgers, The State Univ of New Jersey/New Brunswick	NJ	25,562	VC
Salem State Univ	MA	13,161	LC
Salisbury Univ	MD	19,180	VC
Sam Houston State Univ	TX	17,082	C
Samford Univ	AL	37,060	C+
San Diego State Univ	CA	21,611	C+
San Francisco State Univ	CA	18,514	C
San Jose State Univ	CA	19,133	LC
Shippensburg Univ of Pennsylvania	PA	20,934	C
Slippery Rock Univ of Pennsylvania	PA	10,360	C
Sonoma State Univ	CA	20,541	C
S Dak State Univ	SD	14,296	C
Southern Conn State Univ	CT	18,033	LC
Southern Illinois Univ Carbondale	IL	21,942	C
Southern Illinois Univ Edwardsville	IL	17,532	C
Southern Oregon Univ	OR	17,874	C
St. Cloud State Univ	MN	10,600	C
Stephen F. Austin State Univ	TX	14,668	C
Stetson Univ	FL	51,516	VC
SUNY College at Geneseo	NY	18,670	HC
SUNY Cortland/The SUNY	NY	19,759	C+
SUNY New Paltz	NY	14,348	C
SUNY Oneonta / SUNY	NY	16,919	C
SUNY Plattsburgh / SUNY	NY	18,083	C
Syracuse Univ	NY	56,346	VC
Taylor Univ	IN	37,821	VC+
Temple Univ	PA	24,392	VC
Texas A&M Univ at Commerce	TX	10,496	C
Texas A&M Univ at Corpus Christi	TX	11,544	LC
Texas A&M Univ at Galveston	TX	11,258	C
Texas A&M Univ at Kingsville	TX	7,500	LC
Texas Christian Univ	TX	49,980	HC
Texas State Univ	TX	17,128	C
Texas Tech Univ	TX	14,243	C
Ohio State Univ-Columbus Campus	OH	19,887	HC+
The Pennsylvania State Univ - Univ Park	PA	28,022	VC+
The Univ of Memphis	TN	15,094	C
The Univ of N Car at Greensboro	NC	12,848	C
The Univ of Okla	OK	18,621	VC
The Univ of Utah	UT	16,463	VC
Towson Univ	MD	16,000	VC
United States Air Force Academy	CO		MC
United States Military Academy	NY		MC
Univ at Albany / SUNY	NY	18,674	VC
Univ at Buffalo / The SUNY	NY	20,283	VC
Univ of Akron	OH	20,436	C
Univ of Alabama at Tuscaloosa	AL	17,164	C+
Univ of Alaska Fairbanks	AK	15,130	C
Univ of Arizona	AZ	20,657	C
Univ of Arkansas at Fayetteville	AR	18,352	C
Univ of Calif at Berkeley	CA	23,322	VC
Univ of Calif at Davis	CA		HC
Univ of Calif at Los Angeles	CA	25,686	MC
Univ of Calif at Santa Barbara	CA	27,551	HC
Univ of Central Arkansas	AR	13,667	VC
Univ of Central Missouri	MO	14,605	C
Univ of Central Okla	OK	12,293	C
Univ of Chicago	IL	55,416	MC
Univ of Cincinnati	OH	21,506	VC
Univ of Colo at Colo Springs	CO	15,000	VC
Univ of Colo Boulder	CO	22,605	VC+

School	ST	$IS	SR
Univ of Colo Denver	CO	17,904	C
Univ of Conn	CT	24,706	HC
Univ of Delaware	DE	23,612	VC
Univ of Denver	CO	51,787	VC+
Univ of Florida	FL	15,943	HC
Univ of Georgia	GA	20,082	VC
Univ of Hawaii at Hilo	HI	23,066	C
Univ of Hawaii at Manoa	HI	19,379	C
Univ of Idaho	ID	14,558	C
Univ of Illinois at Urbana-Champaign	IL	26,450	HC
Univ of Iowa	IA	17,693	VC
Univ of Kansas	KS	17,603	C+
Univ of Kentucky	KY	19,868	C
Univ of Louisville	KY	17,946	C
Univ of Maine at Farmington	ME	18,187	LC
Univ of Mary Washington	VA	19,484	VC
Univ of Maryland - College Park	MD	20,060	HC
Univ of Maryland/Baltimore County	MD	18,000	VC
Univ of Mass Amherst	MA	24,215	VC+
Univ of Mass Boston	MA	23,066	VC
Univ of Miami	FL	57,034	MC
Univ of Mich-Flint	MI	17,547	C+
Univ of Minn/Duluth	MN	19,806	C
Univ of Minn/Twin Cities	MN		HC
Univ of Missouri/Columbia	MO	18,201	HC
Univ of Missouri-Kansas City	MO	19,603	C
Univ of Montana	MT	14,105	C
Univ of Nebr - Lincoln	NE	18,031	VC
Univ of Nebr at Kearney	NE	14,855	LC
Univ of Nebr at Omaha	NE	12,700	C
Univ of Nevada/Reno	NV	17,507	C
Univ of New Hampshire	NH	26,912	C
Univ of New Mexico	NM	15,300	C
Univ of New Orleans	LA	9,224	C
Univ of North Alabama	AL	14,950	C
Univ of N Car at Chapel Hill	NC	18,928	MC
Univ of N Car at Charlotte	NC	15,547	C
Univ of N Car at Wilmington	NC	13,572	VC
Univ of N Dak	ND	14,551	C
Univ of North Texas	TX	15,628	C
Univ of Northern Colo	CO	18,446	C
Univ of Northern Iowa	IA	15,795	C
Univ of Oregon	OR	21,360	C+
Univ of Pittsburgh at Johnstown	PA	20,862	LC
Univ of PR Recinto de Rio Piedras	PR	5,750	
Univ of South Alabama	AL	13,510	C
Univ of S Car at Columbia	SC	19,725	VC+
Univ of South Florida/Tampa	FL	13,000	C
Univ of Southern Calif	CA	56,903	MC
Univ of Southern Maine	ME	16,576	C
Univ of Southern Miss	MS	13,170	C
Univ of Tenn at Knoxville	TN	20,364	VC+
Univ of Tenn at Martin	TN	13,734	C
Univ of Texas at Austin	TX	44,074	HC
Univ of Texas at Dallas	TX	21,348	HC+
Univ of Texas at San Antonio	TX	18,372	C
Univ of the District of Columbia	DC	7,244	LC
Univ of Toledo	OH	18,464	C
Univ of Vermont	VT	27,006	VC+
Univ of Washington	WA	14,722	VC
Univ of West Georgia	GA	15,488	LC
Univ of Wisc Whitewater	WI	13,314	C
Univ of Wisc/Eau Claire	WI	15,730	VC
Univ of Wisc/La Crosse	WI	9,304	VC
Univ of Wisc/Madison	WI	18,757	HC+
Univ of Wisc/Oshkosh	WI	10,426	LC
Univ of Wisc/Parkside	WI	10,181	LC
Univ of Wisc/Platteville	WI	14,564	C
Univ of Wisc/River Falls	WI	9,722	LC
Univ of Wisc/Stevens Point	WI	14,043	C
Univ of Wisc-Milwaukee	WI	18,436	C
Univ of Wyoming	WY	14,401	C+
Utah State Univ	UT	12,044	C
Valparaiso Univ	IN	44,940	VC+
Vassar College	NY	61,140	MC
Villanova Univ	PA	58,394	MC
Virginia Polytechnic Inst and State Univ	VA	14,629	HC
Wayne State College	NE	11,764	NC
West Chester Univ of Pennsylvania	PA	17,186	C
West Texas A&M Univ	TX	13,478	C
West Virginia Univ	WV	16,542	C+
Western Carolina Univ	NC	13,965	C
Western Illinois Univ	IL	20,732	C
Western Kentucky Univ	KY	11,000	LC
Western Mich Univ	MI	19,628	C
Western Oregon Univ	OR	15,021	C
Western Washington Univ	WA	18,519	VC
William Paterson Univ of New Jersey	NJ	21,694	C
Worcester State Univ	MA	19,812	C
Wright State Univ	OH	16,983	C
Youngstown State Univ	OH	16,732	C

GEOGRAPHY INFORMATION SCIENCE

School	ST	$IS	SR
Arizona State Univ, at the Tempe Campus	AZ	20,137	C+

ST = STATE $IS = IN-STATE COSTS   SR = SELECTOR RATING

School	ST	$IS	SR
Auburn Univ at Montgomery	AL	14,470	LC
Murray State Univ	KY	15,304	C
Northeastern Illinois Univ	IL	10,318	LC
Ohio Univ	OH	21,080	C
Old Dominion Univ	VA	19,483	LC
The Univ of Okla	OK	18,621	VC

GEOLOGICAL ENGINEERING

School	ST	$IS	SR
Colo School of Mines	CO	18,000	HC
Mich Tech Univ	MI	23,556	HC
Missouri Univ of Science and Technology	MO	18,655	VC+
Montana Tech of The Univ of Montana	MT	14,650	VC
Olivet Nazarene Univ	IL	29,990	C
Oregon State Univ	OR	20,273	VC
Rutgers, The State Univ of New Jersey/Newark Campus	NJ	258,806	C
S Dak School of Mines and Technology	SD	15,260	VC
The Univ of Okla	OK	18,621	VC
The Univ of Utah	UT	16,463	VC
Univ of Akron	OH	20,436	C
Univ of Alaska Fairbanks	AK	15,130	C
Univ of Calif at Los Angeles	CA	25,686	MC
Univ of Idaho	ID	14,558	C
Univ of Illinois at Urbana-Champaign	IL	26,450	HC
Univ of Mich/Ann Arbor	MI	22,102	MC
Univ of Minn/Twin Cities	MN		HC
Univ of Miss	MS	16,704	C+
Univ of Nevada/Reno	NV	17,507	C
Univ of N Dak	ND	14,551	C
Univ of Rochester	NY	60,668	MC
Univ of Wisc/Madison	WI	18,757	HC+

GEOLOGY

School	ST	$IS	SR
Adams State Univ	CO	13,358	LC
Albion College	MI	46,010	C
Alfred Univ	NY	41,770	C
Allegheny College	PA	50,980	HC
Amherst College	MA	58,744	MC
Appalachian State Univ	NC	12,919	VC
Arkansas Tech Univ	AR	13,982	LC
Ashland Univ	OH	25,000	C
Auburn Univ	AL	22,378	VC+
Augustana College	IL	43,398	VC
Ball State Univ	IN	17,850	C
Bates College	ME	60,720	MC
Baylor Univ	TX	50,329	HC
Beloit College	WI	49,970	HC
Bemidji State Univ	MN	13,500	VC
Binghamton Univ/The SUNY	NY	21,648	HC+
Boise State Univ	ID	13,469	LC
Boston College	MA	60,622	MC
Bowling Green State Univ	OH	18,970	C
Brigham Young Univ	UT	12,100	HC
Brown Univ	RI	59,428	MC
Bryn Mawr College	PA	59,890	MC
Bucknell Univ	PA	60,140	MC
Buffalo State College / SUNY	NY	15,733	C+
Calif Inst of Technology	CA	54,045	MC
Calif Lutheran Univ	CA	49,540	C+
Calif State Polytechnic Univ, Pomona	CA	20,156	C
Cal State, Bakersfield	CA	8,000	C
Cal State, Chico	CA	20,158	C
Cal State, Dominguez Hills	CA	17,090	LC
Cal State, East Bay	CA	16,549	C
Cal State, Fresno	CA	17,405	C
Cal State, Fullerton	CA	25,188	C
Cal State, Long Beach	CA	17,502	C
Cal State, Los Angeles	CA	17,186	LC
Cal State, Northridge	CA	28,690	LC
Cal State, Sacramento	CA	16,200	C
Cal State, San Bernardino	CA	12,000	C
Cal State, Stanislaus	CA	18,582	C
Calif Univ of Pennsylvania	PA	14,217	C
Calvin College	MI	39,120	VC
Carleton College	MN	60,102	MC
Case Western Reserve Univ	OH	56,534	MC
Castleton State College	VT	20,186	C
Cedarville Univ	OH	32,860	VC
Centenary College of Louisiana	LA	45,650	C+
Central Washington Univ	WA	11,730	C
Charleston Southern Univ	SC	22,420	C
CUNY/Brooklyn College	NY	5,884	C+
CUNY/City College	NY	20,319	HC+
Clarion Univ of Pennsylvania	PA	17,370	LC
Clemson Univ	SC	19,136	HC
Cleveland State Univ	OH	21,776	C
Colby College	ME	57,510	MC
Colgate Univ	NY	58,135	MC
College of Charleston	SC	22,145	VC
College of William & Mary	VA	28,000	MC
College of Wooster	OH	52,640	MC
Colo College	CO	57,162	MC
Colo State Univ-Fort Collins	CO	20,385	VC
Columbia Univ/City of New York	NY	61,116	MC
Cornell College	IA	44,930	VC
Denison Univ	OH	54,670	HC+
DePauw Univ	IN	48,950	VC+
Duke Univ	NC	50,250	MC
Earlham College	IN	51,470	HC
East Carolina Univ	NC	14,169	C
Eastern Illinois Univ	IL	20,466	C
Eastern Kentucky Univ	KY	11,161	C
Eastern Mich Univ	MI	18,604	C
Eastern New Mexico Univ	NM	10,682	C
Eastern Washington Univ	WA		C
Edinboro Univ of Pennsylvania	PA	15,940	LC
Elizabeth City State Univ	NC	11,638	C
Excelsior College	NY	5,580	SP
Florida Atlantic Univ	FL	17,339	C
Florida International Univ	FL	17,747	C+
Florida State Univ	FL	16,715	VC
Fort Hays State Univ	KS	11,354	C
Fort Lewis College	CO	15,513	C
Franklin and Marshall College	PA	60,799	MC
George Mason Univ	VA	15,724	VC
George Washington Univ	DC	57,108	MC
Georgia Southern Univ	GA	16,942	C
Georgia Southwestern State Univ	GA	13,246	C
Georgia State Univ	GA	15,582	VC
Grand Valley State Univ	MI	17,998	C+
Guilford College	NC	42,800	C
Gustavus Adolphus College	MN	48,170	HC
Hampshire College	MA	58,320	MC
Hanover College	IN	43,073	C
Hardin-Simmons Univ	TX	23,560	C+
Hartwick College	NY	51,270	C
Harvard College/Harvard Univ	MA	49,000	MC
Haverford College	PA	61,564	MC
Hofstra Univ	NY	51,810	VC+
Hope College	MI	38,650	VC
Humboldt State Univ	CA	18,400	C
Idaho State Univ	ID	12,307	C
Illinois State Univ	IL	23,110	VC
Indiana State Univ	IN	16,000	C
Indiana Univ Bloomington	IN	19,801	VC
Indiana Univ Northwest	IN	6,854	LC
Indiana Univ of Pennsylvania	PA	20,846	LC
Indiana Univ-Purdue Univ Fort Wayne	IN	15,521	C
Indiana Univ-Purdue Univ Indianapolis	IN	17,611	C
Iowa State Univ	IA	16,403	C
James Madison Univ	VA	18,049	VC
Juniata College	PA	49,340	VC
Kansas State Univ	KS	15,497	VC
Keene State College	NH	23,232	LC
Kent State Univ	OH	19,920	C
Kutztown Univ of Pennsylvania	PA	16,909	LC
La Salle Univ	PA	50,270	C
Lafayette College	PA	59,155	HC+
Lake Superior State Univ	MI	18,121	C
Lamar Univ	TX	6,820	LC
Lawrence Univ	WI	46,371	HC
Lehman College/The CUNY	NY	5,778	LC
LIU Post	NY	47,660	C
Lock Haven Univ of Pennsylvania	PA	18,028	LC
Louisiana State Univ	LA	18,677	C+
Louisiana Tech Univ	LA	11,302	C
Macalester College	MN	57,691	MC
Marietta College	OH	42,135	C
Marshall Univ	WV	14,820	C
Mercyhurst Univ	PA	40,700	C
Miami Univ	OH	24,191	VC
Mich State Univ	MI	22,450	VC
Mich Tech Univ	MI	23,556	HC
Middlebury College	VT	59,160	MC
Midwestern State Univ	TX	9,722	C
Millersville Univ of Pennsylvania	PA	21,648	C
Millsaps College	MS	43,888	VC+
Minot State Univ	ND	10,915	C
Missouri State Univ	MO	13,996	C+
Missouri Univ of Science and Technology	MO	18,655	VC+
Morehead State Univ	KY	10,900	C
Mount Holyoke College	MA	55,146	MC
Muskingum Univ	OH	30,502	C
New Jersey City Univ	NJ	21,456	LC
New Mexico State Univ	NM	14,050	C
N Car State Univ	NC	16,202	HC
N Dak State Univ	ND		HC
Northern Arizona Univ	AZ	19,010	C
Northern Illinois Univ	IL	19,768	C
Northern Kentucky Univ	KY	21,134	C
Northwest Missouri State Univ	MO	17,347	C
Northwestern Univ	IL	61,640	MC
Norwich Univ	VT	28,212	C
Oberlin College	OH	61,788	MC
Occidental College	CA	60,972	MC
Ohio Univ	OH	21,080	C
Ohio Wesleyan Univ	OH	49,460	C+
Okla State Univ	OK	14,310	VC
Old Dominion Univ	VA	19,483	LC
Oswego / SUNY	NY	20,009	VC
Pomona College	CA	57,680	MC
Portland State Univ	OR	18,672	C
Prescott College	AZ	33,284	C
Purdue Univ/West Lafayette	IN	20,024	HC
Queens College/The CUNY	NY	17,107	VC
Radford Univ	VA	17,766	LC
Rensselaer Polytechnic Inst	NY	61,529	MC
Rice Univ	TX	43,288	MC
Richard Stockton College of New Jersey	NJ	20,000	VC
Rocky Mountain College	MT	32,242	C
Rutgers, The State Univ of New Jersey/New Brunswick	NJ	25,562	VC
Rutgers, The State Univ of New Jersey/Newark Campus	NJ	258,806	C
St. Louis Univ	MO	48,346	HC
Salem State Univ	MA	13,161	LC
Sam Houston State Univ	TX	17,082	C
San Diego State Univ	CA	21,611	C+
San Francisco State Univ	CA	18,514	C
San Jose State Univ	CA	19,133	LC
Scripps College	CA	61,940	MC
Sewanee: The Univ of the South	TN	47,700	HC+
Skidmore College	NY	59,942	HC
Slippery Rock Univ of Pennsylvania	PA	10,360	C
Smith College	MA	59,674	MC
Sonoma State Univ	CA	20,541	C
S Dak School of Mines and Technology	SD	15,260	VC
Southern Illinois Univ Carbondale	IL	21,942	C
Southern Methodist Univ	TX	60,585	MC
St. Cloud State Univ	MN	10,600	C
St. Lawrence Univ	NY	59,972	VC
St. Norbert College	WI	41,478	VC
Stanford Univ	CA	58,388	MC
Stephen F. Austin State Univ	TX	14,668	C
Stony Brook Univ / SUNY	NY	20,078	HC+
Sul Ross State Univ	TX	13,410	LC
SUNY College at Geneseo	NY	18,670	HC
SUNY Cortland/The SUNY	NY	19,759	C+
SUNY Fredonia/The SUNY at Fredonia	NY	19,840	VC
SUNY New Paltz	NY	14,348	C
SUNY Oneonta / SUNY	NY	16,919	C+
SUNY Plattsburgh / SUNY	NY	18,083	C
Syracuse Univ	NY	56,346	VC
Tarleton State Univ	TX	13,489	LC
Temple Univ	PA	24,392	VC
Tenn Tech Univ	TN	11,310	C
Texas A&M Univ	TX	19,207	VC
Texas A&M Univ at Commerce	TX	10,496	C
Texas A&M Univ at Corpus Christi	TX	11,544	LC
Texas A&M Univ at Kingsville	TX	7,500	LC
Texas Christian Univ	TX	49,980	HC
Texas Tech Univ	TX	14,243	C
The College of St. Rose	NY	26,750	C
Ohio State Univ-Columbus Campus	OH	19,887	HC+
The Pennsylvania State Univ - Univ Park	PA	28,022	VC+
The SUNY at Potsdam	NY	18,473	C
The SUNY/College at Brockport	NY	19,002	C
The Univ of Okla	OK	18,621	VC
The Univ of Tenn at Chattanooga	TN	16,883	C
The Univ of Utah	UT	16,463	VC
Towson Univ	MD	16,000	C
Tufts Univ	MA	58,780	MC
Tulane Univ	LA	60,861	MC
Union College	NY	60,240	MC
Unity College	ME	34,054	C
Univ at Buffalo / The SUNY	NY	20,283	VC
Univ of Akron	OH	20,436	C
Univ of Alabama at Tuscaloosa	AL	17,164	C+
Univ of Alaska Fairbanks	AK	15,130	C
Univ of Arizona	AZ	20,657	C
Univ of Arkansas at Fayetteville	AR	18,352	C+
Univ of Arkansas at Little Rock	AR	17,609	C
Univ of Calif at Davis	CA		HC
Univ of Calif at Irvine	CA	25,961	VC
Univ of Calif at Los Angeles	CA	25,686	MC
Univ of Calif at Riverside	CA	27,204	C+
Univ of Calif at Santa Barbara	CA	27,551	HC
Univ of Calif at Santa Cruz	CA	27,807	C+
Univ of Central Missouri	MO	14,605	C
Univ of Cincinnati	OH	21,506	VC
Univ of Colo Boulder	CO	22,605	VC+
Univ of Conn	CT	24,706	HC
Univ of Dayton	OH	49,070	VC
Univ of Delaware	DE	23,612	VC
Univ of Florida	FL	15,943	HC
Univ of Georgia	GA	20,082	VC
Univ of Hawaii at Hilo	HI	23,066	C
Univ of Hawaii at Manoa	HI	19,379	C
Univ of Houston	TX	19,796	VC
Univ of Idaho	ID	14,558	C
Univ of Illinois at Urbana-Champaign	IL	26,450	HC
Univ of Iowa	IA	17,693	VC
Univ of Kansas	KS	17,603	C+
Univ of Kentucky	KY	19,868	C
Univ of Louisiana at Lafayette	LA	6,130	C
Univ of Maine at Farmington	ME	18,187	LC
Univ of Maryland - College Park	MD	20,060	HC
Univ of Mass Amherst	MA	24,215	VC+
Univ of Miami	FL	57,034	MC
Univ of Mich/Ann Arbor	MI	22,102	MC
Univ of Mich/Dearborn	MI	9,885	C
Univ of Minn/Duluth	MN	19,806	C
Univ of Minn/Morris	MN	17,150	C
Univ of Minn/Twin Cities	MN		HC
Univ of Miss	MS	16,704	C+
Univ of Missouri/Columbia	MO	18,201	MC
Univ of Missouri-Kansas City	MO	19,603	C
Univ of Montana	MT	14,105	C
Univ of Montana-Western	MT	9,753	LC
Univ of Mount Union	OH	35,130	C
Univ of Nebr - Lincoln	NE	18,031	VC
Univ of Nebr at Omaha	NE	12,700	C
Univ of Nevada, Las Vegas	NV	17,303	C
Univ of Nevada/Reno	NV	17,507	C
Univ of New Hampshire	NH	26,912	C
Univ of New Orleans	LA	9,224	C
Univ of North Alabama	AL	9,960	C
Univ of N Car at Chapel Hill	NC	18,928	MC
Univ of N Car at Charlotte	NC	15,547	C
Univ of N Car at Wilmington	NC	13,572	VC
Univ of N Dak	ND	14,551	C
Univ of Northern Colo	CO	18,446	C
Univ of Northern Iowa	IA	15,795	C
Univ of Oregon	OR	21,360	C+
Univ of Pennsylvania	PA	61,132	MC
Univ of Pittsburgh at Johnstown	PA	20,862	LC
Univ of Pittsburgh	PA	28,572	HC+
Univ of PR/Mayaguez	PR	1,250	
Univ of Puget Sound	WA	54,608	HC
Univ of Rochester	NY	60,668	MC
Univ of South Alabama	AL	13,510	C
Univ of S Car at Columbia	SC	19,725	VC+
Univ of South Florida/Tampa	FL	13,000	C
Univ of Southern Calif	CA	56,903	MC
Univ of Southern Indiana	IN	14,885	C
Univ of Southern Maine	ME	16,576	C
Univ of Southern Miss	MS	13,170	C
Univ of Tenn at Knoxville	TN	20,364	VC+
Univ of Tenn at Martin	TN	13,734	C
Univ of Texas at Arlington	TX	10,908	LC
Univ of Texas at Austin	TX	44,074	HC
Univ of Texas at El Paso	TX	8,764	NC
Univ of Texas at San Antonio	TX	18,372	C
Univ of the Pacific	CA	52,146	VC
Univ of Toledo	OH	18,464	C
Univ of Tulsa	OK	46,363	MC
Univ of Vermont	VT	27,006	VC+
Univ of Washington	WA	14,722	VC
Univ of West Georgia	GA	15,488	LC
Univ of Wisc/Eau Claire	WI	15,730	VC
Univ of Wisc/Madison	WI	18,757	HC+
Univ of Wisc/Oshkosh	WI	10,426	LC
Univ of Wisc/Parkside	WI	10,181	LC
Univ of Wisc/River Falls	WI	9,722	LC
Univ of Wisc-Milwaukee	WI	18,436	C
Univ of Wyoming	WY	14,401	C+
Utah State Univ	UT	12,044	C
Valparaiso Univ	IN	44,940	VC+
Vassar College	NY	61,140	MC
Virginia Polytechnic Inst and State Univ	VA	14,629	HC
Washington and Lee Univ	VA	52,812	MC
Washington State Univ	WA	20,461	C
Washington Univ in St. Louis	MO	69,844	MC
Wayland Baptist Univ	TX	18,912	LC
Wayne State Univ	MI	22,063	C
Wellesley College	MA	59,038	MC
West Chester Univ of Pennsylvania	PA	17,186	C
West Texas A&M Univ	TX	13,478	C
West Virginia Univ	WV	16,542	C+
Western Carolina Univ	NC	13,965	C
Western Illinois Univ	IL	20,732	C
Western Kentucky Univ	KY	11,000	LC
Western Mich Univ	MI	19,628	C
Western State Colo Univ	CO	16,924	C
Western Washington Univ	WA	18,519	VC
Wheaton College	IL	40,720	MC
Whitman College	WA	55,988	MC
Wichita State Univ	KS	14,607	C+
Williams College	MA	61,070	MC
Wilmington College	OH	29,784	C
Winona State Univ	MN	16,640	C
Wittenberg Univ	OH	47,962	C+
Wright State Univ	OH	16,983	C
Yale Univ	CT	55,300	MC
York College / The CUNY	NY	5,496	VC
Youngstown State Univ	OH	16,732	C

ST = STATE $IS = IN-STATE COSTS   SR = SELECTOR RATING

School	ST	$IS	SR

GEOLOGY & GEOLOGY OCEANOGRAPHY

School	ST	$IS	SR
Univ of Rhode Island	RI	24,002	C

GEOPHYSICAL ENGINEERING

School	ST	$IS	SR
Colo School of Mines	CO	18,000	HC
Montana Tech of The Univ of Montana	MT	14,650	VC
New Jersey Inst of Technology	NJ	26,490	C+
Oregon State Univ	OR	20,273	VC
The Univ of Okla	OK	18,621	VC
Univ of Mich/Ann Arbor	MI	22,102	MC
Univ of Texas at Austin	TX	44,074	HC

GEOPHYSICS AND SEISMOLOGY

School	ST	$IS	SR
Baylor Univ	TX	50,329	HC
Boise State Univ	ID	13,469	LC
Boston College	MA	60,622	MC
Boston Univ	MA	60,694	MC
Calif Inst of Technology	CA	54,045	MC
Colgate Univ	NY	58,135	MC
Columbia Univ/City of New York	NY	61,116	MC
Harvard College/Harvard Univ	MA	49,000	MC
Mich State Univ	MI	22,450	VC
Mich Tech Univ	MI	23,556	VC
Missouri Univ of Science and Technology	MO	18,655	VC+
Rice Univ	TX	43,288	MC
Southern Methodist Univ	TX	60,585	MC
Stanford Univ	CA	58,388	MC
SUNY College at Geneseo	NY	18,670	HC
SUNY Cortland/The SUNY	NY	19,759	C
Texas A&M Univ	TX	19,207	VC
Texas Tech Univ	TX	14,243	VC
The Univ of Okla	OK	18,621	VC
The Univ of Utah	UT	16,463	VC
Univ of Akron	OH	20,436	C
Univ of Calif at Los Angeles	CA	25,686	MC
Univ of Calif at Riverside	CA	27,204	C+
Univ of Calif at Santa Barbara	CA	27,551	HC
Univ of Hawaii at Manoa	HI	19,379	C
Univ of Minn/Twin Cities	MN		HC
Univ of Nevada/Reno	NV	17,507	C
Univ of New Orleans	LA	9,224	C
Univ of S Car at Columbia	SC	19,725	VC+
Univ of Texas at Austin	TX	44,074	HC
Univ of Texas at El Paso	TX	8,764	NC
Univ of the Pacific	CA	52,146	VC
Univ of Tulsa	OK	46,331	MC
Univ of Wisc/Madison	WI	18,757	HC+
Washington Univ in St. Louis	MO	69,844	MC
Western Mich Univ	MI	19,628	C
Wright State Univ	OH	16,983	C

GEOSCIENCE

School	ST	$IS	SR
Angelo State Univ	TX	15,049	NC
Austin Peay State Univ	TN	15,274	C
Bloomsburg Univ of Pennsylvania	PA	13,598	C
Boise State Univ	ID	13,469	LC
Cedarville Univ	OH	32,860	VC
Colby College	ME	57,510	MC
Columbia Univ/School of General Studies	NY	58,231	MC
Eckerd College	FL	43,902	C
Hamilton College	NY	55,620	MC
Hobart and William Smith Colleges	NY	60,034	HC+
Idaho State Univ	ID	12,307	C
Indiana Univ Southeast	IN	16,035	C
Lewis-Clark State College	ID	6,990	C
Mich State Univ	MI	22,450	VC
Minn State Univ, Moorhead	MN	13,392	VC
Miss State Univ	MS	14,750	C
Montclair State Univ	NJ	22,614	C
Northern Illinois Univ	IL	19,768	C
Ohio Univ	OH	21,080	C
Olivet Nazarene Univ	IL	29,990	C
Pacific Lutheran Univ	WA	46,760	C+
Princeton Univ	NJ	53,795	MC
Rider Univ	NJ	45,720	C
Rutgers, The State Univ of New Jersey/Newark Campus	NJ	258,806	C
S Dak State Univ	SD	14,296	C
Stanford Univ	CA	58,388	MC
SUNY Fredonia/The SUNY at Fredonia	NY	19,840	VC
Texas A&M Univ at Galveston	TX	11,258	C
Texas Tech Univ	TX	14,243	VC
The Pennsylvania State Univ - Univ Park	PA	28,022	VC+
The Univ of Utah	UT	16,463	VC
Towson Univ	MD	16,000	VC
Trinity Univ	TX	48,150	HC+
Univ of Alaska Fairbanks	AK	15,130	C
Univ of Arizona	AZ	20,657	C
Univ of Calif at Riverside	CA	27,204	C+
Univ of Chicago	IL	55,416	MC
Univ of Miami	FL	57,034	MC
Univ of Mich/Ann Arbor	MI	22,102	MC
Univ of Montana	MT	14,105	C
Univ of Montana-Western	MT	9,753	LC
Univ of Southern Maine	ME	16,576	C
Univ of Texas at Dallas	TX	21,348	HC+
Univ of Tulsa	OK	46,331	MC
Univ of Wisc/Green Bay	WI	19,074	C
Univ of Wisc/Stevens Point	WI	14,043	C
Utica College	NY	45,670	C
West Chester Univ of Pennsylvania	PA	17,186	C
West Virginia Univ	WV	16,542	C+

GERMAN

School	ST	$IS	SR
Adrian College	MI	42,400	C
Agnes Scott College	GA	45,323	C+
Alabama A&M Univ	AL	10,084	C
Albion College	MI	46,010	C
Allegheny College	PA	50,980	HC
Alma College	MI	44,075	C
American Univ	DC	56,015	HC+
Amherst College	MA	58,744	MC
Aquinas College	MI	33,060	C
Arizona State Univ, at the Tempe Campus	AZ	20,137	C+
Auburn Univ	AL	22,378	VC+
Augsburg College	MN	35,142	C
Augustana College	IL	43,398	VC
Augustana College	SD	36,500	VC
Austin College	TX	45,875	HC
Baker Univ	KS	33,350	C+
Baldwin Wallace Univ	OH	38,318	C
Ball State Univ	IN	17,850	C
Barnard College/Columbia Univ	NY	39,000	MC
Bates College	ME	60,720	MC
Baylor Univ	TX	50,329	HC
Belmont Univ	TN	39,190	VC+
Beloit College	WI	49,970	VC
Bemidji State Univ	MN	13,500	VC
Berea College	KY	7,192	C
Berry College	GA	39,254	VC
Binghamton Univ/The SUNY	NY	21,648	HC+
Birmingham-Southern College	AL	44,168	VC+
Bloomsburg Univ of Pennsylvania	PA	13,598	C
Boise State Univ	ID	13,469	LC
Bowdoin College	ME	59,568	MC
Bowling Green State Univ	OH	18,970	C
Bradley Univ	IL	31,874	VC
Brandeis Univ	MA		MC
Brigham Young Univ	UT	12,100	HC
Bryn Mawr College	PA	59,890	MC
Bucknell Univ	PA	60,140	MC
Butler Univ	IN	47,572	VC+
Calif Lutheran Univ	CA	49,540	C+
Cal State, Chico	CA	20,158	C
Cal State, Fresno	CA	17,405	C
Cal State, Long Beach	CA	17,502	C+
Cal State, Northridge	CA	28,690	LC
Cal State, Sacramento	CA	16,200	C
Calvin College	MI	39,120	VC
Canisius College	NY	44,900	C
Carleton College	MN	60,102	MC
Carnegie Mellon Univ	PA	51,260	MC
Carthage College	WI	33,000	C
Case Western Reserve Univ	OH	56,534	MC
Centenary College of Louisiana	LA	45,650	C+
Central College	IA	42,104	C+
Central Conn State Univ	CT	19,749	C
Central Washington Univ	WA	11,730	C
Centre College	KY	35,000	HC+
Christopher Newport Univ	VA	21,960	VC
Citadel, The	SC		C
Clemson Univ	SC	19,136	HC
Coe College	IA	45,550	VC
Colgate Univ	NY	58,135	MC
College of Charleston	SC	22,145	VC
College of St. Benedict	MN	49,359	VC
College of the Holy Cross	MA	58,042	MC
College of William & Mary	VA	28,000	MC
College of Wooster	OH	52,600	VC
Colo State Univ-Fort Collins	CO	20,385	VC
Columbia Univ/City of New York	NY	61,116	MC
Columbia Univ/School of General Studies	NY	58,231	MC
Concordia College - Moorhead	MN	39,974	VC
Conn College	CT	54,970	MC
Cornell College	IA	44,930	VC
Cornell Univ	NY	60,964	MC
Dartmouth College	NH	57,996	MC
Davidson College	NC	58,146	MC
Denison Univ	OH	54,670	HC+
DePaul Univ	IL	47,623	VC
DePauw Univ	IN	48,950	VC+
Dickinson College	PA	57,662	HC+
Doane College	NE	35,230	C
Dordt College	IA	34,160	C+
Drew Univ/College of Liberal Arts	NJ	57,516	C
Drury Univ	MO	31,909	VC
Earlham College	IN	51,470	HC
East Carolina Univ	NC	14,169	C
Eastern Mennonite Univ	VA	40,660	C
Eastern Mich Univ	MI	18,604	C
Eastern Washington Univ	WA		C
Elizabethtown College	PA	49,740	VC
Elmhurst College	IL	43,336	C
Fairfield Univ	CT	56,960	VC
Florida Atlantic Univ	FL	17,339	C
Florida State Univ	FL	16,715	VC
Fordham Univ	NY	61,588	HC+
Fort Hays State Univ	KS	11,354	C
Franciscan Univ of Steubenville	OH	27,320	VC
Franklin and Marshall College	PA	60,799	MC
Furman Univ	SC	54,006	HC
George Washington Univ	DC	57,108	MC
Georgetown Univ	DC	52,910	MC
Georgia State Univ	GA	15,582	VC
Gettysburg College	PA	58,820	HC
Gordon College	MA	44,320	VC
Grace College and Seminary	IN	28,800	VC
Graceland Univ	IA	28,020	C
Grand Valley State Univ	MI	17,998	C+
Grinnell College	IA	53,654	MC
Guilford College	NC	42,800	C
Hamline Univ	MN	45,678	VC
Hampden-Sydney College	VA	51,758	C
Hanover College	IN	43,073	C+
Hartwick College	NY	51,270	C
Harvard College/Harvard Univ	MA	49,000	MC
Hastings College	NE	27,782	C+
Haverford College	PA	61,564	MC
Heidelberg Univ	OH	34,100	C
Hendrix College	AR	50,202	VC+
Hillsdale College	MI	32,866	MC
Hofstra Univ	NY	51,810	VC+
Hood College	MD	45,730	C
Hope College	MI	38,650	VC
Humboldt State Univ	CA	18,400	C
Hunter College	NY	14,429	VC
Idaho State Univ	ID	12,307	C
Illinois College	IL	25,770	VC
Illinois State Univ	IL	23,110	VC
Illinois Wesleyan Univ	IL	48,452	MC
Indiana State Univ	IN	16,000	C
Indiana Univ-Bloomington	IN	19,801	VC
Indiana Univ South Bend	IN	15,501	C
Indiana Univ Southeast	IN	16,035	C
Indiana Univ-Purdue Univ Fort Wayne	IN	15,521	C
Indiana Univ-Purdue Univ Indianapolis	IN	17,611	C
Iowa State Univ	IA	16,403	C
Ithaca College	NY	53,864	HC
John Carroll Univ	OH	46,300	C+
Johns Hopkins Univ	MD	47,492	MC
Juniata College	PA	49,340	VC
Kalamazoo College	MI	49,740	HC
Kent State Univ	OH	19,920	C
Kenyon College	OH	58,890	MC
Knox College	IL	44,865	VC+
Kutztown Univ of Pennsylvania	PA	16,909	LC
La Salle Univ	PA	50,270	C
Lafayette College	PA	59,155	HC+
Lakeland College	WI	22,990	C
Lawrence Univ	WI	46,371	HC
Lebanon Valley College	PA	38,570	C
Lehigh Univ	PA	56,770	MC
Lehman College/The CUNY	NY	5,778	LC
Lenoir-Rhyne College	NC	35,984	C
Linfield College-McMinnville Campus	OR	47,676	C
Lipscomb Univ	TN	37,490	VC
Lock Haven Univ of Pennsylvania	PA	18,028	LC
Loyola Univ Maryland	MD	56,880	VC+
Luther College	IA	45,720	C+
Lycoming College	PA	45,379	C
Manchester Univ	IN	35,070	C
Marlboro College	VT	35,980	VC
Marquette Univ	WI	46,930	VC+
Marshall Univ	WV	14,820	C
McDaniel College	MD	47,450	VC
Mercer Univ	GA	44,201	VC
Messiah College	PA	40,690	C+
Miami Univ	OH	24,191	VC
Mich State Univ	MI	22,450	VC
Middle Tenn State Univ	TN	8,650	C
Middlebury College	VT	59,160	MC
Millersville Univ of Pennsylvania	PA	21,648	VC
Minn State Univ, Mankato	MN	15,616	C
Minot State Univ	ND	10,915	C
Missouri Southern State Univ	MO	12,061	C
Missouri State Univ	MO	13,996	C+
Moravian College	PA	36,381	VC
Mount St. Mary's Univ	MD	47,996	C
Muhlenberg College	PA	52,837	HC
Murray State Univ	KY	15,304	C
Muskingum Univ	OH	30,502	C
Nazareth College of Rochester	NY	43,028	C+
Nebr Wesleyan Univ	NE	29,774	C+
New York Univ	NY	61,470	MC
Newberry College	SC	26,850	LC
North Central College	IL	38,343	VC
Northern Illinois Univ	IL	19,768	C
Northern Kentucky Univ	KY	21,134	C
Northern State Univ - Aberdeen	SD	14,505	C
Northwestern Univ	IL	61,640	MC
Oakland Univ	MI	19,391	C
Oberlin College	OH	61,788	MC
Ohio Univ	OH	21,080	C
Ohio Wesleyan Univ	OH	49,460	C+
Okla Baptist Univ	OK	28,202	C
Okla State Univ	OK	14,310	VC
Old Dominion Univ	VA	19,483	LC
Oral Roberts Univ	OK	31,734	C
Oregon State Univ	OR	20,273	VC
Oswego / SUNY	NY	20,009	VC
Pacific Lutheran Univ	WA	46,760	C+
Pepperdine Univ	CA	55,372	HC+
Portland State Univ	OR	18,672	C
Princeton Univ	NJ	53,795	MC
Providence College	RI	57,383	VC
Purdue Univ/Calumet	IN	14,336	C
Purdue Univ/West Lafayette	IN	20,024	HC
Queens College/The CUNY	NY	17,107	VC
Randolph-Macon College	VA	49,869	C+
Rhodes College	TN	51,900	HC+
Rider Univ	NJ	45,720	C
Ripon College	WI	36,959	C+
Rockford College	IL	31,000	C
Rosemont College	PA	42,350	C
Rutgers, The State Univ of New Jersey/Camden Campus	NJ	25,121	C
Rutgers, The State Univ of New Jersey/New Brunswick	NJ	25,562	VC
Rutgers, The State Univ of New Jersey/Newark Campus	NJ	258,806	C
St. John's Univ	MN	47,984	C
St. Joseph's Univ	PA	55,006	VC
St. Mary's Univ	TX	33,854	C
Salem College	NC	29,326	VC
Sam Houston State Univ	TX	17,082	C
Samford Univ	AL	37,060	C+
San Diego State Univ	CA	21,611	C+
San Francisco State Univ	CA	18,514	C
San Jose State Univ	CA	19,133	LC
Sarah Lawrence College	NY	48,000	HC
Seattle Pacific Univ	WA	41,559	VC+
Sewanee: The Univ of the South	TN	47,700	HC+
Simpson College	IA	36,086	C+
Skidmore College	NY	59,942	HC
Slippery Rock Univ of Pennsylvania	PA	10,360	C
S Dak State Univ	SD	14,296	C
Southern Conn State Univ	CT	18,033	LC
Southern Illinois Univ Carbondale	IL	21,942	C
Southern Illinois Univ Edwardsville	IL	17,532	C
Southern Methodist Univ	TX	60,585	MC
Southwestern Univ	TX	45,660	VC
St. Ambrose Univ	IA	30,845	C
St. Lawrence Univ	NY	59,972	VC
St. Norbert College	WI	41,478	VC
St. Olaf College	MN	51,200	HC+
Stetson Univ	FL	51,516	VC
SUNY New Paltz	NY	14,348	C
Susquehanna Univ	PA	51,150	C
Swarthmore College	PA	57,870	MC
Temple Univ	PA	24,392	VC
Tenn Tech Univ	TN	11,310	C
Texas A&M Univ	TX	19,207	VC
Texas A&M Univ at Commerce	TX	10,496	C
Texas Christian Univ	TX	49,980	HC
Texas State Univ	TX	17,128	C
Texas Tech Univ	TX	14,243	VC
The Catholic Univ of America	DC	52,852	VC
Ohio State Univ-Columbus Campus	OH	19,887	HC+
The Pennsylvania State Univ - Univ Park	PA	28,022	VC+
The Univ of N Car at Greensboro	NC	12,848	C
The Univ of Okla	OK	18,621	VC
The Univ of Utah	UT	16,463	VC
Thomas Edison State College	NJ	5,700	SP
Towson Univ	MD	16,000	VC
Trinity College	CT		HC+
Trinity Univ	TX	48,150	HC+
Truman State Univ	MO	15,541	HC
Tufts Univ	MA	58,780	MC
Tulane Univ	LA	60,861	MC
Union College	NE	23,270	C
Univ at Buffalo / The SUNY	NY	20,283	VC
Univ of Alabama at Tuscaloosa	AL	17,164	C+

School	ST	$IS	SR
Univ of Alaska Fairbanks	AK	15,130	C
Univ of Arkansas at Fayetteville	AR	18,352	C+
Univ of Calif at Berkeley	CA	23,322	MC
Univ of Calif at Davis	CA		HC
Univ of Calif at Los Angeles	CA	25,686	MC
Univ of Calif at Riverside	CA	27,204	C+
Univ of Calif at Santa Barbara	CA	27,551	HC
Univ of Central Missouri	MO	14,605	C
Univ of Central Okla	OK	12,293	C
Univ of Chicago	IL	55,416	MC
Univ of Cincinnati	OH	21,506	VC
Univ of Conn	CT	24,706	HC
Univ of Dallas	TX	45,500	VC+
Univ of Dayton	OH	49,070	VC
Univ of Denver	CO	51,787	VC+
Univ of Evansville	IN	42,656	VC+
Univ of Florida	FL	15,943	HC
Univ of Georgia	GA	20,082	VC
Univ of Hawaii at Manoa	HI	19,379	C
Univ of Illinois at Chicago	IL	24,505	VC
Univ of Indianapolis	IN	31,740	LC
Univ of Iowa	IA	17,693	VC
Univ of Jamestown	ND	24,738	C
Univ of Kansas	KS	17,603	C+
Univ of Kentucky	KY	19,868	C
Univ of La Verne	CA	47,010	C
Univ of Mary Washington	VA	19,484	VC
Univ of Maryland/Baltimore County	MD	18,000	VC
Univ of Miami	FL	57,034	MC
Univ of Mich/Ann Arbor	MI	22,102	MC
Univ of Minn/Morris	MN	17,150	VC
Univ of Minn/Twin Cities	MN		HC
Univ of Miss	MS	16,704	C+
Univ of Missouri/Columbia	MO	18,201	MC
Univ of Missouri-Kansas City	MO	19,603	C
Univ of Missouri-St. Louis	MO		VC
Univ of Montana	MT	14,105	C
Univ of Montevallo	AL	17,060	C
Univ of Mount Union	OH	35,130	C
Univ of Nebr - Lincoln	NE	18,031	VC
Univ of Nebr at Kearney	NE	14,855	LC
Univ of Nebr at Omaha	NE	12,700	C
Univ of Nevada, Las Vegas	NV	17,303	C
Univ of New Hampshire	NH	26,912	C
Univ of New Mexico	NM	15,300	C
Univ of North Alabama	AL	9,960	C
Univ of N Car at Asheville	NC	13,500	VC
Univ of N Car at Chapel Hill	NC	18,928	MC
Univ of N Car at Charlotte	NC	15,547	C
Univ of N Car at Wilmington	NC	13,572	VC
Univ of N Dak	ND	14,551	C
Univ of North Texas	TX	15,628	C
Univ of Northern Colo	CO	18,446	C
Univ of Notre Dame	IN	57,117	MC
Univ of Oregon	OR	21,360	C+
Univ of Pennsylvania	PA	61,132	MC
Univ of Pittsburgh at Pittsburgh	PA	28,572	HC+
Univ of Puget Sound	WA	54,608	HC
Univ of Redlands	CA	40,500	VC
Univ of Rochester	NY	60,668	MC
Univ of Scranton	PA	51,940	VC
Univ of S Car at Columbia	SC	19,725	VC+
Univ of S Dak	SD	15,111	C
Univ of South Florida/Tampa	FL	13,000	C
Univ of Southern Indiana	IN	14,885	C
Univ of Tenn at Knoxville	TN	20,364	VC+
Univ of Texas at Arlington	TX	10,908	LC
Univ of Texas at Austin	TX	44,074	HC
Univ of Texas at El Paso	TX	8,764	NC
Univ of the Pacific	CA	52,146	VC
Univ of Toledo	OH	18,464	C
Univ of Tulsa	OK	46,331	MC
Univ of Vermont	VT	27,006	VC+
Univ of Virginia	VA	23,050	MC
Univ of Wisc Whitewater	WI	13,314	C
Univ of Wisc/Eau Claire	WI	15,730	VC
Univ of Wisc/Green Bay	WI	19,074	C
Univ of Wisc/Madison	WI	18,757	HC+
Univ of Wisc/Oshkosh	WI	10,426	LC
Univ of Wisc/Parkside	WI	10,181	LC
Univ of Wisc/Platteville	WI	14,564	C
Univ of Wisc/Stevens Point	WI	14,043	C
Univ of Wyoming	WY	14,401	C+
Ursinus College	PA	57,580	VC
Utah State Univ	UT	12,044	C
Valparaiso Univ	IN	44,940	VC+
Vanderbilt Univ	TN	58,220	MC
Vassar College	NY	61,140	MC
Virginia Polytechnic Inst and State Univ	VA	14,629	HC
Virginia Wesleyan College	VA	28,433	LC
Wabash College	IN	46,850	C+
Wake Forest Univ	NC	58,838	MC
Walla Walla Univ	WA	26,256	NC
Wartburg College	IA	41,055	VC
Washburn Univ	KS	12,579	C
Washington and Jefferson College	PA	51,948	VC
Washington and Lee Univ	VA	52,812	MC
Washington College	MD	52,602	VC
Washington Univ in St. Louis	MO	69,844	MC
Wayne State Univ	MI	22,063	C

School	ST	$IS	SR
Webster Univ	MO	35,100	C+
Wellesley College	MA	59,038	MC
Wells College	NY	49,400	VC
West Chester Univ of Pennsylvania	PA	17,186	C
Western Carolina Univ	NC	13,965	C
Western Kentucky Univ	KY	11,000	LC
Western Mich Univ	MI	19,628	C
Western Washington Univ	WA	18,519	VC
Westminster College	PA	31,290	C+
Wheaton College	IL	40,720	MC
Wheaton College	MA	54,934	HC+
Whitman College	WA	55,988	MC
Willamette Univ	OR	56,450	VC+
Williams College	MA	61,070	MC
Winthrop Univ	SC	21,120	C
Wittenberg Univ	OH	47,962	C+
Wofford College	SC	45,795	VC
Wright State Univ	OH	16,983	C
Xavier Univ	OH	44,980	VC

GERMAN AREA STUDIES

School	ST	$IS	SR
American Univ	DC	56,015	HC+
Appalachian State Univ	NC	12,919	VC
Bard College	NY	61,940	HC
Bard College at Simon's Rock	MA	61,749	HC+
Boston College	MA	60,622	MC
Brown Univ	RI	59,428	MC
Cal State, Northridge	CA	28,690	LC
Case Western Reserve Univ	OH	56,534	MC
Coe College	IA	45,550	VC
College of the Holy Cross	MA	58,042	MC
Columbia Univ/School of General Studies	NY	58,231	MC
Cornell Univ	NY	60,964	MC
Dartmouth College	NH	57,996	MC
Emory Univ	GA	56,368	MC
Fordham Univ	NY	61,588	HC+
Hamilton College	NY	55,620	MC
Ithaca College	NY	53,864	HC
Lake Erie College	OH	37,266	C
Lewis & Clark College	OR	54,382	MC
Linfield College-McMinnville Campus	OR	47,676	C
Macalester College	MN	57,691	MC
Moravian College	PA	36,381	VC
Mount Holyoke College	MA	55,146	MC
Muhlenberg College	PA	52,837	HC
New College of Florida	FL	14,504	MC
Pomona College	CA	57,680	MC
Rice Univ	TX	43,288	MC
St. Anselm College	NH	49,376	VC
Scripps College	CA	61,940	MC
Southern Illinois Univ Carbondale	IL	21,942	C
Stanford Univ	CA	58,388	MC
Suffolk Univ	MA	47,298	C
Swarthmore College	PA	57,870	MC
Tufts Univ	MA	58,780	MC
Union College	NY	60,240	MC
Univ of Arizona	AZ	20,657	C
Univ of Calif at Irvine	CA	25,961	VC
Univ of Calif at Santa Cruz	CA	27,807	C+
Univ of Colo Boulder	CO	22,605	VC+
Univ of Illinois at Chicago	IL	24,505	VC
Univ of Minn/Duluth	MN	19,806	C
Univ of N Car at Wilmington	NC	13,572	VC
Univ of Portland	OR	49,964	VC
Univ of Wisc/La Crosse	WI	9,304	VC
Wartburg College	IA	41,055	VC
Wellesley College	MA	59,038	MC
Wesleyan Univ	CT	61,198	MC
Yale Univ	CT	55,300	MC

GERMAN STUDIES

School	ST	$IS	SR
Creighton Univ	NE	45,356	VC
Indiana Univ Bloomington	IN	19,801	VC

GERMANIC LANGUAGES AND LITERATURE

School	ST	$IS	SR
Bard College	NY	61,940	HC
Bennington College	VT	56,990	HC+
Binghamton Univ/The SUNY	NY	21,648	HC+
Boston Univ	MA	60,694	MC
Colby College	ME	57,510	MC
Colo College	CO	57,162	MC
Columbia Univ/City of New York	NY	61,116	MC
Duke Univ	NC	50,250	MC
Kent State Univ	OH	19,920	C
New College of Florida	FL	14,504	MC
New York Univ	NY	61,470	MC
Oberlin College	OH	61,788	MC
Reed College	OR	57,780	MC
St. Louis Univ	MO	48,346	HC
Scripps College	CA	61,940	MC
Smith College	MA	59,674	MC
Stony Brook Univ / SUNY	NY	20,078	HC+
Syracuse Univ	NY	56,346	VC
Ohio State Univ-Columbus Campus	OH	19,887	HC+
Transylvania Univ	KY	42,660	VC+

School	ST	$IS	SR
Univ of Calif at Riverside	CA	27,204	C+
Univ of Calif at San Diego	CA	21,000	VC
Univ of Calif at Santa Barbara	CA	27,551	HC
Univ of Georgia	GA	20,082	VC
Univ of Illinois at Chicago	IL	24,505	VC
Univ of Illinois at Urbana-Champaign	IL	26,450	HC
Univ of Kansas	KS	17,603	C+
Univ of Maryland - College Park	MD	20,060	VC
Univ of Mass Amherst	MA	24,215	VC+
Univ of Mich/Ann Arbor	MI	22,102	MC
Univ of Missouri-St. Louis	MO		VC
Univ of Pittsburgh at Pittsburgh	PA	28,572	HC+
Univ of Washington	WA	14,722	VC
Univ of Wisc/Green Bay	WI	19,074	C
Univ of Wisc-Milwaukee	WI	18,436	C
Vassar College	NY	61,140	MC
Washington and Lee Univ	VA	52,812	MC
Washington Univ in St. Louis	MO	69,844	MC
Yale Univ	CT	55,300	MC

GERONTOLOGY

School	ST	$IS	SR
Alfred Univ	NY	41,770	C
Ashford Univ	CA	10,480	C
Barton Univ	NC	27,660	LC
Bethune-Cookman Univ	FL	22,958	C
Bloomfield College	NJ	37,850	LC
Bowling Green State Univ	OH	18,970	C
Cal State, Fresno	CA	17,405	C
Cal State, San Bernardino	CA	12,000	C
Calif Univ of Pennsylvania	PA	14,217	C
Canisius College	NY	44,900	C
Case Western Reserve Univ	OH	56,534	MC
Central Washington Univ	WA	11,730	C
Eastern Mich Univ	MI	18,604	C
Gwynedd-Mercy College	PA	33,560	C
Ithaca College	NY	53,864	HC
Kent State Univ	OH	19,920	C
Langston Univ	OK	3,000	C
Madonna Univ	MI	24,540	C
Marywood Univ	PA	45,595	C
McKendree Univ	IL	29,920	C+
Metropolitan College of New York	NY	16,720	C
Miami Univ	OH	24,191	VC
Minn State Univ, Moorhead	MN	13,392	VC
Missouri State Univ	MO	13,996	C+
Montclair State Univ	NJ	22,614	C
Mount St. Mary's College - Chalon Campus	CA	43,897	VC+
Northeastern Illinois Univ	IL	10,318	LC
Pontifical Catholic Univ of PR	PR	7,310	
Quinnipiac Univ	CT	55,160	VC
San Diego State Univ	CA	21,611	C+
Shaw Univ	NC	15,488	C
Sojourner-Douglass College	MD	9,160	LC
Southeastern Okla State Univ	OK	7,966	LC
Southern Illinois Univ Edwardsville	IL	17,532	C
Springfield College	MA	25,000	C
St. Bonaventure Univ	NY	41,575	C
SUNY Oneonta / SUNY	NY	16,919	C+
Towson Univ	MD	16,000	VC
Univ of Arkansas at Pine Bluff	AR	13,378	C
Univ of Central Arkansas	AR	13,667	VC
Univ of Central Okla	OK	12,293	C
Univ of Louisiana at Monroe	LA	12,998	C
Univ of Maryland/Univ College	MD	6,168	SP
Univ of Mass Boston	MA	23,066	VC
Univ of Northern Colo	CO	18,446	C
Univ of Northern Iowa	IA	15,795	C
Univ of South Florida/Tampa	FL	13,000	C
Univ of Southern Calif	CA	56,903	MC
Utica College	NY	45,670	C
Wichita State Univ	KS	14,607	C+
York College / The CUNY	NY	5,496	VC
Youngstown State Univ	OH	16,732	C

GLASS

School	ST	$IS	SR
Alfred Univ	NY	41,770	C
Calif College of the Arts	CA	48,334	SP
Cleveland Inst of Art	OH	48,685	SP
College for Creative Studies	MI	45,340	C
Kent State Univ	OH	19,920	C
Rhode Island School of Design	RI	57,234	MC
Rochester Inst of Technology	NY	42,450	VC
Temple Univ	PA	24,392	VC

GLOBAL & PUBLIC HEALTH SCIENCES

School	ST	$IS	SR
Cornell Univ	NY	60,964	MC

GLOBAL MANAGEMENT

School	ST	$IS	SR
Bryant Univ	RI	49,179	VC
Farmingdale State College	NY	19,673	C

GLOBAL STUDIES

School	ST	$IS	SR
Castleton State College	VT	20,186	C
Framingham State Univ	MA	18,854	C
Ohio Univ	OH	21,080	C
Providence College	RI	57,383	VC
St. Leo Univ	FL	30,340	C
Southeast Missouri State Univ	MO	15,370	LC
St. Edward's Univ	TX	47,784	VC
The Pennsylvania State Univ - Univ Park	PA	28,022	VC+

GLOBAL/GENERAL MANAGEMENT

School	ST	$IS	SR
Bryant Univ	RI	49,179	VC
Hamline Univ	MN	45,678	VC
Thomas Edison State College	NJ	5,700	SP
Univ of North Florida	FL	15,870	VC
Univ of Pittsburgh at Pittsburgh	PA	28,572	HC+
Univ of South Florida/St. Petersburg	FL	12,769	C

GOLF ENTERPRISE MANAGEMENT

School	ST	$IS	SR
Univ of Nebr - Lincoln	NE	18,031	VC
Univ of Wisc/Stout	WI	15,459	C

GOVERNMENT

School	ST	$IS	SR
American Univ	DC	56,015	HC+
Cornell Univ	NY	60,964	MC
Mills College	CA	54,119	VC

GRAPHIC AND PRINTING PRODUCTION

School	ST	$IS	SR
Brenau Univ - Women's College	GA	26,650	LC
New York College of Technology/The CUNY	NY	5,769	NC
Pittsburg State Univ	KS	12,032	C
Rochester Inst of Technology	NY	42,450	VC
Univ of Wisc/Stout	WI	15,459	C
Western Mich Univ	MI	19,628	C
Youngstown State Univ	OH	16,732	C

GRAPHIC ARTS TECHNOLOGY

School	ST	$IS	SR
Andrews Univ	MI	28,030	C+
Appalachian State Univ	NC	12,919	VC
Arizona State Univ, at the Polytechnic Campus	AZ	20,531	C
Arizona State Univ, at the Tempe Campus	AZ	20,137	C+
Ball State Univ	IN	17,850	C
Carroll Univ	WI	38,100	C
Central State Univ	OH	9,010	C
Clemson Univ	SC	19,136	HC
College of the Ozarks	MO		VC
Colo Mesa Univ	CO	17,690	LC
Colo Technical Univ	CO	10,500	LC
Emmanuel College	MA	47,985	VC
Florida State Univ	FL	16,715	VC
Idaho State Univ	ID	12,307	C
Minn State Univ, Moorhead	MN	13,392	VC
New York Univ	NY	61,470	MC
North Central College	IL	38,343	VC
Pacific Union College	CA	28,150	VC
Pennsylvania College of Technology	PA	26,286	NC
Pittsburg State Univ	KS	12,032	C
Rochester Inst of Technology	NY	42,450	VC
Univ of Central Missouri	MO	14,605	C
Univ of Wisc/Stout	WI	15,459	C

GRAPHIC COMMUNICATIONS

School	ST	$IS	SR
Bethany College	WV	35,282	LC
Calif Polytechnic State Univ	CA	19,847	HC
Georgia Southern Univ	GA	16,942	C
Illinois State Univ	IL	23,110	VC
Millersville Univ of Pennsylvania	PA	21,648	C
Western Illinois Univ	IL	20,732	C

GRAPHIC COMMUNICATIONS MANAGEMENT

School	ST	$IS	SR
Black Hills State Univ	SD	13,947	C
Ferris State Univ	MI	20,047	C
Univ of Wisc/Stout	WI	15,459	C

GRAPHIC DESIGN

School	ST	$IS	SR
Abilene Christian Univ	TX	38,400	C+
Adams State Univ	CO	13,358	LC
Alabama A&M Univ	AL	10,084	C
American Univ	DC	56,015	HC+
Anderson Univ	IN	36,100	C
Andrews Univ	MI	28,030	C+
Anna Maria College	MA	34,600	C

ST = STATE $IS = IN-STATE COSTS   SR = SELECTOR RATING

School	ST	$IS	SR
Appalachian State Univ	NC	12,919	VC
Arcadia Univ	PA	33,570	C+
Arizona State Univ, at the Tempe Campus	AZ	20,137	C+
Arkansas State Univ	AR	15,470	C
Art Academy of Cincinnati	OH	25,940	SP
Art Center College of Design	CA	34,044	SP
Art Inst of Atlanta	GA	24,000	SP
Art Inst of Portland	OR	23,040	SP
Assumption College	MA	47,122	C
Auburn Univ	AL	22,378	VC+
Barton College	NC	27,660	LC
Becker College	MA	41,420	C
Bethel College	IN	31,560	C
Bethel College	KS	32,160	C
Biola Univ	CA	40,320	C+
Black Hills State Univ	SD	13,947	C
Blackburn College	IL	21,350	C
Bloomfield College	NJ	37,850	LC
Boston Univ	MA	60,694	MC
Bowling Green State Univ	OH	18,970	C
Bradley Univ	IL	31,874	VC
Brescia Univ	KY	26,140	VC+
Briar Cliff Univ	IA	29,514	C
Brigham Young Univ	UT	12,100	HC
Buena Vista Univ	IA	39,188	C
Burlington College	VT	32,510	SP
Cabrini College	PA	40,859	LC
Calif Baptist Univ	CA	38,792	C
Calif College of the Arts	CA	48,334	SP
Calif State Polytechnic Univ, Pomona	CA	20,156	C
Cal State, Chico	CA	20,058	C
Cal State, Fresno	CA	17,405	C
Cal State, Los Angeles	CA	17,186	LC
Cal State, San Bernardino	CA	12,000	C
Calif Univ of Pennsylvania	PA	14,217	C
Calvin College	MI	39,120	VC
Campbell Univ	NC	37,570	VC
Carthage College	WI	33,000	C
Cedarville Univ	OH	32,860	VC
Central Conn State Univ	CT	19,749	C
Champlain College	VT	46,650	VC+
Chapman Univ	CA	58,347	VC+
Cleveland Inst of Art	OH	48,685	SP
Coastal Carolina Univ	SC	18,580	C
Coker College	SC	32,256	LC
Colby-Sawyer College	NH	50,790	C
College for Creative Studies	MI	45,340	C
College of Mount St. Joseph	OH	33,880	C
College of New Jersey	NJ	25,376	HC
Columbia College	MO	24,578	C
Columbus College of Art and Design	OH	37,732	SP
Concordia Univ St. Paul	MN	28,250	C
Concordia Univ Wisc	WI	28,980	C
Cooper Union for the Advancement of Science and Art	NY	55,600	MC
Corcoran College of Art and Design	DC	36,500	SP
Cornerstone Univ and Grand Rapids Theological Seminary	MI	33,338	C
Culver-Stockton College	MO	30,900	C
Curry College	MA	48,925	LC
Daemen College	NY	34,770	C
Dallas Baptist Univ	TX	30,580	VC
Defiance College	OH	30,645	C
DePaul Univ	IL	47,623	VC
Dominican Univ	IL	37,628	C
Dominican Univ of Calif	CA	51,250	C
Dordt College	IA	34,160	C+
Drake Univ	IA	41,516	VC+
Drexel Univ	PA	61,418	VC+
Eastern Mich Univ	MI	18,604	C
Eastern Washington Univ	WA		C
Edgewood College	WI	33,294	C
Edinboro Univ of Pennsylvania	PA	15,940	LC
Elmhurst College	IL	43,336	C
Endicott College	MA	43,228	VC+
Fashion Inst of Technology/SUNY	NY	18,362	SP
Felician College	NJ	41,640	LC
Ferris State Univ	MI	20,047	C
Fitchburg State Univ	MA	18,173	C
Flagler College	FL	25,180	C
Florida Atlantic Univ	FL	17,339	C
Florida Southern College	FL	40,150	C+
Fordham Univ	NY	61,588	HC+
Franklin Pierce Univ	NH	41,598	C
Gallaudet Univ	DC	25,382	SP
Goshen College	IN	35,900	VC
Grace College and Seminary	IN	28,800	VC
Graceland Univ	IA	28,020	C
Grand View Univ	IA	31,050	C
Harding Univ	AR	23,556	C
Hardin-Simmons Univ	TX	23,560	C+
High Point Univ	NC	39,800	C
Howard Univ	DC	13,646	C
Huntington Univ	IN	32,220	C
Indiana Univ–Purdue Univ Fort Wayne	IN	15,521	C
Iowa State Univ	IA	16,403	VC
John Brown Univ	AR	32,056	VC+

School	ST	$IS	SR
Keene State College	NH	23,232	LC
Kutztown Univ of Pennsylvania	PA	16,909	LC
La Roche College	PA	35,824	LC
La Sierra Univ	CA	35,694	VC
Laguna College of Art and Design	CA	27,300	SP
Lasell College	MA	43,750	C
Lenoir-Rhyne College	NC	35,984	C
Limestone College	SC	30,800	C
Lipscomb Univ	TN	37,490	VC
Louisiana College	LA	15,746	C
Loyola Univ New Orleans	LA	46,581	VC
Lyndon State College	VT	14,233	C
Madonna Univ	MI	24,540	VC
Maine College of Art	ME	28,812	SP
Mansfield Univ	PA	19,468	LC
Marian Univ	IN	38,540	C
Marietta College	OH	42,135	C+
Marshall Univ	WV	14,820	C
Maryland Inst College of Art	MD	39,500	SP
Marymount Univ	VA	39,480	C
Maryville Univ of St. Louis	MO	35,856	VC
Marywood Univ	PA	45,595	C
Memphis College of Art	TN	33,550	SP
Mercyhurst Univ	PA	40,700	C
Miami Univ	OH	24,191	VC
MidAmerica Nazarene Univ	KS	28,000	C
Middle Tenn State Univ	TN	8,650	C
Milwaukee Inst of Art and Design	WI	31,938	SP
Minneapolis College of Art and Design	MN	36,700	SP
Miss College	MS	21,998	C
Missouri Southern State Univ	MO	12,061	C
Missouri Western State Univ	MO	12,260	NC
Monmouth Univ	NJ	44,108	C
Montclair State Univ	NJ	22,614	C
Montserrat College of Art	MA	31,000	C
Moore College of Art and Design	PA	50,135	SP
Moravian College	PA	36,381	VC
Morningside College	IA	35,430	C
Mount Ida College	MA	30,115	LC
Mount Mary Univ	WI	33,590	LC
Mount Mercy Univ	IA	35,320	C
Mount Vernon Nazarene Univ	OH	29,590	C
New Mexico Highlands Univ	NM	11,904	NC
New York Inst of Technology	NY	45,010	VC
New York Univ	NY	61,470	MC
Newbury College	MA	43,280	LC
Norfolk State Univ	VA	10,531	LC
N Car State Univ	NC	16,202	HC
Northeastern Univ	MA	55,296	MC
Northwest Nazarene Univ	ID	34,000	C
Northwestern College	MN	24,000	C
Northwestern College of Iowa	IA	36,240	VC
Notre Dame College	OH	34,942	VC
Notre Dame de Namur Univ	CA	44,236	LC
Notre Dame of Maryland Univ	MD	27,700	C
Ohio Dominican Univ	OH	38,380	C+
Ohio Northern Univ	OH	42,075	VC
Ohio Univ	OH	21,080	C
Old Dominion Univ	VA	19,483	LC
Oswego / SUNY	NY	20,009	VC
Otis College of Art and Design	CA	35,404	SP
Ouachita Baptist Univ	AR	30,220	VC
Pacific Northwest College of Art	OR	38,494	C
Pacific Union College	CA	28,150	VC
Palm Beach Atlantic Univ	FL	34,874	C+
Park Univ	MO	17,525	C
Parsons The New School for Design	NY	56,610	SP
Pennsylvania College of Technology	PA	26,286	NC
Philadelphia Univ	PA	44,160	C
Plymouth State Univ	NH	23,148	LC
Point Loma Nazarene Univ	CA	41,006	C+
Purdue Univ/West Lafayette	IN	20,024	HC
Queens College/The CUNY	NY	17,107	VC
Queens Univ of Charlotte	NC	39,543	C+
Quincy Univ	IL	34,980	LC
Rhode Island School of Design	RI	57,234	MC
Ringling College of Art and Design	FL	46,130	SP
Rivier Univ	NH	35,000	LC
Roberts Wesleyan College	NY	38,306	C+
Rochester Inst of Technology	NY	42,450	VC
Rocky Mountain College of Art and Design	CO	22,470	SP
Roger Williams Univ	RI	46,296	VC
Sacred Heart Univ	CT	49,264	VC
St. Mary's Univ of Minn	MN	41,594	C
St. Peter's Univ	NJ	44,240	C
Sam Houston State Univ	TX	17,082	C
Samford Univ	AL	37,060	C+
Santa Fe Univ of Art and Design	NM	39,666	SP
Savannah College of Art and Design	GA	48,005	SP
School of Visual Arts	NY	36,500	VC

School	ST	$IS	SR
Schreiner Univ	TX	32,734	LC
Seton Hall Univ	NJ	45,902	C
Seton Hill Univ	PA	35,172	C
Siena Heights Univ	MI	32,040	C
Simpson College	IA	36,086	C+
S Dak State Univ	SD	14,296	C
South Univ	GA	36,070	LC
Southern Adventist Univ	TN	26,190	C
Southern Nazarene Univ	OK	24,354	C
Southern New Hampshire Univ	NH	38,100	C
Southern Oregon Univ	OR	17,874	C
Southwestern Okla State Univ	OK	9,160	C
Spring Hill College	AL	44,164	VC
St. Ambrose Univ	IA	30,845	C
St. Edward's Univ	TX	47,784	C
St. John's Univ	NY	55,070	C+
St. Norbert College	WI	41,478	VC
Stephens College	MO	38,042	VC
Suffolk Univ	MA	47,298	C
SUNY Fredonia/The SUNY at Fredonia	NY	19,840	VC
SUNY New Paltz	NY	14,348	C
Susquehanna Univ	PA	51,150	C
Syracuse Univ	NY	56,346	VC
Tabor College	KS	29,010	C
Temple Univ	PA	24,392	VC
Texas Christian Univ	TX	49,980	HC
The College of St. Rose	NY	26,752	C
The Pennsylvania State Univ - Univ Park	PA	28,022	VC+
The SUNY College of Agriculture and Tech at Cobleskill	NY	19,749	LC
Union College	NE	23,270	C
Union Univ	TN	28,260	VC
Univ of Bridgeport	CT	39,030	LC
Univ of Central Okla	OK	12,293	C
Univ of Cincinnati	OH	21,506	VC
Univ of Evansville	IN	42,656	VC+
Univ of Florida	FL	15,943	HC
Univ of Illinois at Chicago	IL	24,505	VC
Univ of Illinois at Urbana-Champaign	IL	26,450	HC
Univ of Iowa	IA	17,693	VC
Univ of Kansas	KS	17,603	C+
Univ of Mass Dartmouth	MA	22,223	C
Univ of Miami	FL	57,034	MC
Univ of Mich/Ann Arbor	MI	22,102	MC
Univ of Minn/Duluth	MN	19,806	C
Univ of New Haven	CT	48,940	C
Univ of N Dak	ND	14,551	C
Univ of Northern Colo	CO	18,446	C
Univ of Northern Iowa	IA	15,795	C
Univ of San Francisco	CA	54,770	VC
Univ of S Car Upstate	SC	18,200	LC
Univ of South Florida/St. Petersburg	FL	12,769	C
Univ of Tampa	FL	35,160	VC
Univ of Tenn at Knoxville	TN	20,364	VC+
Univ of the Arts	PA	43,508	SP
Univ of the Pacific	CA	52,146	VC
Univ of Washington	WA	14,722	VC
Upper Iowa Univ	IA	30,426	NC
Ursuline College	OH	33,198	C
Virginia Commonwealth Univ	VA	21,716	C
Viterbo Univ	WI	30,070	C
Walla Walla Univ	WA	26,256	NC
Walsh Univ	OH	35,100	C
Wartburg College	IA	41,055	VC
Washington Univ in St. Louis	MO	69,844	MC
Wayland Baptist Univ	TX	18,912	LC
Wayne State College	NE	11,764	NC
Waynesburg Univ	PA	30,150	C
Webster Univ	MO	35,100	C+
West Liberty Univ	WV	9,142	LC
West Texas A&M Univ	TX	13,478	C
Western Mich Univ	MI	19,628	C
Wichita State Univ	KS	14,607	C+
William Woods Univ	MO	24,260	C
Wilson College	PA	35,080	C
Winona State Univ	MN	16,640	C
Woodbury Univ	CA	34,500	LC
York College of Pennsylvania	PA	26,590	C
Youngstown State Univ	OH	16,732	C

GRAPHIC DESIGN & MEDIA

School	ST	$IS	SR
Baldwin Wallace Univ	OH	38,318	C
Bloomfield College	NJ	37,850	LC
Bluffton Univ	OH	38,948	C
Champlain College	VT	46,650	VC+
Creighton Univ	NE	45,356	VC
Georgian Court Univ	NJ	41,594	LC
Murray State Univ	KY	15,304	C
Southern Oregon Univ	OR	17,874	C
Univ of Illinois at Chicago	IL	24,505	VC
Wilson College	PA	35,080	C

GREAT PLAINS STUDIES

School	ST	$IS	SR
Univ of Nebr - Lincoln	NE	18,031	VC

GREEK

School	ST	$IS	SR
Barnard College/Columbia Univ	NY	39,000	MC
Brigham Young Univ	UT	12,100	HC
Bryn Mawr College	PA	59,890	MC
Calvin College	MI	39,120	VC
Carleton College	MN	60,102	MC
Colgate Univ	NY	58,135	MC
Columbia Univ/City of New York	NY	61,116	MC
Concordia Univ, Ann Arbor	MI	27,220	VC
Creighton Univ	NE	45,356	VC
DePauw Univ	IN	48,950	VC+
Dickinson College	PA	57,662	HC+
Emory Univ	GA	56,368	MC
Florida State Univ	FL	16,715	VC
Franklin and Marshall College	PA	60,799	MC
Furman Univ	SC	54,006	HC
Gettysburg College	PA	58,820	HC
Hampden-Sydney College	VA	51,758	C
Harvard College/Harvard Univ	MA	49,000	MC
Haverford College	PA	61,564	MC
Hobart and William Smith Colleges	NY	60,034	HC+
Hunter College	NY	14,429	VC
John Carroll Univ	OH	46,300	C+
Kent State Univ	OH	19,920	C
Lehman College/The CUNY	NY	5,778	LC
Loyola Marymount Univ	CA	54,649	VC+
Loyola Univ Chicago	IL	51,646	VC+
Marlboro College	VT	43,980	VC
Monmouth College	IL	40,850	C
Mount Holyoke College	MA	55,146	MC
New York Univ	NY	61,470	MC
Northeastern Illinois Univ	IL	10,318	LC
Ohio Univ	OH	21,080	C
Randolph-Macon College	VA	49,869	C+
Samford Univ	AL	37,060	C
Sarah Lawrence College	NY	48,000	HC
Sewanee: The Univ of the South	TN	47,700	HC+
Smith College	MA	59,674	MC
Southwestern Univ	TX	45,660	VC
St. Olaf College	MN	51,200	HC+
Swarthmore College	PA	57,870	MC
Ohio State Univ-Columbus Campus	OH	19,887	HC+
The Univ of Tenn at Chattanooga	TN	16,883	C
Trinity Univ	TX	48,150	HC+
Tufts Univ	MA	58,780	MC
Union Univ	TN	28,260	VC
Univ of Calif at Berkeley	CA	23,322	MC
Univ of Calif at Davis	CA		HC
Univ of Calif at Los Angeles	CA	25,686	MC
Univ of Georgia	GA	20,082	VC
Univ of Iowa	IA	17,693	VC
Univ of Mich/Ann Arbor	MI	22,102	MC
Univ of Minn/Twin Cities	MN		HC
Univ of New Hampshire	NH	26,912	C
Univ of Notre Dame	IN	57,117	MC
Univ of Oregon	OR	21,360	C+
Univ of Scranton	PA	51,940	VC
Univ of Texas at Austin	TX	44,074	HC
Univ of Vermont	VT	27,006	VC+
Wabash College	IN	46,850	VC+
Wake Forest Univ	NC	58,838	MC
Wellesley College	MA	59,038	MC
Wheaton College	MA	54,934	VC+
Wright State Univ	OH	16,983	C

GREEK (CLASSICAL)

School	ST	$IS	SR
Baylor Univ	TX	50,329	HC
Boston Univ	MA	60,694	MC
Butler Univ	IN	47,572	VC+
College of Wooster	OH	52,600	VC
Duquesne Univ	PA	43,720	VC
Indiana Univ Bloomington	IN	19,801	VC
Kenyon College	OH	58,890	MC
Knox College	IL	44,865	VC+
New York Univ	NY	61,470	MC
Ohio Univ	OH	21,080	C
The Catholic Univ of America	DC	52,852	VC
Univ of Miami	FL	57,034	MC
Washington Univ in St. Louis	MO	69,844	MC

GREEK (MODERN)

School	ST	$IS	SR
New York Univ	NY	61,470	VC
Queens College/The CUNY	NY	17,107	VC
Tulane Univ	LA	60,861	MC
Univ of Mich/Ann Arbor	MI	22,102	MC

GUIDANCE EDUCATION

School	ST	$IS	SR
Calif Univ of Pennsylvania	PA	14,217	C
Eastern Washington Univ	WA		C
Prescott College	AZ	33,284	C
S Car State Univ	SC	6,700	LC
St. Cloud State Univ	MN	10,600	C

ST = STATE $IS = IN-STATE COSTS   SR = SELECTOR RATING

School	ST	$IS	SR
Texas A&M Univ at Commerce	TX	10,496	C
Univ of Central Arkansas	AR	13,667	VC
Univ of Cincinnati	OH	21,506	VC
Univ of Southern Miss	MS	13,170	C
Westminster College	PA	31,290	C+

GUITAR

School	ST	$IS	SR
Boston Conservatory	MA	56,380	VC
Central Washington Univ	WA	11,730	C
Illinois Wesleyan Univ	IL	48,452	HC
Indiana Univ Bloomington	IN	19,801	VC
Loyola Univ New Orleans	LA	46,581	VC
Mannes College New School for Music	NY	44,500	SP
Okla City Univ	OK	40,476	VC
Roosevelt Univ	IL	22,605	VC
San Francisco Conservatory of Music	CA	56,428	SP
Stetson Univ	FL	51,516	VC
Wright State Univ	OH	16,983	C

HABILITATION OF THE DEAF

School	ST	$IS	SR
Texas Christian Univ	TX	49,980	HC

HAWAIIAN

School	ST	$IS	SR
Univ of Hawaii at Hilo	HI	23,066	C
Univ of Hawaii at Manoa	HI	19,379	C

HAWAIIAN STUDIES

School	ST	$IS	SR
Brigham Young Univ/Hawaii	HI	10,686	VC
Univ of Hawaii at Hilo	HI	23,066	C
Univ of Hawaii at Manoa	HI	19,379	C

HEALTH

School	ST	$IS	SR
Aquinas College	MI	33,060	C
Averett Univ	VA	37,750	LC
Bentley Univ	MA	56,454	HC+
Buffalo State College / SUNY	NY	15,733	C+
Cal State, Monterey Bay	CA	26,871	LC
Cal State, Northridge	CA	28,690	VC
Chicago State Univ	IL	5,482	C
Coastal Carolina Univ	SC	18,580	C
College of the Ozarks	MO		VC
Concordia College - Moorhead	MN	39,974	VC
Concordia College - New York	NY	39,035	LC
Concordia Univ Nebr	NE	26,000	VC
Coppin State Univ	MD	16,227	VC
DePauw Univ	IN	48,950	VC+
Eastern Illinois Univ	IL	20,466	C
Eastern Oregon Univ	OR	10,400	C
George Fox Univ	OR	40,750	C+
Georgetown Univ	DC	52,910	MC
Georgian Court Univ	NJ	41,594	LC
Goddard College	VT	16,418	VC
Graceland Univ	IA	28,020	C
Harding Univ	AR	23,556	C
Hodges Univ	FL	12,000	LC
Husson Univ	ME	24,194	LC
Idaho State Univ	ID	12,307	C
Indiana Wesleyan Univ	IN	31,815	VC
Ithaca College	NY	53,864	HC
Kentucky Wesleyan College	KY	27,440	C
Lebanon Valley College	PA	38,570	C
LeTourneau Univ	TX	36,210	VC
Luther College	IA	45,720	C+
McKendree Univ	IL	29,920	C+
Missouri Southern State Univ	MO	12,061	C
Molloy College	NY	40,440	C
Montana State Univ	MT	14,068	C
Nebr Wesleyan Univ	NE	29,774	C
New Mexico Highlands Univ	NM	11,904	NC
Northeastern Illinois Univ	IL	10,318	LC
Ohio Northern Univ	OH	42,075	VC
Ohio Valley Univ	WV	17,752	C
Olivet College	MI	19,984	LC
Oregon State Univ	OR	20,273	VC
Prairie View A&M Univ	TX	15,205	LC
Rowan Univ	NJ	24,022	VC+
Rust College	MS	10,600	C
Sam Houston State Univ	TX	17,082	C
Southeast Missouri State Univ	MO	15,370	C
Southeastern Louisiana Univ	LA	13,325	C
Southern Oregon Univ	OR	17,874	C
Southwestern Adventist Univ	TX	23,026	LC
SUNY Polytechnic Inst	NY	19,690	C
SUNY College at Old Westbury	NY	16,324	C
Tenn Wesleyan College	TN	21,250	C
Texas Christian Univ	TX	49,980	HC
Texas Southern Univ	TX	18,212	LC
Texas Tech Univ	TX	14,243	C
The College of Idaho	ID	31,277	C+
Union College	KY	29,955	C
Union Inst & Univ	OH	8,912	SP
Univ of Delaware	DE	23,612	VC
Univ of Houston	TX	19,796	VC
Univ of Louisiana at Monroe	LA	12,998	C
Univ of Louisville	KY	17,946	C
Univ of Mich/Dearborn	MI	9,885	VC
Univ of Minn Crookston	MN	17,834	C
Univ of Missouri-Kansas City	MO	19,603	C
Univ of Mount Union	OH	35,130	C
Univ of New Mexico	NM	15,300	C
Univ of New Orleans	LA	9,224	C
Univ of N Car at Asheville	NC	13,500	VC
Univ of North Texas	TX	15,628	C
Univ of Pennsylvania	PA	61,132	MC
Univ of Rochester	NY	60,668	MC
Univ of Texas - Pan American	TX	11,125	LC
Univ of Texas at San Antonio	TX	18,372	C
Univ of the Cumberlands	KY	27,500	C
Univ of Wisc/Stout	WI	15,459	C
Univ of Wisc/Superior	WI	14,314	C
Upper Iowa Univ	IA	30,426	NC
Voorhees College	SC	18,126	C
Walla Walla Univ	WA	26,256	NC
West Chester Univ of Pennsylvania	PA	17,186	C

HEALTH ADMINISTRATION AND POLICY

School	ST	$IS	SR
Columbia College	MO	24,578	C
Creighton Univ	NE	45,356	VC
Eastern Washington Univ	WA		C
Indiana Univ Bloomington	IN	19,801	VC
Indiana Univ-Purdue Univ Indianapolis	IN	17,611	C
Old Dominion Univ	VA	19,483	LC
Providence College	RI	57,383	VC
The Pennsylvania State Univ - Univ Park	PA	28,022	VC+
Univ of Miami	FL	57,034	MC
Univ of New Hampshire	NH	26,912	C
Univ of St. Francis	IL	37,560	C
Western Illinois Univ	IL	20,732	C
Xavier Univ	OH	44,980	VC

HEALTH AND EDUCATION SCIENCE

School	ST	$IS	SR
Aquinas College	MI	33,060	C
Indiana Univ-Purdue Univ Indianapolis	IN	17,611	C

HEALTH AND PHYSICAL ACTIVITY

School	ST	$IS	SR
Aquinas College	MI	33,060	C
Hanover College	IN	43,073	C+
Millikin Univ	IL	38,940	C
Texas State Univ	TX	17,128	C
Univ of Wisc/Superior	WI	14,314	C

HEALTH AND PHYSICAL EDUCATION

School	ST	$IS	SR
Aquinas College	MI	33,060	C
Baldwin Wallace Univ	OH	38,318	C
Bethel Univ	KS	32,160	C
Bridgewater College	VA	41,450	C
Georgia Southern Univ	GA	16,942	C
Georgia Southwestern State Univ	GA	13,246	C
Morehouse College	GA	39,412	C
Murray State Univ	KY	15,304	C
Oakwood Univ	AL	25,529	NC
Rocky Mountain College	MT	32,242	C
Syracuse Univ	NY	56,346	VC

HEALTH CARE ADMINISTRATION

School	ST	$IS	SR
Adams State Univ	CO	13,358	LC
Alaska Pacific Univ	AK	43,592	VC
Alma College	MI	44,075	C
Appalachian State Univ	NC	12,919	VC
Arcadia Univ	PA	33,570	C+
Ashford Univ	CA	10,480	C
Auburn Univ	AL	22,378	VC+
Baker College of Flint	MI	7,800	NC
Baldwin Wallace Univ	OH	38,318	C
Benedictine Univ	IL	37,820	C
Berkeley College/New Jersey	NJ	27,300	LC
Cabarrus College of Health Sciences	NC	10,000	SP
Calif Baptist Univ	CA	38,792	C
Cal State, Chico	CA	20,158	C
Cal State, Long Beach	CA	17,502	C+
Cal State, Northridge	CA	28,690	VC
Cal State, San Bernardino	CA	12,000	C
Calumet College of St. Joseph	IN	15,000	C
Campbell Univ	NC	37,570	VC
Carlow Univ	PA	30,272	C
Carroll College	MT	28,000	C
Chancellor Univ	OH	11,000	C
Charter Oak State College	CT	8,592	
Chestnut Hill College	PA	42,110	LC
Chicago State Univ	IL	5,482	C
Clayton State Univ	GA	12,000	LC
Coastal Carolina Univ	SC	18,580	C
College of St. Scholastica	MN	41,440	C
Columbia College	MO	24,578	C
Concordia Univ	OR	35,000	C
Corban Univ	OR	37,380	C+
Dallas Baptist Univ	TX	30,580	VC
Dominican College	NY	31,270	LC
Duquesne Univ	PA	43,720	VC
D'Youville College	NY	29,850	C
East Carolina Univ	NC	14,169	C
Eastern Kentucky Univ	KY	11,161	C
Eastern Mich Univ	MI	18,604	C
Eastern Washington Univ	WA		C
Emporia State Univ	KS	12,897	C
Ferris State Univ	MI	20,047	C
Florida Atlantic Univ	FL	17,339	C
Florida International Univ	FL	17,747	C+
Franklin Pierce Univ	NH	41,598	C
Franklin Univ	OH	20,985	SP
Gardner-Webb Univ	NC	34,375	C+
George Fox Univ	OR	40,750	C+
Gwynedd-Mercy College	PA	33,560	C
Harding Univ	AR	23,556	C
Harris-Stowe State Univ	MO	14,360	NC
Hastings College	NE	27,782	C+
Hodges Univ	FL	12,000	LC
Howard Univ	DC	13,646	C
Husson Univ	ME	24,194	LC
Idaho State Univ	ID	12,307	C
Illinois State Univ	IL	23,110	VC
Indiana Univ Bloomington	IN	19,801	VC
Indiana Univ South Bend	IN	15,501	C
Indiana Univ-Purdue Univ Fort Wayne	IN	15,521	C
Indiana Univ-Purdue Univ Indianapolis	IN	17,611	C
Jackson State Univ	MS	13,512	LC
James Madison Univ	VA	18,049	VC
Kent State Univ	OH	19,920	C
Langston Univ	OK	3,000	C
Lebanon Valley College	PA	38,570	C
Lee Univ	TN	18,690	C+
Lehman College/The CUNY	NY	5,778	LC
Lewis Univ	IL	23,050	C
Limestone College	SC	30,800	C
LIU Post	NY	47,660	C
Lourdes Univ	OH	26,055	LC
Mary Baldwin College	VA	38,245	C
Marywood Univ	PA	45,595	C
Mercy College of Health Sciences	IA	14,460	LC
Metropolitan State Univ of Denver	CO	4,835	LC
Midwestern State Univ	TX	9,722	C
Minn State Univ, Moorhead	MN	13,392	VC
Misericordia Univ	PA	41,060	C
Missouri Baptist Univ	MO	31,830	C
Missouri State Univ	MO	13,996	C+
Monroe College	NY	20,240	C
Montana State Univ-Billings	MT	12,425	LC
Mount Aloysius College	PA	29,976	C
Mount Marty College	SD	29,638	C
Mount Mercy Univ	IA	35,320	C
Mount St. Mary's College - Chalon Campus	CA	43,897	VC+
National Louis Univ	IL	16,915	LC
Nebr Methodist College of Nursing and Allied Health	NE	22,690	SP
New York College of Technology/The CUNY	NY	5,769	NC
New York Univ	NY	61,470	MC
Newbury College	MA	43,280	LC
Norfolk State Univ	VA	10,531	LC
Northwest Christian Univ	OR	27,399	C
Ohio Univ	OH	21,080	C
Okla City Univ	OK	40,476	VC
Oregon State Univ	OR	20,273	VC
Park Univ	MO	17,525	C
Pennsylvania College of Technology	PA	26,286	NC
Point Park Univ	PA	36,390	C
Presentation College	SD	14,800	LC
Rhode Island College	RI	17,694	LC
Robert Morris Univ	PA	37,864	C
Roger Williams Univ	RI	46,296	VC
St. Joseph's Univ	PA	55,006	VC
St. Leo Univ	FL	30,340	C
St. Louis Univ	MO	48,346	HC
St. Mary-of-the-Woods College	IN	37,722	LC
St. Peter's Univ	NJ	44,240	C
Salisbury Univ	MD	19,180	VC
Shenandoah Univ	VA	39,916	C
Shippensburg Univ of Pennsylvania	PA	20,934	C
Simpson Univ	CA	28,900	C
Sojourner-Douglass College	MD	9,160	LC
South Univ	GA	36,070	LC
Southeast Missouri State Univ	MO	15,370	C
Southern Adventist Univ	TN	26,190	C
Southern Illinois Univ Carbondale	IL	21,942	C
Southern Univ at New Orleans	LA	2,963	NC
Southern Vermont College	VT	30,740	LC
Southwestern Okla State Univ	OK	9,160	C
Springfield College	MA	25,000	C
St. Catherine Univ	MN	37,782	C+
St. Francis College	NY	34,200	C
St. John's Univ	NY	55,070	C+
St. Joseph's College, New York/Brooklyn Campus	NY	22,630	C
St. Joseph's College, New York/Suffolk Campus	NY	22,630	C
SUNY Polytechnic Inst	NY	19,690	C
SUNY/Empire State College	NY	6,315	SP
Stonehill College	MA	46,780	HC
SUNY Fredonia/The SUNY at Fredonia	NY	19,840	VC
Tenn State Univ	TN	9,048	C
Texas Southern Univ	TX	18,212	LC
Texas State Univ	TX	17,128	C
The Pennsylvania State Univ - Univ Park	PA	28,022	VC+
The Univ of Okla	OK	18,621	VC
Thomas More College	KY	34,760	C
Towson Univ	MD	16,000	VC
Univ of Central Arkansas	AR	13,667	VC
Univ of Central Florida	FL	15,668	VC+
Univ of Colo at Colo Springs	CO	15,000	VC
Univ of Conn	CT	24,706	HC
Univ of Detroit Mercy	MI	30,450	VC
Univ of Evansville	IN	42,656	VC+
Univ of Great Falls	MT	27,970	C
Univ of Illinois at Urbana-Champaign	IL	26,450	HC
Univ of La Verne	CA	47,010	C
Univ of Miami	FL	57,034	MC
Univ of Mich-Flint	MI	17,547	C+
Univ of Minn Crookston	MN	17,834	C
Univ of Nebr at Omaha	NE	12,700	C
Univ of Nevada, Las Vegas	NV	17,303	C
Univ of New England	ME	46,750	C
Univ of N Car at Chapel Hill	NC	18,928	HC
Univ of North Florida	FL	15,870	VC
Univ of Pennsylvania	PA	61,132	MC
Univ of Scranton	PA	51,940	VC
Univ of S Dak	SD	15,111	C
Univ of Southern Indiana	IN	14,885	C
Univ of St. Francis	IL	37,560	C
Univ of Virginia	VA	23,050	MC
Univ of Washington	WA	14,722	VC
Univ of Wisc/Eau Claire	WI	15,730	VC
Upper Iowa Univ	IA	30,426	NC
Ursuline College	OH	33,198	LC
Valparaiso Univ	IN	44,940	VC+
Viterbo Univ	WI	30,070	C
Washburn Univ	KS	12,579	C
Washington Adventist Univ	MD	25,859	LC
Washington Univ in St. Louis	MO	69,844	MC
Wayland Baptist Univ	TX	18,912	LC
West Virginia Univ Inst of Technology	WV	14,094	NC
Western Carolina Univ	NC	13,965	C
Western Conn State Univ	CT	18,327	LC
Western Kentucky Univ	KY	11,000	LC
Wichita State Univ	KS	14,607	C+
Wilberforce Univ	OH	15,100	LC
Winona State Univ	MN	16,640	C
Xavier Univ	OH	44,980	VC

HEALTH COMMUNICATION

School	ST	$IS	SR
Campbell Univ	NC	37,570	VC
N Dak State Univ	ND		C
San Diego State Univ	CA	21,611	C+
Southeast Missouri State Univ	MO	15,370	LC

HEALTH EDUCATION

School	ST	$IS	SR
Albany State Univ	GA	8,500	C
American Univ	DC	56,015	HC+
Anderson Univ	IN	36,100	C
Appalachian State Univ	NC	12,919	VC
Aquinas College	MI	33,060	C
Arizona State Univ, at the Downtown Phoenix Campus	AZ	22,101	C
Arkansas State Univ	AR	15,470	C
Arkansas Tech Univ	AR	13,982	LC
Armstrong State Univ	GA	15,532	C
Ashford Univ	CA	10,480	C
Ashland Univ	OH	25,000	C
Auburn Univ	AL	22,378	VC+
Augsburg College	MN	35,142	C
Austin Peay State Univ	TN	15,274	C
Averett Univ	VA	37,750	LC
Ball State Univ	IN	17,850	C
Baylor Univ	TX	50,329	HC
Bemidji State Univ	MN	13,500	VC
Bethany College	KS	30,605	VC
Bethel Univ	MN	34,940	VC
Briar Cliff Univ	IA	29,514	C
Bridgewater State Univ	MA	18,752	C
Calif Baptist Univ	CA	38,792	C
Cal State, Sacramento	CA	16,200	C
Cal State, San Bernardino	CA	12,000	C
Cal State, Stanislaus	CA	18,582	C
Campbellsville Univ	KY	27,720	C
Carson-Newman Univ	TN	29,058	C+
Castleton State College	VT	20,186	C
Central State Univ	OH	9,010	C
Central Washington Univ	WA	11,730	C
Chadron State College	NE	7,400	NC

ST = STATE $IS = IN-STATE COSTS   SR = SELECTOR RATING

School	ST	$IS	SR
Citadel, The	SC		C
Cleveland State Univ	OH	21,776	C
College of Mount St. Vincent	NY	41,040	MC
College of New Jersey	NJ	25,376	HC
Columbus State Univ	GA	13,176	C
Concordia College - Moorhead	MN	39,974	VC
Concordia Univ, Ann Arbor	MI	27,220	VC
Curry College	MA	48,925	LC
Dakota State Univ	SD	13,811	C
Defiance College	OH	30,645	C
Delaware State Univ	DE	16,722	LC
Delta State Univ	MS	12,292	LC
DePaul Univ	IL	47,623	VC
East Carolina Univ	NC	14,169	C
East Stroudsburg Univ of Pennsylvania	PA	18,868	LC
Eastern Kentucky Univ	KY	11,161	C
Eastern Mich Univ	MI	18,604	C
Eastern Washington Univ	WA		C
Edinboro Univ of Pennsylvania	PA	15,940	LC
Elon Univ	NC	41,914	VC+
Emporia State Univ	KS	12,897	C
Fairmont State Univ	WV	12,098	LC
Fayetteville State Univ	NC	10,816	C
Florida State Univ	FL	16,715	VC
Freed-Hardeman Univ	TN	19,697	VC
Friends Univ	KS	29,100	C
Gardner-Webb Univ	NC	34,375	C+
Georgia Regents Univ	GA		C
Georgia Southern Univ	GA	16,942	C
Glenville State College	WV	11,348	NC
Goddard College	VT	16,418	VC
Goshen College	IN	35,900	VC
Gustavus Adolphus College	MN	48,170	HC
Hofstra Univ	NY	51,810	VC+
Houghton College	NY	36,808	C+
Howard Univ	DC	13,646	C
Hunter College	NY	14,429	VC
Idaho State Univ	ID	12,307	C
Illinois State Univ	IL	23,110	VC
Indiana State Univ	IN	16,000	C
Indiana Univ Bloomington	IN	19,801	VC
Indiana Univ of Pennsylvania	PA	20,846	LC
Inter-American Univ of PR/San Germán	PR	6,720	
Iowa State Univ	IA	16,403	C
Ithaca College	NY	53,864	HC
Jackson State Univ	MS	13,512	LC
Jacksonville State Univ	AL	12,480	LC
Johnson C. Smith Univ	NC	25,336	LC
Kennesaw State Univ	GA		C
Kent State Univ	OH	19,920	C
Lamar Univ	TX	6,820	LC
Lee Univ	TN	18,690	C+
Lehman College/The CUNY	NY	5,778	LC
Lenoir-Rhyne College	NC	35,984	C
Lincoln Memorial Univ	TN	18,144	C
Linfield College-McMinnville Campus	OR	47,676	C
Lipscomb Univ	TN	37,490	VC
LIU Post	NY	47,660	C
Louisiana College	LA	15,746	C
Manchester Univ	IN	35,070	C
Manhattan College	NY	49,588	C+
Mayville State Univ	ND	11,401	NC
McNeese State Univ	LA	2,649	C
MidAmerica Nazarene Univ	KS	28,000	C
Middle Tenn State Univ	TN	8,650	C
Minn State Univ, Mankato	MN	15,616	C
Minn State Univ, Moorhead	MN	13,392	VC
Missouri Baptist Univ	MO	31,830	C
Monmouth Univ	NJ	44,108	C
Montana State Univ-Billings	MT	12,425	LC
Montclair State Univ	NJ	22,614	C
Morehead State Univ	KY	10,900	C
Morgan State Univ	MD	14,500	VC
New Jersey City Univ	NJ	21,456	LC
N Car Central Univ	NC	9,000	C
N Dak State Univ	ND		C
Northeastern Illinois Univ	IL	10,318	LC
Northeastern State Univ	OK	8,615	SC
Northern Illinois Univ	IL	19,768	C
Northern Mich Univ	MI	18,278	C
Northern State Univ - Aberdeen	SD	14,505	C
Northwestern State Univ of Louisiana	LA	14,368	C
Ohio Northern Univ	OH	42,075	VC
Ohio Valley Univ	WV	17,752	C
Okla State Univ	OK	14,310	VC
Oral Roberts Univ	OK	31,734	C
Otterbein College	OH	32,214	C
Pfeiffer Univ	NC	33,700	LC
Plymouth State Univ	NH	23,148	LC
Portland State Univ	OR	18,672	C
Purdue Univ/West Lafayette	IN	20,024	HC
Rhode Island College	RI	17,694	LC
St. Mary's College of Calif	CA	53,550	C
Salisbury Univ	MD	19,180	VC
Shepherd Univ	WV	15,875	C
Slippery Rock Univ of Pennsylvania	PA	10,360	C
S Car State Univ	SC	6,700	LC
S Dak State Univ	SD	14,296	C
Southeastern Louisiana Univ	LA	13,325	C
Southern Arkansas Univ	AR	14,316	C
Southern Conn State Univ	CT	18,033	LC
Southern Illinois Univ Carbondale	IL	21,942	C
Southern Illinois Univ Edwardsville	IL	17,532	C
Southern Methodist Univ	TX	60,585	MC
Southwest Baptist Univ	MO	24,710	C
Southwest Minn State Univ	MN	14,000	C
Southwestern Okla State Univ	OK	9,160	C
Springfield College	MA	25,000	C
St. Cloud State Univ	MN	10,600	C
SUNY Cortland/The SUNY	NY	19,759	C+
Tabor College	KS	29,010	C
Taylor Univ	IN	37,821	VC+
Tenn State Univ	TN	9,048	C
Texas A&M Univ	TX	19,207	VC
Texas A&M Univ at Commerce	TX	10,496	C
Texas A&M Univ at Kingsville	TX	7,500	LC
Texas State Univ	TX	17,128	C
The Lincoln Univ	PA	15,154	LC
The Univ of N Car at Pembroke	NC	13,388	LC
The Univ of Utah	UT	16,463	VC
Troy Univ	AL	10,650	C
Tulane Univ	LA	60,861	MC
Univ of Alabama at Birmingham	AL	18,484	C+
Univ of Arkansas at Little Rock	AR	17,609	LC
Univ of Arkansas at Monticello	AR	12,076	NC
Univ of Cincinnati	OH	21,506	VC
Univ of Florida	FL	15,943	HC
Univ of Georgia	GA	20,082	VC
Univ of Great Falls	MT	27,970	C
Univ of Illinois at Chicago	IL	24,505	VC
Univ of Iowa	IA	17,693	VC
Univ of Kansas	KS	17,603	C+
Univ of Kentucky	KY	19,868	C
Univ of Louisiana at Lafayette	LA	6,130	C
Univ of Louisiana at Monroe	LA	12,998	C
Univ of Maine at Farmington	ME	18,187	LC
Univ of Maine at Presque Isle	ME	15,011	LC
Univ of Maryland/Eastern Shore	MD	14,000	C
Univ of Minn/Duluth	MN	19,806	C
Univ of Montana-Western	MT	9,753	LC
Univ of Nebr at Kearney	NE	14,855	LC
Univ of Nevada, Las Vegas	NV	17,303	C
Univ of New Mexico	NM	15,300	C
Univ of Northern Iowa	IA	15,795	C
Univ of Pittsburgh at Bradford	PA	21,802	C
Univ of Rio Grande	OH	8,750	NC
Univ of St. Francis	IN	29,810	C
Univ of South Alabama	AL	13,510	C
Univ of Southern Miss	MS	13,170	C
Univ of the Cumberlands	KY	27,500	C
Univ of the District of Columbia	DC	7,244	LC
Univ of Toledo	OH	18,464	C
Univ of West Florida	FL	14,656	C
Univ of Wisc/La Crosse	WI	9,304	VC
Univ of Wisc/Stevens Point	WI	14,043	C
Univ of Wisc/Superior	WI	14,314	C
Utah State Univ	UT	12,044	C
Valley City State Univ	ND	12,286	LC
Virginia Commonwealth Univ	VA	21,716	C
Wayne State College	NE	11,764	NC
Wayne State Univ	MI	22,063	C
West Chester Univ of Pennsylvania	PA	17,186	C
West Liberty Univ	WV	9,142	LC
Western Mich Univ	MI	19,628	C
Western Oregon Univ	OR	15,021	C
Western Washington Univ	WA	18,519	VC
William Paterson Univ of New Jersey	NJ	21,694	C
William Penn Univ	IA	26,000	C
Wilmington College	OH	29,784	C
Winona State Univ	MN	16,640	C
Worcester State Univ	MA	19,812	C
Youngstown State Univ	OH	16,732	C

HEALTH INFORMATION MANAGEMENT

School	ST	$IS	SR
Arizona State Univ, at the Polytechnic Campus	AZ	20,531	C+
Arkansas Tech Univ	AR	13,982	LC
Ashford Univ	CA	10,480	C
Bluffton Univ	OH	38,948	C
Champlain College	VT	46,650	VC+
Charter Oak State College	CT	8,592	
College of Mount St. Joseph	OH	33,880	C
Coppin State Univ	MD	16,227	VC
Dakota State Univ	SD	13,811	C
Duquesne Univ	PA	43,720	VC
Ferris State Univ	MI	20,047	C
Gannon Univ	PA	39,608	C
Georgia Regents Univ	GA		C
Idaho State Univ	ID	12,307	C
Illinois State Univ	IL	23,110	VC
Indiana Inst of Technology	IN	34,240	LC
Indiana Univ Northwest	IN	6,854	LC
Indiana Univ Southeast	IN	16,035	C
Indiana Univ-Purdue Univ Indianapolis	IN	17,611	C
John Carroll Univ	OH	46,300	C+
Kean Univ	NJ	23,444	C
Loyola Univ Chicago	IL	51,646	VC+
Marymount Univ	VA	39,480	C
Miami Univ	OH	24,191	VC
Montana Tech of The Univ of Montana	MT	14,650	VC
Murray State Univ	KY	15,304	C
Ohio State Univ at Lima	OH	7,140	C
Rutgers, The State Univ of New Jersey/New Brunswick	NJ	25,562	VC
St. Louis Univ	MO	48,346	HC
Simmons College	MA	49,966	VC
Southern Illinois Univ Carbondale	IL	21,942	C
Southern Illinois Univ Edwardsville	IL	17,532	C
Southern Univ at New Orleans	LA	2,963	NC
Temple Univ	PA	24,392	VC
Texas State Univ	TX	17,128	C
Ohio State Univ-Columbus Campus	OH	19,887	HC+
Thomas Edison State College	NJ	5,700	SP
Univ of Central Florida	FL	15,668	VC+
Univ of Cincinnati	OH	21,506	VC
Univ of Illinois at Chicago	IL	24,505	VC
Univ of Kansas	KS	17,603	C+
Univ of Maine at Farmington	ME	18,187	C
Univ of Miss	MS	16,704	C+
Univ of Pittsburgh at Pittsburgh	PA	28,572	HC+
Univ of S Car Upstate	SC	18,200	LC
Univ of Tenn at Knoxville	TN	20,364	VC+
Univ of Wisc/Green Bay	WI	19,074	C
Western Mich Univ	MI	19,628	C
Xavier Univ	OH	44,980	VC

HEALTH PROMOTION

School	ST	$IS	SR
American Univ	DC	56,015	HC+
Arkansas State Univ	AR	15,470	C
Ashford Univ	CA	10,480	C
Baldwin Wallace Univ	OH	38,318	C
Goddard College	VT	16,418	VC
Lubbock Christian Univ	TX	26,308	C
Lynchburg College	VA	42,645	C
Miami Univ	OH	24,191	VC
Missouri Southern State Univ	MO	12,061	C
Missouri State Univ	MO	13,996	C
Nebr Methodist College of Nursing and Allied Health	NE	22,690	SP
Nova Southeastern Univ	FL	37,280	VC
Samford Univ	AL	37,060	C+
Univ of Georgia	GA	20,082	VC
Univ of Montana	MT	14,105	C
Univ of N Car at Asheville	NC	13,500	VC
Univ of Wisc/Superior	WI	14,314	C
Western Conn State Univ	CT	18,327	LC

HEALTH SCIENCE

School	ST	$IS	SR
Adventist Univ of Health Sciences	FL	16,344	NC
Albany College of Pharmacy and Health Sciences	NY	40,331	SP
Alcorn State Univ	MS	9,500	C
Alderson Broaddus Univ	WV	28,656	C
Alma College	MI	44,075	C
Alvernia Univ	PA	39,250	LC
American Univ	DC	56,015	HC+
Appalachian State Univ	NC	12,919	VC
Arizona State Univ, at the Downtown Phoenix Campus	AZ	22,101	C
Armstrong State Univ	GA	15,532	C
Asbury Univ	KY	32,038	VC
Ashford Univ	CA	10,480	C
Aurora Univ	IL	33,228	C
Baylor Univ	TX	50,329	NC
Benedictine Univ	IL	37,820	C
Bloomsburg Univ of Pennsylvania	PA	13,598	C
Boise State Univ	ID	13,469	LC
Boston Univ	MA	60,694	MC
Bowling Green State Univ	OH	18,970	C
Bradley Univ	IL	31,874	VC
Brandeis Univ	MA		MC
Brigham Young Univ	UT	12,100	HC
Butler Univ	IN	47,572	VC+
Calif Baptist Univ	CA	38,792	C
Cal State, Chico	CA	20,158	C
Cal State, Dominguez Hills	CA	17,090	LC
Cal State, East Bay	CA	16,549	C
Cal State, Fresno	CA	17,405	C
Cal State, Fullerton	CA	25,188	C
Cal State, Long Beach	CA	17,502	C+
Cal State, Los Angeles	CA	17,186	LC
Cal State, Northridge	CA	28,690	LC
Cal State, San Bernardino	CA	12,000	C
Castleton State College	VT	20,186	C
Chapman Univ	CA	58,347	VC+
Chicago State Univ	IL	5,482	C
CUNY/Brooklyn College	NY	5,884	C+
Cleveland State Univ	OH	21,776	C
College of St. Scholastica	MN	41,440	C
College of St Joseph	VT	30,600	LC
College of William & Mary	VA	28,000	MC
Colo State Univ-Fort Collins	CO	20,385	VC
Columbus State Univ	GA	13,176	C
Corban Univ	OR	37,380	C+
Creighton Univ	NE	45,356	VC
Daemen College	NY	34,770	C
DePaul Univ	IL	47,623	VC
Dordt College	IA	34,160	C+
Drury Univ	MO	31,909	VC
East Tenn State Univ	TN	9,000	C
Elms College	MA	23,900	VC
Emporia State Univ	KS	12,897	C
Excelsior College	NY	5,580	SP
Ferrum College	VA	27,740	LC
Fitchburg State Univ	MA	18,173	C
Florida Atlantic Univ	FL	17,339	C
Florida Gulf Coast Univ	FL		C
Franklin Pierce Univ	NH	41,598	C
Friends Univ	KS	29,100	C
Furman Univ	SC	54,006	HC
Gannon Univ	PA	39,608	C
George Mason Univ	VA	15,724	VC
Gettysburg College	PA	58,820	HC
Goddard College	VT	16,418	VC
Goodwin College	CT	19,400	LC
Grand Canyon Univ	AZ	24,540	VC
Grand Valley State Univ	MI	17,998	C+
Guilford College	NC	42,800	C
Hampshire College	MA	58,320	MC
Harding Univ	AR	23,556	C
Hardin-Simmons Univ	TX	23,560	C+
Hofstra Univ	NY	51,810	VC+
Howard Univ	DC	13,646	C
Idaho State Univ	ID	12,307	C
Indiana Univ Bloomington	IN	19,801	VC
Indiana Univ Kokomo	IN	6,811	LC
Indiana Univ Northwest	IN	6,854	C
Indiana Univ-Purdue Univ Indianapolis	IN	17,611	C
Ithaca College	NY	53,864	HC
James Madison Univ	VA	18,049	VC
Johnson State College	VT	16,721	C
Kalamazoo College	MI	49,740	HC
Keene State College	NH	23,232	LC
Kent State Univ	OH	19,920	C
King Univ	TN	33,140	C
La Roche College	PA	35,824	C
La Sierra Univ	CA	35,694	VC
Lee Univ	TN	18,690	C+
LIU Brooklyn	NY	47,182	LC
LIU Post	NY	47,660	C
Lock Haven Univ of Pennsylvania	PA	18,028	LC
Loyola Marymount Univ	CA	54,649	VC+
Marietta College	OH	42,135	C+
Marshall Univ	WV	14,820	C
Marymount Univ	VA	39,480	C
Maryville Univ of St. Louis	MO	35,856	VC
Marywood Univ	PA	45,595	C
Mass College of Pharmacy and Health Sciences	MA	36,450	SP
Mercy College	NY	30,456	C
Mercy College of Health Sciences	IA	14,460	C
Middle Tenn State Univ	TN	8,650	C
Midwestern State Univ	TX	9,722	VC
Minn State Univ, Mankato	MN	15,616	C
Missouri Baptist Univ	MO	31,830	C
Missouri Southern State Univ	MO	12,061	C
Mount St. Mary's Univ	MD	47,996	C
Nazareth College of Rochester	NY	43,028	C+
New England College	NH	45,930	LC
New York Inst of Technology	NY	45,010	VC
Newman Univ	KS	30,380	C
Nicholls State Univ	LA	7,095	C
Norfolk State Univ	VA	10,531	LC
Northeastern Univ	MA	55,296	MC
Northern Arizona Univ	AZ	19,010	C
Northern Illinois Univ	IL	19,768	C
Northern Kentucky Univ	KY	21,134	C
Oakland Univ	MI	19,391	C
Old Dominion Univ	VA	19,483	VC
Oral Roberts Univ	OK	31,734	C
Oregon Inst of Technology	OR	8,910	C
Our Lady of Holy Cross College	LA	8,090	C
Pennsylvania College of Technology	PA	26,286	NC
Point Loma Nazarene Univ	CA	41,006	C+
Purdue Univ/West Lafayette	IN	20,024	HC
Quinnipiac Univ	CT	55,160	VC
Randolph College	VA	45,660	VC
Sacred Heart Univ	CT	49,264	VC
Saginaw Valley State Univ	MI	17,369	C
St. Joseph's Univ	PA	55,006	VC
St. Mary's College of Calif	CA	53,550	C
Samford Univ	AL	37,060	C+
San Diego State Univ	CA	21,611	C+

ST = STATE　　$IS = IN-STATE COSTS　　SR = SELECTOR RATING

School	ST	$IS	SR
San Francisco State Univ	CA	18,514	C
San Jose State Univ	CA	19,133	LC
South Univ	GA	36,070	LC
Southern Adventist Univ	TN	26,190	C
Southwestern Okla State Univ	OK	9,160	C
St. Ambrose Univ	IA	30,845	C
St. Francis College	NY	34,200	C
Stephen F. Austin State Univ	TX	14,668	C
Stetson Univ	FL	51,516	VC
Stony Brook Univ / SUNY	NY	20,078	HC+
SUNY Cortland/The SUNY	NY	19,759	C+
Syracuse Univ	NY	56,346	VC
Taylor Univ	IN	37,821	VC+
Texas A&M Univ at Corpus Christi	TX	11,544	LC
Texas Woman's Univ	TX	13,633	LC
The Lincoln Univ	PA	15,154	LC
Ohio State Univ-Columbus Campus	OH	19,887	HC+
The SUNY/College at Brockport	NY	19,002	C
The Univ of Memphis	TN	15,094	C
Towson Univ	MD	16,000	VC
Truman State Univ	MO	15,541	HC
Universidad Adventista de las Antillas	PR	7,360	
Univ of Alabama at Birmingham	AL	18,484	C+
Univ of Arkansas at Fayetteville	AR	18,352	C+
Univ of Arkansas at Little Rock	AR	17,609	LC
Univ of Calif at Santa Cruz	CA	27,807	C+
Univ of Central Arkansas	AR	13,667	VC
Univ of Central Florida	FL	15,668	VC+
Univ of Delaware	DE	23,612	VC
Univ of Findlay	OH	31,916	C
Univ of Florida	FL	15,943	HC
Univ of Hartford	CT	42,674	C
Univ of Maryland/Baltimore County	MD	18,000	VC
Univ of Mass Dartmouth	MA	22,223	C
Univ of Miami	FL	57,034	MC
Univ of Mich-Flint	MI	17,547	C+
Univ of Minn Crookston	MN	17,834	C
Univ of Miss	MS	16,704	C+
Univ of Missouri-Kansas City	MO	19,603	C
Univ of Nebr - Lincoln	NE	18,031	VC
Univ of New England	ME	46,750	C
Univ of North Florida	FL	15,870	VC
Univ of South Florida/St. Petersburg	FL	12,769	C
Univ of Southern Maine	ME	16,576	C
Univ of Tenn at Martin	TN	13,734	C
Univ of Texas at El Paso	TX	8,764	NC
Univ of the Sciences	PA	48,320	VC+
Univ of Wisc/Stevens Point	WI	14,043	C
Washington Univ in St. Louis	MO	69,844	MC
Wayne State Univ	MI	22,063	C
West Chester Univ of Pennsylvania	PA	17,186	C
Western Conn State Univ	CT	18,327	LC
Western Illinois Univ	IL	20,732	C
Western New England Univ	MA	46,154	C+
Wheaton College	IL	40,720	MC
Whitworth Univ	WA	47,734	VC
William Paterson Univ of New Jersey	NJ	21,694	C
Yeshiva Univ	NY	47,250	VC+

HEALTH SERVICES ADMINISTRATION

School	ST	$IS	SR
Univ of Rhode Island	RI	24,002	C

HEALTH SERVICES TECHNOLOGY

School	ST	$IS	SR
Concordia College - New York	NY	39,035	LC
John Carroll Univ	OH	46,300	C+
St. Louis Univ	MO	48,346	HC
Thomas Edison State College	NJ	5,700	SP
Univ of Pittsburgh at Pittsburgh	PA	28,572	HC+

HEALTHCARE MARKETING

School	ST	$IS	SR
Ferris State Univ	MI	20,047	C

HEAVY EQUIP SERVICE ENGINEERING

School	ST	$IS	SR
Ferris State Univ	MI	20,047	C

HEBREW

School	ST	$IS	SR
American Univ	DC	56,015	HC+
Bard College	NY	61,940	HC
Binghamton Univ/The SUNY	NY	21,648	HC+
Harvard College/Harvard Univ	MA	49,000	MC
Hofstra Univ	NY	51,810	VC
Hunter College	NY	14,429	VC
Lehman College/The CUNY	NY	5,778	LC
New York Univ	NY	61,470	MC

School	ST	$IS	SR
Queens College/The CUNY	NY	17,107	VC
Ohio State Univ-Columbus Campus	OH	19,887	HC+
The Univ of Utah	UT	16,463	VC
Thomas Edison State College	NJ	5,700	SP
Touro College	NY	27,959	VC
Univ of Calif at Los Angeles	CA	25,686	MC
Univ of Cincinnati	OH	21,506	VC
Univ of Illinois at Urbana-Champaign	IL	26,450	HC
Univ of Mich/Ann Arbor	MI	22,102	MC
Univ of Minn/Twin Cities	MN		HC
Univ of Texas at Austin	TX	44,074	MC
Univ of Wisc/Madison	WI	18,757	HC+
Washington Univ in St. Louis	MO	69,844	MC
Yeshiva Univ	NY	47,250	VC+

HISPANIC AMERICAN STUDIES

School	ST	$IS	SR
Boston College	MA	60,622	MC
Boston Univ	MA	60,694	MC
Brown Univ	RI	59,428	MC
Cal State, Long Beach	CA	17,502	C+
CUNY/Brooklyn College	NY	5,884	C+
Claremont McKenna College	CA	62,215	MC
College of St. Benedict	MN	49,359	VC
Colo College	CO	57,162	MC
Columbia Univ/City of New York	NY	61,116	MC
Columbia Univ/School of General Studies	NY	58,231	MC
Conn College	CT	54,970	MC
East Carolina Univ	NC	14,169	C
Hamilton College	NY	55,620	MC
Hofstra Univ	NY	51,810	VC+
Hunter College	NY	14,429	VC
Lewis & Clark College	OR	54,382	MC
Loyola Marymount Univ	CA	54,649	VC+
Mills College	CA	54,119	VC
Mount St. Mary College	NY	41,138	C
Northeastern Illinois Univ	IL	10,318	LC
Pepperdine Univ	CA	55,372	HC+
Pomona College	CA	57,680	MC
Rice Univ	TX	43,288	MC
Rutgers, The State Univ of New Jersey/New Brunswick	NJ	25,562	VC
St. John's Univ	MN	47,984	C
Scripps College	CA	61,940	MC
St. Olaf College	MN	51,200	HC+
Stanford Univ	CA	58,388	MC
SUNY Oneonta / SUNY	NY	16,919	C+
Univ at Albany / SUNY	NY	18,674	VC
Univ of Calif at Berkeley	CA	23,322	MC
Univ of Calif at Irvine	CA	25,961	VC
Univ of Mass Boston	MA	23,066	VC
Univ of Mich/Ann Arbor	MI	22,102	MC
Univ of Mich/Dearborn	MI	9,885	C
Univ of Pennsylvania	PA	61,132	MC
Univ of PR/Cayey	PR	1,504	
Univ of Tenn at Knoxville	TN	20,364	VC
Vassar College	NY	61,140	MC
Wabash College	IN	46,850	C+
Wesleyan Univ	CT	61,198	MC
Western New Mexico Univ	NM	8,500	LC
Wheaton College	MA	54,934	HC+

HISTORIC PRESERVATION

School	ST	$IS	SR
College of Charleston	SC	22,145	VC
Eastern Mich Univ	MI	18,604	C
Roger Williams Univ	RI	46,296	VC
Salve Regina Univ	RI	48,550	VC
Savannah College of Art and Design	GA	48,005	SP
Southeast Missouri State Univ	MO	15,370	LC
Univ of Delaware	DE	23,612	VC
Univ of Georgia	GA	20,082	VC
Univ of Mary Washington	VA	19,484	VC
Univ of Mich/Ann Arbor	MI	22,102	MC
Ursuline College	OH	33,198	LC

HISTORY

School	ST	$IS	SR
Abilene Christian Univ	TX	38,400	C+
Adams State Univ	CO	13,358	LC
Adelphi Univ	NY	44,670	VC
Adrian College	MI	42,400	C
Agnes Scott College	GA	45,323	C+
Alabama A&M Univ	AL	10,084	C
Alabama State Univ	AL	14,142	NC
Albany State Univ	GA	8,500	C
Albertus Magnus College	CT	37,382	LC
Albion College	MI	46,010	C
Albright College	PA	46,660	C
Alcorn State Univ	MS	9,500	C
Alderson Broaddus Univ	WV	28,656	C
Alfred Univ	NY	41,770	C
Alice Lloyd College	KY	14,940	VC
Allegheny College	PA	50,980	HC
Allen Univ	SC	16,124	NC
Alma College	MI	44,075	C
Alvernia Univ	PA	39,250	LC
Alverno College	WI	31,434	LC
American International College	MA	36,100	LC
American Univ	DC	56,015	HC+

School	ST	$IS	SR
Amherst College	MA	58,744	MC
Anderson Univ	IN	36,100	C
Andrews Univ	MI	28,030	C+
Angelo State Univ	TX	15,049	NC
Anna Maria College	MA	34,600	C
Appalachian State Univ	NC	12,919	VC
Aquinas College	MI	33,060	C
Aquinas College	TN	29,250	VC+
Arcadia Univ	PA	33,570	C+
Arizona State Univ, at the Polytechnic Campus	AZ	20,531	C+
Arizona State Univ, at the Tempe Campus	AZ	20,137	C+
Arizona State Univ, at the West Campus	AZ	19,251	C
Arkansas State Univ	AR	15,470	C
Arkansas Tech Univ	AR	13,982	LC
Armstrong State Univ	GA	15,532	C
Asbury Univ	KY	32,038	VC
Ashford Univ	CA	10,480	C
Ashland Univ	OH	25,000	C
Assumption College	MA	47,122	C+
Atlantic Union College	MA	24,600	C
Auburn Univ	AL	22,378	VC+
Auburn Univ at Montgomery	AL	14,470	LC
Augsburg College	MN	35,142	C
Augustana College	IL	43,398	VC
Augustana College	SD	36,500	VC
Aurora Univ	IL	33,228	C
Austin College	TX	45,875	HC
Austin Peay State Univ	TN	15,274	C
Averett Univ	VA	37,750	LC
Avila Univ	MO	26,900	C
Azusa Pacific Univ	CA	42,086	C
Baker Univ	KS	33,350	C+
Baldwin Wallace Univ	OH	38,318	C
Ball State Univ	IN	17,850	C
Bard College	NY	61,940	HC
Bard College at Simon's Rock	MA	61,749	HC+
Barnard College/Columbia Univ	NY	39,000	MC
Barry Univ	FL	38,190	C
Barton College	NC	27,660	LC
Bates College	ME	60,720	MC
Baylor Univ	TX	50,329	HC
Belhaven Univ	MS	27,170	C
Bellarmine Univ	KY	42,950	VC
Bellevue Univ	NE	4,600	NC
Belmont Abbey College	NC	37,716	C
Belmont Univ	TN	39,190	VC+
Beloit College	WI	49,970	HC
Bemidji State Univ	MN	13,500	VC
Benedict College	SC	20,454	NC
Benedictine College	KS	29,180	VC
Benedictine Univ	IL	37,820	C
Bennington College	VT	56,990	HC+
Bentley Univ	MA	56,454	HC+
Berea College	KY	7,192	C
Berry College	GA	39,254	VC
Bethany College	KS	30,605	NC
Bethany College	WV	35,282	LC
Bethel College	IN	31,560	C
Bethel College	KS	32,160	C
Bethel Univ	MN	34,940	VC
Bethel Univ	TN	19,186	C
Bethune-Cookman Univ	FL	22,958	C
Binghamton Univ/The SUNY	NY	21,648	HC+
Biola Univ	CA	40,320	C+
Birmingham-Southern College	AL	44,168	VC+
Black Hills State Univ	SD	13,947	C
Blackburn College	IL	21,350	C
Bloomfield College	NJ	37,850	LC
Bloomsburg Univ of Pennsylvania	PA	13,598	C
Blue Mountain College	MS	15,634	LC
Bluefield College	VA	17,230	C+
Bluffton Univ	OH	38,948	C
Boise State Univ	ID	13,469	LC
Boston College	MA	60,622	MC
Boston Univ	MA	60,694	MC
Bowdoin College	ME	59,568	MC
Bowie State Univ	MD	23,990	LC
Bowling Green State Univ	OH	18,970	C
Bradley Univ	IL	31,874	VC
Brandeis Univ	MA		MC
Brenau Univ - Women's College	GA	26,650	LC
Brescia Univ	KY	26,140	VC+
Brewton-Parker College	GA	33,388	C
Briar Cliff Univ	IA	29,514	C
Bridgewater College	VA	41,450	C
Brigham Young Univ	UT	12,100	VC
Brigham Young Univ/Hawaii	HI	10,686	VC
Brown Univ	RI	59,428	MC
Bryan College	TN	24,194	C
Bryant Univ	RI	49,179	VC
Bryn Athyn College	PA	27,984	C
Bryn Mawr College	PA	59,890	MC
Bucknell Univ	PA	60,140	MC
Buena Vista Univ	IA	39,188	C
Buffalo State College / SUNY	NY	15,733	C+
Butler Univ	IN	47,572	VC+
Cairn Univ	PA	33,270	C
Caldwell College	NJ	35,602	NC
Calif Baptist Univ	CA	38,792	C

School	ST	$IS	SR
Calif Inst of Technology	CA	54,045	MC
Calif Lutheran Univ	CA	49,540	C+
Calif Polytechnic State Univ	CA	19,847	HC
Calif State Polytechnic Univ, Pomona	CA	20,156	C
Cal State, Bakersfield	CA	8,000	C
Cal State, Chico	CA	20,158	C
Cal State, Dominguez Hills	CA	17,090	LC
Cal State, East Bay	CA	16,549	C
Cal State, Fresno	CA	17,405	C
Cal State, Fullerton	CA	25,188	C
Cal State, Long Beach	CA	17,502	C+
Cal State, Los Angeles	CA	17,186	C
Cal State, Northridge	CA	28,690	LC
Cal State, Sacramento	CA	16,200	C
Cal State, San Bernardino	CA	12,000	C
Cal State, San Marcos	CA	14,576	LC
Cal State, Stanislaus	CA	18,582	C
Calif Univ of Pennsylvania	PA	14,217	C
Calvin College	MI	39,120	VC
Cameron Univ	OK	10,004	LC
Campbell Univ	NC	37,570	VC
Campbellsville Univ	KY	27,720	C
Canisius College	NY	44,900	C
Capital Univ	OH	41,050	VC
Cardinal Stritch Univ	WI	24,054	C
Carleton College	MN	60,102	MC
Carlow Univ	PA	30,272	C
Carnegie Mellon Univ	PA	51,260	MC
Carroll College	MT	28,000	C
Carroll Univ	WI	38,100	C
Carson-Newman Univ	TN	29,058	C+
Carthage College	WI	33,000	C
Case Western Reserve Univ	OH	56,534	MC
Castleton State College	VT	20,186	C
Catawba College	NC	37,240	LC
Cedar Crest College	PA	43,240	C
Cedarville Univ	OH	32,860	VC
Centenary College	NJ	38,618	C
Centenary College of Louisiana	LA	45,650	C+
Central College	IA	42,104	C+
Central Conn State Univ	CT	19,749	C
Central Methodist Univ	MO	28,240	VC
Central State Univ	OH	9,010	C
Central Washington Univ	WA	11,730	C
Centre College	KY	35,000	HC+
Chadron State College	NE	7,400	VC
Chaminade Univ of Honolulu	HI	31,664	C
Chapman Univ	CA	58,347	VC+
Charleston Southern Univ	SC	22,420	C
Chatham Univ	PA	43,797	C
Chestnut Hill College	PA	42,110	C
Chicago State Univ	IL	5,482	C
Christendom College	VA	32,600	VC
Christian Brothers Univ	TN	31,670	C
Christopher Newport Univ	VA	21,960	VC
Citadel, The	SC		C
CUNY/Baruch College	NY		HC
CUNY/Brooklyn College	NY	5,884	C+
CUNY/City College	NY	20,319	HC+
Claflin Univ	SC	22,368	LC
Claremont McKenna College	CA	62,215	MC
Clarion Univ of Pennsylvania	PA	17,370	C
Clark Atlanta Univ	GA	30,006	LC
Clark Univ	MA	47,020	HC+
Clarke Univ	IA	37,600	C
Clarkson Univ	NY	57,330	VC
Clayton State Univ	GA	12,000	LC
Clearwater Christian College	FL	23,720	C
Clemson Univ	SC	19,136	VC
Cleveland State Univ	OH	21,776	C
Coastal Carolina Univ	SC	18,580	C
Coe College	IA	45,550	VC
Coker College	SC	32,256	LC
Colby College	ME	57,510	MC
Colby-Sawyer College	NH	50,790	C
Colgate Univ	NY	58,135	MC
College of Charleston	SC	22,145	VC
College of Mount St. Joseph	OH	33,880	C
College of Mount St. Vincent	NY	41,040	MC
College of New Jersey	NJ	25,376	RC
College of St. Benedict	MN	49,359	VC
College of St. Elizabeth	NJ	43,839	LC
College of St. Scholastica	MN	41,440	C
College of St Joseph	VT	30,600	LC
College of Staten Island/The City of New Yok	NY	16,778	NC
College of the Holy Cross	MA	58,042	MC
College of the Ozarks	MO		VC
College of William & Mary	VA	28,000	MC
College of Wooster	OH	52,600	VC
Colo Christian Univ	CO	27,500	VC
Colo College	CO	57,162	MC
Colo Mesa Univ	CO	17,690	LC
Colo State Univ-Fort Collins	CO	20,385	VC
Colo State Univ-Pueblo	CO	16,183	C
Columbia College	MO	24,578	C
Columbia College	SC	27,882	C
Columbia Univ/City of New York	NY	61,116	MC
Columbia Univ/School of General Studies	NY	58,231	MC
Columbus State Univ	GA	13,176	C
Concord Univ	WV	13,102	C

School	ST	$IS	SR	School	ST	$IS	SR	School	ST	$IS	SR	School	ST	$IS	SR
Concordia College - Moorhead	MN	39,974	VC	Fitchburg State Univ	MA	18,173	C	Immaculata Univ	PA	43,000	C	Loyola Univ New Orleans	LA	46,581	VC
Concordia College - New York	NY	39,035	LC	Flagler College	FL	25,180	C	Indiana State Univ	IN	16,000	C	Lubbock Christian Univ	TX	26,308	C
Concordia Univ Irvine	CA	35,390	VC	Florida A&M Univ	FL	14,935	LC	Indiana Univ Bloomington	IN	19,801	VC	Luther College	IA	45,720	C+
Concordia Univ Nebr	NE	26,000	VC	Florida Atlantic Univ	FL	17,339	C	Indiana Univ East	IN	6,783	C	Lycoming College	PA	45,379	C
Concordia Univ St. Paul	MN	28,250	C	Florida Gulf Coast Univ	FL		C	Indiana Univ Northwest	IN	6,854	LC	Lynchburg College	VA	42,645	C
Concordia Univ Texas	TX	23,640	C	Florida International Univ	FL	17,747	C+	Indiana Univ of Pennsylvania	PA	20,846	LC	Lyon College	AR	32,090	C+
Concordia Univ Wisc	WI	28,980	C	Florida Southern College	FL	40,150	C+	Indiana Univ South Bend	IN	15,501	C	Macalester College	MN	57,691	MC
Concordia Univ, Ann Arbor	MI	27,220	VC	Florida State Univ	FL	16,715	VC	Indiana Univ Southeast	IN	16,035	C	MacMurray College	IL	20,755	C
Concordia Univ, River Forest	IL	26,300	C	Fontbonne Univ	MO	31,384	C	Indiana Univ-Purdue Univ Fort Wayne	IN	15,521	C	Madonna Univ	MI	24,540	VC
Conn College	CT	54,970	MC	Fordham Univ	NY	61,588	HC+	Indiana Univ-Purdue Univ Indianapolis	IN	17,611	C	Malone Univ	OH	35,364	C
Converse College	SC	37,130	C	Fort Hays State Univ	KS	11,354	C	Indiana Wesleyan Univ	IN	31,815	VC	Manchester Univ	IN	35,070	C
Coppin State Univ	MD	16,227	VC	Fort Lewis College	CO	15,513	C	Inter-American Univ of PR/Fajardo Campus	PR	4,200		Manhattan College	NY	49,588	C+
Corban Univ	OR	37,380	C+	Framingham State Univ	MA	18,854	C	Inter-American Univ of PR/Metropolitan Campus	PR	4,320		Manhattanville College	NY	50,740	VC
Cornell College	IA	44,930	VC	Francis Marion Univ	SC	16,464	LC	Inter-American Univ of PR/Ponce	PR			Mansfield Univ	PA	19,468	LC
Cornell Univ	NY	60,964	MC	Franciscan Univ of Steubenville	OH	27,320	VC	Inter-American Univ of PR/San Germán	PR	6,720		Marian Univ	IN	38,540	C
Cornerstone Univ and Grand Rapids Theological Seminary	MI	33,338	C	Franklin and Marshall College	PA	60,799	MC	Iona College	NY	44,028	C	Marian Univ	WI	32,420	C
Covenant College	GA	38,990	VC+	Franklin College	IN	36,585	C	Iowa State Univ	IA	16,403	C	Marietta College	OH	42,135	C+
Creighton Univ	NE	45,356	VC	Franklin Pierce Univ	NH	41,598	C	Iowa Wesleyan College	IA	30,850	LC	Marist College	NY	35,500	C
Culver-Stockton College	MO	30,900	C	Freed-Hardeman Univ	TN	19,697	VC	Ithaca College	NY	53,864	HC	Marlboro College	VT	35,980	VC
Cumberland Univ	TN	21,220	C	Fresno Pacific Univ	CA	32,136	C	Jackson State Univ	MS	13,512	LC	Marquette Univ	WI	46,930	VC+
Curry College	MA	48,925	LC	Friends Univ	KS	29,100	C	Jacksonville State Univ	AL	12,480	LC	Mars Hill Univ	NC	22,950	LC
Daemen College	NY	34,770	C	Frostburg State Univ	MD	15,264	LC	Jacksonville Univ	FL	37,780	C	Marshall Univ	WV	14,820	C
Dakota Wesleyan Univ	SD	23,000	C	Furman Univ	SC	54,006	HC	James Madison Univ	VA	18,049	VC	Martin Univ	IN	11,000	SP
Dallas Baptist Univ	TX	30,580	VC	Gallaudet Univ	DC	25,380	SP	Jarvis Christian College	TX	19,552	NC	Mary Baldwin College	VA	38,245	C
Dartmouth College	NH	57,996	MC	Gannon Univ	PA	39,608	C	John Brown Univ	AR	32,056	VC+	Marygrove College	MI	28,926	C
Davidson College	NC	58,146	MC	Gardner-Webb Univ	NC	34,375	C+	John Carroll Univ	OH	46,300	C+	Marymount Manhattan College	NY	40,118	VC
Davis & Elkins College	WV	33,742	C	Geneva College	PA	27,280	C	Johns Hopkins Univ	MD	47,492	MC	Marymount Univ	VA	39,480	C
De Sales Univ	PA	43,970	C	George Fox Univ	OR	40,750	C+	Johnson C. Smith Univ	NC	25,336	C	Maryville College	TN	33,150	C+
Defiance College	OH	30,645	C	George Mason Univ	VA	15,724	VC	Johnson State College	VT	16,721	C	Maryville Univ of St. Louis	MO	35,856	VC
Delaware State Univ	DE	16,722	LC	George Washington Univ	DC	57,108	MC	Judson College	AL	26,794	C	Marywood Univ	PA	45,595	C
Delta State Univ	MS	12,292	LC	Georgetown College	KY	41,440	C+	Judson Univ	IL	25,130	C	Mass College of Liberal Arts	MA	18,613	C
Denison Univ	OH	54,670	HC+	Georgetown Univ	DC	52,910	MC	Juniata College	PA	49,340	VC	Mass Inst of Technology	MA	58,240	MC
DePaul Univ	IL	47,623	VC	Georgia College and State Univ	GA	18,900	C+	Kalamazoo College	MI	49,740	HC	McDaniel College	MD	47,450	VC
DePauw Univ	IN	48,950	VC+	Georgia Regents Univ	GA		C	Kansas State Univ	KS	15,497	VC	McKendree Univ	IL	29,920	C+
Dickinson College	PA	57,662	HC+	Georgia Southern Univ	GA	16,942	C	Kansas Wesleyan Univ	KS	32,000	C	McMurry Univ	TX	25,962	LC
Dickinson State Univ	ND	11,900	NC	Georgia Southwestern State Univ	GA	13,246	C	Kean Univ	NJ	23,444	C	McNeese State Univ	LA	2,649	C
Dillard Univ	LA	22,940	VC	Georgia State Univ	GA	15,582	VC	Keene State College	NH	23,232	LC	McPherson College	KS	28,138	C
Doane College	NE	35,230	C	Georgian Court Univ	NJ	41,594	LC	Kennesaw State Univ	GA		C	Mercer Univ	GA	44,201	VC
Dominican College	NY	31,270	LC	Gettysburg College	PA	58,820	HC	Kent State Univ	OH	19,920	C	Mercy College	NY	30,456	C
Dominican Univ	IL	37,628	C	Glenville State College	WV	11,348	NC	Kentucky Christian Univ	KY	17,622	LC	Mercyhurst Univ	PA	40,700	C
Dominican Univ of Calif	CA	51,250	C	Goddard College	VT	16,418	VC	Kentucky State Univ	KY	11,000	C	Meredith College	NC	31,420	C
Dordt College	IA	34,160	C+	Gonzaga Univ	WA	46,441	HC	Kentucky Wesleyan College	KY	27,440	C	Merrimack College	MA	44,215	C
Dowling College	NY	25,000	LC	Gordon College	MA	44,320	VC	Kenyon College	OH	58,890	MC	Messiah College	PA	40,690	C+
Drake Univ	IA	41,516	VC+	Goshen College	IN	35,900	VC	King Univ	TN	33,140	C	Methodist Univ	NC	37,185	C
Drew Univ/College of Liberal Arts	NJ	57,516	C	Goucher College	MD	52,040	VC+	King's College	PA	43,502	C	Metropolitan State Univ	MN	5,923	
Drexel Univ	PA	61,418	VC+	Graceland Univ	IA	28,020	C	Knox College	IL	44,865	VC+	Metropolitan State Univ of Denver	CO	4,835	LC
Drury Univ	MO	31,909	VC	Grambling State Univ	LA	13,384	LC	Kutztown Univ of Pennsylvania	PA	16,909	LC	Miami Univ	OH	24,191	VC
Duke Univ	NC	50,250	MC	Grand Canyon Univ	AZ	24,540	VC	La Roche College	PA	35,824	LC	Mich State Univ	MI	22,450	VC
Duquesne Univ	PA	43,720	VC	Grand Valley State Univ	MI	17,998	C+	La Salle Univ	PA	50,270	C	Mich Tech Univ	MI	23,556	VC
D'Youville College	NY	29,850	C	Green Mountain College	VT	45,228	LC	La Sierra Univ	CA	35,694	VC	MidAmerica Nazarene Univ	KS	28,000	C
Earlham College	IN	51,470	HC	Greensboro College	NC	28,740	C	Lafayette College	PA	59,155	HC+	Middle Tenn State Univ	TN	8,650	C
East Carolina Univ	NC	14,169	C	Greenville College	IL	27,012	C	LaGrange College	GA	37,670	C	Middlebury College	VT	59,160	MC
East Central Univ	OK	10,223	C	Grinnell College	IA	53,654	HC	Lake Erie College	OH	37,266	C	Midland Univ	NE	34,000	C
East Stroudsburg Univ of Pennsylvania	PA	18,868	LC	Grove City College	PA	24,022	VC	Lake Forest College	IL	50,652	VC	Midwestern State Univ	TX	9,722	C
East Tenn State Univ	TN	9,000	C	Guilford College	NC	42,800	C	Lake Superior State Univ	MI	18,121	C	Miles College	AL	11,164	NC
East Texas Baptist Univ	TX	31,577	LC	Gustavus Adolphus College	MN	48,170	HC	Lakeland College	WI	22,990	C	Millersville Univ of Pennsylvania	PA	21,648	C
Eastern Conn State Univ	CT	20,584	C	Gwynedd-Mercy College	PA	33,560	C	Lamar Univ	TX	6,820	LC	Milligan College	TN	27,510	C
Eastern Illinois Univ	IL	20,466	C	Hamilton College	NY	55,620	MC	Lander Univ	SC	22,514	C+	Millikin Univ	IL	38,940	C
Eastern Kentucky Univ	KY	11,161	VC	Hamline Univ	MN	45,678	VC	Lane College	TN	11,212	C	Mills College	CA	54,119	VC
Eastern Mennonite Univ	VA	40,660	C	Hampden-Sydney College	VA	51,758	C	Langston Univ	OK	3,000	C	Millsaps College	MS	43,888	VC+
Eastern Mich Univ	MI	18,604	C	Hampshire College	MA	58,320	MC	Lasell College	MA	43,750	LC	Minn State Univ, Mankato	MN	15,616	C
Eastern Nazarene College	MA	30,000	C	Hampton Univ	VA	28,528	C	Lawrence Univ	WI	46,371	HC	Minn State Univ, Moorhead	MN	13,392	VC
Eastern New Mexico Univ	NM	10,682	C	Hannibal-LaGrange Univ	MO	24,490	C	Le Moyne College	NY	43,470	C	Minot State Univ	ND	10,915	C
Eastern Oregon Univ	OR	10,400	C	Hanover College	IN	43,073	C+	Lebanon Valley College	PA	38,570	C	Misericordia Univ	PA	41,060	C
Eastern Univ	PA	37,704	C	Harding Univ	AR	23,556	C	Lee Univ	TN	18,690	C+	Miss College	MS	21,998	C
Eastern Washington Univ	WA		C	Hardin-Simmons Univ	TX	23,560	C+	Lees-McRae College	NC	33,944	C	Miss State Univ	MS	14,750	C
Eckerd College	FL	43,902	C	Hartwick College	NY	51,270	C	Lehigh Univ	PA	56,770	MC	Miss Univ for Women	MS	7,400	C
Edgewood College	WI	33,294	C	Harvard College/Harvard Univ	MA	49,000	MC	Lehman College/The CUNY	NY	5,778	C	Miss Valley State Univ	MS	9,706	LC
Edinboro Univ of Pennsylvania	PA	15,940	LC	Hastings College	NE	27,782	C+	LeMoyne-Owen College	TN	13,100	C	Missouri Baptist Univ	MO	31,830	C
Edward Waters College	FL	19,607	LC	Haverford College	PA	61,564	MC	Lenoir-Rhyne College	NC	35,984	C	Missouri Southern State Univ	MO	12,061	C
Elizabeth City State Univ	NC	11,638	C	Hawaii Pacific Univ	HI	34,360	C	LeTourneau Univ	TX	36,210	VC	Missouri State Univ	MO	13,996	C+
Elizabethtown College	PA	49,740	VC	Heidelberg Univ	OH	34,100	C	Lewis & Clark College	OR	54,382	MC	Missouri Univ of Science and Technology	MO	18,655	VC+
Elmhurst College	IL	43,336	C	Hellenic College/Holy Cross Greek Orthodox School of Theology	MA	33,190	C	Lewis Univ	IL	23,050	C	Missouri Valley College	MO	22,200	C
Elmira College	NY	49,950	C+	Henderson State Univ	AR	14,584	C	Lewis-Clark State College	ID	6,990	C	Missouri Western State Univ	MO	12,260	NC
Elon Univ	NC	41,914	VC+	Hendrix College	AR	50,202	VC+	Liberty Univ	VA	19,101	C	Molloy College	NY	40,440	C
Emmanuel College	MA	47,985	VC	High Point Univ	NC	39,800	C	Limestone College	SC	30,800	C	Monmouth College	IL	40,850	C
Emory and Henry College	VA	387,460	C	Hillsdale College	MI	32,866	MC	Lincoln Memorial Univ	TN	18,144	C	Monmouth Univ	NJ	44,108	C
Emory Univ	GA	56,368	MC	Hiram College	OH	37,300	VC	Lincoln Univ	MO	12,904	NC	Montana State Univ	MT	14,068	C
Emporia State Univ	KS	12,897	C	Hobart and William Smith Colleges	NY	60,034	HC+	Lindenwood Univ	MO	20,750	C	Montana State Univ-Billings	MT	12,425	LC
Endicott College	MA	43,228	VC+	Hofstra Univ	NY	51,810	VC+	Lindsey Wilson College	KY	31,220	C	Montana State Univ-Northern	MT	12,500	NC
Erskine College	SC	37,360	C	Hollins Univ	VA	43,295	VC	Linfield College-McMinnville Campus	OR	47,676	C	Montclair State Univ	NJ	22,614	C
Eugene Lang College/The New School for Liberal Arts	NY	55,650	C	Holy Family Univ	PA	40,030	LC	Lipscomb Univ	TN	37,490	VC	Montreat College	NC	31,298	C
Eureka College	IL	19,280	C	Holy Names Univ	CA	40,310	NC	LIU Brooklyn	NY	47,182	LC	Moravian College	PA	36,381	VC
Evangel Univ	MO	23,090	C	Hood College	MD	45,730	C	LIU Post	NY	47,660	C	Morehead State Univ	KY	10,900	C
Excelsior College	NY	5,580	SP	Hope College	MI	38,650	VC	Livingstone College	NC	17,815	LC	Morehouse College	GA	39,412	C
Fairfield Univ	CT	56,960	VC	Houghton College	NY	36,808	C+	Lock Haven Univ of Pennsylvania	PA	18,028	LC	Morgan State Univ	MD	14,500	VC
Fairleigh Dickinson Univ/College at Florham	NJ	42,142	C	Houston Baptist Univ	TX	36,450	C	Longwood Univ	VA	20,924	C	Morningside College	IA	35,430	C
Fairleigh Dickinson Univ/Metropolitan Campus	NJ	40,254	C	Howard Payne Univ	TX	17,115	C	Loras College	IA	37,432	VC	Morris College	SC	16,310	LC
Fairmont State Univ	WV	12,098	LC	Howard Univ	DC	13,646	C	Louisiana College	LA	15,746	C	Mount Aloysius College	PA	29,976	C
Faulkner Univ	AL	25,720	LC	Humboldt State Univ	CA	18,400	C	Louisiana State Univ	LA	18,677	C+	Mount Holyoke College	MA	55,146	MC
Fayetteville State Univ	NC	10,816	C	Hunter College	NY	14,429	VC	Louisiana State Univ in Shreveport	LA	5,606	C	Mount Marty College	SD	29,638	C
Felician College	NJ	41,640	LC	Huntingdon College	AL	33,100	C	Louisiana Tech Univ	LA	11,302	C	Mount Mary Univ	WI	33,590	LC
Ferris State Univ	MI	20,047	C	Huntington Univ	IN	32,220	C+	Lourdes Univ	OH	26,055	LC	Mount Mercy Univ	IA	35,320	C
Ferrum College	VA	27,740	LC	Huston-Tillotson Univ	TX	18,124	C+	Loyola Marymount Univ	CA	54,649	VC+	Mount St. Mary College	NY	41,138	C
Fisk Univ	TN	19,830	C	Idaho State Univ	ID	12,307	C	Loyola Univ Chicago	IL	51,646	VC+	Mount St. Mary's Univ	MD	47,996	C
				Illinois College	IL	25,770	VC	Loyola Univ Maryland	MD	56,880	VC+	Mount St. Mary's College - Chalon Campus	CA	43,897	VC+
				Illinois State Univ	IL	23,110	VC					Mount Vernon Nazarene Univ	OH	29,590	C
				Illinois Wesleyan Univ	IL	48,452	HC					Muhlenberg College	PA	52,837	HC
												Murray State Univ	KY	15,304	C

ST = STATE $IS = IN-STATE COSTS   SR = SELECTOR RATING

School	ST	$IS	SR
Muskingum Univ	OH	30,502	C
National Univ	CA	14,730	SP
Nazareth College of Rochester	NY	43,028	C+
Nebr Wesleyan Univ	NE	29,774	C+
New College of Florida	FL	14,504	MC
New Jersey City Univ	NJ	21,456	LC
New Jersey Inst of Technology	NJ	26,490	C
New Mexico Highlands Univ	NM	11,904	NC
New Mexico State Univ	NM	14,050	C
New York Univ	NY	61,470	MC
Newberry College	SC	26,850	LC
Newman Univ	KS	30,380	C+
Niagara Univ	NY	41,010	C
Nicholls State Univ	LA	7,095	C
Nichols College	MA	37,240	LC
Norfolk State Univ	VA	10,531	LC
N Car Agricultural and Technical State Univ	NC	13,365	LC
N Car Central Univ	NC	9,000	C
N Car State Univ	NC	16,202	HC
N Car Wesleyan College	NC	29,440	C
North Central College	IL	38,343	VC
N Dak State Univ	ND		C
North Park Univ	IL	30,130	C
Northeastern Illinois Univ	IL	10,318	LC
Northeastern State Univ	OK	8,615	VC
Northeastern Univ	MA	55,296	MC
Northern Arizona Univ	AZ	19,010	C
Northern Illinois Univ	IL	19,768	C
Northern Kentucky Univ	KY	21,134	C
Northern Mich Univ	MI	18,278	C
Northern State Univ - Aberdeen	SD	14,505	C
Northland College	WI	26,680	C
Northwest Missouri State Univ	MO	17,347	C
Northwest Nazarene Univ	ID	34,000	C
Northwest Univ	WA	18,854	C
Northwestern College	MN	24,000	C
Northwestern College of Iowa	IA	36,240	VC
Northwestern Okla State Univ	OK	7,275	NC
Northwestern State Univ of Louisiana	LA	14,368	C
Northwestern Univ	IL	61,640	MC
Norwich Univ	VT	28,212	C
Notre Dame College	OH	34,942	VC
Notre Dame de Namur Univ	CA	44,236	LC
Notre Dame of Maryland Univ	MD	27,700	VC
Nyack College	NY	33,250	C
Oakland Univ	MI	19,391	C
Oakwood Univ	AL	25,529	NC
Oberlin College	OH	61,788	MC
Occidental College	CA	60,972	MC
Oglethorpe Univ	GA	44,200	C+
Ohio Dominican Univ	OH	38,380	C+
Ohio Northern Univ	OH	42,075	VC
Ohio State Univ at Lima	OH	7,140	C
Ohio State Univ at Mansfield	OH	13,160	C
Ohio State Univ at Marion	OH	16,990	MC
Ohio State Univ at Newark	OH	17,510	C
Ohio Univ	OH	21,080	C
Ohio Valley Univ	WV	17,752	C
Ohio Wesleyan Univ	OH	49,460	C+
Okla Baptist Univ	OK	28,202	C
Okla Christian Univ	OK	25,870	C
Okla City Univ	OK	40,476	VC
Okla Panhandle State Univ	OK	8,996	C
Okla State Univ	OK	14,310	VC
Okla Wesleyan Univ	OK	21,300	C
Old Dominion Univ	VA	19,483	LC
Olivet College	MI	19,984	LC
Olivet Nazarene Univ	IL	29,990	C
Oral Roberts Univ	OK	31,734	C
Oregon State Univ	OR	20,273	VC
Oswego / SUNY	NY	20,009	VC
Ottawa Univ	KS	15,000	VC
Otterbein College	OH	32,214	C
Ouachita Baptist Univ	AR	30,220	VC
Our Lady of Holy Cross College	LA	8,090	C
Our Lady of the Lake Univ	TX	22,430	LC
Pace Univ	NY	53,367	C
Pacific Lutheran Univ	WA	46,760	C+
Pacific Union College	CA	28,150	VC
Pacific Univ	OR	49,626	C+
Paine College	GA	19,826	LC
Palm Beach Atlantic Univ	FL	34,874	C+
Park Univ	MO	17,525	C
Penn State Erie/The Behrend College	PA	16,256	C
Penn State Univ/Altoona	PA	11,464	C
Pepperdine Univ	CA	55,372	HC+
Peru State College	NE	8,600	NC
Pfeiffer Univ	NC	33,700	LC
Piedmont College	GA	30,136	C
Pine Manor College	MA	32,659	LC
Pittsburg State Univ	KS	12,032	C
Pitzer College	CA	54,988	MC
Plymouth State Univ	NH	23,148	LC
Point Loma Nazarene Univ	CA	41,006	C+
Point Park Univ	PA	36,390	C
Pomona College	CA	57,680	MC

School	ST	$IS	SR
Pontifical Catholic Univ of PR	PR	7,310	
Portland State Univ	OR	18,672	C
Post Univ	CT	35,750	C
Prairie View A&M Univ	TX	15,205	LC
Presbyterian College	SC	42,678	C+
Prescott College	AZ	33,284	C
Princeton Univ	NJ	53,795	MC
Principia College	IL	35,140	C+
Providence College	RI	57,383	VC
Purdue Univ/Calumet	IN	14,336	C
Purdue Univ/West Lafayette	IN	20,024	HC
Queens College/The CUNY	NY	17,107	VC
Queens Univ of Charlotte	NC	39,543	C+
Quincy Univ	IL	34,980	LC
Quinnipiac Univ	CT	55,160	VC
Radford Univ	VA	17,766	LC
Ramapo College of New Jersey	NJ	24,938	C
Randolph College	VA	45,660	VC
Randolph-Macon College	VA	49,869	C+
Reed College	OR	57,780	MC
Regis College	MA	47,565	LC
Regis Univ	CO	41,318	C
Rhode Island College	RI	17,694	LC
Rhodes College	TN	51,900	HC+
Rice Univ	TX	43,288	MC
Richard Stockton College of New Jersey	NJ	20,000	VC
Rider Univ	NJ	45,720	C
Ripon College	WI	36,959	C+
Rivier Univ	NH	35,000	VC
Roanoke College	VA	49,976	C
Roberts Wesleyan College	NY	38,306	C+
Rochester College	MI	18,320	LC
Rockford College	IL	31,000	C
Rockhurst Univ	MO	20,625	C
Rocky Mountain College	MT	32,242	C
Roger Williams Univ	RI	46,296	VC
Rollins College	FL	52,370	HC
Roosevelt Univ	IL	22,605	VC
Rosemont College	PA	42,350	C
Rowan Univ	NJ	24,022	VC+
Russell Sage College	NY	39,370	C
Rutgers, The State Univ of New Jersey/Camden Campus	NJ	25,121	C
Rutgers, The State Univ of New Jersey/New Brunswick	NJ	25,562	VC
Rutgers, The State Univ of New Jersey/Newark Campus	NJ	258,806	C
Sacred Heart Univ	CT	49,264	VC
Saginaw Valley State Univ	MI	17,369	C
St. Anselm College	NH	49,376	VC
St. Augustine's Univ	NC	14,000	C
St. Francis Univ	PA	30,029	LC
St. John's Univ	MN	47,984	C
St. Joseph's College	IN	36,500	C
St. Joseph's College of Maine	ME	31,580	C
St. Joseph's Univ	PA	55,006	VC
St. Leo Univ	FL	30,340	C
St. Louis Univ	MO	48,346	MC
St. Martin's Univ	WA	41,678	C
St. Mary's College	IN	45,160	C+
St. Mary's College of Calif	CA	53,550	C
St. Mary's Univ	TX	33,854	C
St. Mary's Univ of Minn	MN	38,280	C
St. Michael's College	VT	49,975	VC
St. Peter's Univ	NJ	44,240	C
St. Vincent College	PA	40,244	C
St. Xavier Univ	IL	32,840	C
Salem College	NC	29,326	VC
Salem State Univ	MA	13,161	C
Salisbury Univ	MD	19,180	VC
Salve Regina Univ	RI	48,550	VC
Sam Houston State Univ	TX	17,082	C
Samford Univ	AL	37,060	C+
San Diego Christian College	CA	31,012	C
San Diego State Univ	CA	21,611	C+
San Francisco State Univ	CA	18,514	C
San Jose State Univ	CA	19,133	LC
Sarah Lawrence College	NY	48,000	HC
Savannah State Univ	GA	13,156	C
Schreiner Univ	TX	32,734	LC
Scripps College	CA	61,940	MC
Seattle Pacific Univ	WA	41,559	VC+
Seattle Univ	WA	49,035	VC+
Seton Hall Univ	NJ	45,902	C
Seton Hill Univ	PA	35,172	C
Sewanee: The Univ of the South	TN	47,700	HC+
Shawnee State Univ	OH	16,916	C
Shenandoah Univ	VA	39,916	C
Shepherd Univ	WV	15,875	C
Shippensburg Univ of Pennsylvania	PA	20,934	C
Shorter Univ	GA	30,650	LC
Siena College	NY	43,863	VC
Siena Heights Univ	MI	32,040	C
Silver Lake College	WI	22,600	LC
Simmons College	MA	49,966	VC
Simpson College	IA	36,086	C+
Simpson Univ	CA	28,900	C
Skidmore College	NY	59,942	HC

School	ST	$IS	SR
Slippery Rock Univ of Pennsylvania	PA	10,360	C
Smith College	MA	59,674	MC
Sonoma State Univ	CA	20,541	C
S Car State Univ	SC	6,700	LC
S Dak State Univ	SD	14,296	C
Southeast Missouri State Univ	MO	15,370	LC
Southeastern Louisiana Univ	LA	13,325	C
Southeastern Okla State Univ	OK	7,966	LC
Southeastern Univ	FL	27,201	C
Southern Adventist Univ	TN	26,190	C
Southern Arkansas Univ	AR	14,316	C
Southern Conn State Univ	CT	18,033	LC
Southern Illinois Univ Carbondale	IL	21,942	C
Southern Illinois Univ Edwardsville	IL	17,532	C
Southern Methodist Univ	TX	60,585	MC
Southern Nazarene Univ	OK	24,354	C
Southern New Hampshire Univ	NH	38,100	C
Southern Oregon Univ	OR	17,874	C
Southern Univ and A&M College	LA	9,761	LC
Southern Univ at New Orleans	LA	2,963	NC
Southern Vermont College	VT	30,740	LC
Southern Wesleyan Univ	SC	25,600	C
Southwest Baptist Univ	MO	24,710	C
Southwest Minn State Univ	MN	14,000	C
Southwestern Adventist Univ	TX	23,026	LC
Southwestern College	KS	29,270	C
Southwestern Okla State Univ	OK	9,160	C
Southwestern Univ	TX	45,660	VC
Spelman College	GA	24,650	C
Spring Arbor Univ	MI	26,740	C
Spring Hill College	AL	44,164	VC
Springfield College	MA	25,000	C
St. Ambrose Univ	IA	30,845	C
St. Bonaventure Univ	NY	41,575	C
St. Catherine Univ	MN	37,782	C+
St. Cloud State Univ	MN	10,600	C
St. Edward's Univ	TX	47,784	C
St. Francis College	NY	34,200	C
St. John Fisher College	NY	40,708	C+
St. John's Univ	NY	55,070	C+
St. Joseph's College, New York/Brooklyn Campus	NY	22,630	C
St. Joseph's College, New York/Suffolk Campus	NY	22,630	C
St. Lawrence Univ	NY	59,972	VC
St. Mary's College of Maryland	MD	25,754	VC
St. Norbert College	WI	41,478	VC
St. Olaf College	MN	51,200	HC+
St. Thomas Aquinas College	NY	40,230	C
St. Thomas Univ	FL	32,310	LC
Stanford Univ	CA	58,388	MC
SUNY at Purchase	NY	16,951	C
SUNY/Empire State College	NY	6,315	SP
Stephen F. Austin State Univ	TX	14,668	C
Sterling College	KS	27,216	C
Stetson Univ	FL	51,516	VC
Stevens Inst of Technology	NJ	50,130	HC
Stevenson Univ	MD	41,470	C
Stillman College	AL	19,470	C
Stonehill College	MA	46,780	NC
Stony Brook Univ / SUNY	NY	20,078	HC+
Suffolk Univ	MA	47,298	C
Sul Ross State Univ	TX	13,410	LC
SUNY College at Geneseo	NY	18,670	HC
SUNY College at Old Westbury	NY	16,324	C
SUNY Cortland/The SUNY	NY	19,759	C+
SUNY Fredonia/The SUNY at Fredonia	NY	19,840	VC
SUNY New Paltz	NY	14,348	C
SUNY Oneonta / SUNY	NY	16,919	C+
SUNY Plattsburgh / SUNY	NY	18,083	C
Susquehanna Univ	PA	51,150	C
Swarthmore College	PA	57,870	MC
Syracuse Univ	NY	56,346	VC
Tabor College	KS	29,010	C
Talladega College	AL	17,996	C
Tarleton State Univ	TX	13,489	LC
Taylor Univ	IN	37,821	VC+
Temple Univ	PA	24,392	VC
Tenn State Univ	TN	9,048	C
Tenn Tech Univ	TN	11,310	C
Tenn Wesleyan College	TN	21,250	C
Texas A&M Univ	TX	19,207	VC
Texas A&M Univ at Commerce	TX	10,496	C
Texas A&M Univ at Corpus Christi	TX	11,544	LC
Texas A&M Univ at Kingsville	TX	7,500	LC
Texas Christian Univ	TX	49,980	HC
Texas Lutheran Univ	TX	36,040	C
Texas Southern Univ	TX	18,212	LC
Texas State Univ	TX	17,128	C
Texas Tech Univ	TX	14,243	C
Texas Wesleyan Univ	TX	31,382	C
Texas Woman's Univ	TX	13,633	LC
The Catholic Univ of America	DC	52,852	VC

School	ST	$IS	SR
The College of Idaho	ID	31,277	C+
The College of New Rochelle	NY	33,600	VC
The College of St. Rose	NY	26,750	C
The Lincoln Univ	PA	15,154	LC
The Masters College	CA	38,160	C+
Ohio State Univ-Columbus Campus	OH	19,887	HC+
The Pennsylvania State Univ - Univ Park	PA	28,022	VC+
The SUNY at Potsdam	NY	18,473	C
The SUNY/College at Brockport	NY	19,002	C
The Univ of Memphis	TN	15,094	C
The Univ of N Car at Greensboro	NC	12,848	C
The Univ of N Car at Pembroke	NC	13,388	LC
The Univ of Okla	OK	18,621	VC
The Univ of Tenn at Chattanooga	TN	16,883	C
The Univ of Utah	UT	16,463	VC
The Univ of Virginia's College at Wise	VA	11,076	C
Thiel College	PA	38,728	LC
Thomas Edison State College	NJ	5,700	SP
Thomas More College	KY	34,760	C
Tiffin Univ	OH	30,273	LC
Toccoa Falls College	GA	23,210	LC
Tougaloo College	MS	15,275	NC
Touro College	NY	27,959	VC
Towson Univ	MD	16,000	VC
Transylvania Univ	KY	42,660	VC+
Trevecca Nazarene Univ	TN	31,186	C
Trinity Christian College	IL	28,869	C
Trinity College	CT		HC+
Trinity International Univ	IL	31,070	VC
Trinity Univ	TX	43,150	HC+
Trinity Washington Univ	DC	30,250	C+
Troy Univ	AL	10,650	C
Truman State Univ	MO	15,541	HC
Tufts Univ	MA	58,780	MC
Tulane Univ	LA	60,861	MC
Tusculum College	TN	24,295	C
Tuskegee Univ	AL	26,750	C
Union College	KY	29,955	C
Union College	NE	23,270	C
Union College	NY	60,240	MC
Union Univ	TN	28,260	VC
United States Air Force Academy	CO		MC
United States Military Academy	NY		MC
United States Naval Academy	MD		MC
Universidad Adventista de las Antillas	PR	7,360	
Universidad del Turabo	PR	4,110	
Univ at Albany / SUNY	NY	18,674	VC
Univ at Buffalo / The SUNY	NY	20,283	VC
Univ of Akron	OH	20,436	C
Univ of Alabama at Birmingham	AL	18,484	C+
Univ of Alabama at Tuscaloosa	AL	17,164	C+
Univ of Alabama in Huntsville	AL	17,591	VC+
Univ of Alaska Anchorage	AK	16,673	NC
Univ of Alaska Fairbanks	AK	15,130	C
Univ of Arizona	AZ	20,657	C
Univ of Arkansas at Fayetteville	AR	18,352	C
Univ of Arkansas at Little Rock	AR	17,609	LC
Univ of Arkansas at Monticello	AR	12,076	NC
Univ of Arkansas at Pine Bluff	AR	13,378	C
Univ of Calif at Berkeley	CA	23,322	MC
Univ of Calif at Davis	CA		HC
Univ of Calif at Irvine	CA	25,961	VC
Univ of Calif at Los Angeles	CA	25,686	MC
Univ of Calif at Riverside	CA	27,204	C+
Univ of Calif at San Diego	CA	21,000	VC
Univ of Calif at Santa Barbara	CA	27,551	HC
Univ of Calif at Santa Cruz	CA	27,807	C+
Univ of Central Arkansas	AR	13,667	VC
Univ of Central Florida	FL	15,668	VC+
Univ of Central Missouri	MO	14,605	C
Univ of Central Okla	OK	12,293	C
Univ of Charleston	WV	32,300	C
Univ of Chicago	IL	55,416	MC
Univ of Cincinnati	OH	21,506	C
Univ of Colo at Colo Springs	CO	15,000	C
Univ of Colo Boulder	CO	22,605	VC+
Univ of Colo Denver	CO	17,904	C
Univ of Conn	CT	24,706	VC
Univ of Dallas	TX	45,500	VC+
Univ of Dayton	OH	49,070	VC
Univ of Delaware	DE	23,612	VC
Univ of Denver	CO	51,787	VC+
Univ of Detroit Mercy	MI	30,450	VC
Univ of Evansville	IN	42,656	VC+
Univ of Findlay	OH	31,916	C
Univ of Florida	FL	15,943	HC
Univ of Georgia	GA	20,082	VC
Univ of Great Falls	MT	27,970	C
Univ of Hartford	CT	42,674	C

School	ST	$IS	SR
Univ of Hawaii at Hilo	HI	23,066	C
Univ of Hawaii at Manoa	HI	19,379	C
Univ of Houston-Downtown	TX	15,170	LC
Univ of Idaho	ID	14,558	C
Univ of Illinois at Chicago	IL	24,505	VC
Univ of Illinois at Urbana-Champaign	IL	26,450	HC
Univ of Indianapolis	IN	31,740	LC
Univ of Iowa	IA	17,693	VC
Univ of Jamestown	ND	24,738	C
Univ of Kansas	KS	17,603	C+
Univ of Kentucky	KY	19,868	C
Univ of La Verne	CA	47,010	C
Univ of Louisiana at Lafayette	LA	6,130	C
Univ of Louisiana at Monroe	LA	12,998	C
Univ of Louisville	KY	17,946	C
Univ of Maine	ME	19,902	C+
Univ of Maine at Farmington	ME	18,187	LC
Univ of Maine at Machias	ME	10,523	C
Univ of Mary Hardin-Baylor	TX	31,950	C+
Univ of Mary Washington	VA	19,484	VC
Univ of Maryland - College Park	MD	20,060	HC
Univ of Maryland/Baltimore County	MD	18,000	VC
Univ of Maryland/Eastern Shore	MD	14,000	VC
Univ of Maryland/Univ College	MD	6,168	SP
Univ of Mass Amherst	MA	24,215	VC+
Univ of Mass Boston	MA	23,066	C
Univ of Mass Dartmouth	MA	22,223	C
Univ of Mass Lowell	MA	19,316	C
Univ of Miami	FL	57,034	MC
Univ of Mich/Ann Arbor	MI	22,102	MC
Univ of Mich/Dearborn	MI	9,885	VC
Univ of Mich-Flint	MI	17,547	C+
Univ of Minn/Duluth	MN	19,806	C
Univ of Minn/Morris	MN	17,150	VC
Univ of Minn/Twin Cities	MN		HC
Univ of Miss	MS	16,704	C+
Univ of Missouri/Columbia	MO	18,201	MC
Univ of Missouri-Kansas City	MO	19,603	C
Univ of Missouri-St. Louis	MO		VC
Univ of Mobile	AL	28,935	VC
Univ of Montana	MT	14,105	C
Univ of Montana-Western	MT	9,753	LC
Univ of Montevallo	AL	17,060	C
Univ of Mount Olive	NC	18,426	C
Univ of Mount Union	OH	35,130	C
Univ of Nebr - Lincoln	NE	18,031	VC
Univ of Nebr at Kearney	NE	14,855	LC
Univ of Nebr at Omaha	NE	12,700	C
Univ of Nevada, Las Vegas	NV	17,303	C
Univ of Nevada/Reno	NV	17,507	C
Univ of New England	ME	46,750	C
Univ of New Hampshire	NH	26,912	C
Univ of New Haven	CT	48,940	C
Univ of New Mexico	NM	15,300	C
Univ of New Orleans	LA	9,224	C
Univ of North Alabama	AL	9,960	C
Univ of N Car at Asheville	NC	13,500	VC
Univ of N Car at Chapel Hill	NC	18,928	MC
Univ of N Car at Charlotte	NC	15,547	C
Univ of N Car at Wilmington	NC	13,572	VC
Univ of N Dak	ND	14,551	C
Univ of North Florida	FL	15,870	VC
Univ of North Georgia	GA	8,500	C
Univ of North Texas	TX	15,628	C
Univ of Northern Colo	CO	14,800	C
Univ of Northern Iowa	IA	15,795	C
Univ of Notre Dame	IN	57,117	MC
Univ of Oregon	OR	21,360	C+
Univ of Pennsylvania	PA	61,132	MC
Univ of Pikeville	KY	25,500	NC
Univ of Pittsburgh at Bradford	PA	21,802	C
Univ of Pittsburgh at Johnstown	PA	20,862	LC
Univ of Pittsburgh at Pittsburgh	PA	28,572	HC+
Univ of Portland	OR	49,964	VC
Univ of PR Recinto de Rio Piedras	PR	5,750	
Univ of PR/Cayey	PR	1,504	
Univ of PR/Mayaguez	PR	1,250	
Univ of Puget Sound	WA	54,608	HC
Univ of Redlands	CA	40,500	VC
Univ of Rio Grande	OH	8,750	NC
Univ of Rochester	NY	60,668	MC
Univ of St. Francis	IN	29,810	C
Univ of St. Joseph	CT	45,630	C
Univ of St. Mary	KS	28,400	C+
Univ of San Diego	CA	54,818	HC+
Univ of San Francisco	CA	54,770	VC
Univ of Science and Arts of Okla	OK	10,560	VC
Univ of Scranton	PA	51,940	VC
Univ of Sioux Falls	SD	22,990	C
Univ of South Alabama	AL	13,510	C
Univ of S Car Aiken	SC	16,712	C
Univ of S Car at Columbia	SC	19,725	VC+
Univ of S Car Upstate	SC	18,200	LC
Univ of S Dak	SD	15,111	C
Univ of South Florida/St. Petersburg	FL	12,769	C
Univ of South Florida/Tampa	FL	13,000	C
Univ of Southern Calif	CA	56,903	MC
Univ of Southern Indiana	IN	14,885	C
Univ of Southern Maine	ME	16,576	C
Univ of Southern Miss	MS	13,170	C
Univ of St. Francis	IL	37,560	C
Univ of St. Thomas - Houston	TX	37,690	C
Univ of Tampa	FL	35,160	VC
Univ of Tenn at Knoxville	TN	20,364	VC+
Univ of Tenn at Martin	TN	13,734	C
Univ of Texas - Pan American	TX	11,125	LC
Univ of Texas at Arlington	TX	10,908	LC
Univ of Texas at Austin	TX	44,074	HC
Univ of Texas at Dallas	TX	21,348	HC+
Univ of Texas at El Paso	TX	8,764	NC
Univ of Texas at San Antonio	TX	18,372	C
Univ of the Cumberlands	KY	27,500	C
Univ of the District of Columbia	DC	7,244	LC
Univ of the Incarnate Word	TX	37,316	LC
Univ of the Ozarks	AR	31,440	C
Univ of the Pacific	CA	52,146	VC
Univ of the Southwest	NM	15,000	C
Univ of Toledo	OH	18,464	C
Univ of Tulsa	OK	46,331	MC
Univ of Vermont	VT	27,006	VC+
Univ of Virginia	VA	23,050	MC
Univ of Washington	WA	14,722	VC
Univ of West Alabama	AL	14,274	C
Univ of West Florida	FL	14,656	C
Univ of West Georgia	GA	15,488	LC
Univ of Wisc Whitewater	WI	13,314	C
Univ of Wisc/Eau Claire	WI	15,730	C
Univ of Wisc/Green Bay	WI	19,074	C
Univ of Wisc/La Crosse	WI	9,304	VC
Univ of Wisc/Madison	WI	18,757	HC+
Univ of Wisc/Oshkosh	WI	10,426	LC
Univ of Wisc/Parkside	WI	10,181	LC
Univ of Wisc/Platteville	WI	14,564	C
Univ of Wisc/River Falls	WI	9,722	C
Univ of Wisc/Stevens Point	WI	14,043	C
Univ of Wisc/Superior	WI	14,314	C
Univ of Wisc-Milwaukee	WI	18,436	C
Univ of Wyoming	WY	14,401	C+
Urbana Univ	OH	30,820	C
Ursinus College	PA	57,580	VC
Ursuline College	OH	33,198	LC
Utah State Univ	UT	12,044	C
Utica College	NY	45,670	C
Valley City State Univ	ND	12,286	LC
Valparaiso Univ	IN	44,940	VC+
Vanderbilt Univ	TN	58,220	MC
Vanguard Univ of Southern Calif	CA	35,833	VC
Vassar College	NY	61,140	MC
Villanova Univ	PA	58,394	MC
Virginia Commonwealth Univ	VA	21,716	C
Virginia Military Inst	VA	16,156	C
Virginia Polytechnic Inst and State Univ	VA	14,629	HC
Virginia State Univ	VA	11,318	C+
Virginia Union Univ	VA	18,432	C
Virginia Wesleyan College	VA	28,433	LC
Viterbo Univ	WI	30,070	C
Wabash College	IN	46,850	C+
Wagner College	NY	48,600	C+
Wake Forest Univ	NC	58,838	MC
Walla Walla Univ	WA	26,256	NC
Walsh Univ	OH	35,100	C
Warner Pacific College	OR	25,550	C
Warner Univ	FL	18,000	C
Warren Wilson College	NC	40,132	VC
Wartburg College	IA	41,055	VC
Washburn Univ	KS	12,579	C
Washington Adventist Univ	MD	25,859	LC
Washington and Jefferson College	PA	51,948	VC
Washington and Lee Univ	VA	52,812	MC
Washington College	MD	52,602	VC
Washington State Univ	WA	20,461	C
Washington Univ in St. Louis	MO	69,844	MC
Wayland Baptist Univ	TX	18,912	LC
Wayne State College	NE	11,764	NC
Wayne State Univ	MI	22,063	C
Waynesburg Univ	PA	30,150	C
Webster Univ	MO	35,100	C+
Wellesley College	MA	59,038	MC
Wells College	NY	49,400	VC
Wesley College	DE	31,115	LC
Wesleyan College	GA	24,000	C
Wesleyan Univ	CT	61,198	MC
West Chester Univ of Pennsylvania	PA	17,186	C
West Liberty Univ	WV	9,142	LC
West Texas A&M Univ	TX	13,478	C
West Virginia State Univ	WV	8,378	NC
West Virginia Univ	WV	16,542	C+
West Virginia Univ Inst of Technology	WV	14,094	NC
West Virginia Wesleyan College	WV	26,880	C
Western Carolina Univ	NC	13,965	C
Western Conn State Univ	CT	18,327	LC
Western Illinois Univ	IL	20,732	C
Western Kentucky Univ	KY	11,000	LC
Western Mich Univ	MI	19,628	C
Western New England Univ	MA	46,154	C+
Western New Mexico Univ	NM	8,500	C
Western Oregon Univ	OR	15,021	C
Western State Colo Univ	CO	16,924	C
Western Washington Univ	WA	18,519	VC
Westfield State Univ	MA	18,297	C
Westminster College	MO	31,720	VC
Westminster College	PA	31,290	C+
Westminster College	UT	37,708	C+
Westmont College	CA	41,500	HC
Wheaton College	IL	40,720	MC
Wheaton College	MA	54,934	HC+
Wheeling Jesuit Univ	WV	33,500	C
Whitman College	WA	55,988	MC
Whittier College	CA	43,416	C
Whitworth Univ	WA	47,734	VC
Wichita State Univ	KS	14,607	C+
Widener Univ	PA	52,418	C
Wiley College	TX		LC
Wilkes Univ	PA	44,070	C
Willamette Univ	OR	56,450	VC+
William Carey Univ	MS	13,500	LC
William Jewell College	MO	31,000	VC+
William Paterson Univ of New Jersey	NJ	21,694	C
William Penn Univ	IA	26,000	C
William Woods Univ	MO	24,260	C
Williams Baptist College	AR	20,070	C
Williams College	MA	61,070	MC
Wilmington College	OH	29,784	C
Wilson College	PA	35,080	C
Wingate Univ	NC	34,990	C
Winona State Univ	MN	16,640	C
Winston-Salem State Univ	NC	9,418	LC
Winthrop Univ	SC	21,120	C
Wisc Lutheran College	WI	23,510	VC
Wittenberg Univ	OH	47,962	C+
Wofford College	SC	45,795	VC
Woodbury Univ	CA	34,500	LC
Worcester State Univ	MA	19,812	C
Wright State Univ	OH	16,983	C
Xavier Univ	OH	44,980	VC
Xavier Univ of Louisiana	LA	25,300	C
Yale Univ	CT	55,300	MC
Yeshiva Univ	NY	47,250	VC+
York College	NE	19,475	C
York College / The CUNY	NY	5,496	VC
York College of Pennsylvania	PA	26,590	C
Youngstown State Univ	OH	16,732	C

HISTORY AND POLITICAL SCIENCE

School	ST	$IS	SR
Black Hills State Univ	SD	13,947	C
Bridgewater College	VA	41,450	C
Indiana Univ Kokomo	IN	6,811	LC
Mount St. Mary College	NY	41,138	C
Okla Christian Univ	OK	25,870	C
Western Illinois Univ	IL	20,732	C

HISTORY EDUCATION

School	ST	$IS	SR
Bloomfield College	NJ	37,850	LC
Ferris State Univ	MI	20,047	C
Georgetown College	KY	41,440	C+
Hope College	MI	38,650	VC
Huntingdon College	AL	33,100	C
Mount Mary Univ	WI	33,590	LC
Murray State Univ	KY	15,304	C
Nyack College	NY	33,262	C
Shorter Univ	GA	30,650	LC

HISTORY OF ARCHITECTURE / URBAN DEVELOPMENT

School	ST	$IS	SR
Univ of Illinois at Chicago	IL	24,505	VC

HISTORY OF PHILOSOPHY

School	ST	$IS	SR
Colo College	CO	57,162	MC
Univ of Pittsburgh at Pittsburgh	PA	28,572	HC+

HISTORY OF SCIENCE

School	ST	$IS	SR
Calif Inst of Technology	CA	54,045	MC
Case Western Reserve Univ	OH	56,534	MC
Georgia Inst of Technology	GA	21,828	MC
Johns Hopkins Univ	MD	47,492	MC
The Univ of Okla	OK	18,621	VC
Univ of Jamestown	ND	24,738	C
Univ of Pennsylvania	PA	61,132	MC
Univ of Wisc/Madison	WI	18,757	HC+
Yale Univ	CT	55,300	MC

HOME ECONOMICS

School	ST	$IS	SR
Cal State, Fresno	CA	17,405	C
College of the Ozarks	MO		VC
Florida State Univ	FL	16,715	MC
Harding Univ	AR	23,556	C
Illinois State Univ	IL	23,110	VC
Indiana State Univ	IN	16,000	C
Langston Univ	OK	3,000	C
Montclair State Univ	NJ	22,614	C
Morgan State Univ	MD	14,500	VC
Oakwood Univ	AL	25,529	NC
Queens College/The CUNY	NY	17,107	VC
San Diego State Univ	CA	21,611	C+
SUNY Oneonta / SUNY	NY	16,919	C+
SUNY Plattsburgh / SUNY	NY	18,083	C
Tarleton State Univ	TX	13,489	LC
Texas A&M Univ at Kingsville	TX	7,500	LC
Texas Tech Univ	TX	14,243	C
The Masters College	CA	38,160	C+
Univ of Florida	FL	15,943	HC
Univ of Georgia	GA	20,082	VC
Univ of Maryland/Eastern Shore	MD	14,000	VC
Univ of PR Recinto de Rio Piedras	PR	5,750	
Utah State Univ	UT	12,044	C
Virginia State Univ	VA	11,318	C+

HOME ECONOMICS EDUCATION

School	ST	$IS	SR
Alabama A&M Univ	AL	10,084	C
Ashland Univ	OH	25,000	C
Auburn Univ	AL	22,378	VC+
Baylor Univ	TX	50,329	HC
Bluffton Univ	OH	38,948	C
Brigham Young Univ	UT	12,100	HC
Cal State, Northridge	CA	28,690	LC
Carson-Newman Univ	TN	29,058	C+
Central Washington Univ	WA	11,730	C
Cheyney Univ of Pennsylvania	PA	20,372	LC
Concordia Univ Nebr	NE	26,000	VC
Delaware State Univ	DE	16,722	LC
East Carolina Univ	NC	14,169	C
Eastern Kentucky Univ	KY	11,161	C
Eastern New Mexico Univ	NM	10,682	C
Florida State Univ	FL	16,715	MC
Fort Valley State Univ	GA	11,200	VC
Immaculata Univ	PA	43,000	C
Indiana State Univ	IN	16,000	C
Jacksonville State Univ	AL	12,480	LC
Langston Univ	OK	3,000	C
Mercyhurst Univ	PA	40,700	C
Montclair State Univ	NJ	22,614	C
Murray State Univ	KY	15,304	C
New Mexico State Univ	NM	14,050	C
N Car Agricultural and Technical State Univ	NC	13,365	LC
N Dak State Univ	ND		C
Oakwood Univ	AL	25,529	NC
Pittsburg State Univ	KS	12,032	C
Pontifical Catholic Univ of PR	PR	7,310	
Queens College/The CUNY	NY	17,107	VC
San Francisco State Univ	CA	18,514	C
Seattle Pacific Univ	WA	41,559	VC+
Seton Hill Univ	PA	35,172	C
Shepherd Univ	WV	15,875	C
S Car State Univ	SC	6,700	LC
S Dak State Univ	SD	14,296	C
St. Catherine Univ	MN	37,782	C+
SUNY Oneonta / SUNY	NY	16,919	C+
Tarleton State Univ	TX	13,489	LC
Tenn Tech Univ	TN	11,310	C
Univ of Akron	OH	20,436	C
Univ of Arkansas at Pine Bluff	AR	13,378	C
Univ of Louisiana at Lafayette	LA	6,130	C
Univ of Maryland/Eastern Shore	MD	14,000	VC
Univ of Minn/Twin Cities	MN		HC
Univ of Montevallo	AL	17,060	C
Univ of Nebr - Lincoln	NE	18,031	VC
Univ of North Alabama	AL	9,960	C
Univ of Southern Miss	MS	13,170	C
Univ of Wisc/Stout	WI	15,459	C
Utah State Univ	UT	12,044	C
Wayne State College	NE	11,764	NC
Western Kentucky Univ	KY	11,000	LC

HOME FURNISHINGS AND EQUIPMENT MANAGEMENT/ PRODUCTION/SERVICES

School	ST	$IS	SR
Auburn Univ	AL	22,378	VC+
Fashion Inst of Technology/ SUNY	NY	18,362	SP
High Point Univ	NC	39,800	C
Univ of North Texas	TX	15,628	C

HOMELAND SECURITY

School	ST	$IS	SR
Angelo State Univ	TX	15,049	NC
Cal State, Sacramento	CA	16,200	C
Campbell Univ	NC	37,570	VC
Excelsior College	NY	5,580	SP
Marian Univ	WI	32,420	C
Mitchell College	CT	40,983	C
Monmouth Univ	NJ	44,108	C
Savannah State Univ	GA	13,156	C

School	ST	$IS	SR
St. John's Univ	NY	55,070	C+
The Pennsylvania State Univ - Univ Park	PA	28,022	VC+
Univ of Alaska Fairbanks	AK	15,130	C
Virginia Commonwealth Univ	VA	21,716	C
Westminster College	UT	37,708	C+

HOMELAND SECURITY/ EMERGENCY PREPAREDNESS

School	ST	$IS	SR
Ashford Univ	CA	10,480	C
La Roche College	PA	35,824	LC
Thomas Edison State College	NJ	5,700	SP
Tulane Univ	LA	60,861	MC

HORTICULTURE

School	ST	$IS	SR
Alabama A&M Univ	AL	10,084	C
Andrews Univ	MI	28,030	C+
Auburn Univ	AL	22,378	VC+
Clemson Univ	SC	19,136	HC
College of the Ozarks	MO		VC
Colo State Univ-Fort Collins	CO	20,385	VC
Delaware Valley College	PA	29,944	C
Eastern Kentucky Univ	KY	11,161	C
Farmingdale State College	NY	19,673	C
Ferrum College	VA	27,740	LC
Florida A&M Univ	FL	14,935	LC
Florida Southern College	FL	40,150	C+
Fort Valley State Univ	GA	11,200	VC
Iowa State Univ	IA	16,403	C
Kansas State Univ	KS	15,497	VC
Kent State Univ	OH	19,920	C
Mich State Univ	MI	22,450	VC
Miss State Univ	MS	14,750	C
Montana State Univ	MT	14,068	C
New Mexico State Univ	NM	14,050	C
N Car State Univ	NC	16,202	NC
N Dak State Univ	ND		C
Northwest Missouri State	MO	17,347	C
Okla State Univ	OK	14,310	VC
Oregon State Univ	OR	20,273	VC
Purdue Univ/West Lafayette	IN	20,024	HC
Sam Houston State Univ	TX	17,082	C
S Dak State Univ	SD	14,296	C
Stephen F. Austin State Univ	TX	14,668	C
Tarleton State Univ	TX	13,489	LC
Temple Univ	PA	24,392	VC
Texas A&M Univ	TX	19,207	VC
Texas Tech Univ	TX	14,243	C
Truman State Univ	MO	15,541	HC
Tuskegee Univ	AL	26,750	C
Univ of Arkansas at Fayetteville	AR	18,352	C+
Univ of Cincinnati	OH	21,506	VC
Univ of Conn	CT	24,706	HC
Univ of Florida	FL	15,943	HC
Univ of Georgia	GA	20,082	VC
Univ of Idaho	ID	14,558	C
Univ of Illinois at Urbana-Champaign	IL	26,450	HC
Univ of Maine	ME	19,902	C+
Univ of Minn Crookston	MN	17,834	C
Univ of Nebr - Lincoln	NE	18,031	VC
Univ of New Hampshire	NH	26,912	C
Univ of PR/Mayaguez	PR	1,250	
Univ of Vermont	VT	27,006	VC+
Univ of Wisc/Madison	WI	18,757	HC+
Univ of Wisc/Platteville	WI	14,564	C
Univ of Wisc/River Falls	WI	9,722	LC
Virginia Polytechnic Inst and State Univ	VA	14,629	HC
Washington State Univ	WA	20,461	C
West Virginia Univ	WV	16,542	C+

HOSPICE CARE

School	ST	$IS	SR
Madonna Univ	MI	24,540	VC

HOSPITAL ADMINISTRATION

School	ST	$IS	SR
Missouri State Univ	MO	13,996	C+
Thomas Edison State College	NJ	5,700	SP
Univ of Minn/Duluth	MN	19,806	C
Univ of Wisc-Milwaukee	WI	18,436	C

HOSPITALITY MANAGEMENT SERVICES

School	ST	$IS	SR
Appalachian State Univ	NC	12,919	VC
Arkansas Tech Univ	AR	13,982	LC
Ashford Univ	CA	10,480	C
Brigham Young Univ/Hawaii	HI	10,686	VC
Buffalo State College / SUNY	NY	15,733	C+
Burlington College	VT	32,510	SP
Central Conn State Univ	CT	19,749	C
College of Charleston	SC	22,145	VC
Colo State Univ-Fort Collins	CO	20,385	VC
Concordia Univ, Ann Arbor	MI	27,220	VC
Dallas Baptist Univ	TX	30,580	VC
Davis & Elkins College	WV	33,742	C
Delta State Univ	MS	12,292	LC
DePaul Univ	IL	47,623	VC

School	ST	$IS	SR
East Carolina Univ	NC	14,169	C
Eastern Mich Univ	MI	18,604	C
Endicott College	MA	43,228	VC+
Ferris State Univ	MI	20,047	C
Florida Atlantic Univ	FL	17,339	C
Florida International Univ	FL	17,747	C+
Georgia State Univ	GA	15,582	VC
Harris-Stowe State Univ	MO	14,360	NC
Husson Univ	ME	24,194	LC
Indiana Univ-Purdue Univ Fort Wayne	IN	15,521	C
James Madison Univ	VA	18,049	VC
Johnson & Wales Univ/ Charlotte Campus	NC	29,576	C
Johnson & Wales Univ/North Miami Campus	FL		C
Johnson & Wales Univ/ Providence Campus	RI	29,576	C
Johnson State College	VT	16,721	C
Kendall College	IL	32,610	NC
Kent State Univ	OH	19,920	C
Lakeland College	WI	22,990	C
Lasell College	MA	43,750	LC
Livingstone College	NC	17,815	LC
Madonna Univ	MI	24,540	VC
Marywood Univ	PA	45,595	C
Metropolitan State Univ	MN	5,923	
Metropolitan State Univ of Denver	CO	4,835	LC
Mich State Univ	MI	22,450	VC
Mitchell College	CT	40,983	C
Monroe College	NY	20,240	C
Montclair State Univ	NJ	22,614	C
Morgan State Univ	MD	14,500	VC
Mount Ida College	MA	30,115	LC
New York College of Technology/The CUNY	NY	5,769	NC
New York Inst of Technology	NY	45,010	VC
Norfolk State Univ	VA	10,531	LC
N Dak State Univ	ND		C
Northwestern State Univ of Louisiana	LA	14,368	C
Pace Univ	NY	53,367	C
Purdue Univ/West Lafayette	IN	20,024	HC
Robert Morris Univ	PA	37,864	C
Rutgers, The State Univ of New Jersey/Camden Campus	NJ	25,121	C
St. Leo Univ	FL	30,340	C
San Diego State Univ	CA	21,611	C+
San Francisco State Univ	CA	18,514	C
Southeast Missouri State Univ	MO	15,370	LC
Southern New Hampshire Univ	NH	38,100	C
Southern Oregon Univ	OR	17,874	C
St. John's Univ	NY	55,070	C+
St. Joseph's College, New York/Brooklyn Campus	NY	22,630	C
St. Joseph's College, New York/Suffolk Campus	NY	22,630	C
St. Thomas Univ	FL	32,310	LC
Stephen F. Austin State Univ	TX	14,668	C
Ohio State Univ-Columbus Campus	OH	19,887	HC+
The Pennsylvania State Univ - Univ Park	PA	28,022	VC+
The Univ of Memphis	TN	15,094	C
The Univ of N Car at Greensboro	NC	12,848	C
Thomas Edison State College	NJ	5,700	SP
Tougaloo College	MS	15,275	NC
Tuskegee Univ	AL	26,750	C
Univ of Arkansas at Fayetteville	AR	18,352	C+
Univ of Central Florida	FL	15,668	VC+
Univ of Denver	CO	51,787	VC+
Univ of Findlay	OH	31,916	C
Univ of Illinois at Urbana-Champaign	IL	26,450	HC
Univ of Mass Amherst	MA	24,215	VC+
Univ of Miss	MS	16,704	C
Univ of Nebr - Lincoln	NE	18,031	VC
Univ of New Hampshire	NH	26,912	C
Univ of New Haven	CT	48,940	C
Univ of North Texas	TX	15,628	C
Univ of Pittsburgh at Bradford	PA	21,802	C
Univ of San Francisco	CA	54,770	VC
Univ of Wisc/Stout	WI	15,459	C
Webber International Univ	FL	30,147	C
Western Carolina Univ	NC	13,965	C
Western Kentucky Univ	KY	11,000	C
Widener Univ	PA	52,418	C
Youngstown State Univ	OH	16,732	C

HOTEL AND RESTAURANT ADMINISTRATION

School	ST	$IS	SR
Cornell Univ	NY	60,964	MC
Ferris State Univ	MI	20,047	C
N Dak State Univ	ND		C
Southern Oregon Univ	OR	17,874	C

HOTEL/MOTEL AND RESTAURANT MANAGEMENT

School	ST	$IS	SR
Ashland Univ	OH	25,000	C
Auburn Univ	AL	22,378	VC+
Bethune-Cookman Univ	FL	22,958	C
Boston Univ	MA	60,694	MC
Calif State Polytechnic Univ, Pomona	CA	20,156	C
Cheyney Univ of Pennsylvania	PA	20,372	LC
College of the Ozarks	MO		VC
Colo State Univ-Fort Collins	CO	20,385	VC
Concord Univ	WV	13,102	C
Delaware State Univ	DE	16,722	LC
Drexel Univ	PA	61,418	VC+
East Stroudsburg Univ of Pennsylvania	PA	18,868	LC
Eastern Mich Univ	MI	18,604	C
Endicott College	MA	43,228	VC+
Fairleigh Dickinson Univ/ College at Florham	NJ	42,142	C
Fairleigh Dickinson Univ/ Metropolitan Campus	NJ	40,254	C
Ferris State Univ	MI	20,047	C
Florida State Univ	FL	16,715	VC
Grambling State Univ	LA	13,384	LC
Grand Valley State Univ	MI	17,998	C+
Indiana Univ of Pennsylvania	PA	20,846	LC
Inter-American Univ of PR/ Aguadilla Campus	PR	5,578	
Iowa State Univ	IA	16,403	C
Johnson & Wales Univ/ Charlotte Campus	NC	29,576	C
Johnson & Wales Univ/ Denver Campus	CO	29,576	C
Johnson & Wales Univ/North Miami Campus	FL		C
Johnson & Wales Univ/ Providence Campus	RI	29,576	C
Kansas State Univ	KS	15,497	VC
Kendall College	IL	32,610	NC
Keuka College	NY	30,300	C
Lynn Univ	FL	43,500	LC
Mercyhurst Univ	PA	40,700	C
New Mexico State Univ	NM	14,050	C
New York Univ	NY	61,470	MC
Newbury College	MA	43,280	LC
Niagara Univ	NY	41,010	C
N Car Wesleyan College	NC	29,440	C
N Dak State Univ	ND		C
Northern Arizona Univ	AZ	19,010	C
Northwood Univ	FL	33,192	LC
Northwood Univ	MI	26,331	LC
Ohio Univ	OH	21,080	C
Okla State Univ	OK	14,310	VC
Purdue Univ/Calumet	IN	14,336	C
Rochester Inst of Technology	NY	42,450	VC
Roosevelt Univ	IL	22,605	VC
San Francisco State Univ	CA	18,514	C
S Dak State Univ	SD	14,296	C
Southwest Minn State Univ	MN	14,000	C
SUNY Plattsburgh / SUNY	NY	18,083	C
Tenn State Univ	TN	9,048	C
Texas Tech Univ	TX	14,243	C
Univ of Alaska Anchorage	AK	16,673	NC
Univ of Central Missouri	MO	14,605	C
Univ of Delaware	DE	23,612	VC
Univ of Houston	TX	19,796	VC
Univ of Kentucky	KY	19,868	C
Univ of Louisiana at Lafayette	LA	6,130	C
Univ of Maryland/Eastern Shore	MD	14,000	C
Univ of Missouri/Columbia	MO	18,201	MC
Univ of Nevada, Las Vegas	NV	17,303	C
Univ of New Haven	CT	48,940	C
Univ of New Orleans	LA	9,224	C
Univ of San Francisco	CA	54,770	VC
Univ of S Car at Columbia	SC	19,725	VC+
Univ of Southern Miss	MS	13,170	C
Univ of Tenn at Knoxville	TN	20,364	VC+
Univ of Wisc/Stout	WI	15,459	C
Virginia Polytechnic Inst and State Univ	VA	14,629	HC
Virginia State Univ	VA	11,318	C+
Washington State Univ	WA	20,461	C
Wiley College	TX		LC
Youngstown State Univ	OH	16,732	C

HUMAN BIOLOGY

School	ST	$IS	SR
Ohio Univ	OH	21,080	C

HUMAN BIOLOGY, HEALTH, AND SOCIETY

School	ST	$IS	SR
Cornell Univ	NY	60,964	MC
Indiana Univ Bloomington	IN	19,801	C

HUMAN DEVELOPMENT

School	ST	$IS	SR
Alabama A&M Univ	AL	10,084	C
Amridge Univ	AL	6,870	LC
Andrews Univ	MI	28,030	C+
Anna Maria College	MA	34,600	C

School	ST	$IS	SR
Arizona State Univ, at the Tempe Campus	AZ	20,137	C+
Auburn Univ	AL	22,378	VC+
Binghamton Univ/The SUNY	NY	21,648	HC+
Boston College	MA	60,622	MC
Bowling Green State Univ	OH	18,970	C
Brigham Young Univ	UT	12,100	HC
Brown Univ	RI	59,428	MC
Cal State, East Bay	CA	16,549	C
Cal State, Long Beach	CA	17,502	C+
Cal State, San Bernardino	CA	12,000	C
Cal State, San Marcos	CA	14,576	LC
Colo State Univ-Fort Collins	CO	20,385	VC
Conn College	CT	54,970	MC
Cornell Univ	NY	60,964	MC
Earlham College	IN	51,470	HC
East Tenn State Univ	TN	9,000	C
Eckerd College	FL	43,902	C
Goddard College	VT	16,418	VC
Hellenic College/Holy Cross Greek Orthodox School of Theology	MA	33,190	C
Hope International Univ	CA	34,650	C
Howard Univ	DC	13,646	C
Kalamazoo College	MI	49,740	HC
Kent State Univ	OH	19,920	C
Lee Univ	TN	18,690	C+
Marylhurst Univ	OR	20,295	NC
Messiah College	PA	40,690	C
Minn State Univ, Mankato	MN	15,616	C
Mitchell College	CT	40,983	C
Montana State Univ	MT	14,068	C
National Louis Univ	IL	16,915	LC
N Dak State Univ	ND		C
Northwestern Univ	IL	61,640	MC
Nova Southeastern Univ	FL	27,280	C
Oakwood Univ	AL	25,529	NC
Ohio Univ	OH	21,080	C
Okla State Univ	OK	14,310	VC
Oregon State Univ	OR	20,273	VC
Oswego / SUNY	NY	20,009	VC
Penn State Univ/Altoona	PA	11,464	C
Prescott College	AZ	33,284	C
Rivier Univ	NH	35,000	VC
Samford Univ	AL	37,060	C+
San Diego Christian College	CA	31,012	C
Sonoma State Univ	CA	20,541	C
S Dak State Univ	SD	14,296	C
Southern Nazarene Univ	OK	24,354	C
SUNY/Empire State College	NY	6,315	SP
Suffolk Univ	MA	47,298	C
SUNY Plattsburgh / SUNY	NY	18,083	C
Tarleton State Univ	TX	13,489	LC
Tenn Wesleyan College	TN	21,250	C
Texas Tech Univ	TX	14,243	C
Ohio State Univ-Columbus Campus	OH	19,887	HC+
The Pennsylvania State Univ - Univ Park	PA	28,022	VC+
The Univ of Memphis	TN	15,094	C
The Univ of N Car at Greensboro	NC	12,848	C
The Univ of Utah	UT	16,463	VC
Univ of Alabama at Tuscaloosa	AL	17,164	C+
Univ of Arizona	AZ	20,657	C
Univ of Arkansas at Fayetteville	AR	18,352	C+
Univ of Bridgeport	CT	39,030	LC
Univ of Calif at Davis	CA		HC
Univ of Calif at San Diego	CA	21,000	VC
Univ of Chicago	IL	55,416	MC
Univ of Conn	CT	24,706	VC
Univ of Delaware	DE	23,612	VC
Univ of Georgia	GA	20,082	VC
Univ of Idaho	ID	14,558	C
Univ of Illinois at Urbana-Champaign	IL	26,450	HC
Univ of Miami	FL	57,034	MC
Univ of Missouri/Columbia	MO	18,201	MC
Univ of Nebr at Kearney	NE	14,855	LC
Univ of New Mexico	NM	15,300	C
Univ of Pittsburgh at Bradford	PA	21,802	C
Univ of Vermont	VT	27,006	VC+
Univ of Wisc/Green Bay	WI	19,074	C
Univ of Wisc/Madison	WI	18,757	HC+
Univ of Wisc/Stout	WI	15,459	C
Utah State Univ	UT	12,044	C
Vanderbilt Univ	TN	58,220	MC
Virginia Polytechnic Inst and State Univ	VA	14,629	HC
Warner Pacific College	OR	25,550	C
Washington State Univ	WA	20,461	C
Wheelock College	MA	33,075	C

HUMAN DEVELOPMENT & FAMILY STUDIES

School	ST	$IS	SR
Univ of Rhode Island	RI	24,002	C

HUMAN ECOLOGY

School	ST	$IS	SR
College of the Atlantic	ME	48,204	HC+
Goddard College	VT	16,418	VC
Kansas State Univ	KS	15,497	VC

ST = STATE $IS = IN-STATE COSTS   SR = SELECTOR RATING

School	ST	$IS	SR
Montclair State Univ	NJ	22,614	C
Prescott College	AZ	33,284	C
Tenn Tech Univ	TN	11,310	C
Ohio State Univ-Columbus Campus	OH	19,887	HC+
Univ of Calif at Davis	CA		HC
Univ of Texas at Austin	TX	44,074	HC
Virginia Wesleyan College	VA	28,433	LC

HUMAN RESOURCES

School	ST	$IS	SR
Adelphi Univ	NY	44,670	VC
Alderson Broaddus Univ	WV	28,656	C
Alvernia Univ	PA	39,250	LC
American International College	MA	36,100	LC
Amridge Univ	AL	6,870	LC
Aquinas College	MI	33,060	C
Baldwin Wallace Univ	OH	38,318	C
Ball State Univ	IN	17,850	C
Barton College	NC	27,660	LC
Baylor Univ	TX	50,329	HC
Black Hills State Univ	SD	13,947	C
Bluffton Univ	OH	38,948	C
Boston College	MA	60,622	MC
Brescia Univ	KY	26,140	VC+
Briar Cliff Univ	IA	29,514	C
Bryant Univ	RI	49,179	VC
Calif State Polytechnic Univ, Pomona	CA	20,156	C
Cal State, San Bernardino	CA	12,000	C
Carlow Univ	PA	30,272	C
Chestnut Hill College	PA	42,110	LC
Colo Christian Univ	CO	27,500	VC
Columbia College	MO	24,578	C
Davenport Univ	MI	21,002	LC
De Sales Univ	PA	43,970	C
Defiance College	OH	30,645	C
DePaul Univ	IL	47,623	VC
Dominican College	NY	31,270	LC
Elizabethtown College School of Continuing and Professional Studies	PA		VC
Excelsior College	NY	5,580	SP
Faulkner Univ	AL	25,720	LC
Ferris State Univ	MI	20,047	C
Florida Atlantic Univ	FL	17,339	C
Franklin Univ	OH	20,985	SP
Friends Univ	KS	29,100	C
George Washington Univ	DC	57,108	MC
Golden Gate Univ	CA	17,000	C
Goldey-Beacom College	DE	27,493	C
Gwynedd-Mercy College	PA	33,560	C
Hawaii Pacific Univ	HI	34,360	C
Holy Names Univ	CA	40,310	NC
Idaho State Univ	ID	12,307	C
Indiana Univ of Pennsylvania	PA	20,846	LC
Inter-American Univ of PR/ Aguadilla Campus	PR	5,578	
Inter-American Univ of PR/ Bayamon Univ College	PR	4,428	
John Carroll Univ	OH	46,300	C+
Juniata College	PA	49,340	VC
Kentucky Wesleyan College	KY	27,440	C
Lake Erie College	OH	37,266	C
Le Moyne College	NY	43,470	C
Lewis Univ	IL	23,050	C
Limestone College	SC	30,800	C
Lindenwood Univ	MO	20,750	C
Louisiana State Univ	LA	18,677	C+
Lourdes Univ	OH	26,055	LC
Loyola Univ Chicago	IL	51,646	VC+
Lynchburg College	VA	42,645	C
Marietta College	OH	42,135	C+
Marquette Univ	WI	46,930	VC+
Menlo College	CA	49,002	C
Metropolitan State Univ	MN	5,923	
Mich State Univ	MI	22,450	VC
Midway College	KY	20,150	LC
Mount Aloysius College	PA	29,976	C
Mount Mercy Univ	IA	35,320	C
New York Univ	NY	61,490	MC
Niagara Univ	NY	41,010	C
Nichols College	MA	37,240	LC
North Central College	IL	38,343	VC
Northeastern Illinois Univ	IL	10,318	LC
Northern Kentucky Univ	KY	21,134	C
Notre Dame College	OH	34,942	VC
Oakland Univ	MI	19,391	C
Okla Wesleyan Univ	OK	21,300	C
Oswego / SUNY	NY	20,009	VC
Our Lady of the Lake Univ	TX	22,430	LC
Park Univ	MO	17,525	C
Peirce College	PA	12,760	NC
Pennsylvania College of Technology	PA	26,286	NC
Point Park Univ	PA	36,390	C
Purdue Univ/West Lafayette	IN	20,024	HC
Rider Univ	NJ	45,720	C
Rowan Univ	NJ	24,022	VC+
Rutgers, The State Univ of New Jersey/New Brunswick	NJ	25,562	VC
St. Joseph's Univ	PA	55,006	VC
St. Leo Univ	FL	30,340	C
St. Mary-of-the-Woods College	IN	37,722	LC
St. Mary's Univ	TX	33,854	C
Seton Hill Univ	PA	35,172	C
Silver Lake College	WI	22,600	LC
Simpson Univ	CA	28,900	C
Southern Illinois Univ Edwardsville	IL	17,532	C
SUNY/Empire State College	NY	6,315	SP
Tarleton State Univ	TX	13,489	LC
Tenn Wesleyan College	TN	21,250	C
Ohio State Univ-Columbus Campus	OH	19,887	HC+
The Univ of Okla	OK	18,621	VC
Thomas College	ME	33,560	LC
Trinity International Univ	IL	31,070	VC
Univ of Arkansas at Fayetteville	AR	18,352	C+
Univ of Central Missouri	MO	14,605	C
Univ of Central Okla	OK	12,293	C
Univ of Findlay	OH	31,916	C
Univ of Florida	FL	15,943	HC
Univ of Georgia	GA	20,082	VC
Univ of Hawaii at Manoa	HI	19,379	C
Univ of Idaho	ID	14,558	C
Univ of Illinois at Urbana-Champaign	IL	26,450	HC
Univ of Maryland/Univ College	MD	6,168	SP
Univ of Mich-Flint	MI	17,547	C+
Univ of Mount Olive	NC	18,426	C
Univ of Mount Union	OH	35,130	C
Univ of Nebr - Lincoln	NE	18,031	VC
Univ of Nevada, Las Vegas	NV	17,303	C
Univ of N Dak	ND	14,551	C
Univ of North Texas	TX	15,628	C
Univ of Pennsylvania	PA	61,132	MC
Univ of Pittsburgh at Pittsburgh	PA	28,572	HC+
Univ of PR/Humacao	PR	1,877	
Univ of Scranton	PA	51,940	VC
Univ of Tenn at Knoxville	TN	20,364	VC+
Univ of Texas at San Antonio	TX	18,372	C
Univ of the Incarnate Word	TX	37,316	LC
Univ of Wisc/Green Bay	WI	19,074	C
Univ of Wisc/Madison	WI	18,757	HC+
Univ of Wisc/Oshkosh	WI	10,426	LC
Univ of Wisc-Milwaukee	WI	18,436	C
Ursuline College	OH	33,198	LC
Valley City State Univ	ND	12,286	LC
Washington Univ in St. Louis	MO	69,844	MC
Western Mich Univ	MI	19,628	C
Western Washington Univ	WA	18,519	VC
Wichita State Univ	KS	14,607	C+
Xavier Univ	OH	44,980	VC
York College	NE	19,475	C
Youngstown State Univ	OH	16,732	C

HUMAN RESOURCES/ ORGANIZATIONAL MGMT

School	ST	$IS	SR
Ashford Univ	CA	10,480	C
Black Hills State Univ	SD	13,947	C
Bloomfield College	NJ	37,850	LC
Georgia Southwestern State Univ	GA	13,246	C
Indiana Univ Bloomington	IN	19,801	VC
Indiana Univ-Purdue Univ Indianapolis	IN	17,611	C
Lipscomb Univ	TN	37,490	VC
LIU Brooklyn	NY	47,182	LC
Mercy College	NY	30,456	C
Missouri Southern State Univ	MO	12,061	C
Murray State Univ	KY	15,304	C
New York Inst of Technology	NY	45,010	VC
Thomas Edison State College	NJ	5,700	SP
Univ of Miami	FL	57,034	MC
Western Illinois Univ	IL	20,732	C
Winona State Univ	MN	16,640	C

HUMAN SERVICES

School	ST	$IS	SR
Alaska Pacific Univ	AK	43,592	VC
Albertus Magnus College	CT	37,382	LC
Aquinas College	MI	33,060	C
Arkansas Baptist College	AR	15,750	NC
Assumption College	MA	47,122	C+
Beacon College	FL	41,720	C
Bethel College	IN	31,560	C
Bethel Univ	TN	19,186	C
Black Hills State Univ	SD	13,947	C
Bloomfield College	NJ	37,850	LC
Boricua College	NY	8,600	C
Brewton-Parker College	GA	33,388	C
Burlington College	VT	32,510	SP
Cal State, Dominguez Hills	CA	17,090	LC
Cal State, Fullerton	CA	25,188	C
Cal State, Monterey Bay	CA	26,871	C
Cal State, San Bernardino	CA	12,000	C
Calumet College of St. Joseph	IN	15,000	C
Cambridge College	MA	13,392	NC
Cazenovia College	NY	43,464	C
Chestnut Hill College	PA	42,110	LC
College of St Joseph	VT	30,600	LC
Columbia College	MO	24,578	C
Dakota Wesleyan Univ	SD	23,000	C
Drury Univ	MO	31,909	VC
East Central Univ	OK	10,223	LC
Eastern New Mexico Univ	NM	10,682	C
Elizabethtown College School of Continuing and Professional Studies	PA		VC
Elmira College	NY	49,950	C+
Elon Univ	NC	41,914	VC+
Fitchburg State Univ	MA	18,173	C
Fontbonne Univ	MO	31,384	C
Friends Univ	KS	29,100	C
Geneva College	PA	27,280	C
George Washington Univ	DC	57,108	MC
Goodwin College	CT	19,400	LC
Grace Bible College	MI	20,770	C
Graceland Univ	IA	28,020	C
Grand View Univ	IA	31,050	C
Gwynedd-Mercy College	PA	33,560	C
Hastings College	NE	27,782	C+
Hawaii Pacific Univ	HI	34,360	C
Henderson State Univ	AR	14,584	C
High Point Univ	NC	39,800	C
Hilbert College	NY	28,550	C
Holy Names Univ	CA	40,310	NC
Hope International Univ	CA	34,650	C
Indiana Inst of Technology	IN	34,240	LC
Indiana Univ-Purdue Univ Fort Wayne	IN	15,521	C
Kennesaw State Univ	GA		C
Kent State Univ	OH	19,920	C
Lake Superior State Univ	MI	18,121	C
Lasell College	MA	43,750	LC
Le Moyne College	NY	43,470	C
Lenoir-Rhyne College	NC	35,984	C
Lesley Univ	MA	46,350	C
Lindenwood Univ	MO	20,750	C
Lindsey Wilson College	KY	31,220	C
Loyola Univ Chicago	IL	51,646	VC+
Lyndon State College	VT	14,233	C
Metropolitan College of New York	NY	16,720	VC
Metropolitan State Univ	MN	5,923	
Metropolitan State Univ of Denver	CO	4,835	LC
Millikin Univ	IL	38,940	C
Missouri Baptist Univ	MO	31,830	C
Missouri Valley College	MO	22,200	C
Montana State Univ-Billings	MT	12,425	LC
Montreat College	NC	31,298	C
Mount St. Mary College	NY	41,138	C
Mount St. Mary's Univ	MD	47,996	C
National Louis Univ	IL	16,915	LC
New York College of Technology/The CUNY	NY	5,769	NC
N Car Central Univ	NC	9,000	C
Northern State Univ - Aberdeen	SD	14,505	C
Northwest Christian Univ	OR	27,399	C
Notre Dame de Namur Univ	CA	44,236	LC
Nova Southeastern Univ	FL	37,280	VC
Oglala Lakota College	SD	2,000	NC
Old Dominion Univ	VA	19,483	LC
Ottawa Univ	KS	15,000	VC
Park Univ	MO	17,525	C
Pfeiffer Univ	NC	33,700	LC
Prescott College	AZ	33,284	C
Queens Univ of Charlotte	NC	39,543	C+
Quincy Univ	IL	34,980	LC
St. Leo Univ	FL	30,340	C
St. Mary-of-the-Woods College	IN	37,722	LC
St. Mary's Univ of Minn	MN	38,280	C
Salem International Univ	WV	21,090	LC
Seton Hill Univ	PA	35,172	C
Siena Heights Univ	MI	32,040	C
Sinte Gleska Univ	SD	2,300	NC
S Car State Univ	SC	6,700	LC
Southern Oregon Univ	OR	17,874	C
Southern Wesleyan Univ	SC	25,600	C
Southwest Baptist Univ	MO	24,710	C
Springfield College	MA	25,000	C
St. John's Univ	NY	55,070	C+
St. Joseph's College, New York/Brooklyn Campus	NY	22,630	C
St. Joseph's College, New York/Suffolk Campus	NY	22,630	C
St. Thomas Univ	FL	32,310	LC
Stevenson Univ	MD	41,470	C
Suffolk Univ	MA	47,298	C
SUNY Cortland/The SUNY	NY	19,759	C+
Tenn Wesleyan College	TN	21,250	C
Texas Southern Univ	TX	18,212	LC
The Lincoln Univ	PA	15,154	LC
Thomas Edison State College	NJ	5,700	SP
Touro College	NY	27,959	VC
Trinity Washington Univ	DC	30,250	C+
Troy Univ	AL	10,650	C
Univ of Alaska Anchorage	AK	16,673	NC
Univ of Bridgeport	CT	39,030	LC
Univ of Delaware	DE	23,612	VC
Univ of Detroit Mercy	MI	30,450	VC
Univ of Great Falls	MT	27,970	C
Univ of Hartford	CT	42,674	C
Univ of Maine at Machias	ME	10,523	C
Univ of Mass Boston	MA	23,066	VC
Univ of Mount Olive	NC	18,426	C
Univ of New Mexico	NM	15,300	C
Univ of North Texas	TX	15,628	C
Univ of Northern Colo	CO	18,446	C
Univ of Scranton	PA	51,940	VC
Univ of Wisc/Oshkosh	WI	10,426	LC
Upper Iowa Univ	IA	30,426	NC
Washburn Univ	KS	12,579	C
Wayland Baptist Univ	TX	18,912	LC
Waynesburg Univ	PA	30,150	C
Western New Mexico Univ	NM	8,500	LC
Western Washington Univ	WA	18,519	VC
William Penn Univ	IA	26,000	C
Wingate Univ	NC	34,990	C
York College	NE	19,475	C

HUMAN STUDIES

School	ST	$IS	SR
Univ of Rhode Island	RI	24,002	C

HUMANITIES

School	ST	$IS	SR
Albertus Magnus College	CT	37,382	LC
Anna Maria College	MA	34,600	C
Belhaven Univ	MS	27,170	C
Bennington College	VT	56,990	HC+
Biola Univ	CA	40,320	C+
Bloomfield College	NJ	37,850	LC
Bluefield State College	WV	3,140	LC
Brigham Young Univ	UT	12,100	HC
Bucknell Univ	PA	60,140	MC
Buffalo State College / SUNY	NY	15,733	C+
Cal State, Chico	CA	20,158	C
Cal State, Fresno	CA	17,405	C
Cal State, Monterey Bay	CA	26,871	LC
Cal State, Northridge	CA	28,690	LC
Cal State, San Bernardino	CA	12,000	C
Chaminade Univ of Honolulu	HI	31,664	LC
Charleston Southern Univ	SC	22,420	C
Clarkson Univ	NY	57,330	HC
Clearwater Christian College	FL	23,720	C
Colby-Sawyer College	NH	50,790	C
Colgate Univ	NY	58,135	MC
College of St. Benedict	MN	49,359	VC
College of St. Mary	NE	35,184	C
College of St. Scholastica	MN	41,440	C
Concordia College - Moorhead	MN	39,974	VC
Concordia Univ	OR	35,000	C
Concordia Univ Irvine	CA	35,390	VC
Concordia Univ Wisc	WI	28,980	C
Corban Univ	OR	37,380	C+
Cornerstone Univ and Grand Rapids Theological Seminary	MI	33,338	C
Defiance College	OH	30,645	C
DePaul Univ	IL	47,623	VC
Dominican College	NY	31,270	LC
Dominican Univ of Calif	CA	51,250	C
Dowling College	NY	25,000	C
Duquesne Univ	PA	43,720	VC
Eastern Washington Univ	WA		C
Eckerd College	FL	43,902	C
Edinboro Univ of Pennsylvania	PA	15,940	LC
Fairleigh Dickinson Univ/ College at Florham	NJ	42,142	C
Fairleigh Dickinson Univ/ Metropolitan Campus	NJ	40,254	C
Faulkner Univ	AL	25,720	LC
Felician College	NJ	41,640	LC
Florida Inst of Technology	FL	48,290	VC
Florida Southern College	FL	40,150	C+
Florida State Univ	FL	16,715	VC
Fort Lewis College	CO	15,513	C
George Washington Univ	DC	57,108	MC
Georgian Court Univ	NJ	41,594	LC
Hampden-Sydney College	VA	51,758	C
Hampshire College	MA	58,320	MC
Harding Univ	AR	23,556	C
Harvard College/Harvard Univ	MA	49,000	MC
Hawaii Pacific Univ	HI	34,360	C
Holy Family Univ	PA	40,030	LC
Holy Names Univ	CA	40,310	NC
Houghton College	NY	36,808	C+
Illinois Inst of Technology	IL	38,512	HC+
Indiana Univ East	IN	6,783	C
Indiana Univ East	IN	6,783	C
Indiana Univ Kokomo	IN	6,811	LC
Jacksonville Univ	FL	37,780	C
John Carroll Univ	OH	46,300	C+
Johns Hopkins Univ	MD	47,492	MC
Johnson State College	VT	16,721	C
Kansas State Univ	KS	15,497	VC
Kentucky Christian Univ	KY	17,622	LC
Lasell College	MA	43,750	LC
Lawrence Tech Univ	MI	37,630	VC
Lee Univ	TN	18,690	C+
Lees-McRae College	NC	33,944	C
LeMoyne-Owen College	TN	13,100	C
Lesley Univ	MA	46,350	C
LIU Brooklyn	NY	47,182	LC
Loyola Marymount Univ	CA	54,649	VC+
Lubbock Christian Univ	TX	26,308	C
Macalester College	MN	57,691	MC
Maritime College/SUNY	NY	16,020	C
Marshall Univ	WV	14,820	C
Martin Univ	IN	11,000	SP

School	ST	$IS	SR
Mass Inst of Technology	MA	58,240	MC
Mich State Univ	MI	22,450	VC
Midwestern State Univ	TX	9,722	C
Milligan College	TN	27,510	C
Minn State Univ, Mankato	MN	15,616	C
Montana State Univ-Northern	MT	12,500	NC
Montclair State Univ	NJ	22,614	C
Mount Aloysius College	PA	29,976	C
New College of Florida	FL	14,504	C
New York Univ	NY	61,470	MC
N Dak State Univ	ND		C
Northwest Christian Univ	OR	27,399	C
Northwest Missouri State Univ	MO	17,347	C
Northwestern State Univ of Louisiana	LA	14,368	C
Notre Dame de Namur Univ	CA	44,236	LC
Oberlin College	OH	61,788	MC
Ohio Valley Univ	WV	17,752	C
Okla City Univ	OK	40,476	VC
Pacific Univ	OR	49,626	C+
Paul Quinn College	TX	25,350	LC
Pepperdine Univ	CA	55,372	HC+
Plymouth State Univ	NH	23,148	LC
Polytechnic Inst of New York Univ	NY	53,064	HC+
Prescott College	AZ	33,284	C
Providence College	RI	57,383	VC
Quincy Univ	IL	34,980	LC
Roberts Wesleyan College	NY	38,306	C
Rockford College	IL	31,000	C
Roger Williams Univ	RI	46,296	VC
Rollins College	FL	52,370	HC
Rosemont College	PA	42,350	C
Rutgers, The State Univ of New Jersey/New Brunswick	NJ	25,562	VC
St. John's Univ	MN	47,984	C
St. Louis Univ	MO	48,346	HC
St. Mary-of-the-Woods College	IN	37,722	LC
St. Mary's College	IN	45,160	C+
St. Peter's Univ	NJ	44,240	C
San Diego State Univ	CA	21,611	C+
San Francisco State Univ	CA	18,514	C
Schreiner Univ	TX	32,734	LC
Scripps College	CA	61,940	MC
Seattle Univ	WA	49,035	VC+
Shawnee State Univ	OH	16,916	C
Shimer College	IL	32,875	VC
Siena Heights Univ	MI	32,040	C
Sierra Nevada College	NV	32,700	VC
Southern Methodist Univ	TX	60,585	MC
Spring Hill College	AL	44,164	VC
St. Andrews Univ	NC	32,050	LC
St. Norbert College	WI	41,478	VC
Stony Brook Univ / SUNY	NY	20,078	HC+
Suffolk Univ	MA	47,298	C
SUNY College at Old Westbury	NY	16,324	C
Tabor College	KS	29,010	C
Taylor Univ	IN	37,821	VC+
The Univ of Okla	OK	18,621	VC
The Univ of Tenn at Chattanooga	TN	16,883	C
The Univ of Utah	UT	16,463	VC
Thomas Edison State College	NJ	5,700	SP
Thomas More College	KY	34,760	C
Thomas Univ	GA	11,520	NC
Tougaloo College	MS	15,275	NC
Trinity International Univ	IL	31,070	VC
Tulane Univ	LA	60,861	MC
Union College	NY	60,240	MC
United States Air Force Academy	CO		MC
Universidad del Turabo	PR	4,110	
Universidad Metropolitana	PR	3,500	
Univ of Calif at Irvine	CA	25,961	VC
Univ of Central Florida	FL	15,668	VC+
Univ of Central Okla	OK	12,293	C
Univ of Chicago	IL	55,416	MC
Univ of Colo Boulder	CO	22,605	VC+
Univ of Houston-Downtown	TX	15,170	LC
Univ of Illinois at Chicago	IL	24,505	VC
Univ of Illinois at Urbana-Champaign	IL	26,450	HC
Univ of Kansas	KS	17,603	C+
Univ of Louisville	KY	17,946	C
Univ of Maryland/Univ College	MD	6,168	SP
Univ of Mich/Ann Arbor	MI	22,102	MC
Univ of Mich/Dearborn	MI	9,885	VC
Univ of Minn/Twin Cities	MN		HC
Univ of Mobile	AL	28,935	VC
Univ of New Hampshire	NH	26,912	C
Univ of Northern Iowa	IA	15,795	C
Univ of Oregon	OR	21,360	VC
Univ of Pittsburgh at Greensburg	PA	17,640	C
Univ of Pittsburgh at Johnstown	PA	20,862	LC
Univ of Pittsburgh at Pittsburgh	PA	28,572	HC+
Univ of PR/Cayey	PR	1,504	
Univ of Rio Grande	OH	8,750	NC
Univ of San Diego	CA	54,818	HC+
Univ of South Florida/Tampa	FL	13,000	C
Univ of Texas at Austin	TX	44,074	HC
Univ of Texas at Dallas	TX	21,348	HC+
Univ of Texas at San Antonio	TX	18,372	C
Univ of the Southwest	NM	15,000	C
Univ of Toledo	OH	18,464	C
Univ of Wisc/Green Bay	WI	19,074	C
Univ of Wisc/Parkside	WI	10,181	LC
Univ of Wyoming	WY	14,401	C+
Ursuline College	OH	33,198	LC
Valparaiso Univ	IN	44,940	VC+
Villanova Univ	PA	58,394	MC
Virginia Wesleyan College	VA	28,433	LC
Walla Walla Univ	WA	26,256	NC
Washington College	MD	52,602	VC
Washington State Univ	WA	20,461	C
Washington Univ in St. Louis	MO	69,844	MC
Wesleyan College	GA	24,000	C
Western New Mexico Univ	NM	8,500	LC
Western Oregon Univ	OR	15,021	C
Widener Univ	PA	52,418	C
Willamette Univ	OR	56,450	VC+
Wofford College	SC	45,795	VC
Worcester Polytechnic Inst	MA	55,860	MC
Wright State Univ	OH	16,983	C
Xavier Univ	OH	44,980	VC
Yale Univ	CT	55,300	MC
York College of Pennsylvania	PA	26,590	C

HUMANITIES AND SOCIAL SCIENCE

School	ST	$IS	SR
Alabama A&M Univ	AL	10,084	C
Bennington College	VT	56,990	HC+
Bloomfield College	NJ	37,850	LC
Canisius College	NY	44,900	C
Franciscan Univ of Steubenville	OH	27,320	VC
Goddard College	VT	16,418	VC
John Jay College of Criminal Justice/The CUNY	NY	6,359	LC
Lock Haven Univ of Pennsylvania	PA	18,028	LC
Mount Aloysius College	PA	29,976	C
New York Univ	NY	61,470	MC
Northwestern State Univ of Louisiana	LA	14,368	C
Prescott College	AZ	33,284	C
San Francisco State Univ	CA	18,514	C
Spalding Univ	KY	32,287	LC
SUNY/Empire State College	NY	6,315	SP
Texas A&M Univ at Galveston	TX	11,258	C
Univ of Calif at Riverside	CA	27,204	C+
Univ of the Sciences	PA	48,320	VC+

HVACR ENG TECH & ENERGY MANAGEMENT

School	ST	$IS	SR
Ferris State Univ	MI	20,047	C

HVACR ENGINEERING TECHNOLOGY

School	ST	$IS	SR
Ferris State Univ	MI	20,047	C

HYDROGEOLOGY

School	ST	$IS	SR
Eastern Mich Univ	MI	18,604	C
Rensselaer Polytechnic Inst	NY	61,529	HC
Western Mich Univ	MI	19,628	C

HYDROLOGY

School	ST	$IS	SR
Texas A&M Univ at Galveston	TX	11,258	C
Univ of Arizona	AZ	20,657	C
Univ of Calif at Davis	CA		HC
Univ of Calif at Santa Barbara	CA	27,551	HC
Univ of Nevada/Reno	NV	17,507	C
Univ of New Hampshire	NH	26,912	C

IBERIAN STUDIES

School	ST	$IS	SR
New York Univ	NY	61,470	MC
Southern Methodist Univ	TX	60,585	MC
Stanford Univ	CA	58,388	MC
Universidad de Puerto/Arecibo	PR	7,227	
Western New England Univ	MA	46,154	C+

ILLUSTRATION

School	ST	$IS	SR
Arcadia Univ	PA	33,570	C+
Art Academy of Cincinnati	OH	25,940	SP
Art Center College of Design	CA	34,044	SP
Bennington College	VT	56,990	HC+
Brigham Young Univ	UT	12,100	HC
Calif College of the Arts	CA	48,334	SP
Cleveland Inst of Art	OH	48,685	SP
College for Creative Studies	MI	45,340	C
College of Art and Design at Lesley Univ	MA	39,730	SP
Columbus College of Art and Design	OH	37,732	SP
Fashion Inst of Technology/SUNY	NY	18,362	SP
Ferris State Univ	MI	20,047	C
Indiana Wesleyan Univ	IN	31,815	VC
John Brown Univ	AR	32,056	VC+
Kansas City Art Inst	MO	44,308	SP
Kutztown Univ of Pennsylvania	PA	16,909	LC
Laguna College of Art and Design	CA	27,300	SP
Lawrence Tech Univ	MI	37,630	VC
Lewis Univ	IL	23,050	C
Maryland Inst College of Art	MD	39,500	SP
Marywood Univ	PA	45,595	C
Memphis College of Art	TN	33,550	SP
Milwaukee Inst of Art and Design	WI	31,938	SP
Minneapolis College of Art and Design	MN	36,700	SP
Montserrat College of Art	MA	31,000	C
Moore College of Art and Design	PA	50,135	SP
Ohio Univ	OH	21,080	C
Olivet College	MI	19,984	LC
Otis College of Art and Design	CA	35,404	SP
Pacific Northwest College of Art	OR	38,494	C
Parsons The New School for Design	NY	56,610	SP
Rhode Island School of Design	RI	57,234	MC
Ringling College of Art and Design	FL	46,130	SP
Rivier Univ	NH	35,000	C
Rochester Inst of Technology	NY	42,450	VC
Rocky Mountain College of Art and Design	CO	22,470	SP
Savannah College of Art and Design	GA	48,005	SP
School of Visual Arts	NY	36,500	VC
St. John's Univ	NY	55,070	C+
SUNY Fredonia/The SUNY at Fredonia	NY	19,840	VC
Syracuse Univ	NY	56,346	VC
Univ of Bridgeport	CT	39,030	LC
Univ of Findlay	OH	31,916	C
Univ of Hartford	CT	42,674	C
Univ of Kansas	KS	17,603	C+
Univ of Mass Dartmouth	MA	22,223	C
Univ of Mich/Ann Arbor	MI	22,102	MC
Univ of Montana-Western	MT	9,753	LC
Univ of San Francisco	CA	54,770	VC
Univ of the Arts	PA	38,450	SP
Washington Univ in St. Louis	MO	69,844	MC
Western Conn State Univ	CT	18,327	LC

IMAGING SCIENCES

School	ST	$IS	SR
Thomas Edison State College	NJ	5,700	SP

INDUSTRIAL ADMINISTRATION/MANAGEMENT

School	ST	$IS	SR
Chancellor Univ	OH	11,000	C
Clarion Univ of Pennsylvania	PA	17,370	C
Clemson Univ	SC	19,136	HC
Colo State Univ-Pueblo	CO	16,183	C
Gardner-Webb Univ	NC	34,375	C+
Grove City College	PA	24,022	VC
Illinois Inst of Technology	IL	38,512	HC+
Inter-American Univ of PR/Bayamon Univ College	PR	4,428	
Lawrence Tech Univ	MI	37,630	VC
LeTourneau Univ	TX	36,210	VC
Mercer Univ	GA	44,201	VC
Metropolitan State Univ of Denver	CO	4,835	LC
Okla State Univ	OK	14,310	VC
Oregon Inst of Technology	OR	8,910	C
Purdue Univ/West Lafayette	IN	20,024	HC
Saginaw Valley State Univ	MI	17,369	C
St. Augustine's Univ	NC	14,000	C
San Francisco State Univ	CA	18,514	C
S Dak State Univ	SD	14,296	C
Southwestern Okla State Univ	OK	9,160	C
Trine Univ	IN	39,400	HC+
Universidad Politecnica de PR	PR	19,252	
Univ of Alabama at Birmingham	AL	18,484	C+
Univ of Alabama at Tuscaloosa	AL	17,164	C+
Univ of Arkansas at Little Rock	AR	17,609	LC
Univ of Cincinnati	OH	21,506	VC
Univ of Illinois at Urbana-Champaign	IL	26,450	HC
Univ of Iowa	IA	17,693	VC
Univ of Mass Lowell	MA	19,316	C
Univ of Minn Crookston	MN	17,834	C
Univ of Nebr at Kearney	NE	14,855	LC
Univ of N Car at Asheville	NC	13,500	VC
Univ of N Car at Charlotte	NC	15,547	C
Univ of Southern Indiana	IN	14,885	C

INDUSTRIAL AND LABOR RELATIONS

School	ST	$IS	SR
Cornell Univ	NY	60,964	MC
Eastern Conn State Univ	CT	20,584	C
New York Univ	NY	61,470	MC
The Pennsylvania State Univ - Univ Park	PA	28,022	VC+

INDUSTRIAL AND ORGANIZATIONAL PSYCHOLOGY

School	ST	$IS	SR
Albertus Magnus College	CT	37,382	LC
Baldwin Wallace Univ	OH	38,318	C
Cedar Crest College	PA	43,240	C
CUNY/Baruch College	NY		HC
Coe College	IA	45,550	VC
Fitchburg State Univ	MA	18,173	C
Goddard College	VT	16,418	VC
High Point Univ	NC	39,800	C
Holy Family Univ	PA	44,030	LC
Ithaca College	NY	53,864	HC
Kutztown Univ of Pennsylvania	PA	16,909	LC
Marywood Univ	PA	45,595	C
Northwest Missouri State Univ	MO	17,347	C
Oregon Inst of Technology	OR	8,910	C
Point Loma Nazarene Univ	CA	41,006	C+
Texas Wesleyan Univ	TX	31,382	C
Ohio State Univ-Columbus Campus	OH	19,887	HC+
Universidad de Puerto/Arecibo	PR	7,227	
Univ of Georgia	GA	20,082	VC
Washington Univ in St. Louis	MO	69,844	MC

INDUSTRIAL ARTS EDUCATION

School	ST	$IS	SR
Alabama A&M Univ	AL	10,084	C
Auburn Univ	AL	22,378	VC+
Ball State Univ	IN	17,850	C
Bemidji State Univ	MN	13,500	VC
Buffalo State College / SUNY	NY	15,733	C+
Cal State, Los Angeles	CA	17,186	LC
Central Washington Univ	WA	11,730	C
Chicago State Univ	IL	5,482	C
Clemson Univ	SC	19,136	HC
Concordia Univ Nebr	NE	26,000	C
Eastern Kentucky Univ	KY	11,161	C
Eastern Mich Univ	MI	18,604	C
Elizabeth City State Univ	NC	11,638	C
Fitchburg State Univ	MA	18,173	C
Florida A&M Univ	FL	14,935	LC
Humboldt State Univ	CA	18,400	C
Indiana State Univ	IN	16,000	C
Iowa State Univ	IA	16,403	C
Langston Univ	OK	3,000	C
Montana State Univ-Northern	MT	12,500	NC
Morehead State Univ	KY	10,900	C
Murray State Univ	KY	15,304	C
N Car Agricultural and Technical State Univ	NC	13,365	LC
N Car State Univ	NC	16,202	HC
Northeastern State Univ	OK	8,615	VC
Northern Kentucky Univ	KY	21,134	C
Northern Mich Univ	MI	18,278	C
San Diego State Univ	CA	21,611	C+
San Francisco State Univ	CA	18,514	C
S Car State Univ	SC	6,700	C
Southeast Missouri State Univ	MO	15,370	LC
Southwestern Okla State Univ	OK	9,160	C
St. Cloud State Univ	MN	10,600	C
Tarleton State Univ	TX	13,489	LC
Texas A&M Univ at Commerce	TX	10,496	C
Univ of Arkansas at Pine Bluff	AR	13,378	C
Univ of Central Missouri	MO	14,605	C
Univ of Cincinnati	OH	21,506	VC
Univ of Idaho	ID	14,558	C
Univ of Louisiana at Lafayette	LA	6,130	C
Univ of Maryland/Eastern Shore	MD	14,000	VC
Univ of Minn/Twin Cities	MN		HC
Univ of Montana-Western	MT	9,753	LC
Univ of Southern Miss	MS	13,170	C
Utah State Univ	UT	12,044	C
Wayne State College	NE	11,764	NC

INDUSTRIAL DESIGN

School	ST	$IS	SR
Appalachian State Univ	NC	12,919	VC
Arizona State Univ, at the Tempe Campus	AZ	20,137	C+

ST = STATE   **$IS** = IN-STATE COSTS   **SR** = SELECTOR RATING

School	ST	$IS	SR
Art Center College of Design	CA	34,044	SP
Auburn Univ	AL	22,378	VC+
Brigham Young Univ	UT	12,100	HC
Calif College of the Arts	CA	48,334	SP
Cedarville Univ	OH	32,860	VC
Cleveland Inst of Art	OH	48,685	SP
College for Creative Studies	MI	45,340	C
Columbus College of Art and Design	OH	37,732	SP
Escuela de Artes Plasticas de PR	PR	2,660	
Ferris State Univ	MI	20,047	C
Georgia Inst of Technology	GA	21,828	MC
Kean Univ	NJ	23,444	C
Lawrence Tech Univ	MI	37,630	VC
Metropolitan State Univ of Denver	CO	4,835	LC
Milwaukee Inst of Art and Design	WI	31,938	SP
NewSchool of Architecture & Design	CA	24,900	SP
N Car State Univ	NC	16,202	HC
Otis College of Art and Design	CA	35,404	SP
Parsons The New School for Design	NY	56,610	SP
Philadelphia Univ	PA	44,160	C
Pratt Inst	NY	55,956	SP
Purdue Univ/West Lafayette	IN	20,024	HC
Rhode Island School of Design	RI	57,234	MC
Rochester Inst of Technology	NY	42,450	VC
Savannah College of Art and Design	GA	48,005	SP
Syracuse Univ	NY	56,346	VC
Ohio State Univ-Columbus Campus	OH	19,887	HC+
Univ of Bridgeport	CT	39,030	LC
Univ of Houston	TX	19,796	VC
Univ of Illinois at Chicago	IL	24,505	VC
Univ of Illinois at Urbana-Champaign	IL	26,450	HC
Univ of Kansas	KS	17,603	C+
Univ of Mich/Ann Arbor	MI	22,102	MC
Univ of the Arts	PA	38,450	SP
Virginia Polytechnic Inst and State Univ	VA	14,629	HC
Wentworth Inst of Technology	MA	29,800	C

INDUSTRIAL ENGINEERING

School	ST	$IS	SR
Alabama A&M Univ	AL	10,084	C
Arizona State Univ, at the Tempe Campus	AZ	20,137	C+
Auburn Univ	AL	22,378	VC+
Binghamton Univ/The SUNY	NY	21,648	HC+
Bradley Univ	IL	31,874	VC
Calif Polytechnic State Univ	CA	19,847	HC
Calif State Polytechnic Univ, Pomona	CA	20,156	C
Cal State, East Bay	CA	16,549	C
Cal State, Fresno	CA	17,405	C
Clemson Univ	SC	19,136	HC
Colo State Univ-Pueblo	CO	16,183	C
Elizabethtown College	PA	49,740	VC
Florida A&M Univ	FL	14,935	LC
Florida State Univ	FL	16,715	VC
Francis Marion Univ	SC	16,464	LC
George Mason Univ	VA	15,724	VC
Georgia Inst of Technology	GA	21,828	MC
Hofstra Univ	NY	51,810	VC+
Indiana Inst of Technology	IN	34,240	LC
Inter-American Univ of PR/Bayamon Univ College	PR	4,428	
Kansas State Univ	KS	15,497	VC
Kettering Univ	MI	31,456	HC
Lamar Univ	TX	6,820	LC
Lawrence Tech Univ	MI	37,630	VC
Lehigh Univ	PA	56,770	MC
Louisiana State Univ	LA	18,677	C+
Louisiana Tech Univ	LA	11,302	C
Mass Maritime Academy	MA	15,340	C
Milwaukee School of Engineering	WI	39,948	VC+
Miss State Univ	MS	14,750	C
Montana State Univ	MT	14,068	C
New Jersey Inst of Technology	NJ	26,490	C+
New Mexico State Univ	NM	14,050	C
N Car Agricultural and Technical State Univ	NC	13,365	LC
N Car State Univ	NC	16,202	HC
N Dak State Univ	ND		C
Northeastern Univ	MA	55,296	MC
Northern Illinois Univ	IL	19,768	VC
Northwestern State Univ of Louisiana	LA	14,368	C
Northwestern Univ	IL	61,640	MC
Oakland Univ	MI	19,391	C
Okla State Univ	OK	14,310	VC
Oregon State Univ	OR	20,273	VC
Philadelphia Univ	PA	44,160	C
Purdue Univ/West Lafayette	IN	20,024	HC
Quinnipiac Univ	CT	55,160	VC
Rensselaer Polytechnic Inst	NY	61,529	MC
Rochester Inst of Technology	NY	42,450	VC

School	ST	$IS	SR
Rutgers, The State Univ of New Jersey/New Brunswick	NJ	25,562	VC
St. Augustine's Univ	NC	14,000	C
St. Mary's Univ	TX	33,854	VC
San Jose State Univ	CA	19,133	LC
S Dak School of Mines and Technology	SD	15,260	VC
Southern Illinois Univ Edwardsville	IL	17,532	C
St. Ambrose Univ	IA	30,845	C
Stanford Univ	CA	58,388	MC
Tenn Tech Univ	TN	11,310	C
Texas State Univ	TX	17,128	C
Texas State Univ	TX	14,243	C
Ohio State Univ-Columbus Campus	OH	19,887	HC+
The Pennsylvania State Univ - Univ Park	PA	28,022	VC+
The Univ of Okla	OK	18,621	VC
The Univ of Tenn at Chattanooga	TN	16,883	C
Universidad Politecnica de PR	PR	19,252	
Univ at Buffalo / The SUNY	NY	20,283	VC
Univ of Alabama at Tuscaloosa	AL	17,164	C+
Univ of Alabama in Huntsville	AL	17,591	VC+
Univ of Arizona	AZ	20,657	C
Univ of Arkansas at Fayetteville	AR	18,352	C+
Univ of Calif at Berkeley	CA	23,322	MC
Univ of Central Florida	FL	15,668	VC+
Univ of Houston	TX	19,796	VC
Univ of Illinois at Urbana-Champaign	IL	26,450	HC
Univ of Iowa	IA	17,693	VC
Univ of Louisiana at Lafayette	LA	6,130	C
Univ of Louisville	KY	17,946	V
Univ of Mass Amherst	MA	24,215	VC+
Univ of Miami	FL	57,034	MC
Univ of Mich/Ann Arbor	MI	22,102	MC
Univ of Minn/Duluth	MN	19,806	C
Univ of Minn/Twin Cities	MN		HC
Univ of Missouri/Columbia	MO	18,201	MC
Univ of Pittsburgh at Pittsburgh	PA	28,572	HC+
Univ of PR/Mayaguez	PR	1,250	
Univ of San Diego	CA	54,818	HC+
Univ of South Florida/Tampa	FL	13,000	C
Univ of Southern Calif	CA	56,903	MC
Univ of Tenn at Knoxville	TN	20,364	VC+
Univ of Toledo	OH	18,464	C
Univ of Wisc/Madison	WI	18,757	HC+
Univ of Wisc/Platteville	WI	14,564	C
Univ of Wisc-Milwaukee	WI	18,436	C
Utah State Univ	UT	12,044	C
Virginia Polytechnic Inst and State Univ	VA	14,629	HC
Wayne State Univ	MI	22,063	C
Western Mich Univ	MI	19,628	C
Western New England Univ	MA	46,154	C+
Wichita State Univ	KS	14,607	C+
Worcester Polytechnic Inst	MA	55,860	MC
Wright State Univ	OH	16,983	C
Youngstown State Univ	OH	16,732	C

INDUSTRIAL ENGINEERING TECHNOLOGY

School	ST	$IS	SR
Alabama A&M Univ	AL	10,084	C
Appalachian State Univ	NC	12,919	VC
Arizona State Univ, at the Tempe Campus	AZ	20,137	C+
Ball State Univ	IN	17,850	C
Bemidji State Univ	MN	13,500	VC
Berea College	KY	7,192	C
Buffalo State College / SUNY	NY	15,733	C
Cal State, Fresno	CA	17,405	C
Cal State, Los Angeles	CA	17,186	LC
Calif Univ of Pennsylvania	PA	14,217	C
Caribbean Univ	PR	10,375	
Central Conn State Univ	CT	19,749	C
Central Washington Univ	WA	11,730	C
Chadron State College	NE	7,400	NC
Columbia Univ/City of New York	NY	61,116	MC
East Carolina Univ	NC	14,169	C
Eastern Illinois Univ	IL	20,466	C
Elizabeth City State Univ	NC	11,638	C
Farmingdale State College	NY	19,673	C
Fitchburg State Univ	MA	18,173	C
Grand Valley State Univ	MI	17,998	C+
Humboldt State Univ	CA	18,400	C
Illinois State Univ	IL	23,110	VC
Indiana State Univ	IN	16,000	C
Indiana Univ-Purdue Univ Fort Wayne	IN	15,521	C
Iowa State Univ	IA	16,403	C
Jackson State Univ	MS	13,512	LC
Kent State Univ	OH	19,920	C
Lamar Univ	TX	6,820	LC
Langston Univ	OK	3,000	C
Metropolitan State Univ of Denver	CO	4,835	LC
Middle Tenn State Univ	TN	8,650	C

School	ST	$IS	SR
Millersville Univ of Pennsylvania	PA	21,648	C
Minn State Univ, Moorhead	MN	13,392	VC
Miss State Univ	MS	14,750	C
Miss Valley State Univ	MS	9,706	LC
Morehead State Univ	KY	10,900	C
Morgan State Univ	MD	14,500	C
Northern Mich Univ	MI	18,278	N
Northwestern State Univ of Louisiana	LA	14,368	C
Ohio Univ	OH	21,080	C
Okla Panhandle State Univ	OK	8,996	C
Prairie View A&M Univ	TX	15,205	LC
Purdue Univ/Calumet	IN	14,336	C
Purdue Univ/West Lafayette	IN	20,024	HC
Roger Williams Univ	RI	46,296	VC
San Francisco State Univ	CA	18,514	C
Southeastern Louisiana Univ	LA	13,325	C
Southern Illinois Univ Carbondale	IL	21,942	C
Southern Polytechnic State Univ	GA	13,958	C
Southwestern Okla State Univ	OK	9,160	C
Tarleton State Univ	TX	13,489	LC
Tenn Tech Univ	TN	11,310	C
Texas A&M Univ	TX	19,207	VC
Texas A&M Univ at Kingsville	TX	7,500	LC
Texas Southern Univ	TX	18,212	LC
Texas State Univ	TX	17,128	C
Univ of Arkansas at Pine Bluff	AR	13,378	C
Univ of Central Missouri	MO	14,605	C
Univ of Cincinnati	OH	21,506	VC
Univ of Dayton	OH	40,590	VC
Univ of Florida	FL	15,943	HC
Univ of Illinois at Chicago	IL	24,505	VC
Univ of Mass Lowell	MA	19,316	C
Univ of Mich/Dearborn	MI	9,885	VC
Univ of N Dak	ND	14,551	V
Univ of Northern Iowa	IA	15,795	C
Univ of Rio Grande	OH	8,750	NC
Univ of Southern Maine	ME	16,576	C
Univ of Texas at Arlington	TX	10,908	LC
Univ of Texas at El Paso	TX	8,764	NC
Univ of West Alabama	AL	14,274	C
Univ of Wisc/Platteville	WI	14,564	C
Univ of Wisc/Stout	WI	15,459	C
Utah State Univ	UT	12,044	C
Wayne State Univ	MI	22,063	C
West Virginia Univ Inst of Technology	WV	14,094	NC
Western Kentucky Univ	KY	11,000	LC
Western Washington Univ	WA	18,519	VC
William Penn Univ	IA	26,000	C

INDUSTRIAL HYGIENE

School	ST	$IS	SR
Ohio Univ	OH	21,080	C
St. Augustine's Univ	NC	14,000	C
South Univ	GA	36,070	LC
Univ of Central Okla	OK	12,293	C
Univ of North Alabama	AL	9,960	C

INDUSTRIAL PSYCHOLOGY/ SAFETY

School	ST	$IS	SR
Embry-Riddle Aeronautical Univ - Prescott Campus	AZ	40,444	VC+
Faulkner Univ	AL	25,720	LC

INDUSTRIAL TECHNOLOGY

School	ST	$IS	SR
Black Hills State Univ	SD	13,947	C
Calif Polytechnic State Univ	CA	19,847	HC
Ferris State Univ	MI	20,047	C
Missouri Southern State Univ	MO	12,061	C
San Diego State Univ	CA	21,611	C+

INDUSTRY & SYSTEMS ENGINEERING

School	ST	$IS	SR
Univ of Rhode Island	RI	24,002	C

INFORM, SCIENCE, SYSTMS & TECH

School	ST	$IS	SR
Cornell Univ	NY	60,964	MC

INFORMATICS AND COMPUTER SCIENCE

School	ST	$IS	SR
Bloomfield College	NJ	37,850	LC
Bryant Univ	RI	49,179	VC
Creighton Univ	NE	45,356	VC
Faulkner Univ	AL	25,720	LC
Indiana Univ Bloomington	IN	19,801	VC
Indiana Univ East	IN	6,783	C
Indiana Univ Kokomo	IN	6,811	C
Indiana Univ Northwest	IN	6,854	C
Indiana Univ South Bend	IN	15,501	C
Indiana Univ Southeast	IN	16,035	C
Indiana Univ-Purdue Univ Indianapolis	IN	17,611	C

INFORMATION & COMMUNICATION TECHNOLOGY

School	ST	$IS	SR
Abilene Christian Univ	TX	38,400	C+
Aquinas College	MI	33,060	C
Arizona State Univ, at the Polytechnic Campus	AZ	20,531	C+
Bluffton Univ	OH	38,948	C
Cal State, Northridge	CA	28,690	C
Coastal Carolina Univ	SC	18,580	C
Guilford College	NC	42,800	C
Marywood Univ	PA	45,595	C
St. John's Univ	NY	55,070	C+
Univ of Scranton	PA	51,940	VC
Univ of Wisc/Stout	WI	15,459	C

INFORMATION SCIENCE

School	ST	$IS	SR
Bloomfield College	NJ	37,850	LC
Bryant Univ	RI	49,179	VC
Cornell Univ	NY	60,964	MC
Georgia Southern Univ	GA	16,942	C
Niagara Univ	NY	41,010	C
The Pennsylvania State Univ - Univ Park	PA	28,022	VC+

INFORMATION SCIENCES AND SYSTEMS

School	ST	$IS	SR
Abilene Christian Univ	TX	38,400	C+
Alabama State Univ	AL	14,142	NC
Albany State Univ	GA	8,500	C
Albright College	PA	46,660	C
Alfred State/SUNY College of Technology	NY	18,034	C
Andrews Univ	MI	28,030	C
Aquinas College	MI	33,060	C
Arizona State Univ, at the Tempe Campus	AZ	20,137	C+
Arkansas Tech Univ	AR	13,982	LC
Armstrong State Univ	GA	15,532	C
Atlantic Union College	MA	24,600	C
Auburn Univ at Montgomery	AL	14,470	LC
Augustana College	SD	36,500	VC
Averett Univ	VA	37,750	C
Avila Univ	MO	26,900	C
Azusa Pacific Univ	CA	42,086	C
Barton College	NC	27,660	C
Baylor Univ	TX	50,329	NC
Beacon College	FL	41,720	C
Belhaven Univ	MS	27,170	C
Bellevue Univ	NE	4,600	NC
Bentley Univ	MA	56,454	HC+
Bethune-Cookman Univ	FL	22,958	C
Binghamton Univ/The SUNY	NY	21,648	HC+
Biola Univ	CA	40,320	C
Bloomfield College	NJ	37,850	LC
Boise State Univ	ID	13,469	LC
Boston College	MA	60,622	MC
Bradley Univ	IL	31,874	VC
Brewton-Parker College	GA	33,388	C
Briar Cliff Univ	IA	29,514	C
Brigham Young Univ	UT	12,100	HC
Brigham Young Univ/Hawaii	HI	10,686	VC
Bryant Univ	RI	49,179	VC
Buffalo State College / SUNY	NY	15,733	C
Cabrini College	PA	40,859	LC
Caldwell College	NJ	35,602	NC
Calif Lutheran Univ	CA	49,540	VC
Calif State Polytechnic Univ, Pomona	CA	20,156	C
Cal State, Fullerton	CA	25,188	C
Cal State, Los Angeles	CA	17,186	LC
Cal State, Stanislaus	CA	18,582	C
Calif Univ of Pennsylvania	PA	14,217	C
Calumet College of St. Joseph	IN	15,000	C
Calvin College	MI	39,120	VC
Campbell Univ	NC	37,570	VC
Campbellsville Univ	KY	27,720	C
Canisius College	NY	44,900	C
Carlow Univ	PA	30,272	C
Carnegie Mellon Univ	PA	51,260	MC
Carroll Univ	WI	38,100	C
Catawba College	NC	37,240	LC
Cedar Crest College	PA	43,240	C
Cedarville Univ	OH	32,860	VC
Central Washington Univ	WA	11,730	C
Champlain College	VT	46,650	VC+
Chancellor Univ	OH	11,000	C
Chapman Univ	CA	58,347	VC+
Chestnut Hill College	PA	42,110	LC
Chicago State Univ	IL	5,482	C
Christopher Newport Univ	VA	21,960	VC
CUNY/Baruch College	NY		HC
CUNY/Brooklyn College	NY	5,884	C+
Clarion Univ of Pennsylvania	PA	17,370	LC
Clarke Univ	IA	37,600	C
Clarkson Univ	NY	57,330	HC
Clayton State Univ	GA	12,000	VC
Clemson Univ	SC	19,136	HC
Cleveland State Univ	OH	21,776	C
Coastal Carolina Univ	SC	18,580	C
College of the Ozarks	MO		VC

School	ST	$IS	SR
Colo State Univ-Fort Collins	CO	20,385	VC
Colo State Univ-Pueblo	CO	16,183	C
Colo Technical Univ	CO	10,500	LC
Columbia College	MO	24,578	C
Columbia College	SC	27,882	C
Concord Univ	WV	13,102	C
Concordia Univ St. Paul	MN	28,250	C
Corban Univ	OR	37,380	C+
Curry College	MA	48,925	LC
Dakota State Univ	SD	13,811	C
Daniel Webster College	NH	25,380	C
Davenport Univ	MI	21,002	C
Defiance College	OH	30,645	C
Delta State Univ	MS	12,292	LC
DePaul Univ	IL	47,623	VC
Doane College	NE	35,230	C
Dominican College	NY	31,270	LC
Dordt College	IA	34,160	C+
Dowling College	NY	25,000	LC
Drake Univ	IA	41,516	VC+
Drexel Univ	PA	61,418	VC+
D'Youville College	NY	29,850	C
East Carolina Univ	NC	14,169	C
East Tenn State Univ	TN	9,000	C
Eastern Conn State Univ	CT	20,584	C
Eastern Mich Univ	MI	18,604	C
Eastern New Mexico Univ	NM	10,682	C
Eastern Washington Univ	WA		
Edgewood College	WI	33,294	C
Edinboro Univ of Pennsylvania	PA	15,940	LC
Elizabethtown College	PA	49,740	VC
Elmhurst College	IL	43,336	C
Elon Univ	NC	41,914	VC+
Emporia State Univ	KS	12,897	C
Excelsior College	NY	5,580	SP
Fairfield Univ	CT	56,960	VC
Fairleigh Dickinson Univ/ Metropolitan Campus	NJ	40,254	C
Farmingdale State College	NY	19,673	C
Felician College	NJ	41,640	LC
Ferrum College	VA	27,740	LC
Florida Atlantic Univ	FL	17,339	C
Florida Inst of Technology	FL	48,290	VC
Florida State Univ	FL	16,715	VC
Fontbonne Univ	MO	31,384	C
Fordham Univ	NY	61,588	HC+
Fort Hays State Univ	KS	11,354	C
Fort Valley State Univ	GA	11,200	VC
Francis Marion Univ	SC	16,464	LC
Franciscan Univ of Steubenville	OH	27,320	VC
Freed-Hardeman Univ	TN	19,697	VC
Friends Univ	KS	29,100	C
Frostburg State Univ	MD	15,264	LC
Furman Univ	SC	54,006	HC
Gallaudet Univ	DC	25,380	SP
Gannon Univ	PA	39,608	C
Gardner-Webb Univ	NC	34,375	C+
George Fox Univ	OR	40,750	C+
George Mason Univ	VA	15,724	VC
George Washington Univ	DC	57,108	MC
Georgia College and State Univ	GA	18,900	C+
Georgia Regents Univ	GA		
Glenville State College	WV	11,348	NC
Goldey-Beacom College	DE	27,493	C
Goshen College	IN	35,900	VC
Graceland Univ	IA	28,020	C
Grambling State Univ	LA	13,384	LC
Grand Valley State Univ	MI	17,998	C+
Guilford College	NC	42,800	VC
Gwynedd-Mercy College	PA	33,560	C
Hampton Univ	VA	28,528	C
Hannibal-LaGrange Univ	MO	24,490	C
Harding Univ	AR	23,556	C
Hartwick College	NY	51,270	C
Haverford College	PA	61,564	MC
Heidelberg Univ	OH	34,100	C
Henderson State Univ	AR	14,584	C
Hodges Univ	FL	12,000	LC
Hofstra Univ	NY	51,810	VC+
Holy Family Univ	PA	40,030	LC
Houston Baptist Univ	TX	36,450	C
Humboldt State Univ	CA	18,400	C
Huntington Univ	IN	32,220	C+
Idaho State Univ	ID	12,307	C
Illinois College	IL	25,770	VC
Illinois Inst of Technology	IL	38,512	HC+
Illinois State Univ	IL	23,110	VC
Immaculata Univ	PA	43,000	C
Indiana Inst of Technology	IN	34,240	LC
Indiana Univ Kokomo	IN	6,811	C
Indiana Univ-Purdue Univ Fort Wayne	IN	15,521	C
Indiana Wesleyan Univ	IN	31,815	VC
Inter-American Univ of PR/ Aguadilla Campus	PR	5,578	
Iona College	NY	44,028	C
Ithaca College	NY	53,864	HC
Jacksonville Univ	FL	37,780	C
James Madison Univ	VA	18,049	VC
Johnson & Wales Univ/ Providence Campus	RI	29,576	C
Juniata College	PA	49,340	VC
Kansas State Univ	KS	15,497	VC
Kennesaw State Univ	GA		C
Keystone College	PA	28,680	LC
King's College	PA	43,502	C
Kutztown Univ of Pennsylvania	PA	16,909	LC
La Salle Univ	PA	50,270	C
La Sierra Univ	CA	35,694	VC
Lake Superior State Univ	MI	18,121	C
Lamar Univ	TX	6,820	C
Lawrence Tech Univ	MI	37,630	VC
Le Moyne College	NY	43,470	C
Lee Univ	TN	18,690	C+
Limestone College	SC	30,800	C
Lincoln Memorial Univ	TN	18,144	C
Lincoln Univ	MO	12,904	NC
LIU Brooklyn	NY	47,182	LC
LIU Post	NY	47,660	C
Lock Haven Univ of Pennsylvania	PA	18,028	LC
Louisiana State Univ	LA	18,677	C+
Loyola Univ Chicago	IL	51,646	VC+
Lubbock Christian Univ	TX	26,308	C
Madonna Univ	MI	24,540	VC
Manhattan College	NY	49,588	C+
Mansfield Univ	PA	19,468	LC
Marian Univ	WI	32,420	C
Marietta College	OH	42,135	C+
Marist College	NY	35,500	C
Marshall Univ	WV	14,820	C
Marymount Manhattan College	NY	40,118	VC
Maryville Univ of St. Louis	MO	35,856	VC
Marywood Univ	PA	45,595	C
McKendree Univ	IL	29,920	C+
Mercer Univ	GA	44,201	VC
Mercy College	NY	30,456	C
Meredith College	NC	31,420	C
Metropolitan State Univ	MN	5,923	
Metropolitan State Univ of Denver	CO	4,835	LC
Mich State Univ	MI	22,450	VC
Middle Tenn State Univ	TN	8,650	C
Midwestern State Univ	TX	9,722	C
Milligan College	TN	27,510	C
Millikin Univ	IL	38,940	C
Minn State Univ, Mankato	MN	15,616	C
Misericordia Univ	PA	41,060	C
Miss State Univ	MS	14,750	C
Missouri Baptist Univ	MO	31,830	C
Missouri Univ of Science and Technology	MO	18,655	VC+
Missouri Valley College	MO	22,200	C
Missouri Western State Univ	MO	12,260	NC
Monroe College	NY	20,240	C
Montana State Univ-Billings	MT	12,425	LC
Montclair State Univ	NJ	22,614	C
Morgan State Univ	MD	14,500	VC
Mount Aloysius College	PA	29,976	C
Mount St. Mary's Univ	MD	47,996	C
National Louis Univ	IL	16,915	LC
National Univ	CA	14,730	SP
Nebr Wesleyan Univ	NE	29,774	C+
New Jersey Inst of Technology	NJ	26,490	C+
New Mexico Inst of Mining and Technology	NM	13,592	C
New Mexico State Univ	NM	14,050	C
New York College of Technology/The CUNY	NY	5,769	NC
New York Univ	NY	61,470	MC
Newman Univ	KS	30,380	C+
Niagara Univ	NY	41,010	C
Nicholls State Univ	LA	7,095	C
N Car Wesleyan College	NC	29,440	C
Northeastern State Univ	OK	8,615	VC
Northeastern Univ	MA	55,296	MC
Northern Illinois Univ	IL	19,768	C
Northern Kentucky Univ	KY	21,134	C
Northern Mich Univ	MI	18,278	C
Northland College	WI	26,680	C
Northwest Missouri State Univ	MO	17,347	C
Northwestern College of Iowa	IA	36,240	VC
Northwestern State Univ of Louisiana	LA	14,368	C
Northwestern Univ	IL	61,640	MC
Norwich Univ	VT	28,212	C
Notre Dame College	OH	34,942	VC
Notre Dame de Namur Univ	CA	44,236	LC
Notre Dame of Maryland Univ	MD	27,700	VC
Oakland Univ	MI	19,391	C
Oakwood Univ	AL	25,529	NC
Okla Baptist Univ	OK	28,202	C
Okla Christian Univ	OK	25,870	VC
Okla Panhandle State Univ	OK	8,996	C
Old Dominion Univ	VA	19,483	LC
Olivet Nazarene Univ	IL	29,990	C
Oswego / SUNY	NY	20,009	VC
Ottawa Univ	KS	15,000	VC
Our Lady of the Lake Univ	TX	22,430	LC
Pace Univ	NY	53,367	C
Park Univ	MO	17,525	C
Peirce College	PA	12,760	NC
Pennsylvania College of Technology	PA	26,286	NC
Pfeiffer Univ	NC	33,700	LC
Pittsburg State Univ	KS	12,032	C
Plymouth State Univ	NH	23,148	LC
Point Park Univ	PA	36,390	C
Polytechnic Inst of New York Univ	NY	53,064	HC+
Portland State Univ	OR	18,672	C
Purdue Univ/Calumet	IN	14,336	C
Purdue Univ/West Lafayette	IN	20,024	HC
Quincy Univ	IL	34,980	LC
Radford Univ	VA	17,766	LC
Ramapo College of New Jersey	NJ	24,938	C
Rhode Island College	RI	17,694	LC
Richard Stockton College of New Jersey	NJ	20,000	VC
Rider Univ	NJ	45,720	C
Robert Morris Univ	PA	37,864	C
Rochester Inst of Technology	NY	42,450	VC
Roosevelt Univ	IL	22,605	VC
Rutgers, The State Univ of New Jersey/New Brunswick	NJ	25,562	VC
Rutgers, The State Univ of New Jersey/Newark Campus	NJ	258,806	C
Sacred Heart Univ	CT	49,264	VC
Saginaw Valley State Univ	MI	17,369	C
St. Augustine's Univ	NC	14,000	C
St. Joseph's Univ	PA	55,006	VC
St. Leo Univ	FL	30,340	C
St. Michael's College	VT	49,975	VC
Salem International Univ	WV	21,090	LC
Salisbury Univ	MD	19,180	VC
Salve Regina Univ	RI	48,550	VC
San Diego State Univ	CA	21,611	C+
San Francisco State Univ	CA	18,514	C
Seattle Pacific Univ	WA	41,559	VC+
Shepherd Univ	WV	15,875	C
Siena Heights Univ	MI	32,040	C
Silver Lake College	WI	22,600	LC
Simpson College	IA	36,086	C+
Slippery Rock Univ of Pennsylvania	PA	10,360	C
Southeastern Okla State Univ	OK	7,966	LC
Southern Adventist Univ	TN	26,190	C
Southern Illinois Univ Carbondale	IL	21,942	C
Southern New Hampshire Univ	NH	38,100	C
Southwest Baptist Univ	MO	24,710	C
Southwestern Adventist Univ	TX	23,026	LC
Southwestern Okla State Univ	OK	9,160	C
Springfield College	MA	25,000	C
St. Catherine Univ	MN	37,782	C+
St. Edward's Univ	TX	47,784	C
St. Francis College	NY	34,200	C
SUNY/Empire State College	NY	6,315	SP
Stephen F. Austin State Univ	TX	14,668	C
Stevens Inst of Technology	NJ	50,130	HC
Stevenson Univ	MD	41,470	C
Stony Brook Univ / SUNY	NY	20,078	HC+
Suffolk Univ	MA	47,298	C
SUNY College at Old Westbury	NY	16,324	C
Susquehanna Univ	PA	51,150	C
Syracuse Univ	NY	56,346	VC
Tarleton State Univ	TX	13,489	LC
Temple Univ	PA	24,392	VC
Texas Lutheran Univ	TX	36,040	C
The Masters College	CA	38,160	C+
Ohio State Univ-Columbus Campus	OH	19,887	HC+
The SUNY College of Agriculture and Tech at Cobleskill	NY	19,749	LC
The Univ of Okla	OK	18,621	VC
The Univ of Utah	UT	16,463	VC
The Univ of Virginia's College at Wise	VA	11,076	C
Thomas College	ME	33,560	LC
Tiffin Univ	OH	30,273	LC
Towson Univ	MD	16,000	VC
Trevecca Nazarene Univ	TN	31,186	C
Trine Univ	IN	39,400	HC+
Trinity Christian College	IL	28,869	C
Troy Univ	AL	10,650	C
Tulane Univ	LA	60,861	MC
Tusculum College	TN	24,295	C
United States Naval Academy	MD		MC
Univ at Albany / SUNY	NY	18,674	VC
Univ of Alabama at Birmingham	AL	18,484	C+
Univ of Alabama in Huntsville	AL	17,591	VC+
Univ of Arizona	AZ	20,657	C
Univ of Arkansas at Little Rock	AR	17,609	LC
Univ of Arkansas at Monticello	AR	12,076	NC
Univ of Calif at Irvine	CA	25,961	VC
Univ of Calif at Riverside	CA	27,204	C+
Univ of Calif at San Diego	CA	21,000	VC
Univ of Calif at Santa Cruz	CA	27,807	C+
Univ of Central Arkansas	AR	13,667	VC
Univ of Central Florida	FL	15,668	VC+
Univ of Central Missouri	MO	14,605	C
Univ of Cincinnati	OH	21,506	VC
Univ of Dayton	OH	49,070	VC
Univ of Delaware	DE	23,612	VC
Univ of Denver	CO	51,787	VC+
Univ of Detroit Mercy	MI	30,450	VC
Univ of Florida	FL	15,943	HC
Univ of Hartford	CT	42,674	C
Univ of Hawaii at Manoa	HI	19,379	C
Univ of Houston-Downtown	TX	15,170	LC
Univ of Idaho	ID	14,558	C
Univ of Illinois at Chicago	IL	24,505	VC
Univ of Iowa	IA	17,693	VC
Univ of Jamestown	ND	24,738	C
Univ of Kansas	KS	17,603	C+
Univ of Louisiana at Monroe	LA	12,998	C
Univ of Louisville	KY	17,946	C
Univ of Maine at Augusta	ME	6,855	C
Univ of Mary	ND	16,714	C
Univ of Mary Hardin-Baylor	TX	31,950	C+
Univ of Maryland - College Park	MD	20,060	HC
Univ of Maryland/Baltimore County	MD	18,000	VC
Univ of Maryland/Univ College	MD	6,168	SP
Univ of Mass Boston	MA	23,066	VC
Univ of Mass Lowell	MA	19,316	C
Univ of Minn Crookston	MN	17,834	C
Univ of Minn/Duluth	MN	19,806	C
Univ of Missouri-St. Louis	MO		VC
Univ of Mobile	AL	28,935	VC
Univ of Mount Olive	NC	18,426	C
Univ of Mount Union	OH	35,130	C
Univ of Nebr at Kearney	NE	14,855	LC
Univ of Nebr at Omaha	NE	12,700	C
Univ of Nevada/Reno	NV	17,507	C
Univ of North Alabama	AL	9,960	C
Univ of N Car at Chapel Hill	NC	18,928	MC
Univ of N Dak	ND	14,551	C
Univ of North Florida	FL	15,870	VC
Univ of North Texas	TX	15,628	C
Univ of Northern Colo	CO	18,446	C
Univ of Northern Iowa	IA	15,795	C
Univ of Pennsylvania	PA	61,132	MC
Univ of Pittsburgh at Pittsburgh	PA	28,572	HC+
Univ of PR Recinto de Rio Piedras	PR	5,750	
Univ of PR/Bayamon	PR	1,600	
Univ of PR/Mayaguez	PR	1,250	
Univ of Redlands	CA	40,500	VC
Univ of St. Mary	KS	28,400	C+
Univ of San Francisco	CA	54,770	VC
Univ of Scranton	PA	51,940	VC
Univ of S Car Upstate	SC	18,200	LC
Univ of South Florida/St. Petersburg	FL	12,769	C
Univ of Southern Miss	MS	13,170	C
Univ of St. Francis	IL	37,560	C
Univ of Tenn at Martin	TN	13,734	C
Univ of Texas - Pan American	TX	11,125	LC
Univ of Texas at Arlington	TX	10,908	LC
Univ of Texas at Dallas	TX	21,348	HC+
Univ of Texas at San Antonio	TX	18,372	C
Univ of the Cumberlands	KY	27,500	C
Univ of the Incarnate Word	TX	37,316	LC
Univ of the Pacific	CA	52,146	VC
Univ of Toledo	OH	18,464	C
Univ of Tulsa	OK	46,331	MC
Univ of Vermont	VT	27,006	VC+
Univ of Washington	WA	14,722	VC
Univ of Wisc/Eau Claire	WI	15,730	VC
Univ of Wisc/Green Bay	WI	19,074	C
Univ of Wisc/La Crosse	WI	9,304	VC
Univ of Wisc/Madison	WI	18,757	HC+
Univ of Wisc/Stevens Point	WI	14,043	C
Univ of Wisc-Milwaukee	WI	18,436	C
Utah State Univ	UT	12,044	C
Valley City State Univ	ND	12,286	LC
Vermont Technical College	VT	15,751	C
Villanova Univ	PA	58,394	MC
Virginia Commonwealth Univ	VA	21,716	C
Walla Walla Univ	WA	26,256	NC
Warner Univ	FL	18,000	C
Wartburg College	IA	41,055	VC
Washington Adventist Univ	MD	25,859	LC
Washington Univ in St. Louis	MO	69,844	MC
Wayne State Univ	MI	22,063	C
Waynesburg Univ	PA	30,150	C
Webber International Univ	FL	30,147	C
Webster Univ	MO	35,100	C+
Wentworth Inst of Technology	MA	29,800	C
Wesleyan College	GA	24,000	C
West Liberty Univ	WV	9,142	LC
West Texas A&M Univ	TX	13,478	C
Western New England Univ	MA	46,154	C+
Western Oregon Univ	OR	15,021	C
Westfield State Univ	MA	18,297	C
Westminster College	UT	37,708	C+
Widener Univ	PA	52,418	C
Wilberforce Univ	OH	15,100	C
Wilkes Univ	PA	44,070	C
William Woods Univ	MO	24,260	C
Wilmington College	OH	29,784	C

ST = STATE $IS = IN-STATE COSTS   SR = SELECTOR RATING

School	ST	$IS	SR
Woodbury Univ	CA	34,500	LC
Xavier Univ	OH	44,980	VC
York College / The CUNY	NY	5,496	VC
Youngstown State Univ	OH	16,732	C

INFORMATION TECHNOLOGY

School	ST	$IS	SR
Arkansas State Univ	AR	15,470	C
Bloomfield College	NJ	37,850	LC
Bryant Univ	RI	49,179	VC
Cabrini College	PA	40,859	LC
Calvin College	MI	39,120	VC
Cameron Univ	OK	10,004	LC
Campbell Univ	NC	37,570	VC
Cedarville Univ	OH	32,860	VC
Champlain College	VT	46,650	VC+
Dakota State Univ	SD	13,811	C
DePaul Univ	IL	47,623	VC
Elizabethtown College School of Continuing and Professional Studies	PA		VC
Elmhurst College	IL	43,336	C
Faulkner Univ	AL	25,720	LC
Harris-Stowe State Univ	MO	14,360	NC
Kean Univ	NJ	23,444	C
La Roche College	PA	35,824	LC
Lawrence Tech Univ	MI	37,630	VC
LIU Post	NY	47,660	C
Marquette Univ	WI	46,930	VC+
Marshall Univ	WV	14,820	C
Marymount Univ	VA	39,480	C
Missouri State Univ	MO	13,996	C
Mount St. Mary College	NY	41,138	C
Nazareth College of Rochester	NY	43,028	C+
New York Univ	NY	61,470	MC
Simmons College	MA	49,966	VC
Southern Illinois Univ Carbondale	IL	21,942	C
Southern Polytechnic State Univ	GA	13,958	C
The College of St. Rose	NY	26,750	C
The Lincoln Univ	PA	15,154	LC
The Univ of N Car at Greensboro	NC	12,848	C
Thomas Edison State College	NJ	5,700	SP
Univ of Central Florida	FL	15,668	VC+
Univ of Cincinnati	OH	21,506	VC
Univ of Kansas	KS	17,603	C+
Univ of Mass Boston	MA	23,066	VC
Univ of Missouri-Kansas City	MO	19,603	C
Univ of Nebr - Lincoln	NE	18,031	VC
Univ of New Hampshire	NH	26,912	C
Univ of Wisc-Milwaukee	WI	18,436	C
Wayne State Univ	MI	22,063	C
Webster Univ	MO	35,100	C+
Western Illinois Univ	IL	20,732	C
Youngstown State Univ	OH	16,732	C

INSTITUTIONAL MANAGEMENT

School	ST	$IS	SR
Calumet College of St. Joseph	IN	15,000	C
Goshen College	IN	35,900	VC
New York College of Technology/The CUNY	NY	5,769	NC
San Francisco State Univ	CA	18,514	C
SUNY Fredonia/The SUNY at Fredonia	NY	19,840	VC
Univ of La Verne	CA	47,010	C
Warner Univ	FL	18,000	C

INSTRUCTIONAL DESIGN

School	ST	$IS	SR
Ashford Univ	CA	10,480	C
Western Illinois Univ	IL	20,732	C

INSTRUMENTAL MUSIC EDUCATION

School	ST	$IS	SR
Arkansas State Univ	AR	15,470	C
Concordia Univ St. Paul	MN	28,250	C
Missouri Southern State Univ	MO	12,061	C
Murray State Univ	KY	15,304	C
N Dak State Univ	ND		C
Okla City Univ	OK	40,476	VC
Okla City Univ	OK	40,476	VC
Ouachita Baptist Univ	AR	30,220	VC
Texas Christian Univ	TX	49,980	HC
Webster Univ	MO	35,100	C+

INSTRUMENTAL PERFORMANCE

School	ST	$IS	SR
Baldwin Wallace Univ	OH	38,318	C
Bowling Green State Univ	OH	18,970	C
Houghton College	NY	36,808	C+
Kent State Univ	OH	19,920	C
LIU Post	NY	47,660	C
New York Univ	NY	61,470	MC
Okla Christian Univ	OK	25,870	VC
Okla City Univ	OK	40,476	VC
Ouachita Baptist Univ	AR	30,220	VC
Texas Christian Univ	TX	49,980	HC
Univ of Miami	FL	57,034	MC
Webster Univ	MO	35,100	C+
Wright State Univ	OH	16,983	C

INSURANCE

School	ST	$IS	SR
Baylor Univ	TX	50,329	HC
Cal State, Sacramento	CA	16,200	C
Delta State Univ	MS	12,292	LC
Ferris State Univ	MI	20,047	C
Idaho State Univ	ID	12,307	C
Illinois State Univ	IL	23,110	VC
Indiana State Univ	IN	16,000	C
Inter-American Univ of PR/ Fajardo Campus	PR	4,200	
Inter-American Univ of PR/ Ponce	PR		
Kent State Univ	OH	19,920	C
Martin Univ	IN	11,000	SP
Miss State Univ	MS	14,750	C
Old Dominion Univ	VA	19,483	LC
Olivet College	MI	19,984	LC
Roosevelt Univ	IL	22,605	VC
Troy Univ	AL	10,650	C
Univ of Central Okla	OK	12,293	C
Univ of Cincinnati	OH	21,506	VC
Univ of Florida	FL	15,943	HC
Univ of Hartford	CT	42,674	C
Univ of Illinois at Urbana- Champaign	IL	26,450	HC
Univ of Louisiana at Monroe	LA	12,998	C
Univ of Miss	MS	16,704	C+
Univ of North Texas	TX	15,628	C
Univ of S Car at Columbia	SC	19,725	VC+

INSURANCE AND RISK MANAGEMENT

School	ST	$IS	SR
Appalachian State Univ	NC	12,919	VC
Excelsior College	NY	5,580	SP
Ferris State Univ	MI	20,047	C
Florida State Univ	FL	16,715	VC
Gannon Univ	PA	39,608	C
Georgia State Univ	GA	15,582	VC
Illinois Wesleyan Univ	IL	48,452	VC
Mercyhurst Univ	PA	40,700	C
Oswego / SUNY	NY	20,009	VC
Roosevelt Univ	IL	22,605	VC
St. Joseph's Univ	PA	55,006	VC
San Diego State Univ	CA	21,611	C+
Southern Methodist Univ	TX	60,585	MC
St. John's Univ	NY	55,070	C+
Ohio State Univ-Columbus Campus	OH	19,887	HC+
Univ of Central Arkansas	AR	13,667	VC
Univ of Conn	CT	24,706	HC
Univ of Houston-Downtown	TX	15,170	LC
Univ of Louisiana at Monroe	LA	12,998	C
Univ of Nebr - Lincoln	NE	18,031	VC
Univ of Pennsylvania	PA	61,132	MC
Univ of Wisc/Madison	WI	18,757	HC+
Utica College	NY	45,670	C

INTEGRATED LEADERSHIP STUDIES

School	ST	$IS	SR
Creighton Univ	NE	45,356	VC

INTEGRATIVE STUDIES

School	ST	$IS	SR
Arizona State Univ, at the Tempe Campus	AZ	20,137	C
Ferris State Univ	MI	20,047	C
Murray State Univ	KY	15,304	C

INTERDISCIPLINARY STUDIES

School	ST	$IS	SR
Adams State Univ	CO	13,358	LC
Alderson Broaddus Univ	WV	28,656	C
Alfred Univ	NY	41,770	C
American Univ	DC	56,015	HC+
Amherst College	MA	58,744	MC
Andrews Univ	MI	28,030	C+
Angelo State Univ	TX	15,049	NC
Appalachian State Univ	NC	12,919	VC
Aquinas College	MI	33,060	C
Aquinas College	TN	29,250	VC+
Arizona State Univ, at the Downtown Phoenix Campus	AZ	22,101	C
Arizona State Univ, at the Polytechnic Campus	AZ	20,531	C
Arizona State Univ, at the Tempe Campus	AZ	20,137	C
Arizona State Univ, at the West Campus	AZ	19,251	C
Arkansas State Univ	AR	15,470	C
Augustana College	SD	36,500	VC
Austin College	TX	45,875	HC
Austin Peay State Univ	TN	15,274	C
Averett Univ	VA	37,750	LC
Bard College	NY	61,940	MC
Bates College	ME	60,720	MC
Baylor Univ	TX	50,329	HC
Belhaven Univ	MS	27,170	C
Bellarmine Univ	KY	42,950	VC
Beloit College	WI	49,970	HC
Bennett College for Women	NC	21,970	LC
Bennington College	VT	56,990	HC+
Bentley Univ	MA	56,454	HC+
Berry College	GA	39,254	VC
Bethany College	WV	35,282	LC
Bethel College	IN	31,560	C
Binghamton Univ/The SUNY	NY	21,648	HC+
Birmingham-Southern College	AL	44,168	VC+
Blackburn College	IL	21,350	C
Bloomfield College	NJ	37,850	LC
Bluefield College	VA	17,230	C+
Boise State Univ	ID	13,469	LC
Boston Univ	MA	60,694	MC
Bowdoin College	ME	59,568	MC
Bowie State Univ	MD	23,990	LC
Bowling Green State Univ	OH	18,970	C
Brandeis Univ	MA		MC
Brigham Young Univ/Hawaii	HI	10,686	VC
Bryn Athyn College	PA	27,984	C
Bucknell Univ	PA	60,140	MC
Calif Baptist Univ	CA	38,792	C
Calif Lutheran Univ	CA	49,540	C+
Calif Polytechnic State Univ	CA	19,847	HC
Cal State, Dominguez Hills	CA	17,090	LC
Cal State, Long Beach	CA	17,502	C+
Cal State, Los Angeles	CA	17,186	LC
Cal State, Stanislaus	CA	18,582	C
Calvin College	MI	39,120	VC
Cambridge College	MA	13,392	NC
Cameron Univ	OK	10,004	LC
Centenary College	NJ	38,618	C
Centenary College of Louisiana	LA	45,650	C+
Central Methodist Univ	MO	28,240	VC
Chatham Univ	PA	43,797	C
Christopher Newport Univ	VA	21,960	VC
CUNY/Brooklyn College	NY	5,884	C+
Claremont McKenna College	CA	62,215	MC
Clarkson Univ	NY	57,330	HC
Clayton State Univ	GA	12,000	LC
Coastal Carolina Univ	SC	18,580	C
Coe College	IA	45,550	VC
College of the Ozarks	MO		VC
College of William & Mary	VA	28,000	MC
College of Wooster	OH	52,060	MC
Colo College	CO	57,162	MC
Colo State Univ-Fort Collins	CO	20,385	VC
Columbia College	MO	24,578	C
Concordia College - New York	NY	39,035	LC
Coppin State Univ	MD	16,227	VC
Corban Univ	OR	37,380	C+
Cornerstone Univ and Grand Rapids Theological Seminary	MI	33,338	C
Covenant College	GA	38,990	VC+
Dallas Baptist Univ	TX	30,580	VC
Davidson College	NC	58,146	MC
Delta State Univ	MS	12,292	LC
DePauw Univ	IN	48,950	VC+
D'Youville College	NY	29,850	C
East Tenn State Univ	TN	9,000	C
East Texas Baptist Univ	TX	31,577	LC
Eastern Mich Univ	MI	18,604	C
Embry-Riddle Aeronautical Univ - Prescott Campus	AZ	40,444	VC+
Emerson College	MA	52,446	HC+
Emmanuel College	MA	47,985	VC
Emory and Henry College	VA	387,460	VC
Emory Univ	GA	56,368	MC
Eugene Lang College/The New School for Liberal Arts	NY	55,650	C
Fairleigh Dickinson Univ/ Metropolitan Campus	NJ	40,254	C
Fitchburg State Univ	MA	18,173	C
Florida Atlantic Univ	FL	17,339	C
Florida Inst of Technology	FL	48,290	VC
Fort Lewis College	CO	15,513	C
Framingham State Univ	MA	18,854	C
Franklin and Marshall College	PA	60,799	MC
Franklin Pierce Univ	NH	41,598	C
Gannon Univ	PA	39,608	C
Geneva College	PA	27,280	C
George Mason Univ	VA	15,724	VC
George Washington Univ	DC	57,108	MC
Georgetown College	KY	41,440	C+
Georgetown Univ	DC	52,910	MC
Georgia State Univ	GA	15,582	VC
Goddard College	VT	16,418	VC
Gonzaga Univ	WA	46,441	HC
Goshen College	IN	35,900	VC
Goucher College	MD	52,040	VC+
Grace Bible College	MI	20,770	C
Grand Canyon Univ	AZ	24,540	VC
Guilford College	NC	42,800	C
Hamilton College	NY	55,620	MC
Haverford College	PA	61,564	MC
Hendrix College	AR	50,202	VC+
Heritage Univ	WA	17,664	NC
Hodges Univ	FL	12,000	LC
Hollins Univ	VA	43,295	VC
Houghton College	NY	36,808	C+
Howard Univ	DC	13,646	C
Huston-Tillotson Univ	TX	18,124	C+
Illinois State Univ	IL	23,110	VC
Illinois Wesleyan Univ	IL	48,452	HC
Indiana State Univ	IN	16,000	C
Indiana Univ-Purdue Univ Indianapolis	IN	17,611	C
Ithaca College	NY	53,864	HC
John Brown Univ	AR	32,056	VC+
Johns Hopkins Univ	MD	47,492	MC
Judson College	AL	26,794	C
Kalamazoo College	MI	49,740	VC
Kennesaw State Univ	GA		C
King Univ	TN	33,140	C
Lafayette College	PA	59,155	HC+
LaGrange College	GA	37,670	C
Lake Erie College	OH	37,266	C
Lander Univ	SC	22,514	C+
Lane College	TN	11,212	C
Lasell College	MA	43,750	LC
Lee Univ	TN	18,690	C+
Lehigh Univ	PA	56,770	MC
LeTourneau Univ	TX	36,210	VC
Lewis & Clark College	OR	54,382	MC
Liberty Univ	VA	19,101	C
Lipscomb Univ	TN	37,490	VC
LIU Brooklyn	NY	47,182	LC
LIU Post	NY	47,660	C
Louisiana State Univ	LA	18,677	C+
Lourdes Univ	OH	26,055	LC
Lyndon State College	VT	14,233	C
Manchester Univ	IN	35,070	C
Marian Univ	WI	32,420	LC
Marietta College	OH	42,135	C+
Marist College	NY	35,500	C
Marlboro College	VT	35,980	VC
Marquette Univ	WI	46,930	VC+
Marylhurst Univ	OR	20,295	NC
Mass College of Liberal Arts	MA	18,613	C
Mass Inst of Technology	MA	58,240	MC
McMurry Univ	TX	25,962	LC
Mercy College	NY	30,456	C
Messiah College	PA	40,690	C+
Miami Univ	OH	24,191	VC
Mich State Univ	MI	22,450	VC
Middle Tenn State Univ	TN	8,650	C
Midwestern State Univ	TX	9,722	C
Millersville Univ of Pennsylvania	PA	21,648	C
Millikin Univ	IL	38,940	C
Miss State Univ	MS	14,750	C
Molloy College	NY	40,440	C
Montana State Univ- Northern	MT	12,500	NC
Mount St. Mary College	NY	41,138	C
Mount St. Mary's Univ	MD	47,996	C
Naropa Univ	CO	39,166	SP
National Univ	CA	14,730	SP
New York Inst of Technology	NY	45,010	VC
Newman Univ	KS	30,380	C+
Norfolk State Univ	VA	10,531	LC
N Car State Univ	NC	16,202	HC
Northeastern Illinois Univ	IL	10,318	LC
Northeastern Univ	MA	55,296	MC
Northern Arizona Univ	AZ	19,010	C
Northwest Christian Univ	OR	27,399	C
Northwest Univ	WA	18,854	C
Northwestern College	MN	24,000	C
Notre Dame of Maryland Univ	MD	27,700	VC
Nyack College	NY	33,250	C
Ohio Dominican Univ	OH	38,380	C+
Ohio Valley Univ	WV	17,752	C
Okla Christian Univ	OK	25,870	VC
Old Dominion Univ	VA	19,483	LC
Palm Beach Atlantic Univ	FL	34,874	C+
Piedmont College	GA	30,136	C
Plymouth State Univ	NH	23,148	LC
Prairie View A&M Univ	TX	15,205	LC
Queens College/The CUNY	NY	17,107	VC
Radford Univ	VA	17,766	LC
Rensselaer Polytechnic Inst	NY	61,529	MC
Rhodes College	TN	51,900	HC+
Roberts Wesleyan College	NY	38,306	C
Rochester College	MI	18,320	LC
Russell Sage College	NY	39,370	C
Rutgers, The State Univ of New Jersey/Camden Campus	NJ	25,121	C
Rutgers, The State Univ of New Jersey/Newark Campus	NJ	258,806	C
Saginaw Valley State Univ	MI	17,369	C
St. Martin's Univ	WA	41,678	C
St. Peter's Univ	NJ	44,240	C
Salisbury Univ	MD	19,180	VC
San Diego Christian College	CA	31,012	C
San Diego State Univ	CA	21,611	C+
San Francisco State Univ	CA	18,514	C
Shawnee State Univ	OH	16,916	C
Shippensburg Univ of Pennsylvania	PA	20,934	C
Simmons College	MA	49,966	VC
Simpson College	IA	36,086	C+
Sonoma State Univ	CA	20,541	C
S Dak School of Mines and Technology	SD	15,260	VC
Southeast Missouri State Univ	MO	15,370	LC
Southeastern Univ	FL	27,201	C

School	ST	$IS	SR
Southern Oregon Univ	OR	17,874	C
Southwest Baptist Univ	MO	24,710	C
Southwest Minn State Univ	MN	14,000	C
Southwestern College	KS	29,270	C
St. Andrews Univ	NC	32,050	LC
St. Edward's Univ	TX	47,784	C
St. John Fisher College	NY	40,708	C
St. Lawrence Univ	NY	59,972	VC
St. Olaf College	MN	51,200	HC+
SUNY/Empire State College	NY	6,315	SP
Stephen F. Austin State Univ	TX	14,668	C
Stevenson Univ	MD	41,470	C
Stonehill College	MA	46,780	HC
Stony Brook Univ / SUNY	NY	20,078	HC+
SUNY Fredonia/The SUNY at Fredonia	NY	19,840	VC
SUNY Plattsburgh / SUNY	NY	18,083	C
Tarleton State Univ	TX	13,489	LC
Taylor Univ	IN	37,821	VC+
Tenn State Univ	TN	9,048	C
Tenn Wesleyan College	TN	21,250	C
Texas Southern Univ	TX	18,212	LC
Texas State Univ	TX	17,128	C
Texas Wesleyan Univ	TX	31,382	C
Texas Woman's Univ	TX	13,633	LC
The College of St. Rose	NY	26,750	C
The SUNY at Potsdam	NY	18,473	C
The Univ of Memphis	TN	15,094	C
The Univ of N Car at Pembroke	NC	13,388	LC
The Univ of Okla	OK	18,621	VC
Touro College	NY	27,959	VC
Towson Univ	MD	16,000	VC
Trinity College	CT		HC+
Truman State Univ	MO	15,541	HC
Union College	NY	60,240	MC
Univ at Albany / SUNY	NY	18,674	VC
Univ of Akron	OH	20,436	C
Univ of Alabama at Tuscaloosa	AL	17,164	C+
Univ of Alaska Anchorage	AK	16,673	NC
Univ of Alaska Fairbanks	AK	15,130	C
Univ of Arizona	AZ	20,657	C
Univ of Bridgeport	CT	39,030	LC
Univ of Calif at Berkeley	CA	23,322	MC
Univ of Calif at Irvine	CA	25,961	VC
Univ of Calif at Riverside	CA	27,204	C+
Univ of Calif at Santa Barbara	CA	27,551	HC
Univ of Central Florida	FL	15,668	VC+
Univ of Chicago	IL	55,416	MC
Univ of Colo Denver	CO	17,904	C
Univ of Delaware	DE	23,612	VC
Univ of Denver	CO	51,787	VC+
Univ of Evansville	IN	42,656	VC+
Univ of Florida	FL	15,943	HC
Univ of Georgia	GA	20,082	VC
Univ of Hartford	CT	42,674	C
Univ of Hawaii at Manoa	HI	19,379	VC
Univ of Houston	TX	19,796	VC
Univ of Houston-Downtown	TX	15,170	LC
Univ of Idaho	ID	14,558	C
Univ of Maine	ME	19,902	C+
Univ of Maine at Augusta	ME	6,855	C
Univ of Maine at Farmington	ME	18,187	LC
Univ of Maryland - College Park	MD	20,060	HC
Univ of Maryland/Baltimore County	MD	18,000	VC
Univ of Mass Amherst	MA	24,215	VC+
Univ of Mass Dartmouth	MA	22,223	C
Univ of Miami	FL	57,034	MC
Univ of Mich/Ann Arbor	MI	22,102	MC
Univ of Minn/Duluth	MN	19,806	C
Univ of Missouri-St. Louis	MO		VC
Univ of Nebr - Lincoln	NE	18,031	VC
Univ of Nebr at Omaha	NE	12,700	C
Univ of Nevada, Las Vegas	NV	17,303	C
Univ of New Mexico	NM	15,300	C
Univ of N Car at Chapel Hill	NC	18,928	MC
Univ of N Dak	ND	14,551	C
Univ of North Florida	FL	15,870	VC
Univ of North Texas	TX	15,628	C
Univ of Northern Colo	CO	18,446	C
Univ of Pikeville	KY	25,500	NC
Univ of Pittsburgh at Bradford	PA	21,802	C
Univ of Pittsburgh at Pittsburgh	PA	28,572	HC+
Univ of Portland	OR	49,964	VC
Univ of PR Recinto de Rio Piedras	PR	5,750	
Univ of Redlands	CA	40,500	VC
Univ of Rochester	NY	60,668	MC
Univ of St. Mary	KS	28,400	C+
Univ of S Car Aiken	SC	16,712	C
Univ of S Car at Columbia	SC	19,725	VC+
Univ of S Car Upstate	SC	18,200	LC
Univ of Tenn at Knoxville	TN	20,364	VC+
Univ of Texas - Pan American	TX	11,125	LC
Univ of Texas at Arlington	TX	10,908	LC
Univ of Texas at Dallas	TX	21,348	HC+
Univ of Texas at El Paso	TX	8,764	NC
Univ of Texas at San Antonio	TX	18,372	C
Univ of the Sciences	PA	48,320	VC+
Univ of Virginia	VA	23,050	MC
Univ of Wisc/Green Bay	WI	19,074	C
Univ of Wisc/Superior	WI	14,314	C
Univ of Wisc-Milwaukee	WI	18,436	C
Univ of Wyoming	WY	14,401	C+
Valparaiso Univ	IN	44,940	VC+
Vanderbilt Univ	TN	58,220	MC
Villanova Univ	PA	58,394	MC
Virginia Commonwealth Univ	VA	21,716	C
Virginia Polytechnic Inst and State Univ	VA	14,629	HC
Virginia State Univ	VA	11,318	C+
Virginia Wesleyan College	VA	28,433	LC
Warren Wilson College	NC	40,132	VC
Washburn Univ	KS	12,579	C
Washington and Jefferson College	PA	51,948	VC
Washington and Lee Univ	VA	52,812	MC
Washington College	MD	52,602	VC
Washington State Univ	WA	20,461	C
Washington Univ in St. Louis	MO	69,844	MC
Wayland Baptist Univ	TX	18,912	LC
Wayne State College	NE	11,764	NC
Webster Univ	MO	35,100	C+
Wesleyan College	GA	24,000	C
West Liberty Univ	WV	9,142	LC
West Texas A&M Univ	TX	13,478	C
West Virginia Univ	WV	16,542	C+
Western Illinois Univ	IL	20,732	C
Western Mich Univ	MI	19,628	C
Western Oregon Univ	OR	15,021	C
Western Washington Univ	WA	18,519	VC
Wheaton College	IL	40,720	MC
William Woods Univ	MO	24,260	C
Wisc Lutheran College	WI	23,510	VC
Woodbury Univ	CA	34,500	LC
Worcester Polytechnic Inst	MA	55,860	MC

INTERIOR ARCHITECTURE

School	ST	$IS	SR
Cleveland Inst of Art	OH	48,685	SP
Lawrence Tech Univ	MI	37,630	VC

INTERIOR DESIGN

School	ST	$IS	SR
Abilene Christian Univ	TX	38,400	C+
Adrian College	MI	42,400	C
Appalachian State Univ	NC	12,919	VC
Arcadia Univ	PA	33,570	C+
Arizona State Univ, at the Tempe Campus	AZ	20,137	C+
Art Inst of Atlanta	GA	24,000	SP
Art Inst of Portland	OR	23,040	SP
Auburn Univ	AL	22,378	VC+
Baker College of Flint	MI	7,800	NC
Bay Path College	MA	34,565	C
Baylor Univ	TX	50,329	HC
Boston Architectural College	MA	18,622	SP
Bowling Green State Univ	OH	18,970	C
Brenau Univ - Women's College	GA	26,650	LC
Calif College of the Arts	CA	48,334	SP
Cal State, Fresno	CA	17,405	C
Cazenovia College	NY	43,464	C
Chaminade Univ of Honolulu	HI	31,664	LC
Chatham Univ	PA	43,797	C
College for Creative Studies	MI	45,340	C
Colo State Univ-Fort Collins	CO	20,385	VC
Columbus College of Art and Design	OH	37,732	SP
Concordia Univ Wisc	WI	28,980	C
Converse College	SC	37,130	C
Drexel Univ	PA	61,418	VC+
East Carolina Univ	NC	14,169	C
Eastern Kentucky Univ	KY	11,161	C
Eastern Mich Univ	MI	18,604	C
Endicott College	MA	43,228	VC+
Fashion Inst of Technology/ SUNY	NY	18,362	SP
Florida International Univ	FL	17,747	C+
Florida State Univ	FL	16,715	VC
Harding Univ	AR	23,556	C
High Point Univ	NC	39,800	C
Howard Univ	DC	13,646	C
Indiana State Univ	IN	16,000	C
Indiana Univ Bloomington	IN	19,801	VC
Indiana Univ of Pennsylvania	PA	20,846	LC
Indiana Univ-Purdue Univ Fort Wayne	IN	15,521	C
Indiana Univ-Purdue Univ Indianapolis	IN	17,611	C
Indiana Wesleyan Univ	IN	31,815	VC
Iowa State Univ	IA	16,403	C
Kansas State Univ	KS	15,497	VC
Kean Univ	NJ	23,444	C
Kent State Univ	OH	19,920	C
La Roche College	PA	35,824	LC
Lawrence Tech Univ	MI	37,630	VC
Louisiana State Univ	LA	18,677	C+
Marymount Univ	VA	39,480	C
Maryville Univ of St. Louis	MO	35,856	VC
Marywood Univ	PA	45,595	C
Mercyhurst Univ	PA	40,700	C
Meredith College	NC	31,420	C
Miami Univ	OH	24,191	VC
Mich State Univ	MI	22,450	VC
Middle Tenn State Univ	TN	8,650	C
Milwaukee Inst of Art and Design	WI	31,938	SP
Miss College	MS	21,998	C
Missouri State Univ	MO	13,996	C+
Moore College of Art and Design	PA	50,135	SP
Mount Ida College	MA	30,115	LC
Mount Mary Univ	WI	33,590	LC
Murray State Univ	KY	15,304	C
New York Inst of Technology	NY	45,010	VC
Newbury College	MA	43,280	LC
N Dak State Univ	ND		C
Northern Arizona Univ	AZ	19,010	C
Ohio Univ	OH	21,080	C
Okla Christian Univ	OK	25,870	VC
Oregon State Univ	OR	20,273	VC
Park Univ	MO	17,525	C
Parsons The New School for Design	NY	56,610	SP
Philadelphia Univ	PA	44,160	C
Pittsburg State Univ	KS	12,032	C
Pratt Inst	NY	55,956	SP
Purdue Univ/West Lafayette	IN	20,024	HC
Queens Univ of Charlotte	NC	39,543	C+
Rhode Island School of Design	RI	57,234	MC
Ringling College of Art and Design	FL	46,130	SP
Rochester Inst of Technology	NY	42,450	VC
Rocky Mountain College of Art and Design	CO	22,470	SP
Salem College	NC	29,326	VC
Samford Univ	AL	37,060	C+
San Francisco State Univ	CA	18,514	C
San Jose State Univ	CA	19,133	LC
Savannah College of Art and Design	GA	48,005	SP
School of the Art Inst of Chicago	IL	56,230	SP
School of Visual Arts	NY	36,500	VC
Seattle Pacific Univ	WA	41,559	VC+
S Dak State Univ	SD	14,296	C
Southern Illinois Univ Carbondale	IL	21,942	C
Stephen F. Austin State Univ	TX	14,668	C
Stephens College	MO	38,042	VC
Suffolk Univ	MA	47,298	C
Texas A&M Univ at Kingsville	TX	7,500	C
Texas Christian Univ	TX	49,980	HC
Texas State Univ	TX	17,128	C
Texas Tech Univ	TX	14,243	C
Ohio State Univ-Columbus Campus	OH	19,887	HC+
The Univ of N Car at Greensboro	NC	12,848	C
The Univ of Okla	OK	18,621	VC
The Univ of Tenn at Chattanooga	TN	16,883	C
Univ of Akron	OH	20,436	C
Univ of Alabama at Tuscaloosa	AL	17,164	C+
Univ of Arkansas at Fayetteville	AR	18,352	C+
Univ of Bridgeport	CT	39,030	LC
Univ of Central Arkansas	AR	13,667	VC
Univ of Central Missouri	MO	14,605	C
Univ of Central Okla	OK	12,293	C
Univ of Charleston	WV	32,300	C
Univ of Cincinnati	OH	21,506	VC
Univ of Florida	FL	15,943	HC
Univ of Idaho	ID	14,558	C
Univ of Kansas	KS	17,603	C+
Univ of Louisiana at Lafayette	LA	6,130	C
Univ of Minn/Twin Cities	MN		HC
Univ of Nebr - Lincoln	NE	18,031	VC
Univ of Nebr at Kearney	NE	14,855	LC
Univ of Nevada, Las Vegas	NV	17,303	C
Univ of New Haven	CT	48,940	C
Univ of North Alabama	AL	9,960	C
Univ of North Texas	TX	15,628	C
Univ of Tenn at Knoxville	TN	20,364	VC+
Univ of Texas at Arlington	TX	10,908	LC
Univ of Texas at Austin	TX	44,074	HC
Univ of Texas at San Antonio	TX	18,372	C
Univ of the Incarnate Word	TX	37,316	LC
Univ of Wisc/Madison	WI	18,757	HC+
Univ of Wisc/Stevens Point	WI	14,043	C
Utah State Univ	UT	12,044	C
Virginia Commonwealth Univ	VA	21,716	C
Virginia Polytechnic Inst and State Univ	VA	14,629	HC
Washington State Univ	WA	20,461	C
Wentworth Inst of Technology	MA	29,800	C
West Virginia Univ	WV	16,542	C+
Western Carolina Univ	NC	13,965	C
Western Mich Univ	MI	19,628	C
Winthrop Univ	SC	21,120	C
Woodbury Univ	CA	34,500	LC

INTERMEDIA/MULTIMEDIA

School	ST	$IS	SR
Bard College at Simon's Rock	MA	61,749	HC+
Beloit College	WI	49,970	HC
Bloomfield College	NJ	37,850	LC
Goddard College	VT	16,418	VC

INTERNATIONAL ACCOUNTING

School	ST	$IS	SR
Bryant Univ	RI	49,179	VC
Texas Christian Univ	TX	49,980	HC

INTERNATIONAL AGRICULTURE

School	ST	$IS	SR
Eastern Mennonite Univ	VA	40,660	C
Iowa State Univ	IA	16,403	C
MidAmerica Nazarene Univ	KS	28,000	C
Tarleton State Univ	TX	13,489	LC
Univ of Calif at Davis	CA		HC
Utah State Univ	UT	12,044	C

INTERNATIONAL AGRICULTURE / RURAL DEVELOPMENT

School	ST	$IS	SR
Cornell Univ	NY	60,964	MC

INTERNATIONAL BUSINESS

School	ST	$IS	SR
Arkansas State Univ	AR	15,470	C
Ashford Univ	CA	10,480	C
Baldwin Wallace Univ	OH	38,318	C
Bethany College	WV	35,282	LC
Bloomfield College	NJ	37,850	LC
Bryant Univ	RI	49,179	VC
Cal State, Long Beach	CA	17,502	C+
Campbell Univ	NC	37,570	VC
Illinois State Univ	IL	23,110	C
Indiana Univ Bloomington	IN	19,801	VC
Minn State Univ, Mankato	MN	15,616	C
Missouri Southern State Univ	MO	12,061	C
Murray State Univ	KY	15,304	C
Niagara Univ	NY	41,010	C
Northwest Missouri State Univ	MO	17,347	C
St. Mary's Univ of Minn	MN	38,280	C
Taylor Univ	IN	37,821	VC+
Thomas Edison State College	NJ	5,700	SP
Univ of Cincinnati	OH	21,506	VC
Univ of Evansville	IN	42,656	VC+
Univ of Georgia	GA	20,082	VC
Univ of Mary Hardin-Baylor	TX	31,950	C+
Univ of Wisc/Eau Claire	WI	15,730	VC
Univ of Wisc-Milwaukee	WI	18,436	C

INTERNATIONAL BUSINESS INFORMATION SYSTEMS

School	ST	$IS	SR
Bryant Univ	RI	49,179	VC
Concordia College - New York	NY	39,035	LC
Holy Family Univ	PA	40,030	LC
Missouri Southern State Univ	MO	12,061	C
Texas Christian Univ	TX	49,980	HC

INTERNATIONAL BUSINESS MANAGEMENT

School	ST	$IS	SR
Adams State Univ	CO	13,358	LC
Adrian College	MI	42,400	C
Alma College	MI	44,075	C
Alverno College	WI	31,434	C
American International College	MA	36,100	LC
American Univ	DC	56,015	HC+
Angelo State Univ	TX	15,049	NC
Appalachian State Univ	NC	12,919	VC
Aquinas College	MI	33,060	C
Arcadia Univ	PA	33,570	C+
Assumption College	MA	47,122	C+
Auburn Univ	AL	22,378	VC+
Augsburg College	MN	35,142	C
Augustana College	IL	43,398	VC
Avila Univ	MO	26,900	C
Baker Univ	KS	33,350	C+
Barry Univ	FL	38,190	C
Bay Path College	MA	34,565	C
Baylor Univ	TX	50,329	HC
Belmont Univ	TN	39,190	VC+
Benedictine Univ	IL	37,820	C
Berkeley College of New York City	NY	18,300	LC
Berkeley College/New Jersey	NJ	27,300	LC
Berkeley College/Westchester Campus	NY	28,500	LC
Bethel College	IN	31,560	C
Bethune-Cookman Univ	FL	22,958	C
Biola Univ	CA	40,320	C+
Birmingham-Southern College	AL	44,168	VC+
Bloomfield College	NJ	37,850	LC
Boise State Univ	ID	13,469	LC
Bradley Univ	IL	31,874	VC
Brigham Young Univ/Hawaii	HI	10,686	VC
Bryant Univ	RI	49,179	VC
Buena Vista Univ	IA	39,188	C
Butler Univ	IN	47,572	VC+
Caldwell College	NJ	35,602	NC

ST = STATE $IS = IN-STATE COSTS   SR = SELECTOR RATING

School	ST	$IS	SR
Calif State Polytechnic Univ, Pomona	CA	20,156	C
Cal State, Fullerton	CA	25,188	C
Cal State, Long Beach	CA	17,502	C+
Cal State, Sacramento	CA	16,200	C
Cal State, San Bernardino	CA	12,000	C
Campbell Univ	NC	37,570	VC
Canisius College	NY	44,900	C
Cardinal Stritch Univ	WI	24,054	C
Catawba College	NC	37,240	LC
Central Conn State Univ	CT	19,749	C
Central Washington Univ	WA	11,730	C
Champlain College	VT	46,650	VC+
Chatham Univ	PA	43,797	C
Clarion Univ of Pennsylvania	PA	17,370	LC
College of Charleston	SC	22,145	VC
College of the Ozarks	MO		VC
Columbia College	MO	24,578	C
Concordia College - Moorhead	MN	39,974	VC
Cornerstone Univ and Grand Rapids Theological Seminary	MI	33,338	C
Creighton Univ	NE	45,356	VC
Davenport Univ	MI	21,002	LC
Dickinson College	PA	57,662	HC+
Dominican College	NY	31,270	LC
Dominican Univ	IL	37,628	C
Dominican Univ of Calif	CA	51,250	C
Dowling College	NY	25,000	LC
Drake Univ	IA	41,516	VC+
Duquesne Univ	PA	43,720	VC
Eastern Mennonite Univ	VA	40,660	C
Eastern Mich Univ	MI	18,604	C
Eckerd College	FL	43,902	C
Elizabethtown College	PA	49,740	VC
Elmhurst College	IL	43,336	C
Elmira College	NY	49,950	C+
Elms College	MA	23,900	VC
Elon Univ	NC	41,914	VC+
Endicott College	MA	43,228	VC+
Excelsior College	NY	5,580	SP
Felician College	NJ	41,640	LC
Fitchburg State Univ	MA	18,173	C
Florida Atlantic Univ	FL	17,339	C
Florida Inst of Technology	FL	48,290	VC
Florida International Univ	FL	17,747	C+
Florida State Univ	FL	16,715	VC
Fordham Univ	NY	61,588	HC+
Friends Univ	KS	29,100	C
Gannon Univ	PA	39,608	C
Gardner-Webb Univ	NC	34,375	C+
George Washington Univ	DC	57,108	MC
Georgetown College	KY	41,440	C+
Georgetown Univ	DC	52,910	MC
Golden Gate Univ	CA	17,000	C
Goldey-Beacom College	DE	27,493	C
Graceland Univ	IA	28,020	C
Grand Valley State Univ	MI	17,998	C+
Grove City College	PA	24,022	VC
Guilford College	NC	42,800	C
Gustavus Adolphus College	MN	48,170	HC
Gwynedd-Mercy College	PA	33,560	C
Hamline Univ	MN	45,678	VC
Harding Univ	AR	23,556	C
Hawaii Pacific Univ	HI	34,360	C
High Point Univ	NC	39,800	C
Hilbert College	NY	28,550	C
Hillsdale College	MI	32,866	MC
Hofstra Univ	NY	51,810	VC+
Howard Univ	DC	13,646	C
Illinois Wesleyan Univ	IL	48,452	HC
Indiana Univ of Pennsylvania	PA	20,846	LC
Iona College	NY	44,028	C
Iowa State Univ	IA	16,403	C
Jacksonville Univ	FL	37,780	C
James Madison Univ	VA	18,049	VC
John Carroll Univ	OH	46,300	C+
Johnson & Wales Univ/ Denver Campus	CO	29,576	C
Johnson & Wales Univ/ Providence Campus	RI	29,576	C
Judson Univ	IL	25,130	C
Juniata College	PA	49,340	VC
Kean Univ	NJ	23,444	C
Kennesaw State Univ	GA		C
King Univ	TN	33,140	C
King's College	PA	43,502	C
Kutztown Univ of Pennsylvania	PA	16,909	LC
La Roche College	PA	35,824	LC
La Sierra Univ	CA	35,694	VC
Lake Erie College	OH	37,266	C
Lake Superior State Univ	MI	18,121	C
Lakeland College	WI	32,990	C
Lasell College	MA	43,750	C
Lawrence Tech Univ	MI	37,630	VC
Lenoir-Rhyne Univ	NC	35,984	C
Linfield College-McMinnville Campus	OR	47,676	C
Lipscomb Univ	TN	37,490	VC
Loyola Univ Chicago	IL	51,646	VC+
Loyola Univ New Orleans	LA	46,581	VC
Lynn Univ	FL	43,500	LC
Madonna Univ	MI	24,540	VC
Maine Maritime Academy	ME	21,073	C
Manhattan College	NY	49,588	C+
Mansfield Univ	PA	19,468	LC
Marietta College	OH	42,135	C+
Marquette Univ	WI	46,930	VC+
Marshall Univ	WV	14,820	C
Maryville Univ of St. Louis	MO	35,856	VC
Marywood Univ	PA	45,595	C
Mass Maritime Academy	MA	15,340	C
Menlo College	CA	49,002	C
Mercer Univ	GA	44,201	VC
Meredith College	NC	31,420	C
Merrimack College	MA	44,215	C
Messiah College	PA	40,690	C+
Metropolitan State Univ	MN	5,923	
MidAmerica Nazarene Univ	KS	28,000	C
Millikin Univ	IL	38,940	C
Milwaukee School of Engineering	WI	39,948	VC+
Minn State Univ, Mankato	MN	15,616	C
Minn State Univ, Moorhead	MN	13,392	VC
Minot State Univ	ND	10,915	C
Monmouth College	IL	40,850	C
Monmouth Univ	NJ	44,108	C
Montclair State Univ	NJ	22,614	C
Moravian College	PA	36,381	VC
Mount Vernon Nazarene Univ	OH	29,590	C
Muskingum Univ	OH	30,502	C
Nazareth College of Rochester	NY	43,028	C+
Nebr Wesleyan Univ	NE	29,774	C+
Neumann Univ	PA	31,078	LC
New Mexico State Univ	NM	14,050	C
New York Inst of Technology	NY	45,010	VC
New York Univ	NY	61,470	MC
Newbury College	MA	43,280	LC
Nichols College	MA	37,240	LC
North Central College	IL	38,343	VC
North Park Univ	IL	30,130	C
Northeastern Univ	MA	55,296	MC
Northern State Univ - Aberdeen	SD	14,505	C
Northwest Missouri State Univ	MO	17,347	C
Northwestern College	MN	24,000	C
Northwood Univ	FL	33,192	LC
Northwood Univ	MI	26,331	LC
Notre Dame de Namur Univ	CA	44,236	LC
Notre Dame of Maryland Univ	MD	27,700	VC
Ohio Dominican Univ	OH	38,380	C+
Ohio Northern Univ	OH	42,075	VC
Ohio Univ	OH	21,080	C
Ohio Wesleyan Univ	OH	49,460	C+
Okla Christian Univ	OK	25,870	VC
Okla State Univ	OK	14,310	VC
Old Dominion Univ	VA	19,483	C
Olivet College	MI	19,984	C
Olivet Nazarene Univ	IL	29,990	C
Oral Roberts Univ	OK	31,734	C
Pace Univ	NY	53,367	VC
Palm Beach Atlantic Univ	FL	34,874	C+
Pepperdine Univ	CA	55,372	HC+
Pfeiffer Univ	NC	33,700	LC
Philadelphia Univ	PA	44,160	C
Pittsburg State Univ	KS	12,032	C
Queens College/The CUNY	NY	17,107	VC
Quinnipiac Univ	CT	55,160	VC
Ramapo College of New Jersey	NJ	24,938	C
Regis Univ	CO	41,318	C
Rider Univ	NJ	45,720	C
Roberts Wesleyan College	NY	38,306	C+
Rochester Inst of Technology	NY	42,450	VC
Roger Williams Univ	RI	46,296	VC
Rollins College	FL	52,370	HC
Saginaw Valley State Univ	MI	17,369	C
St. Augustine's Univ	NC	14,000	C
St. Joseph's Univ	PA	55,006	VC
St. Mary's Univ	TX	33,854	C
St. Peter's Univ	NJ	44,240	C
St. Vincent College	PA	40,244	C
St. Xavier Univ	IL	32,840	C
Salem College	NC	29,326	VC
Salve Regina Univ	RI	48,550	VC
San Diego State Univ	CA	21,611	C+
San Francisco State Univ	CA	18,514	C
San Jose State Univ	CA	19,133	LC
Seattle Univ	WA	49,035	VC+
Seton Hill Univ	PA	35,172	C
Simpson College	IA	36,086	C+
Slippery Rock Univ of Pennsylvania	PA	10,360	C
Southeast Missouri State Univ	MO	15,370	LC
Southern Adventist Univ	TN	26,190	C
Southern Illinois Univ Edwardsville	IL	17,532	C
Southern New Hampshire Univ	NH	38,100	C
Southwest Baptist Univ	MO	24,710	C
Spring Hill College	AL	44,164	VC
St. Ambrose Univ	IA	30,845	C
St. Catherine Univ	MN	37,782	C+
St. Cloud State Univ	MN	10,600	C
St. Edward's Univ	TX	47,784	C
St. Norbert College	WI	41,478	VC
St. Thomas Univ	FL	32,310	LC
Stephen F. Austin State Univ	TX	14,668	C
Stetson Univ	FL	51,516	VC
Stonehill College	MA	46,780	HC
Suffolk Univ	MA	47,298	C
SUNY New Paltz	NY	14,348	C
SUNY Plattsburgh / SUNY	NY	18,083	C
Taylor Univ	IN	37,821	VC+
Temple Univ	PA	24,392	VC
Texas A&M Univ at Galveston	TX	11,258	C
Texas Tech Univ	TX	14,243	C
Ohio State Univ-Columbus Campus	OH	19,887	HC+
The SUNY/College at Brockport	NY	19,002	C
The Univ of Memphis	TN	15,094	C
The Univ of N Car at Greensboro	NC	12,848	C
Thiel College	PA	38,728	LC
Trinity International Univ	IL	31,070	VC
Truman State Univ	MO	15,541	HC
Union College	KY	29,955	C
Univ of Akron	OH	20,436	C
Univ of Arkansas at Fayetteville	AR	18,352	C+
Univ of Bridgeport	CT	39,030	LC
Univ of Dayton	OH	49,070	VC
Univ of Denver	CO	51,787	VC+
Univ of Findlay	OH	31,916	C
Univ of Hawaii at Manoa	HI	19,379	C
Univ of Houston-Downtown	TX	15,170	LC
Univ of Indianapolis	IN	31,740	LC
Univ of La Verne	CA	47,010	C
Univ of Maryland - College Park	MD	20,060	HC
Univ of Missouri-St. Louis	MO		VC
Univ of Montana	MT	14,105	C
Univ of Mount Union	OH	35,130	C
Univ of Nebr - Lincoln	NE	18,031	VC
Univ of Nevada, Las Vegas	NV	17,303	C
Univ of N Car at Charlotte	NC	15,547	C
Univ of North Florida	FL	15,870	VC
Univ of Pittsburgh at Pittsburgh	PA	28,572	HC+
Univ of Portland	OR	49,964	VC
Univ of PR/Humacao	PR	1,877	
Univ of Rio Grande	OH	8,750	NC
Univ of San Diego	CA	54,818	HC+
Univ of San Francisco	CA	54,770	VC
Univ of Scranton	PA	51,940	VC
Univ of Southern Calif	CA	56,903	MC
Univ of Southern Miss	MS	13,170	C
Univ of St. Francis	IL	37,560	C
Univ of St. Thomas - Houston	TX	37,690	C
Univ of Tampa	FL	35,160	VC
Univ of Texas - Pan American	TX	11,125	LC
Univ of Texas at Dallas	TX	21,348	HC+
Univ of Tulsa	OK	46,331	MC
Univ of Washington	WA	14,722	VC
Univ of Wisc/La Crosse	WI	9,304	VC
Univ of Wisc/Madison	WI	18,757	HC+
Univ of Wisc/Superior	WI	14,314	C
Utah State Univ	UT	12,044	C
Vanguard Univ of Southern Calif	CA	35,833	VC
Villanova Univ	PA	58,394	MC
Walsh Univ	OH	35,100	C
Wartburg College	IA	41,055	VC
Washington and Jefferson College	PA	51,948	VC
Washington State Univ	WA	20,461	C
Washington Univ in St. Louis	MO	69,844	MC
Waynesburg Univ	PA	30,150	C
Wesleyan College	GA	24,000	C
Western Carolina Univ	NC	13,965	C
Western New Mexico Univ	NM	8,500	LC
Western Washington Univ	WA	18,519	VC
Westminster College	MO	31,720	VC
Westminster College	PA	31,290	C+
Westminster College	UT	37,708	C+
Whitworth Univ	WA	47,734	VC
Wichita State Univ	KS	14,607	C+
Widener Univ	PA	52,418	C
William Jewell College	MO	31,000	VC+
Xavier Univ	OH	44,980	VC

INTERNATIONAL ECONOMICS

School	ST	$IS	SR
Austin College	TX	45,875	HC
Belmont Univ	TN	39,190	VC+
Beloit College	WI	49,970	HC
Bethany College	WV	35,282	LC
Bryant Univ	RI	49,179	VC
Carthage College	WI	33,000	C
Colo College	CO	57,162	MC
Cornerstone Univ and Grand Rapids Theological Seminary	MI	33,338	C
Elon Univ	NC	41,914	VC+
Fitchburg State Univ	MA	18,173	C
Georgia Inst of Technology	GA	21,828	MC
La Salle Univ	PA	50,270	C
Lafayette College	PA	59,155	HC+
Louisiana State Univ	LA	18,677	C+

School	ST	$IS	SR
Mary Baldwin College	VA	38,245	C
Middlebury College	VT	59,160	MC
Midwestern State Univ	TX	9,722	C
Pontifical Catholic Univ of PR	PR	7,310	
San Diego State Univ	CA	21,611	C+
Seattle Univ	WA	49,035	VC+
Southwestern Adventist Univ	TX	23,026	LC
St. Catherine Univ	MN	37,782	C+
St. Lawrence Univ	NY	59,972	VC
Suffolk Univ	MA	47,298	C
Texas Christian Univ	TX	49,980	HC
Texas Tech Univ	TX	14,243	C
The Catholic Univ of America	DC	52,852	VC
The College of Idaho	ID	31,277	C+
Univ of Bridgeport	CT	39,030	LC
Univ of Calif at Santa Cruz	CA	27,807	C+
Univ of Puget Sound	WA	54,608	HC
Univ of Vermont	VT	27,006	VC+
Univ of West Georgia	GA	15,488	LC
Valparaiso Univ	IN	44,940	VC+
Washington Univ in St. Louis	MO	69,844	MC
Western Washington Univ	WA	18,519	VC

INTERNATIONAL ENTREPRENEURIAL MANAGEMENT

School	ST	$IS	SR
Bryant Univ	RI	49,179	VC
Texas Christian Univ	TX	49,980	HC

INTERNATIONAL FINANCE

School	ST	$IS	SR
Bryant Univ	RI	49,179	VC
Texas Christian Univ	TX	49,980	HC
Univ of Miami	FL	57,034	MC

INTERNATIONAL MARKETING

School	ST	$IS	SR
Bryant Univ	RI	49,179	VC
Pace Univ	NY	53,367	C
Texas Christian Univ	TX	49,980	HC
Univ of Miami	FL	57,034	MC

INTERNATIONAL POLITICAL SCIENCE

School	ST	$IS	SR
Reed College	OR	57,780	MC
Texas Christian Univ	TX	49,980	HC

INTERNATIONAL PUBLIC SERVICE

School	ST	$IS	SR
Baylor Univ	TX	50,329	HC
Union College	NE	23,270	C
Univ of New Haven	CT	48,940	C
Univ of Texas at Dallas	TX	21,348	HC+
Valparaiso Univ	IN	44,940	VC+

INTERNATIONAL REAL ESTATE FINANCE

School	ST	$IS	SR
Texas Christian Univ	TX	49,980	HC

INTERNATIONAL RELATIONS

School	ST	$IS	SR
Abilene Christian Univ	TX	38,400	C+
Agnes Scott College	GA	45,323	C+
Alverno College	WI	31,434	LC
American International College	MA	36,100	LC
Aquinas College	MI	33,060	C
Augsburg College	MN	35,142	C
Beloit College	WI	49,970	HC
Bennington College	VT	56,990	HC+
Bethany College	WV	35,282	LC
Bethel Univ	MN	34,940	VC
Boston Univ	MA	60,694	MC
Bridgewater College	VA	41,450	C
Brigham Young Univ	UT	12,100	HC
Brown Univ	RI	59,428	MC
Bucknell Univ	PA	60,140	MC
Cal State, Chico	CA	20,158	C
Cal State, Sacramento	CA	16,200	C
Calvin College	MI	39,120	VC
Canisius College	NY	44,900	C
Capital Univ	OH	41,050	VC
Carleton College	MN	60,102	MC
Carroll College	MT	38,000	C
Carroll Univ	WI	38,100	C
Centre College	KY	35,000	HC+
Chaminade Univ of Honolulu	HI	31,664	LC
Chatham Univ	PA	43,797	C
Claremont McKenna College	CA	62,215	MC
Clark Univ	MA	47,020	HC+
Cleveland State Univ	OH	21,776	C
Colgate Univ	NY	58,135	MC
College of William & Mary	VA	28,000	MC
College of Wooster	OH	52,600	VC
Conn College	CT	54,970	VC
Cornell College	IA	44,930	VC
Creighton Univ	NE	45,356	VC
Dominican Univ	IL	37,628	C

School	ST	$IS	SR
Drake Univ	IA	41,516	VC+
Drew Univ/College of Liberal Arts	NJ	57,516	C
Duquesne Univ	PA	43,720	VC
Eastern Mich Univ	MI	18,604	C
Eastern Washington Univ	WA	39,800	C
Eckerd College	FL	43,902	C
Edgewood College	WI	33,294	C
Florida International Univ	FL	17,747	C+
Florida State Univ	FL	16,715	VC
George Mason Univ	VA	15,724	VC
George Washington Univ	DC	57,108	MC
Georgetown Univ	DC	52,910	MC
Georgia Inst of Technology	GA	21,828	MC
Gettysburg College	PA	58,820	HC
Goucher College	MD	52,040	VC+
Grand Valley State Univ	MI	17,998	C
Hamilton College	NY	55,620	MC
Hampshire College	MA	58,320	MC
Hawaii Pacific Univ	HI	34,360	C
Hendrix College	AR	50,202	VC+
High Point Univ	NC	39,800	C
Hobart and William Smith Colleges	NY	60,034	HC+
Hunter College	NY	14,429	VC
Illinois College	IL	25,770	VC
Immaculata Univ	PA	43,000	C
Iowa State Univ	IA	16,403	C
Kent State Univ	OH	19,920	C
Knox College	IL	44,865	VC+
Lafayette College	PA	59,155	HC+
Lake Forest College	IL	50,652	VC
Le Moyne College	NY	43,470	C
Lehigh Univ	PA	56,770	MC
Lehman College/The CUNY	NY	5,778	LC
Lewis & Clark College	OR	54,382	MC
Linfield College-McMinnville Campus	OR	47,676	C
Lynchburg College	VA	42,645	C
Marquette Univ	WI	46,930	VC+
Marshall Univ	WV	14,820	C
Mary Baldwin College	VA	38,245	C
Maryville College	TN	33,150	C
McKendree Univ	IL	29,920	C+
Miami Univ	OH	24,191	VC
Middle Tenn State Univ	TN	8,650	C
Mills College	CA	54,119	VC
Minn State Univ, Mankato	MN	15,616	C
Morningside College	IA	35,430	C
Mount Holyoke College	MA	55,146	MC
Muskingum Univ	OH	30,502	C
New York Univ	NY	61,470	MC
North Park Univ	IL	30,130	C
Northern Arizona Univ	AZ	19,010	C
Northwestern State Univ of Louisiana	LA	14,368	C
Notre Dame of Maryland Univ	MD	27,700	VC
Nova Southeastern Univ	FL	37,280	VC
Oakland Univ	MI	19,391	C
Occidental College	CA	60,972	MC
Ohio Wesleyan Univ	OH	49,460	C+
Oral Roberts Univ	OK	31,734	C
Pitzer College	CA	54,988	MC
Pomona College	CA	57,680	MC
Prescott College	AZ	33,284	C
Princeton Univ	NJ	53,795	MC
Principia College	IL	35,140	C+
Regis Univ	MA	47,565	LC
Roanoke College	VA	49,976	C
Rockhurst Univ	MO	20,625	C
Roger Williams Univ	RI	46,296	VC
Rollins College	FL	52,370	HC
St. Joseph's Univ	PA	55,006	VC
St. Louis Univ	MO	48,346	HC
St. Mary's Univ	TX	33,854	C
St. Michael's College	VT	49,975	VC
Salem College	NC	29,326	VC
Samford Univ	AL	37,060	C+
San Francisco State Univ	CA	18,514	C
Seton Hall Univ	NJ	45,902	C
Shaw Univ	NC	15,488	C
Shawnee State Univ	OH	16,916	C
Simmons College	MA	49,966	VC
Simpson College	IA	36,086	C+
Skidmore College	NY	59,942	HC
Smith College	MA	59,674	MC
Southern Methodist Univ	TX	60,585	MC
Southwestern Adventist Univ	TX	23,026	LC
St. Catherine Univ	MN	37,782	VC+
St. Cloud State Univ	MN	10,600	C
St. Edward's Univ	TX	47,784	C
St. Norbert College	WI	41,478	VC
St. Thomas Univ	FL	32,310	C
Stanford Univ	CA	58,388	MC
Suffolk Univ	MA	47,298	C
SUNY College at Geneseo	NY	18,670	HC
SUNY New Paltz	NY	14,348	C
Syracuse Univ	NY	56,346	VC
Taylor Univ	IN	37,821	VC+
Texas State Univ	TX	17,128	C
Texas Wesleyan Univ	TX	31,382	C
The Pennsylvania State Univ - Univ Park	PA	28,022	VC+
Trinity Univ	TX	48,150	HC+
Tufts Univ	MA	58,780	MC

School	ST	$IS	SR
Univ of Arkansas at Fayetteville	AR	18,352	C+
Univ of Calif at Davis	CA		HC
Univ of Colo Boulder	CO	22,605	VC+
Univ of Delaware	DE	23,612	VC
Univ of Idaho	ID	14,558	C
Univ of Indianapolis	IN	31,740	LC
Univ of Mary Washington	VA	19,484	VC
Univ of Minn/Twin Cities	MN		
Univ of Nevada/Reno	NV	17,507	C
Univ of New Haven	CT	48,940	C
Univ of Northern Colo	CO	18,446	C
Univ of Pennsylvania	PA	61,132	MC
Univ of Redlands	CA	40,500	VC
Univ of Rochester	NY	60,668	MC
Univ of San Diego	CA	54,818	HC+
Univ of South Florida/Tampa	FL	13,000	C
Univ of Southern Calif	CA	56,903	MC
Univ of the Pacific	CA	52,146	VC
Univ of Toledo	OH	18,464	C
Univ of Virginia	VA	23,050	MC
Univ of Washington	WA	14,722	VC
Univ of Wisc/Madison	WI	18,757	HC+
Ursinus College	PA	57,580	VC
Utah State Univ	UT	12,044	C
Valparaiso Univ	IN	44,940	VC+
Virginia Wesleyan College	VA	28,433	LC
Walsh Univ	OH	35,100	C
Wartburg College	IA	41,055	VC
Washington Univ in St. Louis	MO	69,844	MC
Webster Univ	MO	35,100	C
Wellesley College	MA	59,038	MC
Wesleyan College	GA	24,000	C
West Chester Univ of Pennsylvania	PA	17,186	C
Westminster College	PA	31,290	C+
Wheaton College	IL	40,720	MC
Wheaton College	MA	54,934	HC+
Widener Univ	PA	52,418	C
William Jewell College	MO	31,000	VC+
Wilson College	PA	35,080	C
Wittenberg Univ	OH	47,962	C+
Wright State Univ	OH	16,983	C

INTERNATIONAL SECURITY/ CONFLICT RESOLUTION MGMT

School	ST	$IS	SR
Baldwin Wallace Univ	OH	38,318	C
San Diego State Univ	CA	21,611	C+

INTERNATIONAL STUDIES

School	ST	$IS	SR
Adrian College	MI	42,400	C
Albion College	MI	46,010	C
Allegheny College	PA	50,980	HC
American Univ	DC	56,015	HC+
Aquinas College	MI	33,060	C
Arcadia Univ	PA	33,570	C+
Arizona State Univ, at the Tempe Campus	AZ	20,137	C+
Arkansas Tech Univ	AR	13,982	LC
Ashland Univ	OH	25,000	C
Assumption College	MA	47,122	C+
Auburn Univ at Montgomery	AL	14,470	LC
Augustana College	SD	36,500	VC
Austin College	TX	45,875	HC
Azusa Pacific Univ	CA	42,086	C
Baker Univ	KS	33,350	C+
Baldwin Wallace Univ	OH	38,318	C
Bard College	NY	61,940	HC
Barnard College/Columbia Univ	NY	39,000	MC
Barry Univ	FL	38,190	C
Belhaven Univ	MS	27,170	C
Bellarmine Univ	KY	42,950	VC
Benedictine Univ	IL	37,820	C
Bennington College	VT	56,990	HC+
Bentley Univ	MA	56,454	HC+
Berry College	GA	39,254	VC
Bethel College	IN	31,560	C
Bethune-Cookman Univ	FL	22,958	C
Binghamton Univ/The SUNY	NY	21,648	HC+
Birmingham-Southern College	AL	44,168	VC+
Bowling Green State Univ	OH	18,970	C
Bradley Univ	IL	31,874	VC
Brandeis Univ	MA		MC
Brenau Univ - Women's College	GA	26,650	LC
Brigham Young Univ/Hawaii	HI	10,686	VC
Bryant Univ	RI	49,179	VC
Bryn Mawr College	PA	59,890	MC
Butler Univ	IN	41,572	VC+
Calif Baptist Univ	CA	38,792	C
Calif Lutheran Univ	CA	49,540	C+
Cal State, East Bay	CA	16,549	C
Cal State, Long Beach	CA	17,502	C+
Cal State, Monterey Bay	CA	26,871	LC
Calvin College	MI	39,120	VC
Case Western Reserve Univ	OH	56,534	MC
Cedarville Univ	OH	32,860	VC
Centenary College	NJ	38,618	C
Central College	IA	42,104	C+
Central Conn State Univ	CT	19,749	C

School	ST	$IS	SR
Chestnut Hill College	PA	42,110	LC
CUNY/City College	NY	20,319	HC+
Clark Univ	MA	47,020	HC+
College of Charleston	SC	22,145	VC
College of New Jersey	NJ	25,376	HC
College of St. Elizabeth	NJ	43,839	LC
College of Staten Island/The City of New Yok	NY	16,778	NC
Colo State Univ-Fort Collins	CO	20,385	VC
Concordia College - Moorhead	MN	39,974	VC
Concordia College - New York	NY	39,035	LC
Concordia Univ Irvine	CA	35,390	VC
Coppin State Univ	MD	16,227	VC
Defiance College	OH	30,645	C
Denison Univ	OH	54,670	HC+
DePaul Univ	IL	47,623	VC
Dickinson College	PA	57,662	HC+
Doane College	NE	35,230	C
Dominican Univ of Calif	CA	51,250	C
Drexel Univ	PA	61,418	VC+
Drury Univ	MO	31,909	VC
D'Youville College	NY	29,850	C
Earlham College	IN	51,470	HC
East Texas Baptist Univ	TX	31,577	LC
Elmira College	NY	49,950	C+
Elms College	MA	23,900	VC
Elon Univ	NC	41,914	VC+
Emmanuel College	MA	47,985	VC
Emory and Henry College	VA	387,460	VC
Emory Univ	GA	56,368	MC
Endicott College	MA	43,228	VC+
Evangel Univ	MO	23,090	C
Fairfield Univ	CT	56,960	VC
Fairleigh Dickinson Univ/ Metropolitan Campus	NJ	40,254	C
Ferrum College	VA	27,740	LC
Fordham Univ	NY	61,588	HC+
Francis Marion Univ	SC	16,464	LC
Frostburg State Univ	MD	15,264	LC
Gallaudet Univ	DC	25,380	SP
Gannon Univ	PA	39,608	C
George Fox Univ	OR	40,750	C
Georgia Southern Univ	GA	16,942	C
Gonzaga Univ	WA	46,441	HC
Gordon College	MA	44,320	VC
Graceland Univ	IA	28,020	C
Grand Canyon Univ	AZ	24,540	VC
Greenville College	IL	27,012	C
Guilford College	NC	42,800	C
Hampshire College	MA	58,320	MC
Hanover College	IN	43,073	C+
Harding Univ	AR	23,556	C
Hawaii Pacific Univ	HI	34,360	C
Heidelberg Univ	OH	34,100	C
Hollins Univ	VA	43,295	VC
Hood College	MD	45,730	C
Hope College	MI	38,650	VC
Houghton College	NY	36,808	C+
Idaho State Univ	ID	12,307	C
Illinois Wesleyan Univ	IL	48,452	HC
Indiana Univ Bloomington	IN	19,801	VC
Indiana Univ of Pennsylvania	PA	20,846	LC
Indiana Univ Southeast	IN	16,035	C
Indiana Univ-Purdue Univ Indianapolis	IN	17,611	C
Iona College	NY	44,028	C
Jacksonville Univ	FL	37,780	C
James Madison Univ	VA	18,049	VC
John Brown Univ	AR	32,056	VC+
Johns Hopkins Univ	MD	47,492	MC
Juniata College	PA	49,340	VC
Kalamazoo College	MI	49,740	HC
Kennesaw State Univ	GA		C
Kenyon College	OH	58,890	MC
La Roche College	PA	35,824	LC
Lawrence Univ	WI	46,371	HC
Le Moyne College	NY	43,470	C
Liberty Univ	VA	19,101	C
Lindenwood Univ	MO	20,750	C
Lipscomb Univ	TN	37,490	VC
LIU Post	NY	47,660	C
Lock Haven Univ of Pennsylvania	PA	18,028	LC
Loras College	IA	37,432	VC
Louisiana State Univ	LA	18,677	C+
Loyola Univ Chicago	IL	51,646	VC+
Luther College	IA	45,720	C+
Lycoming College	PA	45,379	C
Macalester College	MN	57,691	MC
Malone Univ	OH	35,364	C
Manhattanville College	NY	50,740	VC
Mansfield Univ	PA	19,468	LC
Marlboro College	VT	35,980	VC
Mars Hill Univ	NC	22,950	LC
Marymount Manhattan College	NY	40,118	VC
Maryville Univ of St. Louis	MO	35,856	VC
Meredith College	NC	31,420	C
Methodist Univ	NC	37,185	C
Miami Univ	OH	24,191	VC
Millersville Univ of Pennsylvania	PA	21,648	C
Minn State Univ, Moorhead	MN	13,392	VC
Monmouth College	IL	40,850	C

School	ST	$IS	SR
Morehouse College	GA	39,412	C
Mount Mary Univ	WI	33,590	LC
Mount Mercy Univ	IA	35,320	C
Mount St. Mary's Univ	MD	47,996	C
Muhlenberg College	PA	52,837	HC
Murray State Univ	KY	15,304	C
National Univ	CA	14,730	SP
Nazareth College of Rochester	NY	43,028	C+
Nebr Wesleyan Univ	NE	29,774	C+
New College of Florida	FL	14,504	MC
Niagara Univ	NY	41,010	C
N Dak State Univ	ND		C
Northern Mich Univ	MI	18,278	C
Northwest Christian Univ	OR	27,399	C
Northwest Nazarene Univ	ID	34,000	C
Northwestern Univ	IL	61,640	MC
Norwich Univ	VT	28,212	C
Oakwood Univ	AL	25,529	NC
Oberlin College	OH	61,788	MC
Oglethorpe Univ	GA	44,200	C+
Ohio Northern Univ	OH	42,075	VC
Ohio Univ	OH	21,080	C
Old Dominion Univ	VA	19,483	LC
Oral Roberts Univ	OK	31,734	C
Oregon State Univ	OR	20,273	VC
Oswego / SUNY	NY	20,009	VC
Otterbein College	OH	32,214	C
Pacific Lutheran Univ	WA	46,760	C+
Pepperdine Univ	CA	55,372	HC+
Pittsburg State Univ	KS	12,032	C
Point Loma Nazarene Univ	CA	41,006	C+
Point Park Univ	PA	36,390	C
Portland State Univ	OR	18,672	C
Presbyterian College	SC	42,678	C+
Prescott College	AZ	33,284	C
Ramapo College of New Jersey	NJ	24,938	C
Randolph College	VA	45,660	VC
Randolph-Macon College	VA	49,869	C+
Rhodes College	TN	51,900	HC+
Ripon College	WI	36,959	C+
Rockford College	IL	31,000	C
Roosevelt Univ	IL	22,605	VC
Russell Sage College	NY	39,370	C
Saginaw Valley State Univ	MI	17,369	C
St. Francis Univ	PA	30,029	LC
St. Joseph's College	IN	36,500	C
St. Mary's College	IN	45,160	C+
St. Mary's College of Calif	CA	53,550	C
St. Mary's Univ	TX	33,854	C
St. Peter's Univ	NJ	44,240	C
Salisbury Univ	MD	19,180	VC
Salve Regina Univ	RI	48,550	VC
San Diego State Univ	CA	21,611	C+
Seattle Univ	WA	49,035	VC+
Seton Hill Univ	PA	35,172	C
Sewanee: The Univ of the South	TN	47,700	HC+
Shaw Univ	NC	15,488	C
Shippensburg Univ of Pennsylvania	PA	20,934	C
Sonoma State Univ	CA	20,541	C
Southern Adventist Univ	TN	26,190	C
Southern Illinois Univ Carbondale	IL	21,942	C
Southern Methodist Univ	TX	60,585	MC
Southern Nazarene Univ	OK	24,354	C
Southern Oregon Univ	OR	17,874	C
Southern Polytechnic State Univ	GA	13,958	C
Southwestern Univ	TX	45,660	VC
Spring Hill College	AL	44,164	VC
St. Bonaventure Univ	NY	41,575	C
St. Francis College	NY	34,200	C
St. John Fisher College	NY	40,708	C+
St. Lawrence Univ	NY	59,972	VC
Stetson Univ	FL	51,516	VC
Stonehill College	MA	46,780	HC
SUNY Cortland/The SUNY	NY	19,759	C+
SUNY Oneonta / SUNY	NY	16,919	C+
Susquehanna Univ	PA	51,150	C
Tabor College	KS	29,010	C
Taylor Univ	IN	37,821	VC+
Tenn Wesleyan College	TN	21,250	C
Texas A&M Univ	TX	19,207	VC
Texas Lutheran Univ	TX	36,040	C
Texas State Univ	TX	17,128	C
The College of New Rochelle	NY	33,600	VC
Ohio State Univ-Columbus Campus	OH	19,887	HC+
The SUNY/College at Brockport	NY	19,002	C
The Univ of Memphis	TN	15,094	C
The Univ of Okla	OK	18,621	VC
The Univ of Utah	UT	16,463	VC
The Univ of Virginia's College at Wise	VA	11,076	C
Thomas College	ME	33,560	LC
Thomas Edison State College	NJ	5,700	SP
Thomas More College	KY	34,760	C
Towson Univ	MD	16,000	VC
Trinity College	CT		HC+
Trinity Washington Univ	DC	30,250	C+
Union College	NE	23,270	C
United States Air Force Academy	CO		MC

ST = STATE $IS = IN-STATE COSTS   SR = SELECTOR RATING

School	ST	$IS	SR
United States Military Academy	NY		MC
Univ of Alabama at Birmingham	AL	18,484	C+
Univ of Alabama at Tuscaloosa	AL	17,164	C+
Univ of Arkansas at Little Rock	AR	17,609	LC
Univ of Bridgeport	CT	39,030	LC
Univ of Calif at Irvine	CA	25,961	VC
Univ of Calif at Los Angeles	CA	25,686	MC
Univ of Calif at San Diego	CA	21,000	VC
Univ of Calif at Santa Barbara	CA	27,551	HC
Univ of Central Florida	FL	15,668	VC+
Univ of Chicago	IL	55,416	MC
Univ of Cincinnati	OH	21,506	VC
Univ of Colo Denver	CO	17,904	C
Univ of Dayton	OH	49,070	VC
Univ of Denver	CO	51,787	VC+
Univ of Evansville	IN	42,656	VC+
Univ of Findlay	OH	31,916	C
Univ of Hartford	CT	42,674	C
Univ of Idaho	ID	14,558	C
Univ of Illinois at Urbana-Champaign	IL	26,450	HC
Univ of Iowa	IA	17,693	VC
Univ of Kansas	KS	17,603	C+
Univ of La Verne	CA	47,010	C
Univ of Maine	ME	19,902	C+
Univ of Maine at Farmington	ME	18,187	LC
Univ of Maine at Presque Isle	ME	15,011	LC
Univ of Miami	FL	57,034	MC
Univ of Mich/Ann Arbor	MI	22,102	MC
Univ of Mich/Dearborn	MI	9,885	VC
Univ of Minn/Duluth	MN	19,806	C
Univ of Miss	MS	16,704	C+
Univ of Missouri/Columbia	MO	18,201	MC
Univ of Mount Union	OH	35,130	C
Univ of Nebr - Lincoln	NE	18,031	VC
Univ of Nebr at Kearney	NE	14,855	LC
Univ of Nebr at Omaha	NE	12,700	C
Univ of New Haven	CT	48,940	C
Univ of New Mexico	NM	15,300	C
Univ of New Orleans	LA	9,224	C
Univ of N Car at Chapel Hill	NC	18,928	MC
Univ of N Car at Charlotte	NC	15,547	C
Univ of N Dak	ND	14,551	C
Univ of North Texas	TX	15,628	C
Univ of Oregon	OR	21,360	C+
Univ of Pennsylvania	PA	61,132	MC
Univ of Pittsburgh at Pittsburgh	PA	28,572	HC+
Univ of St. Joseph	CT	45,630	C
Univ of St. Mary	KS	28,400	C+
Univ of Scranton	PA	51,940	VC
Univ of South Alabama	AL	13,510	C
Univ of S Dak	SD	15,111	C
Univ of Southern Indiana	IN	14,885	C
Univ of Southern Miss	MS	13,170	C
Univ of St. Thomas - Houston	TX	37,690	C
Univ of Tampa	FL	35,160	VC
Univ of Tenn at Martin	TN	13,734	C
Univ of the Pacific	CA	52,146	VC
Univ of Wisc Whitewater	WI	13,314	C
Univ of Wisc/Madison	WI	18,757	HC+
Univ of Wisc/Oshkosh	WI	10,426	LC
Univ of Wisc/Parkside	WI	10,181	LC
Univ of Wisc/Platteville	WI	14,564	C
Univ of Wisc/Stevens Point	WI	14,043	C
Univ of Wisc/Superior	WI	14,314	C
Univ of Wisc-Milwaukee	WI	18,436	C
Univ of Wyoming	WY	14,401	C+
Vassar College	NY	61,140	MC
Virginia Commonwealth Univ	VA	21,716	C
Virginia Military Inst	VA	16,156	C
Virginia Polytechnic Inst and State Univ	VA	14,629	HC
Walsh Univ	OH	35,100	C
Washington and Jefferson College	PA	51,948	VC
Washington College	MD	52,602	VC
Washington Univ in St. Louis	MO	69,844	MC
Wells College	NY	49,400	VC
Wesley College	DE	31,115	LC
West Virginia Univ	WV	16,542	C+
West Virginia Wesleyan College	WV	26,880	C
Western Mich Univ	MI	19,628	C
Western New England Univ	MA	46,154	C+
Western Oregon Univ	OR	15,021	C
Westminster College	MO	31,720	VC
Wheeling Jesuit Univ	WV	33,500	C
Whittier College	CA	43,416	C
Whitworth Univ	WA	44,734	VC
Wilkes Univ	PA	44,070	C
Willamette Univ	OR	56,450	VC+
William Woods Univ	MO	24,260	C
Wilson College	PA	35,080	C
Xavier Univ	OH	44,980	VC
Yale Univ	CT	55,300	MC

INTERNATIONAL SUPPLY AND VALUE CHAIN MANAGEMENT

School	ST	$IS	SR
Bryant Univ	RI	49,179	VC
Texas Christian Univ	TX	49,980	HC

INTERPRETER FOR THE DEAF

School	ST	$IS	SR
Bethel College	IN	31,560	C
Columbia College Chicago	IL	30,940	LC
Gallaudet Univ	DC	25,380	SP
Gardner-Webb Univ	NC	34,375	C+
Idaho State Univ	ID	12,307	C
MacMurray College	IL	20,755	C
Madonna Univ	MI	24,540	VC
Maryville College	TN	33,150	C+
Mount Aloysius College	PA	29,976	C
Quincy Univ	IL	34,980	LC
Rochester Inst of Technology	NY	42,450	VC
St. Catherine Univ	MN	37,782	C+
Univ of Arkansas at Little Rock	AR	17,609	LC
Virginia Polytechnic Inst and State Univ	VA	14,629	HC
Western Oregon Univ	OR	15,021	C
William Woods Univ	MO	24,260	C

INVESTMENTS AND SECURITIES

School	ST	$IS	SR
Bryant Univ	RI	49,179	VC
Campbell Univ	NC	37,570	VC
CUNY/Baruch College	NY		HC
Lynn Univ	FL	43,500	LC
St. Joseph's Univ	PA	55,006	VC
Univ of Nebr - Lincoln	NE	18,031	VC
Univ of N Dak	ND	14,551	C
Univ of North Texas	TX	15,628	C
Westminster College	UT	37,708	C+

ISLAMIC STUDIES

School	ST	$IS	SR
Brandeis Univ	MA		MC
DePaul Univ	IL	47,623	VC
Gettysburg College	PA	58,820	HC
New York Univ	NY	61,470	MC
Ohio State Univ-Columbus Campus	OH	19,887	HC+
Univ of Calif at Santa Barbara	CA	27,551	HC
Univ of Mich/Ann Arbor	MI	22,102	MC
Univ of Texas at Austin	TX	44,074	HC
Washington Univ in St. Louis	MO	69,844	MC

ITALIAN

School	ST	$IS	SR
American Univ	DC	56,015	HC+
Arizona State Univ, at the Tempe Campus	AZ	20,137	C+
Bard College	NY	61,940	HC
Barnard College/Columbia Univ	NY	39,000	MC
Bennington College	VT	56,990	HC+
Binghamton Univ/The SUNY	NY	21,648	HC+
Boston College	MA	60,622	MC
Brigham Young Univ	UT	12,100	MC
Bryn Mawr College	PA	59,890	MC
Central Conn State Univ	CT	19,749	C
CUNY/Brooklyn College	NY	5,884	C+
College of the Holy Cross	MA	58,042	MC
Columbia Univ/School of General Studies	NY	58,231	MC
Cornell Univ	NY	60,964	MC
Dartmouth College	NH	57,996	MC
DePaul Univ	IL	47,623	VC
Dominican Univ	IL	37,628	C
Emory Univ	GA	56,368	MC
Fairfield Univ	CT	56,960	VC
Florida Atlantic Univ	FL	17,339	C
Florida International Univ	FL	17,747	C+
Florida State Univ	FL	16,715	VC
Fordham Univ	NY	61,588	HC+
Georgetown Univ	DC	52,910	MC
Harvard College/Harvard Univ	MA	49,000	MC
Haverford College	PA	61,564	MC
Hofstra Univ	NY	51,810	VC+
Hunter College	NY	14,429	VC
Indiana Univ Bloomington	IN	19,801	VC
Iona College	NY	44,028	C
Johns Hopkins Univ	MD	47,492	MC
La Salle Univ	PA	50,270	C
Lehman College/The CUNY	NY	5,778	LC
LIU Post	NY	47,660	C
Loyola Univ Chicago	IL	51,646	VC+
Marlboro College	VT	35,980	VC
Middlebury College	VT	59,160	MC
Montclair State Univ	NJ	22,614	C
Mount Holyoke College	MA	55,146	MC
Nazareth College of Rochester	NY	43,028	C+
New York Univ	NY	61,470	MC
Northeastern Illinois Univ	IL	10,318	LC
Northwestern Univ	IL	61,640	MC
Pepperdine Univ	CA	55,372	HC+
Princeton Univ	NJ	53,795	MC
Providence College	RI	57,383	VC

ISLAMIC STUDIES (col 3 continuation)

School	ST	$IS	SR
Queens College/The CUNY	NY	17,107	VC
Rutgers, The State Univ of New Jersey/New Brunswick	NJ	25,562	VC
Rutgers, The State Univ of New Jersey/Newark Campus	NJ	258,806	C
St. Joseph's Univ	PA	55,006	VC
St. Louis Univ	MO	48,346	HC
St. Mary's College	IN	45,160	C+
San Francisco State Univ	CA	18,514	C
Sarah Lawrence College	NY	48,000	HC
Scripps College	CA	61,940	MC
Seton Hall Univ	NJ	45,902	C
Smith College	MA	59,674	MC
Southern Conn State Univ	CT	18,033	LC
St. John's Univ	NY	55,070	C+
Stanford Univ	CA	58,388	MC
Susquehanna Univ	PA	51,150	C
Temple Univ	PA	24,392	VC
The Catholic Univ of America	DC	52,852	VC
Ohio State Univ-Columbus Campus	OH	19,887	HC+
The Pennsylvania State Univ - Univ Park	PA	28,022	VC+
The Univ of Okla	OK	18,621	VC
Thomas Edison State College	NJ	5,700	SP
Trinity College	CT		HC+
Tufts Univ	MA	58,780	MC
Tulane Univ	LA	60,861	MC
Univ of Buffalo / The SUNY	NY	20,283	VC
Univ of Arizona	AZ	20,657	C
Univ of Calif at Berkeley	CA	23,322	MC
Univ of Calif at Davis	CA		HC
Univ of Calif at Los Angeles	CA	25,686	MC
Univ of Colo Boulder	CO	22,605	VC+
Univ of Delaware	DE	23,612	VC
Univ of Denver	CO	51,787	VC+
Univ of Georgia	GA	20,082	VC
Univ of Illinois at Chicago	IL	24,505	VC
Univ of Illinois at Urbana-Champaign	IL	26,450	HC
Univ of Iowa	IA	17,693	VC
Univ of Kentucky	KY	19,868	C
Univ of Mass Boston	MA	23,066	VC
Univ of Mich/Ann Arbor	MI	22,102	MC
Univ of Minn/Twin Cities	MN		HC
Univ of Notre Dame	IN	57,117	MC
Univ of Oregon	OR	21,360	C+
Univ of Pittsburgh at Pittsburgh	PA	28,572	HC+
Univ of South Florida/Tampa	FL	13,000	C
Univ of Southern Calif	CA	56,903	MC
Univ of Tenn at Knoxville	TN	20,364	VC+
Univ of Texas at Austin	TX	44,074	HC
Univ of Virginia	VA	23,050	MC
Univ of Washington	WA	14,722	VC
Univ of Wisc/Madison	WI	18,757	HC+
Vassar College	NY	61,140	MC
Villanova Univ	PA	58,394	MC
Washington Univ in St. Louis	MO	69,844	MC
Yale Univ	CT	55,300	MC
Youngstown State Univ	OH	16,732	C

ITALIAN STUDIES

School	ST	$IS	SR
Assumption College	MA	47,122	C+
Bard College	NY	61,940	HC
Boston Univ	MA	60,694	MC
Brown Univ	RI	59,428	MC
College of Staten Island/The City of New York	NY	16,778	NC
College of the Holy Cross	MA	58,042	MC
Colo College	CO	57,162	MC
Columbia Univ/City of New York	NY	61,116	MC
Columbia Univ/School of General Studies	NY	58,231	MC
Conn College	CT	54,970	MC
Dickinson College	PA	57,662	HC+
Duke Univ	NC	50,250	MC
Emory Univ	GA	56,368	MC
Fordham Univ	NY	61,588	HC+
Gonzaga Univ	WA	46,441	HC
Ithaca College	NY	53,864	HC
Lake Erie College	OH	37,266	C
Miami Univ	OH	24,191	VC
New York Univ	NY	61,470	MC
Purdue Univ/West Lafayette	IN	20,024	HC
Rosemont College	PA	42,350	C
Scripps College	CA	61,940	MC
Southern Methodist Univ	TX	60,585	MC
Stony Brook Univ / SUNY	NY	20,078	HC+
Syracuse Univ	NY	56,346	VC
Univ of Calif at Los Angeles	CA	25,686	MC
Univ of Calif at San Diego	CA	21,000	VC
Univ of Calif at Santa Barbara	CA	27,551	HC
Univ of Calif at Santa Cruz	CA	27,807	C+
Univ of Conn	CT	24,706	HC
Univ of Houston	TX	19,796	VC
Univ of Illinois at Chicago	IL	24,505	VC
Univ of Maryland - College Park	MD	20,060	HC
Univ of Mass Amherst	MA	24,215	VC+
Univ of Pennsylvania	PA	61,132	MC

JAPANESE

School	ST	$IS	SR
American Univ	DC	56,015	HC+
Ball State Univ	IN	17,850	VC
Bates College	ME	60,720	MC
Bennington College	VT	56,990	HC+
Brigham Young Univ	UT	12,100	MC
Cal State, Fullerton	CA	25,188	C
Cal State, Long Beach	CA	17,502	C+
Cal State, Los Angeles	CA	17,186	LC
Calvin College	MI	39,120	VC
Central Washington Univ	WA	11,730	C
Colgate Univ	NY	58,135	MC
Conn College	CT	54,970	MC
Eastern Mich Univ	MI	18,604	C
Elizabethtown College	PA	49,740	VC
Emory Univ	GA	56,368	MC
George Washington Univ	DC	57,108	MC
Georgetown Univ	DC	52,910	MC
Harvard College/Harvard Univ	MA	49,000	MC
Hofstra Univ	NY	51,810	VC+
Lawrence Univ	WI	46,371	HC
Linfield College-McMinnville Campus	OR	47,676	C
Macalester College	MN	57,691	MC
Marshall Univ	WV	14,820	C
Middlebury College	VT	59,160	MC
Murray State Univ	KY	15,304	C
North Central College	IL	38,343	VC
Northern Kentucky Univ	KY	21,134	C
Oakland Univ	MI	19,391	C
Occidental College	CA	60,972	MC
Pacific Univ	OR	49,626	C+
Pomona College	CA	57,680	MC
Portland State Univ	OR	18,672	C
Purdue Univ/West Lafayette	IN	20,024	HC
San Diego State Univ	CA	21,611	C+
San Francisco State Univ	CA	18,514	C
San Jose State Univ	CA	19,133	LC
Scripps College	CA	61,940	MC
Stanford Univ	CA	58,388	MC
Ohio State Univ-Columbus Campus	OH	19,887	HC+
The Pennsylvania State Univ - Univ Park	PA	28,022	VC+
The Univ of Utah	UT	16,463	VC
Thomas Edison State College	NJ	5,700	SP
Tufts Univ	MA	58,780	MC
Univ of Calif at Berkeley	CA	23,322	MC
Univ of Calif at Davis	CA		HC
Univ of Calif at Irvine	CA	25,961	VC
Univ of Calif at Los Angeles	CA	25,686	MC
Univ of Calif at Riverside	CA	27,204	C+
Univ of Calif at Santa Barbara	CA	27,551	HC
Univ of Colo Boulder	CO	22,605	VC+
Univ of Findlay	OH	31,916	C
Univ of Georgia	GA	20,082	VC
Univ of Hawaii at Hilo	HI	23,066	C
Univ of Hawaii at Manoa	HI	19,379	C
Univ of Iowa	IA	17,693	VC
Univ of Maryland - College Park	MD	20,060	HC
Univ of Mass Amherst	MA	24,215	VC+
Univ of Minn/Twin Cities	MN		HC
Univ of Missouri-St. Louis	MO		VC
Univ of Montana	MT	14,105	C
Univ of Mount Union	OH	35,130	C
Univ of Notre Dame	IN	57,117	MC
Univ of Oregon	OR	21,360	C+
Univ of Pittsburgh at Pittsburgh	PA	28,572	HC+
Univ of Puget Sound	WA	54,608	HC
Univ of Rochester	NY	60,668	MC
Univ of the Pacific	CA	52,146	VC
Univ of Vermont	VT	27,006	VC+
Univ of Washington	WA	14,722	VC
Univ of Wisc/Madison	WI	18,757	HC+
Vassar College	NY	61,140	MC
Wake Forest Univ	NC	58,838	MC
Washington Univ in St. Louis	MO	69,844	MC
Wellesley College	MA	59,038	MC
Western Washington Univ	WA	18,519	VC
Yale Univ	CT	55,300	MC

(Japanese continued — column 4 middle)

School	ST	$IS	SR
Univ of San Diego	CA	54,818	HC+
Univ of Vermont	VT	27,006	VC+
Univ of Wisc-Milwaukee	WI	18,436	C
Vanderbilt Univ	TN	58,220	MC
Wellesley College	MA	59,038	MC
Wesleyan Univ	CT	61,198	MC
Wheaton College	MA	54,934	HC+
Youngstown State Univ	OH	16,732	C

JAPANESE STUDIES

School	ST	$IS	SR
Adrian College	MI	42,400	C
Aquinas College	MI	33,060	C
Binghamton Univ/The SUNY	NY	21,648	HC+
Boston Univ	MA	60,694	MC
Case Western Reserve Univ	OH	56,534	MC
Earlham College	IN	51,470	HC
Gettysburg College	PA	58,820	HC
Hofstra Univ	NY	51,810	VC+
Hope College	MI	38,650	VC

School	ST	$IS	SR
Linfield College-McMinnville Campus	OR	47,676	C
Madonna Univ	MI	24,540	VC
New York Univ	NY	61,470	MC
Purdue Univ/West Lafayette	IN	20,024	HC
Salem International Univ	WV	21,090	LC
Smith College	MA	59,674	MC
Swarthmore College	PA	57,870	MC
Univ of Alaska Fairbanks	AK	15,130	C
Univ of Calif at San Diego	CA	21,000	C
Univ of Hawaii at Hilo	HI	23,066	C
Univ of N Car at Charlotte	NC	15,547	C
Wellesley College	MA	59,038	MC
Willamette Univ	OR	56,450	VC+
William Jewell College	MO	31,000	VC+

JAZZ

School	ST	$IS	SR
Alabama A&M Univ	AL	10,084	C
Aquinas College	MI	33,060	C
Bennington College	VT	56,990	HC+
Berklee College of Music	MA	47,100	SP
Bowling Green State Univ	OH	18,970	C
Brigham Young Univ	UT	12,100	HC
Cal State, Fresno	CA	17,405	C
DePaul Univ	IL	47,623	VC
Eastman School of Music	NY	58,802	SP
Elmhurst College	IL	43,336	VC
Five Towns College	NY	34,550	C
Florida Atlantic Univ	FL	17,339	C
Florida State Univ	FL	16,715	MC
Hofstra Univ	NY	51,810	VC+
Howard Univ	DC	13,646	C
Indiana Univ Bloomington	IN	19,801	VC
Ithaca College	NY	53,864	HC
Johnson State College	VT	16,721	C
Limestone College	SC	30,800	C
LIU Brooklyn	NY	47,182	LC
Loyola Univ New Orleans	LA	46,581	VC
Manhattan School of Music	NY	55,850	SP
Marshall Univ	WV	14,820	C
Mich State Univ	MI	22,450	VC
New England Conservatory of Music	MA	52,550	SP
N Car Central Univ	NC	9,000	C
North Central College	IL	38,343	VC
Northwestern Univ	IL	61,640	MC
Roosevelt Univ	IL	22,605	VC
Rowan Univ	NJ	24,022	VC+
San Jose State Univ	CA	19,133	LC
Shenandoah Univ	VA	39,916	C
Temple Univ	PA	24,392	VC
Texas State Univ	TX	17,128	C
Ohio State Univ-Columbus Campus	OH	19,887	HC+
The Univ of N Car at Greensboro	NC	12,848	C
Tulane Univ	LA	60,861	MC
Univ of Cincinnati	OH	21,506	VC
Univ of Denver	CO	51,787	VC+
Univ of Hartford	CT	42,674	C
Univ of Iowa	IA	17,693	VC
Univ of Maine at Augusta	ME	6,855	C
Univ of Miami	FL	57,034	MC
Univ of Mich/Ann Arbor	MI	22,102	MC
Univ of Minn/Duluth	MN	19,806	C
Univ of North Florida	FL	15,870	VC
Univ of North Texas	TX	15,628	C
Univ of Oregon	OR	21,360	C
Univ of Rochester	NY	60,668	MC
Univ of Southern Calif	CA	56,903	MC
Univ of Washington	WA	14,722	VC
Webster Univ	MO	35,100	C
Western Mich Univ	MI	19,628	C
Youngstown State Univ	OH	16,732	C

JOURNALISM

School	ST	$IS	SR
Abilene Christian Univ	TX	38,400	C+
Adrian College	MI	42,400	C
Alabama A&M Univ	AL	10,084	C
American Jewish Univ - College of A&S	CA	32,600	C
American Univ	DC	56,015	HC+
Andrews Univ	MI	28,030	C+
Angelo State Univ	TX	15,049	NC
Appalachian State Univ	NC	12,919	VC
Aquinas College	MI	33,060	C
Arkansas State Univ	AR	15,470	C
Arkansas Tech Univ	AR	13,982	LC
Asbury Univ	KY	32,038	VC
Ashford Univ	CA	10,480	C
Ashland Univ	OH	25,000	C
Auburn Univ	AL	22,378	VC+
Augustana College	SD	36,500	VC
Averett Univ	VA	37,750	LC
Ball State Univ	IN	17,850	C
Baylor Univ	TX	50,329	HC
Belmont Univ	TN	39,190	VC
Bemidji State Univ	MN	13,500	VC
Benedict College	SC	20,454	NC
Benedictine College	KS	29,180	VC
Bennington College	VT	56,990	HC+
Bethel College	IN	31,560	C
Bethel Univ	MN	34,940	VC
Biola Univ	CA	40,320	C+
Bloomfield College	NJ	37,850	LC
Boston Univ	MA	60,694	MC
Bowling Green State Univ	OH	18,970	C
Briar Cliff Univ	IA	29,514	C
Buffalo State College / SUNY	NY	15,733	C+
Butler Univ	IN	47,572	VC+
Calif Baptist Univ	CA	38,792	C
Calif Polytechnic State Univ	CA	19,847	HC
Cal State, Chico	CA	20,158	C
Cal State, Fresno	CA	17,405	C
Cal State, Fullerton	CA	25,188	C
Cal State, Long Beach	CA	17,502	C+
Cal State, Northridge	CA	28,690	LC
Cal State, Sacramento	CA	16,200	C
Campbell Univ	NC	37,570	VC
Canisius College	NY	44,900	C
Carnegie Mellon Univ	PA	51,260	MC
Cedarville Univ	OH	32,860	VC
Central Conn State Univ	CT	19,749	C
Central State Univ	OH	9,010	C
Central Univ of Bayamon	PR	3,350	
Central Washington Univ	WA	11,730	C
CUNY/Baruch College	NY		HC
CUNY/Brooklyn College	NY	5,884	C+
College of St. Scholastica	MN	41,440	C
College of the Ozarks	MO		VC
Colo State Univ-Fort Collins	CO	20,385	VC
Colo State Univ-Pueblo	CO	16,183	C
Columbia College Chicago	IL	30,940	VC
Concordia College - Moorhead	MN	39,974	VC
Concordia Univ, Ann Arbor	MI	27,220	VC
Corban Univ	OR	37,380	C+
Creighton Univ	NE	45,356	VC
Delaware State Univ	DE	16,722	LC
Delta State Univ	MS	12,292	LC
DePaul Univ	IL	47,623	VC
Dickinson State Univ	ND	11,900	NC
Doane College	NE	35,230	C
Dominican Univ	IL	37,628	C
Dordt College	IA	34,160	C+
Drake Univ	IA	41,516	VC+
Duquesne Univ	PA	43,720	VC
Eastern Illinois Univ	IL	20,466	C
Eastern Kentucky Univ	KY	11,161	C
Eastern Mich Univ	MI	18,604	C
Eastern Nazarene College	MA	30,000	C
Eastern Washington Univ	WA		C
Edinboro Univ of Pennsylvania	PA	15,940	LC
Elon Univ	NC	41,914	VC+
Emerson College	MA	52,446	HC+
Emory and Henry College	VA	387,460	C
Emory Univ	GA	56,368	MC
Evangel Univ	MO	23,090	C
Felician College	NJ	41,640	LC
Florida A&M Univ	FL	14,935	LC
Florida Atlantic Univ	FL	17,339	C
Florida Southern College	FL	40,150	C+
Fordham Univ	NY	61,588	HC+
Franklin College	IN	36,585	C
Freed-Hardeman Univ	TN	19,697	VC
Gannon Univ	PA	39,608	C
George Washington Univ	DC	57,108	MC
Georgia College and State Univ	GA	18,900	C+
Georgia Southern Univ	GA	16,942	C
Georgia State Univ	GA	15,582	VC
Gonzaga Univ	WA	46,441	HC
Goshen College	IN	35,900	VC
Grace College and Seminary	IN	28,800	VC
Grand Valley State Univ	MI	17,998	C+
Grand View Univ	IA	31,050	C
Hampshire College	MA	58,320	MC
Harding Univ	AR	23,556	C
Hawaii Pacific Univ	HI	34,360	C
Hofstra Univ	NY	51,810	VC+
Howard Univ	DC	13,646	C
Humboldt State Univ	CA	18,400	C
Huntington Univ	IN	33,220	C+
Illinois State Univ	IL	23,110	VC
Indiana State Univ	IN	16,000	C
Indiana Univ Bloomington	IN	19,801	VC
Indiana Univ of Pennsylvania	PA	20,846	LC
Indiana Univ South Bend	IN	15,501	C
Indiana Univ Southeast	IN	16,035	C
Indiana-Purdue Univ Indianapolis	IN	17,611	C
Iowa State Univ	IA	16,403	C
Ithaca College	NY	53,864	HC
John Brown Univ	AR	32,056	VC+
Johnson State College	VT	16,721	C
Kansas State Univ	KS	15,497	VC
Keene State College	NH	23,232	LC
Kent State Univ	OH	19,920	C
Lasell College	MA	43,750	LC
Le Moyne College	NY	43,470	C
Lehigh Univ	PA	56,770	HC
Lenoir-Rhyne College	NC	35,984	C
Lewis Univ	IL	23,050	C
Lincoln Univ	MO	12,904	NC
Linfield College-McMinnville Campus	OR	47,676	C
Lipscomb Univ	TN	37,490	VC
LIU Brooklyn	NY	47,182	LC
LIU Post	NY	47,660	C
Lock Haven Univ of Pennsylvania	PA	18,028	LC
Loras College	IA	37,432	VC
Louisiana College	LA	15,746	C
Louisiana State Univ	LA	18,677	C+
Louisiana Tech Univ	LA	11,302	C
Loyola Univ Chicago	IL	51,646	VC+
Lubbock Christian Univ	TX	26,308	C
Lyndon State College	VT	14,233	C
Madonna Univ	MI	24,540	C
Manhattan College	NY	49,588	C+
Mansfield Univ	PA	19,468	LC
Marietta College	OH	42,135	C+
Marquette Univ	WI	46,930	VC+
Marshall Univ	WV	14,820	C
Mercer Univ	GA	44,201	VC
Mercy College	NY	30,456	C
Mercyhurst Univ	PA	40,700	C
Messiah College	PA	40,690	C+
Metropolitan State Univ of Denver	CO	4,835	LC
Miami Univ	OH	24,191	VC
Mich State Univ	MI	22,450	VC
Midland Univ	NE	34,000	C
Millersville Univ of Pennsylvania	PA	21,648	C
Millikin Univ	IL	38,940	C
Minn State Univ, Mankato	MN	15,616	C
Minn State Univ, Moorhead	MN	13,392	VC
Missouri Baptist Univ	MO	31,830	C
Missouri State Univ	MO	13,996	C
Mount Ida College	MA	30,115	LC
Mount Marty College	SD	29,638	C
Mount Mercy Univ	IA	35,320	C
Mount Vernon Nazarene Univ	OH	29,590	C
Murray State Univ	KY	15,304	C
Muskingum Univ	OH	30,502	C
New Mexico State Univ	NM	14,050	C
New York Univ	NY	61,470	MC
Nicholls State Univ	LA	7,095	C
Norfolk State Univ	VA	10,531	LC
North Central College	IL	38,343	VC
Northeastern State Univ	OK	8,615	VC
Northeastern Univ	MA	55,296	MC
Northern Arizona Univ	AZ	19,010	C
Northern Illinois Univ	IL	19,768	C
Northern Kentucky Univ	KY	21,134	C
Northwest Missouri State Univ	MO	17,347	C
Northwest Univ	WA	18,854	C
Northwestern College	MN	24,000	C
Northwestern College of Iowa	IA	36,240	VC
Northwestern Univ	IL	61,640	MC
Oakland Univ	MI	19,391	C
Ohio Northern Univ	OH	42,075	VC
Ohio Univ	OH	21,080	C
Ohio Wesleyan Univ	OH	49,460	C+
Okla Baptist Univ	OK	28,202	C
Okla Christian Univ	OK	25,870	C
Okla State Univ	OK	14,310	VC
Old Dominion Univ	VA	19,483	LC
Olivet College	MI	19,984	LC
Olivet Nazarene Univ	IL	29,990	C
Oswego / SUNY	NY	20,009	VC
Otterbein College	OH	32,214	C
Pacific Union College	CA	28,150	VC
Palm Beach Atlantic Univ	FL	34,874	C+
Pepperdine Univ	CA	55,372	HC+
Pittsburg State Univ	KS	12,032	C
Point Loma Nazarene Univ	CA	41,006	C+
Point Park Univ	PA	36,390	C
Prairie View A&M Univ	TX	15,205	LC
Prescott College	AZ	33,284	C
Purdue Univ/West Lafayette	IN	20,024	HC
Quinnipiac Univ	CT	55,160	VC
Rider Univ	NJ	45,720	C
Roger Williams Univ	RI	46,296	VC
Roosevelt Univ	IL	22,605	VC
Rowan Univ	NJ	24,022	VC+
Rust College	MS	10,600	VC
Rutgers, The State Univ of New Jersey/New Brunswick	NJ	25,562	VC
Rutgers, The State Univ of New Jersey/Newark Campus	NJ	258,806	C
St. Mary-of-the-Woods College	IN	37,722	LC
St. Mary's Univ of Minn	MN	38,280	C
St. Michael's College	VT	49,975	VC
Sam Houston State Univ	TX	17,082	C
Samford Univ	AL	37,060	C+
San Diego State Univ	CA	21,611	C+
San Francisco State Univ	CA	18,514	C
San Jose State Univ	CA	19,133	LC
Seattle Univ	WA	49,035	VC+
Seton Hall Univ	NJ	45,902	C
Seton Hill Univ	PA	35,172	C
Shippensburg Univ of Pennsylvania	PA	20,934	C
Simpson College	IA	36,086	C+
S Dak State Univ	SD	14,296	C
Southeast Missouri State Univ	MO	15,370	LC
Southeastern Univ	FL	27,201	C
Southern Adventist Univ	TN	26,190	C
Southern Arkansas Univ	AR	14,316	C
Southern Conn State Univ	CT	18,033	LC
Southern Illinois Univ Carbondale	IL	21,942	C
Southern Illinois Univ Edwardsville	IL	17,532	C
Southern Methodist Univ	TX	60,585	MC
Southern Nazarene Univ	OK	24,354	C
Southern Univ at New Orleans	LA	2,963	NC
Southwest Baptist Univ	MO	24,710	C
Southwestern Adventist Univ	TX	23,026	LC
Spring Hill College	AL	44,164	VC
St. Bonaventure Univ	NY	41,575	C
St. Cloud State Univ	MN	10,600	C
St. John's Univ	NY	55,070	C+
St. Joseph's College, New York/Brooklyn Campus	NY	22,630	C
St. Joseph's College, New York/Suffolk Campus	NY	22,630	C
SUNY at Purchase	NY	16,951	C
Stephen F. Austin State Univ	TX	14,668	C
Suffolk Univ	MA	47,298	C
SUNY Fredonia/The SUNY at Fredonia	NY	19,840	VC
SUNY New Paltz	NY	14,348	C
SUNY Plattsburgh / SUNY	NY	18,083	C
Syracuse Univ	NY	56,346	VC
Taylor Univ	IN	37,821	VC+
Temple Univ	PA	24,392	VC
Tenn Tech Univ	TN	11,310	C
Texas A&M Univ	TX	19,207	VC
Texas A&M Univ at Commerce	TX	10,496	C
Texas Christian Univ	TX	49,980	HC
Texas State Univ	TX	17,128	C
Texas Tech Univ	TX	14,243	C
Texas Wesleyan Univ	TX	31,382	C
The Lincoln Univ	PA	15,154	LC
Ohio State Univ-Columbus Campus	OH	19,887	HC+
The Pennsylvania State Univ - Univ Park	PA	28,022	VC+
The SUNY/College at Brockport	NY	19,002	C
The Univ of Memphis	TN	15,094	C
The Univ of Okla	OK	18,621	VC
Thomas Edison State College	NJ	5,700	SP
Tougaloo College	MS	15,275	NC
Trevecca Nazarene Univ	TN	31,186	C
Troy Univ	AL	10,650	C
Truman State Univ	MO	15,541	HC
Tulane Univ	LA	60,861	MC
Union College	NE	23,270	C
Union Univ	TN	28,260	VC
Univ of Alabama at Tuscaloosa	AL	17,164	C+
Univ of Alaska Anchorage	AK	16,673	NC
Univ of Alaska Fairbanks	AK	15,130	C
Univ of Arizona	AZ	20,657	C
Univ of Arkansas at Fayetteville	AR	18,352	C+
Univ of Arkansas at Little Rock	AR	17,609	LC
Univ of Arkansas at Pine Bluff	AR	13,378	C
Univ of Bridgeport	CT	39,030	LC
Univ of Calif at Irvine	CA	25,961	VC
Univ of Central Arkansas	AR	13,667	VC
Univ of Central Florida	FL	15,668	VC+
Univ of Central Missouri	MO	14,605	C
Univ of Central Okla	OK	12,293	C
Univ of Cincinnati	OH	21,506	VC
Univ of Colo Boulder	CO	22,605	VC+
Univ of Conn	CT	24,706	HC
Univ of Delaware	DE	23,612	VC
Univ of Denver	CO	51,787	VC+
Univ of Florida	FL	15,943	HC
Univ of Georgia	GA	20,082	VC
Univ of Hawaii at Manoa	HI	19,379	C
Univ of Idaho	ID	14,558	C
Univ of Illinois at Urbana-Champaign	IL	26,450	HC
Univ of Indianapolis	IN	31,740	LC
Univ of Iowa	IA	17,693	VC
Univ of Kansas	KS	17,603	C+
Univ of Kentucky	KY	19,868	C
Univ of La Verne	CA	47,010	C
Univ of Maine	ME	19,902	C+
Univ of Mary Hardin-Baylor	TX	31,950	C+
Univ of Maryland - College Park	MD	20,060	HC
Univ of Mass Amherst	MA	24,215	VC+
Univ of Miami	FL	57,034	MC
Univ of Miss	MS	16,704	C+
Univ of Missouri/Columbia	MO	18,261	NC
Univ of Montana	MT	14,105	C
Univ of Montevallo	AL	17,060	C
Univ of Nebr - Lincoln	NE	18,031	VC
Univ of Nebr at Kearney	NE	14,855	C
Univ of Nebr at Omaha	NE	12,700	C
Univ of Nevada/Reno	NV	17,507	C
Univ of New Haven	CT	48,940	C
Univ of New Mexico	NM	15,300	C
Univ of North Alabama	AL	9,960	C
Univ of N Car at Chapel Hill	NC	18,928	MC
Univ of North Texas	TX	15,628	C

ST = STATE $IS = IN-STATE COSTS SR = SELECTOR RATING

School	ST	$IS	SR
Univ of Northern Colo	CO	18,446	C
Univ of Oregon	OR	21,360	C+
Univ of Pittsburgh at Johnstown	PA	20,862	LC
Univ of PR Recinto de Rio Piedras	PR	5,750	
Univ of S Car at Columbia	SC	19,725	VC+
Univ of S Dak	SD	15,111	C
Univ of Southern Calif	CA	56,903	MC
Univ of Southern Indiana	IN	14,885	C
Univ of Southern Miss	MS	13,170	C
Univ of St. Francis	IL	37,560	C
Univ of Tenn at Knoxville	TN	20,364	VC+
Univ of Texas - Pan American	TX	11,125	LC
Univ of Texas at Arlington	TX	10,908	LC
Univ of Texas at Austin	TX	44,074	HC
Univ of Texas at El Paso	TX	8,764	NC
Univ of the Cumberlands	KY	27,500	C
Univ of West Georgia	GA	15,488	LC
Univ of Wisc Whitewater	WI	13,314	C
Univ of Wisc/Eau Claire	WI	15,730	VC
Univ of Wisc/Madison	WI	18,757	HC+
Univ of Wisc/Oshkosh	WI	10,426	LC
Univ of Wisc/River Falls	WI	9,722	LC
Univ of Wyoming	WY	14,401	C+
Utah State Univ	UT	12,044	C
Utica College	NY	45,670	C
Virginia Union Univ	VA	18,432	C
Virginia Wesleyan College	VA	28,433	LC
Wartburg College	IA	41,055	VC
Washington Adventist Univ	MD	25,859	LC
Washington and Lee Univ	VA	52,812	MC
Washington State Univ	WA	20,461	C
Washington Univ in St. Louis	MO	69,844	MC
Wayne State Univ	MI	22,063	C
Webster Univ	MO	35,100	C+
West Virginia Univ	WV	16,542	C+
Western Illinois Univ	IL	20,732	C
Western Kentucky Univ	KY	11,000	LC
Western Mich Univ	MI	19,628	C
Western Washington Univ	WA	18,519	VC
Whitworth Univ	WA	47,734	VC
William Penn Univ	IA	26,000	C
William Woods Univ	MO	24,260	C
Wilmington College	OH	29,784	C
Wingate Univ	NC	34,990	C
Winona State Univ	MN	16,640	C
Youngstown State Univ	OH	16,732	C

JOURNALISM - MAGAZINE JOURNALISM

School	ST	$IS	SR
Ohio Univ	OH	21,080	C

JOURNALISM - NEWS & INFORMATION

School	ST	$IS	SR
Arizona State Univ, at the Downtown Phoenix Campus	AZ	22,101	C
Bloomfield College	NJ	37,850	LC
N Dak State Univ	ND		C
Ohio Univ	OH	21,080	C
Syracuse Univ	NY	56,346	VC

JOURNALISM - NEWSWRITING / EDIT

School	ST	$IS	SR
Ohio Univ	OH	21,080	C

JOURNALISM & TECHNICAL COMMUNICATIONS

School	ST	$IS	SR
Ferris State Univ	MI	20,047	C
The Pennsylvania State Univ - Univ Park	PA	28,022	VC+

JOURNALISM EDUCATION

School	ST	$IS	SR
Baylor Univ	TX	50,329	HC
Cal State, Northridge	CA	28,690	LC
Carlow Univ	PA	30,272	C
Grace College and Seminary	IN	28,800	VC
Indiana Univ Bloomington	IN	19,801	VC
Univ of Nebr - Lincoln	NE	18,031	VC
Wartburg College	IA	41,055	VC
Webster Univ	MO	35,100	C+

JUDAIC STUDIES

School	ST	$IS	SR
American Jewish Univ - College of A&S	CA	32,600	C
American Univ	DC	56,015	HC+
Arizona State Univ, at the Tempe Campus	AZ	20,137	C+
Bard College	NY	61,940	HC
Bennington College	VT	56,990	HC+
Binghamton Univ/The SUNY	NY	21,648	HC+
Brandeis Univ	MA		MC
Brown Univ	RI	59,428	MC
CUNY/Brooklyn College	NY	5,884	C+
DePaul Univ	IL	47,623	VC
Dickinson College	PA	57,662	HC+
Emory Univ	GA	56,368	MC
Florida Atlantic Univ	FL	17,339	C
George Washington Univ	DC	57,108	MC
Gettysburg College	PA	58,820	HC
Hampshire College	MA	58,320	MC
Hofstra Univ	NY	51,810	VC+
Hunter College	NY	14,429	VC
Indiana Univ Bloomington	IN	19,801	VC
List College	NY	21,600	
New York Univ	NY	61,470	MC
Northeastern Univ	MA	55,296	MC
Oberlin College	OH	61,788	HC
Purdue Univ/West Lafayette	IN	20,024	HC
Queens College/The CUNY	NY	17,107	VC
Rutgers, The State Univ of New Jersey/New Brunswick	NJ	25,562	VC
San Francisco State Univ	CA	18,514	C
Scripps College	CA	61,940	MC
Smith College	MA	59,674	MC
Stanford Univ	CA	58,388	MC
Syracuse Univ	NY	56,346	VC
Ohio State Univ-Columbus Campus	OH	19,887	HC+
The Pennsylvania State Univ - Univ Park	PA	28,022	VC+
The Univ of Okla	OK	18,621	VC
Touro College	NY	27,959	VC
Trinity College	CT		HC+
Tufts Univ	MA	58,780	MC
Tulane Univ	LA	60,861	MC
Univ of Arizona	AZ	20,657	C
Univ of Calif at Los Angeles	CA	25,686	MC
Univ of Calif at San Diego	CA	21,000	VC
Univ of Chicago	IL	55,416	MC
Univ of Cincinnati	OH	21,506	VC
Univ of Colo Boulder	CO	22,605	VC+
Univ of Denver	CO	51,787	VC+
Univ of Florida	FL	15,943	HC
Univ of Hartford	CT	42,674	C
Univ of Illinois at Chicago	IL	24,505	VC
Univ of Maryland - College Park	MD	20,060	HC
Univ of Mass Amherst	MA	24,215	VC+
Univ of Miami	FL	57,034	MC
Univ of Mich/Ann Arbor	MI	22,102	MC
Univ of Missouri-Kansas City	MO	19,603	C
Univ of Oregon	OR	21,360	C+
Univ of Pennsylvania	PA	61,132	MC
Univ of Southern Calif	CA	56,903	MC
Univ of Texas at Austin	TX	44,074	HC
Univ of Washington	WA	14,722	VC
Univ of Wisc/Madison	WI	18,757	HC+
Univ of Wisc-Milwaukee	WI	18,436	VC
Vanderbilt Univ	TN	58,220	MC
Vassar College	NY	61,140	MC
Washington Univ in St. Louis	MO	69,844	MC
Wellesley College	MA	59,038	MC
Yale Univ	CT	55,300	MC

JUSTICE AND SOCIETY

School	ST	$IS	SR
Creighton Univ	NE	45,356	VC
Georgetown College	KY	41,440	C+
Goddard College	VT	16,418	VC
Missouri Southern State Univ	MO	12,061	C
Mount Mary Univ	WI	33,590	LC
Northeastern Illinois Univ	IL	10,318	LC

KEYBOARD - PIANO CONCENTRATION

School	ST	$IS	SR
Aquinas College	MI	33,060	C
Baldwin Wallace Univ	OH	38,318	C
Cedarville Univ	OH	32,860	VC
Chapman Univ	CA	58,347	VC+
Murray State Univ	KY	15,304	C
Ouachita Baptist Univ	AR	30,220	VC
Texas Christian Univ	TX	49,980	HC
Univ of Cincinnati	OH	21,506	VC
Youngstown State Univ	OH	16,732	C

KINESIOLOGY

School	ST	$IS	SR
Aquinas College	MI	33,060	C
Calif Polytechnic State Univ	CA	19,847	HC
Cal State, Fullerton	CA	25,188	C
Cal State, Long Beach	CA	17,502	C+
Chapman Univ	CA	58,347	VC+
East Texas Baptist Univ	TX	31,577	LC
Eastern Illinois Univ	IL	20,466	C
Gannon Univ	PA	39,608	C
Georgia Regents Univ	GA		C
Hanover College	IN	43,073	C+
Indiana Univ Bloomington	IN	19,801	VC
Indiana Univ-Purdue Univ Indianapolis	IN	17,611	C
LIU Brooklyn	NY	47,182	LC
New Mexico State Univ	NM	14,050	C
Nova Southeastern Univ	FL	37,280	VC
St. Louis Univ	MO	48,346	HC
Shenandoah Univ	VA	39,916	C
Taylor Univ	IN	37,821	VC+
The Pennsylvania State Univ - Univ Park	PA	28,022	VC+
The SUNY/College at Brockport	NY	19,002	C
Univ of Alabama at Birmingham	AL	18,484	C+
Univ of Georgia	GA	20,082	VC
Univ of Louisiana at Monroe	LA	12,998	C
Univ of Maine	ME	19,902	C+
Univ of Nevada/Reno	NV	17,507	C
Univ of Wisc/Madison	WI	18,757	HC+
Univ of Wyoming	WY	14,401	C+
Wayne State Univ	MI	22,063	C

KITCHEN AND BATH DESIGN

School	ST	$IS	SR
Thomas Edison State College	NJ	5,700	SP

KOREAN

School	ST	$IS	SR
American Univ	DC	56,015	HC+
Binghamton Univ/The SUNY	NY	21,648	HC+
Brigham Young Univ	UT	12,100	HC
Northeastern Illinois Univ	IL	10,318	LC
Ohio State Univ-Columbus Campus	OH	19,887	HC+
Thomas Edison State College	NJ	5,700	SP
Univ of Calif at Irvine	CA	25,961	VC
Univ of Calif at Los Angeles	CA	25,686	MC
Univ of Hawaii at Manoa	HI	19,379	C

LABOR STUDIES

School	ST	$IS	SR
Cal State, Dominguez Hills	CA	17,090	LC
Cleveland State Univ	OH	21,776	C
Eastern Mich Univ	MI	18,604	C
Hofstra Univ	NY	51,810	VC+
Howard Univ	DC	13,646	C
Indiana Univ Bloomington	IN	19,801	VC
Indiana Univ Kokomo	IN	6,811	LC
Indiana Univ Northwest	IN	6,854	LC
Indiana Univ South Bend	IN	15,501	C
Indiana Univ-Purdue Univ Fort Wayne	IN	15,521	C
Indiana Univ-Purdue Univ Indianapolis	IN	17,611	C
Manhattan College	NY	49,588	C+
Northern Kentucky Univ	KY	21,134	C
Queens College/The CUNY	NY	17,107	VC
Rutgers, The State Univ of New Jersey/New Brunswick	NJ	25,562	VC
San Francisco State Univ	CA	18,514	C
SUNY/Empire State College	NY	6,315	SP
SUNY College at Old Westbury	NY	16,324	C
Thomas Edison State College	NJ	5,700	SP
Univ of Akron	OH	20,436	C
Univ of Illinois at Urbana-Champaign	IL	26,450	HC
Univ of Mass Boston	MA	23,066	VC
Univ of PR Recinto de Rio Piedras	PR	5,750	
Wayne State Univ	MI	22,063	C

LABORATORY ANIMAL SCIENCE

School	ST	$IS	SR
Thomas Edison State College	NJ	5,700	SP

LAND USE MANAGEMENT AND RECLAMATION

School	ST	$IS	SR
Cal State, Bakersfield	CA	8,000	C
Eastern Mich Univ	MI	18,604	C
Humboldt State Univ	CA	18,400	C
Metropolitan State Univ of Denver	CO	4,835	LC
Montana State Univ	MT	14,068	C
Prescott College	AZ	33,284	C
Texas A&M Univ at Galveston	TX	11,258	C
Texas State Univ	TX	17,128	C
Unity College	ME	34,054	C
Univ of Louisiana at Lafayette	LA	6,130	C
Univ of Wisc/Platteville	WI	14,564	C
Univ of Wisc/River Falls	WI	9,722	LC

LANDSCAPE ARCHITECTURE

School	ST	$IS	SR
Calif Polytechnic State Univ	CA	19,847	HC
Cornell Univ	NY	60,964	MC
The Pennsylvania State Univ - Univ Park	PA	28,022	VC+
Univ of Arkansas at Fayetteville	AR	18,352	C+
Univ of Georgia	GA	20,082	VC
Univ of Nebr - Lincoln	NE	18,031	VC

LANDSCAPE ARCHITECTURE/ DESIGN

School	ST	$IS	SR
Andrews Univ	MI	28,030	C+
Arizona State Univ, at the Tempe Campus	AZ	20,137	C+
Auburn Univ	AL	22,378	VC+
Augustana College	IL	43,398	VC
Ball State Univ	IN	17,850	C
Boston Architectural College	MA	18,622	SP
Brigham Young Univ	UT	12,100	HC
Calif State Polytechnic Univ, Pomona	CA	20,156	C
CUNY/City College	NY	20,319	HC+
Clemson Univ	SC	19,136	HC
Colo State Univ-Fort Collins	CO	20,385	VC
Florida International Univ	FL	17,747	C+
Florida Southern College	FL	40,150	C+
Iowa State Univ	IA	16,403	C
Kansas State Univ	KS	15,497	VC
Louisiana State Univ	LA	18,677	C+
Mich State Univ	MI	22,450	VC
Miss State Univ	MS	14,750	C
N Car Agricultural and Technical State Univ	NC	13,365	LC
N Car State Univ	NC	16,202	HC
N Dak State Univ	ND		C
Northeastern Univ	MA	55,296	MC
Okla State Univ	OK	14,310	VC
Philadelphia Univ	PA	44,160	C
Purdue Univ/West Lafayette	IN	20,024	HC
S Dak State Univ	SD	14,296	C
SUNY / College of Environmental Science and Forestry	NY	18,351	VC
Temple Univ	PA	24,392	VC
Texas A&M Univ	TX	19,207	VC
Texas Tech Univ	TX	14,243	C
Ohio State Univ-Columbus Campus	OH	19,887	HC+
The Pennsylvania State Univ - Univ Park	PA	28,022	VC+
The SUNY College of Agriculture and Tech at Cobleskill	NY	19,749	VC
Univ of Arizona	AZ	20,657	C
Univ of Arkansas at Fayetteville	AR	18,352	C+
Univ of Calif at Berkeley	CA	23,322	MC
Univ of Calif at Davis	CA		HC
Univ of Conn	CT	24,706	VC
Univ of Delaware	DE	23,612	VC
Univ of Florida	FL	15,943	HC
Univ of Idaho	ID	14,558	C
Univ of Illinois at Urbana-Champaign	IL	26,450	HC
Univ of Kentucky	KY	19,868	C
Univ of Maryland - College Park	MD	20,060	HC
Univ of Mass Amherst	MA	24,215	VC+
Univ of Minn/Twin Cities	MN		HC
Univ of Nebr - Lincoln	NE	18,031	VC
Univ of Nevada, Las Vegas	NV	17,303	C
Univ of Oregon	OR	21,360	C+
Univ of Texas at Arlington	TX	10,908	LC
Univ of Texas at Austin	TX	44,074	HC
Univ of Vermont	VT	27,006	VC
Univ of Washington	WA	14,722	VC
Univ of Wisc/Madison	WI	18,757	HC+
Utah State Univ	UT	12,044	C
Virginia Polytechnic Inst and State Univ	VA	14,629	HC
Washington State Univ	WA	20,461	C
West Virginia Univ	WV	16,542	C+

LANGUAGE ARTS

School	ST	$IS	SR
Aquinas College	MI	33,060	C
Calvin College	MI	39,120	VC
Catawba College	NC	37,240	LC
Central Washington Univ	WA	11,730	C
College of St. Mary	NE	35,184	C
Concordia Univ, Ann Arbor	MI	27,220	VC
Eastern Mich Univ	MI	18,604	C
Hope College	MI	38,650	VC
Kent State Univ	OH	19,920	C
Lake Erie College	OH	37,266	C
LeMoyne-Owen College	TN	13,100	C
Madonna Univ	MI	24,540	VC
Malone Univ	OH	35,364	C
Marygrove College	MI	28,926	C
Miles College	AL	11,164	NC
Missouri Southern State Univ	MO	12,061	C
Nebr Wesleyan Univ	NE	29,774	C+
Northern Mich Univ	MI	18,278	C
Ohio Northern Univ	OH	42,075	VC
Ohio Univ	OH	21,080	C
Seattle Pacific Univ	WA	41,559	VC+
Spring Arbor Univ	MI	26,740	C
The Univ of Okla	OK	18,621	VC
Univ of Calif at Santa Cruz	CA	27,807	C+
Univ of Mich/Dearborn	MI	9,885	VC
Univ of Nebr - Lincoln	NE	18,031	VC
Wayne State Univ	MI	22,063	C
Wells College	NY	49,400	VC
Western Kentucky Univ	KY	11,000	LC
Wright State Univ	OH	16,983	C

LANGUAGES

School	ST	$IS	SR
Adelphi Univ	NY	44,670	VC
Arkansas Tech Univ	AR	13,982	LC
Assumption College	MA	47,122	C+
Auburn Univ	AL	22,378	VC+
Austin Peay State Univ	TN	15,274	C
Baylor Univ	TX	50,329	HC
Bellarmine Univ	KY	42,950	VC
Bemidji State Univ	MN	13,500	VC
Bennington College	VT	56,990	HC+

School	ST	$IS	SR
Cal State, Northridge	CA	28,690	LC
Cameron Univ	OK	10,004	LC
Carnegie Mellon Univ	PA	51,260	MC
Carson-Newman Univ	TN	29,058	C+
Carthage College	WI	33,000	C
Clark Atlanta Univ	GA	30,006	LC
Clark Univ	MA	47,020	HC+
College of St. Scholastica	MN	41,440	C
Colo State Univ-Fort Collins	CO	20,385	VC
Columbia College	SC	27,882	C
Converse College	SC	37,130	C
Cornell Univ	IA	44,930	VC
Davis & Elkins College	WV	33,742	C
Denison Univ	OH	54,670	HC+
Dordt College	IA	34,160	C+
Dowling College	NY	25,000	LC
Earlham College	IN	51,470	HC
Elmira College	NY	49,950	C+
Excelsior College	NY	5,580	SP
Frostburg State Univ	MD	15,264	LC
Gordon College	MA	44,320	VC
Grand Valley State Univ	MI	17,998	C+
Hamilton College	NY	55,620	MC
Hartwick College	NY	51,270	C
Hunter College	NY	14,429	VC
Ithaca College	NY	53,864	HC
Jackson State Univ	MS	13,512	LC
Lehman College/The CUNY	NY	5,778	LC
Lewis & Clark College	OR	54,382	MC
Louisiana College	LA	15,746	C
McNeese State Univ	LA	2,649	C
Mercyhurst Univ	PA	40,700	C
Miss College	MS	21,998	C
Miss State Univ	MS	14,750	C
New York Univ	NY	61,470	MC
Newberry College	SC	26,850	LC
Northeastern Univ	MA	55,296	MC
Occidental College	CA	60,972	MC
Pomona College	CA	57,680	MC
Portland State Univ	OR	18,672	C
Principia College	IL	35,140	C+
Richard Stockton College of New Jersey	NJ	20,000	VC
Roger Williams Univ	RI	46,296	VC
Roosevelt Univ	IL	22,605	VC
Samford Univ	AL	37,060	C+
San Francisco State Univ	CA	18,514	C
Scripps College	CA	61,940	MC
Southern Illinois Univ Edwardsville	IL	17,532	C
Southern Methodist Univ	TX	60,585	MC
Southern Oregon Univ	OR	17,874	C
St. Cloud State Univ	MN	10,600	C
St. John's Univ	NY	55,070	C+
St. Lawrence Univ	NY	59,972	VC
St. Mary's College of Maryland	MD	25,754	VC
Tenn State Univ	TN	9,048	C
Texas A&M Univ at Commerce	TX	10,496	C
The Univ of Memphis	TN	15,094	C
The Univ of Okla	OK	18,621	VC
United States Military Academy	NY		MC
Univ of Alabama in Huntsville	AL	17,591	VC+
Univ of Alaska Anchorage	AK	16,673	NC
Univ of Calif at Riverside	CA	27,204	C+
Univ of Central Florida	FL	15,668	VC+
Univ of Delaware	DE	23,612	VC
Univ of Denver	CO	51,787	VC+
Univ of Hartford	CT	42,674	C
Univ of Minn/Twin Cities	MN		HC
Univ of New Mexico	NM	15,300	C
Univ of PR Recinto de Rio Piedras	PR	5,750	
Univ of South Alabama	AL	13,510	C
Univ of Southern Miss	MS	13,170	C
Univ of Texas at El Paso	TX	8,764	NC
Virginia Commonwealth Univ	VA	21,716	C
Virginia Wesleyan College	VA	28,433	LC
Washington Univ in St. Louis	MO	69,844	MC
Wilson College	PA	35,080	C
Xavier Univ of Louisiana	LA	25,300	C

LASER ELECTRO-OPTICS TECHNOLOGY

School	ST	$IS	SR
Idaho State Univ	ID	12,307	C
Oregon Inst of Technology	OR	8,910	C

LATIN

School	ST	$IS	SR
Austin College	TX	45,875	HC
Barnard College/Columbia Univ	NY	39,000	MC
Baylor Univ	TX	50,329	HC
Binghamton Univ/The SUNY	NY	21,648	HC+
Boston Univ	MA	60,694	MC
Bowling Green State Univ	OH	18,970	C
Brigham Young Univ	UT	12,100	HC
Bryn Mawr College	PA	59,890	MC
Butler Univ	IN	47,572	VC+
Calvin College	MI	39,120	VC
Carleton College	MN	60,102	MC
Centenary College of Louisiana	LA	45,650	C+
Colgate Univ	NY	58,135	MC
College of Wooster	OH	52,600	VC
Columbia Univ/City of New York	NY	61,116	MC
Concordia College - Moorhead	MN	39,974	VC
Creighton Univ	NE	45,356	VC
Denison Univ	OH	54,670	HC+
DePauw Univ	IN	48,950	VC+
Dickinson College	PA	57,662	HC+
Duquesne Univ	PA	43,720	VC
Emory Univ	GA	56,368	MC
Florida State Univ	FL	16,715	VC
Fordham Univ	NY	61,588	MC
Franklin and Marshall College	PA	60,799	MC
Furman Univ	SC	54,006	HC
Gettysburg College	PA	58,820	HC
Hampden-Sydney College	VA	51,758	C
Harvard College/Harvard Univ	MA	49,000	MC
Haverford College	PA	61,564	MC
Hobart and William Smith Colleges	NY	60,034	HC+
Hofstra Univ	NY	51,810	VC+
Hope College	MI	38,650	VC
Hunter College	NY	14,429	VC
Indiana Univ Bloomington	IN	19,801	VC
John Carroll Univ	OH	46,300	C+
Kent State Univ	OH	19,920	C
Kenyon College	OH	58,890	MC
Knox College	IL	44,865	VC+
Lehman College/The CUNY	NY	5,778	LC
Loyola Marymount Univ	CA	54,649	VC+
Loyola Univ Chicago	IL	51,646	VC
Loyola Univ Maryland	MD	56,880	VC+
Marlboro College	VT	35,980	VC
Mercer Univ	GA	44,201	VC
Mich State Univ	MI	22,450	VC
Missouri State Univ	MO	13,996	C+
Monmouth College	IL	40,850	C
Montclair State Univ	NJ	22,614	C
Mount Holyoke College	MA	55,146	MC
New York Univ	NY	61,470	MC
Ohio Univ	OH	21,080	C
Purdue Univ/West Lafayette	IN	20,024	HC
Purdue Univ/West Lafayette	IN	20,024	HC
Randolph-Macon College	VA	49,869	C+
Rockford College	IL	31,000	C
Rutgers, The State Univ of New Jersey/New Brunswick	NJ	25,562	VC
St. Joseph's Univ	PA	55,006	VC
Samford Univ	AL	37,060	C+
Sarah Lawrence College	NY	48,000	HC
Seattle Pacific Univ	WA	41,559	VC+
Sewanee: The Univ of the South	TN	47,700	HC+
Smith College	MA	59,674	MC
Southwestern Univ	TX	45,660	VC
St. Catherine Univ	MN	37,782	C+
St. Olaf College	MN	51,200	HC+
Swarthmore College	PA	57,870	MC
The Catholic Univ of America	DC	52,852	VC
The Univ of Tenn at Chattanooga	TN	16,883	C
Trinity Univ	TX	48,150	HC+
Tufts Univ	MA	58,780	MC
Univ of Calif at Berkeley	CA	23,322	MC
Univ of Calif at Davis	CA		NC
Univ of Calif at Los Angeles	CA	25,686	VC
Univ of Georgia	GA	20,082	VC
Univ of Iowa	IA	17,693	VC
Univ of Mich/Ann Arbor	MI	22,102	MC
Univ of Minn/Twin Cities	MN		HC
Univ of Nebr - Lincoln	NE	18,031	VC
Univ of New Hampshire	NH	26,912	C
Univ of Oregon	OR	21,360	C+
Univ of Scranton	PA	51,940	VC
Univ of Texas at Austin	TX	44,074	HC
Univ of Vermont	VT	27,006	VC+
Univ of Wisc/Madison	WI	18,757	HC+
Wabash College	IN	46,850	C+
Wake Forest Univ	NC	58,838	MC
Washington Univ in St. Louis	MO	69,844	MC
Wellesley College	MA	59,038	MC
West Chester Univ of Pennsylvania	PA	17,186	C
Western Mich Univ	MI	19,628	C
Westminster College	PA	31,290	C
Wheaton College	MA	54,934	HC+
Wichita State Univ	KS	14,607	C+
Wright State Univ	OH	16,983	C

LATIN AMERICAN STUDIES

School	ST	$IS	SR
Adelphi Univ	NY	44,670	VC
Albright College	PA	46,660	C
American Univ	DC	56,015	HC+
Appalachian State Univ	NC	12,919	VC
Arizona State Univ, at the Tempe Campus	AZ	20,137	C+
Arizona State Univ, at the West Campus	AZ	19,251	C
Assumption College	MA	47,122	C+
Austin College	TX	45,875	HC
Ball State Univ	IN	17,850	C
Bard College	NY	61,940	HC
Bates College	ME	60,720	MC
Baylor Univ	TX	50,329	HC
Bennington College	VT	56,990	HC+
Binghamton Univ/The SUNY	NY	21,648	HC+
Birmingham-Southern College	AL	44,168	VC+
Boston Univ	MA	60,694	MC
Bowdoin College	ME	59,568	MC
Brandeis Univ	MA		MC
Brigham Young Univ	UT	12,100	HC
Brown Univ	RI	59,428	MC
Bucknell Univ	PA	60,140	MC
Cal State, Chico	CA	20,158	C
Cal State, East Bay	CA	16,549	C
Cal State, Fresno	CA	17,405	C
Cal State, Fullerton	CA	25,188	C
Cal State, Los Angeles	CA	17,186	LC
Canisius College	NY	44,900	C
Carleton College	MN	60,102	MC
CUNY/Brooklyn College	NY	5,884	C+
CUNY/City College	NY	20,319	LC
Colby College	ME	57,510	MC
Colgate Univ	NY	58,135	MC
College of Charleston	SC	22,145	VC
College of William & Mary	VA	28,000	MC
Columbia Univ/City of New York	NY	61,116	MC
Columbia Univ/School of General Studies	NY	58,231	MC
Conn College	CT	54,970	MC
Cornell College	IA	44,930	VC
Dartmouth College	NH	57,996	MC
Davidson College	NC	58,146	MC
Denison Univ	OH	54,670	HC+
DePaul Univ	IL	47,623	VC
Dickinson College	PA	57,662	HC+
Earlham College	IN	51,470	HC
Eastern Mich Univ	MI	18,604	C
Emory Univ	GA	56,368	MC
Flagler College	FL	25,180	C
Florida State Univ	FL	16,715	VC
Fordham Univ	NY	61,588	HC+
George Mason Univ	VA	15,724	VC
George Washington Univ	DC	57,108	MC
Gettysburg College	PA	58,820	HC
Hamline Univ	MN	45,678	VC
Hampshire College	MA	58,320	MC
Hobart and William Smith Colleges	NY	60,034	HC+
Hofstra Univ	NY	51,810	VC+
Hood College	MD	45,730	C
Hunter College	NY	14,429	VC
Johns Hopkins Univ	MD	47,492	MC
Kent State Univ	OH	19,920	C
Knox College	IL	44,865	VC+
Lake Forest College	IL	50,652	VC
Linfield College-McMinnville Campus	OR	47,676	C
Lock Haven Univ of Pennsylvania	PA	18,028	LC
Loyola Univ New Orleans	LA	46,581	VC
Macalester College	MN	57,691	MC
Miami Univ	OH	24,191	VC
Middlebury College	VT	59,160	MC
Millsaps College	MS	43,888	VC+
Mount Holyoke College	MA	55,146	MC
New College of Florida	FL	14,504	NC
New York Univ	NY	61,470	MC
Oakland Univ	MI	19,391	C
Oberlin College	OH	61,788	MC
Occidental College	CA	60,972	MC
Ohio Univ	OH	21,080	C
Pace Univ	NY	53,367	C
Pitzer College	CA	54,988	MC
Pomona College	CA	57,680	MC
Prescott College	AZ	33,284	C
Queens College/The CUNY	NY	17,107	VC
Rhode Island College	RI	17,694	LC
Rhodes College	TN	51,900	HC+
Ripon College	WI	36,959	C+
Rollins College	FL	52,370	HC
Rutgers, The State Univ of New Jersey/New Brunswick	NJ	25,562	VC
Sacred Heart Univ	CT	49,264	VC
St. Louis Univ	MO	48,346	HC
St. Mary's Univ	TX	33,854	C
St. Peter's Univ	NJ	44,240	C
Samford Univ	AL	37,060	C+
San Diego State Univ	CA	21,611	VC
Scripps College	CA	61,940	MC
Seattle Pacific Univ	WA	41,559	VC+
Seton Hall Univ	NJ	45,902	C
Smith College	MA	59,674	MC
Sonoma State Univ	CA	20,541	C
Southern Methodist Univ	TX	60,585	MC
Southern Nazarene Univ	OK	24,354	C
Southwestern Univ	TX	45,660	VC
St. Edward's Univ	TX	47,784	C
Stanford Univ	CA	58,388	MC
SUNY New Paltz	NY	14,348	C
SUNY Plattsburgh / SUNY	NY	18,083	C
Syracuse Univ	NY	56,346	VC
Temple Univ	PA	24,392	VC
Texas Tech Univ	TX	14,243	C
The Pennsylvania State Univ - Univ Park	PA	28,022	VC+
The Univ of Utah	UT	16,463	VC
Tufts Univ	MA	58,780	MC
Tulane Univ	LA	60,861	MC
Union College	KY	29,955	C
Univ at Albany / SUNY	NY	18,674	VC
Univ of Arizona	AZ	20,657	C
Univ of Arkansas at Fayetteville	AR	18,352	C+
Univ of Calif at Berkeley	CA	23,322	MC
Univ of Calif at Los Angeles	CA	25,686	MC
Univ of Calif at Riverside	CA	27,204	C+
Univ of Calif at San Diego	CA	21,000	MC
Univ of Calif at Santa Barbara	CA	27,551	HC
Univ of Calif at Santa Cruz	CA	27,807	C+
Univ of Central Florida	FL	15,668	VC+
Univ of Chicago	IL	55,416	MC
Univ of Cincinnati	OH	21,506	VC
Univ of Conn	CT	24,706	HC
Univ of Delaware	DE	23,612	VC
Univ of Georgia	GA	20,082	VC
Univ of Idaho	ID	14,558	C
Univ of Illinois at Chicago	IL	24,505	VC
Univ of Illinois at Urbana-Champaign	IL	26,450	HC
Univ of Kansas	KS	17,603	C+
Univ of Kentucky	KY	19,868	C
Univ of Miami	FL	57,034	MC
Univ of Mich/Ann Arbor	MI	22,102	MC
Univ of Minn/Morris	MN	17,150	VC
Univ of Nebr - Lincoln	NE	18,031	VC
Univ of Nebr at Omaha	NE	12,700	C
Univ of New Mexico	NM	15,300	C
Univ of N Car at Chapel Hill	NC	18,928	MC
Univ of N Car at Charlotte	NC	15,547	C
Univ of Oregon	OR	21,360	C+
Univ of Pennsylvania	PA	61,132	MC
Univ of Rochester	NY	60,668	MC
Univ of San Francisco	CA	54,770	VC
Univ of S Car at Columbia	SC	19,725	VC+
Univ of Southern Calif	CA	56,903	MC
Univ of Texas - Pan American	TX	11,125	LC
Univ of Texas at Austin	TX	44,074	HC
Univ of Texas at El Paso	TX	8,764	NC
Univ of Vermont	VT	27,006	VC+
Univ of Wisc/Eau Claire	WI	15,730	VC
Univ of Wisc/Madison	WI	18,757	HC+
Univ of Wisc-Milwaukee	WI	18,436	C
Vanderbilt Univ	TN	58,220	MC
Vassar College	NY	61,140	MC
Villanova Univ	PA	58,394	MC
Washington Univ in St. Louis	MO	69,844	MC
Wellesley College	MA	59,038	MC
Wesleyan Univ	CT	61,198	MC
Willamette Univ	OR	56,450	VC+
Wofford College	SC	45,795	VC
Yale Univ	CT	55,300	MC

LAW

School	ST	$IS	SR
American Univ	DC	56,015	HC+
Amherst College	MA	58,744	MC
Bay Path College	MA	34,565	C
Bryant Univ	RI	49,179	VC
Dickinson College	PA	57,662	HC+
Florida Gulf Coast Univ	FL		C
Franciscan Univ of Steubenville	OH	27,320	VC
Grand Valley State Univ	MI	17,998	C+
Hampshire College	MA	58,320	MC
Hood College	MD	45,730	C
Howard Univ	DC	13,646	C
Indiana Inst of Technology	IN	34,240	LC
John Jay College of Criminal Justice/The CUNY	NY	6,359	LC
Lasell College	MA	43,750	LC
Minn State Univ, Moorhead	MN	13,392	VC
Montclair State Univ	NJ	22,614	C
Mount Aloysius College	PA	29,976	C
Mount Ida College	MA	30,115	C
New England College	NH	45,930	LC
New York Univ	NY	61,470	MC
Nichols College	MA	37,240	LC
Oberlin College	OH	61,788	MC
Park Univ	MO	17,525	C
Ramapo College of New Jersey	NJ	24,938	C
Regis College	MA	47,565	LC
Scripps College	CA	61,940	MC
South Univ	GA	36,070	C
Southern Illinois Univ Carbondale	IL	21,942	C
The College of St. Rose	NY	26,750	C
Towson Univ	MD	16,000	VC
United States Air Force Academy	CO		MC
United States Military Academy	NY		MC
Univ of Arizona	AZ	20,657	C
Univ of Arkansas at Little Rock	AR	17,609	LC

ST = STATE $IS = IN-STATE COSTS   SR = SELECTOR RATING

School	ST	$IS	SR
Univ of Calif at Berkeley	CA	23,322	MC
Univ of Calif at Santa Cruz	CA	27,807	C+
Univ of Chicago	IL	55,416	MC
Univ of Georgia	GA	20,082	VC
Univ of Hartford	CT	42,674	C
Univ of Mass Amherst	MA	24,215	VC+
Univ of Pennsylvania	PA	61,132	MC
Univ of Wisc/Madison	WI	18,757	HC+
Univ of Wisc/Superior	WI	14,314	C
Ursuline College	OH	33,198	C
Western New England Univ	MA	46,154	C+
Wilson College	PA	35,080	C

LAW ENFORCEMENT AND CORRECTIONS

School	ST	$IS	SR
Adams State Univ	CO	13,358	LC
Amridge Univ	AL	6,870	LC
Ashford Univ	CA	10,480	LC
Calumet College of St. Joseph	IN	15,000	C
College of the Ozarks	MO		VC
Frostburg State Univ	MD	15,264	LC
Idaho State Univ	ID	12,307	C
Indiana Inst of Technology	IN	34,240	LC
Indiana Wesleyan Univ	IN	31,815	VC
Kent State Univ	OH	19,920	C
Le Moyne College	NY	43,470	C
Metropolitan State Univ	MN	5,923	
Minn State Univ, Mankato	MN	15,616	C
Missouri Southern State Univ	MO	12,061	C
Mount Aloysius College	PA	29,976	C
Point Park Univ	PA	36,390	C
Portland State Univ	OR	18,672	C
St. Paul's College	VA	16,030	NC
Sam Houston State Univ	TX	17,082	C
Southwest Minn State Univ	MN	14,000	C
Stephen F. Austin State Univ	TX	14,668	C
Tarleton State Univ	TX	13,489	LC
Texas State Univ	TX	17,128	C
The Univ of Virginia's College at Wise	VA	11,076	C
Tiffin Univ	OH	30,273	LC
Unity College	ME	34,054	C
Univ of Great Falls	MT	27,970	C
Univ of Illinois at Chicago	IL	24,505	VC
Univ of Indianapolis	IN	31,740	LC
Univ of Maine at Augusta	ME	6,855	C
Univ of New Haven	CT	48,940	C
Univ of San Francisco	CA	54,770	VC
Washburn Univ	KS	12,579	C
Western Conn State Univ	CT	18,327	LC
Western Illinois Univ	IL	20,732	C
Western New Mexico Univ	NM	8,500	C
Western Oregon Univ	OR	15,021	C
Youngstown State Univ	OH	16,732	C

LEARNER DESIGNED AREA OF STUDY

School	ST	$IS	SR
Bloomfield College	NJ	37,850	LC
Bowling Green State Univ	OH	18,970	C
Goddard College	VT	16,418	VC
Thomas Edison State College	NJ	5,700	SP
Univ of Illinois at Chicago	IL	24,505	VC

LEGAL STUDIES

School	ST	$IS	SR
Bryant Univ	RI	49,179	VC
Burlington College	VT	32,510	SP
Champlain College	VT	46,650	VC+
Claremont McKenna College	CA	62,215	MC
Culver-Stockton College	MO	30,900	C
Dominican Univ	IL	37,628	C
Elizabethtown College	PA	49,740	VC
Faulkner Univ	AL	25,720	LC
Harding Univ	AR	23,556	VC
Howard Univ	DC	13,646	C
Illinois State Univ	IL	23,110	VC
Indiana Univ Bloomington	IN	19,801	VC
Ithaca College	NY	53,864	HC
Lipscomb Univ	TN	37,490	VC
Manhattanville College	NY	50,740	VC
Mercy College	NY	30,456	C
Monmouth Univ	NJ	44,018	C
Nazareth College of Rochester	NY	43,028	C+
New England College	NH	45,930	LC
Newbury College	MA	43,280	LC
Nova Southeastern Univ	FL	37,280	VC
Old Dominion Univ	VA	19,483	C
Paul Quinn College	TX	25,350	C
Point Park Univ	PA	36,390	C
Roger Williams Univ	RI	46,296	VC
St. John Fisher College	NY	40,708	C+
St. John's Univ	NY	57,034	MC
Temple Univ	PA	24,392	VC
Tulane Univ	LA	60,861	MC
Univ at Buffalo / The SUNY	NY	20,243	VC+
Univ of Central Florida	FL	15,668	VC+
Univ of Central Okla	OK	12,293	C
Univ of Miami	FL	57,034	MC
Univ of New Haven	CT	48,940	C
Univ of Pittsburgh at Pittsburgh	PA	28,572	VC
Webster Univ	MO	35,100	C+
Wesley College	DE	31,115	LC

LIBERAL ARTS, SCIENCES, GENERAL STUDIES, HUMANITIES

School	ST	$IS	SR
Aquinas College	MI	33,060	C
Bloomfield College	NJ	37,850	LC
Excelsior College	NY	5,580	SP
Fairfield Univ	CT	56,960	VC
LIU Post	NY	47,660	C
Murray State Univ	KY	15,304	C
Taylor Univ	IN	37,821	VC+
Washington College	MD	52,602	VC
Western Illinois Univ	IL	20,732	C
Wilson College	PA	35,080	C

LIBERAL ARTS/ENGINEERING STUDIES

School	ST	$IS	SR
Calif Polytechnic State Univ	CA	19,847	HC

LIBERAL ARTS/GENERAL STUDIES

School	ST	$IS	SR
Abilene Christian Univ	TX	38,400	C+
Adams State Univ	CO	13,358	LC
Alaska Pacific Univ	AK	43,592	VC
Albertus Magnus College	CT	37,382	LC
Alvernia Univ	PA	39,250	LC
American International College	MA	36,100	LC
American Jewish Univ - College of A&S	CA	32,600	C
Amridge Univ	AL	6,870	LC
Angelo State Univ	TX	15,049	NC
Anna Maria College	MA	34,600	C
Aquinas College	MI	33,060	C
Aquinas College	TN	29,250	VC+
Arcadia Univ	PA	33,570	C+
Armstrong State Univ	GA	15,532	C
Ashford Univ	CA	10,480	LC
Atlantic Union College	MA	24,600	C
Auburn Univ at Montgomery	AL	14,470	LC
Austin Peay State Univ	TN	15,274	C
Averett Univ	VA	37,750	LC
Azusa Pacific Univ	CA	42,086	C
Ball State Univ	IN	17,850	C
Barry Univ	FL	38,190	C
Bay Path College	MA	34,565	C
Beacon College	FL	41,720	C
Becker College	MA	41,420	C
Bellarmine Univ	KY	42,950	VC
Belmont Abbey College	NC	37,716	C
Belmont Univ	TN	39,190	VC+
Benedictine College	KS	29,180	VC
Bennington College	VT	56,990	HC+
Bentley Univ	MA	56,454	HC+
Bethel Univ	IN	31,560	C
Bethune-Cookman Univ	FL	22,958	C
Biola Univ	CA	40,320	C+
Bloomfield College	NJ	37,850	LC
Boricua College	NY	8,600	C
Bowling Green State Univ	OH	18,970	C
Bradley Univ	IL	31,874	VC
Brenau Univ - Women's College	GA	26,650	LC
Brescia Univ	KY	26,140	VC+
Brewton-Parker College	GA	33,388	C
Bridgewater College	VA	41,450	C
Bryan College	TN	24,194	C
Burlington College	VT	32,510	SP
Cabrini College	PA	40,859	LC
Cairn Univ	PA	33,270	C
Calif Baptist Univ	CA	38,792	C
Calif Lutheran Univ	CA	49,540	C+
Calif Polytechnic State Univ	CA	19,847	HC
Calif State Polytechnic Univ, Pomona	CA	20,156	C
Cal State, Bakersfield	CA	8,000	C
Cal State, Chico	CA	20,158	C
Cal State, Dominguez Hills	CA	17,090	LC
Cal State, East Bay	CA	16,549	C
Cal State, Fresno	CA	17,405	C
Cal State, Fullerton	CA	25,188	C
Cal State, Los Angeles	CA	17,186	LC
Cal State, Monterey Bay	CA	26,871	LC
Cal State, Northridge	CA	28,690	LC
Cal State, San Bernardino	CA	12,000	C
Cal State, San Marcos	CA	14,576	LC
Cal State, Stanislaus	CA	18,582	C
Calif Univ of Pennsylvania	PA	14,217	C
Calumet College of St. Joseph	IN	15,000	C
Canisius College	NY	44,900	C
Carlow Univ	PA	30,272	C
Castleton State College	VT	20,186	C
Cazenovia College	NY	43,464	C
Cedarville Univ	OH	32,860	VC
Centenary College of Louisiana	LA	45,650	C+
Central Washington Univ	WA	11,730	C
Chaminade Univ of Honolulu	HI	31,664	LC
Champlain College	VT	46,650	VC+
Charter Oak State College	CT	8,592	
Chestnut Hill College	PA	42,110	LC
Cheyney Univ of Pennsylvania	PA	20,372	LC
Christian Brothers Univ	TN	31,670	HC
City Univ of Seattle	WA	14,880	NC
Clarion Univ of Pennsylvania	PA	17,370	LC
Clarke Univ	IA	37,600	C
Cleveland State Univ	OH	21,776	C
College of Mount St. Joseph	OH	33,880	C
College of Mount St. Vincent	NY	41,040	MC
College of St. Benedict	MN	49,359	VC
College of St. Mary	NE	35,184	C
College of St Joseph	VT	30,600	LC
Colo Christian Univ	CO	27,500	VC
Colo College	CO	57,162	MC
Colo Mesa Univ	CO	17,690	LC
Colo State Univ-Fort Collins	CO	20,385	VC
Columbia College	MO	24,578	C
Concordia Univ Irvine	CA	35,390	VC
Concordia Univ Texas	TX	23,640	C
Coppin State Univ	MD	16,227	VC
Cornerstone Univ and Grand Rapids Theological Seminary	MI	33,338	C
Curry College	MA	48,925	LC
Dallas Baptist Univ	TX	30,580	VC
De Sales Univ	PA	43,970	C
Dominican Univ of Calif	CA	51,250	C
Dowling College	NY	25,000	LC
Duquesne Univ	PA	43,720	VC
East Carolina Univ	NC	14,169	C
East Central Univ	OK	10,223	C
East Tenn State Univ	TN	9,000	C
Eastern Conn State Univ	CT	20,584	C
Eastern Mennonite Univ	VA	40,660	C
Eastern Oregon Univ	OR	10,400	C
Edinboro Univ of Pennsylvania	PA	15,940	LC
Elmhurst College	IL	43,336	C
Emmanuel College	MA	47,985	VC
Emporia State Univ	KS	12,897	C
Endicott College	MA	43,228	VC+
Eureka College	IL	19,280	C
Excelsior College	NY	5,580	SP
Fairleigh Dickinson Univ/ College at Florham	NJ	42,142	C
Fairleigh Dickinson Univ/ Metropolitan Campus	NJ	40,254	C
Faulkner Univ	AL	25,720	LC
Felician College	NJ	41,640	LC
Ferrum College	VA	27,740	LC
Flagler College	FL	25,180	C
Florida Atlantic Univ	FL	17,339	C
Florida Gulf Coast Univ	FL		C
Florida International Univ	FL	17,747	C+
Fontbonne Univ	MO	31,384	C
Fort Hays State Univ	KS	11,354	C
Francis Marion Univ	SC	16,464	LC
Friends Univ	KS	29,100	C
Frostburg State Univ	MD	15,264	C
Gallaudet Univ	DC	25,380	SP
George Washington Univ	DC	57,108	MC
Georgetown Univ	KY	41,440	LC
Georgia College and State Univ	GA	18,900	C+
Glenville State College	WV	11,348	NC
Goddard College	VT	16,418	VC
Graceland Univ	IA	28,020	C
Grand Valley State Univ	MI	17,998	C+
Granite State College	NH	6,195	NC
Green Mountain College	VT	45,228	LC
Greenville College	IL	27,012	C
Hannibal-LaGrange Univ	MO	24,490	C
Harding Univ	AR	23,556	C
Harris-Stowe State Univ	MO	14,360	NC
Haverford College	PA	61,564	MC
Hilbert College	NY	28,550	C
Hofstra Univ	NY	51,810	VC+
Holy Names Univ	CA	40,310	NC
Hope International Univ	CA	34,650	C
Houghton College	NY	36,808	C+
Houston Baptist Univ	TX	36,450	C
Howard Payne Univ	TX	17,115	C
Humboldt State Univ	CA	18,400	C
Idaho State Univ	ID	12,307	C
Indiana State Univ	IN	16,000	C
Indiana Univ Bloomington	IN	19,801	VC
Indiana Univ-Purdue Univ Fort Wayne	IN	15,521	C
Indiana Wesleyan Univ	IN	31,815	VC
Iona College	NY	44,028	VC
Iowa State Univ	IA	16,043	C
Ithaca College	NY	53,864	HC
James Madison Univ	VA	18,049	VC
John Carroll Univ	OH	46,300	C+
Johnson C. Smith Univ	NC	25,336	LC
Johnson State College	VT	16,721	C
Kentucky Christian Univ	KY	17,622	LC
Kentucky State Univ	KY	11,000	C
Kutztown Univ of Pennsylvania	PA	16,909	LC
La Roche College	PA	35,824	LC
La Sierra Univ	CA	35,694	VC
Lasell College	MA	43,750	C
Lewis Univ	IL	23,050	C
Lewis-Clark State College	ID	6,990	C
Liberty Univ	VA	19,101	C
Limestone College	SC	30,800	C
Lincoln Univ	MO	12,904	NC
Lindenwood Univ	MO	20,750	C
Lindsey Wilson College	KY	31,220	C
Lipscomb Univ	TN	37,490	VC
LIU Brooklyn	NY	47,185	LC
Lock Haven Univ of Pennsylvania	PA	18,028	LC
Longwood Univ	VA	20,924	C
Louisiana State Univ	LA	18,677	C+
Louisiana State Univ in Shreveport	LA	5,606	C
Louisiana Tech Univ	LA	11,302	C
Loyola Marymount Univ	CA	54,649	VC+
Loyola Univ New Orleans	LA	46,581	VC
MacMurray College	IL	20,755	C
Madonna Univ	MI	24,540	VC
Malone Univ	OH	35,364	C
Mansfield Univ	PA	19,468	LC
Marymount Manhattan College	NY	40,118	VC
Marymount Univ	VA	39,480	C
Maryville Univ of St. Louis	MO	35,856	VC
Mass College of Liberal Arts	MA	18,613	C
Mayville State Univ	ND	11,401	NC
McNeese State Univ	LA	2,649	C
Medaille College	NY	35,112	C
Megar Evers College/The CUNY	NY	4,920	NC
Mercy College	NY	30,456	C
Metropolitan State Univ	MN	5,923	
Mich Tech Univ	MI	23,556	VC
Middlebury College	VT	59,160	MC
Midway College	KY	20,150	C
Mills College	CA	54,119	VC
Minot State Univ	ND	10,915	C
Misericordia Univ	PA	41,060	C
Miss State Univ	MS	14,750	C
Missouri Baptist Univ	MO	31,830	C
Missouri Valley College	MO	22,200	C
Mitchell College	CT	40,983	C
Montana State Univ	MT	14,068	C
Montana State Univ-Billings	MT	12,425	C
Montana Tech of The Univ of Montana	MT	14,650	VC
Montreat College	NC	31,298	C
Morehead State Univ	KY	10,900	C
Morris College	SC	16,310	LC
Mount Aloysius College	PA	29,976	C
Mount Ida College	MA	30,115	LC
Mount Mary Univ	WI	33,590	LC
Mount St. Mary's College - Chalon Campus	CA	43,897	VC+
National Univ	CA	14,730	SP
Neumann Univ	PA	31,078	LC
New Mexico Inst of Mining and Technology	NM	13,592	VC
Newman Univ	KS	30,380	C+
Niagara Univ	NY	41,010	C
Northern Arizona Univ	AZ	19,010	C
Northern Illinois Univ	IL	19,768	C
Northern Kentucky Univ	KY	21,134	C
Northwest Nazarene Univ	ID	34,000	C
Northwest Univ	WA	18,854	C
Northwestern State Univ of Louisiana	LA	14,368	C
Norwich Univ	VT	28,212	C
Notre Dame de Namur Univ	CA	44,236	LC
Notre Dame of Maryland Univ	MD	27,700	VC
Oakland Univ	MI	19,391	C
Ohio Dominican Univ	OH	38,380	C+
Okla Christian Univ	OK	25,870	VC
Okla City Univ	OK	40,476	VC
Okla State Univ	OK	14,310	VC
Okla Wesleyan Univ	OK	21,300	C
Oral Roberts Univ	OK	31,734	C
Oregon State Univ	OR	20,273	VC
Otterbein College	OH	32,214	C
Our Lady of Holy Cross College	LA	8,090	C
Our Lady of the Lake Univ	TX	22,430	LC
Palm Beach Atlantic Univ	FL	34,874	C+
Park Univ	MO	17,525	C
Paul Quinn College	TX	25,350	C
Penn State Univ/Altoona	PA	11,464	C
Pepperdine Univ	CA	55,372	HC+
Pittsburg State Univ	KS	12,032	C
Point Loma Nazarene Univ	CA	41,006	C+
Point Park Univ	PA	36,390	C
Polytechnic Inst of New York Univ	NY	53,064	HC+
Pontifical Catholic Univ of PR	PR	7,310	
Portland State Univ	OR	18,672	C
Post Univ	CT	35,750	C
Prescott College	AZ	33,284	C
Providence College	RI	57,383	VC
Purdue Univ/West Lafayette	IN	20,024	HC
Quinnipiac Univ	CT	55,160	VC
Ramapo College of New Jersey	NJ	24,938	C
Regis College	MA	47,565	LC
Reinhardt Univ	GA	25,000	C
Richard Stockton College of New Jersey	NJ	20,000	C

ST = STATE $IS = IN-STATE COSTS   SR = SELECTOR RATING

School	ST	$IS	SR
Rider Univ	NJ	45,720	C
Rivier Univ	NH	35,000	VC
Roberts Wesleyan College	NY	38,306	C+
Roosevelt Univ	IL	22,605	VC
Rosemont College	PA	42,350	C
Rowan Univ	NJ	24,022	VC+
Rutgers, The State Univ of New Jersey/Camden Campus	NJ	25,121	C
Sacred Heart Univ	CT	49,264	VC
St. Anselm College	NH	49,376	VC
St. John's Univ	MN	47,984	C
St. Joseph's Univ	PA	55,006	VC
St. Leo Univ	FL	30,340	C
St. Louis Univ	MO	48,346	HC
St. Mary's College of Calif	CA	53,550	C
St. Vincent College	PA	40,244	C
Salem International Univ	WV	21,090	LC
Samford Univ	AL	37,060	C+
San Diego Christian College	CA	31,012	C
San Diego State Univ	CA	21,611	C+
San Francisco State Univ	CA	18,514	C
Sarah Lawrence College	NY	48,000	HC
Schreiner Univ	TX	32,734	LC
Seattle Pacific Univ	WA	41,559	VC+
Seattle Univ	WA	49,035	VC+
Seton Hall Univ	NJ	45,902	C
Seton Hill Univ	PA	35,172	C
Shaw Univ	NC	15,488	C
Shimer College	IL	32,875	C
Siena Heights Univ	MI	32,040	C
Simpson Univ	CA	28,900	C
Skidmore College	NY	59,942	HC
Sonoma State Univ	CA	20,541	C
S Dak State Univ	SD	14,296	C
Southeastern Louisiana Univ	LA	13,325	C
Southern Illinois Univ Carbondale	IL	21,942	C
Southern Illinois Univ Edwardsville	IL	17,532	C
Southern Methodist Univ	TX	60,585	MC
Southern New Hampshire Univ	NH	38,100	C
Southern Oregon Univ	OR	17,874	C
Southern Vermont College	VT	30,740	LC
Southwestern College	KS	29,270	C
Spalding Univ	KY	32,287	VC
Spring Hill College	AL	44,164	VC
St. Edward's Univ	TX	47,784	VC
St. Francis College	NY	34,200	C
St. John's College, Santa Fe	NM	54,998	HC+
St. John's College-Annapolis	MD	53,590	HC
St. John's Univ	NY	55,070	C+
St. Joseph's College, New York/Brooklyn Campus	NY	22,630	C
St. Joseph's College, New York/Suffolk Campus	NY	22,630	C
St. Thomas Univ	FL	32,310	LC
SUNY at Purchase	NY	16,951	C
SUNY Polytechnic Inst	NY	19,690	C
SUNY/Empire State College	NY	6,315	SP
Stephens College	MO	38,042	VC
Stony Brook Univ / SUNY	NY	20,078	HC+
SUNY Fredonia/The SUNY at Fredonia	NY	19,840	VC
SUNY New Paltz	NY	14,348	C
Susquehanna Univ	PA	51,150	C
Syracuse Univ	NY	56,346	VC
Taylor Univ	IN	37,821	VC+
Texas A&M Univ at Galveston	TX	11,258	C
Texas Southern Univ	TX	18,212	LC
Texas State Univ	TX	17,128	C
Texas Tech Univ	TX	14,243	C
The Catholic Univ of America	DC	52,852	VC
The Evergreen State College	WA	12,969	C+
The Masters College	CA	38,160	C+
The Univ of Memphis	TN	15,094	C
The Univ of N Car at Greensboro	NC	12,848	C
The Univ of Okla	OK	18,621	VC
The Univ of Virginia's College at Wise	VA	11,076	C
Thomas Aquinas College	CA	32,450	HC+
Thomas Edison State College	NJ	5,700	SP
Thomas More College	KY	34,760	C
Thomas More College of Liberal Arts	NH	28,600	C
Thomas Univ	GA	11,520	NC
Touro College	NY	27,959	VC
Trinity International Univ	IL	31,070	VC
Tulane Univ	LA	60,861	MC
Union College	NY	60,240	MC
Union Inst & Univ	OH	8,912	SP
Univ of Alaska Anchorage	AK	16,673	NC
Univ of Alaska Southeast	AK	11,493	C
Univ of Arkansas at Little Rock	AR	17,609	LC
Univ of Arkansas at Monticello	AR	12,076	NC
Univ of Arkansas at Pine Bluff	AR	13,378	C
Univ of Calif at Riverside	CA	27,204	C+
Univ of Central Florida	FL	15,668	VC+
Univ of Central Okla	OK	12,293	C

School	ST	$IS	SR
Univ of Charleston	WV	32,300	C
Univ of Cincinnati	OH	21,506	VC
Univ of Dayton	OH	49,070	VC
Univ of Delaware	DE	23,612	VC
Univ of Detroit Mercy	MI	30,450	VC
Univ of Evansville	IN	42,656	VC+
Univ of Hawaii at Hilo	HI	23,066	C
Univ of Houston	TX	19,796	VC
Univ of Illinois at Urbana-Champaign	IL	26,450	HC
Univ of Iowa	IA	17,693	VC
Univ of Kansas	KS	17,603	C+
Univ of La Verne	CA	47,010	C
Univ of Louisiana at Monroe	LA	12,998	C
Univ of Louisville	KY	17,946	C
Univ of Maine at Augusta	ME	6,855	C
Univ of Maine at Farmington	ME	18,187	LC
Univ of Maine at Fort Kent	ME	15,195	LC
Univ of Maine at Machias	ME	16,523	C
Univ of Maine at Presque Isle	ME	15,011	LC
Univ of Mary	ND	16,714	C
Univ of Mary Washington	VA	19,484	VC
Univ of Maryland/Eastern Shore	MD	14,000	C
Univ of Maryland/Univ College	MD	6,168	SP
Univ of Mass Amherst	MA	24,215	VC+
Univ of Mass Dartmouth	MA	22,223	C
Univ of Mass Lowell	MA	19,316	C
Univ of Miami	FL	57,034	MC
Univ of Mich/Ann Arbor	MI	22,102	MC
Univ of Mich/Dearborn	MI	9,885	VC
Univ of Minn/Morris	MN	17,150	VC
Univ of Miss	MS	16,704	C+
Univ of Missouri/Columbia	MO	18,201	MC
Univ of Missouri-Kansas City	MO	19,603	C
Univ of Missouri-St. Louis	MO		VC
Univ of Mobile	AL	28,935	VC
Univ of Montana	MT	14,105	C
Univ of Montana-Western	MT	9,753	LC
Univ of Mount Olive	NC	18,426	C
Univ of Nebr - Lincoln	NE	18,031	VC
Univ of Nebr at Omaha	NE	12,700	C
Univ of New England	ME	46,750	C
Univ of New Haven	CT	48,940	C
Univ of New Mexico	NM	15,300	C
Univ of North Alabama	AL	9,070	C
Univ of N Car at Asheville	NC	13,500	VC
Univ of N Car at Charlotte	NC	15,547	C
Univ of North Texas	TX	15,628	C
Univ of Northern Iowa	IA	15,795	C
Univ of Notre Dame	IN	57,117	MC
Univ of Pittsburgh at Bradford	PA	21,802	C
Univ of Pittsburgh at Pittsburgh	PA	28,572	HC+
Univ of PR Recinto de Rio Piedras	PR	5,750	
Univ of Redlands	CA	40,500	VC
Univ of St. Francis	IN	29,810	C
Univ of St. Mary	KS	28,400	C+
Univ of San Diego	CA	54,818	HC+
Univ of S Car Upstate	SC	18,220	LC
Univ of S Dak	SD	15,111	C
Univ of South Florida/Tampa	FL	13,000	C
Univ of St. Francis	IL	37,560	C
Univ of St. Thomas - Houston	TX	37,690	C
Univ of Tampa	FL	35,160	VC
Univ of Texas - Pan American	TX	11,125	LC
Univ of Texas at Austin	TX	44,074	HC
Univ of the Ozarks	AR	31,440	C
Univ of the Pacific	CA	52,146	VC
Univ of Washington	WA	14,722	VC
Univ of Wisc/Eau Claire	WI	15,730	VC
Univ of Wisc/Green Bay	WI	19,074	C
Univ of Wisc/Oshkosh	WI	10,426	LC
Univ of Wisc/Platteville	WI	14,564	C
Univ of Wisc/Stevens Point	WI	14,043	C
Univ of Wisc-Milwaukee	WI	18,436	C
Urbana Univ	OH	30,820	C
Utah State Univ	UT	12,044	C
Utica College	NY	45,670	C
Vanguard Univ of Southern Calif	CA	35,833	VC
Villanova Univ	PA	58,394	MC
Virginia Wesleyan College	VA	28,433	LC
Viterbo Univ	WI	30,070	C
Walsh Univ	OH	35,100	C
Warner Pacific College	OR	25,550	C
Washburn Univ	KS	12,579	C
Washington Adventist Univ	MD	25,859	LC
Washington State Univ	WA	20,461	C
Wayne State Univ	MI	22,063	C
Wesley College	DE	31,115	C
West Chester Univ of Pennsylvania	PA	17,186	C
West Texas A&M Univ	TX	13,478	C
West Virginia Univ	WV	16,542	C+
Western Carolina Univ	NC	13,965	C
Western Conn State Univ	CT	18,327	LC
Western Kentucky Univ	KY	11,000	LC
Western New England Univ	MA	46,154	C+
Westfield State Univ	MA	18,297	C
Westmont College	CA	41,500	HC

School	ST	$IS	SR
Wheeling Jesuit Univ	WV	33,500	C
Wichita State Univ	KS	14,607	C+
Wilberforce Univ	OH	15,100	LC
Wiley College	TX		LC
Wilkes Univ	PA	44,070	C
William Carey Univ	MS	13,500	LC
William Peace Univ	NC	32,900	LC
Wilmington College	OH	29,784	C
Wilson College	PA	35,080	C
Wingate Univ	NC	34,990	C
Wright State Univ	OH	16,983	C
Xavier Univ	OH	44,980	VC
York College	NE	19,475	C
York College / The CUNY	NY	5,496	VC

LIBRARY SCIENCE

School	ST	$IS	SR
Ashford Univ	CA	10,480	C
Ball State Univ	IN	17,850	C
Clarion Univ of Pennsylvania	PA	17,370	LC
Kutztown Univ of Pennsylvania	PA	16,909	LC
Northwestern Okla State Univ	OK	7,275	NC
Southern Conn State Univ	CT	18,033	LC
Univ of Arizona	AZ	20,657	C
Univ of Central Arkansas	AR	13,667	VC
Univ of Maine at Augusta	ME	6,855	C
Univ of Nebr at Omaha	NE	12,700	C

LIFE SCIENCE

School	ST	$IS	SR
Arizona State Univ, at the Tempe Campus	AZ	20,137	C+
Arizona State Univ, at the West Campus	AZ	19,251	C
Atlantic Union College	MA	24,600	C
Baylor Univ	TX	50,329	HC
Biola Univ	CA	40,320	C+
Bowling Green State Univ	OH	18,970	C
East Texas Baptist Univ	TX	31,577	LC
Indiana Univ East	IN	6,783	C
Iowa Wesleyan College	IA	30,850	LC
Kansas State Univ	KS	15,497	VC
Kent State Univ	OH	19,920	C
Malone Univ	OH	35,364	C
McMurry Univ	TX	25,962	LC
Minn State Univ, Mankato	MN	15,616	C
Missouri Southern State Univ	MO	12,061	C
Missouri Univ of Science and Technology	MO	18,655	VC+
Mount Vernon Nazarene Univ	OH	29,590	C
National Univ	CA	14,730	SP
New York Inst of Technology	NY	45,010	VC
Niagara Univ	NY	41,010	C
Northwest Univ	WA	18,854	C
Ohio Univ	OH	21,080	C
Otterbein College	OH	32,214	C
Suffolk Univ	MA	47,298	C
United States Military Academy	NY		MC
Wayland Baptist Univ	TX	18,912	LC
Wayne State College	NE	11,764	NC
Western Washington Univ	WA	18,519	VC
Wright State Univ	OH	16,983	C
Xavier Univ	OH	44,980	VC

LIFE SCIENCE SECONDARY SCHOOL EDUCATION

School	ST	$IS	SR
Franklin College	IN	36,585	C
Kent State Univ	OH	19,920	C
Minn State Univ, Mankato	MN	15,616	C
St. Mary's Univ of Minn	MN	38,280	C
Univ of Nebr - Lincoln	NE	18,031	VC

LINGUISTICS

School	ST	$IS	SR
Alabama A&M Univ	AL	10,084	C
Ashford Univ	CA	10,480	C
Bard College at Simon's Rock	MA	61,749	HC+
Barnard College/Columbia Univ	NY	39,000	MC
Binghamton Univ/The SUNY	NY	21,648	HC+
Boston College	MA	60,622	MC
Boston Univ	MA	60,694	MC
Brandeis Univ	MA		MC
Brigham Young Univ	UT	12,100	HC
Brown Univ	RI	59,428	MC
Bryn Mawr College	PA	59,890	MC
Bucknell Univ	PA	60,140	MC
Cal State, Fresno	CA	17,405	C
Cal State, Fullerton	CA	25,188	C
Cal State, Monterey Bay	CA	26,871	C
Cal State, Northridge	CA	28,690	C
Calvin College	MI	39,120	VC
Carleton College	MN	60,102	MC
Central Univ	IA	42,104	C+
CUNY/Brooklyn College	NY	5,884	C
Cleveland State Univ	OH	21,776	C
College of William & Mary	VA	28,000	MC
Columbia Univ/City of New York	NY	61,116	MC
Cornell Univ	NY	60,964	MC
Dartmouth College	NH	57,996	MC

School	ST	$IS	SR
DePauw Univ	IN	48,950	VC+
Duke Univ	NC	50,250	MC
Earlham College	IN	51,470	HC
Eastern Mich Univ	MI	18,604	C
Emory Univ	GA	56,368	MC
Florida Atlantic Univ	FL	17,339	C
Florida State Univ	FL	16,715	VC
Georgetown Univ	DC	52,910	MC
Georgia Southern Univ	GA	16,942	C
Gordon College	MA	44,320	C
Hampshire College	MA	58,320	MC
Harvard College/Harvard Univ	MA	49,000	MC
Haverford College	PA	61,564	MC
Hofstra Univ	NY	51,810	VC+
Indiana Univ Bloomington	IN	19,801	VC
Iowa State Univ	IA	16,403	C
Lawrence Univ	WI	46,371	HC
Lehman College/The CUNY	NY	5,778	C
Macalester College	MN	57,691	MC
Marlboro College	VT	35,980	VC
Mass Inst of Technology	MA	58,240	MC
Miami Univ	OH	24,191	VC
Mich State Univ	MI	22,450	VC
Millersville Univ of Pennsylvania	PA	21,648	C
Montclair State Univ	NJ	22,614	C
New York Univ	NY	61,470	MC
Northeastern Illinois Univ	IL	10,318	LC
Northeastern Univ	MA	55,296	MC
Northwestern Univ	IL	61,640	MC
Oakland Univ	MI	19,391	C
Ohio Univ	OH	21,080	C
Old Dominion Univ	VA	19,483	LC
Oswego / SUNY	NY	20,009	VC
Pitzer College	CA	54,988	MC
Pomona College	CA	57,680	MC
Purdue Univ/West Lafayette	IN	20,024	HC
Queens College/The CUNY	NY	17,107	VC
Reed College	OR	57,780	MC
Rice Univ	TX	43,288	MC
Rutgers, The State Univ of New Jersey/New Brunswick	NJ	25,562	VC
San Diego State Univ	CA	21,611	C+
Seattle Pacific Univ	WA	41,559	VC+
Southern Illinois Univ Carbondale	IL	21,942	C
Stanford Univ	CA	58,388	MC
Stony Brook Univ / SUNY	NY	20,078	HC+
Swarthmore College	PA	57,870	MC
Syracuse Univ	NY	56,346	VC
Temple Univ	PA	24,392	VC
Ohio State Univ-Columbus Campus	OH	19,887	HC+
The Univ of Okla	OK	18,621	VC
The Univ of Utah	UT	16,463	VC
Truman State Univ	MO	15,541	HC
Tulane Univ	LA	60,861	MC
Univ at Albany / SUNY	NY	18,674	VC
Univ at Buffalo / The SUNY	NY	20,283	VC
Univ of Alaska Fairbanks	AK	15,130	C
Univ of Arizona	AZ	20,657	C
Univ of Calif at Berkeley	CA	23,322	MC
Univ of Calif at Davis	CA		HC
Univ of Calif at Los Angeles	CA	25,686	MC
Univ of Calif at Riverside	CA	27,204	C+
Univ of Calif at San Diego	CA	21,000	VC
Univ of Calif at Santa Barbara	CA	27,551	VC
Univ of Calif at Santa Cruz	CA	27,807	C+
Univ of Chicago	IL	55,416	MC
Univ of Cincinnati	OH	21,506	VC
Univ of Colo Boulder	CO	22,605	VC+
Univ of Conn	CT	24,706	VC
Univ of Florida	FL	15,943	VC
Univ of Georgia	GA	20,082	VC
Univ of Hawaii at Hilo	HI	23,066	C
Univ of Hawaii at Manoa	HI	19,379	VC
Univ of Illinois at Urbana-Champaign	IL	26,450	HC
Univ of Iowa	IA	17,693	VC
Univ of Kansas	KS	17,603	C+
Univ of Kentucky	KY	19,868	C
Univ of Louisville	KY	17,946	C
Univ of Maryland - College Park	MD	20,060	HC
Univ of Maryland/Baltimore County	MD	18,000	VC
Univ of Mass Amherst	MA	24,215	VC+
Univ of Mich/Ann Arbor	MI	22,102	MC
Univ of Minn/Twin Cities	MN		HC
Univ of Miss	MS	16,704	C+
Univ of Missouri/Columbia	MO	18,201	VC
Univ of Montana	MT	14,105	C
Univ of New Hampshire	NH	26,912	C
Univ of New Mexico	NM	15,300	C
Univ of N Car at Chapel Hill	NC	18,928	MC
Univ of Oregon	OR	21,360	C+
Univ of Pennsylvania	PA	61,132	MC
Univ of Pittsburgh at Pittsburgh	PA	28,572	HC+
Univ of Rochester	NY	60,668	MC
Univ of Southern Calif	CA	56,903	MC
Univ of Texas at Austin	TX	44,074	HC
Univ of Texas at El Paso	TX	8,764	NC
Univ of Toledo	OH	18,464	C

ST = STATE $IS = IN-STATE COSTS   SR = SELECTOR RATING

School	ST	$IS	SR
Univ of Vermont	VT	27,006	VC+
Univ of Wisc/Madison	WI	18,757	HC+
Univ of Wisc-Milwaukee	WI	18,436	C
Washington State Univ	WA	20,461	C
Washington Univ in St. Louis	MO	69,844	MC
Wayne State Univ	MI	22,063	C
Western Washington Univ	WA	18,519	VC
Yale Univ	CT	55,300	MC

LITERATURE

School	ST	$IS	SR
Adrian College	MI	42,400	C
American Jewish Univ - College of A&S	CA	32,600	C
American Univ	DC	56,015	HC+
Andrews Univ	MI	28,030	C+
Aquinas College	MI	33,060	C
Arizona State Univ, at the Tempe Campus	AZ	20,137	C+
Bard College	NY	61,940	HC
Bard College at Simon's Rock	MA	61,749	HC+
Baylor Univ	TX	50,329	HC
Beloit College	WI	49,970	HC
Benedictine Univ	IL	37,820	C
Bennington College	VT	56,990	HC+
Binghamton Univ/The SUNY	NY	21,648	HC+
Brigham Young Univ	UT	12,100	HC
Bryant Univ	RI	49,179	VC
Calif of the Arts	CA	48,334	SP
Cal State, San Marcos	CA	14,576	LC
Calvin College	MI	39,120	C
Castleton State College	VT	20,186	C
Claremont McKenna College	CA	62,215	MC
Coe College	IA	45,550	VC
College of the Holy Cross	MA	58,042	MC
Columbia Univ/School of General Studies	NY	58,231	MC
Concordia College - New York	NY	39,035	LC
Cornerstone Univ and Grand Rapids Theological Seminary	MI	33,338	C
DePauw Univ	IN	48,950	VC+
Dordt College	IA	34,160	C+
Duke Univ	NC	50,250	MC
Duquesne Univ	PA	43,720	VC
Eastern Mich Univ	MI	18,604	C
Eastern Nazarene College	MA	30,000	C
Eastern Washington Univ	WA		C
Eckerd College	FL	43,902	C
Elon Univ	NC	41,914	VC+
Emory and Henry College	VA	387,460	C
Eugene Lang College/The New School for Liberal Arts	NY	55,650	C
Fairleigh Dickinson Univ/ College at Florham	NJ	42,142	C
Fitchburg State Univ	MA	18,173	C
George Fox Univ	OR	40,750	C+
George Washington Univ	DC	57,108	MC
Goddard College	VT	16,418	VC
Gonzaga Univ	WA	46,441	HC
Graceland Univ	IA	28,020	C
Hampshire College	MA	58,320	MC
Harvard College/Harvard Univ	MA	49,000	MC
Hellenic College/Holy Cross Greek Orthodox School of Theology	MA	33,190	C
John Carroll Univ	OH	46,300	C+
Kutztown Univ of Pennsylvania	PA	16,909	LC
Le Moyne College	NY	43,470	C
Linfield College-McMinnville Campus	OR	47,676	C
Lubbock Christian Univ	TX	26,308	C
Lycoming College	PA	45,379	C
Maharishi Univ of Management	IA	31,000	VC
Marshall Univ	WV	14,820	C
Mass Inst of Technology	MA	58,240	MC
Missouri Southern State Univ	MO	12,061	C
Nazareth College of Rochester	NY	43,028	C+
New College of Florida	FL	14,504	MC
New York Univ	NY	61,470	MC
Northwestern College of Iowa	IA	36,240	VC
Ohio Northern Univ	OH	42,075	VC
Ohio Univ	OH	21,080	C
Old Dominion Univ	VA	19,483	LC
Oral Roberts Univ	OK	31,734	C
Pacific Univ	OR	49,626	C+
Pittsburg State Univ	KS	12,032	C
Point Loma Nazarene Univ	CA	41,006	C+
Pomona College	CA	57,680	MC
Prescott College	AZ	33,284	C
Ramapo College of New Jersey	NJ	24,938	C
Reed College	OR	57,780	MC
Richard Stockton College of New Jersey	NJ	20,000	VC
Roanoke College	VA	49,976	C
Rocky Mountain College	MT	32,242	C
Roosevelt Univ	IL	22,605	VC
St. Mary-of-the-Woods College	IN	37,722	VC
St. Mary's Univ of Minn	MN	38,280	C
San Jose State Univ	CA	19,133	LC

School	ST	$IS	SR
Sarah Lawrence College	NY	48,000	HC
Seattle Pacific Univ	WA	41,559	VC+
Southwest Minn State Univ	MN	14,000	C
SUNY at Purchase	NY	16,951	C
Stevens Inst of Technology	NJ	50,130	HC
Swarthmore College	PA	57,870	MC
The College of Idaho	ID	31,277	C+
The SUNY at Potsdam	NY	18,473	C
The Univ of Okla	OK	18,621	VC
Touro College	NY	27,959	VC
Union College	NE	23,270	C
United States Military Academy	NY		NC
Univ of Alaska Southeast	AK	11,493	C
Univ of Bridgeport	CT	39,030	LC
Univ of Calif at San Diego	CA	21,000	VC
Univ of Calif at Santa Barbara	CA	27,551	HC
Univ of Calif at Santa Cruz	CA	27,807	C+
Univ of Evansville	IN	42,656	VC+
Univ of Mich/Ann Arbor	MI	22,102	MC
Univ of New Haven	CT	48,940	C
Univ of N Car at Asheville	NC	13,500	VC
Univ of Texas at Dallas	TX	21,348	HC+
Washington Univ in St. Louis	MO	69,844	MC
Waynesburg Univ	PA	30,150	C
West Chester Univ of Pennsylvania	PA	17,186	C
Wheaton College	MA	54,934	HC+
Wheeling Jesuit Univ	WV	33,500	C
Wilberforce Univ	OH	15,100	LC
Williams College	MA	61,070	MC
Wright State Univ	OH	16,983	C
Yale Univ	CT	55,300	MC
Youngstown State Univ	OH	16,732	C

LOGISTICS

School	ST	$IS	SR
Bryant Univ	RI	49,179	VC
Georgia Southern Univ	GA	16,942	C
Inter-American Univ of PR/ Bayamon Univ College	PR	4,428	
John Carroll Univ	OH	46,300	C+
Missouri Southern State Univ	MO	12,061	C
Missouri State Univ	MO	13,996	C
Ohio State Univ-Columbus Campus	OH	19,887	HC+
The Univ of Memphis	TN	15,094	C
Univ of Alaska Anchorage	AK	16,673	NC
Univ of Illinois at Urbana-Champaign	IL	26,450	VC
Univ of Maryland - College Park	MD	20,060	HC
Univ of Missouri-St. Louis	MO		VC
Univ of North Texas	TX	15,628	C
Univ of Pennsylvania	PA	61,132	MC
Univ of St. Francis	IL	37,560	C
Univ of Tenn at Knoxville	TN	20,364	VC+

LUSO-BRAZILIAN STUDIES

School	ST	$IS	SR
New York Univ	NY	61,470	MC
Smith College	MA	59,674	MC

MANAGEMENT & STRATEGIC LEADERSHIP

School	ST	$IS	SR
Lehigh Univ	PA	56,770	MC
Ohio Univ	OH	21,080	C
Providence College	RI	57,383	VC

MANAGEMENT ENGINEERING

School	ST	$IS	SR
Appalachian State Univ	NC	12,919	VC
Claremont McKenna College	CA	62,215	MC
Mich Tech Univ	MI	23,556	HC
Pitzer College	CA	54,988	MC
Stanford Univ	CA	58,388	MC
Univ of PR/Bayamon	PR	1,600	
Western Kentucky Univ	KY	11,000	LC
Worcester Polytechnic Inst	MA	55,860	MC

MANAGEMENT INFORMATION SYSTEMS

School	ST	$IS	SR
Adams State Univ	CO	13,358	LC
Adelphi Univ	NY	44,670	VC
Albertus Magnus College	CT	37,382	LC
Alverno College	WI	31,434	LC
Amridge Univ	AL	6,870	LC
Andrews Univ	MI	28,030	C+
Angelo State Univ	TX	15,049	NC
Aquinas College	MI	33,060	C
Ashland Univ	OH	25,000	C
Augsburg College	MN	35,142	C
Aurora Univ	IL	33,228	C
Barry Univ	FL	38,190	C
Baylor Univ	TX	50,329	HC
Benedictine Univ	IL	37,820	C
Binghamton Univ/The SUNY	NY	21,648	HC+
Biola Univ	CA	40,320	C+
Bloomfield College	NJ	37,850	LC
Bowling Green State Univ	OH	18,970	C
Bradley Univ	IL	31,874	VC
Brewton-Parker College	GA	33,388	C
Bridgewater College	VA	41,450	C
Brigham Young Univ	UT	12,100	HC
Bryant Univ	RI	49,179	VC
Butler Univ	IN	47,572	VC+
Cal State, Long Beach	CA	17,502	C+
Cal State, Northridge	CA	28,690	LC
Cal State, Sacramento	CA	16,200	C
Cal State, San Bernardino	CA	12,000	C
Canisius Univ	NY	44,900	C
Cedarville Univ	OH	32,860	VC
Central Conn State Univ	CT	19,749	C
Chatham Univ	PA	43,797	C
Clarkson Univ	NY	57,330	HC
Cleveland State Univ	OH	21,776	C
Colo Christian Univ	CO	27,500	VC
Colo Mesa Univ	CO	17,690	LC
Colo Technical Univ	CO	10,500	LC
Columbus State Univ	GA	13,176	C
Creighton Univ	NE	45,356	VC
Dallas Baptist Univ	TX	30,580	VC
Daniel Webster College	NH	25,380	C
De Sales Univ	PA	43,970	C
DePaul Univ	IL	47,623	VC
Dordt College	IA	34,160	C+
Drury Univ	MO	31,909	VC
Duquesne Univ	PA	43,720	VC
East Carolina Univ	NC	14,169	C
Eastern Illinois Univ	IL	20,466	C
Eastern Mich Univ	MI	18,604	C
Elon Univ	NC	41,914	VC+
Eureka College	IL	19,280	C
Excelsior College	NY	5,580	SP
Fayetteville State Univ	NC	10,816	C
Florida Atlantic Univ	FL	17,339	C
Florida Inst of Technology	FL	48,290	VC
Florida International Univ	FL	17,747	C+
Fort Hays State Univ	KS	11,354	C
Friends Univ	KS	29,100	C
George Fox Univ	OR	40,750	C+
Georgetown College	KY	41,440	C+
Georgia Regents Univ	GA		C
Georgia State Univ	GA	15,582	VC
Goldey-Beacom College	DE	27,493	C
Grace College and Seminary	IN	28,800	VC
Grand View Univ	IA	31,050	C
Greenville College	IL	27,012	C
Hawaii Pacific Univ	HI	34,360	C
Hawaii Pacific Univ	HI	34,360	C
Hawaii Pacific Univ	HI	34,360	C
Hofstra Univ	NY	51,810	VC+
Humphreys College	CA	17,000	NC
Idaho State Univ	ID	12,307	C
Indiana State Univ	IN	16,000	C
Indiana Univ of Pennsylvania	PA	20,846	LC
Inter-American Univ of PR/ Aguadilla Campus	PR	5,578	
Inter-American Univ of PR/ Bayamon Univ College	PR	4,428	
Inter-American Univ of PR/ Fajardo Campus	PR	4,200	
Inter-American Univ of PR/ Metropolitan Campus	PR	4,320	
Inter-American Univ of PR/ Ponce	PR		
John Carroll Univ	OH	46,300	C+
Johnson & Wales Univ/ Providence Campus	RI	29,576	C
Kansas State Univ	KS	15,497	VC
King Univ	TN	33,140	C
La Salle Univ	PA	50,270	C
Le Moyne College	NY	43,470	C
Lenoir-Rhyne College	NC	35,984	C
LeTourneau Univ	TX	36,210	VC
Lewis Univ	IL	23,050	C
Liberty Univ	VA	19,101	C
Lindenwood Univ	MO	20,750	C
Lipscomb Univ	TN	37,490	VC
Loras College	IA	37,432	VC
Loyola Univ Chicago	IL	51,646	VC+
MacMurray College	IL	20,755	C
Marietta College	OH	42,135	C+
Marquette Univ	WI	46,930	VC+
Marshall Univ	WV	14,820	C
McMurry Univ	TX	25,962	LC
Megar Evers College/The CUNY	NY	4,920	NC
Menlo College	CA	49,002	C
Mercyhurst Univ	PA	40,700	C
Messiah College	PA	40,690	C+
Metropolitan State Univ	MN	5,923	
Miami Univ	OH	24,191	VC
Mich Tech Univ	MI	23,556	HC
Midland Univ	NE	34,000	C
Milwaukee School of Engineering	WI	39,948	VC+
Minot State Univ	ND	10,915	C
Missouri Southern State Univ	MO	12,061	C
Missouri Univ of Science and Technology	MO	18,655	VC+
Montclair State Univ	NJ	22,614	C
Morehead State Univ	KY	10,900	C
Morningside College	IA	35,430	C
Mount Aloysius College	PA	29,976	C
Mount Mercy Univ	IA	35,320	C
Mount Vernon Nazarene Univ	OH	29,590	C

School	ST	$IS	SR
New Mexico Highlands Univ	NM	11,904	NC
New Mexico State Univ	NM	14,050	C
New York Univ	NY	61,470	MC
Newman Univ	KS	30,380	C+
Nichols College	MA	37,240	LC
N Dak State Univ	ND		C
Northeastern Univ	MA	55,296	MC
Northwest Christian Univ	OR	27,399	C
Northwestern College	MN	24,000	C
Northwood Univ	MI	26,331	LC
Oakland Univ	MI	19,391	C
Ohio Dominican Univ	OH	38,380	C+
Ohio Univ	OH	21,080	C
Okla State Univ	OK	14,310	VC
Old Dominion Univ	VA	19,483	LC
Oral Roberts Univ	OK	31,734	C
Oregon Inst of Technology	OR	8,910	C
Oregon State Univ	OR	20,270	VC
Ottawa Univ	KS	15,000	VC
Our Lady of the Lake Univ	TX	22,430	LC
Park Univ	MO	17,525	C
Peirce College	PA	12,760	LC
Penn State Erie/The Behrend College	PA	16,256	C
Pennsylvania College of Technology	PA	26,286	NC
Philadelphia Univ	PA	44,160	C
Rensselaer Polytechnic Inst	NY	61,529	MC
Rivier Univ	NH	35,000	VC
Rochester Inst of Technology	NY	42,450	VC
Rockford College	IL	31,000	C
Rutgers, The State Univ of New Jersey/New Brunswick	NJ	25,562	VC
St. Francis Univ	PA	30,029	LC
St. Joseph's Univ	PA	55,006	VC
St. Louis Univ	MO	48,346	HC
St. Mary's College	IN	45,160	C
Salisbury Univ	MD	19,180	VC
Savannah State Univ	GA	13,156	C
Schreiner Univ	TX	32,734	LC
Seton Hall Univ	NJ	45,902	C
Seton Hill Univ	PA	35,172	C
Shippensburg Univ of Pennsylvania	PA	20,934	C
Shorter Univ	GA	30,650	LC
Simmons College	MA	49,966	VC
Southeastern Univ	FL	27,201	C
Southern Illinois Univ Edwardsville	IL	17,532	C
Southern Nazarene Univ	OK	24,354	C
Southwestern Okla State Univ	OK	9,160	C
Spring Arbor Univ	MI	26,740	C
St. Bonaventure Univ	NY	41,575	C
St. Catherine Univ	MN	37,782	C+
St. John's Univ	NY	55,070	C+
SUNY/Empire State College	NY	6,315	SP
Stephen F. Austin State Univ	TX	14,668	C
Stetson Univ	FL	51,516	VC
SUNY College at Old Westbury	NY	16,324	C
SUNY Plattsburgh / SUNY	NY	18,083	C
Temple Univ	PA	24,392	VC
Tenn Wesleyan College	TN	21,250	C
Texas A&M Univ at Corpus Christi	TX	11,544	LC
Texas Tech Univ	TX	14,243	C
Texas Wesleyan Univ	TX	31,382	C
Ohio State Univ-Columbus Campus	OH	19,887	HC+
The Pennsylvania State Univ - Univ Park	PA	28,022	VC+
The Univ of Memphis	TN	15,094	C
The Univ of Okla	OK	18,621	VC
The Univ of Utah	UT	16,463	VC
Thiel College	PA	38,728	C
Thomas College	ME	33,560	LC
Trine Univ	IN	39,400	HC+
Univ of Alabama at Tuscaloosa	AL	17,164	C+
Univ of Alaska Anchorage	AK	16,673	NC
Univ of Arizona	AZ	20,657	C
Univ of Arkansas at Monticello	AR	12,076	NC
Univ of Bridgeport	CT	39,030	LC
Univ of Central Okla	OK	12,293	C
Univ of Conn	CT	24,706	HC
Univ of Dayton	OH	49,070	VC
Univ of Delaware	DE	23,612	VC
Univ of Georgia	GA	20,082	VC
Univ of Hartford	CT	42,674	C
Univ of Hawaii at Manoa	HI	19,379	C
Univ of Houston	TX	19,796	VC
Univ of Idaho	ID	14,558	C
Univ of Illinois at Urbana-Champaign	IL	26,450	VC
Univ of Indianapolis	IN	31,740	LC
Univ of Jamestown	ND	24,738	C
Univ of Kansas	KS	17,603	C+
Univ of Louisiana at Monroe	LA	12,998	C
Univ of Mary	ND	16,714	C
Univ of Maryland - College Park	MD	20,060	HC
Univ of Maryland/University College	MD	6,168	SP
Univ of Mass Dartmouth	MA	22,223	C
Univ of Mich/Dearborn	MI	9,885	VC

ST = STATE   **$IS** = IN-STATE COSTS   **SR** = SELECTOR RATING

School	ST	$IS	SR
Univ of Minn/Duluth	MN	19,806	C
Univ of Miss	MS	16,704	C+
Univ of Missouri-St. Louis	MO		VC
Univ of Montana	MT	14,105	C
Univ of Montana-Western	MT	9,753	LC
Univ of Nebr at Omaha	NE	12,700	C
Univ of Nevada, Las Vegas	NV	17,303	C
Univ of N Car at Charlotte	NC	15,547	C
Univ of North Texas	TX	15,628	C
Univ of Northern Iowa	IA	15,795	C
Univ of Notre Dame	IN	57,117	MC
Univ of Pennsylvania	PA	61,132	MC
Univ of San Francisco	CA	54,770	VC
Univ of South Florida/Tampa	FL	13,000	C
Univ of Southern Indiana	IN	14,885	C
Univ of Tampa	FL	35,160	VC
Univ of Texas at Austin	TX	44,074	HC
Univ of Texas at El Paso	TX	8,764	NC
Univ of the Sacred Heart	PR	5,590	
Univ of Tulsa	OK	46,331	MC
Univ of West Georgia	GA	15,488	LC
Univ of Wisc/Oshkosh	WI	10,426	LC
Univ of Wisc-Milwaukee	WI	18,436	C
Upper Iowa Univ	IA	30,426	NC
Ursuline College	OH	33,198	LC
Utah State Univ	UT	12,044	C
Villanova Univ	PA	58,394	MC
Virginia State Univ	VA	11,318	C+
Viterbo Univ	WI	30,070	C
Washington State Univ	WA	20,461	C
Wayland Baptist Univ	TX	18,912	LC
Wayne State Univ	MI	22,063	C
Western Conn State Univ	CT	18,327	LC
Western Kentucky Univ	KY	11,000	LC
Western Mich Univ	MI	19,628	C
Western New Mexico Univ	NM	8,500	LC
Western Washington Univ	WA	18,519	VC
Westminster College	MO	31,720	VC
Widener Univ	PA	52,418	C
Winona State Univ	MN	16,640	C
Winston-Salem State Univ	NC	9,418	LC
Worcester Polytechnic Inst	MA	58,826	MC
Wright State Univ	OH	16,983	C
York College of Pennsylvania	PA	26,590	C
Youngstown State Univ	OH	16,732	C

MANAGEMENT SCIENCE

School	ST	$IS	SR
Abilene Christian Univ	TX	38,400	C+
Alabama A&M Univ	AL	10,084	C
Anderson Univ	IN	36,100	C
Aurora Univ	IL	33,228	C
Avila Univ	MO	26,900	C
Barry Univ	FL	38,190	C
Belmont Univ	TN	39,190	VC+
Bethany College	WV	35,282	LC
Bethel Univ	TN	19,186	C
Binghamton Univ/The SUNY	NY	21,648	HC+
Biola Univ	CA	40,320	C
Boston College	MA	60,622	MC
Bridgewater State Univ	MA	18,752	C
Brigham Young Univ	UT	12,100	HC
Bryant Univ	RI	49,179	VC
Caldwell College	NJ	35,602	NC
Cal State, Fullerton	CA	25,188	C
Cal State, Monterey Bay	CA	26,871	LC
Cal State, San Bernardino	CA	12,000	C
Calif Univ of Pennsylvania	PA	14,217	C
Cambridge College	MA	13,392	NC
Canisius College	NY	44,900	C
Cazenovia College	NY	43,464	C
Chaminade Univ of Honolulu	HI	31,664	LC
Champlain College	VT	46,650	VC+
Chicago State Univ	IL	5,482	C
CUNY/Baruch College	NY		HC
Claflin Univ	SC	22,368	LC
Clemson Univ	SC	19,136	HC
Cleveland State Univ	OH	21,776	C
College of St. Benedict	MN	49,359	VC
College of St. Scholastica	MN	41,440	C
Colo Christian Univ	CO	27,500	VC
Colo Technical Univ	CO	10,500	LC
Concordia Univ Wisc	WI	28,980	C
Coppin State Univ	MD	16,227	VC
Creighton Univ	NE	36,526	VC
Cumberland Univ	TN	21,220	C
Davenport Univ	MI	21,002	LC
Davis & Elkins College	WV	33,742	C
Defiance College	OH	30,645	C
Delta State Univ	MS	12,292	LC
DePaul Univ	IL	47,623	VC
Drake Univ	IA	41,516	VC+
Duquesne Univ	PA	43,702	VC
East Tenn State Univ	TN	9,000	C
Eastern Mich Univ	MI	18,604	C
Eastern Washington Univ	WA		C
Eckerd College	FL	43,902	C
Elmhurst College	IL	43,336	C
Embry-Riddle Aeronautical Univ - Worldwide	FL	15,512	C
Evangel Univ	MO	23,090	C
Faulkner Univ	AL	25,720	LC
Fitchburg State Univ	MA	18,173	C
Florida State Univ	FL	16,715	VC
Franklin Pierce Univ	NH	41,598	C

School	ST	$IS	SR
Franklin Univ	OH	20,985	SP
Gannon Univ	PA	39,608	C
George Fox Univ	OR	40,750	C+
Georgia College and State Univ	GA	18,900	C+
Georgia Southern Univ	GA	16,942	C
Goodwin College	CT	19,400	LC
Grand Canyon Univ	AZ	24,540	VC
Grand Valley State Univ	MI	17,998	C+
Granite State College	NH	6,195	NC
Gwynedd-Mercy College	PA	33,560	C
Hardin-Simmons Univ	TX	23,560	C+
Hawaii Pacific Univ	HI	34,360	C
Heidelberg Univ	OH	34,100	C
Hiram College	OH	37,300	VC
Idaho State Univ	ID	12,307	C
Indiana Univ-Purdue Univ Fort Wayne	IN	15,521	C
Indiana Univ-Purdue Univ Indianapolis	IN	17,611	C
Indiana Wesleyan Univ	IN	31,815	VC
Iona College	NY	44,028	C
Iowa State Univ	IA	16,403	C
Johnson & Wales Univ/ Denver Campus	CO	29,576	C
Kean Univ	NJ	23,444	C
Kennesaw State Univ	GA		C
Langston Univ	OK	3,000	C
Lehman College/The CUNY	NY	5,778	LC
Lesley Univ	MA	46,350	C
Limestone College	SC	30,800	C
Louisiana State Univ	LA	18,677	C+
Louisiana State Univ in Shreveport	LA	5,606	C
Louisiana Tech Univ	LA	11,302	C
Loyola Univ New Orleans	LA	46,581	VC
Luther College	IA	45,720	C
Lynchburg College	VA	42,645	C
Madonna Univ	MI	24,540	VC
Maharishi Univ of Management	IA	31,000	VC
Marian Univ	WI	32,420	LC
Marylhurst Univ	OR	20,295	NC
Mass Inst of Technology	MA	58,240	MC
Metropolitan State Univ of Denver	CO	4,835	LC
Miami Univ	OH	24,191	VC
Mich Tech Univ	MI	23,556	HC
Midwestern State Univ	TX	9,722	C
Millikin Univ	IL	38,940	C
Milwaukee School of Engineering	WI	39,948	VC+
Minn State Univ, Mankato	MN	15,616	C
Minn State Univ, Moorhead	MN	13,392	VC
Minot State Univ	ND	10,915	C
Missouri Baptist Univ	MO	31,830	C
Missouri State Univ	MO	13,996	C+
Morehead State Univ	KY	10,900	C
Mount Aloysius College	PA	29,976	C
Mount Vernon Nazarene Univ	OH	29,590	C
Murray State Univ	KY	15,304	C
National Louis Univ	IL	16,915	LC
National Univ	CA	14,730	SP
New Jersey Inst of Technology	NJ	26,490	C+
New York Univ	NY	61,470	MC
N Dak State Univ	ND		C
Northeastern Illinois Univ	IL	10,318	LC
Northern Arizona Univ	AZ	19,010	C
Notre Dame College	OH	34,942	VC
Ohio Northern Univ	OH	42,075	VC
Ohio Univ	OH	21,080	C
Okla City Univ	OK	40,476	VC
Oral Roberts Univ	OK	31,734	C
Oregon State Univ	OR	20,273	VC
Oswego / SUNY	NY	20,009	VC
Palm Beach Atlantic Univ	FL	34,874	C+
Pepperdine Univ	CA	55,372	HC+
Philadelphia Univ	PA	44,160	C
Point Park Univ	PA	36,390	C
Portland State Univ	OR	18,672	C
Post Univ	CT	35,750	C
Prescott College	AZ	33,284	C
Quinnipiac Univ	CT	55,160	VC
Regis Univ	MA	47,565	LC
Rensselaer Polytechnic Inst	NY	61,529	MC
Rice Univ	TX	43,288	MC
Richard Stockton College of New Jersey	NJ	20,000	VC
Rider Univ	NJ	45,720	C
Rivier Univ	NH	35,000	VC
Rochester Inst of Technology	NY	42,450	VC
Roger Williams Univ	RI	46,296	VC
Roosevelt Univ	IL	22,605	VC
Rutgers, The State Univ of New Jersey/Camden Campus	NJ	25,121	C
Rutgers, The State Univ of New Jersey/New Brunswick	NJ	25,562	VC
Rutgers, The State Univ of New Jersey/Newark Campus	NJ	258,806	C
St. Francis Univ	PA	30,029	LC
St. John's Univ	MN	47,984	C
St. Leo Univ	FL	30,340	C

School	ST	$IS	SR
Salve Regina Univ	RI	48,550	VC
Samford Univ	AL	37,060	C+
San Francisco State Univ	CA	18,514	C
Southern Illinois Univ Carbondale	IL	21,942	C
Southern Methodist Univ	TX	60,585	MC
Southern Nazarene Univ	OK	24,354	C
Southwestern Adventist Univ	TX	23,026	LC
Southwestern Okla State Univ	OK	9,160	C
St. Ambrose Univ	IA	30,845	C
St. Bonaventure Univ	NY	41,575	C
St. Francis College	NY	34,200	C
St. John's Univ	NY	55,070	C+
SUNY/Empire State College	NY	6,315	SP
Stephen F. Austin State Univ	TX	14,668	C
Suffolk Univ	MA	47,298	C
SUNY Cortland/The SUNY	NY	19,759	C+
Syracuse Univ	NY	56,346	VC
Tarleton State Univ	TX	13,489	C
Tenn Tech Univ	TN	11,310	C
Texas A&M Univ	TX	19,207	VC
Texas A&M Univ at Kingsville	TX	7,500	LC
Texas State Univ	TX	17,128	C
The Catholic Univ of America	DC	52,852	VC
The Lincoln Univ	PA	15,154	LC
The Univ of Memphis	TN	15,094	C
The Univ of Utah	UT	16,463	VC
Thomas College	ME	33,560	LC
Touro College	NY	27,959	VC
Trevecca Nazarene Univ	TN	31,186	C
Trine Univ	IN	39,400	HC+
Troy Univ	AL	10,650	C
Tulane Univ	LA	60,861	MC
Tusculum College	TN	24,295	C
Tuskegee Univ	AL	26,750	C
Union College	NE	23,270	C
Union Univ	TN	28,260	VC
United States Air Force Academy	CO		MC
United States Coast Guard Academy	CT	942	HC
United States Military Academy	NY		MC
Universidad del Turabo	PR	4,110	
Universidad Metropolitana	PR	3,500	
Univ of Akron	OH	20,436	C
Univ of Arizona	AZ	20,657	C
Univ of Arkansas at Little Rock	AR	17,609	LC
Univ of Bridgeport	CT	39,030	LC
Univ of Calif at Berkeley	CA	23,322	MC
Univ of Calif at Riverside	CA	27,204	C+
Univ of Calif at San Diego	CA	21,000	VC
Univ of Central Florida	FL	15,668	VC+
Univ of Central Missouri	MO	14,605	C
Univ of Cincinnati	OH	21,506	VC
Univ of Colo Boulder	CO	22,605	VC+
Univ of Delaware	DE	23,612	VC
Univ of Florida	FL	15,943	HC
Univ of Georgia	GA	20,082	VC
Univ of Great Falls	MT	27,970	C
Univ of Hartford	CT	42,674	C
Univ of Hawaii at Manoa	HI	19,379	VC
Univ of Illinois at Chicago	IL	24,505	VC
Univ of Illinois at Urbana-Champaign	IL	26,450	HC
Univ of Iowa	IA	17,693	VC
Univ of Louisiana at Lafayette	LA	6,130	C
Univ of Louisiana at Monroe	LA	12,998	C
Univ of Louisville	KY	17,946	VC
Univ of Maryland/Univ College	MD	6,168	SP
Univ of Mass Boston	MA	23,066	VC
Univ of Miami	FL	57,034	MC
Univ of Mich/Dearborn	MI	9,885	VC
Univ of Minn/Morris	MN	17,150	VC
Univ of Minn/Twin Cities	MN		HC
Univ of Miss	MS	16,704	C+
Univ of Montevallo	AL	17,060	C
Univ of Nebr - Lincoln	NE	18,031	VC
Univ of Nebr at Omaha	NE	12,700	C
Univ of Nevada, Las Vegas	NV	17,303	C
Univ of Nevada/Reno	NV	17,507	C
Univ of N Car at Chapel Hill	NC	18,928	MC
Univ of North Texas	TX	15,628	C
Univ of Northern Colo	CO	18,446	C
Univ of Northern Iowa	IA	15,795	C
Univ of Notre Dame	IN	57,117	MC
Univ of Pittsburgh at Greensburg	PA	17,640	C
Univ of PR Recinto de Rio Piedras	PR	5,750	
Univ of PR/Cayey	PR	1,504	C
Univ of St. Joseph	CT	45,630	C
Univ of S Car at Columbia	SC	19,725	VC+
Univ of S Dak	SD	15,111	C
Univ of South Florida/St. Petersburg	FL	12,769	C
Univ of South Florida/Tampa	FL	13,000	C
Univ of St. Francis	IL	37,560	C
Univ of Tenn at Knoxville	TN	20,364	VC
Univ of Tenn at Martin	TN	13,734	C
Univ of Texas - Pan American	TX	11,125	LC

School	ST	$IS	SR
Univ of Texas at Arlington	TX	10,908	LC
Univ of Texas at Austin	TX	44,074	HC
Univ of Texas at El Paso	TX	8,764	NC
Univ of Texas at San Antonio	TX	18,372	C
Univ of Tulsa	OK	46,331	MC
Univ of Wisc/Stout	WI	15,459	C
Univ of Wyoming	WY	14,401	C
Upper Iowa Univ	IA	30,426	NC
Valparaiso Univ	IN	44,940	VC+
Virginia Polytechnic Inst and State Univ	VA	14,629	HC
Viterbo Univ	WI	30,070	C
Waynesburg Univ	PA	30,150	C
Webber International Univ	FL	30,147	C
Webster Univ	MO	35,100	C+
West Liberty Univ	WV	9,142	LC
West Texas A&M Univ	TX	13,478	C
Western Carolina Univ	NC	13,965	C
Western Kentucky Univ	KY	11,000	LC
Western New England Univ	MA	46,154	C+
Western Washington Univ	WA	18,519	VC
Wheeling Jesuit Univ	WV	33,500	C
Wichita State Univ	KS	14,607	C+
Wilberforce Univ	OH	15,100	LC
Wilmington College	OH	29,784	C
Wright State Univ	OH	16,983	C
Xavier Univ	OH	44,980	VC

MANUFACTURING ENGINEERING

School	ST	$IS	SR
Arizona State Univ, at the Polytechnic Campus	AZ	20,531	C+
Boston Univ	MA	60,694	MC
Bradley Univ	IL	31,874	VC
Brigham Young Univ	UT	12,100	HC
Calif Polytechnic State Univ	CA	19,847	HC
Calif State Polytechnic Univ, Pomona	CA	20,156	C
Central State Univ	OH	9,010	C
Eastern Mich Univ	MI	18,604	C
Ferris State Univ	MI	20,047	C
Hofstra Univ	NY	51,810	VC+
Kansas State Univ	KS	15,079	C
Miami Univ	OH	24,191	VC
Mich State Univ	MI	22,450	VC
Midwestern State Univ	TX	9,722	C
Minn State Univ, Mankato	MN	15,616	C
Missouri Univ of Science and Technology	MO	18,655	VC+
New Jersey Inst of Technology	NJ	26,490	C+
N Dak State Univ	ND		C
Northern Kentucky Univ	KY	21,134	C
Northwestern Univ	IL	61,640	MC
Oregon State Univ	OR	20,273	VC
Pennsylvania College of Technology	PA	26,286	NC
Purdue Univ/West Lafayette	IN	20,024	HC
Robert Morris Univ	PA	37,864	C
Rochester Inst of Technology	NY	42,450	VC
Southern Illinois Univ Edwardsville	IL	17,532	C
Southwestern Okla State Univ	OK	9,160	C
St. Cloud State Univ	MN	10,600	C
Tenn Tech Univ	TN	11,310	C
Texas State Univ	TX	17,128	C
The Univ of Memphis	TN	15,094	C
Univ of Arkansas at Little Rock	AR	17,609	LC
Univ of Calif at Berkeley	CA	23,322	MC
Univ of Conn	CT	24,706	HC
Univ of Detroit Mercy	MI	30,450	VC
Univ of Mass Dartmouth	MA	22,223	C
Univ of Mich/Dearborn	MI	9,885	VC
Univ of North Texas	TX	15,628	C
Univ of Texas - Pan American	TX	11,125	LC
Univ of Wisc/Stout	WI	15,459	C
Washington State Univ	WA	20,461	C
Western Mich Univ	MI	19,628	C
Wichita State Univ	KS	14,607	C+

MANUFACTURING TECHNOLOGY

School	ST	$IS	SR
Alabama State Univ	AL	14,142	NC
Alfred State/SUNY College of Technology	NY	18,034	C
Arizona State Univ, at the Polytechnic Campus	AZ	20,531	C+
Arizona State Univ, at the Tempe Campus	AZ	20,137	C+
Arkansas State Univ	AR	15,470	C
Black Hills State Univ	SD	13,947	C
Bradley Univ	IL	31,874	VC
Brigham Young Univ	UT	12,100	HC
Cal State, Northridge	CA	28,690	LC
Central Conn State Univ	CT	17,949	C
Eastern Kentucky Univ	KY	11,161	C
Eastern Mich Univ	MI	18,604	C
Edinboro Univ of Pennsylvania	PA	15,940	LC
Fairmont State Univ	WV	12,098	LC
Farmingdale State College	NY	19,673	C
Fitchburg State Univ	MA	18,173	C

School	ST	$IS	SR
Idaho State Univ	ID	12,307	C
Illinois Inst of Technology	IL	38,512	HC+
Indiana State Univ	IN	16,000	C
Indiana Univ-Purdue Univ Indianapolis	IN	17,611	C
Kent State Univ	OH	19,920	C
Lake Superior State Univ	MI	18,121	C
Millersville Univ of Pennsylvania	PA	21,648	C
Minn State Univ, Mankato	MN	15,616	C
Missouri Southern State Univ	MO	12,061	C
Montana State Univ-Northern	MT	12,500	NC
Murray State Univ	KY	15,304	C
Nicholls State Univ	LA	7,095	C
Northern Kentucky Univ	KY	21,134	C
Northern Mich Univ	MI	18,278	C
Oregon Inst of Technology	OR	8,910	C
Pittsburg State Univ	KS	12,032	C
Purdue Univ/West Lafayette	IN	20,024	HC
Rochester Inst of Technology	NY	42,450	C
S Dak State Univ	SD	14,296	C
Southern Arkansas Univ	AR	14,316	C
Southwestern Okla State Univ	OK	9,160	C
Texas State Univ	TX	17,128	C
Univ of Central Missouri	MO	14,605	C
Univ of Dayton	OH	49,070	VC
Univ of Northern Iowa	IA	15,795	C
Univ of Rio Grande	OH	8,750	NC
Univ of Southern Indiana	IN	14,885	C
Wayne State Univ	MI	22,063	C
Western Carolina Univ	NC	13,965	C
Western Mich Univ	MI	19,628	C
Western Washington Univ	WA	18,519	VC

MARINE AFFAIRS

School	ST	$IS	SR
Univ of Rhode Island	RI	24,002	C

MARINE BIOLOGY

School	ST	$IS	SR
Alaska Pacific Univ	AK	43,592	VC
Auburn Univ	AL	22,378	VC+
Barry Univ	FL	38,190	C
Boston Univ	MA	60,694	MC
Brown Univ	RI	59,428	MC
Cal State, Long Beach	CA	17,502	C+
Carroll Univ	WI	38,100	C
Central Methodist Univ	MO	28,240	VC
College of Charleston	SC	22,145	VC
Dowling College	NY	25,000	LC
Eastern Nazarene College	MA	30,000	C
Fairleigh Dickinson Univ/Metropolitan Campus	NJ	40,254	C
Florida Atlantic Univ	FL	17,339	C
Florida Inst of Technology	FL	48,290	VC
Florida International Univ	FL	17,747	C+
Florida Southern College	FL	40,150	C+
Florida State Univ	FL	16,715	VC
Hampshire College	MA	58,320	MC
Hawaii Pacific Univ	HI	34,360	C
Hawaii Pacific Univ	HI	34,360	C
Hawaii Pacific Univ	HI	34,360	C
Missouri Southern State Univ	MO	12,061	C
Monmouth Univ	NJ	44,108	C
Murray State Univ	KY	15,304	C
New College of Florida	FL	14,504	NC
Northeastern Univ	MA	55,296	MC
Northwest Missouri State Univ	MO	17,347	C
Nova Southeastern Univ	FL	37,280	VC
Ohio Univ	OH	21,080	C
Old Dominion Univ	VA	19,483	LC
Prescott College	AZ	33,284	C
Roger Williams Univ	RI	46,296	VC
Rollins College	FL	52,370	HC
St. Paul's College	VA	16,030	NC
San Francisco State Univ	CA	18,514	C
Savannah State Univ	GA	13,156	C
Seattle Univ	WA	49,035	VC+
Southwestern College	KS	29,270	C
Spring Hill College	AL	44,164	VC
Stetson Univ	FL	51,516	VC
Stony Brook Univ / SUNY	NY	20,078	HC+
Texas A&M Univ at Galveston	TX	11,258	C
Texas State Univ	TX	17,128	C
Troy Univ	AL	10,650	C
Unity College	ME	34,054	C
Univ of Alaska Southeast	AK	11,493	C
Univ of Calif at Los Angeles	CA	25,686	MC
Univ of Calif at Santa Barbara	CA	27,551	HC
Univ of Calif at Santa Cruz	CA	27,807	C+
Univ of Hawaii at Manoa	HI	19,379	C
Univ of Maine at Machias	ME	10,523	C
Univ of Mass Dartmouth	MA	22,223	C
Univ of Miami	FL	57,034	MC
Univ of New England	ME	46,750	C
Univ of New Haven	CT	48,940	C
Univ of N Car at Wilmington	NC	13,572	VC
Univ of Oregon	OR	21,360	C+
Univ of PR/Humacao	PR	1,877	
Univ of West Alabama	AL	14,274	C
Univ of West Florida	FL	14,656	C
Waynesburg Univ	PA	30,150	C
Western Washington Univ	WA	18,519	VC

MARINE ENGINEERING

School	ST	$IS	SR
Calif Maritime Academy	CA	15,496	LC
Maine Maritime Academy	ME	21,073	C
Maritime College/SUNY	NY	16,020	C
Mass Maritime Academy	MA	15,340	C
Texas A&M Univ at Galveston	TX	11,258	C
United States Merchant Marine Academy	NY		HC+
United States Naval Academy	MD		MC
Univ of New Orleans	LA	9,224	C

MARINE ENGINEERING SYSTEMS

School	ST	$IS	SR
United States Merchant Marine Academy	NY		HC+

MARINE ENGINEERING/ SHIPYARD MANAGEMENT

School	ST	$IS	SR
United States Merchant Marine Academy	NY		HC+

MARINE SCIENCE

School	ST	$IS	SR
Coastal Carolina Univ	SC	18,580	C
East Stroudsburg Univ of Pennsylvania	PA	18,868	LC
Eckerd College	FL	43,902	C
Florida Gulf Coast Univ	FL		C
Hawaii Pacific Univ	HI	34,360	C
Jacksonville Univ	FL	37,780	C
Kutztown Univ of Pennsylvania	PA	16,909	LC
Maritime College/SUNY	NY	16,020	C
Montclair State Univ	NJ	22,614	C
Nova Southeastern Univ	FL	37,280	VC
Prescott College	AZ	33,284	C
Richard Stockton College of New Jersey	NJ	20,000	VC
Rider Univ	NJ	45,720	C
Rutgers, The State Univ of New Jersey/New Brunswick	NJ	25,562	VC
St. Paul's College	VA	16,030	NC
Samford Univ	AL	37,060	C+
San Jose State Univ	CA	19,133	LC
Suffolk Univ	MA	47,298	C
Texas A&M Univ at Galveston	TX	11,258	C
United States Coast Guard Academy	CT	942	HC
Univ of Alabama at Tuscaloosa	AL	17,164	C+
Univ of Conn	CT	24,706	HC
Univ of Georgia	GA	20,082	VC
Univ of Hawaii at Hilo	HI	23,066	C
Univ of Maine	ME	19,902	C+
Univ of Miami	FL	57,034	MC
Univ of Mobile	AL	28,935	VC
Univ of New England	ME	46,750	C
Univ of N Car at Wilmington	NC	13,572	VC
Univ of San Diego	CA	54,818	HC+
Univ of S Car at Columbia	SC	19,725	VC+
Univ of Tampa	FL	35,160	VC
West Chester Univ of Pennsylvania	PA	17,186	C
Western Washington Univ	WA	18,519	VC

MARINE TRANSPORTATION

School	ST	$IS	SR
United States Merchant Marine Academy	NY		HC+

MARITIME LOGISTICS & SECURITY

School	ST	$IS	SR
United States Merchant Marine Academy	NY		HC+

MARITIME SCIENCE

School	ST	$IS	SR
Calif Maritime Academy	CA	15,496	LC
Maine Maritime Academy	ME	21,073	C
Maritime College/SUNY	NY	16,020	C
Texas A&M Univ at Galveston	TX	11,258	C

MARKETING

School	ST	$IS	SR
Alma College	MI	44,075	C
Arkansas State Univ	AR	15,470	C
Arkansas Tech Univ	AR	13,982	LC
Ashford Univ	CA	10,480	C
Baldwin Wallace Univ	OH	38,318	C
Bloomfield College	NJ	37,850	LC
Bowling Green State Univ	OH	18,970	C
Bryant Univ	RI	49,179	VC
Cabrini College	PA	40,859	LC
Champlain College	VT	46,650	VC+
Christopher Newport Univ	VA	21,960	VC
College of Charleston	SC	22,145	VC
Corban Univ	OR	37,380	C+
Eastern Illinois Univ	IL	20,466	C
Elon Univ	NC	41,914	VC+
Fairfield Univ	CT	56,960	VC
Ferris State Univ	MI	20,047	C
Framingham State Univ	MA	18,854	C
Hood College	MD	45,730	C
Illinois State Univ	IL	23,110	VC
Indiana Univ-Purdue Univ Indianapolis	IN	17,611	C
Kent State Univ	OH	19,920	C
Lehigh Univ	PA	56,770	MC
Limestone College	SC	30,800	C
LIU Brooklyn	NY	47,182	LC
Lubbock Christian Univ	TX	26,308	C
Manhattanville College	NY	50,740	VC
McNeese State Univ	LA	2,649	C
Mich Tech Univ	MI	23,556	HC
Minn State Univ, Mankato	MN	15,616	C
Missouri Southern State Univ	MO	12,061	C
Molloy College	NY	40,440	C
Murray State Univ	KY	15,304	C
New Mexico State Univ	NM	14,050	C
N Dak State Univ	ND		C
Nova Southeastern Univ	FL	37,280	VC
Okla City Univ	OK	40,476	VC
Point Loma Nazarene Univ	CA	41,006	C+
Roberts Wesleyan College	NY	38,306	C+
Rutgers, The State Univ of New Jersey/New Brunswick	NJ	25,562	VC
Rutgers, The State Univ of New Jersey/Newark Campus	NJ	258,806	C
St. Louis Univ	MO	48,346	HC
St. Mary's Univ of Minn	MN	38,280	C
Southeast Missouri State Univ	MO	15,370	C
Southern Oregon Univ	OR	17,874	C
Taylor Univ	IN	37,821	VC+
Texas Christian Univ	TX	49,980	HC
The Pennsylvania State Univ - Univ Park	PA	28,022	VC+
The Univ of Okla	OK	18,621	VC
Tiffin Univ	OH	30,273	LC
Trevecca Nazarene Univ	TN	31,186	C
Univ of Evansville	IN	42,656	VC+
Univ of Georgia	GA	20,082	VC
Univ of Louisiana at Monroe	LA	12,998	C
Univ of Maryland - College Park	MD	20,060	HC
Univ of Miami	FL	57,034	MC
Univ of Nevada/Reno	NV	17,507	C
Univ of N Car at Charlotte	NC	15,547	C
Univ of Rochester	NY	60,668	MC
Univ of St. Thomas - Houston	TX	37,690	C
Univ of Wisc/Eau Claire	WI	15,730	VC
Univ of Wyoming	WY	14,401	C+
Western Illinois Univ	IL	20,732	C
Wheeling Jesuit Univ	WV	33,500	C
Winona State Univ	MN	16,640	C

MARKETING AND DISTRIBUTION

School	ST	$IS	SR
Alvernia Univ	PA	39,250	LC
Aquinas College	MI	33,060	C
Becker College	MA	41,420	C
Bryant Univ	RI	49,179	VC
Caldwell College	NJ	35,602	NC
Clayton State Univ	GA	12,000	LC
Florida Gulf Coast Univ	FL		C
Fort Lewis College	CO	15,513	C
Franklin Univ	OH	20,985	SP
Georgia College and State Univ	GA	18,900	C+
Gwynedd-Mercy College	PA	33,560	C
Indiana State Univ	IN	16,000	C
Indiana Univ-Purdue Univ Indianapolis	IN	17,611	C
Inter-American Univ of PR/Arecibo Campus	PR	3,350	
Johnson & Wales Univ/Charlotte Campus	NC	29,576	C
Johnson & Wales Univ/Providence Campus	RI	29,576	C
Kent State Univ	OH	19,920	C
Lake Erie College	OH	37,266	C
Limestone College	SC	30,800	C
Metropolitan State Univ	MN	5,923	
Nazareth College of Rochester	NY	43,028	C+
Neumann Univ	PA	31,078	LC
New Mexico Highlands Univ	NM	11,904	NC
Northern Kentucky Univ	KY	21,134	C
Our Lady of Holy Cross College	LA	8,090	C
Salve Regina Univ	RI	48,550	VC
Simmons College	MA	49,966	VC
Southern Illinois Univ Edwardsville	IL	17,532	C
Southwest Baptist Univ	MO	24,710	C
SUNY/Empire State College	NY	6,315	SP
Tarleton State Univ	TX	13,489	LC
Texas Tech Univ	TX	14,234	C
The Catholic Univ of America	DC	52,852	VC
Ohio State Univ-Columbus Campus	OH	19,887	HC+
Union College	NE	23,270	C
Univ of Arizona	AZ	20,657	C
Univ of Houston	TX	19,796	VC
Univ of Illinois at Urbana-Champaign	IL	26,450	HC
Univ of South Florida/St. Petersburg	FL	12,769	C
Univ of West Georgia	GA	15,488	LC
West Virginia Univ	WV	16,542	C+
Western Carolina Univ	NC	13,965	C
Western Kentucky Univ	KY	11,000	LC
Wilkes Univ	PA	44,070	C
Wilmington College	OH	29,784	C

MARKETING AND DISTRIBUTION EDUCATION

School	ST	$IS	SR
Central Washington Univ	WA	11,730	C
Dakota State Univ	SD	13,811	C
East Carolina Univ	NC	14,169	C
Eastern Washington Univ	WA		C
Fayetteville State Univ	NC	10,816	C
Johnson & Wales Univ/Providence Campus	RI	29,576	C
Murray State Univ	KY	15,304	C
N Car State Univ	NC	16,202	HC
Rider Univ	NJ	45,720	C
Univ of Nebr - Lincoln	NE	18,031	VC
Univ of Tenn at Knoxville	TN	20,364	VC+
Univ of Wisc/Stout	WI	15,459	C
Western Kentucky Univ	KY	11,000	LC

MARKETING MANAGEMENT

School	ST	$IS	SR
Adrian College	MI	42,400	C
Alverno College	WI	31,434	LC
Aquinas College	MI	33,060	C
Assumption College	MA	47,122	C+
Aurora Univ	IL	33,228	C
Averett Univ	VA	37,750	C
Baker College of Flint	MI	7,800	NC
Benedictine Univ	IL	37,820	C
Berry College	GA	39,254	VC
Bethany College	KS	30,605	NC
Binghamton Univ/The SUNY	NY	21,648	HC+
Biola Univ	CA	40,320	C+
Brigham Young Univ	UT	12,100	HC
Bryant Univ	RI	49,179	VC
Campbellsville Univ	KY	27,720	C
Canisius College	NY	44,900	C
Carthage College	WI	33,000	C
Case Western Reserve Univ	OH	56,534	MC
Catawba College	NC	37,240	C
Champlain College	VT	46,650	VC+
Chatham Univ	PA	43,797	C
CUNY/Baruch College	NY		HC
Clarke Univ	IA	37,600	C
College of St. Scholastica	MN	41,440	C
College of the Ozarks	MO		VC
College of William & Mary	VA	28,000	MC
Columbia College Chicago	IL	30,940	LC
Concordia Univ St. Paul	MN	28,250	C
Corban Univ	OR	37,380	C+
Cumberland Univ	TN	21,220	C
Daniel Webster College	NH	25,380	C
Davenport Univ	MI	21,002	LC
DePaul Univ	IL	47,623	VC
Dominican Univ	IL	37,628	C
Dordt College	IA	34,160	C+
Drake Univ	IA	41,516	VC+
Drury Univ	MO	31,909	VC
East Carolina Univ	NC	14,169	C
Eastern Mich Univ	MI	18,604	C
Elizabethtown College	PA	49,740	VC
Elon Univ	NC	41,914	VC+
Emerson College	MA	52,446	HC+
Endicott College	MA	43,228	VC+
Felician College	NJ	41,640	LC
Fitchburg State Univ	MA	18,173	C
Florida Inst of Technology	FL	48,290	VC
Fontbonne Univ	MO	31,384	C
Fordham Univ	NY	61,588	HC+
George Washington Univ	DC	57,108	MC
Georgia Southern Univ	GA	16,942	C
Georgia Southwestern State Univ	GA	13,246	C
Goldey-Beacom College	DE	27,493	C
Grove City College	PA	24,022	VC
Hardin-Simmons Univ	TX	23,560	C+
Hawaii Pacific Univ	HI	34,360	C
Hofstra Univ	NY	51,810	VC+
Huntington Univ	IN	32,220	C+
Indiana Univ of Pennsylvania	PA	20,846	LC
Iona College	NY	44,028	C
Johnson & Wales Univ/Charlotte Campus	NC	29,576	C
Johnson & Wales Univ/North Miami Campus	FL		C
Johnson & Wales Univ/Providence Campus	RI	29,576	C
Kean Univ	NJ	23,444	C
Kent State Univ	OH	19,920	C
King Univ	TN	33,140	C
La Roche College	PA	35,824	LC
La Sierra Univ	CA	35,694	VC

ST = STATE $IS = IN-STATE COSTS   SR = SELECTOR RATING

School	ST	$IS	SR
Lakeland College	WI	22,990	C
Le Moyne College	NY	43,470	C
LeTourneau Univ	TX	36,210	VC
LIM College	NY	41,575	LC
Linfield College-McMinnville Campus	OR	47,676	C
Lipscomb Univ	TN	37,490	VC
Lourdes Univ	OH	26,055	LC
Lynn Univ	FL	43,500	LC
Mary Baldwin College	VA	38,245	C
Maryville Univ of St. Louis	MO	35,856	VC
Menlo College	CA	49,002	C
Mercer Univ	GA	44,201	VC
Metropolitan State Univ	MN	5,923	
Mich State Univ	MI	22,450	VC
Missouri Baptist Univ	MO	31,830	C
Missouri Southern State Univ	MO	12,061	C
Monmouth Univ	NJ	44,108	C
Montclair State Univ	NJ	22,614	C
Morehead State Univ	KY	10,900	C
Mount Aloysius College	PA	29,976	C
New York Inst of Technology	NY	45,010	VC
New York Univ	NY	61,470	MC
Newbury College	MA	43,280	LC
Northern Arizona Univ	AZ	19,010	C
Northwestern College	MN	24,000	C
Northwood Univ	FL	33,192	LC
Northwood Univ	MI	26,331	LC
Northwood Univ	TX	25,296	LC
Ohio Univ	OH	21,080	C
Okla Christian Univ	OK	25,870	VC
Old Dominion Univ	VA	19,483	LC
Olivet College	MI	19,984	LC
Oregon State Univ	OR	20,273	VC
Our Lady of the Lake Univ	TX	22,430	LC
Palm Beach Atlantic Univ	FL	34,874	C+
Park Univ	MO	17,525	C
Peirce College	PA	12,760	NC
Penn State Erie/The Behrend College	PA	16,256	C
Pennsylvania College of Technology	PA	26,286	NC
Pepperdine Univ	CA	55,372	HC+
Pittsburg State Univ	KS	12,032	C
Plymouth State Univ	NH	23,148	LC
Providence College	RI	57,383	VC
Purdue Univ/West Lafayette	IN	20,024	HC
Quinnipiac Univ	CT	55,160	VC
Rhode Island College	RI	17,694	LC
Rochester College	MI	18,320	LC
Rochester Inst of Technology	NY	42,450	VC
Sacred Heart Univ	CT	49,264	VC
Saginaw Valley State Univ	MI	17,369	C
St. Joseph's Univ	PA	55,006	VC
St. Leo Univ	FL	30,340	C
Samford Univ	AL	37,060	C+
Seattle Univ	WA	49,035	VC+
Seton Hall Univ	NJ	45,902	C
Shippensburg Univ of Pennsylvania	PA	20,934	C
Siena College	NY	43,863	VC
Simpson College	IA	36,086	C+
Southern New Hampshire Univ	NH	38,100	C
Spring Hill College	AL	44,164	VC
St. Edward's Univ	TX	47,784	C
St. John Fisher College	NY	40,708	C+
St. John's Univ	NY	55,070	C+
St. Joseph's College, New York/Brooklyn Campus	NY	22,630	C
St. Joseph's College, New York/Suffolk Campus	NY	22,630	C
Stephen F. Austin State Univ	TX	14,668	C
Stevenson Univ	MD	41,470	C
Syracuse Univ	NY	56,346	VC
Texas Wesleyan Univ	TX	31,382	C
The Pennsylvania State Univ - Univ Park	PA	28,022	VC+
The SUNY/College at Brockport	NY	19,002	C
The Univ of Memphis	TN	15,094	C
The Univ of Utah	UT	16,463	VC
Thomas College	ME	33,560	LC
Troy Univ	AL	10,650	C
Tulane Univ	LA	60,861	MC
Union College	KY	29,955	C
Union Univ	TN	28,260	VC
Univ of Arkansas at Fayetteville	AR	18,352	C+
Univ of Colo Boulder	CO	22,605	VC+
Univ of Idaho	ID	14,558	C
Univ of Illinois at Urbana-Champaign	IL	26,450	HC
Univ of Iowa	IA	17,693	VC
Univ of Maryland/Univ College	MD	6,168	SP
Univ of Mass Amherst	MA	24,215	VC+
Univ of Miami	FL	57,034	MC
Univ of Mich/Dearborn	MI	19,885	VC
Univ of Minn Crookston	MN	17,834	C
Univ of Missouri-St. Louis	MO		VC
Univ of Nebr - Lincoln	NE	18,031	VC
Univ of N Dak	ND	14,551	C
Univ of North Florida	FL	15,870	VC
Univ of PR Recinto de Rio Piedras	PR	5,750	

School	ST	$IS	SR
Univ of Rio Grande	OH	8,750	NC
Univ of San Diego	CA	54,818	HC+
Univ of S Car Upstate	SC	18,200	LC
Univ of Texas at Austin	TX	44,074	NC
Univ of Texas at Dallas	TX	21,348	HC+
Univ of Texas at San Antonio	TX	18,372	C
Univ of the Sciences	PA	48,320	VC+
Univ of Wisc-Milwaukee	WI	18,436	C
Ursuline College	OH	33,198	LC
Virginia Polytechnic Inst and State Univ	VA	14,629	HC
Virginia State Univ	VA	11,318	C+
Walsh Univ	OH	35,100	C
Warner Univ	FL	18,000	C
Washington State Univ	WA	20,461	C
Washington Univ in St. Louis	MO	69,844	MC
Webber International Univ	FL	30,147	C
Webster Univ	MO	35,100	C
West Chester Univ of Pennsylvania	PA	17,186	C
Western Conn State Univ	CT	18,327	LC
Whitworth Univ	WA	47,734	VC
Wilmington College	OH	29,784	C
Wingate Univ	NC	34,990	C
Youngstown State Univ	OH	16,732	C

MARKETING/RETAILING/MERCHANDISING

School	ST	$IS	SR
Abilene Christian Univ	TX	38,400	C+
Adams State Univ	CO	13,358	LC
Alabama A&M Univ	AL	10,084	C
Alabama State Univ	AL	14,142	NC
Albany State Univ	GA	8,500	C
Alderson Broaddus Univ	WV	28,656	C
Alfred Univ	NY	41,770	C
American International College	MA	36,100	LC
Anderson Univ	IN	36,100	C
Andrews Univ	MI	28,030	C+
Angelo State Univ	TX	15,049	NC
Appalachian State Univ	NC	12,919	VC
Arcadia Univ	PA	33,570	C+
Arizona State Univ, at the Tempe Campus	AZ	20,137	C+
Ashland Univ	OH	25,000	C
Auburn Univ	AL	22,378	VC+
Auburn Univ at Montgomery	AL	14,470	LC
Augsburg College	MN	35,142	C
Aurora Univ	IL	33,228	C
Avila Univ	MO	26,900	C
Azusa Pacific Univ	CA	42,086	C
Ball State Univ	IN	17,850	C
Barry Univ	FL	38,190	C
Bay Path College	MA	34,565	C
Baylor Univ	TX	50,329	HC
Belmont Univ	TN	39,190	VC+
Benedictine Univ	IL	37,820	C
Berkeley College of New York City	NY	18,300	LC
Berkeley College/New Jersey	NJ	27,300	LC
Berkeley College/Westchester Campus	NY	28,500	LC
Blackburn College	IL	21,350	C
Bluffton Univ	OH	38,948	C
Boise State Univ	ID	13,469	LC
Boston College	MA	60,622	MC
Bradley Univ	IL	31,874	VC
Brenau Univ - Women's College	GA	26,650	LC
Bryant Univ	RI	49,179	VC
Buena Vista Univ	IA	39,188	C
Butler Univ	IN	47,572	VC+
Calif Baptist Univ	CA	38,792	C
Cal State, Fullerton	CA	25,188	C
Cal State, Long Beach	CA	17,502	C+
Cal State, Northridge	CA	28,690	LC
Cal State, Sacramento	CA	16,200	C
Canisius College	NY	44,900	C
Caribbean Univ	PR	10,375	
Carnegie Mellon Univ	PA	51,260	MC
Cedar Crest College	PA	43,240	C
Cedarville Univ	OH	32,860	VC
Central Conn State Univ	CT	19,749	C
Central State Univ	OH	9,010	C
Central Univ of Bayamon	PR	3,350	
Central Washington Univ	WA	11,730	C
Chancellor Univ	OH	11,000	C
Chestnut Hill College	PA	42,110	LC
Chicago State Univ	IL	5,482	C
CUNY/Baruch College	NY		HC
City Univ of Seattle	WA	14,880	NC
Claflin Univ	SC	22,368	LC
Clarion Univ of Pennsylvania	PA	17,370	LC
Clemson Univ	SC	19,136	HC
Cleveland State Univ	OH	21,776	C
Coastal Carolina Univ	SC	18,580	C
Colo State Univ-Fort Collins	CO	20,385	VC
Columbia College	MO	24,578	C
Columbus State Univ	GA	13,176	C
Concord Univ	WV	13,102	C
Concordia Univ Wisc	WI	28,980	C
Cornerstone Univ and Grand Rapids Theological Seminary	MI	33,338	C
Creighton Univ	NE	45,356	VC

School	ST	$IS	SR
Dallas Baptist Univ	TX	30,580	VC
Davis & Elkins College	WV	33,742	C
De Sales Univ	PA	43,970	C
Defiance College	OH	30,645	C
Delaware State Univ	DE	16,722	LC
Delaware Valley College	PA	29,944	C
Delta State Univ	MS	12,292	LC
Dominican College	NY	31,270	LC
Dowling College	NY	25,000	C
Drexel Univ	PA	61,418	VC+
Duquesne Univ	PA	43,720	VC
East Carolina Univ	NC	14,169	C
East Tenn State Univ	TN	9,000	C
Eastern Kentucky Univ	KY	11,161	C
Eastern Mich Univ	MI	18,604	C
Eastern New Mexico Univ	NM	10,682	C
Eastern Univ	PA	37,704	C
Eastern Washington Univ	WA		C
Elizabethtown College School of Continuing and Professional Studies	PA		VC
Elmhurst College	IL	43,336	C
Elmira College	NY	49,950	C+
Elms College	MA	23,900	VC
Emory Univ	GA	56,368	MC
Emporia State Univ	KS	12,897	C
Evangel Univ	MO	23,090	C
Excelsior College	NY	5,580	SP
Fairleigh Dickinson Univ/ College at Florham	NJ	42,142	C
Fairleigh Dickinson Univ/ Metropolitan Campus	NJ	40,254	C
Fairmont State Univ	WV	12,098	LC
Fashion Inst of Technology/ SUNY	NY	18,362	SP
Ferris State Univ	MI	20,047	C
Florida Atlantic Univ	FL	17,339	C
Florida International Univ	FL	17,747	C+
Florida State Univ	FL	16,715	VC
Fontbonne Univ	MO	31,384	C
Fort Hays State Univ	KS	11,354	C
Fort Valley State Univ	GA	11,200	VC
Francis Marion Univ	SC	16,464	LC
Franklin Pierce Univ	NH	41,598	C
Gannon Univ	PA	39,608	C
George Mason Univ	VA	15,724	VC
Georgetown College	KY	41,440	C+
Georgetown Univ	DC	52,910	MC
Georgia Regents Univ	GA		C
Georgia State Univ	GA	15,582	VC
Glenville State College	WV	11,348	NC
Grambling State Univ	LA	13,384	C
Grand Canyon Univ	AZ	24,540	VC
Grand Valley State Univ	MI	17,998	C+
Greenville College	IL	27,012	C
Hampton Univ	VA	28,528	C
Harding Univ	AR	23,556	C
Hillsdale College	MI	32,866	MC
Holy Family Univ	PA	40,030	LC
Howard Univ	DC	13,646	C
Husson Univ	ME	24,194	LC
Huston-Tillotson Univ	TX	18,124	C+
Idaho State Univ	ID	12,307	C
Indiana State Univ	IN	16,000	C
Indiana Univ-Purdue Univ Fort Wayne	IN	15,521	C
Indiana Wesleyan Univ	IN	31,815	VC
Inter-American Univ of PR/ Aguadilla Campus	PR	5,578	
Inter-American Univ of PR/ Bayamon Univ College	PR	4,428	
Inter-American Univ of PR/ Fajardo Campus	PR	4,200	
Inter-American Univ of PR/ Metropolitan Campus	PR	4,320	
Inter-American Univ of PR/ Ponce	PR		
Inter-American Univ of PR/ San Germán	PR	6,720	
Iowa State Univ	IA	16,403	C
Jackson State Univ	MS	13,512	LC
Jacksonville State Univ	AL	12,480	LC
Jacksonville Univ	FL	37,780	C
James Madison Univ	VA	18,049	VC
John Carroll Univ	OH	46,300	C+
Johnson & Wales Univ/ Charlotte Campus	NC	29,576	C
Johnson & Wales Univ/ Denver Campus	CO	29,576	C
Johnson & Wales Univ/North Miami Campus	FL		C
Johnson & Wales Univ/ Providence Campus	RI	29,576	C
Juniata College	PA	49,340	VC
Kansas State Univ	KS	15,497	VC
Kennesaw State Univ	GA		C
Keuka College	NY	30,300	C
King's College	PA	43,502	C
Kutztown Univ of Pennsylvania	PA	16,909	LC
La Salle Univ	PA	50,270	C
Lake Superior State Univ	MI	18,121	C
Lamar Univ	TX	6,820	LC
Lasell College	MA	43,750	LC
LeTourneau Univ	TX	36,210	LC
Lewis Univ	IL	23,050	C
Lincoln Univ	MO	12,904	NC

School	ST	$IS	SR
Lindenwood Univ	MO	20,750	C
Lipscomb Univ	TN	37,490	C
LIU Post	NY	47,660	C
Loras College	IA	37,432	VC
Louisiana State Univ	LA	18,677	C+
Louisiana State Univ in Shreveport	LA	5,606	C
Louisiana Tech Univ	LA	11,302	C
Loyola Marymount Univ	CA	54,649	VC+
Loyola Univ Chicago	IL	51,646	VC+
Loyola Univ New Orleans	LA	46,581	VC
Lynchburg College	VA	42,645	C
MacMurray College	IL	20,755	C
Madonna Univ	MI	24,540	VC
Manhattan College	NY	49,588	C+
Marian Univ	WI	32,420	LC
Marietta College	OH	42,135	C+
Marquette Univ	WI	46,930	VC+
Marshall Univ	WV	14,820	C
Martin Univ	IN	11,000	SP
Marywood Univ	PA	45,595	C
McKendree Univ	IL	29,920	C+
McMurry Univ	TX	25,962	LC
Mercyhurst Univ	PA	40,700	C
Merrimack College	MA	44,215	C
Messiah College	PA	40,690	C+
Methodist Univ	NC	37,185	C
Metropolitan State Univ of Denver	CO	4,835	LC
Miami Univ	OH	24,191	VC
Mich State Univ	MI	22,450	VC
MidAmerica Nazarene Univ	KS	28,000	C
Middle Tenn State Univ	TN	8,650	C
Midland Univ	NE	34,000	C
Midwestern State Univ	TX	9,722	C
Millikin Univ	IL	38,940	C
Minn State Univ, Moorhead	MN	13,392	VC
Minot State Univ	ND	10,915	C
Misericordia Univ	PA	41,060	C
Miss College	MS	21,998	C
Miss State Univ	MS	14,750	C
Missouri State Univ	MO	13,996	C+
Missouri Western State Univ	MO	12,260	NC
Morgan State Univ	MD	14,500	C
Mount Ida College	MA	30,115	LC
Mount Mary Univ	WI	33,590	LC
Mount Mercy Univ	IA	35,320	C
Mount Vernon Nazarene Univ	OH	29,590	C
New Mexico Highlands Univ	NM	11,904	NC
New Mexico State Univ	NM	14,050	C
New York Univ	NY	61,470	MC
Niagara Univ	NY	41,010	C
Nicholls State Univ	LA	7,095	C
Nichols College	MA	37,240	LC
North Central College	IL	38,343	VC
North Park Univ	IL	30,130	C
Northeastern Illinois Univ	IL	10,318	LC
Northeastern State Univ	OK	8,615	VC
Northern Illinois Univ	IL	19,768	C
Northern Mich Univ	MI	18,278	C
Northern State Univ - Aberdeen	SD	14,505	C
Northwest Missouri State Univ	MO	17,347	C
Notre Dame College	OH	34,942	VC
Notre Dame de Namur Univ	CA	44,236	LC
Notre Dame of Maryland Univ	MD	27,700	C
Oakland Univ	MI	19,391	C
Okla Baptist Univ	OK	28,202	C
Okla Christian Univ	OK	25,870	VC
Okla State Univ	OK	14,310	VC
Olivet Nazarene Univ	IL	29,990	C
Oral Roberts Univ	OK	31,734	C
Oregon State Univ	OR	20,273	VC
Oswego / SUNY	NY	20,009	VC
Pace Univ	NY	53,367	C
Parsons The New School for Design	NY	56,610	SP
Peru State College	NE	8,600	NC
Philadelphia Univ	PA	44,160	C
Pontifical Catholic Univ of PR	PR	7,310	
Portland State Univ	OR	18,672	C
Post Univ	CT	35,750	C
Prairie View A&M Univ	TX	15,205	LC
Purdue Univ/Calumet	IN	14,336	C
Purdue Univ/West Lafayette	IN	20,024	HC
Quincy Univ	IL	34,980	LC
Quinnipiac Univ	CT	55,160	VC
Radford Univ	VA	17,766	LC
Regis Univ	CO	41,318	C
Rider Univ	NJ	45,720	C
Robert Morris Univ	PA	37,864	C
Roger Williams Univ	RI	46,296	VC
Roosevelt Univ	IL	22,605	VC
Rowan Univ	NJ	24,022	VC+
Rutgers, The State Univ of New Jersey/Camden Campus	NJ	25,121	C
Rutgers, The State Univ of New Jersey/New Brunswick	NJ	25,562	VC
Rutgers, The State Univ of New Jersey/Newark Campus	NJ	258,806	C

ST = STATE $IS = IN-STATE COSTS   SR = SELECTOR RATING

School	ST	$IS	SR
St. Joseph's Univ	PA	55,006	VC
St. Mary-of-the-Woods College	IN	37,722	LC
St. Mary's Univ	TX	33,854	C
St. Peter's Univ	NJ	44,240	C
St. Vincent College	PA	40,244	C
St. Xavier Univ	IL	32,840	C
Salem State Univ	MA	13,161	C
Salisbury Univ	MD	19,180	VC
Sam Houston State Univ	TX	17,082	C
San Diego State Univ	CA	21,611	C+
San Francisco State Univ	CA	18,514	C
San Jose State Univ	CA	19,133	LC
Savannah State Univ	GA	13,156	C
Seton Hill Univ	PA	35,172	C
Slippery Rock Univ of Pennsylvania	PA	10,360	C
S Car State Univ	SC	6,700	LC
Southeastern Louisiana Univ	LA	13,325	C
Southeastern Univ	FL	27,201	C
Southern Adventist Univ	TN	26,190	C
Southern Conn State Univ	CT	18,033	LC
Southern Illinois Univ Carbondale	IL	21,942	C
Southern Methodist Univ	TX	60,585	MC
Southern Nazarene Univ	OK	24,354	C
Southern New Hampshire Univ	NH	38,100	C
Southern Oregon Univ	OR	17,874	C
Southern Univ and A&M College	LA	9,761	LC
Southwest Minn State Univ	MN	14,000	C
Southwestern Okla State Univ	OK	9,160	C
St. Ambrose Univ	IA	30,845	C
St. Bonaventure Univ	NY	41,575	C
St. Catherine Univ	MN	37,782	C+
St. Cloud State Univ	MN	10,600	C
St. Thomas Aquinas College	NY	40,230	C
St. Thomas Univ	FL	32,310	LC
Stephen F. Austin State Univ	TX	14,668	C
Stetson Univ	FL	51,546	C
Stonehill College	MA	46,780	HC
Suffolk Univ	MA	47,298	C
SUNY College at Old Westbury	NY	16,324	C
SUNY New Paltz	NY	14,348	C
SUNY Plattsburgh / SUNY	NY	18,083	C
Tabor College	KS	29,010	C
Tarleton State Univ	TX	13,489	LC
Temple Univ	PA	24,392	VC
Tenn Tech Univ	TN	11,310	C
Texas A&M Univ	TX	19,207	VC
Texas A&M Univ at Commerce	TX	10,496	C
Texas A&M Univ at Corpus Christi	TX	11,544	LC
Texas A&M Univ at Kingsville	TX	7,500	LC
Texas Southern Univ	TX	18,212	LC
Texas State Univ	TX	17,128	C
Texas Wesleyan Univ	TX	31,382	C
Texas Woman's Univ	TX	13,633	LC
The Univ of N Car at Greensboro	NC	12,848	C
The Univ of Utah	UT	16,463	VC
Tiffin Univ	OH	30,273	LC
Touro College	NY	27,959	VC
Trevecca Nazarene Univ	TN	31,186	C
Trine Univ	IN	39,400	HC+
Trinity International Univ	IL	31,070	VC
Troy Univ	AL	10,650	C
Tuskegee Univ	AL	26,750	C
Union Univ	TN	28,260	VC
Universidad de Puerto/Arecibo	PR	7,227	
Universidad del Turabo	PR	4,110	
Univ of Akron	OH	20,436	C
Univ of Alabama at Birmingham	AL	18,484	C+
Univ of Alabama in Huntsville	AL	17,591	VC+
Univ of Alaska Anchorage	AK	16,673	NC
Univ of Arkansas at Fayetteville	AR	18,352	C+
Univ of Arkansas at Little Rock	AR	17,609	LC
Univ of Bridgeport	CT	39,030	LC
Univ of Central Arkansas	AR	13,667	VC
Univ of Central Florida	FL	15,668	VC+
Univ of Central Missouri	MO	14,605	C
Univ of Central Okla	OK	12,293	C
Univ of Cincinnati	OH	21,506	VC
Univ of Conn	CT	24,706	HC
Univ of Dayton	OH	49,070	VC
Univ of Delaware	DE	23,612	VC
Univ of Denver	CO	51,737	VC+
Univ of Findlay	OH	31,916	C
Univ of Florida	FL	15,943	HC
Univ of Great Falls	MT	27,970	C
Univ of Hartford	CT	42,674	C
Univ of Hawaii at Manoa	HI	19,379	C
Univ of Houston-Downtown	TX	15,170	C
Univ of Idaho	ID	14,558	C
Univ of Illinois at Chicago	IL	24,505	VC
Univ of Illinois at Urbana-Champaign	IL	26,450	HC
Univ of Indianapolis	IN	31,740	LC
Univ of Kansas	KS	17,603	C+
Univ of Kentucky	KY	19,868	C
Univ of Louisiana at Lafayette	LA	6,130	C
Univ of Louisiana at Monroe	LA	12,998	C
Univ of Louisville	KY	17,946	C
Univ of Maine at Machias	ME	10,523	C
Univ of Mary Hardin-Baylor	TX	31,950	C+
Univ of Mass Dartmouth	MA	22,223	C
Univ of Mich-Flint	MI	17,547	C+
Univ of Minn/Twin Cities	MN		HC
Univ of Miss	MS	16,704	C+
Univ of Missouri/Columbia	MO	18,201	MC
Univ of Montana	MT	14,105	C
Univ of Montevallo	AL	17,060	C
Univ of Nebr - Lincoln	NE	18,031	VC
Univ of Nebr at Kearney	NE	14,855	LC
Univ of Nebr at Omaha	NE	12,700	C
Univ of Nevada, Las Vegas	NV	17,303	C
Univ of Nevada/Reno	NV	17,507	C
Univ of New Haven	CT	48,940	C
Univ of New Orleans	LA	9,224	C
Univ of North Alabama	AL	9,960	C
Univ of N Car at Charlotte	NC	15,547	C
Univ of N Car at Wilmington	NC	13,572	VC
Univ of North Georgia	GA	8,500	C
Univ of North Texas	TX	15,628	C
Univ of Northern Colo	CO	18,446	C
Univ of Northern Iowa	IA	15,795	C
Univ of Notre Dame	IN	57,117	MC
Univ of Pennsylvania	PA	61,132	MC
Univ of Pittsburgh at Pittsburgh	PA	28,572	HC+
Univ of Portland	OR	49,964	VC
Univ of PR/Bayamon	PR	1,600	
Univ of PR/Mayaguez	PR	1,250	
Univ of San Francisco	CA	54,770	VC
Univ of Scranton	PA	51,940	VC
Univ of Sioux Falls	SD	22,990	C
Univ of South Alabama	AL	13,510	C
Univ of S Car at Columbia	SC	19,725	VC+
Univ of South Florida/Tampa	FL	13,000	C
Univ of Southern Indiana	IN	14,885	C
Univ of Southern Miss	MS	13,170	C
Univ of St. Francis	IL	37,560	C
Univ of St. Thomas - Houston	TX	37,690	C
Univ of Tampa	FL	35,160	VC
Univ of Tenn at Martin	TN	13,734	C
Univ of Texas - Pan American	TX	11,125	LC
Univ of Texas at Arlington	TX	10,908	LC
Univ of Texas at El Paso	TX	8,764	NC
Univ of the District of Columbia	DC	7,244	LC
Univ of the Ozarks	AR	31,440	C
Univ of the Sacred Heart	PR	5,590	
Univ of Toledo	OH	18,464	C
Univ of Tulsa	OK	46,331	MC
Univ of Washington	WA	14,722	VC
Univ of West Florida	FL	14,656	C
Univ of Wisc Whitewater	WI	13,314	C
Univ of Wisc/La Crosse	WI	9,304	VC
Univ of Wisc/Madison	WI	18,757	HC+
Univ of Wisc/Oshkosh	WI	10,426	LC
Univ of Wisc/Stout	WI	15,459	C
Upper Iowa Univ	IA	30,426	NC
Utah State Univ	UT	12,044	C
Valparaiso Univ	IN	44,940	VC+
Vanguard Univ of Southern Calif	CA	35,833	VC
Villanova Univ	PA	58,394	MC
Virginia Commonwealth Univ	VA	21,716	C
Viterbo Univ	WI	30,070	C
Wartburg College	IA	41,055	VC
Washburn Univ	KS	12,579	C
Washington Univ in St. Louis	MO	69,844	MC
Wayne State Univ	MI	22,063	C
Waynesburg Univ	PA	30,150	C
West Liberty Univ	WV	9,142	LC
West Texas A&M Univ	TX	13,478	C
West Virginia State Univ	WV	8,378	NC
West Virginia Wesleyan College	WV	26,880	C
Western Mich Univ	MI	19,628	C
Western New England Univ	MA	46,154	C+
Western New Mexico Univ	NM	8,500	LC
Western Washington Univ	WA	18,519	VC
Westminster College	PA	31,290	C+
Westminster College	UT	37,708	C+
Wichita State Univ	KS	14,607	C+
Wilberforce Univ	OH	15,100	LC
Woodbury Univ	CA	34,500	LC
Wright State Univ	OH	16,983	C
Xavier Univ	OH	44,980	VC
Yeshiva Univ	NY	47,250	VC+
York College / The CUNY	NY	5,496	VC
York College of Pennsylvania	PA	26,590	C
Youngstown State Univ	OH	16,732	C

MATERIALS ENGINEERING

School	ST	$IS	SR
Alfred Univ	NY	41,770	C
Auburn Univ	AL	22,378	VC+
Calif Polytechnic State Univ	CA	19,847	HC
Calif State Polytechnic Univ, Pomona	CA	20,156	C
Drexel Univ	PA	61,418	VC+
Florida State Univ	FL	16,715	VC
Georgia Inst of Technology	GA	21,828	MC
Iowa State Univ	IA	16,403	C
Johns Hopkins Univ	MD	47,492	MC
Mass Inst of Technology	MA	58,240	MC
Mich State Univ	MI	22,450	VC
Mich Tech Univ	MI	23,556	NC
Missouri Univ of Science and Technology	MO	18,655	VC+
New Mexico Inst of Mining and Technology	NM	13,592	VC
Northwestern Univ	IL	61,640	MC
Ohio Univ	OH	21,080	C
Rensselaer Polytechnic Inst	NY	61,529	MC
San Jose State Univ	CA	19,133	LC
Ohio State Univ-Columbus Campus	OH	19,887	HC+
The Univ of Utah	UT	16,463	VC
Univ at Albany / SUNY	NY	18,674	VC
Univ of Alabama at Birmingham	AL	18,484	C+
Univ of Arizona	AZ	20,657	C
Univ of Calif at Berkeley	CA	23,322	MC
Univ of Calif at Davis	CA		HC
Univ of Calif at Irvine	CA	25,961	VC
Univ of Calif at Los Angeles	CA	25,686	MC
Univ of Calif at Riverside	CA	27,204	C+
Univ of Cincinnati	OH	21,506	VC
Univ of Conn	CT	24,706	HC
Univ of Florida	FL	15,943	HC
Univ of Idaho	ID	14,558	C
Univ of Illinois at Chicago	IL	24,505	VC
Univ of Illinois at Urbana-Champaign	IL	26,450	MC
Univ of Kentucky	KY	19,868	C
Univ of Maryland - College Park	MD	20,060	VC
Univ of Mich/Ann Arbor	MI	22,102	MC
Univ of Minn/Twin Cities	MN		HC
Univ of Pennsylvania	PA	61,132	MC
Univ of Pittsburgh at Pittsburgh	PA	28,572	HC+
Univ of Tenn at Knoxville	TN	20,364	VC+
Univ of Wisc-Milwaukee	WI	18,436	C
Virginia Polytechnic Inst and State Univ	VA	14,629	HC
Washington State Univ	WA	20,461	C
Winona State Univ	MN	16,640	C
Worcester Polytechnic Inst	MA	55,860	MC
Wright State Univ	OH	16,983	C

MATERIALS SCIENCE

School	ST	$IS	SR
Arizona State Univ, at the Tempe Campus	AZ	20,137	C+
Boise State Univ	ID	13,469	LC
Calif Inst of Technology	CA	54,045	MC
Case Western Reserve Univ	OH	56,534	MC
Columbia Univ/City of New York	NY	61,116	MC
Duke Univ	NC	50,250	MC
Georgia Inst of Technology	GA	21,828	MC
Illinois Inst of Technology	IL	38,512	HC+
Johns Hopkins Univ	MD	47,492	MC
Kent State Univ	OH	19,920	C
Mass Inst of Technology	MA	58,240	MC
Missouri State Univ	MO	13,996	C+
N Car State Univ	NC	16,202	VC
Northwestern Univ	IL	61,640	MC
Purdue Univ/West Lafayette	IN	20,024	HC
Rochester Inst of Technology	NY	42,450	VC
Stanford Univ	CA	58,388	MC
Ohio State Univ-Columbus Campus	OH	19,887	HC+
The Pennsylvania State Univ - Univ Park	PA	28,022	VC+
The Univ of Utah	UT	16,463	VC
Univ at Albany / SUNY	NY	18,674	VC
Univ of Arizona	AZ	20,657	C
Univ of Calif at Berkeley	CA	23,322	MC
Univ of Calif at Los Angeles	CA	25,686	MC
Univ of Denver	CO	51,787	VC+
Univ of Illinois at Urbana-Champaign	IL	26,450	MC
Univ of Mass Dartmouth	MA	22,223	C
Univ of Mich/Ann Arbor	MI	22,102	MC
Univ of Minn/Twin Cities	MN		HC
Univ of Pittsburgh at Pittsburgh	PA	28,572	HC+
Univ of the Ozarks	AR	31,440	C
Univ of Washington	WA	14,722	VC
Univ of Wisc/Eau Claire	WI	15,730	VC
Univ of Wisc/Madison	WI	18,757	HC+

MATERIALS SCIENCE AND ENGINEERING

School	ST	$IS	SR
Cornell Univ	NY	60,964	MC
Georgia Inst of Technology	GA	21,828	MC
Lehigh Univ	PA	56,770	MC
Rutgers, The State Univ of New Jersey/New Brunswick	NJ	25,562	VC

MATHEMATICS

School	ST	$IS	SR
Abilene Christian Univ	TX	38,400	C+
Adams State Univ	CO	13,358	LC
Adelphi Univ	NY	44,670	VC
Adrian College	MI	42,400	C
Agnes Scott College	GA	45,323	C+
Alabama A&M Univ	AL	10,084	C
Alabama State Univ	AL	14,142	NC
Albany State Univ	GA	8,500	C
Albertus Magnus College	CT	37,382	LC
Albion College	MI	46,010	C
Albright College	PA	46,660	C
Alcorn State Univ	MS	9,500	C
Alderson Broaddus Univ	WV	28,656	C
Alfred Univ	NY	41,770	C
Allegheny College	PA	50,980	HC
Allen Univ	SC	16,124	NC
Alma College	MI	28,030	C
Alvernia Univ	PA	39,250	VC
Alverno College	WI	31,434	LC
American International College	MA	36,100	LC
American Univ	DC	56,015	VC+
Amherst College	MA	58,744	MC
Anderson Univ	IN	36,100	C
Andrews Univ	MI	28,030	C
Angelo State Univ	TX	15,049	NC
Appalachian State Univ	NC	12,919	VC
Aquinas College	MI	33,060	C
Arcadia Univ	PA	33,570	C
Arizona State Univ, at the Tempe Campus	AZ	20,137	C+
Arkansas State Univ	AR	15,470	C
Arkansas Tech Univ	AR	13,982	LC
Armstrong State Univ	GA	15,532	C
Asbury Univ	KY	32,038	VC
Ashland Univ	OH	25,000	C
Assumption College	MA	47,122	C+
Atlantic Union College	MA	24,600	C
Auburn Univ	AL	22,378	VC+
Auburn Univ at Montgomery	AL	14,470	LC
Augsburg College	MN	35,142	C
Augustana College	IL	43,398	VC
Augustana College	SD	36,500	VC
Aurora Univ	IL	33,228	C
Austin College	TX	45,875	HC
Austin Peay State Univ	TN	15,274	C
Averett Univ	VA	37,750	LC
Avila Univ	MO	26,900	C
Azusa Pacific Univ	CA	42,086	C
Baker Univ	KS	33,350	C+
Baldwin Wallace Univ	OH	38,318	C
Ball State Univ	IN	17,850	C
Bard College	NY	61,940	HC
Bard College at Simon's Rock	MA	61,749	HC+
Barnard College/Columbia Univ	NY	39,000	MC
Barry Univ	FL	38,190	C
Barton College	NC	27,660	LC
Bates College	ME	60,720	MC
Baylor Univ	TX	50,329	HC
Belhaven Univ	MS	27,170	C
Bellarmine Univ	KY	42,950	VC
Belmont Abbey College	NC	37,716	C
Belmont Univ	TN	39,190	VC+
Beloit College	WI	49,970	HC
Bemidji State Univ	MN	13,500	VC
Benedict College	SC	20,454	NC
Benedictine College	KS	29,180	VC
Benedictine Univ	IL	37,820	C
Bennett College for Women	NC	21,970	C
Bennington College	VT	56,990	HC+
Bentley Univ	MA	56,454	HC+
Berea College	KY	7,192	C
Berry College	GA	39,254	VC
Bethany College	KS	30,605	NC
Bethany College	WV	35,282	LC
Bethel College	IN	31,560	C
Bethel College	KS	32,160	C
Bethel Univ	MN	34,940	VC
Bethel Univ	TN	19,186	C
Bethune-Cookman Univ	FL	22,958	C
Binghamton Univ/The SUNY	NY	21,648	HC+
Biola Univ	CA	40,320	C+
Birmingham-Southern College	AL	44,168	VC+
Black Hills State Univ	SD	13,947	C
Blackburn College	IL	21,350	C
Bloomfield College	NJ	38,362	LC
Bloomsburg Univ of Pennsylvania	PA	13,598	C
Blue Mountain College	MS	15,634	LC
Bluefield College	VA	17,230	C+
Bluffton Univ	OH	38,948	C
Boise State Univ	ID	13,469	LC
Boston College	MA	60,622	MC
Boston Univ	MA	60,694	MC
Bowdoin College	ME	59,568	MC
Bowie State Univ	MD	17,088	
Bowling Green State Univ	OH	18,970	C
Bradley Univ	IL	31,874	VC
Brandeis Univ	MA		MC
Brescia Univ	KY	26,140	VC+
Briar Cliff Univ	IA	29,514	C

ST = STATE $IS = IN-STATE COSTS   SR = SELECTOR RATING

School	ST	$IS	SR
Bridgewater College	VA	41,450	C
Bridgewater State Univ	MA	18,752	C
Brigham Young Univ	UT	12,100	HC
Brigham Young Univ/Hawaii	HI	10,686	HC
Brown Univ	RI	59,428	MC
Bryan College	TN	24,194	C
Bryant Univ	RI	49,179	VC
Bryn Mawr College	PA	59,890	MC
Bucknell Univ	PA	60,140	MC
Buena Vista Univ	IA	39,188	C
Buffalo State College / SUNY	NY	15,733	C+
Butler Univ	IN	47,572	VC+
Cabrini College	PA	40,859	LC
Caldwell College	NJ	35,602	NC
Calif Baptist Univ	CA	38,792	C
Calif Inst of Technology	CA	54,045	MC
Calif Lutheran Univ	CA	49,540	C+
Calif Polytechnic State Univ	CA	19,847	HC
Calif State Polytechnic Univ, Pomona	CA	20,156	C
Cal State, Bakersfield	CA	8,000	C
Cal State, Chico	CA	20,158	C
Cal State, Dominguez Hills	CA	17,090	LC
Cal State, East Bay	CA	16,549	C
Cal State, Fresno	CA	17,405	C
Cal State, Fullerton	CA	25,188	C
Cal State, Long Beach	CA	17,502	C+
Cal State, Los Angeles	CA	17,186	LC
Cal State, Monterey Bay	CA	26,871	C
Cal State, Northridge	CA	28,690	VC
Cal State, Sacramento	CA	16,200	C
Cal State, San Bernardino	CA	12,000	C
Cal State, San Marcos	CA	14,576	LC
Cal State, Stanislaus	CA	18,582	C
Calif Univ of Pennsylvania	PA	14,217	C
Calvin College	MI	39,120	VC
Cameron Univ	OK	10,004	LC
Campbell Univ	NC	37,570	VC
Campbellsville Univ	KY	27,720	C
Canisius College	NY	44,900	C
Capital Univ	OH	41,050	VC
Cardinal Stritch Univ	WI	24,054	C
Caribbean Univ	PR	10,375	
Carleton College	MN	60,102	MC
Carlow Univ	PA	30,272	C
Carnegie Mellon Univ	PA	51,260	MC
Carroll College	MT	28,000	C
Carroll Univ	WI	38,100	C
Carthage College	WI	33,000	C
Case Western Reserve Univ	OH	56,534	MC
Castleton State College	VT	23,000	C
Catawba College	NC	37,240	LC
Cedar Crest College	PA	43,240	C
Cedarville Univ	OH	32,860	VC
Centenary College	NJ	38,618	C
Centenary College of Louisiana	LA	45,650	C+
Central College	IA	42,104	C+
Central Conn State Univ	CT	19,749	C
Central Methodist Univ	MO	28,240	VC
Central State Univ	OH	9,010	C
Central Washington Univ	WA	11,730	C
Centre College	KY	35,000	HC+
Chadron State College	NE	7,400	NC
Chapman Univ	CA	58,347	VC+
Charleston Southern Univ	SC	22,420	C
Chatham Univ	PA	43,797	C
Chestnut Hill College	PA	42,110	C
Cheyney Univ of Pennsylvania	PA	20,372	LC
Chicago State Univ	IL	5,482	C
Christian Brothers Univ	TN	31,670	HC
Christopher Newport Univ	VA	21,960	VC
Citadel, The	SC		C
CUNY/Baruch College	NY		HC
CUNY/Brooklyn College	NY	5,884	C+
CUNY/City College	NY	20,319	HC+
Claflin Univ	SC	22,368	LC
Claremont McKenna College	CA	62,215	MC
Clarion Univ of Pennsylvania	PA	17,370	LC
Clark Atlanta Univ	GA	30,006	LC
Clark Univ	MA	47,020	HC+
Clarke Univ	IA	37,600	C
Clarkson Univ	NY	57,330	HC
Clearwater Christian College	FL	24,720	C
Clemson Univ	SC	19,136	HC
Cleveland State Univ	OH	21,776	C
Coastal Carolina Univ	SC	18,580	C
Coe College	IA	45,550	VC
Coker College	SC	32,256	LC
Colby College	ME	57,510	MC
Colgate Univ	NY	58,135	MC
College of Charleston	SC	22,145	VC
College of Mount St. Joseph	OH	33,880	C
College of Mount St. Vincent	NY	41,040	MC
College of New Jersey	NJ	25,376	HC
College of St. Benedict	MN	49,359	VC
College of St. Elizabeth	NJ	43,838	LC
College of St. Mary	NE	35,184	C
College of St. Scholastica	MN	41,440	C
College of Staten Island/The City of New Yok	NY	16,778	NC
College of the Holy Cross	MA	58,042	MC
College of the Ozarks	MO		VC
College of William & Mary	VA	28,000	MC
College of Wooster	OH	52,600	VC
Colo College	CO	57,162	MC
Colo Mesa Univ	CO	17,690	LC
Colo School of Mines	CO	18,000	HC
Colo State Univ-Fort Collins	CO	20,385	VC
Colo State Univ-Pueblo	CO	16,183	C
Columbia College	MO	24,578	C
Columbia College	SC	27,882	C
Columbia Univ/City of New York	NY	61,116	MC
Columbia Univ/School of General Studies	NY	58,231	MC
Columbus State Univ	GA	13,176	C
Concord Univ	WV	13,102	C
Concordia College - Moorhead	MN	39,974	VC
Concordia College - New York	NY	39,035	LC
Concordia Univ Irvine	CA	35,390	VC
Concordia Univ Nebr	NE	26,000	VC
Concordia Univ St. Paul	MN	28,250	C
Concordia Univ Wisc	WI	28,980	C
Concordia Univ, Ann Arbor	MI	27,220	VC
Concordia Univ, River Forest	IL	26,300	C
Conn College	CT	54,970	MC
Converse College	SC	37,130	C
Coppin State Univ	MD	16,227	VC
Corban Univ	OR	37,380	C+
Cornell College	IA	44,930	VC
Cornell Univ	NY	60,964	MC
Covenant College	GA	38,990	VC+
Creighton Univ	NE	45,356	VC
Culver-Stockton College	MO	30,900	C
Cumberland Univ	TN	21,220	C
Daemen College	NY	34,770	C
Dakota State Univ	SD	13,811	C
Dakota Wesleyan Univ	SD	23,000	C
Dallas Baptist Univ	TX	30,580	VC
Dartmouth College	NH	57,996	MC
Davidson College	NC	58,146	MC
Davis & Elkins College	WV	33,742	C
De Sales Univ	PA	43,970	C
Defiance College	OH	30,645	C
Delaware State Univ	DE	16,722	LC
Delta State Univ	MS	12,292	LC
Denison Univ	OH	54,670	HC+
DePaul Univ	IL	47,623	VC
DePauw Univ	IN	48,950	VC+
Dickinson College	PA	57,662	HC+
Dickinson State Univ	ND	11,900	NC
Doane College	NE	35,230	C
Dominican College	NY	31,270	C
Dominican Univ	IL	37,628	C
Dordt College	IA	34,160	C+
Dowling College	NY	25,000	LC
Drake Univ	IA	41,516	VC+
Drew Univ/College of Liberal Arts	NJ	57,516	C
Drexel Univ	PA	61,418	VC+
Drury Univ	MO	31,909	VC
Duke Univ	NC	50,250	MC
Duquesne Univ	PA	43,720	VC
D'Youville College	NY	53,564	VC
Earlham College	IN	51,470	HC
East Carolina Univ	NC	14,169	C
East Central Univ	OK	10,223	LC
East Stroudsburg Univ of Pennsylvania	PA	18,868	LC
East Tenn State Univ	TN	9,000	C
East Texas Baptist Univ	TX	31,577	LC
Eastern Conn State Univ	CT	20,584	C
Eastern Illinois Univ	IL	20,466	C
Eastern Kentucky Univ	KY	11,161	C
Eastern Mennonite Univ	VA	40,660	C
Eastern Mich Univ	MI	18,604	C
Eastern Nazarene College	MA	30,000	C
Eastern New Mexico Univ	NM	10,682	C
Eastern Oregon Univ	OR	10,400	C
Eastern Univ	PA	37,704	C
Eastern Washington Univ	WA		C
Eckerd College	FL	43,902	C
Edgewood College	WI	33,294	C
Edinboro Univ of Pennsylvania	PA	15,940	LC
Edward Waters College	FL	19,607	LC
Elizabeth City State Univ	NC	11,638	C
Elizabethtown College	PA	49,740	VC
Elmhurst College	IL	43,336	VC
Elmira College	NY	49,950	C+
Elms College	MA	23,900	VC
Elon Univ	NC	41,914	VC+
Embry-Riddle Aeronautical Univ - Daytona Beach	FL	40,884	C+
Emmanuel College	MA	47,985	VC
Emory and Henry College	VA	387,460	C
Emory Univ	GA	56,368	MC
Emporia State Univ	KS	12,897	C
Endicott College	MA	43,228	VC+
Erskine College	SC	37,360	C
Eureka College	IL	19,280	C
Evangel Univ	MO	23,090	C
Excelsior College	NY	5,580	SP
Fairfield Univ	CT	56,960	VC
Fairleigh Dickinson Univ/College at Florham	NJ	42,142	C
Fairleigh Dickinson Univ/Metropolitan Campus	NJ	40,254	C
Fairmont State Univ	WV	12,098	LC
Faulkner Univ	AL	25,720	LC
Fayetteville State Univ	NC	10,816	C
Felician College	NJ	41,640	LC
Ferrum College	VA	27,740	LC
Fisk Univ	TN	19,830	C
Fitchburg State Univ	MA	18,173	C
Florida A&M Univ	FL	14,935	LC
Florida Atlantic Univ	FL	17,339	C
Florida Gulf Coast Univ	FL		C
Florida Inst of Technology	FL	48,290	VC
Florida International Univ	FL	17,747	C+
Florida Memorial Univ	FL	20,888	C
Florida Southern College	FL	40,150	C+
Florida State Univ	FL	16,715	VC
Fontbonne Univ	MO	31,384	C
Fordham Univ	NY	61,588	HC+
Fort Hays State Univ	KS	11,354	C
Fort Lewis College	CO	15,513	C
Fort Valley State Univ	GA	11,200	VC
Framingham State Univ	MA	18,854	C
Francis Marion Univ	SC	16,464	LC
Franciscan Univ of Steubenville	OH	27,320	VC
Franklin and Marshall College	PA	60,799	MC
Franklin College	IN	36,585	C
Franklin Pierce Univ	NH	41,598	C
Freed-Hardeman Univ	TN	19,697	VC
Fresno Pacific Univ	CA	32,136	C
Friends Univ	KS	29,100	C
Frostburg State Univ	MD	15,264	LC
Furman Univ	SC	54,006	HC
Gallaudet Univ	DC	25,380	SP
Gannon Univ	PA	39,608	C
Gardner-Webb Univ	NC	34,375	C+
George Fox Univ	OR	40,750	C+
George Mason Univ	VA	15,724	VC
George Washington Univ	DC	57,108	MC
Georgetown College	KY	41,440	C+
Georgetown Univ	DC	52,910	MC
Georgia College and State Univ	GA	18,900	C+
Georgia Inst of Technology	GA	21,828	MC
Georgia Regents Univ	GA		C
Georgia Southwestern State Univ	GA	13,246	C
Georgia State Univ	GA	15,582	VC
Georgian Court Univ	NJ	41,594	LC
Gettysburg College	PA	58,820	HC
Gonzaga Univ	WA	46,441	HC
Gordon College	MA	44,320	VC
Goshen College	IN	35,900	VC
Goucher College	MD	52,040	VC+
Grace College and Seminary	IN	28,800	VC
Graceland Univ	IA	28,020	C
Grambling State Univ	LA	13,384	C
Grand Valley State Univ	MI	17,998	C+
Grand View Univ	IA	31,050	C
Greensboro College	NC	28,740	LC
Greenville College	IL	27,012	C
Grinnell College	IA	53,654	HC
Grove City College	PA	24,022	VC
Guilford College	NC	42,800	C
Gustavus Adolphus College	MN	48,170	HC
Gwynedd-Mercy College	PA	33,560	C
Hamilton College	NY	55,620	MC
Hamline Univ	MN	45,678	VC
Hampden-Sydney College	VA	51,758	C+
Hampshire College	MA	58,320	MC
Hampton Univ	VA	28,528	C
Hannibal-LaGrange Univ	MO	24,490	C
Hanover College	IN	43,073	C+
Harding Univ	AR	23,556	C
Hardin-Simmons Univ	TX	23,560	C+
Harris-Stowe State Univ	MO	14,360	NC
Hartwick College	NY	51,270	C
Harvard College/Harvard Univ	MA	49,000	MC
Harvey Mudd College	CA	64,527	MC
Hastings College	NE	27,782	C+
Haverford College	PA	61,564	MC
Hawaii Pacific Univ	HI	34,360	C
Heidelberg Univ	OH	34,100	C
Henderson State Univ	AR	14,584	C
Hendrix College	AR	50,202	VC+
Heritage Univ	WA	17,664	NC
High Point Univ	NC	39,800	C
Hillsdale College	MI	32,866	MC
Hiram College	OH	37,300	VC
Hobart and William Smith Colleges	NY	60,034	HC+
Hofstra Univ	NY	51,810	VC+
Hollins Univ	VA	43,295	VC
Holy Family Univ	PA	40,030	LC
Hood College	MD	45,730	C
Hope College	MI	38,650	VC
Houghton College	NY	36,808	C+
Houston Baptist Univ	TX	36,450	C
Howard Payne Univ	TX	17,115	C
Howard Univ	DC	13,646	C
Humboldt State Univ	CA	18,400	C
Hunter College	NY	14,429	VC
Huntingdon College	AL	33,100	C
Huntington Univ	IN	32,220	C+
Huston-Tillotson Univ	TX	18,124	C+
Idaho State Univ	ID	12,307	C
Illinois College	IL	25,770	VC
Illinois State Univ	IL	23,110	VC
Immaculata Univ	PA	43,000	C
Indiana State Univ	IN	16,000	C
Indiana Univ Bloomington	IN	19,801	VC
Indiana Univ East	IN	6,783	C
Indiana Univ Kokomo	IN	6,811	LC
Indiana Univ Northwest	IN	6,854	LC
Indiana Univ of Pennsylvania	PA	20,846	LC
Indiana Univ South Bend	IN	15,501	C
Indiana Univ Southeast	IN	16,035	C
Indiana Univ-Purdue Univ Fort Wayne	IN	15,521	C
Indiana Univ-Purdue Univ Indianapolis	IN	17,611	C
Indiana Wesleyan Univ	IN	31,815	VC
Inter-American Univ of PR/ Bayamon Univ College	PR	4,428	
Inter-American Univ of PR/ Fajardo Campus	PR	4,200	
Inter-American Univ of PR/ Metropolitan Campus	PR	4,320	
Inter-American Univ of PR/ Ponce	PR		
Inter-American Univ of PR/ San Germán	PR	6,720	
Iona College	NY	44,028	C
Iowa State Univ	IA	16,403	C
Iowa Wesleyan College	IA	30,850	LC
Ithaca College	NY	53,864	HC
Jackson State Univ	MS	13,512	LC
Jacksonville State Univ	AL	12,480	LC
Jacksonville Univ	FL	37,780	C
James Madison Univ	VA	18,049	VC
Jarvis Christian College	TX	19,552	NC
John Brown Univ	AR	32,056	VC+
John Carroll Univ	OH	46,300	C+
Johns Hopkins Univ	MD	47,492	MC
Johnson C. Smith Univ	NC	25,336	LC
Johnson State College	VT	16,721	C
Judson College	AL	26,794	C
Judson Univ	IL	25,130	C
Juniata College	PA	49,340	VC
Kalamazoo College	MI	49,740	HC
Kansas State Univ	KS	15,497	VC
Kansas Wesleyan Univ	KS	32,000	C
Kean Univ	NJ	23,444	C
Keene State College	NH	23,232	LC
Kennesaw State Univ	GA		C
Kent State Univ	OH	19,920	C
Kentucky State Univ	KY	11,000	LC
Kenyon College	OH	58,890	MC
King Univ	TN	33,140	C
King's College	PA	43,502	C
Knox College	IL	44,865	VC+
Kutztown Univ of Pennsylvania	PA	16,909	LC
La Roche College	PA	35,824	LC
La Salle Univ	PA	50,270	C
La Sierra Univ	CA	35,694	VC
Lafayette College	PA	59,155	HC+
LaGrange College	GA	37,670	C
Lake Erie College	OH	37,266	C
Lake Forest College	IL	50,652	VC
Lake Superior State Univ	MI	18,121	C
Lakeland College	WI	22,990	C
Lamar Univ	TX	6,820	LC
Lander Univ	SC	22,514	C+
Lane College	TN	11,212	C
Langston Univ	OK	3,000	C
Lawrence Tech Univ	MI	37,630	VC
Lawrence Univ	WI	46,371	HC
Le Moyne College	NY	43,470	C
Lebanon Valley College	PA	38,570	C
Lee Univ	TN	18,690	C+
Lees-McRae College	NC	33,944	C
Lehigh Univ	PA	56,770	MC
Lehman College/The CUNY	NY	5,778	LC
LeMoyne-Owen College	TN	13,100	C
Lenoir-Rhyne College	NC	35,984	C
LeTourneau Univ	TX	36,210	VC
Lewis & Clark College	OR	54,382	MC
Lewis Univ	IL	23,050	C
Lewis-Clark State College	ID	6,990	C
Liberty Univ	VA	19,101	C
Limestone College	SC	30,800	C
Lincoln Memorial Univ	TN	18,144	C
Lincoln Univ	MO	12,904	NC
Lindenwood Univ	MO	20,750	C
Lindsey Wilson College	KY	31,220	C
Linfield College-McMinnville Campus	OR	47,676	C
Lipscomb Univ	TN	37,490	VC
LIU Brooklyn	NY	47,182	LC
LIU Post	NY	47,660	C
Livingstone College	NC	17,815	LC
Lock Haven Univ of Pennsylvania	PA	18,028	LC
Longwood Univ	VA	20,924	C
Loras College	IA	37,432	VC
Louisiana College	LA	15,746	C
Louisiana State Univ	LA	18,677	C+
Louisiana State Univ in Shreveport	LA	5,606	C
Louisiana Tech Univ	LA	11,302	C

ST = STATE $IS = IN-STATE COSTS   SR = SELECTOR RATING

School	ST	$IS	SR
Loyola Marymount Univ	CA	54,649	VC+
Loyola Univ Chicago	IL	51,646	VC+
Loyola Univ Maryland	MD	56,880	VC+
Loyola Univ New Orleans	LA	46,581	VC
Lubbock Christian Univ	TX	26,308	C
Luther College	IA	45,720	C+
Lycoming College	PA	45,379	C
Lynchburg College	VA	42,645	C
Lyndon State College	VT	14,233	C
Lyon College	AR	32,090	C
Macalester College	MN	57,691	MC
MacMurray College	IL	20,755	C
Madonna Univ	MI	24,540	VC
Maharishi Univ of Management	IA	31,000	VC
Malone Univ	OH	35,364	C
Manchester Univ	IN	35,070	C
Manhattan College	NY	49,588	C+
Manhattanville College	NY	50,740	VC
Mansfield Univ	PA	19,468	LC
Marian Univ	IN	38,540	C
Marian Univ	WI	32,420	LC
Marietta College	OH	42,135	C+
Marist College	NY	35,500	C
Marlboro College	VT	53,980	VC
Marquette Univ	WI	46,930	VC+
Mars Hill Univ	NC	22,950	LC
Marshall Univ	WV	14,820	C
Martin Univ	IN	11,000	SP
Mary Baldwin College	VA	38,245	C
Marygrove College	MI	28,926	C
Marymount Univ	VA	39,480	C
Maryville College	TN	33,150	C+
Maryville Univ of St. Louis	MO	35,856	VC
Marywood Univ	PA	45,595	C
Mass College of Liberal Arts	MA	18,613	C
Mass Inst of Technology	MA	58,240	MC
Mayville State Univ	ND	11,401	NC
McDaniel College	MD	47,450	VC
McKendree Univ	IL	29,920	C+
McMurry Univ	TX	25,962	LC
McNeese State Univ	LA	2,649	C
McPherson College	KS	28,138	C
Megar Evers College/The CUNY	NY	4,920	NC
Mercer Univ	GA	44,201	VC
Mercy College	NY	30,456	C
Mercyhurst Univ	PA	40,700	C
Meredith College	NC	31,420	C
Merrimack College	MA	44,215	C
Messiah College	PA	40,690	C+
Methodist Univ	NC	37,185	C
Metropolitan State Univ of Denver	CO	4,835	LC
Miami Univ	OH	24,191	VC
Mich State Univ	MI	22,450	VC
Mich Tech Univ	MI	23,556	HC
MidAmerica Nazarene Univ	KS	28,000	C
Middle Tenn State Univ	TN	8,650	C
Middlebury College	VT	59,160	MC
Midland Univ	NE	34,000	C
Midway Univ	KY	20,150	LC
Midwestern State Univ	TX	9,722	C
Miles College	AL	11,164	NC
Millersville Univ of Pennsylvania	PA	21,648	C
Milligan College	TN	27,510	C
Millikin Univ	IL	38,940	C
Mills College	CA	54,119	VC
Millsaps College	MS	43,888	VC+
Minn State Univ, Mankato	MN	15,616	C
Minn State Univ, Moorhead	MN	13,392	VC
Minot State Univ	ND	10,915	C
Misericordia Univ	PA	41,060	C
Miss College	MS	21,998	C
Miss State Univ	MS	14,750	C
Miss Univ for Women	MS	7,400	C
Miss Valley State Univ	MS	9,706	LC
Missouri Baptist Univ	MO	31,830	C
Missouri Southern State Univ	MO	12,061	C
Missouri State Univ	MO	13,995	C+
Missouri Univ of Science and Technology	MO	18,655	VC+
Missouri Valley College	MO	22,200	C
Missouri Western State Univ	MO	12,260	NC
Molloy College	NY	40,440	C
Monmouth College	IL	40,850	C
Monmouth Univ	NJ	44,108	C
Montana State Univ	MT	14,068	C
Montana State Univ-Billings	MT	12,425	C
Montana Tech of The Univ of Montana	MT	14,650	VC
Montclair State Univ	NJ	22,614	C
Moravian College	PA	36,381	VC
Morehead State Univ	KY	10,900	C
Morehouse College	GA	39,412	C
Morgan State Univ	MD	14,500	VC
Morningside College	IA	35,430	C
Morris College	SC	16,310	LC
Mount Holyoke College	MA	55,146	MC
Mount Marty College	SD	29,638	C
Mount Mary Univ	WI	33,590	LC
Mount Mercy Univ	IA	35,320	C
Mount St. Mary College	NY	41,138	C
Mount St. Mary's Univ	MD	47,996	C

School	ST	$IS	SR
Mount St. Mary's College - Chalon Campus	CA	43,897	VC+
Mount Vernon Nazarene Univ	OH	29,590	C
Muhlenberg College	PA	52,837	HC
Murray State Univ	KY	15,304	C
Muskingum Univ	OH	30,502	C
National Louis Univ	IL	16,915	LC
National Univ	CA	14,730	SP
Nazareth College of Rochester	NY	43,028	C+
Nebr Wesleyan Univ	NE	29,774	C+
New College of Florida	FL	14,504	MC
New England College	NH	45,930	LC
New Jersey City Univ	NJ	21,456	LC
New Jersey Inst of Technology	NJ	26,490	C+
New Mexico Highlands Univ	NM	11,904	NC
New Mexico Inst of Mining and Technology	NM	13,592	VC
New Mexico State Univ	NM	14,050	C
New York Univ	NY	61,470	MC
Newberry College	SC	26,850	LC
Newman Univ	KS	30,380	C+
Niagara Univ	NY	41,010	C
Nicholls State Univ	LA	7,095	C
Nichols College	MA	37,240	LC
Norfolk State Univ	VA	10,531	LC
N Car Agricultural and Technical State Univ	NC	13,365	LC
N Car Central Univ	NC	9,000	C
N Car State Univ	NC	16,202	HC
N Car Wesleyan College	NC	29,440	C
North Central College	IL	38,343	VC
N Dak State Univ	ND		
North Park Univ	IL	30,130	C
Northeastern Illinois Univ	IL	10,318	LC
Northeastern State Univ	OK	8,615	VC
Northeastern Univ	MA	55,296	MC
Northern Arizona Univ	AZ	19,010	C
Northern Illinois Univ	IL	19,768	C
Northern Kentucky Univ	KY	21,134	C
Northern Mich Univ	MI	18,278	C
Northern State Univ - Aberdeen	SD	14,505	C
Northland College	WI	26,680	C
Northwest Missouri State Univ	MO	17,347	C
Northwest Nazarene Univ	ID	34,000	C
Northwestern College	MN	24,000	C
Northwestern College of Iowa	IA	36,240	VC
Northwestern Okla State Univ	OK	7,275	NC
Northwestern State Univ of Louisiana	LA	14,368	C
Northwestern Univ	IL	61,640	MC
Norwich Univ	VT	28,212	C
Notre Dame College	OH	34,942	VC
Notre Dame of Maryland Univ	MD	27,700	VC
Nova Southeastern Univ	FL	37,280	VC
Nyack College	NY	33,250	C
Oakland City Univ	IN	24,500	NC
Oakland Univ	MI	19,391	C
Oakwood Univ	AL	25,529	NC
Oberlin College	OH	61,788	MC
Occidental College	CA	60,972	MC
Oglethorpe Univ	GA	44,200	C+
Ohio Dominican Univ	OH	38,380	C+
Ohio Northern Univ	OH	42,075	VC
Ohio Univ	OH	21,080	C
Ohio Valley Univ	WV	17,752	C
Ohio Wesleyan Univ	OH	49,460	C+
Okla Baptist Univ	OK	28,202	C
Okla Christian Univ	OK	25,870	VC
Okla City Univ	OK	40,476	VC
Okla Panhandle State Univ	OK	8,996	C
Okla State Univ	OK	14,310	VC
Okla Wesleyan Univ	OK	21,300	C
Old Dominion Univ	VA	19,483	LC
Olivet College	MI	19,984	LC
Olivet Nazarene Univ	IL	29,990	C
Oral Roberts Univ	OK	31,734	C
Oregon State Univ	OR	20,273	VC
Oswego / SUNY	NY	20,009	VC
Ottawa Univ	KS	15,000	VC
Otterbein College	OH	32,214	C
Ouachita Baptist Univ	AR	30,220	VC
Our Lady of the Lake Univ	TX	22,430	LC
Pace Univ	NY	53,367	C
Pacific Lutheran Univ	WA	46,760	C+
Pacific Union College	CA	28,150	VC
Pacific Univ	OR	49,626	C+
Paine College	GA	19,826	LC
Palm Beach Atlantic Univ	FL	34,874	C+
Park Univ	MO	17,525	C
Penn State Erie/The Behrend College	PA	16,256	C
Penn State Univ/Altoona	PA	11,464	C
Pepperdine Univ	CA	55,372	HC+
Peru State College	NE	8,600	NC
Pfeiffer Univ	NC	33,700	LC
Philander Smith College	AR	19,760	LC
Piedmont College	GA	30,136	C
Pittsburg State Univ	KS	12,032	C
Pitzer College	CA	54,988	MC
Plymouth State Univ	NH	23,148	LC

School	ST	$IS	SR
Point Loma Nazarene Univ	CA	41,006	C+
Polytechnic Inst of New York Univ	NY	53,064	HC+
Pomona College	CA	57,680	MC
Pontifical Catholic Univ of PR	PR	7,310	
Portland State Univ	OR	18,672	C
Prairie View A&M Univ	TX	15,205	LC
Presbyterian College	SC	42,678	C+
Prescott College	AZ	33,284	C
Princeton Univ	NJ	53,795	MC
Principia College	IL	35,140	C+
Providence College	RI	57,383	VC
Purdue Univ/Calumet	IN	14,336	C
Purdue Univ/West Lafayette	IN	20,024	HC
Queens College/The CUNY	NY	17,107	VC
Queens Univ of Charlotte	NC	39,543	C+
Quincy Univ	IL	34,980	C
Quinnipiac Univ	CT	55,160	VC
Radford Univ	VA	17,766	LC
Ramapo College of New Jersey	NJ	24,938	C
Randolph College	VA	45,660	VC
Randolph-Macon College	VA	49,869	C+
Reed College	OR	57,780	MC
Regis Univ	CO	41,318	C
Rensselaer Polytechnic Inst	NY	61,529	MC
Rhode Island College	RI	17,694	LC
Rhodes College	TN	51,900	HC+
Rice Univ	TX	43,288	MC
Richard Stockton College of New Jersey	NJ	20,000	VC
Rider Univ	NJ	45,720	C
Ripon College	WI	36,959	C+
Rivier Univ	NH	35,000	VC
Roanoke College	VA	49,976	C
Roberts Wesleyan College	NY	38,306	C+
Rochester Inst of Technology	NY	42,450	VC
Rockford Univ	IL	31,000	C
Rockhurst Univ	MO	20,625	C
Rocky Mountain College	MT	32,242	C
Roger Williams Univ	RI	46,296	VC
Rollins College	FL	52,370	HC
Roosevelt Univ	IL	22,605	VC
Rose-Hulman Inst of Technology	IN	53,340	MC
Rosemont College	PA	42,350	C
Rowan Univ	NJ	24,022	VC+
Russell Sage College	NY	39,370	C
Rust College	MS	10,600	C
Rutgers, The State Univ of New Jersey/Camden Campus	NJ	25,121	C
Rutgers, The State Univ of New Jersey/New Brunswick	NJ	25,562	VC
Rutgers, The State Univ of New Jersey/Newark Campus	NJ	258,806	C
Sacred Heart Univ	CT	49,264	VC
Saginaw Valley State Univ	MI	17,369	C
St. Anselm College	NH	49,376	VC
St. Augustine's Univ	NC	14,000	C
St. Francis Univ	PA	30,029	LC
St. John's Univ	MN	47,984	C
St. Joseph's College	IN	36,500	C
St. Joseph's College of Maine	ME	31,580	C
St. Joseph's Univ	PA	55,006	VC
St. Leo Univ	FL	30,340	C
St. Louis Univ	MO	48,346	HC
St. Martin's Univ	WA	41,678	C
St. Mary-of-the-Woods College	IN	37,722	LC
St. Mary's College	IN	45,160	C+
St. Mary's College of Calif	CA	53,550	C
St. Mary's Univ	TX	33,854	C
St. Mary's Univ of Minn	MN	38,280	C
St. Michael's College	VT	49,975	VC
St. Paul's College	VA	16,030	NC
St. Peter's Univ	NJ	44,240	C
St. Vincent College	PA	40,244	C
St. Xavier Univ	IL	32,840	C
Salem College	NC	29,326	VC
Salem State Univ	MA	13,161	LC
Salisbury Univ	MD	19,180	VC
Salve Regina Univ	RI	48,550	VC
Sam Houston State Univ	TX	17,082	C
Samford Univ	AL	37,060	C+
San Diego Christian College	CA	31,012	C
San Diego State Univ	CA	21,611	C+
San Francisco State Univ	CA	18,514	C
San Jose State Univ	CA	19,133	LC
Sarah Lawrence College	NY	48,000	HC
Savannah State Univ	GA	13,156	C
Schreiner Univ	TX	32,734	LC
Scripps College	CA	61,940	MC
Seattle Pacific Univ	WA	41,559	VC+
Seattle Univ	WA	49,035	VC+
Seton Hall Univ	NJ	45,902	C
Seton Hill Univ	PA	35,172	C
Sewanee: The Univ of the South	TN	47,700	HC+
Shaw Univ	NC	15,488	C
Shawnee State Univ	OH	16,916	C
Shenandoah Univ	VA	39,916	C
Shepherd Univ	WV	15,875	C

School	ST	$IS	SR
Shippensburg Univ of Pennsylvania	PA	20,934	C
Shorter Univ	GA	30,650	LC
Siena College	NY	43,863	VC
Siena Heights Univ	MI	32,040	C
Silver Lake College	WI	22,600	LC
Simmons College	MA	49,966	VC
Simpson College	IA	36,086	C+
Simpson Univ	CA	28,900	C
Skidmore College	NY	59,942	HC
Slippery Rock Univ of Pennsylvania	PA	10,360	C
Smith College	MA	59,674	MC
Sonoma State Univ	CA	20,541	C
S Car State Univ	SC	6,700	LC
S Dak School of Mines and Technology	SD	15,260	VC
S Dak State Univ	SD	14,296	C
Southeast Missouri State Univ	MO	15,370	C
Southeastern Louisiana Univ	LA	13,325	C
Southeastern Okla State Univ	OK	7,966	LC
Southeastern Univ	FL	27,201	C
Southern Adventist Univ	TN	26,190	C
Southern Arkansas Univ	AR	14,316	C
Southern Conn State Univ	CT	18,033	LC
Southern Illinois Univ Carbondale	IL	21,942	C
Southern Illinois Univ Edwardsville	IL	17,532	C
Southern Methodist Univ	TX	60,585	MC
Southern Nazarene Univ	OK	24,354	C
Southern Oregon Univ	OR	17,874	C
Southern Polytechnic State Univ	GA	13,958	C
Southern Univ and A&M College	LA	9,761	LC
Southern Univ at New Orleans	LA	2,963	NC
Southern Wesleyan Univ	SC	25,600	C
Southwest Baptist Univ	MO	24,710	C
Southwest Minn State Univ	MN	14,000	C
Southwestern Adventist Univ	TX	23,026	LC
Southwestern College	KS	29,270	C
Southwestern Okla State Univ	OK	9,160	C
Southwestern Univ	TX	45,660	VC
Spelman College	GA	24,650	C
Spring Arbor Univ	MI	26,740	C
Spring Hill College	AL	44,164	VC
Springfield College	MA	25,000	C
St. Ambrose Univ	IA	30,845	C
St. Bonaventure Univ	NY	41,575	C
St. Catherine Univ	MN	37,782	C+
St. Cloud State Univ	MN	10,600	C
St. Edward's Univ	TX	47,784	C
St. Francis College	NY	34,200	C
St. John Fisher College	NY	40,708	C+
St. John's College, Santa Fe	NM	54,998	HC+
St. John's Univ	NY	55,070	C+
St. Joseph's College, New York/Brooklyn Campus	NY	22,630	C
St. Joseph's College, New York/Suffolk Campus	NY	22,630	C
St. Lawrence Univ	NY	59,972	VC
St. Mary's College of Maryland	MD	25,754	VC
St. Norbert College	WI	41,478	VC
St. Olaf College	MN	51,200	HC+
Stanford Univ	CA	58,388	MC
SUNY at Purchase	NY	16,951	C
SUNY/Empire State College	NY	6,315	SP
Stephen F. Austin State Univ	TX	14,668	C
Sterling College	KS	27,216	C
Stetson Univ	FL	51,516	VC
Stevens Inst of Technology	NJ	50,130	HC
Stevenson Univ	MD	41,470	C
Stillman College	AL	19,470	C
Stonehill College	MA	46,780	VC
Stony Brook Univ / SUNY	NY	20,078	HC+
Suffolk Univ	MA	47,298	C
Sul Ross State Univ	TX	13,410	LC
SUNY College at Geneseo	NY	18,670	HC
SUNY College at Old Westbury	NY	16,324	C
SUNY Cortland/The SUNY	NY	19,759	C+
SUNY Fredonia/The SUNY at Fredonia	NY	19,840	VC
SUNY New Paltz	NY	14,348	C
SUNY Oneonta / SUNY	NY	16,919	C+
SUNY Plattsburgh / SUNY	NY	18,083	C
Susquehanna Univ	PA	51,150	C
Swarthmore College	PA	57,870	MC
Syracuse Univ	NY	56,946	VC
Tabor College	KS	29,010	C
Talladega College	AL	17,996	C
Tarleton State Univ	TX	13,489	LC
Taylor Univ	IN	37,821	VC+
Temple Univ	PA	24,392	VC
Tenn State Univ	TN	9,048	C
Tenn Tech Univ	TN	11,310	C
Tenn Wesleyan College	TN	21,250	C
Texas A&M Univ	TX	19,207	VC
Texas A&M Univ at Commerce	TX	10,496	LC
Texas A&M Univ at Corpus Christi	TX	11,544	LC

ST = STATE $IS = IN-STATE COSTS   SR = SELECTOR RATING

School	ST	$IS	SR
Texas A&M Univ at Kingsville	TX	7,500	LC
Texas Christian Univ	TX	49,980	HC
Texas Lutheran Univ	TX	36,040	C
Texas Southern Univ	TX	18,212	LC
Texas State Univ	TX	17,128	C
Texas Tech Univ	TX	14,243	C
Texas Wesleyan Univ	TX	31,382	C
Texas Woman's Univ	TX	13,633	LC
The Catholic Univ of America	DC	52,852	VC
The College of Idaho	ID	31,277	C+
The College of New Rochelle	NY	33,600	VC
The College of St. Rose	NY	26,750	C
The Lincoln Univ	PA	15,154	LC
The Masters College	CA	38,160	C+
Ohio State Univ-Columbus Campus	OH	19,887	HC+
The Pennsylvania State Univ - Univ Park	PA	28,022	VC+
The SUNY at Potsdam	NY	18,473	C
The SUNY/College at Brockport	NY	19,002	C
The Univ of Memphis	TN	15,094	C
The Univ of N Car at Greensboro	NC	12,848	C
The Univ of N Car at Pembroke	NC	13,388	LC
The Univ of Okla	OK	18,621	VC
The Univ of Tenn at Chattanooga	TN	16,883	C
The Univ of Utah	UT	16,463	VC
The Univ of Virginia's College at Wise	VA	11,076	C
Thiel College	PA	38,728	LC
Thomas Edison State College	NJ	5,700	SP
Thomas More College	KY	34,760	C
Tougaloo College	MS	15,275	NC
Touro College	NY	27,959	VC
Towson Univ	MD	16,000	VC
Transylvania Univ	KY	42,660	VC+
Trevecca Nazarene Univ	TN	31,186	C
Trine Univ	IN	39,400	HC+
Trinity Christian College	IL	28,869	C
Trinity College	CT		HC+
Trinity International Univ	IL	31,070	VC
Trinity Univ	TX	48,150	HC+
Trinity Washington Univ	DC	30,250	C+
Troy Univ	AL	10,650	C
Truman State Univ	MO	15,541	HC
Tufts Univ	MA	58,780	MC
Tulane Univ	LA	60,861	MC
Tusculum College	TN	24,295	C
Tuskegee Univ	AL	26,750	C
Union College	KY	29,955	C
Union College	NE	23,270	C
Union College	NY	60,240	MC
Union Univ	TN	28,260	VC
United States Air Force Academy	CO		MC
United States Military Academy	NY		MC
United States Naval Academy	MD		MC
Universidad del Turabo	PR	4,110	
Univ at Albany / SUNY	NY	18,674	VC
Univ at Buffalo / The SUNY	NY	20,283	VC
Univ of Akron	OH	20,436	C
Univ of Alabama at Birmingham	AL	18,484	C+
Univ of Alabama at Tuscaloosa	AL	17,164	C+
Univ of Alabama in Huntsville	AL	17,591	VC+
Univ of Alaska Anchorage	AK	16,673	NC
Univ of Alaska Fairbanks	AK	15,130	C
Univ of Alaska Southeast	AK	11,493	C
Univ of Arizona	AZ	20,657	C
Univ of Arkansas at Fayetteville	AR	18,352	C+
Univ of Arkansas at Little Rock	AR	17,609	LC
Univ of Arkansas at Monticello	AR	12,076	NC
Univ of Arkansas at Pine Bluff	AR	13,378	C
Univ of Bridgeport	CT	39,030	LC
Univ of Calif at Berkeley	CA	23,322	MC
Univ of Calif at Davis	CA		HC
Univ of Calif at Irvine	CA	25,961	VC
Univ of Calif at Los Angeles	CA	25,686	MC
Univ of Calif at Riverside	CA	27,204	C+
Univ of Calif at San Diego	CA	21,000	VC
Univ of Calif at Santa Barbara	CA	27,551	HC
Univ of Calif at Santa Cruz	CA	27,807	C+
Univ of Central Arkansas	AR	13,667	VC
Univ of Central Florida	FL	15,668	VC+
Univ of Central Missouri	MO	14,605	C
Univ of Central Okla	OK	12,293	C
Univ of Chicago	IL	55,416	MC
Univ of Cincinnati	OH	21,506	VC
Univ of Colo at Colo Springs	CO	15,000	VC
Univ of Colo Boulder	CO	22,605	VC+
Univ of Colo Denver	CO	17,904	C
Univ of Conn	CT	24,706	HC
Univ of Dallas	TX	45,500	VC+
Univ of Dayton	OH	49,070	VC
Univ of Delaware	DE	23,612	VC
Univ of Denver	CO	51,787	VC+
Univ of Detroit Mercy	MI	30,450	VC
Univ of Evansville	IN	42,656	VC+
Univ of Findlay	OH	31,916	C
Univ of Florida	FL	15,943	HC
Univ of Georgia	GA	20,082	VC
Univ of Great Falls	MT	27,970	C
Univ of Hartford	CT	42,674	C
Univ of Hawaii at Hilo	HI	23,066	C
Univ of Hawaii at Manoa	HI	19,379	VC
Univ of Houston	TX	19,796	VC
Univ of Houston-Downtown	TX	15,170	LC
Univ of Idaho	ID	14,558	C
Univ of Illinois at Chicago	IL	24,505	VC
Univ of Illinois at Urbana-Champaign	IL	26,450	HC
Univ of Indianapolis	IN	31,740	LC
Univ of Iowa	IA	17,693	VC
Univ of Jamestown	ND	24,738	C
Univ of Kansas	KS	17,603	C+
Univ of Kentucky	KY	19,868	C
Univ of La Verne	CA	47,010	C
Univ of Louisiana at Lafayette	LA	6,130	C
Univ of Louisiana at Monroe	LA	12,998	C
Univ of Louisville	KY	17,946	C
Univ of Maine	ME	19,902	C+
Univ of Maine at Farmington	ME	18,187	LC
Univ of Mary	ND	16,714	C
Univ of Mary Hardin-Baylor	TX	31,950	C+
Univ of Mary Washington	VA	19,484	VC
Univ of Maryland - College Park	MD	20,060	HC
Univ of Maryland/Baltimore County	MD	18,000	VC
Univ of Maryland/Eastern Shore	MD	14,000	VC
Univ of Mass Amherst	MA	24,215	VC+
Univ of Mass Boston	MA	23,066	VC
Univ of Mass Dartmouth	MA	22,223	C
Univ of Mass Lowell	MA	19,316	C
Univ of Miami	FL	57,034	MC
Univ of Mich/Ann Arbor	MI	22,102	MC
Univ of Mich/Dearborn	MI	9,885	VC
Univ of Mich-Flint	MI	17,547	C+
Univ of Minn/Duluth	MN	19,806	C
Univ of Minn/Morris	MN	17,150	VC
Univ of Minn/Twin Cities	MN		NC
Univ of Miss	MS	16,704	C+
Univ of Missouri/Columbia	MO	18,201	MC
Univ of Missouri-Kansas City	MO	19,603	C
Univ of Missouri-St. Louis	MO		VC
Univ of Mobile	AL	28,935	VC
Univ of Montana	MT	14,105	C
Univ of Montana-Western	MT	9,753	LC
Univ of Montevallo	AL	17,060	C
Univ of Mount Olive	NC	18,426	C
Univ of Mount Union	OH	35,130	C
Univ of Nebr - Lincoln	NE	18,031	VC
Univ of Nebr at Kearney	NE	14,855	LC
Univ of Nebr at Omaha	NE	12,700	C
Univ of Nevada, Las Vegas	NV	17,303	C
Univ of Nevada/Reno	NV	17,507	C
Univ of New England	ME	46,750	C
Univ of New Hampshire	NH	26,912	C
Univ of New Haven	CT	48,940	C
Univ of New Mexico	NM	15,300	C
Univ of New Orleans	LA	9,224	C
Univ of North Alabama	AL	9,960	C
Univ of N Car at Asheville	NC	13,500	VC
Univ of N Car at Chapel Hill	NC	18,928	MC
Univ of N Car at Charlotte	NC	15,547	C
Univ of N Car at Wilmington	NC	13,572	VC
Univ of N Dak	ND	14,551	C
Univ of North Florida	FL	15,870	VC
Univ of North Georgia	GA	8,500	C
Univ of North Texas	TX	15,628	C
Univ of Northern Colo	CO	18,446	C
Univ of Northern Iowa	IA	15,795	C
Univ of Notre Dame	IN	57,117	MC
Univ of Oregon	OR	21,360	C+
Univ of Pennsylvania	PA	61,132	MC
Univ of Pikeville	KY	25,500	NC
Univ of Pittsburgh at Bradford	PA	21,802	C
Univ of Pittsburgh at Johnstown	PA	20,862	LC
Univ of Pittsburgh at Pittsburgh	PA	28,572	HC+
Univ of Portland	OR	49,964	VC
Univ of PR/Cayey	PR	1,504	
Univ of PR/Humacao	PR	1,877	
Univ of PR/Mayaguez	PR	1,250	
Univ of Puget Sound	WA	54,608	HC
Univ of Redlands	CA	40,500	VC
Univ of Rio Grande	OH	8,750	NC
Univ of Rochester	NY	60,668	MC
Univ of St. Francis	IN	29,810	C
Univ of St. Joseph	CT	45,630	C
Univ of St. Mary	KS	28,400	C+
Univ of San Diego	CA	54,818	HC+
Univ of San Francisco	CA	54,770	VC
Univ of Science and Arts of Okla	OK	10,560	VC
Univ of Scranton	PA	51,940	VC
Univ of Sioux Falls	SD	22,990	C
Univ of South Alabama	AL	13,510	C
Univ of S Car at Columbia	SC	19,725	VC+
Univ of S Car Upstate	SC	18,200	LC
Univ of S Dak	SD	15,111	C
Univ of South Florida/Tampa	FL	13,000	C
Univ of Southern Calif	CA	56,903	MC
Univ of Southern Indiana	IN	14,885	C
Univ of Southern Maine	ME	16,576	C
Univ of Southern Miss	MS	13,170	C
Univ of St. Francis	IL	37,560	C
Univ of St. Thomas - Houston	TX	37,690	C
Univ of Tampa	FL	35,160	VC
Univ of Tenn at Knoxville	TN	20,364	VC+
Univ of Tenn at Martin	TN	13,734	C
Univ of Texas - Pan American	TX	11,125	LC
Univ of Texas at Arlington	TX	10,908	LC
Univ of Texas at Austin	TX	44,074	NC
Univ of Texas at Dallas	TX	21,348	HC+
Univ of Texas at El Paso	TX	8,764	NC
Univ of Texas at San Antonio	TX	18,372	C
Univ of the Cumberlands	KY	27,500	C
Univ of the District of Columbia	DC	7,244	LC
Univ of the Incarnate Word	TX	37,316	LC
Univ of the Ozarks	AR	31,440	C
Univ of the Pacific	CA	52,146	VC
Univ of the Sacred Heart	PR	5,590	
Univ of the Southwest	NM	15,000	C
Univ of Toledo	OH	18,464	C
Univ of Tulsa	OK	46,331	MC
Univ of Vermont	VT	27,006	VC+
Univ of Virginia	VA	23,050	MC
Univ of Washington	WA	14,722	VC
Univ of West Alabama	AL	14,274	C
Univ of West Florida	FL	14,656	C
Univ of West Georgia	GA	15,488	LC
Univ of Wisc Whitewater	WI	13,314	C
Univ of Wisc/Eau Claire	WI	15,730	VC
Univ of Wisc/Green Bay	WI	19,074	C
Univ of Wisc/La Crosse	WI	9,304	VC
Univ of Wisc/Madison	WI	18,757	HC+
Univ of Wisc/Oshkosh	WI	10,426	LC
Univ of Wisc/Parkside	WI	10,181	LC
Univ of Wisc/Platteville	WI	14,564	C
Univ of Wisc/River Falls	WI	9,722	C
Univ of Wisc/Stevens Point	WI	14,043	C
Univ of Wisc/Superior	WI	14,314	C
Univ of Wisc-Milwaukee	WI	18,436	C
Univ of Wyoming	WY	14,401	C+
Upper Iowa Univ	IA	30,426	NC
Urbana Univ	OH	30,820	C
Ursinus College	PA	57,580	VC
Ursuline College	OH	33,198	LC
Utah State Univ	UT	12,044	C
Utica College	NY	45,670	C
Valley City State Univ	ND	12,286	LC
Valparaiso Univ	IN	44,940	VC+
Vanderbilt Univ	TN	58,220	MC
Vanguard Univ of Southern Calif	CA	35,833	VC
Vassar College	NY	61,140	MC
Villanova Univ	PA	58,394	MC
Virginia Commonwealth Univ	VA	21,716	C
Virginia Military Inst	VA	16,156	C
Virginia Polytechnic Inst and State Univ	VA	14,629	HC
Virginia State Univ	VA	11,318	C+
Virginia Union Univ	VA	18,432	C
Virginia Wesleyan College	VA	28,433	LC
Viterbo Univ	WI	30,070	C
Voorhees College	SC	18,126	C
Wabash College	IN	46,850	C+
Wagner College	NY	48,600	C+
Wake Forest Univ	NC	58,838	MC
Walla Walla Univ	WA	26,256	NC
Walsh Univ	OH	35,100	C
Warren Wilson College	NC	40,132	VC
Wartburg College	IA	41,055	VC
Washburn Univ	KS	12,579	C
Washington Adventist Univ	MD	25,859	LC
Washington and Jefferson College	PA	51,948	VC
Washington and Lee Univ	VA	52,812	MC
Washington College	MD	52,602	VC
Washington State Univ	WA	20,461	C
Washington Univ in St. Louis	MO	69,844	MC
Wayland Baptist Univ	TX	18,912	LC
Wayne State College	NE	11,764	NC
Wayne State Univ	MI	22,063	C
Waynesburg Univ	PA	30,150	C
Webster Univ	MO	35,100	C+
Wellesley College	MA	59,038	MC
Wells College	NY	49,400	VC
Wesley College	DE	31,115	LC
Wesleyan College	GA	24,000	C
Wesleyan Univ	CT	61,198	MC
West Chester Univ of Pennsylvania	PA	17,186	C
West Liberty Univ	WV	9,142	LC
West Texas A&M Univ	TX	13,478	C
West Virginia State Univ	WV	8,378	NC
West Virginia Univ	WV	16,542	C+
West Virginia Wesleyan College	WV	26,880	C
Western Carolina Univ	NC	13,965	C
Western Conn State Univ	CT	18,327	LC
Western Illinois Univ	IL	20,732	C
Western Kentucky Univ	KY	11,000	LC
Western Mich Univ	MI	19,628	C
Western New England Univ	MA	46,154	C+
Western New Mexico Univ	NM	8,500	LC
Western Oregon Univ	OR	15,021	C
Western State Colo Univ	CO	16,924	C
Western Washington Univ	WA	18,519	VC
Westfield State Univ	MA	18,297	C
Westminster College	MO	31,720	VC
Westminster College	PA	31,290	C+
Westminster College	UT	37,708	C+
Westmont College	CA	41,500	HC
Wheaton College	IL	40,720	MC
Wheaton College	MA	54,934	HC+
Wheeling Jesuit Univ	WV	33,500	C
Whitman College	WA	55,988	MC
Whittier College	CA	43,416	C
Whitworth Univ	WA	47,734	VC
Wichita State Univ	KS	14,607	C+
Widener Univ	PA	52,418	C
Wilberforce Univ	OH	15,100	LC
Wiley College	TX		LC
Wilkes Univ	PA	44,070	C
Willamette Univ	OR	56,450	VC+
William Carey Univ	MS	13,500	LC
William Jewell College	MO	31,000	VC+
William Paterson Univ of New Jersey	NJ	21,694	C
William Woods Univ	MO	24,260	C
Williams College	MA	61,070	MC
Wilmington College	OH	29,784	C
Wilson College	PA	35,080	C
Wingate Univ	NC	34,990	C
Winona State Univ	MN	16,640	C
Winston-Salem State Univ	NC	9,418	LC
Winthrop Univ	SC	21,120	C
Wisc Lutheran College	WI	23,510	VC
Wittenberg Univ	OH	47,962	C+
Wofford College	SC	45,795	VC
Worcester Polytechnic Inst	MA	55,860	MC
Worcester State Univ	MA	19,812	C
Wright State Univ	OH	16,983	C
Xavier Univ	OH	44,980	VC
Xavier Univ of Louisiana	LA	25,300	C
Yale Univ	CT	55,300	MC
Yeshiva Univ	NY	47,250	VC+
York College / The CUNY	NY	5,496	VC
York College of Pennsylvania	PA	26,590	C
Youngstown State Univ	OH	16,732	C

MATHEMATICS - ACTUARIAL CONCENTRATION

School	ST	$IS	SR
Bethany College	WV	35,282	LC
Bryant Univ	RI	49,179	VC
Kent State Univ	OH	19,920	C
Murray State Univ	KY	15,304	C
Seattle Univ	WA	49,035	VC+
Texas Christian Univ	TX	49,980	HC
West Chester Univ of Pennsylvania	PA	17,186	C

MATHEMATICS – ECONOMICS

School	ST	$IS	SR
Baldwin Wallace Univ	OH	38,318	C
Bethany College	WV	35,282	LC
Bowdoin College	ME	59,568	MC
Bryant Univ	RI	49,179	VC
Fordham Univ	NY	61,588	HC+
Gettysburg College	PA	58,820	HC
High Point Univ	NC	39,800	C
Ithaca College	NY	53,864	VC
New York Univ	NY	61,470	MC
Reed College	OR	57,780	MC
Southern Oregon Univ	OR	17,874	C
Temple Univ	PA	24,392	C
Univ of Dayton	OH	49,070	VC
Univ of Miami	FL	57,034	MC
Univ of Pittsburgh at Pittsburgh	PA	28,572	HC+
Wake Forest Univ	NC	58,838	MC
Wheaton College	MA	54,934	HC+
Yale Univ	CT	55,300	MC

MATHEMATICS – PHILOSOPHY

School	ST	$IS	SR
Yale Univ	CT	55,300	MC

MATHEMATICS EDUCATION

School	ST	$IS	SR
Adams State Univ	CO	13,358	LC
Alfred Univ	NY	41,770	C
Andrews Univ	MI	28,030	C+
Appalachian State Univ	NC	12,919	VC
Aquinas College	MI	33,060	C
Arizona State Univ, at the Polytechnic Campus	AZ	20,531	C+
Arizona State Univ, at the West Campus	AZ	19,251	C
Arkansas State Univ	AR	15,470	C

ST = STATE $IS = IN-STATE COSTS   SR = SELECTOR RATING

School	ST	$IS	SR
Asbury Univ	KY	32,038	VC
Auburn Univ	AL	22,378	VC+
Averett Univ	VA	37,750	LC
Baker Univ	KS	33,350	C+
Baylor Univ	TX	50,329	HC
Bennett College for Women	NC	21,970	LC
Bennington College	VT	56,990	MC
Berry College	GA	39,254	VC
Bethany College	KS	30,605	NC
Bethany College	WV	35,282	LC
Bethel College	IN	31,560	C
Bethel Univ	MN	34,940	VC
Biola Univ	CA	40,320	C+
Black Hills State Univ	SD	13,947	C
Blackburn College	IL	21,350	C
Bloomfield College	NJ	37,850	LC
Blue Mountain College	MS	15,634	LC
Boston Univ	MA	60,694	MC
Bowdoin College	ME	59,568	MC
Bowling Green State Univ	OH	18,970	C
Brigham Young Univ	UT	12,100	HC
Brigham Young Univ/Hawaii	HI	10,686	VC
Bryant Univ	RI	49,179	VC
Calif Baptist Univ	CA	38,792	C
Cal State, Long Beach	CA	17,502	C+
Calvin College	MI	39,120	C
Cameron Univ	OK	10,004	LC
Canisius College	NY	44,900	C
Carthage College	WI	33,000	C
Catawba College	NC	37,240	LC
Cedarville Univ	OH	32,860	VC
Central Washington Univ	WA	11,730	C
CUNY/Brooklyn College	NY	5,884	C+
CUNY/City College	NY	20,319	HC+
Claflin Univ	SC	22,368	LC
Coker College	SC	32,256	LC
College of New Jersey	NJ	25,376	HC
College of the Ozarks	MO		VC
Colo State Univ-Fort Collins	CO	20,385	VC
Concordia College - Moorhead	MN	39,974	VC
Concordia College - New York	NY	39,035	LC
Concordia Univ St. Paul	MN	28,250	C
Corban Univ	OR	37,380	C
Covenant College	GA	38,990	VC+
Daemen College	NY	34,770	C
Dakota State Univ	SD	13,811	C
Defiance College	OH	30,645	C
Delta State Univ	MS	12,292	LC
Dominican College	NY	31,270	LC
Dordt College	IA	34,160	C+
Drake Univ	IA	41,516	VC+
Duquesne Univ	PA	43,720	VC
East Carolina Univ	NC	14,169	C
East Central Univ	OK	10,223	LC
East Texas Baptist Univ	TX	31,577	LC
Eastern Mich Univ	MI	18,604	C
Eastern Washington Univ	WA		C
Edinboro Univ of Pennsylvania	PA	15,940	LC
Elizabethtown College	PA	49,740	VC
Elmhurst College	IL	43,336	C
Elon Univ	NC	41,914	VC+
Emory and Henry College	VA	387,460	C
Faulkner Univ	AL	25,720	LC
Ferris State Univ	MI	20,047	C
Florida Gulf Coast Univ	FL		C
Florida Inst of Technology	FL	48,290	VC
Florida State Univ	FL	16,715	VC
Fontbonne Univ	MO	31,384	C
Fort Valley State Univ	GA	11,200	VC
Franklin College	IN	36,585	C
Fresno Pacific Univ	CA	32,136	C
Gannon Univ	PA	39,608	C
Geneva College	PA	27,280	C
Georgetown College	KY	41,440	C
Georgia Southern Univ	GA	16,942	C
Glenville State College	WV	11,348	NC
Goshen College	IN	35,900	VC
Grace College and Seminary	IN	28,800	VC
Grambling State Univ	LA	15,294	LC
Greensboro College	NC	28,740	LC
Greenville College	IL	27,012	C
Gwynedd-Mercy College	PA	33,560	C
Hardin-Simmons Univ	TX	23,560	C+
Hofstra Univ	NY	51,810	VC+
Hood College	MD	45,730	C
Houghton College	NY	36,808	C+
Houston Baptist Univ	TX	36,450	C
Humboldt State Univ	CA	18,400	C
Huntingdon College	AL	33,100	C
Huntington Univ	IN	33,220	C+
Indiana Univ Bloomington	IN	19,801	VC
Indiana Univ Northwest	IN	6,854	LC
Indiana Univ South Bend	IN	15,501	C
Indiana Univ Southeast	IN	16,035	C
Indiana Univ-Purdue Univ Fort Wayne	IN	15,521	C
Indiana Univ-Purdue Univ Indianapolis	IN	17,611	C
Indiana Wesleyan Univ	IN	31,815	VC
Ithaca College	NY	53,864	HC
Jackson State Univ	MS	13,512	LC
John Carroll Univ	OH	46,300	C+
Johnson State College	VT	16,721	C
Judson College	AL	26,794	C
Judson Univ	IL	25,130	C
Juniata College	PA	49,340	VC
Keene State College	NH	23,232	LC
Kennesaw State Univ	GA		C
Kent State Univ	OH	19,920	C
Kentucky State Univ	KY	11,000	LC
Keystone College	PA	28,680	LC
Kutztown Univ of Pennsylvania	PA	16,909	LC
Langston Univ	OK	3,000	C
Le Moyne College	NY	43,470	C
Lee Univ	TN	18,690	C+
Limestone College	SC	30,800	C
Lincoln Univ	MO	12,904	NC
Lipscomb Univ	TN	37,490	VC
LIU Post	NY	47,660	C
Louisiana College	LA	15,746	C
Loyola Marymount Univ	CA	54,649	VC+
Loyola Univ Chicago	IL	51,646	VC+
Mansfield Univ	PA	19,468	LC
Marian Univ	WI	32,420	LC
Mars Hill Univ	NC	22,950	LC
Marymount Univ	VA	39,480	C
Marywood Univ	PA	45,595	C
Mass College of Liberal Arts	MA	18,613	C
Mayville State Univ	ND	11,401	NC
Mercyhurst Univ	PA	40,700	C
Messiah College	PA	40,690	C+
MidAmerica Nazarene Univ	KS	28,000	C
Miles College	AL	11,164	NC
Millikin Univ	IL	38,940	C
Minn State Univ, Mankato	MN	15,616	C
Minn State Univ, Moorhead	MN	13,392	VC
Minot State Univ	ND	10,915	C
Miss Valley State Univ	MS	9,706	LC
Missouri Southern State Univ	MO	12,061	C
Monmouth Univ	NJ	44,108	C
Montana State Univ-Billings	MT	12,425	LC
Morningside College	IA	35,430	C
Morris College	SC	16,310	LC
Mount Mary Univ	WI	33,590	LC
Mount Vernon Nazarene Univ	OH	29,590	C
Murray State Univ	KY	15,304	C
Nazareth College of Rochester	NY	43,028	C+
New York College of Technology/The CUNY	NY	5,769	NC
New York Univ	NY	61,470	MC
Niagara Univ	NY	41,010	C
N Car Agricultural and Technical State Univ	NC	13,365	LC
N Car State Univ	NC	16,202	HC
Northern Kentucky Univ	KY	21,134	C
Northwest Missouri State Univ	MO	17,347	C
Northwest Nazarene Univ	ID	34,000	C
Northwestern College	MN	24,000	C
Northwestern Okla State Univ	OK	7,275	NC
Northwestern Univ	IL	61,640	MC
Nyack College	NY	33,250	C
Oakwood Univ	AL	25,529	NC
Ohio Univ	OH	21,080	C
Ohio Valley Univ	WV	17,752	C
Okla Christian Univ	OK	25,870	VC
Okla Wesleyan Univ	OK	21,300	C
Old Dominion Univ	VA	19,483	LC
Olivet Nazarene Univ	IL	29,990	C
Oral Roberts Univ	OK	31,734	C
Oswego / SUNY	NY	20,009	VC
Ouachita Baptist Univ	AR	30,220	VC
Palm Beach Atlantic Univ	FL	34,874	C+
Pepperdine Univ	CA	55,372	HC+
Piedmont College	GA	30,136	C
Pittsburg State Univ	KS	12,032	C
Pontifical Catholic Univ of PR	PR	7,310	
Providence College	RI	57,383	VC
Purdue Univ/West Lafayette	IN	20,024	HC
Regis College	MA	47,565	LC
Rider Univ	NJ	45,720	C
Rivier Univ	NH	35,000	VC
Roberts Wesleyan College	NY	38,306	C+
Rocky Mountain College	MT	32,242	C
Rust College	MS	10,600	C
Sacred Heart Univ	CT	49,264	VC
Saginaw Valley State Univ	MI	17,369	C
St. Augustine's Univ	NC	14,000	C
St. Mary-of-the-Woods College	IN	37,722	LC
St. Mary's Univ of Minn	MN	38,280	C
Salisbury Univ	MD	19,180	VC
Schreiner Univ	TX	32,734	LC
Seattle Pacific Univ	WA	41,559	VC+
Seattle Univ	WA	49,035	VC+
Seton Hill Univ	PA	35,172	C
Shaw Univ	NC	15,488	C
Shepherd Univ	WV	15,875	C
Shippensburg Univ of Pennsylvania	PA	20,934	C
Shorter Univ	GA	30,650	LC
Simpson College	CA	28,900	C
Southeast Missouri State Univ	MO	15,370	LC
Southeastern Okla State Univ	OK	7,966	LC
Southern Illinois Univ Edwardsville	IL	17,532	C
Southern Nazarene Univ	OK	24,354	C
Southern Univ and A&M College	LA	9,761	LC
Southern Univ at New Orleans	LA	2,963	NC
Southern Wesleyan Univ	SC	25,600	C
Southwest Baptist Univ	MO	24,710	C
Southwest Minn State Univ	MN	14,000	C
Southwestern College	KS	29,270	C
Southwestern Okla State Univ	OK	9,160	C
St. Edward's Univ	TX	47,784	C
St. John Fisher College	NY	40,708	C+
St. John's Univ	NY	55,070	C
Suffolk Univ	MA	47,298	C
SUNY College at Old Westbury	NY	16,324	C
SUNY Fredonia/The SUNY at Fredonia	NY	19,840	VC
SUNY New Paltz	NY	14,348	C
SUNY Oneonta / SUNY	NY	16,919	C+
SUNY Plattsburgh / SUNY	NY	18,083	C
Syracuse Univ	NY	56,346	VC
Taylor Univ	IN	37,821	VC+
Temple Univ	PA	24,392	VC
Texas Southern Univ	TX	18,212	LC
Texas Wesleyan Univ	TX	31,382	C
The Catholic Univ of America	DC	52,852	VC
The College of St. Rose	NY	26,750	C
The SUNY at Potsdam	NY	18,473	C
The Univ of N Car at Greensboro	NC	12,848	C
The Univ of Okla	OK	18,621	VC
Tougaloo College	MS	15,275	NC
Trevecca Nazarene Univ	TN	31,186	C
Trine Univ	IN	39,400	HC+
Troy Univ	AL	10,650	C
Union Univ	NE	23,270	C
Universidad del Turabo	PR	4,110	
Univ of Arkansas at Pine Bluff	AR	13,378	C
Univ of Calif at Los Angeles	CA	25,686	MC
Univ of Calif at Riverside	CA	27,204	C+
Univ of Calif at San Diego	CA	21,000	VC
Univ of Central Florida	FL	15,668	VC+
Univ of Central Missouri	MO	14,605	C
Univ of Central Okla	OK	12,293	C
Univ of Conn	CT	24,706	HC
Univ of Delaware	DE	23,612	VC
Univ of Evansville	IN	42,656	VC+
Univ of Georgia	GA	20,082	VC
Univ of Great Falls	MT	27,970	C
Univ of Idaho	ID	14,558	C
Univ of Illinois at Chicago	IL	24,505	VC
Univ of Illinois at Urbana-Champaign	IL	26,450	HC
Univ of Indianapolis	IN	31,740	LC
Univ of Iowa	IA	17,693	VC
Univ of Kentucky	KY	19,868	C
Univ of Louisiana at Lafayette	LA	6,130	C
Univ of Louisiana at Monroe	LA	12,998	C
Univ of Mary	ND	16,714	C
Univ of Mary Hardin-Baylor	TX	31,950	C+
Univ of Maryland/Eastern Shore	MD	14,000	VC
Univ of Miami	FL	57,034	MC
Univ of Mich/Dearborn	MI	9,885	VC
Univ of Minn/Duluth	MN	19,806	C
Univ of Minn/Twin Cities	MN		HC
Univ of Miss	MS	16,704	C+
Univ of Missouri/Columbia	MO	18,201	MC
Univ of Montana-Western	MT	9,753	LC
Univ of Nebr - Lincoln	NE	18,031	VC
Univ of New Hampshire	NH	26,912	C
Univ of New Haven	CT	48,940	C
Univ of New Orleans	LA	9,224	C
Univ of N Car at Charlotte	NC	15,547	C
Univ of North Florida	FL	15,870	VC
Univ of North Georgia	GA	8,500	C
Univ of Pittsburgh at Bradford	PA	21,802	C
Univ of Pittsburgh at Johnstown	PA	20,862	LC
Univ of Rio Grande	OH	8,750	NC
Univ of St. Francis	IN	29,810	C
Univ of S Car Upstate	SC	18,200	LC
Univ of South Florida/Tampa	FL	13,000	C
Univ of Southern Indiana	IN	14,885	C
Univ of the Cumberlands	KY	27,500	C
Univ of Vermont	VT	27,006	VC+
Univ of Wisc/Green Bay	WI	19,074	C
Univ of Wisc/Superior	WI	14,314	C
Utah State Univ	UT	12,044	C
Valparaiso Univ	IN	44,940	VC+
Viterbo Univ	WI	30,070	C
Wartburg College	IA	41,055	VC
Washington Adventist Univ	MD	25,859	LC
Washington Univ in St. Louis	MO	69,844	MC
Wayne State Univ	MI	22,063	C
Webster Univ	MO	35,100	C+
West Chester Univ of Pennsylvania	PA	17,186	C
West Texas A&M Univ	TX	13,478	C
West Virginia Univ	WV	16,542	C
Western Carolina Univ	NC	13,965	C
Westmont College	CA	41,500	HC
Whitworth Univ	WA	47,734	VC
Widener Univ	PA	52,418	C
Wiley College	TX		LC
Wilmington College	OH	29,784	C
Wilson College	PA	35,080	C
Wingate Univ	NC	34,990	C
Winona State Univ	MN	16,640	C
Wright State Univ	OH	16,983	C
Xavier Univ of Louisiana	LA	25,300	C
York College of Pennsylvania	PA	26,590	C
Youngstown State Univ	OH	16,732	C

MATHEMATICS/COMPUTATIONAL

School	ST	$IS	SR
Abilene Christian Univ	TX	38,400	C+
Aquinas College	MI	33,060	C
Bryant Univ	RI	49,179	VC
Hillsdale College	MI	32,866	MC
Keene State College	NH	23,232	LC
Lawrence Tech Univ	MI	37,630	VC
Loyola Univ Chicago	IL	51,646	VC+
Missouri Southern State Univ	MO	12,061	C
Southwestern Univ	TX	45,660	VC
Stanford Univ	CA	58,388	MC
Temple Univ	PA	24,392	VC
Univ of Illinois at Chicago	IL	24,505	VC
Univ of Miami	FL	57,034	MC
West Chester Univ of Pennsylvania	PA	17,186	C

MATHEMATICS/THEORETICAL

School	ST	$IS	SR
Aquinas College	MI	33,060	C
Biola Univ	CA	40,320	C+
Seattle Univ	WA	49,035	VC+

MECHANICAL DESIGN TECHNOLOGY

School	ST	$IS	SR
Pennsylvania College of Technology	PA	26,286	NC
Western Washington Univ	WA	18,519	VC

MECHANICAL ENGINEERING

School	ST	$IS	SR
Alabama A&M Univ	AL	10,084	C
Alfred Univ	NY	41,770	C
Arizona State Univ, at the Tempe Campus	AZ	20,137	C+
Arkansas State Univ	AR	15,470	C
Arkansas Tech Univ	AR	13,982	LC
Auburn Univ	AL	22,378	VC+
Baylor Univ	TX	50,329	HC
Bethel College	IN	31,560	C
Binghamton Univ/The SUNY	NY	21,648	HC+
Boise State Univ	ID	13,469	LC
Boston Univ	MA	60,694	MC
Bradley Univ	IL	31,874	VC
Brigham Young Univ	UT	12,100	HC
Bucknell Univ	PA	60,140	MC
Calif Baptist Univ	CA	38,792	C
Calif Inst of Technology	CA	54,045	MC
Calif Maritime Academy	CA	15,496	LC
Calif Polytechnic State Univ	CA	19,847	VC
Calif State Polytechnic Univ, Pomona	CA	20,156	C
Cal State, Chico	CA	20,158	C
Cal State, Fresno	CA	17,405	C
Cal State, Fullerton	CA	25,188	C
Cal State, Long Beach	CA	17,502	C+
Cal State, Los Angeles	CA	17,186	LC
Cal State, Northridge	CA	28,690	LC
Cal State, Sacramento	CA	16,200	C
Calvin College	MI	39,120	C
Carnegie Mellon Univ	PA	51,260	MC
Case Western Reserve Univ	OH	56,534	MC
Cedarville Univ	OH	32,860	VC
Central Conn State Univ	CT	19,749	C
Central Washington Univ	WA	11,730	C
Christian Brothers Univ	TN	31,670	HC
CUNY/City College	NY	20,319	HC+
Clarkson Univ	NY	57,330	VC
Clemson Univ	SC	19,136	HC
Cleveland State Univ	OH	21,776	C
College of New Jersey	NJ	25,376	HC
Colo State Univ-Fort Collins	CO	20,385	VC
Columbia Univ/City of New York	NY	61,116	MC
Cooper Union for the Advancement of Science and Art	NY	55,600	MC
Cornell Univ	NY	60,964	MC
Daniel Webster College	NH	25,380	C
Delaware State Univ	DE	16,722	LC
Dordt College	IA	34,160	C+
Drexel Univ	PA	61,418	VC+
Duke Univ	NC	50,250	MC
Elizabethtown College	PA	49,740	VC
Embry-Riddle Aeronautical Univ - Daytona Beach	FL	40,884	C+
Embry-Riddle Aeronautical Univ - Prescott Campus	AZ	40,444	VC+

ST = STATE $IS = IN-STATE COSTS   SR = SELECTOR RATING

Mechanical engineering

School	ST	$IS	SR
Fairfield Univ	CT	56,960	VC
Florida A&M Univ	FL	14,935	LC
Florida Atlantic Univ	FL	17,339	VC
Florida Inst of Technology	FL	48,290	VC
Florida International Univ	FL	17,747	C+
Florida State Univ	FL	16,715	VC
Franklin W. Olin College of Engineering	MA	59,225	SP
Gannon Univ	PA	39,608	C
George Washington Univ	DC	57,108	MC
Georgia Inst of Technology	GA	21,828	MC
Georgia Southern Univ	GA	16,942	C
Gonzaga Univ	WA	46,441	HC
Grove City College	PA	24,022	VC
Harding Univ	AR	23,556	C
Hofstra Univ	NY	51,810	VC+
Howard Univ	DC	13,646	C
Idaho State Univ	ID	12,307	C
Illinois Inst of Technology	IL	38,512	HC+
Indiana Univ of Technology	IN	34,240	LC
Indiana Univ-Purdue Univ Fort Wayne	IN	15,521	C
Indiana Univ-Purdue Univ Indianapolis	IN	17,611	C
Inter-American Univ of PR/Bayamon Univ College	PR	4,428	
Iowa State Univ	IA	16,403	C
Jacksonville Univ	FL	37,780	C
Johns Hopkins Univ	MD	47,492	MC
Kansas State Univ	KS	15,497	VC
Kettering Univ	MI	31,456	HC
Lafayette College	PA	59,155	HC+
Lake Superior State Univ	MI	18,121	C
Lamar Univ	TX	6,820	LC
Lawrence Tech Univ	MI	37,630	VC
Lehigh Univ	PA	56,770	MC
LeTourneau Univ	TX	36,210	VC
Lipscomb Univ	TN	37,490	VC
Louisiana State Univ	LA	18,677	C+
Louisiana Tech Univ	LA	11,302	C
Loyola Marymount Univ	CA	54,649	VC+
Manhattan College	NY	49,588	C+
Marquette Univ	WI	46,930	VC+
Mass Inst of Technology	MA	58,240	MC
Miami Univ	OH	24,191	VC
Mich State Univ	MI	22,450	VC
Mich Tech Univ	MI	23,556	HC
Milwaukee School of Engineering	WI	39,948	VC+
Minn State Univ, Mankato	MN	15,616	C
Miss State Univ	MS	14,750	C
Missouri Univ of Science and Technology	MO	18,655	VC+
Montana State Univ	MT	14,068	C
New Jersey Inst of Technology	NJ	26,490	C+
New Mexico Inst of Mining and Technology	NM	13,592	VC
New Mexico State Univ	NM	14,050	C
New York Inst of Technology	NY	45,010	VC
New York Univ	NY	61,470	MC
N Car Agricultural and Technical State Univ	NC	13,365	LC
N Car State Univ	NC	16,202	HC
N Dak State Univ	ND		C
Northeastern Univ	MA	55,296	MC
Northern Arizona Univ	AZ	19,010	C
Northern Illinois Univ	IL	19,768	C
Northwestern Univ	IL	61,640	MC
Norwich Univ	VT	28,212	C
Oakland Univ	MI	19,391	C
Ohio Northern Univ	OH	42,075	VC
Ohio Univ	OH	21,080	C
Okla Christian Univ	OK	25,870	VC
Okla State Univ	OK	14,310	VC
Old Dominion Univ	VA	19,483	LC
Oral Roberts Univ	OK	31,734	C
Oregon State Univ	OR	20,273	VC
Pennsylvania College of Technology	PA	26,286	NC
Point Park Univ	PA	36,390	C
Polytechnic Inst of New York Univ	NY	53,064	HC+
Prairie View A&M Univ	TX	15,205	LC
Princeton Univ	NJ	53,795	MC
Purdue Univ/Calumet	IN	14,336	C
Purdue Univ/West Lafayette	IN	20,024	HC
Quinnipiac Univ	CT	55,160	VC
Rensselaer Polytechnic Inst	NY	61,529	MC
Rice Univ	TX	43,288	MC
Rochester Inst of Technology	NY	42,450	VC
Rose-Hulman Inst of Technology	IN	53,340	MC
Rowan Univ	NJ	24,022	VC+
Rutgers, The State Univ of New Jersey/New Brunswick	NJ	25,562	VC
Saginaw Valley State Univ	MI	17,369	C
St. Louis Univ	MO	48,346	HC
St. Martin's Univ	WA	41,678	C
St. Mary's Univ	TX	33,854	C
San Diego State Univ	CA	21,611	C+
San Francisco State Univ	CA	18,514	C
San Jose State Univ	CA	19,133	LC
Seattle Univ	WA	49,035	VC+
S Dak School of Mines and Technology	SD	15,260	VC
S Dak State Univ	SD	14,296	C
Southern Illinois Univ Carbondale	IL	21,942	C
Southern Illinois Univ Edwardsville	IL	17,532	C
Southern Methodist Univ	TX	60,585	MC
Southern Polytechnic State Univ	GA	13,958	C
Southern Univ and A&M College	LA	9,761	LC
Stanford Univ	CA	58,388	MC
Stevens Inst of Technology	NJ	50,130	HC
Stony Brook Univ / SUNY	NY	20,078	HC+
Syracuse Univ	NY	56,346	VC
Temple Univ	PA	24,392	VC
Tenn State Univ	TN	9,048	C
Tenn Tech Univ	TN	11,310	C
Texas A&M Univ	TX	19,207	VC
Texas A&M Univ at Kingsville	TX	7,500	LC
Texas Christian Univ	TX	49,980	HC
Texas Tech Univ	TX	14,243	C
The Catholic Univ of America	DC	52,852	VC
Ohio State Univ-Columbus Campus	OH	19,887	HC+
The Pennsylvania State Univ - Univ Park	PA	28,022	VC+
The Univ of Memphis	TN	15,094	C
The Univ of Okla	OK	18,621	VC
The Univ of Tenn at Chattanooga	TN	16,883	C
The Univ of Utah	UT	16,463	VC
Trine Univ	IN	39,400	HC+
Tufts Univ	MA	58,780	MC
Tuskegee Univ	AL	26,750	C
Union College	NY	60,240	MC
United States Air Force Academy	CO		MC
United States Coast Guard Academy	CT	942	HC
United States Military Academy	NY		MC
United States Naval Academy	MD		MC
Universidad Politecnica de PR	PR	19,252	
Univ at Buffalo / The SUNY	NY	20,283	VC
Univ of Akron	OH	20,436	C
Univ of Alabama at Birmingham	AL	18,484	C+
Univ of Alabama at Tuscaloosa	AL	17,164	C+
Univ of Alabama in Huntsville	AL	17,591	VC+
Univ of Alaska Fairbanks	AK	15,130	C
Univ of Arizona	AZ	20,657	C
Univ of Arkansas at Fayetteville	AR	18,352	C+
Univ of Calif at Berkeley	CA	23,322	MC
Univ of Calif at Davis	CA		HC
Univ of Calif at Irvine	CA	25,961	VC
Univ of Calif at Los Angeles	CA	25,686	MC
Univ of Calif at Riverside	CA	27,204	C
Univ of Calif at San Diego	CA	21,000	VC
Univ of Calif at Santa Barbara	CA	27,551	VC
Univ of Central Florida	FL	15,668	VC+
Univ of Cincinnati	OH	21,506	VC
Univ of Colo Boulder	CO	22,605	VC+
Univ of Colo Denver	CO	17,904	C
Univ of Conn	CT	24,706	HC
Univ of Dayton	OH	49,070	VC
Univ of Delaware	DE	23,612	VC
Univ of Denver	CO	51,787	VC+
Univ of Detroit Mercy	MI	30,450	VC
Univ of Evansville	IN	42,656	VC+
Univ of Florida	FL	15,943	VC
Univ of Georgia	GA	20,082	VC
Univ of Hartford	CT	42,674	C
Univ of Hawaii at Manoa	HI	19,379	C
Univ of Houston	TX	19,796	VC
Univ of Idaho	ID	14,558	C
Univ of Illinois at Chicago	IL	24,505	VC
Univ of Illinois at Urbana-Champaign	IL	26,450	HC
Univ of Indianapolis	IN	31,740	C
Univ of Iowa	IA	17,693	VC
Univ of Kansas	KS	17,603	C+
Univ of Kentucky	KY	19,868	C
Univ of Louisiana at Lafayette	LA	6,130	C
Univ of Louisville	KY	17,946	C
Univ of Maine	ME	19,902	C+
Univ of Maryland - College Park	MD	20,060	HC
Univ of Maryland/Baltimore County	MD	18,000	VC
Univ of Mass Amherst	MA	24,215	VC+
Univ of Mass Dartmouth	MA	22,223	C
Univ of Mass Lowell	MA	19,316	C
Univ of Miami	FL	57,034	MC
Univ of Mich/Ann Arbor	MI	22,102	MC
Univ of Mich/Dearborn	MI	9,885	VC
Univ of Minn/Duluth	MN	19,806	C
Univ of Minn/Twin Cities	MN		NC
Univ of Miss	MS	16,704	C+
Univ of Missouri/Columbia	MO	18,201	MC
Univ of Missouri-Kansas City	MO	19,603	C
Univ of Missouri-St. Louis	MO		VC
Univ of Mount Union	OH	35,130	C
Univ of Nebr - Lincoln	NE	18,031	VC
Univ of Nevada, Las Vegas	NV	17,303	C
Univ of Nevada/Reno	NV	17,507	C
Univ of New Hampshire	NH	26,912	C
Univ of New Haven	CT	48,940	VC
Univ of New Mexico	NM	15,300	C
Univ of New Orleans	LA	9,224	C
Univ of N Car at Charlotte	NC	15,547	C
Univ of N Dak	ND	14,551	C
Univ of North Florida	FL	15,870	VC
Univ of North Texas	TX	15,628	C
Univ of Notre Dame	IN	57,117	MC
Univ of Pittsburgh at Pittsburgh	PA	28,572	HC+
Univ of Portland	OR	49,964	VC
Univ of PR/Mayaguez	PR	1,250	
Univ of Rochester	NY	60,668	MC
Univ of San Diego	CA	54,818	VC+
Univ of South Alabama	AL	13,510	C
Univ of S Car at Columbia	SC	19,725	VC+
Univ of South Florida/Tampa	FL	13,000	C
Univ of Southern Calif	CA	56,903	MC
Univ of Tenn at Knoxville	TN	20,364	VC+
Univ of Texas - Pan American	TX	11,125	LC
Univ of Texas at Arlington	TX	10,908	LC
Univ of Texas at Austin	TX	44,074	HC
Univ of Texas at Dallas	TX	21,348	HC+
Univ of Texas at El Paso	TX	8,764	NC
Univ of Texas at San Antonio	TX	18,372	C
Univ of the District of Columbia	DC	7,244	LC
Univ of the Pacific	CA	52,146	VC
Univ of Toledo	OH	18,464	C
Univ of Tulsa	OK	46,331	MC
Univ of Vermont	VT	27,006	VC+
Univ of Virginia	VA	23,050	MC
Univ of Wisc/Madison	WI	18,757	HC+
Univ of Wisc/Platteville	WI	14,564	C
Univ of Wisc-Milwaukee	WI	18,436	C
Univ of Wyoming	WY	14,401	C+
Utah State Univ	UT	12,044	C
Valparaiso Univ	IN	44,940	VC+
Vanderbilt Univ	TN	58,220	MC
Villanova Univ	PA	58,394	MC
Virginia Commonwealth Univ	VA	21,716	C
Virginia Military Inst	VA	16,156	C
Virginia Polytechnic Inst and State Univ	VA	14,629	HC
Washington State Univ	WA	20,461	C
Washington Univ in St. Louis	MO	69,844	MC
Wayne State Univ	MI	22,063	C
West Texas A&M Univ	TX	13,478	C
West Virginia Univ	WV	16,542	C+
West Virginia Univ Inst of Technology	WV	14,094	NC
Western Kentucky Univ	KY	11,000	LC
Western Mich Univ	MI	19,628	C
Western New England Univ	MA	46,154	VC
Wichita State Univ	KS	14,607	C+
Widener Univ	PA	52,418	C
Wilkes Univ	PA	44,070	C
Worcester Polytechnic Inst	MA	55,860	MC
Wright State Univ	OH	16,983	C
Yale Univ	CT	55,300	MC
York College of Pennsylvania	PA	26,590	C
Youngstown State Univ	OH	16,732	C

MECHANICAL ENGINEERING TECHNOLOGY

School	ST	$IS	SR
Alabama A&M Univ	AL	10,084	C
Alfred State/SUNY College of Technology	NY	18,034	C
Arizona State Univ, at the Polytechnic Campus	AZ	20,531	C+
Arizona State Univ, at the Tempe Campus	AZ	20,137	C+
Buffalo State College / SUNY	NY	15,733	C+
Central Conn State Univ	CT	17,749	C
Cleveland State Univ	OH	21,776	C
Colo State Univ-Pueblo	CO	16,183	C
Eastern Mich Univ	MI	18,604	C
Eastern Washington Univ	WA		C
Fairleigh Dickinson Univ/Metropolitan Campus	NJ	40,254	C
Fairmont State Univ	WV	12,098	LC
Farmingdale State College	NY	19,673	C
Ferris State Univ	MI	20,047	C
Indiana State Univ	IN	16,000	C
Indiana Univ-Purdue Univ Fort Wayne	IN	15,521	C
Indiana Univ-Purdue Univ Indianapolis	IN	17,611	C
Kent State Univ	OH	19,920	C
Metropolitan State Univ of Denver	CO	4,835	LC
Mich Tech Univ	MI	23,556	HC
Montana State Univ	MT	14,068	C
New York College of Technology/The CUNY	NY	5,769	NC
Northern Kentucky Univ	KY	21,134	C
Okla State Univ	OK	14,310	VC
Old Dominion Univ	VA	19,483	LC
Oregon Inst of Technology	OR	8,910	C
Penn State Erie/The Behrend College	PA	16,256	C
Pennsylvania College of Technology	PA	26,286	NC
Pittsburg State Univ	KS	12,032	C
Point Park Univ	PA	36,390	C
Purdue Univ/Calumet	IN	14,336	C
Purdue Univ/West Lafayette	IN	20,024	HC
Rochester Inst of Technology	NY	42,450	VC
S Car State Univ	SC	6,700	LC
Southern Polytechnic State Univ	GA	13,958	C
SUNY Polytechnic Inst	NY	19,690	C
Texas A&M Univ at Corpus Christi	TX	11,544	LC
Texas A&M Univ at Galveston	TX	11,258	C
Texas Tech Univ	TX	14,243	C
Univ of Akron	OH	20,436	C
Univ of Arkansas at Little Rock	AR	17,609	LC
Univ of Cincinnati	OH	21,506	VC
Univ of Dayton	OH	49,070	VC
Univ of Hartford	CT	42,674	C
Univ of Houston	TX	19,796	VC
Univ of Maine	ME	19,902	C+
Univ of N Car at Charlotte	NC	15,547	C
Univ of North Texas	TX	15,628	C
Univ of Pittsburgh at Johnstown	PA	20,862	LC
Univ of Southern Miss	MS	13,170	C
Univ of Wisc/Green Bay	WI	19,074	C
Vaughn College of Aeronautics and Technology	NY	31,360	C
Wayne State Univ	MI	22,063	C
Wentworth Inst of Technology	MA	29,800	C
Western Washington Univ	WA	18,519	VC
Youngstown State Univ	OH	16,732	C

MECHATRONICS ENGINEERING

School	ST	$IS	SR
Cal State, Chico	CA	20,158	C
Kent State Univ	OH	19,920	C
Southern Polytechnic State Univ	GA	13,958	C
Univ of Denver	CO	51,787	VC+
Vaughn College of Aeronautics and Technology	NY	31,360	C

MEDIA ARTS

School	ST	$IS	SR
Alverno College	WI	31,434	LC
Anna Maria College	MA	34,600	C
Art Inst of Portland	OR	23,040	SP
Ashland Univ	OH	25,000	C
Baker Univ	KS	33,350	C+
Bentley Univ	MA	56,454	HC+
Briar Cliff Univ	IA	29,514	C
Brigham Young Univ	UT	12,100	HC
Brown Univ	RI	59,428	MC
Butler Univ	IN	47,572	VC+
Cal State, Fresno	CA	17,405	C
Cal State, Los Angeles	CA	17,186	LC
Calumet College of St. Joseph	IN	15,000	C
Calvin College	MI	39,120	VC
Canisius College	NY	44,900	C
Carleton College	MN	60,102	MC
Carlow Univ	PA	30,272	C
Champlain College	VT	46,650	VC+
Chatham Univ	PA	43,797	C
Claremont McKenna College	CA	62,215	MC
College of the Ozarks	MO		VC
Cornerstone Univ and Grand Rapids Theological Seminary	MI	33,338	C
De Sales Univ	PA	43,970	C
Denison Univ	OH	54,670	HC+
DePaul Univ	IL	47,623	VC
Drury Univ	MO	31,909	VC
East Stroudsburg Univ of Pennsylvania	PA	18,868	LC
Eastern Mich Univ	MI	18,604	C
Edinboro Univ of Pennsylvania	PA	15,940	LC
Elon Univ	NC	41,914	VC+
Emerson College	MA	52,446	HC+
Florida Atlantic Univ	FL	17,339	C
Goddard College	VT	16,418	VC
Greenville College	IL	27,012	C
Hampshire College	MA	58,320	MC
Harding Univ	AR	23,556	C
Hofstra Univ	NY	51,810	VC+
Houghton College	NY	36,808	C
Howard Univ	DC	13,646	C
Hunter College	NY	14,429	VC
Huntington Univ	IN	32,220	C+
Illinois State Univ	IL	23,110	VC
Indiana Univ Kokomo	IN	6,811	LC
Indiana Univ-Purdue Univ Indianapolis	IN	17,611	C
Ithaca College	NY	53,864	HC
James Madison Univ	VA	18,049	VC

ST = STATE　　$IS = IN-STATE COSTS　　SR = SELECTOR RATING

School	ST	$IS	SR
Johns Hopkins Univ	MD	47,492	MC
Judson Univ	IL	25,130	C
Lake Erie College	OH	37,266	C
Lasell College	MA	43,750	LC
Lawrence Tech Univ	MI	37,630	VC
Le Moyne College	NY	43,470	C
Lindsey Wilson College	KY	31,220	C
LIU Brooklyn	NY	47,182	LC
Loras College	IA	37,432	VC
Loyola Marymount Univ	CA	54,649	VC+
Loyola Univ Chicago	IL	51,646	VC+
Macalester College	MN	57,691	MC
Maine College of Art	ME	28,812	SP
Marquette Univ	WI	46,930	VC+
Maryland Inst College of Art	MD	39,500	SP
Marylhurst Univ	OR	20,295	NC
Mass Inst of Technology	MA	58,240	MC
Mercer Univ	GA	44,201	VC
Mercy College	NY	30,456	C
Messiah College	PA	40,690	C+
Miami Univ	OH	24,191	VC
Mills College	CA	54,119	VC
Montana State Univ	MT	14,068	C
Mount Ida College	MA	30,115	LC
Mount St. Mary College	NY	41,138	C
New Jersey City Univ	NJ	21,456	LC
New York Univ	NY	61,470	MC
NewSchool of Architecture & Design	CA	24,900	SP
Northeastern Illinois Univ	IL	10,318	LC
Ohio Univ	OH	21,080	C
Olivet Nazarene Univ	IL	29,990	C
Pepperdine Univ	CA	55,372	HC+
Pitzer College	CA	54,988	MC
Point Loma Nazarene Univ	CA	41,006	C
Point Park Univ	PA	36,390	C
Pomona College	CA	57,680	MC
Queens College/The CUNY	NY	17,107	VC
Radford Univ	VA	17,766	LC
Rensselaer Polytechnic Inst	NY	61,529	MC
Robert Morris Univ	PA	37,864	C
Rocky Mountain College of Art and Design	CO	22,470	SP
Roger Williams Univ	RI	46,296	VC
Rollins College	FL	52,370	HC
Roosevelt Univ	IL	22,605	VC
Sacred Heart Univ	CT	49,264	VC
Salve Regina Univ	RI	48,550	VC
San Francisco Art Inst	CA	55,762	SP
Savannah College of Art and Design	GA	48,005	SP
Southern Illinois Univ Edwardsville	IL	17,532	C
Southern Methodist Univ	TX	60,585	MC
Southern Polytechnic State Univ	GA	13,958	C
Spalding Univ	KY	32,287	LC
St. Catherine Univ	MN	37,782	C+
Suffolk Univ	MA	47,298	C
SUNY College at Old Westbury	NY	16,324	C
SUNY Fredonia/The SUNY at Fredonia	NY	19,840	VC
Swarthmore College	PA	57,870	MC
Syracuse Univ	NY	56,346	VC
Taylor Univ	IN	37,821	VC+
Temple Univ	PA	24,392	VC
The Univ of N Car at Greensboro	NC	12,848	C
The Univ of Utah	UT	16,463	VC
Thiel College	PA	38,728	LC
Towson Univ	MD	16,000	VC
Tulane Univ	LA	60,861	MC
Univ at Buffalo / The SUNY	NY	20,283	VC
Univ of Akron	OH	20,436	C
Univ of Calif at Irvine	CA	25,961	VC
Univ of Chicago	IL	55,416	MC
Univ of Denver	CO	51,787	VC+
Univ of Georgia	GA	20,082	VC
Univ of Hartford	CT	42,674	C
Univ of Illinois at Urbana-Champaign	IL	26,450	HC
Univ of Maine	ME	19,902	C+
Univ of Maine at Farmington	ME	18,187	LC
Univ of Missouri-St. Louis	MO		VC
Univ of Montana	MT	14,105	C
Univ of Mount Union	OH	35,130	C
Univ of New Mexico	NM	15,300	C
Univ of Pittsburgh at Pittsburgh	PA	28,572	HC+
Univ of Rochester	NY	60,668	MC
Univ of San Francisco	CA	54,770	VC
Univ of S Car at Columbia	SC	19,725	VC+
Univ of Texas at Dallas	TX	21,348	HC+
Univ of the District of Columbia	DC	7,244	LC
Univ of Wisc/Platteville	WI	14,564	C
Vassar College	NY	61,140	MC
Virginia Commonwealth Univ	VA	21,716	C
Washburn Univ	KS	12,579	C
Wayne State Univ	MI	22,063	C
Webster Univ	MO	35,100	C+
Wesley College	DE	31,115	LC
Western Conn State Univ	CT	18,327	LC
Wheeling Jesuit Univ	WV	33,500	C
Widener Univ	PA	52,418	C
Wilkes Univ	PA	44,070	C
Wilmington Univ	DE	8,112	NC
Xavier Univ	OH	44,980	VC

MEDIA MANAGEMENT

School	ST	$IS	SR
Messiah College	PA	40,690	C+
Minn State Univ, Mankato	MN	15,616	C
Ohio Univ	OH	21,080	C
San Diego State Univ	CA	21,611	C+

MEDICAL ANTHROPOLOGY

School	ST	$IS	SR
Creighton Univ	NE	45,356	VC

MEDICAL IMAGING

School	ST	$IS	SR
Indiana Univ Kokomo	IN	6,811	LC
Indiana Univ South Bend	IN	15,501	C
Indiana Univ-Purdue Univ Indianapolis	IN	17,611	C
Thomas Edison State College	NJ	5,700	SP
Univ of Louisiana at Monroe	LA	12,998	C

MEDICAL LABORATORY SCIENCE

School	ST	$IS	SR
Allen College	IA	26,110	SP
Augustana College	SD	36,500	VC
Bloomfield College	NJ	37,850	LC
Eastern Mich Univ	MI	18,604	C
Georgia Regents Univ	GA		
Idaho State Univ	ID	12,307	C
Marquette Univ	WI	46,930	VC+
Mich Tech Univ	MI	23,556	HC
Minn State Univ, Mankato	MN	15,616	C
Monmouth Univ	NJ	44,108	C
Oakland Univ	MI	19,391	C
Rhode Island College	RI	17,694	LC
Saginaw Valley State Univ	MI	17,369	C
St. Louis Univ	MO	48,346	HC
St. Mary's Univ of Minn	MN	38,280	C
S Dak State Univ	SD	14,296	C
Southeast Missouri State Univ	MO	15,370	LC
St. Edward's Univ	TX	47,784	C
Ohio State Univ-Columbus Campus	OH	19,887	HC+
The Univ of Utah	UT	16,463	VC
Univ of Iowa	IA	17,693	VC
Univ of Louisiana at Monroe	LA	12,998	C
Univ of Mass Dartmouth	MA	22,223	C
Univ of Miss	MS	16,704	C+
Univ of New Hampshire	NH	26,912	C
Univ of N Dak	ND	14,551	C
Univ of Vermont	VT	27,006	VC+
Western Carolina Univ	NC	13,965	C
Xavier Univ	OH	44,980	VC
York College of Pennsylvania	PA	26,590	C

MEDICAL LABORATORY TECHNOLOGY

School	ST	$IS	SR
Alabama A&M Univ	AL	10,084	C
American International College	MA	36,100	LC
Anderson Univ	IN	36,100	C
Andrews Univ	MI	28,030	C+
Angelo State Univ	TX	15,049	NC
Arkansas Tech Univ	AR	13,982	LC
Auburn Univ	AL	22,378	VC+
Avila Univ	MO	26,900	C
Ball State Univ	IN	17,850	C
Baylor Univ	TX	50,329	HC
Bemidji State Univ	MN	13,500	VC
Blackburn College	IL	21,350	C
Bloomsburg Univ of Pennsylvania	PA	13,598	C
Brescia Univ	KY	26,140	VC+
Caldwell College	NJ	35,602	NC
Cal State, Northridge	CA	28,690	C
Cal State, Sacramento	CA	16,200	C
Calif Univ of Pennsylvania	PA	14,217	C
Campbellsville Univ	KY	27,720	C
Canisius College	NY	44,900	C
Cheyney Univ of Pennsylvania	PA	20,372	LC
Clemson Univ	SC	19,136	HC
Coker College	SC	32,256	LC
College of St. Mary	NE	35,184	C
Columbia College	SC	27,882	C
Concord Univ	WV	13,102	C
Concordia Univ Nebr	NE	26,000	VC
Defiance College	OH	30,645	C
Dordt College	IA	34,160	C+
East Stroudsburg Univ of Pennsylvania	PA	18,868	LC
Eastern Mennonite Univ	VA	40,660	C
Eastern Mich Univ	MI	18,604	C
Eastern New Mexico Univ	NM	10,682	C
Eastern Washington Univ	WA		C
Edinboro Univ of Pennsylvania	PA	15,940	LC
Elmira College	NY	49,950	C+
Elms College	MA	23,900	VC
Eureka College	IL	19,280	C
Evangel Univ	MO	23,090	C
Fairleigh Dickinson Univ/College at Florham	NJ	42,142	C
Fairleigh Dickinson Univ/Metropolitan Campus	NJ	40,254	C
Fayetteville State Univ	NC	10,816	C
Florida Atlantic Univ	FL	17,339	C
George Washington Univ	DC	57,108	MC
Graceland Univ	IA	28,020	C
Grand Valley State Univ	MI	17,998	C+
Gwynedd-Mercy College	PA	33,560	C
Holy Family Univ	PA	40,030	LC
Hunter College	NY	14,429	VC
Illinois College	IL	25,770	VC
Illinois State Univ	IL	23,110	VC
Indiana State Univ	IN	16,000	C
Indiana Wesleyan Univ	IN	31,815	VC
Inter-American Univ of PR/San Germán	PR	6,720	
Judson Univ	IL	25,130	C
Kent State Univ	OH	19,920	C
Keuka College	NY	30,300	C
King's College	PA	43,502	C
Kutztown Univ of Pennsylvania	PA	16,909	LC
Lake Superior State Univ	MI	18,121	C
Lamar Univ	TX	6,820	LC
Langston Univ	OK	3,000	C
Lebanon Valley College	PA	38,570	C
Lee Univ	TN	18,690	C+
Lenoir-Rhyne College	NC	35,984	C
Lincoln Memorial Univ	TN	18,144	C
LIU Post	NY	47,660	C
Lock Haven Univ of Pennsylvania	PA	18,028	LC
Louisiana College	LA	15,746	C
Louisiana Tech Univ	LA	11,302	C
Madonna Univ	MI	24,540	VC
Malone Univ	OH	35,364	C
Manchester Univ	IN	35,070	C
Marshall Univ	WV	14,820	C
Mayville State Univ	ND	11,401	NC
McKendree Univ	IL	29,920	C+
Mercy College	NY	30,456	C
Mercyhurst Univ	PA	40,700	C
Mich State Univ	MI	22,450	VC
Midwestern State Univ	TX	9,722	C
Minn State Univ, Moorhead	MN	13,392	VC
Misericordia Univ	PA	41,060	C
Missouri Western State Univ	MO	12,260	NC
Monmouth Univ	NJ	44,108	C
Morgan State Univ	MD	14,500	VC
Mount Aloysius College	PA	29,976	C
Mount Mercy Univ	IA	35,320	C
National Louis Univ	IL	16,915	LC
N Car State Univ	NC	16,202	HC
North Park Univ	IL	30,130	C
Northeastern State Univ	OK	8,615	VC
Northern Mich Univ	MI	18,278	C
Northern State Univ - Aberdeen	SD	14,505	C
Northwestern College of Iowa	IA	36,240	VC
Northwestern Okla State Univ	OK	7,275	NC
Norwich Univ	VT	28,212	C
Okla Christian Univ	OK	25,870	VC
Oral Roberts Univ	OK	31,734	C
Pontifical Catholic Univ of PR	PR	7,310	
Purdue Univ/Calumet	IN	14,336	C
Purdue Univ/West Lafayette	IN	20,024	HC
Rutgers, The State Univ of New Jersey/Camden Campus	NJ	25,121	C
Rutgers, The State Univ of New Jersey/New Brunswick	NJ	25,562	VC
Rutgers, The State Univ of New Jersey/Newark Campus	NJ	258,806	C
St. Augustine's Univ	NC	14,000	C
St. Francis Univ	PA	30,029	LC
St. Peter's Univ	NJ	44,240	C
Salem College	NC	29,326	VC
Salem State Univ	MA	13,161	LC
Seton Hill Univ	PA	35,172	C
Shorter Univ	GA	30,450	LC
Slippery Rock Univ of Pennsylvania	PA	10,360	C
Southeastern Okla State Univ	OK	7,966	LC
Southern Arkansas Univ	AR	14,316	C
Southern Wesleyan Univ	SC	25,600	C
St. Francis College	NY	34,200	C
St. Thomas Aquinas College	NY	40,230	C
Stevenson Univ	MD	25,060	C
Suffolk Univ	MA	47,298	C
SUNY Fredonia/The SUNY at Fredonia	NY	19,840	VC
SUNY Plattsburgh / SUNY	NY	18,083	C
Tarleton State Univ	TX	13,489	LC
Texas A&M Univ at Kingsville	TX	7,500	LC
The Catholic Univ of America	DC	52,852	VC
The Univ of Tenn at Chattanooga	TN	16,883	C
The Univ of Utah	UT	16,463	VC
The Univ of Virginia's College at Wise	VA	11,076	C
Thiel College	PA	38,728	LC
Thomas More College	KY	34,760	C
Towson Univ	MD	16,000	VC
Union College	NE	23,270	C
Union Univ	TN	28,260	VC
Univ of Alaska Anchorage	AK	16,673	NC
Univ of Central Florida	FL	15,668	VC+
Univ of Central Missouri	MO	14,605	C
Univ of Cincinnati	OH	21,506	VC
Univ of Conn	CT	24,706	HC
Univ of Delaware	DE	23,612	VC
Univ of Hartford	CT	42,674	C
Univ of Hawaii at Manoa	HI	19,379	C
Univ of Indianapolis	IN	31,740	LC
Univ of Iowa	IA	17,693	VC
Univ of Kansas	KS	17,603	C+
Univ of Louisville	KY	17,946	C
Univ of Maine	ME	19,902	C+
Univ of Mich-Flint	MI	17,547	C
Univ of Minn/Twin Cities	MN		HC
Univ of New Mexico	NM	15,300	C
Univ of North Texas	TX	15,628	C
Univ of Pittsburgh at Johnstown	PA	20,862	LC
Univ of St. Francis	IN	29,810	C
Univ of Scranton	PA	51,940	VC
Univ of Sioux Falls	SD	22,990	C
Univ of Southern Miss	MS	13,170	C
Univ of Texas at El Paso	TX	8,764	NC
Univ of Washington	WA	14,722	VC
Univ of West Florida	FL	14,656	C
Univ of Wisc/La Crosse	WI	9,304	VC
Univ of Wisc/Oshkosh	WI	10,426	LC
Univ of Wyoming	WY	14,401	C+
Utah State Univ	UT	12,044	C
Wartburg College	IA	41,055	VC
Wesley College	DE	31,115	LC
Western Conn State Univ	CT	18,327	LC
Western New Mexico Univ	NM	8,500	LC
Wichita State Univ	KS	14,607	C+
William Carey Univ	MS	13,500	LC
William Jewell College	MO	31,000	VC+
Winthrop Univ	SC	21,120	C
Wright State Univ	OH	16,983	C
York College / The CUNY	NY	5,496	VC

MEDICAL PHYSICS

School	ST	$IS	SR
Belmont Univ	TN	39,190	VC+
Oakland Univ	MI	19,391	C
Oregon State Univ	OR	20,273	VC
Presbyterian College	SC	42,678	C+
Univ of Arizona	AZ	20,657	C
Univ of Notre Dame	IN	57,117	MC

MEDICAL RECORDS ADMINISTRATION/SERVICES

School	ST	$IS	SR
Dakota State Univ	SD	13,811	C
Davenport Univ	MI	21,002	LC
East Carolina Univ	NC	14,169	C
Ferris State Univ	MI	20,047	C
LIU Post	NY	47,660	C
Louisiana Tech Univ	LA	11,302	C
Norfolk State Univ	VA	10,531	C
Pennsylvania College of Technology	PA	26,286	NC
Southwestern Okla State Univ	OK	9,160	C
St. Catherine Univ	MN	37,782	C
Tenn State Univ	TN	9,048	C
Texas State Univ	TX	17,128	C
Univ of Alabama at Birmingham	AL	18,484	C+
Western Carolina Univ	NC	13,965	C

MEDICAL SCIENCE

School	ST	$IS	SR
Bloomfield College	NJ	37,850	LC
Southern Illinois Univ Edwardsville	IL	17,532	C
The Univ of Utah	UT	16,463	VC
Univ of Arizona	AZ	20,657	C
Univ of Chicago	IL	55,416	MC
Univ of Colo Denver	CO	17,904	C
Univ of Louisville	KY	17,946	C
Univ of Wisc/Madison	WI	18,757	HC+

MEDICAL TECHNOLOGY

School	ST	$IS	SR
Armstrong State Univ	GA	15,532	C
Austin Peay State Univ	TN	15,274	C
Ball State Univ	IN	17,850	C
Barry Univ	FL	38,190	C
Bellarmine Univ	KY	42,950	VC
Belmont Univ	TN	39,190	VC+
Bloomfield College	NJ	37,850	LC
Blue Mountain College	MS	15,634	LC
Bradley Univ	IL	31,874	VC
Brescia Univ	KY	26,140	VC+
Briar Cliff Univ	IA	29,514	C
Cameron Univ	OK	10,004	LC
Catawba College	NC	37,240	LC
Clarion Univ of Pennsylvania	PA	17,370	LC

ST = STATE $IS = IN-STATE COSTS   SR = SELECTOR RATING

School	ST	$IS	SR
Cleveland State Univ	OH	21,776	C
College of Staten Island/The City of New Yok	NY	16,778	NC
College of the Ozarks	MO		VC
Colo State Univ-Pueblo	CO	16,183	C
East Carolina Univ	NC	14,169	C
East Central Univ	OK	10,223	LC
Edgewood College	WI	33,294	C
Farmingdale State College	NY	19,673	C
Gannon Univ	PA	39,608	C
Gardner-Webb Univ	NC	34,375	C+
George Mason Univ	VA	15,724	VC
Georgia Regents Univ	GA		C
Gwynedd-Mercy College	PA	33,560	C
Harding Univ	AR	23,556	C
Hartwick College	NY	51,270	C
Henderson State Univ	AR	14,584	C
Houghton College	NY	36,808	C+
Idaho State Univ	ID	12,307	C
Indiana Univ Kokomo	IN	6,811	LC
Indiana Univ South Bend	IN	15,501	C
Indiana Univ-Purdue Univ Fort Wayne	IN	15,521	C
Indiana Univ-Purdue Univ Indianapolis	IN	17,611	C
Inter-American Univ of PR/ Fajardo Campus	PR	4,200	
Inter-American Univ of PR/ Metropolitan Campus	PR	4,320	
Inter-American Univ of PR/ Ponce	PR		
Kansas State Univ	KS	15,497	VC
Kean Univ	NJ	23,444	C
Kutztown Univ of Pennsylvania	PA	16,909	LC
Lincoln Univ	MO	12,904	NC
Lindenwood Univ	MO	20,750	C
Lipscomb Univ	TN	37,490	VC
Lubbock Christian Univ	TX	26,308	C
Mansfield Univ	PA	19,468	LC
Marist College	NY	35,500	C
Marywood Univ	PA	45,595	C
Millersville Univ of Pennsylvania	PA	21,648	C
Miss State Univ	MS	14,750	C
Missouri Southern State Univ	MO	12,061	C
Morehead State Univ	KY	10,900	C
Morningside College	IA	35,430	C
Mount Aloysius College	PA	29,976	C
Mount Marty College	SD	29,638	C
Mount Vernon Nazarene Univ	OH	29,590	C
Norfolk State Univ	VA	10,531	LC
Northern Kentucky Univ	KY	21,134	C
Oakwood Univ	AL	25,529	NC
Ohio Northern Univ	OH	42,075	VC
Old Dominion Univ	VA	19,483	LC
Oregon State Univ	OR	20,273	VC
Pittsburg State Univ	KS	12,032	C
Prairie View A&M Univ	TX	15,205	LC
Roosevelt Univ	IL	22,605	VC
Rutgers, The State Univ of New Jersey/New Brunswick	NJ	25,562	VC
Saginaw Valley State Univ	MI	17,369	C
St. Joseph's College	IN	36,500	C
St. Leo Univ	FL	30,340	C
St. Louis Univ	MO	48,346	HC
St. Mary-of-the-Woods College	IN	37,722	LC
Salisbury Univ	MD	19,180	VC
Sam Houston State Univ	TX	17,082	C
Seattle Univ	WA	49,035	VC+
Southern Adventist Univ	TN	26,190	C
Southern Illinois Univ Edwardsville	IL	17,552	C
Southwest Baptist Univ	MO	24,710	C
Southwest Minn State Univ	MN	14,000	C
Southwestern Adventist Univ	TX	23,026	LC
Southwestern Okla State Univ	OK	9,160	C
St. Joseph's College, New York/Brooklyn Campus	NY	22,630	C
St. Joseph's College, New York/Suffolk Campus	NY	22,630	C
SUNY Plattsburgh / SUNY	NY	18,083	C
Tenn State Univ	TN	9,048	C
Texas Southern Univ	TX	18,212	LC
Texas Woman's Univ	TX	13,633	LC
The Catholic Univ of America	DC	52,852	VC
The College of St. Rose	NY	26,750	C
Ohio State Univ-Columbus Campus	OH	19,887	HC+
The SUNY/College at Brockport	NY	19,002	C
Tusculum College	TN	24,295	C
Univ at Buffalo / The SUNY	NY	20,283	VC
Univ of Alabama at Birmingham	AL	18,484	C+
Univ of Bridgeport	CT	39,030	LC
Univ of Central Arkansas	AR	13,667	VC
Univ of Hawaii at Manoa	HI	19,379	C
Univ of Idaho	ID	14,558	C
Univ of Mass Boston	MA	23,066	VC
Univ of Miss	MS	16,704	C+
Univ of Montana	MT	14,105	C
Univ of Mount Union	OH	35,130	C
Univ of New Orleans	LA	9,224	C

School	ST	$IS	SR
Univ of N Car at Charlotte	NC	15,547	C
Univ of Rio Grande	OH	8,750	NC
Univ of S Dak	SD	15,111	C
Univ of South Florida/Tampa	FL	13,000	C
Univ of St. Francis	IL	37,560	C
Univ of Tenn at Knoxville	TN	20,364	VC+
Univ of Texas at Arlington	TX	10,908	LC
Univ of Texas at Austin	TX	44,074	HC
Univ of the Sacred Heart	PR	5,590	
Univ of the Sciences	PA	48,320	VC+
West Chester Univ of Pennsylvania	PA	17,186	C
West Texas A&M Univ	TX	13,478	C
West Virginia Univ	WV	16,542	C+
Western Kentucky Univ	KY	11,000	LC
Wilkes Univ	PA	44,070	C
Winston-Salem State Univ	NC	9,418	LC

MEDIEVAL STUDIES

School	ST	$IS	SR
Bard College	NY	61,940	HC
Barnard College/Columbia Univ	NY	39,000	MC
Bates College	ME	60,720	MC
Binghamton Univ/The SUNY	NY	21,648	HC+
Brown Univ	RI	59,428	MC
College of the Holy Cross	MA	58,042	MC
College of William & Mary	VA	28,000	MC
Columbia Univ/City of New York	NY	61,116	MC
Cornell College	IA	44,930	VC
Dickinson College	PA	57,662	HC+
Duke Univ	NC	50,250	MC
Emory Univ	GA	56,368	MC
Fordham Univ	NY	61,588	HC+
Hanover College	IN	43,073	C+
Mount Holyoke College	MA	55,146	MC
New College of Florida	FL	14,504	MC
New York Univ	NY	61,470	MC
Pomona College	CA	57,680	MC
Purdue Univ/West Lafayette	IN	20,024	HC
Rice Univ	TX	43,288	MC
Rutgers, The State Univ of New Jersey/New Brunswick	NJ	25,562	VC
Rutgers, The State Univ of New Jersey/Newark Campus	NJ	258,806	C
Sewanee: The Univ of the South	TN	47,700	HC+
Smith College	MA	59,674	MC
Southern Methodist Univ	TX	60,585	MC
St. Olaf College	MN	51,200	HC+
Swarthmore College	PA	57,870	MC
The Catholic Univ of America	DC	52,852	VC
Ohio State Univ-Columbus Campus	OH	19,887	HC+
The Pennsylvania State Univ - Univ Park	PA	28,022	VC+
Tulane Univ	LA	60,861	MC
Univ at Albany / SUNY	NY	18,674	VC
Univ of Calif at Davis	CA		HC
Univ of Calif at Santa Barbara	CA	27,551	HC
Univ of Chicago	IL	55,416	MC
Univ of Mich/Ann Arbor	MI	22,102	MC
Univ of Nebr - Lincoln	NE	18,031	VC
Univ of Notre Dame	IN	57,117	MC
Univ of Oregon	OR	21,360	C+
Vassar College	NY	61,140	MC
Washington and Lee Univ	VA	52,812	MC
Wellesley College	MA	59,038	MC
Wesleyan Univ	CT	61,198	MC

MEETING / SPECIAL EVENT MGMT

School	ST	$IS	SR
College of the Ozarks	MO		VC

MENTAL HEALTH/HUMAN SERVICES

School	ST	$IS	SR
Bloomfield College	NJ	37,850	LC
Calif Univ of Pennsylvania	PA	14,217	C
Franciscan Univ of Steubenville	OH	27,320	VC
Inter-American Univ of PR/ Aguadilla Campus	PR	5,578	
Metropolitan College of New York	NY	16,720	VC
Morgan State Univ	MD	14,500	VC
Northern Kentucky Univ	KY	21,134	C
Pennsylvania College of Technology	PA	26,286	NC
Prescott College	AZ	33,284	C
Sinte Gleska Univ	SD	2,300	NC
Southern Oregon Univ	OR	17,874	C
Univ of Maine at Augusta	ME	6,855	C
Univ of North Florida	FL	15,870	VC
Univ of the Sciences	PA	48,320	VC+

METAL/JEWELRY

School	ST	$IS	SR
Adams State Univ	CO	13,358	LC
Calif College of the Arts	CA	48,334	SP
Cleveland Inst of Art	OH	48,685	SP

School	ST	$IS	SR
College for Creative Studies	MI	45,340	C
Ferris State Univ	MI	20,047	C
Hofstra Univ	NY	51,810	VC+
Maine College of Art	ME	28,812	SP
Memphis College of Art	TN	33,550	SP
Pittsburg State Univ	KS	12,032	C
Rhode Island School of Design	RI	57,234	MC
Rochester Inst of Technology	NY	42,450	VC
Savannah College of Art and Design	GA	48,005	SP
SUNY New Paltz	NY	14,348	C
Syracuse Univ	NY	56,346	VC
Temple Univ	PA	24,392	VC
Univ of Iowa	IA	17,693	VC
Univ of Kansas	KS	17,603	C+
Univ of Mass Dartmouth	MA	22,223	C
Univ of Mich/Ann Arbor	MI	22,102	MC
Univ of Oregon	OR	21,360	C+

METALLURGICAL ENGINEERING

School	ST	$IS	SR
Colo School of Mines	CO	18,000	HC
Columbia Univ/City of New York	NY	61,116	MC
Illinois Inst of Technology	IL	38,512	HC+
Missouri Univ of Science and Technology	MO	18,655	VC+
Montana Tech of The Univ of Montana	MT	14,650	VC
Oregon State Univ	OR	20,273	VC
S Dak School of Mines and Technology	SD	15,260	VC
The Univ of Utah	UT	16,463	VC
Univ of Alabama at Tuscaloosa	AL	17,164	C+
Univ of Cincinnati	OH	21,506	VC
Univ of Illinois at Urbana-Champaign	IL	26,450	HC
Univ of Minn/Twin Cities	MN		HC
Univ of Nevada/Reno	NV	17,507	C
Univ of Texas at El Paso	TX	8,764	NC

MEXICAN-AMERICAN/CHICANO STUDIES

School	ST	$IS	SR
Arizona State Univ, at the Tempe Campus	AZ	20,137	C+
Cal State, Dominguez Hills	CA	17,090	LC
Cal State, Fresno	CA	17,405	C
Cal State, Fullerton	CA	25,188	C
Cal State, Los Angeles	CA	17,186	LC
Cal State, Northridge	CA	28,690	LC
Concordia Univ Texas	TX	23,640	C
Metropolitan State Univ of Denver	CO	4,835	LC
Our Lady of the Lake Univ	TX	22,430	LC
Pitzer College	CA	54,988	MC
Pomona College	CA	57,680	MC
San Diego State Univ	CA	21,611	C+
San Jose State Univ	CA	19,133	C
Scripps College	CA	61,940	MC
Sonoma State Univ	CA	20,541	C
Southern Methodist Univ	TX	60,585	MC
Univ of Arizona	AZ	20,657	C
Univ of Calif at Davis	CA		HC
Univ of Calif at Los Angeles	CA	25,686	MC
Univ of Calif at Riverside	CA	27,204	C+
Univ of Calif at Santa Barbara	CA	27,551	HC
Univ of Mich/Ann Arbor	MI	22,102	MC
Univ of Minn/Twin Cities	MN		HC
Univ of New Mexico	NM	15,300	C
Univ of Northern Colo	CO	18,446	C
Univ of Texas - Pan American	TX	11,125	LC
Univ of Texas at El Paso	TX	8,764	NC
Univ of Texas at San Antonio	TX	18,372	C

MICROBIOLOGY

School	ST	$IS	SR
Albany College of Pharmacy and Health Sciences	NY	40,331	SP
Arizona State Univ, at the Tempe Campus	AZ	20,137	C+
Auburn Univ	AL	22,378	VC+
Brigham Young Univ	UT	12,100	HC
Calif Polytechnic State Univ	CA	19,847	HC
Cal State, Chico	CA	20,158	C
Cal State, Long Beach	CA	17,502	C+
Cal State, Los Angeles	CA	17,186	LC
Cal State, Northridge	CA	28,690	LC
Cal State, Sacramento	CA	16,200	C
Clemson Univ	SC	19,136	HC
Colo State Univ-Fort Collins	CO	20,385	VC
Eastern Kentucky Univ	KY	11,161	C
Eastern Washington Univ	WA		C
Howard Univ	DC	13,646	C
Idaho State Univ	ID	12,307	C
Indiana Univ Bloomington	IN	19,801	VC
Inter-American Univ of PR/ Aguadilla Campus	PR	5,578	
Inter-American Univ of PR/ Arecibo Campus	PR	3,350	
Iowa State Univ	IA	16,403	C
Kansas State Univ	KS	15,497	VC

School	ST	$IS	SR
Kutztown Univ of Pennsylvania	PA	16,909	LC
Louisiana State Univ	LA	18,677	C+
Marlboro College	VT	35,980	VC
Miami Univ	OH	24,191	VC
Mich State Univ	MI	22,450	VC
Mills College	CA	54,119	VC
Miss State Univ	MS	14,750	C
Miss Univ for Women	MS	7,400	C
Missouri Southern State Univ	MO	12,061	C
Montana State Univ	MT	14,068	C
New Mexico State Univ	NM	14,050	C
New York Univ	NY	61,470	MC
N Car State Univ	NC	16,202	HC
N Dak State Univ	ND		C
Northern Arizona Univ	AZ	19,010	C
Northern Mich Univ	MI	18,278	C
Ohio Univ	OH	21,080	C
Ohio Wesleyan Univ	OH	49,460	C+
Okla State Univ	OK	14,310	VC
Oregon State Univ	OR	20,273	VC
Purdue Univ/Calumet	IN	14,336	C
Purdue Univ/West Lafayette	IN	20,024	HC
Quinnipiac Univ	CT	55,160	VC
Rutgers, The State Univ of New Jersey/New Brunswick	NJ	25,562	VC
San Diego State Univ	CA	21,611	C+
San Francisco State Univ	CA	18,514	C
San Jose State Univ	CA	19,133	C
S Dak State Univ	SD	14,296	C
Southern Illinois Univ Carbondale	IL	21,942	C
SUNY / College of Environmental Science and Forestry	NY	18,351	VC
Texas A&M Univ	TX	19,207	VC
Texas State Univ	TX	17,128	C
Texas Tech Univ	TX	14,243	C
Ohio State Univ-Columbus Campus	OH	19,887	HC+
The Pennsylvania State Univ - Univ Park	PA	28,022	VC+
The Univ of Memphis	TN	15,094	C
The Univ of Okla	OK	18,621	VC
Universidad de Puerto/ Arecibo	PR	7,227	
Univ of Alabama at Tuscaloosa	AL	17,164	C+
Univ of Arizona	AZ	20,657	C
Univ of Calif at Berkeley	CA	23,322	MC
Univ of Calif at Davis	CA		HC
Univ of Calif at Irvine	CA	25,961	VC
Univ of Calif at Los Angeles	CA	25,686	MC
Univ of Calif at Riverside	CA	27,204	C+
Univ of Calif at San Diego	CA	21,000	VC
Univ of Calif at Santa Barbara	CA	27,551	HC
Univ of Florida	FL	15,943	HC
Univ of Georgia	GA	20,082	VC
Univ of Great Falls	MT	27,970	C
Univ of Hawaii at Manoa	HI	19,379	C
Univ of Houston-Downtown	TX	15,170	LC
Univ of Idaho	ID	14,558	C
Univ of Illinois at Urbana-Champaign	IL	26,450	HC
Univ of Iowa	IA	17,693	VC
Univ of Kansas	KS	17,603	C+
Univ of Maine	ME	19,902	C
Univ of Maryland - College Park	MD	20,060	HC
Univ of Mass Amherst	MA	24,215	VC+
Univ of Miami	FL	57,034	MC
Univ of Mich/Ann Arbor	MI	22,102	MC
Univ of Mich/Dearborn	MI	9,885	VC
Univ of Minn/Twin Cities	MN		HC
Univ of Missouri/Columbia	MO	18,201	MC
Univ of Montana	MT	14,105	C
Univ of Nebr - Lincoln	NE	18,031	VC
Univ of New Hampshire	NH	26,912	C
Univ of Northern Iowa	IA	15,795	C
Univ of Pittsburgh at Pittsburgh	PA	28,572	HC+
Univ of PR/Humacao	PR	1,877	
Univ of PR/Mayaguez	PR	1,250	
Univ of Rochester	NY	60,668	MC
Univ of South Florida/Tampa	FL	13,000	C
Univ of Texas at Arlington	TX	10,908	LC
Univ of Texas at Austin	TX	44,074	HC
Univ of Texas at El Paso	TX	8,764	NC
Univ of the Sciences	PA	48,320	VC+
Univ of Vermont	VT	27,006	VC+
Univ of Washington	WA	14,722	VC
Univ of Wisc/La Crosse	WI	9,304	VC
Univ of Wisc/Madison	WI	18,757	HC+
Univ of Wisc/Oshkosh	WI	10,426	LC
Univ of Wisc-Milwaukee	WI	18,436	C
Univ of Wyoming	WY	14,401	C+
Utah State Univ	UT	12,044	C
Wagner College	NY	48,600	C+
Washington State Univ	WA	20,461	VC
West Chester Univ of Pennsylvania	PA	17,186	C

MIDDLE EASTERN STUDIES

School	ST	$IS	SR
Appalachian State Univ	NC	12,919	VC

ST = STATE $IS = IN-STATE COSTS   SR = SELECTOR RATING

School	ST	$IS	SR
Bard College	NY	61,940	HC
Barnard College/Columbia Univ	NY	39,000	MC
Baylor Univ	TX	50,329	HC
Boston Univ	MA	60,694	MC
Brandeis Univ	MA		MC
Brigham Young Univ	UT	12,100	HC
Brown Univ	RI	59,428	MC
Claremont McKenna College	CA	62,215	MC
College of the Holy Cross	MA	58,042	MC
Columbia Univ/City of New York	NY	61,116	MC
Columbia Univ/School of General Studies	NY	58,231	MC
Dartmouth College	NH	57,996	MC
Dickinson College	PA	57,662	HC+
Eastern Mich Univ	MI	18,604	C
Emory and Henry College	VA	387,460	C
Emory Univ	GA	56,368	MC
Fordham Univ	NY	61,588	HC+
George Washington Univ	DC	57,108	MC
Gettysburg College	PA	58,820	HC
Hampshire College	MA	58,320	MC
Harvard College/Harvard Univ	MA	49,000	MC
Hood College	MD	45,730	C
McDaniel College	MD	47,450	VC
Middlebury College	VT	59,160	MC
Mount Holyoke College	MA	55,146	MC
New York Univ	NY	61,470	MC
Pomona College	CA	57,680	MC
Rutgers, The State Univ of New Jersey/New Brunswick	NJ	25,562	VC
Sacred Heart Univ	CT	49,264	VC
Smith College	MA	59,674	MC
Syracuse Univ	NY	56,346	MC
Texas State Univ	TX	17,128	C
The Univ of Utah	UT	16,463	VC
Tufts Univ	MA	58,780	MC
Univ of Arizona	AZ	20,657	C
Univ of Arkansas at Fayetteville	AR	18,352	C+
Univ of Calif at Berkeley	CA	23,322	MC
Univ of Calif at Los Angeles	CA	25,686	MC
Univ of Calif at Riverside	CA	27,204	C+
Univ of Calif at Santa Barbara	CA	27,551	VC
Univ of Conn	CT	24,706	HC
Univ of Mass Amherst	MA	24,215	VC+
Univ of Mich/Ann Arbor	MI	22,102	MC
Univ of Minn/Twin Cities	MN		HC
Univ of Pennsylvania	PA	61,132	MC
Univ of Texas at Austin	TX	44,074	VC
Washington Univ in St. Louis	MO	69,844	MC
Wellesley College	MA	59,038	MC
Yale Univ	CT	55,300	MC

MIDDLE SCHOOL EDUCATION

School	ST	$IS	SR
Alabama A&M Univ	AL	10,084	C
Albany State Univ	GA	8,500	C
Alice Lloyd College	KY	4,900	LC
Alvernia Univ	PA	39,250	LC
Alverno College	WI	31,434	LC
American International College	MA	36,100	LC
Appalachian State Univ	NC	12,919	VC
Arkansas State Univ	AR	15,470	C
Arkansas Tech Univ	AR	13,982	LC
Armstrong State Univ	GA	15,532	C
Asbury Univ	KY	32,038	VC
Auburn Univ	AL	22,378	VC+
Augustana College	SD	36,500	VC
Averett Univ	VA	37,750	LC
Avila Univ	MO	26,900	C
Baldwin Wallace Univ	OH	38,318	C
Barton College	NC	27,660	LC
Bellarmine Univ	KY	42,950	VC
Belmont Univ	TN	39,190	VC+
Bemidji State Univ	MN	13,500	VC
Bennett College for Women	NC	21,970	LC
Bennington College	VT	56,990	HC+
Berry College	GA	39,254	VC
Bethany College	KS	30,605	NC
Bethany College	WV	35,282	LC
Bethel Univ	MN	34,940	VC
Bloomsburg Univ of Pennsylvania	PA	13,598	C
Bluefield College	VA	17,230	C+
Bluefield State College	WV	3,140	LC
Bluffton Univ	OH	38,948	C
Bowling Green State Univ	OH	18,970	C
Brenau Univ - Women's College	GA	26,650	LC
Butler Univ	IN	47,572	VC+
Cabrini College	PA	40,859	LC
Campbell Univ	NC	37,570	VC
Campbellsville Univ	KY	27,720	C
Canisius College	NY	44,900	C
Capital Univ	OH	41,050	VC
Cardinal Stritch Univ	WI	24,054	C
Caribbean Univ	PR	10,375	
Carlow Univ	PA	30,072	C
Carson-Newman Univ	TN	29,058	C+
Carthage College	WI	33,000	C
Catawba College	NC	37,240	LC

School	ST	$IS	SR
Cedarville Univ	OH	32,860	VC
Central Methodist Univ	MO	28,240	VC
Central Washington Univ	WA	11,730	C
Champlain College	VT	46,650	VC+
City Univ of Seattle	WA	14,880	NC
Claflin Univ	SC	22,368	LC
Clark Atlanta Univ	GA	30,006	LC
Clayton State Univ	GA	12,000	LC
Coastal Carolina Univ	SC	18,580	C
College of Charleston	SC	22,145	VC
College of Mount St. Joseph	OH	33,880	C
Columbia College	MO	24,578	C
Columbus State Univ	GA	13,176	C
Concord Univ	WV	13,102	C
Concordia Univ Nebr	NE	26,000	VC
Concordia Univ St. Paul	MN	28,250	C
Concordia Univ, River Forest	IL	26,300	C
Cornerstone Univ and Grand Rapids Theological Seminary	MI	33,338	C
Cumberland Univ	TN	21,220	C
Dickinson State Univ	ND	11,900	NC
Dordt College	IA	34,160	C+
Duquesne Univ	PA	43,720	VC
East Carolina Univ	NC	14,169	C
Eastern Illinois Univ	IL	20,466	C
Eastern Kentucky Univ	KY	11,161	C
Eastern Mich Univ	MI	18,604	C
Eastern Univ	PA	37,704	C
Eastern Washington Univ	WA		C
Edinboro Univ of Pennsylvania	PA	15,940	LC
Elizabeth City State Univ	NC	11,638	C
Elms College	MA	23,900	VC
Elon Univ	NC	41,914	VC+
Fairmont State Univ	WV	12,098	LC
Fayetteville State Univ	NC	10,816	C
Fitchburg State Univ	MA	18,173	C
Florida Inst of Technology	FL	48,290	VC
Fontbonne Univ	MO	31,384	C
Fort Valley State Univ	GA	11,200	VC
Francis Marion Univ	SC	16,464	LC
Freed-Hardeman Univ	TN	19,697	VC
Frostburg State Univ	MD	15,264	LC
Gannon Univ	PA	39,608	C
Gardner-Webb Univ	NC	34,375	C+
Georgetown College	KY	41,440	C+
Georgia College and State Univ	GA	18,900	C+
Georgia Regents Univ	GA		C
Georgia Southern Univ	GA	16,942	C
Georgia Southwestern State Univ	GA	13,246	C
Glenville State College	WV	11,348	NC
Goddard College	VT	16,418	VC
Gordon College	MA	44,320	VC
Goshen College	IN	35,900	VC
Grand Valley State Univ	MI	17,998	C+
Greensboro College	NC	28,740	LC
Grove City College	PA	24,022	VC
Gustavus Adolphus College	MN	48,170	HC
Hardin-Simmons Univ	TX	23,560	C+
Harris-Stowe State Univ	MO	14,360	NC
Heidelberg Univ	OH	34,100	C
Henderson State Univ	AR	14,584	C
High Point Univ	NC	39,800	C
Humboldt State Univ	CA	18,400	C
Hunter College	NY	14,429	VC
Illinois State Univ	IL	23,110	VC
Immaculata Univ	PA	43,000	C
Indiana State Univ	IN	16,000	C
Indiana Univ-Purdue Univ Fort Wayne	IN	15,521	C
Ithaca College	NY	53,864	NC
John Brown Univ	AR	32,056	VC+
John Carroll Univ	OH	46,300	C+
Johnson State College	VT	16,721	C
Kean Univ	NJ	23,444	C
Kennesaw State Univ	GA		C
Kent State Univ	OH	19,920	C
Kentucky Christian Univ	KY	17,622	LC
Kentucky Wesleyan College	KY	27,440	C
King's College	PA	43,502	C
Lake Erie College	OH	37,266	C
Lee Univ	TN	18,690	C+
Lenoir-Rhyne College	NC	35,984	C
Lesley Univ	MA	46,350	C
Lincoln Memorial Univ	TN	18,144	C
Lipscomb Univ	TN	37,490	VC
LIU Brooklyn	NY	47,182	LC
Lubbock Christian Univ	TX	26,308	C
Malone Univ	OH	35,364	C
Manchester Univ	IN	35,070	C
Manhattan College	NY	49,588	C+
Marian Univ	WI	32,420	LC
Mars Hill Univ	NC	22,950	LC
Marshall Univ	WV	14,820	C
Maryville Univ of St. Louis	MO	35,856	VC
Mass College of Liberal Arts	MA	18,613	C
McMurry Univ	TX	25,962	LC
Medaille College	NY	35,112	C
Methodist Univ	NC	37,185	C
Miami Univ	OH	24,191	VC
Midland Univ	NE	34,000	C
Millersville Univ of Pennsylvania	PA	21,648	C

School	ST	$IS	SR
Minn State Univ, Mankato	MN	15,616	C
Missouri Baptist Univ	MO	31,830	C
Missouri Southern State Univ	MO	12,061	C
Missouri State Univ	MO	13,996	C+
Montana State Univ-Billings	MT	12,425	LC
Montclair State Univ	NJ	22,614	C
Morehead State Univ	KY	10,900	C
Mount Aloysius College	PA	29,976	C
Mount Mary Univ	WI	33,590	LC
Mount Mercy Univ	IA	35,320	C
Mount Vernon Nazarene Univ	OH	29,590	C
Murray State Univ	KY	15,304	C
Nazareth College of Rochester	NY	43,028	C+
Nebr Wesleyan Univ	NE	29,774	C+
Niagara Univ	NY	41,010	C
N Car Central Univ	NC	9,000	C
N Car State Univ	NC	16,202	HC
N Car Wesleyan College	NC	29,440	C
Northern Kentucky Univ	KY	21,134	C
Northern State Univ - Aberdeen	SD	14,505	C
Northland College	WI	26,680	C
Northwest Missouri State Univ	MO	17,347	C
Northwest Univ	WA	18,854	C
Northwestern College of Iowa	IA	36,240	VC
Notre Dame College	OH	34,942	VC
Nova Southeastern Univ	FL	37,280	VC
Oakland Univ	MI	24,500	NC
Ohio Dominican Univ	OH	38,380	C+
Ohio Northern Univ	OH	42,075	VC
Ohio Univ	OH	49,460	C+
Ohio Wesleyan Univ	OH	49,460	C+
Okla Christian Univ	OK	25,870	VC
Okla Wesleyan Univ	OK	21,300	C
Ouachita Baptist Univ	AR	30,220	VC
Paine College	GA	19,826	LC
Philander Smith College	AR	19,760	LC
Piedmont College	GA	30,136	C
Presbyterian College	SC	42,678	C+
Prescott College	AZ	33,284	C
Ripon College	WI	36,959	C+
Sacred Heart Univ	CT	49,264	VC
St. Joseph's College	IN	36,500	C
St. Leo Univ	FL	30,340	C
St. Vincent College	PA	40,244	C
St. Xavier Univ	IL	32,840	C
Schreiner Univ	TX	32,734	LC
Shippensburg Univ of Pennsylvania	PA	20,934	C
Shorter Univ	GA	30,650	LC
Southeast Missouri State Univ	MO	15,370	LC
Southeastern Louisiana Univ	LA	13,325	C
Southeastern Univ	FL	27,201	C
Southern Arkansas Univ	AR	14,316	C
Southern Univ and A&M	LA	9,761	LC
Southwest Baptist Univ	MO	24,710	C
Springfield College	MA	25,000	C
St. Francis College	NY	34,200	C
St. John Fisher College	NY	40,708	C+
St. John's Univ	NY	55,070	C+
Stevenson Univ	MD	41,470	C
SUNY College at Old Westbury	NY	16,324	C
SUNY Cortland/The SUNY	NY	19,759	C+
SUNY Fredonia/The SUNY at Fredonia	NY	19,840	VC
SUNY New Paltz	NY	14,348	C
Syracuse Univ	NY	56,346	MC
Tabor College	KS	29,010	C
Texas Christian Univ	TX	49,980	HC
Texas Tech Univ	TX	14,243	C
Ohio State Univ-Columbus Campus	OH	19,887	HC+
The Univ of N Car at Greensboro	NC	12,848	C
Thomas More College	KY	34,760	C
Thomas Univ	GA	11,520	NC
Toccoa Falls College	GA	23,210	LC
Transylvania Univ	KY	42,660	VC+
Tusculum College	TN	24,295	C
Union College	KY	29,955	C
Union Univ	TN	28,260	VC
Univ of Akron	OH	20,436	C
Univ of Arizona	AZ	20,657	C
Univ of Arkansas at Fayetteville	AR	18,352	C+
Univ of Arkansas at Monticello	AR	12,076	NC
Univ of Arkansas at Pine Bluff	AR	13,378	C
Univ of Central Arkansas	AR	13,667	VC
Univ of Central Missouri	MO	14,605	C
Univ of Cincinnati	OH	21,506	VC
Univ of Detroit Mercy	MI	30,450	VC
Univ of Findlay	OH	31,916	C
Univ of Georgia	GA	20,082	VC
Univ of Great Falls	MT	27,970	C
Univ of Indianapolis	IN	31,740	LC
Univ of Iowa	IA	17,693	VC
Univ of Kansas	KS	17,603	C+
Univ of Kentucky	KY	19,868	C
Univ of Louisiana at Monroe	LA	12,998	C
Univ of Louisville	KY	17,946	C
Univ of Mary Hardin-Baylor	TX	31,950	C+

School	ST	$IS	SR
Univ of Maryland - College Park	MD	20,060	HC
Univ of Minn/Duluth	MN	19,806	C
Univ of Missouri/Columbia	MO	18,201	MC
Univ of Missouri-Kansas City	MO	19,603	C
Univ of Montana-Western	MT	9,753	LC
Univ of Mount Olive	NC	18,426	C
Univ of Mount Union	OH	35,130	C
Univ of Nebr at Kearney	NE	14,855	LC
Univ of N Car at Chapel Hill	NC	18,928	NC
Univ of N Car at Charlotte	NC	15,547	C
Univ of N Car at Wilmington	NC	13,572	VC
Univ of N Dak	ND	14,551	C
Univ of North Florida	FL	15,870	NC
Univ of North Georgia	GA	8,500	C
Univ of Northern Iowa	IA	15,795	C
Univ of Pikeville	KY	-25,500	NC
Univ of San Francisco	CA	54,770	VC
Univ of Sioux Falls	SD	22,990	C
Univ of S Car Aiken	SC	16,712	C
Univ of S Car at Columbia	SC	19,725	VC+
Univ of S Car Upstate	SC	18,200	LC
Univ of Southern Indiana	IN	14,885	C
Univ of Southern Miss	MS	13,170	C
Univ of the Cumberlands	KY	27,500	C
Univ of the Ozarks	AR	31,440	C
Univ of Vermont	VT	27,006	VC+
Univ of West Alabama	AL	14,274	C
Univ of West Florida	FL	14,656	C
Univ of Wisc Whitewater	WI	13,314	C
Univ of Wisc/Green Bay	WI	19,074	C
Univ of Wisc/Platteville	WI	14,564	C
Urbana Univ	OH	30,820	C
Ursuline College	OH	33,198	LC
Wagner College	NY	48,600	C+
Walsh Univ	OH	35,100	C
Washington Univ in St. Louis	MO	69,844	MC
Wayne State College	NE	11,764	NC
Waynesburg Univ	PA	30,150	C
Webster Univ	MO	35,100	C+
Wesleyan College	GA	24,000	C
West Chester Univ of Pennsylvania	PA	17,186	C
West Liberty Univ	WV	9,142	LC
Western Carolina Univ	NC	13,965	C
Western Kentucky Univ	KY	11,000	LC
Western Mich Univ	MI	19,628	C
Westminster College	MO	31,720	VC
Wilkes Univ	PA	44,070	C
William Woods Univ	MO	24,260	C
Wilmington College	OH	29,784	C
Wingate Univ	NC	34,990	C
Winthrop Univ	SC	21,120	C
Wittenberg Univ	OH	47,962	C+
Wright State Univ	OH	16,983	C
Xavier Univ	OH	44,980	VC
Xavier Univ of Louisiana	LA	25,300	C
York College	NE	19,475	C
Youngstown State Univ	OH	16,732	C

MILITARY SCIENCE

School	ST	$IS	SR
Ashford Univ	CA	10,480	C
Campbell Univ	NC	37,570	VC
Columbia College	MO	24,578	C
Eastern Mich Univ	MI	18,604	C
Eastern Washington Univ	WA		C
Florida Inst of Technology	FL	48,290	VC
Hawaii Pacific Univ	HI	34,360	C
Minn State Univ, Mankato	MN	15,616	C
Norfolk State Univ	VA	10,531	LC
Norwich Univ	VT	28,212	C
Rochester Inst of Technology	NY	42,450	VC
United States Air Force Academy	CO		MC
United States Military Academy	NY		MC

MILITARY TECHNOLOGY LEADERSHIP

School	ST	$IS	SR
Thomas Edison State College	NJ	5,700	SP

MILLING SCIENCE

School	ST	$IS	SR
Kansas State Univ	KS	15,497	VC

MINING AND MINERAL ENGINEERING

School	ST	$IS	SR
Colo School of Mines	CO	18,000	HC
Columbia Univ/City of New York	NY	61,116	MC
Missouri Univ of Science and Technology	MO	18,655	VC+
Montana Tech of The Univ of Montana	MT	14,650	VC
New Mexico Inst of Mining and Technology	NM	13,592	VC
S Dak School of Mines and Technology	SD	15,260	VC
Southern Illinois Univ Carbondale	IL	21,942	C
The Pennsylvania State Univ - Univ Park	PA	28,022	VC+
The Univ of Utah	UT	16,463	VC

ST = STATE $IS = IN-STATE COSTS   SR = SELECTOR RATING

School	ST	$IS	SR
Univ of Alaska Fairbanks	AK	15,130	C
Univ of Arizona	AZ	20,657	C
Univ of Kentucky	KY	19,868	C
Univ of Nevada/Reno	NV	17,507	C
Virginia Polytechnic Inst and State Univ	VA	14,629	HC
West Virginia Univ	WV	16,542	C+

MINISTRIES

School	ST	$IS	SR
Abilene Christian Univ	TX	38,400	C+
American Indian College	AZ	18,142	C
Amridge Univ	AL	6,870	LC
Asbury Univ	KY	32,038	VC
Atlantic Union College	MA	24,600	C
Azusa Pacific Univ	CA	42,086	C
Belmont Univ	TN	39,190	VC+
Bethel College	IN	31,560	C
Biola Univ	CA	40,320	C+
Bluffton Univ	OH	38,948	C
Clearwater Christian College	FL	23,720	C
College of the Ozarks	MO		VC
Concordia Univ Wisc	WI	28,980	C
Corban Univ	OR	37,380	C
Dallas Baptist Univ	TX	30,580	VC
Dominican Univ	IL	37,628	C
Dordt College	IA	34,160	C+
East Texas Baptist Univ	TX	31,577	LC
Eastern Mennonite Univ	VA	40,660	C
Eastern Nazarene College	MA	30,000	C
Faulkner Univ	AL	25,720	LC
Freed-Hardeman Univ	TN	19,697	VC
Fresno Pacific Univ	CA	32,136	C
Geneva College	PA	27,280	C
George Fox Univ	OR	40,750	C+
Greenville College	IL	27,012	C
Harding Univ	AR	23,556	C
Hardin-Simmons Univ	TX	23,560	C+
Hope International Univ	CA	34,650	C
Houghton College	NY	36,808	C+
Huntington Univ	IN	32,220	C+
Indiana Wesleyan Univ	IN	31,815	VC
John Brown Univ	AR	32,056	VC+
Kentucky Christian Univ	KY	17,622	LC
Lee Univ	TN	18,690	C+
Lindenwood Univ	MO	20,750	C
Lindsey Wilson College	KY	31,220	C
Lubbock Christian Univ	TX	26,308	C
Malone Univ	OH	35,364	C
Messiah College	PA	40,690	C+
MidAmerica Nazarene Univ	KS	28,000	C
Missouri Baptist Univ	MO	31,830	C
Mount Vernon Nazarene Univ	OH	29,590	C
North Central Univ	MN	26,400	C
Northwest Christian Univ	OR	27,399	C
Northwest Nazarene Univ	ID	34,000	C
Northwest Univ	WA	18,854	C
Northwestern College	MN	24,000	C
Notre Dame College	OH	34,942	VC
Oakwood Univ	AL	25,529	NC
Okla Christian Univ	OK	25,870	C
Olivet Nazarene Univ	IL	29,990	C
Oral Roberts Univ	OK	31,734	C
Ouachita Baptist Univ	AR	30,220	VC
Palm Beach Atlantic Univ	FL	34,874	C+
Point Loma Nazarene Univ	CA	41,006	C+
Rochester College	MI	18,320	LC
St. Joseph's College	IN	36,500	C
Simpson Univ	CA	28,900	C
Southeastern Univ	FL	27,201	C
Southwest Baptist Univ	MO	24,710	C
Tabor College	KS	29,010	C
Taylor Univ	IN	37,821	VC+
Tenn Wesleyan College	TN	21,250	C
Toccoa Falls College	GA	23,210	LC
Trinity Bible College	ND		
Trinity Christian College	IL	28,869	C
Union College	KY	29,955	C
Union Univ	TN	28,260	VC
Univ of Mary	ND	16,714	C
Univ of Mary Hardin-Baylor	TX	31,950	C+
Univ of Mount Olive	NC	18,426	C
Univ of St. Francis	IN	29,810	C
Valparaiso Univ	IN	44,940	VC+
Vanguard Univ of Southern Calif	CA	35,833	VC
Warner Pacific College	OR	25,550	C
Waynesburg Univ	PA	30,150	C

MISSIONS

School	ST	$IS	SR
Asbury Univ	KY	32,038	VC
Bethel College	IN	31,560	C
Biola Univ	CA	40,320	C+
Cedarville Univ	OH	32,860	VC
Dordt College	IA	34,160	C+
East Texas Baptist Univ	TX	31,577	LC
Eastern Univ	PA	37,704	C
Evangel Univ	MO	23,090	C
Faulkner Univ	AL	25,720	LC
Fresno Pacific Univ	CA	32,136	C
Grace Bible College	MI	20,770	C
Hannibal-LaGrange Univ	MO	24,490	C
Harding Univ	AR	23,556	C
Hardin-Simmons Univ	TX	23,560	C+
Lipscomb Univ	TN	37,490	VC
Lubbock Christian Univ	TX	26,308	C
MidAmerica Nazarene Univ	KS	28,000	C
Mount Vernon Nazarene Univ	OH	29,590	C
Northwest Univ	WA	18,854	C
Okla Christian Univ	OK	25,870	C
Olivet Nazarene Univ	IL	29,990	C
Simpson Univ	CA	28,900	C
Southern Nazarene Univ	OK	24,354	C
Southwest Baptist Univ	MO	24,710	C
Spring Arbor Univ	MI	26,740	C
Trinity Bible College	ND		
Union Univ	TN	28,260	VC
Univ of the Cumberlands	KY	27,500	C
Vanguard Univ of Southern Calif	CA	35,833	VC

MODERN DANCE

School	ST	$IS	SR
Texas Christian Univ	TX	49,980	HC

MODERN JEWISH STUDIES

School	ST	$IS	SR
Cal State, Northridge	CA	28,690	LC
San Diego State Univ	CA	21,611	C+

MODERN LANGUAGE

School	ST	$IS	SR
Anna Maria College	MA	34,600	C
Aquinas College	MI	33,060	C
Augustana College	SD	36,500	VC
Averett Univ	VA	37,750	LC
Beloit College	WI	49,970	HC
Bethune-Cookman Univ	FL	22,958	C
Bryant Univ	RI	49,179	VC
Calif Polytechnic State Univ	CA	19,847	HC
Canisius College	NY	44,900	C
Clemson Univ	SC	19,136	HC
College of Mount St. Vincent	NY	41,040	MC
Converse College	SC	37,130	C
Duquesne Univ	PA	43,720	VC
Elizabethtown College	PA	49,740	VC
Emory and Henry College	VA	387,460	C
Emporia State Univ	KS	12,897	C
Fort Hays State Univ	KS	11,354	C
Framingham State Univ	MA	18,854	C
Francis Marion Univ	SC	16,464	LC
Graceland Univ	IA	28,020	C
Hobart and William Smith Colleges	NY	60,034	HC+
Ithaca College	NY	53,864	NC
James Madison Univ	VA	18,049	VC
John Carroll Univ	OH	46,300	C+
Kansas State Univ	KS	15,497	VC
Kennesaw State Univ	GA		C
Kenyon College	OH	58,890	MC
King Univ	TN	33,140	C
Knox College	IL	44,865	VC+
Longwood Univ	VA	20,924	C
Loyola Marymount Univ	CA	54,649	VC+
Merrimack College	MA	44,215	C
Metropolitan State Univ of Denver	CO	4,835	LC
MidAmerica Nazarene Univ	KS	28,000	VC
Mills College	CA	54,119	VC
Miss College	MS	21,998	C
Monmouth Univ	NJ	44,108	C
Montana State Univ	MT	14,068	C
Northern Arizona Univ	AZ	19,010	C
Notre Dame of Maryland Univ	MD	27,700	C
Ohio Univ	OH	21,080	C
Pace Univ	NY	53,367	C
Presbyterian College	SC	42,678	C+
St. Francis Univ	PA	30,029	LC
St. Peter's Univ	NJ	44,240	C
Seton Hall Univ	NJ	45,902	C
St. Lawrence Univ	NY	59,972	VC
Syracuse Univ	NY	56,346	VC
Trinity College	CT		HC+
Union College	NY	60,240	MC
Univ of Arkansas at Monticello	AR	12,076	NC
Univ of Louisiana at Monroe	LA	12,998	C
Univ of Maine	ME	19,902	C+
Univ of Maryland/Baltimore County	MD	18,000	VC
Univ of Mass Lowell	MA	19,316	C
Univ of Miami	FL	57,034	MC
Univ of Texas at San Antonio	TX	18,372	C
Univ of Wisc/River Falls	WI	9,722	LC
Warren Wilson College	NC	40,132	VC
Wayne State College	NE	11,764	NC
Westmont College	CA	41,500	HC
Widener Univ	PA	52,418	C
Winthrop Univ	SC	21,120	C
Wright State Univ	OH	16,983	C
Xavier Univ	OH	44,980	VC

MOLECULAR BIOLOGY

School	ST	$IS	SR
Adams State Univ	CO	13,358	LC
Alverno College	WI	31,434	LC
Andrews Univ	MI	28,030	C+
Appalachian State Univ	NC	12,919	VC
Arizona State Univ, at the Tempe Campus	AZ	20,137	C+
Assumption College	MA	47,122	C+
Auburn Univ	AL	22,378	VC+
Bellarmine Univ	KY	42,950	VC
Benedictine Univ	IL	37,820	C
Bethel Univ	MN	34,940	VC
Binghamton Univ/The SUNY	NY	21,648	HC+
Bradley Univ	IL	31,874	VC
Brigham Young Univ	UT	12,100	HC
Brown Univ	RI	59,428	MC
Cedarville Univ	OH	32,860	VC
Centre College	KY	35,000	HC+
Chestnut Hill College	PA	42,110	LC
Claremont McKenna College	CA	62,215	MC
Clarion Univ of Pennsylvania	PA	17,370	LC
Clarkson Univ	NY	57,330	HC
Coe College	IA	45,550	VC
Coker College	SC	32,256	LC
Colgate Univ	NY	58,135	MC
Florida Inst of Technology	FL	48,290	VC
Florida Southern College	FL	40,150	C+
Florida State Univ	FL	16,715	VC
Goshen College	IN	35,900	VC
Hardin-Simmons Univ	TX	23,560	C+
Houston Baptist Univ	TX	36,450	C
Illinois Inst of Technology	IL	38,512	HC+
Illinois State Univ	IL	23,110	VC
John Carroll Univ	OH	46,300	C+
Johns Hopkins Univ	MD	47,492	MC
Kent State Univ	OH	19,920	C
Kenyon College	OH	58,890	MC
Kutztown Univ of Pennsylvania	PA	16,909	LC
Lawrence Tech Univ	MI	37,630	VC
Lehigh Univ	PA	56,770	MC
Lipscomb Univ	TN	37,490	VC
Mansfield Univ	PA	19,468	LC
Marquette Univ	WI	46,930	VC+
Marshall Univ	WV	14,820	C
Messiah College	PA	40,690	C
Middlebury College	VT	59,160	MC
Millikin Univ	IL	38,940	C
Mills College	CA	54,119	VC
Milwaukee School of Engineering	WI	39,948	VC+
Montclair State Univ	NJ	22,614	C
Murray State Univ	KY	15,304	C
Muskingum Univ	OH	30,502	C
Nebr Wesleyan Univ	NE	29,774	C+
New Mexico State Univ	NM	14,050	C
Northwestern Univ	IL	61,640	MC
Ohio Northern Univ	OH	42,075	VC
Ohio Univ	OH	21,080	C
Okla State Univ	OK	14,310	VC
Otterbein College	OH	32,214	C
Pittsburg State Univ	KS	12,032	C
Polytechnic Inst of New York Univ	NY	53,064	HC+
Pomona College	CA	57,680	MC
Princeton Univ	NJ	53,795	MC
Purdue Univ/West Lafayette	IN	20,024	HC
Rhodes College	TN	51,900	HC+
Rutgers, The State Univ of New Jersey/New Brunswick	NJ	25,562	VC
Salem International Univ	WV	20,910	LC
Scripps College	CA	61,940	MC
SUNY / College of Environmental Science and Forestry	NY	18,351	VC
Stetson Univ	FL	51,516	VC
Texas Tech Univ	TX	14,243	C
The Lincoln Univ	PA	15,154	LC
Ohio State Univ-Columbus Campus	OH	19,887	HC+
Towson Univ	MD	16,000	VC
Tulane Univ	LA	60,861	MC
Univ of Arizona	AZ	20,657	C
Univ at Albany / SUNY	NY	18,674	VC
Univ of Calif at Berkeley	CA	23,322	MC
Univ of Calif at Los Angeles	CA	25,686	MC
Univ of Calif at San Diego	CA	21,000	VC
Univ of Calif at Santa Barbara	CA	27,551	HC
Univ of Calif at Santa Cruz	CA	27,807	C+
Univ of Colo Boulder	CO	22,605	VC+
Univ of Conn	CT	24,706	VC
Univ of Denver	CO	51,787	VC+
Univ of Great Falls	MT	27,970	C
Univ of Idaho	ID	14,558	C
Univ of Illinois at Urbana-Champaign	IL	26,450	HC
Univ of Kansas	KS	17,603	C+
Univ of Maine	ME	19,902	C+
Univ of Miami	FL	57,034	MC
Univ of Mich/Ann Arbor	MI	22,102	MC
Univ of Minn/Duluth	MN	19,806	C
Univ of New Hampshire	NH	26,912	C
Univ of Pittsburgh at Pittsburgh	PA	28,572	HC+
Univ of Puget Sound	WA	54,608	HC
Univ of Rochester	NY	60,668	MC
Univ of Texas at Austin	TX	44,074	HC
Univ of Texas at Dallas	TX	21,348	HC+
Univ of Vermont	VT	27,006	VC+
Univ of Wisc/Madison	WI	18,757	HC+
Univ of Wisc-Milwaukee	WI	18,436	C
Univ of Wyoming	WY	14,401	C+
Vanderbilt Univ	TN	58,220	MC
Washburn Univ	KS	12,579	C
Wells College	NY	49,400	VC
Wesleyan Univ	CT	61,198	MC
West Chester Univ of Pennsylvania	PA	17,186	C
Western Washington Univ	WA	18,519	VC
Westminster College	PA	31,290	C+
Yale Univ	CT	55,300	MC

MOLECULAR DIAGNOSTICS

School	ST	$IS	SR
Ferris State Univ	MI	20,047	C

MOVEMENT SCIENCE

School	ST	$IS	SR
Texas Christian Univ	TX	49,980	HC
Univ of Idaho	ID	14,558	C
Winona State Univ	MN	16,640	C

MULTIMEDIA

School	ST	$IS	SR
Abilene Christian Univ	TX	38,400	C+
American Univ	DC	56,015	HC+
Arizona State Univ, at the Tempe Campus	AZ	20,137	C+
Art Inst of Atlanta	GA	24,000	SP
Art Inst of Portland	OR	23,040	SP
Belmont Univ	TN	39,190	VC+
Bennington College	VT	56,990	HC+
Bethel Univ	MN	34,940	VC
Bloomfield College	NJ	37,850	LC
Bradley Univ	IL	31,874	VC
Calif Lutheran Univ	CA	49,540	C+
Cameron Univ	OK	10,004	LC
Cedarville Univ	OH	32,860	VC
Champlain College	VT	46,650	VC+
CUNY/Brooklyn College	NY	5,884	C+
CUNY/City College	NY	20,319	VC
College of New Jersey	NJ	25,376	HC
Columbia College Chicago	IL	30,940	LC
Dakota Wesleyan Univ	SD	23,000	C
Duquesne Univ	PA	43,720	VC
Florida Atlantic Univ	FL	17,339	C
Franklin College	IN	36,585	C
George Fox Univ	OR	40,750	C+
George Washington Univ	DC	57,108	MC
Georgia Southern Univ	GA	16,942	C
Hawaii Pacific Univ	HI	34,360	C
Howard Payne Univ	TX	17,115	C
Kent State Univ	OH	19,920	C
La Salle Univ	PA	50,270	C
Lasell College	MA	43,750	LC
Lewis Univ	IL	23,050	C
Louisiana College	LA	15,746	C
Lyndon State College	VT	14,233	C
Lynn Univ	FL	43,500	LC
McMurry Univ	TX	25,962	LC
Minot State Univ	ND	10,915	C
National Univ	CA	14,730	SP
Northeastern Univ	MA	55,296	MC
Ohio Univ	OH	21,080	C
Rider Univ	NJ	45,720	C
St. Leo Univ	FL	30,340	C
Simpson College	IA	36,086	C+
Univ of Mary Hardin-Baylor	TX	31,950	C+
Univ of New Haven	CT	48,940	C
Univ of N Car at Asheville	NC	13,500	VC
Univ of the Arts	PA	38,450	SP
Washington State Univ	WA	20,461	C
Waynesburg Univ	PA	30,150	C
Western Washington Univ	WA	18,519	VC
Wilmington Univ	DE	8,112	NC

MUSEUM STUDIES

School	ST	$IS	SR
Baylor Univ	TX	50,329	HC
Juniata College	PA	49,340	VC
Niagara Univ	NY	41,010	C
Tusculum College	TN	24,295	C
Univ of Central Okla	OK	12,293	C
Univ of Illinois at Chicago	IL	24,505	VC
Walsh Univ	OH	35,100	C
Western Illinois Univ	IL	20,732	C

MUSIC

School	ST	$IS	SR
Abilene Christian Univ	TX	38,400	C+
Adams State Univ	CO	13,358	VC
Adelphi Univ	NY	44,670	VC
Adrian College	MI	42,400	C
Agnes Scott College	GA	45,323	C
Alabama State Univ	AL	14,142	NC
Albany State Univ	GA	8,500	C
Albion College	MI	46,010	C
Alcorn State Univ	MS	9,500	C
Alderson Broaddus Univ	WV	28,656	C
Allegheny College	PA	50,980	VC
Allen Univ	SC	16,124	NC
Alma College	MI	44,075	C
Alverno College	WI	31,434	LC
American Univ	DC	56,015	HC+

ST = STATE $IS = IN-STATE COSTS SR = SELECTOR RATING

School	ST	$IS	SR
Amherst College	MA	58,744	MC
Andrews Univ	MI	28,030	C+
Angelo State Univ	TX	15,049	NC
Anna Maria College	MA	34,600	C
Aquinas College	MI	33,060	C
Arizona State Univ, at the Tempe Campus	AZ	20,137	C+
Arkansas State Univ	AR	15,470	C
Arkansas Tech Univ	AR	13,982	LC
Armstrong State Univ	GA	15,532	C
Asbury Univ	KY	32,038	VC
Ashland Univ	OH	25,000	C
Assumption College	MA	47,122	C+
Atlantic Union College	MA	24,600	C
Augsburg College	MN	35,142	C
Augustana College	IL	43,398	VC
Augustana College	SD	36,500	VC
Austin College	TX	45,875	HC
Austin Peay State Univ	TN	15,274	C
Averett Univ	VA	37,750	LC
Avila Univ	MO	26,900	C
Azusa Pacific Univ	CA	42,086	C
Baker Univ	KS	33,350	C+
Baldwin Wallace Univ	OH	38,318	C
Ball State Univ	IN	17,850	C
Bard College	NY	61,940	HC
Bard College at Simon's Rock	MA	61,749	HC+
Barnard College/Columbia Univ	NY	39,000	MC
Bates College	ME	60,720	MC
Baylor Univ	TX	50,329	HC
Belhaven Univ	MS	27,110	C
Bellarmine Univ	KY	42,950	VC
Belmont Univ	TN	39,190	VC+
Beloit College	WI	49,970	HC
Bemidji State Univ	MN	13,500	C
Benedict College	SC	20,454	NC
Benedictine College	KS	29,180	VC
Benedictine Univ	IL	37,820	C
Bennett College for Women	NC	21,970	LC
Bennington College	VT	56,990	HC+
Berea College	KY	7,192	C
Berklee College of Music	MA	47,100	SP
Berry College	GA	39,254	VC
Bethany College	KS	30,605	NC
Bethany College	WV	35,282	LC
Bethel College	KS	32,160	C
Bethel Univ	MN	34,940	VC
Bethel College	TN	19,186	C
Bethune-Cookman Univ	FL	22,958	C
Binghamton Univ/The SUNY	NY	21,648	HC+
Biola Univ	CA	40,320	C
Birmingham-Southern College	AL	44,168	VC+
Black Hills State Univ	SD	13,947	C
Bloomsburg Univ of Pennsylvania	PA	13,598	C
Blue Mountain College	MS	15,634	LC
Bluefield College	VA	17,230	C
Bluffton Univ	OH	38,948	C
Boise State Univ	ID	13,469	LC
Boston College	MA	60,622	MC
Boston Conservatory	MA	56,380	VC
Boston Univ	MA	60,594	MC
Bowdoin College	ME	59,568	MC
Bowling Green State Univ	OH	18,970	C
Bradley Univ	IL	31,874	VC
Brandeis Univ	MA		MC
Briar Cliff Univ	IA	29,514	C
Bridgewater College	VA	41,450	C
Bridgewater State Univ	MA	18,752	C
Brigham Young Univ	UT	12,100	HC
Brigham Young Univ/Hawaii	HI	10,686	VC
Brown Univ	RI	59,428	MC
Bryan College	TN	24,194	C
Bryn Mawr College	PA	59,890	MC
Bucknell Univ	PA	60,140	MC
Buena Vista Univ	IA	39,188	C
Buffalo State College / SUNY	NY	15,733	C+
Butler Univ	IN	47,572	VC+
Cabrini College	PA	40,859	LC
Cairn Univ	PA	33,270	C
Caldwell College	NJ	35,602	NC
Calif Baptist Univ	CA	38,792	C
Calif Lutheran Univ	CA	49,540	C+
Calif Polytechnic State Univ	CA	19,847	HC
Calif State Polytechnic Univ, Pomona	CA	20,156	C
Cal State, Bakersfield	CA	8,000	C
Cal State, Chico	CA	20,158	C
Cal State, Dominguez Hills	CA	17,090	LC
Cal State, East Bay	CA	16,549	C
Cal State, Fresno	CA	17,405	C
Cal State, Fullerton	CA	25,188	C
Cal State, Long Beach	CA	17,502	C+
Cal State, Los Angeles	CA	17,186	LC
Cal State, Monterey Bay	CA	26,871	LC
Cal State, Northridge	CA	28,690	LC
Cal State, Sacramento	CA	16,200	C
Cal State, San Bernardino	CA	12,000	C
Cal State, Stanislaus	CA	18,582	C
Calvin College	MI	39,120	VC
Cameron Univ	OK	10,004	C
Campbell Univ	NC	37,570	VC
Campbellsville Univ	KY	27,720	C
Canisius College	NY	44,900	C

School	ST	$IS	SR
Capital Univ	OH	41,050	VC
Cardinal Stritch Univ	WI	24,054	C
Carleton College	MN	60,102	MC
Carnegie Mellon Univ	PA	51,260	MC
Carroll Univ	WI	38,100	C
Carson-Newman Univ	TN	29,058	C+
Carthage College	WI	33,000	C
Case Western Reserve Univ	OH	56,534	MC
Castleton State College	VT	20,186	C
Catawba College	NC	37,240	VC
Cedar Crest College	PA	43,240	C
Cedarville Univ	OH	32,860	VC
Centenary College of Louisiana	LA	45,650	C+
Central College	IA	42,104	C+
Central Conn State Univ	CT	19,749	C
Central Methodist Univ	MO	28,240	VC
Central State Univ	OH	9,010	C
Central Washington Univ	WA	11,730	C
Centre College	KY	35,000	HC+
Chadron State College	NE	7,400	NC
Chapman Univ	CA	58,347	VC+
Charleston Southern Univ	SC	22,420	C
Chatham Univ	PA	43,797	C
Chestnut Hill College	PA	42,110	LC
Cheyney Univ of Pennsylvania	PA	20,372	LC
Chicago State Univ	IL	5,482	C
Christopher Newport Univ	VA	21,960	VC
CUNY/Baruch College	NY		HC
CUNY/Brooklyn College	NY	5,884	C+
CUNY/City College	NY	20,319	HC+
Claflin Univ	SC	22,368	LC
Clark Atlanta Univ	GA	30,006	LC
Clark Univ	MA	47,020	HC+
Clarke Univ	IA	37,600	C
Clayton State Univ	GA	12,000	NC
Clearwater Christian College	FL	23,720	C
Cleveland Inst of Music	OH	56,882	SP
Cleveland State Univ	OH	21,776	C
Coastal Carolina Univ	SC	18,580	C
Coe College	IA	45,550	VC
Coker College	SC	32,256	LC
Colby College	ME	57,510	MC
Colgate Univ	NY	58,135	MC
College of Charleston	SC	22,145	VC
College of Mount St. Joseph	OH	33,880	C
College of New Jersey	NJ	25,376	HC
College of St. Benedict	MN	49,359	VC
College of St. Elizabeth	NJ	43,839	LC
College of St. Scholastica	MN	41,440	C
College of Staten Island/The City of New Yok	NY	16,778	NC
College of the Holy Cross	MA	58,042	MC
College of the Ozarks	MO		VC
College of William & Mary	VA	28,000	MC
College of Wooster	OH	52,600	VC
Colo Christian Univ	CO	27,500	VC
Colo College	CO	57,162	MC
Colo Mesa Univ	CO	17,690	C
Colo State Univ-Fort Collins	CO	20,385	VC
Columbia College	SC	27,882	C
Columbia College Chicago	IL	30,940	VC
Columbia Univ/City of New York	NY	61,116	MC
Columbia Univ/School of General Studies	NY	58,231	MC
Columbus State Univ	GA	13,176	C
Concordia College - Moorhead	MN	39,974	VC
Concordia College - New York	NY	39,035	LC
Concordia Univ Irvine	CA	35,390	VC
Concordia Univ Nebr	NE	26,000	VC
Concordia Univ St. Paul	MN	28,250	C
Concordia Univ Texas	TX	23,640	C
Concordia Univ Wisc	WI	28,980	C
Concordia Univ, Ann Arbor	MI	27,220	VC
Concordia Univ, River Forest	IL	26,300	C
Conn College	CT	54,970	MC
Converse College	SC	37,130	C
Corban Univ	OR	37,380	C+
Cornell College	IA	44,930	VC
Cornell Univ	NY	60,964	MC
Cornerstone Univ and Grand Rapids Theological Seminary	MI	33,338	C
Cornish College of the Arts	WA	21,200	SP
Covenant College	GA	38,990	VC+
Creighton Univ	NE	45,356	VC
Culver-Stockton College	MO	30,900	C
Cumberland Univ	TN	21,220	C
Curtis Inst of Music	PA	24,143	SP
Dakota Wesleyan Univ	SD	23,000	C
Dallas Baptist Univ	TX	30,580	VC
Dartmouth College	NH	57,996	MC
Davidson College	NC	58,146	MC
Davis & Elkins College	WV	33,742	C
Delaware State Univ	DE	16,722	LC
Delta State Univ	MS	12,292	LC
Denison Univ	OH	54,670	HC+
DePaul Univ	IL	47,623	VC
DePauw Univ	IN	48,950	VC+
Dickinson College	PA	57,662	HC+
Dickinson State Univ	ND	11,900	NC
Dillard Univ	LA	20,940	VC

School	ST	$IS	SR
Doane College	NE	35,230	C
Dominican Univ	IL	37,628	C
Dominican Univ of Calif	CA	51,250	C
Dordt College	IA	34,160	C+
Dowling College	NY	25,000	LC
Drake Univ	IA	41,516	VC+
Drew Univ/College of Liberal Arts	NJ	57,516	C
Drury Univ	MO	31,909	VC
Duke Univ	NC	50,250	MC
Earlham College	IN	51,470	HC
East Central Univ	OK	10,223	C
East Stroudsburg Univ of Pennsylvania	PA	18,868	LC
East Tenn State Univ	TN	9,000	C
East Texas Baptist Univ	TX	31,577	LC
Eastern Conn State Univ	CT	20,584	C
Eastern Illinois Univ	IL	20,466	C
Eastern Kentucky Univ	KY	11,161	C
Eastern Mennonite Univ	VA	40,660	C
Eastern Mich Univ	MI	18,604	C
Eastern Nazarene College	MA	30,000	C
Eastern New Mexico Univ	NM	10,682	C
Eastern Oregon Univ	OR	10,400	C
Eastern Univ	PA	37,704	C
Eastern Washington Univ	WA		C
Eastman School of Music	NY	58,802	SP
Eckerd College	FL	43,902	C
Edgewood College	WI	33,294	C
Edinboro Univ of Pennsylvania	PA	15,940	LC
Elizabeth City State Univ	NC	11,638	C
Elizabethtown College	PA	49,740	VC
Elmhurst College	IL	43,336	C
Elmira College	NY	49,950	C+
Elon Univ	NC	41,914	VC+
Emory Univ	GA	56,368	MC
Emporia State Univ	KS	12,897	C
Erskine College	SC	37,360	C
Eugene Lang College/The New School for Liberal Arts	NY	55,650	C
Eureka College	IL	19,280	C
Evangel Univ	MO	23,090	C
Excelsior College	NY	5,580	SP
Fairfield Univ	CT	56,960	VC
Faulkner Univ	AL	25,720	C
Felician College	NJ	41,640	LC
Fisk Univ	TN	19,830	C
Florida A&M Univ	FL	14,935	LC
Florida Atlantic Univ	FL	17,339	C
Florida Gulf Coast Univ	FL		C
Florida International Univ	FL	17,747	C+
Florida Memorial Univ	FL	20,888	LC
Florida Southern College	FL	40,150	C+
Florida State Univ	FL	16,715	VC
Fordham Univ	NY	61,588	HC+
Fort Hays State Univ	KS	11,354	C
Fort Lewis College	CO	15,513	C
Francis Marion Univ	SC	16,464	LC
Franklin and Marshall College	PA	60,799	MC
Franklin College	IN	36,585	C
Franklin Pierce Univ	NH	41,598	C
Fresno Pacific Univ	CA	32,136	C
Friends Univ	KS	29,100	C
Frostburg State Univ	MD	15,264	LC
Furman Univ	SC	54,006	HC
Gardner-Webb Univ	NC	34,375	C+
Geneva College	PA	27,280	C
George Fox Univ	OR	40,750	C+
George Mason Univ	VA	15,724	VC
George Washington Univ	DC	57,108	MC
Georgetown Univ	KY	41,440	C+
Georgia College and State Univ	GA	18,900	C+
Georgia Regents Univ	GA		C
Georgia Southern Univ	GA	16,942	C
Georgia Southwestern State Univ	GA	13,246	C
Georgia State Univ	GA	15,582	VC
Gettysburg College	PA	58,820	HC
Gonzaga Univ	WA	46,441	HC
Gordon College	MA	44,320	VC
Goshen College	IN	35,900	VC
Goucher College	MD	52,040	VC+
Grace Bible College	MI	20,750	C
Graceland Univ	IA	28,020	C
Grambling State Univ	LA	13,384	LC
Grand Canyon Univ	AZ	24,540	VC
Grand Valley State Univ	MI	17,998	C+
Grand View Univ	IA	31,050	C
Greensboro College	NC	28,740	LC
Greenville College	IL	27,012	C
Grinnell College	IA	53,654	HC
Grove City College	PA	24,022	VC
Guilford College	NC	42,800	C
Gustavus Adolphus College	MN	48,170	HC
Hamilton College	NY	55,620	MC
Hamline Univ	MN	45,678	VC
Hampshire College	MA	58,320	HC
Hampton Univ	VA	28,528	C
Hannibal-LaGrange Univ	MO	24,490	C
Hanover College	IN	43,073	C+
Harding Univ	AR	23,556	C

School	ST	$IS	SR
Hardin-Simmons Univ	TX	23,560	C+
Hartwick College	NY	51,270	C
Harvard College/Harvard Univ	MA	49,000	MC
Hastings College	NE	27,782	C+
Haverford College	PA	61,564	MC
Heidelberg Univ	OH	34,100	C
Henderson State Univ	AR	14,584	C
Hendrix College	AR	50,202	VC+
High Point Univ	NC	39,800	C
Hillsdale College	MI	32,866	MC
Hiram College	OH	37,300	VC
Hobart and William Smith Colleges	NY	60,034	HC+
Hofstra Univ	NY	51,810	VC+
Hollins Univ	VA	43,295	VC
Holy Names Univ	CA	40,310	NC
Hood College	MD	45,730	C
Hope College	MI	38,650	VC
Houghton College	NY	36,808	C+
Houston Baptist Univ	TX	36,450	C
Howard Payne Univ	TX	17,115	C
Howard Univ	DC	13,646	C
Humboldt State Univ	CA	18,400	C
Hunter College	NY	14,429	VC
Huntingdon College	AL	33,100	C
Huston-Tillotson Univ	TX	18,124	C+
Idaho State Univ	ID	12,307	C
Illinois College	IL	25,770	VC
Illinois State Univ	IL	23,110	VC
Illinois Wesleyan Univ	IL	48,452	HC
Immaculata Univ	PA	43,000	C
Indiana State Univ	IN	16,000	C
Indiana Univ Bloomington	IN	19,801	VC
Indiana Univ of Pennsylvania	PA	20,846	LC
Indiana Univ South Bend	IN	15,501	C
Indiana Univ Southeast	IN	16,035	C
Indiana Univ-Purdue Univ Fort Wayne	IN	15,521	C
Indiana Wesleyan Univ	IN	31,815	VC
Inter-American Univ of PR/ San Germán	PR	6,720	
Iowa State Univ	IA	16,403	C
Iowa Wesleyan College	IA	30,850	LC
Ithaca College	NY	53,864	HC
Jacksonville State Univ	AL	12,480	LC
Jacksonville Univ	FL	37,780	C
James Madison Univ	VA	18,049	VC
John Brown Univ	AR	32,056	VC+
Johnson State College	VT	16,721	C
Judson Univ	IL	25,130	C
Juilliard School	NY	44,460	SP
Kalamazoo College	MI	49,740	HC
Kansas State Univ	KS	15,497	VC
Kansas Wesleyan Univ	KS	32,000	C
Kean Univ	NJ	23,444	C
Keene State College	NH	23,232	LC
Kennesaw State Univ	GA		C
Kent State Univ	OH	19,920	C
Kentucky Christian Univ	KY	17,622	LC
Kentucky Wesleyan College	KY	27,440	C
Kenyon College	OH	58,890	MC
Knox College	IL	44,865	VC+
Kutztown Univ of Pennsylvania	PA	16,909	LC
La Salle Univ	PA	50,270	C
La Sierra Univ	CA	35,694	VC
Lafayette College	PA	59,155	HC+
LaGrange College	GA	37,670	C
Lake Forest College	IL	50,652	VC
Lakeland College	WI	22,990	C
Lamar Univ	TX	6,820	LC
Lander Univ	SC	22,514	C+
Lane College	TN	11,212	C
Langston Univ	OK	3,000	C
Le Moyne College	NY	43,470	C
Lebanon Valley College	PA	38,570	C
Lee Univ	TN	18,690	C
Lehigh Univ	PA	56,770	MC
Lehman College/The CUNY	NY	5,778	LC
LeMoyne-Owen College	TN	13,100	C
Lenoir-Rhyne College	NC	35,984	C
Lewis & Clark College	OR	54,382	MC
Lewis Univ	IL	23,050	C
Liberty Univ	VA	19,101	C
Limestone College	SC	30,800	C
Lindenwood Univ	MO	20,750	C
Linfield College-McMinnville Campus	OR	47,676	C
Lipscomb Univ	TN	37,490	VC
LIU Brooklyn	NY	47,182	LC
LIU Post	NY	47,660	C
Livingstone College	NC	17,815	LC
Lock Haven Univ of Pennsylvania	PA	18,028	LC
Longwood Univ	VA	20,924	C
Loras College	IA	37,432	VC
Louisiana College	LA	15,746	C
Louisiana State Univ	LA	18,677	C+
Louisiana Tech Univ	LA	11,302	C
Loyola Marymount Univ	CA	54,649	VC+
Loyola Univ Chicago	IL	51,646	VC+
Loyola Univ New Orleans	LA	46,581	VC
Lubbock Christian Univ	TX	26,308	C
Luther College	IA	45,720	C+
Lycoming College	PA	45,379	C

ST = STATE $IS = IN-STATE COSTS   SR = SELECTOR RATING

School	ST	$IS	SR
Lynchburg College	VA	42,645	C
Lyon College	AR	32,090	C+
Macalester College	MN	57,691	MC
MacMurray College	IL	20,755	C
Madonna Univ	MI	24,540	VC
Malone Univ	OH	35,364	C
Manchester Univ	IN	35,070	C
Manhattan School of Music	NY	55,850	SP
Manhattanville College	NY	50,740	VC
Mannes College New School for Music	NY	44,500	VC
Mansfield Univ	PA	19,468	LC
Marian Univ	IN	38,540	C
Marian Univ	WI	32,420	LC
Marietta College	OH	42,135	C+
Marlboro College	VT	35,980	VC
Mars Hill Univ	NC	22,950	LC
Marshall Univ	WV	14,820	C
Martin Univ	IN	11,000	SP
Mary Baldwin College	VA	38,245	C
Marygrove College	MI	28,926	C
Marylhurst Univ	OR	20,295	NC
Maryville College	TN	33,150	C+
Mass Inst of Technology	MA	58,240	MC
McDaniel College	MD	47,450	VC
McKendree Univ	IL	29,920	C
McMurry Univ	TX	25,962	LC
McNeese State Univ	LA	2,649	C
McPherson College	KS	28,138	C
Mercer Univ	GA	44,201	VC
Mercy College	NY	30,456	C
Mercyhurst Univ	PA	40,700	C
Meredith College	NC	31,420	C
Messiah College	PA	40,690	C
Methodist Univ	NC	37,185	C
Miami Univ	OH	24,191	VC
Mich State Univ	MI	22,450	VC
MidAmerica Nazarene Univ	KS	28,000	C
Middle Tenn State Univ	TN	8,650	C
Middlebury College	VT	59,160	MC
Midland Univ	NE	34,000	C
Midwestern State Univ	TX	9,722	C
Millersville Univ of Pennsylvania	PA	21,648	C
Milligan College	TN	27,510	C
Millikin Univ	IL	38,940	C
Mills College	CA	54,119	VC
Millsaps College	MS	43,888	VC+
Minn State Univ, Mankato	MN	15,616	C
Minn State Univ, Moorhead	MN	13,392	VC
Minot State Univ	ND	10,915	C
Miss College	MS	21,998	C
Miss Univ for Women	MS	7,400	C
Missouri Baptist Univ	MO	31,830	C
Missouri Southern State Univ	MO	12,061	C
Missouri State Univ	MO	13,996	C+
Missouri Western State Univ	MO	12,260	NC
Molloy College	NY	40,440	C
Monmouth College	IL	40,850	C
Monmouth Univ	NJ	44,108	C
Montana State Univ	MT	14,068	C
Montana State Univ-Billings	MT	12,425	LC
Montana State Univ-Northern	MT	12,500	NC
Montclair State Univ	NJ	22,614	C
Moravian College	PA	36,381	VC
Morehead State Univ	KY	10,900	C
Morehouse College	GA	39,412	C
Morgan State Univ	MD	14,500	VC
Morningside College	IA	35,430	C
Mount Holyoke College	MA	55,146	MC
Mount Marty College	SD	29,638	C
Mount Mercy Univ	IA	35,320	C
Mount St. Mary's College - Chalon Campus	CA	43,897	VC+
Mount Vernon Nazarene Univ	OH	29,590	C
Muhlenberg College	PA	52,837	HC
Murray State Univ	KY	15,304	C
Muskingum Univ	OH	30,502	C
Naropa Univ	CO	39,166	SP
Nazareth College of Rochester	NY	43,028	C+
Nebr Wesleyan Univ	NE	29,774	C+
New College of Florida	FL	14,504	NC
New England Conservatory of Music	MA	52,550	SP
New Jersey City Univ	NJ	21,456	LC
New Mexico Highlands Univ	NM	11,904	NC
New Mexico State Univ	NM	14,050	C
New York Univ	NY	61,470	MC
Newberry College	SC	26,850	LC
Nicholls State Univ	LA	7,095	C
N Car Agricultural and Technical State Univ	NC	13,365	LC
N Car Central Univ	NC	9,000	C
North Central College	IL	38,343	VC
N Dak State Univ	ND		
North Park Univ	IL	30,130	VC
Northeastern Illinois Univ	IL	10,318	LC
Northeastern State Univ	OK	8,615	VC
Northeastern Univ	MA	55,296	MC
Northern Arizona Univ	AZ	19,010	C
Northern Illinois Univ	IL	19,768	VC
Northern Kentucky Univ	KY	21,134	C
Northern Mich Univ	MI	18,278	C
Northern State Univ - Aberdeen	SD	14,505	C
Northwest Christian Univ	OR	27,399	C
Northwest Missouri State Univ	MO	17,347	C
Northwest Nazarene Univ	ID	34,000	C
Northwest Univ	WA	18,854	C
Northwestern College	MN	24,000	C
Northwestern College of Iowa	IA	36,240	VC
Northwestern Okla State	OK	7,275	NC
Northwestern State Univ of Louisiana	LA	14,368	C
Northwestern Univ	IL	61,640	MC
Notre Dame de Namur Univ	CA	44,236	LC
Notre Dame of Maryland Univ	MD	27,700	VC
Nova Southeastern Univ	FL	37,280	VC
Nyack College	NY	33,250	C
Oakland City Univ	IN	24,500	NC
Oakland Univ	MI	19,391	C
Oakwood Univ	AL	25,529	NC
Oberlin College	OH	61,788	MC
Occidental College	CA	60,972	MC
Ohio Northern Univ	OH	42,075	VC
Ohio Univ	OH	21,080	C
Ohio Wesleyan Univ	OH	49,460	C+
Okla Baptist Univ	OK	28,202	C
Okla Christian Univ	OK	25,870	VC
Okla City Univ	OK	40,476	VC
Okla Panhandle State Univ	OK	8,996	C
Okla State Univ	OK	14,310	VC
Okla Wesleyan Univ	OK	21,300	C
Old Dominion Univ	VA	19,483	LC
Olivet Nazarene Univ	IL	29,990	C
Oral Roberts Univ	OK	31,734	C
Oregon State Univ	OR	20,273	VC
Oswego / SUNY	NY	20,009	VC
Ottawa Univ	KS	15,000	NC
Otterbein College	OH	32,214	C
Ouachita Baptist Univ	AR	30,220	VC
Our Lady of the Lake Univ	TX	22,430	LC
Pacific Lutheran Univ	WA	46,760	C+
Pacific Union College	CA	28,150	VC
Pacific Univ	OR	49,626	C+
Palm Beach Atlantic Univ	FL	34,874	C+
Park Univ	MO	17,525	C
Pepperdine Univ	CA	55,372	HC+
Peru State College	NE	8,600	NC
Philander Smith College	AR	19,760	LC
Piedmont College	GA	30,136	C
Pittsburg State Univ	KS	12,032	C
Pitzer College	CA	54,988	MC
Plymouth State Univ	NH	23,148	LC
Point Loma Nazarene Univ	CA	41,006	C+
Pomona College	CA	57,680	MC
Portland State Univ	OR	18,672	C
Prairie View A&M Univ	TX	15,205	LC
Presbyterian College	SC	42,678	C+
Prescott College	AZ	33,284	C
Princeton Univ	NJ	53,795	MC
Principia College	IL	35,140	C+
Providence College	RI	57,383	C+
Queens College/The CUNY	NY	17,107	VC
Queens Univ of Charlotte	NC	39,543	C+
Quincy Univ	IL	34,980	LC
Radford Univ	VA	17,766	LC
Ramapo College of New Jersey	NJ	24,938	C
Randolph College	VA	45,660	VC
Randolph-Macon College	VA	49,869	C+
Reed College	OR	57,780	MC
Regis Univ	CO	41,318	C
Rhode Island College	RI	17,694	LC
Rhodes College	TN	51,900	HC+
Rice Univ	TX	43,288	NC
Richard Stockton College of New Jersey	NJ	20,000	C
Rider Univ	NJ	45,720	C
Ripon College	WI	36,959	C+
Roanoke College	VA	49,976	C
Roberts Wesleyan College	NY	38,306	C+
Rochester College	MI	18,320	LC
Rockford College	IL	31,000	C
Roger Williams Univ	RI	46,296	VC
Rollins College	FL	52,370	HC
Roosevelt Univ	IL	22,605	VC
Rowan Univ	NJ	24,022	VC+
Rust College	MS	10,600	C
Rutgers, The State Univ of New Jersey/Camden Campus	NJ	25,121	C
Rutgers, The State Univ of New Jersey/New Brunswick	NJ	25,562	VC
Rutgers, The State Univ of New Jersey/Newark Campus	NJ	258,806	C
Saginaw Valley State Univ	MI	17,369	C
St. Augustine's Univ	NC	14,000	C
St. John's Univ	MN	47,984	C
St. Joseph's College	IN	36,500	C
St. Joseph's Univ	PA	55,006	VC
St. Louis Univ	MO	48,346	HC
St. Martin's Univ	WA	41,678	C
St. Mary-of-the-Woods College	IN	37,722	LC
St. Mary's College	IN	45,160	C+
St. Mary's Univ	TX	33,854	C
St. Mary's Univ of Minn	MN	38,280	C
St. Michael's College	VT	49,975	VC
St. Vincent College	PA	40,244	C
St. Xavier Univ	IL	32,840	C
Salem College	NC	29,326	VC
Salisbury Univ	MD	19,180	VC
Salve Regina Univ	RI	48,550	VC
Sam Houston State Univ	TX	17,082	C
Samford Univ	AL	37,060	C+
San Diego Christian College	CA	31,012	C
San Diego State Univ	CA	21,611	C+
San Francisco Conservatory of Music	CA	56,428	SP
San Francisco State Univ	CA	18,514	C
San Jose State Univ	CA	19,133	LC
Santa Fe Univ of Art and Design	NM	39,666	SP
Sarah Lawrence College	NY	48,000	HC
Schreiner Univ	TX	32,734	LC
Scripps College	CA	61,940	MC
Seattle Pacific Univ	WA	41,559	VC+
Seattle Univ	WA	49,035	VC+
Seton Hall Univ	NJ	45,902	C
Seton Hill Univ	PA	35,172	C
Sewanee: The Univ of the South	TN	47,700	HC+
Shenandoah Univ	VA	39,916	C
Shepherd Univ	WV	15,875	C
Shorter Univ	GA	30,650	LC
Siena Heights Univ	MI	32,040	C
Sierra Nevada College	NV	32,700	VC
Silver Lake College	WI	22,600	LC
Simmons College	MA	49,966	VC
Simpson College	IA	36,086	C+
Simpson Univ	CA	28,900	C
Skidmore College	NY	59,942	HC
Slippery Rock Univ of Pennsylvania	PA	10,360	C
Smith College	MA	59,674	MC
Sonoma State Univ	CA	20,541	C
S Dak State Univ	SD	14,296	C
Southeast Missouri State Univ	MO	15,370	LC
Southeastern Louisiana Univ	LA	13,325	C
Southeastern Okla State Univ	OK	7,966	LC
Southeastern Univ	FL	37,201	C
Southern Adventist Univ	TN	26,190	C
Southern Illinois Univ Carbondale	IL	21,942	C
Southern Illinois Univ Edwardsville	IL	17,532	C
Southern Nazarene Univ	OK	24,354	C
Southern Oregon Univ	OR	17,874	C
Southern Univ and A&M College	LA	9,761	LC
Southern Wesleyan Univ	SC	25,600	C
Southwest Baptist Univ	MO	24,710	C
Southwest Minn State Univ	MN	14,000	C
Southwestern Adventist Univ	TX	23,026	LC
Southwestern College	KS	29,270	C
Southwestern Univ	TX	45,660	VC
Spelman College	GA	24,650	C
Spring Arbor Univ	MI	26,740	C
St. Ambrose Univ	IA	30,845	C
St. Bonaventure Univ	NY	41,575	C
St. Catherine Univ	MN	37,782	C+
St. Cloud State Univ	MN	10,600	C
St. Lawrence Univ	NY	59,972	VC
St. Mary's College of Maryland	MD	25,754	VC
St. Norbert College	WI	41,478	VC
St. Olaf College	MN	51,200	HC+
Stanford Univ	CA	58,388	MC
SUNY at Purchase	NY	16,951	C
Stephen F. Austin State Univ	TX	14,668	C
Sterling College	KS	27,216	C
Stetson Univ	FL	51,516	VC
Stillman College	AL	19,470	C
Stonehill College	MA	46,780	HC
Stony Brook Univ / SUNY	NY	20,078	HC+
SUNY College at Geneseo	NY	18,670	HC
SUNY Fredonia/The SUNY at Fredonia	NY	19,840	VC
SUNY New Paltz	NY	14,348	C
SUNY Oneonta / SUNY	NY	16,919	C+
SUNY Plattsburgh / SUNY	NY	18,083	C
Susquehanna Univ	PA	51,150	C
Swarthmore College	PA	57,870	MC
Syracuse Univ	NY	56,346	VC
Tabor College	KS	29,010	C
Tarleton State Univ	TX	13,489	LC
Taylor Univ	IN	37,821	VC+
Temple Univ	PA	24,392	VC
Tenn State Univ	TN	9,048	C
Tenn Wesleyan College	TN	21,250	C
Texas A&M Univ at Commerce	TX	10,496	C
Texas A&M Univ at Corpus Christi	TX	11,544	LC
Texas A&M Univ at Kingsville	TX	7,500	LC
Texas Christian Univ	TX	49,980	HC
Texas Lutheran Univ	TX	36,040	C
Texas Southern Univ	TX	18,212	LC
Texas State Univ	TX	17,128	C
Texas Tech Univ	TX	14,243	C
Texas Wesleyan Univ	TX	31,382	C
Texas Woman's Univ	TX	13,633	LC
The Catholic Univ of America	DC	52,852	VC
The College of Idaho	ID	31,277	C+
The College of St. Rose	NY	26,750	C
The Lincoln Univ	PA	15,154	LC
The Masters College	CA	38,160	C+
Ohio State Univ-Columbus Campus	OH	19,887	HC+
The Pennsylvania State Univ - Univ Park	PA	28,022	VC+
The SUNY at Potsdam	NY	18,473	C
The Univ of Memphis	TN	15,094	C
The Univ of N Car at Greensboro	NC	12,848	C
The Univ of N Car at Pembroke	NC	13,388	LC
The Univ of Okla	OK	18,621	VC
The Univ of Tenn at Chattanooga	TN	16,883	C
The Univ of Utah	UT	16,463	VC
Thomas Edison State College	NJ	5,700	SP
Toccoa Falls College	GA	23,210	LC
Towson Univ	MD	16,000	VC
Transylvania Univ	KY	42,660	VC+
Trevecca Nazarene Univ	TN	31,186	C
Trinity Christian College	IL	28,869	C
Trinity College	CT		HC+
Trinity International Univ	IL	31,070	C
Trinity Univ	TX	48,150	HC+
Truman State Univ	MO	15,541	HC
Tufts Univ	MA	58,780	MC
Tulane Univ	LA	60,861	MC
Union College	NE	23,270	C
Union Univ	TN	28,260	VC
Universidad Adventista de las Antillas	PR	7,360	
Univ at Albany / SUNY	NY	18,674	VC
Univ at Buffalo / The SUNY	NY	20,283	VC
Univ of Akron	OH	20,436	C
Univ of Alabama at Birmingham	AL	18,484	C+
Univ of Alabama at Tuscaloosa	AL	17,164	C+
Univ of Alabama in Huntsville	AL	17,591	VC+
Univ of Alaska Anchorage	AK	16,673	NC
Univ of Alaska Fairbanks	AK	15,130	C
Univ of Arizona	AZ	20,657	C
Univ of Arkansas at Fayetteville	AR	18,352	C+
Univ of Arkansas at Little Rock	AR	17,609	LC
Univ of Arkansas at Monticello	AR	12,076	NC
Univ of Arkansas at Pine Bluff	AR	13,378	C
Univ of Bridgeport	CT	39,030	LC
Univ of Calif at Berkeley	CA	23,322	MC
Univ of Calif at Davis	CA		HC
Univ of Calif at Irvine	CA	25,961	VC
Univ of Calif at Los Angeles	CA	25,686	VC
Univ of Calif at Riverside	CA	27,204	C+
Univ of Calif at San Diego	CA	21,000	VC
Univ of Calif at Santa Barbara	CA	27,551	VC
Univ of Calif at Santa Cruz	CA	27,807	C+
Univ of Central Arkansas	AR	13,667	VC
Univ of Central Florida	FL	15,668	VC+
Univ of Central Missouri	MO	14,605	C
Univ of Central Okla	OK	12,293	C
Univ of Chicago	IL	55,416	MC
Univ of Cincinnati	OH	21,506	VC
Univ of Colo Boulder	CO	22,605	VC+
Univ of Colo Denver	CO	17,904	C
Univ of Conn	CT	24,706	HC
Univ of Dayton	OH	49,070	VC
Univ of Delaware	DE	23,612	VC
Univ of Denver	CO	51,787	VC+
Univ of Evansville	IN	42,656	VC+
Univ of Florida	FL	15,943	HC
Univ of Georgia	GA	20,082	VC
Univ of Hartford	CT	42,674	C
Univ of Hawaii at Hilo	HI	23,066	C
Univ of Hawaii at Manoa	HI	19,379	C
Univ of Idaho	ID	14,558	C
Univ of Illinois at Chicago	IL	24,505	VC
Univ of Illinois at Urbana-Champaign	IL	26,450	HC
Univ of Indianapolis	IN	31,740	LC
Univ of Iowa	IA	17,693	VC
Univ of Jamestown	ND	24,738	C
Univ of Kansas	KS	17,603	C+
Univ of Kentucky	KY	19,868	C
Univ of La Verne	CA	47,010	C
Univ of Louisiana at Lafayette	LA	6,130	C
Univ of Louisiana at Monroe	LA	12,998	C
Univ of Louisville	KY	17,946	C
Univ of Maine	ME	19,902	C
Univ of Mary	ND	16,714	C
Univ of Mary Hardin-Baylor	TX	31,950	C+
Univ of Mary Washington	VA	19,484	VC
Univ of Maryland - College Park	MD	20,060	HC

ST = STATE $IS = IN-STATE COSTS   SR = SELECTOR RATING

School	ST	$IS	SR
Univ of Maryland/Baltimore County	MD	18,000	VC
Univ of Mass Amherst	MA	24,215	VC+
Univ of Mass Boston	MA	23,066	VC
Univ of Mass Dartmouth	MA	22,223	C
Univ of Miami	FL	57,034	MC
Univ of Mich/Ann Arbor	MI	22,102	MC
Univ of Mich-Flint	MI	17,547	C+
Univ of Minn/Duluth	MN	19,806	C
Univ of Minn/Morris	MN	17,150	VC
Univ of Minn/Twin Cities	MN		HC
Univ of Miss	MS	16,704	C+
Univ of Missouri/Columbia	MO	18,201	MC
Univ of Missouri-Kansas City	MO	19,603	C
Univ of Missouri-St. Louis	MO		VC
Univ of Mobile	AL	28,935	VC
Univ of Montana	MT	14,105	C
Univ of Montana-Western	MT	9,753	LC
Univ of Montevallo	AL	17,060	C
Univ of Mount Olive	NC	18,426	C
Univ of Mount Union	OH	35,130	C
Univ of Nebr - Lincoln	NE	18,031	VC
Univ of Nebr at Kearney	NE	14,855	LC
Univ of Nebr at Omaha	NE	12,700	C
Univ of Nevada, Las Vegas	NV	17,303	C
Univ of Nevada/Reno	NV	17,507	C
Univ of New Hampshire	NH	26,912	C
Univ of New Haven	CT	48,940	C
Univ of New Mexico	NM	15,300	C
Univ of New Orleans	LA	9,224	C
Univ of North Alabama	AL	9,960	C
Univ of N Car at Asheville	NC	13,500	VC
Univ of N Car at Chapel Hill	NC	18,928	MC
Univ of N Car at Charlotte	NC	15,547	C
Univ of N Car at Wilmington	NC	13,572	VC
Univ of N Car School of the Arts	NC	7,401	SP
Univ of N Dak	ND	14,551	C
Univ of North Florida	FL	15,870	VC
Univ of North Georgia	GA	8,500	C
Univ of North Texas	TX	15,628	C
Univ of Northern Colo	CO	18,446	C
Univ of Northern Iowa	IA	15,795	C
Univ of Notre Dame	IN	57,117	MC
Univ of Oregon	OR	21,360	C+
Univ of Pennsylvania	PA	61,132	MC
Univ of Pittsburgh at Pittsburgh	PA	28,572	HC+
Univ of Portland	OR	49,964	VC
Univ of PR Recinto de Rio Piedras	PR	5,750	
Univ of Puget Sound	WA	54,608	HC
Univ of Redlands	CA	40,500	C
Univ of Rio Grande	OH	8,750	NC
Univ of Rochester	NY	60,668	MC
Univ of San Diego	CA	54,818	HC+
Univ of Science and Arts of Okla	OK	10,560	VC
Univ of Sioux Falls	SD	22,990	C
Univ of South Alabama	AL	13,510	C
Univ of S Car at Columbia	SC	19,725	VC+
Univ of S Dak	SD	15,111	C
Univ of South Florida/Tampa	FL	13,000	C
Univ of Southern Calif	CA	56,903	MC
Univ of Southern Maine	ME	16,576	C
Univ of Southern Miss	MS	13,170	C
Univ of St. Francis	IL	37,560	C
Univ of St. Thomas - Houston	TX	37,690	C
Univ of Tampa	FL	35,160	VC
Univ of Tenn at Knoxville	TN	20,364	VC+
Univ of Tenn at Martin	TN	13,734	C
Univ of Texas - Pan American	TX	11,125	LC
Univ of Texas at Arlington	TX	10,908	LC
Univ of Texas at Austin	TX	44,074	HC
Univ of Texas at El Paso	TX	8,764	NC
Univ of Texas at San Antonio	TX	18,372	C
Univ of the Cumberlands	KY	27,500	C
Univ of the District of Columbia	DC	7,244	LC
Univ of the Incarnate Word	TX	37,316	LC
Univ of the Ozarks	AR	31,440	C
Univ of the Pacific	CA	52,146	VC
Univ of Toledo	OH	18,464	C
Univ of Tulsa	OK	46,331	MC
Univ of Vermont	VT	27,006	VC+
Univ of Virginia	VA	23,050	MC
Univ of West Florida	FL	14,656	C
Univ of Wisc Whitewater	WI	13,314	C
Univ of Wisc/Eau Claire	WI	15,730	VC
Univ of Wisc/Green Bay	WI	19,074	C
Univ of Wisc/La Crosse	WI	9,304	VC
Univ of Wisc/Madison	WI	18,757	HC+
Univ of Wisc/Oshkosh	WI	10,426	VC
Univ of Wisc/Parkside	WI	10,181	LC
Univ of Wisc/Platteville	WI	14,564	C
Univ of Wisc/River Falls	WI	9,722	LC
Univ of Wisc/Stevens Point	WI	14,043	C
Univ of Wisc/Superior	WI	14,314	C
Univ of Wisc-Milwaukee	WI	18,436	C
Univ of Wyoming	WY	14,401	C+
Utah State Univ	UT	12,044	C
Valley City State Univ	ND	12,286	LC
Valparaiso Univ	IN	44,940	VC+
Vanguard Univ of Southern Calif	CA	35,833	VC
Vassar College	NY	61,140	MC
Virginia Commonwealth Univ	VA	21,716	C
Virginia Polytechnic Inst and State Univ	VA	14,629	HC
Virginia Union Univ	VA	18,432	C
Virginia Wesleyan College	VA	28,433	LC
Wabash College	IN	46,850	C+
Wagner College	NY	48,600	C
Wake Forest Univ	NC	58,838	MC
Walla Walla Univ	WA	26,256	NC
Warner Pacific College	OR	25,550	C
Wartburg College	IA	41,055	VC
Washburn Univ	KS	12,579	C
Washington Adventist Univ	MD	25,859	LC
Washington and Jefferson College	PA	51,948	VC
Washington and Lee Univ	VA	52,812	MC
Washington College	MD	52,602	VC
Washington State Univ	WA	20,461	C
Washington Univ in St. Louis	MO	69,844	MC
Wayland Baptist Univ	TX	18,912	LC
Wayne State College	NE	11,764	NC
Wayne State Univ	MI	22,063	C
Webster Univ	MO	35,100	C+
Wellesley College	MA	59,038	MC
Wells College	NY	49,400	VC
Wesley College	DE	31,115	LC
Wesleyan College	GA	24,000	C
Wesleyan Univ	CT	61,198	MC
West Chester Univ of Pennsylvania	PA	17,186	C
West Liberty Univ	WV	9,142	LC
West Texas A&M Univ	TX	13,478	C
West Virginia Univ	WV	16,542	C+
West Virginia Wesleyan College	WV	26,880	C
Western Carolina Univ	NC	13,965	C
Western Conn State Univ	CT	18,327	LC
Western Illinois Univ	IL	20,732	C
Western Kentucky Univ	KY	11,000	LC
Western Mich Univ	MI	19,628	C
Western New Mexico Univ	NM	8,500	LC
Western Oregon Univ	OR	15,021	C
Western State Colo Univ	CO	16,924	C
Western Washington Univ	WA	18,519	VC
Westfield State Univ	MA	18,297	C
Westminster Choir College	NJ	36,000	SP
Westminster College	PA	31,290	C+
Westminster College	UT	37,708	C+
Westmont College	CA	41,500	NC
Wheaton College	IL	40,720	MC
Wheaton College	MA	54,934	HC+
Whitman College	WA	55,988	MC
Whittier College	CA	43,416	C
Whitworth Univ	WA	47,734	VC
Wichita State Univ	KS	14,607	C+
Wilberforce Univ	OH	15,100	LC
Wiley College	TX		LC
Willamette Univ	OR	56,450	VC+
William Carey Univ	MS	13,500	LC
William Jewell College	MO	31,000	VC+
William Paterson Univ of New Jersey	NJ	21,694	C
Williams Baptist College	AR	20,070	C
Williams College	MA	61,070	MC
Wilmington College	OH	29,784	C
Wingate Univ	NC	34,990	C
Winona State Univ	MN	16,640	C
Winthrop Univ	SC	21,120	C
Wisc Lutheran College	WI	23,510	VC
Wittenberg Univ	OH	47,962	C+
Wright State Univ	OH	16,983	C
Xavier Univ	OH	44,980	VC
Xavier Univ of Louisiana	LA	25,300	C
Yale Univ	CT	55,300	MC
Yeshiva Univ	NY	47,250	VC+
York College / The CUNY	NY	5,496	VC
York College of Pennsylvania	PA	26,590	C
Youngstown State Univ	OH	16,732	C

MUSIC BUSINESS MANAGEMENT

School	ST	$IS	SR
Albright College	PA	46,660	C
Anderson Univ	IN	36,100	C
Appalachian State Univ	NC	12,919	VC
Aquinas College	MI	33,060	C
Belmont Univ	TN	39,190	VC+
Berklee College of Music	MA	47,100	SP
Berry College	GA	39,254	VC
Bethel Univ	TN	19,186	C
Bradley Univ	IL	31,874	VC
Central Washington Univ	WA	11,730	C
College of the Ozarks	MO		VC
Columbia College Chicago	IL	30,940	LC
Concordia Univ St. Paul	MN	28,250	C
Dallas Baptist Univ	TX	30,580	VC
Delta State Univ	MS	12,292	LC
DePaul Univ	IL	47,623	VC
DePauw Univ	IN	48,950	VC+
Dillard Univ	LA	20,940	VC
Drake Univ	IA	41,516	VC+
Elmhurst College	IL	43,336	C
Five Towns College	NY	34,550	C

Continued:

School	ST	$IS	SR
Florida Southern College	FL	40,150	C+
Geneva College	PA	27,280	C
Georgia State Univ	GA	15,582	VC
Greenville College	IL	27,012	C
Grove City College	PA	24,022	VC
Hardin-Simmons Univ	TX	23,560	C+
Hofstra Univ	NY	51,810	VC+
Howard Univ	DC	13,646	C
Huntington Univ	IN	32,220	C+
Johnson C. Smith Univ	NC	25,336	LC
Johnson State College	VT	16,721	C
Kentucky Christian Univ	KY	17,622	LC
Kentucky Wesleyan College	KY	27,440	C
Lebanon Valley College	PA	38,570	C
Lee Univ	TN	18,690	C+
Lewis Univ	IL	23,050	C
Loyola Univ New Orleans	LA	46,581	VC
Lubbock Christian Univ	TX	26,308	C
Mansfield Univ	PA	19,468	LC
Marian Univ	WI	32,420	LC
Marywood Univ	PA	45,595	C
McKendree Univ	IL	29,920	C+
Messiah College	PA	40,690	C+
Middle Tenn State Univ	TN	8,650	C
Millikin Univ	IL	38,940	C
Minn State Univ, Mankato	MN	15,616	C
Monmouth Univ	NJ	44,108	C
Montreat College	NC	31,298	C
Murray State Univ	KY	15,304	C
Nazareth College of Rochester	NY	43,028	C+
New York Univ	NY	61,470	MC
Northwest Univ	WA	18,854	C
Northwestern State Univ of Louisiana	LA	14,368	C
Oakwood Univ	AL	25,529	NC
Ohio Northern Univ	OH	42,075	VC
Old Dominion Univ	VA	19,483	LC
Peru State College	NE	8,600	NC
St. Augustine's Univ	NC	14,000	C
St. Joseph's College	IN	36,500	C
S Car State Univ	SC	6,700	LC
Southern Illinois Univ Edwardsville	IL	17,532	C
Southern Nazarene Univ	OK	24,354	C
Southern Oregon Univ	OR	17,874	C
SUNY Oneonta / SUNY	NY	16,919	C+
The SUNY at Potsdam	NY	18,473	C
The Univ of Memphis	TN	15,094	C
Tiffin Univ	OH	30,273	LC
Trevecca Nazarene Univ	TN	31,186	C
Univ of Evansville	IN	42,656	VC+
Univ of Hartford	CT	42,674	C
Univ of Miami	FL	57,034	MC
Univ of New Haven	CT	48,940	C
Univ of the Incarnate Word	TX	37,316	LC
Univ of the Pacific	CA	52,146	VC
Winston-Salem State Univ	NC	9,418	LC

MUSIC COMPOSITION

School	ST	$IS	SR
Baldwin Wallace Univ	OH	38,318	C
Biola Univ	CA	40,320	C+
Cairn Univ	PA	33,270	C
Cedarville Univ	OH	32,860	VC
Keene State College	NH	23,232	LC
Kent State Univ	OH	19,920	C
Lipscomb Univ	TN	37,490	VC
Murray State Univ	KY	15,304	C
New York Univ	NY	61,470	MC
Northern Kentucky Univ	KY	21,134	C
Oberlin College	OH	61,788	MC
Ohio Univ	OH	21,080	C
Okla City Univ	OK	40,476	VC
Ouachita Baptist Univ	AR	30,220	VC
San Francisco Conservatory of Music	CA	56,428	SP
Southern Oregon Univ	OR	17,874	C
Stetson Univ	FL	51,516	VC
Temple Univ	PA	24,392	VC
Tulane Univ	LA	60,861	MC
Univ of Georgia	GA	20,082	VC
Univ of Miami	FL	57,034	MC
Univ of West Georgia	GA	15,488	LC
Youngstown State Univ	OH	16,732	C

MUSIC EDUCATION

School	ST	$IS	SR
Abilene Christian Univ	TX	38,400	C+
Adams State Univ	CO	13,358	LC
Alabama A&M Univ	AL	10,084	C
Alabama State Univ	AL	14,142	NC
Albany State Univ	GA	8,500	C
Albion College	MI	46,010	C
Alderson Broaddus Univ	WV	28,656	C
Anderson Univ	IN	36,100	C
Andrews Univ	MI	28,030	C+
Anna Maria College	MA	34,600	C
Appalachian State Univ	NC	12,919	VC
Aquinas College	MI	33,060	C
Arcadia Univ	PA	33,570	C+
Arizona State Univ, at the Tempe Campus	AZ	20,137	C+
Arkansas Tech Univ	AR	13,982	LC
Armstrong State Univ	GA	15,532	C
Asbury Univ	KY	32,038	VC

Continued:

School	ST	$IS	SR
Ashland Univ	OH	25,000	C
Atlantic Union College	MA	24,600	C
Auburn Univ	AL	22,378	VC+
Augsburg College	MN	35,142	C
Augustana College	IL	43,398	VC
Augustana College	SD	36,500	C
Azusa Pacific Univ	CA	42,086	C
Baker Univ	KS	33,350	C+
Baldwin Wallace Univ	OH	38,318	C
Baylor Univ	TX	50,329	HC
Benedictine College	KS	29,180	VC
Bennett College for Women	NC	21,970	LC
Berklee College of Music	MA	47,100	SP
Berry College	GA	39,254	VC
Bethany College	KS	30,605	NC
Bethel College	IN	31,560	C
Bethel College	MN	34,940	VC
Bethel Univ	TN	19,186	C
Bethune-Cookman Univ	FL	22,958	C
Biola Univ	CA	40,320	C+
Birmingham-Southern College	AL	44,168	VC+
Blue Mountain College	MS	15,634	LC
Bluffton Univ	OH	38,948	C
Boise State Univ	ID	13,469	LC
Boston Conservatory	MA	56,380	VC
Boston Univ	MA	60,694	MC
Bowling Green State Univ	OH	18,970	C
Bradley Univ	IL	31,874	VC
Brenau Univ - Women's College	GA	26,650	LC
Bridgewater State Univ	MA	18,752	C
Brigham Young Univ	UT	12,100	HC
Bucknell Univ	PA	60,140	MC
Buena Vista Univ	IA	39,188	C
Butler Univ	IN	47,572	VC+
Cairn Univ	PA	33,270	C
Calif Baptist Univ	CA	38,792	C
Cal State, Fresno	CA	17,405	C
Cal State, Fullerton	CA	25,188	C
Cal State, San Bernardino	CA	22,000	C
Calvin College	MI	39,120	VC
Cameron Univ	OK	10,004	LC
Campbellsville Univ	KY	27,720	C
Carnegie Mellon Univ	PA	51,260	MC
Carroll Univ	WI	38,100	C
Carson-Newman Univ	TN	29,058	C+
Carthage College	WI	33,000	C
Case Western Reserve Univ	OH	56,534	MC
Castleton State College	VT	20,186	C
Catawba College	NC	37,240	LC
Cedarville Univ	OH	32,860	VC
Central College	IA	42,104	C+
Central Conn State Univ	CT	19,749	C
Central Methodist Univ	MO	28,240	VC
Central State Univ	OH	9,010	C
Central Washington Univ	WA	11,730	C
Chapman Univ	CA	58,347	VC+
Charleston Southern Univ	SC	22,420	C
Chestnut Hill College	PA	42,110	C
Chicago State Univ	IL	5,482	C
CUNY/Brooklyn College	NY	5,884	VC
Chaflin Univ	SC	22,368	LC
Clarion Univ of Pennsylvania	PA	17,370	LC
Clarke Univ	IA	37,600	C
Clearwater Christian College	FL	23,720	C
Cleveland Inst of Music	OH	56,882	SP
Coe College	IA	45,550	VC
Coker College	SC	32,256	LC
College of New Jersey	NJ	25,376	HC
College of the Ozarks	MO		VC
Colo Christian Univ	CO	27,500	VC
Colo State Univ-Fort Collins	CO	20,385	VC
Colo State Univ-Pueblo	CO	16,183	C
Columbia College	SC	27,882	C
Columbus State Univ	GA	13,176	C
Concord Univ	WV	13,102	C
Concordia College - Moorhead	MN	39,974	VC
Concordia College - New York	NY	39,035	LC
Concordia Univ Nebr	NE	26,000	VC
Concordia Univ St. Paul	MN	28,250	C
Concordia Univ, River Forest	IL	26,300	C
Converse College	SC	37,130	C
Corban Univ	OR	37,380	C+
Cornell College	IA	44,930	VC
Cornerstone Univ and Grand Rapids Theological Seminary	MI	33,338	VC
Culver-Stockton College	MO	30,900	C
Cumberland Univ	TN	21,220	C
Delaware State Univ	DE	16,722	LC
Delta State Univ	MS	12,292	LC
DePaul Univ	IL	47,623	VC
DePauw Univ	IN	48,950	VC+
Dickinson State Univ	ND	11,900	NC
Dordt College	IA	34,160	C
Dowling College	NY	25,000	VC
Drake Univ	IA	41,516	VC+
Drury Univ	MO	31,909	VC
Duquesne Univ	PA	43,720	VC
East Carolina Univ	NC	14,169	C
East Central Univ	OK	10,223	VC
East Texas Baptist Univ	TX	31,577	LC
Eastern Kentucky Univ	KY	11,161	C

School	ST	$IS	SR
Eastern Mich Univ	MI	18,604	C
Eastern Nazarene College	MA	30,000	C
Eastern New Mexico Univ	NM	10,682	C
Eastern Washington Univ	WA		C
Eastman School of Music	NY	58,802	SP
Edinboro Univ of Pennsylvania	PA	15,940	LC
Elizabethtown College	PA	49,740	VC
Elmhurst College	IL	43,336	C
Elon Univ	NC	41,914	VC+
Emporia State Univ	KS	12,897	C
Eureka College	IL	19,280	C
Evangel Univ	MO	23,090	C
Fairmont State Univ	WV	12,098	LC
Faulkner Univ	AL	25,720	C
Fayetteville State Univ	NC	10,816	C
Fisk Univ	TN	19,830	C
Five Towns College	NY	34,550	C
Florida A&M Univ	FL	14,935	LC
Florida Gulf Coast Univ	FL		C
Florida Southern College	FL	40,150	C+
Florida State Univ	FL	16,715	VC
Fort Hays State Univ	KS	11,354	C
Freed-Hardeman Univ	TN	19,697	VC
Fresno Pacific Univ	CA	32,136	C
Friends Univ	KS	29,100	C
Furman Univ	SC	54,006	HC
Gardner-Webb Univ	NC	34,375	C+
Geneva College	PA	27,280	C
George Fox Univ	OR	40,750	C+
Georgia College and State Univ	GA	18,900	C+
Georgia Regents Univ	GA		C
Gettysburg College	PA	58,820	HC
Glenville State College	WV	11,348	NC
Gonzaga Univ	WA	46,441	HC
Gordon College	MA	44,320	VC
Goshen College	IN	35,900	VC
Grace College and Seminary	IN	28,800	C
Graceland Univ	IA	28,020	C
Grand Canyon Univ	AZ	24,540	VC
Grand Valley State Univ	MI	17,998	C+
Grand View Univ	IA	31,050	C
Greensboro College	NC	28,740	LC
Greenville College	IL	27,012	C
Grove City College	PA	24,022	VC
Gustavus Adolphus College	MN	48,170	HC
Hamline Univ	MN	45,678	VC
Harding Univ	AR	23,556	C
Hardin-Simmons Univ	TX	23,560	C+
Hartwick College	NY	51,270	C
Hastings College	NE	27,782	C+
Heidelberg Univ	OH	34,100	C
Henderson State Univ	AR	14,584	C
Hofstra Univ	NY	51,810	VC+
Hope College	MI	38,650	VC
Houghton College	NY	36,808	C+
Houston Baptist Univ	TX	36,450	C
Howard Univ	DC	13,646	VC
Humboldt State Univ	CA	18,400	C
Hunter College	NY	14,429	VC
Huntingdon College	AL	33,100	C
Huntington Univ	IN	32,220	C+
Idaho State Univ	ID	12,307	C
Illinois State Univ	IL	23,110	VC
Illinois Wesleyan Univ	IL	48,452	HC
Immaculata Univ	PA	43,000	C
Indiana State Univ	IN	16,000	C
Indiana Univ Bloomington	IN	19,801	VC
Indiana Univ of Pennsylvania	PA	20,846	LC
Indiana Univ South Bend	IN	15,501	C
Indiana Univ-Purdue Univ Fort Wayne	IN	15,521	C
Indiana Wesleyan Univ	IN	31,815	VC
Inter-American Univ of PR/ Fajardo Campus	PR	4,200	
Inter-American Univ of PR/ Ponce	PR		
Inter-American Univ of PR/ San Germán	PR	6,720	
Iowa State Univ	IA	16,403	C
Iowa Wesleyan College	IA	30,850	LC
Ithaca College	NY	53,864	HC
Jackson State Univ	MS	13,512	LC
Jacksonville State Univ	AL	12,480	LC
Jacksonville Univ	FL	37,780	C
John Brown Univ	AR	32,056	VC+
Johnson State College	VT	16,721	C
Judson College	AL	26,794	C
Judson Univ	IL	25,130	C
Kansas State Univ	KS	15,497	VC
Kansas Wesleyan Univ	KS	32,000	C
Kean Univ	NJ	23,444	C
Keene State College	NH	23,232	LC
Kennesaw State Univ	GA		C
Kent State Univ	OH	19,920	C
Kentucky Christian Univ	KY	17,622	LC
Kentucky State Univ	KY	11,000	LC
Kentucky Wesleyan College	KY	27,440	C
King Univ	TN	33,140	C
La Sierra Univ	CA	35,694	VC
Lake Forest College	IL	50,652	VC
Lakeland College	WI	22,990	C
Lamar Univ	TX	6,820	LC
Lander Univ	SC	22,514	C+
Lawrence Univ	WI	46,371	HC
Lebanon Valley College	PA	38,570	C
Lee Univ	TN	18,690	C+
Lenoir-Rhyne College	NC	35,984	C
Limestone College	SC	30,800	C
Lincoln Univ	MO	12,904	NC
Lindenwood Univ	MO	20,750	C
Lindsey Wilson College	KY	31,220	C
Linfield College-McMinnville Campus	OR	47,676	C
Lipscomb Univ	TN	37,490	VC
LIU Brooklyn	NY	47,182	LC
LIU Post	NY	47,660	C
Livingstone College	NC	17,815	LC
Longwood Univ	VA	20,924	C
Louisiana College	LA	15,746	C
Louisiana State Univ	LA	18,677	C+
Louisiana Tech Univ	LA	11,302	C
Loyola Univ New Orleans	LA	46,581	VC
Lubbock Christian Univ	TX	26,308	C
MacMurray College	IL	20,755	C
Madonna Univ	MI	24,540	VC
Malone Univ	OH	35,364	C
Mansfield Univ	PA	19,468	LC
Marian Univ	WI	32,420	LC
Marietta College	OH	42,135	C+
Mars Hill Univ	NC	22,950	LC
Marshall Univ	WV	14,820	C
Maryville College	TN	33,150	C+
Marywood Univ	PA	45,595	C
McKendree Univ	IL	29,920	C+
Mercer Univ	GA	44,201	VC
Mercyhurst Univ	PA	40,700	C
Meredith College	NC	31,420	C
Messiah College	PA	40,690	VC
Methodist Univ	NC	37,185	C
Metropolitan State Univ of Denver	CO	4,835	LC
Miami Univ	OH	24,191	VC
Mich State Univ	MI	22,450	VC
MidAmerica Nazarene Univ	KS	28,000	C
Midland Univ	NE	34,000	C
Midwestern State Univ	TX	9,722	C
Millersville Univ of Pennsylvania	PA	21,648	C
Milligan College	TN	27,510	C
Millikin Univ	IL	38,940	C
Minn State Univ, Mankato	MN	15,616	C
Minn State Univ, Moorhead	MN	13,392	VC
Minot State Univ	ND	10,915	C
Miss College	MS	21,998	C
Miss State Univ	MS	14,750	C
Miss Univ for Women	MS	7,400	C
Miss Valley State Univ	MS	9,706	LC
Missouri Baptist Univ	MO	31,830	C
Missouri Western State Univ	MO	12,260	NC
Molloy College	NY	40,440	C
Monmouth Univ	NJ	44,108	C
Montana State Univ	MT	14,068	C
Montana State Univ-Billings	MT	12,425	LC
Montclair State Univ	NJ	22,614	C
Moravian College	PA	36,381	VC
Morningside College	IA	35,430	C
Mount Vernon Nazarene Univ	OH	29,590	C
Muskingum Univ	OH	30,502	C
Nazareth College of Rochester	NY	43,028	C+
Nebr Wesleyan Univ	NE	29,774	C+
New Jersey City Univ	NJ	21,456	LC
New Mexico State Univ	NM	14,050	C
New York Univ	NY	61,470	MC
Newberry College	SC	26,850	LC
Nicholls State Univ	LA	7,095	C
Norfolk State Univ	VA	10,531	LC
N Car Agricultural and Technical State Univ	NC	13,365	LC
North Central College	IL	38,343	VC
N Dak State Univ	ND		C
Northeastern Illinois Univ	IL	10,318	LC
Northeastern State Univ	OK	8,615	VC
Northern Arizona Univ	AZ	19,010	C
Northern Illinois Univ	IL	19,768	C
Northern Kentucky Univ	KY	21,134	C
Northern Mich Univ	MI	18,278	C
Northern State Univ - Aberdeen	SD	14,505	C
Northland College	WI	26,680	C
Northwest Missouri State Univ	MO	17,347	C
Northwest Nazarene Univ	ID	34,000	C
Northwestern College	MN	24,000	C
Northwestern College of Iowa	IA	36,240	VC
Northwestern Okla State Univ	OK	7,275	NC
Northwestern State Univ of Louisiana	LA	14,368	C
Northwestern Univ	IL	61,640	MC
Notre Dame of Maryland Univ	MD	27,700	VC
Nyack College	NY	33,250	C
Oakland City Univ	IN	24,500	NC
Oakland Univ	MI	19,391	C
Oakwood Univ	AL	25,529	NC
Oberlin College	OH	61,788	MC
Ohio Northern Univ	OH	42,075	VC
Ohio Univ	OH	21,080	C
Ohio Wesleyan Univ	OH	49,460	C+
Okla Baptist Univ	OK	28,202	C
Okla Christian Univ	OK	25,870	VC
Okla City Univ	OK	40,476	VC
Okla State Univ	OK	14,310	VC
Okla Wesleyan Univ	OK	21,300	C
Old Dominion Univ	VA	19,483	LC
Olivet Nazarene Univ	IL	29,990	C
Oral Roberts Univ	OK	31,734	C
Otterbein College	OH	32,214	C
Ouachita Baptist Univ	AR	30,220	C
Pacific Lutheran Univ	WA	46,760	C+
Palm Beach Atlantic Univ	FL	34,874	C+
Peru State College	NE	8,600	NC
Piedmont College	GA	30,136	C
Pittsburg State Univ	KS	12,032	C
Plymouth State Univ	NH	23,148	LC
Point Loma Nazarene Univ	CA	41,006	C+
Pontifical Catholic Univ of PR	PR	7,310	
Presbyterian College	SC	42,678	C+
Prescott College	AZ	33,284	C
Providence College	RI	57,383	VC
Queens College/The CUNY	NY	17,107	VC
Quincy Univ	IL	34,980	LC
Rhode Island College	RI	17,694	LC
Rider Univ	NJ	45,720	C
Roberts Wesleyan College	NY	38,306	C+
Rocky Mountain College	MT	32,242	C
Roosevelt Univ	IL	22,605	VC
Rowan Univ	NJ	24,022	VC+
Saginaw Valley State Univ	MI	17,369	C
St. Augustine's Univ	NC	14,000	C
St. Mary's Univ of Minn	MN	38,280	C
St. Xavier Univ	IL	32,840	C
San Diego State Univ	CA	21,611	C+
San Jose State Univ	CA	19,133	LC
Schreiner Univ	TX	32,734	LC
Seattle Pacific Univ	WA	41,559	VC+
Seton Hill Univ	PA	35,172	C
Shenandoah Univ	VA	39,916	C
Shepherd Univ	WV	15,875	C
Shorter Univ	GA	30,650	LC
Siena Heights Univ	MI	32,040	C
Silver Lake College	WI	22,600	LC
Simpson College	IA	36,086	C+
Simpson Univ	CA	28,900	C
Slippery Rock Univ of Pennsylvania	PA	10,360	C
S Car State Univ	SC	6,700	LC
S Dak State Univ	SD	14,296	C
Southeast Missouri State Univ	MO	15,370	LC
Southeastern Okla State Univ	OK	7,966	C
Southeastern Univ	FL	27,201	C
Southern Adventist Univ	TN	26,190	C
Southern Arkansas Univ	AR	14,316	C
Southern Illinois Univ Edwardsville	IL	17,532	C
Southern Methodist Univ	TX	60,585	MC
Southern Nazarene Univ	OK	24,354	C
Southern Univ and A&M College	LA	9,761	LC
Southern Univ at New Orleans	LA	2,963	NC
Southern Wesleyan Univ	SC	25,600	C
Southwest Baptist Univ	MO	24,710	C
Southwest Minn State Univ	MN	14,000	C
Southwestern College	KS	29,270	C
Southwestern Okla State Univ	OK	9,160	C
Spring Arbor Univ	MI	26,740	C
St. Ambrose Univ	IA	30,845	C
St. Catherine Univ	MN	37,782	C+
St. Cloud State Univ	MN	10,600	C
St. Norbert College	WI	41,478	VC
St. Olaf College	MN	51,200	HC+
Sterling College	KS	27,216	C
Stetson Univ	FL	51,516	VC
SUNY Fredonia/The SUNY at Fredonia	NY	19,840	VC
Susquehanna Univ	PA	51,150	C
Syracuse Univ	NY	56,346	VC
Tabor College	KS	29,010	C
Talladega College	AL	17,996	C
Taylor Univ	IN	37,821	VC+
Temple Univ	PA	24,392	VC
Tenn Tech Univ	TN	11,310	C
Texas A&M Univ at Commerce	TX	10,496	C
Texas A&M Univ at Kingsville	TX	7,500	LC
The Catholic Univ of America	DC	52,852	VC
The College of St. Rose	NY	26,750	C
Ohio State Univ-Columbus Campus	OH	19,887	HC+
The Pennsylvania State Univ - Univ Park	PA	28,022	VC+
The SUNY at Potsdam	NY	18,473	C
The Univ of N Car at Greensboro	NC	12,848	C
The Univ of Okla	OK	18,621	VC
The Univ of Tenn at Chattanooga	TN	16,883	C
Toccoa Falls College	GA	23,210	LC
Tougaloo College	MS	15,275	NC
Towson Univ	MD	16,000	VC
Trevecca Nazarene Univ	TN	31,186	C
Trinity Christian College	IL	28,869	C
Troy Univ	AL	10,650	C
Union College	NE	23,270	C
Union Univ	TN	28,260	VC
Universidad Adventista de las Antillas	PR	7,360	
Univ of Akron	OH	20,436	C
Univ of Alabama at Tuscaloosa	AL	17,164	C+
Univ of Alaska Anchorage	AK	16,673	NC
Univ of Arizona	AZ	20,657	C
Univ of Arkansas at Fayetteville	AR	18,352	C+
Univ of Arkansas at Monticello	AR	12,076	NC
Univ of Arkansas at Pine Bluff	AR	13,378	C
Univ of Central Arkansas	AR	13,667	VC
Univ of Central Florida	FL	15,668	VC+
Univ of Central Missouri	MO	14,605	C
Univ of Central Okla	OK	12,293	C
Univ of Cincinnati	OH	21,506	VC
Univ of Colo Boulder	CO	22,605	VC+
Univ of Conn	CT	24,706	NC
Univ of Dayton	OH	49,070	VC
Univ of Delaware	DE	23,612	VC
Univ of Evansville	IN	42,656	VC+
Univ of Florida	FL	15,943	HC
Univ of Georgia	GA	20,082	VC
Univ of Hartford	CT	42,674	C
Univ of Idaho	ID	14,558	C
Univ of Illinois at Urbana- Champaign	IL	26,450	HC
Univ of Indianapolis	IN	31,740	LC
Univ of Iowa	IA	17,693	VC
Univ of Kansas	KS	17,603	C+
Univ of Kentucky	KY	19,868	C
Univ of Louisiana at Lafayette	LA	6,130	C
Univ of Louisiana at Monroe	LA	12,998	C
Univ of Louisville	KY	17,946	C
Univ of Maine	ME	19,902	C+
Univ of Mary	ND	16,714	C
Univ of Mary Hardin-Baylor	TX	31,950	C+
Univ of Maryland - College Park	MD	20,060	HC
Univ of Maryland/Eastern Shore	MD	14,000	VC
Univ of Miami	FL	57,034	MC
Univ of Mich/Ann Arbor	MI	22,102	MC
Univ of Mich-Flint	MI	17,547	C+
Univ of Minn/Duluth	MN	19,806	C
Univ of Minn/Twin Cities	MN		HC
Univ of Missouri/Columbia	MO	18,201	MC
Univ of Missouri-Kansas City	MO	19,603	C
Univ of Missouri-St. Louis	MO		VC
Univ of Montana	MT	14,105	C
Univ of Montana-Western	MT	9,753	LC
Univ of Montevallo	AL	17,060	C
Univ of Mount Union	OH	35,130	C
Univ of Nebr - Lincoln	NE	18,031	VC
Univ of Nebr at Kearney	NE	14,855	LC
Univ of Nevada/Reno	NV	17,507	C
Univ of New Mexico	NM	15,300	C
Univ of New Orleans	LA	9,224	C
Univ of North Alabama	AL	9,960	C
Univ of N Car at Wilmington	NC	13,572	VC
Univ of N Dak	ND	14,551	C
Univ of North Florida	FL	15,870	VC
Univ of North Georgia	GA	8,500	C
Univ of Northern Colo	CO	18,446	C
Univ of Northern Iowa	IA	15,795	C
Univ of Oregon	OR	21,360	C+
Univ of Puget Sound	WA	54,608	HC
Univ of Redlands	CA	40,500	VC
Univ of Rio Grande	OH	8,750	NC
Univ of Rochester	NY	60,668	MC
Univ of Sioux Falls	SD	22,990	C
Univ of S Car Aiken	SC	16,712	C
Univ of S Car at Columbia	SC	19,725	VC+
Univ of S Dak	SD	15,111	C
Univ of South Florida/Tampa	FL	13,000	C
Univ of Southern Maine	ME	16,576	C
Univ of Southern Miss	MS	13,170	C
Univ of St. Francis	IL	37,560	C
Univ of St. Thomas - Houston	TX	37,690	C
Univ of Tampa	FL	35,160	VC
Univ of the Cumberlands	KY	27,500	C
Univ of the Incarnate Word	TX	37,316	LC
Univ of the Pacific	CA	52,146	VC
Univ of Toledo	OH	18,464	C
Univ of Tulsa	OK	46,331	MC
Univ of Vermont	VT	27,006	VC+
Univ of Washington	WA	14,722	VC
Univ of West Florida	FL	14,656	VC
Univ of West Georgia	GA	15,488	LC
Univ of Wisc Whitewater	WI	13,314	C
Univ of Wisc/Green Bay	WI	19,074	C
Univ of Wisc/Madison	WI	18,757	HC+
Univ of Wisc/Oshkosh	WI	10,426	LC
Univ of Wisc/Platteville	WI	14,564	C
Univ of Wisc/River Falls	WI	9,722	LC
Univ of Wisc/Stevens Point	WI	14,043	C
Univ of Wisc/Superior	WI	14,314	C
Univ of Wisc-Milwaukee	WI	18,436	C
Univ of Wyoming	WY	14,401	C+

ST = STATE $IS = IN-STATE COSTS   SR = SELECTOR RATING

School	ST	$IS	SR
Utah State Univ	UT	12,044	C
Valparaiso Univ	IN	44,940	VC+
Vanderbilt Univ	TN	58,220	MC
VanderCook College of Music	IL	26,360	SP
Virginia Union Univ	VA	18,432	C
Viterbo Univ	WI	30,070	C
Walla Walla Univ	WA	26,256	NC
Warner Pacific College	OR	25,550	C
Warner Univ	FL	18,000	C
Wartburg College	IA	41,055	VC
Washburn Univ	KS	12,579	C
Washington Adventist Univ	MD	25,859	LC
Wayland Baptist Univ	TX	18,912	LC
Wayne State College	NE	11,764	NC
Webster Univ	MO	35,100	C+
West Chester Univ of Pennsylvania	PA	17,186	C
West Liberty Univ	WV	9,142	LC
West Texas A&M Univ	TX	13,478	C
West Virginia Wesleyan College	WV	26,880	C
Western Carolina Univ	NC	13,965	C
Western Conn State Univ	CT	18,327	LC
Western Mich Univ	MI	19,628	C
Western State Colo Univ	CO	16,924	C
Western Washington Univ	WA	18,519	VC
Westminster Choir College	NJ	36,000	SP
Westminster College	PA	31,290	C+
Westmont College	CA	41,500	HC
Wheaton College	IL	40,720	MC
Whitworth Univ	WA	47,734	VC
Wichita State Univ	KS	14,607	C+
Wiley College	TX		LC
Willamette Univ	OR	56,450	VC+
William Carey Univ	MS	13,500	LC
William Jewell College	MO	31,000	VC
William Paterson Univ of New Jersey	NJ	21,694	C
Wingate Univ	NC	34,990	C
Winona State Univ	MN	16,640	C
Winston-Salem State Univ	NC	9,418	LC
Winthrop Univ	SC	21,120	C
Wittenberg Univ	OH	47,962	C+
Wright State Univ	OH	16,983	C
Xavier Univ	OH	44,980	VC
Xavier Univ of Louisiana	LA	25,300	C
York College	NE	19,475	C
York College of Pennsylvania	PA	26,590	C
Youngstown State Univ	OH	16,732	C

MUSIC HISTORY AND APPRECIATION

School	ST	$IS	SR
Aquinas College	MI	33,060	C
Baldwin Wallace Univ	OH	38,318	C
Baylor Univ	TX	50,329	HC
Boston Univ	MA	60,694	MC
Bowling Green State Univ	OH	18,970	C
Bucknell Univ	PA	60,140	MC
Cal State, San Bernardino	CA	12,000	C
Calvin College	MI	39,120	VC
Florida State Univ	FL	16,715	VC
Hardin-Simmons Univ	TX	23,560	C+
Hofstra Univ	NY	51,810	VC+
Howard Univ	DC	13,646	C
Johnson State College	VT	16,721	C
Keene State College	NH	23,232	LC
McKendree Univ	IL	29,920	C+
Nazareth College of Rochester	NY	43,028	C+
New England Conservatory of Music	MA	52,550	SP
Oberlin College	OH	61,788	MC
Ohio Univ	OH	21,080	C
Rice Univ	TX	43,288	MC
Roosevelt Univ	IL	22,605	VC
Southern Illinois Univ Edwardsville	IL	17,532	C
Suffolk Univ	MA	47,298	C
Syracuse Univ	NY	56,346	VC
Temple Univ	PA	24,392	VC
The Catholic Univ of America	DC	52,852	VC
Ohio State Univ-Columbus Campus	OH	19,887	HC+
Univ of Akron	OH	20,436	C
Univ of Calif at Los Angeles	CA	25,686	MC
Univ of Calif at San Diego	CA	21,000	VC
Univ of Cincinnati	OH	21,506	VC
Univ of Hartford	CT	42,674	C
Univ of Idaho	ID	14,558	C
Univ of Illinois at Urbana-Champaign	IL	26,450	HC
Univ of Kansas	KS	17,603	C+
Univ of Mich/Ann Arbor	MI	22,102	MC
Univ of Mich/Dearborn	MI	9,885	VC
Univ of North Texas	TX	15,628	C
Univ of the Pacific	CA	52,146	VC
Univ of Washington	WA	14,722	VC
Vanderbilt Univ	TN	58,220	MC
West Chester Univ of Pennsylvania	PA	17,186	C
Western Washington Univ	WA	18,519	VC
Wright State Univ	OH	16,983	C
Youngstown State Univ	OH	16,732	C

MUSIC INDUSTRY

School	ST	$IS	SR
Cal State, Chico	CA	20,158	C
Drexel Univ	PA	61,418	VC+
Ferris State Univ	MI	20,047	C
Mercy College	NY	30,456	C
Minn State Univ, Mankato	MN	15,616	C
Missouri Southern State Univ	MO	12,061	C
Monmouth Univ	NJ	44,108	C
St. Mary's Univ of Minn	MN	38,280	C
Syracuse Univ	NY	56,346	VC
The College of St. Rose	NY	26,750	C

MUSIC MINISTRY

School	ST	$IS	SR
College of the Ozarks	MO		VC
Lipscomb Univ	TN	37,490	VC
Messiah College	PA	40,690	C+
Missouri Baptist Univ	MO	31,830	C

MUSIC PERFORMANCE

School	ST	$IS	SR
Adams State Univ	CO	13,358	LC
Adrian College	MI	42,400	C
Albion College	MI	46,010	C
Anderson Univ	IN	36,100	C
Andrews Univ	MI	28,030	C+
Anna Maria College	MA	34,600	C
Appalachian State Univ	NC	12,919	VC
Aquinas College	MI	33,060	C
Arizona State Univ, at the Tempe Campus	AZ	20,137	C+
Augustana College	IL	43,398	VC
Averett Univ	VA	37,750	C
Baldwin Wallace Univ	OH	38,318	C
Barry Univ	FL	38,190	C
Baylor Univ	TX	50,329	HC
Belmont Univ	TN	39,190	VC+
Bennington College	VT	56,990	HC+
Berklee College of Music	MA	47,100	SP
Bethel College	IN	31,560	C
Bethel Univ	MN	34,940	VC
Binghamton Univ/The SUNY	NY	21,648	HC+
Biola Univ	CA	40,320	VC+
Blackburn College	IL	21,350	C
Boston Conservatory	MA	56,380	VC
Boston Univ	MA	60,694	MC
Bowling Green State Univ	OH	18,970	C
Bradley Univ	IL	31,874	VC
Brenau Univ - Women's College	GA	26,650	LC
Brigham Young Univ	UT	12,100	HC
Bucknell Univ	PA	60,140	MC
Butler Univ	IN	47,572	VC+
Cairn Univ	PA	33,270	C
Calif Baptist Univ	CA	38,792	C
Calif Inst of the Arts	CA	51,902	SP
Calif Lutheran Univ	CA	49,540	C+
Cal State, Fresno	CA	17,405	C
Cal State, Fullerton	CA	25,188	C
Cal State, Los Angeles	CA	17,186	LC
Cal State, San Bernardino	CA	12,000	C
Cal State, Stanislaus	CA	18,582	C
Calvin College	MI	39,120	VC
Campbellsville Univ	KY	27,720	C
Canisius College	NY	44,900	C
Centenary College of Louisiana	LA	45,650	C+
Chapman Univ	CA	58,347	VC+
CUNY/Brooklyn College	NY	5,884	VC+
Clayton State Univ	GA	12,000	C
Colo State Univ-Fort Collins	CO	20,385	VC
Colo State Univ-Pueblo	CO	16,183	C
Columbia College	SC	27,882	C
Columbus State Univ	GA	13,176	C
Concordia College - Moorhead	MN	39,974	VC
Corban Univ	OR	37,380	C+
Cornerstone Univ and Grand Rapids Theological Seminary	MI	33,338	C
Covenant College	GA	38,990	VC+
Dallas Baptist Univ	TX	30,580	VC
DePaul Univ	IL	47,623	VC
DePauw Univ	IN	48,950	VC+
Dillard Univ	LA	20,940	VC
Dordt College	IA	34,160	C+
Drake Univ	IA	41,516	VC+
Duquesne Univ	PA	43,720	VC
East Carolina Univ	NC	14,169	C
East Texas Baptist Univ	TX	31,577	LC
Eastern Mich Univ	MI	18,604	C
Eastern Nazarene College	MA	30,000	C
Eastern Washington Univ	WA		C
Eastman School of Music	NY	58,802	SP
Elmhurst College	IL	43,336	C
Elon Univ	NC	41,914	VC+
Emory and Henry College	VA	387,460	VC
Evangel Univ	MO	23,090	C
Five Towns College	NY	34,550	C
Florida Southern College	FL	40,150	C+
Florida State Univ	FL	16,715	VC
Fort Hays State Univ	KS	11,354	C
Friends Univ	KS	29,100	C
Furman Univ	SC	54,006	HC
George Washington Univ	DC	57,108	MC
Georgia Regents Univ	GA		C
Gordon College	MA	44,320	VC
Grand Canyon Univ	AZ	24,540	VC
Grove City College	PA	24,022	VC
Hamline Univ	MN	45,678	VC
Hannibal-LaGrange Univ	MO	24,490	C
Hardin-Simmons Univ	TX	23,560	C+
Hofstra Univ	NY	51,810	VC+
Hope College	MI	38,650	VC
Houghton College	NY	36,808	C+
Houston Baptist Univ	TX	36,450	C
Huntington Univ	IN	32,220	C+
Idaho State Univ	ID	12,307	C
Illinois State Univ	IL	23,110	VC
Illinois Wesleyan Univ	IL	48,452	HC
Indiana Univ Bloomington	IN	19,801	VC
Indiana Univ of Pennsylvania	PA	20,846	LC
Indiana Univ-Purdue Univ Fort Wayne	IN	15,521	C
Inter-American Univ of PR/ Metropolitan Campus	PR	4,320	
Ithaca College	NY	53,864	HC
Jacksonville Univ	FL	37,780	C
Johnson State College	VT	16,721	C
Kean Univ	NJ	23,444	C
Keene State College	NH	23,232	LC
Kennesaw State Univ	GA		C
Kentucky Christian Univ	KY	17,622	LC
Kentucky State Univ	KY	11,000	C
La Sierra Univ	CA	35,694	VC
Lawrence Univ	WI	46,371	HC
Lee Univ	TN	18,690	C+
Lenoir-Rhyne College	NC	35,984	C
Lipscomb Univ	TN	37,490	VC
LIU Brooklyn	NY	47,182	LC
LIU Post	NY	47,660	C
Louisiana Tech Univ	LA	11,302	C
Loyola Univ New Orleans	LA	46,581	VC
Lynn Univ	FL	43,500	LC
Manhattan School of Music	NY	55,850	SP
Mannes College New School for Music	NY	44,500	SP
Mansfield Univ	PA	19,468	LC
Mars Hill Univ	NC	22,950	LC
Marshall Univ	WV	14,820	C
Maryville College	TN	33,150	C+
Marywood Univ	PA	45,595	C
Meredith College	NC	31,420	C
Messiah College	PA	40,690	C+
Methodist Univ	NC	37,185	C
Metropolitan State Univ of Denver	CO	4,835	LC
Miami Univ	OH	24,191	VC
Mich State Univ	MI	22,450	VC
MidAmerica Nazarene Univ	KS	28,000	C
Millikin Univ	IL	38,940	C
Missouri Baptist Univ	MO	31,830	C
Montana State Univ-Billings	MT	12,425	LC
Montclair State Univ	NJ	22,614	C
Murray State Univ	KY	15,304	C
Nazareth College of Rochester	NY	43,028	C+
New England Conservatory of Music	MA	52,550	SP
New Mexico State Univ	NM	14,050	C
New York Univ	NY	61,470	MC
Newberry College	SC	26,850	C
Northern Arizona Univ	AZ	19,010	C
Northern Kentucky Univ	KY	21,134	C
Northwestern College	MN	24,000	C
Northwestern Univ	IL	61,640	MC
Nyack College	NY	33,250	C
Oakwood Univ	AL	25,529	NC
Oberlin College	OH	61,788	MC
Ohio Northern Univ	OH	42,075	VC
Ohio Univ	OH	21,080	C
Old Dominion Univ	VA	19,483	LC
Olivet Nazarene Univ	IL	29,990	C
Oral Roberts Univ	OK	31,734	C
Otterbein College	OH	32,214	C
Pacific Lutheran Univ	WA	46,760	C+
Palm Beach Atlantic Univ	FL	34,874	C+
Pittsburg State Univ	KS	12,032	C
Point Loma Nazarene Univ	CA	41,006	C+
Queens College/The CUNY	NY	17,107	VC
Rhode Island College	RI	17,694	LC
Rice Univ	TX	43,288	MC
Roberts Wesleyan College	NY	38,306	C+
Rockford College	IL	31,000	C
Rocky Mountain College	MT	32,242	C
Rollins College	FL	52,370	HC
Roosevelt Univ	IL	22,605	VC
St. Mary's Univ of Minn	MN	38,280	C
St. Vincent College	PA	40,244	C
Sam Houston State Univ	TX	17,082	C
Samford Univ	AL	37,060	C+
San Diego State Univ	CA	21,611	C
San Francisco Conservatory of Music	CA	56,428	SP
Santa Fe Univ of Art and Design	NM	39,666	SP
Shenandoah Univ	VA	39,916	C
Simpson College	IA	36,086	C+
Southern Illinois Univ Edwardsville	IL	17,532	C
Southern Methodist Univ	TX	60,585	MC
Southern Nazarene Univ	OK	24,354	C
Southern Oregon Univ	OR	17,874	C
Southwestern College	KS	29,270	C
St. Olaf College	MN	51,200	HC+
Stetson Univ	FL	51,516	VC
SUNY Fredonia/The SUNY at Fredonia	NY	19,840	VC
Susquehanna Univ	PA	51,150	C
Talladega College	AL	17,996	C
Taylor Univ	IN	37,821	VC+
Temple Univ	PA	24,392	VC
Texas State Univ	TX	17,128	C
Texas Tech Univ	TX	14,243	C
The Catholic Univ of America	DC	52,852	VC
Ohio State Univ-Columbus Campus	OH	19,887	HC+
The Pennsylvania State Univ - Univ Park	PA	28,022	VC+
The SUNY at Potsdam	NY	18,473	C
The Univ of N Car at Greensboro	NC	12,848	C
The Univ of Okla	OK	18,621	VC
Toccoa Falls College	GA	23,210	LC
Tougaloo College	MS	15,275	NC
Trinity Christian College	IL	28,869	C
Truman State Univ	MO	15,541	HC
Union College	NE	23,270	C
Union Univ	TN	28,260	VC
Univ of Akron	OH	20,436	C
Univ of Alaska Anchorage	AK	16,673	NC
Univ of Calif at Irvine	CA	25,961	VC
Univ of Calif at Santa Barbara	CA	27,551	HC
Univ of Central Florida	FL	15,668	VC+
Univ of Cincinnati	OH	21,506	VC
Univ of Colo Boulder	CO	22,605	VC+
Univ of Dayton	OH	49,070	VC
Univ of Denver	CO	51,787	VC+
Univ of Evansville	IN	42,656	VC+
Univ of Georgia	GA	20,082	VC
Univ of Hartford	CT	42,674	C
Univ of Idaho	ID	14,558	C
Univ of Illinois at Chicago	IL	24,505	VC
Univ of Illinois at Urbana-Champaign	IL	26,450	HC
Univ of Indianapolis	IN	31,740	LC
Univ of Kansas	KS	17,603	C+
Univ of Kentucky	KY	19,868	C
Univ of Maine	ME	19,902	C+
Univ of Mary Hardin-Baylor	TX	31,950	C+
Univ of Maryland - College Park	MD	20,060	HC
Univ of Mass Amherst	MA	24,215	VC+
Univ of Mass Lowell	MA	19,316	C
Univ of Miami	FL	57,034	MC
Univ of Mich/Ann Arbor	MI	22,102	MC
Univ of Minn/Duluth	MN	19,806	C
Univ of Missouri-Kansas City	MO	19,603	C
Univ of Mobile	AL	28,935	VC
Univ of Montana	MT	14,105	C
Univ of Montevallo	AL	17,060	C
Univ of Mount Union	OH	35,130	C
Univ of New Haven	CT	48,940	C
Univ of N Car at Chapel Hill	NC	18,928	MC
Univ of N Car at Charlotte	NC	15,547	C
Univ of N Car at Wilmington	NC	13,572	VC
Univ of N Dak	ND	14,551	C
Univ of North Florida	FL	15,870	VC
Univ of North Texas	TX	15,628	C
Univ of Northern Iowa	IA	13,795	C
Univ of Oregon	OR	21,360	C+
Univ of Puget Sound	WA	54,608	HC
Univ of Rochester	NY	60,668	MC
Univ of S Car Upstate	SC	18,200	LC
Univ of S Dak	SD	15,111	C
Univ of Southern Calif	CA	56,903	MC
Univ of Southern Maine	ME	16,576	C
Univ of St. Francis	IL	37,560	C
Univ of Tampa	FL	35,160	VC
Univ of the Arts	PA	38,450	SP
Univ of the Pacific	CA	52,146	VC
Univ of Tulsa	OK	46,331	MC
Univ of Washington	WA	14,722	VC
Univ of West Georgia	GA	15,488	LC
Univ of Wisc/Madison	WI	18,757	HC+
Univ of Wisc/Superior	WI	14,314	C
Univ of Wyoming	WY	14,401	C+
Valparaiso Univ	IN	44,940	VC+
Vanderbilt Univ	TN	58,220	MC
Virginia State Univ	VA	11,318	C+
Viterbo Univ	WI	30,070	C
Walla Walla Univ	WA	26,256	NC
Wartburg College	IA	41,055	VC
Washburn Univ	KS	12,579	C
Washington Adventist Univ	MD	25,859	LC
Washington State Univ	WA	20,461	C
Webster Univ	MO	35,100	C+
West Chester Univ of Pennsylvania	PA	17,186	C
Western Conn State Univ	CT	18,327	LC
Western Mich Univ	MI	19,628	C
Westminster College	PA	31,290	C+
Wiley College	TX		LC
Willamette Univ	OR	56,450	VC+
William Carey Univ	MS	13,500	LC

School	ST	$IS	SR
Winona State Univ	MN	16,640	C
Winthrop Univ	SC	21,120	C
Xavier Univ of Louisiana	LA	25,300	C
York College	NE	19,475	C
Youngstown State Univ	OH	16,732	C

MUSIC PRODUCTION/ RECORDING TECHNOLOGY

School	ST	$IS	SR
Indiana Univ Bloomington	IN	19,801	VC
Kent State Univ	OH	19,920	C
Shenandoah Univ	VA	39,916	C
Syracuse Univ	NY	56,346	VC
Univ of Denver	CO	51,787	VC+

MUSIC TECHNOLOGY

School	ST	$IS	SR
Bellarmine Univ	KY	42,950	VC
Berklee College of Music	MA	47,100	SP
Bloomfield College	NJ	37,850	C
Brigham Young Univ	UT	12,100	HC
Cal State, San Bernardino	CA	12,000	C
Cogswell Polytechnical College	CA	30,531	C
Conn College	CT	54,970	MC
Duquesne Univ	PA	43,720	VC
Elon Univ	NC	41,914	VC+
Indiana Univ-Purdue Univ Indianapolis	IN	17,611	C
Keene State College	NH	23,232	LC
Malone Univ	OH	35,364	C
Mercy College	NY	30,456	C
Minn State Univ, Moorhead	MN	13,392	VC
New York Univ	NY	61,470	MC
Northeastern Univ	MA	55,296	MC
Northwestern Univ	IL	61,640	MC
Santa Fe Univ of Art and Design	NM	39,666	SP
Shenandoah Univ	VA	39,916	C
Stetson Univ	FL	51,516	VC
Stevens Inst of Technology	NJ	50,130	HC
Univ of Calif at San Diego	CA	21,000	VC
Univ of Hartford	CT	42,674	C
Univ of Miami	FL	57,034	MC
Univ of Mich/Ann Arbor	MI	22,102	MC
Univ of New Haven	CT	48,940	C
Univ of N Car at Asheville	NC	13,500	VC
Univ of St. Francis	IN	29,810	C
York College of Pennsylvania	PA	26,590	C

MUSIC THEATRE ACCOMPANYING

School	ST	$IS	SR
College of the Ozarks	MO		VC
Shenandoah Univ	VA	39,916	C

MUSIC THEORY AND COMPOSITION

School	ST	$IS	SR
Adams State Univ	CO	13,358	LC
Aquinas College	MI	33,060	C
Arizona State Univ, at the Tempe Campus	AZ	20,137	C+
Baldwin Wallace Univ	OH	38,318	C
Baylor Univ	TX	50,329	VC
Belmont Univ	TN	39,190	VC+
Bennington College	VT	56,990	HC+
Berklee College of Music	MA	47,100	SP
Biola Univ	CA	40,320	C+
Boston Conservatory	MA	56,380	VC
Boston Univ	MA	60,694	MC
Bowling Green State Univ	OH	18,970	C
Bradley Univ	IL	31,874	VC
Brigham Young Univ	UT	12,100	HC
Bucknell Univ	PA	60,140	MC
Butler Univ	IN	47,572	VC+
Calif Baptist Univ	CA	38,792	C
Calif Inst of the Arts	CA	51,902	SP
Calvin College	MI	39,120	VC
Central Washington Univ	WA	11,730	C
Chapman Univ	CA	58,347	VC+
CUNY/Brooklyn College	NY	5,884	C+
Clayton State Univ	GA	12,000	C
College of the Ozarks	MO		VC
Colo State Univ-Fort Collins	CO	20,385	VC
Colo State Univ-Pueblo	CO	16,183	C
Concordia College - Moorhead	MN	39,974	VC
Dallas Baptist Univ	TX	30,580	VC
DePaul Univ	IL	47,623	VC
DePauw Univ	IN	48,950	VC+
Dordt College	IA	34,160	C+
East Carolina Univ	NC	14,169	C
Eastman School of Music	NY	58,802	SP
Elmhurst College	IL	43,336	C
Emory and Henry College	VA	387,460	C
Five Towns College	NY	34,550	C
Florida State Univ	FL	16,715	VC
Fordham Univ	NY	61,588	HC+
Fort Hays State Univ	KS	11,354	C
Furman Univ	SC	54,006	HC
Hardin-Simmons Univ	TX	23,560	C
Hofstra Univ	NY	51,810	VC+
Houghton College	NY	36,808	C+
Houston Baptist Univ	TX	36,450	C
Huntington Univ	IN	32,220	C+
Illinois Wesleyan Univ	IL	48,452	HC
Indiana Wesleyan Univ	IN	31,815	VC
Ithaca College	NY	53,864	HC
Jacksonville Univ	FL	37,780	C
Lawrence Univ	WI	46,371	C
Lehigh Univ	PA	56,770	MC
Loyola Univ New Orleans	LA	46,581	VC
Manhattan School of Music	NY	55,850	SP
Mannes College New School for Music	NY	44,500	SP
Marshall Univ	WV	14,820	C
Mich State Univ	MI	22,450	VC
Miss College	MS	21,998	C
Montclair State Univ	NJ	22,614	C
Nazareth College of Rochester	NY	43,028	C+
New England Conservatory of Music	MA	22,550	SP
New York Univ	NY	61,470	MC
Newberry College	SC	26,850	LC
North Park Univ	IL	30,130	C
Northwestern College	MN	24,000	C
Northwestern Univ	IL	61,640	MC
Nyack College	NY	33,250	C
Oberlin College	OH	61,788	MC
Ohio Northern Univ	OH	42,075	VC
Ohio Univ	OH	21,080	C
Old Dominion Univ	VA	19,483	LC
Olivet Nazarene Univ	IL	29,990	C
Oral Roberts Univ	OK	31,734	C
Pacific Lutheran Univ	WA	46,760	C+
Palm Beach Atlantic Univ	FL	34,874	C+
Point Loma Nazarene Univ	CA	41,006	C+
Rice Univ	TX	43,288	MC
Roosevelt Univ	IL	22,605	VC
Sam Houston State Univ	TX	17,082	C
Samford Univ	AL	37,060	C+
Santa Fe Univ of Art and Design	NM	39,666	SP
Shenandoah Univ	VA	39,916	C
Southern Illinois Univ Edwardsville	IL	17,532	C
Southern Methodist Univ	TX	60,585	MC
St. Olaf College	MN	51,200	HC+
Stetson Univ	FL	51,516	VC
SUNY Fredonia/The SUNY at Fredonia	NY	19,840	VC
Syracuse Univ	NY	56,346	VC
Taylor Univ	IN	37,821	VC+
Temple Univ	PA	24,392	VC
Texas Christian Univ	TX	49,980	VC
Texas Tech Univ	TX	14,243	C
The Catholic Univ of America	DC	52,852	VC
The College of Idaho	ID	31,277	C+
Ohio State Univ-Columbus Campus	OH	19,887	HC+
The Univ of N Car at Greensboro	NC	12,848	C
Union Univ	TN	28,260	VC
Univ of Akron	OH	20,436	C
Univ of Calif at Santa Barbara	CA	27,551	VC
Univ of Cincinnati	OH	21,506	VC
Univ of Dayton	OH	49,070	VC
Univ of Delaware	DE	23,612	VC
Univ of Georgia	GA	20,082	VC
Univ of Hartford	CT	42,674	C
Univ of Idaho	ID	14,558	C
Univ of Illinois at Urbana-Champaign	IL	26,450	HC
Univ of Kansas	KS	17,603	C+
Univ of Maryland - College Park	MD	20,060	HC
Univ of Mich/Ann Arbor	MI	22,102	MC
Univ of Missouri-Kansas City	MO	19,603	C
Univ of New Haven	CT	48,940	C
Univ of North Texas	TX	15,628	C
Univ of Northern Iowa	IA	15,795	C
Univ of Oregon	OR	21,360	C
Univ of Rochester	NY	60,668	MC
Univ of Texas at Austin	TX	44,074	HC
Univ of the Arts	PA	38,540	SP
Univ of the Pacific	CA	52,146	VC
Valparaiso Univ	IN	44,940	VC+
Vanderbilt Univ	TN	58,220	MC
Wartburg College	IA	41,055	VC
Washington State Univ	WA	20,461	C
Washington Univ in St. Louis	MO	69,844	MC
Webster Univ	MO	35,100	C+
West Chester Univ of Pennsylvania	PA	17,186	C
West Texas A&M Univ	TX	13,478	C
Western Mich Univ	MI	19,628	C
Westminster Choir College	NJ	36,000	SP
Westminster College	PA	31,290	C+
Willamette Univ	OR	56,450	VC+
Wright State Univ	OH	16,983	C
Youngstown State Univ	OH	16,732	C

MUSIC THERAPY

School	ST	$IS	SR
Alverno College	WI	31,434	LC
Anna Maria College	MA	34,600	C
Appalachian State Univ	NC	12,919	VC
Arizona State Univ, at the Tempe Campus	AZ	20,137	C+
Augsburg College	MN	35,142	C
Baldwin Wallace Univ	OH	38,318	C
Berklee College of Music	MA	47,100	SP
Charleston Southern Univ	SC	22,420	C
Drury Univ	MO	31,909	VC
Duquesne Univ	PA	43,720	VC
East Carolina Univ	NC	14,169	C
Eastern Mich Univ	MI	18,604	C
Elizabethtown College	PA	49,740	VC
Florida State Univ	FL	16,715	VC
Georgia College and State Univ	GA	18,900	C
Howard Univ	DC	13,646	C
Immaculata Univ	PA	43,000	C
Indiana Univ-Purdue Univ Fort Wayne	IN	15,521	C
Louisiana State Univ	LA	15,746	C
Loyola Univ New Orleans	LA	46,581	VC
Lubbock Christian Univ	TX	26,308	C
Marylhurst Univ	OR	20,295	NC
Maryville Univ of St. Louis	MO	35,856	VC
Marywood Univ	PA	45,595	C
Mich State Univ	MI	22,450	VC
Molloy College	NY	40,440	C
Montclair State Univ	NJ	22,614	C
Nazareth College of Rochester	NY	43,028	C+
New York Univ	NY	61,470	MC
Queens Univ of Charlotte	NC	39,543	C+
St. Mary-of-the-Woods College	IN	37,722	LC
Sam Houston State Univ	TX	17,082	C
Seton Hill Univ	PA	35,172	C
Shenandoah Univ	VA	39,916	C
Southern Methodist Univ	TX	60,585	MC
Southwestern Okla State Univ	OK	9,160	C
SUNY Fredonia/The SUNY at Fredonia	NY	19,840	VC
SUNY New Paltz	NY	14,348	C
Temple Univ	PA	24,392	VC
Texas Woman's Univ	TX	13,633	LC
Univ of Alabama at Tuscaloosa	AL	17,164	C+
Univ of Dayton	OH	49,070	VC
Univ of Evansville	IN	42,656	VC+
Univ of Georgia	GA	20,082	VC
Univ of Iowa	IA	17,693	VC
Univ of Kansas	KS	17,603	C+
Univ of Louisville	KY	17,946	C
Univ of Miami	FL	57,034	MC
Univ of Minn/Twin Cities	MN		HC
Univ of Missouri-Kansas City	MO	19,603	C
Univ of N Dak	ND	14,551	C
Univ of the Incarnate Word	TX	37,316	LC
Univ of the Pacific	CA	52,146	VC
Univ of Wisc/Oshkosh	WI	10,426	LC
Utah State Univ	UT	12,044	C
Wartburg College	IA	41,055	VC
West Texas A&M Univ	TX	13,478	C
Western Mich Univ	MI	19,628	C
William Carey Univ	MS	13,500	LC

MUSICAL THEATER

School	ST	$IS	SR
Adrian College	MI	42,400	C
American Univ	DC	56,015	HC+
Aquinas College	MI	33,060	C
Arizona State Univ, at the Tempe Campus	AZ	20,137	C+
Ashland Univ	OH	25,000	C
Baldwin Wallace Univ	OH	38,318	C
Belmont Univ	TN	39,190	VC+
Birmingham-Southern College	AL	44,168	VC+
Blackburn College	IL	21,350	C
Boston Conservatory	MA	56,380	VC
Brenau Univ - Women's College	GA	26,650	LC
Brigham Young Univ	UT	12,100	HC
Cal State, Chico	CA	20,158	C
Catawba College	NC	37,240	LC
Clarke Univ	IA	37,600	C
Coastal Carolina Univ	SC	18,580	C
Coker College	SC	32,256	C
College of the Ozarks	MO		VC
Cornerstone Univ and Grand Rapids Theological Seminary	MI	33,338	C
Creighton Univ	NE	45,356	VC
Culver-Stockton College	MO	30,900	C
Elon Univ	NC	41,914	VC+
Emerson College	MA	52,446	HC+
Faulkner Univ	AL	25,720	LC
Florida Southern College	FL	40,150	C+
Florida State Univ	FL	16,715	VC
Friends Univ	KS	29,100	C
Howard Univ	DC	13,646	C
Illinois Wesleyan Univ	IL	48,452	HC
Indiana Univ Bloomington	IN	19,801	VC
Ithaca College	NY	53,864	HC
Kent State Univ	OH	19,920	C
Kutztown Univ of Pennsylvania	PA	16,909	LC
Lees-McRae College	NC	33,944	C
Limestone College	SC	30,800	C
Lipscomb Univ	TN	37,490	VC
Mars Hill Univ	NC	22,950	LC
Marywood Univ	PA	45,595	C
Mercyhurst Univ	PA	40,700	C
Meredith College	NC	31,420	C
Messiah College	PA	40,690	C+
Millikin Univ	IL	38,940	C
Missouri Baptist Univ	MO	31,830	C
Missouri State Univ	MO	13,996	C+
Montclair State Univ	NJ	22,614	C
Nazareth College of Rochester	NY	43,028	C+
Northwestern State Univ of Louisiana	LA	14,368	C
Oswego / SUNY	NY	20,009	VC
Otterbein College	OH	32,214	C
Ouachita Baptist Univ	AR	30,220	VC
Pace Univ	NY	53,367	C
Palm Beach Atlantic Univ	FL	34,874	C+
Piedmont College	GA	30,136	C
Roosevelt Univ	IL	22,605	VC
Russell Sage College	NY	39,370	C
Sam Houston State Univ	TX	17,082	C
Samford Univ	AL	37,060	C+
Santa Fe Univ of Art and Design	NM	39,666	SP
Seton Hill Univ	PA	35,172	C
Shenandoah Univ	VA	39,916	C
Shorter Univ	GA	30,650	LC
Southern Illinois Univ Carbondale	IL	21,942	C
Southern Illinois Univ Edwardsville	IL	17,532	C
St. Catherine Univ	MN	37,782	C+
SUNY College at Geneseo	NY	18,670	HC
SUNY Cortland/The SUNY	NY	19,759	C+
SUNY Fredonia/The SUNY at Fredonia	NY	19,840	VC
Syracuse Univ	NY	56,346	VC
Texas Christian Univ	TX	49,980	HC
Texas State Univ	TX	17,128	C
The Catholic Univ of America	DC	52,852	VC
The Pennsylvania State Univ - Univ Park	PA	28,022	VC+
The Univ of Okla	OK	18,621	VC
Univ at Buffalo / The SUNY	NY	20,283	VC
Univ of Akron	OH	20,436	C
Univ of Alabama at Birmingham	AL	18,484	C+
Univ of Arizona	AZ	20,657	C
Univ of Calif at Irvine	CA	25,961	VC
Univ of Hartford	CT	42,674	C
Univ of Idaho	ID	14,558	C
Univ of Indianapolis	IN	31,740	C
Univ of Miami	FL	57,034	MC
Univ of Mich/Ann Arbor	MI	22,102	MC
Univ of N Dak	ND	14,551	C
Univ of North Texas	TX	15,628	C
Univ of Northern Colo	CO	18,446	C
Univ of the Arts	PA	38,540	SP
Univ of Tulsa	OK	46,331	MC
Webster Univ	MO	35,100	C+
West Chester Univ of Pennsylvania	PA	17,186	C
Western Illinois Univ	IL	20,732	C
Western Mich Univ	MI	19,628	C
Westminster Choir College	NJ	36,000	SP
Wilkes Univ	PA	44,070	C
William Peace Univ	NC	32,900	LC
Wright State Univ	OH	16,983	C
Youngstown State Univ	OH	16,732	C

MUSICOLOGY/ ETHNOMUSICOLOGY

School	ST	$IS	SR
Cal State, San Bernardino	CA	12,000	C
Univ of Calif at Los Angeles	CA	25,686	MC
Univ of Kansas	KS	17,603	C+

NATIVE AMERICAN STUDIES

School	ST	$IS	SR
Black Hills State Univ	SD	13,947	C
Colgate Univ	NY	58,135	MC
College of St. Scholastica	MN	41,440	C
Creighton Univ	NE	45,356	VC
Dartmouth College	NH	57,996	MC
East Central Univ	OK	10,223	LC
Heritage Univ	WA	17,664	NC
Humboldt State Univ	CA	18,400	C
Montana State Univ-Northern	MT	12,500	NC
Northern Arizona Univ	AZ	19,010	C
Southern Oregon Univ	OR	17,874	C
Stanford Univ	CA	58,388	MC
The Univ of Okla	OK	18,621	VC
Univ of Calif at Berkeley	CA	23,322	MC
Univ of Calif at Davis	CA		HC
Univ of Calif at Riverside	CA	27,204	C+
Univ of Minn/Duluth	MN	19,806	C
Univ of Montana	MT	14,105	C
Univ of New Mexico	NM	15,300	C

ST = STATE $IS = IN-STATE COSTS   SR = SELECTOR RATING

NATURAL RESOURCE MANAGEMENT

School	ST	$IS	SR
Alaska Pacific Univ	AK	43,592	NC
Angelo State Univ	TX	15,049	NC
Arizona State Univ, at the Tempe Campus	AZ	20,137	C+
Ball State Univ	IN	17,850	C
Calif Polytechnic State Univ	CA	19,847	HC
Cal State, Sacramento	CA	16,200	C
Colo State Univ-Fort Collins	CO	20,385	VC
Delaware State Univ	DE	16,722	LC
DePauw Univ	IN	48,950	VC+
Drury Univ	MO	31,909	VC
Glenville State College	WV	11,348	NC
Grand Valley State Univ	MI	17,998	C+
Green Mountain College	VT	45,228	LC
Humboldt State Univ	CA	18,400	C
Johnson State College	VT	16,721	C
Keystone College	PA	28,680	LC
Louisiana State Univ	LA	18,677	C+
Lubbock Christian Univ	TX	26,308	C
Marshall Univ	WV	14,820	C
McNeese State Univ	LA	2,649	C
Mich State Univ	MI	22,450	VC
Montana State Univ	MT	14,068	C
New Mexico Highlands Univ	NM	11,904	NC
New Mexico State Univ	NM	14,050	C
N Car State Univ	NC	16,202	HC
N Dak State Univ	ND		C
Northland College	WI	26,680	C
Okla State Univ	OK	14,310	VC
Oregon State Univ	OR	20,273	VC
Purdue Univ/West Lafayette	IN	20,024	HC
Rutgers, The State Univ of New Jersey/New Brunswick	NJ	25,562	VC
San Francisco State Univ	CA	18,514	C
S Dak State Univ	SD	14,296	C
Southern Oregon Univ	OR	17,874	C
SUNY / College of Environmental Science and Forestry	NY	18,351	VC
Sul Ross State Univ	TX	13,410	LC
Texas A&M Univ at Galveston	TX	11,258	C
Ohio State Univ-Columbus Campus	OH	19,887	HC+
The Pennsylvania State Univ - Univ Park	PA	28,022	VC+
Unity College	ME	34,054	C
Univ of Alaska Fairbanks	AK	15,130	C
Univ of Arizona	AZ	20,657	C
Univ of Conn	CT	24,706	HC
Univ of Delaware	DE	23,612	VC
Univ of Florida	FL	15,943	HC
Univ of Hawaii at Manoa	HI	19,379	C
Univ of Idaho	ID	14,558	C
Univ of Illinois at Urbana-Champaign	IL	26,450	VC
Univ of Maryland - College Park	MD	20,060	HC
Univ of Mass Amherst	MA	24,215	VC+
Univ of Minn Crookston	MN	17,834	C
Univ of Minn/Twin Cities	MN		HC
Univ of Montana-Western	MT	9,753	LC
Univ of Nebr - Lincoln	NE	18,031	VC
Univ of Nevada/Reno	NV	17,507	C
Univ of Northern Colo	CO	18,446	C
Univ of PR Recinto de Rio Piedras	PR	5,750	
Univ of Tenn at Martin	TN	13,734	C
Univ of Vermont	VT	27,006	VC+
Univ of Wisc/Stevens Point	WI	14,043	C
Utah State Univ	UT	12,044	C
Washington State Univ	WA	20,461	C
Washington Univ in St. Louis	MO	69,844	MC
West Virginia Univ	WV	16,542	C
Western Carolina Univ	NC	13,965	C

NATURAL RESOURCE/ ENVIRONMENTAL ECONOMICS

School	ST	$IS	SR
Rutgers, The State Univ of New Jersey/New Brunswick	NJ	25,562	VC
Univ of Georgia	GA	20,082	VC
Univ of Nebr - Lincoln	NE	18,031	VC

NATURAL RESOURCES

School	ST	$IS	SR
Austin College	TX	45,875	NC
Sewanee: The Univ of the South	TN	47,700	HC+
The Pennsylvania State Univ - Univ Park	PA	28,022	VC+
Univ of Georgia	GA	20,082	VC
Univ of Tenn at Knoxville	TN	20,364	VC

NATURAL SCIENCES

School	ST	$IS	SR
Alderson Broaddus Univ	WV	28,656	VC
Ashford Univ	CA	10,480	C
Bard College at Simon's Rock	MA	61,749	HC+
Benedictine College	KS	29,180	VC
Bethel College	KS	32,160	C
Biola Univ	CA	40,320	C+
Cal State, Chico	CA	20,158	C
Cal State, Fresno	CA	17,405	C
Cal State, Los Angeles	CA	17,186	LC
Calvin College	MI	39,120	VC
Carthage College	WI	33,000	C
Case Western Reserve Univ	OH	56,534	MC
Castleton State College	VT	20,186	C
Central College	IA	42,104	C+
Charleston Southern Univ	SC	22,420	C
Christian Brothers Univ	TN	31,670	HC
Clarion Univ of Pennsylvania	PA	17,370	LC
Colby-Sawyer College	NH	50,790	C
Colgate Univ	NY	58,135	MC
College of St. Benedict	MN	49,359	VC
College of St. Mary	NE	35,184	C
College of St. Scholastica	MN	41,440	C
Colo State Univ-Fort Collins	CO	20,385	VC
Concordia Univ Nebr	NE	26,000	VC
Concordia Univ, River Forest	IL	26,300	C
Daemen College	NY	34,770	C
Dallas Baptist Univ	TX	30,580	VC
Doane College	NE	35,230	C
Dominican Univ	IL	37,628	C
Dowling College	NY	25,000	LC
Edgewood College	WI	33,294	C
Edinboro Univ of Pennsylvania	PA	15,940	LC
Elms College	MA	23,900	VC
Erskine College	SC	37,360	C
Felician College	NJ	41,640	LC
Fordham Univ	NY	61,588	HC+
Fresno Pacific Univ	CA	32,136	C
Georgian Court Univ	NJ	41,594	C
Gwynedd-Mercy College	PA	33,560	C
Indiana Univ of Pennsylvania	PA	20,846	LC
John Carroll Univ	OH	46,300	C+
Johns Hopkins Univ	MD	47,492	MC
Keystone College	PA	28,680	LC
LeMoyne-Owen College	TN	13,100	C
Lesley Univ	MA	46,350	C
Lewis-Clark State College	ID	6,990	C
Loyola Marymount Univ	CA	54,648	VC+
Lyndon State College	VT	14,233	C
Madonna Univ	MI	24,540	VC
Mercer Univ	GA	44,201	VC
Missouri State Univ	MO	13,996	C+
Missouri Western State Univ	MO	12,260	NC
Muhlenberg College	PA	52,837	HC
New College of Florida	FL	14,504	MC
Oakwood Univ	AL	25,529	NC
Oregon State Univ	OR	20,273	VC
Our Lady of the Lake Univ	TX	22,430	LC
Pacific Union College	CA	28,150	VC
Park Univ	MO	17,525	C
Pepperdine Univ	CA	55,372	HC+
Prescott College	AZ	33,284	C
St. Anselm College	NH	49,376	VC
St. John's Univ	MN	47,984	C
St. Peter's Univ	NJ	44,240	C
San Jose State Univ	CA	19,133	LC
Shawnee State Univ	OH	16,916	C
Shimer College	IL	32,875	VC
Shorter Univ	GA	30,650	LC
Siena Heights Univ	MI	32,040	C
Southwestern Okla State Univ	OK	9,160	C
Spelman College	GA	24,650	C
St. Mary's College of Maryland	MD	25,754	VC
St. Norbert College	WI	41,478	VC
SUNY College at Geneseo	NY	18,670	HC
Tabor College	KS	29,010	C
Taylor Univ	IN	37,821	VC+
Texas A&M Univ at Galveston	TX	11,258	C
The Evergreen State College	WA	12,969	C+
The Masters College	CA	38,160	C+
Unity College	ME	34,054	C
Universidad del Turabo	PR	4,110	
Universidad Metropolitana	PR	3,500	
Univ of Akron	OH	20,436	C
Univ of Alabama at Birmingham	AL	18,484	C+
Univ of Alaska Anchorage	AK	16,673	NC
Univ of Arizona	AZ	20,657	C
Univ of Hawaii at Hilo	HI	23,066	C
Univ of La Verne	CA	47,010	C
Univ of New Haven	CT	48,940	C
Univ of N Dak	ND	14,551	C
Univ of Pittsburgh at Greensburg	PA	17,640	C
Univ of Pittsburgh at Pittsburgh	PA	28,572	HC+
Univ of PR/Cayey	PR	1,504	
Univ of Puget Sound	WA	54,608	HC
Univ of Science and Arts of Okla	OK	10,560	C
Univ of Wisc/Stevens Point	WI	14,043	C
Virginia Wesleyan College	VA	28,433	LC
Viterbo Univ	WI	30,070	C
Washington and Lee Univ	VA	52,812	MC
Western Oregon Univ	OR	15,021	C
Worcester State Univ	MA	19,812	C
Xavier Univ	OH	44,980	VC
York College	NE	19,475	C

NATURAL SCIENCES/ MATHEMATICS

School	ST	$IS	SR
Indiana Univ East	IN	6,783	C
Thomas Edison State College	NJ	5,700	SP

NAVAL ARCHITECTURE AND MARINE ENGINEERING

School	ST	$IS	SR
Maritime College/SUNY	NY	16,020	C
Stevens Inst of Technology	NJ	50,130	HC
Texas A&M Univ at Galveston	TX	11,258	C
United States Coast Guard Academy	CT	942	HC
United States Naval Academy	MD		MC
Univ of Mich/Ann Arbor	MI	22,102	MC
Univ of New Orleans	LA	9,224	C
Univ of Wisc/Madison	WI	18,757	HC+
Webb Inst	NY	14,250	MC

NEAR EASTERN STUDIES

School	ST	$IS	SR
Brandeis Univ	MA		MC
Brigham Young Univ	UT	12,100	HC
Cornell Univ	NY	60,964	MC
Creighton Univ	NE	45,356	VC
Indiana Univ Bloomington	IN	19,801	VC
Johns Hopkins Univ	MD	47,492	MC
Oberlin College	OH	61,788	MC
Princeton Univ	NJ	53,795	MC
Univ of Calif at Berkeley	CA	23,322	MC
Univ of Calif at Los Angeles	CA	25,686	MC
Univ of Chicago	IL	55,416	MC
Univ of Mich/Ann Arbor	MI	22,102	MC
Univ of Mount Union	OH	35,130	C
Univ of Pennsylvania	PA	61,132	MC
Univ of Washington	WA	14,722	VC
Univ of Wisc-Milwaukee	WI	18,436	C
Washington Univ in St. Louis	MO	69,844	MC
Wayne State Univ	MI	22,063	C
Yale Univ	CT	55,300	MC

NEUROSCIENCES

School	ST	$IS	SR
Agnes Scott College	GA	45,323	C+
Alabama A&M Univ	AL	10,084	C
Allegheny College	PA	50,980	VC
Amherst College	MA	58,744	MC
Baldwin Wallace Univ	OH	38,318	C
Bates College	ME	60,720	MC
Baylor Univ	TX	50,329	VC
Belmont Univ	TN	39,190	VC+
Binghamton Univ/The SUNY	NY	21,648	HC+
Boston Univ	MA	60,694	MC
Bowdoin College	ME	59,568	MC
Bowling Green State Univ	OH	18,970	C
Brandeis Univ	MA		MC
Brigham Young Univ	UT	12,100	HC
Brown Univ	RI	59,428	MC
Bucknell Univ	PA	60,140	MC
Canisius College	NY	44,900	C
Cedar Crest College	PA	43,240	C
Centenary College of Louisiana	LA	45,650	C+
Christopher Newport Univ	VA	21,960	VC
Claremont McKenna College	CA	62,215	MC
Coe College	IA	45,550	VC
Colby College	ME	57,510	MC
Colgate Univ	NY	58,135	MC
College of Mount St. Joseph	OH	33,880	C
College of William & Mary	VA	28,000	MC
Colo College	CO	57,162	MC
Columbia Univ/City of New York	NY	61,116	MC
Conn College	CT	54,970	MC
Dartmouth College	NH	57,996	MC
Dickinson College	PA	57,662	HC+
Dominican Univ	IL	37,628	C
Drake Univ	IA	41,516	VC+
Drew Univ/College of Liberal Arts	NJ	57,516	C
Earlham College	IN	51,470	MC
Emmanuel College	MA	47,985	VC
Emory Univ	GA	56,368	MC
Fitchburg State Univ	MA	18,173	C
Fordham Univ	NY	61,588	HC+
Franklin and Marshall College	PA	60,799	MC
Furman Univ	SC	54,006	HC
George Mason Univ	VA	15,724	VC
Hamilton College	NY	55,620	MC
Hiram College	OH	37,300	VC
Indiana Univ Bloomington	IN	19,801	VC
Indiana Univ-Purdue Univ Indianapolis	IN	17,611	C
Johns Hopkins Univ	MD	47,492	MC
Kenyon College	OH	58,890	MC
King Univ	TN	33,140	C
King's College	PA	43,502	C
Knox College	IL	44,865	VC+
Lafayette College	PA	59,155	HC+
Lake Forest College	IL	50,652	VC
Macalester College	MN	57,691	MC
Mass Inst of Technology	MA	58,240	MC
Middlebury College	VT	59,160	MC
Millsaps College	MS	43,888	VC+
Montana State Univ	MT	14,068	C
Moravian College	PA	36,381	VC
Mount Holyoke College	MA	55,146	MC
Muhlenberg College	PA	52,837	HC
Muskingum Univ	OH	30,502	C
New College of Florida	FL	14,504	MC
New York Univ	NY	61,470	MC
Northeastern Univ	MA	55,296	MC
Northwestern Univ	IL	61,640	MC
Nova Southeastern Univ	FL	37,280	VC
Oberlin College	OH	61,788	MC
Ohio Univ	OH	21,080	C
Pitzer College	CA	54,988	MC
Pomona College	CA	57,680	MC
Queens College/The CUNY	NY	17,107	VC
Quinnipiac Univ	CT	55,160	VC
Randolph-Macon College	VA	49,869	C+
Regis Univ	CO	41,318	C
Rhodes College	TN	51,900	HC+
St. Louis Univ	MO	48,346	HC
Scripps College	CA	61,940	MC
Skidmore College	NY	59,942	MC
Smith College	MA	59,674	MC
St. Lawrence Univ	NY	59,972	VC
Stonehill College	MA	46,780	MC
Swarthmore College	PA	57,870	MC
Syracuse Univ	NY	56,346	VC
Texas Christian Univ	TX	49,980	MC
Ohio State Univ-Columbus Campus	OH	19,887	HC+
Thiel College	PA	38,728	LC
Transylvania Univ	KY	42,660	VC+
Trinity College	CT		HC+
Tulane Univ	LA	60,861	MC
Union College	NY	60,240	MC
Univ of Alabama at Birmingham	AL	18,484	C+
Univ of Arizona	AZ	20,657	C
Univ of Calif at Irvine	CA	25,961	VC
Univ of Calif at Los Angeles	CA	25,686	MC
Univ of Calif at Riverside	CA	27,204	C+
Univ of Calif at Santa Cruz	CA	27,807	C+
Univ of Cincinnati	OH	21,506	VC
Univ of Colo Boulder	CO	22,605	VC+
Univ of Evansville	IN	42,656	VC+
Univ of Georgia	GA	20,082	VC
Univ of Illinois at Chicago	IL	24,505	VC
Univ of Miami	FL	57,034	MC
Univ of Mich/Ann Arbor	MI	22,102	MC
Univ of New Hampshire	NH	26,912	C
Univ of Pittsburgh at Pittsburgh	PA	28,572	HC+
Univ of Rochester	NY	60,668	MC
Univ of Scranton	PA	51,940	VC
Univ of Southern Calif	CA	56,903	MC
Univ of Texas at Dallas	TX	21,348	HC+
Univ of Vermont	VT	27,006	VC+
Univ of Washington	WA	14,722	VC
Ursinus College	PA	57,580	VC
Vanderbilt Univ	TN	58,220	MC
Vassar College	NY	61,140	MC
Washington and Jefferson College	PA	51,948	VC
Washington and Lee Univ	VA	52,812	MC
Washington State Univ	WA	20,461	C
Washington Univ in St. Louis	MO	69,844	MC
Wellesley College	MA	59,038	MC
Wesleyan Univ	CT	61,198	MC
Western New England Univ	MA	46,154	C+
Westminster College	UT	37,708	C+
Wheaton College	MA	54,934	HC+

NONPROFIT/PUBLIC ORGANIZATION MANAGEMENT

School	ST	$IS	SR
American Univ	DC	56,015	HC+
Aquinas College	MI	33,060	C
Arizona State Univ, at the Downtown Phoenix Campus	AZ	22,101	C
Bryant Univ	RI	49,179	VC
Duquesne Univ	PA	43,720	VC
High Point Univ	NC	39,800	C
Huntington Univ	IN	32,220	C+
Indiana Univ Bloomington	IN	19,801	VC
Mount Aloysius College	PA	29,976	C
Murray State Univ	KY	15,304	C
Prescott College	AZ	33,284	C
Rockhurst Univ	MO	20,625	C
Southern Adventist Univ	TN	26,190	C
Univ of Georgia	GA	20,082	VC
Univ of S Car Upstate	SC	18,200	LC
Univ of Wisc/Madison	WI	18,757	HC+
Wright State Univ	OH	16,983	C

NORWEGIAN

School	ST	$IS	SR
St. Olaf College	MN	51,200	HC+
Univ of N Dak	ND	14,551	C

ST = STATE $IS = IN-STATE COSTS   SR = SELECTOR RATING

School	ST	$IS	SR

NUCLEAR ENERGY ENGINEERING TECHNOLOGY

School	ST	$IS	SR
Thomas Edison State College	NJ	5,700	SP

NUCLEAR ENGINEERING

School	ST	$IS	SR
Excelsior College	NY	5,580	SP
Georgia Inst of Technology	GA	21,828	MC
Idaho State Univ	ID	12,307	C
Mass Inst of Technology	MA	58,240	MC
Missouri Univ of Science and Technology	MO	18,655	VC+
N Car State Univ	NC	16,202	HC
Oregon State Univ	OR	20,273	VC
Purdue Univ/West Lafayette	IN	20,024	HC
Rensselaer Polytechnic Inst	NY	61,529	MC
Texas A&M Univ	TX	19,207	VC
The Pennsylvania State Univ - Univ Park	PA	28,022	VC+
The Univ of Tenn at Chattanooga	TN	16,883	C
United States Military Academy	NY		MC
United States Naval Academy	MD		MC
Univ of Calif at Berkeley	CA	23,322	MC
Univ of Cincinnati	OH	21,506	VC
Univ of Florida	FL	15,943	HC
Univ of Illinois at Urbana-Champaign	IL	26,450	HC
Univ of Mich/Ann Arbor	MI	22,102	MC
Univ of New Mexico	NM	15,300	C
Univ of Tenn at Knoxville	TN	20,364	VC+
Univ of Wisc/Madison	WI	18,757	HC+

NUCLEAR ENGINEERING TECHNOLOGY

School	ST	$IS	SR
Old Dominion Univ	VA	19,483	LC
Thomas Edison State College	NJ	5,700	SP
Univ of Florida	FL	15,943	HC
Univ of North Texas	TX	15,628	C

NUCLEAR MEDICAL TECHNOLOGY

School	ST	$IS	SR
Adventist Univ of Health Sciences	FL	16,344	NC
Allen College	IA	26,110	SP
Barry Univ	FL	38,190	C
Benedictine Univ	IL	37,820	C
Cedar Crest College	PA	43,240	C
Edinboro Univ of Pennsylvania	PA	15,940	LC
Ferris State Univ	MI	20,047	C
George Washington Univ	DC	57,108	MC
Georgia Regents Univ	GA		C
Indiana Univ of Pennsylvania	PA	20,846	C
Mass College of Pharmacy and Health Sciences	MA	36,450	SP
Mount Aloysius College	PA	29,976	C
North Central College	IL	38,343	VC
Old Dominion Univ	VA	19,483	LC
Rhode Island College	RI	17,694	LC
Robert Morris Univ	PA	37,864	C
Roosevelt Univ	IL	22,605	VC
Univ at Buffalo / The SUNY	NY	20,283	VC
Univ of Alabama at Birmingham	AL	18,484	C+
Univ of Central Arkansas	AR	13,667	VC
Univ of Cincinnati	OH	21,506	VC
Univ of Findlay	OH	31,916	C
Univ of Iowa	IA	17,693	VC
Univ of Nevada, Las Vegas	NV	17,303	C
Univ of St. Francis	IL	37,560	C
Univ of the Incarnate Word	TX	37,316	C
Univ of Vermont	VT	27,006	VC+
Univ of Wisc/La Crosse	WI	9,304	VC
Wheeling Jesuit Univ	WV	33,500	C
York College of Pennsylvania	PA	26,590	C

NUCLEAR MEDICINE

School	ST	$IS	SR
Kent State Univ	OH	19,920	C
Thomas Edison State College	NJ	5,700	SP

NUCLEAR MEDICINE TECHNOLOGY

School	ST	$IS	SR
Indiana Univ-Purdue Univ Indianapolis	IN	17,611	C
Millersville Univ of Pennsylvania	PA	21,648	C
Molloy College	NY	40,440	C
St. Louis Univ	MO	48,346	HC
St. Mary's Univ of Minn	MN	38,280	C
Thomas Edison State College	NJ	5,700	SP

NUCLEAR TECHNOLOGY

School	ST	$IS	SR
Excelsior College	NY	5,580	SP
Peru State College	NE	8,600	NC

NURSING

School	ST	$IS	SR
Abilene Christian Univ	TX	38,400	C+
Adams State Univ	CO	13,358	LC
Adelphi Univ	NY	44,670	VC
Adventist Univ of Health Sciences	FL	16,344	NC
Agnes Scott College	GA	45,323	C+
Alabama A&M Univ	AL	10,084	C
Albany State Univ	GA	8,500	C
Alcorn State Univ	MS	9,500	C
Alderson Broaddus Univ	WV	28,656	C
Allen College	IA	26,110	SP
Alma College	MI	44,075	C
Alvernia Univ	PA	39,250	LC
Alverno College	WI	31,434	LC
American International College	MA	36,100	LC
Anderson Univ	IN	36,100	C
Andrews Univ	MI	28,030	C+
Angelo State Univ	TX	15,049	NC
Anna Maria College	MA	34,600	C
Appalachian State Univ	NC	12,919	VC
Aquinas College	TN	29,250	VC+
Arizona State Univ, at the Downtown Phoenix Campus	AZ	22,101	C
Arkansas State Univ	AR	15,470	C
Arkansas Tech Univ	AR	13,982	LC
Armstrong State Univ	GA	15,532	C
Atlantic Union College	MA	24,600	C
Auburn Univ	AL	22,378	VC+
Auburn Univ at Montgomery	AL	14,470	LC
Augustana College	SD	36,500	VC
Aurora Univ	IL	33,228	C
Austin Peay State Univ	TN	15,274	C
Avila Univ	MO	26,900	C
Azusa Pacific Univ	CA	42,086	C
Baker Univ	KS	33,350	C+
Baldwin Wallace Univ	OH	38,318	C
Ball State Univ	IN	17,850	C
Barry Univ	FL	38,190	C
Barton College	NC	27,660	LC
Baylor Univ	TX	50,329	HC
Becker College	MA	41,420	C
Bellarmine Univ	KY	42,950	VC
Belmont Univ	TN	39,190	VC+
Bemidji State Univ	MN	13,500	VC
Benedictine College	KS	29,180	VC
Benedictine Univ	IL	37,820	C
Berea College	KY	7,192	C
Bethel College	IN	31,560	C
Bethel College	KS	32,160	C
Bethel Univ	MN	34,940	VC
Bethel Univ	TN	19,186	C
Bethune-Cookman Univ	FL	22,958	C
Binghamton Univ/The SUNY	NY	21,648	HC+
Biola Univ	CA	40,320	C+
Bloomfield College	NJ	37,850	LC
Bloomsburg Univ of Pennsylvania	PA	13,598	C
Bluefield State College	WV	3,140	LC
Boise State Univ	ID	13,469	LC
Boston College	MA	60,622	MC
Bowie State Univ	MD	23,990	LC
Bowling Green State Univ	OH	18,970	C
Bradley Univ	IL	31,874	VC
Brenau Univ - Women's College	GA	26,650	LC
Briar Cliff Univ	IA	29,514	C
Brigham Young Univ	UT	12,100	HC
Cabarrus College of Health Sciences	NC	10,000	SP
Caldwell College	NJ	35,602	NC
Calif Baptist Univ	CA	38,792	C
Cal State, Bakersfield	CA	8,000	C
Cal State, Chico	CA	20,158	C
Cal State, Dominguez Hills	CA	17,090	LC
Cal State, East Bay	CA	16,549	C
Cal State, Fresno	CA	17,405	C
Cal State, Fullerton	CA	25,188	C
Cal State, Long Beach	CA	17,502	C+
Cal State, Los Angeles	CA	17,186	LC
Cal State, Northridge	CA	28,690	LC
Cal State, Sacramento	CA	16,200	C
Cal State, San Bernardino	CA	12,000	C
Cal State, San Marcos	CA	14,576	LC
Cal State, Stanislaus	CA	18,582	C
Calif Univ of Pennsylvania	PA	14,217	C
Calvin College	MI	39,120	VC
Campbell Univ	NC	37,570	VC
Campbellsville Univ	KY	27,720	C
Capital Univ	OH	41,050	VC
Cardinal Stritch Univ	WI	24,054	C
Caribbean Univ	PR	10,375	
Carlow Univ	PA	30,272	C
Carroll College	MT	28,000	C
Carroll Univ	WI	38,100	C
Carson-Newman Univ	TN	29,058	C+
Case Western Reserve Univ	OH	56,534	MC
Castleton State College	VT	20,186	C
Cedar Crest College	PA	43,240	C
Cedarville Univ	OH	32,860	VC
Central Conn State Univ	CT	19,749	C
Central Methodist Univ	MO	28,240	VC
Central Univ of Bayamon	PR	3,350	
Chaminade Univ of Honolulu	HI	31,664	LC
Charleston Southern Univ	SC	22,420	C
Chicago State Univ	IL	5,482	C
Clarion Univ of Pennsylvania	PA	17,370	LC
Clarke Univ	IA	37,600	C
Clarkson College	NE	16,300	VC
Clayton State Univ	GA	12,000	LC
Clemson Univ	SC	19,136	HC
Cleveland State Univ	OH	21,776	C
Coastal Carolina Univ	SC	18,580	C
Coe College	IA	45,550	VC
Colby-Sawyer College	NH	50,790	C
College of Mount St. Joseph	OH	33,880	C
College of Mount St. Vincent	NY	41,040	MC
College of New Jersey	NJ	25,376	HC
College of St. Benedict	MN	49,359	VC
College of St. Elizabeth	NJ	43,839	LC
College of St. Mary	NE	35,184	C
College of St. Scholastica	MN	41,440	C
College of Staten Island/The City of New Yok	NY	16,778	NC
College of the Ozarks	MO		VC
Colo Mesa Univ	CO	17,690	LC
Colo State Univ-Pueblo	CO	16,183	C
Columbia College	MO	24,578	C
Columbus State Univ	GA	13,176	C
Concordia College - Moorhead	MN	39,974	VC
Concordia College - New York	NY	39,035	LC
Concordia Univ	OR	35,000	C
Concordia Univ Wisc	WI	28,980	C
Coppin State Univ	MD	16,227	VC
Cox College	MO	15,000	C
Creighton Univ	NE	45,356	VC
Culver-Stockton College	MO	30,900	C
Cumberland Univ	TN	21,220	C
Curry College	MA	48,925	LC
Daemen College	NY	34,770	C
Dakota Wesleyan Univ	SD	23,000	C
Davenport Univ	MI	21,002	LC
De Sales Univ	PA	43,970	C
Defiance College	OH	30,645	C
Delaware State Univ	DE	16,722	LC
Delta State Univ	MS	12,292	LC
DePaul Univ	IL	47,623	VC
Dickinson State Univ	ND	11,900	NC
Dillard Univ	LA	20,940	VC
Dominican College	NY	31,270	LC
Dominican Univ	IL	37,628	C
Dominican Univ of Calif	CA	51,250	C
Dordt College	IA	34,160	C+
Drexel Univ	PA	61,418	VC+
Duquesne Univ	PA	43,720	VC
D'Youville College	NY	29,850	C
East Carolina Univ	NC	14,169	C
East Central Univ	OK	10,223	C
East Stroudsburg Univ of Pennsylvania	PA	18,868	LC
East Tenn State Univ	TN	9,000	C
East Texas Baptist Univ	TX	31,577	LC
Eastern Illinois Univ	IL	20,466	C
Eastern Kentucky Univ	KY	11,161	C
Eastern Mennonite Univ	VA	40,660	C
Eastern Mich Univ	MI	18,604	C
Eastern New Mexico Univ	NM	10,682	C
Eastern Oregon Univ	OR	10,400	C
Eastern Univ	PA	37,704	C
Eastern Washington Univ	WA		C
Edgewood College	WI	33,294	C
Edinboro Univ of Pennsylvania	PA	15,940	LC
Elmhurst College	IL	43,336	C
Elmira College	NY	49,950	C+
Elms College	MA	23,900	VC
Emmanuel College	MA	47,985	VC
Emory Univ	GA	56,368	MC
Emporia State Univ	KS	12,897	C
Endicott College	MA	43,228	VC+
Excelsior College	NY	5,580	SP
Fairfield Univ	CT	56,960	VC
Fairleigh Dickinson Univ/ College at Florham	NJ	42,142	C
Fairleigh Dickinson Univ/ Metropolitan Campus	NJ	40,254	C
Farmingdale State College	NY	19,673	C
Fayetteville State Univ	NC	10,816	C
Felician College	NJ	41,640	LC
Ferris State Univ	MI	20,047	C
Fitchburg State Univ	MA	18,173	C
Florida A&M Univ	FL	14,935	LC
Florida Atlantic Univ	FL	17,339	C
Florida Gulf Coast Univ	FL		C
Florida Southern College	FL	40,150	C+
Florida State Univ	FL	16,715	VC
Fort Hays State Univ	KS	11,354	C
Framingham State Univ	MA	18,854	C
Francis Marion Univ	SC	16,464	LC
Franciscan Univ of Steubenville	OH	27,320	VC
Franklin Pierce Univ	NH	41,598	C
Frostburg State Univ	MD	15,264	LC
Gannon Univ	PA	39,608	C
Gardner-Webb Univ	NC	34,375	C+
George Fox Univ	OR	40,750	C+
George Mason Univ	VA	15,724	VC
Georgetown Univ	DC	52,910	MC
Georgia College and State Univ	GA	18,900	C+
Georgia Regents Univ	GA		C
Georgia Southwestern State Univ	GA	13,246	C
Georgia State Univ	GA	15,582	VC
Georgian Court Univ	NJ	41,594	LC
Glenville State College	WV	11,348	NC
Gonzaga Univ	WA	46,441	HC
Goodwin College	CT	19,400	C
Goshen College	IN	35,900	VC
Graceland Univ	IA	28,020	C
Grambling State Univ	LA	13,384	LC
Grand Canyon Univ	AZ	24,540	VC
Grand Valley State Univ	MI	17,998	C+
Grand View Univ	IA	31,050	C
Gustavus Adolphus College	MN	48,170	HC
Gwynedd-Mercy College	PA	33,560	C
Hampton Univ	VA	28,528	C
Hannibal-LaGrange Univ	MO	24,490	C
Harding Univ	AR	23,556	C
Hardin-Simmons Univ	TX	23,560	C+
Hartwick College	NY	51,270	C
Hawaii Pacific Univ	HI	34,360	C
Henderson State Univ	AR	14,584	C
Hiram College	OH	37,300	VC
Holy Family Univ	PA	40,030	LC
Holy Names Univ	CA	40,310	NC
Hood College	MD	45,730	C
Hope College	MI	38,650	VC
Houston Baptist Univ	TX	36,450	C
Howard Univ	DC	13,646	C
Humboldt State Univ	CA	18,400	C
Hunter College	NY	14,429	NC
Huntington Univ	IN	32,220	C+
Husson Univ	ME	24,194	LC
Idaho State Univ	ID	12,307	C
Illinois State Univ	IL	23,110	VC
Illinois Wesleyan Univ	IL	48,452	HC
Immaculata Univ	PA	43,000	C
Indiana State Univ	IN	16,000	C
Indiana Univ Bloomington	IN	19,801	VC
Indiana Univ East	IN	6,783	C
Indiana Univ Kokomo	IN	6,811	LC
Indiana Univ Northwest	IN	6,854	LC
Indiana Univ of Pennsylvania	PA	20,846	LC
Indiana Univ South Bend	IN	15,501	C
Indiana Univ Southeast	IN	16,035	C
Indiana Univ-Purdue Univ Fort Wayne	IN	15,521	C
Indiana Univ-Purdue Univ Indianapolis	IN	17,611	C
Indiana Wesleyan Univ	IN	31,815	VC
Inter-American Univ of PR/ Aguadilla Campus	PR	5,578	
Inter-American Univ of PR/ Arecibo Campus	PR	3,350	
Inter-American Univ of PR/ Fajardo Campus	PR	4,200	
Inter-American Univ of PR/ Metropolitan Campus	PR	4,320	
Inter-American Univ of PR/ Ponce	PR		
Inter-American Univ of PR/ San Germán	PR	6,720	
Iowa Wesleyan College	IA	30,850	LC
Jacksonville State Univ	AL	12,480	LC
Jacksonville Univ	FL	37,780	C
James Madison Univ	VA	18,049	VC
Johnson C. Smith Univ	NC	25,336	LC
Judson College	AL	26,794	C
Judson Univ	IL	25,130	C
Kansas Wesleyan Univ	KS	32,000	C
Kean Univ	NJ	23,444	C
Keene State College	NH	23,232	LC
Kennesaw State Univ	GA		C
Kent State Univ	OH	19,920	C
Kentucky Christian Univ	KY	17,622	LC
Kentucky State Univ	KY	11,000	LC
Keuka College	NY	30,300	C
King Univ	TN	33,140	C
Kutztown Univ of Pennsylvania	PA	16,909	LC
La Roche College	PA	35,824	LC
La Salle Univ	PA	50,270	C
LaGrange College	GA	37,670	C
Lake Superior State Univ	MI	18,121	C
Lamar Univ	TX	6,820	LC
Lander Univ	SC	22,514	C+
Langston Univ	OK	3,000	C
Le Moyne College	NY	43,470	C
Lehman College/The CUNY	NY	5,778	LC
Lenoir-Rhyne College	NC	35,984	C
Lewis Univ	IL	23,050	C
Lewis-Clark State College	ID	6,990	C
Liberty Univ	VA	19,101	C
Lincoln Memorial Univ	TN	18,144	C
Lincoln Univ	MO	12,904	NC
Lindsey Wilson College	KY	31,220	C
Linfield College-McMinnville Campus	OR	47,676	C
Lipscomb Univ	TN	37,490	VC
LIU Brooklyn	NY	47,182	LC
LIU Post	NY	47,660	C

School	ST	$IS	SR
Longwood Univ	VA	20,924	C
Louisiana College	LA	15,746	C
Lourdes Univ	OH	26,055	LC
Loyola Univ Chicago	IL	51,646	VC+
Loyola Univ New Orleans	LA	46,581	VC
Lubbock Christian Univ	TX	26,308	C
Luther College	IA	45,720	C+
Lynchburg College	VA	42,645	C
MacMurray College	IL	20,755	C
Madonna Univ	MI	24,540	VC
Malone Univ	OH	35,364	C
Mansfield Univ	PA	19,468	LC
Marian Univ	IN	38,540	C
Marian Univ	WI	32,420	LC
Marquette Univ	WI	46,930	VC+
Marshall Univ	WV	14,820	C
Marymount Univ	VA	39,480	C
Maryville College	TN	33,150	C+
Maryville Univ of St. Louis	MO	35,856	VC
Marywood Univ	PA	45,595	C
Mass College of Pharmacy and Health Sciences	MA	36,450	SP
McKendree Univ	IL	29,920	C+
McMurry Univ	TX	25,962	LC
McNeese State Univ	LA	2,649	C
Megar Evers College/The CUNY	NY	4,920	NC
Mercy College	NY	30,456	C
Mercy College of Health Sciences	IA	14,460	VC
Messiah College	PA	40,690	C+
Methodist Univ	NC	37,185	C
Metropolitan State Univ	MN	5,923	
Metropolitan State Univ of Denver	CO	4,835	LC
Miami Univ	OH	24,191	VC
Mich State Univ	MI	22,450	VC
MidAmerica Nazarene Univ	KS	28,000	C
Middle Tenn State Univ	TN	8,650	C
Midland Univ	NE	34,000	C
Midway College	KY	20,150	C
Midwestern State Univ	TX	9,722	C
Millersville Univ of Pennsylvania	PA	21,648	C
Milligan College	TN	27,510	C
Millikin Univ	IL	38,940	C
Mills College	CA	54,119	VC
Milwaukee School of Engineering	WI	39,948	VC+
Minn State Univ, Mankato	MN	15,616	C
Minn State Univ, Moorhead	MN	13,392	VC
Minot State Univ	ND	10,915	C
Misericordia Univ	PA	41,060	C
Miss College	MS	21,998	C
Miss Univ for Women	MS	7,400	C
Missouri State Univ	MO	13,996	C+
Missouri Western State Univ	MO	12,260	NC
Molloy College	NY	40,440	C
Monmouth Univ	NJ	44,108	C
Montana State Univ	MT	14,068	C
Montana State Univ-Northern	MT	12,500	C
Montana Tech of The Univ of Montana	MT	14,650	VC
Moravian College	PA	36,381	C
Morehead State Univ	KY	10,900	C
Morningside College	IA	35,430	C
Mount Aloysius College	PA	29,976	C
Mount Marty College	SD	29,638	C
Mount Mercy Univ	IA	35,320	C
Mount St. Mary College	NY	41,138	C
Mount St. Mary's College - Chalon Campus	CA	43,897	VC+
Mount Vernon Nazarene Univ	OH	29,590	C
Murray State Univ	KY	15,304	C
Muskingum Univ	OH	30,502	C
National Univ	CA	14,730	SP
Nazareth College of Rochester	NY	43,028	C+
Nebr Methodist College of Nursing and Allied Health	NE	22,690	SP
Nebr Wesleyan Univ	NE	29,774	C+
Neumann Univ	PA	31,078	LC
New Jersey City Univ	NJ	12,426	LC
New Mexico State Univ	NM	14,050	C
New York College of Technology/The CUNY	NY	5,769	NC
New York Inst of Technology	NY	45,010	VC
New York Univ	NY	61,470	MC
Newman Univ	KS	30,380	C
Niagara Univ	NY	41,010	C
Nicholls State Univ	LA	7,095	C
Norfolk State Univ	VA	10,531	LC
N Car Agricultural and Technical State Univ	NC	13,365	LC
N Car Central Univ	NC	9,000	C
N Dak State Univ	ND		C
North Park Univ	IL	30,130	C
Northeastern State Univ	OK	8,615	VC
Northeastern Univ	MA	55,296	MC
Northern Arizona Univ	AZ	19,010	C
Northern Illinois Univ	IL	19,600	C
Northern Kentucky Univ	KY	21,134	C
Northern Mich Univ	MI	18,278	C
Northwest Nazarene Univ	ID	34,000	C
Northwest Univ	WA	18,854	C
Northwestern College of Iowa	IA	36,240	VC
Northwestern Okla State Univ	OK	7,275	NC
Northwestern State Univ of Louisiana	LA	14,368	C
Norwich Univ	VT	28,212	C
Notre Dame College	OH	34,942	VC
Notre Dame de Namur Univ	CA	44,236	LC
Notre Dame of Maryland Univ	MD	27,700	VC
Nova Southeastern Univ	FL	37,280	VC
Nyack College	NY	33,250	C
Oakland Univ	MI	19,391	C
Oakwood Univ	AL	25,529	NC
Ohio State Univ at Lima	OH	7,140	C
Ohio State Univ at Mansfield	OH	13,160	C
Ohio State Univ at Marion	OH	16,990	MC
Ohio State Univ at Newark	OH	17,510	C
Ohio Univ	OH	21,080	C
Okla Baptist Univ	OK	28,202	C
Okla Christian Univ	OK	25,870	VC
Okla City Univ	OK	40,476	VC
Okla Panhandle State Univ	OK	8,996	C
Old Dominion Univ	VA	19,483	LC
Olivet Nazarene Univ	IL	29,990	C
Oral Roberts Univ	OK	31,734	C
Otterbein Univ	OH	32,214	C
Our Lady of Holy Cross College	LA	8,090	C
Pace Univ	NY	53,367	C
Pacific Lutheran Univ	WA	46,760	C+
Pacific Union College	CA	28,150	VC
Palm Beach Atlantic Univ	FL	34,874	C+
Penn State Univ/Altoona	PA	11,464	C
Pennsylvania College of Technology	PA	26,286	NC
Pfeiffer Univ	NC	33,700	LC
Piedmont College	GA	30,136	C
Pittsburg State Univ	KS	12,032	C
Plymouth State Univ	NH	23,148	LC
Point Loma Nazarene Univ	CA	41,006	C+
Pontifical Catholic Univ of PR	PR	7,310	
Prairie View A&M Univ	TX	15,205	LC
Presentation College	SD	14,800	LC
Purdue Univ/Calumet	IN	14,336	C
Purdue Univ/West Lafayette	IN	20,024	HC
Queens Univ of Charlotte	NC	39,543	C+
Quincy Univ	IL	34,980	LC
Quinnipiac Univ	CT	55,160	VC
Radford Univ	VA	17,766	LC
Ramapo College of New Jersey	NJ	24,938	C
Regis College	MA	47,565	LC
Regis Univ	CO	41,318	C
Research College of Nursing	MO	33,190	SP
Rhode Island College	RI	17,694	LC
Richard Stockton College of New Jersey	NJ	20,000	VC
Rivier Univ	NH	35,000	VC
Robert Morris Univ	PA	37,864	C
Roberts Wesleyan College	NY	38,306	C+
Rockford College	IL	31,000	C
Rockhurst Univ	MO	20,625	C
Rowan Univ	NJ	24,022	VC+
Russell Sage College	NY	39,370	C
Rutgers, The State Univ of New Jersey/Camden Campus	NJ	25,121	C
Rutgers, The State Univ of New Jersey/New Brunswick	NJ	25,562	VC
Rutgers, The State Univ of New Jersey/Newark Campus	NJ	258,806	C
Sacred Heart Univ	CT	49,264	VC
Saginaw Valley State Univ	MI	17,369	C
St. Anselm College	NH	49,376	VC
St. Francis Univ	PA	30,029	LC
St. John's Univ	MN	47,984	C
St. Joseph's College	IN	36,500	C
St. Joseph's College of Maine	ME	31,580	C
St. Louis Univ	MO	48,346	HC
St. Martin's Univ	WA	41,678	C
St. Mary-of-the-Woods College	IN	37,722	LC
St. Mary's College	IN	45,160	C+
St. Peter's Univ	NJ	44,240	C
St. Xavier Univ	IL	32,840	C
Salem State Univ	MA	13,161	LC
Salisbury Univ	MD	19,180	VC
Salve Regina Univ	RI	48,550	VC
Samford Univ	AL	37,060	C+
San Diego State Univ	CA	21,611	C
San Francisco State Univ	CA	18,514	C
San Jose State Univ	CA	19,133	LC
Schreiner Univ	TX	32,734	LC
Seattle Pacific Univ	WA	41,559	VC+
Seattle Univ	WA	49,035	VC+
Seton Hall Univ	NJ	45,902	C
Shawnee State Univ	OH	16,916	C
Shenandoah Univ	VA	39,916	C
Shepherd Univ	WV	15,875	C
Shorter Univ	GA	30,650	LC
Simmons College	MA	49,946	VC
Simpson Univ	CA	28,900	C
Slippery Rock Univ of Pennsylvania	PA	10,360	C
Sonoma State Univ	CA	20,541	C
S Car State Univ	SC	6,700	LC
S Dak State Univ	SD	14,296	C
South Univ	GA	36,070	LC
Southeast Missouri State Univ	MO	15,370	LC
Southeastern Louisiana Univ	LA	13,325	C
Southern Adventist Univ	TN	26,190	C
Southern Conn State Univ	CT	18,033	LC
Southern Illinois Univ Edwardsville	IL	17,532	C
Southern Nazarene Univ	OK	24,354	C
Southern Oregon Univ	OR	17,874	C
Southern Univ and A&M College	LA	9,761	LC
Southern Vermont College	VT	30,740	LC
Southwest Baptist Univ	MO	24,710	C
Southwestern Adventist Univ	TX	23,026	LC
Southwestern Okla State Univ	OK	9,160	C
Spalding Univ	KY	32,287	LC
Spring Arbor Univ	MI	26,740	C
Spring Hill College	AL	44,164	VC
St. Catherine Univ	MN	37,782	C+
St. Francis College	NY	34,200	C
St. John Fisher College	NY	40,708	C+
St. Joseph's College, New York/Brooklyn Campus	NY	22,630	C
St. Joseph's College, New York/Suffolk Campus	NY	22,630	C
St. Olaf College	MN	51,200	HC+
SUNY Polytechnic Inst	NY	19,690	C
SUNY/Empire State College	NY	6,315	SP
Stephen F. Austin State Univ	TX	14,668	C
Stevenson Univ	MD	41,470	C
Stony Brook Univ / SUNY	NY	20,078	HC+
SUNY New Paltz	NY	14,348	C
SUNY Plattsburgh / SUNY	NY	18,083	C
Tarleton State Univ	TX	13,489	LC
Temple Univ	PA	24,392	VC
Tenn State Univ	TN	9,048	C
Tenn Tech Univ	TN	11,310	C
Tenn Wesleyan College	TN	11,250	C
Texas A&M Univ at Corpus Christi	TX	11,544	LC
Texas A&M Univ at Kingsville	TX	7,500	LC
Texas Christian Univ	TX	49,980	HC
Texas Lutheran Univ	TX	36,040	C
Texas State Univ	TX	17,128	C
Texas Woman's Univ	TX	13,633	LC
The Catholic Univ of America	DC	52,852	VC
The College of Idaho	ID	31,277	C+
The College of New Rochelle	NY	33,600	VC
Ohio State Univ-Columbus Campus	OH	19,887	HC+
The Pennsylvania State Univ - Univ Park	PA	28,022	VC+
The SUNY/College at Brockport	NY	19,002	C
The Univ of Memphis	TN	15,094	C
The Univ of N Car at Greensboro	NC	12,848	C
The Univ of N Car at Pembroke	NC	13,388	C
The Univ of Tenn at Chattanooga	TN	16,883	C
The Univ of Utah	UT	16,463	VC
The Univ of Virginia's College at Wise	VA	11,076	C
Thomas Edison State College	NJ	5,700	SP
Thomas More College	KY	34,760	C
Thomas Univ	GA	11,520	NC
Touro College	NY	27,959	VC
Towson Univ	MD	16,000	VC
Trevecca Nazarene Univ	TN	31,186	C
Trinity Christian College	IL	28,869	C
Trinity College of Nursing and Health Sciences	IL	53,138	SP
Trinity Washington Univ	DC	30,250	C+
Troy Univ	AL	10,650	C
Truman State Univ	MO	15,541	HC
Tuskegee Univ	AL	26,750	C
Union College	KY	29,955	C
Union College	NE	23,270	C
Union Univ	TN	28,260	C
Universidad Adventista de las Antillas	PR	7,360	
Universidad de Puerto/Arecibo	PR	7,227	
Universidad Metropolitana	PR	3,500	
Univ at Buffalo / The SUNY	NY	20,283	VC
Univ of Akron	OH	20,436	C
Univ of Alabama at Birmingham	AL	18,484	C+
Univ of Alabama at Tuscaloosa	AL	17,164	C+
Univ of Alabama in Huntsville	AL	17,591	VC+
Univ of Alaska Anchorage	AK	16,673	NC
Univ of Arizona	AZ	20,657	C
Univ of Arkansas at Fayetteville	AR	18,352	C
Univ of Arkansas at Little Rock	AR	17,609	LC
Univ of Arkansas at Monticello	AR	12,076	NC
Univ of Arkansas at Pine Bluff	AR	13,378	C
Univ of Calif at Irvine	CA	25,961	VC
Univ of Calif at Los Angeles	CA	25,686	MC
Univ of Central Arkansas	AR	13,667	VC
Univ of Central Florida	FL	15,668	VC+
Univ of Central Missouri	MO	14,605	C
Univ of Central Okla	OK	12,293	C
Univ of Charleston	WV	32,300	C
Univ of Cincinnati	OH	21,506	VC
Univ of Colo at Colo Springs	CO	15,000	VC
Univ of Colo Denver	CO	17,904	C
Univ of Conn	CT	24,706	HC
Univ of Dallas	TX	45,500	VC+
Univ of Delaware	DE	23,612	VC
Univ of Detroit Mercy	MI	30,450	VC
Univ of Dubuque	IA	30,200	C
Univ of Evansville	IN	42,656	VC+
Univ of Findlay	OH	31,916	C
Univ of Florida	FL	15,943	HC
Univ of Hartford	CT	42,674	C
Univ of Hawaii at Hilo	HI	23,066	C
Univ of Hawaii at Manoa	HI	19,379	C
Univ of Illinois at Chicago	IL	24,505	VC
Univ of Indianapolis	IN	31,740	C
Univ of Iowa	IA	17,693	VC
Univ of Jamestown	ND	24,738	C
Univ of Kansas	KS	17,603	C+
Univ of Kentucky	KY	19,868	C
Univ of Louisiana at Lafayette	LA	6,130	C
Univ of Louisiana at Monroe	LA	12,998	C
Univ of Louisville	KY	17,946	C
Univ of Maine	ME	19,902	C+
Univ of Maine at Augusta	ME	6,855	C
Univ of Maine at Fort Kent	ME	15,195	LC
Univ of Mary	ND	16,714	C
Univ of Mary Hardin-Baylor	TX	31,950	C+
Univ of Mass Amherst	MA	24,215	VC+
Univ of Mass Boston	MA	23,066	VC
Univ of Mass Dartmouth	MA	22,223	C
Univ of Mass Lowell	MA	19,316	C
Univ of Miami	FL	57,034	MC
Univ of Mich/Ann Arbor	MI	22,102	MC
Univ of Mich-Flint	MI	17,547	C
Univ of Minn/Twin Cities	MN		HC
Univ of Miss	MS	16,704	C+
Univ of Missouri/Columbia	MO	18,201	MC
Univ of Missouri-Kansas City	MO	19,603	C
Univ of Missouri-St. Louis	MO		C
Univ of Mobile	AL	28,935	VC
Univ of Nebr at Kearney	NE	14,855	LC
Univ of Nevada, Las Vegas	NV	17,303	C
Univ of Nevada/Reno	NV	17,507	C
Univ of New England	ME	46,750	C
Univ of New Hampshire	NH	26,912	C
Univ of New Mexico	NM	15,300	C
Univ of North Alabama	AL	9,960	C
Univ of N Car at Chapel Hill	NC	18,928	MC
Univ of N Car at Charlotte	NC	15,547	C
Univ of N Car at Wilmington	NC	13,572	VC
Univ of N Dak	ND	14,551	C
Univ of North Florida	FL	15,870	VC
Univ of North Georgia	GA	8,500	C
Univ of Northern Colo	CO	18,446	C
Univ of Pennsylvania	PA	61,132	MC
Univ of Pikeville	KY	25,500	NC
Univ of Pittsburgh at Bradford	PA	21,802	C
Univ of Pittsburgh at Johnstown	PA	20,862	LC
Univ of Pittsburgh at Pittsburgh	PA	28,572	HC+
Univ of Portland	OR	49,964	VC
Univ of PR/Humacao	PR	1,877	
Univ of PR/Mayaguez	PR	1,250	
Univ of Rio Grande	OH	8,750	NC
Univ of Rochester	NY	60,668	MC
Univ of St. Francis	IN	29,810	C
Univ of St. Joseph	CT	45,630	C
Univ of St. Mary	KS	28,400	C+
Univ of San Francisco	CA	54,770	VC
Univ of Scranton	PA	51,940	VC
Univ of South Alabama	AL	13,510	C
Univ of S Car Aiken	SC	16,712	C
Univ of S Car at Columbia	SC	19,725	VC+
Univ of S Car Upstate	SC	18,200	LC
Univ of South Florida/Tampa	FL	13,000	C
Univ of Southern Indiana	IN	14,885	C
Univ of Southern Maine	ME	16,576	C
Univ of Southern Miss	MS	13,170	C
Univ of St. Francis	IL	37,560	C
Univ of St. Thomas - Houston	TX	37,690	C
Univ of Tampa	FL	35,160	VC
Univ of Tenn at Knoxville	TN	20,364	VC+
Univ of Tenn at Martin	TN	13,734	C
Univ of Texas - Pan American	TX	11,125	LC
Univ of Texas at Arlington	TX	10,908	LC
Univ of Texas at Austin	TX	44,074	HC
Univ of Texas at El Paso	TX	8,764	LC
Univ of the District of Columbia	DC	7,244	LC
Univ of the Incarnate Word	TX	37,316	LC

ST = STATE $IS = IN-STATE COSTS   SR = SELECTOR RATING

School	ST	$IS	SR
Univ of the Sacred Heart	PR	5,590	
Univ of Toledo	OH	18,464	C
Univ of Tulsa	OK	46,331	MC
Univ of Vermont	VT	27,006	VC+
Univ of Virginia	VA	23,050	MC
Univ of Washington	WA	14,722	VC
Univ of West Florida	FL	14,656	C
Univ of West Georgia	GA	15,488	LC
Univ of Wisc/Eau Claire	WI	15,730	VC
Univ of Wisc/Green Bay	WI	19,074	C
Univ of Wisc/Madison	WI	18,757	HC+
Univ of Wisc/Oshkosh	WI	10,426	LC
Univ of Wisc-Milwaukee	WI	18,436	C
Univ of Wyoming	WY	14,401	C+
Urbana Univ	OH	30,820	C
Ursuline College	OH	33,198	LC
Utica College	NY	45,670	C
Valparaiso Univ	IN	44,940	VC+
Vanguard Univ of Southern Calif	CA	35,833	VC
Villanova Univ	PA	58,394	MC
Virginia Commonwealth Univ	VA	21,716	C
Viterbo Univ	WI	30,070	C
Wagner College	NY	48,600	C+
Walla Walla Univ	WA	26,256	NC
Walsh Univ	OH	35,100	C
Washburn Univ	KS	12,579	C
Washington Adventist Univ	MD	25,859	LC
Washington State Univ	WA	20,461	C
Wayland Baptist Univ	TX	18,912	LC
Wayne State Univ	MI	22,063	C
Waynesburg Univ	PA	30,150	C
Webster Univ	MO	35,100	C+
Wesley College	DE	31,115	C
West Chester Univ of Pennsylvania	PA	17,186	C
West Liberty Univ	WV	9,142	LC
West Texas A&M Univ	TX	13,478	C
West Virginia Univ	WV	16,542	C+
West Virginia Univ Inst of Technology	WV	14,094	NC
West Virginia Wesleyan College	WV	26,880	C
Western Carolina Univ	NC	13,965	C
Western Conn State Univ	CT	18,327	LC
Western Illinois Univ	IL	20,732	C
Western Kentucky Univ	KY	11,000	LC
Western Mich Univ	MI	19,628	C
Western Washington Univ	WA	18,519	VC
Westfield State Univ	MA	18,297	C
Westminster College	MO	31,720	VC
Westminster College	UT	37,708	C+
Wheaton College	IL	40,720	MC
Wheeling Jesuit Univ	WV	33,500	C
Whitworth Univ	WA	47,734	VC
Wichita State Univ	KS	14,607	C+
Widener Univ	PA	52,418	C
Wilkes Univ	PA	44,070	C
William Carey Univ	MS	13,500	LC
William Jewell College	MO	31,000	VC+
William Paterson Univ of New Jersey	NJ	21,694	C
Wilmington Univ	DE	8,112	NC
Wingate Univ	NC	34,990	C
Winona State Univ	MN	16,640	C
Winston-Salem State Univ	NC	9,418	LC
Worcester State Univ	MA	19,812	C
Wright State Univ	OH	16,983	C
Xavier Univ	OH	44,980	VC
York College / The CUNY	NY	5,496	VC
York College of Pennsylvania	PA	26,590	C
Youngstown State Univ	OH	16,732	C

NURSING EDUCATION

School	ST	$IS	SR
Allen College	IA	26,110	SP
Aquinas College	TN	29,250	VC+
Cal State, Northridge	CA	28,690	LC
Georgia Southern Univ	GA	16,942	C
Indiana Wesleyan Univ	IN	31,815	VC
New York Univ	NY	61,470	MC
Seattle Pacific Univ	WA	41,559	VC+
Univ of Alaska Anchorage	AK	16,673	NC
Univ of St. Thomas - Houston	TX	37,690	C

NURSING HOME ADMINISTRATION

School	ST	$IS	SR
Kent State Univ	OH	19,920	C
Mount Aloysius College	PA	29,976	C
New York Univ	NY	61,470	MC
Ohio Univ	OH	21,080	C
Univ of Louisiana at Monroe	LA	12,998	C
Youngstown State Univ	OH	16,732	C

NUTRITION

School	ST	$IS	SR
Abilene Christian Univ	TX	38,400	C+
Alabama A&M Univ	AL	10,084	C
Alcorn State Univ	MS	9,500	C
Andrews Univ	MI	28,030	C+
Appalachian State Univ	NC	12,919	VC
Arizona State Univ, at the Downtown Phoenix Campus	AZ	22,101	C
Auburn Univ	AL	22,378	VC+
Baylor Univ	TX	50,329	HC
Benedictine Univ	IL	37,820	C
Boston Univ	MA	60,694	MC
Bowling Green State Univ	OH	18,970	C
Brigham Young Univ	UT	12,100	HC
Calif Polytechnic State Univ	CA	19,847	HC
Case Western Reserve Univ	OH	56,534	MC
Cedar Crest College	PA	43,240	C
College of St. Benedict	MN	49,359	VC
College of St. Elizabeth	NJ	43,839	LC
Colo State Univ-Fort Collins	CO	20,385	VC
Concordia College - Moorhead	MN	39,974	VC
Dominican Univ	IL	37,628	C
Drexel Univ	PA	61,418	VC+
East Carolina Univ	NC	14,169	C
Eastern Mich Univ	MI	18,604	C
Florida State Univ	FL	16,715	VC
Fort Valley State Univ	GA	11,200	VC
Framingham State Univ	MA	18,854	C
Gannon Univ	PA	39,608	C
Georgia Southern Univ	GA	16,942	C
Georgia State Univ	GA	15,582	VC
Goddard College	VT	16,418	VC
Hampshire College	MA	58,320	MC
Howard Univ	DC	13,646	C
Hunter College	NY	14,429	VC
Indiana Univ of Pennsylvania	PA	20,846	LC
Iowa State Univ	IA	16,403	C
Johnson & Wales Univ/ Denver Campus	CO	29,576	C
Kansas State Univ	KS	15,497	VC
Keene State College	NH	23,232	LC
Kent State Univ	OH	19,920	C
La Salle Univ	PA	50,270	C
Langston Univ	OK	3,000	C
LIU Post	NY	47,660	C
Louisiana State Univ	LA	18,677	C+
Madonna Univ	MI	24,540	VC
Marshall Univ	WV	14,820	C
Meredith College	NC	31,420	C
Messiah College	PA	40,690	C+
Miami Univ	OH	24,191	VC
Mich State Univ	MI	22,450	VC
Middle Tenn State Univ	TN	8,650	C
Montclair State Univ	NJ	22,614	C
Murray State Univ	KY	15,304	C
New Mexico State Univ	NM	14,050	C
New York Univ	NY	61,470	MC
N Car Central Univ	NC	9,000	C
N Dak State Univ	ND		C
Northern Illinois Univ	IL	19,768	C
Ohio Univ	OH	21,080	C
Okla State Univ	OK	14,310	VC
Oregon State Univ	OR	20,273	VC
Pepperdine Univ	CA	55,372	HC+
Point Loma Nazarene Univ	CA	41,006	C+
Purdue Univ/West Lafayette	IN	20,024	HC
Queens College/The CUNY	NY	17,107	VC
Rochester Inst of Technology	NY	42,450	VC
Russell Sage College	NY	39,370	C
Rutgers, The State Univ of New Jersey/New Brunswick	NJ	25,562	VC
St. John's Univ	MN	47,984	C
St. Louis Univ	MO	48,346	HC
Samford Univ	AL	37,060	C
San Diego State Univ	CA	21,611	C+
S Car State Univ	SC	6,700	LC
S Dak State Univ	SD	14,296	C
St. Catherine Univ	MN	37,782	C
Stephen F. Austin State Univ	TX	14,668	C
SUNY Plattsburgh / SUNY	NY	18,083	C
Syracuse Univ	NY	56,346	VC
Texas Christian Univ	TX	49,980	VC
Texas Southern Univ	TX	18,212	LC
Texas State Univ	TX	17,128	C
Texas Tech Univ	TX	14,243	C
Ohio State Univ-Columbus Campus	OH	19,887	HC+
The Pennsylvania State Univ - Univ Park	PA	28,022	VC+
The Univ of N Car at Greensboro	NC	12,848	C
Univ of Arizona	AZ	20,657	C
Univ of Arkansas at Fayetteville	AR	18,352	C+
Univ of Calif at Berkeley	CA	23,322	MC
Univ of Calif at Davis	CA		HC
Univ of Central Okla	OK	12,293	C
Univ of Conn	CT	24,706	HC
Univ of Dayton	OH	49,070	VC
Univ of Delaware	DE	23,612	VC
Univ of Illinois at Chicago	IL	24,505	VC
Univ of Illinois at Urbana-Champaign	IL	26,450	HC
Univ of Maine	ME	19,902	C+
Univ of Maryland - College Park	MD	20,060	HC
Univ of Mass Amherst	MA	24,215	VC+
Univ of Minn/Twin Cities	MN		HC
Univ of Missouri/Columbia	MO	18,201	MC
Univ of Nebr - Lincoln	NE	18,031	VC
Univ of Nevada/Reno	NV	17,507	C
Univ of New Hampshire	NH	26,912	C
Univ of New Haven	CT	48,940	C
Univ of New Mexico	NM	15,300	C
Univ of N Car at Chapel Hill	NC	18,928	MC
Univ of North Florida	FL	15,870	VC
Univ of Northern Colo	CO	18,446	C
Univ of Northern Iowa	IA	15,795	C
Univ of PR Recinto de Rio Piedras	PR	5,750	
Univ of St. Joseph	CT	45,630	C
Univ of Southern Indiana	IN	14,885	C
Univ of Tenn at Knoxville	TN	20,364	VC+
Univ of Tenn at Martin	TN	13,734	C
Univ of Texas at Austin	TX	44,074	HC
Univ of the Incarnate Word	TX	37,316	LC
Univ of Vermont	VT	27,006	VC+
Univ of Wisc/Madison	WI	18,757	HC+
Univ of Wisc/Stevens Point	WI	14,043	C
Univ of Wisc-Milwaukee	WI	18,436	C
Virginia Polytechnic Inst and State Univ	VA	14,629	HC
Wayne State Univ	MI	22,063	C
West Chester Univ of Pennsylvania	PA	17,186	C
West Virginia Univ	WV	16,542	C+
West Virginia Wesleyan College	WV	26,880	C
Winthrop Univ	SC	21,120	C
Youngstown State Univ	OH	16,732	C

NUTRITION AND DIETETICS

School	ST	$IS	SR
Arizona State Univ, at the Downtown Phoenix Campus	AZ	22,101	C
Indiana Univ Bloomington	IN	19,801	VC
Kent State Univ	OH	19,920	C
Murray State Univ	KY	15,304	C
St. Louis Univ	MO	48,346	HC
Thomas Edison State College	NJ	5,700	SP
Univ of Nevada/Reno	NV	17,507	C

NUTRITION AND WELLNESS

School	ST	$IS	SR
Bridgewater College	VA	41,450	C
Gannon Univ	PA	39,608	C

NUTRITION EDUCATION

School	ST	$IS	SR
Ohio Univ	OH	21,080	C
Univ of Cincinnati	OH	21,506	VC
Univ of Illinois at Chicago	IL	24,505	VC

NUTRITIONAL SCIENCES

School	ST	$IS	SR
Calif Baptist Univ	CA	38,792	C
Cal State, Long Beach	CA	17,502	C+
Cornell Univ	NY	60,964	MC
Fontbonne Univ	MO	31,384	C
McNeese State Univ	LA	2,649	C
St. Louis Univ	MO	48,346	HC
San Jose State Univ	CA	19,133	C
The Pennsylvania State Univ - Univ Park	PA	28,022	VC+
Univ of Georgia	GA	20,082	VC
Univ of Illinois at Chicago	IL	24,505	VC
Univ of Nevada/Reno	NV	17,507	C

OCCUPATIONAL HYGIENE & SAFETY

School	ST	$IS	SR
Ohio Univ	OH	21,080	C

OCCUPATIONAL SAFETY AND HEALTH

School	ST	$IS	SR
Embry-Riddle Aeronautical Univ - Worldwide	FL	15,512	C
Grand Valley State Univ	MI	17,998	C+
Howard Payne Univ	TX	17,115	C
Keene State College	NH	23,232	LC
Madonna Univ	MI	24,540	VC
Marshall Univ	WV	14,820	C
Millersville Univ of Pennsylvania	PA	21,648	C
Montana Tech of The Univ of Montana	MT	14,650	VC
Murray State Univ	KY	15,304	C
N Car Agricultural and Technical State Univ	NC	13,365	LC
Oakland Univ	MI	19,391	C
Purdue Univ/West Lafayette	IN	20,024	HC
Southeastern Louisiana Univ	LA	13,325	C
Southeastern Okla State Univ	OK	7,966	LC
Southwest Baptist Univ	MO	24,710	C
Univ of Central Missouri	MO	14,605	C
Univ of Findlay	OH	31,916	C
Univ of N Dak	ND	14,551	C

OCCUPATIONAL THERAPY

School	ST	$IS	SR
Allen College	IA	26,110	SP
American International College	MA	36,100	LC
Augustana College	IL	43,398	VC
Baker College of Flint	MI	7,800	NC
Barry Univ	FL	38,190	C
Bay Path College	MA	34,565	C
Bethany College	WV	35,282	LC
Boston Univ	MA	60,694	MC
Brenau Univ - Women's College	GA	26,650	LC
Cal State, Dominguez Hills	CA	17,090	LC
Calvin College	MI	39,120	VC
Cleveland State Univ	OH	21,776	C
College of St. Benedict	MN	49,359	VC
Colo State Univ-Pueblo	CO	16,183	C
Concordia Univ Wisc	WI	28,980	C
Dominican College	NY	31,270	LC
Dominican Univ of Calif	CA	51,250	C
Duquesne Univ	PA	43,720	C
East Carolina Univ	NC	14,169	C
Eastern Kentucky Univ	KY	11,161	C
Eastern Mich Univ	MI	18,604	C
Elizabethtown College	PA	49,740	VC
Florida A&M Univ	FL	14,935	LC
Florida Gulf Coast Univ	FL		C
Gannon Univ	PA	39,608	C
Howard Univ	DC	13,646	C
Husson Univ	ME	24,194	LC
Ithaca College	NY	53,864	HC
Keuka College	NY	30,300	C
Lamar Univ	TX	6,820	LC
Lenoir-Rhyne College	NC	35,984	C
LIU Brooklyn	NY	47,182	LC
Maryville Univ of St. Louis	MO	35,856	VC
Misericordia Univ	PA	41,060	C
Mount Aloysius College	PA	29,976	C
Mount Mary Univ	WI	33,590	LC
New York Univ	NY	61,470	MC
Pennsylvania College of Technology	PA	26,286	NC
Quinnipiac Univ	CT	55,160	VC
Russell Sage College	NY	39,370	C
Sacred Heart Univ	CT	49,264	VC
St. Francis Univ	PA	30,029	C
St. John's Univ	MN	47,984	C
St. Louis Univ	MO	48,346	HC
St. Vincent College	PA	40,244	C
San Jose State Univ	CA	19,133	LC
Spalding Univ	KY	32,287	LC
St. Catherine Univ	MN	37,782	C+
Stony Brook Univ / SUNY	NY	20,078	HC+
Tenn State Univ	TN	9,048	C
Ohio State Univ-Columbus Campus	OH	19,887	HC+
The Univ of Utah	UT	16,463	VC
Touro College	NY	27,959	VC
Towson Univ	MD	16,000	VC
Tuskegee Univ	AL	26,750	C
Univ at Buffalo / The SUNY	NY	20,283	VC
Univ of Central Arkansas	AR	13,667	VC
Univ of Findlay	OH	31,916	C
Univ of Florida	FL	15,943	HC
Univ of Hartford	CT	42,674	C
Univ of Illinois at Chicago	IL	24,505	VC
Univ of Kansas	KS	17,603	C+
Univ of Louisiana at Monroe	LA	12,998	C
Univ of Mary	ND	16,714	C
Univ of Minn/Twin Cities	MN		HC
Univ of Missouri/Columbia	MO	18,201	MC
Univ of New England	ME	46,750	C
Univ of New Hampshire	NH	26,912	C
Univ of Pittsburgh at Pittsburgh	PA	28,572	HC+
Univ of Scranton	PA	51,940	VC
Univ of Southern Calif	CA	56,903	MC
Univ of Southern Indiana	IN	14,885	C
Univ of the Sciences	PA	48,320	VC+
Univ of Wisc/La Crosse	WI	9,304	VC
Univ of Wisc-Milwaukee	WI	18,436	C
Utica College	NY	45,670	C
Wartburg College	IA	41,055	VC
West Virginia Univ	WV	16,542	C+
Western Mich Univ	MI	19,628	C
Worcester State Univ	MA	19,812	C
York College / The CUNY	NY	5,496	VC

OCEAN ENGINEERING

School	ST	$IS	SR
Florida Atlantic Univ	FL	17,339	C
Florida Inst of Technology	FL	48,290	VC
Mass Inst of Technology	MA	58,240	MC
Texas A&M Univ at Galveston	TX	11,258	C
United States Naval Academy	MD		MC
Univ of Washington	WA	14,722	VC
Virginia Polytechnic Inst and State Univ	VA	14,629	HC

OCEANOGRAPHY

School	ST	$IS	SR
Bowdoin College	ME	59,568	MC
Florida Inst of Technology	FL	48,290	VC
Hawaii Pacific Univ	HI	34,360	C
Humboldt State Univ	CA	18,400	C
Maine Maritime Academy	ME	21,073	C
Millersville Univ of Pennsylvania	PA	21,648	C
Old Dominion Univ	VA	19,483	LC
Prescott College	AZ	33,284	C

ST = STATE $IS = IN-STATE COSTS   SR = SELECTOR RATING

School	ST	$IS	SR
Texas A&M Univ at Galveston	TX	11,258	C
United States Naval Academy	MD		MC
Univ of Mich/Ann Arbor	MI	22,102	MC
Univ of Washington	WA	14,722	VC

OFFICE SUPERVISION AND MANAGEMENT

School	ST	$IS	SR
Adams State Univ	CO	13,358	LC
Alabama A&M Univ	AL	10,084	C
Albany State Univ	GA	8,500	C
Baker College of Flint	MI	7,800	NC
Campbellsville Univ	KY	27,720	C
Central Conn State Univ	CT	19,749	C
Chancellor Univ	OH	11,000	C
Concord Univ	WV	13,102	C
Eastern Mich Univ	MI	18,604	C
Fayetteville State Univ	NC	10,816	C
Fort Hays State Univ	KS	11,354	C
Fort Valley State Univ	GA	11,200	VC
Georgia State Univ	GA	15,582	VC
Inter-American Univ of PR/ Bayamon Univ College	PR	4,428	
Johnson & Wales Univ/ Providence Campus	RI	29,576	C
Middle Tenn State Univ	TN	8,650	C
Miss Valley State Univ	MS	9,706	LC
Northwestern Okla State Univ	OK	7,275	NC
Rider Univ	NJ	45,720	C
S Car State Univ	SC	6,700	LC
Southwestern Adventist Univ	TX	23,026	LC
Sul Ross State Univ	TX	13,410	C
Tabor College	KS	29,010	C
Tarleton State Univ	TX	13,489	LC
Universidad Adventista de las Antillas	PR	7,360	
Univ of S Car at Columbia	SC	19,725	VC+
Univ of the Cumberlands	KY	27,500	C
Univ of the District of Columbia	DC	7,244	C
Univ of Wisc Whitewater	WI	13,314	C
Valley City State Univ	ND	12,286	LC
Wiley College	TX		LC

OPERA

School	ST	$IS	SR
Boston Conservatory	MA	56,380	VC
LIU Post	NY	47,660	C

OPERATIONS MANAGEMENT

School	ST	$IS	SR
Ashford Univ	CA	10,480	C
Ball State Univ	IN	17,850	C
Ferris State Univ	MI	20,047	C
George Mason Univ	VA	15,724	VC
Kent State Univ	OH	19,920	C
Le Moyne College	NY	43,470	C
Marquette Univ	WI	46,930	VC+
Metropolitan State Univ	MN	5,923	
Minn State Univ, Moorhead	MN	13,392	VC
New York Univ	NY	61,470	MC
Oakland Univ	MI	19,391	C
Oswego / SUNY	NY	20,009	VC
Ohio State Univ-Columbus Campus	OH	19,887	HC+
The Univ of Utah	UT	16,463	VC
Thomas Edison State College	NJ	5,700	SP
Univ of Arizona	AZ	20,657	VC
Univ of Cincinnati	OH	21,506	VC
Univ of Delaware	DE	23,612	VC
Univ of Idaho	ID	14,558	C
Univ of Maryland - College Park	MD	20,060	HC
Univ of Mass Amherst	MA	24,215	VC+
Univ of Mass Dartmouth	MA	22,223	C
Univ of Missouri-St. Louis	MO		VC
Univ of N Dak	ND	14,551	C
Univ of North Texas	TX	15,628	VC
Univ of Pennsylvania	PA	61,132	MC
Univ of Portland	OR	49,064	VC
Univ of Scranton	PA	51,940	VC
Univ of Wisc/Madison	WI	18,757	HC+
Univ of Wisc-Milwaukee	WI	18,436	C
Washington State Univ	WA	20,461	VC
Western Washington Univ	WA	18,519	VC

OPERATIONS RESEARCH

School	ST	$IS	SR
Boston College	MA	60,622	MC
Canisius College	NY	44,900	C
CUNY/Baruch College	NY		HC
Columbia Univ/City of New York	NY	61,116	MC
LIU Brooklyn	NY	47,182	LC
Milwaukee School of Engineering	WI	39,948	VC+
New York Univ	NY	61,470	MC
Princeton Univ	NJ	53,795	MC
United States Air Force Academy	CO		MC
United States Coast Guard Academy	CT	942	HC
United States Military Academy	NY		MC

School	ST	$IS	SR
United States Naval Academy	MD		MC
Univ of Calif at Berkeley	CA	23,322	MC
Univ of Dayton	OH	49,070	VC
Univ of Illinois at Urbana-Champaign	IL	26,450	HC

OPERATIONS RESEARCH AND ENGINEERING

School	ST	$IS	SR
Cornell Univ	NY	60,964	MC

OPHTHALMIC TECHNOLOGY

School	ST	$IS	SR
Old Dominion Univ	VA	19,483	LC

OPTICAL ENGINEERING

School	ST	$IS	SR
Rose-Hulman Inst of Technology	IN	53,340	MC
Univ of Alabama in Huntsville	AL	17,591	VC+
Univ of Arizona	AZ	20,657	C
Univ of Rochester	NY	60,668	MC

OPTICS

School	ST	$IS	SR
Capitol College	MD	21,250	C
Saginaw Valley State Univ	MI	17,369	C
Univ of Arizona	AZ	20,657	C
Univ of Rochester	NY	60,668	MC

OPTOMETRY

School	ST	$IS	SR
Baylor Univ	TX	50,329	HC
Ferris State Univ	MI	20,047	C
Indiana Univ Bloomington	IN	19,801	VC
Oral Roberts Univ	OK	31,734	C
Purdue Univ/Calumet	IN	14,336	C
Univ of Calif at Berkeley	CA	23,322	MC

ORGAN PERFORMANCE

School	ST	$IS	SR
Embry-Riddle Aeronautical Univ - Prescott Campus	AZ	40,444	VC+
Houghton College	NY	36,808	C+
Indiana Univ Bloomington	IN	19,801	VC
Texas Christian Univ	TX	49,980	HC
Wright State Univ	OH	16,983	C

ORGANIZATIONAL BEHAVIOR

School	ST	$IS	SR
Assumption College	MA	47,122	C+
Benedictine Univ	IL	37,820	C
Coe College	IA	45,550	VC
College of St. Scholastica	MN	41,440	C
DePaul Univ	IL	47,623	VC
Franklin Univ	OH	20,985	SP
Hannibal-LaGrange Univ	MO	24,490	C
Huntington Univ	IN	32,220	C+
Ithaca College	NY	53,864	HC
La Salle Univ	PA	50,270	C
Methodist Univ	NC	37,185	C
National Univ	CA	14,730	SP
New York Univ	NY	61,470	MC
Northwestern Univ	IL	61,640	MC
Oral Roberts Univ	OK	31,734	C
Pitzer College	CA	54,988	MC
Robert Morris Univ	PA	37,864	C
Rollins College	FL	52,370	HC
St. Louis Univ	MO	48,346	HC
The Lincoln Univ	PA	15,154	LC
The Pennsylvania State Univ - Univ Park	PA	28,022	VC+
The Univ of Okla	OK	18,621	VC
Univ of Calif at Davis	CA		HC
Univ of Central Missouri	MO	14,605	C
Univ of Cincinnati	OH	21,506	VC
Univ of Illinois at Urbana-Champaign	IL	26,450	HC
Univ of Mich/Ann Arbor	MI	22,102	MC
Univ of Minn Crookston	MN	17,834	C
Univ of North Texas	TX	15,628	C
Univ of San Francisco	CA	54,770	VC
Univ of Tulsa	OK	46,331	MC
Woodbury Univ	CA	34,500	LC

ORGANIZATIONAL LEADERSHIP AND MANAGEMENT

School	ST	$IS	SR
Adams State Univ	CO	13,358	LC
Alderson Broaddus Univ	WV	28,656	C
Ashford Univ	CA	10,480	C
Aurora Univ	IL	33,228	C
Baldwin Wallace Univ	OH	38,318	C
Blackburn College	IL	21,350	C
Bluffton Univ	OH	38,948	C
Cameron Univ	OK	10,004	LC
Carroll Univ	WI	38,100	C
Claflin Univ	SC	22,368	LC
College of Mount St. Joseph	OH	33,880	C
College of St Joseph	VT	30,600	LC
Concordia Univ St. Paul	MN	28,250	C
Defiance College	OH	30,645	C
Drury Univ	MO	31,909	VC
Eastern Illinois Univ	IL	20,466	C

School	ST	$IS	SR
Eastern Univ	PA	37,704	C
George Fox Univ	OR	40,750	C+
Greenville College	IL	27,012	C
Hilbert College	NY	28,550	C
Indiana Univ-Purdue Univ Fort Wayne	IN	15,521	C
Indiana Univ-Purdue Univ Indianapolis	IN	17,611	C
Keystone College	PA	28,680	LC
Le Moyne College	NY	43,470	C
Loyola Univ Chicago	IL	51,646	VC+
Lubbock Christian Univ	TX	26,308	C
Marquette Univ	WI	46,930	VC+
Maryville Univ of St. Louis	MO	35,856	VC
McNeese State Univ	LA	2,649	C
Millikin Univ	IL	38,940	C
Mount Aloysius College	PA	29,976	C
National Univ	CA	14,730	SP
Northern Kentucky Univ	KY	21,134	C
Northwestern State Univ of Louisiana	LA	14,368	C
Nyack College	NY	33,250	C
Ohio Valley Univ	WV	17,752	C
Palm Beach Atlantic Univ	FL	34,874	C+
Point Park Univ	PA	36,390	C
Prescott College	AZ	33,284	C
Providence College	RI	57,383	VC
Purdue Univ/West Lafayette	IN	20,024	HC
St. Joseph's Univ	PA	55,006	VC
St. Louis Univ	MO	48,346	HC
Samford Univ	AL	37,060	C+
Simpson College	CA	28,900	C
Spring Hill College	AL	44,164	VC
St. Joseph's College, New York/Brooklyn Campus	NY	22,630	C
St. Joseph's College, New York/Suffolk Campus	NY	22,630	C
The Pennsylvania State Univ - Univ Park	PA	28,022	VC+
Thomas Edison State College	NJ	5,700	SP
Union College	KY	29,955	C
Univ of Delaware	DE	23,612	VC
Univ of Louisiana at Monroe	LA	12,998	C
Univ of Minn/Duluth	MN	19,806	C
Univ of Nebr - Lincoln	NE	18,031	VC
Univ of North Texas	TX	15,628	C
Univ of St. Francis	IL	37,560	C
Univ of Wisc/Eau Claire	WI	15,730	VC
Univ of Wyoming	WY	14,401	C+
Viterbo Univ	WI	30,070	C
Voorhees College	SC	18,126	C
Washington Adventist Univ	MD	25,859	LC
Wayne State Univ	MI	22,063	C
Wheeling Jesuit Univ	WV	33,500	C
Wright State Univ	OH	16,983	C

OUTDOOR LEADERSHIP/ EDUCATION

School	ST	$IS	SR
Black Hills State Univ	SD	13,947	C
Montreat College	NC	31,298	C
Shenandoah Univ	VA	39,916	C

PACIFIC AREA STUDIES

School	ST	$IS	SR
Brigham Young Univ/Hawaii	HI	10,686	VC
Hawaii Pacific Univ	HI	34,360	C
New York Univ	NY	61,470	MC
Univ of Hawaii at Manoa	HI	19,379	C

PACKAGING

School	ST	$IS	SR
Univ of Wisc/Stout	WI	15,459	C

PAINTING

School	ST	$IS	SR
Adams State Univ	CO	13,358	LC
Andrews Univ	MI	28,030	C+
Aquinas College	MI	33,060	C
Art Academy of Cincinnati	OH	25,940	SP
Bard College at Simon's Rock	MA	61,749	HC+
Barton College	NC	27,660	LC
Bennington College	VT	56,990	HC+
Binghamton Univ/The SUNY	NY	21,648	HC+
Biola Univ	CA	40,320	C+
Birmingham-Southern College	AL	44,168	VC+
Boston Univ	MA	60,694	MC
Buffalo State College / SUNY	NY	15,733	C+
Calif College of the Arts	CA	48,334	SP
Cal State, San Bernardino	CA	12,000	C
Cleveland Inst of Art	OH	48,685	SP
College for Creative Studies	MI	45,340	C
Columbia College	MO	24,578	C
Dominican Univ	IL	37,628	C
Escuela de Artes Plasticas de PR	PR	2,660	
Ferris State Univ	MI	20,047	C
Harding Univ	AR	23,556	C
Hofstra Univ	NY	51,810	VC+
Howard Univ	DC	13,646	C
Indiana Univ-Purdue Univ Fort Wayne	IN	15,521	C
Indiana Univ-Purdue Univ Indianapolis	IN	17,611	C
Indiana Wesleyan Univ	IN	31,815	VC

School	ST	$IS	SR
Kansas City Art Inst	MO	44,308	SP
Kent State Univ	OH	19,920	C
Kutztown Univ of Pennsylvania	PA	16,909	LC
Laguna College of Art and Design	CA	27,300	SP
Lewis Univ	IL	23,050	C
Maine College of Art	ME	28,812	SP
Marshall Univ	WV	14,820	C
Maryland Inst College of Art	MD	39,500	SP
Marywood Univ	PA	45,595	C
Memphis College of Art	TN	33,550	SP
Milwaukee Inst of Art and Design	WI	31,938	SP
Minneapolis College of Art and Design	MN	36,700	SP
Montserrat College of Art	MA	31,000	C
Moore College of Art and Design	PA	50,135	SP
Oberlin College	OH	61,788	MC
Ohio Univ	OH	21,080	C
Otis College of Art and Design	CA	35,404	SP
Pacific Northwest College of Art	OR	38,494	C
Pittsburg State Univ	KS	12,032	C
Providence College	RI	57,383	VC
Rhode Island School of Design	RI	57,234	MC
Ringling College of Art and Design	FL	46,130	SP
San Francisco Art Inst	CA	55,762	SP
Santa Fe Univ of Art and Design	NM	39,666	SP
Savannah College of Art and Design	GA	48,005	SP
School of the Art Inst of Chicago	IL	56,230	MC
SUNY Fredonia/The SUNY at Fredonia	NY	19,840	C
SUNY New Paltz	NY	14,348	C
Syracuse Univ	NY	56,346	VC
Temple Univ	PA	24,392	VC
The Catholic Univ of America	DC	52,852	VC
Univ of Dallas	TX	45,500	VC+
Univ of Hartford	CT	42,674	C
Univ of Illinois at Chicago	IL	24,505	VC
Univ of Illinois at Urbana-Champaign	IL	26,450	HC
Univ of Iowa	IA	17,693	VC
Univ of Kansas	KS	17,603	C+
Univ of Mass Dartmouth	MA	22,223	C
Univ of Miami	FL	57,034	MC
Univ of Mich/Ann Arbor	MI	22,102	MC
Univ of Oregon	OR	21,360	C+
Univ of San Francisco	CA	54,770	VC
Univ of the Arts	PA	38,450	C
Univ of Washington	WA	14,722	VC
Virginia Commonwealth Univ	VA	21,716	C
Washington Univ in St. Louis	MO	69,844	MC
Webster Univ	MO	35,100	C+
Western Washington Univ	WA	18,519	VC
Youngstown State Univ	OH	16,732	C

PAPER AND PULP SCIENCE

School	ST	$IS	SR
Miami Univ	OH	24,191	VC
N Car State Univ	NC	16,202	HC
SUNY / College of Environmental Science and Forestry	NY	18,351	VC
Univ of Maine	ME	19,902	C+
Univ of Washington	WA	14,722	VC
Univ of Wisc/Stevens Point	WI	14,043	C
Western Mich Univ	MI	19,628	C

PAPER ENGINEERING

School	ST	$IS	SR
SUNY / College of Environmental Science and Forestry	NY	18,351	VC
Western Mich Univ	MI	19,628	C

PARALEGAL STUDIES

School	ST	$IS	SR
Anna Maria College	MA	34,600	C
Avila Univ	MO	26,900	C
Burlington College	VT	32,510	SP
Cal State, San Bernardino	CA	12,000	C
Calumet College of St. Joseph	IN	15,000	C
Central Washington Univ	WA	11,730	C
Chancellor Univ	OH	11,000	C
College of Mount St. Joseph	OH	33,880	C
College of St. Mary	NE	35,184	C
Concordia Univ Wisc	WI	28,980	C
Daemen College	NY	34,770	C
Davenport Univ	MI	21,002	LC
Eastern Kentucky Univ	KY	11,161	C
Eastern Mich Univ	MI	18,604	C
Elms College	MA	23,900	VC
Hamline Univ	MN	45,678	VC
Hilbert College	NY	28,550	C
Hodges Univ	FL	12,000	LC
Humphreys College	CA	17,000	NC
Husson Univ	ME	24,194	LC

School	ST	$IS	SR
Idaho State Univ	ID	12,307	C
Johnson & Wales Univ/North Miami Campus	FL		C
Johnson & Wales Univ/ Providence Campus	RI	29,576	C
Kent State Univ	OH	19,920	C
Kutztown Univ of Pennsylvania	PA	16,909	LC
Lake Erie College	OH	37,266	C
Lake Superior State Univ	MI	18,121	C
Lock Haven Univ of Pennsylvania	PA	18,028	LC
Maryville Univ of St. Louis	MO	35,856	VC
Mercy College	NY	30,456	C
Minn State Univ, Moorhead	MN	13,392	C
Miss College	MS	21,998	C
Miss Univ for Women	MS	7,400	C
Montclair State Univ	NJ	22,614	C
Morehead State Univ	KY	10,900	C
Mount Aloysius College	PA	29,976	C
Nebr Wesleyan Univ	NE	29,774	C+
New York College of Technology/The CUNY	NY	5,769	NC
Nova Southeastern Univ	FL	37,280	VC
Peirce College	PA	12,760	NC
Pennsylvania College of Technology	PA	26,286	NC
Point Park Univ	PA	36,390	C
Quinnipiac Univ	CT	55,160	VC
Roger Williams Univ	RI	46,296	VC
St. Mary-of-the-Woods College	IN	37,722	LC
Samford Univ	AL	37,060	C+
Southern Illinois Univ Carbondale	IL	21,942	C
Stephen F. Austin State Univ	TX	14,668	C
Stevenson Univ	MD	41,470	C
Suffolk Univ	MA	47,298	C
Texas Wesleyan Univ	TX	31,382	C
The Univ of Tenn at Chattanooga	TN	16,883	C
Tiffin Univ	OH	30,273	LC
Tulane Univ	LA	60,861	MC
Univ of Alaska Anchorage	AK	16,673	NC
Univ of Detroit Mercy	MI	30,450	VC
Univ of Great Falls	MT	27,970	C
Univ of La Verne	CA	47,010	C
Univ of Louisville	KY	17,946	C
Univ of Maryland/Univ College	MD	6,168	SP
Univ of Mass Boston	MA	23,066	VC
Univ of Miss	MS	16,704	C+
Washburn Univ	KS	12,579	C
William Woods Univ	MO	24,260	C
Winona State Univ	MN	16,640	C

PARKS AND RECREATION MANAGEMENT

School	ST	$IS	SR
Alabama State Univ	AL	14,142	NC
Arizona State Univ, at the Downtown Phoenix Campus	AZ	22,101	C
Arkansas Tech Univ	AR	13,982	LC
Aurora Univ	IL	33,228	C
Belmont Abbey College	NC	37,716	C
Bemidji State Univ	MN	13,500	VC
Cal State, Sacramento	CA	16,200	C
Calif Univ of Pennsylvania	PA	14,217	C
Central Washington Univ	WA	11,730	C
Cheyney Univ of Pennsylvania	PA	20,372	LC
Clemson Univ	SC	19,136	HC
Concord Univ	WV	13,102	C
Davenport Univ	MI	21,002	LC
Delaware State Univ	DE	16,722	LC
East Carolina Univ	NC	14,169	C
East Stroudsburg Univ of Pennsylvania	PA	18,868	LC
Eastern Washington Univ	WA		C
Evangel Univ	MO	23,090	C
Florida International Univ	FL	17,747	C+
George Mason Univ	VA	15,724	VC
Houghton College	NY	36,808	C+
Humboldt State Univ	CA	18,400	C
Huntington Univ	IN	32,220	C
Illinois State Univ	IL	23,110	VC
Indiana Inst of Technology	IN	34,240	LC
Indiana State Univ	IN	16,000	C
Johnson & Wales Univ/ Charlotte Campus	NC	29,576	C
Johnson & Wales Univ/North Miami Campus	FL		C
Johnson & Wales Univ/ Providence Campus	RI	29,576	C
Kansas State Univ	KS	15,497	VC
Kent State Univ	OH	19,920	C
Lake Superior State Univ	MI	18,121	C
Marshall Univ	WV	14,820	C
Mich State Univ	MI	22,450	VC
Midland Univ	NE	34,000	C
Minn State Univ, Mankato	MN	15,616	C
Missouri Western State Univ	MO	13,996	C
Montclair State Univ	NJ	22,614	C
N Car State Univ	NC	16,202	HC
Northern Arizona Univ	AZ	19,010	C

School	ST	$IS	SR
Northern Mich Univ	MI	18,278	C
Northland College	WI	26,680	C
Ohio Univ	OH	21,080	C
Oregon State Univ	OR	20,273	VC
Prescott College	AZ	33,284	C
Shorter Univ	GA	30,650	LC
Slippery Rock Univ of Pennsylvania	PA	10,360	C
S Dak State Univ	SD	14,296	C
Southwest Baptist Univ	MO	24,710	C
Springfield College	MA	25,000	C
Stephen F. Austin State Univ	TX	14,668	C
Texas A&M Univ	TX	19,207	VC
The Pennsylvania State Univ - Univ Park	PA	28,022	VC+
The Univ of N Car at Greensboro	NC	12,848	C
The Univ of Utah	UT	16,463	VC
Unity College	ME	34,054	C
Univ of Arkansas at Pine Bluff	AR	13,378	C
Univ of Idaho	ID	14,558	C
Univ of Illinois at Urbana-Champaign	IL	26,450	HC
Univ of Iowa	IA	17,693	VC
Univ of Maine	ME	19,902	C+
Univ of Miss	MS	16,704	C+
Univ of Missouri/Columbia	MO	18,201	MC
Univ of Nebr - Lincoln	NE	18,031	VC
Univ of N Car at Wilmington	NC	13,572	VC
Univ of Southern Miss	MS	13,170	C
Univ of Vermont	VT	27,006	VC+
Univ of Wisc/La Crosse	WI	9,304	VC
Utah State Univ	UT	12,044	C
Virginia Polytechnic Inst and State Univ	VA	14,629	HC
Virginia Wesleyan College	VA	28,433	LC
West Virginia Univ	WV	16,542	C
Western Carolina Univ	NC	13,965	C
Western Illinois Univ	IL	20,732	C
Western New England Univ	MA	46,154	C+
Western Washington Univ	WA	18,519	VC
Wingate Univ	NC	34,990	C
York College of Pennsylvania	PA	26,590	C

PASTORAL STUDIES

School	ST	$IS	SR
Andrews Univ	MI	28,030	C
Bethel College	IN	31,560	C
Brescia Univ	KY	26,140	VC+
Calif Baptist Univ	CA	38,792	C
Cedarville Univ	OH	32,860	VC
Clearwater Christian College	FL	23,720	C
Concordia Univ Wisc	WI	28,980	C
Corban Univ	OR	37,380	C
Dallas Baptist Univ	TX	30,580	VC
East Texas Baptist Univ	TX	31,577	LC
Grace Bible College	MI	20,770	C
Greenville College	IL	27,012	C
Hope International Univ	CA	34,650	C
Houghton College	NY	36,808	C+
Kentucky Christian Univ	KY	17,622	LC
Loyola Univ Chicago	IL	51,646	VC+
Madonna Univ	MI	24,540	VC
Marian Univ	IN	38,540	C
Morris College	SC	16,310	LC
Mount Vernon Nazarene Univ	OH	29,590	C
Newman Univ	KS	30,380	C+
North Central Univ	MN	26,400	C
Northwest Univ	WA	18,854	C
Northwestern College	MN	24,000	C
Nyack College	NY	33,250	C
Okla Wesleyan Univ	OK	21,300	C
Olivet Nazarene Univ	IL	29,990	C
St. Mary's Univ of Minn	MN	38,280	C
Simpson Univ	CA	28,900	C
Southeastern Univ	FL	27,201	C
Southwest Baptist Univ	MO	24,710	C
Tenn Wesleyan College	TN	21,250	C
Toccoa Falls College	GA	23,210	LC
Trevecca Nazarene Univ	TN	31,186	C
Union College	NE	23,270	C
Union Univ	TN	28,260	VC
Universidad Adventista de las Antillas	PR	7,360	
Univ of Dallas	TX	45,500	VC+
Univ of Mary	ND	16,714	C
Univ of St. Mary	KS	28,400	C+
Vanguard Univ of Southern Calif	CA	35,833	VC
Warner Univ	FL	18,000	C

PEACE STUDIES

School	ST	$IS	SR
Cal State, Dominguez Hills	CA	17,090	LC
Chapman Univ	CA	58,347	VC+
Colgate Univ	NY	58,135	MC
College of St. Benedict	MN	49,359	VC
College of St. Scholastica	MN	41,440	C
Creighton Univ	NE	45,356	VC
DePaul Univ	IL	47,623	VC
DePauw Univ	IN	48,950	VC+
Earlham College	IN	51,470	HC
Eastern Mennonite Univ	VA	40,660	C
Goshen College	IN	35,900	VC

School	ST	$IS	SR
Goucher College	MD	52,040	VC+
Guilford College	NC	42,800	C
Hamline Univ	MN	45,678	VC
Hampshire College	MA	58,320	MC
John Carroll Univ	OH	46,300	C+
Juniata College	PA	49,340	VC
Le Moyne College	NY	43,470	C
Manchester Univ	IN	35,070	C
Manhattan College	NY	49,588	C+
Marquette Univ	WI	46,930	VC+
Messiah College	PA	40,690	C+
Naropa Univ	CO	39,166	SP
Nazareth College of Rochester	NY	43,028	C+
Northland College	WI	26,680	C
Norwich Univ	VT	28,212	C
Ohio Dominican Univ	OH	38,380	C+
Prescott College	AZ	33,284	C
St. John's Univ	MN	47,984	C
Salisbury Univ	MD	19,180	VC
Swarthmore College	PA	57,870	MC
The Univ of Utah	UT	16,463	VC
Tufts Univ	MA	58,780	MC
Univ of Calif at Berkeley	CA	23,322	MC
Univ of Hawaii at Manoa	HI	19,379	C
Univ of N Car at Chapel Hill	NC	18,928	MC
Univ of Wisc-Milwaukee	WI	18,436	C
Wartburg College	IA	41,055	VC
Wellesley College	MA	59,038	MC
Whitworth Univ	WA	47,734	VC

PERCUSSION

School	ST	$IS	SR
Central Washington Univ	WA	11,730	C
Eastern Mich Univ	MI	18,604	C
Indiana Univ Bloomington	IN	19,801	VC
Indiana Univ-Purdue Univ Fort Wayne	IN	15,521	C
Marshall Univ	WV	14,820	C
Northwestern Univ	IL	61,640	MC
Roosevelt Univ	IL	22,605	VC
San Francisco Conservatory of Music	CA	56,428	SP
Syracuse Univ	NY	56,346	VC
Univ of Iowa	IA	17,693	VC
Univ of Kansas	KS	17,603	C+
Wright State Univ	OH	16,983	C
Youngstown State Univ	OH	16,732	C

PERFORMING AND MEDIA ARTS

School	ST	$IS	SR
Cornell Univ	NY	60,964	MC

PERFORMING ARTS

School	ST	$IS	SR
Adelphi Univ	NY	44,670	VC
American Univ	DC	56,015	HC+
Appalachian State Univ	NC	12,919	VC
Aquinas College	MI	33,060	VC
Arizona State Univ, at the Tempe Campus	AZ	20,137	C+
Arizona State Univ, at the West Campus	AZ	19,251	C
Averett Univ	VA	37,750	LC
Baylor Univ	TX	50,329	HC
Bennington College	VT	56,990	HC+
Bethel College	IN	31,560	C
Biola Univ	CA	40,320	C+
Blackburn College	IL	21,350	C
Boston Univ	MA	60,694	MC
Bowling Green State Univ	OH	18,970	C
Brigham Young Univ	UT	12,100	HC
Brown Univ	RI	59,428	MC
Butler Univ	IN	47,572	VC+
Calif Baptist Univ	CA	38,792	C
Carroll College	MT	28,000	C
Carthage College	WI	33,000	C
CUNY/City College	NY	20,319	HC+
Colby-Sawyer College	NH	50,790	C
College of the Ozarks	MO		VC
Colo State Univ-Fort Collins	CO	20,385	VC
Columbia College	SC	27,882	C
De Sales Univ	PA	43,970	C
DePaul Univ	IL	47,623	VC
Dominican Univ	IL	37,628	C
Eastern Conn State Univ	CT	20,584	C
Eastern Kentucky Univ	KY	11,161	C
Eastern Mich Univ	MI	18,604	C
Edgewood College	WI	33,294	C
Elizabethtown College	PA	49,740	VC
Emerson College	MA	52,446	HC+
Ferrum College	VA	27,740	LC
Fontbonne Univ	MO	31,384	C
Fordham Univ	NY	61,588	HC+
Friends Univ	KS	29,100	C
Georgetown College	KY	41,440	C+
Hampshire College	MA	58,320	MC
Huntington Univ	IN	32,220	C
Illinois Wesleyan Univ	IL	48,452	HC
Ithaca College	NY	53,864	HC
Johnson C. Smith Univ	NC	25,336	LC
Johnson State College	VT	16,721	C
Kean Univ	NJ	23,444	C
Lees-McRae College	NC	33,944	C
Lindenwood Univ	MO	20,750	C
Mars Hill Univ	NC	22,950	LC

School	ST	$IS	SR
Mass College of Liberal Arts	MA	18,613	C
Missouri State Univ	MO	13,996	C+
Naropa Univ	CO	39,166	SP
Neumann Univ	PA	31,078	LC
New York Univ	NY	61,470	MC
N Dak State Univ	ND		C
Northwestern Univ	IL	61,640	MC
Oakland Univ	MI	19,391	C
Oberlin College	OH	61,788	MC
Ohio Univ	OH	21,080	C
Old Dominion Univ	VA	19,483	LC
Plymouth State Univ	NH	23,148	LC
Point Park Univ	PA	36,390	C
Prescott College	AZ	33,284	C
Roosevelt Univ	IL	22,605	VC
Sacred Heart Univ	CT	49,264	VC
St. Mary's College of Calif	CA	53,550	C
Santa Fe Univ of Art and Design	NM	39,666	SP
Savannah College of Art and Design	GA	48,005	SP
Seton Hill Univ	PA	35,172	C
Shenandoah Univ	VA	39,916	C
Southern Methodist Univ	TX	60,585	MC
Southwest Baptist Univ	MO	24,710	C
Suffolk Univ	MA	47,298	C
SUNY College at Geneseo	NY	18,670	HC
Temple Univ	PA	24,392	VC
Texas A&M Univ	TX	19,207	VC
Texas Tech Univ	TX	14,243	C
Univ of Arizona	AZ	20,657	C
Univ of Florida	FL	15,943	HC
Univ of Hartford	CT	42,674	C
Univ of Iowa	IA	17,693	VC
Univ of Mary Hardin-Baylor	TX	31,950	C+
Univ of Mich/Ann Arbor	MI	22,102	MC
Univ of Missouri-Kansas City	MO	19,603	C
Univ of N Car School of the Arts	NC	7,401	SP
Univ of North Texas	TX	15,628	C
Univ of San Francisco	CA	54,770	VC
Univ of Southern Indiana	IN	14,885	C
Univ of Tampa	FL	35,160	VC
Univ of Tenn at Martin	TN	13,734	C
Univ of Texas - Pan American	TX	11,125	LC
Washington Univ in St. Louis	MO	69,844	MC
West Chester Univ of Pennsylvania	PA	17,186	C
West Texas A&M Univ	TX	13,478	C
Western Kentucky Univ	KY	11,000	LC
Western Mich Univ	MI	19,628	C
Youngstown State Univ	OH	16,732	C

PERSONAL FINANCIAL PLANNING

School	ST	$IS	SR
Kansas State Univ	KS	15,497	VC
Lubbock Christian Univ	TX	26,308	C
Univ of Wisc/Madison	WI	18,757	HC+
Western Mich Univ	MI	19,628	C

PERSONNEL MANAGEMENT

School	ST	$IS	SR
Arcadia Univ	PA	33,570	C+
Auburn Univ	AL	22,378	VC+
Auburn Univ at Montgomery	AL	14,470	LC
Ball State Univ	IN	17,850	C
Baylor Univ	TX	50,329	HC
Bellevue Univ	NE	4,600	NC
Bloomfield College	NJ	37,850	LC
Cal State, Long Beach	CA	17,502	C+
CUNY/Baruch College	NY		HC
Dickinson State Univ	ND	11,900	NC
Eastern Mich Univ	MI	18,604	C
Eastern Washington Univ	WA		C
Florida State Univ	FL	16,715	VC
Grand Valley State Univ	MI	17,998	C+
Hawaii Pacific Univ	HI	34,360	C
King's College	PA	43,502	C
Lamar Univ	TX	6,820	LC
Limestone College	SC	30,800	C
Louisiana Tech Univ	LA	11,302	C
Mansfield Univ	PA	19,468	LC
Mich State Univ	MI	22,450	VC
Nicholls State Univ	LA	7,095	C
Northern State Univ - Aberdeen	SD	14,505	C
Oakland Univ	MI	19,391	C
Our Lady of the Lake Univ	TX	22,430	LC
Portland State Univ	OR	18,672	C
Roosevelt Univ	IL	22,605	VC
Rowan Univ	NJ	24,022	VC+
San Francisco State Univ	CA	18,514	C
Seton Hill Univ	PA	35,172	C
Silver Lake College	WI	22,600	C
St. Cloud State Univ	MN	10,600	C
Tarleton State Univ	TX	13,489	LC
Texas A&M Univ	TX	19,207	VC
Troy Univ	AL	10,650	C
Univ of Illinois at Urbana-Champaign	IL	26,450	HC
Univ of Louisiana at Lafayette	LA	6,130	C
Univ of Nebr at Kearney	NE	14,855	LC
Univ of PR Recinto de Rio Piedras	PR	5,750	

ST = STATE $IS = IN-STATE COSTS   SR = SELECTOR RATING

School	ST	$IS	SR
Univ of Southern Miss	MS	13,170	C
Univ of the Sacred Heart	PR	5,590	
Univ of Washington	WA	14,722	VC
Univ of Wisc Whitewater	WI	13,314	C
Utah State Univ	UT	12,044	C
Wilmington Univ	DE	8,112	NC

PETROLEUM SYSTEMS / GEOLOGY

School	ST	$IS	SR
Rocky Mountain College	MT	32,242	C

PETROLEUM/NATURAL GAS ENGINEERING

School	ST	$IS	SR
Colo School of Mines	CO	18,000	HC
Louisiana State Univ	LA	18,677	C+
Marietta College	OH	42,135	VC
Missouri Univ of Science and Technology	MO	18,655	VC+
Montana Tech of The Univ of Montana	MT	14,650	VC
New Mexico Inst of Mining and Technology	NM	13,592	VC
Nicholls State Univ	LA	7,095	C
Stanford Univ	CA	58,388	MC
Texas A&M Univ	TX	19,207	VC
Texas A&M Univ at Kingsville	TX	7,500	LC
The Pennsylvania State Univ - Univ Park	PA	28,022	VC+
The Univ of Okla	OK	18,621	VC
Univ of Alaska Fairbanks	AK	15,130	C
Univ of Houston	TX	19,796	VC
Univ of Kansas	KS	17,603	C+
Univ of Louisiana at Lafayette	LA	6,130	C
Univ of N Dak	ND	14,551	C
Univ of Southern Calif	CA	56,903	MC
Univ of Texas at Austin	TX	44,074	HC
Univ of Tulsa	OK	46,331	VC
Univ of Wyoming	WY	14,401	C+
West Virginia Univ	WV	16,542	C+

PHARMACEUTICAL CHEMISTRY

School	ST	$IS	SR
Lehigh Univ	PA	56,770	MC
Mich Tech Univ	MI	23,556	HC
Pittsburg State Univ	KS	12,032	C
Univ of Dayton	OH	49,070	VC
Univ of Mich/Ann Arbor	MI	22,102	MC
Univ of the Sciences	PA	48,320	VC+

PHARMACEUTICAL SCIENCE

School	ST	$IS	SR
Albany College of Pharmacy and Health Sciences	NY	40,331	SP
Belmont Univ	TN	39,190	VC
Cleveland State Univ	OH	21,776	C
De Sales Univ	PA	43,970	C
Duquesne Univ	PA	43,720	VC
Howard Univ	DC	13,646	C
Mass College of Pharmacy and Health Sciences	MA	36,450	SP
Northeastern Univ	MA	55,296	MC
Purdue Univ/West Lafayette	IN	20,024	HC
S Dak State Univ	SD	14,296	C
Ohio State Univ-Columbus Campus	OH	19,887	HC+
Univ at Buffalo / The SUNY	NY	20,283	C
Univ of Arizona	AZ	20,657	C
Univ of Calif at Irvine	CA	25,961	VC
Univ of Georgia	GA	20,082	VC
Univ of Houston	TX	19,796	VC
Univ of Louisiana at Monroe	LA	12,998	C
Univ of Mich/Ann Arbor	MI	22,102	MC
Univ of Miss	MS	16,704	C+
Univ of N Car at Chapel Hill	NC	18,928	MC
Univ of Pittsburgh at Pittsburgh	PA	28,572	HC+
Univ of the Sciences	PA	48,320	VC+
West Chester Univ of Pennsylvania	PA	17,186	C
York College / The CUNY	NY	5,496	VC

PHARMACOLOGY

School	ST	$IS	SR
Howard Univ	DC	13,646	C
New York Univ	NY	61,470	MC
Stony Brook Univ / SUNY	NY	20,078	HC+
Univ at Buffalo / The SUNY	NY	20,283	VC
Univ of Arizona	AZ	20,657	C
Univ of Illinois at Chicago	IL	24,505	VC
Univ of Louisiana at Monroe	LA	12,998	C
Univ of Montana	MT	14,105	C
Univ of the Sciences	PA	48,320	VC+
Univ of Wisc/Madison	WI	18,757	HC+

PHARMACY

School	ST	$IS	SR
Butler Univ	IN	47,572	VC+
Cedarville Univ	OH	32,860	VC
Drake Univ	IA	41,516	VC+
Duquesne Univ	PA	43,720	VC+
Florida A&M Univ	FL	14,935	LC
Howard Univ	DC	13,646	C

School	ST	$IS	SR
Husson Univ	ME	24,194	LC
Johnson C. Smith Univ	NC	25,336	LC
Lamar Univ	TX	6,820	LC
LIU Brooklyn	NY	47,182	LC
N Dak State Univ	ND		C
Northeastern Univ	MA	55,296	MC
Ohio Northern Univ	OH	42,075	VC
Presbyterian College	SC	42,678	C+
Regis Univ	CO	41,318	C
Roberts Wesleyan College	NY	38,306	C+
Rutgers, The State Univ of New Jersey/New Brunswick	NJ	25,562	VC
Samford Univ	AL	37,060	C+
Seton Hill Univ	PA	35,172	C
S Dak State Univ	SD	14,296	C
St. John's Univ	NY	55,070	C+
The College of Idaho	ID	31,277	C+
The Univ of Utah	UT	16,463	VC
Univ at Buffalo / The SUNY	NY	20,283	VC
Univ of Arizona	AZ	20,657	C
Univ of Calif at Santa Barbara	CA	27,551	HC
Univ of Conn	CT	24,706	HC
Univ of Georgia	GA	20,082	VC
Univ of Illinois at Chicago	IL	24,505	VC
Univ of Iowa	IA	17,693	VC
Univ of Kansas	KS	17,603	C+
Univ of Louisiana at Monroe	LA	12,998	C
Univ of Mich/Ann Arbor	MI	22,102	MC
Univ of Minn/Twin Cities	MN		HC
Univ of Texas at Austin	TX	44,074	MC
Univ of the Sciences	PA	48,320	VC+
Univ of Toledo	OH	18,464	C
Washington Univ in St. Louis	MO	69,844	MC
West Virginia Univ	WV	16,542	C+

PHILOSOPHY

School	ST	$IS	SR
Adelphi Univ	NY	44,670	VC
Adrian College	MI	42,400	C
Agnes Scott College	GA	45,323	C+
Albertus Magnus College	CT	37,382	LC
Albion College	MI	46,010	C
Albright College	PA	46,660	C
Alfred Univ	NY	41,770	C
Allegheny College	PA	50,980	HC
Alma College	MI	44,075	C
Alvernia Univ	PA	39,250	LC
Alverno College	WI	31,434	LC
American International College	MA	36,100	LC
American Univ	DC	56,015	HC+
Amherst College	MA	58,744	MC
Anderson Univ	IN	36,100	C
Angelo State Univ	TX	15,049	NC
Appalachian State Univ	NC	12,919	VC
Aquinas College	MI	33,060	C
Aquinas College	TN	29,250	VC+
Arcadia Univ	PA	33,570	C+
Arizona State Univ, at the Tempe Campus	AZ	20,137	C+
Arkansas State Univ	AR	15,470	C
Asbury Univ	KY	32,038	VC
Ashland Univ	OH	25,000	C
Assumption College	MA	47,122	C+
Auburn Univ	AL	22,378	VC+
Augsburg College	MN	35,142	C
Augustana College	IL	43,398	VC
Augustana College	SD	36,500	VC
Aurora Univ	IL	33,228	C
Austin College	TX	45,875	HC
Austin Peay State Univ	TN	15,274	C
Azusa Pacific Univ	CA	42,086	C
Baker Univ	KS	33,350	C+
Baldwin Wallace Univ	OH	38,318	C
Ball State Univ	IN	17,850	C
Bard College	NY	61,940	HC
Bard College at Simon's Rock	MA	61,749	HC+
Barnard College/Columbia Univ	NY	39,000	MC
Barry Univ	FL	38,190	C
Bates College	ME	60,720	MC
Baylor Univ	TX	50,329	HC
Belhaven Univ	MS	27,170	C
Bellarmine Univ	KY	42,950	VC
Bellevue Univ	NE	4,600	NC
Belmont Abbey College	NC	37,716	C
Belmont Univ	TN	39,190	VC+
Beloit College	WI	49,970	HC
Bemidji State Univ	MN	13,500	VC
Benedict College	SC	20,454	NC
Benedictine College	KS	29,180	VC
Benedictine Univ	IL	37,820	C
Bennington College	VT	56,990	HC+
Bentley Univ	MA	56,454	HC+
Berea College	KY	7,192	C
Berry College	GA	39,254	VC
Bethel College	IN	31,560	C
Bethel Univ	MN	34,940	VC
Binghamton Univ/The SUNY	NY	21,648	HC+
Biola Univ	CA	40,320	C+
Birmingham-Southern College	AL	44,168	VC+
Bloomfield College	NJ	37,850	LC
Bloomsburg Univ of Pennsylvania	PA	13,598	C

School	ST	$IS	SR
Boise State Univ	ID	13,469	LC
Boston College	MA	60,622	MC
Boston Univ	MA	60,694	MC
Bowdoin College	ME	59,568	MC
Bowling Green State Univ	OH	18,970	C
Bradley Univ	IL	31,874	VC
Brandeis Univ	MA		MC
Bridgewater State Univ	MA	18,752	C
Brigham Young Univ	UT	12,100	HC
Brown Univ	RI	59,428	MC
Bryn Mawr College	PA	59,890	MC
Bucknell Univ	PA	60,140	MC
Buena Vista Univ	IA	39,188	C
Buffalo State College / SUNY	NY	15,733	C+
Butler Univ	IN	47,572	VC+
Cabrini College	PA	40,859	LC
Calif Baptist Univ	CA	38,792	C
Calif Inst of Technology	CA	54,045	MC
Calif Lutheran Univ	CA	49,540	C+
Calif Polytechnic State Univ	CA	19,847	HC
Calif State Polytechnic Univ, Pomona	CA	20,156	C
Cal State, Bakersfield	CA	8,000	C
Cal State, Chico	CA	20,158	C
Cal State, Dominguez Hills	CA	17,090	LC
Cal State, East Bay	CA	16,549	C
Cal State, Fresno	CA	17,405	C
Cal State, Fullerton	CA	25,188	C
Cal State, Long Beach	CA	17,502	C
Cal State, Los Angeles	CA	17,186	LC
Cal State, Northridge	CA	28,690	LC
Cal State, Sacramento	CA	16,200	C
Cal State, San Bernardino	CA	12,000	C
Cal State, Stanislaus	CA	18,582	C
Calif Univ of Pennsylvania	PA	14,217	C
Calvin College	MI	39,120	VC
Canisius College	NY	44,900	C
Capital Univ	OH	41,050	VC
Carleton College	MN	60,102	MC
Carlow Univ	PA	30,272	C
Carnegie Mellon Univ	PA	51,260	MC
Carroll College	MT	28,000	C
Carson-Newman Univ	TN	29,058	C+
Carthage College	WI	33,000	C
Case Western Reserve Univ	OH	56,534	MC
Castleton State College	VT	20,186	C
Catawba College	NC	37,240	LC
Cedarville Univ	OH	32,860	VC
Centenary College of Louisiana	LA	45,650	C+
Central Univ	IA	42,104	C
Central Conn State Univ	CT	19,749	C
Central Methodist Univ	MO	28,240	VC
Central Univ of Bayamon	PR	3,350	
Central Washington Univ	WA	11,730	C
Centre College	KY	35,000	HC+
Chapman Univ	CA	58,347	VC+
Christendom College	VA	32,600	VC
Christopher Newport Univ	VA	21,960	VC
CUNY/Baruch College	NY		HC
CUNY/Brooklyn College	NY	5,884	C+
CUNY/City College	NY	20,319	H+
Claremont McKenna College	CA	62,215	MC
Clarion Univ of Pennsylvania	PA	17,370	LC
Clark Atlanta Univ	GA	30,006	C
Clark Univ	MA	47,020	HC+
Clarke Univ	IA	37,600	C
Clemson Univ	SC	19,136	HC
Cleveland State Univ	OH	21,776	C
Coastal Carolina Univ	SC	18,580	C
Coe College	IA	45,550	VC
Colby College	ME	57,510	MC
Colby-Sawyer College	NH	50,790	C
Colgate Univ	NY	58,135	MC
College of Charleston	SC	22,145	VC
College of Mount St. Vincent	NY	41,040	MC
College of New Jersey	NJ	25,376	NC
College of St. Benedict	MN	49,359	VC
College of St. Elizabeth	NJ	43,839	LC
College of St. Scholastica	MN	41,440	C
College of Staten Island/The City of New Yok	NY	16,778	NC
College of the Holy Cross	MA	58,042	MC
College of the Ozarks	MO		VC
College of William & Mary	VA	28,000	MC
College of Wooster	OH	52,600	VC
Colo College	CO	57,162	MC
Colo State Univ-Fort Collins	CO	20,385	VC
Columbia College	MO	24,578	C
Columbia Univ/City of New York	NY	61,116	MC
Columbia Univ/School of General Studies	NY	58,231	MC
Concordia College - Moorhead	MN	39,974	VC
Concordia Univ, Ann Arbor	MI	27,220	VC
Conn College	CT	54,970	MC
Cornell College	IA	44,930	VC
Cornell Univ	NY	60,964	MC
Cornerstone Univ and Grand Rapids Theological Seminary	MI	33,338	C
Covenant College	GA	38,990	VC+
Creighton Univ	NE	45,356	VC
Curry College	MA	48,925	LC
Dallas Baptist Univ	TX	30,580	VC

School	ST	$IS	SR
Dartmouth College	NH	57,996	MC
Davidson College	NC	58,146	MC
De Sales Univ	PA	43,970	C
Denison Univ	OH	54,670	HC+
DePaul Univ	IL	47,623	VC
DePauw Univ	IN	48,950	VC+
Dickinson College	PA	57,662	HC+
Doane College	NE	35,230	C
Dominican Univ	IL	37,628	C
Dordt College	IA	34,160	C+
Dowling College	NY	25,000	LC
Drake Univ	IA	41,516	VC+
Drew Univ/College of Liberal Arts	NJ	57,516	C
Drexel Univ	PA	61,418	VC+
Drury Univ	MO	31,909	VC
Duke Univ	NC	50,250	MC
Duquesne Univ	PA	43,720	VC
D'Youville College	NY	29,850	C
Earlham College	IN	51,470	HC
East Carolina Univ	NC	14,169	C
East Stroudsburg Univ of Pennsylvania	PA	18,868	LC
East Tenn State Univ	TN	9,000	C
Eastern Illinois Univ	IL	20,466	C
Eastern Kentucky Univ	KY	11,161	C
Eastern Mennonite Univ	VA	40,660	C
Eastern Mich Univ	MI	18,604	C
Eastern Univ	PA	37,704	C
Eastern Washington Univ	WA		C
Eckerd College	FL	43,902	C
Edinboro Univ of Pennsylvania	PA	15,940	LC
Edward Waters College	FL	19,607	LC
Elizabethtown College	PA	49,740	VC
Elmhurst College	IL	43,336	C
Elmira College	NY	49,950	C+
Elon Univ	NC	41,914	VC+
Emmanuel College	MA	47,985	VC
Emory and Henry College	VA	387,460	C
Emory Univ	GA	56,368	MC
Erskine College	SC	37,360	C
Eugene Lang College/The New School for Liberal Arts	NY	55,650	C
Eureka College	IL	19,280	C
Excelsior College	NY	5,580	SP
Fairfield Univ	CT	56,960	VC
Fairleigh Dickinson Univ/College at Florham	NJ	42,142	C
Fairleigh Dickinson Univ/Metropolitan Campus	NJ	40,254	C
Felician College	NJ	41,640	LC
Ferrum College	VA	27,740	LC
Fisk Univ	TN	19,830	C
Flagler College	FL	25,180	C
Florida Atlantic Univ	FL	17,339	C
Florida Gulf Coast Univ	FL		C
Florida International Univ	FL	17,747	C+
Florida Memorial Univ	FL	20,888	NC
Florida Southern College	FL	40,150	C+
Florida State Univ	FL	16,715	VC
Fordham Univ	NY	61,588	HC+
Fort Hays State Univ	KS	11,354	C
Fort Lewis College	CO	15,513	C
Franciscan Univ of Steubenville	OH	27,320	VC
Franklin and Marshall College	PA	60,799	MC
Franklin College	IN	36,585	C
Fresno Pacific Univ	CA	32,136	C
Frostburg State Univ	MD	15,264	LC
Furman Univ	SC	54,006	HC
Gallaudet Univ	DC	25,380	SP
Gannon Univ	PA	39,608	C
Geneva College	PA	27,280	C
George Fox Univ	OR	40,750	C+
George Mason Univ	VA	15,724	VC
George Washington Univ	DC	57,108	MC
Georgetown College	KY	41,440	C+
Georgetown Univ	DC	52,910	MC
Georgia College and State Univ	GA	18,900	C+
Georgia Southern Univ	GA	16,942	C
Georgia State Univ	GA	15,582	VC
Gettysburg College	PA	58,820	HC
Gonzaga Univ	WA	46,441	HC
Gordon College	MA	44,320	VC
Goucher College	MD	52,040	VC+
Graceland Univ	IA	28,020	C
Grand Valley State Univ	MI	17,998	C+
Green Mountain College	VT	45,228	LC
Greenville Univ	IL	27,012	C
Grinnell College	IA	53,654	HC
Grove City College	PA	24,022	VC
Guilford College	NC	42,800	C
Gustavus Adolphus College	MN	48,170	HC
Hamilton College	NY	55,620	MC
Hamline Univ	MN	45,678	VC
Hampden-Sydney College	VA	51,758	C+
Hampshire College	MA	58,320	MC
Hanover College	IN	43,073	C+
Hardin-Simmons Univ	TX	23,560	C+
Hartwick College	NY	51,270	C
Harvard College/Harvard Univ	MA	49,000	MC

ST = STATE $IS = IN-STATE COSTS   SR = SELECTOR RATING

School	ST	$IS	SR
Hastings College	NE	27,782	C+
Haverford College	PA	61,564	MC
Heidelberg Univ	OH	34,100	C
Hendrix Univ	AR	50,202	VC+
High Point Univ	NC	39,800	C
Hillsdale College	MI	32,866	MC
Hiram College	OH	37,300	VC
Hobart and William Smith Colleges	NY	60,034	HC+
Hofstra Univ	NY	51,810	VC+
Hollins Univ	VA	43,295	VC
Holy Names Univ	CA	40,310	NC
Hood College	MD	45,730	C
Hope College	MI	38,650	VC
Houghton College	NY	36,808	C+
Howard Univ	DC	13,646	C
Humboldt State Univ	CA	18,400	C
Hunter College	NY	14,429	VC
Huntington Univ	IN	32,220	C+
Idaho State Univ	ID	12,307	C
Illinois College	IL	25,770	VC
Illinois State Univ	IL	23,110	VC
Illinois Wesleyan Univ	IL	48,452	HC
Indiana State Univ	IN	16,000	C
Indiana Univ Bloomington	IN	19,801	VC
Indiana Univ Northwest	IN	6,854	LC
Indiana Univ of Pennsylvania	PA	20,846	LC
Indiana Univ South Bend	IN	15,501	C
Indiana Univ Southeast	IN	16,035	C
Indiana Univ-Purdue Univ Fort Wayne	IN	15,521	C
Indiana Univ-Purdue Univ Indianapolis	IN	17,611	C
Iona College	NY	44,028	C
Iowa State Univ	IA	16,403	C
Ithaca College	NY	53,864	HC
Jacksonville Univ	FL	37,780	C
James Madison Univ	VA	18,049	VC
John Carroll Univ	OH	46,300	C+
John Jay College of Criminal Justice/The CUNY	NY	6,359	LC
Johns Hopkins Univ	MD	47,492	MC
Juniata College	PA	49,340	VC
Kalamazoo College	MI	49,740	HC
Kansas State Univ	KS	15,497	VC
Kennesaw State Univ	GA		C
Kent State Univ	OH	19,920	C
Kenyon College	OH	58,890	MC
King Univ	TN	33,140	C
King's College	PA	43,502	C
Knox College	IL	44,865	VC+
Kutztown Univ of Pennsylvania	PA	16,909	LC
La Salle Univ	PA	50,270	C
Lafayette College	PA	59,155	HC+
Lake Forest College	IL	50,652	VC
Lakeland College	WI	22,990	C
Lawrence Univ	WI	46,371	HC
Le Moyne College	NY	43,470	C
Lebanon Valley College	PA	38,570	C
Lehigh Univ	PA	56,770	MC
Lehman College/The CUNY	NY	5,778	LC
Lenoir-Rhyne College	NC	35,984	C
Lewis & Clark College	OR	54,382	MC
Lewis Univ	IL	23,050	C
Linfield College-McMinnville Campus	OR	47,676	C
Lipscomb Univ	TN	37,490	VC
LIU Brooklyn	NY	47,182	LC
LIU Post	NY	47,660	C
Lock Haven Univ of Pennsylvania	PA	18,028	LC
Loras College	IA	37,432	VC
Louisiana College	LA	15,746	C
Louisiana State Univ	LA	18,677	C+
Loyola Marymount Univ	CA	54,649	VC+
Loyola Univ Chicago	IL	51,646	VC+
Loyola Univ Maryland	MD	56,880	VC+
Loyola Univ New Orleans	LA	46,581	VC
Luther College	IA	45,720	C
Lycoming College	PA	45,379	C
Lynchburg College	VA	42,164	C
Macalester College	MN	57,691	MC
MacMurray College	IL	20,755	C
Malone Univ	OH	35,364	C
Manchester Univ	IN	35,070	C
Manhattan College	NY	49,588	C+
Manhattanville College	NY	50,740	VC
Mansfield Univ	PA	19,468	LC
Marian Univ	IN	38,540	C
Marist College	NY	35,500	C
Marlboro College	VT	35,980	VC
Marquette Univ	WI	46,930	VC+
Marshall Univ	WV	14,820	C
Mary Baldwin College	VA	38,245	C
Marymount Univ	VA	39,480	C
Marywood Univ	PA	45,595	C
Mass College of Liberal Arts	MA	18,613	C
Mass Inst of Technology	MA	58,240	MC
McDaniel College	MD	47,450	VC
McKendree Univ	IL	29,920	C+
McPherson College	KS	28,138	C
Mercer Univ	GA	44,201	VC
Mercyhurst Univ	PA	40,700	C
Merrimack College	MA	44,215	C
Messiah College	PA	40,690	C+
Metropolitan State Univ	MN	5,923	
Metropolitan State Univ of Denver	CO	4,835	LC
Miami Univ	OH	24,191	VC
Mich State Univ	MI	22,450	VC
Middle Tenn State Univ	TN	8,650	C
Middlebury College	VT	59,160	MC
Millersville Univ of Pennsylvania	PA	21,648	C
Millikin Univ	IL	38,940	C
Mills College	CA	54,119	VC
Millsaps College	MS	43,888	VC+
Minn State Univ, Mankato	MN	15,616	C
Minn State Univ, Moorhead	MN	13,392	VC
Misericordia Univ	PA	41,060	C
Miss State Univ	MS	14,750	C
Missouri State Univ	MO	13,996	C+
Missouri Univ of Science and Technology	MO	18,655	VC+
Missouri Valley College	MO	22,200	C
Molloy College	NY	40,440	C
Monmouth College	IL	40,850	C
Montana State Univ	MT	14,068	C
Montclair State Univ	NJ	22,614	C
Moravian College	PA	36,381	VC
Morehead State Univ	KY	10,900	C
Morehouse College	GA	39,412	C
Morgan State Univ	MD	14,500	VC
Morningside College	IA	35,430	C
Mount Holyoke College	MA	55,146	MC
Mount Mary Univ	WI	33,590	C
Mount Mercy Univ	IA	35,320	C
Mount St. Mary's Univ	MD	47,996	C
Mount St. Mary's College - Chalon Campus	CA	43,897	VC+
Mount Vernon Nazarene Univ	OH	29,590	C
Muhlenberg College	PA	52,837	HC
Murray State Univ	KY	15,304	C
Muskingum Univ	OH	30,502	C
Nazareth College of Rochester	NY	43,028	C+
Nebr Wesleyan Univ	NE	29,774	C+
New College of Florida	FL	14,540	VC
New England College	NH	45,930	VC
New Jersey City Univ	NJ	21,456	LC
New Mexico State Univ	NM	14,050	C
New York Univ	NY	61,470	MC
Newberry College	SC	26,850	LC
Newman Univ	KS	30,380	C+
Niagara Univ	NY	41,010	C
N Car State Univ	NC	16,202	VC
North Central College	IL	38,343	VC
North Park Univ	IL	30,130	C
Northeastern Illinois Univ	IL	10,318	LC
Northeastern Univ	MA	55,296	MC
Northern Arizona Univ	AZ	19,010	C
Northern Illinois Univ	IL	19,768	C
Northern Kentucky Univ	KY	21,134	C
Northern Mich Univ	MI	18,278	C
Northwest Missouri State Univ	MO	17,347	C
Northwest Univ	WA	18,854	C
Northwestern College of Iowa	IA	36,240	VC
Northwestern Univ	IL	61,640	MC
Notre Dame de Namur Univ	CA	44,236	LC
Nova Southeastern Univ	FL	37,280	VC
Nyack College	NY	33,250	C
Oakland Univ	MI	19,391	C
Oberlin College	OH	61,788	MC
Occidental College	CA	60,972	MC
Oglethorpe Univ	GA	44,200	C+
Ohio Dominican Univ	OH	38,380	C+
Ohio Northern Univ	OH	42,075	VC
Ohio Univ	OH	21,080	C
Ohio Wesleyan Univ	OH	49,460	C+
Okla City Univ	OK	40,476	VC
Okla State Univ	OK	14,310	VC
Old Dominion Univ	VA	19,483	VC
Olivet Nazarene Univ	IL	29,990	C
Oral Roberts Univ	OK	31,734	C
Oregon State Univ	OR	20,273	VC
Oswego / SUNY	NY	20,009	VC
Otterbein College	OH	32,214	C
Ouachita Baptist Univ	AR	30,220	VC
Our Lady of the Lake Univ	TX	22,430	LC
Pacific Lutheran Univ	WA	46,760	VC
Pacific Univ	OR	49,626	C+
Palm Beach Atlantic Univ	FL	34,874	C+
Pepperdine Univ	CA	55,372	HC+
Piedmont College	GA	30,136	C
Pitzer College	CA	54,988	MC
Plymouth State Univ	NH	23,148	LC
Point Loma Nazarene Univ	CA	41,006	C+
Pomona College	CA	57,680	MC
Pontifical Catholic Univ of PR	PR	7,310	
Portland State Univ	OR	18,672	C
Princeton Univ	NJ	53,795	MC
Principia College	IL	35,140	VC
Providence College	RI	57,383	VC
Purdue Univ/Calumet	IN	14,336	C
Purdue Univ/West Lafayette	IN	20,024	HC
Queens College/The CUNY	NY	17,107	VC
Queens Univ of Charlotte	NC	39,543	C+
Quinnipiac Univ	CT	55,160	VC
Randolph College	VA	45,660	VC
Randolph-Macon College	VA	49,869	C+
Reed College	OR	57,780	MC
Regis Univ	CO	41,318	C
Rensselaer Polytechnic Inst	NY	61,529	MC
Rhode Island College	RI	17,694	LC
Rhodes College	TN	51,900	HC+
Rice Univ	TX	43,288	MC
Richard Stockton College of New Jersey	NJ	20,000	VC
Rider Univ	NJ	45,720	C
Ripon College	WI	36,959	C+
Roanoke College	VA	49,976	C
Roberts Wesleyan College	NY	38,306	C
Rochester Inst of Technology	NY	42,450	VC
Rockford Univ	IL	31,000	C
Rockhurst Univ	MO	20,625	C
Roger Williams Univ	RI	46,296	VC
Rollins College	FL	52,370	HC
Roosevelt Univ	IL	22,605	VC
Rosemont College	PA	42,350	C
Rutgers, The State Univ of New Jersey/Camden Campus	NJ	25,121	C
Rutgers, The State Univ of New Jersey/New Brunswick	NJ	25,562	VC
Rutgers, The State Univ of New Jersey/Newark Campus	NJ	258,806	VC
Sacred Heart Univ	CT	49,264	VC
St. Anselm College	NH	49,376	VC
St. Francis Univ	PA	30,029	LC
St. John's Univ	MN	47,984	C
St. Joseph's College	IN	36,500	C
St. Joseph's College of Maine	ME	31,580	C
St. Joseph's Univ	PA	55,006	VC
St. Louis Univ	MO	48,346	HC
St. Mary's College	IN	45,160	C+
St. Mary's College of Calif	CA	53,550	C
St. Mary's Univ	TX	33,854	C
St. Mary's Univ of Minn	MN	38,280	C
St. Michael's College	VT	49,975	VC
St. Peter's Univ	NJ	44,240	C
St. Vincent College	PA	40,244	C
St. Xavier Univ	IL	32,840	C
Salem College	NC	29,326	VC
Salisbury Univ	MD	19,180	VC
Salve Regina Univ	RI	48,550	VC
Sam Houston State Univ	TX	17,082	C
Samford Univ	AL	37,060	C+
San Diego State Univ	CA	21,611	C+
San Francisco State Univ	CA	18,514	C
San Jose State Univ	CA	19,133	LC
Sarah Lawrence College	NY	48,000	HC
Schreiner Univ	TX	32,734	LC
Scripps College	CA	61,940	MC
Seattle Pacific Univ	WA	41,559	VC+
Seattle Univ	WA	49,035	VC+
Seton Hall Univ	NJ	45,902	C
Sewanee: The Univ of the South	TN	47,700	HC+
Siena College	NY	43,863	VC
Siena Heights Univ	MI	32,040	C
Simmons College	MA	49,966	VC
Simpson College	IA	36,086	C+
Skidmore College	NY	59,942	HC
Slippery Rock Univ of Pennsylvania	PA	10,360	C
Smith College	MA	59,674	MC
Sonoma State Univ	CA	20,541	C
Southeast Missouri State Univ	MO	15,370	LC
Southern Conn State Univ	CT	18,033	LC
Southern Illinois Univ Carbondale	IL	21,942	C
Southern Illinois Univ Edwardsville	IL	17,532	C
Southern Methodist Univ	TX	60,585	MC
Southern Nazarene Univ	OK	24,354	C
Southern Oregon Univ	OR	17,874	C
Southwestern Univ	TX	45,660	VC
Spelman College	GA	24,650	VC
Spring Arbor Univ	MI	26,740	C
Spring Hill College	AL	44,164	VC
St. Ambrose Univ	IA	30,845	C
St. Bonaventure Univ	NY	41,575	C
St. Catherine Univ	MN	37,782	C+
St. Cloud State Univ	MN	10,600	C
St. Edward's Univ	TX	47,784	C
St. Francis College	NY	34,200	C
St. John Fisher College	NY	40,708	C+
St. John's College, Santa Fe	NM	54,998	HC+
St. John's Univ	NY	55,070	C+
St. Lawrence Univ	NY	59,972	VC
St. Mary's College of Maryland	MD	25,754	VC
St. Norbert College	WI	41,478	VC
St. Olaf College	MN	51,200	HC+
St. Thomas Aquinas College	NY	40,230	C
Stanford Univ	CA	58,388	MC
SUNY at Purchase	NY	16,951	C
Stephen F. Austin State Univ	TX	14,668	C
Stetson Univ	FL	51,516	VC
Stevens Inst of Technology	NJ	50,130	HC
Stonehill College	MA	46,780	HC
Stony Brook Univ / SUNY	NY	20,078	HC+
Suffolk Univ	MA	47,298	C
SUNY College at Geneseo	NY	18,670	HC
SUNY College at Old Westbury	NY	16,324	C
SUNY Cortland/The SUNY	NY	19,759	C+
SUNY Fredonia/The SUNY at Fredonia	NY	19,840	VC
SUNY New Paltz	NY	14,348	C
SUNY Oneonta / SUNY	NY	16,919	C+
SUNY Plattsburgh / SUNY	NY	18,083	C
Susquehanna Univ	PA	51,150	C
Swarthmore College	PA	57,870	MC
Syracuse Univ	NY	56,346	VC
Tabor College	KS	29,010	C
Taylor Univ	IN	37,821	VC+
Temple Univ	PA	24,392	VC
Texas A&M Univ	TX	19,207	VC
Texas Christian Univ	TX	49,980	HC
Texas Lutheran Univ	TX	36,040	C
Texas State Univ	TX	17,128	C
Texas Tech Univ	TX	14,243	C
The Catholic Univ of America	DC	52,852	VC
The College of Idaho	ID	31,277	C+
The College of New Rochelle	NY	33,600	C
The College of St. Rose	NY	26,750	C
The Lincoln Univ	PA	15,154	LC
Ohio State Univ-Columbus Campus	OH	19,887	HC+
The Pennsylvania State Univ - Univ Park	PA	28,022	VC+
The SUNY at Potsdam	NY	18,473	C
The SUNY/College at Brockport	NY	19,002	C
The Univ of Memphis	TN	15,094	C
The Univ of N Car at Greensboro	NC	12,848	C
The Univ of Okla	OK	18,621	VC
The Univ of Tenn at Chattanooga	TN	16,883	C
The Univ of Utah	UT	16,463	VC
Thiel College	PA	38,728	LC
Thomas Edison State College	NJ	5,700	SP
Thomas More College	KY	34,760	C
Toccoa Falls College	GA	23,210	LC
Touro College	NY	27,959	VC
Towson Univ	MD	16,000	VC
Transylvania Univ	KY	42,660	VC+
Trinity Christian College	IL	28,869	C
Trinity College	CT		HC+
Trinity International Univ	IL	31,070	VC
Trinity Univ	TX	48,150	HC+
Truman State Univ	MO	15,541	HC
Tufts Univ	MA	58,780	MC
Tulane Univ	LA	60,861	MC
Union College	NY	60,240	MC
Union Univ	TN	28,260	VC
United States Military Academy	NY		MC
Univ at Albany / SUNY	NY	18,674	VC
Univ at Buffalo / The SUNY	NY	20,283	VC
Univ of Akron	OH	20,436	C
Univ of Alabama at Birmingham	AL	18,484	C+
Univ of Alabama at Tuscaloosa	AL	17,164	C+
Univ of Alabama in Huntsville	AL	17,591	VC+
Univ of Alaska Anchorage	AK	16,673	NC
Univ of Alaska Fairbanks	AK	15,130	C
Univ of Arizona	AZ	20,657	C
Univ of Arkansas at Fayetteville	AR	18,352	C
Univ of Arkansas at Little Rock	AR	17,609	LC
Univ of Calif at Davis	CA		HC
Univ of Calif at Irvine	CA	25,961	VC
Univ of Calif at Los Angeles	CA	25,686	MC
Univ of Calif at Riverside	CA	27,204	C+
Univ of Calif at San Diego	CA	21,000	VC
Univ of Calif at Santa Barbara	CA	27,551	HC
Univ of Calif at Santa Cruz	CA	27,807	C+
Univ of Central Arkansas	AR	13,667	VC
Univ of Central Florida	FL	15,668	VC+
Univ of Central Okla	OK	12,293	C
Univ of Chicago	IL	55,416	MC
Univ of Cincinnati	OH	21,506	VC
Univ of Colo at Colo Springs	CO	15,000	VC
Univ of Colo Boulder	CO	22,605	VC+
Univ of Colo Denver	CO	17,904	C
Univ of Conn	CT	24,706	VC
Univ of Dallas	TX	45,500	VC+
Univ of Dayton	OH	49,070	VC
Univ of Delaware	DE	23,612	VC
Univ of Denver	CO	51,787	VC+
Univ of Detroit Mercy	MI	30,450	VC
Univ of Dubuque	IA	30,200	C
Univ of Evansville	IN	42,656	VC+
Univ of Findlay	OH	31,916	C
Univ of Florida	FL	15,943	VC
Univ of Georgia	GA	20,082	VC
Univ of Hartford	CT	42,674	C
Univ of Hawaii at Hilo	HI	23,066	C
Univ of Hawaii at Manoa	HI	19,379	C
Univ of Houston	TX	19,796	VC
Univ of Houston-Downtown	TX	15,170	LC
Univ of Idaho	ID	14,558	C

ST = STATE   **$IS** = IN-STATE COSTS   **SR** = SELECTOR RATING

School	ST	$IS	SR
Univ of Illinois at Chicago	IL	24,505	VC
Univ of Illinois at Urbana-Champaign	IL	26,450	HC
Univ of Indianapolis	IN	31,740	LC
Univ of Iowa	IA	17,693	VC
Univ of Kansas	KS	17,603	C+
Univ of Kentucky	KY	19,868	C
Univ of La Verne	CA	47,010	C
Univ of Louisiana at Lafayette	LA	6,130	C
Univ of Louisville	KY	17,946	C
Univ of Maine	ME	19,902	C+
Univ of Mary Washington	VA	19,484	VC
Univ of Maryland - College Park	MD	20,060	HC
Univ of Maryland/Baltimore County	MD	18,000	VC
Univ of Mass Amherst	MA	24,215	VC+
Univ of Mass Boston	MA	23,066	VC
Univ of Mass Dartmouth	MA	22,223	C
Univ of Mass Lowell	MA	19,316	C
Univ of Miami	FL	57,034	MC
Univ of Mich/Ann Arbor	MI	22,102	MC
Univ of Mich/Dearborn	MI	9,885	C
Univ of Mich-Flint	MI	17,547	C+
Univ of Minn/Duluth	MN	19,806	C
Univ of Minn/Morris	MN	17,150	VC
Univ of Minn/Twin Cities	MN		HC
Univ of Miss	MS	16,704	C+
Univ of Missouri/Columbia	MO	18,201	MC
Univ of Missouri-Kansas City	MO	19,603	C
Univ of Missouri-St. Louis	MO		C
Univ of Montana	MT	14,105	C
Univ of Mount Union	OH	35,130	C
Univ of Nebr - Lincoln	NE	18,031	VC
Univ of Nebr at Omaha	NE	12,700	C
Univ of Nevada, Las Vegas	NV	17,303	C
Univ of Nevada/Reno	NV	17,507	C
Univ of New England	ME	46,750	C
Univ of New Hampshire	NH	26,912	C
Univ of New Mexico	NM	15,300	C
Univ of New Orleans	LA	9,224	C
Univ of N Car at Asheville	NC	13,500	VC
Univ of N Car at Chapel Hill	NC	18,928	MC
Univ of N Car at Charlotte	NC	15,547	C
Univ of N Dak	ND	14,551	C
Univ of North Florida	FL	15,870	VC
Univ of North Texas	TX	15,628	C
Univ of Northern Colo	CO	18,446	C
Univ of Northern Iowa	IA	15,795	C
Univ of Notre Dame	IN	57,117	MC
Univ of Oregon	OR	21,360	C+
Univ of Pennsylvania	PA	61,132	MC
Univ of Pittsburgh at Pittsburgh	PA	28,572	HC+
Univ of Portland	OR	49,964	VC
Univ of PR Recinto de Rio Piedras	PR	5,750	
Univ of PR/Mayaguez	PR	1,250	
Univ of Puget Sound	WA	54,608	HC
Univ of Redlands	CA	40,500	C
Univ of Rochester	NY	60,668	MC
Univ of St. Francis	IN	29,810	C
Univ of St. Joseph	CT	45,630	C
Univ of San Diego	CA	54,818	HC+
Univ of San Francisco	CA	54,770	VC
Univ of Scranton	PA	51,940	VC
Univ of Sioux Falls	SD	22,990	C
Univ of South Alabama	AL	13,510	C
Univ of S Car at Columbia	SC	19,725	VC+
Univ of S Dak	SD	15,111	C
Univ of South Florida/Tampa	FL	13,000	C
Univ of Southern Calif	CA	56,903	MC
Univ of Southern Indiana	IN	14,885	C
Univ of Southern Maine	ME	16,576	C
Univ of Southern Miss	MS	13,170	C
Univ of St. Thomas - Houston	TX	37,690	C
Univ of Tampa	FL	35,160	VC
Univ of Tenn at Knoxville	TN	20,364	VC+
Univ of Tenn at Martin	TN	13,734	C
Univ of Texas - Pan American	TX	11,125	LC
Univ of Texas at Arlington	TX	10,908	LC
Univ of Texas at Austin	TX	44,074	HC
Univ of Texas at El Paso	TX	8,764	NC
Univ of Texas at San Antonio	TX	18,372	C
Univ of the District of Columbia	DC	7,244	LC
Univ of the Incarnate Word	TX	37,316	LC
Univ of the Pacific	CA	52,146	VC
Univ of Toledo	OH	18,464	C
Univ of Tulsa	OK	46,331	MC
Univ of Vermont	VT	27,006	VC+
Univ of Virginia	VA	23,050	MC
Univ of Washington	WA	14,722	VC
Univ of West Florida	FL	14,656	C
Univ of West Georgia	GA	15,488	LC
Univ of Wisc/Eau Claire	WI	15,730	VC
Univ of Wisc/Green Bay	WI	19,074	C
Univ of Wisc/La Crosse	WI	9,304	VC
Univ of Wisc/Madison	WI	18,757	HC+
Univ of Wisc/Oshkosh	WI	10,426	LC
Univ of Wisc/Parkside	WI	10,181	LC
Univ of Wisc/Platteville	WI	14,564	C
Univ of Wisc/Stevens Point	WI	14,043	C
Univ of Wisc-Milwaukee	WI	18,436	C
Univ of Wyoming	WY	14,401	C+
Ursinus College	PA	57,580	VC
Ursuline College	OH	33,198	LC
Utah State Univ	UT	12,044	C
Utica College	NY	45,670	C
Valparaiso Univ	IN	44,940	VC+
Vanderbilt Univ	TN	58,220	MC
Vassar College	NY	61,140	MC
Villanova Univ	PA	58,394	MC
Virginia Commonwealth Univ	VA	21,716	C
Virginia Polytechnic Inst and State Univ	VA	14,629	HC
Virginia Wesleyan College	VA	28,433	LC
Viterbo Univ	WI	30,070	C
Wabash College	IN	46,850	C+
Wagner College	NY	48,600	C+
Wake Forest Univ	NC	58,838	MC
Walsh Univ	OH	35,100	C
Warren Wilson College	NC	40,132	VC
Wartburg College	IA	41,055	C
Washburn Univ	KS	12,579	C
Washington and Jefferson College	PA	51,948	VC
Washington and Lee Univ	VA	52,812	MC
Washington College	MD	52,602	VC
Washington State Univ	WA	20,461	C
Washington Univ in St. Louis	MO	69,844	MC
Wayland Baptist Univ	TX	18,912	LC
Wayne State Univ	MI	22,063	C
Webster Univ	MO	35,100	C
Wellesley College	MA	59,038	MC
Wells College	NY	49,400	VC
Wesleyan College	GA	24,000	C
Wesleyan Univ	CT	61,198	MC
West Chester Univ of Pennsylvania	PA	17,186	C
West Virginia Univ	WV	16,542	C+
West Virginia Wesleyan College	WV	26,880	C
Western Carolina Univ	NC	13,965	C
Western Illinois Univ	IL	20,732	C
Western Kentucky Univ	KY	11,000	LC
Western Mich Univ	MI	19,628	C
Western New England Univ	MA	46,154	C+
Western Oregon Univ	OR	15,021	C
Western Washington Univ	WA	18,519	VC
Westminster College	MO	31,720	VC
Westminster College	PA	31,290	C+
Westminster College	UT	37,708	C+
Westmont College	CA	41,500	HC
Wheaton College	IL	40,720	MC
Wheaton College	MA	54,934	HC+
Wheeling Jesuit Univ	WV	33,500	C
Whitman College	WA	55,988	MC
Whittier College	CA	43,414	VC
Whitworth Univ	WA	47,734	VC
Wichita State Univ	KS	14,607	C+
Wiley College	TX		LC
Wilkes Univ	PA	44,070	C
Willamette Univ	OR	56,450	VC+
William Jewell College	MO	31,000	VC+
William Paterson Univ of New Jersey	NJ	21,694	C
Williams College	MA	61,070	MC
Wilmington College	OH	29,784	C
Wilson College	PA	35,080	C
Wingate Univ	NC	34,990	C
Winthrop Univ	SC	21,120	C
Wittenberg Univ	OH	47,962	C+
Wofford College	SC	45,795	VC
Wright State Univ	OH	16,983	C
Xavier Univ	OH	44,980	VC
Xavier Univ of Louisiana	LA	25,300	C
Yale Univ	CT	55,300	MC
Yeshiva Univ	NY	47,250	VC+
York College / The CUNY	NY	5,496	VC
York College of Pennsylvania	PA	26,590	C
Youngstown State Univ	OH	16,732	C

PHILOSOPHY (AESTHETICS/MEDIA WRITING)

School	ST	$IS	SR
Murray State Univ	KY	15,304	C

PHILOSOPHY (HISTORY/CONTEMPORARY THOUGHT)

School	ST	$IS	SR
Murray State Univ	KY	15,304	C

PHILOSOPHY (POLITICAL THOUGHT)

School	ST	$IS	SR
Murray State Univ	KY	15,304	C

PHILOSOPHY AND RELIGION

School	ST	$IS	SR
Arizona State Univ, at the West Campus	AZ	19,251	C
Augustana College	SD	36,500	VC
Beloit College	WI	49,970	HC
Bethel College	IN	31,560	C
Biola Univ	CA	40,320	C+
Bridgewater College	VA	41,450	C
Cal State, Fresno	CA	17,405	C
Christian Brothers Univ	TN	31,670	HC
Claflin Univ	SC	22,368	LC
Covenant College	GA	38,990	VC+
Dakota Wesleyan Univ	SD	23,000	C
Dordt College	IA	34,160	C+
Friends Univ	KS	29,100	C
Hendrix College	AR	50,202	VC+
Hillsdale College	MI	32,866	MC
Ithaca College	NY	53,864	MC
Kutztown Univ of Pennsylvania	PA	16,909	LC
Marymount Manhattan College	NY	40,118	VC
Mass College of Liberal Arts	MA	18,613	C
Murray State Univ	KY	15,304	C
New York Univ	NY	61,470	MC
N Dak State Univ	ND		C
Northeastern Univ	MA	55,296	MC
Northwest Nazarene Univ	ID	34,000	C
Nova Southeastern Univ	FL	37,280	VC
Nyack College	NY	33,250	C
Okla City Univ	OK	40,476	VC
Ouachita Baptist Univ	AR	30,220	VC
Pace Univ	NY	53,367	C
Paine College	GA	19,826	LC
Philander Smith College	AR	19,760	LC
Point Loma Nazarene Univ	CA	41,006	C+
Prescott College	AZ	33,284	C
Radford Univ	VA	17,766	C
Rocky Mountain College	MT	32,242	C
Rowan Univ	NJ	24,022	VC+
Shawnee State Univ	OH	16,916	C
S Dak State Univ	SD	14,296	C
Southwestern College	KS	29,270	C
Spring Arbor Univ	MI	26,740	C
St. Joseph's College, New York/Brooklyn Campus	NY	22,630	C
St. Joseph's College, New York/Suffolk Campus	NY	22,630	C
Taylor Univ	IN	37,821	VC+
The Univ of N Car at Pembroke	NC	13,388	LC
Univ of Maine at Farmington	ME	18,187	LC
Univ of N Car at Wilmington	NC	13,572	VC
Univ of Notre Dame	IN	57,117	MC
Univ of Texas at San Antonio	TX	18,372	C
Urbana Univ	OH	30,820	C
Virginia Commonwealth Univ	VA	21,716	C
Washington Adventist Univ	MD	25,859	LC
Wesley College	DE	31,115	LC
West Chester Univ of Pennsylvania	PA	17,186	C
Wilson College	PA	35,080	C
Winthrop Univ	SC	21,120	C
Youngstown State Univ	OH	16,732	C

PHOTOGRAPHY

School	ST	$IS	SR
Adams State Univ	CO	13,358	LC
Andrews Univ	MI	28,030	C+
Appalachian State Univ	NC	12,919	VC
Aquinas College	MI	33,060	C
Arcadia Univ	PA	33,570	C+
Art Academy of Cincinnati	OH	25,940	SP
Art Center College of Design	CA	34,044	SP
Art Inst of Atlanta	GA	24,000	SP
Bard College	NY	61,940	HC
Bard College at Simon's Rock	MA	61,749	HC+
Barry Univ	FL	38,190	C
Bellevue Univ	NE	4,600	NC
Bennington College	VT	56,990	HC+
Biola Univ	CA	40,320	C+
Birmingham-Southern College	AL	44,168	VC+
Brigham Young Univ	UT	12,100	HC
Buffalo State College / SUNY	NY	15,733	C+
Calif Baptist Univ	CA	38,792	C
Calif College of the Arts	CA	48,334	SP
Calif Inst of the Arts	CA	51,902	SP
Cal State, San Bernardino	CA	12,000	C
Cleveland Inst of Art	OH	48,685	SP
Coker College	SC	32,256	LC
College for Creative Studies	MI	45,340	C
College of Art and Design at Lesley Univ	MA	39,730	SP
Columbia College	MO	24,578	C
Columbia College Chicago	IL	30,940	LC
Columbus College of Art and Design	OH	37,732	SP
Corcoran College of Art and Design	DC	36,500	SP
Dominican Univ	IL	37,628	C
Drexel Univ	PA	61,418	VC+
Endicott College	MA	43,228	VC+
Ferris State Univ	MI	20,047	C
Fitchburg State Univ	MA	18,173	C
Gallaudet Univ	DC	25,380	SP
Goddard College	VT	16,418	VC
Grand Valley State Univ	MI	17,998	C+
Hampshire College	MA	58,320	MC
Hofstra Univ	NY	51,810	VC+
Howard Univ	DC	13,646	C
Indiana Univ-Purdue Univ Fort Wayne	IN	15,521	C
Indiana Univ-Purdue Univ Indianapolis	IN	17,611	C
Indiana Wesleyan Univ	IN	31,815	VC
Ithaca College	NY	53,864	MC
Kansas City Art Inst	MO	44,308	SP
Kent State Univ	OH	19,920	C
King Univ	TN	33,140	C
Kutztown Univ of Pennsylvania	PA	16,909	LC
LIU Post	NY	47,660	VC
Maine College of Art	ME	28,812	SP
Marlboro College	VT	35,980	VC
Marshall Univ	WV	14,820	C
Maryland Inst College of Art	MD	39,500	SP
Marywood Univ	PA	45,595	C
Memphis College of Art	TN	33,550	SP
Milwaukee Inst of Art and Design	WI	31,938	SP
Minneapolis College of Art and Design	MN	36,700	SP
Montserrat College of Art	MA	31,000	C
Moore College of Art and Design	PA	50,135	SP
Moore College of Art and Design	PA	50,135	SP
Morningside College	IA	35,430	C
New Jersey City Univ	NJ	21,456	LC
New York Univ	NY	61,470	MC
Northern Arizona Univ	AZ	19,010	C
Notre Dame of Maryland Univ	MD	27,700	VC
Oberlin College	OH	61,788	MC
Ohio Univ	OH	21,080	C
Okla Christian Univ	OK	25,870	VC
Okla City Univ	OK	40,476	VC
Otis College of Art and Design	CA	35,404	SP
Pacific Northwest College of Art	OR	38,494	SP
Pacific Union College	CA	28,150	VC
Parsons The New School for Design	NY	56,610	SP
Point Park Univ	PA	36,390	C
Pratt Inst	NY	55,956	SP
Prescott College	AZ	33,284	C
Providence College	RI	57,383	VC
Purdue Univ/West Lafayette	IN	20,024	HC
Rhode Island School of Design	RI	57,234	MC
Ringling College of Art and Design	FL	46,130	SP
Rochester Inst of Technology	NY	42,450	VC
Rocky Mountain College of Art and Design	CO	22,470	SP
Salem State Univ	MA	13,161	LC
Sam Houston State Univ	TX	17,082	C
San Francisco Art Inst	CA	55,762	SP
Santa Fe Univ of Art and Design	NM	39,666	SP
Savannah College of Art and Design	GA	48,005	SP
School of the Art Inst of Chicago	IL	56,230	SP
School of Visual Arts	NY	36,500	VC
Seattle Univ	WA	49,035	VC+
Southern Illinois Univ Carbondale	IL	21,942	C
St. Edward's Univ	TX	47,784	C
St. John's Univ	NY	55,070	C+
SUNY Fredonia/The SUNY at Fredonia	NY	19,840	VC
SUNY New Paltz	NY	14,348	C
Syracuse Univ	NY	56,346	VC
Temple Univ	PA	24,392	VC
Texas A&M Univ at Commerce	TX	10,496	C
Texas Christian Univ	TX	49,980	HC
Texas State Univ	TX	17,128	C
Texas Tech Univ	TX	14,243	C
Thomas Edison State College	NJ	5,700	SP
Univ of Central Florida	FL	15,668	VC+
Univ of Central Missouri	MO	14,605	C
Univ of Central Okla	OK	12,293	C
Univ of Dayton	OH	49,070	VC
Univ of Florida	FL	15,943	HC
Univ of Hartford	CT	42,674	C
Univ of Illinois at Chicago	IL	24,505	VC
Univ of Illinois at Urbana-Champaign	IL	26,450	HC
Univ of Iowa	IA	17,693	VC
Univ of La Verne	CA	47,010	C
Univ of Mass Dartmouth	MA	22,223	C
Univ of Miami	FL	57,034	MC
Univ of Mich/Ann Arbor	MI	22,102	MC
Univ of Oregon	OR	21,360	C+
Univ of the Arts	PA	38,450	SP
Univ of Washington	WA	14,722	VC
Virginia Commonwealth Univ	VA	21,716	C
Washington Univ in St. Louis	MO	69,844	MC
Webster Univ	MO	35,100	C
Western Washington Univ	WA	18,519	VC
Youngstown State Univ	OH	16,732	C

PHYSICAL ACTIVITY

School	ST	$IS	SR
Kent State Univ	OH	19,920	C

ST = STATE　　$IS = IN-STATE COSTS　　SR = SELECTOR RATING

School	ST	$IS	SR
Univ of Pittsburgh at Pittsburgh	PA	28,572	HC+

PHYSICAL CHEMISTRY

School	ST	$IS	SR
Aquinas College	MI	33,060	C
Centre College	KY	35,000	HC+
Kent State Univ	OH	19,920	C
Union Univ	TN	28,260	VC
Univ of Calif at San Diego	CA	21,000	VC

PHYSICAL EDUCATION

School	ST	$IS	SR
Adams State Univ	CO	13,358	LC
Adelphi Univ	NY	44,670	VC
Adrian College	MI	42,400	C
Alabama A&M Univ	AL	10,084	C
Albany State Univ	GA	8,500	C
Alderson Broaddus Univ	WV	28,656	C
Alice Lloyd College	KY	4,900	LC
Anderson Univ	IN	36,100	C
Appalachian State Univ	NC	12,919	VC
Aquinas College	MI	33,060	C
Arkansas State Univ	AR	15,470	C
Arkansas Tech Univ	AR	13,982	LC
Armstrong State Univ	GA	15,532	C
Asbury Univ	KY	32,038	VC
Ashford Univ	CA	10,480	C
Ashland Univ	OH	25,000	C
Auburn Univ	AL	22,378	VC+
Augsburg College	MN	35,142	C
Augustana College	IL	43,398	VC
Augustana College	SD	36,500	VC
Aurora Univ	IL	33,228	C
Averett Univ	VA	37,750	LC
Azusa Pacific Univ	CA	42,086	C
Baker Univ	KS	33,350	C+
Baldwin Wallace Univ	OH	38,318	C
Ball State Univ	IN	17,850	C
Barry Univ	FL	38,190	C
Barton College	NC	27,660	LC
Baylor Univ	TX	50,329	HC
Bellevue Univ	NE	4,600	NC
Belmont Univ	TN	39,190	VC+
Benedictine College	KS	29,180	VC
Berea College	KY	7,192	C
Berry College	GA	39,254	VC
Bethany College	KS	30,605	VC
Bethany College	WV	35,282	LC
Bethel College	IN	31,560	C
Bethel Univ	MN	34,940	VC
Bethel Univ	TN	19,186	C
Bethune-Cookman Univ	FL	22,958	C
Biola Univ	CA	40,320	C+
Black Hills State Univ	SD	13,947	C
Blackburn College	IL	21,350	C
Blue Mountain College	MS	15,634	LC
Bluffton Univ	OH	38,948	C
Boise State Univ	ID	13,469	LC
Boston Univ	MA	60,694	MC
Bowling Green State Univ	OH	18,970	C
Brewton-Parker College	GA	33,388	C
Bridgewater State Univ	MA	18,752	C
Bryan College	TN	24,194	C
Cal State, Dominguez Hills	CA	17,090	LC
Cal State, Los Angeles	CA	17,186	LC
Cal State, Northridge	CA	28,690	LC
Cal State, Stanislaus	CA	18,582	C
Calvin College	MI	39,120	VC
Campbellsville Univ	KY	27,720	C
Canisius College	NY	44,900	C
Capital Univ	OH	41,050	VC
Carroll College	MT	28,000	C
Carroll Univ	WI	38,100	C
Carthage College	WI	33,000	C
Castleton State College	VT	20,186	C
Catawba College	NC	37,240	LC
Cedarville Univ	OH	32,860	VC
Central Conn State Univ	CT	19,749	C
Central Methodist Univ	MO	28,240	VC
Central State Univ	OH	9,010	C
Central Washington Univ	WA	11,730	C
Charleston Southern Univ	SC	22,420	C
Chicago State Univ	IL	5,482	C
Citadel, The	SC		C
CUNY/Brooklyn College	NY	5,884	C+
Clark Atlanta Univ	GA	30,006	LC
Clearwater Christian College	FL	23,720	C
Cleveland State Univ	OH	21,776	C
Coastal Carolina Univ	SC	18,580	C
Coe College	IA	45,550	VC
Coker College	SC	32,256	LC
College of Charleston	SC	22,145	VC
College of Mount St. Vincent	NY	41,040	MC
College of New Jersey	NJ	25,376	HC
College of the Ozarks	MO		VC
Concordia Univ Nebr	NE	26,000	VC
Concordia Univ St. Paul	MN	28,250	C
Concordia Univ Wisc	WI	28,420	C
Concordia Univ, Ann Arbor	MI	27,220	VC
Concordia Univ, River Forest	IL	26,300	C
Corban Univ	OR	37,380	C+

School	ST	$IS	SR
Cornerstone Univ and Grand Rapids Theological Seminary	MI	33,338	C
Culver-Stockton College	MO	30,900	C
Cumberland Univ	TN	21,220	C
Dakota Wesleyan Univ	SD	23,000	C
Dallas Baptist Univ	TX	30,580	VC
Davis & Elkins College	WV	33,742	C
Defiance College	OH	30,645	C
Delaware State Univ	DE	16,722	LC
Denison Univ	OH	54,670	HC+
DePaul Univ	IL	47,623	VC
Doane College	NE	35,230	C
Dordt College	IA	34,160	C+
Drury Univ	MO	31,909	VC
East Carolina Univ	NC	14,169	C
East Central Univ	OK	10,223	LC
East Tenn State Univ	TN	9,000	C
East Texas Baptist Univ	TX	31,577	LC
Eastern Conn State Univ	CT	20,584	C
Eastern Kentucky Univ	KY	11,161	C
Eastern Mennonite Univ	VA	40,660	C
Eastern Mich Univ	MI	18,604	C
Eastern New Mexico Univ	NM	10,682	C
Eastern Oregon Univ	OR	10,400	C
Eastern Washington Univ	WA		C
Edinboro Univ of Pennsylvania	PA	15,940	LC
Edward Waters College	FL	19,607	LC
Elizabeth City State Univ	NC	11,638	C
Elmhurst College	IL	43,336	C
Elon Univ	NC	41,914	VC+
Emory and Henry College	VA	387,460	C
Emporia State Univ	KS	12,897	C
Endicott College	MA	43,228	VC+
Erskine College	SC	37,360	C
Eureka College	IL	19,280	C
Evangel Univ	MO	23,090	C
Faulkner Univ	AL	25,720	C
Ferrum College	VA	27,740	LC
Florida Atlantic Univ	FL	17,339	C
Florida International Univ	FL	17,747	C+
Florida Memorial Univ	FL	20,888	LC
Florida State Univ	FL	16,715	VC
Fort Hays State Univ	KS	11,354	C
Fort Valley State Univ	GA	11,200	VC
Franklin College	IN	36,585	C
Freed-Hardeman Univ	TN	19,697	VC
Fresno Pacific Univ	CA	32,136	C
Frostburg State Univ	MD	15,264	LC
Gallaudet Univ	DC	25,380	SP
Gardner-Webb Univ	NC	34,375	C+
George Mason Univ	VA	15,724	VC
Georgia State Univ	GA	15,582	VC
Glenville State College	WV	11,348	NC
Gonzaga Univ	WA	46,441	HC
Goshen College	IN	35,900	VC
Grace College and Seminary	IN	28,800	VC
Graceland Univ	IA	28,020	C
Grambling State Univ	LA	13,384	C
Grand Canyon Univ	AZ	24,540	VC
Grand View Univ	IA	31,050	C
Greensboro College	NC	28,740	LC
Greenville College	IL	27,012	C
Hampton Univ	VA	28,528	C
Hardin-Simmons Univ	TX	23,560	C+
Heidelberg Univ	OH	34,100	C
Henderson State Univ	AR	14,584	C
High Point Univ	NC	39,800	C
Hillsdale College	MI	32,866	MC
Hofstra Univ	NY	51,810	VC+
Houghton College	NY	36,808	C+
Houston Baptist Univ	TX	36,450	C
Howard Univ	DC	13,646	C
Humboldt State Univ	CA	18,400	C
Huntingdon College	AL	33,100	C
Huntington Univ	IN	33,220	C+
Husson Univ	ME	24,194	LC
Huston-Tillotson Univ	TX	18,124	C+
Idaho State Univ	ID	12,307	C
Indiana Inst of Technology	IN	34,240	LC
Indiana State Univ	IN	16,000	C
Indiana Univ of Pennsylvania	PA	20,846	LC
Indiana Wesleyan Univ	IN	31,815	VC
Inter-American Univ of PR/Aguadilla Campus	PR	5,578	
Iowa State Univ	IA	16,403	C
Iowa Wesleyan College	IA	30,850	C
Ithaca College	NY	53,864	HC
Jacksonville Univ	FL	37,780	C
John Brown Univ	AR	32,056	VC+
John Carroll Univ	OH	46,300	C+
Johnson C. Smith Univ	NC	25,336	LC
Johnson State College	VT	16,721	C
Judson Univ	IL	25,130	C
Kansas Wesleyan Univ	KS	32,000	C
Kean Univ	NJ	23,444	C
Keene State College	NH	23,232	LC
Kennesaw State Univ	GA		C
Kent State Univ	OH	19,920	C
Kentucky State Univ	KY	11,000	LC
Kentucky Wesleyan College	KY	27,440	C
King Univ	TN	33,140	C
La Sierra Univ	CA	35,694	VC
Lander Univ	SC	22,514	C+
Lane College	TN	11,212	C

School	ST	$IS	SR
Langston Univ	OK	3,000	C
Lee Univ	TN	18,690	C+
LeTourneau Univ	TX	36,210	VC
Liberty Univ	VA	19,101	C
Limestone College	SC	30,800	C
Lincoln Univ	MO	12,904	NC
Lindenwood Univ	MO	20,750	C
Linfield College-McMinnville Campus	OR	47,676	C
Lipscomb Univ	TN	37,490	VC
LIU Brooklyn	NY	47,182	LC
LIU Post	NY	47,660	C
Lock Haven Univ of Pennsylvania	PA	18,028	LC
Longwood Univ	VA	20,924	C
Loras College	IA	37,432	VC
Louisiana Tech Univ	LA	11,302	C
Lubbock Christian Univ	TX	26,308	C
Luther College	IA	45,720	C+
Lyndon State College	VT	14,233	C
MacMurray College	IL	20,755	C
Manhattan College	NY	49,588	C+
Marian Univ	IN	38,540	C
Mars Hill Univ	NC	22,950	LC
Marshall Univ	WV	14,820	C
Maryville College	TN	33,150	C+
Marywood Univ	PA	45,595	C
Mayville State Univ	ND	11,401	NC
McDaniel College	MD	47,450	C
McKendree Univ	IL	29,920	C+
McMurry Univ	TX	25,962	LC
McPherson College	KS	28,138	C
Messiah College	PA	40,690	C+
Methodist Univ	NC	37,185	C
Metropolitan State Univ of Denver	CO	4,835	LC
Mich State Univ	MI	22,450	VC
MidAmerica Nazarene Univ	KS	28,000	C
Middle Tenn State Univ	TN	8,650	C
Midwestern State Univ	TX	9,722	C
Millikin Univ	IL	38,940	C
Minn State Univ, Mankato	MN	15,616	C
Minn State Univ, Moorhead	MN	13,392	VC
Minot State Univ	ND	10,915	C
Miss State Univ	MS	14,750	C
Miss Valley State Univ	MS	9,706	LC
Missouri Baptist Univ	MO	31,830	C
Missouri Southern State Univ	MO	12,061	C
Missouri State Univ	MO	13,996	C+
Missouri Valley College	MO	22,200	C
Monmouth College	IL	40,850	C
Monmouth Univ	NJ	44,108	C
Montana State Univ-Billings	MT	12,425	C
Montana State Univ-Northern	MT	12,500	NC
Montclair State Univ	NJ	22,614	C
Morehead State Univ	KY	10,900	C
Morgan State Univ	MD	14,500	VC
Mount Marty College	SD	29,638	C
Mount Vernon Nazarene Univ	OH	29,590	C
Muskingum Univ	OH	30,502	C
Nebr Wesleyan Univ	NE	29,774	C+
New England College	NH	45,930	LC
New Mexico State Univ	NM	14,050	C
Newberry College	SC	26,850	LC
N Car Agricultural and Technical State Univ	NC	13,365	LC
N Car Central Univ	NC	9,000	C
N Dak State Univ	ND		C
Northeastern Illinois Univ	IL	10,318	LC
Northern Illinois Univ	IL	19,768	C
Northern Kentucky Univ	KY	21,134	C
Northern Mich Univ	MI	18,278	C
Northern State Univ - Aberdeen	SD	14,505	C
Northwest Missouri State Univ	MO	17,347	C
Northwest Nazarene Univ	ID	34,000	C
Northwest Univ	WA	18,854	C
Northwestern College	MN	24,000	C
Northwestern College of Iowa	IA	36,240	VC
Northwestern Okla State Univ	OK	7,275	NC
Norwich Univ	VT	28,212	C
Nova Southeastern Univ	FL	37,280	VC
Oakwood Univ	AL	25,529	NC
Ohio Northern Univ	OH	42,075	VC
Ohio Univ	OH	21,080	C
Ohio Wesleyan Univ	OH	49,460	C+
Okla Baptist Univ	OK	28,202	C
Okla Christian Univ	OK	25,870	VC
Okla Panhandle State Univ	OK	8,996	C
Okla State Univ	OK	14,310	VC
Okla Wesleyan Univ	OK	21,300	C
Old Dominion Univ	VA	19,483	LC
Olivet College	MI	19,984	LC
Olivet Nazarene Univ	IL	29,990	C
Oral Roberts Univ	OK	31,734	C
Ottawa Univ	KS	15,000	VC
Otterbein College	OH	32,214	C
Pacific Lutheran Univ	WA	46,760	C+
Pacific Union College	CA	28,150	VC
Palm Beach Atlantic Univ	FL	34,874	C+
Pepperdine Univ	CA	55,372	HC+
Peru State College	NE	8,600	NC

School	ST	$IS	SR
Pfeiffer Univ	NC	33,700	LC
Philander Smith College	AR	19,760	LC
Pittsburg State Univ	KS	12,032	C
Plymouth State Univ	NH	23,148	LC
Pontifical Catholic Univ of PR	PR	7,310	
Prairie View A&M Univ	TX	15,205	LC
Prescott College	AZ	33,284	C
Queens College/The CUNY	NY	17,107	VC
Quincy Univ	IL	34,980	LC
Radford Univ	VA	17,766	LC
Randolph College	VA	45,660	VC
Rhode Island College	RI	17,694	LC
Roanoke College	VA	49,976	C
Roberts Wesleyan College	NY	38,306	C+
Rockford College	IL	31,000	C
Saginaw Valley State Univ	MI	17,369	C
St. Augustine's Univ	NC	14,000	C
St. Joseph's College	IN	36,500	C
St. Joseph's College of Maine	ME	31,580	C
St. Mary's College of Calif	CA	53,550	C
Salisbury Univ	MD	19,180	VC
Sam Houston State Univ	TX	17,082	C
San Diego State Univ	CA	21,611	C+
San Francisco State Univ	CA	18,514	C
Schreiner Univ	TX	32,734	LC
Seattle Pacific Univ	WA	41,559	VC+
Shaw Univ	NC	15,488	C
Shepherd Univ	WV	15,875	C
Simpson College	IA	36,086	C+
S Car State Univ	SC	6,700	LC
S Dak State Univ	SD	14,296	C
Southeastern Louisiana Univ	LA	13,325	C
Southeastern Okla State Univ	OK	7,966	LC
Southern Adventist Univ	TN	26,190	C
Southern Conn State Univ	CT	18,033	LC
Southern Illinois Univ Carbondale	IL	21,942	C
Southern Illinois Univ Edwardsville	IL	17,532	C
Southern Nazarene Univ	OK	24,354	C
Southern Oregon Univ	OR	17,874	C
Southern Univ at New Orleans	LA	2,963	NC
Southern Wesleyan Univ	SC	25,600	C
Southwest Baptist Univ	MO	24,710	C
Southwest Minn State Univ	MN	14,000	C
Southwestern Adventist Univ	TX	23,026	LC
Southwestern College	KS	29,270	C
Southwestern Okla State Univ	OK	9,160	C
Springfield College	MA	25,000	C
St. Ambrose Univ	IA	30,845	C
St. Andrews Univ	NC	32,050	LC
St. Bonaventure Univ	NY	41,575	C
St. Catherine Univ	MN	37,782	C+
St. Edward's Univ	TX	47,784	C
St. Francis College	NY	34,200	C
Stillman College	AL	19,470	C
SUNY Cortland/The SUNY	NY	19,759	C+
Syracuse Univ	NY	56,346	VC
Tabor College	KS	29,010	C
Tarleton State Univ	TX	13,489	LC
Taylor Univ	IN	37,821	VC+
Temple Univ	PA	24,392	VC
Tenn Tech Univ	TN	11,310	C
Tenn Wesleyan College	TN	21,250	C
Texas A&M Univ	TX	19,207	VC
Texas A&M Univ at Kingsville	TX	7,500	LC
Texas Christian Univ	TX	49,980	HC
Texas Lutheran Univ	TX	36,040	C
Texas Southern Univ	TX	18,212	LC
Texas State Univ	TX	17,128	C
Texas Wesleyan Univ	TX	31,382	C
The College of Idaho	ID	31,277	C+
The Masters College	CA	38,160	C
Ohio State Univ-Columbus Campus	OH	19,887	HC+
The SUNY/College at Brockport	NY	19,002	C
The Univ of Memphis	TN	15,094	C
The Univ of N Car at Greensboro	NC	12,848	C
Tougaloo College	MS	15,275	NC
Towson Univ	MD	16,000	VC
Trevecca Nazarene Univ	TN	31,186	C
Trine Univ	IN	39,400	HC+
Trinity International Univ	IL	31,070	VC
Troy Univ	AL	10,650	C
Truman State Univ	MO	15,541	HC
Tusculum College	TN	24,295	C
Tuskegee Univ	AL	26,750	C
Union College	KY	29,955	C
Union College	NE	23,270	C
Union Univ	TN	28,260	VC
Universidad de Puerto/Arecibo	PR	7,227	
Universidad del Turabo	PR	4,110	
Univ of Akron	OH	20,436	C
Univ of Alabama at Tuscaloosa	AL	17,164	C+
Univ of Alaska Anchorage	AK	16,673	NC
Univ of Arkansas at Monticello	AR	12,076	NC
Univ of Arkansas at Pine Bluff	AR	13,378	C

ST = STATE $IS = IN-STATE COSTS   SR = SELECTOR RATING

School	ST	$IS	SR
Univ of Calif at Davis	CA		HC
Univ of Central Arkansas	AR	13,667	VC
Univ of Central Missouri	MO	14,605	C
Univ of Central Okla	OK	12,293	C
Univ of Charleston	WV	32,300	C
Univ of Delaware	DE	23,612	VC
Univ of Dubuque	IA	30,200	C
Univ of Findlay	OH	31,916	C
Univ of Great Falls	MT	27,970	C
Univ of Hawaii at Manoa	HI	19,379	C
Univ of Idaho	ID	14,558	C
Univ of Illinois at Chicago	IL	24,505	C
Univ of Illinois at Urbana-Champaign	IL	26,450	HC
Univ of Indianapolis	IN	31,740	LC
Univ of Jamestown	ND	24,738	C
Univ of Kansas	KS	17,603	C+
Univ of Kentucky	KY	19,868	C
Univ of Louisville	KY	17,946	C
Univ of Maine	ME	19,902	C+
Univ of Maine at Presque Isle	ME	15,011	LC
Univ of Mary	ND	16,714	C
Univ of Mary Hardin-Baylor	TX	31,950	C+
Univ of Maryland - College Park	MD	20,060	HC
Univ of Maryland/Eastern Shore	MD	14,000	VC
Univ of Mich/Ann Arbor	MI	22,102	MC
Univ of Minn/Duluth	MN	19,806	C
Univ of Minn/Twin Cities	MN		HC
Univ of Missouri-St. Louis	MO		VC
Univ of Mobile	AL	28,935	VC
Univ of Montana-Western	MT	9,753	LC
Univ of Montevallo	AL	17,060	C
Univ of Mount Union	OH	35,130	C
Univ of Nebr at Kearney	NE	14,855	LC
Univ of Nebr at Omaha	NE	12,700	C
Univ of Nevada, Las Vegas	NV	17,303	C
Univ of New Hampshire	NH	26,912	C
Univ of New Mexico	NM	15,300	C
Univ of New Orleans	LA	9,224	C
Univ of North Alabama	AL	9,960	C
Univ of N Car at Wilmington	NC	13,572	VC
Univ of N Dak	ND	14,551	C
Univ of North Florida	FL	15,870	VC
Univ of North Georgia	GA	8,500	C
Univ of Northern Colo	CO	18,446	C
Univ of Northern Iowa	IA	15,795	C
Univ of Rio Grande	OH	8,750	NC
Univ of Science and Arts of Okla	OK	10,560	VC
Univ of South Alabama	AL	13,510	C
Univ of S Car at Columbia	SC	19,725	VC+
Univ of S Car Upstate	SC	18,200	LC
Univ of S Dak	SD	15,111	C
Univ of South Florida/Tampa	FL	13,000	VC
Univ of Southern Indiana	IN	14,885	C
Univ of Texas at Arlington	TX	10,908	LC
Univ of the Cumberlands	KY	27,500	C
Univ of the District of Columbia	DC	7,244	LC
Univ of the Incarnate Word	TX	37,316	LC
Univ of the Ozarks	AR	31,440	C
Univ of the Pacific	CA	52,146	VC
Univ of the Sacred Heart	PR	5,590	
Univ of Toledo	OH	18,464	VC
Univ of Vermont	VT	27,006	VC+
Univ of West Alabama	AL	14,274	C
Univ of West Georgia	GA	15,488	LC
Univ of Wisc Whitewater	WI	13,314	C
Univ of Wisc/Eau Claire	WI	15,730	VC
Univ of Wisc/La Crosse	WI	9,304	VC
Univ of Wisc/Madison	WI	18,757	HC+
Univ of Wisc/Oshkosh	WI	10,426	LC
Univ of Wisc/Platteville	WI	14,564	C
Univ of Wisc/River Falls	WI	9,722	LC
Univ of Wisc/Stevens Point	WI	14,043	C
Univ of Wisc/Superior	WI	14,314	C
Univ of Wyoming	WY	14,401	C+
Upper Iowa Univ	IA	30,426	NC
Utah State Univ	UT	12,044	C
Valley City State Univ	ND	12,286	LC
Valparaiso Univ	IN	44,940	VC+
Vanguard Univ of Southern Calif	CA	35,833	VC
Virginia State Univ	VA	11,318	C+
Walla Walla Univ	WA	26,256	NC
Walsh Univ	OH	35,100	C
Warner Pacific College	OR	25,550	C
Warner Univ	FL	18,000	C
Wartburg College	IA	41,055	VC
Washburn Univ	KS	12,579	C
Washington Adventist Univ	MD	25,859	LC
Washington State Univ	WA	20,461	C
Wayland Baptist Univ	TX	18,912	LC
Wayne State Univ	MI	22,063	C
Wesley College	DE	31,115	LC
West Chester Univ of Pennsylvania	PA	17,186	C
West Liberty Univ	WV	9,142	LC
West Texas A&M Univ	TX	13,478	C
West Virginia Univ	WV	16,542	C+
West Virginia Wesleyan College	WV	26,880	C
Western Carolina Univ	NC	13,965	C
Western Illinois Univ	IL	20,732	C

School	ST	$IS	SR
Western Kentucky Univ	KY	11,000	LC
Western Mich Univ	MI	19,628	C
Western New Mexico Univ	NM	8,500	LC
Western Washington Univ	WA	18,519	VC
Westminster College	MO	31,720	VC
Wichita State Univ	KS	14,607	C+
Wiley College	TX		LC
William Carey Univ	MS	13,500	LC
William Paterson Univ of New Jersey	NJ	21,694	C
William Penn Univ	IA	26,000	C
William Woods Univ	MO	24,260	C
Williams Baptist College	AR	20,070	C
Wilmington College	OH	29,784	C
Wilson College	PA	35,080	C
Wingate Univ	NC	34,990	C
Winona State Univ	MN	16,640	C
Winston-Salem State Univ	NC	9,418	VC
Winthrop Univ	SC	21,120	C
Wright State Univ	OH	16,983	C
York College / The CUNY	NY	5,496	VC
Youngstown State Univ	OH	16,732	C

PHYSICAL EDUCATION / EXERCISE SCIENCE

School	ST	$IS	SR
Arizona State Univ, at the Polytechnic Campus	AZ	20,531	C+
College of the Ozarks	MO		VC
Indiana Univ Bloomington	IN	19,801	VC
Southeast Missouri State Univ	MO	15,370	LC
Univ of Montana	MT	14,105	C

PHYSICAL FITNESS/MOVEMENT

School	ST	$IS	SR
Ashland Univ	OH	25,000	C
Auburn Univ	AL	22,378	VC+
Augustana College	SD	36,500	VC
Baylor Univ	TX	50,329	HC
Brigham Young Univ/Hawaii	HI	10,686	VC
Buena Vista Univ	IA	39,188	C
Calif State Polytechnic Univ, Pomona	CA	20,158	C
Cal State, East Bay	CA	16,549	C
Cal State, Fresno	CA	17,405	C
Cal State, Monterey Bay	CA	26,871	LC
Cal State, San Marcos	CA	14,576	LC
Campbell Univ	NC	37,570	VC
Capital Univ	OH	41,050	VC
Clarke Univ	IA	37,600	C
Colo Mesa Univ	CO	17,690	LC
Concordia Univ Nebr	NE	26,000	VC
Concordia Univ St. Paul	MN	28,250	C
Concordia Univ, River Forest	IL	26,300	C
Dallas Baptist Univ	TX	30,580	VC
Defiance College	OH	30,645	C
DePauw Univ	IN	48,950	VC+
East Carolina Univ	NC	14,169	C
East Stroudsburg Univ of Pennsylvania	PA	18,868	LC
East Texas Baptist Univ	TX	31,577	LC
Eastern Nazarene College	MA	30,000	C
Eureka College	IL	19,280	C
George Washington Univ	DC	57,108	MC
Grand Canyon Univ	AZ	24,540	VC
Hope College	MI	38,650	VC
Houston Baptist Univ	TX	36,450	C
Humboldt State Univ	CA	18,400	C
Ithaca College	NY	53,864	HC
James Madison Univ	VA	18,049	VC
Johnson State College	VT	16,721	C
Kansas State Univ	KS	15,497	VC
Lakeland College	WI	22,990	C
Lasell College	MA	43,750	VC
Lewis-Clark State College	ID	6,990	C
Limestone College	SC	30,800	C
Louisiana State Univ	LA	18,677	C+
Lubbock Christian Univ	TX	26,308	C
Lynchburg College	VA	42,645	C
Marshall Univ	WV	14,820	C
Marywood Univ	PA	45,595	C
Metropolitan State Univ of Denver	CO	4,835	LC
Miami Univ	OH	24,191	VC
Minot State Univ	ND	10,915	C
Miss Univ for Women	MS	7,400	C
New England College	NH	45,930	LC
New Mexico Highlands Univ	NM	11,904	NC
New Mexico State Univ	NM	14,050	C
N Dak State Univ	ND		C
Northern Illinois Univ	IL	19,768	C
Northern Mich Univ	MI	18,278	C
Northern State Univ - Aberdeen	SD	14,505	C
Northwestern College of Iowa	IA	36,240	VC
Notre Dame de Namur Univ	CA	44,236	LC
Oakwood Univ	AL	25,529	NC
Occidental College	CA	60,972	MC
Purdue Univ/West Lafayette	IN	20,024	HC
St. Augustine's Univ	NC	14,000	C
Sam Houston State Univ	TX	17,082	C
San Diego Christian College	CA	31,012	C
Seattle Pacific Univ	WA	41,559	VC+
Sonoma State Univ	CA	20,541	C
Southern Methodist Univ	TX	60,585	MC

School	ST	$IS	SR
Southern Nazarene Univ	OK	24,354	C
Spring Arbor Univ	MI	26,740	C
Springfield College	MA	25,000	C
St. Edward's Univ	TX	47,784	C
Stephen F. Austin State Univ	TX	14,668	C
Sul Ross State Univ	TX	13,410	LC
Tarleton State Univ	TX	13,489	LC
Temple Univ	PA	24,392	VC
Texas Southern Univ	TX	18,212	LC
Texas Woman's Univ	TX	13,633	LC
Ohio State Univ-Columbus Campus	OH	19,887	HC+
Truman State Univ	MO	15,541	HC
Union College	NE	23,270	C
Univ of Central Okla	OK	12,293	C
Univ of Florida	FL	15,943	HC
Univ of Illinois at Chicago	IL	24,505	VC
Univ of La Verne	CA	47,010	C
Univ of Mass Boston	MA	23,066	VC
Univ of Mich/Ann Arbor	MI	22,102	MC
Univ of Nevada, Las Vegas	NV	17,303	C
Univ of New Hampshire	NH	26,912	C
Univ of N Car at Charlotte	NC	15,547	C
Univ of North Texas	TX	15,628	C
Univ of Northern Colo	CO	18,446	C
Univ of Rio Grande	OH	8,750	NC
Univ of Texas - Pan American	TX	11,125	LC
Univ of Texas at Austin	TX	44,074	HC
Univ of Texas at El Paso	TX	8,764	NC
Univ of Toledo	OH	18,464	C
Upper Iowa Univ	IA	30,426	NC
Virginia Polytechnic Inst and State Univ	VA	14,629	HC
West Liberty Univ	WV	9,142	LC
Western State Colo Univ	CO	16,924	C
Westfield State Univ	MA	18,297	C
Whittier College	CA	43,416	C
Winona State Univ	MN	16,640	C

PHYSICAL SCIENCE SECONDARY SCHOOL EDUCATION

School	ST	$IS	SR
Aquinas College	MI	33,060	C
Dordt College	IA	34,160	C+
Duquesne Univ	PA	43,720	VC
Kent State Univ	OH	19,920	C
Murray State Univ	KY	15,304	C
Southern Illinois Univ Carbondale	IL	21,942	C
Univ of Nebr - Lincoln	NE	18,031	VC
Youngstown State Univ	OH	16,732	C

PHYSICAL SCIENCES

School	ST	$IS	SR
Arkansas Tech Univ	AR	13,982	LC
Asbury Univ	KY	32,038	VC
Auburn Univ at Montgomery	AL	14,470	LC
Bennington College	VT	56,990	HC+
Bethany College	WV	35,282	LC
Bethel College	IN	31,560	C
Biola Univ	CA	40,320	C
Black Hills State Univ	SD	13,947	C
Bluffton Univ	OH	38,948	C
Brescia Univ	KY	26,140	VC+
Cal State, East Bay	CA	16,549	C
Cal State, Sacramento	CA	16,200	C
Cal State, Stanislaus	CA	18,582	C
Calif Univ of Pennsylvania	PA	14,217	C
Central Conn State Univ	CT	19,749	C
Colgate Univ	NY	58,135	MC
Colo Mesa Univ	CO	17,690	LC
Colo State Univ-Fort Collins	CO	20,385	VC
Concordia Univ Nebr	NE	26,000	VC
Concordia Univ, Ann Arbor	MI	27,220	VC
Concordia Univ, River Forest	IL	26,300	C
Creighton Univ	NE	45,356	VC
Dakota State Univ	SD	13,811	C
DePaul Univ	IL	47,623	VC
Doane College	NE	35,230	C
Dordt College	IA	34,160	C
East Stroudsburg Univ of Pennsylvania	PA	18,868	LC
Embry-Riddle Aeronautical Univ - Daytona Beach	FL	40,884	C+
Emporia State Univ	KS	12,897	C
Eureka College	IL	19,280	C
Fort Hays State Univ	KS	11,354	C
Freed-Hardeman Univ	TN	19,697	VC
Harvard College/Harvard Univ	MA	49,000	MC
Indiana Univ Kokomo	IN	6,811	LC
Indiana Univ-Purdue Univ Fort Wayne	IN	15,521	C
Kansas State Univ	KS	15,497	VC
Kent State Univ	OH	19,920	C
Le Moyne College	NY	43,470	C
Malone Univ	OH	35,364	C
Mayville State Univ	ND	11,401	NC
Mich State Univ	MI	22,450	VC
Minot State Univ	ND	10,915	C
Miss Univ for Women	MS	7,400	C
Muhlenberg College	PA	52,837	HC
Northwestern State Univ of Louisiana	LA	14,368	C
Okla Panhandle State Univ	OK	8,996	C

School	ST	$IS	SR
Olivet Nazarene Univ	IL	29,990	C
Peru State College	NE	8,600	NC
Ripon College	WI	36,959	C+
Rowan Univ	NJ	24,022	VC+
St. Michael's College	VT	49,975	VC
Salisbury Univ	MD	19,180	VC
San Diego State Univ	CA	21,611	C+
St. John's Univ	NY	55,070	C+
Trine Univ	IN	39,400	HC+
Union Univ	TN	28,260	VC
Univ of Arkansas at Monticello	AR	12,076	NC
Univ of Calif at Berkeley	CA	23,322	MC
Univ of Calif at Riverside	CA	27,204	C+
Univ of Dayton	OH	49,070	VC
Univ of Great Falls	MT	27,970	C
Univ of Maryland - College Park	MD	20,060	HC
Univ of Mich-Flint	MI	17,547	C+
Univ of Pittsburgh at Bradford	PA	21,802	C
Univ of Rio Grande	OH	8,750	NC
Univ of South Florida/Tampa	FL	13,000	C
Univ of Southern Calif	CA	56,903	MC
Univ of Texas - Pan American	TX	11,125	LC
Univ of Wisc/Eau Claire	WI	15,730	VC
Univ of Wisc/Platteville	WI	14,564	C
Washington State Univ	WA	20,461	C
Washington Univ in St. Louis	MO	69,844	MC
Wayland Baptist Univ	TX	18,912	LC
Wesleyan College	GA	24,000	C
Youngstown State Univ	OH	16,732	C

PHYSICAL THERAPY

School	ST	$IS	SR
American International College	MA	36,100	LC
Biola Univ	CA	40,320	C+
Boston Univ	MA	60,694	MC
Cal State, Northridge	CA	28,690	LC
Cal State, Sacramento	CA	16,200	C
Carson-Newman Univ	TN	29,058	C+
Chatham Univ	PA	43,797	C
Clarke Univ	IA	37,600	C
Cleveland State Univ	OH	21,776	C
Coe College	IA	45,550	VC
De Sales Univ	PA	43,970	C
Duquesne Univ	PA	43,720	VC
Fairleigh Dickinson Univ/ Metropolitan Campus	NJ	40,254	C
Florida A&M Univ	FL	14,935	LC
Gannon Univ	PA	39,608	C
Gordon College	MA	44,320	VC
Grand Valley State Univ	MI	17,998	C+
Gustavus Adolphus College	MN	48,170	HC
Howard Univ	DC	13,646	C
Hunter College	NY	14,429	VC
Husson Univ	ME	24,194	LC
Ithaca College	NY	53,864	HC
Lamar Univ	TX	6,820	LC
Langston Univ	OK	3,000	C
Lewis Univ	IL	23,050	C
Maryville Univ of St. Louis	MO	35,856	VC
Misericordia Univ	PA	41,060	C
Missouri State Univ	MO	13,996	C+
Mount Aloysius College	PA	29,976	C
New York Univ	NY	61,470	MC
North Park Univ	IL	30,130	C
Northeastern Univ	MA	55,296	MC
Notre Dame College	OH	34,942	VC
Ohio Univ	OH	21,080	C
Okla Baptist Univ	OK	28,202	C
Purdue Univ/Calumet	IN	14,336	C
Quinnipiac Univ	CT	55,160	VC
Regis Univ	CO	41,318	C
Richard Stockton College of New Jersey	NJ	20,000	VC
Russell Sage College	NY	39,370	C
Sacred Heart Univ	CT	49,264	VC
St. Francis Univ	PA	30,029	LC
St. Vincent College	PA	40,244	C
Simmons College	MA	49,966	VC
Stony Brook Univ / SUNY	NY	20,078	HC+
Tarleton State Univ	TX	13,489	LC
Tenn State Univ	TN	9,048	C
Ohio State Univ-Columbus Campus	OH	19,887	HC+
The Univ of Utah	UT	16,463	VC
Thiel College	PA	38,728	LC
Touro College	NY	27,959	VC
Trine Univ	IN	39,400	HC+
Trinity International Univ	IL	31,070	VC
Truman State Univ	MO	15,541	HC
Univ at Buffalo / The SUNY	NY	20,283	VC+
Univ of Akron	OH	20,436	C
Univ of Alaska Anchorage	AK	16,673	NC
Univ of Central Arkansas	AR	13,667	VC
Univ of Conn	CT	24,706	VC
Univ of Florida	FL	15,943	HC
Univ of Hartford	CT	42,674	C
Univ of Illinois at Chicago	IL	24,505	VC
Univ of Kentucky	KY	19,868	C
Univ of Mary	ND	16,714	C
Univ of Maryland/Eastern Shore	MD	14,000	VC

ST = STATE $IS = IN-STATE COSTS SR = SELECTOR RATING

School	ST	$IS	SR
Univ of Mich-Flint	MI	17,547	C+
Univ of Minn/Twin Cities	MN		HC
Univ of Missouri/Columbia	MO	18,201	MC
Univ of N Car at Wilmington	NC	13,572	VC
Univ of N Dak	ND	14,551	C
Univ of North Florida	FL	15,870	VC
Univ of the Sciences	PA	48,320	VC+
Univ of Toledo	OH	18,464	C
Utica College	NY	45,670	C
Vanguard Univ of Southern Calif	CA	35,833	VC
Virginia Polytechnic Inst and State Univ	VA	14,629	HC
Walsh Univ	OH	35,100	C
West Virginia Univ	WV	16,542	C+
Winston-Salem State Univ	NC	9,418	LC

PHYSICAL THERAPY ASSISTANT

School	ST	$IS	SR
Calif Univ of Pennsylvania	PA	14,217	C
Idaho State Univ	ID	12,307	C
Mount Aloysius College	PA	29,976	C
Nebr Methodist College of Nursing and Allied Health	NE	22,690	SP

PHYSICIAN'S ASSISTANT

School	ST	$IS	SR
CUNY/City College	NY	20,319	HC+
Colo State Univ-Pueblo	CO	16,183	C
Daemen College	NY	34,770	C
De Sales Univ	PA	43,970	C
Duquesne Univ	PA	43,720	VC
D'Youville College	NY	29,850	C
Gannon Univ	PA	39,608	C
Gardner-Webb Univ	NC	34,375	C+
George Washington Univ	DC	57,108	MC
Grand Valley State Univ	MI	17,998	C+
Howard Univ	DC	13,646	VC
King's College	PA	43,502	C
Marietta College	OH	42,135	C+
Mars Hill Univ	NC	22,950	LC
Marywood Univ	PA	45,595	C
Methodist Univ	NC	37,185	C
Missouri State Univ	MO	13,996	C+
Mount Aloysius College	PA	29,976	C
Northern Mich Univ	MI	18,278	C
Pennsylvania College of Technology	PA	26,286	NC
Philadelphia Univ	PA	44,160	C
Quinnipiac Univ	CT	55,160	VC
Rochester Inst of Technology	NY	42,450	VC
St. Francis Univ	PA	30,029	LC
St. Vincent College	PA	40,244	C
Seton Hill Univ	PA	35,172	C
South Univ	GA	36,070	LC
Southern Illinois Univ Carbondale	IL	21,942	C
St. Francis College	NY	34,200	C
St. John's Univ	NY	55,070	C+
Union College	NE	23,270	C
Univ of Findlay	OH	31,916	C
Univ of Kentucky	KY	19,868	C
Univ of Miami	FL	57,034	MC
Univ of Texas - Pan American	TX	11,125	LC
Univ of the Sciences	PA	48,320	VC+
Univ of Wisc/La Crosse	WI	9,304	VC
Univ of Wisc/Madison	WI	18,757	HC+
Wagner College	NY	48,600	C+
Wichita State Univ	KS	14,607	C+

PHYSICS

School	ST	$IS	SR
Abilene Christian Univ	TX	38,400	C
Adams State Univ	CO	13,358	LC
Adelphi Univ	NY	44,670	VC
Adrian College	MI	42,400	C
Agnes Scott College	GA	45,323	C+
Alabama A&M Univ	AL	10,084	C
Alabama State Univ	AL	14,142	NC
Albion College	MI	46,010	C
Albright College	PA	46,660	C
Alfred Univ	NY	41,770	C
Allegheny College	PA	50,980	HC
Alma College	MI	44,075	C
American Univ	DC	56,015	HC+
Amherst College	MA	58,744	MC
Anderson Univ	IN	36,100	C
Andrews Univ	MI	28,030	C+
Angelo State Univ	TX	15,049	NC
Appalachian State Univ	NC	12,919	VC
Arizona State Univ, at the Tempe Campus	AZ	20,137	C+
Arkansas State Univ	AR	15,470	C
Arkansas Tech Univ	AR	13,982	LC
Ashland Univ	OH	25,000	C
Auburn Univ	AL	22,378	VC+
Augsburg College	MN	35,142	C
Augustana College	IL	43,398	VC
Augustana College	SD	36,500	VC
Austin College	TX	45,875	HC
Austin Peay State Univ	TN	15,274	C
Azusa Pacific Univ	CA	42,086	C
Baker Univ	KS	33,350	C+
Baldwin Wallace Univ	OH	38,318	C
Ball State Univ	IN	17,850	C
Bard College	NY	61,940	HC
Bard College at Simon's Rock	MA	61,749	HC+
Barnard College/Columbia Univ	NY	39,000	MC
Bates College	ME	60,720	MC
Baylor Univ	TX	50,329	HC
Bellarmine Univ	KY	42,950	VC
Belmont Univ	TN	39,190	VC+
Beloit College	WI	49,970	HC
Bemidji State Univ	MN	13,500	VC
Benedict College	SC	20,454	NC
Benedictine College	KS	29,180	VC
Benedictine Univ	IL	37,820	C
Bennington College	VT	56,990	HC+
Berea College	KY	7,192	C
Berry College	GA	39,254	VC
Bethel Univ	MN	34,940	VC
Binghamton Univ/The SUNY	NY	21,648	HC+
Biola Univ	CA	40,320	C+
Birmingham-Southern College	AL	44,168	VC+
Bloomsburg Univ of Pennsylvania	PA	13,598	C
Bluffton Univ	OH	38,948	C
Boise State Univ	ID	13,469	LC
Boston College	MA	60,622	MC
Boston Univ	MA	60,694	MC
Bowdoin College	ME	59,568	MC
Bowling Green State Univ	OH	18,970	C
Bradley Univ	IL	31,874	VC
Brandeis Univ	MA		MC
Bridgewater College	VA	41,450	C
Bridgewater State Univ	MA	18,752	C
Brigham Young Univ	UT	12,100	HC
Brown Univ	RI	59,428	MC
Bryn Mawr College	PA	59,890	MC
Bucknell Univ	PA	60,140	MC
Buena Vista Univ	IA	39,188	C
Buffalo State College / SUNY	NY	15,733	C+
Butler Univ	IN	47,572	VC+
Calif Inst of Technology	CA	54,045	MC
Calif Lutheran Univ	CA	49,540	C+
Calif Polytechnic State Univ	CA	19,847	HC
Calif State Polytechnic Univ, Pomona	CA	20,156	C
Cal State, Bakersfield	CA	8,000	C
Cal State, Chico	CA	20,158	C
Cal State, Dominguez Hills	CA	17,090	LC
Cal State, East Bay	CA	16,549	C
Cal State, Fresno	CA	17,405	C
Cal State, Fullerton	CA	25,188	C
Cal State, Long Beach	CA	17,502	C+
Cal State, Los Angeles	CA	17,186	VC
Cal State, Northridge	CA	28,690	LC
Cal State, Sacramento	CA	16,200	C
Cal State, San Bernardino	CA	12,000	C
Cal State, Stanislaus	CA	18,582	C
Calif Univ of Pennsylvania	PA	14,217	C
Calvin College	MI	39,120	VC
Cameron Univ	OK	10,004	LC
Canisius College	NY	44,900	C
Carleton College	MN	60,102	MC
Carnegie Mellon Univ	PA	51,260	MC
Carthage College	WI	33,000	C
Case Western Reserve Univ	OH	56,534	MC
Cedarville Univ	OH	32,860	VC
Centenary College of Louisiana	LA	45,650	C+
Central College	IA	42,104	C+
Central Conn State Univ	CT	19,749	C
Central Methodist Univ	MO	28,240	VC
Central Washington Univ	WA	11,730	C
Centre College	KY	35,000	HC+
Chadron State College	NE	7,400	NC
Chapman Univ	CA	58,347	VC+
Chatham Univ	PA	43,797	C
Chicago State Univ	IL	5,482	C
Christian Brothers Univ	TN	31,670	HC
Citadel, The	SC		C
CUNY/Brooklyn College	NY	5,884	C
CUNY/City College	NY	20,319	HC+
Claremont McKenna College	CA	62,215	MC
Clarion Univ of Pennsylvania	PA	17,370	LC
Clark Atlanta Univ	GA	30,006	LC
Clark Univ	MA	47,020	HC+
Clarkson Univ	NY	57,330	HC
Clemson Univ	SC	19,136	HC
Cleveland State Univ	OH	21,776	C
Coastal Carolina Univ	SC	18,580	C
Coe College	IA	45,550	VC
Colby College	ME	57,510	MC
Colgate Univ	NY	58,135	MC
College of Charleston	SC	22,145	VC
College of Mount St. Vincent	NY	41,040	MC
College of New Jersey	NJ	25,376	HC
College of St. Benedict	MN	49,359	VC
College of Staten Island/The City of New Yok	NY	16,778	NC
College of the Holy Cross	MA	58,042	MC
College of William & Mary	VA	38,700	MC
College of Wooster	OH	52,600	VC
Colo College	CO	57,162	MC
Colo School of Mines	CO	18,000	HC
Colo State Univ-Fort Collins	CO	20,385	VC
Colo State Univ-Pueblo	CO	16,183	C
Columbia Univ/City of New York	NY	61,116	MC
Columbia Univ/School of General Studies	NY	58,231	MC
Concordia College - Moorhead	MN	39,974	VC
Concordia Univ, Ann Arbor	MI	27,220	VC
Conn College	CT	54,970	MC
Cornell College	IA	44,930	VC
Cornell Univ	NY	60,964	MC
Covenant College	GA	38,990	VC+
Creighton Univ	NE	45,356	VC
Dartmouth College	NH	57,996	MC
Davidson College	NC	58,146	MC
Delaware State Univ	DE	16,722	LC
Denison Univ	OH	54,670	HC+
DePaul Univ	IL	47,623	VC
DePauw Univ	IN	48,950	VC+
Dickinson College	PA	57,662	HC+
Dillard Univ	LA	20,940	VC
Doane College	NE	35,230	C
Dordt College	IA	34,160	C+
Drake Univ	IA	41,516	VC+
Drew Univ/College of Liberal Arts	NJ	57,516	C
Drexel Univ	PA	61,418	VC+
Drury Univ	MO	31,909	VC
Duke Univ	NC	50,250	MC
Duquesne Univ	PA	43,720	VC
Earlham College	IN	51,470	HC
East Carolina Univ	NC	14,169	C
East Central Univ	OK	10,223	LC
East Tenn State Univ	TN	9,000	C
Eastern Illinois Univ	IL	20,466	C
Eastern Mich Univ	MI	18,604	C
Eastern Nazarene College	MA	30,000	C
Eastern Oregon Univ	OR	10,400	C
Eastern Washington Univ	WA		C
Eckerd College	FL	43,902	C
Edinboro Univ of Pennsylvania	PA	15,940	LC
Elizabeth City State Univ	NC	11,638	C
Elizabethtown College	PA	49,740	VC
Elmhurst College	IL	43,336	C
Elon Univ	NC	41,914	VC+
Emory and Henry College	VA	387,460	C
Emory Univ	GA	56,368	MC
Emporia State Univ	KS	12,897	C
Erskine College	SC	37,360	C
Excelsior College	NY	5,580	SP
Fairfield Univ	CT	56,960	VC
Fisk Univ	TN	19,830	C
Florida A&M Univ	FL	14,935	LC
Florida Atlantic Univ	FL	17,339	C
Florida Inst of Technology	FL	48,290	VC
Florida International Univ	FL	17,747	C+
Florida State Univ	FL	16,715	VC
Fordham Univ	NY	61,588	HC+
Fort Hays State Univ	KS	11,354	C
Fort Lewis College	CO	15,513	C
Francis Marion Univ	SC	16,464	LC
Franklin and Marshall College	PA	60,799	MC
Frostburg State Univ	MD	15,264	LC
Furman Univ	SC	54,006	HC
Geneva College	PA	27,280	C
George Mason Univ	VA	15,724	VC
George Washington Univ	DC	57,108	MC
Georgetown College	KY	41,440	C+
Georgetown Univ	DC	52,910	MC
Georgia College and State Univ	GA	18,900	C+
Georgia Inst of Technology	GA	21,828	MC
Georgia Regents Univ	GA		C
Georgia Southern Univ	GA	16,942	C
Georgia State Univ	GA	15,582	VC
Gettysburg College	PA	58,820	HC
Gonzaga Univ	WA	46,441	HC
Gordon College	MA	44,320	VC
Goshen College	IN	35,900	VC
Goucher College	MD	52,040	VC+
Grambling State Univ	LA	13,384	LC
Grand Valley State Univ	MI	17,998	C+
Greenville College	IL	27,012	C
Grinnell College	IA	53,654	HC
Grove City College	PA	24,022	VC
Guilford College	NC	42,800	C
Gustavus Adolphus College	MN	48,170	HC
Hamilton College	NY	55,620	MC
Hamline Univ	MN	45,674	VC
Hampden-Sydney College	VA	51,758	C
Hampshire College	MA	58,320	MC
Hampton Univ	VA	28,528	C
Hanover College	IN	43,073	C+
Harding Univ	AR	23,556	C
Hardin-Simmons Univ	TX	23,560	C+
Hartwick College	NY	51,270	C
Harvard College/Harvard Univ	MA	49,000	MC
Harvey Mudd College	CA	64,527	MC
Hastings College	NE	27,782	C+
Haverford College	PA	61,564	MC
Heidelberg Univ	OH	34,100	C
Henderson State Univ	AR	14,584	C
Hendrix College	AR	50,202	VC+
Hillsdale College	MI	32,866	MC
Hiram College	OH	37,300	VC
Hobart and William Smith Colleges	NY	60,034	HC+
Hofstra Univ	NY	51,810	VC+
Hollins Univ	VA	43,295	VC
Hope College	MI	38,650	VC
Houghton College	NY	36,808	C+
Houston Baptist Univ	TX	36,450	C
Howard Univ	DC	13,646	VC
Humboldt State Univ	CA	18,400	C
Hunter College	NY	14,429	VC
Huntington Univ	IN	32,220	C
Idaho State Univ	ID	12,307	C
Illinois College	IL	25,770	VC
Illinois Inst of Technology	IL	38,512	HC+
Illinois State Univ	IL	23,110	VC
Illinois Wesleyan Univ	IL	48,452	HC
Indiana State Univ	IN	16,000	C
Indiana Univ Bloomington	IN	19,801	VC
Indiana Univ of Pennsylvania	PA	20,846	LC
Indiana Univ South Bend	IN	15,501	C
Indiana Univ-Purdue Univ Fort Wayne	IN	15,521	C
Indiana Univ-Purdue Univ Indianapolis	IN	17,611	C
Iona College	NY	44,028	C
Iowa State Univ	IA	16,403	C
Ithaca College	NY	53,864	HC
Jackson State Univ	MS	13,512	LC
Jacksonville State Univ	AL	12,480	LC
Jacksonville Univ	FL	37,780	C
James Madison Univ	VA	18,049	VC
John Carroll Univ	OH	46,300	C+
Johns Hopkins Univ	MD	47,492	MC
Johnson C. Smith Univ	NC	25,336	LC
Juniata College	PA	49,340	VC
Kalamazoo College	MI	49,740	HC
Kansas State Univ	KS	15,497	VC
Kansas Wesleyan Univ	KS	32,000	C
Keene State College	NH	23,232	LC
Kent State Univ	OH	19,920	C
Kentucky Wesleyan College	KY	27,440	C
Kenyon College	OH	58,890	MC
King Univ	TN	33,140	C
King's College	PA	43,502	C
Knox College	IL	44,865	VC+
Kutztown Univ of Pennsylvania	PA	16,909	LC
La Sierra Univ	CA	35,694	VC
Lafayette College	PA	59,155	HC+
Lake Forest College	IL	50,652	VC
Lamar Univ	TX	6,820	LC
Lane College	TN	11,212	C
Lawrence Tech Univ	MI	37,630	VC
Lawrence Univ	WI	46,371	HC
Le Moyne College	NY	43,470	C
Lebanon Valley College	PA	38,570	C
Lehigh Univ	PA	56,770	MC
Lehman College/The CUNY	NY	5,778	LC
Lenoir-Rhyne College	NC	35,984	C
Lewis & Clark College	OR	54,382	MC
Lewis Univ	IL	23,050	C
Lincoln Univ	MO	12,904	NC
Linfield College-McMinnville Campus	OR	47,676	C
Lipscomb Univ	TN	37,490	VC
LIU Post	NY	47,660	C
Lock Haven Univ of Pennsylvania	PA	18,028	LC
Longwood Univ	VA	20,924	C
Louisiana State Univ	LA	18,677	C+
Louisiana State Univ in Shreveport	LA	5,606	C
Louisiana Tech Univ	LA	11,302	C
Loyola Marymount Univ	CA	54,649	VC+
Loyola Univ Chicago	IL	51,646	VC+
Loyola Univ Maryland	MD	56,880	VC+
Loyola Univ New Orleans	LA	46,581	VC
Luther College	IA	45,720	C+
Lycoming College	PA	45,379	C
Lynchburg College	VA	42,645	C
Macalester College	MN	57,691	MC
MacMurray College	IL	20,755	C
Manchester Univ	IN	35,070	C
Manhattan College	NY	49,588	C+
Mansfield Univ	PA	19,468	LC
Marietta College	OH	42,135	C+
Marlboro College	VT	35,980	VC
Marquette Univ	WI	46,930	VC+
Marshall Univ	WV	14,820	C
Mary Baldwin College	VA	38,245	C
Mass College of Liberal Arts	MA	18,613	C
Mass Inst of Technology	MA	58,240	MC
McDaniel College	MD	47,450	VC
McMurry Univ	TX	25,962	LC
Mercer Univ	GA	44,201	VC
Merrimack College	MA	44,215	C
Messiah College	PA	40,690	C+
Metropolitan State Univ of Denver	CO	4,835	LC
Miami Univ	OH	24,191	VC
Mich State Univ	MI	22,450	VC
Mich Tech Univ	MI	23,556	HC
MidAmerica Nazarene Univ	KS	28,000	C
Middle Tenn State Univ	TN	8,650	C
Middlebury College	VT	59,160	MC

ST = STATE   **$IS** = IN-STATE COSTS   **SR** = SELECTOR RATING

School	ST	$IS	SR
Millersville Univ of Pennsylvania	PA	21,648	C
Millikin Univ	IL	38,940	C
Millsaps College	MS	43,888	VC+
Minn State Univ, Mankato	MN	15,616	C
Minn State Univ, Moorhead	MN	13,392	VC
Minot State Univ	ND	10,915	C
Miss College	MS	21,998	C
Miss State Univ	MS	14,750	C
Missouri Southern State Univ	MO	12,061	C
Missouri Univ of Science and Technology	MO	18,655	VC+
Monmouth College	IL	40,850	C
Montana State Univ	MT	14,068	C
Montclair State Univ	NJ	22,614	C
Moravian College	PA	36,381	VC
Morehead State Univ	KY	10,900	C
Morehouse College	GA	39,412	C
Morgan State Univ	MD	14,500	VC
Morningside College	IA	35,430	C
Mount Holyoke College	MA	55,146	MC
Muhlenberg College	PA	52,837	MC
Murray State Univ	KY	15,304	C
Muskingum Univ	OH	30,502	C
Nebr Wesleyan Univ	NE	29,777	C+
New College of Florida	FL	14,504	MC
New Jersey City Univ	NJ	21,456	LC
New Mexico Highlands Univ	NM	11,904	NC
New Mexico Inst of Mining and Technology	NM	13,592	VC
New Mexico State Univ	NM	14,050	C
New York Univ	NY	61,470	MC
Norfolk State Univ	VA	10,531	LC
N Car Agricultural and Technical State Univ	NC	13,365	LC
N Car Central Univ	NC	9,000	C
N Car State Univ	NC	16,202	HC
North Central College	IL	38,343	VC
N Dak State Univ	ND		C
North Park Univ	IL	30,130	C
Northeastern Illinois Univ	IL	10,318	LC
Northeastern Univ	MA	55,296	MC
Northern Arizona Univ	AZ	19,010	C
Northern Illinois Univ	IL	19,768	C
Northern Kentucky Univ	KY	21,134	C
Northern Mich Univ	MI	18,278	C
Northwest Missouri State Univ	MO	17,347	C
Northwest Nazarene Univ	ID	34,000	C
Northwestern Okla State Univ	OK	7,275	NC
Northwestern Univ	IL	61,640	MC
Norwich Univ	VT	28,212	C
Notre Dame of Maryland Univ	MD	27,700	VC
Oakland Univ	MI	19,391	C
Oberlin College	OH	61,788	MC
Occidental College	CA	60,972	MC
Oglethorpe Univ	GA	44,200	C+
Ohio Northern Univ	OH	42,075	VC
Ohio Univ	OH	21,080	C
Ohio Wesleyan Univ	OH	49,460	C+
Okla Baptist Univ	OK	28,202	C
Okla City Univ	OK	40,476	VC
Okla State Univ	OK	14,310	C
Old Dominion Univ	VA	19,483	LC
Oral Roberts Univ	OK	31,734	C
Oregon State Univ	OR	20,273	VC
Oswego / SUNY	NY	20,009	VC
Otterbein Univ	OH	32,214	C
Ouachita Baptist Univ	AR	30,220	VC
Pace Univ	NY	53,367	C
Pacific Lutheran Univ	WA	46,760	C
Pacific Union College	CA	28,150	VC
Pacific Univ	OR	49,626	C+
Penn State Erie/The Behrend College	PA	16,256	C
Pepperdine Univ	CA	55,372	HC+
Piedmont College	GA	30,136	C
Pittsburg State Univ	KS	12,032	C
Pitzer College	CA	54,988	MC
Point Loma Nazarene Univ	CA	55,416	MC
Polytechnic Inst of New York Univ	NY	53,064	HC+
Pomona College	CA	57,680	MC
Pontifical Catholic Univ of PR	PR	7,310	
Portland State Univ	OR	18,672	C
Prairie View A&M Univ	TX	15,205	LC
Presbyterian College	SC	42,678	C+
Princeton Univ	NJ	53,795	MC
Principia College	IL	35,140	C+
Purdue Univ/Calumet	IN	14,336	C
Purdue Univ/West Lafayette	IN	20,024	HC
Queens College/The CUNY	NY	17,107	VC
Radford Univ	VA	17,766	C
Randolph College	VA	45,660	VC
Randolph-Macon College	VA	49,869	C+
Reed College	OR	57,780	MC
Rensselaer Polytechnic Inst	NY	61,529	MC
Rhode Island College	RI	17,694	LC
Rhodes College	TN	51,900	HC+
Rice Univ	TX	43,288	MC
Richard Stockton College of New Jersey	NJ	20,000	VC
Rider Univ	NJ	45,720	C
Ripon College	WI	36,959	C+
Roanoke College	VA	49,976	C
Roberts Wesleyan College	NY	38,306	C+
Rochester Inst of Technology	NY	42,450	VC
Rockhurst Univ	MO	20,625	C
Rollins College	FL	52,370	HC
Rose-Hulman Inst of Technology	IN	53,340	MC
Rowan Univ	NJ	24,022	VC+
Rutgers, The State Univ of New Jersey/Camden Campus	NJ	25,121	C
Rutgers, The State Univ of New Jersey/New Brunswick	NJ	25,562	VC
Rutgers, The State Univ of New Jersey/Newark Campus	NJ	258,806	C
Saginaw Valley State Univ	MI	17,369	C
St. John's Univ	MN	47,984	C
St. Joseph's Univ	PA	55,006	VC
St. Louis Univ	MO	48,346	HC
St. Mary's College of Calif	CA	53,550	C
St. Mary's Univ	TX	33,854	C
St. Mary's Univ of Minn	MN	38,280	C
St. Michael's College	VT	49,975	VC
St. Peter's Univ	NJ	44,240	C
St. Vincent College	PA	40,244	C
Salisbury Univ	MD	19,180	VC
Sam Houston State Univ	TX	17,082	C
Samford Univ	AL	37,060	C+
San Diego State Univ	CA	21,611	C+
San Francisco State Univ	CA	18,514	C
San Jose State Univ	CA	19,133	LC
Scripps College	CA	61,940	MC
Seattle Pacific Univ	WA	41,559	VC+
Seattle Univ	WA	49,035	VC+
Seton Hall Univ	NJ	45,902	C
Seton Hill Univ	PA	35,172	C
Sewanee: The Univ of the South	TN	47,700	HC+
Shaw Univ	NC	15,488	C
Shippensburg Univ of Pennsylvania	PA	20,934	C
Siena College	NY	43,863	VC
Simmons College	MA	49,966	VC
Simpson College	IA	36,086	C+
Skidmore College	NY	59,942	HC
Slippery Rock Univ of Pennsylvania	PA	10,360	C
Smith College	MA	59,674	MC
Sonoma State Univ	CA	20,541	C
S Car State Univ	SC	6,700	LC
S Dak School of Mines and Technology	SD	15,260	VC
S Dak State Univ	SD	14,296	C
Southeast Missouri State Univ	MO	15,370	LC
Southeastern Louisiana Univ	LA	13,325	C
Southeastern Okla State Univ	OK	7,966	LC
Southern Adventist Univ	TN	26,190	C
Southern Conn State Univ	CT	18,033	LC
Southern Illinois Univ Carbondale	IL	21,942	C
Southern Illinois Univ Edwardsville	IL	17,532	C
Southern Methodist Univ	TX	60,585	MC
Southern Nazarene Univ	OK	24,354	C
Southern Oregon Univ	OR	17,874	C
Southern Polytechnic State Univ	GA	13,958	C
Southern Univ and A&M College	LA	9,761	LC
Southern Univ at New Orleans	LA	2,963	NC
Southwestern Adventist Univ	TX	23,026	LC
Southwestern Okla State Univ	OK	9,160	C
Southwestern Univ	TX	45,660	VC
Spelman College	GA	24,650	C
Spring Arbor Univ	MI	26,740	C
St. Ambrose Univ	IA	30,845	C
St. Bonaventure Univ	NY	41,575	C
St. Cloud State Univ	MN	10,600	C
St. John Fisher College	NY	40,708	C+
St. John's Univ	NY	55,070	C+
St. Lawrence Univ	NY	59,972	VC
St. Mary's College of Maryland	MD	25,754	VC
St. Norbert College	WI	41,478	VC
St. Olaf College	MN	51,200	HC+
Stanford Univ	CA	58,388	MC
Stephen F. Austin State Univ	TX	14,668	C
Stetson Univ	FL	51,516	VC
Stevens Inst of Technology	NJ	50,130	HC
Stonehill College	MA	46,780	HC
Stony Brook Univ / SUNY	NY	20,078	VC
Suffolk Univ	MA	47,298	C
SUNY College at Geneseo	NY	18,670	HC
SUNY Cortland/The SUNY	NY	19,759	C+
SUNY Fredonia/The SUNY at Fredonia	NY	19,840	VC
SUNY New Paltz	NY	14,348	C
SUNY Oneonta / SUNY	NY	16,919	C+
SUNY Plattsburgh / SUNY	NY	18,083	C
Susquehanna Univ	PA	51,150	C
Swarthmore College	PA	57,870	MC
Syracuse Univ	NY	56,346	VC
Talladega College	AL	17,996	C
Tarleton State Univ	TX	13,489	LC
Taylor Univ	IN	37,821	VC+
Temple Univ	PA	24,392	VC
Tenn State Univ	TN	9,048	C
Tenn Tech Univ	TN	11,310	C
Texas A&M Univ	TX	19,207	VC
Texas A&M Univ at Commerce	TX	10,496	C
Texas A&M Univ at Kingsville	TX	7,500	LC
Texas Christian Univ	TX	49,980	HC
Texas Lutheran Univ	TX	36,040	C
Texas State Univ	TX	17,128	C
Texas Tech Univ	TX	14,243	C
The Catholic Univ of America	DC	52,852	VC
The Lincoln Univ	PA	15,154	LC
Ohio State Univ-Columbus Campus	OH	19,887	HC+
The Pennsylvania State Univ - Univ Park	PA	28,022	VC+
The SUNY at Potsdam	NY	18,473	C
The SUNY/College at Brockport	NY	19,002	C
The Univ of Memphis	TN	15,094	C
The Univ of N Car at Greensboro	NC	12,848	C
The Univ of N Car at Pembroke	NC	13,388	LC
The Univ of Okla	OK	18,621	VC
The Univ of Tenn at Chattanooga	TN	16,883	C
The Univ of Utah	UT	16,463	VC
Thiel College	PA	38,728	LC
Thomas More College	KY	34,760	C
Tougaloo College	MS	15,275	NC
Touro College	NY	27,959	VC
Towson Univ	MD	16,000	VC
Transylvania Univ	KY	42,660	VC+
Trevecca Nazarene Univ	TN	31,186	C
Trinity College	CT		HC+
Trinity Univ	TX	48,150	HC+
Truman State Univ	MO	17,600	VC
Tufts Univ	MA	58,780	MC
Tulane Univ	LA	60,861	MC
Tuskegee Univ	AL	26,750	C
Union College	NE	23,270	C
Union College	NY	60,240	MC
Union Univ	TN	28,260	VC
United States Air Force Academy	CO		MC
United States Military Academy	NY		MC
United States Naval Academy	MD		MC
Univ at Albany / SUNY	NY	18,674	VC
Univ at Buffalo / The SUNY	NY	20,283	VC
Univ of Akron	OH	20,436	C
Univ of Alabama at Birmingham	AL	18,484	C+
Univ of Alabama at Tuscaloosa	AL	17,164	C+
Univ of Alabama in Huntsville	AL	17,591	VC+
Univ of Alaska Fairbanks	AK	15,130	C
Univ of Arizona	AZ	20,657	C
Univ of Arkansas at Fayetteville	AR	18,352	C+
Univ of Arkansas at Little Rock	AR	17,609	LC
Univ of Arkansas at Pine Bluff	AR	13,378	C
Univ of Calif at Berkeley	CA	23,322	MC
Univ of Calif at Davis	CA		HC
Univ of Calif at Irvine	CA	25,961	VC
Univ of Calif at Los Angeles	CA	25,686	MC
Univ of Calif at Riverside	CA	27,204	C+
Univ of Calif at San Diego	CA	21,000	VC
Univ of Calif at Santa Barbara	CA	27,551	HC
Univ of Calif at Santa Cruz	CA	27,807	C+
Univ of Central Arkansas	AR	13,667	VC
Univ of Central Florida	FL	15,668	VC+
Univ of Central Missouri	MO	14,605	C
Univ of Chicago	IL	55,416	MC
Univ of Cincinnati	OH	21,506	VC
Univ of Colo at Colo Springs	CO	15,000	VC
Univ of Colo Boulder	CO	22,605	VC
Univ of Colo Denver	CO	17,904	C
Univ of Conn	CT	24,706	VC
Univ of Dallas	TX	45,500	VC+
Univ of Dayton	OH	49,070	VC
Univ of Delaware	DE	23,612	VC
Univ of Denver	CO	51,787	VC+
Univ of Evansville	IN	42,656	VC+
Univ of Florida	FL	15,943	HC
Univ of Georgia	GA	20,082	VC
Univ of Hartford	CT	43,667	VC
Univ of Hawaii at Hilo	HI	23,066	C
Univ of Hawaii at Manoa	HI	19,379	C
Univ of Houston	TX	19,796	VC
Univ of Idaho	ID	14,558	C
Univ of Illinois at Chicago	IL	24,505	VC
Univ of Illinois at Urbana-Champaign	IL	26,450	VC
Univ of Indianapolis	IN	31,740	LC
Univ of Iowa	IA	17,693	VC
Univ of Kansas	KS	17,603	C+
Univ of Kentucky	KY	19,868	C
Univ of La Verne	CA	47,010	C
Univ of Louisiana at Lafayette	LA	6,130	C
Univ of Louisville	KY	17,946	C
Univ of Maine	ME	19,902	C+
Univ of Mary Washington	VA	19,484	C
Univ of Maryland - College Park	MD	20,060	HC
Univ of Maryland/Baltimore County	MD	18,000	VC
Univ of Mass Amherst	MA	24,215	VC+
Univ of Mass Boston	MA	23,066	VC
Univ of Mass Dartmouth	MA	22,223	C
Univ of Mass Lowell	MA	19,316	C
Univ of Miami	FL	57,034	MC
Univ of Mich/Ann Arbor	MI	22,102	MC
Univ of Mich/Dearborn	MI	9,885	VC
Univ of Mich-Flint	MI	17,547	C+
Univ of Minn/Duluth	MN	19,806	C
Univ of Minn/Morris	MN	17,150	VC
Univ of Minn/Twin Cities	MN		HC
Univ of Miss	MS	16,704	C+
Univ of Missouri/Columbia	MO	18,201	MC
Univ of Missouri-Kansas City	MO	19,603	C
Univ of Missouri-St. Louis	MO		VC
Univ of Montana	MT	14,105	C
Univ of Mount Union	OH	35,130	C
Univ of Nebr - Lincoln	NE	18,031	VC
Univ of Nebr at Kearney	NE	14,855	LC
Univ of Nebr at Omaha	NE	12,700	C
Univ of Nevada, Las Vegas	NV	17,303	C
Univ of Nevada/Reno	NV	17,507	C
Univ of New Hampshire	NH	26,912	C
Univ of New Mexico	NM	15,300	C
Univ of New Orleans	LA	9,224	C
Univ of North Alabama	AL	9,960	C
Univ of N Car at Asheville	NC	13,500	VC
Univ of N Car at Chapel Hill	NC	18,928	MC
Univ of N Car at Charlotte	NC	15,547	C
Univ of N Car at Wilmington	NC	13,572	VC
Univ of N Dak	ND	14,551	C
Univ of North Florida	FL	15,870	VC
Univ of North Georgia	GA	8,500	C
Univ of North Texas	TX	15,628	C
Univ of Northern Colo	CO	18,446	C
Univ of Northern Iowa	IA	15,795	C
Univ of Notre Dame	IN	57,117	MC
Univ of Oregon	OR	21,360	C+
Univ of Pennsylvania	PA	61,132	MC
Univ of Pittsburgh at Pittsburgh	PA	28,572	HC+
Univ of Portland	OR	49,964	VC
Univ of PR/Humacao	PR	1,877	
Univ of PR/Mayaguez	PR	1,250	
Univ of Puget Sound	WA	54,608	HC
Univ of Redlands	CA	40,500	VC
Univ of Rochester	NY	60,668	MC
Univ of San Diego	CA	54,818	HC+
Univ of San Francisco	CA	54,770	VC
Univ of Science and Arts of Okla	OK	10,560	VC
Univ of Scranton	PA	51,940	VC
Univ of South Alabama	AL	13,510	C
Univ of S Car at Columbia	SC	19,725	VC+
Univ of S Dak	SD	15,111	C
Univ of South Florida/Tampa	FL	13,000	VC
Univ of Southern Calif	CA	56,903	MC
Univ of Southern Maine	ME	16,576	C
Univ of Southern Miss	MS	13,170	C
Univ of St. Thomas - Houston	TX	37,690	C
Univ of Tenn at Knoxville	TN	20,364	VC+
Univ of Texas - Pan American	TX	11,125	LC
Univ of Texas at Arlington	TX	10,908	LC
Univ of Texas at Austin	TX	44,074	HC
Univ of Texas at Dallas	TX	21,348	HC+
Univ of Texas at El Paso	TX	8,764	NC
Univ of Texas at San Antonio	TX	18,372	C
Univ of the Cumberlands	KY	27,500	C
Univ of the District of Columbia	DC	7,244	LC
Univ of the Pacific	CA	52,146	VC
Univ of the Sciences	PA	48,320	VC+
Univ of Toledo	OH	18,464	C
Univ of Tulsa	OK	46,331	MC
Univ of Vermont	VT	27,006	VC+
Univ of Virginia	VA	23,050	MC
Univ of Washington	WA	14,722	VC
Univ of West Alabama	AL	14,274	C
Univ of West Florida	FL	14,656	C
Univ of West Georgia	GA	15,488	LC
Univ of Wisc Whitewater	WI	13,314	C
Univ of Wisc/Eau Claire	WI	15,730	VC
Univ of Wisc/La Crosse	WI	9,304	VC
Univ of Wisc/Madison	WI	18,757	HC+
Univ of Wisc/Oshkosh	WI	10,426	LC
Univ of Wisc/Parkside	WI	10,181	LC
Univ of Wisc/Platteville	WI	14,564	C
Univ of Wisc/River Falls	WI	9,722	LC
Univ of Wisc/Stevens Point	WI	14,043	C
Univ of Wisc-Milwaukee	WI	18,436	C
Univ of Wyoming	WY	14,401	C+
Ursinus College	PA	57,580	VC
Utah State Univ	UT	12,044	C
Utica College	NY	45,670	C
Valparaiso Univ	IN	44,940	VC+

ST = STATE $IS = IN-STATE COSTS   SR = SELECTOR RATING

School	ST	$IS	SR
Vanderbilt Univ	TN	58,220	MC
Vassar College	NY	61,140	MC
Villanova Univ	PA	58,394	MC
Virginia Commonwealth Univ	VA	21,716	C
Virginia Military Inst	VA	16,156	C
Virginia Polytechnic Inst and State Univ	VA	14,629	HC
Virginia State Univ	VA	11,318	C+
Wabash College	IN	46,850	C+
Wagner College	NY	48,600	C+
Wake Forest Univ	NC	58,838	MC
Walla Walla Univ	WA	26,256	NC
Wartburg College	IA	41,055	VC
Washburn Univ	KS	12,579	C
Washington and Jefferson College	PA	51,948	VC
Washington and Lee Univ	VA	52,812	MC
Washington College	MD	52,602	VC
Washington State Univ	WA	20,461	C
Washington Univ in St. Louis	MO	69,844	MC
Wayne State Univ	MI	22,063	C
Wellesley College	MA	59,038	MC
Wells College	NY	49,400	VC
Wesleyan College	GA	24,000	C
Wesleyan Univ	CT	61,198	MC
West Chester Univ of Pennsylvania	PA	17,186	C
West Texas A&M Univ	TX	13,478	C
West Virginia Univ	WV	16,542	C+
West Virginia Univ Inst of Technology	WV	14,094	NC
West Virginia Wesleyan College	WV	26,880	C
Western Illinois Univ	IL	20,732	C
Western Kentucky Univ	KY	11,000	LC
Western Mich Univ	MI	19,628	C
Western Washington Univ	WA	18,519	VC
Westminster College	MO	31,720	VC
Westminster College	PA	31,290	C
Westminster College	UT	37,708	C+
Westmont College	CA	41,500	VC
Wheaton College	IL	40,720	MC
Wheaton College	MA	54,934	HC+
Wheeling Jesuit Univ	WV	33,500	C
Whitman College	WA	55,988	MC
Whittier College	CA	43,416	C
Whitworth Univ	WA	47,734	VC
Wichita State Univ	KS	14,607	C+
Widener Univ	PA	52,418	C
Wiley College	TX		LC
Wilkes Univ	PA	44,070	C
Willamette Univ	OR	56,450	VC+
William Jewell College	MO	31,000	VC+
Williams College	MA	61,070	MC
Winona State Univ	MN	16,640	C
Wittenberg Univ	OH	47,962	C+
Wofford College	SC	45,795	VC
Worcester Polytechnic Inst	MA	55,860	MC
Wright State Univ	OH	16,983	C
Xavier Univ	OH	44,980	VC
Xavier Univ of Louisiana	LA	25,300	C
Yale Univ	CT	55,300	MC
York College / The CUNY	NY	5,496	VC
Youngstown State Univ	OH	16,732	C

PHYSICS & PHYSICAL OCEANOGRAPHY

School	ST	$IS	SR
Univ of Rhode Island	RI	24,002	C

PHYSICS AND MATHEMATICS

School	ST	$IS	SR
Bethany College	WV	35,282	LC
Bridgewater College	VA	41,450	C
Missouri Southern State Univ	MO	12,061	C

PHYSICS WITH ASTROPHYSICS OPTION

School	ST	$IS	SR
Univ of Nebr - Lincoln	NE	18,031	VC

PHYSIOLOGY

School	ST	$IS	SR
Boston Univ	MA	60,694	MC
Brigham Young Univ	UT	12,100	HC
Cal State, Long Beach	CA	17,502	C+
Florida State Univ	FL	16,715	VC
Hampshire College	MA	58,320	VC
Howard Univ	DC	13,646	V
Kent State Univ	OH	19,920	V
Marquette Univ	WI	46,930	VC+
Mich State Univ	MI	22,450	VC
Missouri Southern State Univ	MO	12,061	C
Northern Mich Univ	MI	18,278	C
Okla State Univ	OK	14,310	VC
Rutgers, The State Univ of New Jersey/New Brunswick	NJ	25,562	VC
San Francisco State Univ	CA	18,514	C
Southern Illinois Univ Carbondale	IL	21,942	C
Texas State Univ	TX	17,128	C
Univ of Arizona	AZ	20,657	C
Univ of Calif at Davis	CA		HC
Univ of Calif at Los Angeles	CA	25,686	MC

School	ST	$IS	SR
Univ of Calif at San Diego	CA	21,000	VC
Univ of Calif at Santa Barbara	CA	27,551	VC
Univ of Colo Boulder	CO	22,605	VC+
Univ of Conn	CT	24,706	VC
Univ of Great Falls	MT	27,970	C
Univ of Illinois at Urbana-Champaign	IL	26,450	VC
Univ of Minn/Twin Cities	MN		HC
Univ of Montana-Western	MT	9,753	LC
Univ of Oregon	OR	21,360	C+
Univ of Wyoming	WY	14,401	C+

PIANO PEDAGOGY

School	ST	$IS	SR
Ithaca College	NY	53,864	HC
Okla City Univ	OK	40,476	VC
Samford Univ	AL	37,060	C+
Shorter Univ	GA	30,650	LC
Texas Christian Univ	TX	49,980	HC

PIANO PERFORMANCE

School	ST	$IS	SR
Aquinas College	MI	33,060	C
Biola Univ	CA	40,320	C+
Dallas Baptist Univ	TX	30,580	VC
Hope College	MI	38,650	VC
Missouri Southern State Univ	MO	12,061	C
New York Univ	NY	61,470	MC
Okla City Univ	OK	40,476	VC
Ouachita Baptist Univ	AR	30,220	VC
Roberts Wesleyan College	NY	38,306	C+
Samford Univ	AL	37,060	C+
Univ of Central Okla	OK	12,293	C
Webster Univ	MO	35,100	C
West Chester Univ of Pennsylvania	PA	17,186	C
Youngstown State Univ	OH	16,732	C

PIANO/ORGAN

School	ST	$IS	SR
Bennington College	VT	56,990	HC+
Boston Conservatory	MA	56,380	VC
Calif Baptist Univ	CA	38,792	C
Calvin College	MI	39,120	VC
Central Washington Univ	WA	11,730	C
Columbia College	SC	27,882	C
East Central Univ	OK	10,223	LC
East Texas Baptist Univ	TX	31,577	LC
Eastern Mich Univ	MI	18,604	C
Florida State Univ	FL	16,715	VC
Hardin-Simmons Univ	TX	23,560	C+
Hope College	MI	38,650	VC
Illinois Wesleyan Univ	IL	48,452	HC
Indiana Univ Bloomington	IN	19,801	VC
Indiana Univ-Purdue Univ Fort Wayne	IN	15,521	C
Jackson State Univ	MS	13,512	LC
Kent State Univ	OH	19,920	C
Lenoir-Rhyne College	NC	35,984	C
Loyola Univ New Orleans	LA	46,581	VC
Manhattan School of Music	NY	55,850	SP
Mannes College New School for Music	NY	44,500	SP
Marshall Univ	WV	14,820	C
Millikin Univ	IL	38,940	C
Miss College	MS	21,998	C
Northwestern College	MN	24,000	C
Northwestern Univ	IL	61,640	MC
Nyack College	NY	33,250	C
Oberlin College	OH	61,788	MC
Ohio Univ	OH	21,080	C
Okla City Univ	OK	40,476	VC
Ouachita Baptist Univ	AR	30,220	VC
Pacific Lutheran Univ	WA	46,760	C+
Palm Beach Atlantic Univ	FL	34,874	C+
Point Loma Nazarene Univ	CA	41,006	C+
Rider Univ	NJ	45,720	C
Roosevelt Univ	IL	22,605	VC
Samford Univ	AL	37,060	C+
San Francisco Conservatory of Music	CA	56,428	SP
Shorter Univ	GA	30,650	LC
Southern Methodist Univ	TX	60,585	MC
Stetson Univ	FL	51,516	VC
Syracuse Univ	NY	56,346	VC
Temple Univ	PA	24,392	VC
The Catholic Univ of America	DC	52,852	VC
Ohio State Univ-Columbus Campus	OH	19,887	HC+
Union Univ	TN	28,260	VC
Univ of Cincinnati	OH	21,506	VC
Univ of Iowa	IA	17,693	VC
Univ of Kansas	KS	17,603	C+
Univ of Tulsa	OK	46,331	MC
Westminster Choir College	NJ	36,000	SP
Youngstown State Univ	OH	16,732	C

PLANETARY AND SPACE SCIENCE

School	ST	$IS	SR
Boston Univ	MA	60,694	MC
Calif Inst of Technology	CA	54,045	MC
Florida Inst of Technology	FL	48,290	VC
Univ of Arizona	AZ	20,657	C

School	ST	$IS	SR
Virginia Polytechnic Inst and State Univ	VA	14,629	HC
Wilmington College	OH	29,784	C

PLANT GENETICS

School	ST	$IS	SR
Brigham Young Univ	UT	12,100	HC
Purdue Univ/West Lafayette	IN	20,024	HC
SUNY / College of Environmental Science and Forestry	NY	18,351	VC
Univ of Calif at Berkeley	CA	23,322	MC
Univ of Calif at Riverside	CA	27,204	C+
Washington State Univ	WA	20,461	C

PLANT PATHOLOGY

School	ST	$IS	SR
Iowa State Univ	IA	16,403	C
Mich State Univ	MI	22,450	VC
New Mexico State Univ	NM	14,050	C
SUNY / College of Environmental Science and Forestry	NY	18,351	VC
Univ of Arizona	AZ	20,657	C
Univ of Calif at Riverside	CA	27,204	C+
Univ of Delaware	DE	23,612	VC
Univ of Georgia	GA	20,082	VC
Univ of Wisc/Madison	WI	18,757	HC+
Washington State Univ	WA	20,461	C

PLANT PHYSIOLOGY

School	ST	$IS	SR
Brigham Young Univ	UT	12,100	HC
Pittsburg State Univ	KS	12,032	C
Purdue Univ/West Lafayette	IN	20,024	HC
SUNY / College of Environmental Science and Forestry	NY	18,351	VC
Ohio State Univ-Columbus Campus	OH	19,887	HC+
Univ of Illinois at Urbana-Champaign	IL	26,450	VC

PLANT PROTECTION (PEST MANAGEMENT)

School	ST	$IS	SR
Iowa State Univ	IA	16,403	C
Miss State Univ	MS	14,750	C
N Dak State Univ	ND		C
Purdue Univ/West Lafayette	IN	20,024	HC
Texas Tech Univ	TX	14,243	C
Univ of Hawaii at Manoa	HI	19,379	C
Washington State Univ	WA	20,461	C
West Texas A&M Univ	TX	13,478	C

PLANT SCIENCE

School	ST	$IS	SR
Arkansas State Univ	AR	15,470	C
Brigham Young Univ	UT	12,100	HC
Calif State Polytechnic Univ, Pomona	CA	20,156	C
Cal State, Fresno	CA	17,405	C
Cornell Univ	NY	60,964	MC
Florida State Univ	FL	16,715	VC
Fort Valley State Univ	GA	11,200	VC
Iowa State Univ	IA	16,403	C
Louisiana State Univ	LA	18,677	C+
Middle Tenn State Univ	TN	8,650	C
Missouri State Univ	MO	13,996	C+
Montana State Univ	MT	14,068	C
N Dak State Univ	ND		C
Okla State Univ	OK	14,310	VC
Pittsburg State Univ	KS	12,032	C
Purdue Univ/West Lafayette	IN	20,024	HC
Rutgers, The State Univ of New Jersey/New Brunswick	NJ	25,562	VC
S Dak State Univ	SD	14,296	C
Southern Illinois Univ Carbondale	IL	21,942	C
SUNY / College of Environmental Science and Forestry	NY	18,351	VC
Tarleton State Univ	TX	13,489	LC
Tenn Tech Univ	TN	11,310	C
Texas A&M Univ at Kingsville	TX	7,500	LC
Ohio State Univ-Columbus Campus	OH	19,887	HC+
The Pennsylvania State Univ - Univ Park	PA	28,022	VC+
The SUNY College of Agriculture and Tech at Cobleskill	NY	19,749	C
Univ of Arizona	AZ	20,657	C
Univ of Calif at Davis	CA		HC
Univ of Calif at Santa Cruz	CA	27,807	C+
Univ of Delaware	DE	23,612	VC
Univ of Florida	FL	15,943	HC
Univ of Georgia	GA	20,082	VC
Univ of Hawaii at Manoa	HI	19,379	C
Univ of Idaho	ID	14,558	C
Univ of Maryland - College Park	MD	20,060	HC
Univ of Mass Amherst	MA	24,215	VC+
Univ of Missouri/Columbia	MO	18,201	VC
Univ of Nebr - Lincoln	NE	18,031	VC

School	ST	$IS	SR
Univ of Tenn at Knoxville	TN	20,364	VC+
Univ of Tenn at Martin	TN	13,734	C
Univ of Vermont	VT	27,006	VC+
Utah State Univ	UT	12,044	C
Washington State Univ	WA	20,461	C
Washington Univ in St. Louis	MO	69,844	MC
West Texas A&M Univ	TX	13,478	C
West Virginia Univ	WV	16,542	C+

PLASTICS ENGINEERING

School	ST	$IS	SR
Ferris State Univ	MI	20,047	C
Pennsylvania College of Technology	PA	26,286	NC
Univ of Illinois at Urbana-Champaign	IL	26,450	HC
Univ of Mass Lowell	MA	19,316	C
Univ of Wisc/Stout	WI	15,459	C
Western Washington Univ	WA	18,519	VC

PLASTICS TECHNOLOGY

School	ST	$IS	SR
Eastern Mich Univ	MI	18,604	C
Penn State Erie/The Behrend College	PA	16,256	C
Pittsburg State Univ	KS	12,032	C
Shawnee State Univ	OH	16,916	C

PLAYWRITING/SCREENWRITING

School	ST	$IS	SR
Bennington College	VT	56,990	HC+
Biola Univ	CA	40,320	C+
Chapman Univ	CA	58,347	VC+
DePaul Univ	IL	47,623	VC
Goddard College	VT	16,418	VC
Howard Univ	DC	13,646	C
Metropolitan State Univ	MN	5,923	
Ohio Univ	OH	21,080	C
Univ of Southern Calif	CA	56,903	MC
Webster Univ	MO	35,100	C+

POLICY ANALYSIS AND MANAGEMENT

School	ST	$IS	SR
Bloomfield College	NJ	37,850	LC
Cornell Univ	NY	60,964	MC
Indiana Univ Bloomington	IN	19,801	VC

POLISH

School	ST	$IS	SR
Univ of Illinois at Chicago	IL	24,505	VC
Univ of Pittsburgh at Pittsburgh	PA	28,572	HC+
Univ of Wisc/Madison	WI	18,757	HC+

POLITICAL SCIENCE/ GOVERNMENT

School	ST	$IS	SR
Abilene Christian Univ	TX	38,400	C+
Adams State Univ	CO	13,358	LC
Adelphi Univ	NY	44,670	VC
Adrian College	MI	42,400	C
Agnes Scott College	GA	45,323	C+
Alabama A&M Univ	AL	10,084	C
Alabama State Univ	AL	14,142	NC
Albany State Univ	GA	8,500	C
Albertus Magnus College	CT	37,382	C
Albion College	MI	46,010	C
Albright College	PA	46,660	C
Alcorn State Univ	MS	9,500	C
Alderson Broaddus Univ	WV	28,656	C
Alfred Univ	NY	41,770	C
Allegheny College	PA	50,980	VC
Allen Univ	SC	16,124	NC
Alma College	MI	44,075	C
Alvernia Univ	PA	39,250	LC
Alverno College	WI	31,434	C
American International College	MA	36,100	C
American Jewish Univ - College of A&S	CA	32,600	C
American Univ	DC	56,015	HC+
Amherst College	MA	58,744	MC
Anderson Univ	IN	36,100	C
Andrews Univ	MI	28,030	C+
Angelo State Univ	TX	15,049	NC
Anna Maria College	MA	34,600	C
Appalachian State Univ	NC	12,919	VC
Aquinas College	MI	33,060	C
Arcadia Univ	PA	33,570	C+
Arizona State Univ, at the Tempe Campus	AZ	20,137	C+
Arizona State Univ, at the West Campus	AZ	19,251	C
Arkansas State Univ	AR	15,470	C
Arkansas Tech Univ	AR	13,982	LC
Armstrong State Univ	GA	15,532	C
Asbury Univ	KY	32,038	VC
Ashford Univ	CA	10,480	C
Ashland Univ	OH	25,000	C
Assumption College	MA	47,122	C+
Auburn Univ	AL	22,378	VC+
Auburn Univ at Montgomery	AL	14,470	LC
Augsburg College	MN	35,142	C
Augustana College	IL	43,398	VC

ST = STATE   **$IS** = IN-STATE COSTS   **SR** = SELECTOR RATING

School	ST	$IS	SR
Augustana College	SD	36,500	VC
Aurora Univ	IL	33,228	C
Austin College	TX	45,875	HC
Austin Peay State Univ	TN	15,274	C
Averett Univ	VA	37,750	VC
Avila Univ	MO	26,900	C
Azusa Pacific Univ	CA	42,086	C
Baldwin Wallace Univ	OH	38,318	C
Ball State Univ	IN	17,850	C
Bard College	NY	61,940	HC
Bard College at Simon's Rock	MA	61,749	HC+
Barnard College/Columbia Univ	NY	39,000	MC
Barry Univ	FL	38,190	C
Barton College	NC	27,660	C
Bates College	ME	60,720	MC
Baylor Univ	TX	50,329	HC
Belhaven Univ	MS	27,170	C
Bellarmine Univ	KY	42,950	VC
Bellevue Univ	NE	4,600	NC
Belmont Abbey College	NC	37,716	C
Belmont Univ	TN	39,190	VC+
Beloit College	WI	49,970	HC
Bemidji State Univ	MN	13,500	VC
Benedict College	SC	20,454	NC
Benedictine College	KS	29,180	VC
Benedictine Univ	IL	37,820	C
Bennett College for Women	NC	21,970	LC
Bennington College	VT	56,990	HC+
Berea College	KY	7,192	C
Berry College	GA	39,254	VC
Bethany College	WV	35,282	LC
Bethel Univ	MN	34,940	VC
Bethune-Cookman Univ	FL	22,958	C
Binghamton Univ/The SUNY	NY	21,648	HC+
Birmingham-Southern College	AL	44,168	VC+
Black Hills State Univ	SD	13,947	C
Blackburn College	IL	21,350	C
Bloomfield College	NJ	37,850	LC
Bloomsburg Univ of Pennsylvania	PA	13,598	C
Boise State Univ	ID	13,469	LC
Boston College	MA	60,622	MC
Boston Univ	MA	60,694	MC
Bowdoin College	ME	59,568	MC
Bowling Green State Univ	OH	18,970	C
Bradley Univ	IL	31,874	VC
Brandeis Univ	MA		MC
Brenau Univ - Women's College	GA	26,650	LC
Brewton-Parker College	GA	33,388	C
Briar Cliff Univ	IA	29,514	C
Bridgewater College	VA	41,450	C
Bridgewater State Univ	MA	18,752	C
Brigham Young Univ	UT	12,100	HC
Brigham Young Univ/Hawaii	HI	10,686	VC
Brown Univ	RI	59,428	MC
Bryant Univ	RI	49,179	VC
Bryn Mawr College	PA	59,890	MC
Bucknell Univ	PA	60,140	MC
Buena Vista Univ	IA	39,188	C
Buffalo State College / SUNY	NY	15,733	C+
Butler Univ	IN	47,572	VC+
Cabrini College	PA	40,859	LC
Caldwell College	NJ	35,602	NC
Calif Baptist Univ	CA	38,792	C
Calif Inst of Technology	CA	54,045	MC
Calif Lutheran Univ	CA	49,540	C+
Calif Polytechnic State Univ	CA	19,847	HC
Calif State Polytechnic Univ, Pomona	CA	20,156	C
Cal State, Bakersfield	CA	8,000	C
Cal State, Chico	CA	20,158	C
Cal State, Dominguez Hills	CA	17,090	LC
Cal State, East Bay	CA	16,549	C
Cal State, Fresno	CA	17,405	C
Cal State, Fullerton	CA	25,188	C
Cal State, Long Beach	CA	17,502	C+
Cal State, Los Angeles	CA	17,186	LC
Cal State, Northridge	CA	28,690	LC
Cal State, San Bernardino	CA	12,000	C
Cal State, San Marcos	CA	14,576	LC
Cal State, Stanislaus	CA	18,582	C
Calif Univ of Pennsylvania	PA	14,217	C
Calvin College	MI	39,120	VC
Cameron Univ	OK	10,004	LC
Campbell Univ	NC	37,570	VC
Campbellsville Univ	KY	27,720	C
Capital Univ	OH	41,050	VC
Carleton College	MN	60,102	MC
Carlow Univ	PA	30,272	C
Carnegie Mellon Univ	PA	51,260	MC
Carroll College	MT	28,000	C
Carroll Univ	WI	38,100	C
Carthage College	WI	33,000	C
Case Western Reserve Univ	OH	56,534	MC
Castleton State College	VT	20,186	C
Catawba College	NC	37,240	LC
Cedar Crest College	PA	43,240	C
Cedarville Univ	OH	32,860	VC
Centenary College	NJ	38,618	C
Centenary College of Louisiana	LA	45,650	VC
Central College	IA	42,104	C+
Central Conn State Univ	CT	19,749	C
Central Methodist Univ	MO	28,240	VC
Central State Univ	OH	9,010	C
Central Washington Univ	WA	11,730	C
Chadron State College	NE	7,400	NC
Chapman Univ	CA	58,347	VC+
Charleston Southern Univ	SC	22,420	C
Chatham Univ	PA	43,797	C
Chestnut Hill College	PA	42,110	LC
Cheyney Univ of Pennsylvania	PA	20,372	LC
Chicago State Univ	IL	5,482	C
Christendom College	VA	32,600	VC
Christopher Newport Univ	VA	21,960	VC
Citadel, The	SC		C
CUNY/Baruch College	NY		HC
CUNY/Brooklyn College	NY	5,884	C+
CUNY/City College	NY	20,319	HC+
Claflin Univ	SC	22,368	LC
Claremont McKenna College	CA	62,215	MC
Clarion Univ of Pennsylvania	PA	17,370	LC
Clark Atlanta Univ	GA	30,006	LC
Clark Univ	MA	47,020	HC+
Clarke Univ	IA	37,600	C
Clarkson Univ	NY	57,330	HC
Clemson Univ	SC	19,136	HC
Cleveland State Univ	OH	21,776	C
Coastal Carolina Univ	SC	18,580	C
Coe College	IA	45,550	VC
Coker College	SC	32,256	LC
Colby College	ME	57,510	MC
Colgate Univ	NY	58,135	MC
College of Charleston	SC	22,145	VC
College of New Jersey	NJ	25,376	VC
College of the Holy Cross	MA	58,042	MC
College of William & Mary	VA	28,000	MC
College of Wooster	OH	52,600	VC
Colo College	CO	57,162	MC
Colo Mesa Univ	CO	17,690	LC
Colo State Univ-Fort Collins	CO	20,385	VC
Colo State Univ-Pueblo	CO	16,183	C
Columbia College	MO	24,578	C
Columbia College	SC	27,882	C
Columbia Univ/City of New York	NY	61,116	MC
Columbia Univ/School of General Studies	NY	58,231	MC
Columbus State Univ	GA	13,176	C
Concord Univ	WV	13,102	C
Concordia Univ - Moorhead	MN	39,974	VC
Concordia Univ Irvine	CA	35,390	VC
Concordia Univ, River Forest	IL	26,300	C
Conn College	CT	54,970	MC
Converse College	SC	37,130	C
Coppin State Univ	MD	16,227	VC
Corban Univ	OR	37,380	C+
Cornell College	IA	44,930	VC
Creighton Univ	NE	45,356	VC
Culver-Stockton College	MO	30,900	C
Cumberland Univ	TN	21,220	C
Curry College	MA	48,925	LC
Daemen College	NY	34,770	C
Dallas Baptist Univ	TX	30,580	VC
Davidson College	NC	58,146	MC
Davis & Elkins College	WV	33,742	C
De Sales Univ	PA	43,970	C
Delaware State Univ	DE	16,722	LC
Delta State Univ	MS	12,292	LC
Denison Univ	OH	54,670	HC+
DePaul Univ	IL	47,623	VC
DePauw Univ	IN	48,950	VC+
Dickinson College	PA	57,662	HC+
Dickinson State Univ	ND	11,900	NC
Dillard Univ	LA	20,940	VC
Doane College	NE	35,230	C
Dominican Univ	IL	37,628	C
Dominican Univ of Calif	CA	51,250	C
Dordt College	IA	34,160	C+
Dowling College	NY	25,000	LC
Drake Univ	IA	41,516	VC+
Drew Univ/College of Liberal Arts	NJ	57,516	C
Drexel Univ	PA	61,418	VC+
Drury Univ	MO	31,909	VC
Duke Univ	NC	50,250	MC
Duquesne Univ	PA	43,720	VC
Earlham College	IN	51,470	HC
East Carolina Univ	NC	14,169	C
East Central Univ	OK	10,223	LC
East Stroudsburg Univ of Pennsylvania	PA	18,868	LC
East Tenn State Univ	TN	9,000	C
East Texas Baptist Univ	TX	31,577	LC
Eastern Conn State Univ	CT	20,584	C
Eastern Illinois Univ	IL	20,466	C
Eastern Kentucky Univ	KY	11,161	C
Eastern Mich Univ	MI	18,604	C
Eastern New Mexico Univ	NM	10,682	C
Eastern Univ	PA	37,704	C
Eastern Washington Univ	WA		C
Eckerd College	FL	43,902	C
Edgewood College	WI	33,294	C
Edinboro Univ of Pennsylvania	PA	15,940	LC
Edward Waters College	FL	19,607	LC
Elizabeth City State Univ	NC	11,638	C
Elizabethtown College	PA	49,740	VC
Elmhurst College	IL	43,336	C
Elmira College	NY	49,950	C+
Elon Univ	NC	41,914	VC+
Emmanuel College	MA	47,985	VC
Emory and Henry College	VA	387,460	C
Emory Univ	GA	56,368	MC
Emporia State Univ	KS	12,897	C
Endicott College	MA	43,228	VC+
Eugene Lang College/The New School for Liberal Arts	NY	55,650	C
Eureka College	IL	19,280	C
Evangel Univ	MO	23,090	C
Excelsior College	NY	5,580	SP
Fairfield Univ	CT	56,960	VC
Fairleigh Dickinson Univ/College at Florham	NJ	42,142	C
Fairleigh Dickinson Univ/Metropolitan Campus	NJ	40,254	C
Fairmont State Univ	WV	12,098	LC
Faulkner Univ	AL	25,720	LC
Fayetteville State Univ	NC	10,816	C
Ferris State Univ	MI	20,047	C
Ferrum College	VA	27,740	LC
Fisk Univ	TN	19,830	C
Fitchburg State Univ	MA	18,173	C
Flagler College	FL	25,180	C
Florida A&M Univ	FL	14,935	LC
Florida Atlantic Univ	FL	17,339	C
Florida Gulf Coast Univ	FL		C
Florida International Univ	FL	17,747	C+
Florida Memorial Univ	FL	20,888	LC
Florida Southern College	FL	40,150	C+
Florida State Univ	FL	16,715	VC
Fordham Univ	NY	61,588	HC+
Fort Hays State Univ	KS	11,354	C
Fort Lewis College	CO	15,513	C
Fort Valley State Univ	GA	11,200	VC
Framingham State Univ	MA	18,854	C
Francis Marion Univ	SC	16,464	LC
Franciscan Univ of Steubenville	OH	27,320	VC
Franklin and Marshall College	PA	60,799	MC
Franklin College	IN	36,585	C
Franklin Pierce Univ	NH	41,598	C
Friends Univ	KS	29,100	C
Frostburg State Univ	MD	15,264	LC
Furman Univ	SC	54,006	HC
Gallaudet Univ	DC	25,380	SP
Gannon Univ	PA	39,608	C
Geneva College	PA	27,280	C
George Fox Univ	OR	40,750	C+
George Mason Univ	VA	15,724	VC
George Washington Univ	DC	57,108	MC
Georgetown College	KY	41,440	C+
Georgetown Univ	DC	52,910	MC
Georgia College and State Univ	GA	18,900	C+
Georgia Regents Univ	GA		C
Georgia Southern Univ	GA	16,942	C
Georgia Southwestern State Univ	GA	13,246	C
Georgia State Univ	GA	15,582	VC
Gettysburg College	PA	58,820	HC
Gonzaga Univ	WA	46,441	HC
Gordon College	MA	44,320	VC
Goucher College	MD	52,040	VC+
Grambling State Univ	LA	13,384	LC
Grand Valley State Univ	MI	17,998	C
Grand View Univ	IA	31,050	C
Greensboro College	NC	28,740	LC
Grinnell College	IA	53,654	HC
Grove City College	PA	24,022	VC
Guilford College	NC	42,800	C
Gustavus Adolphus College	MN	48,170	HC
Hamilton College	NY	55,620	MC
Hamline Univ	MN	45,678	VC
Hampden-Sydney College	VA	51,758	C
Hampshire College	MA	58,320	MC
Hampton Univ	VA	28,528	C
Hanover College	IN	43,073	C+
Harding Univ	AR	23,556	C
Hardin-Simmons Univ	TX	23,560	C+
Hartwick College	NY	51,270	C
Harvard College/Harvard Univ	MA	49,000	MC
Hastings College	NE	27,782	C+
Haverford College	PA	61,564	MC
Hawaii Pacific Univ	HI	34,360	C
Heidelberg Univ	OH	34,100	C
Henderson State Univ	AR	14,584	C
Hendrix College	AR	50,202	VC+
High Point Univ	NC	39,800	C
Hilbert College	NY	28,550	C
Hillsdale College	MI	32,866	MC
Hiram College	OH	37,300	VC
Hobart and William Smith Colleges	NY	60,034	HC+
Hofstra Univ	NY	51,810	VC+
Hollins Univ	VA	43,295	VC
Holy Family Univ	PA	40,030	LC
Hood College	MD	45,730	C
Hope College	MI	38,650	VC
Houghton College	NY	36,808	C+
Houston Baptist Univ	TX	36,450	C
Howard Payne Univ	TX	17,115	C
Howard Univ	DC	13,646	C
Humboldt State Univ	CA	18,400	C
Hunter College	NY	14,429	VC
Huntingdon College	AL	33,100	C
Huston-Tillotson Univ	TX	18,124	C+
Idaho State Univ	ID	12,307	C
Illinois College	IL	25,770	VC
Illinois Inst of Technology	IL	38,512	HC+
Illinois State Univ	IL	23,110	VC
Illinois Wesleyan Univ	IL	48,452	HC
Indiana State Univ	IN	16,000	C
Indiana Univ Bloomington	IN	19,801	VC
Indiana Univ East	IN	6,783	C
Indiana Univ Northwest	IN	6,854	LC
Indiana Univ of Pennsylvania	PA	20,846	LC
Indiana Univ South Bend	IN	15,501	C
Indiana Univ Southeast	IN	16,035	C
Indiana Univ-Purdue Univ Fort Wayne	IN	15,521	C
Indiana Univ-Purdue Univ Indianapolis	IN	17,611	C
Indiana Wesleyan Univ	IN	31,815	VC
Inter-American Univ of PR/Fajardo Campus	PR	4,200	
Inter-American Univ of PR/Metropolitan Campus	PR	4,320	
Inter-American Univ of PR/Ponce	PR		
Inter-American Univ of PR/San Germán	PR	6,720	
Iona College	NY	44,028	C
Iowa State Univ	IA	16,403	C
Ithaca College	NY	53,864	HC
Jackson State Univ	MS	13,512	LC
Jacksonville State Univ	AL	12,480	LC
Jacksonville Univ	FL	37,780	C
James Madison Univ	VA	18,049	VC
John Brown Univ	AR	32,056	VC+
John Carroll Univ	OH	46,300	C+
John Jay College of Criminal Justice/The CUNY	NY	6,359	C
Johns Hopkins Univ	MD	47,492	MC
Johnson C. Smith Univ	NC	25,336	C
Johnson State College	VT	16,721	C
Judson Univ	IL	25,130	C
Juniata College	PA	49,340	VC
Kalamazoo College	MI	49,740	HC
Kansas State Univ	KS	15,497	VC
Kean Univ	NJ	23,444	C
Keene State College	NH	23,232	LC
Kennesaw State Univ	GA		C
Kent State Univ	OH	19,920	C
Kentucky State Univ	KY	11,000	LC
Kentucky Wesleyan College	KY	27,440	C
Kenyon College	OH	58,890	MC
Keuka College	NY	30,300	C
King Univ	TN	33,140	C
King's College	PA	43,502	C
Knox College	IL	44,865	VC+
Kutztown Univ of Pennsylvania	PA	16,909	LC
La Roche College	PA	35,824	LC
La Salle Univ	PA	50,270	C
La Sierra Univ	CA	35,694	VC
Lafayette College	PA	59,155	HC+
LaGrange College	GA	37,670	C
Lake Erie College	OH	37,266	C
Lake Forest College	IL	50,652	VC
Lake Superior State Univ	MI	18,121	C
Lamar Univ	TX	6,820	C
Lander Univ	SC	22,514	C+
Lawrence Univ	WI	46,371	HC
Le Moyne College	NY	43,470	C
Lebanon Valley College	PA	38,570	C
Lee Univ	TN	18,690	C+
Lehigh Univ	PA	56,770	MC
Lehman College/The CUNY	NY	5,778	LC
LeMoyne-Owen College	TN	13,100	C
Lenoir-Rhyne College	NC	35,984	C
Lewis & Clark College	OR	54,382	MC
Lewis Univ	IL	23,050	C
Liberty Univ	VA	19,101	C
Lincoln Univ	MO	12,904	NC
Lindenwood Univ	MO	20,750	C
Linfield College-McMinnville Campus	OR	47,676	C
Lipscomb Univ	TN	37,490	VC
LIU Brooklyn	NY	47,182	LC
LIU Post	NY	47,660	C
Livingstone College	NC	17,815	LC
Lock Haven Univ of Pennsylvania	PA	18,028	LC
Longwood Univ	VA	20,924	C
Loras College	IA	37,432	VC
Louisiana State Univ	LA	18,677	C+
Louisiana Tech Univ	LA	11,302	C
Loyola Marymount Univ	CA	54,649	VC+
Loyola Univ Chicago	IL	51,646	VC+
Loyola Univ Maryland	MD	56,880	VC+
Loyola Univ New Orleans	LA	46,581	VC

ST = STATE $IS = IN-STATE COSTS   SR = SELECTOR RATING

School	ST	$IS	SR
Luther College	IA	45,720	C+
Lycoming College	PA	45,379	C
Lynchburg College	VA	42,645	C
Lynn Univ	FL	43,500	LC
Lyon College	AR	32,090	C+
Macalester College	MN	57,691	MC
MacMurray College	IL	20,755	C
Malone Univ	OH	35,364	C
Manchester Univ	IN	35,070	C
Manhattan College	NY	49,588	C+
Manhattanville College	NY	50,740	VC
Mansfield Univ	PA	19,468	LC
Marian Univ	IN	38,540	C
Marietta College	OH	42,135	C+
Marist College	NY	35,500	C
Marlboro College	VT	35,980	VC
Marquette Univ	WI	46,930	VC+
Mars Hill Univ	NC	22,950	LC
Marshall Univ	WV	14,820	C
Martin Univ	IN	11,000	SP
Mary Baldwin College	VA	38,245	C
Marygrove College	MI	28,926	C
Marymount Manhattan College	NY	40,118	VC
Marymount Univ	VA	39,480	C
Maryville College	TN	33,150	C+
Marywood Univ	PA	45,595	C
Mass College of Liberal Arts	MA	18,613	C
Mass Inst of Technology	MA	58,240	MC
McDaniel College	MD	47,450	VC
McKendree Univ	IL	29,920	C+
McMurry Univ	TX	25,962	LC
McNeese State Univ	LA	2,649	C
Mercer Univ	GA	44,201	VC
Mercy College	NY	30,456	C
Mercyhurst Univ	PA	40,700	C
Meredith College	NC	31,420	C
Merrimack College	MA	44,215	C
Messiah College	PA	40,690	C+
Methodist Univ	NC	37,185	C
Metropolitan State Univ of Denver	CO	4,835	LC
Miami Univ	OH	24,191	VC
Mich State Univ	MI	22,450	VC
Middle Tenn State Univ	TN	8,650	C
Middlebury College	VT	59,160	MC
Midwestern State Univ	TX	9,722	C
Miles College	AL	11,164	NC
Millersville Univ of Pennsylvania	PA	21,648	C
Millikin Univ	IL	38,940	C
Mills College	CA	54,119	VC
Millsaps College	MS	43,884	VC+
Minn State Univ, Mankato	MN	15,616	C
Minn State Univ, Moorhead	MN	13,392	VC
Miss College	MS	21,998	C
Miss State Univ	MS	14,750	C
Miss Univ for Women	MS	7,400	C
Miss Valley State Univ	MS	9,706	LC
Missouri Southern State Univ	MO	12,061	C
Missouri State Univ	MO	13,996	C+
Missouri Valley College	MO	22,200	C
Missouri Western State Univ	MO	12,260	NC
Molloy College	NY	40,440	C
Monmouth College	IL	40,850	C
Monmouth Univ	NJ	44,108	C
Montana State Univ	MT	14,068	C
Montana State Univ-Billings	MT	12,425	LC
Montclair State Univ	NJ	22,614	C
Moravian College	PA	36,381	C
Morehead State Univ	KY	10,900	C
Morehouse College	GA	39,412	C
Morgan State Univ	MD	14,500	VC
Morningside College	IA	35,430	C
Morris College	SC	16,310	LC
Mount Aloysius College	PA	29,976	C
Mount Holyoke College	MA	55,146	MC
Mount Mercy Univ	IA	35,320	C
Mount St. Mary College	NY	41,138	C
Mount St. Mary's Univ	MD	47,996	C
Mount St. Mary's College - Chalon Campus	CA	43,897	VC+
Mount Vernon Nazarene Univ	OH	29,590	C
Muhlenberg College	PA	52,837	HC
Murray State Univ	KY	15,304	C
Muskingum Univ	OH	30,502	C
Nazareth College of Rochester	NY	43,028	C+
Nebr Wesleyan Univ	NE	29,774	C+
Neumann Univ	PA	31,078	LC
New College of Florida	FL	14,504	MC
New England College	NH	45,930	LC
New Jersey City Univ	NJ	21,456	LC
New Mexico Highlands Univ	NM	11,904	NC
New Mexico State Univ	NM	14,050	C
New York Inst of Technology	NY	45,010	VC
New York Univ	NY	61,470	MC
Newberry College	SC	26,850	LC
Niagara Univ	NY	41,010	C
Nicholls State Univ	LA	7,095	C
Norfolk State Univ	VA	10,531	LC
N Car Agricultural and Technical State Univ	NC	13,365	LC
N Car Central Univ	NC	9,000	C
N Car State Univ	NC	16,202	HC
N Car Wesleyan College	NC	29,440	C

School	ST	$IS	SR
North Central College	IL	38,343	VC
N Dak State Univ	ND		C
North Park Univ	IL	30,130	C
Northeastern Illinois Univ	IL	10,318	LC
Northeastern State Univ	OK	8,615	VC
Northeastern Univ	MA	55,296	MC
Northern Arizona Univ	AZ	19,010	C
Northern Illinois Univ	IL	19,768	C
Northern Kentucky Univ	KY	21,134	C
Northern Mich Univ	MI	18,278	C
Northern State Univ - Aberdeen	SD	14,505	C
Northwest Missouri State Univ	MO	17,347	C
Northwest Nazarene Univ	ID	34,000	C
Northwestern College of Iowa	IA	36,240	VC
Northwestern Okla State Univ	OK	7,275	NC
Northwestern Univ	IL	61,640	MC
Norwich Univ	VT	28,212	C
Notre Dame College	OH	34,942	VC
Notre Dame de Namur Univ	CA	44,236	LC
Notre Dame of Maryland Univ	MD	27,700	VC
Nova Southeastern Univ	FL	37,280	VC
Oakland Univ	MI	19,391	C
Oakwood Univ	AL	25,529	NC
Oberlin College	OH	61,788	MC
Occidental College	CA	60,972	MC
Oglethorpe Univ	GA	44,200	C
Ohio Dominican Univ	OH	38,380	C+
Ohio Northern Univ	OH	42,075	VC
Ohio Univ	OH	21,080	C
Ohio Wesleyan Univ	OH	49,460	C+
Okla Baptist Univ	OK	28,202	C
Okla City Univ	OK	40,476	VC
Okla State Univ	OK	14,310	VC
Okla Wesleyan Univ	OK	21,300	C
Old Dominion Univ	VA	19,483	LC
Olivet Nazarene Univ	IL	29,990	C
Oral Roberts Univ	OK	31,734	C
Oregon State Univ	OR	20,273	VC
Oswego / SUNY	NY	20,009	VC
Ottawa Univ	KS	15,000	VC
Otterbein College	OH	32,214	C
Ouachita Baptist Univ	AR	30,220	VC
Our Lady of the Lake Univ	TX	22,430	LC
Pace Univ	NY	53,367	C
Pacific Lutheran Univ	WA	46,760	C+
Pacific Univ	OR	49,626	C+
Palm Beach Atlantic Univ	FL	34,874	C+
Park Univ	MO	17,525	C
Paul Quinn College	TX	25,350	LC
Penn State Erie/The Behrend College	PA	16,256	C
Pepperdine Univ	CA	55,372	HC+
Pfeiffer Univ	NC	33,700	LC
Philander Smith College	AR	19,760	LC
Piedmont College	GA	30,136	C
Pittsburg State Univ	KS	12,032	C
Pitzer College	CA	54,988	MC
Plymouth State Univ	NH	23,148	LC
Point Loma Nazarene Univ	CA	41,006	C+
Point Park Univ	PA	36,390	C
Pomona College	CA	57,680	MC
Pontifical Catholic Univ of PR	PR	7,310	
Portland State Univ	OR	18,672	C
Prairie View A&M Univ	TX	15,205	LC
Presbyterian College	SC	42,678	C+
Princeton Univ	NJ	53,795	MC
Principia College	IL	35,140	C+
Providence College	RI	57,383	VC
Purdue Univ/Calumet	IN	14,336	C
Purdue Univ/West Lafayette	IN	20,024	HC
Queens College/The CUNY	NY	17,107	VC
Queens Univ of Charlotte	NC	39,543	C+
Quincy Univ	IL	34,980	LC
Quinnipiac Univ	CT	55,160	VC
Radford Univ	VA	17,766	LC
Ramapo College of New Jersey	NJ	24,938	C
Randolph College	VA	45,660	C
Randolph-Macon College	VA	49,869	C+
Reed College	OR	57,780	MC
Regis College	MA	47,565	LC
Regis Univ	CO	41,318	C
Rhode Island College	RI	17,694	LC
Rhodes College	TN	51,900	HC+
Rice Univ	TX	43,288	MC
Richard Stockton College of New Jersey	NJ	20,000	VC
Rider Univ	NJ	45,720	C
Ripon College	WI	36,959	C+
Rivier Univ	NH	35,000	VC
Roanoke College	VA	49,976	C
Rockford College	IL	31,000	C
Rockhurst Univ	MO	20,625	C
Rocky Mountain College	MT	32,242	C
Roger Williams Univ	RI	46,296	VC
Rollins College	FL	52,370	HC
Roosevelt Univ	IL	22,605	VC
Rosemont College	PA	42,350	C
Rowan Univ	NJ	24,022	VC+
Russell Sage College	NY	39,370	C
Rust College	MS	10,600	C

School	ST	$IS	SR
Rutgers, The State Univ of New Jersey/Camden Campus	NJ	25,121	C
Rutgers, The State Univ of New Jersey/New Brunswick	NJ	25,562	VC
Rutgers, The State Univ of New Jersey/Newark Campus	NJ	258,806	C
Sacred Heart Univ	CT	49,264	VC
Saginaw Valley State Univ	MI	17,369	C
St. Anselm College	NH	49,376	VC
St. Augustine's Univ	NC	14,000	C
St. Francis Univ	PA	30,029	LC
St. John's Univ	MN	47,984	C
St. Joseph's College	IN	36,500	C
St. Joseph's Univ	PA	55,006	VC
St. Leo Univ	FL	30,340	C
St. Louis Univ	MO	48,346	HC
St. Martin's Univ	WA	41,678	C
St. Mary's College	IN	45,160	C+
St. Mary's College of Calif	CA	53,550	C
St. Mary's Univ	TX	33,854	C
St. Mary's Univ of Minn	MN	38,280	C
St. Michael's College	VT	49,975	VC
St. Paul's College	VA	16,030	NC
St. Peter's Univ	NJ	44,240	C
St. Vincent College	PA	40,244	C
St. Xavier Univ	IL	32,840	C
Salisbury Univ	MD	19,180	VC
Salve Regina Univ	RI	48,550	VC
Sam Houston State Univ	TX	17,082	C
Samford Univ	AL	37,060	C+
San Diego State Univ	CA	21,611	C+
San Francisco State Univ	CA	18,514	C
San Jose State Univ	CA	19,133	LC
Sarah Lawrence College	NY	48,000	HC
Savannah State Univ	GA	13,156	C
Schreiner Univ	TX	32,734	LC
Scripps College	CA	61,940	MC
Seattle Pacific Univ	WA	41,559	VC+
Seattle Univ	WA	49,035	VC+
Seton Hall Univ	NJ	45,902	C
Seton Hill Univ	PA	35,172	C
Sewanee: The Univ of the South	TN	47,700	HC+
Shaw Univ	NC	15,488	C
Shenandoah Univ	VA	39,916	C
Shepherd Univ	WV	15,875	C
Shippensburg Univ of Pennsylvania	PA	20,934	C
Siena College	NY	43,863	VC
Simmons College	MA	49,966	VC
Simpson College	IA	36,086	C+
Skidmore College	NY	59,942	HC
Slippery Rock Univ of Pennsylvania	PA	10,360	C
Smith College	MA	59,674	MC
Sonoma State Univ	CA	20,541	C
S Car State Univ	SC	6,700	LC
S Dak State Univ	SD	14,296	C
Southeast Missouri State Univ	MO	15,370	LC
Southeastern Louisiana Univ	LA	13,325	C
Southeastern Okla State Univ	OK	7,966	LC
Southern Arkansas Univ	AR	14,316	C
Southern Conn State Univ	CT	18,033	LC
Southern Illinois Univ Carbondale	IL	21,942	C
Southern Illinois Univ Edwardsville	IL	17,532	C
Southern Methodist Univ	TX	60,585	MC
Southern Nazarene Univ	OK	24,354	C
Southern New Hampshire Univ	NH	38,100	C
Southern Oregon Univ	OR	17,874	C
Southern Polytechnic State Univ	GA	13,958	C
Southern Univ and A&M College	LA	9,761	C
Southern Univ at New Orleans	LA	2,963	NC
Southwest Baptist Univ	MO	24,710	C
Southwest Minn State Univ	MN	14,000	C
Southwestern Okla State Univ	OK	9,160	C
Southwestern Univ	TX	45,660	VC
Spelman College	GA	24,650	C
Spring Hill College	AL	44,164	VC
Springfield College	MA	25,000	C
St. Ambrose Univ	IA	30,845	C
St. Bonaventure Univ	NY	41,575	C
St. Catherine Univ	MN	37,782	C+
St. Cloud State Univ	MN	10,600	C
St. Edward's Univ	TX	47,784	C
St. Francis College	NY	34,200	C
St. John Fisher College	NY	40,708	C+
St. John's Univ	NY	55,070	C+
St. Joseph's College, New York/Brooklyn Campus	NY	22,630	C
St. Joseph's College, New York/Suffolk Campus	NY	22,630	C
St. Lawrence Univ	NY	59,972	VC
St. Mary's College of Maryland	MD	25,754	VC
St. Norbert College	WI	41,478	VC
St. Olaf College	MN	51,200	HC
St. Thomas Univ	FL	32,310	LC
Stanford Univ	CA	58,388	MC
SUNY at Purchase	NY	16,951	C

School	ST	$IS	SR
Stephen F. Austin State Univ	TX	14,668	C
Stetson Univ	FL	51,516	VC
Stonehill College	MA	46,780	HC
Stony Brook Univ / SUNY	NY	20,078	HC+
Suffolk Univ	MA	47,298	C
Sul Ross State Univ	TX	13,410	LC
SUNY College at Geneseo	NY	18,670	HC
SUNY College at Old Westbury	NY	16,324	C
SUNY Cortland/The SUNY	NY	19,759	C+
SUNY Fredonia/The SUNY at Fredonia	NY	19,840	VC
SUNY New Paltz	NY	14,348	C
SUNY Oneonta / SUNY	NY	16,919	C+
SUNY Plattsburgh / SUNY	NY	18,083	C
Susquehanna Univ	PA	51,150	C
Swarthmore College	PA	57,870	MC
Syracuse Univ	NY	56,346	VC
Tarleton State Univ	TX	13,489	LC
Taylor Univ	IN	37,821	VC+
Temple Univ	PA	24,392	VC
Tenn State Univ	TN	9,048	C
Tenn Tech Univ	TN	11,310	C
Texas A&M Univ	TX	19,207	VC
Texas A&M Univ at Commerce	TX	10,496	C
Texas A&M Univ at Corpus Christi	TX	11,544	LC
Texas A&M Univ at Kingsville	TX	7,500	LC
Texas Christian Univ	TX	49,980	HC
Texas Lutheran Univ	TX	36,040	C
Texas Southern Univ	TX	18,212	LC
Texas State Univ	TX	17,128	C
Texas Tech Univ	TX	14,243	C
Texas Wesleyan Univ	TX	31,382	C
Texas Woman's Univ	TX	13,633	LC
The Catholic Univ of America	DC	52,852	VC
The College of Idaho	ID	31,277	C+
The College of New Rochelle	NY	33,600	C
The College of St. Rose	NY	26,750	C
The Lincoln Univ	PA	15,154	LC
The Masters College	CA	38,160	C+
Ohio State Univ-Columbus Campus	OH	19,887	HC+
The Pennsylvania State Univ - Univ Park	PA	28,022	VC+
The SUNY at Potsdam	NY	18,473	C
The SUNY/College at Brockport	NY	19,002	C
The Univ of Memphis	TN	15,094	C
The Univ of N Car at Greensboro	NC	12,848	C
The Univ of N Car at Pembroke	NC	13,388	LC
The Univ of Okla	OK	18,621	VC
The Univ of Tenn at Chattanooga	TN	16,883	C
The Univ of Utah	UT	16,463	VC
The Univ of Virginia's College at Wise	VA	11,076	C
Thiel College	PA	38,728	LC
Thomas Edison State College	NJ	5,700	SP
Thomas More College	KY	34,760	C
Tougaloo College	MS	15,275	NC
Touro College	NY	27,959	VC
Towson Univ	MD	16,000	VC
Transylvania Univ	KY	42,660	VC+
Trevecca Nazarene Univ	TN	31,186	C
Trinity College	CT		HC+
Trinity Univ	TX	48,150	HC+
Trinity Washington Univ	DC	30,250	C+
Troy Univ	AL	10,650	C
Truman State Univ	MO	15,541	VC
Tufts Univ	MA	58,780	MC
Tulane Univ	LA	60,861	VC
Tusculum College	TN	24,295	C
Tuskegee Univ	AL	26,750	C
Union College	NY	60,240	MC
Union Univ	TN	28,260	VC
United States Air Force Academy	CO		MC
United States Coast Guard Academy	CT	942	HC
United States Military Academy	NY		MC
United States Naval Academy	MD		MC
Univ at Albany / SUNY	NY	18,674	VC
Univ at Buffalo / The SUNY	NY	20,283	VC
Univ of Akron	OH	20,436	C
Univ of Alabama at Birmingham	AL	18,484	C+
Univ of Alabama at Tuscaloosa	AL	17,164	C
Univ of Alabama in Huntsville	AL	17,591	VC+
Univ of Alaska Anchorage	AK	16,673	NC
Univ of Alaska Fairbanks	AK	15,130	C
Univ of Alaska Southeast	AK	11,493	C
Univ of Arizona	AZ	20,657	C
Univ of Arkansas at Fayetteville	AR	18,352	C
Univ of Arkansas at Little Rock	AR	17,609	LC
Univ of Arkansas at Monticello	AR	12,076	NC

School	ST	$IS	SR
Univ of Arkansas at Pine Bluff	AR	13,378	C
Univ of Calif at Berkeley	CA	23,322	MC
Univ of Calif at Davis	CA		HC
Univ of Calif at Irvine	CA	25,961	VC
Univ of Calif at Los Angeles	CA	25,686	MC
Univ of Calif at Riverside	CA	27,204	C+
Univ of Calif at San Diego	CA	21,000	VC
Univ of Calif at Santa Barbara	CA	27,551	HC
Univ of Calif at Santa Cruz	CA	27,807	C+
Univ of Central Arkansas	AR	13,667	VC
Univ of Central Florida	FL	15,668	VC+
Univ of Central Missouri	MO	14,605	C
Univ of Central Okla	OK	12,293	C
Univ of Charleston	WV	32,300	C
Univ of Chicago	IL	53,416	MC
Univ of Cincinnati	OH	21,506	VC
Univ of Colo at Colo Springs	CO	15,000	VC
Univ of Colo Boulder	CO	22,605	VC+
Univ of Colo Denver	CO	17,904	C
Univ of Conn	CT	24,706	C
Univ of Dallas	TX	45,500	VC
Univ of Dayton	OH	49,070	VC
Univ of Delaware	DE	23,612	VC
Univ of Denver	CO	51,787	VC+
Univ of Detroit Mercy	MI	30,450	VC
Univ of Evansville	IN	42,656	VC+
Univ of Findlay	OH	31,916	C
Univ of Florida	FL	15,943	HC
Univ of Georgia	GA	20,082	VC
Univ of Great Falls	MT	27,970	C
Univ of Hartford	CT	42,674	C
Univ of Hawaii at Hilo	HI	23,066	C
Univ of Hawaii at Manoa	HI	19,379	C
Univ of Houston-Downtown	TX	15,170	LC
Univ of Idaho	ID	14,558	C
Univ of Illinois at Chicago	IL	24,505	VC
Univ of Illinois at Urbana-Champaign	IL	26,450	HC
Univ of Indianapolis	IN	31,740	LC
Univ of Iowa	IA	17,693	VC
Univ of Kansas	KS	17,603	C+
Univ of Kentucky	KY	19,868	C
Univ of La Verne	CA	47,010	C
Univ of Louisiana at Lafayette	LA	6,130	C
Univ of Louisiana at Monroe	LA	12,998	C
Univ of Louisville	KY	17,946	C
Univ of Maine	ME	19,902	C+
Univ of Maine at Farmington	ME	18,187	LC
Univ of Mary Hardin-Baylor	TX	31,950	C+
Univ of Mary Washington	VA	19,484	VC
Univ of Maryland - College Park	MD	20,060	HC
Univ of Maryland/Baltimore County	MD	18,000	VC
Univ of Maryland/Univ College	MD	6,168	SP
Univ of Mass Amherst	MA	24,215	VC+
Univ of Mass Boston	MA	23,066	VC
Univ of Mass Dartmouth	MA	22,223	C
Univ of Mass Lowell	MA	19,316	C
Univ of Miami	FL	57,034	MC
Univ of Mich/Ann Arbor	MI	22,102	MC
Univ of Mich/Dearborn	MI	9,885	VC
Univ of Mich-Flint	MI	17,547	C+
Univ of Minn/Duluth	MN	19,806	C
Univ of Minn/Morris	MN	17,150	VC
Univ of Minn/Twin Cities	MN		HC
Univ of Miss	MS	16,704	C+
Univ of Missouri/Columbia	MO	18,201	MC
Univ of Missouri-Kansas City	MO	19,603	C
Univ of Missouri-St. Louis	MO		VC
Univ of Mobile	AL	28,935	VC
Univ of Montana	MT	14,105	C
Univ of Montana-Western	MT	9,753	LC
Univ of Montevallo	AL	17,060	C
Univ of Mount Union	OH	35,130	C
Univ of Nebr - Lincoln	NE	18,031	VC
Univ of Nebr at Kearney	NE	14,855	LC
Univ of Nebr at Omaha	NE	12,700	C
Univ of Nevada, Las Vegas	NV	17,303	C
Univ of Nevada/Reno	NV	17,507	C
Univ of New England	ME	46,750	C
Univ of New Hampshire	NH	26,912	C
Univ of New Haven	CT	48,940	C
Univ of New Mexico	NM	15,300	C
Univ of New Orleans	LA	9,224	C
Univ of North Alabama	AL	9,960	C
Univ of N Car at Asheville	NC	13,500	VC
Univ of N Car at Chapel Hill	NC	18,928	MC
Univ of N Car at Charlotte	NC	15,547	C
Univ of N Car at Wilmington	NC	13,572	VC
Univ of N Dak	ND	14,551	C
Univ of North Florida	FL	15,870	VC
Univ of North Georgia	GA	8,500	C
Univ of North Texas	TX	15,628	C
Univ of Northern Colo	CO	18,446	C
Univ of Northern Iowa	IA	15,795	C
Univ of Notre Dame	IN	57,117	MC
Univ of Oregon	OR	21,360	C+
Univ of Pennsylvania	PA	61,132	MC
Univ of Pikeville	KY	25,500	NC
Univ of Pittsburgh at Greensburg	PA	17,640	C
Univ of Pittsburgh at Johnstown	PA	20,862	LC
Univ of Pittsburgh at Pittsburgh	PA	28,572	HC+
Univ of Portland	OR	49,964	VC
Univ of PR Recinto de Rio Piedras	PR	5,750	
Univ of PR/Mayaguez	PR	1,250	
Univ of Puget Sound	WA	54,608	HC
Univ of Redlands	CA	40,500	VC
Univ of Rio Grande	OH	8,750	NC
Univ of Rochester	NY	60,668	MC
Univ of St. Mary	KS	28,400	C+
Univ of San Diego	CA	54,818	HC+
Univ of San Francisco	CA	54,770	VC
Univ of Science and Arts of Okla	OK	10,560	VC
Univ of Scranton	PA	51,940	VC
Univ of Sioux Falls	SD	22,990	C
Univ of South Alabama	AL	13,510	C
Univ of S Car Aiken	SC	16,712	C
Univ of S Car at Columbia	SC	19,725	VC+
Univ of S Car Upstate	SC	18,200	LC
Univ of S Dak	SD	15,111	C
Univ of South Florida/St. Petersburg	FL	12,769	C
Univ of South Florida/Tampa	FL	13,000	C
Univ of Southern Calif	CA	56,903	MC
Univ of Southern Indiana	IN	14,885	C
Univ of Southern Maine	ME	16,576	C
Univ of Southern Miss	MS	13,170	C
Univ of St. Francis	IL	37,560	C
Univ of St. Thomas - Houston	TX	37,690	C
Univ of Tampa	FL	35,160	VC
Univ of Tenn at Knoxville	TN	20,364	VC+
Univ of Tenn at Martin	TN	13,734	C
Univ of Texas - Pan American	TX	11,125	LC
Univ of Texas at Arlington	TX	10,908	LC
Univ of Texas at Austin	TX	44,074	HC
Univ of Texas at Dallas	TX	21,348	HC+
Univ of Texas at El Paso	TX	8,764	NC
Univ of Texas at San Antonio	TX	18,372	C
Univ of the Cumberlands	KY	27,500	C
Univ of the District of Columbia	DC	7,244	LC
Univ of the Incarnate Word	TX	37,316	LC
Univ of the Ozarks	AR	31,440	C
Univ of the Pacific	CA	52,146	VC
Univ of Toledo	OH	18,464	C
Univ of Tulsa	OK	46,331	MC
Univ of Vermont	VT	27,006	VC+
Univ of Virginia	VA	23,050	MC
Univ of Washington	WA	14,722	VC
Univ of West Florida	FL	14,656	C
Univ of West Georgia	GA	15,488	LC
Univ of Wisc Whitewater	WI	13,314	C
Univ of Wisc/Eau Claire	WI	15,730	VC
Univ of Wisc/Green Bay	WI	19,074	C
Univ of Wisc/La Crosse	WI	9,304	VC
Univ of Wisc/Madison	WI	18,757	HC+
Univ of Wisc/Oshkosh	WI	10,426	C
Univ of Wisc/Parkside	WI	10,181	C
Univ of Wisc/Platteville	WI	14,564	C
Univ of Wisc/River Falls	WI	9,722	LC
Univ of Wisc/Stevens Point	WI	14,043	C
Univ of Wisc/Superior	WI	14,314	C
Univ of Wisc-Milwaukee	WI	18,436	C
Univ of Wyoming	WY	14,401	C+
Ursinus College	PA	57,580	VC
Utah State Univ	UT	12,044	C
Utica College	NY	45,670	C
Valparaiso Univ	IN	44,940	VC+
Vanderbilt Univ	TN	58,220	MC
Vanguard Univ of Southern Calif	CA	35,833	VC
Vassar College	NY	61,140	MC
Villanova Univ	PA	58,394	MC
Virginia Commonwealth Univ	VA	21,716	C
Virginia Polytechnic Inst and State Univ	VA	14,629	HC
Virginia State Univ	VA	11,318	C+
Virginia Union Univ	VA	18,432	C
Virginia Wesleyan College	VA	28,433	LC
Wabash College	IN	46,850	C+
Wagner College	NY	48,600	C+
Wake Forest Univ	NC	58,838	MC
Walsh Univ	OH	35,100	C
Warren Wilson College	NC	40,132	VC
Wartburg College	IA	41,055	VC
Washburn Univ	KS	12,579	C
Washington Adventist Univ	MD	25,859	LC
Washington and Jefferson College	PA	51,948	VC
Washington and Lee Univ	VA	52,812	MC
Washington College	MD	52,602	VC
Washington State Univ	WA	20,461	C
Washington Univ in St. Louis	MO	69,844	MC
Wayland Baptist Univ	TX	18,912	LC
Wayne State College	NE	11,764	NC
Wayne State Univ	MI	22,063	C
Webster Univ	MO	35,100	C+
Wellesley College	MA	59,038	MC
Wells College	NY	49,400	VC
Wesley College	DE	31,115	LC
Wesleyan College	GA	24,000	C
Wesleyan Univ	CT	61,198	MC
West Chester Univ of Pennsylvania	PA	17,186	C
West Liberty Univ	WV	9,142	LC
West Texas A&M Univ	TX	13,478	C
West Virginia State Univ	WV	8,378	NC
West Virginia Univ	WV	16,542	C+
West Virginia Wesleyan College	WV	26,880	C
Western Carolina Univ	NC	13,965	C
Western Conn State Univ	CT	18,327	LC
Western Kentucky Univ	KY	11,000	LC
Western Mich Univ	MI	19,628	C
Western New England Univ	MA	46,154	C+
Western Oregon Univ	OR	15,021	C
Western State Colo Univ	CO	16,924	C
Western Washington Univ	WA	18,519	VC
Westfield State Univ	MA	18,297	C
Westminster College	MO	31,720	VC
Westminster College	PA	31,290	C+
Westminster College	UT	37,708	C+
Westmont College	CA	41,500	HC
Wheaton College	IL	40,720	MC
Wheaton College	MA	54,934	HC+
Wheeling Jesuit Univ	WV	33,500	C
Whitman College	WA	55,988	MC
Whittier College	CA	43,416	C
Whitworth Univ	WA	47,734	VC
Wichita State Univ	KS	14,607	C+
Widener Univ	PA	52,418	C
Wilberforce Univ	OH	15,100	LC
Wilkes Univ	PA	44,070	C
Willamette Univ	OR	56,450	VC+
William Jewell College	MO	31,000	VC+
William Paterson Univ of New Jersey	NJ	21,694	C
William Peace Univ	NC	32,900	LC
William Penn Univ	IA	26,000	C
William Woods Univ	MO	24,260	C
Williams College	MA	61,070	MC
Wilmington College	OH	29,784	C
Wilson College	PA	35,080	C
Wingate Univ	NC	34,990	C
Winona State Univ	MN	16,640	C
Winston-Salem State Univ	NC	9,418	LC
Winthrop Univ	SC	21,120	C
Wisc Lutheran College	WI	23,510	VC
Wittenberg Univ	OH	47,962	C+
Wofford College	SC	45,795	VC
Woodbury Univ	CA	34,500	LC
Wright State Univ	OH	16,983	C
Xavier Univ	OH	44,980	VC
Xavier Univ of Louisiana	LA	25,300	C
Yale Univ	CT	55,300	MC
Yeshiva Univ	NY	47,250	VC+
York College / The CUNY	NY	5,496	VC
York College of Pennsylvania	PA	26,590	C
Youngstown State Univ	OH	16,732	C

POLYMER SCIENCE

School	ST	$IS	SR
Case Western Reserve Univ	OH	56,534	MC
Eastern Mich Univ	MI	18,604	C
Millersville Univ of Pennsylvania	PA	21,648	C
Murray State Univ	KY	15,304	C
Pittsburg State Univ	KS	12,032	C
Rochester Inst of Technology	NY	42,450	VC
SUNY / College of Environmental Science and Forestry	NY	18,351	VC
Univ of Calif at Davis	CA		HC
Univ of Southern Miss	MS	13,170	C
Western Washington Univ	WA	18,519	VC

PORTUGUESE

School	ST	$IS	SR
Brigham Young Univ	UT	12,100	HC
Brown Univ	RI	59,428	MC
Dartmouth College	NH	57,996	MC
Florida International Univ	FL	17,747	C+
Georgetown Univ	DC	52,910	MC
Harvard College/Harvard Univ	MA	49,000	MC
Indiana Univ Bloomington	IN	19,801	VC
New York Univ	NY	61,470	MC
Princeton Univ	NJ	53,795	MC
Rhode Island College	RI	17,694	LC
Rutgers, The State Univ of New Jersey/New Brunswick	NJ	25,562	VC
Rutgers, The State Univ of New Jersey/Newark Campus	NJ	258,806	C
Ohio State Univ-Columbus Campus	OH	19,887	HC+
Tulane Univ	LA	60,861	MC
Univ of Calif at Los Angeles	CA	25,686	MC
Univ of Calif at Santa Barbara	CA	27,551	VC
Univ of Florida	FL	15,943	HC
Univ of Illinois at Urbana-Champaign	IL	26,450	HC
Univ of Iowa	IA	17,693	VC
Univ of Mass Amherst	MA	24,215	VC+
Univ of Mass Dartmouth	MA	22,223	C
Univ of New Mexico	NM	15,300	C
Univ of Texas at Austin	TX	44,074	HC
Univ of Wisc/Madison	WI	18,757	HC+
Yale Univ	CT	55,300	MC

POULTRY SCIENCE

School	ST	$IS	SR
Auburn Univ	AL	22,378	VC+
Miss State Univ	MS	14,750	C
N Car State Univ	NC	16,202	HC
Stephen F. Austin State Univ	TX	14,668	C
Texas A&M Univ	TX	19,207	HC
Univ of Arkansas at Fayetteville	AR	18,352	C+
Univ of Georgia	GA	20,082	VC
Univ of Maryland/Eastern Shore	MD	14,000	VC
Univ of Wisc/Madison	WI	18,757	HC+
Virginia Polytechnic Inst and State Univ	VA	14,629	VC

PREALLIED HEALTH

School	ST	$IS	SR
Biola Univ	CA	40,320	C+
Ithaca College	NY	53,864	HC
La Salle Univ	PA	50,270	C
Mount Aloysius College	PA	29,976	C
Sacred Heart Univ	CT	49,264	VC
St. Michael's College	VT	49,975	VC
Xavier Univ	OH	44,980	VC

PRECISION PRODUCTION

School	ST	$IS	SR
Calif College of the Arts	CA	48,334	SP

PREDENTISTRY

School	ST	$IS	SR
Albertus Magnus College	CT	37,382	LC
Albion College	MI	46,010	C
American International College	MA	36,100	LC
Aquinas College	MI	33,060	C
Arcadia Univ	PA	33,570	C+
Ashland Univ	OH	25,000	C
Auburn Univ	AL	22,378	VC+
Baldwin Wallace Univ	OH	38,318	C
Ball State Univ	IN	17,850	C
Barry Univ	FL	38,190	C
Baylor Univ	TX	50,329	HC
Bellarmine Univ	KY	42,950	VC
Bemidji State Univ	MN	13,500	VC
Bethel College	IN	31,560	C
Biola Univ	CA	40,320	C
Boise State Univ	ID	13,469	LC
Brigham Young Univ/Hawaii	HI	10,686	VC
Calif Lutheran Univ	CA	49,540	C+
Calvin College	MI	39,120	VC
Campbell Univ	NC	37,570	VC
Campbellsville Univ	KY	27,720	C
Canisius College	NY	44,900	C
Capital Univ	OH	41,050	VC
Cardinal Stritch Univ	WI	24,054	C
Carroll College	MT	28,000	C
Chadron State College	NE	7,400	NC
Chicago State Univ	IL	5,482	C
Christopher Newport Univ	VA	21,960	VC
CUNY/City College	NY	20,319	HC+
Clark Univ	MA	47,020	HC+
Clemson Univ	SC	19,136	HC
Coe College	IA	45,550	VC
College of St. Benedict	MN	49,359	VC
Colo State Univ-Pueblo	CO	16,183	C
Concord Univ	WV	13,102	C
Concordia Univ Nebr	NE	26,000	VC
Concordia Univ, Ann Arbor	MI	27,220	VC
Converse College	SC	37,130	C
Corban Univ	OR	37,380	C
Cornerstone Univ and Grand Rapids Theological Seminary	MI	33,338	C
Davis & Elkins College	WV	33,742	C
Dominican Univ	IL	37,628	C
Dordt College	IA	34,160	C+
Drury Univ	MO	31,909	VC
Eastern Washington Univ	WA		C
Eckerd College	FL	43,902	C
Elizabethtown College	PA	49,740	VC
Elmira College	NY	49,950	C+
Elms College	MA	23,900	VC
Faulkner Univ	AL	25,720	LC
Florida A&M Univ	FL	14,935	LC
Florida Southern College	FL	40,150	C+
Florida State Univ	FL	16,715	VC
Fontbonne Univ	MO	31,384	C
Freed-Hardeman Univ	TN	19,697	VC
Gannon Univ	PA	39,608	C
George Fox Univ	OR	40,750	C+
Georgetown College	KY	41,440	VC
Gettysburg College	PA	58,820	HC
Goshen College	IN	35,900	VC
Grace College and Seminary	IN	28,800	VC
Graceland Univ	IA	28,020	C
Grand Valley State Univ	MI	17,998	C+
Gustavus Adolphus College	MN	48,170	HC
Hardin-Simmons Univ	TX	23,560	C+

ST = STATE $IS = IN-STATE COSTS   SR = SELECTOR RATING

School	ST	$IS	SR
Heidelberg Univ	OH	34,100	C
Hofstra Univ	NY	51,810	VC+
Houghton College	NY	36,808	C+
Howard Univ	DC	13,646	C
Humboldt State Univ	CA	18,400	C
Hunter College	NY	14,429	C
Indiana Univ-Purdue Univ Fort Wayne	IN	15,521	C
Iowa Wesleyan College	IA	30,850	LC
Ithaca College	NY	53,864	HC
Johnson C. Smith Univ	NC	25,336	LC
Judson Univ	IL	25,130	C
Kent State Univ	OH	19,920	C
Kentucky Wesleyan College	KY	27,440	C
Keuka College	NY	30,300	C
King's College	PA	43,502	C
Kutztown Univ of Pennsylvania	PA	16,909	LC
La Salle Univ	PA	50,270	C
Lake Superior State Univ	MI	18,121	C
Lamar Univ	TX	6,820	LC
Le Moyne College	NY	43,470	C
Lehigh Univ	PA	56,770	MC
Lehman College/The CUNY	NY	5,778	LC
Lenoir-Rhyne College	NC	35,984	C
Lewis Univ	IL	23,050	C
Lincoln Memorial Univ	TN	18,144	C
Lipscomb Univ	TN	37,490	VC
Louisiana College	LA	15,746	C
Loyola Univ New Orleans	LA	46,581	VC
MacMurray College	IL	20,755	C
Manhattan College	NY	49,588	C+
Mars Hill Univ	NC	22,950	LC
Marshall Univ	WV	14,820	C
Maryville College	TN	33,150	C+
Mercer Univ	GA	44,201	C
Mercyhurst Univ	PA	40,700	C
Merrimack College	MA	44,215	C
Methodist Univ	NC	37,185	C
Mich Tech Univ	MI	23,556	HC
Midland Univ	NE	34,000	C
Midwestern State Univ	TX	9,722	C
Millikin Univ	IL	38,940	C
Minn State Univ, Mankato	MN	15,616	C
Minn State Univ, Moorhead	MN	13,392	VC
Missouri Southern State Univ	MO	12,061	C
Montclair State Univ	NJ	22,614	C
Mount Aloysius College	PA	29,976	C
Mount Mary Univ	WI	33,590	LC
Murray State Univ	KY	15,304	C
New York Univ	NY	61,470	MC
N Car State Univ	NC	16,202	HC
North Central College	IL	38,343	VC
North Park Univ	IL	30,130	C
Northern Kentucky Univ	KY	21,134	C
Northern Mich Univ	MI	18,278	C
Northern State Univ - Aberdeen	SD	14,505	C
Northwest Missouri State Univ	MO	17,347	C
Notre Dame of Maryland Univ	MD	27,700	VC
Ohio Univ	OH	21,080	C
Ohio Wesleyan Univ	OH	49,460	C+
Okla Baptist Univ	OK	28,202	C
Okla Wesleyan Univ	OK	21,300	C
Olivet College	MI	19,984	LC
Oral Roberts Univ	OK	31,734	C
Oregon State Univ	OR	20,273	VC
Oswego / SUNY	NY	20,009	VC
Ouachita Baptist Univ	AR	30,220	VC
Pittsburg State Univ	KS	12,032	C
Quinnipiac Univ	CT	55,160	VC
Rhode Island College	RI	17,694	LC
Rivier Univ	NH	35,000	VC
Roberts Wesleyan College	NY	38,306	C+
Rochester Inst of Technology	NY	42,450	VC
Roosevelt Univ	IL	22,605	VC
Rosemont College	PA	42,350	C
Sacred Heart Univ	CT	49,264	VC
Saginaw Valley State Univ	MI	17,369	C
St. Anselm College	NH	49,376	VC
St. John's Univ	MN	47,984	C
St. Joseph's College	IN	36,500	C
St. Mary-of-the-Woods College	IN	37,722	LC
St. Mary's Univ	TX	33,854	C
St. Peter's Univ	NJ	44,240	C
St. Vincent College	PA	40,244	C
St. Xavier Univ	IL	32,840	C
Seton Hill Univ	PA	35,172	C
Simpson College	IA	36,086	C+
Spring Hill College	AL	44,164	VC
Springfield College	MA	25,000	C
St. Cloud State Univ	MN	10,600	C
St. Edward's Univ	TX	47,784	C
St. Thomas Univ	FL	32,310	LC
SUNY / College of Environmental Science and Forestry	NY	18,351	VC
SUNY Fredonia/The SUNY at Fredonia	NY	19,840	VC
SUNY Oneonta / SUNY	NY	16,919	C+
Tarleton State Univ	TX	13,489	LC
Temple Univ	PA	24,392	VC
Texas A&M Univ at Commerce	TX	10,496	C
Texas A&M Univ at Kingsville	TX	7,500	LC
The Catholic Univ of America	DC	52,852	VC
Thiel College	PA	38,728	LC
Touro College	NY	27,959	VC
Trinity Christian College	IL	28,869	C
Truman State Univ	MO	15,541	HC
Union Univ	TN	28,260	VC
Univ at Albany / SUNY	NY	18,674	VC
Univ of Arkansas at Pine Bluff	AR	13,378	C
Univ of Bridgeport	CT	39,030	LC
Univ of Central Arkansas	AR	13,667	VC
Univ of Central Missouri	MO	14,605	C
Univ of Central Okla	OK	12,293	C
Univ of Cincinnati	OH	21,506	VC
Univ of Dayton	OH	49,070	VC
Univ of Detroit Mercy	MI	30,450	VC
Univ of Evansville	IN	42,656	VC+
Univ of Great Falls	MT	27,970	C
Univ of Hartford	CT	42,674	C
Univ of Illinois at Chicago	IL	24,505	VC
Univ of Iowa	IA	17,693	VC
Univ of Maryland - College Park	MD	20,060	HC
Univ of Mass Amherst	MA	24,215	VC+
Univ of Miami	FL	57,034	MC
Univ of Minn/Twin Cities	MN		HC
Univ of Nebr - Lincoln	NE	18,031	VC
Univ of Nebr at Kearney	NE	14,855	LC
Univ of New Haven	CT	48,940	C
Univ of N Car at Wilmington	NC	13,572	VC
Univ of North Georgia	GA	8,500	C
Univ of Notre Dame	IN	57,117	MC
Univ of Rio Grande	OH	8,750	NC
Univ of St. Francis	IN	29,810	C
Univ of Southern Miss	MS	13,170	C
Univ of St. Francis	IL	37,560	C
Univ of Tenn at Knoxville	TN	20,364	VC+
Univ of the Cumberlands	KY	27,500	C
Univ of West Alabama	AL	14,274	C
Univ of West Florida	FL	14,656	VC
Univ of Wisc/Eau Claire	WI	15,730	VC
Utah State Univ	UT	12,044	C
Virginia Polytechnic Inst and State Univ	VA	14,629	HC
Walsh Univ	OH	35,100	C
Washington Adventist Univ	MD	25,859	LC
Washington State Univ	WA	20,461	C
Washington Univ in St. Louis	MO	69,844	MC
Waynesburg Univ	PA	30,150	C
West Chester Univ of Pennsylvania	PA	17,186	C
West Liberty Univ	WV	9,142	LC
West Texas A&M Univ	TX	13,478	C
Western Carolina Univ	NC	13,965	C
Western New Mexico Univ	NM	8,500	LC
Western State Colo Univ	CO	16,924	C
Westminster College	PA	31,290	C+
Whitworth Univ	WA	47,734	VC
Wilson College	PA	35,080	C
Wingate Univ	NC	34,990	C
Winona State Univ	MN	16,640	C
Wright State Univ	OH	16,983	C
Youngstown State Univ	OH	16,732	C

PREENGINEERING

School	ST	$IS	SR
Adams State Univ	CO	13,358	LC
Alice Lloyd College	KY	4,900	LC
Aquinas College	MI	33,060	C
Asbury Univ	KY	32,038	VC
Augustana College	IL	43,398	VC
Baldwin Wallace Univ	OH	38,318	C
Ball State Univ	IN	17,850	C
Bard College at Simon's Rock	MA	61,749	HC+
Barry Univ	FL	38,190	C
Bellarmine Univ	KY	42,950	VC
Beloit College	WI	49,970	HC
Bethany College	WV	35,282	LC
Bethel College	IN	31,560	C
Campbellsville Univ	KY	27,720	C
Canisius College	NY	44,900	C
Coe College	IA	45,550	VC
College of St. Benedict	MN	49,359	VC
College of the Ozarks	MO		VC
Colo State Univ-Pueblo	CO	16,183	C
Concordia Univ, Ann Arbor	MI	27,220	VC
DePauw Univ	IN	48,950	VC+
Edgewood College	WI	33,294	C
Elizabethtown College	PA	49,740	VC
Elmhurst College	IL	43,336	C
Embry-Riddle Aeronautical Univ - Worldwide	FL	15,512	C
Ferris State Univ	MI	20,047	C
Freed-Hardeman Univ	TN	19,697	VC
Furman Univ	SC	54,006	HC
Georgetown College	KY	41,440	C+
Goshen College	IN	35,900	VC
Harvard College/Harvard Univ	MA	49,000	MC
Heidelberg Univ	OH	34,100	C
Houghton College	NY	36,808	C+
Hunter College	NY	14,429	VC
Iowa Wesleyan College	IA	30,850	LC
Johnson C. Smith Univ	NC	25,336	LC
Judson Univ	IL	25,130	C
Kentucky Wesleyan College	KY	27,440	C
Kutztown Univ of Pennsylvania	PA	16,909	LC
Le Moyne College	NY	43,470	C
Lenoir-Rhyne College	NC	35,984	C
Lewis Univ	IL	23,050	C
Lipscomb Univ	TN	37,490	VC
Loyola Univ New Orleans	LA	46,581	VC
MacMurray College	IL	20,755	C
Mansfield Univ	PA	19,468	LC
Marshall Univ	WV	14,820	C
Maryville College	TN	33,150	C+
Midwestern State Univ	TX	9,722	C
Millikin Univ	IL	38,940	C
Minn State Univ, Mankato	MN	15,616	C
Mount Vernon Nazarene Univ	OH	29,590	C
North Central College	IL	38,343	VC
Northwest Missouri State Univ	MO	17,347	C
Notre Dame of Maryland Univ	MD	27,700	VC
Oral Roberts Univ	OK	31,734	C
Oswego / SUNY	NY	20,009	VC
Peru State College	NE	8,600	NC
Pfeiffer Univ	NC	33,700	LC
Pittsburg State Univ	KS	12,032	C
Providence College	RI	57,383	VC
Regis Univ	CO	41,318	C
Richard Stockton College of New Jersey	NJ	20,000	VC
Roberts Wesleyan College	NY	38,306	C+
Saginaw Valley State Univ	MI	17,369	C
St. John's Univ	MN	47,984	C
St. Mary's College of Calif	CA	53,550	C
St. Michael's College	VT	49,975	VC
Scripps College	CA	61,940	MC
Shaw Univ	NC	15,488	C
Simpson College	IA	36,086	C+
Southern Oregon Univ	OR	17,874	C
St. Edward's Univ	TX	47,784	C
Texas A&M Univ at Commerce	TX	10,496	C
The College of Idaho	ID	31,277	C+
Thiel College	PA	38,728	LC
Truman State Univ	MO	15,541	HC
Union Univ	TN	28,260	VC
Univ of Arkansas at Pine Bluff	AR	13,378	C
Univ of Central Arkansas	AR	13,667	VC
Univ of N Car at Wilmington	NC	13,572	VC
Univ of North Georgia	GA	8,500	C
Univ of Rio Grande	OH	8,750	NC
Univ of the Cumberlands	KY	27,500	C
Wayland Baptist Univ	TX	18,912	LC
West Liberty Univ	WV	9,142	LC
West Texas A&M Univ	TX	13,478	C
Western Carolina Univ	NC	13,965	C
Western New England Univ	MA	46,154	C+
Western State Colo Univ	CO	16,924	C
Widener Univ	PA	52,418	C
Wilberforce Univ	OH	15,100	LC
Wingate Univ	NC	34,990	C
Winona State Univ	MN	16,640	C
Yeshiva Univ	NY	47,250	VC+

PRE-HEALTH STUDIES

School	ST	$IS	SR
Aquinas College	MI	33,060	C
Asbury Univ	KY	32,038	VC
Bethel College	IN	31,560	C
Binghamton Univ/The SUNY	NY	21,648	HC+
Biola Univ	CA	40,320	C+
Bloomfield College	NJ	37,850	LC
Cornerstone Univ and Grand Rapids Theological Seminary	MI	33,338	C
Elmhurst College	IL	43,336	C
Ferris State Univ	MI	20,047	C
Hofstra Univ	NY	51,810	VC+
Ithaca College	NY	53,864	HC
Marshall Univ	WV	14,820	C
Mass College of Liberal Arts	MA	18,613	C
Messiah College	PA	40,690	C+
Murray State Univ	KY	15,304	C
New York Univ	NY	61,470	MC
Okla City Univ	OK	40,476	VC
Oswego / SUNY	NY	20,009	VC
Point Park Univ	PA	36,390	C
Siena Heights Univ	MI	32,040	C
Texas Christian Univ	TX	49,980	VC
Univ of Arizona	AZ	20,657	C
Univ of Illinois at Chicago	IL	24,505	VC
Univ of Miami	FL	57,034	MC
Valparaiso Univ	IN	44,940	VC+
Wilson College	PA	35,080	C

PRELAW

School	ST	$IS	SR
Adams State Univ	CO	13,358	LC
Albertus Magnus College	CT	37,382	LC
American International College	MA	36,100	LC
Aquinas College	MI	33,060	C
Arcadia Univ	PA	33,570	C+
Ashland Univ	OH	25,000	C
Averett Univ	VA	37,750	C
Ball State Univ	IN	17,850	C
Barry Univ	FL	38,190	C
Beloit College	WI	49,970	HC
Bemidji State Univ	MN	13,500	VC
Bennington College	VT	56,990	HC+
Bethel College	IN	31,560	C
Biola Univ	CA	40,320	C+
Blackburn College	IL	21,350	C
Bryant Univ	RI	49,179	VC
Calif Lutheran Univ	CA	49,540	C+
Calvin College	MI	39,120	VC
Campbell Univ	NC	37,570	VC
Campbellsville Univ	KY	27,720	C
Canisius College	NY	44,900	C
Capital Univ	OH	41,050	VC
Cardinal Stritch Univ	WI	24,054	C
Carroll College	MT	28,000	C
Catawba College	NC	37,240	LC
Cedarville Univ	OH	32,860	VC
Central Washington Univ	WA	11,730	C
Chadron State College	NE	7,400	NC
Chicago State Univ	IL	5,482	C
Christopher Newport Univ	VA	21,960	VC
CUNY/City College	NY	20,319	HC+
Clark Univ	MA	47,020	HC+
Clearwater Christian College	FL	23,720	C
Clemson Univ	SC	19,136	HC
Coe College	IA	45,550	VC
College of St. Benedict	MN	49,359	VC
College of the Ozarks	MO		VC
Colo State Univ-Pueblo	CO	16,183	C
Concord Univ	WV	13,102	C
Concordia Univ Nebr	NE	26,000	VC
Concordia Univ, River Forest	IL	26,300	C
Converse College	SC	37,130	C
Corban Univ	OR	37,380	C+
Davis & Elkins College	WV	33,742	C
Dominican Univ	IL	37,628	C
Dordt College	IA	34,160	C+
Drury Univ	MO	31,909	VC
East Central Univ	OK	10,223	LC
Eastern Washington Univ	WA		C
Eckerd College	FL	43,902	C
Edgewood College	WI	33,294	C
Edinboro Univ of Pennsylvania	PA	15,940	LC
Elmira College	NY	49,950	C+
Elms College	MA	23,900	VC
Faulkner Univ	AL	25,720	C
Fitchburg State Univ	MA	18,173	C
Florida Inst of Technology	FL	48,290	VC
Florida State Univ	FL	16,715	VC
Fontbonne Univ	MO	31,384	C
Fresno Pacific Univ	CA	32,136	C
George Fox Univ	OR	40,750	C+
Georgetown College	KY	41,440	C+
Gettysburg College	PA	58,820	HC
Grace College and Seminary	IN	28,800	VC
Grand Valley State Univ	MI	17,998	C+
Gustavus Adolphus College	MN	48,170	HC
Hamline Univ	MN	45,678	VC
Hardin-Simmons Univ	TX	23,560	C+
Heidelberg Univ	OH	34,100	C
Houghton College	NY	36,808	C+
Humboldt State Univ	CA	18,400	C
Hunter College	NY	14,429	C
Huntington Univ	IN	32,220	C+
Illinois College	IL	25,770	VC
Immaculata Univ	PA	43,000	C
Indiana Inst of Technology	IN	34,240	LC
Indiana Univ-Purdue Univ Fort Wayne	IN	15,521	C
Indiana Univ-Purdue Univ Indianapolis	IN	17,611	C
Indiana Wesleyan Univ	IN	31,815	VC
Iowa Wesleyan College	IA	30,850	LC
Ithaca College	NY	53,864	HC
Johnson C. Smith Univ	NC	25,336	LC
Johnson State College	VT	16,721	C
Judson Univ	IL	25,130	C
Kansas Wesleyan Univ	KS	32,000	C
Kentucky Wesleyan College	KY	27,440	C
Keuka College	NY	30,300	C
King's College	PA	43,502	C
La Salle Univ	PA	50,270	C
Lafayette College	PA	59,155	HC+
Lake Superior State Univ	MI	18,121	C
Lamar Univ	TX	6,820	LC
Le Moyne College	NY	43,470	C
Lehman College/The CUNY	NY	5,778	LC
Lenoir-Rhyne College	NC	35,984	C
LeTourneau Univ	TX	36,210	VC
Lewis Univ	IL	23,050	C
Limestone College	SC	30,800	C
Lincoln Memorial Univ	TN	18,144	C
Lindenwood Univ	MO	20,750	C
Lipscomb Univ	TN	37,490	VC
Louisiana College	LA	15,746	C
Lubbock Christian Univ	TX	26,308	C
MacMurray College	IL	20,755	C

ST = STATE $IS = IN-STATE COSTS   SR = SELECTOR RATING

School	ST	$IS	SR
Manchester Univ	IN	35,070	C
Manhattan College	NY	49,588	C+
Mansfield Univ	PA	19,468	LC
Marlboro College	VT	35,980	VC
Mars Hill Univ	NC	22,950	LC
Marshall Univ	WV	14,820	C
Maryville College	TN	33,150	C+
Marywood Univ	PA	45,595	C
Mayville State Univ	ND	11,401	NC
Mercer Univ	GA	44,201	VC
Mercyhurst Univ	PA	40,700	C
Merrimack College	MA	44,215	C
Methodist Univ	NC	37,185	C
Metropolitan College of New York	NY	16,720	VC
Mich State Univ	MI	22,450	C
Middle Tenn State Univ	TN	8,650	C
Midland Univ	NE	34,000	C
Midwestern State Univ	TX	9,722	C
Millikin Univ	IL	38,940	C
Mills College	CA	54,119	VC
Minn State Univ, Mankato	MN	15,616	C
Minn State Univ, Moorhead	MN	13,392	VC
Missouri Univ of Science and Technology	MO	18,655	VC+
Monmouth Univ	NJ	44,108	C
Mount Aloysius College	PA	29,976	C
Mount Mary Univ	WI	33,590	LC
Mount Vernon Nazarene Univ	OH	29,590	C
National Univ	CA	14,730	SP
N Car State Univ	NC	16,202	HC
North Central College	IL	38,343	VC
North Park Univ	IL	30,130	C
Northern Kentucky Univ	KY	21,134	C
Northern Mich Univ	MI	18,278	C
Northern State Univ - Aberdeen	SD	14,505	C
Northwest Missouri State Univ	MO	17,347	C
Northwestern College of Iowa	IA	36,240	VC
Notre Dame of Maryland Univ	MD	27,700	C
Oakland City Univ	IN	24,500	NC
Oberlin College	OH	61,788	MC
Ohio Univ	OH	21,080	C
Ohio Wesleyan Univ	OH	49,460	C+
Okla Baptist Univ	OK	28,202	C
Okla Christian Univ	OK	25,870	VC
Okla City Univ	OK	40,476	VC
Okla Wesleyan Univ	OK	21,300	C
Olivet College	MI	19,984	LC
Oral Roberts Univ	OK	31,734	C
Oswego / SUNY	NY	20,009	VC
Ouachita Baptist Univ	AR	30,220	VC
Palm Beach Atlantic Univ	FL	34,874	C+
Peru State College	NE	8,600	NC
Pittsburg State Univ	KS	12,032	C
Quinnipiac Univ	CT	55,160	VC
Regis Univ	CO	41,318	C
Rensselaer Polytechnic Inst	NY	61,529	MC
Rhode Island College	RI	17,694	LC
Rider Univ	NJ	45,720	C
Rivier Univ	NH	35,000	VC
Roberts Wesleyan College	NY	38,306	C+
Rochester Inst of Technology	NY	42,450	VC
Roosevelt Univ	IL	22,605	VC
Rosemont College	PA	42,350	C
Sacred Heart Univ	CT	49,264	VC
Saginaw Valley State Univ	MI	17,369	C
St. Anselm College	NH	49,376	VC
St. Augustine's Univ	NC	14,000	C
St. John's Univ	MN	47,984	C
St. Joseph's College	IN	36,500	C
St. Mary-of-the-Woods College	IN	37,722	LC
St. Mary's Univ	TX	33,854	C
St. Michael's College	VT	49,975	VC
St. Peter's Univ	NJ	44,240	C
St. Vincent College	PA	40,244	C
St. Xavier Univ	IL	32,840	C
Schreiner Univ	TX	32,734	LC
Scripps College	CA	61,940	MC
Seattle Pacific Univ	WA	41,559	VC
Seton Hill Univ	PA	35,172	C
Shawnee State Univ	OH	16,916	C
Simpson College	IA	36,086	C+
Southern Oregon Univ	OR	17,874	C
Springfield College	MA	25,000	C
St. Cloud State Univ	MN	10,600	C
St. Edward's Univ	TX	47,784	C
St. John's Univ	NY	55,070	C+
St. Thomas Aquinas College	NY	40,230	C
St. Thomas Univ	FL	32,310	LC
SUNY / College of Environmental Science and Forestry	NY	18,351	VC
Stetson Univ	FL	51,516	VC
Stillman College	AL	19,470	C
SUNY Fredonia/The SUNY at Fredonia	NY	19,840	VC
SUNY Oneonta / SUNY	NY	16,919	C+
Tarleton State Univ	TX	13,489	LC
Temple Univ	PA	24,392	VC
Texas A&M Univ at Commerce	TX	10,496	C
Texas A&M Univ at Kingsville	TX	7,500	LC
Texas Wesleyan Univ	TX	31,382	C
The Catholic Univ of America	DC	52,852	VC
Thiel College	PA	38,728	LC
Touro College	NY	27,959	VC
Trinity Christian College	IL	28,869	C
Truman State Univ	MO	15,541	HC
Union Univ	TN	28,260	VC
Univ at Albany / SUNY	NY	18,674	VC
Univ of Bridgeport	CT	39,030	LC
Univ of Central Missouri	MO	14,605	C
Univ of Cincinnati	OH	21,506	VC
Univ of Detroit Mercy	MI	30,450	VC
Univ of Evansville	IN	42,656	VC+
Univ of Findlay	OH	31,916	C
Univ of Great Falls	MT	27,970	C
Univ of Illinois at Urbana-Champaign	IL	26,450	HC
Univ of Iowa	IA	17,693	VC
Univ of Mary	ND	16,714	C
Univ of Maryland - College Park	MD	20,060	HC
Univ of Miami	FL	57,034	MC
Univ of Minn/Duluth	MN	19,806	C
Univ of Minn/Morris	MN	17,150	VC
Univ of Minn/Twin Cities	MN		HC
Univ of Montana-Western	MT	9,753	LC
Univ of Nebr - Lincoln	NE	18,031	VC
Univ of Nebr at Kearney	NE	14,855	LC
Univ of N Car at Wilmington	NC	13,572	VC
Univ of North Georgia	GA	8,500	C
Univ of Pittsburgh at Pittsburgh	PA	28,572	HC+
Univ of Rio Grande	OH	8,750	NC
Univ of Sioux Falls	SD	22,990	C
Univ of Southern Miss	MS	13,170	C
Univ of the Cumberlands	KY	27,500	C
Univ of the Incarnate Word	TX	37,316	LC
Univ of Tulsa	OK	46,331	MC
Univ of West Alabama	AL	14,274	C
Univ of West Florida	FL	14,656	C
Univ of Wisc Whitewater	WI	13,314	C
Univ of Wisc/Eau Claire	WI	15,730	VC
Univ of Wisc/River Falls	WI	9,722	LC
Urbana Univ	OH	30,820	C
Ursuline College	OH	33,198	LC
Utah State Univ	UT	12,044	C
Valparaiso Univ	IN	44,940	VC+
Vassar College	NY	61,140	MC
Virginia Polytechnic Inst and State Univ	VA	14,629	HC
Walsh Univ	OH	35,100	C
Washington Adventist Univ	MD	25,859	LC
Washington State Univ	WA	20,461	C
Wayland Baptist Univ	TX	18,912	LC
Waynesburg Univ	PA	30,150	C
Webber International Univ	FL	30,147	C
West Chester Univ of Pennsylvania	PA	17,186	C
West Liberty Univ	WV	9,142	LC
West Texas A&M Univ	TX	13,478	C
Western Carolina Univ	NC	13,965	C
Western State Colo Univ	CO	16,924	C
Westminster College	PA	31,290	C+
Westminster College	UT	37,708	C+
Whitworth Univ	WA	47,734	VC
Wilberforce Univ	OH	15,100	LC
William Peace Univ	NC	32,900	LC
Wilmington College	OH	29,784	C
Wilson College	PA	35,080	C
Wingate Univ	NC	34,990	C
Winona State Univ	MN	16,640	C
Wright State Univ	OH	16,983	C
Youngstown State Univ	OH	16,732	C

PREMEDICINE

School	ST	$IS	SR
Adams State Univ	CO	13,358	LC
Albertus Magnus College	CT	37,382	LC
Albion College	MI	46,010	C
American International College	MA	36,100	LC
American Jewish Univ - College of A&S	CA	32,600	C
Aquinas College	MI	33,060	C
Arcadia Univ	PA	33,570	C+
Ashland Univ	OH	25,000	C
Auburn Univ	AL	22,378	VC+
Augustana College	IL	43,398	VC
Avila Univ	MO	26,900	C
Baldwin Wallace Univ	OH	38,318	C
Ball State Univ	IN	17,850	C
Bard College at Simon's Rock	MA	61,749	HC+
Barry Univ	FL	38,190	C
Baylor Univ	TX	50,329	HC
Bellarmine Univ	KY	42,950	VC
Beloit College	WI	49,970	HC
Bemidji State Univ	MN	13,500	C
Bennington College	VT	56,990	HC+
Bethel College	IN	31,560	C
Bethel Univ	TN	19,186	C
Biola Univ	CA	40,320	C+
Blackburn College	IL	21,350	C
Bloomfield College	NJ	37,850	LC
Bluffton Univ	OH	38,948	C
Boise State Univ	ID	13,469	LC
Brigham Young Univ/Hawaii	HI	10,686	VC
Cabrini College	PA	40,859	LC
Calif Lutheran Univ	CA	49,540	C+
Cal State, San Bernardino	CA	12,000	C
Calvin College	MI	39,120	VC
Campbell Univ	NC	37,570	VC
Campbellsville Univ	KY	27,720	C
Canisius College	NY	44,900	C
Capital Univ	OH	41,050	VC
Cardinal Stritch Univ	WI	24,054	C
Carroll College	MT	28,000	C
Central Univ of Bayamon	PR	3,350	
Chadron State College	NE	7,400	NC
Chicago State Univ	IL	5,482	C
Christopher Newport Univ	VA	21,960	VC
CUNY/City College	NY	20,319	HC+
Clark Univ	MA	47,020	HC+
Clearwater Christian College	FL	23,720	C
Clemson Univ	SC	19,136	VC
Cleveland State Univ	OH	21,776	C
Coe College	IA	45,550	VC
Coker College	SC	32,256	LC
College of St. Benedict	MN	49,359	VC
College of the Ozarks	MO		VC
Colo State Univ-Pueblo	CO	16,183	C
Concord Univ	WV	13,102	C
Concordia Univ	OR	35,000	C
Concordia Univ Nebr	NE	26,000	VC
Concordia Univ, Ann Arbor	MI	27,220	VC
Concordia Univ, River Forest	IL	26,300	C
Converse College	SC	37,130	C
Corban Univ	OR	37,380	C+
Cornerstone Univ and Grand Rapids Theological Seminary	MI	33,338	C
Dakota State Univ	SD	13,811	C
Davis & Elkins College	WV	33,742	C
Dominican Univ	IL	37,628	C
Dominican Univ of Calif	CA	51,250	C
Dordt College	IA	34,160	C+
Drexel Univ	PA	61,418	VC+
Drury Univ	MO	31,909	VC
Earlham College	IN	51,470	HC
East Stroudsburg Univ of Pennsylvania	PA	18,868	LC
Eastern Washington Univ	WA		C
Eckerd College	FL	43,902	C
Edinboro Univ of Pennsylvania	PA	15,940	LC
Elizabethtown College	PA	49,740	VC
Elmhurst College	IL	43,336	C
Elmira College	NY	49,950	C+
Elms College	MA	23,900	VC
Faulkner Univ	AL	25,720	LC
Florida A&M Univ	FL	14,935	LC
Florida Inst of Technology	FL	48,290	VC
Florida Southern College	FL	40,150	C+
Florida State Univ	FL	16,715	VC
Fontbonne Univ	MO	31,384	C
Freed-Hardeman Univ	TN	19,697	VC
Fresno Pacific Univ	CA	32,136	C
Friends Univ	KS	29,100	C
Gannon Univ	PA	39,608	C
George Fox Univ	OR	40,750	C+
George Washington Univ	DC	57,108	MC
Georgetown College	KY	41,440	C+
Gettysburg College	PA	58,820	HC
Goshen College	IN	35,900	VC
Grace College and Seminary	IN	28,800	VC
Graceland Univ	IA	28,020	C
Grand Valley State Univ	MI	17,998	C+
Gustavus Adolphus College	MN	48,170	HC
Hamline Univ	MN	45,678	VC
Hampshire College	MA	58,320	MC
Hardin-Simmons Univ	TX	23,560	C+
Hawaii Pacific Univ	HI	34,360	C
Heidelberg Univ	OH	34,100	C
Hofstra Univ	NY	51,810	VC+
Houghton College	NY	36,808	C+
Howard Univ	DC	13,646	C
Humboldt State Univ	CA	18,400	C
Hunter College	NY	14,429	VC
Huntington Univ	IN	32,220	C+
Immaculata Univ	PA	43,000	C
Indiana Univ-Purdue Univ Fort Wayne	IN	15,521	C
Indiana Univ-Purdue Univ Indianapolis	IN	17,611	C
Indiana Wesleyan Univ	IN	31,815	VC
Inter-American Univ of PR/San Germán	PR	6,720	
Iowa Wesleyan College	IA	30,850	LC
Ithaca College	NY	53,864	HC
Jackson State Univ	MS	13,512	LC
Johnson C. Smith Univ	NC	25,336	LC
Johnson State College	VT	16,721	C
Judson Univ	IL	25,130	C
Kent State Univ	OH	19,920	C
Kentucky Wesleyan College	KY	27,440	C
Keuka College	NY	30,300	C
King's College	PA	43,502	C
Kutztown Univ of Pennsylvania	PA	16,909	LC
La Salle Univ	PA	50,270	C
Lake Superior State Univ	MI	18,121	C
Lamar Univ	TX	6,820	LC
Le Moyne College	NY	43,470	C
Lees-McRae College	NC	33,944	C
Lehigh Univ	PA	56,770	MC
Lehman College/The CUNY	NY	5,778	LC
Lenoir-Rhyne College	NC	35,984	C
LeTourneau Univ	TX	36,210	VC
Lewis Univ	IL	23,050	C
Lincoln Memorial Univ	TN	18,144	C
Lipscomb Univ	TN	37,490	VC
Louisiana College	LA	15,746	C
Loyola Univ New Orleans	LA	46,581	VC
Lubbock Christian Univ	TX	26,308	C
MacMurray College	IL	20,755	C
Manhattan College	NY	49,588	C+
Marlboro College	VT	35,980	VC
Marquette Univ	WI	46,930	VC+
Mars Hill Univ	NC	22,950	LC
Marshall Univ	WV	14,820	C
Marymount Manhattan College	NY	40,118	VC
Marymount Univ	VA	39,480	C
Maryville College	TN	33,150	C+
Marywood Univ	PA	45,595	C
Mass College of Pharmacy and Health Sciences	MA	36,450	SP
Mayville State Univ	ND	11,401	NC
Mercer Univ	GA	44,201	VC
Mercy College of Health Sciences	IA	14,460	VC
Mercyhurst Univ	PA	40,700	C
Merrimack College	MA	44,215	C
Mich Tech Univ	MI	23,556	HC
Midland Univ	NE	34,000	C
Midwestern State Univ	TX	9,722	C
Milligan College	TN	27,510	C
Millikin Univ	IL	38,940	C
Minn State Univ, Mankato	MN	15,616	C
Minn State Univ, Moorhead	MN	13,392	VC
Missouri Southern State Univ	MO	12,061	C
Missouri Univ of Science and Technology	MO	18,655	VC+
Monmouth Univ	NJ	44,108	C
Montclair State Univ	NJ	22,614	C
Mount Aloysius College	PA	29,976	C
Mount Mary Univ	WI	33,590	C
Mount Vernon Nazarene Univ	OH	29,590	C
Murray State Univ	KY	15,304	C
New York Inst of Technology	NY	45,010	VC
New York Univ	NY	61,470	VC
N Car State Univ	NC	16,202	HC
N Car Wesleyan College	NC	29,440	C
North Central College	IL	38,343	VC
North Park Univ	IL	30,130	C
Northern Kentucky Univ	KY	21,134	C
Northern Mich Univ	MI	18,278	C
Northern State Univ - Aberdeen	SD	14,505	C
Northwest Missouri State Univ	MO	17,347	C
Northwestern College of Iowa	IA	36,240	VC
Northwestern Univ	IL	61,640	MC
Notre Dame of Maryland Univ	MD	27,700	C
Oakland City Univ	IN	24,500	NC
Oberlin College	OH	61,788	C
Ohio Univ	OH	21,080	C
Ohio Wesleyan Univ	OH	49,460	C
Okla Baptist Univ	OK	28,202	C
Okla City Univ	OK	40,476	VC
Okla Wesleyan Univ	OK	21,300	C
Olivet College	MI	19,984	LC
Oral Roberts Univ	OK	31,734	C
Oregon State Univ	OR	20,273	VC
Oswego / SUNY	NY	20,009	VC
Ouachita Baptist Univ	AR	30,220	VC
Peru State College	NE	8,600	NC
Pfeiffer Univ	NC	33,700	LC
Philadelphia Univ	PA	44,160	C
Pittsburg State Univ	KS	12,032	C
Point Park Univ	PA	36,390	C
Quinnipiac Univ	CT	55,160	VC
Regis Univ	CO	41,318	C
Rensselaer Polytechnic Inst	NY	61,529	MC
Rhode Island College	RI	17,694	LC
Rider Univ	NJ	45,720	C
Rivier Univ	NH	35,000	VC
Roberts Wesleyan College	NY	38,306	C+
Rochester Inst of Technology	NY	42,450	VC
Roosevelt Univ	IL	22,605	VC
Rosemont College	PA	42,350	C
Sacred Heart Univ	CT	49,264	VC
Saginaw Valley State Univ	MI	17,369	C
St. Anselm College	NH	49,376	VC
St. Augustine's Univ	NC	14,000	C
St. John's Univ	MN	47,984	C
St. Joseph's College	IN	36,500	C
St. Mary-of-the-Woods College	IN	37,722	LC
St. Mary's Univ	TX	33,854	C
St. Peter's Univ	NJ	44,240	C
St. Vincent College	PA	40,244	C
St. Xavier Univ	IL	32,840	C
Sarah Lawrence College	NY	48,000	HC

ST = STATE $IS = IN-STATE COSTS   SR = SELECTOR RATING

School	ST	$IS	SR
Seton Hill Univ	PA	35,172	C
Shawnee State Univ	OH	16,916	C
Siena Heights Univ	MI	32,040	C
Simpson College	IA	36,086	C+
Southern Oregon Univ	OR	17,874	C
Spring Hill College	AL	44,164	VC
Springfield College	MA	25,000	C
St. Cloud State Univ	MN	10,600	C
St. Edward's Univ	TX	47,784	C
St. John's Univ	NY	55,070	C+
St. Thomas Aquinas College	NY	40,230	C
St. Thomas Univ	FL	32,310	LC
SUNY / College of Environmental Science and Forestry	NY	18,351	VC
Stillman College	AL	19,470	C
SUNY Fredonia/The SUNY at Fredonia	NY	19,840	VC
SUNY Oneonta / SUNY	NY	16,919	C+
Tarleton State Univ	TX	13,489	LC
Taylor Univ	IN	37,821	VC+
Temple Univ	PA	24,392	VC
Texas A&M Univ at Commerce	TX	10,496	C
Texas A&M Univ at Kingsville	TX	7,500	LC
The Catholic Univ of America	DC	52,852	VC
The Pennsylvania State Univ - Univ Park	PA	28,022	VC+
Thiel College	PA	38,728	LC
Touro College	NY	27,959	VC
Trine Univ	IN	39,400	HC+
Trinity Christian College	IL	28,869	C
Trinity International Univ	IL	31,070	VC
Truman State Univ	MO	15,541	HC
Tusculum College	TN	24,295	C
Union Univ	TN	28,260	VC
Univ at Albany / SUNY	NY	18,674	VC
Univ of Arkansas at Pine Bluff	AR	13,378	C
Univ of Bridgeport	CT	39,030	LC
Univ of Calif at Irvine	CA	25,961	VC
Univ of Central Arkansas	AR	13,667	VC
Univ of Central Missouri	MO	14,605	C
Univ of Central Okla	OK	12,293	C
Univ of Cincinnati	OH	21,506	VC
Univ of Dayton	OH	49,070	VC
Univ of Detroit Mercy	MI	30,450	VC
Univ of Evansville	IN	42,656	VC+
Univ of Findlay	OH	31,916	C
Univ of Great Falls	MT	27,970	C
Univ of Hartford	CT	42,674	C
Univ of Illinois at Chicago	IL	24,505	VC
Univ of Iowa	IA	17,693	VC
Univ of Mary	ND	16,714	C
Univ of Mass Amherst	MA	24,215	VC+
Univ of Miami	FL	57,034	MC
Univ of Minn/Morris	MN	17,150	VC
Univ of Minn/Twin Cities	MN		HC
Univ of Nebr - Lincoln	NE	18,031	VC
Univ of Nebr at Kearney	NE	14,855	LC
Univ of New England	ME	46,750	C
Univ of New Haven	CT	48,940	C
Univ of New Orleans	LA	9,224	C
Univ of N Car at Wilmington	NC	13,572	VC
Univ of North Georgia	GA	8,500	C
Univ of Notre Dame	IN	57,117	MC
Univ of PR/Mayaguez	PR	1,250	
Univ of Rio Grande	OH	8,750	NC
Univ of St. Francis	IN	29,810	C
Univ of Sioux Falls	SD	22,990	C
Univ of Southern Miss	MS	13,170	C
Univ of St. Francis	IL	37,560	C
Univ of Tenn at Knoxville	TN	20,364	VC+
Univ of the Cumberlands	KY	27,500	C
Univ of Tulsa	OK	46,331	MC
Univ of West Alabama	AL	14,274	C
Univ of West Florida	FL	14,656	C
Univ of Wisc/Eau Claire	WI	15,730	VC
Univ of Wisc/River Falls	WI	9,722	LC
Univ of Wisc-Milwaukee	WI	18,436	C
Urbana Univ	OH	30,820	C
Ursuline College	OH	33,198	LC
Utah State Univ	UT	12,044	C
Valparaiso Univ	IN	44,940	VC+
Vanguard Univ of Southern Calif	CA	35,833	VC
Vassar College	NY	61,140	MC
Virginia Polytechnic Inst and State Univ	VA	14,629	HC
Walsh Univ	OH	35,100	C
Washington State Univ	WA	20,461	C
Washington Univ in St. Louis	MO	69,844	MC
Wayland Baptist Univ	TX	18,912	LC
Waynesburg Univ	PA	30,150	C
West Chester Univ of Pennsylvania	PA	17,186	C
West Liberty Univ	WV	9,142	LC
West Texas A&M Univ	TX	13,478	C
Western Carolina Univ	NC	13,965	C
Western New Mexico Univ	NM	8,500	LC
Westminster College	PA	31,290	C
Whitworth Univ	WA	47,734	VC
Wilmington College	OH	29,784	C
Wilson College	PA	35,080	C
Wingate Univ	NC	34,990	C
Winona State Univ	MN	16,640	C
Wright State Univ	OH	16,983	C
Xavier Univ of Louisiana	LA	25,300	C
Youngstown State Univ	OH	16,732	C

PRE-OCCUPATIONAL THERAPY

School	ST	$IS	SR
Indiana Univ-Purdue Univ Indianapolis	IN	17,611	C
Missouri Southern State Univ	MO	12,061	C
Murray State Univ	KY	15,304	C

PREOPTOMETRY

School	ST	$IS	SR
Adams State Univ	CO	13,358	LC
Arcadia Univ	PA	33,570	C+
Ashland Univ	OH	25,000	C
Auburn Univ	AL	22,378	VC+
Ball State Univ	IN	17,850	C
Bethel College	IN	31,560	C
Calvin College	MI	39,120	VC
Campbell Univ	NC	37,570	VC
Cardinal Stritch Univ	WI	24,054	C
Carroll College	MT	28,000	C
Christopher Newport Univ	VA	21,960	VC
College of St. Benedict	MN	49,359	VC
Colo State Univ-Pueblo	CO	16,183	C
Corban Univ	OR	37,380	C+
Dordt College	IA	34,160	C+
Drury Univ	MO	31,909	VC
Faulkner Univ	AL	25,720	LC
Florida State Univ	FL	16,715	VC
Freed-Hardeman Univ	TN	19,697	VC
Gannon Univ	PA	39,608	C
Hofstra Univ	NY	51,810	VC+
Houghton College	NY	36,808	C+
Indiana Univ-Purdue Univ Fort Wayne	IN	15,521	C
Iowa Wesleyan College	IA	30,850	LC
Ithaca College	NY	53,864	HC
Le Moyne College	NY	43,470	C
Lehigh Univ	PA	56,770	MC
Lenoir-Rhyne College	NC	35,984	C
Lewis Univ	IL	23,050	C
Lipscomb Univ	TN	37,490	VC
Louisiana College	LA	15,746	C
Marshall Univ	WV	14,820	C
Millersville Univ of Pennsylvania	PA	21,648	C
Millikin Univ	IL	38,940	C
Missouri Southern State Univ	MO	12,061	C
Mount Aloysius College	PA	29,976	C
Murray State Univ	KY	15,304	C
Northern Kentucky Univ	KY	21,134	C
Oregon State Univ	OR	20,273	VC
Oswego / SUNY	NY	20,009	VC
Pittsburg State Univ	KS	12,032	C
Rhode Island College	RI	17,694	LC
St. John's Univ	MN	47,984	C
Simpson College	IA	36,086	C+
SUNY Fredonia/The SUNY at Fredonia	NY	19,840	VC
Trinity Christian College	IL	28,869	C
Univ of Central Arkansas	AR	13,667	VC
Univ of Central Okla	OK	12,293	C
Univ of Evansville	IN	42,656	VC+
Univ of Hartford	CT	42,674	C
Univ of Iowa	IA	17,693	VC
Univ of N Car at Wilmington	NC	13,572	VC
Univ of St. Francis	IL	37,560	C
Univ of Wisc/Eau Claire	WI	15,730	VC
Walsh Univ	OH	35,100	C
Washington State Univ	WA	20,461	C
Western Carolina Univ	NC	13,965	C
Wilson College	PA	35,080	C
Winona State Univ	MN	16,640	C
Youngstown State Univ	OH	16,732	C

PREOSTEOPATHY

School	ST	$IS	SR
Colo State Univ-Pueblo	CO	16,183	C
Drury Univ	MO	31,909	VC
Hofstra Univ	NY	51,810	VC+
Kent State Univ	OH	19,920	C
Marshall Univ	WV	14,820	C
Marywood Univ	PA	45,595	C
Mercyhurst Univ	PA	40,700	C
Mount Aloysius College	PA	29,976	C
Sacred Heart Univ	CT	49,264	VC
Seton Hill Univ	PA	35,172	C
Wilson College	PA	35,080	C
Youngstown State Univ	OH	16,732	C

PREPHARMACY

School	ST	$IS	SR
Adams State Univ	CO	13,358	LC
Alabama A&M Univ	AL	10,084	C
Alice Lloyd College	KY	4,900	LC
Baldwin Wallace Univ	OH	38,318	C
Ball State Univ	IN	17,850	C
Barry Univ	FL	38,190	C
Biola Univ	CA	40,320	C+
Boise State Univ	ID	13,469	LC
Calvin College	MI	39,120	VC
Campbell Univ	NC	37,570	VC
Campbellsville Univ	KY	27,720	C
Canisius College	NY	44,900	C
Carroll College	MT	28,000	C
Christopher Newport Univ	VA	21,960	VC
Clemson Univ	SC	19,136	HC
College of St. Benedict	MN	49,359	VC
College of the Ozarks	MO		VC
Colo State Univ-Pueblo	CO	16,183	C
Concord Univ	WV	13,102	C
Corban Univ	OR	37,380	C+
Dominican Univ	IL	37,628	C
Dordt College	IA	34,160	C+
Drury Univ	MO	31,909	VC
Florida Southern College	FL	40,150	C+
Florida State Univ	FL	16,715	VC
Freed-Hardeman Univ	TN	19,697	VC
Georgetown College	KY	41,440	C+
Goshen College	IN	35,900	C
Houghton College	NY	36,808	C+
Huntington Univ	IN	32,220	C+
Husson Univ	ME	24,194	LC
Indiana Univ-Purdue Univ Fort Wayne	IN	15,521	C
Indiana Univ-Purdue Univ Indianapolis	IN	17,611	C
Le Moyne College	NY	43,470	C
Lewis Univ	IL	23,050	C
Lipscomb Univ	TN	37,490	VC
Lubbock Christian Univ	TX	26,308	C
Mars Hill Univ	NC	22,950	LC
Marshall Univ	WV	14,820	C
Mercer Univ	GA	44,201	VC
Mercyhurst Univ	PA	40,700	C
Mich Tech Univ	MI	23,556	HC
Midwestern State Univ	TX	9,722	VC
Millersville Univ of Pennsylvania	PA	21,648	C
Millikin Univ	IL	38,940	C
Minn State Univ, Mankato	MN	15,616	C
Minn State Univ, Moorhead	MN	13,392	VC
Missouri Southern State Univ	MO	12,061	C
Montclair State Univ	NJ	22,614	C
Mount Aloysius College	PA	29,976	C
Mount Vernon Nazarene Univ	OH	29,590	C
Murray State Univ	KY	15,304	C
Northern Kentucky Univ	KY	21,134	C
Northwest Missouri State Univ	MO	17,347	C
Notre Dame of Maryland Univ	MD	27,700	VC
Ohio Univ	OH	21,080	C
Oregon State Univ	OR	20,273	VC
Peru State College	NE	8,600	NC
Pittsburg State Univ	KS	12,032	C
Roberts Wesleyan College	NY	38,306	C+
Roosevelt Univ	IL	22,605	VC
Sacred Heart Univ	CT	49,264	VC
St. John's Univ	MN	47,984	C
St. Joseph's College of Maine	ME	31,580	C
St. Michael's College	VT	49,975	VC
St. Vincent College	PA	40,244	C
St. Xavier Univ	IL	32,840	C
Simpson College	IA	36,086	C+
Southern Oregon Univ	OR	17,874	C
SUNY / College of Environmental Science and Forestry	NY	18,351	VC
Tarleton State Univ	TX	13,489	LC
Texas A&M Univ at Commerce	TX	10,496	C
Texas A&M Univ at Kingsville	TX	7,500	LC
Thiel College	PA	38,728	LC
Truman State Univ	MO	15,541	HC
Union Univ	TN	28,260	VC
Univ of Arkansas at Pine Bluff	AR	13,378	C
Univ of Central Arkansas	AR	13,667	VC
Univ of Cincinnati	OH	21,506	VC
Univ of Evansville	IN	42,656	VC+
Univ of Florida	FL	15,943	HC
Univ of Illinois at Chicago	IL	24,505	VC
Univ of Iowa	IA	17,693	VC
Univ of Miami	FL	57,034	MC
Univ of Minn/Twin Cities	MN		HC
Univ of Nebr - Lincoln	NE	18,031	VC
Univ of New England	ME	46,750	C
Univ of N Car at Wilmington	NC	13,572	VC
Univ of North Georgia	GA	8,500	C
Univ of St. Francis	IL	37,560	C
Univ of Tenn at Knoxville	TN	20,364	VC+
Univ of the Cumberlands	KY	27,500	C
Univ of the Pacific	CA	52,146	VC
Univ of Wisc/Eau Claire	WI	15,730	VC
Univ of Wisc/River Falls	WI	9,722	LC
Walsh Univ	OH	35,100	C
Washburn Univ	KS	12,579	C
Washington State Univ	WA	20,461	C
Washington Univ in St. Louis	MO	69,844	MC
West Liberty Univ	WV	9,142	LC
West Texas A&M Univ	TX	13,478	C
Western Carolina Univ	NC	13,965	C
Western New Mexico Univ	NM	8,500	LC
Wilkes Univ	PA	44,070	C
Wilson College	PA	35,080	C
Wingate Univ	NC	34,990	C
Winona State Univ	MN	16,640	C
Xavier Univ	OH	44,980	VC

PREPHYSICAL THERAPY

School	ST	$IS	SR
Asbury Univ	KY	32,038	VC
Baldwin Wallace Univ	OH	38,318	C
Bellarmine Univ	KY	42,950	VC
Bethany College	WV	35,282	LC
Bethel College	IN	31,560	C
Biola Univ	CA	40,320	C+
Boise State Univ	ID	13,469	LC
Calif Baptist Univ	CA	38,792	C
Calvin College	MI	39,120	VC
Christopher Newport Univ	VA	21,960	VC
Coe College	IA	45,550	VC
College of St. Benedict	MN	49,359	VC
Corban Univ	OR	37,380	C+
Dordt College	IA	34,160	C+
Drury Univ	MO	31,909	VC
Elizabethtown College	PA	49,740	VC
Elmhurst College	IL	43,336	C
Faulkner Univ	AL	25,720	LC
Ferris State Univ	MI	20,047	C
Florida Southern College	FL	40,150	C+
Fontbonne Univ	MO	31,384	C
Georgetown College	KY	41,440	C+
Houghton College	NY	36,808	C+
Huntington Univ	IN	32,220	C+
Indiana Univ-Purdue Univ Indianapolis	IN	17,611	C
Lipscomb Univ	TN	37,490	VC
Lubbock Christian Univ	TX	26,308	C
Marshall Univ	WV	14,820	C
Marymount Univ	VA	39,480	C
Mich Tech Univ	MI	23,556	HC
Millikin Univ	IL	38,940	C
Missouri Southern State Univ	MO	12,061	C
Mount Aloysius College	PA	29,976	C
Mount Vernon Nazarene Univ	OH	29,590	C
Murray State Univ	KY	15,304	C
Northern Kentucky Univ	KY	21,134	C
Oregon State Univ	OR	20,273	VC
Oswego / SUNY	NY	20,009	VC
Pittsburg State Univ	KS	12,032	C
Roberts Wesleyan College	NY	38,306	C+
Sacred Heart Univ	CT	49,264	VC
Saginaw Valley State Univ	MI	17,369	C
St. John's Univ	MN	47,984	C
St. Mary's Univ of Minn	MN	38,280	C
Simpson College	IA	36,086	C+
Southern Oregon Univ	OR	17,874	C
St. Edward's Univ	TX	47,784	C
Univ of Dayton	OH	49,070	VC
Univ of Iowa	IA	17,693	VC
Univ of Miami	FL	57,034	MC
Univ of N Car at Wilmington	NC	13,572	VC
Univ of St. Francis	IL	37,560	C
Univ of the Cumberlands	KY	27,500	C
Univ of Wisc/Eau Claire	WI	15,730	VC
Walsh Univ	OH	35,100	C
Washington State Univ	WA	20,461	C
Waynesburg Univ	PA	30,150	C
West Chester Univ of Pennsylvania	PA	17,186	C
Western Carolina Univ	NC	13,965	C
Widener Univ	PA	52,418	C
Wilson College	PA	35,080	C
Winona State Univ	MN	16,640	C

PRE-PHYSICIAN ASSISTANT

School	ST	$IS	SR
Indiana Univ-Purdue Univ Indianapolis	IN	17,611	C
Missouri Southern State Univ	MO	12,061	C
Murray State Univ	KY	15,304	C

PREPODIATRY

School	ST	$IS	SR
Bloomfield College	NJ	37,850	LC
Colo State Univ-Pueblo	CO	16,183	C
Gannon Univ	PA	39,608	C
Hofstra Univ	NY	51,810	VC+
Le Moyne College	NY	43,470	C
Marshall Univ	WV	14,820	C
Millersville Univ of Pennsylvania	PA	21,648	C
Mount Aloysius College	PA	29,976	C
Oregon State Univ	OR	20,273	VC
Univ of Iowa	IA	17,693	VC
Univ of N Car at Wilmington	NC	13,572	VC
Winona State Univ	MN	16,640	C

PREVENTIVE/WELLNESS HEALTH CARE

School	ST	$IS	SR
Appalachian State Univ	NC	12,919	VC
Arizona State Univ, at the Tempe Campus	AZ	20,137	C+
Daemen College	NY	34,770	C
Mount Aloysius College	PA	29,976	C
Oakland Univ	MI	19,391	C

ST = STATE $IS = IN-STATE COSTS   SR = SELECTOR RATING

School	ST	$IS	SR
Univ of New England	ME	46,750	C

PREVETERINARY SCIENCE

School	ST	$IS	SR
Adams State Univ	CO	13,358	C
Alabama A&M Univ	AL	10,084	C
Albertus Magnus College	CT	37,382	LC
Andrews Univ	MI	28,030	C+
Arcadia Univ	PA	33,570	C+
Arizona State Univ, at the Polytechnic Campus	AZ	20,531	C+
Ashland Univ	OH	25,000	C
Auburn Univ	AL	22,378	VC+
Baldwin Wallace Univ	OH	38,318	C
Ball State Univ	IN	17,850	C
Becker College	MA	41,420	C
Bellarmine Univ	KY	42,950	VC
Bethany College	WV	35,282	LC
Boise State Univ	ID	13,469	LC
Calvin College	MI	39,120	VC
Canisius College	NY	44,900	C
Cardinal Stritch Univ	WI	24,054	C
Carroll College	MT	28,000	C
Christopher Newport Univ	VA	21,960	VC
Clemson Univ	SC	19,136	HC
Coe College	IA	45,550	VC
College of St. Benedict	MN	49,359	VC
College of the Ozarks	MO		VC
Colo State Univ-Pueblo	CO	16,183	C
Corban Univ	OR	37,380	C+
Cornerstone Univ and Grand Rapids Theological Seminary	MI	33,338	C
Dordt College	IA	34,160	C+
Drury Univ	MO	31,909	VC
Eastern Washington Univ	WA		C
Elmhurst College	IL	43,336	C
Faulkner Univ	AL	25,720	LC
Florida State Univ	FL	16,715	VC
Freed-Hardeman Univ	TN	19,697	VC
Gannon Univ	PA	39,608	C
George Fox Univ	OR	40,750	C+
Goshen College	IN	35,900	VC
Graceland Univ	IA	28,020	C
Hofstra Univ	NY	51,810	VC+
Houghton College	NY	36,808	C+
Indiana Univ-Purdue Univ Fort Wayne	IN	15,521	C
Indiana Univ-Purdue Univ Indianapolis	IN	17,611	C
Iowa Wesleyan College	IA	30,850	LC
Kansas State Univ	KS	15,497	VC
Kent State Univ	OH	19,920	C
Keuka College	NY	30,300	C
Le Moyne College	NY	43,470	C
Lees-McRae College	NC	33,944	C
Lenoir-Rhyne College	NC	35,984	C
LeTourneau Univ	TX	36,210	VC
Lewis Univ	IL	23,050	C
Lipscomb Univ	TN	37,490	VC
Louisiana College	LA	15,746	C
Loyola Univ New Orleans	LA	46,581	VC
MacMurray College	IL	20,755	C
Mars Hill Univ	NC	22,950	LC
Mercyhurst Univ	PA	40,700	C
Midwestern State Univ	TX	9,722	C
Millikin Univ	IL	38,940	C
Minn State Univ, Mankato	MN	15,616	C
Minn State Univ, Moorhead	MN	13,392	VC
Missouri Southern State Univ	MO	12,061	C
Mount Aloysius College	PA	29,976	C
Mount Mary Univ	WI	33,590	LC
Murray State Univ	KY	15,304	C
N Car State Univ	NC	16,202	HC
North Central College	IL	38,343	VC
N Dak State Univ	ND		C
Northern Kentucky Univ	KY	21,134	C
Northern Mich Univ	MI	18,278	C
Northwest Missouri State Univ	MO	17,347	C
Ohio Wesleyan Univ	OH	49,460	C+
Olivet College	MI	19,984	LC
Oswego / SUNY	NY	20,009	VC
Peru State College	NE	8,600	NC
Pittsburg State Univ	KS	12,032	C
Rhode Island College	RI	17,694	LC
Rivier Univ	NH	35,000	VC
Roberts Wesleyan College	NY	38,306	C+
Rochester Inst of Technology	NY	42,450	VC
Roosevelt Univ	IL	22,605	VC
Sacred Heart Univ	CT	49,264	VC
St. John's Univ	MN	47,984	C
St. Mary-of-the-Woods College	IN	37,722	LC
St. Vincent College	PA	40,244	C
Seton Hill Univ	PA	35,172	C
Simpson College	IA	36,086	C
Spring Hill College	AL	44,164	VC
Tarleton State Univ	TX	13,489	LC
Texas A&M Univ at Kingsville	TX	7,500	LC
The Catholic Univ of America	DC	52,852	VC
The Pennsylvania State Univ - Univ Park	PA	28,022	VC+
Thiel College	PA	38,728	LC
Truman State Univ	MO	15,541	HC
Univ of Central Arkansas	AR	13,667	VC
Univ of Central Missouri	MO	14,605	C
Univ of Evansville	IN	42,656	VC+
Univ of Findlay	OH	31,916	C
Univ of Illinois at Urbana-Champaign	IL	26,450	HC
Univ of Iowa	IA	17,693	VC
Univ of Maryland - College Park	MD	20,060	HC
Univ of Mass Amherst	MA	24,215	VC+
Univ of Miami	FL	57,034	MC
Univ of Minn/Twin Cities	MN		HC
Univ of Montana-Western	MT	9,753	LC
Univ of New Haven	CT	48,940	C
Univ of New Orleans	LA	9,224	C
Univ of N Car at Wilmington	NC	13,572	VC
Univ of North Georgia	GA	8,500	C
Univ of Rio Grande	OH	8,750	NC
Univ of St. Francis	IL	37,560	C
Univ of Tenn at Knoxville	TN	20,364	VC+
Univ of the Cumberlands	KY	27,500	C
Univ of Wisc/Eau Claire	WI	15,730	VC
Walsh Univ	OH	35,100	C
Washington State Univ	WA	20,461	C
Washington Univ in St. Louis	MO	69,844	MC
Waynesburg Univ	PA	30,150	C
West Texas A&M Univ	TX	13,478	C
Western Carolina Univ	NC	13,965	C
Wilmington College	OH	29,784	C
Wilson College	PA	35,080	C
Wingate Univ	NC	34,990	C
Winona State Univ	MN	16,640	C
Youngstown State Univ	OH	16,732	C

PRINTING MANAGEMENT

School	ST	$IS	SR
Ferris State Univ	MI	20,047	C

PRINTING TECHNOLOGY

School	ST	$IS	SR
Pennsylvania College of Technology	PA	26,286	NC
Rochester Inst of Technology	NY	42,450	VC

PRINTMAKING

School	ST	$IS	SR
Adams State Univ	CO	13,358	LC
Aquinas College	MI	33,060	C
Art Academy of Cincinnati	OH	25,940	SP
Bennington College	VT	56,990	HC+
Binghamton Univ/The SUNY	NY	21,648	HC+
Biola Univ	CA	40,320	C+
Birmingham-Southern College	AL	44,168	VC+
Buffalo State College / SUNY	NY	15,733	C+
Calif College of the Arts	CA	48,334	SP
Cal State, San Bernardino	CA	12,000	C
Cleveland Inst of Art	OH	48,685	SP
College for Creative Studies	MI	45,340	C
Columbia College	MO	24,578	C
Drake Univ	IA	41,516	VC+
Escuela de Artes Plasticas de PR	PR	2,660	
Ferris State Univ	MI	20,047	C
Houghton College	NY	36,808	C+
Howard Univ	DC	13,646	C
Indiana Univ-Purdue Univ Fort Wayne	IN	15,521	C
Indiana Univ-Purdue Univ Indianapolis	IN	17,611	C
Indiana Wesleyan Univ	IN	31,815	VC
Kansas City Art Inst	MO	44,308	SP
Kent State Univ	OH	19,920	C
Kutztown Univ of Pennsylvania	PA	16,909	LC
Maine College of Art	ME	28,812	SP
Maryland Inst College of Art	MD	39,500	SP
Milwaukee Inst of Art and Design	WI	31,938	SP
Minneapolis College of Art and Design	MN	36,700	SP
Montserrat College of Art	MA	31,000	C
Ohio Univ	OH	21,080	C
Old Dominion Univ	VA	19,483	LC
Pacific Northwest College of Art	OR	38,494	C
Providence College	RI	57,383	VC
Rhode Island School of Design	RI	57,234	MC
Ringling College of Art and Design	FL	46,130	SP
San Francisco Art Inst	CA	55,762	SP
Savannah College of Art and Design	GA	48,005	SP
School of the Art Inst of Chicago	IL	56,230	SP
Syracuse Univ	NY	56,346	VC
Temple Univ	PA	24,392	VC
Texas A&M Univ at Commerce	TX	10,496	C
Texas Christian Univ	TX	49,980	HC
Univ of Dallas	TX	45,500	VC+
Univ of Hartford	CT	42,674	C
Univ of Iowa	IA	17,693	VC
Univ of Kansas	KS	17,603	C+
Univ of Miami	FL	57,034	MC
Univ of Mich/Ann Arbor	MI	22,102	MC
Univ of Oregon	OR	21,360	C+
Univ of the Arts	PA	38,450	SP
Washington Univ in St. Louis	MO	69,844	MC
Webster Univ	MO	35,100	C+
Youngstown State Univ	OH	16,732	C

PRODUCT DESIGN

School	ST	$IS	SR
Kent State Univ	OH	19,920	C
Stanford Univ	CA	58,388	MC

PRODUCT DESIGN ENGINEERING TECHNOLOGY

School	ST	$IS	SR
Arizona State Univ, at the Polytechnic Campus	AZ	20,531	C+
Ferris State Univ	MI	20,047	C

PRODUCTION AND OPERATIONS MANAGEMENT

School	ST	$IS	SR
Univ of Rhode Island	RI	24,002	C

PROFESSIONAL GOLF MANAGEMENT

School	ST	$IS	SR
Ferris State Univ	MI	20,047	C

PROFESSIONAL PROGRAM IN ACCOUNTING

School	ST	$IS	SR
Black Hills State Univ	SD	13,947	C
Bloomfield College	NJ	37,850	LC
Texas Christian Univ	TX	49,980	HC
Univ of Louisiana at Monroe	LA	12,998	C

PROFESSIONAL STUDIES

School	ST	$IS	SR
College of Charleston	SC	22,145	VC
Old Dominion Univ	VA	19,483	LC
Shippensburg Univ of Pennsylvania	PA	20,934	C

PROFESSIONAL TENNIS MANAGEMENT

School	ST	$IS	SR
Ferris State Univ	MI	20,047	C

PROJECT MANAGEMENT

School	ST	$IS	SR
Ashford Univ	CA	10,480	C

PRO-MO-TED-TECHNICAL EDUCATION

School	ST	$IS	SR
Ferris State Univ	MI	20,047	C

PROPERTY MANAGEMENT

School	ST	$IS	SR
New York Univ	NY	61,470	MC
Univ of Wisc/Stout	WI	15,459	C

PSYCHOBIOLOGY

School	ST	$IS	SR
Albright College	PA	46,660	C
Arcadia Univ	PA	33,570	C+
Binghamton Univ/The SUNY	NY	21,648	HC+
Centre College	KY	35,000	HC+
Florida Atlantic Univ	FL	17,339	C
Hamilton College	NY	55,620	MC
Houghton College	NY	36,808	C+
La Sierra Univ	CA	35,694	VC
Lebanon Valley College	PA	38,570	C
Lindsey Wilson College	KY	31,220	C
Quinnipiac Univ	CT	55,160	VC
Ripon College	WI	36,959	C+
Simmons College	MA	49,966	VC
Swarthmore College	PA	57,870	MC
Tiffin Univ	OH	30,273	LC
Univ of Calif at Los Angeles	CA	25,686	MC
Univ of New England	ME	46,750	C
Wilson College	PA	35,080	C

PSYCHOLOGY

School	ST	$IS	SR
Abilene Christian Univ	TX	38,400	C+
Adams State Univ	CO	13,358	LC
Adelphi Univ	NY	44,670	VC
Adrian College	MI	42,400	C
Agnes Scott College	GA	45,323	C+
Alabama A&M Univ	AL	10,084	C
Alabama State Univ	AL	14,142	NC
Alaska Pacific Univ	AK	43,592	VC
Albany State Univ	GA	8,500	C
Albertus Magnus College	CT	37,382	LC
Albion College	MI	46,010	C
Albright College	PA	46,660	C
Alcorn State Univ	MS	9,500	C
Alderson Broaddus Univ	WV	28,656	C
Alfred Univ	NY	41,770	C
Allegheny College	PA	50,980	HC
Alma College	MI	44,075	C
Alvernia Univ	PA	39,250	LC
Alverno College	WI	31,434	LC
American International College	MA	36,100	LC
American Jewish Univ - College of A&S	CA	32,600	C
American Univ	DC	56,015	HC+
Amherst College	MA	58,744	MC
Anderson Univ	IN	36,100	C
Andrews Univ	MI	28,030	C
Angelo State Univ	TX	15,049	NC
Anna Maria College	MA	34,600	C
Appalachian State Univ	NC	12,919	VC
Aquinas College	MI	33,060	C
Arcadia Univ	PA	33,570	C+
Arizona State Univ, at the Polytechnic Campus	AZ	20,531	C+
Arizona State Univ, at the Tempe Campus	AZ	20,137	C+
Arizona State Univ, at the West Campus	AZ	19,251	C
Arkansas State Univ	AR	15,470	C
Arkansas Tech Univ	AR	13,982	LC
Armstrong State Univ	GA	15,532	C
Asbury Univ	KY	32,038	VC
Ashford Univ	CA	10,480	C
Ashland Univ	OH	25,000	C
Assumption College	MA	47,122	C
Atlantic Union College	MA	24,600	C
Auburn Univ	AL	22,378	VC+
Auburn Univ at Montgomery	AL	14,470	LC
Augsburg College	MN	35,142	C
Augustana College	IL	43,398	VC
Augustana College	SD	36,500	VC
Aurora Univ	IL	33,228	C
Austin College	TX	45,875	HC
Austin Peay State Univ	TN	15,274	C
Averett Univ	VA	37,750	LC
Avila Univ	MO	26,900	C
Azusa Pacific Univ	CA	42,086	C
Baker Univ	KS	33,350	C+
Baldwin Wallace Univ	OH	38,318	C
Ball State Univ	IN	17,850	C
Bard College	NY	61,940	VC
Bard College at Simon's Rock	MA	61,749	HC+
Barnard College/Columbia Univ	NY	39,000	MC
Barry Univ	FL	38,190	C
Barton College	NC	27,660	C
Bates College	ME	60,720	MC
Bay Path College	MA	34,565	C
Baylor Univ	TX	50,329	HC
Becker College	MA	41,420	C
Belhaven Univ	MS	27,170	C
Bellarmine Univ	KY	42,950	VC
Bellevue Univ	NE	4,600	NC
Belmont Abbey College	NC	37,716	C
Belmont Univ	TN	39,190	VC+
Beloit College	WI	49,970	HC
Bemidji State Univ	MN	13,500	VC
Benedictine College	KS	29,180	VC
Benedictine Univ	IL	37,820	C
Bennett College for Women	NC	21,970	LC
Bennington College	VT	56,990	HC+
Berea College	KY	7,192	C
Berry College	GA	39,254	VC
Bethany College	KS	30,605	NC
Bethany College	WV	35,282	LC
Bethel College	IN	31,560	C
Bethel College	KS	32,160	C
Bethel Univ	MN	34,940	VC
Bethel Univ	TN	19,186	C
Bethune-Cookman Univ	FL	22,958	C
Binghamton Univ/The SUNY	NY	21,648	HC+
Biola Univ	CA	40,320	C+
Birmingham-Southern College	AL	44,168	VC+
Black Hills State Univ	SD	13,947	C
Blackburn College	IL	21,350	C
Bloomfield College	NJ	37,850	LC
Bloomsburg Univ of Pennsylvania	PA	13,598	C
Blue Mountain College	MS	15,634	LC
Bluefield College	VA	17,230	C+
Bluffton Univ	OH	38,948	C
Boise State Univ	ID	13,469	LC
Boston College	MA	60,622	MC
Boston Univ	MA	60,694	MC
Bowdoin College	ME	59,568	MC
Bowie State Univ	MD	23,990	LC
Bowling Green State Univ	OH	18,970	C
Bradley Univ	IL	31,874	VC
Brandeis Univ	MA		MC
Brenau Univ - Women's College	GA	26,650	LC
Brescia Univ	KY	26,140	VC+
Brewton-Parker College	GA	33,388	C
Briar Cliff Univ	IA	29,514	C
Bridgewater College	VA	41,450	C
Bridgewater State Univ	MA	18,752	C
Brigham Young Univ	UT	12,100	VC
Brigham Young Univ/Hawaii	HI	10,686	VC
Brown Univ	RI	59,428	MC
Bryan College	TN	24,194	C
Bryant Univ	RI	49,179	VC
Bryn Athyn College	PA	27,984	C

ST = STATE　　$IS = IN-STATE COSTS　　SR = SELECTOR RATING

School	ST	$IS	SR
Bryn Mawr College	PA	59,890	MC
Bucknell Univ	PA	60,140	MC
Buena Vista Univ	IA	39,188	C
Buffalo State College / SUNY	NY	15,733	C+
Burlington College	VT	32,510	SP
Butler Univ	IN	47,572	VC+
Cabrini College	PA	40,859	LC
Cairn Univ	PA	33,270	C
Caldwell College	NJ	35,602	NC
Calif Baptist Univ	CA	38,792	C
Calif Lutheran Univ	CA	49,540	C+
Calif Polytechnic State Univ	CA	19,847	HC
Calif State Polytechnic Univ, Pomona	CA	20,156	C
Cal State, Bakersfield	CA	8,000	C
Cal State, Chico	CA	20,158	C
Cal State, Dominguez Hills	CA	17,090	LC
Cal State, East Bay	CA	16,549	C
Cal State, Fresno	CA	17,405	C
Cal State, Fullerton	CA	25,188	C
Cal State, Long Beach	CA	17,502	C+
Cal State, Los Angeles	CA	17,186	LC
Cal State, Monterey Bay	CA	26,871	LC
Cal State, Northridge	CA	28,690	LC
Cal State, Sacramento	CA	16,200	C
Cal State, San Bernardino	CA	12,000	C
Cal State, San Marcos	CA	14,576	LC
Cal State, Stanislaus	CA	18,582	C
Calif Univ of Pennsylvania	PA	14,217	C
Calumet College of St. Joseph	IN	15,000	C
Calvin College	MI	39,120	VC
Cambridge College	MA	13,392	NC
Cameron Univ	OK	10,004	LC
Campbell Univ	NC	37,570	VC
Campbellsville Univ	KY	27,720	C
Canisius College	NY	44,900	C
Capital Univ	OH	41,050	VC
Cardinal Stritch Univ	WI	24,054	C
Carleton College	MN	60,102	MC
Carlos Albizu Univ	FL	12,053	LC
Carlow Univ	PA	30,272	C
Carnegie Mellon Univ	PA	51,260	MC
Carroll College	MT	28,000	C
Carroll Univ	WI	38,100	C
Carson-Newman Univ	TN	29,058	C+
Carthage College	WI	33,000	C
Case Western Reserve Univ	OH	56,534	MC
Castleton State College	VT	20,186	C
Catawba College	NC	37,240	LC
Cazenovia College	NY	43,464	C
Cedar Crest College	PA	43,240	C
Cedarville Univ	OH	32,860	VC
Centenary College	NJ	38,618	C
Centenary College of Louisiana	LA	45,650	C+
Central College	IA	42,104	C+
Central Conn State Univ	CT	19,749	C
Central Methodist Univ	MO	28,240	VC
Central State Univ	OH	9,010	C
Central Univ of Bayamon	PR	3,350	
Central Washington Univ	WA	11,730	C
Centre College	KY	35,000	HC+
Chadron State College	NE	7,400	NC
Chaminade Univ of Honolulu	HI	31,664	LC
Champlain College	VT	46,650	VC
Chapman Univ	CA	58,347	VC+
Charleston Southern Univ	SC	22,420	C
Chatham Univ	PA	43,797	C
Chestnut Hill College	PA	42,110	LC
Cheyney Univ of Pennsylvania	PA	20,372	LC
Chicago State Univ	IL	5,482	C
Christian Brothers Univ	TN	31,670	HC
Christopher Newport Univ	VA	21,960	VC
Citadel, The	SC		C
CUNY/Baruch College	NY		HC
CUNY/Brooklyn College	NY	5,884	C+
CUNY/City College	NY	20,319	HC+
Claremont McKenna College	CA	62,215	MC
Clarion Univ of Pennsylvania	PA	17,370	LC
Clark Atlanta Univ	GA	30,006	LC
Clark Univ	MA	47,020	HC+
Clarke Univ	IA	37,600	C
Clarkson Univ	NY	57,330	HC
Clearwater Christian College	FL	23,720	C
Clemson Univ	SC	19,136	HC
Cleveland State Univ	OH	21,776	C
Coastal Carolina Univ	SC	18,580	C
Coe College	IA	45,550	VC
Coker College	SC	32,256	LC
Colby College	ME	57,510	MC
Colby-Sawyer College	NH	50,790	C
Colgate Univ	NY	58,135	MC
College of Charleston	SC	22,145	VC
College of Mount St. Joseph	OH	33,880	C
College of Mount St. Vincent	NY	41,040	MC
College of New Jersey	NJ	25,376	HC
College of St. Benedict	MN	49,359	VC
College of St. Elizabeth	NJ	43,839	LC
College of St. Mary	NE	35,184	C
College of St. Scholastica	MN	41,440	C
College of St Joseph	VT	30,600	LC
College of Staten Island/The City of New Yok	NY	16,778	NC
College of the Holy Cross	MA	58,042	MC
College of the Ozarks	MO		VC

School	ST	$IS	SR
College of William & Mary	VA	28,000	MC
College of Wooster	OH	52,600	VC
Colo Christian Univ	CO	27,500	VC
Colo College	CO	57,162	MC
Colo Mesa Univ	CO	17,690	LC
Colo State Univ-Fort Collins	CO	20,385	VC
Colo State Univ-Pueblo	CO	16,183	C
Columbia College	MO	24,578	C
Columbia College	SC	27,882	C
Columbia Univ/City of New York	NY	61,116	MC
Columbia Univ/School of General Studies	NY	58,231	MC
Columbus State Univ	GA	13,176	C
Concord Univ	WV	13,102	C
Concordia College - Moorhead	MN	39,974	VC
Concordia College - New York	NY	39,035	LC
Concordia Univ	OR	35,000	C
Concordia Univ Irvine	CA	35,390	VC
Concordia Univ Nebr	NE	26,000	VC
Concordia Univ St. Paul	MN	28,250	C
Concordia Univ Wisc	WI	28,980	C
Concordia Univ, Ann Arbor	MI	27,220	VC
Concordia Univ, River Forest	IL	26,300	C
Conn College	CT	54,970	MC
Converse College	SC	37,130	C
Coppin State Univ	MD	16,227	NC
Corban Univ	OR	37,380	C+
Cornell College	IA	44,930	VC
Cornell Univ	NY	60,964	MC
Cornerstone Univ and Grand Rapids Theological Seminary	MI	33,338	C
Covenant College	GA	38,990	VC+
Creighton Univ	NE	45,356	VC
Culver-Stockton College	MO	30,900	C
Cumberland Univ	TN	21,220	C
Curry College	MA	48,925	LC
Daemen College	NY	34,770	C
Dakota Wesleyan Univ	SD	23,000	C
Dallas Baptist Univ	TX	30,580	VC
Daniel Webster College	NH	25,380	C
Dartmouth College	NH	57,996	MC
Davidson College	NC	58,146	MC
Davis & Elkins College	WV	33,742	C
De Sales Univ	PA	43,970	C
Defiance College	OH	30,645	C
Delaware State Univ	DE	16,722	LC
Delta State Univ	MS	12,292	LC
Denison Univ	OH	54,670	HC+
DePaul Univ	IL	47,623	VC
DePauw Univ	IN	48,950	VC+
Dickinson College	PA	57,662	HC+
Dillard Univ	LA	20,940	VC
Doane College	NE	35,230	C
Dominican College	NY	31,270	LC
Dominican Univ	IL	37,628	C
Dominican Univ of Calif	CA	51,250	C
Dordt College	IA	34,160	C
Dowling College	NY	25,000	LC
Drake Univ	IA	41,516	VC+
Drew Univ/College of Liberal Arts	NJ	57,516	C
Drexel Univ	PA	61,418	VC+
Drury Univ	MO	31,909	VC
Duke Univ	NC	50,250	MC
Duquesne Univ	PA	43,720	VC
D'Youville College	NY	29,850	C
Earlham College	IN	51,470	HC
East Carolina Univ	NC	14,169	C
East Central Univ	OK	10,223	C
East Stroudsburg Univ of Pennsylvania	PA	18,868	LC
East Tenn State Univ	TN	9,000	C
East Texas Baptist Univ	TX	31,577	LC
Eastern Conn State Univ	CT	20,584	C
Eastern Illinois Univ	IL	20,466	C
Eastern Kentucky Univ	KY	11,161	C
Eastern Mennonite Univ	VA	40,660	C
Eastern Mich Univ	MI	18,604	C
Eastern Nazarene College	MA	30,000	C
Eastern New Mexico Univ	NM	10,682	C
Eastern Oregon Univ	OR	10,400	C
Eastern Univ	PA	37,704	C
Eastern Washington Univ	WA		C
Eckerd College	FL	43,902	C
Edgewood College	WI	33,294	C
Edinboro Univ of Pennsylvania	PA	15,940	LC
Edward Waters College	FL	19,607	LC
Elizabeth City State Univ	NC	11,638	C
Elizabethtown College	PA	49,740	VC
Elmhurst College	IL	43,336	C
Elmira College	NY	49,950	C+
Elms College	MA	23,900	VC
Elon Univ	NC	41,914	VC+
Embry-Riddle Aeronautical Univ - Daytona Beach	FL	40,884	C+
Emmanuel College	MA	47,985	VC
Emory and Henry College	VA	387,460	C
Emory Univ	GA	56,368	MC
Emporia State Univ	KS	12,897	C
Endicott College	MA	43,228	VC+
Erskine College	SC	37,360	C

School	ST	$IS	SR
Eugene Lang College/The New School for Liberal Arts	NY	55,650	C
Eureka College	IL	19,280	C
Evangel Univ	MO	23,090	C
Excelsior College	NY	5,580	SP
Fairfield Univ	CT	56,960	VC
Fairleigh Dickinson Univ/ College at Florham	NJ	42,142	C
Fairleigh Dickinson Univ/ Metropolitan Campus	NJ	40,254	C
Fairmont State Univ	WV	12,098	LC
Fayetteville State Univ	NC	10,816	C
Felician College	NJ	41,640	LC
Ferris State Univ	MI	20,047	C
Ferrum College	VA	27,740	LC
Fisk Univ	TN	19,830	C
Fitchburg State Univ	MA	18,173	C
Flagler College	FL	25,180	C
Florida A&M Univ	FL	14,935	LC
Florida Atlantic Univ	FL	17,339	C
Florida Gulf Coast Univ	FL		C
Florida Inst of Technology	FL	48,290	VC
Florida International Univ	FL	17,747	C+
Florida Memorial Univ	FL	20,888	LC
Florida Southern College	FL	40,150	C+
Florida State Univ	FL	16,715	VC
Fontbonne Univ	MO	31,384	C
Fordham Univ	NY	61,588	HC+
Fort Hays State Univ	KS	11,354	C
Fort Lewis College	CO	15,513	C
Fort Valley State Univ	GA	11,200	VC
Framingham State Univ	MA	18,854	C
Francis Marion Univ	SC	16,464	LC
Franciscan Univ of Steubenville	OH	27,320	VC
Franklin and Marshall College	PA	60,799	MC
Franklin College	IN	36,585	C
Franklin Pierce Univ	NH	41,598	C
Freed-Hardeman Univ	TN	19,697	VC
Fresno Pacific Univ	CA	32,136	C
Friends Univ	KS	29,100	C
Frostburg State Univ	MD	15,264	LC
Furman Univ	SC	54,006	HC
Gallaudet Univ	DC	25,380	SP
Gannon Univ	PA	39,608	C
Gardner-Webb Univ	NC	34,375	C+
Geneva College	PA	27,280	C
George Fox Univ	OR	40,750	C+
George Mason Univ	VA	15,724	VC
George Washington Univ	DC	57,108	MC
Georgetown College	KY	41,440	C+
Georgetown Univ	DC	52,910	MC
Georgia College and State Univ	GA	18,900	C+
Georgia Inst of Technology	GA	21,828	MC
Georgia Regents Univ	GA		C
Georgia Southern Univ	GA	16,942	C
Georgia Southwestern State Univ	GA	13,246	C
Georgia State Univ	GA	15,582	VC
Georgian Court Univ	NJ	41,594	LC
Gettysburg College	PA	58,820	HC
Glenville State College	WV	11,348	NC
Goddard College	VT	16,418	VC
Goldey-Beacom College	DE	27,493	C
Gonzaga Univ	WA	46,441	HC
Gordon College	MA	44,320	VC
Goshen College	IN	35,900	VC
Goucher College	MD	52,040	VC+
Grace College and Seminary	IN	28,800	VC
Graceland Univ	IA	28,020	C
Grambling State Univ	LA	13,384	C
Grand Canyon Univ	AZ	24,540	VC
Grand Valley State Univ	MI	17,998	C+
Grand View Univ	IA	31,050	C
Green Mountain College	VT	45,228	LC
Greensboro College	NC	28,740	LC
Greenville College	IL	27,012	C
Grinnell College	IA	53,654	HC
Grove City College	PA	24,022	VC
Guilford College	NC	42,800	C
Gustavus Adolphus College	MN	48,170	HC
Gwynedd-Mercy College	PA	33,560	C
Hamilton College	NY	55,620	MC
Hamline Univ	MN	45,678	VC
Hampden-Sydney College	VA	51,758	C+
Hampshire College	MA	58,320	MC
Hampton Univ	VA	28,528	C
Hannibal-LaGrange Univ	MO	24,490	C
Hanover College	IN	43,073	C+
Harding Univ	AR	23,556	C
Hardin-Simmons Univ	TX	23,560	C+
Hartwick College	NY	51,270	C
Harvard College/Harvard Univ	MA	49,000	MC
Hastings College	NE	27,782	C+
Haverford College	PA	61,564	MC
Hawaii Pacific Univ	HI	34,360	C
Heidelberg Univ	OH	34,100	C
Henderson State Univ	AR	14,584	C
Hendrix College	AR	50,202	VC+
Heritage Univ	WA	17,664	NC
High Point Univ	NC	39,800	C
Hilbert College	NY	28,550	C

School	ST	$IS	SR
Hillsdale College	MI	32,866	MC
Hiram College	OH	37,300	VC
Hobart and William Smith Colleges	NY	60,034	HC+
Hofstra Univ	NY	51,810	VC+
Hollins Univ	VA	43,295	VC
Holy Family Univ	PA	40,030	LC
Holy Names Univ	CA	40,310	NC
Hood College	MD	45,730	C
Hope College	MI	38,650	VC
Hope International Univ	CA	34,650	C
Houghton College	NY	36,808	C+
Houston Baptist Univ	TX	36,450	C
Howard Payne Univ	TX	17,115	C
Howard Univ	DC	13,646	C
Humboldt State Univ	CA	18,400	C
Hunter College	NY	14,429	VC
Huntingdon College	AL	33,100	C
Huntington Univ	IN	32,220	C+
Husson Univ	ME	24,194	LC
Huston-Tillotson Univ	TX	18,124	C+
Idaho State Univ	ID	12,307	C
Illinois College	IL	25,770	VC
Illinois Inst of Technology	IL	38,512	HC+
Illinois State Univ	IL	23,110	VC
Illinois Wesleyan Univ	IL	48,452	HC
Immaculata Univ	PA	43,000	C
Indiana Inst of Technology	IN	34,240	LC
Indiana State Univ	IN	16,000	C
Indiana Univ Bloomington	IN	19,801	VC
Indiana Univ East	IN	6,783	C
Indiana Univ Kokomo	IN	6,811	LC
Indiana Univ Northwest	IN	6,854	LC
Indiana Univ of Pennsylvania	PA	20,846	LC
Indiana Univ South Bend	IN	15,501	C
Indiana Univ Southeast	IN	16,035	C
Indiana Univ-Purdue Univ Fort Wayne	IN	15,521	C
Indiana Univ-Purdue Univ Indianapolis	IN	17,611	C
Indiana Wesleyan Univ	IN	31,815	VC
Inter-American Univ of PR/ Aguadilla Campus	PR	5,578	
Inter-American Univ of PR/ Fajardo Campus	PR	4,200	
Inter-American Univ of PR/ Metropolitan Campus	PR	4,320	
Inter-American Univ of PR/ Ponce	PR		
Inter-American Univ of PR/ San Germán	PR	6,720	
Iona College	NY	44,028	C
Iowa State Univ	IA	16,403	C
Iowa Wesleyan College	IA	30,850	LC
Ithaca College	NY	53,864	HC
Jackson State Univ	MS	13,512	C
Jacksonville State Univ	AL	12,480	C
Jacksonville Univ	FL	37,780	C
James Madison Univ	VA	18,049	VC
John Brown Univ	AR	32,056	VC+
John Carroll Univ	OH	46,300	C+
John Jay College of Criminal Justice/The CUNY	NY	6,359	LC
Johns Hopkins Univ	MD	47,492	MC
Johnson C. Smith Univ	NC	25,336	LC
Johnson State College	VT	16,721	C
Judson College	AL	26,794	C
Judson Univ	IL	25,130	C
Juniata College	PA	49,340	VC
Kalamazoo College	MI	49,740	HC
Kansas State Univ	KS	15,497	VC
Kansas Wesleyan Univ	KS	32,000	C
Kean Univ	NJ	23,444	C
Keene State College	NH	23,232	LC
Kennesaw State Univ	GA		C
Kent State Univ	OH	19,920	C
Kentucky State Univ	KY	11,000	LC
Kentucky Wesleyan College	KY	27,440	C
Kenyon College	OH	58,890	MC
Keuka College	NY	30,300	C
Keystone College	PA	28,680	LC
King Univ	TN	33,140	C
King's College	PA	43,502	C
Knox College	IL	44,865	VC+
Kutztown Univ of Pennsylvania	PA	16,909	LC
La Roche College	PA	35,824	LC
La Salle Univ	PA	50,270	C
La Sierra Univ	CA	35,694	VC
Lafayette College	PA	59,155	HC+
LaGrange College	GA	37,670	C
Lake Erie College	OH	37,266	C
Lake Forest College	IL	50,652	VC
Lake Superior State Univ	MI	18,121	C
Lakeland College	WI	22,990	C
Lamar Univ	TX	6,820	LC
Lander Univ	SC	22,514	C+
Langston Univ	OK	3,000	C
Lasell College	MA	43,750	LC
Lawrence Tech Univ	MI	37,630	VC
Lawrence Univ	WI	46,371	HC
Le Moyne College	NY	43,470	C
Lebanon Valley College	PA	38,570	C
Lee Univ	TN	18,690	C+
Lees-McRae College	NC	33,944	C
Lehigh Univ	PA	56,770	MC

ST = STATE $IS = IN-STATE COSTS   SR = SELECTOR RATING

School	ST	$IS	SR
Lehman College/The CUNY	NY	5,778	LC
Lenoir-Rhyne College	NC	35,984	C
Lesley Univ	MA	46,350	C
LeTourneau Univ	TX	36,210	VC
Lewis & Clark College	OR	54,382	MC
Lewis Univ	IL	23,050	C
Lewis-Clark State College	ID	6,990	C
Liberty Univ	VA	19,101	C
Limestone College	SC	30,800	C
Lincoln Memorial Univ	TN	18,144	C
Lincoln Univ	MO	12,904	NC
Lindenwood Univ	MO	20,750	C
Lindsey Wilson College	KY	31,220	C
Linfield College-McMinnville Campus	OR	47,676	C
Lipscomb Univ	TN	37,490	VC
LIU Brooklyn	NY	47,182	LC
LIU Post	NY	47,660	C
Livingstone College	NC	17,815	LC
Lock Haven Univ of Pennsylvania	PA	18,028	LC
Longwood Univ	VA	20,924	C
Loras College	IA	37,432	VC
Louisiana College	LA	15,746	C
Louisiana State Univ	LA	18,667	C+
Louisiana State Univ in Shreveport	LA	5,606	C
Louisiana Tech Univ	LA	11,302	C
Lourdes Univ	OH	26,055	LC
Loyola Marymount Univ	CA	54,649	VC+
Loyola Univ Chicago	IL	51,646	VC+
Loyola Univ Maryland	MD	56,880	VC+
Loyola Univ New Orleans	LA	46,581	VC
Lubbock Christian Univ	TX	26,308	C
Luther College	IA	45,720	C+
Lycoming College	PA	45,379	C
Lynchburg College	VA	42,645	C
Lyndon State College	VT	14,233	C
Lynn Univ	FL	43,500	LC
Lyon College	AR	32,090	C+
Macalester College	MN	57,691	MC
MacMurray College	IL	20,755	C
Madonna Univ	MI	24,540	VC
Malone Univ	OH	35,364	C
Manchester Univ	IN	35,070	C
Manhattan College	NY	49,588	C+
Manhattanville College	NY	50,740	VC
Mansfield Univ	PA	19,468	LC
Marian Univ	IN	38,540	C
Marian Univ	WI	32,420	C
Marietta College	OH	42,135	C+
Marist College	NY	35,500	C
Marlboro College	VT	35,980	VC
Marquette Univ	WI	46,930	VC+
Mars Hill Univ	NC	22,950	LC
Marshall Univ	WV	14,820	C
Martin Univ	IN	11,000	SP
Mary Baldwin College	VA	38,245	C
Marygrove College	MI	28,926	C
Marylhurst Univ	OR	20,295	NC
Marymount Manhattan College	NY	40,118	VC
Marymount Univ	VA	39,480	C
Maryville College	TN	33,150	C+
Maryville Univ of St. Louis	MO	35,856	VC
Marywood Univ	PA	45,595	C
Mass College of Liberal Arts	MA	18,613	C
McDaniel College	MD	47,450	VC
McKendree Univ	IL	29,920	C+
McMurry Univ	TX	25,962	LC
McNeese State Univ	LA	2,649	C
McPherson College	KS	28,138	C
Medaille College	NY	35,112	C
Megar Evers College/The CUNY	NY	4,920	NC
Menlo College	CA	49,002	C
Mercer Univ	GA	44,201	VC
Mercy College	NY	30,456	C
Mercyhurst Univ	PA	40,700	C
Meredith College	NC	31,420	C
Merrimack College	MA	44,215	C
Messiah College	PA	40,690	C+
Methodist Univ	NC	37,185	C
Metropolitan College of New York	NY	16,720	VC
Metropolitan State Univ	MN	5,923	
Metropolitan State Univ of Denver	CO	4,835	LC
Miami Univ	OH	24,191	VC
Mich State Univ	MI	22,450	VC
Mich Tech Univ	MI	23,556	HC
MidAmerica Nazarene Univ	KS	28,000	C
Middle Tenn State Univ	TN	8,650	C
Middlebury College	VT	59,160	MC
Midland Univ	NE	34,000	C
Midway College	KY	20,150	LC
Midwestern State Univ	TX	9,722	C
Millersville Univ of Pennsylvania	PA	21,648	C
Milligan College	TN	27,510	C
Millikin Univ	IL	38,940	C
Mills College	CA	54,119	VC
Millsaps College	MS	48,888	VC+
Minn State Univ, Mankato	MN	15,616	C
Minn State Univ, Moorhead	MN	13,392	VC
Minot State Univ	ND	10,915	C

School	ST	$IS	SR
Misericordia Univ	PA	41,060	C
Miss College	MS	21,998	C
Miss State Univ	MS	14,750	C
Miss Univ for Women	MS	7,400	C
Missouri Baptist Univ	MO	31,830	C
Missouri Southern State Univ	MO	12,061	C
Missouri Univ of Science and Technology	MO	18,655	VC+
Missouri Valley College	MO	22,200	C
Missouri Western State Univ	MO	12,260	NC
Mitchell College	CT	40,983	C
Molloy College	NY	40,440	C
Monmouth College	IL	40,850	C
Monmouth Univ	NJ	44,108	C
Montana State Univ	MT	14,068	C
Montana State Univ-Billings	MT	12,425	LC
Montclair State Univ	NJ	22,614	C
Montreat College	NC	31,298	C
Moravian College	PA	36,381	VC
Morehead State Univ	KY	10,900	C
Morehouse College	GA	39,412	C
Morgan State Univ	MD	14,500	VC
Morningside College	IA	35,430	C
Mount Aloysius College	PA	29,976	C
Mount Holyoke College	MA	55,146	MC
Mount Mary Univ	WI	33,590	LC
Mount Mercy Univ	IA	35,320	C
Mount St. Mary College	NY	41,138	C
Mount St. Mary's Univ	MD	47,996	C
Mount St. Mary's College - Chalon Campus	CA	43,897	VC+
Mount Vernon Nazarene Univ	OH	29,590	C
Muhlenberg College	PA	52,837	HC
Murray State Univ	KY	15,304	C
Muskingum Univ	OH	30,502	C
Naropa Univ	CO	39,166	SP
National Louis Univ	IL	16,915	LC
National Univ	CA	14,730	SP
Nazareth College of Rochester	NY	43,028	C+
Nebr Wesleyan Univ	NE	29,774	C+
Neumann Univ	PA	31,078	LC
New College of Florida	FL	14,504	MC
New England College	NH	45,930	LC
New Jersey City Univ	NJ	21,456	LC
New Mexico Highlands Univ	NM	11,904	NC
New Mexico Inst of Mining and Technology	NM	13,592	VC
New Mexico State Univ	NM	14,050	C
New York Inst of Technology	NY	45,010	VC
New York Univ	NY	61,470	MC
Newberry College	SC	26,850	LC
Newbury College	MA	43,280	LC
Newman Univ	KS	30,380	C+
Niagara Univ	NY	41,010	C
Nicholls State Univ	LA	7,095	C
Nichols College	MA	37,240	LC
Norfolk State Univ	VA	10,531	LC
N Car Agricultural and Technical State Univ	NC	13,365	LC
N Car Central Univ	NC	9,000	C
N Car State Univ	NC	16,202	HC
N Car Wesleyan College	NC	29,440	C
North Central College	IL	38,343	VC
N Dak State Univ	ND		C
North Park Univ	IL	30,130	C
Northeastern Illinois Univ	IL	10,318	LC
Northeastern Univ	MA	55,296	MC
Northern Arizona Univ	AZ	19,010	C
Northern Illinois Univ	IL	19,768	C
Northern Kentucky Univ	KY	21,134	C
Northern Mich Univ	MI	18,278	C
Northern State Univ - Aberdeen	SD	14,505	C
Northland College	WI	26,680	C
Northwest Christian Univ	OR	27,399	C
Northwest Missouri State Univ	MO	17,347	C
Northwest Nazarene Univ	ID	34,000	C
Northwest Univ	WA	18,854	C
Northwestern College	MN	24,000	C
Northwestern College of Iowa	IA	36,240	VC
Northwestern Okla State Univ	OK	7,275	NC
Northwestern State Univ of Louisiana	LA	14,368	C
Northwestern Univ	IL	61,640	MC
Norwich Univ	VT	28,212	C
Notre Dame College	OH	34,942	VC
Notre Dame de Namur Univ	CA	44,236	LC
Notre Dame of Maryland Univ	MD	27,700	VC
Nova Southeastern Univ	FL	37,280	VC
Nyack College	NY	33,250	C
Oakland Univ	MI	19,391	C
Oakwood Univ	AL	25,529	NC
Oberlin College	OH	61,788	MC
Occidental College	CA	60,972	MC
Oglethorpe Univ	GA	44,200	C+
Ohio Dominican Univ	OH	38,380	C+
Ohio Northern Univ	OH	42,075	VC
Ohio State Univ at Lima	OH	7,140	C
Ohio State Univ at Mansfield	OH	13,160	C
Ohio State Univ at Marion	OH	16,990	MC
Ohio State Univ at Newark	OH	17,510	C
Ohio Univ	OH	21,080	C

School	ST	$IS	SR
Ohio Valley Univ	WV	17,752	C
Ohio Wesleyan Univ	OH	49,460	C+
Okla Baptist Univ	OK	28,202	C
Okla Christian Univ	OK	25,870	VC
Okla City Univ	OK	40,476	VC
Okla Panhandle State Univ	OK	8,996	C
Okla State Univ	OK	14,310	VC
Old Dominion Univ	VA	19,483	LC
Olivet College	MI	19,984	LC
Olivet Nazarene Univ	IL	29,990	C
Oral Roberts Univ	OK	31,734	C
Oregon State Univ	OR	20,273	VC
Oswego / SUNY	NY	20,009	VC
Ottawa Univ	KS	15,000	VC
Otterbein Univ	OH	32,214	C
Ouachita Baptist Univ	AR	30,220	VC
Our Lady of the Lake Univ	TX	22,430	LC
Pace Univ	NY	53,367	C
Pacific Lutheran Univ	WA	46,760	C+
Pacific Union College	CA	28,150	VC
Pacific Univ	OR	49,626	C+
Paine College	GA	19,826	LC
Palm Beach Atlantic Univ	FL	34,874	C+
Park Univ	MO	17,525	C
Paul Quinn College	TX	25,350	LC
Penn State Erie/The Behrend College	PA	16,256	C
Pepperdine Univ	CA	55,372	HC+
Peru State College	NE	8,600	NC
Pfeiffer Univ	NC	33,700	LC
Philadelphia Univ	PA	44,160	C
Philander Smith College	AR	19,760	LC
Piedmont College	GA	30,136	C
Pine Manor College	MA	32,659	LC
Pittsburg State Univ	KS	12,032	C
Pitzer College	CA	54,988	MC
Plymouth State Univ	NH	23,148	LC
Point Loma Nazarene Univ	CA	41,006	C+
Point Park Univ	PA	36,390	C
Pomona College	CA	57,680	MC
Pontifical Catholic Univ of PR	PR	7,310	
Portland State Univ	OR	18,672	C
Post Univ	CT	35,750	C
Prairie View A&M Univ	TX	15,205	LC
Presbyterian College	SC	42,678	C+
Prescott College	AZ	33,284	C
Princeton Univ	NJ	53,795	MC
Providence College	RI	57,383	VC
Purdue Univ/Calumet	IN	14,336	C
Purdue Univ/West Lafayette	IN	20,024	HC
Queens College/The CUNY	NY	17,107	VC
Queens Univ of Charlotte	NC	39,543	C+
Quincy Univ	IL	34,980	LC
Quinnipiac Univ	CT	55,160	VC
Radford Univ	VA	17,766	C
Ramapo College of New Jersey	NJ	24,938	C
Randolph College	VA	45,660	VC
Randolph-Macon College	VA	45,869	C+
Reed College	OR	57,780	MC
Regis College	MA	47,565	LC
Regis Univ	CO	41,318	C
Rensselaer Polytechnic Inst	NY	61,529	MC
Rhode Island College	RI	17,694	LC
Rhodes College	TN	51,900	HC+
Rice Univ	TX	43,288	MC
Richard Stockton College of New Jersey	NJ	20,000	VC
Rider Univ	NJ	45,720	C
Ripon College	WI	36,959	C+
Rivier Univ	NH	35,000	VC
Roanoke College	VA	44,976	C
Robert Morris Univ	PA	37,864	C
Roberts Wesleyan College	NY	38,306	C+
Rochester College	MI	18,320	LC
Rochester Inst of Technology	NY	42,450	VC
Rockford College	IL	31,000	C
Rockhurst Univ	MO	20,625	C
Rocky Mountain College	MT	32,242	C
Roger Williams Univ	RI	46,296	VC
Rollins College	FL	52,370	HC
Roosevelt Univ	IL	22,605	VC
Rosemont College	PA	42,350	C
Rowan Univ	NJ	24,022	VC+
Russell Sage College	NY	39,370	C
Rutgers, The State Univ of New Jersey/Camden Campus	NJ	25,121	C
Rutgers, The State Univ of New Jersey/New Brunswick	NJ	25,562	VC
Rutgers, The State Univ of New Jersey/Newark Campus	NJ	258,806	C
Sacred Heart Univ	CT	49,264	VC
Saginaw Valley State Univ	MI	17,369	C
St. Anselm College	NH	49,376	VC
St. Augustine's Univ	NC	14,000	C
St. Francis College	NY	30,029	LC
St. John's Univ	MN	47,984	C
St. Joseph's College	IN	36,500	C
St. Joseph's College of Maine	ME	31,580	C
St. Joseph's Univ	PA	55,006	VC
St. Leo Univ	FL	30,340	C
St. Louis Univ	MO	48,346	HC
St. Martin's Univ	WA	41,678	C

School	ST	$IS	SR
St. Mary-of-the-Woods College	IN	37,722	LC
St. Mary's College	IN	45,160	C+
St. Mary's College of Calif	CA	53,550	C
St. Mary's Univ	TX	33,854	C
St. Mary's Univ of Minn	MN	38,280	C
St. Michael's College	VT	49,975	VC
St. Peter's Univ	NJ	44,240	C
St. Vincent College	PA	40,244	C
St. Xavier Univ	IL	32,840	C
Salem College	NC	29,326	VC
Salem State Univ	MA	13,161	LC
Salisbury Univ	MD	19,180	VC
Salve Regina Univ	RI	48,550	VC
Sam Houston State Univ	TX	17,082	C
Samford Univ	AL	37,060	C+
San Diego Christian College	CA	31,012	C
San Diego State Univ	CA	21,611	C+
San Francisco State Univ	CA	18,514	C
San Jose State Univ	CA	19,133	LC
Sarah Lawrence College	NY	48,000	HC
Schreiner Univ	TX	32,734	LC
Scripps College	CA	61,940	MC
Seattle Pacific Univ	WA	41,559	VC+
Seattle Univ	WA	49,035	VC+
Seton Hall Univ	NJ	45,902	C
Seton Hill Univ	PA	35,172	C
Sewanee: The Univ of the South	TN	47,700	HC+
Shaw Univ	NC	15,488	C
Shawnee State Univ	OH	16,916	C
Shenandoah Univ	VA	39,916	C
Shepherd Univ	WV	15,875	C
Shippensburg Univ of Pennsylvania	PA	20,934	C
Shorter Univ	GA	30,650	LC
Siena College	NY	43,863	VC
Siena Heights Univ	MI	32,040	C
Silver Lake College	WI	22,600	LC
Simmons College	MA	49,966	VC
Simpson College	IA	36,086	C+
Simpson Univ	CA	28,900	C
Skidmore College	NY	59,942	HC
Slippery Rock Univ of Pennsylvania	PA	10,360	C
Smith College	MA	59,674	MC
Sojourner-Douglass College	MD	9,160	LC
Sonoma State Univ	CA	20,541	C
S Car State Univ	SC	6,700	LC
S Dak State Univ	SD	14,296	C
Southeast Missouri State Univ	MO	15,370	LC
Southeastern Louisiana Univ	LA	13,325	C
Southeastern Okla State Univ	OK	7,966	LC
Southeastern Univ	FL	27,201	C
Southern Adventist Univ	TN	26,190	C
Southern Arkansas Univ	AR	14,316	C
Southern Conn State Univ	CT	18,033	LC
Southern Illinois Univ Carbondale	IL	21,942	C
Southern Illinois Univ Edwardsville	IL	17,532	C
Southern Methodist Univ	TX	60,585	MC
Southern Nazarene Univ	OK	24,354	C
Southern New Hampshire Univ	NH	38,100	C
Southern Oregon Univ	OR	17,874	C
Southern Polytechnic State Univ	GA	13,958	C
Southern Univ and A&M College	LA	9,761	LC
Southern Univ at New Orleans	LA	2,963	NC
Southern Vermont College	VT	30,740	LC
Southern Wesleyan Univ	SC	25,600	C
Southwest Baptist Univ	MO	24,710	C
Southwest Minn State Univ	MN	14,000	C
Southwestern Adventist Univ	TX	23,026	LC
Southwestern College	KS	29,270	C
Southwestern Okla State Univ	OK	9,160	C
Southwestern Univ	TX	45,660	VC
Spalding Univ	KY	32,287	LC
Spelman College	GA	24,650	C
Spring Arbor Univ	MI	26,740	C
Spring Hill College	AL	44,164	VC
Springfield College	MA	25,000	C
St. Ambrose Univ	IA	30,845	C
St. Andrews Univ	NC	32,050	LC
St. Bonaventure Univ	NY	41,575	C
St. Catherine Univ	MN	37,782	C+
St. Cloud State Univ	MN	10,600	C
St. Edward's Univ	TX	47,784	C
St. Francis College	NY	34,200	C
St. John Fisher College	NY	40,708	C+
St. John's Univ	NY	55,070	C+
St. Joseph's College, New York/Brooklyn Campus	NY	22,630	C
St. Joseph's College, New York/Suffolk Campus	NY	22,630	C
St. Lawrence Univ	NY	59,972	VC
St. Mary's College of Maryland	MD	25,754	VC
St. Norbert College	WI	41,478	VC
St. Olaf College	MN	51,200	HC+
St. Thomas Aquinas College	NY	40,230	C
St. Thomas Univ	FL	32,310	LC
Stanford Univ	CA	58,388	MC

ST = STATE   **$IS** = IN-STATE COSTS   **SR** = SELECTOR RATING

School	ST	$IS	SR
SUNY at Purchase	NY	16,951	C
SUNY Polytechnic Inst	NY	19,690	C
SUNY/Empire State College	NY	6,315	SP
Stephen F. Austin State Univ	TX	14,668	C
Stetson Univ	FL	51,516	VC
Stevenson Univ	MD	41,470	C
Stonehill College	MA	46,780	MC
Stony Brook Univ / SUNY	NY	20,078	HC+
Suffolk Univ	MA	47,298	C
Sul Ross State Univ	TX	13,410	LC
SUNY College at Geneseo	NY	18,670	HC
SUNY College at Old Westbury	NY	16,324	C
SUNY Cortland/The SUNY	NY	19,759	C+
SUNY Fredonia/The SUNY at Fredonia	NY	19,840	VC
SUNY New Paltz	NY	14,348	C
SUNY Oneonta / SUNY	NY	16,919	C+
SUNY Plattsburgh / SUNY	NY	18,083	C
Susquehanna Univ	PA	51,150	C
Swarthmore College	PA	57,870	MC
Syracuse Univ	NY	56,346	VC
Tabor College	KS	29,010	C
Talladega College	AL	17,996	C
Taylor Univ	IN	37,821	VC+
Temple Univ	PA	24,392	VC
Tenn State Univ	TN	9,048	C
Tenn Tech Univ	TN	11,310	C
Tenn Wesleyan College	TN	21,250	C
Texas A&M Univ	TX	19,207	VC
Texas A&M Univ at Commerce	TX	10,496	C
Texas A&M Univ at Corpus Christi	TX	11,544	LC
Texas A&M Univ at Kingsville	TX	7,500	LC
Texas Christian Univ	TX	49,980	HC
Texas Lutheran Univ	TX	36,040	C
Texas Southern Univ	TX	18,212	LC
Texas State Univ	TX	17,128	C
Texas Tech Univ	TX	14,243	C
Texas Wesleyan Univ	TX	31,382	C
Texas Woman's Univ	TX	13,633	LC
The Catholic Univ of America	DC	52,852	VC
The College of Idaho	ID	31,277	C+
The College of New Rochelle	NY	33,600	VC
The College of St. Rose	NY	26,750	C
Ohio State Univ-Columbus Campus	OH	19,887	HC+
The Pennsylvania State Univ - Univ Park	PA	28,022	VC+
The SUNY at Potsdam	NY	18,473	C
The SUNY/College at Brockport	NY	19,002	C
The Univ of Memphis	TN	15,094	C
The Univ of N Car at Greensboro	NC	12,848	C
The Univ of N Car at Pembroke	NC	13,388	LC
The Univ of Okla	OK	18,621	VC
The Univ of Tenn at Chattanooga	TN	16,883	C
The Univ of Utah	UT	16,463	VC
The Univ of Virginia's College at Wise	VA	11,076	C
Thiel College	PA	38,728	LC
Thomas College	ME	33,560	LC
Thomas Edison State College	NJ	5,700	SP
Thomas More College	KY	34,760	C
Thomas Univ	GA	15,275	NC
Tougaloo College	MS	15,275	NC
Touro College	NY	27,959	VC
Towson Univ	MD	16,000	VC
Transylvania Univ	KY	42,660	VC+
Trevecca Nazarene Univ	TN	31,186	C
Trine Univ	IN	39,400	HC+
Trinity Christian College	IL	28,869	C
Trinity College	CT		HC+
Trinity International Univ	IL	31,070	C
Trinity Univ	TX	48,150	HC+
Trinity Washington Univ	DC	30,250	C
Troy Univ	AL	10,650	C
Truman State Univ	MO	15,541	HC
Tufts Univ	MA	58,780	MC
Tulane Univ	LA	60,861	MC
Tusculum College	TN	24,295	C
Tuskegee Univ	AL	26,750	C
Union College	KY	29,955	C
Union College	NE	23,270	C
Union College	NY	60,240	MC
Union Inst & Univ	OH	8,912	SP
Union Univ	TN	28,260	C
United States Air Force Academy	CO		MC
Universidad del Turabo	PR	4,110	
Universidad Metropolitana	PR	3,500	
Univ at Albany / SUNY	NY	18,674	VC
Univ at Buffalo / The SUNY	NY	20,283	VC
Univ of Akron	OH	20,436	C
Univ of Alabama at Birmingham	AL	18,484	C+
Univ of Alabama at Tuscaloosa	AL	17,164	C+
Univ of Alabama in Huntsville	AL	17,591	VC+
Univ of Alaska Anchorage	AK	16,673	NC
Univ of Alaska Fairbanks	AK	15,130	C
Univ of Arizona	AZ	20,657	C
Univ of Arkansas at Fayetteville	AR	18,352	C+
Univ of Arkansas at Little Rock	AR	17,609	LC
Univ of Arkansas at Monticello	AR	12,076	NC
Univ of Arkansas at Pine Bluff	AR	13,378	C
Univ of Bridgeport	CT	39,030	LC
Univ of Calif at Berkeley	CA	23,322	MC
Univ of Calif at Davis	CA		HC
Univ of Calif at Irvine	CA	25,961	VC
Univ of Calif at Los Angeles	CA	25,686	MC
Univ of Calif at Riverside	CA	27,204	C+
Univ of Calif at San Diego	CA	21,000	VC
Univ of Calif at Santa Barbara	CA	27,551	VC
Univ of Calif at Santa Cruz	CA	27,807	C+
Univ of Central Arkansas	AR	13,667	VC
Univ of Central Florida	FL	15,668	VC+
Univ of Central Missouri	MO	14,605	C
Univ of Central Okla	OK	12,293	C
Univ of Charleston	WV	32,300	C
Univ of Chicago	IL	55,416	MC
Univ of Cincinnati	OH	21,506	VC
Univ of Colo at Colo Springs	CO	15,000	VC
Univ of Colo Boulder	CO	22,605	VC+
Univ of Colo Denver	CO	17,904	C
Univ of Conn	CT	24,706	VC
Univ of Dallas	TX	45,500	VC+
Univ of Dayton	OH	49,070	VC
Univ of Delaware	DE	23,612	VC
Univ of Denver	CO	51,787	VC+
Univ of Detroit Mercy	MI	30,450	VC
Univ of Dubuque	IA	30,200	C
Univ of Evansville	IN	42,656	VC+
Univ of Findlay	OH	31,916	C
Univ of Florida	FL	15,943	HC
Univ of Georgia	GA	20,082	VC
Univ of Great Falls	MT	27,970	C
Univ of Hartford	CT	42,674	C
Univ of Hawaii at Hilo	HI	23,066	C
Univ of Hawaii at Manoa	HI	19,379	C
Univ of Houston-Downtown	TX	15,170	LC
Univ of Idaho	ID	14,558	C
Univ of Illinois at Chicago	IL	24,505	VC
Univ of Illinois at Urbana-Champaign	IL	26,450	VC
Univ of Indianapolis	IN	31,740	LC
Univ of Iowa	IA	17,693	VC
Univ of Jamestown	ND	24,738	C
Univ of Kansas	KS	17,603	C+
Univ of Kentucky	KY	19,868	C
Univ of La Verne	CA	47,010	C
Univ of Louisiana at Lafayette	LA	6,130	C
Univ of Louisiana at Monroe	LA	12,998	C
Univ of Louisville	KY	17,946	C
Univ of Maine	ME	19,902	C+
Univ of Maine at Farmington	ME	18,187	LC
Univ of Mary	ND	16,714	C
Univ of Mary Hardin-Baylor	TX	31,950	C+
Univ of Mary Washington	VA	19,484	VC
Univ of Maryland - College Park	MD	20,060	HC
Univ of Maryland/Baltimore County	MD	18,000	VC
Univ of Maryland/Univ College	MD	6,168	SP
Univ of Mass Amherst	MA	24,215	VC+
Univ of Mass Boston	MA	23,066	VC
Univ of Mass Dartmouth	MA	22,223	C
Univ of Mass Lowell	MA	19,316	C
Univ of Miami	FL	57,034	MC
Univ of Mich/Ann Arbor	MI	22,102	MC
Univ of Mich/Dearborn	MI	9,885	VC
Univ of Mich-Flint	MI	17,547	C+
Univ of Minn/Duluth	MN	19,806	C
Univ of Minn/Morris	MN	17,150	VC
Univ of Minn/Twin Cities	MN		HC
Univ of Miss	MS	16,704	C+
Univ of Missouri/Columbia	MO	18,201	MC
Univ of Missouri-Kansas City	MO	19,603	C
Univ of Missouri-St. Louis	MO		VC
Univ of Mobile	AL	28,935	VC
Univ of Montana	MT	14,105	C
Univ of Montevallo	AL	17,060	C
Univ of Mount Olive	NC	18,426	C
Univ of Mount Union	OH	35,130	C
Univ of Nebr - Lincoln	NE	18,031	VC
Univ of Nebr at Kearney	NE	14,855	LC
Univ of Nebr at Omaha	NE	12,700	C
Univ of Nevada, Las Vegas	NV	17,303	C
Univ of Nevada/Reno	NV	17,507	C
Univ of New England	ME	46,750	C
Univ of New Hampshire	NH	26,912	C
Univ of New Haven	CT	48,940	C
Univ of New Mexico	NM	15,300	C
Univ of New Orleans	LA	9,224	C
Univ of North Alabama	AL	9,960	C
Univ of N Car at Asheville	NC	13,500	VC
Univ of N Car at Chapel Hill	NC	18,928	MC
Univ of N Car at Charlotte	NC	15,547	C
Univ of N Car at Wilmington	NC	13,572	VC
Univ of N Dak	ND	14,551	C
Univ of North Florida	FL	15,870	VC
Univ of North Georgia	GA	8,500	C
Univ of North Texas	TX	15,628	C
Univ of Northern Colo	CO	18,446	C
Univ of Northern Iowa	IA	15,795	C
Univ of Notre Dame	IN	57,117	MC
Univ of Oregon	OR	21,360	C+
Univ of Pennsylvania	PA	61,132	MC
Univ of Pikeville	KY	25,500	NC
Univ of Pittsburgh at Bradford	PA	21,802	C
Univ of Pittsburgh at Greensburg	PA	17,640	C
Univ of Pittsburgh at Johnstown	PA	20,862	LC
Univ of Pittsburgh at Pittsburgh	PA	28,572	HC+
Univ of Portland	OR	49,964	VC
Univ of PR Recinto de Rio Piedras	PR	5,750	
Univ of PR/Cayey	PR	1,504	
Univ of PR/Mayaguez	PR	1,250	
Univ of Puget Sound	WA	54,608	HC
Univ of Redlands	CA	40,500	VC
Univ of Rio Grande	OH	8,750	NC
Univ of Rochester	NY	60,668	MC
Univ of St. Francis	IN	29,810	C
Univ of St. Joseph	CT	45,630	C
Univ of St. Mary	KS	28,400	C+
Univ of San Diego	CA	54,818	HC+
Univ of San Francisco	CA	54,770	VC
Univ of Science and Arts of Okla	OK	10,560	VC
Univ of Scranton	PA	51,940	VC
Univ of Sioux Falls	SD	22,990	C
Univ of South Alabama	AL	13,510	C
Univ of S Car Aiken	SC	16,712	C
Univ of S Car at Columbia	SC	19,725	VC+
Univ of S Car Upstate	SC	18,200	LC
Univ of S Dak	SD	15,111	C
Univ of South Florida/St. Petersburg	FL	12,769	C
Univ of South Florida/Tampa	FL	13,000	C
Univ of Southern Calif	CA	56,903	MC
Univ of Southern Indiana	IN	14,885	C
Univ of Southern Maine	ME	16,576	C
Univ of Southern Miss	MS	13,170	C
Univ of St. Francis	IL	37,560	C
Univ of St. Thomas - Houston	TX	37,690	C
Univ of Tampa	FL	35,160	VC
Univ of Tenn at Knoxville	TN	20,364	VC+
Univ of Tenn at Martin	TN	13,734	C
Univ of Texas - Pan American	TX	11,125	LC
Univ of Texas at Arlington	TX	10,908	LC
Univ of Texas at Austin	TX	44,074	MC
Univ of Texas at Dallas	TX	21,348	HC+
Univ of Texas at El Paso	TX	8,764	NC
Univ of the Cumberlands	KY	27,500	C
Univ of the District of Columbia	DC	7,244	LC
Univ of the Incarnate Word	TX	37,316	LC
Univ of the Ozarks	AR	31,440	C
Univ of the Pacific	CA	52,146	VC
Univ of the Sacred Heart	PR	5,590	
Univ of the Sciences	PA	48,320	VC+
Univ of the Southwest	NM	15,000	C
Univ of Toledo	OH	18,464	C
Univ of Tulsa	OK	46,331	MC
Univ of Vermont	VT	27,006	VC+
Univ of Virginia	VA	23,050	MC
Univ of Washington	WA	14,722	VC
Univ of West Alabama	AL	14,274	C
Univ of West Florida	FL	14,656	C
Univ of West Georgia	GA	15,488	LC
Univ of Wisc Whitewater	WI	13,314	C
Univ of Wisc/Eau Claire	WI	15,730	VC
Univ of Wisc/Green Bay	WI	19,074	C
Univ of Wisc/La Crosse	WI	9,304	VC
Univ of Wisc/Madison	WI	18,757	HC+
Univ of Wisc/Oshkosh	WI	10,426	C
Univ of Wisc/Parkside	WI	10,181	LC
Univ of Wisc/Platteville	WI	14,564	C
Univ of Wisc/River Falls	WI	9,722	LC
Univ of Wisc/Stevens Point	WI	14,043	C
Univ of Wisc/Stout	WI	15,459	C
Univ of Wisc/Superior	WI	14,314	C
Univ of Wisc-Milwaukee	WI	18,436	C
Univ of Wyoming	WY	14,401	C+
Upper Iowa Univ	IA	30,426	NC
Urbana Univ	OH	30,820	C
Ursinus College	PA	57,580	VC
Ursuline College	OH	33,198	LC
Utah State Univ	UT	12,044	C
Utica College	NY	45,670	C
Valparaiso Univ	IN	44,940	VC+
Vanderbilt Univ	TN	58,220	MC
Vanguard Univ of Southern Calif	CA	35,833	VC
Vassar College	NY	61,140	MC
Villanova Univ	PA	58,394	MC
Virginia Commonwealth Univ	VA	21,716	C
Virginia Military Inst	VA	16,156	C
Virginia Polytechnic Inst and State Univ	VA	14,629	HC
Virginia State Univ	VA	11,318	C+
Virginia Union Univ	VA	18,432	C
Virginia Wesleyan College	VA	28,433	LC
Viterbo Univ	WI	30,070	C
Wabash College	IN	46,850	C+
Wagner College	NY	48,600	C+
Wake Forest Univ	NC	58,838	MC
Walla Walla Univ	WA	26,256	NC
Walsh Univ	OH	35,100	C
Warner Univ	FL	18,000	C
Warren Wilson College	NC	40,132	VC
Wartburg College	IA	41,055	VC
Washburn Univ	KS	12,579	C
Washington Adventist Univ	MD	25,859	LC
Washington and Jefferson College	PA	51,948	VC
Washington and Lee Univ	VA	52,812	MC
Washington College	MD	52,602	VC
Washington State Univ	WA	20,461	C
Washington Univ in St. Louis	MO	69,844	MC
Wayland Baptist Univ	TX	18,912	LC
Wayne State College	NE	11,764	NC
Wayne State Univ	MI	22,063	C
Waynesburg Univ	PA	30,150	C
Webster Univ	MO	35,100	C
Wellesley College	MA	59,038	MC
Wells College	NY	49,400	VC
Wesley College	DE	31,115	LC
Wesleyan College	GA	24,000	C
Wesleyan Univ	CT	61,198	MC
West Chester Univ of Pennsylvania	PA	17,186	C
West Liberty Univ	WV	9,142	LC
West Texas A&M Univ	TX	13,478	C
West Virginia State Univ	WV	8,378	NC
West Virginia Univ	WV	16,542	C+
West Virginia Wesleyan College	WV	26,880	C
Western Carolina Univ	NC	13,965	C
Western Conn State Univ	CT	18,327	LC
Western Illinois Univ	IL	20,732	C
Western Kentucky Univ	KY	11,000	LC
Western Mich Univ	MI	19,628	C
Western New England Univ	MA	46,154	C+
Western New Mexico Univ	NM	8,500	LC
Western Oregon Univ	OR	15,021	C
Western State Colo Univ	CO	16,924	C
Western Washington Univ	WA	18,519	VC
Westfield State Univ	MA	18,297	C
Westminster College	MO	31,720	VC
Westminster College	PA	31,290	C+
Westminster College	UT	37,708	C
Westmont College	CA	41,500	HC
Wheaton College	IL	40,720	MC
Wheaton College	MA	54,934	HC+
Wheeling Jesuit Univ	WV	33,500	C
Whitman College	WA	55,988	MC
Whittier College	CA	43,416	C
Whitworth Univ	WA	47,734	VC
Wichita State Univ	KS	14,607	C+
Widener Univ	PA	52,418	C
Wilberforce Univ	OH	15,100	LC
Wilkes Univ	PA	44,070	C
Willamette Univ	OR	56,450	VC+
William Carey Univ	MS	13,500	LC
William Jewell College	MO	31,000	VC+
William Paterson Univ of New Jersey	NJ	21,694	C
William Peace Univ	NC	32,900	LC
William Penn Univ	IA	26,000	C
William Woods Univ	MO	24,260	C
Williams Baptist College	AR	20,070	C
Williams College	MA	61,070	MC
Wilmington College	OH	29,784	C
Wilson College	PA	35,080	C
Wingate Univ	NC	34,990	C
Winona State Univ	MN	16,640	C
Winston-Salem State Univ	NC	9,418	LC
Winthrop Univ	SC	21,120	C
Wisc Lutheran College	WI	23,510	VC
Wittenberg Univ	OH	47,962	C+
Wofford College	SC	45,795	VC
Woodbury Univ	CA	34,500	LC
Worcester State Univ	MA	19,812	C
Wright State Univ	OH	16,983	C
Xavier Univ	OH	44,980	VC
Xavier Univ of Louisiana	LA	25,300	C
Yale Univ	CT	55,300	MC
Yeshiva Univ	NY	47,250	VC+
York College	NE	19,475	C
York College / The CUNY	NY	5,496	SP
York College of Pennsylvania	PA	26,590	C
Youngstown State Univ	OH	16,732	C

PSYCHOLOGY EDUCATION

School	ST	$IS	SR
Bethany College	WV	35,282	LC
Bloomfield College	NJ	37,850	LC
Eastern Mich Univ	MI	18,604	C
Kutztown Univ of Pennsylvania	PA	16,909	LC
Mount Holyoke College	MA	55,146	MC
Nazareth College of Rochester	NY	43,028	C+
Pittsburg State Univ	KS	12,032	C

ST = STATE $IS = IN-STATE COSTS   SR = SELECTOR RATING

School	ST	$IS	SR
Rocky Mountain College	MT	32,242	C
St. Vincent College	PA	40,244	C
Tulane Univ	LA	60,861	MC
Univ of Arizona	AZ	20,657	C
Univ of Delaware	DE	23,612	VC
Univ of Rio Grande	OH	8,750	NC
Valparaiso Univ	IN	44,940	VC+
York College	NE	19,475	C

PUBLIC ADMINISTRATION

School	ST	$IS	SR
American International College	MA	36,100	LC
Aquinas College	MI	33,060	C
Ashford Univ	CA	10,480	C
Auburn Univ	AL	22,378	VC+
Augustana College	IL	43,398	VC
Austin Peay State Univ	TN	15,274	C
Baldwin Wallace Univ	OH	38,318	C
Baylor Univ	TX	50,329	MC
Bentley Univ	MA	56,454	HC+
Blackburn College	IL	21,350	C
Bloomfield College	NJ	37,850	LC
Brown Univ	RI	59,428	MC
Buena Vista Univ	IA	39,188	C
Cal State, Bakersfield	CA	8,000	C
Cal State, Chico	CA	20,158	C
Cal State, Dominguez Hills	CA	17,090	LC
Cal State, Fresno	CA	17,405	C
Cal State, Fullerton	CA	25,188	C
Cal State, Sacramento	CA	16,200	C
Cal State, San Bernardino	CA	12,000	C
Calvin College	MI	39,120	VC
Carlow Univ	PA	30,272	C
Carnegie Mellon Univ	PA	51,260	MC
Carroll College	MT	28,000	C
Catawba College	NC	37,240	LC
Cedarville Univ	OH	32,860	VC
Central State Univ	OH	9,010	C
Central Washington Univ	WA	11,730	C
Chancellor Univ	OH	11,000	C
Dakota Wesleyan Univ	SD	23,000	C
DePaul Univ	IL	47,623	VC
Doane College	NE	35,230	C
Dordt College	IA	34,160	C+
Eastern Mich Univ	MI	18,604	C
Edgewood College	WI	33,294	C
Elizabethtown College	PA	49,740	VC
Elizabethtown College School of Continuing and Professional Studies	PA		VC
Elon Univ	NC	41,914	VC+
Evangel Univ	MO	23,090	C
Fayetteville State Univ	NC	10,816	C
Flagler College	FL	25,180	C
Florida A&M Univ	FL	14,935	LC
Florida Atlantic Univ	FL	17,339	C
Florida International Univ	FL	17,747	C+
Florida Memorial Univ	FL	20,888	LC
George Mason Univ	VA	15,724	VC
Grambling State Univ	LA	13,384	LC
Grand Valley State Univ	MI	17,998	C+
Harding Univ	AR	23,556	C
Hawaii Pacific Univ	HI	34,360	C
Heidelberg Univ	OH	34,100	C
Henderson State Univ	AR	14,584	C
Howard Univ	DC	13,646	C
Indiana Univ Kokomo	IN	6,811	LC
Indiana Univ-Purdue Univ Fort Wayne	IN	15,521	C
Inter-American Univ of PR/ Fajardo Campus	PR	4,200	
Inter-American Univ of PR/ Ponce	PR		
Inter-American Univ of PR/ San Germán	PR	6,720	
James Madison Univ	VA	18,049	VC
John Jay College of Criminal Justice/The CUNY	NY	6,359	LC
Juniata College	PA	49,340	VC
Kean Univ	NJ	23,444	C
Kentucky State Univ	KY	11,000	LC
Kutztown Univ of Pennsylvania	PA	16,909	LC
La Salle Univ	PA	50,270	C
Lakeland College	WI	22,990	C
Lamar Univ	TX	6,820	LC
LeTourneau Univ	TX	36,210	VC
Lewis Univ	IL	23,050	C
Lincoln Univ	MO	12,904	NC
Lindenwood Univ	MO	20,750	C
LIU Post	NY	47,660	C
Louisiana College	LA	15,746	C
Mass College of Liberal Arts	MA	18,613	C
Megar Evers College/The CUNY	NY	4,920	NC
Metropolitan State Univ	MN	5,923	
Miami Univ	OH	24,191	VC
Mich State Univ	MI	22,450	VC
Middle Tenn State Univ	TN	8,650	C
Mills College	CA	54,119	VC
Millsaps College	MS	43,888	VC+
Miss Valley State Univ	MS	9,706	LC
Missouri Valley College	MO	22,200	C
Mount Aloysius College	PA	29,976	C
Murray State Univ	KY	15,304	C

School	ST	$IS	SR
New York Univ	NY	61,470	MC
Norfolk State Univ	VA	10,531	LC
Northern Arizona Univ	AZ	19,010	C
Northern Kentucky Univ	KY	21,134	C
Northern Mich Univ	MI	18,278	C
Northland College	WI	26,680	C
Northwest Missouri State Univ	MO	17,347	C
Northwestern State Univ of Louisiana	LA	14,368	C
Nova Southeastern Univ	FL	37,280	VC
Oakland Univ	MI	19,391	C
Ohio Univ	OH	21,080	C
Park Univ	MO	17,525	C
Plymouth State Univ	NH	23,148	LC
Point Park Univ	PA	36,390	C
Pontifical Catholic Univ of PR	PR	7,310	
Rhode Island College	RI	17,694	LC
Roger Williams Univ	RI	46,296	VC
Roosevelt Univ	IL	22,605	VC
Rutgers, The State Univ of New Jersey/Newark Campus	NJ	258,806	C
Saginaw Valley State Univ	MI	17,369	C
St. Francis Univ	PA	30,029	LC
St. Joseph's Univ	PA	55,006	VC
Samford Univ	AL	37,060	C+
San Diego State Univ	CA	21,611	C
Seattle Univ	WA	49,035	VC+
Shaw Univ	NC	15,488	C
Shenandoah Univ	VA	39,916	VC
Shippensburg Univ of Pennsylvania	PA	20,934	C
Siena Heights Univ	MI	32,040	C
Silver Lake College	WI	22,600	LC
Slippery Rock Univ of Pennsylvania	PA	10,360	C
Sojourner-Douglass College	MD	9,160	LC
Southeastern Univ	FL	27,201	C
Southern Adventist Univ	TN	26,190	C
Southwest Minn State Univ	MN	14,000	C
St. Ambrose Univ	IA	30,845	C
St. Cloud State Univ	MN	10,600	C
St. John's Univ	NY	55,070	C+
Stanford Univ	CA	58,388	MC
Stephen F. Austin State Univ	TX	14,668	C
Stonehill College	MA	46,780	HC
Talladega College	AL	17,996	C
Texas A&M Univ at Kingsville	TX	7,500	C
Texas State Univ	TX	17,128	C
The Univ of Okla	OK	18,621	VC
Thomas Edison State College	NJ	5,700	SP
Union Inst & Univ	OH	8,912	SP
Universidad del Turabo	PR	4,110	
Univ of Alaska Southeast	AK	11,493	C
Univ of Arizona	AZ	20,657	C
Univ of Arkansas at Fayetteville	AR	18,352	C+
Univ of Arkansas at Little Rock	AR	17,609	LC
Univ of Central Arkansas	AR	13,667	VC
Univ of Central Florida	FL	15,668	VC+
Univ of Central Okla	OK	12,293	C
Univ of Georgia	GA	20,082	VC
Univ of Illinois at Chicago	IL	24,505	VC
Univ of Kansas	KS	17,603	C+
Univ of La Verne	CA	47,010	C
Univ of Maine at Augusta	ME	6,855	C
Univ of Mich-Flint	MI	17,547	C
Univ of Miss	MS	16,704	C+
Univ of Missouri/Columbia	MO	18,201	MC
Univ of Missouri-St. Louis	MO		VC
Univ of Nebr at Omaha	NE	12,700	C
Univ of Nevada, Las Vegas	NV	17,303	C
Univ of New Haven	CT	48,940	C
Univ of N Dak	ND	14,551	C
Univ of North Florida	FL	15,870	VC
Univ of Northern Iowa	IA	15,795	C
Univ of Oregon	OR	21,360	VC
Univ of Pennsylvania	PA	61,132	MC
Univ of Pittsburgh at Pittsburgh	PA	28,572	HC+
Univ of San Francisco	CA	54,770	VC
Univ of Tenn at Knoxville	TN	20,364	VC+
Univ of Tenn at Martin	TN	13,734	C
Univ of Texas at Dallas	TX	21,348	HC+
Univ of Texas at San Antonio	TX	18,372	C
Univ of the District of Columbia	DC	7,244	LC
Univ of Virginia	VA	23,050	MC
Univ of Wisc Whitewater	WI	13,314	C
Univ of Wisc/Green Bay	WI	19,074	C
Univ of Wisc/La Crosse	WI	9,304	VC
Univ of Wisc/Stevens Point	WI	14,043	C
Univ of Wisc/Superior	WI	14,314	C
Virginia State Univ	VA	11,318	C
Wagner College	NY	48,600	C+
Washburn Univ	KS	12,579	C
West Texas A&M Univ	TX	13,478	C
West Virginia Univ Inst of Technology	WV	14,094	NC
Western New Mexico Univ	NM	8,500	LC
Western Oregon Univ	OR	15,021	C
Winona State Univ	MN	16,640	C

School	ST	$IS	SR
Winston-Salem State Univ	NC	9,418	LC

PUBLIC AFFAIRS

School	ST	$IS	SR
Albion College	MI	46,010	C
Arizona State Univ, at the Tempe Campus	AZ	20,137	C+
Bloomfield College	NJ	37,850	LC
Bryant Univ	RI	49,179	VC
Chatham Univ	PA	43,797	C
CUNY/Baruch College	NY		HC
College of William & Mary	VA	28,000	MC
Columbia College	SC	27,882	C
DePaul Univ	IL	47,623	VC
Dickinson College	PA	57,662	HC+
Duke Univ	NC	50,250	MC
Emory and Henry College	VA	387,460	C
Georgia Inst of Technology	GA	21,828	MC
Hamilton College	NY	55,620	MC
Howard Univ	DC	13,646	C
Indiana Univ Bloomington	IN	19,801	VC
Indiana Univ Northwest	IN	6,854	LC
Indiana Univ South Bend	IN	15,501	C
Indiana Univ-Purdue Univ Fort Wayne	IN	15,521	C
Indiana Univ-Purdue Univ Indianapolis	IN	17,611	C
Meredith College	NC	31,420	C
Mills College	CA	54,119	VC
Muskingum Univ	OH	30,502	C
New College of Florida	FL	14,504	MC
Olivet Nazarene Univ	IL	29,990	C
Pomona College	CA	57,680	MC
Rice Univ	TX	43,288	MC
Rochester Inst of Technology	NY	42,450	VC
St. Vincent College	PA	40,244	C
Southern Methodist Univ	TX	60,585	MC
Southern New Hampshire Univ	NH	38,100	C
St. Mary's College of Maryland	MD	25,754	VC
SUNY/Empire State College	NY	6,315	SP
Stevenson Univ	MD	41,470	C
Texas Southern Univ	TX	18,212	LC
Ohio State Univ-Columbus Campus	OH	19,887	HC+
Trinity College	CT		HC+
Univ of Chicago	IL	55,416	MC
Univ of Denver	CO	51,787	VC+
Univ of Illinois at Chicago	IL	24,505	VC
Univ of Mich/Ann Arbor	MI	22,102	MC
Univ of Missouri/Columbia	MO	18,201	MC
Univ of New Haven	CT	48,940	C
Univ of N Car at Chapel Hill	NC	18,928	MC
Univ of Pittsburgh at Pittsburgh	PA	28,572	HC+
Vanderbilt Univ	TN	58,220	MC
Virginia Polytechnic Inst and State Univ	VA	14,629	HC
Washington and Lee Univ	VA	52,812	MC
Wayne State Univ	MI	22,063	C
Wells College	NY	49,400	VC
Western Washington Univ	WA	18,519	VC

PUBLIC HEALTH

School	ST	$IS	SR
Agnes Scott College	GA	45,323	C+
Allegheny College	PA	50,980	VC
Allen College	IA	26,110	SP
American Univ	DC	56,015	HC+
Andrews Univ	MI	28,030	C+
Arizona State Univ, at the Downtown Phoenix Campus	AZ	22,101	C
Baldwin Wallace Univ	OH	38,318	C
Benedict College	SC	20,454	NC
Bluffton Univ	OH	38,948	C
Bowling Green State Univ	OH	18,970	C
Cal State, Fresno	CA	17,405	C
Calvin College	MI	39,120	VC
Central Washington Univ	WA	11,730	C
Colby-Sawyer College	NH	50,790	C
College of Charleston	SC	22,145	VC
Dillard Univ	LA	20,940	VC
East Carolina Univ	NC	14,169	C
East Tenn State Univ	TN	9,000	C
Edinboro Univ of Pennsylvania	PA	15,940	LC
Elon Univ	NC	41,914	VC+
Ferris State Univ	MI	20,047	C
Fort Lewis College	CO	15,513	C
Hawaii Pacific Univ	HI	34,360	C
Howard Univ	DC	13,646	C
Hunter College	NY	14,429	VC
Indiana Univ Bloomington	IN	19,801	VC
Indiana Univ-Purdue Univ Indianapolis	IN	17,611	C
Ithaca College	NY	53,864	HC
Kent State Univ	OH	19,920	C
Malone Univ	OH	35,364	C
Marshall Univ	WV	14,820	C
Minn State Univ, Mankato	MN	15,616	C
Miss Univ for Women	MS	7,400	C
Montclair State Univ	NJ	22,614	C
New Jersey City Univ	NJ	21,456	LC
New York Univ	NY	61,470	MC

School	ST	$IS	SR
Northeastern Illinois Univ	IL	10,318	LC
Ohio Univ	OH	21,080	C
Old Dominion Univ	VA	19,483	LC
Oregon State Univ	OR	20,273	VC
Regis College	MA	47,565	LC
Richard Stockton College of New Jersey	NJ	20,000	VC
Rutgers, The State Univ of New Jersey/New Brunswick	NJ	25,562	VC
St. Louis Univ	MO	48,346	HC
San Jose State Univ	CA	19,133	LC
Shenandoah Univ	VA	39,916	C
Simmons College	MA	49,966	VC
Southern Conn State Univ	CT	18,033	LC
St. Cloud State Univ	MN	10,600	C
St. Joseph's College, New York/Suffolk Campus	NY	22,630	C
Syracuse Univ	NY	56,346	VC
Taylor Univ	IN	37,821	VC+
Temple Univ	PA	24,392	VC
The Univ of N Car at Greensboro	NC	12,848	C
The Univ of Utah	UT	16,463	VC
Truman State Univ	MO	15,541	HC
Tulane Univ	LA	60,861	MC
Univ of Alabama at Birmingham	AL	18,484	C+
Univ of Arizona	AZ	20,657	C
Univ of Calif at Berkeley	CA	23,322	MC
Univ of Calif at Irvine	CA	25,961	VC
Univ of Colo Denver	CO	17,904	C
Univ of Evansville	IN	42,656	VC+
Univ of Georgia	GA	20,082	VC
Univ of Illinois at Chicago	IL	24,505	VC
Univ of Illinois at Urbana-Champaign	IL	26,450	HC
Univ of Louisville	KY	17,946	C
Univ of Maryland - College Park	MD	20,060	HC
Univ of Mass Amherst	MA	24,215	VC+
Univ of Miami	FL	57,034	MC
Univ of Missouri/Columbia	MO	18,201	MC
Univ of N Car at Charlotte	NC	15,547	C
Univ of Rochester	NY	60,668	MC
Univ of S Car at Columbia	SC	19,725	VC+
Univ of Tampa	FL	35,160	VC
Univ of the Cumberlands	KY	27,500	C
Univ of Wisc/Eau Claire	WI	15,730	VC
Utah State Univ	UT	12,044	C
Wayne State Univ	MI	22,063	C
West Chester Univ of Pennsylvania	PA	17,186	C
Western Illinois Univ	IL	20,732	C
Western Kentucky Univ	KY	11,000	C
Western New Mexico Univ	NM	8,500	LC
Winona State Univ	MN	16,640	C
Youngstown State Univ	OH	16,732	C

PUBLIC HISTORY/ARCHIVES

School	ST	$IS	SR
Arizona State Univ, at the Tempe Campus	AZ	20,137	C+
Arkansas Tech Univ	AR	13,982	LC
Baldwin Wallace Univ	OH	38,318	C
East Carolina Univ	NC	14,169	C
Northern Kentucky Univ	KY	21,134	C
Western Mich Univ	MI	19,628	C

PUBLIC RELATIONS

School	ST	$IS	SR
Abilene Christian Univ	TX	38,400	C+
American Univ	DC	56,015	HC+
Andrews Univ	MI	28,030	C+
Appalachian State Univ	NC	12,919	VC
Ashford Univ	CA	10,480	C
Auburn Univ	AL	22,378	VC+
Baldwin Wallace Univ	OH	38,318	C
Barry Univ	FL	38,190	C
Belmont Univ	TN	39,190	VC+
Bethany College	WV	35,282	C
Biola Univ	CA	40,320	C+
Bluffton Univ	OH	38,948	C
Brigham Young Univ	UT	12,100	HC
Butler Univ	IN	47,572	VC+
Calif Baptist Univ	CA	38,792	C
Cal State, Fresno	CA	17,405	C
Cal State, Fullerton	CA	25,188	C
Capital Univ	OH	41,050	VC
Cardinal Stritch Univ	WI	24,054	C
Carroll College	MT	28,000	C
Central Washington Univ	WA	11,730	C
Champlain College	VT	46,650	VC+
Chapman Univ	CA	58,347	VC+
Coe College	IA	45,550	VC
College of the Ozarks	MO		VC
Columbia College	MO	24,578	C
DePaul Univ	IL	47,623	VC
Drake Univ	IA	41,516	VC+
Drury Univ	MO	31,909	VC
Duquesne Univ	PA	43,720	VC
Eastern Kentucky Univ	KY	11,161	C
Eastern Mich Univ	MI	18,604	C
Emerson College	MA	52,446	HC+
Ferris State Univ	MI	20,047	C
Florida Southern College	FL	40,150	C+
Florida State Univ	FL	16,715	VC

School	ST	$IS	SR
Franklin College	IN	36,585	C
Freed-Hardeman Univ	TN	19,697	VC
George Washington Univ	DC	57,108	MC
Georgia Southern Univ	GA	16,942	C
Gonzaga Univ	WA	46,441	HC
Greenville College	IL	27,012	C
Gwynedd-Mercy College	PA	33,560	C
Hardin-Simmons Univ	TX	23,560	C+
Hawaii Pacific Univ	HI	34,360	C
Heidelberg Univ	OH	34,100	C
Hofstra Univ	NY	51,810	VC+
Howard Univ	DC	13,646	C
Huntington Univ	IN	32,220	C+
Illinois State Univ	IL	23,110	VC
Indiana-Purdue Univ Indianapolis	IN	17,611	C
Ithaca College	NY	53,864	HC
John Brown Univ	AR	32,056	VC+
Kent State Univ	OH	19,920	C
Lasell College	MA	43,750	LC
Le Moyne College	NY	43,470	C
Lee Univ	TN	18,690	C+
Lewis Univ	IL	23,050	C
LIU Post	NY	47,660	C
Loras College	IA	37,432	VC
Malone Univ	OH	35,364	C
Mansfield Univ	PA	19,468	LC
Marietta College	OH	42,135	C+
Marquette Univ	WI	46,930	VC+
Marshall Univ	WV	14,820	C
McKendree Univ	IL	29,920	C+
Mercyhurst Univ	PA	40,700	C
Messiah College	PA	40,690	C+
Middle Tenn State Univ	TN	8,650	C
Millersville Univ of Pennsylvania	PA	21,648	C
Millikin Univ	IL	38,940	VC
Minn State Univ, Moorhead	MN	13,392	VC
Missouri Baptist Univ	MO	31,830	C
Missouri Southern State Univ	MO	12,061	C
Montana State Univ-Billings	MT	12,425	LC
Montclair State Univ	NJ	22,614	C
Mount St. Mary College	NY	41,138	C
Mount Vernon Nazarene Univ	OH	29,590	C
Murray State Univ	KY	15,304	C
New York Univ	NY	61,470	MC
N Dak State Univ	ND		C
Northern Kentucky Univ	KY	21,134	C
Northern Mich Univ	MI	18,278	C
Northwest Missouri State Univ	MO	17,347	C
Northwestern College	MN	24,000	C
Northwestern College of Iowa	IA	36,240	VC
Northwestern Okla State Univ	OK	7,275	NC
Notre Dame College	OH	34,942	VC
Ohio Dominican Univ	OH	38,380	C+
Ohio Northern Univ	OH	42,075	VC
Ohio Univ	OH	21,080	C
Okla Christian Univ	OK	25,870	VC
Okla City Univ	OK	40,476	VC
Oswego / SUNY	NY	20,009	VC
Otterbein College	OH	32,214	C
Pacific Union College	CA	28,150	VC
Park Univ	MO	17,525	C
Pepperdine Univ	CA	55,372	HC+
Pittsburg State Univ	KS	12,032	C
Point Park Univ	PA	36,390	C
Pontifical Catholic Univ of PR	PR	7,310	
Purdue Univ/Calumet	IN	14,336	C
Purdue Univ/West Lafayette	IN	20,024	HC
Quinnipiac Univ	CT	55,160	VC
Rider Univ	NJ	45,720	C
Roosevelt Univ	IL	22,605	VC
Rowan Univ	NJ	24,022	VC+
St. Mary's Univ of Minn	MN	38,280	VC
San Jose State Univ	CA	19,133	LC
Shorter Univ	GA	30,650	LC
Southeast Missouri State Univ	MO	15,370	LC
Southeastern Univ	FL	27,201	C
Southern Adventist Univ	TN	26,190	C
Southern Illinois Univ Edwardsville	IL	17,532	C
Southern Methodist Univ	TX	60,585	MC
Spring Hill College	AL	44,164	VC
St. John's Univ	NY	55,070	C+
Stephens College	MO	38,042	VC
Suffolk Univ	MA	47,298	C
SUNY Fredonia/The SUNY at Fredonia	NY	19,840	VC
SUNY Plattsburgh / SUNY	NY	18,083	C
Syracuse Univ	NY	56,346	VC
Taylor Univ	IN	37,821	VC+
Temple Univ	PA	24,392	VC
Texas State Univ	TX	17,128	C
Texas Tech Univ	TX	14,243	C
Union College	NE	23,270	C
Union Univ	TN	28,260	VC
Univ of Akron	OH	20,436	C
Univ of Alabama at Tuscaloosa	AL	17,164	C+
Univ of Central Florida	FL	15,668	VC+
Univ of Central Missouri	MO	14,605	C
Univ of Central Okla	OK	12,293	C
Univ of Florida	FL	15,943	HC
Univ of Georgia	GA	20,082	VC
Univ of Idaho	ID	14,558	C
Univ of Indianapolis	IN	31,740	LC
Univ of Louisiana at Lafayette	LA	6,130	C
Univ of Miami	FL	57,034	MC
Univ of Nebr - Lincoln	NE	18,031	VC
Univ of North Alabama	AL	9,960	C
Univ of Northern Iowa	IA	15,795	C
Univ of Oregon	OR	21,360	C+
Univ of Pittsburgh at Bradford	PA	21,802	C
Univ of Rio Grande	OH	8,750	NC
Univ of S Car at Columbia	SC	19,725	VC+
Univ of Southern Calif	CA	56,903	MC
Univ of Southern Indiana	IN	14,885	C
Univ of Tenn at Knoxville	TN	20,364	VC+
Univ of Texas at Austin	TX	44,074	HC
Univ of Wisc Whitewater	WI	13,314	C
Ursuline College	OH	33,198	LC
Utica College	NY	45,670	C
Wartburg College	IA	41,055	VC
Washington State Univ	WA	20,461	C
Wayne State Univ	MI	22,063	C
Waynesburg Univ	PA	30,150	C
Webster Univ	MO	35,100	C+
West Texas A&M Univ	TX	13,478	C
West Virginia Univ	WV	16,542	C+
West Virginia Wesleyan College	WV	26,880	C
Western Kentucky Univ	KY	11,000	LC
Western Mich Univ	MI	19,628	C
Western New England Univ	MA	46,154	C+
Westminster College	PA	31,290	C+
William Penn Univ	IA	26,000	C
Wilmington College	OH	29,784	C
Wingate Univ	NC	34,990	C
Winthrop Univ	SC	21,120	C
Xavier Univ	OH	44,980	VC
York College of Pennsylvania	PA	26,590	C
Youngstown State Univ	OH	16,732	C

PUBLISHING

School	ST	$IS	SR
Benedictine Univ	IL	37,820	C
Biola Univ	CA	40,320	C+
Emerson College	MA	52,446	HC+
Hofstra Univ	NY	51,810	VC+
New York Univ	NY	61,470	MC
Rochester Inst of Technology	NY	42,450	VC
West Texas A&M Univ	TX	13,478	C

PUERTO RICAN STUDIES

School	ST	$IS	SR
CUNY/Brooklyn College	NY	5,884	C+
Rutgers, The State Univ of New Jersey/Newark Campus	NJ	258,806	C
Univ of Mich/Ann Arbor	MI	22,102	MC

PURCHASING/INVENTORY MANAGEMENT

School	ST	$IS	SR
Arizona State Univ, at the Tempe Campus	AZ	20,137	C+
Bloomfield College	NJ	37,850	LC
Univ of Illinois at Urbana-Champaign	IL	26,450	HC
Univ of North Texas	TX	15,628	C
Xavier Univ	OH	44,980	VC

QUANTITATIVE METHODS

School	ST	$IS	SR
Bard College at Simon's Rock	MA	61,749	HC+
Bucknell Univ	PA	60,140	MC
CUNY/City College	NY	20,319	HC+
James Madison Univ	VA	18,049	VC
Univ of Cincinnati	OH	21,506	VC
Univ of Washington	WA	14,722	VC
Whitworth Univ	WA	47,734	VC

RADIATION PROTECTION

School	ST	$IS	SR
Thomas Edison State College	NJ	5,700	SP

RADIATION THERAPY

School	ST	$IS	SR
Benedictine Univ	IL	37,820	C
Georgia Regents Univ	GA		C
Gwynedd-Mercy College	PA	33,560	C
Howard Univ	DC	13,646	C
Indiana Univ-Purdue Univ Indianapolis	IN	17,611	C
Mount Aloysius College	PA	29,976	C
North Central College	IL	38,343	VC
Oregon State Univ	OR	20,273	VC
St. Louis Univ	MO	48,346	HC
Texas State Univ	TX	17,128	C
Thomas Edison State College	NJ	5,700	SP
Univ of Mich-Flint	MI	17,547	C+
Univ of St. Francis	IL	37,560	C
Univ of Vermont	VT	27,006	VC+
Univ of Wisc/La Crosse	WI	9,304	C
Wayne State Univ	MI	22,063	C

RADIO/TELEVISION TECHNOLOGY

School	ST	$IS	SR
Arkansas State Univ	AR	15,470	C
Ball State Univ	IN	17,850	C
Biola Univ	CA	40,320	C
Cal State, Fullerton	CA	25,188	C
CUNY/Brooklyn College	NY	5,884	C+
Columbia College Chicago	IL	30,940	LC
De Sales Univ	PA	43,970	C
Drury Univ	MO	31,909	VC
Emerson College	MA	52,446	HC+
Hardin-Simmons Univ	TX	23,560	C+
Hofstra Univ	NY	51,810	VC+
Le Moyne College	NY	43,470	C
Lewis Univ	IL	23,050	C
Lyndon State College	VT	14,233	C
Marshall Univ	WV	14,820	C
Mount Ida College	MA	30,115	LC
Murray State Univ	KY	15,304	C
New York Univ	NY	61,470	MC
Northern Kentucky Univ	KY	21,134	C
Northwestern Univ	IL	61,640	MC
Ohio Univ	OH	21,080	C
Pacific Union College	CA	28,150	VC
Rowan Univ	NJ	24,022	VC+
San Francisco State Univ	CA	18,514	C
Southern Illinois Univ Carbondale	IL	21,942	C
Southern Illinois Univ Edwardsville	IL	17,532	C
St. John's Univ	NY	55,070	C+
Stephen F. Austin State Univ	TX	14,668	C
Univ of Arkansas at Little Rock	AR	17,609	LC
Univ of Central Florida	FL	15,668	VC+
Univ of Montana	MT	14,105	C
Univ of North Texas	TX	15,628	C
Univ of Southern Indiana	IN	14,885	C
Univ of Southern Miss	MS	13,170	C
Vanguard Univ of Southern Calif	CA	35,833	VC

RADIO/TV

School	ST	$IS	SR
Bloomfield College	NJ	37,850	LC
LIU Post	NY	47,660	C
New York Inst of Technology	NY	45,010	VC
San Diego State Univ	CA	21,611	C+
Southern Illinois Univ Carbondale	IL	21,942	C
Univ of Cincinnati	OH	21,506	VC

RADIOGRAPH MEDICAL TECHNOLOGY

School	ST	$IS	SR
Alderson Broaddus Univ	WV	28,656	C
Clarkson College	NE	16,300	VC
Howard Univ	DC	13,646	C
La Roche College	PA	35,824	LC
Misericordia Univ	PA	41,060	C
Mount Aloysius College	PA	29,976	C
Oregon Inst of Technology	OR	8,910	C
Pennsylvania College of Technology	PA	26,286	NC
Ohio State Univ-Columbus Campus	OH	19,887	HC+
Univ of St. Francis	IL	37,560	C

RADIOLOGIC IMAGING MODALITIES

School	ST	$IS	SR
St. Louis Univ	MO	48,346	HC
Thomas Edison State College	NJ	5,700	SP

RADIOLOGICAL SCIENCE

School	ST	$IS	SR
Adventist Univ of Health Sciences	FL	16,344	NC
Arkansas State Univ	AR	15,470	C
Armstrong State Univ	GA	15,532	C
Concordia Univ St. Paul	MN	28,250	C
Friends Univ	KS	29,100	C
George Washington Univ	DC	57,108	MC
Idaho State Univ	ID	12,307	C
Indiana Univ Northwest	IN	6,854	C
Kent State Univ	OH	19,920	C
Manhattan College	NY	49,588	C+
Midwestern State Univ	TX	9,722	C
Missouri State Univ	MO	13,996	C+
Mount Aloysius College	PA	29,976	C
New York College of Technology/The CUNY	NY	5,769	NC
Northwestern State Univ of Louisiana	LA	14,368	C
Purdue Univ/West Lafayette	IN	20,024	HC
Quinnipiac Univ	CT	55,160	C
Regis Univ	CO	47,565	LC
Southern Vermont College	VT	30,740	VC
St. Francis College	NY	34,200	C
St. John's Univ	NY	55,070	C+
Suffolk Univ	MA	47,298	C
Univ of Central Arkansas	AR	13,667	VC
Univ of Charleston	WV	32,300	C
Univ of Iowa	IA	17,693	VC
Univ of Mich/Ann Arbor	MI	22,102	MC
Univ of Miss	MS	16,704	C+
Univ of Missouri/Columbia	MO	18,201	MC
Univ of New Mexico	NM	15,300	C
Univ of N Car at Chapel Hill	NC	18,928	MC
Univ of Pittsburgh at Bradford	PA	21,802	C
Univ of South Alabama	AL	13,510	C
Univ of Southern Indiana	IN	14,885	C

RADIOLOGICAL TECHNOLOGY

School	ST	$IS	SR
Allen College	IA	26,110	SP
Austin Peay State Univ	TN	15,274	C
Avila Univ	MO	26,900	C
Bloomsburg Univ of Pennsylvania	PA	13,598	C
Boise State Univ	ID	13,469	LC
Briar Cliff Univ	IA	29,514	C
Cal State, Northridge	CA	28,690	LC
Carroll Univ	WI	38,100	C
Champlain College	VT	46,650	VC+
Clarion Univ of Pennsylvania	PA	17,370	LC
Clarkson College	NE	16,300	VC
College of St Joseph	VT	30,600	C
Concordia College - New York	NY	39,035	LC
Concordia Univ Wisc	WI	28,980	C
Fairleigh Dickinson Univ/College at Florham	NJ	42,142	C
Fairleigh Dickinson Univ/Metropolitan Campus	NJ	40,254	C
Fort Hays State Univ	KS	11,354	C
Friends Univ	KS	29,100	C
Gwynedd-Mercy College	PA	33,560	C
Henderson State Univ	AR	14,584	C
Holy Family Univ	PA	40,030	LC
Howard Univ	DC	13,646	C
Inter-American Univ of PR/Aguadilla Campus	PR	5,578	
Kent State Univ	OH	19,920	C
LIU Post	NY	47,660	C
Marian Univ	WI	32,420	LC
Mass College of Pharmacy and Health Sciences	MA	36,450	SP
McNeese State Univ	LA	2,649	C
Minot State Univ	ND	10,915	C
Missouri Southern State Univ	MO	12,061	C
Mount Aloysius College	PA	29,976	C
Mount Marty College	SD	29,638	C
Mount Mary Univ	WI	33,590	LC
Nebr Methodist College of Nursing and Allied Health	NE	22,690	SP
N Dak State Univ	ND		C
Northern Kentucky Univ	KY	21,134	C
Presentation College	SD	14,800	LC
Purdue Univ/West Lafayette	IN	20,024	HC
Rhode Island College	RI	17,694	LC
Southern Illinois Univ Carbondale	IL	21,942	C
Univ of Hartford	CT	42,674	C
Univ of Jamestown	ND	24,738	C
Univ of Louisiana at Monroe	LA	12,998	C
Univ of Mary	ND	16,714	C
Univ of Nevada, Las Vegas	NV	17,303	C
Wayne State Univ	MI	22,063	C
William Carey Univ	MS	13,500	LC
Xavier Univ	OH	44,980	VC

RANCH MANAGEMENT

School	ST	$IS	SR
Texas Christian Univ	TX	49,980	HC
Univ of Nebr - Lincoln	NE	18,031	VC

RANGE/FARM MANAGEMENT

School	ST	$IS	SR
Colo State Univ-Fort Collins	CO	20,385	VC
Eastern Oregon Univ	OR	10,400	C
Lake Erie College	OH	37,266	C
New Mexico State Univ	NM	14,050	C
N Dak State Univ	ND		C
Oregon State Univ	OR	20,273	VC
S Dak State Univ	SD	14,296	C
Tarleton State Univ	TX	13,489	LC
Texas A&M Univ	TX	19,207	VC
Texas A&M Univ at Kingsville	TX	7,500	LC
Texas Tech Univ	TX	14,243	C
Unity College	ME	34,054	C
Univ of Calif at Davis	CA		HC
Univ of Idaho	ID	14,558	C
Univ of Illinois at Urbana-Champaign	IL	26,450	HC
Univ of Nebr - Lincoln	NE	18,031	VC
Univ of Wyoming	WY	14,401	C+
Utah State Univ	UT	12,044	C
Washington State Univ	WA	20,461	C
Wilmington College	OH	29,784	C

READING EDUCATION

School	ST	$IS	SR
Baylor Univ	TX	50,329	HC
Black Hills State Univ	SD	13,947	C
Calif Univ of Pennsylvania	PA	14,217	C
Defiance College	OH	30,645	C
Eastern Mich Univ	MI	18,604	C

ST = STATE $IS = IN-STATE COSTS SR = SELECTOR RATING

School	ST	$IS	SR
Florida State Univ	FL	16,715	VC
Hardin-Simmons Univ	TX	23,560	C+
Houston Baptist Univ	TX	36,450	C
Howard Univ	DC	13,646	C
Missouri Southern State Univ	MO	12,061	C
Muskingum Univ	OH	30,502	C
Salisbury Univ	MD	19,180	VC
S Car State Univ	SC	6,700	LC
Univ of Arkansas at Little Rock	AR	17,609	LC
Univ of Georgia	GA	20,082	VC
Univ of Great Falls	MT	27,970	C
Univ of Mary Hardin-Baylor	TX	31,950	C+
Univ of Rio Grande	OH	8,750	NC
West Texas A&M Univ	TX	13,478	C
Western Washington Univ	WA	18,519	VC
Wingate Univ	NC	34,990	C

REAL ESTATE

School	ST	$IS	SR
Angelo State Univ	TX	15,049	NC
Ashford Univ	CA	10,480	C
Baylor Univ	TX	50,329	HC
Cal State, Sacramento	CA	16,200	C
Chancellor Univ	OH	11,000	C
CUNY/Baruch College	NY		HC
Clarion Univ of Pennsylvania	PA	17,370	LC
Colo State Univ-Fort Collins	CO	20,385	VC
DePaul Univ	IL	47,623	VC
Florida Atlantic Univ	FL	17,339	C
Florida International Univ	FL	17,747	C+
Georgia State Univ	GA	15,582	VC
Indiana Univ Bloomington	IN	19,801	VC
Marquette Univ	WI	46,930	VC+
Marylhurst Univ	OR	20,295	VC
Menlo College	CA	49,002	C
Miss State Univ	MS	14,750	C
Monmouth Univ	NJ	44,108	C
Morehead State Univ	KY	10,900	C
New York Univ	NY	61,470	VC
Old Dominion Univ	VA	19,483	LC
Peirce College	PA	12,760	NC
San Diego State Univ	CA	21,611	C+
Southern Methodist Univ	TX	60,585	MC
Syracuse Univ	NY	56,346	VC
Temple Univ	PA	24,392	VC
Texas A&M Univ at Kingsville	TX	7,500	C
Ohio State Univ-Columbus Campus	OH	19,887	HC+
Thomas Edison State College	NJ	5,700	SP
Univ of Central Florida	FL	15,668	VC+
Univ of Cincinnati	OH	21,506	VC
Univ of Conn	CT	24,706	HC
Univ of Denver	CO	51,787	VC+
Univ of Georgia	GA	20,082	VC
Univ of Illinois at Chicago	IL	24,505	VC
Univ of Illinois at Urbana-Champaign	IL	26,450	HC
Univ of Miami	FL	57,034	MC
Univ of Miss	MS	16,704	C+
Univ of Missouri/Columbia	MO	18,201	MC
Univ of Nebr at Omaha	NE	12,700	C
Univ of Nevada, Las Vegas	NV	17,303	C
Univ of N Car at Charlotte	NC	15,547	C
Univ of North Texas	TX	15,628	C
Univ of Northern Iowa	IA	15,795	C
Univ of Pennsylvania	PA	61,132	MC
Univ of San Diego	CA	54,818	HC+
Univ of S Car at Columbia	SC	19,725	VC+
Univ of Texas at Arlington	TX	10,908	LC
Univ of West Georgia	GA	15,488	LC
Univ of Wisc/Madison	WI	18,757	HC+
Univ of Wisc-Milwaukee	WI	18,436	C
Villanova Univ	PA	58,394	MC

REAL ESTATE FINANCE

School	ST	$IS	SR
Southern Methodist Univ	TX	60,585	MC
Texas Christian Univ	TX	49,980	HC
Wright State Univ	OH	16,983	C

RECREATION ADMINISTRATION

School	ST	$IS	SR
Eastern Illinois Univ	IL	20,466	C
Kent State Univ	OH	19,920	C
San Diego State Univ	CA	21,611	C+
Southeast Missouri State Univ	MO	15,370	C
Univ of New Hampshire	NH	26,912	C

RECREATION AND LEISURE SERVICES

School	ST	$IS	SR
Alcorn State Univ	MS	9,500	C
Aquinas College	MI	33,060	C
Arizona State Univ, at the Tempe Campus	AZ	20,137	C+
Asbury Univ	KY	32,038	VC
Aurora Univ	IL	33,228	C
Brigham Young Univ	UT	12,100	HC
Calif Polytechnic State Univ	CA	19,847	HC
Cal State, East Bay	CA	16,549	C
Cal State, Long Beach	CA	17,502	C+
Cal State, Northridge	CA	28,690	LC
Calvin College	MI	39,120	VC

School	ST	$IS	SR
Catawba College	NC	37,240	LC
Central Washington Univ	WA	11,730	C
Chicago State Univ	IL	5,482	C
Colo State Univ-Pueblo	CO	16,183	C
Cumberland Univ	TN	21,220	C
East Central Univ	OK	10,223	LC
Eastern Conn State Univ	CT	20,584	C
Eastern Washington Univ	WA		C
Emporia State Univ	KS	12,897	C
Ferris State Univ	MI	20,047	C
Ferrum College	VA	27,740	LC
Florida State Univ	FL	16,715	VC
Frostburg State Univ	MD	15,264	LC
Gallaudet Univ	DC	25,380	SP
Georgia College and State Univ	GA	18,900	C+
Gordon College	MA	44,320	VC
Graceland Univ	IA	28,020	C
Grambling State Univ	LA	13,384	LC
Green Mountain College	VT	45,228	LC
Greenville College	IL	27,012	C
Hannibal-LaGrange Univ	MO	24,490	C
Henderson State Univ	AR	14,584	C
Houghton College	NY	36,808	C+
Indiana Inst of Technology	IN	34,240	LC
Indiana State Univ	IN	16,000	C
Indiana Univ Bloomington	IN	19,801	VC
Ithaca College	NY	53,864	HC
James Madison Univ	VA	18,049	VC
Johnson & Wales Univ/North Miami Campus	FL		C
Johnson & Wales Univ/Providence Campus	RI	29,576	C
Kent State Univ	OH	19,920	C
Kutztown Univ of Pennsylvania	PA	16,909	LC
Lindsey Wilson College	KY	31,220	C
Lyndon State College	VT	14,233	C
Mars Hill Univ	NC	22,950	LC
Maryville College	TN	33,150	C+
Metropolitan State Univ of Denver	CO	4,835	LC
Middle Tenn State Univ	TN	8,650	C
Minn State Univ, Mankato	MN	15,616	C
Missouri State Univ	MO	13,996	C+
Montclair State Univ	NJ	22,614	C
Morris College	SC	16,310	LC
Murray State Univ	KY	15,304	C
New England College	NH	45,930	LC
New York Univ	NY	61,470	MC
N Car State Univ	NC	16,202	HC
N Dak State Univ	ND		C
Northwest Missouri State Univ	MO	17,347	C
Northwest Nazarene Univ	ID	34,000	C
Ohio Univ	OH	21,080	C
Okla State Univ	OK	14,310	VC
Old Dominion Univ	VA	19,483	LC
Olivet Nazarene Univ	IL	29,990	C
Oral Roberts Univ	OK	31,734	C
Ouachita Baptist Univ	AR	30,220	VC
Pacific Lutheran Univ	WA	46,760	C+
Pittsburg State Univ	KS	12,032	C
Plymouth State Univ	NH	23,148	LC
Radford Univ	VA	17,766	LC
Rensselaer Polytechnic Inst	NY	61,529	MC
Shaw Univ	NC	15,488	C
Shepherd Univ	WV	15,875	C
Simpson Univ	CA	28,900	C
Southeastern Okla State Univ	OK	7,966	LC
Southern Conn State Univ	CT	18,033	LC
Southern Illinois Univ Carbondale	IL	21,942	C
Southern Wesleyan Univ	SC	25,600	C
Southwest Baptist Univ	MO	24,710	C
St. Joseph's College, New York/Brooklyn Campus	NY	22,630	C
St. Joseph's College, New York/Suffolk Campus	NY	22,630	C
St. Thomas Aquinas College	NY	40,230	C
Texas A&M Univ at Galveston	TX	11,258	C
The SUNY/College at Brockport	NY	19,002	C
The Univ of Memphis	TN	15,094	C
The Univ of Tenn at Chattanooga	TN	16,883	C
The Univ of Utah	UT	16,463	VC
Tougaloo College	MS	15,275	NC
Trine Univ	IN	39,400	HC+
Unity College	ME	34,054	C
Univ of Central Missouri	MO	14,605	C
Univ of Florida	FL	15,943	VC
Univ of Georgia	GA	20,082	VC
Univ of Hawaii at Manoa	HI	19,379	C
Univ of Idaho	ID	14,558	C
Univ of Illinois at Urbana-Champaign	IL	26,450	HC
Univ of Iowa	IA	17,693	VC
Univ of Maine at Machias	ME	10,523	C
Univ of Maine at Presque Isle	ME	15,011	LC
Univ of Minn/Twin Cities	MN		HC
Univ of Mount Olive	NC	18,426	C
Univ of Nebr at Omaha	NE	12,700	C
Univ of North Georgia	GA	8,500	C
Univ of North Texas	TX	15,628	C

School	ST	$IS	SR
Univ of Northern Colo	CO	18,446	C
Univ of Northern Iowa	IA	15,795	C
Univ of South Alabama	AL	13,510	C
Univ of S Dak	SD	15,111	C
Univ of Toledo	OH	18,464	C
Upper Iowa Univ	IA	30,426	NC
Voorhees College	SC	18,126	C
Wartburg College	IA	41,055	VC
West Virginia Univ	WV	16,542	C+
Western Kentucky Univ	KY	11,000	LC
Western Mich Univ	MI	19,628	C
Western State Colo Univ	CO	16,924	C
William Penn Univ	IA	26,000	C
Winona State Univ	MN	16,640	C
York College of Pennsylvania	PA	26,590	C

RECREATION EDUCATION

School	ST	$IS	SR
Alderson Broaddus Univ	WV	28,656	C
Baylor Univ	TX	50,329	HC
Benedict College	SC	20,454	NC
Campbellsville Univ	KY	27,720	C
Claflin Univ	SC	22,368	LC
College of the Ozarks	MO		VC
Eastern Washington Univ	WA		C
Friends Univ	KS	29,100	C
Georgia Southern Univ	GA	16,942	C
Johnson State College	VT	16,721	C
Lyndon State College	VT	14,233	C
Messiah College	PA	40,690	C+
Northeastern Illinois Univ	IL	10,318	LC
Northwest Missouri State Univ	MO	17,347	C
Northwest Nazarene Univ	ID	34,000	C
Oral Roberts Univ	OK	31,734	C
Plymouth State Univ	NH	23,148	LC
Prescott College	AZ	33,284	C
St. Mary's College of Calif	CA	53,550	C
San Francisco State Univ	CA	18,514	C
San Jose State Univ	CA	19,133	LC
Southern Adventist Univ	TN	26,190	C
Southern Oregon Univ	OR	17,874	C
Southern Univ at New Orleans	LA	2,963	NC
SUNY Cortland/The SUNY	NY	19,759	C+
Toccoa Falls College	GA	23,210	LC
Univ of Arkansas at Fayetteville	AR	18,352	C+
Univ of Conn	CT	24,706	HC
Univ of Idaho	ID	14,558	C
Univ of Minn/Duluth	MN	19,806	C
Univ of Nevada, Las Vegas	NV	17,303	C
Univ of Tenn at Knoxville	TN	20,364	VC+
Wayne State Univ	MI	22,063	C
Western Washington Univ	WA	18,519	VC

RECREATION THERAPY

School	ST	$IS	SR
Alderson Broaddus Univ	WV	28,656	C
Ashland Univ	OH	25,000	C
Cal State, Northridge	CA	28,690	LC
Calvin College	MI	39,120	VC
Catawba College	NC	37,240	LC
East Carolina Univ	NC	14,169	C
Eastern Mich Univ	MI	18,604	C
Eastern Washington Univ	WA		C
Grand Valley State Univ	MI	17,998	C+
Hampton Univ	VA	28,528	C
Houghton College	NY	36,808	C+
Huntington Univ	IN	33,220	C+
Indiana Inst of Technology	IN	34,240	LC
Indiana Univ Bloomington	IN	19,801	VC
Ithaca College	NY	53,864	HC
Lake Superior State Univ	MI	18,121	C
Longwood Univ	VA	20,924	C
Nova Southeastern Univ	FL	37,280	VC
Pittsburg State Univ	KS	12,032	C
Shaw Univ	NC	15,488	C
Southern Univ and A&M College	LA	9,761	LC
Springfield College	MA	25,000	C
Temple Univ	PA	24,392	VC
Unity College	ME	34,054	C
Univ of Iowa	IA	17,693	VC
Univ of N Car at Wilmington	NC	13,572	VC
Univ of Southern Maine	ME	16,576	C
Univ of Wisc/La Crosse	WI	9,304	VC
Univ of Wisc-Milwaukee	WI	18,436	C
Utica College	NY	45,670	C
West Virginia State Univ	WV	8,378	NC
Western Carolina Univ	NC	13,965	C
Winston-Salem State Univ	NC	9,418	LC

RECREATION/LEISURE (ADVENTURE LEADERSHIP)

School	ST	$IS	SR
Murray State Univ	KY	15,304	C

RECREATION/LEISURE (COMMUNITY RECREATION)

School	ST	$IS	SR
Murray State Univ	KY	15,304	C

RECREATIONAL FACILITIES MANAGEMENT

School	ST	$IS	SR
Alaska Pacific Univ	AK	43,592	VC
Alderson Broaddus Univ	WV	28,656	C
Appalachian State Univ	NC	12,919	VC
Aquinas College	MI	33,060	C
Ashland Univ	OH	25,000	C
Bluffton Univ	OH	38,948	C
Cal State, Fresno	CA	17,405	C
Central Methodist Univ	MO	28,240	VC
Colo State Univ-Fort Collins	CO	20,385	VC
Dordt College	IA	34,160	C+
East Carolina Univ	NC	14,169	C
Eastern Mennonite Univ	VA	40,660	C
Florida Gulf Coast Univ	FL		C
Florida State Univ	FL	16,715	VC
Glenville State College	WV	11,348	NC
Graceland Univ	IA	28,020	C
Houghton College	NY	36,808	C+
Indiana Wesleyan Univ	IN	31,815	VC
Johnson & Wales Univ/Providence Campus	RI	29,576	C
Johnson State College	VT	16,721	C
Kean Univ	NJ	23,444	C
Kent State Univ	OH	19,920	C
Millikin Univ	IL	38,940	C
Missouri Valley College	MO	22,200	C
Ohio Univ	OH	21,080	C
Oregon State Univ	OR	20,273	VC
Oswego / SUNY	NY	20,009	VC
Pittsburg State Univ	KS	12,032	C
San Francisco State Univ	CA	18,514	C
Shorter Univ	GA	30,650	LC
Sierra Nevada College	NV	32,700	VC
Southwestern Okla State Univ	OK	9,160	C
Texas State Univ	TX	17,128	C
Trine Univ	IN	39,400	HC+
Union College	KY	29,955	C
Univ of Iowa	IA	17,693	VC
Univ of Minn/Twin Cities	MN		HC
Univ of Montana	MT	14,105	C
Univ of Nevada, Las Vegas	NV	17,303	C
Univ of N Car at Chapel Hill	NC	18,928	MC
Univ of St. Francis	IL	37,560	C
Univ of the Sciences	PA	48,320	VC+

REHABILITATION THERAPY

School	ST	$IS	SR
Armstrong State Univ	GA	15,532	C
Assumption College	MA	47,122	C+
Cal State, Los Angeles	CA	17,186	LC
Clarion Univ of Pennsylvania	PA	17,370	LC
Coppin State Univ	MD	16,227	VC
East Carolina Univ	NC	14,169	C
Emporia State Univ	KS	12,897	C
Florida State Univ	FL	16,715	VC
Hilbert College	NY	28,550	C
Indiana Univ of Pennsylvania	PA	20,846	LC
Ithaca College	NY	53,864	HC
Maryville Univ of St. Louis	MO	35,856	VC
Montana State Univ-Billings	MT	12,425	LC
Rutgers, The State Univ of New Jersey/New Brunswick	NJ	25,562	VC
Shaw Univ	NC	15,488	C
Southern Illinois Univ Carbondale	IL	21,942	C
Southern Univ and A&M College	LA	9,761	LC
Springfield College	MA	25,000	C
St. Catherine Univ	MN	37,782	C+
Stephen F. Austin State Univ	TX	14,668	C
The Pennsylvania State Univ - Univ Park	PA	28,022	VC+
The Univ of Tenn at Chattanooga	TN	16,883	C
Thomas Univ	GA	11,520	NC
Troy Univ	AL	10,650	C
Univ of Arizona	AZ	20,657	C
Univ of Arkansas at Pine Bluff	AR	13,378	C
Univ of Florida	FL	15,943	HC
Univ of Illinois at Urbana-Champaign	IL	26,450	HC
Univ of Maine at Farmington	ME	18,187	LC
Univ of Maryland/Eastern Shore	MD	14,000	VC
Univ of North Texas	TX	15,628	C
Univ of Northern Colo	CO	18,446	C
Univ of Pittsburgh at Pittsburgh	PA	28,572	HC+
Univ of Texas - Pan American	TX	11,125	LC
Univ of Wisc/Stout	WI	15,459	C
Western Washington Univ	WA	18,519	VC
Wilberforce Univ	OH	15,100	VC
Wright State Univ	OH	16,983	C

RELIGION

School	ST	$IS	SR
Adrian College	MI	42,400	C
Agnes Scott College	GA	45,323	C+
Albertus Magnus College	CT	37,382	LC
Albion College	MI	46,010	C
Albright College	PA	46,660	C

ST = STATE $IS = IN-STATE COSTS   SR = SELECTOR RATING

School	ST	$IS	SR
Allegheny College	PA	50,980	HC
Alma College	MI	44,075	C
Alverno College	WI	31,434	LC
Amherst College	MA	58,744	MC
Anderson Univ	IN	36,100	C
Andrews Univ	MI	28,030	C+
Anna Maria College	MA	34,600	C
Appalachian State Univ	NC	12,919	VC
Aquinas College	MI	33,060	C
Arkansas Baptist College	AR	15,750	NC
Asbury Univ	KY	32,038	C
Ashland Univ	OH	25,000	C
Atlantic Union College	MA	24,600	C
Augsburg College	MN	35,142	C
Augustana College	IL	43,398	VC
Augustana College	SD	36,500	C
Aurora Univ	IL	33,228	C
Austin College	TX	45,875	HC
Averett Univ	VA	37,750	C
Azusa Pacific Univ	CA	42,086	C
Baker Univ	KS	33,350	C+
Baldwin Wallace Univ	OH	38,318	C
Ball State Univ	IN	17,850	C
Bard College	NY	61,940	HC
Barnard College/Columbia Univ	NY	39,000	MC
Barton College	NC	27,660	LC
Baylor Univ	TX	50,329	HC
Belmont Univ	TN	39,190	VC+
Beloit College	WI	49,970	HC
Benedict College	SC	20,454	VC
Benedictine College	KS	29,180	VC
Berea College	KY	7,192	C
Berry College	GA	39,254	VC
Bethany College	WV	35,282	LC
Bethel College	IN	31,560	C
Bethel College	KS	32,160	C
Bethune-Cookman Univ	FL	22,958	C
Birmingham-Southern College	AL	44,168	VC+
Bloomfield College	NJ	37,850	LC
Bluefield College	VA	17,230	C+
Boston Univ	MA	60,694	MC
Bowdoin College	ME	59,568	MC
Bradley Univ	IL	31,874	VC
Brescia Univ	KY	26,140	VC+
Brown Univ	RI	59,428	MC
Bryan College	TN	24,194	C
Bryn Athyn College	PA	27,984	C
Bryn Mawr College	PA	59,890	MC
Bucknell Univ	PA	60,140	MC
Buena Vista Univ	IA	39,188	C
Butler Univ	IN	47,572	VC+
Calif Lutheran Univ	CA	49,540	C+
Cal State, Bakersfield	CA	8,000	C
Cal State, Fullerton	CA	25,188	C
Cal State, Long Beach	CA	17,502	C+
Calumet College of St. Joseph	IN	15,000	C
Calvin College	MI	39,120	VC
Campbell Univ	NC	37,570	VC
Capital Univ	OH	41,050	VC
Cardinal Stritch Univ	WI	24,054	C
Carleton College	MN	60,102	MC
Carroll College	MT	28,000	C
Carroll Univ	WI	38,100	C
Carson-Newman Univ	TN	29,058	C+
Carthage College	WI	33,000	C
Case Western Reserve Univ	OH	56,534	MC
Catawba College	NC	37,240	LC
Centenary College of Louisiana	LA	45,650	C+
Central College	IA	42,104	C+
Central Methodist Univ	MO	28,240	VC
Central Univ of Bayamon	PR	3,350	
Centre College	KY	35,000	HC+
Chaminade Univ of Honolulu	HI	31,664	LC
Chapman Univ	CA	58,347	VC+
Charleston Southern Univ	SC	22,420	C
CUNY/Brooklyn College	NY	5,884	C+
Claremont McKenna College	CA	62,215	MC
Clark Atlanta Univ	GA	30,006	LC
Clarke Univ	IA	37,600	C
Cleveland State Univ	OH	21,776	C
Coe College	IA	45,550	VC
Colby College	ME	57,510	MC
Colgate Univ	NY	58,135	MC
College of Mount St. Joseph	OH	33,880	C
College of Mount St. Vincent	NY	41,040	MC
College of St. Scholastica	MN	41,440	C
College of the Holy Cross	MA	58,042	MC
College of the Ozarks	MO		VC
College of William & Mary	VA	28,000	MC
College of Wooster	OH	52,600	VC
Colo College	CO	57,162	MC
Columbia College	SC	27,882	C
Columbia Univ/City of New York	NY	61,116	MC
Columbia Univ/School of General Studies	NY	58,231	MC
Concordia College - Moorhead	MN	39,974	C
Concordia College - New York	NY	39,035	LC
Concordia Univ St. Paul	MN	28,250	C
Concordia Univ Wisc	WI	28,980	C
Concordia Univ, Ann Arbor	MI	27,220	VC
Concordia Univ, River Forest	IL	26,300	C
Conn College	CT	54,970	MC
Converse College	SC	37,130	C
Cornell College	IA	44,930	VC
Cornerstone Univ and Grand Rapids Theological Seminary	MI	33,338	C
Culver-Stockton College	MO	30,900	C
Daemen College	NY	34,770	C
Dartmouth College	NH	57,996	MC
Davidson College	NC	58,146	MC
Davis & Elkins College	WV	33,742	C
Defiance College	OH	30,645	C
Denison Univ	OH	54,670	HC+
DePaul Univ	IL	47,623	VC
DePauw Univ	IN	48,950	VC+
Dickinson College	PA	57,662	HC+
Doane College	NE	35,230	C
Dominican Univ	IL	37,628	C
Dominican Univ of Calif	CA	51,250	C
Dordt College	IA	34,160	C+
Drake Univ	IA	41,516	VC+
Drew Univ/College of Liberal Arts	NJ	57,516	C
Drury Univ	MO	31,909	VC
Duke Univ	NC	50,250	MC
Earlham College	IN	51,470	HC
East Texas Baptist Univ	TX	31,577	LC
Eastern Mennonite Univ	VA	40,660	C
Eastern Nazarene College	MA	30,000	C
Eastern New Mexico Univ	NM	10,682	C
Eckerd College	FL	43,902	VC
Edgewood College	WI	33,294	C
Edward Waters College	FL	19,607	LC
Elizabethtown College	PA	49,740	VC
Elizabethtown College School of Continuing and Professional Studies	PA		VC
Elmhurst College	IL	43,336	C
Elms College	MA	23,900	VC
Emmanuel College	MA	47,985	VC
Emory and Henry College	VA	387,460	C
Emory Univ	GA	56,368	MC
Erskine College	SC	37,360	C
Eugene Lang College/The New School for Liberal Arts	NY	55,650	C
Eureka College	IL	19,280	C
Evangel Univ	MO	23,090	C
Felician College	NJ	41,640	LC
Ferrum College	VA	27,740	LC
Fisk Univ	TN	19,830	C
Flagler College	FL	25,180	C
Florida International Univ	FL	17,747	C+
Florida Memorial Univ	FL	20,888	LC
Florida Southern College	FL	40,150	C+
Florida State Univ	FL	16,715	VC
Fontbonne Univ	MO	31,384	C
Fordham Univ	NY	61,588	HC+
Franklin and Marshall College	PA	60,799	MC
Franklin College	IN	36,585	C
Fresno Pacific Univ	CA	32,136	C
Friends Univ	KS	29,100	C
Furman Univ	SC	54,006	HC
Gardner-Webb Univ	NC	34,375	C+
George Fox Univ	OR	40,750	C+
George Mason Univ	VA	15,724	VC
George Washington Univ	DC	57,108	MC
Georgetown College	KY	41,440	C+
Georgetown Univ	DC	52,910	MC
Georgian Court Univ	NJ	41,594	LC
Gettysburg College	PA	58,820	HC
Gonzaga Univ	WA	46,441	HC
Goshen College	IN	35,900	VC
Goucher College	MD	52,040	VC+
Grace College and Seminary	IN	28,800	VC
Graceland Univ	IA	28,020	C
Greensboro College	NC	28,740	LC
Greenville College	IL	27,012	C
Grinnell College	IA	53,654	HC
Guilford College	NC	42,800	C
Gustavus Adolphus College	MN	48,170	HC
Hamilton College	NY	55,620	MC
Hamline Univ	MN	45,678	VC
Hampden-Sydney College	VA	51,758	C
Hampshire College	MA	58,320	MC
Harding Univ	AR	23,556	C
Hartwick College	NY	51,270	C
Harvard College/Harvard Univ	MA	49,000	MC
Hastings College	NE	27,782	C+
Haverford College	PA	61,564	MC
Heidelberg Univ	OH	34,100	C
Hellenic College/Holy Cross Greek Orthodox School of Theology	MA	33,190	C
Hendrix College	AR	50,202	VC+
High Point Univ	NC	39,800	C
Hillsdale College	MI	32,866	MC
Hiram College	OH	37,300	VC
Hobart and William Smith Colleges	NY	60,034	HC+
Hofstra Univ	NY	51,810	VC+
Hollins Univ	VA	43,295	VC
Holy Family Univ	PA	40,030	LC
Holy Names Univ	CA	40,310	NC
Hood College	MD	45,730	C
Hope College	MI	38,650	VC
Houghton College	NY	36,808	C+
Howard Univ	DC	13,646	C
Humboldt State Univ	CA	18,400	C
Hunter College	NY	14,429	VC
Huntingdon College	AL	33,100	C
Huntington Univ	IN	32,220	C+
Illinois College	IL	25,770	C
Illinois Wesleyan Univ	IL	48,452	HC
Indiana Wesleyan Univ	IN	31,815	VC
Iona College	NY	44,028	C
Iowa State Univ	IA	16,403	C
Iowa Wesleyan College	IA	30,850	LC
James Madison Univ	VA	18,049	VC
Jarvis Christian College	TX	19,552	NC
John Carroll Univ	OH	46,300	C+
Judson College	AL	26,794	C
Kalamazoo College	MI	49,740	HC
Kansas Wesleyan Univ	KS	32,000	C
La Roche College	PA	35,824	LC
La Salle Univ	PA	50,270	C
La Sierra Univ	CA	35,694	VC
Lafayette College	PA	59,155	HC+
LaGrange College	GA	37,670	C
Lake Forest College	IL	50,652	VC
Lakeland College	WI	22,990	C
Lane College	TN	11,212	C
Le Moyne College	NY	43,470	C
Lebanon Valley College	PA	38,570	C
Lees-McRae College	NC	33,944	C
Lehigh Univ	PA	56,770	MC
Lenoir-Rhyne Univ	NC	35,984	C
Lewis & Clark College	OR	54,382	MC
Lewis Univ	IL	23,050	C
Liberty Univ	VA	19,101	C
Lindenwood Univ	MO	20,750	C
Linfield College-McMinnville Campus	OR	47,676	C
Loras College	IA	37,432	VC
Louisiana College	LA	15,746	C
Loyola Univ New Orleans	LA	46,581	VC
Luther College	IA	45,720	C+
Lycoming College	PA	45,379	C
Lynchburg College	VA	42,645	C
Lyon College	AR	32,090	C
Macalester College	MN	57,691	MC
MacMurray College	IL	20,755	C
Madonna Univ	MI	24,540	VC
Manchester Univ	IN	35,070	C
Manhattan College	NY	49,588	C+
Manhattanville College	NY	50,740	VC
Mars Hill Univ	NC	22,950	LC
Martin Univ	IN	11,000	SP
Mary Baldwin College	VA	38,245	C
Marygrove College	MI	28,926	C
Marylhurst Univ	OR	20,295	NC
Maryville College	TN	33,150	C
Marywood Univ	PA	45,595	C
McDaniel College	MD	47,450	VC
McKendree Univ	IL	29,920	C
McMurry Univ	TX	25,962	LC
McPherson College	KS	28,138	C
Mercer Univ	GA	44,201	VC
Mercyhurst Univ	PA	40,700	C
Meredith College	NC	31,420	C
Merrimack College	MA	44,215	C
Methodist Univ	NC	37,185	C
Miami Univ	OH	24,191	VC
Mich State Univ	MI	22,450	VC
Middlebury College	VT	59,160	MC
Midland Univ	NE	34,000	C
Millsaps College	MS	43,888	VC+
Missouri State Univ	MO	13,996	C
Missouri Valley College	MO	22,200	C
Monmouth College	IL	40,850	C
Montclair State Univ	NJ	22,614	C
Montreat College	NC	31,298	C
Moravian College	PA	46,381	VC
Morehouse College	GA	39,412	VC
Morgan State Univ	MD	14,500	VC
Morningside College	IA	35,430	C
Mount Aloysius College	PA	29,976	C
Mount Holyoke College	MA	55,146	MC
Mount Marty College	SD	29,638	C
Mount Mercy Univ	IA	35,320	C
Mount St. Mary's College - Chalon Campus	CA	43,897	VC+
Mount Vernon Nazarene Univ	OH	29,590	C
Muhlenberg College	PA	52,837	HC
Muskingum Univ	OH	30,502	C
Naropa Univ	CO	39,166	SP
Nazareth College of Rochester	NY	43,028	C+
Nebr Wesleyan Univ	NE	29,774	C
New College of Florida	FL	14,504	MC
New York Univ	NY	61,470	MC
Newberry College	SC	26,850	LC
Niagara Univ	NY	41,010	C
N Car State Univ	NC	16,202	VC
N Car Wesleyan College	NC	29,440	C
North Central College	IL	38,343	VC
North Central Univ	MN	26,400	C
Northeastern Univ	MA	55,296	MC
Northland College	WI	26,680	C
Northwest Univ	WA	18,854	C
Northwestern College of Iowa	IA	36,240	VC
Northwestern Univ	IL	61,640	MC
Notre Dame de Namur Univ	CA	44,236	LC
Notre Dame of Maryland Univ	MD	27,700	VC
Nyack College	NY	33,250	C
Oakland City Univ	IN	24,500	NC
Oakwood Univ	AL	25,529	NC
Oberlin College	OH	61,788	MC
Occidental College	CA	60,972	MC
Ohio Northern Univ	OH	42,075	VC
Ohio Univ	OH	21,080	C
Ohio Wesleyan Univ	OH	49,460	C+
Okla Baptist Univ	OK	28,202	C
Okla City Univ	OK	40,476	VC
Okla Wesleyan Univ	OK	21,300	C
Olivet Nazarene Univ	IL	29,990	C
Oral Roberts Univ	OK	31,734	C
Ottawa Univ	KS	15,000	VC
Otterbein College	OH	32,214	C
Ouachita Baptist Univ	AR	30,220	VC
Our Lady of the Lake Univ	TX	22,430	LC
Pacific Lutheran Univ	WA	46,760	C+
Pacific Union College	CA	28,150	VC
Pepperdine Univ	CA	55,372	HC+
Pfeiffer Univ	NC	33,700	LC
Piedmont College	GA	30,136	C
Pontifical Catholic Univ of PR	PR	7,310	
Presbyterian College	SC	42,678	C+
Prescott College	AZ	33,284	C
Princeton Univ	NJ	53,795	MC
Principia College	IL	35,140	C+
Purdue Univ/West Lafayette	IN	20,024	HC
Queens College/The CUNY	NY	17,107	VC
Queens Univ of Charlotte	NC	39,543	C+
Randolph College	VA	45,660	VC
Randolph-Macon College	VA	49,869	C+
Reed College	OR	57,780	MC
Regis Univ	CO	41,318	C
Rhodes College	TN	51,900	HC+
Rice Univ	TX	43,288	MC
Ripon College	WI	36,959	C+
Roanoke College	VA	49,976	C
Roberts Wesleyan College	NY	38,306	C+
Rollins College	FL	52,370	HC
Rosemont College	PA	42,350	C
Rutgers, The State Univ of New Jersey/Camden Campus	NJ	25,121	C
Rutgers, The State Univ of New Jersey/New Brunswick	NJ	25,562	VC
Sacred Heart Univ	CT	49,264	VC
St. Francis Univ	PA	30,029	LC
St. Joseph's College	IN	36,500	C
St. Leo Univ	FL	30,340	C
St. Mary's Univ	IN	45,160	C+
St. Mary's College of Calif	CA	53,550	C
St. Michael's College	VT	49,975	VC
St. Xavier Univ	IL	32,840	C
Salem College	NC	29,326	VC
Salve Regina Univ	RI	48,550	VC
Samford Univ	AL	37,060	C+
San Francisco State Univ	CA	18,514	C
San Jose State Univ	CA	19,133	LC
Sarah Lawrence College	NY	48,000	HC
Schreiner Univ	TX	32,734	LC
Scripps College	CA	61,940	MC
Seattle Univ	WA	49,035	VC+
Seton Hall Univ	NJ	45,902	C
Seton Hill Univ	PA	35,172	C
Sewanee: The Univ of the South	TN	47,700	HC+
Shaw Univ	NC	15,488	C
Shenandoah Univ	VA	39,916	C
Shorter Univ	GA	30,650	LC
Siena College	NY	43,863	VC
Siena Heights Univ	MI	32,040	C
Silver Lake College	WI	22,600	LC
Simpson College	IA	36,086	C+
Simpson Univ	CA	28,900	C
Skidmore College	NY	59,942	HC
Smith College	MA	59,674	MC
Southeastern Univ	FL	27,201	C
Southern Methodist Univ	TX	60,585	MC
Southern Wesleyan Univ	SC	25,600	C
Southwestern Adventist Univ	TX	23,026	LC
Southwestern Univ	TX	45,660	VC
Spelman College	GA	24,650	C
St. Edward's Univ	TX	47,784	C
St. Francis College	NY	34,200	C
St. John Fisher College	NY	40,708	C+
St. Lawrence Univ	NY	59,972	VC
St. Mary's College of Maryland	MD	25,754	VC
St. Norbert College	WI	41,478	VC
St. Olaf College	MN	51,200	HC+
St. Thomas Aquinas College	NY	40,230	C
St. Thomas Univ	FL	32,310	LC
Stanford Univ	CA	58,388	MC
Stetson Univ	FL	51,516	VC
Stillman College	AL	19,470	C
Stonehill College	MA	46,780	HC
Stony Brook Univ / SUNY	NY	20,078	HC+

ST = STATE $IS = IN-STATE COSTS   SR = SELECTOR RATING

School	ST	$IS	SR
SUNY College at Old Westbury	NY	16,324	C
Susquehanna Univ	PA	51,150	C
Swarthmore College	PA	57,870	MC
Syracuse Univ	NY	56,346	VC
Tabor College	KS	29,010	C
Temple Univ	PA	24,392	VC
Texas A&M Univ at Commerce	TX	10,496	C
Texas Christian Univ	TX	49,980	HC
Texas Wesleyan Univ	TX	31,382	C
The Catholic Univ of America	DC	52,852	VC
The College of Idaho	ID	31,277	C+
The College of New Rochelle	NY	33,600	VC
The College of St. Rose	NY	26,750	C
The Lincoln Univ	PA	15,154	LC
The Univ of N Car at Greensboro	NC	12,848	C
The Univ of Okla	OK	18,621	VC
Thiel College	PA	38,728	LC
Thomas Edison State College	NJ	5,700	SP
Tougaloo College	MS	15,275	NC
Towson Univ	MD	16,000	VC
Transylvania Univ	KY	42,660	VC+
Trevecca Nazarene Univ	TN	31,186	C
Trinity College	CT		HC+
Trinity Univ	TX	48,150	HC+
Truman State Univ	MO	15,541	HC
Tufts Univ	MA	58,780	MC
Tulane Univ	LA	60,861	MC
Union College	KY	29,955	C
Union College	NE	23,270	C
Union College	NY	60,240	VC
Union Univ	TN	28,260	VC
Universidad Adventista de las Antillas	PR	7,360	
Univ at Albany / SUNY	NY	18,674	VC
Univ of Alabama at Tuscaloosa	AL	17,164	C+
Univ of Bridgeport	CT	39,030	LC
Univ of Calif at Berkeley	CA	23,322	MC
Univ of Calif at Davis	CA		HC
Univ of Calif at Irvine	CA	25,961	VC
Univ of Calif at Los Angeles	CA	25,686	MC
Univ of Calif at Riverside	CA	27,204	C+
Univ of Calif at San Diego	CA	21,000	VC
Univ of Calif at Santa Barbara	CA	27,551	HC
Univ of Central Arkansas	AR	13,667	VC
Univ of Central Florida	FL	15,668	VC+
Univ of Chicago	IL	55,416	MC
Univ of Dayton	OH	49,070	VC
Univ of Denver	CO	51,787	VC+
Univ of Detroit Mercy	MI	30,450	VC
Univ of Dubuque	IA	30,200	C
Univ of Findlay	OH	31,916	C
Univ of Florida	FL	15,943	HC
Univ of Georgia	GA	20,082	VC
Univ of Great Falls	MT	27,970	C
Univ of Hawaii at Manoa	HI	19,379	C
Univ of Illinois at Urbana-Champaign	IL	26,450	HC
Univ of Indianapolis	IN	31,740	LC
Univ of Iowa	IA	17,693	VC
Univ of Jamestown	ND	24,738	C
Univ of Kansas	KS	17,603	C+
Univ of La Verne	CA	47,010	C
Univ of Mary Hardin-Baylor	TX	31,950	C+
Univ of Mary Washington	VA	19,484	VC
Univ of Miami	FL	57,034	MC
Univ of Mich/Ann Arbor	MI	22,102	MC
Univ of Miss	MS	16,704	C+
Univ of Missouri/Columbia	MO	18,201	MC
Univ of Mobile	AL	28,935	VC
Univ of Mount Olive	NC	18,426	C
Univ of Mount Union	OH	35,130	C
Univ of New Mexico	NM	15,300	C
Univ of N Car at Asheville	NC	13,500	VC
Univ of N Car at Chapel Hill	NC	18,928	NC
Univ of N Car at Wilmington	NC	13,572	VC
Univ of N Dak	ND	14,551	C
Univ of North Florida	FL	15,870	VC
Univ of Northern Iowa	IA	15,795	C
Univ of Oregon	OR	21,360	C+
Univ of Pennsylvania	PA	61,132	MC
Univ of Pikeville	KY	25,500	NC
Univ of Pittsburgh at Pittsburgh	PA	28,572	HC+
Univ of Puget Sound	WA	54,608	HC
Univ of Redlands	CA	40,500	VC
Univ of Rochester	NY	60,668	MC
Univ of St. Francis	IN	29,810	C
Univ of St. Joseph	CT	45,630	C
Univ of San Francisco	CA	54,770	VC
Univ of Sioux Falls	SD	22,990	C
Univ of S Car at Columbia	SC	19,725	VC+
Univ of South Florida/Tampa	FL	13,000	C
Univ of Southern Calif	CA	56,903	MC
Univ of St. Thomas - Houston	TX	37,690	C
Univ of Tenn at Knoxville	TN	20,364	VC+
Univ of Texas at Austin	TX	44,074	HC
Univ of the Cumberlands	KY	27,500	C
Univ of the Incarnate Word	TX	37,316	LC
Univ of the Ozarks	AR	31,440	C
Univ of the Pacific	CA	52,146	VC
Univ of Tulsa	OK	46,331	MC
Univ of Vermont	VT	27,006	VC+
Univ of Virginia	VA	23,050	MC
Univ of Washington	WA	14,722	VC
Univ of West Florida	FL	14,656	C
Univ of Wisc/Madison	WI	18,757	HC+
Univ of Wisc/Oshkosh	WI	10,426	LC
Univ of Wisc-Milwaukee	WI	18,436	C
Ursuline College	OH	33,198	LC
Valparaiso Univ	IN	44,940	VC+
Vanderbilt Univ	TN	58,220	MC
Vassar College	NY	61,140	MC
Villanova Univ	PA	58,394	MC
Virginia Commonwealth Univ	VA	21,716	C
Virginia Union Univ	VA	18,432	C
Virginia Wesleyan College	VA	28,433	LC
Wabash College	IN	46,850	C+
Wake Forest Univ	NC	58,838	MC
Walla Walla Univ	WA	26,256	NC
Warren Wilson College	NC	40,132	VC
Wartburg College	IA	41,055	VC
Washburn Univ	KS	12,579	C
Washington Adventist Univ	MD	25,859	C
Washington and Lee Univ	VA	52,812	MC
Washington State Univ	WA	20,461	C
Washington Univ in St. Louis	MO	69,844	MC
Wayland Baptist Univ	TX	18,912	LC
Webster Univ	MO	35,100	C+
Wellesley College	MA	59,038	MC
Wells College	NY	49,400	VC
Wesleyan College	GA	24,000	C
Wesleyan Univ	CT	61,198	MC
West Virginia Wesleyan College	WV	26,880	C
Western Kentucky Univ	KY	11,000	LC
Western Mich Univ	MI	19,628	C
Westminster College	MO	31,720	VC
Westminster College	PA	31,290	C+
Westmont College	CA	41,500	HC
Wheaton College	MA	54,934	HC+
Whitman College	WA	55,988	MC
Whittier College	CA	43,416	C
Wiley College	TX		LC
Willamette Univ	OR	56,450	VC+
William Carey Univ	MS	13,500	LC
William Jewell College	MO	31,000	VC+
Williams Baptist College	AR	20,070	C
Williams College	MA	61,070	MC
Wilmington College	OH	29,784	C
Wilson College	PA	35,080	C
Wingate Univ	NC	34,990	C
Winthrop Univ	SC	21,120	C
Wittenberg Univ	OH	47,962	C+
Wofford College	SC	45,795	VC
Wright State Univ	OH	16,983	C
Yale Univ	CT	55,300	MC
Yeshiva Univ	NY	47,250	VC+
Youngstown State Univ	OH	16,732	C

RELIGIOUS EDUCATION

School	ST	$IS	SR
Andrews Univ	MI	28,030	C+
Baylor Univ	TX	50,329	HC
Bloomfield College	NJ	37,850	LC
Cal State, Northridge	CA	28,690	LC
Campbellsville Univ	KY	27,720	C
Clearwater Christian College	FL	23,720	C
College of Mount St. Joseph	OH	33,880	C
Concordia Univ St. Paul	MN	28,250	C
Cornerstone Univ and Grand Rapids Theological Seminary	MI	33,338	C
Dallas Baptist Univ	TX	30,580	VC
East Texas Baptist Univ	TX	31,577	LC
Georgia State Univ	GA	15,582	VC
Grace Bible College	MI	20,770	C
Houghton College	NY	36,808	C+
Indiana Wesleyan Univ	IN	31,815	VC
Kansas Wesleyan Univ	KS	32,000	C
Lenoir-Rhyne College	NC	35,984	C
Louisiana College	LA	15,746	C
Loyola Univ Chicago	IL	51,646	VC+
Loyola Univ New Orleans	LA	46,581	VC
Marian Univ	IN	38,540	C
Mercyhurst Univ	PA	40,700	C
Morris College	SC	16,310	LC
Mount Mary Univ	WI	33,590	LC
Mount Vernon Nazarene Univ	OH	29,590	C
Muskingum Univ	OH	30,502	C
North Central Univ	MN	26,400	C
Northwest Univ	WA	18,854	C
Northwestern College	MN	24,000	C
Oakwood Univ	AL	25,529	NC
Okla Christian Univ	OK	25,870	VC
Okla City Univ	OK	40,476	VC
Oral Roberts Univ	OK	31,734	C
Pfeiffer Univ	NC	33,700	LC
Presbyterian College	SC	42,678	C+
Simpson Univ	CA	28,900	C
Southern Adventist Univ	TN	26,190	C
Southwest Baptist Univ	MO	24,710	C
Sterling College	KS	27,216	C
Texas Wesleyan Univ	TX	31,382	C
Thiel College	PA	38,728	LC
Trinity Bible College	ND		
Union College	NE	23,270	C
Univ of Arizona	AZ	20,657	C
Univ of Calif at Riverside	CA	27,204	C+
Univ of Dayton	OH	49,070	VC
Univ of Jamestown	ND	24,738	C
Vanguard Univ of Southern Calif	CA	35,833	VC
Viterbo Univ	WI	30,070	C
Wayland Baptist Univ	TX	18,912	LC
West Virginia Wesleyan College	WV	26,880	C
Williams Baptist College	AR	20,070	C

RELIGIOUS MUSIC

School	ST	$IS	SR
Aquinas College	MI	33,060	C
Baylor Univ	TX	50,329	HC
Belhaven Univ	MS	27,170	C
Bethel Univ	MN	34,940	VC
Calvin College	MI	39,120	VC
Campbellsville Univ	KY	27,720	C
Centenary College of Louisiana	LA	45,650	C+
Charleston Southern Univ	SC	22,420	C
Clearwater Christian College	FL	23,720	C
College of the Ozarks	MO		VC
Columbia College	SC	27,882	C
Concordia College - New York	NY	39,035	LC
Concordia Univ St. Paul	MN	28,250	C
Concordia Univ Texas	TX	23,640	C
Concordia Univ Wisc	WI	28,980	C
Concordia Univ, Ann Arbor	MI	27,220	VC
Dallas Baptist Univ	TX	30,580	VC
East Texas Baptist Univ	TX	31,577	LC
Eastern Nazarene College	MA	30,000	C
Evangel Univ	MO	23,090	C
Franciscan Univ of Steubenville	OH	27,320	VC
Furman Univ	SC	54,006	HC
Gardner-Webb Univ	NC	34,375	C+
Grove City College	PA	24,022	VC
Hannibal-LaGrange Univ	MO	24,490	C
Hardin-Simmons Univ	TX	23,560	C+
Houghton College	NY	36,808	C+
Houston Baptist Univ	TX	36,450	C
Huntington Univ	IN	32,220	C
Indiana Wesleyan Univ	IN	31,815	VC
Johnson C. Smith Univ	NC	25,336	LC
Kentucky Christian Univ	KY	17,622	LC
Lee Univ	TN	18,690	C+
Lenoir-Rhyne College	NC	35,984	C
Louisiana College	LA	15,746	C
Madonna Univ	MI	24,540	VC
Malone Univ	OH	35,364	C
McKendree Univ	IL	29,920	C+
Milligan College	TN	27,510	C
Miss College	MS	21,998	C
Missouri Baptist Univ	MO	31,830	C
Mount Vernon Nazarene Univ	OH	29,590	C
North Central Univ	MN	26,400	C
Northwest Univ	WA	18,854	C
Northwestern College of Iowa	IA	36,240	VC
Nyack College	NY	33,250	C
Okla Wesleyan Univ	OK	21,300	C
Olivet Nazarene Univ	IL	29,990	C
Oral Roberts Univ	OK	31,734	C
Ouachita Baptist Univ	AR	30,220	VC
Pfeiffer Univ	NC	33,102	NC
Samford Univ	AL	37,060	C+
Seton Hill Univ	PA	35,172	C
Shorter Univ	GA	30,650	LC
Southeastern Univ	FL	27,201	C
Southern Nazarene Univ	OK	24,354	C
Southwest Baptist Univ	MO	24,710	C
St. Olaf College	MN	51,200	HC+
Union Univ	TN	28,260	VC
Univ of Mobile	AL	28,935	VC
Univ of the Cumberlands	KY	27,500	C
Valparaiso Univ	IN	44,940	VC+
Warner Pacific College	OR	25,550	C
Warner Univ	FL	18,000	C
Wartburg College	IA	41,055	VC
Wayland Baptist Univ	TX	18,912	LC
Westminster College	PA	31,290	C+
William Carey Univ	MS	13,500	LC
Williams Baptist College	AR	20,070	C

RELIGIOUS STUDIES

School	ST	$IS	SR
Aquinas College	MI	33,060	C
Arizona State Univ, at the Tempe Campus	AZ	20,137	C+
Bates College	ME	60,720	MC
Beloit College	WI	49,970	HC
Biola Univ	CA	40,320	C
Cabrini College	PA	40,859	LC
Cal State, Chico	CA	20,158	C
Cal State, Long Beach	CA	17,502	C+
College of Charleston	SC	22,145	VC
Cornell Univ	NY	60,964	MC
Dallas Baptist Univ	TX	30,580	VC
Dordt College	IA	34,160	C+
Elon Univ	NC	41,914	VC+
Fairfield Univ	CT	56,960	VC
Fontbonne Univ	MO	31,384	C
Houghton College	NY	36,808	C+
Indiana Univ Bloomington	IN	19,801	VC
Indiana Univ of Pennsylvania	PA	20,846	LC
Indiana Univ-Purdue Univ Indianapolis	IN	17,611	C
Kenyon College	OH	58,890	MC
New York Univ	NY	61,470	MC
Niagara Univ	NY	41,010	C
Old Dominion Univ	VA	19,483	LC
Pomona College	CA	57,680	MC
St. Joseph's Univ	PA	55,006	VC
St. Martin's Univ	WA	41,678	C
San Diego State Univ	CA	21,611	C+
San Jose State Univ	CA	19,133	LC
Univ of Colo Boulder	CO	22,605	VC+
Univ of Miami	FL	57,034	MC
Univ of Nebr - Lincoln	NE	18,031	VC
Univ of N Car at Charlotte	NC	15,547	C
Univ of Wisc/Eau Claire	WI	15,730	VC
Univ of Wyoming	WY	14,401	C+
Viterbo Univ	WI	30,070	C
Webster Univ	MO	35,100	C+
Western Illinois Univ	IL	20,732	C

RESORT MANAGEMENT

School	ST	$IS	SR
Ferris State Univ	MI	20,047	C

RESOURCE ECONOMY & COMMERCE

School	ST	$IS	SR
Univ of Rhode Island	RI	24,002	C

RESPIRATORY THERAPY

School	ST	$IS	SR
Armstrong State Univ	GA	15,532	C
Ball State Univ	IN	17,850	C
Bellarmine Univ	KY	42,950	VC
Boise State Univ	ID	13,469	LC
Dakota State Univ	SD	13,811	C
Drury Univ	MO	31,909	VC
Gannon Univ	PA	39,608	C
Georgia Regents Univ	GA		C
Georgia State Univ	GA	15,582	VC
Gwynedd-Mercy College	PA	33,560	C
Indiana Univ of Pennsylvania	PA	20,846	LC
Indiana Univ-Purdue Univ Indianapolis	IN	17,611	C
LIU Brooklyn	NY	47,182	LC
Marshall Univ	WV	14,820	C
Midwestern State Univ	TX	9,722	C
Millersville Univ of Pennsylvania	PA	21,648	C
Missouri Southern State Univ	MO	12,061	C
Missouri State Univ	MO	13,996	C+
Nebr Methodist College of Nursing and Allied Health	NE	22,690	SP
N Dak State Univ	ND		C
Nova Southeastern Univ	FL	37,280	VC
Point Park Univ	PA	36,390	C
Rhode Island College	RI	17,694	LC
Salisbury Univ	MD	19,180	VC
Shenandoah Univ	VA	39,916	C
Southern Illinois Univ Carbondale	IL	21,942	C
St. Catherine Univ	MN	37,782	C+
Stony Brook Univ / SUNY	NY	20,078	HC+
Tenn State Univ	TN	9,048	C
Texas Southern Univ	TX	18,212	LC
Texas State Univ	TX	17,128	C
Ohio State Univ-Columbus Campus	OH	19,887	HC+
Thomas Edison State College	NJ	5,700	SP
Univ of Akron	OH	20,436	C
Univ of Alabama at Birmingham	AL	18,484	C+
Univ of Cincinnati	OH	21,506	VC
Univ of Indianapolis	IN	31,740	LC
Univ of Kansas	KS	17,603	C+
Univ of Mary	ND	16,714	C
Univ of Missouri/Columbia	MO	18,201	MC
Univ of N Car at Charlotte	NC	15,547	C
Univ of South Alabama	AL	13,510	C
Univ of the Ozarks	AR	31,440	C
Washington Adventist Univ	MD	25,859	LC
West Chester Univ of Pennsylvania	PA	17,186	C
Wheeling Jesuit Univ	WV	33,500	C
York College of Pennsylvania	PA	26,590	C
Youngstown State Univ	OH	16,732	C

RETAILING

School	ST	$IS	SR
Chancellor Univ	OH	11,000	C
East Central Univ	OK	10,223	LC
Johnson & Wales Univ/ Providence Campus	RI	29,576	C
Marywood Univ	PA	45,595	C
Montclair State Univ	NJ	22,614	C
Mount Ida College	MA	30,115	LC
Ohio Univ	OH	21,080	C
Purdue Univ/West Lafayette	IN	20,024	HC
Simmons College	MA	49,966	VC

ST = STATE $IS = IN-STATE COSTS   SR = SELECTOR RATING

School	ST	$IS	SR
Southern New Hampshire Univ	NH	38,100	C
Syracuse Univ	NY	56,346	VC
Texas Tech Univ	TX	14,243	C
Univ of Arizona	AZ	20,657	C
Univ of Minn/Twin Cities	MN		HC
Univ of Pennsylvania	PA	61,132	MC
Univ of S Car at Columbia	SC	19,725	VC+
Univ of Tenn at Knoxville	TN	20,364	VC+
Univ of Wisc/Madison	WI	18,757	HC+
Univ of Wisc/Stout	WI	15,459	C
Youngstown State Univ	OH	16,732	C

ROMANCE LANGUAGES AND LITERATURE

School	ST	$IS	SR
Boston College	MA	60,622	MC
Bowdoin College	ME	59,568	MC
Bowling Green State Univ	OH	18,970	C
Bryn Mawr College	PA	59,890	MC
Carleton Univ	MN	60,102	MC
Christopher Newport Univ	VA	21,960	VC
CUNY/City College	NY	20,319	VC+
Clark Univ	MA	47,020	HC+
Colo College	CO	57,162	MC
Dartmouth College	NH	57,996	MC
DePauw Univ	IN	48,950	VC+
Dowling College	NY	25,000	LC
Haverford College	PA	61,564	MC
Johns Hopkins Univ	MD	47,492	MC
Mount Holyoke College	MA	55,146	MC
New York Univ	NY	61,470	MC
Oberlin College	OH	61,788	MC
Point Loma Nazarene Univ	CA	41,006	C+
Pomona College	CA	57,680	MC
Queens Univ of Charlotte	NC	39,543	C+
Rockford College	IL	31,000	C
St. Thomas Aquinas College	NY	40,230	C
Truman State Univ	MO	15,541	HC
Univ of Chicago	IL	55,416	MC
Univ of Georgia	GA	20,082	VC
Univ of Maine	ME	60,720	MC
Univ of Maryland - College Park	MD	20,060	HC+
Univ of Nevada, Las Vegas	NV	17,303	C
Univ of N Car at Chapel Hill	NC	18,928	MC
Univ of Notre Dame	IN	57,117	MC
Univ of Oregon	OR	21,360	C+
Univ of PR Recinto de Rio Piedras	PR	5,750	
Washington and Lee Univ	VA	52,812	MC
Washington Univ in St. Louis	MO	69,844	MC
Wayne State Univ	MI	22,063	C
Wesleyan Univ	CT	61,198	MC
Wheeling Jesuit Univ	WV	33,500	C

RURAL ECONOMICS

School	ST	$IS	SR
Univ of Alaska Fairbanks	AK	15,130	C
Univ of Idaho	ID	14,558	C

RURAL SOCIOLOGY

School	ST	$IS	SR
S Dak State Univ	SD	14,296	C
Univ of Missouri/Columbia	MO	18,201	MC
Univ of Wisc/Madison	WI	18,757	HC+

RUSSIAN

School	ST	$IS	SR
American Univ	DC	56,015	HC+
Amherst College	MA	58,744	MC
Arizona State Univ, at the Tempe Campus	AZ	20,137	C+
Bard College	NY	61,940	VC
Barnard College/Columbia Univ	NY	39,000	MC
Bates College	ME	60,720	MC
Baylor Univ	TX	50,329	HC
Beloit College	WI	49,970	HC
Bowdoin College	ME	59,568	MC
Bowling Green State Univ	OH	18,970	C
Brigham Young Univ	UT	12,100	HC
Bryn Mawr College	PA	59,890	MC
Bucknell Univ	PA	60,140	MC
Carleton College	MN	60,102	MC
Central Washington Univ	WA	11,730	C
CUNY/Brooklyn College	NY	5,884	C+
Colgate Univ	NY	58,135	MC
College of the Holy Cross	MA	58,042	MC
Columbia Univ/City of New York	NY	61,116	MC
Cornell College	IA	44,930	VC
Dartmouth College	NH	57,996	MC
Dickinson College	PA	57,662	HC+
Ferrum College	VA	27,740	LC
Florida State Univ	FL	16,715	MC
George Washington Univ	DC	57,108	MC
Georgetown Univ	DC	52,910	MC
Goucher College	MD	52,040	VC+
Grinnell College	IA	53,654	VC
Gustavus Adolphus College	MN	48,170	HC
Harvard College/Harvard Univ	MA	49,000	MC
Haverford College	PA	61,564	MC
Hofstra Univ	NY	51,810	VC+

School	ST	$IS	SR
Hunter College	NY	14,429	VC
Indiana Univ Bloomington	IN	19,801	VC
Iowa State Univ	IA	16,403	C
Juniata College	PA	49,340	VC
La Salle Univ	PA	50,270	C
Lawrence Univ	WI	46,371	HC
Lehman College/The CUNY	NY	5,778	LC
Luther College	IA	45,720	C+
Macalester College	MN	57,691	MC
Marlboro College	VT	35,980	VC
Miami Univ	OH	24,191	VC
Mich State Univ	MI	22,450	VC
Middlebury College	VT	59,160	MC
New York Univ	NY	61,470	MC
Northern Illinois Univ	IL	19,768	C
Oberlin College	OH	61,788	MC
Ohio Univ	OH	21,080	C
Pomona College	CA	57,680	MC
Portland State Univ	OR	18,672	C
Purdue Univ/West Lafayette	IN	20,024	HC
Queens College/The CUNY	NY	17,107	VC
Rider Univ	NJ	45,720	C
Rutgers, The State Univ of New Jersey/New Brunswick	NJ	25,562	VC
San Diego State Univ	CA	21,611	C+
Sarah Lawrence College	NY	48,000	HC
Scripps College	CA	61,940	MC
Seattle Pacific Univ	WA	41,559	VC+
Sewanee: The Univ of the South	TN	47,700	HC+
Smith College	MA	59,674	MC
Southern Illinois Univ Carbondale	IL	21,942	C
St. Olaf College	MN	51,200	HC+
Swarthmore College	PA	57,870	MC
Texas A&M Univ	TX	19,207	VC
Ohio State Univ-Columbus Campus	OH	19,887	HC+
The Univ of Utah	UT	16,463	VC
Thomas Edison State College	NJ	5,700	SP
Trinity College	CT		HC+
Trinity Univ	TX	48,150	HC+
Truman State Univ	MO	15,541	HC
Tufts Univ	MA	58,780	MC
Tulane Univ	LA	60,861	MC
Univ of Alabama at Tuscaloosa	AL	17,164	C+
Univ of Arizona	AZ	20,657	C
Univ of Calif at Davis	CA		HC
Univ of Calif at Riverside	CA	27,204	C+
Univ of Chicago	IL	55,416	MC
Univ of Denver	CO	51,787	VC+
Univ of Florida	FL	15,943	HC
Univ of Georgia	GA	20,082	VC
Univ of Hawaii at Manoa	HI	19,379	C
Univ of Illinois at Chicago	IL	24,505	VC
Univ of Iowa	IA	17,693	VC
Univ of Kentucky	KY	19,868	C
Univ of Maryland - College Park	MD	20,060	HC+
Univ of Maryland/Baltimore County	MD	18,000	VC
Univ of Mich/Ann Arbor	MI	22,102	MC
Univ of Minn/Twin Cities	MN		HC
Univ of Missouri/Columbia	MO	18,201	MC
Univ of Montana	MT	14,105	C
Univ of Nebr - Lincoln	NE	18,031	VC
Univ of New Hampshire	NH	26,912	C
Univ of New Mexico	NM	15,300	C
Univ of N Car at Chapel Hill	NC	18,928	MC
Univ of Notre Dame	IN	57,117	MC
Univ of Oregon	OR	21,360	C+
Univ of Pennsylvania	PA	61,132	MC
Univ of Pittsburgh at Pittsburgh	PA	28,572	HC+
Univ of Rochester	NY	60,668	MC
Univ of S Car at Columbia	SC	19,725	VC+
Univ of South Florida/Tampa	FL	13,000	C
Univ of Southern Calif	CA	56,903	MC
Univ of Tenn at Knoxville	TN	20,364	VC+
Univ of Texas at Arlington	TX	10,908	LC
Univ of Texas at Austin	TX	44,074	HC
Univ of Vermont	VT	27,006	VC+
Univ of Wisc/Madison	WI	18,757	HC+
Univ of Wyoming	WY	14,401	C+
Vanderbilt Univ	TN	58,220	MC
Wake Forest Univ	NC	58,838	MC
Wayne State Univ	MI	22,063	C
Wellesley College	MA	59,038	MC
West Chester Univ of Pennsylvania	PA	17,186	C
Western Washington Univ	WA	18,519	VC
Wheaton College	MA	54,934	HC+
Williams College	MA	61,070	MC
Wittenberg Univ	OH	47,962	C+
Yale Univ	CT	55,300	MC

RUSSIAN AND SLAVIC STUDIES

School	ST	$IS	SR
American Univ	DC	56,015	HC+
Augsburg College	MN	35,142	C
Bard College	NY	61,940	VC
Bard College at Simon's Rock	MA	61,749	HC+
Baylor Univ	TX	50,329	HC
Boston College	MA	60,622	MC
Brown Univ	RI	59,428	MC

School	ST	$IS	SR
Colgate Univ	NY	58,135	MC
College of Wooster	OH	52,600	MC
Colo College	CO	57,162	MC
Columbia Univ/City of New York	NY	61,116	MC
Conn College	CT	54,970	MC
Cornell College	IA	44,930	VC
Dartmouth College	NH	57,996	MC
DePauw Univ	IN	48,950	VC+
Eastern Mich Univ	MI	18,604	C
Emory Univ	GA	56,368	MC
Florida State Univ	FL	16,715	VC
George Mason Univ	VA	15,724	VC
Grand Valley State Univ	MI	17,998	C+
Hamilton College	NY	55,620	MC
Harvard College/Harvard Univ	MA	49,000	MC
Hobart and William Smith Colleges	NY	60,034	HC+
Indiana Univ Bloomington	IN	19,801	VC
Kent State Univ	OH	19,920	C
Lafayette College	PA	59,155	HC+
Middlebury College	VT	59,160	MC
Mount Holyoke College	MA	55,146	MC
Muhlenberg College	PA	52,837	HC
New York Univ	NY	61,470	MC
Oakland Univ	MI	19,391	C
Oberlin College	OH	61,788	MC
Pomona College	CA	57,680	MC
Purdue Univ/West Lafayette	IN	20,024	HC
Rhodes College	TN	51,900	HC+
Rutgers, The State Univ of New Jersey/New Brunswick	NJ	25,562	VC
San Diego State Univ	CA	21,611	C+
Sarah Lawrence College	NY	48,000	HC
Smith College	MA	59,674	MC
St. Olaf College	MN	51,200	HC+
Stetson Univ	FL	51,516	VC
Syracuse Univ	NY	56,346	VC
Texas Tech Univ	TX	14,243	C
Tufts Univ	MA	58,780	MC
Tulane Univ	LA	60,861	MC
Univ of Alaska Fairbanks	AK	15,130	C
Univ of Calif at Los Angeles	CA	25,686	MC
Univ of Calif at Riverside	CA	27,204	C+
Univ of Calif at San Diego	CA	21,000	VC
Univ of Illinois at Chicago	IL	24,505	VC
Univ of Illinois at Urbana-Champaign	IL	26,450	HC
Univ of Iowa	IA	17,693	VC
Univ of Kansas	KS	17,603	C+
Univ of Maryland - College Park	MD	20,060	HC+
Univ of Mass Amherst	MA	24,215	VC+
Univ of Mich/Ann Arbor	MI	22,102	MC
Univ of Minn/Twin Cities	MN		HC
Univ of N Car at Chapel Hill	NC	18,928	MC
Univ of Northern Iowa	IA	15,795	C
Univ of Rochester	NY	60,668	MC
Univ of Texas at Austin	TX	44,074	HC
Univ of Tulsa	OK	46,331	MC
Univ of Vermont	VT	27,006	VC+
Univ of Washington	WA	14,722	VC
Wesleyan Univ	CT	61,198	MC
Wheaton College	MA	54,934	HC+
Yale Univ	CT	55,300	MC

RUSSIAN LANGUAGES AND LITERATURE

School	ST	$IS	SR
Boston Univ	MA	60,694	MC
Brandeis Univ	MA		MC
Colby College	ME	57,510	MC
Emory Univ	GA	56,368	MC
Hobart and William Smith Colleges	NY	60,034	HC+
Kent State Univ	OH	19,920	C
New College of Florida	FL	14,504	HC
Oberlin College	OH	61,788	MC
Okla State Univ	OK	14,310	VC
Reed College	OR	57,780	MC
St. Louis Univ	MO	48,346	HC
Stony Brook Univ / SUNY	NY	20,078	HC+
Syracuse Univ	NY	56,346	VC
The Pennsylvania State Univ - Univ Park	PA	28,022	VC+
The Univ of Okla	OK	18,621	VC
Univ of Calif at Los Angeles	CA	25,686	MC
Univ of Calif at Riverside	CA	27,204	C+
Univ of Colo Boulder	CO	22,605	VC+
Univ of Illinois at Chicago	IL	24,505	VC
Univ of Illinois at Urbana-Champaign	IL	26,450	HC
Univ of Mich/Ann Arbor	MI	22,102	MC
Univ of Wisc-Milwaukee	WI	18,436	C
Vassar College	NY	61,140	MC
Washington and Lee Univ	VA	52,812	MC
Wellesley College	MA	59,038	MC
Yale Univ	CT	55,300	MC

SAFETY AND SECURITY TECHNOLOGY

School	ST	$IS	SR
Davenport Univ	MI	21,002	LC
Embry-Riddle Aeronautical Univ - Daytona Beach	FL	40,884	C+
Farmingdale State College	NY	19,673	C
Georgetown College	KY	41,440	C+
Lewis Univ	IL	23,050	C
Madonna Univ	MI	24,540	VC
Marshall Univ	WV	14,820	C
Univ of Wisc Whitewater	WI	13,314	C

SAFETY MANAGEMENT

School	ST	$IS	SR
Amridge Univ	AL	6,870	LC
Concordia Univ, Ann Arbor	MI	27,220	VC
Franklin Univ	OH	20,985	SP
Illinois State Univ	IL	23,110	C
Indiana State Univ	IN	16,000	C
John Jay College of Criminal Justice/The CUNY	NY	6,359	LC
Marshall Univ	WV	14,820	C
Pittsburg State Univ	KS	12,032	C
S Dak State Univ	SD	14,296	C
Univ of Central Missouri	MO	14,605	C
Univ of Houston-Downtown	TX	15,170	C

SAFETY SCIENCE

School	ST	$IS	SR
Central Washington Univ	WA	11,730	C
Embry-Riddle Aeronautical Univ - Daytona Beach	FL	40,884	C+
Indiana Univ of Pennsylvania	PA	20,846	LC
Virginia Commonwealth Univ	VA	21,716	C

SANSKRIT AND INDIAN STUDIES

School	ST	$IS	SR
Bard College	NY	61,940	HC
Harvard College/Harvard Univ	MA	49,000	MC
Univ of Iowa	IA	17,693	VC

SCANDINAVIAN LANGUAGES

School	ST	$IS	SR
Augsburg College	MN	35,142	C
Augustana College	IL	43,398	VC
Gustavus Adolphus College	MN	48,170	HC
North Park Univ	IL	30,130	C
Pacific Lutheran Univ	WA	46,760	C+
Univ of Calif at Berkeley	CA	23,322	MC
Univ of Calif at Los Angeles	CA	25,686	MC
Univ of Minn/Twin Cities	MN		HC
Univ of Texas at Austin	TX	44,074	HC
Univ of Washington	WA	14,722	VC

SCANDINAVIAN STUDIES

School	ST	$IS	SR
Augsburg College	MN	35,142	C
Concordia College - Moorhead	MN	39,974	VC
Minn State Univ, Mankato	MN	15,616	C
Pacific Lutheran Univ	WA	46,760	C+
Univ of Wisc/Madison	WI	18,757	HC+
Univ of Wisc-Milwaukee	WI	18,436	C

SCENIC AND LIGHTING DESIGN

School	ST	$IS	SR
Boston Univ	MA	60,694	MC
Shenandoah Univ	VA	39,916	C
Webster Univ	MO	35,100	C+

SCHOOL PSYCHOLOGY

School	ST	$IS	SR
Adams State Univ	CO	13,358	LC
Calif Univ of Pennsylvania	PA	14,217	C
Eastern Mich Univ	MI	18,604	C
Howard Univ	DC	13,646	C
Lubbock Christian Univ	TX	26,308	C
New York Univ	NY	61,470	MC
Southwestern Okla State Univ	OK	9,160	C
Univ of Arizona	AZ	20,657	C
Univ of Georgia	GA	20,082	VC

SCIENCE

School	ST	$IS	SR
Alfred Univ	NY	41,770	C
Alvernia Univ	PA	39,250	LC
Alverno College	WI	31,434	LC
American International College	MA	36,100	LC
Arcadia Univ	PA	33,570	C+
Bennington College	VT	56,990	HC+
Black Hills State Univ	SD	13,947	C
Bowling Green State Univ	OH	18,970	C
Buena Vista Univ	IA	39,188	C
Caribbean Univ	PR	10,375	
Cedar Crest College	PA	43,240	C
Cheyney Univ of Pennsylvania	PA	20,372	C
Clarkson Univ	NY	57,330	HC
Coe College	IA	45,550	VC
Colo Christian Univ	CO	27,500	VC
Concordia Univ, Ann Arbor	MI	27,220	VC
Drexel Univ	PA	61,418	VC+
East Stroudsburg Univ of Pennsylvania	PA	18,868	LC
Eastern Mich Univ	MI	18,604	C
Eastern Nazarene College	MA	30,000	C

ST = STATE $IS = IN-STATE COSTS   SR = SELECTOR RATING

School	ST	$IS	SR
Fairleigh Dickinson Univ/ Metropolitan Campus	NJ	40,254	C
Fordham Univ	NY	61,588	HC+
Fort Hays State Univ	KS	11,354	C
Gannon Univ	PA	39,608	C
Grace College and Seminary	IN	28,800	VC
Graceland Univ	IA	28,020	C
Grand Valley State Univ	MI	17,998	C+
Grinnell College	IA	53,654	HC
Hampshire College	MA	58,320	MC
Hawaii Pacific Univ	HI	34,360	C
Heritage Univ	WA	17,664	NC
Houghton College	NY	36,808	C+
Indiana Wesleyan Univ	IN	31,815	VC
John Brown Univ	AR	32,056	VC+
Johnson C. Smith Univ	NC	25,336	LC
Keene State College	NH	23,232	LC
Kent State Univ	OH	19,920	C
King's College	PA	43,502	C
La Salle Univ	PA	50,270	C
Le Moyne College	NY	43,470	C
Lee Univ	TN	18,690	C+
LeMoyne-Owen College	TN	13,100	C
Loras College	IA	37,432	VC
Lyndon State College	VT	14,233	C
Madonna Univ	MI	24,540	VC
Marygrove College	MI	28,926	C
Marylhurst Univ	OR	20,295	NC
Maryville Univ of St. Louis	MO	35,856	VC
Marywood Univ	PA	45,595	C
Mayville State Univ	ND	11,401	NC
Middle Tenn State Univ	TN	8,650	C
Miss State Univ	MS	14,750	C
Missouri Southern State Univ	MO	12,061	C
Montana Tech of The Univ of Montana	MT	14,650	VC
Mount Aloysius College	PA	29,976	C
Mount St. Mary College	NY	41,138	C
National Louis Univ	IL	16,915	LC
Northern Kentucky Univ	KY	21,134	C
Northwest Missouri State Univ	MO	17,347	C
Okla City Univ	OK	40,476	VC
Okla Wesleyan Univ	OK	21,300	C
Oregon State Univ	OR	20,273	VC
Penn State Erie/The Behrend College	PA	16,256	C
Penn State Univ/Altoona	PA	11,464	C
Piedmont College	GA	30,136	C
Pitzer College	CA	54,988	MC
Pomona College	CA	57,680	MC
Purdue Univ/West Lafayette	IN	20,024	HC
Rockford College	IL	31,000	C
Rutgers, The State Univ of New Jersey/Camden Campus	NJ	25,121	C
Samford Univ	AL	37,060	C+
Seattle Univ	WA	49,035	VC+
Sierra Nevada College	NV	32,700	VC
Southern Nazarene Univ	OK	24,354	C
Southern Oregon Univ	OR	17,874	C
St. John's College, Santa Fe	NM	54,998	HC+
SUNY/Empire State College	NY	6,315	SP
The Lincoln Univ	PA	15,154	LC
Tiffin Univ	OH	30,273	LC
Trevecca Nazarene Univ	TN	31,186	C
Troy Univ	AL	10,650	C
Tulane Univ	LA	60,861	MC
Union College	NE	23,270	C
Union College	NY	60,240	MC
United States Air Force Academy	CO		MC
United States Naval Academy	MD		MC
Univ of Alabama in Huntsville	AL	17,591	VC+
Univ of Alaska Fairbanks	AK	15,130	C
Univ of Denver	CO	51,787	VC+
Univ of Findlay	OH	31,916	C
Univ of Great Falls	MT	27,970	C
Univ of Mass Amherst	MA	24,215	VC+
Univ of Mich/Dearborn	MI	9,885	VC
Univ of Mich-Flint	MI	17,547	C+
Univ of Nebr - Lincoln	NE	18,031	VC
Univ of N Dak	ND	14,551	C
Univ of Northern Iowa	IA	15,795	C
Univ of Oregon	OR	21,360	C+
Univ of St. Francis	IN	29,810	C
Univ of Texas at El Paso	TX	8,764	NC
Univ of Wisc/Parkside	WI	10,181	LC
Univ of Wisc/River Falls	WI	9,722	LC
Univ of Wisc/Stout	WI	15,459	C
Upper Iowa Univ	IA	30,426	NC
Urbana Univ	OH	30,820	C
Valley City State Univ	ND	12,286	LC
Villanova Univ	PA	58,394	MC
Virginia Commonwealth Univ	VA	21,716	C
Walsh Univ	OH	35,100	C
Washburn Univ	KS	12,579	C
Washington State Univ	WA	20,461	C
Wayland Baptist Univ	TX	18,912	LC
West Virginia Univ	WV	16,542	C+
Western New Mexico Univ	NM	8,500	LC
Westfield State Univ	MA	18,297	C
Widener Univ	PA	52,418	C
Wilberforce Univ	OH	15,100	LC
Willamette Univ	OR	56,450	VC+
William Woods Univ	MO	24,260	C

SCIENCE AND MANAGEMENT

School	ST	$IS	SR
Claremont McKenna College	CA	62,215	MC
George Mason Univ	VA	15,724	VC
Philadelphia Univ	PA	44,160	C
Pitzer College	CA	54,988	MC
Scripps College	CA	61,940	MC
Texas A&M Univ at Galveston	TX	11,258	C

SCIENCE AND SOCIETY

School	ST	$IS	SR
Bard College	NY	61,940	HC
Brown Univ	RI	59,428	MC
Butler Univ	IN	47,572	VC+
College of Staten Island/The City of New Yok	NY	16,778	NC
Northwestern Univ	IL	61,640	MC
Ramapo College of New Jersey	NJ	24,938	C
Rutgers, The State Univ of New Jersey/Newark Campus	NJ	258,806	C
Univ of Puget Sound	WA	54,608	HC
Vassar College	NY	61,140	MC
Walsh Univ	OH	35,100	C
Wesleyan Univ	CT	61,198	MC

SCIENCE AND TECHNOLOGY STUDIES

School	ST	$IS	SR
Cornell Univ	NY	60,964	MC
Kean Univ	NJ	23,444	C

SCIENCE EDUCATION

School	ST	$IS	SR
Adams State Univ	CO	13,358	LC
Alabama A&M Univ	AL	10,084	C
Albany State Univ	GA	8,500	C
Alfred Univ	NY	41,770	C
Alverno College	WI	31,434	LC
American International College	MA	36,100	LC
Anderson Univ	IN	36,100	C
Andrews Univ	MI	28,030	C+
Appalachian State Univ	NC	12,919	VC
Aquinas College	MI	33,060	C
Arizona State Univ, at the Polytechnic Campus	AZ	20,531	C+
Arkansas State Univ	AR	15,470	C
Arkansas Tech Univ	AR	13,982	LC
Asbury Univ	KY	32,038	VC
Ashland Univ	OH	25,000	C
Auburn Univ	AL	22,378	VC+
Averett Univ	VA	37,750	LC
Baker Univ	KS	33,350	C+
Baldwin Wallace Univ	OH	38,318	C
Ball State Univ	IN	17,850	C
Baylor Univ	TX	50,329	HC
Bemidji State Univ	MN	13,500	VC
Bennett College for Women	NC	21,970	LC
Bethany College	KS	30,605	NC
Bethany College	WV	35,282	LC
Bethel College	IN	31,560	C
Bethel Univ	MN	34,940	VC
Bethune-Cookman Univ	FL	22,958	C
Black Hills State Univ	SD	13,947	C
Blackburn College	IL	21,350	C
Bloomfield College	NJ	37,850	LC
Blue Mountain College	MS	15,634	LC
Boston Univ	MA	60,694	MC
Bowie State Univ	MD	23,990	LC
Bowling Green State Univ	OH	18,970	C
Brigham Young Univ	UT	12,100	HC
Brigham Young Univ/Hawaii	HI	10,686	VC
Bryan College	TN	24,194	C
Buena Vista Univ	IA	39,188	C
Buffalo State College / SUNY	NY	15,733	C+
Cal State, Long Beach	CA	17,502	C+
Calvin College	MI	39,120	VC
Cameron Univ	OK	10,004	LC
Canisius College	NY	44,900	C
Caribbean Univ	PR	10,375	
Carroll Univ	WI	38,100	C
Carson-Newman Univ	TN	29,058	C+
Catawba College	NC	37,240	LC
Cedarville Univ	OH	32,860	VC
Central Univ of Bayamon	PR	3,350	
Central Washington Univ	WA	11,730	C
Chadron State College	NE	7,400	NC
Charleston Southern Univ	SC	22,420	C
CUNY/Brooklyn College	NY	5,884	C+
College of New Jersey	NJ	25,376	HC
Colo State Univ-Fort Collins	CO	20,385	VC
Concord Univ	WV	13,102	C
Concordia Univ Nebr	NE	26,000	VC
Concordia Univ St. Paul	MN	28,250	C
Concordia Univ, River Forest	IL	26,300	C
Converse College	SC	37,130	C
Cornell College	IA	44,930	VC
Cornerstone Univ and Grand Rapids Theological Seminary	MI	33,338	C
Covenant College	GA	38,990	VC+
Daemen College	NY	34,770	C
Defiance College	OH	30,645	C
Delaware State Univ	DE	16,722	LC
Dickinson State Univ	ND	11,900	NC
Dominican College	NY	31,270	LC
Dordt College	IA	34,160	C+
East Carolina Univ	NC	14,169	C
East Texas Baptist Univ	TX	31,577	LC
Eastern Illinois Univ	IL	20,466	C
Eastern Mich Univ	MI	18,604	C
Eastern Nazarene College	MA	30,000	C
Eastern Washington Univ	WA		C
Edgewood College	WI	33,294	C
Edinboro Univ of Pennsylvania	PA	15,940	LC
Elizabethtown College	PA	49,740	VC
Elmira College	NY	49,950	C+
Elms College	MA	23,900	VC
Elon Univ	NC	41,914	VC+
Eureka College	IL	19,280	C
Evangel Univ	MO	23,090	C
Fairmont State Univ	WV	12,098	LC
Faulkner Univ	AL	25,720	C
Florida A&M Univ	FL	14,935	LC
Florida Inst of Technology	FL	48,290	VC
Florida International Univ	FL	17,747	C+
Florida State Univ	FL	16,715	VC
Franklin College	IN	36,585	C
Freed-Hardeman Univ	TN	19,697	VC
Fresno Pacific Univ	CA	32,136	C
Friends Univ	KS	29,100	C
Gettysburg College	PA	58,820	HC
Glenville State College	WV	11,348	NC
Goshen College	IN	35,900	VC
Grace College and Seminary	IN	28,800	VC
Grand Valley State Univ	MI	17,998	C+
Greensboro College	NC	28,740	LC
Greenville College	IL	27,012	C
Gustavus Adolphus College	MN	48,170	HC
Gwynedd-Mercy College	PA	33,560	C
Hamline Univ	MN	45,678	VC
Hardin-Simmons Univ	TX	23,560	C+
Hastings College	NE	27,782	C+
Heidelberg Univ	OH	34,100	C
Heritage Univ	WA	17,664	NC
Hofstra Univ	NY	51,810	VC+
Holy Family Univ	PA	40,030	LC
Hood College	MD	45,730	C
Hope College	MI	38,650	VC
Houghton College	NY	36,808	C+
Humboldt State Univ	CA	18,400	C
Hunter College	NY	14,429	VC
Huntington Univ	IN	32,220	C+
Husson Univ	ME	24,194	LC
Illinois College	IL	25,770	VC
Immaculata Univ	PA	43,000	C
Indiana State Univ	IN	16,000	C
Indiana Univ-Purdue Univ Fort Wayne	IN	15,521	C
Indiana Wesleyan Univ	IN	31,815	C
Inter-American Univ of PR/ San Germán	PR	6,720	
Iowa Wesleyan College	IA	30,850	LC
John Brown Univ	AR	32,056	VC+
Johnson State College	VT	16,721	C
Judson College	AL	26,794	C
Judson Univ	IL	25,130	C
Juniata College	PA	49,340	VC
King's College	PA	43,502	C
Kutztown Univ of Pennsylvania	PA	16,909	LC
La Salle Univ	PA	50,270	C
Lamar Univ	TX	6,820	LC
Langston Univ	OK	3,000	C
Le Moyne College	NY	43,470	C
Lehman College/The CUNY	NY	5,778	LC
Lenoir-Rhyne College	NC	35,984	C
LeTourneau Univ	TX	36,210	VC
Lincoln Memorial Univ	TN	18,144	C
Lindenwood Univ	MO	20,750	C
LIU Brooklyn	NY	47,182	LC
Livingstone College	NC	17,815	LC
Lock Haven Univ of Pennsylvania	PA	18,028	LC
Louisiana College	LA	15,746	C
Loyola Univ Chicago	IL	51,646	VC+
Lubbock Christian Univ	TX	26,308	C
Lyndon State College	VT	14,233	C
MacMurray College	IL	20,755	C
Malone Univ	OH	35,364	C
Manhattan College	NY	49,588	C+
Mansfield Univ	PA	19,468	LC
Marian Univ	WI	32,420	LC
Mars Hill Univ	NC	22,950	LC
Maryville College	TN	33,150	C+
Marywood Univ	PA	45,595	C
Mayville State Univ	ND	11,401	NC
Mercyhurst Univ	PA	40,700	C
Messiah College	PA	40,690	C+
Miami Univ	OH	24,191	VC
MidAmerica Nazarene Univ	KS	28,000	C
Midland Univ	NE	34,000	C
Miles College	AL	11,164	NC
Minn State Univ, Mankato	MN	15,616	C
Minn State Univ, Moorhead	MN	13,392	VC
Minot State Univ	ND	10,915	C
Miss Valley State Univ	MS	9,706	LC
Missouri Southern State Univ	MO	12,061	C
Missouri State Univ	MO	13,996	C+
Monmouth Univ	NJ	44,108	C
Montana State Univ-Billings	MT	12,425	LC
Montana State Univ-Northern	MT	12,500	NC
Morningside College	IA	35,430	C
Morris College	SC	16,310	LC
Mount Aloysius College	PA	29,976	C
Mount Mary Univ	WI	33,590	LC
Mount Vernon Nazarene Univ	OH	29,590	C
Muskingum Univ	OH	30,502	C
Nebr Wesleyan Univ	NE	29,774	C+
New Mexico Highlands Univ	NM	11,904	NC
New York Univ	NY	61,470	MC
Niagara Univ	NY	41,010	C
N Car State Univ	NC	16,202	HC
Northeastern State Univ	OK	8,615	VC
Northern Mich Univ	MI	18,278	C
Northern State Univ - Aberdeen	SD	14,505	C
Northwest Missouri State	MO	17,347	C
Northwestern College of Iowa	IA	36,240	VC
Northwestern Okla State Univ	OK	7,275	NC
Notre Dame of Maryland Univ	MD	27,700	VC
Nova Southeastern Univ	FL	37,280	VC
Oakland City Univ	IN	24,500	NC
Oakwood Univ	AL	25,529	NC
Ohio Univ	OH	21,080	C
Ohio Valley Univ	WV	17,752	C
Ohio Wesleyan Univ	OH	49,460	C+
Okla Baptist Univ	OK	28,202	C
Okla Christian Univ	OK	25,870	VC
Okla Wesleyan Univ	OK	21,300	C
Old Dominion Univ	VA	19,483	LC
Olivet Nazarene Univ	IL	29,990	C
Oral Roberts Univ	OK	31,734	C
Ouachita Baptist Univ	AR	30,220	VC
Palm Beach Atlantic Univ	FL	34,874	C+
Peru State College	NE	8,600	NC
Pfeiffer Univ	NC	33,700	LC
Piedmont College	GA	30,136	C
Plymouth State Univ	NH	23,148	LC
Pontifical Catholic Univ of PR	PR	7,310	
Purdue Univ/Calumet	IN	14,336	C
Purdue Univ/West Lafayette	IN	20,024	HC
Queens College/The CUNY	NY	17,107	VC
Rhode Island College	RI	17,694	LC
Rider Univ	NJ	45,720	C
Rocky Mountain College	MT	32,242	C
Rowan Univ	NJ	24,022	VC+
Rust College	MS	10,600	C
Sacred Heart Univ	CT	49,264	VC
Saginaw Valley State Univ	MI	17,369	C
St. Augustine's Univ	NC	14,000	C
St. Mary-of-the-Woods College	IN	37,722	C
St. Mary's Univ	TX	33,854	C
St. Michael's College	VT	49,975	VC
St. Vincent College	PA	40,244	C
St. Xavier Univ	IL	32,840	C
Salem State Univ	MA	13,161	LC
Schreiner Univ	TX	32,734	LC
Seattle Pacific Univ	WA	41,559	VC+
Seton Hill Univ	PA	35,172	C
Shaw Univ	NC	15,488	C
Shepherd Univ	WV	15,875	C
Siena Heights Univ	MI	32,040	C
Slippery Rock Univ of Pennsylvania	PA	10,360	C
Southeast Missouri State Univ	MO	15,370	LC
Southeastern Okla State Univ	OK	7,966	LC
Southern Arkansas Univ	AR	14,316	C
Southern Conn State Univ	CT	18,033	LC
Southern Illinois Univ Edwardsville	IL	17,532	C
Southern Nazarene Univ	OK	24,354	C
Southern Univ at New Orleans	LA	2,963	NC
Southwest Minn State Univ	MN	14,000	C
Southwestern Okla State Univ	OK	9,160	C
Springfield College	MA	25,000	C
St. Cloud State Univ	MN	10,600	C
St. Edward's Univ	TX	47,784	C
St. John Fisher College	NY	40,708	C+
St. John's Univ	NY	55,070	C+
St. Thomas Aquinas College	NY	40,230	C
SUNY / College of Environmental Science and Forestry	NY	18,351	VC
Suffolk Univ	MA	47,298	C
SUNY College at Old Westbury	NY	16,324	C
SUNY Fredonia/The SUNY at Fredonia	NY	19,840	VC
SUNY New Paltz	NY	14,348	C
SUNY Oneonta / SUNY	NY	16,919	C+
Syracuse Univ	NY	56,346	VC
Tabor College	KS	29,010	C

ST = STATE $IS = IN-STATE COSTS   SR = SELECTOR RATING

School	ST	$IS	SR
Taylor Univ	IN	37,821	VC+
Texas A&M Univ at Commerce	TX	10,496	C
Texas Tech Univ	TX	14,243	C
The College of St. Rose	NY	26,750	C
The Univ of N Car at Greensboro	NC	12,848	C
The Univ of N Car at Pembroke	NC	13,388	LC
The Univ of Okla	OK	18,621	VC
Toccoa Falls College	GA	23,210	C
Tougaloo College	MS	15,275	NC
Trevecca Nazarene Univ	TN	31,186	C
Trine Univ	IN	39,400	HC+
Troy Univ	AL	10,650	C
Union College	KY	29,955	C
Universidad del Turabo	PR	4,110	
Univ of Arizona	AZ	20,657	C
Univ of Arkansas at Pine Bluff	AR	13,378	C
Univ of Calif at San Diego	CA	21,000	VC
Univ of Central Arkansas	AR	13,667	VC
Univ of Central Florida	FL	15,668	VC+
Univ of Central Missouri	MO	14,605	C
Univ of Central Okla	OK	12,293	C
Univ of Charleston	WV	32,300	C
Univ of Cincinnati	OH	21,506	VC
Univ of Conn	CT	24,706	HC
Univ of Delaware	DE	23,612	VC
Univ of Evansville	IN	42,656	VC+
Univ of Georgia	GA	20,082	VC
Univ of Great Falls	MT	27,970	C
Univ of Idaho	ID	14,558	C
Univ of Illinois at Urbana-Champaign	IL	26,450	HC
Univ of Indianapolis	IN	31,740	LC
Univ of Iowa	IA	17,693	VC
Univ of Kentucky	KY	19,868	C
Univ of Louisiana at Lafayette	LA	6,130	C
Univ of Louisville	KY	17,946	C
Univ of Mary Hardin-Baylor	TX	31,950	C+
Univ of Maryland/Eastern Shore	MD	14,000	C
Univ of Mich/Dearborn	MI	9,885	VC
Univ of Minn/Duluth	MN	19,806	C
Univ of Minn/Twin Cities	MN		HC
Univ of Miss	MS	16,704	C
Univ of Missouri/Columbia	MO	18,201	MC
Univ of Montana	MT	14,105	C
Univ of Montana-Western	MT	9,753	LC
Univ of Nebr - Lincoln	NE	18,501	VC
Univ of Nebr at Kearney	NE	14,855	LC
Univ of New Haven	CT	48,940	C
Univ of North Alabama	AL	9,960	C
Univ of North Florida	FL	15,870	VC
Univ of North Georgia	GA	8,500	C
Univ of Northern Colo	CO	18,446	C
Univ of Northern Iowa	IA	15,795	C
Univ of Notre Dame	IN	57,117	MC
Univ of Pittsburgh at Bradford	PA	21,802	C
Univ of Pittsburgh at Johnstown	PA	20,862	C
Univ of Rio Grande	OH	8,750	NC
Univ of St. Francis	IN	29,810	C
Univ of Sioux Falls	SD	22,990	C
Univ of South Florida/Tampa	FL	13,000	C
Univ of Southern Indiana	IN	14,885	C
Univ of Southern Miss	MS	13,170	C
Univ of the Cumberlands	KY	27,500	C
Univ of Toledo	OH	18,464	C
Univ of Vermont	VT	27,006	VC+
Univ of West Alabama	AL	14,274	C
Univ of Wisc Whitewater	WI	13,314	C
Univ of Wisc/Eau Claire	WI	15,730	VC
Univ of Wisc/La Crosse	WI	9,304	VC
Univ of Wisc/Oshkosh	WI	10,426	LC
Univ of Wisc/Stout	WI	15,459	C
Univ of Wisc/Superior	WI	14,314	C
Utah State Univ	UT	12,044	C
Valparaiso Univ	IN	44,940	VC+
Vanguard Univ of Southern Calif	CA	35,833	VC
Virginia Polytechnic Inst and State Univ	VA	14,629	HC
Viterbo Univ	WI	30,070	C
Warner Univ	FL	18,000	C
Wartburg College	IA	41,055	VC
Washington State Univ	WA	20,461	C
Washington Univ in St. Louis	MO	69,844	MC
Wayne State College	NE	11,764	NC
Wayne State Univ	MI	22,063	C
West Chester Univ of Pennsylvania	PA	17,186	C
West Liberty Univ	WV	9,142	LC
West Texas A&M Univ	TX	13,478	C
Western Carolina Univ	NC	13,965	C
Western New Mexico Univ	NM	8,543	C
Western State Colo Univ	CO	16,924	C
Western Washington Univ	WA	18,519	VC
Whitworth Univ	WA	47,734	VC
Widener Univ	PA	52,418	C
William Penn Univ	IA	44,910	C
Wilmington College	OH	29,784	C
Wingate Univ	NC	34,990	C
Winona State Univ	MN	16,640	C

School	ST	$IS	SR
Wittenberg Univ	OH	47,962	C+
Wright State Univ	OH	16,983	C
Xavier Univ	OH	44,980	VC
Xavier Univ of Louisiana	LA	25,300	C
York College	NE	19,475	C
York College of Pennsylvania	PA	26,590	C
Youngstown State Univ	OH	16,732	C

SCIENCE OF EARTH SYSTEMS

School	ST	$IS	SR
Cornell Univ	NY	60,964	MC
Univ of Illinois at Chicago	IL	24,505	VC

SCIENCE OF NATURAL AND ENVIRONMENTAL SYSTEMS

School	ST	$IS	SR
Cornell Univ	NY	60,964	MC

SCIENCE TECHNOLOGY

School	ST	$IS	SR
Arizona State Univ, at the Polytechnic Campus	AZ	20,531	C+
Colby College	ME	57,510	MC
James Madison Univ	VA	18,049	VC
Lehigh Univ	PA	56,770	MC
Marshall Univ	WV	14,820	C
Mass Inst of Technology	MA	58,240	MC
Missouri Southern State Univ	MO	12,061	C
Rensselaer Polytechnic Inst	NY	61,529	MC
Scripps College	CA	61,940	MC
Stevens Inst of Technology	NJ	50,130	HC
The Pennsylvania State Univ - Univ Park	PA	28,022	VC+
Univ of Pennsylvania	PA	61,132	MC

SCIENTIFIC/MEDICAL MARKETING

School	ST	$IS	SR
Carlow Univ	PA	30,272	C

SCULPTURE

School	ST	$IS	SR
Adams State Univ	CO	13,358	LC
Aquinas College	MI	33,060	C
Art Academy of Cincinnati	OH	25,940	SP
Bennington College	VT	56,990	HC+
Binghamton Univ/The SUNY	NY	21,648	HC+
Birmingham-Southern College	AL	44,168	VC+
Boston Univ	MA	60,694	MC
Buffalo State College / SUNY	NY	15,733	C+
Calif College of the Arts	CA	48,334	SP
Cal State, San Bernardino	CA	12,000	C
Cleveland Inst of Art	OH	48,685	SP
College for Creative Studies	MI	45,340	C
Escuela de Artes Plasticas de PR	PR	2,660	
Ferris State Univ	MI	20,047	C
Howard Univ	DC	13,646	C
Indiana Univ Bloomington	IN	19,801	VC
Indiana Univ-Purdue Univ Fort Wayne	IN	15,521	C
Indiana Univ-Purdue Univ Indianapolis	IN	17,611	C
Kansas City Art Inst	MO	44,308	SP
Kent State Univ	OH	19,920	C
Kutztown Univ of Pennsylvania	PA	16,909	LC
Maine College of Art	ME	28,812	SP
Marshall Univ	WV	14,820	C
Maryland Inst College of Art	MD	39,500	SP
Marywood Univ	PA	45,595	C
Milwaukee Inst of Art and Design	WI	31,938	SP
Minneapolis College of Art and Design	MN	36,700	SP
Montserrat College of Art	MA	31,000	C
Moore College of Art and Design	PA	50,135	SP
Ohio Univ	OH	21,080	C
Pacific Northwest College of Art	OR	38,494	C
Providence College	RI	57,383	VC
Rhode Island School of Design	RI	57,234	MC
Ringling College of Art and Design	FL	46,130	SP
Rochester Inst of Technology	NY	42,450	VC
San Francisco Art Inst	CA	55,762	SP
Santa Fe Univ of Art and Design	NM	39,666	SP
Savannah College of Art and Design	GA	48,005	SP
School of the Art Inst of Chicago	IL	56,230	SP
SUNY New Paltz	NY	14,348	C
Syracuse Univ	NY	56,346	VC
Temple Univ	PA	24,392	VC
Texas Christian Univ	TX	49,980	VC
Univ of Dallas	TX	45,500	VC+
Univ of Hartford	CT	45,030	C
Univ of Illinois at Chicago	IL	24,505	VC
Univ of Illinois at Urbana-Champaign	IL	26,450	HC
Univ of Iowa	IA	17,693	VC
Univ of Kansas	KS	17,603	C+

School	ST	$IS	SR
Univ of Mass Dartmouth	MA	22,223	C
Univ of Miami	FL	57,034	MC
Univ of Mich/Ann Arbor	MI	22,102	MC
Univ of Oregon	OR	21,360	C
Univ of the Arts	PA	38,450	SP
Univ of Washington	WA	14,722	VC
Virginia Commonwealth Univ	VA	21,716	C
Washington Univ in St. Louis	MO	69,844	MC
Webster Univ	MO	35,100	C+
Western Washington Univ	WA	18,519	VC

SECONDARY EDUCATION

School	ST	$IS	SR
Abilene Christian Univ	TX	38,400	C+
Adams State Univ	CO	13,358	LC
Adrian College	MI	42,400	C
Alabama A&M Univ	AL	10,084	C
Alabama State Univ	AL	14,142	NC
Albright College	PA	46,660	C
Alderson Broaddus Univ	WV	28,656	C
Alfred Univ	NY	41,770	C
Alice Lloyd College	KY	4,900	LC
Alma College	MI	44,075	C
Alvernia Univ	PA	39,261	C
Alverno College	WI	31,434	LC
American International College	MA	36,100	LC
American Univ	DC	56,015	HC+
Andrews Univ	MI	28,030	C
Appalachian State Univ	NC	12,919	VC
Aquinas College	MI	33,060	C
Aquinas College	TN	29,250	VC+
Arcadia Univ	PA	43,570	C
Arizona State Univ, at the Polytechnic Campus	AZ	20,531	C+
Arizona State Univ, at the Tempe Campus	AZ	20,137	C+
Arizona State Univ, at the West Campus	AZ	19,251	C+
Asbury Univ	KY	32,038	VC
Ashland Univ	OH	25,000	C
Auburn Univ	AL	22,378	VC+
Auburn Univ at Montgomery	AL	14,470	LC
Augsburg College	MN	35,142	C
Augustana College	IL	43,398	VC
Aurora Univ	IL	33,228	C
Averett Univ	VA	37,750	LC
Baker Univ	KS	33,350	C+
Baylor Univ	TX	50,329	HC
Bemidji State Univ	MN	13,500	VC
Benedictine College	KS	29,180	VC
Bennington College	VT	56,990	HC+
Bethany College	KS	30,605	NC
Bethany College	WV	35,282	LC
Bethel College	IN	31,560	C
Bethel Univ	MN	34,940	VC
Birmingham-Southern College	AL	44,168	VC+
Blackburn College	IL	21,350	C
Bloomfield College	NJ	37,850	LC
Bloomsburg Univ of Pennsylvania	PA	13,598	C
Bluefield College	VA	17,230	C+
Boise State Univ	ID	13,469	LC
Boston College	MA	60,622	MC
Bowling Green State Univ	OH	18,970	C
Briar Cliff Univ	IA	29,514	C
Bucknell Univ	PA	60,140	MC
Buena Vista Univ	IA	39,188	C
Buffalo State College / SUNY	NY	15,733	C+
Butler Univ	IN	47,572	VC+
Cabrini College	PA	40,859	LC
Calif Univ of Pennsylvania	PA	14,217	C
Calumet College of St. Joseph	IN	15,000	C
Calvin College	MI	39,120	VC
Capital Univ	OH	41,050	VC
Cardinal Stritch Univ	WI	24,054	C
Caribbean Univ	PR	10,375	
Carlow Univ	PA	30,272	C
Carroll College	MT	28,000	C
Carson-Newman Univ	TN	29,058	C+
Carthage College	WI	33,000	C
Centenary College	NJ	38,618	C
Central State Univ	OH	9,010	C
Central Univ of Bayamon	PR	3,350	
Central Washington Univ	WA	11,730	C
Chadron State College	NE	7,400	NC
Chaminade Univ of Honolulu	HI	31,664	LC
Champlain College	VT	46,650	VC+
Chicago State Univ	IL	5,482	C
Citadel, The	SC		C
CUNY/Brooklyn College	NY	5,884	C+
CUNY/City College	NY	20,319	HC+
Clarion Univ of Pennsylvania	PA	17,370	LC
Clarke Univ	IA	37,600	C
Clearwater Christian College	FL	23,720	C
Clemson Univ	SC	19,136	HC
Cleveland State Univ	OH	21,776	C
Coe College	IA	45,550	VC
College of Charleston	SC	22,145	VC
College of St Joseph	VT	30,600	C
College of Staten Island/The City of New Yok	NY	16,778	NC
College of the Ozarks	MO		VC
Colo Christian Univ	CO	27,500	VC

School	ST	$IS	SR
Columbia College	MO	24,578	C
Columbus State Univ	GA	13,176	C
Concord Univ	WV	13,102	C
Concordia College - Moorhead	MN	39,974	VC
Concordia Univ	OR	35,000	C
Concordia Univ Nebr	NE	26,000	VC
Concordia Univ St. Paul	MN	28,250	C
Concordia Univ Texas	TX	23,640	C
Concordia Univ Wisc	WI	28,980	C
Concordia Univ, Ann Arbor	MI	27,220	VC
Concordia Univ, River Forest	IL	26,300	C
Converse College	SC	37,130	C
Cornell College	IA	44,930	VC
Cornerstone Univ and Grand Rapids Theological Seminary	MI	33,338	C
Creighton Univ	NE	45,356	VC
Cumberland Univ	TN	21,220	C
Dakota State Univ	SD	13,811	C
Davis & Elkins College	WV	33,742	C
Defiance College	OH	30,645	C
Delaware Valley College	PA	29,944	C
DePaul Univ	IL	47,623	VC
Dickinson State Univ	ND	11,900	NC
Dominican College	NY	31,270	C
Dominican Univ	IL	37,628	C
Dordt College	IA	34,160	C+
Dowling College	NY	25,000	LC
Drake Univ	IA	41,516	VC+
Drury Univ	MO	31,909	VC
East Stroudsburg Univ of Pennsylvania	PA	18,868	LC
East Texas Baptist Univ	TX	31,577	LC
Eastern Kentucky Univ	KY	11,161	C
Eastern Mennonite Univ	VA	40,660	C
Eastern Mich Univ	MI	18,604	C
Eastern Washington Univ	WA		C
Edinboro Univ of Pennsylvania	PA	15,940	LC
Elizabethtown College	PA	49,740	VC
Elmhurst College	IL	43,336	C
Elmira College	NY	49,950	C+
Elms College	MA	23,900	VC
Elon Univ	NC	41,914	VC+
Emmanuel College	MA	47,985	VC
Emporia State Univ	KS	12,897	C
Eureka College	IL	19,280	C
Evangel Univ	MO	23,090	C
Fairmont State Univ	WV	12,098	LC
Fayetteville State Univ	NC	10,816	C
Felician College	NJ	41,640	LC
Fitchburg State Univ	MA	18,173	C
Flagler College	FL	25,180	C
Florida Gulf Coast Univ	FL		C
Florida Memorial Univ	FL	20,888	LC
Florida Southern College	FL	40,150	C+
Fontbonne Univ	MO	31,384	C
Fort Valley State Univ	GA	11,200	VC
Franklin College	IN	36,585	C
Franklin Pierce Univ	NH	41,598	C
Freed-Hardeman Univ	TN	19,697	VC
Friends Univ	KS	29,100	C
Gallaudet Univ	DC	25,380	SP
Gardner-Webb Univ	NC	34,375	C+
Georgetown College	KY	41,440	C+
Gettysburg College	PA	58,820	HC
Glenville State College	WV	11,348	NC
Goddard College	VT	16,418	VC
Gordon College	MA	44,320	VC
Goshen College	IN	35,900	VC
Grace Bible College	MI	20,770	C
Grambling State Univ	LA	13,384	LC
Grand Canyon Univ	AZ	24,540	VC
Grand Valley State Univ	MI	17,998	C+
Grand View Univ	IA	31,050	C
Green Mountain College	VT	45,228	LC
Greensboro College	NC	28,740	LC
Gustavus Adolphus College	MN	48,170	HC
Gwynedd-Mercy College	PA	33,560	C
Hamline Univ	MN	45,678	VC
Hannibal-LaGrange Univ	MO	24,490	C
Harding Univ	AR	23,556	C
Hardin-Simmons Univ	TX	23,560	C+
Harris-Stowe State Univ	MO	14,360	NC
Hastings College	NE	27,782	C+
Heidelberg Univ	OH	34,100	C
Heritage Univ	WA	17,664	NC
Hofstra Univ	NY	51,810	VC+
Holy Family Univ	PA	40,030	LC
Hood College	MD	45,730	C
Hope College	MI	38,650	VC
Hope International Univ	CA	34,650	C
Houghton College	NY	36,808	C+
Houston Baptist Univ	TX	36,450	C
Howard Payne Univ	TX	17,115	C
Howard Univ	DC	13,646	C
Humboldt State Univ	CA	18,400	C
Hunter College	NY	14,429	VC
Huntington Univ	IN	32,220	C+
Idaho State Univ	ID	12,307	C
Illinois College	IL	25,770	VC
Immaculata Univ	PA	43,000	C
Indiana State Univ	IN	16,000	C
Indiana Univ Bloomington	IN	19,801	VC
Indiana Univ East	IN	6,783	C

School	ST	$IS	SR
Indiana Univ Kokomo	IN	6,811	LC
Indiana Univ Northwest	IN	6,854	LC
Indiana Univ South Bend	IN	15,501	C
Indiana Univ Southeast	IN	16,035	C
Indiana Univ-Purdue Univ Fort Wayne	IN	15,521	C
Indiana Univ-Purdue Univ Indianapolis	IN	17,611	C
Indiana Wesleyan Univ	IN	31,815	VC
Inter-American Univ of PR/ Aguadilla Campus	PR	5,578	
Inter-American Univ of PR/ Arecibo Campus	PR	3,350	
Inter-American Univ of PR/ Barranquitas	PR	3,350	
Inter-American Univ of PR/ Fajardo Campus	PR	4,200	
Inter-American Univ of PR/ Metropolitan Campus	PR	4,320	
Inter-American Univ of PR/ Ponce	PR		
Inter-American Univ of PR/ San Germán	PR	6,720	
Iowa State Univ	IA	16,403	C
Iowa Wesleyan College	IA	30,850	LC
Ithaca College	NY	53,864	HC
Jacksonville State Univ	AL	12,480	LC
Jarvis Christian College	TX	19,552	NC
John Brown Univ	AR	32,056	VC+
John Carroll Univ	OH	46,300	C+
Johnson State College	VT	16,721	C
Judson Univ	IL	25,130	C
Juniata College	PA	49,340	VC
Kansas State Univ	KS	15,497	VC
Kansas Wesleyan Univ	KS	32,000	C
Kean Univ	NJ	23,444	C
Kentucky State Univ	KY	11,000	LC
Kentucky Wesleyan College	KY	27,440	C
Keuka College	NY	30,300	C
King Univ	TN	33,140	C
King's College	PA	43,502	C
Knox College	IL	44,865	VC+
Kutztown Univ of Pennsylvania	PA	16,909	LC
La Salle Univ	PA	50,270	C
La Sierra Univ	CA	35,964	VC
Lake Superior State Univ	MI	18,121	C
Lakeland College	WI	22,990	C
Lamar Univ	TX	6,820	LC
Lasell College	MA	43,750	LC
Le Moyne College	NY	43,470	C
Lehman College/The CUNY	NY	5,778	LC
Lenoir-Rhyne College	NC	35,984	C
LeTourneau Univ	TX	36,210	VC
Lewis Univ	IL	23,050	C
Lewis-Clark State College	ID	6,990	C
Lincoln Memorial Univ	TN	18,144	C
Lindenwood Univ	MO	20,750	C
Lindsey Wilson College	KY	31,220	C
LIU Brooklyn	NY	47,182	LC
LIU Post	NY	47,660	C
Livingstone College	NC	17,815	LC
Lock Haven Univ of Pennsylvania	PA	18,028	LC
Louisiana College	LA	15,746	C
Louisiana State Univ in Shreveport	LA	5,606	C
Louisiana Tech Univ	LA	11,302	C
Loyola Univ Chicago	IL	51,646	VC+
Lubbock Christian Univ	TX	26,308	C
MacMurray College	IL	20,755	C
Madonna Univ	MI	24,540	VC
Malone Univ	OH	35,364	C
Manchester Univ	IN	35,070	C
Manhattan College	NY	49,588	C+
Mansfield Univ	PA	19,468	LC
Marian Univ	WI	32,420	LC
Marquette Univ	WI	46,930	VC+
Marshall Univ	WV	14,820	C
Maryville College	TN	33,150	C+
Maryville Univ of St. Louis	MO	35,956	VC
Marywood Univ	PA	45,595	C
Mass College of Liberal Arts	MA	18,613	C
Mayville State Univ	ND	11,401	NC
McMurry Univ	TX	25,962	LC
McPherson College	KS	28,138	C
Mercer Univ	GA	44,201	VC
Mercyhurst Univ	PA	40,700	C
Merrimack College	MA	44,215	C
Methodist Univ	NC	37,185	C
Miami Univ	OH	24,191	VC
Mich Tech Univ	MI	23,556	HC
Midland Univ	NE	34,000	C
Miles College	AL	11,164	NC
Millikin Univ	IL	38,940	C
Minn State Univ, Mankato	MN	15,616	C
Miss State Univ	MS	14,750	C
Missouri Baptist Univ	MO	31,830	C
Missouri Univ of Science and Technology	MO	18,655	VC+
Missouri Western State Univ	MO	12,260	NC
Monmouth College	IL	40,850	C
Monmouth Univ	NJ	44,108	C
Montana State Univ	MT	14,068	C
Montana State Univ-Billings	MT	12,425	LC
Montana State Univ-Northern	MT	12,500	NC
Moravian College	PA	36,381	VC
Mount Aloysius College	PA	29,976	C
Mount Marty College	SD	29,638	C
Mount Mercy Univ	IA	35,320	C
Muskingum Univ	OH	30,502	C
New England College	NH	45,930	LC
New Jersey City Univ	NJ	21,456	LC
New Mexico State Univ	NM	14,050	C
New York Univ	NY	61,470	MC
Newman Univ	KS	30,380	C+
Niagara Univ	NY	41,010	C
Nicholls State Univ	LA	7,095	C
N Car State Univ	NC	16,202	NC
North Central College	IL	38,343	VC
N Dak State Univ	ND		
North Park Univ	IL	30,130	C
Northeastern Illinois Univ	IL	10,318	LC
Northeastern State Univ	OK	8,615	NC
Northern Arizona Univ	AZ	19,010	C
Northern Kentucky Univ	KY	21,134	C
Northern Mich Univ	MI	18,278	C
Northern State Univ - Aberdeen	SD	14,505	C
Northland College	WI	26,680	C
Northwest Missouri State Univ	MO	17,347	C
Northwest Nazarene Univ	ID	34,000	C
Northwest Univ	WA	18,854	C
Northwestern College of Iowa	IA	36,240	VC
Northwestern Okla State Univ	OK	7,275	VC
Northwestern State Univ of Louisiana	LA	14,368	C
Northwestern Univ	IL	61,640	MC
Notre Dame College	OH	34,942	VC
Notre Dame of Maryland Univ	MD	27,700	VC
Nova Southeastern Univ	FL	37,280	VC
Nyack College	NY	33,250	C
Oakland City Univ	IN	24,500	NC
Okla Baptist Univ	OK	28,202	C
Okla City Univ	OK	40,476	VC
Okla State Univ	OK	14,310	VC
Okla Wesleyan Univ	OK	21,300	C
Old Dominion Univ	VA	19,483	LC
Olivet College	MI	19,984	C
Oswego / SUNY	NY	20,009	VC
Ouachita Baptist Univ	AR	30,220	VC
Our Lady of Holy Cross College	LA	8,090	C
Paine College	GA	19,826	LC
Palm Beach Atlantic Univ	FL	34,874	C+
Pepperdine Univ	CA	55,372	HC+
Peru State College	NE	8,600	NC
Pfeiffer Univ	NC	33,700	LC
Pittsburg State Univ	KS	12,032	C
Point Park Univ	PA	36,390	C
Pontifical Catholic Univ of PR	PR	7,310	
Prescott College	AZ	33,284	C
Providence College	RI	57,383	VC
Purdue Univ/Calumet	IN	14,336	C
Purdue Univ/West Lafayette	IN	20,024	HC
Quinnipiac Univ	CT	55,160	VC
Rhode Island College	RI	17,694	LC
Rider Univ	NJ	45,720	C
Ripon College	WI	36,959	C+
Rivier Univ	NH	35,000	VC
Roberts Wesleyan College	NY	38,306	C+
Rockhurst Univ	MO	20,625	C
Roger Williams Univ	RI	46,296	VC
Roosevelt Univ	IL	22,605	VC
Rosemont College	PA	42,350	C
Rust College	MS	10,600	C
St. Anselm College	NH	49,376	VC
St. Francis Univ	PA	30,029	LC
St. Joseph's College	IN	36,500	C
St. Leo Univ	FL	30,340	C
St. Mary's Univ	TX	33,854	C
St. Mary's Univ of Minn	MN	38,280	C
St. Michael's College	VT	49,975	VC
St. Paul's College	VA	16,030	NC
St. Peter's Univ	NJ	44,240	C
St. Xavier Univ	IL	32,840	C
Salem International Univ	WV	21,090	LC
Salem State Univ	MA	13,161	LC
Salve Regina Univ	RI	48,550	VC
Samford Univ	AL	37,060	C+
Schreiner Univ	TX	32,734	LC
Seattle Pacific Univ	WA	41,559	VC+
Seton Hall Univ	NJ	45,902	C
Seton Hill Univ	PA	35,172	C
Shaw Univ	NC	15,488	C
Shepherd Univ	WV	15,875	C
Shippensburg Univ of Pennsylvania	PA	20,934	C
Silver Lake College	WI	22,600	LC
Simmons College	MA	49,966	VC
Simpson College	IA	36,086	C+
Simpson Univ	CA	28,900	C
Slippery Rock Univ of Pennsylvania	PA	10,360	C
S Dak State Univ	SD	14,296	C
Southeastern Okla State Univ	OK	7,966	C
Southeastern Univ	FL	27,201	C
Southern Conn State Univ	CT	18,033	LC
Southern New Hampshire Univ	NH	38,100	C
Southern Univ and A&M College	LA	9,761	LC
Southern Univ at New Orleans	LA	2,963	NC
Southwest Baptist Univ	MO	24,710	C
Southwestern Adventist Univ	TX	23,026	LC
Southwestern Okla State Univ	OK	9,160	C
Spring Hill College	AL	44,164	VC
Springfield College	MA	25,000	C
St. Ambrose Univ	IA	30,845	C
St. Catherine Univ	MN	37,782	C+
St. Cloud State Univ	MN	10,600	C
St. Francis College	NY	34,200	C
St. John Fisher College	NY	40,708	C+
St. John's Univ	NY	55,070	C+
St. Joseph's College, New York/Brooklyn Campus	NY	22,630	C
St. Joseph's College, New York/Suffolk Campus	NY	22,630	C
St. Thomas Aquinas College	NY	40,230	C
St. Thomas Univ	FL	32,310	LC
Stetson Univ	FL	51,516	VC
SUNY College at Old Westbury	NY	16,324	C
SUNY Cortland/The SUNY	NY	19,759	C+
SUNY Fredonia/The SUNY at Fredonia	NY	19,840	VC
SUNY New Paltz	NY	14,348	C
SUNY Oneonta / SUNY	NY	16,919	C+
Tabor College	KS	29,010	C
Taylor Univ	IN	37,821	VC+
Temple Univ	PA	24,392	VC
Tenn Tech Univ	TN	11,310	C
Tenn Wesleyan College	TN	21,250	C
Texas A&M Univ	TX	19,207	VC
Texas A&M Univ at Commerce	TX	10,496	C
Texas A&M Univ at Kingsville	TX	7,500	LC
Texas Christian Univ	TX	49,980	HC
The Catholic Univ of America	DC	52,852	VC
The Masters College	CA	38,160	C+
The Pennsylvania State Univ - Univ Park	PA	28,022	VC+
The Univ of Tenn at Chattanooga	TN	16,883	C
Thiel College	PA	38,728	C
Thomas More College	KY	34,760	C
Thomas Univ	GA	11,520	NC
Trevecca Nazarene Univ	TN	31,186	C
Trine Univ	IN	39,400	HC+
Trinity International Univ	IL	31,070	C
Troy Univ	AL	10,650	C
Tuskegee Univ	AL	26,750	C
Union College	KY	29,955	C
Union College	NE	23,270	C
Union Univ	TN	28,260	VC
Unity College	ME	34,054	C
Universidad Adventista de las Antillas	PR	7,360	
Universidad del Turabo	PR	4,110	
Universidad Metropolitana	PR	3,500	
Univ of Alabama at Birmingham	AL	18,484	C+
Univ of Alabama at Tuscaloosa	AL	17,164	C+
Univ of Alaska Fairbanks	AK	15,130	C
Univ of Arizona	AZ	20,657	C
Univ of Arkansas at Little Rock	AR	17,609	LC
Univ of Central Arkansas	AR	13,667	VC
Univ of Central Missouri	MO	14,605	C
Univ of Central Okla	OK	12,293	C
Univ of Cincinnati	OH	21,506	VC
Univ of Dayton	OH	49,070	VC
Univ of Delaware	DE	23,612	VC
Univ of Detroit Mercy	MI	30,450	VC
Univ of Findlay	OH	31,916	C
Univ of Great Falls	MT	27,970	C
Univ of Hartford	CT	42,674	C
Univ of Hawaii at Manoa	HI	19,379	C
Univ of Idaho	ID	14,558	C
Univ of Illinois at Chicago	IL	24,505	VC
Univ of Illinois at Urbana-Champaign	IL	26,450	MC
Univ of Indianapolis	IN	31,740	LC
Univ of Iowa	IA	17,693	VC
Univ of Kansas	KS	17,603	C+
Univ of Kentucky	KY	19,868	C
Univ of Louisiana at Lafayette	LA	6,130	C
Univ of Louisiana at Monroe	LA	12,998	C
Univ of Louisville	KY	17,946	C
Univ of Maine	ME	19,902	C+
Univ of Maine at Farmington	ME	18,187	LC
Univ of Maine at Fort Kent	ME	15,195	LC
Univ of Maine at Presque Isle	ME	15,011	LC
Univ of Mary Hardin-Baylor	TX	31,950	C+
Univ of Maryland - College Park	MD	20,060	HC
Univ of Maryland/Eastern Shore	MD	14,000	VC
Univ of Miami	FL	57,034	MC
Univ of Mich/Dearborn	MI	9,885	VC
Univ of Mich-Flint	MI	17,547	C+
Univ of Minn/Duluth	MN	19,806	C
Univ of Minn/Morris	MN	17,150	VC
Univ of Missouri/Columbia	MO	18,201	VC
Univ of Missouri-Kansas City	MO	19,603	C
Univ of Missouri-St. Louis	MO		VC
Univ of Montana	MT	14,105	C
Univ of Montana-Western	MT	9,753	LC
Univ of Mount Olive	NC	18,426	C
Univ of Nebr - Lincoln	NE	18,031	VC
Univ of Nebr at Kearney	NE	14,855	LC
Univ of Nebr at Omaha	NE	12,700	C
Univ of Nevada, Las Vegas	NV	17,303	C
Univ of Nevada/Reno	NV	17,507	C
Univ of New England	ME	46,750	C
Univ of New Haven	CT	48,940	C
Univ of New Mexico	NM	15,300	C
Univ of New Orleans	LA	9,224	C
Univ of North Alabama	AL	9,960	C
Univ of N Car at Wilmington	NC	13,572	VC
Univ of North Florida	FL	15,870	VC
Univ of North Georgia	GA	8,500	C
Univ of Pikeville	KY	25,500	NC
Univ of Pittsburgh at Johnstown	PA	20,862	LC
Univ of Portland	OR	49,964	VC
Univ of PR Recinto de Rio Piedras	PR	5,750	
Univ of PR/Cayey	PR	1,504	
Univ of Rio Grande	OH	8,750	LC
Univ of St. Francis	IN	29,810	C
Univ of San Francisco	CA	54,770	VC
Univ of Scranton	PA	51,940	VC
Univ of Sioux Falls	SD	22,990	C
Univ of South Alabama	AL	13,510	C
Univ of S Car Aiken	SC	16,712	C
Univ of S Car Upstate	SC	18,200	LC
Univ of S Dak	SD	15,111	C
Univ of Southern Indiana	IN	14,885	C
Univ of Southern Miss	MS	13,170	C
Univ of St. Francis	IL	37,560	C
Univ of Tampa	FL	35,160	VC
Univ of Tenn at Martin	TN	13,734	C
Univ of the Incarnate Word	TX	37,316	LC
Univ of the Southwest	NM	15,000	C
Univ of Toledo	OH	18,464	C
Univ of Vermont	VT	27,006	VC+
Univ of West Alabama	AL	14,274	C
Univ of West Florida	FL	14,656	C
Univ of Wisc Whitewater	WI	13,314	C
Univ of Wisc/Green Bay	WI	19,074	C
Univ of Wisc/La Crosse	WI	9,304	VC
Univ of Wisc/Madison	WI	18,757	HC+
Univ of Wisc/Oshkosh	WI	10,426	LC
Univ of Wisc/Platteville	WI	14,564	C
Univ of Wisc/River Falls	WI	9,722	LC
Univ of Wisc/Superior	WI	14,314	C
Univ of Wyoming	WY	14,401	C+
Urbana Univ	OH	30,820	C
Ursuline College	OH	33,198	LC
Utah State Univ	UT	12,044	C
Valparaiso Univ	IN	44,940	VC+
Vanderbilt Univ	TN	58,220	MC
Vanguard Univ of Southern Calif	CA	35,883	VC
Villanova Univ	PA	58,394	MC
Virginia Polytechnic Inst and State Univ	VA	14,629	HC
Virginia Union Univ	VA	18,432	C
Virginia Wesleyan College	VA	28,433	LC
Wagner College	NY	48,600	C+
Walsh Univ	OH	35,100	C
Wartburg College	IA	41,055	VC
Washburn Univ	KS	12,579	C
Washington State Univ	WA	20,461	C
Washington Univ in St. Louis	MO	69,844	MC
Webster Univ	MO	35,100	C
West Chester Univ of Pennsylvania	PA	17,186	C
West Liberty Univ	WV	9,142	LC
West Virginia State Univ	WV	8,378	NC
West Virginia Wesleyan College	WV	26,880	C
Western Carolina Univ	NC	13,965	C
Western Conn State Univ	CT	18,327	LC
Western Mich Univ	MI	19,628	C
Western New England Univ	MA	46,154	C+
Western New Mexico Univ	NM	8,500	LC
Western State Colo Univ	CO	16,924	C
Western Washington Univ	WA	18,519	VC
Westminster College	MO	31,720	VC
Westminster College	PA	31,290	C+
Wheaton College	IL	40,720	MC
Whitworth Univ	WA	47,734	VC
Wichita State Univ	KS	14,607	C+
Wiley College	TX		LC
William Jewell College	MO	31,000	VC+
William Penn Univ	IA	26,000	C
Williams Baptist College	AR	20,070	C
Wilmington College	OH	29,784	C
Wilson College	PA	35,080	C
Winona State Univ	MN	16,640	C
Winthrop Univ	SC	21,120	C
Wittenberg Univ	OH	47,962	C+
Wright State Univ	OH	16,983	C

ST = STATE $IS = IN-STATE COSTS   SR = SELECTOR RATING

School	ST	$IS	SR
York College	NE	19,475	C
York College of Pennsylvania	PA	26,590	C
Youngstown State Univ	OH	16,732	C

SECRETARIAL STUDIES/OFFICE MANAGEMENT

School	ST	$IS	SR
Caribbean Univ	PR	10,375	
Chancellor Univ	OH	11,000	
Dordt College	IA	34,160	C+
Inter-American Univ of PR/ Aguadilla Campus	PR	5,578	
Inter-American Univ of PR/ Barranquitas	PR	3,350	
Inter-American Univ of PR/ Bayamon Univ College	PR	4,428	
Inter-American Univ of PR/ Fajardo Campus	PR	4,200	
Inter-American Univ of PR/ Metropolitan Campus	PR	4,320	
Inter-American Univ of PR/ Ponce	PR		
Inter-American Univ of PR/ San Germán	PR	6,720	
Johnson & Wales Univ/ Providence Campus	RI	29,576	C
Southeastern Okla State Univ	OK	7,966	LC
Southern Univ at New Orleans	LA	2,963	NC
Universidad de Puerto/ Arecibo	PR	7,227	
Universidad del Turabo	PR	4,110	
Univ of PR Recinto de Rio Piedras	PR	5,750	
Univ of PR/Cayey	PR	1,504	
Univ of PR/Humacao	PR	1,877	
Univ of the Sacred Heart	PR	5,590	

SLAVIC LANGUAGES

School	ST	$IS	SR
Columbia Univ/School of General Studies	NY	58,231	MC
Duke Univ	NC	50,250	MC
Indiana Univ Bloomington	IN	19,801	VC
New York Univ	NY	61,470	MC
Northwestern Univ	IL	61,640	MC
Princeton Univ	NJ	53,795	MC
Stanford Univ	CA	58,388	MC
Univ of Calif at Berkeley	CA	23,322	MC
Univ of Calif at Santa Barbara	CA	27,551	HC
Univ of Chicago	IL	55,416	MC
Univ of Illinois at Chicago	IL	24,505	VC
Univ of Kansas	KS	17,603	C+
Univ of Pittsburgh at Pittsburgh	PA	28,572	HC+
Univ of Texas at Austin	TX	44,074	HC
Univ of Virginia	VA	23,050	MC
Univ of Washington	WA	14,722	VC
Wayne State Univ	MI	22,063	C
Yale Univ	CT	55,300	MC

SMALL BUSINESS MANAGEMENT

School	ST	$IS	SR
Adams State Univ	CO	13,358	LC
Cal State, Chico	CA	20,158	C
Cal State, San Bernardino	CA	12,000	C
Carroll Univ	WI	38,100	C
Concord Univ	WV	13,102	C
Florida Atlantic Univ	FL	17,339	C
Florida State Univ	FL	16,715	VC
Hawaii Pacific Univ	HI	34,360	C
Huntington Univ	IN	32,220	C+
Johnson & Wales Univ/ Providence Campus	RI	29,576	C
Johnson State College	VT	16,721	C
Mount Aloysius College	PA	29,976	C
Mount Ida College	MA	30,115	LC
Northern Arizona Univ	AZ	19,010	C
Rowan Univ	NJ	24,022	VC+
Stetson Univ	FL	51,516	C
Tusculum College	TN	24,295	C
Union College	NE	23,270	C
Univ of Montana	MT	14,105	C
Univ of Montana-Western	MT	9,753	LC

SOCIAL FOUNDATIONS

School	ST	$IS	SR
Amridge Univ	AL	6,870	LC
Eastern Mich Univ	MI	18,604	C

SOCIAL PSYCHOLOGY

School	ST	$IS	SR
Bennington College	VT	56,990	HC+
Clarion Univ of Pennsylvania	PA	17,370	LC
Florida Atlantic Univ	FL	17,339	C
Goddard College	VT	16,418	VC
Lehigh Univ	PA	56,770	MC
Northwest Missouri State Univ	MO	17,347	C
Our Lady of Holy Cross College	LA	8,090	C
Park Univ	MO	17,525	C
Univ of Calif at Irvine	CA	25,961	VC

SOCIAL SCIENCE

School	ST	$IS	SR
Adelphi Univ	NY	44,670	VC
Anna Maria College	MA	34,600	C
Aquinas College	MI	33,060	C
Arizona State Univ, at the West Campus	AZ	19,251	C
Ashford Univ	CA	10,480	C
Ashland Univ	OH	25,000	C
Averett Univ	VA	37,750	LC
Azusa Pacific Univ	CA	42,086	C
Bellevue Univ	NE	4,600	NC
Bemidji State Univ	MN	13,500	VC
Benedict College	SC	20,454	NC
Benedictine College	KS	29,180	VC
Benedictine Univ	IL	37,820	C
Bennington College	VT	56,990	HC+
Bethany College	KS	30,605	NC
Bethel College	IN	31,560	C
Biola Univ	CA	40,320	C+
Black Hills State Univ	SD	13,947	C
Bluefield State College	WV	3,140	LC
Bluffton Univ	OH	38,948	C
Boise State Univ	ID	13,469	LC
Bowling Green State Univ	OH	18,970	C
Brewton-Parker College	GA	33,388	C
Buena Vista Univ	IA	39,188	C
Calif Lutheran Univ	CA	49,540	C+
Cal State, Chico	CA	20,158	C
Cal State, Fresno	CA	17,405	C
Cal State, Los Angeles	CA	17,186	LC
Cal State, Monterey Bay	CA	26,871	LC
Cal State, Sacramento	CA	16,200	C
Cal State, San Bernardino	CA	12,000	C
Cal State, San Marcos	CA	14,576	LC
Cal State, Stanislaus	CA	18,582	C
Calif Univ of Pennsylvania	PA	14,217	C
Canisius College	NY	44,900	C
Cardinal Stritch Univ	WI	24,054	C
Caribbean Univ	PR	10,375	
Carnegie Mellon Univ	PA	51,260	MC
Carroll College	MT	28,000	C
Carson-Newman Univ	TN	29,058	C+
Carthage College	WI	33,000	C
Castleton State College	VT	20,186	C
Cazenovia College	NY	43,464	C
Central Washington Univ	WA	11,730	C
Chadron State College	NE	7,400	NC
Chancellor Univ	OH	11,000	C
Charleston Southern Univ	SC	22,420	C
Cheyney Univ of Pennsylvania	PA	20,372	LC
Clarion Univ of Pennsylvania	PA	17,370	LC
Clarkson Univ	NY	57,330	HC
Cleveland State Univ	OH	21,776	C
Colgate Univ	NY	58,135	MC
College of St. Benedict	MN	49,359	VC
College of St. Mary	NE	35,184	C
College of the Ozarks	MO		VC
Colo Christian Univ	CO	27,500	VC
Colo Mesa Univ	CO	17,690	LC
Colo State Univ-Pueblo	CO	16,183	C
Concord Univ	WV	13,102	C
Concordia Univ Wisc	WI	28,980	C
Concordia Univ, River Forest	IL	26,300	C
Coppin State Univ	MD	16,227	C
Corban Univ	OR	37,380	C+
Covenant College	GA	38,990	VC+
Cumberland Univ	TN	21,220	C
Daniel Webster College	NH	25,380	C
Delta State Univ	MS	12,292	LC
DePaul Univ	IL	47,623	VC
Dominican College	NY	31,270	LC
Dominican Univ	IL	37,628	C
Dordt College	IA	34,160	C+
Dowling College	NY	25,000	LC
Eastern Conn State Univ	CT	20,584	C
Eastern Mennonite Univ	VA	40,660	C
Eastern Washington Univ	WA		C
Edinboro Univ of Pennsylvania	PA	15,940	LC
Elizabeth City State Univ	NC	11,638	C
Emporia State Univ	KS	12,897	C
Eureka College	IL	19,280	C
Evangel Univ	MO	23,090	C
Faulkner Univ	AL	25,720	LC
Fayetteville State Univ	NC	10,816	C
Felician College	NJ	41,640	LC
Florida A&M Univ	FL	14,935	LC
Florida Atlantic Univ	FL	17,339	C
Florida State Univ	FL	16,715	VC
Fordham Univ	NY	61,588	HC+
Fresno Pacific Univ	CA	32,136	C
Frostburg State Univ	MD	15,264	LC
Gardner-Webb Univ	NC	34,375	C
George Fox Univ	OR	40,750	C+
Goddard College	VT	16,418	VC
Graceland Univ	IA	28,020	C
Grand Valley State Univ	MI	17,998	C+
Gustavus Adolphus College	MN	48,170	HC
Hamline Univ	MN	45,678	VC
Harding Univ	AR	23,556	C
Harvard College/Harvard Univ	MA	49,000	MC
Hastings College	NE	27,782	C+

School	ST	$IS	SR
Hawaii Pacific Univ	HI	34,360	C
Heidelberg Univ	OH	34,100	C
Hope International Univ	CA	34,650	C
Humboldt State Univ	CA	18,400	C
Hunter College	NY	14,429	VC
Illinois State Univ	IL	23,110	VC
Immaculata Univ	PA	43,000	C
Indiana Univ of Pennsylvania	PA	20,846	LC
Indiana Univ-Purdue Univ Fort Wayne	IN	15,521	C
James Madison Univ	VA	18,049	VC
Johns Hopkins Univ	MD	47,492	MC
Johnson C. Smith Univ	NC	25,336	C
Kansas State Univ	KS	15,497	VC
Keene State College	NH	23,232	LC
Kent State Univ	OH	19,920	C
Keystone College	PA	28,680	LC
Lake Erie College	OH	37,266	C
Lake Superior State Univ	MI	18,121	C
Lamar Univ	TX	6,820	LC
Langston Univ	OK	3,000	C
LeMoyne-Owen College	TN	13,100	C
Lesley Univ	MA	46,350	C
Lewis-Clark State College	ID	6,990	C
Liberty Univ	VA	19,101	C
Lincoln Memorial Univ	TN	18,144	C
Lindsey Wilson College	KY	31,220	C
LIU Brooklyn	NY	47,182	LC
Lock Haven Univ of Pennsylvania	PA	18,028	LC
Loyola Univ New Orleans	LA	46,581	VC
Lyndon State College	VT	14,233	C
Madonna Univ	MI	24,540	VC
Marlboro College	VT	35,980	VC
Marquette Univ	WI	46,930	VC+
Marygrove College	MI	28,926	C
Marylhurst Univ	OR	20,295	VC
Maryville College	TN	33,150	C+
Marywood Univ	PA	45,595	C
Mayville State Univ	ND	11,401	VC
McKendree Univ	IL	29,920	C+
Medaille College	NY	35,112	C
Mercer Univ	GA	44,201	VC
Metropolitan State Univ	MN	5,923	
Mich State Univ	MI	22,450	VC
Mich Tech Univ	MI	23,556	HC
Midland Univ	NE	34,000	C
Minot State Univ	ND	10,915	C
Miss Univ for Women	MS	7,400	C
Missouri Baptist Univ	MO	31,830	C
Montana State Univ- Northern	MT	12,500	NC
Moravian College	PA	36,381	VC
Morehead State Univ	KY	10,900	C
Mount Marty College	SD	29,638	C
Mount St. Mary College	NY	41,138	C
Mount St. Mary's College - Chalon Campus	CA	43,897	VC+
Muskingum Univ	OH	30,502	C
National Louis Univ	IL	16,915	LC
Nazareth College of Rochester	NY	43,028	C
New College of Florida	FL	14,504	NC
New York Univ	NY	61,470	MC
Niagara Univ	NY	41,010	C
N Car State Univ	NC	16,202	NC
North Central College	IL	38,343	VC
N Dak State Univ	ND		C
Northeastern State Univ	OK	8,615	VC
Northern Kentucky Univ	KY	21,134	C
Northern State Univ - Aberdeen	SD	14,505	C
Northwest Christian Univ	OR	27,399	C
Northwest Missouri State Univ	MO	17,347	C
Northwestern Okla State Univ	OK	7,275	NC
Notre Dame de Namur Univ	CA	44,236	LC
Ohio Wesleyan Univ	OH	49,460	C+
Okla Baptist Univ	OK	28,202	C
Olivet Nazarene Univ	IL	29,990	C
Our Lady of Holy Cross College	LA	8,090	C
Pace Univ	NY	53,367	C
Pepperdine Univ	CA	55,372	HC+
Peru State College	NE	8,600	NC
Piedmont College	GA	30,136	C
Plymouth State Univ	NH	23,148	LC
Point Loma Nazarene Univ	CA	41,006	C+
Polytechnic Inst of New York Univ	NY	53,064	HC+
Pontifical Catholic Univ of PR	PR	7,310	
Prescott College	AZ	33,284	C
Providence College	RI	57,383	VC
Quinnipiac Univ	CT	55,160	VC
Radford Univ	VA	17,766	LC
Ramapo College of New Jersey	NJ	24,938	C
Rhode Island College	RI	17,694	LC
Robert Morris Univ	PA	37,864	C
Rockford College	IL	31,000	C
Roger Williams Univ	RI	46,296	VC
Roosevelt Univ	IL	22,605	VC
Rosemont College	PA	42,350	C
St. John's Univ	MN	47,984	C
St. Mary's Univ of Minn	MN	38,280	C

School	ST	$IS	SR
St. Paul's College	VA	16,030	NC
St. Peter's Univ	NJ	44,240	C
St. Xavier Univ	IL	32,840	C
Salisbury Univ	MD	19,180	VC
San Diego State Univ	CA	21,611	C+
San Jose State Univ	CA	19,133	LC
Seattle Pacific Univ	WA	41,559	VC+
Seton Hall Univ	NJ	45,902	C
Shawnee State Univ	OH	16,916	C
Shimer College	IL	32,875	VC
Shorter Univ	GA	30,650	LC
Siena Heights Univ	MI	32,640	C
Silver Lake College	WI	22,600	LC
Simpson Univ	CA	28,900	C
Skidmore College	NY	59,942	HC
Slippery Rock Univ of Pennsylvania	PA	10,360	C
Southeast Missouri State Univ	MO	15,370	LC
Southeastern Okla State Univ	OK	7,966	LC
Southern Illinois Univ Carbondale	IL	21,942	C
Southern New Hampshire Univ	NH	38,100	C
Southern Oregon Univ	OR	17,874	C
Southwestern Adventist Univ	TX	23,026	LC
Spring Arbor Univ	MI	26,740	C
Spring Hill College	AL	44,164	VC
St. Andrews Univ	NC	32,050	LC
St. Cloud State Univ	MN	10,600	C
St. Joseph's College, New York/Brooklyn Campus	NY	22,630	C
St. Joseph's College, New York/Suffolk Campus	NY	22,630	C
St. Thomas Aquinas College	NY	40,230	C
Stetson Univ	FL	51,516	VC
Stony Brook Univ / SUNY	NY	20,078	HC+
Suffolk Univ	MA	47,298	C
Sul Ross State Univ	TX	13,410	LC
SUNY New Paltz	NY	14,348	C
Tabor College	KS	29,010	C
Temple Univ	PA	24,392	VC
The Catholic Univ of America	DC	52,852	VC
The Univ of Utah	UT	16,463	VC
The Univ of Virginia's College at Wise	VA	11,076	C
Thomas Edison State College	NJ	5,700	SP
Thomas Univ	GA	11,520	NC
Touro College	NY	27,959	VC
Towson Univ	MD	16,000	VC
Trine Univ	IN	39,400	HC+
Trinity International Univ	IL	31,070	VC
Troy Univ	AL	10,650	C
Tulane Univ	LA	60,861	MC
Union College	KY	23,270	C
Union College	NY	60,240	MC
Union Inst & Univ	OH	8,912	SP
United States Air Force Academy	CO		MC
Universidad del Turabo	PR	4,110	
Universidad Metropolitana	PR	3,500	
Univ at Buffalo / The SUNY	NY	20,283	VC
Univ of Akron	OH	20,436	C
Univ of Alaska Southeast	AK	11,493	C
Univ of Bridgeport	CT	39,010	LC
Univ of Calif at Berkeley	CA	23,322	MC
Univ of Calif at Davis	CA		HC
Univ of Calif at Irvine	CA	25,961	VC
Univ of Central Florida	FL	15,668	VC+
Univ of Chicago	IL	55,416	MC
Univ of Cincinnati	OH	21,506	VC
Univ of Denver	CO	51,787	VC+
Univ of Great Falls	MT	27,970	C
Univ of Houston-Downtown	TX	15,170	LC
Univ of Indianapolis	IN	31,740	LC
Univ of Iowa	IA	17,693	VC
Univ of La Verne	CA	47,010	C
Univ of Maine at Augusta	ME	6,855	C
Univ of Maine at Fort Kent	ME	15,195	LC
Univ of Mary	ND	16,714	C
Univ of Maryland/Univ College	MD	6,168	SP
Univ of Mich/Ann Arbor	MI	22,102	MC
Univ of Mich-Flint	MI	17,547	C+
Univ of Minn/Morris	MN	17,150	VC
Univ of Missouri/Columbia	MO	18,201	MC
Univ of Mobile	AL	28,935	VC
Univ of Montana-Western	MT	9,753	LC
Univ of Montevallo	AL	17,060	C
Univ of Mount Union	OH	35,130	C
Univ of Nebr at Kearney	NE	14,855	LC
Univ of Nevada, Las Vegas	NV	17,303	C
Univ of New England	ME	46,750	C
Univ of N Dak	ND	14,551	C
Univ of North Georgia	GA	8,500	C
Univ of North Texas	TX	15,628	C
Univ of Northern Colo	CO	18,446	C
Univ of Northern Iowa	IA	15,795	C
Univ of Oregon	OR	21,360	C+
Univ of Pittsburgh at Bradford	PA	21,802	C
Univ of Pittsburgh at Greensburg	PA	17,640	C
Univ of Pittsburgh at Johnstown	PA	20,862	LC

ST = STATE $IS = IN-STATE COSTS   SR = SELECTOR RATING

School	ST	$IS	SR
Univ of Pittsburgh at Pittsburgh	PA	28,572	HC+
Univ of PR Recinto de Rio Piedras	PR	5,750	
Univ of PR/Mayaguez	PR	1,250	
Univ of South Florida/St. Petersburg	FL	12,769	C
Univ of South Florida/Tampa	FL	13,000	C
Univ of Southern Calif	CA	56,903	MC
Univ of Southern Miss	MS	13,170	C
Univ of the Ozarks	AR	31,440	C
Univ of the Pacific	CA	52,146	VC
Univ of West Alabama	AL	14,274	C
Univ of West Florida	FL	14,656	C
Univ of Wisc/Platteville	WI	14,564	C
Univ of Wisc/Stevens Point	WI	14,043	C
Univ of Wyoming	WY	14,401	C
Upper Iowa Univ	IA	30,426	NC
Valley City State Univ	ND	12,286	C
Valparaiso Univ	IN	44,940	VC+
Virginia Wesleyan College	VA	28,433	LC
Warner Pacific College	OR	25,550	C
Washington State Univ	WA	20,461	C
Washington Univ in St. Louis	MO	69,844	MC
Wayland Baptist Univ	TX	18,912	C
Wayne State College	NE	11,764	NC
Waynesburg Univ	PA	30,150	C
Webster Univ	MO	35,100	C+
Wesleyan College	GA	24,000	C
West Liberty Univ	WV	9,142	LC
West Texas A&M Univ	TX	13,478	C
West Virginia Wesleyan College	WV	26,880	C
Western Carolina Univ	NC	13,965	C
Western Conn State Univ	CT	18,327	LC
Western New Mexico Univ	NM	8,500	LC
Western Oregon Univ	OR	15,021	C
Westminster College	PA	31,290	C+
Westminster College	UT	37,708	C+
Westmont College	CA	41,500	HC
Wheaton College	IL	40,720	MC
Wilberforce Univ	OH	15,100	LC
Wiley College	TX		LC
William Carey Univ	MS	13,500	C
Wilmington College	OH	29,784	C
Wisc Lutheran College	WI	23,510	VC
Worcester Polytechnic Inst	MA	55,860	MC

SOCIAL SCIENCE EDUCATION

School	ST	$IS	SR
Appalachian State Univ	NC	12,919	VC
Aquinas College	MI	33,060	C
Arkansas State Univ	AR	15,470	C
Auburn Univ	AL	22,378	VC+
Baylor Univ	TX	50,329	HC
Bethune-Cookman Univ	FL	22,958	C
Black Hills State Univ	SD	13,947	C
Blackburn College	IL	21,350	C
Blue Mountain College	MS	15,634	LC
Boise State Univ	ID	13,469	LC
Bowling Green State Univ	OH	18,967	C
Brigham Young Univ	UT	12,100	HC
Brigham Young Univ/Hawaii	HI	10,686	VC
Campbellsville Univ	KY	27,720	C
Central Methodist Univ	MO	28,240	VC
Coker College	SC	32,256	LC
Colby-Sawyer College	NH	50,790	C
College of New Jersey	NJ	25,376	HC
College of St. Scholastica	MN	41,440	C
Concordia College - New York	NY	39,035	C
Delta State Univ	MS	12,292	LC
Dordt College	IA	34,160	C+
Eastern Illinois Univ	IL	20,466	C
Eastern Nazarene College	MA	30,000	C
Eastern Washington Univ	WA		C
Faulkner Univ	AL	25,720	LC
Fayetteville State Univ	NC	10,816	C
Florida Gulf Coast Univ	FL		C
Florida State Univ	FL	16,715	VC
Fresno Pacific Univ	CA	32,136	C
Friends Univ	KS	29,100	C
Hope International Univ	CA	34,650	C
Humboldt State Univ	CA	18,400	C
Illinois State Univ	IL	23,110	VC
Jackson State Univ	MS	13,512	LC
Kent State Univ	OH	19,920	C
Kutztown Univ of Pennsylvania	PA	16,909	LC
Lincoln Univ	MO	12,904	NC
Marian Univ	WI	32,420	C
Marywood Univ	PA	45,595	C
Mayville State Univ	ND	11,401	NC
Mercyhurst Univ	PA	40,700	C
Miles College	AL	11,164	NC
Millikin Univ	IL	38,940	C
Miss Valley State Univ	MS	9,706	LC
Missouri Southern State Univ	MO	12,061	C
Montana State Univ-Billings	MT	12,425	LC
Montana State Univ-Northern	MT	12,500	NC
Nazareth College of Rochester	NY	43,028	C+
Nebr Wesleyan Univ	NE	29,774	C+
New York Univ	NY	61,470	MC
N Car Agricultural and Technical State Univ	NC	13,365	LC

School	ST	$IS	SR
N Dak State Univ	ND		C
Oakwood Univ	AL	25,529	NC
Okla Christian Univ	OK	25,870	VC
Olivet Nazarene Univ	IL	29,990	C
Piedmont College	GA	30,136	C
Prescott College	AZ	33,284	C
Rocky Mountain College	MT	32,242	C
Rust College	MS	10,600	C
Sacred Heart Univ	CT	49,264	VC
St. Mary-of-the-Woods College	IN	37,722	LC
Schreiner Univ	TX	32,734	LC
Seattle Pacific Univ	WA	41,559	VC+
Seton Hill Univ	PA	35,172	C
Simpson Univ	CA	28,900	C
Southeastern Louisiana Univ	LA	13,325	C
Southern Illinois Univ Edwardsville	IL	17,532	C
Southwestern Okla State Univ	OK	9,160	C
Stetson Univ	FL	51,516	VC
SUNY Oneonta / SUNY	NY	16,919	C+
Texas Wesleyan Univ	TX	31,382	C
The Univ of N Car at Greensboro	NC	12,848	C
The Univ of Utah	UT	16,463	VC
Trine Univ	IN	39,400	HC+
Troy Univ	AL	10,650	C
Union College	NE	23,270	C
Universidad del Turabo	PR	4,110	
Univ of Arkansas at Pine Bluff	AR	13,378	C
Univ of Central Florida	FL	15,668	VC+
Univ of Mary	ND	16,714	C
Univ of Maryland/Eastern Shore	MD	14,000	VC
Univ of Miss	MS	16,704	C
Univ of Montana-Western	MT	9,753	LC
Univ of Nebr - Lincoln	NE	18,031	VC
Univ of North Alabama	AL	9,960	C
Univ of North Georgia	GA	8,500	C
Univ of Northern Colo	CO	18,446	C
Univ of Pittsburgh at Johnstown	PA	20,862	LC
Univ of Rio Grande	OH	8,750	NC
Univ of Southern Indiana	IN	14,885	C
Univ of Wisc/Oshkosh	WI	10,426	C
Univ of Wisc/Superior	WI	14,314	C
Valparaiso Univ	IN	44,940	VC+
Warner Univ	FL	18,000	C
Washington Univ in St. Louis	MO	69,844	MC
Western Carolina Univ	NC	13,965	C
Westmont College	CA	41,500	HC
Wiley College	TX		LC
Wilmington College	OH	29,784	C
Wingate Univ	NC	34,990	C
Wright State Univ	OH	16,983	C
York College	NE	19,475	C
Youngstown State Univ	OH	16,732	C

SOCIAL STUDIES

School	ST	$IS	SR
Andrews Univ	MI	28,030	C+
Aquinas College	MI	33,060	C
Arkansas Tech Univ	AR	13,982	LC
Barton College	NC	27,660	LC
Bethel Univ	MN	34,940	VC
Bluefield College	VA	17,230	C+
Bluffton Univ	OH	38,948	C
Brescia Univ	KY	26,140	VC+
Caldwell College	NJ	35,602	NC
Chaminade Univ of Honolulu	HI	31,664	LC
Cleveland State Univ	OH	21,776	C
Concordia Univ, Ann Arbor	MI	27,220	VC
DePaul Univ	IL	47,623	VC
East Stroudsburg Univ of Pennsylvania	PA	18,868	C
Eastern Mich Univ	MI	18,604	C
Eastern Nazarene College	MA	30,000	C
Eastern New Mexico Univ	NM	10,682	C
Erskine College	SC	37,360	C
Ferris State Univ	MI	20,047	C
Ferrum College	VA	27,740	LC
Hamline Univ	MN	45,678	VC
Harvard College/Harvard Univ	MA	49,000	MC
Hiram College	OH	37,300	C
Indiana Wesleyan Univ	IN	31,815	VC
Ithaca College	NY	53,864	HC
Kent State Univ	OH	19,920	C
Mayville State Univ	ND	11,401	NC
McMurry Univ	TX	25,962	C
Methodist Univ	NC	37,185	C
Millersville Univ of Pennsylvania	PA	21,648	C
Minn State Univ, Mankato	MN	15,616	C
Miss College	MS	21,998	C
Missouri Southern State Univ	MO	12,061	C
Mount Aloysius College	PA	29,976	C
Mount Mary Univ	WI	33,590	LC
Mount St. Mary's Univ	MD	47,996	C
New York Univ	NY	61,470	MC
Northern Kentucky Univ	KY	21,134	C
Ohio Northern Univ	OH	42,075	VC
Okla Christian Univ	OK	25,870	VC
Okla Panhandle State Univ	OK	8,996	C
Okla Wesleyan Univ	OK	21,300	C

School	ST	$IS	SR
Olivet College	MI	19,984	LC
Our Lady of the Lake Univ	TX	22,430	LC
Pacific Union College	CA	28,150	VC
Pfeiffer Univ	NC	33,700	LC
Purdue Univ/West Lafayette	IN	20,024	HC
S Car State Univ	SC	6,700	LC
Southern Wesleyan Univ	SC	25,600	C
Southwestern Adventist Univ	TX	23,026	LC
Spring Arbor Univ	MI	26,740	C
St. Catherine Univ	MN	37,782	C+
St. Francis College	NY	34,200	C
St. John's Univ	NY	55,070	C+
Tulane Univ	LA	60,861	MC
Univ of Mich/Dearborn	MI	9,885	VC
Univ of Texas - Pan American	TX	11,125	LC
Univ of Wisc/Eau Claire	WI	15,730	VC
Univ of Wisc/Madison	WI	18,757	HC+
Univ of Wisc/River Falls	WI	9,722	C
Univ of Wisc/Superior	WI	14,314	C
Utica College	NY	45,670	C
Virginia Wesleyan College	VA	28,433	LC
Viterbo Univ	WI	30,070	C
Washington State Univ	WA	20,461	C
Wayland Baptist Univ	TX	18,912	C
Wesleyan Univ	CT	61,198	MC
Western Kentucky Univ	KY	11,000	LC
Western Washington Univ	WA	18,519	VC
Youngstown State Univ	OH	16,732	C

SOCIAL STUDIES EDUCATION

School	ST	$IS	SR
Adams State Univ	CO	13,358	LC
Alabama State Univ	AL	14,142	NC
Alfred Univ	NY	41,770	C
Alice Lloyd College	KY	4,900	LC
Anderson Univ	IN	36,100	C
Andrews Univ	MI	28,030	C+
Appalachian State Univ	NC	12,919	VC
Aquinas College	MI	33,060	C
Asbury Univ	KY	32,038	VC
Augustana College	SD	36,500	VC
Averett Univ	VA	37,750	LC
Baylor Univ	TX	50,329	HC
Bethany College	WV	35,282	LC
Bethel College	IN	31,560	C
Bethel Univ	MN	34,940	VC
Biola Univ	CA	40,320	C+
Bloomsburg Univ of Pennsylvania	PA	13,598	C
Boston Univ	MA	60,694	MC
Cameron Univ	OK	10,004	LC
Canisius College	NY	44,900	C
Catawba College	NC	37,240	LC
Cedarville Univ	OH	32,860	VC
Central Washington Univ	WA	11,730	C
CUNY/Brooklyn College	NY	5,884	C+
CUNY/City College	NY	20,319	HC+
Clearwater Christian College	FL	23,720	C
Colby-Sawyer College	NH	50,790	C
College of New Jersey	NJ	25,376	HC
Concordia College - Moorhead	MN	39,974	VC
Concordia College - New York	NY	39,035	C
Concordia Univ St. Paul	MN	28,250	C
Corban Univ	OR	37,380	C+
Daemen College	NY	34,770	C
Defiance College	OH	30,645	C
Duquesne Univ	PA	43,720	VC
East Carolina Univ	NC	14,169	C
East Texas Baptist Univ	TX	31,577	LC
Eastern Mich Univ	MI	18,604	C
Edgewood College	WI	33,294	C
Edinboro Univ of Pennsylvania	PA	15,940	LC
Elizabethtown College	PA	49,740	VC
Ferris State Univ	MI	20,047	C
Franklin College	IN	36,585	C
Gannon Univ	PA	39,608	C
Glenville State College	WV	11,348	NC
Grambling State Univ	LA	13,384	C
Green Mountain College	VT	45,228	LC
Greensboro College	NC	28,740	LC
Gwynedd-Mercy College	PA	33,560	C
Hardin-Simmons Univ	TX	23,560	C+
Hofstra Univ	NY	51,810	VC+
Huntington Univ	IN	32,220	C+
Indiana State Univ	IN	16,000	C
Indiana Univ Bloomington	IN	19,801	VC
Indiana Univ South Bend	IN	15,501	C
Indiana Univ Southeast	IN	16,035	C
Indiana Univ-Purdue Univ Indianapolis	IN	17,611	C
Indiana Wesleyan Univ	IN	31,815	VC
Ithaca College	NY	53,864	HC
Judson College	AL	26,794	C
Juniata College	PA	49,340	VC
Kent State Univ	OH	19,920	C
Kentucky Christian Univ	KY	17,622	LC
Kentucky State Univ	KY	11,000	C
Keystone College	PA	28,680	LC
Knox College	IL	44,865	VC+
Kutztown Univ of Pennsylvania	PA	16,909	LC

School	ST	$IS	SR
La Salle Univ	PA	50,270	C
Le Moyne College	NY	43,470	C
LIU Brooklyn	NY	47,182	LC
LIU Post	NY	47,660	C
Louisiana College	LA	15,746	C
Malone Univ	OH	35,364	C
Mansfield Univ	PA	19,468	LC
Mars Hill Univ	NC	22,950	LC
Marshall Univ	WV	14,820	C
Marygrove College	MI	28,926	C
Messiah College	PA	40,690	C+
MidAmerica Nazarene Univ	KS	28,000	C
Millersville Univ of Pennsylvania	PA	21,648	C
Minn State Univ, Mankato	MN	15,616	C
Minn State Univ, Moorhead	MN	13,392	VC
Missouri Southern State Univ	MO	12,061	C
Missouri Valley College	MO	22,200	C
Monmouth Univ	NJ	44,108	C
Montana State Univ-Billings	MT	12,425	LC
Morningside College	IA	35,430	C
Morris College	SC	16,310	LC
Mount Aloysius College	PA	29,976	C
Mount Vernon Nazarene Univ	OH	29,590	C
New York Univ	NY	61,470	MC
Niagara Univ	NY	41,010	C
N Car State Univ	NC	16,202	HC
Northwestern College	MN	24,000	C
Ohio Univ	OH	21,080	C
Okla Christian Univ	OK	25,870	VC
Okla Wesleyan Univ	OK	21,300	C
Old Dominion Univ	VA	19,483	LC
Oral Roberts Univ	OK	31,734	C
Oswego / SUNY	NY	20,009	VC
Ouachita Baptist Univ	AR	30,220	VC
Pfeiffer Univ	NC	33,700	LC
Pittsburg State Univ	KS	12,032	C
Pontifical Catholic Univ of PR	PR	7,310	
Prescott College	AZ	33,284	C
Providence College	RI	57,383	VC
Purdue Univ/West Lafayette	IN	20,024	HC
Rider Univ	NJ	45,720	C
Rivier Univ	NH	35,000	VC
Rocky Mountain College	MT	32,242	C
Sacred Heart Univ	CT	49,264	VC
Saginaw Valley State Univ	MI	17,369	C
St. Augustine's Univ	NC	14,000	C
St. Mary's Univ of Minn	MN	38,280	C
Shaw Univ	NC	15,488	C
Shepherd Univ	WV	15,875	C
Shippensburg Univ of Pennsylvania	PA	20,934	C
Southeast Missouri State Univ	MO	15,370	LC
Southeastern Okla State Univ	OK	7,966	LC
Southern Nazarene Univ	OK	24,354	C
Southern New Hampshire Univ	NH	38,100	C
Southern Univ and A&M College	LA	9,761	LC
Southern Univ at New Orleans	LA	2,963	NC
Southwest Baptist Univ	MO	24,710	C
St. Edward's Univ	TX	47,784	C
St. John Fisher College	NY	40,708	C+
St. John's Univ	NY	55,070	C+
St. Olaf College	MN	51,200	HC+
St. Thomas Univ	FL	32,310	LC
SUNY College at Old Westbury	NY	16,324	C
SUNY Fredonia/The SUNY at Fredonia	NY	19,840	VC
SUNY New Paltz	NY	14,348	C
Syracuse Univ	NY	56,346	VC
Taylor Univ	IN	37,821	VC+
Texas Wesleyan Univ	TX	31,382	C
The SUNY at Potsdam	NY	18,473	C
The Univ of N Car at Greensboro	NC	12,848	C
The Univ of Okla	OK	18,621	VC
Thomas More College	KY	34,760	C
Tiffin Univ	OH	30,273	C
Union College	KY	29,955	C
Univ of Central Missouri	MO	14,605	C
Univ of Central Okla	OK	12,293	C
Univ of Charleston	WV	32,300	C
Univ of Conn	CT	24,706	HC
Univ of Evansville	IN	42,656	VC+
Univ of Georgia	GA	20,082	VC
Univ of Great Falls	MT	27,970	C
Univ of Indianapolis	IN	31,740	LC
Univ of Kentucky	KY	19,868	C
Univ of Louisiana at Lafayette	LA	6,130	C
Univ of Louisiana at Monroe	LA	12,998	C
Univ of Mary Hardin-Baylor	TX	31,950	C+
Univ of Mich/Dearborn	MI	9,885	VC
Univ of Minn/Duluth	MN	19,806	C
Univ of Minn/Twin Cities	MN		HC
Univ of Missouri/Columbia	MO	18,201	MC
Univ of Montana-Western	MT	9,753	LC
Univ of N Car at Charlotte	NC	15,547	C
Univ of North Florida	FL	15,870	C
Univ of Pittsburgh at Bradford	PA	21,802	C
Univ of Rio Grande	OH	8,750	NC

ST = STATE $IS = IN-STATE COSTS SR = SELECTOR RATING

School	ST	$IS	SR
Univ of St. Francis	IN	29,810	C
Univ of S Car Upstate	SC	18,200	LC
Univ of South Florida/Tampa	FL	13,000	C
Univ of the Cumberlands	KY	27,500	C
Univ of Vermont	VT	27,006	VC+
Univ of Wisc Whitewater	WI	13,314	C
Univ of Wisc/La Crosse	WI	9,304	VC
Valparaiso Univ	IN	44,940	VC+
Virginia Wesleyan College	VA	28,433	LC
Viterbo Univ	WI	30,070	C
Wartburg College	IA	41,055	VC
Washington State Univ	WA	20,461	C
Washington Univ in St. Louis	MO	69,844	MC
Wayne State Univ	MI	22,063	C
Webster Univ	MO	35,100	C+
West Chester Univ of Pennsylvania	PA	17,186	C
West Texas A&M Univ	TX	13,478	C
Whitworth Univ	WA	47,734	VC
Wilmington College	OH	29,784	C
Wilson College	PA	35,080	C
Winona State Univ	MN	16,640	LC
Xavier Univ of Louisiana	LA	25,300	C
York College of Pennsylvania	PA	26,590	C
Youngstown State Univ	OH	16,732	C

SOCIAL STUDIES SECONDARY SCHOOL EDUCATION

School	ST	$IS	SR
Aquinas College	MI	33,060	C
Biola Univ	CA	40,320	C+
Concordia Univ St. Paul	MN	28,250	C
East Texas Baptist Univ	TX	31,577	LC
Elizabethtown College	PA	49,740	VC
Georgetown College	KY	41,440	C+
Kent State Univ	OH	19,920	C
Missouri Southern State Univ	MO	12,061	C
Monmouth Univ	NJ	44,108	C
Murray State Univ	KY	15,304	C
New York Univ	NY	61,470	MC
Niagara Univ	NY	41,010	C
Ouachita Baptist Univ	AR	30,220	VC
SUNY Fredonia/The SUNY at Fredonia	NY	19,840	VC
Taylor Univ	IN	37,821	VC+
The College of St. Rose	NY	26,750	C
Univ of Wisc/Superior	WI	14,314	C
Webster Univ	MO	35,100	C+
Youngstown State Univ	OH	16,732	C

SOCIAL WORK

School	ST	$IS	SR
Abilene Christian Univ	TX	38,400	C+
Adams State Univ	CO	13,358	LC
Adelphi Univ	NY	44,670	VC
Adrian College	MI	42,400	C
Alabama A&M Univ	AL	10,084	C
Alabama State Univ	AL	14,142	NC
Albany State Univ	GA	8,500	C
Alcorn State Univ	MS	9,500	C
Alvernia Univ	PA	39,250	LC
Anderson Univ	IN	36,100	C
Andrews Univ	MI	28,030	C+
Angelo State Univ	TX	15,049	NC
Anna Maria College	MA	34,600	C
Appalachian State Univ	NC	12,919	VC
Arizona State Univ, at the Downtown Phoenix Campus	AZ	22,101	C
Arkansas State Univ	AR	15,470	C
Asbury Univ	KY	32,038	VC
Ashland Univ	OH	25,000	C
Atlantic Union College	MA	24,600	C
Auburn Univ	AL	22,378	VC+
Augsburg College	MN	35,142	C
Augustana College	IL	43,398	VC
Aurora Univ	IL	33,228	C
Austin Peay State Univ	TN	15,274	C
Avila Univ	MO	26,900	C
Azusa Pacific Univ	CA	42,086	C
Ball State Univ	IN	17,850	C
Barton College	NC	27,660	LC
Baylor Univ	TX	50,329	HC
Belhaven Univ	MS	27,170	C
Belmont Univ	TN	39,190	VC+
Bemidji State Univ	MN	13,500	VC
Benedict College	SC	20,454	NC
Bennett College for Women	NC	21,970	LC
Bethany College	WV	35,282	LC
Bethel College	KS	32,160	C
Bethel Univ	MN	34,940	VC
Biola Univ	CA	40,320	C+
Bloomfield College	NJ	37,850	LC
Bloomsburg Univ of Pennsylvania	PA	13,598	C
Bluffton Univ	OH	38,948	C
Boise State Univ	ID	13,469	LC
Bowie State Univ	MD	23,990	LC
Bowling Green State Univ	OH	18,970	C
Bradley Univ	IL	31,874	VC
Brescia Univ	KY	26,140	VC+
Briar Cliff Univ	IA	29,514	C
Bridgewater State Univ	MA	18,752	C
Brigham Young Univ	UT	12,100	HC
Brigham Young Univ/Hawaii	HI	10,686	VC
Buena Vista Univ	IA	39,188	C
Buffalo State College / SUNY	NY	15,733	C+
Cabrini College	PA	40,859	LC
Cairn Univ	PA	33,270	C
Cal State, Chico	CA	20,158	C
Cal State, Fresno	CA	17,405	C
Cal State, Long Beach	CA	17,502	C+
Cal State, Los Angeles	CA	17,186	LC
Cal State, Sacramento	CA	16,200	C
Cal State, San Bernardino	CA	12,000	C
Calif Univ of Pennsylvania	PA	14,217	C
Calvin College	MI	39,120	VC
Campbell Univ	NC	37,570	VC
Campbellsville Univ	KY	27,720	C
Capital Univ	OH	41,050	VC
Caribbean Univ	PR	10,375	
Carlow Univ	PA	30,272	C
Carthage College	WI	33,000	C
Castleton State College	VT	20,186	C
Cedar Crest College	PA	43,240	C
Cedarville Univ	OH	32,860	VC
Central Conn State Univ	CT	19,749	C
Central State Univ	OH	9,010	C
Central Univ of Bayamon	PR	3,350	
Central Washington Univ	WA	11,730	C
Chadron State College	NE	7,400	NC
Champlain College	VT	46,650	VC+
Chapman Univ	CA	58,347	VC+
Chatham Univ	PA	43,797	C
Christopher Newport Univ	VA	21,960	VC
Clark Atlanta Univ	GA	30,006	LC
Clarke Univ	IA	37,600	C
Cleveland State Univ	OH	21,776	C
Coker College	SC	32,256	LC
College of Mount St. Joseph	OH	33,880	C
College of St. Scholastica	MN	41,440	C
College of Staten Island/The City of New Yok	NY	16,778	NC
College of the Ozarks	MO		VC
Colo State Univ-Fort Collins	CO	20,385	VC
Colo State Univ-Pueblo	CO	16,183	C
Columbia College	MO	24,578	C
Columbia College	SC	27,882	C
Concord Univ	WV	13,102	C
Concordia College - Moorhead	MN	39,974	VC
Concordia College - New York	NY	39,035	LC
Concordia Univ	OR	35,000	C
Concordia Univ Wisc	WI	28,980	C
Concordia Univ, River Forest	IL	26,300	C
Coppin State Univ	MD	16,227	C
Cornerstone Univ and Grand Rapids Theological Seminary	MI	33,338	C
Creighton Univ	NE	45,356	VC
Daemen College	NY	34,770	C
Defiance College	OH	30,645	C
Delaware State Univ	DE	16,722	LC
Delta State Univ	MS	12,292	C
Dickinson State Univ	ND	11,900	NC
Dominican College	NY	31,270	LC
Dordt College	IA	34,160	C+
East Carolina Univ	NC	14,169	C
East Central Univ	OK	10,223	C
East Tenn State Univ	TN	9,000	C
Eastern Conn State Univ	CT	20,584	C
Eastern Kentucky Univ	KY	11,161	C
Eastern Mennonite Univ	VA	40,660	C
Eastern Mich Univ	MI	18,604	C
Eastern Nazarene College	MA	30,000	C
Eastern New Mexico Univ	NM	10,682	C
Eastern Univ	PA	37,704	C
Eastern Washington Univ	WA		C
Edinboro Univ of Pennsylvania	PA	15,940	LC
Elizabeth City State Univ	NC	11,638	C
Elizabethtown College	PA	49,740	VC
Elms College	MA	23,900	VC
Evangel Univ	MO	23,090	C
Fayetteville State Univ	NC	10,816	C
Ferris State Univ	MI	20,047	C
Ferrum College	VA	27,740	LC
Florida A&M Univ	FL	14,935	LC
Florida Atlantic Univ	FL	17,339	C
Florida Gulf Coast Univ	FL		C
Florida International Univ	FL	17,747	C+
Florida State Univ	FL	16,715	VC
Fontbonne Univ	MO	31,384	C
Fordham Univ	NY	61,588	HC+
Fort Hays State Univ	KS	11,354	C
Fort Valley State Univ	GA	11,200	VC
Franciscan Univ of Steubenville	OH	27,320	VC
Franklin Pierce Univ	NH	41,598	C
Freed-Hardeman Univ	TN	19,697	VC
Fresno Pacific Univ	CA	32,136	C
Frostburg State Univ	MD	15,264	LC
Gallaudet Univ	DC	25,380	SP
Gannon Univ	PA	39,608	C
George Fox Univ	OR	40,750	C+
George Mason Univ	VA	15,724	VC
Georgia Regents Univ	GA		C
Georgia State Univ	GA	15,582	VC
Georgian Court Univ	NJ	41,594	LC
Gordon College	MA	44,320	VC
Goshen College	IN	35,900	VC
Grace College and Seminary	IN	28,800	VC
Grambling State Univ	LA	13,384	LC
Grand Valley State Univ	MI	17,998	C+
Greenville College	IL	27,012	C
Gwynedd-Mercy College	PA	33,560	C
Hannibal-LaGrange Univ	MO	24,490	C
Harding Univ	AR	23,556	C
Hardin-Simmons Univ	TX	23,560	C+
Hawaii Pacific Univ	HI	34,360	C
Heritage Univ	WA	17,664	NC
Hood College	MD	45,730	C
Hope College	MI	38,650	VC
Howard Payne Univ	TX	17,115	C
Howard Univ	DC	13,646	C
Humboldt State Univ	CA	18,400	C
Huntington Univ	IN	32,220	C+
Idaho State Univ	ID	12,307	C
Illinois State Univ	IL	23,110	VC
Indiana State Univ	IN	16,000	C
Indiana Univ Bloomington	IN	19,801	VC
Indiana Univ East	IN	6,783	C
Indiana Univ Northwest	IN	6,854	LC
Indiana Univ South Bend	IN	15,501	C
Indiana Univ-Purdue Univ Indianapolis	IN	17,611	C
Indiana Wesleyan Univ	IN	31,815	VC
Inter-American Univ of PR/ Aguadilla Campus	PR	5,578	
Inter-American Univ of PR/ Arecibo Campus	PR	3,350	
Inter-American Univ of PR/ Fajardo Campus	PR	4,200	
Inter-American Univ of PR/ Metropolitan Campus	PR	4,320	
Inter-American Univ of PR/ Ponce	PR		
Iona College	NY	44,028	C
Jackson State Univ	MS	13,512	LC
Jacksonville State Univ	AL	12,480	LC
James Madison Univ	VA	18,049	VC
Jarvis Christian College	TX	19,552	NC
Johnson C. Smith Univ	NC	25,336	LC
Judson College	AL	26,794	C
Juniata College	PA	49,340	VC
Kansas State Univ	KS	15,497	VC
Kentucky Christian Univ	KY	17,622	LC
Kentucky State Univ	KY	11,000	LC
Keuka College	NY	30,300	C
Kutztown Univ of Pennsylvania	PA	16,909	LC
La Salle Univ	PA	50,270	C
La Sierra Univ	CA	35,694	VC
Lamar Univ	TX	6,820	LC
Lehman College/The CUNY	NY	5,778	LC
LeMoyne-Owen College	TN	13,100	C
Lewis Univ	IL	23,050	C
Lewis-Clark State College	ID	6,990	C
Limestone College	SC	30,800	C
Lincoln Memorial Univ	TN	18,144	C
Lincoln Univ	MO	12,904	NC
Lindenwood Univ	MO	20,750	C
Lipscomb Univ	TN	37,490	VC
LIU Brooklyn	NY	47,182	LC
LIU Post	NY	47,660	C
Livingstone College	NC	17,815	LC
Lock Haven Univ of Pennsylvania	PA	18,028	LC
Longwood Univ	VA	20,924	C
Loras College	IA	37,432	VC
Louisiana College	LA	15,746	C
Lourdes Univ	OH	26,055	LC
Loyola Univ Chicago	IL	51,646	VC+
Lubbock Christian Univ	TX	26,308	C
Luther College	IA	45,720	C+
MacMurray College	IL	20,755	C
Madonna Univ	MI	24,540	VC
Malone Univ	OH	35,364	C
Manchester Univ	IN	35,070	C
Mansfield Univ	PA	19,468	LC
Marian Univ	WI	32,420	LC
Marist College	NY	35,500	C
Mars Hill Univ	NC	22,950	LC
Marshall Univ	WV	14,820	C
Mary Baldwin College	VA	38,245	C
Marygrove College	MI	28,926	C
Marywood Univ	PA	45,595	C
McDaniel College	MD	47,450	VC
McKendree Univ	IL	29,920	C+
Mercy College	NY	30,456	C
Mercyhurst Univ	PA	40,700	C
Meredith College	NC	31,420	C
Messiah College	PA	46,690	C+
Methodist Univ	NC	37,185	C
Metropolitan College of New York	NY	16,720	VC
Metropolitan State Univ	MN	5,923	
Metropolitan State Univ of Denver	CO	4,835	LC
Miami Univ	OH	24,191	VC
Mich State Univ	MI	22,450	VC
Middle Tenn State Univ	TN	8,650	C
Midwestern State Univ	TX	9,722	C
Miles College	AL	11,164	NC
Millersville Univ of Pennsylvania	PA	21,648	C
Minn State Univ, Mankato	MN	15,616	C
Minn State Univ, Moorhead	MN	13,392	VC
Minot State Univ	ND	10,915	C
Misericordia Univ	PA	41,060	C
Miss College	MS	21,998	C
Miss State Univ	MS	14,750	C
Miss Valley State Univ	MS	9,706	LC
Missouri State Univ	MO	13,996	C+
Missouri Western State Univ	MO	12,260	NC
Molloy College	NY	40,440	C
Monmouth Univ	NJ	44,108	C
Morehead State Univ	KY	10,900	C
Morgan State Univ	MD	14,500	VC
Mount Mary Univ	WI	33,590	LC
Mount Mercy Univ	IA	35,320	C
Mount St. Mary's College - Chalon Campus	CA	43,897	VC+
Mount Vernon Nazarene Univ	OH	29,590	C
Murray State Univ	KY	15,304	C
Nazareth College of Rochester	NY	43,028	C+
Nebr Wesleyan Univ	NE	29,774	C+
New Mexico Highlands Univ	NM	11,904	NC
New Mexico State Univ	NM	14,050	C
New York Inst of Technology	NY	45,010	VC
New York Univ	NY	61,470	MC
Niagara Univ	NY	41,010	C
N Car Agricultural and Technical State Univ	NC	13,365	LC
N Car Central Univ	NC	9,000	C
N Car State Univ	NC	16,202	HC
Northeastern Illinois Univ	IL	10,318	LC
Northeastern State Univ	OK	8,615	VC
Northern Arizona Univ	AZ	19,010	C
Northern Kentucky Univ	KY	21,134	C
Northern Mich Univ	MI	18,278	C
Northwest Nazarene Univ	ID	34,000	C
Northwestern College of Iowa	IA	36,240	VC
Northwestern Okla State Univ	OK	7,275	NC
Northwestern State Univ of Louisiana	LA	14,368	C
Nyack College	NY	33,250	C
Oakland Univ	MI	19,391	C
Oakwood Univ	AL	25,529	NC
Oglethorpe Univ	GA	44,200	C+
Ohio Dominican Univ	OH	38,380	C+
Ohio Univ	OH	21,080	C
Okla Baptist Univ	OK	28,202	C
Olivet Nazarene Univ	IL	29,990	C
Oral Roberts Univ	OK	31,734	C
Our Lady of the Lake Univ	TX	22,430	LC
Pacific Lutheran Univ	WA	46,760	C+
Pacific Union College	CA	28,150	VC
Pacific Univ	OR	49,626	C+
Park Univ	MO	17,525	C
Philander Smith College	AR	19,760	LC
Pittsburg State Univ	KS	12,032	C
Plymouth State Univ	NH	23,148	LC
Point Loma Nazarene Univ	CA	41,006	C+
Pontifical Catholic Univ of PR	PR	7,310	
Portland State Univ	OR	18,672	C
Prairie View A&M Univ	TX	15,205	LC
Prescott College	AZ	33,284	C
Presentation College	SD	14,800	LC
Providence College	RI	57,383	VC
Purdue Univ/West Lafayette	IN	20,024	HC
Quincy Univ	IL	34,980	LC
Radford Univ	VA	17,766	LC
Ramapo College of New Jersey	NJ	24,938	C
Regis College	MA	47,565	LC
Rhode Island College	RI	17,694	LC
Richard Stockton College of New Jersey	NJ	20,000	VC
Roberts Wesleyan College	NY	38,306	C+
Rust College	MS	10,600	C
Rutgers, The State Univ of New Jersey/Camden Campus	NJ	25,121	C
Rutgers, The State Univ of New Jersey/New Brunswick	NJ	258,806	C
Rutgers, The State Univ of New Jersey/Newark Campus	NJ	25,562	VC
Sacred Heart Univ	CT	49,264	VC
Saginaw Valley State Univ	MI	17,369	C
St. Francis Univ	PA	30,029	LC
St. Leo Univ	FL	30,340	C
St. Louis Univ	MO	48,346	HC
St. Martin's Univ	WA	41,678	C
St. Mary's College	IN	45,160	C+
Salem State Univ	MA	13,161	LC
Salisbury Univ	MD	19,180	VC
Salve Regina Univ	RI	48,550	VC
San Diego State Univ	CA	21,611	C+
San Francisco State Univ	CA	18,514	C
San Jose State Univ	CA	19,133	LC
Savannah State Univ	GA	13,516	C
Seattle Univ	WA	49,035	VC+
Seton Hall Univ	NJ	45,902	C
Seton Hill Univ	PA	35,172	C
Shaw Univ	NC	15,488	C
Shepherd Univ	WV	15,875	C

ST = STATE $IS = IN-STATE COSTS SR = SELECTOR RATING

School	ST	$IS	SR
Shippensburg Univ of Pennsylvania	PA	20,934	C
Siena College	NY	43,863	VC
Siena Heights Univ	MI	32,040	C
Simmons College	MA	49,966	VC
Skidmore College	NY	59,942	HC
Slippery Rock Univ of Pennsylvania	PA	10,360	C
Sojourner-Douglass College	MD	9,160	LC
S Car State Univ	SC	6,700	LC
Southeast Missouri State Univ	MO	15,370	LC
Southeastern Louisiana Univ	LA	13,325	C
Southeastern Univ	FL	27,201	C
Southern Adventist Univ	TN	26,190	C
Southern Conn State Univ	CT	18,033	LC
Southern Illinois Univ Carbondale	IL	21,942	C
Southern Illinois Univ Edwardsville	IL	17,532	C
Southern Univ and A&M College	LA	9,761	LC
Southern Univ at New Orleans	LA	2,963	NC
Southwest Minn State Univ	MN	14,000	C
Southwestern Adventist Univ	TX	23,026	LC
Southwestern Okla State Univ	OK	9,160	C
Spalding Univ	KY	32,287	LC
Spring Arbor Univ	MI	26,740	C
St. Catherine Univ	MN	37,782	C+
St. Cloud State Univ	MN	10,600	C
St. Edward's Univ	TX	47,784	C
St. Olaf College	MN	51,200	HC+
Stephen F. Austin State Univ	TX	14,668	C
Stony Brook Univ / SUNY	NY	20,078	HC+
SUNY Fredonia/The SUNY at Fredonia	NY	19,840	VC
SUNY Plattsburgh / SUNY	NY	18,083	C
Syracuse Univ	NY	56,346	VC
Talladega College	AL	17,996	C
Tarleton State Univ	TX	13,489	LC
Taylor Univ	IN	37,821	VC+
Temple Univ	PA	24,392	VC
Tenn State Univ	TN	9,048	C
Texas A&M Univ at Commerce	TX	10,496	C
Texas Christian Univ	TX	49,980	HC
Texas Southern Univ	TX	18,212	LC
Texas State Univ	TX	17,128	C
Texas Tech Univ	TX	14,243	C
Texas Woman's Univ	TX	13,633	LC
The Catholic Univ of America	DC	52,852	VC
The College of New Rochelle	NY	33,600	VC
The College of St. Rose	NY	26,750	C
Ohio State Univ-Columbus Campus	OH	19,887	HC+
The SUNY/College at Brockport	NY	19,002	C
The Univ of Memphis	TN	15,094	C
The Univ of N Car at Greensboro	NC	12,848	C
The Univ of N Car at Pembroke	NC	13,388	LC
The Univ of Okla	OK	18,621	VC
The Univ of Tenn at Chattanooga	TN	16,883	C
The Univ of Utah	UT	16,463	VC
Thomas Univ	GA	11,520	NC
Trevecca Nazarene Univ	TN	31,186	C
Trinity Christian College	IL	28,869	C
Troy Univ	AL	10,650	C
Tulane Univ	LA	60,861	MC
Tuskegee Univ	AL	26,750	C
Union College	KY	29,955	C
Union College	NE	23,270	C
Union Inst & Univ	OH	8,912	SP
Union Univ	TN	28,260	C
Univ at Albany / SUNY	NY	18,674	VC
Univ of Akron	OH	20,436	C
Univ of Alabama at Birmingham	AL	18,484	C+
Univ of Alabama at Tuscaloosa	AL	17,164	C+
Univ of Alaska Anchorage	AK	16,673	NC
Univ of Alaska Fairbanks	AK	15,130	C
Univ of Arkansas at Fayetteville	AR	18,352	C+
Univ of Arkansas at Little Rock	AR	17,609	LC
Univ of Arkansas at Monticello	AR	12,076	NC
Univ of Arkansas at Pine Bluff	AR	13,378	C
Univ of Calif at Berkeley	CA	23,322	MC
Univ of Central Florida	FL	15,668	VC+
Univ of Central Missouri	MO	14,605	C
Univ of Charleston	WV	32,300	C
Univ of Cincinnati	OH	21,506	VC
Univ of Detroit Mercy	MI	30,450	VC
Univ of Findlay	OH	31,916	C
Univ of Georgia	GA	20,082	VC
Univ of Hawaii at Manoa	HI	19,379	VC
Univ of Houston-Downtown	TX	15,170	LC
Univ of Indianapolis	IN	30,760	C
Univ of Iowa	IA	17,693	VC
Univ of Kansas	KS	17,603	C+
Univ of Kentucky	KY	19,868	C
Univ of Louisiana at Monroe	LA	12,998	C
Univ of Louisville	KY	17,946	C
Univ of Maine	ME	19,902	C+
Univ of Maine at Presque Isle	ME	15,011	LC
Univ of Mary	ND	16,714	C
Univ of Mary Hardin-Baylor	TX	31,950	C+
Univ of Maryland/Baltimore County	MD	18,000	VC
Univ of Mich-Flint	MI	17,547	C+
Univ of Miss	MS	16,704	C+
Univ of Missouri/Columbia	MO	18,201	MC
Univ of Missouri-St. Louis	MO		VC
Univ of Montana	MT	14,105	C
Univ of Montevallo	AL	17,060	C
Univ of Nebr at Kearney	NE	14,855	C
Univ of Nebr at Omaha	NE	12,700	C
Univ of Nevada, Las Vegas	NV	17,303	C
Univ of Nevada/Reno	NV	17,507	C
Univ of New Hampshire	NH	26,912	C
Univ of North Alabama	AL	9,960	C
Univ of N Car at Charlotte	NC	15,547	C
Univ of N Car at Wilmington	NC	13,572	VC
Univ of N Dak	ND	14,551	C
Univ of North Texas	TX	15,628	C
Univ of Northern Iowa	IA	15,795	C
Univ of Pikeville	KY	25,500	NC
Univ of Pittsburgh at Pittsburgh	PA	28,572	HC+
Univ of Portland	OR	49,964	VC
Univ of PR Recinto de Rio Piedras	PR	5,750	
Univ of PR/Humacao	PR	1,877	
Univ of Rio Grande	OH	8,750	NC
Univ of St. Francis	IN	29,810	C
Univ of St. Joseph	CT	45,630	C
Univ of Sioux Falls	SD	22,990	C
Univ of South Alabama	AL	13,510	C
Univ of S Car at Columbia	SC	19,725	VC+
Univ of S Dak	SD	15,111	C
Univ of South Florida/Tampa	FL	13,000	C
Univ of Southern Indiana	IN	14,885	C
Univ of Southern Maine	ME	16,576	C
Univ of Southern Miss	MS	13,170	C
Univ of St. Francis	IL	37,560	C
Univ of Tenn at Knoxville	TN	20,364	VC+
Univ of Tenn at Martin	TN	13,734	C
Univ of Texas - Pan American	TX	11,125	LC
Univ of Texas at Arlington	TX	10,908	LC
Univ of Texas at Austin	TX	44,074	HC
Univ of Texas at El Paso	TX	8,764	NC
Univ of the Cumberlands	KY	27,500	C
Univ of the District of Columbia	DC	7,244	LC
Univ of the Sacred Heart	PR	5,590	
Univ of Toledo	OH	18,464	C
Univ of Vermont	VT	27,006	VC+
Univ of Washington	WA	14,722	VC
Univ of West Florida	FL	14,656	C
Univ of Wisc Whitewater	WI	13,314	C
Univ of Wisc/Eau Claire	WI	15,730	C
Univ of Wisc/Green Bay	WI	19,074	C
Univ of Wisc/Madison	WI	18,757	HC+
Univ of Wisc/Oshkosh	WI	10,426	LC
Univ of Wisc/River Falls	WI	9,722	C
Univ of Wisc/Stevens Point	WI	14,043	C
Univ of Wisc/Superior	WI	14,314	C
Univ of Wisc-Milwaukee	WI	18,436	C
Univ of Wyoming	WY	14,401	C+
Ursuline College	OH	33,198	LC
Utah State Univ	UT	12,044	C
Valparaiso Univ	IN	44,940	VC+
Virginia Commonwealth Univ	VA	21,716	C
Virginia State Univ	VA	11,318	C+
Virginia Union Univ	VA	18,432	C
Virginia Wesleyan College	VA	28,433	LC
Viterbo Univ	WI	30,070	C
Walla Walla Univ	WA	26,256	NC
Warner Univ	FL	18,000	C
Warren Wilson College	NC	40,132	VC
Wartburg College	IA	41,055	VC
Washburn Univ	KS	12,579	C
Wayne State Univ	MI	22,063	C
West Chester Univ of Pennsylvania	PA	17,186	C
West Texas A&M Univ	TX	13,478	C
West Virginia State Univ	WV	8,378	NC
West Virginia Univ	WV	16,542	C+
Western Carolina Univ	NC	13,965	C
Western Conn State Univ	CT	18,327	LC
Western Illinois Univ	IL	20,732	C
Western Kentucky Univ	KY	11,000	LC
Western Mich Univ	MI	19,628	C
Western New England Univ	MA	46,154	C+
Western New Mexico Univ	NM	8,500	LC
Westfield State Univ	MA	18,297	C
Wheelock College	MA	33,075	C
Whittier College	CA	43,416	C
Wichita State Univ	KS	14,607	C+
Widener Univ	PA	52,418	C
Wilberforce Univ	OH	15,100	LC
William Woods Univ	MO	24,260	C
Wilmington College	OH	29,784	C
Winona State Univ	MN	16,640	C
Winthrop Univ	SC	21,120	C
Wright State Univ	OH	16,983	C
Xavier Univ	OH	44,980	VC
York College / The CUNY	NY	5,496	C
Youngstown State Univ	OH	16,732	C

SOCIOLOGY

School	ST	$IS	SR
Abilene Christian Univ	TX	38,400	C+
Adams State Univ	CO	13,358	LC
Adelphi Univ	NY	44,670	VC
Adrian College	MI	42,400	C
Agnes Scott College	GA	45,323	C+
Alabama A&M Univ	AL	10,084	C
Alabama State Univ	AL	14,142	NC
Albany State Univ	GA	8,500	C
Albertus Magnus College	CT	37,382	LC
Albion College	MI	46,010	C
Albright College	PA	46,660	C
Alcorn State Univ	MS	9,500	C
Alfred Univ	NY	41,770	C
Allen Univ	SC	16,124	NC
Alma College	MI	44,075	C
Alverno College	WI	31,434	LC
American International College	MA	36,100	LC
American Univ	DC	56,015	HC+
Amherst College	MA	58,744	MC
Anderson Univ	IN	36,100	C
Andrews Univ	MI	28,030	C+
Angelo State Univ	TX	15,049	NC
Anna Maria College	MA	34,600	C
Appalachian State Univ	NC	12,919	VC
Aquinas College	MI	33,060	C
Arcadia Univ	PA	33,570	C+
Arizona State Univ, at the Tempe Campus	AZ	20,137	C+
Arizona State Univ, at the West Campus	AZ	19,251	C
Arkansas State Univ	AR	15,470	C
Arkansas Tech Univ	AR	13,982	LC
Asbury Univ	KY	32,038	VC
Ashford Univ	CA	10,480	C
Ashland Univ	OH	25,000	C
Assumption College	MA	47,122	C+
Auburn Univ	AL	22,378	VC+
Auburn Univ at Montgomery	AL	14,470	LC
Augsburg College	MN	35,142	C
Augustana College	IL	43,398	VC
Augustana College	SD	36,500	C
Aurora Univ	IL	33,228	C
Austin College	TX	45,875	HC
Austin Peay State Univ	TN	15,274	C
Averett Univ	VA	37,750	LC
Avila Univ	MO	26,900	C
Azusa Pacific Univ	CA	42,086	C
Baker Univ	KS	33,350	C+
Baldwin Wallace Univ	OH	38,318	C
Ball State Univ	IN	17,850	C
Bard College	NY	61,940	HC
Barnard College/Columbia Univ	NY	39,000	MC
Barry Univ	FL	38,190	C
Bates College	ME	60,720	MC
Baylor Univ	TX	50,329	HC
Bellarmine Univ	KY	42,950	VC
Bellevue Univ	NE	4,600	NC
Belmont Univ	TN	39,190	VC+
Beloit College	WI	49,970	HC
Bemidji State Univ	MN	13,500	VC
Benedict College	SC	20,454	NC
Benedictine College	KS	29,180	C
Benedictine Univ	IL	37,820	C
Bennington College	VT	56,990	HC+
Berea College	KY	7,192	C
Berry College	GA	39,254	VC
Bethel College	IN	31,560	C
Bethel Univ	TN	19,186	C
Bethune-Cookman Univ	FL	22,958	C
Binghamton Univ/The SUNY	NY	21,648	HC+
Biola Univ	CA	40,320	C
Birmingham-Southern College	AL	44,168	VC+
Black Hills State Univ	SD	13,947	C
Bloomfield College	NJ	37,850	LC
Bloomsburg Univ of Pennsylvania	PA	13,598	C
Bluffton Univ	OH	38,948	C
Boise State Univ	ID	13,469	LC
Boston College	MA	60,622	MC
Boston Univ	MA	60,694	MC
Bowdoin College	ME	59,568	MC
Bowie State Univ	MD	23,990	LC
Bowling Green State Univ	OH	18,970	C
Bradley Univ	IL	31,874	VC
Brandeis Univ	MA		MC
Brewton-Parker College	GA	33,388	C
Briar Cliff Univ	IA	29,514	C
Bridgewater College	VA	41,450	C
Bridgewater State Univ	MA	18,752	C
Brigham Young Univ	UT	12,108	HC
Brown Univ	RI	59,428	MC
Bryant Univ	RI	49,179	VC
Bryn Mawr College	PA	59,890	MC
Bucknell Univ	PA	60,140	MC
Buffalo State College / SUNY	NY	15,733	C+
Butler Univ	IN	47,572	VC+
Cabrini College	PA	40,859	LC
Caldwell College	NJ	35,602	NC
Calif Baptist Univ	CA	38,792	C
Calif Lutheran Univ	CA	44,540	C+
Calif Polytechnic State Univ	CA	19,847	HC
Calif State Polytechnic Univ, Pomona	CA	20,156	C
Cal State, Bakersfield	CA	8,000	C
Cal State, Chico	CA	20,158	C
Cal State, Dominguez Hills	CA	17,090	LC
Cal State, East Bay	CA	16,549	C
Cal State, Fresno	CA	17,405	C
Cal State, Long Beach	CA	17,502	C+
Cal State, Los Angeles	CA	17,186	C
Cal State, Northridge	CA	28,690	NC
Cal State, Sacramento	CA	16,200	C
Cal State, San Bernardino	CA	12,000	C
Cal State, San Marcos	CA	14,576	LC
Cal State, Stanislaus	CA	18,582	C
Calvin College	MI	39,120	VC
Cameron Univ	OK	10,004	LC
Campbellsville Univ	KY	27,720	C
Canisius College	NY	44,900	C
Capital Univ	OH	41,050	VC
Cardinal Stritch Univ	WI	24,054	C
Carleton College	MN	60,102	MC
Carlow Univ	PA	30,272	C
Carroll College	MT	28,000	C
Carroll Univ	WI	38,100	C
Carson-Newman Univ	TN	29,058	C+
Carthage College	WI	33,000	C
Case Western Reserve Univ	OH	56,534	MC
Castleton State College	VT	20,186	C
Catawba College	NC	37,240	LC
Cedarville Univ	OH	32,860	VC
Centenary College	NJ	38,618	C
Centenary College of Louisiana	LA	45,650	C+
Central College	IA	42,104	C+
Central Conn State Univ	CT	19,749	C
Central Methodist Univ	MO	28,240	VC
Central State Univ	OH	9,010	C
Central Univ of Bayamon	PR	3,350	
Central Washington Univ	WA	11,730	C
Centre College	KY	35,000	HC+
Chadron State College	NE	7,400	NC
Chapman Univ	CA	58,347	VC+
Charleston Southern Univ	SC	22,420	C
Chestnut Hill College	PA	42,110	LC
Chicago State Univ	IL	5,482	C
Christopher Newport Univ	VA	21,960	VC
CUNY/Baruch College	NY		HC
CUNY/Brooklyn College	NY	5,884	C+
CUNY/City College	NY	20,319	VC+
Claflin Univ	SC	22,368	LC
Clarion Univ of Pennsylvania	PA	17,370	C
Clark Atlanta Univ	GA	30,006	LC
Clark Univ	MA	47,020	HC+
Clarke Univ	IA	37,600	C
Clemson Univ	SC	19,136	HC
Cleveland State Univ	OH	21,776	C
Coastal Carolina Univ	SC	18,580	C
Coe College	IA	45,550	VC
Coker College	SC	32,256	LC
Colby College	ME	57,510	MC
Colby-Sawyer College	NH	50,790	C
Colgate Univ	NY	58,135	MC
College of Charleston	SC	22,145	VC
College of Mount St. Joseph	OH	33,880	C
College of Mount St. Vincent	NY	41,040	VC
College of New Jersey	NJ	25,376	HC
College of St. Benedict	MN	49,359	VC
College of St. Elizabeth	NJ	43,839	LC
College of Staten Island/The City of New Yok	NY	16,778	NC
College of the Holy Cross	MA	58,042	MC
College of the Ozarks	MO		VC
College of William & Mary	VA	28,000	VC
College of Wooster	OH	52,600	VC
Colo College	CO	57,162	MC
Colo Mesa Univ	CO	17,690	LC
Colo State Univ-Fort Collins	CO	20,385	VC
Colo State Univ-Pueblo	CO	16,183	C
Columbia College	MO	24,578	C
Columbia College	SC	27,882	C
Columbia Univ/City of New York	NY	61,116	MC
Columbia Univ/School of General Studies	NY	58,231	MC
Columbus State Univ	GA	13,176	C
Concord Univ	WV	13,102	C
Concordia College - Moorhead	MN	39,974	VC
Concordia College - New York	NY	39,035	LC
Concordia Univ St. Paul	MN	28,250	C
Concordia Univ, Ann Arbor	MI	27,220	VC
Concordia Univ, River Forest	IL	26,360	VC
Conn College	CT	54,970	MC
Cornell College	IA	44,930	VC
Cornell Univ	NY	60,964	MC
Covenant College	GA	38,990	VC+
Creighton Univ	NE	45,356	VC
Cumberland Univ	TN	21,220	C
Curry College	MA	48,925	LC
Dakota Wesleyan Univ	SD	23,000	C

ST = STATE $IS = IN-STATE COSTS   SR = SELECTOR RATING

School	ST	$IS	SR
Dallas Baptist Univ	TX	30,580	VC
Dartmouth College	NH	57,996	MC
Davidson College	NC	58,146	MC
Davis & Elkins College	WV	33,742	C
Delaware State Univ	DE	16,722	LC
Denison Univ	OH	54,670	HC+
DePaul Univ	IL	47,623	VC
DePauw Univ	IN	48,950	VC+
Dickinson College	PA	57,662	HC+
Dickinson State Univ	ND	11,900	NC
Dillard Univ	LA	20,940	VC
Doane College	NE	35,230	C
Dominican Univ	IL	37,628	C
Dordt College	IA	34,160	C+
Dowling College	NY	25,000	LC
Drake Univ	IA	41,516	VC+
Drew Univ/College of Liberal Arts	NJ	57,516	C
Drexel Univ	PA	61,418	VC+
Drury Univ	MO	31,909	VC
Duke Univ	NC	50,250	MC
Duquesne Univ	PA	43,720	VC
D'Youville College	NY	29,850	C
Earlham College	IN	51,470	HC
East Carolina Univ	NC	14,169	C
East Central Univ	OK	10,223	LC
East Stroudsburg Univ of Pennsylvania	PA	18,868	LC
East Tenn State Univ	TN	9,000	C
East Texas Baptist Univ	TX	31,577	LC
Eastern Conn State Univ	CT	20,584	C
Eastern Illinois Univ	IL	20,466	C
Eastern Kentucky Univ	KY	11,161	C
Eastern Mennonite Univ	VA	40,660	C
Eastern Mich Univ	MI	18,604	C
Eastern Nazarene College	MA	30,000	C
Eastern New Mexico Univ	NM	10,682	C
Eastern Oregon Univ	OR	10,400	C
Eastern Univ	PA	37,704	C
Eastern Washington Univ	WA		C
Eckerd College	FL	43,902	C
Edgewood College	WI	33,294	C
Edward Waters College	FL	19,607	LC
Elizabeth City State Univ	NC	11,638	C
Elizabethtown College	PA	49,740	VC
Elmhurst College	IL	43,336	C
Elmira College	NY	49,950	C+
Elms College	MA	23,900	VC
Elon Univ	NC	41,914	VC+
Emmanuel College	MA	47,985	VC
Emory and Henry College	VA	387,460	C
Emory Univ	GA	56,368	MC
Emporia State Univ	KS	12,897	C
Eugene Lang College/The New School for Liberal Arts	NY	55,650	C
Eureka College	IL	19,280	C
Evangel Univ	MO	23,090	C
Excelsior College	NY	5,580	SP
Fairfield Univ	CT	56,960	VC
Fairleigh Dickinson Univ/College at Florham	NJ	42,142	C
Fairmont State Univ	WV	12,098	LC
Faulkner Univ	AL	25,720	LC
Fayetteville State Univ	NC	10,816	C
Ferris State Univ	MI	20,047	C
Fisk Univ	TN	19,830	C
Fitchburg State Univ	MA	18,173	C
Flagler College	FL	25,180	C
Florida A&M Univ	FL	14,935	LC
Florida Atlantic Univ	FL	17,339	C
Florida Gulf Coast Univ	FL		C
Florida International Univ	FL	17,747	C+
Florida Memorial Univ	FL	20,888	LC
Florida State Univ	FL	16,715	VC
Fontbonne Univ	MO	31,384	C
Fordham Univ	NY	61,588	HC+
Fort Hays State Univ	KS	11,354	C
Fort Lewis College	CO	15,513	C
Fort Valley State Univ	GA	11,200	VC
Framingham State Univ	MA	18,854	C
Francis Marion Univ	SC	16,464	LC
Franciscan Univ of Steubenville	OH	27,320	VC
Franklin and Marshall College	PA	60,799	MC
Franklin College	IN	36,585	C
Frostburg State Univ	MD	15,264	LC
Furman Univ	SC	54,006	HC
Gallaudet Univ	DC	25,380	SP
Gardner-Webb Univ	NC	34,375	C
Geneva College	PA	27,280	C
George Fox Univ	OR	40,750	C+
George Mason Univ	VA	15,724	VC
George Washington Univ	DC	57,108	MC
Georgetown College	KY	41,440	C+
Georgetown Univ	DC	52,910	MC
Georgia College and State Univ	GA	18,900	C+
Georgia Regents Univ	GA		C
Georgia Southwestern State Univ	GA	13,246	C
Georgia State Univ	GA	15,582	VC
Gettysburg College	PA	58,820	HC
Gonzaga Univ	WA	46,441	HC
Gordon College	MA	44,320	VC
Goshen College	IN	35,900	VC
Goucher College	MD	52,040	VC+
Grace College and Seminary	IN	28,800	VC
Graceland Univ	IA	28,020	C
Grambling State Univ	LA	13,384	LC
Grand Canyon Univ	AZ	24,540	VC
Grand Valley State Univ	MI	17,998	C+
Green Mountain College	VT	45,228	LC
Greensboro College	NC	28,740	LC
Greenville College	IL	27,012	C
Grinnell College	IA	53,654	HC
Grove City College	PA	24,022	VC
Guilford College	NC	42,800	VC
Gustavus Adolphus College	MN	48,170	HC
Gwynedd-Mercy College	PA	33,560	C
Hamilton College	NY	55,620	MC
Hamline Univ	MN	45,678	VC
Hampshire College	MA	58,320	MC
Hampton Univ	VA	28,528	C
Hannibal-LaGrange Univ	MO	24,490	C
Hanover College	IN	43,073	C+
Hardin-Simmons Univ	TX	23,560	C+
Hartwick College	NY	51,270	C
Harvard College/Harvard Univ	MA	49,000	MC
Hastings College	NE	27,782	C+
Haverford College	PA	61,564	MC
Hawaii Pacific Univ	HI	34,360	C
Henderson State Univ	AR	14,584	C
Hendrix College	AR	50,202	VC+
High Point Univ	NC	39,800	C
Hillsdale College	MI	32,866	MC
Hiram College	OH	37,300	VC
Hobart and William Smith Colleges	NY	60,034	HC+
Hofstra Univ	NY	51,810	VC+
Hollins Univ	VA	43,295	VC
Holy Family Univ	PA	40,030	LC
Holy Names Univ	CA	40,310	NC
Hood College	MD	45,730	C
Hope College	MI	38,650	VC
Houghton College	NY	36,808	C+
Houston Baptist Univ	TX	36,450	C
Howard Payne Univ	TX	17,115	C
Howard Univ	DC	13,646	C
Humboldt State Univ	CA	18,400	C
Hunter College	NY	14,429	VC
Huntington Univ	IN	32,220	C+
Huston-Tillotson Univ	TX	18,124	C+
Idaho State Univ	ID	12,307	C
Illinois College	IL	25,770	VC
Illinois State Univ	IL	23,110	VC
Illinois Wesleyan Univ	IL	48,452	HC
Immaculata Univ	PA	43,000	C
Indiana State Univ	IN	16,000	C
Indiana Univ Bloomington	IN	19,801	VC
Indiana Univ East	IN	6,783	C
Indiana Univ Kokomo	IN	6,811	LC
Indiana Univ Northwest	IN	6,854	LC
Indiana Univ of Pennsylvania	PA	20,846	LC
Indiana Univ South Bend	IN	15,501	C
Indiana Univ Southeast	IN	16,035	C
Indiana Univ-Purdue Univ Fort Wayne	IN	15,521	C
Indiana Univ-Purdue Univ Indianapolis	IN	17,611	C
Indiana Wesleyan Univ	IN	31,815	VC
Inter-American Univ of PR/Fajardo Campus	PR	4,200	
Inter-American Univ of PR/Metropolitan Campus	PR	4,320	
Inter-American Univ of PR/Ponce	PR		
Inter-American Univ of PR/San Germán	PR	6,720	
Iona College	NY	44,028	C
Iowa State Univ	IA	16,643	VC
Iowa Wesleyan College	IA	30,850	LC
Ithaca College	NY	53,864	HC
Jackson State Univ	MS	13,512	LC
Jacksonville State Univ	AL	12,480	LC
Jacksonville Univ	FL	37,780	C
James Madison Univ	VA	18,049	VC
Jarvis Christian College	TX	19,552	NC
John Carroll Univ	OH	46,300	C+
Johns Hopkins Univ	MD	47,492	MC
Johnson C. Smith Univ	NC	25,336	LC
Johnson State College	VT	16,721	C
Judson Univ	IL	25,130	C
Juniata College	PA	49,340	VC
Kalamazoo College	MI	49,740	HC
Kansas State Univ	KS	15,497	VC
Kansas Wesleyan Univ	KS	32,000	C
Kean Univ	NJ	23,444	C
Keene State College	NH	23,232	LC
Kennesaw State Univ	GA		C
Kent State Univ	OH	19,920	C
Kentucky State Univ	KY	11,000	LC
Kentucky Wesleyan College	KY	27,440	C
Kenyon College	OH	58,890	MC
Keuka College	NY	30,300	C
King's College	PA	43,502	C
Knox College	IL	44,865	VC+
Kutztown Univ of Pennsylvania	PA	16,909	LC
La Roche College	PA	35,824	LC
La Salle Univ	PA	50,270	C
La Sierra Univ	CA	35,694	VC
Lafayette College	PA	59,155	HC+
LaGrange College	GA	37,670	C
Lake Forest College	IL	50,652	VC
Lake Superior State Univ	MI	18,121	C
Lakeland College	WI	22,990	C
Lamar Univ	TX	6,820	LC
Lander Univ	SC	22,514	C
Lane College	TN	11,212	C
Langston Univ	OK	3,000	C
Lasell College	MA	43,750	LC
Le Moyne College	NY	43,470	C
Lebanon Valley College	PA	38,570	C
Lee Univ	TN	18,690	C+
Lehigh Univ	PA	56,770	MC
Lehman College/The CUNY	NY	5,778	LC
LeMoyne-Owen College	TN	13,100	C
Lenoir-Rhyne College	NC	35,984	C
Lewis & Clark College	OR	54,382	MC
Lewis Univ	IL	23,050	C
Lincoln Univ	MO	12,904	NC
Lindenwood Univ	MO	20,750	C
Linfield College-McMinnville Campus	OR	47,676	C
LIU Brooklyn	NY	47,182	LC
LIU Post	NY	47,660	VC
Livingstone College	NC	17,815	LC
Lock Haven Univ of Pennsylvania	PA	18,028	LC
Longwood Univ	VA	20,924	C
Loras College	IA	37,432	VC
Louisiana College	LA	15,746	C
Louisiana State Univ	LA	18,677	C+
Louisiana State Univ in Shreveport	LA	5,606	C
Louisiana Tech Univ	LA	11,302	C
Lourdes Univ	OH	26,055	LC
Loyola Marymount Univ	CA	54,649	VC+
Loyola Univ Chicago	IL	51,646	VC+
Loyola Univ Maryland	MD	56,880	VC+
Loyola Univ New Orleans	LA	46,581	VC
Luther College	IA	45,720	C+
Lycoming College	PA	45,379	C
Lynchburg College	VA	42,645	C
Macalester College	MN	57,691	MC
Madonna Univ	MI	24,540	VC
Manchester Univ	IN	35,070	C
Manhattan College	NY	49,588	C+
Manhattanville College	NY	50,740	VC
Mansfield Univ	PA	19,468	LC
Marian Univ	IN	38,540	C
Marlboro College	VT	35,980	VC
Marquette Univ	WI	46,930	VC+
Mars Hill College	NC	22,950	LC
Marshall Univ	WV	14,820	C
Martin Univ	IN	11,000	SP
Mary Baldwin College	VA	38,245	C
Marymount Manhattan College	NY	40,118	VC
Marymount Univ	VA	39,480	C
Maryville College	TN	33,150	C
Maryville Univ of St. Louis	MO	35,856	VC
Mass College of Liberal Arts	MA	18,613	C
McDaniel College	MD	47,450	VC
McKendree Univ	IL	29,920	C+
McMurry Univ	TX	25,962	LC
McNeese State Univ	LA	2,649	C
McPherson College	KS	28,138	C
Mercer Univ	GA	44,201	VC
Mercy College	NY	30,456	C
Mercyhurst Univ	PA	40,700	C
Meredith College	NC	31,420	C
Merrimack College	MA	44,215	C
Messiah College	PA	40,690	C+
Methodist Univ	NC	37,185	C
Metropolitan State Univ of Denver	CO	4,835	LC
Miami Univ	OH	24,191	VC
Mich State Univ	MI	22,450	VC
MidAmerica Nazarene Univ	KS	28,000	C
Middle Tenn State Univ	TN	8,650	C
Middlebury College	VT	59,160	MC
Midland Univ	NE	34,000	C
Midwestern State Univ	TX	9,722	C
Millersville Univ of Pennsylvania	PA	21,648	C
Milligan College	TN	27,510	C
Millikin Univ	IL	38,940	C
Mills College	CA	54,119	VC
Millsaps College	MS	43,888	VC+
Minn State Univ, Mankato	MN	15,616	C
Minn State Univ, Moorhead	MN	13,392	VC
Minot State Univ	ND	10,915	C
Miss College	MS	21,998	C
Miss State Univ	MS	14,750	C
Miss Valley State Univ	MS	9,706	LC
Missouri Southern State Univ	MO	12,061	C
Missouri State Univ	MO	13,996	VC
Missouri Valley College	MO	22,200	C
Molloy College	NY	40,440	C
Monmouth College	IL	40,850	C
Monmouth Univ	NJ	44,108	C
Montana State Univ	MT	14,068	C
Montana State Univ-Billings	MT	12,425	LC
Montclair State Univ	NJ	22,614	C
Moravian College	PA	36,381	VC
Morehead State Univ	KY	10,900	C
Morehouse College	GA	39,412	C
Morgan State Univ	MD	14,500	VC
Morris College	SC	16,310	LC
Mount Holyoke College	MA	55,146	MC
Mount Mary Univ	WI	33,590	LC
Mount Mercy Univ	IA	35,320	C
Mount St. Mary College	NY	41,138	C
Mount St. Mary's Univ	MD	47,996	C
Mount St. Mary's College - Chalon Campus	CA	43,897	VC+
Mount Vernon Nazarene Univ	OH	29,590	C
Muhlenberg College	PA	52,837	HC
Murray State Univ	KY	15,304	C
Muskingum Univ	OH	30,502	C
National Univ	CA	14,730	SP
Nazareth College of Rochester	NY	43,028	C+
Nebr Wesleyan Univ	NE	29,774	C+
New College of Florida	FL	14,504	MC
New England College	NH	45,930	LC
New Jersey City Univ	NJ	21,456	LC
New Mexico Highlands Univ	NM	11,904	NC
New Mexico State Univ	NM	14,050	C
New York Inst of Technology	NY	45,010	VC
New York Univ	NY	61,470	MC
Newberry College	SC	26,850	LC
Newman Univ	KS	30,380	C+
Niagara Univ	NY	41,010	C
Nicholls State Univ	LA	7,095	C
Norfolk State Univ	VA	10,531	LC
N Car Agricultural and Technical State Univ	NC	13,365	LC
N Car Central Univ	NC	9,000	C
N Car State Univ	NC	16,202	HC
N Car Wesleyan College	NC	29,440	C
North Central College	IL	38,343	VC
N Dak State Univ	ND		C
North Park Univ	IL	30,130	C
Northeastern Illinois Univ	IL	10,318	LC
Northeastern State Univ	OK	8,615	VC
Northeastern Univ	MA	55,296	MC
Northern Arizona Univ	AZ	19,010	C
Northern Illinois Univ	IL	19,768	C
Northern Kentucky Univ	KY	21,134	C
Northern Mich Univ	MI	18,278	C
Northern State Univ - Aberdeen	SD	14,505	C
Northland College	WI	26,680	C
Northwest Missouri State Univ	MO	17,347	C
Northwestern College of Iowa	IA	36,240	C
Northwestern Okla State Univ	OK	7,275	NC
Northwestern Univ	IL	61,640	MC
Notre Dame de Namur Univ	CA	44,236	LC
Nova Southeastern Univ	FL	37,280	VC
Nyack College	NY	33,250	C
Oakland Univ	MI	19,391	C
Oberlin College	OH	61,788	MC
Occidental College	CA	60,972	MC
Oglala Lakota College	SD	2,000	NC
Oglethorpe Univ	GA	44,200	C+
Ohio Dominican Univ	OH	38,380	C+
Ohio Northern Univ	OH	42,075	VC
Ohio Univ	OH	21,080	C
Ohio Valley Univ	WV	17,752	C
Ohio Wesleyan Univ	OH	49,460	C+
Okla Baptist Univ	OK	28,202	C
Okla City Univ	OK	40,476	VC
Okla State Univ	OK	14,310	VC
Okla Wesleyan Univ	OK	21,300	C
Old Dominion Univ	VA	19,483	C
Olivet College	MI	19,984	LC
Olivet Nazarene Univ	IL	29,990	C
Oregon State Univ	OR	20,273	VC
Oswego / SUNY	NY	20,009	C
Ottawa Univ	KS	15,000	C
Otterbein College	OH	32,214	C
Ouachita Baptist Univ	AR	30,220	VC
Our Lady of the Lake Univ	TX	22,430	LC
Pace Univ	NY	53,367	C
Pacific Lutheran Univ	WA	46,760	C+
Pacific Univ	OR	49,626	C+
Paine College	GA	19,826	LC
Park Univ	MO	17,525	C
Pepperdine Univ	CA	55,372	HC+
Peru State College	NE	8,600	SC
Philander Smith College	AR	19,760	LC
Piedmont College	GA	30,136	C
Pittsburg State Univ	KS	12,032	C
Pitzer College	CA	54,988	MC
Point Loma Nazarene Univ	CA	41,006	C+
Pomona College	CA	57,680	MC
Pontifical Catholic Univ of PR	PR	7,310	
Portland State Univ	OR	18,672	C
Post Univ	CT	35,750	C
Prairie View A&M Univ	TX	15,205	LC
Presbyterian College	SC	42,678	C+
Prescott College	AZ	33,284	C
Princeton Univ	NJ	53,795	MC
Principia College	IL	35,140	C+
Providence College	RI	57,383	VC
Purdue Univ/Calumet	IN	14,336	C

ST = STATE $IS = IN-STATE COSTS   SR = SELECTOR RATING

School	ST	$IS	SR
Purdue Univ/West Lafayette	IN	20,024	HC
Queens College/The CUNY	NY	17,107	VC
Queens Univ of Charlotte	NC	39,543	C+
Quinnipiac Univ	CT	55,160	VC
Radford Univ	VA	17,766	LC
Ramapo College of New Jersey	NJ	24,938	C
Randolph College	VA	45,660	VC
Randolph-Macon College	VA	49,869	C+
Reed College	OR	57,780	MC
Regis College	MA	47,565	LC
Regis Univ	CO	41,318	C
Rhode Island College	RI	17,694	LC
Rhodes College	TN	51,900	HC+
Rice Univ	TX	43,288	MC
Rider Univ	NJ	45,720	C
Ripon College	WI	36,959	C+
Rivier Univ	NH	35,000	VC
Roanoke College	VA	49,976	C
Rockford College	IL	31,000	C
Rocky Mountain College	MT	32,242	C
Roger Williams Univ	RI	46,296	VC
Rollins College	FL	52,370	HC
Roosevelt Univ	IL	22,605	VC
Rosemont College	PA	42,350	C
Rowan Univ	NJ	24,022	VC+
Russell Sage College	NY	39,370	C
Rust College	MS	10,600	C
Rutgers, The State Univ of New Jersey/Camden Campus	NJ	25,121	C
Rutgers, The State Univ of New Jersey/New Brunswick	NJ	25,562	VC
Rutgers, The State Univ of New Jersey/Newark Campus	NJ	258,806	C
Sacred Heart Univ	CT	49,264	VC
Saginaw Valley State Univ	MI	17,369	C
St. Anselm College	NH	49,376	VC
St. Augustine's Univ	NC	14,000	C
St. Francis Univ	PA	30,029	LC
St. John's Univ	MN	47,984	C
St. Joseph's College	IN	36,500	C
St. Joseph's College of Maine	ME	31,580	C
St. Joseph's Univ	PA	55,006	VC
St. Leo Univ	FL	30,340	C
St. Louis Univ	MO	48,346	HC
St. Martin's Univ	WA	41,678	C
St. Mary's College	IN	45,160	C+
St. Mary's College of Calif	CA	53,550	C
St. Mary's Univ	TX	33,854	C
St. Mary's Univ of Minn	MN	38,280	C
St. Michael's College	VT	49,975	VC
St. Paul's College	VA	16,030	NC
St. Peter's Univ	NJ	44,240	C
St. Vincent College	PA	40,244	C
St. Xavier Univ	IL	32,840	C
Salem College	NC	29,326	VC
Salem State Univ	MA	13,161	LC
Salisbury Univ	MD	19,180	VC
Salve Regina Univ	RI	48,550	VC
Sam Houston State Univ	TX	17,082	C
Samford Univ	AL	37,060	C+
San Diego State Univ	CA	21,611	C+
San Francisco State Univ	CA	18,514	C
San Jose State Univ	CA	19,133	LC
Sarah Lawrence College	NY	48,000	HC
Savannah State Univ	GA	13,156	C
Scripps College	CA	61,940	MC
Seattle Pacific Univ	WA	41,559	VC+
Seattle Univ	WA	49,035	VC+
Seton Hall Univ	NJ	45,902	C
Seton Hill Univ	PA	35,172	C
Shaw Univ	NC	15,488	C
Shawnee State Univ	OH	16,916	C
Shenandoah Univ	VA	39,916	C
Shepherd Univ	WV	15,875	C
Shippensburg Univ of Pennsylvania	PA	20,934	C
Shorter Univ	GA	30,650	LC
Siena College	NY	43,863	VC
Simmons College	MA	49,966	VC
Simpson College	IA	36,082	C
Skidmore College	NY	59,942	HC
Slippery Rock Univ of Pennsylvania	PA	10,360	C
Smith College	MA	59,674	MC
Sonoma State Univ	CA	20,541	C
S Car State Univ	SC	6,700	LC
S Dak State Univ	SD	14,296	C
Southeastern Louisiana Univ	LA	13,325	C
Southeastern Okla State Univ	OK	7,966	LC
Southern Arkansas Univ	AR	14,316	C
Southern Conn State Univ	CT	18,033	LC
Southern Illinois Univ Carbondale	IL	21,942	C
Southern Illinois Univ Edwardsville	IL	17,532	C
Southern Methodist Univ	TX	60,585	MC
Southern Nazarene Univ	OK	24,354	C
Southern Oregon Univ	OR	17,874	C
Southern Univ and A&M College	LA	9,761	LC
Southern Univ at New Orleans	LA	2,963	NC
Southwest Baptist Univ	MO	24,710	C
Southwest Minn State Univ	MN	14,000	C
Southwestern Univ	TX	45,660	VC
Spelman College	GA	24,650	C
Spring Arbor Univ	MI	26,740	C
Spring Hill College	AL	44,164	VC
Springfield College	MA	25,000	C
St. Ambrose Univ	IA	30,845	C
St. Bonaventure Univ	NY	41,575	C
St. Catherine Univ	MN	37,782	C+
St. Cloud State Univ	MN	10,600	C
St. Edward's Univ	TX	47,784	C
St. Francis College	NY	34,200	C
St. John Fisher College	NY	40,708	C+
St. John's Univ	NY	55,070	C+
St. Joseph's College, New York/Brooklyn Campus	NY	22,630	C
St. Joseph's College, New York/Suffolk Campus	NY	22,630	C
St. Lawrence Univ	NY	59,972	VC
St. Mary's College of Maryland	MD	25,754	VC
St. Norbert College	WI	41,478	VC
St. Olaf College	MN	51,200	HC+
Stanford Univ	CA	58,388	MC
SUNY at Purchase	NY	16,951	C
SUNY Polytechnic Inst	NY	19,690	C
SUNY/Empire State College	NY	6,315	SP
Stephen F. Austin State Univ	TX	14,668	C
Stetson Univ	FL	51,516	VC
Stonehill College	MA	46,780	HC
Stony Brook Univ / SUNY	NY	20,078	HC+
Suffolk Univ	MA	47,298	C
SUNY College at Geneseo	NY	18,670	HC
SUNY College at Old Westbury	NY	16,324	C
SUNY Cortland/The SUNY	NY	19,759	C+
SUNY Fredonia/The SUNY at Fredonia	NY	19,840	VC
SUNY New Paltz	NY	14,348	C
SUNY Oneonta / SUNY	NY	16,919	C+
SUNY Plattsburgh / SUNY	NY	18,083	C
Susquehanna Univ	PA	51,150	C
Swarthmore College	PA	57,870	MC
Syracuse Univ	NY	56,346	VC
Tabor College	KS	29,010	C
Talladega College	AL	17,996	C
Tarleton State Univ	TX	13,489	LC
Taylor Univ	IN	37,821	VC+
Temple Univ	PA	24,392	VC
Tenn State Univ	TN	9,048	C
Tenn Tech Univ	TN	11,310	C
Texas A&M Univ	TX	19,207	VC
Texas A&M Univ at Commerce	TX	10,496	C
Texas A&M Univ at Corpus Christi	TX	11,544	LC
Texas A&M Univ at Kingsville	TX	7,500	LC
Texas Christian Univ	TX	49,980	HC
Texas Lutheran Univ	TX	36,040	C
Texas Southern Univ	TX	18,212	LC
Texas State Univ	TX	17,128	C
Texas Tech Univ	TX	14,243	C
Texas Wesleyan Univ	TX	31,382	C
Texas Woman's Univ	TX	13,633	LC
The Catholic Univ of America	DC	52,852	VC
The College of New Rochelle	NY	33,600	VC
The College of St. Rose	NY	26,750	C
The Lincoln Univ	PA	15,161	LC
Ohio State Univ-Columbus Campus	OH	19,887	HC+
The Pennsylvania State Univ - Univ Park	PA	28,022	VC+
The SUNY at Potsdam	NY	18,473	C
The SUNY/College at Brockport	NY	19,002	C
The Univ of Memphis	TN	15,094	C
The Univ of N Car at Greensboro	NC	12,848	C
The Univ of N Car at Pembroke	NC	13,388	LC
The Univ of Okla	OK	18,621	VC
The Univ of Tenn at Chattanooga	TN	16,883	C
The Univ of Utah	UT	16,463	VC
Thiel College	PA	38,728	LC
Thomas Edison State College	NJ	5,700	SP
Thomas More College	KY	34,760	C
Tougaloo College	MS	15,275	NC
Touro College	NY	27,959	VC
Towson Univ	MD	16,000	VC
Transylvania Univ	KY	42,660	VC+
Trevecca Nazarene Univ	TN	31,186	C
Trinity Christian College	IL	28,869	C
Trinity College	CT	65,050	MC
Trinity Univ	TX	48,150	HC+
Trinity Washington Univ	DC	30,250	C+
Troy Univ	AL	10,650	C
Truman State Univ	MO	15,541	HC
Tufts Univ	MA	58,780	MC
Tulane Univ	LA	60,861	MC
Tuskegee Univ	AL	26,750	C
Union College	KY	29,955	C
Union College	NY	60,240	MC
Union Univ	TN	28,260	VC
Universidad del Turabo	PR	4,110	
Universidad Metropolitana	PR	3,500	
Univ at Albany / SUNY	NY	18,674	VC
Univ at Buffalo / The SUNY	NY	20,283	VC
Univ of Akron	OH	20,436	C
Univ of Alabama at Birmingham	AL	18,484	C+
Univ of Alabama in Huntsville	AL	17,591	VC+
Univ of Alaska Anchorage	AK	16,673	NC
Univ of Alaska Fairbanks	AK	15,130	C
Univ of Arizona	AZ	20,657	C
Univ of Arkansas at Fayetteville	AR	18,352	C+
Univ of Arkansas at Little Rock	AR	17,609	LC
Univ of Arkansas at Pine Bluff	AR	13,378	C
Univ of Calif at Berkeley	CA	23,322	MC
Univ of Calif at Davis	CA		HC
Univ of Calif at Irvine	CA	25,961	VC
Univ of Calif at Los Angeles	CA	25,686	MC
Univ of Calif at Riverside	CA	27,204	C+
Univ of Calif at San Diego	CA	21,000	VC
Univ of Calif at Santa Barbara	CA	27,551	HC
Univ of Calif at Santa Cruz	CA	27,807	C+
Univ of Central Arkansas	AR	13,667	VC
Univ of Central Florida	FL	15,668	VC+
Univ of Central Missouri	MO	14,605	C
Univ of Central Okla	OK	12,293	C
Univ of Chicago	IL	55,416	MC
Univ of Cincinnati	OH	21,506	VC
Univ of Colo at Colo Springs	CO	15,000	VC
Univ of Colo Boulder	CO	22,605	VC+
Univ of Colo Denver	CO	17,904	C
Univ of Conn	CT	24,706	HC
Univ of Dayton	OH	49,070	VC
Univ of Delaware	DE	23,612	VC
Univ of Denver	CO	51,787	VC+
Univ of Detroit Mercy	MI	30,450	VC
Univ of Dubuque	IA	30,200	C
Univ of Evansville	IN	42,656	VC+
Univ of Findlay	OH	31,916	C
Univ of Florida	FL	15,943	HC
Univ of Georgia	GA	20,082	VC
Univ of Great Falls	MT	27,970	C
Univ of Hartford	CT	42,674	C
Univ of Hawaii at Hilo	HI	23,066	C
Univ of Hawaii at Manoa	HI	19,379	C
Univ of Houston-Downtown	TX	15,170	LC
Univ of Idaho	ID	14,558	C
Univ of Illinois at Chicago	IL	24,505	VC
Univ of Illinois at Urbana-Champaign	IL	26,450	HC
Univ of Indianapolis	IN	31,740	LC
Univ of Iowa	IA	17,693	VC
Univ of Kansas	KS	17,603	C+
Univ of Kentucky	KY	19,868	C
Univ of La Verne	CA	47,010	C
Univ of Louisiana at Lafayette	LA	6,130	C
Univ of Louisiana at Monroe	LA	12,998	C
Univ of Louisville	KY	17,946	C
Univ of Maine	ME	19,902	C+
Univ of Mary Hardin-Baylor	TX	31,950	C+
Univ of Mary Washington	VA	19,484	VC
Univ of Maryland - College Park	MD	20,060	HC
Univ of Maryland/Baltimore County	MD	18,000	VC
Univ of Maryland/Eastern Shore	MD	14,000	VC
Univ of Mass Amherst	MA	24,215	VC+
Univ of Mass Boston	MA	23,066	VC
Univ of Mass Dartmouth	MA	22,223	C
Univ of Mass Lowell	MA	19,316	C
Univ of Miami	FL	57,034	MC
Univ of Mich/Ann Arbor	MI	22,102	MC
Univ of Mich/Dearborn	MI	9,885	VC
Univ of Mich-Flint	MI	17,547	C+
Univ of Minn/Duluth	MN	19,806	C
Univ of Minn/Morris	MN	17,150	VC
Univ of Minn/Twin Cities	MN		NC
Univ of Miss	MS	16,704	C+
Univ of Missouri/Columbia	MO	18,201	MC
Univ of Missouri-Kansas City	MO	19,603	C
Univ of Missouri-St. Louis	MO		VC
Univ of Mobile	AL	28,935	VC
Univ of Montana	MT	14,105	C
Univ of Montana-Western	MT	9,753	LC
Univ of Montevallo	AL	17,060	VC
Univ of Mount Union	OH	35,130	VC
Univ of Nebr - Lincoln	NE	18,031	VC
Univ of Nebr at Kearney	NE	14,855	LC
Univ of Nebr at Omaha	NE	12,700	C
Univ of Nevada, Las Vegas	NV	17,303	VC
Univ of Nevada/Reno	NV	17,507	C
Univ of New England	ME	46,750	C
Univ of New Hampshire	NH	26,912	C
Univ of New Mexico	NM	15,300	C
Univ of New Orleans	LA	9,224	C
Univ of North Alabama	AL	9,960	C
Univ of N Car at Asheville	NC	13,500	VC
Univ of N Car at Chapel Hill	NC	18,928	NC
Univ of N Car at Charlotte	NC	15,547	C
Univ of N Car at Wilmington	NC	13,572	VC
Univ of N Dak	ND	14,551	C
Univ of North Florida	FL	15,870	VC
Univ of North Georgia	GA	8,500	C
Univ of North Texas	TX	15,628	C
Univ of Northern Colo	CO	18,446	C
Univ of Northern Iowa	IA	15,795	C
Univ of Notre Dame	IN	57,117	MC
Univ of Oregon	OR	21,360	C+
Univ of Pennsylvania	PA	61,132	MC
Univ of Pikeville	KY	25,500	NC
Univ of Pittsburgh at Bradford	PA	21,802	C
Univ of Pittsburgh at Johnstown	PA	20,862	LC
Univ of Pittsburgh at Pittsburgh	PA	28,572	HC+
Univ of Portland	OR	49,964	VC
Univ of PR Recinto de Rio Piedras	PR	5,750	
Univ of PR/Mayaguez	PR	1,250	
Univ of Puget Sound	WA	54,608	HC
Univ of Redlands	CA	40,500	VC
Univ of Rio Grande	OH	8,750	NC
Univ of St. Francis	IN	29,810	C
Univ of St. Mary	KS	28,400	C+
Univ of San Diego	CA	54,818	HC+
Univ of San Francisco	CA	54,770	VC
Univ of Science and Arts of Okla	OK	10,560	VC
Univ of Scranton	PA	51,940	VC
Univ of Sioux Falls	SD	22,990	C
Univ of South Alabama	AL	13,510	C
Univ of S Car Aiken	SC	16,712	C
Univ of S Car at Columbia	SC	19,725	VC+
Univ of S Car Upstate	SC	18,200	LC
Univ of S Dak	SD	15,111	C
Univ of South Florida/Tampa	FL	13,000	C
Univ of Southern Calif	CA	56,903	MC
Univ of Southern Indiana	IN	14,885	C
Univ of Southern Maine	ME	16,576	C
Univ of Southern Miss	MS	13,170	C
Univ of Tampa	FL	35,160	VC
Univ of Tenn at Knoxville	TN	20,364	VC+
Univ of Tenn at Martin	TN	13,734	C
Univ of Texas - Pan American	TX	11,125	LC
Univ of Texas at Arlington	TX	10,908	LC
Univ of Texas at Austin	TX	44,074	HC
Univ of Texas at Dallas	TX	21,348	HC+
Univ of Texas at El Paso	TX	8,764	NC
Univ of Texas at San Antonio	TX	18,372	C
Univ of the District of Columbia	DC	7,244	LC
Univ of the Incarnate Word	TX	37,316	LC
Univ of the Ozarks	AR	31,440	C
Univ of the Pacific	CA	52,146	VC
Univ of the Southwest	NM	15,000	C
Univ of Toledo	OH	18,464	C
Univ of Tulsa	OK	46,331	MC
Univ of Vermont	VT	27,006	VC+
Univ of Virginia	VA	23,050	MC
Univ of Washington	WA	14,722	VC
Univ of West Alabama	AL	14,274	C
Univ of West Georgia	GA	15,488	C
Univ of Wisc Whitewater	WI	13,314	C
Univ of Wisc/Eau Claire	WI	15,730	VC
Univ of Wisc/La Crosse	WI	9,304	VC
Univ of Wisc/Madison	WI	18,757	HC+
Univ of Wisc/Oshkosh	WI	10,426	C
Univ of Wisc/Parkside	WI	10,181	LC
Univ of Wisc/River Falls	WI	9,722	LC
Univ of Wisc/Stevens Point	WI	14,043	C
Univ of Wisc/Superior	WI	14,314	C
Univ of Wisc-Milwaukee	WI	18,436	C
Univ of Wyoming	WY	14,401	C+
Upper Iowa Univ	IA	30,426	NC
Urbana Univ	OH	30,820	C
Ursinus College	PA	57,580	VC
Ursuline College	OH	33,198	LC
Utah State Univ	UT	12,044	C
Utica College	NY	45,670	C
Valparaiso Univ	IN	44,940	VC+
Vanderbilt Univ	TN	58,220	MC
Vanguard Univ of Southern Calif	CA	35,833	VC
Vassar College	NY	61,140	MC
Villanova Univ	PA	58,394	VC
Virginia Commonwealth Univ	VA	21,716	C
Virginia Polytechnic Inst and State Univ	VA	14,629	HC
Virginia State Univ	VA	11,318	C+
Virginia Union Univ	VA	18,432	C
Virginia Wesleyan College	VA	28,433	LC
Viterbo Univ	WI	30,070	C
Voorhees College	SC	18,126	C
Wagner College	NY	48,600	C+
Wake Forest Univ	NC	58,838	MC
Walla Walla Univ	WA	26,256	NC
Walsh Univ	OH	35,100	C
Warner Pacific College	OR	25,550	C
Warren Wilson College	NC	40,132	VC
Wartburg College	IA	41,055	VC
Washburn Univ	KS	12,579	C
Washington and Jefferson College	PA	51,948	VC

ST = STATE $IS = IN-STATE COSTS   SR = SELECTOR RATING

School	ST	$IS	SR
Washington and Lee Univ	VA	52,812	MC
Washington College	MD	52,602	VC
Washington State Univ	WA	20,461	C
Wayland Baptist Univ	TX	18,912	LC
Wayne State College	NE	11,764	NC
Wayne State Univ	MI	22,063	C
Waynesburg Univ	PA	30,150	C
Webster Univ	MO	35,100	C+
Wellesley College	MA	59,038	MC
Wells College	NY	49,400	VC
Wesleyan Univ	CT	61,198	MC
West Chester Univ of Pennsylvania	PA	17,186	C
West Liberty Univ	WV	9,142	LC
West Texas A&M Univ	TX	13,478	C
West Virginia State Univ	WV	8,378	NC
West Virginia Univ	WV	16,542	C+
West Virginia Wesleyan College	WV	26,880	C
Western Carolina Univ	NC	13,965	C
Western Conn State Univ	CT	18,327	LC
Western Illinois Univ	IL	20,732	C
Western Kentucky Univ	KY	11,000	LC
Western Mich Univ	MI	19,628	C
Western New England Univ	MA	46,154	C+
Western New Mexico Univ	NM	8,500	LC
Western Oregon Univ	OR	15,021	C
Western State Colo Univ	CO	16,924	C
Western Washington Univ	WA	18,519	VC
Westfield State Univ	MA	18,297	C
Westminster College	MO	31,720	VC
Westminster College	PA	31,290	C+
Westminster College	UT	37,708	C+
Westmont College	CA	41,500	HC
Wheaton College	IL	40,720	MC
Wheaton College	MA	54,934	MC+
Whitman College	WA	55,988	MC
Whittier College	CA	43,416	C
Whitworth Univ	WA	47,734	VC
Wichita State Univ	KS	14,607	C+
Widener Univ	PA	52,418	C
Wilberforce Univ	OH	15,100	LC
Wiley College	TX		LC
Wilkes Univ	PA	44,070	C
Williams College	MA	61,070	MC
Wilmington College	OH	29,784	C
Wilson College	PA	35,080	C
Wingate Univ	NC	34,990	C
Winona State Univ	MN	16,640	C
Winston-Salem State Univ	NC	9,418	LC
Winthrop Univ	SC	21,120	C
Wittenberg Univ	OH	47,962	C+
Wofford College	SC	45,795	VC
Worcester State Univ	MA	19,812	C
Wright State Univ	OH	16,983	C
Xavier Univ	OH	44,980	VC
Xavier Univ of Louisiana	LA	25,300	C
Yale Univ	CT	55,300	MC
Yeshiva Univ	NY	47,250	VC+
York College / The CUNY	NY	5,496	VC
York College of Pennsylvania	PA	26,590	C
Youngstown State Univ	OH	16,732	C

SOFTWARE ENGINEERING

School	ST	$IS	SR
Allegheny College	PA	50,980	HC
Arizona State Univ, at the Polytechnic Campus	AZ	20,531	C+
Auburn Univ	AL	22,378	VC+
Baldwin Wallace Univ	OH	38,318	C
Butler Univ	IN	47,572	VC+
Calif Polytechnic State Univ	CA	19,847	HC
Central Washington Univ	WA	11,730	C
Chapman Univ	CA	58,347	VC+
Clarkson Univ	NY	57,330	HC
Drexel Univ	PA	61,418	VC+
Embry-Riddle Aeronautical Univ - Daytona Beach	FL	40,884	C+
Embry-Riddle Aeronautical Univ - Prescott Campus	AZ	40,444	VC+
Fairfield Univ	CT	56,960	VC
Florida Inst of Technology	FL	48,290	VC
Gannon Univ	PA	39,608	C
George Mason Univ	VA	15,724	VC
Husson Univ	ME	24,194	LC
Indiana Inst of Technology	IN	34,240	LC
Keene State College	NH	23,232	LC
Kutztown Univ of Pennsylvania	PA	16,909	LC
Lipscomb Univ	TN	37,490	VC
Loyola Univ Chicago	IL	51,646	VC+
Miami Univ	OH	24,191	VC
Mich Tech Univ	MI	23,556	HC
Milwaukee School of Engineering	WI	39,948	VC+
Monmouth Univ	NJ	44,108	C
National Univ	CA	14,730	SP
Okla City Univ	OK	40,476	VC
Oswego / SUNY	NY	20,009	VC
Purdue Univ/West Lafayette	IN	20,024	HC
Quinnipiac Univ	CT	55,160	VC
Rochester Inst of Technology	NY	42,450	VC

School	ST	$IS	SR
Rose-Hulman Inst of Technology	IN	53,340	MC
San Jose State Univ	CA	19,133	LC
Shippensburg Univ of Pennsylvania	PA	20,934	C
S Dak State Univ	SD	14,296	C
Southern Polytechnic State Univ	GA	13,958	C
Univ of Calif at Irvine	CA	25,961	VC
Univ of Mass Dartmouth	MA	22,223	C
Univ of Miami	FL	57,034	MC
Univ of Mich/Dearborn	MI	9,885	VC
Univ of Minn Crookston	MN	17,834	C
Univ of N Car at Charlotte	NC	15,547	C
Univ of Texas at Dallas	TX	21,348	HC+
Univ of Wisc/Platteville	WI	14,564	C
Vermont Technical College	VT	15,751	C

SOIL SCIENCE

School	ST	$IS	SR
Alabama A&M Univ	AL	10,084	C
Auburn Univ	AL	22,378	VC+
Calif Polytechnic State Univ	CA	19,847	HC
Clemson Univ	SC	19,136	HC
Colo State Univ-Fort Collins	CO	20,385	VC
Eastern Oregon Univ	OR	10,400	C
Mich State Univ	MI	22,450	VC
New Mexico State Univ	NM	14,050	C
N Car State Univ	NC	16,202	HC
N Dak State Univ	ND		C
Okla State Univ	OK	14,310	VC
Purdue Univ/West Lafayette	IN	20,024	HC
SUNY / College of Environmental Science and Forestry	NY	18,351	VC
Tenn Tech Univ	TN	11,310	C
Texas A&M Univ at Kingsville	TX	7,500	LC
Univ of Arizona	AZ	20,657	C
Univ of Arkansas at Fayetteville	AR	18,352	C+
Univ of Calif at Davis	CA		HC
Univ of Calif at Riverside	CA	27,204	C+
Univ of Delaware	DE	23,612	VC
Univ of Florida	FL	15,943	HC
Univ of Georgia	GA	20,082	VC
Univ of Hawaii at Manoa	HI	19,379	C
Univ of Idaho	ID	14,558	C
Univ of Mass Amherst	MA	24,215	VC+
Univ of Missouri/Columbia	MO	18,201	MC
Univ of Tenn at Knoxville	TN	20,364	VC+
Univ of Wisc/Madison	WI	18,757	HC+
Univ of Wisc/Platteville	WI	14,564	C
Univ of Wisc/River Falls	WI	9,722	LC
Univ of Wisc/Stevens Point	WI	14,043	C
Utah State Univ	UT	12,044	C
Virginia Polytechnic Inst and State Univ	VA	14,629	HC
Washington State Univ	WA	20,461	C
West Texas A&M Univ	TX	13,478	C

SOUTH ASIAN STUDIES

School	ST	$IS	SR
Appalachian State Univ	NC	12,919	VC
Binghamton Univ/The SUNY	NY	21,648	HC+
Brown Univ	RI	59,428	MC
Indiana Univ Bloomington	IN	19,801	VC
Middlebury College	VT	59,160	MC
Mount Holyoke College	MA	55,146	MC
Oakland Univ	MI	19,391	C
Univ of Calif at Berkeley	CA	23,322	MC
Univ of Calif at Los Angeles	CA	25,686	MC
Univ of Chicago	IL	55,416	MC
Univ of Minn/Twin Cities	MN		HC
Univ of Pennsylvania	PA	61,132	MC
Univ of Washington	WA	14,722	VC
Washington Univ in St. Louis	MO	69,844	MC
Yale Univ	CT	55,300	MC

SOUTHWEST AMERICAN STUDIES

School	ST	$IS	SR
Colo College	CO	57,162	MC
Fort Lewis College	CO	15,513	C

SPANISH

School	ST	$IS	SR
Abilene Christian Univ	TX	38,400	C+
Adams State Univ	CO	13,358	LC
Adelphi Univ	NY	44,670	VC
Adrian College	MI	42,400	C
Agnes Scott College	GA	45,323	C+
Alabama State Univ	AL	14,142	NC
Albany State Univ	GA	8,500	C
Albion College	MI	46,010	C
Albright College	PA	46,660	C
Alfred Univ	NY	41,770	C
Allegheny College	PA	50,980	HC
Alma College	MI	44,075	C
American International College	MA	36,100	LC
American Univ	DC	56,015	HC+
Amherst College	MA	58,744	MC
Anderson Univ	IN	36,100	C
Andrews Univ	MI	28,030	C+
Angelo State Univ	TX	15,049	NC

School	ST	$IS	SR
Appalachian State Univ	NC	12,919	VC
Aquinas College	MI	33,060	C
Arizona State Univ, at the Tempe Campus	AZ	20,137	C+
Arizona State Univ, at the West Campus	AZ	19,251	C+
Armstrong State Univ	GA	15,532	C
Asbury Univ	KY	32,038	VC
Ashland Univ	OH	25,000	C
Assumption College	MA	47,122	C+
Auburn Univ	AL	22,378	VC+
Augsburg College	MN	35,142	C
Augustana College	IL	43,398	VC
Augustana College	SD	36,500	VC
Aurora Univ	IL	33,228	C
Austin College	TX	45,875	HC
Azusa Pacific Univ	CA	42,086	C
Baker Univ	KS	33,350	C+
Baldwin Wallace Univ	OH	38,318	C
Ball State Univ	IN	17,850	C
Bard College	NY	61,940	MC
Barnard College/Columbia Univ	NY	39,000	MC
Barry Univ	FL	38,190	C
Bates College	ME	60,720	MC
Baylor Univ	TX	50,329	HC
Bellarmine Univ	KY	42,950	VC
Belmont Univ	TN	39,190	VC+
Beloit College	WI	49,970	VC
Bemidji State Univ	MN	13,500	C
Benedictine College	KS	29,180	VC
Benedictine Univ	IL	37,820	C
Bennington College	VT	56,990	HC+
Berea College	KY	7,192	C
Berry College	GA	39,254	VC
Bethany College	WV	35,282	LC
Bethel College	IN	31,560	C
Bethel Univ	MN	34,940	VC
Binghamton Univ/The SUNY	NY	21,648	HC+
Biola Univ	CA	40,320	C+
Birmingham-Southern College	AL	44,168	VC+
Black Hills State Univ	SD	13,947	C
Blackburn College	IL	21,350	C
Bloomsburg Univ of Pennsylvania	PA	13,598	C
Bluffton Univ	OH	38,948	C
Boise State Univ	ID	13,469	LC
Boston Univ	MA	60,694	MC
Bowdoin College	ME	59,568	MC
Bowling Green State Univ	OH	18,970	C
Bradley Univ	IL	31,874	VC
Brandeis Univ	MA		MC
Brescia Univ	KY	26,140	VC+
Briar Cliff Univ	IA	29,514	C
Bridgewater College	VA	41,450	C
Bridgewater State Univ	MA	18,752	C
Brigham Young Univ	UT	12,100	HC
Bryan College	TN	24,194	C
Bryant Univ	RI	49,179	VC
Bryn Mawr College	PA	59,890	MC
Bucknell Univ	PA	60,140	MC
Buena Vista Univ	IA	39,188	C
Buffalo State College / SUNY	NY	15,733	C+
Butler Univ	IN	47,572	VC+
Cabrini College	PA	40,859	LC
Caldwell College	NJ	35,602	NC
Calif Baptist Univ	CA	38,792	C
Calif Lutheran Univ	CA	49,540	C+
Calif State Polytechnic Univ, Pomona	CA	20,156	C
Cal State, Bakersfield	CA	8,000	C
Cal State, Chico	CA	20,158	C
Cal State, Dominguez Hills	CA	17,090	LC
Cal State, East Bay	CA	16,549	C
Cal State, Fresno	CA	17,405	C
Cal State, Fullerton	CA	25,188	C
Cal State, Long Beach	CA	17,502	C+
Cal State, Los Angeles	CA	17,186	LC
Cal State, Monterey Bay	CA	26,871	LC
Cal State, Northridge	CA	28,690	LC
Cal State, Sacramento	CA	16,200	C
Cal State, San Bernardino	CA	12,000	C
Cal State, San Marcos	CA	14,576	LC
Cal State, Stanislaus	CA	18,582	C
Calif Univ of Pennsylvania	PA	14,217	C
Calvin College	MI	39,120	VC
Campbell Univ	NC	37,570	VC
Canisius College	NY	44,900	C
Capital Univ	OH	41,050	VC
Cardinal Stritch Univ	WI	24,054	C
Carleton College	MN	60,102	MC
Carlow Univ	PA	30,272	C
Carnegie Mellon Univ	PA	51,260	MC
Carroll College	MT	28,000	C
Carroll Univ	WI	38,100	C
Carson-Newman Univ	TN	29,058	C+
Carthage College	WI	33,000	C
Case Western Reserve Univ	OH	56,534	MC
Castleton State College	VT	20,186	C
Catawba College	NC	37,240	LC
Cedarville Univ	OH	32,860	VC
Centenary College of Louisiana	LA	45,650	C+
Central College	IA	42,104	C+
Central Conn State Univ	CT	19,749	C

School	ST	$IS	SR
Central Methodist Univ	MO	28,240	VC
Central Univ of Bayamon	PR	3,350	
Central Washington Univ	WA	11,730	C
Centre College	KY	35,000	HC+
Chapman Univ	CA	58,347	VC+
Charleston Southern Univ	SC	22,420	C
Chatham Univ	PA	43,797	C
Chestnut Hill College	PA	42,110	LC
Chicago State Univ	IL	5,482	C
Christopher Newport Univ	VA	21,960	VC
Citadel, The	SC		C
CUNY/Baruch College	NY		HC
CUNY/Brooklyn College	NY	5,884	C
CUNY/City College	NY	20,319	HC+
Claremont McKenna College	CA	62,215	MC
Clarion Univ of Pennsylvania	PA	17,370	LC
Clark Univ	MA	47,020	HC+
Clarke Univ	IA	37,600	C
Clemson Univ	SC	19,136	HC
Cleveland State Univ	OH	21,776	C
Coastal Carolina Univ	SC	18,580	C
Coe College	IA	45,550	VC
Coker College	SC	32,256	LC
Colby College	ME	57,510	MC
Colgate Univ	NY	58,135	MC
College of Charleston	SC	22,145	VC
College of Mount St. Vincent	NY	41,040	MC
College of New Jersey	NJ	25,376	HC
College of St. Benedict	MN	49,359	VC
College of St. Elizabeth	NJ	43,839	LC
College of St. Mary	NE	35,184	C
College of Staten Island/The City of New Yok	NY	16,778	NC
College of the Holy Cross	MA	58,042	MC
College of the Ozarks	MO		VC
College of Wooster	OH	52,600	VC
Colo Mesa Univ	CO	17,690	LC
Colo State Univ-Fort Collins	CO	20,385	VC
Colo State Univ-Pueblo	CO	16,183	C
Columbia College	SC	27,882	C
Columbia Univ/City of New York	NY	61,116	MC
Columbia Univ/School of General Studies	NY	58,231	MC
Columbus State Univ	GA	13,176	C
Concordia College - Moorhead	MN	39,974	VC
Concordia Univ Texas	TX	23,640	C
Concordia Univ Wisc	WI	28,980	C
Concordia Univ, Ann Arbor	MI	27,220	VC
Converse College	SC	37,130	C
Cornell College	IA	44,930	VC
Cornell Univ	NY	60,964	MC
Covenant College	GA	38,990	VC+
Daemen College	NY	34,770	C
Dartmouth College	NH	57,996	MC
Davidson College	NC	58,146	MC
De Sales Univ	PA	43,970	C
Delaware State Univ	DE	16,722	LC
Denison Univ	OH	54,670	HC+
DePaul Univ	IL	47,623	VC
DePauw Univ	IN	48,950	VC+
Dickinson College	PA	57,662	HC+
Dickinson State Univ	ND	11,900	NC
Doane College	NE	35,230	C
Dominican College	NY	31,270	LC
Dominican Univ	IL	37,628	C
Dordt College	IA	34,160	C+
Drew Univ/College of Liberal Arts	NJ	57,516	C
Drury Univ	MO	31,909	VC
Duke Univ	NC	50,250	MC
Duquesne Univ	PA	43,720	VC
Earlham College	IN	51,470	HC
East Stroudsburg Univ of Pennsylvania	PA	18,868	LC
East Texas Baptist Univ	TX	31,577	LC
Eastern Conn State Univ	CT	20,584	C
Eastern Kentucky Univ	KY	11,161	C
Eastern Mennonite Univ	VA	40,660	C
Eastern Mich Univ	MI	18,604	C
Eastern Nazarene College	MA	30,000	C
Eastern New Mexico Univ	NM	10,682	C
Eastern Univ	PA	37,704	C
Eastern Washington Univ	WA		C
Eckerd College	FL	43,902	C
Edgewood College	WI	33,294	C
Elizabethtown College	PA	49,740	VC
Elmhurst College	IL	43,336	C
Elmira College	NY	49,950	C+
Elms College	MA	33,900	C
Elon Univ	NC	41,914	VC+
Emmanuel College	MA	47,985	VC
Emory Univ	GA	56,368	MC
Evangel Univ	MO	23,090	C
Fairfield Univ	CT	56,960	VC
Fayetteville State Univ	NC	10,816	C
Ferrum College	VA	27,740	LC
Fisk Univ	TN	19,830	C
Flagler College	FL	25,180	C
Florida Atlantic Univ	FL	17,339	C
Florida Gulf Coast Univ	FL		C
Florida International Univ	FL	17,747	C+
Florida Southern College	FL	40,150	C
Florida State Univ	FL	16,715	VC
Fordham Univ	NY	61,588	HC+

ST = STATE　　　$IS = IN-STATE COSTS　　　SR = SELECTOR RATING

School	ST	$IS	SR
Fort Hays State Univ	KS	11,354	C
Fort Lewis College	CO	15,513	C
Franciscan Univ of Steubenville	OH	27,320	VC
Franklin and Marshall College	PA	60,799	MC
Franklin College	IN	36,585	C
Fresno Pacific Univ	CA	32,136	C
Friends Univ	KS	29,100	C
Furman Univ	SC	54,006	HC
Gallaudet Univ	DC	25,380	SP
Gardner-Webb Univ	NC	34,375	C+
Geneva College	PA	27,280	C
George Fox Univ	OR	40,750	C+
George Mason Univ	VA	15,724	C
George Washington Univ	DC	57,108	MC
Georgetown College	KY	41,440	C+
Georgetown Univ	DC	52,910	MC
Georgia College and State Univ	GA	18,900	C+
Georgia State Univ	GA	15,582	VC
Georgian Court Univ	NJ	41,594	LC
Gettysburg College	PA	58,820	HC
Gonzaga Univ	WA	46,441	HC
Gordon College	MA	44,320	VC
Goshen College	IN	35,900	C
Goucher College	MD	52,040	VC+
Grace College and Seminary	IN	28,800	VC
Graceland Univ	IA	28,020	C
Grand Valley State Univ	MI	17,998	C+
Greensboro College	NC	28,740	LC
Greenville College	IL	27,012	C
Grinnell College	IA	53,654	VC
Grove City College	PA	24,022	VC
Guilford College	NC	42,800	C
Gustavus Adolphus College	MN	48,170	HC
Hamline Univ	MN	45,678	VC
Hampden-Sydney College	VA	51,758	C
Hanover College	IN	43,073	C+
Harding Univ	AR	23,556	C
Hardin-Simmons Univ	TX	23,560	C
Hartwick College	NY	51,270	C
Harvard College/Harvard Univ	MA	49,000	MC
Hastings College	NE	27,782	C+
Haverford College	PA	61,564	MC
Heidelberg Univ	OH	34,100	C
Henderson State Univ	AR	14,584	C
Hendrix College	AR	50,202	VC+
High Point Univ	NC	39,800	C
Hillsdale College	MI	32,866	MC
Hiram College	OH	37,300	VC
Hofstra Univ	NY	51,810	VC+
Hollins Univ	VA	43,295	VC
Hood College	MD	45,730	C
Hope College	MI	38,650	VC
Houghton College	NY	36,808	C+
Houston Baptist Univ	TX	36,450	C
Howard Payne Univ	TX	17,115	C
Howard Univ	DC	13,646	C
Humboldt State Univ	CA	18,400	C
Hunter College	NY	14,429	VC
Idaho State Univ	ID	12,307	C
Illinois College	IL	25,770	VC
Illinois State Univ	IL	23,110	VC
Immaculata Univ	PA	43,000	C
Indiana State Univ	IN	16,000	C
Indiana Univ Bloomington	IN	19,801	VC
Indiana Univ Northwest	IN	6,854	LC
Indiana Univ of Pennsylvania	PA	20,846	LC
Indiana Univ South Bend	IN	15,501	C
Indiana Univ Southeast	IN	16,035	C
Indiana Univ-Purdue Univ Fort Wayne	IN	15,521	C
Indiana Univ-Purdue Univ Indianapolis	IN	17,611	C
Indiana Wesleyan Univ	IN	31,815	VC
Inter-American Univ of PR/ Fajardo Campus	PR	4,200	
Inter-American Univ of PR/ Metropolitan Campus	PR	4,320	
Inter-American Univ of PR/ Ponce	PR		
Inter-American Univ of PR/ San Germán	PR	6,720	
Iona College	NY	44,028	C
Iowa State Univ	IA	16,403	C
Ithaca College	NY	53,864	HC
Jacksonville Univ	FL	37,780	C
John Brown Univ	AR	32,056	VC+
John Carroll Univ	OH	46,300	C+
Johns Hopkins Univ	MD	47,492	MC
Johnson C. Smith Univ	NC	25,336	LC
Judson College	AL	26,794	C
Juniata College	PA	49,340	VC
Kalamazoo College	MI	49,740	HC
Kansas Wesleyan Univ	KS	32,000	C
Kean Univ	NJ	23,444	C
Keene State College	NH	23,232	LC
Kent State Univ	OH	19,920	C
Kentucky Wesleyan College	KY	27,440	C
Kenyon College	OH	58,890	MC
King Univ	TN	33,140	C
King's College	PA	43,502	C
Knox College	IL	44,865	VC+
Kutztown Univ of Pennsylvania	PA	16,909	LC
La Salle Univ	PA	50,270	C
La Sierra Univ	CA	35,694	VC
Lafayette College	PA	59,155	HC+
LaGrange College	GA	37,670	C
Lake Forest College	IL	50,652	VC
Lake Superior State Univ	MI	18,121	C
Lakeland College	WI	22,990	C
Lamar Univ	TX	6,820	LC
Lander Univ	SC	22,514	C+
Lawrence Univ	WI	46,371	HC
Le Moyne College	NY	43,470	C
Lebanon Valley College	PA	38,570	C
Lee Univ	TN	18,690	C+
Lehigh Univ	PA	56,770	MC
Lehman College/The CUNY	NY	5,778	LC
Lenoir-Rhyne College	NC	35,984	C
Liberty Univ	VA	19,101	C
Lincoln Univ	MO	12,904	NC
Lindenwood Univ	MO	20,750	C
Linfield College-McMinnville Campus	OR	47,676	C
Lipscomb Univ	TN	37,490	VC
LIU Brooklyn	NY	47,182	LC
LIU Post	NY	47,660	C
Lock Haven Univ of Pennsylvania	PA	18,028	LC
Loras College	IA	37,432	VC
Louisiana State Univ	LA	18,677	C+
Louisiana Tech Univ	LA	11,302	C
Loyola Marymount Univ	CA	54,649	VC+
Loyola Univ Chicago	IL	51,646	VC+
Loyola Univ Maryland	MD	56,880	VC+
Loyola Univ New Orleans	LA	46,581	VC
Luther College	IA	45,720	C+
Lycoming College	PA	45,379	C
Lynchburg College	VA	42,645	C
Lyon College	AR	32,090	C+
Macalester College	MN	57,691	MC
MacMurray College	IL	20,755	C
Madonna Univ	MI	24,540	VC
Manchester Univ	IN	35,070	C
Manhattan College	NY	49,588	C+
Manhattanville College	NY	50,740	VC
Mansfield Univ	PA	19,468	LC
Marian Univ	IN	38,540	C
Marian Univ	WI	32,420	LC
Marietta College	OH	42,135	C
Marist College	NY	35,500	C
Marlboro College	VT	35,980	VC
Marquette Univ	WI	46,930	VC+
Mars Hill Univ	NC	22,950	LC
Marshall Univ	WV	14,820	C
Martin Univ	IN	11,000	SP
Maryville College	TN	33,150	C+
Marywood Univ	PA	45,595	C
McDaniel College	MD	47,450	VC
McMurry Univ	TX	25,962	C
McPherson College	KS	28,138	C
Mercer Univ	GA	44,201	VC
Mercy College	NY	30,456	C
Meredith College	NC	31,420	C
Messiah College	PA	40,690	C+
Methodist Univ	NC	37,185	C
Metropolitan State Univ of Denver	CO	4,835	LC
Miami Univ	OH	24,191	VC
Mich State Univ	MI	22,450	VC
MidAmerica Nazarene Univ	KS	28,000	C
Middle Tenn State Univ	TN	8,650	C
Middlebury College	VT	59,160	MC
Midwestern State Univ	TX	9,722	C
Millersville Univ of Pennsylvania	PA	21,648	C
Millikin Univ	IL	38,940	C
Mills College	CA	54,119	VC
Millsaps College	MS	43,888	VC+
Minn State Univ, Mankato	MN	15,616	C
Minn State Univ, Moorhead	MN	13,392	VC
Minot State Univ	ND	10,915	C
Miss College	MS	21,998	C
Miss Univ for Women	MS	7,400	C
Missouri State Univ	MO	13,996	C+
Missouri Western State Univ	MO	12,260	NC
Monmouth College	IL	40,850	C
Monmouth Univ	NJ	44,108	C
Montclair State Univ	NJ	22,614	C
Moravian College	PA	36,381	C
Morehouse College	GA	39,412	C
Morningside College	IA	35,430	C
Mount Holyoke College	MA	55,146	MC
Mount Mary Univ	WI	33,590	LC
Mount St. Mary's Univ	MD	47,996	C
Mount St. Mary's College - Chalon Campus	CA	43,897	VC+
Mount Vernon Nazarene Univ	OH	29,590	C
Muhlenberg College	PA	52,837	HC
Murray State Univ	KY	15,304	C
Muskingum Univ	OH	30,502	C
Nazareth College of Rochester	NY	43,028	C+
Nebr Wesleyan Univ	NE	29,774	C+
New College of Florida	FL	14,504	MC
New Jersey City Univ	NJ	21,456	LC
New Mexico Highlands Univ	NM	11,904	NC
New York Univ	NY	61,470	MC
Newberry College	SC	26,850	LC
Niagara Univ	NY	41,010	C
N Car Central Univ	NC	9,000	C
N Car State Univ	NC	16,202	HC
North Central College	IL	38,343	VC
N Dak State Univ	ND		C
North Park Univ	IL	30,130	C
Northeastern Illinois Univ	IL	10,318	LC
Northeastern State Univ	OK	8,615	VC
Northern Arizona Univ	AZ	19,010	C
Northern Illinois Univ	IL	19,768	C
Northern Kentucky Univ	KY	21,134	C
Northern Mich Univ	MI	18,278	C
Northern State Univ - Aberdeen	SD	14,505	C
Northwest Missouri State Univ	MO	17,347	C
Northwestern College	MN	24,000	C
Northwest Nazarene Univ	ID	34,000	C
Northwestern College of Iowa	IA	36,240	VC
Northwestern Univ	IL	61,640	MC
Oakland Univ	MI	19,391	C
Oakwood Univ	AL	25,529	NC
Oberlin College	OH	61,788	MC
Occidental College	CA	60,972	MC
Oglethorpe Univ	GA	44,200	C+
Ohio Northern Univ	OH	42,075	VC
Ohio Univ	OH	21,080	C
Ohio Wesleyan Univ	OH	49,460	C+
Okla Baptist Univ	OK	28,202	C
Okla Christian Univ	OK	25,870	VC
Okla City Univ	OK	40,476	VC
Okla State Univ	OK	14,310	VC
Old Dominion Univ	VA	19,483	LC
Olivet Nazarene Univ	IL	29,990	C
Oral Roberts Univ	OK	31,734	C
Oregon State Univ	OR	20,273	VC
Oswego / SUNY	NY	20,009	VC
Otterbein College	OH	32,214	C
Ouachita Baptist Univ	AR	30,220	VC
Our Lady of the Lake Univ	TX	22,430	LC
Pace Univ	NY	53,367	C
Pacific Lutheran Univ	WA	46,760	C+
Pacific Union College	CA	28,150	VC
Pacific Univ	OR	49,626	C+
Park Univ	MO	17,525	C
Pepperdine Univ	CA	55,372	HC+
Piedmont College	GA	30,136	C
Pittsburg State Univ	KS	12,032	C
Pitzer College	CA	54,988	MC
Plymouth State Univ	NH	23,148	LC
Point Loma Nazarene Univ	CA	41,006	C+
Pomona College	CA	57,680	MC
Pontifical Catholic Univ of PR	PR	7,310	
Portland State Univ	OR	18,672	C
Prairie View A&M Univ	TX	15,205	LC
Presbyterian College	SC	42,678	C+
Prescott College	AZ	33,284	C
Princeton Univ	NJ	53,795	MC
Principia College	IL	35,140	C+
Providence College	RI	57,383	VC
Purdue Univ/Calumet	IN	14,336	C
Purdue Univ/West Lafayette	IN	20,024	HC
Queens College/The CUNY	NY	17,107	VC
Queens Univ of Charlotte	NC	39,543	C+
Quinnipiac Univ	CT	55,160	VC
Randolph College	VA	45,660	VC
Randolph-Macon College	VA	49,869	C+
Regis College	MA	47,565	LC
Regis Univ	CO	41,318	C
Rhode Island College	RI	17,694	LC
Rhodes College	TN	51,900	HC+
Rider Univ	NJ	45,720	C
Ripon College	WI	36,959	C+
Roanoke College	VA	49,976	C
Roberts Wesleyan College	NY	38,306	C+
Rockford College	IL	31,000	C
Rockhurst Univ	MO	20,625	C
Rollins College	FL	52,370	HC
Roosevelt Univ	IL	22,605	VC
Rosemont College	PA	42,350	C
Rowan Univ	NJ	24,022	VC+
Russell Sage College	NY	39,370	C
Rutgers, The State Univ of New Jersey/Camden Campus	NJ	25,121	C
Rutgers, The State Univ of New Jersey/New Brunswick	NJ	25,562	VC
Rutgers, The State Univ of New Jersey/Newark Campus	NJ	258,806	C
Sacred Heart Univ	CT	49,264	VC
Saginaw Valley State Univ	MI	17,369	C
St. Anselm College	NH	49,376	VC
St. Augustine's Univ	NC	14,000	C
St. Francis Univ	PA	30,029	LC
St. John's Univ	MN	47,984	C
St. Joseph's Univ	PA	55,006	VC
St. Louis Univ	MO	48,346	HC
St. Mary's College	IN	45,160	C+
St. Mary's College of Calif	CA	53,550	C
St. Mary's Univ	TX	33,854	C
St. Mary's Univ of Minn	MN	38,280	C
St. Michael's College	VT	49,975	VC
St. Peter's Univ	NJ	44,240	C
St. Vincent College	PA	40,244	C
St. Xavier Univ	IL	32,840	C
Salem College	NC	29,326	VC
Salisbury Univ	MD	19,180	VC
Salve Regina Univ	RI	48,550	VC
Sam Houston State Univ	TX	17,082	C
Samford Univ	AL	37,060	C+
San Diego State Univ	CA	21,611	C+
San Francisco State Univ	CA	18,514	C
San Jose State Univ	CA	19,133	LC
Sarah Lawrence College	NY	40,008	MC
Scripps College	CA	61,940	MC
Seattle Pacific Univ	WA	41,559	VC+
Seattle Univ	WA	49,035	VC+
Seton Hall Univ	NJ	45,902	C
Seton Hill Univ	PA	35,172	C
Sewanee: The Univ of the South	TN	47,700	HC+
Shenandoah Univ	VA	39,916	C
Shepherd Univ	WV	15,875	C
Shippensburg Univ of Pennsylvania	PA	20,934	C
Shorter Univ	GA	30,650	LC
Siena College	NY	43,863	VC
Siena Heights Univ	MI	32,040	C
Simmons College	MA	49,966	VC
Simpson College	IA	36,086	C
Skidmore College	NY	59,942	HC
Slippery Rock Univ of Pennsylvania	PA	10,360	C
Smith College	MA	59,674	MC
Sonoma State Univ	CA	20,541	C
S Car State Univ	SC	6,700	LC
S Dak State Univ	SD	14,296	C
Southeastern Louisiana Univ	LA	13,325	C
Southern Arkansas Univ	AR	14,316	C
Southern Conn State Univ	CT	18,033	LC
Southern Illinois Univ Carbondale	IL	21,942	C
Southern Illinois Univ Edwardsville	IL	17,532	C
Southern Methodist Univ	TX	60,585	MC
Southern Nazarene Univ	OK	24,354	C
Southern Oregon Univ	OR	17,874	C
Southern Univ and A&M College	LA	9,761	LC
Southern Univ at New Orleans	LA	2,963	NC
Southwest Baptist Univ	MO	24,710	C
Southwest Minn State Univ	MN	14,000	C
Southwestern Univ	TX	45,660	VC
Spelman College	GA	24,650	C
Spring Arbor Univ	MI	26,740	C
St. Ambrose Univ	IA	30,845	C
St. Bonaventure Univ	NY	41,575	C
St. Catherine Univ	MN	37,782	C+
St. Edward's Univ	TX	47,784	C
St. Francis College	NY	34,200	C
St. John Fisher College	NY	40,708	C+
St. John's Univ	NY	55,070	C+
St. Joseph's College, New York/Brooklyn Campus	NY	22,630	C
St. Joseph's College, New York/Suffolk Campus	NY	22,630	C
St. Lawrence Univ	NY	59,972	VC
St. Norbert College	WI	41,478	VC
St. Olaf College	MN	51,200	HC+
St. Thomas Aquinas College	NY	40,230	C
Stanford Univ	CA	58,388	MC
Stephen F. Austin State Univ	TX	14,668	C
Stetson Univ	FL	51,516	VC
Stonehill College	MA	46,780	VC
Suffolk Univ	MA	47,298	C
Sul Ross State Univ	TX	13,410	LC
SUNY College at Geneseo	NY	18,670	HC
SUNY College at Old Westbury	NY	16,324	C
SUNY Fredonia/The SUNY at Fredonia	NY	19,840	VC
SUNY New Paltz	NY	14,348	C
SUNY Oneonta / SUNY	NY	16,919	C+
SUNY Plattsburgh / SUNY	NY	18,083	C
Susquehanna Univ	PA	51,150	C
Swarthmore College	PA	57,870	MC
Tarleton State Univ	TX	13,489	LC
Taylor Univ	IN	37,821	VC+
Temple Univ	PA	24,392	VC
Tenn Tech Univ	TN	11,310	C
Texas A&M Univ	TX	19,207	VC
Texas A&M Univ at Commerce	TX	10,496	C
Texas A&M Univ at Corpus Christi	TX	11,544	LC
Texas A&M Univ at Kingsville	TX	7,500	LC
Texas Christian Univ	TX	49,980	HC
Texas Lutheran Univ	TX	36,040	C
Texas Southern Univ	TX	18,212	LC
Texas State Univ	TX	17,128	C
Texas Tech Univ	TX	14,243	C
Texas Wesleyan Univ	TX	31,382	C
The Catholic Univ of America	DC	52,852	VC
The College of Idaho	ID	31,277	C+
The College of New Rochelle	NY	33,600	VC

ST = STATE $IS = IN-STATE COSTS   SR = SELECTOR RATING

School	ST	$IS	SR
The College of St. Rose	NY	26,750	C
The Lincoln Univ	PA	15,154	LC
Ohio State Univ-Columbus Campus	OH	19,887	HC+
The Pennsylvania State Univ - Univ Park	PA	28,022	VC+
The SUNY at Potsdam	NY	18,473	C
The SUNY/College at Brockport	NY	19,002	C
The Univ of N Car at Greensboro	NC	12,848	C
The Univ of N Car at Pembroke	NC	13,388	LC
The Univ of Okla	OK	18,621	C
The Univ of Tenn at Chattanooga	TN	16,883	C
The Univ of Utah	UT	16,463	VC
The Univ of Virginia's College at Wise	VA	11,076	C
Thomas Edison State College	NJ	5,700	SP
Thomas More College	KY	34,760	C
Towson Univ	MD	16,000	VC
Transylvania Univ	KY	42,660	VC+
Trinity Christian College	IL	28,869	C
Trinity College	CT		HC+
Trinity Univ	TX	48,150	HC+
Truman State Univ	MO	15,541	HC
Tufts Univ	MA	58,780	MC
Tulane Univ	LA	60,861	MC
Union College	NE	23,270	C
Union Univ	TN	28,260	VC
Universidad Adventista de las Antillas	PR	7,360	
Universidad del Turabo	PR	4,110	
Univ at Albany / SUNY	NY	18,674	VC
Univ at Buffalo / The SUNY	NY	20,283	VC
Univ of Akron	OH	20,436	C
Univ of Alabama at Tuscaloosa	AL	17,164	C+
Univ of Alaska Fairbanks	AK	15,130	C
Univ of Arizona	AZ	20,657	VC
Univ of Arkansas at Fayetteville	AR	18,352	C+
Univ of Arkansas at Little Rock	AR	17,609	LC
Univ of Calif at Berkeley	CA	23,322	MC
Univ of Calif at Davis	CA		HC
Univ of Calif at Irvine	CA	25,961	VC
Univ of Calif at Los Angeles	CA	25,686	MC
Univ of Calif at Riverside	CA	27,204	C+
Univ of Calif at Santa Barbara	CA	27,551	VC
Univ of Central Arkansas	AR	13,667	VC
Univ of Central Florida	FL	15,668	VC+
Univ of Central Missouri	MO	14,605	C
Univ of Central Okla	OK	12,293	C
Univ of Cincinnati	OH	21,506	VC
Univ of Colo at Colo Springs	CO	15,000	VC
Univ of Colo Boulder	CO	22,605	VC+
Univ of Colo Denver	CO	17,904	C
Univ of Conn	CT	24,706	HC
Univ of Dallas	TX	45,500	VC+
Univ of Dayton	OH	49,070	VC
Univ of Denver	CO	51,787	VC+
Univ of Evansville	IN	42,656	VC+
Univ of Findlay	OH	31,916	C
Univ of Florida	FL	15,943	HC
Univ of Georgia	GA	20,082	VC
Univ of Hawaii at Manoa	HI	19,379	VC
Univ of Houston	TX	19,796	VC
Univ of Houston-Downtown	TX	15,170	LC
Univ of Idaho	ID	14,558	C
Univ of Illinois at Chicago	IL	24,505	VC
Univ of Illinois at Urbana-Champaign	IL	26,450	HC
Univ of Indianapolis	IN	31,740	LC
Univ of Iowa	IA	17,693	VC
Univ of Jamestown	ND	24,738	C
Univ of Kansas	KS	17,603	C+
Univ of Kentucky	KY	19,868	C
Univ of La Verne	CA	47,010	C
Univ of Louisiana at Lafayette	LA	6,130	C
Univ of Louisiana at Monroe	LA	12,998	C
Univ of Louisville	KY	17,946	C
Univ of Maine	ME	19,902	C+
Univ of Mary Hardin-Baylor	TX	31,950	C+
Univ of Mary Washington	VA	19,484	VC
Univ of Maryland - College Park	MD	20,060	HC
Univ of Maryland/Baltimore County	MD	18,000	VC
Univ of Maryland/Univ College	MD	6,168	SP
Univ of Mass Amherst	MA	24,215	VC+
Univ of Mass Boston	MA	23,066	VC
Univ of Mass Dartmouth	MA	22,223	C
Univ of Miami	FL	57,034	MC
Univ of Mich/Ann Arbor	MI	22,102	MC
Univ of Mich-Flint	MI	17,547	C+
Univ of Minn/Duluth	MN	19,806	C
Univ of Minn/Morris	MN	17,150	C
Univ of Minn/Twin Cities	MN		VC
Univ of Miss	MS	16,704	C+
Univ of Missouri/Columbia	MO	18,201	VC
Univ of Missouri-Kansas City	MO	19,603	C
Univ of Missouri-St. Louis	MO		VC

School	ST	$IS	SR
Univ of Montana	MT	14,105	C
Univ of Montevallo	AL	17,060	C
Univ of Mount Union	OH	35,130	C
Univ of Nebr - Lincoln	NE	18,031	VC
Univ of Nebr at Kearney	NE	14,855	LC
Univ of Nebr at Omaha	NE	12,700	C
Univ of Nevada, Las Vegas	NV	17,303	C
Univ of Nevada/Reno	NV	17,507	C
Univ of New Hampshire	NH	26,912	C
Univ of New Mexico	NM	15,300	C
Univ of New Orleans	LA	9,224	C
Univ of North Alabama	AL	9,960	C
Univ of N Car at Asheville	NC	13,500	VC
Univ of N Car at Charlotte	NC	15,547	C
Univ of N Car at Wilmington	NC	13,572	VC
Univ of N Dak	ND	14,551	C
Univ of North Florida	FL	15,870	VC
Univ of North Georgia	GA	8,500	C
Univ of North Texas	TX	15,628	C
Univ of Northern Colo	CO	18,446	C
Univ of Northern Iowa	IA	15,795	C
Univ of Notre Dame	IN	57,117	MC
Univ of Oregon	OR	21,360	C+
Univ of Pikeville	KY	25,500	NC
Univ of Pittsburgh at Pittsburgh	PA	28,572	HC+
Univ of Portland	OR	49,964	VC
Univ of Puget Sound	WA	54,608	VC
Univ of Redlands	CA	40,500	VC
Univ of Rochester	NY	60,668	MC
Univ of St. Joseph	CT	45,630	C
Univ of San Diego	CA	54,818	HC+
Univ of San Francisco	CA	54,770	VC
Univ of Scranton	PA	51,940	VC
Univ of S Car at Columbia	SC	19,725	VC+
Univ of S Car Upstate	SC	18,200	LC
Univ of S Dak	SD	15,111	C
Univ of South Florida/Tampa	FL	13,000	C
Univ of Southern Calif	CA	56,903	MC
Univ of Southern Indiana	IN	14,885	C
Univ of St. Thomas - Houston	TX	37,690	C
Univ of Tampa	FL	35,160	VC
Univ of Tenn at Martin	TN	13,734	C
Univ of Texas - Pan American	TX	11,125	LC
Univ of Texas at Arlington	TX	10,908	LC
Univ of Texas at Austin	TX	44,074	HC
Univ of Texas at El Paso	TX	8,764	NC
Univ of Texas at San Antonio	TX	18,372	C
Univ of the Cumberlands	KY	27,500	C
Univ of the District of Columbia	DC	7,244	LC
Univ of the Incarnate Word	TX	37,316	LC
Univ of the Pacific	CA	52,146	VC
Univ of Toledo	OH	18,464	C
Univ of Tulsa	OK	46,331	MC
Univ of Vermont	VT	27,006	VC+
Univ of Virginia	VA	23,050	MC
Univ of Washington	WA	14,722	VC
Univ of Wisc Whitewater	WI	13,314	C
Univ of Wisc/Eau Claire	WI	15,730	VC
Univ of Wisc/Green Bay	WI	19,074	C
Univ of Wisc/La Crosse	WI	9,304	VC
Univ of Wisc/Madison	WI	18,757	HC+
Univ of Wisc/Oshkosh	WI	10,426	C
Univ of Wisc/Parkside	WI	10,181	LC
Univ of Wisc/Platteville	WI	14,564	C
Univ of Wisc/Stevens Point	WI	14,043	C
Univ of Wyoming	WY	14,401	C+
Ursinus College	PA	57,580	VC
Utah State Univ	UT	12,044	C
Valley City State Univ	ND	12,286	LC
Valparaiso Univ	IN	44,940	VC+
Vanderbilt Univ	TN	58,220	MC
Vanguard Univ of Southern Calif	CA	35,833	VC
Villanova Univ	PA	58,394	MC
Virginia Polytechnic Inst and State Univ	VA	14,629	HC
Virginia Wesleyan College	VA	28,433	LC
Viterbo Univ	WI	30,070	C
Wabash College	IN	46,850	C+
Wake Forest Univ	NC	58,838	MC
Walla Walla Univ	WA	26,256	NC
Walsh Univ	OH	35,100	C
Wartburg College	IA	41,055	VC
Washburn Univ	KS	12,579	C
Washington and Jefferson College	PA	51,948	VC
Washington and Lee Univ	VA	52,812	MC
Washington College	MD	52,602	VC
Washington State Univ	WA	20,461	C
Washington Univ in St. Louis	MO	69,844	MC
Wayland Baptist Univ	TX	18,912	LC
Wayne State College	NE	11,764	NC
Webster Univ	MO	35,100	C
Wellesley College	MA	59,038	MC
Wells College	NY	49,400	VC
Wesleyan College	GA	24,000	C
West Chester Univ of Pennsylvania	PA	17,186	C
West Texas A&M Univ	TX	13,478	C
Western Carolina Univ	NC	13,965	C
Western Conn State Univ	CT	18,327	LC
Western Illinois Univ	IL	20,732	C

School	ST	$IS	SR
Western Kentucky Univ	KY	11,000	LC
Western Mich Univ	MI	19,628	C
Western New Mexico Univ	NM	8,500	LC
Western Oregon Univ	OR	15,021	C
Western State Colo Univ	CO	16,924	C
Western Washington Univ	WA	18,519	VC
Westfield State Univ	MA	18,297	C
Westminster College	MO	31,720	VC
Westminster College	PA	31,290	C+
Westmont College	CA	41,500	HC
Wheaton College	IL	40,720	MC
Wheeling Jesuit Univ	WV	33,500	C
Whitman College	WA	55,988	MC
Whittier College	CA	43,416	C
Whitworth Univ	WA	47,734	VC
Wichita State Univ	KS	14,607	C+
Widener Univ	PA	52,418	C
Wilkes Univ	PA	44,070	C
Willamette Univ	OR	56,450	VC+
William Carey Univ	MS	13,500	LC
William Jewell College	MO	31,000	VC+
William Paterson Univ of New Jersey	NJ	21,694	C
Williams College	MA	61,070	MC
Wilmington College	OH	29,784	C
Wilson College	PA	35,080	C
Winona State Univ	MN	16,640	C
Winston-Salem State Univ	NC	9,418	LC
Winthrop Univ	SC	21,120	C
Wisc Lutheran College	WI	23,510	VC
Wittenberg Univ	OH	47,962	C+
Wofford College	SC	45,795	VC
Worcester State Univ	MA	19,812	C
Wright State Univ	OH	16,983	C
Xavier Univ	OH	44,980	VC
Xavier Univ of Louisiana	LA	25,300	C
Yale Univ	CT	55,300	MC
York College / The CUNY	NY	5,496	VC
York College of Pennsylvania	PA	26,590	C
Youngstown State Univ	OH	16,732	C

SPANISH / ADOLESCENCE EDUCATION

School	ST	$IS	SR
Arizona State Univ, at the Polytechnic Campus	AZ	20,531	C+
Arizona State Univ, at the West Campus	AZ	19,251	C
Bethany College	WV	35,282	LC
Blue Mountain College	MS	15,634	LC
Indiana Univ of Pennsylvania	PA	20,846	LC
LIU Post	NY	47,660	C
Messiah College	PA	40,690	C+
Nazareth College of Rochester	NY	43,028	C+
Niagara Univ	NY	41,010	C
Northern Kentucky Univ	KY	21,134	C
Old Dominion Univ	VA	19,483	LC
Oswego / SUNY	NY	20,009	VC
St. Mary's Univ of Minn	MN	38,280	C
SUNY Plattsburgh / SUNY	NY	18,083	C
The College of St. Rose	NY	26,750	C
Youngstown State Univ	OH	16,732	C

SPANISH AND HISPANIC STUDIES

School	ST	$IS	SR
Creighton Univ	NE	45,356	VC
Hobart and William Smith Colleges	NY	60,034	HC+
Molloy College	NY	40,440	C
Oberlin College	OH	61,788	MC

SPANISH EDUCATION K-12

School	ST	$IS	SR
Aquinas College	MI	33,060	C
Black Hills State Univ	SD	13,947	C
College of the Ozarks	MO		VC
Indiana Univ Bloomington	IN	19,801	VC
Indiana Univ Northwest	IN	6,854	LC
Indiana Univ South Bend	IN	15,501	C
Indiana Univ-Purdue Univ Indianapolis	IN	17,611	C
Lubbock Christian Univ	TX	26,308	C
Missouri Southern State Univ	MO	12,061	C
Monmouth Univ	NJ	44,108	C
Murray State Univ	KY	15,304	C
Niagara Univ	NY	41,010	C
Univ of the Cumberlands	KY	27,500	C

SPANISH STUDIES

School	ST	$IS	SR
American Univ	DC	56,015	HC+
Bard College	NY	61,940	HC
Bard College at Simon's Rock	MA	61,749	HC+
Barton College	NC	27,660	C
Bentley Univ	MA	56,454	HC+
Blue Mountain College	MS	15,634	LC
Cal State, San Bernardino	CA	12,000	C
Cedar Crest College	PA	43,240	C
Coe College	IA	45,550	VC
College of William & Mary	VA	28,000	MC
Creighton Univ	NE	45,356	VC
Dartmouth College	NH	57,996	MC
Drury Univ	MO	31,909	VC

School	ST	$IS	SR
Fairleigh Dickinson Univ/ College at Florham	NJ	42,142	C
Fairleigh Dickinson Univ/ Metropolitan Campus	NJ	40,254	C
Fordham Univ	NY	61,588	HC+
Hobart and William Smith Colleges	NY	60,034	HC+
Holy Names Univ	CA	40,310	NC
Howard Univ	DC	13,646	C
Lake Erie College	OH	37,266	C
Messiah College	PA	40,690	C+
Mills College	CA	54,119	VC
Minn State Univ, Moorhead	MN	13,392	VC
Montana State Univ-Billings	MT	12,425	LC
New College of Florida	FL	14,504	MC
Olivet Nazarene Univ	IL	29,990	C
Purdue Univ/West Lafayette	IN	20,024	HC
Ramapo College of New Jersey	NJ	24,938	C
Reed College	OR	57,780	MC
Southern Nazarene Univ	OK	24,354	C
Spring Hill College	AL	44,164	VC
Stony Brook Univ / SUNY	NY	20,078	HC+
Syracuse Univ	NY	56,346	VC
The Catholic Univ of America	DC	52,852	VC
The SUNY at Potsdam	NY	18,473	C
Union College	NY	60,240	MC
Univ of Calif at Los Angeles	CA	25,686	MC
Univ of Calif at San Diego	CA	21,000	VC
Univ of Illinois at Chicago	IL	24,505	VC
Univ of Wisc-Milwaukee	WI	18,436	C
Vassar College	NY	61,140	MC
Westminster College	UT	37,708	C+
Winthrop Univ	SC	21,120	C
Youngstown State Univ	OH	16,732	C

SPECIAL EDUCATION

School	ST	$IS	SR
Abilene Christian Univ	TX	38,400	C+
Adams State Univ	CO	13,358	LC
Alabama A&M Univ	AL	10,084	C
Alabama State Univ	AL	14,142	NC
Albany State Univ	GA	8,500	C
Albright College	PA	46,660	C
Alcorn State Univ	MS	9,500	C
Alma College	MI	44,075	C
American International College	MA	36,100	LC
Appalachian State Univ	NC	12,919	VC
Aquinas College	MI	33,060	C
Arcadia Univ	PA	33,570	C+
Arizona State Univ, at the Polytechnic Campus	AZ	20,531	C+
Arizona State Univ, at the Tempe Campus	AZ	20,137	C+
Arizona State Univ, at the West Campus	AZ	19,251	C
Armstrong State Univ	GA	15,532	C
Auburn Univ	AL	22,378	VC+
Augustana College	SD	36,500	VC
Aurora Univ	IL	33,228	C
Austin Peay State Univ	TN	15,274	C
Avila Univ	MO	26,900	C
Baylor Univ	TX	50,329	HC
Bellarmine Univ	KY	42,950	VC
Benedictine College	KS	29,180	VC
Benedictine Univ	IL	37,820	C
Bennett College for Women	NC	21,970	LC
Black Hills State Univ	SD	13,947	C
Bloomfield College	NJ	37,850	LC
Bloomsburg Univ of Pennsylvania	PA	13,598	C
Bluffton Univ	OH	38,948	C
Boise State Univ	ID	13,469	LC
Boston College	MA	60,622	HC
Boston Univ	MA	60,694	MC
Bowling Green State Univ	OH	18,970	C
Bradley Univ	IL	31,874	VC
Brenau Univ - Women's College	GA	26,650	LC
Brescia Univ	KY	26,140	VC+
Bridgewater State Univ	MA	18,752	C
Brigham Young Univ	UT	12,100	HC
Brigham Young Univ/Hawaii	HI	10,686	VC
Buena Vista Univ	IA	39,188	C
Buffalo State College / SUNY	NY	15,733	C+
Butler Univ	IN	47,572	VC+
Cabrini College	PA	40,859	LC
Cal State, Long Beach	CA	17,502	C+
Calif Univ of Pennsylvania	PA	14,217	C
Calvin College	MI	39,120	VC
Canisius College	NY	44,900	C
Cardinal Stritch Univ	WI	24,054	C
Caribbean Univ	PR	10,375	
Carlow Univ	PA	30,272	C
Cedarville Univ	OH	32,860	VC
Central Methodist Univ	MO	28,240	VC
Central State Univ	OH	9,010	C
Central Washington Univ	WA	11,730	C
Cheyney Univ of Pennsylvania	PA	20,372	LC
Christian Brothers Univ	TN	31,670	HC
CUNY/City College	NY	20,319	HC+
Clarion Univ of Pennsylvania	PA	17,370	C
Clarke Univ	IA	37,600	C

ST = STATE $IS = IN-STATE COSTS   SR = SELECTOR RATING

School	ST	$IS	SR
Clearwater Christian College	FL	23,720	C
Clemson Univ	SC	19,136	HC
Cleveland State Univ	OH	21,776	C
Coastal Carolina Univ	SC	18,580	C
College of Charleston	SC	22,145	VC
College of Mount St. Joseph	OH	33,880	C
College of Mount St. Vincent	NY	41,040	MC
College of New Jersey	NJ	25,376	C
College of St. Mary	NE	35,184	C
Columbia College	SC	27,882	C
Columbus State Univ	GA	13,176	C
Concord Univ	WV	13,102	C
Concordia Univ Nebr	NE	26,000	VC
Concordia Univ St. Paul	MN	28,250	C
Coppin State Univ	MD	16,227	VC
Cumberland Univ	TN	21,220	C
Curry College	MA	48,925	LC
Dakota Wesleyan Univ	SD	23,000	C
Delaware State Univ	DE	16,722	LC
DePaul Univ	IL	47,623	VC
Doane College	NE	35,230	C
Dominican College	NY	31,270	LC
Dordt College	IA	34,160	C+
Dowling College	NY	25,000	LC
East Carolina Univ	NC	14,169	C
East Central Univ	OK	10,223	LC
East Stroudsburg Univ of Pennsylvania	PA	18,868	LC
East Tenn State Univ	TN	9,000	C
Eastern Illinois Univ	IL	20,466	C
Eastern Kentucky Univ	KY	11,161	C
Eastern Mennonite Univ	VA	40,660	C
Eastern Mich Univ	MI	18,604	C
Eastern New Mexico Univ	NM	10,682	C
Edinboro Univ of Pennsylvania	PA	15,940	LC
Elizabeth City State Univ	NC	11,638	C
Elmhurst College	IL	43,336	C
Elms College	MA	23,900	VC
Elon Univ	NC	41,914	VC+
Erskine College	SC	37,360	C
Evangel Univ	MO	23,090	C
Felician College	NJ	41,640	LC
Fitchburg State Univ	MA	18,173	C
Florida Atlantic Univ	FL	17,339	C
Florida Gulf Coast Univ	FL		
Florida International Univ	FL	17,747	C+
Fontbonne Univ	MO	31,384	C
Freed-Hardeman Univ	TN	19,697	VC
Gannon Univ	PA	39,608	C
Georgia College and State Univ	GA	18,900	C
Georgia Regents Univ	GA		C
Georgia Southern Univ	GA	16,942	C
Georgia Southwestern State Univ	GA	13,246	C
Glenville State College	WV	11,348	NC
Gonzaga Univ	WA	46,441	HC
Gordon College	MA	44,320	VC
Goucher College	MD	52,040	VC+
Grace College and Seminary	IN	28,800	VC
Grambling State Univ	LA	13,384	LC
Grand Valley State Univ	MI	17,998	C
Greensboro College	NC	28,740	LC
Greenville College	IL	27,012	C
Grove City College	PA	24,022	VC
Gwynedd-Mercy College	PA	33,560	C
Hastings College	NE	27,782	C+
High Point Univ	NC	39,800	C
Holy Family Univ	PA	40,030	LC
Hood College	MD	45,730	C
Hope College	MI	38,650	C
Houghton College	NY	36,808	C+
Houston Baptist Univ	TX	36,450	C
Illinois State Univ	IL	23,110	VC
Indiana State Univ	IN	16,000	C
Indiana Univ Bloomington	IN	19,801	VC
Indiana Univ of Pennsylvania	PA	20,846	LC
Indiana Univ South Bend	IN	15,501	C
Indiana Univ Southeast	IN	16,035	C
Indiana Wesleyan Univ	IN	31,815	VC
Inter-American Univ of PR/ Aguadilla Campus	PR	5,578	
Inter-American Univ of PR/ Arecibo Campus	PR	3,350	
Inter-American Univ of PR/ Fajardo Campus	PR	4,200	
Inter-American Univ of PR/ Metropolitan Campus	PR	4,320	
Inter-American Univ of PR/ Ponce	PR		
Inter-American Univ of PR/ San Germán	PR	6,720	
Jackson State Univ	MS	13,512	LC
Jacksonville State Univ	AL	12,480	LC
Jarvis Christian College	TX	19,552	NC
Juniata College	PA	49,340	VC
Kansas Wesleyan Univ	KS	32,000	C
Kean Univ	NJ	23,444	C
Kent State Univ	OH	19,920	C
King's College	PA	43,502	C
Kutztown Univ of Pennsylvania	PA	16,909	LC
La Salle Univ	PA	50,270	C
Lake Erie College	OH	37,266	C
Lamar Univ	TX	6,820	LC
Lander Univ	SC	22,514	C+
Le Moyne College	NY	43,470	C
Lebanon Valley College	PA	38,570	C
Lee Univ	TN	18,690	C+
LeMoyne-Owen College	TN	13,100	C
Lesley Univ	MA	46,350	C
Lewis Univ	IL	23,050	C
Lincoln Univ	MO	12,904	NC
Lock Haven Univ of Pennsylvania	PA	18,028	LC
Longwood Univ	VA	20,924	C
Loras College	IA	37,432	VC
Louisiana College	LA	15,746	C
Louisiana State Univ	LA	18,677	C+
Louisiana Tech Univ	LA	11,302	C
Loyola Univ Chicago	IL	51,646	VC+
MacMurray College	IL	20,755	C
Malone Univ	OH	35,364	C
Manhattan College	NY	49,588	C+
Mansfield Univ	PA	19,468	LC
Marian Univ	IN	38,540	C
Marist College	NY	35,500	C
Marshall Univ	WV	14,820	C
Marygrove College	MI	28,926	C
Marymount Univ	VA	39,480	C
Marywood Univ	PA	45,595	C
McPherson College	KS	28,138	C
Megar Evers College/The CUNY	NY	4,920	NC
Mercer Univ	GA	44,201	VC
Mercy College	NY	30,456	C
Mercyhurst Univ	PA	40,700	C
Methodist Univ	NC	37,185	C
Miami Univ	OH	24,191	VC
Mich State Univ	MI	22,450	VC
Middle Tenn State Univ	TN	8,650	C
Millersville Univ of Pennsylvania	PA	21,648	C
Minn State Univ, Mankato	MN	15,616	C
Minn State Univ, Moorhead	MN	13,392	VC
Miss College	MS	21,998	C
Miss State Univ	MS	14,750	C
Missouri Southern State Univ	MO	12,061	C
Missouri State Univ	MO	13,996	C+
Monmouth Univ	NJ	44,108	C
Montana State Univ-Billings	MT	12,425	LC
Morehead State Univ	KY	10,900	C
Morningside College	IA	35,430	C
Mount Marty College	SD	29,638	C
Mount Vernon Nazarene Univ	OH	29,590	C
Muskingum Univ	OH	30,502	C
Nebr Wesleyan Univ	NE	29,774	C+
New England College	NH	45,930	LC
New Jersey City Univ	NJ	21,456	LC
New Mexico Highlands Univ	NM	11,904	NC
New Mexico State Univ	NM	14,050	C
New York Univ	NY	61,470	MC
Niagara Univ	NY	41,010	C
Nicholls State Univ	LA	7,095	C
N Car Agricultural and Technical State Univ	NC	13,365	LC
Northeastern Illinois Univ	IL	10,318	LC
Northeastern State Univ	OK	8,615	VC
Northern Arizona Univ	AZ	19,010	C
Northern Illinois Univ	IL	19,768	C
Northern Kentucky Univ	KY	21,134	C
Northern State Univ - Aberdeen	SD	14,505	C
Northwest Missouri State Univ	MO	17,347	C
Northwest Univ	WA	18,854	C
Northwestern College of Iowa	IA	36,240	VC
Northwestern Okla State Univ	OK	7,275	NC
Notre Dame College	OH	34,942	VC
Notre Dame of Maryland Univ	MD	27,700	VC
Ohio Dominican Univ	OH	38,380	C+
Ohio Univ	OH	21,080	C
Old Dominion Univ	VA	19,483	LC
Oral Roberts Univ	OK	31,734	C
Our Lady of the Lake Univ	TX	22,430	LC
Peru State College	NE	8,600	NC
Pfeiffer Univ	NC	33,700	LC
Piedmont College	GA	30,136	C
Point Park Univ	PA	36,390	C
Pontifical Catholic Univ of PR	PR	7,310	
Prescott College	AZ	33,284	C
Providence College	RI	57,383	VC
Purdue Univ/West Lafayette	IN	20,024	HC
Quincy Univ	IL	34,980	C
Rhode Island College	RI	17,664	LC
Roberts Wesleyan College	NY	38,306	C+
Rockford College	IL	31,000	C
Saginaw Valley State Univ	MI	17,369	C
St. Joseph's Univ	PA	55,006	VC
St. Martin's Univ	WA	41,678	C
St. Mary-of-the-Woods College	IN	37,722	LC
Salve Regina Univ	RI	48,550	VC
Seattle Pacific Univ	WA	41,559	VC+
Seton Hall Univ	NJ	45,902	C
Seton Hill Univ	PA	35,172	C
Shaw Univ	NC	15,488	C
Shawnee State Univ	OH	16,916	C
Shippensburg Univ of Pennsylvania	PA	20,934	C
Siena Heights Univ	MI	32,040	C
Silver Lake College	WI	22,600	LC
Simmons College	MA	49,966	VC
Slippery Rock Univ of Pennsylvania	PA	10,360	C
S Car State Univ	SC	6,700	LC
Southeastern Louisiana Univ	LA	13,325	C
Southern Conn State Univ	CT	18,033	LC
Southern Illinois Univ Carbondale	IL	21,942	C
Southern Illinois Univ Edwardsville	IL	17,532	C
Southern New Hampshire Univ	NH	38,100	C
Southern Univ and A&M College	LA	9,761	LC
Southern Wesleyan Univ	SC	25,600	C
Southwestern Okla State Univ	OK	9,160	C
Spring Arbor Univ	MI	26,740	C
St. Bonaventure Univ	NY	41,575	C
St. Edward's Univ	TX	47,784	C
St. John Fisher College	NY	40,708	C+
St. John's Univ	NY	55,070	C+
St. Joseph's College, New York/Brooklyn Campus	NY	22,630	C
St. Joseph's College, New York/Suffolk Campus	NY	22,630	C
St. Thomas Aquinas College	NY	40,230	C
SUNY College at Geneseo	NY	18,670	HC
SUNY College at Old Westbury	NY	16,324	C
SUNY Plattsburgh / SUNY	NY	18,083	C
Syracuse Univ	NY	56,346	VC
Tabor College	KS	29,010	C
Tenn State Univ	TN	9,048	C
Tenn Tech Univ	TN	11,310	C
Texas State Univ	TX	17,128	C
The College of St. Rose	NY	26,750	C
The Pennsylvania State Univ - Univ Park	PA	28,022	VC+
The Univ of Memphis	TN	15,094	C
The Univ of N Car at Greensboro	NC	12,848	C
The Univ of Okla	OK	18,621	VC
The Univ of Tenn at Chattanooga	TN	16,883	C
The Univ of Utah	UT	16,463	VC
Thiel College	PA	38,728	LC
Tougaloo College	MS	15,275	NC
Touro College	NY	27,959	VC
Towson Univ	MD	16,000	VC
Trevecca Nazarene Univ	TN	31,186	C
Trinity Christian College	IL	28,869	C
Troy Univ	AL	10,650	C
Tusculum College	TN	24,295	C
Tuskegee Univ	AL	26,750	C
Union College	KY	29,955	C
Union Univ	TN	28,260	VC
Universidad del Turabo	PR	4,110	
Univ of Akron	OH	20,436	C
Univ of Alabama at Tuscaloosa	AL	17,164	C+
Univ of Arizona	AZ	20,657	C
Univ of Arkansas at Little Rock	AR	17,609	LC
Univ of Arkansas at Pine Bluff	AR	13,378	C
Univ of Central Arkansas	AR	13,667	VC
Univ of Central Missouri	MO	14,605	C
Univ of Central Okla	OK	12,293	C
Univ of Charleston	WV	32,300	C
Univ of Cincinnati	OH	21,506	VC
Univ of Conn	CT	24,706	HC
Univ of Dayton	OH	49,070	VC
Univ of Delaware	DE	23,612	VC
Univ of Detroit Mercy	MI	30,450	VC
Univ of Evansville	IN	42,656	VC+
Univ of Georgia	GA	20,082	VC
Univ of Great Falls	MT	27,970	C
Univ of Hartford	CT	42,674	C
Univ of Idaho	ID	14,558	C
Univ of Kentucky	KY	19,868	C
Univ of Louisiana at Lafayette	LA	6,130	C
Univ of Louisiana at Monroe	LA	12,998	C
Univ of Maine at Farmington	ME	18,187	LC
Univ of Mary	ND	16,714	C
Univ of Mary Hardin-Baylor	TX	31,950	C+
Univ of Maryland - College Park	MD	20,060	HC
Univ of Mich/Dearborn	MI	9,885	VC
Univ of Miss	MS	16,704	C+
Univ of Missouri-St. Louis	MO		VC
Univ of Montana-Western	MT	9,753	LC
Univ of Nebr - Lincoln	NE	18,031	VC
Univ of Nebr at Kearney	NE	14,855	LC
Univ of Nevada, Las Vegas	NV	17,303	C
Univ of Nevada/Reno	NV	17,507	C
Univ of New Mexico	NM	15,300	C
Univ of N Car at Charlotte	NC	15,547	C
Univ of N Car at Wilmington	NC	13,572	VC
Univ of North Florida	FL	13,905	VC
Univ of North Georgia	GA	8,500	C
Univ of Northern Colo	CO	18,446	C
Univ of Northern Iowa	IA	15,795	C
Univ of PR Recinto de Rio Piedras	PR	5,750	
Univ of PR/Cayey	PR	1,504	
Univ of St. Francis	IN	29,810	C
Univ of St. Joseph	CT	45,630	C
Univ of South Alabama	AL	13,510	C
Univ of S Car Aiken	SC	16,712	C
Univ of S Car Upstate	SC	18,200	LC
Univ of S Dak	SD	15,111	C
Univ of South Florida/Tampa	FL	13,000	C
Univ of Southern Indiana	IN	14,885	C
Univ of St. Francis	IL	37,560	C
Univ of Tenn at Knoxville	TN	20,364	VC+
Univ of Tenn at Martin	TN	13,734	C
Univ of the Cumberlands	KY	27,500	C
Univ of the Southwest	NM	15,000	C
Univ of Toledo	OH	18,464	C
Univ of Vermont	VT	27,006	VC+
Univ of West Alabama	AL	14,274	C
Univ of West Georgia	GA	15,488	LC
Univ of Wisc Whitewater	WI	13,314	C
Univ of Wisc/Eau Claire	WI	15,730	VC
Univ of Wisc/Madison	WI	18,757	HC+
Univ of Wisc/Oshkosh	WI	10,426	LC
Univ of Wisc/Stout	WI	15,459	C
Univ of Wisc-Milwaukee	WI	18,436	C
Univ of Wyoming	WY	14,401	C+
Ursuline College	OH	33,198	LC
Utah State Univ	UT	12,044	C
Vanderbilt Univ	TN	58,220	MC
Virginia Union Univ	VA	18,432	C
Walla Walla Univ	WA	26,256	NC
Walsh Univ	OH	35,100	C
Washington State Univ	WA	20,461	C
Wayne State College	NE	11,764	NC
Wayne State Univ	MI	22,063	C
Waynesburg Univ	PA	30,150	C
Webster Univ	MO	35,100	C+
West Chester Univ of Pennsylvania	PA	17,186	C
West Liberty Univ	WV	9,142	LC
West Texas A&M Univ	TX	13,478	C
Western Carolina Univ	NC	13,965	C
Western Illinois Univ	IL	20,732	C
Western Mich Univ	MI	19,628	C
Western New Mexico Univ	NM	8,500	LC
Western Washington Univ	WA	18,519	VC
Westfield State Univ	MA	18,297	C
Westminster College	UT	37,708	C+
Wheelock College	MA	33,075	C
Wichita State Univ	KS	14,607	C
Widener Univ	PA	52,418	C
Wiley College	TX		LC
William Paterson Univ of New Jersey	NJ	21,694	C
William Penn Univ	IA	26,000	C
William Woods Univ	MO	24,260	C
Winona State Univ	MN	16,640	C
Winston-Salem State Univ	NC	9,418	LC
Winthrop Univ	SC	21,120	C
Wittenberg Univ	OH	47,962	C+
Wright State Univ	OH	16,983	C
Xavier Univ	OH	44,980	VC
York College	NE	19,475	C
York College of Pennsylvania	PA	26,590	C
Youngstown State Univ	OH	16,732	C

SPECIFIC LEARNING DISABILITIES

School	ST	$IS	SR
Aquinas College	MI	33,060	C
Baldwin Wallace Univ	OH	38,318	C
Barton College	NC	27,660	LC
Florida International Univ	FL	17,747	C+
Florida State Univ	FL	16,715	VC
Idaho State Univ	ID	12,307	C
Murray State Univ	KY	15,304	C
Northwest Missouri State Univ	MO	17,347	C
Univ of South Florida/Tampa	FL	13,000	C
Winona State Univ	MN	16,640	C

SPEECH AND THEATRE EDUCATION

School	ST	$IS	SR
College of the Ozarks	MO		VC
Missouri Southern State Univ	MO	12,061	C

SPEECH CORRECTION

School	ST	$IS	SR
Columbia College	SC	27,882	C
East Texas Baptist Univ	TX	31,577	LC
Ithaca College	NY	53,864	HC
Kutztown Univ of Pennsylvania	PA	16,909	LC
Lewis Univ	IL	23,050	C
MidAmerica Nazarene Univ	KS	28,000	C
New York Univ	NY	61,470	MC
Western Carolina Univ	NC	13,965	C

SPEECH PATHOLOGY/ AUDIOLOGY

School	ST	$IS	SR
Adelphi Univ	NY	44,670	VC

ST = STATE $IS = IN-STATE COSTS   SR = SELECTOR RATING

School	ST	$IS	SR
Alabama A&M Univ	AL	10,084	C
Andrews Univ	MI	28,030	C+
Appalachian State Univ	NC	12,919	VC
Arizona State Univ, at the Tempe Campus	AZ	20,137	C+
Auburn Univ	AL	22,378	VC+
Augustana College	IL	43,398	VC
Ball State Univ	IN	17,850	C
Baylor Univ	TX	50,329	HC
Biola Univ	CA	40,320	C+
Bloomsburg Univ of Pennsylvania	PA	13,598	C
Boston Univ	MA	60,694	MC
Brescia Univ	KY	26,140	VC+
Brigham Young Univ	UT	12,100	HC
Buffalo State College / SUNY	NY	15,733	C+
Butler Univ	IN	47,572	VC+
Cal State, East Bay	CA	16,549	C
Cal State, Fresno	CA	17,405	C
Cal State, Fullerton	CA	25,188	C
Cal State, Los Angeles	CA	17,186	LC
Cal State, Northridge	CA	28,690	LC
Cal State, Sacramento	CA	16,200	C
Calvin College	MI	39,120	VC
Case Western Reserve Univ	OH	56,534	MC
CUNY/Brooklyn College	NY	5,884	C
Clarion Univ of Pennsylvania	PA	17,370	LC
Clemson Univ	SC	19,136	HC
Cleveland State Univ	OH	21,776	C
Colo State Univ-Pueblo	CO	16,183	C
Delta State Univ	MS	12,292	LC
Duquesne Univ	PA	43,720	VC
East Carolina Univ	NC	14,169	C
East Stroudsburg Univ of Pennsylvania	PA	18,868	LC
Eastern Mich Univ	MI	18,604	C
Eastern New Mexico Univ	NM	10,682	C
Eastern Washington Univ	WA		C
Edinboro Univ of Pennsylvania	PA	15,940	LC
Elmhurst College	IL	43,336	C
Elmira College	NY	49,950	C+
Elms College	MA	23,900	VC
Emerson College	MA	52,446	HC+
Florida State Univ	FL	16,715	VC
Fontbonne Univ	MO	31,384	C
Fort Hays State Univ	KS	11,354	C
Geneva College	PA	27,280	C
George Washington Univ	DC	57,108	MC
Hampton Univ	VA	28,528	C
Harding Univ	AR	23,556	C
Hardin-Simmons Univ	TX	23,560	C+
Hofstra Univ	NY	51,810	VC+
Howard Univ	DC	13,646	C
Idaho State Univ	ID	12,307	C
Illinois State Univ	IL	23,110	VC
Indiana State Univ	IN	16,000	C
Indiana Univ Bloomington	IN	19,801	VC
Indiana Univ of Pennsylvania	PA	20,846	LC
Indiana Univ-Purdue Univ Fort Wayne	IN	15,521	C
Iona College	NY	44,028	C
Ithaca College	NY	53,864	HC
James Madison Univ	VA	18,049	VC
Kansas State Univ	KS	15,497	VC
Kean Univ	NJ	23,444	C
Kent State Univ	OH	19,920	C
Kutztown Univ of Pennsylvania	PA	16,909	LC
La Salle Univ	PA	50,270	C
Lamar Univ	TX	6,820	LC
Lehman College/The CUNY	NY	5,778	LC
LIU Post	NY	47,660	C
Louisiana State Univ	LA	18,677	C+
Louisiana Tech Univ	LA	11,302	C
Loyola Univ Maryland	MD	56,880	VC+
Marquette Univ	WI	46,930	VC+
Marshall Univ	WV	14,820	C
Marymount Manhattan College	NY	40,118	VC
Marywood Univ	PA	45,595	C
Mercy College	NY	30,456	C
Miami Univ	OH	24,191	VC
Mich State Univ	MI	22,450	VC
Minn State Univ, Mankato	MN	15,616	C
Minn State Univ, Moorhead	MN	13,392	VC
Minot State Univ	ND	10,915	C
Miss Univ for Women	MS	7,400	C
Missouri State Univ	MO	13,996	C+
Molloy College	NY	40,440	C
Murray State Univ	KY	15,304	C
Nazareth College of Rochester	NY	43,028	C+
New Mexico State Univ	NM	14,050	C
New York Univ	NY	61,470	MC
Nicholls State Univ	LA	7,095	C
N Car State Univ	NC	16,202	HC
Northeastern Univ	MA	55,296	MC
Northern Illinois Univ	IL	19,768	C
Northern Mich Univ	MI	18,278	C
Northern State Univ - Aberdeen	SD	14,505	C
Northwestern Univ	IL	61,640	MC
Nova Southeastern Univ	FL	37,280	VC
Okla State Univ	OK	14,310	VC
Old Dominion Univ	VA	19,483	LC
Ouachita Baptist Univ	AR	30,220	VC
Our Lady of the Lake Univ	TX	22,430	LC
Pace Univ	NY	53,367	LC
Purdue Univ/West Lafayette	IN	20,024	HC
Queens College/The CUNY	NY	17,107	VC
Radford Univ	VA	17,766	LC
Richard Stockton College of New Jersey	NJ	20,000	VC
Rockhurst Univ	MO	20,625	C
St. Louis Univ	MO	48,346	HC
St. Mary's College	IN	45,160	C+
St. Xavier Univ	IL	32,840	C
San Diego State Univ	CA	21,611	C+
San Francisco State Univ	CA	18,514	C
San Jose State Univ	CA	19,133	LC
Shaw Univ	NC	15,488	C
S Car State Univ	SC	6,700	LC
Southern Illinois Univ Carbondale	IL	21,942	C
Southern Illinois Univ Edwardsville	IL	17,532	C
Southern Univ and A&M College	LA	9,761	LC
St. Cloud State Univ	MN	10,600	C
St. John's Univ	NY	55,070	C+
SUNY Cortland/The SUNY	NY	19,759	C+
SUNY Fredonia/The SUNY at Fredonia	NY	19,840	VC
SUNY New Paltz	NY	14,348	C
Syracuse Univ	NY	56,346	VC
Tenn State Univ	TN	9,048	C
Texas A&M Univ at Kingsville	TX	7,500	LC
Texas Christian Univ	TX	49,980	HC
Texas State Univ	TX	17,128	C
The College of Idaho	ID	31,277	C+
Ohio State Univ-Columbus Campus	OH	19,887	HC+
The Univ of N Car at Greensboro	NC	12,848	C
The Univ of Utah	UT	16,463	VC
Thiel College	PA	38,728	LC
Towson Univ	MD	16,000	VC
Truman State Univ	MO	15,541	HC
Univ at Buffalo / The SUNY	NY	20,283	VC
Univ of Akron	OH	20,436	C
Univ of Arizona	AZ	20,657	C
Univ of Arkansas at Little Rock	AR	17,609	LC
Univ of Central Arkansas	AR	13,667	VC
Univ of Central Florida	FL	15,668	VC+
Univ of Central Missouri	MO	14,605	C
Univ of Central Okla	OK	12,293	C
Univ of Cincinnati	OH	21,506	VC
Univ of Colo Boulder	CO	22,605	VC+
Univ of Florida	FL	15,943	HC
Univ of Hawaii at Manoa	HI	19,379	C
Univ of Iowa	IA	17,693	VC
Univ of Louisiana at Lafayette	LA	6,130	C
Univ of Louisiana at Monroe	LA	12,998	C
Univ of Maine	ME	19,902	C+
Univ of Maryland - College Park	MD	20,060	HC
Univ of Mass Amherst	MA	24,215	VC+
Univ of Minn/Twin Cities	MN		HC
Univ of Montevallo	AL	17,060	C
Univ of Nebr - Lincoln	NE	18,031	VC
Univ of Nevada/Reno	NV	17,507	C
Univ of New Hampshire	NH	26,912	C
Univ of New Mexico	NM	15,300	C
Univ of North Texas	TX	15,628	C
Univ of Northern Colo	CO	18,446	C
Univ of Northern Iowa	IA	15,795	C
Univ of Oregon	OR	21,360	C+
Univ of Science and Arts of Okla	OK	10,560	VC
Univ of South Alabama	AL	13,510	C
Univ of S Dak	SD	15,111	C
Univ of Southern Miss	MS	13,170	C
Univ of Texas - Pan American	TX	11,125	LC
Univ of Texas at Austin	TX	44,074	HC
Univ of Texas at Dallas	TX	21,348	HC+
Univ of the District of Columbia	DC	7,244	LC
Univ of the Pacific	CA	52,146	VC
Univ of Toledo	OH	18,464	C
Univ of Tulsa	OK	46,331	MC
Univ of Vermont	VT	27,006	VC+
Univ of Virginia	VA	23,050	MC
Univ of Washington	WA	14,722	VC
Univ of West Georgia	GA	15,488	LC
Univ of Wisc/Madison	WI	18,757	HC+
Univ of Wisc/Oshkosh	WI	10,426	LC
Univ of Wisc/River Falls	WI	9,722	LC
Univ of Wisc/Stevens Point	WI	14,043	C
Univ of Wisc-Milwaukee	WI	18,436	C
Univ of Wyoming	WY	14,401	C+
Utah State Univ	UT	12,044	C
Washington State Univ	WA	20,461	C
Wayne State Univ	MI	22,063	C
West Chester Univ of Pennsylvania	PA	17,186	C
West Liberty Univ	WV	9,142	LC
West Texas A&M Univ	TX	13,478	C
West Virginia Univ	WV	16,542	C+
Western Kentucky Univ	KY	11,000	C
Western Mich Univ	MI	19,628	C
Western Washington Univ	WA	18,519	VC
Wichita State Univ	KS	14,607	C+
Worcester State Univ	MA	19,812	C
Xavier Univ of Louisiana	LA	25,300	C

SPEECH THERAPY

School	ST	$IS	SR
Baylor Univ	TX	50,329	HC
Biola Univ	CA	40,320	C+
Cal State, Fresno	CA	17,405	C
Cleveland State Univ	OH	21,776	C
Ithaca College	NY	53,864	HC
Misericordia Univ	PA	41,060	C
Southern Univ and A&M College	LA	9,761	LC
Stephen F. Austin State Univ	TX	14,668	C
Temple Univ	PA	24,392	VC
Ohio State Univ-Columbus Campus	OH	19,887	HC+

SPEECH/DEBATE/RHETORIC

School	ST	$IS	SR
Albany State Univ	GA	8,500	C
Arkansas Tech Univ	AR	13,982	LC
Ashland Univ	OH	25,000	C
Auburn Univ	AL	22,378	VC+
Augsburg College	MN	35,142	C
Augustana College	IL	43,398	VC
Ball State Univ	IN	17,850	C
Bates College	ME	60,720	MC
Baylor Univ	TX	50,329	HC
Bellarmine Univ	KY	42,950	VC
Binghamton Univ/The SUNY	NY	21,648	HC+
Black Hills State Univ	SD	13,947	C
Bloomsburg Univ of Pennsylvania	PA	13,598	C
Bridgewater State Univ	MA	18,752	C
Butler Univ	IN	47,572	VC+
Cal State, East Bay	CA	16,549	C
Cal State, Fresno	CA	17,405	C
Cal State, Fullerton	CA	25,188	C
Cal State, Los Angeles	CA	17,186	LC
Cal State, Northridge	CA	28,690	LC
Calif Univ of Pennsylvania	PA	14,217	C
Canisius College	NY	44,900	C
Capital Univ	OH	41,050	VC
Central Washington Univ	WA	11,730	C
Chadron State College	NE	7,400	NC
Charleston Southern Univ	SC	22,420	C
Chicago State Univ	IL	5,482	C
CUNY/Brooklyn College	NY	5,884	C+
Clarion Univ of Pennsylvania	PA	17,370	LC
Clark Atlanta Univ	GA	30,006	LC
Concordia Univ Nebr	NE	26,000	VC
Concordia Univ Wisc	WI	28,980	C
Cornerstone Univ and Grand Rapids Theological Seminary	MI	33,338	C
Denison Univ	OH	54,670	HC+
DePaul Univ	IL	47,623	VC
Dickinson State Univ	ND	11,900	NC
Dordt College	IA	34,160	C+
Dowling College	NY	25,000	C
Drake Univ	IA	41,516	VC+
Duquesne Univ	PA	43,720	VC
East Carolina Univ	NC	14,169	C
East Central Univ	OK	10,223	LC
East Tenn State Univ	TN	9,000	C
East Texas Baptist Univ	TX	31,577	LC
Eastern Kentucky Univ	KY	11,161	C
Eastern Mich Univ	MI	18,604	C
Eastern Nazarene College	MA	30,000	C
Eastern Washington Univ	WA		C
Emerson College	MA	52,446	HC+
Evangel Univ	MO	23,090	C
Fairmont State Univ	WV	12,098	LC
Fayetteville State Univ	NC	10,816	C
Fisk Univ	TN	19,830	C
Florida State Univ	FL	16,715	VC
Freed-Hardeman Univ	TN	19,697	VC
Geneva College	PA	27,280	C
Georgia College and State Univ	GA	18,900	C+
Georgia State Univ	GA	15,582	VC
Gonzaga Univ	WA	46,441	HC
Graceland Univ	IA	28,020	C
Greenville College	IL	27,012	C
Gustavus Adolphus College	MN	48,170	HC
Hannibal-LaGrange Univ	MO	24,490	C
Hardin-Simmons Univ	TX	23,560	C+
Hastings College	NE	27,782	C+
Hillsdale College	MI	32,866	MC
Hofstra Univ	NY	51,810	VC+
Humboldt State Univ	CA	18,400	C
Illinois College	IL	25,770	VC
Illinois State Univ	IL	23,110	VC
Indiana Univ-Purdue Univ Fort Wayne	IN	15,521	C
Iona College	NY	44,028	C
Iowa State Univ	IA	16,403	C
Jackson State Univ	MS	13,512	LC
James Madison Univ	VA	18,049	VC
Kansas Wesleyan Univ	KS	32,000	C
Kutztown Univ of Pennsylvania	PA	16,909	LC
Lamar Univ	TX	6,820	LC
Lander Univ	SC	22,514	C+
Langston Univ	OK	3,000	C
Lehman College/The CUNY	NY	5,778	LC
Lock Haven Univ of Pennsylvania	PA	18,028	LC
Louisiana College	LA	15,746	C
Louisiana Tech Univ	LA	11,302	C
Madonna Univ	MI	24,540	VC
Marietta College	OH	42,135	C+
McKendree Univ	IL	29,920	C+
McPherson College	KS	28,138	C
Metropolitan State Univ of Denver	CO	4,835	LC
Miami Univ	OH	24,191	VC
Minn State Univ, Mankato	MN	15,616	C
Minn State Univ, Moorhead	MN	13,392	VC
Miss Valley State Univ	MS	9,706	LC
Missouri State Univ	MO	13,996	C+
Missouri Valley College	MO	22,200	C
Missouri Western State Univ	MO	12,260	NC
Montclair State Univ	NJ	22,614	C
Morehead State Univ	KY	10,900	C
Morgan State Univ	MD	14,500	VC
Muskingum Univ	OH	30,502	C
New York Univ	NY	61,470	MC
N Car Agricultural and Technical State Univ	NC	13,365	LC
North Central College	IL	38,343	VC
Northeastern State Univ	OK	8,615	VC
Northern Kentucky Univ	KY	21,134	C
Northern Mich Univ	MI	18,278	C
Northwest Missouri State Univ	MO	17,347	C
Northwestern Okla State Univ	OK	7,275	NC
Ohio Univ	OH	21,080	C
Okla Baptist Univ	OK	28,202	C
Oral Roberts Univ	OK	31,734	C
Oregon State Univ	OR	20,273	VC
Otterbein College	OH	32,214	C
Ouachita Baptist Univ	AR	30,220	VC
Pepperdine Univ	CA	55,372	HC+
Portland State Univ	OR	18,672	C
Prairie View A&M Univ	TX	15,205	LC
Radford Univ	VA	17,766	LC
Rowan Univ	NJ	24,022	VC+
St. Mary's Univ	TX	33,854	C
Sam Houston State Univ	TX	17,082	C
San Francisco State Univ	CA	18,514	C
San Jose State Univ	CA	19,133	LC
Shippensburg Univ of Pennsylvania	PA	20,934	C
Southeastern Okla State Univ	OK	7,966	LC
Southern Illinois Univ Carbondale	IL	21,942	C
Southern Illinois Univ Edwardsville	IL	17,532	C
Southern Nazarene Univ	OK	24,354	C
Southern Univ at New Orleans	LA	2,963	NC
Southwestern Adventist Univ	TX	23,026	LC
St. Ambrose Univ	IA	30,845	C
St. Catherine Univ	MN	37,782	C+
St. Cloud State Univ	MN	10,600	C
St. John's Univ	NY	55,070	C+
St. Joseph's College, New York/Brooklyn Campus	NY	22,630	C
St. Joseph's College, New York/Suffolk Campus	NY	22,630	C
Stephen F. Austin State Univ	TX	14,668	C
Suffolk Univ	MA	47,298	C
SUNY New Paltz	NY	14,348	C
Syracuse Univ	NY	56,346	VC
Tarleton State Univ	TX	13,489	LC
Temple Univ	PA	24,392	VC
Tenn State Univ	TN	9,048	C
Texas A&M Univ	TX	19,207	VC
Texas A&M Univ at Corpus Christi	TX	11,544	LC
The Pennsylvania State Univ - Univ Park	PA	28,022	VC+
Touro College	NY	27,959	VC
Univ of Alaska Southeast	AK	11,493	C
Univ of Arkansas at Monticello	AR	12,076	NC
Univ of Arkansas at Pine Bluff	AR	13,378	C
Univ of Calif at Berkeley	CA	23,322	MC
Univ of Calif at Davis	CA		HC
Univ of Central Arkansas	AR	13,667	VC
Univ of Central Missouri	MO	14,605	C
Univ of Cincinnati	OH	21,506	VC
Univ of Dubuque	IA	30,200	C
Univ of Florida	FL	15,943	HC
Univ of Hawaii at Manoa	HI	19,379	C
Univ of Illinois at Urbana-Champaign	IL	26,450	VC
Univ of Indianapolis	IN	31,740	LC
Univ of Iowa	IA	17,693	VC
Univ of Kansas	KS	17,603	C+
Univ of La Verne	CA	47,010	C
Univ of Mary Hardin-Baylor	TX	31,950	C+
Univ of Mich/Ann Arbor	MI	22,102	MC
Univ of Minn/Morris	MN	17,150	C
Univ of Minn/Twin Cities	MN		HC

ST = STATE $IS = IN-STATE COSTS SR = SELECTOR RATING

School	ST	$IS	SR
Univ of Nebr - Lincoln	NE	18,031	VC
Univ of Nebr at Kearney	NE	14,855	LC
Univ of Nebr at Omaha	NE	12,700	C
Univ of N Car at Wilmington	NC	13,572	VC
Univ of Northern Iowa	IA	15,795	C
Univ of Sioux Falls	SD	22,990	C
Univ of S Car at Columbia	SC	19,725	VC+
Univ of South Florida/Tampa	FL	13,000	C
Univ of Southern Indiana	IN	14,885	C
Univ of Southern Miss	MS	13,170	C
Univ of Texas at Arlington	TX	10,908	LC
Univ of Texas at Austin	TX	44,074	HC
Univ of Texas at El Paso	TX	8,764	NC
Univ of Washington	WA	14,722	VC
Univ of Wisc Whitewater	WI	13,314	C
Univ of Wisc/La Crosse	WI	9,304	C
Univ of Wisc/Oshkosh	WI	10,426	LC
Univ of Wisc/River Falls	WI	9,722	LC
Univ of Wisc/Superior	WI	14,314	C
Wabash College	IN	46,850	C+
Walla Walla Univ	WA	26,256	NC
Washburn Univ	KS	12,579	C
Wayne State College	NE	11,764	NC
West Texas A&M Univ	TX	13,478	C
West Virginia Univ	WV	16,542	C+
West Virginia Wesleyan College	WV	26,880	C
Western Carolina Univ	NC	13,965	C
Western Oregon Univ	OR	15,021	C
Whitman College	WA	55,988	MC
Whitworth Univ	WA	47,734	VC
Willamette Univ	OR	56,450	VC+
Wilmington College	OH	29,784	C
Winona State Univ	MN	16,640	C
Yeshiva Univ	NY	47,250	VC+
York College / The CUNY	NY	5,496	VC

SPORT & LIFESTYLE STUDIES

School	ST	$IS	SR
Ohio Univ	OH	21,080	C

SPORTS ADMINISTRATION

School	ST	$IS	SR
Bethany College	WV	35,282	LC
Ohio Univ	OH	21,080	C
Southern Illinois Univ Carbondale	IL	21,942	C
Southern Methodist Univ	TX	60,585	MC

SPORTS AND WELLNESS STUDIES

School	ST	$IS	SR
Adams State Univ	CO	13,358	LC
Aquinas College	MI	33,060	C
Averett Univ	VA	37,750	C
Corban Univ	OR	37,380	C+
Dakota Wesleyan Univ	SD	23,000	C
Ithaca College	NY	53,864	HC
Mercy College	NY	30,456	C
Nova Southeastern Univ	FL	37,280	VC
Okla Christian Univ	OK	25,870	VC
Southwestern College	KS	29,270	C
SUNY Plattsburgh / SUNY	NY	18,083	C
Univ of Illinois at Chicago	IL	24,505	VC
Univ of Montana-Western	MT	9,753	LC
Westminster College	MO	31,720	VC
Winthrop Univ	SC	21,120	C

SPORTS COMMUNICATION

School	ST	$IS	SR
Bethany College	WV	35,282	LC
Ferris State Univ	MI	20,047	C
Indiana Univ Bloomington	IN	19,801	VC

SPORTS MANAGEMENT

School	ST	$IS	SR
Adams State Univ	CO	13,358	LC
Adrian College	MI	42,400	C
Alvernia Univ	PA	39,250	LC
Anderson Univ	IN	36,100	C
Anna Maria College	MA	34,600	C
Aquinas College	MI	33,060	C
Arkansas State Univ	AR	15,470	C
Asbury Univ	KY	32,038	VC
Ashford Univ	CA	10,480	C
Augustana College	SD	36,500	VC
Baker Univ	KS	33,350	C+
Baldwin Wallace Univ	OH	38,318	C
Barry Univ	FL	38,190	C
Barton College	NC	27,660	LC
Becker College	MA	41,420	C
Belmont Abbey College	NC	37,716	C
Bethany College	KS	30,605	NC
Bethany College	WV	35,282	LC
Bethel College	IN	31,560	C
Blackburn College	IL	21,350	C
Bluffton Univ	OH	38,948	C
Bowling Green State Univ	OH	18,970	C
Buena Vista Univ	IA	39,188	C
Cabrini College	PA	40,859	LC
Calif Univ of Pennsylvania	PA	14,217	C
Calvin College	MI	39,120	VC
Cameron Univ	OK	10,004	LC
Campbell Univ	NC	37,570	VC
Campbellsville Univ	KY	27,720	C
Canisius College	NY	44,900	C
Castleton State College	VT	20,186	C
Catawba College	NC	37,240	LC
Cedarville Univ	OH	32,860	VC
Central Methodist Univ	MO	28,240	VC
Claflin Univ	SC	22,368	LC
Clarke Univ	IA	37,600	C
Coastal Carolina Univ	SC	18,580	C
Colby-Sawyer College	NH	50,790	C
College of Mount St. Joseph	OH	33,880	C
College of St Joseph	VT	30,600	LC
Columbia College	MO	24,578	C
Concordia Univ Nebr	NE	26,000	VC
Concordia Univ St. Paul	MN	28,250	C
Coppin State Univ	MD	16,227	VC
Corban Univ	OR	37,380	C+
Cornerstone Univ and Grand Rapids Theological Seminary	MI	33,338	C
Culver-Stockton College	MO	30,900	C
Dakota Wesleyan Univ	SD	23,000	C
Dallas Baptist Univ	TX	30,580	VC
Daniel Webster College	NH	25,380	C
De Sales Univ	PA	43,970	C
Defiance College	OH	30,645	C
Delaware Valley College	PA	29,944	C
Dordt College	IA	34,160	C+
Dowling College	NY	25,000	LC
Drexel Univ	PA	61,418	VC+
Drury Univ	MO	31,909	VC
Eastern Conn State Univ	CT	20,584	C
Edinboro Univ of Pennsylvania	PA	15,940	LC
Elmhurst College	IL	43,336	C
Elon Univ	NC	41,914	VC+
Emmanuel College	MA	47,985	VC
Endicott College	MA	43,228	VC+
Erskine College	SC	37,360	C
Farmingdale State College	NY	19,673	C
Faulkner Univ	AL	25,720	C
Ferrum College	VA	27,740	LC
Flagler College	FL	25,180	C
Florida Inst of Technology	FL	48,290	VC
Florida State Univ	FL	16,715	VC
Fontbonne Univ	MO	31,384	C
Franklin Pierce Univ	NH	41,598	C
Fresno Pacific Univ	CA	32,136	C
Gannon Univ	PA	39,608	C
Gardner-Webb Univ	NC	34,375	C+
Georgetown College	KY	41,440	C+
Georgia Southern Univ	GA	16,942	C
Glenville State College	WV	11,348	NC
Goldey-Beacom College	DE	27,493	C
Gonzaga Univ	WA	46,441	HC
Grand Canyon Univ	AZ	24,540	VC
Grand View Univ	IA	31,050	C
Guilford College	NC	42,800	C
Gwynedd-Mercy College	PA	33,560	C
Hampton Univ	VA	28,528	C
Harding Univ	AR	23,556	C
Heidelberg Univ	OH	34,100	C
Hilbert College	NY	28,550	C
Hillsdale College	MI	32,866	MC
Holy Family Univ	PA	40,030	LC
Hope International Univ	CA	34,650	C
Howard Univ	DC	13,646	C
Huntingdon College	AL	33,100	C
Huntington Univ	IN	32,220	C+
Husson Univ	ME	24,194	LC
Indiana Inst of Technology	IN	34,240	LC
Indiana State Univ	IN	16,000	C
Indiana Univ Bloomington	IN	19,801	VC
Indiana Univ-Purdue Univ Indianapolis	IN	17,611	C
Iowa Wesleyan College	IA	30,850	LC
Ithaca College	NY	53,864	HC
Johnson & Wales Univ/ Charlotte Campus	NC	29,576	C
Johnson & Wales Univ/ Denver Campus	CO	29,576	C
Johnson & Wales Univ/North Miami Campus	FL		C
Johnson & Wales Univ/ Providence Campus	RI	29,576	C
Johnson C. Smith Univ	NC	25,336	LC
Judson Univ	IL	25,130	C
Kent State Univ	OH	19,920	C
Kentucky Wesleyan College	KY	27,440	C
Keystone College	PA	28,680	LC
King Univ	TN	33,140	C
Lake Erie College	OH	37,266	C
Lasell College	MA	43,750	LC
Lees-McRae College	NC	33,944	C
Lenoir-Rhyne College	NC	35,984	C
Lewis Univ	IL	23,050	C
Liberty Univ	VA	19,101	C
Limestone College	SC	30,800	C
Lindenwood Univ	MO	20,750	C
Lipscomb Univ	TN	37,490	VC
Livingstone College	NC	17,815	C
Louisiana State Univ	LA	18,677	C+
Loyola Univ Chicago	IL	51,646	VC+
Lubbock Christian Univ	TX	26,308	C
Lynchburg College	VA	42,645	C
Lyndon State College	VT	14,233	C
Lynn Univ	FL	43,500	LC
MacMurray College	IL	20,755	C
Madonna Univ	MI	24,540	VC
Malone Univ	OH	35,364	C
Marian Univ	IN	38,540	C
Marian Univ	WI	32,420	LC
Marietta College	OH	42,135	C+
Marshall Univ	WV	14,820	C
Maryville Univ of St. Louis	MO	35,856	VC
Mayville State Univ	ND	11,401	NC
Medaille College	NY	35,112	C
Menlo College	CA	49,002	C
Messiah College	PA	40,690	C+
Methodist Univ	NC	37,185	C
Miami Univ	OH	24,191	VC
Mich Tech Univ	MI	23,556	HC
MidAmerica Nazarene Univ	KS	28,000	C
Midway College	KY	20,150	LC
Millikin Univ	IL	38,940	C
Minn State Univ, Mankato	MN	15,616	C
Misericordia Univ	PA	41,060	C
Miss Univ for Women	MS	7,400	C
Missouri Baptist Univ	MO	31,830	C
Mitchell College	CT	40,983	C
Mount St. Mary's Univ	MD	47,996	C
Mount Vernon Nazarene Univ	OH	29,590	C
Nebr Wesleyan Univ	NE	29,774	C+
Neumann Univ	PA	31,078	LC
New England College	NH	45,930	LC
New York Univ	NY	61,470	MC
Newbury College	MA	43,280	LC
Niagara Univ	NY	41,010	C
Nichols College	MA	37,240	LC
North Central College	IL	38,343	VC
N Dak State Univ	ND		C
Northern Kentucky Univ	KY	21,134	C
Northwood Univ	FL	33,192	LC
Northwood Univ	MI	26,331	LC
Ohio Dominican Univ	OH	38,380	C+
Ohio Northern Univ	OH	42,075	VC
Ohio Univ	OH	21,080	C
Ohio Valley Univ	WV	17,752	C
Old Dominion Univ	VA	19,483	LC
Olivet Nazarene Univ	IL	29,990	C
Ouachita Baptist Univ	AR	30,220	VC
Peru State College	NE	8,600	NC
Pfeiffer Univ	NC	33,700	LC
Point Park Univ	PA	36,390	C
Principia College	IL	35,140	C+
Queens Univ of Charlotte	NC	39,543	C+
Quincy Univ	IL	34,980	LC
Roanoke College	VA	49,976	C
Robert Morris Univ	PA	37,864	C
Rochester College	MI	18,320	LC
Rocky Mountain College	MT	32,242	C
Sacred Heart Univ	CT	49,264	VC
St. Joseph's College	IN	36,500	C
St. Leo Univ	FL	30,340	C
St. Mary's Univ of Minn	MN	38,280	C
Salem International Univ	WV	21,090	LC
Samford Univ	AL	37,060	C+
Seton Hall Univ	NJ	45,902	C
Seton Hill Univ	PA	35,172	C
Shawnee State Univ	OH	16,916	C
Shenandoah Univ	VA	39,916	C
Shorter Univ	GA	30,650	LC
Simpson College	IA	36,086	C+
Southeast Missouri State Univ	MO	15,370	LC
Southeastern Louisiana Univ	LA	13,325	C
Southeastern Univ	FL	27,201	C
Southern Nazarene Univ	OK	24,354	C
Southern New Hampshire Univ	NH	38,100	C
Southern Vermont College	VT	30,740	LC
Southern Wesleyan Univ	SC	25,600	C
Southwest Baptist Univ	MO	24,710	C
Southwestern College	KS	29,270	C
Springfield College	MA	25,000	C
St. Ambrose Univ	IA	30,845	C
St. John Fisher College	NY	40,708	C+
St. John's Univ	NY	55,070	C+
St. Thomas Univ	FL	32,310	LC
Sterling College	KS	27,216	C
Stetson Univ	FL	51,516	VC
SUNY Cortland/The SUNY	NY	19,759	C+
SUNY Fredonia/The SUNY at Fredonia	NY	19,840	VC
Syracuse Univ	NY	56,346	VC
Taylor Univ	IN	37,821	VC+
Temple Univ	PA	24,392	VC
Tenn Wesleyan College	TN	21,250	C
Texas Wesleyan Univ	TX	31,382	C
The SUNY/College at Brockport	NY	19,002	C
Thomas College	ME	33,560	LC
Towson Univ	MD	16,000	VC
Trevecca Nazarene Univ	TN	31,186	C
Trine Univ	IN	39,400	HC+
Trinity International Univ	IL	31,070	VC
Troy Univ	AL	10,650	C
Tusculum College	TN	24,295	C
Union College	KY	29,955	C
Union Univ	TN	28,260	VC
Univ of Arkansas at Little Rock	AR	17,609	LC
Univ of Charleston	WV	32,300	C
Univ of Cincinnati	OH	21,506	VC
Univ of Dayton	OH	49,070	VC
Univ of Delaware	DE	23,612	VC
Univ of Evansville	IN	42,656	VC+
Univ of Georgia	GA	20,082	VC
Univ of Idaho	ID	14,558	C
Univ of Indianapolis	IN	31,740	LC
Univ of Kansas	KS	17,603	C+
Univ of Louisville	KY	17,946	C
Univ of Mary Hardin-Baylor	TX	31,950	C+
Univ of Mass Amherst	MA	24,215	VC+
Univ of Miami	FL	57,034	MC
Univ of Mich/Ann Arbor	MI	22,102	MC
Univ of Minn Crookston	MN	17,834	C
Univ of Montana-Western	MT	9,753	LC
Univ of Mount Union	OH	35,130	C
Univ of New England	ME	46,750	C
Univ of New Haven	CT	48,940	C
Univ of North Florida	FL	15,870	VC
Univ of Pittsburgh at Bradford	PA	21,802	C
Univ of St. Mary	KS	28,400	C+
Univ of S Car at Columbia	SC	19,725	VC+
Univ of Southern Indiana	IN	14,885	C
Univ of Tampa	FL	35,160	VC
Univ of Tenn at Knoxville	TN	20,364	VC+
Univ of the Cumberlands	KY	27,500	C
Univ of the Incarnate Word	TX	37,316	LC
Univ of Tulsa	OK	46,331	MC
Univ of West Georgia	GA	15,488	LC
Urbana Univ	OH	30,820	C
Valparaiso Univ	IN	44,940	VC+
Virginia Commonwealth Univ	VA	21,716	C
Viterbo Univ	WI	30,070	C
Warner Univ	FL	18,000	C
Washington State Univ	WA	20,461	C
Wayne State College	NE	11,764	NC
Webber International Univ	FL	30,147	C
Wesley College	DE	31,115	LC
West Virginia Univ	WV	16,542	C+
Western Carolina Univ	NC	13,965	C
Western New England Univ	MA	46,154	C+
Westminster College	MO	31,720	VC
Wichita State Univ	KS	14,607	C+
Wilkes Univ	PA	44,070	C
William Penn Univ	IA	26,000	C
Wilmington College	OH	29,784	C
Wilmington Univ	DE	8,112	NC
Wilson College	PA	35,080	C
Wingate Univ	NC	34,990	C
Winston-Salem State Univ	NC	9,418	LC
Winthrop Univ	SC	21,120	C
Xavier Univ	OH	44,980	VC
York College of Pennsylvania	PA	26,590	C

SPORTS MARKETING

School	ST	$IS	SR
Baylor Univ	TX	50,329	HC
Duquesne Univ	PA	43,720	VC
Miami Univ	OH	24,191	VC
St. Joseph's Univ	PA	55,006	VC
Southern Nazarene Univ	OK	24,354	C
Thomas More College	KY	34,760	C
Xavier Univ	OH	44,980	VC

SPORTS MEDIA

School	ST	$IS	SR
Bethany College	WV	35,282	LC
Ithaca College	NY	53,864	HC
Lasell College	MA	43,750	LC
Marshall Univ	WV	14,820	C
Newman Univ	KS	30,380	C+
Southern Nazarene Univ	OK	24,354	C
Texas Christian Univ	TX	49,980	HC

SPORTS MEDICINE

School	ST	$IS	SR
Alcorn State Univ	MS	9,500	C
Aquinas College	MI	33,060	C
Arizona State Univ, at the Downtown Phoenix Campus	AZ	22,101	C
Avila Univ	MO	26,900	C
Belhaven Univ	MS	27,170	C
Briar Cliff Univ	IA	29,514	C
Campbellsville Univ	KY	27,720	C
Canisius College	NY	44,900	C
Capital Univ	OH	41,050	VC
Concordia Univ Wisc	WI	28,980	C
Eastern Mich Univ	MI	18,604	C
Eastern Nazarene College	MA	30,000	C
Elon Univ	NC	41,914	VC+
Florida State Univ	FL	16,715	VC
Howard Univ	DC	13,646	C
Ithaca College	NY	53,864	HC
John Brown Univ	AR	32,056	VC+
King's College	PA	43,502	C
Lander Univ	SC	22,514	C+
Mercyhurst Univ	PA	40,700	C
Merrimack College	MA	44,215	C
Norwich Univ	VT	28,212	C
Ohio Univ	OH	21,080	C
Pepperdine Univ	CA	55,372	HC+
Samford Univ	AL	37,060	C+

ST = STATE $IS = IN-STATE COSTS   SR = SELECTOR RATING

School	ST	$IS	SR
Southern Oregon Univ	OR	17,874	C
Towson Univ	MD	16,000	VC
Trinity International Univ	IL	31,070	VC
Tusculum College	TN	24,295	C
Union Univ	TN	28,260	VC
Univ of Detroit Mercy	MI	30,450	VC
Univ of Kansas	KS	17,603	C+
Univ of Nevada, Las Vegas	NV	17,303	C
Univ of Pittsburgh at Bradford	PA	21,802	C
Univ of Southern Maine	ME	16,576	C
Western Carolina Univ	NC	13,965	C

SPORTS PSYCHOLOGY

School	ST	$IS	SR
Faulkner Univ	AL	25,720	LC
Hillsdale Univ	MI	32,866	MC
Lubbock Christian Univ	TX	26,308	C
Texas Christian Univ	TX	49,980	HC

SPORTS STUDIES

School	ST	$IS	SR
Bethel College	IN	31,560	C
Brewton-Parker College	GA	33,388	C
Bryant Univ	RI	49,179	VC
Guilford College	NC	42,800	C
Huntingdon College	AL	33,100	C
Huntington Univ	IN	32,220	C+
Ithaca College	NY	53,864	HC
John Carroll Univ	OH	46,300	C+
Lake Erie College	OH	37,266	C
Lasell College	MA	43,750	LC
Manhattanville College	NY	50,740	VC
Miami Univ	OH	24,191	VC
Southern Nazarene Univ	OK	24,354	C
St. Andrews Univ	NC	32,050	LC
St. Bonaventure Univ	NY	41,575	C
Trinity Christian College	IL	28,869	C
Univ of Iowa	IA	17,693	VC
Univ of Kansas	KS	17,603	C+
Univ of Montana-Western	MT	9,753	LC
Vanguard Univ of Southern Calif	CA	35,833	VC

STAGE MANAGEMENT

School	ST	$IS	SR
Ohio Univ	OH	21,080	C

STATISTICS

School	ST	$IS	SR
American Univ	DC	56,015	HC+
Appalachian State Univ	NC	12,919	VC
Arizona State Univ, at the Tempe Campus	AZ	20,137	C+
Arizona State Univ, at the West Campus	AZ	19,251	C
Barnard College/Columbia Univ	NY	39,000	MC
Biola Univ	CA	40,320	C+
Bowling Green State Univ	OH	18,970	C
Brigham Young Univ	UT	12,100	HC
Brown Univ	RI	59,428	MC
Bryant Univ	RI	49,179	VC
Calif Baptist Univ	CA	38,792	C
Calif Polytechnic State Univ	CA	19,847	HC
Cal State, East Bay	CA	16,549	C
Cal State, Fullerton	CA	25,188	C
Cal State, Long Beach	CA	17,502	C+
Carnegie Mellon Univ	PA	51,260	MC
Case Western Reserve Univ	OH	56,534	MC
CUNY/Baruch College	NY		HC
Colo State Univ-Fort Collins	CO	20,385	VC
Columbia Univ/City of New York	NY	61,116	MC
Columbia Univ/School of General Studies	NY	58,231	MC
Cornell Univ	NY	60,964	MC
Eastern Kentucky Univ	KY	11,161	C
Eastern Mich Univ	MI	18,604	C
Elon Univ	NC	41,914	VC+
Florida International Univ	FL	17,747	C+
Florida State Univ	FL	16,715	VC
Fordham Univ	NY	61,588	HC+
George Washington Univ	DC	57,108	MC
Georgia State Univ	GA	15,582	VC
Grand Valley State Univ	MI	17,998	C+
Harvard College/Harvard Univ	MA	49,000	MC
Hunter College	NY	14,429	VC
Idaho State Univ	ID	12,307	C
Indiana Univ Bloomington	IN	19,801	VC
Indiana Univ-Purdue Univ Fort Wayne	IN	15,521	C
Iowa State Univ	IA	16,403	C
James Madison Univ	VA	18,049	VC
Kansas State Univ	KS	15,497	VC
Kent State Univ	OH	19,920	C
Le Moyne College	NY	43,470	C
Lehigh Univ	PA	56,770	MC
Loyola Univ Chicago	IL	51,646	VC+
Luther College	IA	45,720	C+
Marquette Univ	WI	46,930	VC+
Miami Univ	OH	24,191	VC
Mich State Univ	MI	22,450	VC
Mich Tech Univ	MI	23,556	HC
Millersville Univ of Pennsylvania	PA	21,648	C
Missouri Univ of Science and Technology	MO	18,655	VC+
Montana Tech of The Univ of Montana	MT	14,650	VC
Mount Holyoke College	MA	55,146	MC
New York Univ	NY	61,470	MC
N Car State Univ	NC	16,202	HC
N Dak State Univ	ND		C
Northern Kentucky Univ	KY	21,134	C
Northwest Missouri State Univ	MO	17,347	C
Northwestern Univ	IL	61,640	MC
Oakland Univ	MI	19,391	C
Ohio Northern Univ	OH	42,075	VC
Ohio Univ	OH	21,080	C
Okla State Univ	OK	14,310	VC
Old Dominion Univ	VA	19,483	LC
Purdue Univ/West Lafayette	IN	20,024	HC
Rice Univ	TX	43,288	MC
Rochester Inst of Technology	NY	42,450	VC
Roosevelt Univ	IL	22,605	VC
Rutgers, The State Univ of New Jersey/New Brunswick	NJ	25,562	VC
St. Mary's College	IN	45,160	C+
San Diego State Univ	CA	21,611	C+
San Francisco State Univ	CA	18,514	C
San Jose State Univ	CA	19,133	LC
Southern Illinois Univ Edwardsville	IL	17,532	C
Southern Methodist Univ	TX	60,585	MC
St. Cloud State Univ	MN	10,600	C
St. John Fisher College	NY	40,708	C+
SUNY Oneonta / SUNY	NY	16,919	C
The Pennsylvania State Univ - Univ Park	PA	28,022	VC+
Univ of Akron	OH	20,436	C
Univ of Alaska Fairbanks	AK	15,130	C
Univ of Arizona	AZ	20,657	C
Univ of Arkansas at Fayetteville	AR	18,352	C
Univ of Calif at Berkeley	CA	23,322	MC
Univ of Calif at Davis	CA		HC
Univ of Calif at Los Angeles	CA	25,686	MC
Univ of Calif at Riverside	CA	27,204	C+
Univ of Calif at Santa Barbara	CA	27,551	HC
Univ of Central Florida	FL	15,668	VC+
Univ of Chicago	IL	55,416	MC
Univ of Conn	CT	24,706	HC
Univ of Delaware	DE	23,612	VC
Univ of Denver	CO	51,787	VC+
Univ of Florida	FL	15,943	HC
Univ of Georgia	GA	20,082	VC
Univ of Houston-Downtown	TX	15,170	LC
Univ of Illinois at Chicago	IL	24,505	VC
Univ of Illinois at Urbana-Champaign	IL	26,450	HC
Univ of Iowa	IA	17,693	VC
Univ of Louisiana at Lafayette	LA	6,130	C
Univ of Maryland/Baltimore County	MD	18,000	VC
Univ of Miami	FL	57,034	MC
Univ of Mich/Ann Arbor	MI	22,102	MC
Univ of Minn/Duluth	MN	19,806	C
Univ of Minn/Morris	MN	17,150	VC
Univ of Minn/Twin Cities	MN		HC
Univ of Missouri/Columbia	MO	18,201	MC
Univ of Nebr at Kearney	NE	14,855	LC
Univ of New Mexico	NM	15,300	C
Univ of N Car at Wilmington	NC	13,572	VC
Univ of North Florida	FL	15,870	VC
Univ of Northern Colo	CO	18,446	C
Univ of Pennsylvania	PA	61,132	MC
Univ of Pittsburgh at Pittsburgh	PA	28,572	HC+
Univ of Rochester	NY	60,668	MC
Univ of S Car at Columbia	SC	19,725	VC+
Univ of Southern Miss	MS	13,170	C
Univ of Tenn at Knoxville	TN	20,364	VC+
Univ of Texas at El Paso	TX	8,764	NC
Univ of Texas at San Antonio	TX	18,372	C
Univ of Vermont	VT	27,006	VC+
Univ of Washington	WA	14,722	VC
Univ of West Florida	FL	14,656	C
Univ of Wisc/Madison	WI	18,757	HC+
Univ of Wyoming	WY	14,401	C+
Utah State Univ	UT	12,044	C
Virginia Polytechnic Inst and State Univ	VA	14,629	HC
Washington Univ in St. Louis	MO	69,844	MC
West Chester Univ of Pennsylvania	PA	17,186	C
Western Mich Univ	MI	19,628	C
Williams College	MA	61,070	MC
Winona State Univ	MN	16,640	C
Wright State Univ	OH	16,983	C
Xavier Univ of Louisiana	LA	25,300	C
Yale Univ	CT	55,300	MC
Youngstown State Univ	OH	16,732	C

STRATEGIC COMMUNICATION

School	ST	$IS	SR
American Univ	DC	56,015	HC+
Calvin College	MI	39,120	VC
Chapman Univ	CA	58,347	VC+
Concordia Univ St. Paul	MN	28,250	C
Elon Univ	NC	41,914	VC+
Texas Christian Univ	TX	49,980	HC
Univ of Denver	CO	51,787	VC+

STRINGS

School	ST	$IS	SR
Bennington College	VT	56,990	HC+
Central Washington Univ	WA	11,730	C
Eastern Mich Univ	MI	18,604	C
Florida State Univ	FL	16,715	VC
Hardin-Simmons Univ	TX	23,560	C+
Indiana Univ-Purdue Univ Fort Wayne	IN	15,521	C
Manhattan School of Music	NY	55,850	SP
Mannes College New School for Music	NY	44,500	SP
Marshall Univ	WV	14,820	C
Northwestern College	MN	24,000	C
Northwestern Univ	IL	61,640	MC
Oberlin College	OH	61,788	MC
Roosevelt Univ	IL	22,605	VC
San Francisco Conservatory of Music	CA	56,428	SP
Seattle Univ	WA	49,035	VC+
Syracuse Univ	NY	56,346	VC
Texas Christian Univ	TX	49,980	HC
Univ of Iowa	IA	17,693	VC
Univ of Kansas	KS	17,603	C+
Wright State Univ	OH	16,983	C
Youngstown State Univ	OH	16,732	C

STUDIO ART

School	ST	$IS	SR
Adrian College	MI	42,400	C
Agnes Scott College	GA	45,323	C+
Allegheny College	PA	50,980	NC
American Univ	DC	56,015	HC+
Angelo State Univ	TX	15,049	NC
Anna Maria College	MA	34,600	C
Appalachian State Univ	NC	12,919	VC
Assumption College	MA	47,122	C+
Augsburg College	MN	35,142	C
Augustana College	IL	43,398	VC
Baker Univ	KS	33,350	C+
Baldwin Wallace Univ	OH	38,318	C
Bard College	NY	61,940	HC
Barton College	NC	27,660	LC
Baylor Univ	TX	50,329	HC
Bellarmine Univ	KY	42,950	VC
Belmont Univ	TN	39,190	VC+
Beloit College	WI	49,970	HC
Benedict College	SC	20,454	NC
Benedictine Univ	IL	37,820	C
Bennington College	VT	56,990	HC+
Berry College	GA	39,254	VC
Bethany College	WV	35,282	LC
Bethel College	IN	31,560	C
Binghamton Univ/The SUNY	NY	21,648	HC+
Biola Univ	CA	40,320	C+
Birmingham-Southern College	AL	44,168	VC+
Bloomsburg Univ of Pennsylvania	PA	13,598	C
Boston College	MA	60,622	MC
Bowdoin College	ME	59,568	MC
Bradley Univ	IL	31,874	VC
Brandeis Univ	MA		MC
Brenau Univ - Women's College	GA	26,650	LC
Brigham Young Univ	UT	12,100	HC
Cabrini College	PA	40,859	LC
Caldwell College	NJ	35,602	NC
Campbell Univ	NC	37,570	VC
Carleton College	MN	60,102	MC
Carthage College	WI	33,000	C
Cazenovia College	NY	43,464	C
Centenary College of Louisiana	LA	45,650	C+
Central Washington Univ	WA	11,730	C
Christian Brothers Univ	TN	31,670	HC
Clark Univ	MA	47,020	HC+
Clarke Univ	IA	37,600	C
Coastal Carolina Univ	SC	18,500	C
Colby College	ME	57,510	MC
Colby-Sawyer College	NH	50,790	C
Colgate Univ	NY	58,135	MC
College of Charleston	SC	22,145	VC
College of the Holy Cross	MA	58,042	MC
College of the Ozarks	MO		VC
Colo College	CO	57,162	MC
Columbia College	SC	27,882	C
Concordia Univ Nebr	NE	26,000	VC
Concordia Univ St. Paul	MN	28,250	C
Cornell College	IA	44,930	VC
Creighton Univ	NE	45,356	VC
Dartmouth College	NH	57,996	MC
Denison Univ	OH	54,670	HC+
DePauw Univ	IN	48,950	VC+
Drake Univ	IA	41,516	VC+
East Carolina Univ	NC	14,169	C
Eastern Washington Univ	WA		C
Elizabethtown College	PA	49,740	VC
Emmanuel College	MA	47,985	VC
Endicott College	MA	43,228	VC+
Fairfield Univ	CT	56,960	VC
Florida Southern College	FL	40,150	C+
Florida State Univ	FL	16,715	VC
Fordham Univ	NY	61,588	HC+
Framingham State Univ	MA	18,854	C
Franklin and Marshall College	PA	60,799	MC
Franklin College	IN	36,585	C
Gallaudet Univ	DC	25,380	SP
Georgia State Univ	GA	15,582	VC
Gettysburg College	PA	58,820	HC
Graceland Univ	IA	28,020	C
Hamilton College	NY	55,620	MC
Henderson State Univ	AR	14,584	C
Hiram College	OH	37,300	VC
Hobart and William Smith Colleges	NY	60,034	HC+
Hollins Univ	VA	43,295	VC
Houghton College	NY	36,808	C+
Huntington Univ	IN	32,220	C+
Indiana State Univ	IN	16,000	C
Indiana Univ Bloomington	IN	19,801	VC
Indiana Univ of Pennsylvania	PA	20,846	LC
Indiana Wesleyan Univ	IN	31,815	VC
Ithaca College	NY	53,864	HC
Jacksonville Univ	FL	37,780	C
Johnson State College	VT	16,721	C
Juniata College	PA	49,340	VC
Kansas Wesleyan Univ	KS	32,000	C
Kean Univ	NJ	23,444	C
Keene State College	NH	23,232	LC
Kentucky State Univ	KY	11,000	LC
Knox College	IL	44,865	VC+
Kutztown Univ of Pennsylvania	PA	16,909	LC
Lawrence Univ	WI	46,371	HC
Lewis & Clark College	OR	54,382	MC
Lewis Univ	IL	23,050	C
Limestone College	SC	30,800	C
Lindenwood Univ	MO	20,750	C
Linfield College-McMinnville Campus	OR	47,676	C
Lipscomb Univ	TN	37,490	VC
LIU Brooklyn	NY	47,182	VC
Loras College	IA	37,432	VC
Louisiana College	LA	15,746	C
Louisiana State Univ	LA	18,677	C+
Loyola Marymount Univ	CA	54,649	VC+
Loyola Univ Chicago	IL	51,646	VC+
Loyola Univ New Orleans	LA	46,581	VC
Lycoming College	PA	45,379	C
Manhattanville College	NY	50,740	VC
Marian Univ	IN	38,540	C
Marietta College	OH	42,135	C+
Mary Baldwin College	VA	38,245	C
Maryville Univ of St. Louis	MO	35,856	VC
Marywood Univ	PA	45,595	C
Memphis College of Art	TN	33,550	SP
Mercyhurst Univ	PA	40,700	C
Messiah College	PA	40,690	C+
Mich State Univ	MI	22,450	VC
Middle Tenn State Univ	TN	8,650	C
Middlebury College	VT	59,160	MC
Millikin Univ	IL	38,940	C
Mills College	CA	54,119	VC
Millsaps College	MS	43,888	VC+
Minneapolis College of Art and Design	MN	36,700	SP
Missouri Southern State Univ	MO	12,061	C
Montclair State Univ	NJ	22,614	C
Moravian College	PA	36,381	VC
Mount Holyoke College	MA	55,146	MC
Murray State Univ	KY	15,304	C
Nazareth College of Rochester	NY	43,028	C+
Nebr Wesleyan Univ	NE	29,774	C+
New York Univ	NY	61,470	MC
North Central College	IL	38,343	VC
Northeastern Univ	MA	55,296	MC
Northern Arizona Univ	AZ	19,010	C
Northern Illinois Univ	IL	19,768	C
Northern Kentucky Univ	KY	21,134	C
Northwestern College	MN	24,000	C
Notre Dame College	OH	34,942	VC
Notre Dame of Maryland Univ	MD	27,700	VC
Oakland Univ	MI	19,391	C
Oberlin College	OH	61,788	MC
Ohio Univ	OH	21,080	C
Okla City Univ	OK	40,476	VC
Old Dominion Univ	VA	19,483	LC
Oral Roberts Univ	OK	31,734	C
Parsons The New School for Design	NY	56,610	SP
Pomona College	CA	57,680	MC
Prescott College	AZ	33,284	C
Principia College	IL	35,140	C+
Providence College	RI	57,383	VC
Queens College/The CUNY	NY	17,107	VC
Randolph-Macon College	VA	49,869	C+
Rhode Island College	RI	17,694	LC
Rivier Univ	NH	35,000	C
Roberts Wesleyan College	NY	38,306	C+
Rochester Inst of Technology	NY	42,450	VC
Rollins College	FL	52,370	HC
St. Louis Univ	MO	48,346	HC
St. Mary's Univ of Minn	MN	38,280	C

ST = STATE $IS = IN-STATE COSTS SR = SELECTOR RATING

School	ST	$IS	SR
St. Vincent College	PA	40,244	C
Salem College	NC	29,326	VC
Salve Regina Univ	RI	48,550	VC
San Diego State Univ	CA	21,611	C+
Santa Fe Univ of Art and Design	NM	39,666	SP
Scripps College	CA	61,940	MC
Seton Hill Univ	PA	35,172	C
Siena Heights Univ	MI	32,040	C
Silver Lake College	WI	22,600	LC
Smith College	MA	59,674	MC
Southern Conn State Univ	CT	18,033	LC
Southern Illinois Univ Edwardsville	IL	17,532	C
Southern Methodist Univ	TX	60,585	MC
Southern Oregon Univ	OR	17,874	C
Spring Hill College	AL	44,164	VC
St. Lawrence Univ	NY	59,972	VC
St. Olaf College	MN	51,200	HC+
Stanford Univ	CA	58,388	MC
Stetson Univ	FL	51,516	VC
Stony Brook Univ / SUNY	NY	20,078	HC+
SUNY New Paltz	NY	14,348	C
Susquehanna Univ	PA	51,150	C
Texas Christian Univ	TX	49,980	HC
Texas State Univ	TX	17,128	C
Texas Tech Univ	TX	14,243	C
The Catholic Univ of America	DC	52,852	VC
The College of St. Rose	NY	26,750	C
The SUNY at Potsdam	NY	18,473	C
The SUNY/College at Brockport	NY	19,002	C
Transylvania Univ	KY	42,660	VC+
Trinity Christian College	IL	28,869	C
Trinity College	CT		HC+
Troy Univ	AL	10,650	C
Truman State Univ	MO	15,541	HC
Tulane Univ	LA	60,861	MC
Union College	NE	23,270	C
Union College	NY	60,240	MC
Univ at Albany / SUNY	NY	18,674	VC
Univ at Buffalo / The SUNY	NY	20,283	VC
Univ of Akron	OH	20,436	C
Univ of Arizona	AZ	20,657	C
Univ of Calif at Davis	CA		HC
Univ of Calif at Irvine	CA	25,961	VC
Univ of Calif at San Diego	CA	21,000	VC
Univ of Central Missouri	MO	14,605	C
Univ of Colo Boulder	CO	22,605	VC+
Univ of Findlay	OH	31,916	C
Univ of Georgia	GA	20,082	VC
Univ of Houston	TX	19,796	VC
Univ of Idaho	ID	14,558	C
Univ of Illinois at Chicago	IL	24,505	VC
Univ of Indianapolis	IN	31,740	LC
Univ of Maine	ME	19,902	C+
Univ of Mary Washington	VA	19,484	VC
Univ of Maryland - College Park	MD	20,060	HC
Univ of Mass Amherst	MA	24,215	VC+
Univ of Miami	FL	57,034	MC
Univ of Minn/Duluth	MN	19,806	C
Univ of Minn/Morris	MN	17,150	VC
Univ of Minn/Twin Cities	MN		HC
Univ of Missouri-Kansas City	MO	19,603	C
Univ of Missouri-St. Louis	MO		VC
Univ of Montevallo	AL	17,060	C
Univ of Nebr - Lincoln	NE	18,031	VC
Univ of New Hampshire	NH	26,912	C
Univ of New Mexico	NM	15,300	C
Univ of New Orleans	LA	9,224	C
Univ of N Car at Chapel Hill	NC	18,928	MC
Univ of N Car at Wilmington	NC	13,572	VC
Univ of North Texas	TX	15,628	C
Univ of Northern Iowa	IA	15,795	C
Univ of Notre Dame	IN	57,117	MC
Univ of Pittsburgh at Pittsburgh	PA	28,572	HC+
Univ of Redlands	CA	40,500	C
Univ of Rochester	NY	60,668	MC
Univ of St. Francis	IN	29,810	C
Univ of S Car at Columbia	SC	19,725	VC+
Univ of S Car Upstate	SC	18,200	LC
Univ of Southern Calif	CA	56,903	MC
Univ of St. Thomas - Houston	TX	37,690	C
Univ of Tenn at Knoxville	TN	20,364	VC+
Univ of Texas at Arlington	TX	10,908	LC
Univ of Texas at Austin	TX	34,074	HC
Univ of the Pacific	CA	52,146	VC
Univ of Washington	WA	14,722	VC
Univ of West Florida	FL	14,656	C
Univ of Wisc/Stout	WI	15,459	C
Univ of Wisc/Superior	WI	14,314	C
Viterbo Univ	WI	30,070	C
Wake Forest Univ	NC	58,838	MC
Washington and Lee Univ	VA	52,812	MC
Washington Univ in St. Louis	MO	69,844	MC
Webster Univ	MO	35,100	C+
Wellesley College	MA	59,038	MC
Wesleyan College	GA	24,000	C
Wesleyan Univ	CT	61,198	MC
West Chester Univ of Pennsylvania	PA	17,186	C
West Texas A&M Univ	TX	13,478	C

School	ST	$IS	SR
Wheaton College	MA	54,934	HC+
Whitman College	WA	55,988	MC
Wichita State Univ	KS	14,607	C+
Willamette Univ	OR	56,450	VC
William Paterson Univ of New Jersey	NJ	21,694	C
William Woods Univ	MO	24,260	C
Wofford College	SC	45,795	VC
Wright State Univ	OH	16,983	C
York College / The CUNY	NY	5,496	VC
Youngstown State Univ	OH	16,732	C

STUDIO ART CERAMICS

School	ST	$IS	SR
College of the Ozarks	MO		VC
Texas Christian Univ	TX	49,980	HC

STUDIO ART COMPUTER ART

School	ST	$IS	SR
College of the Ozarks	MO		VC

STUDIO ART FIBERS

School	ST	$IS	SR
College of the Ozarks	MO		VC
Old Dominion Univ	VA	19,483	LC

STUDIO ART GRAPHIC DESIGN

School	ST	$IS	SR
Campbell Univ	NC	37,570	VC
College of the Ozarks	MO		VC
Franklin College	IN	36,585	C
Keene State College	NH	23,232	LC

STUDIO ART PAINTING

School	ST	$IS	SR
College of the Ozarks	MO		VC
Franklin College	IN	36,585	C
Missouri Southern State Univ	MO	12,061	C
Oberlin College	OH	61,788	MC
Old Dominion Univ	VA	19,483	LC
Texas Christian Univ	TX	49,980	HC

SUPPLY CHAIN MANAGEMENT

School	ST	$IS	SR
Arizona State Univ, at the Tempe Campus	AZ	20,137	C+
Arizona State Univ, at the West Campus	AZ	19,251	C
Arkansas State Univ	AR	15,470	C
Ashford Univ	CA	10,480	C
Binghamton Univ/The SUNY	NY	21,648	HC+
Bloomfield College	NJ	37,850	LC
Boise State Univ	ID	13,469	LC
Bryant Univ	RI	49,179	VC
Clarkson Univ	NY	57,330	HC
Duquesne Univ	PA	43,720	VC
Eastern Mich Univ	MI	18,604	C
Elmhurst College	IL	43,336	C
Embry-Riddle Aeronautical Univ - Worldwide	FL	15,512	C
Fontbonne Univ	MO	31,384	C
Gannon Univ	PA	39,608	C
Hofstra Univ	NY	51,810	VC+
Howard Univ	DC	13,646	C
Indiana Univ Bloomington	IN	19,801	VC
Indiana Univ-Purdue Univ Indianapolis	IN	17,611	C
Lehigh Univ	PA	56,770	MC
Lipscomb Univ	TN	37,490	VC
Marquette Univ	WI	46,930	VC+
Miami Univ	OH	24,191	VC
Murray State Univ	KY	15,304	C
Old Dominion Univ	VA	19,483	LC
Rutgers, The State Univ of New Jersey/Newark Campus	NJ	258,806	C
Shippensburg Univ of Pennsylvania	PA	20,934	C
Southeastern Louisiana Univ	LA	13,325	C
SUNY Plattsburgh / SUNY	NY	18,083	C
Syracuse Univ	NY	56,346	VC
Texas Christian Univ	TX	49,980	HC
The Pennsylvania State Univ - Univ Park	PA	28,022	VC+
Tuskegee Univ	AL	26,750	C
Univ of Houston	TX	19,796	VC
Univ of Houston-Downtown	TX	15,170	LC
Univ of Kansas	KS	17,603	C+
Univ of Maryland - College Park	MD	20,060	HC
Univ of Mich/Dearborn	MI	9,885	VC
Univ of Nebr - Lincoln	NE	18,031	VC
Univ of N Car at Charlotte	NC	15,547	C
Univ of Pittsburgh at Pittsburgh	PA	28,572	HC+
Univ of Wisc/Stout	WI	15,459	C
Wayne State Univ	MI	22,063	C
Western Illinois Univ	IL	20,732	C
Western Mich Univ	MI	19,628	C
Wright State Univ	OH	16,983	C

SURVEY AND MAPPING TECHNOLOGY

School	ST	$IS	SR
Alfred State/SUNY College of Technology	NY	18,034	C

School	ST	$IS	SR
East Tenn State Univ	TN	9,000	C
Glenville State College	WV	11,348	NC
Metropolitan State Univ of Denver	CO	4,835	LC
Southern Polytechnic State Univ	GA	13,958	C
SUNY / College of Environmental Science and Forestry	NY	18,351	VC
Univ of Akron	OH	20,436	C
Univ of Alaska Anchorage	AK	16,673	NC

SURVEYING ENGINEERING

School	ST	$IS	SR
Cal State, Fresno	CA	17,405	C
Ferris State Univ	MI	20,047	C
Metropolitan State Univ of Denver	CO	4,835	LC
Mich Tech Univ	MI	23,556	HC
New Mexico State Univ	NM	14,050	C
Oregon Inst of Technology	OR	8,910	C
Purdue Univ/West Lafayette	IN	20,024	VC
Universidad Metropolitana	PR	3,500	
Universidad Politecnica de PR	PR	19,252	
Univ of Arkansas at Little Rock	AR	17,609	LC
Univ of Maine	ME	19,902	C+
Univ of PR/Mayaguez	PR	1,250	

SUSTAINABLE MANAGEMENT

School	ST	$IS	SR
American Univ	DC	56,015	HC+
Arizona State Univ, at the West Campus	AZ	19,251	C
Ashford Univ	CA	10,480	C
Aurora Univ	IL	33,228	C
Baldwin Wallace Univ	OH	38,318	C
Catawba College	NC	37,240	LC
Chatham Univ	PA	43,797	C
Goddard College	VT	16,418	VC
Indiana-Purdue Univ Indianapolis	IN	17,611	C
Kean Univ	NJ	23,444	C
Lipscomb Univ	TN	37,490	VC
Marylhurst Univ	OR	20,295	NC
Messiah College	PA	40,690	C+
Univ of Wisc/Green Bay	WI	19,074	C
Univ of Wisc/Stout	WI	15,459	C
Univ of Wisc/Superior	WI	14,314	C
Viterbo Univ	WI	30,070	C
Xavier Univ	OH	44,980	VC

SYSTEMS ANALYSIS

School	ST	$IS	SR
Baldwin Wallace Univ	OH	38,318	C
George Washington Univ	DC	57,108	MC
Johnson & Wales Univ/ Providence Campus	RI	29,576	C
Rochester Inst of Technology	NY	42,450	VC

SYSTEMS ENGINEERING

School	ST	$IS	SR
Binghamton Univ/The SUNY	NY	21,648	HC+
Case Western Reserve Univ	OH	56,534	MC
Embry-Riddle Aeronautical Univ - Worldwide	FL	15,512	C
George Mason Univ	VA	15,724	VC
Missouri Univ of Science and Technology	MO	18,655	VC+
Point Park Univ	PA	36,390	C
Southern Nazarene Univ	OK	24,354	C
Southern Polytechnic State Univ	GA	13,958	C
Stanford Univ	CA	58,388	MC
Stevens Inst of Technology	NJ	50,130	HC
Taylor Univ	IN	37,821	VC+
Texas A&M Univ at Galveston	TX	11,258	C
United States Military Academy	NY		MC
United States Naval Academy	MD		MC
Univ of Arizona	AZ	20,657	C
Univ of New Haven	CT	48,940	C
Univ of N Car at Charlotte	NC	15,547	C
Univ of Southern Calif	CA	56,903	MC
Univ of Virginia	VA	23,050	MC
Washington Univ in St. Louis	MO	69,844	MC
West Virginia Univ	WV	16,542	C+
Wright State Univ	OH	16,983	C

SYSTEMS SCIENCE

School	ST	$IS	SR
Case Western Reserve Univ	OH	56,534	MC
Johnson & Wales Univ/ Providence Campus	RI	29,576	C
Stanford Univ	CA	58,388	MC
Washington Univ in St. Louis	MO	69,844	MC
Worcester Polytechnic Inst	MA	55,860	MC

TEACHING ENGLISH AS A SECOND/FOREIGN LANGUAGE (TESOL/TEFOL)

School	ST	$IS	SR
Andrews Univ	MI	28,030	C+
Aquinas College	MI	33,060	C

School	ST	$IS	SR
Bethel Univ	MN	34,940	VC
Brigham Young Univ/Hawaii	HI	10,686	VC
Campbellsville Univ	KY	27,720	C
Canisius College	NY	44,900	C
Caribbean Univ	PR	10,375	
Carroll College	MT	28,000	C
Elms College	MA	23,900	VC
Goshen College	IN	35,900	VC
Hawaii Pacific Univ	HI	34,360	C
Houghton College	NY	36,808	C+
Houston Baptist Univ	TX	36,450	C
Howard Payne Univ	TX	17,115	C
Huntington Univ	IN	32,220	C+
Inter-American Univ of PR/ Arecibo Campus	PR	3,350	
Inter-American Univ of PR/ San Germán	PR	6,720	
Kent State Univ	OH	19,920	C
Le Moyne College	NY	43,470	C
Mercy College	NY	30,456	C
Missouri Southern State Univ	MO	12,061	C
Murray State Univ	KY	15,304	C
Niagara Univ	NY	41,010	C
Northeastern Illinois Univ	IL	10,318	LC
Nyack College	NY	33,250	C
Okla Christian Univ	OK	25,870	VC
Oswego / SUNY	NY	20,009	VC
Pontifical Catholic Univ of PR	PR	7,310	
Salisbury Univ	MD	19,180	VC
San Jose State Univ	CA	19,133	LC
Seattle Pacific Univ	WA	41,559	VC+
Simmons College	MA	49,966	VC
Taylor Univ	IN	37,821	VC+
Texas Wesleyan Univ	TX	31,382	C
The Univ of Utah	UT	16,463	VC
Union Univ	TN	28,260	VC
Univ of Arizona	AZ	20,657	C
Univ of Georgia	GA	20,082	VC
Univ of Louisville	KY	17,946	C
Univ of Minn/Twin Cities	MN		HC
Univ of Nebr - Lincoln	NE	18,031	VC
Univ of Nebr at Kearney	NE	14,855	LC
Univ of Northern Iowa	IA	15,795	C
Univ of PR/Mayaguez	PR	1,250	
Western Carolina Univ	NC	13,965	C
Winona State Univ	MN	16,640	C

TECHNICAL & APPLIED STUDIES

School	ST	$IS	SR
Ohio Univ	OH	21,080	C

TECHNICAL AND BUSINESS WRITING

School	ST	$IS	SR
Carlow Univ	PA	30,272	C
Cedarville Univ	OH	32,860	VC
Clarkson Univ	NY	57,330	HC
Eastern Mich Univ	MI	18,604	C
Illinois Inst of Technology	IL	38,512	HC+
Indiana Univ-Purdue Univ Fort Wayne	IN	15,521	C
King Univ	TN	33,140	C
Lawrence Tech Univ	MI	37,630	C
Madonna Univ	MI	24,540	VC
Metropolitan State Univ	MN	5,923	
Mich Tech Univ	MI	23,556	HC
Milwaukee School of Engineering	WI	39,948	VC+
Missouri Univ of Science and Technology	MO	18,655	VC+
Mount Mary Univ	WI	33,590	LC
New Jersey Inst of Technology	NJ	26,490	C
New Mexico Inst of Mining and Technology	NM	13,592	VC
New York Univ	NY	61,470	MC
Pittsburg State Univ	KS	12,032	C
Saginaw Valley State Univ	MI	17,369	C
Taylor Univ	IN	37,821	VC+
Tenn Tech Univ	TN	11,310	C
Univ of Arkansas at Little Rock	AR	17,609	LC
Univ of Findlay	OH	31,916	C
Univ of Hartford	CT	42,674	C
Univ of Houston-Downtown	TX	15,170	LC
Univ of Montana-Western	MT	9,753	LC
Univ of Washington	WA	14,722	VC
Valparaiso Univ	IN	44,940	VC+
Winthrop Univ	SC	21,120	C
Worcester Polytechnic Inst	MA	55,860	MC
Youngstown State Univ	OH	16,732	C

TECHNICAL COMMUNICATION

School	ST	$IS	SR
Bowling Green State Univ	OH	18,970	C
Cedarville Univ	OH	32,860	VC
Ferris State Univ	MI	20,047	C
Indiana Univ-Purdue Univ Indianapolis	IN	17,611	C
Mercer Univ	GA	44,201	VC
Minn State Univ, Mankato	MN	15,616	C
Southern Polytechnic State Univ	GA	13,958	C

School	ST	$IS	SR

TECHNICAL EDUCATION

School	ST	$IS	SR
Bowling Green State Univ	OH	18,970	C
Brigham Young Univ	UT	12,100	HC
Central Conn State Univ	CT	19,749	C
College of New Jersey	NJ	25,376	HC
Eastern Illinois Univ	IL	20,466	C
Eastern Kentucky Univ	KY	11,161	C
Eastern Mich Univ	MI	18,604	C
Eastern New Mexico Univ	NM	10,682	C
Elizabeth City State Univ	NC	11,638	C
Ferris State Univ	MI	20,047	C
Fitchburg State Univ	MA	18,173	C
Fort Hays State Univ	KS	11,354	C
Illinois State Univ	IL	23,110	VC
Kent State Univ	OH	19,920	C
Millersville Univ of Pennsylvania	PA	21,648	C
Miss State Univ	MS	14,750	C
Montana State Univ	MT	14,068	C
Murray State Univ	KY	15,304	C
New York College of Technology/The CUNY	NY	5,769	NC
Norfolk State Univ	VA	10,531	LC
N Car State Univ	NC	16,202	HC
Oswego / SUNY	NY	20,009	VC
Pittsburg State Univ	KS	12,032	C
Purdue Univ/West Lafayette	IN	20,024	HC
Rhode Island College	RI	17,694	LC
Rochester College	MI	18,320	LC
S Dak State Univ	SD	14,296	C
Southwestern Okla State Univ	OK	9,160	C
Temple Univ	PA	24,392	VC
Texas State Univ	TX	17,128	C
Ohio State Univ-Columbus Campus	OH	19,887	HC+
Thomas Edison State College	NJ	5,700	SP
Tuskegee Univ	AL	26,750	C
Univ of Akron	OH	20,436	C
Univ of Arkansas at Fayetteville	AR	18,352	C+
Univ of Central Florida	FL	15,668	VC+
Univ of Idaho	ID	14,558	C
Univ of New Mexico	NM	15,300	C
Univ of Northern Iowa	IA	15,795	C
Univ of Southern Maine	ME	16,576	C
Univ of Wisc/Platteville	WI	14,564	C
Univ of Wisc/Stout	WI	15,459	C
Univ of Wyoming	WY	14,401	C+
Valley City State Univ	ND	12,286	LC
Wayne State Univ	MI	22,063	C
Western Kentucky Univ	KY	11,000	LC
Western Washington Univ	WA	18,519	VC

TECHNICAL OPERATIONS MANAGEMENT

School	ST	$IS	SR
Ohio Univ	OH	21,080	C

TECHNOLOGICAL MANAGEMENT

School	ST	$IS	SR
Alfred State/SUNY College of Technology	NY	18,034	C
Arkansas State Univ	AR	15,470	C
Brewton-Parker College	GA	33,388	C
Clayton State Univ	GA	12,000	LC
Colo Technical Univ	CO	10,500	LC
Davenport Univ	MI	21,002	LC
Embry-Riddle Aeronautical Univ - Worldwide	FL	15,512	C
Excelsior College	NY	5,580	SP
Franklin Univ	OH	20,985	SP
Golden Gate Univ	CA	17,000	C
Indiana Univ Bloomington	IN	19,801	VC
Johnson & Wales Univ/ Providence Campus	RI	29,576	C
Lawrence Tech Univ	MI	37,630	VC
LIU Brooklyn	NY	47,182	LC
New Jersey Inst of Technology	NJ	26,490	C+
Northern Illinois Univ	IL	19,768	C
Ohio Northern Univ	OH	42,075	VC
Okla Panhandle State Univ	OK	8,996	C
Oswego / SUNY	NY	20,009	VC
Pennsylvania College of Technology	PA	26,286	NC
Pittsburg State Univ	KS	12,032	C
Roger Williams Univ	RI	46,296	VC
Southeast Missouri State Univ	MO	15,370	LC
Southern New Hampshire Univ	NH	38,100	C
Southern Univ at New Orleans	LA	2,963	NC
Stony Brook Univ / SUNY	NY	20,078	HC+
The SUNY College of Agriculture and Tech at Cobleskill	NY	19,749	LC
Troy Univ	AL	10,650	C
Univ of Alaska Anchorage	AK	16,673	NC
Univ of Findlay	OH	31,916	C
Washburn Univ	KS	12,579	C
Wayne State College	NE	11,764	NC
Wentworth Inst of Technology	MA	29,800	C

TECHNOLOGY & SCIENCE EDUCATION

School	ST	$IS	SR
Colo State Univ-Fort Collins	CO	20,385	VC
Excelsior College	NY	5,580	SP
Univ of Wisc/Stout	WI	15,459	C
Viterbo Univ	WI	30,070	C

TECHNOLOGY AND PUBLIC AFFAIRS

School	ST	$IS	SR
Georgia Inst of Technology	GA	21,828	MC
New Jersey Inst of Technology	NJ	26,490	C+
Pomona College	CA	57,680	MC
Washington Univ in St. Louis	MO	69,844	MC
Western Kentucky Univ	KY	11,000	C
Western Washington Univ	WA	18,519	VC
Worcester Polytechnic Inst	MA	55,860	MC

TELECOMMUNICATIONS

School	ST	$IS	SR
Alabama A&M Univ	AL	10,084	C
Baylor Univ	TX	50,329	HC
Bowling Green State Univ	OH	18,970	C
Cal State, Monterey Bay	CA	26,871	LC
Capitol College	MD	21,250	C
Colo Technical Univ	CO	10,500	LC
Concordia Univ Wisc	WI	28,980	C
Eastern Mich Univ	MI	18,604	C
Fort Hays State Univ	KS	11,354	C
Howard Univ	DC	13,646	C
Illinois State Univ	IL	23,110	VC
Indiana Univ Bloomington	IN	19,801	VC
Indiana-Purdue Univ Fort Wayne	IN	15,521	C
Ithaca College	NY	53,864	HC
Kutztown Univ of Pennsylvania	PA	16,909	LC
Lee Univ	TN	18,690	C+
Mich State Univ	MI	22,450	VC
Morgan State Univ	MD	14,500	VC
New York College of Technology/The CUNY	NY	5,769	NC
New York Inst of Technology	NY	45,010	VC
Ohio Univ	OH	21,080	C
Okla Baptist Univ	OK	28,202	C
Pepperdine Univ	CA	55,372	HC+
Rochester Inst of Technology	NY	42,450	VC
Roosevelt Univ	IL	22,605	VC
San Diego State Univ	CA	21,611	C+
St. John's Univ	NY	55,070	C+
SUNY Polytechnic Inst	NY	19,690	C
Syracuse Univ	NY	56,346	VC
Temple Univ	PA	24,392	VC
Texas Tech Univ	TX	14,243	C
Universidad de Puerto/ Arecibo	PR	7,227	
Univ of Alabama at Tuscaloosa	AL	17,164	C+
Univ of Florida	FL	15,943	HC
Univ of Idaho	ID	14,558	C
Univ of Kentucky	KY	19,868	C
Univ of Louisiana at Lafayette	LA	6,130	C
Univ of Nebr at Kearney	NE	14,855	LC
Univ of North Texas	TX	15,628	C
Univ of Northern Colo	CO	18,446	C
Univ of Texas at Dallas	TX	21,348	HC+
Univ of the Sacred Heart	PR	5,590	
Univ of Wisc/Stout	WI	15,459	C
Western Mich Univ	MI	19,628	C
Youngstown State Univ	OH	16,732	C

TELECOMMUNICATIONS ENGINEERING TECHNOLOGY

School	ST	$IS	SR
Farmingdale State College	NY	19,673	C
Jackson State Univ	MS	13,512	LC
Southern Polytechnic State Univ	GA	13,958	C
Univ of Texas at Dallas	TX	21,348	HC+

TELECOMMUNICATIONS SYSTEMS MGMT

School	ST	$IS	SR
Murray State Univ	KY	15,304	C

TELEVISION & DIGITAL MEDIA PRODUCTION

School	ST	$IS	SR
Bloomfield College	NJ	37,850	LC
Ferris State Univ	MI	20,047	C

TEXTILE ENGINEERING

School	ST	$IS	SR
Auburn Univ	AL	22,378	VC+
Georgia Inst of Technology	GA	21,828	MC
N Car State Univ	NC	16,202	HC
Philadelphia Univ	PA	44,160	C

TEXTILE MARKETING

School	ST	$IS	SR
Univ of Rhode Island	RI	24,002	C

TEXTILE TECHNOLOGY

School	ST	$IS	SR
Clemson Univ	SC	19,136	HC
Fashion Inst of Technology/ SUNY	NY	18,362	SP
Mich State Univ	MI	22,450	VC
Philadelphia Univ	PA	44,160	C
Univ of Wisc/Madison	WI	18,757	HC+

TEXTILE, FASHION MERCHANDISING & DESIGN

School	ST	$IS	SR
Univ of Rhode Island	RI	24,002	C

TEXTILES AND CLOTHING

School	ST	$IS	SR
Albright College	PA	46,660	C
Auburn Univ	AL	22,378	VC+
Calif College of the Arts	CA	48,334	SP
College for Creative Studies	MI	45,340	C
Eastern Mich Univ	MI	18,604	C
Fashion Inst of Technology/ SUNY	NY	18,362	SP
Framingham State Univ	MA	18,854	C
Howard Univ	DC	13,646	C
Indiana State Univ	IN	16,000	C
Iowa State Univ	IA	16,403	C
Kansas State Univ	KS	15,497	VC
Kent State Univ	OH	19,920	C
Lipscomb Univ	TN	37,490	VC
Louisiana State Univ	LA	18,677	C+
Middle Tenn State Univ	TN	8,650	C
Moore College of Art and Design	PA	50,135	SP
New Mexico State Univ	NM	14,050	C
N Car State Univ	NC	16,202	HC
N Dak State Univ	ND		C
Northern Illinois Univ	IL	19,768	C
Northwest Missouri State Univ	MO	17,347	C
Rhode Island School of Design	RI	57,234	MC
Univ of Calif at Davis	CA		HC
Univ of Central Missouri	MO	14,605	C
Univ of Idaho	ID	14,558	C
Univ of Illinois at Urbana-Champaign	IL	26,450	VC
Univ of Kentucky	KY	19,868	C
Univ of Minn/Twin Cities	MN		HC
Univ of Missouri/Columbia	MO	18,201	MC
Univ of Nebr - Lincoln	NE	18,031	VC
Univ of Texas at Austin	TX	44,074	MC
Univ of Wisc/Madison	WI	18,757	HC+
Western Kentucky Univ	KY	11,000	LC
Western Mich Univ	MI	19,628	C

THEATER DESIGN

School	ST	$IS	SR
Adelphi Univ	NY	44,670	VC
Alabama A&M Univ	AL	10,084	C
Arcadia Univ	PA	33,570	C+
Arizona State Univ, at the Tempe Campus	AZ	20,137	C+
Baldwin Wallace Univ	OH	38,318	C
Baylor Univ	TX	50,329	HC
Belmont Univ	TN	39,190	VC+
Bennington College	VT	56,990	HC+
Binghamton Univ/The SUNY	NY	21,648	HC+
Biola Univ	CA	40,320	C+
Boston Univ	MA	60,694	MC
Calif Inst of the Arts	CA	51,902	SP
Cal State, Fresno	CA	17,405	C
Cal State, Fullerton	CA	25,188	C
College of the Ozarks	MO		VC
Colo State Univ-Fort Collins	CO	20,385	VC
Cornish College of the Arts	WA	21,200	SP
De Sales Univ	PA	43,970	C
DePaul Univ	IL	47,623	VC
Elon Univ	NC	41,914	VC+
Emerson College	MA	52,446	HC+
Eugene Lang College/The New School for Liberal Arts	NY	55,650	C
Faulkner Univ	AL	25,720	LC
Florida Southern College	FL	40,150	C+
Florida State Univ	FL	16,715	VC
Fordham Univ	NY	61,588	HC+
Grand Canyon Univ	AZ	24,540	VC
Hofstra Univ	NY	51,810	VC+
Huntington Univ	IN	32,220	C+
Illinois Wesleyan Univ	IL	48,452	HC
Ithaca College	NY	53,864	HC
Johnson State College	VT	16,721	C
Kean Univ	NJ	23,444	C
Lehigh Univ	PA	56,770	MC
Marshall Univ	WV	14,820	C
Mich Tech Univ	MI	23,556	HC
Millikin Univ	IL	38,940	C
Montclair State Univ	NJ	22,614	C
Niagara Univ	NY	41,010	C
Oberlin College	OH	61,788	MC
Ohio Univ	OH	21,080	C
Okla City Univ	OK	40,476	VC
Old Dominion Univ	VA	19,483	LC
Pace Univ	NY	53,367	C+

School	ST	$IS	SR
Palm Beach Atlantic Univ	FL	34,874	C+
Piedmont College	GA	30,136	C
Roosevelt Univ	IL	22,605	VC
Santa Fe Univ of Art and Design	NM	39,666	SP
Seton Hill Univ	PA	35,172	C
Shenandoah Univ	VA	39,916	C
Southern Illinois Univ Edwardsville	IL	17,532	C
SUNY at Purchase	NY	16,951	C
Stephens Univ	MO	38,042	VC
SUNY College at Geneseo	NY	18,670	VC
SUNY Fredonia/The SUNY at Fredonia	NY	19,840	VC
SUNY New Paltz	NY	14,348	C
Syracuse Univ	NY	56,346	VC
Temple Univ	PA	24,392	VC
Texas Christian Univ	TX	49,980	VC
Texas Tech Univ	TX	14,243	C
Texas Wesleyan Univ	TX	31,382	C
Ohio State Univ-Columbus Campus	OH	19,887	HC+
The Pennsylvania State Univ - Univ Park	PA	28,022	VC+
Towson Univ	MD	16,000	VC
Tulane Univ	LA	60,861	MC
Univ of Central Missouri	MO	14,605	C
Univ of Central Okla	OK	12,293	C
Univ of Cincinnati	OH	21,506	VC
Univ of Conn	CT	24,706	MC
Univ of Florida	FL	15,943	HC
Univ of Illinois at Chicago	IL	24,505	VC
Univ of Kansas	KS	17,603	C+
Univ of Maryland/Baltimore County	MD	18,000	C
Univ of Miami	FL	57,034	MC
Univ of Mich/Ann Arbor	MI	22,102	MC
Univ of Nebr - Lincoln	NE	18,031	VC
Univ of New Mexico	NM	15,300	C
Univ of N Car at Wilmington	NC	13,572	VC
Univ of N Car School of the Arts	NC	7,401	SP
Univ of North Texas	TX	15,628	C
Univ of Northern Iowa	IA	15,795	C
Univ of Southern Calif	CA	56,903	MC
Wagner College	NY	48,600	C+
Washburn Univ	KS	12,579	C
Webster Univ	MO	35,100	C+
Western Mich Univ	MI	19,628	C
Western Washington Univ	WA	18,519	VC
Wright State Univ	OH	16,983	C

THEATER MANAGEMENT

School	ST	$IS	SR
Aquinas College	MI	33,060	C
Baldwin Wallace Univ	OH	38,318	C
Barry Univ	FL	38,190	C
Benedictine College	KS	29,180	VC
Bethel Univ	TN	19,186	C
Biola Univ	CA	40,320	C+
Boston Univ	MA	60,694	MC
Cal State, Fullerton	CA	25,188	C
Catawba College	NC	37,240	LC
CUNY/Brooklyn College	NY	5,884	C+
Colo Mesa Univ	CO	17,690	LC
De Sales Univ	PA	43,970	C
DePaul Univ	IL	47,623	VC
Emerson College	MA	52,446	HC+
Fitchburg State Univ	MA	18,173	C
Fontbonne Univ	MO	31,384	C
Grand Canyon Univ	AZ	24,540	VC
Hofstra Univ	NY	51,810	VC+
Illinois Wesleyan Univ	IL	48,452	HC
Ithaca College	NY	53,864	HC
Johnson State College	VT	16,721	C
Marywood Univ	PA	45,595	C
Messiah College	PA	40,690	C+
New York Univ	NY	61,470	MC
Ohio Univ	OH	21,080	C
Pace Univ	NY	53,367	C+
Roosevelt Univ	IL	22,605	VC
St. Louis Univ	MO	48,346	HC
Salisbury Univ	MD	19,180	VC
Santa Fe Univ of Art and Design	NM	39,666	SP
Seton Hill Univ	PA	35,172	C
Syracuse Univ	NY	56,346	VC
Temple Univ	PA	24,392	VC
Trinity College	CT		HC+
Univ of Akron	OH	20,436	C
Univ of Delaware	DE	23,612	VC
Univ of Evansville	IN	42,656	VC+
Univ of Hartford	CT	42,674	C
Univ of Idaho	ID	14,558	C
Univ of Miami	FL	57,034	MC
Univ of North Texas	TX	15,628	C
Univ of Southern Calif	CA	56,903	MC
Univ of Texas at El Paso	TX	8,764	NC
Wright State Univ	OH	16,983	C

THEATRE ACTING

School	ST	$IS	SR
Asbury Univ	KY	32,038	VC
Baldwin Wallace Univ	OH	38,318	C
Bates College	ME	60,720	MC
Bethany College	WV	35,282	LC

School	ST	$IS	SR
Biola Univ	CA	40,320	C+
Colo State Univ-Fort Collins	CO	20,385	VC
De Sales Univ	PA	43,970	C
Dordt College	IA	34,160	C
Eastern Conn State Univ	CT	20,584	C
Elon Univ	NC	41,914	VC+
Eugene Lang College/The New School for Liberal Arts	NY	55,650	C
Florida Southern College	FL	40,150	C+
Fontbonne Univ	MO	31,384	C
Fordham Univ	NY	61,588	HC+
Gonzaga Univ	WA	46,441	HC
Illinois State Univ	IL	23,110	VC
Kent State Univ	OH	19,920	C
Lycoming College	PA	45,379	C
Millersville Univ of Pennsylvania	PA	21,648	C
Nova Southeastern Univ	FL	37,280	VC
Oberlin College	OH	61,788	MC
Okla City Univ	OK	40,476	VC
Oswego / SUNY	NY	20,009	VC
Pace Univ	NY	53,367	C
Southeast Missouri State Univ	MO	15,370	LC
Texas Christian Univ	TX	49,980	HC
The SUNY/College at Brockport	NY	19,002	C
Univ of Central Okla	OK	12,293	VC
Univ of Illinois at Chicago	IL	24,505	VC
Univ of Miami	FL	57,034	MC
Univ of New Hampshire	NH	26,912	C
Univ of Wyoming	WY	14,401	C+
Wright State Univ	OH	16,983	C
Youngstown State Univ	OH	16,732	C

THEATRE ARTS

School	ST	$IS	SR
Adams State Univ	CO	13,358	C
Albion College	MI	46,010	C
Alfred Univ	NY	41,770	C
Alma College	MI	44,075	C
Alvernia Univ	PA	39,250	LC
Angelo State Univ	TX	15,049	NC
Aquinas College	MI	33,060	C
Arizona State Univ, at the Tempe Campus	AZ	20,137	C+
Arkansas State Univ	AR	15,470	C
Armstrong State Univ	GA	15,532	C
Augustana College	SD	36,500	VC
Bard College	NY	61,940	HC
Belmont Univ	TN	39,190	VC+
Berea College	KY	7,192	C
Berry College	GA	39,254	VC
Bethany College	KS	30,605	NC
Bethel College	IN	31,560	C
Binghamton Univ/The SUNY	NY	21,648	HC+
Biola Univ	CA	40,320	C
Boise State Univ	ID	13,469	LC
Boston Univ	MA	60,694	MC
Bowdoin College	ME	59,568	MC
Brandeis Univ	MA		MC
Brescia Univ	KY	26,140	VC+
Buena Vista Univ	IA	39,188	C
Butler Univ	IN	47,572	VC+
Calif Baptist Univ	CA	38,792	C
Calif Lutheran Univ	CA	49,540	C+
Calif Polytechnic State Univ	CA	19,847	HC
Cal State, Chico	CA	20,158	C
Cal State, Fresno	CA	17,405	C
Cal State, Long Beach	CA	17,502	C+
Calvin College	MI	39,120	VC
Cameron Univ	OK	10,004	LC
Campbell Univ	NC	37,570	VC
Campbellsville Univ	KY	27,720	C
Canisius College	NY	44,900	C
Carroll Univ	WI	38,100	C
Castleton State College	VT	20,186	C
Catawba College	NC	37,240	VC
Cedarville Univ	OH	32,860	VC
Central Conn State Univ	CT	19,749	C
Christopher Newport Univ	VA	21,960	VC
Claremont McKenna College	CA	62,215	MC
Coe College	IA	45,550	VC
Colby College	ME	57,510	MC
College of Charleston	SC	22,145	VC
College of St. Benedict	MN	49,359	VC
College of William & Mary	VA	28,000	MC
Colo Mesa Univ	CO	17,690	LC
Concordia Univ St. Paul	MN	28,250	C
Creighton Univ	NE	45,356	VC
DePaul Univ	IL	47,623	VC
Dickinson College	PA	57,662	HC+
Dominican Univ	IL	37,628	C
Dordt College	IA	34,160	C
Drew Univ/College of Liberal Arts	NJ	57,516	C
East Texas Baptist Univ	TX	31,577	LC
Eastern Illinois Univ	IL	20,466	C
Elmhurst College	IL	43,336	C
Elon Univ	NC	41,914	VC+
Emporia State Univ	KS	12,897	C
Fairfield Univ	CT	56,960	VC
Florida Southern College	FL	40,150	C+
Fontbonne Univ	MO	31,384	C
Franklin College	IN	36,585	C
Franklin Pierce Univ	NH	41,598	C
Gallaudet Univ	DC	25,380	SP
Georgia College and State Univ	GA	18,900	C+
Goshen College	IN	35,900	VC
Goucher College	MD	52,040	VC+
Grand Canyon Univ	AZ	34,160	VC
Guilford College	NC	42,800	C
Hamline Univ	MN	45,678	VC
High Point Univ	NC	39,800	C
Hillsdale College	MI	32,866	MC
Hope College	MI	38,650	VC
Howard Univ	DC	13,646	C
Huntington Univ	IN	32,220	C+
Indiana Univ Bloomington	IN	19,801	VC
Indiana Univ Northwest	IN	6,854	LC
Indiana Univ of Pennsylvania	PA	20,846	LC
Indiana Univ South Bend	IN	15,501	C
John Carroll Univ	OH	46,300	C+
Kean Univ	NJ	23,444	C
Kennesaw State Univ	GA		C
King Univ	TN	33,140	C
LaGrange College	GA	37,670	C
Lake Forest College	IL	50,652	VC
Limestone College	SC	30,800	C
Linfield College-McMinnville Campus	OR	47,676	C
Lipscomb Univ	TN	37,490	VC
LIU Post	NY	47,660	C
Loyola Univ Chicago	IL	51,646	VC+
Lubbock Christian Univ	TX	26,308	C
Luther College	IA	45,720	C+
Lynchburg College	VA	42,645	C
Marquette Univ	WI	46,930	VC+
Marshall Univ	WV	14,820	C
Mary Baldwin College	VA	38,245	C
Missouri Baptist Univ	MO	31,830	C
Missouri Southern State Univ	MO	12,061	C
Missouri State Univ	MO	13,996	C+
Molloy College	NY	40,440	C
Montreat College	NC	31,298	C
Murray State Univ	KY	15,304	C
Nazareth College of Rochester	NY	43,028	C+
New Mexico State Univ	NM	14,050	C
Niagara Univ	NY	41,010	C
North Central College	IL	38,343	VC
N Dak State Univ	ND		C
Northeastern Illinois Univ	IL	10,318	LC
Northeastern Univ	MA	55,296	MC
Northern Arizona Univ	AZ	19,010	C
Northern Kentucky Univ	KY	21,134	C
Occidental College	CA	60,972	MC
Okla City Univ	OK	40,476	VC
Oswego / SUNY	NY	20,009	VC
Ouachita Baptist Univ	AR	30,220	VC
Pace Univ	NY	53,367	C
Piedmont College	GA	30,136	C
Plymouth State Univ	NH	23,148	LC
Point Park Univ	PA	36,390	C
Pomona College	CA	57,680	MC
Providence College	RI	57,383	VC
Quinnipiac Univ	CT	55,160	VC
Radford Univ	VA	17,766	LC
Rhodes College	TN	51,900	HC+
Roanoke College	VA	49,976	C
Rocky Mountain College	MT	32,242	C
Roger Williams Univ	RI	46,294	VC
Rollins College	FL	52,370	HC
Rowan Univ	NJ	24,022	VC+
St. John's Univ	MN	47,984	C
St. Joseph's College	IN	36,500	C
St. Joseph's Univ	PA	55,006	VC
St. Louis Univ	MO	48,346	HC
St. Martin's Univ	WA	41,678	C
St. Mary's Univ of Minn	MN	38,280	C
Samford Univ	AL	37,060	C+
San Diego State Univ	CA	21,611	C+
Schreiner Univ	TX	32,734	LC
Seattle Univ	WA	49,035	VC+
Seton Hall Univ	NJ	45,902	C
Sewanee: The Univ of the South	TN	47,700	HC+
Siena Heights Univ	MI	32,040	C
Southern Oregon Univ	OR	17,874	C
Spring Hill College	AL	44,164	VC
St. Edward's Univ	TX	47,784	C
St. Norbert College	WI	41,478	VC
St. Olaf College	MN	51,200	HC+
SUNY Fredonia/The SUNY at Fredonia	NY	19,840	VC
Swarthmore College	PA	57,870	MC
Taylor Univ	IN	37,821	VC+
Texas Christian Univ	TX	49,980	HC
Texas State Univ	TX	17,128	C
The College of Idaho	ID	31,277	C+
Ohio State Univ-Columbus Campus	OH	19,887	VC+
The Pennsylvania State Univ - Univ Park	PA	28,022	VC+
The SUNY at Potsdam	NY	18,473	C
The Univ of Utah	UT	16,463	VC
Thomas Edison State College	NJ	5,700	SP
Transylvania Univ	KY	42,660	VC+
Univ at Buffalo / The SUNY	NY	20,283	VC
Univ of Alaska Fairbanks	AK	15,130	C
Univ of Arizona	AZ	20,657	C
Univ of Arkansas at Little Rock	AR	17,609	LC
Univ of Calif at Riverside	CA	27,204	C+
Univ of Central Florida	FL	15,668	VC+
Univ of Central Okla	OK	12,293	C
Univ of Colo Boulder	CO	22,605	VC+
Univ of Georgia	GA	20,082	VC
Univ of Illinois at Chicago	IL	24,505	VC
Univ of Iowa	IA	17,693	VC
Univ of Maryland - College Park	MD	20,060	HC
Univ of Miami	FL	57,034	MC
Univ of Miss	MS	16,704	C+
Univ of Nebr - Lincoln	NE	18,031	VC
Univ of New Haven	CT	48,940	C
Univ of N Car at Charlotte	NC	15,547	C
Univ of Oregon	OR	21,360	C+
Univ of Pittsburgh at Pittsburgh	PA	28,572	HC+
Univ of Rochester	NY	60,668	MC
Univ of San Diego	CA	54,818	HC+
Univ of Scranton	PA	51,940	VC
Univ of Southern Indiana	IN	14,885	C
Univ of Tenn at Knoxville	TN	20,364	VC+
Univ of Tulsa	OK	46,331	MC
Univ of West Georgia	GA	15,488	LC
Univ of Wisc/Eau Claire	WI	15,730	VC
Univ of Wisc/Green Bay	WI	19,074	C
Univ of Wisc/Madison	WI	18,757	HC+
Univ of Wisc/Superior	WI	14,314	C
Valparaiso Univ	IN	44,940	VC+
Vanderbilt Univ	TN	58,220	MC
Vanguard Univ of Southern Calif	CA	35,833	VC
Warren Wilson College	NC	40,132	VC
Wayne State Univ	MI	22,063	C
Western Illinois Univ	IL	20,732	C
Westfield State Univ	MA	18,297	C
Whitman College	WA	55,988	MC
William Peace Univ	NC	32,900	LC
Winthrop Univ	SC	21,120	C
Wofford College	SC	45,795	VC
Xavier Univ	OH	44,980	VC
Youngstown State Univ	OH	16,732	C

THEATRE MINISTRY

School	ST	$IS	SR
College of the Ozarks	MO		VC

THEATRE PRODUCTION

School	ST	$IS	SR
Aquinas College	MI	33,060	C
Bethany College	WV	35,282	LC
Colo State Univ-Fort Collins	CO	20,385	VC
De Sales Univ	PA	43,970	C
Elon Univ	NC	41,914	VC+
Fontbonne Univ	MO	31,384	C
Fordham Univ	NY	61,588	HC+
Okla City Univ	OK	40,476	VC
Oswego / SUNY	NY	20,009	VC
Pace Univ	NY	53,367	C
Shenandoah Univ	VA	39,916	C
Southern Oregon Univ	OR	17,874	C
SUNY Fredonia/The SUNY at Fredonia	NY	19,840	VC
Texas Christian Univ	TX	49,980	HC
Univ of Illinois at Chicago	IL	24,505	VC
Youngstown State Univ	OH	16,732	C

THEATRE STUDIES

School	ST	$IS	SR
Amherst College	MA	58,744	MC
Aquinas College	MI	33,060	C
Baylor Univ	TX	50,329	HC
Bowling Green State Univ	OH	18,970	C
Capital Univ	OH	41,050	VC
Chapman Univ	CA	58,347	VC+
Chatham Univ	PA	43,797	C
College of the Ozarks	MO		VC
Colo State Univ-Fort Collins	CO	20,385	VC
Elon Univ	NC	41,914	VC+
Eugene Lang College/The New School for Liberal Arts	NY	55,650	C
Faulkner Univ	AL	25,720	LC
John Carroll Univ	OH	46,300	C+
Keene State College	NH	23,232	LC
Lindsey Wilson College	KY	31,220	C
Malone Univ	OH	35,364	C
Mich Tech Univ	MI	23,556	HC
Minn State Univ, Mankato	MN	15,616	C
Missouri Southern State Univ	MO	12,061	C
Oberlin College	OH	61,788	MC
Southern Oregon Univ	OR	17,874	C
SUNY Fredonia/The SUNY at Fredonia	NY	19,840	VC
Texas Christian Univ	TX	49,980	HC
Univ of Central Florida	FL	15,668	VC+
Univ of Central Okla	OK	12,293	C
Univ of Chicago	IL	55,416	MC
Univ of Denver	CO	51,787	VC+
Univ of Illinois at Chicago	IL	24,505	VC
Univ of New Mexico	NM	15,300	C
Viterbo Univ	WI	30,070	C
Wake Forest Univ	NC	58,838	MC
Western Mich Univ	MI	19,628	C
Wright State Univ	OH	16,983	C
Xavier Univ	OH	44,980	VC
Youngstown State Univ	OH	16,732	C

THEOLOGICAL STUDIES

School	ST	$IS	SR
Alvernia Univ	PA	39,250	LC
Andrews Univ	MI	28,030	C+
Aquinas College	MI	33,060	C
Aquinas College	TN	29,250	VC+
Assumption College	MA	47,122	C+
Atlantic Union College	MA	24,600	C
Avila Univ	MO	26,900	C
Bard College	NY	61,940	HC
Barry Univ	FL	38,190	C
Bellarmine Univ	KY	42,950	VC
Belmont Abbey College	NC	37,716	C
Benedictine Univ	IL	37,820	C
Bethel Univ	MN	34,940	VC
Boston College	MA	60,622	MC
Briar Cliff Univ	IA	29,514	C
Caldwell College	NJ	35,602	NC
Calif Lutheran Univ	CA	49,540	C+
Calumet College of St. Joseph	IN	15,000	C
Calvin College	MI	39,120	VC
Carlow Univ	PA	30,272	C
Christendom College	VA	32,600	VC
College of St. Benedict	MN	49,359	VC
College of St. Elizabeth	NJ	43,839	LC
College of St. Mary	NE	35,184	C
Colo Christian Univ	CO	27,500	VC
Concordia Univ	OR	35,000	C
Concordia Univ Irvine	CA	35,390	VC
Concordia Univ Nebr	NE	26,000	VC
Concordia Univ St. Paul	MN	28,250	C
Concordia Univ Wisc	WI	28,980	C
Concordia Univ, River Forest	IL	26,300	C
De Sales Univ	PA	43,970	C
Dominican Univ	IL	37,628	C
Duquesne Univ	PA	43,720	VC
Eastern Mennonite Univ	VA	40,660	C
Eastern Univ	PA	37,704	C
Elmhurst College	IL	43,336	C
Fordham Univ	NY	61,588	HC+
Franciscan Univ of Steubenville	OH	27,320	VC
Gannon Univ	PA	39,608	C
Hanover College	IN	43,073	C+
Hardin-Simmons Univ	TX	23,560	C+
Immaculata Univ	PA	43,000	C
John Brown Univ	AR	32,056	VC
John Carroll Univ	OH	46,300	C+
Juniata College	PA	49,340	VC
King's College	PA	43,502	C
Lenoir-Rhyne College	NC	35,984	C
Livingstone College	NC	17,815	LC
Lourdes Univ	OH	26,055	LC
Loyola Marymount Univ	CA	54,649	VC+
Loyola Univ Chicago	IL	51,646	VC+
Loyola Univ Maryland	MD	56,880	VC+
Malone Univ	OH	35,364	C
Marian Univ	IN	38,540	C
Marquette Univ	WI	46,930	VC+
Marymount Univ	VA	39,480	C
Messiah College	PA	40,690	C
Mount Mary Univ	WI	33,590	LC
Mount St. Mary's Univ	MD	47,996	C
Mount Vernon Nazarene Univ	OH	29,590	C
Newman Univ	KS	30,380	C+
Northwest Univ	WA	18,854	C
Notre Dame College	OH	34,942	VC
Nyack College	NY	33,250	C
Ohio Dominican Univ	OH	38,380	C
Ouachita Baptist Univ	AR	30,220	VC
Pacific Union College	CA	28,150	VC
Pontifical Catholic Univ of PR	PR	7,310	
Providence College	RI	57,383	VC
Quincy Univ	IL	34,980	LC
Rockhurst Univ	MO	20,625	C
St. Anselm College	NH	49,376	VC
St. John's Univ	MN	47,984	C
St. Joseph's College of Maine	ME	31,580	C
St. Joseph's Univ	PA	55,006	VC
St. Louis Univ	MO	48,346	HC
St. Mary-of-the-Woods College	IN	37,722	LC
St. Mary's Univ	TX	33,854	C
St. Peter's Univ	NJ	44,240	C
St. Vincent College	PA	40,244	C
Seattle Pacific Univ	WA	41,559	VC+
Seattle Univ	WA	49,035	VC+
Seton Hall Univ	NJ	45,902	C
Southern Adventist Univ	TN	26,190	C
Southern Nazarene Univ	OK	24,354	C
Southwestern Adventist Univ	TX	23,026	LC
Spring Arbor Univ	MI	26,740	C
Spring Hill College	AL	44,164	VC
St. Ambrose Univ	IA	30,845	C
St. Bonaventure Univ	NY	41,575	C
St. Catherine Univ	MN	37,782	C+
St. John's Univ	NY	55,070	C+
Sterling College	KS	27,216	C
Texas Lutheran Univ	TX	36,040	C

ST = STATE $IS = IN-STATE COSTS   SR = SELECTOR RATING

School	ST	$IS	SR
The Catholic Univ of America	DC	52,852	VC
Thomas More College	KY	34,760	C
Trinity Christian College	IL	28,869	C
Union College	NE	23,270	C
Universidad Adventista de las Antillas	PR	7,360	
Univ of Chicago	IL	55,416	MC
Univ of Dallas	TX	45,500	VC+
Univ of Evansville	IN	42,656	VC+
Univ of Great Falls	MT	27,970	C
Univ of Mary	ND	16,714	C
Univ of Mobile	AL	28,935	VC
Univ of Notre Dame	IN	57,117	MC
Univ of Portland	OR	49,964	VC
Univ of St. Mary	KS	28,400	C+
Univ of San Diego	CA	54,818	HC+
Univ of San Francisco	CA	54,770	VC
Univ of Scranton	PA	51,940	VC
Univ of St. Francis	IL	37,560	C
Univ of St. Thomas - Houston	TX	37,690	C
Valparaiso Univ	IN	44,940	VC+
Vanguard Univ of Southern Calif	CA	35,833	VC
Villanova Univ	PA	58,394	MC
Walla Walla Univ	WA	26,256	NC
Walsh Univ	OH	35,100	C
Washington Adventist Univ	MD	25,859	LC
Wheeling Jesuit Univ	WV	33,500	C
Whitworth Univ	WA	47,734	VC
Wisc Lutheran College	WI	23,510	VC
Xavier Univ	OH	44,980	VC
Xavier Univ of Louisiana	LA	25,300	C

THEOLOGY

School	ST	$IS	SR
Aquinas College	MI	33,060	C
Calif Baptist Univ	CA	38,792	C
Calvin College	MI	39,120	VC
Creighton Univ	NE	45,356	VC
Molloy College	NY	40,440	C
St. Louis Univ	MO	48,346	HC
St. Mary's Univ of Minn	MN	38,280	C

THERAPEUTIC RIDING

School	ST	$IS	SR
St. Andrews Univ	NC	32,050	LC
Wilson College	PA	35,080	C

THIRD WORLD STUDIES

School	ST	$IS	SR
Appalachian State Univ	NC	12,919	VC
Bethel Univ	MN	34,940	VC
Pitzer College	CA	54,988	MC
Univ of Calif at San Diego	CA	21,000	VC

TOTAL QUALITY MANAGEMENT (TQM)

School	ST	$IS	SR
Cal State, Dominguez Hills	CA	17,090	LC
San Diego State Univ	CA	21,611	C+

TOURISM

School	ST	$IS	SR
Arizona State Univ, at the Downtown Phoenix Campus	AZ	22,101	C
Black Hills State Univ	SD	13,947	C
Bowling Green State Univ	OH	18,970	C
Brigham Young Univ	UT	12,100	HC
Brigham Young Univ/Hawaii	HI	10,686	VC
Cal State, Dominguez Hills	CA	17,090	LC
Cal State, Fullerton	CA	25,188	C
Central Washington Univ	WA	11,730	VC
Coastal Carolina Univ	SC	18,580	C
Colo State Univ-Fort Collins	CO	20,385	VC
Dowling College	NY	25,000	LC
Eastern Mich Univ	MI	18,604	C
George Mason Univ	VA	15,724	VC
George Washington Univ	DC	57,108	MC
Hawaii Pacific Univ	HI	34,360	C
Indiana Univ Bloomington	IN	19,801	VC
Indiana Univ Kokomo	IN	6,811	LC
Indiana Univ-Purdue Univ Indianapolis	IN	17,611	C
James Madison Univ	VA	18,049	VC
Johnson & Wales Univ/ Charlotte Campus	NC	29,576	C
Johnson & Wales Univ/North Miami Campus	FL		C
Johnson & Wales Univ/ Providence Campus	RI	29,576	C
Johnson State College	VT	16,721	C
Kent State Univ	OH	19,920	C
Lasell College	MA	43,750	LC
Mich State Univ	MI	22,450	VC
Montclair State Univ	NJ	22,614	C
New Mexico State Univ	NM	14,050	C
Niagara Univ	NY	41,010	C
Ohio Univ	OH	21,080	C
Plymouth State Univ	NH	23,148	LC
Purdue Univ/West Lafayette	IN	20,024	HC
Rochester Inst of Technology	NY	42,450	VC
Seton Hill Univ	PA	35,172	C
Sojourner-Douglass College	MD	9,160	LC

School	ST	$IS	SR
Southern New Hampshire Univ	NH	38,100	C
St. Joseph's College, New York/Brooklyn Campus	NY	22,630	C
St. Joseph's College, New York/Suffolk Campus	NY	22,630	C
St. Thomas Univ	FL	32,310	LC
Temple Univ	PA	24,392	VC
Texas State Univ	TX	17,128	C
Univ of Central Missouri	MO	14,605	C
Univ of Hawaii at Manoa	HI	19,379	C
Univ of Missouri/Columbia	MO	18,201	MC
Univ of Montana-Western	MT	9,753	LC
Univ of New Hampshire	NH	26,912	C
Univ of New Haven	CT	48,940	C
Univ of New Orleans	LA	9,224	C
Univ of the Sacred Heart	PR	5,590	
Virginia Polytechnic Inst and State Univ	VA	14,629	HC
West Liberty Univ	WV	9,142	LC
West Virginia Univ	WV	16,542	C+
Western Mich Univ	MI	19,628	C

TOXICOLOGY

School	ST	$IS	SR
Ashland Univ	OH	25,000	C
Bloomfield College	NJ	37,850	LC
Nazareth College of Rochester	NY	43,028	C+
St. John's Univ	NY	55,051	C+
The Pennsylvania State Univ - Univ Park	PA	28,022	VC+
Univ of Calif at Davis	CA		HC
Univ of Georgia	GA	20,082	VC
Univ of Louisiana at Monroe	LA	12,998	C
Univ of the Sciences	PA	48,320	VC+

TOY DESIGN

School	ST	$IS	SR
Fashion Inst of Technology/ SUNY	NY	18,362	SP
Otis College of Art and Design	CA	35,404	SP

TRADE AND INDUSTRIAL EDUCATION

School	ST	$IS	SR
Alabama A&M Univ	AL	10,084	C
Eastern Mich Univ	MI	18,604	C
Kent State Univ	OH	19,920	C
Oswego / SUNY	NY	20,009	VC
Siena Heights Univ	MI	32,040	C
Univ of Nevada, Las Vegas	NV	17,303	C
Univ of Wyoming	WY	14,401	C+
Virginia State Univ	VA	11,318	C+

TRADE AND INDUSTRIAL SUPERVISION AND MANAGEMENT

School	ST	$IS	SR
Cal State, Dominguez Hills	CA	17,090	C
Eastern Mich Univ	MI	18,604	C
Metropolitan State Univ	MN	5,923	
Miss State Univ	MS	14,750	C
Washington Univ in St. Louis	MO	69,844	MC

TRANSPORTATION AND TRAVEL MARKETING

School	ST	$IS	SR
Johnson & Wales Univ/ Providence Campus	RI	29,576	C
Northwood Univ	FL	33,192	LC
Northwood Univ	MI	26,331	LC

TRANSPORTATION ENGINEERING

School	ST	$IS	SR
Calif Polytechnic State Univ	CA	19,847	VC
Lawrence Tech Univ	MI	37,630	VC
Texas A&M Univ at Galveston	TX	11,258	C

TRANSPORTATION MANAGEMENT

School	ST	$IS	SR
Auburn Univ	AL	22,378	VC+
Calif Maritime Academy	CA	15,496	LC
Dowling College	NY	25,000	LC
Embry-Riddle Aeronautical Univ - Daytona Beach	FL	40,884	C+
Embry-Riddle Aeronautical Univ - Worldwide	FL	15,512	C
Florida Memorial Univ	FL	20,888	LC
Iowa State Univ	IA	16,403	C
Maritime College/SUNY	NY	16,020	C
Mass Maritime Academy	MA	15,340	C
Niagara Univ	NY	41,010	C
Southern Univ at New Orleans	LA	2,963	NC
Texas A&M Univ at Galveston	TX	11,258	C
Ohio State Univ-Columbus Campus	OH	19,887	HC+
Univ of Alaska Anchorage	AK	16,673	NC
Univ of Arkansas at Fayetteville	AR	18,352	C+

School	ST	$IS	SR
Univ of North Florida	FL	15,870	VC
Univ of Pennsylvania	PA	61,132	MC
Univ of Wisc/Superior	WI	14,314	C

TRANSPORTATION TECHNOLOGY

School	ST	$IS	SR
Maine Maritime Academy	ME	21,073	C
Missouri Southern State Univ	MO	12,061	C

TURFGRASS AND LANDSCAPE MANAGEMENT

School	ST	$IS	SR
New Mexico State Univ	NM	14,050	C
The Pennsylvania State Univ - Univ Park	PA	28,022	VC+
Univ of Georgia	GA	20,082	C
Univ of Nebr - Lincoln	NE	18,031	VC

ULTRASOUND TECHNOLOGY

School	ST	$IS	SR
Barry Univ	FL	38,190	C
Mount Aloysius College	PA	29,976	C
Newman Univ	KS	30,380	C+
Oregon Inst of Technology	OR	8,910	C
Rochester Inst of Technology	NY	42,450	VC
Seattle Univ	WA	49,035	VC+
Washburn Univ	KS	12,579	C

UNIVERSITY STUDIES

School	ST	$IS	SR
Shenandoah Univ	VA	39,916	C
Univ of Maine	ME	19,902	C+

URBAN ADMINISTRATION

School	ST	$IS	SR
New York Inst of Technology	NY	45,010	VC

URBAN AND REGIONAL STUDIES

School	ST	$IS	SR
Arizona State Univ, at the Downtown Phoenix Campus	AZ	22,101	C
Cornell Univ	NY	60,964	MC

URBAN DESIGN

School	ST	$IS	SR
New York Univ	NY	61,470	MC
Parsons The New School for Design	NY	56,610	SP
Univ at Albany / SUNY	NY	18,674	VC
Univ of Virginia	VA	23,050	VC

URBAN ECOLOGY

School	ST	$IS	SR
Hofstra Univ	NY	51,810	VC+
Seattle Univ	WA	49,035	VC+
Xavier Univ	OH	44,980	VC

URBAN PLANNING TECHNOLOGY

School	ST	$IS	SR
Ball State Univ	IN	17,850	C
Calif State Polytechnic Univ, Pomona	CA	20,156	C
Eastern Mich Univ	MI	18,604	C
Florida Atlantic Univ	FL	17,339	C
Mich State Univ	MI	22,450	VC
San Jose State Univ	CA	19,133	LC
Texas State Univ	TX	17,128	C
The Univ of Utah	UT	16,463	VC
Univ of Nevada, Las Vegas	NV	17,303	C
Univ of Wisc-Milwaukee	WI	18,436	C
West Chester Univ of Pennsylvania	PA	17,186	C

URBAN STUDIES

School	ST	$IS	SR
Albertus Magnus College	CT	37,382	LC
Arizona State Univ, at the Tempe Campus	AZ	20,137	C+
Augsburg College	MN	35,142	C
Ball State Univ	IN	17,850	C
Barnard College/Columbia Univ	NY	39,000	MC
Baylor Univ	TX	50,329	HC
Bellevue Univ	NE	4,600	NC
Boston Univ	MA	60,694	MC
Brown Univ	RI	59,428	MC
Bryn Mawr College	PA	59,890	MC
Buffalo State College / SUNY	NY	15,733	C+
Calif State Polytechnic Univ, Pomona	CA	20,156	C
Cal State, Fresno	CA	17,405	C
Cal State, Northridge	CA	28,690	LC
Calumet College of St. Joseph	IN	15,000	C
Canisius College	NY	44,900	C
Carnegie Mellon Univ	PA	51,260	MC
CUNY/City College	NY	20,319	HC+
Cleveland State Univ	OH	21,776	C
College of Charleston	SC	22,145	VC
College of Mount St. Vincent	NY	41,040	MC
College of Wooster	OH	52,600	MC

School	ST	$IS	SR
Columbia Univ/City of New York	NY	61,116	MC
Columbia Univ/School of General Studies	NY	58,231	MC
Conn College	CT	54,970	MC
Coppin State Univ	MD	16,227	VC
DePaul Univ	IL	47,623	VC
Dillard Univ	LA	20,940	VC
Eastern Mich Univ	MI	18,604	VC
Eastern Washington Univ	WA		C
Elmhurst College	IL	43,336	C
Eugene Lang College/The New School for Liberal Arts	NY	55,650	C
Fordham Univ	NY	61,588	HC+
Furman Univ	SC	54,006	HC
Georgia State Univ	GA	15,582	VC
Hamline Univ	MN	45,678	VC
Hampshire College	MA	58,320	MC
Haverford College	PA	61,564	MC
Hobart and William Smith Colleges	NY	60,034	HC+
Howard Univ	DC	13,646	C
Hunter College	NY	14,429	VC
Jackson State Univ	MS	13,512	LC
Langston Univ	OK	3,000	C
Lipscomb Univ	TN	37,490	VC
Loyola Marymount Univ	CA	54,649	VC+
Manhattan College	NY	49,588	C+
Mass Inst of Technology	MA	58,240	MC
Metropolitan State Univ of Denver	CO	4,835	LC
Miami Univ	OH	24,191	VC
MidAmerica Nazarene Univ	KS	28,000	C
Minn State Univ, Mankato	MN	15,616	C
Morehouse College	GA	39,412	C
New College of Florida	FL	14,504	MC
New York Univ	NY	61,470	MC
Northeastern Illinois Univ	IL	10,318	LC
Northwestern College	MN	24,000	C
Northwestern Univ	IL	61,640	MC
Occidental College	CA	60,972	MC
Ohio Univ	OH	21,080	C
Queens College/The CUNY	NY	17,107	VC
Rhodes College	TN	51,900	HC+
Roosevelt Univ	IL	22,605	VC
Rutgers, The State Univ of New Jersey/Camden Campus	NJ	25,121	C
Rutgers, The State Univ of New Jersey/New Brunswick	NJ	25,562	VC
St. Augustine's Univ	NC	14,000	C
St. Louis Univ	MO	48,346	HC
St. Peter's Univ	NJ	44,240	C
San Diego State Univ	CA	21,611	C+
San Francisco State Univ	CA	18,514	C
Smith College	MA	59,674	MC
Southern Nazarene Univ	OK	24,354	C
St. Cloud State Univ	MN	10,600	C
Stanford Univ	CA	58,388	MC
The Univ of Utah	UT	16,463	VC
Trinity Univ	TX	48,150	HC+
Tufts Univ	MA	58,780	MC
Univ of Calif at Berkeley	CA	23,322	MC
Univ of Calif at Irvine	CA	25,961	VC
Univ of Calif at San Diego	CA	21,000	VC
Univ of Cincinnati	OH	21,506	C
Univ of Conn	CT	24,706	VC
Univ of Illinois at Chicago	IL	24,505	VC
Univ of Mich/Dearborn	MI	9,885	VC
Univ of Mich-Flint	MI	17,547	C+
Univ of Minn/Duluth	MN	19,806	C
Univ of Minn/Twin Cities	MN		HC
Univ of Missouri-Kansas City	MO	19,603	C
Univ of New Orleans	LA	9,224	C
Univ of Pennsylvania	PA	61,132	MC
Univ of Pittsburgh at Pittsburgh	PA	28,572	HC+
Univ of Texas at Austin	TX	44,074	HC
Univ of the District of Columbia	DC	7,244	LC
Univ of the Sacred Heart	PR	5,590	
Univ of Wisc/Green Bay	WI	19,074	C
Univ of Wisc/Oshkosh	WI	10,426	LC
Univ of Wisc-Milwaukee	WI	18,436	C
Vassar College	NY	61,140	MC
Virginia Commonwealth Univ	VA	21,716	C
Virginia Polytechnic Inst and State Univ	VA	14,629	HC
Washington Univ in St. Louis	MO	69,844	MC
Wayne State Univ	MI	22,063	C
Wheaton College	IL	40,720	MC
Worcester State Univ	MA	19,812	C
Wright State Univ	OH	16,983	C

VASCULAR SONOGRAPHY

School	ST	$IS	SR
Thomas Edison State College	NJ	5,700	SP

VETERINARY SCIENCE

School	ST	$IS	SR
Becker College	MA	41,420	C
Fort Valley State Univ	GA	11,200	VC
Lincoln Memorial Univ	TN	18,144	C
Medaille College	NY	35,112	C

School	ST	$IS	SR
Mercy College	NY	30,456	C
Mich State Univ	MI	22,450	VC
Mount Ida College	MA	30,115	LC
Newberry College	SC	26,850	LC
N Dak State Univ	ND		C
The Pennsylvania State Univ - Univ Park	PA	28,022	VC+
Tuskegee Univ	AL	26,750	C
Univ of Arizona	AZ	20,657	C
Univ of Georgia	GA	20,082	VC
Univ of Idaho	ID	14,558	C
Univ of Maine	ME	19,902	C+
Univ of Maryland - College Park	MD	20,060	HC
Univ of Missouri/Columbia	MO	18,201	MC
Univ of Montana-Western	MT	9,753	LC
Univ of Nebr - Lincoln	NE	18,031	VC
Univ of New Hampshire	NH	26,912	C
Utah State Univ	UT	12,044	C
West Virginia Univ	WV	16,542	C+
Wilson College	PA	35,080	C

VETERINARY TECHNOLOGY

School	ST	$IS	SR
Murray State Univ	KY	15,304	C

VICTORIAN STUDIES

School	ST	$IS	SR
Bard College	NY	61,940	HC
Vassar College	NY	61,140	MC

VIDEO

School	ST	$IS	SR
Art Inst of Atlanta	GA	24,000	SP
Bennington College	VT	56,990	HC+
Bloomfield College	NJ	37,850	LC
Calif Inst of the Arts	CA	51,902	SP
Calvin College	MI	39,120	VC
CUNY/City College	NY	20,319	HC+
Cornerstone Univ and Grand Rapids Theological Seminary	MI	33,338	C
Drexel Univ	PA	61,418	VC+
Fairleigh Dickinson Univ/ College at Florham	NJ	42,142	C
Fitchburg State Univ	MA	18,173	C
Five Towns College	NY	34,550	C
George Mason Univ	VA	15,724	VC
Hampshire College	MA	58,320	MC
Hofstra Univ	NY	51,810	VC+
Ithaca College	NY	53,864	HC
Lasell College	MA	43,750	LC
Madonna Univ	MI	24,540	VC
Maryland Inst College of Art	MD	39,500	SP
Minneapolis College of Art and Design	MN	36,700	SP
New Mexico State Univ	NM	14,050	C
Ohio Univ	OH	21,080	C
Point Park Univ	PA	36,390	C
Rochester Inst of Technology	NY	42,450	VC
School of the Art Inst of Chicago	IL	56,230	MC
School of Visual Arts	NY	36,500	VC
Spring Arbor Univ	MI	26,740	C
Stevenson Univ	MD	41,470	C
SUNY Fredonia/The SUNY at Fredonia	NY	19,840	VC
Syracuse Univ	NY	56,346	VC
The Univ of Okla	OK	18,621	VC
Univ of Hartford	CT	42,674	C
Univ of Mich/Ann Arbor	MI	22,102	MC
Univ of Southern Calif	CA	56,903	MC
Webster Univ	MO	35,100	C+
Wilmington Univ	DE	8,112	NC

VISUAL AND PERFORMING ARTS

School	ST	$IS	SR
Albion College	MI	46,010	C
Alderson Broaddus Univ	WV	28,656	C
Andrews Univ	MI	28,030	C+
Anna Maria College	MA	34,600	C
Aquinas College	MI	33,060	C
Arizona State Univ, at the Tempe Campus	AZ	20,137	C+
Armstrong State Univ	GA	15,532	C
Belmont Univ	TN	39,190	VC+
Bennett College for Women	NC	21,970	LC
Bennington College	VT	56,990	HC+
Bethel Univ	MN	34,940	VC
Binghamton Univ/The SUNY	NY	21,648	HC+
Bowling Green State Univ	OH	18,970	C
Brigham Young Univ	UT	12,100	HC
Brown Univ	RI	59,428	MC
Bucknell Univ	PA	60,140	MC
Burlington College	VT	32,510	SP
Calif Baptist Univ	CA	38,792	C
Calif College of the Arts	CA	48,334	SP
Calif Inst of the Arts	CA	51,902	SP
Cal State, Fullerton	CA	25,188	C
Cal State, Monterey Bay	CA	26,871	LC
Cal State, San Marcos	CA	14,576	LC
Central Washington Univ	WA	11,730	C
Chatham Univ	PA	43,797	C
CUNY/Brooklyn College	NY	5,884	C+
Clark Univ	MA	47,020	HC+

School	ST	$IS	SR
Columbia Univ/City of New York	NY	61,116	MC
Columbia Univ/School of General Studies	NY	58,231	MC
Columbus State Univ	GA	13,176	C
Coppin State Univ	MD	16,227	VC
Creighton Univ	NE	45,356	VC
Curry College	MA	48,925	LC
Dordt College	IA	34,160	C+
Dowling College	NY	25,000	C
Duke Univ	NC	50,250	MC
East Texas Baptist Univ	TX	31,577	LC
Eastern Conn State Univ	CT	20,584	C
Eastern Mich Univ	MI	18,604	C
Eckerd College	FL	43,902	C
Erskine College	SC	37,360	C
Fayetteville State Univ	NC	10,816	C
Florida Atlantic Univ	FL	17,339	C
Fordham Univ	NY	61,588	HC+
George Mason Univ	VA	15,724	VC
Goddard College	VT	16,418	VC
Grambling State Univ	LA	13,384	LC
Grand View Univ	IA	31,050	C
Guilford College	NC	42,800	C
Haverford College	PA	61,564	MC
Hofstra Univ	NY	51,810	VC+
Indiana Univ Bloomington	IN	19,801	VC
Inter-American Univ of PR/ Bayamon Univ College	PR	4,428	
Inter-American Univ of PR/ Fajardo Campus	PR	4,200	
Inter-American Univ of PR/ Ponce	PR		
Ithaca College	NY	53,864	HC
Johnson State College	VT	16,721	C
Kean Univ	NJ	23,444	C
Kent State Univ	OH	19,920	C
Keystone College	PA	28,680	LC
King Univ	TN	33,140	C
Kutztown Univ of Pennsylvania	PA	16,909	LC
Lander Univ	SC	22,514	C+
Lees-McRae College	NC	33,944	C
Lesley Univ	MA	46,350	C
Lipscomb Univ	TN	37,490	VC
LIU Brooklyn	NY	47,182	LC
Longwood Univ	VA	20,924	C
Loras College	IA	37,432	VC
Loyola Univ New Orleans	LA	46,581	VC
Mass College of Liberal Arts	MA	18,613	C
Millikin Univ	IL	38,940	C
Naropa Univ	CO	39,166	SP
New England Conservatory of Music	MA	52,550	SP
New Mexico State Univ	NM	14,050	C
Notre Dame College	OH	34,942	VC
Ohio Univ	OH	21,080	C
Oregon State Univ	OR	20,273	VC
Otterbein College	OH	32,214	C
Ouachita Baptist Univ	AR	30,220	VC
Penn State Univ/Altoona	PA	11,464	C
Point Loma Nazarene Univ	CA	41,006	C+
Presbyterian College	SC	42,678	C+
Prescott College	AZ	33,284	C
Purdue Univ/West Lafayette	IN	20,024	HC
Ramapo College of New Jersey	NJ	24,938	C
Regis Univ	CO	41,318	C
Rice Univ	TX	43,288	MC
Roger Williams Univ	RI	46,296	VC
Rutgers, The State Univ of New Jersey/New Brunswick	NJ	25,562	VC
Rutgers, The State Univ of New Jersey/Newark Campus	NJ	258,806	C
St. Augustine's Univ	NC	14,000	C
St. Mary's College	IN	45,160	C+
St. Peter's Univ	NJ	44,240	C
St. Vincent College	PA	40,244	C
Sarah Lawrence College	NY	48,000	HC
Savannah State Univ	GA	13,156	C
School of the Art Inst of Chicago	IL	56,230	SP
Schreiner Univ	TX	32,734	LC
Seattle Univ	WA	49,035	VC+
Shaw Univ	NC	15,488	C
Siena College	NY	43,863	VC
Siena Heights Univ	MI	32,040	C
Sonoma State Univ	CA	20,541	C
Southern Oregon Univ	OR	17,874	C
Spring Arbor Univ	MI	26,740	C
St. Andrews Univ	NC	32,050	LC
St. Bonaventure Univ	NY	41,575	C
St. Lawrence Univ	NY	59,972	VC
St. Mary's College of Maryland	MD	25,754	VC
SUNY at Purchase	NY	16,951	C
SUNY College at Old Westbury	NY	16,324	C
SUNY New Paltz	NY	14,348	C
Susquehanna Univ	PA	51,150	C
Taylor Univ	IN	37,821	VC+
Temple Univ	PA	24,392	VC
Texas Tech Univ	TX	14,243	C
The Lincoln Univ	PA	15,154	LC

School	ST	$IS	SR
The Pennsylvania State Univ - Univ Park	PA	28,022	VC+
The SUNY at Potsdam	NY	18,473	C
The Univ of Utah	UT	16,463	VC
Univ of Alaska Anchorage	AK	16,673	NC
Univ of Arkansas at Little Rock	AR	17,609	LC
Univ of Calif at Riverside	CA	27,204	C+
Univ of Calif at San Diego	CA	21,000	VC
Univ of Chicago	IL	55,416	MC
Univ of Cincinnati	OH	21,506	VC
Univ of Colo Denver	CO	17,904	C
Univ of Conn	CT	24,706	HC
Univ of Florida	FL	15,943	HC
Univ of Hartford	CT	42,674	C
Univ of Illinois at Chicago	IL	24,505	VC
Univ of Maine at Farmington	ME	18,187	LC
Univ of Maryland/Baltimore County	MD	18,000	VC
Univ of Montana-Western	MT	9,753	LC
Univ of New Haven	CT	48,940	C
Univ of N Dak	ND	14,551	C
Univ of North Texas	TX	15,628	C
Univ of Northern Colo	CO	18,446	C
Univ of Pennsylvania	PA	61,132	MC
Univ of San Diego	CA	54,818	HC+
Univ of San Francisco	CA	54,770	VC
Univ of Southern Calif	CA	56,903	MC
Univ of St. Francis	IL	37,560	C
Univ of Texas at Austin	TX	44,074	HC
Univ of Texas at Dallas	TX	21,348	HC+
Univ of the Sacred Heart	PR	5,590	
Univ of Wisc/Platteville	WI	14,564	C
Univ of Wisc/Superior	WI	14,314	C
Virginia State Univ	VA	11,318	C
Wagner College	NY	48,600	C+
Washington Univ in St. Louis	MO	69,844	MC
Wells College	NY	49,400	VC
West Chester Univ of Pennsylvania	PA	17,186	C
West Virginia Univ	WV	16,542	C+
Western Kentucky Univ	KY	11,000	LC
Western Washington Univ	WA	18,519	VC
Wichita State Univ	KS	14,607	C+
Worcester State Univ	MA	19,812	C

VISUAL DESIGN

School	ST	$IS	SR
Art Academy of Cincinnati	OH	25,940	SP
Calif Inst of the Arts	CA	51,902	SP
Cal State, Fullerton	CA	25,188	C
Cazenovia College	NY	43,464	C
Drury Univ	MO	31,909	VC
Eastern New Mexico Univ	NM	10,682	C
Farmingdale State College	NY	19,673	C
Indiana-Purdue Univ Fort Wayne	IN	15,521	C
Kent State Univ	OH	19,920	C
Loyola Univ Chicago	IL	51,646	VC+
Nazareth College of Rochester	NY	43,028	C+
Okla Christian Univ	OK	25,870	VC
San Francisco State Univ	CA	18,514	C
Stevenson Univ	MD	41,470	C
Ohio State Univ-Columbus Campus	OH	19,887	HC+
Truman State Univ	MO	15,541	HC
Univ of Dayton	OH	49,070	VC
Univ of Delaware	DE	23,612	VC
Univ of Mary Hardin-Baylor	TX	31,950	C+
Univ of Mass Dartmouth	MA	22,223	C
Univ of New Haven	CT	48,940	C

VISUAL EFFECTS

School	ST	$IS	SR
Otis College of Art and Design	CA	35,404	SP
Savannah College of Art and Design	GA	48,005	SP
School of Visual Arts	NY	36,500	VC

VITICULTURE AND ENOLOGY

School	ST	$IS	SR
Cornell Univ	NY	60,964	MC

VOCAL MUSIC EDUCATION

School	ST	$IS	SR
Aquinas College	MI	33,060	VC
Calvin College	MI	39,120	VC
Concordia Univ St. Paul	MN	28,250	C
Dordt College	IA	34,160	C+
Hope College	MI	38,650	VC
Houghton College	NY	36,808	C+
Murray State Univ	KY	15,304	C
Texas Christian Univ	TX	49,980	HC
Webster Univ	MO	35,100	C+
Youngstown State Univ	OH	16,732	C

VOCAL PERFORMANCE

School	ST	$IS	SR
Aquinas College	MI	33,060	VC
Arkansas State Univ	AR	15,470	C
Dallas Baptist Univ	TX	30,580	VC
Houghton College	NY	36,808	C+
LIU Post	NY	47,660	C
Missouri Southern State Univ	MO	12,061	C
New York Univ	NY	61,470	MC

School	ST	$IS	SR
Okla Christian Univ	OK	25,870	VC
Okla City Univ	OK	40,476	VC
Roberts Wesleyan College	NY	38,306	C+
Taylor Univ	IN	37,821	VC
Texas Christian Univ	TX	49,980	HC
Univ of Miami	FL	57,034	MC
Webster Univ	MO	35,100	C+
Wright State Univ	OH	16,983	C
Youngstown State Univ	OH	16,732	C

VOCATIONAL EDUCATION

School	ST	$IS	SR
Auburn Univ	AL	22,378	VC+
Cal State, Los Angeles	CA	17,186	LC
Cal State, San Bernardino	CA	12,000	C
Central Conn State Univ	CT	19,749	C
Chicago State Univ	IL	5,482	C
College of the Ozarks	MO		VC
Fitchburg State Univ	MA	18,173	C
Indiana Univ of Pennsylvania	PA	20,846	LC
Martin Univ	IN	11,000	C
New York College of Technology/The CUNY	NY	5,769	NC
N Car State Univ	NC	16,202	HC
Okla State Univ	OK	14,310	VC
Oswego / SUNY	NY	20,009	VC
Pittsburg State Univ	KS	12,032	C
San Diego State Univ	CA	21,611	C+
S Dak State Univ	SD	14,296	C
Southern Illinois Univ Carbondale	IL	21,942	C
Univ of Illinois at Urbana-Champaign	IL	26,450	HC
Univ of Toledo	OH	18,464	C
Univ of Wisc/Stout	WI	15,459	C
Valley City State Univ	ND	12,286	LC
Wayland Baptist Univ	TX	18,912	LC
Western Kentucky Univ	KY	11,000	LC
Western New Mexico Univ	NM	8,500	LC
Youngstown State Univ	OH	16,732	C

VOICE

School	ST	$IS	SR
Aquinas College	MI	33,060	VC
Baldwin Wallace Univ	OH	38,318	C
Bennington College	VT	56,990	HC+
Butler Univ	IN	47,572	VC+
Calif Baptist Univ	CA	38,792	C
Calvin College	MI	39,120	VC
Campbellsville Univ	KY	27,720	C
Central Washington Univ	WA	11,730	C
East Central Univ	OK	10,223	LC
East Texas Baptist Univ	TX	31,577	LC
Eastern Mich Univ	MI	18,604	C
Florida State Univ	FL	16,715	VC
Hardin-Simmons Univ	TX	23,560	C+
Houghton College	NY	36,808	C+
Illinois Wesleyan Univ	IL	48,452	HC
Indiana Univ Bloomington	IN	19,801	VC
Indiana Univ-Purdue Univ Fort Wayne	IN	15,521	C
Loyola Univ New Orleans	LA	46,581	VC
Manhattan School of Music	NY	55,850	SP
Mannes College New School for Music	NY	44,500	SP
Marshall Univ	WV	14,820	C
Millikin Univ	IL	38,940	C
Miss College	MS	21,998	C
Mount Aloysius College	PA	29,976	C
New York Univ	NY	61,470	MC
Northwestern College	MN	24,000	C
Northwestern Univ	IL	61,640	MC
Nyack College	NY	33,250	C
Ohio Univ	OH	21,080	C
Ouachita Baptist Univ	AR	30,220	VC
Pacific Lutheran Univ	WA	46,760	C+
Palm Beach Atlantic Univ	FL	34,874	C+
Point Loma Nazarene Univ	CA	41,006	C+
Rider Univ	NJ	45,720	C
Roosevelt Univ	IL	22,605	VC
Samford Univ	AL	37,060	C+
San Francisco Conservatory of Music	CA	56,428	SP
Shorter Univ	GA	30,650	LC
Stetson Univ	FL	51,516	VC
Syracuse Univ	NY	56,346	VC
The Catholic Univ of America	DC	52,852	VC
Union Univ	TN	28,260	VC
Univ of Cincinnati	OH	21,506	VC
Univ of Illinois at Urbana-Champaign	IL	26,450	HC
Univ of Iowa	IA	17,693	VC
Univ of Kansas	KS	17,603	C+
Univ of Mobile	AL	28,935	VC
Univ of Tulsa	OK	46,331	VC
Valparaiso Univ	IN	44,940	VC+
Webster Univ	MO	35,100	C+
West Chester Univ of Pennsylvania	PA	17,186	C
Westminster Choir College	NJ	36,000	SP
York College	NE	19,475	C
Youngstown State Univ	OH	16,732	C

WATER AND WASTEWATER TECHNOLOGY

School	ST	$IS	SR
Texas State Univ	TX	17,128	C
Wright State Univ	OH	16,983	C

WATER RESOURCES

School	ST	$IS	SR
Central State Univ	OH	9,010	C
Colo State Univ-Fort Collins	CO	20,385	VC
Heidelberg Univ	OH	34,100	C
Northern Mich Univ	MI	18,278	C
Prescott College	AZ	33,284	C
SUNY Oneonta / SUNY	NY	16,919	C+
Tarleton State Univ	TX	13,489	LC
Texas A&M Univ at Galveston	TX	11,258	C
The SUNY/College at Brockport	NY	19,002	C
Univ of Georgia	GA	20,082	VC
Univ of Nebr - Lincoln	NE	18,031	VC

WEB SERVICES

School	ST	$IS	SR
Bloomfield College	NJ	37,850	LC
Champlain College	VT	46,650	VC+
Idaho State Univ	ID	12,307	C
Indiana Inst of Technology	IN	34,240	LC
Johnson & Wales Univ/Providence Campus	RI	29,576	C
Keene State College	NH	23,232	LC
Limestone College	SC	30,800	C
Lipscomb Univ	TN	37,490	VC
Marymount Univ	VA	39,480	C
Mercyhurst Univ	PA	40,700	C
Roger Williams Univ	RI	46,296	VC
Southern Adventist Univ	TN	26,190	C
Taylor Univ	IN	37,821	VC+
Thiel College	PA	38,728	LC
Univ of Wisc/Stevens Point	WI	14,043	C
Univ of Wisc-Milwaukee	WI	18,436	C

WEB TECHNOLOGY

School	ST	$IS	SR
Belmont Univ	TN	39,190	VC+
Bloomfield College	NJ	37,850	LC
Cogswell Polytechnical College	CA	30,531	C
Davenport Univ	MI	21,002	LC
Drexel Univ	PA	61,418	VC+
Illinois Inst of Technology	IL	38,512	HC+
Lasell College	MA	43,750	LC
Limestone College	SC	30,800	C
Mercyhurst Univ	PA	40,700	C
Mount Aloysius College	PA	29,976	C
Pennsylvania College of Technology	PA	26,286	NC
Quinnipiac Univ	CT	55,160	VC
Roger Williams Univ	RI	46,296	VC
Tenn Tech Univ	TN	11,310	C
Tulane Univ	LA	60,861	MC
Univ of St. Francis	IL	37,560	C

WELDING ENGINEERING

School	ST	$IS	SR
Ferris State Univ	MI	20,047	C
Idaho State Univ	ID	12,307	C
LeTourneau Univ	TX	36,210	VC
Pennsylvania College of Technology	PA	26,286	NC
Ohio State Univ-Columbus Campus	OH	19,887	HC+

WESTERN CIVILIZATION/ CULTURE

School	ST	$IS	SR
St. John's College-Annapolis	MD	53,590	HC
Univ of Montana-Western	MT	9,753	LC

WESTERN EUROPEAN STUDIES

School	ST	$IS	SR
Denison Univ	OH	54,670	HC+
St. John's College-Annapolis	MD	53,590	HC
Univ of Mich/Ann Arbor	MI	22,102	MC
Washington Univ in St. Louis	MO	69,844	MC

WILDLIFE BIOLOGY

School	ST	$IS	SR
Adams State Univ	CO	13,358	LC
Auburn Univ	AL	22,378	VC+
Colo State Univ-Fort Collins	CO	20,385	VC
Friends Univ	KS	29,100	C
Humboldt State Univ	CA	18,400	C
Kansas State Univ	KS	15,497	VC
Lees-McRae College	NC	33,944	C
Murray State Univ	KY	15,304	C
Ohio Univ	OH	21,080	VC
Oregon State Univ	OR	20,273	VC
Pittsburg State Univ	KS	12,032	C
Prescott College	AZ	33,284	C
Purdue Univ/West Lafayette	IN	20,024	HC
S Dak State Univ	SD	14,296	C
SUNY / College of Environmental Science and Forestry	NY	18,351	VC
Tarleton State Univ	TX	13,489	LC
Texas State Univ	TX	17,128	C
Unity College	ME	34,054	C
Univ of Alaska Fairbanks	AK	15,130	C
Univ of Calif at Davis	CA		HC
Univ of Florida	FL	15,943	HC
Univ of Illinois at Urbana-Champaign	IL	26,450	HC
Univ of Minn/Twin Cities	MN		HC
Univ of Montana	MT	14,105	C
Univ of Montana-Western	MT	9,753	LC
Univ of Tenn at Knoxville	TN	20,364	VC+
Univ of Vermont	VT	27,006	VC+
Univ of Wisc/Madison	WI	18,757	HC+
Univ of Wisc/Stevens Point	WI	14,043	C
Univ of Wyoming	WY	14,401	C+
Washington State Univ	WA	20,461	C
West Texas A&M Univ	TX	13,478	C

WILDLIFE CONSERVATION BIOLOGY

School	ST	$IS	SR
Univ of Rhode Island	RI	24,002	C

WILDLIFE MANAGEMENT

School	ST	$IS	SR
Arkansas State Univ	AR	15,470	C
Brigham Young Univ	UT	12,100	HC
Dakota Wesleyan Univ	SD	23,000	C
Delaware Valley College	PA	29,944	C
Eastern Kentucky Univ	KY	11,161	C
Eastern New Mexico Univ	NM	10,682	C
Frostburg State Univ	MD	15,264	LC
Kansas State Univ	KS	15,497	VC
Lake Superior State Univ	MI	18,121	C
Lincoln Memorial Univ	TN	18,144	C
Louisiana Tech Univ	LA	11,302	C
Mich State Univ	MI	22,450	VC
Mich Tech Univ	MI	23,556	HC
Miss State Univ	MS	14,750	C
Missouri State Univ	MO	13,996	C+
Northwest Missouri State Univ	MO	17,347	C
Oregon State Univ	OR	20,273	VC
Peru State College	NE	8,600	NC
Prescott College	AZ	33,284	C
Stephen F. Austin State Univ	TX	14,668	C
Sul Ross State Univ	TX	13,410	LC
Tenn Tech Univ	TN	11,310	C
Texas A&M Univ at Commerce	TX	10,496	C
Texas Tech Univ	TX	14,243	C
The SUNY College of Agriculture and Tech at Cobleskill	NY	19,749	LC
Unity College	ME	34,054	C
Univ of Arkansas at Monticello	AR	12,076	NC
Univ of Delaware	DE	23,612	VC
Univ of Idaho	ID	14,558	C
Univ of Illinois at Urbana-Champaign	IL	26,450	HC
Univ of Maine	ME	19,902	C+
Univ of Nebr - Lincoln	NE	18,031	VC
Univ of Nevada/Reno	NV	17,507	C
Univ of New Hampshire	NH	26,912	C
Univ of PR/Humacao	PR	1,877	
Utah State Univ	UT	12,044	C
Washington State Univ	WA	20,461	C

WILDLIFE SCIENCE

School	ST	$IS	SR
Embry-Riddle Aeronautical Univ - Prescott Campus	AZ	40,444	VC+
New Mexico State Univ	NM	14,050	C

WINDS

School	ST	$IS	SR
Eastern Mich Univ	MI	18,604	C
Florida State Univ	FL	16,715	VC
Mannes College New School for Music	NY	44,500	SP
Miss College	MS	21,998	C
Northwestern Univ	IL	61,640	MC
Oberlin College	OH	61,788	MC
Roosevelt Univ	IL	22,605	VC
San Francisco Conservatory of Music	CA	56,428	SP
Stetson Univ	FL	51,516	VC
Syracuse Univ	NY	56,346	VC
Univ of Kansas	KS	17,603	C+
Univ of Mich/Ann Arbor	MI	22,102	MC
Wright State Univ	OH	16,983	C
Youngstown State Univ	OH	16,732	C

WINE AND VITICULTURE

School	ST	$IS	SR
Calif Polytechnic State Univ	CA	19,847	HC

WOMEN & GENDER STUDIES

School	ST	$IS	SR
Allegheny College	PA	50,980	HC
Amherst College	MA	58,744	HC
Aquinas College	MI	33,060	C
Arizona State Univ, at the West Campus	AZ	19,251	C
Armstrong State Univ	GA	15,532	C
Austin College	TX	45,875	HC
Bates College	ME	60,720	MC
Cal State, Chico	CA	20,158	C
Cal State, Long Beach	CA	17,502	C+
Castleton State College	VT	20,186	C
College of Staten Island/The City of New Yok	NY	16,778	NC
Duquesne Univ	PA	43,720	VC
Eastern Conn State Univ	CT	20,584	C
Goddard College	VT	16,418	VC
Illinois Wesleyan Univ	IL	48,452	HC
Indiana Univ South Bend	IN	15,501	C
Keene State College	NH	23,232	LC
Kenyon College	OH	58,890	MC
Lycoming College	PA	45,379	C
Mills College	CA	54,119	VC
New Jersey City Univ	NJ	21,456	C
N Dak State Univ	ND		C
Northern Arizona Univ	AZ	19,010	C
Oberlin College	OH	61,788	MC
Ohio Univ	OH	21,080	C
Oswego / SUNY	NY	20,009	VC
Pace Univ	NY	53,367	C
Seattle Univ	WA	49,035	VC+
Southern Oregon Univ	OR	17,874	C
Syracuse Univ	NY	56,346	VC
The College of St. Rose	NY	26,750	C
Univ of Colo Boulder	CO	22,605	VC+
Univ of Illinois at Chicago	IL	24,505	VC
Univ of Maine	ME	19,902	C+
Univ of Mass Dartmouth	MA	22,223	C
Univ of Mich/Dearborn	MI	9,885	VC
Univ of Nebr - Lincoln	NE	18,031	VC
Univ of Tulsa	OK	46,331	MC
Univ of Wyoming	WY	14,401	C+
Vanderbilt Univ	TN	58,220	MC
Winona State Univ	MN	16,640	C

WOMEN'S STUDIES

School	ST	$IS	SR
Agnes Scott College	GA	45,323	C+
Albion College	MI	46,010	C
Albright College	PA	46,660	C
Alverno College	WI	31,434	LC
American Univ	DC	56,015	HC+
Appalachian State Univ	NC	12,919	VC
Aquinas College	MI	33,060	C
Arizona State Univ, at the Tempe Campus	AZ	20,137	C+
Augsburg College	MN	35,142	C
Augustana College	IL	43,398	VC
Ball State Univ	IN	17,850	C
Barnard College/Columbia Univ	NY	39,000	MC
Beloit College	WI	49,970	HC
Bennington College	VT	56,990	HC+
Berea College	KY	7,192	C
Bloomfield College	NJ	37,850	LC
Bowdoin College	ME	59,568	MC
Bowling Green State Univ	OH	18,970	C
Brandeis Univ	MA		MC
Bucknell Univ	PA	60,140	MC
Cal State, Fresno	CA	17,405	C
Cal State, Fullerton	CA	25,188	C
Cal State, Long Beach	CA	17,502	C+
Cal State, Northridge	CA	28,690	LC
Cal State, San Marcos	CA	14,576	LC
Canisius College	NY	44,900	C
Carleton College	MN	60,102	MC
Case Western Reserve Univ	OH	56,534	MC
Chatham Univ	PA	43,797	C
CUNY/Brooklyn College	NY	5,884	C+
Clark Univ	MA	47,020	HC+
Cleveland State Univ	OH	21,776	C
Coe College	IA	45,550	VC
Colby College	ME	57,510	MC
Colgate Univ	NY	58,135	MC
College of Charleston	SC	22,145	VC
College of New Jersey	NJ	25,376	HC
College of William & Mary	VA	28,000	MC
College of Wooster	OH	52,600	VC
Colo College	CO	57,162	MC
Columbia Univ/City of New York	NY	61,116	MC
Columbia Univ/School of General Studies	NY	58,231	MC
Cornell Univ	IA	44,930	VC
Dartmouth College	NH	57,996	MC
Denison Univ	OH	54,670	HC+
DePaul Univ	IL	47,623	VC
DePauw Univ	IN	48,950	VC+
Dickinson College	PA	57,662	HC+
Dominican Univ	IL	37,628	C
Dominican Univ of Calif	CA	51,250	C
Drew Univ/College of Liberal Arts	NJ	57,516	C
Duke Univ	NC	50,250	MC
Earlham College	IN	51,470	MC
East Carolina Univ	NC	14,169	C
Eastern Mich Univ	MI	18,604	C
Eckerd College	FL	43,902	C
Emory Univ	GA	56,368	MC
Florida International Univ	FL	17,747	C+
Florida State Univ	FL	16,715	VC
Fordham Univ	NY	61,588	HC+
Georgia State Univ	GA	15,582	VC
Gettysburg College	PA	58,820	HC
Goucher College	MD	52,040	VC+
Grinnell College	IA	63,654	HC
Guilford College	NC	42,800	C
Gustavus Adolphus College	MN	48,170	HC
Hamilton College	NY	55,620	MC
Hamline Univ	MN	45,678	VC
Hampshire College	MA	58,320	MC
Harvard College/Harvard Univ	MA	49,000	MC
Hobart and William Smith Colleges	NY	60,034	HC+
Hofstra Univ	NY	51,810	VC+
Hope College	MI	38,650	VC
Howard Univ	DC	13,646	C
Hunter College	NY	14,429	VC
Indiana Univ-Purdue Univ Fort Wayne	IN	15,521	C
John Carroll Univ	OH	46,300	C+
Kansas State Univ	KS	15,497	VC
Knox College	IL	44,865	VC+
Lehigh Univ	PA	56,770	MC
Loyola Marymount Univ	CA	54,649	VC+
Loyola Univ Chicago	IL	51,646	VC+
Luther College	IA	45,720	C
Macalester College	MN	57,691	MC
Marshall Univ	WV	14,820	C
Mercer Univ	GA	44,201	VC
Metropolitan State Univ	MN	5,923	
Miami Univ	OH	24,191	VC
Mich State Univ	MI	22,450	VC
Middlebury College	VT	59,160	MC
Minn State Univ, Mankato	MN	15,616	C
Minn State Univ, Moorhead	MN	13,392	VC
Montclair State Univ	NJ	22,614	C
Mount Aloysius College	PA	29,976	C
Nazareth College of Rochester	NY	43,028	C+
Nebr Wesleyan Univ	NE	29,774	C+
New England College	NH	45,930	LC
New Mexico State Univ	NM	14,050	C
Northeastern Illinois Univ	IL	10,318	C
Northern Kentucky Univ	KY	21,134	C
Oakland Univ	MI	19,391	C
Oberlin College	OH	61,788	MC
Ohio Univ	OH	21,080	C
Ohio Wesleyan Univ	OH	49,460	VC
Old Dominion Univ	VA	19,483	LC
Oregon State Univ	OR	20,273	VC
Oswego / SUNY	NY	20,009	VC
Pacific Lutheran Univ	WA	46,760	C+
Pitzer College	CA	54,988	MC
Pomona College	CA	57,680	MC
Portland State Univ	OR	18,672	C
Prescott College	AZ	33,284	C
Providence College	RI	57,383	VC
Purdue Univ/West Lafayette	IN	20,024	HC
Queens College/The CUNY	NY	17,107	VC
Randolph-Macon College	VA	49,869	C+
Regis Univ	CO	41,318	C
Rhode Island College	RI	17,694	LC
Rice Univ	TX	43,288	MC
Roosevelt Univ	IL	22,605	VC
Rosemont College	PA	42,350	C
Rutgers, The State Univ of New Jersey/New Brunswick	NJ	25,562	C
Rutgers, The State Univ of New Jersey/Newark Campus	NJ	258,806	C
Sacred Heart Univ	CT	49,264	VC
St. Louis Univ	MO	48,346	HC
San Diego State Univ	CA	21,611	C+
San Francisco State Univ	CA	18,514	C
Sarah Lawrence College	NY	48,000	HC
Scripps College	CA	61,940	MC
Simmons College	MA	49,966	VC
Smith College	MA	59,674	MC
Sonoma State Univ	CA	20,541	C
Southwestern Univ	TX	45,660	VC
Spelman College	GA	24,650	C
St. Bonaventure Univ	NY	41,575	C
St. Catherine Univ	MN	37,782	C+
St. Olaf College	MN	51,200	HC+
Stanford Univ	CA	58,388	MC
SUNY at Purchase	NY	16,951	C
Stony Brook Univ / SUNY	NY	20,078	VC+
Suffolk Univ	MA	47,298	C
SUNY Fredonia/The SUNY at Fredonia	NY	19,840	VC
SUNY New Paltz	NY	14,348	C
SUNY Plattsburgh / SUNY	NY	18,083	C
Temple Univ	PA	24,392	VC
The College of New Rochelle	NY	33,600	VC
Ohio State Univ-Columbus Campus	OH	19,887	HC+
The Pennsylvania State Univ - Univ Park	PA	28,022	VC+
The SUNY at Potsdam	NY	18,473	C
The SUNY/College at Brockport	NY	19,002	C
The Univ of N Car at Greensboro	NC	12,848	C
The Univ of Okla	OK	18,621	VC
The Univ of Utah	UT	16,463	VC
Towson Univ	MD	16,000	VC
Trinity College	CT		HC

ST = STATE $IS = IN-STATE COSTS   SR = SELECTOR RATING

PART IV

A CLOSE LOOK AT

THE COLLEGES

This section will help you understand the college Profiles that are at the heart of this directory, so you can get the most out of them.

The College Admissions Selector explains Barron's unique system of comparing every school's degree of admissions competitiveness. Colleges are rated from Most Competitive to Less Competitive, and more.

Explanations of the ratings are followed by an in-depth look at the college capsule and essay.

Next come the Profiles—over 1600 four-year accredited colleges and universities in the United States—followed by encapsulated descriptions of about fifty religious schools. Universities outside the boundaries of this country are profiled here, too, including Canadian, European, and more.

COLLEGE ADMISSIONS SELECTOR

This index groups all the colleges listed in this book according to degree of admissions competitiveness. The *Selector* is not a rating of colleges by academic standards or quality of education; it is rather an attempt to describe, in general terms, the situation a prospective student will meet when applying for admission.

THE CRITERIA USED

The factors used in determining the category for each college were: median entrance examination scores for the 2014–2015 freshman class (the SAT score used was derived by averaging the median critical reading, math, and writing scores; the ACT score used was the median composite score); percentages of 2014–2015 freshmen scoring 500 and above and 600 and above on the critical reading, math, and writing sections of the SAT; percentages of 2014–2015 freshmen scoring 21 and above and 27 and above on the ACT; percentage of 2014–2015 freshmen who ranked in the upper fifth and the upper two-fifths of their high school graduating classes; minimum class rank and grade point average required for admission (if any); and percentage of applicants to the 2014–2015 freshman class who were accepted. The *Selector* cannot and does not take into account all the other factors that each college considers when making admissions decisions. Colleges place varying degrees of emphasis on the factors that comprise each of these categories.

USING THE SELECTOR

To use the *Selector* effectively, the prospective student's records should be compared realistically with the freshmen enrolled by the colleges in each category, as shown by the SAT or ACT scores, the quality of high school record emphasized by the colleges in each category, and the kinds of risks that the applicant wishes to take.

The student should also be aware of what importance a particular school places on various nonacademic factors; when available, this information is presented in the profile of the school. If a student has unusual qualifications that may compensate for exam scores or high school record, the student should examine admissions policies of the colleges in the next higher category than the one that encompasses his or her score and consider those colleges that give major consideration to factors other than exam scores and high school grades. The "safety" college should usually be chosen from the next lower category, where the student can be reasonably sure that his or her scores and high school record will fall above the median scores and records of the freshmen enrolled in the college.

The listing within each category is alphabetical and not in any qualitative order. State-supported institutions have been classified according to the requirements for state residents, but standards for admission of out-of-state students are usually higher. Colleges that are experimenting with the admission of students of higher potential but lower achievement may appear in a less competitive category because of this fact.

A WORD OF CAUTION

The *Selector* is intended primarily for preliminary screening, to eliminate the majority of colleges that are not suitable for a particular student. Be sure to examine the admissions policies spelled out in the *Admissions* section of each profile. And remember that many colleges have to reject *qualified* students; the *Selector* will tell you what your chances are, not which college will accept you.

MOST COMPETITIVE

Even superior students will encounter a great deal of competition for admission to the colleges in this category. In general, these colleges require high school rank in the top 10% to 20% and grade averages of A to B+. Median freshman test scores at these colleges are generally between 655 and 800 on the SAT and 29 and above on the ACT. In addition, many of these colleges admit only a small percentage of those who apply—usually fewer than one third.

Amherst College, MA
Bates College, ME
Boston College, MA
Bowdoin College, ME
Brown University, RI
Bryn Mawr College, PA
Bucknell University, PA
California Institute of Technology, CA
Carleton College, MN
Carnegie Mellon University, PA
Case Western Reserve University, OH
Claremont McKenna College, CA
Colby College, ME
Colgate University, NY
College of Mount Saint Vincent, NY
College of the Holy Cross, MA
College of William & Mary, VA
Colorado College, CO
Columbia University in the City of New York, NY
Columbia University/Barnard College, NY
Columbia University/School of General Studies, NY
Connecticut College, CT
Cooper Union for the Advancement of Science and Art, NY
Cornell University, NY
Dartmouth College, NH
Davidson College, NC
Duke University, NC
Emory University, GA
Franklin and Marshall College, PA
George Washington University, DC
Georgetown University, DC
Georgia Institute of Technology, GA
Hamilton College, NY

Hampshire College, MA
Harvard University/Harvard College, MA
Harvey Mudd College, CA
Haverford College, PA
Johns Hopkins University, MD
Kenyon College, OH
Lehigh University, PA
Macalester College, MN
Massachusetts Institute of Technology, MA
Middlebury College, VT
New York University, NY
Northeastern University, MA
Northwestern University, IL
Oberlin College, OH
Occidental College, CA
The Ohio State University, OH
Ohio State University at Marion, OH
Pitzer College, CA
Pomona College, CA
Princeton University, NJ
Reed College, OR
Rensselaer Polytechnic Institute, NY
Rice University, TX
Rose-Hulman Institute of Technology, IN
Santa Clara University, CA
Scripps College, CA
Smith College, MA
Southern Methodist University, TX
Stanford University, CA
Swarthmore College, PA
Tufts University, MA
Tulane University, LA
Union College, NY

United States Air Force Academy, CO
United States Military Academy, NY
United States Naval Academy, MD
University of California at Berkeley, CA
University of California at Los Angeles, CA
University of Chicago, IL
University of Miami, FL
University of Missouri/Columbia, MO
University of North Carolina at Chapel Hill, NC
University of Notre Dame, IN
University of Pennsylvania, PA
University of Richmond, VA
University of Rochester, NY
University of Southern California, CA

University of Virginia, VA
Vanderbilt University, TN
Vassar College, NY
Villanova University, PA
Wake Forest University, NC
Washington and Lee University, VA
Washington University in St. Louis, MO
Webb Institute, NY
Wellesley College, MA
Wesleyan University, CT
Whitman College, WA
Williams College, MA
Yale University, CT

HIGHLY COMPETITIVE

Colleges in this group generally look for students with grade averages of B+ to B and accept most of their students from the top 20% to 35% of the high school class. Median freshman test scores at these colleges generally range from 620 to 654 on the SAT and 27 or 28 on the ACT. These schools generally accept between one third and one half of their applicants.

To provide for finer distinctions within this admissions category, a plus (+) symbol has been placed before some entries. These are colleges with median freshman scores of 645 or more on the SAT or 28 or more on the ACT (depending on which test the college prefers), and colleges that accept fewer than one quarter of their applicants.

Allegheny College, PA
+American University, DC
Augustana College, IL
Austin College, TX
Babson College, MA
Bard College, NY
+Bard College at Simon's Rock, MA
Baylor University, TX
Beloit College, WI
+Bennington College, VT
+Bentley University, MA
Berea College, KY
Berry College, GA
+Binghamton University / The State University of New York, NY
+Boston University, MA
Brandeis University, MA
Brigham Young University, UT
California Polytechnic State University, CA
+Centre College, KY
Christian Brothers University, TN
+Clark University, MA
Clarkson University, NY
Clemson University, SC
College of New Jersey, NJ
+College of the Atlantic, ME
Colorado School of Mines, CO
Cornell College, IA
+CUNY-City College, NY
+Denison University, OH
+Dickinson College, PA
Drexel University, PA
Elon University, NC
Emerson College, MA
Florida State University, FL
Fordham University, NY
Furman University, SC
Gettysburg College, PA
Gonzaga University, WA
Grinnell College, IA
Grove City College, PA
Gustavus Adolphus College, MN
+Hendrix College, AR
+Hillsdale College, MI
+Illinois Institute of Technology, IL
Indiana University Bloomington, IN
Ithaca College, NY
+Kalamazoo College, MI
Kettering University, MI
+Lafayette College, PA
Lawrence University, WI
Miami University, OH
Mills College, CA

+Mount Holyoke College, MA
Muhlenberg College, PA
+New College of Florida, FL
New Mexico Institute of Mining and Technology, NM
North Carolina State University, NC
+Pepperdine University, CA
+Polytechnic Institute of New York University, NY
Providence College, RI
Purdue University/West Lafayette, IN
+Rhodes College, TN
Rollins College, FL
Sarah Lawrence College, NY
+Sewanee: The University of the South, TN
Skidmore College, NY
+St. John's College, Santa Fe, NM
St. John's College-Annapolis, MD
St. Lawrence University, NY
St. Mary's College of Maryland, MD
+St. Olaf College, MN
State University of New York / College of Environmental Science and Forestry, NY
Stevens Institute of Technology, NJ
Stony Brook University / State University of New York, NY
+SUNY College at Geneseo , NY
Syracuse University, NY
Texas Christian University, TX
+Thomas Aquinas College, CA
+Trinity College, CT
+Trinity University, TX
Truman State University, MO
United States Coast Guard Academy, CT
+United States Merchant Marine Academy, NY
University of California at Davis, CA
University of California at Santa Barbara, CA
University of Connecticut, CT
+University of Florida, FL
University of Illinois at Urbana-Champaign, IL
University of Maryland, MD
+University of Michigan/Ann Arbor, MI
University of Minnesota/Twin Cities, MN
+University of Pittsburgh at Pittsburgh, PA
+University of Puget Sound, WA
+University of San Diego, CA
University of Texas at Austin, TX
University of Texas at Dallas, TX
+University of Tulsa, OK
University of Wisconsin/Madison, WI
Virginia Polytechnic Institute and State University, VA
Westmont College, CA
+Wheaton College, IL
+Wheaton College, MA
+Worcester Polytechnic Institute, MA

VERY COMPETITIVE

The colleges in this category generally admit students whose averages are no less than B- and who rank in the top 35% to 50% of their graduating class. They generally report median freshman test scores in the 573 to 619 range on the SAT and from 24 to 26 on the ACT. These schools generally accept between one half and three quarters of their applicants.

The plus (+) has been placed before colleges with median freshman scores of 610 or above on the SAT or 26 or better on the ACT (depending on which test the college prefers), and colleges that accept fewer than one third of their applicants.

Abilene Christian University, TX
Adelphi University, NY
+Agnes Scott College, GA
Alaska Pacific University, AK
Albion College, MI
Alfred University, NY
Alma College, MI
Appalachian State University, NC
Asbury University, KY
Assumption College, MA
+Auburn University, AL
Augustana College, SD
Baldwin Wallace University, OH
Bellarmine University, KY
+Belmont University, TN
Benedictine College, KS
Bethel University, MN
Biola University, CA
+Birmingham-Southern College, AL
Bradley University, IL
+Brescia University, KY
Brigham Young University/Hawaii, HI
Bryant University, RI
+Butler University, IN
+Calvin College, MI
Canisius College, NY
Capital University, OH
The Catholic University of America, DC
+Cedarville University, OH
Central College, IA
Central Methodist University, MO
Champlain College, VT
+Chapman University, CA
Chatham University, PA
Christendom College, VA
Christopher Newport University, VA
City University of New York/Baruch College, NY
Clarkson College, NE
Coe College, IA
The College at Brockport / State University of New York, NY
College of Charleston, SC
The College of Idaho, ID
The College of New Rochelle, NY
College of New Rochelle - School of New Resources, NY
College of Saint Benedict , MN
College of the Ozarks, MO
College of Wooster, OH
Colorado Christian University, CO
Colorado State University-Fort Collins, CO
Concordia College New York, NY
Concordia University - Irvine, CA
Concordia University Nebraska, NE
Concordia University, Ann Arbor, MI
Coppin State University, MD
+Covenant College, GA
+Creighton University, NE
DePaul University, IL
+DePauw University, IN
Dillard University, LA
Doane College, NE
Dordt College, IA
+Drake University, IA
Drew University/College of Liberal Arts, NJ
Drury University, MO
Duquesne University, PA
+Earlham College, IN
Eastern Mennonite University, VA
Eckerd College, FL
Elizabethtown College, PA

Elizabethtown College School of Continuing and Professional Studies, PA
Elms College, MA
Embry-Riddle Aeronautical University - Prescott Campus, AZ
Emmanuel College, MA
Eugene Lang College - The New School for Liberal Arts, NY
Fairfield University, CT
Flagler College, FL
Florida Institute of Technology, FL
Florida International University, FL
Florida Southern College, FL
Fort Valley State University, GA
Franciscan University of Steubenville, OH
Freed-Hardeman University, TN
George Mason University, VA
Georgia College and State University, GA
Georgia State University, GA
Goddard College, VT
+Gordon College, MA
Goshen College, IN
+Goucher College, MD
Grand Canyon University, AZ
Grand Valley State University, MI
Hamline University, MN
Hanover College, IN
Hellenic College/Holy Cross Greek Orthodox School of Theology, MA
Hiram College, OH
Hobart and William Smith Colleges, NY
+Hofstra University, NY
Hollins University, VA
+Hope College, MI
Houghton College, NY
Hunter College / The City University of New York, NY
Illinois College, IL
Illinois State University, IL
+Illinois Wesleyan University, IL
Indiana Wesleyan University, IN
James Madison University, VA
+John Brown University, AR
Juniata College, PA
Kansas State University, KS
Kennesaw State University, GA
+Kentucky Wesleyan College, KY
Knox College, IL
La Sierra University, CA
Lake Forest College, IL
Lawrence Technological University, MI
Le Moyne College, NY
Lewis & Clark College, OR
Lindsey Wilson College, KY
Lipscomb University, TN
Loras College, IA
+Louisiana State University, LA
+Loyola Marymount University, CA
+Loyola University Chicago, IL
Loyola University Maryland, MD
Loyola University New Orleans, LA
+Luther College, IA
Lyon College, AR
Madonna University, MI
Maharishi University of Management, IA
Manhattan College, NY
Manhattanville College, NY
Marietta College, OH
Marlboro College, VT
+Marquette University, WI
Marymount Manhattan College, NY
Maryville College, TN

Maryville University of Saint Louis, MO
McDaniel College, MD
Medaille College, NY
+Mercer University, GA
Messiah College, PA
Metropolitan College of New York, NY
Michigan State University, MI
Michigan Technological University, MI
+Millsaps College, MS
+Milwaukee School of Engineering, WI
Mississippi College, MS
Missouri State University, MO
+Missouri University of Science and Technology, MO
Montana State University, MT
Montana Tech of The University of Montana, MT
Montreat College, NC
Moravian College, PA
Morgan State University, MD
+Mount St. Mary's College/Chalon Campus, CA
Nazareth College of Rochester, NY
New Jersey Institute of Technology, NJ
New York Institute of Technology, NY
North Central College, IL
Northeastern State University, OK
Northern Michigan University, MI
Notre Dame College, OH
Nova Southeastern University, FL
Oakland University, MI
Oglethorpe University, GA
Ohio Northern University, OH
Ohio University, OH
Oklahoma Baptist University, OK
Oklahoma Christian University, OK
Oklahoma City University, OK
Oklahoma State University, OK
Oswego / State University of New York, NY
Ottawa University, KS
Ouachita Baptist University, AR
Pace University, NY
Pacific Lutheran University, WA
Pacific Union College, CA
Penn State University/University Park , PA
Point Loma Nazarene University, CA
Presbyterian College, SC
Queens College / The City University of New York, NY
Queens University of Charlotte, NC
Quinnipiac University, CT
Randolph College, VA
Richard Stockton College of New Jersey, NJ
Rivier College, NH
+Rochester Institute of Technology, NY
Roosevelt University, IL
Rowan University, NJ
Rutgers, The State University of New Jersey/New Brunswick, NJ
Sacred Heart University, CT
Saint Anselm College, NH
Saint Joseph's University, PA
+Saint Louis University, MO
Saint Mary's College, IN
Saint Michael's College, VT
Salem College, NC
Salisbury University, MD
Salve Regina University, RI
+Samford University, AL
San Diego State University, CA
+Seattle Pacific University, WA
+Seattle University, WA
Shimer College, IL
Siena College, NY
Sierra Nevada College, NV
Simmons College, MA
Simpson College, IA
South Dakota School of Mines and Technology, SD
Southern Polytechnic State University, GA
Southwestern University, TX
Spelman College, GA
Spring Hill College, AL
St. Edward's University, TX
St. Joseph's College, New York / Suffolk Campus, NY
St. Norbert College, WI
The State University of New York College of Agriculture and
    Tech at Cobleskill, NY

Stephens College, MO
+Stetson University, FL
+Stonehill College, MA
SUNY Fredonia / The State University of New York at Fredonia,
    NY
SUNY Oneonta / State University of New York, NY
SUNY Plattsburgh / State University of New York, NY
+Taylor University, IN
Temple University, PA
+Texas A&M University, TX
Texas State University, TX
Touro College, NY
Towson University, MD
+Transylvania University, KY
Trine University, IN
Union College, NE
Union University, TN
University at Albany / SUNY, NY
University at Buffalo / The State University of New York, NY
University of Alabama at Huntsville, AL
University of Arkansas at Fayetteville, AR
University of California at Irvine, CA
University of California at San Diego, CA
University of California at Santa Cruz, CA
University of Central Arkansas, AR
+University of Central Florida, FL
University of Cincinnati, OH
University of Colorado at Colorado Springs, CO
+University of Colorado Boulder, CO
+University of Dallas, TX
University of Dayton, OH
University of Delaware, DE
+University of Denver, CO
+University of Evansville, IN
University of Georgia, GA
University of Hawaii at Manoa, HI
University of Houston, TX
University of Illinois at Chicago, IL
University of Iowa, IA
University of La Verne, CA
University of Louisville, KY
University of Mary Washington, VA
University of Maryland/Baltimore County, MD
+University of Massachusetts Amherst, MA
University of Michigan/Dearborn, MI
University of Minnesota/Morris, MN
University of Mississippi, MS
University of Missouri-St. Louis, MO
University of Mobile, AL
University of Nebraska - Lincoln, NE
University of New Hampshire, NH
University of New Orleans, LA
+University of North Carolina at Asheville, NC
+University of North Carolina at Wilmington, NC
University of North Florida, FL
+University of Oklahoma, OK
University of Oregon, OR
University of Portland, OR
University of Redlands, CA
University of Saint Thomas, MN
University of San Francisco, CA
University of Science and Arts of Oklahoma, OK
University of Scranton, PA
+University of South Carolina at Columbia, SC
University of South Florida/St. Petersburg, FL
University of St. Thomas - Houston, TX
University of Tampa, FL
+University of Tennessee at Knoxville, TN
University of the Pacific, CA
+University of the Sciences , PA
University of Utah, UT
+University of Vermont, VT
University of Washington, WA
University of Wisconsin/Eau Claire, WI
University of Wisconsin/La Crosse, WI
+Ursinus College, PA
+Valparaiso University, IN
Vanguard University of Southern California, CA
Wabash College, IN
Wagner College, NY
Warren Wilson College, NC
Wartburg College, IA

Washington and Jefferson College, PA
Washington College, MD
Wells College, NY
Western Washington University, WA
Westminster College, MO
Westminster College, UT
+Whitworth University, WA
+Willamette University, OR

+William Jewell College, MO
Winthrop University, SC
Wisconsin Lutheran College, WI
Wittenberg University, OH
Wofford College, SC
Xavier University, OH
+Yeshiva University, NY

COMPETITIVE

This category is a very broad one, covering colleges that generally have median freshman test scores between 500 and 572 on the SAT and between 21 and 23 on the ACT. Some of these colleges require that students have high school averages of B- or better, although others state a minimum of C+ or C. Generally, these colleges prefer students in the top 50% to 65% of the graduating class and accept between 75% and 85% of their applicants.

Colleges with a plus (+) are those with median freshman SAT scores of 563 or more or median freshman ACT scores of 24 or more (depending on which test the colleges prefers), and those that admit fewer than half of their applicants.

Adrian College, MI
Alabama Agricultural and Mechanical University, AL
Albany State University, GA
Albright College, PA
Alcorn State University, MS
Alderson Broaddus University, WV
Alfred State / SUNY College of Technology , NY
Alice Lloyd College, KY
Alvernia University, PA
American Indian College , AZ
American Jewish University , CA
Anderson University, IN
+Andrews University, MI
Aquinas College, MI
+Aquinas College, TN
+Arcadia University, PA
+Arizona State University, AZ
Arkansas State University, AR
Armstrong Atlantic State University, GA
Ashford University, IA
Ashland University, OH
Auburn University at Montgomery, AL
Augsburg College, MN
Aurora University, IL
Austin Peay State University, TN
Avila University, MO
Azusa Pacific University, CA
+Baker University, KS
Ball State University, IN
Barry University, FL
Barton College, NC
Bay Path College, MA
Beacon College, FL
Belhaven University, MS
Belmont Abbey College, NC
Bemidji State University, MN
Benedictine University, IL
Bethany College, WV
Bethel College, IN
Bethel College, KS
Bethel University, TN
Blackburn College, IL
Bloomfield College, NJ
Bloomsburg University of Pennsylvania, PA
+Bluefield College, VA
Bluffton University, OH
Boise State University, ID
Boricua College, NY
Bowling Green State University, OH
+Brenau University Women's College, GA
Briar Cliff University, IA
Bridgewater College, VA
Bridgewater State University, MA
Bryan College, TN
Bryn Athyn College , PA
Buena Vista University, IA
+Buffalo State/State University of Buffalo, NY

Cairn University, PA
California Baptist University, CA
California Lutheran University, CA
California Maritime Academy, CA
California State Polytechnic University, Pomona, CA
California State University, Chico, CA
California State University, East Bay, CA
California State University, Fresno, CA
+California State University, Fullerton, CA
+California State University, Long Beach, CA
California State University, Los Angeles, CA
California State University, Northridge, CA
California State University, Sacramento, CA
California State University, San Bernardino, CA
California State University, San Marcos, CA
California State University, Stanislaus, CA
California University of Pennsylvania, PA
Campbell University, NC
Campbellsville University, KY
Capitol College, MD
Cardinal Stritch University, WI
Carlow University, PA
Carroll College, MT
Carroll University, WI
+Carson-Newman University, TN
Carthage College, WI
Castleton State College, VT
Catawba College, NC
Cazenovia College, NY
Cedar Crest College, PA
+Centenary College of Louisiana, LA
Central Connecticut State University, CT
Central Michigan University, MI
Central State University, OH
Central Washington University, WA
Chaminade University of Honolulu, HI
Chancellor University, OH
Charleston Southern University, SC
Chicago State University, IL
Citadel, The, SC
+City University of New York/Brooklyn College, NY
+Claflin University, SC
Clarion University of Pennsylvania, PA
Clark Atlanta University, GA
Clarke University, IA
Clearwater Christian College, FL
Cleary University, MI
Cleveland State University, OH
Coastal Carolina University, SC
Cogswell Polytechnical College, CA
College of Mount Saint Joseph, OH
College of Saint Mary, NE
The College of Saint Rose, NY
College of Saint Scholastica, MN
Columbia College, MO
Columbia College, SC

Columbus State University, GA
Concord University, WV
+Concordia College, Moorhead, MN
Concordia University, OR
Concordia University Saint Paul, MN
Concordia University Texas, TX
Concordia University Wisconsin, WI
Concordia University, River Forest, IL
Converse College, SC
Corban University, OR
Cornerstone University and Grand Rapids Theological
    Seminary, MI
Culver-Stockton College, MO
Cumberland University, TN
Daemen College, NY
Dakota State University, SD
Dakota Wesleyan University, SD
Dallas Baptist University, TX
Daniel Webster College, NH
Davis and Elkins College, WV
De Sales University, PA
Defiance College, OH
Delaware Valley College, PA
Dominican College, NY
Dominican University, IL
Dominican University of California, CA
D'Youville College, NY
East Carolina University, NC
East Stroudsburg University of Pennsylvania, PA
East Tennessee State University, TN
East Texas Baptist University, TX
Eastern Connecticut State University, CT
Eastern Illinois University, IL
Eastern Kentucky University, KY
Eastern Michigan University, MI
Eastern Nazarene College, MA
Eastern New Mexico University, NM
Eastern Oregon University, OR
Eastern University, PA
Eastern Washington University, WA
East-West University, IL
Edgewood College, WI
Elizabeth City State University, NC
+Elmhurst College, IL
+Elmira College, NY
+Embry-Riddle Aeronautical University - Daytona Beach, FL
Embry-Riddle Aeronautical University - Worldwide, FL
Emory and Henry College, VA
Emporia State University, KS
Endicott College, MA
Erskine College, SC
Eureka College, IL
Evangel University, MO
+Evergreen State College, WA
Fairleigh Dickinson University/College at Florham, NJ
Fairleigh Dickinson University/Metropolitan Campus, NJ
Farmingdale State College, NY
Fayetteville State University, NC
Felician College, NJ
Ferris State University, MI
Fisk University, TN
Fitchburg State University, MA
Florida Atlantic University, FL
Florida Gulf Coast University, FL
Fontbonne University, MO
Fort Hays State University, KS
Fort Lewis College, CO
Framingham State University, MA
Franklin College, IN
Franklin Pierce University, NH
Fresno Pacific University, CA
Friends University, KS
Gannon University, PA
+Gardner-Webb University, NC
Geneva College, PA
+George Fox University, OR
Georgetown College, KY
Georgia Regents University, GA
Georgia Southern University, GA
Georgia Southwestern State Seliversity, GA
Golden Gate University, CA
Goldey-Beacom College, DE

Grace Bible College, MI
Grace College and Theological Seminary, IN
Graceland University, IA
Grand View University, IA
Greenville College, IL
Guilford College, NC
Gwynedd-Mercy College, PA
Hampden-Sydney College, VA
Hampton University, VA
Hannibal-LaGrange University, MO
+Harding University, AR
+Hardin-Simmons University, TX
+Hartwick College, NY
+Hastings College, NE
Hawaii Pacific University, HI
Heidelberg University, OH
Henderson State University, AR
High Point University, NC
Hilbert College, NY
Hood College, MD
Hope International University, CA
+Houston Baptist University, TX
Howard Payne University, TX
Howard University, DC
Humboldt State University, CA
Huntingdon College, AL
Huntington University, IN
+Huston-Tillotson University, TX
Idaho State University, ID
Immaculata University, PA
Indiana State University, IN
Indiana University South Bend, IN
Indiana University-Purdue University Fort Wayne, IN
Indiana University-Purdue University Indianapolis, IN
Iona College, NY
Iowa State University, IA
Jacksonville University, FL
+John Carroll University, OH
John Jay College of Criminal Justice / The City University of
    New York, NY
Johnson and Wales University/Charlotte Campus, NC
Johnson and Wales University/Denver Campus, CO
Johnson and Wales University/North Miami Campus, FL
Johnson and Wales University/Providence Campus, RI
Johnson State College, VT
Judson College, AL
Judson University, IL
Kansas Wesleyan University, KS
Keene State College, NH
Kent State University, OH
Keuka College, NY
King University, TN
King's College, PA
La Salle University, PA
LaGrange College, GA
Lake Erie College, OH
Lake Superior State University, MI
Lakeland College, WI
+Lander University, SC
Lane College, TN
Lebanon Valley College, PA
+Lee University, TN
Lees-McRae College, NC
LeMoyne-Owen College, TN
Lenoir-Rhyne College, NC
Lesley University, MA
LeTourneau University, TX
Lewis University, IL
Lewis-Clark State College, ID
Liberty University, VA
Limestone College, SC
Lincoln Memorial University, TN
Lindenwood University, MO
Linfield College-McMinnville Campus, OR
Long Island University/Brooklyn Campus, NY
Long Island University/C.W. Post Campus, NY
Longwood University, VA
Louisiana College, LA
Louisiana State University in Shreveport, LA
Louisiana Tech University, LA
Lubbock Christian University, TX
Lycoming College, PA

Lynchburg College, VA
Lyndon State College, VT
Lynn University, FL
MacMurray College, IL
Maine Maritime Academy, ME
Malone University, OH
Manchester College, IN
Mannes College New School for Music, NY
Marian University/Indianapolis, IN
Marist College, NY
Maritime College / State University of New York, NY
Marshall University, WV
Mary Baldwin College, VA
Marygrove College, MI
Marymount University, VA
Marywood University, PA
Massachusetts College of Liberal Arts, MA
Massachusetts Maritime Academy, MA
+The Masters College, CA
+McKendree University, IL
McNeese State University, LA
McPherson College, KS
Menlo College, CA
Mercy College, NY
Mercyhurst University, PA
Meredith College, NC
Merrimack College, MA
Methodist University, NC
MidAmerica Nazarene University, KS
Middle Tennessee State University, TN
Midland University, NE
Midway College, KY
Midwestern State University, TX
Millersville University of Pennsylvania, PA
Milligan College, TN
Millikin University, IL
Minnesota State University, Mankato, MN
Minnesota State University, Moorhead, MN
Minot State University, ND
Misericordia University, PA
Mississippi State University, MS
Missouri Baptist University, MO
Missouri Southern State University, MO
Missouri Valley College, MO
Mitchell College, CT
Molloy College, NY
Monmouth College, IL
Monmouth University, NJ
Monroe College, NY
Montclair State University, NJ
Morehead State University, KY
Morehouse College, GA
Morningside College, IA
Mount Aloysius College, PA
Mount Marty College, SD
Mount Mercy University, IA
Mount Olive College, NC
Mount Saint Mary College, NY
Mount Saint Mary's University, MD
Mount Vernon Nazarene University, OH
Murray State University, KY
Muskingum University, OH
+Nebraska Wesleyan University, NE
+New Jersey City University, NJ
Newbury College, MA
+Newman University, KS
Niagara University, NY
Nicholls State University, LA
North Carolina Wesleyan College, NC
North Central University, MN
North Dakota State University, ND
North Georgia College & State University, GA
North Park University, IL
Northeastern Illinois University, IL
Northern Arizona University, AZ
Northern Illinois University, IL
Northern State University, SD
Northland College, WI
Northwest Christian University, OR
Northwest Missouri State University, MO
Northwest University, WA
Northwestern College, MN

+Northwestern College of Iowa, IA
Northwestern State University of Louisiana, LA
Norwich University, VT
Notre Dame of Maryland University, MD
Nyack College, NY
Oakwood University, AL
+Ohio Dominican University, OH
Ohio State University at Lima, OH
Ohio State University at Mansfield, OH
Ohio State University at Newark, OH
Ohio Valley University, WV
+Ohio Wesleyan University, OH
Oklahoma Wesleyan University, OK
Old Dominion University, VA
Olivet College, MI
Olivet Nazarene University, IL
Oral Roberts University, OK
Oregon Institute of Technology, OR
+Oregon State University, OR
Otterbein College, OH
Pacific University, OR
Park University, MO
Penn State Erie/The Behrend College, PA
Penn State University/Altoona, PA
Pfeiffer University, NC
Philadelphia University, PA
Piedmont College, GA
Pittsburg State University, KS
Point Park University, PA
Portland State University, OR
Post University, CT
+Prescott College, AZ
+Principia College, IL
Purchase College / State University of New York , NY
Purdue University/Calumet, IN
+Ramapo College of New Jersey, NJ
Randolph-Macon College, VA
Regis University, CO
Reinhardt College, GA
Rider University, NJ
+Ripon College, WI
+Roanoke College, VA
Robert Morris University, PA
+Roberts Wesleyan College, NY
Rochester College, MI
Rockford College, IL
Rockhurst University, MO
Rocky Mountain College, MT
Roger Williams University, RI
Rosemont College, PA
Russell Sage College, NY
Rust College, MS
Rutgers, The State University of New Jersey/Camden Campus, NJ
Rutgers, The State University of New Jersey/Newark Campus, NJ
Saginaw Valley State University, MI
Saint Augustine's University, NC
Saint John's University, MN
Saint Joseph's College, IN
Saint Joseph's College of Maine, ME
Saint Leo University, FL
Saint Martin's University, WA
Saint Mary's College of California, CA
Saint Mary's University , TX
Saint Mary's University of Minnesota, MN
Saint Peter's College, NJ
Saint Vincent College, PA
Saint Xavier University, IL
Salem International University, WV
Sam Houston State University, TX
San Diego Christian College, CA
San Francisco State University, CA
San Jose State University, CA
Savannah State University, GA
Seton Hall University, NJ
Seton Hill University, PA
Shenandoah University, VA
Shepherd University, WV
Shorter University, GA
Simpson University, CA
Sonoma State University, CA

South Dakota State University, SD
Southeastern Louisiana University, LA
Southeastern Oklahoma State University, OK
+Southeastern University, FL
Southern Adventist University, TN
Southern Arkansas University, AR
Southern Connecticut State University, CT
Southern Illinois University Carbondale, IL
Southern Illinois University Edwardsville, IL
Southern New Hampshire University, NH
Southern Oregon University, OR
+Southern University and A&M College, LA
Southern Utah University, UT
Southern Wesleyan University, SC
Southwest Baptist University, MO
Southwest Minnesota State University, MN
Southwestern College, KS
Southwestern Oklahoma State University, OK
Spring Arbor University, MI
Springfield College, MA
St. Ambrose University, IA
St. Bonaventure University, NY
+St. Catherine University, MN
St. Cloud State University, MN
+St. John Fisher College, NY
+St. John's University, NY
St. Joseph's College, New York / Brooklyn Campus, NY
St. Thomas Aquinas College, NY
+St. Thomas University, FL
The State University of New York at Potsdam, NY
State University of New York Institute of Technology at Utica / Rome, NY
Stephen F. Austin State University, TX
Sterling College, KS
Sterling College, VT
Stevenson University, MD
Stillman College, AL
Suffolk University, MA
SUNY College at Old Westbury, NY
SUNY Cortland / The State University of New York, NY
SUNY New Paltz, NY
Susquehanna University, PA
+Sweet Briar College, VA
Talladega College, AL
Tennessee State University, TN
Tennessee Technological University, TN
Tennessee Wesleyan College, TN
Texas A&M University at Commerce, TX
Texas A&M University at Galveston, TX
Texas Lutheran University, TX
Texas Tech University, TX
Texas Wesleyan University, TX
Thomas More College, KY
Thomas More College of Liberal Arts, NH
Toccoa Falls College, GA
Trevecca Nazarene University, TN
Trinity Christian College, IL
Trinity International University, IL
+Trinity Washington University, DC
Troy University, AL
Tusculum College, TN
Tuskegee University, AL
Union College, KY
Unity College, ME
University of Akron, OH
+University of Alabama at Birmingham, AL
+University of Alabama at Tuscaloosa, AL
University of Alaska Fairbanks, AK
University of Alaska Southeast, AK
University of Arizona, AZ
University of Arkansas at Little Rock, AR
University of Arkansas at Pine Bluff, AR
University of California at Riverside, CA
University of Central Missouri, MO
University of Central Oklahoma, OK
University of Charleston, WV
University of Colorado Denver , CO
University of Detroit Mercy, MI
University of Dubuque, IA
University of Findlay, OH
University of Great Falls, MT
University of Hartford, CT

University of Hawaii at Hilo, HI
University of Idaho, ID
University of Jamestown, ND
+University of Kansas, KS
University of Kentucky, KY
University of Louisiana at Lafayette, LA
University of Louisiana at Monroe, LA
+University of Maine, ME
University of Maine at Augusta, ME
University of Maine at Farmington, ME
University of Maine at Machias, ME
University of Mary, ND
+University of Mary Hardin-Baylor, TX
University of Maryland/Eastern Shore, MD
University of Massachusetts Boston, MA
University of Massachusetts Dartmouth, MA
University of Massachusetts Lowell, MA
University of Memphis, TN
+University of Michigan-Flint, MI
University of Minnesota Crookston, MN
+University of Minnesota/Duluth, MN
University of Missouri-Kansas City, MO
University of Montana, MT
University of Montevallo, AL
University of Mount Union , OH
University of Nebraska at Omaha, NE
University of Nevada, Las Vegas, NV
+University of New England, ME
University of New Haven, CT
University of New Mexico, NM
University of North Alabama, AL
University of North Carolina at Charlotte, NC
University of North Carolina at Greensboro, NC
University of North Carolina at Pembroke, NC
University of North Dakota, ND
University of North Texas, TX
University of Northern Colorado, CO
University of Northern Iowa, IA
University of Pittsburgh at Greensburg, PA
+University of Rhode Island, RI
University of Saint Francis, IN
+University of Saint Mary, KS
University of Sioux Falls, SD
University of South Alabama, AL
University of South Carolina at Aiken, SC
University of South Dakota, SD
University of South Florida, FL
University of Southern Indiana, IN
University of Southern Maine, ME
University of Southern Mississippi, MS
University of St. Francis, IL
University of Tennessee at Chattanooga, TN
University of Tennessee at Martin, TN
University of Texas at San Antonio, TX
University of the Ozarks, AR
University of the Southwest, NM
University of Toledo, OH
University of Virginia's College at Wise, VA
University of West Alabama, AL
University of West Florida, FL
University of Wisconsin Whitewater, WI
University of Wisconsin/Green Bay, WI
University of Wisconsin/Platteville, WI
University of Wisconsin/Stevens Point, WI
University of Wisconsin/Stout, WI
University of Wisconsin/Superior, WI
University of Wisconsin-Milwaukee, WI
+University of Wyoming, WY
Urbana University, OH
Utah State University, UT
Utica College, NY
Valdosta State University, GA
Vermont Technical College, VT
Victory University, TN
Virginia Commonwealth University, VA
Virginia Military Institute, VA
+Virginia State University, VA
Virginia Union University, VA
Viterbo University, WI
Voorhees College, SC
Walsh University, OH
Warner Pacific College, OR

Warner University, FL
+Washington Adventist University, MD
Washington State University, WA
Wayne State University, MI
Waynesburg University, PA
Webber International University, FL
+Webster University, MO
+Wesleyan College, GA
West Chester University of Pennsylvania, PA
West Texas A&M University, TX
+West Virginia University, WV
West Virginia Wesleyan College, WV
+Western Carolina University, NC
Western Connecticut State University, CT
Western Illinois University, IL
Western Michigan University, MI
Western New England University, MA
Western Oregon University, OR
Western State Colorado University, CO
Westfield State University, MA

+Westminster College, PA
Wheeling Jesuit University, WV
Wheelock College, MA
Whittier College, CA
Wichita State University, KS
Widener University, PA
Wilkes University, PA
William Paterson University of New Jersey, NJ
William Penn University, IA
William Woods University, MO
Williams Baptist College, AR
Wilmington College, OH
Wilson College, PA
Wingate University, NC
Winona State University, MN
Worcester State University, MA
Wright State University, OH
Xavier University of Louisiana, LA
York College, NE
York College of Pennsylvania, PA

LESS COMPETITIVE

Included in this category are colleges with median freshman test scores generally below 500 on the SAT and below 21 on the ACT; some colleges that require entrance examinations but do not report median scores; and colleges that admit students with averages gen-erally below C who rank in the top 65% of the graduating class. These colleges usually admit 85% or more of their applicants. For detailed profiles of these colleges, please go to *barronspac.com*.

Adams State College, CO
Albertus Magnus College, CT
Alverno College, WI
American International College, MA
Amridge University, AL
Anna Maria College, MA
Arkansas Tech University, AR
Atlantic Union College, MA
Averett University, VA
Becker College, MA
Bennett College, NC
Berkeley College, NY
Berkeley College/New Jersey, NJ
Berkeley College/Westchester Campus, NY
Bethune-Cookman University, FL
Black Hills State University, SD
Blue Mountain College, MS
Bluefield State College, WV
Bowie State University, MD
Brewton-Parker College, GA
Cabrini College, PA
Caldwell College, NJ
California State University, Bakersfield, CA
California State University, Dominguez Hills, CA
California State University, Monterey Bay, CA
Calumet College of St. Joseph, IN
Cameron University, OK
Carlos Albizu University, FL
Centenary College, NJ
Chestnut Hill College, PA
Cheyney University of Pennsylvania, PA
Clayton State University, GA
Coker College, SC
College of Saint Elizabeth, NJ
College of St Joseph, VT
Colorado Mesa University, CO
Colorado State University-Pueblo, CO
Colorado Technical University, CO
Columbia College Chicago, IL
Cox College, MO
Curry College, MA
Davenport University, MI
Delaware State University, DE
Delta State University, MS
Dowling College, NY
East Central University, OK

Edinboro University of Pennsylvania, PA
Edward Waters College, FL
Fairmont State University, WV
Faulkner University, AL
Ferrum College, VA
Florida Agricultural and Mechanical University, FL
Florida Memorial University, FL
Francis Marion University, SC
Frostburg State University, MD
Georgian Court University, NJ
Goodwin College, CT
Grambling State University, LA
Green Mountain College, VT
Greensboro College, NC
Hodges University, FL
Holy Family University, PA
Husson University, ME
Indiana Institute of Technology, IN
Indiana University East, IN
Indiana University Kokomo, IN
Indiana University Northwest, IN
Indiana University of Pennsylvania, PA
Indiana University Southeast, IN
Iowa Wesleyan College, IA
Jackson State University, MS
Jacksonville State University, AL
Johnson C. Smith University, NC
Kean University, NJ
Kentucky Christian University, KY
Kentucky State University, KY
Keystone College, PA
Kutztown University of Pennsylvania, PA
La Roche College, PA
Lamar University, TX
Langston University, OK
Lasell College, MA
Lehman College / The City University of New York, NY
LIM College, NY
The Lincoln University, PA
Livingstone College, NC
Lock Haven University of Pennsylvania, PA
Lourdes University, OH
Mansfield University, PA
Marian University, WI
Mars Hill College, NC
McMurry University, TX

Metropolitan State University of Denver, CO
Mississippi University for Women, MS
Mississippi Valley State University, MS
Montana State University-Billings, MT
Morris College, SC
Mount Ida College, MA
Mount Mary University, WI
National Louis University, IL
Neumann University, PA
New England College, NH
New Mexico State University, NM
Newberry College, SC
Nichols College, MA
Norfolk State University, VA
North Carolina Agricultural and Technical State University, NC
North Carolina Central University, NC
Northern Kentucky University, KY
Northwood University, FL
Northwood University, MI
Northwood University, TX
Notre Dame de Namur University, CA
Our Lady of Holy Cross College, LA
Our Lady of the Lake University of San Antonio, TX
Paine College, GA
Palm Beach Atlantic University, FL
Paul Quinn College, TX
Philander Smith College, AR
Pine Manor College, MA
Plymouth State University, NH
Prairie View A&M University, TX
Presentation College, SD
Quincy University, IL
Radford University, VA
Regis College, MA
Rhode Island College, RI
Saint Francis University, PA
Saint Joseph College, CT
Saint Mary-of-the-Woods College, IN
Salem State College, MA
Schreiner University, TX
Shaw University, NC
Shippensburg University of Pennsylvania, PA
Siena Heights University, MI
Silver Lake College, WI
Slippery Rock University of Pennsylvania, PA
Sojourner-Douglass College, MD
South Carolina State University, SC
South University, GA
Southeast Missouri State University, MO
Southern Vermont College, VT

Southwestern Adventist University, TX
Spalding University, KY
St. Andrews University, NC
St. Francis College, NY
Sul Ross State University, TX
Tabor College, KS
Tarleton State University, TX
Texas A&M University at Corpus Christi, TX
Texas A&M University at Kingsville, TX
Texas Southern University, TX
Texas Woman's University, TX
Thiel College, PA
Thomas College, ME
Tiffin University, OH
University of Bridgeport, CT
University of Houston-Downtown, TX
University of Indianapolis, IN
University of Maine at Fort Kent, ME
University of Maine at Presque Isle, ME
University of Montana-Western, MT
University of Nebraska at Kearney, NE
University of Pittsburgh at Bradford, PA
University of Pittsburgh at Johnstown, PA
University of South Carolina Upstate, SC
University of Texas at Arlington, TX
University of Texas-Pan American, TX
University of the Cumberlands, KY
University of the District of Columbia, DC
University of the Incarnate Word, TX
University of West Georgia, GA
University of Wisconsin/Oshkosh, WI
University of Wisconsin/Parkside, WI
University of Wisconsin/River Falls, WI
Ursuline College, OH
Valley City State University, ND
Virginia Intermont College, VA
Virginia Wesleyan College, VA
Wayland Baptist University, TX
Wesley College, DE
West Liberty University, WV
Western Kentucky University, KY
Western New Mexico University, NM
Wilberforce University, OH
Wiley College, TX
William Carey University, MS
William Peace University, NC
Winston-Salem State University, NC
Woodbury Institute of Champlain College in Burlington, VT
Woodbury University, CA
Youngstown State University, OH

NONCOMPETITIVE

The colleges in this category generally only require evidence of graduation from an accredited high school (although they may also require completion of a certain number of high school units). Some require that entrance examinations be taken for placement purposes only, or only by graduates of unaccredited high schools or only by out-of-state students. In some cases, insufficient capacity may compel a college in this category to limit the number of students that are accepted; generally, however, if a college accepts 98% or more of its applicants, it automatically falls in this category. Colleges are also rated Noncompetitive if they admit all state residents, but have some requirements for nonresidents. For detailed profiles of these colleges, please go to *barronspac.com*.

Adventist Universtiy of Health Sciences, FL
Alabama State University, AL
Allen University, SC
American InterContinental University, GA
Angelo State University, TX
Arkansas Baptist College, AR
Baker College of Flint, MI
Bellevue University, NE
Benedict College, SC
Bethany College, KS
Cambridge College, MA
Chadron State College, NE
City University of Seattle, WA
College of Staten Island / The City University of New York, NY
Concordia College - Alabama, AL
Dickinson State University, ND
Glenville State College, WV
Harris-Stowe State University, MO
Heritage University, WA
Holy Names University, CA
Humphreys College, CA
Jarvis Christian College, TX
Kaplan University, IA
Kendall College, IL
Lincoln University, MO
Marylhurst University, OR
Mayville State University, ND
Medgar Evers College / The City University of New York, NY
Miles College, AL
Missouri Western State University, MO
Montana State University-Northern, MT
Mount Washington College, NH
Mountain State University, WV
National American University, SD
New Mexico Highlands University, NM

New York City College of Technology / The City University of New York, NY
Northwest Nazarene University, ID
Northwestern Oklahoma State University, OK
Oakland City University, IN
Oglala Lakota College, SD
Oklahoma Panhandle State University, OK
Peirce College, PA
Pennsylvania College of Technology, PA
Peru State College, NE
Rocky Mountain College of Art and Design, CO
Saint Paul's College, VA
Shawnee State University, OH
Sinte Gleska University, SD
Southern Nazarene University, OK
Southern University at New Orleans, LA
St. Gregory's University, OK
Thomas University, GA
Tougaloo College, MS
University of Alaska Anchorage, AK
University of Arkansas at Monticello, AR
University of Nevada/Reno, NV
University of Pikeville, KY
University of Rio Grande, OH
University of Texas at El Paso, TX
Upper Iowa University, IA
Walla Walla University, WA
Washburn University, KS
Wayne State College, NE
Weber State University, UT
West Virginia State University, WV
West Virginia University Institute of Technology, WV
Wilmington University, DE
York College / City University of New York, NY

SPECIAL

Listed here are colleges whose programs of study are specialized; professional schools of art, music, nursing, and other disciplines. In general, the admissions requirements are not based primarily on academic criteria, but on evidence of talent or special interest in the field. Many other colleges and universities offer special-interest pro- grams *in addition* to regular academic curricula, but such institutions have been given a regular competitive rating based on academic cri- teria. Schools oriented toward working adults have also been assigned this rating. For detailed profiles of these colleges, please go to *barronspac.com*.

Albany College of Pharmacy and Health Sciences, NY
Allen College, IA
Art Academy of Cincinnati, OH
Art Center College of Design, CA
Art Institute of Atlanta, GA
Art Institute of Portland, OR
Benjamin Franklin Institute of Technology, MA
Berklee College of Music, MA
Boston Architectural College, MA
Boston Conservatory, MA
Burlington College, VT
Cabarrus College of Health Sciences, NC
California College of the Arts, CA
California Institute of the Arts, CA
Chamberlain College of Nursing, MO
Charter Oak State College, CT
Cincinnati College of Mortuary Science, OH
Cleveland Institute of Art, OH
Cleveland Institute of Music, OH
College for Creative Studies, MI
College of Art and Design at Lesley University, MA
College of Visual Arts - School is Closed, MN
Columbus College of Art and Design, OH
Corcoran College of Art and Design, DC
Cornish College of the Arts, WA
Curtis Institute of Music, PA
Eastman School of Music, NY
Excelsior College, NY
Fashion Institute of Technology/State University of New York, NY
Five Towns College, NY
Franklin University, OH
Franklin W. Olin College of Engineering, MA
Gallaudet University, DC
Granite State College, NH
Juilliard School, NY
Kansas City Art Institute, MO
Kendall College of Art and Design of Ferris State University, MI
Laguna College of Art and Design, CA
Maine College of Art, ME

Manhattan School of Music, NY
Martin University, IN
Maryland Institute College of Art, MD
Massachusetts College of Art and Design, MA
Massachusetts College of Pharmacy and Health Sciences, MA
Memphis College of Art, TN
Mercy College of Health Sciences, IA
Metropolitan State University, MN
Milwaukee Institute of Art and Design, WI
Minneapolis College of Art and Design, MN
Montserrat College of Art, MA
Moore College of Art and Design, PA
Naropa University, CO
National University, CA
Nebraska Methodist College of Nursing and Allied Health, NE
New England Conservatory of Music, MA
Otis College of Art and Design, CA
Pacific Northwest College of Art, OR
Parsons The New School for Design, NY
Pratt Institute, NY
Research College of Nursing, MO
Rhode Island School of Design, RI
Ringling College of Art and Design, FL
San Francisco Art Institute, CA
San Francisco Conservatory of Music, CA
Santa Fe University of Art and Design, NM
Savannah College of Art and Design, GA
School of the Art Institute of Chicago, IL
School of Visual Arts, NY
State University of New York/Empire State College, NY
Thomas Edison State College, NJ
Trinity College of Nursing & Health Sciences, IL
Union Institute & University, OH
University of Maryland/University College, MD
University of North Carolina School of the Arts, NC
University of the Arts, PA
VanderCook College of Music, IL
Vaughn College of Aeronautics and Technology, NY
Wentworth Institute of Technology, MA
Westminster Choir College, NJ

THE BASICS

Over 1600 U.S. colleges and universities, public and private college systems, and Canadian and other foreign universities are described in detail in the Profiles that follow, as well as our web site, BarronsPAC.com.

The Choice of Schools

Colleges and universities in this country may achieve recognition from a number of professional organizations, but we have based our choice of U.S. colleges on accreditation from the U.S. regional accrediting associations.

Accreditation amounts to a stamp of approval given to a college. The accreditation process evaluates institutions and programs to determine whether they meet established standards of educational quality. The regional associations listed below supervise an aspect of the accrediting procedure—the study of a detailed report submitted by the institution applying for accreditation, and then an inspection visit by members of the accrediting agency. The six agencies are associated with the Commission on Recognition of Postsecondary Accreditation (CORPA). They include:

Middle States Association of Colleges and Schools
New England Association of Schools and Colleges
North Central Association of Colleges and Schools
Northwest Commission on Colleges and Universities
Southern Association of Colleges and Schools
Western Association of Schools and Colleges

Getting accreditation for the first time can take a school several years. To acknowledge that schools have begun this process, the agencies accord them candidate status. Most candidates eventually are awarded full accreditation.

The U.S. schools included in this book are fully accredited or are candidates for that status. If the latter is the case, it is indicated below the address of the school. Because the U.S. regional accrediting bodies do not officially accredit Canadian colleges and universities, and because there is no equivalent accrediting system in Canada, we have chosen to include only the larger, English-language Canadian schools—those with total full-time undergraduate enrollment of more than 10,000. It should be understood that size in no way relates to quality; there are many excellent Canadian colleges and universities with fewer than 10,000 students.

Four-Year Colleges Only

This book presents Profiles for all accredited four-year colleges that grant bachelor's degrees and admit freshmen with no previous college experience. Most of these colleges also accept transfer students. Profiles of upper-division schools, which offer only the junior or senior year of undergraduate study, are not included, nor are junior or community colleges.

Consistent Entries

Each Profile of a U.S. college is organized in the same way; the only Profiles that vary are those of Canada, schools abroad, and religious schools. The following discussion applies to the U.S. college Profiles, but refers to the other Profiles as well.

Every Profile begins with a capsule and is followed by separate sections covering the campus environment, student life, programs of study, admissions, financial aid, information for international students, computers, graduates, and the admissions contact. These categories are always introduced in the same sequence, so you can find data and compare specific points easily. The following commentary will help you evaluate and interpret the information given for each college.

Data Collection

Barron's *Profiles of American Colleges* was first published in 1964. Since then, it has been revised every year online; comprehensive revisions are undertaken every two years for the print edition. Such frequent updating is necessary because so much information about colleges—particularly enrollment figures, costs, programs of study, and admissions standards—changes rapidly.

The facts in the capsule portion of each Profile in this edition were gathered in the fall of 2014 and apply to the 2014–2015 academic year. Figures on tuition and room-and-board costs generally change soon after the book is published. For the most up-to-date information on such items, you should always check with the colleges. Other information—such as the basic nature of the school, its campus, and the educational goals of its students—changes less rapidly. A few new programs of study might be added or new services made available, but the basic educational offerings generally will remain constant.

THE CAPSULE

The capsule of each Profile provides basic information about the college at a glance. An explanation of the standard capsule is shown in the accompanying box.

All toll-free phone numbers are presumed to be out-of-state or both in-state and out-of-state, unless noted.

A former name is given if the name has been changed recently. To use the map code to the right of the college name, turn to the appropriate college-locator map at the beginning of each chapter. Wherever "n/av" is used in the capsule, it means the information was not available. The abbreviation "n/app" means not applicable.

Full-time, Part-time, Graduate

Enrollment figures are the clearest indication of the size of a college, and show whether or not it is coeducational and what the

---

COMPLETE NAME OF SCHOOL
(Former Name, if any)
City, State, Zip Code

MAP CODE

Phone Numbers, Fax and E-mail

Full-time: Full-time undergraduate enrollment
Part-time: Part-time undergraduate enrollment
Graduate: Graduate enrollment
Year: Semesters, quarters, summer sessions
Application Deadline: Fall admission deadline
CEEB Code: 0101
Freshman Class: Number of students who applied, number accepted, number enrolled
SAT: Median Critical Reading, Median Math, Median Writing
(abbreviated CR/M/W)

Faculty: Number of full-time faculty; AAUP category
of school, salary-level symbol
Ph.D.s: Percentage of faculty holding Ph.D.
Student/Faculty: Full-time student/full-time faculty ratio
Tuition: Yearly tuition and fees (out-of-state if different)
Room & Board: Yearly room-and-board costs

ACT: Median composite ACT

ADMISSIONS SELECTOR RATING

male-female ratio is. Graduate enrollment is presented to give a better idea of the size of the entire student body; some schools have far more graduate students enrolled than undergraduates.

Year

Some of the more innovative college calendars include the 4-1-4, 3-2-3, 3-3-1, and 1-3-1-4-3 terms. College administrators sometimes utilize various intersessions or interims—special short terms—for projects, independent study, short courses, or travel programs. The early semester calendar, which allows students to finish spring semesters earlier than those of the traditional semester calendar, gives students a head start on finding summer jobs. A modified semester (4-1-4) system provides a January or winter term, approximately four weeks long, for special projects that usually earn the same credit as one semester-long course. The trimester calendar divides the year into three equal parts; students may attend college during all three but generally take a vacation during any one. The quarter calendar divides the year into four equal parts; students usually attend for three quarters each year. The capsule also indicates schools that offer a summer session.

Application Deadline

Indicated here is the deadline for applications for admission to the fall semester. If there are no specific deadlines, it will say "open." Application deadlines for admission to other semesters are, where available, given in the admissions section of the profile.

CEEB Code

This is a standardized identification number assigned to a college or university by the Educational Testing Service (ETS).

Faculty

The first number given refers to the number of full-time faculty members at the college or university.

The Roman numeral and symbol that follow represent the salary level of faculty at the entire institution as compared with faculty salaries nationally. This information is based on the salary report* published by the American Association of University Professors (AAUP). The Roman numeral refers to the AAUP category to which the particular college or university is assigned. (This allows for comparison of faculty salaries at the same types of schools.) Category I includes "institutions that offer the doctorate degree, and that conferred in the most recent three years an annual average of fifteen or more earned doctorates covering a minimum of three nonrelated disciplines." Category IIA includes "institutions awarding degrees above the baccalaureate, but not included in Category I." Category IIB includes "institutions awarding only the baccalaureate or equivalent degree." Category III includes "institutions with academic ranks, mostly two-year institutions." Category IV includes "institutions without academic ranks." (With the exception of a few liberal arts colleges, this category includes mostly two-year institutions.)

The symbol that follows the Roman numeral indicates into which percentile range the average salary of professors, associate professors, assistant professors, and instructors at the school falls, as compared with other schools in the same AAUP category. The symbols used in this book represent the following:

++$	95th percentile and above
+$	80th–94.9th percentile
av$	60th–79.9th percentile
–$	40th–59.9th percentile
––$	39.9th percentile and below

If the school is not a member of AAUP, nothing will appear.

---

*Source: Annual Report on the Economic Status of the Profession published in the March-April 2013 issue of *Academe: Bulletin of the AAUP*, American Association of University Professors, 1133 Nineteenth Street N.W., Suite 200, Washington, DC 20036

Ph.D.s

The figure here indicates the percentage of full-time faculty who have Ph.D.s or the highest terminal degree.

Student/Faculty

Student/faculty ratios may be deceptive because the faculties of many large universities include scholars and scientists who do little or no teaching. Nearly every college has some large lecture classes, usually in required or popular subjects, and many small classes in advanced or specialized fields. Here, the ratio reflects full-time students and full-time faculty, and some colleges utilize the services of a large part-time faculty. Additionally, some institutions factor in an FTE component in determining this ratio. We do not, and thus the Student/Faculty ratio that we report may differ somewhat from what the college reports. In general, a student/faculty ratio of 10 to 1 is very good.

If the faculty and student body are both mostly part-time, the entry will say "n/app."

Tuition

It is important to remember that tuition costs change continually and that in many cases, these changes are substantial. Particularly heavy increases have occurred recently and will continue to occur. On the other hand, some smaller colleges are being encouraged to lower tuitions, in order to make higher education more affordable. Students are therefore urged to contact individual colleges for the most current tuition figures.

The figure given here includes tuition and student fees for the school's standard academic year. If costs differ for state residents and out-of-state residents, the figure for nonresidents is given in parentheses. Where tuition costs are listed per credit hour (p/c), per course (p/course), or per unit (p/unit), student fees are not included. In some university systems, tuition is the same for all schools. However, student fees, and therefore the total tuition figure, may vary from school to school.

Room and Board

It is suggested that students check with individual schools for the most current room-and-board figures because, like tuition figures, they increase continually. The room-and-board figures given here represent the annual cost of a double room and all meals. The word "none" indicates that the college does not charge for room and board; "n/app" indicates that room and board are not provided.

Freshman Class

The numbers apply to the number of students who applied, were accepted, and enrolled in the 2014–2015 freshman class or in a recent class.

SAT, ACT

Whenever available, the median SAT scores—Critical Reading, Math, and Writing—and the median ACT composite score for the 2014–2015 freshman class are given. If the school has not reported median SAT or ACT scores, the capsule indicates whether the SAT or ACT is required. Note: Test scores are reported for mainstream students.

Admissions Selector Rating

The College Admissions Selector Rating indicates the degree of competitiveness of admission to the college.

THE GENERAL DESCRIPTION

The Introductory Paragraph

This paragraph indicates, in general, what types of programs the college offers, when it was founded, whether it is public or private, and its religious affiliation. Baccalaureate program accreditation and information on the size of the school's library collection are also provided.

In evaluating the size of the collection, keep in mind the difference between college and university libraries: A university's graduate and professional schools require many specialized books that would be of no value to an undergraduate. For a university, a ratio of one undergraduate to 500 books generally means an outstanding library, one to 200 an adequate library, one to 100 an inferior library. For a college, a ratio of one to 400 is outstanding, one to 300 superior, one to 200 adequate, one to 50 inferior.

These figures are somewhat arbitrary, because a large university with many professional schools or campuses requires more books than a smaller university. Furthermore, a recently founded college would be expected to have fewer books than an older school, since it has not inherited from the past what might be a great quantity of outdated and useless books. Most libraries can make up for deficiencies through interlibrary loans.

The ratio of students to the number of subscriptions to periodicals is less meaningful, and again, a university requires more periodicals than a college. But for a university, subscription to more than 15,000 periodicals is outstanding, and 6000 is generally more than adequate. For a college, 1500 subscriptions is exceptional, 700 very good, and 400 adequate. Subscription to fewer than 200 periodicals generally implies an inferior library with a very tight budget. Microform items are assuming greater importance within a library's holdings, and this information is included when available. Services of a Learning Resource Center and special facilities, such as a museum, radio or TV station, and Internet access are also described in this paragraph.

This paragraph also provides information on the campus: its size, the type of area in which it is located, and its proximity to a large city.

At most institutions, the existence of classrooms, administrative offices, and dining facilities may be taken for granted, and they generally are not mentioned in the entries unless they have been recently constructed or are considered exceptional.

Student Life

This section, with subdivisions that detail housing, campus activities, sports, facilities for disabled students, services offered to students, and campus safety concentrates on the everyday life of students.

The introductory paragraph, which includes various characteristics of the student body, gives an idea of the mix of attitudes and backgrounds. It includes, where available, percentages of students from out-of-state and from private or public high schools. It also indicates what percentage of the students belong to minority groups and what percentages are Protestant, Catholic, and Jewish. Finally, it tells the average age of all enrolled freshmen and of all undergraduates, and gives data on the freshman dropout rate and the percentage of freshmen who remain to graduate.

Male to Female Ratio. When available, the ratio of male to female students on the college campus is provided for the school.

Housing. Availability of on-campus housing is described here. If you plan to live on campus, note the type, quantity, and capacity of the dormitory accommodations. Some colleges provide dormitory rooms for freshmen, but require upperclass students to make their own arrangements to live in fraternity or sorority houses, off-campus apartments, or rented rooms in private houses. Some small colleges require all students who do not live with parents or other relatives to live on campus. And some colleges have no residence halls.

This paragraph tells whether special housing is available and whether campus housing is single-sex or coed. It gives the percentage of those who live on campus and those who remain on campus on weekends. Finally, it states if alcohol is not permitted on campus and whether students may keep cars on campus.

Faculty/Classrooms. The percentage of male and female faculty is mentioned here if provided by the college, along with the percentage of introductory courses taught by

graduate students (if any). The average class size in an introductory lecture, laboratory, and regular class offering may also be indicated.

Programs of Study

Listed here are the bachelor's degrees granted, strongest and most popular majors, and whether associate, master's, and doctoral degrees are awarded. Major areas of study have been included under broader general areas (shown in capital letters in the profiles) for quicker reference; however, the general areas do not necessarily correspond to the academic divisions of the college or university but are more career-oriented.

Activities

Campus organizations play a vital part in students' social lives. This subsection lists types of activities, including student government, special interest or academic clubs, fraternities and sororities, and cultural and popular campus events sponsored at the college.

Sports. Sports are important on campus, so we indicate the extent of the athletic program by giving the number of intercollegiate and intramural sports offered for men and for women. We have also included the athletic and recreation facilities and campus stadium seating capacity.

Graduates. This section gives the number of graduates in the 2013–2014 class, the most popular majors and percentage of graduates earning degrees in those fields, and the percentages of graduates in the 2014 class who enrolled in graduate school or found employment within 6 months of graduation.

Services

Services that may be available to students—free or for a fee—include counseling, tutoring, remedial instruction, and reader service for the blind.

Library/Resources. This section describes the number of publications and media in the library collection of the college. In addition, you will also find computerized library services available to students, as well as any special learning facilities.

Physically Challenged Students. The colleges' own estimates of how accessible their campuses are to the physically disabled are provided. This information should be considered along with the specific kinds of special facilities available. If a Profile does not include a subsection on the disabled, the college did not provide the information.

Special. Special programs are described here. Students at almost every college now have the opportunity to study abroad, either through their college or through other institutions. Internships with businesses, schools, hospitals, and public agencies permit students to gain work experience as they learn. The pass/fail grading option, now quite prevalent, allows students to take courses in unfamiliar areas without threatening their academic average. Many schools offer students the opportunity to earn a combined B.A.-B.S. degree, pursue a general studies (no major) degree, or design their own major. Frequently students may take advantage of a cooperative program offered by two or more universities. Such a program might be referred to, for instance, as a 3-2 engineering program; a student in this program would spend three years at one institution and two at another. The number of national honor societies represented on campus is included. Schools also may conduct honors programs for qualified students, either university-wide or in specific major fields, and these also are listed.

Visiting. Some colleges hold special orientation programs for prospective students to give them a better idea of what the school is like. Many also will provide guides for informal visits, often allowing students to spend a night in the residence halls. You should make arrangements with the college before visiting.

Campus Safety and Security. This section lists the safety and security measures that are in place on the campus. These vary among schools, but may include 24-hour foot and vehicle patrol, self-defense education, security escort services, shuttle buses, informal discussions, pamphlets/posters/films, emergency telephones, and lighted pathways/sidewalks.

Requirements

Wherever possible, information on specific required courses and distribution requirements is supplied, in addition to the number of credits or hours required for graduation. If the college requires students to maintain a certain grade point average (GPA) or pass comprehensive exams to graduate, that also is given.

This section also specifies the minimum high school class rank and GPA, if any, required by the college for freshman applicants. It indicates what standardized tests (if any) are required, specifically the SAT or ACT, or for Puerto Rican schools, the CEEB (the Spanish-language version of the SAT). Additional requirements are given such as whether an essay, interview, or audition is necessary, and if AP*/CLEP credit is given. If a college accepts applications on computer disk or on-line, those facts are so noted and described. Other factors used by the school in the admissions decision are also listed.

Procedures. This subsection indicates when you should take entrance exams, the application deadlines for various sessions, the application fee, and when students are notified of the admissions decision. Some schools note that their application deadlines are open; this can mean either that they will consider applications until a class is filled, or that applications are considered right up until registration for the term in which the student wishes to enroll. If a waiting list is an active part of the admissions procedure, the college may indicate the number of applicants placed on that list and the number of wait-listed applicants accepted.

Transfer Students. Nearly every college admits some transfer students. These students may have earned associate degrees at two-year colleges and want to continue their education at a four-year college or wish to attend a different school. One important thing to consider when transferring is how many credits earned at one school will be accepted at another, so entire semesters won't be spent making up lost work. Because most schools require students to spend a specified number of hours in residence to earn a degree, it is best not to wait too long to transfer if you decide to do so.

International Students. This section begins by telling how many of the school's students come from outside the United States. It tells which English proficiency exam, if any, applicants must take. Any necessary college entrance exams, including SAT Subject tests, are listed.

Admissions

The admissions section gives detailed information on standards so you can evaluate your chances for acceptance. Where the SAT or ACT scores of the 2013–2014 freshman class are broken down, you may compare your own scores. Because the role of standardized tests in the admissions process has been subject to criticism, more colleges are considering other factors such as recommendations from high school officials, leadership record, special talents, extracurricular activities, and advanced placement or honors courses completed. A few schools may consider education of parents, ability to pay for college, and relationship to alumni. Some give preference to state residents; others seek a geographically diverse student body.

If a college indicates that it follows an open admissions policy, it is noncompetitive and generally accepts all applicants who meet certain basic requirements, such as graduation from an accredited high school. If a college has rolling admissions, it decides on each application as soon as possible if the applicant's file is complete and does not specify a notification deadline. As a general rule, it is best to submit applications as early as possible.

Some colleges offer special admissions programs for nontraditional applicants. Early admissions programs allow students to begin college either during the summer before their freshman year or during what would have been their last year of high school; in the latter case, a high school diploma is not required. These programs are designed for students who are emotionally and educationally prepared for college at an earlier age than usual.

Deferred admissions plans permit students to spend a year at another activity, such as working or traveling, before beginning college. Students who take advantage of this option can relax during the year off, because they already have been accepted at a college and have a space reserved. During the year off from study, many students become clearer about their educational goals, and they perform better when they do begin study.

Early decision plans allow students to be notified by their first-choice school during the first term of the senior year. This plan may eliminate the anxiety of deciding whether or not to send a deposit to a second-choice college that offers admission before the first-choice college responds.

Admissions Contact. When provided, this is the name or title of the person to whom all correspondence regarding your application should be sent. In addition, internet addresses are included here.

Financial Aid

This paragraph in each Profile describes the availability of financial aid. It includes the percentage of freshmen and continuing students who receive aid, the average freshman award, and average and maximum amounts for various types of need-based and non-need-based financial aid. Aid application deadlines and required forms are also indicated.

---

* Advanced Placement and AP are registered trademarks owned by the College Entrance Examination Board. No endorsement of this product is implied or given.

PROFILES OF

AMERICAN

COLLEGES

A B C D E

1 Normal
• Florence Huntsville

59

2 65 Jacksonville
20

Birmingham
Talladega

Livingston

3 20 Tuscaloosa
Marion • Montevallo Auburn
85

Selma • Tuskegee
4 Montgomery •

65 Troy

5

Mobile 10

6
• College Location

0   20   40   60   80   100
Miles

ALABAMA

ALABAMA AGRICULTURAL AND MECHANICAL UNIVERSITY C-1

www.aamu.edu

Normal, AL 35762	(256) 372-5245
	(800) 553-0816
Fax: (256) 372-9747	Email: venita.king@aamu.edu
Full-time: 2015 men, 2015 women	Faculty: n/av
Part-time: 180 men, 205 women	Ph.D.s: 70%
Graduate: 385 men, 810 women	Student/Faculty: n/av
Year: semesters, summer session	Tuition: $4984 ($9178)
Room & Board: $5100	Freshman Class: n/av
SAT or ACT: required	CEEB CODE: 1003
Application Deadline: July 15	COMPETITIVE

Alabama Agricultural and Mechanical University, founded in 1875, is a public land-grant institution offering undergraduate and graduate studies in agriculture, home economics, arts and sciences, business, education, engineering, and technology. The figures in the above capsule and in this profile are approximate. There are 5 undergraduate schools and 1 graduate school. In addition to regional accreditation, A&M has baccalaureate program accreditation with ABET, ADA, AHEA, CSWE, FIDER, NCATE, and AAMU. The 2001-acre campus is in a suburban area 90 miles north of Birmingham and 95 miles south of Nashville. Including any residence halls, there are 55 buildings.

STUDENT LIFE: 70% of undergraduates are from Alabama. Others are from 42 states, 29 foreign countries, and Canada. 90% are from public schools. 90% are African American. 98% are Protestant. The average age of freshmen is 18; all undergraduates, 20. 30% do not continue beyond their first year; 60% remain to graduate. **Housing:** 3100 students can be accommodated in college housing, which includes single-sex dorms. On-campus housing is guaranteed for all 4 years. 60% of students live on campus; of those, 60% remain on campus on weekends. Alcohol is not permitted. All students may keep cars.

FACULTY/CLASSROOMS: 70% of faculty are male; 30% are female.

50% teach undergraduates, 30% do research, and 30% do both. No introductory courses are taught by graduate students. The average class size in an introductory lecture is 90; in a laboratory is 20; and in a regular course is 30.

PROGRAMS OF STUDY: A&M confers B.A., B.S., B.S.C.E., B.S.E.E., B.S.E.T., B.S.M.E. and B.S.W. degrees. Associate, Master's, and Doctoral degrees are also awarded. Bachelor's degrees are awarded in AGRICULTURE (agricultural business management, agricultural economics, agronomy, animal science, forestry and related sciences, horticulture, and soil science), BIOLOGICAL SCIENCE (biology/biological science, neurosciences, nutrition, and zoology), BUSINESS (accounting, banking and finance, business administration and management, management science, marketing/retailing/merchandising, and office supervision and management), COMMUNICATIONS AND THE ARTS (art, classics, dramatic arts, English, French, German, graphic design, jazz, journalism, linguistics, telecommunications, and theater design), COMPUTER AND PHYSICAL SCIENCE (chemistry, computer science, mathematics, and physics), EDUCATION (agricultural education, art education, early childhood education, elementary education, home economics education, industrial arts education, middle school education, music education, physical education, science education, secondary education, special education, and trade and industrial education), ENGINEERING AND ENVIRONMENTAL DESIGN (city/community/regional planning, civil engineering, civil engineering technology, drafting and design technology, electrical/electronics engineering, electrical/electronics engineering technology, environmental engineering, industrial engineering, industrial engineering technology, mechanical engineering, and mechanical engineering technology), HEALTH PROFESSIONS (medical laboratory technology, nursing, prepharmacy, preveterinary science, and speech pathology/audiology), SOCIAL SCIENCE (criminology, economics, family/consumer studies, food science, history, human development, humanities and social science, political science/government, psychology, social work, and sociology). Physics, food science, and teacher education are the strongest academically. Business administration, education, and computer science have the largest enrollments.

ACTIVITIES: 7% of men belong to 4 national fraternities; 9% of women belong to 4 national sororities. There are 109 groups on campus, including band, cheerleading, choir, chorus, computers, dance, debate, drama, drill team, ethnic, forensics, gay, honors, international, jazz band, marching band, newspaper, orchestra, pep band, political, professional, radio and TV, religious, social, student government, symphony, and yearbook. Popular campus events include Magic City Classic, Women's Week, and Men's Week. **Sports:** There are 7 intercollegiate sports for men and 7 for women, and 7 intramural sports for men and 7 for women. Facilities include a 7000-seat gym, an Olympic-size pool, track and playing fields, and a 21,000-seat stadium/health education complex.

SERVICES: Counseling and information services are available, as is tutoring in most subjects. There is a reader service for the blind. **Library/Resources:** The library contains 253,620 volumes, 48,300 microform items, and 3,010 audio/video tapes/CDs/DVDs, and subscribes to 2,070 periodicals including electronic. Computerized library services include interlibrary loans and database searching. Special learning facilities include an art gallery, radio/TV station, and state black archives. **Physically Challenged Students:** 85% of the campus is accessible. Facilities include wheelchair ramps, elevators, special parking, specially equipped restrooms, and lowered drinking fountains. **Special:** Co-op programs with Georgia Institute of Technology and Tuskegee University, cross-registration with the University of Alabama in Huntsville, Oakwood College, Calhoun Community College, and Athens State College, internships with various government agencies, dual majors, and work-study programs are available. There is a 3-2 engineering degree program with Georgia Institute of Technology. There are 5 national honor societies, a freshman honors program, and 5 departmental honors programs. **Visiting:** There are regularly scheduled orientations for prospective students, consisting of sessions in June, July, and November. There are guides for informal visits and visitors may stay overnight. To schedule a visit, contact the Director of Admissions. **Campus Safety**

and Security: Measures include 24-hour foot and vehicle patrol, self-defense education, and security escort services. There are lighted pathways/sidewalks.

REQUIREMENTS: The SAT or ACT is required, with a satisfactory score on the ACT. Applicants must have 4 years each of English, math, science, social studies, and history. An interview is recommended. The GED is accepted. AP and CLEP credits are accepted. Important factors in the admissions decision are advanced placement or honors courses, leadership record, and recommendations by school officials. All students are required to take at least 52 hours of general studies, including phys ed, music, and art, and to maintain a minimum GPA of 2.0. Students must complete a total of 120 to 126 credit hours, with 30 to 36 in the major. A comprehensive exam is required for some majors. **Procedure:** Freshmen are admitted to all sessions. There are early decision, early admissions, deferred admissions, and rolling admissions plans. Applications should be filed by July 15 for fall entry; December 1 for spring entry; and May 15 for summer entry. The fall 2014 application fee was $10. Applications are accepted on-line. **Transfer Students:** Transfer students must have a minimum GPA of 2.0 and have earned at least 12 semester credit hours. 30 of 128 credits required for the bachelor's degree must be completed at A&M. **International Students:** The school actively recruits these students. They must take the TOEFL.

ADMISSIONS: A. Boyle, Director of Admissions. E-Mail: *aboyle@asnaam.aamu.edu* Web: *www.aamu.edu*

FINANCIAL AID: In 2014-2015, 72% of all full-time freshmen and 68% of continuing full-time students received some form of financial aid. 75% of all full-time freshmen and 61% of continuing full-time students received need-based aid. The average freshman award was $12,018. Need-based scholarships or need-based grants averaged $11,937 ($14,450 maximum); need-based self-help aid (loans and jobs) averaged $2,884 ($2,884 maximum); and non-need-based athletic scholarships averaged $2,659 ($3,250 maximum). 50% of undergraduate students work part-time. Average annual earnings from campus work are $3,600. The average financial indebtedness of the 2014 graduate was $6,060. The CCS/Profile, or FAFSA, or FFS, or SFS and the college's own financial statement are required. Check with the school for current application deadlines.

ALABAMA STATE UNIVERSITY *(The complete profile is made available exclusively on our website, www.barronspac.com)*

AMRIDGE UNIVERSITY *(The complete profile is made available exclusively on our website, www.barronspac.com)*

AUBURN UNIVERSITY SYSTEM

The Auburn University System, established in 1856, is a land-grant system in Alabama. It is governed by a board of trustees, whose chief administrator is the president. The primary goal of the system is to provide outstanding, economical instruction to its undergraduate, graduate, and professional students. The main priorities are to expand and diversify overall research efforts, and to disseminate and apply knowledge through extension and public service programs. The total student enrollment is usually 24,864 with 1701 faculty members. Altogether there are 120 baccalaureate, 75 master's, and 42 doctoral programs offered in the Auburn University System. Profiles of the 4-year campuses are included in this section.

AUBURN UNIVERSITY   D-3
www.auburn.edu

Auburn, AL 36849	(334) 844-4080
Fax: (334) 844-4773	**Email:** admissions@auburn.edu
Full-time: 9420 men, 9433 women	**Faculty:** I, -$
Part-time: 1116 men, 660 women	**Ph.D.s:** 95%
Graduate: 2578 men, 2705 women	**Student/Faculty:** 18 to 1
Year: semesters, summer session	**Tuition:** $10,200 ($27,384)
Room & Board: $12,178	**Freshman Class:** 16958 applied, 14154 accepted, 4592 enrolled
SAT CR/M/W: 570/590/560 **ACT:** 27	**CEEB CODE:** 1005
Application Deadline: February 1	**VERY COMPETITIVE+**

Auburn University, founded in 1856, is a state-supported land grant institution offering undergraduate, first professional, and graduate degrees in agriculture, business, education, engineering, liberal arts, sciences and math, veterinary medicine, architecture/design and construction, forestry, human sciences, nursing, and pharmacy. There are 11 undergraduate schools and 1 graduate school. In addition to regional accreditation, Auburn has baccalaureate program accreditation with AACSB, ABET, ACCE, ACEJMC, ACPE, ADA, AHEA, ASLA, CSAB, CSWE, FIDER, NAAB, NASAD, NASM, NCATE, NLN, and SAF. The 1875-acre campus is in a small town 110 miles southwest of Atlanta, GA. Including any residence halls, there are 392 buildings.

STUDENT LIFE: 63% of undergraduates are from Alabama. Others are from 51 states, 85 foreign countries, and Canada. 86% are from public schools. 85% are White. The average age of freshmen is 18; all undergraduates, 20. 10% do not continue beyond their first year; 71% remain to graduate. **Housing:** 4702 students can be accommodated in college housing, which includes single-sex and coed dorms, on-campus apartments, and married student housing. In addition, there are honors houses, fraternity houses, learning communities. On-campus housing is available on a first-come and first-served basis. 78% of students commute. Alcohol is not permitted. All students may keep cars.

FACULTY/CLASSROOMS: 63% of faculty are male; 37% are female. Graduate students teach 17% of introductory courses.

PROGRAMS OF STUDY: Auburn confers B.A., B.S., B.A.E., B.Arch., B.B.E., B.C.E., B.Che.E., B.E.E., B.F.A., B.Int. Arch., B.Int.Design, B.I.S.E., B.M.E., B.Mus.Ed., B.M., B.W.E., B.Mtl.E., B.P.F.E., and B.SW.E. degrees. Master's and doctoral degrees are also awarded. Bachelor's degrees are awarded in AGRICULTURE (agricultural business management, agricultural communications, agricultural economics, agriculture, agronomy, animal science, equine science, fishing and fisheries, forest engineering, forestry production and processing, horticulture, poultry science, and soil science), BIOLOGICAL SCIENCE (biochemistry, biology/biological science, botany, cell biology, marine biology, microbiology, molecular biology, nutrition, wildlife biology, and zoology), BUSINESS (accounting, apparel and accessories marketing, banking and finance, business administration and management, business economics, fashion merchandising, hotel/motel and restaurant management, international business management, marketing/retailing/merchandising, personnel management, and transportation management), COMMUNICATIONS AND THE ARTS (apparel design, art, communications, design, dramatic arts, English, fine arts, French, German, graphic design, industrial design, journalism, languages, public relations, Spanish, and speech/debate/rhetoric), COMPUTER AND PHYSICAL SCIENCE (actuarial science, applied mathematics, chemistry, computer science, geology, mathematics, physics, and software engineering), EDUCATION (business education, early childhood education, education, education administration, elementary education, English education, foreign languages education, health education, home economics education, industrial arts education, mathematics education, middle school education, music education, physical education, science education, secondary education, social science education, special education, and vocational education), ENGINEERING AND ENVIRONMENTAL DESIGN (aeronautical engineering, agricultural engineering, architecture, aviation administration/management, chemical engineering, civil engineering, computer engineering, construction management, electrical/electronics engineering, environmental science, industrial engineering, interior design, landscape architecture/design, materials engineering, mechanical engineering, and textile engineering), HEALTH PROFESSIONS (biomedical science, health care administration, medical laboratory technology, nursing, predentistry, premedicine, preoptometry, preveterinary science, and speech pathology/audiology), SOCIAL SCIENCE (anthropology, criminology, economics, food science, geography, history, home furnishings and equipment management/production/services, human development, philosophy, physical fitness/movement, political science/government, psychology, public administration, social work, sociology, and textiles and clothing). Engineering, education, and architecture are the strongest academically. Engineering, business, and liberal arts are the largest.

ACTIVITIES: 21% of men belong to 35 national fraternities; 31% of

women belong to 21 national sororities. There are 399 groups on campus, including art, band, cheerleading, chess, choir, chorale, chorus, computers, dance, drama, drill team, environmental, ethnic, film, gay, honors, international, jazz band, literary magazine, marching band, musical theater, newspaper, opera, orchestra, pep band, photography, political, professional, radio and TV, religious, social, social service, student government, symphony, and yearbook. Popular campus events include A Day, Pep Rallies, and Tiger Nights. **Sports:** There are 8 intercollegiate sports for men and 11 for women, and 15 intramural sports for men and 15 for women. Facilities include an 87,451-seat stadium, 10,500-seat coliseum, baseball and softball stadiums, a women's athletics center, tennis center, aquatics center, soccer complex, track, intramural field houses, golf course, 2 equestrian arenas, student activities center with a volleyball arena, racquetball, tennis, basketball courts, fitness/weight room, and an aerobics/cardio theater. **Graduates:** From July 1, 2013 to June 30, 2014, 4485 bachelor's degrees were awarded. The most popular majors were business (19%), engineering (16%), and education (9%). 326 companies recruited on campus in 2013-2014. In an average class, 2% graduate in 3 years or less, 42% graduate in 4 years or less, 65% graduate in 5 years or less, and 71% graduate in 6 years or less. Of the 2013 graduating class, 41% were enrolled in graduate school within 6 months of graduation, and 81% were employed.

SERVICES: Counseling and information services are available, as is tutoring in most subjects. There is a reader service for the blind, and remedial writing. Auburn's Academic Support Services provides supplemental instruction and study partners through regularly scheduled peer-review sessions by students selected by the faculty. **Library/Resources:** The 3 libraries contain 4.4 million volumes, 2.7 million microform items, and 123,086 audio/video tapes/CDs/DVDs, and subscribe to 65,711 periodicals including electronic. Computerized library services include interlibrary loans, database searching, Internet access, and Wi-Fi capability. Special learning facilities include an art gallery, radio station, TV station, a nuclear science center, an arboretum, electron microscope laboratory, MRI research center and a museum of fine arts. **Physically Challenged Students:** All of the campus is accessible. Facilities include wheelchair ramps, elevators, special parking, specially equipped restrooms, special class scheduling, lowered drinking fountains, special housing. Elevators with Braille controls, wheelchair lifts and assistive technology lab. **Special:** Opportunities are available for co-op programs, internships, work-study, and dual majors on a program-by-program basis; students should contact their advisers for specific information. 3-2 engineering degrees are offered with numerous other liberal arts colleges or with Auburn's colleges of Agriculture, Liberal Arts, or Sciences and Mathematics. Other options available to students include study abroad in more than 47 countries, credit by exam, nondegree study, and pass/fail grading on select courses. There are 42 national honor societies, including Phi Beta Kappa, a freshman honors program, and 26 departmental honors programs. **Visiting:** There are regularly scheduled orientations for prospective students, including War Eagle Days, held in the fall and spring and offering students and their families an opportunity to meet with representatives from admissions, financial aid, housing, residence life, and various academic departments. There are guides for informal visits and visitors may sit in on classes. To schedule a visit, contact the Office of Admissions at admissions@auburn.edu. **Campus Safety and Security:** Measures include 24-hour foot and vehicle patrol, emergency notification system, self-defense education, and security escort services. There are shuttle buses, emergency telephones, lighted pathways/sidewalks, and controlled access to dorms/residences.

REQUIREMENTS: The SAT or ACT is required. Favorable consideration for admission will be given to accredited secondary school graduates whose college ability test scores and high school grades give promise of the greatest level of success in college courses. Secondary school students planning to apply for admission are required to complete 4 years of English, 3 years each of social studies and math, and 2 years of science. Applicants of a mature age who are not high school graduates may be considered for admission if their educational attainments are shown through testing to be equivalent to those of high school graduates. Tests include the USAFI General Education Development Test, the American College Test, or other tests recommended by the Admissions Committee. AP credits are accepted.

Auburn University's Core Curriculum sets a foundation for learning by requiring students to complete 41-2 credit hours in courses that provide a broad-based academic foundation and that ensure students receive grounding in the competencies articulated in our general education student learning outcomes. The Core Curriculum consists of an 8 hour sequence in science, 6 hour sequence in English composition, 3-4 hour course in mathematics, 12 hours of social science (including at least 3 hours in history), and 12 hours of humanities (including at least 3 hours of fine arts, and 3 hours of literature). Each student is also required to complete a 6 hour sequence in either literature or history. Students must also choose a major curriculum and complete its requirements and those of the college or school with at least a 2.0 GPA. The total number of credit hours required is at least 120; some majors require more. **Procedure:** Freshmen are admitted to all sessions. There are deferred admissions and rolling admissions plans. Applications should be filed by February 1 for fall entry; October 1 for spring entry; and February 1 for summer entry, along with a $50 fee. Notification is sent on a rolling basis. Applications are accepted on-line. **Transfer Students:** 1270 transfer students enrolled in 2013-2014. Transfer applicants must provide official transcripts from each college attended. A satisfactory citizenship record, a minimum 2.5 GPA on all college work, and eligibility to re-enter the institution last attended are required for transfer admission. All transfer students who have attempted 32 semester hours of college work must have earned a cumulative 2.5 GPA in at least 20 semester hours of standard academic courses, in addition to the overall 2.5 cumulative average. These 20 semester hours must include at least 1 course in English (college-level composition or literature) and 1 in natural science with a lab. 30 of 120 credits required for the bachelor's degree must be completed at Auburn. **International Students:** There are 314 international students enrolled. The school actively recruits these students. They must take the TOEFL with a minimum score of 550 on the paper-based TOEFL (PBT) or 79 on the Internet-based version (iBT). They must also take the SAT or ACT.

ADMISSIONS: 83% of the 2014-2015 applicants were accepted. The SAT scores for the 2014-2015 freshman class were: Critical Reading--13% below 500, 51% between 500 and 599, 28% between 600 and 699, and 8% between 700 and 800; Math--10% below 500, 45% between 500 and 599, 35% between 600 and 699, and 11% between 700 and 800; Writing--17% below 500, 50% between 500 and 599, 26% between 600 and 699, and 7% between 700 and 800. The ACT scores were 2% below 21, 18% between 21 and 23, 27% between 24 and 26, 15% between 27 and 28, and 37% above 28. 52% of the current freshmen were in the top fifth of their class; 80% were in the top two fifths. There were 70 National Merit finalists. **Admissions Contact:** Dr. Wayne Alderman, Dean of Enrollment Services. E-Mail: *admissions@auburn.edu* Web: *www.auburn.edu*

FINANCIAL AID: In 2014-2015, 78% of all full-time freshmen and 70% of continuing full-time students received some form of financial aid. 37% of all full-time freshmen and 38% of continuing full-time students received need-based aid. The average freshman award was $12,069. Need-based scholarships or need-based grants averaged $7,277; need-based self-help aid (loans and jobs) averaged $3,814; and non-need-based athletic scholarships averaged $35,023. 13% of undergraduate students work part-time. Average annual earnings from campus work are $4500. The average financial indebtedness of the 2014 graduate was $27,146. Auburn is a member of CSS. The FAFSA is required. The deadline for filing freshman financial aid applications for fall entry is March 1.

AUBURN UNIVERSITY AT MONTGOMERY *(The complete profile is made available exclusively on our website, www.barronspac.com)*

BIRMINGHAM-SOUTHERN COLLEGE C-2
www.bsc.edu

Birmingham, AL 35254	(205) 226-4696
	(800) 523-5793
Fax: (205) 523-3074	Email: admission@bsc.edu
Full-time: n/av	Faculty: IIB, av$
Part-time: n/av	Ph.D.s: 96%
Graduate: n/av	Student/Faculty: 13 to 1
Year: 4-1-4, summer session	Tuition: $31,888
Room & Board: $12,280	Freshman Class: 1638 applied, 931 accepted, 356 enrolled
SAT CR/M/W: 570/580/570 ACT: 26	CEEB CODE: 1064
Application Deadline: February 1	VERY COMPETITIVE+

Birmingham-Southern College, founded in 1856, is a private liberal arts college affiliated with the United Methodist Church. BSC offers 30 undergraduate majors, 23 minors, and 10 special programs. There is 1 undergraduate school and 1 graduate school. In addition to regional accreditation, BSC has baccalaureate program accreditation with NASM and NCATE. The 192-acre campus is in an urban area 3 miles west of downtown Birmingham. Including any residence halls, there are 45 buildings.

STUDENT LIFE: 75% of undergraduates are from Alabama. Others are from 33 states, and 16 foreign countries. 65% are from public schools. 83% are White. 54% are Protestant; 16% claim no religious affiliation; 13% Catholic. The average age of freshmen is 18; all undergraduates, 21. 19% do not continue beyond their first year; 71% remain to graduate. **Housing:** 1429 students can be accommodated in college housing, which includes single-sex dorms, on-campus apartments, and married student housing. In addition, there are fraternity houses, sorority houses, international, community service, and environmental areas in residence halls. On-campus housing is guaranteed for all 4 years. 84% of students live on campus; of those, 55% remain on campus on weekends. All students may keep cars.

FACULTY/CLASSROOMS: 57% of faculty are male; 43% are female. 92% teach undergraduates. No introductory courses are taught by graduate students. The average class size in an introductory lecture is 17 and in a laboratory is 20.

PROGRAMS OF STUDY: BSC confers B.A., B.F.A., B.Mus., B.Mus.Ed. and B.S. degrees. Bachelor's degrees are awarded in AGRICULTURE (environmental studies), BIOLOGICAL SCIENCE (biology/biological science), BUSINESS (accounting, business administration and management, and international business management), COMMUNICATIONS AND THE ARTS (art history and appreciation, dance, dramatic arts, English, French, German, music, musical theater, painting, photography, printmaking, sculpture, Spanish, and studio art), COMPUTER AND PHYSICAL SCIENCE (chemistry, computer science, mathematics, and physics), EDUCATION (art education, collaborative education, dance education, education services, music education, and secondary education), SOCIAL SCIENCE (Asian/Oriental studies, biopsychology, economics, history, interdisciplinary studies, international studies, Latin American studies, philosophy, political science/government, psychology, religion, and sociology). Biology, English, and psychology are the strongest academically. Business administration, accounting, and history have the largest enrollments.

ACTIVITIES: 43% of men belong to 6 national fraternities; 52% of women belong to 7 national sororities. There are 79 groups on campus, including art, cheerleading, choir, chorale, chorus, computers, dance, drama, environmental, ethnic, gay, honors, international, jazz band, literary magazine, marching band, musical theater, newspaper, opera, orchestra, pep band, political, professional, religious, social, social service, student government, symphony, and yearbook. Popular campus events include Honors Day, Halloween on the Hilltop and Entertainment Fest. **Sports:** There are 11 intercollegiate sports for men and 11 for women, and 19 intramural sports for men and 19 for women. Facilities include a football stadium, urban environmental park, a coliseum, baseball field, racquetball and tennis courts, 2 soccer fields, weight room, intramural athletic field, indoor pool, game room, indoor jogging track, 3 gyms, and an aerobics studio. **Graduates:** From July 1, 2013 to June 30, 2014, 239 bachelor's degrees were awarded. The most popular majors were business administration (18%), biology (11%), and English (9%). 200 companies recruited on campus in 2013-2014. In an average class, 1% graduate in 3 years or less, 58% graduate in 4 years or less, 68% graduate in 5 years or less, and 72% graduate in 6 years or less.

SERVICES: Counseling and information services are available, as is tutoring in some subjects, math, English, and computer science. Through the use of peer tutors and one-on-one assistance, the Academic Resource Center also promotes the Foundation's general education goal of collaborative learning and peer-teaching. **Library/Resources:** The library contains 263,024 volumes, 90,675 microform items, and 38,261 audio/video tapes/CDs/DVDs, and subscribes to 40,000 periodicals including electronic. Computerized library services include interlibrary loans, database searching, Internet access, and Wi-Fi capability. Special learning facilities include an art gallery, planetarium, an environmental center, and an outdoor educational center. **Physically Challenged Students:** 90% of the campus is accessible. Facilities include wheelchair ramps, elevators, special parking, specially equipped restrooms, special class scheduling, lowered drinking fountains, lowered telephones, and special housing. **Special:** There is cross-registration with the University of Alabama at Birmingham, Miles College, the University of Montevallo, and Samford University. Student-designed, dual, and interdisciplinary majors, internships, work-study programs, and study abroad are offered. There is a 3-2 nursing program with Vanderbilt University and a 3-2 environmental studies program wih Duke University. A 3-2 engineering degree is offered with the University of Alabama at Birmingham, Auburn University, Columbia University, and Washington University. There are 19 national honor societies, including Phi Beta Kappa, a freshman honors program, and 5 departmental honors programs. **Visiting:** There are regularly scheduled orientations for prospective students, including preview and scholarship days, and individual visits. There are guides for informal visits, visitors may sit in on classes, and stay overnight. To schedule a visit, contact Becky Baxter at bbaxter@bsc.edu. **Campus Safety and Security:** Measures include 24-hour foot and vehicle patrol, emergency notification system, self-defense education, and security escort services. There are shuttle buses, emergency telephones, and lighted pathways/sidewalks.

REQUIREMENTS: The SAT or ACT is required. The minimum SAT score should be 970 combined, and the minimum ACT score, 21. Applicants should have graduated from an accredited secondary school with 4 courses in English, 4 each in math, science, and social studies, and a recommended 2 in foreign language. The GED is also accepted. An essay is required and an interview is recommended. Fine arts majors are advised to submit a portfolio or arrange an interview with the fine arts department. BSC requires applicants to be in the upper 50% of their class. A GPA of 2.3 is required. AP and CLEP credits are accepted. Important factors in the admissions decision are advanced placement or honors courses, leadership record, and recommendations by school officials. All students must complete 32 regular units with courses in English composition and literature, lab sciences, math, fine arts, foreign language, social sciences, history, and philosophy or religion as well as 4 interim projects. A total of 128 credits with a GPA of at least 2.0 is required to graduate. **Procedure:** Freshmen are admitted fall, spring, and summer. Entrance exams should be taken in the spring of the junior year. There are early admissions and deferred admissions plans. Applications should be filed by February 1 for fall entry; December 15 for winter entry; January 15 for spring entry; and May 1 for summer entry, along with a $50 fee. Notification is sent on a rolling basis. Applications are accepted on-line. **Transfer Students:** 27 transfer students enrolled in 2013-2014. Transfer applicants must have a minimum GPA of 2.0 and leave their former school in good standing. An essay and a school recommendation are required. An interview is recommended. 72 of 144 credits required for the bachelor's degree must be completed at BSC. **International Students:** There are 36 international students enrolled. The school actively recruits these students. They must take the TOEFL with a minimum score of 500 on the paper-based TOEFL (PBT) or 61 on the Internet-based version (iBT). The SAT or ACT is required instead of the TOEFL for students whose primary language is English, with minimum English or verbal scores of 21 or 475. **ADMISSIONS:** 57% of the 2014-2015 applicants were accepted. The

SAT scores for the 2014-2015 freshman class were: Critical Reading--18% below 500, 44% between 500 and 599, 32% between 600 and 699, and 6% between 700 and 800; Math--12% below 500, 44% between 500 and 599, 32% between 600 and 699, and 11% between 700 and 800; Writing--16% below 500, 45% between 500 and 599, 28% between 600 and 699, and 12% between 700 and 800. The ACT scores were 4% below 21, 23% between 21 and 23, 27% between 24 and 26, 19% between 27 and 28, and 25% above 28. 40% of the current freshmen were in the top fifth of their class; 81% were in the top two fifths. There was 1 National Merit finalist. 5 freshmen graduated first in their class. **Admissions Contact:** Sheri S. Salmon, Assoc. VP for Enrollment Management. E-Mail: *admission@bsc.edu* Web: *www.bsc.edu*

FINANCIAL AID: In 2014-2015, 99% of all full-time freshmen and 99% of continuing full-time students received some form of financial aid. 51% of all full-time freshmen and 51% of continuing full-time students received need-based aid. The average freshman award was $26,844. Need-based scholarships or need-based grants averaged $6,290 ($16,000 maximum); need-based self-help aid (loans and jobs) averaged $2,549 ($6,500 maximum); and other non-need-based awards and non-need-based scholarships averaged $18,005 ($45,162 maximum). 28% of undergraduate students work part-time. Average annual earnings from campus work are $972. The average financial indebtedness of the 2014 graduate was $32,250. The FAFSA is required. The priority date for freshman financial aid applications for fall entry is March 1.

CONCORDIA COLLEGE - ALABAMA (*The complete profile is made available exclusively on our website, www.barronspac.com*)

FAULKNER UNIVERSITY (*The complete profile is made available exclusively on our website, www.barronspac.com*)

HUNTINGDON COLLEGE   C-4
www.huntingdon.edu

Montgomery, AL 36106	(334) 833-4497
	(800) 763-0313
Fax: (334) 833-4347	Email: admiss@huntingdon.edu
Full-time: 504 men, 408 women	Faculty: 41; IIB, --$
Part-time: 84 men, 164 women	Ph.D.s: 85%
Graduate: n/av	Student/Faculty: 22 to 1
Year: semesters, summer session	Tuition: $24,550
Room & Board: $8550	Freshman Class: 1437 applied, 839 accepted, 227 enrolled
SAT CR/M: 480/480 ACT: 22	CEEB CODE: 1303
Application Deadline:	COMPETITIVE

Huntingdon College, founded in 1854 and affiliated with the United Methodist Church, is a private institution offering a liberal arts curriculum that focuses on the development of critical thinking skills. Through its Huntingdon plan, the college provides hands-on experience through internships, service, and student-faculty research and exploration of the world through travel/study with faculty and fellow students, each student is also provided with a laptop computer. There is 1 undergraduate school. In addition to regional accreditation, Huntingdon has baccalaureate program accreditation with NASM. The 71-acre campus is in a suburban area 90 miles south of Birmingham. Including any residence halls, there are 23 buildings. **STUDENT LIFE:** 81% of undergraduates are from Alabama. Others are from 30 states, 8 foreign countries, and Canada. 78% are from public schools. 64% are White; 20% African American. 32% are Protestant; 24% claim no religious affiliation; 19% Nondenominational, Christian, Pentecostal, and Church of Christ. The average age of freshmen is 18; all undergraduates, 24. 29% do not continue beyond their first year; 45% remain to graduate. **Housing:** 594 students can be accommodated in college housing, which includes single-sex and coed dorms. In addition, there are fraternity houses, sorority houses, special housing for disabled students. On-campus housing is guaranteed for all 4 years. 62% of students live on campus; of those, 70% remain on campus on weekends. Alcohol is not permitted. All students may keep cars.

FACULTY/CLASSROOMS: 58% of faculty are male; 42% are female. All teach undergraduates. No introductory courses are taught by graduate students. The average class size in an introductory lecture is 23; in a laboratory is 15; and in a regular course is 14.

PROGRAMS OF STUDY: Huntingdon confers B.A., and B.S. (B.S. degrees can be earned in the evening studies program only) degrees. Bachelor's degrees are awarded in BIOLOGICAL SCIENCE (biochemistry, biology/adolescence education, biology/biological science, and cell biology), BUSINESS (accounting, business administration and management, and sports management), COMMUNICATIONS AND THE ARTS (art, communication rhetoric/communication, English, and music), COMPUTER AND PHYSICAL SCIENCE (chemistry, chemistry/adolescence education, digital arts/technology, and mathematics), EDUCATION (collaborative education, elementary education, English education, history education, mathematics education, music education, physical education, and sports studies), HEALTH PROFESSIONS (exercise science), SOCIAL SCIENCE (Christian studies, history, political science/government, psychology, and religion). Biology and chemistry are the strongest academically. Sport studies, biology, and business administration have the largest enrollments.

ACTIVITIES: 26% of men belong to 4 national fraternities; 42% of women belong to 3 national sororities. Groups on campus include art, band, cheerleading, choir, chorale, chorus, drama, environmental, ethnic, honors, international, literary magazine, marching band, newspaper, pep band, political, professional, religious, social, social service, student government, and yearbook. Popular campus events include Home Sweet Huntingdon, Stallworth Lecture Series, Clover-Jam, Scarlet and Gray Victory Days, Welcome Back Week, Homecoming, Countess of Huntingdon Ball. **Sports:** There are 8 intercollegiate sports for men and 7 for women, and 6 intramural sports for men and 6 for women. Facilities include a multipurpose student center with a refurbished gym for basketball and a fitness training facility with fixed and free weight machines; an athletic center with a gym used primarily for volleyball; sports medicine and athletic training facilities; a 3,000-seat football stadium; and state-of-the-art weight training and conditioning facilities. There are also outdoor tennis courts, softball, baseball, and soccer fields, an outdoor basketball court and a sand volleyball court. **Graduates:** From July 1, 2013 to June 30, 2014, 236 bachelor's degrees were awarded. The most popular majors were business administration/business management (46%), biology/cell biology (12%), and human performance/sport studies (10%). Of the 2013 graduating class, 30% were enrolled in graduate school within 6 months of graduation, and 62% were employed.

SERVICES: Counseling and information services are available, as is tutoring in some subjects, writing, mathematics, history, english, business, political science and religion. **Library/Resources:** The library contains 109,564 volumes, 61,448 microform items, 4,476 audio/video tapes/CDs/DVDs, and subscribes to 190 periodicals including electronic. Computerized library services include interlibrary loans, database searching, Internet access, and Wi-Fi capability. Special learning facilities include an art gallery, the Bowman Ecological Center, Sybil Smith Hall, the Dr. Laurie Jean Weil Center for Human Performance, and The Methodist Archives Center. **Physically Challenged Students:** 85% of the campus is accessible. Facilities include wheelchair ramps, elevators, special parking, specially equipped restrooms, special class scheduling, lowered drinking fountains, lowered telephones, special housing. **Special:** Huntingdon currently offers more than 20 majors, the opportunity for travel/study experiences offered as part of regular educational costs, hands-on learning experiences in every program of study, dual majors, internships, and preprofessional advising. Cross-registration is available with Auburn University Montgomery, Faulkner University, and the Marine Environmental Sciences Consortium in Dauphin Island, Alabama. Work-study options are also available to qualifying students. There are 15 national honor societies, a freshman honors program, and 12 departmental honors programs. **Visiting:** There are regularly scheduled orientations for prospective students, the Office of Admissions offers personal campus visits during the week (Monday-Friday) and select Saturdays. There are guides for informal visits, visitors may sit in on classes, and stay overnight. To schedule a visit, contact the Office of Admission at (334) 833-4497. **Campus Safety and Security:**

Measures include 24-hour foot and vehicle patrol, emergency notification system, self-defense education, and security escort services. There are emergency telephones, lighted pathways/sidewalks, controlled access to dorms/residences, weather alert broadcasts, and parking lot cameras in most lots.

REQUIREMENTS: The SAT or ACT is required. Prospective students must have received a high school diploma or its equivalency. AP, CLEP, IB and dual enrollment credits are considered for acceptance. Huntingdon's core curriculum includes 36 hours of required courses, including 9 hours of religion/history of the church, 6 hours of writing/communication, and 3 hours each of fine art appreciation, history, literature, mathematics, natural sciences, social science, and critical thinking. Students must maintain a minimum GPA of 2.0 over 120 credits for the bachelor's degree. Major requirements range from 30 to 60+ hours. **Procedure:** Freshmen are admitted fall, spring, and summer. Entrance exams should be taken in the spring of the junior year. There are deferred admissions and rolling admissions plans. Application deadlines are open. Applications are accepted online. **Transfer Students:** 62 transfer students enrolled in 2013-2014. Transfer students must have successfully completed 24 semester hours of non-remedial courses at a regionally accredited college or university and be in good standing at previously attended institutions; otherwise, students must meet the regular freshman admission requirements. Transfer admission to the Evening Studies Program should be referenced in the college catalog. 30 of 120 credits required for the bachelor's degree must be completed at Huntingdon. **International Students:** There are 11 international students enrolled. They must take the TOEFL with a minimum score of 500 on the paper-based TOEFL (PBT) or 45 on the Internet-based version (iBT). They must also take the SAT or ACT.

ADMISSIONS: 58% of the 2014-2015 applicants were accepted. The SAT scores for the 2014-2015 freshman class were: Critical Reading--55% below 500, 36% between 500 and 599, 6% between 600 and 699, and 3% between 700 and 800; Math--58% below 500, 27% between 500 and 599, and 15% between 600 and 699. The ACT scores were 33% below 21, 38% between 21 and 23, 17% between 24 and 26, 9% between 27 and 28, and 3% above 28. 28% of the current freshmen were in the top fifth of their class; 66% were in the top two fifths. 1 freshman graduated first in the class. **Admissions Contact:** Laura Duncan, VP for Enrollment Management. E-Mail: *admiss@huntingdon.edu* Web: *http://www.huntingdon.edu/future-students/*

FINANCIAL AID: In 2014-2015, 100% of all full-time freshmen and 100% of continuing full-time students received some form of financial aid. 68% of all full-time freshmen and 68% of continuing full-time students received need-based aid. The average freshman award was $18,215. Need-based scholarships or need-based grants averaged $15,159; need-based self-help aid (loans and jobs) averaged $3,769; and other non-need-based awards and non-need-based scholarships averaged $11,647. 25% of undergraduate students work part-time. Average annual earnings from campus work are $776. The average financial indebtedness of the 2014 graduate was $25,714. The FAFSA and the college's own financial statement are required. The priority date for freshman financial aid applications for fall entry is March 1. The deadline for filing freshman financial aid applications for fall entry is rolling.

JACKSONVILLE STATE UNIVERSITY (*The complete profile is made available exclusively on our website, www.barronspac.com*)

JUDSON COLLEGE   **B-3**
www.judson.edu

Marion, AL 36756	(334) 683-5110
	(800) 447-9472
Fax: (334) 683-5282	Email: admissions@judson.edu
Full-time: 1 men, 261 women	Faculty: 31
Part-time: 15 men, 70 women	Ph.D.s: 81%
Graduate: n/av	Student/Faculty: 9 to 1
Year: semesters, summer session	Tuition: $16,286
Room & Board: $10,508	Freshman Class: 268 applied, 198 accepted, 68 enrolled
SAT or ACT: required	CEEB CODE: 1349
Application Deadline: open	**COMPETITIVE**

Judson College, founded in 1838, is a private women's liberal arts college affiliated with the Alabama Baptist Convention. Men are accepted only in the Distance Learning division of the college. Figures in the above capsule and in this profile are approximate. There is one undergraduate school. In addition to regional accreditation, Judson has baccalaureate program accreditation with NASM. The 118-acre campus is in a small town 75 miles southwest of Birmingham. Including any residence halls, there are 18 buildings.

STUDENT LIFE: 82% of undergraduates are from Alabama. Others are from 19 states, and 4 foreign countries. 77% are from public schools. 75% are White; 14% African American. 90% are Protestant. The average age of freshmen is 18; all undergraduates, 25. 39% do not continue beyond their first year; 37% remain to graduate. **Housing:** 264 students can be accommodated in college housing, which includes single-sex dorms. On-campus housing is guaranteed for all 4 years. 57% of students live on campus; of those, 25% remain on campus on weekends. Alcohol is not permitted. All students may keep cars.

FACULTY/CLASSROOMS: 53% of faculty are male; 47% are female. All teach undergraduates. No introductory courses are taught by graduate students. The average class size in an introductory lecture is 23; in a laboratory is 12; and in a regular course is 7.

PROGRAMS OF STUDY: Judson confers B.A, B.Min., B.S. and B.S.W. degrees. Associate degrees are also awarded. Bachelor's degrees are awarded in AGRICULTURE (equine science), BIOLOGICAL SCIENCE (biology/biological science), BUSINESS (business administration and management), COMMUNICATIONS AND THE ARTS (applied music, art, English, and Spanish), COMPUTER AND PHYSICAL SCIENCE (chemistry and mathematics), EDUCATION (elementary education, English education, mathematics education, music education, science education, and social studies education), HEALTH PROFESSIONS (nursing), SOCIAL SCIENCE (criminal justice, history, interdisciplinary studies, psychology, religion, and social work). Biology, education, business, nursing, art, and English are the strongest academically. Biology, nursing, and psychology have the largest enrollments.

ACTIVITIES: There are no fraternities or sororities. There are 26 groups on campus, including art, band, choir, chorale, chorus, computers, departmental clubs, drama, environmental, honors, literary magazine, marching band, musical theater, newspaper, orchestra, photography, political, professional, religious, social, social service, student government, and yearbook. Popular campus events include Hockey Day, Junior-Sophomore Dance, Pageant, Christmas Tea and Vespers, and Rose Sunday. **Sports:** There are 6 intercollegiate sports for women, and 3 intramural sports for women. Facilities include an indoor swimming pool, equine center with class rooms, tack rooms, stalls, and a covered riding arena, tennis courts, wellness center, gym with an aerobics room and weight training facility, hockey field, softball field, soccer field, and a game room. **Graduates:** From July 1, 2013 to June 30, 2014, 58 bachelor's degrees were awarded. The most popular majors were nursing (34%), biology (12%), and English (9%). 10 companies recruited on campus in 2013-2014. In an average class, 3% graduate in 3 years or less, 10% graduate in 4 years or less, 68% graduate in 5 years or less, and 19% graduate in 6 years or less. Of the 2013 graduating class, 9% were enrolled in graduate school within 6 months of graduation, and 47% were employed.

SERVICES: Counseling and information services are available, as is tutoring in most subjects, Math, English, history, business and others on request There is remedial math and writing. **Library/Resources:** The library contains 59,096 volumes, 2,012 microform items, 1,359 audio/video tapes/CDs/DVDs, and subscribes to 32,679 periodicals including electronic. Computerized library services include interlibrary loans, database searching, Internet access, and Wi-Fi capability. **Physically Challenged Students:** 75% of the campus is accessible. Facilities include wheelchair ramps, elevators, special parking, specially equipped restrooms, lowered drinking fountains, lowered telephones, and special housing. **Special:** Cross-registration with the Marion Military Institute is available for ROTC students. B.A.-B.S. degrees are offered in criminal justice, math, business, biology, psychology, and chemistry. Students study abroad in such places as Salzburg, China, India, Oxford, Uganda, Australia, Latin America, and the Middle East. Dual majors, an equine science program, an accelerated degree program, an interdisciplinary major, work-study programs, and internships are offered. Students may combine their Associate Degree in Nursing with Biology for a B.S. degree. There are preprofessional programs in health areas, engineering, and law. The Distance Learning program offers credit for prior learning experience and provides individually paced instruction leading to a baccalaureate degree. There are 7 national honor societies, a freshman honors program, and 19 departmental honors programs. **Visiting:** There are regularly scheduled orientations for prospective students, consisting of 3 college Scholarship Days, 1 in September, 1 in November and 1 in February, and a Junior Day in May. Activities include scholarship testing, an equine show, campus tours, faculty meetings, and financial aid planning. There are guides for informal visits, visitors may sit in on classes, and stay overnight. To schedule a visit, contact the Admissions Office at (334) 683-511. **Campus Safety and Security:** Measures include 24-hour foot and vehicle patrol, emergency notification system, self-defense education, and security escort services. There are emergency telephones, lighted pathways/sidewalks, controlled access to dorms/residences, card access systems are on classroom and administrative buildings.

REQUIREMENTS: Judson College requires either the SAT or the ACT. Along with a minimum composite score of 18 on the ACT (SAT), applicants should have completed 17 high school credits, including 4 in English. Non-high school graduates must provide the GED equivalent. A GPA of 2.0 is required. AP and CLEP credits are accepted. All students are required to complete courses in English, history, multicultural studies, speech, religion, social science, math, science, humanities, computer literacy, health/phys ed, and women's studies. A total of 128 credit hours, with a minimum GPA of 2.0 (2.5 for education majors) is required to graduate. B.A. students must also complete at least 6 hours of foreign languages at the 200-level or above; B.S. students must complete at least 12 hours of math or science electives in addition to the core competency. A passing score is required on the English Language Usage Test and on the senior essay that meets the requirements of the Judson Quality Enhancement Plan. **Procedure:** Freshmen are admitted fall, winter, and summer. Entrance exams should be taken in the spring of the junior year. There are early admissions, deferred admissions, and rolling admissions plans. Application deadlines are open. The fall 2014 application fee was $35. Notification is sent on a rolling basis. Applications are accepted on-line. **Transfer Students:** 56 transfer students enrolled in 2013-2014. Transfer students must have a minimum GPA of 2.0 and be eligible to return to the school from which they transfer. 32 of 128 credits required for the bachelor's degree must be completed at Judson. **International Students:** There are 4 international students enrolled. The school actively recruits these students. They must take the TOEFL with a minimum score of 500 on the paper-based TOEFL (PBT) or 61 on the Internet-based version (iBT) and the college's own test.

ADMISSIONS: 74% of the 2014-2015 applicants were accepted. 42% of the current freshmen were in the top fifth of their class; 67% were in the top two fifths. **Admissions Contact:** Layne Calhoun, Executive Director of Enrollment Service. E-Mail: *admissions@judson.edu* Web: *www.judson.edu*

FINANCIAL AID: In 2014-2015, 100% of all full-time freshmen and 99% of continuing full-time students received some form of financial aid. 89% of all full-time freshmen and 87% of continuing full-time students received need-based aid. The average freshman award was $10,512. Need-based scholarships or need-based grants averaged $5,812 ($35,222 maximum); need-based self-help aid (loans and jobs) averaged $7,416 ($26,250 maximum); non-need-based athletic scholarships averaged $3,990 ($9,000 maximum); and other non-need-based awards and non-need-based scholarships averaged $8,037 ($35,222 maximum). 31% of undergraduate students work part-time. Average annual earnings from campus work are $899. The average financial indebtedness of the 2014 graduate was $24,374. The FAFSA is required. The priority date for freshman financial aid applications for fall entry is March 1. The deadline for filing freshman financial aid applications for fall entry is July 1.

MILES COLLEGE (*The complete profile is made available exclusively on our website, www.barronspac.com*)

OAKWOOD UNIVERSITY   C-1
www.oakwood.edu

Huntsville, AL 35896	(256) 726-7000
	(800) 824-5312
Fax: (256) 726-7154	Email: admission@oakwood.edu
Full-time: n/av	Faculty: n/av
Part-time: n/av	Ph.D.s: 54%
Graduate: n/av	Student/Faculty: n/av
Year: semesters, summer session	Tuition: $16,217
Room & Board: $9312	Freshman Class: n/av
SAT or ACT: recommended	CEEB CODE: 1586
Application Deadline: open	COMPETITIVE

Oakwood University, founded in 1896, is a private, historically black, Seventh-day Adventist institution offering undergraduate programs in business and education, humanities, natural sciences and math, religion and theology, and social sciences. The figures in the above capsule and in this profile are approximate. In addition to regional accreditation, Oakwood has baccalaureate program accreditation with ACBSP, ADA, CSWE, and NCATE. The 1186-acre campus is in a suburban area 5 miles northwest of Huntsville. Including any residence halls, there are 30 buildings.

STUDENT LIFE: 79% of undergraduates are from out of state, mostly the South. Students are from 39 states, 22 foreign countries, and Canada. 52% are from public schools. 79% are African American; 12% Foreign. The average age of freshmen is 19; all undergraduates, 23. 27% do not continue beyond their first year. **Housing:** 1173 students can be accommodated in college housing, which includes single-sex dorms and married student housing. On-campus housing is available on a first-come and first-served basis. Priority is given to out-of-town students. 71% of students live on campus; of those, 98% remain on campus on weekends. Alcohol is not permitted. Upperclassmen may keep cars.

FACULTY/CLASSROOMS: 51% of faculty are male; 49% are female. All teach undergraduates. No introductory courses are taught by graduate students. The average class size in an introductory lecture is 30; in a laboratory is 30; and in a regular course is 40.

PROGRAMS OF STUDY: Oakwood confers B.A., B.S., B.B.A., B.M. and B.S.W. degrees. Associate degrees are also awarded. Bachelor's degrees are awarded in BIOLOGICAL SCIENCE (biochemistry and biology/biological science), BUSINESS (accounting and business administration and management), COMMUNICATIONS AND THE ARTS (communications, English, foreign language, French, music, music business management, music performance, and Spanish), COMPUTER AND PHYSICAL SCIENCE (chemistry, chemistry education, computer mathematics, computer science, information sciences and systems, mathematics, and natural sciences), EDUCATION (business education, education, elementary education, English education, health and physical education, home economics education, mathematics education, music education, physical education, science education, and social science education), HEALTH PROFESSIONS (allied health, medical technology, and nursing), SOCIAL SCIENCE (dietetics, family/consumer studies, history, home economics, human development, international studies, ministries, physical fitness/movement, political science/government, psychology, religion, religious education, and social work). Biochemistry, chemistry, and nursing are the strongest academically. Business and biology have the largest enrollments.

ACTIVITIES: There are 20 groups on campus, including band, choir, chorale, drama, honors, international, newspaper, professional, radio and TV, religious, student government, and yearbook. Popular campus events include Convocations, Arts and Lecture Series and Centennial. **Sports:** There are 4 intramural sports for men and 3 for women. Facilities include a gym, skating rink, an Olympic-size pool, tennis courts, playing fields, racquetball courts, and a weight room.

SERVICES: Counseling and information services are available, as is tutoring in most subjects. There is remedial math, reading, and writing. Testing, counseling, and developmental guidance services are available through the counseling center. **Library/Resources:** The library contains 125,373 volumes, 2,140 microform items, 4,816 audio/video tapes/CDs/DVDs, and subscribes to 630 periodicals including electronic. Computerized library services include database searching. Special learning facilities include a radio station, a black history museum. **Physically Challenged Students:** 80% of the campus is accessible. Facilities include wheelchair ramps, elevators, special parking, and specially equipped restrooms. **Special:** Students may cross-register with Alabama A&M, Athens State, or the University of Alabama at Huntsville. The college offers a student missionary abroad program as well as a study abroad program through the Adventist College Consortium. Internships, work-study, dual majors, independent study, life experience credit, and pass/fail options are also available. A second bachelor's degree is offered to students completing at least 160 semester credits. There is 1 national honor society and 2 departmental honors programs. **Visiting:** There are guides for informal visits, visitors may sit in on classes, and stay overnight. To schedule a visit, contact the Enrollment Management. **Campus Safety and Security:** Measures include 24-hour foot and vehicle patrol and security escort services. There are lighted pathways/sidewalks.

REQUIREMENTS: The SAT or ACT is recommended. Applicants should be high school graduates with a minimum GPA of 2.0 and at least 11 academic units, distributed as follows: 4 in English, 2 each in math, science, and social studies, and 1 in typing. The GED is accepted. Two character references are required. Students with GPAs between 1.7 and 2.0 may be admitted on probation. Applicants admitted without test scores must take the ACT during freshman orientation. A GPA of 2.0 is required. AP and CLEP credits are accepted. Important factors in the admissions decision are recommendations by school officials, ability to finance college education, and leadership record. To graduate, students must complete 128 semester hours, including 30 in the major and 40 in upper-division courses, with a GPA of 2.0. Regular chapel attendance is required. All students must complete a liberal arts core, and must meet English oral and written proficiency requirements. **Procedure:** Freshmen are admitted to all sessions. Entrance exams should be taken before high school graduation. There are early decision and rolling admissions plans. Application deadlines are open. Application fee is $20. **Transfer Students:** Applicants must submit a college transcript and a statement of honorable dismissal. Grades of C minus or better transfer for credit. 32 of 128 credits required for the bachelor's degree must be completed at Oakwood. **International Students:** They must take the TOEFL and the college's own test. They must also take the SAT or ACT. Students may take the ACT on campus prior to registration.

ADMISSIONS: Fred Pullins, Enrollment Management Director. E-Mail: *admission@oakwood.edu* Web: *www.oakwood.edu*

FINANCIAL AID: In 2014-2015, 60% of all full-time freshmen and continuing full-time students received some form of financial aid. 60% of all full-time freshmen and continuing full-time students received need-based aid. Oakwood is a member of CSS. The FAFSA and the college's own financial statement, and student and parent federal income tax returns are required. Check with the school for current application deadlines.

SAMFORD UNIVERSITY   C-2
www.samford.edu

Birmingham, AL 35229   (205) 726-2871
                                              (800) 888-7218
Fax: (205) 726-2171   Email: admission@samford.edu
Full-time: 1026 men, 1889 women   Faculty: 200; IIA, av$
Part-time: 44 men, 92 women   Ph.D.s: 87%
Graduate: 781 men, 1101 women   Student/Faculty: 15 to 1
Year: 4-1-4, summer session   Tuition: $27,324
Room & Board: $9736   Freshman Class: 4704
                                     applied, 2725 accepted,
                                     728 enrolled
SAT CR/M/W: 560/560/550 ACT: 25   CEEB CODE: 1302
Application Deadline: July 1   COMPETITIVE+

Samford University is Alabama's top-ranked private university. Samford was founded in 1841. The university is organized in 10 academic units: arts, arts and sciences, business, divinity, education, health professions, law, nursing, pharmacy and public health. Samford offers 32 undergraduate and graduate degree programs, with 155 undergradu-

ate majors, minors and concentrations. The figures in the above capsule and in this profile are approximate. In addition to regional accreditation, Samford has baccalaureate program accreditation with AACSB, ACPE, ADA, NASM, and NCATE. The 318-acre campus is in a suburban area 4 miles south of Birmingham. Including any residence halls, there are 105 buildings.

STUDENT LIFE: 65% of undergraduates are from out of state, mostly the South. Students are from 39 states, 17 foreign countries, and Canada. 48% are from public schools. 82% are White. 36% claim no religious affiliation; 18% Protestant. The average age of freshmen is 18; all undergraduates, 21. 12% do not continue beyond their first year; 66% remain to graduate. **Housing:** 2301 students can be accommodated in college housing, which includes single-sex dorms and on-campus apartments. In addition, there are fraternity houses, sorority houses, and special housing accommodations for disabled and international students. On-campus housing is guaranteed for the freshman year only, and is available on a first-come, first-served basis. 71% of students live on campus. Alcohol is not permitted. All students may keep cars.

FACULTY/CLASSROOMS: 50% of faculty are male; 50% are female. 61% teach undergraduates. No introductory courses are taught by graduate students. The average class size in an introductory lecture is 21 and in a laboratory is 12.

PROGRAMS OF STUDY: Samford confers B.S.B.A., B.S.E., B.S.N., B.A., B.F.A., B.M., B.M.E. and B.S degrees. Master's and doctoral degrees are also awarded. Bachelor's degrees are awarded in BIOLOGICAL SCIENCE (biochemistry, biology/biological science, marine science, and nutrition), BUSINESS (accounting, entrepreneurial studies, finance, management science, marketing management, organizational leadership and management, and sports management), COMMUNICATIONS AND THE ARTS (art, church music, classics, communications, English, French, German, graphic design, Greek, journalism, languages, Latin, music, music performance, music theory and composition, musical theater, piano/organ, piano pedagogy, piano performance, Spanish, theatre arts, and voice), COMPUTER AND PHYSICAL SCIENCE (chemistry, computer science, mathematics, physics, and science), EDUCATION (athletic training, early childhood education, elementary education, English education, and secondary education), ENGINEERING AND ENVIRONMENTAL DESIGN (engineering physics, environmental science, and interior design), HEALTH PROFESSIONS (exercise science, health promotion, health science, nursing, pharmacy, and sports medicine), SOCIAL SCIENCE (criminal justice, dietetics, early childhood studies, economics, geography, (Social Science) Global Studies, history, human development, international relations, Latin American studies, liberal arts/general studies, paralegal studies, philosophy, political science/government, psychology, public administration, religion, religious music, and sociology). Business, nursing, pharmacy, liberal arts, and education are the strongest academically. Business, nursing, journalism, and mass communications have the largest enrollments.

ACTIVITIES: 36% of men belong to 6 national fraternities; 49% of women belong to 8 national sororities. There are 101 groups on campus, including academic organizations/clubs and university sponsored organizations/clubs, art, band, cheerleading, choir, chorale, chorus, computers, dance, debate, drama, environmental, ethnic, film, honors, international, jazz band, literary magazine, marching band, musical theater, newspaper, opera, orchestra, pep band, photography, political, professional, radio and TV, religious, social, social service, student government, symphony, and yearbook. Popular campus events include Homecoming, Family Weekend, Hanging of the Green, Lighting of the Way, Step Sing, NCAA Division I Athletics, Samford Gives Back, Spring Fling, Greek Week, Harry's Coffeehouse Series, Leadership Lunches, and Intramurals. **Sports:** There are 8 intercollegiate sports for men and 9 for women, and 22 intramural sports for men and 22 for women. Facilities include a 6700-seat football stadium, a 4000-seat basketball gym, tennis complex and a state-of-the-art student fitness/wellness center, track and soccer stadium, sand volleyball, outdoor basketball, and 2 grass fields. Also available is a 50-foot-high climbing wall offering more than 35 different climbing routes with varying degrees of challenge involved. **Graduates:** From July 1, 2013 to June 30, 2014, 650 bachelor's degrees were awarded. The most popular majors were business and marketing (19%), health professions and related sciences (17%), and visual and performing arts (9%). 180 companies recruited on campus in 2013-2014. In an average class, 48% graduate in 4 years or less, 62% graduate in 5 years or less, and 66% graduate in 6 years or less.

SERVICES: Counseling and information services are available, as is tutoring in most subjects. There is a reader service for the blind. **Library/Resources:** The 6 libraries contain 1.1 million volumes, 1.4 million microform items, and 51,132 audio/video tapes/CDs/DVDs, and subscribe to 46,629 periodicals including electronic. Computerized library services include interlibrary loans, database searching, Internet access, and Wi-Fi capability. Special learning facilities include an art gallery, planetarium, radio station, a global center, drug information center, a nursing school state-of-the-art human simulation center, business school investment trading room and conservatory. **Physically Challenged Students:** All of the campus is accessible. Facilities include wheelchair ramps, elevators, special parking, specially equipped restrooms, special class scheduling, lowered drinking fountains, lowered telephones. **Special:** The Department of Physics offers a dual-degree engineering program jointly with the following universities: University of Alabama at Birmingham, Auburn University, and Mercer University (Georgia). The five-year program leads to two degrees: a bachelor of science degree from Samford with a major in engineering physics, and a bachelor of engineering degree from the participating university. Students in this five-year program will first pursue a three-year general curriculum at Samford, followed by a two-year general technical curriculum at one of the participating engineering schools. Samford University cooperates with the University of Alabama at Birmingham (UAB), Miles College, University of Montevallo, and Birmingham-Southern College in a student exchange program known as the Birmingham Area Consortium for Higher Education (BACHE). The program is designed to expand the undergraduate educational opportunities for students at these institutions. As part of its commitment to internationalization of the curriculum, Samford University provides a special opportunity for students and faculty to live and study in one of the most cosmopolitan and culturally rich cities of the world—London. Daniel House, Samford's London Study Centre, serves as home and classroom to students and faculty throughout the year in a variety of academic programs. Samford offers opportunities to travel and study in foreign countries for credit. The purpose of these programs is to prepare Samford students for global citizenship in the 21st century. More specifically, Samford seeks to expose students and faculty to the peoples and cultures of other nations; to provide on-site observation of historical, scientific, and cultural phenomena; and to provide opportunities for foreign language study within the cultural context of the target languages. There are 23 national honor societies, a freshman honors program, and 21 departmental honors programs. **Visiting:** There are regularly scheduled orientations for prospective students, campus tours offered 6 days a week. Tours last 90-minutes followed by a 30-minute information session. Special arrangements can be made for overnight stay, class visitation, and/or meeting with admission and financial aid counselors. There are guides for informal visits, visitors may sit in on classes, and stay overnight. To schedule a visit, contact The Office of Admission. **Campus Safety and Security:** Measures include 24-hour foot and vehicle patrol, emergency notification system, self-defense education, and security escort services. There are emergency telephones, lighted pathways/sidewalks, and controlled access to dorms/residences.

REQUIREMENTS: The SAT or ACT is required. Samford University seeks to enroll students capable of success in a challenging academic environment. Every applicant is evaluated individually on the basis of academic preparedness and potential, as well as personal fit with the mission and purpose of the university. The Admission Committee considers factors such as the rigor of the high school curriculum, grade point average, standardized test scores, and recommendations. AP and CLEP credits are accepted. The academic requirements for all students are to earn a minimum of 128 successfully completed credits, at least 50% of the credit for the first undergraduate degree from Samford. All undergraduates are required to take the University Core Curriculum at Samford (22 credits). **Procedure:** Freshmen are admitted fall, winter, spring, and summer. Entrance exams should be taken in the junior year. There are deferred admissions and rolling admissions plans. Applications should be filed by July 1 for fall entry, along with a $40 fee. Notifications are sent November 1. 178 applicants were on the 2014 waiting list; 113 were admitted. Applications are accepted on-line. **Transfer Students:** 187 transfer students enrolled in 2013-2014. Transfer students generally receive favorable admission review when they present a minimum cumulative 2.50 grade point average on all college-level coursework, provided they have attempted at least 24 credits, or 36 quarter credits, at institutions accredited by one of the regional accrediting agencies. If a student has attempted less than 24 credits of college-level coursework, an official high school transcript and official test scores must also be submitted in order to be considered for admission. 64 of 128 credits required for the bachelor's degree must be completed at Samford. **International Students:** There are 97 international students enrolled. The school actively recruits these students. They must take the TOEFL with a minimum score of 575 on the paper-based TOEFL (PBT) or 90 on the Internet-based version (iBT). TOEFL requirement may be waived if submitting the SAT or ACT.

ADMISSIONS: 58% of the 2014-2015 applicants were accepted. The SAT scores for the 2014-2015 freshman class were: Critical Reading--18% below 500, 47% between 500 and 599, 29% between 600 and 699, and 6% between 700 and 800; Math--21% below 500, 47% between 500 and 599, 26% between 600 and 699, and 6% between 700 and 800; Writing--23% below 500, 45% between 500 and 599, 27% between 600 and 699, and 5% between 700 and 800. The ACT scores were 9% below 21, 19% between 21 and 23, 32% between 24 and 26, 15% between 27 and 28, and 25% above 28. There was 1 National Merit finalist. **Admissions Contact:** Jason E. Black, Dean of Admission. E-Mail: *admission@samford.edu* Web: *www.samford.edu*

FINANCIAL AID: In 2014-2015, 98% of all full-time freshmen and 90% of continuing full-time students received some form of financial aid. 53% of all full-time freshmen and 44% of continuing full-time students received need-based aid. The average freshman award was $19,266. Need-based scholarships or need-based grants averaged $3,930 ($37,060 maximum); need-based self-help aid (loans and jobs) averaged $2,863 ($24,120 maximum); non-need-based athletic scholarships averaged $14,055 ($37,186 maximum); and other non-need-based awards and non-need-based scholarships averaged $4,889 ($39,300 maximum). 22% of undergraduate students work part-time. Average annual earnings from campus work are $2227. The average financial indebtedness of the 2014 graduate was $30,635. The FAFSA and the state aid form are required. The priority date for freshman financial aid applications for fall entry is March 1.

SPRING HILL COLLEGE A-5
www.shc.edu

Mobile, AL 36608	**(251) 380-3030**
	(800) 742-6704
Fax: (251) 460-2186	Email: admit@shc.edu
Full-time: 480 men, 735 women	**Faculty:** 81
Part-time: 26 men, 33 women	**Ph.D.s:** 95%
Graduate: 58 men, 80 women	**Student/Faculty:** 15 to 1
Year: semesters, summer session	**Tuition:** $32,468
Room & Board: $11,696	**Freshman Class:** 365 enrolled
SAT CR/M: 550/530 **ACT:** 24	**CEEB CODE:** 1733
Application Deadline: July 15	**VERY COMPETITIVE**

Spring Hill College, Founded in 1830, is the oldest Catholic college in the Southeast as well as the third oldest Jesuit college and fifth oldest Catholic college in the United States. Ranked among the top 20 Southern colleges and universities "America's Best Colleges," its mission is to form students to become responsible leaders in service to others. There are 8 undergraduate schools and 5 graduate schools. The 381-acre campus is in a suburban area in Mobile, Alabama. Including any residence halls, there are 33 buildings.

STUDENT LIFE: 61% of undergraduates are from out of state, mostly the South. Students are from 35 states, 18 foreign countries, and Canada. 67% are White; 15% African American. 51% are Catholic; 24% Protestant; 24% claim no religious affiliation. **Male To**

Female Ratio: 1.5:1. The average age of freshmen is 18; all undergraduates, 20. 27% do not continue beyond their first year; 58% remain to graduate. **Housing:** 1055 students can be accommodated in college housing, which includes coed dorms and on-campus apartments. In addition, there are special-interest houses. On-campus housing is guaranteed for all 4 years. 80% of students live on campus. All students may keep cars.

FACULTY/CLASSROOMS: 52% of faculty are male; 48% are female. 97% teach undergraduates. No introductory courses are taught by graduate students. The average class size in an introductory lecture is 23; in a laboratory is 13; and in a regular course is 17.

PROGRAMS OF STUDY: Spring Hill confers B.A., B.S. and B.S.N. degrees. Master's degrees are also awarded. Bachelor's degrees are awarded in BIOLOGICAL SCIENCE (biochemistry, biology/ biological science, and marine biology), BUSINESS (accounting, business administration and management, international business management, marketing management, and organizational leadership and management), COMMUNICATIONS AND THE ARTS (arts administration/management, communications, digital communications, English, English Writing, graphic design, journalism, public relations, studio art, and theatre arts), COMPUTER AND PHYSICAL SCIENCE (chemistry, computer science, and mathematics), EDUCATION (early childhood education, elementary education, and secondary education), ENGINEERING AND ENVIRONMENTAL DESIGN (engineering), HEALTH PROFESSIONS (nursing, predentistry, premedicine, and preveterinary science), SOCIAL SCIENCE (biopsychology, economics, history, humanities, international studies, liberal arts/general studies, philosophy, political science/ government, psychology, social science, sociology, Spanish studies, and theological studies). Business, biology, and psychology have the largest enrollments.

ACTIVITIES: 24% of men belong to 4 national fraternities; 31% of women belong to 6 national sororities. There are 46 groups on campus, including art, cheerleading, chorale, communications, computers, dance, drama, environmental, ethnic, film, gay, honors, international, literary magazine, newspaper, photography, political, professional, radio and TV, religious, social, social service, and student government. Popular campus events include Weeks of Welcome/Badger Expo, Christmas on the Hill, Free Art Fridays, Mardi Gras Week/Ball, Badger Brawl, Cajun Fest, McKinney Mixers, Family Weekend,Food for Thought Series, and RHA Best Dance Crew massages). **Sports:** There are 7 intercollegiate sports for men and 8 for women, and 12 intramural sports for men and 12 for women. Facilities include an 18-hole golf course, basketball courts, outdoor sand volleyball area, baseball, softball, rugby, and soccer fields. A recreation center houses the intercollegiate basketball arena, racquetball courts, weight-training and exercise facilities, an aerobic exercise room, and a running track. **Graduates:** From July 1, 2013 to June 30, 2014, 239 bachelor's degrees were awarded. The most popular majors were business (22%), psychology (15%), and public relations (7%). In an average class, 51% graduate in 4 years or less, 57% graduate in 5 years or less, and 58% graduate in 6 years or less.

SERVICES: Counseling and information services are available, as is tutoring in some subjects, English, theology, math, languages, philosophy, economics, biology, chemistry, psychology, history and accounting There is remedial math, reading, and writing. **Library/ Resources:** The 2 libraries contain 186,696 volumes, 314,677 microform items, 3,082 audio/video tapes/CDs/DVDs, and subscribe to 4,847 periodicals including electronic. Computerized library services include interlibrary loans, database searching, Internet access, and Wi-Fi capability. Special learning facilities include an art gallery, radio station, a theater. **Physically Challenged Students:** 90% of the campus is accessible. Facilities include wheelchair ramps, elevators, special parking, specially equipped restrooms, special class scheduling, and special housing. **Special:** SHC offers 3-2 engineering programs with the University of Alabama-Birmingham, Auburn University, the University of Florida, Marquette University, and Texas A & M University. The college is a member of the Marine Environmental Sciences Consortium and offers marine biology courses at the Dauphin Island Sea Lab. The college offers a study-abroad experience at its Italy Center in Bologna, Italy; other study abroad options are available through the CCSA (Cooperative Center for Study Abroad) consortium and the foreign study programs of other Ameri-

can Jesuit and non-Jesuit colleges and universities. Internships are available in many majors. There are 16 national honor societies and a freshman honors program. **Visiting:** There are regularly scheduled orientations for prospective students, campus tours, faculty appointments, attending classes, and interviews with admission counselors. There are guides for informal visits, visitors may sit in on classes, and stay overnight. To schedule a visit, contact the Office of Admissions. **Campus Safety and Security:** Measures include 24-hour foot and vehicle patrol, emergency notification system, self-defense education, and security escort services. There are emergency telephones, lighted pathways/sidewalks, and controlled access to dorms/residences.

REQUIREMENTS: The SAT or ACT is required. The ACT is preferred. Applicants should have completed at least 16 high school units, including 4 in English; 3 each in math, science, and social studies, 2 in foreign languages, and 1 academic elective. The GED equivalent is accepted. AP and CLEP credits are accepted. All students must take core curriculum courses in English composition and literature, history, philosophy, theology, math, science, social science, fine art, and foreign language. Students must also take: one cultural diversity course; at least 3 writing-enriched courses (including one in the major) beyond the required 4 core curriculum English courses; and one LEAP (Learning, Engagement and Awareness, Personal Growth) course. Graduation requirements include completion of a minimum of 128 semester hours with a minimum GPA of 2.0 and 30 to 36 upper-division semester hours in the major with a minimum grade of C/C- (see department policy) in each of the major courses and prerequisites. **Procedure:** Freshmen are admitted fall, spring, and summer. Entrance exams should be taken in spring of the junior year or fall of the senior year. There are deferred admissions and rolling admissions plans. Applications should be filed by July 15 for fall entry; December 1 for spring entry, along with a $25 fee. Notification is sent on a rolling basis. Applications are accepted on-line. **Transfer Students:** 47 transfer students enrolled in 2013-2014. Transfer applicants must have at least 20 semester hours of college credit, a minimum college cumulative GPA of 2.5, good academic standing at the last college or university attended, and satisfactory recommendations. 32 of 128 credits required for the bachelor's degree must be completed at Spring Hill. **International Students:** There are 27 international students enrolled. The school actively recruits these students. They must take the TOEFL with a minimum score of 550 on the paper-based TOEFL (PBT) or 80 on the Internet-based version (iBT) or take the MELAB, or IELTS. Students whose first language is English must take the ACT or SAT.

ADMISSIONS: The SAT scores for the 2014-2015 freshman class were: Critical Reading--35% below 500, 39% between 500 and 599, 20% between 600 and 699, and 6% between 700 and 800; Math--27% below 500, 48% between 500 and 599, 25% between 600 and 699. The ACT scores were 14% below 21, 32% between 21 and 23, 26% between 24 and 26, 15% between 27 and 28, and 13% above 28. 49% of the current freshmen were in the top fifth of their class; 78% were in the top two fifths. 8 freshmen graduated first in their class. **Admissions Contact:** Robert Stewart, Vice Pres for Admissions & Financial Aid. E-Mail: *admit@shc.edu* Web: *www.shc.edu/admissions*

FINANCIAL AID: Spring Hill is a member of CSS. The FAFSA and the state aid form are required. The priority date for freshman financial aid applications for fall entry is March 1.

STILLMAN COLLEGE   B-3
www.stillman.edu

Tuscaloosa, AL 35403

(404) 679-4501
(800) 841-5722

Fax: (205) 366-8817

Email: admissions@stillman.edu

Full-time: 700 men, 800 women

Faculty: n/av

Part-time: 40 men, 40 women

Ph.D.s: 70%

Graduate: n/av

Student/Faculty: n/av

Year: semesters, summer session

Tuition: $13,526

Room & Board: $5944

Freshman Class: n/av

SAT or ACT: required

CEEB CODE: 1739

Application Deadline: n/av

COMPETITIVE

Stillman College, founded in 1876, is a small, private liberal arts institution affiliated with the Presbyterian Church. Figures in the above capsule and in this profile are approximate. There are no undergraduate schools. In addition to regional accreditation, Stillman has baccalaureate program accreditation with NASM, NCATE, NCAA, and SIAC. The 105-acre campus is in a small town 52 miles from Birmingham and 105 miles from Montgomery. Including any residence halls, there are 26 buildings.

STUDENT LIFE: 70% of undergraduates are from Alabama. Others are from 27 states, and 8 foreign countries. 95% are from public schools. 98% are African American. 99% are Protestant. **Female To Male Ratio:** 1.1:1. The average age of freshmen is 19. **Housing:** 750 students can be accommodated in college housing, which includes single-sex dorms and off-campus apartments. On-campus housing is available on a first-come and first-served basis. 50% of students commute. Alcohol is not permitted. All students may keep cars.

FACULTY/CLASSROOMS: 40% of faculty are male; 60% are female. All teach undergraduates. No introductory courses are taught by graduate students. The average class size in an introductory lecture is 40; in a laboratory is 40; and in a regular course is 35.

PROGRAMS OF STUDY: Stillman confers B.A., and B.S. degrees. Bachelor's degrees are awarded in BIOLOGICAL SCIENCE (biology/biological science), BUSINESS (business administration and management), COMMUNICATIONS AND THE ARTS (art, English, and music), COMPUTER AND PHYSICAL SCIENCE (computer science and mathematics), EDUCATION (elementary education and physical education), HEALTH PROFESSIONS (premedicine), SOCIAL SCIENCE (history, prelaw, and religion).

ACTIVITIES: 10% of men belong to 4 national fraternities; 20% of women belong to 4 national sororities. There are 19 groups on campus, including art, band, cheerleading, choir, chorus, dance, debate, drama, honors, international, jazz band, marching band, newspaper, pep band, radio and TV, religious, social, social service, student government, and yearbook. **Sports:** There are 6 intercollegiate sports for men and 6 for women. Facilities include a college center, tennis courts, stress center, bowling lanes, billiards, a swimming pool, a gym, a football field, and a weight room.

REQUIREMENTS: The SAT or ACT is required. Applicants should be high school graduates or have earned the GED. Secondary preparation should include 4 units of English and 1 unit each of math, science, and history. All applicants must have an interview. Music majors must audition. A GPA of 2.0 is required. AP and CLEP credits are accepted. To graduate, students must complete a minimum of 124 credit hours, with at least 30 in the major, and maintain a minimum GPA of 2.0 overall and in the major. The 53-credit-hour general education core includes courses in religion, logic, English composition, public speaking, African heritage, African American experience, history, social science, physical and life sciences, math, computer literacy, health, and phys ed. All students must submit a senior thesis and take a senior departmental exam. **Procedure:** Freshmen are admitted to all sessions. There is a rolling admissions plan. Check with the school for current application deadlines. The fall 2014 application fee was $25. **Transfer Students:** Transfer applicants should present at least a C average in previous college work and must plan to spend at least a year in residence. 64 of 124 credits required for the bachelor's degree must be completed at Stillman. **International Students:** The school actively recruits these students. They must take the TOEFL. They must also take the SAT or ACT.

ADMISSIONS: Lu Ann Baker, Director of Admissions. E-Mail: *admissions@stillman.edu* Web: *www.stillman.edu*

FINANCIAL AID: The CCS/Profile, FAFSA, FFS, or SFS and the college's own financial statement are required. Check with the school for current application deadlines.

TALLADEGA COLLEGE — C-2
www.talladega.edu

Talladega, AL 35160	(256) 761-6416
	(800) 633-2440
Fax: n/av	Email: admissions@talladega.edu
Full-time: 270 men, 420 women	Faculty: n/av
Part-time: 20 men, 30 women	Ph.D.s: 60%
Graduate: n/av	Student/Faculty: 12 to 1
Year: semesters	Tuition: $11,492
Room & Board: $6504	Freshman Class: n/av
SAT or ACT: required	CEEB CODE: 1800
Application Deadline: open	COMPETITIVE

Talladega College, founded in 1867, is a private liberal arts institution offering emphases on business, sciences, and social work. The figures in above capsule and in this profile are approximate. In addition to regional accreditation, Dega has baccalaureate program accreditation with CSWE. The 50-acre campus is in a small town 55 miles east of Birmingham and 115 miles west of Atlanta. Including any residence halls, there are 41 buildings.

STUDENT LIFE: 60% of undergraduates are from Alabama. Others are from 29 states and 2 foreign countries. 99% are African American. 90% are Protestant. **Male To Female Ratio:** 1.6:1. The average age of freshmen is 18; all undergraduates, 20. 22% do not continue beyond their first year; 45% remain to graduate. **Housing:** 580 students can be accommodated in college housing, which includes single-sex dorms and on-campus apartments. In addition, there are honors houses. On-campus housing is guaranteed for all 4 years. 70% of students live on campus; of those, 90% remain on campus on weekends. Alcohol is not permitted. All students may keep cars.

FACULTY/CLASSROOMS: 60% of faculty are male; 40% are female. All teach undergraduates, and 25% do both. No introductory courses are taught by graduate students. The average class size in an introductory lecture is 30; in a laboratory is 20; and in a regular course is 18.

PROGRAMS OF STUDY: Dega confers B.A. degrees. Bachelor's degrees are awarded in BIOLOGICAL SCIENCE (biology/biological science), BUSINESS (accounting, banking and finance, and business administration and management), COMMUNICATIONS AND THE ARTS (English and music performance), COMPUTER AND PHYSICAL SCIENCE (chemistry, computer science, mathematics, and physics), EDUCATION (music education), SOCIAL SCIENCE (economics, history, psychology, public administration, social work, and sociology). Business, biology, and chemistry are the strongest academically. Biology has the largest enrollment.

ACTIVITIES: 14% of men belong to 4 national fraternities; 40% of women belong to 4 national sororities. There are 23 groups on campus, including art, cheerleading, choir, chorus, computers, dance, drama, honors, jazz band, newspaper, professional, social, student government, and yearbook. Popular campus events include Spring Concert, Carnival and Coronation. **Sports:** There are 4 intercollegiate sports for men and 4 for women, and 8 intramural sports for men and 3 for women. Facilities include a swimming pool, a 150-seat gym, lounges, game rooms, tennis courts, and a baseball field.

SERVICES: Counseling and information services are available, as is tutoring in every subject. There is remedial math, reading, and writing. **Library/Resources:** The library contains 87,960 volumes, 350 audio/video tapes/CDs/DVDs, and subscribes to 330 periodicals including electronic. Computerized library services include interlibrary loans. Special learning facilities include an art gallery, science drop-in center, curriculum and writing labs, and financial computer lab. **Physically Challenged Students:** 50% of the campus is accessible. Facilities include wheelchair ramps, elevators, special parking, and specially equipped restrooms. **Special:** Talladega offers co-op programs with other schools through individual departments, a 3-2 engineering degree with Auburn University, internships involving historic preservation work, work-study plans with Adopt-a-Family and Adult Literacy, and B.A.-B.S. degrees in biology, business administration, chemistry, and computer science. There are dual majors available in law, nursing, engineering, and allied health. There are 4 national honor societies. **Visiting:** There are guides for informal visits, visitors may sit in on classes, and stay overnight. To schedule a visit, contact the Admissions Office. **Campus Safety and Security:** Measures include 24-hour foot and vehicle patrol and security escort services. There are lighted pathways/sidewalks.

REQUIREMENTS: The SAT or ACT is required. Applicants must be graduates of an accredited secondary school with 22 academic units, including 4 in English, 3 in social studies, and 2 each in math, science, health/phys ed, and electives. The GED is considered. An essay and interview are recommended. An audition is required for music majors. A GPA of 2.5 is required. CLEP credits are accepted. Important factors in the admissions decision are advanced placement or honors courses, recommendations by school officials, and recommendations by alumni. To graduate, students must maintain a minimum GPA of 2.5 while taking 124 to 127 total semester hours, including 60 in the major and completion of a core curriculum. Distribution requirements at the freshman level include 8 semester hours in natural sciences, 6 each in communications, social sciences, and humanities, 2 in phys ed, and 1 in freshman orientation; additional hours in these subjects vary by major at the sophomore level. **Procedure:** Freshmen are admitted fall and spring. Entrance exams should be taken in the junior year. There are deferred admissions and rolling admissions plans. Application deadlines are open. The fall 2014 application fee was $10. Applications are accepted on-line. **Transfer Students:** Applicants must have a cumulative GPA of 2.0 in college work. The SAT or ACT is recommended. 60 of 124 credits required for the bachelor's degree must be completed at Dega. **International Students:** The school actively recruits these students. They must take the TOEFL and the college's own test. They must also take the SAT or ACT.

ADMISSIONS: Monroe Thornton, Admissions Office. E-Mail: *admissions@talladega.edu* Web: *www.talladega.edu*

FINANCIAL AID: The FAFSA, CCS/Profile, FFS, or SFS and the college's own financial statement are required. Check with the school for current application deadlines.

TROY UNIVERSITY   C-4
www.troy.edu

Troy, AL 36082	**(334) 670-3179**
	(800) 551-9716
Fax: (334) 670-3733	**Email: bstar@troy.edu**
Full-time: 4050 men, 6300 women	**Faculty:** n/av
Part-time: 5550 men, 6000 women	**Ph.D.s:** n/av
Graduate: 2575 men, 5260 women	**Student/Faculty:** n/av
Year: semesters, summer session	**Tuition:** $4650 ($9550)
Room & Board: $6000	**Freshman Class:** n/av
SAT or ACT: required	**CEEB CODE:** 1738
Application Deadline: open	**COMPETITIVE**

Troy University, founded in 1887, is a public institution composed of a network of campuses throughout Alabama and worldwide. International in scope, Troy University provides a variety of educational programs at the undergraduate and graduate levels for a diverse student body. Academic programs are offered in traditional, nontraditional and emerging electronic formats. Information in this profile applies to the Troy, Phenix City, Dothan, and Montgomery campuses and University College sites. The figures in the above capsule and in this profile are approximate. There are 5 undergraduate schools and 5 graduate schools. In addition to regional accreditation, Troy has baccalaureate program accreditation with ACBSP, CSWE, NASM, NCATE, NLN, and CAAHEP. The 768-acre campus is in a rural area is 50 miles south of Montgomery. Including any residence halls, there are 111 buildings.

STUDENT LIFE: 48% are White; 40% African American. **Female To Male Ratio:** 1.4:1. **Housing:** 1525 students can be accommodated in college housing, which includes single-sex and coed dorms, on-campus apartments, off-campus apartments, and married student housing. In addition, there are honors houses, special-interest houses, fraternity houses, sorority houses, an international house, and substance-free housing. On-campus housing is guaranteed for all 4 years. 66% of students commute. Alcohol is not permitted. All students may keep cars.

FACULTY/CLASSROOMS: All teach undergraduates. No introductory courses are taught by graduate students.

PROGRAMS OF STUDY: Troy confers B.A., B.S., B.A.B.A., B.A.Ed., B.Applied Sc., F.F.A., B.M.Ed., B.S.B.A., B.S.Ed. and B.S.N. degrees. Associate and master's degrees are also awarded. Bachelor's degrees are awarded in BIOLOGICAL SCIENCE (biology/biological science and marine biology), BUSINESS (accounting, banking and finance, business administration and management, business economics, insurance, management science, marketing management, marketing/retailing/merchandising, personnel management, and sports management), COMMUNICATIONS AND THE ARTS (art, art history and appreciation, broadcasting, communications, design, dramatic arts, English, journalism, and studio art), COMPUTER AND PHYSICAL SCIENCE (chemistry, computer science, information sciences and systems, mathematics, and science), EDUCATION (art education, athletic training, collaborative education, early childhood education, elementary education, English education, health education, mathematics education, music education, physical education, science education, secondary education, social science education, and special education), ENGINEERING AND ENVIRONMENTAL DESIGN (environmental science and technological management), HEALTH PROFESSIONS (nursing and rehabilitation therapy), SOCIAL SCIENCE (criminal justice, history, human services, political science/government, psychology, social science, social work, and sociology). Business and education are the strongest academically. Business has the largest enrollment.

ACTIVITIES: 19% of men belong to 12 national fraternities; 18% of women belong to 9 national sororities. There are 147 groups on campus, including art, band, cheerleading, choir, chorale, chorus, computers, dance, debate, drama, drill team, ethnic, film, forensics, gay, honors, international, jazz band, literary magazine, marching band, musical theater, newspaper, opera, orchestra, pep band, photography, political, professional, radio and TV, religious, social, social service, student government, and symphony. Popular campus events include ISCO Festival, Spring Picnic, and Heritage Week. **Sports:** There are 7 intercollegiate sports for men and 9 for women, and 11 intramural sports for men and 11 for women. Facilities include a 150-seat auditorium, a 3,000-square-foot weight training center, the 2,250-seat Pace-Riddle baseball stadium, a 9-hole golf course, the 30,000-seat Movie Gallery Veteran's Stadium, and 2 football practice fields. Other nearby facilities include a softball and soccer/track complex. The 4,000-seat Trojan Arena is home to both basketball teams and the volleyball team. Also available for student use is the natatorium with an indoor swimming pool, the recreational gym with an outdoor swimming pool and fitness centers, and intramural fields.

SERVICES: Counseling and information services are available, as is tutoring in some subjects. There is a reader service for the blind, and remedial math, reading, and writing. Tutors may be provided for students upon request. **Library/Resources:** The 4 libraries contain 594,716 volumes, 2.1 million microform items, and 19,532 audio/video tapes/CDs/DVDs, and subscribe to 3,263 periodicals including electronic. Computerized library services include interlibrary loans, database searching, Internet access, and Wi-Fi capability. Special learning facilities include an art gallery, planetarium, radio station, TV station, an arboretum, the Davis theater, and the Rosa L. Parks Library, a museum and children's annex. **Physically Challenged Students:** 95% of the campus is accessible. Facilities include wheelchair ramps, elevators, special parking, specially equipped restrooms, special class scheduling, lowered drinking fountains, lowered telephones. **Special:** Cross-registration with the Marine Biological Consortium, internships in education, journalism, and nursing, study abroad in 5 countries, work-study programs at the university, and student-designed majors in public relations, advertising, and other fields are offered. Credit for life experience and nondegree study are also offered. There is a dual-degree program with Vyatka State University of Humanities in Kirov, Russia. There are 28 national honor societies, including Phi Beta Kappa, a freshman honors program, and 14 departmental honors programs. **Visiting:** There are regularly scheduled orientations for prospective students, including a campus tour, classroom visitation, academic consultation, and interviews. There are guides for informal visits and visitors may sit in on classes. To schedule a visit, contact the Office of Enrollment Services. **Campus Safety and Security:** Measures include 24-hour foot and vehicle patrol, self-defense education, and security escort services. There are lighted pathways/sidewalks, foot and vehicle patrols during class hours.

REQUIREMENTS: The SAT or ACT is required. Applicants must have earned at least 15 Carnegie units, with 11 in academic courses and 3 to 4 in English. An interview is recommended, along with a portfolio or audition for some programs. The GED is accepted. A GPA of 2.0 is required. AP and CLEP credits are accepted. Important factors in the admissions decision are ability to finance college education, evidence of special talent, and extracurricular activities record. All students must maintain a minimum GPA of 2.0 while taking 120 to 140 semester credit hours, 54 of which must be in their major field. Distribution requirements include 48 hours of general studies, covering such subjects as English, math, history, science, and fine arts. **Procedure:** Freshmen are admitted fall, spring, and summer. Entrance exams should be taken in the spring of junior year of high school. There is a rolling admissions plan. Application deadlines are open. Application fee is $30. Applications are accepted on-line. **Transfer Students:** Transfer applicants need 20 semester hours attempted at their previous institution, with a GPA of 2.0. **International Students:** The school actively recruits these students. They must take the TOEFL with a minimum score of 500 on the paper-based TOEFL (PBT) or 61 on the Internet-based version (iBT), or take the IELTS. They must also take the SAT, scoring 18.

ADMISSIONS: Buddy Starling, Dean of Enrollment Services. E-Mail: *bstar@troy.edu* Web: *www.troy.edu*

FINANCIAL AID: Average annual earnings from campus work are $2050. The FAFSA and the college's own financial statement are required. Check with the school for current application deadlines.

TUSKEGEE UNIVERSITY D-4
www.tuskegee.edu

Tuskegee, AL 36088	(334) 727-8289
	(800) 622-6531
Fax: (334) 727 5750	Email: admissions@tuskegee.edu
Full-time: 1085 men, 1436 women	Faculty: 280
Part-time: 38 men, 39 women	Ph.D.s: 70%
Graduate: 161 men, 358 women	Student/Faculty: 12 to 1
Year: semesters, summer session	Tuition: $18,800
Room & Board: $7950	Freshman Class: 5147 applied, 3519 accepted, 650 enrolled
SAT CR/M: 500/480 ACT: 21	CEEB CODE: 1813
Application Deadline: open	COMPETITIVE

Tuskegee University, founded in 1881 by Booker T. Washington, is an independent professional and technical institution offering degree programs in liberal arts and sciences, agriculture, architecture, business, education, engineering, and health professions. Figures in the above capsule and in this profile are approximate. There are 7 undergraduate schools and 4 graduate schools. In addition to regional accreditation, Tuskegee has baccalaureate program accreditation with ABET, CSWE, NAAB, NCATE, and NLN. The 5200-acre campus is in a rural area 40 miles east of Montgomery, and 20 miles west of Auburn. Including any residence halls, there are 160 buildings.

STUDENT LIFE: 67% of undergraduates are from out of state, mostly the South. Students are from 42 states, 31 foreign countries, and Canada. 90% are from public schools. 80% are African American. **Male To Female Ratio:** 1.4:1. The average age of freshmen is 19; all undergraduates, 22. 22% do not continue beyond their first year; 46% remain to graduate. **Housing:** 2300 students can be accommodated in college housing, which includes single-sex dorms, on-campus apartments, and married student housing. In addition, there are honors houses. On-campus housing is guaranteed for the freshman year only, and is available on a first-come, first-served basis. Alcohol is not permitted. All students may keep cars.

FACULTY/CLASSROOMS: 70% of faculty are male; 30% are female. No introductory courses are taught by graduate students.

PROGRAMS OF STUDY: Tuskegee confers B.A., B.S. and B.S.N. degrees. Master's and doctoral degrees are also awarded. Bachelor's degrees are awarded in AGRICULTURE (agricultural economics, animal science, and horticulture), BIOLOGICAL SCIENCE (biology/biological science), BUSINESS (accounting, banking and finance,

business administration and management, business economics, hospitality management services, management science, marketing/retailing/merchandising, and supply chain management), COMMUNICATIONS AND THE ARTS (English), COMPUTER AND PHYSICAL SCIENCE (chemistry, computer science, mathematics, and physics), EDUCATION (early childhood education, elementary education, physical education, secondary education, special education, and technical education), ENGINEERING AND ENVIRONMENTAL DESIGN (aeronautical engineering, architecture, biomedical engineering, chemical engineering, construction management, electrical/electronics engineering, electrical/electronics engineering technology, and mechanical engineering), HEALTH PROFESSIONS (allied health, nursing, occupational therapy, and veterinary science), SOCIAL SCIENCE (dietetics, economics, food science, history, political science/government, psychology, social work, and sociology). Engineering, nursing, veterinary science, and business are the strongest academically. Engineering, biology, and veterinary science have the largest enrollments.

ACTIVITIES: 4% of men belong to 6 local and 4 national fraternities; 4% of women belong to 5 local and 4 national sororities. There are 60 groups on campus, including band, cheerleading, choir, chorus, drama, honors, international, jazz band, marching band, newspaper, orchestra, religious, social service, and student government. Popular campus events include Spring Pageant, Campus All-Star Challenge, and Student Leadership Retreat. **Sports:** There are 5 intercollegiate sports for men and 5 for women, and 7 intramural sports for men and 6 for women. Facilities include a 10,000-seat stadium, a 5000-seat arena, a student center, tennis courts, a rifle range, playing fields, and an Olympic-size natatorium. **Graduates:** From July 1, 2013 to June 30, 2014, 356 bachelor's degrees were awarded. The most popular majors were engineering (11%), biology (11%), and business (8%). 87 companies recruited on campus in 2013-2014. In an average class, 17% graduate in 4 years or less, 28% graduate in 5 years or less, and 43% graduate in 6 years or less.

SERVICES: Counseling and information services are available, as is tutoring in some subjects. There is a reader service for the blind. **Library/Resources:** The 4 libraries contain 380,000 volumes, 2,500 microform items, and 3,000 audio/video tapes/CDs/DVDs, and subscribe to 1,150 periodicals including electronic. Computerized library services include interlibrary loans, database searching, Internet access, and Wi-Fi capability. **Physically Challenged Students:** Facilities include wheelchair ramps, elevators, special parking, specially equipped restrooms, special class scheduling, lowered drinking fountains, and lowered telephones. **Special:** Cooperative programs, internships, work-study programs, dual majors, nondegree study, and a B.A.-B.S. degree are offered. There are 17 national honor societies, a freshman honors program, and 9 departmental honors programs. **Visiting:** There are guides for informal visits, visitors may sit in on classes, and stay overnight. To schedule a visit, contact the Office of Admissions. **Campus Safety and Security:** Measures include 24-hour foot and vehicle patrol and security escort services. There are lighted pathways/sidewalks.

REQUIREMENTS: The SAT or ACT is required. In addition, a GPA of 3.0 is recommended. Applicants should be graduates of an accredited secondary school or hold the GED. They should have completed 4 units of English, 3 each of social science and math, and 1 each of physical science and biological science. SAT: Subject tests in mathematics (level I or II) and 1 other subject are recommended. An essay is not required. A GPA of 3.0 is required. AP and CLEP credits are accepted. Important factors in the admissions decision are advanced placement or honors courses, ability to finance college education, and geographical diversity. All students must complete a general education curriculum, including courses in history, sociology, philosophy, art, English, humanities, political science, math, natural sciences, and phys ed. A minimum of 124 semester credits with a GPA of 2.0 is required for graduation. **Procedure:** Freshmen are admitted to all sessions. Entrance exams should be taken starting in the junior year. There are early admissions and rolling admissions plans. Application deadlines are open. Application fee is $25. Applications are accepted on-line. **Transfer Students:** 166 transfer students enrolled in 2013-2014. Applicants must be in good standing at all previously attended institutions and have completed 12 or more semester hours with a GPA of 2.5. 44 of 124 credits required for the bachelor's degree must be completed at Tuskegee. **International Students:** There are 27 international students enrolled. They must take the TOEFL with a minimum score of 500 on the paper-based TOEFL (PBT) or 62 on the Internet-based version (iBT). They must also take the SAT or ACT, scoring 1000.

ADMISSIONS: 68% of the 2014-2015 applicants were accepted. The SAT scores for the 2014-2015 freshman class were: Critical Reading--67% below 500, 27% between 500 and 599, and 4% between 600 and 699; Math--64% below 500, 26% between 500 and 599, and 8% between 600 and 699. The ACT scores were 17% below 21, 61% between 21 and 23, 15% between 24 and 26, 6% between 27 and 28, and 1% above 28. 60% of the current freshmen were in the top fifth of their class; 80% were in the top two fifths. **Admissions Contact:** Elizabeth Dadzie, Associate VP of Admissions . E-Mail: *admissions@ tuskegee.edu* Web: *www.tuskegee.edu*

FINANCIAL AID: In 2014-2015, 87% of all full-time freshmen and 91% of continuing full-time students received some form of financial aid. 71% of all full-time freshmen and 74% of continuing full-time students received need-based aid. The average freshman award was $19,250. Need-based scholarships or need-based grants averaged $2,500 ($5,550 maximum); need-based self-help aid (loans and jobs) averaged $2,400 ($5,500 maximum); non-need-based athletic scholarships averaged $12,000 ($25,000 maximum); and other non-need-based awards and non-need-based scholarships averaged $3,500 ($10,000 maximum). 59% of undergraduate students work part-time. Average annual earnings from campus work are $2610. The average financial indebtedness of the 2014 graduate was $20,000. Tuskegee is a member of CSS. The CSS/Profile and federal tax returns are required. The priority date for freshman financial aid applications for fall entry is March 31. The deadline for filing freshman financial aid applications for fall entry is March 31.

UNIVERSITY OF ALABAMA SYSTEM

The University of Alabama System, established in 1900, is a public system in Alabama. It is governed by a board of trustees, whose chief administrator is the chancellor. The primary goal of the system is to serve all the people of the state through teaching, research, and public service. The main priorities are to promote the economic, cultural, and social welfare of Alabama through higher education; to educate and train the leasers and citizens of tomorrow; and to conduct research in all fields that address the critical needs of mankind. The total student enrollment for all three campuses is usually 44,500 with 3400 faculty members. Altogether there are 194 baccalaureate, 169 master's, 93 doctoral programs offered in the University of Alabama System. Profiles of the 4-year campuses are included in this section.

UNIVERSITY OF ALABAMA AT BIRMINGHAM
C-2

www.uab.edu

Birmingham, AL 35294

(205) 934-8221
(800) 421-8743

Fax: (205) 975-7114   Email: chooseuab@uab.edu

Full-time: 3501 men, 4856 women	Faculty: I, -$
Part-time: 1279 men, 1866 women	Ph.D.s: 86%
Graduate: 2529 men, 4537 women	Student/Faculty: 18 to 1
Year: semesters, summer session	Tuition: $8904 ($20,394)
Room & Board: $9580	Freshman Class: 5710 applied, 4893 accepted, 1748 enrolled
SAT: required	CEEB CODE: 1856
Application Deadline: June 1	COMPETITIVE+

The University of Alabama at Birmingham, founded in 1969, is a public institution offering degrees in the arts and sciences, business, dentistry, education, engineering, health professions, joint health sciences, medicine, nursing, optometry, and public health. There are 9 undergraduate schools and 11 graduate schools. In addition to regional accreditation, UAB has baccalaureate program accreditation with AACSB, ABET, CSWE, NASAD, NASM, and NCATE. The 323-acre campus is in an urban area in Birmingham. Including any residence halls, there are 206 buildings.

STUDENT LIFE: 90% of undergraduates are from Alabama. Others are from 48 states, 53 foreign countries, and Canada. 92% are from public schools. 64% are White; 21% African American. **Male To Female Ratio:** 1.5:1. The average age of freshmen is 18; all undergraduates, 24. 20% do not continue beyond their first year; 48% remain to graduate. **Housing:** 2260 students can be accommodated in college housing, which includes single-sex and coed dorms, on-campus apartments, and married student housing. Housing for disabled students is available on a first-come and first-served basis. 80% of students commute. Alcohol is not permitted. All students may keep cars.

FACULTY/CLASSROOMS: 54% of faculty are male; 46% are female. No introductory courses are taught by graduate students.

PROGRAMS OF STUDY: UAB confers B.A., B.S., B.F.A., B.S.B.M.E., B.S.C.E., B.S.E.E., B.S.M.E., B.S.Mt.E., B.S.N. and B.S.S.W. degrees. Master's and doctoral degrees are also awarded. Bachelor's degrees are awarded in BIOLOGICAL SCIENCE (biology/biological science and neurosciences), BUSINESS (accounting, banking and finance, and marketing/retailing/merchandising), COMMUNICATIONS AND THE ARTS (art, communications, dramatic arts, English, foreign language, music, and musical theater), COMPUTER AND PHYSICAL SCIENCE (chemistry, computer science, information sciences and systems, mathematics, natural sciences, and physics), EDUCATION (early childhood education, elementary education, health education, and secondary education), ENGINEERING AND ENVIRONMENTAL DESIGN (biomedical engineering, civil engineering, electrical/electronics engineering, industrial administration/management, materials engineering, and mechanical engineering), HEALTH PROFESSIONS (biomedical science, health science, kinesiology, medical records administration/services, medical technology, nuclear medical technology, nursing, public health, and respiratory therapy), SOCIAL SCIENCE (African American studies, anthropology, criminal justice, economics, history, international studies, philosophy, political science/government, psychology, social work, and sociology). Biology, accounting, and psychology have the largest enrollments.

ACTIVITIES: 4% of men belong to 12 national fraternities; 4% of women belong to 10 national sororities. There are 150 groups on campus, including band, cheerleading, chess, choir, chorale, chorus, computers, dance, drama, environmental, ethnic, gay, honors, international, jazz band, literary magazine, marching band, musical theater, newspaper, opera, orchestra, pep band, political, professional, radio and TV, religious, social, social service, and student government. Popular campus events include Springfest, Homecoming, Camille Armstrong Memorial Scholarship Stepshow, and Talent Search. **Sports:** There are 6 intercollegiate sports for men and 10 for women, and 35 intramural sports for men and 35 for women. Facilities include a 150,000-square-foot recreation center with 4 basketball/volleyball courts, 5 racquetball courts (1 of which can be converted to squash and 4 for wallyball), 4 aerobics studios, 18,000 square feet of weight and cardio-fitness areas, a game room, a KidsZone, an aquatics center with both lap and leisure components, a gym used for indoor soccer, floor hockey, and badminton, a juice bar, an indoor track, and a climbing wall. **Graduates:** From July 1, 2013 to June 30, 2014, 2042 bachelor's degrees were awarded. The most popular majors were nursing (14%), psychology (8%), and biology (7%). 254 companies recruited on campus in 2013-2014. In an average class, 25% graduate in 4 years or less, 42% graduate in 5 years or less, and 48% graduate in 6 years or less.

SERVICES: Counseling and information services are available, as is tutoring in some subjects, including biology, chemistry, physics, psychology, and mathematics. There is a reader service for the blind, and remedial math, reading, and writing. **Library/Resources:** The 3 libraries contain 1.3 million volumes, 1.3 million microform items, 29,744 audio/video tapes/CDs/DVDs, and subscribe to 35,622 periodicals including electronic. Computerized library services include interlibrary loans, database searching, Internet access, and Wi-Fi capability. Special learning facilities include an art gallery, radio station, TV station, Reynolds Historical Library, Alabama Museum of the Health Sciences, Alys Stephens Performing Art Center. **Physically Challenged Students:** All of the campus is accessible. Facilities include wheelchair ramps, elevators, special parking, specially equipped restrooms, lowered drinking fountains, lowered telephones, and special housing. **Special:** UAB offers student-designed majors, cross-registration with the Birmingham Area Consortium for Higher Education, internships, study abroad in 32 countries, work-study programs, nondegree study, pass/fail options, and credit by exam and for life experience. Cooperative education programs in the student's area of interest provide full- or part-time work. Additionally, there are several special programs such as the Industrial Scholars Program (provides financial support and industry experience for engineering students), Fifth Year Master of Science program in biology, Mathematics Fast Track Program, and the Early Medical School Acceptance Program. There are 32 national honor societies, a freshman honors program, and 33 departmental honors programs. **Visiting:** There are regularly scheduled orientations for prospective students, including a question-and-answer session, academic advising, sessions for parents, and presentations on student life, financial aid, housing, and student development. There are guides for informal visits and visitors may sit in on classes. To schedule a visit, contact Jessica Bobo at campustours@uab.edu. **Campus Safety and Security:** Measures include 24-hour foot and vehicle patrol, emergency notification system, self-defense education, and security escort services. There are shuttle buses, emergency telephones, and lighted pathways/sidewalks.

REQUIREMENTS: The SAT or ACT is required. Applicants should have completed 17 Carnegie units and a college prep diploma, including 4 units in English, 3 each in math, science, and social studies, 1 in foreign language, and 3 in electives. The GED is accepted. A GPA of 2.0 is required. AP and CLEP credits are accepted. All students must complete a core curriculum that includes courses in math, computers, English, history, science and technology, social sciences, philosophy, fine arts, foreign language or culture, and literature. To receive a bachelor's degree, students must complete 128 semester hours for most programs, with a GPA of at least 2.0. **Procedure:** Freshmen are admitted to all sessions. Entrance exams should be taken during the beginning of the senior year. There are early admissions, deferred admissions, and rolling admissions plans. Applications should be filed by June 1 for fall entry, along with a $30 fee. Notification is sent on a rolling basis. Applications are accepted online. **Transfer Students:** 1449 transfer students enrolled in 2013-2014. Transfer applicants must have a GPA of 2.0 after completing 24 semester hours (or 36 quarter hours) of college-level work. College transcripts are required of all students. Applicants who have completed fewer than 24 semester hours must meet the requirements of beginning freshmen. **International Students:** There are 180 international students enrolled. The school actively recruits these students. They must take the TOEFL with a minimum score of 77 on the Internet-based version (iBT), or take the IELTS. They must also take the SAT or ACT, scoring 20.

ADMISSIONS: 86% of the 2014-2015 applicants were accepted. 46% of the current freshmen were in the top fifth of their class; 74% were in the top two fifths. There were 16 National Merit finalists. 10 freshmen graduated first in their class. **Admissions Contact:** Kirk Kluver, Director of Admissions. E-Mail: *chooseuab@uab.edu* Web: *http://www.uab.edu/apply*

FINANCIAL AID: In 2014-2015, 84% of all full-time freshmen and continuing full-time students received some form of financial aid. 59% of all full-time freshmen and continuing full-time students received need-based aid. The average freshman award was $9,966. Need-based scholarships or need-based grants averaged $4,776; need-based self-help aid (loans and jobs) averaged $3,580; non-need-based athletic scholarships averaged $18,767; and other non-need-based awards and non-need-based scholarships averaged $8,020. The average financial indebtedness of the 2014 graduate was $28,164. The FAFSA is required. The priority date for freshman financial aid applications for fall entry is March 1.

UNIVERSITY OF ALABAMA AT TUSCALOOSA
B-3

www.ua.edu

Tuscaloosa, AL 35487

(205) 348-6010
(800) 933-BAMA

Fax: (205) 348-9046
Full-time: 11253 men, 12692 women
Part-time: 1022 men, 1267 women
Graduate: 2244 men, 3169 women
Year: semesters, summer session
Room & Board: $8564

Email: admissions@ua.edu
Faculty: n/av
Ph.D.s: n/av
Student/Faculty: 19 to 1
Tuition: $8600 ($21,900)
Freshman Class: 22136 applied, 9636 accepted, 5728 enrolled

SAT or ACT: required
Application Deadline: March 1

CEEB CODE: 1830
COMPETITIVE+

The University of Alabama, the state of Alabama's first public university is a senior comprehensive doctoral level institution. The university was established by constitutional provision under statutory mandates and authorizations. It's mission is to advance the intellectual and social condition of the people of the state through quality programs of teaching, research and service. Figures in the above capsule and in this profile are approximate. There are 9 undergraduate schools and 11 graduate schools. In addition to regional accreditation, UA has baccalaureate program accreditation with AACSB, ABET, ACEJMC, ADA, CSWE, FIDER, NASAD, NASM, and NCATE. The 1000-acre campus is in a suburban area 50 miles southwest of Birmingham. Including any residence halls, there are 216 buildings.

STUDENT LIFE: 50% of undergraduates are from out of state, mostly the South. Students are from 50 states, 79 foreign countries, and Canada. 89% are from public schools. 81% are White; 12% African American. 56% are Protestant; 32% claim no religious affiliation. The average age of freshmen is 18; all undergraduates, 21. 14% do not continue beyond their first year; 87% remain to graduate. **Housing:** 5800 students can be accommodated in college housing, which includes single-sex and coed dorms, on-campus apartments, and married student housing. In addition, there are honors houses, language houses, special-interest houses, fraternity houses, and sorority houses. On-campus housing is guaranteed for the freshman year only, and is available on a first-come, first-served basis. 92% of students live on campus; of those, 35% remain on campus on weekends. All students may keep cars.

FACULTY/CLASSROOMS: 60% of faculty are male; 40% are female. 71% teach undergraduates, 5% do research, and 4% do both. Graduate students teach 28% of introductory courses. The average class size in an introductory lecture is 52; in a laboratory is 19; and in a regular course is 26.

PROGRAMS OF STUDY: UA confers B.A., B.S., B.A.Com., B.F.A., B.M., B.S.A.E., B.S.C.B.A., B.S.C.E., B.S.Che.E., B.S.Chem., B.S.C.S., B.S.Ed., B.S.E.E., B.S.Geo., B.S.H.E.S., B.S.I.E., B.S.M.E., B.S.Met., B.S. Micr., B.S.N. and B.S.W. degrees. Master's and doctoral degrees are also awarded. Bachelor's degrees are awarded in BIOLOGICAL SCIENCE (biology/biological science, marine science, and microbiology), BUSINESS (accounting and management information systems), COMMUNICATIONS AND THE ARTS (advertising, art history and appreciation, classics, communications, dance, English, French, German, journalism, music, public relations, Russian, Spanish, and telecommunications), COMPUTER AND PHYSICAL SCIENCE (chemistry, computer science, geology, mathematics, and physics), EDUCATION (athletic training, early childhood education, elementary education, music education, physical education, secondary education, and special education), ENGINEERING AND ENVIRONMENTAL DESIGN (aerospace studies, chemical engineering, civil engineering, electrical/electronics engineering, environmental science, industrial administration/management, industrial engineering, interior design, mechanical engineering, and metallurgical engineering), HEALTH PROFESSIONS (music therapy and nursing), SOCIAL SCIENCE (American studies, anthropology, clothing and textiles management/production/services, criminal justice, economics, food science, geography, history, human development, interdisciplinary studies, international studies, philosophy, political science/government, psychology, religion, and social work). Advertising, accounting, and engineering are the strongest academically. Business, elementary education and nursing have the largest enrollments.

ACTIVITIES: 28% of men belong to 1 local and 26 national fraternities; 43% of women belong to 1 local and 20 national sororities. There are 391 groups on campus, including leadership and other national honoraries, academic service, art, band, cheerleading, chess, choir, chorale, chorus, computers, dance, debate, drama, drill team, ethnic, film, forensics, gay, honors, international, jazz band, literary magazine, marching band, musical theater, newspaper, opera, orchestra, pep band, photography, political, professional, radio and TV, religious, social, social service, student government, symphony, and yearbook. Popular campus events include Honors Week, Get on Board Day and Family Weekend. **Sports:** There are 9 intercollegiate sports for men and 12 for women, and 17 intramural sports for men and 16 for women. Facilities include an 83,000-seat football stadium, a 15,000-seat basketball arena, a track and field facility, a 6,100-seat baseball stadium, a 1,600-foot softball stadium, an indoor football practice facility, lighted varsity and public tennis courts, an aquatic complex with Olympic-size and standard pools and a weight-lifting facility, a soccer field, racquetball, basketball, and volleyball courts, weight and exercise rooms, an indoor/outdoor pool, and an 18-hole golf course with clubhouse and driving range. **Graduates:** From July 1, 2013 to June 30, 2014, 4463 bachelor's degrees were awarded. The most popular majors were business/marketing (29%), health professions and related programs (10%), and communication/journalism (9%). In an average class, 59% graduate in 3 years or less, 24% graduate in 5 years or less, and 67% graduate in 6 years or less. Of the 2013 graduating class, 87% were enrolled in graduate school within 6 months of graduation.

SERVICES: Counseling and information services are available, as is tutoring in some subjects, including statistics math, chemistry, physics, computer science, accounting, finance, economics, and foreign languages. There is a reader service for the blind, and remedial math, reading, and writing. There is a center for teaching and learning, a writing lab, a career center, computer-based self-tutoring, and a math computer lab. Many departments and colleges offer tutorial services or tutorial reference. **Library/Resources:** The 10 libraries contain 2.5 million volumes, 4.0 million microform items, 526,856 audio/video tapes/CDs/DVDs, and subscribe to 23,222 periodicals including electronic. Computerized library services include interlibrary loans, database searching, and Internet access. Special learning facilities include an art gallery, natural history museum, radio station, TV station, special collections department, map library, observatory, specialized computer labs, and archeological site. For **Physically Challenged Students:** 90% of the campus is accessible. Facilities include wheelchair ramps, elevators, special parking, specially equipped restrooms, special class scheduling, lowered drinking fountains, lowered telephones, special housing. automatic doors, TDD, adaptive technology, and areas of rescue assistance. **Special:** UA offers cross-registration with Stillman College and Shelton State Community College, internships, international study programs, a Washington semester, a 3-week May-June interim term, exchange study within the United States, work-study, co-op programs, accelerated programs, B.A.-B.S. degrees, dual majors, student-designed majors, interdisciplinary majors in the New College arts and sciences program, credit for life experiences, nondegree study, and pass/fail options. There are 27 national honor societies, including Phi Beta Kappa, a freshman honors program, and 17 departmental honors programs. **Visiting:** There are regularly scheduled orientations for prospective students, consisting of a campus tour followed by meetings with admissions counselors and faculty and staff. Customized visits to suit student and parent needs are possible. University Day (4 times a year) offers tours and information sessions. There are guides for informal visits, visitors may sit in on classes, and stay overnight. To schedule a visit, contact the Office of Undergraduate Admissions. **Campus Safety and Security:** Measures include 24-hour foot and vehicle patrol, self-defense education, and security escort services. There are emergency telephones, lighted pathways/sidewalks, community-oriented police service, UA police bike patrol, educational awareness for personal safety, alcohol awareness, child seat installations and domestic violence awareness programs.

REQUIREMENTS: The SAT or ACT is required. A minimum GPA

of 2.0 is required; admission is based on a sliding scale of test scores and high school GPA. The GED is accepted. High school preparation should include 4 units each of English and social studies, 3 each of math and science, 1 of foreign language, and history and 5 of academic electives. Students with a 3.0 cumulative GPA and a satisfactory ACT or SAT (verbal and math only) score will generally be admitted. A GPA of 2.0 is required. AP and CLEP credits are accepted. Important factors in the admissions decision are advanced placement or honors courses, evidence of special talent, and leadership record.To graduate, all students must complete a minimum of 120 semester hours, including at least 27 in the major, with a minimum GPA of 2.0. Core curriculum requirements include 12 hours each of humanities/fine arts and history/social science, 11 of natural science/math, 6 of computer studies or a foreign language, 6 of English composition, and 6 of upper-level courses with a writing component. **Procedure:** Freshmen are admitted fall, spring, and summer. Entrance exams should be taken in the spring of the junior year. There are early admissions and rolling admissions plans. Applications should be filed by March 1 for fall entry; December 1 for spring entry; and March 1 for summer entry, along with a $40 fee. Notification is sent on a rolling basis. Applications are accepted online. **Transfer Students:** 1463 transfer students enrolled in 2013-2014. Applicants need an overall minimum GPA of 2.0 with at least 24 semester hours earned. Those with fewer than 24 hours must meet freshman standards. 30 of 120 credits required for the bachelor's degree must be completed at UA. **International Students:** The school actively recruits these students. They must take the TOEFL, or earn a proficiency certificate from the university's English Language Institute. They must also take the SAT or ACT.

ADMISSIONS: 44% of the 2014-2015 applicants were accepted. **Admissions Contact:** Mary K. Spiegel, Director of Undergraduate Admissions. E-Mail: *admissions@ua.edu* Web: *www.ua.edu*

FINANCIAL AID: The average freshman award was $10,780. Need-based scholarships or need-based grants averaged $8,500; need-based self-help aid (loans and jobs) averaged $3,614; non-need-based athletic scholarships averaged $22,990; and other non-need-based awards and non-need-based scholarships averaged $8,495. The average financial indebtedness of the 2014 graduate was $26,714. The FAFSA is required. Check with the school for current application deadlines.

UNIVERSITY OF ALABAMA IN HUNTSVILLE   C-1
www.uah.edu

Huntsville, AL 35899

(256) 824-2773
(800) UAH-CALL

Fax: (256) 824-4539
Full-time: 2392 men, 1912 women
Part-time: 818 men, 496 women
Graduate: 967 men, 763 women
Year: semesters, summer session
Room & Board: $8433

Email: uahadmissions@uah.edu
Faculty: 309; I, -$
Ph.Ds: 86%
Student/Faculty: 14 to 1
Tuition: $9158 ($21,232)
Freshman Class: 2104 applied, 1726 accepted, 724 enrolled

SAT CR/M: 587/598 **ACT:** 27
Application Deadline: June 1

CEEB CODE: 1854
VERY COMPETITIVE+

The University of Alabama in Huntsville, founded in 1950 and part of the University of Alabama system, is a public institution offering programs in liberal arts, sciences, business administration, nursing, and engineering. Figures in the above capsule and in this profile are approximate. There are 5 undergraduate schools and 1 graduate school. In addition to regional accreditation, UAH, UAHuntsville has baccalaureate program accreditation with AACSB, ABET, ACCE, CSAB, NASAD, NASM, and NCATE. The 400-acre campus is in a suburban area 100 miles north of Birmingham and 90 miles south of Nashville. Including any residence halls, there are 59 buildings.

STUDENT LIFE: 90% of undergraduates are from Alabama. Others are from 46 states, 75 foreign countries, and Canada. 90% are from public schools. 69% are White; 11% African American. 72% are Protestant; 11% Catholic. The average age of freshmen is 18; all undergraduates, 23. 23% do not continue beyond their first year; 46% remain to graduate. **Housing:** 1680 students can be accommodated in college housing, which includes coed dorms, on-campus apartments, and married student housing. In addition, there are honors houses, fraternity houses, and sorority houses. On-campus housing is guaranteed for the freshman year only, and is available on a first-come, first-served basis. 79% of students commute. Alcohol is not permitted. All students may keep cars.

FACULTY/CLASSROOMS: All teach and do research. No introductory courses are taught by graduate students.

PROGRAMS OF STUDY: UAH, UAHuntsville confers B.A., B.F.A., B.S., B.S.B.A., B.S.A.E., B.S.Che.E., B.S.C.E., B.S.Cp.E., B.S.E.E., B.S.M.E., B.S.I.S.E., B.S.O.E. and B.S.N. degrees. Master's and doctoral degrees are also awarded. Bachelor's degrees are awarded in BIOLOGICAL SCIENCE (biology/biological science), BUSINESS (accounting, banking and finance, business administration and management, economics – statistics, and marketing/retailing/merchandising), COMMUNICATIONS AND THE ARTS (art, communications, English, languages, and music), COMPUTER AND PHYSICAL SCIENCE (chemistry, computer science, earth science, information sciences and systems, mathematics, physics, and science), EDUCATION (elementary education), ENGINEERING AND ENVIRONMENTAL DESIGN (chemical engineering, civil engineering, computer engineering, electrical/electronics engineering, industrial engineering, mechanical engineering, and optical engineering), HEALTH PROFESSIONS (nursing), SOCIAL SCIENCE (history, philosophy, political science/government, psychology, and sociology). Nursing, mechanical engineering, and biological sciences have the largest enrollments.

ACTIVITIES: There are 125 groups on campus, including community service, honor societies, multicultural, special interest, academic, art, band, cheerleading, choir, chorale, chorus, computers, dance, drama, environmental, ethnic, gay, honors, international, jazz band, musical theater, newspaper, opera, pep band, political, professional, religious, social, social service, student government, and symphony. Popular campus events include Week of Welcome, Homecoming, Family Weekend, Late Night Breakfast, ChargerCon, The Big Event, Sandella Sounds, and Spring Fling. **Sports:** There are 8 intercollegiate sports for men and 8 for women, and 11 intramural sports for men and 11 for women. Facilities include a 2800-seat gym, swimming pool, racquetball and tennis courts, disc golf course, soccer fields, softball diamonds, a fitness center with cardio equipment, indoor track, weight room, fitness classes, aquatics, sand volleyball, basketball courts and a sports nutrition center. **Graduates:** From July 1, 2013 to June 30, 2014, 1070 bachelor's degrees were awarded. The most popular majors were nursing (21%), mechanical engineering (8%), and biology (8%). In an average class, 15% graduate in 4 years or less, 38% graduate in 5 years or less, and 46% graduate in 6 years or less.

SERVICES: Counseling and information services are available, as is tutoring in most subjects. Tutoring services are available for most 100-200 level classes, most undergraduate math classes, and undergraduate writing in any discipline. **Library/Resources:** The library contains 289,500 volumes, 571,000 microform items, and 1,489 audio/video tapes/CDs/DVDs, and subscribes to 339 periodicals including electronic. Computerized library services include interlibrary loans, database searching, Internet access, and Wi-Fi capability. Special learning facilities include an art gallery, an optical observatory and a radio telescope, the National Space Science and Technology center, shared between UAHuntsville, NASA and the National Weather service, and a rooftop greenhouse used for research and laboratory experiences. **Physically Challenged Students:** 98% of the campus is accessible. Facilities include wheelchair ramps, elevators, special parking, specially equipped restrooms, special class scheduling, lowered drinking fountains, special housing, a swimming pool lift, and sign language interpreters. **Special:** UAH offers co-op programs in all majors, cross-registration with Alabama Agricultural and Mechanical University, Athens State University, and Calhoun Community College, and internships in business, communications, education, and political science. A 3-2 engineering degree is available with Oakwood College. Dual majors, B.A.-B.S. degrees in math and biology, study abroad in 28 countries, nondegree study, and a pass/fail

option are also offered. Joint Undergraduate Masters Program (JUMP) available in many disciplines. There are 15 national honor societies and a freshman honors program. **Visiting:** There are regularly scheduled orientations for prospective students, including sessions on academics, campus life, financial aid and other important topics are provided as well as time dedicated to advising and class registration. Social activities are available for participants to meet both new and current students. There are guides for informal visits, visitors may sit in on classes, and stay overnight. To schedule a visit, contact Vangie Harris at (800) 824-2773. **Campus Safety and Security:** Measures include 24-hour foot and vehicle patrol, emergency notification system, self-defense education, and security escort services. There are emergency telephones, lighted pathways/sidewalks, controlled access to dorms/residences, emergency management plan, 911 system and digitally recorded security cameras.

REQUIREMENTS: The SAT or ACT is required. A sliding scale with the GPA determines the minimum test score needed. The GED is accepted. Students should present a minimum of 20 Carnegie units, including 4 years of English and social studies, and 3 each of math and science. A GPA of 2.0 is required. AP and CLEP credits are accepted. All students must earn a minimum GPA of 2.0 and over 120 to 134 credit hours, including 21 to 36 in their major. The core curriculum includes courses in English composition, literature, world history, foreign language and communications, fine arts, math, science and social sciences. **Procedure:** Freshmen are admitted fall, spring, and summer. Entrance exams should be taken during the junior year. There are early admissions, deferred admissions, and rolling admissions plans. Applications should be filed by June 1 for fall entry; December 15 for spring entry; and May 15 for summer entry, along with a $30 fee. Applications are accepted on-line. **Transfer Students:** 705 transfer students enrolled in 2013-2014. Applicants need a minimum cumulative GPA of 2.0 and at least 24 hours of credit from a regionally accredited college or university. 32 of 128 credits required for the bachelor's degree must be completed at UAH, UAHuntsville. **International Students:** There are 203 international students enrolled. The school actively recruits these students. They must take the TOEFL with a minimum score of 500 on the paper-based TOEFL (PBT) or 62 on the Internet-based version (iBT) and the college's own test. They must also take the SAT or ACT.

ADMISSIONS: 82% of the 2014-2015 applicants were accepted. The SAT scores for the 2014-2015 freshman class were: Critical Reading--17% below 500, 37% between 500 and 599, 32% between 600 and 699, and 14% between 700 and 800; Math--12% below 500, 41% between 500 and 599, 31% between 600 and 699, and 17% between 700 and 800. The ACT scores were 11% below 21, 10% between 21 and 23, 26% between 24 and 26, 16% between 27 and 28, and 36% above 28. 32% of the current freshmen were in the top fifth of their class; 64% were in the top two fifths. 21 freshmen graduated first in their class. **Admissions Contact:** Sally Badoud, Interim Director of Admissions. E-Mail: *uahadmissions@uah.edu* Web: *http://www.uah.edu/admissions*

FINANCIAL AID: In 2014-2015, 90% of all full-time freshmen and 75% of continuing full-time students received some form of financial aid. 55% of all full-time freshmen and 55% of continuing full-time students received need-based aid. The average freshman award was $11,617. Need-based scholarships or need-based grants averaged $9,367 ($35,308 maximum); need-based self-help aid (loans and jobs) averaged $5,741 ($33,589 maximum); non-need-based athletic scholarships averaged $8,803 ($33,392 maximum); and other non-need-based awards and non-need-based scholarships averaged $8,806 ($34,276 maximum). The average financial indebtedness of the 2014 graduate was $29,421. The FAFSA is required. The priority date for freshman financial aid applications for fall entry is April 1. The deadline for filing freshman financial aid applications for fall entry is July 31.

UNIVERSITY OF MOBILE
www.umobile.edu

A-5

Mobile, AL 36613

(251) 442-2249
(800) 946-7267

Fax: (251) 675-6329
Email: jmcgehee@mail.umobile.edu

Full-time: 473 men, 809 women
Part-time: 40 men, 144 women
Graduate: 25 men, 109 women
Year: semesters, summer session
Room & Board: $9550

Faculty: 84
Ph.D.s: 62%
Student/Faculty: 12 to 1
Tuition: $19,385
Freshman Class: 1009 applied, 590 accepted, 275 enrolled

ACT: 22
Application Deadline: August 1

CEEB CODE: 1515
VERY COMPETITIVE

University of Mobile, founded in 1961, is a private liberal arts institution affiliated with the Southern Baptists. There are 7 undergraduate schools and 5 graduate schools. In addition to regional accreditation, UMobile has baccalaureate program accreditation with ACBSP and NASM. The 880-acre campus is in a suburban area 10 miles northwest of Mobile. Including any residence halls, there are 60 buildings.

STUDENT LIFE: 74% of undergraduates are from Alabama. Others are from 39 states, 23 foreign countries, and Canada. 63% are White; 24% African American. The average age of freshmen is 18; all undergraduates, 24. 23% do not continue beyond their first year; 46% remain to graduate. **Housing:** 734 students can be accommodated in college housing, which includes single-sex dorms and on-campus apartments. On-campus housing is guaranteed for the freshman year only, and is available on a first-come, first-served basis. 51% of students commute. Alcohol is not permitted. All students may keep cars.

FACULTY/CLASSROOMS: 50% of faculty are male; 50% are female. 98% teach undergraduates. No introductory courses are taught by graduate students. The average class size in an introductory lecture is 16; in a laboratory is 16; and in a regular course is 16.

PROGRAMS OF STUDY: UMobile confers B.A., B.S., B.B.A., B.M. and B.S.N. degrees. Associate and master's degrees are also awarded. Bachelor's degrees are awarded in BIOLOGICAL SCIENCE (biology/biological science and marine science), BUSINESS (accounting and business administration and management), COMMUNICATIONS AND THE ARTS (art, communications, English, music, music performance, and voice), COMPUTER AND PHYSICAL SCIENCE (information sciences and systems and mathematics), EDUCATION (athletic training, early childhood education, elementary education, and physical education), HEALTH PROFESSIONS (nursing), SOCIAL SCIENCE (history, humanities, liberal arts/general studies, political science/government, psychology, religion, religious music, social science, sociology, and theological studies). Business, education, nursing, music, and worship leadership are the strongest academically. Business administration, education, and nursing have the largest enrollments.

ACTIVITIES: There are no fraternities or sororities. There are 52 groups on campus, including art, band, cheerleading, choir, chorale, chorus, computers, dance, drama, drum and bugle corps, honors, international, jazz band, musical theater, opera, orchestra, pep band, political, professional, religious, social, social service, student government, and symphony. Popular campus events include College Preview Day and Christmas Spectacular. **Sports:** There are 7 intercollegiate sports for men and 8 for women, and 5 intramural sports for men and 5 for women. Facilities include an 800-seat gym, tennis complex with 10 courts, swimming pool, track, baseball, softball, 2 soccer fields, and a golf driving range with 2 putting greens. **Graduates:** From July 1, 2013 to June 30, 2014, 272 bachelor's degrees were awarded. The most popular majors were education (22%), nursing (21%), and business (15%). In an average class, 26% graduate in 4 years or less, 14% graduate in 5 years or less, and 42% graduate in 6 years or less. Of the 2013 graduating class, 26% were enrolled in graduate school within 6 months of graduation, and 72% were employed.

SERVICES: Counseling and information services are available, as is tutoring in some subjects, including writing, English and math. There is remedial math, reading, and writing. Additional tutoring provided in other subjects as needed. **Library/Resources:** The library contains 110,005 volumes, 1,733 audio/video tapes/CDs/DVDs, and subscribes to 258 periodicals including electronic. Computerized library services include interlibrary loans, database searching, Internet access, and Wi-Fi capability. Special learning facilities include an art gallery. **Physically Challenged Students:** All of the campus is accessible. Facilities include wheelchair ramps, elevators, special parking, specially equipped restrooms, special class scheduling, lowered drinking fountains. Special housing can be arranged on an as-needed basis. **Special:** A variety of internships and work-study programs, a five-year B.S./M.B.A. degree, adult programs in business, education, nursing, and leadership/cultural studies, and dual majors are available, as is a 3-2 engineering degree with the University of South Alabama. There are 13 national honor societies, a freshman honors program, and 1 departmental honors program. **Visiting:** There are regularly scheduled orientations for prospective students, including financial aid seminars, academic seminars, faculty advising, campus tours, and admissions counseling. There are guides for informal visits, visitors may sit in on classes, and stay overnight. To schedule a visit, contact Justin McGehee at (251) 442-2638. **Campus Safety and Security:** Measures include 24-hour foot and vehicle patrol and emergency notification system. There are lighted pathways/sidewalks, controlled access to dorms/residences. A professional campus security service is available 24 hours per day.

REQUIREMENTS: Applicants must have 22 Carnegie units and a minimum composite score of 21 on the ACT. The GED is accepted. The ACT is not required of applicants over age 25. A GPA of 2.8 is required. AP and CLEP credits are accepted. Important factors in the admissions decision are advanced placement or honors courses, ability to finance college education, and leadership record. All students are required to complete 123 credit hours, with at least 30 in their major field, and earn a minimum GPA of 2.0. Distribution requirements include 9 hours in English, 4 hours in lab science, 6 hours in Christian ministries, and 3 hours each in math, history, and public speaking or philosophy. Students select an additional 18 hours of electives from among art, literature, psychology, sociology, political science, philosophy, science, history, economics, music, and Christian ministries. Chapel attendance is also required. **Procedure:** Freshmen are admitted fall, spring, and summer. Entrance exams should be taken in August before the junior year. There are deferred admissions and rolling admissions plans. Applications should be filed by August 1 for fall entry; January 4 for spring entry; and May 1 for summer entry. The fall 2014 application fee was $25. Notification is sent on a rolling basis. Applications are accepted on-line. **Transfer Students:** 113 transfer students enrolled in 2013-2014. Transfer students need to have earned a minimum GPA of 2.0 for previous college work. If fewer than 24 semester hours are accepted, a minimum score of 21 on the ACT and a high school transcript, or GED, are required. 32 of 123 credits required for the bachelor's degree must be completed at UMobile. **International Students:** There are 64 international students enrolled. The school actively recruits these students. They must take the TOEFL with a minimum score of 500 on the paper-based TOEFL (PBT) or 61 on the Internet-based version (iBT). They must also take the SAT or ACT, scoring 21.

ADMISSIONS: 58% of the 2014-2015 applicants were accepted. The SAT scores for the 2014-2015 freshman class were: Critical Reading--67% below 500, 24% between 500 and 599, 9% between 600 and 699; Math--64% below 500, 33% between 500 and 599, and 3% between 600 and 699. 50% of the current freshmen were in the top fifth of their class; 84% were in the top two fifths. **Admissions Contact:** Justin McGehee, Assistant Director of Enrollment. E-Mail: *jmcgehee@mail.umobile.edu* Web: *www.umobile.edu*

FINANCIAL AID: In 2014-2015, 82% of all full-time freshmen and 76% of continuing full-time students received some form of financial aid. 58% of all full-time freshmen and 45% of continuing full-time students received need-based aid. The average freshman award was $18,602. Need-based scholarships or need-based grants averaged $5,219; need-based self-help aid (loans and jobs) averaged $2,175; non-need-based athletic scholarships averaged $16,508; and other non-need-based awards and non-need-based scholarships averaged $9,377. Average annual earnings from campus work are $2175. The average financial indebtedness of the 2014 graduate was $28,250. The FAFSA, the state aid form, and the college's own financial statement are required. The deadline for filing freshman financial aid applications for fall entry is August 1.

UNIVERSITY OF MONTEVALLO — C-3

go.montevallo.edu

Montevallo, AL 35115   (205) 665-6034

Fax: (205) 665-6032	Email: admissions@montevallo.edu
Full-time: n/av	Faculty: IIA, --$
Part-time: n/av	Ph.D.s: n/av
Graduate: n/av	Student/Faculty: 16 to 1
Year: semesters, summer session	Tuition: $10,660 ($21,220)
Room & Board: $6400	Freshman Class: 531 enrolled
ACT: 23	CEEB CODE: 1004
Application Deadline: August 1	COMPETITIVE

The University of Montevallo, founded in 1896, is a public, liberal arts institution offering courses in business, fine arts, music, teacher preparation and preprofessional training. Figures in the above capsule and in this profile are approximate. There are 4 undergraduate schools and 2 graduate schools. In addition to regional accreditation, UM has baccalaureate program accreditation with AACSB, ADA, AHEA, CSWE, NASAD, NASM, and NCATE. The 160-acre campus is in a small town 35 miles south of Birmingham. Including any residence halls, there are 40 buildings.

STUDENT LIFE: 95% of undergraduates are from Alabama. Others are from 6 states, 17 foreign countries, and Canada. 74% are White; 14% African American. The average age of freshmen is 18; all undergraduates, 20. 26% do not continue beyond their first year; 47% remain to graduate. **Housing:** 1253 students can be accommodated in college housing, which includes single-sex and coed dorms and on-campus apartments. In addition, there are fraternity houses. On-campus housing is available on a first-come and first-served basis. 53% of students commute. All students may keep cars.

FACULTY/CLASSROOMS: 99% teach undergraduates. No introductory courses are taught by graduate students. The average class size in an introductory lecture is 24; in a laboratory is 23; and in a regular course is 24.

PROGRAMS OF STUDY: UM confers B.A., B.S., B.B.A., B.F.A., B.M. and B.M.E. degrees. Master's degrees are also awarded. Bachelor's degrees are awarded in BIOLOGICAL SCIENCE (biology/biological science), BUSINESS (accounting, banking and finance, business administration and management, management science, and marketing/retailing/merchandising), COMMUNICATIONS AND THE ARTS (art, communications, dramatic arts, English, French, German, journalism, music, music performance, Spanish, and studio art), COMPUTER AND PHYSICAL SCIENCE (chemistry and mathematics), EDUCATION (art education, education of the deaf and hearing impaired, elementary education, home economics education, music education, and physical education), ENGINEERING AND ENVIRONMENTAL DESIGN (environmental science), HEALTH PROFESSIONS (speech pathology/audiology), SOCIAL SCIENCE (family/consumer studies, history, political science/government, psychology, social science, social work, and sociology). Elementary/early childhood education, business and art have the largest enrollments.

ACTIVITIES: 19% of men belong to 7 national fraternities; 24% of women belong to 8 national sororities. There are 93 groups on campus, including art, cheerleading, choir, chorus, computers, dance, debate, drama, environmental, ethnic, forensics, gay, honors, international, jazz band, literary magazine, musical theater, newspaper, pep band, photography, political, professional, radio and TV, religious, social, social service, student government, and yearbook. Popular campus events include College Night, and Honors Day. **Sports:** There are 4 intercollegiate sports for men and 7 for women, and 7 intramural sports for men and 4 for women. Facilities include a 97,000-square-foot student activity center with a 6-lane collegiate competition size pool, 6000-square-foot weight training and cardio-conditioning theater, 3500-seat arena, several athletic fields, tennis courts, sand volleyball facility, a lake, camping area, an 18-hole golf

course and driving range. **Graduates:** From July 1, 2013 to June 30, 2014, 326 bachelor's degrees were awarded. The most popular majors were business/marketing (17%), education (13%), and visual and performing arts (12%). In an average class, 21% graduate in 4 years or less, 41% graduate in 5 years or less, and 47% graduate in 6 years or less.

SERVICES: Counseling and information services are available, as is tutoring in some subjects. There is a reader service for the blind, and remedial math, reading, and writing. **Library/Resources:** The library contains 266,236 volumes, 795,344 microform items, 4,673 audio/video tapes/CDs/DVDs, and subscribes to 27,962 periodicals including electronic. Computerized library services include interlibrary loans, database searching, Internet access, and Wi-Fi capability. Special learning facilities include an art gallery, radio, and TV station, all-Steinway music department, Center for Innovative Teaching and Technology, digital cafe, distance learning classroom, glass-blowing studio, painting and drawing Studios, Ebeneezer Swamp Ecological Preserve, speech and hearing center, observatory, and traffic safety center. **Physically Challenged Students:** Facilities include wheelchair ramps, elevators, special parking, specially equipped restrooms, special class scheduling, lowered drinking fountains, and lowered telephones. **Special:** A 3-2 engineering degree is offered with Auburn University, the University of Alabama at Birmingham, and the University of Alabama at Tuscaloosa. Internships are required for some majors. Study abroad, B.A.-B.S. degrees, dual degrees, a Washington semester, and pass/fail options are available. There are 26 national honor societies, a freshman honors program, and 1 departmental honors program. **Visiting:** There are regularly scheduled orientations for prospective students, consisting of a program of orientation, advising, and academic counseling prior to enrollment. There are guides for informal visits, visitors may sit in on classes, and stay overnight. To schedule a visit, contact the Office of Admissions. **Campus Safety and Security:** Measures include 24-hour foot and vehicle patrol, emergency notification system, self-defense education, and security escort services. There are emergency telephones, lighted pathways/sidewalks, controlled access to dorms/residences, campus lighting, and electronic access into residence halls.

REQUIREMENTS: The ACT is required. Applicants must present a high school transcript with a minimum GPA of 2.5 and successful completion of a minimum of 16 academic or college-preparatory credits from 9th to 12th grade, including 4 units each of English, social studies, and math, 2 units of science, and 4 units of foreign language or electives. Applicants who have earned a GED should have an official copy of their score report sent in lieu of a high school transcript. A GPA of 2.0 is required. AP and CLEP credits are accepted. Important factors in the admissions decision are advanced placement or honors courses, evidence of special talent, and geographical diversity. To graduate, students must complete a minimum of 130 semester hours with an overall 2.0 GPA while meeting core, major, and minor requirements. Core requirements include 12 hours of writing reinforcement courses (usually met with literature and major/minor courses), 7 hours of sciences (2 branches), 6 hours each in foundations in writing, world literature, world civilizations, and institutions and issues courses, 4 hours of health/phys ed, 3 hours each of oral communications, math, computer science, fine arts, and humanities, and 1 additional fine arts or humanity elective. **Procedure:** Freshmen are admitted to all sessions. Entrance exams should be taken in spring of the junior year or fall of the senior year. There are deferred admissions and rolling admissions plans. Applications should be filed by August 1 for fall entry; December 1 for spring entry; and May 1 for summer entry. The fall 2014 application fee was $25. Notification is sent on a rolling basis. Applications are accepted on-line. **Transfer Students:** 192 transfer students enrolled in 2013-2014. A minimum of a cumulative C average on all college-level study attempted must have been attained. This is a cumulative GPA of 2.0 or better on a 4.0 scale. Applicants must be in good standing-neither probation nor suspension can be in effect at the previous or current college of university attended. Transcripts of all previous study attempted must be submitted and evaluated before an application review can be conducted. Collegiate work from post-secondary institutions not accredited nor in candidacy status for accreditation by a regional accrediting association is not transferable to the University of Montevallo. Students who have completed less than 24 semester hours (or 36 quarter hours) of college-level study must also submit a secondary-school transcript and either an ACT or SAT score report and must satisfy all requirements for freshman admission. A maximum of 64 semester hours (or 96 quarter hours) may be transferred for credit from either a community or junior college. 33 of 130 credits required for the bachelor's degree must be completed at UM. **International Students:** There are 35 international students enrolled. They must take the TOEFL with a minimum score of 525 on the paper-based TOEFL (PBT) or 71 on the Internet-based version (iBT). They must also take the SAT or ACT.

ADMISSIONS: Greg Embry, Director of Admissions. E-Mail: *admissions@montevallo.edu* Web: *go.montevallo.edu*

FINANCIAL AID: 17% of undergraduate students work part-time. Average annual earnings from campus work are $4640. The FAFSA is required. The priority date for freshman financial aid applications for fall entry is March 1.

UNIVERSITY OF NORTH ALABAMA   B-1
www.una.edu

Florence, AL 35632	(256) 765-4608
	(800) TALKUNA
Fax: (256) 765-4960	Email: admissions@una.edu
Full-time: 2170 men, 2885 women	Faculty: 269; IIA, --$
Part-time: 429 men, 677 women	Ph.D.s: 68%
Graduate: 443 men, 605 women	Student/Faculty: 18 to 1
Year: semesters, summer session	Tuition: $5500 ($9500)
Room & Board: $4460	Freshman Class: n/av
ACT: required	CEEB CODE: 1735
Application Deadline: n/av	COMPETITIVE

The University of North Alabama, founded in 1872, is a public institution offering degree programs in arts and sciences, business, education, and nursing. Figures in the above capsule and in this profile are approximate. There are 4 undergraduate schools and 3 graduate schools. In addition to regional accreditation, UNA has baccalaureate program accreditation with AACSB, ABET, ACBSP, CSWE, NASAD, NASM, NCATE, and NLN. The 200-acre campus is in an urban area 116 miles north of Birmingham. Including any residence halls, there are 77 buildings.

STUDENT LIFE: 74% of undergraduates are from Alabama. Others are from 36 states, 53 foreign countries, and Canada. 89% are from public schools. 69% are White. The average age of freshmen is 20; all undergraduates, 23. 32% do not continue beyond their first year; 56% remain to graduate. **Housing:** 1563 students can be accommodated in college housing, which includes single-sex and coed dorms, on-campus apartments, off-campus apartments, and married student housing. In addition, there are fraternity houses, and an international house. On-campus housing is available on a first-come, first-served basis. 77% of students commute. Alcohol is not permitted. All students may keep cars.

FACULTY/CLASSROOMS: 53% of faculty are male; 47% are female. All teach undergraduates. No introductory courses are taught by graduate students.

PROGRAMS OF STUDY: UNA confers B.A., B.S., B.A.M., B.B.A., B.F.A., B.G.S., B.S.Ed., B.S.M., B.S.N. and B.S.W. degrees. Master's degrees are also awarded. Bachelor's degrees are awarded in BIOLOGICAL SCIENCE (biology/biological science and environmental biology), BUSINESS (accounting, banking and finance, business economics, and marketing/retailing/merchandising), COMMUNICATIONS AND THE ARTS (art, communications, dramatic arts, English, French, German, journalism, music, public relations, and Spanish), COMPUTER AND PHYSICAL SCIENCE (chemistry, computer science, geology, information sciences and systems, mathematics, and physics), EDUCATION (art education, business education, early childhood education, elementary education, foreign languages education, home economics education, music education, physical education, science education, secondary education, and social science education), ENGINEERING AND ENVIRONMENTAL DESIGN (interior design), HEALTH PROFESSIONS (industrial hygiene and nursing), SOCIAL SCIENCE (criminal justice, geography, history,

liberal arts/general studies, political science/government, psychology, social work, and sociology). Physical sciences, biological sciences and math are the strongest academically. Management, accounting, and marketing have the largest enrollments.

ACTIVITIES: 7% of men belong to 8 national fraternities; 13% of women belong to 7 national sororities. There are 91 groups on campus, including band, cheerleading, choir, chorus, computers, debate, drama, drill team, ethnic, film, honors, international, jazz band, literary magazine, marching band, musical theater, newspaper, pep band, photography, political, professional, radio and TV, religious, social, social service, and student government. Popular campus events include Spring Fling and George Lindsey Film Festival. **Sports:** There are 6 intercollegiate sports for men and 6 for women, and 20 intramural sports for men and 20 for women. Facilities include a 13,500-seat football stadium, a 4000-seat gym, baseball and softball fields, an outdoor track, indoor swimming pool, tennis courts, fitness center with a cardio theater, weights and machines, aerobics studio, gaming lounge, intramural field with 3 multipurpose courts, 2-lane track, and equipment checkout. **Graduates:** From July 1, 2013 to June 30, 2014, 915 bachelor's degrees were awarded. The most popular majors were business (30%), education (18%), and nursing (17%). 100 companies recruited on campus in 2013-2014. In an average class, 17% graduate in 4 years or less, 34% graduate in 5 years or less, and 39% graduate in 6 years or less.

SERVICES: Counseling and information services are available, as is tutoring in some subjects, including math, English, history, biology, chemistry, accounting, finance, and economics. There is a reader service for the blind, and remedial math and writing. An academic resource center features computer-assisted tutoring and faculty mentoring. **Library/Resources:** The 3 libraries contain 405,406 volumes, 1.1 million microform items, 14,236 audio/video tapes/CDs/DVDs, and subscribe to 3,711 periodicals including electronic. Computerized library services include interlibrary loans, database searching, Internet access, and Wi-Fi capability. Special learning facilities include an art gallery, planetarium, and radio station. **Physically Challenged Students:** 96% of the campus is accessible. Facilities include wheelchair ramps, elevators, special parking, specially equipped restrooms, special class scheduling, lowered drinking fountains, and lowered telephones. **Special:** University of North Alabama offers cooperative programs in all majors, work-study programs, various B.A.-B.S. degrees, dual majors and a general studies degree. Non-degree study is possible. There are 13 national honor societies, including Phi Beta Kappa, a freshman honors program, and 2 departmental honors programs. **Visiting:** There are regularly scheduled orientations for prospective students, including orientation programs conducted each summer prior to the fall semester. There are guides for informal visits. To schedule a visit, contact the Office of Admissions. **Campus Safety and Security:** Measures include 24-hour foot and vehicle patrol and emergency notification system. There are shuttle buses, emergency telephones, lighted pathways/sidewalks, and controlled access to dorms/residences.

REQUIREMENTS: The ACT is required. Applicants should be graduates of an accredited high school or have earned a GED. A GPA of 2.0 is required. AP and CLEP credits are accepted. Students must complete a core curriculum, which includes 12 semester hours in history, social and behavioral sciences, humanities, and fine arts, 11 in natural sciences and math, and 6 in language composition. Total number of hours in majors vary. Passing grades in 1 writing emphasis and 1 computer course also are needed. A minimum of 128 semester hours and a minimum GPA of 2.0 are required to graduate. **Procedure:** Freshmen are admitted fall, spring, and summer. Entrance exams should be taken in the senior year. There are deferred admissions and rolling admissions plans. Application deadlines are open. The fall 2014 application fee was $25. Applications are accepted online. **Transfer Students:** 707 transfer students enrolled in 2013-2014. Applicants should be eligible to return to the school last attended. 30 of 128 credits required for the bachelor's degree must be completed at UNA. **International Students:** There are 259 international students enrolled. The school actively recruits these students. They must take the TOEFL with a minimum score of 500 on the paper-based TOEFL (PBT).

ADMISSIONS CONTACT: Kim Mauldin, Director of Admissions. E-Mail: *admissions@una.edu* Web: *www.una.edu*

FINANCIAL AID: In 2014-2015, 59% of all full-time freshmen and

62% of continuing full-time students received some form of financial aid. 47% of all full-time freshmen and 52% of continuing full-time students received need-based aid. The average freshman award was $6,254. Need-based scholarships or need-based grants averaged $4,237; need-based self-help aid (loans and jobs) averaged $3,034; and non-need-based athletic scholarships averaged $2,598. 8% of undergraduate students work part-time. Average annual earnings from campus work are $2250. The FAFSA is required. Check with the school for current application deadlines.

UNIVERSITY OF SOUTH ALABAMA	A-5
www.southalabama.edu	

Mobile, AL 36688	**(251) 460-6141**
	(800) 872-5247
Fax: (251) 460-7023	Email: admiss@.usouthal.edu
Full-time: 3895 men, 4813 women	Faculty: 437; IIA, -$
Part-time: 1077 men, 1530 women	Ph.D.s: 76%
Graduate: 809 men, 2512 women	Student/Faculty: 21 to 1
Year: semesters, summer session	Tuition: $6360 ($12,720)
Room & Board: $7150	Freshman Class: 4770 applied, 4159 accepted, 1944 enrolled
SAT CR/M/W: 514/513/501 ACT: 23	CEEB CODE: 1880
Application Deadline: August 10	COMPETITIVE

The University of South Alabama, a state-supported institution established in 1963, offers undergraduate and graduate degrees in the allied health professions, arts and sciences, business and management studies, education, engineering, nursing, computer and information sciences, and medicine. Figures in the above capsule and in this profile are approximate. There are 9 undergraduate schools and 9 graduate schools. In addition to regional accreditation, USA has baccalaureate program accreditation with AACSB, ABET, AHEA, APTA, CAHEA, CSAB, NASAD, NASM, NCATE, and NLN. The 1224-acre campus is in a suburban area 150 miles east of New Orleans. Including any residence halls, there are 111 buildings.

STUDENT LIFE: 79% of undergraduates are from Alabama. Others are from 50 states, 87 foreign countries, and Canada. 67% are White; 19% African American. **Male To Female Ratio:** 1.5:1. The average age of all undergraduates is 23. 34% do not continue beyond their first year; 37% remain to graduate. **Housing:** 3098 students can be accommodated in college housing, which includes coed dorms, on-campus apartments, and married student housing. In addition, there are special-interest houses and fraternity houses. On-campus housing is available on a first-come and first-served basis. 75% of students commute. Alcohol is not permitted. All students may keep cars.

FACULTY/CLASSROOMS: 51% of faculty are male; 49% are female. No introductory courses are taught by graduate students.

PROGRAMS OF STUDY: USA confers B.A., B.S., B.F.A., B.Mus., B.S.B.A., B.S.Cardioresp.Sc., B.S.C.E., B.S.Ch.E., B.S.C.L.S., B.S.Comp.Eng., B.S.Ed., B.S.E.E., B.S.M.E., B.S.N., B.S.Preprof.Hlth.Sc., B.S.R.S. and B.S.Sp.Hear.Sc. degrees. Master's and doctoral degrees are also awarded. Bachelor's degrees are awarded in BIOLOGICAL SCIENCE (biology/biological science), BUSINESS (accounting, banking and finance, business administration and management, business economics, marketing/retailing/merchandising, and recreation and leisure services), COMMUNICATIONS AND THE ARTS (communications, dramatic arts, English, fine arts, languages, and music), COMPUTER AND PHYSICAL SCIENCE (atmospheric sciences and meteorology, chemistry, computer science, geology, mathematics, and physics), EDUCATION (early childhood education, education, elementary education, health education, physical education, secondary education, and special education), ENGINEERING AND ENVIRONMENTAL DESIGN (chemical engineering, civil engineering, computer engineering, electrical/electronics engineering, and mechanical engineering), HEALTH PROFESSIONS (biomedical science, emergency medical technologies, nursing, radiological science, respiratory therapy, and speech pathology/audiology), SOCIAL SCIENCE (anthropology, criminal justice, geography, history, international studies, philosophy, political science/government, psychology, social work, and soci-

ology). Business administration, nursing, and elementary education have the largest enrollments.

ACTIVITIES: There are 155 groups on campus, including art, band, cheerleading, chess, choir, chorale, chorus, computers, dance, debate, drama, ethnic, film, gay, honors, international, jazz band, literary magazine, marching band, musical theater, newspaper, opera, orchestra, pep band, political, professional, radio and TV, religious, social, social service, student government, and symphony. Popular campus events include Club South, Greek Week, and Chi Omega Songfest. **Sports:** There are 7 intercollegiate sports for men and 8 for women, and 15 intramural sports for men and 15 for women. Facilities include a 10,000-seat arena, 49,000-square-foot student recreation center, including 6 handball courts, fitness rooms, 2 basketball/volleyball courts, and an indoor track, several intramural fields, and an outdoor swimming pool. **Graduates:** From July 1, 2013 to June 30, 2014, 1669 bachelor's degrees were awarded. The most popular majors were nursing (20%), elementary education (7%), and interdisciplinary studies (6%). In an average class, 14% graduate in 4 years or less, 30% graduate in 5 years or less, and 37% graduate in 6 years or less.

SERVICES: Counseling and information services are available, as is tutoring in some subjects. There is a reader service for the blind, and remedial math, reading, and writing. **Library/Resources:** The 2 libraries contain 515,914 volumes, 723,399 microform items, and 14,413 audio/video tapes/CDs/DVDs. Computerized library services include interlibrary loans and database searching. Special learning facilities include an art gallery, radio station, TV station, the Dauphin Island Sea Lab. **Physically Challenged Students:** 90% of the campus is accessible. Facilities include wheelchair ramps, elevators, special parking, specially equipped restrooms, lowered drinking fountains, and lowered telephones. **Special:** University of South Alabama, offers co-op programs in most majors, federal work-study, internships, study abroad in many countries, dual majors, an adult degree program, and a personalized studies program. There are 43 national honor societies and a freshman honors program. **Visiting:** There are regularly scheduled orientations for prospective students, including 3 Saturday visiting days in November, February and April. There are guides for informal visits and visitors may sit in on classes. To schedule a visit, contact the Director of Admissions. **Campus Safety and Security:** Measures include 24-hour foot and vehicle patrol, emergency notification system, self-defense education, and security escort services. There are emergency telephones and lighted pathways/sidewalks.

REQUIREMENTS: The ACT is required. Applicants should be high school graduates or have a GED certificate. A minimum ACT score of 19 is required for regular admission. AP and CLEP credits are accepted. General education requirements consist of 12 hours in written composition, 12 hours in humanities and fine arts, at least 12 hours in history and the social and behavioral sciences, and 11 hours in natural science and math. A minimum of 128 semester hours, with a minimum GPA of 2.0, are required for graduation. **Procedure:** Freshmen are admitted to all sessions. Entrance exams should be taken during the junior year or early in the senior year. There are early admissions and rolling admissions plans. Applications should be filed by August 10 for fall entry; December 1 for spring entry; and May 1 for summer entry. The fall 2014 application fee was $35. **Transfer Students:** 1002 transfer students enrolled in 2013-2014. Transfer applicants must have at least a 2.0 GPA on all college work attempted for regular admission. 32 of 128 credits required for the bachelor's degree must be completed at USA. **International Students:** There are 377 international students enrolled. The school actively recruits these students. They must take the TOEFL with a minimum score of 61 on the Internet-based version (iBT) and the college's own test.

ADMISSIONS: 87% of the 2014-2015 applicants were accepted. The ACT scores were 33% below 21, 26% between 21 and 23, 23% between 24 and 26, 9% between 27 and 28, and 9% above 28. **Admissions Contact:** Norma Jean Tanner, Director of Admissions. E-Mail: *admiss@.usouthal.edu* Web: *www.southalabama.edu*

FINANCIAL AID: The FAFSA and the college's own financial statement are required. Check with the school for current application deadlines.

UNIVERSITY OF WEST ALABAMA   A-3
www.uwa.edu

Livingston, AL 35470	**(205) 652-3581**
	800-621-8044
Fax: (205) 652-3881	**Email: admissions@uwa.edu**
Full-time: 789 men, 1084 women	**Faculty:** n/av
Part-time: n/av	**Ph.D.s:** n/av
Graduate: 879 men, 1387 women	**Student/Faculty:** n/av
Year: semesters, summer session	**Tuition:** $8018 ($14,886)
Room & Board: $6256	**Freshman Class:** n/av
SAT or ACT: required	**CEEB CODE:** 1737
Application Deadline: open	**COMPETITIVE**

University of West Alabama, founded in 1835, is a state-controlled institution offering programs in liberal arts, sciences and mathematics, business and commerce, nursing, and education. There are 5 undergraduate schools and 1 graduate school. In addition to regional accreditation, UWA has baccalaureate program accreditation with ACBSP, NCATE, and NLN. The 514-acre campus is in a small town 35 miles east of Meridian, Mississippi. Including any residence halls, there are 51 buildings.

STUDENT LIFE: Male To Female Ratio: 1.5:1. **Housing:** 851 students can be accommodated in college housing, which includes single-sex dorms and on-campus apartments. In addition, there are honors houses. On-campus housing is guaranteed for all 4 years. Alcohol is not permitted. All students may keep cars.

FACULTY/CLASSROOMS: No introductory courses are taught by graduate students.

PROGRAMS OF STUDY: UWA confers B.A., B.S. and B.B.A. degrees. Associate and master's degrees are also awarded. Bachelor's degrees are awarded in BIOLOGICAL SCIENCE (biology/biological science and marine biology), BUSINESS (accounting and business administration and management), COMMUNICATIONS AND THE ARTS (English), COMPUTER AND PHYSICAL SCIENCE (chemistry, computer science, mathematics, and physics), EDUCATION (athletic training, early childhood education, elementary education, middle school education, physical education, science education, secondary education, and special education), ENGINEERING AND ENVIRONMENTAL DESIGN (environmental science and industrial engineering technology), HEALTH PROFESSIONS (predentistry and premedicine), SOCIAL SCIENCE (history, prelaw, psychology, social science, and sociology). English, business, and sciences are the strongest academically. Education, business, and biology comprehensive have the largest enrollments.

ACTIVITIES: Groups on campus include band, cheerleading, choir, chorus, communications, drama, drill team, ethnic, honors, international, jazz band, marching band, newspaper, pep band, photography, political, professional, radio and TV, religious, social, student government, symphony, and yearbook. Popular campus events include Springfest, Serendipity Talent Show, and Homecoming. **Sports:** There are 9 intercollegiate sports for men and 9 for women, and 12 intramural sports for men and 12 for women. Facilities include an 800-seat gym, 7500-seat football stadium, baseball field, tennis and racquetball courts, a pool, weight rooms, a lake, and hiking trails. **Graduates:** From July 1, 2013 to June 30, 2014, 226

bachelor's degrees were awarded. 128 companies recruited on campus in 2013-2014.

SERVICES: Counseling and information services are available, as is tutoring in most subjects. There is remedial math, reading, and writing. **Library/Resources:** Computerized library services include interlibrary loans, database searching, and Internet access. Special learning facilities include an art gallery, radio station, and TV station. **Physically Challenged Students:** All of the campus is accessible. Facilities include wheelchair ramps, elevators, special parking, specially equipped restrooms, special class scheduling, lowered drinking fountains, and special housing. **Special:** There are B.A., B.S. degrees in accounting, athletic training, biology, business administration, chemistry, computer information systems, early childhood education, elementary education, English, environmental science, history, industrial technology, integrated marketing communications, interdisciplinary arts, management, marine biology, marketing, mathematics, mathematics/ computer information systems, physical education, psychology, social work, sociology, special education, and technology. There are 3-2 programs in engineering with Auburn University, The University of Alabama at Birmingham, Mississippi State University, and the University of Alabama, forestry with Auburn University, nursing with the University of Alabama, and social work with the University of Alabama. There are 17 national honor societies, a freshman honors program, and 4 departmental honors programs. **Visiting:** There are regularly scheduled orientations for prospective students. There are guides for informal visits, visitors may sit in on classes, and stay overnight. To schedule a visit, contact the Admissions Office at admissions@uwa.edu. **Campus Safety and Security:** Measures include 24-hour foot and vehicle patrol. There are lighted pathways/sidewalks, controlled access to dorms/residences, SNAP night time student patrol.

REQUIREMENTS: The SAT or ACT is required. Students with a minimum composite score of 19 on the ACT can be admitted unconditionally. Students may be admitted conditionally with a ACT score of 17-18. In addition, applicants should have completed 15 high school credits or the GED equivalent. Applications are accepted online. AP and CLEP credits are accepted. To graduate, all students must complete at least 120 semester hours with a minimum GPA of 2.0. **Procedure:** Freshmen are admitted to all sessions. Entrance exams should be taken during the junior or senior year. There are early admissions, deferred admissions, and rolling admissions plans. Application deadlines are open. The fall 2014 application fee was $25. Notification is sent on a rolling basis. Applications are accepted online. **Transfer Students:** 254 transfer students enrolled in 2013-2014. Transfer applicants must have maintained a minimum GPA of 2.0 in all previous college courses. 30 of 120 credits required for the bachelor's degree must be completed at UWA. **International Students:** They must take the TOEFL with a minimum score of 500 on the paper-based TOEFL (PBT) or 61 on the Internet-based version (iBT). They must also take the SAT or ACT, scoring 19.

ADMISSIONS: Danny Buckalew, Vice President of Student Affairs. E-Mail: *admissions@uwa.edu* Web: *www.uwa.edu*

FINANCIAL AID: The FAFSA and CCS/Profile, or FFS, or SFS are required. The priority date for freshman financial aid applications for fall entry is February 15. The deadline for filing freshman financial aid applications for fall entry is rolling.

ALASKA

ALASKA PACIFIC UNIVERSITY   D-3
www.alaskapacific.edu

Anchorage, AK 99508   (907) 564-8248
                                                           (800) 252-7528
Fax: (907) 564-8317   Email: BMcDermott@alaskapacific.edu

Full-time: 125 men, 200 women	**Faculty:** n/av
Part-time: 60 men, 160 women	**Ph.D.s:** 60%
Graduate: 85 men, 190 women	**Student/Faculty:** 10 to 1
Year: 4-1-4, summer session	**Tuition:** $29,592
Room & Board: $14,000	**Freshman Class:** n/av
SAT or ACT: required	**CEEB CODE:** 4201
Application Deadline: n/av	**VERY COMPETITIVE**

Alaska Pacific University, founded in 1957 and affiliated with the United Methodist Church, is a private institution offering undergraduate, graduate, and adult degree-completion programs. Figures in the above capsule and in this profile are approximate. There are 6 undergraduate schools and 6 graduate schools. The 170-acre campus is in a suburban area in midtown Anchorage. Including any residence halls, there are 13 buildings.

STUDENT LIFE: 73% of undergraduates are from Alaska. Others are from 37 states, and 2 foreign countries. 68% are White; 18% American Indian/Alaska Native. **Male To Female Ratio:** 2.0:1. The average age of freshmen is 25; all undergraduates, 30. 25% do not continue beyond their first year; 36% remain to graduate. **Housing:** 170 students can be accommodated in college housing, which includes coed dorms and on-campus apartments. In addition, there are special-interest houses. On-campus housing is guaranteed for the freshman year only, is available on a first-come, first-served basis, and is available on a lottery system for upperclassmen. 73% of students commute. Alcohol is not permitted. All students may keep cars.

FACULTY/CLASSROOMS: 42% of faculty are male; 58% are female. 98% teach undergraduates. No introductory courses are taught by graduate students. The average class size in an introductory lecture is 12; in a laboratory is 9; and in a regular course is 10.

PROGRAMS OF STUDY: APU confers B.A., and B.S. degrees. Associate and master's degrees are also awarded. Bachelor's degrees are awarded in AGRICULTURE (environmental studies and natural resource management), BIOLOGICAL SCIENCE (marine biology), BUSINESS (business administration and management and recreational facilities management), COMPUTER AND PHYSICAL SCIENCE (earth science), EDUCATION (elementary education), ENGINEERING AND ENVIRONMENTAL DESIGN (environmental science), HEALTH PROFESSIONS (health care administration), SOCIAL SCIENCE (human services, liberal arts/general studies, and psychology). Environmental science, outdoor studies, and psychology have the largest enrollments.

ACTIVITIES: There are no fraternities or sororities. There are 18 groups on campus, including departmental, art, band, chorus, drama, ethnic, international, newspaper, photography, professional, religious, social service, student government, and students in free enterprise. Popular campus events include Earth Day, Spring Honors Convocation and Fall Academic Convocation. **Sports:** There is no sports program at APU. Facilities include a 300-seat sports center, an indoor swimming pool, cross-country skiing and running trails, climbing wall, soccer field, lake for boating, and a weight/exercise room.

SERVICES: Counseling and information services are available, as is tutoring in some subjects, math, writing, and other subjects as needed. There is remedial math and writing. **Library/Resources:** The library contains 891,103 volumes, 627,916 microform items, 13,324 audio/video tapes/CDs/DVDs, and subscribes to 3,840 periodicals including electronic. Computerized library services include interlibrary loans and Internet access. Special learning facilities include an art gallery, TV station, the Alaskana collection located in the Consortium Library. **Physically Challenged Students:** 75% of the campus is accessible. Facilities include wheelchair ramps, elevators, special parking, specially equipped restrooms, lowered drinking fountains, and lowered telephones. **Special:** Internships are required, and study abroad, student-designed majors, and B.A.-B.S. degrees in earth sciences, environmental science, and marine biology are possible. Accelerated degrees are offered through the Degree Completion Program for working adults in business administration management, accounting information for management, human services, and health services administration. There are 2 national honor societies and 2 departmental honors programs. **Visiting:** There are guides for informal visits, visitors may sit in on classes, and stay overnight. To schedule a visit, contact the Admissions Office. **Campus Safety and Security:** Measures include 24-hour foot and vehicle patrol, self-defense education, and security escort services. There are emergency telephones, lighted pathways/sidewalks, safety signs are posted as needed.

REQUIREMENTS: The SAT or ACT is required, with a satisfactory score on the SAT or at least 19 on the ACT. Two teacher recommendations and an essay are required. A GED is acceptable in lieu of a high school transcript. A GPA of 2.5 is required. AP and CLEP credits are accepted. Important factors in the admissions decision are advanced placement or honors courses, leadership record, and recommendations by school officials. All students must complete at least 128 semester hours, with 39 to 61 in the major, and maintain a minimum GPA of 2.0. Distribution requirements include 4 semester hours each in Orientation to Active Learning, a lab science, a course in social/behavioral science, and a course in ethics or religion; 2 courses in humanities; a sophomore seminar in the major; and a world language course that includes American Sign Language. Courses to meet writing, speech, and quantitative skills competencies are also required, as well as a 3-semester-hour practicum, portfolio, and senior project. **Procedure:** Freshmen are admitted to all sessions. Entrance exams should be taken before January of the senior year. There is a rolling admissions plan. Check with the school for current application deadlines. The application fee is $25. Applications are accepted on-line. **Transfer Students:** 80 transfer students enrolled in 2013-2014. Transfer applicants must have a 2.0 cumulative GPA. 32 of 128 credits required for the bachelor's degree must be completed at APU. **International Students:** They must take the TOEFL with a minimum score of 550 on the paper-based TOEFL (PBT) or 79 on the Internet-based version (iBT). They must also take the SAT or ACT.

ADMISSIONS: 1 freshman graduated first in the class. **Admissions Contact:** Brian McDermott, Assistant Director of Admissions. E-Mail: *BMcDermott@alaskapacific.edu* Web: *www.alaskapacific.edu*

FINANCIAL AID: APU is a member of CSS. The FAFSA is required. Check with the school for current application deadlines.

UNIVERSITY OF ALASKA SYSTEM

The University of Alaska, established in 1975, is a private system in Alaska. It is governed by a board of regents whose chief administrator is the president. The primary goal of the system is teaching, research, and public service. The main priorities are maintaining open access to students to prepare them for and provide rigorous postsecondary programs; providing the cultural populations of Alaska with appropriate vocational and academic education; and conducting research with emphasis on arctic areas and issues. The total student enrollment is usually about 27,500 with 2000 faculty members. Altogether there are 120 baccalaureate, 85 master's, 13 doctoral programs offered in the University of Alaska System. Profiles of the 4-year campuses are included in this section.

UNIVERSITY OF ALASKA ANCHORAGE *(The complete profile is made available exclusively on our website, www.barronspac.com)*

UNIVERSITY OF ALASKA FAIRBANKS   D-2
www.uaf.edu

Fairbanks, AK 99775	(907) 474-7500
	(800) 478-1823
Fax: (907) 474-7097	Email: admissions@uaf.edu
Full-time: 1768 men, 1723 women	Faculty: 361; I, --$
Part-time: 1437 men, 2635 women	Ph.D.s: 71%
Graduate: 466 men, 671 women	Student/Faculty: 7 to 1
Year: semesters, summer session	Tuition: $6890 ($20,600)
Room & Board: $8240	Freshman Class: 1216 applied, 751 accepted, 519 enrolled
SAT CR/M/W: 560/560/530 ACT: 24	CEEB CODE: 4866
Application Deadline: June 15	COMPETITIVE

The University of Alaska Fairbanks, founded in 1917, is the nation's northernmost Land, Sea, and Space Grant university and international research center. The institution advances and disseminates knowledge through teaching, research, and public service with an emphasis on Alaska and circumpolar regions. There are 8 undergraduate schools and 8 graduate schools. In addition to regional accreditation, UAF has baccalaureate program accreditation with AACSB, ABET, ACEJMC, CSWE, NASM, and SAF. The 2250-acre campus is in a small town 4 miles northwest of Fairbanks. Including any residence halls, there are 67 buildings.

STUDENT LIFE: 83% of undergraduates are from Alaska. Others are from 46 states, 24 foreign countries, and Canada. 48% are White; 32% race unknown. The average age of freshmen is 18; all undergraduates, 23. 22% do not continue beyond their first year; 42% remain to graduate. **Housing:** 1578 students can be accommodated in college housing, which includes coed dorms, on-campus apartments, and married student housing, first-year experience residence, and Alaska native cultural housing. On-campus housing is available on a first-come and first-served basis. 57% of students live on campus. All students may keep cars.

FACULTY/CLASSROOMS: 59% of faculty are male; 41% are female. 54% teach undergraduates, 76% do research, and 40% do both. No introductory courses are taught by graduate students. The average class size in an introductory lecture is 20; in a laboratory is 15; and in a regular course is 18.

PROGRAMS OF STUDY: UAF confers B.A., B.S., B.B.A., B.A.S., B.E.M., B.F.A., B.M. and B.T. degrees. Associate, master's, and doctoral degrees are also awarded. Bachelor's degrees are awarded in AGRICULTURE (fishing and fisheries and natural resource management), BIOLOGICAL SCIENCE (biology/biological science and wildlife biology), BUSINESS (accounting and business administration and management), COMMUNICATIONS AND THE ARTS (art, communications, English, Eskimo, film arts, French, German, journalism, linguistics, music, Spanish, and theatre arts), COMPUTER AND PHYSICAL SCIENCE (applied physics, chemistry, computer science, earth science, geology, geoscience, mathematics, physics, science, and statistics), EDUCATION (education, elementary education, and secondary education), ENGINEERING AND ENVIRONMENTAL DESIGN (civil engineering, computer engineering, electrical/electronics engineering, emergency/disaster science, engineering, geological engineering, mechanical engineering, mining and mineral engineering, and petroleum/natural gas engineering), SOCIAL SCIENCE (anthropology, area studies, child care/child and family studies, economics, geography, history, homeland security, interdisciplinary studies, Japanese studies, philosophy, political science/government, psychology, rural economics, Russian and Slavic studies, social work, and sociology). Engineering, fisheries, and biology are the strongest academically. Biological sciences, mechanical engineering, and business administration have the largest enrollments.

ACTIVITIES: There are 160 groups on campus, including art, band, chess, choir, chorus, communications, computers, dance, drama, environmental, ethnic, film, gay, honors, international, jazz band, literary magazine, newspaper, orchestra, photography, political, professional, radio and TV, religious, social, student government, and symphony. Popular campus events include Starvation Gulch, All-Campus Day, and Meltdown. **Sports:** There are 5 intercollegiate sports for men and 6 for women, and 7 intramural sports for men and 7 for women. Facilities include a 4500-seat arena, 2000-seat gym, 1500-seat skating rink, 2 racquetball courts, 2 weight rooms, 4 basketball courts, an Olympic-size swimming pool, small-bore rifle range, and a lighted 30-mile ski trail. **Graduates:** From July 1, 2013 to June 30, 2014, 579 bachelor's degrees were awarded. The most popular majors were biological sciences (8%), business administration (7%), and psychology (6%). 89 companies recruited on campus in 2013-2014. In an average class, 1% graduate in 3 years or less, 15% graduate in 4 years or less, 33% graduate in 5 years or less, and 42% graduate in 6 years or less.

SERVICES: Counseling and information services are available, as is tutoring in some subjects, chemistry, calculus, languages, biology, math, physics, geology, and English. There is a reader service for the blind, and remedial math, reading, and writing. **Library/Resources:** The 3 libraries contain 1.2 million volumes, 133,755 microform items, 95,528 audio/video tapes/CDs/DVDs, and subscribe to 55,685 periodicals including electronic. Computerized library services include interlibrary loans, database searching, Internet access, and Wi-Fi capability. Special learning facilities include an art gallery, natural history museum, radio station, TV station, several research institutes and labs for study in the physical and natural sciences are associated with the university. **Physically Challenged Students:** 90% of the campus is accessible. Facilities include wheelchair ramps, elevators, special parking, specially equipped restrooms, special class scheduling, lowered drinking fountains, lowered telephones, special housing, shuttle bus, and a swimming pool equipped with hydraulic lifts. **Special:** The university's Office of eLearning and Distance Education offers satellite education programs to Alaska residents to reach students at remote sites. Study abroad is offered in 42 countries. Internships are offered through the Rural Alaska Honors Institute. Student-designed majors, credit/no credit options, nondegree study, and credit for life, military, and work experience are also available. There are 7 national honor societies and a freshman honors program. **Visiting:** There are regularly scheduled orientations for prospective students tours generally include academic facilities, dorms, and student recreation center, and may also include meeting with an admissions counselor, professors, advisors, and students, and classroom visits. There are guides for informal visits, visitors may sit in on classes, and stay overnight. To schedule a visit, contact UAF Office of Admissions. **Campus Safety and Security:** Measures include 24-hour foot and vehicle patrol, emergency notification system, self-defense education, and security escort services. There are shuttle buses, emergency telephones, lighted pathways/sidewalks, controlled access to dorms/residences, 24-hour crisis line, evening patrols inside dorms.

REQUIREMENTS: The SAT or ACT is required. Applicants should be graduates of an accredited secondary school with 16 academic credits, including 4 in English and 3 each in math, natural or physical sciences, and social sciences, with a minimum GPA of 2.5 in these courses. Applicants should have an overall high school GPA of at least 3.0 or an overall GPA of at least 2.5 along with an ACT Plus Writing score of at least 18 or SAT total score of at least 1290. The GED is not accepted. A GPA of 2.5 is required. AP and CLEP credits are accepted. All students must complete core courses in English and oral communication, library skills, humanities, social science, natural science, and math. A minimum of 120 credit hours, with 27 to 30 in the major, and a 2.0 GPA are required for graduation. **Procedure:** Freshmen are admitted fall, spring, and summer. Entrance exams should be taken during one year of applying. There are early admissions, deferred admissions, and rolling admissions plans. Applications should be filed by June 15 for fall entry; November 1 for spring entry; and May 1 for summer entry, along with a $50 fee. Notification is sent on a rolling basis. Applications are accepted on-line. **Transfer Students:** 254 transfer students enrolled in 2013-2014. A GPA of 2.0 in all previous college work and an honorable dismissal from all schools attended are required. Applicants with fewer than 30 semester hours of transferable credit also must have a high school GPA of 2.0 and ACT or SAT scores. 30 of 120 credits required for the bachelor's degree must be completed at UAF. **International Students:** There are 48 international students enrolled. The school actively recruits these students. They must take the TOEFL with a minimum score of 550 on the paper-based TOEFL (PBT) or 79 on the Internet-based version (iBT), or take the IELTS. They must also take the SAT or ACT.

ADMISSIONS: 62% of the 2014-2015 applicants were accepted. The SAT scores for the 2014-2015 freshman class were: Critical Reading--21% below 500, 39% between 500 and 599, 33% between 600 and 699, and 7% between 700 and 800; Math--21% below 500, 42% between 500 and 599, 30% between 600 and 699, and 6% between 700 and 800; Writing--38% below 500, 39% between 500 and 599, 22% between 600 and 699, and 1% between 700 and 800. The ACT scores were 23% below 21, 26% between 21 and 23, 24% between 24 and 26, 15% between 27 and 28, and 12% above 28. 43% of the current freshmen were in the top fifth of their class; 73% were in the top two fifths. 20 freshmen graduated first in their class. **Admissions Contact:** Libby Eddy, Registrar and Director of Admissions. E-Mail: *admissions@uaf.edu* Web: *http://www.uaf.edu/admissions/*

FINANCIAL AID: In 2014-2015, 92% of all full-time freshmen and 77% of continuing full-time students received some form of financial aid. 48% of all full-time freshmen and 51% of continuing full-time students received need-based aid. The average freshman award was $9,290. Need-based scholarships or need-based grants averaged $7,172 ($22,684 maximum); need-based self-help aid (loans and jobs) averaged $5,913 ($13,749 maximum); non-need-based athletic scholarships averaged $16,838 ($37,050 maximum); and other non-need-based awards and non-need-based scholarships averaged $9,490 ($43,304 maximum). 18% of undergraduate students work part-time. Average annual earnings from campus work are $5320. The average financial indebtedness of the 2014 graduate was $29,906. The FAFSA is required. The priority date for freshman financial aid applications for fall entry is February 15. The deadline for filing freshman financial aid applications for fall entry is June 30.

UNIVERSITY OF ALASKA SOUTHEAST   F-3
www.usa.alaska.edu

Juneau, AK 99801	(907) 465-6457
	(877) 465-4827
Fax: (907) 465-6365	Email: jyuas@alaska.edu
Full-time: 270 men, 325 women	Faculty: IIA, -$
Part-time: 625 men, 875 women	Ph.D.s: n/av
Graduate: 70 men, 80 women	Student/Faculty: n/av
Year: semesters, summer session	Tuition: $5693
Room & Board: $8317	Freshman Class: n/av
SAT or ACT: recommended	CEEB CODE: 4897
Application Deadline: open	COMPETITIVE

The University of Alaska Southeast, a multicampus institution founded in 1972, is part of the University of Alaska statewide system, with baccalaureate programs offered in business and public administration, education, and liberal arts and science. There are 4 undergraduate schools and 2 graduate schools. The 198-acre campus is in a suburban area 10 miles north of Juneau. Including any residence halls, there are 18 buildings.

STUDENT LIFE: 75% of undergraduates are from Alaska. Others are from 37 states, 12 foreign countries, and Canada. 95% are from public schools. 70% are White; 17% American Indian/Alaska Native. **Male To Female Ratio:** 1.3:1. The average age of freshmen is 18; all undergraduates, 24. **Housing:** 400 students can be accommodated in college housing, which includes single-sex dorms, on-campus apartments, and married student housing. On-campus housing is available on a first-come and first-served basis. Priority is given to out-of-town students. 90% of students commute. All students may keep cars.

FACULTY/CLASSROOMS: 98% teach undergraduates. No introductory courses are taught by graduate students. The average class size in an introductory lecture is 20 and in a laboratory is 12.

PROGRAMS OF STUDY: UAS confers B.A., B.S., B.B.A., B.Ed. and B.L.A. degrees. Associate and master's degrees are also awarded. Bachelor's degrees are awarded in BIOLOGICAL SCIENCE (biology/biological science and marine biology), BUSINESS (accounting and business administration and management), COMMUNICATIONS AND THE ARTS (art, communications, literature, and speech/debate/rhetoric), COMPUTER AND PHYSICAL SCIENCE (mathematics), EDUCATION (elementary education), ENGINEERING AND ENVIRONMENTAL DESIGN (environmental science), SOCIAL SCIENCE (liberal arts/general studies, political science/government, public administration, and social science). Accounting, marine biology and environmental science are the strongest academically. Liberal arts has the largest enrollment.

ACTIVITIES: There are no fraternities or sororities. There are 16 groups on campus, including choir, ethnic, gay, honors, literary magazine, newspaper, political, professional, religious, and student government. Popular campus events include Ski Day, Whale-watching, and Eagle Preserve Field Trips. **Sports:** There are 3 intramural sports for men and 3 for women. Facilities include a community gym and pool, an activity center, and access to health club facilities.

SERVICES: Counseling and information services are available, as is tutoring in most subjects. There is a reader service for the blind, and remedial math, reading, and writing. **Library/Resources:** The library contains 250,000 volumes, 250,000 microform items, 1,850 audio/

video tapes/CDs/DVDs, and subscribes to 1,500 periodicals including electronic. Computerized library services include interlibrary loans, database searching, and Internet access. **Physically Challenged Students:** 95% of the campus is accessible. Facilities include wheelchair ramps, elevators, special parking, specially equipped restrooms, lowered drinking fountains, and lowered telephones. **Special:** UAS offers cross-registration through the National Student Exchange, and internships with federal and state agencies. Study abroad, work-study, dual and student-designed majors, credit/no credit options, and credit for military experience are also available. The School of Career and Continuing Education offers courses and certificate programs in technological skills. **Visiting:** There are regularly scheduled orientations for prospective students. There are guides for informal visits and visitors may sit in on classes. **Campus Safety and Security:** There are shuttle buses, emergency telephones, lighted pathways/sidewalks, late-night security at student housing.

REQUIREMENTS: The SAT or ACT is recommended. Applicants should be graduates of an accredited secondary school or have the GED. A GPA of 2.0 is required. AP and CLEP credits are accepted.

All students are required to complete general education courses, including 15 credits in humanities and social science, 10 in math and natural sciences, 6 in written communication skills, and 3 in speech. A total of 120 semester credits, with at least 36 in the major, and a minimum GPA of 2.0 are required in order to graduate. In the liberal arts program, a portfolio is required. **Procedure:** Freshmen are admitted fall and spring. There are early admissions, deferred admissions, and rolling admissions plans. Application deadlines are open. The fall 2014 application fee was $35. **Transfer Students:** A minimum GPA of 2.0 from an accredited institution is required. 30 of 120 credits required for the bachelor's degree must be completed at UAS. **International Students:** They must take the TOEFL. They must also take the SAT or ACT.

ADMISSIONS: Greg Wagner, Director of Admissions. E-Mail: *jyuas@alaska.edu* Web: *www.usa.alaska.edu*

FINANCIAL AID: UAS is a member of CSS. The FAFSA and the college's own financial statement are required. Check with the school for current application deadlines.

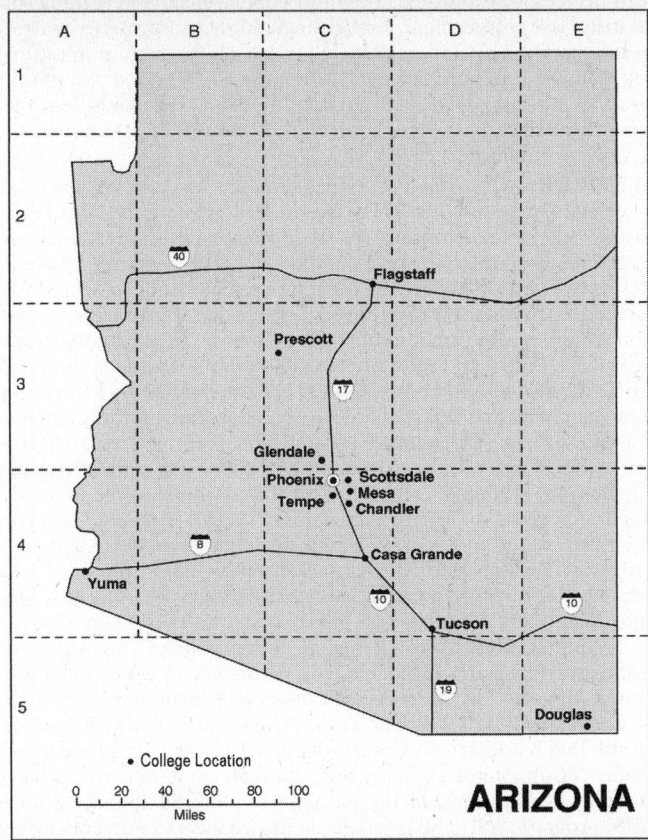

- College Location

```
0   20  40  60  80  100
        Miles
```

ARIZONA

AMERICAN INDIAN COLLEGE   C-4
www.aicag.edu

Phoenix, AZ 85021	(602) 944-3335, ext.244
	(800) 933-3828
Fax: (602) 943-8299	Email: jsaggio@aicag.edu
Full-time: 50 men, 45 women	Faculty: n/av
Part-time: 15 men, 20 women	Ph.D.s: n/av
Graduate: n/av	Student/Faculty: n/av
Year: semesters	Tuition: $11,940
Room & Board: $6202	Freshman Class: n/av
SAT or ACT: required	CEEB CODE: 2597
Application Deadline: open	COMPETITIVE

American Indian College, founded in 1957, is a Christian college with a specific mission of preparing American Indians for leadership in churches, education, and the community. The figures in the above capsule and in this profile are approximate. The 10-acre campus is in a small town in north Phoenix, just east of I17 and the Metrocenter area. Including any residence halls, there are 9 buildings.

STUDENT LIFE: 72% of undergraduates are from Arizona. Others are from 10 states, and 1 foreign country. 85% are from public schools. 67% are American Indian/Alaska Native; 18% White. 100% are Protestant. **Male To Female Ratio:** Is 1:1. The average age of freshmen is 23; all undergraduates, 26. **Housing:** 80 students can be accommodated in college housing, which includes single-sex dorms and off-campus apartments. 52% of students live on campus; of those, 100% remain on campus on weekends. Alcohol is not permitted. All students may keep cars.

FACULTY/CLASSROOMS: 65% of faculty are male; 35% are female. All teach undergraduates. No introductory courses are taught by graduate students. The average class size in an introductory lecture is 11; in a laboratory is 6; and in a regular course is 6.

PROGRAMS OF STUDY: AIC confers B.A. degrees. Associate degrees are also awarded. Bachelor's degrees are awarded in EDUCATION (elementary education), SOCIAL SCIENCE (ministries).

ACTIVITIES: There are no fraternities or sororities. Groups on campus include band, cheerleading, drama, ethnic, religious, student government, and yearbook. Popular campus events include Missions Conventions, and College Days. **Sports:** There is no sports program at AIC. Facilities include a full-size gym with a locker room and a weight room.

SERVICES: Counseling and information services are available, as is tutoring in most subjects. There is remedial math, reading, and writing. **Library/Resources:** The library contains 20,000 volumes, 35 audio/video tapes/CDs/DVDs, and subscribes to 102 periodicals including electronic. Computerized library services include Internet access. **Physically Challenged Students:** All of the campus is accessible. Facilities include wheelchair ramps, special parking, specially equipped restrooms, and lowered drinking fountains. **Special:** Internships and dual majors are available. **Visiting:** There are regularly scheduled orientations for prospective students, consisting of College Days in the fall and spring semesters that include class visits, overnight stays in dorms, and meals in the cafeteria for 2 days. There are guides for informal visits, visitors may sit in on classes, and stay overnight. To schedule a visit, contact the Admissions Office. **Campus Safety and Security:** There are lighted pathways/sidewalks, night security.

REQUIREMENTS: The SAT or ACT is required. Transcripts from high school and any other secondary schools attended are required along with a pastor's reference form. Applicants are required to take placement tests with satisfactory results. A 2.0 GPA is required and the GED is accepted. A GPA of 2.0 is required. AP and CLEP credits are accepted. Important factors in the admissions decision are advanced placement or honors courses, evidence of special talent, and extracurricular activities record.To graduate, all students must maintain a GPA of 2.0 and complete 128 total credits. Students must complete courses in history, science, math, computer, and bible studies. A comprehensive bible exam is required. **Procedure:** Freshmen are admitted to all sessions. Entrance exams should be taken prior to acceptance. There are early decision, early admissions, and deferred admissions plans. Application deadlines are open. **Transfer Students:** Official transcripts from high school and each college attended, plus a pastor's reference form are required. Students must demonstrate proficiency in English, writing, math, and reading. 30 of 128 credits required for the bachelor's degree must be completed at AIC. **International Students:** They must take the TOEFL. They must also take the SAT or ACT.

ADMISSIONS: Dr. Joseph Saggio, Vice President for Academic Affairs. E-Mail: *jsaggio@aicag.edu* Web: *www.aicag.edu*

FINANCIAL AID: The FAFSA is required. Check with the school for current application deadlines.

ARIZONA BOARD OF REGENTS

The Arizona Board of Regents, established in 1945, is a private system in Arizona. It is governed by a board of regents, whose chief administrator is the executive director and chief executive officer. The primary goal of the system is teaching, research, and service. The main priorities are to provide strong undergraduate instruction programs; to conduct extensive research and graduate instruction programs; and to ensure access for qualified Arizona residents, especially underrepresented ethnic minorities. The total student enrollment is usually about 116,166 with 3550 faculty members. Altogether there are 389 baccalaureate, 311 masters, and 180 doctoral programs offered in the Arizona Board of Regents. Profiles of the 4-year campuses are included in this section.

ARIZONA STATE UNIVERSITY, AT THE DOWNTOWN PHOENIX CAMPUS
www.campus.asu.edu/downtown

Phoenix, AZ 85004   **(480) 965-7788**

Fax: (480) 965-3610   **Email:** admissions@asu.edu
Full-time: 2672 men, 5395 women   **Faculty:** n/av
Part-time: 416 men, 667 women   **Ph.D.s:** n/av
Graduate: 547 men, 1520 women   **Student/Faculty:** n/av
Year: semesters, summer session   **Tuition:** $10,127 ($24,503)
Room & Board: $11,974   **Freshman Class:** 4835 applied, 3813 accepted, 1154 enrolled
SAT CR/M: 540/540 **ACT:** 23   **CEEB CODE:** 4007
Application Deadline: February 1   **COMPETITIVE**

Arizona State University at the Downtown Phoenix Campus in metropolitan Phoenix, the nation's sixth-largest city, creates strong academic and career connections for students with media, health care, corporate and government organizations. State-of-the-art living and learning facilities offer students a high-quality academic experience woven into the Valley's metropolitan core. The campus is near Phoenix's major sports, performing arts and cultural venues. ASU's vision is to establish ASU as the model for a New American University, measured not by who we exclude, but by who we include and how they succeed; pursuing research and discovery that benefits the public good; and assuming major responsibility for the economic, social, and cultural vitality and health and well-being of the community. ASU champions intellectual and cultural diversity. Its research is inspired by real-world application, blurring the boundaries that traditionally separate academic disciplines. There are 6 undergraduate schools and 6 graduate schools. In addition to regional accreditation, Downtown Phoenix campus has baccalaureate program accreditation with ACEJMC, ADA, CCNE, NAACLS, COAPRT and CSWE. The 17-acre campus is in an urban area in Phoenix, AZ. Including any residence halls, there are 21 buildings.

STUDENT LIFE: 75% of undergraduates are from Arizona. Others are from all 50 states, 26 foreign countries, and Canada. 94% of the resident undergraduates are from public schools. 53% are White; 27% Hispanic. **Male To Female Ratio:** 2.1:1. The average age of freshmen is 18; all undergraduates, 23. **Housing:** 1253 students can be accommodated in college housing, which includes coed dorms. In addition, there are honors houses and special-interest houses. On-campus housing is guaranteed for the freshman year only, is available on a first-come, and first-served basis. 84% of students commute. Alcohol is not permitted. All students may keep cars.

FACULTY/CLASSROOMS: The average class size in an introductory lecture is 35; in a laboratory is 21; and in a regular course is 31.

PROGRAMS OF STUDY: Downtown Phoenix campus confers B.A.S., B.A., B.A.E., B.S., B.G.S., B.I.S., B.S.N. and B.S.W. degrees. Master's and doctoral degrees are also awarded. Bachelor's degrees are awarded in BIOLOGICAL SCIENCE (nutrition), BUSINESS (nonprofit/public organization management and tourism), COMMUNICATIONS AND THE ARTS (communication and journalism - news & information), COMPUTER AND PHYSICAL SCIENCE (applied science), EDUCATION (health education), HEALTH PROFESSIONS (health science, nursing, nutrition and dietetics, public health, and sports medicine), SOCIAL SCIENCE (criminal justice, interdisciplinary studies, parks and recreation management, social work, and urban and regional studies). Criminal justice and criminology, journalism and mass communication, and health sciences have the largest enrollments.

ACTIVITIES: There are 93 groups on campus, including health, technology and sports, art, band, communications, debate, entrepreneurship, ethnic, gay, honors, international, musical theater, newspaper, photography, political, professional, radio and TV, religious, social, and social service. Popular campus events include Taylor Fest, Sparky's Carnival, Welcome Back BBQ, Homecoming Dance, Spring Luau, Movies in the Park. **Sports:** There are 10 intercollegiate sports for men and 13 for women, and 15 intramural sports for men and 15 for women. Facilities include a fitness complex and recreation

center. **Graduates:** From July 1, 2013 to June 30, 2014, 2128 bachelor's degrees were awarded. The most popular majors were homeland security, law enforcement, firefighting and related protective (18%), health professions and related programs (17%), communications, journalism, and and related programs (17%). 166 companies recruited on campus in 2013-2014. Of the 2013 graduating class, 18% were enrolled in graduate school within 6 months of graduation, and 84% were employed.

SERVICES: Counseling and information services are available, as is tutoring in most subjects. There is a reader service for the blind. Face-to-face and online tutoring are free to students. Academic success courses and graduate test preparation are also available. Disability Resource Centers support the learning needs of students with documented disabilities. **Library/Resources:** The library contains 4.5 million volumes, 7.8 million microform items, 152,490 audio/video tapes/CDs/DVDs, and subscribes to 60,941 periodicals including electronic. Computerized library services include interlibrary loans, database searching, and Internet access. Special learning facilities include a radio station, TV station, writing labs, tutoring, research labs, instructional kitchen, news studio, and news museum. **Physically Challenged Students:** 99% of the campus is accessible. Facilities include wheelchair ramps, elevators, special parking, specially equipped restrooms, special class scheduling, lowered telephones. There are flashing alarms for the deaf, braille maps, modified residence hall rooms and an adaptive exercise program and facility. **Special:** ASU offers domestic and international internships in a variety of disciplines, study abroad programs in more than 55 countries and work study programs. Students may participate in educational programs supported by a variety of centers and institutes, such as the Morrison Institute for Public Policy, Center for Applied Behavioral Health Policy and Knight Center for Digital Media Entrepreneurship. Students gain interdisciplinary skills through combining two areas of study from disciplines in the Bachelors of Interdisciplinary Studies (BIS) program. ASU also offers students two ways to earn concurrent degrees; students can choose to create their own combination degree programs to match their personal or professional interest or choose from a special, predetermined combination. Accelerated degree options are also available for many degree programs. ASU has Semesters (15 week schedule) and Sessions (7.5 week schedule) allowing students flexibility in choosing their schedule. There are 2 national honor societies and an undergraduate honors program. **Visiting:** There are regularly scheduled orientations for prospective students. There are guides for informal visits and visitors may sit in on classes. **Campus Safety and Security:** Measures include 24-hour foot and vehicle patrol, emergency notification system, self-defense education, and security escort services. There are shuttle buses, emergency telephones, lighted pathways/sidewalks, controlled access to dorms/residences, in-room safes, A text messaging alert system (limited to those who sign up); surveillance cameras may be located in residence halls.

REQUIREMENTS: The SAT is recommended. Applicants must successfully complete ASU competency requirements. 4-years English (composition/literature based), 4 years Math (Algebra l, Geometry, Algebra ll and one course requiring Algebra ll as a prerequisite), 3 years Laboratory Science- 3 year total (1 year each from any of the following areas are accepted: Biology, Chemistry, Earth Science, Integrated Science, and Physics), 2 years Social Science (including one year American History), 2 years Foreign Language (same language) and 1 year Fine Arts. Applicants must also meet at least one of the following: top 25% in high school graduating class, 3.0 GPA in competency courses (4.0=A), ACT 22 (24 nonresidents), SAT Reasoning 1040 (1110 nonresidents). All students who don't meet the above standards will be evaluated through a process called Individual Review. Through this process Undergraduate Admissions will review all available information about a student's application, carefully considering all aspects of a student's academic background and accomplishments. Submission of an ACT or SAT test score is highly recommended. In some cases, additional information might be requested. ASU welcomes home school students and recognizes the unique academic experiences they contribute to our rich community of scholars. A GPA of 3.0 is required. AP and CLEP credits are accepted.In order to graduate, students must have a minimum cumulative grade point average of 2.0 (some programs may require a higher

GPA) and a minimum total of 120 credit hours, including a minimum of 45 hours in upper division courses. The number of hours in the major varies by degree program, some programs may require more upper division work. All students must satisfy a minimum of 35 credit hours of approved General Studies course work in five core areas and three awareness areas: mathematics studies, literacy and critical inquiry, humanities, fine arts, design, social and behavioral sciences, natural sciences, global awareness, historical awareness, and cultural diversity in the United States. **Procedure:** Freshmen are admitted fall and spring. There is a rolling admissions plan. Applications should be filed by February 1 for fall entry; December 1 for spring entry, along with a $50 fee. Applications are accepted on-line. **Transfer Students:** 1285 transfer students enrolled in 2013-2014. Requirements are one of the following: official high school transcript with high school graduation date; GED with acceptable score of 500 or above; official college transcript with Associate degree posted (including award date); official college transcript with Associate degree in progress posted (including expected award date). 30 of 120 credits required for the bachelor's degree must be completed at Downtown Phoenix campus. **International Students:** There are 119 international students enrolled. The school actively recruits these students. The SAT or ACT are required for some.

ADMISSIONS: 79% of the 2014-2015 applicants were accepted. The SAT scores for the 2014-2015 freshman class were: Critical Reading--31% below 500, 46% between 500 and 599, 20% between 600 and 699, and 4% between 700 and 800; Math--29% below 500, 49% between 500 and 599, 21% between 600 and 699, and 2% between 700 and 800. The ACT scores were 21% below 21, 31% between 21 and 23, 24% between 24 and 26, 12% between 27 and 28, and 13% above 28. 54% of the current freshmen were in the top fifth of their class; 86% were in the top two fifths. There were 5 National Merit finalists. **Admissions Contact:** David Burge, Executive Director Undergrad Admissions. E-Mail: *admissions@asu.edu* Web: *http:/ students.asu.edu/admissions*

FINANCIAL AID: The FAFSA is required. The priority date for freshman financial aid applications for fall entry is March 1.

ARIZONA STATE UNIVERSITY, AT THE POLYTECHNIC CAMPUS   C-4

www.campus.asu.edu/polytechnic

Mesa, AZ 85212	(480) 965-7788
Fax: (480) 965-3610	**Email:** admissions@asu.edu
Full-time: 2364 men, 866 women	**Faculty:** IIA, --$
Part-time: 381 men, 139 women	**Ph.Ds:** n/av
Graduate: 218 men, 126 women	**Student/Faculty:** n/av
Year: semesters, summer session	**Tuition:** $9811 ($23,312)
Room & Board: $10,720	**Freshman Class:** 2136 applied, 1639 accepted, 535 enrolled
SAT CR/M: 550/570 **ACT:** 25	**CEEB CODE:** 4007
Application Deadline: February 1	**COMPETITIVE+**

Arizona State University at the Polytechnic Campus, located in a peaceful desert arboretum setting in east Mesa, is home to students who are exploring interdisciplinary science, engineering, management, technology and education. Thousands of square feet of innovative laboratory space make way for exciting hands-on, project-based learning. A freshman residence hall, dining facility and student recreation center complement the growing campus community. ASU's vision is to establish ASU as the model for a New American University, measured not by who we exclude, but by who we include and how they succeed; pursing research and discovery that benefits the public good; and assuming major responsibility for the economic, social and cultural vitality and health and well-being of the community. There are 5 undergraduate schools and 4 graduate schools. In addition to regional accreditation, Polytechnic campus has baccalaureate program accreditation with ABET. The 581-acre campus is in a suburban area in Mesa, AZ. Including any residence halls, there are 86 buildings.

STUDENT LIFE: 74% of undergraduates are from Arizona. Others are from 45 states, 39 foreign countries, and Canada. 94% of the resident undergraduates are from public schools. 57% are White; 19% Hispanic. The average age of freshmen is 18; all undergraduates, 24.
Housing: 1136 students can be accommodated in college housing, which includes coed dorms, on-campus apartments, and married student housing. In addition, there are honors houses and special-interest houses. On-campus housing is guaranteed for the freshman year only, is available on a first-come, first-served basis. 76% of students commute. Alcohol is not permitted. All students may keep cars.

FACULTY/CLASSROOMS: The average class size in an introductory lecture is 31; in a laboratory is 19; and in a regular course is 29.

PROGRAMS OF STUDY: Polytechnic campus confers B.A., B.A.E., B.A.S., B.I.S., B.S. and B.S.E degrees. Master's and doctoral degrees are also awarded. Bachelor's degrees are awarded in AGRICULTURE (agricultural business management), BIOLOGICAL SCIENCE (biology/adolescence education), BUSINESS (business administration and management, business administration - international, business communications, business and technology, environment and natural resource economics, and information and communication technology), COMMUNICATIONS AND THE ARTS (communication, English, English as a second/foreign language, and spanish / adolescence education), COMPUTER AND PHYSICAL SCIENCE (applied science, chemistry/adolescence education, computer information systems, earth science / adolescence education, science technology, and software engineering), EDUCATION (business education, educational studies, elementary education, English education, health information management, mathematics education, physical education / exercise science, science education, secondary education, and special education), ENGINEERING AND ENVIRONMENTAL DESIGN (aeronautical technology, air traffic management, electrical/electronics engineering technology, engineering, graphic arts technology, manufacturing engineering, manufacturing technology, mechanical engineering technology, and product design engineering technology), HEALTH PROFESSIONS (preveterinary science), SOCIAL SCIENCE (food production/management/services, history, interdisciplinary studies, and psychology). Engineering, business, and applied biological sciences have the largest enrollments.

ACTIVITIES: There are 69 groups on campus, including health, technology and sports, band, computers, dance, entrepreneurship, environmental, ethnic, honors, international, newspaper, photography, professional, religious, social service, and student government. Popular campus events include Fall Fest, Homecoming Devils Royale, Innovation Showcase, Sun Devil Drumstix Dash. **Sports:** There are 10 intercollegiate sports for men and 13 for women, and 17 intramural sports for men and 17 for women. Facilities include 60,000 sq ft workout and fitness space, 3 multisport courts, 3 fitness rooms, heated swimming pool, 2 racquetball courts, 10,000 sq ft of weight and cardio space. The outdoor space includes 2 multisport fields, 2 softball fields, sand volleyball, tennis and basketball courts. **Graduates:** From July 1, 2013 to June 30, 2014, 685 bachelor's degrees were awarded. The most popular majors were engineering technologies and engineering-related fields (15%), engineering (14%), business, management, and marketing (13%). 158 companies recruited on campus in 2013-2014. Of the 2013 graduating class, 14% were enrolled in graduate school within 6 months of graduation, and 82% were employed.

SERVICES: Counseling and information services are available, as is tutoring in most subjects. There is a reader service for the blind. Face-to-face and online tutoring are free to students on all campuses. Academic success courses and graduate test preparation are also available. Disability Resource Centers support the learning needs of students with documented disabilities. **Library/Resources:** The library contains 4.5 million volumes, 7.8 million microform items, 152,490 audio/video tapes/CDs/DVDs, and subscribes to 60,941 periodicals including electronic. Computerized library services include interlibrary loans, database searching, and Internet access. **Physically Challenged Students:** 99% of the campus is accessible. Facilities include wheelchair ramps, elevators, special parking, specially equipped restrooms, special class scheduling, lowered drinking fountains, lowered telephones. There are flashing alarms for the deaf, braille maps, modified residence hall rooms and an adaptive exercise program and facility. **Special:** ASU's many undergraduate programs offer students a variety of special academic opportunities. ASU offers domestic and international internships in a variety of disciplines, study abroad programs in more than 55 countries and work study programs. Students may participate in educational programs supported by a variety of centers and institutes. Students gain interdisciplinary skills through combining two areas of study from disciplines in the Bachelors of Interdisciplinary Studies (BIS) program. ASU also offers students two ways to earn concurrent degrees; students can choose to create their own combination degree programs to match their personal or professional interest or choose from a special, predetermined combination. Accelerated degree options are also available for many degree programs. Also available are continuing education programs and summer math, sciences, and journalism programs for high school students. Students who attend Barrett, the Honors College, can choose from more than 300 majors and concentrations. ASU has semesters (15 week schedule) and sessions (7.5 week schedule) allowing students flexibility in choosing their schedule. There is 1 national honor society and an undergraduate honors program. **Visiting:** There are regularly scheduled orientations for prospective students. There are guides for informal visits and visitors may sit in on classes. **Campus Safety and Security:** Measures include 24-hour foot and vehicle patrol, emergency notification system, self-defense education, and security escort services. There are shuttle buses, emergency telephones, lighted pathways/sidewalks, controlled access to dorms/residences, in-room safes, a text messaging alert system (limited to those who sign up); surveillance cameras may be located in residence halls.

REQUIREMENTS: The SAT or ACT is recommended. ASU requirements are; English - 4 years (composition/literature based), Math - 4 years- Algebra l, Geometry, Algebra ll as a prerequisite, Laboratory Science - 3 years total (1 year each from any of the following areas are accepted; Biology, Chemistry, Earth Science, Integrated Science, and Physics), Social Science - 2 years (including 1 year American History), Foreign Language - 2 years (same language), and Fine Arts - 1 year. Applicants must also meet at least one of the following: Top 25 in high school graduating class, 3.0 GPA in competency courses (4.0=A), ACT 22 (24 nonresidents), SAT Reasoning 1040 (1110 nonresidents). All students who don't meet the above standards will be evaluated through a process called Individual Review. Through this process Undergraduate Admissions will review all available information about a student's application, carefully considering all aspects of a student's academic background and accomplishments. Submission of an ACT of SAT test scores is highly recommended. In some cases, additional information might be requested. ASU welcomes home school students and recognizes the unique academic experiences they contribute to our rich community of scholars. A GPA of 3.0 is required. AP and CLEP credits are accepted. To graduate, students must have a minimum cumulative grade point average of 2.0 (some programs may require a higher GPA) and a minimum of total of 120 credit hours, including a minimum total of 45 hours in upper division courses. The number of hours in the major varies by degree program, and some programs may require more upper division work. All students must satisfy a minimum of 35 credit hours of approved General Studies course work in five core areas and three awareness areas: mathematics studies; literacy and critical inquiry; humanities, fine arts, design, social and behavioral sciences; natural sciences, global awareness, historical awareness, and cultural diversity in the United States. **Procedure:** Freshmen are admitted fall and spring. There is a rolling admissions plan. Applications should be filed by February 1 for fall entry; December 1 for spring entry, along with a $50 fee. Applications are accepted on-line. **Transfer Students:** 518 transfer students enrolled in 2013-2014. All transfer students must meet ASU's transfer requirements, providing one of the following: official high school transcript with high school graduation date; GED with acceptable score of 500 or above; official transcript with Associate degree (including award date), official college transcript with Associate degree in progress posted (including expected award date). 30 of 120 credits required for the bachelor's degree must be completed at Polytechnic campus. **International Students:** There are 295 international students enrolled. The school actively recruits these students. They must take the TOEFL with a minimum score of 500 on the paper-based TOEFL (PBT) or 61 on the Internet-based version (iBT), or take the IELTS. The SAT or ACT are required for some.

ADMISSIONS: 77% of the 2014-2015 applicants were accepted. The SAT scores for the 2014-2015 freshman class were: Critical Reading--26% below 500, 43% between 500 and 599, 25% between 600 and 699, and 7% between 700 and 800; Math--19% below 500, 39% between 500 and 599, 33% between 600 and 699, and 9% between 700 and 800. The ACT scores were 16% below 21, 26% between 21 and 23, 23% between 24 and 26, 16% between 27 and 28, and 19% above 28. 45% of the current freshmen were in the top fifth of their class; 77% were in the top two fifths. There were 3 National Merit finalists. **Admissions Contact:** David Burge, Executive Director Undergrad Admissions. E-Mail: *admissions@asu.edu* Web: *https://students.asu.edu/admission*

FINANCIAL AID: The FAFSA is required. The priority date for freshman financial aid applications for fall entry is March 1.

ARIZONA STATE UNIVERSITY, AT THE TEMPE CAMPUS
C-4

www.campus.asu.edu/tempe

Tempe, AZ 85287   (480) 965-7788

Fax: (480) 965-3610
Full-time: 20310 men, 15955 women
Part-time: 2149 men, 1554 women
Graduate: 6262 men, 4128 women
Year: semesters, summer session
Room & Board: $10,010

Email: admissions@asu.edu
Faculty: n/av
Ph.D.s: n/av
Student/Faculty: n/av
Tuition: $10,127 ($24,503)
Freshman Class: 22581 applied, 19042 accepted, 7647 enrolled

SAT CR/M: 560/580 **ACT:** 25
Application Deadline: February 1

CEEB CODE: 4007
COMPETITIVE+

Arizona State University at the Tempe Campus, welcomes students pursuing a wide range of majors including business, liberal arts, engineering and the sciences. Modern classrooms and high-tech laboratories create a dynamic and engaging learning environment. The newly expanded fitness complex allows students to take a break from their studies and focus on their health, while the Sun Devil Athletics facilities, performing arts venues, museums and vibrant downtown Tempe location complement this diverse university environment. ASU's vision is to establish ASU as the model for a New American University, measured not by who we exclude, but by who we include and how they succeed; pursuing research and discovery that benefits the public good; and assuming major responsibility for the economic, social, and cultural vitality and health and well-being of the community. Its research is inspired by real-world application, blurring the boundaries that traditionally separate academic disciplines. There are 8 undergraduate schools and 10 graduate schools. In addition to regional accreditation, ASU at the Tempe campus has baccalaureate program accreditation with AABI, AACSB, ABET, ACCE, CAHME, CIDA, EAC, LAAB, NASAD, NASM AND PAB. The 592-acre campus is in an urban area in Tempe, AZ. Including any residence halls, there are 211 buildings.

STUDENT LIFE: 69% of undergraduates are from Arizona. Others are from all 50 states, 97 foreign countries, and Canada. 92% of the resident undergraduates are from public schools. 54% are White; 19% Hispanic; 11% Foreign. **Male To Female Ratio:** 0.8:1. The average age of freshmen is 18; all undergraduates, 22. **Housing:** 9458 students can be accommodated in college housing, which includes coed dorms and on-campus apartments. In addition, there are honors houses, special-interest houses, residence is available for freshmen and students in particular academic areas. On-campus housing is guaranteed for the freshman year only, and available on a first-come, first-served basis. 77% of students commute. Alcohol is not permitted. All students may keep cars.

FACULTY/CLASSROOMS: The average class size in an introductory lecture is 40; in a laboratory is 25; and in a regular course is 36.

PROGRAMS OF STUDY: ASU at the Tempe campus confers B.A., B.A.E., B.F.A., B.I.S., B.Mus., B.S., B.S.D., B.S.E., B.S.LA. and B.S.P. degrees. Master's and doctoral degrees are also awarded. Bachelor's degrees are awarded in AGRICULTURE (conservation and regulation and natural resource management), BIOLOGICAL SCIENCE (biochemistry, biology/biological science, biology and society, biophysics, life science, microbiology, and molecular biology), BUSINESS (accounting, banking and finance, business administration and management, business administration - international, business administration marketing, business communications, business information systems, business law, business statistics, business systems analysis, integrative studies, marketing/retailing/merchandising, purchasing/inventory management, recreation and leisure services, and supply chain management), COMMUNICATIONS AND THE ARTS (art history, art, art/art studies, ceramic art and design, communications, dance, design, digital media, digital media software engineering, dramatic arts, English, English as a second/foreign language, English literature, English Writing, film arts, fine arts, French, German, graphic design, industrial design, Italian, literature, multimedia, music, music performance, music theory and composition, musical theater, performing arts, Russian, Spanish, theatre arts, theater design, and visual and performing arts), COMPUTER AND PHYSICAL SCIENCE (actuarial science, applied mathematics, chemistry, computer mathematics, computer networks & systems, computer programming, computer information systems, computer science, digital animation & game design, digital arts/technology, earth science, information sciences and systems, mathematics, physics, and statistics), EDUCATION (art education, early childhood education, education, educational studies, elementary education, foreign languages education, music education, secondary education, and special education), ENGINEERING AND ENVIRONMENTAL DESIGN (aerospace engineering, biomedical engineering, chemical engineering, city/community/regional planning, civil engineering, civil and environmental engineering, computer engineering, construction engineering, construction management, electrical/electronics engineering, electrical/electronics engineering technology, engineering, engineering management, environmental design, graphic arts technology, industrial engineering, industrial engineering technology, interior design, landscape architecture/design, manufacturing technology, materials science, mechanical engineering, and mechanical engineering technology), HEALTH PROFESSIONS (biomedical science, music therapy, preventive/wellness health care, and speech pathology/audiology), SOCIAL SCIENCE (African American studies, American Indian studies, anthropology, architectural studies, Asian/American studies, Asian/Oriental studies, economics, geography, geography information science, history, human development, interdisciplinary studies, international studies, Judaic studies, Latin American studies, Mexican-American/Chicano studies, philosophy, political science/government, psychology, public affairs, public history/archives, religious studies, sociology, urban studies, and women's studies). Supply chain management (logistics), geography, and electrical engineering are the strongest academically. Business, biological sciences, and psychology have the largest enrollments.

ACTIVITIES: 9% of men belong to 1 local and 33 national fraternities; 15% of women belong to 25 national sororities. There are 673 groups on campus, including health, technology and sports, art, band, cheerleading, chess, choir, chorus, communications, computers, dance, debate, drama, drill team, entrepreneurship, environmental, ethnic, film, forensics, gay, honors, international, jazz band, marching band, musical theater, newspaper, orchestra, pep band, photography, political, professional, radio and TV, religious, social, social service, student government, and symphony. Popular campus events include Devils on Mill, Sorority and Fraternity Recruitment, Passport to ASU, Homecoming, MU After Dark, MU Takeover, Finals Breakfast, Post Football Game Concert. **Sports:** There are 10 intercollegiate sports for men and 13 for women, and 28 intramural sports for men and 27 for women. Facilities include 5 stadiums (including football, baseball, softball, track, and soccer), a basketball, volleyball, gymnastics and wrestling arena, tennis facilities, an aquatic complex, golf course, athletic and activity centers, student recreation complex, weight rooms, circuit training room, exercise rooms, tennis courts, basketball courts, indoor gyms (used for basketball, volleyball, badminton), racquetball courts, outside sand volleyball courts, badminton courts, squash court, table tennis courts, MAC court (multiactivity court with dasherboards), outdoor fields, indoor and outdoor running track. **Graduates:** From July 1, 2013 to June 30, 2014, 9319 bachelor's degrees were awarded. The most popular majors were business, management, marketing, and related support services

(22%), social sciences (10%), and biological and biomedical sciences (9%). 1175 companies recruited on campus in 2013-2014. Of the 2013 graduating class, 18% were enrolled in graduate school within 6 months of graduation, and 85% were employed.

SERVICES: Counseling and information services are available, as is tutoring in most subjects. There is a reader service for the blind. Face-to-face and online tutoring are free to students on all campuses. Academic success courses and graduate test preparation are also available. Disability Resource Centers support the learning needs of students with documented disabilities. **Library/Resources:** The 5 libraries contain 4.5 million volumes, 7.8 million microform items, 152,490 audio/video tapes/CDs/DVDs, and subscribe to 60,941 periodicals including electronic. Computerized library services include interlibrary loans, database searching, and Internet access. Special learning facilities include an art gallery, natural history museum, planetarium, museums, galleries, collections, research labs, digital labs, art, dance and development studios. **Physically Challenged Students:** 99% of the campus is accessible. Facilities include wheelchair ramps, elevators, special parking, specially equipped restrooms, special class scheduling, lowered drinking fountains, lowered telephones. There are flashing alarms for the deaf, braille maps, modified residence hall rooms and an adaptive exercise program and facility. **Special:** ASU's many undergraduate programs offer students a variety of special academic opportunities. ASU offers domestic and international internships in a variety of disciplines, more than 250 study abroad programs in over 55 countries and work study programs. Students gain interdisciplinary skills through combining two areas of study from a list of more than 140 disciplines in the Bachelors of Interdisciplinary Studies (BIS) program. The Ira A. Fulton Schools of Engineering offer co-operative education experiences. The McCain Institute for International Leadership in Washington, D.C. offers students the opportunity to gain experience in foreign policy and international relations through winter and semester courses with the Washington Policy Design Studio. ASU also offers students two ways to earn concurrent degrees; students can choose to create their own combination degrees programs to match their personal or professional interests or choose from a special, predetermined combinations. Accelerated degree options are also available for more than 30 degree programs. ASU has Semesters (15-week schedule) and Sessions (7.5 week schedule) allowing student's flexibility in choosing their schedule. There are 27 national honor societies and an undergraduate honors program. **Visiting:** There are regularly scheduled orientations for prospective students. There are guides for informal visits and visitors may sit in on classes. **Campus Safety and Security:** Measures include 24-hour foot and vehicle patrol, emergency notification system, self-defense education, and security escort services. There are shuttle buses, emergency telephones, lighted pathways/sidewalks, controlled access to dorms/residences, in-room safes, text messaging alert system (limited to those who sign up); surveillance cameras may be located in residence halls.

REQUIREMENTS: The SAT or ACT is recommended. Applicants must successfully complete ASU competency requirement; English 4 years (composition/literature based), Math, 4 years (Algebra I, Geometry, Algebra II and one course requiring Algebra II as a prerequisite), Laboratory Science, 3 years total (1 year each from any of the following areas are accepted: Biology, Chemistry, Earth Science, Integrated Sciences, and Physics), Social Science, 2 years (including one year American History), Foreign Language, 2 years (same language), and Fine Art, 1 year. Applicants must also meet at least one of the following: Top 25% in high school graduating class, 3.0 GPA in competency courses (4.0 = A), ACT 22 (24 nonresidents), SAT Reasoning 1040 (1110 nonresidents). All students who don't meet the above standards will be evaluated through a process called Individual Review. Through this process Undergraduate Admissions will review all available information about a student's application, carefully considering all aspects of a student's academic background and accomplishments. Submission of an ACT or SAT test score is highly recommended. In some cases, additional information might be requested. ASU welcomes home school students and recognizes the unique academic experiences they contribute to our rich community of scholars. A GPA of 3.0 is required. AP and CLEP credits are accepted. To graduate, students must have a minimum cumulative grade point average of 2.0 (some programs may require a higher GPA) and a minimum total of 120 credit hours, including a minimum of 45 hours in upper-division courses. The number of hours in the major varies by degree program, and some programs may require more upper-division work. All students must satisfy a minimum of 35 credit hours of approved General Studies course work in five core areas and three awareness areas: mathematics studies; literacy and critical inquiry; humanities, fine arts, design, social and behavioral sciences; natural sciences; global awareness; historical awareness, and cultural diversity in the United States. **Procedure:** Freshmen are admitted fall and spring. There is a rolling admissions plan. Applications should be filed by February 1 for fall entry; December 1 for spring entry, along with a $50 fee. Notification is sent on a rolling basis. Applications are accepted on-line. **Transfer Students:** 3417 transfer students enrolled in 2013-2014. All transfer students must meet ASU's transfer requirement by providing one of the following: official high school transcript with high school graduation date; GED with acceptable score of 500 or above; official college transcript with Associate degree posted (including award date); official college transcript with Associate degree in progress posted (including expected award date). Please note that some ASU colleges and schools have higher requirements for admission to their majors. Arizona transfer students must meet one of the following requirements: Associate degree with a 2.00 cumulative GPA or higher (4.00=A); Arizona General Education Curriculum (AGEC) with a 2.50 cumulative GPA or higher (4.00=A); complete a transfer pathway program through an accredited Arizona community college. Nonresident transfer students must meet one of the following requirements: Associate degree with a 2.50 cumulative GPA or higher (4.00=A); AGEC with a 2.50 cumulative GPA or higher (4.00=A). (For those students transferring from a California community college, ASU accepts the Intersegmental General Education Transfer Curriculum/California State University General Education [IGETC/CSU GE] patterns). Students with fewer than 24 transferable credit hours must have a minimum 2.50 cumulative GPA and meet freshman aptitude requirements to be considered through individual review. Some ASU colleges and schools have higher requirements for admission to their majors. See degree search for detailed admission information for your desired program of study. 30 of 120 credits required for the bachelor's degree must be completed at ASU at the Tempe campus. **International Students:** There are 4124 international students enrolled. The school actively recruits these students. They must take the TOEFL with a minimum score of 500 on the paper-based TOEFL (PBT) or 61 on the Internet-based version (iBT), or take the IELTS. SAT or ACT is required for the W.P. Carey School of Business.

ADMISSIONS: 84% of the 2014-2015 applicants were accepted. The SAT scores for the 2014-2015 freshman class were: Critical Reading--23% below 500, 42% between 500 and 599, 28% between 600 and 699, and 8% between 700 and 800; Math--16% below 500, 40% between 500 and 599, 34% between 600 and 699, and 10% between 700 and 800. The ACT scores were 13% below 21, 22% between 21 and 23, 29% between 24 and 26, 15% between 27 and 28, and 21% above 28. 51% of the current freshmen were in the top fifth of their class; 80% were in the top two fifths. There were 109 National Merit finalists. **Admissions Contact:** David Burge, Executive Director Undergrad Admissions. E-Mail: *admissions@asu.edu* Web: *https://students.asu.edu/admission*

FINANCIAL AID: The FAFSA is required. The priority date for freshman financial aid applications for fall entry is March 1.

ARIZONA STATE UNIVERSITY, AT THE WEST CAMPUS   C-4

www.campus.asu.edu/west

Phoenix, AZ 85036   (480) 965-7788

Fax: (480) 965-3610   Email: admissions@asu.edu
Full-time: 1067 men, 1701 women   Faculty: IIA, --$
Part-time: 219 men, 309 women   Ph.D.s: n/av
Graduate: 134 men, 263 women   Student/Faculty: n/av
Year: semesters, summer session   Tuition: $9811 ($23,312)
Room & Board: $9440   Freshman Class: 1288
                                        applied, 1002 accepted,
                                        342 enrolled
SAT CR/M: 540/540 ACT: 23   CEEB CODE: 4007
Application Deadline: February 1   COMPETITIVE

Arizona State University at the West Campus, in northwest Phoenix, welcomes students studying business, education, and interdisciplinary arts and sciences. Patterned after the University of Oxford's architecture, this inviting campus creates a close-knit community. ASU's vision is to establish ASU as the model for a New American University, measured not by who we exclude, but by who we include and how they succeed; pursuing research and discovery that benefits the public good; and assuming major responsibility for the economic, social, and cultural vitality and health and well-being of the community. There are 4 undergraduate schools and 3 graduate schools. The 278-acre campus is in an urban area in Phoenix, AZ. Including any residence halls, there are 21 buildings.

STUDENT LIFE: 85% of undergraduates are from Arizona. Others are from 41 states, 17 foreign countries, and Canada. 95% of the resident undergraduates are from public schools. 52% are White; 28% Hispanic.. **Male To Female Ratio:** 1.6:1. The average age of freshmen is 18; all undergraduates, 25. **Housing:** 437 students can be accommodated in college housing, which includes coed dorms and on-campus apartments. In addition, there are honors houses and special-interest houses. On-campus housing is guaranteed for the freshman year only, is available on a first-come, and first-served basis. 89% of students commute. Alcohol is not permitted. All students may keep cars.

FACULTY/CLASSROOMS: The average class size in an introductory lecture is 32; in a laboratory is 19; and in a regular course is 28.

PROGRAMS OF STUDY: ASU at the West campus confers B.A., B.A.E., B.A.S. and B.S. degrees. Master's and doctoral degrees are also awarded. Bachelor's degrees are awarded in BIOLOGICAL SCIENCE (forensic science and life science), BUSINESS (accounting, business administration and management, business administration - international, business communications, business statistics, supply chain management, and sustainable management), COMMUNICATIONS AND THE ARTS (communications, English, English as a second/foreign language, performing arts, Spanish, and Spanish/adolescence education), COMPUTER AND PHYSICAL SCIENCE (applied mathematics, applied science, chemistry education, earth science/adolescence education, and statistics), EDUCATION (business education, education, elementary education, English education, mathematics education, secondary education, and special education), ENGINEERING AND ENVIRONMENTAL DESIGN (environmental science), SOCIAL SCIENCE (American studies, cultural studies/critical theory and analysis, ethnic studies, forensic studies, (Social Science) Global Studies, history, interdisciplinary studies, Latin American studies, philosophy and religion, political science/government, psychology, social science, sociology, and women and gender studies). Psychology, business, and life sciences have the largest enrollments.

ACTIVITIES: There are 50 groups on campus, including health, technology and sports, art, chess, communications, computers, entrepreneurship, film, forensics, gay, honors, international, newspaper, political, professional, religious, social, social service, and student government. Popular campus events include Sparky's Big Top Carnival and Fun Run, Midnight Breakfast, and Market on the Move. **Sports:** There are 10 intercollegiate sports for men and 13 for women, and 16 intramural sports for men and 16 for women. Facilities include Social Gaming-Wii and Xbox 360 gaming stations, ping pong tables, lounge seating, flat screen TVs, wellness-demonstration kitchen, conference room, cam studios, facility-indoor basketball courts, indoor running track, weight area, stretching area, selectorized machines, multipurpose aerobic rooms, racquetball courts, cardio loft, sunrise yoga terrace, locker rooms, outdoor facilities, competition fields, softball field, sand volleyball courts, basketball courts, and a heated pool. **Graduates:** From July 1, 2013 to June 30, 2014, 848 bachelor's degrees were awarded. The most popular majors were psychology (20%), education (19%), and communication and journalism (11%). 106 companies recruited on campus in 2013-2014. Of the 2013 graduating class, 21% were enrolled in graduate school within 6 months of graduation, and 81% were employed.

SERVICES: Counseling and information services are available, as is tutoring in most subjects, face-to-face and on-line tutoring are free to students. Academic success courses and graduate test preparation are also availlable. Disability resource centers support the learning needs of students with documented disabilities. There is a reader service for the blind. **Library/Resources:** The library contains 4.5 million volumes, 7.8 million microform items, 152,490 audio/video tapes/CDs/DVDs, and subscribes to 60,941 periodicals including electronic. Computerized library services include interlibrary loans, database searching, and Internet access. Special learning facilities include an art gallery, Herberger Young Scholars Academy-school for 7th grade thru 12th grade, art collections, galleries, dance studios, little theatre, black box, communications assessment learning lab, research lab, cooking labs, performing arts studios, and writing labs. For **Physically Challenged Students:** 99% of the campus is accessible. Facilities include wheelchair ramps, elevators, special parking, specially equipped restrooms, special class scheduling, lowered drinking fountains, lowered telephones. There are flashing alarms for the deaf, braille maps, modified residence hall rooms and an adaptive exercise program and facility. **Special:** ASU's many undergraduate programs offer students a variety of special academic opportunities. ASU offers domestic and international internships in a variety of disciplines, study abroad programs in more than 55 countries and work study programs. Students may participate in educational programs supported by a variety of centers and institutes, such as the Center for Critical Inquiry and Cultural Studies. Students gain interdisciplinary skills through combining two areas of study from disciplines in the Bachelors of Interdisciplinary Studies (BIS) program. ASU also offers students two ways to earn concurrent degrees; students can choose to create their own combination degree programs to match their personal or professional interest or choose from a special, predetermined combination. Accelerated degree options are also available for many degree programs. ASU has semesters (15 week schedule) and sessions (7.5 week schedule) allowing students flexibility in choosing their schedule. There are 2 national honor societies and an undergraduate honors program. **Visiting:** There are regularly scheduled orientations for prospective students. There are guides for informal visits and visitors may sit in on classes. **Campus Safety and Security:** Measures include 24-hour foot and vehicle patrol, emergency notification system, self-defense education, and security escort services. There are shuttle buses, emergency telephones, lighted pathways/sidewalks, controlled access to dorms/residences, in-room safes, a text messaging alert system (limited to those who sign up); surveillance cameras may be located in residence halls.

REQUIREMENTS: The SAT or ACT is recommended. ASU requirements, 4 years of English, 4 years of Math, 3 years total (1 year each from any of the following) Biology, Chemistry, Earth Science, Integrated Science, and Physics, 2 years of Social Studies (including 1 year of American History), 2 years of Foreign Language (same language), and 1 year of Fine Arts. Applicants must also meet at least one of the following: top 25% in high school graduating class, 3.0 GPA in competency courses (4.0=A), ACT 22 (24 nonresidents), SAT Reasoning 1040 (1110 nonresidents). All students who don't meet the above standards will be evaluated through a process called Individual Review. Through this process Undergraduate Admissions will review all available information about a student's application, carefully considering all aspects of a student's academic background and accomplishments. Submission of an ACT or SAT test score is highly recommended. In some cases, additional information might be requested. ASU welcomes home school students and recognizes the unique academic experiences they contribute to our rich community of scholars. A GPA of 3.0 is required. AP and CLEP credits are accepted. To graduate, students must have a minimum cumulative grade point average of 2.0 (some programs may require a higher GPA) and a minimum total of 120 credit hours, including a minimum of 45 hours in upper division courses. The number of hours in the major varies by degree program, and some programs may require more upper-division work. All students must satisfy a minimum of 35 credit hours of approved General Studies course work in five core areas and three awareness areas: mathematics studies; literacy and critical inquiry; humanities, fine arts, design, social and behavioral sciences; natural sciences; global awareness, historical awareness, and cultural diversity in the United States. **Procedure:** Freshmen are admitted in the fall and spring. There is a rolling admissions plan. Applications should be filed by February 1 for fall entry; December 1 for spring entry, along with a $50 fee. Applications are accepted online. **Transfer Students:** 549 transfer students enrolled in 2013-2014. All transfer students must meet ASU's transfer requirement by pro-

viding one of the following: official high school transcript with high school graduation date; GED with acceptable score of 500 or above; official college transcript with Associate degree posted (including award date); official college transcript with Associate degree in progress posted (including expected award date). Please note that some ASU colleges and schools have higher requirements for admission to their majors. Arizona transfer students must meet one of the following requirements: Associate degree with a 2.00 cumulative GPA or higher (4.00=A); Arizona General Education Curriculum (AGEC) with a 2.50 cumulative GPA or higher (4.00=A); complete a transfer pathway program through an accredited Arizona community college. Nonresident transfer students must meet one of the following requirements: Associate degree with a 2.50 cumulative GPA or higher (4.00=A); AGEC with a 2.50 cumulative GPA or higher (4.00=A). (For those students transferring from a California community college, ASU accepts the Intersegmental General Education Transfer Curriculum/California State University General Education [IGETC/CSU GE] patterns). Students with fewer than 24 transferable credit hours must have a minimum 2.50 cumulative GPA and meet freshman aptitude requirements to be considered through individual review. Some ASU colleges and schools have higher requirements for admission to their majors. 30 of 120 credits required for the bachelor's degree must be completed at ASU at the West campus. **International Students:** There are 71 international students enrolled. The school actively recruits these students. They must take the TOEFL with a minimum score of 500 on the paper-based TOEFL (PBT) or 61 on the Internet-based version (iBT), or take the IELTS. SAT or ACT required for some.

ADMISSIONS: 78% of the 2014-2015 applicants were accepted. The SAT scores for the 2014-2015 freshman class were: Critical Reading--30% below 500, 44% between 500 and 599, 23% between 600 and 699, and 2% between 700 and 800; Math--29% below 500, 47% between 500 and 599, 23% between 600 and 699, and 2% between 700 and 800. The ACT scores were 22% below 21, 31% between 21 and 23, 22% between 24 and 26, 15% between 27 and 28, and 10% above 28. 55% of the current freshmen were in the top fifth of their class; 86% were in the top two fifths. **Admissions Contact:** David Burge, Executive Director Undergrad Admissions. E-Mail: *admissions@asu.edu* Web: *http://students.asu.edu/admissions*

FINANCIAL AID: The FAFSA is required. The priority date for freshman financial aid applications for fall entry is March 1.

EMBRY-RIDDLE AERONAUTICAL UNIVERSITY - PRESCOTT CAMPUS

C-3

www.erau.edu

Prescott, AZ 86301

(928) 777-6600
(800) 888-3728
Email: pradmit@erau.edu

Full-time: 1320 men, 367 women	**Faculty:** 100; IIB, +$
Part-time: 99 men, 27 women	**Ph.D.s:** 70%
Graduate: 32 men, 10 women	**Student/Faculty:** 16 to 1
Year: semesters, summer session	**Tuition:** $31,034
Room & Board: $9410	**Freshman Class:** 1689 applied, 1334 accepted, 448 enrolled
SAT CR/M/W: 570/600/530 **ACT:** 26	**CEEB CODE:** 4305
Application Deadline: July 1	**VERY COMPETITIVE+**

Embry-Riddle Aeronautical University, founded in 1926, is a private institution offering undergraduate programs in aviation, engineering, business, and professional training on 2 campuses: the Prescott campus, founded in 1978, and the Daytona Beach, Florida, campus. Graduate programs are also offered at both campuses. The figures in the above capsule and in this profile are approximate. There are 4 undergraduate schools and 1 graduate school. In addition to regional accreditation, ERAU has baccalaureate program accreditation with ABET and ACBSP. The 539-acre campus is in a rural area 100 miles north of Phoenix. Including any residence halls, there are 28 buildings.

STUDENT LIFE: 76% of undergraduates are from out of state, mostly the Southwest. Students are from 48 states, and 30 foreign countries. 60% are White. **Male To Female Ratio:** 0.3:1. The average age of freshmen is 18; all undergraduates, 21. 21% do not continue beyond their first year; 59% remain to graduate. **Housing:** 849 students can be accommodated in college housing, which includes coed dorms and on-campus apartments. In addition, there are honors houses. On-campus housing is guaranteed for the freshman year only and is available on a lottery system for upperclassmen. 50% of students commute. All students may keep cars.

FACULTY/CLASSROOMS: 76% of faculty are male; 24% are female. All teach undergraduates. No introductory courses are taught by graduate students. The average class size in an introductory lecture is 24; in a laboratory is 19; and in a regular course is 23.

PROGRAMS OF STUDY: ERAU confers B.S. degrees. Master's degrees are also awarded. Bachelor's degrees are awarded in AGRICULTURE (wildlife science), BIOLOGICAL SCIENCE (forensic science), COMMUNICATIONS AND THE ARTS (organ performance), COMPUTER AND PHYSICAL SCIENCE (applied meteorology, astronomy, atmospheric sciences and meteorology, cyber intelligence/security studies, industrial psychology/safety, and software engineering), ENGINEERING AND ENVIRONMENTAL DESIGN (aeronautical science, aerospace engineering, air traffic management, aviation business administration, computer engineering, electrical/electronics engineering, and mechanical engineering), SOCIAL SCIENCE (interdisciplinary studies). Aviation environmental science, applied meteorology, and air traffic management are the strongest academically. Aerospace engineering, aeronautical science, global security, and intelligence studies have the largest enrollments.

ACTIVITIES: 10% of men belong to 5 national fraternities; 9% of women belong to 2 national sororities. There are 105 groups on campus, including academic, jet dragster, military, band, computers, dance, debate, environmental, ethnic, forensics, gay, honors, international, jazz band, literary magazine, newspaper, political, professional, radio and TV, religious, social, social service, special interest: UAV, and student government. Popular campus events include Hypnotist, Casino Night, OctoberWest, Activity Fair, GreekWeek, Finals Breakfast, Carpe Notcem Events, Smores, and Friday Night Entertainment. **Sports:** There are 4 intercollegiate sports for men and 5 for women, and 16 intramural sports for men and 15 for women. Facilities include an activity center with 3 basketball courts and 3 volleyball courts, gym/weight room, multipurpose athletic playing field, game room, swimming pool complex, and a fitness facility. **Graduates:** From July 1, 2013 to June 30, 2014, 339 bachelor's degrees were awarded. The most popular majors were aerospace engineering (26%), aeronautics (17%), and aeronautical science (15%).

SERVICES: Counseling and information services are available, as is tutoring in most subjects. There is remedial math, reading, and writing. **Library/Resources:** The library contains 30,168 volumes, 100,077 microform items, 2,256 audio/video tapes/CDs/DVDs, and subscribes to 174 periodicals including electronic. Computerized library services include interlibrary loans, database searching, Internet access, and Wi-Fi capability. Special learning facilities include a radio station, 4 wind tunnels, an aviation safety center, and an aircraft structures lab. The Flight Training Center at Ernest A. Love Field offers a simulator lab and flight operations center. **Physically Challenged Students:** 95% of the campus is accessible. Facilities include wheelchair ramps, special parking, specially equipped restrooms, special class scheduling, lowered drinking fountains, lowered telephones, special housing, and pneumatic doors. **Special:** Cooperative and work-study programs, nondegree study, internships in all majors, and study abroad in 21 countries are offered. Flight training may be taken in conjunction with aeronautical science and other degree programs. Credit is given for life and military experience. There is 1 national honor society and a freshman honors program. **Visiting:** There are regularly scheduled orientations for prospective students. There are guides for informal visits and visitors may sit in on classes. To schedule a visit, contact the Admissions Office at pradmit@erau.edu. **Campus Safety and Security:** Measures include 24-hour foot and vehicle patrol, emergency notification system, self-defense education, and security escort services. There are shuttle buses, emergency telephones, and lighted pathways/sidewalks.

REQUIREMENTS: The SAT or ACT is recommended. AP and CLEP credits are accepted. Important factors in the admissions decision are advanced placement or honors courses, recommendations by school officials, and evidence of special talent. All students must complete 36 credits of general education requirements, including courses in communication skills, technical report writing, humanities/social sciences, math, physical science, economics, and computer science. A total of 120 to 136 credit hours with a minimum GPA of 2.0 is required to graduate. **Procedure:** Freshmen are admitted fall, spring, and summer. Entrance exams should be taken by the fall of the senior year. There are deferred admissions and rolling admissions plans. Early decision applications should be filed by December 1; regular applications, by July 1 for fall entry; November 1 for spring entry; and April 1 for summer entry, along with a $50 fee. Notification is sent on a rolling basis. Applications are accepted on-line. **Transfer Students:** 109 transfer students enrolled in 2013-2014. A G.P.A. of 2.5 is preferred. 30 of 120 credits required for the bachelor's degree must be completed at ERAU. **International Students:** There are 148 international students enrolled. The school actively recruits these students. They must take the TOEFL with a minimum score of 550 on the paper-based TOEFL (PBT) or 79 on the Internet-based version (iBT). SAT or ACT is strongly recommended.

ADMISSIONS: 79% of the 2014-2015 applicants were accepted. The SAT scores for the 2014-2015 freshman class were: Critical Reading--19% below 500, 42% between 500 and 599, 31% between 600 and 699, and 8% between 700 and 800; Math--13% below 500, 35% between 500 and 599, 43% between 600 and 699, and 9% between 700 and 800; Writing--29% below 500, 44% between 500 and 599, 25% between 600 and 699, and 2% between 700 and 800. The ACT scores were 6% below 21, 19% between 21 and 23, 27% between 24 and 26, 16% between 27 and 28, and 32% above 28. 50% of the current freshmen were in the top fifth of their class; 78% were in the top two fifths. **Admissions Contact:** Sara Bofferding, Director, Prescott Admissions . E-Mail: *pradmit@erau.edu* Web: *www.erau.edu*

FINANCIAL AID: In 2014-2015, 95% of all full-time freshmen and 87% of continuing full-time students received some form of financial aid. 86% of all full-time freshmen and 81% of continuing full-time students received need-based aid. The average freshman award was $17,904. Need-based scholarships or need-based grants averaged $12,046; need-based self-help aid (loans and jobs) averaged $4,810; and non-need-based athletic scholarships averaged $9,124. 33% of undergraduate students work part-time. Average annual earnings from campus work are $2106. The FAFSA is required. The priority date for freshman financial aid applications for fall entry is March 1.

GRAND CANYON UNIVERSITY   C-4
www.gcu.edu

Phoenix, AZ 85017

Full-time: 1767 men, 3568 women	**Faculty:** 223
Part-time: 4997 men, 17348 women	**Ph.D.s:** 19%
Graduate: 3052 men, 10025 women	**Student/Faculty:** 25 to 1
Year: semesters, summer session	**Tuition:** $16,640
Room & Board: $7900	**Freshman Class:** n/av
SAT or ACT: recommended	**CEEB CODE:** 4331
Application Deadline: open	**VERY COMPETITIVE**

Grand Canyon University, founded in 1949, is a small, private, publicly traded nonsectarian liberal arts institution. Figures in the above capsule and in this profile are approximate. There are 5 undergraduate schools and 5 graduate schools. In addition to regional accreditation, GCU has baccalaureate program accreditation with ACBSP. The 100-acre campus is in a suburban area in Phoenix, AZ. Including any residence halls, there are 50 buildings.

STUDENT LIFE: 73% of undergraduates are from out of state, mostly the Southwest. Students are from 50 states, 12 foreign countries, and Canada. 41% are White; 25% African American. 98% claim no religious affiliation. **Male To Female Ratio:** 3.2:1. The average age of freshmen is 18; all undergraduates, 33. **Housing:** 1600 students can be accommodated in college housing, which includes single-sex dorms, on-campus apartments, and married student housing. On-campus housing is available on a first-come and first-served basis. 52% of students commute. Alcohol is not permitted. All students may keep cars.

FACULTY/CLASSROOMS: 85% teach undergraduates. No introductory courses are taught by graduate students. The average class size in an introductory lecture is 18; in a laboratory is 14; and in a regular course is 18.

PROGRAMS OF STUDY: GCU confers B.A., B.S. and B.S.N. degrees. Master's and doctoral degrees are also awarded. Bachelor's degrees are awarded in BIOLOGICAL SCIENCE (biology/biological science), BUSINESS (accounting, business administration and management, entrepreneurial studies, management science, marketing/retailing/merchandising, and sports management), COMMUNICATIONS AND THE ARTS (communications, communications technology, English, music, music performance, theatre arts, theater design, and theater management), COMPUTER AND PHYSICAL SCIENCE (digital arts/technology), EDUCATION (athletic training, dance education, education, elementary education, music education, physical education, and secondary education), HEALTH PROFESSIONS (exercise science, health science, and nursing), SOCIAL SCIENCE (addiction studies, Christian studies, forensic studies, history, interdisciplinary studies, international studies, physical fitness/movement, psychology, and sociology). Education, business, and nursing are the strongest academically, and have the largest enrollments.

ACTIVITIES: There are no fraternities or sororities. There are 12 groups on campus, including art, band, cheerleading, choir, chorale, chorus, dance, drama, ethnic, film, honors, international, literary magazine, musical theater, newspaper, pep band, photography, political, professional, religious, social, social service, and student government. Popular campus events include Spiritual Emphasis Week, Harvest Festival and Spring Formal. **Sports:** There are 10 intercollegiate sports for men and 11 for women, and 6 intramural sports for men and 6 for women. Facilities include a 5,000 seat arena, intramural fields, a 1500-seat baseball stadium, a 1550-seat gymnasium, athlete performance center, a 300-seat soccer/track and field venue, a 150-seat softball venue, 55,000 square foot student recreation center (includes recreational basketball courts-2; student fitness center, aerobics/dance room, cardio/weight facilities, locker facilities, wrestling and basketball intercollegiate training areas). **Graduates:** From July 1, 2013 to June 30, 2014, 2279 bachelor's degrees were awarded. The most popular majors were nusing (17%), curriculum and instruction (5%), and special education (4%). 100 companies recruited on campus in 2013-2014.

SERVICES: Counseling and information services are available, as is tutoring in every subject. There is remedial math, reading, and writing. Tutors are also trained in test-taking techniques, study skills, and time management. **Library/Resources:** The library contains 140,456 volumes, 53,459 microform items, 527 audio/video tapes/CDs/DVDs, and subscribes to 9,502 periodicals including electronic. Computerized library services include interlibrary loans, database searching, Internet access, and Wi-Fi capability. Special learning facilities include an art gallery. **Physically Challenged Students:** 99% of the campus is accessible. Facilities include wheelchair ramps, elevators, special parking, specially equipped restrooms, lowered drinking fountains, and special housing. **Special:** Internships are offered for most majors through organizations, corporations, and agencies in the Phoenix area. Study abroad in 5 countries and a Washington semester are possible. There are 3 national honor societies and a freshman honors program. **Visiting:** There are regularly scheduled orientations for prospective students, including student orientation and registration in the summer. There are guides for informal visits, visitors may sit in on classes, and stay overnight. To schedule a visit, contact the Admission Office. **Campus Safety and Security:** Measures include 24-hour foot and vehicle patrol, emergency notification system, self-defense education, and security escort services. There are emergency telephones, lighted pathways/sidewalks, and controlled access to dorms/residences.

REQUIREMENTS: The SAT or ACT is recommended. Applicants need to be graduates of an accredited high school or have a GED. A GPA of 3.0 is required. AP and CLEP credits are accepted. Important factors in the admissions decision are evidence of special talent, extracurricular activities record, and leadership record. All students are required to complete 40 hours of general studies, including 12 hours each in Effective Communication and Critical Thinking, 8 hours in Global Awareness, and 4 hours each in University Foundation and Christian Worldview. A total of 120 semester hours, with a minimum

GPA of 2.0, are required to graduate. **Procedure:** Freshmen are admitted to all sessions. Entrance exams should be taken during the junior or senior year of high school. There are early decision and rolling admissions plans. Application deadlines are open. Applications are accepted on-line. **Transfer Students:** 30 of 120 credits required for the bachelor's degree must be completed at GCU. **International Students:** There are 102 international students enrolled. The school actively recruits these students. They must take the TOEFL with a minimum score of 500 on the paper-based TOEFL (PBT) or 61 on the Internet-based version (iBT) and the college's own test.

ADMISSIONS: Dr. Brian McGuire, Executive Director . E-Mail: *admissiononline@gcu.edu* Web: *www.gcu.edu*

FINANCIAL AID: 14% of undergraduate students work part-time. Average annual earnings from campus work are $4800. Check with the school for current application deadlines.

NORTHERN ARIZONA UNIVERSITY C-2
nau.edu

Flagstaff, AZ 86011

(928) 523-1428
(888) 628-2968
Email: Anika.Olsen@nau.edu

Full-time: 8288 men, 11066 women	**Faculty:** I, --$
Part-time: 1701 men, 2650 women	**Ph.D.s:** n/av
Graduate: 1338 men, 2532 women	**Student/Faculty:** n/av
Year: semesters, summer session	**Tuition:** $9990 ($22,510)
Room & Board: $9020	**Freshman Class:** 27780 applied, 25153 accepted, 5035 enrolled
SAT CR/M/W: 523/520/503 **ACT:** 23	**CEEB CODE:** 4006
Application Deadline: n/av	**COMPETITIVE**

Northern Arizona University, founded in 1899, is a comprehensive public university in the heart of the southern Colorado Plateau. At Northern Arizona University, we fully prepare students for meaningful life and work through our commitment to learning and teaching in an unparalleled environment. Through our main campus in Flagstaff and our distance-education opportunities throughout Arizona and online, we offer excellence in teaching, research, and public service to the citizens of Arizona and beyond. Northern Arizona University is a doctoral-intensive institution with undergraduate education at our core and significant research opportunities as well as select master's and doctoral programs. We offer undergraduate and graduate degrees in a full range of disciplines from liberal arts and sciences to professional and career-related fields. Our commitment to high-quality education at all levels is exemplified by small class size and close interaction between students and faculty. Figures in the above capsule and in this profile are approximate. There are 8 undergraduate schools and 1 graduate school. In addition to regional accreditation, NAU has baccalaureate program accreditation with AACSB, ABET, ACBSP, ACCE, ADA, CSWE, NASM, NCATE, NRPA, and SAF. The 740-acre campus is in a rural area 140 miles north of Flagstaff and 80 miles from the Grand Canyon's South Rim. Including any residence halls, there are 109 buildings.

STUDENT LIFE: 70% of undergraduates are from Arizona. Others are from 50 states, 65 foreign countries, and Canada. 62% are White; 19% Hispanic. The average age of freshmen is 18; all undergraduates, 23. **Housing:** 7500 students can be accommodated in college housing, which includes single-sex and coed dorms, on-campus apartments, and married student housing. In addition, there are honors houses, fraternity houses, and sorority houses. On-campus housing is guaranteed for the freshman year only, is available on a first-come, first-served basis. 71% of students commute. All students may keep cars.

FACULTY/CLASSROOMS: No introductory courses are taught by graduate students.

PROGRAMS OF STUDY: NAU confers B., B.A., B.A.S., B.B.A., B.F.A., B.M.Ed., B.Mus., B.P.S., B.S., B.S.Accy., B.S.B.A., B.S.C.S., B.S.D.H., B.S.E., B.S.Ed., B.S.F., B.S.Jour., B.S.N., B.S.S., B.S.W. and B.U.S. degrees. Master's and doctoral degrees are also awarded. Bachelor's degrees are awarded in AGRICULTURE (environmental studies and forestry and related sciences), BIOLOGICAL SCIENCE (biology/biological science and microbiology), BUSINESS (accounting, business administration and management, business economics, finance, hotel/motel and restaurant management, management science, marketing management, and small business management), COMMUNICATIONS AND THE ARTS (communications, English, film, television and digital media, journalism, modern language, music, music performance, photography, Spanish, studio art, and theatre arts), COMPUTER AND PHYSICAL SCIENCE (applied science, astronomy, chemistry, computer information technology, computer science, geology, mathematics, and physics), EDUCATION (early childhood education, elementary education, music education, secondary education, and special education), ENGINEERING AND ENVIRONMENTAL DESIGN (civil engineering, construction management, electrical and computer engineering, environmental engineering, environmental science, interior design, and mechanical engineering), HEALTH PROFESSIONS (biomedical science, dental hygiene, exercise science, health science, and nursing), SOCIAL SCIENCE (anthropology, criminal justice, criminology, crosscultural studies, geography, history, interdisciplinary studies, international relations, liberal arts/general studies, Native American studies, parks and recreation management, philosophy, political science/government, psychology, public administration, social work, sociology, and women and gender studies). Biology, elementary education, and nursing have the largest enrollments.

ACTIVITIES: There are 337 groups on campus, including art, band, cheerleading, chess, choir, chorale, chorus, computers, dance, debate, drama, environmental, ethnic, film, forensics, gay, honors, international, jazz band, literary magazine, marching band, musical theater, newspaper, opera, orchestra, pep band, photography, political, professional, radio and TV, religious, social, social service, student government, and symphony. Popular campus events include Welcome Week, Family Weekend and Homecoming. **Sports:** There are 6 intercollegiate sports for men and 9 for women, and 11 intramural sports for men and 9 for women. Facilities include a skydome for football, basketball, and indoor track and field; three recreation centers with basketball and racquetball courts and weight rooms, a 50-meter indoor swimming pool with diving facilities, and numerous outdoor grass fields for soccer, rugby, and lacrosse. The Health and Learning Center (272,000 square foot) engages students in holistic learning by integrating recreation, health services, athletics, and academics into one central location. **Graduates:** From July 1, 2013 to June 30, 2014, 4984 bachelor's degrees were awarded. The most popular majors were elementary education, psychology, and nursing. 200 companies recruited on campus in 2013-2014. In an average class, 33% graduate in 4 years or less, 48% graduate in 5 years or less, and 52% graduate in 6 years or less.

SERVICES: Counseling and information services are available, as is tutoring in most subjects. There is a reader service for the blind, and remedial math, reading, and writing. **Library/Resources:** The library contains 1.2 million volumes, and subscribes to 63,429 periodicals including electronic. Computerized library services include interlibrary loans, database searching, Internet access, and Wi-Fi capability. Special learning facilities include an art gallery, radio station, TV station, an observatory, research centers, and the Centennial Forest. **Physically Challenged Students:** 90% of the campus is accessible. Facilities include wheelchair ramps, elevators, special parking, specially equipped restrooms, special class scheduling, lowered drinking fountains, lowered telephones, and special housing. **Special:** NAU offers co-op programs in business and hotel/restaurant management, cross-registration with many universities through the National Student Exchange, and internships in most majors. Legislative internships are offered through the Arizona State Senate and House of Representatives. Students may study abroad in over 50 countries. Work-study programs are available in numerous fields, including engineering, business, and park services. NAU now also offers a Personalized Learning program. There is a freshman honors program. **Visiting:** There are regularly scheduled orientations for prospective students. There are guides for informal visits and visitors may sit in on classes. To schedule a visit, contact the Office of Undergraduate Admissions and Orientation at (928) 523-0922. **Campus Safety and Security:** Measures include 24-hour foot and vehicle patrol, emergency notification system, self-defense education, and security escort services. There are shuttle buses, emergency telephones, lighted pathways/sidewalks, and controlled access to dorms/residences.

REQUIREMENTS: The SAT or ACT is recommended. Students will be offered admission if they meet the following: 3.0 or higher core GPA, or top 50 percent class rank and have no deficiencies in the required college preparatory courses. Home school students must meet aptitude requirements through ACT or SATI composite test scores. ACT score of 22 (Arizona resident) or 24 (non-resident) or SATI score of 1040 (Arizona resident) or 1110 (non-resident). *GPA is calculated using only the 16 core courses listed under course requirements. NAU requires applicants to be in the upper 50% of their class. A GPA of 3.0 is required. AP and CLEP credits are accepted.To receive a bachelor's degree at Northern Arizona University, you must complete at least 120 units of credit. Within those total units, you must complete: all of Northern Arizona University's liberal studies requirements; all requirements for your specific academic plan(s); at least 30 units of upper-division courses, which may include transfer work; at least 30 units taken through Northern Arizona University, of which at least 18 must be upper-division courses (300 level or above); and a cumulative grade point average of at least 2.0 on all work attempted at Northern Arizona University. **Procedure:** Freshmen are admitted fall, spring, and summer. Entrance exams should be taken before the last semester of the senior year. There are deferred admissions and rolling admissions plans. Application deadlines are open. Application fee is $25. Applications are accepted on-line. **Transfer Students:** 2478 transfer students enrolled in 2013-2014. Transfer students will be offered admission if they have earned more than 12 college credits in the Arizona General Education Curriculum (AGEC) or the California inter-segmental General Education Transfer Curriculum (IEGTC) with a cumulative GPA of 2.0; or earn an associate's degree with a cumulative GPA of 2.0. Transfer students must be eligible to re-enter the institution they last attended. 30 of 120 credits required for the bachelor's degree must be completed at NAU. **International Students:** There are 1053 international students enrolled. The school actively recruits these students. They must take the TOEFL with a minimum score of 525 on the paper-based TOEFL (PBT) or 70 on the Internet-based version (iBT).

ADMISSIONS: 91% of the 2014-2015 applicants were accepted. The SAT scores for the 2014-2015 freshman class were: Critical Reading-36% below 500, 45% between 500 and 599, 17% between 600 and 699, and 2% between 700 and 800; Math--36% below 500, 45% between 500 and 599, 17% between 600 and 699, and 2% between 700 and 800; Writing--47% below 500, 39% between 500 and 599, 12% between 600 and 699, and 1% between 700 and 800. The ACT scores were 30% below 21, 27% between 21 and 23, 26% between 24 and 26, 10% between 27 and 28, and 7% above 28. **Admissions Contact:** Anika Olsen, Director of Admissions. E-Mail: *Anika.Olsen@nau.edu* Web: *nau.edu*

FINANCIAL AID: 63% of all full-time freshmen and 63% of continuing full-time students received need-based aid. The average freshman award was $11,167. Need-based scholarships or need-based grants averaged $6,541; need-based self-help aid (loans and jobs) averaged $3,464; non-need-based athletic scholarships averaged $13,005; and other non-need-based awards and non-need-based scholarships averaged $6,373. The FAFSA is required. The priority date for freshman financial aid applications for fall entry is February 14.

PRESCOTT COLLEGE C-3
www.prescott.edu

Prescott, AZ 86301

(928) 350-2100
(800) 628-6364

Fax: (928) 776-5242

Email: admissions@prescott.edu

Full-time: 204 men, 240 women

Faculty: 60

Part-time: 40 men, 61 women

Ph.D.s: 58%

Graduate: 90 men, 308 women

Student/Faculty: 9 to 1

Year: semesters, summer session

Tuition: $26,819

Room & Board: $6465

Freshman Class: 399 applied, 291 accepted, 49 enrolled

SAT CR/M/W: 565/520/534 ACT: 23

CEEB CODE: 0484

Application Deadline: August 15

COMPETITIVE

Prescott College, founded in 1960, is a private liberal arts institution offering a nontraditional undergraduate program complemented with experiential learning focused on sustainability, the environment, and social justice. The curriculum is organized into multidisciplinary courses that allow students to pursue individual areas of competency. Evaluations of a student's work are conducted through a portfolio/contract system and an ongoing series of student self-evaluations. Grades are optional. Figures in the above capsule and in this profile are approximate. There are 2 undergraduate schools and 2 graduate schools. In addition to regional accreditation, Prescott has baccalaureate program accreditation with NASDTEC. The 13-acre campus is in a small town 100 miles northwest of Phoenix. Including any residence halls, there are 29 buildings.

STUDENT LIFE: 75% of undergraduates are from out of state, mostly the West. Students are from 42 states, 6 foreign countries, and Canada. 73% are White; 12% race unknown. The average age of freshmen is 19; all undergraduates, 23. 27% do not continue beyond their first year; 37% remain to graduate. **Housing:** 120 students can be accommodated in college housing, which includes coed dorms, on-campus houses, and coed housing. On-campus housing is guaranteed for the freshman year only, is available on a first-come, first-served basis. 80% of students commute. Alcohol is not permitted. All students may keep cars.

FACULTY/CLASSROOMS: 44% of faculty are male; 56% are female. 82% teach undergraduates. No introductory courses are taught by graduate students. The average class size in an introductory lecture is 12; in a laboratory is 12; and in a regular course is 12.

PROGRAMS OF STUDY: Prescott confers B.A., B.S. and B.F.A degrees. Master's and doctoral degrees are also awarded. Bachelor's degrees are awarded in AGRICULTURE (agriculture, environmental studies, forestry and related sciences, and wildlife management), BIOLOGICAL SCIENCE (biology/biological science, ecology, environmental biology, marine biology, marine science, and wildlife biology), BUSINESS (management science, nonprofit/public organization management, and organizational leadership and management), COMMUNICATIONS AND THE ARTS (art, arts administration/management, communications, creative writing, dance, dramatic arts, English, fine arts, journalism, literature, music, performing arts, photography, Spanish, studio art, and visual and performing arts), COMPUTER AND PHYSICAL SCIENCE (earth science, environmental geology, geology, mathematics, natural sciences, and oceanography), EDUCATION (agricultural education, art education, early childhood education, education, education of the emotionally handicapped, education of the exceptional child, education of the mentally handicapped, elementary education, environmental education, foreign languages education, guidance education, middle school education, music education, physical education, recreation education, secondary education, social science education, social studies education, and special education), ENGINEERING AND ENVIRONMENTAL DESIGN (environmental design, environmental science, and land use management and reclamation), HEALTH PROFESSIONS (art therapy, community health work, and mental health/human services), SOCIAL SCIENCE (addiction studies, anthropology, archeology, area studies, community services, counseling/psychology, economics, ethics, politics, and social policy, experimental psychology, gender studies, geography, history, human development, human ecology, human services, humanities, humanities and social science, international relations, international studies, Latin American studies, liberal arts/general studies, parks and recreation management, peace studies, philosophy and religion, psychology, religion, social science, social work, sociology, water resources, and women's studies). Environmental studies, and adventure education are the strongest academically. Environmental studies has the largest enrollment.

ACTIVITIES: There are no fraternities or sororities. There are 12 groups on campus, including bicycle, book club, dance and garden club, jugglers and hoopers, meditation club, agriculture, art, dance, drama, environmental, film, gay, international, literary magazine, newspaper, photography, political, social, social service, and student government. Popular campus events include Earth Day, and Southwest Writers Series. **Sports:** There is no sports program at Prescott. There are no sports facilities on campus, but students have access to the local community pool, a weight room, gym, and city league

sports. **Graduates:** From July 1, 2013 to June 30, 2014, 196 bachelor's degrees were awarded. The most popular majors were human development (23%), environmental studies/natural resources (22%), and education (16%). In an average class, 23% graduate in 4 years or less, 34% graduate in 5 years or less, and 37% graduate in 6 years or less.

SERVICES: Counseling and information services are available, as is tutoring in every subject. There is a learning specialist on staff, and untimed tests are available. There are recordings for the blind and dyslexic. **Library/Resources:** The library contains 131,524 volumes, 155 microform items, and 1,732 audio/video tapes/CDs/DVDs, and subscribes to 31,330 periodicals including electronic. Computerized library services include interlibrary loans, database searching, Internet access, and Wi-Fi capability. Special learning facilities include an art gallery, a library annexes at Kino Bay, Mexico and Tucson Center; an experimental agroecology farm, a field station in Kino Bay, Mexico, a GIS station, state of the art visual arts classrooms and a functioning gallery, equipment gear warehouse, and a recycling center. In the library, access to 96,521 electronic books and a learning commons for writing and math help. **Physically Challenged Students:** 90% of the campus is accessible. Facilities include wheelchair ramps, elevators, special parking, specially equipped restrooms, and special housing. **Special:** Cross-registration with Eco-League colleges and the Consortium for Innovative Environments in Learning is possible. Student-coordinated internships, study abroad in almost any country, dual majors, a general studies degree, pass/fail options, and credit for life experience are offered. All majors are student-designed. **Visiting:** There are regularly scheduled orientations for prospective students, including a campus tour, an interview with an admissions counselor, opportunities to sit in classes, faculty interviews, and informational meetings with financial aid and library staff. There are guides for informal visits and visitors may sit in on classes. To schedule a visit, contact the Admissions Office at admissions@prescott.edu. **Campus Safety and Security:** Measures include emergency notification system and security escort services. There are emergency telephones, controlled access to dorms/residences, after hours patrol.

REQUIREMENTS: The SAT is required. The ACT is recommended. In addition, a high school diploma is required, the GED is accepted. The school requires a completed application form, 1 essay, official transcripts, and 1 letter of recommendation. Students may also submit portfolios and writing samples. A GPA of 2.0 is required. AP and CLEP credits are accepted. Important factors in the admissions decision are extracurricular activities record, leadership record, and evidence of special talent. Students must complete an orientation course, fulfill a minimum residency requirement, demonstrate proficiency in college-level writing and math, and meet course and credit requirements. Students design an individual program of studies within 7 multidisciplinary areas: adventure education, arts and letters, cultural and regional studies, education, environmental studies, humanities, and human development. Each student is required to submit a graduation proposal at the end of the junior year to a graduation review committee. **Procedure:** Freshmen are admitted fall and spring. There are early decision, deferred admissions, and rolling admissions plans. Early decision applications should be filed by December 1; regular applications, by August 15 for fall entry; and December 15 for spring entry. Notification of early decision is sent December 15; regular decision, on a rolling basis. 11 early decision candidates were accepted for the 2014-2015 class. Applications are accepted on-line. **Transfer Students:** 119 transfer students enrolled in 2013-2014. Transfer applicants must meet the same requirements as entering freshmen and must also submit official college transcripts and an essay or personal statement. Students who successfully completed 2 years of college work (60 semester hours or 90 quarter credits) need not submit high school transcripts. There is a 2-year residency requirement. 60 of 120 credits required for the bachelor's degree must be completed at Prescott. **International Students:** There are 8 international students enrolled. They must take the TOEFL with a minimum score of 500 on the paper-based TOEFL (PBT) or 61 on the Internet-based version (iBT).

ADMISSIONS: 73% of the 2014-2015 applicants were accepted. The SAT scores for the 2014-2015 freshman class were: Critical Reading--29% below 500, 41% between 500 and 599, 18% between 600 and 699, and 12% between 700 and 800; Math--44% below 500, 26% between 500 and 599, 24% between 600 and 699, and 6% between

700 and 800; Writing--33% below 500, 50% between 500 and 599, 11% between 600 and 699, and 6% between 700 and 800. The ACT scores were 8% below 21, 42% between 21 and 23, % between 24 and 26, 33% between 27 and 28, and 17% above 28. **Admissions Contact:** Nancy Simmons, Receptionist. E-Mail: *admissions@prescott.edu* Web: *www.prescott.edu*

FINANCIAL AID: In 2014-2015, 78% of all full-time freshmen and 70% of continuing full-time students received some form of financial aid. 77% of all full-time freshmen and 69% of continuing full-time students received need-based aid. The average freshman award was $19,706. Need-based scholarships or need-based grants averaged $14,569; need-based self-help aid (loans and jobs) averaged $5,493; other non-need-based awards and non-need-based scholarships averaged $8,642; and $4,821 from other forms of aid. 31% of undergraduate students work part-time. Average annual earnings from campus work are $800. The average financial indebtedness of the 2014 graduate was $27,213. The FAFSA is required. The priority date for freshman financial aid applications for fall entry is March 1.

UNIVERSITY OF ARIZONA — D-4
www.arizona.edu

Tucson, AZ 85721   (520) 621-3705

Email: kasandra@email.arizona.edu

Full-time: 14054 men, 15475 women	**Faculty:** 1509
Part-time: 1781 men, 1677 women	**Ph.D.s:** 90%
Graduate: 4510 men, 4739 women	**Student/Faculty:** n/av
Year: semesters, summer session	**Tuition:** $10,957 ($29,421)
Room & Board: $9700	**Freshman Class:** n/av
SAT or ACT: recommended	**CEEB CODE:** 4832
Application Deadline: n/av	**COMPETITIVE**

The University of Arizona, founded in 1885, is a public land-grant institution controlled by the state of Arizona. Undergraduate programs are offered in agriculture, architecture, arts and sciences, business and public administration, education, engineering and mines, nursing, pharmacy and other health-related professions. There are 41 undergraduate schools and 1 graduate school. In addition to regional accreditation, UA has baccalaureate program accreditation with ACPE, ADA, NASAD, and NASM. The 392-acre campus is in an urban area in Tucson, AZ. Including any residence halls, there are 103 buildings.

STUDENT LIFE: 66% of undergraduates are from Arizona. Others are from 50 states, 138 foreign countries, and Canada. 86% are from public schools. 52% are White; 22% Hispanic. **Male To Female Ratio:** 1.1:1. The average age of freshmen is 18; all undergraduates, 21. **Housing:** 7254 students can be accommodated in college housing, which includes single-sex and coed dorms, on-campus apartments, and off-campus apartments. In addition, there are honors houses, special-interest houses, fraternity houses, and sorority houses. On-campus housing is available on a first-come and first-served basis. 80% of students commute. Alcohol is not permitted. All students may keep cars.

FACULTY/CLASSROOMS: 61% of faculty are male; 39% are female. No introductory courses are taught by graduate students.

PROGRAMS OF STUDY: UA confers B.A., B.A.E., B.Arch., B.A.S., B.E.S., B.F.A., B.G.S., B.Mu., B.S., B.S.Ae.E., B.S.B.A., B.S.Bm.E., B.S.Bs.E., B.S.Ch.E., B.S.Cv.E., B.S.E., B.S.E.C.E., B.S.E.Mg., B.S.H.S., B.S.In.E., B.S.Me.E., B.S.Mn.E., B.S.M.S.E., B.S.N., B.S.O.S.E., B.S.S.B.E., B.S.S.Ed. and B.S.Sy.E. degrees. Master's and doctoral degrees are also awarded. Bachelor's degrees are awarded in AGRICULTURE (agricultural business management, agricultural economics, animal science, environmental studies, natural resource management, plant science, and soil science), BIOLOGICAL SCIENCE (biochemistry, biology/biological science, biometrics and biostatistics, cell biology, ecology, entomology, genetics, microbiology, molecular biology, neurosciences, nutrition, physiology, and plant pathology), BUSINESS (accounting, business administration and management, business economics, entrepreneurial studies,

finance, management information systems, management science, marketing and distribution, operations management, and retailing), COMMUNICATIONS AND THE ARTS (art history, art, classics, communications, creative writing, dance, English, English as a second/foreign language, film arts, fine arts, French, Italian, journalism, linguistics, music, musical theater, performing arts, Russian, Spanish, studio art, and theatre arts), COMPUTER AND PHYSICAL SCIENCE (applied mathematics, applied science, astronomy, atmospheric sciences and meteorology, chemistry, computer science, geology, geoscience, hydrology, information sciences and systems, mathematics, medical physics, natural sciences, optics, physics, planetary and space science, and statistics), EDUCATION (agricultural education, art education, early childhood education, education, elementary education, library science, middle school education, music education, psychology education, school psychology, science education, secondary education, special education, and teaching English as a second/foreign language (TESOL/TEFOL)), ENGINEERING AND ENVIRONMENTAL DESIGN (aeronautical engineering, agricultural engineering, architecture, biomedical engineering, chemical engineering, civil engineering, electrical/electronics engineering, engineering, environmental engineering, environmental science, industrial engineering, landscape architecture/design, materials engineering, materials science, mechanical engineering, mining and mineral engineering, optical engineering, and systems engineering), HEALTH PROFESSIONS (environmental health science, medical science, nursing, pharmaceutical science, pharmacology, pharmacy, Pre-Health Studies, public health, rehabilitation therapy, speech pathology/audiology, and veterinary science), SOCIAL SCIENCE (African studies, American Indian studies, anthropology, counseling/psychology, East Asian studies, economics, family/consumer studies, gender studies, geography, German area studies, history, human development, interdisciplinary studies, Judaic studies, Latin American studies, law, Mexican-American/Chicano studies, Middle Eastern studies, philosophy, political science/government, psychology, public administration, religious education, sociology, and women's studies). Sciences, social sciences, and business administration are the strongest academically. Business, and sciences have the largest enrollments.

ACTIVITIES: 15% of men belong to 24 national fraternities; 20% of women belong to 24 national sororities. There are 411 groups on campus, including art, band, cheerleading, chess, choir, chorale, chorus, computers, dance, debate, drama, drill team, environmental, ethnic, film, gay, honors, international, jazz band, literary magazine, marching band, musical theater, newspaper, orchestra, pep band, photography, political, professional, radio and TV, religious, social, student government, and yearbook. Popular campus events include Spring Fling Carnival, Cultural Programs and Family Weekend. **Sports:** There are 7 intercollegiate sports for men and 10 for women. Facilities include an athletic center, stadium, arena, student recreation facility with a weight room, a wave-less swimming pool, two gyms, aerobics facilities, treadmills, stair climbers, stationary bicycles, racquetball, squash, handball courts, hiking, backpacking, skiing trails as well as facilities for kayaking, caving, and scuba diving are available. **Graduates:** From July 1, 2013 to June 30, 2014, 6370 bachelor's degrees were awarded.

SERVICES: Counseling and information services are available, as is tutoring in most subjects. There is a reader service for the blind, and remedial math, reading, and writing. **Library/Resources:** The 7 libraries contain 6.4 million volumes, 5.6 million microform items, 86,067 audio/video tapes/CDs/DVDs, and subscribe to 76,605 periodicals including electronic. Computerized library services include interlibrary loans, database searching, Internet access, and Wi-Fi capability. Special learning facilities include an art gallery, natural history museum, planetarium, radio station, TV station, the Ansel Adams center for creative photography, and the integrated learning center. **Physically Challenged Students:** 95% of the campus is accessible. Facilities include wheelchair ramps, elevators, special parking, specially equipped restrooms, lowered drinking fountains, lowered telephones, special housing, physical therapy, counseling, interpreters, equipment maintenance and an adaptive athletics program. **Special:** Co-op programs are available in almost all majors. Internships in almost all disciplines. Washington semester for certain internships related to government. Accelerated Masters programs-MBA, MIS, and Entrepreneurship programs. 119 B.A.-B.S. degrees, dual majors, interdisciplinary degrees such as engineering-math and theater arts-education, a 3-2 arts and sciences-business degree, and student designed majors are offered. Study abroad in numerous countries, work-study programs on campus, a general studies degree, and pass/fail options are offered. Non-degree study is possible. There are 33 national honor societies, including Phi Beta Kappa, and a freshman honors program. **Visiting:** There are regularly scheduled orientations for prospective students, consisting of an admissions presentation and tour. There are guides for informal visits and visitors may sit in on classes. To schedule a visit, contact the Admissions Office. **Campus Safety and Security:** Measures include 24-hour foot and vehicle patrol, emergency notification system, self-defense education, and security escort services. There are shuttle buses, emergency telephones, lighted pathways/sidewalks, and controlled access to dorms/residences.

REQUIREMENTS: The SAT or ACT is recommended. Applicants should have completed 4 years each in high school English and math, 3 in science, 2 of a foreign language, and 1 each in history, fine arts, and social studies. A GED may be considered in place of a high school diploma. Some fine arts programs require auditions prior to admission. A GPA of 2.0 is required. AP and CLEP credits are accepted.Opportunities for engagement, i.e. real-world experiences, outside of the classroom to support classroom learning available and supported to enhance the educational experience, including internships, study aboard around the world, exchange programs, practicums and work options. Accelerated Masters programs available in a variety of disciplines, including a new 3+3 law program. Dual majors and interdisciplinary degree options available, in addition to a multitude of minor options. **Procedure:** Freshmen are admitted to all sessions. There is a rolling admissions plan. Check with the school for current application deadlines. The application fee is $50. Notification is sent on a rolling basis. Applications are accepted on-line. **Transfer Students:** 2049 transfer students enrolled in 2013-2014. Resident transfer applicants must have a minimum GPA of 2.00; and nonresidents must have a minimum GPA of 2.5. Some university divisions have higher requirements. Admission is competitive for out-of-state students. 30 of 120 credits required for the bachelor's degree must be completed at UA. **International Students:** There are 1876 international students enrolled. The school actively recruits these students. They must take the TOEFL with a minimum score of 550 on the paper-based TOEFL (PBT) or 70 on the Internet-based version (iBT) and the Comprehensive English Language Test. They must also take the SAT or ACT, scoring 1110.

ADMISSIONS: There were 68 National Merit finalists. **Admissions Contact:** Kasandra Urquidez, Dean of Undergraduate Admissions . E-Mail: *kasandra@email.arizona.edu* Web: *www.arizona.edu*

FINANCIAL AID: In 2014-2015, 82% of all full-time freshmen and 74% of continuing full-time students received some form of financial aid. 54% of all full-time freshmen and 49% of continuing full-time students received need-based aid. UA is a member of CSS. The FAFSA is required. Check with the school for current application deadlines.

ARKANSAS

A B C D E

1
• Saloan Springs
Fayetteville!
• Walnut Ridge

Batesville •
Jonesboro •

Clarksville •
40
• Russellville
Searcy •
55

2

Conway •
40

3
Little Rock •

Arkadelphia •
Pine Bluff •
30

4
Monticello •

Magnolia •

5

• College Location

0 20 40 60 80 100
Miles

ARKANSAS BAPTIST COLLEGE (*The complete profile is made available exclusively on our website, www.barronspac.com*)

ARKANSAS STATE UNIVERSITY   D-2
www.astate.edu

State University, AR 72467   **(870) 972-2782**

Fax: (870) 972-3545   **Email:** recruitment@astate.edu

Full-time: 3275 men, 4190 women   **Faculty:** 440; IIA, --$
Part-time: 933 men, 1459 women   **Ph.D.s:** 85%
Graduate: 1139 men, 2148 women   **Student/Faculty:** 17 to 1
Year: semesters, summer session   **Tuition:** $7720 ($13,480)
Room & Board: $7750   **Freshman Class:** 5086
                                        applied, 3682 accepted,
                                        1698 enrolled
SAT CR/M/W: 470/510/440 **ACT:** 24 **CEEB CODE:** 6011
Application Deadline: August 17   **COMPETITIVE**

Arkansas State University, founded in 1909, and part of the Arkansas State University System, is a state-supported institution offering undergraduate and graduate degrees in Agriculture and Technology, Business, Education and Behavioral Sciences, Engineering, Fine Arts, Humanities and Social Sciences, Media and Communication, Nursing and Health Professions, Sciences and Mathematics. There are 11 undergraduate schools and 1 graduate school. In addition to regional accreditation, ASU has baccalaureate program accreditation with AACSB, ABET, ACEJMC, CSWE, NASAD, NASM, NCATE, and NLN. The 1376-acre campus is in a small town 70 miles west of Memphis, TN. Including any residence halls, there are 152 buildings.

STUDENT LIFE: 85% of undergraduates are from Arkansas. Others are from 40 states, 46 foreign countries, and Canada. 93% are from public schools. 75% are White; 14% African American. **Male To Female Ratio:** 1.5:1. The average age of freshmen is 18; all undergraduates, 23. 26% do not continue beyond their first year; 41% remain

to graduate. **Housing:** 3218 students can be accommodated in college housing, which includes single-sex and coed dorms, on-campus apartments, and married student housing. In addition, there are honors houses, special-interest houses, fraternity houses, sorority houses, living learning communities (Honors, STEM, ROTC) and first-year residential experience wing. On-campus housing is available on a first-come and first-served basis. 70% of students commute. Alcohol is not permitted. All students may keep cars.

FACULTY/CLASSROOMS: 45% of faculty are male; 55% are female. 90% teach undergraduates, 20% do research, and 20% do both. Graduate students teach 5% of introductory courses. The average class size in an introductory lecture is 30; in a laboratory is 24; and in a regular course is 27.

PROGRAMS OF STUDY: ASU confers B.A., B.G.S., B.S., B.A.S., B.F.A., B.M., B.M.E., B.S.A., B.S.E., B.S.C.E., B.S.E.E., B.S.M.E., B.S.N., B.S.E.N., B.S.R.S. and B.S.W. degrees. Associate, master's, and doctoral degrees are also awarded. Bachelor's degrees are awarded in AGRICULTURE (agricultural business management, agriculture, animal science, plant science, and wildlife management), BIOLOGICAL SCIENCE (biology/biological science and biotechnology), BUSINESS (accounting, banking and finance, business administration and management, business economics, international business, marketing, sports management, and supply chain management), COMMUNICATIONS AND THE ARTS (art, communications, English, foreign language, graphic design, information technology, instrumental music education, journalism, music, radio/television technology, theatre arts, and vocal performance), COMPUTER AND PHYSICAL SCIENCE (chemistry, clinical laboratory science, chemistry education, computer science, mathematics, and physics), EDUCATION (athletic training, business education, early childhood education, English education, foreign languages education, general studies, health education, mathematics education, middle school education, physical education, science education, and social science education), ENGINEERING AND ENVIRONMENTAL DESIGN (civil engineering technology, electrical/electronics engineering, emergency/disaster science, engineering, manufacturing technology, mechanical engineering, and technological management), HEALTH PROFESSIONS (exercise science, health promotion, nursing, and radiological science), SOCIAL SCIENCE (communication sciences and disorders, criminology, dietetics, economics, history, interdisciplinary studies, philosophy, political science/government, psychology, social work, and sociology). Engineering, nursing, and biological sciences are the strongest academically. Nursing, early childhood education, and interdisciplinary studies have the largest enrollments.

ACTIVITIES: 15% of men belong to 13 national fraternities; 12% of women belong to 7 national sororities. There are 165 groups on campus, including academic, art, cheerleading, choir, computers, dance, debate, drama, drill team, environmental, ethnic, forensics, gay, honors, international, jazz band, marching band, musical theater, newspaper, pep band, photography, political, professional, radio and TV, religious, social, social service, student government, symphony, and yearbook. Popular campus events include Welcome Week, Order of the Pack, Homecoming, Mardi Gras Celebration, Springfest, and Black History Month Celebration. **Sports:** There are 7 intercollegiate sports for men and 9 for women, and 16 intramural sports for men and 16 for women. Facilities include a 10,563-seat convocation center for basketball games or 10,704-seats for concerts, a 30,708-seat football stadium, 1,200-seat baseball complex, 400-seat track facility, and a 500-seat soccer field. **Graduates:** From July 1, 2013 to June 30, 2014, 1824 bachelor's degrees were awarded. The most popular majors were interdisciplinary studies (10%), nursing (8%), and early childhood education (8%). 207 companies recruited on campus in 2013-2014. In an average class, 11% graduate in 3 years or less, 28% graduate in 4 years or less, 37% graduate in 5 years or less, and 39% graduate in 6 years or less. Of the 2013 graduating class, 19% were enrolled in graduate school within 6 months of graduation, and 34% were employed.

SERVICES: Counseling and information services are available, as is tutoring in most subjects. There is a reader service for the blind, and remedial math, reading, and writing. Tutoring is provided in virtually all general education subjects. Student Support Services tries to provide as much tutoring as possible for upper level courses when tutors are available for the subject areas. **Library/Resources:** The library contains 1.4 million volumes, 28,736 audio/video tapes/CDs/DVDs, and subscribes to 33,952 periodicals including electronic. Computerized library services include interlibrary loans, database searching, Internet access, and Wi-Fi capability. Special learning facilities include an art gallery, natural history museum, radio station, TV station, Facilities for Agriculture and Environmental Ecotoxicology Research, the Arkansas Biosciences Institute, the Fowler Center for Performing Arts, distance learning, the Hemingway-Pfeiffer Museum and Educational Center,a geographic information system facility, an electron microscope lab, and the Delta Studies Center. **Physically Challenged Students:** 90% of the campus is accessible. Facilities include wheelchair ramps, elevators, special parking, specially equipped restrooms, special class scheduling, lowered drinking fountains, lowered telephones. **Special:** An interdisciplinary studies degree, study abroad, and work-study programs are offered. Dual majors and internships are available in many areas. Non-degree study is possible. There are 31 national honor societies and a freshman honors program. **Visiting:** There are regularly scheduled orientations for prospective students, consisting of various sessions held throughout the year. There are guides for informal visits, visitors may sit in on classes, and stay overnight. To schedule a visit, contact the Office of Recruitment at (870) 972-2782. **Campus Safety and Security:** Measures include 24-hour foot and vehicle patrol, emergency notification system, self-defense education, and security escort services. There are shuttle buses, emergency telephones, and lighted pathways/sidewalks.

REQUIREMENTS: ACT, SAT, ASSET, or COMPASS scores are required, with ACT scores recommended. Applicants should have completed 14 academic high school units, including 4 each in English and math, 3 in social studies, 3 in science (must be labs), and it is recommended to take 2 in 1 foreign language. Applicants must have an ACT composite score of 21 and a high school GPA of 2.75 for unconditional admission. Recommend 2 units of a foreign language. A GPA of 2.8 is required. AP and CLEP credits are accepted. All students must complete a 35 hour credit distribution of general education courses. A total of at least 120 credits, with a minimum GPA of 2.0, is required to graduate. **Procedure:** Freshmen are admitted fall, spring, and summer. Entrance exams should be taken before April 1 of the high school senior year. There are early admissions and rolling admissions plans. Applications should be filed by August 17 for fall entry; January 11 for spring entry; and June 1 for summer entry, along with a $15 fee. Applications are accepted on-line. **Transfer Students:** 867 transfer students enrolled in 2013-2014. Transfer applicants should have a minimum GPA of 2.0. Those having completed 12 or fewer credit hours will be admitted on the same basis as freshmen. Official transcripts from every institution attended are required. 32 of 120 credits required for the bachelor's degree must be completed at ASU. **International Students:** There are 475 international students enrolled. The school actively recruits these students. They must take the TOEFL with a minimum score of 500 on the paper-based TOEFL (PBT) or 61 on the Internet-based version (iBT).

ADMISSIONS: 72% of the 2014-2015 applicants were accepted. The SAT scores for the 2014-2015 freshman class were: Critical Reading--68% below 500, 29% between 500 and 599, 3% between 600 and 699, and % between 700 and 800; Math--38% below 500, 41% between 500 and 599, 21% between 600 and 699, and 13% between 700 and 800; Writing--82% below 500, 18% between 500 and 599, % between 600 and 699, and % between 700 and 800. The ACT scores were 20% below 21, 30% between 21 and 23, 26% between 24 and 26, 13% between 27 and 28, and 11% above 28. 43% of the current freshmen were in the top fifth of their class; 66% were in the top two fifths. 49 freshmen graduated first in their class. **Admissions Contact:** Tammy Fowler, Director of Recruitment. E-Mail: *recruitment@astate.edu* Web: *www.astate.edu*

FINANCIAL AID: In 2014-2015, 93% of all full-time freshmen and 75% of continuing full-time students received some form of financial aid. 82% of all full-time freshmen and 74% of continuing full-time students received need-based aid. The average freshman award was $13,250. Need-based scholarships or need-based grants averaged $7,800 ($9,000 maximum); need-based self-help aid (loans and jobs) averaged $6,200 ($8,500 maximum); non-need-based athletic schol-

arships averaged $9,500 ($10,000 maximum); and other non-need-based awards and non-need-based scholarships averaged $6,000 ($12,000 maximum). 9% of undergraduate students work part-time. Average annual earnings from campus work are $5880. The average financial indebtedness of the 2014 graduate was $25,000. ASU is a member of CSS. The FAFSA and the college's own financial statement are required. The priority date for freshman financial aid applications for fall entry is February 15. The deadline for filing freshman financial aid applications for fall entry is July 1.

ARKANSAS TECH UNIVERSITY (*The complete profile is made available exclusively on our website, www.barronspac.com*)

HARDING UNIVERSITY C-2
www.harding.edu

Searcy, AR 72149	(501) 279-4407
	(800) 477-4407
Fax: (501) 279-4129	Email: gdillard@harding.edu
Full-time: 1857 men, 2301 women	Faculty: 225
Part-time: 160 men, 174 women	Ph.D.s: 67%
Graduate: 579 men, 1004 women	Student/Faculty: 16 to 1
Year: semesters, summer session	Tuition: $17,040
Room & Board: $6516	Freshman Class: 2269 applied, 2249 accepted, 1067 enrolled
SAT CR/M: 540/530 ACT: 25	CEEB CODE: 6267
Application Deadline: June 1	COMPETITIVE

Harding University, founded in 1924, is a private Christian institution comprised of the Colleges of Allied Health, Arts and Humanities, Sciences, Bible and Religion, Business, Education, Nursing, and Pharmacy. There are 7 undergraduate schools and 5 graduate schools. In addition to regional accreditation, Harding has baccalaureate program accreditation with ABET, ACBSP, CSWE, NASM, NCATE, and NLN. The 350-acre campus is in a small town 50 miles northeast of Little Rock and 105 miles west of Memphis, TN. Including any residence halls, there are 65 buildings.

STUDENT LIFE: 72% of undergraduates are from out of state, mostly the South. Students are from 49 states, 44 foreign countries, and Canada. 64% are from public schools. 83% are White. 93% are Protestant. **Male To Female Ratio:** 1.3:1. The average age of freshmen is 18; all undergraduates, 21. 18% do not continue beyond their first year; 64% remain to graduate. **Housing:** 3220 students can be accommodated in college housing, which includes single-sex dorms, on-campus apartments, off-campus apartments, and married student housing. On-campus housing is guaranteed for all 4 years, is available on a first-come, and first-served basis. 74% of students live on campus; of those, 75% remain on campus on weekends. Alcohol is not permitted. All students may keep cars.

FACULTY/CLASSROOMS: 62% of faculty are male; 38% are female. 78% teach undergraduates. No introductory courses are taught by graduate students. The average class size in an introductory lecture is 17 and in a laboratory is 14.

PROGRAMS OF STUDY: Harding confers B.A., B.S., B.B.A., B.F.A., B.M.E., B.M.N., B.S.N., B.S.W., M.S., M.A.T., M.B.A., M.S.E., M.ED., E.D.D. and E.D.S. degrees. Master's and doctoral degrees are also awarded. Bachelor's degrees are awarded in BIOLOGICAL SCIENCE (biochemistry and biology/biological science), BUSINESS (accounting, banking and finance, business administration and management, fashion merchandising, international business management, marketing/retailing/merchandising, and sports management), COMMUNICATIONS AND THE ARTS (advertising, art, broadcasting, communications, design, dramatic arts, English, fine arts, French, graphic design, journalism, media arts, music, painting, and Spanish), COMPUTER AND PHYSICAL SCIENCE (chemistry, computer science, information sciences and systems, mathematics, and physics), EDUCATION (athletic training, Christian education, early childhood education, elementary education, foreign languages education, music education, and secondary education), ENGINEERING AND ENVIRONMENTAL DESIGN (biomedical engineering, computer engineering, electrical/electronics engineering, interior design, and mechanical engineering), HEALTH PROFESSIONS (exercise science, health, health care administration, health science, medical technology, nursing, and speech pathology/audiology), SOCIAL SCIENCE (American studies, biblical languages, biblical studies, child care/child and family studies, criminal justice, dietetics, economics, history, home economics, humanities, international studies, legal studies, liberal arts/general studies, ministries, missions, political science/government, psychology, public administration, religion, social science, social work, and youth ministry). Engineering, pharmacy, physical therphy, premedicine and nursing are the strongest academically. Business, education and nursing have the largest enrollments.

ACTIVITIES: 48% of men belong to 15 local fraternities; 55% of women belong to 16 local sororities. There are 103 groups on campus, including art, band, cheerleading, choir, chorale, chorus, computers, debate, drama, ethnic, film, honors, international, jazz band, literary magazine, marching band, musical theater, newspaper, orchestra, pep band, photography, political, professional, radio and TV, religious, social, social service, student government, symphony, and yearbook. Popular campus events include Spring Sing, Homecoming, Bison Days and Lectureship. **Sports:** There are 8 intercollegiate sports for men and 8 for women, and 11 intramural sports for men and 9 for women. Facilities include baseball and softball fields, racquetball, handball, and tennis courts, a football stadium, indoor and outdoor track, golf practice range, gymnastics room, weight rooms, an Olympic-size swimming pool, and 2 gyms. The football and athletic training complex provides state of the art weight room, locker room, office space, as well as rehabilitation area and hydrotherapy area. Harding owns a 2000-acre camp in the Ozark Mountains with horses, 25 rustic cabins, streams, and hiking trails. **Graduates:** From July 1, 2013 to June 30, 2014, 856 bachelor's degrees were awarded. The most popular majors were business/marketing (16%), early childhood licensure (14%), and health professions and related programs (14%). 263 companies recruited on campus in 2013-2014. In an average class, 43% graduate in 4 years or less, 59% graduate in 5 years or less, and 63% graduate in 6 years or less. Of the 2013 graduating class, 30% were enrolled in graduate school within 6 months of graduation.

SERVICES: Counseling and information services are available, as is tutoring in most subjects. There is a reader service for the blind, and remedial math, reading, and writing. **Library/Resources:** The library contains 337,421 volumes, 238,445 microform items, 13,313 audio/video tapes/CDs/DVDs, and subscribes to 49,918 periodicals including electronic. Computerized library services include interlibrary loans, database searching, Internet access, and Wi-Fi capability. Special learning facilities include an art gallery, radio station, and TV station. **Physically Challenged Students:** 95% of the campus is accessible. Facilities include wheelchair ramps, elevators, special parking, specially equipped restrooms, special class scheduling, lowered drinking fountains, lowered telephones, and special housing. **Special:** The Harding campus in Florence, Italy, and programs in Greece, England, Latin America, France/Switzerland, Australia, and Zambia offer international studies. Internships are given in social work, teaching, nursing, and international missions. Co-op programs in all majors, work-study programs, dual majors, a general studies degree, and non-degree study are available. There are 11 national honor societies and a freshman honors program. **Visiting:** There are regularly scheduled orientations for prospective students. There are guides for informal visits, visitors may sit in on classes, and stay overnight. To schedule a visit, contact the Admissions Office. **Campus Safety and Security:** Measures include 24-hour foot and vehicle patrol, emergency notification system, self-defense education, and security escort services. There are emergency telephones, lighted pathways/sidewalks, and controlled access to dorms/residences.

REQUIREMENTS: The SAT or ACT is required. A lower GPA can be offset by higher test scores. Applicants should be graduates of an accredited secondary school and have completed 15 high school hours, including 4 in English, 3 each in math, and social studies, 3 in art, history, or music, and 2 in a science. An interview is highly recommended. AP and CLEP credits are accepted. Important factors in the admissions decision are leadership record, recommendations by school officials, and advanced placement or honors courses. All students must complete 53 hours of general education courses, including

religion, English composition, history, speech communications, social sciences, biology, physical science, math, Western literature, music and art appreciation, and phys ed. A total of 128 semester hours, with a minimum GPA of 2.0, is required to graduate. 32 hours must be completed in residence and 45 must be upper-level. **Procedure:** Freshmen are admitted to all sessions. Entrance exams should be taken in the junior year or early in the senior year. There are early admissions, deferred admissions, and rolling admissions plans. Applications should be filed by June 1 for fall entry; November 1 for spring entry, along with a $50 fee. Notifications are sent May 1. Applications are accepted on-line. **Transfer Students:** Applicants with a minimum GPA of 2.0 and at least 14 semester hours earned are considered for admission. An interview is highly recommended. 32 of 128 credits required for the bachelor's degree must be completed at Harding. **International Students:** There are 288 international students enrolled. The school actively recruits these students. They must take the TOEFL with a minimum score of 550 on the paper-based TOEFL (PBT) or 79 on the Internet-based version (iBT). They must also take the SAT or ACT.

ADMISSIONS: 99% of the 2014-2015 applicants were accepted. The SAT scores for the 2014-2015 freshman class were: Critical Reading--26% below 500, 41% between 500 and 599, 24% between 600 and 699, and 9% between 700 and 800; Math--27% below 500, 39% between 500 and 599, 28% between 600 and 699, and 6% between 700 and 800. The ACT scores were 16% below 21, 21% between 21 and 23, 26% between 24 and 26, 14% between 27 and 28, and 23% above 28. 46% of the current freshmen were in the top fifth of their class; 74% were in the top two fifths. There were 7 National Merit finalists. **Admissions Contact:** Glen Dillard, Assistant Vice President for Enrollment Management. E-Mail: *gdillard@harding.edu* Web: *www.harding.edu*

FINANCIAL AID: In 2014-2015, 95% of all full-time freshmen and 92% of continuing full-time students received some form of financial aid. The average freshman award was $16,314. 35% of undergraduate students work part-time. Average annual earnings from campus work are $1700. The average financial indebtedness of the 2014 graduate was $24,120. The FAFSA is required. The priority date for freshman financial aid applications for fall entry is February 15. The deadline for filing freshman financial aid applications for fall entry is April 1.

HENDERSON STATE UNIVERSITY   B-4
www.hsu.edu

Arkadelphia, AR 71999   (870) 230-5028

Fax: (870) 230-5066	Email: admissions@hsu.edu
Full-time: 1268 men, 1610 women	Faculty: 167; IIA, --$
Part-time: 142 men, 179 women	Ph.D.s: 67%
Graduate: 122 men, 262 women	Student/Faculty: 17 to 1
Year: semesters, summer session	Tuition: $7562 ($13,404)
Room & Board: $7022	Freshman Class: 3388 applied, 2106 accepted, 705 enrolled
SAT CR/M: 500/536 ACT: 21	CEEB CODE: 6272
Application Deadline: open	COMPETITIVE

Henderson State University, founded in 1890 as Arkadelphia Methodist College, became a state institution in 1929 and offers liberal arts courses. Figures in the above capsule and in this profile are approximate. There are 3 undergraduate schools and 1 graduate school. In addition to regional accreditation, HSU has baccalaureate program accreditation with AACSB, ADA, NASM, and NCATE. The 152-acre campus is in a small town in Arkadelphia, a small town in southwest Arkansas, 35 miles from Hot Spring. Including any residence halls, there are 61 buildings.

STUDENT LIFE: 86% of undergraduates are from Arkansas. Others are from 27 states, 23 foreign countries, and Canada. 66% are White; 24% African American. **Male To Female Ratio:** 1.3:1. The average age of freshmen is 18; all undergraduates, 22. 45% do not continue beyond their first year; 29% remain to graduate. **Housing:** 1378 students can be accommodated in college housing, which includes single-sex and coed dorms and off-campus apartments. In addition, there are honors houses, international student housing and apartments on campus that are managed by an outside group. On-campus housing is available on a first-come and first-served basis. 59% of students commute. Alcohol is not permitted. All students may keep cars. **FACULTY/CLASSROOMS:** 49% of faculty are male; 51% are female. 95% teach undergraduates. No introductory courses are taught by graduate students. The average class size in an introductory lecture is 50; in a laboratory is 20; and in a regular course is 30.

PROGRAMS OF STUDY: HSU confers B.A., B.S., B.B.A., B.F.A., B.G.S., B.M., B.S.E. and B.S.N. degrees. Master's degrees are also awarded. Bachelor's degrees are awarded in BIOLOGICAL SCIENCE (biology/biological science), BUSINESS (accounting, business administration and management, recreation and leisure services), COMMUNICATIONS AND THE ARTS (communications, dramatic arts, English, music, Spanish, and studio art), COMPUTER AND PHYSICAL SCIENCE (chemistry, computer science, information sciences and systems, mathematics, physics, and radiological technology), EDUCATION (art education, athletic training, business education, early childhood education, education, middle school education, music education, and physical education), ENGINEERING AND ENVIRONMENTAL DESIGN (aviation administration/management and engineering physics), HEALTH PROFESSIONS (medical technology and nursing), SOCIAL SCIENCE (criminal justice, family/consumer studies, history, human services, political science/government, psychology, public administration, and sociology). Education, business administration, and biology have the largest enrollments.

ACTIVITIES: There are 90 groups on campus, including art, band, cheerleading, choir, chorale, chorus, dance, debate, drama, ethnic, gay, honors, international, jazz band, marching band, musical theater, newspaper, pep band, political, professional, radio and TV, religious, social, social service, student government, and yearbook. Popular campus events include Spring Fling, Orientation and Family Day. **Sports:** There are 5 intercollegiate sports for men and 7 for women. Facilities include a 9600-seat football stadium, gym, an auxiliary gym, weight room, intramural practice field for football, swimming pool, 6 tennis courts, women's volleyball, baseball, basketball, golf, softball fields, and a track. **Graduates:** From July 1, 2013 to June 30, 2014, 486 bachelor's degrees were awarded. The most popular majors were education (22%), business administration (14%), and general studies (13%). 75 companies recruited on campus in 2013-2014. In an average class, 18% graduate in 4 years or less, 30% graduate in 5 years or less, and 35% graduate in 6 years or less.

SERVICES: Counseling and information services are available, as is tutoring in most subjects. There is a reader service for the blind, and remedial math and reading. **Library/Resources:** The library contains 269,000 volumes, 213,000 microform items, and 20,600 audio/video tapes/CDs/DVDs. Computerized library services include interlibrary loans, database searching, and Internet access. Special learning facilities include an art gallery, planetarium, radio station, and TV station. **Physically Challenged Students:** 90% of the campus is accessible. Facilities include wheelchair ramps, elevators, special parking, specially equipped restrooms, special class scheduling, lowered drinking fountains, lowered telephones. **Special:** HSU offers co-op programs and cross-registration with Ouachita Baptist University, internships in business, psychology, political science, recreation, and education, work-study programs, credit for military experience, nondegree study, and pass/fail options. There are a freshman honors program. **Visiting:** There are regularly scheduled orientations for prospective students, campus tours are given Monday through Friday at 10 a.m. and 1 p.m. Give us a call at 800-228-7333 or register for the tour online. There are guides for informal visits and visitors may stay overnight. To schedule a visit, contact the Admissions Office at admissions@hsu.edu. **Campus Safety and Security:** Measures include 24-hour foot and vehicle patrol and emergency notification system. There are lighted pathways/sidewalks and controlled access to dorms/residences.

REQUIREMENTS: The SAT or ACT is required. The ACT is recommended. Applicants need at least 15 academic credits or 15 Carnegie units. Students with a predicted GPA of 1.5 or below will be admitted conditionally. 4 units of English, 3 of history, civics, or American government, 2 each of natural science, math, and foreign language, and a half unit of computer science are recommended. AP and CLEP

credits are accepted. All students must complete a total of 120 credit hours, including 30 in the major, with a minimum GPA of 2.0. Core requirements include 12 semester hours in social science, 11 in natural science, 9 in English, 6 in humanities, 3 each in non-Western culture, math, and oral communication, and 2 in phys ed or military science. Students must take the comprehensive Rising Junior Examination. **Procedure:** Freshmen are admitted fall, spring, and summer. Entrance exams should be taken during the senior year. There is a rolling admissions plan. Application deadlines are open. Applications are accepted on-line. **Transfer Students:** 297 transfer students enrolled in 2013-2014. Applicants with a cumulative GPA below 2.0 will be admitted conditionally. The entire academic record is considered. 30 of 124 credits required for the bachelor's degree must be completed at HSU. **International Students:** There are 28 international students enrolled. The school actively recruits these students. They must take the TOEFL with a minimum score of 500 on the paper-based TOEFL (PBT) or 61 on the Internet-based version (iBT) or take the MELAB. They must also take the SAT or ACT, scoring 19.

ADMISSIONS: 62% of the 2014-2015 applicants were accepted. The SAT scores for the 2014-2015 freshman class were: Critical Reading--58% below 500, and 42% between 500 and 599; Math--37% below 500, 42% between 500 and 599, and 21% between 600 and 699. The ACT scores were 45% below 21, 26% between 21 and 23, 19% between 24 and 26, 6% between 27 and 28, and 4% above 28. 26% of the current freshmen were in the top fifth of their class; 52% were in the top two fifths. 8 freshmen graduated first in their class. **Admissions Contact:** Vikita Hardwrick, Director of University Relations/Admissions. E-Mail: *admissions@hsu.edu* Web: *www.hsu.edu*

FINANCIAL AID: The FAFSA and FFS are required. Check with the school for current application deadlines.

HENDRIX COLLEGE   C-3
www.hendrix.edu

Conway, AR 72032	**(501) 450-1362**
	(800) 277-9017
Fax: (501) 450-3843	
Full-time: 602 men, 737 women	**Faculty:** 108; IIB, -$
Part-time: 5 men, 4 women	**Ph.D.s:** 92%
Graduate: 5 men, 5 women	**Student/Faculty:** 11 to 1
Year: semesters	**Tuition:** $39,290
Room & Board: $10,912	**Freshman Class:** 1511 applied, 1278 accepted, 314 enrolled
SAT CR/M: 595/594 **ACT:** 28	**CEEB CODE:** 6273
Application Deadline: n/av	**VERY COMPETITIVE+**

Hendrix College, founded in 1876, is a private liberal arts college affiliated with the United Methodist Church. There is 1 undergraduate school and 1 graduate school. In addition to regional accreditation, Hendrix has baccalaureate program accreditation with NASM and NCATE. The 180-acre campus is in a suburban area 25 miles northwest of Little Rock. Including any residence halls, there are 65 buildings.

STUDENT LIFE: 56% of undergraduates are from out of state, mostly the Mid-West. Students are from 35 states, and 25 foreign countries. 80% are from public schools. 76% are White. 42% claim no religious affiliation; 26% Protestant; 12% Catholic. **Male To Female Ratio:** 1.2:1. The average age of freshmen is 18; all undergraduates, 20. 13% do not continue beyond their first year; 63% remain to graduate. **Housing:** 1257 students can be accommodated in college housing, which includes single-sex and coed dorms and on-campus apartments. In addition, there are language houses, a substance-free house, ecology, various academic interests. On-campus housing is guaranteed for all 4 years, is available on a first-come, first-served basis, and is available on a lottery system for upperclassmen. 90% of students live on campus; of those, 80% remain on campus on weekends. All students may keep cars.

FACULTY/CLASSROOMS: 52% of faculty are male; 48% are female. All teach undergraduates, 75% do research, and 75% do both. No introductory courses are taught by graduate students. The average

class size in an introductory lecture is 19; in a laboratory is 20; and in a regular course is 16.

PROGRAMS OF STUDY: Hendrix confers B.A. degrees. Master's degrees are also awarded. Bachelor's degrees are awarded in AGRI-CULTURE (environmental studies), BIOLOGICAL SCIENCE (biochemistry and biology/biological science), BUSINESS (accounting and business economics), COMMUNICATIONS AND THE ARTS (art, dramatic arts, English, French, German, music, and Spanish), COMPUTER AND PHYSICAL SCIENCE (chemical physics, chemistry, computer science, mathematics, and physics), EDUCATION (early childhood education), HEALTH PROFESSIONS (allied health and exercise science), SOCIAL SCIENCE (American studies, anthropology, economics, history, interdisciplinary studies, international relations, philosophy, philosophy and religion, political science/government, psychology, religion, and sociology). Psychology, chemistry and philosophy are the strongest academically. Psychology, biology and biochemstry/molecular biology have the largest enrollments.

ACTIVITIES: There are no fraternities or sororities. There are 70 groups on campus, including art, band, cheerleading, chess, choir, chorale, chorus, dance, debate, drama, environmental, ethnic, film, gay, honors, international, jazz band, literary magazine, musical theater, newspaper, orchestra, pep band, photography, political, professional, radio and TV, religious, social, social service, student government, Ultimate Frisbee, and yearbook. Popular campus events include Kampus Kitty, Themed Dance Parties, Shirttails, and Dance Competition. **Sports:** There are 10 intercollegiate sports for men and 11 for women, and 12 intramural sports for men and 12 for women. Facilities include the Wellness and Athletic center is a 100,000 square foot building which includes a 1,200 seat competition gym, a fitness center with free weights/weight equipment as well as cardiovascular machines, an indoor climbing wall, a dance/movement studio and an indoor track. In addition, there is an indoor 25 meter pool with diving boards and a retractable roof, baseball, softball and soccer fields, a multi-purpose turf field and 5 outdoor tennis courts. Athletic facilities also include a 1,500 seat stadium, a multi-purpose field house with additional locker rooms and a weight room, an additional multi-purpose turf field and a tennis bubble with three indoor courts. **Graduates:** From July 1, 2013 to June 30, 2014, 358 bachelor's degrees were awarded. The most popular majors were psychology (13%), biology (11%), biochemistry, biophysics, and and molecular biology (7%). 92 companies recruited on campus in 2013-2014. In an average class, 63% graduate in 4 years or less, 67% graduate in 5 years or less, and 71% graduate in 6 years or less. Of the 2013 graduating class, 32% were enrolled in graduate school within 6 months of graduation.

SERVICES: Counseling and information services are available, as is tutoring in some subjects, math, biology, writing, chemistry, foreign languanges, accounting, physics, genetics and zoology. **Library/Resources:** The library contains 264,400 volumes, 67,497 microform items, 4,088 audio/video tapes/CDs/DVDs, and subscribes to 65,518 periodicals including electronic. Computerized library services include interlibrary loans, database searching, internet access, and Wi-Fi capability. Special learning facilities include an art gallery, radio station, and a writing lab. **Physically Challenged Students:** 90% of the campus is accessible. Facilities include wheelchair ramps, elevators, special parking, specially equipped restrooms, lowered drinking fountains, and push-button door openers. **Special:** Internships and work-study may be arranged in all fields. The college offers 3-2 engineering programs with Columbia, Vanderbilt, and Washington Universities. Also available are a Washington semester, study abroad, dual majors, and student-designed interdisciplinary studies. Students can pursue minors in all academic departments, as well as African studies, art history, Asian studies, dance, secondary education, gender studies, international business, medical humanities, neuroscience, public health, and applied mathmatics. There are 12 national honor societies including Phi Beta Kappa. **Visiting:** There are regularly scheduled orientations for prospective students, Student visits include attending a class, visits with current students and faculty, a campus tour, and a luncheon with speakers. Students may also stay overnight in a residence hall. There are guides for informal visits, visitors may sit in on classes, and stay overnight. To schedule a visit, contact the Office of Admission. **Campus Safety and Security:** Measures include 24-hour foot and vehicle patrol, emergency notification system, self-defense education, and security escort services. There are emergency telephones, lighted pathways/sidewalks, and controlled access to dorms/residences.

REQUIREMENTS: The SAT or ACT is required. Hendrix recommends that applicants have completed 4 high school units in English, 3 to 4 each in math and social studies, 2 or more in science, and 2 or more in a foreign language. The GED is accepted. AP and CLEP credits are accepted. Important factors in the admissions decision are extracurricular activities record, advanced placement or honors courses, and leadership record. The Collegiate Center is the general education program at Hendrix College and it has four distinct parts: First-Year Experience (consists of The Engaged Citizen course that is grouped in faculty dyads and an Explorations seminar that meets weekly); Capacities (consists of a bi-level writing program, foreign language (equivalent to two semesters), a quantitative skills course, and two physical activities); Learning Domains (consists of 7 courses across 7 disciplines) including one course in Expressive Arts, one course in Historical Perspectives, one course in Literary Studies, two courses (one a lab) in Natural Science Inquiry, one course in Social and Behavioral Analysis, and one course in Values, Beliefs and Ethics; The Odyssey Program (consists of 3 reflective, engaged experiences across the six categories of Artistic Creativity, Global Awareness, Professional and Leadership Development, Service to the World, Undergraduate Research, and Special Programs). All majors include a senior capstone experience that varies by major and 32 courses are required for graduation. **Procedure:** Freshmen are admitted fall and spring. Entrance exams should be taken during the junior and senior years. There is an early admissions plan. Check with the school for current application deadlines. The application fee is $40. Notification of early decision is sent December 15; regular decision, March 1. Applications are accepted on-line. **Transfer Students:** 21 transfer students enrolled in 2013-2014. Complete the Common Application online for free, or mail a completed Common Application along with $40 nonrefundable application fee. Submit an official transcript starting in 9th grade. Request your ACT or SAT scores be sent to Hendrix. Have each college or university previously or currently attended send official transcript and a Dean of Student Affairs Recommendation Form. 16 of 32 credits required for the bachelor's degree must be completed at Hendrix. **International Students:** There are 54 international students enrolled. The school actively recruits these students. They must take the TOEFL with a minimum score of 550 on the paper-based TOEFL (PBT) or 79 on the Internet-based version (iBT).

ADMISSIONS: 85% of the 2014-2015 applicants were accepted. The SAT scores for the 2014-2015 freshman class were: Critical Reading--15% below 500, 39% between 500 and 599, 33% between 600 and 699, and 13% between 700 and 800; Math--12% below 500, 34% between 500 and 599, 45% between 600 and 699, and 9% between 700 and 800. The ACT scores were 2% below 21, 13% between 21 and 23, 23% between 24 and 26, 17% between 27 and 28, and 45% above 28. 65% of the current freshmen were in the top fifth of their class; 86% were in the top two fifths. There were 2 National Merit finalists. 16 freshmen graduated first in their class. **Admissions Contact:** Karen Foust, EVP Strategic Initiatives & VP Enrollmen. Web: *www.hendrix.edu*

FINANCIAL AID: In 2014-2015, 100% of all full-time freshmen and 100% of continuing full-time students received some form of financial aid. 67% of all full-time freshmen and 61% of continuing full-time students received need-based aid. The average freshman award was $32,106. Need-based scholarships or need-based grants averaged $28,606 ($50,202 maximum); and need-based self-help aid (loans and jobs) averaged $5,430 ($7,500 maximum). 32% of undergraduate students work part-time. Average annual earnings from campus work are $1548. The average financial indebtedness of the 2014 graduate was $26,203. The FAFSA is required. The priority date for freshman financial aid applications for fall entry is March 1.

JOHN BROWN UNIVERSITY

A-1

www.jbu.edu

Siloam Springs, AR 72761

(479) 524-7150
(877) JBU-INFO

Fax: (479) 524-4196

Email: jbuinfo@jbu.edu

Full-time: 669 men, 896 women

Faculty: IIB, --$

Part-time: 102 men, 114 women

Ph.D.s: 51%

Graduate: 216 men, 403 women

Student/Faculty: 15 to 1

Year: semesters, summer session

Tuition: $23,588

Room & Board: $8468

Freshman Class: 1201 applied, 828 accepted, 318 enrolled

SAT CR/M/W: 577/563/545 ACT: 26

CEEB CODE: 6311

Application Deadline: May 1

VERY COMPETITIVE+

John Brown University, founded in 1919, is a private, interdenominational Christian university offering nearly 50 undergraduate degree programs, 3 degree completion programs, and 9 graduate degree programs. Figures in the above capsule and in this profile are approximate. There are 2 undergraduate schools and 2 graduate schools. In addition to regional accreditation, JBU has baccalaureate program accreditation with ABET, ACBSP, ACCE, and NCATE. The 200-acre campus is in a small town in Siloam Springs, AR, 25 miles west of Rogers, AR and 80 mile east of Tulsa, Oklahoma. Including any residence halls, there are 33 buildings.

STUDENT LIFE: 57% of undergraduates are from out of state, mostly the Mid-West. Students are from 42 states, 40 foreign countries, and Canada. 80% are White. 90% are Protestant. **Male To Female Ratio:** 1.4:1. The average age of freshmen is 19; all undergraduates, 21. 20% do not continue beyond their first year; 70% remain to graduate. **Housing:** 1100 students can be accommodated in college housing, which includes single-sex and coed dorms, on-campus apartments, off-campus apartments, and married student housing. On-campus housing is guaranteed for all 4 years. 77% of students live on campus; of those, 65% remain on campus on weekends. Alcohol is not permitted. All students may keep cars.

FACULTY/CLASSROOMS: 67% of faculty are male; 33% are female. No introductory courses are taught by graduate students. The average class size in an introductory lecture is 22; in a laboratory is 15; and in a regular course is 20.

PROGRAMS OF STUDY: JBU confers B.A., B.S., B.Mus.Ed., B.S.E. and B.S.Eng. degrees. Associate and master's degrees are also awarded. Bachelor's degrees are awarded in BIOLOGICAL SCIENCE (biochemistry and biology/biological science), BUSINESS (accounting and business administration and management), COMMUNICATIONS AND THE ARTS (broadcasting, design, English, graphic design, illustration, journalism, music, public relations, and Spanish), COMPUTER AND PHYSICAL SCIENCE (chemistry, computer science, digital arts/technology, mathematics, and science), EDUCATION (early childhood education, elementary education, middle school education, music education, physical education, science education, and secondary education), ENGINEERING AND ENVIRONMENTAL DESIGN (construction management, electrical/electronics engineering, engineering, and environmental science), HEALTH PROFESSIONS (community health work and sports medicine), SOCIAL SCIENCE (biblical studies, crosscultural studies, family and community services, history, interdisciplinary studies, international studies, ministries, political science/government, psychology, theological studies, and youth ministry). Engineering, teacher education, visual arts and business are the strongest academically. Business, digital media, engineering and graphic design have the largest enrollments.

ACTIVITIES: There are no fraternities or sororities. Groups on campus include art, cheerleading, choir, chorale, chorus, dance, debate, drama, ethnic, forensics, honors, international, jazz band, musical theater, newspaper, orchestra, pep band, photography, radio and TV, religious, student government, and yearbook. Popular campus events include Fall Breakway, Christmas Candlelight Service and Toilet Paper Game. **Sports:** There are 6 intercollegiate sports for men and 6 for women, and 10 intramural sports for men and 8 for women. Facilities include a 2000-seat gym, soccer and softball fields,

a baseball diamond, training room, and a swimming pool. The Lifetime Health Complex includes an indoor track, 4 racquetball courts, a nautilus fitness center, an aerobics room, tennis courts, a rugby pitch, and a 3-court recreation center. **Graduates:** From July 1, 2013 to June 30, 2014, 421 bachelor's degrees were awarded. The most popular majors were business/marketing (50%), education (10%), and visual and performing arts (7%). 63 companies recruited on campus in 2013-2014. In an average class, 1% graduate in 3 years or less, 66% graduate in 4 years or less, 58% graduate in 5 years or less, and 68% graduate in 6 years or less. Of the 2013 graduating class, 27% were enrolled in graduate school within 6 months of graduation, and 98% were employed.

SERVICES: Counseling and information services are available, as is tutoring in most subjects. There is remedial math, reading, and writing. **Library/Resources:** The library contains 118,980 volumes, 67,000 microform items, and 5,437 audio/video tapes/CDs/DVDs. Computerized library services include interlibrary loans, database searching, and Internet access. Special learning facilities include an art gallery, radio station, TV station, a wellness assessment laboratory. **Physically Challenged Students:** 95% of the campus is accessible. Facilities include wheelchair ramps, elevators, special parking, specially equipped restrooms, special class scheduling, lowered drinking fountains, lowered telephones, and special housing. **Special:** Internships or field experiences are available in most majors. Study abroad in 15 countries, a Washington semester, work-study, and accelerated degree programs in organizational management and early childhood education are offered. There are a freshman honors program and 12 departmental honors programs. **Visiting:** There are regularly scheduled orientations for prospective students, including campus tours, consultations with faculty and coaches, and examination of financial aid opportunities. There are guides for informal visits, visitors may sit in on classes, and stay overnight. To schedule a visit, contact the Admissions Office. **Campus Safety and Security:** Measures include 24-hour foot and vehicle patrol, emergency notification system, self-defense education, and security escort services. There are lighted pathways/sidewalks and controlled access to dorms/residences.

REQUIREMENTS: The SAT or ACT is recommended. Applicants should have completed 14 high school units, including 4 in English, 3 in math, 2 each in science, social studies, and foreign language, and 1 in history. 2 references are required: 1 from a high school counselor or teacher, the other from a pastor or church leader. An essay and an interview are recommended. Applicants 21 years of age or older may be admitted without ACT or SAT scores. A GPA of 2.5 is required. AP and CLEP credits are accepted. All students must complete 25 hours of lower-level core courses, 19 to 22 of elective courses in wellness, natural science, mathematics, philosophy, arts, social studies, and global studies, and 8 hours in upper-level core courses. A total of 142 to 145 credit hours (includes hours for minor) with a minimum GPA of 2.25 (2.5 in profession education, teaching, and other state-required courses) is required to graduate. Students must complete an exit assessment before graduation. **Procedure:** Freshmen are admitted fall and spring. Entrance exams should be taken during the spring of the junior year or fall of the senior year. There is a rolling admissions plan. Applications should be filed by May 1 for fall entry, along with a $25 fee. Applications are accepted on-line. **Transfer Students:** 65 transfer students enrolled in 2013-2014. Transfer applicants must have completed at least 12 units of college work, with a minimum 2.5 GPA. 36 of 124 credits required for the bachelor's degree must be completed at JBU. **International Students:** They must take the TOEFL.

ADMISSIONS: 69% of the 2014-2015 applicants were accepted. The SAT scores for the 2014-2015 freshman class were: Critical Reading--18% below 500, 39% between 500 and 599, 36% between 600 and 699, and 7% between 700 and 800; Math--17% below 500, 47% between 500 and 599, 33% between 600 and 699, and 4% between 700 and 800; Writing--31% below 500, 41% between 500 and 599, 28% between 600 and 699, and % between 700 and 800. The ACT scores were 1% below 21, 29% between 21 and 23, 26% between 24 and 26, 26% between 27 and 28, and 17% above 28. 30% of the current freshmen were in the top fifth of their class; 59% were in the top two fifths. **Admissions Contact:** Don Crandall, Vice President for Enrollment. E-Mail: *jbuinfo@jbu.edu* Web: *www.jbu.edu*

FINANCIAL AID: 77% of all full-time freshmen and 71% of continuing full-time students received need-based aid. The average freshman award was $19,242. Need-based scholarships or need-based grants averaged $16,076; need-based self-help aid (loans and jobs) averaged $605; non-need-based athletic scholarships averaged $9,736; and other non-need-based awards and non-need-based scholarships averaged $16,202. The CSS/Profile, FAFSA, and FFS are required. The priority date for freshman financial aid applications for fall entry is March 1.

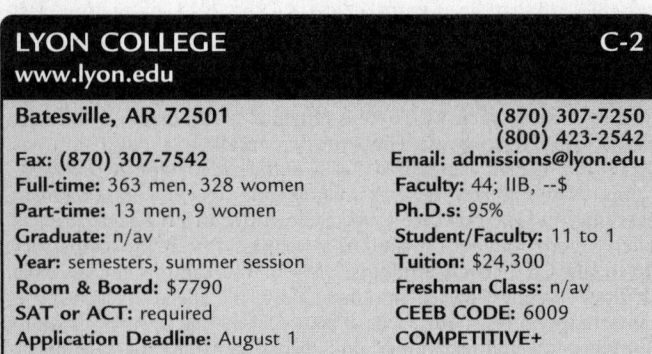

LYON COLLEGE — C-2
www.lyon.edu

Batesville, AR 72501

(870) 307-7250
(800) 423-2542

Fax: (870) 307-7542
Email: admissions@lyon.edu
Full-time: 363 men, 328 women — Faculty: 44; IIB, --$
Part-time: 13 men, 9 women — Ph.D.s: 95%
Graduate: n/av — Student/Faculty: 11 to 1
Year: semesters, summer session — Tuition: $24,300
Room & Board: $7790 — Freshman Class: n/av
SAT or ACT: required — CEEB CODE: 6009
Application Deadline: August 1 — COMPETITIVE+

Lyon College, founded in 1872, is a selective, private, residential, liberal arts college affiliated with the Presbyterian Church. Figures in the above capsule and in this profile are approximate. There is one undergraduate school. In addition to regional accreditation, Lyon has baccalaureate program accreditation with NCATE. The 136-acre campus is in a small town 90 miles north of Little Rock. Including any residence halls, there are 30 buildings.

STUDENT LIFE: 73% of undergraduates are from Arkansas. Others are from 21 states, and 11 foreign countries. 74% are White. **Male To Female Ratio:** 0.9:1. The average age of freshmen is 18; all undergraduates, 21. 26% do not continue beyond their first year; 55% remain to graduate. **Housing:** 500 students can be accommodated in college housing, which includes single-sex and coed dorms, on-campus apartments, and off-campus apartments. In addition, there are special-interest houses, Freshman-only housing. On-campus housing is guaranteed for all 4 years. 77% of students live on campus; of those, 70% remain on campus on weekends. All students may keep cars.

FACULTY/CLASSROOMS: 52% of faculty are male; 48% are female. All teach and do research. No introductory courses are taught by graduate students. The average class size in an introductory lecture is 23; in a laboratory is 19; and in a regular course is 17.

PROGRAMS OF STUDY: Lyon confers B.A., and B.S. degrees. Bachelor's degrees are awarded in AGRICULTURE (environmental studies), BIOLOGICAL SCIENCE (biology/biological science), BUSINESS (accounting and business administration and management), COMMUNICATIONS AND THE ARTS (art, dramatic arts, English, music, and Spanish), COMPUTER AND PHYSICAL SCIENCE (chemistry and mathematics), EDUCATION (early childhood education), SOCIAL SCIENCE (economics, history, political science/government, psychology, and religion). Psychology, biology, and English have the largest enrollments.

ACTIVITIES: 28% of men belong to 3 national fraternities; 28% of women belong to 2 national sororities. There are 40 groups on campus, including art, bagpipe, band, cheerleading, choir, drama, ethnic, gay, honors, international, literary magazine, newspaper, orchestra, political, professional, religious, social, social service, student government, and yearbook. Popular campus events include Arkansas Scottish Festival, Service Day and Baccalaureate. **Sports:** There are 4 intercollegiate sports for men and 5 for women, and 14 intramural sports for men and 14 for women. Facilities include an 1100-seat gym, softball, baseball, soccer fields, cross-country trail, indoor swimming pool, 6 tennis courts, indoor baseball practice facility, and a weight room. **Graduates:** From July 1, 2013 to June 30, 2014, 100 bachelor's degrees were awarded. The most popular majors were psychology (21%), biology (12%), and English (11%). 30 companies recruited on campus in 2013-2014. In an average class, 43% graduate in 4 years or less, 49% graduate in 5 years or less, and 47% graduate in 6 years or less.

SERVICES: Counseling and information services are available, as is

tutoring in most subjects, foreign language, chemistry, math, english, political science, history, economics, biology, religion and philosophy. Writing and math labs are available. **Library/Resources:** The library contains 169,177 volumes, 2,928 microform items, 6,921 audio/video tapes/CDs/DVDs, and subscribes to 31,799 periodicals including electronic. Computerized library services include interlibrary loans, database searching, Internet access, and Wi-Fi capability. Special learning facilities include an art gallery, a language lab, math and science tutoring lab, and a computer lab. **Physically Challenged Students:** 80% of the campus is accessible. Facilities include wheelchair ramps, elevators, special parking, specially equipped restrooms, and special housing. **Special:** Internships are offered as is cross-registration (for certain courses) with the University of Arkansas Community College at Batesville. A 2-2 engineering program is offered with the University of Missouri in Rolla, and a 3-2 program is offered with the University of Arkansas at Fayetteville. Work-study courses, study abroad in 4 countries, dual majors, student-designed majors, pass/fail options, a Washington semester, and credit for military experience are available. A 3-2 program is available with the University of Minnesota. There are 14 national honor societies. **Visiting:** There are regularly scheduled orientations for prospective students, consisting of a campus tour, admission and financial aid orientation, and information sessions with faculty and students. There are guides for informal visits and visitors may sit in on classes. To schedule a visit, contact the Admission Office at (800) 423-2542. **Campus Safety and Security:** Measures include 24-hour foot and vehicle patrol, emergency notification system, and security escort services. There are lighted pathways/sidewalks.

REQUIREMENTS: The SAT or ACT is required. Applicants should have completed a minimum of 16 high school units, including 4 in English, 3 each in science, math, and social sciences, and 2 in a foreign language. A letter of recommendation and an admission interview are recommended. AP credits are accepted. All students are required to demonstrate proficiency in English composition, math, and foreign language; meet distribution requirements in social sciences, arts and literature, natural science and math, and religion and philosophy; take the 2-semester Western Tradition course sequence; complete the freshman orientation program; and take 1 semester of phys ed in each of the 4 years. The core curriculum requires 31 to 49 credit hours. A total of 120 credits, with a minimum GPA of 2.0, is required to graduate. **Procedure:** Freshmen are admitted fall and spring. Entrance exams should be taken in spring of the junior year and fall of the senior year. There are deferred admissions and rolling admissions plans. Applications should be filed by August 1 for fall entry; January 1 for spring entry, along with a $25 fee. Notification is sent on a rolling basis. Applications are accepted on-line. **Transfer Students:** 54 transfer students enrolled in 2013-2014. Transfer applicants with 24 or more semester hours must submit a transcript and statement of good standing from each institution attended. Students with fewer than 24 semester hours must submit their final high school transcript and ACT or SAT scores. 30 of 120 credits required for the bachelor's degree must be completed at Lyon. **International Students:** There are 27 international students enrolled. The school actively recruits these students. They must take the TOEFL with a minimum score of 550 on the paper-based TOEFL (PBT) or 79 on the Internet-based version (iBT), or take the IELTS. They must also take the SAT or ACT.

ADMISSIONS: 56% of the current freshmen were in the top fifth of their class; 79% were in the top two fifths. 12 freshmen graduated first in their class. **Admissions Contact:** Josh Manning, Director of Enrollment Services. E-Mail: admissions@lyon.edu Web: www.lyon.edu

FINANCIAL AID: In 2014-2015, 100% of all full-time freshmen and 99% of continuing full-time students received some form of financial aid. 63% of all full-time freshmen and 62% of continuing full-time students received need-based aid. The average freshman award was $26,559. Need-based scholarships or need-based grants averaged $6,262 ($8,500 maximum); need-based self-help aid (loans and jobs) averaged $7,243 ($10,500 maximum); non-need-based athletic scholarships averaged $13,322 ($31,154 maximum); and other non-need-based awards and non-need-based scholarships averaged $13,416 ($61,154 maximum). 26% of undergraduate students work part-time. Average annual earnings from campus work are $998. The average financial indebtedness of the 2014 graduate was $17,179. The FAFSA is required. The priority date for freshman financial aid applications for fall entry is March 1.

OUACHITA BAPTIST UNIVERSITY   B-4
www.obu.edu

Arkadelphia, AR 71998

(870) 245-5110
(800) 342-5628

Fax: (870) 245-5500

Email: admissions@obu.edu

Full-time: 697 men, 755 women

Faculty: 103; IIB, --$

Part-time: 35 men, 14 women

Ph.D.s: 87%

Graduate: n/av

Student/Faculty: 12 to 1

Year: semesters, summer session

Tuition: $23,320

Room & Board: $6900

Freshman Class: 1732 applied, 1223 accepted, 420 enrolled

SAT CR/M: 531/540 ACT: 25

CEEB CODE: 6549

Application Deadline: open

VERY COMPETITIVE

Ouachita Baptist University, founded in 1886, is a private liberal arts institution affiliated with the Arkansas Baptist State Convention. There are 7 undergraduate schools. In addition to regional accreditation, Ouachita has baccalaureate program accreditation with AACSB, ADA, NASM, and NCATE. The 200-acre campus is in a small town 65 miles southwest of Little Rock. Including any residence halls, there are 35 buildings.

STUDENT LIFE: 61% of undergraduates are from Arkansas. Others are from 25 states, and 29 foreign countries. 90% are from public schools. 82% are White. 80% are Protestant; 15% Unknown. **Male To Female Ratio:** 1.1:1. The average age of freshmen is 18; all undergraduates, 21. 20% do not continue beyond their first year; 60% remain to graduate. **Housing:** 1598 students can be accommodated in college housing, which includes single-sex dorms, on-campus apartments, off-campus apartments, and married student housing. On-campus housing is guaranteed for all 4 years. 96% of students live on campus; of those, 50% remain on campus on weekends. Alcohol is not permitted. All students may keep cars.

FACULTY/CLASSROOMS: 56% of faculty are male; 44% are female. All teach undergraduates, 45% do research, and 45% do both. No introductory courses are taught by graduate students. The average class size in an introductory lecture is 30; in a laboratory is 12; and in a regular course is 19.

PROGRAMS OF STUDY: Ouachita confers B.A., B.F.A., B.S., B.M. and B.M.E. degrees. Associate degrees are also awarded. Bachelor's degrees are awarded in BIOLOGICAL SCIENCE (biology/biological science), BUSINESS (accounting, business administration and management, recreation and leisure services, and sports management), COMMUNICATIONS AND THE ARTS (applied music, art, church music, communications, dramatic arts, English, graphic design, instrumental performance, instrumental music education, keyboard - piano concentration, music, music composition, musical theater, piano/organ, piano performance, Spanish, speech/debate/rhetoric, theatre arts, visual and performing arts, and voice), COMPUTER AND PHYSICAL SCIENCE (chemistry, computer science, mathematics, and physics), EDUCATION (art education, business education, early childhood education, elementary education, foreign languages education, mathematics education, middle school education, music education, science education, secondary education, social studies education, and social studies secondary school education), HEALTH PROFESSIONS (predentistry, premedicine, and speech pathology/audiology), SOCIAL SCIENCE (biblical languages, biblical studies, Christian studies, dietetics, history, ministries, philosophy, philosophy and religion, political science/government, prelaw, psychology, religion, religious music, sociology, theological studies, and youth ministry). Biology, business administration, and Christian studies have the largest enrollments.

ACTIVITIES: 20% of men belong to 4 local fraternities; 35% of women belong to 5 local sororities. There are 60 groups on campus, including band, cheerleading, choir, chorale, chorus, computers, drama, drill team, ethnic, film, honors, international, jazz band, literary magazine, marching band, musical theater, newspaper, opera, orchestra, pep band, photography, political, professional, radio and TV, religious, social, social service, student government, and yearbook. Popular campus events include International Student Fair, Tiger Tunes and Tiger Traks. **Sports:** There are 8 intercollegiate sports for men and 8 for women, and 5 intramural sports for men and 5 for women. Facilities include a 6000-seat football stadium, an indoor/outdoor tennis center, indoor complex featuring a 2500-seat basketball arena, a swimming pool, a weight room, racquetball courts, and volleyball courts. **Graduates:** From July 1, 2013 to June 30, 2014, 355 bachelor's degrees were awarded. The most popular majors were business (18%), biology (13%), and visual and performing arts (11%). 35 companies recruited on campus in 2013-2014. In an average class, 1% graduate in 3 years or less, 50% graduate in 4 years or less, 59% graduate in 5 years or less, and 60% graduate in 6 years or less. Of the 2013 graduating class, 45% were enrolled in graduate school within 6 months of graduation, and 92% were employed.

SERVICES: Counseling and information services are available, as is tutoring in most subjects. There is a reader service for the blind, and remedial math, reading, and writing. **Library/Resources:** The 2 libraries contain 848,710 volumes, 325,275 microform items, 3,560 audio/video tapes/CDs/DVDs, and subscribe to 7,608 periodicals including electronic. Computerized library services include interlibrary loans and database searching. Special learning facilities include an art gallery, planetarium, and radio station. **Physically Challenged Students:** 95% of the campus is accessible. Facilities include wheelchair ramps, elevators, special parking, specially equipped restrooms, special class scheduling, and lowered drinking fountains. **Special:** Ouachita offers cross-registration with Henderson State University, a Washington semester for political science majors, internships for business majors and some mass communications and Christian studies majors, B.A.-B.S. degrees, dual majors, pass/fail options, and non-degree study. Study-abroad opportunities are available in Germany, England, France, Italy, Russia, Japan, China, Hong Kong, Australia, Austria, Belize, Scotland, Spain, South Africa, Costa Rica, and Morocco. There are 8 national honor societies and a freshman honors program. **Visiting:** There are regularly scheduled orientations for prospective students, include a campus tour, a question-and-answer session, and meetings with professors and students. There are guides for informal visits, visitors may sit in on classes, and stay overnight. To schedule a visit, contact the Admissions Counseling Office at admissions@obu.edu. **Campus Safety and Security:** Measures include 24-hour foot and vehicle patrol and emergency notification system. There are emergency telephones, lighted pathways/sidewalks, and controlled access to dorms/residences.

REQUIREMENTS: The SAT or ACT is required. Applicants should have completed 19 high school units, including 4 in English, 3 in social science, and 2 each in natural science and math, 2 in a foreign language and 1/2 in computer science are also recommended. A GPA of 2.8 is required. AP and CLEP credits are accepted. All students must fulfill 48 semester hours of general education courses, including 2 semesters of 1 foreign language and 7 chapel credits. A total of 120 semester hours, with a minimum GPA of 2.0, is required for graduation. **Procedure:** Freshmen are admitted fall, spring, and summer. Entrance exams should be taken in the junior year. There are deferred admissions and rolling admissions plans. Application deadlines are open. Applications are accepted on-line. **Transfer Students:** 46 transfer students enrolled in 2013-2014. Applicants must be eligible to return to their previous school. 60 of 120 credits required for the bachelor's degree must be completed at Ouachita. **International Students:** There are 37 international students enrolled. The school actively recruits these students. They must take the TOEFL with a minimum score of 550 on the paper-based TOEFL (PBT) or 80 on the Internet-based version (iBT).

ADMISSIONS: 71% of the 2014-2015 applicants were accepted. The SAT scores for the 2014-2015 freshman class were: Critical Reading--33% below 500, 46% between 500 and 599, 18% between 600 and 699, and 3% between 700 and 800; Math--28% below 500, 47% between 500 and 599, 22% between 600 and 699, and 3% between 700 and 800. The ACT scores were 20% below 21, 24% between 21 and 23, 23% between 24 and 26, 13% between 27 and 28, and 20% above 28. 49% of the current freshmen were in the top fifth of their class; 72% were in the top two fifths. There were 16 National Merit finalists. 17 freshmen graduated first in their class. **Admissions Contact:** Lori Motl, Director of Admissions Counseling. E-Mail: *admissions@obu.edu* Web: *www.obu.edu*

FINANCIAL AID: In 2014-2015, 98% of all full-time freshmen and 97% of continuing full-time students received some form of financial aid. 70% of all full-time freshmen and 80% of continuing full-time students received need-based aid. The average freshman award was $20,358. Need-based scholarships or need-based grants averaged $14,158; need-based self-help aid (loans and jobs) averaged $4,223; and other non-need-based awards and non-need-based scholarships averaged $1,977. 50% of undergraduate students work part-time. Average annual earnings from campus work are $1800. The average financial indebtedness of the 2014 graduate was $25,823. The FAFSA and the college's own financial statement are required. The priority date for freshman financial aid applications for fall entry is January 15.

PHILANDER SMITH COLLEGE (*The complete profile is made available exclusively on our website, www.barronspac.com*)

SOUTHERN ARKANSAS UNIVERSITY B-5
www.saumag.edu

Magnolia, AR 71754	(870) 235-4040
	(800) 332-SAUM
Fax: (870) 235-4931	Email: sejennings@saumag.edu
Full-time: 1130 men, 1450 women	Faculty: IIB, --$
Part-time: 150 men, 400 women	Ph.D.s: n/av
Graduate: 65 men, 225 women	Student/Faculty: n/av
Year: semesters, summer session	Tuition: $9616
Room & Board: $4700	Freshman Class: n/av
ACT: required	CEEB CODE: 6661
Application Deadline: open	COMPETITIVE

Southern Arkansas University, founded in 1909, is a state-supported liberal arts institution offering degrees in business administration, education, liberal and performing arts, and science and technology. The figures in the above capsule and in this profile are approximate. There are 4 undergraduate schools and one graduate school. In addition to regional accreditation, SAU has baccalaureate program accreditation with CSWE, NASAD, NASM, NCATE, and NLN. The 781-acre campus is in a small town. Including any residence halls, there are 27 buildings.

STUDENT LIFE: 71% of undergraduates are from Arkansas. Others are from 22 states, 40 foreign countries, and Canada. 97% are from public schools. 69% are White; 24% African American. **Male To Female Ratio:** 1.5:1. The average age of freshmen is 18; all undergraduates, 28. 32% do not continue beyond their first year. **Housing:** 1043 students can be accommodated in college housing, which includes single-sex and coed dorms. In addition, there are honors houses, including an International house. On-campus housing is guaranteed for all 4 years. 66% of students commute. Alcohol is not permitted. All students may keep cars.

FACULTY/CLASSROOMS: 56% of faculty are male; 44% are female. 97% teach undergraduates, 10% do research, and 10% do both. No introductory courses are taught by graduate students. The average class size in an introductory lecture is 23; in a laboratory is 18; and in a regular course is 20.

PROGRAMS OF STUDY: SAU confers B.A., B.S., B.A.S., B.B.A., B.M.E., B.S.E. and B.S.W. degrees. Associate and master's degrees are also awarded. Bachelor's degrees are awarded in AGRICULTURE (agricultural business management and agriculture), BIOLOGICAL SCIENCE (biology/biological science), BUSINESS (accounting and business administration and management), COMMUNICATIONS AND THE ARTS (art, broadcasting, communications, English, journalism, and Spanish), COMPUTER AND PHYSICAL SCIENCE (chemistry, computer science, and mathematics), EDUCATION (agricultural education, art education, business education, elementary education, health education, middle school education, music education, and science education), ENGINEERING AND ENVI-

RONMENTAL DESIGN (manufacturing technology), HEALTH PROFESSIONS (medical laboratory technology), SOCIAL SCIENCE (community services, history, political science/government, psychology, and sociology). Accounting and physical science is the strongest academically. Business administration and health education/ kinesiology have the largest enrollments.

ACTIVITIES: 6% of men belong to 7 national fraternities; 5% of women belong to 7 national sororities. There are 80 groups on campus, including art, band, cheerleading, choir, chorale, computers, dance, drama, drill team, ethnic, honors, international, jazz band, literary magazine, marching band, musical theater, newspaper, pep band, photography, political, professional, radio and TV, religious, social, and student government. Popular campus events include Spring Fling and Celebration of Lights (Christmas). **Sports:** There are 8 intercollegiate sports for men and 8 for women, and 7 intramural sports for men and 7 for women. Facilities include a 6500-seat stadium, 1450-seat gym, 10 lighted tennis courts, baseball and softball fields, a track, indoor pool, dance studio, multipurpose building with basketball and volleyball courts, and a wellness center.

SERVICES: Counseling and information services are available, as is tutoring in most subjects. There is remedial math, reading, and writing. Supplemental instruction in courses with high drop/failure rates. **Library/Resources:** The library contains 150,341 volumes, 669,721 microform items, and 12,214 audio/video tapes/CDs/DVDs, subscribes to 725 periodicals including electronic. Computerized library services include interlibrary loans, database searching, and Internet access. Special learning facilities include an art gallery, radio station, an biological field station, and university farm. **Physically Challenged Students:** 95% of the campus is accessible. Facilities include wheelchair ramps, elevators, special parking, specially equipped restrooms, special class scheduling, lowered drinking fountains, and lowered telephones. **Special:** Work-study programs at SAU, business and Spanish internships, study abroad in Russia and Mexico, and a general studies degree are offered. There is 1 national honor society, a freshman honors program, and 6 departmental honors programs. **Visiting:** There are regularly scheduled orientations for prospective students. There are guides for informal visits, visitors may sit in on classes, and stay overnight. To schedule a visit, contact the Admissions Office. **Campus Safety and Security:** Measures include 24-hour foot and vehicle patrol and security escort services. There are emergency telephones and lighted pathways/sidewalks.

REQUIREMENTS: The ACT is required, with a minimum composite of 19. Applicants should have completed 4 high school units in English, 3 each in math and social studies, and 2 each in natural science and a foreign language. The GED is accepted. AP and CLEP credits are accepted. All students must complete 43 semester hours of general education courses, including 18 in humanities, 12 in social sciences, 4 each in biological and physical science, 3 in math, and 2 to 3 in physical and health education. A minimum of 124 total semester hours, with a minimum GPA of 2.0, is required to graduate. **Procedure:** Freshmen are admitted to all sessions. Entrance exams should be taken in the fall prior to enrollment. There are deferred admissions and rolling admissions plans. Application deadlines are open. Notification is sent on a rolling basis. Applications are accepted on-line. **Transfer Students:** Applicants must be eligible to return to their previous school and meet GPA requirements. Those with fewer than 24 credit hours must submit ACT or SAT scores and a high school transcript or GED. 30 of 124 credits required for the bachelor's degree must be completed at SAU. **International Students:** The school actively recruits these students. They must take the TOEFL. They must also take the ACT.

ADMISSIONS: Sarah Jennings, Dean of Enrollment Services. E-Mail: *sejennings@saumag.edu* Web: *www.saumag.edu*

FINANCIAL AID: The FAFSA is required. Check with the school for current application deadlines.

UNIVERSITY OF ARKANSAS SYSTEM

The University of Arkansas System, established in 1871, is a system in Arkansas. It is governed by a board of trustees, whose chief administrator is the president. The primary goal of the system is teaching, research, and public service. The student enrollment for all five campuses is usually 33,000 with 2500 faculty members. Altogether there are 240 baccalaureate, 112 master's, and 30 doctoral programs offered in the University of Arkansas System. Profiles of the 4-year campuses are included in this section.

UNIVERSITY OF ARKANSAS AT FAYETTEVILLE

A-1

www.arkansas.edu

Fayetteville, AR 72701

(479) 575-5346
(800) 377-8632

Fax: (479) 575-7515
Full-time: 9044 men, 9521 women
Part-time: 1303 men, 1141 women
Graduate: 2244 men, 2078 women
Year: semesters, summer session
Room & Board: $9454

Email: uofa@uark.edu
Faculty: I, -$
Ph.D.s: 75%
Student/Faculty: 19 to 1
Tuition: $8898 ($20,988)
Freshman Class: 18908 applied, 11066 accepted, 4339 enrolled

SAT CR/M: 540/560 ACT: 25
Application Deadline: August 1

CEEB CODE: 6866
COMPETITIVE+

The University of Arkansas, founded in 1871, is a land-grant institution offering undergraduate and graduate programs in liberal arts and sciences, agricultural, food, social and natural sciences, life sciences, business administration, engineering, architecture, education, law, and human environmental sciences. Figures in the above capsule and in this profile are approximate. There are 8 undergraduate schools and 2 graduate schools. In addition to regional accreditation, U of A has baccalaureate program accreditation with AACSB, ABET, ACEJMC, ADA, CSWE, FIDER, NAAB, NASM, and NCATE. The 510-acre campus is in an urban area 190 miles northwest of Little Rock. Including any residence halls, there are 189 buildings.
STUDENT LIFE: 58% of undergraduates are from Arkansas. Others are from 50 states, 120 foreign countries, and Canada. 85% are from public schools. 77% are White. **Male To Female Ratio:** 1.0:1. The average age of freshmen is 18; all undergraduates, 21. 18% do not continue beyond their first year; 60% remain to graduate. **Housing:** 5652 students can be accommodated in college housing, which includes single-sex and coed dorms and on-campus apartments. In addition, there are honors houses, special-interest houses, fraternity houses, sorority houses, International living/learning community, and First-year experience program. On-campus housing is guaranteed for the freshman year only, is available on a first-come, and first-served basis. 75% of students commute. All students may keep cars.
FACULTY/CLASSROOMS: 64% of faculty are male; 36% are female. 93% teach undergraduates. Graduate students teach 42% of introductory courses. The average class size in an introductory lecture is 39; in a laboratory is 16; and in a regular course is 31.
PROGRAMS OF STUDY: U of A confers B.A., B.S., B.Arch., B.E.A., B.I.D., B.L.A., B.M., B.S.A., B.S.B.A., B.S.B.E., B.S.C.E., B.S.Ch.E., B.S.C.S.E., B.S.Cmp.E., B.S.E., B.S.E.E., B.S.H.E.S., B.S.I.B., B.S.I.E., B.S.M.E., B.S.N. and B.S.P.A. degrees. Master's and doctoral degrees are also awarded. Bachelor's degrees are awarded in AGRICULTURE (agricultural business management, agricultural communications, agricultural economics, animal science, horticulture, poultry science, and soil science), BIOLOGICAL SCIENCE (biology/biological science and nutrition), BUSINESS (accounting, apparel and accessories marketing, banking and finance, business administration and management, business economics, business information systems, finance, hospitality management services, human resources, international business management, marketing management, marketing/retailing/merchandising, and transportation management), COMMUNICATIONS AND THE ARTS (advertising, art, communication, dramatic arts, English, French, German, journalism, music, and Spanish), COMPUTER AND PHYSICAL SCIENCE (chemistry, computer science, earth science, geology, mathematics, physics, and statistics), EDUCATION (agricultural education, business education, (Education) Childhood Education, career, technical education & training, childhood education: 1-6, early childhood education, elementary education, middle school education, music education, recreation education, and technical education), ENGINEERING AND ENVI-

RONMENTAL DESIGN (architecture, bioengineering, chemical engineering, civil engineering, computer engineering, electrical/electronics engineering, environmental science, industrial engineering, interior design, landscape architecture, landscape architecture/design, and mechanical engineering), HEALTH PROFESSIONS (exercise science, health science, and nursing), SOCIAL SCIENCE (African studies, African American studies, American studies, anthropology, architectural studies, asian studies, classical/ancient civilization, criminal justice, dietetics, economics, European studies, food science, geography, history, human development, international relations, Latin American studies, Middle Eastern studies, philosophy, political science/government, psychology, public administration, social work, and sociology). Business, chemical and electrical engineering, and computer science are the strongest academically. Nursing, kinesiology, and biology have the largest enrollments.
ACTIVITIES: 23% of men belong to 19 national fraternities; 36% of women belong to 14 national sororities. There are 469 groups on campus, including art, band, cheerleading, chess, choir, chorale, chorus, computers, dance, drama, drill team, ethnic, gay, honors, international, jazz band, literary magazine, marching band, musical theater, newspaper, opera, orchestra, pep band, photography, political, professional, radio and TV, religious, social, social service, student government, symphony, and yearbook. Popular campus events include Academic Festival, International Banquet and Fashion Show, and Martin Luther King Jr. Event. **Sports:** There are 8 intercollegiate sports for men and 11 for women, and 56 intramural sports for men and 56 for women. Facilities include a 72,000-seat stadium, a 20,000-seat basketball arena, a 10,700-seat baseball stadium, a 9000-seat volleyball arena, a 1500-seat soccer stadium, 4 gyms, indoor and outdoor jogging tracks, 2 dance studios, 10 racquetball courts, a fitness and weight training center, a swimming pool, an outdoor recreation center, 10 outdoor and 6 indoor tennis courts, 10 multipurpose playing fields, an indoor practice football field, a 5000-seat indoor running track, a 7,000 seat outdoor track, a 1,500-seat softball stadium, and a gym/weight training and conditioning facility. **Graduates:** From July 1, 2013 to June 30, 2014, 3363 bachelor's degrees were awarded. The most popular majors were kinesiology (5%), marketing (5%), and finance (4%). 265 companies recruited on campus in 2013-2014. In an average class, 37% graduate in 4 years or less, 55% graduate in 5 years or less, and 62% graduate in 6 years or less.
SERVICES: Counseling and information services are available, as is tutoring in some subjects, mathematical sciences and statistics, biological sciences, physics, chemistry, biochemistry, geosciences, anthropology, political science, sustainability, and world languages. There is a reader service for the blind, and remedial math, reading, and writing. There is a math resource center and a writing center. Student Support Services and individual colleges have labs and other facilities. **Library/Resources:** The 4 libraries contain 2.0 million volumes, 5.8 million microform items, 37,256 audio/video tapes/CDs/DVDs, and subscribe to 27,518 periodicals including electronic. Computerized library services include interlibrary loans, database searching, Internet access, and Wi-Fi capability. Special learning facilities include a planetarium, radio station, TV station, numerous research centers. **Physically Challenged Students:** All of the campus is accessible. Facilities include wheelchair ramps, elevators, special parking, specially equipped restrooms, special class scheduling, lowered drinking fountains, lowered telephones. **Special:** Co-op programs and internships are available, as well as dual majors and B.A.-B.S. degrees in many majors, and study abroad in 47 countries. There are 3-2 engineering degrees with several universities, a combined medical/dental degree, and a 6-year B.S./J.D. degree for highly qualified students. Non-degree study is possible. There are 40 national honor societies, including Phi Beta Kappa, a freshman honors program, and 84 departmental honors programs. **Visiting:** There are regularly scheduled orientations for prospective students, visit consists of individual or group campus tours, meetings with an academic adviser, residence hall tours, and a meeting with an admissions counselor. Appointments are strongly encouraged for the best experience but not required. There are guides for informal visits and visitors may sit in on classes. To schedule a visit, contact Kristen Davidson at visit@uark.edu. **Campus Safety and Security:** Measures include 24-hour foot and vehicle patrol, emergency notification system, self-defense education, and security escort services. There are shuttle

buses, emergency telephones, lighted pathways/sidewalks, controlled access to dorms/residences, crime prevention lectures, rape defense program, property engraving, bicycle patrol, and electronic card access in residence halls.

REQUIREMENTS: The SAT or ACT is required. Additional requirements: 4 years of English and math, 3 years each of social science and natural science. AP and honors level courses will enhance the applicant's opportunity for admission. A GPA of 3.0 is required. AP and CLEP credits are accepted. Important factors in the admissions decision are advanced placement or honors courses, leadership record, and extracurricular activities record. To graduate, all students must complete 35 hours of general education courses, including 9 in social sciences, 8 in science, 6 in English, and 3 each in fine arts, math, humanities, and history/government. No more than 25% of the minimum total of 120 hours may be D or below. **Procedure:** Freshmen are admitted fall, spring, and summer. Entrance exams should be taken in the junior year or early in the senior year. There are early admissions, deferred admissions, and rolling admissions plans. Applications should be filed by August 1 for fall entry; December 20 for spring entry; and May 1 for summer entry, along with a $40 fee. Notification of early decision is sent December 15; regular decision, on a rolling basis. Applications are accepted on-line. **Transfer Students:** 1383 transfer students enrolled in 2013-2014. Applicants must present a GPA of 2.0 on all college course work attempted and be in good standing at the last institution attended. Those with fewer than 24 transferable semester credits must meet the requirements of entering freshmen in addition to those of transfer students. 30 of 120 credits required for the bachelor's degree must be completed at U of A. **International Students:** There are 619 international students enrolled. The school actively recruits these students. They must take the TOEFL with a minimum score of 550 on the paper-based TOEFL (PBT) or 79 on the Internet-based version (iBT) and the college's own test. They must also take the SAT or ACT.

ADMISSIONS: 59% of the 2014-2015 applicants were accepted. The SAT scores for the 2014-2015 freshman class were: Critical Reading--21% below 500, 48% between 500 and 599, 25% between 600 and 699, and 6% between 700 and 800; Math--15% below 500, 45% between 500 and 599, 34% between 600 and 699, and 6% between 700 and 800. The ACT scores were 5% below 21, 21% between 21 and 23, 33% between 24 and 26, 16% between 27 and 28, and 25% above 28. 58% of the current freshmen were in the top fifth of their class; 87% were in the top two fifths. **Admissions Contact:** Suzanne McCray, Vice Provost of Enrollment. E-Mail: *uofa@uark.edu* Web: *www.arkansas.edu*

FINANCIAL AID: In 2014-2015, 81% of all full-time freshmen and 66% of continuing full-time students received some form of financial aid. 40% of all full-time freshmen and 37% of continuing full-time students received need-based aid. The average freshman award was $10,004. Need-based scholarships or need-based grants averaged $7,547; need-based self-help aid (loans and jobs) averaged $3,954; non-need-based athletic scholarships averaged $9,007; and other non-need-based awards and non-need-based scholarships averaged $4,494. 5% of undergraduate students work part-time. Average annual earnings from campus work are $1301. The average financial indebtedness of the 2014 graduate was $22,695. The FAFSA is required. The priority date for freshman financial aid applications for fall entry is March 15.

UNIVERSITY OF ARKANSAS AT LITTLE ROCK (*The complete profile is made available exclusively on our website, www. barronspac.com*)

UNIVERSITY OF ARKANSAS AT MONTICELLO (*The complete profile is made available exclusively on our website, www. barronspac.com*)

UNIVERSITY OF ARKANSAS AT PINE BLUFF		C-4
www.uapb.edu		
Pine Bluff, AR 71601		**(870) 575-8492**
Fax: (870) 543-8014	**Email:** fulton_e@4500.uapb.edu	
Full-time: 1260 men, 1520 women	**Faculty:** n/av	
Part-time: 130 men, 205 women	**Ph.D.s:** n/av	
Graduate: 50 men, 135 women	**Student/Faculty:** n/av	
Year: semesters, summer session	**Tuition:** $6178 ($11,908)	
Room & Board: $7200	**Freshman Class:** n/av	
SAT or ACT: required	**CEEB CODE:** 6004	
Application Deadline: n/av	**COMPETITIVE**	

The University of Arkansas at Pine Bluff, established in 1873, is a historically black land-grant institution providing a liberal arts education as part of the public University of Arkansas system. The figures in the above capsule and in this profile are approximate. There are 5 undergraduate schools and one graduate school. In addition to regional accreditation, UAPB has baccalaureate program accreditation with AHEA, CSWE, NASM, NCATE, and NLN. The 318-acre campus is in a small town 40 miles southeast of Little Rock and approximately 142 miles southwest of Memphis. Including any residence halls, there are 49 buildings.

STUDENT LIFE: 80% of undergraduates are from Arkansas. Others are from 28 states, 17 foreign countries, and Canada. 94% are African American. **Male To Female Ratio:** 1.3:1. The average age of freshmen is 18; all undergraduates, 22. 61% do not continue beyond their first year. **Housing:** 1099 students can be accommodated in college housing, which includes single-sex dorms. Honors clusters in the dorms. On-campus housing is guaranteed for all 4 years. 65% of students commute. Alcohol is not permitted. All students may keep cars.

FACULTY/CLASSROOMS: 54% of faculty are male; 46% are female. No introductory courses are taught by graduate students. The average class size in a laboratory is 20 and in a regular course is 21.

PROGRAMS OF STUDY: UAPB confers B.A., and B.S. degrees. Associate and master's degrees are also awarded. Bachelor's degrees are awarded in AGRICULTURE (agriculture, conservation and regulation, and fishing and fisheries), BIOLOGICAL SCIENCE (biology/biological science), BUSINESS (accounting and business administration and management), COMMUNICATIONS AND THE ARTS (art, English, journalism, music, and speech/debate/rhetoric), COMPUTER AND PHYSICAL SCIENCE (applied mathematics, chemistry, computer science, mathematics, and physics), EDUCATION (agricultural education, art education, business education, early childhood education, English education, home economics education, industrial arts education, mathematics education, middle school education, music education, physical education, science education, social science education, and special education), ENGINEERING AND ENVIRONMENTAL DESIGN (industrial engineering technology and preengineering), HEALTH PROFESSIONS (nursing, predentistry, premedicine, prepharmacy, and rehabilitation therapy), SOCIAL SCIENCE (criminal justice, family/consumer studies, gerontology, history, liberal arts/general studies, parks and recreation management, political science/government, psychology, social work, and sociology). Business administration, biology and computer science are the strongest academically and have the largest enrollments.

ACTIVITIES: There are 65 groups on campus, including art, band, cheerleading, choir, computers, drama, drill team, honors, jazz band, marching band, newspaper, orchestra, photography, political, professional, radio and TV, religious, social, social service, student government, and yearbook. Popular campus events include Founders Day, Spring Emphasis, and Unity Fest. **Sports:** There are 7 intercollegiate sports for men and 8 for women, and 20 intramural sports for men and 19 for women. Facilities include a phys ed complex that provides activities such as flag football, basketball, volleyball, softball, tennis, handball, racquetball, track and field, and badminton. There is also a swimming pool and a 6,000-seat football stadium.

SERVICES: Counseling and information services are available, as is tutoring in most subjects. There is a reader service for the blind, and remedial math, reading, and writing. **Library/Resources:** The library contains 271,547 volumes, 119,205 microform items, 4,299 audio/video tapes/CDs/DVDs, and subscribes to 1,050 periodicals including electronic. Computerized library services include interlibrary loans and database searching. Special learning facilities include an art gallery, radio station, and TV station. **Physically Challenged Students:** 98% of the campus is accessible. Facilities include wheelchair ramps, elevators, special parking, specially equipped restrooms, special class scheduling, lowered drinking fountains, and lowered telephones. **Special:** The university offers formal co-op education and work-study programs, concurrent registration with members of the University of Arkansas system, internships, B.A.-B.S. degrees, and dual and student-designed majors. Also offered are credit for military experience, nondegree study, individualized programs of study for honors college students, and study abroad. There are 4 national honor societies, a freshman honors program, and 6 departmental honors programs. **Visiting:** There are regularly scheduled orientations for prospective students. There are guides for informal visits, visitors may sit in on classes, and stay overnight. To schedule a visit, contact the Director of Recruitment at (501) 575-8961 or (800) 525-5272. **Campus Safety and Security:** Measures include 24-hour foot and vehicle patrol, self-defense education, and security escort services. There are emergency telephones, lighted pathways/sidewalks, There is a department of public safety and security on campus.

REQUIREMENTS: The SAT or ACT is required, with a satisfactory score is preferred. Applicants must have earned 15 credits, including 4 units of English and 3 each in social studies, math, and science. The GED is accepted. Students not meeting these requirements may apply for conditional admission. A GPA of 2.0 is required. AP and CLEP credits are accepted. All students must complete at least 124 hours of credit, including 30 hours in their major, while earning an overall 2.0 GPA (2.5 for teacher education majors) and a C or better in all major courses. Distribution requirements include English, math, social and natural science, and phys ed courses. Students must pass a comprehensive exam in their major. **Procedure:** Freshmen are admitted fall, spring, and summer. Entrance exams should be taken during the junior or senior year. There are early admissions, deferred admissions, and rolling admissions plans. Check with the school for current application deadlines. **Transfer Students:** Transfer students must have a minimum GPA of 2.0. Applicants with fewer than 60 semester hours of college credit must submit an application, ACT or SAT I scores, and all college transcripts. 30 of 124 credits required for the bachelor's degree must be completed at UAPB. **International Students:** They must take the TOEFL. They must also take the SAT or ACT. The ACT is preferred. SAT scores may be used.

ADMISSIONS: Erica Fulton, Director of Admissions and Academic Records. E-Mail: *fulton_e@4500.uapb.edu* Web: *www.uapb.edu*

FINANCIAL AID: UAPB is a member of CSS. The FAFSA is required. Check with the school for current application deadlines.

UNIVERSITY OF CENTRAL ARKANSAS C-3
www.uca.edu

Conway, AR 72035

(501) 450-3663
(800) 243-8245
Email: amberh@uca.edu

Full-time: 3306 men, 4866 women	**Faculty:** IIA, --$
Part-time: 779 men, 891 women	**Ph.D.s:** n/av
Graduate: 467 men, 1389 women	**Student/Faculty:** n/av
Year: semesters, summer session	**Tuition:** $7889 ($13,806)
Room & Board: $5778	**Freshman Class:** n/av
SAT or ACT: required	**CEEB CODE:** 6012
Application Deadline: n/av	**VERY COMPETITIVE**

The University of Central Arkansas, established in 1907, is a comprehensive public institution offering undergraduate and graduate degrees in liberal arts, business, health-related sciences, and education. The figures given in the above capsule and in this profile are approximate. There are 7 undergraduate schools and 1 graduate school. In addition to regional accreditation, UCA has baccalaureate program accreditation with AACSB, ADA, APTA, CAHEA, NASAD, NASM, NCATE, and NLN. The 350-acre campus is in a small town

29 miles north of Little Rock. Including any residence halls, there are 118 buildings.

STUDENT LIFE: **Male To Female Ratio:** 1.6:1. 30% do not continue beyond their first year; 40% remain to graduate. **Housing:** 3612 students can be accommodated in college housing, which includes single-sex and coed dorms, on-campus apartments, off-campus apartments, and married student housing. In addition, there are honors houses, international students' residence hall, as well as residential colleges. On-campus housing is guaranteed for all 4 years. Alcohol is not permitted. All students may keep cars.

FACULTY/CLASSROOMS: No introductory courses are taught by graduate students.

PROGRAMS OF STUDY: UCA confers B.A., B.S., B.S.E., B.P.S., B.B.A., B.F.A., B.M. and B.S.N. degrees. Associate, master's, and doctoral degrees are also awarded. Bachelor's degrees are awarded in BIOLOGICAL SCIENCE (biology/biological science), BUSINESS (accounting, banking and finance, business administration and management, business economics, insurance and risk management, and marketing/retailing/merchandising), COMMUNICATIONS AND THE ARTS (communications, English, French, journalism, music, Spanish, and speech/debate/rhetoric), COMPUTER AND PHYSICAL SCIENCE (applied mathematics, chemistry, computer science, information sciences and systems, mathematics, and physics), EDUCATION (art education, athletic training, early childhood education, education of the exceptional child, elementary education, foreign languages education, guidance education, library science, middle school education, music education, physical education, science education, secondary education, and special education), ENGINEERING AND ENVIRONMENTAL DESIGN (environmental science, interior design, and preengineering), HEALTH PROFESSIONS (exercise science, health care administration, health science, medical technology, nuclear medical technology, nursing, occupational therapy, physical therapy, predentistry, premedicine, preoptometry, prepharmacy, preveterinary science, radiological science, and speech pathology/audiology), SOCIAL SCIENCE (African American studies, dietetics, economics, family/consumer studies, geography, gerontology, history, philosophy, political science/government, psychology, public administration, religion, and sociology). Business, health-related sciences, and education are the strongest academically. Health professions and related sciences, business/marketing, and education have the largest enrollments.

ACTIVITIES: Groups on campus include art, band, cheerleading, choir, chorale, chorus, computers, dance, debate, drama, environmental, ethnic, film, forensics, gay, honors, international, jazz band, literary magazine, marching band, musical theater, newspaper, orchestra, pep band, photography, political, professional, radio and TV, religious, social, social service, student government, symphony, and yearbook. Popular campus events include Bear Facts Day, Greek God and Miss UCA. **Sports:** There are 7 intercollegiate sports for men and 8 for women, and 10 intramural sports for men and 10 for women. Facilities include a gym, swimming pool, fitness center, racquetball and tennis courts, a track, soccer fields, football field, basketball court, and an indoor athletic facility. **Graduates:** From July 1, 2013 to June 30, 2014, 1554 bachelor's degrees were awarded. The most popular majors were health professions and related sciences (21%), business/marketing (21%), and education (9%).

SERVICES: Counseling and information services are available, as is tutoring in some subjects, biology, chemistry, physics, algebra, trigonometry, calculus, geometry, sociology, writing, literature, Spanish, accounting, business statistics, French, German, writing and technology There is a reader service for the blind, and remedial math, reading, and writing. **Library/Resources:** The library contains 554,180 volumes, 618,378 microform items, 2,191 audio/video tapes/CDs/DVDs, and subscribes to 59,937 periodicals including electronic. Computerized library services include interlibrary loans, database searching, Internet access, and Wi-Fi capability. Special learning facilities include an art gallery, planetarium, radio station, and TV station. **Physically Challenged Students:** Facilities include wheelchair ramps, elevators, special parking, specially equipped restrooms, special class scheduling, lowered drinking fountains, lowered telephones, and special housing. **Special:** Study abroad, work-study programs, a B.S.-B.A. degree, a 3-2 engineering degree with the University of Arkansas at Fayetteville, dual majors, nondegree study, and pass/fail options are available. Co-op programs in business, computer science, and health sciences and internships in education are also possible. There is a freshman honors program. **Visiting:** There are regularly scheduled orientations for prospective students, including tours at 11 a.m. and 2 p.m.; departments and dormitories may be visited. There are also special visitation days that include a campus tour, departmental session, lunch, parents' session, optional residence hall tour, and classroom visit or planetarium show. Visitors may sit in on classes. To schedule a visit, contact the Admissions Office at admissions@uca .edu. **Campus Safety and Security:** Measures include 24-hour foot and vehicle patrol, emergency notification system, self-defense education, and security escort services. There are shuttle buses, emergency telephones, lighted pathways/sidewalks, and controlled access to dorms/residences.

REQUIREMENTS: The SAT or ACT is required. AP and CLEP credits are accepted. Important factors in the admissions decision are advanced placement or honors courses, evidence of special talent, and recommendations by school officials. All students must earn a minimum of 124 semester hours, including 40 in upper-division courses. A minimum GPA of 2.25 is needed for the B.B.A., 2.5 for most education programs. Minimum requirements also include 3 semester hours in phys ed. **Procedure:** Freshmen are admitted to all sessions. There is a rolling admissions plan. Application deadlines are open. Applications are accepted on-line. **Transfer Students:** Applicants need, on UCA's scale, a minimum cumulative GPA of 2.0. 15 of 120 credits required for the bachelor's degree must be completed at UCA. **International Students:** The school actively recruits these students. They must take the TOEFL.

ADMISSIONS: Amber Hall, Director of Institutional Research. E-Mail: *amberh@uca.edu* Web: *www.uca.edu*

FINANCIAL AID: The FAFSA is required. Check with the school for current application deadlines.

UNIVERSITY OF THE OZARKS B-2
www.ozarks.edu

Clarksville, AR 72830

(479) 979-1227
(800) 264-8636

Fax: (479) 979-1417

Email: emorrow@ozarks.edu.

Full-time: 280 men, 325 women	**Faculty:** n/av
Part-time: 20 men, 35 women	**Ph.D.s:** 77%
Graduate: n/av	**Student/Faculty:** 12 to 1
Year: semesters, summer session	**Tuition:** $24,440
Room & Board: $7000	**Freshman Class:** n/av
SAT or ACT: required	**CEEB CODE:** 6111
Application Deadline: April 1	**COMPETITIVE**

The University of the Ozarks, founded in 1834, is a private, comprehensive liberal arts, and professional programs affiliated with the Presbyterian Church. The figures in the above capsule and in this profile are approximate. There are 4 undergraduate schools. In addition to regional accreditation, Ozarks has baccalaureate program accreditation with NCATE. The 30-acre campus is in a small town in Clarksville, Arkansas, 1 hour east of Fort Smith, and 100 miles northwest of Little Rock. Including any residence halls, there are 16 buildings.

STUDENT LIFE: 59% of undergraduates are from Arkansas. Others are from 22 states, 20 foreign countries, and Canada. 93% are from public schools. 69% are White; 18% Foreign. 60% are Protestant; 20% claim no religious affiliation; 18% Catholic. **Male To Female Ratio:** 1.2:1. The average age of freshmen is 18; all undergraduates, 20. 33% do not continue beyond their first year; 46% remain to graduate. **Housing:** 447 students can be accommodated in college housing, which includes single-sex and coed dorms. On-campus housing is guaranteed for the freshman year only, is available on a first-come, and first-served basis. Priority is given to out-of-town students. 64% of students live on campus; of those, 51% remain on campus on weekends. Alcohol is not permitted. All students may keep cars.

FACULTY/CLASSROOMS: 70% of faculty are male; 30% are female. All teach undergraduates. No introductory courses are taught by graduate students. The average class size in an introductory lecture is 14; in a laboratory is 11; and in a regular course is 15.

PROGRAMS OF STUDY: Ozarks confers B.A., B.S. and B.G.S. degrees. Bachelor's degrees are awarded in BIOLOGICAL SCIENCE (biology/biological science), BUSINESS (accounting, business administration and management, and marketing/retailing/merchandising), COMMUNICATIONS AND THE ARTS (art, communications, dramatic arts, English, and music), COMPUTER AND PHYSICAL SCIENCE (chemistry and mathematics), EDUCATION (business education, early childhood education, middle school education, and physical education), ENGINEERING AND ENVIRONMENTAL DESIGN (environmental science and materials science), HEALTH PROFESSIONS (respiratory therapy), SOCIAL SCIENCE (economics, history, liberal arts/general studies, political science/government, psychology, religion, social science, and sociology). Business and biology have the largest enrollments.

ACTIVITIES: There are no fraternities or sororities. There are 30 groups on campus, including special interest groups, university-sponsored groups, art, cheerleading, choir, chorale, chorus, dance, debate, drama, environmental, film, forensics, honors, international, literary magazine, newspaper, political, professional, radio and TV, recreational organizations, religious, social, social service, and student government. Popular campus events include International Fair and Banquet, Family Weekend and Freshman Matriculation Ceremony. **Sports:** There are 5 intercollegiate sports for men and 5 for women, and 6 intramural sports for men and 5 for women. Facilities include a sports complex housing racquetball courts, a pool, and a 2,200-seat basketball arena. In addition, there are badminton, dodgeball, flag football, golf, volleyball, ping pong, and sand vollyball, softball, soccer, weight room, wrestling facility, shooting sports facility, baseball fields, tennis courts, and a 700-seat soccer stadium. **Graduates:** From July 1, 2013 to June 30, 2014, 106 bachelor's degrees were awarded. The most popular majors were business administration/management (15%), biology (13%), and marketing (11%). 50 companies recruited on campus in 2013-2014. In an average class, 32% graduate in 4 years or less, 45% graduate in 5 years or less, and 46% graduate in 6 years or less. Of the 2013 graduating class, 11% were enrolled in graduate school within 6 months of graduation, and 68% were employed.

SERVICES: Counseling and information services are available, as is tutoring in every subject. There is remedial math, reading, and writing. **Library/Resources:** The library contains 69,960 volumes, 6,927 microform items, 2,955 audio/video tapes/CDs/DVDs, and subscribes to 611 periodicals including electronic. Computerized library services include interlibrary loans, database searching, Internet access, and Wi-Fi capability. Special learning facilities include an art gallery, radio station, TV station, the Jones Learning Center for students with diagnosed learning disabilities. **Physically Challenged Students:** 90% of the campus is accessible. Facilities include elevators, special parking, specially equipped restrooms, special class scheduling, and lowered drinking fountains. **Special:** Internships, study abroad in 8 countries including Japan, numerous work-study programs, dual majors, a general studies degree, and a 3-2 engineering degree with the University of Arkansas are available. There are 3 national honor societies. **Visiting:** There are regularly scheduled orientations for prospective students, including a campus tour and meetings with faculty and students, admissions, and financial aid. In most cases, prospective students may meet with the president and coaches as requested. There are guides for informal visits, visitors may sit in on classes, and stay overnight. To schedule a visit, contact the Admissions Office. **Campus Safety and Security:** Measures include 24-hour foot and vehicle patrol. There are emergency telephones and lighted pathways/sidewalks.

REQUIREMENTS: The SAT or ACT is required, with a satisfactory score on the SAT or on the ACT. An interview is recommended. The GED is accepted. A GPA of 2.0 is required. AP and CLEP credits are accepted. Important factors in the admissions decision are personality/intangible qualities, advanced placement or honors courses, and evidence of special talent. Students are required to earn 124 hours, with 30 to 54 in the major, and maintain a minimum GPA of 2.0. Distribution requirements include 9 hours in civic awareness and social science, 7 to 10 hours in math and science, 4 hours in phys ed and wellness, 3 hours in literature, fine arts, and religion, and up to 6 hours in global awareness. **Procedure:** Freshmen are admitted to all sessions. Entrance exams should be taken as early as possible.

There are deferred admissions and rolling admissions plans. Applications should be filed by April 1 for fall entry; December 1 for spring entry, along with a $30 fee. Applications are accepted on-line. **Transfer Students:** 41 transfer students enrolled in 2013-2014. A GPA of 2.0 and college transcripts are required. Applicants with a GPA of less than 2.0 or fewer than 30 hours of college work must furnish high school transcripts and ACT or SAT results. 30 of 124 credits required for the bachelor's degree must be completed at Ozarks. **International Students:** There are 118 international students enrolled. The school actively recruits these students. They must take the TOEFL and the college's own test.

ADMISSIONS: Emma Lee Morrow, Admissions Coordinator. E-Mail: *emorrow@ozarks.edu*. Web: *www.ozarks.edu*

FINANCIAL AID: In 2014-2015, 99% of all full-time freshmen and 91% of continuing full-time students received some form of financial aid. 66% of all full-time freshmen and 47% of continuing full-time students received need-based aid. The average freshman award was $11,800. 41% of undergraduate students work part-time. Average annual earnings from campus work are $4900. The average financial indebtedness of the 2014 graduate was $16,000. The FAFSA is required. Check with the school for current application deadlines.

WILLIAMS BAPTIST COLLEGE D-1
www.wbcoll.edu

Walnut Ridge, AR 72476

(870) 759-4120
(800) 722-4434

Fax: (870) 886-3924
Email: admissions@wbclab.edu

Full-time: 230 men, 270 women	Faculty: 25
Part-time: 21 men, 29 women	Ph.D.s: 76%
Graduate: n/av	Student/Faculty: 15 to 1
Year: semesters, summer session	Tuition: $13,750
Room & Board: $6320	Freshman Class: n/app
SAT: required ACT: 21	CEEB CODE: 6658
Application Deadline: n/av	COMPETITIVE

Williams Baptist College, founded in 1941, is a private liberal arts institution providing undergraduate education in business, education, humanities, natural sciences, religion, and social sciences. WBC is affiliated with the Southern Baptist Church and is sponsored by the Arkansas Baptist Convention. Figures in the above capsule and in this profile are approximate. In addition to regional accreditation, WBC has baccalaureate program accreditation with NCATE. The 180-acre campus is in a rural area 100 miles northwest of Memphis, TN and 125 miles north of Little Rock. Including any residence halls, there are 41 buildings.

STUDENT LIFE: 69% of undergraduates are from Arkansas. Others are from 22 states, and 6 foreign countries. 90% are from public schools. 87% are White. 89% are Protestant. **Male To Female Ratio:** 1.2:1. The average age of freshmen is 18; all undergraduates, 24. 40% do not continue beyond their first year; 43% remain to graduate. **Housing:** 473 students can be accommodated in college housing, which includes single-sex dorms, on-campus apartments, and married student housing. On-campus housing is guaranteed for all 4 years. 70% of students live on campus; of those, 50% remain on campus on weekends. Alcohol is not permitted. All students may keep cars.

FACULTY/CLASSROOMS: 54% of faculty are male; 46% are female. All teach and do research. No introductory courses are taught by graduate students.

PROGRAMS OF STUDY: WBC confers B.A., B.S. and B.S.Ed. degrees. Associate degrees are also awarded. Bachelor's degrees are awarded in BIOLOGICAL SCIENCE (biology/biological science), BUSINESS (business administration and management), COMMUNICATIONS AND THE ARTS (art, English, and music), COMPUTER AND PHYSICAL SCIENCE (computer science), EDUCATION (elementary education, physical education, and secondary education), SOCIAL SCIENCE (counseling/psychology, history, psychology, religion, religious education, and religious music). Education, psychology, and biology have the largest enrollments.

ACTIVITIES: There are no fraternities or sororities. There are 32 groups on campus, including art, cheerleading, choir, chorale, drama, international, literary magazine, professional, religious, social, social service, and student government. Popular campus events include Harvest Fest, Christmas in the Cove, and Spring Fling. **Sports:** There are 3 intercollegiate sports for men and 4 for women, and 4 intramural sports for men and 4 for women. Facilities include a gym, weight room, racquetball and tennis courts, a jogging track, sand volleyball, disc golf, and a student center. **Graduates:** From July 1, 2013 to June 30, 2014, 101 bachelor's degrees were awarded. The most popular majors were psychology (20%), early childhood education (14%), and business/finance (13%). In an average class, 29% graduate in 4 years or less, 37% graduate in 5 years or less, and 40% graduate in 6 years or less.

SERVICES: Counseling and information services are available, as is tutoring in most subjects. There is remedial math. **Library/Resources:** The library contains 60,131 volumes, 41 microform items, and 172 audio/video tapes/CDs/DVDs, and subscribes to 37 periodicals including electronic. Computerized library services include interlibrary loans, database searching, Internet access, and Wi-Fi capability. Special learning facilities include an art gallery, an education curriculum lab. **Physically Challenged Students:** 90% of the campus is accessible. Facilities include wheelchair ramps, elevators, special parking, specially equipped restrooms, and lowered drinking fountains. **Special:** WBC offers study abroad in England, Latin America, the Middle East, and Russia, a Washington semester through the American Studies Program, and a general studies major. There are 9 national honor societies and 10 departmental honors programs. **Visiting:** There are regularly scheduled orientations for prospective students. There are guides for informal visits, visitors may sit in on classes, and stay overnight. To schedule a visit, contact Andrew Watson at (800) 722-4434. **Campus Safety and Security:** Measures include 24-hour foot and vehicle patrol and emergency notification system. There are lighted pathways/sidewalks and controlled access to dorms/residences.

REQUIREMENTS: The SAT or ACT is required. First-time freshmen must have a minimum composite score of 19 and 2.5 cumulative high school GPA for unconditional admission. A GPA of 2.5 is required. AP and CLEP credits are accepted.To graduate, all students must follow a core curriculum including humanities, social science and religion, natural science and math, and physical activity. Chapel attendance is mandatory. A total of 123 credits, with 36 to 64 hours in the major, and a minimum GPA of 2.0 are required to graduate. **Procedure:** Freshmen are admitted to all sessions. There is a rolling admissions plan. Application deadlines are open. Applications are accepted on-line. Application fees are waived if application is completed on-line. **Transfer Students:** 58 transfer students enrolled in 2013-2014. Transfer students must have a GPA of 2.0 for unconditional admission. 32 of 123 credits required for the bachelor's degree must be completed at WBC. **International Students:** There are 19 international students enrolled. The school actively recruits these students. They must also take the SAT or ACT, scoring 19.

ADMISSIONS: Andrew Watson, Director of Admissions. E-Mail: *admissions@wbclab.edu* Web: *www.wbcoll.edu*

FINANCIAL AID: In 2014-2015, 100% of all full-time freshmen and 99% of continuing full-time students received some form of financial aid. 65% of all full-time freshmen and 71% of continuing full-time students received need-based aid. The average freshman award was $15,131. Need-based scholarships or need-based grants averaged $4,377 ($7,245 maximum); need-based self-help aid (loans and jobs) averaged $3,439 ($6,581 maximum); non-need-based athletic scholarships averaged $3,793 ($16,000 maximum); and other non-need-based awards and non-need-based scholarships averaged $6,727 ($21,600 maximum). 40% of undergraduate students work part-time. Average annual earnings from campus work are $1317. The average financial indebtedness of the 2014 graduate was $19,024. The FAFSA is required. The priority date for freshman financial aid applications for fall entry is February 1. The deadline for filing freshman financial aid applications for fall entry is May 1.

CALIFORNIA

• College Location

0 20 40 60 80 100 120 140 160 180 200
Miles

AMERICAN JEWISH UNIVERSITY - COLLEGE OF ARTS AND SCIENCES
www.ajula.edu

Los Angeles, CA 90077	**(310) 476-9777, ext. 250**
	(877) GO-2-AJULA
Fax: (310) 471-3657	**Email:** mdavidson@ajula.edu
Full-time: 40 men, 60 women	**Faculty:** n/av
Part-time: 5 men, 5 women	**Ph.D.s:** 100%
Graduate: 65 men, 75 women	**Student/Faculty:** n/av
Year: semesters	**Tuition:** $21,500
Room & Board: $11,000	**Freshman Class:** n/av
SAT or ACT: required	**CEEB CODE:** 4876
Application Deadline: May 31	**COMPETITIVE**

American Jewish University, College of Arts and Science, founded in 2007, is distinguished by its core curriculum integrating the study of Western and Jewish civilizations. It prepares students for careers and graduate studies in law, business, psychology, education, and other fields. The figures in the above capsule and in this profile are approximate. There are 3 graduate schools. The 28-acre campus is in a suburban area in Los Angeles. Including any residence halls, there are 9 buildings.

STUDENT LIFE: 71% of undergraduates are from California. Others are from 22 states, and 2 foreign countries. 70% are from public schools. 81% are White. 94% are Jewish. **Male To Female Ratio:** 1.3:1. The average age of freshmen is 18; all undergraduates, 23. 5% do not continue beyond their first year; 90% remain to graduate. **Housing:** 192 students can be accommodated in college housing, which includes coed dorms, on-campus apartments, and married student housing. On-campus housing is guaranteed for all 4 years. 70% of students live on campus; of those, 70% remain on campus on weekends. All students may keep cars.

FACULTY/CLASSROOMS: 45% of faculty are male; 55% are female. All teach and do research. No introductory courses are taught by graduate students. The average class size in an introductory lecture is 7 and in a laboratory is 7.

PROGRAMS OF STUDY: AJU confers B.A. degrees. Master's degrees are also awarded. Bachelor's degrees are awarded in BUSINESS (business administration and management), COMMUNICATIONS AND THE ARTS (journalism and literature), HEALTH PROFESSIONS (premedicine), SOCIAL SCIENCE (ethics, politics, and social policy, Judaic studies, liberal arts/general studies, political science/government, and psychology).

ACTIVITIES: There are no fraternities or sororities. There are 15 groups on campus, including Tikkum Olam, bioethics, Hillel, peer mentoring, psychology, art, choir, dance, drama, Israel action, literary magazine, newspaper, political, radio and TV, religious, social, social service, and student government. Popular campus events include Israel Memorial Day (Yom Hazikaron), and Israel Independence Day (Yom Ha'atzmaut). **Sports:** There is no sports program at AJU. Facilities include a gym, a basketball court, and a soccer field at the Familian campus in Los Angeles and horseback riding, swimming pools, and a ropes course at the Brandeis-Bardin campus in Simi Valley.

SERVICES: Counseling and information services are available, as is tutoring in most subjects. There is remedial math and writing. **Library/Resources:** The library contains 105,000 volumes, and subscribes to 400 periodicals including electronic. Computerized library services include interlibrary loans. Special learning facilities include an art gallery and radio station. **Physically Challenged Students:** All of the campus is accessible. Facilities include elevators, special parking, specially equipped restrooms, lowered drinking fountains, lowered telephones. **Special:** There is a 5-year joint business management program with American Jewish University's Lieber School of Graduate Studies and a 5-year joint master's degree in Jewish education with AJU's Fingerhut School of Education. Student designed and dual majors are available. Internships in all available majors, study abroad, work-study programs, accelerated degree programs, and pass/fail options are offered. Students may apply for independent study projects. There is 1 national honor society. **Visiting:** There are regularly scheduled orientations for prospective students, including meeting with admissions representatives, department chairs, and the Dean of the College of Arts and Sciences, sitting in on classes, sleeping over in the dorms, eating meals in the Berg dining hall, meeting current students and touring the campus. There are guides for informal visits, visitors may sit in on classes, and stay overnight. To schedule a visit, contact the Director of Undergraduate Admissions. **Campus Safety and Security:** Measures include 24-hour foot and vehicle patrol, self-defense education, and security escort services. There are emergency telephones and lighted pathways/sidewalks.

REQUIREMENTS: The SAT or ACT is required. Applicants must be graduates of an accredited secondary school or have a GED. A visit and an interview are recommended for all students. 2 letters of recommendation, an autobiographical essay, and official high school transcripts are required. A GPA of 2.0 is required. AP credits are accepted. Important factors in the admissions decision are extracurricular activities record. All students must complete a core curriculum combining the study of Jewish and Western civilizations, as well as courses in communications and foreign language and 1 in computer science. There are distribution requirements in math, natural and behavioral sciences, English, and fine arts. Other requirements vary according to the major, with at least 32 to 36 upper-division credits needed. A total of 120 semester units, with a minimum GPA of 2.0, is required to graduate. **Procedure:** Freshmen are admitted fall and spring. Entrance exams should be taken no later than November of the year prior to enrollment. There are early decision, deferred admissions, and rolling admissions plans. Applications should be filed by May 31 for fall entry; November 30 for spring entry. The fall 2014 application fee was $35. Notification is sent on a rolling basis. Applications are accepted on-line. **Transfer Students:** 19 transfer students enrolled in 2013-2014. Previous college work should be at the B level to transfer. Students with fewer than 60 college credits should also have a minimum 3.0 high school GPA, at least 1700 on the SAT or 24 on the ACT, recommendations, and an autobiographical essay. The SAT or ACT requirement is waived if the applicant has 60 or more transferable credits. A visit and an interview are recommended. 34 of 120 credits required for the bachelor's degree must be completed at AJU. **International Students:** They must take the TOEFL with a minimum score of 79 on the Internet-based version (iBT). They must also take the SAT or ACT, scoring 1700.

ADMISSIONS: Jyllian Siegal, Director of Undergraduate Admissions. E-Mail: *mdavidson@ajula.edu* Web: *www.ajula.edu*

FINANCIAL AID: The FAFSA and the college's own financial statement, tax returns, and W2s are required. Check with the school for current application deadlines.

ART CENTER COLLEGE OF DESIGN (*The complete profile is made available exclusively on our website, www.barronspac.com*)

AZUSA PACIFIC UNIVERSITY	D-5
www.apu.edu	

Azusa, CA 91702	(626) 812-3016
	(800) TALK-APU
Fax: (626) 812-3096	Email: admissions@apu.edu
Full-time: 1929 men, 3471 women	Faculty: I, -$
Part-time: 263 men, 497 women	Ph.D.s: n/av
Graduate: 1191 men, 2974 women	Student/Faculty: n/av
Year: semesters, summer session	Tuition: $33,096
Room & Board: $8990	Freshman Class: n/av
	CEEB CODE: 4596
Application Deadline: May 1	COMPETITIVE

Azusa Pacific University, founded in 1899, is a private (non-profit), interdenominational Christian institution offering undergraduate and graduate programs in the liberal arts and emphasizing spiritual growth. There are 7 undergraduate schools and 8 graduate schools. In addition to regional accreditation, APU has baccalaureate program accreditation with CSWE, NASAD, NASM, NCATE, and NLN. The 60-acre campus is in a small town 26 miles east of Los Angeles. Including any residence halls, there are 67 buildings.

STUDENT LIFE: 82% of undergraduates are from California. Others are from 47 states, 19 foreign countries, and Canada. 47% are White; 26% Hispanic. 58% are Protestant; 37% unknown denominations. **Male To Female Ratio:** 2.1:1. The average age of freshmen is 18; all undergraduates, 31. 15% do not continue beyond their first year; 67% remain to graduate. **Housing:** 3077 students can be accommodated in college housing, which includes single-sex and coed dorms, on-campus apartments, and off-campus apartments. In addition, there are honors houses and special-interest houses. On-campus housing is available on a first-come, first-served basis, and is available on a lottery system for upperclassmen. 57% of students live on campus. Alcohol is not permitted. All students may keep cars.

FACULTY/CLASSROOMS: No introductory courses are taught by graduate students.

PROGRAMS OF STUDY: APU confers B.A., B.S., B.M., B.F.A, B.S.N. and B.S.W. degrees. Master's and doctoral degrees are also awarded. Bachelor's degrees are awarded in BIOLOGICAL SCIENCE (biochemistry and biology/biological science), BUSINESS (accounting, business administration and management, and marketing/retailing/merchandising), COMMUNICATIONS AND THE ARTS (communications, English, music, and Spanish), COMPUTER AND PHYSICAL SCIENCE (chemistry, computer science, information sciences and systems, mathematics, and physics), EDUCATION (art education, music education, and physical education), HEALTH PROFESSIONS (nursing), SOCIAL SCIENCE (biblical studies, history, international studies, liberal arts/general studies, ministries, philosophy, political science/government, psychology, religion, social science, social work, and sociology). Nursing, education, and religion are the strongest academically. Business, nursing, and psychology have the largest enrollments.

ACTIVITIES: There are no fraternities or sororities. There are 48 groups on campus, including art, band, cheerleading, choir, chorale, chorus, computers, dance, debate, drama, ethnic, film, honors, international, jazz band, literary magazine, marching band, musical theater, newspaper, opera, orchestra, pep band, photography, political, radio and TV, religious, social, social service, student government, and yearbook. Popular campus events include Missions Week, Mega

Weekend-Homecoming/Dinner Rally and Night of Champions. **Sports:** There are 8 intercollegiate sports for men and 10 for women, and 7 intramural sports for men and 7 for women. Facilities include an all-weather track, 3000-seat football stadium, baseball field, 1200-seat gym, residence hall lounge, turf recreation field, sand volleyball courts, indoor/outdoor basketball courts, and a recreation room. **Graduates:** From July 1, 2013 to June 30, 2014, 1764 bachelor's degrees were awarded. The most popular majors were business/marketing (23%), health professions and related programs (20%). In an average class, 47% graduate in 4 years or less, 63% graduate in 5 years or less, and 67% graduate in 6 years or less.

SERVICES: Counseling and information services are available, as is tutoring in most subjects. There is remedial math, reading, and writing. **Library/Resources:** The 3 libraries contain 247,700 volumes, and subscribe to 64,590 periodicals including electronic. Computerized library services include interlibrary loans, database searching, Internet access, and Wi-Fi capability. Special learning facilities include an art gallery, radio station, and TV station. **Physically Challenged Students:** All of the campus is accessible. Facilities include wheelchair ramps, elevators, special parking, specially equipped restrooms, lowered drinking fountains, lowered telephones, and special housing. **Special:** Internships in ministerial and American studies, study abroad in Japan, Latin America, Taiwan, England, Australia, China, Tanzania, Italy, Israel, France, Lithuania, Spain, Uganda, and South Africa, and a Washington semester are available. In addition work-study with the university, a B.A.-B.S. degree, dual majors in all programs, and a 3-2 engineering degree are offered. Accelerated degree programs are available in Christian leadership, computer information systems, management information systems, human development, and organizational leadership; there is also a Registered Nurse to Bachelor of Science in Nursing Program. APU awards credit for life experience and allows nondegree study. There are 2 national honor societies and a freshman honors program. **Visiting:** There are regularly scheduled orientations for prospective students, including Seniors Only Day in November, and a brother/sister weekend in February that is open to both juniors and seniors. There are guides for informal visits, visitors may sit in on classes, and stay overnight. To schedule a visit, contact the Admissions Office. **Campus Safety and Security:** Measures include 24-hour foot and vehicle patrol, emergency notification system, self-defense education, and security escort services. There are shuttle buses, emergency telephones, lighted pathways/sidewalks, and controlled access to dorms/residences.

REQUIREMENTS: The SAT and ACT are required, but no minimum score is necessary. An essay is required. A portfolio and an interview are recommended for certain programs. The GED is accepted. A GPA of 2.8 is required. AP and CLEP credits are accepted. Important factors in the admissions decision are personality/intangible qualities, evidence of special talent, and advanced placement or honors courses. All students must take 120 semester units and earn a minimum GPA of 2.0. 18 units of Bible courses, 120 hours of community ministry, and 2 units of health are required. General education requirements include courses in public speaking, fine arts, religion and philosophy, English, algebra, foreign language, and phys ed. heritage and institution, identity and relationships, and nature are also required courses. **Procedure:** Freshmen are admitted to all sessions. Entrance exams should be taken prior to enrollment. There are early admissions, deferred admissions, and rolling admissions plans. Early decision applications should be filed by February 15; regular applications, by May 1 for fall entry, along with a $45 fee. Notification of early decision is sent October 1; regular decision, April 1. Applications are accepted on-line. Application fees are waived if application is completed on-line. **Transfer Students:** 658 transfer students enrolled in 2013-2014. Applicants must have a minimum GPA of 2.20 on previous college work. The SAT or ACT is not required if 30 or more semester units have been completed. An associate degree and an interview are recommended. 30 of 120 credits required for the bachelor's degree must be completed at APU. **International Students:** There are 113 international students enrolled. The school actively recruits these students. They must take the TOEFL.

ADMISSIONS: David Burke, Director of Undergraduate Admissions. E-Mail: *admissions@apu.edu* Web: *www.apu.edu*

FINANCIAL AID: The FAFSA and the college's own financial statement are required. Check with the school for current application deadlines.

BIOLA UNIVERSITY   **D-5**
www.biola.edu

La Mirada, CA 90639	(562) 903-4752
	(800) OK-BIOLA
Fax: (562) 903-4709	Email: admissions@biola.edu
Full-time: 1582 men, 2575 women	Faculty: IIA, +$
Part-time: 88 men, 92 women	Ph.D.s: 74%
Graduate: 1294 men, 671 women	Student/Faculty: 16 to 1
Year: 4-1-4, summer session	Tuition: $32,142
Room & Board: $9316	Freshman Class: 3528 applied, 2634 accepted, 930 enrolled
SAT CR/M/W: 556/559/550 ACT: 24	CEEB CODE: 4017
Application Deadline: March 1	COMPETITIVE+

Biola University, founded in 1908, is a private, interdenominational Christian institution offering undergraduate and graduate degrees in arts and sciences, psychology, theology, intercultural studies, and business. Figures in the above capsule and in this profile are approximate. There are 7 undergraduate schools and 6 graduate schools. In addition to regional accreditation, Biola has baccalaureate program accreditation with ACBSP, NASAD, NASM, and NLN. The 95-acre campus is in a suburban area 22 miles southeast of Los Angeles. Including any residence halls, there are 53 buildings.

STUDENT LIFE: 78% of undergraduates are from California. Others are from 40 states, 28 foreign countries, and Canada. 69% are from public schools. 56% are White; 17% Hispanic; 15% Asian American. 99% are Protestant. **Male To Female Ratio:** 1.1:1. The average age of freshmen is 18; all undergraduates, 20. 14% do not continue beyond their first year; 65% remain to graduate. **Housing:** 2307 students can be accommodated in college housing, which includes single-sex and coed dorms, on-campus apartments, and off-campus apartments. On-campus housing is guaranteed for the freshman year only, is available on a first-come, first-served basis, and is available on a lottery system for upperclassmen. 61% of students live on campus; of those, 73% remain on campus on weekends. Alcohol is not permitted. All students may keep cars.

FACULTY/CLASSROOMS: 63% of faculty are male; 37% are female. No introductory courses are taught by graduate students.

PROGRAMS OF STUDY: Biola confers B.A., B.S., B.F.A. and B.M. degrees. Master's and doctoral degrees are also awarded. Bachelor's degrees are awarded in BIOLOGICAL SCIENCE (biochemistry, biology/adolescence education, biology/biological science, and life science), BUSINESS (accounting, business administration and management, business communications, business economics, business information systems, economics – statistics, international business management, management information systems, management science, and marketing management), COMMUNICATIONS AND THE ARTS (advertising, American literature, American Sign Language, art, broadcasting, communications, dramatic arts, drawing, English, film arts, fine arts, graphic design, journalism, music, music composition, music performance, music theory and composition, painting, performing arts, photography, piano performance, playwriting/screenwriting, printmaking, public relations, publishing, radio/television technology, Spanish, studio art, theatre acting, theatre arts, theater design, and theater management), COMPUTER AND PHYSICAL SCIENCE (applied mathematics, chemistry, computer mathematics, computer information technology, computer science, information sciences and systems, mathematics, mathematics/theoretical, natural sciences, physical sciences, physics, and statistics), EDUCATION (Christian education, early childhood education, mathematics education, music education, physical education, social studies education, and social studies secondary school education), ENGINEERING AND ENVIRONMENTAL DESIGN (computational sciences, computer technology, engineering, and environmental science), HEALTH PROFESSIONS (nursing, physical therapy, preallied health, Pre-Health Studies, predentistry, premedicine, prepharmacy, prephysical therapy, speech pathology/audiology, and speech therapy), SOCIAL SCIENCE (anthropology, applied psychology, archeology, biblical studies, counseling/psychology, crosscultural studies, early childhood studies, economics, history, humanities, liberal arts/general studies, ministries, missions, philosophy, philosophy and reli-

gion, prelaw, psychology, religious studies, social science, social work, and sociology). Biblical studies, business administration, journalism/communication, and psychology are the strongest academically. Biblical studies, business, psychology have the largest enrollments.

ACTIVITIES: There are no fraternities or sororities. There are 52 groups on campus, including dance clubs, gospel choir, missionary and ministries groups, adventure club, art, band, cheerleading, chess, choir, chorale, dance, debate, drama, environmental, ethnic, film, forensics, honors, international, jazz band, literary magazine, musical theater, newspaper, opera, orchestra, political, professional, radio and TV, religious, social, social service, student government, symphony, and yearbook. Popular campus events include Multicultural Week, Christmas Celebration, Biola Weekend, Missions Conference and Torrey Conference. **Sports:** There are 12 intercollegiate sports for men and 12 for women, and 10 intramural sports for men and 10 for women. Facilities include a gym/swimming complex, a 450-seat auditorium, athletic fields, including 1 for soccer, a quarter-mile track, a baseball diamond, tennis, sand volleyball, basketball courts, and a fitness center. **Graduates:** From July 1, 2013 to June 30, 2014, 898 bachelor's degrees were awarded. The most popular majors were business/marketing (19%), theology and religious vocations (14%), and visual and performing arts (11%). In an average class, 47% graduate in 4 years or less, 62% graduate in 5 years or less, and 65% graduate in 6 years or less. Of the 2013 graduating class, 50% were employed within 6 months of graduation.

SERVICES: Counseling and information services are available, as is tutoring in most subjects. There is a reader service for the blind. A Writing Center is available to all students. **Library/Resources:** The library contains 315,000 volumes, 580,000 microform items, 9,232 audio/video tapes/CDs/DVDs, and subscribes to 30,000 periodicals including electronic. Computerized library services include interlibrary loans, database searching, Internet access, and Wi-Fi capability. Special learning facilities include an art gallery, radio station, TV station, film studio and a 3-D art facility, MIDI lab for music composition majors, electronic piano lab, listening lab with music archives, physical science labs, and scanning electron microscope, including an archeological dig-site on. **Physically Challenged Students:** 90% of the campus is accessible. Facilities include wheelchair ramps, elevators, special parking, specially equipped restrooms, special class scheduling, lowered drinking fountains, and lowered telephones. **Special:** Cross-registration with the Au Sable Institute of Environmental Studies is possible. Biola offers internships, summer travel tours, study abroad in 11 countries, and an American studies program in Washington D.C., sponsored by the Christian College Coalition. Special programs include L.A. Film Studies, a semester in Hollywood working in the film industry; Biola Baja, a 3-week program at Vermillion Sea Field, Baja; a family studies course at Focus on the Family Institute in Colorado Springs; a China studies program at Fudan University in Shanghai, China; and a development theory studies program in Honduras. Also available are on- and off-campus work-study programs, a B.A.- B.S. degree, a 3-2 engineering degree with the University of Southern California, dual majors, and nondegree study. There are several preprofessional programs available, including prelaw, prephysical therapy, and prechiropractic. A 3-1 program with Los Angeles College of Chiropractic is offered. Students can also attend a semester at Martha's Vineyard with the Contemporary Music Center and explore the many areas of the Christian music industry. There are 2 national honor societies, a freshman honors program, and 7 departmental honors programs. **Visiting:** There are regularly scheduled orientations for prospective students, including class visits; orientation with the departments of admissions, financial aid, and student affairs; chapel; a sporting event; and a Disneyland or Knott's Berry Farm visit. There are guides for informal visits, visitors may sit in on classes, and stay overnight. To schedule a visit, contact the Admissions Office at admissions@biola.edu. **Campus Safety and Security:** Measures include 24-hour foot and vehicle patrol, emergency notification system, self-defense education, and security escort services. There are shuttle buses, emergency telephones, lighted pathways/sidewalks, controlled access to dorms/residences, bicycle patrol, and Segway patrol.

REQUIREMENTS: The SAT or ACT is required. Applicants need not be graduates of an accredited secondary school. The GED is accepted. Students should have completed 15 academic credits, including 4 years of English and foreign language, 3 years of math, and 2 each of social studies and science. All students must be evangelical Christians who can demonstrate Christian character, leadership ability, and the aptitude for possible success in college. Applicants must submit 1 reference from their pastor or someone on the pastoral staff. A personal essay is required. A GPA of 3.0 is required. AP and CLEP credits are accepted. Important factors in the admissions decision are personality/intangible qualities, recommendations by school officials, and leadership record. To graduate, students must pass a writing competency exam, complete 30 units of biblical studies and theology, and fulfill the general education and phys ed requirements. At least 130 semester hours must be completed, with 30 hours in the major and 24 of these in upper-division work. Other requirements vary by major. A minimum 2.0 GPA is required. **Procedure:** Freshmen are admitted to all sessions. There are early decision and rolling admissions plans. Early decision applications should be filed by November 15; regular applications, by March 1 for fall entry; and November 15 for spring entry, along with a $45 fee. Notification of early decision is sent January 15; regular decision, April 1. Applications are accepted on-line. **Transfer Students:** 322 transfer students enrolled in 2013-2014. Applicants with fewer than 15 credit hours must submit both college transcripts and SAT scores. All students must provide high school transcripts. A minimum 2.0 GPA and an interview are required. 30 of 130 credits required for the bachelor's degree must be completed at Biola. **International Students:** There are 180 international students enrolled. The school actively recruits these students. They must take the TOEFL with a minimum score of 600 on the paper-based TOEFL (PBT) or 100 on the Internet-based version (iBT). They must also take the SAT or ACT.

ADMISSIONS: 75% of the 2014-2015 applicants were accepted. The SAT scores for the 2014-2015 freshman class were: Critical Reading--24% below 500, 42% between 500 and 599, 27% between 600 and 699, and 7% between 700 and 800; Math--26% below 500, 42% between 500 and 599, 29% between 600 and 699, and 3% between 700 and 800; Writing--25% below 500, 44% between 500 and 599, 25% between 600 and 699, and 6% between 700 and 800. The ACT scores were 7% below 21, 35% between 21 and 23, 28% between 24 and 26, 19% between 27 and 28, and 11% above 28. **Admissions Contact:** André Stephens, Senior Director/Undergraduate Admissions. E-Mail: *admissions@biola.edu* Web: *undergrad.biola.edu*

FINANCIAL AID: In 2014-2015, 69% of all full-time freshmen and 70% of continuing full-time students received some form of financial aid. 68% of all full-time freshmen and 67% of continuing full-time students received need-based aid. The average freshman award was $16,773. Need-based scholarships or need-based grants averaged $12,990; need-based self-help aid (loans and jobs) averaged $7,011; non-need-based athletic scholarships averaged $11,165; and other non-need-based awards and non-need-based scholarships averaged $6,523. 34% of undergraduate students work part-time. The average financial indebtedness of the 2014 graduate was $34,587. Biola is a member of CSS. The FAFSA and the college's own financial statement, and California residents should submit the Cal Grant GPA verification form. are required. The priority date for freshman financial aid applications for fall entry is May 15. The deadline for filing freshman financial aid applications for fall entry is June 15.

CALIFORNIA BAPTIST UNIVERSITY   D-5
www.calbaptist.edu

Riverside, CA 92504

(951) 343-4212
(877) 228-8866

Fax: (951) 343-4525   Email: admissions@calbaptist.edu

Full-time: 1861 men, 3225 women   **Faculty:** 254

Part-time: 244 men, 467 women   **Ph.D.s:** 73%

Graduate: 350 men, 997 women   **Student/Faculty:** 20 to 1

Year: semesters, summer session   **Tuition:** $28,122

Room & Board: $9220   **Freshman Class:** 3853 applied, 3036 accepted, 993 enrolled

SAT CR/M/W: 487/491/476 **ACT:** 21   **CEEB CODE:** 4094

Application Deadline: rolling   **COMPETITIVE**

California Baptist University (CBU) is one of the top private Christian colleges and universities in Southern California. CBU offers bachelor's, master's and credential programs in Riverside, San Bernardino and online. California Baptist University believes each person has been created for a purpose. CBU strives to help students understand and engage this purpose by providing a Christ-centered educational experience that integrates academics with spiritual and social development opportunities. Graduates are challenged to become individuals whose skills, integrity and sense of purpose glorify God and distinguish them in the workplace and in the world. There are 11 undergraduate schools and 9 graduate schools. In addition to regional accreditation, CBU has baccalaureate program accreditation with ABET, ACBSP, and NASM. The 160-acre campus is located 60 miles east of Los Angeles. Including any residence halls, there are 138 buildings.

STUDENT LIFE: 95% of undergraduates are from California. Others are from 43 states, 22 foreign countries, and Canada. 90% are from public schools. 45% are White; 30% Hispanic. 59% are Protestant; 30% Latter Day Saints, Buddhist, Muslim, and unknown. **Male To Female Ratio:** 1.9:1. The average age of freshmen is 19; all undergraduates, 23. 23% do not continue beyond their first year; 58% remain to graduate. **Housing:** 2482 students can be accommodated in college housing, which includes single-sex dorms, on-campus apartments, and married student housing. In addition, there are special-interest houses, Global Village for students interested in living with multicultural residents. On-campus housing is available on a first-come and first-served basis. 60% of students commute. Alcohol is not permitted. All students may keep cars.

FACULTY/CLASSROOMS: 51% of faculty are male; 49% are female. 95% teach undergraduates. No introductory courses are taught by graduate students. The average class size in an introductory lecture is 24 and in a laboratory is 16.

PROGRAMS OF STUDY: CBU confers B.A., B.S., B.Ch.E., B.S.C.E., B.S.E.C.E., B.S.E., B.S.M.E., B.S.N., B.A.T. and B.M. degrees. Master's degrees are also awarded. Bachelor's degrees are awarded in BIOLOGICAL SCIENCE (biochemistry, biology/biological science, and nutritional sciences), BUSINESS (accounting, business administration and management, and marketing/retailing/merchandising), COMMUNICATIONS AND THE ARTS (communications, dramatic arts, English, film arts, graphic design, journalism, music, music performance, music theory and composition, piano/organ, public relations, Spanish, visual and performing arts, and voice), COMPUTER AND PHYSICAL SCIENCE (chemistry, digital arts/technology, mathematics, and statistics), EDUCATION (health education, mathematics education, and music education), ENGINEERING AND ENVIRONMENTAL DESIGN (applied aviation, architecture, aviation administration/management, aviation flight technology, civil engineering, construction management, electrical and computer engineering, engineering, environmental science, and mechanical engineering), HEALTH PROFESSIONS (exercise science, health care administration, health science, nursing, and prephysical therapy), SOCIAL SCIENCE (anthropology, behavioral science, Christian studies, communication sciences and disorders, criminal justice, early childhood studies, history, interdisciplinary studies, international studies, liberal arts/general studies, pastoral studies, philosophy, political science/government, psychology, and sociology). Engineering, nursing, business administration, psychology and education are the strongest academically. Business administration, nursing and psychology have the largest enrollments.

ACTIVITIES: There are no fraternities or sororities. There are 34 groups on campus, including Caihong Campus Ministry and Bible Study, art, band, cheerleading, choir, chorale, chorus, communications, computers, debate, drama, drill team, environmental, ethnic, FAITH Club, film, forensics, honors, international, jazz band, literary magazine, musical theater, newspaper, orchestra, pep band, photography, political, professional, religious, social, social service, student government, symphony, and yearbook. Popular campus events include Twirp Week, Octoberfest, CBU CRAZIES, Annual YuleFest, Intramural Sports, and Spiritual Emphasis Week. **Sports:** There are 9 intercollegiate sports for men and 9 for women, and 6 intramural sports for men and 6 for women. Facilities include 1,100-seat gym; 40,682-square-foot recreation center with indoor basketball courts, racquetball courts, climbing wall, and rooftop running track and soccer field, aquatics center with Olympic-size pool, outdoor athletic complex with baseball, softball, and soccer fields, athletic performance center, athletic training clinic, tennis center, and sand volleyball courts. **Graduates:** From July 1, 2013 to June 30, 2014, 929 bachelor's degrees were awarded. The most popular majors were psychology (11%), business administration (10%), and nursing (9%). 165 companies recruited on campus in 2013-2014. In an average class, 9% graduate in 3 years or less, 41% graduate in 4 years or less, 54% graduate in 5 years or less, and 58% graduate in 6 years or less.

SERVICES: Counseling and information services are available, as is tutoring in most subjects. There is remedial math, reading, and writing. **Library/Resources:** The library contains 257,674 volumes, 54,853 microform items, 22,020 audio/video tapes/CDs/DVDs, and subscribes to 29,680 periodicals including electronic. Computerized library services include interlibrary loans, database searching, and Internet access. Special learning facilities include an art gallery, a music production and recording studios, language lab, digital design and photography studio, theater arts stage production workshop, Bourns engineering laboratories, athletic performance center, recreation and fitness center, and a aquatic center. **Physically Challenged Students:** 95% of the campus is accessible. Facilities include wheelchair ramps, elevators, special parking, specially equipped restrooms, and lowered drinking fountains. **Special:** CBU offers accelerated programs in accounting, business administration, Christian ministries, communication studies, computer information technology, criminal justice, early childhood studies, English, graphic design and digital media, interdisciplinary studies, kinesiology, liberal studies, organizational leadership, political science, psychology, public administration, public relations, and sociology. Study abroad, internships, work-study programs, a Washington semester, double majors, and credit for military/work experience are available. There are 3 national honor societies, a freshman honors program, and 1 departmental honors programs. **Visiting:** There are regularly scheduled orientations for prospective students, consisting of a welcome, orientation, academic fair, and tours. There are guides for informal visits, visitors may sit in on classes, and stay overnight. To schedule a visit, contact Allen Johnson at (877) 228-8866. **Campus Safety and Security:** Measures include 24-hour foot and vehicle patrol, emergency notification system, self-defense education, and security escort services. There are emergency telephones, lighted pathways/sidewalks, and controlled access to dorms/residences.

REQUIREMENTS: The SAT or ACT is required. Applicants should be graduates of an accredited high school or have a GED. Required academic units: English-4, mathematics-3, Lab Science-2; foreign language-2, social studies-2, history-2. An essay and interview are recommended, and two references, preferably from a church leader and an official of an academic institution, are required. A GPA of 2.0 is required. AP and CLEP credits are accepted. Important factors in the admissions decision are evidence of special talent, leadership record, and advanced placement or honors courses. All students must be proficient in English and complete courses in English, Communication Arts, Math, Behavioral/Social Science, Art or Music, Philosophy, U.S. History, Study Abroad or Non-U.S. History, Political Science, Laboratory Science, science or Kinesiology, and Christian Studies. A total of 124 units, with a minimum GPA of 2.0, is required to graduate. **Procedure:** Freshmen are admitted fall, spring, and summer. Entrance exams should be taken during the junior year. There are deferred admissions and rolling admissions plans. Early decision applications should be filed by December 15, along with a $45 fee. Notification of early decision is sent January 31; regular decision, Nov 9. Applications are accepted on-line. **Transfer Students:** 886 transfer students enrolled in 2013-2014. Applicants must have a minimum GPA of 2.0 if they are transferring at least 30 transferable semester units. Only courses with a grade of C- or better may transfer. Applicants transferring less than 30 units must have a high school GPA of at least 2.5 and must submit SAT or ACT scores. 36 of 124 credits required for the bachelor's degree must be completed at CBU. **International Students:** There are 111 international students enrolled. The school actively recruits these students. They must take the TOEFL with a minimum score of 71 on the Internet-based version (iBT). They must also take the SAT or ACT, scoring 920.

ADMISSIONS: 79% of the 2014-2015 applicants were accepted. The SAT scores for the 2014-2015 freshman class were: Critical Reading-53% below 500, 35% between 500 and 599, 10% between 600 and 699, and 2% between 700 and 800; Math--52% below 500, 32% between 500 and 599, 15% between 600 and 699, and 1% between 700 and 800; Writing--57% below 500, 35% between 500 and 599, 7% between 600 and 699, and 1% between 700 and 800. The ACT scores were 45% below 21, 28% between 21 and 23, 19% between 24 and 26, 5% between 27 and 28, and 3% above 28. 40% of the current freshmen were in the top fifth of their class; 75% were in the top two fifths. 6 freshmen graduated first in their class. **Admissions Contact:** Allen Johnson, Dean of Admissions. E-Mail: *admissions@calbaptist .edu* Web: *www.calbaptist.edu*

FINANCIAL AID: In 2014-2015, 75% of all full-time freshmen and 73% of continuing full-time students received some form of financial aid. 57% of all full-time freshmen and 63% of continuing full-time students received need-based aid. The average freshman award was $15,861. Need-based scholarships or need-based grants averaged $11,266; need-based self-help aid (loans and jobs) averaged $11,796; non-need-based athletic scholarships averaged $5,875; and other non-need-based awards and non-need-based scholarships averaged $4,188. 20% of undergraduate students work part-time. Average annual earnings from campus work are $3900. The average financial indebtedness of the 2014 graduate was $36,773. The FAFSA is required. The priority date for freshman financial aid applications for fall entry is March 2.

CALIFORNIA COLLEGE OF THE ARTS (*The complete profile is made available exclusively on our website, www.barronspac.com*)

CALIFORNIA INSTITUTE OF TECHNOLOGY	C-5
www.caltech.edu	
Pasadena, CA 91125	**(626) 395-6341**
Fax: (626) 683-3026	Email: ugadmissions@caltech.edu
Full-time: 615 men, 382 women	Faculty: 302; I, ++$
Part-time: n/av	Ph.D.s: 97%
Graduate: 888 men, 358 women	Student/Faculty: 3 to 1
Year: quarters	Tuition: $41,538
Room & Board: $12,507	Freshman Class: 5535 applied, 587 accepted, 249 enrolled
SAT or ACT: required	CEEB CODE: 4034
Application Deadline: January 3	MOST COMPETITIVE

California Institute of Technology, founded in 1891, is a private institution offering programs in engineering, science, and math. Figures in the above capsule and in this profile are approximate. There are no undergraduate schools and 6 graduate schools. In addition to regional accreditation, Caltech has baccalaureate program accreditation with ABET. The 124-acre campus is in a suburban area 12 miles northeast of Los Angeles. Including any residence halls, there are 105 buildings.

STUDENT LIFE: 69% of undergraduates are from out of state, mostly the West. Students are from 46 states, 28 foreign countries, and Canada. 85% are from public schools. 40% are Asian American; 31% White; 11% Foreign. The average age of freshmen is 18; all undergraduates, 20. 2% do not continue beyond their first year; 90% remain to graduate. **Housing:** 879 students can be accommodated in college housing, which includes coed dorms, off-campus apartments, and married student housing. On-campus housing is guaranteed for the freshman year only. Alcohol is not permitted. All students may keep cars.

FACULTY/CLASSROOMS: 82% of faculty are male; 18% are female. All teach and do research. No introductory courses are taught by graduate students. The average class size in an introductory lecture is 200 and in a regular course is 15.

PROGRAMS OF STUDY: Caltech confers B.S. degrees. Master's and doctoral degrees are also awarded. Bachelor's degrees are awarded in BIOLOGICAL SCIENCE (biology/biological science), BUSINESS (business administration and management), COMPUTER AND

PHYSICAL SCIENCE (applied mathematics, astrophysics, chemistry, computer mathematics, computer science, geochemistry, geology, geophysics and seismology, mathematics, physics, and planetary and space science), ENGINEERING AND ENVIRONMENTAL DESIGN (chemical engineering, computer engineering, electrical/electronics engineering, engineering and applied science, materials science, and mechanical engineering), HEALTH PROFESSIONS (environmental health science), SOCIAL SCIENCE (economics, history, history of science, philosophy, and political science/government). Engineering, physical science, and computer science have the largest enrollments.

ACTIVITIES: There are no fraternities or sororities. There are 150 groups on campus, including art, band, cheerleading, chess, choir, chorale, chorus, computers, dance, drama, ethnic, film, gay, honors, international, jazz band, literary magazine, musical theater, newspaper, opera, orchestra, pep band, photography, political, professional, religious, social, social service, student government, symphony, and yearbook. Popular campus events include Ditch Day, International Day, and Pre-Frosh Weekend. **Sports:** There are 9 intercollegiate sports for men and 8 for women, and 19 intramural sports for men and 15 for women. Facilities include 2 Olympic-size swimming pools, a 300-seat gym, a 440-meter track, a football field, 4 baseball fields, and 8 tennis courts. Another athletic facility includes a gym, a 4000-square-foot exercise room with equipment, and racquetball courts. **Graduates:** From July 1, 2013 to June 30, 2014, 192 bachelor's degrees were awarded. The most popular majors were engineering (34%), physical sciences (25%), and mathematics (18%). 85 companies recruited on campus in 2013-2014. In an average class, 82% graduate in 4 years or less and 89% graduate in 6 years or less. Of the 2013 graduating class, 55% were enrolled in graduate school within 6 months of graduation.

SERVICES: Counseling and information services are available, as is tutoring in every subject. There is a reader service for the blind. **Library/Resources:** The 7 libraries contain 624,136 volumes, 10,586 microform items, 3,033 audio/video tapes/CDs/DVDs, and subscribe to 2,641 periodicals including electronic. Computerized library services include inter-library loans, database searching, and Internet access. **Physically Challenged Students:** 98% of the campus is accessible. Facilities include wheelchair ramps, elevators, special parking, specially equipped restrooms, and lowered telephones. **Special:** Caltech offers cross-registration with Scripps College, Occidental College, and Art Center College of Design, various work-study programs, including those with NASA's Jet Propulsion Laboratory, dual majors in any major, and independent studies degrees with faculty-approved student-designed majors. A 3-2 engineering degree is possible with several institutions. Pass/fail options are available for freshmen. A summer undergraduate research fellowship program is offered. Study abroad at University College in London, Cambridge University, and University of Copenhagen, in Denmark. **Visiting:** There are regularly scheduled orientations for prospective students, including a student-led campus tour followed by an information session . There are guides for informal visits and visitors may sit in on classes. To schedule a visit, contact the Undergraduate Admissions Office. **Campus Safety and Security:** Measures include 24-hour foot and vehicle patrol, emergency notification system, self-defense education, and security escort services. There are emergency telephones, lighted pathways/sidewalks, and controlled access to dorms/residences.

REQUIREMENTS: The SAT or ACT is required. In addition, SAT II: Subject tests in math level II and one in physics, biology, or chemistry are required. Applicants should have completed 4 years of high school math (including a year of calculus), 3 years of English, 1 year of chemistry, 1 year of physics, and 1 year of U.S. History or Government (waived for international students) Important factors in the admissions decision are advanced placement or honors courses, recommendations by school officials, and evidence of special talent. Caltech's core curriculum consists of the following: (27 units) of mathematics, (27 units) of physics, (15 units) of chemistry, (9 units) of biology, (9 units) freshman menu course, (12 units) of introductory lab courses, (3 units) of scientific writing, (108 units) of humanities courses, (9 units) Physical Education. All grades are issued pass/fail. **Procedure:** Freshmen are admitted fall. Entrance exams should be taken through December of the senior year. There are early admissions and deferred admissions plans. Early decision applications should be filed by November 1; regular applications, by January 3 for

fall entry, along with a $65 fee. Notification of early decision is sent December 15; regular decision, April 1. 556 applicants were on the 2014 waiting list; 40 were admitted. Applications are accepted online. **Transfer Students:** 8 transfer students enrolled in 2013-2014. Transfers, admitted only into sophomore and junior classes, need a minimum GPA of 3.0. Applicants must have completed 1 year (2 years for juniors) of calculus and calculus-based physics, and must take Caltech's entrance exams in math and physics. Chemistry or chemical engineering majors also should have completed 1 year of chemistry and must take an additional entrance exam. 216 of 780 credits required for the bachelor's degree must be completed at Caltech. **International Students:** There are 116 international students enrolled. The school actively recruits these students. They must also take the SAT or ACT.

ADMISSIONS: 11% of the 2014-2015 applicants were accepted. The SAT scores for the 2014-2015 freshman class were: Critical Reading--1% between 500 and 599, 20% between 600 and 699, and 79% between 700 and 800; Math--1% between 600 and 699, and 99% between 700 and 800; Writing--22% between 600 and 699, and 78% between 700 and 800. The ACT scores were 100% above 28. 100% of the current freshmen were in the top fifth of their class; 100% were in the top two fifths. **Admissions Contact:** Jarrid Whitney, Executive Director of Admissions and Fin. E-Mail: *ugadmissions@caltech.edu* Web: *admissions.caltech.edu*

FINANCIAL AID: In 2014-2015, 56% of all full-time freshmen and 54% of continuing full-time students received some form of financial aid. 56% of all full-time freshmen and 54% of continuing full-time students received need-based aid. The average financial indebtedness of the 2014 graduate was $9,561. Caltech is a member of CSS. The CSS/Profile, FAFSA, the state aid form, and the college's own financial statement are required. The deadline for filing freshman financial aid applications for fall entry is Febuary 1.

CALIFORNIA INSTITUTE OF THE ARTS (*The complete profile is made available exclusively on our website, www.barronspac.com*)

CALIFORNIA LUTHERAN UNIVERSITY C-5
www.callutheran.edu

Thousand Oaks, CA 91360

(805) 493-3049
(877) 258-3678

Fax: (805) 493-3645
Email: elgarico@callutheran.edu

Full-time: 1184 men, 1464 women	**Faculty:** 125; IIA, +$
Part-time: 62 men, 98 women	**Ph.Ds:** 85%
Graduate: 524 men, 828 women	**Student/Faculty:** 16 to 1
Year: semesters, summer session	**Tuition:** $37,140
Room & Board: $12,400	**Freshman Class:** 6490 applied, 3958 accepted, 556 enrolled
SAT CR/M/W: 540/550/540 **ACT:** 24	**CEEB CODE:** 4088
Application Deadline: January 15	**COMPETITIVE+**

California Lutheran University is a diverse, scholarly community dedicated to excellence in the liberal arts and sciences and professional studies. Rooted in the Lutheran tradition of Christian faith, the University encourages critical inquiry into matters of both faith and reason. The mission of the University is to educate leaders for a global society who are strong in character and judgment, confident in their identity and vocation, and committed to service and justice. There are 2 undergraduate schools and 4 graduate schools. The 225-acre campus is in a suburban area 45 miles north of downtown Los Angeles in Ventura County, 50 miles south of Santa Barbara. Including any residence halls, there are 53 buildings.

STUDENT LIFE: 81% of undergraduates are from California. Others are from 33 states, 52 foreign countries, and Canada. 75% are from public schools. 51% are White; 25% Hispanic. 33% are Islam, Buddhist and Hindu; 30% claim no religious affiliation; 24% Catholic. **Male To Female Ratio:** 1.4:1. The average age of freshmen is 18; all undergraduates, 20. 17% do not continue beyond their first year; 70% remain to graduate. **Housing:** 1398 students can be accommodated in college housing, which includes coed dorms and on-campus apartments. On-campus housing is guaranteed for all 4 years. 51% of students commute. Alcohol is not permitted. All students may keep cars.

FACULTY/CLASSROOMS: 56% of faculty are male; 44% are female. 60% teach undergraduates. No introductory courses are taught by graduate students. The average class size in an introductory lecture is 17; in a laboratory is 14; and in a regular course is 17.

PROGRAMS OF STUDY: Cal Lutheran confers B.A., and B.S. degrees. Master's and doctoral degrees are also awarded. Bachelor's degrees are awarded in AGRICULTURE (environmental studies), BIOLOGICAL SCIENCE (biochemistry and biology/biological science), BUSINESS (accounting and business administration and management), COMMUNICATIONS AND THE ARTS (art, communications, English, French, German, multimedia, music, music performance, Spanish, and theatre arts), COMPUTER AND PHYSICAL SCIENCE (chemistry, computer science, geology, information sciences and systems, mathematics, and physics), HEALTH PROFESSIONS (exercise science, predentistry, and premedicine), SOCIAL SCIENCE (criminal justice, economics, history, interdisciplinary studies, international studies, liberal arts/general studies, philosophy, political science/government, prelaw, psychology, religion, social science, sociology, and theological studies). Biology, accounting and economics are the strongest academically. Business, communication, and psychology have the largest enrollments.

ACTIVITIES: There are no fraternities or sororities. There are 80 groups on campus, including Model United Nations, art, band, cheerleading, choir, chorale, chorus, computers, dance, debate, drama, environmental, ethnic, film, forensics, gay, honors, international, jazz band, literary magazine, musical theater, newspaper, orchestra, pep band, photography, political, professional, radio and TV, religious, social, social service, student alumni, student government, symphony, and yearbook. Popular campus events include Santa Lucia, Scandinavian Festival, Chinese New Year, World Fair and Service Day. **Sports:** There are 10 intercollegiate sports for men and 10 for women, and 10 intramural sports for men and 10 for women. Facilities include a sports and fitness center, includes an arena for home basketball and volleyball games, dance studio, training room and the CLU Athletic Hall of Fame, football and soccer teams, a 50-meter pool. **Graduates:** From July 1, 2013 to June 30, 2014, 778 bachelor's degrees were awarded. The most popular majors were business (22%), communication (18%), and psychology (11%). 86 companies recruited on campus in 2013-2014. In an average class, 2% graduate in 3 years or less, 58% graduate in 4 years or less, 65% graduate in 5 years or less, and 66% graduate in 6 years or less. Of the 2013 graduating class, 23% were enrolled in graduate school within 6 months of graduation, and 68% were employed.

SERVICES: Counseling and information services are available, as is tutoring in every subject. The learning resources and writing centers offer help with study and writing skills. There is a reader service for the blind, and remedial math, reading, and writing. A student support services program helps low-income first-generation students adapt to the academic and social life of the campus. We have a coordinator for students with disabilities. **Library/Resources:** The library contains 335,783 volumes, 22,000 microform items, and 2,932 audio/video tapes/CDs/DVDs, and subscribes to 80 periodicals including electronic. Computerized library services include interlibrary loans, database searching, Internet access, and Wi-Fi capability. Special learning facilities include an art gallery, radio station, TV station, a human performance lab, and SEEd project garden. **Physically Challenged Students:** 95% of the campus is accessible. Facilities include wheelchair ramps, elevators, special parking, specially equipped restrooms, lowered drinking fountains, lowered telephones, and special housing. **Special:** Cal Lutheran offers co-op programs, internships, a Washington semester, and study abroad in over 80 countries. Also available are work-study and student-designed interdisciplinary degree majors, redit for experiential learning, special student status for non degree study, pass/fail options and continuing education. A bachelor's degree for professionals program offers accelerated degrees in accounting, business, computer science, communication, liberal studies, organizational leadership and psychology. There are 9 national honor societies and a freshman honors program. **Visiting:** There are regularly scheduled orientations for prospective students, including an admission and financial aid interview, a tour, visits with faculty or coaches, and lunch. There are guides for informal visits, visitors may sit in on classes, and stay overnight. To schedule a visit, contact the Presidential Host Coordinators at prehost@callutheran

.edu. **Campus Safety and Security:** Measures include 24-hour foot and vehicle patrol, emergency notification system, self-defense education, and security escort services. There are emergency telephones, lighted pathways/sidewalks, controlled access to dorms/residences, and all residence halls are equipped with security systems.

REQUIREMENTS: The SAT or ACT is required. Applicants must be graduates of an accredited secondary school and have completed a minimum of four years of English, two years of math, and two years each of foreign language, social studies, and lab science. The GED is accepted. An essay is required and an interview is recommended. AP and CLEP credits are accepted. Important factors in the admissions decision are advanced placement or honors courses, recommendations by school officials, and evidence of special talent. To graduate, all students must complete a core curriculum including 16 to 20 units in social science, 8 each in religion, foreign language, and science, 7 in English, 4 to 6 in creative arts, 4 in math, and 1 in phys ed. Students must also fulfill content requirements of a freshman cluster and take one course of each: writing-intensive, speaking intensive, global studies, U.S diversity, and senior level capstone. Also needed are a total of 124 units, 40 of which must be upper division with 32 hours in the major for a B.A. and a minimum of 36 hours for a B.S. The final 30 credits before graduation must be completed at Cal Lutheran. Students must have a minimum 2.0 GPA. **Procedure:** Freshmen are admitted fall and spring. Entrance exams should be taken during spring of junior year, or early fall of senior year. There is an early admissions plan. Early decision applications should be filed by November 15; regular applications, by January 15 for fall entry; and December 15 for spring entry, along with a $25 fee. Notification of early decision is sent January 15; regular decision, on a rolling basis. 510 applicants were on the 2014 waiting list; 189 were admitted. Applications are accepted on-line. **Transfer Students:** 341 transfer students enrolled in 2013-2014. Transfers should have at least a 2.75 transferable GPA and 28 transferable units. An application is required. An interview is recommended. Applicants must be in good standing at the previous college and may submit a recommendation from a college professor in lieu of a high school recommendation. 30 of 124 credits required for the bachelor's degree must be completed at Cal Lutheran. **International Students:** There are 117 international students enrolled. The school actively recruits these students. They must take the TOEFL with a minimum score of 550 on the paper-based TOEFL (PBT) or 79 on the Internet-based version (iBT). They must also take the SAT or ACT.

ADMISSIONS: 61% of the 2014-2015 applicants were accepted. The SAT scores for the 2014-2015 freshman class were: Critical Reading--24% below 500, 51% between 500 and 599, 22% between 600 and 699, and 3% between 700 and 800; Math--21% below 500, 50% between 500 and 599, 25% between 600 and 699, and 4% between 700 and 800; Writing--25% below 500, 52% between 500 and 599, 20% between 600 and 699, and 3% between 700 and 800. The ACT scores were 13% below 21, 26% between 21 and 23, 31% between 24 and 26, 17% between 27 and 28, and 13% above 28. **Admissions Contact:** Michael Elgarico, Director of Undergraduate Admissions. E-Mail: *elgarico@callutheran.edu* Web: *www.callutheran.edu*

FINANCIAL AID: In 2014-2015, 95% of all full-time freshmen and 91% of continuing full-time students received some form of financial aid. 80% of all full-time freshmen and 61% of continuing full-time students received need-based aid. The average freshman award was $26,470. Need-based scholarships or need-based grants averaged $23,870 ($47,314 maximum); need-based self-help aid (loans and jobs) averaged $2,500 ($4,000 maximum); and other non-need-based awards and non-need-based scholarships averaged $16,970 ($38,690 maximum). 55% of undergraduate students work part-time. Average annual earnings from campus work are $2500. The average financial indebtedness of the 2014 graduate was $24,150. The FAFSA is required. The priority date for freshman financial aid applications for fall entry is March 1.

CALIFORNIA MARITIME ACADEMY (*The complete profile is made available exclusively on our website, www.barronspac.com*)

CALIFORNIA POLYTECHNIC STATE UNIVERSITY

B-4

www.calpoly.edu

San Luis Obispo, CA 93407	(805) 756-2311

Fax: (805) 756-5400	Email: admissions@calpoly.edu
Full-time: 9836 men, 8222 women	Faculty: 843; IIA, --$
Part-time: 427 men, 254 women	Ph.D.s: 76%
Graduate: 509 men, 455 women	Student/Faculty: 21 to 1
Year: quarters, summer session	Tuition: $8724 ($19,884)
Room & Board: $11,123	Freshman Class: 40402 applied, 13953 accepted, 4871 enrolled
SAT CR/M: 595/630 ACT: 28	CEEB CODE: 4038
Application Deadline: November 30	**HIGHLY COMPETITIVE**

California Polytechnic State University, founded in 1901, is a public institution that is part of the California State University system. It offers programs in agriculture, architecture and environmental design, business, education, engineering, liberal arts, sciences and math, and preprofessional studies. There are 6 undergraduate schools. In addition to regional accreditation, Cal Poly has baccalaureate program accreditation with AACSB, ABET, ACCE, ASLA, NAAB, NASAD, NASM, NRPA, and SAF. The 6000-acre campus is in a suburban area 200 miles north of Los Angeles, and 230 miles south of San Francisco. Including any residence halls, there are 125 buildings.

STUDENT LIFE: 90% of undergraduates are from California. 60% are White; 15% Hispanic; 11% Asian American. The average age of freshmen is 17; all undergraduates, 19. 7% do not continue beyond their first year. **Housing:** 6239 students can be accommodated in college housing, which includes single-sex and coed dorms and on-campus apartments. In addition, there are honors houses, special-interest houses, living/learning residence halls with an academic theme affiliated with University's six academic colleges (Engineering, Science and Math, Architecture, Agriculture, Liberal Arts, Business). On-campus housing is available on a first-come, first-served basis, and is available on a lottery system for upperclassmen. 62% of students commute. Alcohol is not permitted. All students may keep cars.

FACULTY/CLASSROOMS: 62% of faculty are male; 38% are female. No introductory courses are taught by graduate students.

PROGRAMS OF STUDY: Cal Poly confers B.A., B.S., B.Arch., B.F.A. and B.L.A. degrees. Master's degrees are also awarded. Bachelor's degrees are awarded in AGRICULTURE (agricultural business management, agricultural communications, agricultural mechanics, agricultural sciences, agronomy, animal science, dairy science, forestry and related sciences, natural resource management, soil science, and wine and viticulture), BIOLOGICAL SCIENCE (biochemistry, biology/biological science, microbiology, and nutrition), BUSINESS (business administration and management and recreation and leisure services), COMMUNICATIONS AND THE ARTS (art and design, communication studies, English, graphic communications, journalism, modern language, music, and theatre arts), COMPUTER AND PHYSICAL SCIENCE (chemistry, computer science, earth science, industrial technology, mathematics, physics, software engineering, and statistics), EDUCATION (agricultural education and education), ENGINEERING AND ENVIRONMENTAL DESIGN (aeronautical engineering, architectural engineering, architecture, biomedical engineering, bioresource engineering, city/community/regional planning, civil engineering, computer engineering, construction management, electrical/electronics engineering, engineering science, environmental engineering, environmental science, industrial engineering, landscape architecture, manufacturing engineering, materials engineering, mechanical engineering, and transportation engineering), HEALTH PROFESSIONS (kinesiology), SOCIAL SCIENCE (anthropology, child psychology/development, economics, ethnic studies, food science, history, interdisciplinary studies, liberal arts/general studies, liberal arts/engineering studies, philosophy, political science/government, psychology, and sociology).

ACTIVITIES: 13% of men belong to 1 local and 21 national fraternities; 18% of women belong to 13 national sororities. There are 400 groups on campus, including art, band, cheerleading, chess, choir, chorale, chorus, computers, dance, debate, drama, environmental, ethnic, film, gay, honors, international, jazz band, literary magazine, marching band, musical theater, newspaper, opera, orchestra, pep band, photography, political, professional, radio and TV, religious, social, social service, student government, symphony, and various engineering clubs. Popular campus events include Rose Float, Open House, Week of Welcome, and SOAR. **Sports:** There are 10 intercollegiate sports for men and 10 for women, and 7 intramural sports for men and 7 for women. Facilities include outdoor track, outdoor swimming pools, indoor and sand volleyball, tennis, indoor and outdoor basketball and racquetball courts, weight rooms, cardio exercise rooms, martial arts room, synthetic and natural turf playing fields, baseball stadium, softball stadium, and football/soccer stadium. **Graduates:** From July 1, 2013 to June 30, 2014, 3997 bachelor's degrees were awarded. The most popular majors were engineering technologies (27%), business/marketing (13%), and agriculture (12%). Of the 2013 graduating class, 13% were enrolled in graduate school within 6 months of graduation, and 73% were employed.

SERVICES: Counseling and information services are available, as is tutoring in most subjects. There is a reader service for the blind, writing skills lab and test office. Psychological and career services are available. **Library/Resources:** The library contains 795,216 volumes, 1.8 million microform items, and 3,000 audio/video tapes/CDs/DVDs, and subscribes to 60,000 periodicals including electronic. Computerized library services include interlibrary loans, database searching, Internet access, and Wi-Fi capability. Special learning facilities include an art gallery, radio station, and TV station. For **Physically Challenged Students:** 80% of the campus is accessible. Facilities include wheelchair ramps, elevators, special parking, specially equipped restrooms, special class scheduling, lowered drinking fountains, lowered telephones, special housing. **Special:** Cal Poly offers work-study programs, co-op programs in numerous majors, study abroad, and dual majors. Credit for military experience and pass/fail options are available. There are a freshman honors program. **Visiting:** There are regularly scheduled orientations for prospective students, campus tours are offered Monday through Friday at 11:00 AM. Admissions presentations for all freshmen and transfer prospective students are offered Monday through Friday at 1:00 PM. There are guides for informal visits. To schedule a visit, contact Admissions Office at admissions@calpoly.edu. **Campus Safety and Security:** Measures include 24-hour foot and vehicle patrol, emergency notification system, self-defense education, and security escort services. There are emergency telephones, lighted pathways/sidewalks, and controlled access to dorms/residences.

REQUIREMENTS: The SAT or ACT is required. Applicants must be graduates of an accredited high school or have a GED. Required are 15 academic credits, including 4 years of English, 3 of math, 2 of science (2 lab), 2 of foreign language, and 1 each of social studies, history, visual and performing arts, and academic electives. AP and CLEP credits are accepted. Students must have a minimum 2.0 GPA, 72 quarter units of general education, a minimum of 180 total units, a United States Cultural Pluralism course, completion of the Graduation Writing Requirement, a minimum of 50 units in residence and a senior project are required. **Procedure:** Freshmen are admitted fall. Entrance exams should be taken mid-June every year. There are early decision and early admissions plans. Early decision applications should be filed by October 31; regular applications, by November 30 for fall entry, along with a $55 fee. Notification of early decision is sent December 15; regular decision, April 1. 1343 early decision candidates were accepted for the 2014-2015 class. 1603 applicants were on the 2014 waiting list; 15 were admitted. Applications are accepted on-line. **Transfer Students:** 947 transfer students enrolled in 2013-2014. Applicants must meet general education and breadth requirements and submit college transcripts with a minimum GPA of 2.0 50 of 180 credits required for the bachelor's degree must be completed at Cal Poly. **International Students:** There are 211 international students enrolled. The school actively recruits these students. They must take the TOEFL with a minimum score of 550 on the paper-based TOEFL (PBT) or 80 on the Internet-based version (iBT), or take the IELTS.

ADMISSIONS: 35% of the 2014-2015 applicants were accepted. The SAT scores for the 2014-2015 freshman class were: Critical Reading--8% below 500, 43% between 500 and 599, 39% between 600 and 699, and 10% between 700 and 800; Math--2% below 500, 29% between 500 and 599, 48% between 600 and 699, and 21% between 700 and 800. The ACT scores were 14% between 21 and 23, 59% between 24 and 26, and 27% above 28. 83% of the current freshmen were in the top fifth of their class; 98% were in the top two fifths.

Admissions Contact: James L. Maraviglia, Assoc. VP, Marketing & Enroll. Develop.. E-Mail: *admissions@calpoly.edu* Web: *http:/admissions.calpoly.edu/*

FINANCIAL AID: The average freshman award was $10,129. Need-based scholarships or need-based grants averaged $3,567; need-based self-help aid (loans and jobs) averaged $3,773; non-need-based athletic scholarships averaged $5,029; other non-need-based awards and non-need-based scholarships averaged $1,946; and $3,854 from other forms of aid. The FAFSA is required. The priority date for freshman financial aid applications for fall entry is March 2.

CALIFORNIA STATE POLYTECHNIC UNIVERSITY, POMONA	D-5
www.csupomona.edu	

Pomona, CA 91768	(909) 869-3130
Fax: (909) 869-5315	Email: awright@cpp.edu
Full-time: 10938 men, 8779 women	Faculty: IIA, +$
Part-time: 1650 men, 1028 women	Ph.D.s: 81%
Graduate: 747 men, 824 women	Student/Faculty: 25 to 1
Year: quarters, summer session	Tuition: $6872 ($18,032)
Room & Board: $13,284	Freshman Class: 32801 applied, 17014 accepted, 3658 enrolled
SAT CR/M: 510/540 ACT: 23	CEEB CODE: 4082
Application Deadline: November 1	COMPETITIVE

California State Polytechnic University, Pomona, an occupationally oriented institution founded in 1938, is part of the state-supported university system. It offers undergraduate and graduate programs in agriculture, liberal arts and sciences, business, engineering, and technical and professional training. Figures in the above capsule and in this profile are approximate. There are 8 undergraduate schools and 7 graduate schools. In addition to regional accreditation, Cal Poly Pomona has baccalaureate program accreditation with AACSB, ABET, ADA, ASLA, CSAB, and NAAB. The 1438-acre campus is in a suburban area 30 miles east of Los Angeles. Including any residence halls, there are 80 buildings.

STUDENT LIFE: 99% of undergraduates are from California. Others are from 34 states, 50 foreign countries, and Canada. 88% are from public schools. 37% are Hispanic; 25% Asian American; 22% White. **Male To Female Ratio:** 0.8:1. The average age of freshmen is 18; all undergraduates, 21. 12% do not continue beyond their first year; 57% remain to graduate. **Housing:** 3500 students can be accommodated in college housing, which includes coed dorms and off-campus apartments. In addition, there are special-interest houses, and a center for regenerative studies. On-campus housing is available on a first-come and first-served basis. 89% of students commute. All students may keep cars.

FACULTY/CLASSROOMS: 61% of faculty are male; 39% are female. No introductory courses are taught by graduate students. The average class size in an introductory lecture is 37; in a laboratory is 22; and in a regular course is 37.

PROGRAMS OF STUDY: Cal Poly Pomona confers B.A., B.S., BArch. and B.F.A. degrees. Master's and doctoral degrees are also awarded. Bachelor's degrees are awarded in AGRICULTURE (agricultural business management, agriculture, animal science, and plant science), BIOLOGICAL SCIENCE (biology/biological science and biotechnology), BUSINESS (apparel and accessories marketing, business administration and management, hotel/motel and restaurant management, human resources, and international business management), COMMUNICATIONS AND THE ARTS (art, communications, dramatic arts, English, graphic design, music, and Spanish), COMPUTER AND PHYSICAL SCIENCE (chemistry, computer sci-

ence, geology, information sciences and systems, mathematics, and physics), ENGINEERING AND ENVIRONMENTAL DESIGN (architecture, chemical engineering, civil engineering, computer technology, construction technology, electrical/electronics engineering, engineering, engineering technology, industrial engineering, landscape architecture/design, manufacturing engineering, materials engineering, mechanical engineering, and urban planning technology), SOCIAL SCIENCE (anthropology, economics, food science, gender studies, geography, history, liberal arts/general studies, philosophy, physical fitness/movement, political science/government, psychology, sociology, and urban studies). Engineering, architecture and business are the strongest academically. Mechanical engineering, hospitality management and accounting (BUS) have the largest enrollments.

ACTIVITIES: 2% of men belong to 6 local and 12 national fraternities; 1% of women belong to 4 local and 8 national sororities. There are 288 groups on campus, including art, band, cheerleading, choir, chorale, chorus, computers, drama, ethnic, film, gay, honors, international, jazz band, literary magazine, musical theater, newspaper, opera, orchestra, pep band, photography, political, professional, religious, social, social service, and student government. Popular campus events include Rose Float, Broncofest and Founders Day. **Sports:** There are 6 intercollegiate sports for men and 6 for women. Facilities include a 5000-seat stadium, tennis and racquetball courts, basketball and volleyball courts, soccer, baseball, and softball fields, a track, swimming pool, gymnastics and weight rooms, a horse arena, and dance studios, Bronco Recreation and Intramural Complex (BRIC) rock wall, fitness studios, basketball courts, MAC, racquetball courts, running track, lap pool, cardio and strength equipment. **Graduates:** From July 1, 2013 to June 30, 2014, 4137 bachelor's degrees were awarded. The most popular majors were hotel and restaurant management (6%), management and human resources (6%), and accounting (5%). 230 companies recruited on campus in 2013-2014. In an average class, 12% graduate in 4 years or less, 39% graduate in 5 years or less, and 57% graduate in 6 years or less.

SERVICES: Counseling and information services are available, as is tutoring in most subjects. There is a reader service for the blind, and remedial math and writing. **Library/Resources:** The library contains 855,565 volumes, 1.4 million microform items, 11,390 audio/video tapes/CDs/DVDs, and subscribes to 89,315 periodicals including electronic. Computerized library services include interlibrary loans, database searching, and Internet access. Special learning facilities include an art gallery, TV station, an interactive TV studio. **Physically Challenged Students:** 96% of the campus is accessible. Facilities include wheelchair ramps, elevators, special parking, specially equipped restrooms, special class scheduling, lowered drinking fountains, lowered telephones, a specialized tram, van and shuttle transportation. **Special:** Cross-registration is possible with any California State University school. Internships and co-op programs are available in agriculture, business, environmental design, engineering, science, political science, behavioral science, and phys ed. An international study program in 17 countries, work-study programs, B.A.-B.S. degrees, a liberal studies degree, credit for military experience, an external degree program, and credit/no credit options are offered. Nondegree study is possible. There are 30 national honor societies and a freshman honors program. **Visiting:** There are regularly scheduled orientations for prospective students, consisting of tours of the campus led by current undergraduate students and a 90-minute walking tour. There are guides for informal visits, visitors may sit in on classes, and stay overnight. To schedule a visit, contact the Admissions and Outreach at (909) 869-3529. **Campus Safety and Security:** Measures include 24-hour foot and vehicle patrol, emergency notification system, self-defense education, and security escort services. There are shuttle buses, emergency telephones, lighted pathways/sidewalks, vehicle assists, and crime prevention programs.

REQUIREMENTS: The SAT or ACT is recommended. Applicants must be graduates of an accredited secondary school or have a GED equivalent. Secondary school courses must include 4 years of high school English, 3 each of math and electives, 2 of foreign language, and 1 each of science, history, and art. A GPA of 2.0 is required. AP and CLEP credits are accepted. All students must complete general education requirements, including courses in written and oral communications, critical thinking, math, humanities, natural sciences, and social sciences, and must pass a graduation writing test. A total of 180 (B.A.) to 246 (B.S.) quarter units with a minimum GPA of 2.0 is required to graduate. **Procedure:** Freshmen are admitted fall. Entrance exams should be taken during the fall of the senior year. There is a rolling admissions plan. Applications should be filed by November 1 for fall entry; June 1 for winter entry; August 1 for spring entry; and February 1 for summer entry, along with a $55 fee. Notification is sent on a rolling basis. Applications are accepted on-line. **Transfer Students:** 2487 transfer students enrolled in 2013-2014. Applicants must have completed 56 semester or 90 quarter units including college preparatory subjects. A 2.0 GPA (2.4 for nonresidents) is required. 50 of 180 credits required for the bachelor's degree must be completed at Cal Poly Pomona. **International Students:** There are 1080 international students enrolled. They must take the TOEFL with a minimum score of 525 on the paper-based TOEFL (PBT) or 70 on the Internet-based version (iBT). They must also take the SAT or ACT.

ADMISSIONS: 52% of the 2014-2015 applicants were accepted. The SAT scores for the 2014-2015 freshman class were: Critical Reading--41% below 500, 40% between 500 and 599, 17% between 600 and 699, and 2% between 700 and 800; Math--30% below 500, 35% between 500 and 599, 28% between 600 and 699, and 7% between 700 and 800. The ACT scores were 27% below 21, 24% between 21 and 23, 23% between 24 and 26, 13% between 27 and 28, and 13% above 28. **Admissions Contact:** Andrew M. Wright, Director of Admissions. E-Mail: *awright@cpp.edu* Web: *www.csupomona.edu*

FINANCIAL AID: In 2014-2015, 65% of all full-time freshmen and 64% of continuing full-time students received some form of financial aid. 52% of all full-time freshmen and 60% of continuing full-time students received need-based aid. The average freshman award was $10,429. Need-based scholarships or need-based grants averaged $8,871; need-based self-help aid (loans and jobs) averaged $3,622; non-need-based athletic scholarships averaged $1,563; and other non-need-based awards and non-need-based scholarships averaged $2,125. Average annual earnings from campus work are $2000. The average financial indebtedness of the 2014 graduate was $20,795. The FAFSA is required. The deadline for filing freshman financial aid applications for fall entry is March 2.

CALIFORNIA STATE UNIVERSITY SYSTEM

The California State University System, established in 1961, is a public system in California. It is governed by a board of trustees, whose chief administrator is the chancellor. The primary goal of the system is teaching. The main priorities are to emphasize quality in instruction; to provide an environment in which scholarship, research, creative, artistic, and professional activity are valued and supported; and to stress the importance of the liberal arts and sciences. The total student enrollment is usually about 447,000 with about 45,000 faculty members. Altogether there are 1233 baccalaureate, 783 master's, and 29 doctoral programs offered in the California State University System. Profiles of the 4-year campuses are included in this section.

CALIFORNIA STATE UNIVERSITY, BAKERSFIELD	C-4
www.csub.edu	
Bakersfield, CA 93311	**(661) 664-2160**
Fax: (661) 664-3389	Email: hmontalvo@csubak.edu
Full-time: 1500 men, 2750 women	Faculty: IIA, av$
Part-time: 410 men, 710 women	Ph.D.s: n/av
Graduate: 585 men, 1310 women	Student/Faculty: n/av
Year: trimesters, summer session	Tuition: $6682 ($11,000)
Room & Board: $7120	Freshman Class: n/av
SAT or ACT: required	CEEB CODE: 4110
Application Deadline: open	**COMPETITIVE**

California State University/Bakersfield, founded in 1965, is part of the California State University System. It offers graduate and undergrad-

uate programs in liberal arts and sciences, business, public administration, education, health fields, preengineering, and preprofessional training. The figures in the above capsule and in this profile are approximate. There are 3 undergraduate schools and 10 graduate schools. In addition to regional accreditation, Cal State Bakersfield has baccalaureate program accreditation with AACSB, NCATE, and NLN. The 375-acre campus is in a small town in southwest Bakersfield. Including any residence halls, there are 30 buildings.

STUDENT LIFE: 98% of undergraduates are from California. Others are from 25 states, 50 foreign countries, and Canada. 98% are from public schools. 51% are White; 25% Hispanic. The average age of freshmen is 19; all undergraduates, 25. 15% do not continue beyond their first year. **Housing:** 330 students can be accommodated in college housing, which includes single-sex and coed dorms. On-campus housing is guaranteed for all 4 years. 98% of students commute. Alcohol is not permitted. All students may keep cars.

FACULTY/CLASSROOMS: 62% of faculty are male; 38% are female. All teach and do research. No introductory courses are taught by graduate students. The average class size in an introductory lecture is 40; in a laboratory is 24; and in a regular course is 30.

PROGRAMS OF STUDY: Cal State Bakersfield confers B.A., and B.S. degrees. Master's degrees are also awarded. Bachelor's degrees are awarded in BIOLOGICAL SCIENCE (biology/biological science), BUSINESS (business administration and management), COMMUNICATIONS AND THE ARTS (art, communications, dramatic arts, English, music, and Spanish), COMPUTER AND PHYSICAL SCIENCE (chemistry, computer science, geology, mathematics, and physics), ENGINEERING AND ENVIRONMENTAL DESIGN (land use management and reclamation), HEALTH PROFESSIONS (clinical science and nursing), SOCIAL SCIENCE (anthropology, child psychology/development, criminal justice, economics, history, liberal arts/general studies, philosophy, political science/government, psychology, public administration, religion, and sociology). Business, education, and public administration are the strongest academically. Business has the largest enrollment.

ACTIVITIES: 2% of men belong to 3 national fraternities; 2% of women belong to 4 national sororities. There are 74 groups on campus, including art, band, cheerleading, chess, choir, chorale, computers, dance, drama, ethnic, film, gay, honors, international, jazz band, literary magazine, musical theater, newspaper, opera, orchestra, pep band, photography, political, professional, radio and TV, religious, social, social service, student government, and symphony. Popular campus events include Cinco de Mayo, Open Campus and Jazz Festival. **Sports:** There are 7 intercollegiate sports for men and 6 for women, and 12 intramural sports for men and 12 for women. Facilities include a 4000-seat gym, a wrestling sport center, aquatic center, tennis and racquetball courts, softball and soccer fields.

SERVICES: Counseling and information services are available, as is tutoring in most subjects, as well as in study skills. There is a reader service for the blind, and remedial math, reading, and writing. **Library/Resources:** The library contains 339,900 volumes, 603,300 microform items, 5,180 audio/video tapes/CDs/DVDs, and subscribes to 2,700 periodicals including electronic. Computerized library services include interlibrary loans and database searching. Special learning facilities include an art gallery, natural history museum, radio station, a geological data sample repository, an archeological information center, instructional television network, applied research center, and animal care and treatment facility. **Physically Challenged Students:** Facilities include wheelchair ramps, elevators, special parking, specially equipped restrooms, special class scheduling, lowered drinking fountains, and lowered telephones. **Special:** Cal State Bakersfield offers co-op programs in education and business administration, cross-registration through the National Student Exchange Program, study abroad at 36 universities in 16 countries, a 3-2 engineering degree with California Polytechnic State University/San Luis Obispo, and student-designed majors. Credit for life experience, pass/fail options, and nondegree study are available. Students may also earn credits as interns and participate in work-study programs on and off campus. There is a freshman honors program. **Visiting:** There are regularly scheduled orientations for prospective students, consisting of a day-long orientation that includes meetings with faculty advisers and school deans. There are guides for informal visits and visitors may sit in on classes. To schedule a visit, contact the Office of Outreach Services at (805) 664-3138. **Campus Safety and Security:** Measures include 24-hour foot and vehicle patrol, self-defense education, and security escort services. There are emergency telephones and lighted pathways/sidewalks.

REQUIREMENTS: The SAT or ACT is required. Admission is based on an eligibility index that weights the GPA and standardized test scores. In addition, applicants must be graduates of an accredited secondary school or GED equivalent, and have a total of 15 academic units, including 4 years of English, 3 of math, 2 of foreign language, 1 each of lab science, U.S. history/government, and visual and performing arts, and 3 of electives. A GPA of 2.0 is required. AP and CLEP credits are accepted.All students must complete 72 quarter units of general education requirements in basic skills, Western civilization, non-Western culture, philosophy, fine arts, literature, technology, and physical, social, and life sciences. They must also take a comprehensive writing examination or complete an upper-division writing course with a grade of C or better, demonstrate understanding of American history and government institutions, and complete a senior seminar. A total of 186 quarter units with a minimum GPA of 2.0 is required in order to graduate. **Procedure:** Freshmen are admitted fall, winter, and spring. Entrance exams should be taken by December of the senior year. There are early decision, early admissions, deferred admissions, and rolling admissions plans. Application deadlines are open. Application fee is $55. **Transfer Students:** A 2.0 GPA (2.4 for nonresidents) is required in a minimum of 56 semester or 84 quarter units earned, including English and math. 45 of 186 credits required for the bachelor's degree must be completed at Cal State Bakersfield. **International Students:** The school actively recruits these students. They must take the TOEFL. The SAT or ACT is required if the GPA is below 3.0.

ADMISSIONS: Dr. Homer Montalvo, Dean of Admissions. E-Mail: *hmontalvo@csubak.edu* Web: *www.csub.edu*

FINANCIAL AID: Cal State Bakersfield is a member of CSS. The FAFSA is required. Check with the school for current application deadlines.

CALIFORNIA STATE UNIVERSITY, CHICO   **B-2**
www.csuchico.edu

Chico, CA 95929	(530) 898-4428
	(800) 542-4426
Fax: (530) 898-6456	Email: info@csuchico.edu
Full-time: 6806 men, 7403 women	Faculty: 496; IIA, av$
Part-time: 543 men, 540 women	Ph.D.s: 84%
Graduate: 336 men, 728 women	Student/Faculty: 24 to 1
Year: semesters, summer session	Tuition: $8472 ($19,632)
Room & Board: $10,480	Freshman Class: 19217 applied, 12905 accepted, 2340 enrolled
SAT CR/M: 501/512 ACT: 21	CEEB CODE: 4048
Application Deadline: November 30	COMPETITIVE

California State University, Chico, founded in 1887, is a public institution offering undergraduate programs in behavioral and social sciences, business, communication and education, engineering, computer science and technology, humanities and fine arts, natural sciences, agriculture, and nursing. The university offers Web-based classes. Figures in the above capsule and in this profile are approximate. There are 7 undergraduate schools and 1 graduate school. In addition to regional accreditation, Chico State has baccalaureate program accreditation with AACSB, ABET, ACCE, ACEJMC, ADA, CSAB, CSWE, NASAD, NASM, and NRPA. The 130-acre campus is in a small town 90 miles north of Sacramento, and 174 miles northeast of San Francisco. Including any residence halls, there are 77 buildings.

STUDENT LIFE: 97% of undergraduates are from California. Others are from 36 states, 47 foreign countries, and Canada. 91% are from public schools. 52% are White; 22% Hispanic. **Male To Female Ratio:** 1.1:1. The average age of freshmen is 18; all undergraduates, 24. 15% do not continue beyond their first year; 85% remain to graduate. **Housing:** 2000 students can be accommodated in college housing,

which includes coed dorms, on-campus apartments, and off-campus apartments. In addition, there are honors houses, language houses, special-interest houses, fraternity houses, sorority houses, thematic housing for minorities in engineering and science, math, and business. Theme floors include community service, recreational sports, leadership, adventure outings, and sustainability. On-campus housing is available on a first-come and first-served basis. 99% of students commute. Alcohol is not permitted. All students may keep cars.

FACULTY/CLASSROOMS: 52% of faculty are male; 48% are female. 97% teach undergraduates, and 21% do research. No introductory courses are taught by graduate students. The average class size in an introductory lecture is 25; in a laboratory is 21; and in a regular course is 22.

PROGRAMS OF STUDY: Chico State confers B.A., B.S. and B.F.A. degrees. Master's degrees are also awarded. Bachelor's degrees are awarded in AGRICULTURE (agricultural business management, agriculture, animal science, and horticulture), BIOLOGICAL SCIENCE (biochemistry, biology/biological science, botany, ecology, and microbiology), BUSINESS (accounting, business administration and management, finance, international economics, management information systems, small business management, and supply chain management), COMMUNICATIONS AND THE ARTS (art history, art, communication design , communication, communications, communication rhetoric/communication, communication science, English, English literature, fine arts, German, graphic design, journalism, linguistics, media arts, music, music industry, musical theater, public relations, Spanish, and theatre arts), COMPUTER AND PHYSICAL SCIENCE (applied mathematics, atmospheric sciences and meteorology, chemistry, computer science, geology, geoscience, mathematics, physical sciences, physics, and statistics), EDUCATION (agricultural education, art education, education, English education, health education, and mathematics education), ENGINEERING AND ENVIRONMENTAL DESIGN (civil engineering, computer engineering, computer graphics, construction management, electrical/electronics engineering, environmental science, interior design, mechanical engineering, and Mechatronics Engineering), HEALTH PROFESSIONS (environmental health science, health care administration, health science, and nursing), SOCIAL SCIENCE (anthropology, applied psychology, Asian studies, child psychology/development, communication sciences and disorders, community services, criminal justice, dietetics, economics, French studies, geography, gerontology, history, humanities, international relations, Latin American studies, legal studies, liberal arts/general studies, philosophy, political science/government, public administration, public affairs, religious studies, social science, social work, sociology, and women and gender studies). Business administration, nursing, and psychology are the strongest academically, and have the largest enrollments.

ACTIVITIES: 1% of men belong to 3 local and 11 national fraternities; 1% of women belong to 1 local and 11 national sororities. There are 186 groups on campus, including art, band, cheerleading, choir, chorale, chorus, computers, dance, debate, drama, environmental, ethnic, film, forensics, gay, honors, international, jazz band, literary magazine, musical theater, newspaper, opera, orchestra, pep band, political, professional, radio and TV, religious, social, social service, student government, symphony, and yearbook. Popular campus events include International Festival, Greek Week Community Challenge, and Up 'Til Dawn St. Jude Hospital Fund-raiser. **Sports:** There are 6 intercollegiate sports for men and 7 for women, and 8 intramural sports for men and 8 for women. Facilities include 2 gyms, athletic training rooms, a dance studio, swimming and diving pools, a par course, putting greens and sand trap, handball/racquetball courts, baseball/softball fields, an all-weather track, a soccer stadium, 7500-seat football stadium, a residence hall sports center. A recreation center includes a climbing wall, pool, fitness and weight rooms, a concert/events facility, and a computer lab. **Graduates:** From July 1, 2013 to June 30, 2014, 3495 bachelor's degrees were awarded. The most popular majors were business administration (17%), health professions (9%), and social sciences (9%). 480 companies recruited on campus in 2013-2014. In an average class, 21% graduate in 4 years or less, 48% graduate in 5 years or less, and 56% graduate in 6 years or less.

SERVICES: Counseling and information services are available, as is tutoring in most subjects, including accounting, anthropology,

Arabic, business administration, biology, chemistry, economics, finance, French, German, history, Italian, Japanese, math, management information systems, music, philosophy, physics, political science, psychology. There is a reader service for the blind, and remedial math and writing. A student learning center offers a tutorial program, study skills development, learning assistance workshops, and writing resources. **Library/Resources:** The library contains 924,410 volumes, 1.2 million microform items, and 25,744 audio/video tapes/CDs/DVDs, and subscribes to 515 periodicals including electronic. Computerized library services include interlibrary loans, database searching, and Internet access. Special learning facilities include an art gallery, planetarium, radio station, an instructional media center, a university farm, a biological field station, a media preparation lab, a computer graphics lab, a recording arts studio, a writing center, and distributed learning technologies, anthropology museum, science museum. **Physically Challenged Students:** 95% of the campus is accessible. Facilities include wheelchair ramps, elevators, special parking, specially equipped restrooms, special class scheduling, lowered drinking fountains, lowered telephones, special housing. **Special:** The university offers co-op programs and cross-registration as part of the National Student Exchange. In addition, internships, distance learning, teacher certification, study abroad in 32 countries, work-study, student-designed majors, independent study, credit for experience, non-degree study, and pass/fail options are available. Chico State has a nationally recognized sustainability program and an established Institute for Sustainable Development. There are 15 national honor societies, including Phi Beta Kappa, a freshman honors program, and 40 departmental honors programs. **Visiting:** There are regularly scheduled orientations for prospective students, consisting of a 1-hour tour given at 11:30 a.m. Monday through Saturday. There are guides for informal visits and visitors may sit in on classes. To schedule a visit, contact the Office of Admissions. **Campus Safety and Security:** Measures include 24-hour foot and vehicle patrol, emergency notification system, self-defense education, and security escort services. There are shuttle buses, emergency telephones, lighted pathways/sidewalks, controlled access to dorms/residences, a freshman safe start program, a victim awareness program, and crime prevention workshops.

REQUIREMENTS: The SAT or ACT is required. An index combining GPA and SAT and ACT scores is used to determine eligibility for admission. Applicants must be graduates of a secondary school or have a GED and have completed 4 years of English, 3 years of math, 2 years of lab sciences (1 physical and 1 life), 2 years of the same foreign language, 2 years of social science, 1 year of a visual or performing art course, and 1 year of electives. A GPA of 2.0 is required. AP and CLEP credits are accepted. Graduation requirements include: complete a total of 120 to 132 units; 40 units of upper division coursework; a minimum of 12 units must be in their major; 30 units in residence at California State University, Chico; 48 units of prescribed General Education (9 units as a resident at Chico State); minimum of two courses with focus on cultural diversity; demonstrate competent understanding of the Constitution of the United States, U.S. History, mathematics and writing; complete an approved major; and have a G.P.A of 2.0 or better. General education coursework includes: oral communications, writing, critical thinking, mathematics, two laboratory sciences (one physical science and one in the life sciences), US History, US Governmental Institutions, four writing intensive courses, and a GE Capstone course. In addition, each student must complete a Pathway, which consists of 18 units of lower division and 9 units of upper division coursework. **Procedure:** Freshmen are admitted fall and spring. Entrance exams should be taken in fall of the senior year. There are deferred admissions and rolling admissions plans. Early decision applications should be filed by October 30; regular applications, by November 30 for fall entry, along with a $55 fee. Notifications are sent March 1. Applications are accepted on-line. **Transfer Students:** 1601 transfer students enrolled in 2013-2014. Transfer students who are California residents must have a minimum 2.0 GPA, and nonresidents need 2.4. Students must have made up any missing college preparatory subjects and provide a statement of good standing and transcripts from prior institutions. 30 of 124 credits required for the bachelor's degree must be completed at Chico State. **International Students:** There are 515 international students enrolled. The school actively recruits these students. They must take the TOEFL with a minimum score of 500 on the paper-based TOEFL (PBT) or 61 on the Internet-based version (iBT), or take the IELTS. They must also take the SAT or ACT.

ADMISSIONS: 67% of the 2014-2015 applicants were accepted. The SAT scores for the 2014-2015 freshman class were: Critical Reading--39% below 500, 42% between 500 and 599, 10% between 600 and 699, and 1% between 700 and 800; Math--33% below 500, 45% between 500 and 599, 14% between 600 and 699, and 1% between 700 and 800. **Admissions Contact:** Allan Bee, Director of Admissions. E-Mail: *info@csuchico.edu* Web: *www.csuchico.edu*

FINANCIAL AID: In 2014-2015, 41% of all full-time freshmen and 44% of continuing full-time students received some form of financial aid. 25% of all full-time freshmen and 32% of continuing full-time students received need-based aid. The average freshman award was $10,851. Need-based scholarships or need-based grants averaged $7,387; need-based self-help aid (loans and jobs) averaged $4,581; non-need-based athletic scholarships averaged $2,710; and other non-need-based awards and non-need-based scholarships averaged $5,711. The FAFSA, and scholarship application form is required. The priority date for freshman financial aid applications for fall entry is March 2. The deadline for filing freshman financial aid applications for fall entry is rolling.

CALIFORNIA STATE UNIVERSITY, DOMINGUEZ HILLS (*The complete profile is made available exclusively on our website, www. barronspac.com*)

CALIFORNIA STATE UNIVERSITY, EAST BAY   B-3

www.csueastbay.edu

Hayward, CA 94542   (510) 885-2310

Email: annette.walker@csueastbay.edu

Full-time: 3985 men, 6313 women	**Faculty:** IIA, av$
Part-time: 617 men, 938 women	**Ph.D.s:** n/av
Graduate: 738 men, 1260 women	**Student/Faculty:** n/av
Year: quarters, summer session	**Tuition:** $6549 ($15,477)
Room & Board: $10,000	**Freshman Class:** n/av
SAT or ACT: recommended	**CEEB CODE:** 4011
Application Deadline: n/av	**COMPETITIVE**

California State University, East Bay, founded in 1957, is part of the California State University system. The institution offers degree programs in the arts, sciences, business and economics, and education to a primarily commuter student body. The figures given in the above capsule and in this profile are approximate. There are 4 undergraduate schools and 4 graduate schools. In addition to regional accreditation, Cal. State East Bay has baccalaureate program accreditation with AACSB, NASAD, NASM, NCATE, and NLN. The 342-acre campus is in a small town 20 miles southeast of San Francisco in the Hayward Hills. Including any residence halls, there are 19 buildings.

STUDENT LIFE: 92% of undergraduates are from California. Others are from 31 states, 63 foreign countries, and Canada. 85% are from public schools. 23% are Asian American; 23% Hispanic; 21% White; 11% African American. **Male To Female Ratio:** 1.6:1. The average age of all undergraduates is 25. 25% do not continue beyond their first year; 50% remain to graduate. **Housing:** 1300 students can be accommodated in college housing, which includes coed on-campus apartments. In addition, there are special-interest houses. On-campus housing is available on a first-come and first-served basis. 90% of students commute. All students may keep cars.

FACULTY/CLASSROOMS: 45% of faculty are male; 55% are female. No introductory courses are taught by graduate students.

PROGRAMS OF STUDY: Cal. State East Bay confers B.A., and B.S. degrees. Master's and doctoral degrees are also awarded. Bachelor's degrees are awarded in AGRICULTURE (environmental studies), BIOLOGICAL SCIENCE (biology/biological science), BUSINESS (accounting, business administration and management, and recreation and leisure services), COMMUNICATIONS AND THE ARTS (advertising, art, communications, dramatic arts, English, music,

Spanish, and speech/debate/rhetoric), COMPUTER AND PHYSICAL SCIENCE (chemistry, computer science, geology, mathematics, physical sciences, physics, and statistics), ENGINEERING AND ENVIRONMENTAL DESIGN (engineering, environmental science, and industrial engineering), HEALTH PROFESSIONS (health science, nursing, and speech pathology/audiology), SOCIAL SCIENCE (anthropology, criminal justice, economics, ethnic studies, geography, history, human development, international studies, Latin American studies, liberal arts/general studies, philosophy, physical fitness/movement, political science/government, psychology, and sociology).

ACTIVITIES: 1% of men belong to 4 national fraternities; 1% of women belong to 3 national sororities. There are 90 groups on campus, including art, cheerleading, choir, chorale, chorus, computers, dance, drama, environmental, ethnic, film, gay, honors, international, jazz band, literary magazine, musical theater, newspaper, opera, orchestra, pep band, photography, political, professional, radio and TV, religious, social, social service, student government, and symphony. Popular campus events include Science Fair, Leadership Conferences and Al Fresco. **Sports:** There are 5 intercollegiate sports for men and 8 for women. Facilities include tennis and racquetball courts, 2 swimming pools, a track, a soccer field, a martial arts facility, a dance studio, baseball and softball diamonds, a 9000-seat stadium, a 500-seat gym, and a 500-seat theater. **Graduates:** From July 1, 2013 to June 30, 2014, 2700 bachelor's degrees were awarded. The most popular majors were business administration (30%), health sciences (7%), and nursing (7%). In an average class, 25% graduate in 4 years or less, 35% graduate in 5 years or less, and 45% graduate in 6 years or less.

SERVICES: Counseling and information services are available, as is tutoring in most subjects. There is a reader service for the blind, and remedial math, reading, and writing. **Library/Resources:** The 2 libraries contain 912,912 volumes, 873,177 microform items, 29,768 audio/video tapes/CDs/DVDs, and subscribe to 2,000 periodicals including electronic. Computerized library services include interlibrary loans, database searching, Internet access, and Wi-Fi capability. Special learning facilities include an art gallery, natural history museum, radio station, TV station, marine biology lab, and geology summer field camp. **Physically Challenged Students:** 95% of the campus is accessible. Facilities include wheelchair ramps, elevators, special parking, specially equipped restrooms, special class scheduling, lowered drinking fountains, lowered telephones, special housing. The Disabled Student Services Center provides scribe, interpretive, and translation services. **Special:** California State East Bay offers cross-registration with local community colleges, other CSU campuses, and the University of California, Berkeley. Internships, study abroad in 20 countries, work-study programs, and student-designed majors are also available. The PACE program provides degree opportunities in liberal studies, hospitality and leisure services, and in human development to working adults. There is 1 national honor society, a freshman honors program, and 1 departmental honors programs. **Visiting:** There are regularly scheduled orientations for prospective students. There are guides for informal visits and visitors may sit in on classes. To schedule a visit, contact Welcome Center at admissions@csueastbay.edu. **Campus Safety and Security:** Measures include 24-hour foot and vehicle patrol, self-defense education, and security escort services. There are shuttle buses, emergency telephones, and lighted pathways/sidewalks.

REQUIREMENTS: The SAT or ACT is recommended. All students must meet the eligibility index, a combination of the high school GPA and SAT or ACT scores. Applicants must be graduates of an accredited secondary school or have a GED certificate. Secondary school courses must include 4 years of English, 3 of math, 2 each of a language other than English, social science, and science with a lab, and 1 elective. A GPA of 2.0 is required. AP and CLEP credits are accepted. In order to graduate, students must fulfill the university writing skills requirement, have a 2.0 minimum GPA, and complete 186 quarter units. **Procedure:** Freshmen are admitted to all sessions. Entrance exams should be taken prior to orientation. There is a rolling admissions plan. Check with the school for current application deadlines. The fall 2014 application fee was $55. Notification is sent on a rolling basis. Applications are accepted on-line. **Transfer Students:** Applicants must have a minimum 2.0 GPA (2.45 for nonresidents), be in good standing at the last college attended, and either

meet freshman admission requirements or have completed at least 56 transferable semester (84 quarter) units. 45 of 186 credits required for the bachelor's degree must be completed at Cal. State East Bay. **International Students:** The school actively recruits these students. They must take the TOEFL. They must also take the SAT or ACT.

ADMISSIONS: Director of Graduate Programs. E-Mail: *annette.walker@csueastbay.edu* Web: *www.csueastbay.edu*

FINANCIAL AID: Cal. State East Bay is a member of CSS. The FAFSA is required. Check with the school for current application deadlines.

CALIFORNIA STATE UNIVERSITY, FRESNO
C-3

www.csufresno.edu

Fresno, CA 93740	(559) 278-6067
Fax: (559) 278-4812	Email: tinab@csufresno.edu
Full-time: 7314 men, 9836 women	Faculty: IIA, av$
Part-time: 1186 men, 1368 women	Ph.D.s: n/av
Graduate: 969 men, 1892 women	Student/Faculty: n/av
Year: semesters, summer session	Tuition: $6762 ($14,400)
Room & Board: $10,192	Freshman Class: 16242 applied, 9444 accepted, 3139 enrolled
SAT or ACT: required	CEEB CODE: 4312
Application Deadline: November 30	COMPETITIVE

California State University, Fresno, founded in 1911, is part of the state-supported university system. The school offers undergraduate and graduate programs in agriculture and technology, liberal arts and sciences, business administration, education, engineering, health fields, and preprofessional training. The figures given in the above capsule and in this profile are approximate. There are 8 undergraduate schools and 8 graduate schools. In addition to regional accreditation, Fresno State has baccalaureate program accreditation with AACSB, ABET, ACCE, ACEJMC, ADA, APTA, ASLA, CSWE, FIDER, NCATE, NLN, and NRPA. The 388-acre campus is in an urban area 200 miles southeast of San Francisco in the Central Valley of California.

STUDENT LIFE: 97% of undergraduates are from California. Others are from 32 states, 53 foreign countries, and Canada. 98% are from public schools. 39% are Hispanic; 29% White; 15% Asian American. **Male To Female Ratio:** 1.4:1. The average age of freshmen is 18; all undergraduates, 22. 17% do not continue beyond their first year; 83% remain to graduate. **Housing:** 1100 students can be accommodated in college housing, which includes single-sex and coed dorms. In addition, there are special-interest houses. On-campus housing is available on a first-come and first-served basis. 95% of students commute. Alcohol is not permitted. All students may keep cars.

FACULTY/CLASSROOMS: 53% of faculty are male; 47% are female. All teach undergraduates, and all do research. No introductory courses are taught by graduate students.

PROGRAMS OF STUDY: Fresno State confers B.A., and B.S. degrees. Master's and doctoral degrees are also awarded. Bachelor's degrees are awarded in AGRICULTURE (agricultural business management, agricultural communications, animal science, dairy science, and plant science), BIOLOGICAL SCIENCE (biology/biological science and biophysics), BUSINESS (accounting, business administration and management, business data processing, business law, and recreational facilities management), COMMUNICATIONS AND THE ARTS (art, communications, dramatic arts, English, French, German, graphic design, jazz, journalism, linguistics, media arts, music, music performance, public relations, Spanish, speech/debate/rhetoric, theatre arts, and theater design), COMPUTER AND PHYSICAL SCIENCE (chemistry, Computer Engineering Technology, computer science, geology, mathematics, natural sciences, and physics), EDUCATION (agricultural education and music education), ENGINEERING AND ENVIRONMENTAL DESIGN (civil engineering, civil engineering technology, computer engineering, construction management, electrical/electronics engineering, furniture design, industrial engineering, industrial engineering technology, interior design, mechanical engineering, and surveying engineering), HEALTH PROFESSIONS (health science, nursing, public health, speech pathology/audiology, and speech therapy), SOCIAL SCIENCE (African American studies, anthropology, child care/child and family studies, child psychology/development, counseling/psychology, criminology, economics, family/consumer studies, food science, forensic studies, French studies, geography, gerontology, history, home economics, humanities, Latin American studies, liberal arts/general studies, Mexican-American/Chicano studies, philosophy, philosophy and religion, physical fitness/movement, political science/government, psychology, public administration, social science, social work, sociology, urban studies, and women's studies). Business and liberal arts have the largest enrollments.

ACTIVITIES: 6% of women belong to 4 local and 9 national sororities. There are 413 groups on campus, including art, band, cheerleading, chess, choir, chorale, chorus, computers, dance, drama, drill team, ethnic, film, gay, honors, international, jazz band, marching band, musical theater, newspaper, opera, orchestra, pep band, photography, political, professional, radio and TV, religious, social, social service, student government, and symphony. Popular campus events include Vintage Days, International Week and Black History Month. **Sports:** There are 7 intercollegiate sports for men and 11 for women. Facilities include football and women's soccer teams, a 5,422-seat baseball stadium, is considered one of the finest collegiate complexes in the country and home to the 2008 NCAA National Champion baseball team. Bulldog Diamond, home of the 1998 NCAA champion Fresno state softball team, seats 3,288 and is the finest on-campus facility of its kind in the nation. Fresno State has track and field facilities, two gymnasiums, and putting greens and driving areas complete with sand traps for golf. The strength and conditioning center is one of the best weight rooms on the West Coast with 10,800 square feet, and the resplendent Spalding G. Wathen Tennis Center is home to the men's and women's tennis teams. Fresno State opened the Save Mart Center, the largest on-campus arena on the West Coast with a capacity of 15,596. **Graduates:** From July 1, 2013 to June 30, 2014, 3441 bachelor's degrees were awarded. The most popular majors were liberal studies-blended program (8%), psychology (6%), and criminology-law enforcement option (5%). In an average class, 15% graduate in 4 years or less, 36% graduate in 5 years or less, and 48% graduate in 6 years or less.

SERVICES: Counseling and information services are available, as is tutoring in most subjects. There is a reader service for the blind, and remedial math, reading, and writing. **Library/Resources:** The library contains 1.2 million volumes, 1.6 million microform items, 92,426 audio/video tapes/CDs/DVDs, and subscribes to 25,534 periodicals including electronic. Computerized library services include interlibrary loans, database searching, and Internet access. Special learning facilities include an art gallery, planetarium, radio station, various farm lab units. **Physically Challenged Students:** All of the campus is accessible. Facilities include wheelchair ramps, elevators, special parking, specially equipped restrooms, special class scheduling, lowered drinking fountains, and lowered telephones. **Special:** Study abroad in 17 countries, including England, New Zealand, China, and the South Pacific, co-op programs, internships, work-study programs, B.A.-B.S. degrees, dual majors, and student-designed majors are offered. A liberal studies major, credit for military experience, pass/fail options, and nondegree study are available. There are 10 national honor societies, including Phi Beta Kappa, a freshman honors program, and 4 departmental honors programs. **Visiting:** There are regularly scheduled orientations for prospective students, including 1- and 2-day overnight programs for entering students. There are guides for informal visits and visitors may stay overnight. To schedule a visit, contact the University Outreach Services at (559) 278-7533 . **Campus Safety and Security:** Measures include 24-hour foot and vehicle patrol, emergency notification system, self-defense education, and security escort services. There are emergency telephones, lighted pathways/sidewalks, closed circuit television cameras, and bicycle safety patrols.

REQUIREMENTS: The SAT or ACT is required. Students with a GPA below 3.0 are required to submit the SAT or ACT scores. Applicants must be graduates of an accredited secondary school or have a GED. Secondary school courses must include 15 academic credits:

4 years of high school English, 3 each of math and electives, 2 of a foreign language, and 1 each of science, history/government, and visual/performing arts. A GPA of 2.0 is required. AP and CLEP credits are accepted. All students must complete general education requirements. A minimum of 120 semester units, with a GPA of 2.0, is required to graduate. The number of required hours in the major varies. **Procedure:** Freshmen are admitted fall and spring. Entrance exams should be taken as early as possible, by the first semester of the senior year. There is a rolling admissions plan. Applications should be filed by November 30 for fall entry, along with a $55 fee. Applications are accepted on-line. **Transfer Students:** 2574 transfer students enrolled in 2013-2014. Transfer applicants must have a minimum GPA of 2.0 and 56 transferable semester units earned, including English and math. 30 of 124 credits required for the bachelor's degree must be completed at Fresno State. **International Students:** There are 255 international students enrolled. The school actively recruits these students. They must take the TOEFL. They must also take the SAT or ACT.

ADMISSIONS: 58% of the 2014-2015 applicants were accepted. The SAT scores for the 2014-2015 freshman class were: Critical Reading--68% below 500, 24% between 500 and 599, 6% between 600 and 699, and 1% between 700 and 800; Math--61% below 500, 24% between 500 and 599, 6% between 600 and 699, and 1% between 700 and 800; Writing--69% below 500, 25% between 500 and 599, 5% between 600 and 699, and 1% between 700 and 800. **Admissions Contact:** Tina Beddall, Interim Director of Admissions. E-Mail: *tinab@csufresno.edu* Web: *www.csufresno.edu*

FINANCIAL AID: In 2014-2015, 69% of all full-time freshmen and continuing full-time students received some form of financial aid. 76% of all full-time freshmen continuing full-time students received need-based aid. The average freshman award was $11,194. Need-based scholarships or need-based grants averaged $1,024; need-based self-help aid (loans and jobs) averaged $3,243; non-need-based athletic scholarships averaged $14,332; and other non-need-based awards and non-need-based scholarships averaged $3,421. The average financial indebtedness of the 2014 graduate was $16,100. Fresno State is a member of CSS. The FAFSA is required. The priority date for freshman financial aid applications for fall entry is March 3.

CALIFORNIA STATE UNIVERSITY, FULLERTON   **D-5**
www.fullerton.edu

Fullerton, CA 92834	(657) 278-2371
Fax: (657) 278-2356	Email: admissions@fullerton.edu
Full-time: 11721 men, 14931 women	Faculty: 891; IIA, av$
	Ph.D.s: 87%
Part-time: 2999 men, 3435 women	Student/Faculty: 26 to 1
Graduate: 2104 men, 3105 women	Tuition: $6186 ($17,346)
Year: semesters, summer session	Freshman Class: 41013 applied, 19614 accepted, 4667 enrolled
Room & Board: $12,816	
SAT CR/M: 490/520 ACT: 21	CEEB CODE: 4589
Application Deadline: November 30	COMPETITIVE

California State University, Fullerton, founded in 1957, is part of the California State University system. Figures in the above capsule and in this profile are approximate. The school offers programs in the arts, business and economics, communications, engineering and computer science, education, health and human development, humanities and social science, natural science and math. The institution provides a comprehensive teaching credential program. There are 8 undergraduate schools and 8 graduate schools. In addition to regional accreditation, Cal State Fullerton has baccalaureate program accreditation with AACSB, ABET, ACEJMC, NASAD, NASM, NCATE, and NLN. The 240-acre campus is in a suburban area 30 miles southeast of Los Angeles. Including any residence halls, there are 29 buildings.

STUDENT LIFE: 98% of undergraduates are from California. Others are from 36 states, 59 foreign countries, and Canada. 95% are from public schools. 37% are Hispanic; 26% White; 22% Asian American. **Male To Female Ratio:** 1.3:1. The average age of freshmen is 18; all undergraduates, 22. 11% do not continue beyond their first year; 89% remain to graduate. **Housing:** 2000 students can be accommodated in college housing, which includes coed on-campus apartments and off-campus apartments. In addition, there are fraternity houses and sorority houses. On-campus housing is available on a first-come and first-served basis. 94% of students commute. All students may keep cars.

FACULTY/CLASSROOMS: 50% of faculty are male; 50% are female. All teach and do research. No introductory courses are taught by graduate students. The average class size in an introductory lecture is 35; in a laboratory is 20; and in a regular course is 33.

PROGRAMS OF STUDY: Cal State Fullerton confers B.A., B.S., B.F.A. and B.M. degrees. Master's and doctoral degrees are also awarded. Bachelor's degrees are awarded in BIOLOGICAL SCIENCE (biochemistry and biology/biological science), BUSINESS (business administration and management, business economics, entrepreneurial studies, finance, international business management, management science, marketing/retailing/merchandising, and tourism), COMMUNICATIONS AND THE ARTS (advertising, art history, art, communications, comparative literature, dance, dramatic arts, English, fine arts, French, Japanese, journalism, linguistics, music, music performance, public relations, radio/television technology, Spanish, speech/debate/rhetoric, theater design, theater management, visual and performing arts, and visual design), COMPUTER AND PHYSICAL SCIENCE (applied mathematics, chemistry, computer science, geology, information sciences and systems, mathematics, physics, and statistics), EDUCATION (athletic training and music education), ENGINEERING AND ENVIRONMENTAL DESIGN (civil engineering, computer engineering, electrical/electronics engineering, engineering and applied science, and mechanical engineering), HEALTH PROFESSIONS (exercise science, health science, kinesiology, nursing, and speech pathology/audiology), SOCIAL SCIENCE (African American studies, American studies, anthropology, Asian/American studies, child care/child and family studies, criminal justice, economics, ethnic studies, European studies, geography, history, human services, Latin American studies, liberal arts/general studies, Mexican-American/Chicano studies, philosophy, political science/government, psychology, public administration, religion, and women's studies). Business, economics and teacher credential program are the strongest academically. Business, economics, humanities, social sciences, health and human development have the largest enrollments.

ACTIVITIES: 2% of men belong to 5 local and 13 national fraternities; 2% of women belong to 1 local and 8 national sororities. There are 250 groups on campus, including art, band, cheerleading, choir, chorus, communications, computers, dance, debate, drama, ethnic, film, forensics, gay, honors, international, jazz band, literary magazine, musical theater, newspaper, opera, orchestra, pep band, photography, political, professional, radio and TV, religious, social, social service, and student government. Popular campus events include Block Party, Spring Concert, and Snow Day. **Sports:** There are 6 intercollegiate sports for men and 9 for women, and 15 intramural sports for men and 11 for women. Facilities include a gym, a swimming pool, tennis and racquetball courts, baseball/softball, track, and soccer fields, a bowling alley, and a stadium. **Graduates:** From July 1, 2013 to June 30, 2014, 7472 bachelor's degrees were awarded. The most popular majors were business/marketing (24%), communication/journalism (13%), and health professions and related programs (8%). In an average class, 14% graduate in 4 years or less, 40% graduate in 5 years or less, and 53% graduate in 6 years or less.

SERVICES: Counseling and information services are available, as is tutoring in most subjects. There is a reader service for the blind, and remedial math, reading, and writing. **Library/Resources:** The library contains 2.3 million volumes, 1.2 million microform items, 65,305 audio/video tapes/CDs/DVDs, and subscribes to 80,890 periodicals including electronic. Computerized library services include interlibrary loans, database searching, Internet access, and Wi-Fi capability. Special learning facilities include an art gallery, radio station, TV station, a wildlife sanctuary, an arboretum, a desert studies center, a demographic research center, and a number of centers for studies in

economics and business, the environment, aging, education, land use, oral and public history, and religion in American life. **Physically Challenged Students:** All of the campus is accessible. Facilities include wheelchair ramps, elevators, special parking, specially equipped restrooms, lowered drinking fountains, lowered telephones and automatic doors. **Special:** The university offers distance learning, honors program, freshman program, internships and co-op programs in 45 academic areas, study abroad in 18 countries, and work-study programs both on and off campus. Double majors, pass/fail options, teacher credential programs, and service learning are also available. There is a freshman honors program. **Visiting:** There are regularly scheduled orientations for prospective students, consisting of daily campus tours and information on academic colleges, student services, student life, and the history of Cal State Fullerton. There are guides for informal visits. To schedule a visit, contact New Student and Parent Programs at (657) 278-2501. **Campus Safety and Security:** Measures include 24-hour foot and vehicle patrol, emergency notification system, self-defense education, and security escort services. There are shuttle buses, emergency telephones, and lighted pathways/sidewalks.

REQUIREMENTS: The SAT or ACT is required. Applicants must be graduates of an accredited secondary school or have a GED certificate. Secondary school courses must include 4 years of English, 3 of math, 2 each of a foreign language, science, and history, and 1 of visual or performing arts. Admission is based on the Qualifiable Eligibility Index, a combination of the high school GPA and either the SAT or ACT score. Auditions are required for music majors. A GPA of 2.0 is required. AP and CLEP credits are accepted. Graduation requirements for all students include completion of a minimum of 51 units of general education courses, a 2.0 GPA, and an upper-division writing course designated by the major department. 120 to 135 credit hours must be completed for graduation. **Procedure:** Freshmen are admitted fall. Entrance exams should be taken during the senior year of high school. There is a rolling admissions plan. Applications should be filed by November 30 for fall entry, along with a $55 fee. Notification is sent on a rolling basis. Applications are accepted on-line. **Transfer Students:** 4752 transfer students enrolled in 2013-2014. Applicants must have a minimum 2.0 GPA. The SAT or ACT is required for students with fewer than 60 transferable units earned. Students with 60 transferable units or more must have 30 units of general education completed with a C or better, including English composition, math, speech, and critical thinking. 30 of 120 credits required for the bachelor's degree must be completed at Cal State Fullerton. **International Students:** There are 791 international students enrolled. They must take the TOEFL with a minimum score of 500 on the paper-based TOEFL (PBT) or 61 on the Internet-based version (iBT).

ADMISSIONS: 48% of the 2014-2015 applicants were accepted. The SAT scores for the 2014-2015 freshman class were: Critical Reading--51% below 500, 39% between 500 and 599, 9% between 600 and 699, and 1% between 700 and 800; Math--38% below 500, 45% between 500 and 599, 15% between 600 and 699, and 2% between 700 and 800. The ACT scores were 43% below 21, 32% between 21 and 23, 19% between 24 and 26, 4% between 27 and 28, and 3% above 28. 49% of the current freshmen were in the top fifth of their class; 88% were in the top two fifths. 2 freshmen graduated first in their class. **Admissions Contact:** Admissions Office E-Mail: *admissions@fullerton.edu* Web: *www.fullerton.edu*

FINANCIAL AID: In 2014-2015, 60% of all full-time freshmen and 60% of continuing full-time students received some form of financial aid. 49% of all full-time freshmen and 47% of continuing full-time students received need-based aid. The average freshman award was $11,010. Need-based scholarships or need-based grants averaged $6,635; need-based self-help aid (loans and jobs) averaged $5,756; non-need-based athletic scholarships averaged $5,177; and other non-need-based awards and non-need-based scholarships averaged $7,301. The average financial indebtedness of the 2014 graduate was $14,983. The FAFSA is required. The priority date for freshman financial aid applications for fall entry is March 2. The deadline for filing freshman financial aid applications for fall entry is June 6.

CALIFORNIA STATE UNIVERSITY, LONG BEACH   D-5
www.csulb.edu

Long Beach, CA 90840	**(562) 985-5471**

Fax: (562) 985-4973	Email: Tom.Enders@csulb.edu
Full-time: 11436 men, 14621 women	Faculty: IIA, av$
	Ph.D.s: 87%
Part-time: 2294 men, 3172 women	Student/Faculty: n/av
Graduate: 2089 men, 3285 women	Tuition: $6452 ($15,380)
Year: semesters, summer session	Freshman Class: 55896
Room & Board: $11,050	applied, 19681 accepted, 4343 enrolled
SAT CR/M: 512/537 ACT: 21	CEEB CODE: 4389
Application Deadline: November 30	COMPETITIVE+

California State University, Long Beach, is a diverse, student-centered, globally-engaged public university committed to providing highly-valued undergraduate and graduate educational opportunities through superior teaching, research, creative activity and service for the people of California and the world. CSULB is one of the largest campuses in the CSU system and in the state of California. It is nationally recognized as one of the nations' best values in higher education, offering a high-quality, low-cost education. There are 7 undergraduate schools and 7 graduate schools. In addition to regional accreditation, CSULB has baccalaureate program accreditation with AACSB, AALE, ABET, ACEJMC, AHEA, APTA, CAHEA, CSAB, CSWE, FIDER, NASAD, NASM, NCATE, NLN, and NRPA. The 322-acre campus is in an urban area just 25 miles southeast of Los Angeles and a short drive to Orange County. Including any residence halls, there are 86 buildings.

STUDENT LIFE: 95% of undergraduates are from California. Others are from 47 states, 100 foreign countries, and Canada. 46% are from public schools. 36% are Hispanic; 22% Asian American; 21% White. **Male To Female Ratio:** 1.3:1. The average age of freshmen is 18; all undergraduates, 22. 10% do not continue beyond their first year; 65% remain to graduate. **Housing:** 2672 students can be accommodated in college housing, which includes single-sex and coed dorms. In addition, there are honors houses and special-interest houses. On-campus housing is available on a first-come and first-served basis. 91% of students commute. Alcohol is not permitted. All students may keep cars.

FACULTY/CLASSROOMS: No introductory courses are taught by graduate students.

PROGRAMS OF STUDY: CSULB confers B.A., B.S., B.F.A. and B.M. degrees. Master's and doctoral degrees are also awarded. Bachelor's degrees are awarded in BIOLOGICAL SCIENCE (biochemistry, biology/biological science, botany, cell biology, ecology, marine biology, microbiology, nutritional sciences, physiology, and zoology), BUSINESS (accounting, banking and finance, business administration and management, business economics, finance, international business, international business management, management information systems, marketing/retailing/merchandising, personnel management, and recreation and leisure services), COMMUNICATIONS AND THE ARTS (art history, art, Chinese, classics, communications, comparative literature, creative writing, dance, design, dramatic arts, English, film arts, French, french and francophone studies, German, Japanese, journalism, music, Spanish, and theatre arts), COMPUTER AND PHYSICAL SCIENCE (applied mathematics, chemistry, Computer Engineering Technology, computer science, earth science, geology, mathematics, physics, and statistics), EDUCATION (elementary education, mathematics education, science education, and special education), ENGINEERING AND ENVIRONMENTAL DESIGN (aerospace engineering, chemical engineering, civil engineering, computer engineering, electrical/electronics engineering, engineering technology, environmental science, and mechanical engineering), HEALTH PROFESSIONS (health care administration, health science, kinesiology, and nursing), SOCIAL SCIENCE (African studies, American studies, anthropology, Asian/Oriental studies, child care/child and family studies, child psychology/development, criminal justice, criminology, economics, family/consumer studies, geography,

Hispanic American studies, history, human development, interdisciplinary studies, international studies, philosophy, political science/government, psychology, religion, religious studies, social work, sociology, women and gender studies, and women's studies). Art, biological sciences, and music are the strongest academically. Business administration, psychology, and speech communication have the largest enrollments.

ACTIVITIES: 7% of men belong to 24 national fraternities; 6% of women belong to 15 national sororities. There are 395 groups on campus, including art, band, cheerleading, choir, chorale, chorus, communications, computers, dance, debate, drama, drill team, ethnic, film, forensics, gay, honors, international, jazz band, literary magazine, musical theater, newspaper, opera, orchestra, pep band, photography, political, professional, radio and TV, religious, social, social service, student government, and symphony. Popular campus events include Homecoming, and Smorgasport. **Sports:** There are 7 intercollegiate sports for men and 11 for women, and 14 intramural sports for men and 12 for women. Facilities include The Walter Pyramid, a nationally recognized icon for the university and the city of Long Beach it is home to the university's basketball and volleyball teams. Its floor space accommodates nine volleyball courts or three full basketball courts and four additional half basketball courts on the "activity" level. Blair Field, one of America's best amateur baseball facilities, is home to the baseball team. The 49er Softball Complex is an 800-seat facility. The Women's Soccer Team plays on George Allen Field. Jack Rose Stadium is an 850-seat facility that features 400-meter all-weather track and runways and grass turf throughout the infield. The Rhodes Tennis Center is a 12-court complex that is home to the nationally ranked 49er women's tennis program. The Student Recreation and Wellness Center (SRWC) is a two-story, 126,500 square-foot recreation facility that contains a three-court gym, a multi-activity court gym, an indoor jogging track, 20,000 square feet of weight lifting and cardio equipment, racquetball courts, activity rooms, a custom-made rock climbing wall, and an outdoor pool and spa to take advantage of the year-round sunshine in Long Beach. **Graduates:** From July 1, 2013 to June 30, 2014, 6831 bachelor's degrees were awarded. The most popular majors were business/marketing (15%), visual and performing arts (10%), and communications/journalism (10%). In an average class, 12% graduate in 4 years or less and 64% graduate in 6 years or less.

SERVICES: Counseling and information services are available, as is tutoring in most subjects. There is a reader service for the blind, and remedial math, reading, and writing. **Library/Resources:** The library contains 1.1 million volumes, 1.5 million microform items, and 29,948 audio/video tapes/CDs/DVDs, and subscribes to 21,002 periodicals including electronic. Computerized library services include interlibrary loans, database searching, and Internet access. Special learning facilities include an art gallery, radio station, and TV station. **Physically Challenged Students:** 99% of the campus is accessible. Facilities include wheelchair ramps, elevators, special parking, specially equipped restrooms, special class scheduling, lowered drinking fountains, lowered telephones. The university also offers registration and mobility assistance, adaptive equipment, counseling, community referrals, and services to the learning-disabled. **Special:** There are 23 national honor societies, including Phi Beta Kappa, and a freshman honors program. **Visiting:** There are regularly scheduled orientations for prospective students, consisting of a one hour walking tour showcases campus distinctions and facilities, provides a general overview of campus academic programs, student support services and campus life. There are guides for informal visits. To schedule a visit, contact the Office of University Outreach and School Relations at (562) 985-5358. **Campus Safety and Security:** Measures include 24-hour foot and vehicle patrol, emergency notification system, and security escort services. There are shuttle buses, emergency telephones, and lighted pathways/sidewalks.

REQUIREMENTS: The SAT or ACT is required. Applicants must be graduates of an accredited secondary school and have completed 4 years of English, 3 years of math, 2 years of the same foreign language, 2 years of lab science, 2 years of history and social science, 1 year of visual and performing arts and 1 year of electives. Students are admitted on the basis of the eligibility index, a formula that combines students' achievement in high school college preparatory courses with the results of the SAT I or ACT. California residents with a minimum

3.0 GPA are automatically admissible. A portfolio is required for art and design students. An audition is required for dance, music, and theater students. A GPA of 2.0 is required. AP and CLEP credits are accepted. Graduation requirements for all students include the completion of 40 units of upper-division course work and 30 units in residence at the university. Students must have a minimum 2.0 GPA and a total of 120 to 132 units, depending on the major. Students must also satisfy the Graduation Writing Assessment Requirement. **Procedure:** Freshmen are admitted fall and spring. Entrance exams should be taken during the fall semester of the senior year. There is a rolling admissions plan. Applications should be filed by November 30 for fall entry; August 31 for spring entry. The fall 2014 application fee was $55. Applications are accepted on-line. **Transfer Students:** 3284 transfer students enrolled in 2013-2014. Upper-division students must have completed a minimum of 56 semester units and have a minimum 2.0 GPA; lower-division students must meet the same requirements as entering freshmen. 30 of 120 credits required for the bachelor's degree must be completed at CSULB. **International Students:** There are 1740 international students enrolled. The school actively recruits these students. They must take the TOEFL with a minimum score of 500 on the paper-based TOEFL (PBT) or 61 on the Internet-based version (iBT).

ADMISSIONS: 35% of the 2014-2015 applicants were accepted. The SAT scores for the 2014-2015 freshman class were: Critical Reading--42% below 500, 44% between 500 and 599, 13% between 600 and 699, and 2% between 700 and 800; Math--32% below 500, 42% between 500 and 599, 24% between 600 and 699, and 3% between 700 and 800. The ACT scores were 42% below 21, 25% between 21 and 23, 20% between 24 and 26, 7% between 27 and 28, and 6% above 28. **Admissions Contact:** Tom Enders, Associate Vice Pres. Enrollment Services. E-Mail: *Tom.Enders@csulb.edu* Web: *www.csulb.edu*

FINANCIAL AID: CSULB is a member of CSS. The FAFSA is required. The deadline for filing freshman financial aid applications for fall entry is March 2.

CALIFORNIA STATE UNIVERSITY, LOS ANGELES *(The complete profile is made available exclusively on our website, www.barronspac.com)*

CALIFORNIA STATE UNIVERSITY, MONTEREY BAY *(The complete profile is made available exclusively on our website, www.barronspac.com)*

CALIFORNIA STATE UNIVERSITY, NORTHRIDGE *(The complete profile is made available exclusively on our website, www.barronspac.com)*

CALIFORNIA STATE UNIVERSITY, SACRAMENTO	B-3
www.csus.edu	

Sacramento, CA 95819	(916) 278-7362
	(800) 722-4748
Fax: (916) 278-5603	Email: outreach@csus.edu
Full-time: 8697 men, 11713 women	Faculty: IIA, +$
Part-time: 1971 men, 2320 women	Ph.D.s: n/av
Graduate: 1071 men, 2244 women	Student/Faculty: n/av
Year: semesters, summer session	Tuition: $6572 ($17,732)
Room & Board: $9628	Freshman Class: 18617 applied, 12496 accepted, 4671 enrolled
SAT or ACT: required	CEEB CODE: 4671
Application Deadline: November 30	COMPETITIVE

California State University, Sacramento is an integral part of the community, committed to access, excellence and diversity. California State University, Sacramento is dedicated to the life-altering potential of learning that balances a liberal arts education with depth of knowledge in a discipline. We are committed to providing an excellent education to all eligible applicants who aspire to expand their knowledge

and prepare themselves for meaningful lives, careers, and service to their community. The figures in the above capsule and in this profile are approximate. California State University, Sacramento is a richly diverse community. As such, the University is committed to fostering in all its members a sense of inclusiveness, respect for human differences, and concern for others. In doing so, we strive to create a pluralistic community in which members participate collaboratively in all aspects of university life. There are 7 undergraduate schools and 7 graduate schools. In addition to regional accreditation, Sacramento State has baccalaureate program accreditation with AACSB, ABET, ACBSP, ACCE, ADA, AHEA, APTA, ASLA, CSWE, FIDER, NASAD, NASM, NCATE, NLN, NRPA, and TEAC. The 300-acre campus is in a suburban area 90 miles northeast of San Francisco. Including any residence halls, there are 52 buildings.

STUDENT LIFE: 99% of undergraduates are from California. Others are from 37 states, 36 foreign countries, and Canada. 96% are from public schools. 44% are White; 18% Asian American; 14% Hispanic. **Male To Female Ratio:** 1.4:1. **Housing:** 1100 students can be accommodated in college housing, which includes coed dorms and off-campus apartments. On-campus housing is available on a first-come and first-served basis. 95% of students commute. All students may keep cars.

FACULTY/CLASSROOMS: 51% of faculty are male; 49% are female. All teach and do research. No introductory courses are taught by graduate students. The average class size in an introductory lecture is 38; in a laboratory is 19; and in a regular course is 34.

PROGRAMS OF STUDY: Sacramento State confers B.A., B.S., B.M. and B.V.E. degrees. Master's and doctoral degrees are also awarded. Bachelor's degrees are awarded in AGRICULTURE (natural resource management), BIOLOGICAL SCIENCE (biology/biological science and microbiology), BUSINESS (accounting, banking and finance, business administration and management, insurance, international business management, management information systems, marketing/retailing/merchandising, and real estate), COMMUNICATIONS AND THE ARTS (communications, dramatic arts, English, French, German, journalism, music, and Spanish), COMPUTER AND PHYSICAL SCIENCE (chemistry, computer science, geology, mathematics, physical sciences, and physics), EDUCATION (business education, early childhood education, and health education), ENGINEERING AND ENVIRONMENTAL DESIGN (civil engineering, computer engineering, electrical/electronics engineering, engineering technology, and mechanical engineering), HEALTH PROFESSIONS (environmental health science, medical laboratory technology, nursing, physical therapy, and speech pathology/audiology), SOCIAL SCIENCE (anthropology, criminal justice, economics, geography, history, homeland security, international relations, parks and recreation management, philosophy, psychology, public administration, social science, social work, and sociology). Nursing, criminal justice, and business administration. are the strongest academically. Business administration, and communications have the largest enrollment.

ACTIVITIES: 7% of men belong to 3 local and 18 national fraternities; 5% of women belong to 1 local and 20 national sororities. There are 230 groups on campus, including art, band, cheerleading, chess, choir, chorale, chorus, computers, dance, debate, drama, ethnic, film, gay, honors, international, jazz band, literary magazine, marching band, musical theater, newspaper, opera, orchestra, pep band, photography, political, professional, radio and TV, religious, social, social service, student government, and symphony. Popular campus events include Greek Week, Festival of New American Music and River City Days. **Sports:** Facilities include a 17000-seat stadium, 2 gyms, 2 swimming pools, an all-weather outdoor track, 16 tennis courts, baseball, softball, and soccer fields, and an aquatic center, with sailing, windsurfing, rowing, and canoeing. **Graduates:** From July 1, 2013 to June 30, 2014, 5075 bachelor's degrees were awarded. The most popular majors were business/marketing (21%), homeland security (11%), and communication/journalism (8%).

SERVICES: Counseling and information services are available, as is tutoring in most subjects. There is a reader service for the blind, and remedial math, reading, and writing. **Library/Resources:** The library contains 1.4 million volumes, 2.4 million microform items, 53,515 audio/video tapes/CDs/DVDs, and subscribes to 2,171 periodicals including electronic. Computerized library services include interlibrary loans, database searching, and Internet access. Special learning facilities include an art gallery, radio station, an aquatic center, an anthropology museum, several art galleries, and a brand new wellness center. **Physically Challenged Students:** 90% of the campus is accessible. Facilities include wheelchair ramps, elevators, special parking, specially equipped restrooms, special class scheduling, lowered drinking fountains, and lowered telephones. **Special:** The university offers cross-registration with other California State University schools, co-op programs in many academic programs, internships, a Washington semester, study abroad in 12 countries, and dual and student-designed majors. A joint Ph.D. program in public history is available with the university of California at Santa Barbara. There is a freshman honors program, including Phi Beta Kappa. **Visiting:** There are regularly scheduled orientations for prospective students. There are guides for informal visits and visitors may sit in on classes. To schedule a visit, contact the University Outreach Services Office. **Campus Safety and Security:** Measures include 24-hour foot and vehicle patrol, self-defense education, and security escort services. There are shuttle buses, emergency telephones, and lighted pathways/sidewalks.

REQUIREMENTS: The SAT or ACT is required of applicants with a high school GPA below 3.0. Applicants should have completed 4 years of high school English, 3 years of math, 2 years of a foreign language, 1 year each of lab science, history, and visual/performing arts and 3 years of college preparatory electives. A GPA of 2.0 is required. AP and CLEP credits are accepted. In order to graduate, students must complete a minimum of 120 semester hours, including 30 to 86 hours in the major, with a minimum 2.0 GPA. Students must complete 51 units in general education requirements and take proficiency exams in writing and a foreign language. Distribution requirements include 15 units in the individual and society; 12 each in arts and humanities and physical universe/life forms, 9 in English language communication, and 3 in understanding personal development. A course in race and ethnicity in American society is required. **Procedure:** Freshmen are admitted fall and spring. Entrance exams should be taken before December of the senior year. There are deferred admissions and rolling admissions plans. Applications should be filed by November 30 for fall entry. The fall 2014 application fee was $55. Notifications are sent November 1. Applications are accepted on-line. **Transfer Students:** 3556 transfer students enrolled in 2013-2014. Applicants must have a 2.0 GPA and 56 transferable semester units, including 30 units of specific general education courses to include oral and written communication, critical thinking, and math. 30 of 120 credits required for the bachelor's degree must be completed at Sacramento State. **International Students:** There are 333 international students enrolled. The school actively recruits these students. They must take the TOEFL. They must also take the SAT or ACT.

ADMISSIONS: 67% of the 2014-2015 applicants were accepted. **Admissions Contact:** Emiliano Diaz, Director of University Outreach Services. E-Mail: *outreach@csus.edu* Web: *www.csus.edu*

FINANCIAL AID: Sacramento State is a member of CSS. The FAFSA, and SAAC is required. Check with the school for current application deadlines.

CALIFORNIA STATE UNIVERSITY, SAN BERNARDINO — D-5
www.csusb.edu

San Bernardino, CA 92407	(909) 537-5188
Fax: (909) 537-7034	
Full-time: 4817 men, 8163 women	**Faculty:** IIA, +$
Part-time: 707 men, 1045 women	**Ph.D.s:** n/av
Graduate: 919 men, 1599 women	**Student/Faculty:** n/av
Year: quarters, summer session	**Tuition:** $6453 ($12,150)
Room & Board: $9796	**Freshman Class:** n/av
	CEEB CODE: 4099
Application Deadline: open	**COMPETITIVE**

California State University, San Bernardino, founded in 1965, is a public, comprehensive regional university offering programs in business and public administration, natural sciences, education, arts and letters, and social and behavioral sciences. The figures in the above capsule and in this profile are approximate. There are 5 undergraduate schools and 19 graduate schools. In addition to regional accreditation, CSUSB has baccalaureate program accreditation with AACSB, ABET, ADA, CSAB, CSWE, NASAD, NASM, NCATE, and NLN. The 430-acre campus is in a suburban area 60 miles east of Los Angeles and 60 miles west of Palm Springs. Including any residence halls, there are 45 buildings.

STUDENT LIFE: 99% of undergraduates are from California. 46% are Hispanic; 24% White. **Male To Female Ratio:** 1.7:1. The average age of freshmen is 18; all undergraduates, 22. 18% do not continue beyond their first year; 82% remain to graduate. **Housing:** College-sponsored housing includes single-sex and coed dorms and on-campus apartments. In addition, there are special-interest houses, and an all-women dorm. On-campus housing is available on a first-come and first-served basis. All students may keep cars.

FACULTY/CLASSROOMS: No introductory courses are taught by graduate students. The average class size in an introductory lecture is 40; in a laboratory is 18; and in a regular course is 24.

PROGRAMS OF STUDY: CSUSB confers B.A., B.S. and B.V.E. degrees. Master's degrees are also awarded. Bachelor's degrees are awarded in AGRICULTURE (environmental studies), BIOLOGICAL SCIENCE (biochemistry and biology/biological science), BUSINESS (accounting, banking and finance, business administration and management, business economics, human resources, international business management, management information systems, management science, and small business management), COMMUNICATIONS AND THE ARTS (art, art history and appreciation, ceramic art and design, communications, dance, dramatic arts, English, French, graphic design, music, music history and appreciation, music performance, music technology, musicology/ethnomusicology, painting, photography, printmaking, sculpture, and Spanish), COMPUTER AND PHYSICAL SCIENCE (applied physics, chemistry, computer science, geology, mathematics, and physics), EDUCATION (bilingual/bicultural education, health education, music education, and vocational education), HEALTH PROFESSIONS (environmental health science, exercise science, health care administration, health science, nursing, and premedicine), SOCIAL SCIENCE (American studies, anthropology, child psychology/development, criminal justice, economics, ethnic studies, food science, geography, gerontology, history, human development, human services, humanities, liberal arts/general studies, paralegal studies, philosophy, political science/government, psychology, public administration, social science, social work, sociology, and Spanish studies). Liberal studies, nursing, and psychology have the largest enrollments.

ACTIVITIES: 4% of men belong to 1 local and 8 national fraternities; 3% of women belong to 6 national sororities. There are 80 groups on campus, including art, cheerleading, choir, chorale, chorus, computers, dance, drama, ethnic, gay, honors, international, jazz band, musical theater, newspaper, orchestra, political, professional, radio and TV, religious, social, social service, and student government. Popular campus events include Annual Picnic and California Indian Cultural Awareness Conference. **Sports:** There are 4 intercollegiate sports for men and 7 for women. Facilities include an arena for basketball and volleyball, baseball, softball, soccer fields, tennis courts, swimming pools for water polo and recreational swimming, and a gym for recreational workouts. **Graduates:** From July 1, 2013 to June 30, 2014, 2868 bachelor's degrees were awarded. The most popular majors were psychology (10%), criminal justice (7%), and liberal studies (7%).

SERVICES: Counseling and information services are available, as is tutoring in most subjects. There is a reader service for the blind, remedial math and writing. **Library/Resources:** Computerized library services include interlibrary loans and database searching. Special learning facilities include an art gallery, radio station, observatory. **Physically Challenged Students:** 95% of the campus is accessible. Facilities include wheelchair ramps, elevators, special parking, specially equipped restrooms, lowered drinking fountains, lowered telephones. **Special:** The university offers cross-registration with other CSU campuses and study abroad in 18 countries. Also available are internships, accelerated study, campus and community work-study programs, B.A.-B.S. degrees, dual and student-designed majors, credit for vocational education and military experience, and nondegree study. There are 3 national honor societies, including Phi Beta

Kappa, and a freshman honors program. <u>Visiting:</u> There are regularly scheduled orientations for prospective students, including sessions on admissions requirements, financial aid information, and campus (student) life information. There are guides for informal visits, visitors may sit in on classes, and stay overnight. To schedule a visit, contact the Outreach Services Office. <u>Campus Safety and Security:</u> Measures include 24-hour foot and vehicle patrol, self-defense education, and security escort services. There are emergency telephones, lighted pathways/sidewalks, E-mail and web site alerts.

<u>REQUIREMENTS:</u> Applicants must be graduates of an accredited secondary school. Preparatory work should include 4 years of English, 3 of math, 2 of foreign language, 1 each of U.S. history/ government, lab science, and visual and performing arts, and 3 of electives. Admission is based on an eligibility index that weighs the high school GPA and the SAT or ACT score. Students with GPAs of 3.0 or better (3.6 for nonresidents) are exempt from test score requirements. AP and CLEP credits are accepted. Important factors in the admissions decision are advanced placement or honors courses, recommendations by school officials, and leadership record. To graduate, students must complete 180 to 198 quarter hours, including 60 in upper-division courses and requirements for the major, with a minimum GPA of 2.0. The 82-credit general education program includes courses in basic skills, natural sciences, humanities, social and behavioral sciences, lifelong understanding, upper-division writing, multicultural/gender studies, and electives. Students must also demonstrate an understanding of the U.S. Constitution, American history, and California government. <u>Procedure:</u> Freshmen are admitted to all sessions. Entrance exams should be taken prior to applying. There is a rolling admissions plan. Application deadlines are open. The fall 2014 application fee was $55. Notification is sent on a rolling basis. Applications are accepted on-line. <u>Transfer Students:</u> 1676 transfer students enrolled in 2013-2014. Applicants must have a minimum college GPA of 2.0 (2.4 for nonresidents) and be in good standing at the previously attended institution. Those with fewer than 56 transferable semester units must submit ACT or SAT scores. 45 of 180 credits required for the bachelor's degree must be completed at CSUSB. <u>International Students:</u> There are 557 international students enrolled. The school actively recruits these students.

<u>ADMISSIONS:</u> Olivia Rosas, Director. Web: *www.csusb.edu*

<u>FINANCIAL AID:</u> The FAFSA is required. Check with the school for current application deadlines.

CALIFORNIA STATE UNIVERSITY, SAN MARCOS (*The complete profile is made available exclusively on our website, www. barronspac.com*)

CALIFORNIA STATE UNIVERSITY, STANISLAUS
B-3

www.csustan.edu

Turlock, CA 95382   (209) 667-3070

Fax: (209) 667-3788	Email: outreach_help_desk@csustan.edu
Full-time: 1610 men, 3010 women	Faculty: IIA, av$
Part-time: 665 men, 1355 women	Ph.D.s: n/av
Graduate: 520 men, 1190 women	Student/Faculty: n/av
Year: 4-1-4, summer session	Tuition: $6582 ($15,500)
Room & Board: $12,000	Freshman Class: n/av
	CEEB CODE: 4713
Application Deadline: n/av	**COMPETITIVE**

California State University, Stanislaus, founded in 1957, is a state-supported institution offering undergraduate and graduate programs in liberal and fine arts, business, health science, and teacher preparation. The figures in the above capsule and in this survey are approximate. There are 3 undergraduate schools and 1 graduate school. In addition to regional accreditation, CSU Stanislaus has baccalaureate program accreditation with AACSB, CSWE, NASAD, NASM, and NCATE. The 228-acre campus is in a suburban area in the San Joaquin Valley, about 100 miles south of San Francisco. Including any residence halls, there are 26 buildings.

STUDENT LIFE: 94% of undergraduates are from California. Others are from 21 states, 46 foreign countries, and Canada. 95% are from public schools. 43% are White; 27% Hispanic; 11% Asian American. <u>Male To Female Ratio:</u> 2.0:1. The average age of freshmen is 18; all undergraduates, 25. 18% do not continue beyond their first year; 50% remain to graduate. <u>Housing:</u> 650 students can be accommodated in college housing, which includes coed dorms and on-campus apartments. On-campus housing is available on a first-come and first-served basis. 90% of students commute. All students may keep cars.

FACULTY/CLASSROOMS: 53% of faculty are male; 47% are female. All teach undergraduates. No introductory courses are taught by graduate students.

PROGRAMS OF STUDY: CSU Stanislaus confers B.A., B.S., B.F.A. and B.M. degrees. Master's degrees are also awarded. Bachelor's degrees are awarded in AGRICULTURE (agriculture), BIOLOGICAL SCIENCE (biology/biological science), BUSINESS (business administration and management), COMMUNICATIONS AND THE ARTS (art, art history and appreciation, communications, dramatic arts, English, fine arts, French, music, music performance, and Spanish), COMPUTER AND PHYSICAL SCIENCE (applied physics, chemistry, computer science, geology, information sciences and systems, mathematics, physical sciences, and physics), EDUCATION (health education and physical education), HEALTH PROFESSIONS (nursing), SOCIAL SCIENCE (anthropology, child psychology/ development, cognitive science, criminal justice, developmental psychology, economics, ethnic studies, geography, history, interdisciplinary studies, liberal arts/general studies, philosophy, political science/government, psychology, social science, and sociology). Liberal studies, business administration, and psychology have the largest enrollments.

ACTIVITIES: 3% of men belong to 1 local and 4 national fraternities; 3% of women belong to 5 local and 3 national sororities. There are 64 groups on campus, including art, band, cheerleading, choir, chorale, chorus, computers, dance, drama, ethnic, gay, honors, international, jazz band, newspaper, opera, orchestra, photography, political, professional, radio and TV, religious, social, social service, student government, and symphony. Popular campus events include Warrior Day, College Day, and Wellness Day. <u>Sports:</u> There are 6 intercollegiate sports for men and 6 for women, and 9 intramural sports for men and 9 for women. Facilities include a field house, 2300-seat gym, softball and baseball diamonds, soccer field, tennis courts, an all-weather track, swimming pool, and a weight room.

SERVICES: Counseling and information services are available, as is tutoring in most subjects. There is a reader service for the blind, and remedial math, reading, and writing. <u>Library/Resources:</u> The library contains 363,479 volumes, 1.3 million microform items, 4,288 audio/ video tapes/CDs/DVDs, and subscribes to 1,398 periodicals including electronic. Computerized library services include interlibrary loans, database searching, Internet access, and Wi-Fi capability. Special learning facilities include an art gallery, radio station, laser lab, marine sciences station, greenhouse, art gallery, main stage theater, recital hall, observatory, art complex, and distance learning studios. <u>Physically Challenged Students:</u> 99% of the campus is accessible. Facilities include wheelchair ramps, elevators, special parking, specially equipped restrooms, lowered drinking fountains, lowered telephones, special housing. <u>Special:</u> Numerous co-op programs and internships are offered. Cross-registration with the Higher Education Consortium of Central California, study abroad, work-study programs, nondegree study, an accelerated degree program, B.A.-B.S. degrees, dual majors, student-designed majors, and pass/fail options are also available. There are 10 national honor societies, including Phi Beta Kappa, a freshman honors program, and 99 departmental honors programs. <u>Visiting:</u> There are regularly scheduled orientations for prospective students. There are guides for informal visits and visitors may sit in on classes. To schedule a visit, contact the University Outreach. <u>Campus Safety and Security:</u> Measures include 24-hour foot and vehicle patrol, self-defense education, and security escort services. There are shuttle buses, emergency telephones, lighted pathways/sidewalks, CPR and first-aid training.

REQUIREMENTS: Admission is based on an eligibility index that weights GPA and the SAT or ACT scores. Applicants with a GPA of 3.0 (3.4 for nonresidents) are exempt from test score requirements. Applicants should be graduates of an accredited secondary school.

Preparatory course work should include 4 years of English, 3 of math, 2 each of foreign language, history/social sciences, and lab science, 1 of visual and performing arts, and 1 academic elective. A GPA of 3.0 is required. AP and CLEP credits are accepted. Important factors in the admissions decision are advanced placement or honors courses, evidence of special talent, and geographical diversity. To graduate, students must complete at least 120 semester units, including 51 in the general education program and 40 in upper-division courses, with a minimum GPA of 2.0. Distribution requirements consist of 12 units of Social, Economic, and Political Institutions and Human Behavior, 9 each of Communication Skills, Natural Sciences and Mathematics, and Humanities, and 3 of Individual Resources for Modern Living. **Procedure:** Freshmen are admitted to all sessions. Entrance exams should be taken in fall of the senior year. There is a rolling admissions plan. Check with the school for current application deadlines. The application fee is $55. Notification is sent on a rolling basis. Applications are accepted on-line. **Transfer Students:** Applicants must have a college GPA of 2.0 (2.4 for nonresidents) and have completed their lower-division general education English and math courses. Those with fewer than 60 transferable semester credits must meet freshman entrance requirements. 30 of 120 credits required for the bachelor's degree must be completed at CSU Stanislaus. **International Students:** They must take the TOEFL. They must also take the SAT or ACT or EPT/ELM.

ADMISSIONS: Lisa Bernardo, Director of Admissions and Records. E-Mail: *outreach_help_desk@csustan.edu* Web: *www.csustan.edu*

FINANCIAL AID: The FAFSA, and the SAAC for California residents, is required. Check with the school for current application deadlines.

CHAPMAN UNIVERSITY — D-5
www.chapman.edu

Orange, CA 92866

(714) 997-6711
(888) CU-APPLY

Fax: (714) 997-6713
Email: admit@chapman.edu

Full-time: 2393 men, 3611 women
Faculty: 348; IIA, ++$

Part-time: 144 men, 133 women
Ph.D.s: 87%

Graduate: 775 men, 1076 women
Student/Faculty: 14 to 1

Year: 4-1-4, summer session
Tuition: $45,393

Room & Board: $12,954
Freshman Class: 12507 applied, 5883 accepted, 1422 enrolled

SAT CR/M/W: 600/600/610 ACT: 27
CEEB CODE: 4047

Application Deadline: January 15
VERY COMPETITIVE+

Chapman University, founded in 1861, is one of the oldest, most prestigious private universities in California. Chapman's picturesque campus is located in the heart of Orange County, one of the nation's most exciting centers of arts, business, science and technology, and draws outstanding students from across the United States and around the world. Known for its blend of liberal arts and professional programs, Chapman University encompasses seven schools and colleges. The university's mission is to provide personalized education of distinction that leads to inquiring, ethical and productive lives as global citizens. There are 7 undergraduate schools and 8 graduate schools. In addition to regional accreditation, Chapman has baccalaureate program accreditation with AACSB and NASM. The 79-acre campus is in a suburban area 35 miles southeast of Los Angeles. Including any residence halls, there are 52 buildings.

STUDENT LIFE: 74% of undergraduates are from California. Others are from 45 states, 84 foreign countries, and Canada. 60% are White; 14% Hispanic. 30% are Catholic; 25% Protestant; 18% claim no religious affiliation; 17% Other Christian, Buddhist, Baha'i, Hindu, and Muslim. **Male To Female Ratio:** 1.5:1. The average age of freshmen is 18; all undergraduates, 20. 9% do not continue beyond their first year; 74% remain to graduate. **Housing:** 1958 students can be accommodated in college housing, which includes coed dorms, on-campus apartments, off-campus apartments, and married student housing. In addition, there are special-interest houses. On-campus housing is guaranteed for the freshman year only, is available on a first-come, first-served basis, and is available on a lottery system for upperclass-

men. Priority is given to out-of-town students. 68% of students commute. All students may keep cars.

FACULTY/CLASSROOMS: 58% of faculty are male; 42% are female. 89% teach undergraduates. Graduate students teach 2% of introductory courses. The average class size in an introductory lecture is 24 and in a laboratory is 24.

PROGRAMS OF STUDY: Chapman confers B.A., B.S., B.F.A. and B.M. degrees. Master's and doctoral degrees are also awarded. Bachelor's degrees are awarded in BIOLOGICAL SCIENCE (biochemistry and biology/biological science), BUSINESS (accounting and business administration and management), COMMUNICATIONS AND THE ARTS (acting, art, art history and appreciation, broadcasting, communications, creative writing, dance, dramatic arts, English, film arts, film, television and digital media, French, graphic design, keyboard - piano concentration, music, music performance, music theory and composition, playwriting/screenwriting, public relations, Spanish, strategic communication, and theatre studies), COMPUTER AND PHYSICAL SCIENCE (chemistry, computer science, digital arts/technology, information sciences and systems, mathematics, physics, and software engineering), EDUCATION (athletic training, education, and music education), ENGINEERING AND ENVIRONMENTAL DESIGN (environmental science), HEALTH PROFESSIONS (health science and kinesiology), SOCIAL SCIENCE (economics, history, peace studies, philosophy, political science/government, psychology, religion, social work, and sociology). Business, computational science, and history are the strongest academically. Business, communication studies, and psychology have the largest enrollments.

ACTIVITIES: 28% of men belong to 9 national fraternities; 38% of women belong to 8 national sororities. Groups on campus include art, band, cheerleading, choir, chorale, chorus, computers, dance, debate, drama, environmental, ethnic, film, forensics, gay, honors, international, jazz band, literary magazine, musical theater, newspaper, opera, orchestra, pep band, photography, political, professional, radio and TV, religious, social, social service, student government, symphony, and yearbook. **Sports:** There are 11 intercollegiate sports for men and 11 for women, and 4 intramural sports for men and 4 for women. Facilities include gym, weight room, soccer/football field, aquatic center, tennis courts, baseball and softball fields are also available for student use nearby in the city of Orange. **Graduates:** From July 1, 2013 to June 30, 2014, 1352 bachelor's degrees were awarded. The most popular majors were business administration (17%), communication studies (10%), and film studies (10%). In an average class, 2% graduate in 3 years or less, 58% graduate in 4 years or less, 71% graduate in 5 years or less, and 74% graduate in 6 years or less.

SERVICES: Counseling and information services are available, as is tutoring in most subjects. There is a reader service for the blind, and remedial math, reading, and writing. **Library/Resources:** The 2 libraries contain 322,793 volumes, 689,946 microform items, 25,594 audio/video tapes/CDs/DVDs, and subscribe to 62,917 periodicals including electronic. Computerized library services include interlibrary loans, database searching, Internet access, and Wi-Fi capability. Special learning facilities include a radio station, food science sensory lab, and economic sciences lab. **Physically Challenged Students:** 75% of the campus is accessible. Facilities include wheelchair ramps, elevators, special parking, specially equipped restrooms, special class scheduling, lowered drinking fountains, lowered telephones, and special housing. **Special:** Internship programs are available. Students are encouraged to study abroad for a semester or spend a semester in Washington, D.C. Dual and student-designed majors are possible. A general studies degree, B.A.-B.S. degrees, nondegree study options, and pass/fail options are also permitted. A 3-2 engineering degree with the University of California, Irvine, is possible. There are 13 national honor societies and a freshman honors program. **Visiting:** There are regularly scheduled orientations for prospective students, consisting of Fall and Spring Campus Exploration Day events. Weekday appointments and campus tours are also available. There are guides for informal visits, and visitors may sit in on classes. To schedule a visit, contact the Office of Admissions at (888) CU-APPLY. **Campus Safety and Security:** Measures include 24-hour foot and vehicle patrol, emergency notification system, self-defense education, and security escort services. There are shuttle buses, emergency telephones, lighted pathways/sidewalks, controlled access to dorms/residences, rape awareness, and victim assistance programs.

REQUIREMENTS: The SAT or ACT is required. The ACT Optional Writing test is also required. Applicants should be graduates of accredited high schools or have earned the GED. Secondary preparation should include 4 years of English, foreign language, math, and social science; and 2 years of science. Prospective art or music majors should show some preparation in those fields. A personal essay is required. An on-campus interview is recommended. Entry to the film school requires portfolio acceptance. Dance performance and theater performance require audition. AP and CLEP credits are accepted. Important factors in the admissions decision are advanced placement or honors courses, evidence of special talent, and leadership record. Students in the baccalaureate program must complete a total of 124 credits with at least a 2.0 GPA. The general education program includes courses in artistic inquiry, natural science inquiry, quantitative inquiry, social inquiry, values and ethical inquiry, and written inquiry. Freshman foundation, global citizenship, and interdisciplinary courses are also required. **Procedure:** Freshmen are admitted fall and spring. Entrance exams should be taken by fall of the senior year. Applications should be filed by January 15 for fall entry; November 1 for spring entry, along with a $65 fee. Notifications are sent March 15. 455 applicants were on the 2014 waiting list; 92 were admitted. Applications are accepted on-line. **Transfer Students:** 358 transfer students enrolled in 2013-2014. Transfer applicants should have completed at least 12 credits of transferable college work with a 2.25 minimum GPA. High school records and SAT or ACT scores should be submitted if fewer than 30 transferable credits have been completed. 48 of 124 credits required for the bachelor's degree must be completed at Chapman. **International Students:** There are 256 international students enrolled. The school actively recruits these students. They must take the TOEFL with a minimum score of 550 on the paper-based TOEFL (PBT) or 80 on the Internet-based version (iBT). They must also take the SAT or ACT.

ADMISSIONS: 47% of the 2014-2015 applicants were accepted. The SAT scores for the 2014-2015 freshman class were: Critical Reading--6% below 500, 41% between 500 and 599, 45% between 600 and 699, and 8% between 700 and 800; Math--4% below 500, 41% between 500 and 599, 45% between 600 and 699, and 10% between 700 and 800; Writing--4% below 500, 38% between 500 and 599, 46% between 600 and 699, and 12% between 700 and 800. The ACT scores were 2% below 21, 12% between 21 and 23, 28% between 24 and 26, 26% between 27 and 28, and 33% above 28. **Admissions Contact:** Mike Drummy, Assistant Vice President and Chief Admission Officer. E-Mail: *admit@chapman.edu* Web: *www.chapman.edu*

FINANCIAL AID: Chapman is a member of CSS. The FAFSA and the state aid form are required. The priority date for freshman financial aid applications for fall entry is March 2.

CLAREMONT COLLEGES, THE

The Claremont Colleges, is a consortium of five undergraduate liberal arts colleges and two graduate institutions, established in 1925, is a private system in California. It is governed by the council of the Claremont Colleges, whose chief administrator is the chief executive officer. The primary goal of the system is to provide outstanding instruction to its undergraduate, graduate, and professional students. The total student enrollment is usually 6,900 and 3600 faculty members. Altogether there are 194 baccalaureate, 24 master's, and 15 doctoral programs offered in Claremont Colleges. Profiles of the 4-year campuses are included in this section.

CLAREMONT MCKENNA COLLEGE	D-5
www.cmc.edu	
Claremont, CA 91711	**(909) 621-8088**
Fax: (909) 621-8516	Email: admission@cmc.edu
Full-time: 673 men, 625 women	Faculty: 145; IIB, ++$
Part-time: 3 women	Ph.D.s: 98%
Graduate: 21 men, 2 women	Student/Faculty: 8 to 1
Year: semesters	Tuition: $47,395
Room & Board: $14,820	Freshman Class: 6043 applied, 651 accepted, 327 enrolled
SAT CR/M/W: 710/740/710 ACT: 32	CEEB CODE: 4054
Application Deadline: January 1	MOST COMPETITIVE

Established in 1946, Claremont McKenna College (CMC) is a highly selective, independent, coeducational, residential, undergraduate liberal arts college with a curricular emphasis on economics, government, and public affairs. Unlike so many other colleges, which champion either a traditional liberal arts education or the acquisition of professional and technical skills, CMC builds bridges between the two. By combining the intellectual breadth of the liberal arts with the more pragmatic concerns of public affairs, based on principles established by founding President George C. S. Benson, CMC helps students acquire the vision, skills, and values they will need to lead society. As expressed in the College's mission statement CMC seeks to "educate its students for thoughtful and productive lives and responsible leadership in business, government, and the professions, and to support faculty and student scholarship that contribute to intellectual vitality and the understanding of public policy issues." There is one graduate school. The 69-acre campus is in a suburban area 35 miles east of downtown Los Angeles.

STUDENT LIFE: 63% of undergraduates are from out of state, mostly the West. Students are from 46 states, 31 foreign countries, and Canada. 43% are White; 17% Foreign; 12% Hispanic. **Male To Female Ratio:** 0.9:1. The average age of freshmen is 18; all undergraduates, 20. 4% do not continue beyond their first year; 96% remain to graduate. **Housing:** 1183 students can be accommodated in college housing, which includes single-sex and coed dorms and on-campus apartments. Substance-free housing. On-campus housing is guaranteed for the freshman year only and is available on a lottery system for upperclassmen. 97% of students live on campus. Upperclassmen may keep cars.

FACULTY/CLASSROOMS: 67% of faculty are male; 33% are female. No introductory courses are taught by graduate students. The average class size in a regular course is 18.

PROGRAMS OF STUDY: CMC confers B.A. degrees. Master's degrees are also awarded. Bachelor's degrees are awarded in AGRICULTURE (environmental studies), BIOLOGICAL SCIENCE (biochemistry, biology/biological science, biophysics, molecular biology, and neurosciences), BUSINESS (accounting and management engineering), COMMUNICATIONS AND THE ARTS (classics, film arts, French, literature, media arts, Spanish, and theatre arts), COMPUTER AND PHYSICAL SCIENCE (chemistry, mathematics, physics, and science and management), ENGINEERING AND ENVIRONMENTAL DESIGN (environmental science), SOCIAL SCIENCE (African studies, American studies, Asian/Oriental studies, economics, Hispanic American studies, history, interdisciplinary studies, International relations, legal studies, Middle Eastern studies, philosophy, political science/government, psychology, and religion). Economics, international relations, and government have the largest enrollments.

ACTIVITIES: There are no fraternities or sororities. There are 200 groups on campus, including Army ROTC, band, chorale, communications, computers, dance, debate, drama, environmental, ethnic, film, gay, honors, international, jazz band, literary magazine, musical theater, newspaper, political, professional, religious, social, social service, student government, symphony, and yearbook. Popular campus events include International Festival, Athenaeum Speakers, and Monte Carlo Night (Homecoming). **Sports:** There are 10 intercollegiate sports for men and 11 for women, and 8 intramural sports for men and 8 for women. Facilities include basketball courts, a weight room, a fitness center, squash, volleyball, a track and football field, an aquatic center, tennis courts, baseball, softball, lacrosse, and soccer fields, an archery range, and squash and volleyball courts. **Graduates:** From July 1, 2013 to June 30, 2014, 354 bachelor's degrees were awarded. The most popular majors were economics (27%), government (14%), and psychology (14%). 73 companies recruited on campus in 2013-2014. In an average class, 86% graduate in 4 years or less, 89% graduate in 5 years or less, and 90% graduate in 6 years or less.

SERVICES: The Center for Writing and Public Discourse offers writing assistance and specialized workshops. **Library/Resources:** The library contains 1.1 million volumes, 980,340 microform items, and 13,171 audio/video tapes/CDs/DVDs. Computerized library services include interlibrary loans, database searching, Internet access, and Wi-Fi capability. **Physically Challenged Students:** All of the campus is accessible. Facilities include wheelchair ramps, elevators, special parking, specially equipped restrooms. The campus complies with ADA requirements and reasonably accommodates students with physical disabilities as necessary to meet their access needs. **Special:** Internships, Washington DC and Silicon Valley programs, BA/MA program in Finance, 3-2 engineering degree, cross registration with the Claremont Colleges, study abroad programs, ten research institutes, and the Robert Day Scholars program. There is a chapter of Phi Beta Kappa. **Visiting:** There are regularly scheduled orientations for prospective students. There are guides for informal visits, visitors may sit in on classes, and stay overnight. To schedule a visit, contact the Office of Admission at (909) 621-8088. **Campus Safety and Security:** Measures include 24-hour foot and vehicle patrol, emergency notification system, and security escort services. There are emergency telephones, lighted pathways/sidewalks, and controlled access to dorms/residences.

REQUIREMENTS: The SAT or ACT is required. The ACT Optional Writing test is also required. AP credits are accepted. All students must complete 32 courses (128 semester hours), including General Education, major and grade-point requirements. **Procedure:** Freshmen are admitted fall. Entrance exams should be taken no later than fall of senior year. There is a early decision plan. Early decision applications should be filed by November 1; regular applications, by January 1 for fall entry; and November 1 for spring entry, along with a $60 fee. Notification of early decision is sent December 15; regular decision, April 1. 181 early decision candidates were accepted for the 2014-2015 class. 614 applicants were on the 2014 waiting list; 38 were admitted. Applications are accepted on-line. **Transfer Students:** 21 transfer students enrolled in 2013-2014. 64 of 128 credits required for the bachelor's degree must be completed at CMC. **International Students:** There are 215 international students enrolled. The school actively recruits these students. They must take the TOEFL with a minimum score of 600 on the paper-based TOEFL (PBT) or 100 on the Internet-based version (iBT). They must also take the SAT or ACT.

ADMISSIONS: 11% of the 2014-2015 applicants were accepted. The SAT scores for the 2014-2015 freshman class were: Critical Reading--2% between 500 and 599, 41% between 600 and 699, and 57% between 700 and 800; Math--3% between 500 and 599, 26% between 600 and 699, and 71% between 700 and 800; Writing--1% between 500 and 599, 38% between 600 and 699, and 61% between 700 and 800. **Admissions Contact:** Georgette R. DeVeres, AVP and Dean of Admission and Financial Aid. E-Mail: *admission@cmc.edu* Web: *www.cmc.edu*

FINANCIAL AID: In 2014-2015, 43% of all full-time freshmen and 45% of continuing full-time students received some form of financial aid. 39% of all full-time freshmen and 39% of continuing full-time students received need-based aid. The average freshman award was $41,556. Need-based scholarships or need-based grants averaged $38,850; need-based self-help aid (loans and jobs) averaged $4,456; and other non-need-based awards and non-need-based scholarships averaged $9,829. The average financial indebtedness of the 2014 graduate was $23,232. CMC is a member of CSS. The CSS/Profile, FAFSA, and the state aid form are required. The priority date for freshman financial aid applications for fall entry is January 1. The deadline for filing freshman financial aid applications for fall entry is February 1.

COGSWELL POLYTECHNICAL COLLEGE   **B-3**
www.cogswell.edu

Sunnyvale, CA 94089	(408) 541-0100, ext.147
	(800)-264-7955
Fax: (408) 747-0764	Email: admissions@cogswell.edu
Full-time: 142 men, 45 women	Faculty: 11
Part-time: 87 men, 14 women	Ph.D.s: 35%
Graduate: n/av	Student/Faculty: 12 to 1
Year: semesters, summer session	Tuition: $19,668
Room & Board: $10,863	Freshman Class: 146 applied, 79 accepted, 45 enrolled
SAT or ACT: recommended	CEEB CODE: 4057
Application Deadline: n/av	COMPETITIVE

Strategically located in Silicon Valley and with over one hundred and twenty years of academic history, Cogswell College provides accredited higher education that empowers students to innovate through the integration of art, engineering and entrepreneurship. The figures in the above capsule and in this profile are approximate. There is 1 undergraduate school and 1 graduate school. The 4-acre campus is in a suburban area 40 miles south of San Francisco in California's Silicon Valley. Including any residence halls, there is 1 building.

STUDENT LIFE: 88% of undergraduates are from California. Others are from 13 states, and 2 foreign countries. 65% are from public schools. 49% are White; 15% Hispanic. The average age of freshmen is 19; all undergraduates, 28. 29% do not continue beyond their first year; 71% remain to graduate. **Housing:** 70 students can be accommodated in college housing, which includes off-campus apartments. Arrangements can be made to accommodate students in private houses or at nearby corporate apartments. Alcohol is not permitted. All students commute. All students may keep cars.

FACULTY/CLASSROOMS: 65% of faculty are male; 35% are female. No introductory courses are taught by graduate students. The average class size in an introductory lecture is 15; in a laboratory is 8; and in a regular course is 25.

PROGRAMS OF STUDY: Cogswell College confers B.A.D.A.A., B.S.D.A.T., B.S.D.A.E., B.S.(Comp Eng), B.S.S.E., B.S.F.A., B.S.F.P.T. and B.A.E.I. degrees. Master's degrees are also awarded. Bachelor's degrees are awarded in BUSINESS (entrepreneurial studies), COMMUNICATIONS AND THE ARTS (animation, audio technology, and music technology), COMPUTER AND PHYSICAL SCIENCE (computer programming, digital arts/technology, and web technology), ENGINEERING AND ENVIRONMENTAL DESIGN (computer engineering and computer graphics), SOCIAL SCIENCE (fire control and safety technology and fire protection). Digital art and animation, digital audio technology, are the strongest academically, and have the largest enrollments.

ACTIVITIES: There are no fraternities or sororities. Groups on campus include art, computers, honors, international, jazz band, radio and TV, and student government. Popular campus events include Founders Day, Club Competitions, and Friday Concerts. **Sports:** There is no sports program at Cogswell College. Facilities include a game room, a student lounge, and access to community athletic facilities. **Graduates:** From July 1, 2013 to June 30, 2014, 47 bachelor's degrees were awarded. The most popular majors were digital art and animation (43%), fire administration (34%), and digital audio technology (15%). In an average class, 33% graduate in 4 years or less, 44% graduate in 5 years or less, and 55% graduate in 6 years or less.

SERVICES: There is remedial math and writing. On campus tutoring is available if needed for any subjects **Library/Resources:** The library contains 103,000 volumes, 250 microform items, 831 audio/video tapes/CDs/DVDs, and subscribes to 16 periodicals including electronic. Computerized library services include database searching. Special learning facilities include an art gallery, radio station, drawing and sculpture studios, digital arts labs, audio labs, and a recording studio. **Physically Challenged Students:** Facilities include wheelchair ramps, special parking, specially equipped restrooms, special class scheduling, lowered drinking fountains, and lowered telephones. **Special:** Cogswell offers various internships and work-study programs. The college administers the Degree at a Distance Program (DDP) for the Fire Service program for Arizona, California, and Nevada, through which nonresident students can earn a B.S. in Fire Administration or Fire Prevention and Technology. There is a freshman honors program. **Visiting:** Visitors may sit in on classes. **Campus Safety and Security:** Measures include emergency notification system. There are emergency telephones, lighted pathways/sidewalks, controlled access to dorms/residences, an emergency evacuation plan, and maps in the classrooms.

REQUIREMENTS: The SAT or ACT is recommended. Applicants must be high school graduates or have the GED. Secondary preparation must include 3 years of English, 2 to 3 of math, including algebra, geometry, and trigonometry, and 1 year of science. Cogswell requires a personal essay and recommends a personal interview. A portfolio is required for computer and video imaging programs. A GPA of 2.7 is required. AP and CLEP credits are accepted. Important factors in the admissions decision are evidence of special talent, recommendations by school officials, and ability to finance college education. To graduate, students must complete a total of 120 to 131 credits with 18 to 27 in the major and have a 2.0 GPA. 45 to 56 credits in general education core courses are required, depending on the major, and include courses in English, math, natural sciences, social sciences, and humanities. **Procedure:** Freshmen are admitted to all sessions. There is a rolling admissions plan. Application deadlines are open. Applications are accepted on-line. **Transfer Students:** Applicants must have completed at least 12 college credits with a 2.2 GPA. An interview is recommended. 40 of 120 credits required for the bachelor's degree must be completed at Cogswell College. **International Students:** There are 11 international students enrolled. They must take the TOEFL with a minimum score of 525 on the paper-based TOEFL (PBT).

ADMISSIONS: 54% of the 2014-2015 applicants were accepted. **Admissions Contact:** Abraham Chacko, Director of Admissions. E-Mail: *admissions@cogswell.edu* Web: *www.cogswell.edu*

FINANCIAL AID: In 2014-2015, 77% of all full-time freshmen and 75% of continuing full-time students received some form of financial aid. 75% of all full-time freshmen and 72% of continuing full-time students received need-based aid. 4% of undergraduate students work part-time. Average annual earnings from campus work are $2500. The average financial indebtedness of the 2014 graduate was $22,352. Cogswell College is a member of CSS. The FAFSA and the college's own financial statement are required. The deadline for filing freshman financial aid applications for fall entry is March 1.

CONCORDIA UNIVERSITY IRVINE   D-5
www.cui.edu

Irvine, CA 92612	(949) 854-8002, ext. 1118
	(800) 229-1200
Fax: (949) 854-6894	Email: scott.rhodes@cui.edu
Full-time: 618 men, 974 women	Faculty: n/av
Part-time: 39 men, 107 women	Ph.D.s: n/av
Graduate: 837 men, 944 women	Student/Faculty: n/av
Year: semesters, summer session	Tuition: $26,800
Room & Board: $8590	Freshman Class: n/av
SAT or ACT: required	CEEB CODE: 4069
Application Deadline: n/av	**VERY COMPETITIVE**

Concordia University, founded in 1972, is a private liberal arts college affiliated with the Lutheran Church-Missouri Synod. Figures in the above capsule and in this profile are approximate. There are 5 undergraduate schools and 4 graduate schools. The 70-acre campus is in a suburban area 40 miles south of Los Angeles. Including any residence halls, there are 26 buildings.

STUDENT LIFE: 89% of undergraduates are from California. Others are from 34 states, 18 foreign countries, and Canada. 66% are White; 13% Hispanic. 16% are Catholic; 15% Non-denominational. **Male To Female Ratio:** 1.4:1. The average age of freshmen is 18; all undergraduates, 22. 73% remain to graduate. **Housing:** 1077 students can be accommodated in college housing, which includes single-sex dorms. On-campus housing is guaranteed for all 4 years. 69% of students live on campus; of those, 95% remain on campus on weekends. All students may keep cars.

FACULTY/CLASSROOMS: 63% of faculty are male; 37% are female. No introductory courses are taught by graduate students.

PROGRAMS OF STUDY: Concordia Irvine confers B.A. degrees. Associate and master's degrees are also awarded. Bachelor's degrees are awarded in BIOLOGICAL SCIENCE (biology/biological science), BUSINESS (business administration and management), COMMUNICATIONS AND THE ARTS (art, communications, dramatic arts, English, film arts, and music), COMPUTER AND PHYSICAL SCIENCE (chemistry and mathematics), EDUCATION (Christian education and early childhood education), HEALTH PROFESSIONS (exercise science), SOCIAL SCIENCE (behavioral science, biblical languages, history, humanities, international studies, liberal arts/general studies, political science/government, psychology, and theological studies). Business administration, education and social science are the strongest academically.

ACTIVITIES: There are no fraternities or sororities. There are 20 groups on campus, including art, choir, chorale, chorus, communications, dance, debate, drama, ethnic, film, forensics, honors, literary magazine, newspaper, political, radio and TV, religious, social, social service, student government, and yearbook. Popular campus events include Closing Banquet, Christmas Dance and Oktoberfest. **Sports:** There are 9 intercollegiate sports for men and 10 for women, and 7 intramural sports for men and 6 for women. Facilities include a 1800-seat gym, soccer field, baseball/softball diamond, volleyball, tennis, and racquetball courts, track field, weight room, dance room, team rooms, and locker rooms.

SERVICES: Counseling and information services are available, as is tutoring in math, chemistry, critical thinking, Spanish, biology and calculus. **Library/Resources:** The library contains 82,600 volumes, 54,550 microform items, 2,000 audio/video tapes/CDs/DVDs, and subscribes to 10,513 periodicals including electronic. Computerized library services include interlibrary loans, database searching, and Internet access. Special learning facilities include an art gallery, radio station, newspaper. **Physically Challenged Students:** 90% of the campus is accessible. Facilities include wheelchair ramps, elevators, special parking, and specially equipped restrooms. **Special:** Cross-registration is possible with 9 Concordia University institutions nationwide. An accelerated degree program in either applied liberal arts or business administration and leadership. Internships, study abroad, and dual and student-designed majors are available. There are 6 national honor societies, a freshman honors program, and 2 departmental honors programs. **Visiting:** There are regularly scheduled orientations for prospective students. There are guides for informal visits, visitors may sit in on classes, and stay overnight. To schedule a visit, contact the Admission Office. **Campus Safety and Security:** Measures include 24-hour foot and vehicle patrol and security escort services. There are lighted pathways/sidewalks.

REQUIREMENTS: The SAT or ACT is required. Applicants should be high school graduates with 4 years of English, 3 each of math and science, and 2 each of social studies and a foreign language. The GED is accepted. A school reference is also required. A GPA of 2.8 is required. AP and CLEP credits are accepted. All students must complete 49 semester hours of general education requirements, including courses in humanities and fine arts, math and science, social science, religion, and exercise and sport science. A total of 128 credits is required to graduate. A GPA of 2.0 in major and program course work must be maintained. For the CU Accelerate program, 120 semester units are required to graduate. **Procedure:** Freshmen are admitted fall and spring. Entrance exams should be taken by the fall of the senior year. There are deferred admissions and rolling admissions plans. Check with the school for current application deadlines. The fall 2014 application fee was $50. Notification is sent on a rolling basis. Applications are accepted on-line. **Transfer Students:** A GPA of 2.3 is required in a minimum of 24 semester or 36 quarter units completed. An academic reference is required, as are official high school transcripts. 32 of 128 credits required for the bachelor's degree must be completed at Concordia Irvine. **International Students:** The school actively recruits these students. They must take the TOEFL. They must also take the SAT or ACT.

ADMISSIONS: Scott Rhodes, Executive Director of Admissions. E-Mail: *scott.rhodes@cui.edu* Web: *www.cui.edu*

FINANCIAL AID: The FAFSA and the college's own financial statement are required. Check with the school for current application deadlines.

DOMINICAN UNIVERSITY OF CALIFORNIA   B-3
www.dominican.edu

San Rafael, CA 94901	(888) 323-6763
	(888) 323-6763
Fax: (415) 485-3214	Email: enroll@dominican.edu
Full-time: 350 men, 1000 women	Faculty: IIA, +$
Part-time: 75 men, 200 women	Ph.D.s: 74%
Graduate: 215 men, 500 women	Student/Faculty: n/av
Year: semesters, summer session	Tuition: $37,350
Room & Board: $13,900	Freshman Class: n/av
SAT or ACT: required	CEEB CODE: 4284
Application Deadline: open	**COMPETITIVE**

Dominican University of California, founded in 1890, is an independent, international, learner-centered university of Catholic heritage. The figures in the above capsule and in this profile are approximate. There are 4 undergraduate schools and 4 graduate schools. The 80-acre campus is in a suburban area 12 miles north of San Francisco. Including any residence halls, there are 25 buildings.

STUDENT LIFE: 91% of undergraduates are from California. Others are from 31 states, 15 foreign countries, and Canada. 48% are from public schools. 33% are White; 25% Asian American; 18% Hispanic. 38% are Catholic. **Male To Female Ratio:** 2.7:1. The average age of freshmen is 18; all undergraduates, 24. 16% do not continue beyond their first year; 34% remain to graduate. **Housing:** 600 students can be accommodated in college housing, which includes coed dorms. On-campus housing is available on a first-come, first-served basis, and is available on a lottery system for upperclassmen. 55% of students commute. Upperclassmen may keep cars.

FACULTY/CLASSROOMS: 47% of faculty are male; 53% are female. All teach undergraduates, 75% do research, and 75% do both. No introductory courses are taught by graduate students. The average class size in an introductory lecture is 19; in a laboratory is 15; and in a regular course is 15.

PROGRAMS OF STUDY: Dominican confers B.A., B.S., B.F.A. and B.S.N. degrees. Master's degrees are also awarded. Bachelor's degrees are awarded in AGRICULTURE (environmental studies), BIOLOGICAL SCIENCE (biology/biological science), BUSINESS (business administration and management and international business management), COMMUNICATIONS AND THE ARTS (art, art history and appreciation, communications, creative writing, dance, English literature, graphic design, and music), HEALTH PROFESSIONS (nursing, occupational therapy, and premedicine), SOCIAL SCIENCE (history, humanities, international studies, liberal arts/general studies, political science/government, psychology, religion, and women's studies). Nursing, biology, psychology, and business management have the largest enrollments.

ACTIVITIES: There are no fraternities or sororities. There are 27 groups on campus, including art, band, cheerleading, choir, chorale, dance, drama, environmental, ethnic, film, gay, honors, international, jazz band, literary magazine, musical theater, newspaper, orchestra, photography, political, professional, radio and TV, religious, social service, and student government. Popular campus events include Shield Day (welcoming the freshman class), Boat Dance and Penguin Ball. **Sports:** There are 5 intercollegiate sports for men and 7 for women, and 5 intramural sports for men and 5 for women. Facilities include a gym, fitness center, 6-lane swimming pool, 2 full-sized basketball courts, a multipurpose room for dance and exercise classes, tennis courts, and a soccer field. **Graduates:** From July 1, 2013 to June 30, 2014, 283 bachelor's degrees were awarded. The most popular majors were nursing (27%), psychology (15%), and business (11%). In an average class, 44% graduate in 4 years or less, 46% graduate in 5 years or less, and 51% graduate in 6 years or less.

SERVICES: Counseling and information services are available, as is tutoring in most subjects, writing, math, chemistry, economics, time management, study skills, anatomy, physiology, algebra, and physics. There is a reader service for the blind, and remedial math and writing. **Library/Resources:** The library contains 92,536 volumes, 3,500 microform items, 1,640 audio/video tapes/CDs/DVDs, and subscribes to 597 periodicals including electronic. Computerized library services include interlibrary loans, database searching, Internet access, and Wi-Fi capability. Special learning facilities include an art gallery, radio station, a music library, and art history slide and print collection. **Physically Challenged Students:** 50% of the campus is accessible. Facilities include wheelchair ramps, elevators, special parking, specially equipped restrooms, special class scheduling, and lowered drinking fountains. **Special:** There is a semester interchange program with colleges in Michigan, Florida, or New York. Dominican also offers study abroad, dual majors for students with a 3.0 GPA or better, B.A.-B.S. degrees, student-designed majors, a Washington semester, internships, pass/fail options outside of major and general education courses, and an evening/weekend bachelor's degree program. There are 3 national honor societies, including Phi Beta Kappa, a freshman honors program, and 3 departmental honors programs. **Visiting:** There are regularly scheduled orientations for prospective students, including financial aid conferences, lunch on campus,

meeting with the prospective academic adviser, and a campus tour. There are guides for informal visits and visitors may sit in on classes. To schedule a visit, contact the Admissions Office. **Campus Safety and Security:** Measures include 24-hour foot and vehicle patrol, emergency notification system, and security escort services. There are emergency telephones, lighted pathways/sidewalks, and controlled access to dorms/residences.

REQUIREMENTS: The SAT or ACT is required. Applicants must be graduates of an accredited high school or have earned the GED. Secondary preparation must include 4 years of English, 2 each of math and a foreign language, and 1 each of lab science and history. An essay and a recommendation are required. An interview and a visit to the campus are highly recommended. Prospective music majors are encouraged to schedule an audition. AP and CLEP credits are accepted. Important factors in the admissions decision are recommendations by school officials, extracurricular activities record, and evidence of special talent. All students must complete 124 credit hours including at least 24 in upper-division work, with a minimum 2.0 GPA. Core requirements include a cultural heritage colloquium of 9 units, 6 units each in religion and first-year interdisciplinary studies, 3 to 4 units each of math and quantitative reasoning, natural science, social science, moral philosophy and ethics, and creative and performing arts, and 1 unit of information and research. Students must pass a computer competency test, and a senior thesis, project, recital, or comprehensive exam is required. **Procedure:** Freshmen are admitted fall and spring. Entrance exams should be taken in the late fall or early spring of the senior year. There are deferred admissions and rolling admissions plans. Application deadlines are open. Application fee is $50. Applications are accepted on-line. **Transfer Students:** 110 transfer students enrolled in 2013-2014. Applicants must have a 2.0 GPA at an accredited college. They must also submit official high school and college transcripts and a letter of recommendation from a professor, academic dean, or counselor. 30 of 124 credits required for the bachelor's degree must be completed at Dominican. **International Students:** There are 30 international students enrolled. The school actively recruits these students. They must take the TOEFL with a minimum score of 550 on the paper-based TOEFL (PBT) or 80 on the Internet-based version (iBT). They must also take the SAT or ACT.

ADMISSIONS: Rebecca Finn Kenney, Asst. VP of Undergraduate Admissions. E-Mail: *enroll@dominican.edu* Web: *www.dominican.edu*

FINANCIAL AID: In 2014-2015, 97% of all full-time freshmen and 85% of continuing full-time students received some form of financial aid. 70% of all full-time freshmen and 72% of continuing full-time students received need-based aid. The average freshman award was $34,561. Need-based scholarships or need-based grants averaged $14,006 ($28,922 maximum); need-based self-help aid (loans and jobs) averaged $4,646 ($7,375 maximum); non-need-based athletic scholarships averaged $2,567 ($6,000 maximum); and other non-need-based awards and non-need-based scholarships averaged $7,660 ($15,500 maximum). 17% of undergraduate students work part-time. Average annual earnings from campus work are $2254. The average financial indebtedness of the 2014 graduate was $19,092. Dominican is a member of CSS. The FAFSA and the college's own financial statement are required. Check with the school for current application deadlines.

FRESNO PACIFIC UNIVERSITY   C-3
www.fresno.edu

Fresno, CA 93702   (559) 453-2039
                                                      (800) 660-6089
Fax: (559) 453-2007   Email: ugadmis@fresno.edu
Full-time: 701 men, 1448 women   **Faculty:** IIA, --$
Part-time: 108 men, 182 women   **Ph.D.s:** n/av
Graduate: 320 men, 701 women   **Student/Faculty:** n/av
Year: semesters, summer session   **Tuition:** $25,236
Room & Board: $6900   **Freshman Class:** n/av
SAT or ACT: required   **CEEB CODE:** 4616
Application Deadline: n/av   **COMPETITIVE**

Fresno Pacific University, founded in 1944, is a private Christian liberal arts college offering both undergraduate and graduate degrees, affiliated with the Mennonite Brethren. Figures in the above capsule and in this profile are approximate. There are 4 undergraduate schools and 5 graduate schools. The 42-acre campus is in a suburban area 150 miles southeast of San Francisco. Including any residence halls, there are 20 buildings.

STUDENT LIFE: 97% of undergraduates are from California. Others are from 14 states, 12 foreign countries, and Canada. 86% are from public schools. 50% are White; 29% Hispanic. 79% are Protestant; 15% Catholic. **Male To Female Ratio:** 2.1:1. The average age of freshmen is 20; all undergraduates, 21. 20% do not continue beyond their first year; 62% remain to graduate. **Housing:** 550 students can be accommodated in college housing, which includes single-sex dorms, on-campus apartments, and off-campus apartments. In addition, there are special-interest houses. On-campus housing is available on a first-come, first-served basis, and is available on a lottery system for upperclassmen. Priority is given to out-of-town students. 51% of students commute. Alcohol is not permitted. All students may keep cars.

FACULTY/CLASSROOMS: 66% of faculty are male; 34% are female. 78% teach undergraduates. No introductory courses are taught by graduate students. The average class size in a laboratory is 14 and in a regular course is 18.

PROGRAMS OF STUDY: FPU confers B.A., and B.S. degrees. Associate and master's degrees are also awarded. Bachelor's degrees are awarded in BIOLOGICAL SCIENCE (biology/biological science), BUSINESS (accounting, business administration and management, and sports management), COMMUNICATIONS AND THE ARTS (English, music, and Spanish), COMPUTER AND PHYSICAL SCIENCE (chemistry, mathematics, and natural sciences), EDUCATION (English education, mathematics education, music education, physical education, science education, and social science education), ENGINEERING AND ENVIRONMENTAL DESIGN (environmental science), HEALTH PROFESSIONS (premedicine), SOCIAL SCIENCE (history, ministries, missions, philosophy, prelaw, psychology, religion, social science, and social work). Business, education and religion are the strongest academically. Business, education and psychology have the largest enrollments.

ACTIVITIES: There are no fraternities or sororities. There are 20 groups on campus, including art, cheerleading, choir, chorale, chorus, communications, dance, drama, ethnic, honors, international, jazz band, newspaper, pep band, political, professional, religious, social, social service, and student government. Popular campus events include Carol Sing, Winter Ball, and Junior/Senior Banquet. **Sports:** There are 8 intercollegiate sports for men and 8 for women, and 9 intramural sports for men and 9 for women. Facilities include a gym, 3 soccer fields, swimming pool, track and field facility, weight room, 2 racquetball courts, and 7 tennis courts.

SERVICES: Counseling and information services are available, as is tutoring in every subject. There is a reader service for the blind, remedial math, reading, and writing, including audio books. **Library/Resources:** The library contains 197,532 volumes, 315,000 microform items, 7,840 audio/video tapes/CDs/DVDs, and subscribes to 3,200 periodicals including electronic. Computerized library services include interlibrary loans, database searching, and Internet access. **Physically Challenged Students:** All of the campus is accessible. Facilities include wheelchair ramps, elevators, special parking, specially equipped restrooms, lowered drinking fountains, lowered telephones, and special housing. **Special:** Accelerated degrees and internships are available as is a 1-semester cooperative program with the University of California, Davis. Cross-registration is possible with San Joaquin College of Law and California State University, Fresno. A B.A. in management and organizational development is offered to working adults. Other off-campus learning opportunities include programs in American studies in Washington, D.C., urban studies in Chicago, and study abroad in Israel, Japan, and Costa Rica, and at Brethren Colleges in England, Spain, France, Germany, or China. There are 2 national honor societies, a freshman honors program, and 1 departmental honors program. **Visiting:** There are regularly scheduled orientations for prospective students. There are guides for informal visits, visitors may sit in on classes, and stay overnight. To schedule a visit, contact the Admissions Office at (559) 453-2000. **Campus Safety and Security:** Measures include 24-hour foot and

vehicle patrol, self-defense education, and security escort services. There are shuttle buses, emergency telephones, lighted pathways/sidewalks, 24-hour CCTV monitored in real-time closed-circuit security cameras. 16 cameras create a virtual perimeter patrol of the campus with 5 emergency telephones and 8 regular telephones.

REQUIREMENTS: The SAT or ACT is required. Applicants should be graduates of an accredited high school or have the GED. Required secondary preparation includes 4 years of college prep English, 2 years of social studies, algebra 1 and 2, and geometry, and at least 1 year of a lab science. The college recommends that applicants also take courses in art, music, and 2 years of the same foreign language, all with a grade of C or better. An essay is required, and an audition is recommended for prospective music majors. A GPA of 3.1 is required. AP and CLEP credits are accepted. Important factors in the admissions decision are recommendations by school officials, advanced placement or honors courses, and extracurricular activities record. Students must complete 124 semester units, 40 of which are in upper-division courses, with at least a 2.0 GPA. General education requirements include a biblical studies/world civilization series, and 2 courses each in humanities, natural sciences, social sciences, and phys ed and math. Students are required to attend College Hour, a twice-weekly program of lectures, films, and concerts. Students are encouraged to volunteer 2 hours of community service per week. Several majors require internships. **Procedure:** Freshmen are admitted fall and spring. Entrance exams should be taken during the fall of their senior year. There are early admissions and rolling admissions plans. Check with the school for current application deadlines. The application fee is $40. Notification is sent on a rolling basis. Applications are accepted on-line. **Transfer Students:** Applicants should have completed at least 24 transferable units of college work with a 2.4 GPA. Those with fewer credits may apply any time but must meet freshman admission requirements. The SAT or ACT scores are recommended. 30 of 124 credits required for the bachelor's degree must be completed at FPU. **International Students:** The school actively recruits these students. They must take the TOEFL.

ADMISSIONS: 4 freshmen graduated first in their class. **Admissions Contact:** Yammilette Rodriguez, Undergraduate College Admission. E-Mail: *ugadmis@fresno.edu* Web: *www.fresno.edu*

FINANCIAL AID: The FAFSA is required. Check with the school for current application deadlines.

GOLDEN GATE UNIVERSITY   B-3
www.ggu.edu

San Francisco, CA 94105

(415) 442-7800
(800) 448-4968

Fax: (415) 442-7807
Email: info@ggu.edu

Full-time: 85 men, 110 women
Part-time: 215 men, 235 women
Graduate: 1555 men, 1795 women
Year: varies, summer session
Room & Board: n/av

Faculty: n/av
Ph.D.s: n/av
Student/Faculty: n/av
Tuition: $17,000
Freshman Class: n/av
CEEB CODE: 4329

Application Deadline: n/av

COMPETITIVE

Golden Gate University, founded in 1901, is a private, independent, commuter institution offering undergraduate and graduate degrees in business administration, accounting, human and social sciences, and special programs. The figures given in the above capsule and in this profile are approximate. There are 3 undergraduate schools and 4 graduate schools. The 1-acre campus is in an urban area in San Francisco. Including any residence halls, there are 2 buildings.

STUDENT LIFE: 51% are White; 19% Asian American; 18% Foreign. The average age of freshmen is 21; all undergraduates, 37. 12% do not continue beyond their first year. Alcohol is not permitted. All students commute.

FACULTY/CLASSROOMS: All teach undergraduates. No introductory courses are taught by graduate students. The average class size in an introductory lecture is 25; in a laboratory is 15; and in a regular course is 20.

PROGRAMS OF STUDY: Golden Gate confers B.S., and B.B.A.

degrees. Master's and doctoral degrees are also awarded. Bachelor's degrees are awarded in BUSINESS (accounting, banking and finance, human resources, and international business management), ENGINEERING AND ENVIRONMENTAL DESIGN (technological management). Accounting, finance, and information systems are the strongest academically. Finance, accounting, and management have the largest enrollments.

ACTIVITIES: There are 5 groups on campus, including ethnic, international, newspaper, professional, and social. Popular campus events include Commencement Ball. **Sports:** There is no sports program at Golden Gate.

SERVICES: Counseling and information services are available, as is tutoring in some subjects. There is remedial math, reading, and writing. **Library/Resources:** The 2 libraries contain 300,000 volumes, and subscribe to 2,500 periodicals including electronic. Computerized library services include interlibrary loans and database searching. **Physically Challenged Students:** All of the campus is accessible. Facilities include wheelchair ramps, elevators, special parking, and specially equipped restrooms. **Special:** The university offers cooperative programs, cross-registration with the San Francisco Consortium, internships, an accelerated degree program, dual majors, credit for military experience, nondegree study, and credit/no credit options. Also available are weekend classes and 10-week terms. **Visiting:** Visitors may sit in on classes. To schedule a visit, contact the Student Affairs Office. **Campus Safety and Security:** Measures include security escort services.

REQUIREMENTS: Applicants must be graduates of an accredited secondary school or have a GED. A GPA of 3.0 is required. AP and CLEP credits are accepted. A total of 123 trimester hours, with 21 to 33 in the major, are required to graduate. A minimum GPA of 2.0 is also required. **Procedure:** Freshmen are admitted fall, spring, and summer. There is a rolling admissions plan. Check with the school for current application deadlines. Notification is sent on a rolling basis. Applications are accepted on-line. **Transfer Students:** At least 24 transferable units and a 2.0 overall GPA are required. A minimum of 30 units out of 123, including 21 in the major, must be completed at GGU. **International Students:** The school actively recruits these students. They must take the TOEFL.

ADMISSIONS: Office of Admissions and Student Affairs. E-Mail: *info@ggu.edu* Web: *www.ggu.edu*

FINANCIAL AID: The FAFSA is required. Check with the school for current application deadlines.

HARVEY MUDD COLLEGE — D-5
www.hmc.edu

Claremont, CA 91711 — (909) 621-8011

Fax: (909) 607-7046	Email: admission@hmc.edu
Full-time: 436 men, 369 women	Faculty: 93; IIB, ++$
Part-time: 1 men, 1 women	Ph.D.s: 100%
Graduate: n/av	Student/Faculty: 8 to 1
Year: semesters	Tuition: $48,694
Room & Board: $15,833	Freshman Class: 3678 applied, 524 accepted, 195 enrolled
SAT CR/M/W: 730/770/730 ACT: 34	CEEB CODE: 4341
Application Deadline: January 1	MOST COMPETITIVE

Harvey Mudd College, founded in 1955, is one of the Claremont Colleges. It is a private college specializing in a math, science, and engineering education within a liberal arts tradition. There are 5 undergraduate schools and 2 graduate schools. In addition to regional accreditation, Harvey Mudd has baccalaureate program accreditation with ABET. The 33-acre campus is in a suburban area 35 miles east of Los Angeles. Including any residence halls, there are 18 buildings.

STUDENT LIFE: 50% of undergraduates are from out of state, mostly the Middle Atlantic. Students are from 41 states, 24 foreign countries, and Canada. 66% are from public schools. 43% are White; 20% Asian American; 12% Foreign. **Male To Female Ratio:** 0.8:1. The average age of freshmen is 18; all undergraduates, 19. **Housing:**

College-sponsored housing includes single-sex and coed dorms, on-campus apartments, off-campus apartments, and married student housing. On-campus housing is guaranteed for the freshman year only and is available on a lottery system for upperclassmen. Upperclassmen may keep cars.

FACULTY/CLASSROOMS: 62% of faculty are male; 38% are female. All teach undergraduates, and all do research. No introductory courses are taught by graduate students. The average class size in an introductory lecture is 65; in a laboratory is 20; and in a regular course is 20.

PROGRAMS OF STUDY: Harvey Mudd confers B.S. degrees. Bachelor's degrees are awarded in BIOLOGICAL SCIENCE (biology/biological science), COMPUTER AND PHYSICAL SCIENCE (chemistry, computer science, mathematics, and physics), ENGINEERING AND ENVIRONMENTAL DESIGN (engineering). Engineering, computer science, and mathematics have the larges enrollments.

ACTIVITIES: There are 46 groups on campus, including art, band, chess, choir, chorale, chorus, computers, dance, drama, environmental, ethnic, film, gay, international, jazz band, literary magazine, musical theater, newspaper, orchestra, photography, political, professional, radio and TV, religious, social, social service, student government, symphony, and yearbook. Popular campus events include 5-Class Competition, Wednesday Nighters, Crib Races, Frosh Soph Games, and Inner Tube Water Polo. **Sports:** There are 10 intercollegiate sports for men and 11 for women, and 9 intramural sports for men and 9 for women. The Claremont McKenna, Harvey Mudd, and Scripps Colleges share an athletic facility housing 2 gym floors, a weight room, a 400-meter track, a swimming pool, 9 tennis courts, and sports fields. The HMC campus recreation facility houses a full-size gym floor, an aerobics/dance room, and a fitness room with cardio and weight equipment. **Graduates:** From July 1, 2013 to June 30, 2014, 181 bachelor's degrees were awarded. The most popular majors were engineering (36%), computer science and math (18%), and physics (14%). 150 companies recruited on campus in 2013-2014. In an average class, 86% graduate in 4 years or less, 89% graduate in 5 years or less, and 91% graduate in 6 years or less. Of the 2013 graduating class, 36% were enrolled in graduate school within 6 months of graduation, and 56% were employed.

SERVICES: Counseling and information services are available, as is tutoring in most subjects. Additional support is offered on a case-by-case basis in coordination with the Associate Dean of Academic Affairs, the Associate Dean of Student Life, the Academic Excellence Program, and our faculty. **Library/Resources:** The library contains 2.0 million volumes, and subscribes to 70,000 periodicals including electronic. Computerized library services include interlibrary loans, database searching, Internet access, and Wi-Fi capability. Special learning facilities include an art gallery, planetarium, and radio station. **Physically Challenged Students:** Facilities include wheelchair ramps, elevators, special parking, specially equipped restrooms, special class scheduling, and lowered drinking fountains. **Special:** Students may cross-register at any of the other Claremont Colleges. Industry-sponsored projects (the Clinic Program) are available for all students, and required for Engineering and Computer Science majors. All students may choose to study abroad and an on-campus office supports these students. We offer dual and special majors in Computer Science and Math, Mathematical and Computational Biology, Chemistry and Biology, and student-designed majors are available. A 3-2 engineering degree with Claremont McKenna College or Scripps College is possible. The first semester for freshmen is taken on a pass/fail basis. There is 1 national honor society and 7 departmental honors programs. **Visiting:** There are regularly scheduled orientations for prospective students, campus tours and admission interviews are offered Monday through Friday and some Saturday mornings during the fall. There are guides for informal visits, visitors may sit in on classes, and stay overnight. To schedule a visit, contact the Office of Admission. **Campus Safety and Security:** Measures include 24-hour foot and vehicle patrol, emergency notification system, self-defense education, and security escort services. There are emergency telephones, lighted pathways/sidewalks, and controlled access to dorms/residences.

REQUIREMENTS: The SAT or ACT is required. The ACT Optional Writing test is also required. Applicants must have completed 4 years each of English and Mathematics (including algebra, demonstrative and analytic geometry, trigonometry, and calculus), 3 years of science (including 1 year each of Physics and Chemistry), and 1 year of history. The college recommends applicants take 2 years of a foreign language and 2 additional years each of history and social sciences. Students are required to take the SAT or ACT, and SAT subject tests in Math (level 2) and 1 other subject are required. Letters of recommendation are required from the student's counselor, a Math or science teacher, and an English, social science, or foreign language teacher. Applicants must submit 2 personal essays and are encouraged to seek an interview. Important factors in the admissions decision are advanced placement or honors courses, recommendations by school officials, and extracurricular activities record. The required curriculum is divided into three components: the Common Core, which provides the foundation for advanced study; the program in Humanities, Social Sciences, and the Arts, which completes the liberal arts nature of a Harvey Mudd College education by providing humanistic, social scientific, and aesthetic perspectives; and the Major, which builds depth and technical competence. Unifying all of these is an emphasis on strong oral and written communications, the development of computational skills, and direct experience with a research or design project. In order to be recommended by the faculty for the Bachelor of Science degree, students are required to complete satisfactorily a minimum of 128 credit hours of courses (including approved transfer credits for courses taken at other colleges). **Procedure:** Freshmen are admitted fall. Entrance exams should be taken ED I- Nov test date, ED II- Dec test date, RD- Jan test date. There are early decision and deferred admissions plans. Early decision applications should be filed by November 15; regular applications, by January 1 for fall entry, along with a $70 fee. Notification of early decision is sent December 15; regular decision, April 1. 63 early decision candidates were accepted for the 2014-2015 class. 596 applicants were on the 2014 waiting list; 14 were admitted. Applications are accepted on-line. **Transfer Students:** 1 transfer student enrolled in 2013-2014. Applicants must submit test scores, transcripts, course descriptions, and references from a college math, science, or engineering teacher, and from a counselor. Students should aim to complete courses equivalent to the courses in our Common Core. 64 of 128 credits required for the bachelor's degree must be completed at Harvey Mudd. **International Students:** There are 98 international students enrolled. The school actively recruits these students. They must take the TOEFL with a minimum score of 600 on the paper-based TOEFL (PBT) or 100 on the Internet-based version (iBT), Or take the IELTS if English has not been their primary language of instruction for the last 5 years. They must also take the SAT or ACT. For the ACT, the optional writing section must be taken.

ADMISSIONS: 14% of the 2014-2015 applicants were accepted. The SAT scores for the 2014-2015 freshman class were: Critical Reading--2% between 500 and 599, 30% between 600 and 699, and 68% between 700 and 800; Math--7% between 600 and 699, and 93% between 700 and 800; Writing--3% between 500 and 599, 29% between 600 and 699, and 67% between 700 and 800. The ACT scores were 1% between 24 and 26, 2% between 27 and 28, and 97% above 28. 99% of the current freshmen were in the top fifth of their class. There were 53 National Merit finalists. 20 freshmen graduated first in their class. **Admissions Contact:** Peter Osgood, Director of Admission. E-Mail: admission@hmc.edu Web: www.hmc.edu

FINANCIAL AID: In 2014-2015, 76% of all full-time freshmen and 74% of continuing full-time students received some form of financial aid. 48% of all full-time freshmen and 47% of continuing full-time students received need-based aid. The average freshman award was $38,113. Need-based scholarships or need-based grants averaged $41,953 ($72,602 maximum); need-based self-help aid (loans and jobs) averaged $6,638 ($11,225 maximum); and other non-need-based awards and non-need-based scholarships averaged $11,011 ($55,655 maximum). 67% of undergraduate students work part-time. Average annual earnings from campus work are $693. The average financial indebtedness of the 2014 graduate was $24,503. Harvey Mudd is a member of CSS. The CSS/Profile, FAFSA, and the state aid form are required. The deadline for filing freshman financial aid applications for fall entry is February 1.

HOLY NAMES UNIVERSITY (*The complete profile is made available exclusively on our website, www.barronspac.com*)

HOPE INTERNATIONAL UNIVERSITY D-5
www.hiu.edu

Fullerton, CA 92831
(714) 879-3901
(800) 762-1294

Fax: (714) 524-0231	Email: dkbutler@hiu.edu
Full-time: 289 men, 361 women	Faculty: 42
Part-time: 100 men, 111 women	Ph.D.s: 71%
Graduate: 199 men, 274 women	Student/Faculty: 13 to 1
Year: 4-1-4, summer session	Tuition: $26,050
Room & Board: $8600	Freshman Class: 635 applied, 196 accepted, 86 enrolled
SAT or ACT: required	CEEB CODE: 4614
Application Deadline: n/av	COMPETITIVE

Hope International University, founded in 1928, is a small, private liberal arts institution affiliated with the Independent Christian Churches/Churches of Christ. There are 5 undergraduate schools and 4 graduate schools. The 15-acre campus is in an urban area 45 miles southeast of Los Angeles. Including any residence halls, there are 9 buildings.

STUDENT LIFE: 76% of undergraduates are from California. Others are from 44 states, 12 foreign countries, and Canada. 88% are from public schools. 40% are White; 20% race unknown; 17% Hispanic. 65% are Protestant; 20% Catholic; 15% claim no Religious affiliation. **Male To Female Ratio:** 1.3:1. The average age of freshmen is 18; all undergraduates, 21. 20% do not continue beyond their first year; 47% remain to graduate. **Housing:** 530 students can be accommodated in college housing, which includes single-sex dorms and on-campus apartments. On-campus housing is guaranteed for all 4 years. 54% of students commute. Alcohol is not permitted. All students may keep cars.

FACULTY/CLASSROOMS: 59% of faculty are male; 41% are female. All teach undergraduates. No introductory courses are taught by graduate students. The average class size in an introductory lecture is 33; in a laboratory is 20; and in a regular course is 30.

PROGRAMS OF STUDY: HIU confers B.A., B.S. and B.Mus. degrees. Associate and master's degrees are also awarded. Bachelor's degrees are awarded in BUSINESS (business administration and management and sports management), COMMUNICATIONS AND THE ARTS (church music, communications, and English literature), EDUCATION (education, secondary education, and social science education), SOCIAL SCIENCE (biblical studies, child psychology/development, crosscultural studies, human development, human services, liberal arts/general studies, ministries, pastoral studies, psychology, social science, and youth ministry). Psychology is the strongest academically. Ministry/Biblical studies, psychology and counseling, and business have the larges enrollments.

ACTIVITIES: There are no fraternities or sororities. There are 17 groups on campus, including cheerleading, choir, chorale, communications, drama, international, jazz band, musical theater, newspaper, religious, social service, student government, Students participate in Model UN at Harvard and Security Council at Yale., and yearbook. Popular campus events include Happy House (community Halloween outreach), Spring Formal and Intercultural Awareness Events. **Sports:** There are 8 intercollegiate sports for men and 8 for women, and 4 intramural sports for men and 4 for women. Facilities include a 2500-seat gym with basketball and volleyball courts, fitness center, and recreation room. An outdoor swimming pool is adjacent to the residence halls. **Graduates:** From July 1, 2013 to June 30, 2014, 185 bachelor's degrees were awarded. The most popular majors were psychology, social science and human services (36%), ministries and biblical studies (31%), and business (19%). In an average class, 21% graduate in 4 years or less, 39% graduate in 5 years or less, and 47% graduate in 6 years or less.

SERVICES: Counseling and information services are available, as is tutoring in, history, English, mathematics, science, Bible, and financial accounting. There is a reader service for the blind, and remedial math, reading, and writing. **Library/Resources:** The library contains 193,398 volumes, 100 microform items, and 2,287 audio/video tapes/CDs/DVDs, and subscribes to 500 periodicals including electronic.

Computerized library services include interlibrary loans, database searching, Internet access, and Wi-Fi capability. **Physically Challenged Students:** 95% of the campus is accessible. Facilities include elevators, special parking, specially equipped restrooms. Priority is given to disabled students for first-floor housing. **Special:** Hope International offers cross-registration with California State University, Fullerton. Internships, study abroad in 7 countries, work-study programs, dual and student-designed majors, non-degree study, pass/fail options, and credit for life, military, and work experience are also offered. Most Leadership and Ethics Curriculum courses are available in the online modality as well. There is 1 national honor society and 1 departmental honors program. **Visiting:** There are guides for informal visits, visitors may sit in on classes, and stay overnight. To schedule a visit, contact Pam Ellis at pjellis@hiu.edu. **Campus Safety and Security:** Measures include 24-hour foot and vehicle patrol, emergency notification system, and security escort services. There are emergency telephones, lighted pathways/sidewalks, and controlled access to dorms/residences.

REQUIREMENTS: The SAT or ACT is required. Applicants must be high school graduates. The GED is accepted. A personal essay and references from a church leader and an academic counselor are required. A GPA of 2.0 is required. AP and CLEP credits are accepted. Regular attendance at chapel and participation in Christian service is required. To graduate, students must complete at least 122 credit units with 36 to 51 in the major. A minimum GPA of 2.0 must be maintained. The Leadership and Ethics Core curriculum includes required and elective courses in biblical studies, leadership, written and oral communication, social sciences, humanities, natural sciences, and math. **Procedure:** Freshmen are admitted fall and spring. There are early admissions, deferred admissions, and rolling admissions plans. Application deadlines are open. Application fee is $40. Applications are accepted on-line. **Transfer Students:** 54 transfer students enrolled in 2013-2014. Transfer students must submit copies of college transcripts and SAT or ACT scores if fewer than 30 college units have been completed. A minimum GPA of 2.0 is required. 30 of 122 credits required for the bachelor's degree must be completed at HIU. **International Students:** There are 22 international students enrolled. The school actively recruits these students. They must take the TOEFL with a minimum score of 83 on the Internet-based version (iBT).

ADMISSIONS: 31% of the 2014-2015 applicants were accepted. The SAT scores for the 2014-2015 freshman class were: Critical Reading--74% below 500, 25% between 500 and 599, and 1% between 600 and 699; Math--78% below 500, 19% between 500 and 599, 3% between 600 and 699, and % between 700 and 800; Writing--81% below 500, and 19% between 500 and 599. The ACT scores were 60% below 21, 32% between 21 and 23, 4% between 24 and 26, and 4% between 27 and 28. 4% of the current freshmen were in the top fifth of their class; 76% were in the top two fifths. **Admissions Contact:** Dionne Butler, Director of Undergraduate Admissions. E-Mail: *dkbutler@hiu.edu* Web: *www.hiu.edu*

FINANCIAL AID: The FAFSA and the college's own financial statement are required. Check with the school for current application deadlines.

system. The figures given in the above capsule and in this profile are approximate. There are 3 undergraduate schools and 1 graduate school. In addition to regional accreditation, Humboldt has baccalaureate program accreditation with ABET, CSWE, NASAD, NASM, NLN, and SAF. The 161-acre campus is in a small town 275 miles north of San Francisco. Including any residence halls, there are 93 buildings.

STUDENT LIFE: 83% of undergraduates are from California. Others are from 50 states, 28 foreign countries, and Canada. 95% are from public schools. 53% are White. The average age of freshmen is 19; all undergraduates, 24. 25% do not continue beyond their first year; 49% remain to graduate. **Housing:** 1400 students can be accommodated in college housing, which includes single-sex and coed dorms and on-campus apartments. In addition, there are special-interest houses, and living learning houses. On-campus housing is available on a first-come and first-served basis. 82% of students commute. All students may keep cars.

FACULTY/CLASSROOMS: 53% of faculty are male; 47% are female. All teach undergraduates. No introductory courses are taught by graduate students. The average class size in an introductory lecture is 33; in a laboratory is 21; and in a regular course is 24.

PROGRAMS OF STUDY: Humboldt confers B.A., and B.S. degrees. Master's degrees are also awarded. Bachelor's degrees are awarded in AGRICULTURE (fishing and fisheries, forestry and related sciences, and natural resource management), BIOLOGICAL SCIENCE (biology/biological science, botany, wildlife biology, and zoology), BUSINESS (business administration and management and business economics), COMMUNICATIONS AND THE ARTS (art, communications, dramatic arts, English, fine arts, French, German, journalism, music, Spanish, and speech/debate/rhetoric), COMPUTER AND PHYSICAL SCIENCE (chemistry, geology, information sciences and systems, mathematics, oceanography, and physics), EDUCATION (business education, elementary education, English education, industrial arts education, mathematics education, middle school education, music education, physical education, science education, secondary education, and social science education), ENGINEERING AND ENVIRONMENTAL DESIGN (environmental engineering, environmental science, industrial engineering technology, and land use management and reclamation), HEALTH PROFESSIONS (nursing, predentistry, and premedicine), SOCIAL SCIENCE (anthropology, child psychology/development, geography, history, liberal arts/general studies, Native American studies, parks and recreation management, philosophy, physical fitness/movement, political science/government, prelaw, psychology, religion, social science, social work, and sociology). Environmental resources engineering, natural resources, and performing arts are the strongest academically. Biological sciences has the largest enrollment.

ACTIVITIES: There are 178 groups on campus, including art, band, cheerleading, chorale, chorus, computers, dance, debate, drama, environmental, ethnic, film, gay, honors, international, jazz band, literary magazine, marching band, musical theater, newspaper, opera, orchestra, pep band, photography, political, professional, radio and TV, religious, social, social service, student government, and symphony. Popular campus events include Campus Dialogue on Race, International Education week and International Cultural Festival. **Sports:** There are 5 intercollegiate sports for men and 7 for women, and 4 intramural sports for men and 4 for women. Facilities include a 7000-seat stadium, an all-weather track, a swimming pool, tennis and racquetball courts, playing fields, 2 gyms, a student recreation center with exercise equipment and weight room, and a rock-climbing wall.

SERVICES: Counseling and information services are available, as is tutoring in every subject. There is a reader service for the blind, and remedial math, reading, and writing. **Library/Resources:** The library contains 566,531 volumes, 610,992 microform items, 21,955 audio/video tapes/CDs/DVDs, and subscribes to 1,413 periodicals including electronic. Computerized library services include interlibrary loans, database searching, Internet access, and Wi-Fi capability. Special learning facilities include an art gallery, natural history museum, radio station, observatory, greenhouse, solar hydrogen project, wildlife sanctuaries, the Center for Appropriate Technology, child development lab, ceramics lab, jewelry lab, marine lab, marine research vessel, fish hatchery, and wildlife care center. **Physically Challenged**

HUMBOLDT STATE UNIVERSITY · A-1
www.humboldt.edu

Arcata, CA 95521

(707) 826-4402
(866) 850-9556

Fax: (707) 826-6194

Email: hsuinfo@.humboldt.edu

Full-time: 2855 men, 3255 women — Faculty: n/av

Part-time: 355 men, 365 women — Ph.D.s: n/av

Graduate: 415 men, 635 women — Student/Faculty: n/av

Year: semesters, summer session — Tuition: $8400 ($16,200)

Room & Board: $10,000 — Freshman Class: n/av

SAT or ACT: recommended — CEEB CODE: 4345

Application Deadline: n/av — **COMPETITIVE**

Humboldt State University, founded in 1913, is a liberal arts institution and the northernmost campus of the California State University

Students: 60% of the campus is accessible. Facilities include wheelchair ramps, elevators, special parking, specially equipped restrooms, special class scheduling, lowered drinking fountains, lowered telephones. Wheelchair-accessible transportation, and a study center. **Special:** HSU offers campus work-study programs and co-op programs with a variety of public and private agencies, fisheries, biology, geology, botany, engineering, soil science, hydrology, and range and soil conservation. Internships and study abroad in 25 countries, with semesters in London, China, and Greece, are also offered. Dual majors, student-designed majors, credit for life and military experience, and credit/no credit grading options are also available. **Visiting:** There are regularly scheduled orientations for prospective students, including Preview Day in the spring and mandatory summer orientation for new students, which provides peer and academic counseling, registration, and a variety of social activities. There are guides for informal visits, visitors may sit in on classes, and stay overnight. To schedule a visit, contact the Office of Admissions. **Campus Safety and Security:** Measures include 24-hour foot and vehicle patrol, emergency notification system, self-defense education, and security escort services. There are emergency telephones, lighted pathways/sidewalks, emergency transportation services.

REQUIREMENTS: The SAT or ACT is recommended. Applicants must be high school graduates with a minimum of 15 academic credits, to include 4 years in English, 3 years in college prep math, 2 years each in foreign language, social science, and lab science, including 1 year physical and 1 year life science, and 1 year each of U.S. history/government and visual and performing arts. The GED is accepted. HSU uses an eligibility index that combines GPA and ACT or SAT scores for admission. Requirements are higher for out-of-state applicants. Contact the Office of Admissions for further information. A GPA of 2.0 is required. AP and CLEP credits are accepted. To graduate, students must complete 120 to 132 semester credits, including 48 in general education courses, 24 to 36 in the major, and up to 40 in electives, with a minimum overall GPA of 2.0. Requirements include freshman reading and composition, diversity and common ground course work, and U.S. history course work as required by the California legislature. **Procedure:** Freshmen are admitted fall and spring. Entrance exams should be taken prior to admission. There are early decision and rolling admissions plans. Check with the school for current application deadlines. The application fee is $55. Notification is sent on a rolling basis. Applications are accepted on-line. **Transfer Students:** Applicants must have a minimum college GPA of 2.0 (2.4 for nonresidents). To enter, students need 30 general education units with a grade of C or better, including courses in written and speech communication, critical thinking, and math. Students with fewer than 56 transferable semester units must meet freshman requirements. 30 of 132 credits required for the bachelor's degree must be completed at Humboldt. **International Students:** There are 61 international students enrolled. The school actively recruits these students. They must take the TOEFL.

ADMISSIONS: Rebecca Kalal, Assistant Director of Admissions. E-Mail: *hsuinfo@humboldt.edu* Web: *www.humboldt.edu*

FINANCIAL AID: The FAFSA is required. Check with the school for current application deadlines.

HUMPHREYS COLLEGE (*The complete profile is made available exclusively on our website, www.barronspac.com*)

LA SIERRA UNIVERSITY	D-5
www.lasierra.edu	
Riverside, CA 92515	(951) 785-2957
	(800) 874-5587
Fax: (951) 785-2447	Email: admissions@lasierra.edu
Full-time: 615 men, 865 women	Faculty: n/av
Part-time: 90 men, 110 women	Ph.D.s: n/av
Graduate: 160 men, 175 women	Student/Faculty: n/av
Year: trimesters, summer session	Tuition: $28,314
Room & Board: $7380	Freshman Class: n/av
SAT or ACT: required	CEEB CODE: 4380
Application Deadline: n/av	VERY COMPETITIVE

La Sierra University, founded originally as La Sierra Academy in 1922, is a Seventh-day Adventist, private university, offering undergraduate and graduate programs in applied and liberal arts and sciences, business and management, religion, and education. The figures given in the above capsule and in this profile are approximate. There are 5 undergraduate schools and 4 graduate schools. In addition to regional accreditation, La Sierra has baccalaureate program accreditation with ABET, CSWE, and NASM. The 300-acre campus is in a suburban area 40 miles east of Los Angeles. Including any residence halls, there are 48 buildings.

STUDENT LIFE: 201% of undergraduates are from California. Others are from 34 states, 58 foreign countries, and Canada. 39% are from public schools. 35% are White; 31% Asian American; 19% Hispanic. 90% are Protestant; 12% claim no religious affiliation. **Male To Female Ratio:** 1.3:1. The average age of freshmen is 19; all undergraduates, 22. **Housing:** 650 students can be accommodated in college housing, which includes single-sex dorms, on-campus apartments, off-campus apartments, and married student housing. In addition, there are honors houses. On-campus housing is guaranteed for all 4 years, is guaranteed for the freshman year only. Priority is given to out-of-town students. 56% of students commute. Alcohol is not permitted. All students may keep cars.

FACULTY/CLASSROOMS: All teach undergraduates, and 70% do research. Graduate students teach 1% of introductory courses. The average class size in an introductory lecture is 30; in a laboratory is 21; and in a regular course is 20.

PROGRAMS OF STUDY: La Sierra confers B.A., B.S., B.F.A., B.Mus. and B.S.W. degrees. Master's and doctoral degrees are also awarded. Bachelor's degrees are awarded in BIOLOGICAL SCIENCE (biochemistry, biology/biological science, biometrics and biostatistics, and biophysics), BUSINESS (accounting, banking and finance, business administration and management, electronic business, international business management, and marketing management), COMMUNICATIONS AND THE ARTS (art, communications, English, English as a second/foreign language, fine arts, graphic design, music, music performance, and Spanish), COMPUTER AND PHYSICAL SCIENCE (chemistry, computer science, information sciences and systems, mathematics, and physics), EDUCATION (elementary education, music education, physical education, and secondary education), HEALTH PROFESSIONS (exercise science and health science), SOCIAL SCIENCE (history, liberal arts/general studies, political science/government, psychobiology, psychology, religion, social work, and sociology). Biology, criminal justice and business are the strongest academically and has the largest enrollments.

ACTIVITIES: There are 30 groups on campus, including art, band, choir, chorale, chorus, computers, debate, drama, environmental, ethnic, film, honors, international, literary magazine, newspaper, orchestra, photography, professional, religious, social service, student government, symphony, and yearbook. Popular campus events include University Experience, Academic Expo and Community Service Day. **Sports:** There are 3 intercollegiate sports for men and 3 for women, and 9 intramural sports for men and 9 for women. Facilities include a gym, soccer and flag football fields, running track, swimming pool, and a fitness center. **Graduates:** From July 1, 2013 to June 30, 2014, 208 bachelor's degrees were awarded. The most popular majors were biomedical science (9%), management (7%), and exercise science/scientific basis (5%). In an average class, 35% graduate in 4 years or less and 45% graduate in 6 years or less.

SERVICES: Counseling and information services are available, as is tutoring in most subjects. There is a reader service for the blind, and remedial math, reading, and writing. A learning support center. **Library/Resources:** The library contains 262,554 volumes, 648,664 microform items, and subscribes to 825 periodicals including electronic. Computerized library services include interlibrary loans, database searching, Internet access, and Wi-Fi capability. Special learning facilities include an art gallery, natural history museum, observatory, missionary museum, and arboretum. **Physically Challenged Students:** 99% of the campus is accessible. Facilities include wheelchair ramps, elevators, special parking, specially equipped restrooms, and special class scheduling. **Special:** Cross-registration with Walla Walla College is necessary for engineering students. Study abroad is available in 3 countries through the Adventist Colleges Abroad Consortium. Liberal studies students work with an adviser to design their own major. There is a freshman honors program. **Visiting:** There are regularly scheduled orientations for prospective students, including a tour and meetings with faculty and administrators. There are guides for informal visits, visitors may sit in on classes, and stay overnight. To schedule a visit, contact the Admissions Department. **Campus Safety and Security:** Measures include 24-hour foot and vehicle patrol, emergency notification system, and security escort services. There are emergency telephones, lighted pathways/sidewalks, and controlled access to dorms/residences.

REQUIREMENTS: The SAT or ACT is required. In addition, prospective students should have a high school diploma or equivalent. Completion of college preparatory work is required. A recommendation is also required. A GPA of 2.5 is required. AP and CLEP credits are accepted. Important factors in the admissions decision are recommendations by school officials, leadership record, and evidence of special talent.To graduate, students must complete 190 units, at least 60 of which must be upper-division, with a GPA of 2.0. All students must complete a University Studies curriculum requirements and 3 community service courses. **Procedure:** Freshmen are admitted to all sessions. Entrance exams should be taken during the senior year. There are deferred admissions and rolling admissions plans. Check with the school for current application deadlines. The fall 2014 application fee was $30. **Transfer Students:** Transcripts from all previous colleges are required. 36 of 190 credits required for the bachelor's degree must be completed at La Sierra. **International Students:** There are 283 international students enrolled. The school actively recruits these students. They must take the TOEFL with a minimum score of 500 on the paper-based TOEFL (PBT). They must also take the SAT or ACT.

ADMISSIONS: Ivy Tejeda, Associate Director of Admissions. E-Mail: *admissions@lasierra.edu* Web: *www.lasierra.edu*

FINANCIAL AID: La Sierra is a member of CSS. The FAFSA is required. Check with the school for current application deadlines.

LAGUNA COLLEGE OF ART AND DESIGN (*The complete profile is made available exclusively on our website, www.barronspac.com*)

LOYOLA MARYMOUNT UNIVERSITY C-5
www.lmu.edu

Los Angeles, CA 90045

(310) 338-2750
(800) LMU-INFO

Fax: (310) 338-2797
Email: admissions@lmu.edu
Full-time: 2515 men, 3410 women
Faculty: 429
Part-time: 141 men, 118 women
Ph.D.s: 96%
Graduate: 1301 men, 2030 women
Student/Faculty: 11 to 1
Year: semesters, summer session
Tuition: $41,372
Room & Board: $13,277
Freshman Class: 12115 applied, 6385 accepted, 1348 enrolled
SAT CR/M/W: 590/610/600 **ACT:** 27
CEEB CODE: 4403
Application Deadline: January 15
VERY COMPETITIVE+

Loyola Marymount University is one of the largest Catholic universities in the West and one of 28 Jesuit universities in the United States. LMU, founded in 1911, is a comprehensive university offering 60 major programs and 56 minor programs for undergraduates. There are 5 undergraduate schools and 2 graduate schools. In addition to regional accreditation, LMU has baccalaureate program accreditation with AACSB, ABET, NASAD, NASM, and NCATE. The 142-acre campus is in a suburban area 15 miles southwest of downtown Los Angeles. Including any residence halls, there are 60 buildings.

STUDENT LIFE: 78% of undergraduates are from California. Others are from 47 states, 70 foreign countries, and Canada. 50% are from public schools. 46% are White; 22% Hispanic; 11% Asian American. 43% are Catholic; 29% claim no religious affiliation; 25% Christian, Muslim, Buddhist and Hindu. **Male To Female Ratio:** 1.4:1. The average age of freshmen is 18; all undergraduates, 20. 10% do not continue beyond their first year; 78% remain to graduate. **Housing:** 3210 students can be accommodated in college housing, which

includes single-sex and coed dorms and on-campus apartments. In addition, there are honors houses and special-interest houses. On-campus housing is guaranteed for the freshman year only and is available on a lottery system for upperclassmen. 53% of students live on campus. All students may keep cars.

FACULTY/CLASSROOMS: 54% of faculty are male; 46% are female. All teach and do research. Graduate students teach 4% of introductory courses. The average class size in an introductory lecture is 24 and in a laboratory is 52.

PROGRAMS OF STUDY: LMU confers B.A., B.S., B.B.A., B.S.A. and B.S.E. degrees. Master's and doctoral degrees are also awarded. Bachelor's degrees are awarded in BIOLOGICAL SCIENCE (biochemistry and biology/biological science), BUSINESS (accounting, business administration and management, entrepreneurial studies, and marketing/retailing/merchandising), COMMUNICATIONS AND THE ARTS (animation, art history and appreciation, classics, communications, dance, dramatic arts, English, French, Greek, Latin, media arts, modern language, music, Spanish, and studio art), COMPUTER AND PHYSICAL SCIENCE (chemistry, computer science, mathematics, natural sciences, and physics), EDUCATION (athletic training and mathematics education), ENGINEERING AND ENVIRONMENTAL DESIGN (civil engineering, electrical/electronics engineering, engineering physics, environmental science, and mechanical engineering), HEALTH PROFESSIONS (health science), SOCIAL SCIENCE (African American studies, Asian/Oriental studies, classical/ancient civilization, economics, European studies, Hispanic American studies, history, humanities, liberal arts/general studies, philosophy, political science/government, psychology, sociology, theological studies, urban studies, and women's studies). Engineering, entrepreneurship, school of film and television are the strongest academically. Communication studies, marketing and psychology have the largest enrollments.

ACTIVITIES: 22% of men belong to 9 national fraternities; 33% of women belong to 12 national sororities. There are 140 groups on campus, including art, cheerleading, chess, choir, chorale, chorus, computers, dance, debate, drama, ethnic, film, gay, honors, international, literary magazine, newspaper, orchestra, pep band, political, professional, radio and TV, religious, social, social service, student government, and yearbook. Popular campus events include College Fest, Madness at Midnight, Charity Ball and Club Fest. **Sports:** There are 8 intercollegiate sports for men and 10 for women, and 5 intramural sports for men and 5 for women. Facilities include an athletic pavilion, a 4166-seat gym, a swimming pool, tennis, handball, and racquetball courts, a baseball stadium, a floating crew shell house, soccer, rugby, and football fields, and a recreation center. **Graduates:** From July 1, 2013 to June 30, 2014, 1579 bachelor's degrees were awarded. The most popular majors were communication studies (9%), finance (7%), and psychology (6%). 175 companies recruited on campus in 2013-2014. In an average class, 2% graduate in 3 years or less, 69% graduate in 4 years or less, 77% graduate in 5 years or less, and 78% graduate in 6 years or less. Of the 2013 graduating class, 23% were enrolled in graduate school within 6 months of graduation, and 47% were employed.

SERVICES: Counseling and information services are available, as is tutoring in most subjects. There is a reader service for the blind, and remedial math, reading, and writing. There is an extensive learning resource center with full-time specialists in reading, writing, and study skills, as well as a peer tutoring staff and computer-aided instruction. **Library/Resources:** The library contains 598,443 volumes, 130,185 microform items, and 29,700 audio/video tapes/CDs/DVDs. Computerized library services include interlibrary loans, database searching, Internet access, and Wi-Fi capability. Special learning facilities include an art gallery, radio station, TV station, the Burns Fine Arts Center, and the Little Theatre. **Physically Challenged Students:** 95% of the campus is accessible. Facilities include wheelchair ramps, elevators, special parking, specially equipped restrooms, special class scheduling, lowered drinking fountains, lowered telephones, special housing. special test and registration arrangements, and hearing aid equipment in the library. **Special:** LMU offers internships and volunteer work experience with local firms, study abroad in over 20 countries, a Washington semester, dual majors, work-study, student-designed and individualized studies majors, a general studies degree, non-degree study, and some pass/fail options for electives. There are

19 national honor societies and a freshman honors program. **Visiting:** There are regularly scheduled orientations for prospective students, and student visits consist of an open house in the fall. There are guides for informal visits and visitors may sit in on classes. To schedule a visit, contact the Admissions Office. **Campus Safety and Security:** Measures include 24-hour foot and vehicle patrol, emergency notification system, and security escort services. There are emergency telephones, lighted pathways/sidewalks, and controlled access to dorms/residences.

REQUIREMENTS: The SAT is required. The ACT is recommended. Prospective students must be graduates of an accredited secondary school and have completed 4 years of English, 3 each of a foreign language, math, and social studies, 2 of science, and 1 of an academic elective. A recommendation from an official of a previous school and essays are required. An interview is recommended. AP credits are accepted. Important factors in the admissions decision are advanced placement or honors courses, evidence of special talent, and personality/intangible qualities. Regardless of major, all undergraduates must take courses in the following core areas: American cultures; college writing; communication/critical thinking; critical and creative arts; history; literature, math, science, and technology; philosophy; social sciences; and theological studies. A minimum 2.0 GPA is required, as are at least 120 semester hours, with at least 45 semester hours in upper-division courses. At least 30 of the last 36 semester hours of academic work and at least two thirds of the upper-division semester hours of the major must be completed at LMU. **Procedure:** Freshmen are admitted fall and spring. Entrance exams should be taken during the spring of the junior year or fall of senior year. There are early admissions, deferred admissions, and rolling admissions plans. Applications should be filed by January 15 for fall entry; October 15 for spring entry, along with a $60 fee. 1354 applicants were on the 2014 waiting list; 29 were admitted. Applications are accepted online. **Transfer Students:** 479 transfer students enrolled in 2013-2014. Applicants must have a minimum 3.00 GPA in college work and most recent college work. Students who were not academically eligible for admission as freshmen must have at least 30 semester hours of college work. Grades below C (2.0) do not transfer. No minimum credit hours are necessary for students who meet freshman requirements. The SAT I is required for those with fewer than 30 transfer hours, and letters of recommendation are recommended for all transfer students. 30 of 120 credits required for the bachelor's degree must be completed at LMU. **International Students:** There are 409 international students enrolled. The school actively recruits these students. They must take the TOEFL with a minimum score of 550 on the paper-based TOEFL (PBT) or 80 on the Internet-based version (iBT). They must also take the SAT or ACT.

ADMISSIONS: 53% of the 2014-2015 applicants were accepted. The SAT scores for the 2014-2015 freshman class were: Critical Reading--8% below 500, 44% between 500 and 599, 42% between 600 and 699, and 6% between 700 and 800; Math--8% below 500, 33% between 500 and 599, 50% between 600 and 699, and 9% between 700 and 800; Writing--8% below 500, 41% between 500 and 599, 43% between 600 and 699, and 8% between 700 and 800. The ACT scores were 3% below 21, 13% between 21 and 23, 29% between 24 and 26, 21% between 27 and 28, and 34% above 28. 63% of the current freshmen were in the top fifth of their class; 89% were in the top two fifths. **Admissions Contact:** Matthew Fissinger, Director of Undergraduate Admissions. E-Mail: *admissions@lmu.edu* Web: *http:/admission.lmu.edu/*

FINANCIAL AID: In 2014-2015, 95% of all full-time freshmen and 85% of continuing full-time students received some form of financial aid. 59% of all full-time freshmen and 60% of continuing full-time students received need-based aid. The average freshman award was $24,792. Need-based scholarships or need-based grants averaged $7,339 ($49,552 maximum); need-based self-help aid (loans and jobs) averaged $4,187 ($50,939 maximum); non-need-based athletic scholarships averaged $1,436 ($68,219 maximum); other non-need-based awards and non-need-based scholarships averaged $6,207 ($54,160 maximum); and $5,623 from other forms of aid. 52% of undergraduate students work part-time. Average annual earnings from campus work are $1187. The average financial indebtedness of the 2014 graduate was $30,243. The FAFSA and the college's own financial statement are required. Check with the school for current application deadlines.

MENLO COLLEGE
www.menlo.edu

B-3

Atherton, CA 94027

(650) 543-3910
(800) 55-MENLO

Fax: (650) 543-4476
Email: holly.dalton@menlo.edu

Full-time: 438 men, 266 women
Faculty: 32; IIB, ++$

Part-time: 7 men, 2 women
Ph.D.s: 88%

Graduate: n/av
Student/Faculty: 22 to 1

Year: semesters, summer session
Tuition: $37,100

Room & Board: $11,902
Freshman Class: 1717 applied, 1519 accepted, 139 enrolled

SAT CR/M/W: 470/500/480 ACT: 20
CEEB CODE: 4403

Application Deadline: Open
COMPETITIVE

Menlo College, founded in 1927, is a private college offering programs in business management and psychology with a strong liberal arts foundation. Figures in the above capsule and in this profile are approximate. There is one undergraduate school. The 45-acre campus is in a suburban area 30 miles south of San Francisco and 30 miles north of San Jose. Including any residence halls, there are 13 buildings.

STUDENT LIFE: 69% of undergraduates are from California. Others are from 23 states, 30 foreign countries, and Canada. 35% are White; 21% Hispanic; 13% Foreign. **Male To Female Ratio:** 0.6:1. The average age of freshmen is 18; all undergraduates, 21. 18% do not continue beyond their first year; 55% remain to graduate. **Housing:** 503 students can be accommodated in college housing, which includes single-sex and coed dorms. On-campus housing is guaranteed for the freshman year only. 61% of students live on campus; of those, 80% remain on campus on weekends. All students may keep cars.

FACULTY/CLASSROOMS: 55% of faculty are male; 45% are female. All teach undergraduates, and 88% do both. No introductory courses are taught by graduate students. The average class size in an introductory lecture is 19; in a laboratory is 27; and in a regular course is 19.

PROGRAMS OF STUDY: Menlo confers B.A. in Business and B.A in Psychology and B.S. in Business degrees. Bachelor's degrees are awarded in BUSINESS (accounting, entrepreneurial studies, finance, human resources, international business management, management information systems, marketing management, real estate, and sports management), SOCIAL SCIENCE (psychology). Business and psychology is the strongest academically. Business has the largest enrollment.

ACTIVITIES: There are 35 groups on campus, including art, band, cheerleading, chess, chorale, communications, computers, environmental, ethnic, film, finance and investment club, gay, honors, international, photography, political, professional, religious, social, social service, and student government. Popular campus events include School of Business Administration Day, Luau, Homecoming and Mystery Dance. **Sports:** There are 8 intercollegiate sports for men and 8 for women, and 2 intramural sports for men and 2 for women. Facilities include 2 swimming pools, soccer and football fields, tennis courts, a track, 600-seat gym, fitness center, weight facility, and a baseball diamond. The campus stadium seats 1000, the largest auditorium/arena. **Graduates:** From July 1, 2013 to June 30, 2014, 139 bachelor's degrees were awarded. The most popular majors were management (42%), marketing (14%), and accounting (7%). In an average class, 55% graduate in 6 years or less. Of the 2013 graduating class, 87% were employed within 6 months of graduation.

SERVICES: Counseling and information services are available, as is tutoring in most subjects. There is a reader service for the blind, and remedial reading. **Library/Resources:** 1,020 audio/video tapes/CDs/DVDs, and subscribes to 41,050 periodicals including electronic. Computerized library services include interlibrary loans, database searching, Internet access, and Wi-Fi capability. Special learning facilities include an art gallery, dedicated computer labs, social media labs, academic success center, writing lab, math lab, and study slam sessions. **Physically Challenged Students:** 95% of the campus is accessible. Facilities include wheelchair ramps, elevators, special parking, specially equipped restrooms, lowered drinking fountains, lowered telephones, and special housing. **Special:** Business students are required to earn 6 credits through internships. Menlo also offers study abroad in Spain, China, Chile, and Japan; dual and student-designed majors, B.A.-B.S. degrees. There are 2 national honor societies and 1 departmental honors program. **Visiting:** There are regularly scheduled orientations for prospective students, There are two Open Houses, one in early Fall and one in early Spring, where prospective students can meet with key faculty and staff and tour the campus. In late Spring there is a Preview Day interactive event culminating with the Student Luau. There are guides for informal visits, visitors may sit in on classes, and stay overnight. To schedule a visit, contact the Office of Admissions. **Campus Safety and Security:** Measures include 24-hour foot and vehicle patrol, emergency notification system, and security escort services. There are emergency telephones, lighted pathways/sidewalks, and controlled access to dorms/residences.

REQUIREMENTS: The SAT or ACT is required. A personal essay and letter of recommendation should be submitted. The GED is accepted. A GPA of 2.5 is required. AP and CLEP credits are accepted. Important factors in the admissions decision are advanced placement or honors courses, evidence of special talent, and leadership record.Students must complete 124 units with a cumulative GPA above 2.0 to earn a Bachelor's degree. All students must complete 49 credit hours of general education courses and 39-63 hours of major courses depending on the specific major. The remaining courses are free electives. **Procedure:** Freshmen are admitted fall and spring. Entrance exams should be taken During a junior or a senior year of high school. There are early admissions, deferred admissions, and rolling admissions plans. Early decision applications should be filed by December 1, along with a $40 fee. Notification of early decision is sent December 15; regular decision, on a rolling basis. Applications are accepted online. **Transfer Students:** 89 transfer students enrolled in 2013-2014. Transfer applicants must show potential for success indicated by a 2.0 GPA at the college level. Those with fewer than 12 credits must meet freshman requirements. 30 of 124 credits required for the bachelor's degree must be completed at Menlo. **International Students:** There are 96 international students enrolled. The school actively recruits these students. They must take the TOEFL with a minimum score of 500 on the paper-based TOEFL (PBT) or 61 on the Internet-based version (iBT), or take the SAT or ACT if English is their first language.

ADMISSIONS: 88% of the 2014-2015 applicants were accepted. The SAT scores for the 2014-2015 freshman class were: Critical Reading--63% below 500, 33% between 500 and 599, 3% between 600 and 699, and 1% between 700 and 800; Math--46% below 500, 43% between 500 and 599, 9% between 600 and 699, and 2% between 700 and 800; Writing--64% below 500, 30% between 500 and 599, 6% between 600 and 699, and % between 700 and 800. The ACT scores were 50% below 21, 12% between 21 and 23, 25% between 24 and 26, 10% between 27 and 28, and 3% above 28. 1 freshman graduated first in the class. **Admissions Contact:** Dean of Enrollment Management. Web: *www.menlo.edu*

FINANCIAL AID: In 2014-2015, 98% of all full-time freshmen and 97% of continuing full-time students received some form of financial aid. 64% of all full-time freshmen and 63% of continuing full-time students received need-based aid. The average freshman award was $28,041. Need-based scholarships or need-based grants averaged $24,979 ($36,500 maximum); need-based self-help aid (loans and jobs) averaged $3,585 ($4,500 maximum); non-need-based athletic scholarships averaged $5,591 ($21,527 maximum); and other non-need-based awards and non-need-based scholarships averaged $14,014 ($19,000 maximum). 52% of undergraduate students work part-time. Average annual earnings from campus work are $1800. The average financial indebtedness of the 2014 graduate was $28,972. The FAFSA is required. The priority date for freshman financial aid applications for fall entry is March 2.

MILLS COLLEGE
www.mills.edu

B-3

Oakland, CA 94613

(510) 430-2135
(800) 87-MILLS

Fax: (510) 430-3314
Full-time: 922 women
Part-time: 63 women
Graduate: 126 men, 484 women
Year: semesters
Room & Board: $12,625

Email: admission@mills.edu
Faculty: 94; IIA, ++$
Ph.D.s: 92%
Student/Faculty: 9 to 1
Tuition: $41,494
Freshman Class: 1827 applied, 1242 accepted, 217 enrolled

SAT CR/M/W: 600/560/570 ACT: 26
Application Deadline: January 15

CEEB CODE: 4485
VERY COMPETITIVE

Located in the heart of the San Francisco Bay Area, Mills College has shaped women's lives for more than 160 years. Offering a progressive liberal arts and sciences curriculum taught by renowned faculty, Mills gives students the personal attention that leads to extraordinary learning. Figures in the above capsule and in this profile are approximate. There is 1 undergraduate school and 4 graduate schools. The 135-acre campus is in an urban area in the San Francisco Bay area, 12 miles east of San Francisco and 8 miles from Berkeley. Including any residence halls, there are 64 buildings.

STUDENT LIFE: 82% of undergraduates are from California. Others are from 48 states, and 12 foreign countries. 84% are from public schools. 47% are White; 22% Hispanic; 12% Asian American. 52% claim no religious affiliation; 17% Buddhist, Hindu, and Muslim; 14% Catholic; 13% Protestant. **Male To Female Ratio:** 11.7:1. The average age of freshmen is 18; all undergraduates, 22. 19% do not continue beyond their first year; 62% remain to graduate. **Housing:** 810 students can be accommodated in college housing, which includes single-sex and coed dorms, on-campus apartments, and married student housing. In addition, there are language houses, special-interest houses, married-student housing is offered on an equal basis to domestic partners of lesbian and gay students, and a student co-op house is available for juniors and seniors. On-campus housing is guaranteed for all 4 years, is available on a first-come, first-served basis. 58% of students live on campus; of those, 77% remain on campus on weekends. All students may keep cars.

FACULTY/CLASSROOMS: 30% of faculty are male; 70% are female. All teach and do research. No introductory courses are taught by graduate students. The average class size in an introductory lecture is 25; in a laboratory is 15; and in a regular course is 16.

PROGRAMS OF STUDY: Mills confers B.A. and B.S. degrees. Master's and doctoral degrees are also awarded. Bachelor's degrees are awarded in AGRICULTURE (environmental studies), BIOLOGICAL SCIENCE (biochemistry, biology/biological science, microbiology, and molecular biology), BUSINESS (business economics), COMMUNICATIONS AND THE ARTS (art history, comparative literature, creative writing, dance, English, English literature, English Writing, French, media arts, modern language, music, Spanish, and studio art), COMPUTER AND PHYSICAL SCIENCE (chemistry, computer science, and mathematics), ENGINEERING AND ENVIRONMENTAL DESIGN (environmental science), HEALTH PROFESSIONS (nursing), SOCIAL SCIENCE (American studies, anthropology, biopsychology, child psychology/development, early childhood studies, economics, ethnic studies, government, French studies, Hispanic American studies, history, international relations, liberal arts/general studies, philosophy, political science/government, prelaw, psychology, public administration, public affairs, sociology, Spanish studies, and women & gender studies). English, psychology, political, legal, economic analysis and computer science are the strongest academically. Psychology, English, and biology have the largest enrollments.

ACTIVITIES: There are 63 groups on campus, including art, cheerleading, choir, dance, drama, environmental, ethnic, film, gay, honors, international, literary magazine, newspaper, political, professional, religious, social, social service, student government, and yearbook. Popular campus events include Black and White Ball, Spring Fling, Heritage Months, Fetish Ball, Choir Winter Celebration,

Vagina Monologues, Final Snacks and Midnight Breakfast, Final Fridays, and Second Saturdays. **Sports:** There are 6 intercollegiate sports for women, and 9 intramural sports for women. Mills College athletic and recreational facilities include a multi-purpose gymnasium, fitness center with a complete array of cardio-fitness and strength training equipment, staffed and equipped training room, activity rooms, dance studios, state-of-the-art aquatic center and therapy spa, 6 newly refurbished lighted tennis courts, grass soccer field, and on-campus running trail. Just minutes away are miles of wooded trails for hiking and running, and the Mills boathouse at Briones Reservoir provides for year-round rowing. **Graduates:** From July 1, 2013 to June 30, 2014, 240 bachelor's degrees were awarded. The most popular majors were English (40%), psychology (25%), and biology (18%). 63 companies recruited on campus in 2013-2014. In an average class, 53% graduate in 4 years or less, 61% graduate in 5 years or less, and 64% graduate in 6 years or less. Of the 2013 graduating class, 20% were enrolled in graduate school within 6 months of graduation, and 36% were employed.

SERVICES: Counseling and information services are available, as is tutoring in every subject. There is a reader service for the blind, and remedial writing. **Library/Resources:** The library contains 244,110 volumes, 28,315 microform items, and 14,057 audio/video tapes/CDs/DVDs, and subscribes to 50,202 periodicals including electronic. Computerized library services include interlibrary loans, database searching, Internet access, and Wi-Fi capability. Special learning facilities include an art gallery, children's school, a small book press, an electronic/computer music studio, botanical garden, computer learning studio, and a radio broadcasting room. **Physically Challenged Students:** All of the campus is accessible. Facilities include wheelchair ramps, elevators, special parking, specially equipped restrooms, special class scheduling, lowered drinking fountains, lowered telephones, and special housing. **Special:** There is cross-registration with the University of California at Berkeley, California State University, and California College of the Arts, among others. Mills offers co-op programs, internships, study abroad, a Washington semester, work-study programs, dual majors, student-designed majors, and interdisciplinary majors, including political, legal, and economic analysis. Accelerated degree programs include 3-2 engineering, 4+1 M.B.A., 4+1 M.P.P., a 4+1 B.A./M.A. program in which students graduate in 5 years with a bachelor's degree in psychology and a master's in infant mental health, and a 4+1 program in which students earn a B.A., an M.A. in education, and complete a program qualifying them for a teaching credential. A general studies degree, credit by exam, and pass/fail options are also available. Mills also offers a a 3-2 engineering degree with USC and a prenursing program leading to a bachelor's degree in nursing at Samuel Merritt College. There are 5 national honor societies including Phi Beta Kappa. **Visiting:** There are regularly scheduled orientations for prospective students, consisting of class visits, campus tours, lunch with faculty, financial aid workshops, an admissions interview, and an overnight stay. There are guides for informal visits, visitors may sit in on classes, and stay overnight. To schedule a visit, contact Kathleen Mulvey at kmulvey@mills.edu. **Campus Safety and Security:** Measures include 24-hour foot and vehicle patrol, emergency notification system, self-defense education, and security escort services. There are shuttle buses, emergency telephones, lighted pathways/sidewalks, controlled access to dorms/residences, AED units, vehicle jumps.

REQUIREMENTS: The SAT or ACT is required. Students are required to submit a high school transcript, two letters of recommendation, a school report, official SAT or ACT test scores, and a writing sample or personal statement. Interviews are recommended but not required. GED or High School Proficiency are accepted in lieu of a High School Transcript. We recommend a cumulative GPA of 3.0 or higher and SAT scores above 1500 combined. AP and CLEP credits are accepted. Important factors in the admissions decision are advanced placement or honors courses, personality/intangible qualities, and recommendations by school officials. To graduate, students must fulfill general education requirements, earn a total of 34 semester course credits, with 10 to 17 in the major, and maintain a minimum GPA of 2.0. Required courses include English, a second-semester writing course, and 1 course in the following: quantitative and computational reasoning, information literacy/information technology, interdisciplinary perspectives, women and gender, multicul-

tural perspectives, creation and criticism in the arts, historical perspectives, natural sciences, and human institutions and behavior. **Procedure:** Freshmen are admitted fall and spring. Entrance exams should be taken at least 1 month prior to application. There are early decision and deferred admissions plans. Early decision applications should be filed by November 15; regular applications, by January 15 for fall entry; and November 1 for spring entry, along with a $50 fee. Notification of early decision is sent December 1; regular decision, February 15. 496 early decision candidates were accepted for the 2014-2015 class. Applications are accepted on-line. **Transfer Students:** 117 transfer students enrolled in 2013-2014. A writing sample, two letters of recommendation, a high school transcript, and official transcripts from all colleges attended are required. The recommended minimum GPA to apply to Mills is 3.0. We consider other factors such as writing skills, strength of curriculum, and number of credit hours. 12 of 34 credits required for the bachelor's degree must be completed at Mills. **International Students:** There are 14 international students enrolled. They must take the TOEFL with a minimum score of 550 on the paper-based TOEFL (PBT) or 80 on the Internet-based version (iBT).

ADMISSIONS: 68% of the 2014-2015 applicants were accepted. The SAT scores for the 2014-2015 freshman class were: Critical Reading--13% below 500, 36% between 500 and 599, 40% between 600 and 699, and 11% between 700 and 800; Math--22% below 500, 45% between 500 and 599, 30% between 600 and 699, and 3% between 700 and 800; Writing--20% below 500, 38% between 500 and 599, 37% between 600 and 699, and 5% between 700 and 800. The ACT scores were 7% below 21, 33% between 21 and 23, 16% between 24 and 26, 26% between 27 and 28, and 18% above 28. 62% of the current freshmen were in the top fifth of their class; 91% were in the top two fifths. 3 freshmen graduated first in their class. **Admissions Contact:** Director of Undergraduate Admission. E-Mail: *admission@mills .edu* Web: *www.mills.edu*

FINANCIAL AID: In 2014-2015, 99% of all full-time freshmen and 95% of continuing full-time students received some form of financial aid. 88% of all full-time freshmen and 84% of continuing full-time students received need-based aid. The average freshman award was $40,894. Need-based scholarships or need-based grants averaged $27,603; and need-based self-help aid (loans and jobs) averaged $6,297. 104% of undergraduate students work part-time. Average annual earnings from campus work are $2292. The average financial indebtedness of the 2014 graduate was $29,349. The FAFSA and the college's own financial statement are required. The priority date for freshman financial aid applications for fall entry is February 1. The deadline for filing freshman financial aid applications for fall entry is February 15.

MOUNT ST. MARY'S COLLEGE - CHALON CAMPUS   C-5
www.msmc.la.edu

Los Angeles, CA 90049	(310) 954-4250
	(800) 999-9893
Fax: (310) 954-4259	Email: admissions@msmc.la.edu
Full-time: 91 men, 1712 women	Faculty: 88
Part-time: 83 men, 402 women	Ph.D.s: 61%
Graduate: 126 men, 448 women	Student/Faculty: 12 to 1
Year: semesters	Tuition: $33,367
Room & Board: $10,530	Freshman Class: 1799 applied, 309 accepted, 528 enrolled
SAT or ACT: required	CEEB CODE: 4493
Application Deadline: February 15	VERY COMPETITIVE+

Mount Saint Mary's College, founded in 1925 and affiliated with the Catholic Church, is a private, primarily women's institution that offers programs in the liberal arts and sciences. Figures in the above capsule and in this profile are approximate. There is 1 undergraduate school and 1 graduate school. In addition to regional accreditation, The Mount has baccalaureate program accreditation with NLN. The 72-acre campus is in an urban area 10 miles west of Los Angeles. Including any residence halls, there are 31 buildings.

STUDENT LIFE: 97% of undergraduates are from California. Others are from 19 states, 5 foreign countries, and Canada. 70% are from public schools. 49% are Hispanic; 17% Asian American; 15% White. 53% are Catholic; 14% Protestant; 13% claim no religious affiliation. **Male To Female Ratio:** 8.5:1. The average age of freshmen is 18; all undergraduates, 23. 16% do not continue beyond their first year; 84% remain to graduate. **Housing:** 668 students can be accommodated in college housing, which includes single-sex dorms. On-campus housing is available on a first-come and first-served basis. 71% of students commute. All students may keep cars.

FACULTY/CLASSROOMS: 27% of faculty are male; 73% are female. 92% teach undergraduates. No introductory courses are taught by graduate students. The average class size in an introductory lecture is 23; in a laboratory is 18; and in a regular course is 23.

PROGRAMS OF STUDY: The Mount confers B.A., B.S. and B.S.N. degrees. Associate, master's, and doctoral degrees are also awarded. Bachelor's degrees are awarded in BIOLOGICAL SCIENCE (biochemistry and biology/biological science), BUSINESS (business administration and management), COMMUNICATIONS AND THE ARTS (art, English, film arts, French, music, and Spanish), COMPUTER AND PHYSICAL SCIENCE (chemistry and mathematics), EDUCATION (elementary education), HEALTH PROFESSIONS (health care administration and nursing), SOCIAL SCIENCE (American studies, child psychology/development, counseling/psychology, gerontology, history, liberal arts/general studies, philosophy, political science/government, psychology, religion, social science, social work, and sociology). Nursing is the strongest academically and have the largest enrollments.

ACTIVITIES: There are no fraternities; 1% of women belong to 2 local and 1 national sorority. There are 28 groups on campus, including art, choir, drama, environmental, ethnic, film, gay, Greek cultural, honors, international, newspaper, political, professional, religious, social, social service, student government, and yearbook. Popular campus events include Leadership Boot Camp, Charity Ball and Spring Carnival. **Sports:** There is 1 intramural sports for men and 2 for women. Facilities include a basketball court, tennis courts, volleyball court, swimming pool, fitness workout room, and dance studio. **Graduates:** From July 1, 2013 to June 30, 2014, 360 bachelor's degrees were awarded. The most popular majors were nursing (50%), sociology (13%), and business (11%). In an average class, 54% graduate in 4 years or less, 59% graduate in 5 years or less, and 62% graduate in 6 years or less. Of the 2013 graduating class, 26% were enrolled in graduate school within 6 months of graduation, and 31% were employed.

SERVICES: Counseling and information services are available, as is tutoring in most subjects. A peer tutoring program is available. **Library/Resources:** The 2 libraries contain 140,000 volumes, and 2,520 audio/video tapes/CDs/DVDs, and subscribe to 25,000 periodicals including electronic. Computerized library services include interlibrary loans, database searching, Internet access, and Wi-Fi capability. Special learning facilities include an art gallery, and an film studio. **Physically Challenged Students:** All of the campus is accessible. Facilities include wheelchair ramps, elevators, special parking, specially equipped restrooms, lowered drinking fountains, lowered telephones, and special housing. **Special:** The Mount offers cross-registration with UCLA, the University of Judaism, internships, study abroad in 17 countries, a Washington semester through American University, dual and student-designed majors, work-study programs, and an accelerated degree program in nursing. There are 20 national honor societies, including Phi Beta Kappa, and a freshman honors program. **Visiting:** There are regularly scheduled orientations for prospective students, including workshops, student panels, tours, class visits, and faculty presentations. There are guides for informal visits, visitors may sit in on classes, and stay overnight. To schedule a visit, contact the Admissions Office. **Campus Safety and Security:** Measures include 24-hour foot and vehicle patrol, emergency notification system, self-defense education, and security escort services. There are shuttle buses, emergency telephones, lighted pathways/sidewalks, and controlled access to dorms/residences.

REQUIREMENTS: The SAT or ACT is required. Applicants must be graduates of an accredited secondary school or have earned the GED, with 16 academic credits and 16 Carnegie units, including 4 years of English literature and composition, 2 or 3 years each of math, science, and social studies, and 1 or 2 years of history. An essay is required,

and an interview is recommended. A GPA of 2.5 is required. AP and CLEP credits are accepted. Important factors in the admissions decision are advanced placement or honors courses, extracurricular activities record, and leadership record. To graduate, students must complete at least 124 semester units with a GPA of 2.0 (C average); a minimum of 45 semester units must be in upper-division work. The total number of hours students must complete in their major varies. All students must satisfy a senior residence requirement and complete a general studies program. Freshmen entering the college with fewer than 24 units must complete Introduction to College Studies. Students must file a graduation application in the Registrar's Office by the end of the term prior to the term of projected completion. **Procedure:** Freshmen are admitted fall and spring. Entrance exams should be taken at the end of the junior year or the beginning of the senior year. There is a rolling admissions plan. Applications should be filed by February 15 for fall entry; November 1 for spring entry, along with a $50 fee. Notification is sent on a rolling basis. Applications are accepted on-line. **Transfer Students:** 254 transfer students enrolled in 2013-2014. Transfer students must have a minimum 2.40 GPA with at least 24 completed credit hours. 30 of 124 credits required for the bachelor's degree must be completed at The Mount. **International Students:** There are 22 international students enrolled. They must take the TOEFL with a minimum score of 530 on the paper-based TOEFL (PBT) or 75 on the Internet-based version (iBT). They must also take the SAT or ACT.

ADMISSIONS: 17% of the 2014-2015 applicants were accepted. **Admissions Contact:** Director of Admissions. E-Mail: *admissions@msmc.la.edu* Web: *www.msmc.la.edu*

FINANCIAL AID: In 2014-2015, 92% of all full-time freshmen and 80% of continuing full-time students received some form of financial aid. 86% of all full-time freshmen and 77% of continuing full-time students received need-based aid. The average freshman award was $29,900. Need-based scholarships or need-based grants averaged $11,000; and need-based self-help aid (loans and jobs) averaged $5,500 ($12,000 maximum). 45% of undergraduate students work part-time. Average annual earnings from campus work are $2723. The average financial indebtedness of the 2014 graduate was $26,500. The Mount is a member of CSS. The FAFSA and the college's own financial statement are required. The priority date for freshman financial aid applications for fall entry is February 15.

NATIONAL UNIVERSITY (*The complete profile is made available exclusively on our website, www.barronspac.com*)

NEWSCHOOL OF ARCHITECTURE & DESIGN (*The complete profile is made available exclusively on our website, www.barronspac.com*)

NOTRE DAME DE NAMUR UNIVERSITY (*The complete profile is made available exclusively on our website, www.barronspac.com*)

OCCIDENTAL COLLEGE   C-5
www.oxy.edu

Los Angeles, CA 90041	(323) 259-2700 / (800) 825-5262
Fax: (323) 341-4875	Email: admission@oxy.edu
Full-time: 915 men, 1186 women	Faculty: 172; IIB, ++$
Part-time: 10 men, 6 women	Ph.D.s: 95%
Graduate: n/av	Student/Faculty: 12 to 1
Year: semesters	Tuition: $47,522
Room & Board: $13,450	Freshman Class: 6071 applied, 2552 accepted, 546 enrolled
SAT CR/M/W: 640/650/660 ACT: 29	CEEB CODE: 4581
Application Deadline: January 10	MOST COMPETITIVE

Founded in 1887, Occidental College is a private, nonsectarian school of liberal arts and sciences, one of the few top liberal arts colleges in a major city. Even more distinctive is Occidental's ability to sustain its traditional commitment to high achievement while enrolling a diverse student body and faculty. There is 1 undergraduate school.

The 120-acre campus is in an urban area in the city of Los Angeles. Including any residence halls, there are 44 buildings.

STUDENT LIFE: 53% of undergraduates are from out of state, mostly the Northwest. Students are from 45 states, 34 foreign countries, and Canada. 58% are from public schools. 51% are White; 15% Hispanic; 12% Asian American. 35% are Protestant; 30% claim no religious affiliation; 19% Catholic; 11% Jewish. **Male To Female Ratio:** 1.3:1. The average age of freshmen is 18; all undergraduates, 20. 7% do not continue beyond their first year; 88% remain to graduate. **Housing:** 1671 students can be accommodated in college housing, which includes single-sex and coed dorms. In addition, there are special-interest houses, fraternity houses, multicultural, food justice, pet, all-women, and gender neutral. On-campus housing is available on a lottery system for upperclassmen. 76% of students live on campus; of those, 60% remain on campus on weekends. All students may keep cars.

FACULTY/CLASSROOMS: 50% of faculty are male; 50% are female. All teach and do research. No introductory courses are taught by graduate students. The average class size in an introductory lecture is 20; in a laboratory is 12; and in a regular course is 15.

PROGRAMS OF STUDY: Oxy confers A.B. degrees. Master's degrees are also awarded. Bachelor's degrees are awarded in BIOLOGICAL SCIENCE (biochemistry and biology/biological science), COMMUNICATIONS AND THE ARTS (art history, Chinese, English, French, Japanese, languages, music, Spanish, and theatre arts), COMPUTER AND PHYSICAL SCIENCE (chemistry, geology, mathematics, and physics), SOCIAL SCIENCE (American studies, asian studies, cognitive science, cultural studies/critical theory & analysis, East Asian studies, economics, history, international relations, Latin American studies, philosophy, physical fitness/movement, political science/government, psychology, religion, sociology, and urban studies). Social sciences, biology, and chemistry are the strongest academically. Economics, diplomacy and world affairs, and biology have the largest enrollments.

ACTIVITIES: 10% of men belong to 4 national fraternities; 13% of women belong to 2 local and 2 national sororities. There are 116 groups on campus, including art, cheerleading, choir, chorus, dance, debate, drama, environmental, ethnic, film, gay, honors, international, jazz band, literary magazine, musical theater, newspaper, orchestra, photography, political, professional, radio and TV, religious, social, social service, student government, student investment fund; entrepreneurs, symphony, and yearbook. Popular campus events include Dance Production, New Play Festival, and Taste of Oxy. **Sports:** There are 10 intercollegiate sports for men and 11 for women, and 6 intramural sports for men and 6 for women. Facilities include a football, soccer, baseball, and softball fields, an all-weather track, tennis courts, an outdoor pool, outdoor basketball courts, a dance studio, a sports medicine center, gym, weight room, and a fitness center. **Graduates:** From July 1, 2013 to June 30, 2014, 554 bachelor's degrees were awarded. The most popular majors were economics (15%), diplomacy and world affairs (8%), and biology (7%). 50 companies recruited on campus in 2013-2014. In an average class, 83% graduate in 4 years or less, 87% graduate in 5 years or less, and 88% graduate in 6 years or less. Of the 2013 graduating class, 22% were enrolled in graduate school within 6 months of graduation, and 64% were employed.

SERVICES: Counseling and information services are available, as is tutoring in some subjects, peer tutors are available in biology, chemistry, geology, kinesiology, mathematics and physics. Peer and faculty advisers are available through the Center for Academic Excellence. **Library/Resources:** The library contains 431,586 volumes, 6,839 microform items, and 12,338 audio/video tapes/CDs/DVDs, and subscribes to 55,322 periodicals including electronic. Computerized library services include interlibrary loans, database searching, Internet access, and Wi-Fi capability. Special learning facilities include an art gallery, radio station, student newspaper and yearbook, fully equipped theater, art studio and gallery, ornithology, conchology and geology collections, physics, plasma, paleomagnetic and optic labs, library special collections. **Physically Challenged Students:** 80% of the campus is accessible. Facilities include wheelchair ramps, elevators, special parking, specially equipped restrooms, lowered drinking fountains. Occidental has a hillside campus. **Special:** Cross-registration is permitted with the California Institute of Technology

and the Art Center College of Design. Students may study abroad in 41 countries in Europe, Asia, Africa, and Latin America. Opportunities are provided for internships, a Washington semester, a residential U.N. semester in New York City, dual and student-designed majors, a 3-2 engineering degree with the California Institute of Technology, a 3-3 law program with Columbia, and a 4-2 biotech program with Keck. There are 8 national honor societies, including Phi Beta Kappa, and 32 departmental honors programs. **Visiting:** There are regularly scheduled orientations for prospective students, including campus tours Monday through Friday at 10:15 a.m. and 1:30 p.m., followed by info sessions with an admission officer at 11:30 a.m. and 4 p.m. There are guides for informal visits, visitors may sit in on classes, and stay overnight. To schedule a visit, contact the Office of Admission at admission@oxy.edu. **Campus Safety and Security:** Measures include 24-hour foot and vehicle patrol, emergency notification system, self-defense education, and security escort services. There are shuttle buses, emergency telephones, lighted pathways/sidewalks, controlled access to dorms/residences, and an whistle alert program.

REQUIREMENTS: The SAT or ACT is required. Applicants should be high school graduates of high academic standing with 4 years of English, 4 of math, 3 each of foreign language and science, and 2 each of social studies and history. The GED is accepted. An essay is required and an interview is recommended. AP credits are accepted. Important factors in the admissions decision are extracurricular activities record, advanced placement or honors courses, and recommendations by school officials. To graduate, students must complete 32 courses of 4 semester hours each and maintain a minimum GPA of 2.0. In addition, all students must fulfill core course requirements in foreign language, fine arts, writing proficiency; 12 units are required in science and mathematics, foreign language, and cultural studies. To graduate, all students must complete a comprehensive exam; some majors require a thesis. **Procedure:** Freshmen are admitted fall. Entrance exams should be taken no later than December of the senior year. There are early decision and deferred admissions plans. Early decision applications should be filed by November 15; regular applications, by January 10 for fall entry, along with a $60 fee. Notification of early decision is sent December 15; regular decision, April 1. 130 early decision candidates were accepted for the 2014-2015 class. 792 applicants were on the 2014 waiting list; 65 were admitted. Applications are accepted on-line. **Transfer Students:** 41 transfer students enrolled in 2013-2014. Students must have at least a B average (3.0 GPA) in all courses submitted for transfer credit. The SAT or ACT is required. The application deadline is March 15 for the fall, October 15 for the spring. 64 of 128 credits required for the bachelor's degree must be completed at Oxy. **International Students:** There are 121 international students enrolled. The school actively recruits these students. They must take the TOEFL with a minimum score of 600 on the paper-based TOEFL (PBT). They must also take the SAT or ACT.

ADMISSIONS: 42% of the 2014-2015 applicants were accepted. The SAT scores for the 2014-2015 freshman class were: Critical Reading--1% below 500, 20% between 500 and 599, 56% between 600 and 699, and 22% between 700 and 800; Math--1% below 500, 19% between 500 and 599, 51% between 600 and 699, and 28% between 700 and 800; Writing--1% below 500, 18% between 500 and 599, 55% between 600 and 699, and 26% between 700 and 800. The ACT scores were 2% between 21 and 23, 16% between 24 and 26, 19% between 27 and 28, and 63% above 28. 79% of the current freshmen were in the top fifth of their class; 96% were in the top two fifths. **Admissions Contact:** Sally Richmond, Dean of Admission. E-Mail: *admission@oxy.edu* Web: *www.oxy.edu*

FINANCIAL AID: In 2014-2015, 72% of all full-time freshmen and 75% of continuing full-time students received some form of financial aid. 56% of all full-time freshmen and 57% of continuing full-time students received need-based aid. The average freshman award was $39,377. Need-based scholarships or need-based grants averaged $30,947 ($59,592 maximum); need-based self-help aid (loans and jobs) averaged $7,398 ($10,000 maximum); and other non-need-based awards and non-need-based scholarships averaged $7,761 ($60,822 maximum). 57% of undergraduate students work part-time. Average annual earnings from campus work are $1546. The average financial indebtedness of the 2014 graduate was $22,786. The CSS/Profile, FAFSA, and the state aid form, and non-custodial parent's statement are required. The deadline for filing freshman financial aid applications for fall entry is February 1.

OTIS COLLEGE OF ART AND DESIGN (*The complete profile is made available exclusively on our website, www.barronspac.com*)

PACIFIC UNION COLLEGE	B-2
www.puc.edu	
Angwin, CA 94508	(707) 965-6336
	(800) 862-7080
Fax: (707) 965-6432	Email: enroll@puc.edu
Full-time: 500 men, 575 women	Faculty: n/av
Part-time: 135 men, 165 women	Ph.Ds: n/av
Graduate: 1 women	Student/Faculty: n/av
Year: trimesters, summer session	Tuition: $22,150
Room & Board: $6000	Freshman Class: n/av
SAT or ACT: recommended	CEEB CODE: 4600
Application Deadline: open	**VERY COMPETITIVE**

Pacific Union College, founded in 1888, is a private college affiliated with the Seventh-day Adventist Church, offering programs in liberal arts, religion, business, health science, and teacher preparation, among others. The figures in the above capsule and in this profile are approximate. There is one graduate school. In addition to regional accreditation, PUC has baccalaureate program accreditation with CSWE, NASM, and NLN. The 1500-acre campus is in a rural area 70 miles north of San Francisco. Including any residence halls, there are 60 buildings.

STUDENT LIFE: 76% of undergraduates are from California. Others are from 42 states, 26 foreign countries, and Canada. 40% are White; 29% Asian American; and 15% Hispanic. **Male To Female Ratio:** 1.2:1. The average age of freshmen is 19; all undergraduates, 21. 32% do not continue beyond their first year; 40% remain to graduate. **Housing:** 1344 students can be accommodated in college housing, which includes single-sex dorms and married student housing. On-campus housing is guaranteed for the freshman year only. 76% of students live on campus. Alcohol is not permitted. All students may keep cars.

FACULTY/CLASSROOMS: 56% of faculty are male; 44% are female. All teach undergraduates. No introductory courses are taught by graduate students. The average class size in an introductory lecture is 19; in a laboratory is 18; and in a regular course is 17.

PROGRAMS OF STUDY: PUC confers B.A., B.S., B.B.A., B.Mus. and B.S.W. degrees. Associate and master's degrees are also awarded. Bachelor's degrees are awarded in BIOLOGICAL SCIENCE (biology/biological science and biophysics), BUSINESS (business administration and management), COMMUNICATIONS AND THE ARTS (communications, English, fine arts, French, graphic design, journalism, music, photography, public relations, radio/television technology, and Spanish), COMPUTER AND PHYSICAL SCIENCE (applied mathematics, chemistry, computer science, mathematics, natural sciences, and physics), EDUCATION (early childhood education and physical education), ENGINEERING AND ENVIRONMENTAL DESIGN (airline piloting and navigation and graphic arts technology), HEALTH PROFESSIONS (nursing), SOCIAL SCIENCE (history, psychology, religion, social studies, social work, and theological studies). Sciences and behavioral science is the strongest academically. Nursing and business administration has the largest enrollments.

ACTIVITIES: There are 50 groups on campus, including and campus ministries, academic interest groups, art, band, chess, choir, chorale, computers, drama, ethnic, film, honors, jazz band, literary magazine, newspaper, orchestra, photography, political, radio and TV, religious, social, student government, symphony, and yearbook. Popular campus events include Picnic and Ski Days, All-College Get-Acquainted Party, Fall and Spring Festivals. **Sports:** There are 3 intercollegiate sports for men and 3 for women, and 6 intramural sports for men and 6 for women. Facilities include a gym, a pool, lighted tennis courts, and 3 athletic fields for softball, soccer, volleyball, flag ball, and track and field. **Graduates:** From July 1, 2013 to June 30,

2014, 325 bachelor's degrees were awarded. The most popular majors were nursing (36%), business (19%), and chemistry (5%). In an average class, 12% graduate in 4 years or less, 19% graduate in 5 years or less, and 36% graduate in 6 years or less.

SERVICES: Counseling and information services are available, as is tutoring in most subjects. There is a reader service for the blind, and remedial math and writing. **Library/Resources:** The library contains 148,218 volumes, 125,268 microform items, and 6,623 audio/video tapes/CDs/DVDs, and subscribes to 10,637 periodicals including electronic. Computerized library services include interlibrary loans, database searching, Internet access, and Wi-Fi capability. Special learning facilities include an art gallery, natural history museum, radio station, a video production studio, an observatory and a marine field station. **Physically Challenged Students:** 95% of the campus is accessible. Facilities include wheelchair ramps, elevators, special parking, specially equipped restrooms, and special class scheduling. **Special:** Students may study abroad in Austria, Spain, France, Argentina, and Italy, earn B.A.-B.S. degrees, take dual majors, and pursue a major in interdisciplinary studies. Internships, social work, education, ministerial field experiences, and accelerated degree programs in business management and early childhood education are also offered. The college offers nondegree study and credit for life, military, and work experience. There are 2 national honor societies and a freshman honors program. **Visiting:** There are regularly scheduled orientations for prospective students. There are guides for informal visits, visitors may sit in on classes, and stay overnight. To schedule a visit, contact the Admissions Office. **Campus Safety and Security:** Measures include 24-hour foot and vehicle patrol, emergency notification system, self-defense education, and security escort services. There are emergency telephones, lighted pathways/sidewalks, and a safety committee.

REQUIREMENTS: The SAT or ACT is recommended. Scores are used only for advising purposes. Candidates for admission should have completed 4 years of English, 2 of math, and 1 each of science and history. A GPA of 2.3 is required. AP and CLEP credits are accepted. Important factors in the admissions decision are recommendations by school officials, leadership record, and advanced placement or honors courses.To graduate, a student must complete a minimum of 192 quarter hours, including 60 in upper-level courses, and maintain a minimum GPA of 2.0. Distribution requirements include courses in rhetoric, statistics, historic, philosophy, social science, foreign language, literature, visual and applied arts, music, math, science, and health and fitness. A religion course is required, as is a thesis in some programs. **Procedure:** Freshmen are admitted to all sessions. Entrance exams should be taken in the junior or senior year. There is a rolling admissions plan. Application deadlines are open. Application fee is $30. Applications are accepted on-line. **Transfer Students:** Admission requirements are the same as for non-transfer students. 36 of 192 credits required for the bachelor's degree must be completed at PUC. **International Students:** There are 92 international students enrolled. They must take the TOEFL. They must also take the SAT or ACT.

ADMISSIONS: Director of Enrollment Services. E-Mail: *enroll@puc.edu* Web: *www.puc.edu*

FINANCIAL AID: In 2014-2015, 100% of all full-time freshmen and 99% of continuing full-time students received some form of financial aid. 95% of all full-time freshmen and 64% of continuing full-time students received need-based aid. The average freshman award was $15,899. 80% of undergraduate students work part-time. Average annual earnings from campus work are $1500. The average financial indebtedness of the 2014 graduate was $13,000. The FAFSA and the college's own financial statement are required. Check with the school for current application deadlines.

PEPPERDINE UNIVERSITY — C-4

www.pepperdine.edu

Malibu, CA 90263	(310) 506-4369

Fax: (310) 506-4861	Email: admission-seaver@pepperdine.edu
Full-time: 1262 men, 1824 women	Faculty: IIA, ++$
Part-time: 232 men, 170 women	Ph.D.s: 100%
Graduate: 1499 men, 2332 women	Student/Faculty: 15 to 1
Year: semesters, summer session	Tuition: $42,772
Room & Board: $12,600	Freshman Class: 9222 applied, 3497 accepted, 777 enrolled
SAT CR/M/W: 604/623/610 ACT: 29	CEEB CODE: 4630
Application Deadline: January 5	HIGHLY COMPETITIVE+

Pepperdine University, founded in 1937, is a private liberal arts university affiliated with the Church of Christ. Figures in the above capsule and in this profile are approximate. There is 1 undergraduate school and 4 graduate schools. In addition to regional accreditation, Pepperdine has baccalaureate program accreditation with AACSB and NCATE. The 830-acre campus is in a suburban area 35 miles northwest of Los Angeles, overlooking the Pacific Ocean. Including any residence halls, there are 76 buildings.

STUDENT LIFE: 53% of undergraduates are from California. Others are from 50 states, 60 foreign countries, and Canada. 65% are from public schools. 45% are White; 15% Hispanic; 12% Asian American. 16% are Catholic. The average age of freshmen is 18; all undergraduates, 20. **Housing:** College-sponsored housing includes single-sex dorms, on-campus apartments, off-campus apartments, and married student housing. In addition, there are honors houses and special-interest houses. On-campus housing is guaranteed for the freshman year only and is available on a lottery system for upperclassmen. Alcohol is not permitted. All students may keep cars.

FACULTY/CLASSROOMS: 58% of faculty are male; 42% are female. All teach and do research. No introductory courses are taught by graduate students. The average class size in an introductory lecture is 18; in a laboratory is 15; and in a regular course is 17.

PROGRAMS OF STUDY: Pepperdine confers B.A., B.S. and B.S.M. degrees. Master's and doctoral degrees are also awarded. Bachelor's degrees are awarded in BIOLOGICAL SCIENCE (biology/biological science and nutrition), BUSINESS (accounting, business administration and management, international business management, management science, and marketing management), COMMUNICATIONS AND THE ARTS (advertising, art, art history and appreciation, communications, creative writing, dramatic arts, English, film arts, French, German, Italian, journalism, media arts, music, public relations, Spanish, speech/debate/rhetoric, and telecommunications), COMPUTER AND PHYSICAL SCIENCE (chemistry, computer science, mathematics, natural sciences, and physics), EDUCATION (elementary education, mathematics education, physical education, and secondary education), ENGINEERING AND ENVIRONMENTAL DESIGN (engineering), HEALTH PROFESSIONS (sports medicine), SOCIAL SCIENCE (economics, Hispanic American studies, history, humanities, international studies, liberal arts/general studies, philosophy, political science/government, psychology, religion, social science, and sociology). Natural sciences (premedical), sports medicine, business administration, economics and political science are the strongest academically. Communication and business has the largest enrollments.

ACTIVITIES: There are 60 groups on campus, including Hawaiian, women's leadership, art, band, cheerleading, chess, choir, chorale, chorus, computers, dance, debate, drama, environmental, ethnic, film, honors, international, jazz band, literary magazine, medical, musical theater, newspaper, opera, orchestra, pep band, photography, political, professional, radio and TV, religious, social, social service, student government, and symphony. Popular campus events include Waves Weekend, C2F (Culture and Club Fair), Songfest and REEL Stories Student Film Festival. **Sports:** There are 8 intercollegiate sports for men and 9 for women, and 7 intramural sports for men and 7 for women. Facilities include a field house, pool, weight room, basketball, racquetball, tennis courts, playing fields, an all-weather track, an aerobics room, and a whirlpool/hot tub. **Graduates:** From July 1, 2013 to June 30, 2014, 891 bachelor's degrees were awarded. The most popular majors were business administration (9%), international business (6%), and advertising (4%). In an average class, 3% graduate in 3 years or less, 69% graduate in 4 years or less, 80% graduate in 5 years or less, and 81% graduate in 6 years or less.

SERVICES: Counseling and information services are available, as is tutoring in most subjects. **Library/Resources:** The 4 libraries contain 551,502 volumes, 505,458 microform items, 15,402 audio/video tapes/CDs/DVDs, and subscribe to 51,798 periodicals including electronic. Computerized library services include interlibrary loans, database searching, and Internet access. Special learning facilities include an art gallery, radio station, TV station, a writing center, and the academic center for excellence. **Physically Challenged Students:** 90% of the campus is accessible. Facilities include wheelchair ramps, elevators, special parking, specially equipped restrooms, special class scheduling, lowered drinking fountains, lowered telephones, and special housing. **Special:** Students may earn 1 to 4 units for an internship, available in most majors, participate in a Washington semester, and study abroad in 8 countries. The school offers a 3-2 engineering degree with Washington University in St. Louis and the University of Southern California. There are dual majors in any discipline, student-designed contract majors, federal work-study programs, nondegree study, and pass/fail options. There are 14 national honor societies and 6 departmental honors programs. **Visiting:** There are regularly scheduled orientations for prospective students, information sessions, campus tours, classroom visits, admission counselor meetings, and meeting faculty member. There are guides for informal visits, visitors may sit in on classes, and stay overnight. To schedule a visit, contact the Housing and Residence Life Office at (310) 506-7586. **Campus Safety and Security:** Measures include 24-hour foot and vehicle patrol, emergency notification system, self-defense education, and security escort services. There are shuttle buses, emergency telephones, lighted pathways/sidewalks, in-room safes, guarded entrances to campus, security cameras, and a campus crime watch program.

REQUIREMENTS: The SAT or ACT is required. It is strongly recommended that candidates for admission present a college preparatory program that includes 4 years of English, 3 of math, 2 each of foreign language and science, and courses in speech communication, humanities, and social science. AP and CLEP credits are accepted. Important factors in the admissions decision are advanced placement or honors courses, recommendations by school officials, and evidence of special talent. To graduate, students must complete 128 units, including 64 units of general education requirements. 2 years of a broad liberal arts core curriculum are needed. Courses are required in English, religion, Western heritage, non-Western heritage, American heritage, behavioral science, foreign language, lab science, math, speech and rhetoric, freshman seminar, and phys ed. Students must take at least 40 upper-division units and complete a 28-unit residency requirement. Pepperdine requires a minimum GPA of 2.0 for graduation. **Procedure:** Freshmen are admitted fall and spring. Entrance exams should be taken in the fall. There is a deferred admissions plan. Applications should be filed by January 5 for fall entry; October 15 for spring entry, along with a $65 fee. Notifications are sent April 1. **Transfer Students:** Transfer applicants should have a minimum GPA of 3.0 from an accredited college. SAT or ACT scores are required for applicants who have completed fewer than 30 transferable semester hours at an accredited college. 28 of 128 credits required for the bachelor's degree must be completed at Pepperdine. **International Students:** There are 290 international students enrolled. The school actively recruits these students. They must take the TOEFL with a minimum score of 550 on the paper-based TOEFL (PBT) or 80 on the Internet-based version (iBT) and the college's own test. They must also take the SAT.

ADMISSIONS: 38% of the 2014-2015 applicants were accepted. The SAT scores for the 2014-2015 freshman class were: Critical Reading--6% below 500, 39% between 500 and 599, 42% between 600 and 699, and 13% between 700 and 800; Math--5% below 500, 28% between 500 and 599, 46% between 600 and 699, and 21% between 700 and 800; Writing--5% below 500, 34% between 500 and 599, 43% between 600 and 699, and 18% between 700 and 800. The ACT scores were 6% below 21, 8% between 21 and 23, 19% between 24 and 26, 21% between 27 and 28, and 46% above 28. 74% of the current freshmen were in the top fifth of their class; 93% were in the top two fifths.

Admissions Contact: Dean of Admission and Enrollment Management. E-Mail: *admission-seaver@pepperdine.edu* Web: *www.pepperdine.edu*

FINANCIAL AID: In 2014-2015, 76% of all full-time freshmen and 73% of continuing full-time students received some form of financial aid. 53% of all full-time freshmen and 53% of continuing full-time students received need-based aid. The average freshman award was $33,178. Need-based scholarships or need-based grants averaged $29,916 ($54,172 maximum); need-based self-help aid (loans and jobs) averaged $9,208 ($55,296 maximum); non-need-based athletic scholarships averaged $40,028 ($54,272 maximum); other non-need-based awards and non-need-based scholarships averaged $22,857 ($46,816 maximum); and $9,102 from other forms of aid. 40% of undergraduate students work part-time. Average annual earnings from campus work are $2100. The average financial indebtedness of the 2014 graduate was $29,823. The FAFSA and the college's own financial statement, and the federal income tax form, the state scholarship/grant form (California residents), and W-2 wage statements are required. The priority date for freshman financial aid applications for fall entry is February 15.

PITZER COLLEGE · D-5
www.pitzer.edu

Claremont, CA 91711	(909) 621-8129
	(800) PITZER-1
Fax: (909) 621-8770	Email: admission@pitzer.edu
Full-time: 411 men, 647 women	Faculty: 74; IIB, ++$
Part-time: 12 men, 29 women	Ph.D.s: 100%
Graduate: n/av	Student/Faculty: 12 to 1
Year: semesters, summer session	Tuition: $42,550
Room & Board: $12,438	Freshman Class: 3743 applied, 903 accepted, 272 enrolled
SAT CR/M: 652/641 ACT: 30	CEEB CODE: 4619
Application Deadline: January 1	MOST COMPETITIVE

Pitzer College, founded in 1963, is a private liberal arts college that through an interdisciplinary approach emphasizes social justice, intercultural understanding, and environmental sensitivity. It is one of the Claremont Colleges. The figures in the above capsule and in this profile are approximate. The 31-acre campus is in a suburban area 35 miles east of Los Angeles. Including any residence halls, there are 17 buildings.

STUDENT LIFE: 50% of undergraduates are from out of state, mostly the Northwest. Students are from 42 states, 14 foreign countries, and Canada. 46% are White; 16% Hispanic. **Male To Female Ratio:** 1.6:1. The average age of freshmen is 18; all undergraduates, 21. 7% do not continue beyond their first year; 80% remain to graduate. **Housing:** 734 students can be accommodated in college housing, which includes coed dorms and off-campus apartments. In addition, there are special-interest houses, a quiet hall, an involvement tower, and food co-op, substance-free, and all-female floors. On-campus housing is guaranteed for the freshman year only. 75% of students live on campus; of those, 75% remain on campus on weekends. Upperclassmen may keep cars.

FACULTY/CLASSROOMS: 54% of faculty are male; 46% are female. All teach and do research. No introductory courses are taught by graduate students. The average class size in an introductory lecture is 20; in a laboratory is 18; and in a regular course is 18.

PROGRAMS OF STUDY: Pitzer confers B.A. degrees. Bachelor's degrees are awarded in BIOLOGICAL SCIENCE (biochemistry, biology/biological science, and neurosciences), BUSINESS (management engineering and organizational behavior), COMMUNICATIONS AND THE ARTS (art, classics, dance, dramatic arts, English, film arts, French, linguistics, media arts, music, and Spanish), COMPUTER AND PHYSICAL SCIENCE (chemistry, mathematics, physics, science, and science and management), ENGINEERING AND ENVIRONMENTAL DESIGN (environmental science), SOCIAL SCIENCE (African American studies, American studies, anthropol-

ogy, Asian/American studies, Asian/Oriental studies, Caribbean studies, economics, European studies, history, international relations, Latin American studies, Mexican-American/Chicano studies, philosophy, political science/government, psychology, sociology, Third World studies, and women's studies). Social and behavioral sciences are the strongest academically and have the largest enrollments.

ACTIVITIES: There are 50 groups on campus, including art, band, chess, choir, chorale, chorus, computers, dance, debate, drama, environmental, ethnic, film, gay, honors, international, jazz band, literary magazine, newspaper, orchestra, photography, political, professional, radio and TV, religious, social, social service, student government, and symphony. Popular campus events include the Kohoutek Festival, Hammock on the Mounds and Reggae Festival. **Sports:** There are 10 intercollegiate sports for men and 11 for women. Facilities include 3 gyms, 5 swimming pools, 20 tennis courts, numerous playing fields, and lighted volleyball courts. The campus stadium seats 1200. There are also shared intercollegiate sports with Pomona College. The Gold Student Center features a fitness room, lap pool, frisbee field, and basketball and volleyball courts. **Graduates:** From July 1, 2013 to June 30, 2014, 244 bachelor's degrees were awarded. The most popular majors were psychology (17%), political studies (11%), and sociology (11%). 25 companies recruited on campus in 2013-2014. In an average class, 75% graduate in 4 years or less, 80% graduate in 5 years or less, and 85% graduate in 6 years or less. Of the 2013 graduating class, 17% were enrolled in graduate school within 6 months of graduation, and 56% were employed.

SERVICES: Counseling and information services are available, as is tutoring in most subjects, tutoring software and programs for the learning disabled. There is a reader service for the blind, and remedial writing. **Library/Resources:** The library contains 250,000 volumes, 1.2 million microform items, 17,000 audio/video tapes/CDs/DVDs, and subscribes to 35,000 periodicals including electronic. Computerized library services include interlibrary loans, database searching, Internet access, and Wi-Fi capability. Special learning facilities include an art gallery, radio station, a social science lab, an arboretum, and a farm in Costa Rica. **Physically Challenged Students:** 95% of the campus is accessible. Facilities include wheelchair ramps, elevators, special parking, specially equipped restrooms, lowered drinking fountains, lowered telephones, and special housing. **Special:** Students may cross-register at any of the other Claremont Colleges, or study abroad in 60 countries in Africa, Asia, Europe, Latin America, North America, or Oceania. There are co-op programs, work-study, internships, dual majors, student-designed majors, an extensive first-year seminar program, and interdisciplinary study offered in science and technology, and international or intercultural studies. Joint advanced degrees are offered in math, economics, M.I.S., psychology, and public policy, as is a 7-year B.A./D.O. program with the College of Western Health Sciences. There are independent study and limited pass/fail options. There is 1 national honor society and 18 departmental honors programs. **Visiting:** There are regularly scheduled orientations for prospective students. There are guides for informal visits, visitors may sit in on classes, and stay overnight. To schedule a visit, contact the Office of Admissions. **Campus Safety and Security:** Measures include 24-hour foot and vehicle patrol, emergency notification system, self-defense education, and security escort services. There are emergency telephones and lighted pathways/sidewalks.

REQUIREMENTS: Applicants must be graduates of an accredited secondary school or have earned the GED. Secondary school courses must include 4 years of English courses requiring extensive writing, and 3 years each of social and behavioral sciences including history, lab science, foreign language, and math. A personal essay is required and a personal interview is recommended. Students in the top 10% of their class or those with an unweighted GPA in academic subjects of 3.5 are not required to submit ACT or SAT scores. Students without these qualifications must submit either ACT or SAT scores, 2 SAT subject tests, 2 AP test scores of at least 4 (1 in English, 1 in math or science), 2 IB exams (English 1A and Mathematics Methods Standard Level or a higher-level course), or a recent analytical writing sample from a humanities or social science course and a math exam from a course at the algebra II level or higher, both including teacher's comments and grades. AP credits are accepted. Important factors in the admissions decision are advanced placement or honors courses, leadership record, and evidence of special talent. Students must complete a total of 32 courses with a 2.0 GPA. Although requirements vary according to major, most students take introductory or preparatory courses in their first 2 years and courses in or related to their major in the last 2 years. All students must fulfill educational objectives in the following areas: interdisciplinary and intercultural exploration; social responsibility and the ethical implications of knowledge and action; breadth of knowledge; and written expression. More than 10 courses are required in the major. **Procedure:** Freshmen are admitted fall and spring. Entrance exams should be taken by January 1. There are early decision and deferred admissions plans. Early decision applications should be filed by November 1; regular applications, by January 1 for fall entry; and October 15 for spring entry. The fall 2014 application fee was $50. Notifications are sent April 1. Applications are accepted on-line. **Transfer Students:** 21 transfer students enrolled in 2013-2014. No more than 2 years of previous credits may be transferred. 64 of 128 credits required for the bachelor's degree must be completed at Pitzer. **International Students:** There are 36 international students enrolled. The school actively recruits these students. They must take the TOEFL with a minimum score of 520 on the paper-based TOEFL (PBT) or 70 on the Internet-based version (iBT).

ADMISSIONS: 24% of the 2014-2015 applicants were accepted. The SAT scores for the 2014-2015 freshman class were: Critical Reading--15% between 500 and 599, 60% between 600 and 699, and 25% between 700 and 800; Math-24% between 500 and 599, 60% between 600 and 699, and 16% between 700 and 800. 75% of the current freshmen were in the top fifth of their class; 98% were in the top two fifths. **Admissions Contact:** Vice President, Admission and Financial Aid. E-Mail: *admission@pitzer.edu* Web: *www.pitzer.edu*

FINANCIAL AID: In 2014-2015, 34% of all full-time freshmen and 40% of continuing full-time students received some form of financial aid. 32% of all full-time freshmen and 39% of continuing full-time students received need-based aid. The average freshman award was $35,509. Need-based scholarships or need-based grants averaged $32,873; need-based self-help aid (loans and jobs) averaged $4,914; and other non-need-based awards and non-need-based scholarships averaged $5,000. Pitzer is a member of CSS. The CSS/Profile, FAFSA, and the state aid form are required. The deadline for filing freshman financial aid applications for fall entry is February 1.

POINT LOMA NAZARENE UNIVERSITY   **D-5**
www.pointloma.edu

San Diego, CA 92106	**(619) 849-2541**
	(800) 733-7770
Fax: (619) 849-2601	Email: admissions@pointloma.edu
Full-time: 890 men, 1603 women	Faculty: IIB, +$
Part-time: 39 men, 36 women	Ph.D.s: 82%
Graduate: 223 men, 583 women	Student/Faculty: 14 to 1
Year: semesters, summer session	Tuition: $31,406
Room & Board: $9600	Freshman Class: 3036 applied, 2111 accepted, 588 enrolled
SAT CR/M/W: 560/560/550 ACT: 25	CEEB CODE: 4605
Application Deadline: March 1	COMPETITIVE+

Point Loma Nazarene University, founded in 1902, is a private liberal arts university affiliated with the Church of the Nazarene. There are 2 undergraduate schools and 5 graduate schools. In addition to regional accreditation, PLNU has baccalaureate program accreditation with ACBSP and NCATE. The 90-acre campus is in a suburban area in San Diego. Including any residence halls, there are 51 buildings.

STUDENT LIFE: 83% of undergraduates are from California. 62% are White; 22% Hispanic. **Male To Female Ratio:** 1.9:1. The average age of freshmen is 18; all undergraduates, 20. 15% do not continue beyond their first year; 74% remain to graduate. **Housing:** 1762 students can be accommodated in college housing, which includes single-sex and coed dorms, on-campus apartments, and off-campus apartments. On-campus housing is available on a first-come, first-served basis, and is available on a lottery system for upperclassmen. 67% of students live on campus. Alcohol is not permitted. Upperclassmen may keep cars.

FACULTY/CLASSROOMS: 45% of faculty are male; 55% are female. No introductory courses are taught by graduate students. The average class size in an introductory lecture is 25 and in a laboratory is 18.

PROGRAMS OF STUDY: PLNU confers B.A., B.S., B.Mus. B.S.N. and B.S.Bus Admin degrees. Master's degrees are also awarded. Bachelor's degrees are awarded in BIOLOGICAL SCIENCE (biochemistry, biology/biological science, and nutrition), BUSINESS (accounting, business administration and management, business communications, finance, and marketing), COMMUNICATIONS AND THE ARTS (broadcasting, communications, graphic design, journalism, literature, media arts, music, music performance, music theory and composition, piano/organ, romance languages and literature, Spanish, visual and performing arts, voice, and writing), COMPUTER AND PHYSICAL SCIENCE (chemistry, computer information systems, computer science, mathematics, and physics), EDUCATION (art education, athletic training, education, and music education), ENGINEERING AND ENVIRONMENTAL DESIGN (engineering physics and environmental science), HEALTH PROFESSIONS (exercise science, health science, and nursing), SOCIAL SCIENCE (biblical studies, child psychology/development, Christian studies, dietetics, economics, family and community services, history, industrial and organizational psychology, international studies, liberal arts/general studies, ministries, philosophy, philosophy and religion, political science/government, psychology, social science, social work, and sociology). Nursing, business administration, and biology are the strongest academically and have the largest enrollments.

ACTIVITIES: There are no fraternities or sororities. Groups on campus include art, band, cheerleading, choir, chorale, computers, debate, drama, ethnic, film, forensics, honors, international, jazz band, literary magazine, musical theater, newspaper, opera, orchestra, political, professional, radio and TV, religious, social, social service, student government, and yearbook. Popular campus events include Spiritual Emphasis Week and Christmas Messiah Concert. **Sports:** Facilities include a gym, baseball and soccer fields, a track, tennis courts, dorm lounges, and table tennis and pool tables. **Graduates:** From July 1, 2013 to June 30, 2014, 588 bachelor's degrees were awarded. The most popular majors were business/marketing (21%), health professions and related programs (17%), and biological and life sciences (9%). In an average class, 59% graduate in 4 years or less, 72% graduate in 5 years or less, and 73% graduate in 6 years or less.

SERVICES: Counseling and information services are available, as is tutoring in most subjects. There is a reader service for the blind, and remedial math, reading, and writing. **Library/Resources:** Computerized library services include interlibrary loans, database searching, and Internet access. Special learning facilities include an art gallery, radio station, TV station, a lab preschool. **Physically Challenged Students:** All of the campus is accessible. Facilities include wheelchair ramps, elevators, special parking, specially equipped restrooms, special class scheduling, lowered drinking fountains, and lowered telephones. **Special:** PLNU offers internships in the church, in state and national governments, in journalism, in small business, and in the film industry. Students may study abroad in several world capitals and in more than 40 countries. There are Washington and United Nations semester programs. Various dual or interdepartmental majors are offered, including biology-chemistry, graphic communications, human environmental science-business, and church music-youth ministries. There are pre-professional programs in medicine/dentistry, law, and engineering. A general studies degree in liberal studies is available, as is credit for life, military, and work experience for nursing students. There are 6 national honor societies, a freshman honors program, and 10 departmental honors programs. **Visiting:** There are regularly scheduled orientations for prospective students, including campus tours and appointments with major advisers. There are guides for informal visits, visitors may sit in on classes, and stay overnight. To schedule a visit, contact the Admissions Office. **Campus Safety and Security:** Measures include 24-hour foot and vehicle patrol, emergency notification system, self-defense education, and security escort services. There are shuttle buses, emergency telephones, and lighted pathways/sidewalks.

REQUIREMENTS: The SAT or ACT is required. Candidates for admission should have completed 4 years of English, 3 of math, 2 each of a lab science and the same foreign language, and 1 of history. A GPA of 2.8 is required. AP and CLEP credits are accepted. Important factors in the admissions decision are personality/intangible qualities, leadership record, and advanced placement or honors courses. To graduate, students must complete a minimum of 128 semester units. At least 24 upper-division semester units are needed for the major. A minimum GPA of 2.0 is required. Students must complete the general education requirements, though B.S.N. candidates need not take a foreign language. General education requirements include 9 courses in cultural studies, 5 in the sciences, 4 in cognitive studies, and 3 in religious studies. Students must demonstrate proficiency in writing and math. **Procedure:** Freshmen are admitted fall and spring. Entrance exams should be taken in the junior year or early in the senior year. Applications should be filed by March 1 for fall entry, along with a $50 fee. Notifications are sent April 1. Applications are accepted on-line. **Transfer Students:** Transfer students must have a minimum cumulative GPA of 2.0 (based on transferable units) to be considered for admission. Applicants with at least 36 transferable units at the time of application need only submit college transcripts (high school transcripts are not required for these applicants). 24 of 128 credits required for the bachelor's degree must be completed at PLNU. **International Students:** There are 14 international students enrolled. They must take the TOEFL with a minimum score of 550 on the paper-based TOEFL (PBT) or 80 on the Internet-based version (iBT).

ADMISSIONS: 70% of the 2014-2015 applicants were accepted. The SAT scores for the 2014-2015 freshman class were: Critical Reading--18% below 500, 52% between 500 and 599, 27% between 600 and 699, and 4% between 700 and 800; Math--17% below 500, 46% between 500 and 599, 31% between 600 and 699, and 5% between 700 and 800; Writing--21% below 500, 53% between 500 and 599, 22% between 600 and 699, and 4% between 700 and 800. **Admissions Contact:** Shannon Hutchison, Director, Undergrad Admissions. E-Mail: *admissions@pointloma.edu* Web: *www.pointloma.edu*

FINANCIAL AID: The average financial indebtedness of the 2014 graduate was $32,649. PLNU is a member of CSS. The FAFSA is required. The priority date for freshman financial aid applications for fall entry is March 2.

POMONA COLLEGE — D-5
www.pomona.edu

Claremont, CA 91711   (909) 621-8134

Fax: (909) 621-8952	Email: admissions@pomona.edu
Full-time: 766 men, 830 women	Faculty: 190; IIB, ++$
Part-time: 7 men, 9 women	Ph.D.s: 99%
Graduate: n/av	Student/Faculty: 8 to 1
Year: semesters	Tuition: $43,580
Room & Board: $14,100	Freshman Class: 7153 applied, 996 accepted, 397 enrolled
SAT CR/M/W: 730/730/730 ACT: 33	CEEB CODE: 4607
Application Deadline: January 1	MOST COMPETITIVE

Established in 1887, Pomona College is one of the nation's leading liberal arts colleges and the founding member of The Claremont Colleges, a consortium of 5 undergraduate and 2 graduate schools. The 140-acre campus is in a suburban area 35 miles east of Los Angeles, and 20 miles east of Pasadena. Including any residence halls, there are 63 buildings.

STUDENT LIFE: 68% of undergraduates are from out of state, mostly the Northeast. Students are from 46 states, 24 foreign countries, and Canada. 65% are from public schools. 44% are White; 15% Hispanic; 12% Asian American. The average age of freshmen is 18; all undergraduates, 20. 3% do not continue beyond their first year; 96% remain to graduate. **Housing:** 1500 students can be accommodated in college housing, which includes coed dorms and on-campus apartments. In addition, there are language houses. On-campus housing is guaranteed for all 4 years. 98% of students live on campus. Upperclassmen may keep cars.

FACULTY/CLASSROOMS: 54% of faculty are male; 46% are female. All teach undergraduates and do research. No introductory courses

are taught by graduate students. The average class size in a regular course is 15.

PROGRAMS OF STUDY: Pomona confers B.A. degrees. Bachelor's degrees are awarded in AGRICULTURE (environmental studies), BIOLOGICAL SCIENCE (biology/biological science, molecular biology, and neurosciences), COMMUNICATIONS AND THE ARTS (art history and appreciation, Chinese, classics, dance, English, fine arts, French, Japanese, languages, linguistics, literature, media arts, music, romance languages and literature, Russian, Spanish, studio art, and theatre arts), COMPUTER AND PHYSICAL SCIENCE (chemistry, computer science, geology, mathematics, physics, and science), ENGINEERING AND ENVIRONMENTAL DESIGN (technology and public affairs), SOCIAL SCIENCE (africana studies, American studies, anthropology, Asian/American studies, Asian/Oriental studies, cognitive science, economics, German area studies, Hispanic American studies, history, international relations, Latin American studies, medieval studies, Mexican-American/Chicano studies, Middle Eastern studies, philosophy, political science/government, psychology, public affairs, religious studies, Russian and Slavic studies, sociology, and women's studies).

ACTIVITIES: 4% of men and 4% of women belong to 3 local fraternities. There are no sororities. There are 200 groups on campus, including the outdoors club of the Claremont Colleges, art, band, chess, choir, chorus, dance, debate, drama, environmental, ethnic, film, gay, honors, international, jazz band, literary magazine, musical theater, newspaper, on the Loose, orchestra, pep band, photography, political, professional, radio and TV, religious, social, social service, student government, symphony, and yearbook. **Sports:** There are 10 intercollegiate sports for men and 11 for women, and 13 intramural sports for men and 13 for women. Facilities include an all-weather track, 2 swimming pools, weight room, fitness center, dance studio, various playing fields, and courts for tennis, squash, racquetball, basketball, volleyball, and badminton. **Graduates:** From July 1, 2013 to June 30, 2014, 362 bachelor's degrees were awarded. The most popular majors were economics (13%), math (11%), and neuroscience (9%). 500 companies recruited on campus in 2013-2014. In an average class, 93% graduate in 4 years or less, 95% graduate in 5 years or less, and 96% graduate in 6 years or less. Of the 2013 graduating class, 20% were enrolled in graduate school within 6 months of graduation, and 35% were employed.

SERVICES: Counseling and information services are available, as is tutoring in most subjects. There is a reader service for the blind. **Library/Resources:** The 3 libraries contain 2.0 million volumes, 1.4 million microform items, 777 audio/video tapes/CDs/DVDs, and subscribe to 6,624 periodicals including electronic. Computerized library services include interlibrary loans, database searching, and Internet access. Special learning facilities include an art gallery, radio station, observatory, modern languages and international relations center, organic farm. **Physically Challenged Students:** 80% of the campus is accessible. Facilities include wheelchair ramps, elevators, special parking, specially equipped restrooms, special class scheduling, lowered drinking fountains, and lowered telephones. **Special:** Students may cross-register at any of The Claremont Colleges, which are on adjacent campuses and follow the same academic schedule. Study abroad is offered through 49 programs in 31 countries. The Pomona College Internship Program provides students with paid part-time internships in the greater Los Angeles area. Paid internship opportunities are also offered in the summer. The college's Summer Undergraduate Research Program enables students to conduct extended, focused research in close cooperation with a Pomona faculty member. SURP funding includes room and board, a supply budget, and a stipend. Other opportunities include spending a semester in Washington, D.C.; a 3-2 engineering program offered with the California Institute of Technology, Washington University in St. Louis, and Dartmouth College; spending one semester at Colby, Smith, Spellman, or Swarthmore colleges; independent study options; and dual and student-designed majors. There is a Phi Beta Kappa chapter. **Visiting:** There are regularly scheduled orientations for prospective students, including interviews, information sessions, and guided tours. Visitors may sit in on classes and stay overnight. To schedule a visit, contact the Office of Admissions. **Campus Safety and Security:** Measures include 24-hour foot and vehicle patrol, emergency notification system, self-defense education, and security escort services. There are emergency telephones, lighted pathways/sidewalks, and controlled access to dorms/residences.

REQUIREMENTS: The SAT or ACT is required. Although applicants need not be graduates of accredited high schools (some may be admitted after the junior year), most are, or have earned the GED. Secondary preparation must include 4 years of English, 3 years each of math and foreign languages, and 2 years each of lab and social sciences. An interview is strongly recommended. AP credits are accepted. Important factors in the admissions decision are advanced placement or honors courses, recommendations by school officials, and extracurricular activities record. The B.A. requires 32 credits, 30 of which must be completed post-matriculation. Students must satisfy the Breadth of Study requirement (one course in each of five areas), complete a first-year Critical Inquiry seminar, take one P.E. course in the first year, demonstrate proficiency in 3 semesters of the same foreign language, and satisfy the requirements for a major (including a senior exercise). **Procedure:** Freshmen are admitted fall. Entrance exams should be taken before December of the senior year. Early decision applications should be filed by November 1; regular applications, by January 1 for fall entry, along with a $70 fee. Notification of early decision is sent December 15; regular decision, April 1. 140 early decision candidates were accepted for the 2014-2015 class. 253 applicants were on the 2014 waiting list; 73 were admitted. Applications are accepted on-line. **Transfer Students:** 13 transfer students enrolled in 2013-2014. Applicants must have completed at least 1 year (24 semester hours) of college-level courses at the time of enrollment. 16 of 32 credits required for the bachelor's degree must be completed at Pomona. **International Students:** There are 121 international students enrolled. The school actively recruits these students. They must take the TOEFL with a minimum score of 600 on the paper-based TOEFL (PBT) or 100 on the Internet-based version (iBT). They must also take the SAT or ACT.

ADMISSIONS: 14% of the 2014-2015 applicants were accepted. 97% of the current freshmen were in the top fifth of their class; 100% were in the top two fifths. 21 freshmen graduated first in their class. **Admissions Contact:** Seth Allen, Dean of Admissions. E-Mail: *admissions@pomona.edu* Web: *www.pomona.edu/admissions*

FINANCIAL AID: In 2014-2015, 57% of all full-time freshmen and 54% of continuing full-time students received some form of financial aid. 57% of all full-time freshmen and 54% of continuing full-time students received need-based aid. The average freshman award was $46,477. Need-based scholarships or need-based grants averaged $44,703 and need-based self-help aid (loans and jobs) averaged $1,774. The average financial indebtedness of the 2014 graduate was $13,441. Pomona is a member of CSS. The CSS/Profile and FAFSA are required. The priority date for freshman financial aid applications for fall entry is February 1. The deadline for filing freshman financial aid applications for fall entry is June 1.

SAINT MARY'S COLLEGE OF CALIFORNIA B-3
www.stmarys-ca.edu

Moraga, CA 94575

(925) 631-4224
(800) 800-4SMC

Fax: (925) 376-7193
Email: smcadmit@stmarys-ca.edu

Full-time: 1106 men, 1675 women
Faculty: 194; IIA, ++$

Part-time: 101 men, 153 women
Ph.D.s: 95%

Graduate: 396 men, 797 women
Student/Faculty: 14 to 1

Year: 4-1-4, summer session
Tuition: $39,890

Room & Board: $13,660
Freshman Class: 5256 applied, 3448 accepted, 623 enrolled

SAT CR/M: 552/558 ACT: 24
CEEB CODE: 4675

Application Deadline: February 1
COMPETITIVE

Saint Mary's College of California, founded in 1863, is a private, independent, liberal arts college affiliated with the Roman Catholic Church. The school offers undergraduate and graduate programs in liberal arts, nursing, economics and business administration, education, and preprofessional studies. Figures in the above capsule and in this profile are approximate. There are 4 undergraduate schools and 3 graduate schools. In addition to regional accreditation, SMC has

baccalaureate program accreditation with NLN. The 420-acre campus is in a suburban area 20 miles east of San Francisco. Including any residence halls, there are 77 buildings.

STUDENT LIFE: 84% of undergraduates are from California. Others are from 40 states, 18 foreign countries, and Canada. 57% are from public schools. 48% are White; 24% Hispanic; 11% Asian American. 43% are Catholic; 39% claim no religious affiliation; 13% Protestant. **Male To Female Ratio:** 1.6:1. The average age of freshmen is 19; all undergraduates, 21. 13% do not continue beyond their first year; 87% remain to graduate. **Housing:** 1557 students can be accommodated in college housing, which includes single-sex and coed dorms, on-campus apartments, and off-campus apartments. In addition, there are honors houses, special-interest houses, Lasallian and Santiago living communities. On-campus housing is guaranteed for the freshman year only and is available on a lottery system for upperclassmen. 62% of students live on campus; of those, 50% remain on campus on weekends. All students may keep cars.

FACULTY/CLASSROOMS: 48% of faculty are male; 52% are female. All teach and do research. No introductory courses are taught by graduate students. The average class size in an introductory lecture is 25; in a laboratory is 16; and in a regular course is 20.

PROGRAMS OF STUDY: SMC confers B.A., and B.S. degrees. Master's and doctoral degrees are also awarded. Bachelor's degrees are awarded in AGRICULTURE (environmental studies), BIOLOGICAL SCIENCE (biology/biological science), BUSINESS (accounting and business administration and management), COMMUNICATIONS AND THE ARTS (art, classical languages, communications, English, French, performing arts, and Spanish), COMPUTER AND PHYSICAL SCIENCE (chemistry, computer science, mathematics, and physics), EDUCATION (health education, physical education, and recreation education), ENGINEERING AND ENVIRONMENTAL DESIGN (environmental science and preengineering), HEALTH PROFESSIONS (health science), SOCIAL SCIENCE (anthropology, economics, history, international studies, liberal arts/general studies, philosophy, political science/government, psychology, religion, and sociology). Business administration, communications and psychology have the largest enrollments.

ACTIVITIES: There are 41 groups on campus, including art, cheerleading, choir, chorale, chorus, dance, debate, drama, environmental, ethnic, forensics, gay, honors, international, jazz band, literary magazine, musical theater, newspaper, pep band, political, professional, radio and TV, religious, social, social service, and student government. Popular campus events include Cultural Nights, and Coffee House events. **Sports:** There are 7 intercollegiate sports for men and 9 for women, and 7 intramural sports for men and 7 for women. Facilities include a gym, football, baseball and recreational fields, swimming pool, lighted tennis courts, soccer field and rugby pitch, weight room, and workout facility. **Graduates:** From July 1, 2013 to June 30, 2014, 598 bachelor's degrees were awarded. The most popular majors were business administration (19%), communication (12%), and psychology (10%). 92 companies recruited on campus in 2013-2014. In an average class, 52% graduate in 4 years or less, 56% graduate in 5 years or less, and 57% graduate in 6 years or less. Of the 2013 graduating class, 14% were enrolled in graduate school within 6 months of graduation, and 64% were employed.

SERVICES: Counseling and information services are available, as is tutoring in most subjects. There is a reader service for the blind, and remedial writing. Tutoring is available in 1-on-1 sessions or group workshops. Readers, note takers, and other services are provided to learning or physically disabled students. **Library/Resources:** The library contains 309,615 volumes, 446,888 microform items, 9,611 audio/video tapes/CDs/DVDs, and subscribes to 58,339 periodicals including electronic. Computerized library services include interlibrary loans, database searching, Internet access, and Wi-Fi capability. Special learning facilities include an art gallery, radio station, an observatory. **Physically Challenged Students:** 90% of the campus is accessible. Facilities include wheelchair ramps, elevators, special parking, specially equipped restrooms, special class scheduling, lowered drinking fountains, lowered telephones, and special housing. **Special:** The college offers seminars in all fields, dual and student-designed majors, study abroad in 8 countries, a Washington semester, work-study, cross-registration with the Regional Association of East Bay Colleges and Universities, and B.A.-B.S. liberal arts degree. There are

3-2 engineering programs with Washington University, the University of Southern California, and Boston University. There are a freshman honors program and 2 departmental honors programs. **Visiting:** There are regularly scheduled orientations for prospective students, Weekdays: 9 a.m. presentation and 10 a.m. tour & 1 p.m. presentation and 2 p.m. tour. Weekends (Sept.-May): 10 a.m. presentation and 11 a.m. tour. There are guides for informal visits, visitors may sit in on classes, and stay overnight. To schedule a visit, contact Patrick Lorenzo at (925) 631-4106. **Campus Safety and Security:** Measures include 24-hour foot and vehicle patrol, emergency notification system, and security escort services. There are emergency telephones, lighted pathways/sidewalks, controlled access to dorms/residences, late night transport/escort service.

REQUIREMENTS: The SAT or ACT is required, with the SAT preferred. Candidates should be graduates of an accredited secondary school, with 16 academic units, including 4 in English and 1 each in algebra, advanced algebra, geometry, and U.S. history. It is recommended that the remaining units be made up of foreign language, lab science, and additional academic electives in the student's areas of strength. The GED is accepted. An essay is required. A GPA of 2.0 is required. AP and CLEP credits are accepted. Important factors in the admissions decision are recommendations by school officials, advanced placement or honors courses, and parents or siblings attended your school.To graduate, students must complete 36 course credits, including 17 at the upper-division level, with a GPA of 2.0 overall and in the major. Specific requirements include a 4-course Great Books seminar and 2 courses each in religious studies, humanities, math/science, written English, and social sciences. All students must demonstrate proficiency in a second language. **Procedure:** Freshmen are admitted to all sessions. Entrance exams should be taken by December of the senior year. There are early admissions and deferred admissions plans. Early decision applications should be filed by November 15; regular applications, by February 1 for fall entry; and January 1 for spring entry, along with a $55 fee. Notification of early decision is sent December 15; regular decision, March 15. 894 applicants were on the 2014 waiting list; 167 were admitted. Applications are accepted on-line. **Transfer Students:** 199 transfer students enrolled in 2013-2014. Applicants must have a GPA of 2.3 and a minimum of 23 transferable academic semester units. 9 of 36 credits required for the bachelor's degree must be completed at SMC. **International Students:** There are 70 international students enrolled. The school actively recruits these students. They must take the TOEFL with a minimum score of 550 on the paper-based TOEFL (PBT) or 79 on the Internet-based version (iBT) and the Comprehensive English Language Test. Nonactive English speakers who submit a minimum score or higher on the TOEFL may be admitted as full-time undergraduates.

ADMISSIONS: 66% of the 2014-2015 applicants were accepted. The SAT scores for the 2014-2015 freshman class were: Critical Reading--23% below 500, 49% between 500 and 599, 23% between 600 and 699, and 5% between 700 and 800; Math--23% below 500, 46% between 500 and 599, 29% between 600 and 699, and 4% between 700 and 800. The ACT scores were 13% below 21, 33% between 21 and 23, 27% between 24 and 26, 14% between 27 and 28, and 11% above 28. 51% of the current freshmen were in the top fifth of their class; 79% were in the top two fifths. 6 freshmen graduated first in their class. **Admissions Contact:** Dean of Admissions. Web: *www.stmarys-ca.edu*

FINANCIAL AID: In 2014-2015, 94% of all full-time freshmen and 96% of continuing full-time students received some form of financial aid. 89% of all full-time freshmen and 76% of continuing full-time students received need-based aid. The average freshman award was $31,979. Need-based scholarships or need-based grants averaged $24,082 ($31,200 maximum); need-based self-help aid (loans and jobs) averaged $6,640 ($7,500 maximum); non-need-based athletic scholarships averaged $36,486 ($59,470 maximum); and other non-need-based awards and non-need-based scholarships averaged $14,946 ($39,740 maximum). 60% of undergraduate students work part-time. Average annual earnings from campus work are $2007. The average financial indebtedness of the 2014 graduate was $33,000. SMC is a member of CSS. The FAFSA, and California GPA verification form for residents only is required. The priority date for freshman financial aid applications for fall entry is February 15.

SAN DIEGO CHRISTIAN COLLEGE   D-5
www.sdcc.edu

El Cajon, CA 92019   **(619) 588-7747**
                                                (800) 676-2242
Fax: (619) 590-1739   **Email: chcadm@adm.christianheritage.edu**

Full-time: n/av	Faculty: n/av
Part-time: n/av	Ph.D.s: n/av
Graduate: n/av	Student/Faculty: n/av
Year: semesters, summer session	Tuition: $22,690
Room & Board: $8322	Freshman Class: n/av
SAT or ACT: required	CEEB CODE: 4150
Application Deadline: open	**COMPETITIVE**

San Diego Christian College is a small, private institution founded in 1970 by the Scott Memorial Baptist Church of San Diego, with which it is still affiliated. It offers programs in the liberal arts, business, and education. Figures given in the above capsule and in this profile are approximate. There is one undergraduate school. The 32-acre campus is in a suburban area 15 miles east of San Diego. Including any residence halls, there are 14 buildings.

STUDENT LIFE: 80% of undergraduates are from California. Others are from states. 75% are from public schools. 70% are White. 100% are Protestant. **Male To Female Ratio:** Is 1:1. The average age of freshmen is 18; all undergraduates, 21. 40% do not continue beyond their first year; 30% remain to graduate. **Housing:** 200 students can be accommodated in college housing, which includes single-sex dorms and off-campus apartments. In addition, there are language houses. On-campus housing is guaranteed for all 4 years, is available on a first-come, and first-served basis. 50% of students commute. Alcohol is not permitted. All students may keep cars.

FACULTY/CLASSROOMS: 60% of faculty are male; 40% are female. All teach undergraduates. No introductory courses are taught by graduate students. The average class size in an introductory lecture is 40; in a laboratory is 15; and in a regular course is 16.

PROGRAMS OF STUDY: SDCC confers B.A., and B.S. degrees. Associate degrees are also awarded. Bachelor's degrees are awarded in BIOLOGICAL SCIENCE (biology/biological science), BUSINESS (business administration and management), COMMUNICATIONS AND THE ARTS (communications, English, and music), COMPUTER AND PHYSICAL SCIENCE (mathematics), EDUCATION (education), ENGINEERING AND ENVIRONMENTAL DESIGN (aviation administration/management), SOCIAL SCIENCE (biblical studies, history, human development, interdisciplinary studies, liberal arts/general studies, physical fitness/movement, and psychology). Counseling psychology, education, and business are the strongest academically. Business, education, and human development have the largest enrollments.

ACTIVITIES: There are no fraternities or sororities. There are 16 groups on campus, including art, cheerleading, choir, chorale, chorus, computers, drama, honors, international, musical theater, newspaper, pep band, political, religious, social, student government, and yearbook. Popular campus events include Spring, Winter, and Valentine's Day Banquets and the Missions Conference. **Sports:** There are 3 intercollegiate sports for men and 4 for women, 5 intramural sports for men and 4 for women. Facilities include a swimming pool, gym, outdoor courts for tennis, volleyball, and basketball, soccer and softball fields.

SERVICES: Counseling and information services are available, as is tutoring in some subjects, tutors recruited as needed for most general education courses. There is remedial math, reading, and writing. **Library/Resources:** The library contains 69,435 volumes, 80 microform items, 61,522 audio/video tapes/CDs/DVDs, and subscribes to 30,475 periodicals including electronic. Computerized library services include interlibrary loans, database searching, and Internet access. **Physically Challenged Students:** 90% of the campus is accessible. Facilities include wheelchair ramps, elevators, special parking, and special class scheduling. **Special:** Students attend chapel 3 times each week, participate in an annual Bible conference, and complete a student ministry assignment each semester. Independent study for 1 to 3 credits can be arranged. There are internships in psychology, pastoral studies, and education. **Visiting:** There are regularly scheduled orientations for prospective students, including a campus tour, cafeteria meal, and class and chapel attendance. There are guides for informal visits, visitors may sit in on classes, and stay overnight. To schedule a visit, contact the Admissions Office. **Campus Safety and Security:** Measures include 24-hour foot and vehicle patrol and emergency notification system. There are lighted pathways/sidewalks, and a fenced campus.

REQUIREMENTS: The SAT or ACT is required. The ACT is preferred. Applicants must have a high school diploma or the GED, or have successfully completed the California State High School Proficiency Exam. Secondary preparation should include 4 units of English, 3 each of math, natural science, and social studies, and 2 of a single foreign language. A personal essay is also required. In addition, applicants must meet certain spiritual requirements. A GPA of 2.3 is required. AP and CLEP credits are accepted. Important factors in the admissions decision are recommendations by school officials, leadership record, and extracurricular activities record. The required credits for graduation vary by degree program and major. All students must take 46 to 52 credits in sciences and math, social science, and humanities; 20 credits in personal Christian development and biblical studies; and the balance in major field requirements and electives. A 2.0 GPA is required for graduation. **Procedure:** Freshmen are admitted fall and spring. Entrance exams should be taken during the junior year. There is a rolling admissions plan. Application deadlines are open. The fall 2014 application fee was $25. Notification is sent on a rolling basis. **Transfer Students:** 30 of 124 credits required for the bachelor's degree must be completed at SDCC. **International Students:** The school actively recruits these students. They must take the TOEFL and the college's own test. They must also take the SAT or ACT, scoring 900.

ADMISSIONS: Misty Chappelle, Director of Admissions. E-Mail: *chcadm@adm.christianheritage.edu* Web: *www.sdcc.edu*

FINANCIAL AID: SDCC is a member of CSS. The FAFSA and the college's own financial statement are required. Check with the school for current application deadlines.

SAN DIEGO STATE UNIVERSITY D-5
www.sdsu.edu

San Diego, CA 92182	(619) 594-6336
Fax: (619) 594-1250	Email: admissions@sdsu.edu
Full-time: 11269 men, 13819 women	Faculty: IIA, +$
Part-time: 1521 men, 1753 women	Ph.D.s: 87%
Graduate: 2031 men, 3090 women	Student/Faculty: n/av
Year: semesters, summer session	Tuition: $6866 ($18,026)
Room & Board: $14,745	Freshman Class: 56921 applied, 19625 accepted, 5054 enrolled
SAT CR/M: 544/568 ACT: 24	CEEB CODE: 4682
Application Deadline: November 30	COMPETITIVE+

San Diego State University, founded in 1897, is a public research university that is part of the California State University system. There are 8 undergraduate schools. In addition to regional accreditation, SDSU has baccalaureate program accreditation with AACSB, ABET, ACEJMC, CSWE, NASAD, and NRPA. The 283-acre campus is in an urban area 8 miles east of downtown San Diego. Including any residence halls, there are 108 buildings.

STUDENT LIFE: 93% of undergraduates are from California. Others are from 50 states, 114 foreign countries, and Canada. 92% are from public schools. 35% are White; 31% Hispanic; 14% Asian American. **Male To Female Ratio:** 1.3:1. The average age of freshmen is 19; all undergraduates, 22. 12% do not continue beyond their first year. **Housing:** 4260 students can be accommodated in college housing, which includes coed dorms and on-campus apartments. In addition, there are honors houses, language houses, special-interest houses, gender neutral housing, international housing, a living/learning center, Aztec engineering residence, and substance-free and quiet-study housing. On-campus housing is available on a first-come and first-served basis. 86% of students commute. All students may keep cars.

FACULTY/CLASSROOMS: 50% of faculty are male; 50% are female. No introductory courses are taught by graduate students. The average class size in an introductory lecture is 74; in a laboratory is 17; and in a regular course is 53.

PROGRAMS OF STUDY: SDSU confers B.A., B.F.A., B.S. and B.M. degrees. Master's and doctoral degrees are also awarded. Bachelor's degrees are awarded in AGRICULTURE (agricultural business management and environmental studies), BIOLOGICAL SCIENCE (biology/biological science, botany, ecology, microbiology, nutrition, and zoology), BUSINESS (accounting, business administration and management, finance, financial services, hospitality management services, insurance and risk management, international business management, international economics, international security/conflict resolution management, marketing/retailing/merchandising, real estate, and total quality management (TQM)), COMMUNICATIONS AND THE ARTS (art, classics, communications, comparative literature, dance, English, French, German, Japanese, journalism, linguistics, media management, music, music performance, radio/tv, recreation administration, Russian, Spanish, studio art, telecommunications, theatre arts, and writing), COMPUTER AND PHYSICAL SCIENCE (applied mathematics, astronomy, chemical physics, chemistry, computer science, geology, industrial technology, information sciences and systems, mathematics, physical sciences, physics, and statistics), EDUCATION (athletic training, industrial arts education, music education, physical education, and vocational education), ENGINEERING AND ENVIRONMENTAL DESIGN (aerospace engineering, civil engineering, computer engineering, construction engineering, electrical/electronics engineering, engineering, environmental engineering, environmental science, and mechanical engineering), HEALTH PROFESSIONS (environmental health science, exercise science, health communication, health science, nursing, and speech pathology/audiology), SOCIAL SCIENCE (African American studies, American Indian studies, American studies, anthropology, Asian/Oriental studies, child psychology/development, criminal justice, economics, European studies, gender studies, geography, gerontology, history, home economics, humanities, interdisciplinary studies, international studies, Latin American studies, liberal arts/general studies, Mexican-American/Chicano studies, modern Jewish studies, philosophy, political science/government, psychology, public administration, religious studies, Russian and Slavic studies, social science, social work, sociology, urban studies, and women's studies). Psychology, management, physical education/kinesiology have the largest enrollments.

ACTIVITIES: There are 300 groups on campus, including art, band, cheerleading, choir, chorale, chorus, dance, debate, drama, drill team, environmental, ethnic, film, gay, honors, international, jazz band, literary magazine, marching band, musical theater, newspaper, opera, orchestra, pep band, political, professional, radio and TV, religious, social, social service, student government, and symphony. Popular campus events include Student Involvement Expo, Welcome Week, Aztec Nights, Midnight Breakfast Finals Week, and Explore SDSU. **Sports:** There are 6 intercollegiate sports for men and 13 for women, and 8 intramural sports for men and 8 for women. Facilities include a gym, basketball, racquetball, tennis, and volleyball courts, a swimming pool/aquaplex, track, soccer, softball, baseball, football fields, an aquatic center, weight room, bowling and gymnastic equipment, cardio room, and a 30-foot climbing wall. **Graduates:** From July 1, 2013 to June 30, 2014, 6563 bachelor's degrees were awarded. The most popular majors were psychology (8%), criminal justice administration (6%), and general communication studies (3%). 760 companies recruited on campus in 2013-2014. In an average class, 30% graduate in 4 years or less, 56% graduate in 5 years or less, and 67% graduate in 6 years or less.

SERVICES: Counseling and information services are available, as is tutoring in most subjects. There is a reader service for the blind. **Library/Resources:** The library contains 2.2 million volumes, 4.6 million microform items, 42,724 audio/video tapes/CDs/DVDs, and subscribes to 75,661 periodicals including electronic. Computerized library services include interlibrary loans, database searching, Internet access, and Wi-Fi capability. Special learning facilities include an art gallery, planetarium, radio station, TV station, performing arts theatres and recital halls, seismology and weather stations. **Physically Challenged Students:** 99% of the campus is accessible. Facilities include wheelchair ramps, elevators, special parking, specially equipped restrooms, special class scheduling, lowered drinking fountains, lowered telephones. **Special:** There are 25 national honor societies, including Phi Beta Kappa, and a freshman honors program. **Visiting:** There are regularly scheduled orientations for prospective students, including tours that can be scheduled with SDSU ambassadors. **Campus Safety and Security:** Measures include 24-hour foot and vehicle patrol, emergency notification system, self-defense education, and security escort services. There are shuttle buses, emergency telephones, lighted pathways/sidewalks, and controlled access to dorms/residences.

REQUIREMENTS: The SAT or ACT is required. Applicants must have a qualifying CSU eligibility index, based on a combination of GPA and standardized test scores. Candidates for admission should have completed 4 years of English, 3 years of math, 2 years each of science and foreign language, and 1 year each of social studies, U.S. history, visual/performing arts, and academic elective. AP and CLEP credits are accepted.To graduate, students must complete a minimum of 120 units, including 49 general education units. The number of units in the major varies by program. A 2.0 or higher GPA must be maintained, depending on the major. Students must demonstrate math and writing competency and fulfill requirements in upper-division writing and in American Institutions. Certain majors require a senior thesis. **Procedure:** Freshmen are admitted fall. Entrance exams should be taken by October of the senior year. Applications should be filed by November 30 for fall entry, along with a $55 fee. Notifications are sent in March. 1945 applicants were on the 2014 waiting list; 47 were admitted. Applications are accepted on-line. **Transfer Students:** 3179 transfer students enrolled in 2013-2014. Transfer applicants are required to declare a major and have completed all preparation for the major courses and pre-major requirements if applicable. In addition, all lower division general education courses must be completed. Must have "C" grades in four required classes: Oral Communication, Written Communication, Critical Thinking, and Mathematics (above the level of intermediate Algebra). Different application policies apply for applicants in and out of SDSU service area and for applicants in impacted majors. Refer to the Office of Admission website for more information. 30 of 120 credits required for the bachelor's degree must be completed at SDSU. **International Students:** There are 2265 international students enrolled. The school actively recruits these students. They must take the TOEFL with a minimum score of 550 on the paper-based TOEFL (PBT) or 80 on the Internet-based version (iBT) and the college's own test, or take the IELTS, scoring 6.5 or higher. They must also take the SAT or ACT.

ADMISSIONS: 34% of the 2014-2015 applicants were accepted. The SAT scores for the 2014-2015 freshman class were: Critical Reading--26% below 500, 49% between 500 and 599, 23% between 600 and 699, and 2% between 700 and 800; Math--18% below 500, 44% between 500 and 599, 33% between 600 and 699, and 5% between 700 and 800; Writing--28% below 500, 49% between 500 and 599, 22% between 600 and 699, and 2% between 700 and 800. The ACT scores were 16% below 21, 25% between 21 and 23, 31% between 24 and 26, 16% between 27 and 28, and 14% above 28. 65% of the current freshmen were in the top fifth of their class; 92% were in the top two fifths. **Admissions Contact:** Sabrina Cortell, Director of Admissions. E-Mail: *admissions@sdsu.edu* Web: *www.sdsu.edu/apply*

FINANCIAL AID: In 2014-2015, 60% of all full-time freshmen and 61% of continuing full-time students received some form of financial aid. The average freshman award was $8,000. The average financial indebtedness of the 2014 graduate was $18,400. SDSU is a member of CSS. The FAFSA and the state aid form are required. Check with the school for current application deadlines.

SAN FRANCISCO ART INSTITUTE (*The complete profile is made available exclusively on our website, www.barronspac.com*)

SAN FRANCISCO CONSERVATORY OF MUSIC (*The complete profile is made available exclusively on our website, www. barronspac.com*)

SAN FRANCISCO STATE UNIVERSITY   B-3
www.sfsu.edu

San Francisco, CA 94132   (415) 338-6486

Fax: (415) 338-3880	**Email:** ugadmit@sfsu.edu
Full-time: 9399 men, 12712 women	**Faculty:** IIA, +$
Part-time: 1951 men, 2094 women	**Ph.D.s:** 36%
Graduate: 1471 men, 2278 women	**Student/Faculty:** n/av
Year: semesters, summer session	**Tuition:** $6938 ($18,098)
Room & Board: $11,576	**Freshman Class:** 34930 applied, 20889 accepted, 3612 enrolled
SAT CR/M: 490/505 **ACT:** required	**CEEB CODE:** 4684
Application Deadline: November 30	**COMPETITIVE**

San Francisco State University, founded in 1899, is a public liberal arts institution offering graduate and undergraduate programs as part of the California State University system. There are 6 undergraduate schools and 6 graduate schools. In addition to regional accreditation, SF State, San Francsico State has baccalaureate program accreditation with AACSB, ACEJMC, ADA, AHEA, NASM, and NLN. The 142-acre campus is in an urban area in San Francisco. Including any residence halls, there are 23 buildings.

STUDENT LIFE: 92% of undergraduates are from California. Others are from 37 states, 97 foreign countries, and Canada. 32% are Asian American; 27% White; 23% Hispanic. The average age of freshmen is 18; all undergraduates, 23. **Housing:** 3200 students can be accommodated in college housing, which includes coed dorms, off-campus apartments, and married student housing. In addition, there are language houses, special-interest houses, theme housing. On-campus housing is available on a first-come and first-served basis. 88% of students commute. Alcohol is not permitted. All students may keep cars.

FACULTY/CLASSROOMS: 47% of faculty are male; 53% are female. No introductory courses are taught by graduate students.

PROGRAMS OF STUDY: San Francsico State confers B.A., B.S. and B.M. degrees. Master's and Doctoral degrees are also awarded. Bachelor's degrees are awarded in AGRICULTURE (environmental studies and natural resource management), BIOLOGICAL SCIENCE (biochemistry, biology/biological science, botany, cell biology, ecology, marine biology, microbiology, physiology, and zoology), BUSINESS (accounting, banking and finance, business administration and management, electronic business, entrepreneurial studies, hospitality management services, hotel/motel and restaurant management, institutional management, international business management, labor studies, management science, marketing/retailing/merchandising, personnel management, and recreational facilities management), COMMUNICATIONS AND THE ARTS (apparel design, art, broadcasting, Chinese, classics, communications, comparative literature, creative writing, dance, design, dramatic arts, English, film arts, French, German, Italian, Japanese, journalism, languages, music, radio/television technology, Spanish, speech/debate/rhetoric, and visual design), COMPUTER AND PHYSICAL SCIENCE (applied mathematics, astronomy, astrophysics, atmospheric sciences and meteorology, chemistry, computer science, earth science, geology, information sciences and systems, mathematics, physics, and statistics), EDUCATION (elementary education, home economics education, industrial arts education, physical education, and recreation education), ENGINEERING AND ENVIRONMENTAL DESIGN (civil engineering, computer engineering, electrical/electronics engineering, industrial administration/management, industrial engineering technology, interior design, and mechanical engineering), HEALTH PROFESSIONS (clinical science, exercise science, health science, nursing, and speech pathology/audiology), SOCIAL SCIENCE (African studies, American studies, anthropology, Asian/American studies, clothing and textiles management/production/services, consumer services, criminal justice, dietetics, economics, family/consumer studies, geography, history, humanities, humanities and social science, interdisciplinary studies, international relations, Judaic studies, liberal arts/general studies, philosophy, political science/government, psychology, religion, social work, sociology, urban studies, and women's studies).

ACTIVITIES: 3% of men belong to 1 local and 10 national fraterni-

ties; 4% of women belong to 6 local and 10 national sororities. There are 200 groups on campus, including model UN, art, band, cheerleading, choir, chorale, chorus, communications, computers, dance, debate, drama, environmental, ethnic, film, forensics, gay, honors, international, jazz band, literary magazine, music ensembles, musical theater, newspaper, opera, orchestra, political, professional, radio and TV, religious, social, social service, student government, and symphony. Popular campus events include Activities Fair and Crafts Festival, Morrison Artists' Series Chamber Music Program and the Alexander String Quartet. **Sports:** There are 5 intercollegiate sports for men and 6 for women, and 3 intramural sports for men and 3 for women. Facilities include a 6500-seat stadium, 2 gyms, an indoor pool, a weight room, a training room, wrestling and gymnastics areas, a dance studio, an all-weather track, 14 tennis courts, softball and baseball fields, and auxiliary practice fields. **Graduates:** From July 1, 2013 to June 30, 2014, 6344 bachelor's degrees were awarded. The most popular majors were business/marketing (24%), social sciences (10%), and visual and performing arts (9%). In an average class, 34% graduate in 5 years or less and 46% graduate in 6 years or less.

SERVICES: Counseling and information services are available, as is tutoring in every subject. **Library/Resources:** The library contains 921,744 volumes, 1.7 million microform items, 264,128 audio/video tapes/CDs/DVDs, and subscribes to 73,735 periodicals including electronic. Computerized library services include interlibrary loans, database searching, and Internet access. Special learning facilities include an art gallery, natural history museum, planetarium, radio station, TV station, a field campus, the labor archives and research center, a media access center, and an anthropology museum. **Physically Challenged Students:** Facilities include wheelchair ramps, elevators, special parking, specially equipped restrooms, special class scheduling, lowered drinking fountains, lowered telephones, special housing. **Special:** Students may cross-register with the California College of Podiatric Medicine, the City College of San Francisco, Cogswell College of Engineering, and several other area universities. Study abroad in 23 countries, a Washington semester, campus work-study, a general studies degree, dual and student-designed majors, credit for life experience, nondegree study, and pass/fail options are also offered. There is a Phi Beta Kappa chapter, a freshman honors program, and 1 departmental honors program. **Visiting:** There are regularly scheduled orientations for prospective students. There are guides for informal visits and visitors may sit in on classes. To schedule a visit, contact the Student Outreach Services at (415) 338-2355. **Campus Safety and Security:** Measures include 24-hour foot and vehicle patrol, emergency notification system, self-defense education, and security escort services. There are shuttle buses, emergency telephones, lighted pathways/sidewalks, and controlled access to dorms/residences.

REQUIREMENTS: The SAT or ACT is required. Applicants should be graduates of an accredited secondary school with a minimum GPA of 2.0. The GED is accepted. High school courses should include 4 years of English, 3 of math, 2 of foreign language, and 1 each of U.S. history or government, lab science, and visual and performing arts. A GPA of 2.0 is required. AP and CLEP credits are accepted. To graduate, students must complete 120 to 132 credits with a minimum GPA of 2.0. The required general education core includes 27 credits in arts and sciences, 12 in basic skills subjects, and 9 in upper-division courses. English composition and U.S. history and government competency requirements may be fulfilled by either exam or course work. **Procedure:** Freshmen are admitted fall and spring. There is a rolling admissions plan. Applications should be filed by November 30 for fall entry, along with a $55 fee. Notification is sent on a rolling basis. Applications are accepted on-line. **Transfer Students:** 3766 transfer students enrolled in 2013-2014. Applicants must have a college GPA of 2.0 (2.4 for nonresidents). Those with fewer than 56 transferable semester credits must meet freshman entrance requirements. 30 of 120 credits required for the bachelor's degree must be completed at San Francsico State. **International Students:** There are 1666 international students enrolled. The school actively recruits these students. They must take the TOEFL with a minimum score of 500 on the paper-based TOEFL (PBT) or 61 on the Internet-based version (iBT). They must also take the SAT or ACT.

ADMISSIONS: 60% of the 2014-2015 applicants were accepted. The SAT scores for the 2014-2015 freshman class were: Critical Reading -54% below 500, 35% between 500 and 599, 10% between 600 and 699, and 1% between 700 and 800; Math--46% below 500, 40% between 500 and 599, and 13% between 600 and 699. **Admissions Contact:** Director. E-Mail: ugadmit@sfsu.edu Web: http://www.sfsu.edu/

FINANCIAL AID: The average freshman award was $11,932. Need-based scholarships or need-based grants averaged $10,404; need-based self-help aid (loans and jobs) averaged $4,242; non-need-based athletic scholarships averaged $3,449; and other non-need-based awards and non-need-based scholarships averaged $2,536. The average financial indebtedness of the 2014 graduate was $20,493. San Francsico State is a member of CSS. The FAFSA is required. The priority date for freshman financial aid applications for fall entry is March 2.

SAN JOSE STATE UNIVERSITY (*The complete profile is made available exclusively on our website, www.barronspac.com*)

SANTA CLARA UNIVERSITY (*Information is not available*)

SCRIPPS COLLEGE — D-5
www.scrippscollege.edu

Claremont, CA 91711	(909) 621-8578
	(800) 770-1333
Fax: (909) 607-7508	**Email:** VRomero@scrippscollege.edu
Full-time: 968 women	**Faculty:** 88; IIB, ++$
Part-time: 4 women	**Ph.D.s:** n/av
Graduate: 6 men, 10 women	**Student/Faculty:** 10 to 1
Year: semesters	**Tuition:** $47,378
Room & Board: $14,562	**Freshman Class:** 2782 applied, 758 accepted, 250 enrolled
SAT or ACT: required	**CEEB CODE:** 4693
Application Deadline: January 2	**MOST COMPETITIVE**

Scripps College, founded in 1926, is a private liberal arts institution for women. A member of the Claremont Colleges, Scripps emphasizes a challenging core curriculum based on interdisciplinary humanistic studies. There are 5 undergraduate schools. The 37-acre campus is in a suburban area 35 miles east of Los Angeles. Including any residence halls, there are 27 buildings.

STUDENT LIFE: 55% of undergraduates are from out of state, mostly the Northwest. 49% are White; 19% Asian American. The average age of freshmen is 18; all undergraduates, 20. **Housing:** 834 students can be accommodated in college housing, which includes single-sex dorms, on-campus apartments, and off-campus apartments, and foreign language corridors. On-campus housing is guaranteed for all 4 years. 97% of students live on campus. All students may keep cars.

FACULTY/CLASSROOMS: All teach and do research. No introductory courses are taught by graduate students.

PROGRAMS OF STUDY: Scripps confers B.A., and B.S. degrees. Bachelor's degrees are awarded in AGRICULTURE (environmental studies), BIOLOGICAL SCIENCE (biology/biological science, molecular biology, and neurosciences), COMMUNICATIONS AND THE ARTS (art history and appreciation, Chinese, classical languages, communications, dance, dramatic arts, English, Germanic languages and literature, Italian, Japanese, languages, music, Russian, Spanish, and studio art), COMPUTER AND PHYSICAL SCIENCE (chemistry, computer science, geology, mathematics, physics, science and management, and science technology), ENGINEERING AND ENVIRONMENTAL DESIGN (environmental science and preengineering), SOCIAL SCIENCE (African American studies, American studies, anthropology, Asian/American studies, Asian/Oriental studies, classical/ancient civilization, economics, European studies, French studies, German area studies, Hispanic American studies, history, humanities, Italian studies, Judaic studies, Latin American studies, law, Mexican-American/Chicano studies, philosophy, political science/government, prelaw, psychology, religion, sociology, and women's studies). Psychology, biology, and economics have the largest enrollments.

ACTIVITIES: There are no fraternities or sororities. There are 200 groups on campus, including art, chess, choir, chorale, chorus, computers, dance, debate, drama, environmental, ethnic, film, gay, honors, international, literary magazine, musical theater, newspaper, orchestra, photography, political, professional, radio and TV, radio only, religious, social, social service, student government, symphony, and yearbook. Popular campus events include Spring Fling Carnival, Levitt on the Lawn, Break Away Series, Scripps Outdoor Adventure Program and Holiday Dinner. **Sports:** There are 11 intercollegiate sports for women, and 6 intramural sports for women. The Sallie Tiernan Field House is a state-of-the art 24,000 square-foot facility with an aerobics studio, cardio machine room, weight room, and other spaces for fitness and health education. The facility also includes the swimming pool and soccer/lacrosse fields. There are also tennis courts, a climbing wall, an outdoor track, and fields for baseball and softball. **Graduates:** From July 1, 2013 to June 30, 2014, 209 bachelor's degrees were awarded. 300 companies recruited on campus in 2013-2014. In an average class, 80% graduate in 4 years or less, 84% graduate in 5 years or less, and 84% graduate in 6 years or less.

SERVICES: Counseling and information services are available, as is tutoring in every subject. There is a reader service for the blind. **Library/Resources:** The library contains 1.1 million volumes, 84,084 microform items, 10,287 audio/video tapes/CDs/DVDs, and subscribes to 394,952 periodicals including electronic. Computerized library services include interlibrary loans, database searching, Internet access, and Wi-Fi capability. Special learning facilities include an art gallery, radio station, an humanities museum and biological field station. **Physically Challenged Students:** Facilities include wheelchair ramps, elevators, special parking, specially equipped restrooms, special class scheduling, lowered drinking fountains, and special housing. **Special:** Students may cross-register with any of the other Claremont Colleges. Scripps also offers study abroad in 36 countries, a Washington semester, and student-designed, dual, and interdisciplinary majors, including organizational studies and science, technology, and society. Many courses are offered as seminars. There are 4-1 accelerated degree programs in the arts and business administration. A 3-2 engineering program (B.A.-B.S.) is offered with Harvey Mudd College, USC, UC Berkeley, Columbia, Stanford, and Boston Universities, and others. There are 7 national honor societies including Phi Beta Kappa. **Visiting:** There are guides for informal visits, visitors may sit in on classes, and stay overnight. To schedule a visit, contact the Admission Office. **Campus Safety and Security:** Measures include 24-hour foot and vehicle patrol, emergency notification system, self-defense education, and security escort services. There are emergency telephones, lighted pathways/sidewalks, and controlled access to dorms/residences.

REQUIREMENTS: The SAT or ACT is required. Applicants must have completed 4 units each of high school English and math, 3 each of lab science and social studies, and either 3 of a single foreign language or 2 each of 2 languages. SAT Subject Tests and an interview are recommended. An essay and a graded writing assignment from the junior or senior year are required. AP and CLEP credits are accepted. Important factors in the admissions decision are advanced placement or honors courses, evidence of special talent, and leadership record.Students must complete a total of 32 courses, or 128 units, with at least a C average. Requirements include a 3-semester humanities core, a first-year writing/critical thinking course, and 1 course each in fine arts, letters, natural science, social science, gender and women's studies, and race and ethnic studies. A senior thesis or project is also required. **Procedure:** Freshmen are admitted fall and spring. Entrance exams should be taken by December of the senior year. There are early decision, early admissions, and deferred admissions plans. Early decision applications should be filed by November 15; regular applications, by January 2 for fall entry; and November 1 for spring entry, along with a $60 fee. Notification of early decision is sent December 15; regular decision, April 1. 683 applicants were on the 2014 waiting list. Applications are accepted on-line. **Transfer Students:** A cumulative college GPA of 3.0 is required. **International Students:** There are 41 international students enrolled. The school actively recruits these students. They must take the TOEFL with a minimum score of 600 on the paper-based TOEFL (PBT) or 100 on the Internet-based version (iBT). They must also take the SAT or ACT.

ADMISSIONS: 27% of the 2014-2015 applicants were accepted. The SAT scores for the 2014-2015 freshman class were: Critical Reading--8% between 500 and 599, 40% between 600 and 699, and 43% between 700 and 800; Math--14% between 500 and 599, 54% between 600 and 699, and 32% between 700 and 800; Writing--5% between 500 and 599, 50% between 600 and 699, and 45% between 700 and 800. **Admissions Contact:** Victoria Romero, VP for Enrollment. E-Mail: *VRomero@scrippscollege.edu* Web: *www.scrippscollege.edu*

FINANCIAL AID: Scripps is a member of CSS. The CSS/Profile, FAFSA, and the state aid form are required. The priority date for freshman financial aid applications for fall entry is February 1.

SIMPSON UNIVERSITY   B-2
www.simpsonu.edu

Redding, CA 96003	(530) 224-5600
	(888) 9-SIMPSON
Fax: (530) 226-4861	Email: admissions@simpsonu.edu
Full-time: 322 men, 665 women	Faculty: 43
Part-time: 12 men, 20 women	Ph.D.s: 56%
Graduate: 102 men, 176 women	Student/Faculty: 15 to 1
Year: semesters, summer session	Tuition: $21,600
Room & Board: $7300	Freshman Class: 533 applied, 317 accepted, 158 enrolled
SAT CR/M/W: 500/500/490 ACT: 21	CEEB CODE: 4698
Application Deadline: open	COMPETITIVE

Simpson University, founded in 1921, is a Christian university offering undergraduate, graduate, and teaching credential programs. Simpson University is an official institution of the Christian and Missionary Alliance, and the student population represents more than 25 evangelical denominations. Figures in the above capsule and in this profile are approximate. There are 3 graduate schools. The 92-acre campus is in a suburban area in the northeast city limits of Redding. Including any residence halls, there are 17 buildings.

STUDENT LIFE: 87% of undergraduates are from California. Others are from 27 states, and 7 foreign countries. 59% are from public schools. 60% are White. 99% are Protestant. The average age of freshmen is 18; all undergraduates, 25. 35% do not continue beyond their first year; 45% remain to graduate. **Housing:** 590 students can be accommodated in college housing, which includes single-sex dorms, off-campus apartments, and married student housing. In addition, there are special-interest houses, and Gatehouse Missionary Kid Housing. On-campus housing is guaranteed for all 4 years. 55% of students commute. Alcohol is not permitted. All students may keep cars.

FACULTY/CLASSROOMS: 52% of faculty are male; 48% are female. 65% teach undergraduates. No introductory courses are taught by graduate students. The average class size in an introductory lecture is 42; in a laboratory is 11; and in a regular course is 11.

PROGRAMS OF STUDY: Simpson confers B.A., and B.S. degrees. Associate and master's degrees are also awarded. Bachelor's degrees are awarded in BIOLOGICAL SCIENCE (biology/biological science), BUSINESS (accounting, business administration and management, human resources, organizational leadership and management, and recreation and leisure services), COMMUNICATIONS AND THE ARTS (communications, English, and music), COMPUTER AND PHYSICAL SCIENCE (mathematics), EDUCATION (elementary education, English education, mathematics education, music education, secondary education, and social science education), HEALTH PROFESSIONS (health care administration and nursing), SOCIAL SCIENCE (biblical studies, crosscultural studies, history, liberal arts/general studies, ministries, missions, pastoral studies, psychology, religion, religious education, social science, and youth ministry). Biology, nursing, and music are the strongest academically. Psychology, business administration, and liberal studies have the largest enrollments.

ACTIVITIES: There are 20 groups on campus, including commuter students association, psychology, band, choir, chorale, computers, drama, ethnic, film, golf, international, jazz band, newspaper, orchestra, photography, professional, religious, social, social service, student government, symphony, and yearbook. Popular campus events include Spring Banquet, Missions Emphasis Week and Airband. **Sports:** There are 5 intercollegiate sports for men and 6 for women, and 2 intramural sports for men and 1 for women. Facilities include a soccer field, a 1450-seat gym, weight and training rooms, softball field, outdoor volleyball and basketball courts. Students have access to nearby facilities for swimming, boating, mountain climbing, and skiing. **Graduates:** From July 1, 2013 to June 30, 2014, 300 bachelor's degrees were awarded. The most popular majors were liberal arts (18%), psychology (18%), and human resources management (9%). In an average class, 1% graduate in 3 years or less, 32% graduate in 4 years or less, 43% graduate in 5 years or less, and 45% graduate in 6 years or less.

SERVICES: Counseling and information services are available, as is tutoring in every subject. There is remedial math and writing. **Library/Resources:** The library contains 176,640 volumes, 242,910 microform items, 3,253 audio/video tapes/CDs/DVDs, and subscribes to 24,334 periodicals including electronic. Computerized library services include interlibrary loans, database searching, Internet access, and Wi-Fi capability. **Physically Challenged Students:** 95% of the campus is accessible. Facilities include wheelchair ramps, elevators, special parking, specially equipped restrooms, lowered drinking fountains, lowered telephones, and special housing. **Special:** Off-campus educational programs are offered through the China Studies Program, Contemporary Music Program in Martha's Vineyard, Latin American Studies Program, Los Angeles Film Studies Center, Middle East Studies Program, Oxford Honors Program, and the Russian Studies Program. Students may study abroad in a variety of countries. Internships are available in Christian education, pastoral studies, youth ministries, business, and psychology. Work-study programs in elementary education and with the federal government are also available. There is also a 1-year, nondegree certificate program in Bible and contemporary church music. There are 2 national honor societies and 1 departmental honors program. **Visiting:** There are regularly scheduled orientations for prospective students. There are guides for informal visits, visitors may sit in on classes, and stay overnight. To schedule a visit, contact the Visit Coordinator at (530) 226-4769. **Campus Safety and Security:** Measures include 24-hour foot and vehicle patrol, emergency notification system, and security escort services. There are emergency telephones, lighted pathways/sidewalks, controlled access to dorms/residences, emergency whistle program, local police patrols, and monthly campus safety meetings.

REQUIREMENTS: The SAT or ACT is required. Applicants must be graduates of an accredited high school or have a GED. It is recommended that applicants have completed 4 years of high school English, 3 each of math, science, and social studies/history, and 2 of a foreign language. A GPA of 2.0 is required. AP and CLEP credits are accepted. Important factors in the admissions decision are leadership record, personality/intangible qualities, and recommendations by school officials. Students must complete at least 124 credits, with a minimum of 36 upper-division credits and at least 42 major credits (of which 24 must be upper division). A minimum GPA of 2.0 must be maintained. Foundational studies requirements include 24 credits in biblical studies and theology and 41 credits in human expression, human history and behavior, and global environment. **Procedure:** Freshmen are admitted to all sessions. Entrance exams should be taken during the junior year or in the fall of the senior year. There are deferred admissions and rolling admissions plans. Application deadlines are open. Application fee is $25. Notification is sent on a rolling basis. Applications are accepted on-line. **Transfer Students:** 98 transfer students enrolled in 2013-2014. Transfer applicants with at least 30 semester college credits need not submit SAT or ACT scores. 30 of 124 credits required for the bachelor's degree must be completed at Simpson. **International Students:** There are 7 international students enrolled. They must take the TOEFL with a minimum score of 500 on the paper-based TOEFL (PBT) or 79 on the Internet-based version (iBT). They must also take the SAT or ACT.

ADMISSIONS: 59% of the 2014-2015 applicants were accepted. The SAT scores for the 2014-2015 freshman class were: Critical Reading--35% below 500, 41% between 500 and 599, 22% between 600 and 699, and 2% between 700 and 800; Math--36% below 500, 50% between 500 and 599, and 14% between 600 and 699; Writing--42% below 500, 43% between 500 and 599, and 15% between 600 and 699. The ACT scores were 44% below 21, 26% between 21 and 23, 13% between 24 and 26, 11% between 27 and 28, and 4% above 28. 53% of the current freshmen were in the top fifth of their class; 71% were in the top two fifths. **Admissions Contact:** Director of Admissions. E-Mail: *admissions@simpsonu.edu* Web: *www.simpsonu.edu*

FINANCIAL AID: In 2014-2015, 100% of all full-time freshmen and 99% of continuing full-time students received some form of financial aid. 91% of all full-time freshmen and 94% of continuing full-time students received need-based aid. The average freshman award was $14,815. Need-based scholarships or need-based grants averaged $15,600 ($25,400 maximum); need-based self-help aid (loans and jobs) averaged $4,300 ($9,000 maximum); non-need-based athletic scholarships averaged $7,227 ($9,000 maximum); and other non-need-based awards and non-need-based scholarships averaged $7,610 ($21,600 maximum). 27% of undergraduate students work part-time. Average annual earnings from campus work are $3452. The average financial indebtedness of the 2014 graduate was $17,524. Simpson is a member of CSS. The FAFSA and the college's own financial statement are required. The priority date for freshman financial aid applications for fall entry is March 2.

SONOMA STATE UNIVERSITY — B-3
www.sonoma.edu

Rohnert Park, CA 94952   (707) 664-2778

Email: student.outreach@sonoma.edu

Full-time: 2931 men, 4721 women	**Faculty:** 175; IIA, av$
Part-time: 311 men, 388 women	**Ph.D.s:** 60%
Graduate: 216 men, 553 women	**Student/Faculty:** 25 to 1
Year: semesters, summer session	**Tuition:** $8996 ($17,824)
Room & Board: $11,545	**Freshman Class:** 14272 applied, 12870 accepted, 1807 enrolled
SAT CR/M: 490/495 **ACT:** 21	**CEEB CODE:** 4723
Application Deadline: November 30	**COMPETITIVE**

Sonoma State University, founded in 1960, and part of the California State University system, offers undergraduate programs in business and economics, natural sciences, social sciences, and arts and humanities, and graduate programs in education, counseling, and business. There are 5 undergraduate schools and 1 graduate school. In addition to regional accreditation, Sonoma State has baccalaureate program accreditation with AACSB, NASAD, NASM, NCATE, and NLN. The 269-acre campus is in a suburban area 45 miles north of San Francisco. Including any residence halls, there are 62 buildings.

STUDENT LIFE: 98% of undergraduates are from California. Others are from 31 states, 26 foreign countries, and Canada. 83% are from public schools. 59% are White; 19% Hispanic. The average age of freshmen is 21; all undergraduates, 21. 27% do not continue beyond their first year; 54% remain to graduate. **Housing:** 3054 students can be accommodated in college housing, which includes single-sex and coed dorms and on-campus apartments. In addition, there are special-interest houses, women in math/science, housing for focused learning communities- freshman seminar dorms, special housing for disabled students, wellness housing, substance-free and intensive-study houses. On-campus housing is guaranteed for the freshman year only, is available on a first-come, first-served basis. 63% of students commute. All students may keep cars.

FACULTY/CLASSROOMS: 46% of faculty are male; 54% are female. 87% teach undergraduates. Graduate students teach 1% of introductory courses. The average class size in an introductory lecture is 40; in a laboratory is 18; and in a regular course is 30.

PROGRAMS OF STUDY: Sonoma State confers B.A., B.F.A. and B.S. degrees. Master's degrees are also awarded. Bachelor's degrees are awarded in BIOLOGICAL SCIENCE (biochemistry and biology/biological science), BUSINESS (business administration and management), COMMUNICATIONS AND THE ARTS (art, communications, English, fine arts, French, music, Spanish, and visual and performing arts), COMPUTER AND PHYSICAL SCIENCE (chemistry, computer science, geology, mathematics, and physics), ENGINEERING AND ENVIRONMENTAL DESIGN (environmental science), HEALTH PROFESSIONS (nursing), SOCIAL SCIENCE (African American studies, American Indian studies, anthropology, criminal justice, economics, ethnic studies, gender studies, geography, history, human development, interdisciplinary studies, international studies, Latin American studies, liberal arts/general studies, Mexican-American/Chicano studies, philosophy, physical fitness/movement, political science/government, psychology, sociology, and women's studies). Liberal arts, physics and math are the strongest academically. Business, psychology and liberal studies have the largest enrollments.

ACTIVITIES: 5% of men belong to 5 national fraternities; 11% of women belong to 9 national sororities. There are 100 groups on campus, including art, cheerleading, chess, choir, chorale, chorus, computers, dance, drama, ethnic, gay, honors, jazz band, literary magazine, musical theater, newspaper, opera, orchestra, pep band, political, professional, radio station, religious, social, social service, student government, and symphony. Popular campus events include Science Night, Parents Day, and Unity Through Diversity Week. **Sports:** There are 14 intercollegiate sports for men and 9 for women, and 8 intramural sports for men and 8 for women. Facilities include a 5,000-seat stadium, a 3,000-seat gym, a field house, tennis courts, a pool, a 500-seat auditorium, and various playing fields. The Sonoma State University Recreation Center, a 59,000 square-foot facility includes a two-court gymnasium, one-court gymnasium/soccer arena, fitness center, climbing wall, outdoor adventure resource and equipment rental area, game room, exercise studios, locker rooms, and spa. **Graduates:** From July 1, 2013 to June 30, 2014, 1727 bachelor's degrees were awarded. The most popular majors were business and marketing (22%), psychology (12%), and social sciences (9%). 720 companies recruited on campus in 2013-2014. In an average class, 23% graduate in 3 years or less, 28% graduate in 4 years or less, 22% graduate in 5 years or less, and 54% graduate in 6 years or less.

SERVICES: Counseling and information services are available, as is tutoring in most subjects. There is a reader service for the blind, remedial math, reading, and writing. Learning disability assessment is also available. **Library/Resources:** The library contains 505,306 volumes, 1.7 million microform items, 39,114 audio/video tapes/CDs/DVDs, and subscribes to 131,000 periodicals including electronic. Computerized library services include interlibrary loans, database searching, Internet access, and Wi-Fi capability. Special learning facilities include an art gallery, a performing arts center, an observatory, electron microscope, seismograph, environmental technology center, green music center and natural preserves. **Physically Challenged Students:** All of the campus is accessible. Facilities include wheelchair ramps, elevators, special parking, specially equipped restrooms, special class scheduling, lowered drinking fountains, lowered telephones. A reading machine, phonic listening devices, PC and mainframe access, and interpreters are also available. **Special:** Students may cross-register at Mills College, Oakland, and University of California, Berkeley. Study-abroad programs are available in 17 countries. Community service internships, work-study, nondegree study through Open University, and pass/fail grading options are available. B.A. and B.S. options in biology, chemistry, environmental studies, geology, interdisciplinary studies, math, and physics are offered. The Hutchins School B.A. in liberal studies offers small seminar classes and an interdisciplinary curriculum. Distance learning programs in nursing are available at 3 off-site centers. There are 6 national honor societies and 5 departmental honors programs. **Visiting:** There are regularly scheduled orientations for prospective students, consisting of programs in the spring and summer. There are guides for informal visits and visitors may sit in on classes. To schedule a visit, contact the Admissions Development Office at (707) 664-3032. **Campus Safety and Security:** Measures include 24-hour foot and vehicle patrol, emergency notification system, self-defense education, and security escort services. There are emergency telephones and lighted pathways/sidewalks.

REQUIREMENTS: The SAT or ACT is required. Applicants should be graduates of accredited high school or have earned the GED. Secondary school preparation should include 4 years of English, 3 year of math, 2 years each of science, foreign language and history, and 1 each of visual/performing arts, academic electives, science with lab. A GPA of 2.0 is required. AP and CLEP credits are accepted. Important factors in the admissions decision are geographical diversity, parents or siblings attended your school, and evidence of special talent. Undergraduate students must complete 120 to 132 units, depending on the degree program, consisting of 48 to 51 units of general education, a concentration of study in a specific major, and electives. General education programs require experience in oral and written communications, critical thinking, natural science and math, arts and humanities, social sciences, and personal integration. All students must take an ethnic studies course and the equivalent of courses in U.S. government, U.S. history, and California government. **Procedure:** Freshmen are admitted fall and spring. There is a rolling admissions plan. Applications should be filed by November 30 for fall entry, along with a $55 fee. Applications are accepted on-line. **Transfer Students:** 1026 transfer students enrolled in 2013-2014. Applicants must have a minimum 2.0 GPA. The maximum number of transferable credits is 70. 30 of 120 credits required for the bachelor's degree must be completed at Sonoma State. **International Students:** There are 148 international students enrolled. The school actively recruits these students. They must take the TOEFL with a minimum score of 500 on the paper-based TOEFL (PBT) or 61 on the Internet-based version (iBT). They must also take the SAT or ACT.

ADMISSIONS: 90% of the 2014-2015 applicants were accepted. The SAT scores for the 2014-2015 freshman class were: Critical Reading--51% below 500, 39% between 500 and 599, 10% between 600 and 699, and 1% between 700 and 800; Math--49% below 500, 41% between 500 and 599, and 10% between 600 and 699. The ACT scores were 14% below 21, 63% between 21 and 23, % between 24 and 26, % between 27 and 28, and 23% above 28. **Admissions Contact:** Gustavo Flores, Director of Admissions and Records. E-Mail: *student.outreach@sonoma.edu* Web: *www.sonoma.edu*

FINANCIAL AID: In 2014-2015, 40% of all full-time freshmen and 20% of continuing full-time students received some form of financial aid. 36% of all full-time freshmen and 21% of continuing full-time students received need-based aid. The average freshman award was $9,620. Need-based scholarships or need-based grants averaged $10,023; need-based self-help aid (loans and jobs) averaged $3,390; non-need-based athletic scholarships averaged $2,085; and other non-need-based awards and non-need-based scholarships averaged $1,654. 15% of undergraduate students work part-time. Average annual earnings from campus work are $4373. The average financial indebtedness of the 2014 graduate was $20,568. The FAFSA is required. The priority date for freshman financial aid applications for fall entry is January 31. The deadline for filing freshman financial aid applications for fall entry is rolling.

STANFORD UNIVERSITY   B-3
www.stanford.edu

Stanford, CA 94305	(650) 723-2091
Fax: (650) 723-6050	Email: admission@stanford.edu
Full-time: 3704 men, 3315 women	Faculty: I, ++$
Part-time: 30 men, 40 women	Ph.D.s: 99%
Graduate: 6687 men, 4693 women	Student/Faculty: 4 to 1
Year: quarters, summer session	Tuition: $44,757
Room & Board: $13,631	Freshman Class: 42167 applied, 2145 accepted, 1678 enrolled
SAT or ACT: required	CEEB CODE: 4704
Application Deadline: January 3	MOST COMPETITIVE

Stanford is a research university, located in one of the most culturally dynamic and diverse areas of the nation with seven schools: Business, Earth Sciences, Education, Engineering, Humanities and Sciences, Law, and Medicine. Stanford's campus is considered among the most beautiful worldwide. Stanford's entrepreneurial character draws from the legacy of its founders, Jane and Leland Stanford, and its relationship to Silicon Valley. Current faculty have won 21 Nobels and 5 Pulitzers. Areas of academic excellence cross disciplines, ranging from humanities to social sciences to engineering and the sciences. Students, distinguished by initiative, love of learning and commitment to public service, are talented in many areas, including academics, art, music and athletics. There are 3 undergraduate schools and 7 graduate schools. In addition to regional accreditation, Stanford has baccalaureate program accreditation with AACSB and ABET. The 8180-acre campus is in an urban area 30 miles south of San Francisco, 20 miles north of San Jose and adjacent to the cities of Palo Alto and Menlo Park. Including any residence halls, there are 700 buildings.

STUDENT LIFE: 53% of undergraduates are from out of state, mostly the South. Students are from 50 states, 90 foreign countries, and Canada. 58% are from public schools. 43% are White; 23% Asian American; 13% Hispanic. **Male To Female Ratio:** 0.8:1. The average age of freshmen is 18; all undergraduates, 20. 1% do not continue beyond their first year; 95% remain to graduate. **Housing:** 6503 students can be accommodated in college housing, which includes single-sex and coed dorms, on-campus apartments, off-campus apartments, and married student housing. In addition, there are language houses, special-interest houses, fraternity houses, sorority houses, ethnic theme houses, substance free housing, academic interest housing. On-campus housing is guaranteed for all 4 years. 92% of students live on campus; of those, 95% remain on campus on weekends. Upperclassmen may keep cars.

FACULTY/CLASSROOMS: 73% of faculty are male; 27% are female. All teach undergraduates, all do research. No introductory courses are taught by graduate students.

PROGRAMS OF STUDY: Stanford confers A.B., B.S. and B.A.S. degrees. Master's and doctoral degrees are also awarded. Bachelor's degrees are awarded in BIOLOGICAL SCIENCE (biology/biological science), BUSINESS (management engineering and product design), COMMUNICATIONS AND THE ARTS (art, art history and appreciation, Chinese, classics, communications, comparative literature, dramatic arts, English, film arts, fine arts, French, Italian, Japanese, linguistics, music, Slavic languages, Spanish, and studio art), COMPUTER AND PHYSICAL SCIENCE (chemistry, computer science, earth science, geology, geophysics and seismology, geoscience, mathematics, mathematics/computational, and physics), ENGINEERING AND ENVIRONMENTAL DESIGN (aeronautical engineering, architectural engineering, bioengineering, chemical engineering, civil engineering, electrical/electronics engineering, engineering, engineering physics, environmental engineering, industrial engineering, materials science, mechanical engineering, petroleum/natural gas engineering, and systems engineering), SOCIAL SCIENCE (African American studies, American studies, anthropology, archeology, area studies, Asian/American studies, crosscultural studies, East Asian studies, economics, German area studies, Hispanic American studies, history, Iberian studies, international relations, Judaic studies, Latin American studies, Native American studies, philosophy, political science/government, psychology, public administration, religion, sociology, systems science, urban studies, and women's studies). Computer science, human biology, and engineering have the largest enrollments.

ACTIVITIES: 24% of men belong to 16 national fraternities; 28% of women belong to 14 national sororities. There are 625 groups on campus, including art, band, cheerleading, chess, choir, chorale, chorus, computers, dance, debate, drama, environmental, ethnic, film, gay, honors, international, jazz band, literary magazine, marching band, musical theater, newspaper, opera, orchestra, pep band, photography, political, professional, radio and TV, religious, social, social service, student government, symphony, and yearbook. Popular campus events include The Big Game, Full Moon on the Quad, Gaities, Fountain Hopping, and Viennese Ball. **Sports:** There are 16 intercollegiate sports for men and 20 for women. Facilities include club sports, intramural sports, athletic fields, gyms, swimming pools, volleyball courts, lighted tennis courts, dance studios, climbing wall, weight rooms, an 18-hole golf course, a sailing facility, a rowing facility, handball, racquetball, squash courts, baseball diamond, football stadium, softball stadium, soccer stadium field hockey and lacrosse fields. **Graduates:** From July 1, 2013 to June 30, 2014, 1723 bachelor's degrees were awarded. The most popular majors were interdisciplinary studies (18%), engineering (16%), and social sciences (15%). 350 companies recruited on campus in 2013-2014. In an average class, 95% graduate in 6 years or less.

SERVICES: Counseling and information services are available, as is tutoring in most subjects. There is a reader service for the blind.

Schwab Learning Center offers services for students with learning disabilities and attention-deficit hyperactivity disorder. **Library/Resources:** The 20 libraries contain 9.3 million volumes, 6.0 million microform items, 2.5 million audio/video tapes/CDs/DVDs, and subscribe to 77,000 periodicals including electronic. Computerized library services include interlibrary loans, database searching, Internet access, and Wi-Fi capability. Special learning facilities include an art gallery, radio station, TV station, 3 art museums, a concert hall, a biological preserve, a linear accelerator, an observatory. **Physically Challenged Students:** 98% of the campus is accessible. Facilities include wheelchair ramps, elevators, special parking, specially equipped restrooms, special class scheduling, lowered drinking fountains, lowered telephones, special housing. Stanford has a Diversity and Access Office and an Office of Accessible Education to provide help. **Special:** Internships, study abroad, a Washington semester, a New York City program, marine research center, semester at sea, 12 overseas study programs, dual majors, a B.A.-B.S. degree, research opportunities, honors programs and co-terminal bachelor's and master's programs are available. Also offered on a pilot basis are joint majors that integrate humanities and computer science. There is a Phi Beta Kappa chapter. **Visiting:** There are regularly scheduled orientations for prospective students, including group information sessions and campus tours. There are guides for informal visits, visitors may sit in on classes, and stay overnight. To schedule a visit, contact the Office of Undergraduate Admission at admission@stanford.edu. **Campus Safety and Security:** Measures include 24-hour foot and vehicle patrol, emergency notification system, self-defense education, and security escort services. There are shuttle buses, emergency telephones, lighted pathways/sidewalks, controlled access to dorms/residences, AlertSU notifies students immediately of safety threats on campus.

REQUIREMENTS: The SAT or ACT is required. The ACT Optional Writing test is also required. The SAT (Critical Reading, Math and Writing) or ACT Plus Writing is required. SAT Subject Tests are recommended. The university recommends that applicants have strong preparation in high school English, math, a foreign language, science and social studies. If English is not your native language, we recommend, but do not require, the Test of English as a Foreign Language. Generally speaking, Stanford students have taken the most rigorous classes available to them. Applicants must complete the Common Application, the Stanford University Questions and arrange for recommendations. Candidates choose one topic from the Common Application, as well as complete three Stanford short essays. AP credits are accepted. Important factors in the admissions decision are advanced placement or honors courses, personality/intangible qualities, and recommendations by school officials. To graduate, students must complete 180 units, including requirements for the major, a writing and rhetoric requirement, and 1 year of a foreign language. General education requirements include the one-quarter freshman class Thinking Matters. Also required is Ways of Thinking, Ways of Doing, which includes eleven courses in eight subject areas, including aesthetic and interpretive inquiry, applied quantitative reasoning, creative expression, engaging diversity, ethical reasoning, formal reasoning, scientific method and analysis and social inquiry. **Procedure:** Freshmen are admitted fall. Entrance exams should be taken by Nov. 1 for early decision; Jan. 15 for regular admission. There are early decision and deferred admissions plans. Early decision applications should be filed by November 1; regular applications, by January 3 for fall entry, along with a $90 fee. Notification of early decision is sent December 15; regular decision, April 1. 748 early decision candidates were accepted for the 2014-2015 class. 958 applicants were on the 2014 waiting list; 7 were admitted. Applications are accepted on-line. **Transfer Students:** 29 transfer students enrolled in 2013-2014. Transfer students must complete 1 full year of academic work prior to enrollment. There is only fall quarter enrollment for transfer students. The application deadline is March 15. 90 of 180 credits required for the bachelor's degree must be completed at Stanford. **International Students:** There are 574 international students enrolled. The school actively recruits these students. They must also take the SAT or ACT. SAT Subject tests are recommended.

ADMISSIONS: 5% of the 2014-2015 applicants were accepted. The SAT scores for the 2014-2015 freshman class were: Critical Reading--5% between 500 and 599, 26% between 600 and 699, and 69%

between 700 and 800; Math--3% between 500 and 599, 19% between 600 and 699, and 78% between 700 and 800; Writing--4% between 500 and 599, 22% between 600 and 699, and 74% between 700 and 800. The ACT scores were 1% below 21, 11% between 24 and 26, and 88% above 28. 99% of the current freshmen were in the top fifth of their class; 100% were in the top two fifths. **Admissions Contact:** Richard H. Shaw, Dean of Admissions. E-Mail: *admission@stanford .edu* Web: *www.stanford.edu*

FINANCIAL AID: In 2014-2015, 82% of continuing full-time students received some form of financial aid. 67% of continuing full-time students received need-based aid. The average freshman award was $42,514. Need-based scholarships or need-based grants averaged $44,790; need-based self-help aid (loans and jobs) averaged $2,168; and non-need-based athletic scholarships averaged $41,935. The average financial indebtedness of the 2014 graduate was $19,230. Stanford is a member of CSS. The CSS/Profile and FAFSA are required. The priority date for freshman financial aid applications for fall entry is February 15.

THE MASTERS COLLEGE   **D-4**
www.masters.edu

Santa Clarita, CA 91321   **(661) 362-2608**
                             (800) 568-6248
Fax: (661) 362-2718   **Email: admissions@masters.edu**
Full-time: 477 men, 490 women   **Faculty:** 58
Part-time: 98 men, 33 women   **Ph.D.s:** 74%
Graduate: 352 men, 35 women   **Student/Faculty:** 10 to 1
Year: semesters, summer session   **Tuition:** $28,800
Room & Board: $9360   **Freshman Class:** 757 applied, 590 accepted, 256 enrolled
SAT CR/M/W: 552/536/538 **ACT:** 24   **CEEB CODE:** 4411
Application Deadline: March 2   **COMPETITIVE+**

The Master's College, founded in 1927, is a Christ centered liberal arts college that exists to advance the kingdom of God by equipping students for moral integrity and lives of service in strategic fields of ministry and vocation. Figures in the above capsule and in this profile are approximate. Within this authentic and life-changing community students from around the globe gather to be challenged academically, culturally engaged and to embrace Biblical fidelity in all things. There is 1 undergraduate school and 1 graduate school. In addition to regional accreditation, TMC has baccalaureate program accreditation with ABHES and NASM. The 110-acre campus is in a suburban area 35 miles north of Los Angeles. Including any residence halls, there are 32 buildings.

STUDENT LIFE: 73% of undergraduates are from California. Others are from 43 states, 19 foreign countries, and Canada. 26% are from public schools. 66% are White. 100% are Protestant. The average age of freshmen is 19; all undergraduates, 20. 20% do not continue beyond their first year; 56% remain to graduate. **Housing:** 808 students can be accommodated in college housing, which includes single-sex dorms and off-campus apartments. On-campus housing is guaranteed for all 4 years, is guaranteed for the freshman year only, is available on a first-come, first-served basis. 75% of students live on campus; of those, 80% remain on campus on weekends. Alcohol is not permitted. All students may keep cars.

FACULTY/CLASSROOMS: 76% of faculty are male; 24% are female. All teach undergraduates. No introductory courses are taught by graduate students. The average class size in an introductory lecture is 30; in a laboratory is 11; and in a regular course is 14.

PROGRAMS OF STUDY: TMC confers B.A., B.M. and B.S. degrees. Master's degrees are also awarded. Bachelor's degrees are awarded in BIOLOGICAL SCIENCE (biology/biological science), BUSINESS (business administration and management), COMMUNICATIONS AND THE ARTS (communications, English, and music), COMPUTER AND PHYSICAL SCIENCE (information sciences and systems, mathematics, and natural sciences), EDUCATION (elementary education, physical education, and secondary education), SOCIAL SCIENCE (biblical studies, history, home economics, liberal arts/

general studies, and political science/government). Biological sciences, Biblical studies, and business administration are the strongest academically. Biblical studies, business administration, and communication have the largest enrollments.

ACTIVITIES: There are 15 groups on campus, including band, choir, chorale, drama, film, jazz band, musical theater, newspaper, opera, orchestra, pep band, political, radio and TV, religious, social service, and student government. Popular campus events include College View Weekend, Community Day, and Truth and Life Conference. **Sports:** There are 6 intercollegiate sports for men and 5 for women, and 6 intramural sports for men and 6 for women. Facilities include a gym, sports field, tennis and volleyball courts, an intramural field, swimming pool, and a fitness facility. **Graduates:** From July 1, 2013 to June 30, 2014, 224 bachelor's degrees were awarded. The most popular majors were Biblical studies (30%), business (13%), and liberal studies (11%). In an average class, 8% graduate in 3 years or less, 48% graduate in 4 years or less, 55% graduate in 5 years or less, and 56% graduate in 6 years or less. Of the 2013 graduating class, 10% were enrolled in graduate school within 6 months of graduation.

SERVICES: Counseling and information services are available, as is tutoring in most subjects. There is remedial math. **Library/ Resources:** The library contains 193,130 volumes, 38,349 microform items, 2,723 audio/video tapes/CDs/DVDs, and subscribes to 34,685 periodicals including electronic. Computerized library services include interlibrary loans, database searching, Internet access, and Wi-Fi capability. Special learning facilities include a radio station, a modular, computerized music rehearsal rooms and a technology recording facility. **Physically Challenged Students:** All of the campus is accessible. Facilities include wheelchair ramps, elevators, special parking, specially equipped restrooms, lowered drinking fountains, and lowered telephones. **Special:** Students may cross-register with the Coalition of Christian Colleges and Universities and may participate in a co-op program with the College of the Canyons. Internships are offered with local churches, radio stations, and newspapers. A Washington semester, study abroad, dual majors in music plus a second discipline, and a general studies degree are available. The Master's Institute, a 1-year certificate Bible program, is also offered. **Visiting:** There are regularly scheduled orientations for prospective students, including class visitation, meetings with faculty, interviews, athletic events, an overnight stay, and college activities. There are guides for informal visits, visitors may sit in on classes, and stay overnight. To schedule a visit, contact the Admissions Office. **Campus Safety and Security:** Measures include 24-hour foot and vehicle patrol, emergency notification system, and security escort services. There are shuttle buses and lighted pathways/sidewalks.

REQUIREMENTS: The SAT or ACT is required. Applicants must have completed 4 years of English, 3 each of math and science, 2 of history, and 8 units of electives. A GPA of 2.8 is required. AP and CLEP credits are accepted. Important factors in the admissions decision are personality/intangible qualities, recommendations by school officials, and leadership record. Students must complete at least 122 semester hours, including 78 distributed as follows: 24 hours in Biblical studies, 18 in social sciences, 9 in English, 7 in natural science, 6 in cross-cultural studies, and 3 each in communication, business, logical reasoning, and fine arts. Students must complete at least 40 semester hours in upper-division courses and at least 40 in the major and must maintain a minimum GPA of 2.0. **Procedure:** Freshmen are admitted fall and spring. Entrance exams should be taken In the fall. There are early admissions and deferred admissions plans. Early decision applications should be filed by November 15; regular applications, by March 2 for fall entry, along with a $40 fee. Notification of early decision is sent December 22; regular decision, April 1. 303 early decision candidates were accepted for the 2014-2015 class. Applications are accepted on-line. **Transfer Students:** 90 transfer students enrolled in 2013-2014. Applicants must meet freshman requirements. A maximum of 70 units can be transferred from a junior college and 94 units from a 4-year college. 28 of 122 credits required for the bachelor's degree must be completed at TMC. **International Students:** There are 47 international students enrolled. The school actively recruits these students. They must take the TOEFL.

ADMISSIONS: 78% of the 2014-2015 applicants were accepted. The SAT scores for the 2014-2015 freshman class were: Critical Reading--24% below 500, 50% between 500 and 599, 17% between 600 and

699, and 7% between 700 and 800; Math--31% below 500, 37% between 500 and 599, 20% between 600 and 699, and 7% between 700 and 800; Writing--27% below 500, 38% between 500 and 599, 22% between 600 and 699, and 5% between 700 and 800. The ACT scores were 23% below 21, 32% between 21 and 23, 24% between 24 and 26, 6% between 27 and 28, and 15% above 28. 48% of the current freshmen were in the top fifth of their class; 73% were in the top two fifths. 2 freshmen graduated first in their class. **Admissions Contact:** Director of Admissions. E-Mail: *admissions@masters.edu* Web: *www. masters.edu*

FINANCIAL AID: In 2014-2015, 98% of all full-time freshmen and 92% of continuing full-time students received some form of financial aid. 61% of all full-time freshmen and 41% of continuing full-time students received need-based aid. The average freshman award was $22,295. Need-based scholarships or need-based grants averaged $13,918 ($5,645 maximum); need-based self-help aid (loans and jobs) averaged $6,619 ($5,500 maximum); non-need-based athletic scholarships averaged $21,063 ($37,740 maximum); and other non-need-based awards and non-need-based scholarships averaged $7,893 ($14,000 maximum). 48% of undergraduate students work part-time. Average annual earnings from campus work are $2000. The average financial indebtedness of the 2014 graduate was $11,500. TMC is a member of CSS. The FAFSA and the college's own financial statement are required. Check with the school for current application deadlines.

THOMAS AQUINAS COLLEGE   **C-4**
www.thomasaquinas.edu

Santa Paula, CA 93060

(800) 634-9797
(800) 634-9797

Fax: (805) 421-5905   Email: admissions@thomasaquinas.edu

Full-time: 191 men, 187 women	Faculty: 32
Part-time: n/av	Ph.D.s: 88%
Graduate: n/av	Student/Faculty: 11 to 1
Year: semesters	Tuition: $24,500
Room & Board: $7950	Freshman Class: 210 applied, 175 accepted, 102 enrolled
SAT CR/M/W: 660/610/630 ACT: 28	CEEB CODE: 4828
Application Deadline: n/av	**HIGHLY COMPETITIVE+**

Thomas Aquinas College, founded in 1971 and affiliated with the Roman Catholic Church, is a small, private, liberal arts college offering an integrated studies curriculum based on the Great Books. All classes are conducted as conversations directed by teachers using the Socratic method. Figures in the above capsule and in this profile are approximate. There is one undergraduate school. The 131-acre campus is in a rural area 70 miles northwest of Los Angeles. Including any residence halls, there are 20 buildings.

STUDENT LIFE: 61% of undergraduates are from out of state, mostly the Mid-West. Students are from 36 states, 10 foreign countries, and Canada. 17% are from public schools. 71% are White; 15% Hispanic. 97% are Catholic. **Male To Female Ratio:** 1.0:1. The average age of freshmen is 18; all undergraduates, 20. 5% do not continue beyond their first year; 70% remain to graduate. **Housing:** 398 students can be accommodated in college housing, which includes single-sex dorms. On-campus housing is guaranteed for all 4 years. 99% of students live on campus; of those, 95% remain on campus on weekends. Alcohol is not permitted. All students may keep cars.

FACULTY/CLASSROOMS: 89% of faculty are male; 11% are female. All teach undergraduates. No introductory courses are taught by graduate students. The average class size in a laboratory is 17 and in a regular course is 17.

PROGRAMS OF STUDY: TAC confers B.A. degrees. Bachelor's degrees are awarded in SOCIAL SCIENCE (liberal arts/general studies).

ACTIVITIES: There are no fraternities or sororities. There are 6 groups on campus, including Tocqueville Political Forum, art, choir, chorale, chorus, drama, literary magazine, Medical Society, and orchestra. Popular campus events include St. Thomas Aquinas Day, President's Day, St. Patrick's Day and Easter. **Sports:** There are 7

intramural sports for men and 6 for women. Facilities include a tennis, basketball, and volleyball courts, a soccer field, swimming area, weight-lifting rooms, and a softball field. **Graduates:** From July 1, 2013 to June 30, 2014, 82 bachelor's degrees were awarded. The most popular majors were liberal arts (100%). 16 companies recruited on campus in 2013-2014. In an average class, 61% graduate in 4 years or less, 69% graduate in 5 years or less, and 70% graduate in 6 years or less. Of the 2013 graduating class, 12% were enrolled in graduate school within 6 months of graduation, and 73% were employed.

SERVICES: There is remedial writing. All students may be tutored by the full-time teaching faculty. **Library/Resources:** The library contains 64,783 volumes, 6,674 audio/video tapes/CDs/DVDs, and subscribes to 61 periodicals including electronic. Computerized library services include database searching and Internet access. **Physically Challenged Students:** All of the campus is accessible. Facilities include wheelchair ramps, elevators, special parking, specially equipped restrooms, special class scheduling, lowered drinking fountains, lowered telephones, and special housing. **Visiting:** There are regularly scheduled orientations for prospective students, includes a campus tour and the hosting of prospective students by current students. Visits are for up to 3 days and consist of observing classes, attending lectures and concerts, enjoying community meals and events. There are guides for informal visits, visitors may sit in on classes, and stay overnight. To schedule a visit, contact the Admissions Office.

REQUIREMENTS: The SAT or ACT is required. Candidates for Admission are expected to have completed four years of English and a minimum of 2 years of natural science, 2 years of a foreign language, 2 years of algebra, and 1 year of geometry. Additional work in science, mathematics and language study is recommended. Important factors in the admissions decision are personality/intangible qualities, advanced placement or honors courses, and recommendations by school officials. The entire curriculum is required of all students: it includes four years each of Philosophy, Theology, Mathematics, Science and Seminar (Seminar covers philosophical works not covered in the Philosophy courses, Literature, History, and Social Science, among others), 2 years of Language (Latin), and 1 year of Music. Seniors are required to write and defend a thesis. A total of 146 semester hours, with a minimum GPA of 2.0, is required to graduate. **Procedure:** Freshmen are admitted in fall. There is a rolling admissions plan. Application deadlines are open. 39 applicants were on the 2014 waiting list; 14 were admitted. Applications are accepted online. **Transfer Students:** The integrated nature of the program requires that all students start as freshmen, and so, regardless of past education Thomas Aquinas College only admits students as freshmen. 15-20% of each freshman class has attended college elsewhere prior to enrolling in Thomas Aquinas College. 146 of 146 credits required for the bachelor's degree must be completed at TAC. **International Students:** There are 15 international students enrolled. They must take the TOEFL with a minimum score of 570 on the paper-based TOEFL (PBT). They must also take the SAT or ACT.

ADMISSIONS: 83% of the 2014-2015 applicants were accepted. The SAT scores for the 2014-2015 freshman class were: Critical Reading--16% between 500 and 599, 50% between 600 and 699, and 34% between 700 and 800; Math--1% below 500, 46% between 500 and 599, 44% between 600 and 699, and 9% between 700 and 800; Writing--3% below 500, 29% between 500 and 599, 46% between 600 and 699, and 23% between 700 and 800. The ACT scores were 18% between 21 and 23, 18% between 24 and 26, 18% between 27 and 28, and 45% above 28. 64% of the current freshmen were in the top fifth of their class; 88% were in the top two fifths. There were 6 National Merit finalists. 2 freshmen graduated first in their class. **Admissions Contact:** Jonathan P. Daly, Director of Admissions. E-Mail: *admissions@thomasaquinas.edu* Web: *www.thomasaquinas.edu*

FINANCIAL AID: In 2014-2015, 75% of all full-time freshmen and 82% of continuing full-time students received some form of financial aid. 70% of all full-time freshmen and 79% of continuing full-time students received need-based aid. The average freshman award was $20,883. Need-based scholarships or need-based grants averaged $13,666 ($23,234 maximum); need-based self-help aid (loans and jobs) averaged $6,119 ($9,000 maximum); and other non-need-based awards and non-need-based scholarships averaged $20 ($1,500 maximum). 76% of undergraduate students work part-time. Average annual earnings from campus work are $3982. The average financial indebtedness of the 2014 graduate was $13,329. The FAFSA and the college's own financial statement, and parent and student federal tax returns are required. The deadline for filing freshman financial aid applications for fall entry is March 2.

UNIVERSITY OF CALIFORNIA SYSTEM

The University of California System, established in 1868, is a public system in California. It is governed by a board of regents, whose chief administrator is the president. The primary goal of the system is teaching, research, and public service. The total enrollment in a recent year of all 10 campuses is about 233,000 with approximately 9500 faculty members. Altogether there are 565 baccalaureate, 250 master's, and 200 doctoral programs offered in the University of California System. 4-year campuses are located in Berkeley, Davis, Irvine, Los Angeles, Riverside, San Diego, Santa Barbara, Merced, and Santa Cruz. Profiles of the 4-year campuses are included in this section.

UNIVERSITY OF CALIFORNIA AT BERKELEY
B-3

www.berkeley.edu

Berkeley, CA 94720	(510) 642-2316
Full-time: n/av	Faculty: I, ++$
Part-time: n/av	Ph.D.s: 99%
Graduate: n/av	Student/Faculty: n/av
Year: semesters, summer session	Tuition: $8938 ($31,665)
Room & Board: $14,384	Freshman Class: 48650 applied, 10561 accepted, 4356 enrolled
SAT CR/M/W: 660/700/670 ACT: 30	CEEB CODE: 4833
Application Deadline: November 30	MOST COMPETITIVE

The University of California at Berkeley, founded in 1868, is a public institution offering a wide variety of programs in the social and physical sciences, liberal arts, and professional fields. It is the oldest campus of the University of California system. There are 7 undergraduate schools and 14 graduate schools. In addition to regional accreditation, Cal has baccalaureate program accreditation with AACSB, ABET, ADA, ASLA, and SAF. The 1232-acre campus is in an urban area 10 miles east of San Francisco. Including any residence halls, there are 300 buildings.

STUDENT LIFE: 90% of undergraduates are from California. Others are from 50 states, 80 foreign countries, and Canada. 85% are from public schools. 43% are Asian American; 32% White; 13% Hispanic. **Male To Female Ratio:** Is 1:1. The average age of freshmen is 19; all undergraduates, 21. 4% do not continue beyond their first year; 90% remain to graduate. **Housing:** 8800 students can be accommodated in college housing, which includes single-sex and coed dorms, off-campus apartments, and married student housing. In addition, there are honors houses, language houses, special-interest houses, fraternity houses, sorority houses, substance-free housing, an international house, theme housing, and co-ops. On-campus housing is guaranteed for the freshman year only and is available on a lottery system for upperclassmen. All students may keep cars.

FACULTY/CLASSROOMS: 65% of faculty are male; 35% are female. No introductory courses are taught by graduate students.

PROGRAMS OF STUDY: Cal confers A.B., and B.S. degrees. Master's and doctoral degrees are also awarded. Bachelor's degrees are awarded in AGRICULTURE (conservation and regulation and forestry and related sciences), BIOLOGICAL SCIENCE (biology/biological science, microbiology, molecular biology, nutrition, and plant genetics), BUSINESS (business administration and management, management science, and operations research), COMMUNICATIONS AND THE ARTS (art, art history and appreciation, Chinese, classical languages, communications, comparative literature, dance, dramatic arts, Dutch, English, film arts, French, German, Greek, Italian, Japanese, Latin, linguistics, music, Scandinavian languages, Slavic languages, Spanish, and speech/debate/rhetoric), COMPUTER AND PHYSICAL SCIENCE (applied mathematics, astrophysics, chemistry, computer science, earth science, mathematics, physical sciences, physics, and statistics), ENGINEERING AND ENVIRONMENTAL DESIGN (architecture, bioengineering, chemical engineering, civil engineering, computer engineering, electrical/electronics engineering, engineering and applied science, engineering physics, environmental engineering, environmental science, industrial engineering, landscape architecture/design, manufacturing engineering, materials engineering, materials science, mechanical engineering, and nuclear engineering), HEALTH PROFESSIONS (optometry and public health), SOCIAL SCIENCE (African American studies, American studies, anthropology, Asian/American studies, Asian/Oriental studies, Celtic studies, classical/ancient civilization, cognitive science, economics, ethnic studies, geography, Hispanic American studies, history, interdisciplinary studies, Latin American studies, law, Middle Eastern studies, Native American studies, Near Eastern studies, peace studies, political science/government, psychology, religion, social science, social work, sociology, South Asian studies, urban studies, and women's studies). Electrical engineering and computer science, political science and economics have the largest enrollments.

ACTIVITIES: There are 400 groups on campus, including art, band, cheerleading, chess, choir, chorale, chorus, computers, dance, debate, drama, ethnic, film, forensics, gay, honors, international, jazz band, literary magazine, marching band, musical theater, newspaper, orchestra, pep band, photography, political, professional, radio and TV, religious, social, social service, student government, and symphony. Popular campus events include The Big Game, Cal Performances, and E-Week. **Sports:** Facilities include a football stadium, track stadium, basketball pavilion, 4 gyms, martial arts room, 7 swimming pools, 3 weight rooms, squash, racquetball, handball, volleyball, tennis courts, baseball and softball fields. **Graduates:** From July 1, 2013 to June 30, 2014, 7247 bachelor's degrees were awarded. The most popular majors were molecular biology (10%), economics (7%), and political science (7%). 600 companies recruited on campus in 2013-2014. In an average class, 3% graduate in 3 years or less, 69% graduate in 4 years or less, 88% graduate in 5 years or less, and 90% graduate in 6 years or less.

SERVICES: Counseling and information services are available, as is tutoring in most subjects. There is a reader service for the blind. **Library/Resources:** The 35 libraries contain 10.4 million volumes, 6.6 million microform items, 46,162 audio/video tapes/CDs/DVDs, and subscribe to 82,151 periodicals including electronic. Computerized library services include interlibrary loans and database searching. Special learning facilities include an art gallery, natural history museum, radio station, TV station, a botanical garden, an anthropology museum, a hall of science, the University Art Museum and Pacific Film Archive, seismographic station, an herbaria, the Hall for the Performing Arts, an observatory, and many off-campus facilities. **Physically Challenged Students:** 95% of the campus is accessible. Facilities include wheelchair ramps, elevators, special parking, specially equipped restrooms, special class scheduling, lowered drinking fountains, and lowered telephones. **Special:** Co-op programs, cross-registration with many area schools, internships, work-study programs, and study abroad programs in 35 countries are available. Interdisciplinary majors are also available, as are pass/fail options, independent study, an independent research and undergraduate research program, and a freshman seminar program, in which 15 to 25 students meet with professors to explore a wide range of majors. There is a 3-2 engineering program with the University of California, Santa Cruz. There is a Phi Beta Kappa chapter and a freshman honors program. **Visiting:** There are regularly scheduled orientations for prospective students, including 1 1/2 hour student-led walking tours, usually followed by an admissions information presentation; self-guided tours are also available. There are guides for informal visits and visitors may sit in on classes. To schedule a visit, contact the Visitor Services at (510) 642-5215. **Campus Safety and Security:** Measures include 24-hour foot and vehicle patrol, emergency notification system, self-defense education, and security escort services. There are shuttle buses, emergency telephones, lighted pathways/sidewalks, controlled access to dorms/residences, a rape prevention peer education program, an earthquake emergency preparedness program, and safety, threats and alerts reports via computer.

REQUIREMENTS: The SAT or ACT is required. Applicants must submit scores from 2 SAT Subject Tests. Also required are 4 years of English, 3 of math (4 recommended), 2 each of history/social sciences, lab science (3 recommended), foreign language (3 recommended), and college preparatory electives. AP credits are accepted. Important factors in the admissions decision are advanced placement or honors courses, evidence of special talent, and leadership record. All undergraduate students are required to satisfy the general university requirements of English and writing proficiency and take integrative and comparative courses in American history, institutions, and cultures. Students must complete 120 units with a minimum GPA of 2.0. **Procedure:** Freshmen are admitted in fall. Entrance exams should be taken no later than December test dates in the senior year. There is a deferred admissions plan. Applications should be filed by November 30 for fall entry, along with a $60 fee. Notifications are sent March 30. Applications are accepted on-line. **Transfer Students:** 2012 transfer students enrolled in 2013-2014. 24 of 120 credits required for the bachelor's degree must be completed at Cal. **International Students:** There are 1073 international students enrolled. They must take the TOEFL with a minimum score of 550 on the paper-based TOEFL (PBT) or 83 on the Internet-based version (iBT). They must also take the SAT or ACT.

ADMISSIONS: 22% of the 2014-2015 applicants were accepted. The SAT scores for the 2014-2015 freshman class were: Critical Reading--8% below 500, 20% between 500 and 599, 43% between 600 and 699, and 29% between 700 and 800; Math--4% below 500, 14% between 500 and 599, 32% between 600 and 699, and 51% between 700 and 800; Writing--6% below 500, 18% between 500 and 599, 42% between 600 and 699, and 34% between 700 and 800. **Admissions Contact:** Director of Undergraduate Admission. Web: *www.berkeley.edu*

FINANCIAL AID: In 2014-2015, 50% of all full-time freshmen and 49% of continuing full-time students received some form of financial aid. 48% of all full-time freshmen and 48% of continuing full-time students received need-based aid. The average freshman award was $17,250. Need-based scholarships or need-based grants averaged $12,651; need-based self-help aid (loans and jobs) averaged $6,037; non-need-based athletic scholarships averaged $12,873; and other non-need-based awards and non-need-based scholarships averaged $2,136. The average financial indebtedness of the 2014 graduate was $14,751. The FAFSA is required. The deadline for filing freshman financial aid applications for fall entry is March 2.

UNIVERSITY OF CALIFORNIA AT DAVIS   B-2
www.ucdavis.edu

Davis, CA 95616 (530) 752-2971

Fax: (530) 752-1280	Email: undergraduateadmissions@ucdavis
Full-time: 11140 men, 13647 women	Faculty: I, +$
	Ph.D.s: 98%
Part-time: 142 men, 167 women	Student/Faculty: 15 to 1
Graduate: 3292 men, 3344 women	Tuition: $13,860 ($36,738)
Year: quarters, summer session	Freshman Class: 43295
Room & Board: $12,697	applied, 19460 accepted, 4501 enrolled
SAT CR/M/W: 600/640/600 ACT: 27	CEEB CODE: 4834
Application Deadline: November 30	HIGHLY COMPETITIVE

University of California at Davis, founded in 1908, is a land-grant, comprehensive institution offering programs in arts and science, agricultural and environmental sciences, and engineering. There are 4 undergraduate schools and 5 graduate schools. In addition to regional accreditation, UC Davis has baccalaureate program accreditation with ABET, ADA, and ASLA. The 5300-acre campus is in a suburban area 15 miles west of Sacramento, and 72 miles northeast of San Francisco. Including any residence halls, there are 1186 buildings.

STUDENT LIFE: 98% of undergraduates are from California. Others are from 47 states, 113 foreign countries, and Canada. 90% are from public schools. 38% are Asian American; 34% White; 15% Hispanic. **Male To Female Ratio:** 1.2:1. The average age of freshmen is 18; all undergraduates, 21. 8% do not continue beyond their first year; 82%

remain to graduate. **Housing:** 5653 students can be accommodated in college housing, which includes single-sex and coed dorms, on-campus apartments, off-campus apartments, and married student housing. In addition, there are honors houses, language houses, and special-interest houses. On-campus housing is guaranteed for the freshman year only. 75% of students commute. Alcohol is not permitted. No one may keep cars.

FACULTY/CLASSROOMS: 63% of faculty are male; 37% are female. No introductory courses are taught by graduate students.

PROGRAMS OF STUDY: UC Davis confers B.S., A.B. and B.A.S. degrees. Master's and doctoral degrees are also awarded. Bachelor's degrees are awarded in AGRICULTURE (agricultural business management, agricultural economics, animal science, international agriculture, plant science, range/farm management, and soil science), BIOLOGICAL SCIENCE (avian sciences, bacteriology, biochemistry, biology/biological science, botany, ecology, entomology, environmental biology, genetics, microbiology, nutrition, physiology, toxicology, wildlife biology, and zoology), BUSINESS (organizational behavior), COMMUNICATIONS AND THE ARTS (art history and appreciation, Chinese, communications, comparative literature, design, dramatic arts, English, fine arts, French, German, Greek, Italian, Japanese, Latin, linguistics, music, Russian, Spanish, speech/debate/rhetoric, and studio art), COMPUTER AND PHYSICAL SCIENCE (atmospheric sciences and meteorology, chemistry, computer science, geology, hydrology, mathematics, physics, polymer science, and statistics), EDUCATION (physical education), ENGINEERING AND ENVIRONMENTAL DESIGN (aeronautical engineering, agricultural engineering, bioengineering, chemical engineering, civil engineering, computer engineering, electrical/electronics engineering, environmental design, environmental science, landscape architecture/design, materials engineering, and mechanical engineering), HEALTH PROFESSIONS (community health work and environmental health science), SOCIAL SCIENCE (African studies, American studies, anthropology, behavioral science, classical/ancient civilization, dietetics, East Asian studies, economics, food science, geography, history, human development, human ecology, international relations, medieval studies, Mexican-American/Chicano studies, Native American studies, philosophy, political science/government, psychology, religion, social science, sociology, textiles and clothing, and women's studies). Agricultural, biological, and biotechnical sciences are the strongest academically. Biological science, biochemistry, and psychology have the largest enrollments.

ACTIVITIES: There are 320 groups on campus, including art, band, cheerleading, chess, choir, chorus, computers, dance, debate, drama, ethnic, film, gay, honors, international, jazz band, literary magazine, marching band, musical theater, newspaper, orchestra, pep band, photography, political, professional, radio and TV, religious, social, social service, student government, and symphony. Popular campus events include Picnic Day, Whole Earth Festival, and Asian Pacific Cultural Week. **Sports:** There are 9 intercollegiate sports for men and 14 for women. Facilities include a football stadium, tennis and basketball courts, equestrian trails, a track field, baseball, soccer, and softball fields, a recreation hall, 2 gyms, 2 swimming pools, bowling alleys, weight-training facilities, and an outdoor roller hockey rink. **Graduates:** From July 1, 2013 to June 30, 2014, 6369 bachelor's degrees were awarded. The most popular majors were psychology (10%), biological sciences (6%), and economics (6%). In an average class, 2% graduate in 3 years or less, 51% graduate in 4 years or less, 78% graduate in 5 years or less, and 82% graduate in 6 years or less. Of the 2013 graduating class, 38% were enrolled in graduate school within 6 months of graduation, and 79% were employed.

SERVICES: Counseling and information services are available, as is tutoring in most subjects. There is a reader service for the blind, and remedial math and writing. **Library/Resources:** The 6 libraries contain 4.2 million volumes, 4.3 million microform items, and 19,581 audio/video tapes/CDs/DVDs, and subscribe to 74,836 periodicals including electronic. Computerized library services include database searching. Special learning facilities include an art gallery, radio station, an experimental farm, a 150-acre arboretum, a raptor center, an equestrian center, a primate research center, and the Crocker Nuclear Laboratory. **Physically Challenged Students:** All of the campus is accessible. Facilities include wheelchair ramps, elevators, special parking, specially equipped restrooms, special class scheduling, lowered drinking fountains, lowered telephones. **Special:** There are credit and noncredit internship programs. Study abroad in more than 32 countries and a Washington semester are offered. Students may participate in college work-study, federal work-study, and California work-study programs. Several A.B.-B.S. degrees are offered. Students may design their own majors, take dual majors, and elect pass/fail options. Interdisciplinary majors are offered in African American and African studies, American studies, Mexican American studies, comparative literature, East Asian studies, exercise science, international relations, linguistics, medieval studies, Native American studies, religious studies, and women's studies. There are 24 national honor societies, including a Phi Beta Kappa chapter, a freshman honors program, and 3 departmental honors programs. **Visiting:** There are regularly scheduled orientations for prospective students, including weekend tours of the campus, weekday tours by appointment, and drop-in counseling with staff and faculty. The campus also offers a 1-day preview for prospective students and their families. There are guides for informal visits, visitors may sit in on classes, and stay overnight. To schedule a visit, contact UC Davis Visitor Services at visit@ucdavis.edu. **Campus Safety and Security:** Measures include 24-hour foot and vehicle patrol, emergency notification system, self-defense education, and security escort services. There are shuttle buses, emergency telephones, and lighted pathways/sidewalks. There is also a rape prevention program, a crime prevention unit, a bike patrol unit, and a K-9 program.

REQUIREMENTS: The SAT or ACT is required. Candidates for admission should have completed 4 units of English, 3 of math, and 2 each of foreign language, history/social science, lab science, and college preparatory electives, for a total of 15 units. Two SAT Subject Tests are required in two different areas. A GPA of 3.0 is required. AP credits are accepted. Important factors in the admissions decision are advanced placement or honors courses, evidence of special talent, and leadership record. General education requirements vary by college but are based on 3 components: topical breadth, social-cultural diversity, and writing experience. A minimum of 180 quarter units with a minimum GPA of 2.0 are required for graduation, as is proficiency in English composition and an American History and Institutions requirement. **Procedure:** Freshmen are admitted fall, winter, and spring. Entrance exams should be taken by December of the senior year. There is a deferred admissions plan. Applications should be filed by November 30 for fall entry. The fall 2014 application fee was $60. Notifications are sent March 15. 1510 applicants were on the 2014 waiting list; 595 were admitted. Applications are accepted online. **Transfer Students:** 2756 transfer students enrolled in 2013-2014. Junior-level transfers have priority. Requirements vary by college, discipline, and major. 35 of 180 credits required for the bachelor's degree must be completed at UC Davis. **International Students:** They must take the TOEFL with a minimum score of 550 on the paper-based TOEFL (PBT) or 60 on the Internet-based version (iBT). They must also take the SAT or ACT.

ADMISSIONS: 45% of the 2014-2015 applicants were accepted. The SAT scores for the 2014-2015 freshman class were: Critical Reading--14% below 500, 34% between 500 and 599, 40% between 600 and 699, and 11% between 700 and 800; Math--8% below 500, 23% between 500 and 599, 46% between 600 and 699, and 22% between 700 and 800; Writing--12% below 500, 34% between 500 and 599, 40% between 600 and 699, and 13% between 700 and 800. 100% of the current freshmen were in the top fifth of their class. **Admissions Contact:** Walter Robinson, Director, Undergraduate Admissions. E-Mail: *undergraduateadmissions@ucdavis.edu* Web: *www.ucdavis.edu*

FINANCIAL AID: In 2014-2015, 54% of all full-time freshmen and continuing full-time students received some form of financial aid. 51% of all full-time freshmen and continuing full-time students received need-based aid. The average freshman award was $15,811. Need-based scholarships or need-based grants averaged $12,361; need-based self-help aid (loans and jobs) averaged $5,305; non-need-based athletic scholarships averaged $10,804; and other non-need-based awards and non-need-based scholarships averaged $4,763. The average financial indebtedness of the 2014 graduate was $15,155. UC Davis is a member of CSS. The FAFSA is required. The deadline for filing freshman financial aid applications for fall entry is March 2.

UNIVERSITY OF CALIFORNIA AT IRVINE   D-5
www.uci.edu

Irvine, CA 92697	(949) 824-6703

Fax: (949) 824-2951	Email: admissions@uci.edu
Full-time: 9965 men, 11913 women	Faculty: 1467; I, +$
Part-time: 196 men, 142 women	Ph.D.s: 98%
Graduate: 3108 men, 2155 women	Student/Faculty: 19 to 1
Year: quarters, summer session	Tuition: $14,226 ($37,104)
Room & Board: $11,735	Freshman Class: 56508 applied, 23956 accepted, 5077 enrolled
SAT CR/M/W: 540/610/550 ACT: required	CEEB CODE: 4859
Application Deadline: November 30	VERY COMPETITIVE

The University of California, Irvine, founded in 1965, is a public research university and part of the University of California System. There are 13 undergraduate schools and 15 graduate schools. In addition to regional accreditation, UCI has baccalaureate program accreditation with AACSB and ABET. The 1489-acre campus is in a suburban area 40 miles south of Los Angeles. Including any residence halls, there are 492 buildings.

STUDENT LIFE: 91% of undergraduates are from California. Others are from 40 states, 70 foreign countries, and Canada. 86% are from public schools. 52% are Asian American; 20% Hispanic; 19% White. **Male To Female Ratio:** 1.1:1. The average age of freshmen is 18; all undergraduates, 21. 7% do not continue beyond their first year; 93% remain to graduate. **Housing:** 10199 students can be accommodated in college housing, which includes single-sex and coed dorms, on-campus apartments, and married student housing. In addition, there are honors houses, special-interest houses, fraternity houses, and sorority houses. On-campus housing is available on a first-come, first-served basis, and is available on a lottery system for upperclassmen. 62% of students commute. All students may keep cars.

FACULTY/CLASSROOMS: 64% of faculty are male; 36% are female. All teach and do research. No introductory courses are taught by graduate students. The average class size in an introductory lecture is 107; in a laboratory is 20; and in a regular course is 31.

PROGRAMS OF STUDY: UCI confers B.A., B.S., B.F.A. and B.Mus. degrees. Master's and doctoral degrees are also awarded. Bachelor's degrees are awarded in AGRICULTURE (environmental studies), BIOLOGICAL SCIENCE (biochemistry, bioinformatics, biology/biological science, botany, cell biology, ecology, genetics, microbiology, and neurosciences), BUSINESS (business administration and management, business economics, and economics – statistics), COMMUNICATIONS AND THE ARTS (art history, classics, comparative literature, creative writing, dance, dramatic arts, English, film arts, French, Japanese, journalism, Korean, media arts, music, music performance, musical theater, Spanish, and studio art), COMPUTER AND PHYSICAL SCIENCE (chemistry, computer science, earth science, environmental geology, geology, information sciences and systems, mathematics, physics, and software engineering), ENGINEERING AND ENVIRONMENTAL DESIGN (aeronautical engineering, biomedical engineering, chemical engineering, civil engineering, computer engineering, electrical/electronics engineering, engineering, environmental engineering, environmental science, materials engineering, and mechanical engineering), HEALTH PROFESSIONS (nursing, pharmaceutical science, premedicine, and public health), SOCIAL SCIENCE (African American studies, anthropology, Asian/American studies, Chinese Studies, classical/ancient civilization, criminology, East Asian studies, economics, European studies, German area studies, (Social Science) Global Studies, Hispanic American studies, history, humanities, interdisciplinary studies, international studies, philosophy, political science/government, psychology, religion, social psychology, social science, sociology, urban studies, and women's studies). Biological sciences, psychology and social behavior, and business economics have the largest enrollments.

ACTIVITIES: 9% of men belong to 21 national fraternities; 10% of women belong to 3 local and 23 national sororities. There are 543 groups on campus, including art, band, cheerleading, chess, choir, chorus, communications, computers, dance, debate, drama, environmental, ethnic, film, gay, honors, international, jazz band, literary magazine, marching band, musical theater, newspaper, opera, orchestra, pep band, political, professional, radio and TV, religious, social, social service, student government, symphony, and yearbook. Popular campus events include Celebrate UCI, Shocktoberfest, Homecoming, Reggae and Wayzgoose Festivals, Welcome Week's All-UCI Dance Battle. **Sports:** There are 35 intercollegiate sports for men and 33 for women, and 23 intramural sports for men and 23 for women. Facilities include a 2500-seat track stadium, 5000-seat events center, 1000-seat soccer field, 500-seat tennis stadium, baseball and other fields, swimming pool, 6 indoor handball/racquetball/squash courts, and an activities hall with areas for badminton, basketball, volleyball, combaitives, fencing, and weight training. A sailing and crew base is located in nearby Newport Beach. **Graduates:** From July 1, 2013 to June 30, 2014, 6766 bachelor's degrees were awarded. The most popular majors were biological sciences (14%), business economics (8%), and pyschology and social behavior (6%). In an average class, 4% graduate in 3 years or less, 68% graduate in 4 years or less, 84% graduate in 5 years or less, and 86% graduate in 6 years or less.

SERVICES: Counseling and information services are available, as is tutoring in some subjects, varies by quarter. There is a reader service for the blind, remedial reading and writing. **Library/Resources:** The 4 libraries contain 3.2 million volumes, 2.2 million microform items, 123,396 audio/video tapes/CDs/DVDs, and subscribe to 132,134 periodicals including electronic. Computerized library services include interlibrary loans, database searching, and Internet access. Special learning facilities include an art gallery, planetarium, radio station, a freshwater marsh reserve, an arboretum, a laser institute, and numerous research centers. **Physically Challenged Students:** 95% of the campus is accessible. Facilities include wheelchair ramps, elevators, special parking, specially equipped restrooms, special class scheduling, lowered drinking fountains, lowered telephones, special housing. **Special:** Students may study abroad in dozens of locations. UCI also offers internships, a Washington semester, semester at sea, work-study programs with the university, B.A.-B.S. degrees, dual majors, and pass/fail options. There are 7 national honor societies, including a Phi Beta Kappa, and a freshman honors program. **Visiting:** There are regularly scheduled orientations for prospective students. There are guides for informal visits, visitors may sit in on classes, and stay overnight. To schedule a visit, contact the Visitor Center at (949) 824.4636. **Campus Safety and Security:** Measures include 24-hour foot and vehicle patrol, emergency notification system, self-defense education, and security escort services. There are shuttle buses, emergency telephones, and lighted pathways/sidewalks.

REQUIREMENTS: The SAT or ACT is required. Required minimum scores are determined by an eligibility index. Applicants need 15 academic credits, including 4 years of English, 3 in math, and 2 each in foreign language, history/social science, lab science, and electives. An additional year each in foreign language, math, and science is recommended. An essay also is needed. The GED is accepted. AP credits are accepted. To graduate, students must maintain a GPA of at least 2.0, earn 180 quarter units, satisfy all the requirements for their majors, and fulfill requirements in English composition and in American history and institutions. Further, students must also meet the following General Education requirements: I. Writing (two lower-division plus one upper-division course) II. Science and Technology (three courses) III. Social and Behavioral Sciences (three courses) IV. Arts and Humanities (three courses) V. Quantitative, Symbolic, and Computational Reasoning (three courses that may also satisfy another GE category) VI. Language Other Than English (one course) VII. Multicultural Studies (one course that may also satisfy another GE category) VIII. International/Global Issues (one course that may also satisfy another GE category) **Procedure:** Freshmen are admitted fall. Entrance exams should be taken no later than December of the senior year. Applications should be filed by November 30 for fall entry, along with a $70 fee. Notifications are sent March 31. Applications are accepted on-line. **Transfer Students:** 1727 transfer students enrolled in 2013-2014. UC requirements for admission as a tranfer applicant vary according to the high school record. Please see catalog for full details. 36 of 180 credits required for the bachelor's degree must be completed at UCI. **International Students:** There are 1292 international students enrolled. They must take the TOEFL with a

minimum score of 550 on the paper-based TOEFL (PBT) or 80 on the Internet-based version (iBT). They must also take the SAT or ACT.

ADMISSIONS: 42% of the 2014-2015 applicants were accepted. The SAT scores for the 2014-2015 freshman class were: Critical Reading--34% below 500, 37% between 500 and 599, 24% between 600 and 699, and 5% between 700 and 800; Math--15% below 500, 30% between 500 and 599, 40% between 600 and 699, and 15% between 700 and 800; Writing--27% below 500, 40% between 500 and 599, 28% between 600 and 699, and 5% between 700 and 800. **Admissions Contact:** Assistant Vice Chancellor E-Mail: *admissions@uci.edu* Web: *www.uci.edu*

FINANCIAL AID: UCI is a member of CSS. The FAFSA, and GPA verification form to state agency is required. The priority date for freshman financial aid applications for fall entry is March 2. The deadline for filing freshman financial aid applications for fall entry is May 2.

UNIVERSITY OF CALIFORNIA AT LOS ANGELES   C-5

www.admissions.ucla.edu

Los Angeles, CA 90095   **(310) 825-3101**

Fax: (310) 206-1206	**Email:** ugadm@saonet.ucla.edu
Full-time: 11378 men, 14056 women	**Faculty:** I
	Ph.D.s: 98%
Part-time: 386 men, 342 women	**Student/Faculty:** n/av
Graduate: 7128 men, 6303 women	**Tuition:** $11,618 ($34,496)
Year: quarters, summer session	**Freshman Class:** 57670 applied, 13088 accepted, 4636 enrolled
Room & Board: $13,968	
SAT CR/M/W: 640/680/660 **ACT:** 29	**CEEB CODE:** 4837
Application Deadline: November 30	**MOST COMPETITIVE**

University of California at Los Angeles (UCLA), founded in 1919, is a public institution offering undergraduate and graduate degrees. Its disciplines include arts and sciences, engineering, applied science, health sciences, law, management, and theater, film, and television. The figures in the above capsule and in this profile are approximate. There are 5 undergraduate schools and 12 graduate schools. In addition to regional accreditation, UCLA has baccalaureate program accreditation with AACSB, ABET, ADA, CSAB, CSWE, FIDER, NAAB, and NLN. The 419-acre campus is in an urban area in Los Angeles. Including any residence halls, there are 190 buildings.

STUDENT LIFE: 89% of undergraduates are from California. Others are from 46 states, 71 foreign countries, and Canada. 77% are from public schools. 36% are Asian American; 32% White; 16% Hispanic. **Male To Female Ratio:** 1.1:1. The average age of freshmen is 18; all undergraduates, 21. 3% do not continue beyond their first year; 92% remain to graduate. **Housing:** 13300 students can be accommodated in college housing, which includes coed dorms, off-campus apartments, and married student housing. In addition, there are special-interest houses, fraternity houses, and sorority houses. On-campus housing is available on a lottery system for upperclassmen. 64% of students commute. Alcohol is not permitted. Some may keep cars.

FACULTY/CLASSROOMS: 65% of faculty are male; 35% are female. All teach and do research. No introductory courses are taught by graduate students.

PROGRAMS OF STUDY: UCLA confers B.A., and B.S degrees. Master's and doctoral degrees are also awarded. Bachelor's degrees are awarded in AGRICULTURE (environmental studies), BIOLOGICAL SCIENCE (biochemistry, biology/biological science, biophysics, cell biology, ecology, marine biology, microbiology, molecular biology, neurosciences, and physiology), BUSINESS (business economics), COMMUNICATIONS AND THE ARTS (American literature, Arabic, art, art history and appreciation, Chinese, classics, communications, dramatic arts, English, film arts, French, German, Greek, Hebrew, Italian, Japanese, Korean, Latin, linguistics, music, music history and appreciation, musicology/ethnomusicology, Portuguese, Russian languages and literature, Scandinavian languages, and Spanish), COMPUTER AND PHYSICAL SCIENCE (applied mathematics, astrophysics, atmospheric sciences and meteorology, chemistry, computer science, earth science, geology, geophysics and seismology, mathematics, physics, and statistics), EDUCATION (mathematics education), ENGINEERING AND ENVIRONMENTAL DESIGN (aeronautical engineering, aerospace studies, architecture, bioengineering, biomedical engineering, chemical engineering, civil engineering, computer engineering, electrical/electronics engineering, environmental science, geological engineering, materials engineering, materials science, and mechanical engineering), HEALTH PROFESSIONS (nursing), SOCIAL SCIENCE (African studies, African American studies, American Indian studies, anthropology, Asian/American studies, Asian/Oriental studies, classical/ancient civilization, cognitive science, East Asian studies, economics, European studies, French studies, geography, history, international studies, Italian studies, Judaic studies, Latin American studies, Mexican-American/Chicano studies, Middle Eastern studies, Near Eastern studies, philosophy, political science/government, psychobiology, psychology, religion, Russian and Slavic studies, sociology, South Asian studies, Spanish studies, and women's studies). Economics, psychology, and political science have the largest enrollments.

ACTIVITIES: 13% of men belong to 32 national fraternities; 13% of women belong to 33 national sororities. There are 1000 groups on campus, including art, band, cheerleading, chess, choir, chorale, chorus, computers, dance, debate, drama, environmental, ethnic, film, forensics, gay, honors, international, jazz band, literary magazine, marching band, musical theater, newspaper, opera, orchestra, pep band, photography, political, professional, radio and TV, religious, social, social service, student government, symphony, and yearbook. Popular campus events include Career Week, Casino Night, and Welcome Week. **Sports:** There are 10 intercollegiate sports for men and 12 for women, and 21 intramural sports for men and 19 for women. Facilities include a pavilion, a stadium, tennis center, and a recreation and sports center. **Graduates:** From July 1, 2013 to June 30, 2014, 7518 bachelor's degrees were awarded. The most popular majors were political science (9%), history (8%), and psychology (8%). In an average class, 3% graduate in 3 years or less, 70% graduate in 4 years or less, 87% graduate in 5 years or less, and 90% graduate in 6 years or less.

SERVICES: Counseling and information services are available, as is tutoring in most subjects. There is a reader service for the blind. **Library/Resources:** The 13 libraries contain 9.2 million volumes, 6.2 million microform items, 5.0 million audio/video tapes/CDs/DVDs, and subscribe to 78,463 periodicals including electronic. Computerized library services include interlibrary loans, database searching, and Internet access. Special learning facilities include an art gallery, natural history museum, planetarium, radio station, TV station, air photo archives, arts library, biomed library; Young Research library; Clark Memorial library; college library; Cuneiform digital library; Darling biomedical library; Darling law library; film and television archive; folklore and mythology archive; ethnomusicology archive; institute for social science library; libraries of the ethnic studies centers; music library; Rudolph East Asian library; Rosenfeld management library; science and engineering library; UES Gonda library; university archives; performing arts special collections. MUSEUMS--Fowler Museum, Hammer Museum of Art and Culture Center, Grunwald Center for Graphic Arts, New Wright Gallery; GARDENS--Mildred E. Mathias Botanical Garden, Franklin D. Murphy Sculpture Garden, Hannah Carter Japanese Garden; ART--Eli and Edythe Broad Art Center; DANCE--Glorya Kaufman Hall; THEATER--Geffen Playhouse, Macgowan Little Theater, Freud Playhouse, Billy Wilder Theater; MUSIC--Royce Hall, Schoenberg Hall, Pauley Pavilion, Los Angeles Tennis Center; FILM--James Bridges Theater. **Physically Challenged Students:** All of the campus is accessible. Facilities include wheelchair ramps, elevators, special parking, specially equipped restrooms, special class scheduling, lowered drinking fountains, and lowered telephones. **Special:** Opportunities are provided for internships, work-study programs, study abroad in 33 countries, student-designed majors, dual majors, and interdisciplinary majors, including chemistry and materials science, Chicana and Chicano studies, and math and engineering. There is a Washington, D.C., program for 20 to 30 students selected each fall and spring. There are 21 national honor societies, including Phi Beta Kappa, a freshman

honors program, and 100 departmental honors programs. **Visiting:** There are regularly scheduled orientations for prospective students, including campus tours by current UCLA students, offered weekdays at 10:15 a.m. and 2:15 p.m. Reservations are required. Visitors may sit in on classes. To schedule a visit, contact the Undergraduate Admissions. **Campus Safety and Security:** Measures include 24-hour foot and vehicle patrol, emergency notification system, self-defense education, and security escort services. There are shuttle buses, emergency telephones, lighted pathways/sidewalks, and controlled access to dorms/residences.

REQUIREMENTS: The SAT or ACT is required. The ACT Optional Writing test is also required. NOTE: For freshmen applicants applying for admission to Fall Quarter 2012 or later, we will no longer require two SAT subject exams. (We will still review these exams if applicants choose to send them to us, and certain SAT subject exams may be recommended for some majors). We will continue to require either the SAT Reasoning or ACT with Writing examination. AP credits are accepted. Important factors in the admissions decision are advanced placement or honors courses, evidence of special talent, and leadership record. Students must complete a minimum of 180 quarter units and maintain a minimum GPA of 2.0 in all courses. All students must demonstrate a proficiency in English composition, or take specific courses to achieve this proficiency, and must also meet course requirements in American history and institutions. Other requirements vary by major and college or school. **Procedure:** Freshmen are admitted fall. Entrance exams should be taken preferably in the junior year, but no later than December of the senior year. Applications should be filed by November 30 for fall entry. The fall 2014 application fee was $60. Notifications are sent March 15. Applications are accepted on-line. **Transfer Students:** 3229 transfer students enrolled in 2013-2014. For minimum requirements, transfer students must have earned 90 quarter units at the previous college and have completed preparatory courses for the selected major. Most students selected present a GPA of 3.0 or better. 68 of 180 credits required for the bachelor's degree must be completed at UCLA. **International Students:** There are 1498 international students enrolled. They must take the TOEFL with a minimum score of 550 on the paper-based TOEFL (PBT) or 83 on the Internet-based version (iBT), or take the IELTS, scoring at least 7. They must also take the SAT or ACT.

ADMISSIONS: 23% of the 2014-2015 applicants were accepted. The SAT scores for the 2014-2015 freshman class were: Critical Reading--8% below 500, 24% between 500 and 599, 45% between 600 and 699, and 23% between 700 and 800; Math--6% below 500, 16% between 500 and 599, 36% between 600 and 699, and 42% between 700 and 800; Writing--6% below 500, 21% between 500 and 599, 40% between 600 and 699, and 33% between 700 and 800. The ACT scores were 8% below 21, 13% between 21 and 23, 16% between 24 and 26, 14% between 27 and 28, and 53% above 28. **Admissions Contact:** Director of Undergraduate Admissions Office. E-Mail: *ugadm@ saonet.ucla.edu* Web: *www.admissions.ucla.edu*

FINANCIAL AID: In 2014-2015, 56% of all full-time freshmen and 55% of continuing full-time students received some form of financial aid. 54% of all full-time freshmen and 52% of continuing full-time students received need-based aid. The average freshman award was $19,561. Need-based scholarships or need-based grants averaged $16,080 need-based self-help aid (loans and jobs) averaged $6,144; non-need-based athletic scholarships averaged $18,580; and other non-need-based awards and non-need-based scholarships averaged $5,493. The average financial indebtedness of the 2014 graduate was $18,203. The FAFSA and the college's own financial statement are required. The deadline for filing freshman financial aid applications for fall entry is March 2.

UNIVERSITY OF CALIFORNIA AT RIVERSIDE   D-5
www.ucr.edu

Riverside, CA 92521   **(951) 827-4531**

Fax: (951) 827-6346   Email: discover@ucr.edu
Full-time: 8817 men, 9380 women   Faculty: 751; I, av$
Part-time: 248 men, 167 women   Ph.D.s: 98%
Graduate: 1470 men, 1206 women   Student/Faculty: 21 to 1
Year: quarters, summer session   Tuition: $14,004 ($36,882)
Room & Board: $13,200   Freshman Class: 34816
                                      applied, 20973 accepted,
                                      4201 enrolled

SAT CR/M/W: 540/540/580 ACT: 23   CEEB CODE: 4839
Application Deadline: November 30   COMPETITIVE+

The University of California at Riverside, founded in 1954, is a public research university with undergraduate and graduate programs in engineering, humanities, arts, social sciences, natural and agricultural sciences, medicine, public policy, health sciences, education and business. There are 3 undergraduate schools and 9 graduate schools. In addition to regional accreditation, UCR has baccalaureate program accreditation with AACSB and ABET. The 1200-acre campus is in a suburban area 50 miles east of Los Angeles. Including any residence halls, there are 668 buildings.

STUDENT LIFE: 98% of undergraduates are from California. Others are from 35 states, 43 foreign countries, and Canada. 92% are from public schools. 35% are Asian American; 32% Hispanic; 17% White. The average age of freshmen is 18; all undergraduates, 20.3. 11% do not continue beyond their first year; 89% remain to graduate. **Housing:** 6045 students can be accommodated in college housing, which includes coed dorms, on-campus apartments, and married student housing. In addition, there are honors houses, special-interest houses, and an international village. On-campus housing is guaranteed for the freshman year only, is available on a first-come, first-served basis, and is available on a lottery system for upperclassmen. 70% of students commute. All students may keep cars.

FACULTY/CLASSROOMS: 65% of faculty are male; 35% are female. All teach undergraduates, 74% do research, and 74% do both. No introductory courses are taught by graduate students.

PROGRAMS OF STUDY: UCR confers B.A., and B.S. degrees. Master's and doctoral degrees are also awarded. Bachelor's degrees are awarded in AGRICULTURE (soil science), BIOLOGICAL SCIENCE (biochemistry, biology/biological science, cell biology, entomology, genetics, microbiology, neurosciences, plant genetics, and plant pathology), BUSINESS (business administration and management, business economics, and management science), COMMUNICATIONS AND THE ARTS (art history, art, art history and appreciation, Chinese, classical languages, comparative literature, creative writing, dance, dramatic arts, English, film arts, French, German, Germanic languages and literature, Japanese, languages, linguistics, music, Russian, Russian languages and literature, Spanish, theatre arts, and visual and performing arts), COMPUTER AND PHYSICAL SCIENCE (chemistry, computer science, geology, geophysics and seismology, geoscience, information sciences and systems, mathematics, physical sciences, physics, and statistics), EDUCATION (mathematics education), ENGINEERING AND ENVIRONMENTAL DESIGN (bioengineering, chemical engineering, electrical/electronics engineering, engineering and applied science, engineering mechanics, environmental engineering, environmental science, materials engineering, and mechanical engineering), HEALTH PROFESSIONS (biomedical science), SOCIAL SCIENCE (African American studies, anthropology, Asian/American studies, Asian/Oriental studies, classical/ancient civilization, economics, ethnic studies, history, humanities and social science, interdisciplinary studies, Latin American studies, liberal arts/general studies, Mexican-American/Chicano studies, Middle Eastern studies, Native American studies, philosophy, political science/government, psychology, religion, religious education, Russian and Slavic studies, sociology, and women's studies). Engineering is the strongest academically. Business administration, biology and psychology have the largest enrollments.

ACTIVITIES: 1% of men belong to 6 local and 14 national fraternities; 1% of women belong to 8 local and 12 national sororities. There are 470 groups on campus, including art, bagpipe, cheerleading, computers, dance, drama, ethnic, film, gay, honors, international, literary magazine, musical theater, newspaper, pep band, photography, political, professional, radio and TV, social, social service, and student government. Popular campus events include HEAT Festival, Block Party and Spring Splash. **Sports:** There are 7 intercollegiate sports for men and 8 for women, and 8 intramural sports for men and 9 for women. Facilities include UCR competes in the NCAA Division I. The campus has a heated Olympic-size pool, an 80,000 square foot student recreation center with a weight room/fitness center, 4 indoor multi-use courts, 4 racquetball courts, 1 squash court, 3 fitness studios, 10 tennis courts, a roller hockey rink, challenge ropes course, and a jogging trail. **Graduates:** From July 1, 2013 to June 30, 2014, 4196 bachelor's degrees were awarded. The most popular majors were business/marketing (15%), psychology (10%), and biology (7%). 248 companies recruited on campus in 2013-2014. In an average class, 2% graduate in 3 years or less, 42% graduate in 4 years or less, 62% graduate in 5 years or less, and 69% graduate in 6 years or less. Of the 2013 graduating class, 39% were enrolled in graduate school within 6 months of graduation, and 78% were employed.

SERVICES: Counseling and information services are available, as is tutoring in most subjects, individual and group tutoring. There is a reader service for the blind. There are also study skills classes, preparation sessions for graduate entrance exams, study groups, individual counseling and lab work, and speed-reading classes. **Library/Resources:** The 4 libraries contain 3.2 million volumes, 2.3 million microform items, and subscribe to 97,678 periodicals including electronic. Computerized library services include interlibrary loans, database searching, Internet access, and Wi-Fi capability. Special learning facilities include an Art Gallery, Radio Station, Culver Center for the Arts; Sweeney Art Gallery; UCR/California Museum of Photography; College of Engineering-Center for Environmental Research and Technology; Air Pollution Research Center; Agricultural Research Institute for Deserts; Citrus Variety Collection; Agricultural Experiment Station; Botanic Gardens; Entomology Museum; George E. Brown Salinity Lab; Core Instrumentation Facility for Genomics Research. **Physically Challenged Students:** Facilities include wheelchair ramps, elevators, special parking, specially equipped restrooms, special class scheduling, lowered drinking fountains, lowered telephones, special housing, and automatic doors. **Special:** Internships, work-study programs with various agencies and employers on and off campus, study abroad in 35 countries, and a semester in Washington are available. The campus has a School of Medicine now accepting students, and a School of Public Policy. Student-dual majors, opportunities for undergraduate research, and pass/fail options in elective subjects are possible. Grants are available for research, fieldwork, or other creative activity. Academic internships and co-op programs are offered in all majors. There are 14 national honor societies, including Phi Beta Kappa, a freshman honors program, and 13 departmental honors programs. **Visiting:** There are regularly scheduled orientations for prospective students, Discover Days; Highlander Day: College Week Live Virtual UCR Day; Chancellor's receptions in the spring, tours are available throughout the year on weekdays and some Saturdays. There are guides for informal visits, visitors may sit in on classes, and stay overnight. To schedule a visit, contact Griselda Rodriguez at (951) 827-4531. **Campus Safety and Security:** Measures include 24-hour foot and vehicle patrol, emergency notification system, self-defense education, and security escort services. There are shuttle buses, emergency telephones, lighted pathways/sidewalks, off campus Point to Point Shuttle Service; 24/7 University of California police department.

REQUIREMENTS: The SAT or ACT is required. The ACT Optional Writing test is also required. In addition, the minimum GPA varies depending on SAT or ACT scores. Candidates for admission should have completed 4 years of English, 3 of math, and 2 of foreign language, history, science, 1 visual/performing arts and electives. UCR requires applicants to be in the upper 25% of their class. AP credits are accepted. Students must demonstrate proficiency in English and a knowledge of American history and institutions. A total of 180 quarter credit hours with a minimum GPA of 2.0 is required in order to graduate. The number of hours in the major varies. All students must complete a 1-year sequence in English composition, in computers, math, or statistics, and in concepts/issues of ethnicity. There are breadth requirements in humanities, social sciences, and natural sciences/math for all students; the number of units/courses in each group depends on the student's college and major. A thesis is required for honors program students. **Procedure:** Freshmen are admitted fall. Entrance exams should be taken by December of the senior year. Applications should be filed by November 30 for fall entry, along with a $70 fee. Notifications are sent February 1. 3748 applicants were on the 2014 waiting list; 1412 were admitted. Applications are accepted on-line. **Transfer Students:** 1235 transfer students enrolled in 2013-2014. Transfer students applying to selecting majors must meet major preparation and GPA requirements for that major. 45 of 180 credits required for the bachelor's degree must be completed at UCR. **International Students:** There are 586 international students enrolled. The school actively recruits these students. They must take the TOEFL with a minimum score of 550 on the paper-based TOEFL (PBT) or 80 on the Internet-based version (iBT), or take the IELTS. They must also take the SAT or ACT.

ADMISSIONS: 60% of the 2014-2015 applicants were accepted. The SAT scores for the 2014-2015 freshman class were: Critical Reading--26% below 500, 45% between 500 and 599, 22% between 600 and 699, and 6% between 700 and 800; Math--17% below 500, 39% between 500 and 599, 34% between 600 and 699, and 9% between 700 and 800; Writing--26% below 500, 48% between 500 and 599, 23% between 600 and 699, and 2% between 700 and 800. The ACT scores were 27% below 21, 29% between 21 and 23, 25% between 24 and 26, 10% between 27 and 28, and 9% above 28. 100% of the current freshmen were in the top fifth of their class. **Admissions Contact:** Undergraduate Admissions Director. E-Mail: *discover@ucr.edu* Web: *www.ucr.edu*

FINANCIAL AID: In 2014-2015, 89% of all full-time freshmen and 85% of continuing full-time students received some form of financial aid. 77% of all full-time freshmen and 78% of continuing full-time students received need-based aid. The average freshman award was $23,102. Need-based scholarships or need-based grants averaged $18,133; need-based self-help aid (loans and jobs) averaged $6,484; non-need-based athletic scholarships averaged $13,828; and other non-need-based awards and non-need-based scholarships averaged $2,882. 27% of undergraduate students work part-time. The average financial indebtedness of the 2014 graduate was $21,300. The FAFSA is required. The priority date for freshman financial aid applications for fall entry is March 2. The deadline for filing freshman financial aid applications for fall entry is May 1.

UNIVERSITY OF CALIFORNIA AT SAN DIEGO — D-5
www.sandiego.edu

La Jolla, CA 92093   (858) 534-4831

Email: admissionsinfo@sandiego.edu

Full-time: 9775 men, 10700 women	**Faculty:** I, +$
Part-time: n/av	**Ph.D.s:** n/av
Graduate: 2160 men, 1475 women	**Student/Faculty:** n/av
Year: trimesters, summer session	**Tuition:** $9000 ($22,000)
Room & Board: $12,000	**Freshman Class:** n/av
SAT or ACT: required	**CEEB CODE:** 4836
Application Deadline: November 30	**VERY COMPETITIVE**

University of California at San Diego, founded in 1960, is a public liberal arts institution. The figures in the above capsule and in this profile are approximate. There are 6 undergraduate schools and 5 graduate schools. In addition to regional accreditation, UCSD has baccalaureate program accreditation with ABET. The 1976-acre campus is in a suburban area 12 miles north of downtown San Diego. Including any residence halls, there are 501 buildings.

STUDENT LIFE: 95% of undergraduates are from California. Others are from 70 foreign countries, and Canada. 88% are from public schools. 41% are Asian American; 34% White. **Male To Female Ratio:** 1.0:1. The average age of freshmen is 18; all undergraduates,

21. 7% do not continue beyond their first year; 93% remain to graduate. **Housing:** 6352 students can be accommodated in college housing, which includes coed dorms, on-campus apartments, off-campus apartments, and married student housing. In addition, there are language houses, special-interest houses, international house. On-campus housing is available on a lottery system for upperclassmen. 64% of students commute. All students may keep cars.

FACULTY/CLASSROOMS: 73% of faculty are male; 27% are female. 98% teach undergraduates, and all do research. Graduate students teach 2% of introductory courses. The average class size in an introductory lecture is 300; in a laboratory is 40; and in a regular course is 100.

PROGRAMS OF STUDY: UCSD confers B.A., and B.S. degrees. Master's and doctoral degrees are also awarded. Bachelor's degrees are awarded in AGRICULTURE (animal science and environmental studies), BIOLOGICAL SCIENCE (biochemistry, bioinformatics, biology/biological science, biophysics, biotechnology, ecology, microbiology, molecular biology, and physiology), BUSINESS (management science), COMMUNICATIONS AND THE ARTS (art history and appreciation, Chinese, classics, communications, dance, dramatic arts, English literature, Germanic languages and literature, linguistics, literature, music, music history and appreciation, music technology, studio art, and visual and performing arts), COMPUTER AND PHYSICAL SCIENCE (applied mathematics, applied physics, chemistry, computer science, earth science, information sciences and systems, mathematics, physical chemistry, and physics), EDUCATION (mathematics education and science education), ENGINEERING AND ENVIRONMENTAL DESIGN (aerospace studies, bioengineering, chemical engineering, computer engineering, electrical/electronics engineering, engineering, engineering physics, environmental engineering, environmental science, and mechanical engineering), SOCIAL SCIENCE (anthropology, cognitive science, economics, ethnic studies, French studies, gender studies, history, human development, international studies, Italian studies, Japanese studies, Judaic studies, Latin American studies, philosophy, political science/government, psychology, religion, Russian and Slavic studies, sociology, Spanish studies, Third World studies, and urban studies). Sciences, engineering, and the arts are the strongest academically. Biology, economics, and psychology have the largest enrollments.

ACTIVITIES: 10% of men belong to 14 national fraternities; 10% of women belong to 19 national sororities. There are 450 groups on campus, including academic, art, band, cheerleading, chess, choir, chorale, chorus, computers, dance, debate, drama, ethnic, film, gay, honors, international, jazz band, literary magazine, musical theater, newspaper, opera, orchestra, pep band, photography, political, professional, radio and TV, religious, social, social service, student government, symphony, and yearbook. Popular campus events include Fall Festival on the Green, Spring Sun God Festival, and Asian Pacific Awareness Week. **Sports:** There are 12 intercollegiate sports for men and 12 for women, and 27 intramural sports for men and 23 for women. Facilities include a 9-lane, all-weather track, soccer and softball fields, an athletic training facility, 2 pools, a spa, a weight room, tennis courts, playing fields, and a golf driving range. An 188,000-square-foot recreation complex features a 5000-seat arena, 8 handball/racquetball courts, 2 squash courts, a 12,000-square-foot weight-training facility, a climbing wall, and basketball, volleyball, and badminton courts.

SERVICES: Counseling and information services are available, as is tutoring in most subjects. There is a reader service for the blind. **Library/Resources:** The 10 libraries contain 2.6 million volumes, 2.9 million microform items, 87,625 audio/video tapes/CDs/DVDs, and subscribe to 24,986 periodicals including electronic. Computerized library services include interlibrary loans, database searching, and Internet access. Special learning facilities include an art gallery, radio station, TV station, an aquarium-museum, a supercomputer center, and theater. **Physically Challenged Students:** 95% of the campus is accessible. Facilities include wheelchair ramps, elevators, special parking, specially equipped restrooms, special class scheduling, lowered drinking fountains, lowered telephones, special accommodations, and administrative support services. **Special:** Internships in many fields, work-study, study abroad in more than 30 countries, and a Washington semester are offered. B.A.-B.S. degrees, an accelerated degree, dual majors, student-designed majors, and exchange programs with Dartmouth College, Spelman College, and Morehouse College are available. Nondegree study, credit for military experience, and pass/fail options are possible. There are 2 national honor societies, including Phi Beta Kappa, a freshman honors program, and 14 departmental honors programs. **Visiting:** There are regularly scheduled orientations for prospective students. There are guides for informal visits and visitors may sit in on classes. To schedule a visit, contact Campus Tours at (858) 822-1455. **Campus Safety and Security:** Measures include 24-hour foot and vehicle patrol, self-defense education, and security escort services. There are shuttle buses, emergency telephones, lighted pathways/sidewalks, student safety awareness program, peer educators, and an on-campus police department.

REQUIREMENTS: The SAT or ACT is required. The SAT Reasoning Test with critical reading, math and writing, or ACT Assesment plus Writing, and 2 SAT Subject Tests in two different areas: history/social science, literature, math (Level 2 only), science or language other than English, are required. Tests must be taken by December of senior year. A GPA of 2.8 is required. AP credits are accepted. Important factors in the admissions decision are advanced placement or honors courses, leadership record, and extracurricular activities record. Graduation requirements vary by undergraduate college but students must complete 180 to 184 total quarter units or 45 to 46 courses, with a minimum of 60 credit hours or 12 to 22 courses in the major. Students must maintain a minimum GPA of 2.0. **Procedure:** Freshmen are admitted fall. Entrance exams should be taken by December of the senior year. Applications should be filed by November 30 for fall entry, along with a $55 fee. Notifications are sent March 30. Applications are accepted on-line. **Transfer Students:** California residents should have a competitive GPA; average 2004 GPA was 3.42. Transfers should have completed 90 quarter units. Preference is given to applicants from state community colleges. 36 of 180 credits required for the bachelor's degree must be completed at UCSD. **International Students:** They must take the TOEFL. They must also take the SAT or ACT.

ADMISSIONS: Admissions and Enrollment. E-Mail: *admissionsinfo@sandiego.edu* Web: *www.sandiego.edu*

FINANCIAL AID: UCSD is a member of CSS. The FAFSA and the state aid form are required. Check with the school for current application deadlines.

UNIVERSITY OF CALIFORNIA AT SANTA BARBARA   C-5

www.ucsb.edu

Santa Barbara, CA 93106	(805) 893-2881
Fax: (805) 893-2676	Email: appinfo@sa.ucsb.edu
Full-time: 9065 men, 10011 women	Faculty: 885; I, +$
Part-time: 172 men, 114 women	Ph.D.s: 100%
Graduate: 1611 men, 1252 women	Student/Faculty: 17 to 1
Year: quarters, summer session	Tuition: $13,746 ($35,767)
Room & Board: $13,805	Freshman Class: 62427 applied, 24813 accepted, 4624 enrolled
SAT CR/M/W: 610/640/630 ACT: 27	CEEB CODE: 4835
Application Deadline: November 30	HIGHLY COMPETITIVE

The University of California at Santa Barbara, founded in 1909, is a public liberal arts institution offering programs in creative studies, engineering, and letters and science. Figures in the above capsule and in this profile are approximate. There are 3 undergraduate schools and one graduate school. In addition to regional accreditation, UCSB has baccalaureate program accreditation with ABET and CSAB. The 1055-acre campus is in a suburban area 10 miles north of Santa Barbara. Including any residence halls, there are 399 buildings.

STUDENT LIFE: 93% of undergraduates are from California. Others are from 48 states, 80 foreign countries, and Canada. 86% are from public schools. 40% are White; 24% Asian American; 24% Hispanic. **Male To Female Ratio:** 1.0:1. The average age of freshmen is 18; all undergraduates, 20. 9% do not continue beyond their first year; 91% remain to graduate. **Housing:** 6300 students can be accommodated

in college housing, which includes coed dorms, on-campus apartments, off-campus apartments, and married student housing. In addition, there are special-interest houses, and special interest floors. On-campus housing is guaranteed for the freshman year only, is available on a first-come, first-served basis. 66% of students commute. All students may keep cars.

FACULTY/CLASSROOMS: 63% of faculty are male; 37% are female. All teach and do research. No introductory courses are taught by graduate students. The average class size in an introductory lecture is 100; in a laboratory is 17; and in a regular course is 40.

PROGRAMS OF STUDY: UCSB confers B.A., B.F.A., B.M. and B.S. degrees. Master's and doctoral degrees are also awarded. Bachelor's degrees are awarded in BIOLOGICAL SCIENCE (biochemistry, biology/biological science, cell biology, ecology, evolutionary biology, marine biology, microbiology, molecular biology, physiology, and zoology), BUSINESS (accounting), COMMUNICATIONS AND THE ARTS (art, art history and appreciation, Chinese, classics, communications, comparative literature, dance, dramatic arts, English, film arts, French, German, Germanic languages and literature, Japanese, linguistics, literature, music, music performance, music theory and composition, Portuguese, Slavic languages, and Spanish), COMPUTER AND PHYSICAL SCIENCE (actuarial science, chemistry, computer science, earth science, geology, geophysics and seismology, hydrology, mathematics, physics, and statistics), ENGINEERING AND ENVIRONMENTAL DESIGN (chemical engineering, computer engineering, electrical/electronics engineering, environmental science, and mechanical engineering), HEALTH PROFESSIONS (pharmacy), SOCIAL SCIENCE (African American studies, anthropology, Asian/American studies, Asian/Oriental studies, biopsychology, economics, geography, history, interdisciplinary studies, international studies, Islamic studies, Italian studies, Latin American studies, medieval studies, Mexican-American/Chicano studies, Middle Eastern studies, philosophy, political science/government, psychology, religion, sociology, and women's studies). Economics, biological science and psychology have the largest enrollments.

ACTIVITIES: 8% of men belong to 20 national fraternities; 12% of women belong to 24 national sororities. There are 455 groups on campus, including art, band, cheerleading, chess, choir, chorale, chorus, computers, dance, drama, environmental, ethnic, film, gay, honors, international, jazz band, literary magazine, musical theater, newspaper, opera, pep band, photography, political, professional, radio and TV, religious, social, social service, student government, symphony, and yearbook. Popular campus events include Club Day, Activities Fair, and UCEN Cultural Festival, and Extravaganza. **Sports:** There are 10 intercollegiate sports for men and 10 for women, and 19 intramural sports for men and 19 for women. Facilities include 4 gyms, a gymnastics facility, rock-climbing walls, indoor and outdoor basketball courts, outdoor tennis and sand volleyball courts, 3 swimming pools, including 1 Olympic-sized, a football/soccer stadium, softball diamond, baseball stadium, indoor/outdoor racquetball/squash courts, extensive playing fields, weight rooms, fitness center, and a synthetic track. **Graduates:** From July 1, 2013 to June 30, 2014, 5775 bachelor's degrees were awarded. The most popular majors were biological sciences (15%), economics (9%), and psychology (8%). 475 companies recruited on campus in 2013-2014. In an average class, 69% graduate in 4 years or less, 83% graduate in 5 years or less, and 86% graduate in 6 years or less.

SERVICES: Counseling and information services are available, as is tutoring in most subjects. There is a reader service for the blind, and remedial reading and writing. **Library/Resources:** The library contains 3.0 million volumes, 3.8 million microform items, and 5.5 million audio/video tapes/CDs/DVDs, and subscribes to 92,139 periodicals including electronic. Computerized library services include interlibrary loans, database searching, Internet access, and Wi-Fi capability. Special learning facilities include an art gallery, radio station, a language and learning lab, and numerous national and multicampus research institutes. **Physically Challenged Students:** All of the campus is accessible. Facilities include wheelchair ramps, elevators, special parking, specially equipped restrooms, special class scheduling, lowered drinking fountains, and lowered telephones. **Special:** A Washington semester, internships, cross-registration with all University of California campuses, study abroad in 34 countries, work-study programs, dual majors, student-designed majors, the B.A.-B.S. degree, and an accelerated degree program in electrical engineering are offered. There are 3 national honor societies, including Phi Beta Kappa, and a freshman honors program. **Visiting:** There are regularly scheduled orientations for prospective students, consisting of a campus film, an information session, and a walking tour of the campus led by a student guide. There are guides for informal visits, visitors may sit in on classes, and stay overnight. To schedule a visit, contact the Office of Relations at (805) 893-2485. **Campus Safety and Security:** Measures include 24-hour foot and vehicle patrol, emergency notification system, self-defense education, and security escort services. There are emergency telephones and lighted pathways/sidewalks.

REQUIREMENTS: The SAT is required. The ACT and ACT Writing Test are recommended. SAT Subject tests in math and 1 other choice. Candidates for admission must have completed 4 years of English, 3 of math, and 2 each of foreign language, lab science, history/social science, and college-preparatory electives. An additional year each in foreign language, math, and science is recommended. A GPA of 3.3 is required. AP credits are accepted. Graduation requirements vary by college. Generally, students will take one third of their distribution in the major subject, one third in general education courses, and one third in elective courses. General subject requirements include courses in English, foreign language, science/math/technology, social sciences, civilization and thought, literature, and the arts; specific subject requirements include 6 writing-intensive courses and 1 course each in non-Western culture, quantitative relationships, and ethnic studies. To graduate, students must earn at least 180 quarter units, with a minimum GPA of 2.0, and have completed the American History and Institutions requirement. **Procedure:** Freshmen are admitted fall. Entrance exams should be taken by December of the senior year. Applications should be filed by November 30 for fall entry, along with a $70 fee. Notifications are sent March 1. Applications are accepted on-line. **Transfer Students:** 1651 transfer students enrolled in 2013-2014. High school transcripts, college transcripts, and an essay or personal statement are required for all transfer applicants. Standardized test scores are required of all lower division transfers. An applicant must be in good standing at prior institution but no statement to this request is required. Preference is given to students who have completed 90 quarter (60 a semester) units and who transfer from community colleges. California residents should have a minimum 2.0 GPA in transferable course work; nonresidents, a 2.8 GPA. Students with fewer than 12 quarter or semester units of transferable course work must provide standardized test scores. 35 of 180 credits required for the bachelor's degree must be completed at UCSB. **International Students:** There are 552 international students enrolled. They must take the TOEFL with a minimum score of 550 on the paper-based TOEFL (PBT) or 80 on the Internet-based version (iBT). They must also take the SAT or ACT.

ADMISSIONS: 40% of the 2014-2015 applicants were accepted. The SAT scores for the 2014-2015 freshman class were: Critical Reading--10% below 500, 32% between 500 and 599, 42% between 600 and 699, and 16% between 700 and 800; Math--6% below 500, 23% between 500 and 599, 45% between 600 and 699, and 27% between 700 and 800; Writing--6% below 500, 29% between 500 and 599, 45% between 600 and 699, and 19% between 700 and 800. The ACT scores were 7% below 21, 14% between 21 and 23, 21% between 24 and 26, 17% between 27 and 28, and 41% above 28. 100% of the current freshmen were in the top fifth of their class; 100% were in the top two fifths. **Admissions Contact:** Office of Admissions E-Mail: *appinfo@sa.ucsb.edu* Web: *www.ucsb.edu*

FINANCIAL AID: In 2014-2015, 62% of all full-time freshmen and 58% of continuing full-time students received some form of financial aid. 58% of all full-time freshmen and 53% of continuing full-time students received need-based aid. The average freshman award was $23,996. Need-based scholarships or need-based grants averaged $19,295 need-based self-help aid (loans and jobs) averaged $6,583; non-need-based athletic scholarships averaged $12,907; and other non-need-based awards and non-need-based scholarships averaged $10,886. 19% of undergraduate students work part-time. The average financial indebtedness of the 2014 graduate was $18,361. UCSB is a member of CSS. The FAFSA is required. The deadline for filing freshman financial aid applications for fall entry is March 2.

UNIVERSITY OF CALIFORNIA AT SANTA CRUZ
B-3

www.uscs.edu

Santa Cruz, CA 95064   (831) 459-4008

Fax: (831) 459-4452	Email: admissions@ucsc.edu
Full-time: 7197 men, 8253 women	Faculty: I, +$
Part-time: 114 men, 131 women	Ph.D.s: 98%
Graduate: 818 men, 690 women	Student/Faculty: 18 to 1
Year: trimesters, summer session	Tuition: $13,398 ($36,276)
Room & Board: $14,409	Freshman Class: 38640 applied, 20039 accepted, 3303 enrolled
SAT CR/M/W: 550/560/550 ACT: 24	CEEB CODE: 4860
Application Deadline: November 30	COMPETITIVE+

The University of California, Santa Cruz is a public university, one of 10 campuses in the University of California. Located 80 miles south of San Francisco in coastal community of Santa Cruz, the campus lies on 2,001 acres of rolling hills overlooking the Pacific Ocean and Monterey Bay. Founded in 1965, UC Santa Cruz began as a showcase for progressive, cross-disciplinary undergraduate education, innovative teaching methods and contemporary architecture. Since then, it has evolved into a modern research university with a wide variety of undergraduate and graduate programs, while retaining its reputation for strong undergraduate support and political activism. The residential college system, consisting of 10 small colleges, combines the student support of a small college with the resources of a major university. There are 10 undergraduate schools and 1 graduate school. In addition to regional accreditation, UCSC has baccalaureate program accreditation with ABET. The campus is in a small town. Including any residence halls, there are 559 buildings.

STUDENT LIFE: 96% of undergraduates are from California. Others are from 46 states, 79 foreign countries, and Canada. 90% are from public schools. 37% are White; 30% Hispanic; 20% Asian American. The average age of freshmen is 19; all undergraduates, 21. 9% do not continue beyond their first year; 75% remain to graduate. **Housing:** 8415 students can be accommodated in college housing, which includes single-sex and coed dorms, on-campus apartments, off-campus apartments, and married student housing. In addition, there are language houses, special-interest houses, Multicultural residence halls. On-campus housing is available on a lottery system for upperclassmen. 53% of students commute. Alcohol is not permitted. Upperclassmen may keep cars.

FACULTY/CLASSROOMS: 58% of faculty are male; 42% are female. All teach and do research. Graduate students teach 1% of introductory courses.

PROGRAMS OF STUDY: UCSC confers B.A., B.S. and B.M. degrees. Master's and Doctoral degrees are also awarded. Bachelor's degrees are awarded in AGRICULTURE (environmental studies and plant science), BIOLOGICAL SCIENCE (biochemistry, bioinformatics, biology/biological science, cell biology, ecology, evolutionary biology, marine biology, molecular biology, and neurosciences), BUSINESS (business economics and international economics), COMMUNICATIONS AND THE ARTS (art, art history and appreciation, classical languages, dramatic arts, film arts, language arts, linguistics, literature, and music), COMPUTER AND PHYSICAL SCIENCE (chemistry, computer game design/development, computer science, earth science, geology, information sciences and systems, mathematics, and physics), ENGINEERING AND ENVIRONMENTAL DESIGN (computer engineering and electrical/electronics engineering), HEALTH PROFESSIONS (health science), SOCIAL SCIENCE (American studies, anthropology, community services, economics, German area studies, history, Italian studies, Latin American studies, law, philosophy, political science/government, psychology, sociology, and women's studies). Psychology, business management economics and biology have the largest enrollments.

ACTIVITIES: There are 157 groups on campus, including art, band, cheerleading, chess, choir, chorale, chorus, computers, dance, debate, drama, ethnic, film, gay, honors, international, jazz band, literary magazine, musical theater, newspaper, opera, orchestra, photography, political, professional, radio and TV, religious, social, social service, student government, and symphony. Popular campus events include Multicultural Festival and Martin Luther King Convocation. **Sports:** There are 5 intercollegiate sports for men and 7 for women, and 10 intramural sports for men and 6 for women. Facilities include a 50-meter pool, 2 playing fields, a weight room, an all-weather jogging track, fully equipped gyms, a fitness course, racquetball, tennis, and basketball courts, and a 12,000-square-foot fitness center. **Graduates:** From July 1, 2013 to June 30, 2014, 3958 bachelor's degrees were awarded. The most popular majors were biological and life sciences (16%), social sciences (15%), and psychology (13%). In an average class, 4% graduate in 3 years or less, 55% graduate in 4 years or less, 70% graduate in 5 years or less, and 74% graduate in 6 years or less. **SERVICES:** Counseling and information services are available, as is tutoring in most subjects. There is a reader service for the blind. A learning center helps SAA/EOP students with math and writing skills. There is also a program to help any student who is having trouble with certain courses. **Library/Resources:** The 2 libraries contain 2.3 million volumes, 68,573 microform items, 56,757 audio/video tapes/CDs/DVDs, and subscribe to 46,433 periodicals including electronic. Computerized library services include interlibrary loans, database searching, and Internet access. Special learning facilities include an art gallery, natural history museum, radio station, TV station, Agroecology Program The Farm, Arboretum, Long Marine Lab, Seymour Marine Discovery Center, Lick Observatory on Mt. Hamilton, Silicon Valley Center, Digital Arts Research Center, Genome Bioinformatics Project, and a Computer Game Design . **Physically Challenged Students:** 90% of the campus is accessible. Facilities include wheelchair ramps, elevators, special parking, specially equipped restrooms, special class scheduling, lowered drinking fountains, lowered telephones. Wheelchair lift-equipped transportation. **Special:** Cross-registration is possible with other University of California campuses, Hampshire College, the University of New Hampshire, and the University of New Mexico. UCSC also offers work-study, a Washington semester, internships in many arenas, study abroad in 34 countries, student-designed majors, dual majors, and a B.A.-B.S. degree in earth sciences, chemistry, and computer science. There is a Phi Beta Kappa chapter and a freshman honors program. **Visiting:** There are regularly scheduled orientations for prospective students. There are guides for informal visits and visitors may sit in on classes. To schedule a visit, contact the Office of Admissions at (831) 459-4008. **Campus Safety and Security:** Measures include 24-hour foot and vehicle patrol, emergency notification system, self-defense education, and security escort services. There are shuttle buses, emergency telephones, lighted pathways/sidewalks, a rape prevention program, seminars for residential staff, and guards at each entrance from 8 p.m. until dawn.

REQUIREMENTS: The SAT or ACT is required. The ACT Optional Writing test is also required. Applicants must be graduates of an accredited secondary school or have a GED certificate. They should have completed 15 academic credits, including 4 years of English, 3 of math, and 2 each of foreign language, history, lab science, visual or performing arts, and college preparatory electives. Auditions are required for music majors, and portfolios are required for art majors. All students must submit a personal statement. Nonresidents must meet additional requirements. A GPA of 2.8 is required. AP credits are accepted. Important factors in the admissions decision are advanced placement or honors courses, evidence of special talent, and extracurricular activities record. To graduate, all students must complete 36 full-credit courses (180 quarter units) with a minimum GPA of 2.0. Courses are required in arts, English, history, writing-intensive, U.S. ethnic minorities/non-Western society, humanities, math, sciences, and social sciences. They must satisfy university requirements in U.S. history and institutions and in English composition, the residence requirement, the core course, and a comprehensive exam or equivalent body of work, or a senior thesis. Particular college requirements and those of an approved major vary. All students must also satisfy each of the UCSC general education requirements with a course graded C or better. **Procedure:** Freshmen are admitted fall and winter. Entrance exams should be taken by December of the senior year. Applications should be filed by November 30 for fall entry, along with a $70 fee. Notifications are sent March 31. Applications are accepted on-line. **Transfer Students:** 1005 transfer

students enrolled in 2013-2014. Applicants should have completed 84 quarter credits, with a GPA of 2.4 required for California residents and 2.8 for nonresidents, and all subject areas must be completed. No senior transfers are accepted. 35 of 180 credits required for the bachelor's degree must be completed at UCSC. **International Students:** There are 806 international students enrolled. They must take the TOEFL with a minimum score of 550 on the paper-based TOEFL (PBT) or 83 on the Internet-based version (iBT). They must also take the SAT or ACT.

ADMISSIONS: 52% of the 2014-2015 applicants were accepted. The SAT scores for the 2014-2015 freshman class were: Critical Reading--27% below 500, 36% between 500 and 599, 29% between 600 and 699, and 8% between 700 and 800; Math--21% below 500, 34% between 500 and 599, 33% between 600 and 699, and 11% between 700 and 800; Writing--26% below 500, 38% between 500 and 599, 30% between 600 and 699, and 6% between 700 and 800. The ACT scores were 23% below 21, 21% between 21 and 23, 24% between 24 and 26, 12% between 27 and 28, and 18% above 28. 100% of the current freshmen were in the top fifth of their class; 100% were in the top two fifths. **Admissions Contact:** Director of Admissions. E-Mail: *admissions@ucsc.edu* Web: *www.uscs.edu*

FINANCIAL AID: In 2014-2015, 68% of continuing full-time students received some form of financial aid, and 56% of continuing full-time students received need-based aid. The average freshman award was $23,293. Need-based scholarships or need-based grants averaged $18,108; need-based self-help aid (loans and jobs) averaged $6,663; and other non-need-based awards and non-need-based scholarships averaged $10,897. The average financial indebtedness of the 2014 graduate was $19,851. The FAFSA is required. The priority date for freshman financial aid applications for fall entry is January 1. The deadline for filing freshman financial aid applications for fall entry is March 2.

UNIVERSITY OF LA VERNE D-5
www.laverne.edu

La Verne, CA 91750	(909) 392-2800
	(800) 876-4858
Fax: (909) 392-2714	Email: admission@laverne.edu
Full-time: 1054 men, 1541 women	Faculty: 214
Part-time: 37 men, 50 women	Ph.D.s: 81%
Graduate: 961 men, 1468 women	Student/Faculty: 14 to 1
Year: 4-1-4, summer session	Tuition: $35,000
Room & Board: $12,010	Freshman Class: 8264 applied, 2843 accepted, 563 enrolled
SAT CR/M/W: 510/520/510 **ACT:** 22	CEEB CODE: 4381
Application Deadline: February 1	**COMPETITIVE**

Since 1891, the University of La Verne has been dedicated to the belief that a quality, values-based education enriches the human condition by engendering service, scholarly accomplishment, and professionalism. Though decades of growth have changed its appearance and reach, La Verne has retained its sense of purpose, seeking to provide students with individual attention to spark personal growth through intellectual challenge and development. Figures in the above capsule and in this profile are approximate. There are 3 undergraduate schools and 4 graduate schools. In addition to regional accreditation, La Verne has baccalaureate program accreditation with NCATE. The 38-acre campus is in a suburban area on the eastern edge of Los Angeles County, some 30 miles from downtown Los Angeles. Including any residence halls, there are 35 buildings.

STUDENT LIFE: 97% of undergraduates are from California. Others are from 19 states, and 10 foreign countries. 51% are Hispanic; 26% White. **Male To Female Ratio:** 1.5:1. The average age of freshmen is 18; all undergraduates, 20. 13% do not continue beyond their first year; 59% remain to graduate. **Housing:** 837 students can be accommodated in college housing, which includes single-sex and coed dorms. In addition, there are special-interest houses. On-campus housing is available on a first-come, first-served basis, and is available on a lottery system for upperclassmen. Priority is given to out-of-town students. 68% of students commute. Alcohol is not permitted. All students may keep cars.

FACULTY/CLASSROOMS: 50% of faculty are male; 50% are female. No introductory courses are taught by graduate students. The average class size in an introductory lecture is 17 and in a regular course is 17.

PROGRAMS OF STUDY: La Verne confers B.A., and B.S. degrees. Associate, master's, and doctoral degrees are also awarded. Bachelor's degrees are awarded in BIOLOGICAL SCIENCE (biology/biological science and environmental biology), BUSINESS (accounting, business administration and management, business economics, electronic business, institutional management, and international business management), COMMUNICATIONS AND THE ARTS (art, art history and appreciation, broadcasting, communications, comparative literature, dramatic arts, English, French, German, journalism, music, photography, Spanish, and speech/debate/rhetoric), COMPUTER AND PHYSICAL SCIENCE (chemistry, computer science, mathematics, natural sciences, and physics), EDUCATION (athletic training and education), ENGINEERING AND ENVIRONMENTAL DESIGN (computer engineering and environmental science), HEALTH PROFESSIONS (health care administration), SOCIAL SCIENCE (anthropology, behavioral science, child psychology/development, criminology, history, international studies, liberal arts/general studies, paralegal studies, philosophy, physical fitness/movement, political science/government, psychology, public administration, religion, social science, and sociology). Business administration, natural science, education and psychology are the strongest academically. Business administration, organizational management, liberal studies, child development and psychology have the largest enrollments.

ACTIVITIES: 7% of men belong to 1 local and 2 national fraternities; 16% of women belong to 2 local and 3 national sororities. There are 66 groups on campus, including art, band, choir, chorale, chorus, communications, computers, dance, debate, drama, environmental, ethnic, forensics, gay, honors, international, jazz band, literary magazine, musical theater, newspaper, pep band, photography, political, professional, radio and TV, religious, social, social service, and student government. Popular campus events include Homecoming, Club Day, and Greek Week. **Sports:** There are 11 intercollegiate sports for men and 9 for women. Facilities include a football field, soccer field, and track. Indoor gym with a weight and fitness centers. **Graduates:** From July 1, 2013 to June 30, 2014, 414 bachelor's degrees were awarded. The most popular majors were business administration (14%), psychology (10%), and liberal studies (10%). In an average class, 42% graduate in 4 years or less, 55% graduate in 5 years or less, and 59% graduate in 6 years or less.

SERVICES: Counseling and information services are available, as is tutoring in most subjects. There is a reader service for the blind, and remedial math and writing. Students may use the Learning Enhancement Center or schedule tutoring free of charge. **Library/Resources:** The library contains 181,576 volumes, 1,068 microform items, 1,640 audio/video tapes/CDs/DVDs, and subscribes to 37,287 periodicals including electronic. Computerized library services include interlibrary loans, database searching, Internet access, and Wi-Fi capability. Special learning facilities include an art gallery, natural history museum, radio station, TV station, a theater, archeology lab, and nuclear magnetic resonance (NMR) facility. **Physically Challenged Students:** Facilities include wheelchair ramps, elevators, special parking, specially equipped restrooms, lowered drinking fountains, and lowered telephones. **Special:** Study abroad programs, work-study programs, student-designed majors, and accelerated programs for adults are available. There are 9 national honor societies and a freshman honors program. **Visiting:** There are regularly scheduled orientations for prospective students, student visits include campus tours, faculty and student panels, and meals. There are guides for informal visits, visitors may sit in on classes, and stay overnight. To schedule a visit, contact the Admissions Office. **Campus Safety and Security:** Measures include 24-hour foot and vehicle patrol, emergency notification system, and security escort services. There are shuttle buses, emergency telephones, lighted pathways/sidewalks, and controlled access to dorms/residences.

REQUIREMENTS: The ACT Optional Writing test is required. The SAT or ACT is recommended. Applicants must be graduates of an accredited secondary school. To apply for admission to the University, the following documents must be submitted to the Office of Admission: Application for Admission and Application Fee (using the La Verne Application for Admission or the Common Application); Personal Statement; High School Transcripts; SAT I or ACT Test Scores; Letter of Recommendation. AP and CLEP credits are accepted. 128 semester hours, 44 must be taken at La Verne. At least 16 semester hours of the last 32 must be taken at La Verne. The La Verne Experience integrates curricular, co-curricular, and community engagement activities for traditional undergraduates and spans throughout their four years at La Verne. **Procedure:** Freshmen are admitted fall and spring. Entrance exams should be taken during the junior or senior year. There are deferred admissions and rolling admissions plans. Applications should be filed by February 1 for fall entry; December 1 for spring entry, along with a $50 fee. Notifications are sent December 1. Applications are accepted on-line. **Transfer Students:** 221 transfer students enrolled in 2013-2014. Transfer requirements include: 28 college semester units completed upon enrollment at La Verne, 2.7 GPA, College-level English and college-level math (typically college algebra or statistics or pre-calculus and higher). 44 of 128 credits required for the bachelor's degree must be completed at La Verne. **International Students:** There are 123 international students enrolled. The school actively recruits these students. They must take the TOEFL with a minimum score of 550 on the paper-based TOEFL (PBT) or 80 on the Internet-based version (iBT), the Comprehensive English Language Test, and the college's own test, SAT critical reading score of 550, a minimum score of 6.5 on IELTS. They must also take the SAT or ACT.

ADMISSIONS: 34% of the 2014-2015 applicants were accepted. The SAT scores for the 2014-2015 freshman class were: Critical Reading--42% below 500, 44% between 500 and 599, 14% between 600 and 699, and 1% between 700 and 800; Math--34% below 500, 51% between 500 and 599, 14% between 600 and 699, and 1% between 700 and 800; Writing--45% below 500, 44% between 500 and 599, 10% between 600 and 699, and 1% between 700 and 800. The ACT scores were 35% below 21, 35% between 21 and 23, 21% between 24 and 26, 7% between 27 and 28, and 3% above 28. 49% of the current freshmen were in the top fifth of their class; 80% were in the top two fifths. 3 freshmen graduated first in their class. **Admissions Contact:** Associate Dean of Undergraduate Admissions. E-Mail: *admission@laverne.edu* Web: *www.laverne.edu*

FINANCIAL AID: In 2014-2015, 86% of all full-time freshmen and 83% of continuing full-time students received some form of financial aid. 82% of all full-time freshmen and 77% of continuing full-time students received need-based aid. The average freshman award was $29,569. Need-based scholarships or need-based grants averaged $9,600; and need-based self-help aid (loans and jobs) averaged $8,073. The average financial indebtedness of the 2014 graduate was $30,677. The FAFSA, and Cal Grant Application is required. The priority date for freshman financial aid applications for fall entry is March 2.

UNIVERSITY OF REDLANDS E-5
www.redlands.edu

Redlands, CA 92373	(909) 335-4074
	(800) 455-5064
Fax: (909) 335-4089	Email: admissions@uor.edu
Full-time: 975 men, 1375 women	Faculty: IIA, +$
Part-time: 10 men, 15 women	Ph.D.s: 86%
Graduate: 30 men, 20 women	Student/Faculty: n/av
Year: 4-1-4	Tuition: $30,500
Room & Board: $10,000	Freshman Class: n/av
SAT or ACT: required	CEEB CODE: 4848
Application Deadline: n/av	VERY COMPETITIVE

University of Redlands, founded in 1907, is a private institution that offers programs in liberal and fine arts, business, and teacher preparation. The figures in the above capsule and in this profile are approximate. There are 2 undergraduate schools and 4 graduate schools. The 160-acre campus is in a suburban area 60 miles east of Los Angeles. Including any residence halls, there are 86 buildings.

STUDENT LIFE: 71% of undergraduates are from California. Others are from 45 states, 8 foreign countries, and Canada. 60% are White; 12% Hispanic. **Male To Female Ratio:** 1.4:1. The average age of freshmen is 18; all undergraduates, 20. 15% do not continue beyond their first year; 60% remain to graduate. **Housing:** 1621 students can be accommodated in college housing, which includes single-sex and coed dorms, on-campus apartments, and off-campus apartments. In addition, there are honors houses, special-interest houses, fraternity houses, and sorority houses. On-campus housing is guaranteed for all 4 years. 70% of students live on campus. All students may keep cars.

FACULTY/CLASSROOMS: 48% of faculty are male; 52% are female. All teach undergraduates. No introductory courses are taught by graduate students. The average class size in an introductory lecture is 20; in a laboratory is 10; and in a regular course is 12.

PROGRAMS OF STUDY: Redlands confers B.A., B.S. and B.Mus. degrees. Master's degrees are also awarded. Bachelor's degrees are awarded in AGRICULTURE (environmental studies), BIOLOGICAL SCIENCE (biochemistry and biology/biological science), BUSINESS (accounting and business administration and management), COMMUNICATIONS AND THE ARTS (art, creative writing, dramatic arts, English, English literature, French, German, music, Spanish, and studio art), COMPUTER AND PHYSICAL SCIENCE (chemistry, computer science, information sciences and systems, mathematics, and physics), EDUCATION (music education), ENGINEERING AND ENVIRONMENTAL DESIGN (environmental science), SOCIAL SCIENCE (anthropology, Asian/Oriental studies, economics, history, interdisciplinary studies, international relations, liberal arts/general studies, philosophy, political science/government, psychology, religion, and sociology). Liberal arts is the strongest academically. Business has the largest enrollment.

ACTIVITIES: 3% of men belong to 6 local fraternities; 6% of women belong to 5 local sororities. There are 105 groups on campus, including art, band, cheerleading, chess, choir, chorale, chorus, dance, debate, drama, drill team, ethnic, film, gay, honors, international, jazz band, literary magazine, musical theater, newspaper, opera, orchestra, pep band, photography, political, professional, radio and TV, religious, social, social service, student government, symphony, and yearbook. Popular campus events include Mayfest, Multicultural Festival, and Feast of Lights. **Sports:** There are 10 intercollegiate sports for men and 10 for women, and 7 intramural sports for men and 7 for women. Facilities include a fitness center, an aquatic center, a football stadium, tennis courts, and baseball, softball, soccer, and lacrosse fields.

SERVICES: Counseling and information services are available, as is tutoring in every subject. There is a reader service for the blind. **Library/Resources:** The library contains 421,219 volumes, 317,465 microform items, 6,091 audio/video tapes/CDs/DVDs, and subscribes to 12,800 periodicals including electronic. Computerized library services include interlibrary loans, database searching, and Internet access. Special learning facilities include an art gallery, radio station, a language lab, a computer center, and a geographic information systems lab. **Physically Challenged Students:** 25% of the campus is accessible. Facilities include wheelchair ramps, elevators, special parking, specially equipped restrooms, special class scheduling, lowered drinking fountains, and lowered telephones. **Special:** Cross-registration with sister colleges, various internships, and study abroad in 50 countries are offered. A Washington semester, a Sacramento program, various work-study programs, B.A.-B.S. degrees, a liberal studies degree, dual majors, and accelerated degree programs are available. Students may pursue nondegree study, take advantage of pass/fail options, and receive credit for life or work experience. At the Johnston Center for Integrative Studies, students design their own majors and courses of study. There are 4 national honor societies, including Phi Beta Kappa, a freshman honors program, and 23 departmental honors programs. **Visiting:** There are regularly scheduled orientations for prospective students, including campus tours at 10 a.m., 1 p.m., and 4 p.m., on weekdays and 11 a.m. and 1 p.m. on Saturdays during the school year, interviews with counselors, department heads, and coaches, and sitting in on classes. There are guides for informal visits, visitors may sit in on classes, and stay overnight. To schedule a visit, contact the Admissions office. **Campus Safety and Security:** Measures include 24-hour foot and vehicle patrol, self-defense education, and security escort services. There are shuttle buses, emergency telephones, lighted pathways/sidewalks, and safety whistles.

REQUIREMENTS: The SAT or ACT is required. Applicants should complete at least 16 credits in academic areas, including 4 years of English, 3 years of math, up to and including Algebra II, and 2 to 3 years of foreign language, sciences, and social studies. AP and CLEP credits are accepted. Important factors in the admissions decision are advanced placement or honors courses, leadership record, and personality/intangible qualities. Requirements for graduation vary according to the degree and major. Students must complete at least 128 units with at least 32 in residence and maintain a minimum GPA of 2.0. Students pursuing a B.S. degree must fulfill an additional field requirement or a minor. A comprehensive exam is required for some programs. A liberal arts core curriculum, first-year seminar, community service, and participation in 2 May terms are required. **Procedure:** Freshmen are admitted fall and spring. Entrance exams should be taken prior to application. There are deferred admissions and rolling admissions plans. Check with the school for current application deadlines. The fall 2014 application fee was $45. Applications are accepted on-line. **Transfer Students:** The SAT or the ACT may be required of transfer applicants, depending on how many units are accepted. 32 of 128 credits required for the bachelor's degree must be completed at Redlands. **International Students:** The school actively recruits these students. They must take the TOEFL. They must also take the SAT or ACT.

ADMISSIONS: Dean of Admissions. E-Mail: *admissions@uor.edu* Web: *www.redlands.edu*

FINANCIAL AID: The FAFSA and the college's own financial statement, and the GPA verification form for California residents are required. Check with the school for current application deadlines.

UNIVERSITY OF SAN DIEGO   D-5

www.sandiego.edu/admissions/undergraduate

San Diego, CA 92110

(619) 260-4506
(800) 248-4873

Fax: (619) 260-6836

Email: admissions@sandiego.edu

Full-time: 2469 men, 3072 women   **Faculty:** 305; I, ++$

Part-time: 105 men, 95 women   **Ph.D.s:** 96%

Graduate: 1014 men, 1594 women   **Student/Faculty:** 15 to 1

Year: 4-1-4, summer session   **Tuition:** $42,908

Room & Board: $11,910   **Freshman Class:** 14247 applied, 6589 accepted, 1129 enrolled

SAT CR/M/W: 600/620/610 **ACT:** 28   **CEEB CODE:** 4849

Application Deadline: December 15   **HIGHLY COMPETITIVE+**

The University of San Diego, founded in 1949, is a private, Catholic liberal arts university. There are 3 undergraduate schools and 6 graduate schools. In addition to regional accreditation, USD has baccalaureate program accreditation with AACSB, ABET, and NCATE. The 180-acre campus is in an urban area 5 miles north of downtown San Diego. Including any residence halls, there are 85 buildings.

STUDENT LIFE: 63% of undergraduates are from California. Others are from 47 states, 61 foreign countries, and Canada. 58% are from public schools. 53% are White; 19% Hispanic. 48% are Catholic; 25% Protestant; 21% claim no religious affiliation. **Male To Female Ratio:** 1.3:1. The average age of freshmen is 18; all undergraduates, 20. 10% do not continue beyond their first year; 75% remain to graduate. **Housing:** 2500 students can be accommodated in college housing, which includes single-sex and coed dorms and on-campus apartments. In addition, there are honors houses and special-interest houses. On-campus housing is guaranteed for the freshman year only, is available on a first-come, first-served basis, and is available on a lottery system for upperclassmen. 60% of students commute. All students may keep cars.

FACULTY/CLASSROOMS: 50% of faculty are male; 50% are female. No introductory courses are taught by graduate students. The average class size in a laboratory is 15 and in a regular course is 22.

PROGRAMS OF STUDY: USD confers B.A., B.A./B.S., B.Acc. and B.B.A. degrees. Master's and doctoral degrees are also awarded. Bachelor's degrees are awarded in AGRICULTURE (environmental studies), BIOLOGICAL SCIENCE (biochemistry, biology/biological science, biophysics, and marine science), BUSINESS (accounting, business administration and management, business economics, finance, international business management, marketing management, and real estate), COMMUNICATIONS AND THE ARTS (art history, art and design, communications, English, French, music, Spanish, theatre arts, and visual and performing arts), COMPUTER AND PHYSICAL SCIENCE (chemistry, computer science, mathematics, and physics), ENGINEERING AND ENVIRONMENTAL DESIGN (electrical/electronics engineering, industrial engineering, and mechanical engineering), SOCIAL SCIENCE (anthropology, architectural studies, behavioral science, economics, ethnic studies, history, humanities, international relations, Italian studies, liberal arts/general studies, philosophy, political science/government, psychology, sociology, and theological studies). Business administration, finance and accountancy have the largest enrollments.

ACTIVITIES: 24% of men belong to 7 national fraternities; 37% of women belong to 8 national sororities. There are 75 groups on campus, including academic club, art, cheerleading, choir, chorale, dance, debate, drama, environmental, ethnic, gay, honors, international, jazz band, musical theater, newspaper, pep band, political, professional, radio and TV, religious, social, social service, and student government. Popular campus events include Alcala bazaar, Orientation week, Sponsored Concerts and Events. **Sports:** There are 8 intercollegiate sports for men and 9 for women, and 10 intramural sports for men and 10 for women. Facilities include a sports center, 6000 seat stadium for football and soccer, tennis courts, swimming pools, 1700 seat baseball facility, and an aquatic center. **Graduates:** From July 1, 2013 to June 30, 2014, 1281 bachelor's degrees were awarded. The most popular majors were finance (12%), business administration (9%), and communications (9%). 115 companies recruited on campus in 2013-2014. In an average class, 67% graduate in 4 years or less, 76% graduate in 5 years or less, and 76% graduate in 6 years or less. Of the 2013 graduating class, 13% were enrolled in graduate school within 6 months of graduation, and 90% were employed.

SERVICES: Counseling and information services are available, as is tutoring in most subjects. **Library/Resources:** The 2 libraries contain 1.1 million volumes, 1.2 million microform items, 17,442 audio/video tapes/CDs/DVDs, and subscribe to 69,687 periodicals including electronic. Computerized library services include interlibrary loans, database searching, Internet access, and Wi-Fi capability. **Physically Challenged Students:** 85% of the campus is accessible. Facilities include wheelchair ramps, elevators, special parking, specially equipped restrooms, lowered drinking fountains. Individual needs can be accommodated. **Special:** A B.A.-B.S. degree is offered in electrical, industrial and mechanical engineering. Internships in all disciplines, study abroad in over 30 countries and work-study programs on campus are available. Undergraduate research is a focus and available in many disciplines. The Washington Center Academic Seminar takes place each January in Washington, DC. The Department of Political Science and International Relations offers an intersession course (PS434) which enables students to earn 3 units for attending the seminar. There are 22 national honor societies, including Phi Beta Kappa, and a freshman honors program. **Visiting:** There are regularly scheduled orientations for prospective students, tours and information sessions offered by the Admissions Office Monday through Friday 10 a.m. and 1:30 p.m., and most Saturdays from November through April at 11:00 a.m. There are guides for informal visits, visitors may sit in on classes, and stay overnight. To schedule a visit, contact the Undergraduate Admissions Office. **Campus Safety and Security:** Measures include 24-hour foot and vehicle patrol, emergency notification system, self-defense education, and security escort services. There are shuttle buses, emergency telephones, lighted pathways/sidewalks, and controlled access to dorms/residences.

REQUIREMENTS: The SAT is required. Applicants should present a well-balanced secondary school program of college preparatory courses in English, foreign language, math, laboratory science, history, and social science. Both the content of the academic program as well as the quality of performance is considered. In addition, SAT/ACT results are used to broaden understanding of the applicant's potential. Participation in extracurricular activities at the school and

in the community or church is taken into consideration in the admission decision. AP and CLEP credits are accepted. Important factors in the admissions decision are advanced placement or honors courses, extracurricular activities record, and ability to finance college education. All students must take 124 credit hours,including 36 to 72 in their major, while maintaining a minimum GPA of 2.0. Distribution requirements include 9 units each of religious studies and humanities and fine arts, 6 each of philosophy, natural sciences, and social sciences, 3 or 4 of math, 3 of composition and literature, 3 semesters of foreign language, as well as 3 units upper division writing and 3 units in diversity of the human experience. **Procedure:** Freshmen are admitted fall, spring, and summer. Applications should be filed by December 15 for fall entry; October 1 for spring entry, along with a $55 fee. 2028 applicants were on the 2014 waiting list; 772 were admitted. Applications are accepted on-line. **Transfer Students:** 484 transfer students enrolled in 2013-2014. Transfer students must have a minimum GPA of 3.0 and have earned 24 credit hours. 30 of 124 credits required for the bachelor's degree must be completed at USD. **International Students:** There are 433 international students enrolled. The school actively recruits these students. They must take the TOEFL with a minimum score of 550 on the paper-based TOEFL (PBT) or 80 on the Internet-based version (iBT). They must also take the SAT or ACT.

ADMISSIONS: 46% of the 2014-2015 applicants were accepted. The SAT scores for the 2014-2015 freshman class were: Critical Reading--7% below 500, 36% between 500 and 599, 48% between 600 and 699, and 9% between 700 and 800; Math--4% below 500, 31% between 500 and 599, 50% between 600 and 699, and 15% between 700 and 800; Writing--7% below 500, 34% between 500 and 599, 47% between 600 and 699, and 12% between 700 and 800. The ACT scores were 2% below 21, 9% between 21 and 23, 21% between 24 and 26, 23% between 27 and 28, and 46% above 28. 72% of the current freshmen were in the top fifth of their class; 91% were in the top two fifths. **Admissions Contact:** Minh-Ha Hoang, Director of Admissions. E-Mail: *admissions@sandiego.edu* Web: *www.sandiego.edu/admissions/undergraduate*

FINANCIAL AID: In 2014-2015, 81% of all full-time freshmen and 72% of continuing full-time students received some form of financial aid. 57% of all full-time freshmen and 52% of continuing full-time students received need-based aid. The average freshman award was $30,579. Need-based scholarships or need-based grants averaged $24,971; need-based self-help aid (loans and jobs) averaged $6,978; non-need-based athletic scholarships averaged $25,401; and other non-need-based awards and non-need-based scholarships averaged $12,795. 17% of undergraduate students work part-time. Average annual earnings from campus work are $3000. The average financial indebtedness of the 2014 graduate was $30,225. The FAFSA is required. The priority date for freshman financial aid applications for fall entry is March 2. The deadline for filing freshman financial aid applications for fall entry is March 2.

UNIVERSITY OF SAN FRANCISCO   B-3
www.usfca.edu

San Francisco, CA 94117	**(415) 422-2465**
	(800) CALL USF
Fax: (415) 422-2217	**Email:** admissions@usfca.edu
Full-time: 2462 men, 4067 women	**Faculty:** 480
Part-time: 139 men, 177 women	**Ph.D.s:** 93%
Graduate: 1370 men, 2486 women	**Student/Faculty:** 15 to 1
Year: 4-1-4, summer session	**Tuition:** $41,450
Room & Board: $13,320	**Freshman Class:** 15434 applied, 10478 accepted, 1502 enrolled
SAT or ACT: required	**CEEB CODE:** 4850
Application Deadline: January 15	**VERY COMPETITIVE**

The University of San Francisco, founded in 1855, is a private Roman Catholic institution run by the Jesuit Fathers and offering degree programs in the arts and sciences, business, education, nursing, and law. There are 3 undergraduate schools and 5 graduate schools. In addition to regional accreditation, USF has baccalaureate program accreditation with AACSB, CSAB, and NLN. The 55-acre campus is in an urban area in the heart of the city. Including any residence halls, there are 21 buildings.

STUDENT LIFE: 79% of undergraduates are from California. Others are from 47 states, 67 foreign countries, and Canada. 60% are from public schools. 29% are White; 21% Asian American; 20% Hispanic; 19% Foreign. 30% are Catholic; 17% claim no religious affiliation. The average age of freshmen is 18; all undergraduates, 21. 13% do not continue beyond their first year; 70% remain to graduate. **Housing:** 2250 students can be accommodated in college housing, which includes single-sex and coed dorms, on-campus apartments, and off-campus apartments. In addition, there are special-interest houses, multicultural floor, an academic interest floor, a freshman experiences floor, and a quiet floor. On-campus housing is guaranteed for the freshman year only. 65% of students commute. Alcohol is not permitted. All students may keep cars.

FACULTY/CLASSROOMS: 54% of faculty are male; 46% are female. 90% teach undergraduates, 75% do research, and 90% do both. No introductory courses are taught by graduate students. The average class size in an introductory lecture is 28; in a laboratory is 14; and in a regular course is 20.

PROGRAMS OF STUDY: USF confers B.B.A., B.A., B.S., B.Arch., B.F.A., B.P.A., B.S.B.A., B.H.S. and B.S.N. degrees. Master's and doctoral degrees are also awarded. Bachelor's degrees are awarded in BIOLOGICAL SCIENCE (biology/biological science), BUSINESS (accounting, banking and finance, business administration and management, entrepreneurial studies, finance, hospitality management services, hotel/motel and restaurant management, international business management, management information systems, marketing/retailing/merchandising, and organizational behavior), COMMUNICATIONS AND THE ARTS (advertising, art history and appreciation, arts administration/management, communications, comparative literature, design, drawing, English, fine arts, French, graphic design, illustration, media arts, painting, performing arts, Spanish, and visual and performing arts), COMPUTER AND PHYSICAL SCIENCE (chemistry, computer science, information sciences and systems, mathematics, and physics), EDUCATION (athletic training, elementary education, middle school education, and secondary education), ENGINEERING AND ENVIRONMENTAL DESIGN (architecture and environmental science), HEALTH PROFESSIONS (exercise science and nursing), SOCIAL SCIENCE (economics, history, Latin American studies, law enforcement and corrections, philosophy, political science/government, psychology, public administration, religion, sociology, and theological studies). Sciences and business is the strongest academically. Business, communications, nursing, and psychology have the largest enrollments.

ACTIVITIES: 4% of men belong to 3 national fraternities; 6% of women belong to 4 national sororities. There are 118 groups on campus, including art, band, cheerleading, choir, chorale, chorus, communications, computers, dance, drama, environmental, ethnic, honors, international, jazz band, literary magazine, marching band, musical theater, newspaper, orchestra, pep band, political, professional, radio and TV, religious, social, social service, student government, and yearbook. Popular campus events include Founders Day and International Week. **Sports:** There are 7 intercollegiate sports for men and 8 for women, and 8 intramural sports for men and 8 for women. Facilities include a 600-seat soccer stadium, a recreation center with a 50-meter swimming pool, a multipurpose gym, a weight room, a dance and aerobics room, a martial arts room, and 5 racquetball/handball courts. **Graduates:** From July 1, 2013 to June 30, 2014, 1506 bachelor's degrees were awarded. The most popular majors were nursing (11%), psychology (7%), and finance (7%). 100 companies recruited on campus in 2013-2014. In an average class, 3% graduate in 3 years or less, 60% graduate in 4 years or less, 68% graduate in 5 years or less, and 70% graduate in 6 years or less.

SERVICES: Counseling and information services are available, as is tutoring in every subject. There is a reader service for the blind. There is a full-time counselor for learning-disabled students, as well as a learning and writing center for students in need of academic assistance. **Library/Resources:** The 2 libraries contain 1,000,000 volumes, 900,000 microform items, 6,000 audio/video tapes/CDs/DVDs, and subscribe to 2,500 periodicals including electronic. Computerized library services include interlibrary loans, database searching, Inter-

net access, and Wi-Fi capability. Special learning facilities include an art gallery, radio station, TV station, rare book room, the institute for Chinese-Western Cultural History, and the Center for Pacific Rim Studies. **Physically Challenged Students:** 95% of the campus is accessible. Facilities include wheelchair ramps, elevators, special parking, specially equipped restrooms, lowered drinking fountains. **Special:** Cross-registration with the San Francisco Consortium, internships with local business, social services, and research opportunities are available. Study abroad in Europe and Japan, work-study programs on and off campus and with social service agencies, a B.A.-B.S. degree in exercise and sports science, dual majors in liberal arts and education, 3-2 engineering degrees with the University of Southern California, student-designed majors, nondegree study, and limited pass/fail options are also available. The College of Professional Studies is a degree completion program for working adults. There are 5 national honor societies, a freshman honors program, and 1 departmental honors programs. **Visiting:** There are regularly scheduled orientations for prospective students, including a tour of campus, academic buildings, library, residence halls, recreation centers, and a group information session hosted by an admissions staff member. There are guides for informal visits, visitors may sit in on classes, and stay overnight. To schedule a visit, contact the Office of Admissions at admission@usfca.edu. **Campus Safety and Security:** Measures include 24-hour foot and vehicle patrol, emergency notification system, self-defense education, and security escort services. There are shuttle buses, emergency telephones, lighted pathways/sidewalks, and controlled access to dorms/residences.

REQUIREMENTS: The SAT or ACT is required. Applicants are required to have 20 academic units, based on 6 years of academic electives, 4 of English, 3 each of math and social studies, and 2 each of foreign language and lab science. An essay is required. The GED is accepted. A GPA of 3.0 is required. AP and CLEP credits are accepted. Important factors in the admissions decision are extracurricular activities record, evidence of special talent, and leadership record. All students must maintain a GPA of at least 2.0 and take 128 credit hours, including 58 in upper-division courses. 36 to 58 hours are required in the major. The current general education requirements include 9 units each of basic skills and history/social science, 6 each of philosophy, religious studies, cultural perspectives, natural science, and literature and fine arts, and 3 of ethics. **Procedure:** Freshmen are admitted fall and spring. Entrance exams should be taken during the first half of the senior year. There are early admissions, deferred admissions, and rolling admissions plans. Early decision applications should be filed by November 15; regular applications, by January 15 for fall entry; and December 15 for spring entry, along with a $55 fee. Notification of early decision is sent January 1; regular decision, on a rolling basis. 386 early decision candidates were accepted for the 2014-2015 class. 1607 applicants were on the 2014 waiting list; were admitted. Applications are accepted online. **Transfer Students:** 510 transfer students enrolled in 2013-2014. Applicants need a minimum GPA of 3.0, with minimum 2.5 in sciences. 45 of 128 credits required for the bachelor's degree must be completed at USF. **International Students:** There are 1279 international students enrolled. The school actively recruits these students. They must take the TOEFL with a minimum score of 550 on the paper-based TOEFL (PBT) or 79 on the Internet-based version (iBT). They must also take the SAT.

ADMISSIONS: 68% of the 2014-2015 applicants were accepted. 59% of the current freshmen were in the top fifth of their class; 87% were in the top two fifths. 5 freshmen graduated first in their class. **Admissions Contact:** Michael Hughes, Associate Dean and Director of Admissions. E-Mail: *admissions@usfca.edu* Web: *www.usfca.edu*

FINANCIAL AID: In 2014-2015, 74% of all full-time freshmen and 66% of continuing full-time students received some form of financial aid. The average freshman award was $27,982. Need-based scholarships or need-based grants averaged $23,971 ($62,666 maximum); need-based self-help aid (loans and jobs) averaged $6,100 ($54,000 maximum); non-need-based athletic scholarships averaged $40,420 ($59,196 maximum); and other non-need-based awards and non-need-based scholarships averaged $8,558 ($25,000 maximum). 40% of undergraduate students work part-time. Average annual earnings from campus work are $3742. The average financial indebtedness of the 2014 graduate was $327,331. The FAFSA is required. The deadline for filing freshman financial aid applications for fall entry is February 1.

UNIVERSITY OF SOUTHERN CALIFORNIA C-5
www.usc.edu

Los Angeles, CA 90089   (213) 740-1111

Fax: (213) 740-6364   Email: admdean@usc.edu
Full-time: 8637 men, 8982 women   Faculty: 1572; I, +$
Part-time: 395 men, 302 women   Ph.D.s: 90%
Graduate: 10313 men, 11329 women   Student/Faculty: 9 to 1
Year: semesters, summer session   Tuition: $44,463
Room & Board: $12,440   Freshman Class: 46104 applied, 9187 accepted, 3021 enrolled
SAT or ACT: required   CEEB CODE: 4852
Application Deadline: January 10   MOST COMPETITIVE

University of Southern California, founded in 1880, is a private institution offering undergraduate and graduate programs in liberal arts, fine arts, education, business, law, dentistry, engineering, communications, and health professions. Figures in the above capsule and in this profile are approximate. There are 13 undergraduate schools and 18 graduate schools. In addition to regional accreditation, USC has baccalaureate program accreditation with AACSB, ABET, ACEJMC, ACPE, ADA, APTA, CSWE, NAAB, NASM, and NLN. The 226-acre campus is in an urban area 3 miles south of the Los Angeles Civic Center. Including any residence halls, there are 166 buildings.

STUDENT LIFE: 68% of undergraduates are from California. Others are from 50 states, and 87 foreign countries. 39% are White; 23% Asian American; 14% Hispanic; 12% Foreign. **Male To Female Ratio:** 1.1:1. The average age of freshmen is 18; all undergraduates, 20. 3% do not continue beyond their first year; 97% remain to graduate. **Housing:** 6990 students can be accommodated in college housing, which includes coed dorms, on-campus apartments, off-campus apartments, and married student housing. In addition, there are special-interest houses, fraternity houses, sorority houses, Greek honors house, African American, Jewish, Latino, LGBT, multicultural floors; substance-free housing; business, cinema, environmental, law and women in science and engineering floors; and an international residential hall. On-campus housing is guaranteed for the freshman year only, is available on a first-come, first-served basis, and is available on a lottery system for upperclassmen. 62% of students commute. All students may keep cars.

FACULTY/CLASSROOMS: 60% of faculty are male; 40% are female. 84% teach undergraduates. No introductory courses are taught by graduate students.

PROGRAMS OF STUDY: USC confers B.A., B.S., B.Arch., B.F.A., B.Land.Arch. and B.M. degrees. Master's and doctoral degrees are also awarded. Bachelor's degrees are awarded in AGRICULTURE (environmental studies), BIOLOGICAL SCIENCE (biology/ biological science, biophysics, and neurosciences), BUSINESS (accounting, business administration and management, and international business management), COMMUNICATIONS AND THE ARTS (art history and appreciation, broadcasting, classics, communications, comparative literature, creative writing, dramatic arts, East Asian languages and literature, English, English literature, film arts, fine arts, French, Italian, jazz, journalism, linguistics, music, music performance, playwriting/screenwriting, public relations, Russian, Spanish, studio art, theater design, theater management, video, and visual and performing arts), COMPUTER AND PHYSICAL SCIENCE (applied mathematics, astronomy, chemistry, computer science, geology, mathematics, physical sciences, and physics), ENGINEERING AND ENVIRONMENTAL DESIGN (aeronautical engineering, aerospace studies, architecture, biomedical engineering, chemical engineering, civil engineering, computer engineering, construction engineering, electrical/electronics engineering, environmental engineering, environmental science, industrial engineering, mechanical engineering, petroleum/natural gas engineering, and systems engineering), HEALTH PROFESSIONS (dental hygiene, exercise science, and occupational therapy), SOCIAL SCIENCE (African

American studies, American studies, anthropology, Asian/American studies, classical/ancient civilization, East Asian studies, economics, ethics, politics, and social policy, geography, gerontology, history, international relations, Judaic studies, Latin American studies, philosophy, political science/government, psychology, religion, social science, sociology, and women's studies). Business, communications and biological sciences have the largest enrollments.

ACTIVITIES: 25% of men belong to 6 local and 30 national fraternities; 21% of women belong to 7 local and 18 national sororities. There are 769 groups on campus, including art, band, cheerleading, chess, choir, chorale, chorus, computers, dance, debate, drama, drill team, environmental, ethnic, film, forensics, gay, honors, international, jazz band, literary magazine, marching band, musical theater, newspaper, opera, orchestra, pep band, photography, political, professional, radio and TV, religious, social, social service, student government, symphony, and yearbook. Popular campus events include Springfest, International Food and Cultural Fair and Spectrum Concert Series. **Sports:** There are 10 intercollegiate sports for men and 12 for women, and 30 intramural sports for men and 23 for women. Facilities include a student athletic center, a track, a gym, 2 Olympic pools, and tennis, swimming, and baseball stadiums. **Graduates:** From July 1, 2013 to June 30, 2014, 4539 bachelor's degrees were awarded. The most popular majors were business (19%), communication (6%), and psychology (5%). In an average class, 3% graduate in 3 years or less, 75% graduate in 4 years or less, 89% graduate in 5 years or less, and 90% graduate in 6 years or less.

SERVICES: Counseling and information services are available, as is tutoring in every subject. There is a reader service for the blind. Accommodations are made for students with disabilities. **Library/ Resources:** The 23 libraries contain 4.8 million volumes, 6.6 million microform items, and 84,953 audio/video tapes/CDs/DVDs. Computerized library services include interlibrary loans, database searching, Internet access, and Wi-Fi capability. Special learning facilities include an art gallery, natural history museum, radio station, TV station, state-of-the-art cinema/film-making facilities, labs, wind tunnel, and a marine science center. **Physically Challenged Students:** 97% of the campus is accessible. Facilities include wheelchair ramps, elevators, special parking, specially equipped restrooms, special housing, and shuttle service for students with temporary disabilities. **Special:** Cross-registration is permitted with Hebrew Union College and Howard University. Internships in various majors, a Washington semester, work-study programs, study abroad in 29 countries, dual majors, a general studies degree, student-designed majors, a 3-2 engineering degree, and pass/fail options are available. Students are encouraged to pursue interdisciplinary study linking core art and science disciplines to professional programs. There are 50 national honor societies, including Phi Beta Kappa, and a freshman honors program. **Visiting:** There are regularly scheduled orientations for prospective students. There are guides for informal visits, visitors may sit in on classes, and stay overnight. To schedule a visit, contact The Admission Office. **Campus Safety and Security:** Measures include 24-hour foot and vehicle patrol, emergency notification system, self-defense education, and security escort services. There are shuttle buses, emergency telephones, and lighted pathways/sidewalks. The safety department responds to calls for service on and off campus.

REQUIREMENTS: The SAT or ACT is required. The ACT Optional Writing test is also required. In addition, 3 SAT Subject Tests are recommended. Graduation from an accredited secondary school is required. Applicants must have completed at least 13 year-long courses in English, humanities, math, natural sciences, social sciences, and foreign languages, plus 3 additional year-long courses in those areas or in computer science and, with some exceptions, theater, fine arts, journalism, music or speech. AP credits are accepted. Important factors in the admissions decision are advanced placement or honors courses, recommendations by school officials, and evidence of special talent. All students must satisfy requirements in foreign language, freshman writing, general education, and take 1 multicultural course. Graduation requirements include a minimum of 128 credit hours and a minimum GPA of 2.0. **Procedure:** Freshmen are admitted fall and spring. Entrance exams should be taken by November of the senior year for scholarship applicants; by December for all others. Applications should be filed by January 10 for fall entry, along with a $80 fee. Notifications are sent April 1. Applications are accepted on-line.

Transfer Students: 1658 transfer students enrolled in 2013-2014. Transfer applicants must submit 30 units of transferable work with a strong GPA in a rigorous selection of courses. SAT or ACT scores are considered if 30 units have not been completed. 64 of 128 credits required for the bachelor's degree must be completed at USC. **International Students:** There are 2237 international students enrolled. The school actively recruits these students. They must take the TOEFL. Undergraduate students who score 500 or better on the verbal portion of the SAT are exempted from providing TOEFL scores. Upon arrival students with low TOEFL scores are required to take our local English proficiency examination. They must also take the SAT or ACT.

ADMISSIONS: 20% of the 2014-2015 applicants were accepted. The SAT scores for the 2014-2015 freshman class were: Critical Reading--3% below 500, 14% between 500 and 599, 47% between 600 and 699, and 36% between 700 and 800; Math--1% below 500, 8% between 500 and 599, 34% between 600 and 699, and 57% between 700 and 800; Writing--1% below 500, 9% between 500 and 599, 39% between 600 and 699, and 50% between 700 and 800. There were 251 National Merit finalists. **Admissions Contact:** Dean of Admission. E-Mail: *admdean@usc.edu* Web: *www.usc.edu*

FINANCIAL AID: In 2014-2015, 74% of all full-time freshmen and 69% of continuing full-time students received some form of financial aid. 41% of all full-time freshmen and 45% of continuing full-time students received need-based aid. The average freshman award was $32,811. Need-based scholarships or need-based grants averaged $30,378; need-based self-help aid (loans and jobs) averaged $5,720; non-need-based athletic scholarships averaged $36,606; and other non-need-based awards and non-need-based scholarships averaged $19,924. The average financial indebtedness of the 2014 graduate was $28,575. USC is a member of CSS. The CSS/Profile and FAFSA, and Parent and Student Federal Income Tax forms and all schedules are required. The priority date for freshman financial aid applications for fall entry is February 2.

UNIVERSITY OF THE PACIFIC   B-3
www.pacific.edu

Stockton, CA 95211

(209) 946-2211
(800) 959-2867

Fax: (209) 946-2413

Email: madkins@pacific.edu

Full-time: 1811 men, 1969 women

Faculty: IIA, ++$

Part-time: 48 men, 49 women

Ph.D.s: 74%

Graduate: 1101 men, 1443 women

Student/Faculty: 14 to 1

Year: semesters, summer session

Tuition: $39,810

Room & Board: $12,336

Freshman Class: 14222 applied, 10332 accepted, 958 enrolled

SAT CR/M/W: 570/605/570 **ACT:** 25

CEEB CODE: 4065

Application Deadline: February 15

VERY COMPETITIVE

The University of the Pacific, founded in 1851, is a private institution that offers undergraduate and graduate programs in the arts and sciences, and professional programs in pharmacy, law, and dentistry. The figures in the above capsule and in this profile are approximate. There are 8 undergraduate schools and one graduate school. In addition to regional accreditation, Pacific has baccalaureate program accreditation with AACSB, ABET, NASAD, NASM, and NCATE. The 175-acre campus is in a suburban area 80 miles east of San Francisco, and 40 miles south of Sacramento. Including any residence halls, there are 68 buildings.

STUDENT LIFE: 85% of undergraduates are from California. 36% are Asian American; 35% White; 12% Hispanic. The average age of freshmen is 18; all undergraduates, 20. 13% do not continue beyond their first year; 82% remain to graduate. **Housing:** 2208 students can be accommodated in college housing, which includes coed dorms, on-campus apartments, and married student housing. In addition, there are honors houses, special-interest houses, fraternity houses, sorority houses, Intercultural, wellness, pharmacy, honors, and learning involvement theme houses. On-campus housing is guaranteed for the freshman year only, is available on a first-come, first-served basis, and is available on a lottery system for upperclassmen. Priority is given to out-of-town students. 57% of students live on campus. Alcohol is not permitted. All students may keep cars.

FACULTY/CLASSROOMS: 55% of faculty are male; 45% are female. All teach undergraduates. No introductory courses are taught by graduate students. The average class size in a regular course is 19.

PROGRAMS OF STUDY: Pacific confers B.A., B.S., B.F.A., B.M., B.S.B.A., B.S.B.E., B.S.C.E., B.S.E.E., B.S.E.M., B.S.E.P. and B.S.M.E. degrees. Master's and doctoral degrees are also awarded. Bachelor's degrees are awarded in BIOLOGICAL SCIENCE (biochemistry and biology/biological science), BUSINESS (business administration and management), COMMUNICATIONS AND THE ARTS (art, communications, dramatic arts, English, French, German, graphic design, Japanese, music, music business management, music history and appreciation, music performance, music theory and composition, Spanish, and studio art), COMPUTER AND PHYSICAL SCIENCE (applied mathematics, chemistry, computer science, geology, geophysics and seismology, information sciences and systems, mathematics, and physics), EDUCATION (education, music education, and physical education), ENGINEERING AND ENVIRONMENTAL DESIGN (civil engineering, computer engineering, electrical/electronics engineering, engineering management, engineering physics, environmental science, and mechanical engineering), HEALTH PROFESSIONS (music therapy, prepharmacy, and speech pathology/audiology), SOCIAL SCIENCE (economics, history, international relations, international studies, liberal arts/general studies, philosophy, political science/government, psychology, religion, social science, and sociology). Natural sciences and the professions is the strongest academically. Arts and sciences, pharmacy, and business have the largest enrollments.

ACTIVITIES: 15% of men and 16% of women belong to 1 local and 7 national fraternities; 22% of women belong to 1 local and 6 national sororities. There are 100 groups on campus, including intramurals, Model UN, resident hall association and campus ministries, residential learning, band, cheerleading, choir, chorale, chorus, club sports, computers, dance, debate, drama, ethnic, forensics, gay, honors, international, jazz band, literary magazine, musical theater, newspaper, opera, orchestra, pep band, photography, political, professional, radio and TV, religious, social, social service, student government, symphony, and yearbook. Popular campus events include Alumni Weekend, Pacific Boardwalk Carnival and Cultural Diversity Week. **Sports:** There are 7 intercollegiate sports for men and 9 for women, and 30 intramural sports for men and 30 for women. Facilities include a 6000-seat sports arena, an Olympic-size pool, tennis courts, a softball field, and a fitness center. **Graduates:** From July 1, 2013 to June 30, 2014, 823 bachelor's degrees were awarded. The most popular majors were business/marketing (24%), biological/life sciences (16%), and engineering/engineering tech (8%).

SERVICES: Counseling and information services are available, as is tutoring in every subject. There is a reader service for the blind, remedial math, reading, and writing. **Library/Resources:** The 2 libraries contain 381,686 volumes, 691,985 microform items, 12,732 audio/video tapes/CDs/DVDs, and subscribe to 12,732 periodicals including electronic. Computerized library services include interlibrary loans, database searching, and Internet access. Special learning facilities include an art gallery, radio station, and the Brubeck Institute. **Physically Challenged Students:** 90% of the campus is accessible. Facilities include wheelchair ramps, elevators, special parking, specially equipped restrooms, special class scheduling, lowered drinking fountains, and lowered telephones. **Special:** The engineering school requires and guarantees a co-op program for specialized training in the field. Internships for credit or pay in all majors, more than 230 study-abroad programs in more than 80 countries, a Washington semester, and more than 20 work-study programs also are available. Student-designed majors, B.A./B.S. degrees, dual majors in most disciplines, and pass/fail options are possible. There are 18 national honor societies, a freshman honors program, and 42 departmental honors programs. **Visiting:** There are regularly scheduled orientations for prospective students, visiting students can take a tour, and schedule appointments with faculty, admissions, financial aid personnel, and class visits. There are guides for informal visits, visitors may sit in on classes, and stay overnight. To schedule a visit, contact the Admissions Office. **Campus Safety and Security:** Measures include 24-hour foot and vehicle patrol and security escort services. There are emergency telephones and lighted pathways/sidewalks.

REQUIREMENTS: The SAT or ACT is required. Applicants must have 16 academic credits, including a recommended 4 years of high school English, 3 of math, 2 in the same foreign language, 2 of lab science, 1 of U.S history or government, 1 of fine or performing arts, and 4 additional academic courses. An essay is required and an interview is recommended. In addition, music students must audition. The GED is accepted plus one year of math and science for science and health related majors. A GPA of 2.5 is required. AP and CLEP credits are accepted. Important factors in the admissions decision are advanced placement or honors courses, leadership record, and extracurricular activities record. Students must complete at least 124 credit hours to graduate. The required general education program consists of 3 "mentor seminars" and 6 to 9 other courses chosen from categories such as the Individual and Society, the Human Heritage, and the Natural World and Formal Systems of Thought. **Procedure:** Freshmen are admitted fall and spring. Entrance exams should be taken in the spring of the junior year or fall of the senior year. There are early decision, early admissions, deferred admissions, and rolling admissions plans. Early decision applications should be filed by November 15; regular applications, by February 15 for fall entry; and November 15 for spring entry, along with a $35 fee. Notification of early decision is sent January 15; regular decision, March 15. 1100 applicants were on the 2014 waiting list; 34 were admitted. Applications are accepted on-line. **Transfer Students:** 178 transfer students enrolled in 2013-2014. Applicants should have a minimum GPA of 3.0 and at least 16 credit hours. The SAT or ACT and high school transcripts are required if fewer than 30 units of college work have been completed. 32 of 124 credits required for the bachelor's degree must be completed at Pacific. **International Students:** There are 125 international students enrolled. The school actively recruits these students. They must take the TOEFL. The SAT or ACT is required if the student has attended a U.S.high school.

ADMISSIONS: 73% of the 2014-2015 applicants were accepted. The SAT scores for the 2014-2015 freshman class were: Critical Reading--21% below 500, 38% between 500 and 599, 31% between 600 and 699, and 10% between 700 and 800; Math--15% below 500, 29% between 500 and 599, 34% between 600 and 699, and 22% between 700 and 800; Writing--23% below 500, 37% between 500 and 599, 29% between 600 and 699, and 11% between 700 and 800. The ACT scores were 4% below 21, 30% between 24 and 26, and 66% above 28. **Admissions Contact:** Margaret Adkins, Director of Admissions. E-Mail: *madkins@pacific.edu* Web: *www.pacific.edu*

FINANCIAL AID: The average freshman award was $29,290. Need-based scholarships or need-based grants averaged $21,932; need-based self-help aid (loans and jobs) averaged $8,630; non-need-based athletic scholarships averaged $35,468; and other non-need-based awards and non-need-based scholarships averaged $7,611. Pacific is a member of CSS. The FAFSA is required. The deadline for filing freshman financial aid applications for fall entry is February 15.

VANGUARD UNIVERSITY OF SOUTHERN CALIFORNIA   D-5
www.vanguard.edu

Costa Mesa, CA 92626	(714) 556-3610
	(800) 722-6279
Fax: (714) 966-5471	Email: admissions@vanguard.edu
Full-time: 532 men, 962 women	Faculty: n/av
Part-time: 156 men, 391 women	Ph.D.s: 81%
Graduate: 79 men, 189 women	Student/Faculty: 19 to 1
Year: semesters, summer session	Tuition: $27,400
Room & Board: $8433	Freshman Class: 1244 applied, 917 accepted, 412 enrolled
SAT or ACT: required	CEEB CODE: 4701
Application Deadline: March 2	VERY COMPETITIVE

Vanguard University of Southern California, founded in 1920, is a private Christian comprehensive university of liberal arts and professional studies affiliated with the Assemblies of God. Figures in the above capsule and in this profile are approximate. There are 4 graduate schools. The 38-acre campus is in a suburban area 40 miles south-

east of Los Angeles, and 5 miles north of Newport Beach. Including any residence halls, there are 25 buildings.

STUDENT LIFE: 95% of undergraduates are from California. Others are from 29 states, 8 foreign countries, and Canada. 75% are from public schools. 56% are White; 27% Hispanic. 74% are Protestant; 22% unknown denominations. **Male To Female Ratio:** 2.0:1. The average age of freshmen is 22; all undergraduates, 24. 25% do not continue beyond their first year; 55% remain to graduate. **Housing:** 1074 students can be accommodated in college housing, which includes single-sex and coed dorms, on-campus apartments, off-campus apartments, and married student housing. On-campus housing is available on a first-come, first-served basis, and is available on a lottery system for upperclassmen. Priority is given to out-of-town students. 74% of students live on campus; of those, 75% remain on campus on weekends. Alcohol is not permitted. All students may keep cars.

FACULTY/CLASSROOMS: 54% of faculty are male; 46% are female. 57% teach undergraduates. No introductory courses are taught by graduate students. The average class size in an introductory lecture is 40; in a laboratory is 12; and in a regular course is 19.

PROGRAMS OF STUDY: VUSC confers B.A., and B.S. degrees. Associate and Master's degrees are also awarded. Bachelor's degrees are awarded in BIOLOGICAL SCIENCE (biochemistry and biology/biological science), BUSINESS (accounting, business administration and management, international business management, and marketing/retailing/merchandising), COMMUNICATIONS AND THE ARTS (broadcasting, communications, digital communications, dramatic arts, English, music, radio/television technology, Spanish, and theatre arts), COMPUTER AND PHYSICAL SCIENCE (chemistry and mathematics), EDUCATION (athletic training, education, elementary education, physical education, science education, secondary education, and sports studies), HEALTH PROFESSIONS (exercise science, nursing, physical therapy, and premedicine), SOCIAL SCIENCE (anthropology, biblical studies, Christian studies, history, liberal arts/general studies, ministries, missions, pastoral studies, political science/government, psychology, religious education, sociology, theological studies, and youth ministry). Religion, social sciences, natural sciences and kinesiology are the strongest academically. Business, psychology and communication have the largest enrollments.

ACTIVITIES: There are 30 groups on campus, including art, band, choir, chorale, chorus, computers, dance, debate, drama, ethnic, film, forensics, international, jazz band, literary magazine, musical theater, newspaper, opera, orchestra, photography, political, professional, radio and TV, religious, social, social service, student government, student ministries, symphony, and yearbook. Popular campus events include Harvest Party, International Missions Week and Christmas Party. **Sports:** There are 7 intercollegiate sports for men and 8 for women, and 4 intramural sports for men and 4 for women. Facilities include a gym, baseball, softball, and soccer fields, a weight room, and contracted off-campus tennis courts and track course. **Graduates:** From July 1, 2013 to June 30, 2014, 432 bachelor's degrees were awarded. The most popular majors were psychology (20%), business administration (17%), and communications (11%). In an average class, 45% graduate in 4 years or less and 54% graduate in 6 years or less.

SERVICES: Counseling and information services are available, as is tutoring in most subjects. Time management, organization skill, writing center, and learning strategy **Library/Resources:** The library contains 175,877 volumes, 20,795 microform items, 7,962 audio/video tapes/CDs/DVDs, and subscribes to 10,000 periodicals including electronic. Computerized library services include interlibrary loans, database searching, and Internet access. Special learning facilities include a radio station. **Physically Challenged Students:** 95% of the campus is accessible. Facilities include wheelchair ramps, elevators, special parking, specially equipped restrooms, special class scheduling, and special housing. **Special:** Study abroad in cooperation with Assemblies of God programs and programs in the CCCU with placement in over 100 countries, a general studies degree, work-study, accelerated degree programs in business, psychology, and religion, and pass/fail options are available. 3 summer sessions are offered. There are 9 national honor societies and 6 departmental honors programs. **Visiting:** There are regularly scheduled orientations for prospective students, durning fall and spring university visit days with schedules for students and parents. There are guides for informal visits, visitors may sit in on classes, and stay overnight. To schedule a visit, contact the Undergraduate Admissions. **Campus Safety and Security:** Measures include 24-hour foot and vehicle patrol, emergency notification system, and security escort services. There are emergency telephones, lighted pathways/sidewalks, controlled access to dorms/residences, room and vehicle locks.

REQUIREMENTS: The SAT or ACT is required. High school courses should include 4 years of English, 3 of social studies, and 2 of math and science. Applicants are required to write an application essay and submit 2 references--1 academic and 1 from a pastor/minister. A GPA of 2.8 is required. AP and CLEP credits are accepted. Important factors in the admissions decision are leadership record, advanced placement or honors courses, and evidence of special talent. Students must complete a minimum of 124 credits, with 40 to 70 in the major. General education requirements include 16 credits in religion, 15 in humanities and fine arts, 12 in social science, 7 in natural sciences and math, and 2 in phys ed. **Procedure:** Freshmen are admitted fall and spring. Entrance exams should be taken in the junior year. There is a rolling admissions plan. Early decision applications should be filed by December 1; regular applications, by March 2 for fall entry; and December 1 for spring entry, along with a $45 fee. **Transfer Students:** 173 transfer students enrolled in 2013-2014. Transfer applicants must submit college transcripts and have a minimum college GPA of 2.5. 24 of 124 credits required for the bachelor's degree must be completed at VUSC. **International Students:** They must take the TOEFL with a minimum score of 550 on the paper-based TOEFL (PBT) or 80 on the Internet-based version (iBT).

ADMISSIONS: 74% of the 2014-2015 applicants were accepted. There is 1 National Merit finalist. 5 freshmen graduated first in their class. **Admissions Contact:** Assoc Director Admissions. E-Mail: *admissions@vanguard.edu* Web: *www.vanguard.edu*

FINANCIAL AID: In 2014-2015, 92% of all full-time freshmen and % of continuing full-time students received some form of financial aid. The FAFSA, and state scholarship/grant forms is required. Check with the school for current application deadlines.

WESTMONT COLLEGE C-5
www.westmont.edu

Santa Barbara, CA 93108	(805) 565-6005
	(800) 777-9011
Fax: (805) 565-6234	Email: admissions@westmont.edu
Full-time: 515 men, 800 women	Faculty: IIB, +$
Part-time: 5 men, 20 women	Ph.Ds: 89%
Graduate: n/av	Student/Faculty: n/av
Year: semesters, summer session	Tuition: $31,500
Room & Board: $10,000	Freshman Class: n/av
SAT or ACT: required	CEEB CODE: 4950
Application Deadline: n/av	HIGHLY COMPETITIVE

Westmont College, founded in 1937, is a private, nondenominational Christian institution offering undergraduate liberal arts degrees. The figures in the above capsule and in this profile are approximate. The 111-acre campus is in a suburban area 90 miles north of Los Angeles. Including any residence halls, there are 30 buildings.

STUDENT LIFE: 69% of undergraduates are from California. Others are from 41 states, 8 foreign countries, and Canada. 70% are from public schools. 69% are White. 95% are Protestant. **Male To Female Ratio:** 1.6:1. The average age of freshmen is 18; all undergraduates, 20. 13% do not continue beyond their first year; 70% remain to graduate. **Housing:** 1113 students can be accommodated in college housing, which includes single-sex and coed dorms and off-campus apartments. On-campus housing is guaranteed for all 4 years. 84% of students live on campus; of those, 65% remain on campus on weekends. Alcohol is not permitted. Upperclassmen may keep cars.

FACULTY/CLASSROOMS: 67% of faculty are male; 33% are female. All teach and do research. No introductory courses are taught by graduate students. The average class size in an introductory lecture is 30; in a laboratory is 15; and in a regular course is 20.

PROGRAMS OF STUDY: Westmont confers B.A., and B.S. degrees.

Bachelor's degrees are awarded in BIOLOGICAL SCIENCE (biology/biological science), BUSINESS (business economics), COMMUNICATIONS AND THE ARTS (art, communications, dramatic arts, English, French, modern language, music, and Spanish), COMPUTER AND PHYSICAL SCIENCE (chemistry, computer science, mathematics, and physics), EDUCATION (art education, English education, mathematics education, music education, and social science education), ENGINEERING AND ENVIRONMENTAL DESIGN (engineering physics), HEALTH PROFESSIONS (exercise science), SOCIAL SCIENCE (European studies, history, liberal arts/general studies, philosophy, political science/government, psychology, religion, social science, and sociology). Biology, communication studies, and economics/business have the largest enrollments.

ACTIVITIES: There are 50 groups on campus, including art, band, chess, choir, chorale, chorus, computers, dance, debate, drama, ethnic, film, honors, international, jazz band, leadership, literary magazine, musical theater, newspaper, opera, orchestra, pep band, photography, political, professional, radio and TV, religious, social, social service, student government, symphony, and yearbook. Popular campus events include Spring Sing Musical/Talent Show, Multicultural Fellowship Week, and Theatrical and Musical Productions. **Sports:** There are 6 intercollegiate sports for men and 6 for women, and 10 intramural sports for men and 10 for women. Facilities include a 2133-seat gym, a soccer/baseball field, a swimming pool, a fitness room, a dance studio, a track, and volleyball, tennis, basketball, and racquetball courts. **Graduates:** From July 1, 2013 to June 30, 2014, 326 bachelor's degrees were awarded. The most popular majors were business/economics (14%), English (12%), and social sciences (9%). 50 companies recruited on campus in 2013-2014. In an average class, 54% graduate in 3 years or less, 68% graduate in 4 years or less, 70% graduate in 5 years or less, and 73% graduate in 6 years or less. Of the 2013 graduating class, 48% were enrolled in graduate school within 6 months of graduation, and 85% were employed.

SERVICES: Counseling and information services are available, as is tutoring in every subject. There is a reader service for the blind, and remedial math. A writers' corner supervised by tutors is available. **Library/Resources:** The library contains 162,274 volumes, 20,687 microform items, 7,926 audio/video tapes/CDs/DVDs, and subscribes to 3,211 periodicals including electronic. Computerized library services include interlibrary loans, database searching, and Internet access. Special learning facilities include an art gallery, radio station, an observatory, a science center with a premedical center, and a physiology lab. **Physically Challenged Students:** 60% of the campus is accessible. Facilities include wheelchair ramps, elevators, special parking, specially equipped restrooms, special class scheduling, lowered drinking fountains, lowered telephones, and special housing. **Special:** Westmont offers cross-registration with 12 Christian colleges in the Christian College Consortium, internships in local businesses and social agencies, study abroad in 11 countries, and semesters in Washington, D.C., San Francisco, and Los Angeles. B.A.-B.S. degrees, student-designed majors, work-study programs, a 3-2 engineering program with several California universities, the University of Washington, and Boston University, and pass/fail options are also available. There are preprofessional programs in sports medicine, dentistry, engineering, law, medicine, ministry/missions, optometry, pharmacology, physical therapy, teaching, and veterinary medicine. There are 8 national honor societies, a freshman honors program, and 9 departmental honors programs. **Visiting:** There are regularly scheduled orientations for prospective students, consisting of meeting faculty and administrators and attending classes, academic seminars, student/parent panels, academic open houses, admission and financial aid sessions, student led small groups, campus tours, and various cultural events. There are guides for informal visits, visitors may sit in on classes, and stay overnight. To schedule a visit, contact Admissions/Campus Visit Coordinator. **Campus Safety and Security:** Measures include 24-hour foot and vehicle patrol, self-defense education, and security escort services. There are shuttle buses, emergency telephones, and lighted pathways/sidewalks.

REQUIREMENTS: The SAT or ACT is required. The ACT Optional Writing test is also required. Applicants need 16 academic credits, including 4 years of high school English, 3 of math, 2 each of a foreign language, social science, and physical science, and 1 each of history and biological science. Interviews are recommended. Essays are required. The GED is accepted. AP and CLEP credits are accepted. Important factors in the admissions decision are advanced placement or honors courses, leadership record, and extracurricular activities record. Of the 124 semester units required for graduation, the college's general education requirements include 20 semester units of Common Context courses and 32 semester units of Common Inquiries courses. In addition, students must complete Common Skills courses and courses relating to Competent and Compassionate Action. Courses in religions studies and phys ed are required, as are courses in the history of Western civilization and English composition. Math proficiency is also required. There are distribution requirements in social sciences, humanities, and natural sciences. The total number of hours in the major varies from 36 to 66. A GPA of 2.0 must be maintained. **Procedure:** Freshmen are admitted fall and spring. Entrance exams should be taken during the spring of the junior year or the beginning of the senior year. Check with the school for current application deadlines. The fall 2014 application fee was $35. Applications are accepted on-line. **Transfer Students:** 55 transfer students enrolled in 2013-2014. Transfer students from 2-year colleges should have a minimum GPA of 2.8 and students from 4-year colleges or universities, a 2.5. The college will not accept more than 64 transferable units from a community college; there is no maximum number of transferable units from a 4-year college. High school transcripts and test scores are required if the student has fewer than 24 transferable units. 32 of 124 credits required for the bachelor's degree must be completed at Westmont. **International Students:** There are 9 international students enrolled. The school actively recruits these students. They must take the TOEFL with a minimum score of 560 on the paper-based TOEFL (PBT) or 83 on the Internet-based version (iBT). They must also take the SAT or ACT.

ADMISSIONS: Dean of Admissions. E-Mail: *admissions@westmont .edu* Web: *www.westmont.edu*

FINANCIAL AID: In 2014-2015, 83% of all full-time freshmen and 85% of continuing full-time students received some form of financial aid. 83% of all full-time freshmen and 85% of continuing full-time students received need-based aid. The average freshman award was $22,476. 54% of undergraduate students work part-time. Average annual earnings from campus work are $909. The average financial indebtedness of the 2014 graduate was $25,008. The FAFSA is required. Check with the school for current application deadlines.

WHITTIER COLLEGE   D-5
www.whittier.edu

Whittier, CA 90608   **(562) 907-4238**

Fax: (562) 907-4870   Email: admission@whittier.edu
Full-time: 634 men, 720 women   Faculty: 92; IIB, +$
Part-time: 7 men, 7 women   Ph.D.s: 100%
Graduate: 258 men, 286 women   Student/Faculty: 15 to 1
Year: 4-1-4, summer session   Tuition: $33,868
Room & Board: $9548   Freshman Class: 1970
                                   applied, 1639 accepted,
                                   358 enrolled
SAT CR/M: 526/532 ACT: 22   CEEB CODE: 4952
Application Deadline: February 1   COMPETITIVE

Whittier College, founded in 1887 by the Society of Friends and chartered by the State of California in 1901, is an independent, secular, liberal arts institution. The figures in the above capsule and in this profile are approximate. There is 1 undergraduate school and 2 graduate schools. In addition to regional accreditation, Whittier has baccalaureate program accreditation with CSWE. The 75-acre campus is in a suburban area 18 miles southeast of Los Angeles, in the foothills of the San Gabriel Mountains. Including any residence halls, there are 51 buildings.

STUDENT LIFE: 71% of undergraduates are from California. Others are from 25 states, 16 foreign countries, and Canada. 40% are White; 29% Hispanic. The average age of freshmen is 18; all undergraduates, 20. 26% do not continue beyond their first year; 54% remain to graduate. **Housing:** 840 students can be accommodated in college housing, which includes coed dorms. In addition, there are special-interest

houses. On-campus housing is guaranteed for all 4 years. 61% of students live on campus; of those, 85% remain on campus on weekends. All students may keep cars.

FACULTY/CLASSROOMS: 47% of faculty are male; 53% are female. All teach and do research. No introductory courses are taught by graduate students. The average class size in an introductory lecture is 20; in a laboratory is 24; and in a regular course is 22.

PROGRAMS OF STUDY: Whittier confers B.A. degrees. Master's and doctoral degrees are also awarded. Bachelor's degrees are awarded in BIOLOGICAL SCIENCE (biochemistry and biology/ biological science), BUSINESS (business administration and management), COMMUNICATIONS AND THE ARTS (art, Chinese, dramatic arts, English, French, music, and Spanish), COMPUTER AND PHYSICAL SCIENCE (chemistry, mathematics, and physics), ENGINEERING AND ENVIRONMENTAL DESIGN (environmental science), SOCIAL SCIENCE (child psychology/development, economics, history, international studies, philosophy, physical fitness/movement, political science/government, psychology, religion, social work, and sociology). Business administration, political science, and English have the largest enrollments.

ACTIVITIES: 13% of men belong to 4 local fraternities; 21% of women belong to 6 local sororities. There are 90 groups on campus, including art, band, cheerleading, choir, chorale, chorus, computers, dance, drama, ethnic, film, gay, honors, international, jazz band, literary magazine, musical theater, newspaper, photography, political, professional, radio and TV, religious, social, social service, and student government. Popular campus events include Helping Hands Day, Tardeada-Latino Cultural Celebration, and MLK Jr., and Oratorical Contest. **Sports:** There are 11 intercollegiate sports for men and 10 for women, and 5 intramural sports for men and 5 for women. Facilities include a 7000-seat stadium, a 2000-seat gym, 4 playing fields, an athletics center, an aquatics center, a fitness center, and tennis courts. **Graduates:** From July 1, 2013 to June 30, 2014, 259 bachelor's degrees were awarded. The most popular majors were business (12%), political science (10%), and English (10%). 38 companies recruited on campus in 2013-2014. In an average class, 49% graduate in 4 years or less, 62% graduate in 5 years or less, and 64% graduate in 6 years or less. Of the 2013 graduating class, 37% were enrolled in graduate school within 6 months of graduation, and 57% were employed.

SERVICES: Counseling and information services are available, as is tutoring in every subject. **Library/Resources:** The library contains 127,410 volumes, 6,877 microform items, 1,793 audio/video tapes/ CDs/DVDs, and subscribes to 26,365 periodicals including electronic. Computerized library services include interlibrary loans, database searching, Internet access, and Wi-Fi capability. Special learning facilities include an art gallery, radio station, an performing arts center, and writing center. **Physically Challenged Students:** 75% of the campus is accessible. Facilities include wheelchair ramps, elevators, special parking, specially equipped restrooms, special class scheduling, lowered drinking fountains, lowered telephones, and special housing. **Special:** Internships are possible fall, spring, and summer. Study abroad is offered in 30 countries. The Whittier Scholars Program offers self-designed interdisciplinary curricula, and dual majors are possible in all majors. Nondegree study and pass/fail options are available. Whittier offers a 3-2 engineering program with the Universities of Southern California and Minnesota, and a 3-3 law degree with Whittier Law School. There are 17 national honor societies and 16 departmental honors programs. **Visiting:** There are regularly scheduled orientations for prospective students, consisting of an interview with an admission officer and a campus tour. Customized visits can be arranged to include faculty, coaches, extracurricular activities, class visits, and residence hall tours. There are guides for informal visits, visitors may sit in on classes, and stay overnight. To schedule a visit, contact the Office of Admissions. **Campus Safety and Security:** Measures include 24-hour foot and vehicle patrol, emergency notification system, self-defense education, and security escort services. There are emergency telephones and lighted pathways/ sidewalks.

REQUIREMENTS: The SAT or ACT is required. The SAT I is preferred. The college recommends that applicants have 4 years of high school English, 3 years each of history, math, and science, and 2 years of a foreign language. An essay is required. An interview is recommended. A GPA of 2.5 is required. AP credits are accepted. Important factors in the admissions decision are advanced placement or honors courses, recommendations by school officials, and leadership record. All students must take a total of 120 credits, including at least 30 in the major field, with a minimum GPA of 2.0. Distribution requirements include 4 courses in 4 distinct areas of communication, 4 courses in culture from 4 distinct areas, and a pair of courses in science and society. **Procedure:** Freshmen are admitted fall and spring. Entrance exams should be taken during the junior year or fall of the senior year. There are early admissions, deferred admissions, and rolling admissions plans. Early decision applications should be filed by December 1; regular applications, by February 1 for fall entry; and December 1 for spring entry, along with a $50 fee. Notification of early decision is sent December 29; regular decision, March 1. Applications are accepted on-line. **Transfer Students:** 95 transfer students enrolled in 2013-2014. Transfer applicants are considered on a case-by-case basis, but a minimum GPA of 2.5 is recommended in academic course work. The SAT or the ACT is required for students with fewer than 30 academic units. The GED is accepted for transfer applicants with at least 30 academic units. 30 of 120 credits required for the bachelor's degree must be completed at Whittier. **International Students:** There are 32 international students enrolled. The school actively recruits these students. They must take the TOEFL. They must also take the SAT or ACT.

ADMISSIONS: 83% of the 2014-2015 applicants were accepted. The SAT scores for the 2014-2015 freshman class were: Critical Reading--38% below 500, 42% between 500 and 599, 17% between 600 and 699, and 3% between 700 and 800; Math--36% below 500, 41% between 500 and 599, 21% between 600 and 699, and 2% between 700 and 800; Writing--40% below 500, 42% between 500 and 599, 16% between 600 and 699, and 2% between 700 and 800. The ACT scores were 36% below 21, 27% between 21 and 23, 23% between 24 and 26, 8% between 27 and 28, and 6% above 28. 54% of the current freshmen were in the top fifth of their class; 75% were in the top two fifths. 16 freshmen graduated first in their class. **Admissions Contact:** Vice President of Enrollment. E-Mail: *admission@whittier.edu* Web: *www.whittier.edu*

FINANCIAL AID: In 2014-2015, 83% of all full-time freshmen and 75% of continuing full-time students received some form of financial aid. 67% of all full-time freshmen and 64% of continuing full-time students received need-based aid. The average freshman award was $31,970. 64% of undergraduate students work part-time. Average annual earnings from campus work are $1280. The average financial indebtedness of the 2014 graduate was $30,970. Whittier is a member of CSS. The FAFSA and the college's own financial statement are required. The deadline for filing freshman financial aid applications for fall entry is February 15.

WOODBURY UNIVERSITY *(The complete profile is made available exclusively on our website, www.barronspac.com)*

A B C D E

Fort Collins

Greely

Boulder
Westminster
Golden
Lakewood

Aurora
Denver

Grant
Junction

Colorado Springs

Gunnison

Pueblo

Durango · Alamosa

COLORADO
· College Location

0 20 40 60 80 100
Miles

ADAMS STATE UNIVERSITY (*The complete profile is made available exclusively on our website, www.barronspac.com*)

COLORADO CHRISTIAN UNIVERSITY   C-2
www.ccu.edu

Lakewood, CO 80226

(303) 963-3207
(800) 44 FAITH

Fax: (303) 963-3401 — **Email:** sturner@ccu.edu

Full-time: 425 men, 700 women — **Faculty:** n/av

Part-time: 175 men, 175 women — **Ph.D.s:** 85%

Graduate: 55 men, 80 women — **Student/Faculty:** n/av

Year: semesters, summer session — **Tuition:** $20,000

Room & Board: $7500 — **Freshman Class:** n/av

SAT or ACT: required — **CEEB CODE:** 4659

Application Deadline: n/av — **VERY COMPETITIVE**

Colorado Christian University, founded in 1914, is a private, Christian interdenominational institution offering undergraduate and graduate programs in the arts and sciences, biblical studies, music, and education. The figures in the above capsule and in this profile are approximate. There are 4 undergraduate schools and 3 graduate schools. The 29-acre campus is in a suburban area 10 miles west of Denver. Including any residence halls, there are 21 buildings.

STUDENT LIFE: 59% of undergraduates are from Colorado. Others are from 44 states, 16 foreign countries, and Canada. 81% are White. 99% are Protestant. **Male To Female Ratio:** 1.5:1. The average age of freshmen is 19; all undergraduates, 20. 33% do not continue beyond their first year. **Housing:** 732 students can be accommodated in college housing, which includes single-sex dorms, on-campus apartments, off-campus apartments, and married student housing. In addition, there are special-interest houses. On-campus housing is guaranteed for the freshman year only, is available on a first-come, first-served basis, and is available on a lottery system for upperclassmen. Priority is given to out-of-town students. 65% of students live on campus; of those, 38% remain on campus on weekends. Alcohol is not permitted. All students may keep cars.

FACULTY/CLASSROOMS: 65% of faculty are male; 35% are female. No introductory courses are taught by graduate students. The average class size in an introductory lecture is 25; in a laboratory is 18; and in a regular course is 30.

PROGRAMS OF STUDY: CCU confers B.A., B.S. and B.M. degrees.

Associate and master's degrees are also awarded. Bachelor's degrees are awarded in BIOLOGICAL SCIENCE (biology/biological science), BUSINESS (accounting, business administration and management, human resources, management information systems, and management science), COMMUNICATIONS AND THE ARTS (art, communications, English, and music), COMPUTER AND PHYSICAL SCIENCE (computer management and science), EDUCATION (elementary education, music education, and secondary education), SOCIAL SCIENCE (biblical studies, history, liberal arts/general studies, psychology, social science, theological studies, and youth ministry). Science, biology, and education are the strongest academically. Human resources management, computer/information technology, and liberal arts have the largest enrollments.

ACTIVITIES: There are 21 groups on campus, including band, cheerleading, choir, chorus, computers, drama, honors, international, jazz band, literary magazine, musical theater, newspaper, orchestra, photography, professional, religious, social, social service, student government, symphony, and yearbook. Popular campus events include Preview Days, Spring Retreat, and New Student Retreat. **Sports:** There are 5 intercollegiate sports for men and 5 for women, and 6 intramural sports for men and 6 for women. Facilities include a gym, soccer and practice fields.

SERVICES: Counseling and information services are available, as is tutoring in every subject. There is remedial math, reading, and writing. **Library/Resources:** The library contains 53,532 volumes, 281,234 microform items, 3,917 audio/video tapes/CDs/DVDs, and subscribes to 415 periodicals including electronic. Computerized library services include interlibrary loans, database searching, and Internet access. Special learning facilities include an art gallery. **Physically Challenged Students:** 85% of the campus is accessible. Facilities include wheelchair ramps, special parking, specially equipped restrooms, special class scheduling, lowered drinking fountains, lowered telephones, and special housing. **Special:** The school offers an ROTC program in cooperation with CU Boulder, cross-registration with the Focus on the Family Institute, internships, study abroad in 7 countries, a Washington semester, and work-study programs. Accelerated degree programs are available in Christian leadership, organizational management, and management of information systems. Dual and student-designed majors, nondegree study, pass/fail options, and credit for life, military, and work experience are also available. There are 2 national honor societies, a freshman honors program, and 1 departmental honors program. **Visiting:** There are regularly scheduled orientations for prospective students. There are guides for informal visits, visitors may sit in on classes, and stay overnight. To schedule a visit, contact the Office of Admissions. **Campus Safety and Security:** Measures include 24-hour foot and vehicle patrol and security escort services. There are emergency telephones and lighted pathways/sidewalks.

REQUIREMENTS: The SAT or ACT is required. Applicants must be graduates of an accredited secondary school. The GED is accepted. An essay is required. A campus visit is recommended. A GPA of 2.8 is required. AP and CLEP credits are accepted. To graduate, students must complete at least 128 semester hours, including the 48-hour general education requirement and courses specified for the major, with a minimum cumulative GPA of 2.0, 2.5 in the major. The university requires 4 semesters of Christian service and regular chapel attendance. All students must complete 12 credits in biblical studies. **Procedure:** Freshmen are admitted to all sessions. There are deferred admissions and rolling admissions plans. Check with the school for current application deadlines. The fall 2014 application fee was $40. Applications are accepted on-line. **Transfer Students:** Applicants for transfer should have completed 12 college credits with a minimum GPA of 2.0. 30 of 128 credits required for the bachelor's degree must be completed at CCU. **International Students:** The school actively recruits these students. They must take the TOEFL and the college's own test. They must also take the SAT or ACT.

ADMISSIONS: Associate Director of Admissions. Web: *www.ccu.edu*

FINANCIAL AID: The FAFSA is required. Check with the school for current application deadlines.

COLORADO COLLEGE D-3
www.coloradocollege.edu

Colorado Springs, CO 80903

(719) 389-6344
(800) 542-7214

Fax: (719) 389-6816 Email: admission@coloradocollege.edu

Full-time: 948 men, 1088 women **Faculty:** IIB, ++$
Part-time: 7 men, 7 women **Ph.D.s:** 98%
Graduate: 2 men, 15 women **Student/Faculty:** 10 to 1
Year: other, summer session **Tuition:** $46,410
Room & Board: $10,752 **Freshman Class:** 7602 applied, 1361 accepted, 549 enrolled

SAT CR/M/W: 660/670/670 **ACT:** 30 **CEEB CODE:** 4072
Application Deadline: January 15 **MOST COMPETITIVE**

Colorado College, founded in 1874, is an independent liberal arts and sciences institution. The academic year is based on a block plan, under which students take only 1 course during each of the 8 3-1/2-week-long blocks of study; there is also a 9-week 3-block summer session. There is 1 undergraduate school and 1 graduate school. The 90-acre campus is in an urban area in Colorado Springs, 70 miles south of Denver. Including any residence halls, there are 77 buildings. **STUDENT LIFE:** 83% of undergraduates are from out of state, mostly the Northeast. Students are from 49 states, 57 foreign countries, and Canada. 66% are White. The average age of freshmen is 18; all undergraduates, 20. 6% do not continue beyond their first year; 87% remain to graduate. **Housing:** 1550 students can be accommodated in college housing, which includes single-sex and coed dorms, on-campus apartments, and off-campus apartments. In addition, there are language houses, special-interest houses, fraternity houses, substance-free, smoke-free, diversity, community arts, arts and crafts, and sustainable living houses. On-campus housing is guaranteed for all 4 years. 76% of students live on campus. Upperclassmen may keep cars.

FACULTY/CLASSROOMS: 57% of faculty are male; 43% are female. All teach undergraduates. No introductory courses are taught by graduate students. The average class size in a regular course is 15.
PROGRAMS OF STUDY: CC confers B.A. degrees. Master's degrees are also awarded. Bachelor's degrees are awarded in BIOLOGICAL SCIENCE (biochemistry, biology/biological science, and neurosciences), BUSINESS (international economics), COMMUNICATIONS AND THE ARTS (art history and appreciation, classics, comparative literature, creative writing, dance, dramatic arts, English, film arts, Germanic languages and literature, music, romance languages and literature, and studio art), COMPUTER AND PHYSICAL SCIENCE (chemistry, computer science, geology, mathematics, and physics), EDUCATION (education), ENGINEERING AND ENVIRONMENTAL DESIGN (environmental science), SOCIAL SCIENCE (anthropology, Asian/Oriental studies, economics, French studies, gender studies, Hispanic American studies, history, history of philosophy, interdisciplinary studies, Italian studies, liberal arts/general studies, philosophy, political science/government, psychology, religion, Russian and Slavic studies, sociology, Southwest American studies, and women's studies). Economics, biology, and sociology have the largest enrollments.
ACTIVITIES: There are 144 groups on campus, including health awareness, science, art, band, chess, choir, chorale, chorus, communications, computers, dance, debate, drama, environmental, ethnic, film, forensics, gay, honors, international, jazz band, literary magazine, musical theater, newspaper, orchestra, outdoor, photography, political, professional, religious, social, social service, student government, symphony, and yearbook. Popular campus events include Afternoon and Evening Blues, Rock, Folk, Jazz, World Music Concerts and an Annual Arts and Crafts Sale, Winter Ball and Homecoming. **Sports:** There are 8 intercollegiate sports for men and 8 for women, and 9 intramural sports for men and 9 for women. Facilities include a sports center with 2 gyms, weight and exercise rooms, squash, tennis, and racquetball courts, a pool, an ice rink, and playing fields. **Graduates:** From July 1, 2013 to June 30, 2014, 554 bachelor's degrees were awarded. The most popular majors were economics (8%), ecology and evolutinary biology (8%), and studio art (5%). 30

companies recruited on campus in 2013-2014. In an average class, 2% graduate in 3 years or less, 82% graduate in 4 years or less, 86% graduate in 5 years or less, and 86% graduate in 6 years or less.
SERVICES: Colorado college offers a variety of services and resources to help students succeed. **Library/Resources:** The 2 libraries contain 645,456 volumes, 137,651 microform items, 41,953 audio/video tapes/CDs/DVDs, and subscribe to 56,523 periodicals including electronic. Computerized library services include interlibrary loans, database searching, Internet access, and Wi-Fi capability. Special learning facilities include an art gallery, an electronic music studio, music library, telescope dome, multimedia computer lab, the Colorado College Press, an herbarium, Fourier transform nuclear magnetic resonance spectrometer, a scanning electronic microscope and transmission electronic microscope, an environmental service van equipped for field research, petrographic microscopes, an X-ray diffractometer, sedimentology lab, metabolic equipment, hydrostatic weighing equipment, and a cadaver study in sports science. **Physically Challenged Students:** Colorado college staff members work closely with students who have documented disabilities requiring accommodation to ensure equal access to the college's programs, activities, and services. **Special:** CC offers study abroad in many countries, a Washington semester, student-designed majors, 3-3 law program opportunity with Columbia University School of Law, and 3-2/4-2 engineering degrees with Columbia University, Rensselaer Polytechnic Institute, University of Southern California, and Washington University. There are 12 national honor societies, including Phi Beta Kappa. **Visiting:** There are regularly scheduled orientations for prospective students, including a class visit, an information session with an admissions director, and a student-led tour. There are guides for informal visits, visitors may sit in on classes, and stay overnight. To schedule a visit, contact the Admission Office. **Campus Safety and Security:** Measures include 24-hour foot and vehicle patrol, emergency notification system, self-defense education, and security escort services. There are emergency telephones, lighted pathways/sidewalks, controlled access to dorms/residences, whistle stop program, and fire safety inspections.
REQUIREMENTS: Applicants should have completed at least 16 (18 to 20 recommended) high school academic credits. The GED is accepted. An essay is required.Colorado College has adopted a new flexible testing policy which allows applicants an expanded set of choices for meeting standardized test requirements. AP credits are accepted. Important factors in the admissions decision are advanced placement or honors courses, extracurricular activities record, and evidence of special talent. To graduate, students must complete 32 units with a cumulative GPA of 2.0. No major may require more than 14 units in any one department and no more than 16 overall (including prerequisites). Students must take and pass at least 1 full unit in each academic division. They must complete a Critical Perspectives requirement, consisting of "West in Time" units (one two-block course, 2 units); a "Global Cultures" unit (1 unit); a "Social Inequality" unit (1 unit); Scientific Investigation of the Natural World (2 units, including at least one lab or field course); Quantitative Reasoning (1 unit). Courses may meet more than one designation (for example, a course may be designated both "West in Time" and "Global Cultures") but students must choose one designation or the other, except in the case of "Quantitative Reasoning," which may be fulfilled along with any of the other Critical Perspectives requirements. Basic competency in a foreign language is also required, as is 2 units of a First Year Experience course. **Procedure:** Freshmen are admitted fall and spring. Entrance exams should be taken by January 15 for fall entry. There are early decision, early admissions, and deferred admissions plans. Early decision applications should be filed by November 10; regular applications, by January 15 for fall entry, along with a $60 fee. Notification of early decision is sent December 15; regular decision, April 1. 233 early decision candidates were accepted for the 2014-2015 class. 198 applicants were on the 2014 waiting list; 24 were admitted. Applications are accepted online. **Transfer Students:** 35 transfer students enrolled in 2013-2014. 64 of 128 credits required for the bachelor's degree must be completed at CC. **International Students:** There are 130 international students enrolled. The school actively recruits these students. Applicants must submit either the SAT Reasoning, ACT test, or three exams of the applicant's choice chosen from a list.
ADMISSIONS: 18% of the 2014-2015 applicants were accepted. The

SAT scores for the 2014-2015 freshman class were: Critical Reading--1% below 500, 14% between 500 and 599, 51% between 600 and 699, and 34% between 700 and 800; Math--10% between 500 and 599, 51% between 600 and 699, and 39% between 700 and 800; Writing--1% below 500, 13% between 500 and 599, 53% between 600 and 699, and 33% between 700 and 800. The ACT scores were 2% below 21, 2% between 21 and 23, 10% between 24 and 26, 17% between 27 and 28, and 69% above 28. 87% of the current freshmen were in the top fifth of their class; 98% were in the top two fifths. 19 freshmen graduated first in their class. **Admissions Contact:** Matthew Bonser, Director of Admissions. E-Mail: *admission@coloradocollege.edu* Web: *www.coloradocollege.edu*

FINANCIAL AID: In 2014-2015, 54% of all full-time freshmen and 58% of continuing full-time students received some form of financial aid. 41% of all full-time freshmen and 43% of continuing full-time students received need-based aid. 40% of undergraduate students work part-time. Average annual earnings from campus work are $1412. The average financial indebtedness of the 2014 graduate was $19,230. CC is a member of CSS. The CSS/Profile and FAFSA, non-custodial parents' form, and parent and student tax return, are required. The priority date for freshman financial aid applications for fall entry is November 15. The deadline for filing freshman financial aid applications for fall entry is February 15.

COLORADO MESA UNIVERSITY (*The complete profile is made available exclusively on our website, www.barronspac.com*)

COLORADO SCHOOL OF MINES	C-2
www.mines.edu	
Golden, CO 80401	(303) 273-3220
	(888) 446-9489
Fax: (303) 273-3509	Email: admit@mines.edu
Full-time: 2125 men, 590 women	Faculty: I, av$
Part-time: 470 men, 135 women	Ph.D.s: 90%
Graduate: 635 men, 270 women	Student/Faculty: n/av
Year: semesters, summer session	Tuition: $10,500 ($23,500)
Room & Board: $7500	Freshman Class: n/av
SAT or ACT: required	CEEB CODE: 4073
Application Deadline: n/av	HIGHLY COMPETITIVE

The Colorado School of Mines, founded in 1874, is a public institution offering programs in math, science, economics, and engineering. Figures in the above capsule and in this profile are approximate. In addition to regional accreditation, Mines has baccalaureate program accreditation with ABET. The 373-acre campus is in a small town 20 miles west of Denver. Including any residence halls, there are 40 buildings.

STUDENT LIFE: 76% of undergraduates are from Colorado. Others are from 44 states, 52 foreign countries, and Canada. 90% are from public schools. 79% are White. 52% are Protestant; 21% Catholic; 20% claim no religious affiliation. The average age of freshmen is 18; all undergraduates, 20. 14% do not continue beyond their first year; 67% remain to graduate. **Housing:** 855 students can be accommodated in college housing, which includes single-sex and coed dorms, on-campus apartments, and married student housing. In addition, there are fraternity houses. On-campus housing is guaranteed for the freshman year only, and is available on a first-come, first-served basis. 10% of students commute. All students may keep cars.

FACULTY/CLASSROOMS: 80% of faculty are male; 20% are female. 93% teach undergraduates, 50% do research, and 50% do both. No introductory courses are taught by graduate students. The average class size in an introductory lecture is 100; in a laboratory is 22; and in a regular course is 29.

PROGRAMS OF STUDY: Mines confers B.S. degrees. Master's and doctoral degrees are also awarded. Bachelor's degrees are awarded in COMPUTER AND PHYSICAL SCIENCE (chemistry, mathematics, and physics), ENGINEERING AND ENVIRONMENTAL DESIGN (chemical engineering, engineering, geological engineering, geophysical engineering, metallurgical engineering, mining and mineral engineering, and petroleum/natural gas engineering), SOCIAL SCIENCE

(economics). Chemical engineering, geological engineering, and petroleum engineering are the strongest academically. General engineering, chemical engineering, and engineering physics have the largest enrollments.

ACTIVITIES: 19% of men belong to 7 national fraternities; 19% of women belong to 3 national sororities. There are 95 groups on campus, including band, cheerleading, choir, chorus, computers, drama, ethnic, honors, international, jazz band, literary magazine, marching band, musical theater, newspaper, political, professional, religious, social, social service, student government, and yearbook. Popular campus events include International Day and Parents Day. **Sports:** There are 9 intercollegiate sports for men and 7 for women, and 20 intramural sports for men and 20 for women. Facilities include a 10,000-seat stadium, a recreation center, gym, numerous intramural fields, tennis courts, and a field house. **Graduates:** From July 1, 2013 to June 30, 2014, 563 bachelor's degrees were awarded. The most popular majors were general engineering (34%), petroleum engineering (12%), and chemical engineering (11%). 267 companies recruited on campus in 2013-2014. In an average class, 1% graduate in 3 years or less, 40% graduate in 4 years or less, 66% graduate in 5 years or less, and 69% graduate in 6 years or less. Of the 2013 graduating class, 20% were enrolled in graduate school within 6 months of graduation, and 95% were employed.

SERVICES: Counseling and information services are available, as is tutoring in most subjects. There is a reader service for the blind, and remedial math and writing. **Library/Resources:** The library contains 356,000 volumes, 236,000 microform items, and subscribes to 2,700 periodicals including electronic. Computerized library services include interlibrary loans, database searching, and Internet access. **Physically Challenged Students:** All of the campus is accessible. Facilities include wheelchair ramps, elevators, special parking, specially equipped restrooms, special class scheduling, lowered drinking fountains, lowered telephones, and special housing. **Special:** Co-op programs, internships in the McBride honors program in the humanities, accelerated degree programs in all majors, dual majors, study abroad in 20 countries, and nondegree study are offered. There is 1 national honor society, a freshman honors program, and 3 departmental honors programs. **Visiting:** There are regularly scheduled orientations for prospective students, including a half day-long visitation program twice each fall where students may visit departments and talk with faculty. Sessions in admissions and financial aid also are given. There are guides for informal visits and visitors may sit in on classes. To schedule a visit, contact the Admissions Office. **Campus Safety and Security:** Measures include 24-hour foot and vehicle patrol, emergency notification system, and self-defense education. There are emergency telephones and lighted pathways/sidewalks.

REQUIREMENTS: The SAT or ACT is required. Applicants must be graduates of an accredited secondary school. The GED is accepted. Students should have completed 16 high school academic credits, including 4 credits each of English and math, 3 of science, 2 of social studies, and 3 academic electives. AP credits are accepted. Important factors in the admissions decision are advanced placement or honors courses, leadership record, and recommendations by school officials.Students must complete 138 to 148 credit hours, with 35 to 40 hours in the major and a GPA of 2.0. Required courses include humanities, calculus, physics, computer science, chemistry, and phys ed. **Procedure:** Freshmen are admitted to all sessions. Entrance exams should be taken by late in the junior year or early in the senior year. There are deferred admissions and rolling admissions plans. Check with the school for current application deadlines. The fall 2014 application fee was $45. Applications are accepted on-line. **Transfer Students:** 79 transfer students enrolled in 2013-2014. Transfer applicants must have a minimum GPA of 2.75 30 of 138 credits required for the bachelor's degree must be completed at Mines. **International Students:** There are 204 international students enrolled. The school actively recruits these students. They must take the TOEFL and the Comprehensive English Language Test.

ADMISSIONS: 75 freshmen graduated first in their class. **Admissions Contact:** Director of Admissions. E-Mail: *admit@mines.edu* Web: *www.mines.edu*

FINANCIAL AID: In 2014-2015, 85% of all full-time freshmen and 85% of continuing full-time students received some form of financial aid. 74% of all full-time freshmen and 74% of continuing full-time students received need-based aid. The average freshman award was $15,540. Need-based scholarships or need-based grants averaged $8,350; and need-based self-help aid (loans and jobs) averaged $7,190. 70% of undergraduate students work part-time. Average annual earnings from campus work are $900. The average financial indebtedness of the 2014 graduate was $18,500. Mines is a member of CSS. The FAFSA is required. Check with the school for current application deadlines.

COLORADO STATE UNIVERSITY-FORT COLLINS   C-1
www.colostate.edu

Fort Collins, CO 80523   **(970) 491-6909**

Fax: (970) 491-7799   Email: admissions@colostate.edu

Full-time: 10098 men, 10790 women   Faculty: 1004; I, av$

Part-time: 930 men, 688 women   Ph.D.s: 99%

Graduate: 2167 men, 2413 women   Student/Faculty: 16 to 1

Year: semesters, summer session   Tuition: $9897 ($26,076)

Room & Board: $10,488   Freshman Class: 16667 applied, 13416 accepted, 4353 enrolled

SAT CR/M: 570/580 ACT: 25   CEEB CODE: 4075

Application Deadline: February 1   **VERY COMPETITIVE**

Colorado State University, founded in 1870 and part of the Colorado State University system, is a public, land-grant institution offering 71 undergraduate degrees in 53 departments within 8 colleges. There is 1 graduate school. In addition to regional accreditation, Colorado State has baccalaureate program accreditation with AACSB, ABET, ACCE, ACEJMC, CSWE, NASM, and SAF. The 586-acre campus is in a suburban area about 65 miles north of Denver. Including any residence halls, there are 157 buildings.

STUDENT LIFE: 77% of undergraduates are from Colorado. Others are from 50 states, 91 foreign countries, and Canada. 72% are White. **Male To Female Ratio:** 1.1:1. The average age of freshmen is 18; all undergraduates, 21. 14% do not continue beyond their first year; 67% remain to graduate. **Housing:** 6659 students can be accommodated in college housing, which includes coed dorms, on-campus apartments, off-campus apartments, married student housing, honors floors, and more than 10 different residential learning communities. On-campus housing is guaranteed for the freshman year only, is available on a first-come, first-served basis. 75% of students commute. All students may keep cars.

FACULTY/CLASSROOMS: 64% of faculty are male; 36% are female. All teach and do research. Graduate students teach 17% of introductory courses. The average class size in an introductory lecture is 58; in a laboratory is 23; and in a regular course is 38.

PROGRAMS OF STUDY: Colorado State confers B.A., B.S., B.F.A., B.S.W. and B.M. degrees. Master's and doctoral degrees are also awarded. Bachelor's degrees are awarded in AGRICULTURE (agricultural business management, agricultural economics, animal science, equine science, fishing and fisheries, forestry and related sciences, horticulture, natural resource management, range/farm management, and soil science), BIOLOGICAL SCIENCE (biochemistry, biology/biological science, botany, ecology, microbiology, nutrition, wildlife biology, and zoology), BUSINESS (apparel and accessories marketing, banking and finance, business administration and management, hospitality management services, hotel/motel and restaurant management, marketing/retailing/merchandising, real estate, recreational facilities management, and tourism), COMMUNICATIONS AND THE ARTS (apparel design, art, art history and appreciation, communications, creative writing, dance, dramatic arts, English, fine arts, French, German, journalism, languages, music, music performance, music theory and composition, performing arts, Spanish, theatre acting, theater design, theatre production, and theatre studies), COMPUTER AND PHYSICAL SCIENCE (applied mathematics, chemistry, computer science, geology, information sciences and systems, mathematics, natural sciences, physical sciences,

physics, and statistics), EDUCATION (agricultural education, art education, education, English education, foreign languages education, mathematics education, music education, science education, and technology & science education), ENGINEERING AND ENVIRONMENTAL DESIGN (bioengineering, biomedical engineering, chemical engineering, civil engineering, computer engineering, computer technology, construction management, electrical/electronics engineering, engineering, engineering and applied science, engineering physics, environmental engineering, interior design, landscape architecture/design, and mechanical engineering), HEALTH PROFESSIONS (biomedical science, environmental health science, exercise science, and health science), SOCIAL SCIENCE (anthropology, economics, ethnic studies, family/consumer studies, fire services administration, food science, history, human development, interdisciplinary studies, international studies, liberal arts/general studies, philosophy, political science/government, psychology, social work, sociology, and water resources). Electrical and computer engineering, chemistry, and biology are the strongest academically. Health and exercise science, biology, and psychology have the largest enrollments.

ACTIVITIES: 8% of men belong to 24 national fraternities; 12% of women belong to 17 national sororities. There are 646 groups on campus, including art, band, cheerleading, choir, chorale, chorus, computers, dance, drama, drill team, environmental, ethnic, film, gay, honors, international, jazz band, literary magazine, marching band, musical theater, newspaper, opera, orchestra, pep band, photography, political, professional, radio and TV, religious, social, social service, student government, and symphony. Popular campus events include Homecoming, Ag Day, President's Annual Address and a Picnic. **Sports:** There are 5 intercollegiate sports for men and 9 for women, and 22 intramural sports for men and 22 for women. Facilities include an athletic and recreation facilities include a renovated 30,000-seat stadium, an 8745-seat arena, indoor and outdoor tracks, tennis courts, intramural fields, indoor swimming pools, a comprehensive student recreation center (featuring free weights, state-of-the-art fitness equipment, and sports courts), and a ropes course. **Graduates:** From July 1, 2013 to June 30, 2014, 4962 bachelor's degrees were awarded. The most popular majors were business/marketing (14%), biological/life sciences (10%), and social sciences (9%). 700 companies recruited on campus in 2013-2014. In an average class, 2% graduate in 3 years or less, 39% graduate in 4 years or less, 63% graduate in 5 years or less, and 67% graduate in 6 years or less. Of the 2013 graduating class, 28% were enrolled in graduate school within 6 months of graduation, and 52% were employed.

SERVICES: Counseling and information services are available, as is tutoring in most subjects. There is a reader service for the blind. Interpreters and note takers are available **Library/Resources:** The 2 libraries contain 2.8 million volumes, 86,614 microform items, 2,890 audio/video tapes/CDs/DVDs, and subscribe to 77,181 periodicals including electronic. Computerized library services include interlibrary loans, database searching, Internet access, and Wi-Fi capability. Special learning facilities include an art gallery, radio station, TV station, concert hall, thrust theatre, music hall, engineering research center, equine center, veterinary teaching hospital, environmental learning center, and a plant environmental research center. **Physically Challenged Students:** 98% of the campus is accessible. Facilities include wheelchair ramps, elevators, special parking, specially equipped restrooms, special class scheduling, lowered drinking fountains, lowered telephones, special housing. **Special:** Colorado State offers a co-op program in Engineering. Study abroad, a semester at sea, work-study programs, internships, B.A.-B.S. degrees, dual majors, and pass/fail options are available. Teaching certification students receive a bachelor's degree in their chosen subject and also complete a certification sequence through the School of Education. There are 38 national honor societies, including Phi Beta Kappa, a freshman honors program, and 19 departmental honors programs. **Visiting:** There are regularly scheduled orientations for prospective students, regularly scheduled visit days provide specialized information for particular groups including high school seniors and juniors, transfer students, special interests and others. A daily information session and campus tour are presented each weekday. There are guides for informal visits and visitors may sit in on classes. To schedule a visit, contact the Office of Admissions. **Campus Safety and**

Security: Measures include 24-hour foot and vehicle patrol, emergency notification system, self-defense education, and security escort services. There are shuttle buses, emergency telephones, lighted pathways/sidewalks, controlled access to dorms/residences, Lectures by campus police on a variety of safety issues, a crime victim support unit and a bike patrol.

REQUIREMENTS: The SAT or ACT is required. Graduation from secondary school is required, but the GED is accepted. Priority consideration is given to applicants who have earned a minimum 3.25 GPA with no D/F grades and who will have successfully satisfied our academic course work standards before enrolling at CSU. Applicants with a GPA below 3.25, occasional D/F grades, and/or fewer than the 18 recommended high school units are encouraged to apply, since many factors are considered in the holistic review process. The 18 recommended high school credits are to include 4 English, 4 math (algebra I and II, geometry, and an advanced math), 3 natural sciences (at least 2 must include a lab), 2 social studies, 1 history, 2 foreign language (must be the same language), and 2 academic electives. An essay (minimum 250 words) and 1 recommendation are required. The most recent freshman class entered with an average GPA of 3.61; ACT Composite score of 24.7; SAT Critical Reading score of 566; and SAT Math score of 574. AP and CLEP credits are accepted. To graduate, students must complete at least 120 credit hours (more for some programs) of which 42 must be upper division. The minimum GPA for graduation is 2.0. Students must complete the All University Core and all curricular requirements as described in the current catalog. **Procedure:** Freshmen are admitted to all sessions. Entrance exams should be taken during the junior year or early fall of the senior year. There are deferred admissions and rolling admissions plans. Applications should be filed by February 1 for fall entry; November 1 for spring entry, along with a $50 fee. Notification is sent on a rolling basis. Applications are accepted on-line. **Transfer Students:** 1952 transfer students enrolled in 2013-2014. Strong candidates for transfer admission have earned a minimum 2.5 cumulative GPA in 30 or more college-level academic semester credits and have satisfied the transfer admissions requirement in mathematics. Students holding an Associate Degree from an accredited Colorado institution are guaranteed admission provided that it is the last institution attended and that a cumulative 2.0 GPA has been achieved from all institutions attended. Specific majors may require additional course work and a higher GPA. 30 of 120 credits required for the bachelor's degree must be completed at Colorado State. **International Students:** There are 809 international students enrolled. The school actively recruits these students. They must take the TOEFL with a minimum score of 550 on the paper-based TOEFL (PBT) or 79 on the Internet-based version (iBT). Scores from other English language proficiency exams may be considered in lieu of the TOEFL. They must also take the SAT or ACT.

ADMISSIONS: 80% of the 2014-2015 applicants were accepted. The SAT scores for the 2014-2015 freshman class were: Critical Reading--18% below 500, 44% between 500 and 599, 33% between 600 and 699, and 5% between 700 and 800; Math--15% below 500, 45% between 500 and 599, 34% between 600 and 699, and 6% between 700 and 800. The ACT scores were 11% below 21, 27% between 21 and 23, 30% between 24 and 26, 15% between 27 and 28, and 17% above 28. 50% of the current freshmen were in the top fifth of their class; 85% were in the top two fifths. There were 5 National Merit finalists. 54 freshmen graduated first in their class. **Admissions Contact:** Bryan Whish, Director of Undergraduate Admission. E-Mail: *admissions@colostate.edu* Web: *http://admissions.colostate.edu/*

FINANCIAL AID: In 2014-2015, 72% of all full-time freshmen and 73% of continuing full-time students received some form of financial aid. 46% of all full-time freshmen and 48% of continuing full-time students received need-based aid. The average freshman award was $10,158. Need-based scholarships or need-based grants averaged $7,653; need-based self-help aid (loans and jobs) averaged $5,446; non-need-based athletic scholarships averaged $20,682; and other non-need-based awards and non-need-based scholarships averaged $3,996. 32% of undergraduate students work part-time. Average annual earnings from campus work are $3432. The average financial indebtedness of the 2014 graduate was $21,240. The FAFSA is required. The priority date for freshman financial aid applications for fall entry is March 1. The deadline for filing freshman financial aid applications for fall entry is March 1.

COLORADO STATE UNIVERSITY-PUEBLO   D-3
www.colostate-pueblo.edu

Pueblo, CO 81001

(719) 549-2462
(877) 872-9653

Fax: (719) 549-2419
Email: info@colostate-pueblo.edu

Full-time: 1774 men, 1968 women
Part-time: 540 men, 925 women
Graduate: 374 men, 1508 women
Year: semesters, summer session
Room & Board: $8856
SAT: required ACT: 21
Application Deadline: n/av

Faculty: II, --$
Ph.Ds: 70%
Student/Faculty: n/av
Tuition: $7327 ($17,649)
Freshman Class: n/av
CEEB CODE: 4611

COMPETITIVE

Colorado State University - Pueblo, founded in 1933, is part of the Colorado State University System. The public institution offers undergraduate programs in humanities and social sciences, fine arts, business administration, nursing, the natural sciences, technology, engineering, and education. There are 4 undergraduate schools and 1 graduate school. In addition to regional accreditation, CSU-Pueblo has baccalaureate program accreditation with AACSB, ABET, CSWE, NASM, NLN, and TEAC. The 275-acre campus is in an urban area 100 miles south of Denver, 50 miles south of Colorado Springs, 100 miles north of New Mexico. Including any residence halls, there are 23 buildings.

STUDENT LIFE: 87% of undergraduates are from Colorado. Others are from 41 states, 40 foreign countries, and Canada. 51% are White; 30% Hispanic. **Male To Female Ratio:** 1.6:1. The average age of freshmen is 19; all undergraduates, 26. 39% do not continue beyond their first year; 27% remain to graduate. **Housing:** 652 students can be accommodated in college housing, which includes coed dorms and on-campus apartments. On-campus housing is guaranteed for the freshman year only, and is available on a first-come, first-served basis. 81% of students commute. Alcohol is not permitted. All students may keep cars.

FACULTY/CLASSROOMS: 57% of faculty are male; 43% are female. 99% teach undergraduates, 10% do research, and 4% do both. No introductory courses are taught by graduate students. The average class size in an introductory lecture is 70; in a laboratory is 24; and in a regular course is 22.

PROGRAMS OF STUDY: CSU-Pueblo confers B.A., B.S., B.S.B.A., B.F.A., B.S.C.E.T., B.S.I.En., B.S.N. and B.S.W. degrees. Master's degrees are also awarded. Bachelor's degrees are awarded in BIOLOGICAL SCIENCE (biochemistry, biology/biological science, and biotechnology), BUSINESS (accounting, business administration and management, and recreation and leisure services), COMMUNICATIONS AND THE ARTS (art, broadcasting, communications, English, journalism, music performance, music theory and composition, and Spanish), COMPUTER AND PHYSICAL SCIENCE (chemistry, information sciences and systems, mathematics, and physics), EDUCATION (music education), ENGINEERING AND ENVIRONMENTAL DESIGN (automotive technology, civil engineering technology, electrical/electronics engineering technology, industrial administration/management, industrial engineering, mechanical engineering technology, and preengineering), HEALTH PROFESSIONS (chiropractic, environmental health science, exercise science, medical technology, nursing, occupational therapy, physician's assistant, predentistry, premedicine, preoptometry, preosteopathy, prepharmacy, prepodiatry, preveterinary science, and speech pathology/audiology), SOCIAL SCIENCE (criminology, economics, history, political science/government, prelaw, psychology, social science, social work.

ACTIVITIES: 1% of men belong to 2 national fraternities; 1% of women belong to 1 local sorority. There are 68 groups on campus, including art, cheerleading, choir, chorale, computers, drama, ethnic, forensics, gay, honors, international, jazz band, literary magazine, marching band, newspaper, pep band, political, professional, radio and TV, religious, social, social service, student government, and symphony. Popular campus events include Distinguished Lecture Series and Departmental Lecture Series, Pueblo Symphony, Career Fair, and Homecoming. **Sports:** There are 7 intercollegiate sports for men and 8 for women, and 7 intramural sports for men and 7 for women. Facilities include an arena with an indoor swimming pool, a weight room, rock-climbing wall, racquetball, basketball, and volleyball courts, a sports complex with tennis courts, baseball, softball, football and soccer fields, bike trails, and a rope course. **Graduates:** From July 1, 2013 to June 30, 2014, 889 bachelor's degrees were awarded. In an average class, 18% graduate in 4 years or less, 28% graduate in 5 years or less, and 33% graduate in 6 years or less.

SERVICES: Counseling and information services are available, as is tutoring in most subjects. **Library/Resources:** The library contains 350,000 volumes, 10,000 microform items, 16,862 audio/video tapes/CDs/DVDs, and subscribes to 1,327 periodicals including electronic. Computerized library services include interlibrary loans and database searching. Special learning facilities include an art gallery, radio station, TV station, observatory at nature center. **Physically Challenged Students:** All of the campus is accessible. Facilities include wheelchair ramps, elevators, special parking, specially equipped restrooms, special class scheduling, lowered drinking fountains, and lowered telephones. **Special:** CSU-Pueblo offers co-op programs, internships, study abroad in 8 countries, and on-campus work-study programs. Also available are 5-year combined B.S.B.A./M.B.A. degrees, a 3-2 engineering degree with Colorado State University, dual majors, non-degree study, and preprofessional programs in forestry, physical therapy, and wildlife management. CSU-Pueblo is a member of the National Student Exchange. There are 10 national honor societies, a freshman honors program, and 10 departmental honors programs. **Visiting:** There are regularly scheduled orientations for prospective students, including a tour, lunch, and mini-sessions on financial aid, athletics, scholarships, and student services. There are guides for informal visits and visitors may sit in on classes. To schedule a visit, contact Tiffany Kingrey at tiffany.kingrey@colostate-pueblo.edu. **Campus Safety and Security:** Measures include 24-hour foot and vehicle patrol, self-defense education, and security escort services. There are emergency telephones and lighted pathways/sidewalks.

REQUIREMENTS: The SAT or ACT is required. Applicants must be graduates of an accredited secondary school or have a GED certificate with a minimum score of 45. CSU-Pueblo computes a CCHE admission index, comprised of the high school GPA and SAT or ACT scores. Students scoring below the minimum will still be considered by an admissions committee. Academic preparation should consist of 4 years of English, 3 of math including algebra and geometry, 2 of natural science including physical science, 3 years of social studies including American government, and 1 year of a foreign language. A GPA of 2.0 is required. AP and CLEP credits are accepted. Important factors in the admissions decision are advanced placement or honors courses, leadership record, and recommendations by school officials.To graduate, all students must complete at least 120 semester hours, including 40 in upper-division courses and 30 to 48 in the major, with a minimum GPA of 2.0. General education requirements include a 14-credit skills component of courses in communication, computer literacy, and quantitative skills, as well as a 19-credit knowledge component of courses in humanities, social sciences, and science and technology. Other requirements vary with the major. **Procedure:** Freshmen are admitted to all sessions. Entrance exams should be taken during spring of the junior year or fall of the senior year. There is a rolling admissions plan. Check with the school for current application deadlines. The fall 2014 application fee was $25. Notification is sent on a rolling basis. **Transfer Students:** A minimum GPA of 2.0 and official transcripts of previous college work are required. Applicants with fewer than 30 credit hours must submit ACT or SAT scores and high school transcripts. 30 of 120 credits required for the bachelor's degree must be completed at CSU-Pueblo. **International Students:** The school actively recruits these students. They must take the TOEFL or MELAB.

ADMISSIONS: Chrissy Holliday, Director of Admissions. E-Mail: *info@colostate-pueblo.edu* Web: *www.colostate-pueblo.edu*

FINANCIAL AID: 54% of all full-time freshmen received need-based aid. The average freshman award was $8,637. Need-based scholarships or need-based grants averaged $6,610; need-based self-help aid (loans and jobs) averaged $3,336; non-need-based athletic scholarships averaged $3,688; and other non-need-based awards and non-need-based scholarships averaged $3,483. The FAFSA is required. Check with the school for current application deadlines.

COLORADO TECHNICAL UNIVERSITY (*The complete profile is made available exclusively on our website, www.barronspac.com*)

FORT LEWIS COLLEGE	B-4
www.explore.fortlewis.edu	

Durango, CO 81301	**(970) 247-7180**

Fax: (970) 247-7179	Email: admission@fortlewis.edu
Full-time: 1881 men, 1817 women	Faculty: 158; IIB, av$
Part-time: 185 men, 145 women	Ph.D.s: 87%
Graduate: 7 men, 30 women	Student/Faculty: 21 to 1
Year: varies, summer session	Tuition: $6923 ($17,763)
Room & Board: $8590	Freshman Class: 2560 applied, 2240 accepted, 876 enrolled
SAT: required ACT: 22	CEEB CODE: 4310
Application Deadline: August 1	COMPETITIVE

Fort Lewis College, founded in 1911, is a public institution with undergraduate programs in arts and sciences, business and education. Figures in the above capsule and in this profile are approximate. There are 2 undergraduate schools and 1 graduate school. In addition to regional accreditation, FLC has baccalaureate program accreditation with AACSB, ABET, NASM, and TEAC. The 362-acre campus is in a small town the southwestern corner of Colorado, about 330 southwest of Denver. Including any residence halls, there are 58 buildings.

STUDENT LIFE: 59% of undergraduates are from Colorado. Others are from 50 states, 20 foreign countries, and Canada. 85% are from public schools. 60% are White; 20% American Indian/Alaska Native. **Male To Female Ratio:** 1.0:1. The average age of freshmen is 18; all undergraduates, 21. 35% do not continue beyond their first year; 38% remain to graduate. **Housing:** 1572 students can be accommodated in college housing, which includes coed dorms, on-campus apartments, and married student housing. On-campus housing is guaranteed for the freshman year only, is available on a first-come, first-served basis. 63% of students commute. Alcohol is not permitted. All students may keep cars.

FACULTY/CLASSROOMS: 50% of faculty are male; 50% are female. All teach undergraduates. No introductory courses are taught by graduate students. The average class size in an introductory lecture is 21; in a laboratory is 20; and in a regular course is 21.

PROGRAMS OF STUDY: FLC confers B.A., and B.S. degrees. Master's degrees are also awarded. Bachelor's degrees are awarded in AGRICULTURE (environmental studies), BIOLOGICAL SCIENCE (biochemistry and biology/biological science), BUSINESS (accounting, business administration and management, business economics, and marketing and distribution), COMMUNICATIONS AND THE ARTS (art, dramatic arts, English, music, and Spanish), COMPUTER AND PHYSICAL SCIENCE (chemistry, geology, mathematics, and physics), EDUCATION (athletic training), HEALTH PROFESSIONS (exercise science and public health), SOCIAL SCIENCE (American Indian studies, anthropology, economics, gender studies, history, humanities, interdisciplinary studies, philosophy, political science/government, psychology, sociology, and Southwest American studies). Business, psychology and biology have the largest enrollments.

ACTIVITIES: There are 65 groups on campus, including art, band, cheerleading, choir, chorale, chorus, computers, dance, drama, environmental, ethnic, gay, honors, international, jazz band, literary magazine, newspaper, pep band, political, professional, radio and TV, religious, social, social service, student government, and symphony. Popular campus events include Fiesta on the Mesa, Fall Blaze, Homecoming and Hozhoni Days. **Sports:** There are 5 intercollegiate sports for men and 6 for women, and 16 intramural sports for men and 16 for women. Facilities include a field house, an outdoor sports complex, an indoor swimming pool, and a student life center, which includes a 3-court gym, racquetball court, aerobic/dance studio, track, climbing wall, and cardio/weight area. **Graduates:** From July 1, 2013 to June 30, 2014, 697 bachelor's degrees were awarded. The most popular majors were business administration (16%), biology (7%), and psychology (7%). 140 companies recruited on campus in 2013-2014. In an average class, 17% graduate in 4 years or less, 33% graduate in 5 years or less, and 37% graduate in 6 years or less. Of the 2013 graduating class, 17% were enrolled in graduate school within 6 months of graduation.

SERVICES: Counseling and information services are available, as is tutoring in most subjects. There is a reader service for the blind, and remedial math, reading, and writing. **Library/Resources:** The library contains 257,653 volumes, 344,803 microform items, and 10,300 audio/video tapes/CDs/DVDs, and subscribes to 26,820 periodicals including electronic. Computerized library services include interlibrary loans, database searching, Internet access, and Wi-Fi capability. Special learning facilities include an art gallery, radio station, a center for Southwest studies. **Physically Challenged Students:** All of the campus is accessible. Facilities include wheelchair ramps, elevators, special parking, specially equipped restrooms, special class scheduling, lowered drinking fountains, lowered telephones, special housing, and workstations modified for individual needs. **Special:** The college offers cooperative programs in most majors, numerous internships, a Washington semester for political science majors, study abroad in 32 countries, student-designed majors, a general studies degree, non-degree study, pass/fail option, and B.A.-B.S. degrees. There are 3-2 engineering degrees with 4 universities and a preforestry degree with Colorado State and Northern Arizona Universities. There are 5 national honor societies and a freshman honors program. **Visiting:** There are regularly scheduled orientations for prospective students. There are guides for informal visits, visitors may sit in on classes, and stay overnight. To schedule a visit, contact the Office of Admission at (877) 352-2656. **Campus Safety and Security:** Measures include 24-hour foot and vehicle patrol, emergency notification system, self-defense education, and security escort services. There are shuttle buses, emergency telephones, lighted pathways/sidewalks, and controlled access to dorms/residences.

REQUIREMENTS: The SAT or ACT is required. Applicants must be graduates of an accredited secondary school or have a GED certificate. An interview is recommended. AP and CLEP credits are accepted.To graduate, students must complete 120 semester hours with 30 to 40 hours in the major, 50 credits outside the major, and a minimum GPA of 2.0 overall and in the major. A total of 32 to 44 hours in general distribution courses is required. **Procedure:** Freshmen are admitted to all sessions. Entrance exams should be taken in spring of the junior year. There are deferred admissions and rolling admissions plans. Early decision applications should be filed by January 15; regular applications, by August 1 for fall entry. The fall 2014 application fee was $40. Notification is sent on a rolling basis. Applications are accepted on-line. **Transfer Students:** 416 transfer students enrolled in 2013-2014. Applicants for transfer should have completed a minimum of 12 credit hours and have a GPA of 2.40. Courses completed with a grade of C- or better may transfer. An interview is recommended. 30 of 120 credits required for the bachelor's degree must be completed at FLC. **International Students:** There are 61 international students enrolled. They must take the TOEFL with a minimum score of 500 on the paper-based TOEFL (PBT) or 61 on the Internet-based version (iBT).

ADMISSIONS: 88% of the 2014-2015 applicants were accepted. The SAT scores for the 2014-2015 freshman class were: Critical Reading--38% below 500, 44% between 500 and 599, 14% between 600 and 699, and 3% between 700 and 800; Math--33% below 500, 48% between 500 and 599, 17% between 600 and 699, and 1% between 700 and 800; Writing--43% below 500, 39% between 500 and 599, and 16% between 600 and 699. The ACT scores were 37% below 21, 30% between 21 and 23, 21% between 24 and 25, 8% between 27 and 28, and 5% above 28. 32% of the current freshmen were in the top fifth of their class; 65% were in the top two fifths. **Admissions Contact:** Director of Admissions. E-Mail: *admission@fortlewis.edu* Web: *www.explore.fortlewis.edu*

FINANCIAL AID: In 2014-2015, 95% of all full-time freshmen and 80% of continuing full-time students received some form of financial aid. 65% of all full-time freshmen and 60% of continuing full-time students received need-based aid. The average freshman award was $12,131. Need-based scholarships or need-based grants averaged $5,840 ($16,000 maximum); need-based self-help aid (loans and jobs) averaged $4,304 ($5,500 maximum); non-need-based athletic scholarships averaged $10,635 ($16,000 maximum); other non-need-based awards and non-need-based scholarships averaged $6,000 ($16,000 maximum); and $1,400 from other forms of aid. 90% of

undergraduate students work part-time. The average financial indebtedness of the 2014 graduate was $25,313. FLC is a member of CSS. The FAFSA is required. The priority date for freshman financial aid applications for fall entry is February 15.

JOHNSON & WALES UNIVERSITY/ DENVER CAMPUS
www.jwu.edu

C-2

Denver, CO 80220	(877) 598-3368
Fax: (303) 256-9333	Email: admissions.den@jwu.edu
Full-time: 497 men, 758 women	Faculty: 48
Part-time: 47 men, 61 women	Ph.Ds: n/av
Graduate: 7 men, 21 women	Student/Faculty: 24 to 1
Year: quarters, summer session	Tuition: $29,576
Room & Board: n/app	Freshman Class: 1990 applied, 1636 accepted, 322 enrolled
	CEEB CODE: 3567
Application Deadline: n/av	COMPETITIVE

Johnson & Wales University/Denver Campus, founded in 2000, offers degree programs in its College of Business, College of Culinary Arts, Hospitality College, and School of Education. There are 4 undergraduate schools. In addition to regional accreditation, JWU has baccalaureate program accreditation with NEASC. The 26-acre campus is in a suburban area. Including any residence halls, there are 19 buildings.

STUDENT LIFE: 60% of undergraduates are from out of state, mostly the West. Students are from 50 states, 11 foreign countries, and Canada. 48% are White; 11% Hispanic. **Female To Male Ratio:** 1.5:1. The average age of freshmen is 18; all undergraduates, 18. 67% remain to graduate. **Housing:** college-sponsored housing includes coed dorms and on-campus apartments. On-campus housing is available on a lottery system for upperclassmen. 69% of students commute. Alcohol is not permitted. All students may keep cars.

FACULTY/CLASSROOMS: No introductory courses are taught by graduate students.

PROGRAMS OF STUDY: JWU confers B.S. degrees. Associate degrees are also awarded. Bachelor's degrees are awarded in BIOLOGICAL SCIENCE (nutrition), BUSINESS (accounting, banking and finance, entrepreneurial studies, hotel/motel and restaurant management, international business management, management science, marketing/retailing/merchandising, and sports management), SOCIAL SCIENCE (criminal justice and food production/management/services). Culinary, sports entertainment event management, and food service management have the largest enrollments.

ACTIVITIES: 1% of women belong to 1 national sorority. There are 26 groups on campus, including leadership academy, campus activities board, cheerleading, dance, drama, gay, international, literary magazine, musical theater, newspaper, professional, social, student government, and yearbook. Popular campus events include Winter Week, Love Fest, and Spring Fling. **Sports:** Facilities include a gym, weight room, cardio room, a sand volleyball pit, and an outdoor basketball court.

SERVICES: Counseling and information services are available, as is tutoring in every subject. **Library/Resources:** The library contains 29,000 volumes, 1,200 audio/video tapes/CDs/DVDs, and subscribes to 215 periodicals including electronic. Computerized library services include interlibrary loans, database searching, Internet access, and Wi-Fi capability. **Physically Challenged Students:** All of the campus is accessible. Facilities include wheelchair ramps, elevators, special parking, specially equipped restrooms, special class scheduling, lowered drinking fountains, and lowered telephones. **Special:** The university offers co-op programs, accelerated degree programs, dual majors, study abroad, and worldwide work-study opportunities in business, hospitality, technology, and culinary arts. Most majors require 11-week internships. There is a freshman honors program. **Visiting:** There are guides for informal visits, visitors may sit in on classes, and stay overnight. To schedule a visit, contact the Admissions Office. **Campus Safety and Security:** Measures include 24-hour foot and vehicle patrol and security escort services. There are shuttle buses and emergency telephones.

REQUIREMENTS: Although SAT and ACT scores are required only for students applying for honors admissions, students who have taken these tests are encouraged to submit their scores. High school diploma is required and the GED is accepted. Requirements are 4 years of English, 3 years each of mathematics, science, and 2 years of social studies. A GPA of 2.0 is required. AP and CLEP credits are accepted. Important factors in the admissions decision are advanced placement or honors courses, extracurricular activities record, parents or siblings attended your school, and recommendations by school officials. To graduate, students must complete 180 quarter credit hours, including at least 36 in the major, with a minimum GPA of 2.0. Required classes include English, math, history, psychology, sociology, economics, science, and professional development. **Procedure:** Freshmen are admitted to all sessions. There are deferred admissions and rolling admissions plans. Application deadlines are open. Applications are accepted on-line. **Transfer Students:** 95 transfer students enrolled in 2013-2014. Applicants are required to submit official high school and college transcripts and must have earned a minimum college GPA of 2.0. 45 of 180 credits required for the bachelor's degree must be completed at JWU. **International Students:** The school actively recruits these students.

ADMISSIONS: 82% of the 2014-2015 applicants were accepted. **Admissions Contact:** Kim Medina, Director of Admissions. E-Mail: *admissions.den@jwu.edu* Web: *www.jwu.edu*

FINANCIAL AID: JWU is a member of CSS. The FAFSA is required. The priority date for freshman financial aid applications for fall entry is March 1.

METROPOLITAN STATE UNIVERSITY OF DENVER *(The complete profile is made available exclusively on our website, www.barronspac.com)*

NAROPA UNIVERSITY *(The complete profile is made available exclusively on our website, www.barronspac.com)*

REGIS UNIVERSITY   C-2
www.regis.edu

Denver, CO 80221   (303) 458-4900
                                              (800) 388-2366
Fax: (303) 964-5534   **Email:** regisadm@regis.edu
Full-time: 530 men, 940 women   **Faculty:** 100
Part-time: 25 men, 25 women   **Ph.D.s:** 95%
Graduate: n/av   **Student/Faculty:** n/av
Year: semesters, summer session **Tuition:** $31,888
Room & Board: $9430   **Freshman Class:** 1946
                                     applied, 1546 accepted,
                                     377 enrolled
SAT: required **ACT:** 23   **CEEB CODE:** 4656
Application Deadline: open   **COMPETITIVE**

Regis University, founded in 1877, is a private, Roman Catholic liberal arts institution operated by the Society of Jesus, the Jesuits. The figures in the above capsule and in this profile are approximate. There are 3 undergraduate schools. In addition to regional accreditation, Regis has baccalaureate program accreditation with CAHEA, NCATE, and NLN. The 90-acre campus is in a suburban area in north Denver. Including any residence halls, there are 16 buildings. **STUDENT LIFE:** 58% of undergraduates are from Colorado. Others are from 45 states, 6 foreign countries, and Canada. 55% are from public schools. 75% are White; 16% Hispanic. 43% are Catholic; 11% Protestant. **Male To Female Ratio:** 1.7:1. The average age of freshmen is 18; all undergraduates, 21. 20% do not continue beyond their first year; 65% remain to graduate. **Housing:** 680 students can be accommodated in college housing, which includes coed dorms and on-campus apartments. In addition, there are honors houses and special-interest houses. On-campus housing is guaranteed for all 4 years. 60% of students live on campus; of those, 80% remain on campus on weekends. All students may keep cars.

FACULTY/CLASSROOMS: 52% of faculty are male; 48% are female.

All teach and do research. No introductory courses are taught by graduate students. The average class size in an introductory lecture is 26 and in a laboratory is 16.

PROGRAMS OF STUDY: Regis confers B.A., B.S. and B.S.N. degrees. Master's and doctoral degrees are also awarded. Bachelor's degrees are awarded in AGRICULTURE (environmental studies), BIOLOGICAL SCIENCE (biochemistry, biology/biological science, and neurosciences), BUSINESS (accounting, business administration and management, business economics, international business management, and marketing/retailing/merchandising), COMMUNICATIONS AND THE ARTS (communications, English, French, music, Spanish, and visual and performing arts), COMPUTER AND PHYSICAL SCIENCE (chemistry, computer science, and mathematics), EDUCATION (education), ENGINEERING AND ENVIRONMENTAL DESIGN (preengineering), HEALTH PROFESSIONS (nursing, pharmacy, physical therapy, and premedicine), SOCIAL SCIENCE (economics, history, philosophy, political science/government, prelaw, psychology, religion, sociology, and women's studies). Business has the largest enrollment.

ACTIVITIES: There are no fraternities or sororities. There are 54 groups on campus, including art, cheerleading, chess, choir, chorus, dance, debate, environmental, ethnic, forensics, gay, honors, international, jazz band, leadership, literary magazine, musical theater, newspaper, orchestra, photography, political, professional, radio and TV, religious, social, social service, student government, and yearbook. Popular campus events include Mistletoe Madness, Ranger Week and Hall Olympics. **Sports:** There are 5 intercollegiate sports for men and 7 for women, and 8 intramural sports for men and 7 for women. Facilities include a 2800-seat gym, a pool, and playing fields. **Graduates:** From July 1, 2013 to June 30, 2014, 279 bachelor's degrees were awarded. The most popular majors were business administration, English, and biology. In an average class, 47% graduate in 4 years or less, 62% graduate in 5 years or less, and 65% graduate in 6 years or less.

SERVICES: Counseling and information services are available, as is tutoring in every subject. There is a reader service for the blind. **Library/Resources:** The library contains 425,000 volumes, 140,000 microform items, 110,000 audio/video tapes/CDs/DVDs, and subscribes to 4,000 periodicals including electronic. Computerized library services include interlibrary loans, database searching, Internet access, and Wi-Fi capability. Special learning facilities include an art gallery, radio station, nursing labs, physical therapy labs, cadaver lab, music labs, classrooms in residence halls. **Physically Challenged Students:** 80% of the campus is accessible. Facilities include wheelchair ramps, elevators, special parking, specially equipped restrooms, special class scheduling, lowered drinking fountains, and lowered telephones. **Special:** Cross-registration is possible with Denver University and Metropolitan State. Internships, study abroad, and work-study programs are available. The college offers B.A.-B.S. degrees, dual majors, student-designed majors, a 3-2 engineering degree with Washington University, and pass/fail options. An accelerated degree program in nursing is also offered. There are 3 national honor societies and a freshman honors program. **Visiting:** There are guides for informal visits, visitors may sit in on classes, and stay overnight. To schedule a visit, contact the Admissions Office. **Campus Safety and Security:** Measures include 24-hour foot and vehicle patrol, emergency notification system, self-defense education, and security escort services. There are shuttle buses, emergency telephones, lighted pathways/sidewalks, and controlled access to dorms/residences.

REQUIREMENTS: The SAT or ACT is required. Applicants should be graduates of an accredited secondary school. The GED is accepted. Students should have completed 16 high school academic credits, including 4 years of English, 3 each of math, science, and history, 2 of a foreign language, and 1 to 2 of social studies. A recommendation from the high school counselor and an essay are required. An interview is recommended. A GPA of 2.3 is required. AP and CLEP credits are accepted. Important factors in the admissions decision are recommendations by school officials, leadership record, and extracurricular activities record. Students must complete 128 credit hours with a minimum GPA of 2.0. Required courses include 58 credit hours in the core curriculum, of which 12 are seminars, 7 to 8 are math and natural science, 6 are in literature/humanities, social science, religious studies, and philosophy, and 3 each are in economics, communication arts, and fine arts. **Procedure:** Freshmen are admitted fall and spring. Entrance exams should be taken in the fall. There are deferred admissions and rolling admissions plans. Application deadlines are open. Application fee is $40. Notification is sent on a rolling basis. Applications are accepted online. **Transfer Students:** 81 transfer students enrolled in 2013-2014. Applicants must have a GPA of 2.5. All previous college work is considered. The college reviews each applicant individually. 30 of 128 credits required for the bachelor's degree must be completed at Regis. **International Students:** The school actively recruits these students. They must take the TOEFL, MELAB, or the ELS.

ADMISSIONS: 79% of the 2014-2015 applicants were accepted. The SAT scores for the 2014-2015 freshman class were: Critical Reading--32% below 500, 42% between 500 and 599, 22% between 600 and 699, and 4% between 700 and 800; Math--31% below 500, 40% between 500 and 599, 25% between 600 and 699, and 4% between 700 and 800. The ACT scores were 23% below 21, 27% between 21 and 23, 26% between 24 and 26, 12% between 27 and 28, and 12% above 28. 48% of the current freshmen were in the top fifth of their class; 74% were in the top two fifths. 30 freshmen graduated first in their class. **Admissions Contact:** Director of Admissions E-Mail: *regisadm@regis.edu* Web: *www.regis.edu*

FINANCIAL AID: In 2014-2015, 90% of all full-time freshmen and 90% of continuing full-time students received some form of financial aid. 63% of all full-time freshmen and 65% of continuing full-time students received need-based aid. The FAFSA and the college's own financial statement are required. Check with the school for current application deadlines.

ROCKY MOUNTAIN COLLEGE OF ART AND DESIGN (*The complete profile is made available exclusively on our website, www. barronspac.com*)

UNITED STATES AIR FORCE ACADEMY   D-3
www.academyadmissions.com

Colorado Springs, CO 80840

	(719) 333-2520
	(800) 443-9266
Fax: (719) 333-3012	Email: almattson@verizon.net
Full-time: 3635 men, 835 women	Faculty: n/av
Part-time: n/av	Ph.D.s: 49%
Graduate: n/av	Student/Faculty: n/av
Year: semesters, summer session	Tuition: see profile
Room & Board: see profile	Freshman Class: n/av
SAT or ACT: required	CEEB CODE: 4830
Application Deadline: n/av	**MOST COMPETITIVE**

The United States Air Force Academy, was founded in 1954 and is a public institution. Graduates receive the B.S. degree and a second lieutenant's commission in the regular Air Force. All graduates are obligated to serve at least 5 years of active duty military service. Tuition, room, board, medical, and dental expenses are paid by the U.S. government. Each cadet receives a monthly salary from which to pay for uniforms, supplies, and personal expenses. Entering freshmen are required to deposit $2,500 to defray the initial costs of uniforms and personal expenses incurred upon entry. Students who are unable to submit the full deposit will receive a reduced monthly cash allotment until prescribed levels are reached. The figures in the above capsule and in this profile are approximate. In addition to regional accreditation, USAFA has baccalaureate program accreditation with ABET and CSAB. The 18000-acre campus is in a suburban area 70 miles south of downtown Denver and 8 miles north of downtown Colorado Springs. Including any residence halls, there are 13 buildings.

STUDENT LIFE: 95% of undergraduates are from out of state, mostly the South. Students are from 30 foreign countries. 77% are White. 58% are Protestant; 30% Catholic. **Male To Female Ratio:** 0.2:1. The average age of freshmen is 18; all undergraduates, 20. 15% do not continue beyond their first year; 85% remain to graduate. **Housing:** 4550 students can be accommodated in college housing, which includes coed dorms. On-campus housing is guaranteed for all 4 years. Alcohol is not permitted. Upperclassmen may keep cars.

FACULTY/CLASSROOMS: 85% of faculty are male; 15% are female. All teach undergraduates, and 10% do research. No introductory courses are taught by graduate students. The average class size in an introductory lecture is 17; in a laboratory is 17; and in a regular course is 17.

PROGRAMS OF STUDY: USAFA confers B.S. degrees. Bachelor's degrees are awarded in BIOLOGICAL SCIENCE (biology/biological science), BUSINESS (management science and operations research), COMMUNICATIONS AND THE ARTS (English), COMPUTER AND PHYSICAL SCIENCE (atmospheric sciences and meteorology, chemistry, computer science, mathematics, physics, and science), ENGINEERING AND ENVIRONMENTAL DESIGN (aeronautical engineering, aerospace studies, civil engineering, computer engineering, electrical/electronics engineering, engineering, engineering and applied science, engineering mechanics, environmental engineering, mechanical engineering, and military science), SOCIAL SCIENCE (behavioral science, economics, geography, history, humanities, international studies, law, political science/government, psychology, and social science). Engineering and basic sciences are the strongest academically. Engineering, management, and social sciences have the largest enrollments.

ACTIVITIES: There are no fraternities or sororities. There are 87 groups on campus, including show choir, band, chamber music, cheerleading, chess, choir, chorale, chorus, computers, drama, drill team, drum and bugle corps, ethnic, film, forensics, honors, marching band, musical theater, pep band, photography, professional, radio and TV, religious, social, social service, and student government. Popular campus events include Acceptance Parade and Christmas events. **Sports:** There are 17 intercollegiate sports for men and 10 for women, and 14 intramural sports for men and 13 for women. Facilities include a 47,000-seat stadium, a cadet gym, a field house, 143 acres of athletic facilities and recreational areas, 3 basketball gyms, 4 indoor tennis courts, an Olympic-size swimming pool, a water polo pool, 3 squash and 19 racquetball/handball courts, 3 weight-training rooms, and 2 18-hole golf courses. **Graduates:** From July 1, 2013 to June 30, 2014, 986 bachelor's degrees were awarded. The most popular majors were social sciences (36%), engineering (35%), and basic sciences (15%). In an average class, 71% graduate in 4 years or less and 77% graduate in 5 years or less. Of the 2013 graduating class, 3% were enrolled in graduate school within 6 months of graduation, and 97% were employed.

SERVICES: Counseling and information services are available, as is tutoring in every subject. There is remedial math, reading, and writing. **Library/Resources:** The 2 libraries contain 551,476 volumes, 729,880 microform items, 3,643 audio/video tapes/CDs/DVDs, and subscribe to 36,252 periodicals including electronic. Computerized library services include interlibrary loans, database searching, Internet access, and Wi-Fi capability. Special learning facilities include an art gallery, planetarium, radio station, TV station, a field engineering and readiness lab, and an aeronautics lab/aeronautical research center. **Physically Challenged Students:** All of the campus is accessible. Facilities include wheelchair ramps, elevators, special parking, specially equipped restrooms, and lowered drinking fountains. **Special:** All cadets receive orientation flights in Air Force aircraft and take aviation science courses. A semester exchange program is available with the French Air Force Academy and U.S. Army, Naval, and Coast Guard academies. Freshman classes start in June, and basic cadet training must be completed before academics begin in August. Work-study programs are available, and dual majors are possible in all areas. There is an interdisciplinary space operations major. There are 2 national honor societies and a freshman honors program. **Visiting:** There are regularly scheduled orientations for prospective students, consisting of a 2-day orientation held in March and April. Students are given briefings by the superintendent, the commandant of cadets, the dean of cadets, and the director of athletics. Students stay overnight in the dormitories and shadow their escort cadets the second day, attending classes, training, and meals. There is also a daily tour. There are guides for informal visits. To schedule a visit, contact the Director of Admissions. **Campus Safety and Security:** Measures include 24-hour foot and vehicle patrol, self-defense education, and security escort services. There are emergency telephones and lighted pathways/sidewalks.

REQUIREMENTS: The SAT or ACT is required. Candidates must be

U.S. citizens between 17 and 22 years of age, unmarried and with no dependents, and nominated from a legal source. Students should have completed 4 years each of English, math, and lab sciences and 2 years each of social sciences and foreign languages. A computer course is recommended. A personal interview is required, as is an essay and a drug and alcohol abuse certificate. A GPA of 2.0 is required. AP credits are accepted. Important factors in the admissions decision are advanced placement or honors courses, leadership record, and personality/intangible qualities. Cadets must complete the requirements for the core curriculum and for an academic major. They must be proficient in phys ed and military training and demonstrate an aptitude for commissioned service and leadership. A total of 145 to 161 semester hours are required, with a minimum GPA of 2.0, to graduate. The required curriculum includes 9 hours of military arts and sciences, 6 hours of phys ed, and 1 hour of aviation. **Procedure:** Freshmen are admitted summer. Entrance exams should be taken in the spring of the junior year. Check with the school for current application deadlines. Applications are accepted on-line. **Transfer Students:** All students must enter as freshmen and attend 4 years. 145 of 145 credits required for the bachelor's degree must be completed at USAFA. **International Students:** There are 52 international students enrolled. They must also take the SAT or ACT.

ADMISSIONS: 45 freshmen graduated first in their class. **Admissions Contact:** Associate Director, Admissions Web: *www.academyadmissions.com*

FINANCIAL AID: Check with the school for current application deadlines.

UNIVERSITY OF COLORADO SYSTEM

The University of Colorado System, established in 1876, is a private system in Colorado. It is governed by a board of regents whose chief administrator is the president. The primary goal of the system is comprehensive research. The main priorities are research, teaching, and public service. The total student enrollment for all four campuses is usually about 45,000 with 4750 faculty members. Profiles of the 4-year campuses are included in this section.

UNIVERSITY OF COLORADO AT COLORADO SPRINGS www.uccs.edu	D-3
Colorado Springs, CO 80918	(719) 255-3317 (800) 990-8227 Email: ugapp@uccs.edu
Full-time: 1900 men, 3500 women	Faculty: IIA, -$
Part-time: 550 men, 800 women	Ph.D.s: 64%
Graduate: 630 men, 900 women	Student/Faculty: n/av
Year: semesters, summer session	Tuition: $6000 ($17,500)
Room & Board: $9000	Freshman Class: n/av
SAT or ACT: required	CEEB CODE: 4874
Application Deadline: n/av	VERY COMPETITIVE

The University of Colorado at Colorado Springs, established in 1965, is a public institution, with programs in liberal arts, business, engineering, education, and nursing. The figures in the above capsule and in this profile are approximate. There are 4 undergraduate schools and 5 graduate schools. In addition to regional accreditation, UCCS has baccalaureate program accreditation with AACSB, ABET, CSAB, NCATE, and NLN. The 504-acre campus is in a small town 70 miles south of Denver. Including any residence halls, there are 24 buildings.

STUDENT LIFE: 92% of undergraduates are from Colorado. Others are from 48 states, 35 foreign countries, and Canada. 76% are White. The average age of freshmen is 18; all undergraduates, 28. 35% do not continue beyond their first year; 40% remain to graduate. **Housing:** 900 students can be accommodated in college housing, which includes single-sex and coed dorms and on-campus apartments. On-campus housing is available on a first-come and first-served basis. 88% of students commute. All students may keep cars.

FACULTY/CLASSROOMS: 51% of faculty are male; 49% are female. 93% teach undergraduates, 80% do research, and 80% do both.

Graduate students teach 1% of introductory courses. The average class size in an introductory lecture is 32; in a laboratory is 45; and in a regular course is 22.

PROGRAMS OF STUDY: UCCS confers B.A., and B.S. degrees. Master's and doctoral degrees are also awarded. Bachelor's degrees are awarded in BIOLOGICAL SCIENCE (biology/biological science), BUSINESS (business administration and management), COMMUNICATIONS AND THE ARTS (communications, English, fine arts, and Spanish), COMPUTER AND PHYSICAL SCIENCE (chemistry, computer science, mathematics, and physics), ENGINEERING AND ENVIRONMENTAL DESIGN (electrical/electronics engineering), HEALTH PROFESSIONS (health care administration and nursing), SOCIAL SCIENCE (anthropology, economics, geography, history, philosophy, political science/government, psychology, and sociology). Business, engineering, and psychology are the strongest academically.

ACTIVITIES: 1% of men and 1 of women belong to 1 national fraternity; 1% of women belong to 1 local sororities. There are 50 groups on campus, including art, choir, computers, dance, drama, ethnic, film, gay, honors, international, literary magazine, newspaper, photography, political, professional, radio and TV, religious, social, and student government. Popular campus events include Winter Holiday Festival, and Comedy Night. **Sports:** There are 5 intercollegiate sports for men and 5 for women, and 13 intramural sports for men and 12 for women. Facilities include a gym, softball and soccer fields, a multipurpose field, tennis and volleyball courts, and a fitness center.

SERVICES: Counseling and information services are available, as is tutoring in most subjects. There is a reader service for the blind. **Library/Resources:** The library contains 669,757 volumes, 432,872 microform items, 5,979 audio/video tapes/CDs/DVDs, and subscribes to 2,247 periodicals including electronic. Computerized library services include interlibrary loans, database searching, and Internet access. Special learning facilities include an art gallery, radio station, a center for excellence in oral communication, a math learning center, a science learning center, a writing center, and a language technology center. **Physically Challenged Students:** 95% of the campus is accessible. Facilities include wheelchair ramps, elevators, special parking, specially equipped restrooms, lowered drinking fountains, and lowered telephones. **Special:** The university offers work-study, dual majors, nondegree study, and pass/fail options. There are 3 national honor societies including a Phi Beta Kappa chapter. **Visiting:** There are regularly scheduled orientations for prospective students. There are guides for informal visits and visitors may sit in on classes. To schedule a visit, contact the Marketing Office at visitcu@uccs.edu. **Campus Safety and Security:** Measures include 24-hour foot and vehicle patrol, self-defense education, and security escort services. There are shuttle buses, emergency telephones, and lighted pathways/sidewalks.

REQUIREMENTS: The SAT or ACT is required. Applicants must be graduates of an accredited secondary school. The GED is accepted. Secondary school courses must include 15 high school credits, including 4 years of English, 3 years each of math and science, 2 years each of foreign language and social studies, and 1 academic elective. AP and CLEP credits are accepted. Important factors in the admissions decision are advanced placement or honors courses, evidence of special talent, and recommendations by school officials. To graduate, students must complete 124 credit hours, with at least 30 of them in the major, with a minimum GPA of 2.0. All students must take English and a computer literacy course. Other requirements vary with the program. **Procedure:** Freshmen are admitted to all sessions. Entrance exams should be taken during the senior year. There are deferred admissions and rolling admissions plans. Check with the school for current application deadlines. Applications are accepted on-line. **Transfer Students:** Applicants must have a minimum GPA of 2.5 and a minimum of 12 credit hours earned. 30 of 124 credits required for the bachelor's degree must be completed at UCCS. **International Students:** They must take the TOEFL. They must also take the SAT or ACT.

ADMISSIONS: ugapp@uccs.edu

FINANCIAL AID: The FAFSA is required. Check with the school for current application deadlines.

UNIVERSITY OF COLORADO BOULDER C-2
www.colorado.edu

Boulder, CO 80309 (303) 492-6301

Fax: (303) 492-7115
Full-time: 12960 men, 10799 women
Part-time: 1016 men, 686 women
Graduate: 2096 men, 2217 women
Year: semesters, summer session
Room & Board: $12,258

Email: apply@colorado.edu
Faculty: 1382; I, av$
Ph.D.s: 90%
Student/Faculty: 17 to 1
Tuition: $10,347 ($32,115)
Freshman Class: 22477 applied, 19710 accepted, 5846 enrolled

SAT CR/M: 570/600 ACT: 27
Application Deadline: January 15

CEEB CODE: 4841
VERY COMPETITIVE+

The University of Colorado Boulder, established in 1876, is a public institution offering undergraduate and graduate programs in arts and sciences, business, engineering, environmental design, music, education, journalism and mass communication, and law. Figures in the above capsule and in this profile are approximate. There are 5 undergraduate schools and 3 graduate schools. In addition to regional accreditation, CU-Boulder has baccalaureate program accreditation with AACSB, ABET, ACEJMC, NASM, and NCATE. The 600-acre campus is in a suburban area 30 miles northwest of Denver. Including any residence halls, there are 200 buildings.

STUDENT LIFE: 63% of undergraduates are from Colorado. Others are from 50 states, 100 foreign countries, and Canada. 91% are from public schools. 74% are White. **Male To Female Ratio:** 0.9:1. The average age of freshmen is 18; all undergraduates, 21. 15% do not continue beyond their first year; 70% remain to graduate. **Housing:** 7392 students can be accommodated in college housing, which includes coed dorms, on-campus apartments, off-campus apartments, and married student housing. In addition, there are honors houses, special-interest houses, and 14 residential academic programs that include housing in the dorms. On-campus housing is guaranteed for the freshman year only, and is available on a first-come, first-served basis. 72% of students commute. All students may keep cars.

FACULTY/CLASSROOMS: 62% of faculty are male; 38% are female. 89% teach undergraduates, and all do research. Graduate students teach 11% of introductory courses. The average class size in an introductory lecture is 37; in a laboratory is 20; and in a regular course is 23.

PROGRAMS OF STUDY: CU-Boulder confers B.A., B.Envd., B.F.A., B.A.Mus., B.Mus., B.Mus.Ed., B.S., and I.B.A. degrees. Master's and doctoral degrees are also awarded. Bachelor's degrees are awarded in BIOLOGICAL SCIENCE (biochemistry, ecology, evolutionary biology, molecular biology, neurosciences, and physiology), BUSINESS (accounting, business administration and management, finance, management science, and marketing management), COMMUNICATIONS AND THE ARTS (advertising, art history, art history and appreciation, broadcasting, Chinese, classics, communications, creative writing, dance, English, film arts, fine arts, French, Italian, Japanese, journalism, linguistics, music, music performance, Russian languages and literature, Spanish, studio art, and theatre arts), COMPUTER AND PHYSICAL SCIENCE (applied mathematics, astronomy, chemistry, computer science, geology, mathematics, and physics), EDUCATION (music education), ENGINEERING AND ENVIRONMENTAL DESIGN (aeronautical engineering, architectural engineering, bioengineering, chemical engineering, civil engineering, computer engineering, electrical/electronics engineering, engineering physics, environmental design, environmental engineering, environmental science, and mechanical engineering), HEALTH PROFESSIONS (speech pathology/audiology), SOCIAL SCIENCE (anthropology, Asian/Oriental studies, asian studies, economics, ethnic studies, geography, German area studies, history, humanities, international relations, Judaic studies, philosophy, political science/government, psychology, religious studies, sociology, and women & gender studies). Psychology, integrative physiology, and communication have the largest enrollments.

ACTIVITIES: 11% of men belong to 21 national fraternities; 17% of women belong to 2 local and 14 national sororities. There are 400 groups on campus, including art, band, cheerleading, chess, choir, chorale, chorus, communications, computers, dance, debate, drama, drill team, environmental, ethnic, film, gay, honors, international, jazz band, literary magazine, marching band, musical theater, newspaper, opera, orchestra, pep band, photography, political, professional, radio and TV, religious, social, social service, student government, and symphony. Popular campus events include Conference on World Affairs, Colorado Shakespeare Festival, Holiday Festival (orchestra, choir, & other musical group performances), Football Games, International Festival, and Global Jam. **Sports:** There are 6 intercollegiate sports for men and 9 for women, and 13 intramural sports for men and 13 for women. Facilities include CU-Boulder has a 53,500-seat stadium, an 8,700-seat events center, 4 outdoor lighted basketball courts, and five outdoor recreational fields to accommodate rugby, ultimate frisbee, and soccer. The student recreation center features include expanded weight training and cardio space; fitness and wellness amenities that include a wellness suite, massage studio, private area for health screenings, and five fitness studios including mind body, indoor cycling, and functional training; a new ice rink with cutting edge 200X85 sheet and stadium seating; three outdoor tennis courts on the roof of the ice rink (in addition to five other courts on campus); a buffalo-shaped, 2-yard, 2-lane outdoor leisure pool; state-of-the-art climbing wall; and new locker rooms with dry heat saunas. Rec center facilities also include an 8-lane swimming pool; diving pool; two large general purpose gyms; three indoor basketball courts; a 1/10th-mile indoor running track; courts for handball, racquetball, and squash; and aerobics studio. Additionally, four program areas are offered   instruction, outdoor program, intramurals, and club sports that provide organized sports and classes.
Graduates: From July 1, 2013 to June 30, 2014, 5729 bachelor's degrees were awarded. The most popular majors were psychology (11%), integrative physiology (5%), and communcation (4%). 614 companies recruited on campus in 2013-2014. In an average class, 44% graduate in 4 years or less, 66% graduate in 5 years or less, and 70% graduate in 6 years or less. Of the 2013 graduating class, 20% were enrolled in graduate school within 6 months of graduation, and 74% were employed.

SERVICES: Counseling and information services are available, as is tutoring in most subjects. There is a reader service for the blind, and remedial writing. Academic Excellence Program/Student Support Services offers a number of services supportive of low-income and first-generation college students and individuals with disabilities. Services include academic skill building, tutoring, technology and computer skill building, and study groups. **Library/Resources:** The 7 libraries contain 6.5 million volumes, 9.1 million microform items, 95,046 audio/video tapes/CDs/DVDs. Computerized library services include interlibrary loans, database searching, Internet access, and Wi-Fi capability. Special learning facilities include an art gallery, natural history museum, planetarium, radio station, an interactive foreign language video center, a mountain research station, integrated teaching and learning lab in engineering, and multidisciplinary information technology center. **Physically Challenged Students:** 85% of the campus is accessible. Facilities include wheelchair ramps, elevators, special parking, specially equipped restrooms, special class scheduling, lowered drinking fountains, lowered telephones, special housing. Power-assisted doors, assisted classroom listening devices, TTY phone support systems, and an assistive technology lab to enable students with disabilities to access computer systems, information resources, and online services. **Special:** Fourteen residential programs for freshmen and sophomores offer a small liberal arts college atmosphere while taking advantage of the resources of a major university. Student-designed and dual majors, internships, 5-year B.A.-M.A. degrees, and cooperative programs in engineering and computer science are available. Study abroad in 65 countries, work-study programs in federal labs, internships, and cross-registration with other University of Colorado campuses are also offered. There are 27 national honor societies, including Phi Beta Kappa, a freshman honors program, and 60 departmental honors programs. **Visiting:** There are regularly scheduled orientations for prospective students. Visit includes a 1-hour information session hosted by an admission representative, followed by a student-led, 90-minute walking tour of campus. CU-Boulder also offers all-day visit programs. There are guides for informal visits and visitors may sit in on classes. To schedule a visit, contact the Admissions Office. **Campus Safety and Security:** Measures include 24-hour foot and vehicle patrol, emergency notification system, self-defense education, and security escort services. There are shuttle buses, emergency telephones, lighted pathways/sidewalks, controlled access to dorms/residences. Campus police are academy-trained and commissioned officers of the Boulder police force.

REQUIREMENTS: The SAT or ACT is required. Applicants must send an official score report for either the SAT or the ACT and either an official high school transcript or an official copy of certificate of high school equivalency and official GED scores. They are expected to have completed 17 credits of high school work as identified by the CU-Boulder Minimum Academic Preparation Standards. Required application materials include 2 short-answer essay questions and one academic letter of recommendation. Interviews are not used in the decision-making process. Auditions are required for consideration to the College of Music. Portfolios are discouraged. A GPA of 2.0 is required. AP and CLEP credits are accepted. Undergraduate degree requirements (e.g., number of credits overall and in the major, minimum GPA, core curriculum requirements) vary by degree program (e.g., B.A., B.F.A) and by undergraduate college and program. **Procedure:** Freshmen are admitted fall, spring, and summer. Entrance exams should be taken no later than December of the senior year. There are early admissions and deferred admissions plans. Early decision applications should be filed by November 15; regular applications, by January 15 for fall entry; October 1 for spring entry; and January 15 for summer entry, along with a $50 fee. Notification of early decision is sent February 1; regular decision, April 1. 469 applicants were on the 2014 waiting list; 0 were admitted. Applications are accepted online. **Transfer Students:** 1219 transfer students enrolled in 2013-2014. Transfer applicants must submit official high school and college transcripts. Students who have completed fewer than 24 semester hours of transferable college work must also submit SAT or ACT results. Required application materials include 2 short-answer essay questions. Starting with Spring 2014 applications, one academic letter of recommendation will be required. College of Music applicants must also complete a College of Music application after their admission application has been submitted, provide a letter of reference, and schedule an audition. 45 of 120 credits required for the bachelor's degree must be completed at CU-Boulder. **International Students:** There are 918 international students enrolled. The school actively recruits these students.

ADMISSIONS: 88% of the 2014-2015 applicants were accepted. The SAT scores for the 2014-2015 freshman class were: Critical Reading--16% below 500, 44% between 500 and 599, 32% between 600 and 699, and 9% between 700 and 800; Math--11% below 500, 38% between 500 and 599, 39% between 600 and 699, and 12% between 700 and 800. The ACT scores were 4% below 21, 16% between 21 and 23, 29% between 24 and 26, 19% between 27 and 28, and 32% above 28. 46% of the current freshmen were in the top fifth of their class; 77% were in the top two fifths. There were 13 National Merit finalists. 123 freshmen graduated first in their class. **Admissions Contact:** Director of Admissions. E-Mail: *apply@colorado.edu* Web: *www.colorado.edu*

FINANCIAL AID: In 2014-2015, 72% of all full-time freshmen and 58% of continuing full-time students received some form of financial aid. 44% of all full-time freshmen and 36% of continuing full-time students received need-based aid. The average freshman award was $22,860. Need-based scholarships or need-based grants averaged $14,303 ($61,290 maximum); need-based self-help aid (loans and jobs) averaged $9,972 ($33,600 maximum); non-need-based athletic scholarships averaged $42,120 ($99,578 maximum); and other non-need-based awards and non-need-based scholarships averaged $6,879 ($50,500 maximum). 18% of undergraduate students work part-time. Average annual earnings from campus work are $4410. The average financial indebtedness of the 2014 graduate was $24,880. The FAFSA, tax returns are required. The priority date for freshman financial aid applications for fall entry is March 1.

UNIVERSITY OF COLORADO DENVER   **C-2**
www.ucdenver.edu

Denver, CO 80217   (303) 556-3287

Fax: (303) 556-4838	Email: admissions@cudenver.edu
Full-time: 3625 men, 4116 women	**Faculty:** I, -$
Part-time: 2436 men, 2926 women	**Ph.D.s:** 72%
Graduate: 3671 men, 5622 women	**Student/Faculty:** 17 to 1
Year: semesters, summer session	**Tuition:** $7494 ($21,006)
Room & Board: $10,410	**Freshman Class:** 3075 applied, 2333 accepted, 991 enrolled
SAT CR/M: 540/540 **ACT:** 23	**CEEB CODE:** 4875
Application Deadline: July 22	**COMPETITIVE**

The University of Colorado at Denver, formerly known as the University of Colorado at Denver and Health Sciences Center, is a public institution that was established in 1912. The University has two campuses. The downtown Denver campus is a commuter school with programs in the liberal arts and sciences, business, engineering and applied sciences, music, architecture and planning, and education. The Anschutz Medical Campus is a commuter school with programs in medicine, nursing, pharmacy, and dentistry. There are 5 undergraduate schools and 7 graduate schools. In addition to regional accreditation, CU Denver has baccalaureate program accreditation with AACSB, ABET, NAAB, NASM, and NCATE. The 151-acre campus is in an urban area in downtown Denver.

STUDENT LIFE: 93% of undergraduates are from Colorado. Others are from 50 states, 67 foreign countries, and Canada. 52% are White; 15% Hispanic. The average age of freshmen is 18; all undergraduates, 24. 29% do not continue beyond their first year; 45% remain to graduate. **Housing:** 685 students can be accommodated in college housing, which includes coed dorms and off-campus apartments. On-campus housing is guaranteed for the freshman year only. 95% of students commute. Alcohol is not permitted. All students may keep cars.

FACULTY/CLASSROOMS: 48% of faculty are male; 52% are female. No introductory courses are taught by graduate students. The average class size in an introductory lecture is 27; in a laboratory is 20; and in a regular course is 27.

PROGRAMS OF STUDY: CU Denver confers B.A., B.S. and B.F.A degrees. Master's and doctoral degrees are also awarded. Bachelor's degrees are awarded in BIOLOGICAL SCIENCE (biology/biological science), BUSINESS (business administration and management), COMMUNICATIONS AND THE ARTS (communications, English, English writing, fine arts, French, music, Spanish, and visual and performing arts), COMPUTER AND PHYSICAL SCIENCE (chemistry, computer science, mathematics, and physics), EDUCATION (education), ENGINEERING AND ENVIRONMENTAL DESIGN (architecture, bioengineering, civil engineering, electrical/electronics engineering, and mechanical engineering), HEALTH PROFESSIONS (medical science, nursing, and public health), SOCIAL SCIENCE (anthropology, criminal justice, economics, ethnic studies, geography, history, interdisciplinary studies, international studies, philosophy, political science/government, psychology, and sociology). Business, nursing, and psychology are the strongest academically. Business administration, biology, and psychology have the largest enrollments.

ACTIVITIES: There are no fraternities or sororities. There are 228 groups on campus, including art, cheerleading, chorale, computers, dance, drama, environmental, ethnic, film, gay, honors, international, jazz band, men's hockey club, musical theater, newspaper, political, professional, radio and TV, religious, social, social service, and student government. Popular campus events include Fall Festival. **Sports:** There are 10 intramural sports for men and 12 for women. Facilities include a facility that includes a diving well, a weight room, squash, racquetball/handball, and tennis courts and a basketball half-court, a dance studio, 3 gym arenas, a fitness center and a green room, a 400-meter track, a football, rugby, and lacrosse field, softball fields, a baseball field, a soccer field, and a sand volleyball court. **Graduates:** From July 1, 2013 to June 30, 2014, 2184 bachelor's degrees were awarded. The most popular majors were business administration (16%), nursing (11%), and psychology (10%). In an average class, 18% graduate in 4 years or less, 39% graduate in 5 years or less, and 45% graduate in 6 years or less.

SERVICES: Counseling and information services are available, as is tutoring in most subjects. There is a reader service for the blind. There are ESL classes and study skills courses. **Library/Resources:** The library contains 683,089 volumes, 1.0 million microform items, 15,491 audio/video tapes/CDs/DVDs, and subscribes to 93,559 periodicals including electronic. Computerized library services include interlibrary loans, database searching, Internet access, and Wi-Fi capability. Special learning facilities include an art gallery, radio station, a writing center. **Physically Challenged Students:** All of the campus is accessible. Facilities include wheelchair ramps, elevators, special parking, specially equipped restrooms, special class scheduling, lowered drinking fountains, lowered telephones. **Special:** Students can cross-register with Metropolitan State College, Community College of Denver, and Red Rocks Community College. Concurrent enrollment with any University of Colorado campus is possible. Cooperative programs, 1-semester internships, study abroad in 12 countries, work-study programs, an accelerated degree program in liberal arts and arts and media, and B.A.-B.S. degrees are available. The university offers dual majors, a general studies degree, nondegree study, and pass/fail options. There are small individualized classes, peer advocates, and workshops. There are 10 national honor societies and a freshman honors program. **Visiting:** There are regularly scheduled orientations for prospective students, Student visits include a mini-lecture, campus tour, and financial aid and academic advising. There are guides for informal visits and visitors may sit in on classes. To schedule a visit, contact the Office of Admissions. **Campus Safety and Security:** Measures include 24-hour foot and vehicle patrol, emergency notification system, self-defense education, and security escort services. There are shuttle buses, emergency telephones, lighted pathways/sidewalks, crime prevention programs, and emergency response.

REQUIREMENTS: The SAT or ACT is required. Preference for admission is given to applicants who rank in the top 30% of their high school graduating class and present a composite score of 21 or higher on the ACT, or a combined score of 950 or higher on the SAT. CU Denver requires applicants to be in the upper 30% of their class. A GPA of 2.5 is required. AP and CLEP credits are accepted. Important factors in the admissions decision are advanced placement or honors courses, evidence of special talent, and extracurricular activities record. To graduate, students must complete 120 credit hours with a minimum GPA of 2.0. All students must complete the core curriculum courses in addition to the requirements for the major. **Procedure:** Freshmen are admitted fall, spring, and summer. Entrance exams should be taken in the junior or senior year of high school. There are deferred admissions and rolling admissions plans. Applications should be filed by July 22 for fall entry; December 1 for spring entry; and May 3 for summer entry, along with a $50 fee. Notification is sent on a rolling basis. Applications are accepted online. **Transfer Students:** 1531 transfer students enrolled in 2013-2014. Students transferring less than 30 approved college credits are required to submit standardized test scores and high school GPA and rank. Students transferring 30 approved credits or more from an accredited college only need to submit their current college transcript and proof of good-standing. 60 of 120 credits required for the bachelor's degree must be completed at CU Denver. **International Students:** There are 1017 international students enrolled. The school actively recruits these students. They must take the TOEFL with a minimum score of 537 on the paper-based TOEFL (PBT) or 75 on the Internet-based version (iBT). They must also take the SAT or ACT.

ADMISSIONS: 76% of the 2014-2015 applicants were accepted. The SAT scores for the 2014-2015 freshman class were: Critical Reading--26% below 500, 47% between 500 and 599, 21% between 600 and 699, and 6% between 700 and 800; Math--30% below 500, 40% between 500 and 599, 23% between 600 and 699, and 7% between 700 and 800. 47% of the current freshmen were in the top fifth of their class; 75% were in the top two fifths. **Admissions Contact:** Director of Admissions. E-Mail: *admissions@cudenver.edu* Web: *www.ucdenver.edu*

FINANCIAL AID: In 2014-2015, 60% of all full-time freshmen and 58% of continuing full-time students received some form of financial aid. 51% of all full-time freshmen and 45% of continuing full-time students received need-based aid. The average freshman award was $8,120. Need-based scholarships or need-based grants averaged $7,500; need-based self-help aid (loans and jobs) averaged $3,343; and other non-need-based awards and non-need-based scholarships averaged $3,125. The average financial indebtedness of the 2014 graduate was $19,480. The FAFSA, the college's own financial statement, and tax returns are required. The priority date for freshman financial aid applications for fall entry is April 1.

UNIVERSITY OF DENVER · C-2
www.du.edu

Denver, CO 80208 · (303) 871-2036

Fax: (303) 871-3301 · Email: admission@du.edu

Full-time: 2353 men, 2776 women · Faculty: 480; I, av$
Part-time: 146 men, 242 women · Ph.D.s: 90%
Graduate: 2628 men, 3633 women · Student/Faculty: 10 to 1
Year: quarters, summer session · Tuition: $40,707
Room & Board: $11,080 · Freshman Class: 13735 applied, 10539 accepted, 1399 enrolled

SAT CR/M/W: 610/610/580 ACT: 28 · CEEB CODE: 4852
Application Deadline: January 15 · VERY COMPETITIVE+

The University of Denver, established in 1864, is a private institution offering degrees in arts and sciences, fine arts, music, business, engineering, and education. Figures in the above capsule and in this profile are approximate. There are 8 undergraduate schools and 10 graduate schools. In addition to regional accreditation, DU has baccalaureate program accreditation with AACSB, ABET, NASAD, and NASM. The 125-acre campus is in an urban area 8 miles south of downtown Denver. Including any residence halls, there are 74 buildings.

STUDENT LIFE: 59% of undergraduates are from out of state, mostly the Mid-West. Students are from 50 states, 47 foreign countries, and Canada. 68% are White. **Male To Female Ratio:** 1.3:1. The average age of freshmen is 18; all undergraduates, 21. 14% do not continue beyond their first year; 78% remain to graduate. **Housing:** 2422 students can be accommodated in college housing, which includes single-sex and coed dorms, on-campus apartments, off-campus apartments, and married student housing. In addition, there are honors houses, special-interest houses, fraternity houses, sorority houses, 5 living and learning communities, a pioneer leadership program floor, and an honors floor. On-campus housing is guaranteed for the freshman year only and is available on a lottery system for upperclassmen. 55% of students commute. All students may keep cars.

FACULTY/CLASSROOMS: 53% of faculty are male; 47% are female. 71% teach undergraduates, 70% do research, and 53% do both. Graduate students teach 5% of introductory courses. The average class size in an introductory lecture is 23; in a laboratory is 18; and in a regular course is 19.

PROGRAMS OF STUDY: DU confers B.A., B.S., B.B.A., B.F.A., B.M., B.S.A.C.C., B.S.B.A., B.S.C.H., B.S.C.P.E., B.S.E.E. and B.S.M.E. degrees. Master's and doctoral degrees are also awarded. Bachelor's degrees are awarded in BIOLOGICAL SCIENCE (biochemistry, bioinformatics, biology/biological science, ecology, and molecular biology), BUSINESS (accounting, banking and finance, business administration and management, business economics, business statistics, finance, hospitality management services, international business management, marketing/retailing/merchandising, and real estate), COMMUNICATIONS AND THE ARTS (animation, art history, art, art/art studies, art history and appreciation, communication studies, dramatic arts, English, film arts, French, German, Italian, jazz, journalism, languages, media arts, music, music production/recording technology, music performance, Russian, Spanish, strategic communication, and theatre studies), COMPUTER AND PHYSICAL SCIENCE (chemistry, computer game design/development, computer science, digital arts/technology, environmental chemistry, information sciences and systems, mathematics, physics, science, and statistics), ENGINEERING AND ENVIRONMENTAL DESIGN (bioengineering, computer engineering, construction management, electrical and computer engineering, electrical/electronics engineering, environmental science, materials science, mechanical engineering, and Mechatronics Engineering), HEALTH PROFESSIONS (biology), SOCIAL SCIENCE (anthropology, Asian/American studies, cognitive science, criminology, economics, geography, history, interdisciplinary studies, international studies, Judaic studies, philosophy, political science/government, psychology, public affairs, religion, social science, sociology, and women's studies). Information technology studies, real estate and construction management, and accounting are the strongest academically. Management, biology, and general business have the largest enrollments.

ACTIVITIES: 24% of men belong to 9 national fraternities; 28% of women belong to 5 national sororities. There are 160 groups on campus, including art, band, cheerleading, chess, choir, chorale, chorus, communications, computers, dance, debate, drama, drum and bugle corps, environmental, ethnic, film, forensics, gay, honors, international, jazz band, literary magazine, musical theater, newspaper, opera, orchestra, pep band, photography, political, professional, radio and TV, religious, social, social service, student government, and symphony. Popular campus events include Winter Carnival, May Days, and Festival of Nations Celebration. **Sports:** There are 8 intercollegiate sports for men and 9 for women. Facilities include a sports and wellness center housing 2 ice arenas, a gym, a multipurpose field house, an Olympic-size swimming pool, a fitness center, racquetball courts, studios for yoga, dance, cycling, and karate, a 25-foot climbing wall, a health clinic, a soccer field, a lacrosse stadium, and a tennis pavilion. **Graduates:** From July 1, 2013 to June 30, 2014, 1223 bachelor's degrees were awarded. The most popular majors were finance (11%), international studies (7%), and international business (6%). 200 companies recruited on campus in 2013-2014. In an average class, 2% graduate in 3 years or less, 66% graduate in 4 years or less, 76% graduate in 5 years or less, and 78% graduate in 6 years or less.

SERVICES: Counseling and information services are available, as is tutoring in most subjects. There is a reader service for the blind. **Library/Resources:** The 2 libraries contain 2.3 million volumes, 1.1 million microform items, 24,425 audio/video tapes/CDs/DVDs, and subscribe to 282,209 periodicals including electronic. Computerized library services include interlibrary loans, database searching, Internet access, and Wi-Fi capability. Special learning facilities include an art gallery, radio station, a high-altitude lab, an observatory, and an elementary and early learning center. **Physically Challenged Students:** 85% of the campus is accessible. Facilities include wheelchair ramps, elevators, special parking, specially equipped restrooms, special class scheduling, lowered drinking fountains, lowered telephones, and special housing. **Special:** DU offers co-op programs, study abroad through more than 59 programs, internships across the country and internationally, a Washington quarter, work-study programs, accelerated degree programs, and dual majors. Non-degree study and pass/fail options are also available. There are 19 national honor societies, including Phi Beta Kappa, and a freshman honors program. **Visiting:** There are regularly scheduled orientations for prospective students, including tours and information sessions throughout the year, and 2 day-long open houses in the fall. Visitors may sit in on classes and stay overnight. To schedule a visit, contact the Office of Undergraduate Admission at admission@du.edu. **Campus Safety and Security:** Measures include 24-hour foot and vehicle patrol, emergency notification system, self-defense education, and security escort services. There are shuttle buses, emergency telephones, lighted pathways/sidewalks, controlled access to dorms/residences, and in-room safes.

REQUIREMENTS: The SAT or ACT is required. Applicants must be graduates of an accredited secondary school. The GED is accepted. DU recommends that applicants have 4 years in English, 3 to 4 in math, and 2 to 4 each in foreign language, social sciences, and natural sciences (2 with lab). An essay and a counselor recommendation are required, and a Hyde interview is strongly encouraged. AP and CLEP credits are accepted. Important factors in the admissions decision are advanced placement or honors courses, personality/intangible qualities, and evidence of special talent. For graduation, students must complete 183 to 194 quarter hours, including 40 to 135 in the major,

with a minimum GPA of 2.0. They must fulfill foundational requirements in the freshman and sophomore years, and with junior standing take core courses in communities and environments, self and identities, and change and continuity, and must complete a writing-intensive course. Distribution requirements include 12 quarter hours each of English, natural sciences, arts and humanities, and social sciences, 8 of math and computer science, and 4 of oral communication. **Procedure:** Freshmen are admitted to all sessions. Entrance exams should be taken by January of the senior year. There are early admissions and deferred admissions plans. Early decision applications should be filed by November 1; regular applications, by January 15 for fall entry; December 1 for winter entry; February 15 for spring entry; and May 1 for summer entry, along with a $60 fee. Notification of early decision is sent January 15; regular decision, March 15. 1659 applicants were on the 2014 waiting list; 108 were admitted. Applications are accepted online. **Transfer Students:** 182 transfer students enrolled in 2013-2014. Applicants must submit an official transcript from all colleges attended. Those students with fewer than 30 semester hours of college credit must submit a high school transcript and test scores. A minimum GPA of 2.0 is required, but a GPA of 3.0 is recommended. 45 of 183 credits required for the bachelor's degree must be completed at DU. **International Students:** There are 475 international students enrolled. The school actively recruits these students. They must take the TOEFL with a minimum score of 550 on the paper-based TOEFL (PBT) or 80 on the Internet-based version (iBT), or take the IELTS. They must also take the SAT or ACT.

ADMISSIONS: 77% of the 2014-2015 applicants were accepted. The SAT scores for the 2014-2015 freshman class were: Critical Reading--12% below 500, 34% between 500 and 599, 42% between 600 and 699, and 12% between 700 and 800; Math--5% below 500, 36% between 500 and 599, 48% between 600 and 699, and 11% between 700 and 800; Writing--15% below 500, 44% between 500 and 599, 35% between 600 and 699, and 6% between 700 and 800. The ACT scores were 2% below 21, 10% between 21 and 23, 26% between 24 and 26, 20% between 27 and 28, and 42% above 28. 70% of the current freshmen were in the top fifth of their class; 92% were in the top two fifths. 22 freshmen graduated first in their class. **Admissions Contact:** Office of Admission E-Mail: *admission@du.edu* Web: *www.du.edu*

FINANCIAL AID: In 2014-2015, 79% of all full-time freshmen and 81% of continuing full-time students received some form of financial aid. 44% of all full-time freshmen and 42% of continuing full-time students received need-based aid. The average freshman award was $32,229. Need-based scholarships or need-based grants averaged $27,121; need-based self-help aid (loans and jobs) averaged $7,368; non-need-based athletic scholarships averaged $33,742; and other non-need-based awards and non-need-based scholarships averaged $14,880. Average annual earnings from campus work are $3000. The average financial indebtedness of the 2014 graduate was $22,106. DU is a member of CSS. The CSS/Profile and FAFSA are required. The deadline for filing freshman financial aid applications for fall entry is March 1.

UNIVERSITY OF NORTHERN COLORADO   D-1
www.unco.edu

Greeley, CO 80639	(970) 351-2881
	(888) 700-4UNC
Fax: (970) 351-2984	Email: admissions.help@unco.edu
Full-time: 3584 men, 5715 women	Faculty: 428; I, --$
Part-time: 321 men, 611 women	Ph.D.s: n/av
Graduate: 609 men, 1759 women	Student/Faculty: 22 to 1
Year: semesters, summer session	Tuition: $8896 ($17,745)
Room & Board: $9550	Freshman Class: 8092 applied, 5939 accepted, 2274 enrolled
SAT CR/M/W: 531/533/516 ACT: 23	CEEB CODE: 4074
Application Deadline: August 1	COMPETITIVE

The University of Northern Colorado, founded in 1890, is a state-supported public institution offering undergraduate and graduate programs in liberal arts and sciences, business, education, health and human sciences, and performing and visual arts. Figures in the above capsule and in this profile are approximate. There are 6 undergraduate schools and 1 graduate school. In addition to regional accreditation, UNC has baccalaureate program accreditation with AACSB, ADA, NASM, NCATE, and NLN. The 260-acre campus is in a suburban area 50 miles north of Denver. Including any residence halls, there are 86 buildings.

STUDENT LIFE: 88% of undergraduates are from Colorado. Others are from 50 states, 23 foreign countries, and Canada. 55% are White; 13% Hispanic. The average age of freshmen is 18; all undergraduates, 22. **Housing:** 3176 students can be accommodated in college housing, which includes single-sex and coed dorms, on-campus apartments, married student housing, off-campus houses, graduate women's houses, and special-interest floors. On-campus housing is guaranteed for the freshman year only, is available on a first-come, first-served basis, and is available on a lottery system for upperclassmen. 68% of students commute. All students may keep cars.

FACULTY/CLASSROOMS: 45% of faculty are male; 55% are female. All teach and do research. Graduate students teach 17% of introductory courses. The average class size in an introductory lecture is 46; in a laboratory is 27; and in a regular course is 28.

PROGRAMS OF STUDY: UNC confers B.A., B.M., B.M.E. and B.S. degrees. Master's and doctoral degrees are also awarded. Bachelor's degrees are awarded in AGRICULTURE (natural resource management), BIOLOGICAL SCIENCE (biology/biological science and nutrition), BUSINESS (business administration and management, management science, marketing/retailing/merchandising, and recreation and leisure services), COMMUNICATIONS AND THE ARTS (American Sign Language, art, communications, English, fine arts, French, German, graphic design, journalism, music, musical theater, Spanish, telecommunications, and visual and performing arts), COMPUTER AND PHYSICAL SCIENCE (chemistry, earth science, geology, information sciences and systems, mathematics, physics, and statistics), EDUCATION (athletic training, education, music education, physical education, science education, social science education, and special education), HEALTH PROFESSIONS (exercise science, nursing, rehabilitation therapy, and speech pathology/audiology), SOCIAL SCIENCE (African American studies, anthropology, Asian/American studies, criminal justice, dietetics, economics, ethics, politics, and social policy, geography, gerontology, history, human services, interdisciplinary studies, international relations, Mexican-American/Chicano studies, philosophy, physical fitness/movement, political science/government, psychology, social science, and sociology). Business, music, and nursing are the strongest academically. Business, interdisciplinary studies, and sport and exercise science have the largest enrollments.

ACTIVITIES: 6% of men belong to 11 national fraternities; 7% of women belong to 9 national sororities. There are 138 groups on campus, including art, band, cheerleading, chess, choir, chorale, chorus, computers, dance, drama, drill team, ethnic, film, gay, honors, international, jazz band, literary magazine, marching band, musical theater, newspaper, opera, orchestra, pep band, photography, political, professional, radio and TV, religious, social, social service, student government, and symphony. Popular campus events include Hawaiian Luau, Academic Excellence Week, and International Dinner. **Sports:** There are 8 intercollegiate sports for men and 9 for women, and 16 intramural sports for men and 16 for women. Maxcy Hall is the center of the sports world on campus: it's a modern facility that's got a 50-foot rock climbing wall, full high ropes course and bouldering cave, 8,000 square-foot fitness center, $300,000 worth of treadmills, spin cycles, ellipticals, strength equipment and free weights, 4,000-seat gymnasium 2,200-seat hockey rink, Olympic-size swimming pool with a diving well, 33,000 square-foot field house, complete with indoor track, basketball, volleyball and indoor lacrosse courts,6 racquetball courts and 3 squash courts, dance studio, and physical therapy/training room. Maxcy is surrounded by 50 acres of athletic fields and courts for tennis and basketball and a quarter-mile track. Plus, there is a new field for softball and a modern turf field for soccer, lacrosse and intramural competition. **Graduates:** From July 1, 2013 to June 30, 2014, 1921 bachelor's degrees were awarded. The most popular majors were interdisciplinary studies (15%), business administration (12%), and nursing (7%). 469 companies recruited on campus in 2013-2014. In an average class, 87% graduate

in 4 years or less, 92% graduate in 5 years or less, and 94% graduate in 6 years or less. Of the 2013 graduating class, 3% were enrolled in graduate school within 6 months of graduation, and 87% were employed.

SERVICES: Counseling and information services are available, as is tutoring in most subjects. There is a reader service for the blind, and remedial math, reading, and writing. **Library/Resources:** The 2 libraries contain 1.1 million volumes, 2.1 million microform items, 36,009 audio/video tapes/CDs/DVDs, and subscribe to 40,304 periodicals including electronic. Computerized library services include interlibrary loans, database searching, Internet access, and Wi-Fi capability. Special learning facilities include an art gallery and radio station. **Physically Challenged Students:** All of the campus is accessible. Facilities include wheelchair ramps, elevators, special parking, specially equipped restrooms, special class scheduling, lowered drinking fountains, lowered telephones. There are academic support services such as note taking, transportation, interpreters, adaptive computer instruction, and library assistance. **Special:** UNC offers internships and co-op programs in many majors and study abroad in England, Australia, Spain, France, and Germany or through the International Student Exchange Program. Dual majors, student-designed majors, credit by exam, and pass/fail options are also available. There are 7 national honor societies and a freshman honors program. **Visiting:** There are regularly scheduled orientations for prospective students, including academic advising, registration, tours, and special activities. There are guides for informal visits and visitors may sit in on classes. To schedule a visit, contact the UNC Visitors Center at visitors.center@unco.edu. **Campus Safety and Security:** Measures include 24-hour foot and vehicle patrol, emergency notification system, and security escort services. There are shuttle buses, emergency telephones, and lighted pathways/sidewalks.

REQUIREMENTS: The SAT or ACT is required. Admission standards are set by the Colorado Commission on Higher Education, but each applicant is evaluated on an individual basis. In general, an ACT score of 22, or an SAT composite score of 1000, and a cumulative GPA of 2.9, are required. Graduation from an accredited high school is required. A GPA of 3.2 is required. AP and CLEP credits are accepted. Important factors in the admissions decision are recommendations by school officials, evidence of special talent, and advanced placement or honors courses. Students must earn a minimum of 120 semester hours (some majors require additional hours) with a minimum GPA of 2.0. All students must complete 40 semester hours in required general education courses and meet all degree requirements in the major. **Procedure:** Freshmen are admitted fall, spring, and summer. Entrance exams should be taken as early as possible. There are deferred admissions and rolling admissions plans. Applications should be filed by August 1 for fall entry; December 20 for spring entry; and May 1 for summer entry, along with a $45 fee. Applications are accepted online. **Transfer Students:** 817 transfer students enrolled in 2013-2014. Transfer students who have completed 12 or fewer hours of college must meet the same criteria for admission as entering freshmen. Transfers with 13 or more semester hours must have a minimum 2.4 GPA. 30 of 120 credits required for the bachelor's degree must be completed at UNC. **International Students:** There are 130 international students enrolled. They must take the TOEFL with a minimum score of 520 on the paper-based TOEFL (PBT) or 70 on the Internet-based version (iBT) or take the MELAB. They must also take the SAT or ACT.

ADMISSIONS: 73% of the 2014-2015 applicants were accepted. The SAT scores for the 2014-2015 freshman class were: Critical Reading--33% below 500, 46% between 500 and 599, 18% between 600 and 699, and 3% between 700 and 800; Math--34% below 500, 43% between 500 and 599, 20% between 600 and 699, and 3% between 700 and 800; Writing--43% below 500, 36% between 500 and 599, and 21% between 600 and 699. The ACT scores were 47% below 21, 57% between 21 and 23, 18% between 24 and 26, 15% between 27 and 28, and 3% above 28. 32% of the current freshmen were in the top fifth of their class; 69% were in the top two fifths. 29 freshmen graduated first in their class. **Admissions Contact:** Director of Admissions. E-Mail: *admissions.help@unco.edu* Web: *www.unco.edu*

FINANCIAL AID: In 2014-2015, 56% of all full-time freshmen and 72% of continuing full-time students received some form of financial aid. 36% of all full-time freshmen and 50% of continuing full-time

students received need-based aid. The average freshman award was $2,238. Need-based scholarships or need-based grants averaged $2,097; need-based self-help aid (loans and jobs) averaged $1,659; non-need-based athletic scholarships averaged $5,434; and other non-need-based awards and non-need-based scholarships averaged $838. The FAFSA is required. The deadline for filing freshman financial aid applications for fall entry is March 1.

WESTERN STATE COLORADO UNIVERSITY
B-3

www.western.edu

Gunnison, CO 81231

(970) 943-2119
(800) 876-5309

Fax: (970) 943-2212

Email: admissions@western.edu

Full-time: 1117 men, 738 women	Faculty: 109
Part-time: 248 men, 235 women	Ph.D.s: n/av
Graduate: 91 men, 152 women	Student/Faculty: 17 to 1
Year: semesters, summer session	Tuition: $7874 ($18,319)
Room & Board: $9050	Freshman Class: n/av
SAT CR/M: 509/516 ACT: 22	CEEB CODE: 4946
Application Deadline: June 1	COMPETITIVE

Western State Colorado University, founded in 1901, is a public institution offering undergraduate programs in liberal arts and sciences, business, recreation, and education. There are 8 undergraduate schools and 2 graduate schools. In addition to regional accreditation, Western has baccalaureate program accreditation with NASM. The 228-acre campus is in a rural area 210 miles southwest of Denver. Including any residence halls, there are 31 buildings.

STUDENT LIFE: 75% of undergraduates are from Colorado. Others are from 50 states, 8 foreign countries, and Canada. 85% are from public schools. 75% are White. The average age of freshmen is 18; all undergraduates, 21. 30% do not continue beyond their first year; 39% remain to graduate. **Housing:** 1234 students can be accommodated in college housing, which includes single-sex and coed dorms, on-campus apartments, and married student housing. In addition, there are special-interest houses, theme floors on art, science, and outdoor pursuits. On-campus housing is guaranteed for the freshman year only, and is available on a first-come, first-served basis. 55% of students commute. All students may keep cars.

FACULTY/CLASSROOMS: 53% of faculty are male; 47% are female. 97% do both. No introductory courses are taught by graduate students. The average class size in an introductory lecture is 22; in a laboratory is 15; and in a regular course is 19.

PROGRAMS OF STUDY: Western confers B.A., and B.F.A. degrees. Master's degrees are also awarded. Bachelor's degrees are awarded in AGRICULTURE (environmental studies), BIOLOGICAL SCIENCE (biology/biological science), BUSINESS (accounting, business administration and management, and recreation and leisure services), COMMUNICATIONS AND THE ARTS (art, communications, dramatic arts, English, fine arts, music, and Spanish), COMPUTER AND PHYSICAL SCIENCE (chemistry, computer science, geology, and mathematics), EDUCATION (art education, elementary education, foreign languages education, music education, science education, and secondary education), ENGINEERING AND ENVIRONMENTAL DESIGN (preengineering), HEALTH PROFESSIONS (predentistry), SOCIAL SCIENCE (anthropology, economics, history, physical fitness/movement, political science/government, prelaw, psychology, and sociology). Business, biological sciences and communications are the strongest academically. Business, exercise and sports science, recreation and outdoor education have the largest enrollments.

ACTIVITIES: There are no fraternities or sororities. There are 60 groups on campus, including adventure race team, alpine ski, wilderness pursuits, baseball, climbing, English performance poetry club, hockey, men's and women's rugby, men's and women's soccer, mountain bike/road cycling, art, band, cheerleading, choir, chorale, chorus, dance, drama, environmental, ethnic, gay, honors, international, jazz band, literary magazine, marching band, musical theater, newspaper, nordic, opera, orchestra, pep band, photography, politi-

cal, professional, radio and TV, religious, social, social service, student government, and symphony. Popular campus events include Family Weekend, Spring Carnival and Winter Fest. **Sports:** There are 15 intercollegiate sports for men and 14 for women, and 9 intramural sports for men and 9 for women. Facilities include a fitness center, 2 gyms, a 5000-seat football stadium, an all-weather track, a number of playing fields, a weight room, an indoor swimming pool, a games/pool area, and tennis and volleyball courts. **Graduates:** From July 1, 2013 to June 30, 2014, 394 bachelor's degrees were awarded. The most popular majors were business (23%), parks and recreation (14%), and social sciences (11%). 45 companies recruited on campus in 2013-2014. In an average class, 1% graduate in 3 years or less, 24% graduate in 4 years or less, 33% graduate in 5 years or less, and 36% graduate in 6 years or less. Of the 2013 graduating class, 12% were enrolled in graduate school within 6 months of graduation, and 25% were employed.

SERVICES: Counseling and information services are available, as is tutoring in most subjects. There is a reader service for the blind, and remedial math and writing. **Library/Resources:** The library contains 252,757 volumes, 105,363 microform items, 10,268 audio/video tapes/CDs/DVDs, and subscribes to 211 periodicals including electronic. Computerized library services include interlibrary loans and database searching. Special learning facilities include an art gallery, radio station, TV station, a greenhouse, Westen mountain archeological site, and media production studio. **Physically Challenged Students:** 90% of the campus is accessible. Facilities include wheelchair ramps, elevators, special parking, specially equipped restrooms, special class scheduling, lowered drinking fountains, lowered telephones, special housing, screen reader programs available on all student lab computers, ADA compliant rooms in residence halls, and an audio device that increases telephone volume. **Special:** The Department of Business and Accounting offers a co-op program. Study abroad, internships, work-study programs, an accelerated degree program in teacher education, dual and student-designed majors, and credit for military and work experience are available. There are 9 national honor societies and a freshman honors program. **Visiting:** There are regularly scheduled orientations for prospective students, consisting of campus tours, and meetings with faculty, coaches, and admissions counselors are available. There are guides for informal visits and visitors may sit in on classes. To schedule a visit, contact the Admissions Office. **Campus Safety and Security:** Measures include 24-hour foot and vehicle patrol and security escort services. There are emergency telephones, lighted pathways/sidewalks, and a special event van shuttle service.

REQUIREMENTS: The SAT or ACT is required. An essay required and interview is recommended. Applicants must be graduates of an accredited secondary school. Western recommends that in high school students complete 4 units of English, 4 units of math, 3 units of laboratory science, 3 units of social science, and at least 1 unit of foreign language. A GPA of 2.5 is required. AP and CLEP credits are accepted. Important factors in the admissions decision are advanced placement or honors courses, leadership record, and extracurricular activities record. To be eligible to graduate, students must complete 120 credit hours and attain a minimum GPA of 2.0. Students must complete 35 core curriculum credits, 26 of which must be fulfilled through liberal arts credits in human relationships, natural sciences, and creative arts, as well as completing competencies in written expression, oral communication, and math. **Procedure:** Freshmen are admitted to all sessions. Entrance exams should be taken during spring of junior year or fall of senior year. There are deferred admissions and rolling admissions plans. Applications should be filed by June 1 for fall entry; November 1 for spring entry, along with a $30 fee. Notification is sent on a rolling basis. Applications are accepted on-line. **Transfer Students:** 159 transfer students enrolled in 2013-2014. Transfer applicants must have a minimum GPA of 2.0, and may be asked to submit SAT or ACT test scores. 30 of 120 credits required for the bachelor's degree must be completed at Western. **International Students:** There are 14 international students enrolled. They must take the TOEFL with a minimum score of 550 on the paper-based TOEFL (PBT) or 96 on the Internet-based version (iBT).

ADMISSIONS: The SAT scores for the 2014-2015 freshman class were: Critical Reading--51% below 500, 36% between 500 and 599, 12% between 600 and 699, and 1% between 700 and 800; Math--43%

below 500, 43% between 500 and 599, 13% between 600 and 699, and 1% between 700 and 800. The ACT scores were 43% below 21, 28% between 21 and 23, 17% between 24 and 26, 8% between 27 and 28, and 4% above 28. **Admissions Contact:** Admissions Officer E-Mail: *admissions@western.edu* Web: *www.western.edu*

FINANCIAL AID: In 2014-2015, 82% of all full-time freshmen and 74% of continuing full-time students received some form of financial aid. 82% of all full-time freshmen and 74% of continuing full-time students received need-based aid. The average freshman award was $13,054. Need-based scholarships or need-based grants averaged $5,909; need-based self-help aid (loans and jobs) averaged $4,097; and non-need-based athletic scholarships averaged $5,300. 30% of undergraduate students work part-time. Average annual earnings from campus work are $1400. The average financial indebtedness of the 2014 graduate was $19,000. The FAFSA is required. The priority date for freshman financial aid applications for fall entry is March 1.

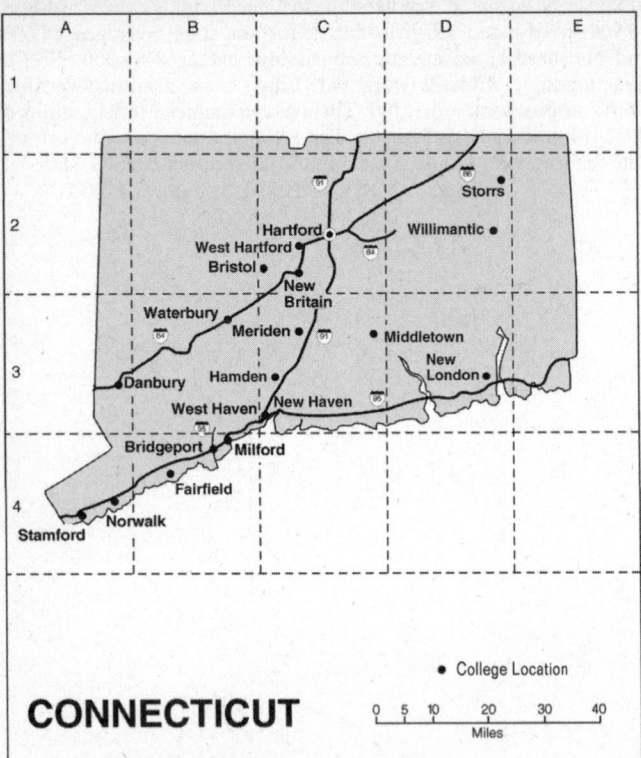

CONNECTICUT

College Location

0 5 10 20 30 40
Miles

ALBERTUS MAGNUS COLLEGE (*The complete profile is made available exclusively on our website, www.barronspac.com*)

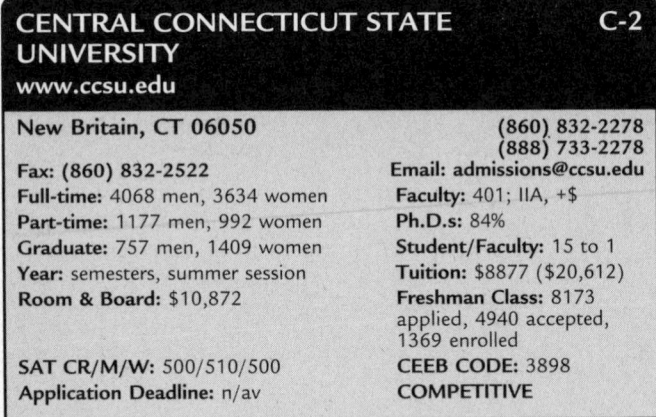

CENTRAL CONNECTICUT STATE UNIVERSITY   C-2
www.ccsu.edu

New Britain, CT 06050	(860) 832-2278
	(888) 733-2278
Fax: (860) 832-2522	Email: admissions@ccsu.edu
Full-time: 4068 men, 3634 women	Faculty: 401; IIA, +$
Part-time: 1177 men, 992 women	Ph.D.s: 84%
Graduate: 757 men, 1409 women	Student/Faculty: 15 to 1
Year: semesters, summer session	Tuition: $8877 ($20,612)
Room & Board: $10,872	Freshman Class: 8173 applied, 4940 accepted, 1369 enrolled
SAT CR/M/W: 500/510/500	CEEB CODE: 3898
Application Deadline: n/av	COMPETITIVE

Central Connecticut State University, has 4 undergraduate schools and 1 graduate school. In addition to regional accreditation, CCSU has a baccalaureate program accreditation with AACSB, ABET, CSAB, CSWE, NCATE, and NLN. The 314-acre campus is in a suburban area 10 miles west of Hartford. Including any residence halls, there are 63 buildings.

STUDENT LIFE: 96% of undergraduates are from Connecticut. Others are from 38 states, 21 foreign countries, and Canada. 68% are White; 11% Hispanic. **Male To Female Ratio:** 1.0:1. The average age of freshmen is 18; all undergraduates, 23. 20% do not continue beyond their first year; 52% remain to graduate. **Housing:** 2142 students can be accommodated in college housing, which includes single-sex and coed dorms. On-campus housing is guaranteed for all 4 years, is available on a first-come, and first-served basis. 79% of students commute. All students may keep cars.

FACULTY/CLASSROOMS: 55% of faculty are male; 45% are female. 90% teach undergraduates. No introductory courses are taught by graduate students.

PROGRAMS OF STUDY: CCSU confers B.A., B.S., B.F.A. and B.S.N.

degrees. Master's and doctoral degrees are also awarded. Bachelor's degrees are awarded in BIOLOGICAL SCIENCE (biochemistry and biology/biological science), BUSINESS (accounting, business administration and management, finance, hospitality management services, international business management, management information systems, marketing/retailing/merchandising, and office supervision and management), COMMUNICATIONS AND THE ARTS (art, communications, dramatic arts, English, French, German, graphic design, Italian, journalism, music, Spanish, and theatre arts), COMPUTER AND PHYSICAL SCIENCE (chemistry, Computer Engineering Technology, computer science, earth science, mathematics, physical sciences, and physics), EDUCATION (art education, athletic training, elementary education, music education, physical education, technical education, and vocational education), ENGINEERING AND ENVIRONMENTAL DESIGN (civil engineering, civil engineering technology, construction management, electrical/electronics engineering technology, industrial engineering technology, manufacturing technology, mechanical engineering, and mechanical engineering technology), HEALTH PROFESSIONS (nursing), SOCIAL SCIENCE (anthropology, criminology, economics, geography, history, international studies, philosophy, political science/government, psychology, social work, and sociology). Psychology, criminology, and accounting have the largest enrollments.

ACTIVITIES: 1% of men belong to 2 national fraternities; 1% of women belong to 1 national sorority. There are 100 groups on campus, including art, band, cheerleading, choir, chorale, chorus, computers, dance, drama, ethnic, gay, honors, international, jazz band, literary magazine, marching band, newspaper, orchestra, pep band, photography, political, professional, radio and TV, religious, social, social service, student government, and symphony. Popular campus events include Winter and Spring Weekends, First Week and Vance Lectures. **Sports:** There are 7 intercollegiate sports for men and 8 for women. Facilities include a 3,800-seat gym, 8 tennis courts, 6,000-seat football stadium, 37,000-square-foot air-supported recreation facility, a natatorium, weight training rooms, softball, baseball, touch football, and soccer fields. **Graduates:** From July 1, 2013 to June 30, 2014, 1865 bachelor's degrees were awarded. The most popular majors were business/marketing (24%), social sciences (15%), and education (11%). In an average class, 21% graduate in 4 years or less, 45% graduate in 5 years or less, and 52% graduate in 6 years or less.

SERVICES: Counseling and information services are available, as is tutoring in some subjects. There is a reader service for the blind, and remedial math, reading, and writing. **Library/Resources:** The library contains 588,349 volumes, 84,571 microform items, and 11,895 audio/video tapes/CDs/DVDs, and subscribes to 43,582 periodicals including electronic. Computerized library services include interlibrary loans, database searching, Internet access, and Wi-Fi capability. Special learning facilities include an art gallery, planetarium, radio station, TV station, writing and math centers. **Physically Challenged Students:** 90% of the campus is accessible. Facilities include wheelchair ramps, elevators, special parking, specially equipped restrooms, special class scheduling, lowered drinking fountains, lowered telephones. There are personal care attendants who serve as roommates for physically disabled resident students. **Special:** The university offers co-op programs and cross-registration with several other Connecticut educational institutions, study abroad in more than 45 countries, internships in most departments, work-study programs, dual majors, and student-designed majors. There are 7 national honor societies, a freshman honors program, and 1 departmental honors program. **Visiting:** There are regularly scheduled orientations for prospective students, including a fall open house in October and daily and select Saturday visits throughout the fall and spring. There are guides for informal visits and visitors may sit in on classes. To schedule a visit, contact the Admissions Office. **Campus Safety and Security:** Measures include 24-hour foot and vehicle patrol, emergency notification system, self-defense education, and security escort services. There are shuttle buses, emergency telephones, lighted pathways/sidewalks, and controlled access to dorms/residences.

REQUIREMENTS: The SAT is required. The ACT Optional Writing test is also required. Applicants must be graduates of an accredited secondary school or have earned a GED. An interview is recommended. CCSU also recommends that applicants have 14 academic credits: 4 in English, 3 each in math and a foreign language, and 2 each in science and social sciences, including 1 in U.S. history. AP and CLEP credits are accepted. Important factors in the admissions decision are extracurricular activities record, recommendations by school officials, and advanced placement or honors courses.To graduate, all students must complete at least 122 to 130 credit hours, depending on the major, with a minimum GPA of 2.0. General education requirements total 44 to 46 credits in arts and humanities, sciences, math, communications, and fitness/wellness studies. Students must also demonstrate foreign language proficiency, complete 6 credits in courses with a global context, and satisfy a First-Year Experience requirement. **Procedure:** Freshmen are admitted fall and spring. Entrance exams should be taken in May of the junior year or November of the senior year. There are deferred admissions and rolling admissions plans. Check with the school for current application deadlines. The application fee is $50. Notifications are sent April 1. 123 applicants were on the 2014 waiting list; 116 were admitted. Applications are accepted on-line. **Transfer Students:** 1072 transfer students enrolled in 2013-2014. Applicants must have a minimum of 12 transferable credits and a GPA of 2.0, and must submit official transcripts from previous schools attended. 30 of 122 credits required for the bachelor's degree must be completed at CCSU. **International Students:** There are 58 international students enrolled. They must take the TOEFL with a minimum score of 500 on the paper-based TOEFL (PBT).

ADMISSIONS: 60% of the 2014-2015 applicants were accepted. The SAT scores for the 2014-2015 freshman class were: Critical Reading--45% below 500, 44% between 500 and 599, 10% between 600 and 699, and 1% between 700 and 800; Math--43% below 500, 46% between 500 and 599, 10% between 600 and 699, and 1% between 700 and 800; Writing--47% below 500, 43% between 500 and 599, 9% between 600 and 699, and 1% between 700 and 800. **Admissions Contact:** Larry Hall, Director of Recruitment and Admissions. E-Mail: *admissions@ccsu.edu* Web: *www.ccsu.edu*

FINANCIAL AID: 80% of undergraduate students work part-time. Average annual earnings from campus work are $2500. CCSU is a member of CSS. The FAFSA and federal income tax returns are required. The priority date for freshman financial aid applications for fall entry is March 1.

CHARTER OAK STATE COLLEGE *(The complete profile is made available exclusively on our website, www.barronspac.com)*

CONNECTICUT COLLEGE   D-3
www.connecticutcollege.edu

New London, CT 06320	(860) 439-2200
Fax: (860) 439-4301	Email: admissions@conncoll.edu
Full-time: 763 men, 1121 women	Faculty: 179; IIB, +$
Part-time: 16 men, 26 women	Ph.D.s: 91%
Graduate: 3 men, 4 women	Student/Faculty: 9 to 1
Year: semesters	Tuition: $43,990
Room & Board: $10,980	Freshman Class: 4838 applied, 1734 accepted, 503 enrolled
SAT CR/M/W: 670/650/690 ACT: 29	CEEB CODE: 3284
Application Deadline: January 1	MOST COMPETITIVE

Connecticut College is a highly selective residential liberal arts college known for interdisciplinary studies, international programs, funded internships, strong student-faculty relationships, and service learning. Institutional values include commitment to diversity, academic excellence, shared governance, and sustainability. Figures in the above capsule and in this profile are approximate. The College operates under a student-adjudicated honor code, has no Greek system, and is a member of the New England Small College Athletic Conference. The scenic 750-acre campus overlooks Long Island Sound. There is 1 graduate school. The 750-acre campus is in a small town midway between Boston and New York City, just off Interstate 95. Including any residence halls, there are 103 buildings.

STUDENT LIFE: 83% of undergraduates are from out of state, mostly the Northeast. Students are from 42 states, 46 foreign countries, and Canada. 50% are from public schools. 74% are White. 27% are Protestant; 26% Catholic; 17% claim no religious affiliation; 14% Jewish. **Male To Female Ratio:** 1.5:1. The average age of freshmen is 18; all undergraduates, 20. 8% do not continue beyond their first year; 85% remain to graduate. **Housing:** 1790 students can be accommodated in college housing, which includes coed dorms and on-campus apartments. In addition, there are language houses, special-interest houses, quiet housing, theme housing, substance-free housing and gender-neutral housing. On-campus housing is guaranteed for all 4 years and is available on a lottery system for upperclassmen. 99% of students live on campus. Upperclassmen may keep cars.

FACULTY/CLASSROOMS: 49% of faculty are male; 51% are female. All teach undergraduates, all do research, and all teach and do research. No introductory courses are taught by graduate students. The average class size in an introductory lecture is 25; in a laboratory is 13; and in a regular course is 19.

PROGRAMS OF STUDY: Connecticut College confers B.A. degrees. Master's degrees are also awarded. Bachelor's degrees are awarded in BIOLOGICAL SCIENCE (biochemistry, biology/biological science, botany, and neurosciences), COMMUNICATIONS AND THE ARTS (art, art history and appreciation, Chinese, classics, dance, dramatic arts, English, film arts, French, German, Japanese, music, and music technology), COMPUTER AND PHYSICAL SCIENCE (chemistry, mathematics, and physics), ENGINEERING AND ENVIRONMENTAL DESIGN (architecture and environmental science), SOCIAL SCIENCE (African studies, American studies, anthropology, East Asian studies, economics, gender studies, Hispanic American studies, history, human development, international relations, Italian studies, Latin American studies, philosophy, political science/government, psychology, religion, Russian and Slavic studies, sociology, and urban studies). Economics, English, government, international relations, psychology, biological sciences, environmental studies, human development and history have the largest enrollments.

ACTIVITIES: There are no fraternities or sororities. There are 55 groups on campus, including a capella, art, band, choir, chorus, communications, computers, dance, drama, environmental, ethnic, film, gay, international, jazz band, literary magazine, newspaper, orchestra, photography, political, professional, radio and TV, religious, social, social service, student government, and symphony. Popular campus events include Eclipse Weekend, Harvestfest and Floralia. **Sports:** There are 12 intercollegiate sports for men and 14 for women, and 12 intramural sports for men and 10 for women. Facilities include the Charles B. Luce Field House, Dayton Arena, a 10,000-square-foot fitness/wellness center, Lott Natatorium, a lighted artificial-turf field, an eight-lane all-weather track, new tennis courts, and playing fields on Tempel Green at the center of campus. **Graduates:** From July 1, 2013 to June 30, 2014, 453 bachelor's degrees were awarded. The most popular majors were economics (16%), government (10%), and international relations (8%). In an average class, 83% graduate in 4 years or less, 85% graduate in 5 years or less, and 85% graduate in 6 years or less. Of the 2013 graduating class, 25% were enrolled in graduate school within 6 months of graduation, and 75% were employed.

SERVICES: Counseling and information services are available, as is tutoring in some subjects, including math, writing, and biological sciences. **Library/Resources:** Computerized library services include interlibrary loans, database searching, Internet access, and Wi-Fi capability. Special learning facilities include an art gallery, radio station, 750-acre arboretum, greenhouse, ion accelerator, refracting telescope and observatory, scanning and transmission electron microscopes, nuclear magnetic resonance spectrometer, tunable diode laser spectroscopy laboratory, center for electronic and digital sound, neuroscience and animal behavior laboratories, clinical and social psychology research observation suites. **Physically Challenged Students:** Facilities include wheelchair ramps, elevators, special parking, specially equipped restrooms, special class scheduling, lowered drinking fountains, lowered telephones, special housing. Case-by-case accommodations are made for housing. **Special:** Cross-registration with 12 area colleges, internships in government, human services, and other fields, a Washington semester at American University, dual majors, student-designed majors, a 3-2 engineering degree with Washington University in St. Louis and Boston University, non-degree study, and satisfactory/unsatisfactory options are available. About half of the junior class studies abroad. Students may supplement their majors by earning certificates from one of our four interdisciplinary centers (focused on international studies, arts and technology, community action and public policy, or the environment. Students can also earn a certificate in museum studies or earn Connecticut teacher certification. There are 5 national honor societies and a Phi Beta Kappa chapter. **Visiting:** There are regularly scheduled orientations for prospective students, Student visits include an introduction to the college, student perspectives, academic programs, a luncheon for parents and students, tours, and a reception. There are guides for informal visits, visitors may sit in on classes, and stay overnight. To schedule a visit, contact The Office of Admission. **Campus Safety and Security:** Measures include 24-hour foot and vehicle patrol, emergency notification system, and security escort services. There are shuttle buses, emergency telephones, lighted pathways/sidewalks, controlled access to dorms/residences, campus-wide emergency communications system.

REQUIREMENTS: The submission of standardized test scores is optional, although students whose primary language is not English are required to submit the TOEFL or its equivalent. In addition, applicants must be graduates of an accredited secondary school. An essay is required and an interview is recommended. AP credits are accepted.To graduate, students must complete at least 128 credit hours with a minimum GPA of 2.0. The number of courses required for our majors varies somewhat. Our General Education distribution requirements cover 7 courses from 7 academic areas, plus a foreign language and 2 writing-intensive courses. **Procedure:** Freshmen are admitted fall and spring. Entrance exams should be taken by January of the senior year. There are early decision and deferred admissions plans. Early decision applications should be filed by November 15; regular applications, by January 1 for fall entry; and December 1 for spring entry, along with a $60 fee. Notification of early decision is sent December 15; regular decision, April 1. 268 early decision candidates were accepted for the 2014-2015 class. 213 applicants were on the 2014 waiting list; 31 were admitted. Applications are accepted online. **Transfer Students:** 18 transfer students enrolled in 2013-2014. Applicants must have a minimum college GPA of 3.0 and be in good standing at the previous school attended. SAT or ACT scores are required and an interview is recommended. 64 of 128 credits required for the bachelor's degree must be completed at Connecticut College. **International Students:** There are 90 international students enrolled. The school actively recruits these students. They must take the TOEFL with a minimum score of 600 on the paper-based TOEFL (PBT) or 100 on the Internet-based version (iBT). Students must take either the APIEL, IELTS, MELAB, or ELPT or an equivalent.

ADMISSIONS: 36% of the 2014-2015 applicants were accepted. The SAT scores for the 2014-2015 freshman class were: Critical Reading--1% below 500, 14% between 500 and 599, 49% between 600 and 699, and 36% between 700 and 800; Math--1% below 500, 14% between 500 and 599, 59% between 600 and 699, and 26% between 700 and 800; Writing--1% below 500, 6% between 500 and 599, 49% between 600 and 699, and 44% between 700 and 800. **Admissions Contact:** Dean of Admissions. E-Mail: *admissions@conncoll.edu* Web: *www.connecticutcollege.edu*

FINANCIAL AID: In 2014-2015, 48% of all full-time freshmen and 48% of continuing full-time students received some form of financial aid. 48% of all full-time freshmen and 48% of continuing full-time students received need-based aid. The average freshman award was $32,993.. The average financial indebtedness of the 2014 graduate was $22,790. Connecticut College is a member of CSS. The CSS/Profile, FAFSA, and parent and student tax forms, including noncustodial parent's statement, are required. The deadline for filing freshman financial aid applications for fall entry is January 15.

CONNECTICUT STATE UNIVERSITY SYSTEM

The Connecticut State University System, established in 1983, is a public system in Connecticut. It is governed by a board of trustees, whose chief administrator is the president. The primary goal of the system is teaching. The main priorities are access, with emphasis on a multi-cultural experience; quality, within a context of curriculum diversity and a range of delivery systems; and public service, including linkages with schools, state government, and private enterprise. CSUS is the largest public university system in Connecticut, and offers 90 baccalaureate, 77 graduate and numerous professional degrees. The total student enrollment is about 38,000 with 2005 faculty members. Profiles of the 4-year campuses are included in this section.

EASTERN CONNECTICUT STATE UNIVERSITY	**D-2**
www1.easternct.edu	

Willimantic, CT 06226	(860) 465-5286

Email: admissions@easternct.edu

Full-time: 2023 men, 2372 women	**Faculty:** 194; IIA, ++$
Part-time: 373 men, 411 women	**Ph.D.s:** 94%
Graduate: 48 men, 141 women	**Student/Faculty:** 22 to 1
Year: semesters, summer session	**Tuition:** $9376 ($21,241)
Room & Board: $11,208	**Freshman Class:** 5112 applied, 3299 accepted, 985 enrolled
SAT CR/M/W: 510/510/520 **ACT:** 22	**CEEB CODE:** 3966
Application Deadline: May 1	**COMPETITIVE**

Eastern Connecticut State University, founded in 1889, is the state's public liberal arts university. Figures in the above capsule and in this profile are approximate. There are 3 undergraduate schools and 1 graduate school. In addition to regional accreditation, Eastern has baccalaureate program accreditation with CSWE and NCATE. The 182-acre campus is in a small town 29 miles east of Hartford and 90 miles southwest of Boston. Including any residence halls, there are 54 buildings.

STUDENT LIFE: 95% of undergraduates are from Connecticut. Others are from 24 states, 50 foreign countries, and Canada. 95% are from public schools. 70% are White. **Male To Female Ratio:** 1.2:1. The average age of freshmen is 18; all undergraduates, 22. 22% do not continue beyond their first year; 51% remain to graduate. **Housing:** 2655 students can be accommodated in college housing, which includes coed dorms and on-campus apartments. In addition, there are honors houses and special-interest houses. 53% of students live on campus. Alcohol is not permitted. Upperclassmen may keep cars.

FACULTY/CLASSROOMS: 51% of faculty are male; 49% are female. 98% teach undergraduates. No introductory courses are taught by graduate students. The average class size in an introductory lecture is 23.

PROGRAMS OF STUDY: Eastern confers B.A., B.S. and B.G.S. degrees. Associate and master's degrees are also awarded. Bachelor's degrees are awarded in BIOLOGICAL SCIENCE (biochemistry and biology/biological science), BUSINESS (accounting, business administration and management, industrial and labor relations, recreation and leisure services, and sports management), COMMUNICATIONS AND THE ARTS (communications, English, music, performing arts, Spanish, theatre acting, and visual and performing arts), COMPUTER AND PHYSICAL SCIENCE (computer science, information sciences and systems, and mathematics), EDUCATION (early childhood education, elementary education, and physical education), ENGINEERING AND ENVIRONMENTAL DESIGN (environmental science), SOCIAL SCIENCE (economics, history, liberal arts/general studies, political science/government, psychology, social science, social work, sociology, and women and gender studies). Business administration, psychology, and social sciences have the largest enrollments.

ACTIVITIES: There are 77 groups on campus, including and ice hockey, fencing, football, art, cheerleading, club sports include rugby, computers, dance, debate, drama, environmental, ethnic, gay, honors, international, newspaper, photography, political, professional, radio and TV, religious, social, social service, student government, and yearbook. Popular campus events include Open Rec Night, Springfest and Arts and Lecture Series. **Sports:** There are 7 intercollegiate sports for men and 10 for women, and 15 intramural sports for men and 15 for women. Facilities include a student center with theaters, café, billiards, fitness center, a 2800-seat field house, a 6-lane swimming pool, soccer field, baseball complex, softball stadium, 400 meter 8-lane track, field hockey field, intramural field, tennis, basketball, racquetball, and squash courts, weight room, matted rooms for yoga and martial arts, and trails in an arboretum. **SERVICES:** Counseling and information services are available, as is tutoring in every subject. **Library/Resources:** The library contains 408,479 volumes, 973,594 microform items, 9,006 audio/video tapes/CDs/DVDs, and subscribes to 44,778 periodicals including electronic. Computerized library services include interlibrary loans, database searching, Internet access, and Wi-Fi capability. Special learning facilities include an art gallery, planetarium, radio station, TV station, an arboretum, child and family development resource center, church farm center for the arts and sciences. **Physically Challenged Students:** Facilities include wheelchair ramps, elevators, special parking, specially equipped restrooms, special class scheduling, and lowered drinking fountains. **Special:** The University Honors Program promotes undergraduate scholarship by providing academically talented students with opportunities to participate in specially designed courses that prepare them to conduct independent research and/or scholarly activity under the oversight of a faculty mentor. The Individualized Major Plan is a student's self-designed interdisciplinary plan of study, which consists of courses from two or more disciplines and results in a B.A. or B.S. degree. The self-designed plan of study allows the student to take courses in areas that naturally complement each other in today's workplace and to develop a strong educational base in at least one subject to facilitate entrance into a graduate program. There are 8 national honor societies and a freshman honors program. **Visiting:** There are regularly scheduled orientations for prospective students, including small group discussions, a tour of the campus, and a personal interview. There are guides for informal visits and visitors may sit in on classes. To schedule a visit, contact the Office of Admissions at admissions@easternct.edu. **Campus Safety and Security:** Measures include 24-hour foot and vehicle patrol, emergency notification system, and security escort services. There are shuttle buses, emergency telephones, lighted pathways/sidewalks, and controlled access to dorms/residences.

REQUIREMENTS: The SAT or ACT is required. Applicants must be graduates of an accredited secondary school or have a GED. They should have completed 15 high school academic credits, including 4 years of English, 4 of math, and 2 each of foreign language, social studies, and science (including 1 of lab science). While interviews are not generally required of students applying for admission, the admission staff may request an interview with certain applicants to obtain additional information or clarify information. AP and CLEP credits are accepted. Important factors in the admissions decision are advanced placement or honors courses, personality/intangible qualities, and extracurricular activities record.To graduate, students must complete 120 credit hours, including the requirements of an academic major, with a GPA of 2.0. Liberal Arts Core Curriculum requirements include 26 credits in Methods and Concepts, 15 in Synthesis and Application, and 3 credits in Independent Inquiry. **Procedure:** Freshmen are admitted fall and spring. Entrance exams should be taken in November or December of the senior year. There are deferred admissions and rolling admissions plans. Applications should be filed by May 1 for fall entry, along with a $50 fee. Notification is sent on a rolling basis. Applications are accepted on-line. **Transfer Students:** 499 transfer students enrolled in 2013-2014. Official college and high school transcripts are required. 30 of 120 credits required for the bachelor's degree must be completed at Eastern. **International Students:** The school actively recruits these students. They must take the TOEFL. They must also take the SAT or ACT.

ADMISSIONS: 65% of the 2014-2015 applicants were accepted. The SAT scores for the 2014-2015 freshman class were: Critical Reading--44% below 500, 45% between 500 and 599, 9% between 600 and 699, and 2% between 700 and 800; Math--42% below 500, 45% between 500 and 599, 12% between 600 and 699, and 1% between 700 and 800; Writing--39% below 500, 46% between 500 and 599, 13% between 600 and 699, and 1% between 700 and 800. The ACT scores were 32% below 21, 41% between 21 and 23, 20% between 24 and 26, 6% between 27 and 28, and 1% above 28. 23% of the current freshmen were in the top fifth of their class; 56% were in the top two fifths. 3 freshmen graduated first in their class. **Admissions Contact:**

Director of Enrollment Management. E-Mail: *admissions@easternct .edu* Web: *www1.easternct.edu/admissions/*

FINANCIAL AID: Eastern is a member of CSS. The FAFSA is required. The deadline for filing freshman financial aid applications for fall entry is March 15.

FAIRFIELD UNIVERSITY　　　　　　　　　　B-4
www.fairfield.edu

Fairfield, CT 06824	(203) 254-4100
Fax: (203) 254-4199	Email: admis@fairfield.edu
Full-time: 1489 men, 2199 women	Faculty: 258; IIA, +$
Part-time: 141 men, 153 women	Ph.D.s: 93%
Graduate: 412 men, 729 women	Student/Faculty: 14 to 1
Year: semesters, summer session	Tuition: $43,770
Room & Board: $13,190	Freshman Class: 9978 applied, 7137 accepted, 1056 enrolled
SAT CR/M/W: 580/600/600 ACT: 26	CEEB CODE: 3390
Application Deadline: January 15	VERY COMPETITIVE

Fairfield University was founded by the Society of Jesus (the Jesuits) in 1942 and is rooted in one of the world's oldest intellectual and spiritual traditions. There are 4 undergraduate schools and 5 graduate schools. In addition to regional accreditation, Fairfield has baccalaureate program accreditation with AACSB, ABET, NCATE, and NLN. The 200-acre campus is in a suburban area 60 miles northeast of New York City and 1 mile from Long Island Sound. Including any residence halls, there are 48 buildings.

STUDENT LIFE: 71% of undergraduates are from out of state, mostly the Northeast. Students are from 33 states, 34 foreign countries, and Canada. 57% are from public schools. 75% are White. The average age of freshmen is 18; all undergraduates, 20. 11% do not continue beyond their first year; 89% remain to graduate. **Housing:** 2912 students can be accommodated in college housing, which includes single-sex, coed dorms and on-campus apartments. In addition, there are special-interest houses, including a substance-free floor. On-campus housing is guaranteed for all 4 years and is available on a lottery system for upperclassmen. 76% of students live on campus. Upperclassmen may keep cars.

FACULTY/CLASSROOMS: 50% of faculty are male; 50% are female. 86% teach undergraduates. No introductory courses are taught by graduate students. The average class size in an introductory lecture is 18 and in a laboratory is 13.

PROGRAMS OF STUDY: Fairfield confers B.A., B.S. and B.S.N. degrees. Master's and doctoral degrees are also awarded. Bachelor's degrees are awarded in BIOLOGICAL SCIENCE (biochemistry and biology/biological science), BUSINESS (accounting, business administration, mgmt, operations, finance, and marketing), COMMUNICATIONS AND THE ARTS (art history, communication, English, film, television and digital media, French, German, Italian, music, Spanish, studio art, and theatre arts), COMPUTER AND PHYSICAL SCIENCE (chemistry, computer science, information sciences and systems, mathematics, physics, and software engineering), ENGINEERING AND ENVIRONMENTAL DESIGN (bioengineering, computer engineering, electrical and computer engineering, and mechanical engineering), HEALTH PROFESSIONS (nursing), SOCIAL SCIENCE (American studies, anthropology, economics, history, international studies, liberal arts, sciences, general studies, humanities, philosophy, political science/government, psychology, religious studies, and sociology). Accounting, finance, biology, communication, nursing, and international studies are the strongest academically. Nursing, psychology, and finance have the largest enrollments.

ACTIVITIES: There are no fraternities or sororities. There are 92 groups on campus, including art, band, cheerleading, chess, choir, chorale, chorus, communications, computers, dance, debate, drama, environmental, ethnic, film, gay, honors, international, jazz band, literary magazine, musical theater, newspaper, orchestra, pep band, photography, political, professional, radio and TV, religious, social,

social service, student government, and yearbook. Popular campus events include Presidential Ball, Midnight Breakfast, Fall Concert, Relay for Life, Glee Club Pops Concert, Hunger Clean-up, Noche Caliente, Pride and Purpose, Rep Ya Flag, Remixx Showcase, Late Night @ Barone, Extreme Bowling, South Side Cafe, and Senior Week. **Sports:** There are 9 intercollegiate sports for men and 11 for women, and 18 intramural sports for men and 11 for women. Facilities include The RecPlex, which is primarily used for open recreation, physical conditioning, and intramural sports. Numerous classes are coordinated within the RecPlex such as; fitness classes, tennis, pilates, yoga, 25-meter pool, jazz dance, aqua aerobics, cardio, weight training. Three racquetball courts, saunas, whirlpools, and a field house that houses four courts interchangeable used for basketball, tennis, and volleyball are available. Membership is included in tuition and fees for all full-time undergraduates. Fairfield also sponsors 20 varsity sports which all compete in the NCAA's Division I. Varsity programs include nine men's and 11 women's sports teams. The Walsh Athletic Center offers a high-tech academic study center, a multimedia recruitment center, equipment rooms, strength and conditioning center, practice courts, and indoor batting cages. The 3,500 seat state-of-the-art Rafferty Stadium is the home of Fairfield lacrosse, equipped with a full service production suite among the amenities. Additionally, Fairfield has an artificial surface field, a grass soccer field, baseball and softball fields, state of the art tennis courts, an on campus basketball facility, as well as an off campus basketball arena, rowing facility and golf facility. **Graduates:** From July 1, 2013 to June 30, 2014, 899 bachelor's degrees were awarded. The most popular majors were nursing (14%), communication (11%), and marketing (8%). 188 companies recruited on campus in 2013-2014. In an average class, 78% graduate in 4 years or less, 81% graduate in 5 years or less, and 80% graduate in 6 years or less. Of the 2013 graduating class, 22% were enrolled in graduate school within 6 months of graduation, and 75% were employed.

SERVICES: Counseling and information services are available, as is tutoring in some subjects. Group based peer tutoring is offered in the following courses: chemistry, biology, finance, physics, psychology, and nursing as well as modern languages courses in French, Italian and Spanish. Additional tutoring is offered in accounting and economics. There is a reader service for the blind. Fairfield University also offers tutoring at both the writing and math center. **Library/Resources:** The library contains 379,941 volumes, 945,373 microform items, 15,810 audio/video tapes/CDs/DVDs, and subscribes to 67,386 periodicals including electronic. Computerized library services include interlibrary loans, database searching, Internet access, and Wi-Fi capability. Special learning facilities include an art gallery, radio station, TV station, a media center, 750-seat concert hall/theater, a rehearsal and improvisation theater, language learning lab, business education simulation training (BEST) classroom, SIM/simulated hospital environment and human patient simulators in the nursing facility, an art gallery and an art museum, model interactive high technology classrooms, resource center for core science. **Physically Challenged Students:** 95% of the campus is accessible. Facilities include wheelchair ramps, elevators, special parking, specially equipped restrooms, special class scheduling, lowered drinking fountains, lowered telephones, special housing. Accommodations for seeing-eye dogs and a library computer station for physically challenged students are also available. **Special:** Fairfield administers its own study abroad program in several countries and has affiliations with 17 programs, a Washington semester, a federal work-study program, B.A.-B.S. degrees in economics, international studies, and psychology, individually-designed majors, and dual majors in all subjects. The university offers 5th year graduate degree programs in education, psychology, and engineering. Fairfield university offers a four year Honors Program across the University open, by special admission, to all undergraduates regardless of the school in which they are enrolled. A bachelor of Arts/Sciences in Liberal Studies is offered for part time students through the College of Arts and Sciences. Internships, both credit and noncredit, are offered at area corporations, publications, banks, and other organizations nationally and internationally. Interdisciplinary minors include women's studies, entrepreneurship, marine science, Black studies, environmental studies, jazz, classical performance, Italian studies, Russian and Eastern European studies, Catholic studies and Judaic studies,

applied ethics, Asian studies, Irish studies, Latin American and Caribbean studies, and peace and justice. Fairfield University offers a comprehensive study abroad program through our office of International Programs which includes: Italy, France, Spain, Ireland, Nicaragua, Tanzania, Australia, and Brazil. There are 22 national honor societies, including Phi Beta Kappa, and a freshman honors program. **Visiting:** There are regularly scheduled orientations for prospective students, information sessions and tours offered weekdays and some weekends. Individualized class visits are available. There are guides for informal visits, visitors may sit in on classes, and stay overnight. To schedule a visit, contact the Office of Admission. **Campus Safety and Security:** Measures include 24-hour foot and vehicle patrol, emergency notification system, self-defense education, and security escort services. There are shuttle buses, emergency telephones, lighted pathways/sidewalks, controlled access to dorms/residences, EMT public safety officers, bike patrol, closed circuit television system, crime prevention seminars and information via campus television network.

REQUIREMENTS: Fairfield has test optional admission. There is no additional information required if students choose not to submit test scores. There is no required grade point average, although most admitted students have a B+ average or better in a solid college preparatory program, which should include advanced and/or honors classes. Students should have completed 15 academic credits, including 4 credits of English, 3 to 4 credits each of history, math, and lab science, and 2 to 4 credits of a foreign language. AP and CLEP credits are accepted. Important factors in the admissions decision are advanced placement or honors courses, recommendations by school officials, and extracurricular activities record. To graduate, students must complete a minimum of 120 credits and completed at least 38 three or four credit courses with a minimum GPA of 2.0 both overall and in the major. Sixty of the 120 credits are in general education core requirements. Distribution requirements include 15 credits in philosophy, religious studies, and ethics, 15 credits in English and fine arts, 12 credits in math and natural sciences, 12 credits in history and social sciences, and 6 credits in foreign languages. Students are also required to take courses in US and world diversity. **Procedure:** Freshmen are admitted fall. Entrance exams should be taken In the spring of the junior year or fall of the senior year. There are early decision, early admissions, and deferred admissions plans. Early decision applications should be filed by November 15; regular applications, by January 15 for fall entry, along with a $60 fee. Notification of early decision is sent January 1; regular decision, April 1. 88 early decision candidates were accepted for the 2014-2015 class. 1690 applicants were on the 2014 waiting list; 15 were admitted. Applications are accepted on-line. **Transfer Students:** 41 transfer students enrolled in 2013-2014. The following are needed to complete the transfer application: common application for transfer students, application fee, personal statement/essay addressing why you are seeking transfer, official high school transcript (Fairfield does not accept the GED), official college transcript from all universities attended (whether or not credit was earned), SAT or ACT results (If you choose to submit them). Refer to our Standardized Test Optional Policy for more details, mid-term grade progress report, Dean of Students Certification Form, and course catalog/descriptions of all classes taken. 60 of 120 credits required for the bachelor's degree must be completed at Fairfield. **International Students:** There are 88 international students enrolled. The school actively recruits these students. They must take the TOEFL with a minimum score of 550 on the paper-based TOEFL (PBT) or 80 on the Internet-based version (iBT), or take the IELTS (International English Language Testing System)

ADMISSIONS: 72% of the 2014-2015 applicants were accepted. The SAT scores for the 2014-2015 freshman class were: Critical Reading--6% below 500, 52% between 500 and 599, 37% between 600 and 699, and 4% between 700 and 800; Math--5% below 500, 40% between 500 and 599, 50% between 600 and 699, and 5% between 700 and 800; Writing--6% below 500, 42% between 500 and 599, 44% between 600 and 699, and 8% between 700 and 800. The ACT scores were 2% below 21, 14% between 21 and 23, 36% between 24 and 26, 26% between 27 and 28, and 22% above 28. **Admissions Contact:** Karen Pellegrino, Dean of Enrollment. E-Mail: *admis@fairfield.edu* Web: *www.fairfield.edu*

FINANCIAL AID: In 2014-2015, 92% of all full-time freshmen and 80% of continuing full-time students received some form of financial aid. 51% of all full-time freshmen and 55% of continuing full-time students received need-based aid. The average freshman award was $18,984. Need-based scholarships or need-based grants averaged $24,615 ($55,800 maximum); need-based self-help aid (loans and jobs) averaged $3,320 ($5,750 maximum); non-need-based athletic scholarships averaged $20,733 ($58,985 maximum); and other non-need-based awards and non-need-based scholarships averaged $11,001 ($43,170 maximum). 90% of undergraduate students work part-time. Average annual earnings from campus work are $876. The average financial indebtedness of the 2014 graduate was $24,061. Fairfield is a member of CSS. The CSS/Profile and FAFSA are required. The priority date for freshman financial aid applications for fall entry is February 15.

GOODWIN COLLEGE (*The complete profile is made available exclusively on our website, www.barronspac.com*)

MITCHELL COLLEGE	D-3
www.mitchell.edu	

New London, CT 06320	(800) 443-2811
	(800) 443-2811
Fax: (860) 444-1209	Email: gorneault_g@mitchell.edu
Full-time: 395 men, 336 women	Faculty: 35
Part-time: 59 men, 68 women	Ph.D.s: 74%
Graduate: n/av	Student/Faculty: 14 to 1
Year: semesters, summer session	Tuition: $28,491
Room & Board: $12,492	Freshman Class: n/av
	CEEB CODE: 3582
Application Deadline: rolling	COMPETITIVE

Mitchell College, founded in 1938, is a private institution offering associate and bachelor degree programs in the liberal arts and professional areas. Figures in the above capsule and in this profile are approximate. The 68-acre campus is in a suburban area in southeastern Connecticut, on the shore of the Thames River where it meets Long Island Sound. Including any residence halls, there are 26 buildings.

STUDENT LIFE: 54% of undergraduates are from Connecticut. Others are from 26 states, and 5 foreign countries. 50% are from public schools. 66% are White; 12% Hispanic. 61% claim no religious affiliation; 18% Catholic; 12% Protestant. **Male To Female Ratio:** 0.9:1. The average age of freshmen is 19; all undergraduates, 20. 43% do not continue beyond their first year; 47% remain to graduate. **Housing:** 598 students can be accommodated in college housing, which includes single-sex and coed dorms and on-campus apartments. On-campus housing is guaranteed for all 4 years. 80% of students live on campus; of those, 60% remain on campus on weekends. All students may keep cars.

FACULTY/CLASSROOMS: 49% of faculty are male; 51% are female. All teach undergraduates. No introductory courses are taught by graduate students. The average class size in an introductory lecture is 14; in a laboratory is 10; and in a regular course is 14.

PROGRAMS OF STUDY: confers B.A. and B.S. degrees. Associate degrees are also awarded. Bachelor's degrees are awarded in AGRICULTURE (environmental studies), BUSINESS (business administration and management, hospitality management services, and sports management), COMMUNICATIONS AND THE ARTS (communications), EDUCATION (early childhood education), SOCIAL SCIENCE (criminal justice, homeland security, human development, liberal arts/general studies, and psychology). Early childhood education is the strongest academically. Business administration, criminal justice, sport and fitness management have the largest enrollments.

ACTIVITIES: There are 35 groups on campus, including art, cheerleading, choir, chorus, computers, dance, drama, ethnic, gay, honors, international, professional, radio and TV, religious, social, social service, and student government. **Sports:** There are 8 intercollegiate sports for men and 7 for women, and 4 intramural sports for men and 4 for women. Facilities include an basketball court, fitness center, two beaches, woods with natural and groomed trails, tennis courts, and athletic fields for all varsity teams. **Graduates:** From July 1, 2013

to June 30, 2014, 190 bachelor's degrees were awarded. The most popular majors were liberal and pressional studies (23%), business administration (22%), and criminal justice (18%).

SERVICES: Counseling and information services are available, as is tutoring in most subjects. There is a reader service for the blind. **Library/Resources:** The library contains 94,542 volumes, 1,658 audio/video tapes/CDs/DVDs, and subscribes to 90 periodicals including electronic. Computerized library services include interlibrary loans, database searching, Internet access, and Wi-Fi capability. Special learning facilities include a radio station. **Physically Challenged Students:** 50% of the campus is accessible. Facilities include wheelchair ramps, elevators, special parking, specially equipped restrooms, and special class scheduling. **Special:** Internships are available through Academic Department Chairs. Liberal and Prefessional Studies offers an Individualized (student-designed) option. Work study jobs are available. There are 8 national honor societies, including Phi Beta Kappa, and 1 departmental honors program. **Visiting:** There are regularly scheduled orientations for prospective students, with a student-guided tour and an interview with an admissions counselor. There are guides for informal visits and visitors may sit in on classes. To schedule a visit, contact Visit Coordinator, Admissions Office. **Campus Safety and Security:** Measures include 24-hour foot and vehicle patrol, emergency notification system, and security escort services. There are shuttle buses, emergency telephones, lighted pathways/sidewalks, and controlled access to dorms/residences.

REQUIREMENTS: The GED is accepted. A recommendation and a personal statement are required. A personal interview is recommended but not required. A GPA of 2.0 is required. AP and CLEP credits are accepted. Important factors in the admissions decision are personality/intangible qualities, recommendations by school officials, and extracurricular activities record. To graduate bachelor-degree-seeking students must complete 120 credits (associate-degree-seeking 60 credits) with a minimum GPA of 2.0 (2.67 for early childhood education). Required general education curriculum. Several majors contain a cumulating experience (a capstone, senior project, or internship). **Procedure:** Freshmen are admitted fall and spring. Entrance exams should be taken during summer orientation. There are early decision, deferred admissions, and rolling admissions plans. Early decision applications should be filed by November 15, along with a $30 fee. Notification of early decision is sent December 15; regular decision, on a rolling basis. Applications are accepted on-line. **Transfer Students:** 74 transfer students enrolled in 2013-2014. In addition to fulfilling regular application requirements, transfer applicants must submit official college transcripts from all colleges/universities attended. 30 of 120 credits required for the bachelor's degree must be completed at Mitchell. **International Students:** There are 7 international students enrolled. The school actively recruits these students. They must take the TOEFL with a minimum score of 500 on the paper-based TOEFL (PBT) or take the APIEL.

ADMISSIONS: **Admissions Contact:** Director of Admissions. Web: *www.mitchell.edu*

FINANCIAL AID: In 2014-2015, 83% of all full-time freshmen and 73% of continuing full-time students received some form of financial aid. 83% of all full-time freshmen and 73% of continuing full-time students received need-based aid. The average freshman award was $20,235. Need-based scholarships or need-based grants averaged $16,739 need-based self-help aid (loans and jobs) averaged $7,281; and other non-need-based awards and non-need-based scholarships averaged $7,636. The FAFSA is required. The priority date for freshman financial aid applications for fall entry is April 1.

POST UNIVERSITY	B-3
www.post.edu	

Waterbury, CT 06723	(203) 596-4520
	(800) 345-2562
Fax: (203) 756-5810	Email: tpuadmis@teikyopost.edu
Full-time: 325 men, 400 women	Faculty: n/av
Part-time: 200 men, 350 women	Ph.D.s: 61%
Graduate: n/av	Student/Faculty: n/av
Year: semesters, summer session	Tuition: $25,900
Room & Board: $9850	Freshman Class: n/av
SAT or ACT: required	CEEB CODE: 3698
Application Deadline: open	COMPETITIVE

Post University, founded in 1890, is a private institution offering liberal arts and business programs. The figures in the above capsule and in this profile are approximate. There are 2 undergraduate schools. The 70-acre campus is in an urban area 1 mile west of Waterbury. Including any residence halls, there are 13 buildings.

STUDENT LIFE: 83% of undergraduates are from Connecticut. Others are from 12 states, 20 foreign countries, and Canada. 75% are from public schools. 63% are White; 17% African American. **Male To Female Ratio:** 1.4:1. The average age of freshmen is 19; all undergraduates, 26. 23% do not continue beyond their first year; 39% remain to graduate. **Housing:** 424 students can be accommodated in college housing, which includes coed dorms and off-campus apartments. On-campus housing is guaranteed for all 4 years. 58% of students live on campus; of those, 60% remain on campus on weekends. All students may keep cars.

FACULTY/CLASSROOMS: 57% of faculty are male; 43% are female. All teach undergraduates. No introductory courses are taught by graduate students. The average class size in an introductory lecture is 20; in a laboratory is 15; and in a regular course is 35.

PROGRAMS OF STUDY: TPU confers B.A. and B.S. degrees. Associate degrees are also awarded. Bachelor's degrees are awarded in BUSINESS (accounting, banking and finance, business administration and management, management science, and marketing/retailing/merchandising), COMMUNICATIONS AND THE ARTS (English), SOCIAL SCIENCE (criminal justice, history, liberal arts/general studies, psychology, and sociology). Biology is the strongest academically. Management and general studies have the largest enrollments.

ACTIVITIES: There are 30 groups on campus, including cheerleading, chorale, chorus, computers, drama, ethnic, gay, honors, international, literary magazine, musical theater, social, social service, student government, and yearbook. Popular campus events include dances, concerts, and international food festivals. **Sports:** There are 5 intercollegiate sports for men and 5 for women, and 4 intramural sports for men and 4 for women. Facilities include a soccer field, a fitness center, a weight room, a racquetball court, a swimming pool, and tennis courts.

SERVICES: Counseling and information services are available, as is tutoring in most subjects. There is a reader service for the blind, and remedial math, reading, and writing. **Library/Resources:** The library contains 85,000 volumes, 75,158 microform items, 1,027 audio/video tapes/CDs/DVDs, and subscribes to 427 periodicals including electronic. Computerized library services include interlibrary loans and database searching. **Physically Challenged Students:** 70% of the campus is accessible. Facilities include wheelchair ramps, elevators, special parking, specially equipped restrooms, and special class scheduling. **Special:** Co-op programs in all majors, cross-registration with Naugatuck Valley Community College, study abroad in England, the Netherlands, and Japan, internships with area businesses, general studies degrees, accelerated degree programs, B.A.-B.S. degrees, and credit for life experience are available. There are 2 national honor societies and 1 departmental honors programs. **Visiting:** There are regularly scheduled orientations for prospective students, including tours, interviews with admissions counselors, and meetings with faculty and students. There are guides for informal visits, visitors may sit in on classes, and stay overnight. To schedule a visit, contact the Admissions Office. **Campus Safety and Security:** Measures include 24-hour foot and vehicle patrol, self-defense education, and security escort services. There are shuttle buses and lighted pathways/sidewalks.

REQUIREMENTS: The SAT or ACT is required. Applicants must be graduates of an accredited secondary school, with 4 years of English and at least 16 total academic credits. The GED is accepted. A GPA of 2.0 is required. AP and CLEP credits are accepted. Important factors in the admissions decision are personality/intangible qualities, extracurricular activities record, and recommendations by school officials. To graduate, all students must maintain a minimum GPA of 2.0, earn a total of 120 credits, including at least 33 in the major, and take a computer course. **Procedure:** Freshmen are admitted to all sessions. There are early admissions, deferred admissions, and rolling admissions plans. Check with the school for current application deadlines. The fall 2014 application fee was $40. Notification is sent on a rolling basis. Applications are accepted on-line. **Transfer Stu-**

dents: Applicants must have a minimum college GPA of 2.0, submit an official college transcript, and have an interview. The SAT is recommended. 30 of 120 credits required for the bachelor's degree must be completed at TPU. **International Students:** There are 48 international students enrolled. The school actively recruits these students. They must take the TOEFL with a minimum score of 500 on the paper-based TOEFL (PBT) or 79 on the Internet-based version (iBT).

ADMISSIONS: Dean of Admissions. Web: *www.post.edu*

FINANCIAL AID: In 2014-2015, 100% of all full-time freshmen and 98% of continuing full-time students received some form of financial aid. 53% of all full-time freshmen and 54% of continuing full-time students received need-based aid. The average freshman award was $14,491. Need-based scholarships or need-based grants averaged $14,491; need-based self-help aid (loans and jobs) averaged $4,684; and non-need-based athletic scholarships averaged $10,890. The average financial indebtedness of the 2014 graduate was $33,377. The FAFSA and the college's own financial statement, and parent and student federal tax returns are required. Check with the school for current application deadlines.

QUINNIPIAC UNIVERSITY   C-3
www.quinnipiac.edu

Hamden, CT 06518

	(203) 582-8600
	(800) 462-1944
Fax: (203) 582-8906	Email: admissions@quinnipiac.edu
Full-time: 2524 men, 3811 women	Faculty: 369; IIA
Part-time: 80 men, 138 women	Ph.D.s: 86%
Graduate: 854 men, 1628 women	Student/Faculty: 17 to 1
Year: semesters, summer session	Tuition: $40,670
Room & Board: $14,490	Freshman Class: 23259 applied, 15328 accepted, 1656 enrolled
SAT CR/M/W: 540/560/550 ACT: 25	CEEB CODE: 3712
Application Deadline: February 1	VERY COMPETITIVE

Quinnipiac University, founded in 1929, is a private institution offering 58 plus undergraduate majors and 22 graduate programs through the schools of health sciences, nursing, business and engineering, communications, education, the college of arts and sciences, the school of law and the Frank H. Netter MD school of medicine. There are 5 undergraduate schools and 8 graduate schools. In addition to regional accreditation, Quinnipiac has baccalaureate program accreditation with AACSB, ABET, APTA, CAHEA, NCATE, and NLN. The 600-acre campus is in a suburban area in Hamden, just 8 miles north of New Haven. Including any residence halls, there are 80 buildings.

STUDENT LIFE: 77% of undergraduates are from out of state, mostly the Middle Atlantic. Students are from 30 states, 30 foreign countries, and Canada. 75% are from public schools. 76% are White. 51% are Catholic; 26% Protestant. **Male To Female Ratio:** 1.6:1. The average age of freshmen is 19; all undergraduates, 21. 13% do not continue beyond their first year; 78% remain to graduate. **Housing:** 5020 students can be accommodated in college housing, which includes coed dorms, on-campus apartments, and off-campus apartments. In addition, there are honors houses, special-interest houses, wellness housing. On-campus housing is guaranteed for all 4 years. 80% of students live on campus; of those, 75% remain on campus on weekends. Upperclassmen may keep cars.

FACULTY/CLASSROOMS: 48% of faculty are male; 52% are female. 85% teach undergraduates, 30% do research, and 30% do both. No introductory courses are taught by graduate students. The average class size in an introductory lecture is 24; in a laboratory is 15; and in a regular course is 22.

PROGRAMS OF STUDY: Quinnipiac confers B.A., B.S. and B.F.A. degrees. Master's and doctoral degrees are also awarded. Bachelor's degrees are awarded in BIOLOGICAL SCIENCE (biochemistry, biology/biological science, biotechnology, microbiology, and neurosciences), BUSINESS (accounting, banking and finance, business administration and management, entrepreneurial studies, finance, international business management, management science, marketing management, and marketing/retailing/merchandising), COMMUNI-

CATIONS AND THE ARTS (advertising, communications, dramatic arts, English, journalism, public relations, Spanish, and theatre arts), COMPUTER AND PHYSICAL SCIENCE (chemistry, computer science, digital arts/technology, mathematics, software engineering, and web technology), EDUCATION (athletic training, elementary education, and secondary education), ENGINEERING AND ENVIRONMENTAL DESIGN (civil engineering, engineering, industrial engineering, and mechanical engineering), HEALTH PROFESSIONS (biomedical science, health science, nursing, occupational therapy, physical therapy, physician's assistant, predentistry, premedicine, and radiological science), SOCIAL SCIENCE (criminal justice, economics, gerontology, history, liberal arts/general studies, paralegal studies, philosophy, political science/government, prelaw, psychobiology, psychology, social science, and sociology). Psychology, physical therapy and nursing are the strongest academically. Communications, physical therapy and management have the largest enrollments.

ACTIVITIES: 12% of men belong to 8 national fraternities; 11% of women belong to 9 national sororities. There are 120 groups on campus, including cheerleading, choir, chorus, dance, drama, environmental, ethnic, film, gay, honors, international, literary magazine, newspaper, pep band, political, professional, radio and TV, religious, social, social service, student government, and yearbook. Popular campus events include The BIG Event, Parents Weekend, Relay for Life, Holiday Party, and Fall and Spring Concerts. **Sports:** There are 7 intercollegiate sports for men and 14 for women, and 6 intramural sports for men and 6 for women. Facilities include a sports center with twin arenas, each seating more than 3000 for ice hockey and basketball, more than 20 acres of playing fields, and a recreation center with a weight training room, a steam room, a large multipurpose room for indoor tennis, basketball, volleyball, and aerobics, and a suspended indoor track. Weight room and 'spinning' room on the York Hill campus plus exercise and yoga space in North Haven provide a range of options for student. **Graduates:** From July 1, 2013 to June 30, 2014, 1484 bachelor's degrees were awarded. The most popular majors were health professions (30%), business (21%), and communications (19%). 250 companies recruited on campus in 2013-2014. In an average class, 71% graduate in 4 years or less, 75% graduate in 5 years or less, and 77% graduate in 6 years or less. Of the 2013 graduating class, 22% were enrolled in graduate school within 6 months of graduation, and 72% were employed.

SERVICES: Counseling and information services are available, as is tutoring in most subjects, all freshman-level courses and others by request. Special workshops on work study skills, library resources, and time management are available. **Library/Resources:** The 3 libraries contain 311,000 volumes, 592,900 microform items, 6,000 audio/video tapes/CDs/DVDs, and subscribe to 44,700 periodicals including electronic. Computerized library services include interlibrary loans, database searching, Internet access, and Wi-Fi capability. Special learning facilities include an art gallery, radio station, TV station, an Gorta Mor an exhibit on the Irish famine, part of Quinnipiac's Ireland's Great Hunger Museum, which is located on Whitney Avenue and the Albert Schweitzer Institute. **Physically Challenged Students:** All of the campus is accessible. Facilities include wheelchair ramps, elevators, special parking, specially equipped restrooms, special class scheduling, and lowered drinking fountains. **Special:** Internships or clinical placements are available in all majors. Students can choose to study abroad in more than 25 countries - particularly Ireland and Australia. A 6 or 7-year freshman entry-level doctorate (BS/DPT) in physical therapy and a 5 1/2 year freshman entry-level master's (BS/MOT) in occupational therapy are offered, as well as a 6-year BS in Health Sciences/MHS in a physician assistant master's program. For those interested in teaching elementary or secondary education, a 5-year BA in an academic major plus a master of arts in teaching (MAT) which includes student teaching. An innovative BS/MBA is offered to academically talented business students in a 3+1 format to complete both degrees in 4 years is a new 3+3 BA or BS/JD degree with the School of Law that invites academically talented students to complete both degrees in 6 rather than 7 years. There are 11 national honor societies, a freshman honors program, and 20 departmental honors programs. **Visiting:** There are regularly scheduled orientations for prospective students, consisting of interviews, a group information session, student-guided tours, financial aid sessions, an opportunity to speak with faculty, and open houses. There

are guides for informal visits and visitors may sit in on classes. To schedule a visit, contact the Admissions Office. **Campus Safety and Security:** Measures include 24-hour foot and vehicle patrol, emergency notification system, self-defense education, and security escort services. There are shuttle buses, emergency telephones, lighted pathways/sidewalks, controlled access to dorms/residences, perimeter security in the form of contract security officers at all entrances, and vehicle and occupant check-in identification.

REQUIREMENTS: The SAT or ACT is required. The ACT Optional Writing test is also required. A minimum composite score of 1050 on the SAT (critical reading plus math) or 23 composite on the ACT is recommended. The scores are used for admission and scholarship purposes. All students must have completed 16 academic credits, including 4 in English, 3 in math, 2 each in science and social studies, and 5 in electives. The GED is accepted. An interview is recommended, and an essay and at least one letter of recommendation are required. For majors in the health sciences, 4 years each of math and science are required. Quinnipiac requires applicants to be in the upper 40% of their class. A GPA of 2.9 is required. AP and CLEP credits are accepted. Important factors in the admissions decision are advanced placement or honors courses, extracurricular activities record, and personality/intangible qualities. All students must complete 46 semester hours of the core curriculum, which includes a series of 3 seminars that explore community as it relates to the individual and the world, plus English, math, fine arts, social sciences, humanities and science. To graduate, students must maintain a GPA of 2.0 over 120 total semester hours. **Procedure:** Freshmen are admitted fall and spring. Entrance exams should be taken in the junior year and early in the senior year. There are early decision, deferred admissions, and rolling admissions plans. Early decision applications should be filed by November 1; regular applications, by February 1 for fall entry; and December 15 for spring entry, along with a $65 fee. Notification of early decision is sent December 1; regular decision, December 15. 170 early decision candidates were accepted for the 2014-2015 class. 1650 applicants were on the 2014 waiting list; 250 were admitted. Applications are accepted on-line. **Transfer Students:** 178 transfer students enrolled in 2013-2014. Transfer students must have a minimum college GPA of 2.5 (some programs require a minimum of 3.0) and must submit SAT scores and high school or college transcripts if they have not received an associate degree prior to enrollment. An interview is recommended. 45 of 120 credits required for the bachelor's degree must be completed at Quinnipiac. **International Students:** There are 145 international students enrolled. The school actively recruits these students. They must take the TOEFL with a minimum score of 550 on the paper-based TOEFL (PBT) or 80 on the Internet-based version (iBT), or take the IELTS. They must also take the SAT or ACT only if the language of instruction is in English.

ADMISSIONS: 66% of the 2014-2015 applicants were accepted. The SAT scores for the 2014-2015 freshman class were: Critical Reading--26% below 500, 52% between 500 and 599, 20% between 600 and 699, and 2% between 700 and 800; Math--19% below 500, 51% between 500 and 599, 27% between 600 and 699, and 3% between 700 and 800; Writing--21% below 500, 49% between 500 and 599, 28% between 600 and 699, and 2% between 700 and 800. The ACT scores were 11% below 21, 19% between 21 and 23, 36% between 24 and 26, 25% between 27 and 28, and 9% above 28. 55% of the current freshmen were in the top fifth of their class; 88% were in the top two fifths. 26 freshmen graduated first in their class. **Admissions Contact:** Joan Isaac Mohr, VP for Admissions/Financial Aid. E-Mail: *admissions@quinnipiac.edu* Web: *www.quinnipiac.edu*

FINANCIAL AID: In 2014-2015, 88% of all full-time freshmen and 81% of continuing full-time students received some form of financial aid. 62% of all full-time freshmen and 58% of continuing full-time students received need-based aid. The average freshman award was $24,923. Need-based scholarships or need-based grants averaged $19,707 ($55,780 maximum); need-based self-help aid (loans and jobs) averaged $4,808 ($11,000 maximum); non-need-based athletic scholarships averaged $29,231 ($57,734 maximum); and other non-need-based awards and non-need-based scholarships averaged $14,959 ($38,000 maximum). 28% of undergraduate students work part-time. Average annual earnings from campus work are $2078. The average financial indebtedness of the 2014 graduate was $44,552.

Quinnipiac is a member of CSS. The CSS/Profile and FAFSA are required. The priority date for freshman financial aid applications for fall entry is March 1. The deadline for filing freshman financial aid applications for fall entry is April 1.

SACRED HEART UNIVERSITY   **B-4**
www.sacredheart.edu

Fairfield, CT 06825	(203) 371-7881

Fax: (203) 365-7607   Email: osullivank6@sacredheart.edu
Full-time: 1587 men, 2645 women   **Faculty:** 191
Part-time: 216 men, 549 women   **Ph.D.s:** 77%
Graduate: 790 men, 1994 women   **Student/Faculty:** 14 to 1
Year: semesters, summer session   **Tuition:** $35,750
Room & Board: $13,514   **Freshman Class:** 9114
                                       applied, 5209 accepted,
                                       1385 enrolled
                                       CEEB CODE: 3780
Application Deadline: rolling   **VERY COMPETITIVE**

Sacred Heart University, founded in 1963, is a private Catholic institution that offers majors within health sciences, liberal arts and sciences, business, education, and information technology. There are 4 undergraduate schools and 4 graduate schools. In addition to regional accreditation, SHU has baccalaureate program accreditation with AACSB, APTA, CSWE, NCATE, and NLN. The 100-acre campus is in a suburban area 60 minutes from Manhattan and 150 minutes from Boston. Including any residence halls, there are 25 buildings. **STUDENT LIFE:** 59% of undergraduates are from out of state, mostly the Northeast. Students are from 49 states, 27 foreign countries, and Canada. 68% are White; 13% race unknown. The average age of freshmen is 18; all undergraduates, 22. 18% do not continue beyond their first year; 82% remain to graduate. **Housing:** 2948 students can be accommodated in college housing, which includes coed dorms, on-campus apartments, and off-campus apartments. In addition, there are honors houses, special-interest houses, living and learning communities with themes such as honors, business, wellness and community service. On-campus housing is guaranteed for all 4 years, is available on a first-come, first-served basis, and is available on a lottery system for upperclassmen. 53% of students live on campus. Upperclassmen may keep cars.

FACULTY/CLASSROOMS: 44% of faculty are male; 56% are female. 61% teach undergraduates. No introductory courses are taught by graduate students. The average class size in an introductory lecture is 25; in a laboratory is 15; and in a regular course is 21.

PROGRAMS OF STUDY: SHU confers B.A., B.S., B.S.W. and B.S.N. degrees. Associate, master's, and doctoral degrees are also awarded. Bachelor's degrees are awarded in BIOLOGICAL SCIENCE (biology/biological science and ecology), BUSINESS (accounting, banking and finance, business administration and management, business economics, fashion merchandising, marketing management, and sports management), COMMUNICATIONS AND THE ARTS (communications, communications technology, creative writing, English, graphic design, media arts, performing arts, and Spanish), COMPUTER AND PHYSICAL SCIENCE (chemistry, computer science, computer security and information assurance, information sciences and systems, and mathematics), EDUCATION (athletic training, business education, education, elementary education, English education, foreign languages education, mathematics education, middle school education, science education, social science education, and social studies education), ENGINEERING AND ENVIRONMENTAL DESIGN (computer graphics), HEALTH PROFESSIONS (exercise science, health science, nursing, occupational therapy, physical therapy, preallied health, predentistry, premedicine, preosteopathy, prepharmacy, prephysical therapy, and preveterinary science), SOCIAL SCIENCE (criminal justice, history, Latin American studies, liberal arts/general studies, Middle Eastern studies, philosophy, political science/government, prelaw, psychology, religion, social work, sociology, and women's studies). Physical therapy, nursing, and business management are the strongest academically. Nursing, exercise science, and business management have the largest enrollments.

ACTIVITIES: 16% of men belong to 5 local and 1 national fraternities; 30% of women belong to 7 national sororities. There are 110 groups on campus, including Habitat for Humanity, spectrum newspaper, student events team, radio station, academic clubs, art, bagpipe, band, cheerleading, chess, choir, chorale, chorus, communications, computers, dance, debate, drama, drill team, environmental, ethnic, film, gay, honors, international, jazz band, literary magazine, marching band, musical theater, newspaper, orchestra, pep band, photography, political, professional, radio and TV, religious, social, social service, student government, and yearbook. Popular campus events include Spring Concert, Family Weekend, Pack the Pitt, SHU Hoops Madness, President's Gala, and Just SHU it! **Sports:** There are 14 intercollegiate sports for men and 19 for women, and 26 intramural sports for men and 24 for women. Facilities include the William H. Pitt Health and Recreation Center features a 2,300-seat arena, four basketball courts, state-of-the-art fitness center, aerobics and fencing room, varsity wrestling room, and much more – including an outstanding Sports Medicine and Rehabilitation Center. Other facilities include a Spinturf athletic field, eight-lane outdoor running track and six superior Deco II tennis courts. **Graduates:** From July 1, 2013 to June 30, 2014, 858 bachelor's degrees were awarded. The most popular majors were business (28%), health professions (28%), and psychology (12%). 109 companies recruited on campus in 2013-2014. In an average class, 1% graduate in 3 years or less, 63% graduate in 4 years or less, 69% graduate in 5 years or less, and 70% graduate in 6 years or less. Of the 2013 graduating class, 11% were enrolled in graduate school within 6 months of graduation.

SERVICES: Counseling and information services are available, as is tutoring in every subject. There is a reader service for the blind, and remedial math, reading, and writing. **Library/Resources:** The 2 libraries contain 126,290 volumes, 223,059 microform items, 1,249 audio/video tapes/CDs/DVDs, and subscribe to 47,366 periodicals including electronic. Computerized library services include interlibrary loans, database searching, Internet access, and Wi-Fi capability. Special learning facilities include an art gallery, radio station, TV station, the Edgerton center for performing arts, a media studies lab, a fashion design studio, Jandrisevits learning center, 3D printing lab, life and sport analysis clinic, physical therapy clinics, cadaver lab and nursing simulators in the College of Health Professions, Markerless motion lab and Microsoft Kinnect for computer science. **Physically Challenged Students:** Facilities include wheelchair ramps, elevators, special parking, specially equipped restrooms, special class scheduling, lowered drinking fountains, lowered telephones, special housing. Special housing rooms are equipped with special audible alarms for students with hearing disabilities and other special accommodations can be made through Res Life. **Special:** SHU offers paid and unpaid internships at local, regional, and national organizations, including Fortune 500 and 1000 companies, hospitals, media outlets, social service agencies, and schools. Study abroad opportunities exist worldwide and year-round, and on-campus employment is available through the university's work-study program. There are 10 national honor societies, a freshman honors program, and 1 departmental honors program. **Visiting:** There are regularly scheduled orientations for prospective students, including Monday-Friday tours and interviews, weekend tours, interviews and information sessions, and open house programs during the academic year and summer. There are guides for informal visits, visitors may sit in on classes, and stay overnight. To schedule a visit, contact the Office of Undergraduate Admissions. **Campus Safety and Security:** Measures include 24-hour foot and vehicle patrol, emergency notification system, self-defense education, and security escort services. There are shuttle buses, emergency telephones, lighted pathways/sidewalks, controlled access to dorms/residences. All campus-owned residence halls have sprinklers and alarms, and are designated nonsmoking.

REQUIREMENTS: A completed application, essay, and 1 letter of recommendation are required. An interview is required for early decision candidates and recommended for all other candidates. Required are 4 years of English and 3 years of math, science, history, and language, with 4 years preferred. A GPA of 3.0 is required. AP and CLEP credits are accepted. Important factors in the admissions decision are advanced placement or honors courses, recommendations by school officials, and leadership record. A central component of undergraduate study is the university's core curriculum, which embodies the university's commitment to academic excellence, social responsibility, and ethical awareness. All candidates for the baccalaureate degree must complete at least 120 credits, with a minimum of 30 credits taken at Sacred Heart University. A minimum cumulative grade point average (GPA) of 2.0 is required. **Procedure:** Freshmen are admitted fall and spring. Entrance exams should be taken in May of the junior year through November of the senior year. There are early decision, early admissions, deferred admissions, and rolling admissions plans. Early decision applications should be filed by December 1. The fall 2014 application fee was $50. Notification of early decision is sent December 15; regular decision, April 1. 187 early decision candidates were accepted for the 2014-2015 class. Applications are accepted on-line. **Transfer Students:** 141 transfer students enrolled in 2013-2014. A minimum GPA of 2.0 is required. 30 of 120 credits required for the bachelor's degree must be completed at SHU. **International Students:** There are 52 international students enrolled. The school actively recruits these students. They must take the TOEFL with a minimum score of 570 on the paper-based TOEFL (PBT) or 80 on the Internet-based version (iBT).

ADMISSIONS: 57% of the 2014-2015 applicants were accepted. **Admissions Contact:** Kevin O'Sullivan, Executive Director Admissions. E-Mail: *osullivank6@sacredheart.edu* Web: *www.sacredheart.edu*

FINANCIAL AID: In 2014-2015, 72% of all full-time freshmen and 69% of continuing full-time students received some form of financial aid. 72% of all full-time freshmen and 68% of continuing full-time students received need-based aid. The average freshman award was $19,506. Need-based scholarships or need-based grants averaged $15,942; need-based self-help aid (loans and jobs) averaged $4,484; non-need-based athletic scholarships averaged $16,269; and other non-need-based awards and non-need-based scholarships averaged $11,893. The average financial indebtedness of the 2014 graduate was $23,901. SHU is a member of CSS. The CSS/Profile and FAFSA are required. The priority date for freshman financial aid applications for fall entry is February 15.

SOUTHERN CONNECTICUT STATE UNIVERSITY (*The complete profile is made available exclusively on our website, www. barronspac.com*)

TRINITY COLLEGE   C-2
www.trincoll.edu

Hartford, CT 06106   (860) 297-2180

Fax: (860) 297-2287	Email: admissions.office@mail.trincoll.edu
Full-time: 1145 men, 1069 women	Faculty: 198; IIB, ++$
Part-time: 51 men, 43 women	Ph.D.s: 92%
Graduate: 42 men, 49 women	Student/Faculty: 9 to 1
Year: semesters	Tuition: $50826
Room & Board: $13,144	Freshman Class: 7653 applied, 2432 accepted, 604 enrolled
SAT CR/M/W: 610/650/630 ACT: 28	CEEB CODE: 3899
Application Deadline: January 1	HIGHLY COMPETITIVE+

Founded in 1823, Trinity College in Hartford is an independent, nonsectarian liberal arts college. Figures in the above capsule and in this profile are approximate. There is 1 graduate school. In addition to regional accreditation, Trinity has baccalaureate program accreditation with ABET. The 100-acre campus is in an urban area southwest of downtown Hartford. Including any residence halls, there are 78 buildings.

STUDENT LIFE: 83% of undergraduates are from out of state, mostly the Northeast. Students are from 49 states, 57 foreign countries, and Canada. 42% are from public schools. 65% are White. 30% claim no religious affiliation; 28% Protestant; 27% Catholic. **Male To Female Ratio:** 0.9:1. The average age of freshmen is 18; all undergraduates, 20. 9% do not continue beyond their first year; 86% remain to graduate. **Housing:** 2000 students can be accommodated in college housing, which includes coed dorms, on-campus apartments, and off-campus apartments. In addition, there are special-interest houses. On-campus housing is guaranteed for all 4 years. 90% of students live on campus; of those, 70% remain on campus on weekends. Upperclassmen may keep cars.

FACULTY/CLASSROOMS: 55% of faculty are male; 45% are female. All teach undergraduates, all do research, and all teach and do research. No introductory courses are taught by graduate students. The average class size in an introductory lecture is 20; in a laboratory is 16; and in a regular course is 13.

PROGRAMS OF STUDY: Trinity confers B.A., and B.S. degrees. Master's degrees are also awarded. Bachelor's degrees are awarded in BIOLOGICAL SCIENCE (biochemistry, biology/biological science, and neurosciences), COMMUNICATIONS AND THE ARTS (art history and appreciation, classics, comparative literature, dance, dramatic arts, English, fine arts, French, German, Italian, modern language, music, Russian, Spanish, studio art, and theater management), COMPUTER AND PHYSICAL SCIENCE (chemistry, computer science, mathematics, and physics), EDUCATION (education), ENGINEERING AND ENVIRONMENTAL DESIGN (engineering and environmental science), SOCIAL SCIENCE (American studies, anthropology, classical/ancient civilization, economics, history, interdisciplinary studies, international studies, Judaic studies, philosophy, political science/government, psychology, public affairs, religion, sociology, and women's studies). Political science, economics, English and psychology have the largest enrollments.

ACTIVITIES: 20% of men and 16 of women belong to 5 local and 2 national fraternities. There are no sororities. There are 120 groups on campus, including art, bagpipe, band, cheerleading, chess, choir, chorale, chorus, dance, debate, drama, ethnic, film, gay, honors, international, jazz band, literary magazine, musical theater, newspaper, pep band, photography, political, professional, radio and TV, religious, social, social service, student government, and yearbook. Popular campus events include Human Rights Lecture Series, Black History Month and Latino Heritage Week. **Sports:** There are 15 intercollegiate sports for men and 13 for women, and 14 intramural sports for men and 14 for women. Facilities include a pool, outdoor and indoor tracks, playing fields, a weight room, a fitness center, and tennis, squash, and basketball courts. **Graduates:** From July 1, 2013 to June 30, 2014, 543 bachelor's degrees were awarded. The most popular majors were economics (16%), political science (12%), and history (7%). 200 companies recruited on campus in 2013-2014. In an average class, 81% graduate in 4 years or less, 83% graduate in 5 years or less, and 86% graduate in 6 years or less.

SERVICES: Counseling and information services are available, as is tutoring in every subject. There is a reader service for the blind. The writing center offers instruction in all forms of writing, and the math center provides individual tutoring on topics related to math and other courses involving quantitative reasoning. **Library/Resources:** The library contains 992,817 volumes, 399,394 microform items, 225,477 audio/video tapes/CDs/DVDs, and subscribes to 2,438 periodicals including electronic. Computerized library services include interlibrary loans, database searching, Internet access, and Wi-Fi capability. Special learning facilities include an art gallery, radio station, and TV station. **Physically Challenged Students:** 60% of the campus is accessible. Facilities include wheelchair ramps, elevators, special parking, specially equipped restrooms, special class scheduling, lowered drinking fountains, and lowered telephones. **Special:** Trinity offers special freshman programs for exceptional students, including interdisciplinary programs in the sciences and the humanities. There is an intensive study program under which students can devote a semester to 1 subject. Cross-registration through such programs as the Hartford Consortium and the Twelve-College Exchange Program, hundreds of internships (some with Connecticut Public Radio and TV on campus), study abroad virtually worldwide, including Rome, South Africa, Trinidad, Russia, and Nepal, a Washington semester, dual majors in all disciplines, student-designed majors, nondegree study, and pass/fail options also are offered. A 5-year advanced degree in electrical or mechanical engineering with Rensselaer Polytechnic Institute is available. There are 4 national honor societies including Phi Beta Kappa chapter. **Visiting:** There are regularly scheduled orientations for prospective students. There are guides for informal visits, visitors may sit in on classes, and stay overnight. To schedule a visit, contact the Admissions Office. **Campus Safety and Security:** Measures include 24-hour foot and vehicle patrol, self-defense education, and security escort services. There are shuttle buses, emergency telephones, and lighted pathways/sidewalks.

REQUIREMENTS: The SAT or ACT is required. Trinity strongly emphasizes individual character and personal qualities in admission. Consequently, an interview and essay are recommended. The college requires 4 years of English, 2 years each in foreign language and algebra, and 1 year each in geometry, history, and lab science. AP credits are accepted. Important factors in the admissions decision are advanced placement or honors courses, extracurricular activities record, and evidence of special talent. All students must complete 36 course credits, including 10 to 15 in the major and 1 from each of 5 distribution areas: arts, humanities, natural sciences, numerical and symbolic reasoning, and social sciences. Students must maintain at least a C average overall. **Procedure:** Freshmen are admitted fall. Entrance exams should be taken in the fall of the senior year. There are early decision and deferred admissions plans. Early decision applications should be filed by November 15; regular applications, by January 1 for fall entry, along with a $60 fee. Notification of early decision is sent December 15; regular decision, April 1. 311 early decision candidates were accepted for the 2014-2015 class. Applications are accepted on-line. **Transfer Students:** 15 transfer students enrolled in 2013-2014. Transfer applicants must take the SAT or ACT. A minimum college GPA of 3.0 is recommended. 18 of 36 credits required for the bachelor's degree must be completed at Trinity. **International Students:** There are 195 international students enrolled. The school actively recruits these students. They must take the TOEFL. They must also take the SAT or ACT.

ADMISSIONS: 32% of the 2014-2015 applicants were accepted. The SAT scores for the 2014-2015 freshman class were: Critical Reading--2% below 500, 22% between 500 and 599, 49% between 600 and 699, and 27% between 700 and 800; Math--3% below 500, 32% between 500 and 599, 48% between 600 and 699, and 17% between 700 and 800; Writing--4% below 500, 25% between 500 and 599, 54% between 600 and 699, and 16% between 700 and 800. The ACT scores were 1% below 21, 11% between 21 and 23, 24% between 24 and 26, 34% between 27 and 28, and 30% above 28. **Admissions Contact:** Dean of Admissions/Financial Aid. E-Mail: *admissions.office@ mail.trincoll.edu* Web: *www.trincoll.edu*

FINANCIAL AID: In 2014-2015, 42% of all full-time freshmen and 42% of continuing full-time students received some form of financial aid. 40% of all full-time freshmen and 39% of continuing full-time students received need-based aid. The average freshman award was $39,282. Need-based scholarships or need-based grants averaged $35,580 ($62,350 maximum); need-based self-help aid (loans and jobs) averaged $10,121 ($11,000 maximum); and other non-need-based awards and non-need-based scholarships averaged $25,810 ($60,810 maximum). 29% of undergraduate students work part-time. Average annual earnings from campus work are $2500. The average financial indebtedness of the 2014 graduate was $4,538. Trinity is a member of CSS. The CSS/Profile and FAFSA are required. The priority date for freshman financial aid applications for fall entry is February 1. The deadline for filing freshman financial aid applications for fall entry is March 1.

ernment provides a yearly allowance of $12,192 to help cover cadet expenses. There is 1 undergraduate school. In addition to regional accreditation, USCGA has baccalaureate program accreditation with AACSB and ABET. The 103-acre campus is in a suburban area next to New London, 2 hours South of Boston, 2 hours North of NYC. Including any residence halls, there are 28 buildings.

STUDENT LIFE: 94% of undergraduates are from out of state, mostly the Northeast. Students are from 49 states, and 23 foreign countries. 76% are from public schools. 65% are White; 12% Hispanic. **Male To Female Ratio:** 0.5:1. The average age of freshmen is 18; all undergraduates, 20. 2% do not continue beyond their first year; 85% remain to graduate. **Housing:** 961 students can be accommodated in college housing, which includes coed dorms. On-campus housing is guaranteed for all 4 years. Alcohol is not permitted. Upperclassmen may keep cars.

FACULTY/CLASSROOMS: 70% of faculty are male; 30% are female. All teach undergraduates, 50% do research, and 50% do both. No introductory courses are taught by graduate students. The average class size in an introductory lecture is 25; in a laboratory is 14; and in a regular course is 18.

PROGRAMS OF STUDY: USCGA confers B.S. degrees. Bachelor's degrees are awarded in BIOLOGICAL SCIENCE (marine science), BUSINESS (management science and operations research), ENGINEERING AND ENVIRONMENTAL DESIGN (civil engineering, electrical/electronics engineering, mechanical engineering, and naval architecture and marine engineering), SOCIAL SCIENCE (political science/government). Engineering, marine science, and government have the largest enrollments.

ACTIVITIES: There are no fraternities or sororities. There are 51 groups on campus, including art, band, cheerleading, choir, chorale, chorus, computers, dance, debate, drama, drill team, drum and bugle corps, environmental, ethnic, gay, honors, international, jazz band, marching band, musical theater, newspaper, pep band, political, professional, religious, social, social service, student government, and yearbook. Popular campus events include Parents' weekend, Coast Guard Day, Homecoming, Graduation, Cultural History and Heritage Events and Sporting Events. **Sports:** There are 15 intercollegiate sports for men and 13 for women, and 22 intramural sports for men and 22 for women. Facilities include a field house with 3 basketball courts, a 6-lane swimming pool, 5 racquetball courts, and facilities for track meets, tennis matches, baseball and softball games, an additional athletic facility with wrestling and weight rooms, basketball courts, gymnastics areas, swimming pool, saunas, a 4500-seat stadium, practice and playing fields, outdoor tennis courts, rowing and seamanship-sailing centers. **Graduates:** From July 1, 2013 to June 30, 2014, 221 bachelor's degrees were awarded. The most popular majors were civil engineering (18%), management (16%), and government (14%). In an average class, 76% graduate in 4 years or less, 85% graduate in 5 years or less, and 85% graduate in 6 years or less. Of the 2013 graduating class, 100% were employed within 6 months of graduation.

SERVICES: Counseling and information services are available, as is tutoring in every subject. There is remedial math, reading, and writing. **Library/Resources:** The library contains 247,000 volumes, 410,000 microform items, 2,400 audio/video tapes/CDs/DVDs, and subscribes to 74,000 periodicals including electronic. Computerized library services include interlibrary loans, database searching, Internet access, and Wi-Fi capability. **Physically Challenged Students:** 24% of the campus is accessible. Facilities include wheelchair ramps, elevators, special parking, and specially equipped restrooms. **Special:** Cross-registration with Connecticut College, summer cruises to foreign ports, 6-week internships with various government agencies and some engineering and science organizations, and 1-semester exchange program with the 3 other military academies are available. All U.S. citizen graduates are commissioned in the U.S. Coast Guard (Foreign nationals are not commissioned in the U.S. Coast Guard). There are 2 national honor societies, a freshman honors program, and 3 departmental honors programs. **Visiting:** There are regularly scheduled orientations for prospective students, including an admissions briefing and tour of the academy every Monday, Wednesday, and Friday from 1 p.m. To schedule a visit, contact the Admissions Receptionist or register online; www.uscga.edu. **Campus Safety and Security:** Measures include 24-hour foot and vehicle patrol, emer-

---

UNITED STATES COAST GUARD ACADEMY   D-3
www.uscga.edu

New London, CT 06320

(860) 444-8500
(800) 883-8724

Fax: (860) 701-6700   Email: uscga.admissions@uscga.edu

Full-time: 586 men, 310 women	Faculty: 118
Part-time: n/av	Ph.D.s: 52%
Graduate: n/av	Student/Faculty: 8 to 1
Year: semesters, summer session	Tuition: see profile
Room & Board: n/app	Freshman Class: 2096 applied, 379 accepted, 249 enrolled
SAT CR/M/W: 620/660/610 ACT: 28	CEEB CODE: 5807
Application Deadline: February 1	HIGHLY COMPETITIVE

The U.S. Coast Guard Academy, founded in 1876, is an Armed Forces Service Academy for men and women. Appointments are made solely on the basis of an annual nationwide competition. The federal gov-gency notification system, self-defense education, and security escort services. There are lighted pathways/sidewalks and controlled access to dorms/residences.

REQUIREMENTS: The SAT or ACT is required. The ACT Optional Writing test is also required. Applicants must have reached the age of 17 but not the age of 23 by July 1 of the year of admission, be citizens of the United States, and be single at the time of appointment and remain single while attending the academy. Required secondary school courses include 4 years each of English and math. International students must apply through their consulate.These requirements for the degree of Bachelor of Science and a commission as an Ensign in the United States Coast Guard are as follows: a. Pass or validate every course in the core curriculum. b. Pass at least 37 courses of 3.00 credits or greater. c. Attain an average of at least a 2.00 in all required "upper-division" courses in the major, as specified in the official catalog of courses. For repeated courses, all grades earned are included in the average. d. Satisfy the academic requirements for one of the majors as specified in the official catalog of courses. e. Attain a cumulative GPA of at least a 2.00. f. Be in residence at the Academy for at least four academic years. g. Successfully complete all required portions of the physical education program, including meeting minimum swimming and physical fitness standards. h. Meet all military performance standards, demonstrating all aspects of personal and professional development necessary to serve as Ensigns in the United States Coast Guard, unless a commission will not be offered due to a medical disqualification. International cadets must meet the same standards of personal and professional development as all other graduates, notwithstanding that they are not entitled to appointment in the U.S. Coast Guard. **Procedure:** Freshmen are admitted fall. Entrance exams should be taken must receive by March 1, 2015. There are early admissions, deferred admissions, and rolling admissions plans. Applications should be filed by February 1 for fall entry. Notification is sent on a rolling basis. 174 applicants were on the 2014 waiting list; 47 were admitted. Applications are accepted on-line. **Transfer Students:** All transfer students must meet the same standards as incoming freshmen and must begin as freshmen no matter how many semesters or years of college they have completed. 126 of 126 credits required for the bachelor's degree must be completed at USCGA. **International Students:** There are 25 international students enrolled. They must take the TOEFL with a minimum score of 560 on the paper-based TOEFL (PBT). They must also take the SAT or ACT.

ADMISSIONS: 18% of the 2014-2015 applicants were accepted. The SAT scores for the 2014-2015 freshman class were: Critical Reading--2% below 500, 35% between 500 and 599, 50% between 600 and 699, and 13% between 700 and 800; Math--1% below 500, 20% between 500 and 599, 58% between 600 and 699, and 21% between 700 and 800; Writing--4% below 500, 36% between 500 and 599, 50% between 600 and 699, and 10% between 700 and 800. The ACT scores were 4% between 21 and 23, 26% between 24 and 26, 28% between 27 and 28, and 42% above 28. 66% of the current freshmen were in the top fifth of their class; 90% were in the top two fifths. 14 freshmen graduated first in their class. **Admissions Contact:** Captain McKenna, Director of Admissions. E-Mail: *uscga.admissions@uscga.edu* Web: *www.uscga.edu*

FINANCIAL AID: Check with the school for current application deadlines.

UNIVERSITY OF BRIDGEPORT *(The complete profile is made available exclusively on our website, www.barronspac.com)*

UNIVERSITY OF CONNECTICUT   D-2
www.uconn.edu

Storrs, CT 06269	**(860) 486-3137**
Fax: (860) 486-1476	Email: beahusky@uconn.edu
Full-time: 8707 men, 8512 women	Faculty: I, +$
Part-time: 470 men, 343 women	Ph.D.s: 94%
Graduate: 3780 men, 4099 women	Student/Faculty: 16 to 1
Year: semesters, summer session	Tuition: $12,700 ($32,880)
Room & Board: $12,006	Freshman Class: 27479 applied, 14745 accepted, 3755 enrolled
SAT CR/M/W: 600/630/610 ACT: 27	CEEB CODE: 3915
Application Deadline: n/av	**HIGHLY COMPETITIVE**

The University of Connecticut, founded in 1881, is a public, land-grant, sea-grant, multicampus research institution offering degree programs in liberal arts and sciences and professional studies. There are 9 undergraduate schools and 5 graduate schools. In addition to regional accreditation, UConn has baccalaureate program accreditation with AACSB, ABET, ASLA, NASAD, NASM, and NCATE. The 4093-acre campus is in a rural area 25 miles east of Hartford. Including any residence halls, there are 350 buildings.

STUDENT LIFE: 79% of undergraduates are from Connecticut. Others are from 43 states, 60 foreign countries, and Canada. 87% are from public schools. 63% are White. **Male To Female Ratio:** 1.0:1. The average age of freshmen is 18; all undergraduates, 20. 6% do not continue beyond their first year; 83% remain to graduate. **Housing:** 12668 students can be accommodated in college housing, which includes single-sex and coed dorms, on-campus apartments, off-campus apartments, and married student housing. In addition, there are honors houses, language houses, special-interest houses, fraternity houses, sorority houses, living and learning communities, business connections, Eco-house, global house, humanities house, public health house, women in math, science, and engineering. On-campus housing is guaranteed for the freshman year only. 72% of students live on campus; of those, 70% remain on campus on weekends. Upperclassmen may keep cars.

FACULTY/CLASSROOMS: 63% of faculty are male; 37% are female. Graduate students teach 33% of introductory courses. The average class size in an introductory lecture is 48; in a laboratory is 20; and in a regular course is 38.

PROGRAMS OF STUDY: UConn confers B.A., B.S., B.F.A., B.G.S., B.Mus., B.S.E., B.S.N. and B.S.Pharm. degrees. Associate, master's, and doctoral degrees are also awarded. Bachelor's degrees are awarded in AGRICULTURE (agricultural economics, agriculture, agronomy, animal science, horticulture, and natural resource management), BIOLOGICAL SCIENCE (biology/biological science, biophysics, evolutionary biology, genetics, marine science, molecular biology, nutrition, and physiology), BUSINESS (accounting, banking and finance, business administration and management, insurance and risk management, management information systems, marketing/retailing/merchandising, and real estate), COMMUNICATIONS AND THE ARTS (art, art history and appreciation, classics, communications, dramatic arts, English, French, German, journalism, linguistics, music, Spanish, theater design, and visual and performing arts), COMPUTER AND PHYSICAL SCIENCE (chemistry, computer science, geology, mathematics, physics, and statistics), EDUCATION (agricultural education, athletic training, education, elementary education, English education, foreign languages education, mathematics education, music education, recreation education, science education, social studies education, and special education), ENGINEERING AND ENVIRONMENTAL DESIGN (biomedical engineering, chemical engineering, civil engineering, computer engineering, electrical/electronics engineering, environmental engineering, environmental science, landscape architecture/design, manufacturing engineering, materials engineering, and mechanical engineering), HEALTH PROFESSIONS (cytotechnology, exercise science, health care administration, medical laboratory technology, nursing, pharmacy, and physical therapy), SOCIAL SCIENCE (anthropology, dietetics, economics, geography, history, human development, Italian studies, Latin American studies, Middle Eastern studies, philosophy, political science/government, psychology, sociology, urban studies, and women's studies). Biological sciences, psychology, and political science have the largest enrollments.

ACTIVITIES: 11% of men belong to 16 national fraternities; 15% of women belong to 16 national sororities. There are 656 groups on campus, including art, band, cheerleading, chess, choir, chorale, chorus, communications, computers, dance, debate, drama, drill team, environmental, ethnic, film, gay, honors, international, jazz band, literary magazine, marching band, musical theater, newspaper, opera, orchestra, pep band, photography, political, professional, radio and TV, religious, social, social service, student government, symphony, and yearbook. Popular campus events include Husky WOW (Week of Welcome,) Homecoming, Winter Weekend/One Ton Sundae, Lipsync, Oozeball, Huskymania/Midnight Madness, Family Weekend, UConn Late Night, and Midnight Breakfast. **Sports:** There are 11 intercollegiate sports for men and 13 for women, and 29 intramural sports for men and 28 for women. Facilities include a sports center, a field house, a 16,000-seat football stadium, a 10,000-seat basketball stadium, and a student, faculty, and staff workout center. **Graduates:** From July 1, 2013 to June 30, 2014, 5122 bachelor's degrees were awarded. The most popular majors were social sciences (12%), business, management, marketing, and related support services (12%), and health professions and related programs (11%). In an average class, 70% graduate in 4 years or less, 80% graduate in 5 years or less, and 83% graduate in 6 years or less. Of the 2013 graduating class, 30% were enrolled in graduate school within 6 months of graduation, and 82% were employed.

SERVICES: Counseling and information services are available, as is tutoring in most subjects. There is a reader service for the blind. Also available are a Braille printer, a Kurzweil reading machine and Mac computer with voice synthesizer, a machine to enlarge printed material, a talking calculator, and a TDD. **Library/Resources:** The library contains 3.3 million volumes, 3.2 million microform items, 106,017 audio/video tapes/CDs/DVDs, and subscribes to 424,922 periodicals including electronic. Computerized library services include interlibrary loans, database searching, and Internet access. Special learning facilities include an art gallery, natural history museum, planetarium, radio station, and TV station. **Physically Challenged Students:** 90% of the campus is accessible. Facilities include wheelchair ramps, elevators, special parking, specially equipped restrooms, special class scheduling, lowered drinking fountains, lowered telephones, special housing, a tactile map, and 4 specially equipped transportation vans. **Special:** UConn offers co-op programs in most majors, internships, more than 200 study-abroad programs in 65 countries, dual majors, general studies degrees, student-designed majors, work-study programs, nondegree study, and pass/fail options. There are 31 national honor societies, including Phi Beta Kappa, a freshman honors program, and 8 departmental honors programs. **Visiting:** There are regularly scheduled orientations for prospective students, including daily tours and information sessions. Visitors may sit in on classes. To schedule a visit, contact Lodewick Visitors Center at (860) 486-4900 . **Campus Safety and Security:** Measures include 24-hour foot and vehicle patrol, emergency notification system, self-defense education, and security escort services. There are shuttle buses, emergency telephones, and lighted pathways/sidewalks.

REQUIREMENTS: The SAT or ACT is required. Applicants must be graduates of an approved secondary school and should rank in the upper range of their class. The GED is accepted. Students must complete 16 high school academic units, including 4 years of English, 3 of math, 2 each of foreign language, science, and social studies, and 3 of electives. An essay is required. An audition is required for music and theater students and a portfolio for art students. AP credits are accepted. Important factors in the admissions decision are advanced placement or honors courses, evidence of special talent, and leadership record. To graduate, students must complete 120 credits with a GPA of 2.0. There are general education requirements in foreign language, expository writing, math, literature and the arts, culture and modern society, philosophical and ethical analysis, social scientific and comparative analysis, and science and technology. Students must complete a course that provides hands-on experience in a major computer application. **Procedure:** Freshmen are admitted fall and spring. Entrance exams should be taken in the spring of the junior year or fall of the senior year. There are deferred admissions and rolling admissions plans. Check with the school for current application deadlines. The application fee is $70. Notifications are sent in March. 1271 applicants were on the 2014 waiting list; 24 were admitted. Applications are accepted on-line. **Transfer Students:** 786 transfer students enrolled in 2013-2014. Applicants should have a minimum GPA of 2.7 and submit official transcripts from all colleges previously attended, the high school transcript, and SAT or ACT scores as needed. An associate degree or a minimum of 54 credit hours is recommended. 30 of 120 credits required for the bachelor's degree must be completed at UConn. **International Students:** There are 632 international students enrolled. The school actively recruits these students. They must take the TOEFL with a minimum score of 550 on the paper-based TOEFL (PBT) or 79 on the Internet-based version (iBT) and the college's own test. They must also take the SAT or ACT.

ADMISSIONS: 54% of the 2014-2015 applicants were accepted. The SAT scores for the 2014-2015 freshman class were: Critical Read-

ing--4% below 500, 41% between 500 and 599, 46% between 600 and 699, and 9% between 700 and 800; Math--3% below 500, 25% between 500 and 599, 58% between 600 and 699, and 14% between 700 and 800; Writing--5% below 500, 36% between 500 and 599, 50% between 600 and 699, and 9% between 700 and 800. The ACT scores were 2% below 21, 6% between 21 and 23, 32% between 24 and 26, 25% between 27 and 28, and 35% above 28. 73% of the current freshmen were in the top fifth of their class; 95% were in the top two fifths. 81 freshmen graduated first in their class. **Admissions Contact:** Director of Admissions. Web: *www.uconn.edu*

FINANCIAL AID: In 2014-2015, 53% of all full-time freshmen and 55% of continuing full-time students received some form of financial aid. 61% of all full-time freshmen and 64% of continuing full-time students received need-based aid. The average freshman award was $12,086. 49% of undergraduate students work part-time. Average annual earnings from campus work are $2025. The average financial indebtedness of the 2014 graduate was $24,373. The FAFSA is required. The priority date for freshman financial aid applications for fall entry is March 1.

UNIVERSITY OF HARTFORD   C-2
www.hartford.edu

West Hartford, CT 06117	(860) 243-4296
	(800) 947-4303
Fax: (860) 768-4961	**Email:** admission@hartford.edu
Full-time: 2281 men, 2222 women	**Faculty:** 347; IIA, av$
Part-time: 315 men, 466 women	**Ph.D.s:** 86%
Graduate: 651 men, 959 women	**Student/Faculty:** 12 to 1
Year: semesters, summer session	**Tuition:** $30,754
Room & Board: $11,920	**Freshman Class:** 14683 applied, 9086 accepted, 1289 enrolled
SAT CR/M: 521/530 **ACT:** 22	**CEEB CODE:** 3436
Application Deadline: open	**COMPETITIVE**

The University of Hartford, founded in 1877, is an independent, nonsectarian institution offering extensive undergraduate and graduate programs ranging from liberal arts to business. Figures in the above capsule and in this profile are approximate. There are 7 undergraduate schools and 6 graduate schools. In addition to regional accreditation, has baccalaureate program accreditation with AACSB, ABET, APTA, CAHEA, NASAD, NASM, NCATE, and NLN. The 320-acre campus is in a suburban area 4 miles northwest of Hartford. Including any residence halls, there are 32 buildings.

STUDENT LIFE: 58% of undergraduates are from out of state, mostly the Northeast. Students are from 45 states, 37 foreign countries, and Canada. 80% are from public schools. 61% are White; 14% African American. 91% claim no religious affiliation. **Male To Female Ratio:** 1.1:1. The average age of freshmen is 18; all undergraduates, 22. 27% do not continue beyond their first year; 57% remain to graduate. **Housing:** 3530 students can be accommodated in college housing, which includes coed dorms and on-campus apartments. In addition, there are honors houses, special-interest houses, the residential college for the arts, and the international residential college. On-campus housing is guaranteed for all 4 years. 61% of students live on campus; of those, 85% remain on campus on weekends. All students may keep cars.

FACULTY/CLASSROOMS: 61% of faculty are male; 39% are female. All teach undergraduates, and 97% do research. No introductory courses are taught by graduate students. The average class size in an introductory lecture is 43; in a laboratory is 21; and in a regular course is 24.

PROGRAMS OF STUDY: University of Hartford confers B.A., B.F.A., B.Mus., B.S., B.S.A.E.T., B.S.B.A., B.S.C.E., B.S.Comp.E., B.S.Ed., B.S.E.E. and B.S.M.E. degrees. Associate, master's, and doctoral degrees are also awarded. Bachelor's degrees are awarded in BIOLOGICAL SCIENCE (biology/biological science), BUSINESS (accounting, banking and finance, business administration and management, entrepreneurial studies, insurance, management information systems, management science, and marketing/retailing/

merchandising), COMMUNICATIONS AND THE ARTS (art history and appreciation, audio technology, ceramic art and design, communications, dance, design, dramatic arts, drawing, English, film arts, illustration, jazz, languages, media arts, music, music business management, music history and appreciation, music performance, music technology, music theory and composition, musical theater, painting, performing arts, photography, printmaking, sculpture, technical and business writing, theater management, video, and visual and performing arts), COMPUTER AND PHYSICAL SCIENCE (chemistry, computer science, information sciences and systems, mathematics, physics, and radiological technology), EDUCATION (early childhood education, elementary education, music education, secondary education, and special education), ENGINEERING AND ENVIRONMENTAL DESIGN (architectural engineering, biomedical engineering, chemical engineering technology, civil engineering, computer engineering, electrical/electronics engineering, electrical/electronics engineering technology, engineering, engineering technology, mechanical engineering, and mechanical engineering technology), HEALTH PROFESSIONS (health science, medical laboratory technology, nursing, occupational therapy, physical therapy, predentistry, premedicine, and preoptometry), SOCIAL SCIENCE (criminal justice, economics, history, human services, interdisciplinary studies, international studies, Judaic studies, law, philosophy, political science/government, psychology, and sociology). Accounting, management, and engineering are the strongest academically. Communication, architectural engineering technology and psychology have the largest enrollments.

ACTIVITIES: 17% of men belong to 7 national fraternities; 21% of women belong to 7 national sororities. There are 45 groups on campus, including art, band, cheerleading, choir, chorale, chorus, computers, drama, ethnic, gay, honors, international, jazz band, literary magazine, musical theater, newspaper, opera, orchestra, pep band, political, professional, radio and TV, religious, social, social service, student government, and symphony. Popular campus events include Welcome Weekend, Spring Weekend and Winter Carnival.

Sports: There are 9 intercollegiate sports for men and 9 for women, and 15 intramural sports for men and 15 for women. Facilities include playing fields, a 25-meter outdoor pool, tennis courts, golf practice cages, a fitness trail, and a sports center with a 4,600-seat multipurpose court, an 8-lane swimming pool, a weight room, racquetball courts, a squash court, and saunas. **Graduates:** From July 1, 2013 to June 30, 2014, 955 bachelor's degrees were awarded. The most popular majors were communications (7%), psychology (4%), and architectural engineering tech. (4%). 182 companies recruited on campus in 2013-2014. In an average class, 53% graduate in 4 years or less, 58% graduate in 5 years or less, and 59% graduate in 6 years or less. Of the 2013 graduating class, 35% were enrolled in graduate school within 6 months of graduation, and 75% were employed.

SERVICES: Counseling and information services are available, as is tutoring in most subjects. There is a reader service for the blind, and remedial math, reading, and writing. The health education office offers peer counseling and workshops on health-related topics. Professional counseling is available. **Library/Resources:** The 3 libraries contain 590,724 volumes, 383,386 microform items, 5,921 audio/video tapes/CDs/DVDs, and subscribe to 49,600 periodicals including electronic. Computerized library services include interlibrary loans, database searching, Internet access, and Wi-Fi capability. Special learning facilities include an art gallery, radio station, TV station, the Museum of American Political Life. **Physically Challenged Students:** Facilities include wheelchair ramps, elevators, special parking, specially equipped restrooms, lowered drinking fountains, lowered telephones, and special housing. **Special:** Cross-registration with the Greater Hartford Consortium, internships in all majors, study abroad, a Washington semester, work-study programs, credit for life experience, nondegree study, and pass/fail options are available. In addition, students may pursue accelerated degrees, B.A.-B.S. degrees, dual majors, or their own individually designed majors. There are interdisciplinary majors in acoustics and music and in experimental studio combining performing, literary, and visual arts. Also available are preprofessional programs in biology/preoptometry with the New England College of Optometry, predentistry with the New York University School of Dentistry, prechiropractic with the New York Chiropractic College, preosteopathic with the University of New England

College of Osteopathic Medicine, and prepodiatry with the New York College of Podiatric Medicine. There are 19 national honor societies, a freshman honors program, and 7 departmental honors programs. **Visiting:** There are regularly scheduled orientations for prospective students. There are guides for informal visits, visitors may sit in on classes, and stay overnight. To schedule a visit, contact the Office of Admissions. **Campus Safety and Security:** Measures include 24-hour foot and vehicle patrol, emergency notification system, self-defense education, and security escort services. There are shuttle buses, emergency telephones, lighted pathways/sidewalks, and a bicycle patrol.

REQUIREMENTS: The SAT is required. Applicants should have 16 academic high school credits and 16 Carnegie units, including 4 units in English, 3 in math (3.5 for B.S. candidates), and 2 each in foreign language, science, and social studies. A portfolio and an audition are required for B.F.A. and B.Mus. candidates, respectively. A personal statement is required, and an interview is recommended for all students. AP and CLEP credits are accepted. Important factors in the admissions decision are advanced placement or honors courses, recommendations by school officials, and leadership record. To graduate, students must complete at least 120 credit hours, fulfill the university's core curriculum requirements, and maintain an overall GPA of 2.0. Specific core and course requirements vary with the major. **Procedure:** Freshmen are admitted fall and spring. Entrance exams should be taken in the spring of the junior year or the fall of the senior year. There are deferred admissions and rolling admissions plans. Application deadlines are open. The fall 2014 application fee was $40. Notification is sent on a rolling basis. Applications are accepted online. **Transfer Students:** 232 transfer students enrolled in 2013-2014. Transfer students must have a minimum college GPA of 2.25, with 2.5 recommended, and must submit SAT or ACT scores if they have fewer than 30 transferable college-level credits. An interview is also recommended. 30 of 120 credits required for the bachelor's degree must be completed at the University of Hartford. **International Students:** There are 195 international students enrolled. The school actively recruits these students. They must take the TOEFL with a minimum score of 550 on the paper-based TOEFL (PBT). The SAT or the ACT is recommended.

ADMISSIONS: 62% of the 2014-2015 applicants were accepted. The SAT scores for the 2014-2015 freshman class were: Critical Reading--46% below 500, 39% between 500 and 599, 14% between 600 and 699, and 1% between 700 and 800; Math--44% below 500, 37% between 500 and 599, 17% between 600 and 699, and 2% between 700 and 800. The ACT scores were 38% below 21, 28% between 21 and 23, 20% between 24 and 26, 6% between 27 and 28, and 8% above 28. 12% of the current freshmen were in the top fifth of their class; 27% were in the top two fifths. **Admissions Contact:** Dean of Admissions. E-Mail: *admission@hartford.edu* Web: *www.hartford.edu*

FINANCIAL AID: In 2014-2015, 94% of all full-time freshmen and 97% of continuing full-time students received some form of financial aid. 80% of all full-time freshmen and 78% of continuing full-time students received need-based aid. The average freshman award was $9,592. Need-based scholarships or need-based grants averaged $14,834; need-based self-help aid (loans and jobs) averaged $16,846; non-need-based athletic scholarships averaged $38,648; and other non-need-based awards and non-need-based scholarships averaged $14,101. 22% of undergraduate students work part-time. Average annual earnings from campus work are $3200. The average financial indebtedness of the 2014 graduate was $26,652. The FAFSA is required. The priority date for freshman financial aid applications for fall entry is February 1. The deadline for filing freshman financial aid applications for fall entry is March 1.

UNIVERSITY OF NEW HAVEN C-3
www.newhaven.edu

West Haven, CT 06516 (203) 932-7319
(800) 342-5864 ext. 7319
Fax: (203) 931-6093 Email: admissions@newhaven.edu
Full-time: 2343 men, 2331 women Faculty: IIA, +$
Part-time: 201 men, 173 women Ph.D.s: 82%
Graduate: 930 men, 833 women Student/Faculty: n/av
Year: 4-1-4, summer session Tuition: $34,630
Room & Board: $14,310 Freshman Class: 9006 applied, 7282 accepted, 1221 enrolled
SAT CR/M/W: 520/530/510 ACT: required
CEEB CODE: 3663
Application Deadline: open COMPETITIVE

The University of New Haven is a private, top-tier comprehensive institution recognized as a national leader in experiential education. Founded in 1920, the University provides its students with a unique combination of a solid liberal arts education and real-world, hands-on career and research opportunities. There are 5 undergraduate schools and 4 graduate schools. In addition to regional accreditation, UNH has baccalaureate program accreditation with ABET, ADA, and NCATE. The 82-acre campus is in a suburban area 90 minutes from New York City and approximately 2 1/2 hours from Boston.

STUDENT LIFE: 57% of undergraduates are from out of state, mostly the Northeast. Students are from 39 states, 30 foreign countries, and Canada. 59% are White. **Male To Female Ratio:** 1.0:1. The average age of freshmen is 18; all undergraduates, 20. 20% do not continue beyond their first year; 49% remain to graduate. **Housing:** 2852 students can be accommodated in college housing, which includes coed dorms, on-campus apartments, and off-campus apartments. On-campus housing is available on a first-come, first-served basis, and is available on a lottery system for upperclassmen. 53% of students live on campus. Upperclassmen may keep cars.

FACULTY/CLASSROOMS: 67% of faculty are male; 33% are female. No introductory courses are taught by graduate students.

PROGRAMS OF STUDY: UNH confers B.A., B.S. and B.F.A. degrees. Associate, master's, and doctoral degrees are also awarded. Bachelor's degrees are awarded in BIOLOGICAL SCIENCE (biochemistry, biology/biological science, biotechnology, marine biology, and nutrition), BUSINESS (accounting, banking and finance, business administration and management, hospitality management services, hotel/motel and restaurant management, marketing/retailing/merchandising, sports management, and tourism), COMMUNICATIONS AND THE ARTS (advertising, art, audio technology, communications, communications technology, creative writing, design, English, fine arts, fine/studio arts, general, graphic design, journalism, literature, multimedia, music, music business management, music performance, music technology, music theory and composition, theatre arts, visual and performing arts, and visual design), COMPUTER AND PHYSICAL SCIENCE (applied mathematics, chemistry, computer management, computer mathematics, computer programming, computer science, mathematics, and natural sciences), EDUCATION (mathematics education, science education, and secondary education), ENGINEERING AND ENVIRONMENTAL DESIGN (chemical engineering, civil engineering, computer engineering, electrical/electronics engineering, engineering, environmental science, fire protection engineering, interior design, mechanical engineering, and systems engineering), HEALTH PROFESSIONS (dental hygiene, predentistry, premedicine, and preveterinary science), SOCIAL SCIENCE (behavioral science, clinical psychology, community psychology, corrections, counseling/psychology, criminal justice, criminology, dietetics, economics, family and community services, family/juvenile justice, fire control and safety technology, fire protection, fire science, fire services administration, forensic studies, (Social Science) Global Studies, history, international public service, international relations, international studies, law enforcement and corrections, legal studies, liberal arts/general studies, political science/government, psychology, public administration, and public affairs). Criminal justice, forensic science, and psychology have the largest enrollments.

ACTIVITIES: There are 134 groups on campus, including and fire science club, forensic science and chemistry club, band, cheerleading, choir, communications, computers, criminal justice club, dance, debate, drama, ethnic, film, forensics, gay, honors, international, jazz band, literary magazine, marching band, newspaper, pep band, photography, political, professional, radio and TV, religious, social, social service, student government, symphony, and yearbook. Popular campus events include Homecoming, Snow Ball Formal, and Spring Weekend. **Sports:** There are 7 intercollegiate sports for men and 9 for women, and 11 intramural sports for men and 11 for women. Facilities include baseball, softball, intramural playing fields, tennis courts, a gym with basketball courts, weight training room, racquetball court, a 56000-square-foot recreation center, an outdoor stadium for football, soccer, and lacrosse. **Graduates:** From July 1, 2013 to June 30, 2014, 930 bachelor's degrees were awarded. The most popular majors were criminal justice (25%), forensic sciences (8%), and psychology (5%). In an average class, 49% graduate in 6 years or less.

SERVICES: Counseling and information services are available, as is tutoring in every subject. There is a reader service for the blind, and remedial math, reading, and writing. **Library/Resources:** The library contains 386,358 volumes, 407,212 microform items, 1,444 audio/video tapes/CDs/DVDs, and subscribes to 36,057 periodicals including electronic. Computerized library services include interlibrary loans, database searching, Internet access, and Wi-Fi capability. Special learning facilities include an art gallery, radio station, TV station, Institute of Forensic Science, crime scene training and technology center, nutrition lab, dental center, finance and technology center, communication studios, and music and sound recording facilities. **Physically Challenged Students:** 6% of the campus is accessible. Facilities include wheelchair ramps, elevators, special parking, specially equipped restrooms, special class scheduling, lowered drinking fountains, lowered telephones, special housing. **Special:** UNH offers co-op programs in some majors, internships in all majors, work-study programs, interdisciplinary majors, fast-track business programs leading to bachelor's degrees in 3 years, 5-year B.S.-M.S. programs in education and in environmental science, and nondegree study programs. Study-abroad programs are available. There is a freshman honors program. **Visiting:** There are regularly scheduled orientations for prospective students, including daily information sessions, open houses, accepted student days, charger days, and summer preview days. There are guides for informal visits, visitors may sit in on classes, and stay overnight. To schedule a visit, contact the Office of Undergraduate Admissions at admissions@newhaven.edu. **Campus Safety and Security:** Measures include 24-hour foot and vehicle patrol, emergency notification system, self-defense education, and security escort services. There are shuttle buses, emergency telephones, lighted pathways/sidewalks, controlled access to dorms/residences, required programs during orientation for new students as well as a crime prevention program.

REQUIREMENTS: The SAT or ACT is required. Applicants should be graduates of an accredited secondary school. The GED is accepted. An interview is recommended. A letter of recommendation is required along with a personal essay. AP and CLEP credits are accepted. Important factors in the admissions decision are advanced placement or honors courses, extracurricular activities record, and recommendations by school officials. To graduate, all students must maintain a GPA of 2.0, pass a writing proficiency exam, and complete a total of 120 to 132 credits, depending on the major. Students must complete at least 40 credits from the university core curriculum, including a total of 28 credits in lab science, social sciences, history, literature or philosophy, and art, music, or theater, 9 credits in communication skills, and 3 credits each in quantitative skills, computers, and scientific methodology. **Procedure:** Freshmen are admitted fall and spring. Entrance exams should be taken in the fall or winter of the senior year. There are early admissions and rolling admissions plans. Application deadlines are open. The fall 2014 application fee was $50. Applications are accepted on-line. **Transfer Students:** 347 transfer students enrolled in 2013-2014. Applicants should have a minimum college GPA of 2.3 and should submit all official transcripts. An interview is recommended, and the SAT is required for students with fewer than 24 college credits. 30 of 120 credits required for the bachelor's degree must be completed at UNH. **International Students:** There are 412 international students enrolled. The school actively recruits these students. They must take the TOEFL with a minimum score of 75 on the Internet-based version (iBT). They must also take the SAT or ACT. English-speaking students may submit the SAT or ACT scores instead.

ADMISSIONS: 81% of the 2014-2015 applicants were accepted. The SAT scores for the 2014-2015 freshman class were: Critical Reading--36% below 500, 48% between 500 and 599, 15% between 600 and 699, and 1% between 700 and 800; Math--32% below 500, 45% between 500 and 599, 20% between 600 and 699, and 3% between 700 and 800; Writing--39% below 500, 45% between 500 and 599, 15% between 600 and 699, and 1% between 700 and 800. **Admissions Contact:** Kevin J. Phillips, Associate Vice President for Enrollment. E-Mail: *admissions@newhaven.edu* Web: *www.newhaven.edu*

FINANCIAL AID: UNH is a member of CSS. The FAFSA, and copies of the student's and parents' 1040 tax forms and W-2 forms are required. Check with the school for current application deadlines.

UNIVERSITY OF SAINT JOSEPH — C-2
www.sjc.edu

West Hartford, CT 06117	(860) 231-5223
	(866) 442-8752
	Email: admissions@sjc.edu
Full-time: 10 men, 810 women	Faculty: IIA, av$
Part-time: 15 men, 225 women	Ph.D.s: n/av
Graduate: 215 men, 1350 women	Student/Faculty: n/av
Year: semesters, summer session	Tuition: $31,500
Room & Board: $14,130	Freshman Class: 1335 applied, 1047 accepted, 158 enrolled
SAT CR/M: 500/500	CEEB CODE: 3754
Application Deadline: n/av	COMPETITIVE

University of Saint Joseph, is a private institution consisting of an undergraduate women's program, a coed bachelor's degree completion program for adults, and a coed graduate school. The figures in the above capsule and in this profile are approximate. The 84-acre campus is in a suburban area 3 miles from Hartford. Including any residence halls, there are 17 buildings. **STUDENT LIFE:** 94% of undergraduates are from Connecticut. 76% are White. **Male To Female Ratio:** 9.9:1. The average age of freshmen is 18; all undergraduates, 25. 25% do not continue beyond their first year. **Housing:** College-sponsored housing includes single-sex dorms. On-campus housing is available on a first-come and first-served basis. 60% of students commute. All students may keep cars. **FACULTY/CLASSROOMS:** No introductory courses are taught by graduate students. **PROGRAMS OF STUDY:** SJC confers B.A., and B.S. degrees. Master's and Doctoral degrees are also awarded. Bachelor's degrees are awarded in BIOLOGICAL SCIENCE (biochemistry, biology/biological science, and nutrition), BUSINESS (accounting and management science), COMMUNICATIONS AND THE ARTS (art history and appreciation, English, and Spanish), COMPUTER AND PHYSICAL SCIENCE (chemistry and mathematics), EDUCATION (special education), HEALTH PROFESSIONS (nursing), SOCIAL SCIENCE (child psychology/development, family/consumer studies, history, international studies, philosophy, psychology, religion, social work, and women's studies). Nursing has the largest enrollment. **ACTIVITIES:** Groups on campus include dance, drama, ethnic, gay, honors, international, political, professional, religious, social, social service, and student government. **Sports:** There are 8 intercollegiate sports for women. Facilities include a fitness center, basketball court, a pool, indoor and outdoor tracks, tennis courts, softball field, soccer field, and dance studio. **SERVICES:** Counseling and information services are available, as is tutoring in most subjects. **Library/Resources:** Computerized library services include interlibrary loans, database searching, Internet access, and Wi-Fi capability. Special learning facilities include an art gallery. **Physically Challenged Students:** Facilities include wheelchair ramps, elevators, special parking, specially equipped restrooms, special class scheduling, and special housing. **Special:** Saint Joseph College offers cross-registration at member colleges through the Hartford Consortium for Higher Education. Internship opportunities, study abroad, double majors, and student-designed majors are also available. There is a freshman honors program. **Visiting:** There are regularly scheduled orientations for prospective students. There are guides for informal visits, visitors may sit in on classes, and stay overnight. To schedule a visit, contact the Director of Admissions. **Campus Safety and Security:** Measures include 24-hour foot and vehicle patrol, emergency notification system, and security escort services. There are shuttle buses, emergency telephones, lighted pathways/sidewalks, and controlled access to dorms/residences. **REQUIREMENTS:** The SAT is required. SAT scores and high school GPA are important considerations for admission. A high school plan of study focused on college preparation is strongly suggested. AP and CLEP credits are accepted. To earn a bachelor's degree, students must have a minimum 2.0 GPA and 120 earned credits. In addition, requirements must be fulfilled in the general education curriculum and major area of study. **Procedure:** Freshmen are admitted fall and spring. There are deferred admissions and rolling admissions plans. Application deadlines are open. Application fee is $50. Applications are accepted on-line. **Transfer Students:** 45 of 120 credits required for the bachelor's degree must be completed at SJC. **International Students:** They must take the TOEFL. They must also take the SAT or ACT.

ADMISSIONS: 78% of the 2014-2015 applicants were accepted. The SAT scores for the 2014-2015 freshman class were: Critical Reading--46% below 500, 44% between 500 and 599, and 10% between 600 and 699; Math--49% below 500, 39% between 500 and 599, and 12% between 600 and 699. **Admissions Contact: Director of Admissions.** E-Mail: *admissions@sjc.edu* Web: *www.sjc.edu*

FINANCIAL AID: In 2014-2015, 90% of all full-time freshmen and continuing full-time students received some form of financial aid. 90% of all full-time freshmen and continuing full-time students received need-based aid. The average freshman award was $23,527. Need-based scholarships or need-based grants averaged $19,320; and need-based self-help aid (loans and jobs) averaged $4,666. SJC is a member of CSS. The FAFSA is required. The priority date for freshman financial aid applications for fall entry is February 15.

WESLEYAN UNIVERSITY — C-3
www.wesleyan.edu

Middletown, CT 06459	(860) 685-3000
Fax: (860) 685-3001	Email: www.wesleyan.edu
Full-time: 1388 men, 1526 women	Faculty: 352; IIA, ++$
Part-time: 9 men, 5 women	Ph.D.s: 95%
Graduate: 137 men, 159 women	Student/Faculty: 8 to 1
Year: semesters, summer session	Tuition: $47,972
Room & Board: $13,226	Freshman Class: 9390 applied, 2245 accepted, 750 enrolled
SAT CR/M/W: 700/690/710 ACT: 31	CEEB CODE: 3959
Application Deadline: January 1	MOST COMPETITIVE

Wesleyan University, founded in 1831, is a private institution offering programs in the liberal arts and sciences. There is 1 undergraduate school and 1 graduate school. The 316-acre campus is in a suburban area 15 miles south of Hartford, and 2 hours from both Boston and New York City. Including any residence halls, there are 301 buildings. **STUDENT LIFE:** 92% of undergraduates are from out of state, mostly the Northeast. Students are from 47 states, 48 foreign countries, and Canada. 48% are from public schools. 53% are White. **Male To Female Ratio:** 1.1:1. The average age of freshmen is 19; all undergraduates, 20. 4% do not continue beyond their first year; 93% remain to graduate. **Housing:** 2915 students can be accommodated in college housing, which includes single-sex and coed dorms and on-campus apartments. In addition, there are language houses, special-interest houses, and fraternity houses. On-campus housing is guaranteed for all 4 years. 99% of students live on campus; of those, 99% remain on campus on weekends. All students may keep cars. **FACULTY/CLASSROOMS:** 54% of faculty are male; 46% are female. All teach and do research. No introductory courses are taught by graduate students. The average class size in an introductory lecture is 37; in a laboratory is 28; and in a regular course is 18. **PROGRAMS OF STUDY:** Wesleyan confers B.A. degrees. Master's and doctoral degrees are also awarded. Bachelor's degrees are awarded in AGRICULTURE (environmental studies), BIOLOGICAL SCIENCE (biology/biological science, molecular biology, and neurosciences), COMMUNICATIONS AND THE ARTS (art history and appreciation, classics, dance, dramatic arts, English, English literature, film arts, music, romance languages and literature, and studio art), COMPUTER AND PHYSICAL SCIENCE (astronomy, chemistry, computer science, earth science, mathematics, and physics), SOCIAL SCIENCE (African American studies, American studies, anthropology, archeology, classical/ancient civilization, East Asian studies, economics, French studies, gender studies, German area studies, Hispanic American studies, history, Italian studies, Latin American studies, medieval studies, philosophy, political science/

government, psychology, religion, Russian and Slavic studies, science and society, social studies, and sociology). Sciences, economics and history are the strongest academically. Psychology, chemistry, and music have the largest enrollments.

ACTIVITIES: 4% of men and 1 of women belong to 4 local and 3 national fraternities; 1% of women belong to 1 local sororities. There are 230 groups on campus, including art, band, cheerleading, chess, choir, chorale, chorus, communications, computers, dance, debate, drama, environmental, ethnic, film, gay, honors, international, jazz band, literary magazine, musical theater, newspaper, opera, orchestra, pep band, photography, political, professional, radio and TV, religious, social, social service, student government, symphony, and yearbook. Popular campus events include Cultural Shows, and Spring Fling. **Sports:** There are 15 intercollegiate sports for men and 14 for women, and 7 intramural sports for men and 7 for women. Facilities include a 5000-seat stadium, a 1200-seat gym, 50-meter Olympic-size pool, 400-meter outdoor track, cross-country trail, hockey arena, strength and fitness center, 12 outdoor tennis courts, eight squash courts, three soccer fields, two football practice fields, rugby pitch, boathouse, baseball diamond, softball diamond, and two artificial turf fields. The field house contains a 200-meter indoor track, four indoor tennis courts, three recreational basketball courts, three volleyball courts, and three badminton courts. **Graduates:** From July 1, 2013 to June 30, 2014, 785 bachelor's degrees were awarded. The most popular majors were psychology (9%), economics (9%), and English (7%). 658 companies recruited on campus in 2013-2014. In an average class, 87% graduate in 4 years or less, 91% graduate in 5 years or less, and 93% graduate in 6 years or less.

SERVICES: Counseling and information services are available, as is tutoring in most subjects. Peer advisor assistance in time management and academic skills development, writing tutors, math tutoring, quantitative skills and quantitative analysis, as well as supplemental instruction in biology and chemistry are available for students. **Library/Resources:** The 2 libraries contain 1.5 million volumes, 373,192 microform items, 75,824 audio/video tapes/CDs/DVDs, and subscribe to 16,746 periodicals including electronic. Computerized library services include interlibrary loans, database searching, Internet access, and Wi-Fi capability. Special learning facilities include an art gallery, radio station, an observatory. **Physically Challenged Students:** 53% of the campus is accessible. Facilities include wheelchair ramps, elevators, special parking, specially equipped restrooms, special class scheduling, lowered drinking fountains, lowered telephones, special housing. **Special:** Wesleyan offers exchange programs with 11 northeastern colleges, cross-registration with 2 area colleges, study abroad in 45 countries on 6 continents, internships, dual and student-designed majors, and pass/fail options. 3-2 engineering programs with Cal Tech, Columbia University, and Dartmouth College are also available. There are 2 national honor societies, including Phi Beta Kappa, and 48 departmental honors programs. **Visiting:** There are regularly scheduled orientations for prospective students, consisting of student visits with hour-long campus tours and group information sessions. There are guides for informal visits, visitors may sit in on classes, and stay overnight. To schedule a visit, contact the Office of Admissions. **Campus Safety and Security:** Measures include 24-hour foot and vehicle patrol, emergency notification system, self-defense education, and security escort services. There are shuttle buses, emergency telephones, lighted pathways/sidewalks, and controlled access to dorms/residences.

REQUIREMENTS: Applicants must submit the common application, transcript, and recommendations. Standardized tests are optional. Students should have a minimum of 20 academic credits, including 4 years each of English, foreign language, math, science, and social studies. AP credits are accepted. Important factors in the admissions decision are advanced placement or honors courses, recommendations by school officials, and personality/intangible qualities.To graduate, all students must complete 128 credit hours. All students are expected, but not required, to take courses each in humanities and arts, social and behavioral sciences, and natural science and math. A minimum academic average of 74 must be maintained, with at least 6 semesters of full-time residency. **Procedure:** Freshmen are admitted fall. Entrance exams should be taken in the spring of the junior year or the fall of the senior year. There are early decision, early admissions, and deferred admissions plans. Early deci-

sion applications should be filed by November 15; regular applications, by January 1 for fall entry, along with a $55 fee. Notification of early decision is sent December 15; regular decision, April 1. 367 early decision candidates were accepted for the 2014-2015 class. Applications are accepted on-line. **Transfer Students:** 74 transfer students enrolled in 2013-2014. Applicants need a strong academic record. Standardized tests are optional. An interview is recommended. 64 of 128 credits required for the bachelor's degree must be completed at Wesleyan. **International Students:** There are 253 international students enrolled. The school actively recruits these students. They must take the TOEFL with a minimum score of 600 on the paper-based TOEFL (PBT) or 100 on the Internet-based version (iBT), or take the IELTS.

ADMISSIONS: 24% of the 2014-2015 applicants were accepted. The SAT scores for the 2014-2015 freshman class were: Critical Reading--11% between 500 and 599, 35% between 600 and 699, and 54% between 700 and 800; Math--9% between 500 and 599, 42% between 600 and 699, and 49% between 700 and 800; Writing--9% between 500 and 599, 30% between 600 and 699, and 60% between 700 and 800. The ACT scores were 8% between 24 and 26, 10% between 27 and 28, and 81% above 28. **Admissions Contact:** Dean of Admissions and Financial Aid. E-Mail: *www.wesleyan.edu* Web: *www.wesleyan.edu/admission*

FINANCIAL AID: Wesleyan is a member of CSS. The CSS/Profile, FAFSA, and parent and student 1040 forms, W-2s, business tax returns are required. The priority date for freshman financial aid applications for fall entry is February 15. The deadline for filing freshman financial aid applications for fall entry is February 15.

WESTERN CONNECTICUT STATE UNIVERSITY (*The complete profile is made available exclusively on our website, www.barronspac.com*)

YALE UNIVERSITY	C-3
www.yale.edu	

New Haven, CT 06520	(203) 432-9316
Fax: (203) 432-9370	Email: student.questions@yale.edu
Full-time: 2710 men, 2683 women	Faculty: 885; I, ++$
Part-time: 8 men, 4 women	Ph.D.s: 92%
Graduate: 3275 men, 3226 women	Student/Faculty: 6 to 1
Year: semesters, summer session	Tuition: $42,300
Room & Board: $13,000	Freshman Class: 28977 applied, 2043 accepted, 1356 enrolled
SAT CR/M/W: 750/750/760 ACT: 33	CEEB CODE: 3987
Application Deadline: December 31	MOST COMPETITIVE

Yale University, founded in 1701, is a private liberal arts institution. Figures in the above capsule and in this profile are approximate. There is 1 undergraduate school and 13 graduate schools. In addition to regional accreditation, Yale has baccalaureate program accreditation with AACSB, ABET, CAHEA, NAAB, NASM, NLN, and SAF. The 342-acre campus is in an urban area 75 miles northeast of New York City. Including any residence halls, there are 440 buildings.

STUDENT LIFE: 93% of undergraduates are from out of state, mostly the West. Students are from 49 states, 74 foreign countries, and Canada. 57% are from public schools. 53% are White; 17% Asian American; 11% Hispanic. **Male To Female Ratio:** 1.0:1. The average age of freshmen is 18; all undergraduates, 20. 1% do not continue beyond their first year; 96% remain to graduate. **Housing:** College-sponsored housing includes coed dorms. Students are ramdomly assigned to 1 of 12 residential colleges where they live, eat, socialize, and pursue varius academic and extracurricular activities. All undergraduate housing is provided through the residential college system. On-campus housing is guaranteed for the freshman year only and is available on a lottery system for upperclassmen. 88% of students live on campus. All students may keep cars.

FACULTY/CLASSROOMS: 64% of faculty are male; 36% are female. All teach undergraduates. No introductory courses are taught by graduate students.

PROGRAMS OF STUDY: Yale confers B.A., and B.S. degrees. Master's and Doctoral degrees are also awarded. Bachelor's degrees are awarded in AGRICULTURE (environmental studies), BIOLOGICAL SCIENCE (biochemistry, biology/biological science, biophysics, evolutionary biology, and molecular biology), COMMUNICATIONS AND THE ARTS (art history, art, Chinese, classics, dramatic arts, East Asian languages and literature, English, film arts, French, Germanic languages and literature, Italian, Japanese, linguistics, literature, music, Portuguese, Russian, Russian languages and literature, Slavic languages, and Spanish), COMPUTER AND PHYSICAL SCIENCE (applied mathematics, applied physics, astronomy, chemistry, computer science, geology, mathematics, mathematics – economics, mathematics – philosophy, physics, and statistics), ENGINEERING AND ENVIRONMENTAL DESIGN (architecture, biomedical engineering, chemical engineering, electrical/electronics engineering, engineering, engineering and applied science, environmental engineering, and mechanical engineering), SOCIAL SCIENCE (African studies, African American studies, American studies, anthropology, archeology, classical/ancient civilization, cognitive science, East Asian studies, Eastern European studies, economics, ethics, politics, and social policy, ethnic studies, German area studies, history, history of science, humanities, international studies, Judaic studies, Latin American studies, Middle Eastern studies, Near Eastern studies, philosophy, political science/government, psychology, religion, Russian and Slavic studies, sociology, South Asian studies, and women's studies). History, political science, and economics have the largest enrollments.

ACTIVITIES: There are 400 groups on campus, including art, band, cheerleading, chess, choir, chorale, chorus, communications, computers, dance, debate, drama, environmental, ethnic, film, gay, honors, international, jazz band, literary magazine, marching band, musical theater, newspaper, opera, orchestra, pep band, photography, political, professional, radio and TV, religious, social, social service, student government, symphony, and yearbook. Popular campus events include Freshman Dinner, Spring Fling Concert, Fall Show, Yale Symphony Orchestra Halloween Show, Yale Top Chef Competition, Yale-Harvard Football Game and special cultural dinners in the residential colleges. **Sports:** There are 16 intercollegiate sports for men and 18 for women, and 25 intramural sports for men and 21 for women. Facilities include an 71,000-seat Yale Bowl (football), sports complex, gymnasium, 2 swimming pools, fitness center, ice rink, sailing center, squash center, tennis center, golf course, boathouse. **Graduates:** From July 1, 2013 to June 30, 2014, 1285 bachelor's degrees were awarded. The most popular majors were political science (14%), economics (12%), and history (10%). In an average class, 96% graduate in 6 years or less. Of the 2013 graduating class, 21% were enrolled in graduate school within 6 months of graduation, and 75% were employed.

SERVICES: Counseling and information services are available, as is tutoring in every subject. There is a reader service for the blind. **Library/Resources:** The 15 libraries contain 15.0 million volumes, 10.0 million microform items, 400,000 audio/video tapes/CDs/DVDs, and subscribe to 450,000 periodicals including electronic. Computerized library services include interlibrary loans, database searching, Internet access, and Wi-Fi capability. Special learning facilities include an art gallery, natural history museum, planetarium, radio station, Yale Center for British Art, Beinecke Rare Book and Manuscript Library, Film Study Center, Center for Engineering Innovation and Design, Marsh Botanical Gardens and Yale Natural Preserves, and numerous research centers. **Physically Challenged Students:** Facilities include wheelchair ramps, elevators, special parking, specially equipped restrooms, special class scheduling, lowered drinking fountains, lowered telephones, a door-to-door lift-van service. **Special:** The university runs a study abroad program in England and offers opportunities for term-time or summer study in many other countries. It also offers an accelerated degree program, B.A.-B.S. degrees, dual majors, and student-designed majors. Directed Studies, a special freshman program in the humanities, affords outstanding students the opportunity to survey the Western cultural tradition. Perspectives on Science is a special freshmen program for students who are especially strong in science and mathematics. Freshmen

Seminars offer the opportunity for first-year students the opportunity to enroll in small classes with some of Yale's most distinguished faculty members. The STARS (Science, Technology and Research Scholars) program offers research opportunities, mentoring and support to students historically under-represented in fields of natural science and quantitative reasoning. There is a Phi Beta Kappa chapter. **Visiting:** There are regularly scheduled orientations for prospective students, Flexible: admissions information sessions, campus tours, in summer Student Forums. There are guides for informal visits and visitors may sit in on classes. To schedule a visit, contact the Receptionist Office at (203) 432-9300. **Campus Safety and Security:** Measures include 24-hour foot and vehicle patrol, emergency notification system, self-defense education, and security escort services. There are shuttle buses, emergency telephones, lighted pathways/sidewalks, and controlled access to dorms/residences.

REQUIREMENTS: The SAT or ACT is required. The ACT Optional Writing test is also required. Only those applicants submitting SAT scores must also take any 2 SAT Subject tests. ACT submitters must take the ACT with Writing. Most successful applicants rank in the top 10% of their high school class. All students must have completed a rigorous high school program encompassing all academic disciplines. 2 essays, 2 teacher recommendations and a counselor letter are required, and an interview is recommended. Yale offers a non-binding Single Choice Early Action option (not Early Decision.) AP credits are accepted. Important factors in the admissions decision are leadership record, extracurricular activities record, and advanced placement or honors courses. To graduate, students must complete at least 36 semester courses, including 2 course credits in the humanities, 2 in the social sciences and 2 in the sciences; 2 writing courses; 2 in quantitative reasoning; and courses to further proficiency in a foreign language. All students complete requirements for an academic major. Yale does not have a 'minor' program but students may have two majors. **Procedure:** Freshmen are admitted fall. Entrance exams should be taken at any time up to and including the January test date in the year of application. There is a deferred admissions plan. Early decision applications should be filed by November 1; regular applications, by December 31 for fall entry, along with a $75 fee. Notifications are sent April 1. 617 applicants were on the 2014 waiting list; 70 were admitted. Applications are accepted on-line. **Transfer Students:** 22 transfer students enrolled in 2013-2014. Applicants must take either the SAT or ACT and have 1 full year of credit. An essay and 3 letters of recommendation are required. (One Yale credit = one semester-long course.) 18 of 36 credits required for the bachelor's degree must be completed at Yale. **International Students:** There are 555 international students enrolled. The school actively recruits these students. They must take the TOEFL with a minimum score of 600 on the paper-based TOEFL (PBT) or 100 on the Internet-based version (iBT), or take the ELTS or Pearson Test of English. the SAT and 2 SAT Subject tests, or the ACT with Writing.

ADMISSIONS: 7% of the 2014-2015 applicants were accepted. The SAT scores for the 2014-2015 freshman class were: Critical Reading--2% between 500 and 599, 22% between 600 and 699, and 76% between 700 and 800; Math--2% between 500 and 599, 7% between 600 and 699, and 81% between 700 and 800; Writing--2% between 500 and 599, 16% between 600 and 699, and 81% between 700 and 800. **Admissions Contact:** Margit Dahl, Director of Admissions. E-Mail: *student.questions@yale.edu* Web: *http://admissions.yale.edu*

FINANCIAL AID: In 2014-2015, 50% of all full-time freshmen and 55% of continuing full-time students received some form of financial aid. 50% of all full-time freshmen and 55% of continuing full-time students received need-based aid. The average freshman award was $46,530. Need-based scholarships or need-based grants averaged $41,230 ($55,900 maximum); and need-based self-help aid (loans and jobs) averaged $2,700 ($2,700 maximum). 56% of undergraduate students work part-time. Average annual earnings from campus work are $1433. The average financial indebtedness of the 2014 graduate was $12,626. Yale is a member of CSS. The CSS/Profile and FAFSA, and Student and parent tax returns; CSS divorced/separated parents statement and business/farm supplement if appropriate are required. The deadline for filing freshman financial aid applications for fall entry is March 1.

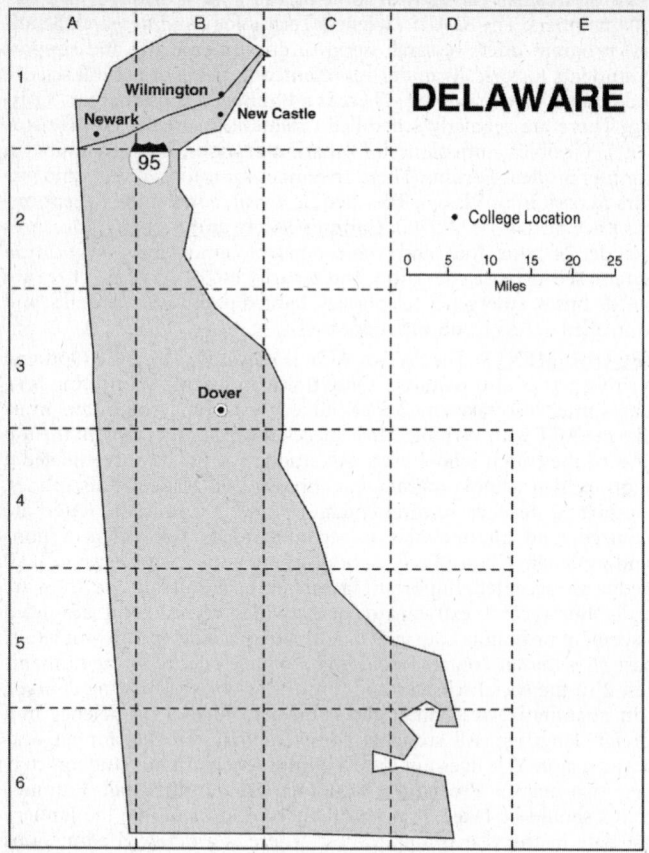

DELAWARE

● College Location

0   5   10   15   20   25
Miles

DELAWARE STATE UNIVERSITY *(The complete profile is made available exclusively on our website, www.barronspac.com)*

GOLDEY-BEACOM COLLEGE   B-1
www.gbc.edu

Wilmington, DE 19808	(302) 225-6248
	(800) 833-4877
Fax: (302) 996-5408	Email: admissions@gbc.edu
Full-time: 208 men, 254 women	Faculty: 18
Part-time: 70 men, 93 women	Ph.D.s: 100%
Graduate: 458 men, 269 women	Student/Faculty: 24 to 1
Year: semesters, summer session	Tuition: $22,140
Room & Board: $5353	Freshman Class: 717 applied, 385 accepted, 128 enrolled
SAT: required	CEEB CODE: 5255
Application Deadline: n/av	COMPETITIVE

Goldey-Beacom College, founded in 1886, is a private coeducational college offering programs in psychology, criminal justice, english, economics, and other areas of business. Figures in the above capsule and in this profile are approximate. There is 1 undergraduate school and 1 graduate school. In addition to regional accreditation, has baccalaureate program accreditation with ACBSP. The 24-acre campus is in a suburban area in the Pike Creek Valley suburb of Wilmington, Delaware. Including any residence halls, there are 6 buildings.

STUDENT LIFE: 67% of undergraduates are from Delaware. Others are from 19 states, 60 foreign countries, and Canada. 75% are from public schools. 41% are White; 28% Foreign; 15% African American. **Male To Female Ratio:** 0.8:1. The average age of freshmen is 19; all undergraduates, 21. 24% do not continue beyond their first year; 62% remain to graduate. **Housing:** 271 students can be accommodated in college housing, which includes coed on-campus apartments. In addition, there are special-interest houses. On-campus housing is guaranteed for all 4 years, is available on a first-come, and first-served basis. 64% of students commute. All students may keep cars.

FACULTY/CLASSROOMS: 59% of faculty are male; 41% are female. 89% teach undergraduates. No introductory courses are taught by graduate students. The average class size in an introductory lecture is 28 and in a regular course is 21.

PROGRAMS OF STUDY: confers B.A., and B.S. degrees. Associate and master's degrees are also awarded. Bachelor's degrees are awarded in BUSINESS (accounting, banking and finance, business administration and management, human resources, international business management, management information systems, marketing management, and sports management), COMPUTER AND PHYSICAL SCIENCE (information sciences and systems), SOCIAL SCIENCE (economics and psychology). Accounting, economics, and finance are the strongest academically. Accounting, management, and business administration have the largest enrollments.

ACTIVITIES: There are no fraternities or sororities. There are 14 groups on campus, including computers, drama, ethnic, honors, international, newspaper, professional, religious, social service, and student government. Popular campus events include Spring Fest, Karaoke Night, Casino Night and Homecoming. **Sports:** There are 4 intercollegiate sports for men and 6 for women. Facilities include soccer and softball fields, tennis and handball courts, a gym with basketball and volleyball courts, and a fitness center available to all students and staff. When there is a student interest, an intermural sports team is established. **Graduates:** From July 1, 2013 to June 30, 2014, 119 bachelor's degrees were awarded. The most popular majors were business administration (63%), accounting (26%), and psychology (5%). 81 companies recruited on campus in 2013-2014. In an average class, 41% graduate in 6 years or less. Of the 2013 graduating class, 45% were enrolled in graduate school within 6 months of graduation, and 90% were employed.

SERVICES: Counseling and information services are available, as is tutoring in most subjects. There is a reader service for the blind, and remedial math, reading, and writing. Computer-based tutorials. **Library/Resources:** The library contains 191,268 volumes, 3,793 audio/video tapes/CDs/DVDs, and subscribes to 17,434 periodicals including electronic. Computerized library services include interlibrary loans, database searching, Internet access, and Wi-Fi capability. **Physically Challenged Students:** All of the campus is accessible. Facilities include wheelchair ramps, elevators, special parking, specially equipped restrooms, lowered drinking fountains, and lowered telephones. **Special:** A 5-year B.S/M.B.A degree, dual majors, internships, and work-study programs are available. There are 1 national honor society, a freshman honors program, and 1 departmental honors program. **Visiting:** There are regularly scheduled orientations for prospective students, consisting of a meeting with an admissions representative which includes a campus tour. There are guides for informal visits, visitors may sit in on classes, and stay overnight. To schedule a visit, contact the College's Admissions Office. **Campus Safety and Security:** Measures include 24-hour foot and vehicle patrol, emergency notification system, self-defense education, and security escort services. There are lighted pathways/sidewalks and controlled access to dorms/residences.

REQUIREMENTS: The SAT is required. Applicants must be high school graduates or have a GED and submit their official high school transcripts and SAT scores A GPA of 2.0 is required. AP and CLEP credits are accepted. Important factors in the admissions decision are advanced placement or honors courses, extracurricular activities record, and recommendations by school officials.To graduate, students must complete a minimum of 136 credit hours with an overall GPA of 2.0. Students must also fulfill the College's degree requirements. **Procedure:** Freshmen are admitted to all sessions. There are early admissions, deferred admissions, and rolling admissions plans. Application deadlines are open. Applications are accepted on-line. **Transfer Students:** 77 transfer students enrolled in 2013-2014. Transfer applicants must submit high school and college transcripts. 65 of 136 credits required for the bachelor's degree must be completed at Gpldey-Beacon. **International Students:** There are 55 international students enrolled. The school actively recruits these students. They must take the TOEFL with a minimum score of 500 on the paper-based TOEFL (PBT) or 60 on the Internet-based version (iBT), or take the IELTS. They must also take the SAT or ACT, scoring 1200.

ADMISSIONS: 54% of the 2014-2015 applicants were accepted. **Admissions Contact:** Director of Admissions. E-Mail: *admissions@gbc.edu* Web: *www.gbc.edu*

FINANCIAL AID: In 2014-2015, 100% of all full-time freshmen and 80% of continuing full-time students received some form of financial aid. 99% of all full-time freshmen and continuing full-time students received need-based aid. 90% of undergraduate students work part-time. Average annual earnings from campus work are $1200. The FAFSA is required. The priority date for freshman financial aid applications for fall entry is April 15. The deadline for filing freshman financial aid applications for fall entry is July 15.

UNIVERSITY OF DELAWARE   A-1
www.udel.edu

Newark, DE 19716   (302) 831-8123

Fax: (302) 831-6905	Email: hkelly@udel.edu
Full-time: 6762 men, 9269 women	Faculty: 1165; I, +$
Part-time: 402 men, 435 women	Ph.D.s: 86%
Graduate: 1756 men, 1836 women	Student/Faculty: 13 to 1
Year: 4-1-4, summer session	Tuition: $12,112 ($29,932)
Room & Board: $11,500	Freshman Class: 24657 applied, 15621 accepted, 3806 enrolled
SAT CR/M/W: 590/605/590 ACT: 26	CEEB CODE: 5811
Application Deadline: January 15	VERY COMPETITIVE

The University of Delaware, founded in 1743 and chartered in 1833, is a State-Assisted, Land-Grant, Sea-Grant, Space-Grant, Carnegie Research University offering programs in agriculture and natural resources, arts and sciences, business and economics, engineering, health sciences, and education and public policy. The figures in the above capsule and in this profile are approximate. There are 7 undergraduate schools and 7 graduate schools. In addition to regional accreditation, Delaware has baccalaureate program accreditation with AACSB, ABET, ADA, APTA, CAHEA, NASM, NCATE, and NLN. The 969-acre campus is in a small town 12 miles southwest of Wilmington. Including any residence halls, there are 347 buildings.

STUDENT LIFE: 64% of undergraduates are from out of state, mostly the Middle Atlantic. Students are from 47 states, 77 foreign countries, and Canada. 77% are White. 36% are Catholic; 26% claim no religious affiliation. **Male To Female Ratio:** 1.3:1. The average age of freshmen is 18; all undergraduates, 20. 10% do not continue beyond their first year; 80% remain to graduate. **Housing:** 7214 students can be accommodated in college housing, which includes single-sex and coed dorms, on-campus apartments, and married student housing. In addition, there are honors houses, special-interest houses, fraternity houses, sorority houses, alcohol/smoke-free residence halls, and suites, coed dorms, women's dorms, and theme housing for gender-neutral. On-campus housing is guaranteed for all 4 years. 54% of students commute. All students may keep cars.

FACULTY/CLASSROOMS: 61% of faculty are male; 39% are female. All teach undergraduates. No introductory courses are taught by graduate students. The average class size in a laboratory is 18 and in a regular course is 35.

PROGRAMS OF STUDY: Delaware confers B.A., B.S., B.A.E.S., B.A. Liberal Studies, B.C.E., B.Ch.E., B.C.P.E., B.E.E., B.En.E., B.F.A., B.M.E., B.Mus., B.R.N., B.S.Ed. and B.S.N. degrees. Associate, master's, and doctoral degrees are also awarded. Bachelor's degrees are awarded in AGRICULTURE (agricultural business management, agricultural economics, agriculture, animal science, natural resource management, plant science, soil science, and wildlife management), BIOLOGICAL SCIENCE (biochemistry, biology/biological science, biotechnology, entomology, nutrition, and plant pathology), BUSINESS (accounting, banking and finance, business administration and management, hotel/motel and restaurant management, management information systems, management science, marketing/retailing/merchandising, operations management, organizational leadership

and management, and sports management), COMMUNICATIONS AND THE ARTS (apparel design, applied music, art, art history and appreciation, communications, comparative literature, English, fine arts, historic preservation, Italian, journalism, languages, music, music theory and composition, theater management, and visual design), COMPUTER AND PHYSICAL SCIENCE (astronomy, chemistry, computer science, geology, information sciences and systems, mathematics, physics, and statistics), EDUCATION (athletic training, early childhood education, education, elementary education, English education, foreign languages education, mathematics education, music education, physical education, psychology education, science education, secondary education, and special education), ENGINEERING AND ENVIRONMENTAL DESIGN (bioengineering, chemical engineering, civil engineering, computer engineering, electrical/electronics engineering, engineering, engineering technology, environmental engineering, environmental science, landscape architecture/design, and mechanical engineering), HEALTH PROFESSIONS (health, health science, medical laboratory technology, and nursing), SOCIAL SCIENCE (anthropology, criminal justice, dietetics, East Asian studies, economics, European studies, family and community services, fashion design and technology, food production/management/services, food science, geography, history, human development, human services, interdisciplinary studies, international relations, Latin American studies, liberal arts/general studies, philosophy, political science/government, psychology, sociology, and women's studies). Biological sciences, psychology, and nursing hare the largest enrollments.

ACTIVITIES: 15% of men belong to 20 national fraternities; 17% of women belong to 15 national sororities. There are 310 groups on campus, including art, band, cheerleading, chess, choir, chorale, chorus, computers, dance, debate, drama, drill team, drum and bugle corps, environmental, ethnic, film, gay, honors, international, jazz band, literary magazine, marching band, musical theater, newspaper, opera, orchestra, pep band, political, professional, radio and TV, religious, social service, student government, and symphony. Popular campus events include Greek Week, Convocation and Commencement. **Sports:** There are 11 intercollegiate sports for men and 12 for women, and 32 intramural sports for men and 32 for women. Facilities include a 23,000-seat football stadium, 3 multipurpose gyms, 6 outdoor multipurpose fields, 8 outdoor basketball courts, 1 squash court, 15 racquetball courts, 21 outdoor tennis courts, indoor and outdoor pools, a universal weight room, a 5,000-seat basketball arena, a rock-climbing wall, a high-ropes challenge course, 4 student fitness centers, a strength and conditioning room with free weights, outdoor and indoor tracks, softball, baseball, lacrosse, and soccer fields, 2 ice arenas, and an outdoor hockey rink. **Graduates:** From July 1, 2013 to June 30, 2014, 3827 bachelor's degrees were awarded. The most popular majors were business/marketing (20%), social sciences (12%), and health professions and related programs (9%). 491 companies recruited on campus in 2013-2014. In an average class, 79% graduate in 4 years or less, 67% graduate in 5 years or less, and 82% graduate in 6 years or less. Of the 2013 graduating class, 15% were enrolled in graduate school within 6 months of graduation, and 75% were employed.

SERVICES: Counseling and information services are available, as is tutoring in every subject. There is a reader service for the blind, and remedial math, reading, and writing. There is also a writing center, a math center, an academic services center for assistance with academic self-management development, critical thinking, and problem solving, as well as individual assistance for learning-disabled students. **Library/Resources:** The 5 libraries contain 2.8 million volumes, 3.4 million microform items, 600,000 audio/video tapes/CDs/DVDs, and subscribe to 30,000 periodicals including electronic. Computerized library services include interlibrary loans, database searching, Internet access, and Wi-Fi capability. Special learning facilities include an art gallery, radio station, TV station, a preschool lab, development ice skating science center, computer-controlled greenhouse, nursing practice labs, physical therapy clinic, agricultural research complex, exercise physiology biomechanics labs, foreign language media center, and composite materials center. **Physically Challenged Students:** 95% of the campus is accessible. Facilities include wheelchair ramps, elevators, special parking, specially equipped restrooms, special class scheduling, lowered drinking fountains, lowered telephones, and special housing. **Special:** Students may participate in cooperative programs, internships, study abroad in 55 countries, a Washington semester, and work-study programs. The university offers accelerated degree programs, B.A. and B.S. degrees, dual majors, minors, student-designed majors (Bachelor of Arts in Liberal Studies), and pass/fail options. There are 4-1 degree programs in engineering, and hotel and restaurant management. Non-degree study is available through the Division of Continuing Education. There is an extensive undergraduate research program. Students may earn an enriched degree through the University Honors Program. There are 35 national honor societies, including Phi Beta Kappa, and a freshman honors program. **Visiting:** There are regularly scheduled orientations for prospective students, student visits consist of a 40-minute admissions information session and a 90-minute walking tour of campus. There are guides for informal visits and visitors may sit in on classes. To schedule a visit, contact the Admissions Office. **Campus Safety and Security:** Measures include 24-hour foot and vehicle patrol, emergency notification system, self-defense education, and security escort services. There are shuttle buses, emergency telephones, lighted pathways/sidewalks, controlled access to dorms/residences, ongoing student-awareness programs in the residence halls, community policing, and keycard access to residence halls.

REQUIREMENTS: The SAT or ACT is required. The ACT Optional Writing test is also required. Applicants should be graduates of an accredited secondary school. The GED is accepted. Students should have completed a minimum of 18 high school academic units, including 4 units of English, 3 units of math, 3 units of science with 2 lab units, 2 units each of foreign language, history, and social studies, and 2 units of academic course electives. SAT Subject Tests are recommended, especially for honors program applicants. A writing sample and at least 1 letter of recommendation are required for all. AP credits are accepted. Important factors in the admissions decision are advanced placement or honors courses, evidence of special talent, extracurricular activities record, leadership record, parents or siblings attended your school, recommendations by alumni, geographical diversity, recommendations by school officials, and personality/intangible qualities. For graduation, students must complete at least 120 credits with a minimum GPA of 2.0. All students must take freshman English and 3 credits of course work with multicultural, ethnic, and/or gender-related content. Most majors require more than 120 credits. Most degree programs require that half of the courses be in the major field of study. Students must also have 1 incoming semester of First Year Experience (FYE) and 3 credits of Discovery Learning Experience (DLE). **Procedure:** Freshmen are admitted fall and spring. Entrance exams should be taken by junior year or the beginning of the senior year. There are early admissions and deferred admissions plans. Applications should be filed by January 15 for fall entry; December 15 for spring entry, along with a $75 fee. Notifications are sent in mid-March. Applications are accepted on-line. **Transfer Students:** 461 transfer students enrolled in 2013-2014. Applicants for transfer should have completed at least 24 credits with a minimum GPA of 2.5 for most majors. Some majors require a GPA of 3.0 or better and/or specific course work. All transfer students must submit high school and college transcripts, an essay, and a statement of good standing from their prior institution. In some cases, an interview and standardized test scores are required. 30 of 120 credits required for the bachelor's degree must be completed at Delaware. **International Students:** There are 716 international students enrolled. The school actively recruits these students. They must take the TOEFL with a minimum score of 550 on the paper-based TOEFL (PBT) or 80 on the Internet-based version (iBT), or take the IELTS. The SAT is recommended.

ADMISSIONS: 63% of the 2014-2015 applicants were accepted. The SAT scores for the 2014-2015 freshman class were: Critical Reading--11% below 500, 44% between 500 and 599, 34% between 600 and 699, and 10% between 700 and 800; Math--9% below 500, 36% between 500 and 599, 43% between 600 and 699, and 12% between 700 and 800; Writing--11% below 500, 42% between 500 and 599, 39% between 600 and 699, and 7% between 700 and 800. The ACT scores were 20% below 21, 63% between 27 and 28, and 17% above 28. 97 freshmen graduated first in their class. **Admissions Contact:** Lou Hirsh, Director of Admissions. E-Mail: *admissions@udel.edu* Web: *http://admissions.udel.edu/*

FINANCIAL AID: In 2014-2015, 62% of all full-time freshmen and continuing full-time students received some form of financial aid. 62% of all full-time freshmen and continuing full-time students received need-based aid. The average freshman award was $15,928. Need-based scholarships or need-based grants averaged $9,321; need-based self-help aid (loans and jobs) averaged $7,114; non-need-based athletic scholarships averaged $13,385; and other non-need-based awards and non-need-based scholarships averaged $6,074. The average financial indebtedness of the 2014 graduate was $32,571. The FAFSA is required. The priority date for freshman financial aid applications for fall entry is February 1. The deadline for filing freshman financial aid applications for fall entry is March 15.

WESLEY COLLEGE (*The complete profile is made available exclusively on our website, www.barronspac.com*)

WILMINGTON UNIVERSITY (*The complete profile is made available exclusively on our website, www.barronspac.com*)

DISTRICT of COLUMBIA

0   1   2   3
Miles

AMERICAN UNIVERSITY   A-2
www.american.edu

Washington, DC 20016	(202) 885-6000
Fax: (202) 885-1025	Email: admissions@american.edu
Full-time: 2782 men, 4604 women	Faculty: I, av$
Part-time: 162 men, 158 women	Ph.D.s: n/av
Graduate: 2104 men, 3251 women	Student/Faculty: n/av
Year: semesters, summer session	Tuition: $41,833
Room & Board: $14,182	Freshman Class: 15119 applied, 6931 accepted, 1787 enrolled
SAT CR/M/W: 640/610/620 ACT: 28	CEEB CODE: 5007
Application Deadline: January 15	HIGHLY COMPETITIVE+

American University, students learn from award-winning scholars and researchers, policy makers, authors, artists, filmmakers, lawyers, scientists, and journalists. AU's faculty are both thought leaders and committed teachers, 94 percent of whom hold the highest degree in their field. Balancing theory and practice, they take full advantage of the university's location in the nation's capital, a remarkable laboratory for applying knowledge. Faculty and students are deeply connected through research partnerships and networking with pinnacle organizations in government, business, and the nonprofit worlds. Active and engaged, AU students strive to serve the world around them, learning how to create change and address major issues - from health care to human rights and global economics to the environment - through internships, as well as hands-on community and volunteer service and study abroad, in more than 145 locations in 44 countries on 6 continents. AU's award-winning Career Center helps students land unique internships and careers. American University offers five schools for undergraduate study: the School of Public Affairs, one of the nation's oldest and finest; the School of International Service, the world's largest of its kind; Kogod School of Business, the School of Communication, which has gained prominence for innovating new models of investigative journalism and news media and excels in campaign communication and documentary film; and the College of Arts and Sciences, the university's liberal arts core and home to distinguished artists and writers, scientists, and presidential and judicial historians. Students may elect to double major, pursue an interdisciplinary program, or custom design an interdepartmental or inter-school major. AU's beautiful campus - itself an arboretum - provides an attractive collegiate setting, characterized by federal-style architec-

ture and the striking, contemporary Katzen Arts Center, a state-of-the-art exhibition and performance space that serves both the AU and greater DC communities. LEED Gold Certified building, further enhancing the opportunities for one of the world's most renowned international programs. There are 6 undergraduate schools and 7 graduate schools. In addition to regional accreditation, AU has baccalaureate program accreditation with AACSB, ACEJMC, NASDTEC, NASM, and NCATE. The 84-acre campus is in a suburban area 5 miles northwest of downtown Washington D.C. Including any residence halls, there are 54 buildings.

STUDENT LIFE: 81% of undergraduates are from out of state, mostly the Middle Atlantic. Students are from 50 states, 122 foreign countries, and Canada. 55% are White. **Male To Female Ratio:** 1.6:1. The average age of freshmen is 18; all undergraduates, 20. 11% do not continue beyond their first year; 82% remain to graduate. **Housing:** 3825 students can be accommodated in college housing, which includes coed dorms and off-campus apartments. In addition, there are honors houses, special-interest houses, International-intercultural hall, honors hall, living learning community halls and floors, housing for students with disabilities handled on an individual basis. On-campus housing is guaranteed for the freshman year only, is available on a first-come, and first-served basis. Alcohol is not permitted. Upperclassmen may keep cars.

FACULTY/CLASSROOMS: No introductory courses are taught by graduate students.

PROGRAMS OF STUDY: AU confers B.A., B.F.A., B.S. and B.S.B.A. degrees. Associate, Master's, and Doctoral degrees are also awarded. Bachelor's degrees are awarded in AGRICULTURE (environmental studies), BIOLOGICAL SCIENCE (biochemistry and biology/biological science), BUSINESS (business administration and management, international business management, nonprofit/public organization management, and sustainable management), COMMUNICATIONS AND THE ARTS (American literature, Arabic, art, art history and appreciation, audio technology, Chinese, communication, communications, creative writing, dramatic arts, film arts, fine arts, French, German, graphic design, Hebrew, Italian, Japanese, journalism, Korean, literature, multimedia, music, musical theater, performing arts, public relations, Russian, Spanish, strategic communication, and studio art), COMPUTER AND PHYSICAL SCIENCE (applied mathematics, chemistry, computer science, mathematics, physics, and statistics), EDUCATION (early childhood education, elementary education, foreign languages education, health education, and secondary education), ENGINEERING AND ENVIRONMENTAL DESIGN (environmental science), HEALTH PROFESSIONS (health promotion, health science, and public health), SOCIAL SCIENCE (American studies, anthropology, area studies, clinical psychology, criminal justice, economics, government, French studies, gender studies, German area studies, history, interdisciplinary studies, international studies, Judaic studies, Latin American studies, law, philosophy, political science/government, psychology, Russian and Slavic studies, sociology, Spanish studies, and women's studies). International studies, business administration and political science have the largest enrollments.

ACTIVITIES: 18% of men belong to 15 national fraternities; 18% of women belong to 11 national sororities. There are 200 groups on campus, including art, band, cheerleading, chess, choir, chorale, chorus, computers, dance, debate, drama, environmental, ethnic, film, gay, honors, international, jazz band, literary magazine, musical theater, newspaper, opera, orchestra, pep band, photography, political, professional, radio and TV, religious, social, social service, student government, symphony, various athletic clubs, and yearbook. Popular campus events include Family Weekend, Founders Day Ball and Campus Beautification Day. **Sports:** There are 6 intercollegiate sports for men and 8 for women. Facilities include a 6,000-seat sports arena, main fitness center, 2 swimming pools, hockey and soccer fields, a softball diamond, an all-purpose field, cardiovascular and strength training equipment, weight rooms, courts for tennis, basketball, and volleyball, an aerobics studio, an indoor jogging track, an outdoor 6-lane tartan track, and fitness centers within residence halls. **Graduates:** From July 1, 2013 to June 30, 2014, 1713 bachelor's degrees were awarded. The most popular majors were international studies (26%), business administration (13%), and political science (9%). In an average class, 5% graduate in 3 years or less, 76% graduate in 4 years or less, 81% graduate in 5 years or less, and 52% graduate in 6 years or less.

SERVICES: Counseling and information services are available, as is tutoring in every subject. There is a reader service for the blind, and remedial math, reading, and writing. Academic Support and Access Center is available to help students develop the tools needed for college success. In addition, a math and statistics tutoring lab, a writing center, and a foreign language resource center are available. **Library/Resources:** The library contains 1,000,000 volumes, 1.1 million microform items, 66,000 audio/video tapes/CDs/DVDs, and subscribes to 125,000 periodicals including electronic. Computerized library services include interlibrary loans, database searching, Internet access, and Wi-Fi capability. Special learning facilities include an art gallery, radio station, TV station, American University's Washington College of law library, a state-of-the-art language resource center, multimedia design and development labs, science and computer science labs, and well-equipped buildings for art and the performing arts, National Public Radio station (WAMU 88.5FM). The American University Game Lab serves as a hub for experiential education, persuasive play research, and innovative production in the fields of games for change and rhetorical play. Part of a university-wide commitment to high-impact research, this multidisciplinary initiative combines the expertise of the School of Communication and the College of Arts and Sciences. AU's Kreeger Building is the site of the Audio Technology Program new recording studios. For **Physically Challenged Students:** 95% of the campus is accessible. Facilities include wheelchair ramps, elevators, special parking, specially equipped restrooms, special class scheduling, lowered drinking fountains, lowered telephones, special housing. The Academic Support and Access Center is committed to providing access for individuals with disabilities within the university's diverse community. Also, university shuttles are equipped to accommodate students in wheelchairs. **Special:** AU offers co-op programs and internships in all majors, over 155 distinct study abroad programs in more than 45 countries, and the Washington Semester and Gateway programs. Work-study is available on campus and with local community service agencies. Dual majors, interdisciplinary programs, student-designed majors, 3-year B.A. degree programs, 3-2 engineering degrees, and B.A./B.S.degrees are also available. Combined bachelor's/master's programs are available in most majors. Cross-registration may be arranged through the Consortium of Universities of the Washington Metropolitan Area. Credit for life experience, nondegree study, and pass/fail options are available. There are preprofessional programs in engineering, law, and medicine (the medical program is aimed at strengthening credentials for applying to programs in medicine, dentistry, optometry, podiatry, oral survey, veterinary medicine, and public health). There are 12 national honor societies, including Phi Beta Kappa, and a freshman honors program. **Visiting:** There are regularly scheduled orientations for prospective students, including student-led daily tours and information sessions, open houses, and overnight programs. There are guides for informal visits, visitors may sit in on classes, and stay overnight. To schedule a visit, contact the Admissions Office Tours and Infromation Program at admissions@american.edu. **Campus Safety and Security:** Measures include 24-hour foot and vehicle patrol, emergency notification system, self-defense education, and security escort services. There are shuttle buses, emergency telephones, lighted pathways/sidewalks, controlled access to dorms/residences, crime prevention programs, building alarms, video surveillance, posted crime alerts, on-line annual crime reports, escorts, laptop security protocols, RAD courses, emergency preparedness protocols and alerting system.

REQUIREMENTS: The SAT or ACT is required. Students must have graduated from an accredited secondary school with at least 16 Carnegie units, including at least 4 units in English, 3 units in college preparatory math (including the equivalent of 2 units in algebra), 3 units in science, 2 units in social sciences, and 2 units in foreign language(s). Applicants who have satisfactory scores on the GED may also apply. All students must submit an essay and 2 letters of recommendation. American University (AU) is continuing its test-optional pilot program for the 2015 fall semester. This program is open to all applicants (Early Decision and Regular Decision) for fall 2015. AP and

CLEP credits are accepted. Important factors in the admissions decision are advanced placement or honors courses, recommendations by school officials, and extracurricular activities record.To graduate, students must complete 120 credit hours with a minimum GPA of 2.0. In addition, students must complete 31 credit hours of general education requirements in 5 curricular areas and fulfill the school's competency requirements in English composition and mathematics by either passing an exam or taking a course in each area. Please see program specific websites for additional requirements. **Procedure:** Freshmen are admitted to all sessions. Entrance exams should be taken in the spring of the junior year or the fall of the senior year. There are early decision and deferred admissions plans. Early decision applications should be filed by November 15; regular applications, by January 15 for fall entry; December 1 for spring entry; and April 1 for summer entry, along with a $70 fee. Notification of early decision is sent December 31; regular decision, April 1. 728 early decision candidates were accepted for the 2014-2015 class. 73 applicants were on the 2014 waiting list. Applications are accepted on-line. **Transfer Students:** 287 transfer students enrolled in 2013-2014. Transfer applicants who wish to be considered competitive candidates should have a cumulative GPA of at least 2.5 from all schools attended. All applicants with a cumulative GPA of 2.0 or above will be considered. 45 of 120 credits required for the bachelor's degree must be completed at AU. **International Students:** There are 786 international students enrolled. The school actively recruits these students. They must take the TOEFL with a minimum score of 550 on the paper-based TOEFL (PBT) or 80 on the Internet-based version (iBT) and the college's own test, May also take the IELTS composite with a score 6.5 or higher, or the Pearson Test of English with score 53 or higher.

ADMISSIONS: 46% of the 2014-2015 applicants were accepted. The SAT scores for the 2014-2015 freshman class were: Critical Reading--3% below 500, 26% between 500 and 599, 52% between 600 and 699, and 20% between 700 and 800; Math--5% below 500, 37% between 500 and 599, 46% between 600 and 699, and 12% between 700 and 800; Writing--5% below 500, 30% between 500 and 599, 50% between 600 and 699, and 16% between 700 and 800. The ACT scores were 2% below 21, 7% between 21 and 23, 21% between 24 and 26, 24% between 27 and 28, and 46% above 28. **Admissions Contact:** Greg Grauman, Asst Vice Provost Undergrad Admissions. E-Mail: *admissions@american.edu* Web: *www.american.edu*

FINANCIAL AID: The FAFSA and the college's own financial statement are required. The deadline for filing freshman financial aid applications for fall entry is February 15.

CORCORAN COLLEGE OF ART AND DESIGN (*The complete profile is made available exclusively on our website, www.barronspac.com*)

GALLAUDET UNIVERSITY (*The complete profile is made available exclusively on our website, www.barronspac.com*)

GEORGE WASHINGTON UNIVERSITY	**B-3**
www.gwu.edu	
Washington, DC 20052	(202) 994-6040
	(800) 447-3765
Fax: (202) 994-0325	Email: gwadm@gwu.edu
Full-time: 4215 men, 5533 women	Faculty: n/av
Part-time: 343 men, 352 women	Ph.D.s: n/av
Graduate: 6521 men, 8296 women	Student/Faculty: 13 to 1
Year: semesters, summer session	Tuition: $44,148
Room & Board: $12,960	Freshman Class: n/av
SAT or ACT: required	CEEB CODE: 5246
Application Deadline: n/av	**MOST COMPETITIVE**

George Washington University, founded in 1821, is a private institution providing degree programs in arts and sciences, business, engineering, international affairs, health sciences, education, law, and public health. Figures in the above capsle and in this profile are approximate. There are 7 undergraduate schools and 10 graduate schools. In addition to regional accreditation, GW has baccalaureate program accreditation with AACSB, ABET, CAHEA, CSAB, NASAD, NASM, and NCATE. The 37-acre campus is in an urban area 3 blocks west of the White House. Including any residence halls, there are 123 buildings.

STUDENT LIFE: 98% of undergraduates are from out of state, mostly the Middle Atlantic. Students are from 50 states, 137 foreign countries, and Canada. 70% are from public schools. 65% are White. **Male To Female Ratio:** 1.3:1. The average age of freshmen is 18; all undergraduates, 20. 7% do not continue beyond their first year; 81% remain to graduate. **Housing:** 8245 students can be accommodated in college housing, which includes coed dorms and on-campus apartments. In addition, there are special-interest houses, fraternity houses, sorority houses, Sorority floors. On-campus housing is available on a lottery system for upperclassmen. 70% of students live on campus. All students may keep cars.

FACULTY/CLASSROOMS: 61% of faculty are male; 39% are female. No introductory courses are taught by graduate students.

PROGRAMS OF STUDY: GW confers B.A., B.S., B.Accy., B.B.A., B.Mus., B.S.C.E., B.S.C.Eng., B.S.C.S., B.S.E.E., B.S.H.S., B.S.M.E. and B.S.S.A. degrees. Associate, master's, and doctoral degrees are also awarded. Bachelor's degrees are awarded in BIOLOGICAL SCIENCE (biology/biological science), BUSINESS (accounting, banking and finance, business administration and management, business economics, human resources, international business management, marketing management, and tourism), COMMUNICATIONS AND THE ARTS (art history and appreciation, broadcasting, Chinese, classics, communications, dance, dramatic arts, English, fine arts, French, German, Japanese, journalism, literature, multimedia, music, music performance, public relations, Russian, and Spanish), COMPUTER AND PHYSICAL SCIENCE (applied mathematics, chemistry, computer science, geology, information sciences and systems, mathematics, physics, statistics, and systems analysis), ENGINEERING AND ENVIRONMENTAL DESIGN (civil engineering, computer engineering, electrical/electronics engineering, engineering, environmental science, and mechanical engineering), HEALTH PROFESSIONS (clinical science, emergency medical technologies, medical laboratory technology, nuclear medical technology, physician's assistant, premedicine, radiological science, and speech pathology/audiology), SOCIAL SCIENCE (American studies, anthropology, archeology, criminal justice, East Asian studies, economics, European studies, geography, history, human services, humanities, interdisciplinary studies, international relations, Judaic studies, Latin American studies, liberal arts/general studies, Middle Eastern studies, philosophy, physical fitness/movement, political science/government, psychology, religion, and sociology). Political communication, international affairs, and biological sciences are the strongest academically. Psychology, and political science have the largest enrollments.

ACTIVITIES: 23% of men belong to 11 national fraternities; 23% of women belong to 7 national sororities. There are 257 groups on campus, including and folk life, art, band, cheerleading, chess, choir, chorale, chorus, computers, dance, debate, drama, ethnic, film, forensics, gay, geology, honors, international, jazz band, literary magazine, marching band, musical theater, newspaper, opera, orchestra, pep band, photography, political, professional, radio and TV, religious, social, social service, and student government. Popular campus events include Spring Fling, Fall Fest and a yearly Benefit Auction. **Sports:** There are 9 intercollegiate sports for men and 8 for women, and 16 intramural sports for men and 16 for women. Facilities include a 5000-seat gym with 2 auxiliary gyms, an AAU swimming pool, weight rooms, a jogging track, squash and racquetball courts, and soccer and baseball fields.

SERVICES: Counseling and information services are available, as is tutoring in every subject. There is a reader service for the blind. **Library/Resources:** Computerized library services include interlibrary loans and database searching. Special learning facilities include an art gallery, radio station, and TV station. **Physically Challenged Students:** 95% of the campus is accessible. Facilities include wheelchair ramps, elevators, special parking, specially equipped restrooms, special class scheduling, lowered drinking fountains, and lowered telephones. **Special:** Cross-registration is available through the Consortium of Colleges and Universities. There are co-op programs in education, business, engineering, arts and sciences, and international affairs and internships in the Washington metropolitan area. Study

abroad in locations throughout the world, work-study programs, dual majors, student-designed majors, and a 3-2 engineering degree program with 8 colleges are also available. Nondegree study, a general studies degree, credit by exam, and pass/fail options are possible. There are 12 national honor societies, including Phi Beta Kappa, a freshman honors program, and 21 departmental honors programs. **Visiting:** There are regularly scheduled orientations for prospective students, including group information sessions and campus tours. Class visitation, lunch with current students, and other activities can be arranged, if requested in advance. There are guides for informal visits, visitors may sit in on classes, and stay overnight. To schedule a visit, contact the University Visitor Center at (202) 994-6602. **Campus Safety and Security:** Measures include 24-hour foot and vehicle patrol, self-defense education, and security escort services. There are emergency telephones, lighted pathways/sidewalks, a bike patrol.

REQUIREMENTS: The SAT or ACT is required. Students must have successfully completed a strong academic program in high school. SAT: Subject tests are strongly recommended. An essay, 1 teacher recommendation, and 1 counselor recommendation are required. An interview is encouraged. AP and CLEP credits are accepted. Important factors in the admissions decision are advanced placement or honors courses, recommendations by school officials, and leadership record. Students must complete 120 semester hours with a minimum GPA of 2.0 for most majors. Arts and sciences majors must meet general curriculum requirements that include literacy, quantitative and logical reasoning, natural sciences, social and behavioral sciences, creative and performing arts, literature, Western civilization, and foreign languages or culture. Other specific course requirements vary with the different divisions of the university. **Procedure:** Freshmen are admitted to all sessions. Entrance exams should be taken in the junior year and the fall semester of the senior year. There are early decision and deferred admissions plans. Check with the school for current application deadlines. The fall 2014 application fee was $60. applicants were on the 2014 waiting list; were admitted. Applications are accepted on-line. **Transfer Students:** In addition to a record of high grades and exam scores, applicants must submit official transcripts of all postsecondary work. Minimum GPA requirements vary from 2.5 to 3.0, depending on the major. The SAT or ACT is required, and an interview is encouraged. 30 of 120 credits required for the bachelor's degree must be completed at GW. **International Students:** The school actively recruits these students. They must take the TOEFL and the college's own test. They must also take the SAT or ACT.

ADMISSIONS: Executive Dean for Undergraduate Admissions. Web: *www.gwu.edu*

FINANCIAL AID: GW is a member of CSS. The CSS/Profile and FAFSA are required. Check with the school for current application deadlines.

GEORGETOWN UNIVERSITY   B-3
www.georgetown.edu

Washington, DC 20057   (202) 687-3600

Fax: (202) 687-5084   Email: guadmiss@georgetown.edu

Full-time: 3212 men, 4030 women	**Faculty:** I, +$
Part-time: 142 men, 168 women	**Ph.D.s:** 74%
Graduate: 4798 men, 5007 women	**Student/Faculty:** 12 to 1
Year: semesters, summer session	**Tuition:** $41,393
Room & Board: $12,517	**Freshman Class:** 20115 applied, 3413 accepted, 1570 enrolled
SAT or ACT: required	**CEEB CODE:** 5422
Application Deadline: January 10	**MOST COMPETITIVE**

Georgetown University, founded in 1789, is a private institution affiliated with the Roman Catholic Church and offers programs in arts and sciences, business administration, foreign service, languages and linguistics, and nursing. Figures in the above capsule and in this profile are approximate. There are 4 undergraduate schools and 3 graduate schools. In addition to regional accreditation, Georgetown has baccalaureate program accreditation with AACSB. The 104-acre campus is in an urban area 1.5 miles northwest of downtown Washington D.C. Including any residence halls, there are 64 buildings.

STUDENT LIFE: 96% of undergraduates are from out of state, mostly the Middle Atlantic. Students are from 50 states, 91 foreign countries, and Canada. 46% are from public schools. 60% are White; 11% Foreign. 42% are Catholic; 21% Protestant. **Male To Female Ratio:** 1.1:1. The average age of freshmen is 18; all undergraduates, 21. 4% do not continue beyond their first year; 94% remain to graduate. **Housing:** 5053 students can be accommodated in college housing, which includes coed dorms and on-campus apartments. Special interest floors are available in some residence halls. On-campus housing is available on a lottery system for upperclassmen. 63% of students live on campus. No one may keep cars.

FACULTY/CLASSROOMS: 62% of faculty are male; 38% are female. All teach and do research. No introductory courses are taught by graduate students.

PROGRAMS OF STUDY: Georgetown confers A.B., B.S., B.A.L.S., B.S.B.A., B.S.F.S. and B.S.N. degrees. Master's and Doctoral degrees are also awarded. Bachelor's degrees are awarded in BIOLOGICAL SCIENCE (biochemistry, biology/biological science, and environmental biology), BUSINESS (accounting, banking and finance, business administration and management, finance, international business management, and marketing/retailing/merchandising), COMMUNICATIONS AND THE ARTS (Arabic, art history, art, Chinese, classics, comparative literature, English, fine arts, French, German, Italian, Japanese, linguistics, Portuguese, Russian, and Spanish), COMPUTER AND PHYSICAL SCIENCE (chemistry, computer science, mathematics, and physics), HEALTH PROFESSIONS (health and nursing), SOCIAL SCIENCE (American studies, anthropology, economics, history, interdisciplinary studies, international relations, philosophy, political science/government, psychology, religion, and sociology). International politics, government, and international politics have the largest.

ACTIVITIES: There are 171 groups on campus, including art, band, cheerleading, chess, choir, chorale, chorus, computers, dance, debate, drama, ethnic, film, gay, honors, international, jazz band, literary magazine, musical theater, newspaper, orchestra, pep band, photography, political, professional, radio and TV, religious, social, social service, student government, and symphony. Popular campus events include GU Day, Career Week, and Senior Salute. **Sports:** There are 11 intercollegiate sports for men and 12 for women. Facilities include a 5,000-seat gym for basketball and volleyball, along with sports medicine and training room facilities, a 2,500-seat multi-sport field for football and lacrosse, and a 4-level sports and recreation facility that houses a swimming pool, basketball courts, aerobics rooms, a weight area, cardiovascular equipment, a wellness center, locker rooms, and racquetball courts. **Graduates:** From July 1, 2013 to June 30, 2014, 1871 bachelor's degrees were awarded. The most popular majors were government (11%), international politics (9%), and nursing (9%). In an average class, 90% graduate in 4 years or less, 93% graduate in 5 years or less, and 94% graduate in 6 years or less.

SERVICES: Counseling and information services are available, as is tutoring in some subjects, accounting, finance, biological sciences, math, Spanish, French and Arabic There is a reader service for the blind. **Library/Resources:** The 6 libraries contain 3.0 million volumes, 4.0 million microform items, 54,513 audio/video tapes/CDs/DVDs, and subscribe to 61,257 periodicals including electronic. Computerized library services include interlibrary loans, database searching, Internet access, and Wi-Fi capability. Special learning facilities include an art gallery, planetarium, radio station, and TV station. **Physically Challenged Students:** 94% of the campus is accessible. Facilities include wheelchair ramps, elevators, special parking, specially equipped restrooms, special class scheduling, lowered drinking fountains, lowered telephones, special housing, A special map of the campus with accessibility routes, a tactile map of the campus for visually disabled students, and a paratransit vehicle for mobility on the main campus. **Special:** Cross-registration is available with a consortium of universities in the Washington Metropolitan area. Opportunities are provided for internships, study abroad in 30 countries, work-study programs, student-designed majors, and dual majors. A liberal studies degree, B.A. and B.S. degrees, non-degree study, credit by examination, and pass/fail options are also offered. There is a chapter of Phi Beta Kappa and a freshman honors program. **Visiting:**

There are regularly scheduled orientations for prospective students, throughout the year, including a question and answer period led by an admissions officer, followed by a campus tour led by a student guide. There are guides for informal visits and visitors may sit in on classes. To schedule a visit, contact the Office of Undergraduate Admissions. **Campus Safety and Security:** Measures include 24-hour foot and vehicle patrol, emergency notification system, and security escort services. There are shuttle buses, emergency telephones, lighted pathways/sidewalks, controlled access to dorms/residences, Laptop computer registration, bicycle registration, and off-campus security assestments.

REQUIREMENTS: The SAT or ACT is required. Graduation from an accredited secondary school is required, including 4 years of English, a minimum of 2 each of a foreign language, math, and social studies, and 1 of natural science. An additional 2 years each of math and science is required for students intending to major in math, science, nursing, or business. SAT subject tests are strongly recommended. AP credits are accepted. Important factors in the admissions decision are recommendations by school officials, leadership record, and advanced placement or honors courses. Students must complete 120 credits and maintain a minimum GPA of 2.0. A core of liberal arts courses is required, consisting of 2 courses each in philosophy and theology. Additional requirements are specific to undergraduate school as well as major concentration. **Procedure:** Freshmen are admitted fall. Entrance exams should be taken in the junior year and again at the beginning of the senior year. There is a deferred admissions plan. Early decision applications should be filed by November 1; regular applications, by January 10 for fall entry, along with a $70 fee. Notification of early decision is sent December 15; regular decision, April 1. Applications are accepted on-line. **Transfer Students:** 168 transfer students enrolled in 2013-2014. Transfer students must have successfully completed a minimum of 12 credit hours with a minimum GPA of 3.0. Either the SAT or the ACT is required. An interview is recommended. Transfers must complete their last 2 years at Georgetown. 60 of 120 credits required for the bachelor's degree must be completed at Georgetown. **International Students:** There are 781 international students enrolled. The school actively recruits these students. They must take the TOEFL. They must also take the SAT or ACT.

ADMISSIONS: 17% of the 2014-2015 applicants were accepted. The SAT scores for the 2014-2015 freshman class were: Critical Reading--1% below 500, 9% between 500 and 599, 33% between 600 and 699, and 57% between 700 and 800; Math--1% below 500, 8% between 500 and 599, 36% between 600 and 699, and 56% between 700 and 800. **Admissions Contact:** Dean of Admissions. E-Mail: *guadmiss@georgetown.edu* Web: *www.georgetown.edu*

FINANCIAL AID: Georgetown is a member of CSS. The CSS/Profile and FAFSA, and non-custodial profile, business/farm supplement, and tax returns are required. The deadline for filing freshman financial aid applications for fall entry is February 1.

HOWARD UNIVERSITY — C-3
www.howard.edu

Washington, DC 20059

(202) 806-2864
1-800-822-6363

Fax: (202) 806-2818
Email: dkindle@howard.edu

Full-time: 2093 men, 4420 women
Faculty: 746; I, --$

Part-time: 204 men, 296 women
Ph.D.s: 73%

Graduate: 1262 men, 1990 women
Student/Faculty: 8 to 1

Year: semesters, summer session
Tuition: $23,970

Room & Board: $13,274
Freshman Class: n/av
CEEB CODE: 5297

Application Deadline: February 15
COMPETITIVE

Howard University, founded in 1867, is the largest predominantly Black University in the United States. As a culturally diverse, comprehensive, nonsectarian, research intensive, and historically Black private university, Howard University provides an educational experience of exceptional quality at the undergraduate, graduate, and professional levels to students of high academic standing and potential, with particular emphasis upon educational opportunities for

Black students. Moreover, the University is dedicated to attracting and sustaining a cadre of faculty who are, through their teaching, research and service, committed to the development of distinguished, historically aware, and compassionate graduates and to the discovery of solutions to human problems in the United States and throughout the world. With an abiding interest in both domestic and international affairs, the University is committed to continuing to produce leaders for America and the global community. There are 6 undergraduate schools and 12 graduate schools. In addition to regional accreditation, Howard has baccalaureate program accreditation with AACSB, ABET, ACEJMC, ACPE, ADA, APTA, CSWE, NAAB, NASAD, NASDTEC, NASM, and NCATE. The 258-acre campus is in an urban area in Northwest Washington, D.C. Including any residence halls, there are 127 buildings.

STUDENT LIFE: 96% of undergraduates are from out of state, mostly the Middle Atlantic. Students are from 45 states, 38 foreign countries, and Canada. 87% are African American. **Male To Female Ratio:** 1.9:1. The average age of freshmen is 18; all undergraduates, 21. 17% do not continue beyond their first year; 83% remain to graduate. **Housing:** 5748 students can be accommodated in college housing, which includes single-sex and coed dorms, on-campus apartments, and off-campus apartments. In addition, there are honors houses and special-interest houses. On-campus housing is guaranteed for the freshman year only, is available on a first-come, first-served basis, and is available on a lottery system for upperclassmen. 56% of students live on campus; of those, 40% remain on campus on weekends. Alcohol is not permitted. All students may keep cars.

FACULTY/CLASSROOMS: 55% of faculty are male; 45% are female. 65% teach undergraduates, 35% do research, and 40% do both. No introductory courses are taught by graduate students. The average class size in an introductory lecture is 35; in a laboratory is 20; and in a regular course is 20.

PROGRAMS OF STUDY: Howard confers B.B.A., B.A., B.S. and B.F.A. degrees. Master's and doctoral degrees are also awarded. Bachelor's degrees are awarded in BIOLOGICAL SCIENCE (anatomy, biochemistry, biology/biological science, genetics, microbiology, nutrition, and physiology), BUSINESS (accounting, banking and finance, business administration and management, fashion merchandising, international business management, labor studies, marketing/retailing/merchandising, sports management, and supply chain management), COMMUNICATIONS AND THE ARTS (acting, advertising, art history and appreciation, broadcasting, ceramic art and design, communications, communication science, dance, design, dramatic arts, English, film arts, French, graphic design, jazz, journalism, media arts, music, music business management, music history and appreciation, musical theater, painting, photography, playwriting/screenwriting, printmaking, public relations, sculpture, Spanish, telecommunications, and theatre arts), COMPUTER AND PHYSICAL SCIENCE (atmospheric sciences and meteorology, chemistry, Computer Engineering Technology, computer science, mathematics, physics, and radiological technology), EDUCATION (art education, early childhood education, education, education administration, elementary education, health education, music education, physical education, reading education, school psychology, and secondary education), ENGINEERING AND ENVIRONMENTAL DESIGN (architecture, chemical engineering, civil engineering, computer engineering, electrical/electronics engineering, environmental science, interior design, and mechanical engineering), HEALTH PROFESSIONS (allied health, clinical science, community health work, dental hygiene, health care administration, health science, music therapy, nursing, occupational therapy, pharmaceutical science, pharmacology, pharmacy, physical therapy, physician's assistant, predentistry, premedicine, public health, radiation therapy, radiograph medical technology, speech pathology/audiology, and sports medicine), SOCIAL SCIENCE (administration of justice, African studies, African American studies, anthropology, child psychology/development, classical/ancient civilization, counseling/psychology, criminal justice, economics, fashion design and technology, geography, history, human development, interdisciplinary studies, law, legal studies, philosophy, political science/government, psychology, public administration, public affairs, religion, social work, sociology, Spanish studies, textiles and clothing, urban studies, and women's

studies). Chemical engineering, computer engineering, and physics are the strongest academically. Biology, psychology, and political science have the largest enrollments.

ACTIVITIES: 3% of men belong to 10 local fraternities; 5% of women belong to 8 local sororities. There are 155 groups on campus, including programming boards (residence halls and activities); step teams; entertainment industry clubs, art, band, cheerleading, chess, choir, chorus, communications, community service; youth/peer mentorship; residence hall councils, computers, dance, debate, drama, drill team, drum and bugle corps, environmental, ethnic, film, gay, honors, international, jazz band, marching band, musical theater, newspaper, opera, orchestra, pep band, photography, political, professional, radio and TV, religious, social, social service, student government, symphony, and yearbook. Popular campus events include Orientation, Freshman Welcome Pep Rally and Pinning Ceremony, Opening Convocation, Charter Day Dinner, Global Community Week, Howard Homecoming, Spring Black Arts Festival (Springfest), MLK Day of Service and Student Leadership Conference. **Sports:** There are 8 intercollegiate sports for men and 10 for women, and 6 intramural sports for men and 5 for women. Facilities include Greene Stadium (outdoor track, football/soccer/lacrosse field); Burr Gymnasium (basketball courts, swimming pool, indoor track, classrooms, weight room, cardio fitness center); Blackburn Recreational Center (bowling alley and pool hall); and several practice fields. **Graduates:** From July 1, 2013 to June 30, 2014, 2153 bachelor's degrees were awarded. The most popular majors were biology health professions and related programs (22%), business, management, marketing, and related support services (18%), communication, journalism, and and related programs (16%). 211 companies recruited on campus in 2013-2014. In an average class, 49% graduate in 4 years or less, 62% graduate in 5 years or less, and 61% graduate in 6 years or less. Of the 2013 graduating class, 54% were enrolled in graduate school within 6 months of graduation, and 65% were employed.

SERVICES: Counseling and information services are available, as is tutoring in most subjects. There is a reader service for the blind, and remedial math, reading, and writing. Tutoring is also available for the following subjects: Humanities, Research, Mathematics, Foreign Languages, English, Science, Psychology, Statistics **Library/Resources:** The 8 libraries contain 2.5 million volumes, 4.2 million microform items, 194,000 audio/video tapes/CDs/DVDs, and subscribe to 82,758 periodicals including electronic. Computerized library services include interlibrary loans, database searching, Internet access, and Wi-Fi capability. Special learning facilities include an art gallery, radio station, TV station, a history and culture research centers (e.g. Moorland-Spingarn Research Center (MSRC); Ralph Bunche International Center; E. Franklin Frazier Reading Room). **Physically Challenged Students:** All of the campus is accessible. Facilities include wheelchair ramps, elevators, special parking, specially equipped restrooms, special class scheduling, lowered drinking fountains, lowered telephones, and special housing. **Special:** Cross-registration is available with the Consortium of Universities in the Washington Metropolitan Area. Opportunities are also provided for internships, work-study, co-op programs, study abroad in 5 countries in Europe and Africa, B.A.-B.S. degrees in engineering and business, student-designed majors, pass/fail options, and accelerated degree programs in medicine and dentistry. There are 20 national honor societies, including Phi Beta Kappa, and a freshman honors program. **Visiting:** There are regularly scheduled orientations for prospective students, consisting of a verbal presentation by an admission staff member, followed by a walking guided tour. There are guides for informal visits and visitors may sit in on classes. To schedule a visit, contact the Office of Admissions. **Campus Safety and Security:** Measures include 24-hour foot and vehicle patrol, emergency notification system, self-defense education, and security escort services. There are shuttle buses, emergency telephones, lighted pathways/sidewalks, controlled access to dorms/residences, Biweekly checks of calls for service and response time, blue light emergency system, fingerprinting services, town-hall meetings, and a crime prevention program.

REQUIREMENTS: The SAT or ACT is required. Evaluation of an applicant's qualifications for admission is based on high school course work, grade point average, class rank, test scores, extracurricular activities and letters of recommendation. An essay, audition, portfolio, or interview also may be required. Academic Eligibility; we consider the applicant's secondary school academic record, standardized college entrance exams (SAT or ACT), leadership in school and community activities, unique talents and skills, and educational objectives. For admission consideration, an applicant should have a well-balanced college preparatory program that includes the following course work; 4 years English, 3 years mathematics, 2 years social science, 2 years science (w/ lab), 2 years foreign language. Admission Requirements Package; A complete application package includes the following credentials; Application for Admission, Nonrefundable $45 application fee payable by credit card, money order, or cashier's check, (personal checks are not accepted). Howard University does not waive application fees, Official high school transcript or GED certificate, score results from the Scholastic Aptitude Test (SAT) or the American College Test (ACT), One letter of recommendation from a high school counselor, Guidance Counselor Recommendation Form; One letter of recommendation from a high school teacher, Teacher Recommendation Form, an Admission essay, and a Resume (optional). A GPA of 3.0 is required. AP and CLEP credits are accepted. Important factors in the admissions decision are leadership record, advanced placement or honors courses, and extracurricular activities record.To graduate, students must complete a total of 120 semester hours, exclusive of courses taken through the Center for Academic Reinforcement (CAR); maintain grades of C or better in all courses used to satisfy the minimum credit-hour requirement for departmental majors; maintain grades higher than C for courses used to satisfy requirements for departmental majors in any department stipulating this requirement; and maintain a cumulative grade point average of 2.0 or better in departmental majors, as well as in the minor fields of concentration. **Procedure:** Freshmen are admitted fall, spring, and summer. Entrance exams should be taken by January of Senior Year. There are early decision, deferred admissions, and rolling admissions plans. Early decision applications should be filed by November 1; regular applications, by February 15 for fall entry; November 1 for spring entry; and April 1 for summer entry, along with a $45 fee. Notification of early decision is sent December 20; regular decision, January 15. 636 early decision candidates were accepted for the 2014-2015 class. Applications are accepted on-line. **Transfer Students:** 469 transfer students enrolled in 2013-2014. Admission criteria vary among Howard University's schools and colleges. As a transfer applicant, you must meet the following minimum requirements for admission consideration: 15 transferrable credit hours (30 credit hours for the School of Business) from a regionally accredited postsecondary institution, earned a 2.5 cumulative GPA (3.0 GPA for the School of Business) and received a passing grade of C or better in both a college-level English and college-level math course, additional credentials such as a high school transcript and SAT scores may be requested for admission. 30 of 120 credits required for the bachelor's degree must be completed at Howard. **International Students:** There are 187 international students enrolled. The school actively recruits these students. They must take the TOEFL with a minimum score of 550 on the paper-based TOEFL (PBT) or 79 on the Internet-based version (iBT), If TOEFL is not offered in your country, applicants may submit results from IELTS (International English Language). They must also take the SAT or ACT.

ADMISSIONS: 51% of the current freshmen were in the top fifth of their class; 77% were in the top two fifths. **Admissions Contact:** Derek Kindle, Director of Student Financial Services. E-Mail: *dkindle@howard.edu* Web: *http://www.howard.edu/*

FINANCIAL AID: In 2014-2015, 93% of all full-time freshmen and 90% of continuing full-time students received some form of financial aid. 50% of all full-time freshmen and 53% of continuing full-time students received need-based aid. The average freshman award was $35,045. Need-based scholarships or need-based grants averaged $8,839 ($15,188 maximum); need-based self-help aid (loans and jobs) averaged $5,000 ($5,000 maximum); non-need-based athletic scholarships averaged $24,439 ($23,970 maximum); and other non-need-based awards and non-need-based scholarships averaged $28,555 ($41,983 maximum). 4% of undergraduate students work part-time. Average annual earnings from campus work are $4900. The average financial indebtedness of the 2014 graduate was $47,784. The FAFSA is required. The priority date for freshman financial aid applications for fall entry is February 1.

THE CATHOLIC UNIVERSITY OF AMERICA   C-2
www.cua.edu

Washington, DC 20064

(202) 319-5305
(800) 673-2772

Fax: (202) 319-6533
Email: cua-admissions@cua.edu

Full-time: 1601 men, 1972 women
Faculty: 270; I, -$

Part-time: 102 men, 124 women
Ph.D.s: 98%

Graduate: n/av
Student/Faculty: 10 to 1

Year: semesters, summer session
Tuition: $38,526

Room & Board: $14,326
Freshman Class: n/av

SAT or ACT: required
CEEB CODE: 5104

Application Deadline: February 15
VERY COMPETITIVE

The Catholic University of America, founded in 1887 and affiliated with the Roman Catholic Church, offers undergraduate programs in arts and sciences, engineering, architecture, nursing, philosophy, social service, and music and through the Metropolitan College. CUA's location provides a unique college experience and a wide spectrum of internship opportunities. Figures in the above capsule and in this profile are approximate. There are 8 undergraduate schools and 11 graduate schools. In addition to regional accreditation, CUA has baccalaureate program accreditation with AACSB, ABET, ACPE, CSWE, NAAB, NASM, NCATE, and NLN. The 180-acre campus is in an urban area in Washington, DC. Including any residence halls, there are 52 buildings.

STUDENT LIFE: 96% of undergraduates are from out of state, mostly the Middle Atlantic. Students are from 50 states, 90 foreign countries, and Canada. 56% are from public schools. 62% are White. 80% are Catholic. **Male To Female Ratio:** 1.2:1. The average age of freshmen is 18; all undergraduates, 20. 20% do not continue beyond their first year; 73% remain to graduate. **Housing:** College-sponsored housing includes single-sex dorms and on-campus apartments. In addition, there are honors houses, special-interest houses, a freshman residential college, and a residential college for upperclassmen, living and learning communities based on common interest. On-campus housing is available on a first-come, first-served basis, and is available on a lottery system for upperclassmen. 62% of students live on campus. Upperclassmen may keep cars.

FACULTY/CLASSROOMS: 70% teach undergraduates, and all do research. No introductory courses are taught by graduate students. The average class size in an introductory lecture is 21; in a laboratory is 20; and in a regular course is 19.

PROGRAMS OF STUDY: CUA confers B.A., B.S., B.A.G.S., B.Arch., B.B.E., B.C.E., B.E.E., B.M., B.M.E., B.S.Arch., B.S.N. and B.S.B.A. degrees. Master's and doctoral degrees are also awarded. Bachelor's degrees are awarded in BIOLOGICAL SCIENCE (biochemistry, biology/biological science, and biotechnology), BUSINESS (accounting, banking and finance, business administration and management, finance, international economics, management science, and marketing and distribution), COMMUNICATIONS AND THE ARTS (art history, art, art history and appreciation, ceramic art and design, classics, communications, dramatic arts, English, English literature, French, German, Greek (classical), Italian, Latin, music, music history and appreciation, music performance, music theory and composition, musical theater, painting, piano/organ, Spanish, studio art, and voice), COMPUTER AND PHYSICAL SCIENCE (chemical physics, chemistry, computer science, elementary particle physics, mathematics, and physics), EDUCATION (art education, drama education, early childhood education, education, elementary education, English education, mathematics education, music education, and secondary education), ENGINEERING AND ENVIRONMENTAL DESIGN (architecture, biomedical engineering, civil engineering, computer engineering, construction engineering, electrical/electronics engineering, engineering, environmental engineering, environmental science, and mechanical engineering), HEALTH PROFESSIONS (medical laboratory technology, medical technology, nursing, predentistry, premedicine, and preveterinary science), SOCIAL SCIENCE (anthropology, economics, French studies, history, liberal arts/general studies, medieval studies, philosophy, political science/government, prelaw, psychology, religion, social science, social work, sociology, Spanish studies, and theological studies). Politics is the strongest academically. Architecture has the largest enrollment.

ACTIVITIES: 1% of men belong to 2 national fraternities. There are 90 groups on campus, including art, cheerleading, choir, chorale, chorus, computers, dance, debate, drama, ethnic, film, honors, international, jazz band, literary magazine, musical theater, newspaper, opera, orchestra, pep band, political, professional, radio and TV, religious, social, social service, student government, symphony, and yearbook. Popular campus events include Luaupalooza, Movies on the Mall, Fall Fiesta, Beaux Arts Ball and Mistletoe Ball. **Sports:** There are 10 intercollegiate sports for men and 11 for women, and 9 intramural sports for men and 9 for women. Facilities include an DuFour Athletic Center houses 4 basketball and 5 handball/racquetball courts, a 6-lane, 25-meter swimming pool, a weight training room, an aerobics room, men's and women's saunas, 2 dance studios, an indoor jogging track, and 3 volleyball courts. Outdoor facilities include Cardinal Stadium made with state-of-the-art FieldTurf, adjoining grass playing fields, baseball and softball facilities, and 6 tennis courts. **Graduates:** The most popular majors were architecture, nursing, and politics. In an average class, 62% graduate in 4 years or less and 68% graduate in 6 years or less. Of the 2013 graduating class, 36% were enrolled in graduate school within 6 months of graduation.

SERVICES: Counseling and information services are available, as is tutoring in most subjects, Center for Academic Success: drop-in tutoring, individual tutoring, smartthinking online service, and Writing Center. There is a reader service for the blind, and remedial math, reading, and writing. Taped books/scanned books, assistive technology, including reading software and screen readers, test accommodations, and sign language interpreters are available. **Library/Resources:** The 3 libraries contain 1.6 million volumes, 1.2 million microform items, 40,697 audio/video tapes/CDs/DVDs, and subscribe to 10,448 periodicals including electronic. Computerized library services include interlibrary loans, database searching, Internet access, and Wi-Fi capability. Special learning facilities include an art gallery and radio station. **Physically Challenged Students:** 78% of the campus is accessible. Facilities include wheelchair ramps, elevators, special parking, specially equipped restrooms, special class scheduling, lowered drinking fountains, lowered telephones, special housing. **Special:** Cross-registration is available with the Consortium of Universities of the Washington Metropolitan Area. Opportunities are also provided for internships, accelerated degree programs, dual majors, B.A.-B.S. degrees, work study, pass/fail options, and study abroad in 13 countries. There are 15 national honor societies, including Phi Beta Kappa, and a freshman honors program. **Visiting:** There are regularly scheduled orientations for prospective students, visits include an information session with an admissions counselor and a guided campus tour. There are guides for informal visits, visitors may sit in on classes, and stay overnight. To schedule a visit, contact the Admissions Office. **Campus Safety and Security:** Measures include 24-hour foot and vehicle patrol, emergency notification system, self-defense education, and security escort services. There are shuttle buses, emergency telephones, lighted pathways/sidewalks, controlled access to dorms/residences, fixed security posts, emergency whistles, watch captains in every building, and an access control system.

REQUIREMENTS: The SAT or ACT is required. Applicants must be graduates of an accredited secondary school. Students should present 17 academic credits, including 4 each in English and social studies, 3 each in math and science, 2 in foreign languages, and 1 in fine arts or humanities. An essay is required, one letter of recommendation, official high school transcripts, and either an SAT or ACT score. An audition is required for music applicants, and a portfolio for architecture applicants is recommended. A GPA of 3.0 is required. AP credits are accepted. Important factors in the admissions decision are extracurricular activities record, leadership record, and advanced placement or honors courses.To graduate, students must complete 120 credit hours, including 36 to 42 hours in the major, with a minimum GPA of 2.0. Courses must meet distribution requirements in theology and religious studies, philosophy, English composition, humanities, language and literature, math and natural sciences, and social and behavioral sciences. A comprehensive exam is required in most majors. **Procedure:** Freshmen are admitted fall and spring. Entrance exams should be taken by February of the senior year of high school. There are early admissions and deferred admissions plans. Early deci-

sion applications should be filed by November 15; regular applications, by February 15 for fall entry. The fall 2014 application fee was $55. Notification of early decision is sent December 20; regular decision, March 15. applicants were on the 2014 waiting list; were admitted. Applications are accepted on-line. **Transfer Students:** Applicants must submit a high school transcript, SAT or ACT scores, and a college transcript. A letter of recommendation and an essay are required. Terms of admission are finalized by the dean of the appropriate school. 60 of 120 credits required for the bachelor's degree must be completed at CUA. **International Students:** There are 66 international students enrolled. The school actively recruits these students. They must take the TOEFL. They must also take the SAT or ACT.

ADMISSIONS: Dean of University Admissions. E-Mail: *cua-admissions@cua.edu* Web: *www.cua.edu*

FINANCIAL AID: In 2014-2015, 90% of all full-time freshmen and % of continuing full-time students received some form of financial aid. CUA is a member of CSS. The FAFSA is required. The priority date for freshman financial aid applications for fall entry is February 15.

TRINITY WASHINGTON UNIVERSITY   C-2
www.trinitydc.edu

Washington, DC 20017	(202) 884-9400
	(800) 492-6882
Fax: (202) 884-9403	**Email:** admissions@trinitydc.edu
Full-time: 17 men, 841 women	**Faculty:** 48; IIB, -$
Part-time: 45 men, 488 women	**Ph.D.s:** 98%
Graduate: 107 men, 515 women	**Student/Faculty:** 12 to 1
Year: semesters	**Tuition:** $21,040
Room & Board: $9210	**Freshman Class:** n/av
SAT or ACT: recommended	**CEEB CODE:** 5796
Application Deadline: n/av	**COMPETITIVE+**

Trinity Washington University, founded in 1897, is a private, women's liberal arts college in the nation's capital. The school year consists of traditional semesters plus 1-week courses during January and May. The School of Professional Studies and School of Education are both co-ed and offer adult students bachelor's and master's degrees with evening and weekend classes. Figures in the above capsule and in this profile are approximate. There are 4 undergraduate schools and 2 graduate schools. In addition to regional accreditation, Trinity has baccalaureate program accreditation with NCATE. The 26-acre campus is in an urban area 2 1/2 miles north of the U.S. Capitol. Including any residence halls, there are 7 buildings.

STUDENT LIFE: 51% of undergraduates are from out of state, mostly the Middle Atlantic. Students are from 21 states, and 2 foreign countries. 90% are from public schools. 68% are African American. 52% claim no religious affiliation; 35% Protestant; 12% Catholic. **Male To Female Ratio:** 10.9:1. The average age of freshmen is 18; all undergraduates, 22. 30% do not continue beyond their first year; 50% remain to graduate. **Housing:** 275 students can be accommodated in college housing, which includes single-sex dorms. On-campus housing is available on a first-come, first-served basis, and is available on a lottery system for upperclassmen. Priority is given to out-of-town students. 75% of students commute. Alcohol is not permitted. All students may keep cars.

FACULTY/CLASSROOMS: 35% of faculty are male; 65% are female. 72% teach undergraduates. No introductory courses are taught by graduate students. The average class size in an introductory lecture is 16; in a laboratory is 16; and in a regular course is 13.

PROGRAMS OF STUDY: Trinity confers B.A., and B.S. degrees. Associate and Master's degrees are also awarded. Bachelor's degrees are awarded in BIOLOGICAL SCIENCE (biochemistry and biology/biological science), BUSINESS (business administration and management and business economics), COMMUNICATIONS AND THE ARTS (communications and English), COMPUTER AND PHYSICAL SCIENCE (chemistry and mathematics), EDUCATION (early childhood education, education, and elementary education), HEALTH PROFESSIONS (exercise science and nursing), SOCIAL SCIENCE (criminal justice, economics, history, human services, international studies, political science/government, psychology, and sociology). Nursing, exercise science, biology, chemistry, and biochemistry are the strongest academically. Psychology, business administration, nursing, and criminal justice have the largest enrollments.

ACTIVITIES: There are 23 groups on campus, including choir, computers, dance, debate, drama, ethnic, honors, international, literary magazine, newspaper, political, professional, religious, social, social service, student government, and yearbook. Popular campus events include Founders Day, Class Days, Junior Ring Day, and Cap and Gown. **Sports:** There are 5 intercollegiate sports for women, and 2 intramural sports for women. Facilities include 2 athletic fields for soccer and lacrosse, a fitness center, 6 tennis courts, a state-of-the-art sports center with pool, weight room, basketball court and volleyball court. **Graduates:** From July 1, 2013 to June 30, 2014, 130 bachelor's degrees were awarded. The most popular majors were psychology (36%), business administration (15%), and English (10%).

SERVICES: Counseling and information services are available, as is tutoring in every subject. There is a reader service for the blind. Signing for hearing-impaired students. **Library/Resources:** The library contains 215,338 volumes, 6,826 microform items, 13,797 audio/video tapes/CDs/DVDs, and subscribes to 509 periodicals including electronic. Computerized library services include interlibrary loans, database searching, and Internet access. Special learning facilities include an art gallery. **Physically Challenged Students:** 85% of the campus is accessible. Facilities include wheelchair ramps, elevators, special parking, and specially equipped restrooms. **Special:** Cross-registration is offered through the Consortium of Universities of the Washington Metropolitan Area. Trinity offers internships in all majors and minors, as well as work-study programs. Students may study in France, Italy, and various other countries by arrangement with their faculty adviser. B.A.-B.S. degrees, a 5-year accelerated degree in teaching, dual and student-designed majors, a general studies degree, credit for life experience, nondegree study, and pass/fail options are also available. There are 7 national honor societies, including Phi Beta Kappa, and a freshman honors program. **Visiting:** There are regularly scheduled orientations for prospective students, consisting of a half-day program, including an overview of the college, the curriculum, and financing. There are guides for informal visits, visitors may sit in on classes, and stay overnight. To schedule a visit, contact the Office of Admissions. **Campus Safety and Security:** Measures include 24-hour foot and vehicle patrol, self-defense education, and security escort services. There are shuttle buses, emergency telephones, lighted pathways/sidewalks, and controlled access to dorms/residences.

REQUIREMENTS: The SAT or ACT is recommended. Graduation from an accredited secondary school or satisfactory scores on the GED are required for admission. A total of 16 academic credits is required, including 4 years of English and 3 to 4 years each of a foreign language, history, math, and science. An essay or graded writing sample is required, as are two letters of recommendation from faculty/guidance counselor. An interview is optional, but may be required of some applicants. Standardized tests are not required, but are recommended. A GPA of 2.0 is required. AP and CLEP credits are accepted. Important factors in the admissions decision are leadership record, extracurricular activities record, and recommendations by school officials. To graduate, students must complete a total of 128 credit hours with a minimum GPA of 2.0. Between 42 and 60 hours are required in the major. All students must take the courses required in the general education curriculum and must complete a senior seminar. **Procedure:** Freshmen are admitted fall and spring. Entrance exams should be taken by the junior year is preferred. There are deferred admissions and rolling admissions plans. Application deadlines are open. Application fee is $40. Applications are accepted online. **Transfer Students:** 130 transfer students enrolled in 2013-2014. Transfer applicants must have a GPA of 2.5. An interview is recommended, and an essay and recommendation are required. 45 of 128 credits required for the Bachelor's degree must be completed at Trinity. **International Students:** There are 2 international students enrolled. They must take the TOEFL with a minimum score of 543 on the paper-based TOEFL (PBT) or 76 on the Internet-based version (iBT).

ADMISSIONS: 2 freshmen graduated first in their class. **Admissions Contact:** Vice President of Admissions. E-Mail: *admissions@trinitydc.edu* Web: *www.trinitydc.edu*

FINANCIAL AID: In 2014-2015, 98% of all full-time freshmen and 95% of continuing full-time students received some form of financial aid. 83% of all full-time freshmen and 82% of continuing full-time students received need-based aid. The average freshman award was $23,280. Need-based scholarships or need-based grants averaged $14,000; need-based self-help aid (loans and jobs) averaged $7,000; and other non-need-based awards and non-need-based scholarships averaged $2,280. 7% of undergraduate students work part-time. Average annual earnings from campus work are $1400. The average financial indebtedness of the 2014 graduate was $17,000. Trinity is a member of CSS. The FAFSA is required. The priority date for freshman financial aid applications for fall entry is March 1.

UNIVERSITY OF THE DISTRICT OF COLUMBIA *(The complete profile is made available exclusively on our website, www.barronspac.com)*

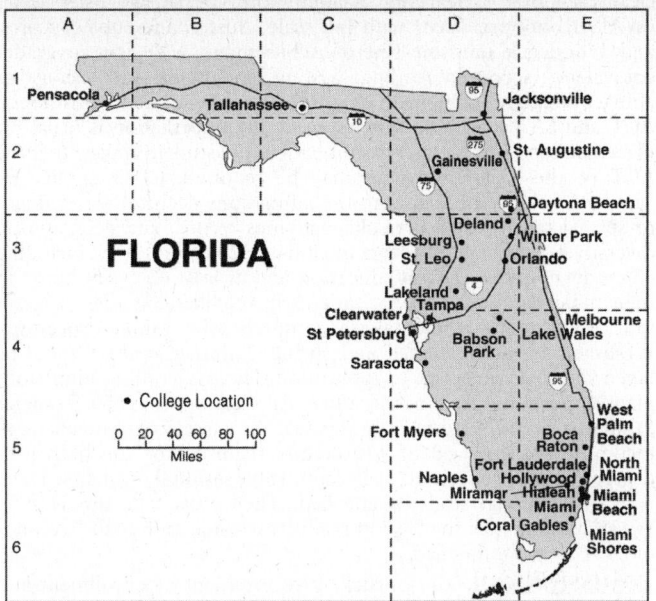

ADVENTIST UNIVERSITY OF HEALTH SCIENCES (*The complete profile is made available exclusively on our website, www.barronspac.com*)

BARRY UNIVERSITY   E-5
www.barry.edu

Miami Shores, FL 33161	(305) 899-3134
	(800) 695-2279
Fax: (305) 899-2971	Email: admissions@mail.barry.edu
Full-time: 1270 men, 2900 women	Faculty: IIA, av$
Part-time: 350 men, 630 women	Ph.D.s: 80%
Graduate: 1270 men, 2400 women	Student/Faculty: n/av
Year: semesters, summer session	Tuition: $28,160
Room & Board: $9030	Freshman Class: n/av
SAT or ACT: required	CEEB CODE: 5053
Application Deadline: open	**COMPETITIVE**

Barry University is an independent Roman Catholic institution of liberal arts and professional studies. The figures in the above capsule and in this profile are approximate. There are 6 undergraduate schools and 10 graduate schools. In addition to regional accreditation, Barry has baccalaureate program accreditation with CAHEA and NLN. The 122-acre campus is in a suburban area 14 miles from Fort Lauderdale and 7 miles north of downtown Miami. Including any residence halls, there are 26 buildings.

STUDENT LIFE: 63% of undergraduates are from Florida. Others are from 47 states, 81 foreign countries, and Canada. 80% are from public schools. 31% are Hispanic; 26% White; 24% African American. 24% are Catholic. **Male To Female Ratio:** 2.1:1. The average age of freshmen is 18; all undergraduates, 23. **Housing:** 750 students can be accommodated in college housing, which includes single-sex and coed dorms and off-campus apartments. In addition, there are special-interest houses. On-campus housing is guaranteed for the freshman year only, is available on a first-come, first-served basis, and is available on a lottery system for upperclassmen. Priority is given to out-of-town students. 65% of students commute. All students may keep cars.

FACULTY/CLASSROOMS: 49% of faculty are male; 51% are female. 72% teach undergraduates. No introductory courses are taught by graduate students. The average class size in an introductory lecture is 17; in a laboratory is 14; and in a regular course is 17.

PROGRAMS OF STUDY: Barry confers B.A., B.S., B.F.A., B.L.S., B.P.A., B.P.S., B.S.L.S., B.S.N., B.S.T. and B.S.W. degrees. Master's

and Doctoral degrees are also awarded. Bachelor's degrees are awarded in BIOLOGICAL SCIENCE (biology/biological science and marine biology), BUSINESS (accounting, international business management, management information systems, management science, marketing/retailing/merchandising, and sports management), COMMUNICATIONS AND THE ARTS (advertising, art, broadcasting, communications, dramatic arts, English, French, music performance, photography, public relations, Spanish, and theater management), COMPUTER AND PHYSICAL SCIENCE (chemistry, computer science, and mathematics), EDUCATION (early childhood education and physical education), ENGINEERING AND ENVIRONMENTAL DESIGN (preengineering), HEALTH PROFESSIONS (cytotechnology, medical technology, nuclear medical technology, nursing, occupational therapy, predentistry, premedicine, prepharmacy, and ultrasound technology), SOCIAL SCIENCE (criminology, economics, history, international studies, liberal arts/general studies, philosophy, political science/government, prelaw, psychology, sociology, and theological studies). Biology, chemistry, and elementary and early childhood education are the strongest academically. Nursing, elementary and early childhood education, and biology have the largest enrollments.

ACTIVITIES: 11% of men belong to 3 national fraternities; 6% of women belong to 2 national sororities. There are 85 groups on campus, including cheerleading, chorale, computers, dance, drama, ethnic, honors, international, literary magazine, musical theater, newspaper, photography, political, professional, radio and TV, religious, social, social service, and student government. Popular campus events include Halloween Dance, Festival of Nations and World AIDS Day. **Sports:** There are 5 intercollegiate sports for men and 7 for women. Facilities include baseball, softball, and soccer fields, a health and sports center with an indoor gym, outdoor basketball courts, and racquetball and tennis courts, an outdoor swimming pool, a strength and conditioning center, an athletic training room, a human performance lab, and a biomechanics lab.

SERVICES: Counseling and information services are available, as is tutoring in most subjects. There is remedial math, reading, and writing. **Library/Resources:** The library contains 322,079 volumes, 617,792 microform items, 7,706 audio/video tapes/CDs/DVDs, and subscribes to 1,851 periodicals including electronic. Computerized library services include interlibrary loans and database searching. Special learning facilities include an art gallery, radio station, a human performance lab, biotechnology lab, photography studios, TV studio, theater, biomechanics lab, and multimedia business classrooms. **Physically Challenged Students:** 85% of the campus is accessible. Facilities include wheelchair ramps, elevators, special parking, specially equipped restrooms, special class scheduling, lowered drinking fountains, and lowered telephones. **Special:** Barry offers junior- or senior-year internships, a Washington semester for prelaw/political science students, on-campus work-study programs in all departments, dual majors, a liberal studies degree, an accelerated degree program in nursing, nondegree study, and pass/fail options. Students may study in 25 European countries. Barry is a member of the College Consortium for International Studies; students can participate in more than 50 programs offered by members. There are 15 national honor societies and a freshman honors program. **Visiting:** There are guides for informal visits and visitors may sit in on classes. To schedule a visit, contact the Undergraduate Admissions. **Campus Safety and Security:** Measures include 24-hour foot and vehicle patrol, self-defense education, and security escort services. There are shuttle buses, emergency telephones, and lighted pathways/sidewalks.

REQUIREMENTS: The SAT or ACT is required. Graduation from an accredited secondary school or satisfactory scores on the GED are required for admission. A GPA of 2.0 is required. AP and CLEP credits are accepted. To graduate, students must complete 120 credit hours, including at least 48 in upper-division courses, 40 to 60 in the major, and 45 distributed in these curricular divisions: theology and philosophy, written and oral communication, physical or natural science and math, social and behavior sciences, and humanities and the arts. A minimum GPA of 2.0 must be maintained. **Procedure:** Freshmen are admitted to all sessions. Entrance exams should be taken as early as possible. There is a rolling admissions plan. Application deadlines are open. The fall 2014 application fee was $30. Applications are accepted on-line. **Transfer Students:** Applicants must have earned at least 12 acceptable credit hours with a minimum GPA of 2.0. 30 of 120 credits required for the bachelor's degree must be completed at Barry. **International Students:** The school actively recruits these students. They must take the TOEFL.

ADMISSIONS: Director of Admissions. E-Mail: *admissions@ mail.barry.edu* Web: *www.barry.edu*

FINANCIAL AID: Barry is a member of CSS. The FAFSA is required. Check with the school for current application deadlines.

BEACON COLLEGE   D-3
www.beaconcollege.edu

Leesburg, FL 34748	(352) 787-7249
Fax: (352) 787-0721	Email: admissions@beaconcollege.edu
Full-time: 80 men, 60 women	Faculty: n/av
Part-time: n/av	Ph.D.s: n/av
Graduate: n/av	Student/Faculty: n/av
Year: semesters, summer session	Tuition: $32,416
Room & Board: $9304	Freshman Class: n/av
	CEEB CODE: 3611
Application Deadline: n/av	COMPETITIVE

Beacon College, founded in 1989, is a private institution that offers undergraduate degrees in liberal studies, human services, and computer information systems exclusively for students with language-based learning disabilities and or ADHD. The figures in the above capsule and in this profile are approximate. The 2-acre campus is in a small town in the downtown historic district. Including any residence halls, there are 11 buildings.

STUDENT LIFE: 84% of undergraduates are from out of state, mostly the South. Students are from 25 states, and 1 foreign countries. 48% are from public schools. 81% are White; 14% African American. **Male To Female Ratio:** 0.8:1. The average age of freshmen is 21. 23% do not continue beyond their first year; 76% remain to graduate. **Housing:** 130 students can be accommodated in college housing, which includes coed on-campus apartments and off-campus apartments. On-campus housing is guaranteed for all 4 years. Alcohol is not permitted. All students may keep cars.

FACULTY/CLASSROOMS: All teach undergraduates, 15% do research, and 15% do both. No introductory courses are taught by graduate students. The average class size in an introductory lecture is 8; in a laboratory is 10; and in a regular course is 8.

PROGRAMS OF STUDY: confers B.A., and B.S. degrees. Associate degrees are also awarded. Bachelor's degrees are awarded in COMPUTER AND PHYSICAL SCIENCE (information sciences and systems), SOCIAL SCIENCE (human services and liberal arts/general studies). Information sciences and systems and liberal studies has the largest enrollments.

ACTIVITIES: 38% of women belong to 1 local sororities. There are 15 groups on campus, including art, choir, computers, drama, literary magazine, musical theater, newspaper, social, social service, student government, and yearbook. **Sports:** There is no sports program at Beacon.

SERVICES: Counseling and information services are available, as is tutoring in every subject. There is remedial math, reading, and writing. There is an academic mentoring program. **Library/Resources:** The library contains 20,075 volumes, 554 audio/video tapes/CDs/DVDs, and subscribes to 182 periodicals including electronic. Computerized library services include interlibrary loans, database searching, and Internet access. Special learning facilities include an art gallery. **Physically Challenged Students:** 90% of the campus is accessible. Facilities include wheelchair ramps, special parking, specially equipped restrooms, special class scheduling, and special housing. **Special:** Internships, B.A.-B.S. degrees, dual majors, and study abroad are possible. **Visiting:** There are regularly scheduled orientations for prospective students. There are guides for informal visits. To schedule a visit, contact the Admissions Office. **Campus Safety and Security:** Measures include emergency notification system. There are lighted pathways/sidewalks, and a van transportation.

REQUIREMENTS: Required testing and documentation include a clear diagnosis of learning disability or ADHD; Wechsler scales (WAIS-III are preferred) with full scale, cluster, and subtest scores; and Woodcock Johnson Test of Achievement with age- or grade-equivalency scores in reading, writing, and math; and average or above average IQ range with diagnosed learning disability. Although ACT and SAT scores are not required, the information is usual for placement and it is highly recommended that students take either the ACT or the SAT. Interviews may be required. CLEP credits are accepted. Important factors in the admissions decision are evidence of special talent, extracurricular activities record, and geographical diversity. To graduate, students must have 120 credit hours, including 33 credit hours of general education and at least 63 credit hours in their major, and a 2.0 GPA. Students in the liberal studies program must write a thesis and take a comprehensive exam. **Procedure:** Freshmen are admitted fall and spring. Entrance exams should be taken within 3 years prior to application. There is a rolling admissions plan. Application deadlines are open. Application fee is $50. **Transfer Students:** Transfer students must meet the same requirements as all incoming students. 60 of 120 credits required for the bachelor's degree must be completed at Beacon. **International Students:** There is 1 International students enrolled. They must take the TOEFL. WAIS subtests with the GLE in reading, writing, and math. SATand/ or ACT is recommended.

ADMISSIONS: Dr. Mary Bruck, Vice President of Enrollment and Admissions. E-Mail: *admissions@beaconcollege.edu* Web: *www. beaconcollege.edu*

FINANCIAL AID: The FAFSA and the college's own financial statement are required. Check with the school for current application deadlines.

BETHUNE-COOKMAN UNIVERSITY   D-2
www.cookman.edu

Daytona Beach, FL 32114	(386) 481-2600
	(800) 448-0228
Fax: (386) 481-2601	Email: mccoyf@cookman.edu
Full-time: 1305 men, 2013 women	Faculty: 183; IIB, -$
Part-time: 101 men, 108 women	Ph.D.s: 58%
Graduate: 28 men, 23 women	Student/Faculty: 17 to 1
Year: semesters, summer session	Tuition: $14,410
Room & Board: $9600	Freshman Class: 4707 applied, 3152 accepted, 886 enrolled
SAT or ACT: required	CEEB CODE: 5061
Application Deadline: July 30	COMPETITIVE

Bethune-Cookman College, founded in 1904, is a private liberal arts institution affiliated with the United Methodist Church. Figures in the above capsule and in this profile are approximate. There are 6 undergraduate schools and 2 graduate schools. In addition to regional accreditation, B-CC or B-CU has baccalaureate program accreditation with NCATE. The 84-acre campus is in a small town 65 miles east of Orlando. Including any residence halls, there are 63 buildings.

STUDENT LIFE: 67% of undergraduates are from Florida. Others are from 39 states, 21 foreign countries, and Canada. 90% are from public schools. 92% are African American. 56% are Protestant; 28% Seventh Day Adventist, Muslim, and Jehovah Witness. **Male To Female Ratio:** 1.5:1. The average age of freshmen is 18; all undergraduates, 21. 31% do not continue beyond their first year; 69% remain to graduate. **Housing:** 1961 students can be accommodated in college housing, which includes single-sex and coed dorms. In addition, there are honors houses, and a leadership house. On-campus housing is guaranteed for the freshman year only, is available on a first-come, and first-served basis. Priority is given to out-of-town students. 53% of students commute. Alcohol is not permitted. Upperclassmen may keep cars.

FACULTY/CLASSROOMS: 46% of faculty are male; 54% are female. No introductory courses are taught by graduate students. The average class size in an introductory lecture is 20; in a laboratory is 20; and in a regular course is 25.

PROGRAMS OF STUDY: B-CC or B-CU confers B.A., and B.S.

degrees. Master's degrees are also awarded. Bachelor's degrees are awarded in BIOLOGICAL SCIENCE (biology/biological science), BUSINESS (accounting, business administration and management, hotel/motel and restaurant management, and international business management), COMMUNICATIONS AND THE ARTS (communications, dramatic arts, English, modern language, and music), COMPUTER AND PHYSICAL SCIENCE (chemistry, computer science, information sciences and systems, and mathematics), EDUCATION (business education, education, education of the exceptional child, elementary education, English education, music education, physical education, science education, and social science education), ENGINEERING AND ENVIRONMENTAL DESIGN (computer engineering), HEALTH PROFESSIONS (clinical science and nursing), SOCIAL SCIENCE (criminal justice, gerontology, history, international studies, liberal arts/general studies, political science/government, psychology, religion, and sociology). Business administration, Education, and Nursing are the strongest academically. Criminal justice has the largest enrollment.

ACTIVITIES: 25% of men belong to 5 national fraternities; 35% of women belong to 4 national sororities. There are 60 groups on campus, including band, cheerleading, choir, chorale, computers, dance, drama, drill team, honors, international, jazz band, literary magazine, marching band, newspaper, pep band, political, professional, radio and TV, religious, social, social service, student government, symphony, and yearbook. Popular campus events include Religious Outreach, Career Day and Founders Day. **Sports:** There are 8 intercollegiate sports for men and 9 for women, and 6 intramural sports for men and 8 for women. Facilities include a gym, weightrooms, and practice fields. **Graduates:** From July 1, 2013 to June 30, 2014, 561 bachelor's degrees were awarded. The most popular majors were education (15%), criminal justice (14%), and business administration (12%). 240 companies recruited on campus in 2013-2014. In an average class, 2% graduate in 3 years or less, 15% graduate in 4 years or less, 31% graduate in 5 years or less, and 37% graduate in 6 years or less. Of the 2013 graduating class, 20% were enrolled in graduate school within 6 months of graduation, and 17% were employed.

SERVICES: Counseling and information services are available, as is tutoring in most subjects. There is remedial math, reading, and writing. **Library/Resources:** The library contains 127,930 volumes, 45,000 microform items, 6,345 audio/video tapes/CDs/DVDs, and subscribes to 118 periodicals including electronic. Computerized library services include interlibrary loans, database searching, Internet access, and Wi-Fi capability. Special learning facilities include an art gallery, radio station, TV station, an observatory and founders' home and gravesite. **Physically Challenged Students:** 35% of the campus is accessible. Facilities include wheelchair ramps, elevators, special parking, specially equipped restrooms, special class scheduling, lowered drinking fountains, and lowered telephones. **Special:** Students may take courses at other institutions with the approval of the area adviser or registrar. B-CU offers cooperative courses in all divisions, internships related to the student's major, work-study programs, an accelerated degree program in business administration, non-degree-study, and 3-2 engineering degrees. Study abroad is available in South Africa, Ghana, Cuba, Brazil and Zimbabwe. There are 11 national honor societies, a freshman honors program, and 1 departmental honors programs. **Visiting:** There are guides for informal visits and visitors may sit in on classes. To schedule a visit, contact the Office of Admissions at (800) 448-0228. **Campus Safety and Security:** Measures include 24-hour foot and vehicle patrol and security escort services. There are lighted pathways/sidewalks, controlled access to dorms/residences, surveillance cameras and autolock door.

REQUIREMENTS: The SAT or ACT is required. Graduation from an accredited secondary school or satisfactory scores on the GED are required for admission. High school courses must include 24 credits with 4 of English, 3 each of math and science, 3 of social science and history, and 6 electives; 2 years of a modern language and 1 year of computer literacy are strongly recommended. Students must submit an essay and a letter of recommendation. A GPA of 2.3 is required. AP and CLEP credits are accepted. Important factors in the admissions decision are recommendations by school officials, leadership record, and geographical diversity. To graduate, students must have a minimum of 120 credit hours with a minimum GPA of 2.0. All students must complete a total of 39 hours in general education requirements, and pass at a specified level a senior exit exam that may include a standardized exam and/or senior area comprehensive exam. They must also complete a senior seminar and senior research paper, and must have 1 year residency, especially the last semester of study at B-CU. **Procedure:** Freshmen are admitted to all sessions. Entrance exams should be taken during the fall prior to application. There are deferred admissions and rolling admissions plans. Applications should be filed by July 30 for fall entry; November 30 for spring entry; and April 30 for summer entry, along with a $25 fee. Notification is sent on a rolling basis. **Transfer Students:** 108 transfer students enrolled in 2013-2014. Applicants must submit transcripts from previous institutions attended and a statement of good standing and eligibility to return. A minimum GPA of 2.25 is required. Students having fewer than 24 credit hours must meet the requirements for entering freshmen. 30 of 120 credits required for the bachelor's degree must be completed at B-CC or B-CU. **International Students:** There are 70 international students enrolled. The school actively recruits these students. They must take the TOEFL with a minimum score of 550 on the paper-based TOEFL (PBT) or 73 on the Internet-based version (iBT). They must also take the SAT or ACT.

ADMISSIONS: 67% of the 2014-2015 applicants were accepted. **Admissions Contact:** Director of Admissions. Web: *www.cookman.edu*

FINANCIAL AID: In 2014-2015, 82% of all full-time freshmen and 92% of continuing full-time students received some form of financial aid. 80% of all full-time freshmen and 89% of continuing full-time students received need-based aid. The average freshman award was $13,190. Need-based scholarships or need-based grants averaged $9,903 ($19,000 maximum); need-based self-help aid (loans and jobs) averaged $3,796 ($5,500 maximum); non-need-based athletic scholarships averaged $10,338 ($22,300 maximum); and other non-need-based awards and non-need-based scholarships averaged $8,380 ($20,000 maximum). 23% of undergraduate students work part-time. Average annual earnings from campus work are $2100. The average financial indebtedness of the 2014 graduate was $21,435. The FAFSA is required. The priority date for freshman financial aid applications for fall entry is April 1.

CARLOS ALBIZU UNIVERSITY (*The complete profile is made available exclusively on our website, www.barronspac.com*)

CLEARWATER CHRISTIAN COLLEGE   D-4
www.clearwater.edu

Clearwater, FL 33759	(727) 726-1153, ext. 220
	(800) 348-4463
Fax: (727) 726-8597	Email: admissions@clearwater.edu
Full-time: 290 men, 280 women	Faculty: 32
Part-time: 10 men, 10 women	Ph.D.s: 63%
Graduate: 5 men, 10 women	Student/Faculty: 17 to 1
Year: semesters, summer session	Tuition: $16,250
Room & Board: $7470	Freshman Class: n/av
SAT or ACT: required	CEEB CODE: 5142
Application Deadline: July 1	COMPETITIVE

Clearwater Christian College, founded in 1966, is a private, nondenominational institution offering 30 majors in graduate and undergraduate programs. The figures in the above capsule and in this profile are approximate. There are 6 undergraduate schools and one graduate school. The 138-acre campus is in a rural area 10 miles west of Tampa. Including any residence halls, there are 8 buildings.

STUDENT LIFE: 55% of undergraduates are from out of state, mostly the South. Students are from 37 states, 9 foreign countries, and Canada. 25% are from public schools. 89% are White. 100% are Protestant. **Male To Female Ratio:** 1.0:1. The average age of freshmen is 19; all undergraduates, 20. 30% do not continue beyond their first year; 44% remain to graduate. **Housing:** 600 students can be accommodated in college housing, which includes single-sex dorms. On-campus housing is guaranteed for all 4 years. 79% of students live on campus; of those, 67% remain on campus on weekends. Alcohol is not permitted. All students may keep cars.

FACULTY/CLASSROOMS: 69% of faculty are male; 31% are female. All teach undergraduates. No introductory courses are taught by graduate students. The average class size in an introductory lecture is 42; in a laboratory is 10; and in a regular course is 12.

PROGRAMS OF STUDY: CCC confers B.A., and B.S. degrees. Associate and Master's degrees are also awarded. Bachelor's degrees are awarded in BIOLOGICAL SCIENCE (biology/biological science), BUSINESS (accounting and business administration and management), COMMUNICATIONS AND THE ARTS (communications, English, and music), COMPUTER AND PHYSICAL SCIENCE (mathematics), EDUCATION (elementary education, music education, physical education, secondary education, social studies education, and special education), HEALTH PROFESSIONS (premedicine), SOCIAL SCIENCE (biblical studies, history, humanities, ministries, pastoral studies, prelaw, psychology, religious education, and religious music). Biology and premed is the strongest academically. Education and business has the largest enrollments.

ACTIVITIES: 100% of men and 100% of women belong to 6 local fraternities; 100% of women belong to 6 local sororities. There are 20 groups on campus, including band, cheerleading, choir, chorale, chorus, drama, film, honors, newspaper, orchestra, pep band, political, professional, religious, social, social service, student government, symphony, and yearbook. Popular campus events include Junior Senior Banquet, Film Festival, and Midnight Madness. **Sports:** There are 4 intercollegiate sports for men and 4 for women, and 4 intramural sports for men and 3 for women. Facilities include a 12,000-square-foot gym, a lighted outdoor soccer field, and outdoor basketball and tennis courts. **Graduates:** From July 1, 2013 to June 30, 2014, 123 bachelor's degrees were awarded. The most popular majors were general studies (15%), education (14%), and psychology (11%). 60 companies recruited on campus in 2013-2014. In an average class, 3% graduate in 3 years or less, 37% graduate in 4 years or less, 42% graduate in 5 years or less, and 42% graduate in 6 years or less. Of the 2013 graduating class, 25% were enrolled in graduate school within 6 months of graduation, and 82% were employed.

SERVICES: There is a reader service for the blind, and remedial math, reading, and writing. **Library/Resources:** The library contains 113,000 volumes, 100,000 microform items, 7,570 audio/video tapes/CDs/DVDs, and subscribes to 12,000 periodicals including electronic. Computerized library services include interlibrary loans, database searching, Internet access, and Wi-Fi capability. **Physically Challenged Students:** Facilities include wheelchair ramps, elevators, special parking, and specially equipped restrooms. **Special:** Students may cross-register for ROTC with the University of Florida. The college also offers internships, study abroad in 14 countries, and student-designed majors in interdisciplinary studies. There are 1 national honor society. **Visiting:** There are regularly scheduled orientations for prospective students, consisting of campus tours, classroom visits, sessions on admissions and financial aid, lunch, and meeting administrators, faculty, and coaches. There are guides for informal visits, visitors may sit in on classes, and stay overnight. To schedule a visit, contact the Admissions Office. **Campus Safety and Security:** Measures include 24-hour foot and vehicle patrol and emergency notification system. There are lighted pathways/sidewalks.

REQUIREMENTS: The SAT or ACT is required. In addition, with a minimum score of 870 on the SAT or 18 composite on the ACT. Applicants must be high school graduates or have a GED certificate. An essay is required, and an interview is recommended. A GPA of 2.0 is required. AP and CLEP credits are accepted. Important factors in the admissions decision are personality/intangible qualities, recommendations by school officials, leadership record, parents or siblings attended your school, extracurricular activities record, ability to finance college education, advanced placement or honors courses, evidence of special talent, recommendations by alumni, and geographical diversity.Students must complete courses in computer science, English, humanities, math, science, social science, and theology/Bible. A total of 128 credit hours is required, including more than 60 in the major, with a minimum GPA of 2.0. Students may have no grade lower than a C- in any major course. **Procedure:** Freshmen are admitted fall, spring, and summer. Entrance exams should be taken during the junior or senior year. There are deferred admissions and

rolling admissions plans. Applications should be filed by July 1 for fall entry; December 1 for spring entry, along with a $35 fee. Applications are accepted on-line. **Transfer Students:** 65 transfer students enrolled in 2013-2014. Transfer applicants must submit transcripts from all postsecondary schools attended. Grades of C or better transfer. Applicants must have a minimum cumulative postsecondary GPA of 2.0. 30 of 128 credits required for the bachelor's degree must be completed at CCC. **International Students:** There are 17 international students enrolled. They must take the TOEFL, Applicants must also submit a Foreign Student Data Form. They must also take the SAT or ACT, scoring 18.

ADMISSIONS: 8 freshmen graduated first in their class. **Admissions Contact:** Director of Admissions. E-Mail: *admissions@clearwater.edu* Web: *www.clearwater.edu*

FINANCIAL AID: In 2014-2015, 99% of all full-time freshmen and 95% of continuing full-time students received some form of financial aid. The average freshman award was $13,609. 45% of undergraduate students work part-time. Average annual earnings from campus work are $1600. The average financial indebtedness of the 2014 graduate was $13,051. The CSS/Profile, FAFSA, and FFS, and The FFS is preferred. are required. Check with the school for current application deadlines.

ECKERD COLLEGE   D-4
www.eckerd.edu

St. Petersburg, FL 33711   (727) 864-8331
   (800) 456-9009
Fax: (727) 866-2304   Email: admissions@eckerd.edu
Full-time: 755 men, 1094 women   **Faculty:** 117; IIB, av$
Part-time: 17 men, 27 women   **Ph.D.s:** 93%
Graduate: n/av   **Student/Faculty:** 13 to 1
Year: 4-1-4, summer session   **Tuition:** $34,546
Room & Board: $9652   **Freshman Class:** 3910 applied, 2776 accepted, 532 enrolled
SAT CR/M: 565/550 **ACT:** 25   **CEEB CODE:** 5223
Application Deadline: April 1   **COMPETITIVE**

Eckerd College, founded in 1958, is a private liberal arts institution affiliated with the Presbyterian Church. Interdisciplinary programs are an important part of the school's curriculum, thus faculty are organized into collegia, rather than into traditional departments. Figures in the above capsule and in this profile are approximate. The 188-acre campus is in a suburban area 1 1/4 miles of Waterfront, 5 miles south of St. Petersburg. Including any residence halls, there are 87 buildings.

STUDENT LIFE: 76% of undergraduates are from out of state, mostly the Middle Atlantic. Students are from 45 states, 35 foreign countries, and Canada. 79% are White. 61% claim no religious affiliation; 13% Catholic. **Male To Female Ratio:** 1.5:1. The average age of freshmen is 18; all undergraduates, 20. 19% do not continue beyond their first year; 60% remain to graduate. **Housing:** 1501 students can be accommodated in college housing, which includes single-sex and coed dorms and on-campus apartments. In addition, there are language houses, Community service, pet dorms and substance-free houses. On-campus housing is guaranteed for the freshman year only, is available on a first-come, first-served basis, and is available on a lottery system for upperclassmen. 81% of students live on campus; of those, 92% remain on campus on weekends. All students may keep cars.

FACULTY/CLASSROOMS: 58% of faculty are male; 42% are female. All teach and do research. No introductory courses are taught by graduate students. The average class size in an introductory lecture is 20; in a laboratory is 15; and in a regular course is 20.

PROGRAMS OF STUDY: Eckerd confers B.A., and B.S. degrees. Bachelor's degrees are awarded in AGRICULTURE (environmental studies), BIOLOGICAL SCIENCE (biochemistry, biology/biological science, and marine science), BUSINESS (business administration and management, international business management, and management science), COMMUNICATIONS AND THE ARTS (communications, comparative literature, creative writing, dramatic arts, French, literature, music, Spanish, and visual and performing arts), COMPUTER AND PHYSICAL SCIENCE (chemistry, computer science, geoscience, mathematics, and physics), HEALTH PROFESSIONS (predentistry and premedicine), SOCIAL SCIENCE (American studies, anthropology, classical/ancient civilization, East Asian studies, economics, history, human development, humanities, international relations, philosophy, political science/government, prelaw, psychology, religion, sociology, and women's studies). Marine science, environmental studies, psychology have the largest enrollments.

ACTIVITIES: There are 90 groups on campus, including art, cheerleading, chess, choir, chorale, chorus, communications, computers, dance, drama, environmental, ethnic, film, gay, honors, international, literary magazine, musical theater, newspaper, photography, political, professional, radio and TV, religious, social, social service, student government, water search and rescue, and yearbook. Popular campus events include Festival of Hope, EC Surreal-fest in partnership with the Dali Museum, Festival of Cultures and Earth Fest. **Sports:** There are 5 intercollegiate sports for men and 6 for women, and 13 intramural sports for men and 13 for women. Facilities include a gym, baseball and softball complex, soccer fields, tennis courts, an open-air multi-purpose sports pavilion, a weight room, fitness room, swimming pool, and waterfront facilities. **Graduates:** From July 1, 2013 to June 30, 2014, 439 bachelor's degrees were awarded. The most popular majors were marine science (10%), environmental studies (10%), and biology (8%). 120 companies recruited on campus in 2013-2014. In an average class, 60% graduate in 6 years or less. Of the 2013 graduating class, 35% were enrolled in graduate school within 6 months of graduation, and 60% were employed.

SERVICES: Counseling and information services are available, as is tutoring in some subjects, math, sciences and foreign languages. **Library/Resources:** The library contains 181,031 volumes, 14,338 microform items, 3,415 audio/video tapes/CDs/DVDs, and subscribes to 6,775 periodicals including electronic. Computerized library services include interlibrary loans, database searching, and Internet access. Special learning facilities include an art gallery and radio station. **Physically Challenged Students:** 95% of the campus is accessible. Facilities include wheelchair ramps, elevators, special parking, specially equipped restrooms, special class scheduling, lowered drinking fountains, and lowered telephones. **Special:** Eckerd offers internships, study abroad, work-study programs, and dual majors in all subjects, interdisciplinary majors in international relations and environmental studies, student-designed majors, nondegree study, and pass/fail options. Students may earn B.A.-B.S. degrees in biology, chemistry, and marine science. A 3-2 engineering degree is offered with Washington and Columbia Universities. There are 8 national honor societies, including Phi Beta Kappa, and a freshman honors program. **Visiting:** There are regularly scheduled orientations for prospective students, consisting of an interview and a tour. There are guides for informal visits, visitors may sit in on classes, and stay overnight. To schedule a visit, contact the Admissions Office at admissions@eckerd.edu. **Campus Safety and Security:** Measures include 24-hour foot and vehicle patrol, emergency notification system, and security escort services. There are emergency telephones and lighted pathways/sidewalks.

REQUIREMENTS: The SAT or ACT is required. Graduation from an accredited secondary school or satisfactory scores on the GED is required. High school courses must include 4 years of English, 3 each of math and science, 2 each of a foreign language and social studies, and 1 of history. SAT: Subject tests in writing, literature, and math are recommended. An essay is required and an interview is recommended. A GPA of 2.0 is required. AP and CLEP credits are accepted. Important factors in the admissions decision are advanced placement or honors courses, leadership record, and personality/intangible qualities. To graduate, students must complete a total of 36 courses or 126 semester hours with a minimum GPA of 2.0. Required courses include 1 each in the arts, humanities, natural and social sciences, and environmental and global perspectives. Students must also demonstrate competencies in writing, speaking, foreign language, computation, and technology and must take a comprehensive exam or submit a thesis or project in the senior year. **Procedure:** Freshmen are admitted fall, winter, and spring. Entrance exams should be taken in Octo-

ber, November or December. There are early admissions, deferred admissions, and rolling admissions plans. Applications should be filed by April 1 for fall entry; December 1 for winter entry; and December 1 for spring entry, along with a $40 fee. 111 applicants were on the 2014 waiting list; 34 were admitted. Applications are accepted on-line. **Transfer Students:** 66 transfer students enrolled in 2013-2014. Applicants must have a minimum GPA of 2.5. The SAT or ACT is required. An interview is recommended. A faculty recommendation is required. 63 of 126 credits required for the bachelor's degree must be completed at Eckerd. **International Students:** There are 83 international students enrolled. The school actively recruits these students. They must take the TOEFL with a minimum score of 550 on the paper-based TOEFL (PBT) or 79 on the Internet-based version (iBT). They must also take the SAT or ACT.

ADMISSIONS: 71% of the 2014-2015 applicants were accepted. The SAT scores for the 2014-2015 freshman class were: Critical Reading--20% below 500, 45% between 500 and 599, 27% between 600 and 699, and 8% between 700 and 800; Math--25% below 500, 41% between 500 and 599, 30% between 600 and 699, and 4% between 700 and 800. The ACT scores were 14% below 21, 24% between 21 and 23, 29% between 24 and 26, 16% between 27 and 28, and 18% above 28. **Admissions Contact:** John Sullivan, Dean of Admissions and Financial Aid. E-Mail: *admissions@eckerd.edu* Web: *www.eckerd.edu*

FINANCIAL AID: The FAFSA is required. The priority date for freshman financial aid applications for fall entry is March 1.

EDWARD WATERS COLLEGE (*The complete profile is made available exclusively on our website, www.barronspac.com*)

EMBRY-RIDDLE AERONAUTICAL UNIVERSITY - DAYTONA BEACH   D-2
www.erau.edu

Daytona Beach, FL 32114	386-226-6100
	(800) 862-2416
	Email: dbadmit@db.erau.edu
Full-time: 3619 men, 740 women	**Faculty:** 328; IIA, +$
Part-time: 266 men, 54 women	**Ph.D.s:** 65%
Graduate: 438 men, 162 women	**Student/Faculty:** 13 to 1
Year: semesters, summer session	**Tuition:** $31,334
Room & Board: $9550	**Freshman Class:** 4074 applied, 3017 accepted, 944 enrolled
SAT CR/M/W: 530/580/510 **ACT:** 24	**CEEB CODE:** 5190
Application Deadline: July 1	**COMPETITIVE+**

Embry-Riddle Aeronautical University, founded in 1926, is a private institution offering undergraduate programs in aviation, engineering, and business on 2 campuses: one in Daytona Beach and the other, founded in 1978, in Prescott, Arizona. Figures in the above capsule and in this profile are approximate. There are 4 undergraduate schools and 1 graduate school. In addition to regional accreditation, ERAU has baccalaureate program accreditation with ABET and ACBSP. The 185-acre campus is in an urban area 48 miles northeast of Orlando. Including any residence halls, there are 45 buildings.

STUDENT LIFE: 65% of undergraduates are from out of state, mostly the South. Students are from 50 states, 97 foreign countries, and Canada. 53% are White; 16% Foreign. **Male To Female Ratio:** 0.2:1. The average age of freshmen is 18; all undergraduates, 21. **Housing:** 1994 students can be accommodated in college housing, which includes coed dorms, on-campus apartments, and off-campus apartments. On-campus housing is guaranteed for the freshman year only, is available on a first-come, first-served basis, and is available on a lottery system for upperclassmen. 64% of students commute. All students may keep cars.

FACULTY/CLASSROOMS: 73% of faculty are male; 27% are female. All teach undergraduates. No introductory courses are taught by graduate students. The average class size in an introductory lecture is 28; in a laboratory is 15; and in a regular course is 23.

PROGRAMS OF STUDY: ERAU confers B.S. degrees. Associate,

Master's, and Doctoral degrees are also awarded. Bachelor's degrees are awarded in BUSINESS (business administration and management and transportation management), COMMUNICATIONS AND THE ARTS (communications), COMPUTER AND PHYSICAL SCIENCE (atmospheric sciences and meteorology, computer science, mathematics, physical sciences, and software engineering), ENGINEERING AND ENVIRONMENTAL DESIGN (aeronautical engineering, aeronautical science, aerospace studies, air traffic control, airline piloting and navigation, aviation maintenance management, civil engineering, computer engineering, electrical/electronics engineering, engineering, engineering physics, engineering technology, and mechanical engineering), SOCIAL SCIENCE (psychology, safety and security technology, and safety science). Aerospace engine have the largest enrollments.

ACTIVITIES: There are 140 groups on campus, including cheerleading, chess, chorale, computers, dance, debate, drama, drill team, environmental, ethnic, film, gay, honors, international, literary magazine, musical theater, newspaper, pep band, photography, political, professional, radio and TV, religious, social, social service, and student government. Popular campus events include Homecoming, Touch-n-Go events that includes Bands, Comedians, Magicians, Movies every Thursday night, Student Activities Fair and Annual Arts and Letters Shakespeare Production. **Sports:** There are 7 intercollegiate sports for men and 8 for women. Facilities include 50,000+ square-foot facility; men's basketball and women's volleyball teams and is the centerpiece for campus recreation, state-of-the-art fitness center, swimming pool with shower and locker room facilities, tennis and basketball courts, tennis complex, racquetball courts, intercollegiate soccer stadium and softball fields, baseball stadium and NCAA-approved track and field complex. **Graduates:** From July 1, 2013 to June 30, 2014, 818 bachelor's degrees were awarded. The most popular majors were aerospace engineering and aeronautics. 120 companies recruited on campus in 2013-2014.

SERVICES: Counseling and information services are available, as is tutoring in some subjects, first year math, physics, chemistry and writing (composition) There is remedial math, reading, and writing. Lower level engineering courses **Library/Resources:** The library contains 102,374 volumes, 308,127 microform items, 5,331 audio/video tapes/CDs/DVDs, and subscribes to 1,039 periodicals including electronic. Computerized library services include interlibrary loans, database searching, Internet access, and Wi-Fi capability. Special learning facilities include a radio station, State-of-the-Art Advanced Flight Simulation Center; Chandler Titus Engine Repair Station (AMS Engine Test); Clean Energy Systems Lab; Electrical Engineering Laboratory; Airport Technology and Operations Lab; Applied Aviation Simulation Lab; Business Process Lab; Radio-Frequency Identification Lab; Transportation and Logistics Lab. **Physically Challenged Students:** 95% of the campus is accessible. Facilities include wheelchair ramps, elevators, special parking, specially equipped restrooms, lowered drinking fountains, lowered telephones. **Special:** ERAU offers co-op programs and internships in all majors, study abroad in 21 countries, work-study programs, accelerated degree programs in aerospace engineering and engineering physics, credit for life experience, and non-degree study. There are 9 national honor societies and a freshman honors program. **Visiting:** There are regularly scheduled orientations for prospective students. There are guides for informal visits and visitors may sit in on classes. To schedule a visit, contact the Admissions Office. **Campus Safety and Security:** Measures include 24-hour foot and vehicle patrol, emergency notification system, self-defense education, and security escort services. There are emergency telephones, lighted pathways/sidewalks, controlled access to dorms/residences, and in-room safes.

REQUIREMENTS: The SAT or ACT is recommended. In addition, Students should complete a competitive academic program in high school, including 16 Carnegie units with at least 3 years of math. Admissions decisions are based on the strength of the academic record, rank in class, standardized test scores, recommendations, and the written statement. A GPA of 2.0 is required. AP and CLEP credits are accepted. Important factors in the admissions decision are advanced placement or honors courses, recommendations by school officials, and evidence of special talent. To graduate, students must complete a total of 120 to 136 credit hours, including 60 in the major, with a minimum GPA of 2.0. All students must complete 36 credits

of general education requirements, including courses in communication skills, technical report writing, humanities/social sciences, math, physical science, economics, and computer science. **Procedure:** Freshmen are admitted fall, spring, and summer. Entrance exams should be taken During spring of the junior year or fall of the senior year. There are deferred admissions and rolling admissions plans. Early decision applications should be filed by December 1; regular applications, by July 1 for fall entry; November 1 for spring entry; and April 1 for summer entry, along with a $50 fee. Notification is sent on a rolling basis. Applications are accepted on-line. **Transfer Students:** 1003 transfer students enrolled in 2013-2014. A GPA of 2.5 is preferred. 30 of 120 credits required for the bachelor's degree must be completed at ERAU. **International Students:** There are 698 international students enrolled. The school actively recruits these students. They must take the TOEFL with a minimum score of 550 on the paper-based TOEFL (PBT) or 79 on the Internet-based version (iBT). They must also take the SAT or ACT.

ADMISSIONS: 74% of the 2014-2015 applicants were accepted. The SAT scores for the 2014-2015 freshman class were: Critical Reading--33% below 500, 43% between 500 and 599, 21% between 600 and 699, and 3% between 700 and 800; Math--19% below 500, 40% between 500 and 599, 31% between 600 and 699, and 10% between 700 and 800; Writing--41% below 500, 40% between 500 and 599, 17% between 600 and 699, and 13% between 700 and 800. The ACT scores were 19% below 21, 24% between 21 and 23, 24% between 24 and 26, 14% between 27 and 28, and 19% above 28. 43% of the current freshmen were in the top fifth of their class; 70% were in the top two fifths. **Admissions Contact:** Robert J. Adams, Director of Undergraduate Admissions. E-Mail: *dbadmit@db.erau.edu* Web: *www.erau .edu*

FINANCIAL AID: In 2014-2015, 79% of all full-time freshmen and 81% of continuing full-time students received some form of financial aid. 80% of all full-time freshmen and 81% of continuing full-time students received need-based aid. The average freshman award was $16,066. Need-based scholarships or need-based grants averaged $11,732; need-based self-help aid (loans and jobs) averaged $4,068; and non-need-based athletic scholarships averaged $15,298. 32% of undergraduate students work part-time. Average annual earnings from campus work are $2436. The FAFSA is required. The priority date for freshman financial aid applications for fall entry is March 1.

EMBRY-RIDDLE AERONAUTICAL UNIVERSITY - WORLD-WIDE (*The complete profile is made available exclusively on our website, www.barronspac.com*)

FLAGLER COLLEGE	**D-2**
www.flagler.edu	
St. Augustine, FL 32084	**(904) 829-6481**
	(800) 304-4208
Fax: (904) 819-6466	**Email:** admissions@flagler.edu
Full-time: 1071 men, 1611 women	**Faculty:** 228; IIB, -$
Part-time: 41 men, 51 women	**Ph.D.s:** 73%
Graduate: n/av	**Student/Faculty:** 23 to 1
Year: semesters, summer session	**Tuition:** $16,180
Room & Board: $9000	**Freshman Class:** 4063 applied, 3153 accepted, 673 enrolled
SAT CR/M/W: 530/510/510 **ACT:** 23	**CEEB CODE:** 5235
Application Deadline: March 1	**COMPETITIVE**

Flagler College, founded in 1968, is an independent liberal arts college that emphasizes undergraduate education in select liberal and pre-professional studies. There is 1 undergraduate school. The 47-acre campus is in a small town 35 miles south of Jacksonville and 45 miles north of Daytona Beach. Including any residence halls, there are 34 buildings.

STUDENT LIFE: 61% of undergraduates are from Florida. Others are from 41 states, 44 foreign countries, and Canada. 75% are from public schools. 74% are White. **Male To Female Ratio:** 1.5:1. The average age of freshmen is 18; all undergraduates, 21. 32% do not continue beyond their first year; 58% remain to graduate. **Housing:** 1029 students can be accommodated in college housing, which includes single-sex dorms. On-campus housing is guaranteed for the freshman year only, is available on a first-come, and first-served basis. 63% of students commute. Alcohol is not permitted. All students may keep cars.

FACULTY/CLASSROOMS: 49% of faculty are male; 51% are female. All teach undergraduates. No introductory courses are taught by graduate students. The average class size in an introductory lecture is 20; in a laboratory is 20; and in a regular course is 19.

PROGRAMS OF STUDY: Flagler confers B.A., B.S. and B.F.A. degrees. Bachelor's degrees are awarded in BUSINESS (accounting, business administration and management, and sports management), COMMUNICATIONS AND THE ARTS (art history, communications, dramatic arts, English, fine arts, graphic design, and Spanish), EDUCATION (art education, education of the deaf and hearing impaired, education of the exceptional child, elementary education, and secondary education), ENGINEERING AND ENVIRONMENTAL DESIGN (environmental science), SOCIAL SCIENCE (economics, history, Latin American studies, liberal arts/general studies, philosophy, political science/government, psychology, public administration, religion, and sociology). Business, education, communication, and coastal environmental science are the strongest academically. Psychology, communication, and business administration have the largest enrollments.

ACTIVITIES: There are no fraternities or sororities. There are 45 groups on campus, including art, cheerleading, choir, chorus, dance, drama, environmental, ethnic, film, gay, honors, international, literary magazine, musical theater, newspaper, photography, political, professional, radio and TV, religious, social, social service, and student government. Popular campus events include De-Stress Day, Bachelor Bids, and Hogwarts House Parties. **Sports:** There are 7 intercollegiate sports for men and 8 for women, and 44 intramural sports for men and 44 for women. Facilities include a 20-acre complex for baseball and soccer, 6 tennis courts, a swimming pool, a multipurpose gym, and an outdoor volleyball court. **Graduates:** From July 1, 2013 to June 30, 2014, 677 bachelor's degrees were awarded. The most popular majors were business administration (14%), communication (14%), and art (13%). In an average class, 45% graduate in 4 years or less, 60% graduate in 5 years or less, and 57% graduate in 6 years or less.

SERVICES: There is a reader service for the blind, and remedial math, reading, and writing. **Library/Resources:** The library contains 276,120 volumes, 1,813 microform items, 5,578 audio/video tapes/CDs/DVDs, and subscribes to 182 periodicals including electronic. Computerized library services include interlibrary loans, database searching, Internet access, and Wi-Fi capability. Special learning facilities include an art gallery, radio station, the Learning Center for assistance in writing, mathematics, and study skills. **Physically Challenged Students:** 90% of the campus is accessible. Facilities include wheelchair ramps, elevators, special parking, specially equipped restrooms, special class scheduling, lowered drinking fountains, lowered telephones, and special housing. **Special:** The school offers internships, work-study, and dual majors. Students may participate in study-abroad programs in almost any country. Students majoring in deaf education can work directly with students at the Florida State School for the Deaf and Blind. There are 12 national honor societies and 7 departmental honors programs. **Visiting:** There are regularly scheduled orientations for prospective students, including visitation weekend. There are guides for informal visits and visitors may sit in on classes. To schedule a visit, contact the Office of Admissions at admissions@flagler.edu. **Campus Safety and Security:** Measures include 24-hour foot and vehicle patrol, emergency notification system, self-defense education, and security escort services. There are shuttle buses, emergency telephones, lighted pathways/sidewalks, controlled access to dorms/residences, uniformed police officer from 6 pm to 6 am.

REQUIREMENTS: The SAT or ACT is required. The ACT Optional Writing test is also required. Student must have graduated from an accredited secondary school or have a satisfactory score on the GED. Students must have a total of 19 academic credits. High school courses must include 4 credits of English, 3 credits each of math and science, and 2 credits of a foreign language. An essay is required, and

an interview is recommended. A GPA of 2.5 is required. AP and CLEP credits are accepted. Important factors in the admissions decision are advanced placement or honors courses, leadership record, and extracurricular activities record.To graduate a student must complete 120 semester hours with at least a 2.0 grade point average. Completion of one major in accordance with the requirements set forth by the academic department. Completion of 36 hours in General Education. Students are required to take a minimum of five courses designated Writing Intensive within the General Education curriculum. **Procedure:** Freshmen are admitted fall and spring. Entrance exams should be taken during the fall of the senior year at the latest. There are early decision, early admissions, and deferred admissions plans. Early decision applications should be filed by January 1; regular applications, by March 1 for fall entry; and December 15 for spring entry, along with a $50 fee. Notification of early decision is sent December 15; regular decision, March 31. 288 early decision candidates were accepted for the 2014-2015 class. 164 applicants were on the 2014 waiting list; 19 were admitted. Applications are accepted on-line. **Transfer Students:** 170 transfer students enrolled in 2013-2014. Transfer students must have a minimum of 24 semester hours with a satisfactory GPA. Transfers must also present satisfactory scores from the SAT or ACT. 45 of 120 credits required for the bachelor's degree must be completed at Flagler. **International Students:** There are 103 international students enrolled. They must take the TOEFL with a minimum score of 550 on the paper-based TOEFL (PBT) or 75 on the Internet-based version (iBT). They must also take the SAT or ACT or take the IELTS.

ADMISSIONS: 78% of the 2014-2015 applicants were accepted. The SAT scores for the 2014-2015 freshman class were: Critical Reading--29% below 500, 53% between 500 and 599, 16% between 600 and 699, and 2% between 700 and 800; Math--37% below 500, 50% between 500 and 599, 12% between 600 and 699, and 1% between 700 and 800; Writing--35% below 500, 50% between 500 and 599, 14% between 600 and 699, and 1% between 700 and 800. The ACT scores were 18% below 21, 41% between 21 and 23, 24% between 24 and 26, 14% between 27 and 28, and 3% above 28. 27% of the current freshmen were in the top fifth of their class; 57% were in the top two fifths. 2 freshmen graduated first in their class. **Admissions Contact:** Deborah Thompson, Vice President of Enrollment Management. E-Mail: *admissions@flagler.edu* Web: *www.flagler.edu*

FINANCIAL AID: In 2014-2015, 88% of all full-time freshmen and 88% of continuing full-time students received some form of financial aid. 61% of all full-time freshmen and 58% of continuing full-time students received need-based aid. The average freshman award was $15,452. Need-based scholarships or need-based grants averaged $5,638; need-based self-help aid (loans and jobs) averaged $3,406; non-need-based athletic scholarships averaged $8,391; and other non-need-based awards and non-need-based scholarships averaged $9,445. 61% of undergraduate students work part-time. Average annual earnings from campus work are $1400. The average financial indebtedness of the 2014 graduate was $25,948. The FAFSA, and Florida resident affidavit if applying for the Florida Resident Access Grant is required. The priority date for freshman financial aid applications for fall entry is April 1.

FLORIDA AGRICULTURAL AND MECHANICAL UNIVERSITY
(The complete profile is made available exclusively on our website, www.barronspac.com)

FLORIDA ATLANTIC UNIVERSITY	E-5
www.fau.edu	
Boca Raton, FL 33431	**(561) 297-3040**
	(800) 299-4FAU
Fax: (561) 297-2758	Email: Admissions@fau.edu
Full-time: 7085 men, 8508 women	Faculty: 875; I, --$
Part-time: 3843 men, 5387 women	Ph.Ds: 90%
Graduate: 1991 men, 3224 women	Student/Faculty: 20 to 1
Year: semesters, summer session	Tuition: $5986 ($21,543)
Room & Board: $11,353	Freshman Class: 27888 applied, 10876 accepted, 3237 enrolled
	CEEB CODE: 5529
Application Deadline: May 1	COMPETITIVE

Florida Atlantic University, founded in 1964, was one of the few universities in the country to offer only upper-division and graduate-level work, on the theory that freshmen and sophomores could be served by the community college system. Located in rapidly growing Southeast Florida, the University responded to the need to provide increased access to educational opportunities by opening its doors to freshmen in 1984. Today, with its well developed system of distributed campuses and sites that offer students high-quality degree programs at seven locations, FAU serves as a model for America's urban, regional universities. FAU offers a comprehensive array of undergraduate and graduate programs, enrolling more than 29,000 students who bring rich cultural diversity to campus life. Figures in the above capsule and in this profile are approximate. There are 9 undergraduate schools and 8 graduate schools. In addition to regional accreditation, FAU has baccalaureate program accreditation with AACSB, ABET, CSAB, CSWE, NAAB, NASM, NCATE, and NLN. The 850-acre campus is in a suburban area 17 miles north of Ft. Lauderdale, 45 miles north of Miami, and 22 miles south of Palm Beach. Including any residence halls, there are 160 buildings.

STUDENT LIFE: 96% of undergraduates are from Florida. Others are from 49 states, 135 foreign countries, and Canada. 73% are from public schools. 50% are White; 22% Hispanic; 18% African American. **Male To Female Ratio:** 1.3:1. The average age of freshmen is 18; all undergraduates, 24. 22% do not continue beyond their first year; 43% remain to graduate. **Housing:** 3750 students can be accommodated in college housing, which includes single-sex and coed dorms and on-campus apartments. In addition, there are honors houses, special-interest houses, living- Learning communities. On-campus housing is guaranteed for the freshman year only, is available on a first-come, and first-served basis. 85% of students commute. All students may keep cars.

FACULTY/CLASSROOMS: 54% of faculty are male; 46% are female. All teach and do research. Graduate students teach 5% of introductory courses. The average class size in an introductory lecture is 38; in a laboratory is 21; and in a regular course is 29.

PROGRAMS OF STUDY: FAU confers B.A., B.S., B.A.E., B.Arch., B.B.A., B.E.C.E. B.F.A., B.H.S., B.I.E.T., B.Mus., B.P.M., B.S.C.E., B.S.C.V., B.S.E., B.S.E.E., B.S.G.E., B.S.H.S., B.S.M.E., B.S.M.T., B.S.N., B.S.O.E., B.S.W. and B.U.R.P. degrees. Associate, Master's, and Doctoral degrees are also awarded. Bachelor's degrees are awarded in BIOLOGICAL SCIENCE (biology/biological science and marine biology), BUSINESS (accounting, banking and finance, business administration and management, business economics, hospitality management services, human resources, international business management, management information systems, marketing/retailing/merchandising, real estate, and small business management), COMMUNICATIONS AND THE ARTS (art, communications, dramatic arts, English, fine arts, French, German, graphic design, Italian, jazz, journalism, linguistics, media arts, multimedia, music, Spanish, and visual and performing arts), COMPUTER AND PHYSICAL SCIENCE (chemistry, computer science, computer security and information assurance, geology, information sciences and systems, mathematics, and physics), EDUCATION (education of the exceptional child, elementary education, English education, foreign languages education, physical education, and special education), ENGINEERING AND ENVIRONMENTAL DESIGN (architecture, civil engineering, computer engineering, electrical/electronics engineering, engineering, mechanical engineering, ocean engineering, and urban planning technology), HEALTH PROFESSIONS (health care administration, health science, medical laboratory technology, and nursing), SOCIAL SCIENCE (anthropology, criminal justice, economics, geography, history, interdisciplinary studies, Judaic studies, liberal arts/general studies, philosophy, political science/government, psychobiology, psychology, public administration, social psychology, social science, social work, and sociology). Engineering, education and business are the strongest academically. biological science, psychology and elementary education have the largest enrollments.

ACTIVITIES: 1% of men belong to 11 national fraternities; 1% of women belong to 8 national sororities. There are 250 groups on campus, including art, band, cheerleading, chess, choir, chorale, chorus, computers, dance, debate, drama, drill team, environmental, ethnic, film, forensics, gay, honors, international, jazz band, literary magazine, marching band, musical theater, newspaper, opera, orchestra, pep band, photography, political, professional, radio and TV, religious, social, social service, and student government. Popular campus events include Luau, African American Festival, Festival of Nations and Homecoming. **Sports:** There are 8 intercollegiate sports for men and 9 for women, and 10 intramural sports for men and 10 for women. Facilities include a 54,000 sq. ft. facility that houses weight rooms, training rooms, lighted baseball, softball, and soccer stadiums: arena for volleyball and basketball, cross country and track field complex; football practice field; aquatic center tennis courts, fitness center with cardio; outdoor basketball courts, practice fields, and a football stadium. **Graduates:** From July 1, 2013 to June 30, 2014, 4892 bachelor's degrees were awarded. The most popular majors were elementary education (8%), accounting (8%), and criminal justics (7%). 200 companies recruited on campus in 2013-2014. In an average class, 17% graduate in 4 years or less, 35% graduate in 5 years or less, and 43% graduate in 6 years or less.

SERVICES: Counseling and information services are available, as is tutoring in most subjects. There is a reader service for the blind. Remedial work must be taken at the community college level. **Library/Resources:** The 4 libraries contain 206,615 volumes, 2.1 million microform items, 22,414 audio/video tapes/CDs/DVDs, and subscribe to 12,549 periodicals including electronic. Computerized library services include interlibrary loans, database searching, Internet access, and Wi-Fi capability. Special learning facilities include an art gallery, planetarium, radio station, TV station, engineering research labs, a marine sciences research center, a K-12 developmental research school, a nonnative fish research lab, and an environmental sciences center, and medical school. **Physically Challenged Students:** All of the campus is accessible. Facilities include wheelchair ramps, elevators, special parking, specially equipped restrooms, lowered drinking fountains, and lowered telephones. **Special:** FAU offers cooperative programs and internships in most majors. Work-study programs, dual and student-designed majors, a general studies degree, credit for military experience, nondegree study, and pass/fail options are available. The school offers a Washington semester, study abroad through all state university system of Florida programs. There are 21 national honor societies, a freshman honors program, and 9 departmental honors programs. **Visiting:** There are regularly scheduled orientations for prospective students, consisting of a group tour. There are guides for informal visits. To schedule a visit, contact the Admissions Office. **Campus Safety and Security:** Measures include 24-hour foot and vehicle patrol, emergency notification system, self-defense education, and security escort services. There are shuttle buses, emergency telephones, lighted pathways/sidewalks, and controlled access to dorms/residences.

REQUIREMENTS: The SAT or ACT is required, with a satisfactory score on the SAT Critical Reading and Math sections or on the ACT. In addition, graduation from an accredited secondary school or satisfactory scores on the GED are required. Students must have 19 academic credits, including 4 units of English, 3 each of math (algebra I and higher), science (including 2 with substantial lab work), and social studies, and 2 of a foreign language, plus 4 of electives in computer science, fine arts, or humanities. A portfolio or an audition may be requested by individual departments. An essay and an interview are required. A GPA of 2.0 is required. AP and CLEP credits are accepted. Important factors in the admissions decision are advanced placement or honors courses, evidence of special talent, and recommendations by school officials. All students must take the College Level Academic Skills Test (CLAST) required by the state. To graduate, students must complete a total of 120 credit hours, with a minimum GPA of 2.0. All students must take the required courses in the core curriculum, including 9 credits each of humanities and social sciences, and 6 each of math, communication, and natural sciences, and must demonstrate proficiency in a foreign language. **Procedure:** Freshmen are admitted fall, spring, and summer. There are early decision, early admissions, deferred admissions, and rolling admissions plans. Applications should be filed by May 1 for fall entry; October 15 for spring entry; and March 15 for summer entry, along with a $30 fee. Applications are accepted on-line. **Transfer Students:** 3425 transfer students enrolled in 2013-2014. Students must have a minimum GPA of 2.0, submit official transcripts from the previous schools attended, and be in good standing at those institutions. Applicants from a community or junior college in Florida with an associate degree are automatically admitted. Students with fewer than 60 transferable hours must meet the same criteria as entering freshmen. 30 of 120 credits required for the bachelor's degree must be completed at FAU. **International Students:** There are 268 international students enrolled. The school actively recruits these students. They must take the TOEFL with a minimum score of 550 on the paper-based TOEFL (PBT). They must also take the SAT or ACT.

ADMISSIONS: 39% of the 2014-2015 applicants were accepted. 51% of the current freshmen were in the top fifth of their class; 80% were in the top two fifths. There were 2 National Merit finalists. **Admissions Contact:** Barbar Pletcher, Director of Admissions. E-Mail: *Admissions@fau.edu* Web: *www.fau.edu*

FINANCIAL AID: In 2014-2015, 63% of all full-time freshmen and 65% of continuing full-time students received some form of financial aid. 58% of all full-time freshmen and 49% of continuing full-time students received need-based aid. The average freshman award was $6,000. Need-based scholarships or need-based grants averaged $6,078; need-based self-help aid (loans and jobs) averaged $5,356; and non-need-based athletic scholarships averaged $9,892. FAU is a member of CSS. The FAFSA is required. The deadline for filing freshman financial aid applications for fall entry is March 1.

FLORIDA GULF COAST UNIVERSITY   D-5
www.fgcu.edu

Fort Myers, FL 33965	**(239) 590-7891**
	(888) 889-1095
Fax: (239) 590-7894	Email: oar@fgcu.edu
Full-time: 4429 men, 5709 women	Faculty: IIA, -$
Part-time: 1291 men, 1432 women	Ph.Ds: 72%
Graduate: 401 men, 836 women	Student/Faculty: 23 to 1
Year: semesters, summer session	Tuition: n/av
Room & Board: n/app	Freshman Class: 10804 applied, 7108 accepted, 2761 enrolled
SAT: required	CEEB CODE: 5221
Application Deadline: May 1	COMPETITIVE

Florida Gulf Coast University, founded in 1991, is part of the State University System of Florida. Figures in the above capsule and in this profile are approximate. There are 5 undergraduate schools. In addition to regional accreditation, FGCU has baccalaureate program accreditation with AACSB, APTA, CSWE, and NLN. The 760-acre campus is in a suburban area in southwest Florida in southern Lee County. Including any residence halls, there are 112 buildings.

STUDENT LIFE: 93% of undergraduates are from Florida. Others are from 46 states, 87 foreign countries, and Canada. 67% are White; 19% Hispanic. **Male To Female Ratio:** 1.3:1. The average age of freshmen is 18; all undergraduates, 22. **Housing:** 4200 students can be accommodated in college housing, which includes coed dorms, on-campus apartments, and off-campus apartments. On-campus housing is available on a first-come and first-served basis. 67% of students commute. Alcohol is not permitted. Some may keep cars.

FACULTY/CLASSROOMS: 55% of faculty are male; 45% are female. All teach and do research. No introductory courses are taught by graduate students. The average class size in a regular course is 25.

PROGRAMS OF STUDY: FGCU confers B.A., and B.S. degrees. Associate, Master's, and Doctoral degrees are also awarded. Bachelor's degrees are awarded in AGRICULTURE (environmental studies), BIOLOGICAL SCIENCE (biology/biological science, biotechnology, and marine science), BUSINESS (accounting, banking and finance, marketing and distribution, and recreational facilities management), COMMUNICATIONS AND THE ARTS (art, communications, English, music, and Spanish), COMPUTER AND PHYSICAL SCIENCE (applied science, chemistry, computer science, and mathematics), EDUCATION (athletic training, early childhood education, elementary education, mathematics education, music education, secondary education, social science education, and special education), ENGINEERING AND ENVIRONMENTAL DESIGN (civil engineering and environmental engineering), HEALTH PRO-

FESSIONS (clinical science, community health work, exercise science, health science, nursing, and occupational therapy), SOCIAL SCIENCE (anthropology, child psychology/development, counseling/psychology, criminal justice, criminology, economics, forensic studies, history, law, liberal arts/general studies, philosophy, political science/government, psychology, social work, and sociology). Management, communication, and psychology have the largest enrollments.

ACTIVITIES: 1% of men and 3 of women belong to 7 national fraternities; 7% of women belong to 5 national sororities. There are 125 groups on campus, including art, cheerleading, chess, computers, dance, debate, drama, environmental, ethnic, film, gay, honors, international, literary magazine, musical theater, newspaper, political, professional, religious, social, social service, and student government. Popular campus events include Eagle Expo, and President's Lecture Series. **Sports:** There are 6 intercollegiate sports for men and 8 for women, and 9 intramural sports for men and 9 for women. Facilities include a fitness center, a lakefront, a 4500-seat teaching gym, 2 playing fields, 12 tennis courts, softball complex seating 2500, baseball field, Swanson Stadium seating 2500, and Aquatics Center with a 50-meter Olympic sized pool and 25 yard recreational pool. **Graduates:** From July 1, 2013 to June 30, 2014, 1873 bachelor's degrees were awarded. The most popular majors were communication/journalism (10%), management (8%), and psychology (6%). In an average class, 47% graduate in 6 years or less.

SERVICES: Counseling and information services are available, as is tutoring in most subjects. **Library/Resources:** The library contains 276,638 volumes, 843,772 microform items, 319,258 audio/video tapes/CDs/DVDs, and subscribes to 409,967 periodicals including electronic. Computerized library services include interlibrary loans, database searching, Internet access, and Wi-Fi capability. Special learning facilities include an art gallery, TV station, chickee huts, computer labs, and a family resource center. **Physically Challenged Students:** All of the campus is accessible. Facilities include wheelchair ramps, elevators, special parking, specially equipped restrooms, special class scheduling, lowered drinking fountains, lowered telephones, and special housing. **Special:** The university offers cross-registration with the University of Central Florida, study abroad in China, a Washington semester, accelerated degree in biology, and work-study programs. There is 1 national honor society, including Phi Beta Kappa, a freshman honors program, and 1 departmental honors program. **Visiting:** There are regularly scheduled orientations for prospective students. There are guides for informal visits and visitors may sit in on classes. To schedule a visit, contact the Admissions Office. **Campus Safety and Security:** Measures include 24-hour foot and vehicle patrol, self-defense education, and security escort services. There are shuttle buses, emergency telephones, and lighted pathways/sidewalks.

REQUIREMENTS: The SAT is required. The ACT Optional Writing test is also required. A GPA of 2.0 is required. AP and CLEP credits are accepted. To graduate, students must have a 2.0 minimum GPA and 120 credit hours that include courses in phys ed, computer science, general education, service learning, and university colloquium. **Procedure:** Freshmen are admitted fall, spring, and summer. Entrance exams should be taken in the junior year. There is a deferred admissions plan. Applications should be filed by May 1 for fall entry; November 9 for spring entry; and February 1 for summer entry, along with a $30 fee. Applications are accepted on-line. **Transfer Students:** 1058 transfer students enrolled in 2013-2014. Lower level transfers must meet the same requirements as regular admissions. Upper level transfers must have a 2.0 GPA and 60 hours of transferable credit, and be in good standing at their last institution. 30 of 120 credits required for the bachelor's degree must be completed at FGCU. **International Students:** There are 206 international students enrolled. The school actively recruits these students. They must take the TOEFL with a minimum score of 550 on the paper-based TOEFL (PBT) or 79 on the Internet-based version (iBT). They must also take the SAT or ACT, scoring 440.

ADMISSIONS: 66% of the 2014-2015 applicants were accepted. The SAT scores for the 2014-2015 freshman class were: Critical Reading--43% below 500, 46% between 500 and 599, 10% between 600 and 699, and 1% between 700 and 800; Math--41% below 500, 46% between 500 and 599, 12% between 600 and 699, and 1% between

700 and 800; Writing--52% below 500, 40% between 500 and 599, 7% between 600 and 699, and 1% between 700 and 800. The ACT scores were 5% below 21, 70% between 21 and 23, 23% between 27 and 28, and 2% above 28. 27% of the current freshmen were in the top fifth of their class; 61% were in the top two fifths. 4 freshmen graduated first in their class. **Admissions Contact:** Marc Maviolette, Director of Admissions. E-Mail: *oar@fgcu.edu* Web: *www.fgcu.edu*

FINANCIAL AID: In 2014-2015, 57% of all full-time freshmen students received some form of financial aid. 36% of all full-time freshmen students received need-based aid. The average freshman award was $9,135. Need-based scholarships or need-based grants averaged $5,080; need-based self-help aid (loans and jobs) averaged $6,887; and non-need-based athletic scholarships averaged $6,774. The average financial indebtedness of the 2014 graduate was $23,863. FGCU is a member of CSS. The FAFSA is required. The deadline for filing freshman financial aid applications for fall entry is March 1.

FLORIDA INSTITUTE OF TECHNOLOGY   E-4
www.fit.edu

Melbourne, FL 32901	(321) 674-8030
	(800) 888-4348
Fax: (321) 674-8004	Email: perrymj@fit.edu
Full-time: 2028 men, 766 women	Faculty: 231; I, --$
Part-time: 128 men, 56 women	Ph.D.s: 91%
Graduate: 1398 men, 1008 women	Student/Faculty: 11 to 1
Year: semesters, summer session	Tuition: $36,020
Room & Board: $12,270	Freshman Class: 7428 applied, 4386 accepted, 756 enrolled
SAT CR/M: 550/590 ACT: 25	CEEB CODE: 5080
Application Deadline:	VERY COMPETITIVE

Florida Institute of Technology, founded in 1958, offers undergraduate degrees in engineering, science, business, psychology, liberal arts, and aeronautics. Figures in the above capsule and in this profile are approximate. There are 5 undergraduate schools and 6 graduate schools. In addition to regional accreditation, Florida Tech has baccalaureate program accreditation with ABET and CSAB. The 130-acre campus is in a suburban area 70 miles east of Orlando. Including any residence halls, there are 86 buildings.

STUDENT LIFE: 33% of undergraduates are from out of state, mostly the Middle Atlantic. Students are from 47 states, 97 foreign countries, and Canada. 49% are from public schools. 45% are White; 24% Foreign. **Male To Female Ratio:** 0.5:1. The average age of freshmen is 18; all undergraduates, 21. 21% do not continue beyond their first year; 55% remain to graduate. **Housing:** 1676 students can be accommodated in college housing, which includes single-sex and coed dorms and on-campus apartments. On-campus housing is guaranteed for the freshman year only, is available on a first-come, and first-served basis. 53% of students commute. All students may keep cars.

FACULTY/CLASSROOMS: 75% of faculty are male; 25% are female. 7% teach undergraduates, 5% do research, and 88% do both. Graduate students teach 4% of introductory courses. The average class size in an introductory lecture is 22; in a laboratory is 20; and in a regular course is 21.

PROGRAMS OF STUDY: Florida Tech confers B.A., and B.S. degrees. Master's and doctoral degrees are also awarded. Bachelor's degrees are awarded in AGRICULTURE (conservation and regulation and environmental studies), BIOLOGICAL SCIENCE (biochemistry, biology/biological science, biomathematics, ecology, marine biology, and molecular biology), BUSINESS (accounting, business administration and management, electronic business, international business management, management information systems, marketing management, and sports management), COMMUNICATIONS AND THE ARTS (communications), COMPUTER AND PHYSICAL SCIENCE (applied mathematics, astronomy, astrophysics, atmospheric sciences and meteorology, chemistry, computer science, information sciences and systems, mathematics, oceanography, physics, planetary and space science, and software engineering), EDUCATION (mathematics education, middle school education, and science education), ENGINEERING AND ENVIRONMENTAL DESIGN (aeronautical engineering, aeronautical science, aviation administration/management, aviation computer technology, biomedical engineering, chemical engineering, civil engineering, computer engineering, construction engineering, construction management, electrical/electronics engineering, environmental science, mechanical engineering, military science, and ocean engineering), HEALTH PROFESSIONS (premedicine), SOCIAL SCIENCE (forensic studies, humanities, interdisciplinary studies, prelaw, and psychology). Engineering, science, and aeronautics are the strongest academically. Aerospace engineering, mechanical engineering, and electrical engineering have the largest enrollments.

ACTIVITIES: 14% of men belong to 8 national fraternities; 11% of women belong to 3 national sororities. There are 147 groups on campus, including cheerleading, chess, chorus, computers, dance, drama, drill team, ethnic, film, gay, honors, international, jazz band, literary magazine, newspaper, pep band, photography, political, professional, radio and TV, religious, social, social service, and student government. Popular campus events include International Festival, Homecoming, Campus Cleanup, Relay for Life, Engineering Week, and Greek Week. **Sports:** There are 10 intercollegiate sports for men and 10 for women, and 9 intramural sports for men and 9 for women. Facilities include The Charles and Ruth Clemente Center for Sports and Recreation is equipped with 2 basketball courts, a racquetball court, group fitness rooms, volleyball and badminton courts, and a 5000-square-foot weight and fitness area with cardiovascular machines, free weights, and specialized weight equipment. The Panther Aquatic Center is a 32,000-sq.-ft. facility that features a competition pool and a recreation pool. The competition pool includes nine 25-yard lanes complete with one- and three-meter diving boards. The depth ranges from 5.5 to 13 feet. The recreation pool varies in depth from three to six feet and includes three 25-yard lanes, stair entry and wading benches. Both pools are equipped with geothermal heating and cooling systems. **Graduates:** From July 1, 2013 to June 30, 2014, 521 Bachelor's degrees were awarded. The most popular majors were aerospace engineering (12%), electrical engineering (8%), and mechanical engineering (8%). 154 companies recruited on campus in 2013-2014. In an average class, 2% graduate in 3 years or less, 37% graduate in 4 years or less, 52% graduate in 5 years or less, and 55% graduate in 6 years or less. Of the 2013 graduating class, 42% were enrolled in graduate school within 6 months of graduation, and 49% were employed.

SERVICES: Counseling and information services are available, as is tutoring in every subject. There is a reader service for the blind, and remedial math, reading, and writing. **Library/Resources:** The library contains 527,223 volumes, 310,337 microform items, 10,319 audio/video tapes/CDs/DVDs, and subscribes to 68,007 periodicals including electronic. Computerized library services include interlibrary loans, database searching, Internet access, and Wi-Fi capability. Special learning facilities include an art gallery, radio station, TV station, the 3,000 square foot Ruth Funk Center for Textile Arts is the only textiles gallery in the state of Florida. **Physically Challenged Students:** 90% of the campus is accessible. Facilities include wheelchair ramps, elevators, special parking, specially equipped restrooms, special class scheduling, lowered drinking fountains, and lowered telephones. **Special:** The ProTrack cooperative education program allows students in the College of Engineering to complete three semester-long (amounting to one year) paid work experiences within the four years it takes to earn a bachelor's degree. Students graduate with their employers' names on their final transcripts. The FastTrack accelerated master's degree program allows students to take graduate coursework as undergraduates, so students can complete a master's degree in as little as one additional year of study. Earned scholarships carry over to the fifth year. Florida Tech offers co-op programs in all majors. Students may choose to pursue more than 1 degree by completing degree requirements for each major. Internships are available in the senior year for many majors, including psychology, engineering, and aeronautics. Study abroad and work-study programs are available. There are 8 national honor societies and 1 departmental honors programs. **Visiting:** There are regularly scheduled orientations for prospective students, including tours and interviews with admissions staff, faculty, or department heads upon request. There are guides for informal visits and visitors may sit in on classes. To schedule a visit, contact The Office of Undergraduate Admissions at admission@fit.edu. **Campus Safety and Security:** Measures include 24-hour foot and vehicle patrol, emergency notification system, self-defense education, and security escort services. There are shuttle buses, emergency telephones, lighted pathways/sidewalks, and controlled access to dorms/residences.

REQUIREMENTS: The SAT or ACT is required. Applicants must be graduates of an accredited secondary school or have a GED certificate. At least 18 academic credits or Carnegie units are required, including 4 years each of English, math, and science. An experiential essay is required and an interview is recommended. A GPA of 2.8 is required. AP and CLEP credits are accepted. Important factors in the admissions decision are advanced placement or honors courses, recommendations by school officials, and extracurricular activities record.To graduate, students must have a minimum 2.0 GPA and 120 to 135 credit hours. The required number of hours in the major varies. All students must take 9 hours in communication and humanities and 3 in English composition. The core curriculum also requires 6 credit hours each in physical or life sciences and math and 3 hours in computer science and social sciences. **Procedure:** Freshmen are admitted fall and spring. Entrance exams should be taken during the junior year or the beginning of the senior year of high school. There are deferred admissions and rolling admissions plans. Application deadlines are open. Applications are accepted on-line. **Transfer Students:** 207 transfer students enrolled in 2013-2014. Applicants must have a minimum 2.5 GPA. If transfer students have fewer than 30 semester hours, high school transcripts and SAT or ACT scores are required. A personal statement is recommended. 25 of 120 credits required for the bachelor's degree must be completed at Florida Tech. **International Students:** There are 791 international students enrolled. The school actively recruits these students. They must take the TOEFL with a minimum score of 550 on the paper-based TOEFL (PBT) or 79 on the Internet-based version (iBT), and a math entrance qualifying exam. If students score below the minimum, they take language courses on campus.

ADMISSIONS: 59% of the 2014-2015 applicants were accepted. The SAT scores for the 2014-2015 freshman class were: Critical Reading--24% below 500, 44% between 500 and 599, 25% between 600 and 699, and 7% between 700 and 800; Math--12% below 500, 40% between 500 and 599, 36% between 600 and 699, and 12% between 700 and 800. The ACT scores were 12% below 21, 23% between 21 and 23, 25% between 24 and 26, 17% between 27 and 28, and 23% above 28. 52% of the current freshmen were in the top fifth of their class; 74% were in the top two fifths. 17 freshmen graduated first in their class. **Admissions Contact:** Michael J. Perry, Director, Undergraduate Admissions. E-Mail: *perrymj@fit.edu* Web: *www.fit.edu*

FINANCIAL AID: In 2014-2015, 63% of all full-time freshmen and 58% of continuing full-time students received some form of financial aid. 63% of all full-time freshmen and 58% of continuing full-time students received need-based aid. The average freshman award was $32,855. Need-based scholarships or need-based grants averaged $21,560 ($48,297 maximum); need-based self-help aid (loans and jobs) averaged $4,419 ($11,000 maximum); non-need-based athletic scholarships averaged $16,636 ($48,650 maximum); and other non-need-based awards and non-need-based scholarships averaged $13,696 ($49,927 maximum). 21% of undergraduate students work part-time. Average annual earnings from campus work are $8300. The average financial indebtedness of the 2014 graduate was $22,161. The FAFSA is required. The priority date for freshman financial aid applications for fall entry is March 1.

Florida International University (FIU) is a multi-campus public research university offering a broad array of undergraduate, graduate, and professional programs. FIU offers more than 180 baccalaureate, masters, professional and research doctorate programs and conducts basic and applied research. Interdisciplinary centers and institutes conduct collaborative research to seek innovative solutions to economic, technological, and social problems. FIU is dynamic. We have a can-do spirit that you will feel on our campuses. This vibrancy is reflected in the campus through modern architecture and the energy of our students. Figures in the above capsule and in this profile are approximate. There are 10 undergraduate schools. In addition to regional accreditation, FIU has baccalaureate program accreditation with AACSB, ABET, ACCE, ACEJMC, APTA, ASLA, CSWE, NAAB, NASAD, NASM, NCATE, NLN, and NRPA. The 582-acre campus is in an urban area 2 main campuses, Modesto A. Maidique campus in western Miami-Dade County, and the Biscayne Bay Campus in northeast Miami-Dade County. Including any residence halls, there are 129 buildings.

STUDENT LIFE: 93% of undergraduates are from Florida. Others are from 50 states, 146 foreign countries, and Canada. 62% are Hispanic; 13% White; 13% African American. **Male To Female Ratio:** 1.3:1. The average age of freshmen is 18; all undergraduates, 23. **Housing:** 3011 students can be accommodated in college housing, which includes coed dorms, on-campus apartments, and married student housing. In addition, there are fraternity houses. On-campus housing is available on a first-come and first-served basis. 93% of students commute. All students may keep cars.

FACULTY/CLASSROOMS: 54% of faculty are male; 46% are female. No introductory courses are taught by graduate students.

PROGRAMS OF STUDY: FIU confers B.A., B.S., B.Ac., B.B.A., B.F.A., B.H.S.A., B.M., B.P.A. and B.S.N. degrees. Master's and Doctoral degrees are also awarded. Bachelor's degrees are awarded in BIOLOGICAL SCIENCE (biology/biological science and marine biology), BUSINESS (accounting, banking and finance, business administration and management, hospitality management services, international business management, management information systems, marketing/retailing/merchandising, and real estate), COMMUNICATIONS AND THE ARTS (art, art history and appreciation, dramatic arts, English, fine arts, French, Italian, music, Portuguese, and Spanish), COMPUTER AND PHYSICAL SCIENCE (chemistry, computer science, geology, mathematics, physics, and statistics), EDUCATION (art education, early childhood education, education, elementary education, physical education, science education, special education, and specific learning disabilities), ENGINEERING AND ENVIRONMENTAL DESIGN (architecture, biomedical engineering, civil engineering, computer engineering, construction engineering, construction technology, electrical/electronics engineering, environmental engineering, environmental science, interior design, landscape architecture/design, and mechanical engineering), HEALTH PROFESSIONS (exercise science and health care administration), SOCIAL SCIENCE (Asian/Oriental studies, criminal justice, dietetics, economics, geography, history, international relations, liberal arts/general studies, parks and recreation management, philosophy, political science/government, psychology, public administration, religion, social work, sociology, and women's studies).

ACTIVITIES: Men belong to 6 local and 17 national fraternities; Women belong to 2 local and 10 national sororities. There are 192 groups on campus, including band, cheerleading, chorus, drama, environmental, ethnic, gay, honors, international, jazz band, marching band, newspaper, opera, political, professional, radio and TV, religious, social, social service, student government, and symphony. Popular campus events include Welcome Week, Homecoming and Dance Marathon. **Sports:** There are 5 intercollegiate sports for men and 9 for women, and 14 intramural sports for men and 15 for women. Facilities include a 20,000 seat football stadium, a 5000-seat arena with basketball and racquetball courts, an aquatic center, baseball and soccer fields, a fitness center with Nautilus machines, and a racquet sports center with lighted tennis and racquetball courts. **Graduates:** From July 1, 2013 to June 30, 2014, 7077 bachelor's degrees were awarded. The most popular majors were business administration (35%), social sciences (9%), and psychology (8%). **SERVICES:** Counseling and information services are available, as is tutoring in most subjects. There is a reader service for the blind, and

---

FLORIDA INTERNATIONAL UNIVERSITY E-5
www.fiu.edu

Miami, FL 33199 (305) 348-3675

Fax: (305) 348-3648	Email: admissions@fiu.edu
Full-time: 10521 men, 13480 women	Faculty: I, -$
	Ph.Ds: 87%
Part-time: 6192 men, 7275 women	Student/Faculty: n/av
Graduate: 3699 men, 5094 women	Tuition: $6417 ($18,816)
Year: semesters, summer session	Freshman Class: 15863
Room & Board: $11,330	applied, 6418 accepted, 2636 enrolled
SAT CR/M/W: 571/569/563 ACT: 25	CEEB CODE: 5206
Application Deadline: January 18	COMPETITIVE+

remedial math, reading, and writing. Note taking, adapted testing, and special registration may be arranged for disabled students. **Library/Resources:** The 5 libraries contain 2.2 million volumes, 4.3 million microform items, 57,466 audio/video tapes/CDs/DVDs, and subscribe to 61,891 periodicals including electronic. Computerized library services include interlibrary loans, database searching, Internet access, and Wi-Fi capability. Special learning facilities include an art gallery, radio station, including a Frost art museum, nature preserve, Biscayne Bay preserve, and an Wolfsonian art museum. **Physically Challenged Students:** All of the campus is accessible. Facilities include wheelchair ramps, elevators, special parking, specially equipped restrooms, special class scheduling, lowered drinking fountains, lowered telephones. There is also accessible computer equipment for visually impaired students, including talking and large-print computers. **Special:** FIU offers co-op and work-study programs, and study abroad in 30 countries. Accelerated degree programs, nondegree study, dual majors, and several combined Bachelor's-Master's programs. There are 40 national honor societies, including Phi Beta Kappa, and a freshman honors program. **Visiting:** There are regularly scheduled orientations for prospective students, tours are available on both the Modesto Maidique campus and Biscayne Bay campuses. There are guides for informal visits and visitors may sit in on classes. To schedule a visit, contact the Undgergraduate Admissions. **Campus Safety and Security:** Measures include 24-hour foot and vehicle patrol, emergency notification system, and security escort services. There are emergency telephones and lighted pathways/sidewalks.

REQUIREMENTS: The SAT or ACT is required. In addition to the application, the following credentials are required: Official secondary school transcripts and appropriate test scores: Scholastic Aptitude Test (SAT) or the American College Test (ACT with writing). Proof of graduation from an accredited secondary school must be submitted before enrolling. High School diplomas accepted for undergraduate degree-seeking admission to FIU must be completed at a secondary institution accredited by a regional accrediting body or at an institution accredited by a national accrediting agency recognized by the United States Department of Education. Eighteen academic units in college preparatory courses are required as follows: 4 English, 4 Mathematics, 3 Natural Science, 3 Social Science, 2 Foreign Languages, 2 Academic Electives (see notes). Freshman admission decisions are made based on the student's strong academic preparation. Competition for placement in the freshman class includes a review of all academic credentials and a completed file. Applicants are encouraged to complete the MyMajorMatch assessment to match their interest with FIU majors, find an appropriate major, and explore possible careers. Students who apply to majors in Theatre and Music must meet University academic standards and receive the approval of the respective department through an audition. Students should contact the specific department for audition dates. Notes: (1) Two units in the same foreign language are required, (2) Academic Electives are from the fields of mathematics, English, natural science, social science, and a foreign language. The academic grade point average will be computed only on the units listed above. Grades in honors courses, International Baccalaureate (IB), and advanced placement (AP) courses will be given additional weight. Admission to the University is a selective process and satisfying the general requirements does not guarantee acceptance. A GPA of 2.0 is required. AP and CLEP credits are accepted. Important factors in the admissions decision are advanced placement or honors courses, evidence of special talent, and recommendations by school officials.To graduate, students must complete between 120 and 152 hours with a 2.0 GPA. There are also general education and writing requirements. **Procedure:** Freshmen are admitted fall, spring, and summer. Entrance exams should be taken during the spring of the junior year. There is a rolling admissions plan. Application deadlines are open. Application fee is $30. Applications are accepted on-line. **Transfer Students:** 4248 transfer students enrolled in 2013-2014. Degree seeking applicants with fewer than 60 semester hours of transfer credits must meet the same requirements as beginning freshmen students. In addition, they must demonstrate satisfactory performance in their college work. Applicants who receive an Associate in Arts (A.A.) degree from a Florida Public Community College or State University in Florida will be considered for admission without restriction except for published limited access programs within the University. Students trans-

ferring from independent Florida and out-of-state colleges into the University's upper division must have maintained a minimum 2.0 grade point average using a 4.0 scale (with the exception of some limited access programs). All applicants must meet the criteria published for limited access programs and should consult the specific college and major for requirements. Applicants who meet the above admissions requirements, but have not completed the University's core curriculum requirements, or the prerequisites of their proposed major, may complete this college work at FIU, or at any other accredited institution. Students may also fulfill general education requirements through the College Level Examination Program (CLEP). Official transcripts from all previous post secondary institutions must be forwarded to the Office of initiating this request directly from the academic institution. All students seeking admission to the University regardless of whether the student holds an A.A., should have completed two years of credit in one foreign language at the high school level or 8-10 credits in one foreign language at the college level (American Sign Language is acceptable). If a student is admitted to the University without this requirement, the credits must be completed prior to graduation. Students who can demonstrate continuous enrollment in a degree program at a SUS institution or Florida Community College since Fall Term 1989 (continuous enrollment is defined by the state to be the completion of at least one course per academic year) can be exempt from this requirement. Students holding an A.A. degree from a Florida Community College or SUS institution prior to Fall Term 1989 will also be exempt. Students, who are applying to majors in Theatre and Music, in addition to meeting university academic standards, must meet the approval of the respective department through an audition. Students should contact the department for audition dates. Admission to the University is a selective process and satisfying the general requirements does not guarantee acceptance. 30 of 120 credits required for the bachelor's degree must be completed at FIU. **International Students:** There are 1461 international students enrolled. The school actively recruits these students. They must take the TOEFL with a minimum score of 500 on the paper-based TOEFL (PBT) or 63 on the Internet-based version (iBT). They must also take the SAT or ACT.

ADMISSIONS: 40% of the 2014-2015 applicants were accepted. The SAT scores for the 2014-2015 freshman class were: Critical Reading--6% below 500, 63% between 500 and 599, 28% between 600 and 699, and 3% between 700 and 800; Math--9% below 500, 58% between 500 and 599, 31% between 600 and 699, and 2% between 700 and 800; Writing--10% below 500, 64% between 500 and 599, 24% between 600 and 699, and 2% between 700 and 800. The ACT scores were 1% below 21, 24% between 21 and 23, 46% between 24 and 26, 16% between 27 and 28, and 13% above 28. **Admissions Contact:** Barry Taylor, Admissions Director. E-Mail: *admissions@fiu.edu* Web: *www.fiu.edu*

FINANCIAL AID: FIU is a member of CSS. The FAFSA is required. The deadline for filing freshman financial aid applications for fall entry is March 1.

FLORIDA MEMORIAL UNIVERSITY (*The complete profile is made available exclusively on our website, www.barronspac.com*)

FLORIDA SOUTHERN COLLEGE   D-3
www.flsouthern.edu

Lakeland, FL 33801	(863) 680-4131
	(800) 274-4131
Fax: (863) 680-4120	Email: fscadm@flsouthern.edu
Full-time: 824 men, 1291 women	Faculty: 130; IIB, av$
Part-time: 27 men, 30 women	Ph.D.s: 77%
Graduate: 89 men, 178 women	Student/Faculty: 16 to 1
Year: semesters, summer session	Tuition: $29,990
Room & Board: $10,160	Freshman Class: 5590 applied, 2505 accepted, 665 enrolled
SAT CR/M/W: 560/560/535 ACT: 26	CEEB CODE: 5218
Application Deadline: May 1	COMPETITIVE+

Founded in 1885, Florida Southern College, is a private, comprehensive college that maintains its commitment to academic excellence through 52 undergraduate programs and distinctive graduate programs in business administration, accounting, education, and nursing. Florida Southern is a national leader in engaged learning; and boasts 27 NCAA Division II National Championships. FSC is home to the world's largest single-site collection of Frank Lloyd Wright architecture. Figures in the above capsule and in this profile are approximate. There are 4 undergraduate schools and 3 graduate schools. In addition to regional accreditation, Florida Southern has baccalaureate program accreditation with AACSB and NASM. The 113-acre campus is in a suburban area off of Interstate 4, FSC is 30 miles east of Tampa, 40 miles west of Orlando, with easy access to two international airports. Including any residence halls, there are 48 buildings.

STUDENT LIFE: 64% of undergraduates are from Florida. Others are from 49 states, 38 foreign countries, and Canada. 80% are from public schools. 73% are White. 40% are Protestant; 22% claim no religious affiliation; 21% Catholic. **Male To Female Ratio:** 1.6:1. The average age of freshmen is 18; all undergraduates, 21. 19% do not continue beyond their first year; 65% remain to graduate. **Housing:** 1803 students can be accommodated in college housing, which includes single-sex and coed dorms and off-campus apartments. In addition, there are honors houses, special-interest houses, fraternity houses, and sorority houses. On-campus housing is guaranteed for all 4 years. 80% of students live on campus; of those, 90% remain on campus on weekends. Alcohol is not permitted. All students may keep cars.

FACULTY/CLASSROOMS: 51% of faculty are male; 49% are female. All teach undergraduates, 75% do research, and 75% do both. No introductory courses are taught by graduate students. The average class size in an introductory lecture is 18; in a laboratory is 15; and in a regular course is 18.

PROGRAMS OF STUDY: Florida Southern confers B.A., B.S., B.F.A., B.M., B.M.E. and B.S.N. degrees. Master's and doctoral degrees are also awarded. Bachelor's degrees are awarded in AGRICULTURE (agricultural business management, agriculture, environmental studies, and horticulture), BIOLOGICAL SCIENCE (biochemistry, biology/biological science, marine biology, and molecular biology), BUSINESS (accounting and business administration and management), COMMUNICATIONS AND THE ARTS (advertising, art history and appreciation, broadcasting, communications, communication rhetoric/communication, creative writing, dance, digital communications, dramatic arts, English, graphic design, journalism, music, music business management, music performance, musical theater, public relations, Spanish, studio art, theatre acting, theatre arts, and theater design), COMPUTER AND PHYSICAL SCIENCE (chemistry, computer mathematics, computer science, and mathematics), EDUCATION (art education, athletic training, elementary education, music education, and secondary education), ENGINEERING AND ENVIRONMENTAL DESIGN (landscape architecture/design), HEALTH PROFESSIONS (exercise science, nursing, predentistry, premedicine, prepharmacy, and prephysical therapy), SOCIAL SCIENCE (criminology, economics, history, humanities, philosophy, political science/government, psychology, religion, and youth ministry). Biological sciences, nursing, business, communication, and psychology are the strongest academically. Business administration, biology, and nursing have the largest enrollments.

ACTIVITIES: 30% of men belong to 7 national fraternities; 35% of women belong to 6 national sororities. There are 102 groups on campus, including and honor societies., community service and shared interest groups, Greek organizations, intramurals, art, band, cheerleading, chess, choir, chorale, chorus, clubs and organizations include a variety of campus ministries, dance, drama, environmental, ethnic, film, forensics, honors, international, jazz band, literary magazine, musical theater, newspaper, opera, orchestra, pep band, photography, political, professional, radio and TV, religious, social, social service, student government, symphony, and yearbook. Popular campus events include Graduating Class Water Dome Splash, Greek Week, Flick 'n' Float movies in the pool, FSC's Got Talent, Flap Jack Fling, annual Winter Carnival and Farewell Festival, Homecoming, Festival of Fine Arts, and Founders Day. **Sports:** There are 10 intercollegiate sports for men and 11 for women, and 25 intramural sports

for men and 25 for women. Facilities include a variety of outdoor recreational areas, including intramural fields for softball, soccer, lacrosse, flag football, frisbee, golf, gardens and plazas, a waterfront program offering water-skiing, canoeing, kayaking, and a 3-mile walk/run path around Lake Hollingsworth. The Hollis Wellness Center provides a fully-equipped weight room with personal trainers, an aerobics, Pilates, and yoga studio, a large gymnasium for basketball and volleyball and other intramural sports, a heated competition-size swimming pool. The College's 1,800-seat Jenkins Field House is used for intercollegiate basketball and volleyball, and features locker rooms, weight rooms, and athletic training facilities. Facilities for baseball, lacrosse, and golf are conveniently located near campus. The Warden Tennis Center with a grandstand, two championship courts and eight tournament courts, a 2.3-acre central open space ideal for recreational and social events. With 27 national championships, the College's NCAA Division II athletic program is among the best in the nation. **Graduates:** From July 1, 2013 to June 30, 2014, 643 bachelor's degrees were awarded. The most popular majors were business/marketing (23%), social sciences (11%), and nursing (10%). In an average class, 56% graduate in 4 years or less, 64% graduate in 5 years or less, and 65% graduate in 6 years or less. Of the 2013 graduating class, 24% were enrolled in graduate school within 6 months of graduation, and 70% were employed.

SERVICES: Counseling and information services are available, as is tutoring in most subjects. The Student Solutions Center provides tutoring in various subjects Monday through Friday as well as peer-assisted study sessions in select areas. The center also offers support for navigating financial aid, academic advising, student life, and billing. Additional resources include the Center for English Proficiency and Academic Success to assist international students. **Library/Resources:** The 2 libraries contain 687,698 volumes, 448,346 microform items, 7,566 audio/video tapes/CDs/DVDs, and subscribe to 97,746 periodicals including electronic. Computerized library services include interlibrary loans, database searching, Internet access, and Wi-Fi capability. Special learning facilities include an art gallery, planetarium, radio station, TV station, Other: Special learning facilities include the Rinker Technology Center; numerous computer labs across campus, including the popular TuTu's Cyber Café; the Christoverson Humanities Building with a film studies theater and modern language lab; the Chatlos Communication Building houses a newly renovated television studio; the state-of-the-art Blanton Nursing Building with high-tech classrooms and a learning lab featuring a full complement of patient simulators; the McKay Archives Center, which houses the College's original Frank Lloyd Wright drawings and documents, the Florida Citrus Hall of Fame, and the Center for Florida History; and the Davis Performing Arts Center, including the nationally renowned Branscomb Auditorium, modern Buckner Theatre, and Melvin Art Gallery. The campus also is home to The Roberts Center for Learning and Literacy and The Roberts Academy, a transitional school for gifted elementary-age students with dyslexia that also serves as a learning lab for education students. 4,700 square-foot Wynee Warden Dance Studio, 45,000 square-foot facility that will include a simulated trading floor, high-tech classrooms, and a dedicated career center for students in the Barney Barnett School of Business and Free Enterprise. **Physically Challenged Students:** 68% of the campus is accessible. Facilities include wheelchair ramps, elevators, special parking, specially equipped restrooms, special class scheduling, lowered drinking fountains, lowered telephones, and special housing. **Special:** Florida Southern College offers a dynamic, transformational curriculum complemented by a variety of exciting experiential opportunities, including guaranteed internships for all students, numerous travel-study programs, student-faculty research, service learning, and music/theater performances. FSC is the only private college in the state affiliated with the prestigious Washington Center, a D.C.-based internship provider supporting students to study and work in the nation's capital, as well as other major cities around the world. The Honors Program offers innovative curriculum options to talented students seeking extraordinary inter-disciplinary learning opportunities. Honors students receive priority registration and are able to take course overloads without paying additional fees. An agreement with the University of South Florida's School of Medicine guarantees admission to all Honors Students who complete the undergraduate requirements. A self-designed major provides motivated students with the option to create a degree program to suit a unique interest or career path, such as art therapy, politics and justice, technology management, and more. All FSC students are encouraged to participate in an international or domestic travel-study experience at little to no additional cost as part of their educational journey. Month- and semester-long internships have taken FSC students to England, France, Italy, Spain, China, the Bahamas, Peru, Greece, and Turkey. The College also offers yearlong study through Regent's College in London and a popular modern language school in Spain. In fall 2013, the College launched the Hollingsworth Scholars program, a full-tuition scholarship offered to select students of extraordinary academic talent and vision. There are 27 national honor societies, a freshman honors program, and 9 departmental honors programs. **Visiting:** There are regularly scheduled orientations for prospective students, including a meeting with faculty, a campus tour, and class visits, as well as special programming for parents with a brief history of Frank Lloyd Wright, the architect of FSC's West Campus. There are guides for informal visits, visitors may sit in on classes, and stay overnight. To schedule a visit, contact the Admissions Office at fscadm@flsouthern.edu. **Campus Safety and Security:** Measures include 24-hour foot and vehicle patrol, emergency notification system, self-defense education, and security escort services. There are shuttle buses, emergency telephones, lighted pathways/sidewalks, controlled access to dorms/residences, Safety key fobs that students can use in emergency.

REQUIREMENTS: The SAT or ACT is required. Applicants are expected to have earned credit in at least 18 units of college preparatory courses and graduated from an accredited secondary school. It is recommended that students have a 3.0 GPA. An essay is required, and an interview is recommended. Applicants must submit either the SAT or ACT. A GPA of 2.0 is required. AP and CLEP credits are accepted. Important factors in the admissions decision are leadership record, geographical diversity, and recommendations by school officials.To gradate, a student needs a minimum of 124 semester credit hours from Florida Southern College and other regionally accredited colleges or universities. A maximum 62 of the required semester credit hours may have been earned at a junior/community college. After completing 96 hours, a student must finish the remaining credits at Florida Southern College. Some degree programs require more than 124 semester hours. **Procedure:** Freshmen are admitted to all sessions. Entrance exams should be taken starting in the junior year of high school. There are early decision, early admissions, deferred admissions, and rolling admissions plans. Early decision applications should be filed by December 1; regular applications, by May 1 for fall entry; and December 1 for spring entry, along with a $30 fee. Notification of early decision is sent December 15; regular decision, on a rolling basis. 48 early decision candidates were accepted for the 2014-2015 class. Applications are accepted on-line. **Transfer Students:** 111 transfer students enrolled in 2013-2014. Students who have successfully completed work at a regionally accredited college or university may apply for admission to Florida Southern College. Applicants should submit SAT or ACT scores, if available, along with a personal statement indicating the reason for the transfer. Official transcripts are required from each postsecondary institution attended. Transfer students must have a minimum 2.5 GPA in all college work attempted. An associate degree and an interview are recommended. 32 of 124 credits required for the bachelor's degree must be completed at Florida Southern. **International Students:** There are 108 international students enrolled. The school actively recruits these students. They must take the TOEFL with a minimum score of 550 on the paper-based TOEFL (PBT) or 79 on the Internet-based version (iBT). They must also take the SAT or ACT.

ADMISSIONS: 45% of the 2014-2015 applicants were accepted. The SAT scores for the 2014-2015 freshman class were: Critical Reading--14% below 500, 51% between 500 and 599, 28% between 600 and 699, and 7% between 700 and 800; Math--14% below 500, 58% between 500 and 599, 25% between 600 and 699, and 3% between 700 and 800; Writing--24% below 500, 55% between 500 and 599, 18% between 600 and 699, and 3% between 700 and 800. The ACT scores were 2% below 21, 27% between 21 and 23, 34% between 24 and 26, 13% between 27 and 28, and 24% above 28. 48% of the current freshmen were in the top fifth of their class; 77% were in the top two fifths. 3 freshmen graduated first in their class. **Admissions Con-**

tact: Erin Ervin, Director of Admissions. E-Mail: *fscadm@flsouthern .edu* Web: *http://www.flsouthern.edu*

FINANCIAL AID: In 2014-2015, 99% of all full-time freshmen and 99% of continuing full-time students received some form of financial aid. 74% of all full-time freshmen and 70% of continuing full-time students received need-based aid. The average freshman award was $29,031. Need-based scholarships or need-based grants averaged $20,122 ($45,191 maximum); need-based self-help aid (loans and jobs) averaged $1,781 ($3,094 maximum); non-need-based athletic scholarships averaged $12,758 ($34,000 maximum); and other non-need-based awards and non-need-based scholarships averaged $16,908 ($39,872 maximum). 61% of undergraduate students work part-time. Average annual earnings from campus work are $1993. The average financial indebtedness of the 2014 graduate was $24,314. The FAFSA and the college's own financial statement, and the parents' and student's tax returns are required. The priority date for freshman financial aid applications for fall entry is March 1. The deadline for filing freshman financial aid applications for fall entry is July 1.

FLORIDA STATE UNIVERSITY   C-1
www.fsu.edu

Tallahassee, FL 32306   (850) 644-6200

Fax: (850) 644-0197	Email: abrady@fsu.edu
Full-time: 12669 men, 16241 women	Faculty: 747; I, -$
	Ph.D.s: 92%
Part-time: 1958 men, 1660 women	Student/Faculty: 26 to 1
Graduate: 3780 men, 4601 women	Tuition: $6507 ($21,673)
Year: semesters, summer session	Freshman Class: 30040 applied, 16124 accepted, 5738 enrolled
Room & Board: $10,208	
SAT CR/M/W: 600/595/600 ACT: 27	CEEB CODE: 5219
Application Deadline: January 25	VERY COMPETITIVE

Florida State University, a public institution founded in 1851, is a residential university designated as a Doctoral Research (Extensive) University by the Carnegie Foundation for the Advancement of Teaching. Figures in the above capsule and in this profile are approximate. There are 15 undergraduate schools and 16 graduate schools. In addition to regional accreditation, FSU has baccalaureate program accreditation with AACSB, ABET, ADA, AHEA, ASLA, CSWE, FIDER, NASAD, NASM, NCATE, NLN, and NRPA. The 475-acre campus is in a suburban area 163 miles west of Jacksonville. Including any residence halls, there are 237 buildings.

STUDENT LIFE: 87% of undergraduates are from Florida. Others are from 50 states, 128 foreign countries, and Canada. 81% are from public schools. 67% are White; 17% Hispanic. **Male To Female Ratio:** 1.2:1. The average age of freshmen is 18; all undergraduates, 21. 8% do not continue beyond their first year; 91% remain to graduate.

Housing: 6570 students can be accommodated in college housing, which includes single-sex and coed dorms, on-campus apartments, and married student housing. In addition, there are honors houses, special-interest houses, fraternity houses, sorority houses, living and learning centers, music residence, scholarship houses, and academic discipline houses, wellness housing, Cooperative living through the southern scholarship foundation and several private residence halls. On-campus housing is available on a first-come and first-served basis. 80% of students commute. All students may keep cars.

FACULTY/CLASSROOMS: 62% of faculty are male; 38% are female. Graduate students teach 49% of introductory courses. The average class size in an introductory lecture is 40; in a laboratory is 18; and in a regular course is 36.

PROGRAMS OF STUDY: FSU confers B.A., B.S., B.S.N., B.F.A, B.M. and B.M.Ed. degrees. Associate, Master's, and Doctoral degrees are also awarded. Bachelor's degrees are awarded in AGRICULTURE (environmental studies and plant science), BIOLOGICAL SCIENCE (biochemistry, biology/biological science, cell biology, ecology, evolutionary biology, genetics, marine biology, molecular biology, nutrition, physiology, and zoology), BUSINESS (accounting, banking and finance, business administration and management, entrepreneurial studies, fashion merchandising, hotel/motel and restaurant management, insurance and risk management, international business management, management science, marketing/retailing/merchandising, personnel management, recreation and leisure services, recreational facilities management, small business management, and sports management), COMMUNICATIONS AND THE ARTS (advertising, American literature, apparel design, art history and appreciation, broadcasting, classics, communications, creative writing, dance, dramatic arts, English, fiber/textiles/weaving, film arts, French, German, Greek, Italian, jazz, Latin, linguistics, music, music history and appreciation, music performance, music theory and composition, musical theater, piano/organ, public relations, Russian, Spanish, speech/debate/rhetoric, strings, studio art, theater design, voice, and winds), COMPUTER AND PHYSICAL SCIENCE (actuarial science, applied mathematics, atmospheric sciences and meteorology, chemical technology, chemistry, computer science, geology, information sciences and systems, mathematics, physics, and statistics), EDUCATION (art education, athletic training, early childhood education, education of the emotionally handicapped, education of the mentally handicapped, education of the visually handicapped, elementary education, English education, foreign languages education, health education, home economics education, mathematics education, music education, physical education, reading education, science education, social science education, and specific learning disabilities), ENGINEERING AND ENVIRONMENTAL DESIGN (bioengineering, biomedical engineering, chemical engineering, civil engineering, computer engineering, electrical/electronics engineering, environmental engineering, environmental science, graphic arts technology, industrial engineering, interior design, materials engineering, and mechanical engineering), HEALTH PROFESSIONS (community health work, music therapy, nursing, predentistry, premedicine, preoptometry, prepharmacy, preveterinary science, rehabilitation therapy, speech pathology/audiology, and sports medicine), SOCIAL SCIENCE (American studies, anthropology, Asian/Oriental studies, Caribbean studies, child care/child and family studies, classical/ancient civilization, clothing and textiles management/production/services, criminology, dietetics, Eastern European studies, economics, family/consumer studies, fashion design and technology, food science, geography, history, home economics, humanities, international relations, Latin American studies, philosophy, political science/government, prelaw, psychology, religion, Russian and Slavic studies, social science, social work, sociology, and women's studies). Biology, meteorology, and physics are the strongest academically. Psychology, political science and business have the largest enrollments.

ACTIVITIES: 16% of men belong to 31 national fraternities; 22% of women belong to 26 national sororities. There are 628 groups on campus, including art, band, cheerleading, chess, choir, chorale, chorus, computers, dance, debate, drama, drill team, ethnic, forensics, gay, honors, international, jazz band, literary magazine, marching band, musical theater, newspaper, opera, orchestra, pep band, political, professional, radio and TV, religious, social, social service, student government, and symphony. Popular campus events include Twelve Days of Dance, Parents Weekend and Seven Days of Opening Nights. **Sports:** There are 9 intercollegiate sports for men and 10 for women, and 27 intramural sports for men and 27 for women. Facilities include an 80,000-seat stadium, an aquatic center with a heated outdoor swimming pool, a golf course, a track, courts for basketball, tennis, racquetball, and handball, a student recreation center with an indoor Olympic-size swimming pool, 2 Jacuzzis, a steam room, a sauna, 10 racquetball courts, a squash court, a multipurpose gym, a 3-lane jogging track, aerobic rooms, aerobic exercise machines, free and fixed weights, and a lakefront recreation area for outdoor water sports. **Graduates:** From July 1, 2013 to June 30, 2014, 8011 bachelor's degrees were awarded. The most popular majors were business/marketing (19%), social sciences (18%), and psychology and English (6%). In an average class, 4% graduate in 3 years or less, 57% graduate in 4 years or less, 74% graduate in 5 years or less, and 77% graduate in 6 years or less. Of the 2013 graduating class, 48% were enrolled in graduate school within 6 months of graduation, and 63% were employed.

SERVICES: Counseling and information services are available, as is tutoring in most subjects. There is a reader service for the blind, and remedial math, reading, and writing. **Library/Resources:** The 8 libraries contain 3.2 million volumes, 9.8 million microform items, 257,419 audio/video tapes/CDs/DVDs, and subscribe to 72,825 periodicals including electronic. Computerized library services include interlibrary loans, database searching, and Internet access. Special learning facilities include an art gallery, planetarium, radio station, TV station, an nuclear accelerator, x-ray emission lab, marine lab, supercomputers, and the national high magnetic field laboratory. **Physically Challenged Students:** 99% of the campus is accessible. Facilities include wheelchair ramps, elevators, special parking, specially equipped restrooms, special class scheduling, lowered drinking fountains, and lowered telephones. **Special:** Cross-registration with Florida Agricultural and Mechanical University and Tallahassee Community College is possible, as is study at FSU centers in London or Florence and in programs in Costa Rica, France, Russia, Spain, Switzerland, and Vietnam, among other countries. FSU offers cooperative programs in Engineering, Computer Science, Business, and Communication, work-study programs, general studies and combined B.A.-B.S. degrees, dual majors, and accelerated degree programs. Internships are required in Criminology, Human Science, Education, Nursing, Business (PMG), and Social Work. There are pre-professional programs in Health and Law. There are 34 national honor societies, including Phi Beta Kappa, a freshman honors program, and 60 departmental honors programs. **Visiting:** There are regularly scheduled orientations for prospective students, including campus tours several times daily on weekdays. Walking and riding tours are available and tours are coordinated around an 11:00 admissions information session. There are guides for informal visits and visitors may sit in on classes. To schedule a visit, contact the Visitor Services at visitorservices@admin.fsu.edu. **Campus Safety and Security:** Measures include 24-hour foot and vehicle patrol, emergency notification system, self-defense education, and security escort services. There are shuttle buses, emergency telephones, lighted pathways/sidewalks, a full-time police force, a bicycle identification program, a valuables identification program, and a victim advocate program.

REQUIREMENTS: The SAT or ACT is required. It is recommended that in-state students have at least an A-/B+ weighted average and a satisfactory SAT or ACT score. Out-of-state students must meet higher standards. Applicants should have at least the following high school units; 4 in English and math, 3 in natural science, and social science, and 2 in a foreign language. Other factors include the number of honors, AP, and IB classes, strength of academic curriculum, class rank, among others. FSU requires applicants to be in the upper 77% of their class. A GPA of 3.9 is required. AP and CLEP credits are accepted. Important factors in the admissions decision are advanced placement or honors courses, evidence of special talent, and recommendations by school officials. Students must satisfy the Florida College-Level Academic Skills (CLAS) requirement or an approved alternative. The required core curriculum includes 6 semester hours in Mathematics, 6 in English composition, 6 to 12 in history/social science, 5 to 11 humanities/fine arts, and 7 in natural sciences. Students must satisfy major requirements of their chosen degree program, including additional requirements set by the college offering the degree. All academic areas require at least 120 semester hours for graduation. Additional information is available in the General Bulletin. **Procedure:** Freshmen are admitted fall, spring, and summer. Entrance exams should be taken beginning in the second semester of the junior year. There is a rolling admissions plan. Applications should be filed by January 25 for fall entry; November 1 for spring entry; and February 13 for summer entry, along with a $30 fee. Applications are accepted on-line. **Transfer Students:** 2115 transfer students enrolled in 2013-2014. Transfer applicants should present at least a 3.0 cumulative college GPA unless transferring from a Florida public community college with an associate in arts degree, in which case the minimum college GPA needed varies according to major. Applicants with less than 60 semester hours of transferable credit must also meet freshman admission requirements. All transfers must have completed 2 years of the same foreign language in high school or have 8 semester hours at the college level. Students must pass the Florida CLAST. 30 of 120 credits required for the bachelor's degree must be completed at FSU. **International Students:** There are 486 international students enrolled. They must take the TOEFL with a minimum score of 550 on the paper-based TOEFL (PBT) or 80 on the Internet-based version (iBT). They must also take the SAT or ACT.

ADMISSIONS: 54% of the 2014-2015 applicants were accepted. The SAT scores for the 2014-2015 freshman class were: Critical Reading--2% below 500, 48% between 500 and 599, 42% between 600 and 699, and 8% between 700 and 800; Math--3% below 500, 46% between 500 and 599, 43% between 600 and 699, and 6% between 700 and 800; Writing--3% below 500, 49% between 500 and 599, 43% between 600 and 699, and 5% between 700 and 800. The ACT scores were 6% between 21 and 23, and 94% above 28. 88% of the current freshmen were in the top fifth of their class. There were 13 National Merit finalists. **Admissions Contact:** Andrew Brady, Statistical Coodinator. E-Mail: *abrady@fsu.edu* Web: *www.fsu.edu*

FINANCIAL AID: In 2014-2015, 99% of all full-time freshmen and 90% of continuing full-time students received some form of financial aid. 45% of all full-time freshmen and 53% of continuing full-time students received need-based aid. The average freshman award was $8,319. Need-based scholarships or need-based grants averaged $4,508; need-based self-help aid (loans and jobs) averaged $3,254; non-need-based athletic scholarships averaged $7,118; and other non-need-based awards and non-need-based scholarships averaged $3,602. 2% of undergraduate students work part-time. Average annual earnings from campus work are $1746. The average financial indebtedness of the 2014 graduate was $22,722. The FAFSA and the college's own financial statement are required. The priority date for freshman financial aid applications for fall entry is January 15.

HODGES UNIVERSITY (*The complete profile is made available exclusively on our website, www.barronspac.com*)

JACKSONVILLE UNIVERSITY · D-1
www.ju.edu

Jacksonville, FL 32211 · (904) 256-7000 / (800) 225-2027

Fax: (904) 256-7012	Email: admissions@ju.edu
Full-time: 1075 men, 1125 women	Faculty: IIA, -$
Part-time: 165 men, 675 women	Ph.D.s: 78%
Graduate: 190 men, 295 women	Student/Faculty: n/av
Year: semesters, summer session	Tuition: $27,900
Room & Board: $9880	Freshman Class: n/av
SAT or ACT: required	CEEB CODE: 5331
Application Deadline: open	COMPETITIVE

Jacksonville University, founded in 1934, is a private institution offering undergraduate and graduate degree programs in the arts and sciences, fine arts, and business. The figures in the above capsule and in this profile are approximate. There are 3 undergraduate schools and 4 graduate schools. In addition to regional accreditation, JU has baccalaureate program accreditation with NASAD, NASM, and NLN. The 198-acre campus is in a suburban area 10 minutes from downtown Jacksonville, near the St. Johns River. Including any residence halls, there are 48 buildings.

STUDENT LIFE: 60% of undergraduates are from Florida. Others are from 45 states, 50 foreign countries, and Canada. 56% are White; 20% African American. 35% claim no religious affiliation; 18% Protestant; 16% Catholic. **Male To Female Ratio:** 1.5:1. The average age of freshmen is 19; all undergraduates, 22. 35% do not continue beyond their first year; 49% remain to graduate. **Housing:** 1342 students can be accommodated in college housing, which includes single-sex dorms and on-campus apartments. On-campus housing is guaranteed for the freshman year only, is available on a first-come, first-served basis, and is available on a lottery system for upperclassmen. 59% of students live on campus; of those, 60% remain on campus on weekends. All students may keep cars.

FACULTY/CLASSROOMS: 53% of faculty are male; 47% are female. No introductory courses are taught by graduate students. The average class size in an introductory lecture is 18; in a laboratory is 16; and in a regular course is 14.

PROGRAMS OF STUDY: JU confers B.A., B.S., B.B.A., B.F.A.,

B.G.S., B.Mus., B.Mus.Ed. and B.S.N. degrees. Master's degrees are also awarded. Bachelor's degrees are awarded in BIOLOGICAL SCIENCE (biology/biological science and marine science), BUSINESS (accounting, banking and finance, business administration and management, international business management, and marketing/retailing/merchandising), COMMUNICATIONS AND THE ARTS (art history and appreciation, communications, dance, dramatic arts, English, French, music, music performance, music theory and composition, Spanish, and studio art), COMPUTER AND PHYSICAL SCIENCE (chemistry, computer science, information sciences and systems, mathematics, and physics), EDUCATION (art education, dance education, education of the exceptional child, elementary education, music education, and physical education), ENGINEERING AND ENVIRONMENTAL DESIGN (aviation administration/management, computer graphics, electrical/electronics engineering, engineering physics, environmental science, and mechanical engineering), HEALTH PROFESSIONS (nursing), SOCIAL SCIENCE (economics, geography, history, humanities, international studies, philosophy, political science/government, psychology, and sociology). Business administration, nursing, and biology have the largest enrollments.

ACTIVITIES: 20% of men belong to 8 national fraternities; 15% of women belong to 7 national sororities. There are 100 groups on campus, including art, band, cheerleading, choir, chorale, chorus, computers, dance, debate, drama, drill team, environmental, ethnic, film, gay, honors, international, jazz band, literary magazine, musical theater, newspaper, orchestra, pep band, photography, political, professional, radio and TV, religious, social, social service, student government, and symphony. Popular campus events include FIN Fest and Campus Movie Fest. **Sports:** There are 8 intercollegiate sports for men and 9 for women. Facilities include a 1500-seat stadium, a gym, a swimming pool, a boathouse, baseball and softball diamonds, soccer and football fields, and an archery range. There are also tennis, basketball, handball/racquetball, volleyball, and shuffleboard courts, an all-purpose playing field, a 440-yard track, a 540-seat auditorium, a 220-seat recital hall, and a dance pavilion.

SERVICES: Counseling and information services are available, as is tutoring in most subjects. There is a reader service for the blind, and remedial math, reading, and writing. The library contains 24,919 audio/video tapes/CDs/DVDs, and subscribes to 19,740 periodicals including electronic. Computerized library services include interlibrary loans, database searching, and Internet access. Special learning facilities include an art gallery, planetarium, radio station, TV station, a chemistry research lab, and a marine science center. **Physically Challenged Students:** Facilities include wheelchair ramps, elevators, special parking, specially equipped restrooms, special class scheduling, lowered drinking fountains. Accommodation for all students regardless of disability. **Special:** Internships and work-study are available, as are student-designed majors and a dual major in music and business. There is a co-op program in art, and a 3-2 engineering degree is available with 7 other universities and technological institutes. There is a Washington semester and study abroad in 12 countries. Credit is granted for military experience. There are 16 national honor societies, including Phi Beta Kappa, and a freshman honors program. **Visiting:** There are regularly scheduled orientations for prospective students, consisting of an interview, a campus tour, advisement, area presentations, registration, a parents program, and mock classes. There are guides for informal visits, visitors may sit in on classes, and stay overnight. To schedule a visit, contact the Admissions Office. **Campus Safety and Security:** Measures include 24-hour foot and vehicle patrol, self-defense education, and security escort services. There are emergency telephones and lighted pathways/sidewalks.

REQUIREMENTS: The SAT or ACT is required. Applicants must be graduates of an accredited secondary school and provide an official copy of their secondary school transcripts or have a GED. At least 18 academic credits are required, including 4 in English, 3 each in math, natural science, and social sciences, and 2 of the same foreign language. Art students must submit a portfolio. Music, theater, and dance students must audition. A GPA of 2.0 is required. AP and CLEP credits are accepted. Important factors in the admissions decision are advanced placement or honors courses, extracurricular activities record, and leadership record. All students must complete a core curriculum, which provides the liberal arts foundation for all bachelor's degrees. The core includes 4 hours of lab science and 3 hours each of English composition, world literature, economics, fine arts, global studies, humanities, modern world history, math, philosophy, social science, and technology. The B.A. degree requires completion of a foreign language component in place of 3 hours of global studies. A minimum of 120 credit hours, with a minimum GPA of 2.0, is needed to graduate. **Procedure:** Freshmen are admitted to all sessions. Entrance exams should be taken in the spring of the junior year or the fall or spring of the senior year. There are early admissions, deferred admissions, and rolling admissions plans. Application deadlines are open. The fall 2014 application fee was $30. Applications are accepted on-line. **Transfer Students:** Transfer students must submit official transcripts from all colleges attended. Art students must submit a portfolio; music and dance students must audition. Transfer applicants must have completed at least 1 semester at an accredited college or university, be in good standing at the last institution attended, and have a minimum GPA of 2.0. 30 of 120 credits required for the bachelor's degree must be completed at JU. **International Students:** The school actively recruits these students. They must take the TOEFL with a minimum score of 540 on the paper-based TOEFL (PBT) or 76 on the Internet-based version (iBT). They must also take the SAT or ACT.

ADMISSIONS: Director of Admissions. E-Mail: *admissions@ju.edu* Web: *www.ju.edu*

FINANCIAL AID: JU is a member of CSS. The FAFSA and the college's own financial statement, and a federal tax return and W-2 are required. Check with the school for current application deadlines.

JOHNSON & WALES UNIVERSITY/NORTH MIAMI CAMPUS   E-5
www.jwu.edu

North Miami, FL 33181	(866) 598-3567 (800) 342-5598
Fax: (305) 892-7020	Email: admissions.fla@jwu.edu
Full-time: 211 men, 382 women	Faculty: 58
Part-time: 25 men, 24 women	Ph.Ds: n/av
Graduate: n/av	Student/Faculty: 25 to 1
Year: trimesters	Tuition: $29,576
Room & Board: n/app	Freshman Class: n/av CEEB CODE: 3441
Application Deadline: n/av	COMPETITIVE

Johnson & Wales University/North Miami Campus, founded in 1992, offers degree programs in its College of Culinary Arts, College of Business, and Hospitality College. Figures in the above capsule and in this profile are approximate. There are 3 undergraduate schools. In addition to regional accreditation, JWU has baccalaureate program accreditation with NEASCE-CIHE. The campus is in a small town in the heart of North Miami, between Miami and Fort Lauderdale. Including any residence halls, there are 13 buildings.

STUDENT LIFE: 52% of undergraduates are from Florida. Others are from 44 states, 54 foreign countries, and Canada. 24% are African American; 23% White; 21% Hispanic. **Female To Male Ratio:** 1.7:1. The average age of freshmen is 19; all undergraduates, 20. **Housing:** 1184 students can be accommodated in college housing, which includes coed dorms, on-campus apartments, apartments for single students, special housing for disabled, wellness housing, and theme housing. On-campus housing is available on a lottery system for upperclassmen. All students may keep cars.

FACULTY/CLASSROOMS: 61% of faculty are male; 37% are female. No introductory courses are taught by graduate students.

PROGRAMS OF STUDY: JWU confers B.S. degrees. Associate degrees are also awarded. Bachelor's degrees are awarded in BUSINESS (accounting, business administration and management, entrepreneurial studies, hospitality management services, hotel/motel and restaurant management, marketing management, marketing/retailing/merchandising, recreation and leisure services, sports management, and tourism), ENGINEERING AND ENVIRONMENTAL DESIGN (electrical/electronics engineering and food services technology), SOCIAL SCIENCE (clothing and textiles management/production/services, criminal justice, food production/management/services, paralegal studies, and parks and recreation management).

ACTIVITIES: Groups on campus include cheerleading, dance, ethnic, gay, honors, international, music ensembles and campus ministries, newspaper, pep band, professional, religious, social, and student government. **Sports:** There are 4 intercollegiate sports for men and 4 for women, and 5 intramural sports for men and 5 for women. Facilities include a fitness center is equipped with cardio machines, free weights, universal machines, treadmills. **Graduates:** From July 1, 2013 to June 30, 2014, 287 bachelor's degrees were awarded. The most popular majors were business/marketing (41%), family and consumer sciences (36%), and parks and recreation (13%).

SERVICES: Counseling and information services are available, as is tutoring in every subject. **Library/Resources:** The library contains 12,525 volumes, and subscribes to 232 periodicals including electronic. Computerized library services include interlibrary loans, database searching, Internet access, and Wi-Fi capability. **Physically Challenged Students:** Facilities include wheelchair ramps, elevators, special parking, specially equipped restrooms, special class scheduling, lowered drinking fountains, lowered telephones, and special housing. **Special:** The university offers co-op programs, accelerated degree programs, dual majors, study abroad, and worldwide work-study opportunities in business, hospitality, technology, and culinary arts. Most majors require 11-week internships. **Visiting:** There are regularly scheduled orientations for prospective students, including an introduction to the academic and social aspects of the campus experience through interactive sessions. There are guides for informal visits, visitors may sit in on classes, and stay overnight. To schedule a visit, contact Admissions. **Campus Safety and Security:** Measures include 24-hour foot and vehicle patrol and security escort services. There are shuttle buses and emergency telephones.

REQUIREMENTS: SAT and ACT scores are required only for students applying for honors admissions, students who have taken these test are encouraged to submit their scores. High school diploma is required the GED is accepted. Student requirements are 4 years of English, 3 years each of mathematics, and science, and 2 years of social studies. A GPA of 2.0 is required. AP and CLEP credits are accepted. Important factors in the admissions decision are leadership record, advanced placement or honors courses, extracurricular activities record, evidence of special talent, personality/intangible qualities, and recommendations by school officials. To graduate, students must complete 180 quarter credit hours, including at least 36 in the major, with a minimum GPA of 2.0. Required classes include English, math history, economics, science, psychology, sociology, and professional development. **Procedure:** Freshmen are admitted to all sessions. There are deferred admissions and rolling admissions plans. Application deadlines are open. **Transfer Students:** 142 transfer students enrolled in 2013-2014. Applicants are required to submit official high school and college transcripts and must have earned a minimum college GPA of 2.0. **International Students:** There are 192 international students enrolled. The school actively recruits these students. They must take the TOEFL.

ADMISSIONS: Jeff Greenip, Director of Admissions. E-Mail: *admissions.fla@jwu.edu* Web: *www.jwu.edu*

FINANCIAL AID: JWU is a member of CSS. The FAFSA is required. Check with the school for current application deadlines.

LYNN UNIVERSITY (*The complete profile is made available exclusively on our website, www.barronspac.com*)

NEW COLLEGE OF FLORIDA   D-4
www.ncf.edu

Sarasota, FL 34243	(941) 487-5000
Fax: (941) 487-5010	Email: admissions@ncf.edu
Full-time: 320 men, 481 women	Faculty: 71; IIB, +$
Part-time: n/av	Ph.Ds: 97%
Graduate: n/av	Student/Faculty: 10 to 1
Year: 4-1-4	Tuition: $6032 ($28,949)
Room & Board: $8472	Freshman Class: 1414 applied, 751 accepted, 183 enrolled
SAT CR/M/W: 680/620/640 ACT: 29	CEEB CODE: 5506
Application Deadline: February 15	MOST COMPETITIVE

New College of Florida, established in 1960, is the honors college for the liberal arts and sciences of the State University System of Florida. There is one undergraduate school. The 119-acre campus is in a suburban area is 50 miles south of Tampa, Florida on Sarasota Bay. Including any residence halls, there are 53 buildings.

STUDENT LIFE: 83% of undergraduates are from Florida. Others are from 40 states, 22 foreign countries, and Canada. 83% are from public schools. 76% are White; 13% Hispanic. **Male To Female Ratio:** 1.5:1. The average age of freshmen is 18; all undergraduates, 20. 18% do not continue beyond their first year; 68% remain to graduate. **Housing:** 636 students can be accommodated in college housing, which includes coed dorms and on-campus apartments. Specialized housing options may be arranged in response to student interest. On-campus housing is guaranteed for all 4 years and is available on a lottery system for upperclassmen. 76% of students live on campus. All students may keep cars.

FACULTY/CLASSROOMS: 47% of faculty are male; 53% are female. 30% teach undergraduates, and 70% do both. No introductory courses are taught by graduate students. The average class size in an introductory lecture is 22; in a laboratory is 14; and in a regular course is 22.

PROGRAMS OF STUDY: New College confers B.A. degrees. Bachelor's degrees are awarded in AGRICULTURE (environmental studies), BIOLOGICAL SCIENCE (biochemistry, biology/biological science, marine biology, and neurosciences), COMMUNICATIONS AND THE ARTS (art, art history and appreciation, Chinese, classics, English, French, Germanic languages and literature, literature, music, Russian languages and literature, and Spanish), COMPUTER AND PHYSICAL SCIENCE (applied mathematics, chemistry, mathematics, natural sciences, and physics), ENGINEERING AND ENVIRONMENTAL DESIGN (computational sciences), SOCIAL SCIENCE (anthropology, economics, French studies, gender studies, German area studies, history, humanities, international studies, Latin American studies, medieval studies, philosophy, political science/government, psychology, public affairs, religion, social science, sociology, Spanish studies, and urban studies). Biology, psychology, economics, anthropology, English, political science have the largest enrollments.

ACTIVITIES: There are no fraternities or sororities. There are 60 groups on campus, including art, chess, chorale, chorus, computers, dance, debate, drama, environmental, ethnic, film, gay, international, jazz band, literary magazine, newspaper, photography, political, radio and TV, religious, social, social service, and student government. Popular campus events include Halloween and Graduation Parties, Diversity Discussion Service, and a Kickball Tournament. **Sports:** There are 1 intercollegiate sports for men and 1 for women, and 20 intramural sports for men and 20 for women. Facilities include an soccer field, a softball diamond, a fitness path, outdoor tennis and basketball courts, a volleyball pit, playground equipment, a swimming pool, and a fitness center with Cybex equipment and indoor facilities for racquetball, aerobics, dance, and yoga. **Graduates:** From July 1, 2013 to June 30, 2014, 153 Bachelor's degrees were awarded. The most popular majors were biology (12%), psychology (10%), and economics (9%). In an average class, 1% graduate in 3 years or less, 57% graduate in 4 years or less, 67% graduate in 5 years or less, and 68% graduate in 6 years or less. Of the 2013 graduating class, 29% were enrolled in graduate school within 6 months of graduation.

SERVICES: There is a reader service for the blind. A writing resouce center provides assistance in developing writing skills and strategies. A Quantitative Resource center provides assistance in math and statistics as well as the technology needed in these fields. **Library/Resources:** The library contains 281,794 volumes, 198,287 microform items, 6,001 audio/video tapes/CDs/DVDs, and subscribes to 1,086 periodicals including electronic. Computerized library services include interlibrary loans, database searching, Internet access, and Wi-Fi capability. Special learning facilities include an art gallery, radio station, a media and educational technology center, public archaeology lab, writing resource center, quantitative resource center, language resource center, marine biology research center, black box theater, fine arts complex, and a living ecosystem teaching and research aquarium. **Physically Challenged Students:** 80% of the campus is accessible. Facilities include wheelchair ramps, elevators, special parking, specially equipped restrooms, special class schedul-

ing, lowered drinking fountains, lowered telephones, and special housing. **Special:** Domestic and international internships, study abroad, accelerated degree programs, student-designed interdisciplinary and dual majors, and independent study are available. There are a freshman honors program. **Visiting:** There are regularly scheduled orientations for prospective students, Including a campus tour, admissions information session, and/or class visits, which must be scheduled individually by the student through Admissions. Visitors may sit in on classes. To schedule a visit, contact Campus Visit Facilitator at admissions@ncf.edu. **Campus Safety and Security:** Measures include 24-hour foot and vehicle patrol, emergency notification system, self-defense education, and security escort services. There are emergency telephones, lighted pathways/sidewalks, controlled access to dorms/residences, 24-hour dispatch/information services, and fire/smoke alarm systems in all dorms.

REQUIREMENTS: The SAT or ACT is required. The ACT Optional Writing test is also required. Graduation from an accredited secondary school (preferred) or the GED. High school students should pursue at least 5 academic courses each year, at the most rigorous level available, with a minimum distribution of 4 years of English and Mathematics; 3 years each of sciences and social sciences; 2 consecutive years of the same foreign language; and 3 other academic courses. Application essays must be submitted. AP credits are accepted. Important factors in the admissions decision are advanced placement or honors courses, evidence of special talent, and recommendations by school officials.An academic credit system is not used. To qualify for graduation, students must complete 7 semester contracts, which are designed by the student in consultation with faculty; 3 independent study projects completed during January each year, between the fall and spring semesters; a senior thesis, that involves original research or creative work and includes working closely with a faculty committee of the student's choice; and an oral baccalaureate exam, which is primarily a defense of the senior thesis. To fulfill the liberal arts curriculum requirements, students must complete 8 LAC-designated courses, including 1 each in humanities, natural sciences, and social sciences. Exemptions from the LAC requirements are possible through AP exam scores of 3 or above, IB exam scores of 5 to 7, and transferable college course work at the general education level. Students also must use on-line training to sign up for a college e-mail account and complete the College Level Academic Skills Test or be exempted by appropriate college course work or SAT or ACT scores. **Procedure:** Freshmen are admitted fall and spring. Entrance exams should be taken By fall of the senior year. There is a deferred admissions plan. Applications should be filed by February 15 for fall entry; December 15 for spring entry, along with a $30 fee. Notifications are sent April 1. 56 applicants were on the 2014 waiting list; 22 were admitted. Applications are accepted on-line. **Transfer Students:** 38 transfer students enrolled in 2013-2014. Transfers must be in good academic and financial standing with their previous college(s). Transfers with less than 60 semester hours must submit SAT or ACT scores. **International Students:** There are 31 international students enrolled. The school actively recruits these students. They must take the TOEFL with a minimum score of 560 on the paper-based TOEFL (PBT) or 83 on the Internet-based version (iBT). They must also take the SAT or ACT.

ADMISSIONS: 53% of the 2014-2015 applicants were accepted. The SAT scores for the 2014-2015 freshman class were: Critical Reading--1% below 500, 8% between 500 and 599, 48% between 600 and 699, and 43% between 700 and 800; Math--2% below 500, 28% between 500 and 599, 54% between 600 and 699, and 17% between 700 and 800; Writing--1% below 500, 21% between 500 and 599, 57% between 600 and 699, and 21% between 700 and 800. The ACT scores were 4% between 21 and 23, 14% between 24 and 26, 24% between 27 and 28, and 58% above 28. 74% of the current freshmen were in the top fifth of their class; 91% were in the top two fifths. There were 21 National Merit finalists. 3 freshmen graduated first in their class. **Admissions Contact:** Kathy Killion, Dean of Admissions and Financial Aid. E-Mail: *admissions@ncf.edu* Web: *www.ncf.edu*

FINANCIAL AID: In 2014-2015, 100% of all full-time freshmen and 98% of continuing full-time students received some form of financial aid. 36% of all full-time freshmen and 43% of continuing full-time students received need-based aid. The average freshman award was $10,521. Need-based scholarships or need-based grants averaged

$1,929 ($23,300 maximum); need-based self-help aid (loans and jobs) averaged $888 ($7,000 maximum); and other non-need-based awards and non-need-based scholarships averaged $7,704 ($40,199 maximum). 21% of undergraduate students work part-time. Average annual earnings from campus work are $2449. The average financial indebtedness of the 2014 graduate was $15,438. The FAFSA is required. The priority date for freshman financial aid applications for fall entry is February 15.

NORTHWOOD UNIVERSITY (*The complete profile is made available exclusively on our website, www.barronspac.com*)

NOVA SOUTHEASTERN UNIVERSITY	E-5
www.nova.edu	

Fort Lauderdale, FL 33314	(954) 262-8000
	(800) 338-4723
	Email: admissions@nova.edu
Full-time: 1044 men, 2118 women	Faculty: n/av
Part-time: 382 men, 1155 women	Ph.Ds: 85%
Graduate: 5886 men, 13563 women	Student/Faculty: 16 to 1
Year: trimesters, summer session	Tuition: $26,700
Room & Board: $10,580	Freshman Class: 4364 applied, 2130 accepted, 611 enrolled
SAT CR/M: 560/560 ACT: 25	CEEB CODE: 5514
Application Deadline: open	VERY COMPETITIVE

Nova Southeastern University, founded in 1964, is an independent institution offering degree programs in liberal arts, sciences, business, health sciences, education, and preprofessional studies. The university also offers graduate and first-professional programs. Figures in the above capsule and in this profile are approximate. There are 7 undergraduate schools and 16 graduate schools. In addition to regional accreditation, NSU has baccalaureate program accreditation with APTA, CAHEA, and NCATE. The 314-acre campus is in a suburban area 10 miles west of downtown Fort Lauderdale. Including any residence halls, there are 39 buildings.

STUDENT LIFE: 84% of undergraduates are from Florida. Others are from 47 states, 73 foreign countries, and Canada. 33% are Hispanic; 32% White; 18% African American. **Male To Female Ratio:** 2.3:1. The average age of freshmen is 19; all undergraduates, 26. 26% do not continue beyond their first year; 42% remain to graduate. **Housing:** 1472 students can be accommodated in college housing, which includes coed dorms, on-campus apartments, and married student housing. Theme housing, Leadership, CoEd Greek and Quiet. On-campus housing is guaranteed for all 4 years. All students may keep cars.

FACULTY/CLASSROOMS: 46% of faculty are male; 54% are female. No introductory courses are taught by graduate students. The average class size in an introductory lecture is 15.

PROGRAMS OF STUDY: NSU confers B.A., B.H.Sc., B.S., B.B.A. and B.S.N. degrees. Associate, Master's, and Doctoral degrees are also awarded. Bachelor's degrees are awarded in BIOLOGICAL SCIENCE (marine biology, marine science, and neurosciences), BUSINESS (accounting, business administration and management, finance, and marketing), COMMUNICATIONS AND THE ARTS (communication studies, dance, dramatic arts, fine arts, music, and theatre acting), COMPUTER AND PHYSICAL SCIENCE (chemistry, Computer Engineering Technology, computer information systems, computer science, and mathematics), EDUCATION (art education, education, education of the exceptional child, elementary education, English education, general studies, middle school education, physical education, science education, secondary education, and sports and wellness studies), ENGINEERING AND ENVIRONMENTAL DESIGN (computer engineering and environmental science), HEALTH PROFESSIONS (biology, diagnostic medical sonography, exercise science, health promotion, kinesiology, nursing, recreation therapy, respiratory therapy, and speech pathology/audiology), SOCIAL SCIENCE (anthropology, behavioral science, criminal justice, human development, human services, international relations, legal studies, paralegal studies, philosophy, philosophy and religion,

political science/government, psychology, public administration, and sociology). Biology, nursing, and business have the largest enrollments.

ACTIVITIES: 8% of men belong to 6 national fraternities; 7% of women belong to 6 national sororities. There are 316 groups on campus, including band, cheerleading, chorale, chorus, computers, dance, drama, environmental, ethnic, gay, honors, international, literary magazine, musical theater, newspaper, orchestra, political, professional, radio and TV, religious, social, social service, and student government. Popular campus events include Homecoming, Sharkapalooza and Student Life Achievement Awards. **Sports:** There are 7 intercollegiate sports for men and 10 for women, and 7 intramural sports for men and 7 for women. Facilities include baseball and soccer fields and a recreational complex with a swimming pool and basketball and tennis courts. **Graduates:** From July 1, 2013 to June 30, 2014, 1376 bachelor's degrees were awarded. The most popular majors were nursing (23%), biology (premedical) (15%), and business administration (10%). In an average class, 5% graduate in 3 years or less, 32% graduate in 4 years or less, 43% graduate in 5 years or less, and 46% graduate in 6 years or less.

SERVICES: Counseling and information services are available, as is tutoring in some subjects, science, math, and writing. **Library/Resources:** The 5 libraries contain 823,797 volumes, 2.3 million microform items, 62,388 audio/video tapes/CDs/DVDs, and subscribe to 50,033 periodicals including electronic. Computerized library services include interlibrary loans, database searching, Internet access, and Wi-Fi capability. Special learning facilities include an art gallery, radio station, including a center of excellence for coral reef ecosystems science, dryland training. Palm Beach student educational center, nursing simulation labs, the Huizenga Sales Institute, neuro immune medicine clinic, health professions division museum, hall of fame, performing arts center, oceanographic center, law center, family village center, and Preschool. **Physically Challenged Students:** All of the campus is accessible. Facilities include wheelchair ramps, elevators, special parking, specially equipped restrooms, special class scheduling, lowered drinking fountains, and special housing. **Special:** NSU offers internships, study abroad, work-study, accelerated degree programs, nondegree study, Washington Semester, Undergraduate Honors Program, and undergraduate research experience. Combined bachelor-professional degree programs and a dual admission program are also available. There are 9 national honor societies and a freshman honors program. **Visiting:** There are regularly scheduled orientations for prospective students. There are guides for informal visits and visitors may sit in on classes. **Campus Safety and Security:** Measures include 24-hour foot and vehicle patrol, emergency notification system, and security escort services. There are shuttle buses, emergency telephones, lighted pathways/sidewalks, and controlled access to dorms/residences.

REQUIREMENTS: The SAT or ACT is required. Applicants must be graduates of an accredited secondary school or have a GED certificate. An interview is recommended. AP and CLEP credits are accepted. Important factors in the admissions decision are advanced placement or honors courses, leadership record, evidence of special talent, and extracurricular activities record.To graduate, all students must complete at least 120 credit hours, at least 30 of the credits must be earned at NSU and at least 50% of the credits in the major area must be earned at NSU. A minimum 2.25 GPA is needed for courses in the major, and a 2.0 for all other courses. **Procedure:** Freshmen are admitted to all sessions. Entrance exams should be taken exams must be received by 7/15/15 for the fall-term. There are deferred admissions and rolling admissions plans. Application deadlines are open. Application fee is $50. Notification is sent on a rolling basis. Applications are accepted on-line. **Transfer Students:** 731 transfer students enrolled in 2013-2014. Students transfering in good standing with AA or 60 credits from SACS accredited college are accepted and guaranteed junior standing. 30 of 120 credits required for the bachelor's degree must be completed at NSU. **International Students:** There are 288 international students enrolled. The school actively recruits these students. They must take the TOEFL with a minimum score of 550 on the paper-based TOEFL (PBT) or 79 on the Internet-based version (iBT) or take the MELAB, the Comprehensive English Language Test, and the college's own test, or take the IELTS, or the PTE-Academic.

ADMISSIONS: 49% of the 2014-2015 applicants were accepted. The

SAT scores for the 2014-2015 freshman class were: Critical Reading--20% below 500, 47% between 500 and 599, 29% between 600 and 699, and 3% between 700 and 800; Math--22% below 500, 39% between 500 and 599, 32% between 600 and 699, and 6% between 700 and 800. The ACT scores were 8% below 21, 29% between 21 and 23, 21% between 24 and 26, 11% between 27 and 28, and 32% above 28. 57% of the current freshmen were in the top fifth of their class; 81% were in the top two fifths. 8 freshmen graduated first in their class. **Admissions Contact:** Maria Dillard, Undergraduate Admissions. E-Mail: *admissions@nova.edu* Web: *www.nova.edu*

FINANCIAL AID: Check with the school for current application deadlines.

PALM BEACH ATLANTIC UNIVERSITY — E-5
www.pba.edu

West Palm Beach, FL 33416	(561) 803-2101
	(888) GO TO PBA
Fax: (561) 803-2115	Email: admissions_admissions@pba.edu
Full-time: 811 men, 1613 women	**Faculty:** 130
Part-time: 259 men, 338 women	**Ph.D.s:** 80%
Graduate: 299 men, 545 women	**Student/Faculty:** 15 to 1
Year: semesters, summer session	**Tuition:** $26,274
Room & Board: $8600	**Freshman Class:** 1802 applied, 1270 accepted, 524 enrolled
SAT CR/M/W: 530/550/525 **ACT:** 26	**CEEB CODE:** 5553
Application Deadline: n/av	**COMPETITIVE+**

Founded in 1968, PBA is an interdenominational Christian university with some 48 undergraduate majors (including nursing). Graduate degrees in business, leadership, counseling psychology, divinity, pharmacy, and nursing practice are offered. PBA is an ideal place to grow and explore your faith with young people of many races, nationalities, and creeds. There are 9 undergraduate schools and 4 graduate schools. In addition to regional accreditation, PBA has baccalaureate program accreditation with ACPE and NASM. The 106-acre campus is in an urban area 60 miles north of Miami, 180 miles south of Orlando. Including any residence halls, there are 48 buildings.

STUDENT LIFE: 64% of undergraduates are from Florida. Others are from 47 states, 43 foreign countries, and Canada. 62% are White; 16% Hispanic; 12% African American. 12% are Catholic. **Male To Female Ratio:** 1.8:1. The average age of freshmen is 18; all undergraduates, 23. 26% do not continue beyond their first year; 55% remain to graduate. **Housing:** 1237 students can be accommodated in college housing, which includes single-sex and coed dorms and on-campus apartments. In addition, there are honors houses and special-interest houses. On-campus housing is available on a first-come and first-served basis. 54% of students commute. Alcohol is not permitted. All students may keep cars.

FACULTY/CLASSROOMS: 52% of faculty are male; 48% are female. 85% teach undergraduates. No introductory courses are taught by graduate students. The average class size in an introductory lecture is 19; in a laboratory is 17; and in a regular course is 18.

PROGRAMS OF STUDY: PBA confers B.A., B.S., B.G.S., B.Mus. and B.S.N. degrees. Associate, Master's, and Doctoral degrees are also awarded. Bachelor's degrees are awarded in BIOLOGICAL SCIENCE (biology/biological science), BUSINESS (banking and finance, business administration and management, international business management, management science, marketing management, and organizational leadership and management), COMMUNICATIONS AND THE ARTS (art, communications, dance, English, film arts, graphic design, journalism, music, music performance, music theory and composition, musical theater, piano/organ, theater design, and voice), COMPUTER AND PHYSICAL SCIENCE (chemistry, computer science, and mathematics), EDUCATION (art education, athletic training, elementary education, English education, mathematics education, music education, physical education, science education, and secondary education), HEALTH PROFESSIONS (exercise science and nursing), SOCIAL SCIENCE (biblical studies, crosscultural studies, history, interdisciplinary studies, liberal arts/general studies,

ministries, philosophy, political science/government, prelaw, and psychology). English, biology, and medicinal and biological chemistry are the strongest academically. Business, phamacy, and psychology have the largest enrollments.

ACTIVITIES: There are no fraternities or sororities. There are 39 groups on campus, including and music ensembles, campus ministries, concert band, international organizations, Army ROTC, art, band, choir, chorale, chorus, communications, computers, dance, drama, environmental, ethnic, film, honors, international, jazz band, literary magazine, musical theater, newspaper, orchestra, pep band, photography, political, professional, radio and TV, religious, social, social service, student government, and symphony. Popular campus events include American Free Enterprise Day and Christival. **Sports:** There are 5 intercollegiate sports for men and 7 for women, and 8 intramural sports for men and 8 for women. Facilities include 65,000 square foot facility known as the Greene Complex for Sports and Recreation. The Greene complex houses the Rubin Arena, locker rooms, athletic training facility, fitness center, and recreational space for both its varsity and club level sports programs. Currently, Rinker Athletic Complex which will house all of PBA's outside sports including baseball, softball, tennis and soccer. **Graduates:** From July 1, 2013 to June 30, 2014, 482 bachelor's degrees were awarded. The most popular majors were business/marketing (31%), ministry (11%), and music and fine arts (10%). In an average class, 43% graduate in 4 years or less, 53% graduate in 5 years or less, and 55% graduate in 6 years or less.

SERVICES: Counseling and information services are available, as is tutoring in most subjects. There is a reader service for the blind, and remedial math and writing. Center for Writing Excellence **Library/Resources:** The library contains 265,143 volumes, 79,094 microform items, 6,254 audio/video tapes/CDs/DVDs, and subscribes to 32,000 periodicals including electronic. Computerized library services include interlibrary loans, database searching, Internet access, and Wi-Fi capability. Special learning facilities include an art gallery, radio station, center for writing excellence (writing assistance); student success center (peer tutoring, first year experience, and ADA accomodations). **Physically Challenged Students:** 60% of the campus is accessible. Facilities include wheelchair ramps, elevators, special parking, specially equipped restrooms, and special class scheduling. **Special:** PBA offers work-study, internships, a student-designed interdisciplinary major, accelerated degree programs in organizational management (evening program only) and ministry, a London semester, study abroad through the Coalition of Christian Colleges and Universities, and teacher certification. There are 13 national honor societies, a freshman honors program, and 1 departmental honors program. **Visiting:** There are regularly scheduled orientations for prospective students, including a general open house and a school-specific open house. There are guides for informal visits, visitors may sit in on classes, and stay overnight. To schedule a visit, contact the Admissions Office at (561) 803-2100. **Campus Safety and Security:** Measures include 24-hour foot and vehicle patrol, emergency notification system, self-defense education, and security escort services. There are emergency telephones, lighted pathways/sidewalks, controlled access to dorms/residences, closed circuit television system.

REQUIREMENTS: The SAT or ACT is required. Applicants must be graduates of an accredited secondary school or have a GED certificate, and have completed 18 academic credits: 4 in English, 3 in math, science, 2 in a foreign language, and 5 in electives. An essay and an interview are required. A portfolio is recommended for art students. A GPA of 2.0 is required. AP and CLEP credits are accepted. Important factors in the admissions decision are advanced placement or honors courses, leadership record, and personality/intangible qualities.Students must complete general education requirements and a minimum of 120 credit hours. Students must complete 42 credit hours in courses numbered 3000 or above (Bachelor of Music students, 33 hours). The last 32 credit hours must be completed at PBA and a minimum 2.0 GPA is required. **Procedure:** Freshmen are admitted to all sessions. Entrance exams should be taken in the junior year of high school. There are deferred admissions and rolling admissions plans. Application deadlines are open. Application fee is $50. Notifications are sent September 1. Applications are accepted on-line. **Transfer Students:** 344 transfer students enrolled in 2013-2014.

Transfer students must have a minimum 2.5 GPA on at least 12 semester hours, 300-500 word essay, and 2 letters of recommendation. An interview is required. 32 of 120 credits required for the bachelor's degree must be completed at PBA. **International Students:** There are 112 international students enrolled. The school actively recruits these students. They must take the TOEFL with a minimum score of 79 on the Internet-based version (iBT). They must also take the SAT or ACT.

ADMISSIONS: 70% of the 2014-2015 applicants were accepted. The SAT scores for the 2014-2015 freshman class were: Critical Reading--41% below 500, 33% between 500 and 599, 25% between 600 and 699, and 2% between 700 and 800; Math--43% below 500, 39% between 500 and 599, 16% between 600 and 699, and 3% between 700 and 800; Writing--43% below 500, 38% between 500 and 599, 18% between 600 and 699, and 2% between 700 and 800. The ACT scores were 4% below 21, 32% between 21 and 23, 24% between 24 and 26, 18% between 27 and 28, and 22% above 28. **Admissions Contact:** Jamie Zugelder, Director of Admissions. E-Mail: *admissions_admissions@pba.edu* Web: *www.pba.edu*

FINANCIAL AID: In 2014-2015, 100% of all full-time freshmen and 100% of continuing full-time students received some form of financial aid. 73% of all full-time freshmen and 74% of continuing full-time students received need-based aid. The average freshman award was $19,439. Need-based scholarships or need-based grants averaged $17,244 ($10,760 maximum); need-based self-help aid (loans and jobs) averaged $3,229 ($8,500 maximum); non-need-based athletic scholarships averaged $10,455 ($36,726 maximum); and other non-need-based awards and non-need-based scholarships averaged $1,846 ($26,700 maximum). 13% of undergraduate students work part-time. Average annual earnings from campus work are $2600. The average financial indebtedness of the 2014 graduate was $27,374. The FAFSA and the state aid form are required. The priority date for freshman financial aid applications for fall entry is May 1.

RINGLING COLLEGE OF ART AND DESIGN (*The complete profile is made available exclusively on our website, www.barronspac.com*)

ROLLINS COLLEGE	D-3
www.rollins.edu	

Winter Park, FL 32789	(407) 691-2573
Fax: 407-646-2351	Email: ir@rollins.edu
Full-time: 765 men, 1119 women	Faculty: IIA, av$
Part-time: n/av	Ph.D.s: 90%
Graduate: 262 men, 313 women	Student/Faculty: 10 to 1
Year: semesters	Tuition: $39,900
Room & Board: $12,470	Freshman Class: 4542 applied, 2533 accepted, 518 enrolled
	CEEB CODE: 5572
Application Deadline: February 15	HIGHLY COMPETITIVE

Founded through innovation, focused on excellence, fueled by dedication to pragmatic liberal arts - Rollins College has transformed lives by educating responsible, global citizens since 1885. Rollins provides small-town community and proximity to neighboring Orlando, a premier international destination. Beneath Spanish moss and inside the arched doorways of Spanish Mediterranean buildings, students experience small classes led by faculty nationally recognized for innovative teaching and scholarship. Figures in the above capsule and in this profile are approximate. There are 2 graduate schools. In addition to regional accreditation, Rollins has baccalaureate program accreditation with AACSB and NASM. The 80-acre campus is in a suburban area 5 miles north of Orlando.

STUDENT LIFE: 54% of undergraduates are from Florida. Others are from 42 states, 49 foreign countries, and Canada. 54% are from public schools. 69% are White; 13% Hispanic. **Male To Female Ratio:** 1.4:1. The average age of freshmen is 18; all undergraduates, 20. 16% do not continue beyond their first year; 62% remain to graduate. **Housing:** 1264 students can be accommodated in college housing, which includes single-sex and coed dorms and on-campus apart-

ments. In addition, there are honors houses, special-interest houses, fraternity houses, and sorority houses. On-campus housing is guaranteed for the freshman year only. 68% of students live on campus. Upperclassmen may keep cars.

FACULTY/CLASSROOMS: 57% of faculty are male; 43% are female. No introductory courses are taught by graduate students.

PROGRAMS OF STUDY: Rollins confers A.B. degrees. Master's degrees are also awarded. Bachelor's degrees are awarded in BIOLOGICAL SCIENCE (biochemistry, biology/biological science, and marine biology), BUSINESS (international business management and organizational behavior), COMMUNICATIONS AND THE ARTS (art history and appreciation, communications, dramatic arts, English, French, media arts, music, music performance, Spanish, studio art, and theatre arts), COMPUTER AND PHYSICAL SCIENCE (chemistry, computer science, mathematics, and physics), EDUCATION (elementary education), ENGINEERING AND ENVIRONMENTAL DESIGN (environmental science), SOCIAL SCIENCE (anthropology, Asian/Oriental studies, classical/ancient civilization, crosscultural studies, economics, history, humanities, international relations, Latin American studies, philosophy, political science/government, psychology, religion, and sociology). International business, psychology, and economics have the largest enrollments.

ACTIVITIES: 29% of men belong to 1 local and 4 national fraternities; 35% of women belong to 1 local and 6 national sororities. There are 121 groups on campus, including art, band, cheerleading, chess, choir, chorale, chorus, computers, dance, debate, drama, drum and bugle corps, environmental, ethnic, film, gay, honors, international, jazz band, literary magazine, musical theater, newspaper, orchestra, pep band, photography, political, professional, radio and TV, religious, social, social service, student government, symphony, and yearbook. Popular campus events include WPRK 91.5 Marathon, Civic Engagement Week and Sexual Assault Awareness Week. **Sports:** There are 11 intercollegiate sports for men and 12 for women, and 9 intramural sports for men and 10 for women. Facilities include a 2500-seat auditorium, a 600-seat stadium, tennis courts, baseball and soccer fields, a field house with a gym that seats 2500, a weight room, a boat house, and a swimming pool. **Graduates:** From July 1, 2013 to June 30, 2014, 389 bachelor's degrees were awarded. The most popular majors were economics (12%), psychology (10%), and English (8%). In an average class, 62% graduate in 4 years or less, 70% graduate in 5 years or less, and 71% graduate in 6 years or less.

SERVICES: Counseling and information services are available, as is tutoring in every subject. There is a reader service for the blind, and remedial math, reading, and writing. **Library/Resources:** The library contains 366,684 volumes, and 494 microform items. Computerized library services include interlibrary loans, database searching, Internet access, and Wi-Fi capability. Special learning facilities include an art gallery, radio station, TV station, an art museum, theaters, writing center, and student resource center. **Physically Challenged Students:** 80% of the campus is accessible. Facilities include wheelchair ramps, elevators, special parking, specially equipped restrooms, special class scheduling, lowered drinking fountains, lowered telephones, and special housing. **Special:** Rollins offers cross-registration with the evening studies division, co-op programs with American University in Washington, D.C., and Duke University School of Forestry and Environmental Studies. Departmental and professional internships, study abroad in 9 countries, and a Washington semester are also options. Also available are an accelerated (3-2) MBA program, a B.A.-B.S. degree in preengineering with Washington University (St. Louis), Auburn, and Columbia Universities, an interdepartmental biochemistry/molecular biology major, dual majors in any combination, and student-designed majors. Nondegree study and pass/fail options are possible. There are 5 national honor societies, a freshman honors program, and 30 departmental honors programs. **Visiting:** There are regularly scheduled orientations for prospective students, Fall Open House . There are guides for informal visits and visitors may sit in on classes. To schedule a visit, contact The Office of Admissions. **Campus Safety and Security:** Measures include 24-hour foot and vehicle patrol, emergency notification system, self-defense education, and security escort services. There are shuttle buses, emergency telephones, lighted pathways/sidewalks, controlled access to dorms/residences, 24-hour locked residential units.

REQUIREMENTS: Applicants must be graduates of an accredited secondary school or have a GED certificate and have completed 4 years of English, 3 of math, and 2 each of foreign language, science, and social studies. An essay is required. SAT Subject tests in writing, math, and foreign language and an interview are recommended. AP and CLEP credits are accepted. Important factors in the admissions decision are advanced placement or honors courses, evidence of special talent, and extracurricular activities record. Students must complete a minimum of 140 semester hours of academic work, of which at least sixty-four (64) semester hours must be outside a single departmental prefix. All students must complete a minimum of sixteen (16) semester hours that are not used to meet either a general education curriculum or major requirement. Students must earn a minimum academic average of a 2.00 ('C') for all courses taken at Rollins and achieve a minimum academic average of a 2.00 ('C') for all courses taken to fulfill major requirements. **Procedure:** Freshmen are admitted fall and spring. Entrance exams should be taken by the first semester of the senior year. There are early decision and deferred admissions plans. Early decision applications should be filed by November 15; regular applications, by February 15 for fall entry; and November 1 for spring entry. The fall 2014 application fee was $40. Notification of early decision is sent December 15; regular decision, April 1. 200 early decision candidates were accepted for the 2014-2015 class. 188 applicants were on the 2014 waiting list; 13 were admitted. Applications are accepted on-line. **Transfer Students:** 62 transfer students enrolled in 2013-2014. Transfer students must satisfy all regular admission requirements and submit official transcripts of college and high school work and SAT or ACT scores. A recommended 3.0 GPA and a year's worth of credit hours earned are required. An interview is recommended. 64 of 140 credits required for the bachelor's degree must be completed at Rollins. **International Students:** There are 101 international students enrolled. The school actively recruits these students. They must take the TOEFL with a minimum score of 550 on the paper-based TOEFL (PBT) or 80 on the Internet-based version (iBT). They must also take the SAT or ACT.

ADMISSIONS: 56% of the 2014-2015 applicants were accepted. The SAT scores for the 2014-2015 freshman class were: Critical Reading--5% below 500, 46% between 500 and 599, 41% between 600 and 699, and 9% between 700 and 800; Math--7% below 500, 39% between 500 and 599, 43% between 600 and 699, and 9% between 700 and 800; Writing--9% below 500, 46% between 500 and 599, 35% between 600 and 699, and 9% between 700 and 800. **Admissions Contact:** Udeth Lugo, Director of Institutional Research. E-Mail: *ir@rollins.edu* Web: *www.rollins.edu*

FINANCIAL AID: In 2014-2015, 77% of all full-time freshmen and 83% of continuing full-time students received some form of financial aid. 54% of all full-time freshmen and 62% of continuing full-time students received need-based aid. The average freshman award was $29,800.. The average financial indebtedness of the 2014 graduate was $24,096. Rollins is a member of CSS. The FAFSA and the college's own financial statement are required. The priority date for freshman financial aid applications for fall entry is March 1.

SAINT LEO UNIVERSITY   **D-3**
www.saintleo.edu

Saint Leo, FL 33574	**(352) 588-8283**
	(800) 334-5532
Fax: (352) 588-8257	Email: admission@saintleo.edu
Full-time: 1040 men, 1153 women	Faculty: 121
Part-time: 53 men, 44 women	Ph.D.s: 85%
Graduate: 1552 men, 2216 women	Student/Faculty: 18 to 1
Year: semesters, summer session	Tuition: $20,420
Room & Board: $9920	Freshman Class: 3490 applied, 2511 accepted, 617 enrolled
SAT CR/M/W: 510/500/480 ACT: 22	CEEB CODE: 5638
Application Deadline: n/av	COMPETITIVE

Saint Leo University was founded in 1889. Undergraduate students benefit from a rewarding, values-based education that integrates caring faculty, state-of-the-art technology and active learning as they choose from more than 50 outstanding academic programs and endorsements. There are 3 undergraduate schools and 5 graduate schools. In addition to regional accreditation, Saint Leo has baccalaureate program accreditation with ACBSP and CSWE. The 297-acre campus is in a rural area 40 miles north of Tampa. Including any residence halls, there are 34 buildings.

STUDENT LIFE: 72% of undergraduates are from Florida. Others are from 45 states, 61 foreign countries, and Canada. 77% are from public schools. 46% are White; 17% Hispanic; 13% African American; 13% Foreign. 43% claim no religious affiliation; 30% Catholic; 20% Protestant. **Male To Female Ratio:** 1.3:1. The average age of freshmen is 19; all undergraduates, 21. 32% do not continue beyond their first year; 40% remain to graduate. **Housing:** 1582 students can be accommodated in college housing, which includes single-sex and coed dorms, on-campus apartments, and off-campus apartments. On-campus housing is guaranteed for all 4 years. 63% of students live on campus; of those, 85% remain on campus on weekends. All students may keep cars.

FACULTY/CLASSROOMS: 54% of faculty are male; 46% are female. All teach undergraduates. No introductory courses are taught by graduate students. The average class size in a laboratory is 14 and in a regular course is 19.

PROGRAMS OF STUDY: Saint Leo confers B.A., B.S., B.A.S. and B.S.W. degrees. Associate, Master's, and Doctoral degrees are also awarded. Bachelor's degrees are awarded in BIOLOGICAL SCIENCE (biology/biological science), BUSINESS (accounting, business administration and management, business communications, hospitality management services, human resources, management science, marketing management, and sports management), COMMUNICATIONS AND THE ARTS (English and multimedia), COMPUTER AND PHYSICAL SCIENCE (information sciences and systems and mathematics), EDUCATION (education services, elementary education, global studies, middle school education, and secondary education), HEALTH PROFESSIONS (health care administration and medical technology), SOCIAL SCIENCE (criminal justice, economics, history, human services, liberal arts/general studies, political science/government, psychology, religion, social work, and sociology). Accounting, biology, and education are the strongest academically. Criminal justice, biology, and sport business have the largest enrollments.

ACTIVITIES: 13% of men belong to 2 local and 4 national fraternities; 21% of women belong to 1 local and 5 national sororities. There are 80 groups on campus, including and Caribbean Student Association, the Quest, Campus Activities Board, cheerleading, chorus, computers, drama, environmental, ethnic, honors, international, literary magazine, musical theater, newspaper, political, professional, radio and TV, religious, social, social service, student government, and yearbook. Popular campus events include Spring Fling, Winter Formal, Family Fall Festival, and Halloween Horror Nights Trip. **Sports:** There are 8 intercollegiate sports for men and 9 for women, and 10 intramural sports for men and 10 for women. Facilities include a 1500-seat indoor gym, fitness center, an outdoor swimming pool, golf course, soccer, softball, baseball, and practice fields, basketball, volleyball, racquetball, and lighted tennis courts, turf field, sailing, and canoeing. **Graduates:** From July 1, 2013 to June 30, 2014, 360 bachelor's degrees were awarded. The most popular majors were criminal justice (14%), sport business (11%), and psychology (9%). 67 companies recruited on campus in 2013-2014. In an average class, 27% graduate in 4 years or less, 38% graduate in 5 years or less, and 40% graduate in 6 years or less.

SERVICES: Counseling and information services are available, as is tutoring in most subjects. There is a reader service for the blind, and remedial math and writing. **Library/Resources:** The library contains 507,125 volumes, 26,288 microform items, 778 audio/video tapes/CDs/DVDs, and subscribes to 104,521 periodicals including electronic. Computerized library services include interlibrary loans, database searching, Internet access, and Wi-Fi capability. Special learning facilities include an art gallery, radio station, and TV station. **Physically Challenged Students:** 95% of the campus is accessible. Facilities include wheelchair ramps, elevators, special parking, specially equipped restrooms, lowered drinking fountains, special housing. Students with disabilities are available on a case-by-case basis with proper documentation. **Special:** Saint Leo offers internships in most majors, study abroad in 11 countries, work-study programs on campus, dual majors, and credit for military experience. There is a prelaw program, preprofessional programs in medicine, dentistry, and veterinary science, learning enhancement for academic progress, and Air Force and Army ROTC programs. Saint Leo also offers articulation agreements with Nova Southeastern University (osteopathy, dental, pharmacy, and nursing), University of St. Augustine for Health Sciences (occupational and physical therapy), Life Chiropractic School, and an affiliation agreement with Bayfront Medical Center (St. Petersburg). There are 19 national honor societies, a freshman honors program, and 1 departmental honors program. **Visiting:** There are regularly scheduled orientations for prospective students, consisting of overnight campus visitation programs. There are guides for informal visits, visitors may sit in on classes, and stay overnight. To schedule a visit, contact the Office of Admission at (352) 334-5532. **Campus Safety and Security:** Measures include 24-hour foot and vehicle patrol, emergency notification system, and security escort services. There are shuttle buses, emergency telephones, lighted pathways/sidewalks, and controlled access to dorms/residences.

REQUIREMENTS: The SAT or ACT is recommended. Applicants for regular admission status are recommended to have successfully completed the following high school courses by the time they enroll at Saint Leo University: English (4 years), Mathematics and History/Social Science (3 years each), Science, Foreign Language, and Electives (2 years each). Students must submit an application, official high school transcript, letter of recommendation from a high school guidance counselor or teacher, essay or graded writing sample, and standardized test scores if not applying as test optional. Students who do not meet the minimum regular admission requirements but who exhibit potential for academic success may be eligible for admission to our LEAP program. AP and CLEP credits are accepted. Important factors in the admissions decision are advanced placement or honors courses, leadership record, and recommendations by school officials. To graduate, all students must complete a minimum of 120 academic credits with 30 to 60 hours in the major, all the requirements of their division and major, and 42 hours in the University Explorations program. The honors program may be substituted for general education requirements. A minimum 2.0 GPA and capstone course are required, and there is a 30-hour residency requirement. **Procedure:** Freshmen are admitted fall and spring. Entrance exams should be taken March 1. There are deferred admissions and rolling admissions plans. Application deadlines are open. Application fee is $40. Notification is sent on a rolling basis. Applications are accepted on-line. Application fees are waived if application is completed on-line. **Transfer Students:** 155 transfer students enrolled in 2013-2014. Applicants for transfer admission must have a minimum cumulative college GPA of 2.5. Students are classified according to the number of credits earned at their previous institution(s): Freshman (fewer than 30 credits), Sophomore (at least 30 and fewer than 60 credits), Junior (at least 60 and fewer than 90 credits), and Senior (at least 90 credits). Transfer applicants must submit an application along with an official college transcript from each institution attended, a recommendation from the Dean of Students or equivalent, and an essay or graded writing sample. 30 of 120 credits required for the bachelor's degree must be completed at Saint Leo. **International Students:** There are 282 international students enrolled. The school actively recruits these students. They must take the TOEFL with a minimum score of 547 on the paper-based TOEFL (PBT) or 78 on the Internet-based version (iBT), SAT Verbal (minimum score 450 required) or IELTS (minimum score 6 required) may be substituted for TOEFL.

ADMISSIONS: 72% of the 2014-2015 applicants were accepted. The SAT scores for the 2014-2015 freshman class were: Critical Reading--40% below 500, 50% between 500 and 599, 9% between 600 and 699, and 1% between 700 and 800; Math--45% below 500, 42% between 500 and 599, 12% between 600 and 699, and 1% between 700 and 800; Writing--58% below 500, 37% between 500 and 599, 4% between 600 and 699, and 1% between 700 and 800. The ACT scores were 28% below 21, 33% between 21 and 23, 27% between 24 and 26, 9% between 27 and 28, and 3% above 28. 17% of the current freshmen were in the top fifth of their class; 39% were in the top two fifths. 4 freshmen graduated first in their class. **Admissions Contact:** Peter Littlefield, Director of Undergraduate Admission. E-Mail: *admission@saintleo.edu* Web: *www.saintleo.edu*

FINANCIAL AID: In 2014-2015, 100% of all full-time freshmen and 91% of continuing full-time students received some form of financial aid. 90% of all full-time freshmen and 87% of continuing full-time students received need-based aid. The average freshman award was $22,191. Need-based scholarships or need-based grants averaged $4,842 ($22,730 maximum); need-based self-help aid (loans and jobs) averaged $4,500 ($7,000 maximum); non-need-based athletic scholarships averaged $11,265 ($30,000 maximum); and other non-need-based awards and non-need-based scholarships averaged $8,737 ($30,180 maximum). 26% of undergraduate students work part-time. Average annual earnings from campus work are $2480. The average financial indebtedness of the 2014 graduate was $12,280. Saint Leo is a member of CSS. The FAFSA is required. The priority date for freshman financial aid applications for fall entry is March 1.

SOUTHEASTERN UNIVERSITY D-3
www.seuniversity.edu

Lakeland, FL 33801	(863) 667-5018
	(800) 500-8760
Fax: (863) 667-5200	Email: admission@seuniversity.edu
Full-time: 896 men, 1210 women	Faculty: 93; IIB, -$
Part-time: 184 men, 158 women	Ph.D.s: 67%
Graduate: 106 men, 149 women	Student/Faculty: 22 to 1
Year: semesters, summer session	Tuition: $18,596
Room & Board: $8605	Freshman Class: 1442 applied, 707 accepted, 592 enrolled
SAT CR/M/W: 509/487/494 ACT: 21	CEEB CODE: 5621
Application Deadline: n/av	COMPETITIVE

Southeastern University, founded in 1935, is a Christian liberal arts institution offering 43 degree programs that equip students to serve in both professional careers and ministry-related fields. The figures in the above capsule and in this profile are approximate. There are 5 undergraduate schools and 4 graduate schools. The 88-acre campus is in a suburban area 30 miles east of Tampa and 45 miles west of Orlando. Including any residence halls, there are 30 buildings.

STUDENT LIFE: 65% of undergraduates are from Florida. Others are from 47 states, 21 foreign countries, and Canada. 67% are White; 13% Hispanic. 99% are Protestant. **Male To Female Ratio:** 1.3:1. The average age of freshmen is 20; all undergraduates, 23. 36% do not continue beyond their first year; 39% remain to graduate. **Housing:** 1355 students can be accommodated in college housing, which includes single-sex dorms and on-campus apartments. On-campus housing is available on a first-come and first-served basis. 51% of students live on campus; of those, 60% remain on campus on weekends. Alcohol is not permitted. All students may keep cars.

FACULTY/CLASSROOMS: 66% of faculty are male; 34% are female. All teach undergraduates. No introductory courses are taught by graduate students. The average class size in an introductory lecture is 60; in a laboratory is 20; and in a regular course is 32.

PROGRAMS OF STUDY: Southeastern confers B.A., B.S., B.M. and B.S.W. degrees. Associate, Master's, and Doctoral degrees are also awarded. Bachelor's degrees are awarded in BIOLOGICAL SCIENCE (biology/biological science), BUSINESS (accounting, banking and finance, business administration and management, management information systems, marketing/retailing/merchandising, and sports management), COMMUNICATIONS AND THE ARTS (broadcasting, communications, dramatic arts, English, journalism, music, and public relations), COMPUTER AND PHYSICAL SCIENCE (mathematics), EDUCATION (education of the exceptional child, elementary education, middle school education, music education, and secondary education), SOCIAL SCIENCE (biblical studies, criminal justice, history, interdisciplinary studies, ministries, pastoral studies, psychology, public administration, religion, religious music, and social work). Religion, education, and business are the strongest academically. Religion and business have the largest enrollments.

ACTIVITIES: There are no fraternities or sororities. There are 30 groups on campus, including band, cheerleading, choir, chorale, chorus, communications, computers, drama, ethnic, honors, international, jazz band, musical theater, newspaper, opera, orchestra, political, professional, radio and TV, religious, social, social service, student government, symphony, and yearbook. <u>Sports:</u> There are 6 intercollegiate sports for men and 7 for women, and 8 intramural sports for men and 8 for women. Facilities include a gym, baseball and soccer fields, tennis, racquetball, and beach volleyball courts, a weight room, and intramural fields.

<u>SERVICES:</u> Counseling and information services are available, as is tutoring in most subjects, Science, English, Math, Religion, History, Music, Communication There is remedial math, reading, and writing. <u>Library/Resources:</u> The 2 libraries contain 131,072 volumes, 2,163 microform items, and 8,046 audio/video tapes/CDs/DVDs, and subscribe to 1,223 periodicals including electronic. Computerized library services include interlibrary loans, database searching, and Internet access. Special learning facilities include a radio station, TV station, Pentecostal Research Library. <u>Physically Challenged Students:</u> 90% of the campus is accessible. Facilities include wheelchair ramps, elevators, special parking, specially equipped restrooms, special class scheduling, and lowered drinking fountains. <u>Special:</u> Internships are available in communications, education, ministry, psychology, pastoral studies, Christian education, and business. There are accelerated degree programs in church leadership and in business and professional leadership, study abroad in 7 countries, and a Washington semester. There are 2 national honor societies, a freshman honors program, and 2 departmental honors programs. <u>Visiting:</u> There are regularly scheduled orientations for prospective students, Preview Days (fall and spring), which consist of a 24-hour overview of campus life with class visits, faculty reception, admission/financial aid workshops, student panel discussion, and a worship service. There are guides for informal visits, visitors may sit in on classes, and stay overnight. To schedule a visit, contact the Admission Office. <u>Campus Safety and Security:</u> Measures include 24-hour foot and vehicle patrol, emergency notification system, and security escort services. There are emergency telephones, lighted pathways/sidewalks, controlled access to dorms/residences, and a main entrance security booth attendant.

<u>REQUIREMENTS:</u> The SAT or ACT is required. The GED is accepted. A GPA of 1.5 is required. AP and CLEP credits are accepted. Important factors in the admissions decision are extracurricular activities record, recommendations by school officials, and personality/intangible qualities.Every degree student must complete 125 to 130 hours, including 36 hours of general education and up to 20 hours of religion (transfer students may have fewer required, based on transfer hours). Distribution requirements include 6 to 12 hours each in arts and communications, human adjustment, science and math, social sciences, and humanities and fine arts. A minimum GPA of 2.0 must be maintained. <u>Procedure:</u> Freshmen are admitted to all sessions. Entrance exams should be taken prior to enrollment. There is a rolling admissions plan. Check with the school for current application deadlines. The application fee is $40. Applications are accepted on-line. <u>Transfer Students:</u> 257 transfer students enrolled in 2013-2014. Admission requirements for transfer applicants are the same as for first-time students. 30 of 124 credits required for the bachelor's degree must be completed at Southeastern. <u>International Students:</u> The school actively recruits these students. They must take the TOEFL. They must also take the SAT or ACT.

<u>ADMISSIONS:</u> 49% of the 2014-2015 applicants were accepted. The SAT scores for the 2014-2015 freshman class were: Critical Reading--45% below 500, 39% between 500 and 599, 15% between 600 and 699, and 2% between 700 and 800; Math--53% below 500, 35% between 500 and 599, 12% between 600 and 699, and 1% between 700 and 800; Writing--52% below 500, 35% between 500 and 599, 12% between 600 and 699, and 2% between 700 and 800. The ACT scores were 50% below 21, 22% between 21 and 23, 18% between 24 and 26, 6% between 27 and 28, and 4% above 28. <u>Admissions Contact:</u> Omar Rashed, Director of Admissions. E-Mail: *admission@seuniversity.edu* Web: *www.seuniversity.edu*

<u>FINANCIAL AID:</u> The FAFSA and the college's own financial statement are required. Check with the school for current application deadlines.

ST. THOMAS UNIVERSITY *(The complete profile is made available exclusively on our website, www.barronspac.com)*

STATE UNIVERSITY SYSTEM OF FLORIDA

The State University System of Florida, established in 1906, is a public system in Florida. It is governed by a constitutional board of governors, whose chief administrator is the chancellor. The primary goal of the system is teaching, research, and public service. The main priorities are to improve the quality of undergraduate education, to solve critical state problems, to forge public-private partnerships, and to increase the efficiency of the system. The total student enrollment of all 12 campuses is usually about 335,000 with over 17,377 faculty members. Altogether there are 746 baccalaureate, 677 master's, and 292 doctoral programs offered in the State University System of Florida. 4-year campuses are located in Gainesville, Tallahassee, Tampa, Boca Raton, Pensacola, Orlando, Jacksonville, Miami, Fort Myers, and Sarasota. Profiles of the 4-year campuses are included in this section.

STETSON UNIVERSITY D-3
www.stetson.edu

DeLand, FL 32723	**(386) 822-7100**
	(800) 688-0101
Fax: (386) 822-7112	**Email: admissions@stetson.edu**
Full-time: 1188 men, 1616 women	**Faculty:** 208; IIA, ++$
Part-time: 18 men, 19 women	**Ph.D.s:** 94%
Graduate: 605 men, 691 women	**Student/Faculty:** 12 to 1
Year: semesters, summer session	**Tuition:** $40,040
Room & Board: $11,476	**Freshman Class:** 10986 applied, 6728 accepted, 773 enrolled
SAT CR/M/W: 590/580/570 **ACT:** 26	**CEEB CODE:** 5630
Application Deadline: March 15	**VERY COMPETITIVE**

Stetson University, is the oldest private university in the State of Florida. Located in DeLand with a second campus in Gulfport and two satellite centers -- one in Celebration and the other in Tampa -- Stetson indeed spans Central Florida from coast to coast. Founded in 1883 by Henry A. DeLand as the DeLand Academy and later renamed Stetson University to honor its benefactor, John B. Stetson, the university has a storied history of leadership, values and significance. The university is home to many Florida firsts, including the first collegiate newspaper, the first chapter of Phi Beta Kappa (the nation's oldest and most prestigious undergraduate honor society), the oldest schools of business administration and music and the first college of law. Stetson also was Florida's first private university to integrate. Stetson is about more than the buildings and those who helped build them; it's really about a vibrant, growing institution where students are prepared to lead lives of significance. The university is led by its ninth president, Wendy B. Libby and is home to 73 undergraduate academic programs in law, music, arts and sciences and business with graduate studies offered in business and education. Undergraduate leadership, research, social justice, advocacy and volunteer service, and participatory activities flourish at all four of the university's locations. Figures in the above capsule and in this profile are approximate. There are 3 undergraduate schools and 2 graduate schools. In addition to regional accreditation, Stetson has baccalaureate program accreditation with AACSB, NASM, and NCATE. The 155-acre campus is in a small town 35 miles north of Orlando and 25 miles west of Daytona Beach. Including any residence halls, there are 93 buildings.

<u>STUDENT LIFE:</u> 72% of undergraduates are from Florida. Others are from 42 states, 51 foreign countries, and Canada. 78% are from public schools. 64% are White; 14% Hispanic. 48% claim no religious affiliation; 25% Protestant; 18% Catholic. <u>Male To Female Ratio:</u> 1.3:1. The average age of freshmen is 18; all undergraduates, 20. 22% do not continue beyond their first year; 64% remain to graduate. <u>Housing:</u> 2005 students can be accommodated in college housing, which includes single-sex and coed dorms and on-campus apartments. In addition, there are honors houses, language houses, special-interest houses, fraternity houses, sorority houses, Family and Partnered housing, Gender-neutral housing, Pet-friendly options (pets allowed), Living-Learning Communities: First-Year Experience, Women's Leadership, Wellness, and Honors Houses. On-campus housing is guaranteed for all 4 years. 64% of students live on campus; of those, 80% remain on campus on weekends. All students may keep cars.

FACULTY/CLASSROOMS: 55% of faculty are male; 45% are female. All teach undergraduates. No introductory courses are taught by graduate students. The average class size in an introductory lecture is 20; in a laboratory is 17; and in a regular course is 18.

PROGRAMS OF STUDY: Stetson confers B.A., B.S., B.B.A., B.M. and B.M.E. degrees. Master's and doctoral degrees are also awarded. Bachelor's degrees are awarded in BIOLOGICAL SCIENCE (biochemistry, biology/biological science, marine biology, and molecular biology), BUSINESS (accounting, banking and finance, business administration and management, business economics, international business management, management information systems, marketing/retailing/merchandising, small business management, and sports management), COMMUNICATIONS AND THE ARTS (art history, communications, dramatic arts, English, French, German, guitar, music, music composition, music performance, music technology, music theory and composition, piano/organ, Spanish, studio art, voice, and winds), COMPUTER AND PHYSICAL SCIENCE (chemistry, computer science, digital arts/technology, mathematics, and physics), EDUCATION (elementary education, music education, secondary education, and social science education), ENGINEERING AND ENVIRONMENTAL DESIGN (environmental science), HEALTH PROFESSIONS (health science), SOCIAL SCIENCE (American studies, economics, geography, history, international studies, philosophy, political science/government, prelaw, psychology, religion, Russian and Slavic studies, social science, and sociology). Environmental science, biology, chemistry, finance, mathematics, computer science, creative writing and the arts, music, and education are the strongest academically. Psychology, business administration, and integrative health science have the largest enrollments.

ACTIVITIES: 27% of men belong to 7 national fraternities; 28% of women belong to 6 national sororities. There are 124 groups on campus, including band, cheerleading, chess, choir, chorus, computers, dance, drama, environmental, ethnic, gay, honors, international, jazz band, literary magazine, Model UN, musical theater, newspaper, opera, orchestra, pep band, political, professional, radio and TV, religious, social, social service, student government, symphony, and yearbook. Popular campus events include Undergraduate Research Showcase, Greenfeather Service Week, and Homecoming. **Sports:** There are 8 intercollegiate sports for men and 10 for women, and 19 intramural sports for men and 19 for women. Facilities include weightroom and exercise facilities, fieldhouse, basketball courts, volleyball courts, tennis courts, handball courts, softball fields, soccer fields, baseball fields, running trail, swimming pool. **Graduates:** From July 1, 2013 to June 30, 2014, 492 bachelor's degrees were awarded. The most popular majors were business (29%), visual/performing arts (10%), and social sciences (10%). 58 companies recruited on campus in 2013-2014. In an average class, 4% graduate in 3 years or less, 56% graduate in 4 years or less, 60% graduate in 5 years or less, and 61% graduate in 6 years or less. Of the 2013 graduating class, 27% were enrolled in graduate school within 6 months of graduation, and 46% were employed.

SERVICES: Counseling and information services are available, as is tutoring in most subjects. There is a reader service for the blind, and remedial writing. **Library/Resources:** The 3 libraries contain 473,418 volumes, 285,355 microform items, 19,281 audio/video tapes/CDs/DVDs, and subscribe to 117,905 periodicals including electronic. Computerized library services include interlibrary loans, database searching, Internet access, and Wi-Fi capability. Special learning facilities include an art gallery, radio station, a museum of minerals. **Physically Challenged Students:** 80% of the campus is accessible. Facilities include wheelchair ramps, elevators, special parking, specially equipped restrooms, special class scheduling, lowered drinking fountains, and lowered telephones. **Special:** Stetson's curriculum is designed to provide students with a high quality education that includes high-impact practices such as experiential learning, internships that are available to all students, and community engagement throughout the curriculum. Stetson offers interdisciplinary programs, including environmental studies, entrepreneurship, music education, and others. The 3+3 BA/JD program offers accelerated admission to the College of Law. In finance, the Roland George Investments Program gives students the experience of managing over $3.4 million in stocks and bonds. Through the David and Leighan

Rinker Center for International Learning, students study throughout the world, including Argentina, Cayman Islands, China, Spain, South Africa, India, United Kingdom, Australia, South Korea, Japan, Sweden, Russia, Italy, Taiwan, Vietnam, France, New Zealand, and a host of other nations. Students in Stetson University's Honors Program take a uniquely integrated curriculum, receive special funding for personal research and travel, may design their major and some courses, and work closely with their advisor to be especially competitive for national scholarships and fellowships. There are 27 national honor societies, including Phi Beta Kappa, and a freshman honors program. **Visiting:** There are regularly scheduled orientations for prospective students, consisting of a campus tour and orientation, interviews, class visits, and presentations. There are guides for informal visits, visitors may sit in on classes, and stay overnight. To schedule a visit, contact the Admissions Office at admissions@stetson.edu. **Campus Safety and Security:** Measures include 24-hour foot and vehicle patrol, emergency notification system, self-defense education, and security escort services. There are emergency telephones, lighted pathways/sidewalks, and controlled access to dorms/residences.

REQUIREMENTS: Applicants must be graduates of an accredited secondary school or have a GED, and have completed 4 years of English, 3 of math and science, and 2 each of foreign language, social sciences, and electives. Auditions are required for music students. A GPA of 2.0 is required. AP and CLEP credits are accepted. Important factors in the admissions decision are advanced placement or honors courses, leadership record, and evidence of special talent. Stetson University provides an integrated, comprehensive learning experience for all students through a combination of courses in the major and general education. General education requirements are based on a set of highly desirable learning outcomes that enable students to succeed academically and in future endeavors. These learning outcomes include communication skills, quantitative reasoning skills, critical thinking, personal and social responsibility, and specific knowledge areas such as the physical world and creative arts. All students at Stetson University accomplish this learning through our First Year Seminars, courses in quantitative reasoning, writing, personal and social responsibility, a selection of knowledge-area courses, the interdisciplinary junior seminar, and senior research capstone courses. Students have a wide range of options from which to select these and other general education courses. To graduate, all students must complete 32 units/courses, equivalent to 128 credits. **Procedure:** Freshmen are admitted fall, spring, and summer. Entrance exams should be taken in the spring of the junior year or the fall of the senior y. There are deferred admissions and rolling admissions plans. Application deadlines are open. Application fee is $50. Notification is sent on a rolling basis. Applications are accepted on-line. **Transfer Students:** 105 transfer students enrolled in 2013-2014. Transfer students must have completed a semester of academic work in good standing at an accredited college with a minimum 2.0 GPA. A 2.75 GPA and an interview (in person or remotely) are encouraged but not required. They must submit college transcripts and also an essay or personal statement at the time of application. High School transcripts may be requested as part of the application process if less than 30 college credits have been earned prior to the time of application. 64 of 128 credits required for the bachelor's degree must be completed at Stetson. **International Students:** There are 156 international students enrolled. The school actively recruits these students. They must take the TOEFL with a minimum score of 550 on the paper-based TOEFL (PBT) or 79 on the Internet-based version (iBT), Student may take either the TOEFL or the IELTS. Minimum score for IELTS is 6.0. They must also take the SAT or ACT.

ADMISSIONS: 61% of the 2014-2015 applicants were accepted. The SAT scores for the 2014-2015 freshman class were: Critical Reading--10% below 500, 42% between 500 and 599, 37% between 600 and 699, and 11% between 700 and 800; Math--12% below 500, 46% between 500 and 599, 37% between 600 and 699, and 6% between 700 and 800; Writing--17% below 500, 46% between 500 and 599, 31% between 600 and 699, and 7% between 700 and 800. The ACT scores were 4% below 21, 20% between 21 and 23, 30% between 24 and 26, 22% between 27 and 28, and 24% above 28. 49% of the current freshmen were in the top fifth of their class; 81% were in the top two fifths. 10 freshmen graduated first in their class. **Admissions Contact:** Robert B. Andrews, Director of Admissions. E-Mail: *admissions@stetson.edu* Web: *www.stetson.edu*

FINANCIAL AID: In 2014-2015, 100% of all full-time freshmen and 99% of continuing full-time students received some form of financial aid. 78% of all full-time freshmen and 71% of continuing full-time students received need-based aid. The average freshman award was $38,345. Need-based scholarships or need-based grants averaged $27,486 ($57,014 maximum); need-based self-help aid (loans and jobs) averaged $4,869 ($10,000 maximum); non-need-based athletic scholarships averaged $26,683 ($52,718 maximum); and other non-need-based awards and non-need-based scholarships averaged $21,120 ($48,025 maximum). 41% of undergraduate students work part-time. Average annual earnings from campus work are $2455. The average financial indebtedness of the 2014 graduate was $32,302. Stetson is a member of CSS. The FAFSA is required. The priority date for freshman financial aid applications for fall entry is March 15.

UNIVERSITY OF CENTRAL FLORIDA   D-3
www.ucf.edu

Orlando, FL 32816   (407) 823-3000

Fax: (407) 823-5625	Email: admission@ucf.edu
Full-time: 16571 men, 19857 women	Faculty: I, --$
	Ph.D.s: 79%
Part-time: 7194 men, 8910 women	Student/Faculty: 31 to 1
Graduate: 3549 men, 4729 women	Tuition: $6368 ($22,467)
Year: semesters, summer session	Freshman Class: 33226
Room & Board: $9300	applied, 16483 accepted, 6467 enrolled
SAT CR/M/W: 591/596/564 ACT: 26	CEEB CODE: 5233
Application Deadline: May 1	VERY COMPETITIVE+

The University of Central Florida, founded in 1963, is the nation's second-largest university. Offering 177 bachelor's and master's degrees and 30 doctoral programs. The Carnegie Foundation for the Advancement of Teaching named UCF a "Curricular Engagement and Outreach and Partnerships University" and a university with "very high research activity." There are 10 undergraduate schools and 11 graduate schools. In addition to regional accreditation, UCF has baccalaureate program accreditation with AACSB, ABET, CAHEA, CSWE, NASM, and NCATE. The 1415-acre campus is in a suburban area 13 miles northeast of downtown Orlando. Including any residence halls, there are 173 buildings.

STUDENT LIFE: 95% of undergraduates are from Florida. Others are from 50 states, 151 foreign countries, and Canada. 55% are White; 23% Hispanic; 11% African American. **Male To Female Ratio:** 1.2:1. The average age of freshmen is 18; all undergraduates, 22. 13% do not continue beyond their first year; 70% remain to graduate. **Housing:** 11593 students can be accommodated in college housing, which includes single-sex and coed dorms, on-campus apartments, and off-campus apartments. In addition, there are honors houses, special-interest houses, fraternity houses, and sorority houses. On-campus housing is available on a first-come and first-served basis. 82% of students commute. All students may keep cars.

FACULTY/CLASSROOMS: 55% of faculty are male; 45% are female. 69% teach undergraduates, 67% do research, and 40% do both. Graduate students teach 12% of introductory courses. The average class size in an introductory lecture is 42; in a laboratory is 15; and in a regular course is 41.

PROGRAMS OF STUDY: UCF confers B.A., B.S., B.A.B.A., B.A.S., B.F.A., B.M., B.M.E., B.S.A.E., B.S.B.A., B.S.C.E., B.S.Con.E., B.S.Cp.E., B.S.E.E., B.S.E.E.T., B.S.Env.E., B.S.E.T., B.S.I.E., B.S.M.E., B.S.N., B.Des., B.S.P.S.E., and B.S.W. degrees. Associate, Master's, and Doctoral degrees are also awarded. Bachelor's degrees are awarded in BIOLOGICAL SCIENCE (biology/biological science, biotechnology, and forensic science), BUSINESS (accounting, banking and finance, business administration and management, business economics, hospitality management services, management science, marketing/retailing/merchandising, and real estate), COMMUNICATIONS AND THE ARTS (advertising, art, broadcasting, communications, dramatic arts, English, film arts, fine arts, French, information technology, journalism, languages, music, music performance, photography, public relations, radio/television technology, Spanish, the-

atre arts, theatre studies, and writing), COMPUTER AND PHYSICAL SCIENCE (applied science, chemistry, computer science, digital arts/technology, information sciences and systems, mathematics, physics, and statistics), EDUCATION (art education, athletic training, business education, early childhood education, education of the exceptional child, elementary education, English education, foreign languages education, health information management, mathematics education, music education, science education, social science education, and technical education), ENGINEERING AND ENVIRONMENTAL DESIGN (aeronautical engineering, aerospace studies, architecture, civil engineering, computer engineering, construction engineering, electrical/electronics engineering, environmental engineering, food services technology, industrial engineering, and mechanical engineering), HEALTH PROFESSIONS (biomedical science, exercise science, health care administration, health science, medical laboratory technology, nursing, and speech pathology/audiology), SOCIAL SCIENCE (anthropology, criminal justice, economics, food production/management/services, forensic studies, (Social Science) Global Studies, history, humanities, interdisciplinary studies, international studies, Latin American studies, legal studies, liberal arts/general studies, philosophy, political science/government, psychology, public administration, religion, social science, social work, and sociology). Engineering, business administration and computer science are the strongest academically. Psychology, biomedical sciences, and health related fields have the largest enrollments.

ACTIVITIES: 7% of men belong to 27 national fraternities; 11% of women belong to 22 national sororities. There are 605 groups on campus, including and sports, pre-professional medical society, art, band, cheerleading, chess, choir, chorus, communications, computers, dance, debate, drama, drill team, environmental, ethnic, film, forensics, gay, honors, international, jazz band, literary magazine, marching band, musical theater, newspaper, opera, orchestra, pep band, photography, political, professional, radio and TV, religious, social, social service, student government, symphony, and volunteer UCF. Popular campus events include Homecoming Events, Spirit Splash, Pegasuspalloza, Symphony Under the Stars, Concerts, Comedians and Movies on the Plaza. **Sports:** There are 6 intercollegiate sports for men and 9 for women, and 20 intramural sports for men and 20 for women. Facilities include football, men's and women's basketball, volleyball, baseball, locker rooms, a weight room, training room and equipment room with complete laundry facilities, 3 batting cages and 2 pitching mounds, softball complex, game day ticketing, retail, marketing and concessions, a lighted indoor batting cage, bullpen area and roomy home dugout, soccer, track complex, rowing facility, tennis complex and a golf facility. **Graduates:** From July 1, 2013 to June 30, 2014, 12592 bachelor's degrees were awarded. The most popular majors were business (23%), health professions (14%), and psychology (9%). 1027 companies recruited on campus in 2013-2014. In an average class, 3% graduate in 3 years or less, 40% graduate in 4 years or less, 63% graduate in 5 years or less, and 70% graduate in 6 years or less. Of the 2013 graduating class, 19% were enrolled in graduate school within 6 months of graduation, and 69% were employed.

SERVICES: Counseling and information services are available, as is tutoring in some subjects, Bio & Microbio, Chem (inc- Organic & Biochem), Genetics, Human Anat & Physio, Astronomy, Accounting, Finance, Stats, C Programming, Object-oriented Program, Comp Eng Statics & Dynamics, Thermodynamics, Physics, Quant Bus Tools, Elec Networks, Phy Sci Geo. **Library/Resources:** The library contains 2.8 million volumes, 3.3 million microform items, 63,536 audio/video tapes/CDs/DVDs, and subscribes to 50,677 periodicals including electronic. Computerized library services include interlibrary loans, database searching, Internet access, and Wi-Fi capability. Special learning facilities include an art gallery, radio station, TV station, University Writing Center, Robinson Observatory, an arboretum, Townes Laser Institute, Siemens Energy Center, Morgridge International Reading Center, Center for Research and Education in Optics and Lasers, Toni Jennings Exceptional Education Institute, Communication Disorders Clinic, Institute for Simulation and Training, Florida Solar Energy Center, Biomolecular Science Center, fine art research facility and non-profit publisher, Florida Space Institute, Community Counseling and Research Center, Florida Photonics Center of Excellence, Institute for Diversity and Ethics in Sport,

Blackstone LaunchPad, Business Incubation Program, Center for Entrepreneurship and Innovation, Small Business Development Center, Center for Advanced Turbomachinery and Energy Research, Center for Computer Vision, Coastal Dynamics of Sea Level Research Cluster of Excellence, Dick Pope Sr. Institute for Tourism Studies, Lou Frey Institute of Politics and Government, NanoScience Technology Center, Advanced Materials Processing and Analysis Center, and a partnership with the Central Florida Research Park, one of the nation's largest research parks located adjacent to campus. **Physically Challenged Students:** 97% of the campus is accessible. Facilities include wheelchair ramps, elevators, special parking, specially equipped restrooms, special class scheduling, lowered drinking fountains, lowered telephones. **Special:** Internships are available in most majors through UCF's extensive partnerships with area businesses and industries such as NASA, Disney, Universal Studios, and AT&T. Students may participate in study abroad and co-op and work-study programs, earn B.A.-B.S. degrees or a liberal studies degree, or pursue dual majors. Nondegree study and pass/fail options are available. There are 23 national honor societies, a freshman honors program, and 59 departmental honors programs. **Visiting:** There are regularly scheduled orientations for prospective students, including tours offered twice a day, Monday through Friday, followed by a group information session or personal interview. There are guides for informal visits and visitors may sit in on classes. To schedule a visit, contact the Undergraduate Admissions Office. **Campus Safety and Security:** Measures include 24-hour foot and vehicle patrol, emergency notification system, self-defense education, and security escort services. There are shuttle buses, emergency telephones, lighted pathways/sidewalks, controlled access to dorms/residences, including a college-sponsored transportation system that buses students to and from apartment complexes within a 2- or 3-mile radius of the school.

REQUIREMENTS: The SAT or ACT is required. The ACT Optional Writing test is also required. GPA and standardized test scores are rated on a sliding scale. A high school diploma or GED is required. Applicants should have completed 4 units of English, 4 each of math, 3 units of science (2 with labs), and social studies, and 2 of a foreign language, plus 2 of academic electives. A GPA of 2.0 is required. AP and CLEP credits are accepted. Important factors in the admissions decision are advanced placement or honors courses, evidence of special talent, and leadership record. To graduate, students must complete at least 120 semester hours, with 36 hours in general education program courses, including 9 each in communication foundations and cultural and historical foundations and 6 each in math foundations, science foundations, and social foundations. Students must maintain a minimum GPA of 2.0. There is a 30-hour residency requirement, and the last semester is required in residence. **Procedure:** Freshmen are admitted fall, spring, and summer. Entrance exams should be taken during the junior year or the first semester of the senior year. There is a rolling admissions plan. Applications should be filed by May 1 for fall entry; November 1 for spring entry; and March 1 for summer entry, along with a $30 fee. Notification is sent on a rolling basis. 1800 applicants were on the 2014 waiting list; 200 were admitted. Applications are accepted on-line. **Transfer Students:** 10930 transfer students enrolled in 2013-2014. A minimum GPA of 2.0 is required in all college work. Either the SAT or the ACT is required of applicants with fewer than 60 credit hours. Other transfer requirements vary widely. 30 of 120 credits required for the bachelor's degree must be completed at UCF. **International Students:** There are 603 international students enrolled. They must take the TOEFL with a minimum score of 550 on the paper-based TOEFL (PBT) or 80 on the Internet-based version (iBT). They must also take the SAT or ACT. Students with fewer than 60 semester hours of college credit must take either the SAT or the ACT.

ADMISSIONS: 50% of the 2014-2015 applicants were accepted. The SAT scores for the 2014-2015 freshman class were: Critical Reading--8% below 500, 45% between 500 and 599, 40% between 600 and 699, and 7% between 700 and 800; Math--6% below 500, 44% between 500 and 599, 42% between 600 and 699, and 8% between 700 and 800; Writing--16% below 500, 52% between 500 and 599, 28% between 600 and 699, and 4% between 700 and 800. The ACT scores were 2% below 21, 19% between 21 and 23, 38% between 24 and 26, 20% between 27 and 28, and 21% above 28. 59% of the current freshmen were in the top fifth of their class; 91% were in the top

two fifths. There were 79 National Merit finalists. 51 freshmen graduated first in their class. **Admissions Contact:** Undergraduate Admissions E-Mail: *admission@ucf.edu* Web: *www.ucf.edu*

FINANCIAL AID: In 2014-2015, 91% of all full-time freshmen and 82% of continuing full-time students received some form of financial aid. 51% of all full-time freshmen and 59% of continuing full-time students received need-based aid. The average freshman award was $8,200. Need-based scholarships or need-based grants averaged $4,961 ($11,344 maximum); need-based self-help aid (loans and jobs) averaged $3,482 ($10,696 maximum); non-need-based athletic scholarships averaged $9,628 ($22,820 maximum); and other non-need-based awards and non-need-based scholarships averaged $3,356 ($35,450 maximum). Average annual earnings from campus work are $6000. The average financial indebtedness of the 2014 graduate was $23,378. The FAFSA is required. The priority date for freshman financial aid applications for fall entry is March 1. The deadline for filing freshman financial aid applications for fall entry is June 30.

UNIVERSITY OF FLORIDA   D-2
www.ufl.edu

Gainesville, FL 32611   (352) 294-3683

Full-time: 13373 men, 16875 women	**Faculty:** 3468; I, --$
Part-time: 1811 men, 1611 women	**Ph.D.s:** 80%
Graduate: 7889 men, 8741 women	**Student/Faculty:** n/av
Year: semesters, summer session	**Tuition:** $6313 ($28,590)
Room & Board: $9630	**Freshman Class:** 26356 applied, 13072 accepted, 6514 enrolled
SAT CR/M/W: 629/637/625 **ACT:** 28	**CEEB CODE:** 5812
Application Deadline: November 1	**HIGHLY COMPETITIVE**

The University of Florida, founded in 1853, is a public liberal arts institution that is part of the state university system of Florida. There are 16 undergraduate schools. In addition to regional accreditation, UF has baccalaureate program accreditation with AACSB, ABET, ACCE, ACEJMC, ACPE, ADA, APTA, ASLA, FIDER, NAAB, NASAD, NASM, NCATE, and SAF. The 1955-acre campus is in a suburban area 75 miles from Jacksonville, FL. Including any residence halls, there are 887 buildings.

STUDENT LIFE: 94% of undergraduates are from Florida. Others are from 50 states, 152 foreign countries, and Canada. 58% are White; 19% Hispanic. **Male To Female Ratio:** 1.2:1. The average age of freshmen is 18; all undergraduates, 21. **Housing:** 8894 students can be accommodated in college housing, which includes coed dorms, on-campus apartments, off-campus apartments, and married student housing. In addition, there are honors houses, special-interest houses, fraternity houses, sorority houses, Honors residential college, career exploration community, wellness communities, faculty-in-residence communities, first-year experience program, engineering community, fine arts living learning community, global living learning community, sophomore experience program, pre-health community, ROTC community, and a international house. On-campus housing is available on a first-come and first-served basis. All students may keep cars.

FACULTY/CLASSROOMS: 64% of faculty are male; 36% are female. No introductory courses are taught by graduate students.

PROGRAMS OF STUDY: UF confers B.A., and B.S. degrees. Associate, Master's, and Doctoral degrees are also awarded. Bachelor's degrees are awarded in AGRICULTURE (agricultural business management, agronomy, animal science, dairy science, forestry and related sciences, horticulture, natural resource management, plant science, and soil science), BIOLOGICAL SCIENCE (botany, entomology, microbiology, wildlife biology, and zoology), BUSINESS (accounting, banking and finance, business administration and management, human resources, insurance, management science, marketing/retailing/merchandising, and recreation and leisure services), COMMUNICATIONS AND THE ARTS (advertising, art, art history and appreciation, creative writing, dance, East Asian languages and literature, English, French, German, graphic design, journalism, linguistics, music, performing arts, photography, Portuguese, public relations, Russian, Spanish, speech/debate/rhetoric, telecommunications, theater design, and visual and performing arts), COMPUTER AND PHYSICAL SCIENCE (astronomy, chemistry, computer science, earth science, geology, information sciences and systems, mathematics, physics, and statistics), EDUCATION (agricultural education, art education, elementary education, health education, and music education), ENGINEERING AND ENVIRONMENTAL DESIGN (aeronautical engineering, agricultural engineering, architecture, chemical engineering, civil engineering, computer engineering, construction engineering, electrical/electronics engineering, emergency/disaster science, engineering and applied science, environmental engineering, industrial engineering technology, interior design, landscape architecture/design, materials engineering, mechanical engineering, nuclear engineering, and nuclear engineering technology), HEALTH PROFESSIONS (allied health, exercise science, health science, nursing, occupational therapy, physical therapy, prepharmacy, rehabilitation therapy, and speech pathology/audiology), SOCIAL SCIENCE (American studies, anthropology, Asian/Oriental studies, classical/ancient civilization, criminology, economics, food science, geography, history, home economics, interdisciplinary studies, Judaic studies, philosophy, physical fitness/movement, political science/government, psychology, religion, and sociology). Biology, psychology and political science are the strongest academically. Biology, psychology and finance have the largest enrollments.

ACTIVITIES: 23% of men belong to 38 national fraternities; 23% of women belong to 26 national sororities. There are 1000 groups on campus, including art, band, cheerleading, chess, choir, chorale, chorus, computers, dance, debate, drama, environmental, ethnic, film, forensics, gay, honors, international, jazz band, literary magazine, marching band, newspaper, opera, orchestra, pep band, photography, political, professional, radio and TV, religious, social, social service, student government, and symphony. Popular campus events include Homecoming Parade, Annual Dance Marathon and ACCENT Speaker's Bureau, Gator Growl Student Run Pep Rally, and Florida Invitational Step Show. **Sports:** There are 9 intercollegiate sports for men and 12 for women, and 45 intramural sports for men and 45 for women. Facilities include state-of-the-art football stadium with a capacity of 88,548, and the 25,000-square-foot strength and conditioning weight room, basketball, volleyball, gymnastics meets, indoor track, commencements, concerts and shows, Olympic-size pool inside with one- and three-meter diving boards, a gymnastics arena, dance studio, martial arts studio, and an outdoor training facility with another 50-meter pool, baseball stadium, three full-size volleyball courts, training and sports medicine, locker rooms, softball stadium, all-weather batting cage, lacrosse, and a soccer field. **Graduates:** From July 1, 2013 to June 30, 2014, 8244 bachelor's degrees were awarded. The most popular majors were biology (6%), psychology (5%), and finance (4%). 800 companies recruited on campus in 2013-2014. In an average class, 4% graduate in 3 years or less, 66% graduate in 4 years or less, 84% graduate in 5 years or less, and 87% graduate in 6 years or less.

SERVICES: Counseling and information services are available, as is tutoring in every subject. There is a reader service for the blind. In addition to a free centralized tutoring service, UF provides subject specific tutoring including a Writing Center, Math tutoring lab, sciences tutoring lab, and others. **Library/Resources:** The 7 libraries contain 4.9 million volumes, 6.6 million microform items, 84,716 audio/video tapes/CDs/DVDs, and subscribe to 165,339 periodicals including electronic. Computerized library services include interlibrary loans, database searching, Internet access, and Wi-Fi capability. Special learning facilities include an art gallery, natural history museum, radio station, TV station, performing arts center, and a teaching hospital. **Physically Challenged Students:** 95% of the campus is accessible. Facilities include wheelchair ramps, elevators, special parking, specially equipped restrooms, special class scheduling, lowered drinking fountains, lowered telephones, special housing. **Special:** Hundreds of internships and study abroad opportunities are available. Students should consult their major departments. UF offers the Washington semester and work study programs. Accelerated degree programs vary by major. Dual majors vary by colleges. Interdisciplinary Studies in the college of Liberal Arts and Sciences, Inno-

vation Academy at UF: A groundbreaking living/learning community that offers a flexible spring-summer cohort, enlightening guest speakers, diverse internship opportunities, co-curricular environment, and a minor in Innovation. 3-2 engineering degree with the University of the Virgin Islands. There are 100 national honor societies, including Phi Beta Kappa, a freshman honors program, and 100 departmental honors programs. **Visiting:** There are regularly scheduled orientations for prospective students, consisting of the Welcome Center calendar for tour, as tours are based on the time of the year. There are guides for informal visits, visitors may sit in on classes, and stay overnight. To schedule a visit, contact the UF Welcome Center. **Campus Safety and Security:** Measures include 24-hour foot and vehicle patrol, emergency notification system, self-defense education, and security escort services. There are shuttle buses, emergency telephones, lighted pathways/sidewalks, and controlled access to dorms/residences.

REQUIREMENTS: The SAT or ACT is required. The ACT Optional Writing test is also required. A satisfactory score on the SAT and a minimum score of 19 on the ACT are required. Candidates should have graduated from an accredited secondary school or have a GED, and have completed 4 years of English, 4 years of math, 3 science, and 3 social studies, 2 years of a foreign language, and 4 units of academic electives. A GPA of 2.5 is required. AP and CLEP credits are accepted. Important factors in the admissions decision are advanced placement or honors courses, extracurricular activities record, and evidence of special talent. UNDERGRADUATE: Requirements for graduation vary depending on the major elected, but all students are required to complete a minimum of 120 credits and maintain a minimum 2.0 GPA, including 36 credits of general education courses. GRADUATE: All graduate degrees require the minimum stipulated number of credits for the type of degree, and a 3.0 GPA in the major, in the minor if applicable, and overall. Master's Degrees; Most require a minimum of 30 credits, with curriculum and requirements dictated by each degree program. **Procedure:** Freshmen are admitted to all sessions. Entrance exams should be taken in the junior year. Applications should be filed by November 1 for fall entry; November 1 for spring entry; and November 1 for summer entry, along with a $30 fee. Notifications are sent February 13. Applications are accepted online. **Transfer Students:** 2589 transfer students enrolled in 2013-2014. Admission requirements for transfer students vary by college. Students must have 60 hours or AA degree. 30 of 120 credits required for the bachelor's degree must be completed at UF. **International Students:** There are 353 international students enrolled. The school actively recruits these students. They must take the TOEFL with a minimum score of 550 on the paper-based TOEFL (PBT) or 80 on the Internet-based version (iBT) or take the MELAB, or take the IELTS. They must also take the SAT or ACT. Freshmen and lower-division transfers must take the SAT or ACT.

ADMISSIONS: 50% of the 2014-2015 applicants were accepted. The SAT scores for the 2014-2015 freshman class were: Critical Reading--3% below 500, 28% between 500 and 599, 53% between 600 and 699, and 16% between 700 and 800; Math--2% below 500, 23% between 500 and 599, 53% between 600 and 699, and 22% between 700 and 800; Writing--3% below 500, 28% between 500 and 599, 51% between 600 and 699, and 18% between 700 and 800. The ACT scores were 6% between 21 and 23, 17% between 24 and 26, 24% between 27 and 28, and 54% above 28. **Admissions Contact:** Zina Evans, Vice President for Enrollment Management. Web: *www.ufl.edu*

FINANCIAL AID: In 2014-2015, 98% of all full-time freshmen and 98% of continuing full-time students received some form of financial aid. 38% of all full-time freshmen and 39% of continuing full-time students received need-based aid. The average freshman award was $12,154. Need-based scholarships or need-based grants averaged $7,599; need-based self-help aid (loans and jobs) averaged $4,555; non-need-based athletic scholarships averaged $14,111; and other non-need-based awards and non-need-based scholarships averaged $5,335. 10% of undergraduate students work part-time. Average annual earnings from campus work are $1266. The average financial indebtedness of the 2014 graduate was $20,642. UF is a member of CSS. The FAFSA is required. The priority date for freshman financial aid applications for fall entry is March 15.

UNIVERSITY OF MIAMI   E-6
www.miami.edu

Coral Gables, FL 33124   (305) 284-4323

Fax: (305) 284-6605
Full-time: 5229 men, 5408 women
Part-time: 304 men, 439 women
Graduate: 2735 men, 2820 women
Year: semesters, summer session
Room & Board: $12,684

Email: admission@miami.edu
Faculty: I, av$
Ph.D.s: 91%
Student/Faculty: 12 to 1
Tuition: $44,350
Freshman Class: 28907 applied, 11691 accepted, 2140 enrolled

SAT CR/M/W: 640/680/640 ACT: 30
Application Deadline: January 1

CEEB CODE: 5815
MOST COMPETITIVE

The mission of the University of Miami encompasses two primary goals: empowering the discoveries that enhance civilization and preparing our students for success in their careers and in life. A brilliant faculty corps draws exceptional students, and the cumulative impact of the two has made the University one of the fastest-rising research universities in the nation. Dynamic courses are offered in more than 180 majors and programs and students have the freedom to cross disciplines and carve an educational path unique to their aptitudes and interests. At UM, a student can construct learning around individual strengths, interests, curiosities, passions, and goals by taking advantage of an array of learning options in our nine undergraduate schools and two graduate professional schools. The Cognates Program of General Education allows a student to use those options to create an education that is both broad and deep and that displays who the student is and what the student cares about. Our approach nurtures curiosity and exploration of the world outside the classroom while also bringing the world to the University of Miami campus. The value of a University of Miami education is the ability to become part of this vast and renewable resource, gaining knowledge, inspiration, camaraderie and connections that will prove invaluable for years to come. Figures in the above capsule and in this profile are approximate. There are 9 undergraduate schools and 3 graduate schools. In addition to regional accreditation, UM has baccalaureate program accreditation with AACSB, ABET, APTA, NAAB, NASM, and TEAC. The 239-acre campus is in a suburban area 7 miles from Miami International Airport. Including any residence halls, there are 130 buildings.

STUDENT LIFE: 54% of undergraduates are from out of state, mostly the Middle Atlantic. Students are from 50 states, 105 foreign countries, and Canada. 61% are from public schools. 43% are White; 22% Hispanic; 14% Foreign. 40% are Protestant; 33% Catholic; 15% Hindu, Muslim, Buddhism, and 12% Jewish. **Male To Female Ratio:** 1.0:1. The average age of freshmen is 18; all undergraduates, 21. 9% do not continue beyond their first year; 91% remain to graduate. **Housing:** 4310 students can be accommodated in college housing, which includes single-sex and coed dorms and on-campus apartments. In addition, there are special-interest houses, fraternity houses, Freshmen are required to live on campus, and they live in residential colleges with live-in resident faculty. On-campus housing is guaranteed for the freshman year only, is available on a first-come, first-served basis, and is available on a lottery system for upperclassmen. 62% of students commute. Some may keep cars.

FACULTY/CLASSROOMS: 62% of faculty are male; 38% are female. No introductory courses are taught by graduate students.

PROGRAMS OF STUDY: UM confers A.B., B.A., B.S., B.A.M., B.A.M.A., B.Arch., B.B.A., B.F.A., B.G.S., B.L.A., B.M., B.S.A.E., B.S.A.S.E., B.S.B.A., B.S.B.E., B.S.C., B.S.C.E., B.S.Cp.E., B.S.Ed., B.S.E.E., B.S.E.S., B.S.En.E., B.S.H.S., B.S.I.E., B.S.M.A.S., B.S.M.E., B.S.N. and B.S.P.H. degrees. Master's and doctoral degrees are also awarded. Bachelor's degrees are awarded in BIOLOGICAL SCIENCE (biochemistry, marine biology, marine science, microbiology, molecular biology, and neurosciences), BUSINESS (accounting, entrepreneurial studies, finance, human resources/organizational mgmt, international finance, international marketing, management science, marketing, marketing management, real estate, and sports management), COMMUNICATIONS AND THE ARTS (advertising, art history, art, ceramic art and design, classical languages, classics,

communication, communication studies, English, film arts, fine arts, French, German, graphic design, Greek (classical), instrumental performance, jazz, journalism, modern language, music, music business management, music composition, music performance, music technology, musical theater, painting, photography, printmaking, public relations, sculpture, Spanish, studio art, theatre acting, theatre arts, theater design, theater management, and vocal performance), COMPUTER AND PHYSICAL SCIENCE (applied mathematics, atmospheric sciences and meteorology, chemistry, computer game design/development, computer information systems, computer science, geology, geoscience, mathematics, mathematics/computational, mathematics – economics, physics, software engineering, and statistics), EDUCATION (athletic training, education of the exceptional child, elementary education, mathematics education, music education, and secondary education), ENGINEERING AND ENVIRONMENTAL DESIGN (aerospace studies, architectural engineering, architecture, biomedical engineering, civil engineering, computer engineering, computer graphics, electrical/electronics engineering, engineering science, environmental engineering, environmental science, industrial engineering, and mechanical engineering), HEALTH PROFESSIONS (biology, exercise science, health administration and policy, health care administration, health science, music therapy, nursing, physician's assistant, Pre-Health Studies, predentistry, premedicine, prepharmacy, prephysical therapy, preveterinary science, and public health), SOCIAL SCIENCE (africana studies, American studies, anthropology, classical/ancient civilization, criminology, economics, gender studies, geography, history, human development, interdisciplinary studies, international studies, Judaic studies, Latin American studies, legal studies, liberal arts/general studies, philosophy, political science/government, prelaw, psychology, religion, religious studies, sociology, and women's studies). Business/marketing, biological/life sciences, and social sciences have the largest enrollments.

ACTIVITIES: 14% of men belong to 21 national fraternities; 17% of women belong to 15 national sororities. There are 260 groups on campus, including art, athletic organizations, band, cheerleading, chess, choir, chorale, chorus, computers, dance, debate, drama, environmental, ethnic, film, gay, honors, international, jazz band, literary magazine, marching band, musical theater, newspaper, opera, orchestra, pep band, political, professional, radio and TV, religious, social, social service, student government, symphony, and yearbook. Popular campus events include Homecoming, Alumni Weekend, 'Canes Spirit Day, International Week, SportsFest, Miami International Film Festival, CaneFest, Hug the Lake, and Thanksgiving Day Matchup Program. **Sports:** There are 8 intercollegiate sports for men and 10 for women, and 28 intramural sports for men and 28 for women. Facilities include The Cobb Stadium, a soccer and track and field facility; the BankUnited Center, home of UM's basketball program and the University's first large-capacity venue for other educational, cultural and community events; Hecht Center Athletic Training Facility, equipped with the latest in diagnostic and rehabilitative equipment and serves as the main lab for the Athletic Training Major; Schwartz Center for Athletic Excellence, serves the University's more than 400 student-athletes with resources such as a new academic center and expanded training facilities; Mark Light Baseball Stadium, home to UM's baseball program; Alex Rodriguez Park, the newly renovated facility at Mark Light Baseball Stadium; Neil Schiff Tennis Center, 16-court facility with seating for 1,000 spectators; University Center Pool, this double-Olympic-size swimming pool is home to UM's swimming and diving teams and is enjoyed recreationally by UM students and faculty; Sun Life Stadium, a world-class sports and entertainment facility that hosts a wide variety of events, including the Miami Hurricanes football games; Herbert Wellness Center, a premier fitness, recreation and wellness facility that includes a fitness room, aerobic classes, indoor track, gymnasium with basketball, volleyball and badminton courts, racquetball and squash courts, tennis, indoor pool, spa, sauna and community and cooking classes. **Graduates:** From July 1, 2013 to June 30, 2014, 2451 bachelor's degrees were awarded. The most popular majors were psychology (6%), biology (6%), and finance (5%). 362 companies recruited on campus in 2013-2014. In an average class, 4% graduate in 3 years or less, 71% graduate in 4 years or less, 81% graduate in 5 years or less, and 82% graduate in 6 years or less. Of the 2013 graduating class, 28% were enrolled in graduate school within 6 months of graduation, and 59% were employed.

SERVICES: Counseling and information services are available, as is tutoring in some subjects. There is a reader service for the blind. Remedial study skills **Library/Resources:** The 10 libraries contain 3.5 million volumes, 4.1 million microform items, 106,136 audio/video tapes/CDs/DVDs, and subscribe to 92,958 periodicals including electronic. Computerized library services include interlibrary loans, database searching, Internet access, and Wi-Fi capability. Special learning facilities include an art gallery, radio station, TV station, Cinema, observatory, palmetum, marine science research vessels, broadcasting studios, concert hall, arboretum, performing arts theater, film studios, sound stage, museum, wellness center and state-of-the-art student activities center. **Physically Challenged Students:** 4% of the campus is accessible. Facilities include wheelchair ramps, elevators, special parking, specially equipped restrooms, special class scheduling, lowered drinking fountains, lowered telephones, special housing, and lowered elevator controls. **Special:** Our internships, work-study programs, and study-abroad programs provide the opportunity for UM students to acquire an expansive perspective in their academic career. Opportunities to learn and grow flourish through our special programs such as our accelerated degree programs as well as our dual degree programs. There are 52 national honor societies, including Phi Beta Kappa, and a freshman honors program. **Visiting:** There are regularly scheduled orientations for prospective students, Several open house programs that enable students to tour the campus and meet with representatives from admission, financial aid, and various university departments. Daily information sessions are offered on campus as well as walking tours. There are guides for informal visits and visitors may sit in on classes.. **Campus Safety and Security:** Measures include 24-hour foot and vehicle patrol, emergency notification system, self-defense education, and security escort services. There are shuttle buses, emergency telephones, lighted pathways/sidewalks, controlled access to dorms/residences, There has been a comprehensive crime prevention program since 1981.

REQUIREMENTS: The SAT or ACT is required. It is recommended that applicants have completed 4 units of English, 4 units of Mathematics, 3 units of Science with 2 of the 3 units being in lab, 2 units of Foreign Language, 3 units of Social Studies, 2 units of History, and 2 units of Academic Electives with 1 unit being in Computer Science and 1 unit being in Visual/Performing Arts. Applicants are based on the strength of their high school curriculum and grades earned, standardized test scores, letters of recommendation, essay, extracurricular activities and awards/achievements. The GED is accepted. Portfolios are required for the Arts and Architecture programs. Auditions are required for the Music and Theatre Programs. Supplemental applications are required for the Frost School of Music, BFA Theatre, BFA Art, Architecture, and Dual Degree Programs. AP and CLEP credits are accepted. Important factors in the admissions decision are extra-curricular activities record, recommendations by school officials, and advanced placement or honors courses. To receive a Bachelor's degree from the University, the student must earn at least 120 semester hours of credit, more in some schools, with a C average or better as well as a C average for all work done at the University of Miami. The student must fulfill the general education requirements as well as meet all of the degree requirements of their respective school or college. Each student must complete the final 45 credits that are applied to his or her baccalaureate degree in residence at the University of Miami. In addition, each student must complete at least half of the credits specified for his or her major in residence at the University of Miami. **Procedure:** Freshmen are admitted fall and spring. Entrance exams should be taken the summer before the senior year in high school. There are early decision, early admissions, and deferred admissions plans. Early decision applications should be filed by November 1; regular applications, by January 1 for fall entry; and November 1 for spring entry, along with a $70 fee. Notification of early decision is sent December 20; regular decision, April 15. 157 early decision candidates were accepted for the 2014-2015 class. Applications are accepted online. **Transfer Students:** 599 transfer students enrolled in 2013-2014. Only credits from a regionally accredited institution are transferable to the University of Miami. The average accepted transfer student has a 3.4 GPA. Courses with a grade lower than a C will not transfer, however these grades will still be used

to compute an admission GPA. If the student has fewer than 30 college credits when submitting the application, official high school transcripts, the Common Application Secondary School Final Report and SAT/ACT scores must be submitted in addition to the core application documents. Portfolios are required for BFA Art and Architecture programs. Supplemental applications are required for the Frost School of Music, BFA Theatre, BFA Art and Architecture programs. 45 of 120 credits required for the bachelor's degree must be completed at UM. **International Students:** There are 1510 international students enrolled. The school actively recruits these students. They must take the TOEFL with a minimum score of 550 on the paper-based TOEFL (PBT) or 80 on the Internet-based version (iBT). All students whose native language is not English are required to submit official results of the TOEFL or IELTS. SAT/ACT not required and shouldn't be submitted for admission consideration from applicants attending school outside US.

ADMISSIONS: 40% of the 2014-2015 applicants were accepted. The SAT scores for the 2014-2015 freshman class were: Critical Reading--4% below 500, 21% between 500 and 599, 49% between 600 and 699, and 26% between 700 and 800; Math--2% below 500, 12% between 500 and 599, 48% between 600 and 699, and 38% between 700 and 800; Writing--3% below 500, 23% between 500 and 599, 50% between 600 and 699, and 24% between 700 and 800. The ACT scores were 74% above 28. 89% of the current freshmen were in the top fifth of their class; 96% were in the top two fifths. There were 51 National Merit finalists. 53 freshmen graduated first in their class. **Admissions Contact:** Deanna L. Voss, Executive Director of Admission. E-Mail: *admission@miami.edu* Web: *www.miami.edu/ug*

FINANCIAL AID: In 2014-2015, 79% of all full-time freshmen and 72% of continuing full-time students received some form of financial aid. 50% of all full-time freshmen and 45% of continuing full-time students received need-based aid. The average freshman award was $33,811. Need-based scholarships or need-based grants averaged $26,119 ($61,603 maximum); need-based self-help aid (loans and jobs) averaged $7,760 ($39,392 maximum); non-need-based athletic scholarships averaged $33,262 ($60,906 maximum); other non-need-based awards and non-need-based scholarships averaged $18,404 ($60,960 maximum); and $22,872 from other forms of aid. 56% of undergraduate students work part-time. Average annual earnings from campus work are $2000. The average financial indebtedness of the 2014 graduate was $27,827. UM is a member of CSS. The CSS/Profile and FAFSA are required. The priority date for freshman financial aid applications for fall entry is February 1.

UNIVERSITY OF NORTH FLORIDA   D-1
www.unf.edu

Jacksonville, FL 32224   (904) 620-2624

Fax: (904) 620-2414	Email: osprey@unf.edu
Full-time: 4376 men, 5525 women	Faculty: 381; IIA, -$
Part-time: 1956 men, 2264 women	Ph.D.s: 92%
Graduate: 675 men, 1188 women	Student/Faculty: 20 to 1
Year: semesters, summer session	Tuition: $6386 ($20,789)
Room & Board: $9484	Freshman Class: 7288 applied, 3681 accepted, 964 enrolled
SAT CR/M: 601/615 ACT: 26	CEEB CODE: 5490
Application Deadline: n/av	VERY COMPETITIVE

The University of North Florida, founded in 1965, is a public university that is part of the state university system. There are 5 undergraduate schools and 5 graduate schools. In addition to regional accreditation, UNF has baccalaureate program accreditation with AACSB, ABET, ACCE, NASM, NCATE, and NLN. The 1300-acre campus is in an urban area 12 miles southeast of downtown Jacksonville. Including any residence halls, there are 85 buildings.

STUDENT LIFE: 95% of undergraduates are from Florida. Others are from 47 states, 109 foreign countries, and Canada. 69% are White. 99% claim no religious affiliation. **Male To Female Ratio:** 1.3:1. The average age of freshmen is 18; all undergraduates, 23. 17% do not continue beyond their first year; 50% remain to graduate. **Housing:**

3130 students can be accommodated in college housing, which includes coed dorms and on-campus apartments. In addition, there are honors houses. On-campus housing is guaranteed for the freshman year only, is available on a first-come, and first-served basis. 78% of students commute. All students may keep cars.

FACULTY/CLASSROOMS: 54% of faculty are male; 46% are female. 90% teach undergraduates, 71% do research, and 64% do both. Graduate students teach 15% of introductory courses. The average class size in an introductory lecture is 38; in a laboratory is 20; and in a regular course is 33.

PROGRAMS OF STUDY: UNF confers B.A., B.S., B.A.E., B.B.A., B.F.A., B.H.A., B.M., B.M.E., B.S.A.T., B.S.E.E., B.S.H. and B.S.N. degrees. Associate, Master's, and Doctoral degrees are also awarded. Bachelor's degrees are awarded in BIOLOGICAL SCIENCE (biology/biological science and nutrition), BUSINESS (accounting, banking and finance, business administration and management, business economics, finance, global/general management, international business management, marketing management, sports management, and transportation management), COMMUNICATIONS AND THE ARTS (American Sign Language, art, communications, English, English literature, fine arts, jazz, music, music performance, and Spanish), COMPUTER AND PHYSICAL SCIENCE (applied mathematics, chemistry, computer science, information sciences and systems, mathematics, physics, and statistics), EDUCATION (art education, athletic training, elementary education, English education, mathematics education, middle school education, music education, physical education, science education, secondary education, social studies education, and special education), ENGINEERING AND ENVIRONMENTAL DESIGN (civil engineering, construction engineering, construction management, electrical/electronics engineering, and mechanical engineering), HEALTH PROFESSIONS (health care administration, health science, mental health/human services, nursing, and physical therapy), SOCIAL SCIENCE (anthropology, counseling/psychology, criminal justice, dietetics, economics, ethnic studies, French studies, history, interdisciplinary studies, philosophy, political science/government, psychology, public administration, religion, and sociology). Nursing, fine arts, and elementary education are the strongest academically. Psychology, communication and biology have the largest enrollments.

ACTIVITIES: 2% of men belong to 10 national fraternities; 4% of women belong to 8 national sororities. There are 196 groups on campus, including art, band, cheerleading, choir, chorale, chorus, computers, dance, drama, drum and bugle corps, environmental, ethnic, film, gay, honors, international, jazz band, literary magazine, newspaper, photography, political, professional, radio and TV, religious, social, social service, and student government. Popular campus events include Clubfest, Spring Bash and Earth Music Fest. **Sports:** There are 7 intercollegiate sports for men and 10 for women, and 11 intramural sports for men and 11 for women. Facilities include a baseball stadium, softball, soccer, and multipurpose fields, 9800-seat soccer stadium, an aquatic center, a fitness center, jogging trails, racquetball, basketball, volleyball, tennis courts, 6000-seat multipurpose arena, and lakes for canoeing and fishing. Student Wellness Complex contains 34' climbing wall, indoor 3-lane rubber track, 3 dedicated group fitness rooms, and wheelchair-accessible equipment including, weight machines. **Graduates:** From July 1, 2013 to June 30, 2014, 3177 bachelor's degrees were awarded. The most popular majors were psychology (11%), communications (8%), and criminal justice (6%). 281 companies recruited on campus in 2013-2014. In an average class, 2% graduate in 3 years or less, 20% graduate in 4 years or less, 42% graduate in 5 years or less, and 49% graduate in 6 years or less.

SERVICES: Counseling and information services are available, as is tutoring in some subjects, accounting, biology, chemistry, comping science, economics, history, mathematics, physics, psychology, statistics, and world languages. Writing tutoring is available by appointment through the Writing Center **Library/Resources:** The library contains 864,706 volumes, 1.5 million microform items, 35,263 audio/video tapes/CDs/DVDs, and subscribes to 38,246 periodicals including electronic. Computerized library services include interlibrary loans, database searching, Internet access, and Wi-Fi capability. Special learning facilities include an art gallery, radio station, TV station, a theater, auditorium, nature preserve, Museum of Science and History (MOSH). **Physically Challenged Students:** Facilities include wheelchair ramps, elevators, special parking, specially equipped restrooms, special class scheduling, lowered drinking fountains, lowered telephones, special housing. The Disability Resource Center provides specialized assistance and equipment, including priority registration, interpreters for the hearing impaired, and proctored testing. **Special:** There are cooperative programs and internships in most majors and work-study programs with several Jacksonville businesses. Study abroad, an accelerated degree program in nursing, B.A.-B.S. degrees in math, statistics, and psychology, dual majors, and student-designed majors also are available. Credit is given for military experience. There are 6 national honor societies, a freshman honors program, and 14 departmental honors programs. **Visiting:** There are regularly scheduled orientations for prospective students, consisting of open houses which include tours of the campus and housing, a general information session, financial aid sessions, academic advising, and personal interviews by request. There are guides for informal visits. To schedule a visit, contact the Admissions Office. **Campus Safety and Security:** Measures include 24-hour foot and vehicle patrol, emergency notification system, self-defense education, and security escort services. There are shuttle buses, emergency telephones, lighted pathways/sidewalks, university police presentations at new student orientation.

REQUIREMENTS: The SAT or ACT is required. The Office of Admissions will recalculate a grade point average (GPA) based on the following eighteen (18) academic units in college preparatory courses. Additional weight is given to grades of "C" or higher earned in honors, Dual Enrollment, Advanced Placement, IB, or AICE courses. While students may not have completed all the required courses at the time an application is submitted, they are required to complete them prior to high school graduation and entrance into UNF. The State of Florida has implemented new minimum admission standards for freshmen applicants to all state universities. In order to be considered, students must have a minimum 2.5 recalculated GPA, on a 4.0 scale, and meet minimum test score requirements (460 SAT Critical Reading, 460 SAT Math, 440 SAT Writing; or 19 ACT Reading, 19 ACT Math, 18 ACT English/Writing). Please keep in mind that these standards only outline potential eligibility for admission to a state university. UNF's admission criteria depend on the applicant pool and will be higher than these minimums. A GPA of 2.5 is required. AP and CLEP credits are accepted. Important factors in the admissions decision are advanced placement or honors courses, recommendations by school officials, and evidence of special talent.Students are required to take general education distribution requirements, including 9 hours of composition and humanities and 6 each of natural science, math, and social science. There is a core curriculum in Western civilization and cultural diversity. A minimum 2.0 GPA and 120 credit hours, with a minimum of 60 hours in the major, are needed for graduation. **Procedure:** Freshmen are admitted to all sessions. Entrance exams should be taken during the spring of the junior year or the fall of the senior year. There are deferred admissions and rolling admissions plans. Application deadlines are open. Application fee is $30. Notification is sent on a rolling basis. Applications are accepted on-line. **Transfer Students:** 2834 transfer students enrolled in 2013-2014. Upper-level transfer students are defined as those with at least 60 transferable credit hours or an Associate of Arts degree from a Florida public or postsecondary institution. Admission requirements will vary by major, term, and space-availability. In order to be considered, applicants must meet or exceed a cumulative college GPA of 2.0 or higher, including a "C" or higher average and "good standing" status at the most recent college attended. Listed below are the minimum required materials for upper-level students to submit in order to be evaluated for a decision. Additional requirements will exist for students applying to limited access/selective admission programs or as international students. 30 of 120 credits required for the Bachelor's degree must be completed at UNF. **International Students:** There are 270 international students enrolled. The school actively recruits these students. They must take the TOEFL. They must also take the SAT or ACT.

ADMISSIONS: 51% of the 2014-2015 applicants were accepted. The SAT scores for the 2014-2015 freshman class were: Critical Reading--2% below 500, 36% between 500 and 599, 55% between 600 and 699, and 7% between 700 and 800; Math--3% below 500, 44% between 500 and 599, 49% between 600 and 699, and 4% between

700 and 800; Writing--10% below 500, 51% between 500 and 599, 36% between 600 and 699, and 3% between 700 and 800. The ACT scores were 1% below 21, 17% between 21 and 23, 46% between 24 and 26, 18% between 27 and 28, and 18% above 28. 45% of the current freshmen were in the top fifth of their class; 75% were in the top two fifths. 5 freshmen graduated first in their class. **Admissions Contact:** John Yancey, Director of Admissions. E-Mail: *osprey@unf.edu* Web: *www.unf.edu*

FINANCIAL AID: In 2014-2015, 77% of all full-time freshmen and 79% of continuing full-time students received some form of financial aid. 49% of all full-time freshmen and 47% of continuing full-time students received need-based aid. The average freshman award was $10,013. Need-based scholarships or need-based grants averaged $6,742 ($18,746 maximum); need-based self-help aid (loans and jobs) averaged $4,176 ($11,016 maximum); non-need-based athletic scholarships averaged $9,965 ($23,669 maximum); and other non-need-based awards and non-need-based scholarships averaged $5,843 ($35,192 maximum). 5% of undergraduate students work part-time. The average financial indebtedness of the 2014 graduate was $17,118. The FAFSA is required. The deadline for filing freshman financial aid applications for fall entry is April 1.

UNIVERSITY OF SOUTH FLORIDA/ST. PETERSBURG   D-4
www.usfsp.edu

St. Petersburg, FL 33701	727-873-4142
Fax: 727-873-4525	Email: admissions@mail.usf.edu
Full-time: 1134 men, 1654 women	Faculty: 107; I, --$
Part-time: 462 men, 756 women	Ph.D.s: n/av
Graduate: 155 men, 303 women	Student/Faculty: 24 to 1
Year: semesters, summer session	Tuition: $5199 ($14,387)
Room & Board: $7570	Freshman Class: 1996 applied, 914 accepted, 474 enrolled
SAT CR/M/W: 530/530/510 ACT: 23	CEEB CODE: 5828
Application Deadline: March 15	COMPETITIVE

University of South Florida St. Petersburg, offers master's level and undergraduate programs in the arts and sciences, business and education within a student-centered environment. The first regional institution in the USF System with separate accreditation, USFSP distinguishes itself by its urban waterfront location in downtown St. Petersburg and its focus on undergraduate research, civic engagement and small classes. Most faculty members hold the highest degree in their field and teach courses from the freshman to graduate level. USFSP retains its separate identity and mission while contributing to and benefiting from the associations, cooperation, and shared resources of a premier national research university. Figures in the above capsule and in this profile are approximate. There are 3 undergraduate schools and one graduate school. In addition to regional accreditation, USF St. Petersburg has baccalaureate program accreditation with AACSB, ACEJMC, and NCATE. The 50-acre campus is in an urban area on Bayboro Harbor in downtown St. Petersburg.

STUDENT LIFE: 97% of undergraduates are from Florida. 74% are White; 13% Hispanic. **Male To Female Ratio:** 1.5:1. **Housing:** 600 students can be accommodated in college housing, which includes coed dorms. On-campus housing is guaranteed for the freshman year only. Priority is given to out-of-town students. 85% of students commute. Alcohol is not permitted. All students may keep cars.

FACULTY/CLASSROOMS: 48% of faculty are male; 52% are female. No introductory courses are taught by graduate students. The average class size in an introductory lecture is 36 and in a laboratory is 23.

PROGRAMS OF STUDY: USF St. Petersburg confers B.A., B.S. and B.F.A. degrees. Master's degrees are also awarded. Bachelor's degrees are awarded in BIOLOGICAL SCIENCE (biology/biological science), BUSINESS (accounting, business administration and management, entrepreneurial studies, finance, global/general management, management science, and marketing and distribution), COMMUNICATIONS AND THE ARTS (communications, English, and graphic design), COMPUTER AND PHYSICAL SCIENCE (information sciences and systems), EDUCATION (education), ENGINEERING AND ENVIRONMENTAL DESIGN (environmental science), HEALTH PROFESSIONS (health science), SOCIAL SCIENCE (anthropology, criminology, economics, history, political science/government, psychology, and social science).

ACTIVITIES: There are no fraternities or sororities. There are 100 groups on campus, including debate, environmental, ethnic, gay, newspaper, professional, religious, social service, and student government. Popular campus events include Welcome Week, Homecoming Week, Spring Fling and Leadership Retreats. **Sports:** There are 5 intramural sports for men and 5 for women. Facilities include Recreation center, aquatics center and waterfront activities; sailing, kayaking and paddle boarding. **Graduates:** From July 1, 2013 to June 30, 2014, 705 bachelor's degrees were awarded. The most popular majors were accounting (15%), psychology (10%), and general business (10%). In an average class, 11% graduate in 4 years or less, 26% graduate in 5 years or less, and 33% graduate in 6 years or less.

SERVICES: Counseling and information services are available, as is tutoring in some subjects. There is remedial math and writing. **Library/Resources:** The library contains 236,793 volumes, 899,329 microform items, 10,329 audio/video tapes/CDs/DVDs, and subscribes to 52,812 periodicals including electronic. Computerized library services include interlibrary loans, database searching, Internet access, and Wi-Fi capability. **Physically Challenged Students:** Facilities include wheelchair ramps, elevators, special parking, specially equipped restrooms, special class scheduling, lowered drinking fountains, lowered telephones, and special housing. **Special:** There are 7 national honor societies, a freshman honors program, and 3 departmental honors programs. **Visiting:** There are regularly scheduled orientations for prospective students. There are guides for informal visits. To schedule a visit, contact Prospective Student Outreach at (727) USF-4802. **Campus Safety and Security:** Measures include 24-hour foot and vehicle patrol, emergency notification system, and security escort services. There are emergency telephones, lighted pathways/sidewalks, and controlled access to dorms/residences.

REQUIREMENTS: The SAT or ACT is required. The ACT Optional Writing test is also required. AP and CLEP credits are accepted. **Procedure:** Freshmen are admitted fall and spring. Entrance exams should be taken Junior year in high school. There are deferred admissions and rolling admissions plans. Applications should be filed by March 15 for fall entry; November 15 for spring entry, along with a $30 fee. Applications are accepted on-line. **Transfer Students:** 582 transfer students enrolled in 2013-2014. Courses taken at a regionally accredited school, minimum GPA of 2.5 (or a GPA of 2.0 if holding an AA degree). **International Students:** They must take the TOEFL.

ADMISSIONS: 46% of the 2014-2015 applicants were accepted. 6% of the current freshmen were in the top fifth of their class. **Admissions Contact:** Holly Kickliter, Director, Admissions and Marketing. E-Mail: *admissions@mail.usf.edu* Web: *www.usfsp.edu/enrollment*

FINANCIAL AID: In 2014-2015, 73% of all full-time freshmen and 70% of continuing full-time students received some form of financial aid. 38% of all full-time freshmen and 43% of continuing full-time students received need-based aid. The average freshman award was $6,932. Need-based scholarships or need-based grants averaged $5,024; need-based self-help aid (loans and jobs) averaged $3,098; and other non-need-based awards and non-need-based scholarships averaged $2,058. The average financial indebtedness of the 2014 graduate was $23,665. The FAFSA is required. Check with the school for current application deadlines.

UNIVERSITY OF SOUTH FLORIDA/ TAMPA   D-4
www.usf.edu

Tampa, FL 33620	(813) 974-3350
Fax: (813) 974-9689	Email: dhollema@admin.usf.edu
Full-time: 10100 men, 14575 women	Faculty: I, --$
	Ph.D.s: 90%
Part-time: 4390 men, 5920 women	Student/Faculty: n/av
Graduate: 3850 men, 6400 women	Tuition: $4000 ($17,000)
Year: semesters, summer session	Freshman Class: n/av
Room & Board: $9000	
SAT or ACT: required	CEEB CODE: 5828
Application Deadline: n/av	COMPETITIVE

The University of South Florida, founded in 1956, is a comprehensive public institution and part of the Florida Division of Colleges and Universities, offering programs in liberal and fine arts, business, engineering, health science, and education. USF also maintains campuses at Lakeland, Sarasota, and St. Petersburg. The figures in the above capsule and in this profile are approximate. There are 6 undergraduate schools and 11 graduate schools. In addition to regional accreditation, USF has baccalaureate program accreditation with AACSB, ABET, ACEJMC, ASLA, CSAB, CSWE, NAAB, NASAD, NASM, NCATE, and NLN. The 1941-acre campus is in an urban area 10 miles northeast of downtown Tampa. Including any residence halls, there are 434 buildings.

STUDENT LIFE: 96% of undergraduates are from Florida. Others are from 50 states, 132 foreign countries, and Canada. 91% are from public schools. 65% are White; 13% African American; 13% Hispanic. **Male To Female Ratio:** 1.5:1. The average age of freshmen is 19; all undergraduates, 22. 18% do not continue beyond their first year; 47% remain to graduate. **Housing:** 4326 students can be accommodated in college housing, which includes single-sex and coed dorms, on-campus apartments, and married student housing. In addition, there are honors houses, special-interest houses, fraternity houses, sorority houses, Graduate students only, medical students, and an international hall. On-campus housing is available on a first-come and first-served basis. 87% of students commute. All students may keep cars.

FACULTY/CLASSROOMS: 57% of faculty are male; 43% are female. 48% teach undergraduates, and 16% do research. No introductory courses are taught by graduate students. The average class size in an introductory lecture is 39; in a laboratory is 21; and in a regular course is 26.

PROGRAMS OF STUDY: USF confers B.A., B.S., B.F.A., B.I.S., B.M. and B.S.W. degrees. Associate, Master's, and Doctoral degrees are also awarded. Bachelor's degrees are awarded in BIOLOGICAL SCIENCE (biology/biological science and microbiology), BUSINESS (accounting, banking and finance, business administration and management, business economics, management information systems, management science, and marketing/retailing/merchandising), COMMUNICATIONS AND THE ARTS (classics, communications, dance, dramatic arts, English literature, French, German, Italian, music, Russian, Spanish, and speech/debate/rhetoric), COMPUTER AND PHYSICAL SCIENCE (chemistry, geology, mathematics, physical sciences, and physics), EDUCATION (art education, business education, education, education of the emotionally handicapped, education of the mentally handicapped, elementary education, English education, foreign languages education, mathematics education, music education, physical education, science education, social studies education, special education, and specific learning disabilities), ENGINEERING AND ENVIRONMENTAL DESIGN (chemical engineering, civil engineering, computer engineering, electrical/electronics engineering, engineering, environmental science, industrial engineering, and mechanical engineering), HEALTH PROFESSIONS (medical technology and nursing), SOCIAL SCIENCE (African American studies, American studies, anthropology, criminology, economics, geography, gerontology, history, humanities, international relations, liberal arts/general studies, philosophy, political science/government, psychology, religion, social science, social work, and sociology). Education, business and arts and sciences, are the strongest academically. Business and education have the largest enrollments.

ACTIVITIES: 7% of men belong to 19 national fraternities; 6% of women belong to 11 national sororities. There are 200 groups on campus, including art, band, cheerleading, chess, choir, chorale, chorus, computers, dance, drama, drill team, ethnic, film, gay, honors, international, jazz band, literary magazine, marching band, musical theater, newspaper, opera, orchestra, pep band, photography, political, professional, radio and TV, religious, social, social service, student government, and symphony. Popular campus events include Minority and International events, and the University Lecture Series. **Sports:** There are 9 intercollegiate sports for men and 9 for women, and 20 intramural sports for men and 19 for women. Facilities include a 10,000-seat multipurpose arena, 4 pools, tennis and indoor racquetball courts, a track, a jogging course, an indoor recreation center with weight training and aerobics rooms, a soccer stadium, a softball complex, a baseball stadium, and an 18-hole golf course. **SERVICES:** Counseling and information services are available, as is

tutoring in most subjects. There is a reader service for the blind. **Library/Resources:** The 5 libraries contain 2.3 million volumes, 4.4 million microform items, 55,762 audio/video tapes/CDs/DVDs, and subscribe to 32,423 periodicals including electronic. Computerized library services include interlibrary loans, database searching, and Internet access. Special learning facilities include an art gallery, radio station, TV station, an mock broadcasting studio, a anthropology museum, and botanical gardens. **Physically Challenged Students:** All of the campus is accessible. Facilities include wheelchair ramps, elevators, special parking, specially equipped restrooms, special class scheduling, lowered drinking fountains, and lowered telephones. **Special:** USF offers co-op programs in business and engineering, study abroad, cross-registration, work-study programs, accelerated degree programs in public health and medicine, internships, a Washington semester, dual and student-designed majors, a liberal arts degree, nondegree study, and pass/fail options for some courses. There are 21 national honor societies, a freshman honors program, and 18 departmental honors programs. **Visiting:** There are regularly scheduled orientations for prospective students, including a 2-day program. There are guides for informal visits and visitors may sit in on classes. To schedule a visit, contact the Admissions Office/New Student Orientation. **Campus Safety and Security:** Measures include 24-hour foot and vehicle patrol, self-defense education, and security escort services. There are shuttle buses, emergency telephones, lighted pathways/sidewalks, university police.

REQUIREMENTS: The SAT or ACT is required. Candidates for admission should have completed 4 units each of English and academic electives, 3 each of math, science, and social studies, and 2 of a foreign language. The GED is accepted. Applicants who do not meet minimum requirements but have important attributes, special talents, or unique circumstances are considered for admission by an academic faculty committee. A GPA of 2.0 is required. AP and CLEP credits are accepted. Important factors in the admissions decision are advanced placement or honors courses, evidence of special talent, and recommendations by school officials. To graduate, all students are required to complete at least 120 credit hours, including 36 distributed among English, math, science, social science, historical perspectives, fine arts, and humanities and 9 of exit requirements in major works/major issues and literature/writing. The number of hours required for each major varies. Students must maintain a minimum GPA of 2.0. **Procedure:** Freshmen are admitted to all sessions. Entrance exams should be taken at the end of the junior year or the beginning of the senior year. There is a rolling admissions plan. Check with the school for current application deadlines. The fall 2014 application fee was $30. Notification is sent on a rolling basis. Applications are accepted on-line. **Transfer Students:** Applicants must have a cumulative college GPA of 2.0 and be in good standing at their last institution. 30 of 120 credits required for the bachelor's degree must be completed at USF. **International Students:** The school actively recruits these students. They must take the TOEFL. They must also take the SAT or ACT.

ADMISSIONS: There were 12 National Merit finalists. **Admissions Contact:** J. Robert Spatig, Director of Admissions. E-Mail: *dhollema@admin.usf.edu* Web: *www.usf.edu*

FINANCIAL AID: The FAFSA is required. Check with the school for current application deadlines.

UNIVERSITY OF TAMPA   **D-4**
www.ut.edu

Tampa, FL 33606   (813) 257-1808
                                             (888) 646-2738
Fax: (813) 258-7398   Email: admissions@ut.edu
Full-time: 2759 men, 3429 women   **Faculty:** 277; IIA, av$
Part-time: 151 men, 160 women   **Ph.Ds:** 87%
Graduate: 364 men, 397 women   **Student/Faculty:** n/av
Year: semesters, summer session   **Tuition:** $25,772
Room & Board: $9388   **Freshman Class:** 15345
                                    applied, 8011 accepted,
                                    1590 enrolled
SAT CR/M/W: 525/540/520 **ACT:** 24   **CEEB CODE:** 5819
Application Deadline: **VERY COMPETITIVE**

The University of Tampa, founded in 1931, is a comprehensive, independent institution that offers degree programs in more than 100 undergraduate and preprofessional areas of study and graduate and evening programs. The figures in the above capsule and in this profile are approximate. There are 4 undergraduate schools and one graduate school. In addition to regional accreditation, UT has baccalaureate program accreditation with AACSB, NASM, and NLN. The 105-acre campus is in an urban area in Tampa. Including any residence halls, there are 54 buildings.

STUDENT LIFE: 70% of undergraduates are from out of state, mostly the Northeast. Students are from 50 states, 122 foreign countries, and Canada. 59% are White; 12% Hispanic. **Male To Female Ratio:** 1.2:1. The average age of freshmen is 18; all undergraduates, 21. 26% do not continue beyond their first year; 57% remain to graduate. **Housing:** 3747 students can be accommodated in college housing, which includes single-sex and coed dorms and on-campus apartments. a special honors floor, a nontraditional floor, a leadership floor and a substance-free floor. 59% of students live on campus; of those, 75% remain on campus on weekends. All students may keep cars.

FACULTY/CLASSROOMS: 42% of faculty are male; 58% are female. All teach undergraduates. No introductory courses are taught by graduate students. The average class size in an introductory lecture is 24; in a laboratory is 16; and in a regular course is 22.

PROGRAMS OF STUDY: UT confers B.A., B.S., B.F.A., B.L.S., B.M. and B.S.N. degrees. Associate and master's degrees are also awarded. Bachelor's degrees are awarded in BIOLOGICAL SCIENCE (biochemistry, biology/biological science, and marine science), BUSINESS (accounting, banking and finance, business administration and management, business economics, entrepreneurial studies, international business management, management information systems, marketing/retailing/merchandising, and sports management), COMMUNICATIONS AND THE ARTS (advertising, art, communications, creative writing, dramatic arts, English, film arts, graphic design, music, music performance, performing arts, and Spanish), COMPUTER AND PHYSICAL SCIENCE (chemistry, digital arts/technology, and mathematics), EDUCATION (athletic training, elementary education, music education, and secondary education), ENGINEERING AND ENVIRONMENTAL DESIGN (computer graphics and environmental science), HEALTH PROFESSIONS (exercise science, nursing, and public health), SOCIAL SCIENCE (criminology, economics, forensic studies, history, international studies, liberal arts/general studies, philosophy, political science/government, psychology, and sociology). Performing arts, mathematics and philosophy are the strongest academically. Management, communication and psychology are the largest.

ACTIVITIES: 10% of men belong to 11 national fraternities; 21% of women belong to 10 national sororities. There are 180 groups on campus, including leadership, media and special interest., academic, art, band, cheerleading, chess, chorale, chorus, computers, dance, drama, ethnic, gay, honors, international, jazz band, literary magazine, musical theater, newspaper, orchestra, pep band, political, professional, religious, social, social service, student government, symphony, and yearbook. Popular campus events include Into the Streets (volunteer program), Greek Sing and Leadership Awards Night. **Sports:** There are 8 intercollegiate sports for men and 11 for women, and 22 intramural sports for men and 22 for women. Facilities include 2 outdoor basketball courts, 2 outdoor sand volleyball courts. Athletic Facilities (shared with Campus Recreation): Intramural Field (1 field); The Art and Poly Pepin Stadium (1 field); Bob Martinez Athletic Center (3 courts/locker rooms/academic study lounge); softball field (1 field); Cass Gymnasium (1 court); Naimoli and Young Family Tennis Complex (6 courts); Aquatic Center (pool); Naimoli Family Athletic and Intramural Complex (1 field plus side practice field). Athletic Department (Exclusive): Bailey Baseball Field; McNeel Boathouse. **Graduates:** From July 1, 2013 to June 30, 2014, 1319 bachelor's degrees were awarded. The most popular majors were business/marketing (26%), social sciences (12%), and communications (12%). 328 companies recruited on campus in 2013-2014. In an average class, 2% graduate in 3 years or less, 51% graduate in 4 years or less, 60% graduate in 5 years or less, and 61% graduate in 6 years or less. Of the 2013 graduating class, 16% were enrolled in graduate school within 6 months of graduation, and 85% were employed.

SERVICES: Counseling and information services are available, as is tutoring in every subject. There is remedial math, reading, and writing. **Library/Resources:** The library contains 238,320 volumes, 68,718 microform items, and 13,938 audio/video tapes/CDs/DVDs, and subscribes to 56,657 periodicals including electronic. Computerized library services include interlibrary loans, database searching, Internet access, and Wi-Fi capability. Special learning facilities include an art gallery, TV station, a fully equipped research vessel for marine science studies, a music facility, writing and language labs, an academic center for excellence, a graphic design studio, a marine science lab, and art studios. **Physically Challenged Students:** All of the campus is accessible. Facilities include wheelchair ramps, elevators, special parking, specially equipped restrooms, lowered drinking fountains, lowered telephones, and special housing. **Special:** Students may participate in internships, work-study programs on campus, study abroad in 14 countries, a Washington Center internship, and an Oxford semester program. UT also offers summer marine science courses at the Gulf Coast Research Laboratory, nondegree study, pass/fail options, dual majors, accelerated degree programs, and credit for life, military, and work experience. There are 19 national honor societies, a freshman honors program, and 16 departmental honors programs. **Visiting:** There are regularly scheduled orientations for prospective students, including a campus tour and an interview with an admissions counselor, faculty, and others as requested. There are guides for informal visits, visitors may sit in on classes, and stay overnight. To schedule a visit, contact the Admissions Office. **Campus Safety and Security:** Measures include 24-hour foot and vehicle patrol, emergency notification system, self-defense education, and security escort services. There are shuttle buses, emergency telephones, lighted pathways/sidewalks, Full-service, and on-campus security office.

REQUIREMENTS: The SAT or ACT is required. In addition, Candidates for admission should have completed 4 credits in English, 3 each in math, science, and social studies, and 3 in college-preparatory electives. Of the science units, 2 must be labs. The GED is accepted. A portfolio or an audition is required for specific art and music programs. A GPA of 2.5 is required. AP and CLEP credits are accepted. Important factors in the admissions decision are recommendations by school officials, evidence of special talent, and personality/intangible qualities.To graduate, students must maintain a minimum GPA of 2.0 in at least 124 credit hours, including the 2-year learning community, 11 hours each in humanities/fine arts and social science, 6 in natural science, global issues, nonWestern studies, and art/aesthetics as well as writing-intensive course work. The requirements for individual majors vary. **Procedure:** Freshmen are admitted fall, spring, and summer. Entrance exams should be taken by the end of the junior year or early in the senior year. There are deferred admissions and rolling admissions plans. Application deadlines are open. Application fee is $40. Notifications are sent October 1. 1290 applicants were on the 2014 waiting list; 56 were admitted. Applications are accepted on-line. **Transfer Students:** 471 transfer students enrolled in 2013-2014. Applicants should have earned 17 or more college credits with a minimum GPA of 2.0. 31 of 124 credits required for the bachelor's degree must be completed at UT. **International Students:** There are 673 international students enrolled. The school actively recruits these students. They must take the TOEFL with a minimum score of 550 on the paper-based TOEFL (PBT) or 79 on the Internet-based version (iBT).

ADMISSIONS: 52% of the 2014-2015 applicants were accepted. The SAT scores for the 2014-2015 freshman class were: Critical Reading--32% below 500, 54% between 500 and 599, 13% between 600 and 699, and 1% between 700 and 800; Math--24% below 500, 55% between 500 and 599, 19% between 600 and 699, and 1% between 700 and 800; Writing--37% below 500, 49% between 500 and 599, 13% between 600 and 699, and 2% between 700 and 800. The ACT scores were 15% below 21, 36% between 21 and 23, 30% between 24 and 26, 13% between 27 and 28, and 6% above 28. 32% of the current freshmen were in the top fifth of their class; 74% were in the top two fifths. **Admissions Contact:** Dennis Nostrand, Vice President for Enrollment. E-Mail: *admissions@ut.edu* Web: *www.ut.edu*

FINANCIAL AID: In 2014-2015, 93% of all full-time freshmen and 90% of continuing full-time students received some form of financial aid. 63% of all full-time freshmen and 59% of continuing full-time

students received need-based aid. The average freshman award was $15,712. Need-based scholarships or need-based grants averaged $10,912 ($43,645 maximum); need-based self-help aid (loans and jobs) averaged $7,566 ($32,008 maximum); non-need-based athletic scholarships averaged $8,323 ($34,018 maximum); and other non-need-based awards and non-need-based scholarships averaged $6,766 ($40,739 maximum). 21% of undergraduate students work part-time. Average annual earnings from campus work is $1701. The average financial indebtedness of the 2014 graduate was $23,977. The FAFSA is required. The priority date for freshman financial aid applications for fall entry is February 1.

UNIVERSITY OF WEST FLORIDA   A-1
www.uwf.edu

Pensacola, FL 32514	(850) 474-2230
	(800) 263-1074
Fax: (850) 474-3360	Email: admissions@uwf.edu
Full-time: 3227 men, 4332 women	Faculty: IIA, -$
Part-time: 1164 men, 1609 women	Ph.D.s: n/av
Graduate: 836 men, 1483 women	Student/Faculty: 24 to 1
Year: semesters, summer session	Tuition: $6238 ($19,120)
Room & Board: $8418	Freshman Class: 13623 applied, 8284 accepted, 1797 enrolled
SAT or ACT: required	CEEB CODE: 5833
Application Deadline: June 30	COMPETITIVE

The University of West Florida, founded in 1967, is a public, regional comprehensive institution, that is part of the State University System of Florida. The figures in the above capsule and in this profile are approximate. There are 3 undergraduate schools and 3 graduate schools. In addition to regional accreditation, UWF has baccalaureate program accreditation with AACSB, ABET, CSWE, NASM, NCATE, and NLN. The 1600-acre campus is in a suburban area 10 miles north of downtown Pensacola. Including any residence halls, there are 205 buildings.

STUDENT LIFE: 95% of undergraduates are from Florida. Others are from 48 states, 70 foreign countries, and Canada. 70% are White; 12% African American. **Male To Female Ratio:** 1.4:1. The average age of freshmen is 19; all undergraduates, 24. 16% do not continue beyond their first year; 74% remain to graduate. **Housing:** 1800 students can be accommodated in college housing, which includes coed dorms and on-campus apartments. In addition, there are honors houses. On-campus housing is available on a first-come and first-served basis. 82% of students commute. All students may keep cars.

FACULTY/CLASSROOMS: 53% of faculty are male; 47% are female. No introductory courses are taught by graduate students. The average class size in an introductory lecture is 34; in a laboratory is 21; and in a regular course is 26.

PROGRAMS OF STUDY: UWF confers B.A., B.S., B.F.A., B.S.B.A., B.S.C.E., B.S.E.E. and B.S.N degrees. Associate, Master's, and Doctoral degrees are also awarded. Bachelor's degrees are awarded in BIOLOGICAL SCIENCE (biology/biological science and marine biology), BUSINESS (accounting, banking and finance, business administration and management, business economics, and marketing/retailing/merchandising), COMMUNICATIONS AND THE ARTS (communications, English, music, and studio art), COMPUTER AND PHYSICAL SCIENCE (chemistry, computer science, mathematics, physics, and statistics), EDUCATION (art education, early childhood education, elementary education, health education, middle school education, music education, and secondary education), ENGINEERING AND ENVIRONMENTAL DESIGN (computer engineering and electrical/electronics engineering), HEALTH PROFESSIONS (medical laboratory technology, nursing, predentistry, and premedicine), SOCIAL SCIENCE (criminal justice, history, philosophy, political science/government, prelaw, psychology, religion, social science, and social work). Accounting, communication arts and management are the strongest academically. Communication arts, psychology and business have the largest enrollments.

ACTIVITIES: There are 158 groups on campus, including art, band,

cheerleading, chess, choir, chorale, chorus, communications, computers, dance, debate, drama, environmental, ethnic, film, forensics, gay, honors, international, jazz band, literary magazine, musical theater, newspaper, orchestra, political, professional, radio and TV, religious, social, social service, student government, and symphony. **Sports:** There are 6 intercollegiate sports for men and 8 for women, and 12 intramural sports for men and 12 for women. Facilities include facilities for baseball, track, tennis, racquetball, handball, softball, soccer, swimming, diving, weight lifting, and aerobics. **Graduates:** From July 1, 2013 to June 30, 2014, 2082 bachelor's degrees were awarded. The most popular majors were psychology (8%), nursing (5%), and criminal justice (5%).

SERVICES: Counseling and information services are available, as is tutoring in most subjects. There is remedial math. Remedial courses are offered on campus by the local community college. **Library/Resources:** The library contains 767,633 volumes, 1.2 million microform items, 5,224 audio/video tapes/CDs/DVDs, and subscribes to 5,056 periodicals including electronic. Computerized library services include interlibrary loans and database searching. Special learning facilities include an art gallery, radio station, TV station, an archeology museum. **Physically Challenged Students:** 80% of the campus is accessible. Facilities include wheelchair ramps, elevators, special parking, specially equipped restrooms, special class scheduling, lowered drinking fountains, and special housing. **Special:** Internships are arranged on an individual basis through a student's major department. The college offers pass/fail options and credit for military experience. A 3-2 engineering degree is also offered. There are 5 national honor societies and a freshman honors program. **Visiting:** There are regularly scheduled orientations for prospective students, including 5 Open House Programs per year. There are guides for informal visits and visitors may sit in on classes. To schedule a visit, contact the Admissions Office. **Campus Safety and Security:** Measures include 24-hour foot and vehicle patrol, emergency notification system, self-defense education, and security escort services. There are emergency telephones, lighted pathways/sidewalks, a trolley system.

REQUIREMENTS: The SAT or ACT is required. Students must have completed 4 years of English, 3 each of math (algebra 1 and higher), science, and social studies, and 2 of a foreign language. A GPA of 2.0 is required. AP and CLEP credits are accepted. Important factors in the admissions decision are advanced placement or honors courses, evidence of special talent, and geographical diversity. To graduate, students must maintain a 2.0 GPA and complete 120 semester hours with a minimum of 24 hours in the major and 24 hours in upper-division courses. **Procedure:** Freshmen are admitted to all sessions. Entrance exams should be taken by the fall of the senior year. There are early admissions and rolling admissions plans. Early decision applications should be filed by June 30; regular applications, by June 30 for fall entry, along with a $30 fee. Applications are accepted online. **Transfer Students:** Applicants must have a 2.0 GPA and a 2.0 at their last institution. Transfer students with fewer than 60 semester hours of transferable credit must meet freshman admission requirements. 30 of 120 credits required for the bachelor's degree must be completed at UWF. **International Students:** There are 228 international students enrolled. They must take the TOEFL with a minimum score of 525 on the paper-based TOEFL (PBT) or 69 on the Internet-based version (iBT) or take the MELAB. They must also take the SAT or ACT, scoring 970.

ADMISSIONS: 61% of the 2014-2015 applicants were accepted. The SAT scores for the 2014-2015 freshman class were: Critical Reading--44% below 500, 44% between 500 and 599, 10% between 600 and 699, and 1% between 700 and 800; Math--49% below 500, 41% between 500 and 599, 9% between 600 and 699, and 1% between 700 and 800; Writing--60% below 500, 34% between 500 and 599, 5% between 600 and 699, and 1% between 700 and 800. The ACT scores were 8% below 21, 56% between 21 and 23, 32% between 24 and 26, 2% between 27 and 28, and 2% above 28. 4 freshmen graduated first in their class. **Admissions Contact:** Katherine Condon, Interim Director of Admissions. E-Mail: *admissions@uwf.edu* Web: *www.uwf.edu*

FINANCIAL AID: In 2014-2015, 23% of all full-time freshmen and 54% of continuing full-time students received some form of financial aid. 15% of all full-time freshmen and 57% of continuing full-time students received need-based aid. The average freshman award was

$2,034. Need-based scholarships or need-based grants averaged $1,735 ($4,000 maximum); need-based self-help aid (loans and jobs) averaged $2,352 ($3,500 maximum); non-need-based athletic scholarships averaged $626 ($1,500 maximum); and other non-need-based awards and non-need-based scholarships averaged $2,276 ($10,900 maximum). The FAFSA and the college's own financial statement are required. Check with the school for current application deadlines.

WARNER UNIVERSITY — D-4
www.warner.edu

Lake Wales, FL 33859

(863) 638-7212
(800) 309-9563

Fax: (863) 638-7290 — Email: admissions@warner.edu

Full-time: 340 men, 450 women	Faculty: 52
Part-time: 65 men, 235 women	Ph.D.s: 54%
Graduate: 40 men, 20 women	Student/Faculty: 15 to 1
Year: semesters, summer session	Tuition: $12,000
Room & Board: $6000	Freshman Class: n/av
SAT or ACT: required	CEEB CODE: 5883
Application Deadline: open	COMPETITIVE

Warner Southern College is a Christian college in the liberal arts tradition committed to the search for truth in the context of Christian faith and academic excellence. Figures in the above capsule and in this profile are approximate. There are 2 undergraduate schools and one graduate school. The 380-acre campus is in a rural area 5 miles south of Lake Wales. Including any residence halls, there are 20 buildings.

STUDENT LIFE: 88% of undergraduates are from Florida. Others are from 26 states, 18 foreign countries, and Canada. 68% are White; 17% African American. 61% are Protestant; 29% claim no religious affiliation. **Male To Female Ratio:** 1.6:1. The average age of freshmen is 19; all undergraduates, 22. 62% do not continue beyond their first year; 50% remain to graduate. **Housing:** 235 students can be accommodated in college housing, which includes single-sex dorms and off-campus apartments. On-campus housing is guaranteed for all 4 years. 58% of students commute. Alcohol is not permitted. All students may keep cars.

FACULTY/CLASSROOMS: 72% of faculty are male; 28% are female. All teach undergraduates, 20% do research, and 20% do both. No introductory courses are taught by graduate students. The average class size in an introductory lecture is 28; in a laboratory is 20; and in a regular course is 18.

PROGRAMS OF STUDY: Warner confers B.A. degrees. Associate and Master's degrees are also awarded. Bachelor's degrees are awarded in BIOLOGICAL SCIENCE (biology/biological science), BUSINESS (accounting, banking and finance, business administration and management, business law, institutional management, marketing management, and sports management), COMMUNICATIONS AND THE ARTS (communications and English), COMPUTER AND PHYSICAL SCIENCE (information sciences and systems), EDUCATION (business education, education of the exceptional child, elementary education, English education, music education, physical education, science education, and social science education), HEALTH PROFESSIONS (exercise science), SOCIAL SCIENCE (biblical studies, history, pastoral studies, psychology, religious music, and social work). Biblical studies, social work, and teacher education are the strongest academically. Organizational management, church ministry, and teacher education have the largest enrollments.

ACTIVITIES: There are no fraternities or sororities. There are 14 groups on campus, including band, cheerleading, choir, chorale, chorus, computers, honors, newspaper, pep band, photography, religious, social, social service, and student government. Popular campus events include Christmas Banquet, Barn Party, and Spring Banquet. **Sports:** There are 7 intercollegiate sports for men and 8 for women, and 4 intramural sports for men and 3 for women. **Graduates:** From July 1, 2013 to June 30, 2014, 368 bachelor's degrees were awarded. The most popular majors were organizational management (63%), elementary education (6%), and business administration (3%). In an average class, 25% graduate in 4 years or less, 32% graduate in 5 years or less, and 35% graduate in 6 years or less.

SERVICES: Counseling and information services are available, as is tutoring in most subjects. There is remedial math, reading, and writing. **Library/Resources:** The library contains 74,000 volumes, 7,267 microform items, 15,200 audio/video tapes/CDs/DVDs, and subscribes to 178 periodicals including electronic. Computerized library services include interlibrary loans, database searching, and Internet access. **Physically Challenged Students:** 90% of the campus is accessible. Facilities include wheelchair ramps, special parking, specially equipped restrooms, lowered drinking fountains, and lowered telephones. **Special:** Internships are required in many majors, including teacher education, social work, sports management, and church ministry. An accelerated degree program is available in organizational management. HEART (Hunger Education and Resoure Training) is a missionary training program designed to equip students to serve in missions, community development work, or crosscultural assignments in developing countries. There are 5 national honor societies and 1 departmental honors programs. **Visiting:** There are regularly scheduled orientations for prospective students, consisiting of Warner Weekend held in the spring. There are guides for informal visits, visitors may sit in on classes, and stay overnight. To schedule a visit, contact the Admissions Office. **Campus Safety and Security:** Measures include 24-hour foot and vehicle patrol and security escort services. There are shuttle buses, emergency telephones, lighted pathways/sidewalks, and special training in CPR/First Aid and emergency response.

REQUIREMENTS: The SAT or ACT is required. A GPA of 2.3 is required. AP and CLEP credits are accepted. To graduate, students must complete 128 credit hours with a GPA of 2.0 to 2.5, depending on the major. 30 to 80 hours are required in the major. 48 hours of upper-division courses are required, as is a computer application course in the major. **Procedure:** Freshmen are admitted fall and spring. Entrance exams should be taken in the junior or senior year. There are early admissions, deferred admissions, and rolling admissions plans. Application deadlines are open. Application fee is $20. Applications are accepted on-line. **Transfer Students:** 39 transfer students enrolled in 2013-2014. Applicants may transfer 24 or more hours from a regionally accredited school and must present a GPA of 2.0 or higher. 36 of 128 credits required for the bachelor's degree must be completed at Warner. **International Students:** There are 31 international students enrolled. The school actively recruits these students. They must take the TOEFL. They must also take the SAT or ACT, scoring 870.

ADMISSIONS: There were 1 National Merit finalists. 2 freshmen graduated first in their class. **Admissions Contact:** Jason Roe, Director of Admissions. E-Mail: *admissions@warner.edu* Web: *www.warner.edu*

FINANCIAL AID: In 2014-2015, 93% of all full-time freshmen and 98% of continuing full-time students received some form of financial aid. 91% of all full-time freshmen and 52% of continuing full-time students received need-based aid. 47% of undergraduate students work part-time. Average annual earnings from campus work are $1528. The FAFSA and the state aid form are required. The priority date for freshman financial aid applications for fall entry is May 10. The deadline for filing freshman financial aid applications for fall entry is October 1.

WEBBER INTERNATIONAL UNIVERSITY — D-4
www.webber.edu

Babson Park, FL 33827

(863) 638-2927
(800) 741-1844

Fax: (863) 638-1591 — Email: admissions@webber.edu

Full-time: 426 men, 202 women	Faculty: 20
Part-time: 16 men, 11 women	Ph.D.s: 60%
Graduate: 28 men, 34 women	Student/Faculty: 27 to 1
Year: semesters, summer session	Tuition: $21,686
Room & Board: $8462	Freshman Class: 521 applied, 380 accepted, 263 enrolled
SAT or ACT: required	CEEB CODE: 5893
Application Deadline: August 1	COMPETITIVE

Webber International University, founded in 1927, is a privately endowed, institution offering undergraduate and graduate degrees in business. There is 1 undergraduate school and 1 graduate school. The 110-acre campus is in a small town 50 miles east of Tampa and 50 miles south of Orlando. Including any residence halls, there are 12 buildings.

STUDENT LIFE: 69% of undergraduates are from Florida. Others are from 24 states, 41 foreign countries, and Canada. 41% are White; 24% African American; 23% Foreign. **Male To Female Ratio:** 0.5:1. The average age of freshmen is 19; all undergraduates, 22. 14% do not continue beyond their first year; 86% remain to graduate. **Housing:** 419 students can be accommodated in college housing, which includes single-sex and coed dorms and off-campus apartments. On-campus housing is guaranteed for all 4 years, is guaranteed for the freshman year only, is available on a first-come, and first-served basis. 53% of students live on campus. All students may keep cars.

FACULTY/CLASSROOMS: 56% of faculty are male; 44% are female. All teach undergraduates. No introductory courses are taught by graduate students. The average class size in a regular course is 21.

PROGRAMS OF STUDY: Webber confers B.S. degrees. Associate and Master's degrees are also awarded. Bachelor's degrees are awarded in BUSINESS (accounting, banking and finance, business administration and management, business communications, hospitality management services, management science, marketing management, and sports management), COMPUTER AND PHYSICAL SCIENCE (computer security and information assurance and information sciences and systems), SOCIAL SCIENCE (prelaw). General business studies is the strongest academically and has the largest enrollment.

ACTIVITIES: There are no fraternities or sororities. There are 11 groups on campus, including band, cheerleading, debate, honors, international, marching band, newspaper, pep band, photography, political, professional, religious, social, social service, and student government. Popular campus events include Webber Weekend, International Day, and End-of-the-Year Beach Party. **Sports:** There are 9 intercollegiate sports for men and 9 for women, and 6 intramural sports for men and 6 for women. Facilities include a gym, 2 weight rooms, 6 tennis courts, a football practice field, swimming pool, softball, baseball, and soccer fields, 4 beach volleyball courts, and a pier for fishing on the lake. **Graduates:** From July 1, 2013 to June 30, 2014, 131 bachelor's degrees were awarded. The most popular majors were general business (73%), sport management (18%), and communications (1%). 40 companies recruited on campus in 2013-2014. In an average class, 1% graduate in 3 years or less, 48% graduate in 4 years or less, 50% graduate in 5 years or less, and 54% graduate in 6 years or less.

SERVICES: Counseling and information services are available, as is tutoring in most subjects. There is remedial math, reading, and writing. **Library/Resources:** The library contains 15,000 volumes, 200 audio/video tapes/CDs/DVDs, and subscribes to 2 periodicals including electronic. Computerized library services include interlibrary loans, database searching, Internet access, and Wi-Fi capability. **Physically Challenged Students:** 90% of the campus is accessible. Facilities include wheelchair ramps, special parking, specially equipped restrooms, special class scheduling, and special housing. **Special:** Internships, study abroad in 5 countries, work study, and B.S. degrees are offered. Any combination of majors requires an additional 30 credit hours for a total of 150 to graduate. There are a freshman honors program. **Visiting:** There are regularly scheduled orientations for prospective students, including a campus tour and individual attention from admission counselors and other office representatives such as financial aid, coaches, and professors. There are guides for informal visits, visitors may sit in on classes, and stay overnight. To schedule a visit, contact Vice President Enrollment Management at PicardRP@webber.edu. **Campus Safety and Security:** Measures include 24-hour foot and vehicle patrol, emergency notification system, self-defense education, and security escort services. There are lighted pathways/sidewalks, a security patrol nights and all weekend.

REQUIREMENTS: The SAT or ACT is required. Applicants should be graduates of accredited secondary schools and have completed 3 years each of English, math, and science and 2 years of social studies. An essay is also required. The GED is accepted. A GPA of 2.0 is required. AP and CLEP credits are accepted. To graduate, all students must complete 120 credit hours, including courses in their major, a 36-credit general curriculum, and a 36-credit business core, 18-credit tailored electives, and 30-credit area of concentration. A GPA of 2.0 or better must be maintained. Students must pass the college's required English courses and meet its writing requirements. All students must take at least 3 computer courses. **Procedure:** Freshmen are admitted to all sessions. Entrance exams should be taken during the senior year. There are deferred admissions and rolling admissions plans. Applications should be filed by August 1 for fall entry; December 1 for spring entry; and April 1 for summer entry, along with a $35 fee. Applications are accepted on-line. **Transfer Students:** 42 transfer students enrolled in 2013-2014. Applicants must have a minimum GPA of 2.0 with 15 credit hours and leave their previous institution in good academic standing. Students with fewer than 15 credits must meet freshman requirements. 30 of 120 credits required for the bachelor's degree must be completed at Webber. **International Students:** There are 170 international students enrolled. The school actively recruits these students. They must take the TOEFL. We consider each application on a case by case basis.

ADMISSIONS: 73% of the 2014-2015 applicants were accepted. The SAT scores for the 2014-2015 freshman class were: Critical Reading--68% below 500, 29% between 500 and 599, and 3% between 600 and 699; Math--63% below 500, 32% between 500 and 599, 4% between 600 and 699, and 1% between 700 and 800. The ACT scores were 70% below 21, 20% between 21 and 23, and 1% between 27 and 28. **Admissions Contact:** Ryan P Picard, Director of Admissions. E-Mail: *admissions@webber.edu* Web: *www.webber.edu*

FINANCIAL AID: In 2014-2015, 98% of all full-time freshmen and 99% of continuing full-time students received some form of financial aid. 62% of all full-time freshmen and 60% of continuing full-time students received need-based aid. The average freshman award was $18,697. Need-based scholarships or need-based grants averaged $15,812 ($24,550 maximum); need-based self-help aid (loans and jobs) averaged $3,139 ($11,000 maximum); non-need-based athletic scholarships averaged $3,755 ($12,000 maximum); and other non-need-based awards and non-need-based scholarships averaged $12,973 ($16,000 maximum). 40% of undergraduate students work part-time. Average annual earnings from campus work are $1300. The average financial indebtedness of the 2014 graduate was $26,676. Webber is a member of CSS. The FAFSA is required. The priority date for freshman financial aid applications for fall entry is April 1. The deadline for filing freshman financial aid applications for fall entry is August 1.

GEORGIA

• College Location

0 20 40 60 80 100
Miles

AGNES SCOTT COLLEGE   B-2
www.agnesscott.edu

Decatur, GA 30030

Fax: (404) 471-6414
Full-time: 8 men, 889 women
Part-time: 2 men, 16 women
Graduate: n/av
Year: semesters, summer session
Room & Board: $10,535

(404) 471-6423
(800) 868-8602
Email: admission@agnesscott.edu
Faculty: 70; IIB, +$
Ph.Ds: 97%
Student/Faculty: 11 to 1
Tuition: $34,788
Freshman Class: 1340 applied, 896 accepted, 254 enrolled

SAT CR/M/W: 590/570/570 ACT: 26
Application Deadline: March 1
CEEB CODE: 5002
COMPETITIVE+

Agnes Scott College, founded in 1889, is an independent liberal arts college for women and is affiliated with the Presbyterian Church. Figures in the above capsule and in this profile are approximate. There is one undergraduate school. In addition to regional accreditation, Agnes Scott has baccalaureate program accreditation with SACS. The 100-acre campus is in an urban area 6 miles from downtown Atlanta. Including any residence halls, there are 27 buildings.

STUDENT LIFE: 63% of undergraduates are from Georgia. Others are from 37 states, and 32 foreign countries. 75% are from public schools. 33% are African American; 31% White; 12% Foreign. 38% are Protestant. **Male To Female Ratio:** 90.5:1. The average age of freshmen is 18; all undergraduates, 20. 17% do not continue beyond their first year; 72% remain to graduate. **Housing:** 795 students can be accommodated in college housing, which includes single-sex dorms and on-campus apartments. In addition, there are special-interest houses, language wings within residence halls for French and German and CHOICE housing (Choosing Healthy Options in a Community Environment). On-campus housing is guaranteed for all 4 years. 82% of students live on campus; of those, 70% remain on campus on weekends. All students may keep cars.

FACULTY/CLASSROOMS: 37% of faculty are male; 63% are female.

All teach and do research. No introductory courses are taught by graduate students. The average class size in a regular course is 21.

PROGRAMS OF STUDY: Agnes Scott confers B.A., and B.S. degrees. Bachelor's degrees are awarded in BIOLOGICAL SCIENCE (biochemistry, biology/biological science, and neurosciences), BUSINESS (business administration and management), COMMUNICATIONS AND THE ARTS (art history and appreciation, classical languages, creative writing, dance, dramatic arts, English literature, French, German, music, Spanish, and studio art), COMPUTER AND PHYSICAL SCIENCE (astrophysics, chemistry, computer science, mathematics, and physics), ENGINEERING AND ENVIRONMENTAL DESIGN (engineering), HEALTH PROFESSIONS (nursing and public health), SOCIAL SCIENCE (African studies, anthropology, classical/ancient civilization, economics, history, international relations, philosophy, political science/government, psychology, religion, sociology, and women's studies). Psychology, English literature-creative writing, and economics are the largest.

ACTIVITIES: There are no fraternities or sororities. There are 81 groups on campus, including art, cheerleading, choir, chorale, chorus, communications, dance, drama, environmental, ethnic, gay, honors, international, literary magazine, musical theater, newspaper, orchestra, pep band, photography, political, professional, religious, social, social service, student government, and yearbook. Popular campus events include Black Cat, Holiday Parties and Senior Investiture. **Sports:** There are 6 intercollegiate sports for women, and 3 intramural sports for women. Facilities include a fitness center, a gym with a regulation basketball court, an 8-lane indoor pool, a soccer field, a tennis facility, a weight room, a track, an aerobics room, and dance studios. **Graduates:** From July 1, 2013 to June 30, 2014, 175 bachelor's degrees were awarded. The most popular majors were psychology (17%), economics and organizational management (7%), and English lit-creative writing (6%). 55 companies recruited on campus in 2013-2014. In an average class, 2% graduate in 3 years or less, 70% graduate in 4 years or less, 66% graduate in 5 years or less, and 72% graduate in 6 years or less. Of the 2013 graduating class, 21% were enrolled in graduate school within 6 months of graduation, and 46% were employed.

SERVICES: Counseling and information services are available, as is tutoring in some subjects, classical languages, English, math, physics, biology, psychology, chemistry, economics and foreign languages. There is a reader service for the blind, center for writing and speaking, and a resource center for math and science. **Library/Resources:** The library contains 284,856 volumes, 33,621 microform items, 23,354 audio/video tapes/CDs/DVDs, and subscribes to 28,598 periodicals including electronic. Computerized library services include interlibrary loans, database searching, Internet access, and Wi-Fi capability. Special learning facilities include an art gallery, planetarium, TV station, an educational technology center, multimedia classrooms, and centers for writing and speaking. **Physically Challenged Students:** 90% of the campus is accessible. Facilities include wheelchair ramps, elevators, special parking, specially equipped restrooms, special class scheduling, lowered drinking fountains, lowered telephones, special housing, and lifts. **Special:** There is cross-registration through ARCHE (a 19-member consortium), and more than 300 credit and noncredit internships are available. There is a 3-2 engineering program with the Georgia Institute of Technology, a Computer Science dual-degree program with Emory University, a 3-2 nursing program with Emory University and the college also offers student-designed interdisciplinary majors. Pass/fail options are also available. Opportunities for study abroad include exchange programs, a Global Awareness program, and Global Connections. Also offered are a Washington semester, the PLEN Public Policy Semester, the Mills College Exchange, and work-study programs. B.A. degree requirements may be completed in 3 years. There are 14 national honor societies, including Phi Beta Kappa, and 13 departmental honors programs. **Visiting:** There are regularly scheduled orientations for prospective students, including tours, interviews, residence hall experiences, and informational sessions. There are guides for informal visits, visitors may sit in on classes, and stay overnight. To schedule a visit, contact the Admissions Office at admission@agnesscott .edu. **Campus Safety and Security:** Measures include 24-hour foot and vehicle patrol, emergency notification system, self-defense education, and security escort services. There are emergency telephones, lighted pathways/sidewalks, controlled access to dorms/residences, reimbursement for emergency taxi service.

REQUIREMENTS: Applications must include at least one of the following: SAT/ACT scores; an interview with an Agnes Scott College representative; a graded writing sample. All home-schooled students must submit SAT I or ACT scores and SAT II Subject tests. All applicants (except early admission) must graduate from an accredited secondary school or have a GED. A total of 16 academic credits is recommended, including 4 years of English, 3 of math, and 2 each of a foreign language, science, and social studies. An essay is required, and an interview is recommended. An audition is required for those seeking a music scholarship. AP credits are accepted. Important factors in the admissions decision are leadership record, recommendations by school officials, and advanced placement or honors courses. Requirements for graduation include first-year seminar and courses in English composition and reading, foreign language, and phys ed, as well as courses in literature and fine arts, religious or philosophical thought, historical studies or classical civilization, natural science, math, social science, and social and cultural analysis. Students must complete 128 credit hours, including 32 to 52 in the major, with a 2.0 GPA. **Procedure:** Freshmen are admitted fall and spring. Entrance exams should be taken late in the junior year or by January of the senior year. There are early admissions and deferred admissions plans. Early decision applications should be filed by November 15; regular applications, by March 1 for fall entry; and November 1 for spring entry, along with a $35 fee. Notification of early decision is sent December 15; regular decision, March 1. applicants were on the 2014 waiting list; were admitted. Applications are accepted on-line. Application fees are waived if application is completed on-line. **Transfer Students:** 14 transfer students enrolled in 2013-2014. A minimum college GPA of 3.0 is required, as is an interview and a letter of recommendation from a professor. 64 of 128 credits required for the bachelor's degree must be completed at Agnes Scott. **International Students:** There are 105 international students enrolled. The school actively recruits these students. They must take the TOEFL, with a score of 600 recommended. They must also take the SAT or ACT.

ADMISSIONS: 67% of the 2014-2015 applicants were accepted. The SAT scores for the 2014-2015 freshman class were: Critical Reading--17% below 500, 38% between 500 and 599, 33% between 600 and 699, and 12% between 700 and 800; Math--19% below 500, 40% between 500 and 599, 27% between 600 and 699, and 14% between 700 and 800; Writing--16% below 500, 40% between 500 and 599, 36% between 600 and 699, and 8% between 700 and 800. The ACT scores were 16% below 21, 19% between 21 and 23, 26% between 24 and 26, 16% between 27 and 28, and 23% above 28. 60% of the current freshmen were in the top fifth of their class; 83% were in the top two fifths. 3 freshmen graduated first in their class. **Admissions Contact:** Alexa Gaeta, Director of Admissions. E-Mail: *admission@ agnesscott.edu* Web: *www.agnesscott.edu*

FINANCIAL AID: In 2014-2015, 100% of all full-time freshmen and 99% of continuing full-time students received some form of financial aid. 73% of all full-time freshmen and 78% of continuing full-time students received need-based aid. The average freshman award was $32,641. Need-based scholarships or need-based grants averaged $27,030; need-based self-help aid (loans and jobs) averaged $4,285; and other non-need-based awards and non-need-based scholarships averaged $20,681. 90% of undergraduate students work part-time. Average annual earnings from campus work are $2000. The average financial indebtedness of the 2014 graduate was $30,139. Agnes Scott is a member of CSS. The FAFSA and the college's own financial statement, and previous year's tax return are required. The priority date for freshman financial aid applications for fall entry is February 15. The deadline for filing freshman financial aid applications for fall entry is May 1.

ALBANY STATE UNIVERSITY   B-4
www.albany.edu

Albany, GA 31705

(229) 430-4646
(800) 822-RAMS

Fax: (229) 430-4105

Full-time: 855 men, 1610 women
Part-time: 150 men, 410 women
Graduate: 115 men, 330 women
Year: semesters, summer session
Room & Board: $5000
SAT or ACT: required
Application Deadline: June 1

Email: fsuttles@asurams.edu
Faculty: n/av
Ph.D.s: 52%
Student/Faculty: n/av
Tuition: $3500 ($10,500)
Freshman Class: n/av
CEEB CODE: 5004
COMPETITIVE

Albany State University, founded in 1903, is a state-supported institution within the University System of Georgia, offering programs in liberal arts, business, health fields, and teacher education. The figures in the above capsule and in this profile are approximate. There are 4 undergraduate schools and 1 graduate school. In addition to regional accreditation, Albany State has baccalaureate program accreditation with ACBSP, NCATE, and NLN. The 144-acre campus is in an urban area 175 miles south of Atlanta. Including any residence halls, there are 28 buildings.

STUDENT LIFE: 98% of undergraduates are from Georgia. Others are from states. 91% are African American. **Male To Female Ratio:** 2.1:1. The average age of all undergraduates is 24. **Housing:** College-sponsored housing includes single-sex dorms. On-campus housing is available on a first-come, first-served basis, and is available on a lottery system for upperclassmen. Alcohol is not permitted. All students may keep cars.

FACULTY/CLASSROOMS: 56% of faculty are male; 44% are female. No introductory courses are taught by graduate students.

PROGRAMS OF STUDY: Associate and Master's degrees are also awarded. Bachelor's degrees are awarded in BIOLOGICAL SCIENCE (biology/biological science), BUSINESS (accounting, marketing/retailing/merchandising, and office supervision and management), COMMUNICATIONS AND THE ARTS (art, dramatic arts, English, fine arts, French, music, Spanish, and speech/debate/rhetoric), COMPUTER AND PHYSICAL SCIENCE (chemistry, computer science, information sciences and systems, and mathematics), EDUCATION (early childhood education, health education, middle school education, music education, physical education, science education, and special education), HEALTH PROFESSIONS (allied health and nursing), SOCIAL SCIENCE (criminal justice, forensic studies, history, political science/government, psychology, social work, and sociology).

ACTIVITIES: Men belong to 3 national fraternities; Women belong to 3 national sororities. Groups on campus include art, band, cheerleading, choir, chorale, computers, dance, debate, drama, drill team, honors, jazz band, marching band, musical theater, pep band, political, professional, religious, social, social service, student government, and yearbook. Popular campus events include Honors Day and Founders Day. **Sports:** There are 5 intercollegiate sports for men and 6 for women, and 2 intramural sports for men and 1 for women. Facilities include tennis courts, baseball and softball fields, an Olympic-size pool, a recreation room, and an all-weather track. **Graduates:** From July 1, 2013 to June 30, 2014, 485 bachelor's degrees were awarded. The most popular majors were criminal justice (9%), sociology (7%), and allied health science (6%).

SERVICES: There is remedial math, reading, and writing. **Library/Resources:** The library contains 351,467 volumes, 743,621 microform items, 3,431 audio/video tapes/CDs/DVDs, and subscribes to 169,097 periodicals including electronic. Computerized library services include interlibrary loans and database searching. **Physically Challenged Students:** 90% of the campus is accessible. Facilities include wheelchair ramps, elevators, special parking, specially equipped restrooms, lowered drinking fountains, and lowered telephones. **Special:** The university offers co-op programs in all majors, 2+2 programs with Darton College, dual majors in social sciences, and 3-2 engineering degrees with the Georgia Institute of Technology. Several work-study programs and a gerontology training program are available. Albany State participates in the Georgian Intern Programs. All language majors are eligible to study abroad. There are 5 national honor societies, a freshman honors program, and 4 departmental honors programs. **Visiting:** There are regularly scheduled orientations for prospective students, consisting of summer and fall orientations and planned campus visitations. There are guides for informal visits and visitors may sit in on classes. To schedule a visit, contact the Office of Student Affairs. **Campus Safety and Security:** Measures include 24-hour foot and vehicle patrol and security escort services. There are emergency telephones and lighted pathways/sidewalks.

REQUIREMENTS: The SAT or ACT is required. Applicants must be graduates of an accredited secondary school and have completed 4 years each of English and math, 3 each of science and social sciences, and 2 of a foreign language. A GED is accepted; however, GED students must take and pass SAT: Subject tests in areas where college-preparatory courses are deficient. A GPA of 2.0 is required. AP and CLEP credits are accepted. To graduate, all students must complete 120 semester hours, including 30 in the major. The core curriculum includes 12 hours of social science, 10 to 11 of science, math and technology, 9 of essential composition and math skills, 6 of humanities and fine arts, 5 of leadership and global awareness, and 3 of phys ed. Most majors require a minimum GPA of 2.25. Students must take a Regents exam to assess English language skills competency, pass a comprehensive exam in their major, and/or score satisfactorily on the aptitude section of the GRE. **Procedure:** Freshmen are admitted to all sessions. Entrance exams should be taken by December of the senior year. There is an early admissions plan. Applications should be filed by June 1 for fall entry; November 1 for spring entry; and April 1 for summer entry. The fall 2014 application fee was $20. **Transfer Students:** Students must provide official transcripts of all previous college work. Students with fewer than 30 transferable semester hours must meet freshman requirements. 30 of 120 credits required for the bachelor's degree must be completed at Albany State. **International Students:** They must take the TOEFL. They must also take the SAT or ACT, scoring 830, and the college's own entrance exam.

ADMISSIONS: Admissions Contact: Fred Suttles, Assistant Director of Recruitment. E-Mail: *fsuttles@asurams.edu* Web: *www.albany.edu*

FINANCIAL AID: The FAFSA is required. Check with the school for current application deadlines.

ARMSTRONG STATE UNIVERSITY　　　E-4
www.armstrong.edu

Savannah, GA 31419

912-344-2503
(800) 633-2349

Fax: (912) 344-3417　　Email: adm-info@armstrong.edu

Full-time: 1559 men, 3143 women	Faculty: 280
Part-time: 561 men, 1083 women	Ph.D.s: n/av
Graduate: 167 men, 581 women	Student/Faculty: 17 to 1
Year: semesters, summer session	Tuition: $5266 ($15,271)
Room & Board: $10,266	Freshman Class: 2719 applied, 1944 accepted, 1016 enrolled
SAT CR/M/W: 519/494/489 ACT: 21	CEEB CODE: 5012
Application Deadline: July 1	COMPETITIVE

Armstrong State University is "teaching-centered and student-focused, providing diverse learning experiences and professional programs grounded in the liberal arts." Armstrong is governed by the Board of Regents of the University System of Georgia. Recognized as a state university, Armstrong offers more than 100 academic programs and majors in the College of Education, College of Health Professions, College of Liberal Arts, College of Science and Technology, and Graduate Studies. The university grants more than 60 academic credentials including undergraduate and graduate certificates, as well as associate, bachelor, and master's degrees. Armstrong offers an Doctor of Physical Therapy degree. There are 4 undergraduate schools and 4 graduate schools. In addition to regional accreditation, Armstrong has baccalaureate program accreditation with ABET, NASM, NCATE, ACS, NAACLS, CAPTE, CoARC, CAHME, JRCERT, JRCNMT, CEPH, and CCNE. The 267-acre campus is in a suburban area 250 miles from Atlanta and 150 miles from Jacksonville, FL. Including any residence halls, there are 27 buildings.

STUDENT LIFE: 92% of undergraduates are from Georgia. Others are from 46 states, 71 foreign countries, and Canada. 60% are White; 25% African American. **Male To Female Ratio:** 2.1:1. The average age of freshmen is 19; all undergraduates, 24. 33% do not continue beyond their first year; 31% remain to graduate. **Housing:** 1411 students can be accommodated in college housing, which includes coed dorms and on-campus apartments. On-campus housing is guaranteed for the freshman year only, is available on a first-come, first-served basis, and is available on a lottery system for upperclassmen. 81% of students commute. Alcohol is not permitted. All students may keep cars.

FACULTY/CLASSROOMS: 40% of faculty are male; 60% are female. 94% teach undergraduates. No introductory courses are taught by graduate students. The average class size in an introductory lecture is 24; in a laboratory is 20; and in a regular course is 20.

PROGRAMS OF STUDY: Armstrong confers B.A., B.S., B.F.A., B.H.S., B.I.T., B.L.S., B.M.E., B.S.Ed., B.S.I.T., B.S.M.L.S., B.S.N., B.S.N.C., B.S.P. and B.S.R.S. degrees. Associate, Master's, and Doctoral degrees are also awarded. Bachelor's degrees are awarded in BIOLOGICAL SCIENCE (biochemistry and biology/biological science), COMMUNICATIONS AND THE ARTS (art, English, music, Spanish, theatre arts, and visual and performing arts), COMPUTER AND PHYSICAL SCIENCE (applied physics, chemistry, computer science, information sciences and systems, and mathematics), EDUCATION (art education, early childhood education, health education, middle school education, music education, physical education, and special education), HEALTH PROFESSIONS (health science, medical technology, nursing, radiological science, rehabilitation therapy, and respiratory therapy), SOCIAL SCIENCE (communication sciences and disorders, criminal justice, economics, history, liberal arts/general studies, political science/government, psychology, and women & gender studies). Biology, nursing, and rehabilitation sciences have the largest enrollments.

ACTIVITIES: There are 80 groups on campus, including band, cheerleading, choir, chorus, computers, dance, debate, drama, ethnic, gay, honors, international, jazz band, literary magazine, musical theater, newspaper, political, professional, religious, social, social service, and student government. Popular campus events include Celebrate Armstrong, International Week and HOLA (Hispanic Outreach and Leadership), Treasure Savannah. **Sports:** There are 6 intercollegiate sports for men and 6 for women, and 34 intramural sports for men and 34 for women. Facilities include an outdoor soccer, softball and baseball fields. The ARC houses the volleyball program where our volleyball team practices and competes, the facility seats approximately 800 people. The Alumni Arena has a full court basketball court where both the men's and women's teams practice and compete. Alumni Arena seats approximately 3,500. Student Recreation Center, 38,000 square feet. 2 Basketball courts, 1 multipurpose room, 1 weight room area, 2 locker rooms. Outdoor Field space: 4 acre lighted area, can hold 3 flag football fields or 2 softball fields. **Graduates:** From July 1, 2013 to June 30, 2014, 1023 Bachelor's degrees were awarded. The most popular majors were nursing (15%), liberal studies (9%), and health sciences (8%). In an average class, 11% graduate in 4 years or less, 24% graduate in 5 years or less, and 34% graduate in 6 years or less.

SERVICES: Counseling and information services are available, as is tutoring in most subjects. There is a reader service for the blind, and remedial math, reading, and writing. **Library/Resources:** The library contains 216,484 volumes, 535,080 microform items, 1,529 audio/video tapes/CDs/DVDs, and subscribes to 496 periodicals including electronic. Computerized library services include interlibrary loans, database searching, Internet access, and Wi-Fi capability. Special learning facilities include an art gallery. **Physically Challenged Students:** Facilities include wheelchair ramps, elevators, special parking, specially equipped restrooms, special class scheduling, lowered drinking fountains, and special housing. **Special:** There are 14 national honor societies and a freshman honors program. **Visiting:** There are regularly scheduled orientations for prospective students, including a tour of the campus and departments. There are guides for informal visits. To schedule a visit, contact Campus Tours at (912) 344-2503. **Campus Safety and Security:** Measures include 24-hour foot and vehicle patrol, emergency notification system, self-defense education, and security escort services. There are emergency telephones, lighted pathways/sidewalks, and controlled access to dorms/residences.

REQUIREMENTS: The SAT or ACT is required. Applicants should graduate from an accredited secondary school. A GED may be accepted. College preparatory work should include 4 units of English and science, 3 units of math, and social studies, and 2 of foreign language. Art students must submit a portfolio. A GPA of 2.5 is required. AP and CLEP credits are accepted. The core curriculum consists of 60 hours in humanities, math, natural sciences, and social sciences and 3 in phys ed. A minimum GPA of 2.0 overall and a grade of C or better in each major course is required. Each student must complete 123 hours, with 29 hours in the major, and must take a comprehensive exam. **Procedure:** Freshmen are admitted to all sessions. There are deferred admissions and rolling admissions plans. Applications should be filed by July 1 for fall entry; December 1 for spring entry; and April 15 for summer entry, along with a $25 fee. Applications are accepted on-line. **Transfer Students:** 631 transfer students enrolled in 2013-2014. Transfer applicants must submit all transcripts and must be in good standing at the last college attended. 30 of 124 credits required for the bachelor's degree must be completed at Armstrong. **International Students:** There are 192 international students enrolled. They must take the TOEFL with a minimum score of 523 on the paper-based TOEFL (PBT) or 70 on the Internet-based version (iBT). They must also take the SAT or ACT.

ADMISSIONS: 71% of the 2014-2015 applicants were accepted. The SAT scores for the 2014-2015 freshman class were: Critical Reading--39% below 500, 47% between 500 and 599, 13% between 600 and 699, and 1% between 700 and 800; Math--55% below 500, 37% between 500 and 599, 7% between 600 and 699, and 1% between 700 and 800; Writing--56% below 500, 37% between 500 and 599, 7% between 600 and 699, and 1% between 700 and 800. The ACT scores were 45% below 21, 31% between 21 and 23, 13% between 24 and 26, 7% between 27 and 28, and 4% above 28. **Admissions Contact:** Georj Lewis, Interim Director of Admissions. E-Mail: *adm-info@armstrong.edu* Web: *www.armstrong.edu*

FINANCIAL AID: The FAFSA is required. The priority date for freshman financial aid applications for fall entry is March 15. The deadline for filing freshman financial aid applications for fall entry is April 20.

ART INSTITUTE OF ATLANTA (*The complete profile is made available exclusively on our website, www.barronspac.com*)

BERRY COLLEGE   A-2
www.berry.edu

Mount Berry, GA 30149	**(706) 236-2215**
	(800) BERRYGA
Fax: (706) 290-2178	**Email: admissions@berry.edu**
Full-time: 798 men, 1309 women	**Faculty:** 165; IIA, -$
Part-time: 11 men, 23 women	**Ph.D.s:** 89%
Graduate: 22 men, 60 women	**Student/Faculty:** 12 to 1
Year: semesters, summer session	**Tuition:** $29,090
Room & Board: $10,164	**Freshman Class:** 3901 applied, 2353 accepted, 672 enrolled
SAT CR/M/W: 590/580/550 **ACT:** 26	**CEEB CODE:** 5059
Application Deadline: February 1	**VERY COMPETITIVE**

Berry College, founded in 1902, is a private nonsectarian college offering programs in fine and liberal arts and preprofessional programs in education and business. Figures in the above capsule and in this profile are approximate. There are 4 undergraduate schools and 2 graduate schools. In addition to regional accreditation, Berry has baccalaureate program accreditation with AACSB, NASM, NCATE, and ACS. The 27000-acre campus is in a suburban area north of Rome on U.S. 27 in northwest Georgia, 72 miles northwest of Atlanta and 75 miles from Chattanooga, TN. Including any residence halls, there are 47 buildings.

STUDENT LIFE: 68% of undergraduates are from Georgia. Others are from 33 states, 13 foreign countries, and Canada. 76% are from public schools. 84% are White. **Male To Female Ratio:** 1.7:1. The average age of freshmen is 19; all undergraduates, 20. 21% do not continue beyond their first year; 60% remain to graduate. **Housing:**

1843 students can be accommodated in college housing, which includes single-sex and coed dorms and on-campus apartments. On-campus housing is guaranteed for all 4 years. 86% of students live on campus; of those, 60% remain on campus on weekends. Alcohol is not permitted. All students may keep cars.

FACULTY/CLASSROOMS: 57% of faculty are male; 43% are female. 99% do both. No introductory courses are taught by graduate students. The average class size in an introductory lecture is 19 and in a laboratory is 17.

PROGRAMS OF STUDY: Berry confers B.A., B.S., B.Mus. and B.S.N. degrees. Master's degrees are also awarded. Bachelor's degrees are awarded in AGRICULTURE (animal science), BIOLOGICAL SCIENCE (biochemistry and biology/biological science), BUSINESS (accounting, business administration and management, finance, and marketing management), COMMUNICATIONS AND THE ARTS (art, art history and appreciation, communications, English, English literature, French, German, music, music business management, Spanish, studio art, and theatre arts), COMPUTER AND PHYSICAL SCIENCE (chemistry, mathematics, and physics), EDUCATION (art education, early childhood education, mathematics education, middle school education, music education, and physical education), ENGINEERING AND ENVIRONMENTAL DESIGN (environmental science), HEALTH PROFESSIONS (exercise science), SOCIAL SCIENCE (anthropology, economics, history, interdisciplinary studies, international studies, philosophy, political science/government, psychology, religion, and sociology). Animal science, psychology and biology have the largest enrollments.

ACTIVITIES: There are no fraternities or sororities. There are 80 groups on campus, including art, cheerleading, chess, choir, chorus, communications, computers, dance, drama, environmental, ethnic, forensics, honors, international, jazz band, literary magazine, musical theater, newspaper, orchestra, pep band, political, professional, religious, social, social service, student government, symphony, and yearbook. Popular campus events include Mountain Day, Conson Wilson Lecture Series and BCTC Theatre Season. **Sports:** There are 11 intercollegiate sports for men and 12 for women, and 21 intramural sports for men and 21 for women. Facilities include Athletic and recreational facility with six-lane 25-yard competitive swimming pool, multipurpose athletic court, basketball court, racquetball courts, and a performance gym in a 1,900+ seat arena; tennis courts; equine center; baseball, softball, and soccer/lacrosse fields; numerous running and biking trails; 6 camping pads, including 1 ADA pad; an 18-hole disc golf course; and 10 tennis courts. **Graduates:** From July 1, 2013 to June 30, 2014, 406 bachelor's degrees were awarded. The most popular majors were biology/biological sciences and general (13%), animal science, general (10%), and psychology (10%). 90 companies recruited on campus in 2013-2014. In an average class, 2% graduate in 3 years or less, 55% graduate in 4 years or less, 61% graduate in 5 years or less, and 60% graduate in 6 years or less.

SERVICES: Counseling and information services are available, as is tutoring in most subjects. There is a reader service for the blind, and remedial writing. **Library/Resources:** The library contains 391,135 volumes, 341,621 microform items, 5,732 audio/video tapes/CDs/DVDs, and subscribes to 40,392 periodicals including electronic. Computerized library services include interlibrary loans, database searching, Internet access, and Wi-Fi capability. Special learning facilities include an art gallery, an observatory, an equine center, a forestry center, beef-and-dairy-cattle operations, BOLD (Berry Outdoor Leadership Development), Wildlife Management Area, Longleaf Pine Project, student-only campsites, and a trail system for hiking, biking, and horseback riding. **Physically Challenged Students:** 80% of the campus is accessible. Facilities include wheelchair ramps, elevators, special parking, specially equipped restrooms, lowered drinking fountains, and special housing. **Special:** The college offers internships, study abroad in more than 20 countries, work-study programs, student-designed majors, co-op programs, cross-registration with Shorter College, dual majors, credit by exam, and nondegree study. There are 3-2 engineering degrees and dual-degree programs in several fields with the Georgia Institute of Technology. There is also a dual-degree program in nursing with Emory University. There are 12 national honor societies, a freshman honors program, and 20 departmental honors programs. **Visiting:** There are regularly scheduled orientations for prospective students, including weekdays and Saturday mornings. Students should schedule campus visits in advance. . There are guides for informal visits, visitors may sit in on classes, and stay overnight. To schedule a visit, contact The Office of Admissions at (706) 236-2215. **Campus Safety and Security:** Measures include 24-hour foot and vehicle patrol and emergency notification system. There are emergency telephones, lighted pathways/sidewalks, controlled access to dorms/residences, and a gated campus, mobile police patrols, identification of valuables, limited access to campus.

REQUIREMENTS: The SAT or ACT is required. Applicants should be graduates of an accredited high school or have a GED. 20 academic credits are required, including 4 units each of English and math (to include algebra I, algebra II, and either geometry or trigonometry), 3 each of science and social studies, and 2 of a foreign language. Either SAT or ACT is required. AP credits are accepted. Important factors in the admissions decision are advanced placement or honors courses, leadership record, and recommendations by school officials.General education requirements include 5 courses in the humanities and fine arts, 3 each in behavioral science, math and natural sciences, communication, and health and phys ed, and 2 in electives. A 2.0 GPA and a total of 124 credits, including at least 30 hours in the major, are required for graduation. All students are also required to attend at least 3 approved cultural events per semester and pass a comprehensive exam or other senior assessment in the major. **Procedure:** Freshmen are admitted to all sessions. Entrance exams should be taken by the fall of the senior year. There is a rolling admissions plan. Applications should be filed by February 1 for fall entry. Notifications are sent November 1. 33 applicants were on the 2014 waiting list; 1 was admitted. Applications are accepted on-line. **Transfer Students:** 40 transfer students enrolled in 2013-2014. Applicants must submit official transcripts from all colleges previously attended, have a minimum GPA of 2.5, and be in good standing at the last school attended. 62 of 124 credits required for the bachelor's degree must be completed at Berry. **International Students:** There are 19 international students enrolled. The school actively recruits these students. They must take the TOEFL with a minimum score of 550 on the paper-based TOEFL (PBT) or 80 on the Internet-based version (iBT), or take the IELTS. They must also take the SAT or ACT, if the student is from an English-speaking country.

ADMISSIONS: 60% of the 2014-2015 applicants were accepted. The SAT scores for the 2014-2015 freshman class were: Critical Reading--8% below 500, 46% between 500 and 599, 38% between 600 and 699, and 8% between 700 and 800; Math--7% below 500, 52% between 500 and 599, 36% between 600 and 699, and 4% between 700 and 800; Writing--18% below 500, 51% between 500 and 599, 27% between 600 and 699, and 4% between 700 and 800. The ACT scores were 1% below 21, 22% between 21 and 23, 30% between 24 and 26, 18% between 27 and 28, and 28% above 28. 58% of the current freshmen were in the top fifth of their class; 86% were in the top two fifths. There were 1 National Merit finalists. 19 freshmen graduated first in their class. **Admissions Contact:** Brett Kennedy, Director of Admissions. E-Mail: *admissions@berry.edu* Web: *www.berry.edu*

FINANCIAL AID: In 2014-2015, 100% of all full-time freshmen and 99% of continuing full-time students received some form of financial aid. 77% of all full-time freshmen and 73% of continuing full-time students received need-based aid. The average freshman award was $23,432. Need-based scholarships or need-based grants averaged $20,093; need-based self-help aid (loans and jobs) averaged $4,296; and other non-need-based awards and non-need-based scholarships averaged $11,140. 91% of undergraduate students work part-time. Average annual earnings from campus work are $2358. The average financial indebtedness of the 2014 graduate was $25,335. The FAFSA is required. The priority date for freshman financial aid applications for fall entry is March 1.

BRENAU UNIVERSITY - WOMEN'S COLLEGE (*The complete profile is made available exclusively on our website, www.barronspac.com*)

BREWTON-PARKER COLLEGE	D-4
www.bpc.edu	

Mt. Vernon, GA 30445	(912) 583-3247
	(800) 342-1087
Fax: (912) 583-4498	Email: admissions@bpc.edu
Full-time: 237 men, 231 women	Faculty: 31
Part-time: 79 men, 82 women	Ph.D.s: 45%
Graduate: n/av	Student/Faculty: 9 to 1
Year: semesters, summer session	Tuition: $26,080
Room & Board: $7308	Freshman Class: n/av
SAT: required	CEEB CODE: 5068
Application Deadline: n/av	**COMPETITIVE**

Brewton-Parker College is a four-year Christian college located on the main campus in Mount Vernon, Georgia, and one external site in Newnan. Affiliated with the Georgia Baptist Convention, the College offers four baccalaureate degrees in a caring, Christian environment that nurtures the whole student. Students enjoy challenging academic programs in an unapologetically Christian setting. Residential students participate in a comprehensive campus life program involving student organizations, intramural sports, campus ministry opportunities, and weekend activities. There are no undergraduate schools. In addition to regional accreditation, BPC has baccalaureate program accreditation with NCATE. The 270-acre campus is in a rural area on Hwy 280 in the adjoining towns of Mt. Vernon and Ailey. Including any residence halls, there are 36 buildings.

STUDENT LIFE: 95% of undergraduates are from Georgia. **Male To Female Ratio:** 1.0:1. The average age of freshmen is 20; all undergraduates, 26. **Housing:** 410 students can be accommodated in college housing, which includes single-sex dorms. On-campus housing is guaranteed for all 4 years. 50% of students commute. Alcohol is not permitted. All students may keep cars.

FACULTY/CLASSROOMS: 54% of faculty are male; 46% are female. No introductory courses are taught by graduate students. The average class size in an introductory lecture is 20; in a laboratory is 24; and in a regular course is 17.

PROGRAMS OF STUDY: BPC confers B.A., B.S. and B.Min. degrees. Associate degrees are also awarded. Bachelor's degrees are awarded in BIOLOGICAL SCIENCE (biology/biological science), BUSINESS (accounting, business administration and management, and management information systems), COMMUNICATIONS AND THE ARTS (communications, dramatic arts, and English), COMPUTER AND PHYSICAL SCIENCE (information sciences and systems), EDUCATION (early childhood education, physical education, and sports studies), ENGINEERING AND ENVIRONMENTAL DESIGN (technological management), SOCIAL SCIENCE (Christian studies, history, human services, liberal arts/general studies, political science/government, psychology, social science, and sociology). Business, education, and psychology have the largest enrollments.

ACTIVITIES: There are no fraternities or sororities. There are 22 groups on campus, including cheerleading, choir, Circle K, film, honors, international, professional, religious, social, social service, and student government. Popular campus events include Homecoming, Alumni Weekend, and Fall Festival. **Sports:** There are 4 intercollegiate sports for men and 5 for women, and 8 intramural sports for men and 8 for women. Facilities include softball, baseball, and soccer fields, tennis courts, a swimming pool, a gym, a track, an intramural field, an outdoor volleyball court, a physical fitness building, a game room, and a campus lake. **Graduates:** From July 1, 2013 to June 30, 2014, 124 bachelor's degrees were awarded. The most popular majors were early childhood education (10%), business (9%), and psychology (8%).

SERVICES: Counseling and information services are available, as is tutoring in most subjects. There is remedial math, reading, and writing. Tutoring in Spanish is available. **Library/Resources:** The library contains 98,045 volumes, 1,562 microform items, 6,941 audio/video tapes/CDs/DVDs, and subscribes to 132 periodicals including electronic. Computerized library services include interlibrary loans, database searching, Internet access, and Wi-Fi capability. Special learning facilities include a **Physically Challenged Students:** 80% of the campus is accessible. Facilities include wheelchair ramps, special parking, specially equipped restrooms, and special housing. **Special:** The college offers internships, a general studies degree, B.A.-B.S. degrees, B.Min. degree, and nondegree study. There are 3 national honor societies. **Visiting:** There are regularly scheduled orientations for prospective students, consisting of a campus tour and academic and financial aid sessions. There are guides for informal visits, visitors may sit in on classes, and stay overnight. To schedule a visit, contact the Office of Admissions. **Campus Safety and Security:** There are lighted pathways/sidewalks, controlled access to dorms/residences, evening security guard on campus.

REQUIREMENTS: The SAT is required. The ACT and ACT Writing Test are recommended. A GED is accepted. Students should prepare with 4 years of English, 3 of social studies, and 2 each of foreign language, math, and science. A GPA of 2.0 is required. AP and CLEP credits are accepted. Important factors in the admissions decision are personality/intangible qualities, leadership record, and advanced placement or honors courses.The required core curriculum consists of humanities, math, natural science, social science, phys ed, and computer science. Students must maintain a minimum 2.0 GPA with half of the major taken at Brewton Parker. **Procedure:** Freshmen are admitted to all sessions. Entrance exams should be taken during the senior year of high school. There is a deferred admissions plan. Application deadlines are open. Application fee is $25. Applications are accepted on-line. **Transfer Students:** 81 transfer students enrolled in 2013-2014. Applicants must submit transcripts from previously attended institutions, along with high school transcripts, if they have completed fewer than 30 semester hours. **International Students:** There are 13 international students enrolled. They must also take the SAT, scoring 880.

ADMISSIONS: The SAT scores for the 2014-2015 freshman class were: Critical Reading--65% below 500, 29% between 500 and 599, 5% between 600 and 699, and 1% between 700 and 800; Math--65% below 500, 29% between 500 and 599, and 6% between 600 and 699; Writing--65% below 500, 29% between 500 and 599, and 6% between 600 and 699. The ACT scores were 87% between 21 and 23, 11% between 27 and 28, and 2% above 28. **Admissions Contact:** Sandra Clay, Director of Admissions. E-Mail: *admissions@bpc.edu* Web: *www.bpc.edu*

FINANCIAL AID: In 2014-2015, 95% of all full-time freshmen and 95% of continuing full-time students received some form of financial aid. BPC is a member of CSS. The FAFSA and the college's own financial statement are required. Check with the school for current application deadlines.

CLARK ATLANTA UNIVERSITY (*The complete profile is made available exclusively on our website, www.barronspac.com*)

CLAYTON STATE UNIVERSITY (*The complete profile is made available exclusively on our website, www.barronspac.com*)

COLUMBUS STATE UNIVERSITY　　　A-3
www.colstate.edu

Columbus, GA 31907	(706) 507-8800
	(866) 264-2035
Fax: (706) 568-2462	Email: lovell_susan@columbusstate.com
Full-time: 1917 men, 3078 women	Faculty: 265; IIA, -$
Part-time: 895 men, 1179 women	Ph.D.s: 78%
Graduate: 503 men, 726 women	Student/Faculty: 19 to 1
Year: semesters, summer session	Tuition: $5896 ($17,872)
Room & Board: $7280	Freshman Class: 3454 applied, 2075 accepted, 1240 enrolled
SAT CR/M/W: 508/496/490 **ACT:** 21	CEEB CODE: 5123
Application Deadline: June 30	COMPETITIVE

Columbus State University, established in 1958, is a public liberal arts institution within the University System of Georgia. Figures in the above capsule and in this profile are approximate. There are 4 undergraduate schools and 1 graduate school. In addition to regional accreditation, Columbus State has baccalaureate program accredita-

tion with AACSB, APTA, NASAD, NASM, NCATE, NLN, and CACREP. The 150-acre campus is in a suburban area in Columbus, Georgia, 100 miles south of Atlanta. Including any residence halls, there are 55 buildings.

STUDENT LIFE: 86% of undergraduates are from Georgia. Others are from 40 states, 41 foreign countries, and Canada. 55% are White; 35% African American. **Male To Female Ratio:** 1.5:1. The average age of freshmen is 19; all undergraduates, 24. 32% do not continue beyond their first year; 32% remain to graduate. **Housing:** 1200 students can be accommodated in college housing, which includes single-sex on-campus apartments and off-campus apartments. In addition, there are special-interest houses. On-campus housing is guaranteed for all 4 years. 81% of students commute. Alcohol is not permitted. All students may keep cars.

FACULTY/CLASSROOMS: 53% of faculty are male; 47% are female. 98% teach undergraduates, and 90% do both. No introductory courses are taught by graduate students. The average class size in an introductory lecture is 27; in a laboratory is 17; and in a regular course is 26.

PROGRAMS OF STUDY: Columbus State confers B.A., B.S.. B.B.A., B.M., B.S.Ed. and B.S.N. degrees. Associate, Master's, and Doctoral degrees are also awarded. Bachelor's degrees are awarded in BIOLOGICAL SCIENCE (biology/biological science), BUSINESS (accounting, banking and finance, business administration and management, management information systems, and marketing/retailing/merchandising), COMMUNICATIONS AND THE ARTS (art, communications, dramatic arts, English, French, music, music performance, Spanish, and visual and performing arts), COMPUTER AND PHYSICAL SCIENCE (chemistry, computer science, earth science, and mathematics), EDUCATION (art education, drama education, early childhood education, foreign languages education, health education, middle school education, music education, secondary education, and special education), HEALTH PROFESSIONS (exercise science, health science, and nursing), SOCIAL SCIENCE (criminal justice, history, political science/government, psychology, and sociology). nursing, biology, and music are the strongest academically. Nursing, business, and early childhood education have the largest enrollments.

ACTIVITIES: 2% of men belong to 1 local and 8 national fraternities; 2% of women belong to 3 local and 5 national sororities. There are 51 groups on campus, including art, band, cheerleading, choir, chorale, chorus, computers, dance, debate, drama, drill team, environmental, ethnic, film, honors, international, jazz band, literary magazine, musical theater, newspaper, orchestra, pep band, photography, political, professional, religious, social, social service, student government, and symphony. Popular campus events include Black History Month, Halloween, and Greek Week. **Sports:** There are 6 intercollegiate sports for men and 7 for women, and 16 intramural sports for men and 16 for women. Facilities include Art Student Recreation Center with physical fitness rooms, racketball courts, swimming pools, basketball courts climbing wall, tennis courts, baseball, soccer, softball, and intramural multipurpose fields, a walking trail, volleyball and basketball courts. **Graduates:** From July 1, 2013 to June 30, 2014, 872 bachelor's degrees were awarded. The most popular majors were nursing (11%), management (8%), and criminal justice (8%). In an average class, 12% graduate in 4 years or less, 23% graduate in 5 years or less, and 33% graduate in 6 years or less.

SERVICES: Counseling and information services are available, as is tutoring in most subjects. There is a reader service for the blind, and remedial math, reading, and writing. Scribe and braille services are also available. **Library/Resources:** The 2 libraries contain 263,110 volumes, 1.1 million microform items, 12,122 audio/video tapes/CDs/DVDs, and subscribe to 1,394 periodicals including electronic. Computerized library services include interlibrary loans, database searching, and Internet access. Special learning facilities include an art gallery, planetarium, archives. **Physically Challenged Students:** All of the campus is accessible. Facilities include wheelchair ramps, elevators, special parking, specially equipped restrooms, special class scheduling, lowered drinking fountains, lowered telephones. **Special:** Internships, a Washington semester, work-study, and study abroad in 14 countries is possible. A 3-2 engineering degree with the Georgia Institute of Technology and a B.A.-B.S. degree in biology, chemistry, math, or psychology are also available. There are 19 national honor societies and a freshman honors program. **Visiting:** There are regularly scheduled orientations for prospective students, during the fall and spring semesters, there are college visitation programs. Prospective students may arrange a tour on any weekday. There are guides for informal visits and visitors may sit in on classes. To schedule a visit, contact the Admissions Office at www.colstate.edu/future/. **Campus Safety and Security:** Measures include 24-hour foot and vehicle patrol, emergency notification system, self-defense education, and security escort services. There are shuttle buses, emergency telephones, lighted pathways/sidewalks, shuttles for evening students.

REQUIREMENTS: The SAT or ACT is required. The SAT is preferred, with a minimum Critical Reading score of 440 and Math score of 410. A minimum ACT score of 17 English and 17 math is accepted. Applicants must be graduates of accredited secondary schools. 16 academic credits are required, including 4 each in English and math, 3 each in science and social studies, and 2 in a foreign language. A GPA of 2.3 is required. AP and CLEP credits are accepted.To graduate, all students must maintain a 2.0 GPA and complete a minimum of 123 semester hours, 63 of them in a core curriculum and 60 in the major. Three semester hours of phys ed are required. All students must complete English 1101, English 1102, and Math 1111 with a C or better, and satisfy the Georgia History and Constitution and U.S. History and Constitution requirement by taking specified courses at a University System of Georgia institution or, for transfers from outside the system, by passing an exemption test. Some majors require a comprehensive exam. **Procedure:** Freshmen are admitted to all sessions. Entrance exams should be taken in the fall of the senior year. There are early admissions and rolling admissions plans. Applications should be filed by June 30 for fall entry; November 1 for spring entry; and March 1 for summer entry, along with a $30 fee. Applications are accepted on-line. **Transfer Students:** 604 transfer students enrolled in 2013-2014. Transfer students with fewer than 30 hours of credit must meet the same requirements as entering freshmen. Transfer students must have a 2.0 GPA and be eligible to return to the institution last attended. 30 of 123 credits required for the bachelor's degree must be completed at Columbus State. **International Students:** There are 68 international students enrolled. The school actively recruits these students. They must take the TOEFL with a minimum score of 550 on the paper-based TOEFL (PBT) or 79 on the Internet-based version (iBT). They must also take the SAT or ACT, scoring 17.

ADMISSIONS: 60% of the 2014-2015 applicants were accepted. The SAT scores for the 2014-2015 freshman class were: Critical Reading--48% below 500, 38% between 500 and 599, 13% between 600 and 699, and 1% between 700 and 800; Math--54% below 500, 36% between 500 and 599, 9% between 600 and 699, and 1% between 700 and 800; Writing--57% below 500, 34% between 500 and 599, 8% between 600 and 699, and 1% between 700 and 800. The ACT scores were 59% below 21, 25% between 21 and 23, 12% between 24 and 26, 3% between 27 and 28, and 1% above 28. **Admissions Contact:** Susan Lovell, Director of Enrollment Services. E-Mail: *lovell_susan@columbusstate.edu* Web: *www.colstate.edu*

FINANCIAL AID: In 2014-2015, 88% of all full-time freshmen and 83% of continuing full-time students received some form of financial aid. 58% of all full-time freshmen and 58% of continuing full-time students received need-based aid. The average freshman award was $10,477. Need-based scholarships or need-based grants averaged $4,926; need-based self-help aid (loans and jobs) averaged $3,228; non-need-based athletic scholarships averaged $4,486; and other non-need-based awards and non-need-based scholarships averaged $5,433. The average financial indebtedness of the 2014 graduate was $21,486. The FAFSA is required. The priority date for freshman financial aid applications for fall entry is May 1.

COVENANT COLLEGE	A-1
www.covenant.edu	

Lookout Mountain, GA 30750

(706) 820-2398
(888) 451-2683

Fax: (706) 820-0893   Email: admissions@covenant.edu

Full-time: 440 men, 609 women	Faculty: 62; IIB, av$
Part-time: 11 men, 6 women	Ph.D.s: 90%
Graduate: 17 men, 51 women	Student/Faculty: 14 to 1
Year: semesters, summer session	Tuition: $30,160
Room & Board: $8830	Freshman Class: 655 applied, 633 accepted, 265 enrolled

SAT CR/M/W: 610/570/590 **ACT:** 26   CEEB CODE: 6124
Application Deadline: May 1   **VERY COMPETITIVE+**

Covenant College, founded in 1955, is a private liberal arts college affiliated with the Presbyterian Church in America. At Covenant, we seek to inspire and equip our students to be faithful stewards of their God-given abilities- all of our programs are designed with this in mind. There is 1 undergraduate school and 1 graduate school. In addition to regional accreditation, Covenant has baccalaureate program accreditation with SACS-COC. The 350-acre campus is in a suburban area 12 miles southwest of Chattanooga, Tennessee. Including any residence halls, there are 15 buildings.

STUDENT LIFE: 78% of undergraduates are from out of state, mostly the South. Students are from 48 states, 23 foreign countries, and Canada. 90% are White. 49% are Protestant. **Male To Female Ratio:** 1.4:1. The average age of freshmen is 18; all undergraduates, 20. 15% do not continue beyond their first year; 58% remain to graduate. **Housing:** 917 students can be accommodated in college housing, which includes single-sex dorms and on-campus apartments. Coed dorms, and apartments for single students. On-campus housing is guaranteed for all 4 years. 98% of students live on campus. Alcohol is not permitted. All students may keep cars.

FACULTY/CLASSROOMS: 75% of faculty are male; 26% are female. All teach undergraduates. No introductory courses are taught by graduate students. The average class size in an introductory lecture is 19; in a laboratory is 16; and in a regular course is 18.

PROGRAMS OF STUDY: Covenant confers B.A., and B.S. degrees. Master's degrees are also awarded. Bachelor's degrees are awarded in BIOLOGICAL SCIENCE (biology/biological science), BUSINESS (business administration and management), COMMUNICATIONS AND THE ARTS (art, dramatic arts, English, French, music, music performance, and Spanish), COMPUTER AND PHYSICAL SCIENCE (chemistry, computer science, mathematics, and physics), EDUCATION (elementary education, English education, mathematics education, and science education), SOCIAL SCIENCE (biblical studies, economics, history, interdisciplinary studies, philosophy, philosophy and religion, psychology, social science, and sociology). English, history, sociology and education have the largest enrollments.

ACTIVITIES: There are no fraternities or sororities. There are 43 groups on campus, including campus ministries, music ensembles and student-run film society, radio station, bagpipe, choir, chorale, concert band, dance, debate, drama, film, honors, international, jazz band, literary magazine, musical theater, newspaper, photography, professional, religious, social, social service, student government, and yearbook. Popular campus events include Madrigal Dinner, Spring Banquet and Kilter Night. **Sports:** There are 6 intercollegiate sports for men and 7 for women, and 9 intramural sports for men and 9 for women. Facilities include a gym, weight room, swimming pool, tennis courts, 3 soccer fields, running trails, an aerobics room, and a wellness room equipped with a variety of fitness machines. **Graduates:** From July 1, 2013 to June 30, 2014, 243 bachelor's degrees were awarded. The most popular majors were social sciences (14%), English (13%), and education (10%).

SERVICES: Counseling and information services are available, as is tutoring in some subjects, math and writing. There is remedial math, reading, and writing. **Library/Resources:** The library contains 89,449 volumes, 121,159 microform items, 4,500 audio/video tapes/CDs/DVDs, and subscribes to 525 periodicals including electronic. Computerized library services include interlibrary loans, database searching, Internet access, and Wi-Fi capability. Special learning facilities include an art gallery. **Physically Challenged Students:** All of the campus is accessible. Facilities include wheelchair ramps, elevators, special parking, specially equipped restrooms, lowered drinking fountains, lowered telephones. **Special:** Cross-registration is possible with the Council for Christian Colleges and Universities (CCCU). Students may study abroad in 9 countries or spend a semester in Washington. There is a 3-2 engineering program with Georgia Tech; and a cooperative nursing program with Emory; Bridge program for MSN with Vanderbilt. Juniors and seniors may take classes on a pass/fail basis. There are 5 national honor societies and 5 departmental honors programs. **Visiting:** There are regularly scheduled orientations for prospective students, consisting of a campus preview weekend during which high school students stay in dormitories and attend classes, seminars, and other college activities. There are guides for informal visits, visitors may sit in on classes, and stay overnight.. **Campus Safety and Security:** Measures include 24-hour foot and vehicle patrol, emergency notification system, and security escort services. There are lighted pathways/sidewalks, A watchman who maintains campus security at night.

REQUIREMENTS: The SAT or ACT is required. Students must submit the following: application for admission, application fee, Christian testimony, official high school transcript, minimum GPA of 2.50, a combined SAT score of at least 1000 (sum of critical reading and math section scores) or composite ACT score of at least 21, academic references, and a church reference. Applicants must graduate from an accredited high school or have a GED. Applicants should have 14 total units, including 4 years of high school English, 3 years of math, and 2 years each of science, and social studies, and academic electives. An essay and an interview are required. A GPA of 2.5 is required. AP and CLEP credits are accepted. Important factors in the admissions decision are advanced placement or honors courses, personality/intangible qualities, recommendations by school officials, leadership record, parents or siblings attended your school, extracurricular activities record, and recommendations by alumni.All students must complete 55 to 63 hours of core and distribution requirements, including course work in Bible studies, interdisciplinary studies, English composition, cross-cultural experience, language, phys ed, lab science, social science, and history. A minimum total of 126 credits and a GPA of 2.0 are required for graduation. All students must also complete an oral interview and a senior integration project, in which they explore a problem in their major field in light of Christian philosophy. **Procedure:** Freshmen are admitted fall and spring. Entrance exams should be taken by January of the senior year. There is a rolling admissions plan. Applications should be filed by May 1 for fall entry; November 1 for spring entry, along with a $35 fee. Notification of early decision is sent August 15; regular decision, in rolling. Applications are accepted on-line. Application fees are waived if application is completed on-line. **Transfer Students:** 39 transfer students enrolled in 2013-2014. Transfer applicants must take either the SAT, with a minimum satisfactory score, or the ACT, with a minimum composite of 21. Courses with a grade of C or better that apply toward the selected Covenant program will receive transfer credit. 32 of 126 credits required for the bachelor's degree must be completed at Covenant. **International Students:** There are 23 international students enrolled. The school actively recruits these students. They must take the TOEFL with a minimum score of 540 on the paper-based TOEFL (PBT) or 76 on the Internet-based version (iBT). Applicants are encouraged to take the SAT or ACT if it is available in their country.

ADMISSIONS: 97% of the 2014-2015 applicants were accepted. The SAT scores for the 2014-2015 freshman class were: Critical Reading--10% below 500, 38% between 500 and 599, 35% between 600 and 699, and 17% between 700 and 800; Math--17% below 500, 45% between 500 and 599, 32% between 600 and 699, and 6% between 700 and 800; Writing--19% below 500, 35% between 500 and 599, 37% between 600 and 699, and 9% between 700 and 800. The ACT scores were 7% below 21, 18% between 21 and 23, 25% between 24 and 26, 21% between 27 and 28, and 28% above 28. 46% of the current freshmen were in the top fifth of their class; 65% were in the top two fifths. **Admissions Contact:** Scott Schindler, Assoc. Director of Admissions. E-Mail: *admissions@covenant.edu* Web: *www.covenant.edu*

FINANCIAL AID: In 2014-2015, 100% of all full-time freshmen and continuing full-time students received some form of financial aid. 70% of all full-time freshmen and 68% of continuing full-time students received need-based aid. The average freshman award was $21,771. Need-based scholarships or need-based grants averaged $17,722 ($30,430 maximum); need-based self-help aid (loans and jobs) averaged $5,450 ($33,522 maximum); and other non-need-based awards and non-need-based scholarships averaged $12,131 ($27,850 maximum). 56% of undergraduate students work part-time. Average annual earnings from campus work are $2427. The average financial indebtedness of the 2014 graduate was $22,208. The FAFSA, the state aid form, and the college's own financial statement are required. The priority date for freshman financial aid applications for fall entry is March 1. The deadline for filing freshman financial aid applications for fall entry is March 31.

EMORY UNIVERSITY
B-2
www.emory.edu

Atlanta, GA 30322	(404) 727-6036

Email: admission@emory.edu

Full-time: 3321 men, 4355 women	**Faculty:** 780; I, ++$
Part-time: 72 men, 88 women	**Ph.D.s:** 100%
Graduate: 2935 men, 3742 women	**Student/Faculty:** 8 to 1
Year: semesters, summer session	**Tuition:** $44,008
Room & Board: $12,360	**Freshman Class:** 17681 applied, 4685 accepted, 1354 enrolled
SAT CR/M/W: 660/700/690 **ACT:** 31	**CEEB CODE:** 5187
Application Deadline: January 15	**MOST COMPETITIVE**

Emory University, founded in 1836, is a private institution affiliated with the United Methodist Church. There are 5 undergraduate schools and 8 graduate schools. In addition to regional accreditation, Emory has baccalaureate program accreditation with SACS. The 634-acre campus is in a suburban area 5 miles northeast of downtown Atlanta. Including any residence halls, there are 150 buildings.

STUDENT LIFE: 73% of undergraduates are from out of state, mostly the South. Students are from 50 states, 48 foreign countries, and Canada. 60% are from public schools. 41% are White; 22% Asian American; 15% Foreign. 43% claim no religious affiliation; 18% Protestant; 13% Muslim, Hindu, and Buddhist.; 12% Catholic; 11% Jewish. **Male To Female Ratio:** 1.3:1. The average age of freshmen is 18; all undergraduates, 20. 6% do not continue beyond their first year; 89% remain to graduate. **Housing:** 4425 students can be accommodated in college housing, which includes single-sex and coed dorms, on-campus apartments, and married student housing. In addition, there are honors houses, language houses, special-interest houses, fraternity houses, sorority houses, Theme housing. On-campus housing is guaranteed for all 4 years. 67% of students live on campus; of those, 95% remain on campus on weekends. Upperclassmen may keep cars.

FACULTY/CLASSROOMS: 59% of faculty are male; 41% are female. No introductory courses are taught by graduate students.

PROGRAMS OF STUDY: Emory confers B.A., B.S., B.B.A. and B.S.N. degrees. Associate, Master's, and Doctoral degrees are also awarded. Bachelor's degrees are awarded in AGRICULTURE (environmental studies), BIOLOGICAL SCIENCE (biology/biological science and neurosciences), BUSINESS (accounting, banking and finance, business administration and management, business economics, and marketing/retailing/merchandising), COMMUNICATIONS AND THE ARTS (art, art history and appreciation, Chinese, classics, comparative literature, creative writing, dance, dramatic arts, English, film arts, fine arts, French, Greek, Italian, Japanese, journalism, Latin, linguistics, music, Russian languages and literature, and Spanish), COMPUTER AND PHYSICAL SCIENCE (chemistry, computer science, mathematics, and physics), EDUCATION (educational statistics and research), HEALTH PROFESSIONS (nursing), SOCIAL SCIENCE (African studies, African American studies, American studies, anthropology, Asian/American studies, Asian/Oriental studies, Caribbean studies, classical/ancient civilization, economics,

French studies, German area studies, history, interdisciplinary studies, international studies, Italian studies, Judaic studies, Latin American studies, medieval studies, Middle Eastern studies, philosophy, political science/government, psychology, religion, Russian and Slavic studies, sociology, and women's studies). Business administration, biology, neuroscience and behavioral biology have the largest enrollments.

ACTIVITIES: 30% of men belong to 12 national fraternities; 31% of women belong to 13 national sororities. There are 220 groups on campus, including art, bagpipe, band, cheerleading, chess, choir, chorale, chorus, computers, dance, debate, drama, ethnic, film, gay, honors, international, jazz band, literary magazine, musical theater, newspaper, orchestra, pep band, photography, political, professional, radio and TV, religious, social, social service, student government, symphony, and yearbook. Popular campus events include Heritage Ball, Dooley's Week, and Festival of Nine Lessons. **Sports:** There are 8 intercollegiate sports for men and 8 for women, and 20 intramural sports for men and 20 for women. Facilities include a recreation center, which contains a 3000-seat gym with 4 basketball courts, 5 volleyball courts, an Olympic-size swimming pool, indoor track, 2 Nautilus weight rooms, a sheer rock wall, and tennis, racquetball, and squash courts. In addition, there is a soccer field and a 400-meter track, with seating for 2000 spectators. **Graduates:** The most popular majors were business administration and management, general (14%), biology/biological sciences, general (9%), economics, and general (9%). Of the 2013 graduating class, 43% were enrolled in graduate school within 6 months of graduation, and 31% were employed.

SERVICES: Counseling and information services are available, as is tutoring in most subjects. There is a reader service for the blind. **Library/Resources:** The 9 libraries contain 3.9 million volumes, 6.3 million microform items, 117,143 audio/video tapes/CDs/DVDs, and subscribe to 0 periodicals including electronic. Computerized library services include interlibrary loans, database searching, Internet access, and Wi-Fi capability. Special learning facilities include an art gallery, planetarium, radio station, TV station, the Michael C. Carlos museum, and the Carter center. **Physically Challenged Students:** 90% of the campus is accessible. Facilities include wheelchair ramps, elevators, special parking, specially equipped restrooms, special class scheduling, lowered drinking fountains, lowered telephones, and special housing. **Special:** Special academic programs include cross-registration with Atlanta area colleges and universities, departmental internships, work-study programs, dual majors, 3-2 and 4-2 engineering degrees with Georgia Tech, and pass/fail options. A Washington semester and B.A.-B.S. degrees are available, and students may study abroad in many countries. There are accelerated degree programs offered in chemistry, math, math and computer science, English, history, philosophy, political science, and sociology. There are 30 national honor societies and including Phi Beta Kappa chapter. **Visiting:** There are regularly scheduled orientations for prospective students, including a student-led campus tour and an informational focus session led by a member of our Admission staff. Prospective students may also arrange to sit in on classes, as well as meet with faculty or athletic coaches. There are guides for informal visits and visitors may sit in on classes. To schedule a visit, contact the Office of Undergraduate Admission. **Campus Safety and Security:** Measures include 24-hour foot and vehicle patrol, self-defense education, and security escort services. There are shuttle buses, emergency telephones, lighted pathways/sidewalks, the campus patrol is a fully accredited police department.

REQUIREMENTS: The SAT or ACT is required. Students must submit a high school transcript. Students may submit SAT results, but they are not required unless a student is home-schooled. A recommendation from a high school counselor and up to 2 additional letters of recommendation are required. The student must have acquired 16 academic credits in secondary school, including 4 years of English, 3 years of math, and 2 years each of history, science, and foreign language. AP credits are accepted. Important factors in the admissions decision are advanced placement or honors courses, recommendations by school officials, and extracurricular activities record. To graduate, students must complete 127 semester hours, including courses during the first 2 years in English, science, math, history, the social sciences, health, and phys ed. Students must main-

tain at least a C (2.0) average in any major or minor they complete. The number of hours required for the major varies by department. A thesis is required for students in honors or dual B.A.-M.A. or B.S.-M.S. programs. **Procedure:** Freshmen are admitted fall. Entrance exams should be taken prior to applying. There are early decision, early admissions, and deferred admissions plans. Early decision applications should be filed by November 1; regular applications, by January 15 for fall entry, along with a $75 fee. Notification of early decision is sent 12 15; regular decision, 4 1. Applications are accepted on-line. **Transfer Students:** 164 transfer students enrolled in 2013-2014. Applicants must have taken the SAT or ACT and completed at least 1 year of college, with a GPA of 3.0. 64 of 127 credits required for the bachelor's degree must be completed at Emory. **International Students:** The school actively recruits these students. They must take the TOEFL. They must also take the SAT or ACT.

ADMISSIONS: 26% of the 2014-2015 applicants were accepted. The SAT scores for the 2014-2015 freshman class were: Critical Reading--1% below 500, 19% between 500 and 599, 47% between 600 and 699, and 33% between 700 and 800; Math--10% between 500 and 599, 36% between 600 and 699, and 54% between 700 and 800; Writing--1% below 500, 10% between 500 and 599, 44% between 600 and 699, and 45% between 700 and 800. The ACT scores were 2% between 24 and 26, 32% between 27 and 28, and 66% above 28. There were 43 National Merit finalists. **Admissions Contact:** Admissions Department, Dean of Admissions. E-Mail: *admission@emory.edu* Web: *www.emory.edu*

FINANCIAL AID: In 2014-2015, 45% of all full-time freshmen and 49% of continuing full-time students received some form of financial aid. 43% of all full-time freshmen and 44% of continuing full-time students received need-based aid. 17% of undergraduate students work part-time. Average annual earnings from campus work are $1090. The average financial indebtedness of the 2014 graduate was $19,397. Emory is a member of CSS. The CSS/Profile and FAFSA are required. Check with the school for current application deadlines.

FORT VALLEY STATE UNIVERSITY   B-3
www.fvsu.edu

Fort Valley, GA 31030   (478) 825-6307

Fax: (478) 825-6169

Full-time: 1313 men, 1688 women	**Faculty:** 153
Part-time: 175 men, 245 women	**Ph.D.s:** 64%
Graduate: 64 men, 86 women	**Student/Faculty:** 20 to 1
Year: semesters, summer session	**Tuition:** $5012 ($16,626)
Room & Board: $6188	**Freshman Class:** 5343 applied, 2161 accepted, 960 enrolled
SAT or ACT: required	**CEEB CODE:** 5220
Application Deadline: n/av	**VERY COMPETITIVE**

Fort Valley State University, founded in 1895, is a public land-grant member of the University System of Georgia. The university offers undergraduate programs in the arts and sciences, business, education, agriculture, engineering, and other vocational and technical fields. Graduate programs are offered in early childhood, middle grades education, mental health and rehabilitation counseling, and guidance counseling. The figures in the above capsule and in this profile are approximate. There are 3 undergraduate schools and 1 graduate school. In addition to regional accreditation, FVSU has baccalaureate program accreditation with NCATE. The 1375-acre campus is in a rural area 30 miles southwest of Macon. Including any residence halls, there are 35 buildings.

STUDENT LIFE: 96% of undergraduates are from Georgia. Others are from 29 states, and 5 foreign countries. 92% are African American. **Male To Female Ratio:** 1.3:1. The average age of freshmen is 19; all undergraduates, 21. 27% do not continue beyond their first year; 39% remain to graduate. **Housing:** 1450 students can be accommodated in college housing, which includes single-sex and coed dorms and on-campus apartments. On-campus housing is guaranteed for the freshman year only, is available on a first-come, and first-served basis. 62% of students live on campus. Alcohol is not permitted. All students may keep cars.

FACULTY/CLASSROOMS: 50% of faculty are male; 50% are female. No introductory courses are taught by graduate students. The average class size in a regular course is 25.

PROGRAMS OF STUDY: FVSU confers B.A., B.S., B.B.A. and B.S.W. degrees. Associate and Master's degrees are also awarded. Bachelor's degrees are awarded in AGRICULTURE (agricultural economics, animal science, horticulture, and plant science), BIOLOGICAL SCIENCE (biology/biological science, nutrition, and zoology), BUSINESS (accounting, business administration and management, marketing/retailing/merchandising, and office supervision and management), COMMUNICATIONS AND THE ARTS (communications and English), COMPUTER AND PHYSICAL SCIENCE (chemistry, computer science, information sciences and systems, and mathematics), EDUCATION (agricultural education, early childhood education, home economics education, mathematics education, middle school education, physical education, and secondary education), ENGINEERING AND ENVIRONMENTAL DESIGN (agricultural engineering technology, commercial art, and electrical/electronics engineering technology), HEALTH PROFESSIONS (veterinary science), SOCIAL SCIENCE (child psychology/development, criminal justice, economics, political science/government, psychology, social work, and sociology).

ACTIVITIES: 5% of men belong to 4 national fraternities; 2% of women belong to 5 national sororities. There are 73 groups on campus, including band, cheerleading, choir, chorus, dance, drama, honors, international, jazz band, marching band, newspaper, opera, orchestra, political, radio and TV, religious, social service, and student government. Popular campus events include Black History month. **Sports:** There are 5 intercollegiate sports for men and 6 for women, and 3 intramural sports for men and 3 for women. Facilities include a stadium, a gym, a baseball field, lighted tennis courts, an indoor swimming pool, indoor and outdoor tracks, and shuffleboard courts. **Graduates:** From July 1, 2013 to June 30, 2014, 230 bachelor's degrees were awarded. The most popular majors were mathmatics (43%), visual/performing arts (17%), and psychology (10%). In an average class, 13% graduate in 4 years or less, 33% graduate in 5 years or less, and 39% graduate in 6 years or less.

SERVICES: Counseling and information services are available, as is tutoring in most subjects. There is remedial math, reading, and writing. **Library/Resources:** The library contains 250,000 volumes, 172,000 microform items, and subscribes to 1,168 periodicals including electronic. Computerized library services include interlibrary loans and database searching. Special learning facilities include a radio station, TV station, experimental agricultural plots, animal research centers, and greenhouse complex. **Physically Challenged Students:** All of the campus is accessible. Facilities include wheelchair ramps, elevators, special parking, specially equipped restrooms, and special housing. **Special:** Students may participate in cooperative work-study programs with local industries, cross-register for courses at Robins Residence Center, and study abroad. Fort Valley also offers a 3-2 dual degree program in chemistry, geosciences with University of Oklahoma, in engineering or other technical fields with Georgia Institute of Technology, and a 3-2 engineering degree with University of Nevada, Las Vegas. There are 5 national honor societies and a freshman honors program. **Visiting:** There are regularly scheduled orientations for prospective students, including an overview, an introduction of administration and faculty, and a tour. There are guides for informal visits and visitors may sit in on classes. To schedule a visit, contact the Office of Enrollment Management. **Campus Safety and Security:** Measures include 24-hour foot and vehicle patrol. There are emergency telephones.

REQUIREMENTS: The SAT or ACT is required. Applicants must be graduates of an accredited secondary school or have earned a GED. The university requires at least 17 academic units of study, including 4 in English, 3 in social science, 3 each in math and science, and 2 of foreign language. A GPA of 2.7 is required. AP and CLEP credits are accepted. Students must complete a minimum of 120 credit hours, plus 5 additional hours to satisfy requirements for freshmen orientation and for military science or phys ed. General education requirements include courses in humanities, social science, math, science, and courses in the major. The bachelor's degree requires a minimum GPA of 2.0 and no grade below C in the major. **Procedure:** Freshmen are admitted to all sessions. There are early admissions,

deferred admissions, and rolling admissions plans. Check with the school for current application deadlines. The application fee is $30. Applications are accepted on-line. **Transfer Students:** 135 transfer students enrolled in 2013-2014. In addition to meeting standard admission requirements, transfers must submit transcripts from all colleges previously attended. Transfer credit is accepted based on a 2.0 minimum GPA, and only courses with a C or better will be accepted. 45 of 125 credits required for the bachelor's degree must be completed at FVSU. **International Students:** There are 23 international students enrolled. They must take the TOEFL and the college's own test. They must also take the SAT or ACT.

ADMISSIONS: 40% of the 2014-2015 applicants were accepted. **Admissions Contact:** Donovan Coley, Interim Director of Admissions. Web: *www.fvsu.edu*

FINANCIAL AID: In 2014-2015, 94% of all full-time freshmen students received some form of financial aid. 8% of all full-time freshmen students received need-based aid. The average freshman award was $2,300. Need-based scholarships or need-based grants averaged $2,300; need-based self-help aid (loans and jobs) averaged $2,425; and other non-need-based awards and non-need-based scholarships averaged $1,850. The FAFSA is required. Check with the school for current application deadlines.

GEORGIA COLLEGE AND STATE UNIVERSITY   C-3
www.gcsu.edu

Milledgeville, GA 31061	(478) 445-1283
	n/av
Fax: (478) 445-1914	Email: admissions@gcsu.edu
Full-time: 2144 men, 3377 women	Faculty: n/av
Part-time: 175 men, 231 women	Ph.D.s: n/av
Graduate: 303 men, 542 women	Student/Faculty: n/av
Year: semesters, summer session	Tuition: $8960 ($27,308)
Room & Board: $9940	Freshman Class: 3979 applied, 3034 accepted, 1463 enrolled
SAT CR/M/W: 570/560/550 ACT: 24	CEEB CODE: 5252
Application Deadline: April 1	COMPETITIVE+

Georgia College and State University, founded in 1889, is the public liberal arts university of Georgia. There are 4 undergraduate schools and 1 graduate school. In addition to regional accreditation, Georgia College has baccalaureate program accreditation with AACSB, NCATE, NMSA, AMTA, and AEE. The 602-acre campus is in a small town 30 miles from Macon. Including any residence halls, there are 91 buildings.

STUDENT LIFE: 99% of undergraduates are from Georgia. Others are from 22 states, 26 foreign countries, and Canada. 85% are White; 12% two or more races. **Male To Female Ratio:** 1.6:1. The average age of freshmen is 18; all undergraduates, 20. 14% do not continue beyond their first year; 86% remain to graduate. **Housing:** 2237 students can be accommodated in college housing, which includes single-sex and coed dorms and off-campus apartments. In addition, there are honors houses and special-interest houses. On-campus housing is guaranteed for the freshman year only, is available on a first-come, and first-served basis. 64% of students commute. All students may keep cars.

FACULTY/CLASSROOMS: No introductory courses are taught by graduate students.

PROGRAMS OF STUDY: Georgia College confers B.A., B.S., B.B.A., B.M.E., B.M.T. and B.S.N. degrees. Master's and Doctoral degrees are also awarded. Bachelor's degrees are awarded in BIOLOGICAL SCIENCE (biology/biological science), BUSINESS (accounting, business administration and management, management science, marketing and distribution, and recreation and leisure services), COMMUNICATIONS AND THE ARTS (art, English, French, journalism, music, Spanish, speech/debate/rhetoric, and theatre arts), COMPUTER AND PHYSICAL SCIENCE (chemistry, computer science, information sciences and systems, mathematics, and physics), EDUCATION (athletic training, early childhood education, middle school education, music education, and special education), ENGINEERING AND ENVIRONMENTAL DESIGN (environmental science), HEALTH PROFESSIONS (community health work, exercise science, music therapy, and nursing), SOCIAL SCIENCE (criminal justice, economics, geography, history, liberal arts/general studies, philosophy, political science/government, psychology, and sociology). Biology, nursing, and management have the largest enrollments.

ACTIVITIES: 6% of men belong to 11 national fraternities; 12% of women belong to 10 national sororities. There are 160 groups on campus, including band, cheerleading, choir, chorale, chorus, dance, debate, drama, ethnic, gay, honors, international, jazz band, literary magazine, musical theater, photography, political, professional, radio and TV, religious, residence student association, social, social service, student government, and yearbook. Popular campus events include Week of Welcome, Progressive Dinner and International Week. **Sports:** There are 5 intercollegiate sports for men and 6 for women, and 10 intramural sports for men and 10 for women. Facilities include Georgia College Wellness and recreation Center is LEED Silver certified and encompasses 101,000 square feet. Reflecting the university's commitment to a holistic approach to health and wellness, the center combines fitness and recreation activities, health education programs and formal wellness courses with health services and counseling services all in one centralized. Also available is the 95,000 square foot, over 4,000 capacity Centennial Center, home of the basketball and volleyball teams. **Graduates:** From July 1, 2013 to June 30, 2014, 1183 bachelor's degrees were awarded. The most popular majors were psychology (10%), management (9%), and nursing (8%). In an average class, 33% graduate in 4 years or less, 51% graduate in 5 years or less, and 57% graduate in 6 years or less.

SERVICES: Counseling and information services are available, as is tutoring in some subjects. Including math, calculus, statistics, economics, chemistry, biology, physics, accounting, and management **Library/Resources:** The library contains 201,389 volumes, 24,459 microform items, and 11,666 audio/video tapes/CDs/DVDs, and subscribes to 42,613 periodicals including electronic. Computerized library services include interlibrary loans, database searching, Internet access, and Wi-Fi capability. Special learning facilities include an art gallery, natural history museum, planetarium, radio station, TV station, campus theatre an art deco theatre adjacent to the campus serves as a performance space and bookstore for both the college and the community. **Physically Challenged Students:** 90% of the campus is accessible. Facilities include wheelchair ramps, elevators, special parking, specially equipped restrooms, special class scheduling, lowered drinking fountains, lowered telephones, and special housing. **Special:** GCSU has study-abroad agreements with institutions worldwide, a Washington semester, co-op programs, internships, work-study programs, dual majors, independent study, and student-designed majors. There is a 3-2 engineering degree program with the Georgia Institute of Technology. **Visiting:** There are regularly scheduled orientations for prospective students, including receptions, tours, school meetings, information sessions, academic and cocurricular advising, and registration. There are guides for informal visits and visitors may sit in on classes. To schedule a visit, contact the Office of Admissions at admissions@gcsu.edu. **Campus Safety and Security:** Measures include 24-hour foot and vehicle patrol, emergency notification system, self-defense education, and security escort services. There are shuttle buses, emergency telephones, lighted pathways/sidewalks, and controlled access to dorms/residences.

REQUIREMENTS: The SAT or ACT is required. The ACT Optional Writing test is also required. Applicants must be graduates of an accredited or recognized secondary school and must complete the Georgia college preparatory curriculum requirements, including 4 units each of English and math (with math I or algebra I being the minimum level for consideration), 4 of science, (including 2 lab sciences), 2 of the same foreign language, and 3 of social science. A GPA of 2.0 is required. AP and CLEP credits are accepted. Important factors in the admissions decision are advanced placement or honors courses, extracurricular activities record, and evidence of special talent. To graduate, students must complete at least 120 semester hours, of which 40 must be completed in residence. Complete 21 of the last 30 credit hours at the upper level. All B.A. candidates and some B.S. candidates must demonstrate a foreign language proficiency. All students must pass an exam on the history and Constitu-

tion of both the United States and Georgia, and a senior exit exam in the major. They must also earn a C or better in English 1101. **Procedure:** Freshmen are admitted to all sessions. Entrance exams should be taken ACT in February and SAT in March. There are early admissions, deferred admissions, and rolling admissions plans. Applications should be filed by April 1 for fall entry; November 1 for spring entry; and May 1 for summer entry, along with a $35 fee. Notification is sent on a rolling basis. Applications are accepted on-line. **Transfer Students:** 401 transfer students enrolled in 2013-2014. To transfer applicants must submit official transcripts from all colleges attended and be eligible to return to their previous institution. Those who have completed fewer than 30 semester hours must meet all freshman admissions requirements. 40 of 120 credits required for the bachelor's degree must be completed at Georgia College. **International Students:** There are 72 international students enrolled. The school actively recruits these students. They must take the TOEFL with a minimum score of 500 on the paper-based TOEFL (PBT) or 61 on the Internet-based version (iBT), SAT Verbal score of 440, ACT English score of 17, or IELTS score of 6.0. To comply with NCAA regulations, international students who will compete in intercollegiate athletics must take either the SAT or ACT.

ADMISSIONS: 76% of the 2014-2015 applicants were accepted. The SAT scores for the 2014-2015 freshman class were: Critical Reading--11% below 500, 53% between 500 and 599, 33% between 600 and 699, and 3% between 700 and 800; Math--13% below 500, 55% between 500 and 599, 29% between 600 and 699, and 2% between 700 and 800; Writing--18% below 500, 54% between 500 and 599, 26% between 600 and 699, and 1% between 700 and 800. The ACT scores were 8% below 21, 29% between 21 and 23, 40% between 24 and 26, 16% between 27 and 28, and 7% above 28. **Admissions Contact:** Suzanne Pittman, AVP for Enrollment Management. E-Mail: *admissions@gcsu.edu* Web: *www.gcsu.edu*

FINANCIAL AID: In 2014-2015, 60% of all full-time freshmen and continuing full-time students received some form of financial aid. The average freshman award was $9,430. Need-based scholarships or need-based grants averaged $4,284; need-based self-help aid (loans and jobs) averaged $3,430; and non-need-based athletic scholarships averaged $3,717. 11% of undergraduate students work part-time. Average annual earnings from campus work are $7962. The average financial indebtedness of the 2014 graduate was $23,153. The FAFSA is required. The priority date for freshman financial aid applications for fall entry is March. The deadline for filing freshman financial aid applications for fall entry is July 1.

GEORGIA INSTITUTE OF TECHNOLOGY   B-2
www.gatech.edu

Atlanta, GA 30332	(404) 894-4154
	n/av
Fax: (404) 894-9511	Email: admission@gatech.edu
Full-time: 8708 men, 4545 women	Faculty: n/av
Part-time: 1007 men, 422 women	Ph.D.s: n/av
Graduate: 6425 men, 2002 women	Student/Faculty: n/av
Year: semesters, summer session	Tuition: $11,394 ($30,698)
Room & Board: $10,434	Freshman Class: 25884 applied, 8641 accepted, 2809 enrolled
SAT CR/M/W: 670/730/680 **ACT:** 32	CEEB CODE: 5248
Application Deadline: January 10	MOST COMPETITIVE

Georgia Institute of Technology, founded in 1885, is a public technological institution offering programs in architecture, management, policy, international affairs, engineering, computing, and science. There are 6 undergraduate schools and 6 graduate schools. In addition to regional accreditation, Georgia Tech has baccalaureate program accreditation with AACSB, ABET, ACCE, NAAB, NASAD, ACS, APA, HFES, CAAHEP, IFMA, PAB, IDSA, CAMPEP, NCOPE, and RICS. The 400-acre campus is in an urban area in Atlanta, GA. Including any residence halls, there are 242 buildings.

STUDENT LIFE: 62% of undergraduates are from Georgia. Others are from 50 states, 98 foreign countries, and Canada. 52% are White; 19% Asian American; 11% Foreign. **Male To Female Ratio:** 0.4:1.

The average age of freshmen is 18; all undergraduates, 20. 4% do not continue beyond their first year; 82% remain to graduate. **Housing:** 9744 students can be accommodated in college housing, which includes single-sex and coed dorms, on-campus apartments, and married student housing. In addition, there are honors houses, language houses, special-interest houses, fraternity houses, sorority houses, Freshman experience. On-campus housing is guaranteed for all 4 years, is available on a first-come, and first-served basis. 54% of students live on campus; of those, 74% remain on campus on weekends. All students may keep cars.

FACULTY/CLASSROOMS: No introductory courses are taught by graduate students.

PROGRAMS OF STUDY: Georgia Tech confers B.S. degrees. Master's and Doctoral degrees are also awarded. Bachelor's degrees are awarded in BIOLOGICAL SCIENCE (biochemistry and biology/biological science), BUSINESS (business administration and management and international economics), COMMUNICATIONS AND THE ARTS (digital communications and industrial design), COMPUTER AND PHYSICAL SCIENCE (applied mathematics, applied physics, chemistry, computer science, earth science, mathematics, and physics), ENGINEERING AND ENVIRONMENTAL DESIGN (aeronautical engineering, architecture, biomedical engineering, chemical engineering, civil engineering, computer engineering, construction management, electrical/electronics engineering, environmental engineering, industrial engineering, materials engineering, materials science, materials science and engineering, mechanical engineering, nuclear engineering, technology and public affairs, and textile engineering), SOCIAL SCIENCE (economics, history of science, international relations, psychology, and public affairs). Engineering, business administration and computer science. are the strongest academically. Computer science, mechanical engineering, and industrial engineering have the largest enrollments.

ACTIVITIES: 23% of men belong to 40 national fraternities; 30% of women belong to 16 national sororities. There are 548 groups on campus, including athletic and outdoor, cultural, art, band, cheerleading, chess, choir, chorale, chorus, communications, computers, debate, departmental, drama, drill team, environmental, ethnic, film, gay, honors, international, jazz band, literary magazine, marching band, musical theater, newspaper, orchestra, pep band, photography, political, professional, radio and TV, religious, social, social service, student government, symphony, and yearbook. Popular campus events include Team Buzz, Tech Beautification Day, and Dance Marathon. **Sports:** There are 9 intercollegiate sports for men and 8 for women, and 7 intramural sports for men and 7 for women. Facilities include a 4,000-seat baseball stadium, a 55,000-seat football stadium, softball fields, an 8,600-seat basketball arena, a golf practice facility, an 88,000-square-foot football practice facility, a basketball practice center with a 2,000-square-foot weight room, an Olympic aquatic center for swimming and diving, an eight-lane outdoor track with a state-of-the-art Mondo surface and 1,500-seat grandstand, a state-of-the-art 6-court indoor tennis complex that seats 232 spectators, outdoor tennis courts, and outdoor turf field featuring flag football fields, 2 outdoor sand volleyball courts, and a 300,659 square foot recreation center with 6 multipurpose indoor courts, strength training and cardio-fitness, 4 racquetball/wallyball/squash courts, a running track, a climbing wall, co-ed sauna, 3 studios for aerobic fitness programs. **Graduates:** From July 1, 2013 to June 30, 2014, 3267 bachelor's degrees were awarded. The most popular majors were mechanical engineering (14%), industrial engineering (11%), and management (9%). 924 companies recruited on campus in 2013-2014. In an average class, 40% graduate in 4 years or less, 75% graduate in 5 years or less, and 82% graduate in 6 years or less. Of the 2013 graduating class, 67% were employed within 6 months of graduation.

SERVICES: Counseling and information services are available, as is tutoring in most subjects. There is a reader service for the blind, and remedial math, reading, and writing. The Learning Assistance Program provides tutors for calculus, chemistry, and physics through call-in Tutor-Vision, which airs live on the GT Cable Network. One to One Tutoring is offered in addition to success workshops, Peer Led Undergraduate Study (PLUS), walk-in tutoring and academic coaching. **Library/Resources:** The 2 libraries contain 2.5 million volumes, 4.8 million microform items, 328,178 audio/video tapes/CDs/DVDs, and subscribe to 25,765 periodicals including electronic. Computerized library services include interlibrary loans, database searching, Internet access, and Wi-Fi capability. Special learning facilities include an art gallery, radio station, TV station, G. Wayne Clough Undergraduate Learning Commons, Center for Academic Enrichment, Center for Academic Success, Center for the Enhancement of Teaching and Learning, Communication Center, and Center for Career Discovery and Development. **Physically Challenged Students:** 75% of the campus is accessible. Facilities include wheelchair ramps, elevators, special parking, specially equipped restrooms, special class scheduling, lowered drinking fountains, special housing. Visual alarms in housing, assistive listening devices, and adaptable living space. **Special:** Extensive co-op programs, cross-registration with other Atlanta-area colleges, internships, and undergraduate research opportunities are available. Numerous study abroad opportunities available. An engineering transfer program is offered within the university system, and a liberal arts-engineering dual degree program serves area colleges and institutions nationwide. Students have access to multidisciplinary and certificate programs outside their major field of study. The College of Engineering offers the opportunity to transfer to Georgia Tech via the Dual Degree Engineering Program (DDEP) and the Regional Engineering Transfer Program (RETP). There are 22 national honor societies, a freshman honors program, and 12 departmental honors programs. **Visiting:** There are regularly scheduled orientations for prospective students, the session is conducted by a counselor from the Office of Undergraduate Admission who discusses the admission process, majors, opportunities outside of the classroom, campus activities, and student life. There are guides for informal visits, visitors may sit in on classes, and stay overnight. To schedule a visit, contact the Office of Undergraduate Admissions at (404) 894-4154. **Campus Safety and Security:** Measures include 24-hour foot and vehicle patrol, emergency notification system, self-defense education, and security escort services. There are shuttle buses, emergency telephones, lighted pathways/sidewalks, controlled access to dorms/residences, foot patrol, bike patrol, limited access to dorms, mobile security patrol, video cameras, K-9 force, and bike and laptop registration is offered.

REQUIREMENTS: The SAT or ACT is required. The ACT Optional Writing test is also required. Candidates for admission must have completed 4 units each of English and Math, 3 units of Social Studies, 4 units of Science, including 2 units of lab sciences, and 2 units of a foreign language. An essay is required. AP credits are accepted.All students must fulfill the core curriculum requirements and maintain a 2.0 GPA for their entire academic program. Core curriculum requirements include 12 hours of science, math, and technology; 12 hours of social sciences, 13 hours of essential skills courses (English composition, calculus, and computing), 6 hours of humanities, and 5 or more hours of electives depending on the major. Other course requirements include a U.S. and Georgia history/constitution course, a global perspectives course, a U.S perspectives course, an ethics course, and a wellness course. **Procedure:** Freshmen are admitted fall and summer. Entrance exams should be taken by the end of the junior year. There are early admissions and deferred admissions plans. Applications should be filed by January 10 for fall entry; January 10 for summer entry. The fall 2014 application fee was $85. Notifications are sent March 14. Applications are accepted on-line. **Transfer Students:** 788 transfer students enrolled in 2013-2014. Transfer applicants must have completed a minimum of 30 semester hours or 45 quarter hours of course work. All of the specifically required courses on the course requirements chart for the prospective major must be completed. Grades and academic standing must be satisfactory for the last term of enrollment at the prior college. The minimum transfer GPA requirement for most majors is 3.00. Some programs require a higher transfer GPA. 36 of 122 credits required for the bachelor's degree must be completed at Georgia Tech. **International Students:** There are 1586 international students enrolled. They must also take the SAT or ACT.

ADMISSIONS: 33% of the 2014-2015 applicants were accepted. The SAT scores for the 2014-2015 freshman class were: Critical Reading--1% below 500, 9% between 500 and 599, 53% between 600 and 699, and 37% between 700 and 800; Math--4% between 500 and 599, 29% between 600 and 699, and 67% between 700 and 800; Writing--1% below 500, 9% between 500 and 599, 48% between 600 and 699, and 42% between 700 and 800. The ACT scores were 1% below

21, 4% between 24 and 26, 9% between 27 and 28, and 86% above 28. There were 161 National Merit finalists. **Admissions Contact:** Rick Clark, Director of Undergraduate Admissions. E-Mail: *admission@gatech.edu* Web: *www.gatech.edu*

FINANCIAL AID: In 2014-2015, 42% of all full-time freshmen and 44% of continuing full-time students received some form of financial aid. 40% of all full-time freshmen and 39% of continuing full-time students received need-based aid. The average freshman award was $12,900. Need-based scholarships or need-based grants averaged $11,168; need-based self-help aid (loans and jobs) averaged $6,032; non-need-based athletic scholarships averaged $17,152; and other non-need-based awards and non-need-based scholarships averaged $4,393. The average financial indebtedness of the 2014 graduate was $24,891. Georgia Tech is a member of CSS. The CSS/Profile, FAFSA, and the college's own financial statement are required. The deadline for filing freshman financial aid applications for fall entry is February 15.

GEORGIA REGENTS UNIVERSITY   D-2
www.gru.edu

Augusta, GA 30912	(706) 667-4095
	n/av
Fax: (706) 721-7279	Email: admissions@gruedu
Full-time: 1431 men, 2646 women	Faculty: n/av
Part-time: 449 men, 698 women	Ph.D.s: 88%
Graduate: 1129 men, 1624 women	Student/Faculty: n/av
Year: semesters, summer session	Tuition: n/av
Room & Board: n/app	Freshman Class: n/av
SAT or ACT: required	CEEB CODE: 5406
Application Deadline: n/av	COMPETITIVE

Georgia Regents University is a public comprehensive research institution as well as an academic health center. There are 6 undergraduate schools and 3 graduate schools. In addition to regional accreditation, GRU has baccalaureate program accreditation with AACSB, CSWE, NASAD, NASM, NCATE, NLN, and SACS COC. The 650-acre campus is in an urban area 140 miles east of Atlanta on the Georgia-South Carolina border. Including any residence halls, there are 150 buildings.

STUDENT LIFE: 52% are White; 25% African American. **Male To Female Ratio:** 1.7:1. **Housing:** 825 students can be accommodated in college housing, which includes coed dorms, on-campus apartments, and married student housing. On-campus housing is available on a first-come and first-served basis. Alcohol is not permitted. All students may keep cars.

FACULTY/CLASSROOMS: 57% of faculty are male; 43% are female. And 16% do research. No introductory courses are taught by graduate students.

PROGRAMS OF STUDY: GRU confers B.A., B.A.F.L, B.S., B.B.A., B.F.A., B.M., B.S.A.I.T., B.S.Ed., B.S.W., B.S.N., B.S.C.L.S, B.S.D.H., B.S.H.I.A., B.S.R.P.T., B.S.R.S. and B.S.K. degrees. Associate, Master's, and Doctoral degrees are also awarded. Bachelor's degrees are awarded in BIOLOGICAL SCIENCE (biology/biological science, cell biology, and ecology), BUSINESS (accounting, banking and finance, business administration and management, management information systems, and marketing/retailing/merchandising), COMMUNICATIONS AND THE ARTS (art, communications, English, music, and music performance), COMPUTER AND PHYSICAL SCIENCE (chemistry, computer science, information sciences and systems, mathematics, and physics), EDUCATION (elementary education, foreign languages education, health education, health information management, middle school education, music education, and special education), HEALTH PROFESSIONS (dental hygiene, kinesiology, medical laboratory science, medical technology, nuclear medical technology, nursing, radiation therapy, and respiratory therapy), SOCIAL SCIENCE (anthropology, criminal justice, history, political science/government, psychology, social work, and sociology). Chemistry, nursing, psychology have the largest enrollments.

ACTIVITIES: 1% of men belong to 5 national fraternities; 1% of women belong to 5 national sororities. Groups on campus include art, band, cheerleading, choir, chorus, drama, ethnic, film, gay, honors, international, jazz band, literary magazine, musical theater, newspaper, orchestra, pep band, photography, political, professional, radio and TV, religious, social, social service, student government, and symphony. Popular campus events include Homecoming, Lyceum Series and Family Fun Days. **Sports:** There are 6 intercollegiate sports for men and 7 for women. Facilities include a 2000-seat gym and fitness center, baseball, soccer, softball fields, a tennis center, an 18-hole golf course with club house, golf house, and a fitness center in the student activites center. **Graduates:** The most popular majors were elementary education, communications, and psychology. In an average class, 32% graduate in 6 years or less.

SERVICES: Counseling and information services are available, as is tutoring in most subjects. There is a reader service for the blind, and remedial math. **Library/Resources:** Computerized library services include interlibrary loans, database searching, Internet access, and Wi-Fi capability. Special learning facilities include an art gallery, radio station, a history walk and guardhouse museum. **Physically Challenged Students:** 95% of the campus is accessible. Facilities include wheelchair ramps, elevators, special parking, specially equipped restrooms, special class scheduling, lowered drinking fountains, and lowered telephones. **Special:** The school offers co-op programs and internships with area companies, work-study programs, dual majors, nondegree study, and cross-registration with Paine College. There are 5 national honor societies, a freshman honors program, and 7 departmental honors programs. **Visiting:** There are regularly scheduled orientations for prospective students, including a meal, campus tour, discussion of schedules, deadlines, and registration. There are guides for informal visits and visitors may sit in on classes. To schedule a visit, contact the Admissions Office. **Campus Safety and Security:** Measures include 24-hour foot and vehicle patrol, emergency notification system, self-defense education, and security escort services. There are shuttle buses, emergency telephones, lighted pathways/sidewalks, controlled access to dorms/residences, Controlled access to labs after hours.

REQUIREMENTS: The SAT or ACT is required. Applicants must have at least a 2.0 HSGPA,with a verbal score of 430 and math score of 400 on the SAT or a comparable score on the ACT. Applicants must be graduates of an accredited secondary school. The GED is accepted. Secondary school courses must include 4 units each of English and math, 3 each of science and social science, and 2 of a foreign language. AP and CLEP credits are accepted. Students must complete 125 hours with a minimum GPA of 2.0. All students are required to take 6 courses in phys ed, pass the Regents test in reading and composition, and demonstrate, through course completion or exam, a knowledge of U.S. and Georgia history and their constitutions. **Procedure:** Freshmen are admitted fall, spring, and summer. There are deferred admissions and rolling admissions plans. Check with the school for current application deadlines. Applications are accepted on-line. **Transfer Students:** **International Students:** The school actively recruits these students. They must take the TOEFL. They must also take the SAT or ACT.

ADMISSIONS: Scott Argo, Intermin Director of Admissions. E-Mail: *admissions@gruedu* Web: *www.gru.edu*

FINANCIAL AID: In 2014-2015, 84% of all full-time freshmen and 85% of continuing full-time students received some form of financial aid. 53% of all full-time freshmen and 61% of continuing full-time students received need-based aid. The average freshman award was $4,796. Need-based scholarships or need-based grants averaged $2,510 ($2,865 maximum); need-based self-help aid (loans and jobs) averaged $1,726 ($1,732 maximum); non-need-based athletic scholarships averaged $3,019 ($4,185 maximum); and other non-need-based awards and non-need-based scholarships averaged $2,944 ($10,529 maximum). 2% of undergraduate students work part-time. Average annual earnings from campus work are $721. The average financial indebtedness of the 2014 graduate was $18,425. The FAFSA is required. The priority date for freshman financial aid applications for fall entry is April 1.

GEORGIA SOUTHERN UNIVERSITY   D-3
www.georgiasouthern.edu

Statesboro, GA 30458	(912) 478-5391
	n/av
Fax: (912) 478-7240 Email: admissions@georgiasouthern.edu	
Full-time: 7906 men, 7938 women	Faculty: 696; IIA, --$
Part-time: 1061 men, 1099 women	Ph.D.s: 82%
Graduate: 834 men, 1679 women	Student/Faculty: 22 to 1
Year: semesters, summer session	Tuition: $7190 ($20,086)
Room & Board: $9752	Freshman Class: 9679 applied, 6107 accepted, 3498 enrolled
SAT CR/M/W: 550/550/520 **ACT:** 23	CEEB CODE: 5253
Application Deadline: May 1	**COMPETITIVE**

Georgia Southern University is the state's largest and most comprehensive center of higher education south of Atlanta. With 124 degree programs at the baccalaureate, master's and doctoral levels, Georgia Southern has been designated a Carnegie Doctoral-Research university and provides the classic residential campus experience and online learning options. Georgia Southern's nationally accredited academic programs prepare diverse scholars for leadership and service as world citizens. A unit of the University System of Georgia, the University boasts 200-plus student organizations, outstanding Division I athletics, and state-of-the art residence halls and campus facilities. Since 1906, the University's hallmark has been a culture of engagement that bridges theory with practice, extends the learning environment beyond the classroom, and promotes student growth and life success. Central to the University's mission is the faculty's dedication to excellence in teaching and the development of a fertile learning environment exemplified by a free exchange of ideas, high academic expectations, and individual responsibility for academic achievement. Faculty, staff, and students embrace core values expressed through integrity, civility, kindness, collaboration, and a commitment to lifelong learning, wellness, and social responsibility. There are 7 undergraduate schools and 1 graduate school. In addition to regional accreditation, Georgia Southern has baccalaureate program accreditation with AACSB, ABET, ACCE, NASAD, NASM, NCATE, NRPA, NCAA, IACS, AAM, ACCE, NASP, NCACE, CIDA, GPSC, NAEYC, CACREP, CADE, CAATE, CEPH, CCNE, GBN, NASPAA, NAST, ACS, and AALRCA. The 900-acre campus is in a small town 1 hour from Savannah, 2 hours from Florida, and about 3 hours from metropolitan Atlanta. Including any residence halls, there are 204 buildings.

STUDENT LIFE: 95% of undergraduates are from Georgia. Others are from 49 states, 69 foreign countries, and Canada. 62% are White; 26% African American. 95% claim no religious affiliation. **Male To Female Ratio:** 1.1:1. The average age of freshmen is 18; all undergraduates, 21. 19% do not continue beyond their first year; 51% remain to graduate. **Housing:** 4935 students can be accommodated in college housing, which includes coed dorms, on-campus apartments, and off-campus apartments. In addition, there are honors houses and special-interest houses. On-campus housing is guaranteed for the freshman year only, is available on a first-come, first-served basis, and is available on a lottery system for upperclassmen. 72% of students commute. All students may keep cars.

FACULTY/CLASSROOMS: 50% of faculty are male; 50% are female. 91% teach undergraduates, 75% do research, and 65% do both. Graduate students teach 6% of introductory courses. The average class size in an introductory lecture is 23; in a laboratory is 20; and in a regular course is 35.

PROGRAMS OF STUDY: Georgia Southern confers B.A., B.B.A., B.F.A., B.G.S., B.M., B.S.A.T., B.S., B.S.B., B.S.C.E., B.S.Chem., B.S.Cons., B.S.Ed., B.S.E.E., B.S.GraphCom., B.S.P.H., B.S.I.T., B.S.J.S., B.S.K., B.S.Mat., B.S.M.E., B.S.N. and B.S.P. degrees. Master's and Doctoral degrees are also awarded. Bachelor's degrees are awarded in BIOLOGICAL SCIENCE (biology/biological science and nutrition), BUSINESS (accounting, finance, logistics, management science, marketing management, and sports management), COMMUNICATIONS AND THE ARTS (art, communications, English, graphic communications, journalism, linguistics, multimedia, music, public relations, and writing), COMPUTER AND PHYSICAL SCIENCE (chemistry, chemistry education, computer science, geology,

information science, and physics), EDUCATION (athletic training, early childhood education, health education, health and physical education, mathematics education, middle school education, nursing education, recreation education, and special education), ENGINEERING AND ENVIRONMENTAL DESIGN (civil engineering, construction management, electrical/electronics engineering, and mechanical engineering), HEALTH PROFESSIONS (exercise science), SOCIAL SCIENCE (anthropology, child care/child and family studies, economics, geography, history, international studies, philosophy, political science/government, and psychology). Family nurse practitioner, geology, geography, chemistry, and undergraduate game design program are the strongest academically. Bilolgy, general studies, and psychology have the largest enrollments.

ACTIVITIES: 13% of men and 6% of women belong to 48 national fraternities; 16% of women belong to 12 national sororities. There are 280 groups on campus, including art, band, cheerleading, choir, chorale, chorus, communications, computers, dance, drama, environmental, ethnic, film, gay, honors, international, jazz band, literary magazine, marching band, musical theater, newspaper, opera, orchestra, political, professional, radio and TV staion, religious, social, social service, student government, and symphony. Popular campus events include Homecoming, Concerts, and Final Feast. **Sports:** There are 6 intercollegiate sports for men and 9 for women, and 23 intramural sports for men and 23 for women. Facilities include a baseball, football, and softball stadiums, volleyball and basketball field house, natatorium, tennis courts, track/soccer stadium and golf practice facility, and a rifle shooting range. **Graduates:** From July 1, 2013 to June 30, 2014, 2973 bachelor's degrees were awarded. The most popular majors were business/marketing (18%), parks and recreation (8%), and liberal arts/general studies (8%). 120 companies recruited on campus in 2013-2014. In an average class, 1% graduate in 3 years or less, 27% graduate in 4 years or less, 47% graduate in 5 years or less, and 51% graduate in 6 years or less.

SERVICES: Counseling and information services are available, as is tutoring in most subjects. There is a reader service for the blind, and remedial math, reading, and writing. **Library/Resources:** The library contains 649,338 volumes, 896,632 microform items, 29,759 audio/video tapes/CDs/DVDs, and subscribes to 48,288 periodicals including electronic. Computerized library services include interlibrary loans, database searching, Internet access, and Wi-Fi capability. Special learning facilities include an art gallery, natural history museum, planetarium, radio station, Bureau of Business Research and Economic Development, Center for Addiction Recovery, The Center for Africana Studies, Karl E. Peace Center for Bio-statistics and Survey, Center for Education Leadership, Center for Entrepreneurial Learning and Leadership, Center for Forensic Studies in Accounting, Center for International Schooling, Center for International Studies, Center for Irish Studies, Center for Retail Studies, Center for Sustainability, Center for Wildlife Education, Center for Women's and Gender Studies, Child Development Center, Graduate Academic Services Center (GASC), Instructional Resources Center (IRC), Institute for Coastal Plain Science, Magnolia Coastlands AHEC, National Youth-At-Risk Center (NYAR), Small Business Development Center, Student Success Center (SSC), Black Box Theatre, Performing Arts Center, and Garden of the Coastal Plain. **Physically Challenged Students:** 97% of the campus is accessible. Facilities include wheelchair ramps, elevators, special parking, specially equipped restrooms, special class scheduling, lowered drinking fountains, and special housing. **Special:** Co-op programs in: Accounting, finance, construction management, biology, geology, engineering technology (civil, electrical, and mechanical) information technology, industrial management, engineering (electrical, civil, and mechanical), and logistics. Internships: A number of academic degree programs require internships as part of the program requirements and offer academic credit for internship experiences. Non-academic internships are offered for all majors through the Office of career Services. There is a Washington Semester. Accelerated degree program in (name of major): is a state-funded program for public and private high school students that provide dual enrollment tuition assistance in Georgia. The program offers the opportunity to earn dual credit, satisfying high school and college core curriculum requirements. Joint Enrollment is not a state-funded program and does not guarantee satisfaction of the high school core curriculum. Admissions requirements for Accel of joint enrollment are: Have earned an academic GPA of 3.0. Submit SAT scores of at least 1000 or 21 ACT. Excel in the field in which the student plans to enroll. Have written consent of parent and guardian. Must be on track to complete College Preparatory Curriculum (CPC) requirements. Dual majors in (name of majors): students may be granted a second baccalaureate degree if the following conditions are met: if the first degree is earned at GSU, a student may seek a second degree if it is different from the first degree. The student must satisfy all major requirements. The student must complete the history and constitution requirements. Take a minimum of 30 additional credit hours at GSU. 5. The student must earn at least 50% of the credits toward the major at GSU. The student may work on two degrees at the same time. 3-2 engineering degree with (name of university): Georgia Institute of Technology. Cross registration with (name of consortium): Georgia Southern has cross-registration available with East Georgia and GOML (Georgia OnMyLine) programs. Study abroad in (name of countries): Argentina, Australia, Austria, Belgium, Botswana, Brazil, Bulgaria, Canada, Chile, China, Colombia, Costa Rica, Czech Republic, Denmark, Ecuador, Estonia, Finland, France, Germany, Ghana, India, Indonesia, Ireland, Italy, Japan, Korea, Latvia, Lithuania, Malawi, Malaysia, Mexico, Morocco, the Netherlands, Norway, Poland, Russia, South Africa, Spain, Sweden, Switzerland, Thailand, Turkey, United Arab Emirates, United Kingdom, Uruguay, and Vietnam. Work- study programs with (name of employer): Career Services assists students in relevant work experience through several different formats. Through our Experiential Education program, students can participate in job shadowing, non-academic internships, and cooperative education assignments. The student's assignments vary based on their majors and interests. Some of the companies that students are currently participating with are The Southern Company, Bell South, BMW, the United States Army Corps, Target, and Coca-Cola. B.A. degrees include: Modern Languages, English, Writing and Linguistics, Biology, Philosophy, Chemistry, Geology, Physics, Anthropology, Economics, Geography, International Studies, Political Science, Theatre, Art, Music, and History. B.S. degrees include: Journalism, Multimedia Communication, Public Relations and Organizational Communications, Computer Science, Nutrition and Food Science, Child and Family Development, Fashion Merchandising and Apparel Design, Communication Studies, Mathematics. Recreation, Sport Management, Geology, Psychology, Geography, Political Science, Sociology, Interior Design, and International Trade. Student Designed Majors: Yes. Accelerated degree program is a state-funded program for public and private high school students that provide dual enrollment tuition assistance in Georgia. The program offers the opportunity to earn dual credit, satisfying high school and college core curriculum requirements. Joint Enrollment is not a state-funded program and does not guarantee satisfaction of the high school core curriculum. Admissions requirements for Accel of joint enrollment are; earned an academic GPA of 3.0., submit SAT scores of at least 1000 or 21 ACT, Excel in the field in which the student plans to enroll, have written consent of parent and guardian, and must be on track to complete College Preparatory Curriculum (CPC) requirements. Dual majors; Students may be granted a second baccalaureate degree if the following conditions are met; if the first degree is earned at GSU, a student may seek a second degree if it is different from the first degree; must satisfy all major requirements, and must complete the history and constitution requirements; take a minimum of 30 additional credit hours at GSU, also earn at least 50% of the credits toward the major at GSU, and may work on two degrees at the same time. 3-2 engineering degree with Georgia Institute of Technology.Cross registration with Georgia Southern has cross-registration available with East Georgia and GOML (Georgia OnMyLine) programs. Study abroad in Argentina, Australia, Austria, Belgium, Botswana, Brazil, Bulgaria, Canada, Chile, China, Colombia, Costa Rica, Czech Republic, Denmark, Ecuador, Estonia, Finland, France, Germany, Ghana, India, Indonesia, Ireland, Italy, Japan, Korea, Latvia, Lithuania, Malawi, Malaysia, Mexico, Morocco, the Netherlands, Norway, Poland, Russia, South Africa, Spain, Sweden, Switzerland, Thailand, Turkey, United Arab Emirates, United Kingdom, Uruguay, and Vietnam. Work- study programs with; Career Services assists students in relevant work experience through several different formats. Through our Experiential Education program, students can participate in job shadowing, non-academic internships, and cooperative education assignments. The student's assignments vary based on their majors and interests. Some of the companies that students are currently participating with are; The Southern Company, Bell South, BMW, the United States Army Corps, Target, and Coca-Cola. B.A. degrees include: Modern Languages, English, Writing and Linguistics, Biology, Philosophy, Chemistry, Geology, Physics, Anthropology, Economics, Geography, International Studies, Political Science, Theatre, Art, Music, and History. B.S. degrees include: Journalism, Multimedia Communication, Public Relations and Organizational Communications, Computer Science, Nutrition and Food Science, Child and Family Development, Fashion Merchandising and Apparel Design, Communication Studies, Mathematics. Recreation, Sport Management, Geology, Psychology, Geography, Political Science, Sociology, Interior Design, and International Trade. There are 17 national honor societies, a freshman honors program, and 24 departmental honors programs. **Visiting:** There are regularly scheduled orientations for prospective students. There are guides for informal visits and visitors may sit in on classes. To schedule a visit, contact Kathryn Lockwood at (912) 478-5851. **Campus Safety and Security:** Measures include 24-hour foot and vehicle patrol, emergency notification system, self-defense education, and security escort services. There are shuttle buses, emergency telephones, lighted pathways/sidewalks, controlled access to dorms/residences, panic button alarms in all residence hall rooms.

REQUIREMENTS: The SAT or ACT is required. Applicants must have a high school diploma or the equivalent is required. A minimum of 17 credits in college preparatory courses should include 4 each in English and math, 3 each in social studies, 4 in science, and 2 in a foreign language. A GPA of 2.0 is required. AP and CLEP credits are accepted. All students must complete a total of 126 semester credit hours, including at least 30 in the major, with a minimum GPA of 2.0. Students must complete specific courses in English, math, humanities, science, and social sciences, a healthful living class, 2 physical activity courses, orientation course, and interdisciplinary studies class. **Procedure:** Freshmen are admitted fall, spring, and summer. Entrance exams should be taken during the junior year. There are deferred admissions and rolling admissions plans. Applications should be filed by May 1 for fall entry; December 1 for spring entry; and April 1 for summer entry, along with a $30 fee. Notification is sent on a rolling basis. Applications are accepted on-line. **Transfer Students:** 1071 transfer students enrolled in 2013-2014. Applicants must have completed at least 30 semester credit hours of college courses with a minimum GPA of 2.0. Those with fewer than 30 hours must meet freshman requirements. Students transferring with an associate degree must have a minimum GPA of 2.0 in a school with a parallel curriculum. 30 of 126 credits required for the bachelor's degree must be completed at Georgia Southern. **International Students:** There are 245 international students enrolled. The school actively recruits these students. They must take the TOEFL with a minimum score of 523 on the paper-based TOEFL (PBT) or 69 on the Internet-based version (iBT), or take the IELTS. They must also take the SAT or ACT, scoring 1010. International students whose native language is not English, but whose secondary instruction was exclusively in English, must submit TOEFL or SAT/ACT.

ADMISSIONS: 63% of the 2014-2015 applicants were accepted. The SAT scores for the 2014-2015 freshman class were: Critical Reading- -12% below 500, 63% between 500 and 599, 22% between 600 and 699, and 2% between 700 and 800; Math--13% below 500, 63% between 500 and 599, 22% between 600 and 699, and 1% between 700 and 800; Writing--33% below 500, 52% between 500 and 599, 14% between 600 and 699, and 1% between 700 and 800. The ACT scores were 1% below 21, 58% between 21 and 23, 26% between 24 and 26, 8% between 27 and 28, and 7% above 28. 38% of the current freshmen were in the top fifth of their class; 66% were in the top two fifths. **Admissions Contact:** Amy Smith, Director. E-Mail: *admissions@georgiasouthern.edu* Web: *www.georgiasouthern.edu*

FINANCIAL AID: In 2014-2015, 92% of all full-time freshmen and 89% of continuing full-time students received some form of financial aid. 60% of all full-time freshmen and 57% of continuing full-time students received need-based aid. The average freshman award was $9,390. Need-based scholarships or need-based grants averaged $6,927 ($37,766 maximum); need-based self-help aid (loans and jobs) averaged $4,157 ($29,500 maximum); non-need-based athletic scholarships averaged $7,516 ($20,381 maximum); and other non-need-based awards and non-need-based scholarships averaged $1,624 ($6,974 maximum). Average annual earnings from campus work are $2109. The average financial indebtedness of the 2014 graduate was $24,201. Georgia Southern is a member of CSS. The FAFSA is required. The priority date for freshman financial aid applications for fall entry is April 20.

GEORGIA SOUTHWESTERN STATE UNIVERSITY
B-4
www.gsw.edu

Americus, GA 31709

(229) 928-1273
(800) 338-0082

Fax: (229) 931-2983

Email: Admissions@gsw.edu

Full-time: 672 men, 1080 women

Faculty: 107

Part-time: 269 men, 506 women

Ph.D.s: 74%

Graduate: 40 men, 99 women

Student/Faculty: 19 to 1

Year: semesters, summer session

Tuition: $6126 ($18,612)

Room & Board: $7140

Freshman Class: 1999 applied, 813 accepted, 392 enrolled

SAT CR/M/W: 480/480/470 ACT: 20

CEEB CODE: 5250

Application Deadline: July 21

COMPETITIVE

Georgia Southwestern State University, founded in 1906, is a comprehensive state university within the University System of Georgia. The mission of Georgia Southwestern State University is to cultivate excellence in learning and teaching that encourages intellectual, personal, and social growth for students, faculty, staff, and the community. Georgia Southwestern fulfills its commitment to research and public service through the individual efforts of an outstanding faculty and the focused activities of specific centers. GSW offers a full range of bachelor degree programs, along with selected master's degree programs in English, computer science, business, education, and nursing. As a residential, comprehensive university, GSW serves a diverse student body, primarily drawn from southwest Georgia, with a growing number of students from across the state as well as out-of-state, international, and on-line students. There are 5 undergraduate schools and 4 graduate schools. In addition to regional accreditation, GSW has baccalaureate program accreditation with AACSB, NCATE, NLN, and CCNE. The 250-acre campus is in a small town 38 miles north of Albany, Georgia and 135 miles south of Atlanta, Georgia. Including any residence halls, there are 33 buildings.

STUDENT LIFE: 96% of undergraduates are from Georgia. Others are from 18 states, 34 foreign countries, and Canada. 82% are from public schools. 63% are White; 27% African American. **Male To Female Ratio:** 1.7:1. The average age of freshmen is 18; all undergraduates, 25. 30% do not continue beyond their first year; 30% remain to graduate. **Housing:** 950 students can be accommodated in college housing, which includes coed dorms and on-campus apartments. In addition, there are special-interest houses, independent fraternity and sorority houses. On-campus housing is guaranteed for all 4 years. 69% of students commute. All students may keep cars.

FACULTY/CLASSROOMS: 46% of faculty are male; 54% are female. All teach undergraduates. No introductory courses are taught by graduate students. The average class size in an introductory lecture is 28; in a laboratory is 26; and in a regular course is 23.

PROGRAMS OF STUDY: GSW confers B.A., B.S., B.B.A., B.F.A., B.S.Ed. and B.S.N. degrees. Master's degrees are also awarded. Bachelor's degrees are awarded in BIOLOGICAL SCIENCE (biology/ biological science), BUSINESS (accounting, business administration and management, human resources/organizational mgmt, and marketing management), COMMUNICATIONS AND THE ARTS (art, dramatic arts, English, fine arts, and music), COMPUTER AND PHYSICAL SCIENCE (chemistry, computer information technology, computer science, geology, and mathematics), EDUCATION (early childhood education, health and physical education, middle school education, and special education), HEALTH PROFESSIONS (exercise science and nursing), SOCIAL SCIENCE (history, political science/government, psychology, and sociology). Business, nursing, education, and biology are the strongest academically. Business, education, and nursing have the largest enrollments.

ACTIVITIES: Men belong to 5 national fraternities; Women belong to 6 national sororities. There are 60 groups on campus, including art, band, cheerleading, choir, chorale, chorus, computers, dance, drama, ethnic, gay, honors, international, jazz band, literary magazine, musical theater, newspaper, orchestra, political, professional, radio and TV, religious, social, social service, and student government. Popular campus events include Welcome Week, FallFest, Student Appreciation Day, and Convocation Series. **Sports:** There are 4 intercollegiate sports for men and 4 for women, and 4 intramural sports for men and 4 for women. Facilities include 2 gyms, tennis courts, indoor climbing wall, fitness center, group exercise room, racquetball courts, game room, lake for canoeing, and playing fields for baseball, softball, flag football, and soccer. The larger gym seats 3000, the smaller seats 500. **Graduates:** From July 1, 2013 to June 30, 2014, 546 bachelor's degrees were awarded. The most popular majors were management (17%), nursing (17%), and accounting (12%). In an average class, 1% graduate in 3 years or less, 10% graduate in 4 years or less, 26% graduate in 5 years or less, and 32% graduate in 6 years or less.

SERVICES: Counseling and information services are available, as is tutoring in most subjects. There is a reader service for the blind, and remedial math, reading, and writing. **Library/Resources:** The library contains 181,952 volumes, 1.6 million microform items, 14,335 audio/video tapes/CDs/DVDs, and subscribes to 190 periodicals including electronic. Computerized library services include interlibrary loans, database searching, Internet access, and Wi-Fi capability. Special learning facilities include an art gallery, radio station, TV station, a glass-blowing facility and state of the art simulation technology labs in nursing. **Physically Challenged Students:** 95% of the campus is accessible. Facilities include wheelchair ramps, elevators, special parking, specially equipped restrooms, special class scheduling, lowered drinking fountains. **Special:** GSW and Georgia Institute of Technology offer a dual degree program that results in students who complete a BS in Civil Engineering, a BS in Electrical Engineering, or a BS in Mechanical Engineering receiving a BS in Mathematics from GSW. The dual degree student enrolls at GSW for approximately 3 years and upon acceptance to Georgia Teach, enrolls for an additional 2 years. The Bachelor of Business Administration degree is offered entirely online to students who transfer in having already completed an Associate of Science or Associate of Arts degree in Business. There are 3 national honor societies, a freshman honors program, and 1 departmental honors program. **Visiting:** There are regularly scheduled orientations for prospective students. There are guides for informal visits. **Campus Safety and Security:** Measures include 24-hour foot and vehicle patrol, emergency notification system, self-defense education, and security escort services. There are emergency telephones, lighted pathways/sidewalks, and controlled access to dorms/residences.

REQUIREMENTS: The SAT or ACT is required. Freshmen applicants must submit transcripts of his/her high school record. 17 required high school curriculum courses, based on 4 units of English, 4 of science and 4 of math, 3 units of social science (including one focusing on world studies) and 2 units in the same foreign language are required of students who graduated from high school spring 2012 or later. All new students are required to submit proof of required immunizations on the form provided by GSW prior to their enrollment. An art portfolio and a music audition are recommended for appropriate majors. Non-traditional, transfer, international students and beginning freshmen applicants from home schools or graduates of non-accredited high schools should contact Admissions for additional requirements. A GPA of 2.0 is required. AP and CLEP credits are accepted. To graduate, students must complete 120 credit hours consisting of 60 hours in the Core Curriculum and 60 hour in upper division with a minimum GPA of 2.0. The Core curriculum requires 42 hours in general education courses (English, math, humanities, social sciences, sciences, institutional options) and 18 hours in a major area of study. Students are also required to complete 3 courses in physical education. **Procedure:** Freshmen are admitted fall, spring, and summer. Entrance exams should be taken before the end of the senior year. There is a rolling admissions plan. Applications should be filed by July 21 for fall entry; December 10 for spring entry; and May 15 for summer entry, along with a $25 fee. Applications are accepted on-line. **Transfer Students:** 574 transfer students enrolled in 2013-2014. Applicants should be in good standing at their former institutions, with a cumulative GPA of 2.0 or higher on a 4.0 scale. Students with fewer than 30 hours of transfer credit must meet freshman requirements. 30 of 120 credits required for the bachelor's degree must be completed at GSW. **International Students:** There are 42 international students enrolled. The school actively recruits these students. They must take the TOEFL with a minimum score of 523 on the paper-based TOEFL (PBT) or 70 on the Internet-based version (iBT), or take the IELTS.

ADMISSIONS: 41% of the 2014-2015 applicants were accepted. The SAT scores for the 2014-2015 freshman class were: Critical Reading--56% below 500, 34% between 500 and 599, 9% between 600 and 699, and 1% between 700 and 800; Math--58% below 500, 36% between 500 and 599, and 6% between 600 and 699; Writing--66% below 500, 29% between 500 and 599, and 5% between 600 and 699. The ACT scores were 61% below 21, 20% between 21 and 23, 12% between 24 and 26, 4% between 27 and 28, and 3% above 28. 15% of the current freshmen were in the top fifth of their class; 33% were in the top two fifths. **Admissions Contact:** David Jenkins, Assistant Director of Admissions. E-Mail: *Admissions@gsw.edu* Web: *www.gsw.edu*

FINANCIAL AID: In 2014-2015, 95% of all full-time freshmen and 90% of continuing full-time students received some form of financial aid. 65% of all full-time freshmen and 68% of continuing full-time students received need-based aid. The average freshman award was $9,085. Need-based scholarships or need-based grants averaged $4,855 ($6,330 maximum); need-based self-help aid (loans and jobs) averaged $3,462 ($10,446 maximum); non-need-based athletic scholarships averaged $2,730 ($10,600 maximum); and other non-need-based awards and non-need-based scholarships averaged $4,609 ($12,240 maximum). The average financial indebtedness of the 2014 graduate was $26,294. The FAFSA is required. The priority date for freshman financial aid applications for fall entry is April 15. The deadline for filing freshman financial aid applications for fall entry is June 15.

GEORGIA STATE UNIVERSITY	B-2
www.gsu.edu	
Atlanta, GA 30302	**(404) 413-2500**
	n/av
Fax: (404) 413-2002	Email: admissions@gsu.edu
Full-time: 5455 men, 8305 women	Faculty: I, -$
Part-time: 2020 men, 3195 women	Ph.D.s: 85%
Graduate: 2880 men, 4110 women	Student/Faculty: n/av
Year: semesters, summer session	Tuition: $5000 ($16,000)
Room & Board: $7000	Freshman Class: n/av
SAT or ACT: required	CEEB CODE: 5251
Application Deadline: n/av	**VERY COMPETITIVE**

Georgia State University, founded in 1913 and a part of the University System of Georgia, is a public residential university offering programs in liberal arts and sciences, business administration, education, law, health sciences, and public policy. Figures in the above capsule are approximate. There are 5 undergraduate schools and 6 graduate schools. In addition to regional accreditation, Georgia State has baccalaureate program accreditation with AACSB, ADA, APTA, CAHEA, CSWE, NASAD, NASM, NCATE, NLN, ABA, ACS, APA, CADE, CACREP, and CAPTE. The 33-acre campus is in an urban area in downtown Atlanta. Including any residence halls, there are 46 buildings.

STUDENT LIFE: 92% of undergraduates are from Georgia. Others are from 48 states, 139 foreign countries, and Canada. 37% are White; 31% African American. **Male To Female Ratio:** 1.5:1. The average age of freshmen is 20; all undergraduates, 24. 24% do not continue beyond their first year; 44% remain to graduate. **Housing:** 2435 students can be accommodated in college housing, which includes coed on-campus apartments. In addition, there are honors houses and special-interest houses. On-campus housing is available on a first-come and first-served basis. 90% of students commute. All students may keep cars.

FACULTY/CLASSROOMS: 56% of faculty are male; 44% are female. No introductory courses are taught by graduate students.

PROGRAMS OF STUDY: Georgia State confers B.A., B.S., B.B.A., B.F.A., B.I.S., B.M., B.S.Ed. and B.S.W. degrees. Master's and Doctoral degrees are also awarded. Bachelor's degrees are awarded in BIOLOGICAL SCIENCE (biology/biological science and nutrition), BUSINESS (accounting, banking and finance, business administration and management, business economics, hospitality management services, insurance and risk management, management information systems, marketing/retailing/merchandising, office supervision and management, and real estate), COMMUNICATIONS AND THE ARTS (art, art history and appreciation, classics, English, film arts, fine arts, French, German, journalism, music, music business management, Spanish, speech/debate/rhetoric, and studio art), COMPUTER AND PHYSICAL SCIENCE (actuarial science, chemistry, computer science, geology, mathematics, physics, and statistics), EDUCATION (art education, early childhood education, and physical education), HEALTH PROFESSIONS (exercise science, nursing, and respiratory therapy), SOCIAL SCIENCE (African American studies, anthropology, criminal justice, economics, geography, history, interdisciplinary studies, philosophy, political science/government, psychology, religious education, social work, sociology, urban studies, and women's studies). Biological sciences, psychology, and management have the largest enrollments.

ACTIVITIES: 3% of men belong to 10 national fraternities; 4% of women belong to 11 national sororities. There are 203 groups on campus, including art, band, cheerleading, chess, chorale, chorus, computers, dance, debate, drama, ethnic, film, gay, honors, international, jazz band, literary magazine, musical theater, newspaper, opera, orchestra, outdoor, pep band, photography, political, professional, radio and TV, religious, social, social service, and student government. Popular campus events include International Student Festival, Honors Day and Greek Week. **Sports:** There are 7 intercollegiate sports for men and 8 for women, and 30 intramural sports for men and 30 for women. Facilities include a phys ed complex with 3 gyms, a pool, a diving well, a weight room, indoor and outdoor tennis courts, a climbing wall, a jogging track, exercise rooms, a dance studio, and racquetball courts. In addition, the Indian Creek recreation area has a pool, 3 tennis courts, picnic facilities, regular and sand volleyball, basketball courts, and a rope challenge course. There are also athletic fields.

SERVICES: Counseling and information services are available, as is tutoring in most subjects. There is a reader service for the blind, and remedial math, reading, and writing. Programs are available in effective studying, reading comprehension, speed reading, test and note taking, test anxiety, fear of public speaking, and organization and planning. **Library/Resources:** The 2 libraries contain 1.4 million volumes, 1.7 million microform items, 22,551 audio/video tapes/CDs/DVDs, and subscribe to 7,788 periodicals including electronic. Computerized library services include interlibrary loans, database searching, Internet access, and Wi-Fi capability. Special learning facilities include an art gallery, radio station, TV station, digital arts lab, observatory, instructional technology center, and distance learning classrooms. **Physically Challenged Students:** All of the campus is accessible. Facilities include wheelchair ramps, elevators, special parking, specially equipped restrooms, special class scheduling, lowered drinking fountains, and lowered telephones. **Special:** There is cross-registration with the Atlanta Regional Consortium for Higher Education (ARCHE). Internships with numerous employers and government agencies can be arranged. Study abroad is available in various countries. Work-study, an accelerated degree program in nursing, and dual majors are available. The Summer Scholar program allows high school seniors to take college-level course work. There are a freshman honors program. **Visiting:** There are guides for informal visits and visitors may sit in on classes. To schedule a visit, contact Welcome Center at (404) 651-3900. **Campus Safety and Security:** Measures include 24-hour foot and vehicle patrol, self-defense education, and security escort services. There are shuttle buses, emergency telephones, lighted pathways/sidewalks, 24-hour security at university housing, and a bicycle patrol.

REQUIREMENTS: The SAT or ACT is required. The ACT Optional Writing test is also required. Applicants must graduate from a regionally accredited high school. A total of 16 academic credits is required. Students should prepare with 4 years each of English and math, 3 years each of science and social science, and 2 years of the same foreign language. They must have a minimum 2.80 high school GPA calculated on the 16 courses listed above. A GPA of 2.8 is required. AP and CLEP credits are accepted. Important factors in the admissions decision are evidence of special talent, advanced placement or honors courses, and extracurricular activities record.Students must complete distribution requirements, including courses in English composition, humanities, natural science and math, social science, U.S. history, and political science. A minimum of 120 hours must be completed for graduation with a minimum GPA of 2.0. **Procedure:** Freshmen are admitted fall, spring, and summer. Entrance exams should be taken during the first semester of the senior year. There is a rolling admissions plan. Check with the school for current application deadlines. The fall 2014 application fee was $50. Applications are accepted online. **Transfer Students:** 1962 transfer students enrolled in 2013-2014. Transfer applicants must submit official transcripts of all college-level work, have a minimum GPA of 2.5, have earned 30 semester hours, and be in good academic standing. Those with fewer than 30 semester hours earned must meet freshman requirements. 39 of 120 credits required for the bachelor's degree must be completed at Georgia State. **International Students:** The school actively recruits these students. They must take the TOEFL and the college's own test, or take the GSTEP with a score of 6, or SAT with verbal score 430 or the ACT with an English subtest score of 17. They must also take the SAT or ACT.

ADMISSIONS: Admissions Contact: Stephanie Buchanan, Associate Director. E-Mail: *admissions@gsu.edu* Web: *www.gsu.edu*

FINANCIAL AID: The FAFSA is required. Check with the school for current application deadlines.

KENNESAW STATE UNIVERSITY — B-2
www.kennesaw.edu

Kennesaw, GA 30144	(770) 423-6300 n/av
Fax: (770) 420-4435	Email: ksuadmit@kennesaw.edu
Full-time: 2455 men, 3297 women	Faculty: 755; IIA, -$
Part-time: 6994 men, 9875 women	Ph.D.s: n/av
Graduate: 754 men, 1254 women	Student/Faculty: 21 to 1
Year: semesters, summer session	Tuition: $6807 ($19,390)
Room & Board: $6210	Freshman Class: 10058 applied, 5572 accepted, 3146 enrolled
SAT CR/M/W: 540/530/510 ACT: 22	CEEB CODE: 5359
Application Deadline: May 8	COMPETITIVE

Kennesaw State University (KSU) is the third-largest university in Georgia with more than 24,600 undergraduate and graduate students representing 121 countries. Accredited by the Southern Association of Colleges and Schools (SACS), KSU offers 80 bachelor's, master's and doctorate degree programs including undergraduate degrees in education, health, business, the humanities, the arts, science and math. The university's graduate degree programs include nursing, business, information systems, conflict management, public administration, education and professional writing. KSU's expanding doctoral programs currently offer doctorates in education, business and nursing, as well as KSU's first Ph.D program in International Conflict Management. There are 7 undergraduate schools and 6 graduate schools. In addition to regional accreditation, Kennesaw State has baccalaureate program accreditation with AACSB, ABET, CSWE, NASAD, NASM, NCATE, NLN, NAST, NASAD, CCNE, ACEI, NMSA, NCTE, ACTFL, NCSS, AAHPERD, NASPE, ACS, NSTA, and NCTM. The 384-acre campus is in a suburban area 25 miles north of Atlanta. Including any residence halls, there are 91 buildings.

STUDENT LIFE: 97% of undergraduates are from Georgia. Others are from 48 states, 120 foreign countries, and Canada. 65% are White; 17% African American. **Male To Female Ratio:** 1.4:1. The average age of freshmen is 18; all undergraduates, 24. **Housing:** 3497 students can be accommodated in college housing, which includes coed on-campus apartments. On-campus housing is available on a first-come and first-served basis. 86% of students commute. Alcohol is not permitted. All students may keep cars.

FACULTY/CLASSROOMS: 42% of faculty are male; 58% are female.

All teach and do research. No introductory courses are taught by graduate students. The average class size in an introductory lecture is 41; in a laboratory is 22; and in a regular course is 35.

PROGRAMS OF STUDY: Kennesaw State confers B.A., B.S., B.B.A., B.F.A., B.M., B.S.N., and B.S.N.C. degrees. Master's and Doctoral degrees are also awarded. Bachelor's degrees are awarded in BIOLOGICAL SCIENCE (biochemistry, biology/biological science, and biotechnology), BUSINESS (accounting, business administration and management, finance, international business management, management science, and marketing/retailing/merchandising), COMMUNICATIONS AND THE ARTS (art history, art, communications, dance, English, modern language, music, music performance, and theatre arts), COMPUTER AND PHYSICAL SCIENCE (chemistry, computer science, computer security and information assurance, information sciences and systems, and mathematics), EDUCATION (art education, (Education) Childhood Education, early childhood education, English education, health education, mathematics education, middle school education, music education, and physical education), HEALTH PROFESSIONS (exercise science and nursing), SOCIAL SCIENCE (African studies, anthropology, criminal justice, economics, geography, history, human services, interdisciplinary studies, international studies, philosophy, political science/government, psychology, and sociology). Business, nursing and biology are the strongest academically. Communication, nursing, and psychology have the largest enrollments.

ACTIVITIES: 4% of men belong to 9 national fraternities; 5% of women belong to 10 national sororities. There are 180 groups on campus, including art, band, cheerleading, choir, chorale, chorus, computers, dance, drama, ethnic, gay, honors, international, jazz band, literary magazine, musical theater, newspaper, pep band, political, professional, radio and TV, religious, social, social service, student government, and symphony. Popular campus events include KSU College Colors Day, Black History Month, Country Study Program, Tricycle Derby, and Turkey Trot. **Sports:** There are 6 intercollegiate sports for men and 9 for women, and 9 intramural sports for men and 9 for women. Facilities include Athletic Complex for softball, a stadium for soccer, lacrosse, and football. A convocation center for men's and women's basketball and volleyball, indoor golf practice facility, outdoor track and field facility, rehabilitation facility, baseball stadium, strength and conditioning facility. **Graduates:** From July 1, 2013 to June 30, 2014, 3488 bachelor's degrees were awarded. The most popular majors were communication (8%), early childhood education (8%), and management (7%). In an average class, 15% graduate in 4 years or less, 35% graduate in 5 years or less, and 43% graduate in 6 years or less. Of the 2013 graduating class, 24% were enrolled in graduate school within 6 months of graduation, and 43% were employed.

SERVICES: Counseling and information services are available, as is tutoring in some subjects, Math, Foreign Languages, and English. Academic Coaching for Writing/Research Skills There is a reader service for the blind, and remedial math, reading, and writing. **Library/Resources:** The 2 libraries contain 614,198 volumes, 125,000 microform items, and 9,000 audio/video tapes/CDs/DVDs, and subscribe to 55,000 periodicals including electronic. Computerized library services include interlibrary loans, database searching, Internet access, and Wi-Fi capability. Special learning facilities include an art gallery, radio station, The Museum of History and Holocaust Education, The Civil War Center, Center for Regional History and Culture, Center for African and African Diaspora Studies, Center for Hispanic Studies. Confucius Institute at Kennesaw State University. **Physically Challenged Students:** All of the campus is accessible. Facilities include wheelchair ramps, elevators, special parking, specially equipped restrooms, special class scheduling, lowered drinking fountains, lowered telephones. **Special:** Students may register for courses with any of the colleges in the University System of Georgia, study abroad in over 60 countries, and participate in work-study programs and internships, some with pass/fail options. Dual majors, student-designed majors, and nondegree programs also are offered. There are 21 national honor societies and a freshman honors program. **Visiting:** There are regularly scheduled orientations for prospective students, Mondays, Wednesdays and Fridays: 10 a.m. and 2 p.m. Information session followed by a student led walking tour of the academic areas of campus with a tour of University Housing and optional post-tour meal in The Commons. Tuesdays and Thursdays. There are guides for informal visits. To schedule a visit, contact the Office of Undergraduate Admissions. **Campus Safety and Security:** Measures include 24-hour foot and vehicle patrol, emergency notification system, self-defense education, and security escort services. There are shuttle buses, emergency telephones, lighted pathways/sidewalks, Full-service police department, siren system with messages, pop-up computer notification on the KSU network, telephone emergency message system, email emergency notification, security badges, electronic access control, intrusion alarms and video surveillance.

REQUIREMENTS: The SAT or ACT is required. For applicants graduating from high school prior to 2012, a minimum of 16 RHSC units (Carnegie units which equate to four years of completed high school study) are required in the following subject areas: English (4), Mathematics (4), Science (3), Social Science (3), Foreign Language (2), Applicants graduating from high school in 2012 or later must meet the above requirements with the following changes (17 units): Mathematics (4), Science (4). KSU's minimum requirements for admission as a regular first year freshman include the following: Graduation from a regionally accredited high school or a high school accredited by the Georgia Accreditation Commission (GAC), or from a public school under the authority of the state department of education. Completion of at least the 17 required units for graduates 2012 or later (16 units for graduates 2011 or earlier) in the University System's Required High School Curriculum. Have a combined Critical Reading and Math total of 950 on the SAT (20 ACT Composite), Freshman Index of at least 1940, with a SAT-Critical Reading/Verbal of at least 490 (ACT 20) and a SAT-Math of at least 460 (ACT 19), and an academic HSGPA of at least 2.5 in the Required High School Curriculum as calculated by KSU. (The SAT essay portion must be submitted, but will not be used in the decision.) A GPA of 2.5 is required. AP and CLEP credits are accepted.Requirements vary by degree program. Generally, all students must complete 123 semester hours, including 45 to 47 in core curriculum courses and 39 in upper-level courses, with a minimum GPA of 2.0 and grades of C or better in the major and in required English courses. Students must also successfully complete the University System of Georgia Regents' Testing Program and demonstrate (by course or exam) competency in the history and constitutions of the United States and Georgia. 3 hours of Fitness for Living are also required. **Procedure:** Freshmen are admitted fall, spring, and summer. Entrance exams should be taken before June 1. There is a rolling admissions plan. Applications should be filed by May 8 for fall entry; November 1 for spring entry; and April 4 for summer entry. The fall 2014 application fee was $40. Applications are accepted on-line. **Transfer Students:** 2205 transfer students enrolled in 2013-2014. Applicants with fewer than 30 semester hours of acceptable transfer credit must meet the same admissions requirements identified earlier for freshmen admitted from high school. Freshman transfer applicants may be required to take the COMPASS in English and/or math depending upon SAT/ACT scores, and are held to appropriate standards based upon results. Transfer freshmen must be in good standing at previous institutions. Transfer applicants with sufficient transferable hours to be classified as a sophomore, junior or senior at KSU must have completed any and all learning support requirements prior to admission and have a cumulative GPA of at least 2.0 in the previous institutions attended. Students transferring from another institution in the University System of Georgia must have satisfied any and all learning support requirements before being admitted to KSU. Transferring students taking physical education hours at one institution will not be required to duplicate these hours at KSU. However, students taking an orientation course at another institution may be required to take the KSU 1101 orientation course. All admission application deadlines cited earlier apply to transfer applicants. All of the documents cited earlier and required for a complete application file apply to transfer applicants with the following exceptions: High school transcripts are not required for applicants with 30 or more earned semester hours of acceptable transfer credit. (All college and university transcripts are required, however); SAT I or ACT scores are not required for applicants with 30 or more earned semester hours of acceptable transfer credit; Freshman transfer applicants (less than 30 semester hours of transferable credit) may be required to take the COMPASS in English and/or math depending upon SAT/ACT scores. 30 of 123 credits

required for the bachelor's degree must be completed at Kennesaw State. **International Students:** There are 971 international students enrolled. The school actively recruits these students. They must take the TOEFL with a minimum score of 527 on the paper-based TOEFL (PBT) or 75 on the Internet-based version (iBT), or take the IELTS score of 6.0. They must also take the SAT or ACT, scoring SAT 950 combined. SAT scores a minimum of 950 points combined, minimum score of 430 in the verbal section and 400 in math.

ADMISSIONS: 55% of the 2014-2015 applicants were accepted. The SAT scores for the 2014-2015 freshman class were: Critical Reading--18% below 500, 60% between 500 and 599, 20% between 600 and 699, and 2% between 700 and 800; Math--26% below 500, 56% between 500 and 599, 17% between 600 and 699, and 1% between 700 and 800; Writing--39% below 500, 47% between 500 and 599, 13% between 600 and 699, and 1% between 700 and 800. The ACT scores were 22% below 21, 52% between 21 and 23, 21% between 24 and 26, 4% between 27 and 28, and 1% above 28. **Admissions Contact:** Angela Evans, Director of Admissions. E-Mail: *ksuadmit@ kennesaw.edu* Web: *http:/www.kennesaw.edu/*

FINANCIAL AID: In 2014-2015, 94% of all full-time freshmen and 44% of continuing full-time students received some form of financial aid. 96% of all full-time freshmen and 49% of continuing full-time students received need-based aid. The average freshman award was $7,990. Need-based scholarships or need-based grants averaged $4,242 ($6,626 maximum); need-based self-help aid (loans and jobs) averaged $2,494 ($2,884 maximum); non-need-based athletic scholarships averaged $4,055 ($7,565 maximum); and other non-need-based awards and non-need-based scholarships averaged $5,303 ($18,981 maximum). 4% of undergraduate students work part-time. Average annual earnings from campus work are $7924. The average financial indebtedness of the 2014 graduate was $22,407. Kennesaw State is a member of CSS. The FAFSA is required. The priority date for freshman financial aid applications for fall entry is April 1.

LAGRANGE COLLEGE   A-3
www.lagrange.edu

LaGrange, GA 30240   (706) 880-8261
    (800) 593-2885

Fax: (706) 880-8010   Email: dmcgreal@lagrange.edu

Full-time: 400 men, 404 women   **Faculty:** 72

Part-time: 13 men, 63 women   **Ph.D.s:** 83%

Graduate: 30 men, 54 women   **Student/Faculty:** 11 to 1

Year: 4-1-4, summer session   **Tuition:** $26,620

Room & Board: $11,050   **Freshman Class:** 1343 applied, 742 accepted, 238 enrolled

SAT CR/M/W: 520/510/490 **ACT:** 21   **CEEB CODE:** 5362

Application Deadline: n/av   **COMPETITIVE**

LaGrange College, founded in 1831, is a private liberal arts institution affiliated with the United Methodist Church. Major undergraduate programs include business, visual and performing arts, education, biology, psychology, and exercise science. Figures in the above capsule and in this profile are approximate. There are no undergraduate schools and one graduate school. In addition to regional accreditation, LaGrange has baccalaureate program accreditation with ACBSP, NLN, and GPSC. The 120-acre campus is in a small town 70 miles southwest of Atlanta. Including any residence halls, there are 26 buildings.

STUDENT LIFE: 83% of undergraduates are from Georgia. Others are from 18 states, and 4 foreign countries. 82% are from public schools. 70% are White; 22% African American. 67% are Protestant; 25% Unknown Religious affiliation. **Male To Female Ratio:** 1.2:1. The average age of freshmen is 18; all undergraduates, 22. 39% do not continue beyond their first year; 53% remain to graduate. **Housing:** 632 students can be accommodated in college housing, which includes single-sex and coed dorms, on-campus apartments, and married student housing. In addition, there are special-interest houses, fraternity houses, and sorority houses. On-campus housing is guaranteed for all 4 years. 60% of students live on campus; of those, 63% remain on campus on weekends. Alcohol is not permitted. All students may keep cars.

FACULTY/CLASSROOMS: 49% of faculty are male; 51% are female. All teach undergraduates. No introductory courses are taught by graduate students. The average class size in an introductory lecture is 18 and in a laboratory is 18.

PROGRAMS OF STUDY: LaGrange confers B.A., B.S., B.S.N., B.B.A. and B.M. degrees. Master's degrees are also awarded. Bachelor's degrees are awarded in BIOLOGICAL SCIENCE (biochemistry and biology/biological science), BUSINESS (accounting and business administration and management), COMMUNICATIONS AND THE ARTS (art, English, music, Spanish, and theatre arts), COMPUTER AND PHYSICAL SCIENCE (chemistry, computer science, and mathematics), EDUCATION (early childhood education and education), HEALTH PROFESSIONS (exercise science and nursing), SOCIAL SCIENCE (history, interdisciplinary studies, political science/government, psychology, religion, and sociology). Nursing, biology, and early childhood education are the largest.

ACTIVITIES: 22% of men belong to 3 national fraternities; 28% of women belong to 3 national sororities. There are 55 groups on campus, including art, cheerleading, choir, chorale, chorus, drama, environmental, ethnic, gay, honors, international, literary magazine, musical theater, newspaper, orchestra, pep band, political, professional, religious, social, social service, and student government. Popular campus events include Homecoming, Spirit and Traditions Kickoff, May Day, Family Weekend, Vegas on the Hill, Christmas on the Hill, and Halloween on the Hill. **Sports:** There are 8 intercollegiate sports for men and 9 for women, and 8 intramural sports for men and 8 for women. Facilities include a fitness center, West Point Lake, an auditorium, indoor and outdoor pools, 2 gyms, 10 lighted tennis courts, lighted softball, baseball stadium, soccer fields, a football practice field, and a football stadium. **Graduates:** From July 1, 2013 to June 30, 2014, 165 bachelor's degrees were awarded. The most popular majors were nursing (22%), biology (11%), and art and design and early childhood education (8%). 177 companies recruited on campus in 2013-2014. In an average class, 45% graduate in 4 years or less, 53% graduate in 5 years or less, and 53% graduate in 6 years or less. Of the 2013 graduating class, 19% were enrolled in graduate school within 6 months of graduation, and 53% were employed.

SERVICES: Counseling and information services are available, as is tutoring in most subjects, Chemistry, French, Religion, Spanish, nursing, political science, American experience, psychology, art history, statistics, problem solving, biology, economics, and history There is remedial math and reading. Writing center **Library/Resources:** The library contains 421,924 volumes, 119,677 microform items, 7,570 audio/video tapes/CDs/DVDs, and subscribes to 493 periodicals including electronic. Computerized library services include interlibrary loans, database searching, Internet access, and Wi-Fi capability. Special learning facilities include an art gallery, 2 music technology labs, an exercise science lab, and a performing arts theater and auditorium. **Physically Challenged Students:** 85% of the campus is accessible. Facilities include wheelchair ramps, elevators, special parking, specially equipped restrooms, special class scheduling, lowered drinking fountains, and special housing. **Special:** Students may participate in an international study tour progam currently offered through the Interim Program in January. A 3-2 engineering degree is offered with Georgia Institute of Technology and Auburn University. A self-designed B.A. in Interdisciplinary Studies is also available to qualifying students. Internships and work-study programs are offered in numerous disciplines. The CHIP program allows students to work and study in Washington, D.C. Cross-registration relationships have been established with postsecondary institutions in Japan. There are 13 national honor societies. **Visiting:** There are regularly scheduled orientations for prospective students, Preview Day consists of a welcome and introduction to the college, guided campus tour, showcase sessions (including major departments and financial aid). There are guides for informal visits, visitors may sit in on classes, and stay overnight. To schedule a visit, contact David McGreal at (760) 880-8005. **Campus Safety and Security:** Measures include 24-hour foot and vehicle patrol, emergency notification system, and security escort services. There are emergency telephones, lighted pathways/sidewalks, and controlled access to dorms/residences.

REQUIREMENTS: The SAT or ACT is required. Applicants should be graduates of accredited secondary schools or have a GED certificate. They should have completed a minimum of 4 units of English and math, 3 of social studies, 3 of science, and 2 units of a foreign language is recommended. A GPA of 2.5 is required. AP and CLEP credits are accepted. Important factors in the admissions decision are personality/intangible qualities, leadership record, evidence of special talent, extracurricular activities record, recommendations by alumni, recommendations by school officials, parents or siblings attended your school, and geographical diversity. To graduate, all students must complete 120 semester hours. The core curriculum includes First-Year Cornerstone, rhetoric and composition, math, world languages and culture, laboratory science, problem solving, computer applications, humanities, fine arts, religion, and the American experience. All students must have a minimum GPA of 2.0. **Procedure:** Freshmen are admitted to all sessions. There are early admissions, deferred admissions, and rolling admissions plans. Application deadlines are open. Application fee is $30. Applications are accepted on-line. Application fees are waived if application is completed on-line. **Transfer Students:** 84 transfer students enrolled in 2013-2014. Transfer students must have a minimum 2.5 College GPA and be in good standing with the previous college. Transfer students must also have a minimum high school GPA of 2.5 if less than 30 hours of college credit is transferred. 39 of 120 credits required for the bachelor's degree must be completed at LaGrange. **International Students:** There are 5 international students enrolled. They must take the TOEFL with a minimum score of 500 on the paper-based TOEFL (PBT) or 61 on the Internet-based version (iBT). They must also take the SAT or ACT, scoring 450.

ADMISSIONS: 55% of the 2014-2015 applicants were accepted. The SAT scores for the 2014-2015 freshman class were: Critical Reading--39% below 500, 48% between 500 and 599, 12% between 600 and 699, and 1% between 700 and 800; Math--39% below 500, 44% between 500 and 599, 15% between 600 and 699, and 1% between 700 and 800; Writing--60% below 500, 38% between 500 and 599, and 2% between 600 and 699. The ACT scores were 35% below 21, 37% between 21 and 23, 19% between 24 and 26, 5% between 27 and 28, and 4% above 28. **Admissions Contact:** David McGreal, Director of Admission. E-Mail: *dmcgreal@lagrange.edu* Web: *www.lagrange.edu*

FINANCIAL AID: In 2014-2015, 99% of all full-time freshmen and 98% of continuing full-time students received some form of financial aid. 88% of all full-time freshmen and 81% of continuing full-time students received need-based aid. The average freshman award was $29,729. Need-based scholarships or need-based grants averaged $3,754 ($15,890 maximum); need-based self-help aid (loans and jobs) averaged $3,455 ($15,200 maximum); other non-need-based awards and non-need-based scholarships averaged $5,525 ($36,640 maximum); and $4,238 from other forms of aid. 34% of undergraduate students work part-time. Average annual earnings from campus work are $1750. The average financial indebtedness of the 2014 graduate was $21,700. The FAFSA and the college's own financial statement are required. The priority date for freshman financial aid applications for fall entry is March 1.

MERCER UNIVERSITY   **C-3**
www.mercer.edu

Macon, GA 31207	(478) 301-2650
	(800) 840-8577
Fax: (478) 301-2828	Email: admissions@mercer.edu
Full-time: 1258 men, 1214 women	Faculty: IIA, av$
Part-time: 35 men, 31 women	Ph.D.s: 94%
Graduate: 1410 men, 2522 women	Student/Faculty: 12 to 1
Year: semesters, summer session	Tuition: $33,120
Room & Board: $11,081	Freshman Class: 3864 applied, 2666 accepted, 727 enrolled
SAT CR/M/W: 580/590/560 ACT: 26	CEEB CODE: 5025
Application Deadline: April 1	VERY COMPETITIVE

Mercer University, founded in 1833, is a private institution of higher learning that seeks to achieve excellence and scholarly discipline in the fields of liberal learning and professional knowledge. The university offers degree programs in liberal arts, music, business and economics, education, engineering, nursing and professional studies. Mercer also offers a Great Books program as an alternative to the traditional core curriculum. Figures in the above capsule and in this profile are approximate. There are 5 undergraduate schools and 11 graduate schools. In addition to regional accreditation, Mercer has baccalaureate program accreditation with AACSB, ABET, NASM, NCATE, ACS, CCNE, and NCAA. The 130-acre campus is in a suburban area 85 miles south of Atlanta.

STUDENT LIFE: 83% of undergraduates are from Georgia. Others are from 37 states, 42 foreign countries, and Canada. 59% are White; 19% African American. 50% are Protestant; 23% claim no religious affiliation; 11% Catholic. **Male To Female Ratio:** 1.4:1. The average age of freshmen is 18; all undergraduates, 20. 18% do not continue beyond their first year; 61% remain to graduate. **Housing:** 1647 students can be accommodated in college housing, which includes single-sex and coed dorms, on-campus apartments, off-campus apartments, and married student housing. In addition, there are special-interest houses and fraternity houses. On-campus housing is available on a first-come, first-served basis, and is available on a lottery system for upperclassmen. Priority is given to out-of-town students. 65% of students live on campus. Alcohol is not permitted. All students may keep cars.

FACULTY/CLASSROOMS: 50% of faculty are male; 50% are female. No introductory courses are taught by graduate students. The average class size in a laboratory is 20 and in a regular course is 20.

PROGRAMS OF STUDY: Mercer confers B.A., B.S., B.B.A., B.M., B.M.E., B.S.E., B.S.E.D., B.S.M. and B.S.N. degrees. Master's and Doctoral degrees are also awarded. Bachelor's degrees are awarded in AGRICULTURE (environmental studies), BIOLOGICAL SCIENCE (biochemistry, biology/biological science, and environmental biology), BUSINESS (accounting, business administration and management, finance, international business management, and marketing management), COMMUNICATIONS AND THE ARTS (art, communications, communication rhetoric/communication, creative writing, dramatic arts, English literature, French, German, journalism, Latin, media arts, music, Technical Communication, and Spanish), COMPUTER AND PHYSICAL SCIENCE (chemistry, computer science, earth science, information sciences and systems, mathematics, natural sciences, and physics), EDUCATION (early childhood education, education, elementary education, music education, secondary education, and special education), ENGINEERING AND ENVIRONMENTAL DESIGN (computational sciences, engineering, and industrial administration/management), HEALTH PROFESSIONS (predentistry, premedicine, and prepharmacy), SOCIAL SCIENCE (African studies, anthropology, area studies, Christian studies, criminal justice, economics, gender studies, history, philosophy, political science/government, prelaw, psychology, religion, social science, sociology, and women's studies). Engineering, business, and biology have the largest enrollments.

ACTIVITIES: 22% of men belong to 8 national fraternities; 24% of women belong to 7 national sororities. There are 115 groups on campus, including bagpipe, band, cheerleading, choir, chorale, chorus, computers, dance, debate, drama, environmental, ethnic, film, gay, honors, international, jazz band, literary magazine, marching band, musical theater, newspaper, opera, orchestra, pep band, photography, political, professional, radio and TV, religious, social, social service, student government, and symphony. Popular campus events include Bearstock (outdoor concert), Pilgrimage to Penfield, Homecoming and Mercer Madness. **Sports:** There are 8 intercollegiate sports for men and 10 for women, and 10 intramural sports for men and 10 for women. Facilities include 2 gyms, 3 playing fields, a student center, a swimming pool, a lighted intramural complex, and tennis, volleyball, and racquetball courts. **Graduates:** From July 1, 2013 to June 30, 2014, 446 bachelor's degrees were awarded. The most popular majors were business (18%), biology (12%), and engineering (10%). In an average class, 45% graduate in 4 years or less, 59% graduate in 5 years or less, and 61% graduate in 6 years or less.

SERVICES: Counseling and information services are available, as is tutoring in most subjects. There is a reader service for the blind, and remedial math. **Library/Resources:** The 2 libraries contain 864,793 volumes, 3.4 million microform items, 70,477 audio/video tapes/CDs/DVDs, and subscribe to 14,491 periodicals including electronic. Computerized library services include interlibrary loans, database

searching, and Internet access. Special learning facilities include a radio station, TV station, music building. **Physically Challenged Students:** 85% of the campus is accessible. Facilities include wheelchair ramps, elevators, special parking, specially equipped restrooms, special class scheduling, lowered drinking fountains, lowered telephones. Assistance with registration. **Special:** Mercer offers co-op programs in all majors, cross-registration with Wesleyan and Macon State Colleges, B.A.-B.S. degrees in various science and math fields, internships, student-designed majors, work-study programs, and satisfactory-unsatisfactory options for elective courses. Mercer offers a wide variety of study-abroad opportunities, including independent semester or year-long programs, faculty-led programs, or Mercer on Mission. There are 2 national honor societies, a freshman honors program, and 20 departmental honors programs. **Visiting:** There are regularly scheduled orientations for prospective students. There are guides for informal visits, visitors may sit in on classes, and stay overnight. To schedule a visit, contact the Office of Admissions. **Campus Safety and Security:** Measures include 24-hour foot and vehicle patrol, emergency notification system, self-defense education, and security escort services. There are shuttle buses, emergency telephones, lighted pathways/sidewalks, controlled access to dorms/residences, External CCTV cameras monitored by the police department.

REQUIREMENTS: The SAT or ACT is required. Applicants must be graduates of an accredited secondary school and have completed 16 academic units. Students should submit their transcript and class rank, a recommendation from a guidance counselor, and a list of extracurricular activities, including employment. A GPA of 3.0 is required. AP and CLEP credits are accepted. To graduate, all students must complete at least 120 semester hours with a minimum GPA of 2.0. **Procedure:** Freshmen are admitted fall, spring, and summer. Entrance exams should be taken in the spring of the junior year or fall of the senior year. There are deferred admissions and rolling admissions plans. Applications should be filed by April 1 for fall entry. The fall 2014 application fee was $50. Notification is sent on a rolling basis. Applications are accepted on-line. **Transfer Students:** A minimum GPA of 2.0 is required for all transfer students. Applicants with fewer than 9 semester hours must meet freshman entrance requirements. Those with fewer than 20 semester hours must submit a high school transcript and SAT or ACT scores, and those with more than 20 semester hours must submit transcripts from all colleges attended and be in good academic standing at their present school, or present evidence of satisfactory work in a previously attended college. 30 of 120 credits required for the bachelor's degree must be completed at Mercer. **International Students:** There are 103 international students enrolled. The school actively recruits these students. They must take the TOEFL, or Mercer's ELI exit examination. They must also take the SAT or ACT, scoring 1000.

ADMISSIONS: 69% of the 2014-2015 applicants were accepted. The SAT scores for the 2014-2015 freshman class were: Critical Reading--9% below 500, 47% between 500 and 599, 35% between 600 and 699, and 9% between 700 and 800; Math--7% below 500, 48% between 500 and 599, 37% between 600 and 699, and 8% between 700 and 800; Writing--19% below 500, 46% between 500 and 599, 29% between 600 and 699, and 6% between 700 and 800. **Admissions Contact:** Alejandra Sosa, Director of Freshman Admissions. E-Mail: admissions@mercer.edu Web: www.mercer.edu

FINANCIAL AID: In 2014-2015, 99% of all full-time freshmen and 97% of continuing full-time students received some form of financial aid. 81% of all full-time freshmen and 73% of continuing full-time students received need-based aid. The average financial indebtedness of the 2014 graduate was $29,101. The FAFSA and the college's own financial statement are required. The deadline for filing freshman financial aid applications for fall entry is April 1.

MOREHOUSE COLLEGE B-2
www.morehouse.edu

Atlanta, GA 30314	(404) 215-2632
	(800) 851-1254
Fax: (404) 572-3668	Email: admissions@morehouse.edu
Full-time: 2002 men	Faculty: 162; IIB, av$
Part-time: 104 men	Ph.D.s: 84%
Graduate: n/av	Student/Faculty: 12 to 1
Year: semesters, summer session	Tuition: $26,090
Room & Board: $13,322	Freshman Class: 1678 applied, 1410 accepted, 540 enrolled
SAT CR/M/W: 500/500/480 ACT: 21	CEEB CODE: 5415
Application Deadline: February 15	COMPETITIVE

Morehouse is the nation's historically black college for men of exceptional ambition and promise. Our students engage with renowned faculty members in an intensive liberal arts and sciences program that inspires intellectual growth, character development and the pursuit of social justice. Supported and enriched by a close-knit, diverse brotherhood like none other, Morehouse students build their skills and networks through extensive internship opportunities, push their boundaries through a residential experience that spurs lively debate and constant interaction, and hone their leadership capabilities through a wide variety of student-run organizations, formal and informal discussions with nationally known speakers and scholars, and boundless international travel opportunities. There is one undergraduate school. In addition to regional accreditation, Morehouse has baccalaureate program accreditation with AACSB, NASM, and ACS. The 66-acre campus is in an urban area in Atlanta, Georgia. Including any residence halls, there are 36 buildings.

STUDENT LIFE: 73% of undergraduates are from out of state, mostly the South. Students are from 43 states, and 23 foreign countries. 94% are African American. The student base is all male. The average age of freshmen is 18; all undergraduates, 20. 17% do not continue beyond their first year; 54% remain to graduate. **Housing:** 1580 students can be accommodated in college housing, which includes single-sex dorms and on-campus apartments. In addition, there are special-interest houses. On-campus housing is guaranteed for the freshman year only, is available on a first-come, first-served basis, and is available on a lottery system for upperclassmen. 72% of students live on campus; of those, 90% remain on campus on weekends. Alcohol is not permitted. All students may keep cars.

FACULTY/CLASSROOMS: 65% of faculty are male; 35% are female. All teach and do research. No introductory courses are taught by graduate students. The average class size in an introductory lecture is 25; in a laboratory is 30; and in a regular course is 20.

PROGRAMS OF STUDY: Morehouse confers B.A., B.S. and B.S.G.S. degrees. Bachelor's degrees are awarded in BIOLOGICAL SCIENCE (biology/biological science), BUSINESS (business administration and management), COMMUNICATIONS AND THE ARTS (art, dramatic arts, English, film, television and digital media, French, music, and Spanish), COMPUTER AND PHYSICAL SCIENCE (chemistry, computer science, mathematics, and physics), EDUCATION (early childhood education and health and physical education), ENGINEERING AND ENVIRONMENTAL DESIGN (engineering physics and engineering science), SOCIAL SCIENCE (African American studies, economics, history, international studies, philosophy, political science/government, psychology, religion, sociology, and urban studies). Political science, business administration, and dual degree engineering are the strongest academically. Business administration, biology, and political science have the largest enrollments.

ACTIVITIES: 4% of men belong to 7 national fraternities.there are no sororities. There are 60 groups on campus, including Campus Alliance for Student Activities (CASA), Morehouse Debate Team, band, cheerleading, chess, choir, chorus, communications, computers, dance, debate, drama, drill team, environmental, ethnic, film, forensics, gay, honors, international, jazz band, literary magazine, marching band, Morehouse Glee Club, musical theater, newspaper, orchestra, pep band, photography, political, professional, religious, social, social service, student government, symphony, and yearbook.

Popular campus events include New Student Orientation, Homecoming, Founder's Day, Parent's Weekend, Admitted Students Day, Martin Luther King Jr. Commemoration, Spring Fest. **Sports:** There are 7 intercollegiate sports for men, and 9 intramural sports for men. Facilities include Samuel H. Archer Hall is a 54,000 sq. ft. facility that houses a swimming pool, television lounge, game room, weight room, cardio room, locker rooms, gymnasium/basketball courts, conference rooms, and a multipurpose room. Forbes Arena, the home of the Maroon Tigers Basketball Team, is a 6000-seat, 3-level facility with four locker rooms, a first-aid station, a training room, a weight room, and four concession stands. Other facilities include the 9000-seat B.T. Harvey Football Stadium, the Edwin Moses Track, and the tennis center. **Graduates:** From July 1, 2013 to June 30, 2014, 339 Bachelor's degrees were awarded. The most popular majors were business administration (29%), political science (7%), and psychology (7%). In an average class, 39% graduate in 4 years or less, 51% graduate in 5 years or less, and 54% graduate in 6 years or less.

SERVICES: Counseling and information services are available, as is tutoring in most subjects. There is a reader service for the blind, and remedial math and reading. **Library/Resources:** The library contains 361,066 volumes, 841,506 microform items, 8,192 audio/video tapes/CDs/DVDs, and subscribes to 3,286 periodicals including electronic. Computerized library services include interlibrary loans, database searching, Internet access, and Wi-Fi capability. Special learning facilities include a **Physically Challenged Students:** 85% of the campus is accessible. Facilities include wheelchair ramps, elevators, special parking, specially equipped restrooms, lowered drinking fountains, lowered telephones, and special housing. **Special:** Morehouse is a member of the Atlanta University Center and Morehouse students may register for courses at any of other member institutions (i.e, Clark Atlanta University, Spelman College, and Morehouse School of Medicine). Morehouse students can complete a major at Spelman College. Moreover, through the Atlanta Regional Consortium for Higher Education (ARCHE), students can take courses at Atlanta-area colleges and universities such as Agnes Scott College, Kennesaw State University, Emory University, Georgia Institute of Technology, Georgia State University, and many others. In addition, students may elect to participate in a wide range of study abroad and domestic exchange programs. Morehouse also offers students the option to study engineering through the Dual Degree Engineering Program (DDEP); participating engineering institutions include the University of Michigan, Columbia University, Dartmouth College, Georgia Institute of Technology, Rensselaer Polytechnic Institute, and nine other institutions. Other opportunities that Morehouse students engage include summer internships, semester at sea, work study, and undergraduate research programs. There are 15 national honor societies, including Phi Beta Kappa, a freshman honors program, and 12 departmental honors programs. **Visiting:** There are regularly scheduled orientations for prospective students. There are guides for informal visits and visitors may sit in on classes. To schedule a visit, contact Director of On-Campus Recruitment at (404) 653-7736. **Campus Safety and Security:** Measures include 24-hour foot and vehicle patrol, emergency notification system, self-defense education, and security escort services. There are shuttle buses, emergency telephones, lighted pathways/sidewalks, and controlled access to dorms/residences.

REQUIREMENTS: The SAT or ACT is required. Entering students must have a high school diploma or GED. A general college-preparatory high school curriculum is recommended, including 4 units in English, 3 in math, 2 each in natural and social sciences, and 5 in other disciplines. Applicants must write an essay and are urged to seek an interview. AP and CLEP credits are accepted. Important factors in the admissions decision are advanced placement or honors courses, leadership record, and recommendations by school officials. Students must complete a minimum of 120 semester hours, including 53 hours in general studies, plus 8 noncredit hours in Freshman Orientation and College Assembly. A 2.0 GPA is required, with no grade below C in the major. **Procedure:** Freshmen are admitted fall and spring. Entrance exams should be taken by the fall of the senior year. There are early decision, early admissions, and deferred admissions plans. Early decision applications should be filed by November 1; regular applications, by February 15 for fall entry; and November 1 for spring entry. The fall 2014 application fee was $50. Notification of early decision is sent December 15; regular decision, April 1. Applications are accepted on-line. **Transfer Students:** 72 transfer students enrolled in 2013-2014. Transfer applicants must have at least a 2.5 GPA and a minimum of 26 semester hours of credit. 60 of 120 credits required for the bachelor's degree must be completed at Morehouse. **International Students:** There are 66 international students enrolled. The school actively recruits these students. They must take the TOEFL. They must also take the SAT or ACT.

ADMISSIONS: 84% of the 2014-2015 applicants were accepted. The SAT scores for the 2014-2015 freshman class were: Critical Reading--49% below 500, 35% between 500 and 599, 15% between 600 and 699, and 1% between 700 and 800; Math--48% below 500, 37% between 500 and 599, 14% between 600 and 699, and 1% between 700 and 800; Writing--58% below 500, 31% between 500 and 599, 10% between 600 and 699, and 1% between 700 and 800. The ACT scores were 43% below 21, 29% between 21 and 23, 19% between 24 and 26, 6% between 27 and 28, and 4% above 28. 35% of the current freshmen were in the top fifth of their class; 62% were in the top two fifths. 6 freshmen graduated first in their class. **Admissions Contact:** Darryl Isom, Director of Admissions and Recruitment. E-Mail: *admissions@morehouse.edu* Web: *www.morehouse.edu*

FINANCIAL AID: In 2014-2015, 94% of all full-time freshmen and 90% of continuing full-time students received some form of financial aid. 94% of all full-time freshmen and 90% of continuing full-time students received need-based aid. The average freshman award was $37,348. 12% of undergraduate students work part-time. Average annual earnings from campus work are $2800. The average financial indebtedness of the 2014 graduate was $30,167. Morehouse is a member of CSS. The FAFSA and the college's own financial statement are required. The priority date for freshman financial aid applications for fall entry is Febuary 15.

OGLETHORPE UNIVERSITY B-2
www.oglethorpe.edu

Atlanta, GA 30319 (404) 364-8307
(800) 428-8491
Fax: (404) 364-8500 Email: admission@oglethorpe.edu
Full-time: 435 men, 600 women Faculty: 60; IIB
Part-time: 21 men, 39 women Ph.D.s: n/av
Graduate: n/av Student/Faculty: n/av
Year: semesters, summer session Tuition: $32,500
Room & Board: $11,700 Freshman Class: 2768 applied, 2172 accepted, 277 enrolled
SAT CR/M/W: 570/550/550 ACT: 24 CEEB CODE: 5521
Application Deadline: open COMPETITIVE+

Oglethorpe University, founded in 1835, is an independent institution offering programs in the liberal arts and science, business, and preprofessional studies. The figures in the above capsule and in this profile are approximate. There are 2 undergraduate schools. The 102-acre campus is in a suburban area 10 miles northeast of downtown Atlanta. Including any residence halls, there are 25 buildings.

STUDENT LIFE: 74% of undergraduates are from Georgia. Others are from 33 states, 36 foreign countries, and Canada. 74% are from public schools. 34% are White; 25% race unknown; 18% African American. **Male To Female Ratio:** 1.4:1. The average age of freshmen is 18; all undergraduates, 21. 28% do not continue beyond their first year; 55% remain to graduate. **Housing:** 803 students can be accommodated in college housing, which includes single-sex and coed dorms. In addition, there are fraternity houses and sorority houses. On-campus housing is guaranteed for the freshman year only, is available on a first-come, and first-served basis. Priority is given to out-of-town students. 65% of students live on campus; of those, 75% remain on campus on weekends. All students may keep cars.

FACULTY/CLASSROOMS: 58% of faculty are male; 42% are female. No introductory courses are taught by graduate students. The average class size in an introductory lecture is 20; in a laboratory is 18; and in a regular course is 15.

PROGRAMS OF STUDY: Oglethorpe confers B.A., B.S., B.A.L.S. and

B.B.A. degrees. Bachelor's degrees are awarded in BIOLOGICAL SCIENCE (biology/biological science), BUSINESS (accounting and business administration and management), COMMUNICATIONS AND THE ARTS (art, art history and appreciation, communications, English, French, and Spanish), COMPUTER AND PHYSICAL SCIENCE (chemistry, mathematics, and physics), SOCIAL SCIENCE (American studies, behavioral science, biopsychology, economics, history, international studies, philosophy, political science/government, psychology, social work, and sociology). Biology, Business, Pyschology are the strongest academically. Business administration, biology, communications and rhetoric have the largest enrollments.

ACTIVITIES: 26% of men belong to 5 national fraternities; 22% of women belong to 1 local and 4 national sororities. There are 51 groups on campus, including art, cheerleading, choir, chorale, chorus, computers, dance, drama, ethnic, gay, honors, international, literary magazine, newspaper, orchestra, pep band, photography, political, professional, radio and TV, religious, social, social service, student government, and yearbook. Popular campus events include Oglethorpe Day, and Liberal Arts Symposium. **Sports:** There are 8 intercollegiate sports for men and 8 for women, and 6 intramural sports for men and 6 for women. Facilities include a field house and recreation center housing basketball and volleyball courts, a running track, handball courts, and a weight room. Outdoor facilities include 6 tennis courts, an all-weather track, a sand volleyball court, and soccer, baseball, and intramural fields. **Graduates:** From July 1, 2013 to June 30, 2014, 154 bachelor's degrees were awarded. The most popular majors were business and accounting (18%), English and communications (14%), and social sciences (14%).

SERVICES: Counseling and information services are available, as is tutoring in most subjects, including all core (general education) courses, English, writing, accounting, and math. **Library/Resources:** The library contains 157,000 volumes, 4,189 microform items, and 6,786 audio/video tapes/CDs/DVDs, and subscribes to 775 periodicals including electronic. Computerized library services include interlibrary loans, database searching, Internet access, and Wi-Fi capability. Special learning facilities include an art gallery, radio station, Atlanta Laboratory for Learning which includes the Center for Civic Engagement, Global Education Opportunities, and Professional Development. Additionally, Oglethorpe has an in-residence, professional theatre program. **Physically Challenged Students:** 80% of the campus is accessible. Facilities include wheelchair ramps, elevators, special parking, specially equipped restrooms, special class scheduling, lowered drinking fountains, and special housing. **Special:** Oglethorpe offers co-op programs in all majors, cross-registration through the Atlanta Regional Consortium for Higher Education, international exchange agreements with several universities in Europe, Asia, and South America, and other study-abroad options. Internships are available in all areas of study for up to 15 credit hours for upperclassmen with a minimum 2.8 GPA, and a Washington semester offers internships with Georgia senators and others. There is a 3-2 engineering program with Georgia Institute of Technology, the Universities of Florida and Southern California, and Auburn University. Accelerated degrees, dual majors, student-designed majors, federal work-study programs, and nondegree study are offered. There are 7 national honor societies, a freshman honors program, and 99 departmental honors programs. **Visiting:** There are regularly scheduled orientations for prospective students, including placement tests, class registration, an activities fair, and group activities. There are guides for informal visits, visitors may sit in on classes, and stay overnight. To schedule a visit, contact the Admissions Office at admissions@oglethorpe.edu. **Campus Safety and Security:** Measures include 24-hour foot and vehicle patrol, emergency notification system, self-defense education, and security escort services. There are lighted pathways/sidewalks, controlled access to dorms/residences, Entrance to residence halls is on an ID card-swipe system.

REQUIREMENTS: The SAT or ACT is required. Students should graduate from an accredited high school or have a GED certificate. They should have completed 4 courses in English, 3 each in science and social studies, and a math sequence of algebra I and II and geometry. A counselor's or teacher's recommendation is required, and an essay is required for a scholarship. An interview is recommended. AP and CLEP credits are accepted. Important factors in the admissions decision are recommendations by school officials, extracurricular activities record, and advanced placement or honors courses.To graduate with a B.A. or B.S., all students must complete at least 128 credit hours (120 for B.B.A. and B.A.L.S.). They must fulfill a major as well as complete the core curriculum and achieve a minimum GPA of 2.0. The core curriculum is a unique 4-year sequence of related interdisciplinary courses, 1 per semester. All freshman must complete the first-year experience program. **Procedure:** Freshmen are admitted to all sessions. Entrance exams should be taken late in the junior year or early in the senior year. There are early decision, early admissions, deferred admissions, and rolling admissions plans. Check with the school for current application deadlines. The application fee is $50. Notification is sent on a rolling basis. Applications are accepted online. **Transfer Students:** 42 transfer students enrolled in 2013-2014. Applicants who have completed less than a full year of college work must take the SAT or ACT. All transfers must be in good academic standing with a minimum GPA of 2.5. An interview is recommended. 64 of 128 credits required for the bachelor's degree must be completed at Oglethorpe. **International Students:** There are 66 international students enrolled. The school actively recruits these students. They must take the TOEFL with a minimum score of 550 on the paper-based TOEFL (PBT), or demonstrate proficiency in English by other means. They must also take the SAT or ACT.

ADMISSIONS: 78% of the 2014-2015 applicants were accepted. The SAT scores for the 2014-2015 freshman class were: Critical Reading--8% below 500, 51% between 500 and 599, 35% between 600 and 699, and 6% between 700 and 800; Math--20% below 500, 52% between 500 and 599, 23% between 600 and 699, and 4% between 700 and 800; Writing--24% below 500, 49% between 500 and 599, 24% between 600 and 699, and 3% between 700 and 800. The ACT scores were 12% below 21, 30% between 21 and 23, 25% between 24 and 26, 14% between 27 and 28, and 19% above 28. 45% of the current freshmen were in the top fifth of their class; 78% were in the top two fifths. **Admissions Contact:** Lucy Leusch, Vice President for Enrollment. E-Mail: *admission@oglethorpe.edu* Web: *www.oglethorpe .edu*

FINANCIAL AID: In 2014-2015, 98% of all full-time freshmen and 97% of continuing full-time students received some form of financial aid. 73% of all full-time freshmen and 71% of continuing full-time students received need-based aid. The average freshman award was $33,046. Need-based scholarships or need-based grants averaged $7,062; need-based self-help aid (loans and jobs) averaged $3,062; other non-need-based awards and non-need-based scholarships averaged $20,887; and $2,034 from other forms of aid. 12% of undergraduate students work part-time. Average annual earnings from campus work are $1750. The average financial indebtedness of the 2014 graduate was $27,650. Oglethorpe is a member of CSS. The FAFSA is required. The priority date for freshman financial aid applications for fall entry is February 15.

PAINE COLLEGE *(The complete profile is made available exclusively on our website, www.barronspac.com)*

PIEDMONT COLLEGE   C-1
www.piedmont.edu

Demorest, GA 30535	**(706) 778-3000**
	(800) 277-7020
Fax: (706) 776-6635	Email: bboonstra@piedmont.edu
Full-time: 389 men, 748 women	**Faculty:** n/av
Part-time: 52 men, 97 women	**Ph.D.s:** 79%
Graduate: 166 men, 668 women	**Student/Faculty:** n/av
Year: semesters, summer session	**Tuition:** $21,350
Room & Board: $8786	**Freshman Class:** 994 applied, 572 accepted, 273 enrolled
	CEEB CODE: 5537
Application Deadline: n/av	**COMPETITIVE**

Piedmont College is an independent, comprehensive, co-educational liberal arts college that offers bachelors, masters and doctoral degrees. Campuses in Demorest and Athens, students are challenged to

immerse themselves in discovery, analysis, and communication. The college maintains affiliation with the National Association of Congregational Christian Churches and United Church of Christ. There are 4 undergraduate schools and 2 graduate schools. In addition to regional accreditation, Piedmont College has baccalaureate program accreditation with ACBSP and NLN. The 186-acre campus is in a small town 75 miles northeast of Atlanta. Including any residence halls, there are 35 buildings.

STUDENT LIFE: 93% of undergraduates are from Georgia. Others are from 19 states, 8 foreign countries, and Canada. 75% are White. **Male To Female Ratio:** 2.5:1. The average age of freshmen is 19; all undergraduates, 24. 27% do not continue beyond their first year; 53% remain to graduate. **Housing:** 605 students can be accommodated in college housing, which includes single-sex and coed dorms and on-campus apartments. On-campus housing is guaranteed for all 4 years, is available on a first-come, and first-served basis. 69% of students live on campus; of those, 50% remain on campus on weekends. Alcohol is not permitted. All students may keep cars.

FACULTY/CLASSROOMS: 45% of faculty are male; 55% are female. No introductory courses are taught by graduate students. The average class size in a regular course is 15.

PROGRAMS OF STUDY: Piedmont College confers B.A., B.S., B.F.A. and B.S.N. degrees. Master's and Doctoral degrees are also awarded. Bachelor's degrees are awarded in AGRICULTURE (environmental studies), BIOLOGICAL SCIENCE (biology/biological science), BUSINESS (business administration and management), COMMUNICATIONS AND THE ARTS (art, arts administration/management, communications, dramatic arts, English, fine arts, music, musical theater, Spanish, theatre arts, and theater design), COMPUTER AND PHYSICAL SCIENCE (applied mathematics, applied physics, chemistry, mathematics, physics, and science), EDUCATION (art education, athletic training, early childhood education, education, English education, mathematics education, middle school education, music education, science education, social science education, and special education), ENGINEERING AND ENVIRONMENTAL DESIGN (environmental science), HEALTH PROFESSIONS (nursing), SOCIAL SCIENCE (criminal justice, history, interdisciplinary studies, philosophy, political science/government, psychology, religion, social science, and sociology). Education, nursing, social sciences, and business are the strongest academically. Education, business administration, nursing and social sciences are the largest.

ACTIVITIES: There are no fraternities or sororities. There are 32 groups on campus, including art, cheerleading, choir, chorale, chorus, debate, drama, environmental, film, honors, jazz band, musical theater, newspaper, pep band, photography, professional, radio and TV, religious, social, social service, student government, and yearbook. Popular campus events include Arrendale Amphitheatre: Festivals, Bands, Athletic events, Music Recitals, and Art Museum Receptions. **Sports:** There are 8 intercollegiate sports for men and 9 for women, and 5 intramural sports for men and 5 for women. Facilities include an athletic center, 8 tennis courts, beach volleyball courts, and regulation baseball, softball, and soccer fields, indoor training facilty for baseball and softball. **Graduates:** From July 1, 2013 to June 30, 2014, 326 bachelor's degrees were awarded. The most popular majors were education/early childhood/middle grades (26%), business administration (25%), and social sciences (18%). In an average class, 39% graduate in 4 years or less, 47% graduate in 5 years or less, and 53% graduate in 6 years or less.

SERVICES: Counseling and information services are available, as is tutoring in most subjects, the Learning Center offers academic support, including accounting, foreign languages, math, science, and writing. **Library/Resources:** The 2 libraries contain 272,600 volumes, 18,279 audio/video tapes/CDs/DVDs, and subscribe to 21,400 periodicals including electronic. Computerized library services include interlibrary loans, database searching, Internet access, and Wi-Fi capability. Special learning facilities include an art gallery, radio station, and TV station. **Physically Challenged Students:** 85% of the campus is accessible. Facilities include wheelchair ramps, elevators, special parking, specially equipped restrooms, special class scheduling, and special housing. **Special:** Piedmont College assists students with internships in business, psychology, education, art management, criminal justice, sociology, political science and other academic majors. Study abroad and interdisciplinary majors are available. There are 4 national honor societies and 1 departmental honors programs. **Visiting:** There are regularly scheduled orientations for prospective students, includes a campus tour, introduction to student activities, academic overview, admissions counseling, resident orientation, and a financial aid presentation. There are guides for informal visits, visitors may sit in on classes, and stay overnight. To schedule a visit, contact the Undergraduate Admissions Office at ugrad@piedmont.edu. **Campus Safety and Security:** Measures include 24-hour foot and vehicle patrol, emergency notification system, self-defense education, and security escort services. There are shuttle buses, emergency telephones, lighted pathways/sidewalks, controlled access to dorms/residences, Campus also patrolled by the local police department; Student security hosts in each residence hall.

REQUIREMENTS: The SAT is required. Applicants must be graduates of an accredited secondary school or have a GED certificate. Students must have completed a minimum of 21 academic units. A portfolio is required for art scholarship applicants and an audition for music scholarship applicants. An interview is recommended for all students. AP and CLEP credits are accepted. Important factors in the admissions decision are leadership record, advanced placement or honors courses, and extracurricular activities record.To graduate with a bachelor's degree a minimum of 120 credit hours is required. Students must complete credit hours for their major, including general education coursework in the humanities, fine arts, math, natural sciences, social sciences, and in computer science. **Procedure:** Freshmen are admitted to all sessions. There are deferred admissions and rolling admissions plans. Application deadlines are open. Applications are accepted on-line. **Transfer Students:** 110 transfer students enrolled in 2013-2014. Applicants must have a GPA of 2.0 at each institution attended. An interview is recommended. 30 of 120 credits required for the bachelor's degree must be completed at Piedmont College. **International Students:** There are 8 international students enrolled. They must take the TOEFL with a minimum score of 550 on the paper-based TOEFL (PBT) or 80 on the Internet-based version (iBT). They must also take the SAT or ACT.

ADMISSIONS: Brenda Boonstra, Director of Undergraduate Admissions. E-Mail: *bboonstra@piedmont.edu* Web: *www.piedmont.edu*

FINANCIAL AID: In 2014-2015, 100% of all full-time freshmen and 98% of continuing full-time students received some form of financial aid. 67% of all full-time freshmen and 71% of continuing full-time students received need-based aid. The average freshman award was $22,216. Need-based scholarships or need-based grants averaged $5,363 ($16,214 maximum); need-based self-help aid (loans and jobs) averaged $3,292 ($5,442 maximum); other non-need-based awards and non-need-based scholarships averaged $12,538 ($30,136 maximum); and $7,288 from other forms of aid. 33% of undergraduate students work part-time. Average annual earnings from campus work are $2490. The average financial indebtedness of the 2014 graduate was $19,521. The FAFSA and the state aid form are required. Check with the school for current application deadlines.

REINHARDT COLLEGE   B-1

www.reinhardt.edu

Waleska, GA 30183	(770) 720-5526
	1-87REINHARDT
Fax: (770) 720-5899	Email: admissions@reinhardt.edu
Full-time: 390 men, 575 women	Faculty: n/av
Part-time: 65 men, 90 women	Ph.D.s: n/av
Graduate: n/av	Student/Faculty: n/av
Year: semesters, summer session	Tuition: $15,000
Room & Board: $10,000	Freshman Class: n/av
SAT or ACT: required	CEEB CODE: 5568
Application Deadline: n/av	COMPETITIVE

Reinhardt College, founded in 1883, is a private institution affiliated with the Methodist Church and offering undergraduate degrees. The figures in the above capsule and in this profile are approximate. There are 4 undergraduate schools. In addition to regional accreditation, Reinhardt has baccalaureate program accreditation with SACS. The 600-acre campus is in a small town 40 miles north of Atlanta. Including any residence halls, there are 31 buildings.

STUDENT LIFE: 98% of undergraduates are from Georgia. Others are from 4 states, 6 foreign countries, and Canada. 90% are from public schools. 82% are White. 70% are Protestant; 23% claim no religious affiliation. **Male To Female Ratio:** 1.5:1. The average age of freshmen is 18; all undergraduates, 23. 36% do not continue beyond their first year; 50% remain to graduate. **Housing:** 404 students can be accommodated in college housing, which includes single-sex dorms. On-campus housing is guaranteed for all 4 years. 64% of students commute. Alcohol is not permitted. All students may keep cars.

FACULTY/CLASSROOMS: 45% of faculty are male; 55% are female. All teach undergraduates. No introductory courses are taught by graduate students. The average class size in an introductory lecture is 17; in a laboratory is 17; and in a regular course is 17.

PROGRAMS OF STUDY: Reinhardt confers B.A., B.S., B.F.A. and B.S.B.A. degrees. Associate degrees are also awarded. Bachelor's degrees are awarded in BIOLOGICAL SCIENCE (biology/biological science), BUSINESS (business administration and management), COMMUNICATIONS AND THE ARTS (communications), SOCIAL SCIENCE (liberal arts/general studies). Business and liberal studies have the largest enrpllments.

ACTIVITIES: There are no fraternities or sororities. There are 14 groups on campus, including cheerleading, honors, newspaper, professional, radio and TV, religious, social, social service, student government, and yearbook. Popular campus events include Spring Day, Spring Formal and Diversity Days. **Sports:** There are 5 intercollegiate sports for men and 4 for women, and 4 intramural sports for men and 4 for women. Facilities include parks, jogging trails, outdoor volleyball, tennis, and basketball courts, soccer and softball fields, a pool, weight room, bowling alley, and racquetball courts.

SERVICES: Counseling and information services are available, as is tutoring in every subject. **Library/Resources:** The library contains 48,000 volumes, 1,983 microform items, 3,598 audio/video tapes/CDs/DVDs, and subscribes to 315 periodicals including electronic. Computerized library services include interlibrary loans, database searching, and Internet access. Special learning facilities include an art gallery, natural history museum, radio station, and TV station. **Physically Challenged Students:** 90% of the campus is accessible. Facilities include wheelchair ramps, elevators, special parking, specially equipped restrooms, special class scheduling, and lowered drinking fountains. **Special:** Internships, study abroad, and work-study programs are available. There is an accelerated degree program in organizational leadership. There are 1 national honor societies and a freshman honors program. **Visiting:** There are regularly scheduled orientations for prospective students. There are guides for informal visits and visitors may sit in on classes. **Campus Safety and Security:** Measures include 24-hour foot and vehicle patrol and self-defense education. There are lighted pathways/sidewalks.

REQUIREMENTS: The SAT or ACT is required. The GED is accepted and a placement test may be required. A GPA of 2.0 is required. AP and CLEP credits are accepted. Important factors in the admissions decision are recommendations by alumni, recommendations by school officials, and parents or siblings attended your school.To graduate, students must have a core curriculum in the humanities, math and science, social science, language, phys ed, and wellness. A total of 120 semester hours is required, including 65 in the major. A 2.0 GPA must be maintained. **Procedure:** Freshmen are admitted to all sessions. Entrance exams should be taken before acceptance. There are early admissions and rolling admissions plans. Application deadlines are open. Application fee is $25. Applications are accepted on-line. **Transfer Students:** A GPA of 2.0 or better may be considered for transfer applicants. 40 of 120 credits required for the bachelor's degree must be completed at Reinhardt. **International Students:** They must take the TOEFL.

ADMISSIONS: Julie Cook, Director of Admissions. E-Mail: *admissions@reinhardt.edu* Web: *www.reinhardt.edu*

FINANCIAL AID: Reinhardt is a member of CSS. The FAFSA is required. Check with the school for current application deadlines.

SAVANNAH COLLEGE OF ART AND DESIGN (*The complete profile is made available exclusively on our website, www.barronspac.com*)

SAVANNAH STATE UNIVERSITY E-4
www.savannahstate.edu

Savannah, GA 31404

912-358-4338
(800) 788-0478

Fax: 912-358-3171 Email: admissions@savannahstate.edu

Full-time: 1727 men, 2077 women Faculty: n/av

Part-time: 277 men, 332 women Ph.D.s: n/av

Graduate: 38 men, 131 women Student/Faculty: 23 to 1

Year: semesters, summer session Tuition: $6192 ($18,096)

Room & Board: $6964 Freshman Class: 3374 applied, 2134 accepted, 1104 enrolled

SAT or ACT: required CEEB CODE: 5609

Application Deadline: July 15 **COMPETITIVE**

Savannah State University, founded in 1890, is a liberal arts institution that is part of the University System of Georgia. Undergraduate and graduate degrees are offered through the colleges of business, liberal arts and social sciences, and sciences and technology. Preprofessional programs are available. Figures in the above capsule and in this profile are approximate. There are 3 undergraduate schools and 5 graduate schools. In addition to regional accreditation, Savannah State has baccalaureate program accreditation with ABET, CSWE, and NCATE. The 165-acre campus is in a suburban area 265 miles southeast of Atlanta. Including any residence halls, there are 45 buildings.

STUDENT LIFE: Undergraduates are mostly from the South. Students are also from 38 states, 33 foreign countries, and Canada. 87% are African American. **Male To Female Ratio:** 1.2:1. The average age of freshmen is 19; all undergraduates, 21. 28% do not continue beyond their first year; 32% remain to graduate. **Housing:** 2745 students can be accommodated in college housing, which includes single-sex dorms, on-campus apartments, and married student housing. On-campus housing is available on a first-come and first-served basis. Alcohol is not permitted. All students may keep cars.

FACULTY/CLASSROOMS: 54% of faculty are male; 46% are female. No introductory courses are taught by graduate students.

PROGRAMS OF STUDY: Savannah State confers B.A., B.S., B.B.A. and B.S.W. degrees. Associate and Master's degrees are also awarded. Bachelor's degrees are awarded in BIOLOGICAL SCIENCE (biology/biological science and marine biology), BUSINESS (accounting, business administration and management, management information systems, and marketing/retailing/merchandising), COMMUNICATIONS AND THE ARTS (communications, English, and visual and performing arts), COMPUTER AND PHYSICAL SCIENCE (chemistry, computer science, and mathematics), ENGINEERING AND ENVIRONMENTAL DESIGN (civil engineering, electrical/electronics engineering technology, and environmental science), SOCIAL SCIENCE (African studies, behavioral science, criminal justice, history, homeland security, political science/government, social work, and sociology). Marine science, social work, and computer information systems are the strongest academically. Biology, mass communications and management have the largest enrollments.

ACTIVITIES: 2% of men belong to 7 national fraternities; 3% of women belong to 6 national sororities. Groups on campus include art, band, cheerleading, choir, chorale, computers, dance, debate, drama, drill team, ethnic, international, jazz band, literary magazine, marching band, newspaper, political, professional, radio and TV, religious, and student government. Popular campus events include Drama Presentations, a Fine Arts Festival, and Christmas and Spring Concerts. **Sports:** There are 5 intercollegiate sports for men and 4 for women, and 1 intramural sports for men. Facilities include a student center, a gym complex, a swimming pool, a stadium, a field house, a tennis court, a track, and a field. **Graduates:** From July 1, 2013 to June 30, 2014, 395 bachelor's degrees were awarded. The most popular majors were mass communications (10%), business management (10%), and criminal justice (8%). In an average class, 32% graduate in 6 years or less.

SERVICES: Counseling and information services are available, as is tutoring in every subject. There is remedial math, reading, and writing. **Library/Resources:** The library contains 209,714 volumes, 586,633 microform items, 3,725 audio/video tapes/CDs/DVDs, and subscribes to 360 periodicals including electronic. Computerized library services include interlibrary loans, database searching, and Internet access. Special learning facilities include a radio station, arts center, and marine science lab. **Physically Challenged Students:** Facilities include wheelchair ramps, elevators, special parking, specially equipped restrooms, lowered drinking fountains, and special housing. **Special:** The college offers co-op programs, cross-registration with Armstrong Atlantic State University, study abroad, a dual-degree program with Georgia Institute of Technology, the Georgia Legislative Internship Program, and a variety of other internship programs across the curriculum, on- and off-campus work-study programs, correspondence study, credit for military experience, and non-degree study. There are a freshman honors program. **Visiting:** There are guides for informal visits and visitors may sit in on classes. To schedule a visit, contact The Office of Admissions. **Campus Safety and Security:** Measures include 24-hour foot and vehicle patrol and emergency notification system. There are shuttle buses, emergency telephones, lighted pathways/sidewalks, the campus police department is staffed with public safety officers, building attendants, security guards, safety inspectors, and telephone operators.

REQUIREMENTS: The SAT or ACT is required. A minimum composite score of 830 on the SAT, or 17 on the ACT is required. In addition, applicants must be graduates of an accredited secondary school. Students should have completed 4 units each of English, math and science, 3 units of social science, and 2 units of 1 foreign language. A GPA of 2.0 is required. AP and CLEP credits are accepted. To graduate, all students must complete a minimum of 120 credit hours with satisfactory completion of the core curriculum requirements. Students must maintain a minimum 2.0 GPA. Exit competency exams and other requirements may be required. **Procedure:** Freshmen are admitted fall, spring, and summer. Entrance exams should be taken Early in the senior year. There are early admissions and deferred admissions plans. Applications should be filed by July 15 for fall entry; November 15 for spring entry; and May 1 for summer entry, along with a $20 fee. Notification is sent on a rolling basis. Applications are accepted on-line. **Transfer Students:** Applicants with at least 45 quarter hours or 30 semester hours of core curriculum credit do not need to submit high school transcripts, but must have a 2.0 average. All transfers must submit college transcripts, standardized test scores, and proof of good standing at the previous institution. 30 of 120 credits required for the bachelor's degree must be completed at Savannah State. **International Students:** There are 50 international students enrolled. The school actively recruits these students. They must take the TOEFL with a minimum score of 530 on the paper-based TOEFL (PBT). They must also take the SAT or ACT, and the college's own entrance exam or the collegiate placement exams.

ADMISSIONS: 63% of the 2014-2015 applicants were accepted. **Admissions Contact:** Cynthia Stephens, Interim Director of Admissions. E-Mail: *admissions@savannahstate.edu* Web: *www.savannahstate.edu*

FINANCIAL AID: The CSS/Profile, FAFSA, and the college's own financial statement, and Scholarship Application Form are required. The priority date for freshman financial aid applications for fall entry is July 15. The deadline for filing freshman financial aid applications for fall entry is July 15.

SHORTER UNIVERSITY (*The complete profile is made available exclusively on our website, www.barronspac.com*)

SOUTH UNIVERSITY (*The complete profile is made available exclusively on our website, www.barronspac.com*)

SOUTHERN POLYTECHNIC STATE UNIVERSITY

B-2

www.spsu.edu

Marietta, GA 30060	(678) 915-7778
	(800) 635-3204
Fax: (678) 915-7496	Email: admiss@spsu.edu
Full-time: 3206 men, 657 women	Faculty: 209
Part-time: 1210 men, 329 women	Ph.D.s: 71%
Graduate: 483 men, 317 women	Student/Faculty: 18 to 1
Year: semesters, summer session	Tuition: $6678 ($20,126)
Room & Board: $7280	Freshman Class: 1507 applied, 1189 accepted, 778 enrolled
SAT CR/M/W: 550/590/520 ACT: 24	CEEB CODE: 5626
Application Deadline: July 1	COMPETITIVE

Southern Polytechnic State University, founded in 1948, is a member of the University System of Georgia. Through a fusion of technology with the liberal arts and sciences, SPSU creates a learning community that encourages thoughtful inquiry, diverse perspectives, and strong preparation of its graduates to be leaders in an increasingly technological world. The university offers degree programs in accounting, applied science, architecture, biology, business administration, chemistry, computer science, computer game design and development, construction management, education, English and professional communication, engineering, engineering technology, fashion design, information and instructional design, information design and communication, information technology, international studies, math, new media arts, physics, political science, psychology, quality assurance, surveying and mapping, and technical communication. Figures in the above capsule and in this profile are approximate. There are 5 undergraduate schools and 5 graduate schools. In addition to regional accreditation, Southern Poly has baccalaureate program accreditation with ABET, ACBSP, ACCE, and NAAB. The 198-acre campus is in a suburban area 15 miles northwest of Atlanta. Including any residence halls, there are 64 buildings.

STUDENT LIFE: 98% of undergraduates are from Georgia. Others are from 38 states, 51 foreign countries, and Canada. 96% are from public schools. 55% are White; 21% African American. **Male To Female Ratio:** 0.3:1. The average age of freshmen is 20; all undergraduates, 25. 25% do not continue beyond their first year; 37% remain to graduate. **Housing:** 1673 students can be accommodated in college housing, which includes single-sex and coed dorms and on-campus apartments. In addition, there are honors houses, special-interest houses, fraternity houses, and sorority houses. On-campus housing is guaranteed for the freshman year only, is available on a first-come, and first-served basis. 75% of students commute. All students may keep cars.

FACULTY/CLASSROOMS: 66% of faculty are male; 34% are female. All teach undergraduates, 81% do research, and 81% do both. No introductory courses are taught by graduate students. The average class size in an introductory lecture is 23; in a laboratory is 18; and in a regular course is 20.

PROGRAMS OF STUDY: Southern Poly confers B.A., B.S., B.ARCH., B.A.S., B.A.T., B.S.A, B.S.C.E, B.S.C.G.D.D., B.S.C.V.E., B.S.E.E., B.S.I.T., B.S.M.E., B.S.P., B.S.P.S., B.S.S.E.N.G., B.S.S.W.E. and B.S.T.E.T. degrees. Associate and Master's degrees are also awarded. Bachelor's degrees are awarded in BIOLOGICAL SCIENCE (biology/biological science), BUSINESS (accounting, apparel and textiles, and business administration and management), COMMUNICATIONS AND THE ARTS (information technology, media arts, English and Professional Communication, Technical Communication, and Telecommunications Engineering Technology), COMPUTER AND PHYSICAL SCIENCE (applied science, chemistry, Computer Engineering Technology, computer game design/development, computer science, mathematics, physics, and software engineering), EDUCATION (education), ENGINEERING AND ENVIRONMENTAL DESIGN (architecture, civil engineering, civil engineering technology, construction engineering, construction management, electrical/electronics engineering, electrical/electronics engineering technology, industrial engineering technology, mechani-

cal engineering, mechanical engineering technology, Mechatronics Engineering, survey and mapping technology, and systems engineering), SOCIAL SCIENCE (international studies, political science/government, and psychology). Engineering, engineering technology, computer science, information technology, and architecture have the largest enrollments.

ACTIVITIES: 7% of men belong to 10 national fraternities; 8% of women belong to 4 national sororities. There are 128 groups on campus, including cheerleading, computers, debate, drama, environmental, ethnic, forensics, gay, honors, international, newspaper, pep band, political, professional, religious, social, social service, and student government. Popular campus events include SPSU Live Fall Concert, Goat Night, Fall Carnival, Pumpkin Launch and Bathtub Race. **Sports:** There are 3 intercollegiate sports for men and 1 for women, and 14 intramural sports for men and 14 for women. Facilities include a 1000-seat gym, a baseball field, softball fields, outdoor areas for basketball and volleyball, a multipurpose soccer field, an outdoor running track, an indoor health/wellness facility with a swimming pool, racquetball courts, exercise and weight training rooms, and basketball courts that are suitable for badminton and volleyball. **Graduates:** From July 1, 2013 to June 30, 2014, 729 bachelor's degrees were awarded. The most popular majors were mechanical engineering technology (12%), construction management (10%), and business admisistration (9%). 176 companies recruited on campus in 2013-2014. In an average class, 7% graduate in 4 years or less, 26% graduate in 5 years or less, and 37% graduate in 6 years or less.

SERVICES: Counseling and information services are available, as is tutoring in some subjects, English, core math, physics, chemistry, computer science, and biology There is a reader service for the blind. **Library/Resources:** The library contains 126,779 volumes, 3,493 microform items, 355 audio/video tapes/CDs/DVDs, and subscribes to 510 periodicals including electronic. Computerized library services include interlibrary loans, database searching, Internet access, and Wi-Fi capability. **Physically Challenged Students:** All of the campus is accessible. Facilities include wheelchair ramps, elevators, special parking, specially equipped restrooms, special class scheduling, lowered drinking fountains, lowered telephones, and special housing. **Special:** Southern Polytechnic offers cross-registration through ARCHE cooperative programs, dual majors in all disciplines, internships, and co-ops. There are 4 national honor societies and a freshman honors program. **Visiting:** There are regularly scheduled orientations for prospective students, orientations cover the following areas and more: Advising, Registration, Housing/Board, Financial Aid, Student Activities, Student Government, Payments, Library, Parent Sessions, Location of Faculty and Staff Offices, Classroom Locations. There are guides for informal visits and visitors may sit in on classes. To schedule a visit, contact Becca Tuck at (678) 915-3521. **Campus Safety and Security:** Measures include 24-hour foot and vehicle patrol, emergency notification system, self-defense education, and security escort services. There are emergency telephones, lighted pathways/sidewalks, controlled access to dorms/residences, audits of campus lighting and emergency call boxes are conducted monthly.

REQUIREMENTS: The SAT or ACT is required. The ACT Optional Writing test is also required. Applicants must be graduates of an accredited secondary school. Students must have completed 19 CPC units in high school, including 4 years each of English, math, and science, 3 years of social studies, and 2 years of a foreign language, plus 2 additional units. A GPA of 2.5 is required. AP and CLEP credits are accepted. Southern Polytechnic minimum requirements for admission as a regular freshman include the following: Graduation from a regionally accredited high school, or a high school accredited by the Georgia Accreditation Commission, or an approved University System of Georgia agency, or from a public school under the authority of the State Department of Education. Completion of the 17 required CPC units, plus 2 additional academic units. Have an academic high school GPA of at least a 2.5 and minimum scores on the ACT or SAT as follows: Minimum Score SAT I Critical Reading 500; SAT I Math 500; ACT-English 21; ACT-Math 21. Curriculum Framework for the Common Core; Essential Skills (9-10 hours), English Composition I, English Composition II, College Algebra, Pre-Calculus or Calculus I, depending on major, Institutional Options (4 hours) these courses address institution-wide general education outcomes chosen by the University. Examples include, but are not limited to, global issues, oral communication, information technology, critical thinking, wellness, geography, and foreign languages. At Southern Polytechnic State University, the Institutional Option courses are: Public Speaking (COMM 2400), Science, Technology and Society (STS 2400), Humanities/Fine Arts (6 hours). These are courses that address humanities/fine arts learning outcomes and which the undergraduate curriculum committee has approved. Interdisciplinary courses are acceptable. Science, Mathematics, and Technology (10-11 hours). These are courses approved by the undergraduate curriculum committee that address learning outcomes in the sciences, mathematics, and technology. These need not be sequential courses. Interdisciplinary courses are acceptable. Required are: Two four-hour laboratory science courses, Three additional credit hours in mathematics, science, or technology, Social Sciences (12 hours). These are courses approved by the undergraduate curriculum committee that address learning outcomes in the social sciences, including, but not limited to, history and American government. Interdisciplinary courses are acceptable. If credit course work is used to satisfy the U.S./Georgia history and constitution requirement, course(s) shall be part of this area. Courses Related to the Program of Study (18 hour). These are courses numbered below 3000 that are related to your program of study, and courses which are prerequisites to major courses at higher levels. **Procedure:** Freshmen are admitted fall, spring, and summer. Entrance exams should be taken by the end of the junior year or early in the senior year. There is a rolling admissions plan. Applications should be filed by July 1 for fall entry; November 1 for spring entry; and April 1 for summer entry, along with a $40 fee. Notification is sent on a rolling basis. Applications are accepted on-line. **Transfer Students:** 547 transfer students enrolled in 2013-2014. Transfer applicants must have a minimum cumulative college GPA of 2.0 and must submit all college transcripts. Transfer applicants must have completed and exited all required remedial courses at their previous institution. Transfer applicants with less than 30 transferable hours must meet Freshmen requirements and have completed and exited all required remedial courses at their previous institution. **International Students:** There are 195 international students enrolled. The school actively recruits these students. They must take the TOEFL with a minimum score of 550 on the paper-based TOEFL (PBT) or 79 on the Internet-based version (iBT), or Minimum overall band of 6.5 on the International English Language Testing System (IELTS). They must also take the SAT or ACT.

ADMISSIONS: 79% of the 2014-2015 applicants were accepted. The SAT scores for the 2014-2015 freshman class were: Critical Reading--20% below 500, 52% between 500 and 599, 24% between 600 and 699, and 4% between 700 and 800; Math--9% below 500, 45% between 500 and 599, 39% between 600 and 699, and 7% between 700 and 800; Writing--39% below 500, 46% between 500 and 599, 14% between 600 and 699, and 1% between 700 and 800. The ACT scores were 17% below 21, 29% between 21 and 23, 29% between 24 and 26, 12% between 27 and 28, and 13% above 28. **Admissions Contact:** Gary Bush, Director of Admissions. E-Mail: *admiss@spsu.edu* Web: *www.spsu.edu*

FINANCIAL AID: In 2014-2015, 91% of all full-time freshmen and 83% of continuing full-time students received some form of financial aid. 40% of all full-time freshmen and 44% of continuing full-time students received need-based aid. The average freshman award was $1,970. Need-based scholarships or need-based grants averaged $2,217 ($2,775 maximum); need-based self-help aid (loans and jobs) averaged $1,656 ($3,342 maximum); non-need-based athletic scholarships averaged $2,867 ($4,500 maximum); and other non-need-based awards and non-need-based scholarships averaged $2,006 ($7,070 maximum). 26% of undergraduate students work part-time. The average financial indebtedness of the 2014 graduate was $16,624. Southern Poly is a member of CSS. The FAFSA is required. The priority date for freshman financial aid applications for fall entry is April 1.

SPELMAN COLLEGE B-2
www.spelman.edu

Atlanta, GA 30314

(404) 681-3643
(800) 982-2411

Fax: (404) 215-7788
Full-time: 18 men, 2203 women
Part-time: 97 women
Graduate: n/av
Year: semesters
Room & Board: $8455

Email: admiss@spelman.edu
Faculty: IIB, av$
Ph.D.s: n/av
Student/Faculty: 14 to 1
Tuition: $18,615
Freshman Class: 4534 applied, 1771 accepted, 531 enrolled

SAT: required ACT: 23
Application Deadline: February 1

CEEB CODE: 5628
COMPETITIVE

Spelman College, founded in 1881, is a private, nonsectarian, liberal arts college for black women. The figures in the above capsule and in this profile are approximate. In addition to regional accreditation, Spelman has baccalaureate program accreditation with NASM and NCATE. The 32-acre campus is in an urban area 3 miles southwest of downtown Atlanta. Including any residence halls, there are 24 buildings.

STUDENT LIFE: 71% of undergraduates are from out of state, mostly the South. Students are from 46 states, 21 foreign countries, and Canada. 86% are from public schools. 96% are African American. **Male To Female Ratio:** 127.8:1. The average age of freshmen is 18; all undergraduates, 20. 10% do not continue beyond their first year; 72% remain to graduate. **Housing:** 1169 students can be accommodated in college housing, which includes dorms. In addition, there are honors houses. On-campus housing is guaranteed for the freshman year only, is available on a first-come, first-served basis, and is available on a lottery system for upperclassmen. Priority is given to out-of-town students. 60% of students live on campus; of those, 67% remain on campus on weekends. Alcohol is not permitted. Upperclassmen may keep cars.

FACULTY/CLASSROOMS: 36% of faculty are male; 64% are female. No introductory courses are taught by graduate students.

PROGRAMS OF STUDY: Spelman confers B.A. and B.S. degrees. Bachelor's degrees are awarded in BIOLOGICAL SCIENCE (biochemistry and biology/biological science), COMMUNICATIONS AND THE ARTS (art, dramatic arts, English, fine arts, French, music, and Spanish), COMPUTER AND PHYSICAL SCIENCE (chemistry, computer science, mathematics, natural sciences, and physics), EDUCATION (art education), ENGINEERING AND ENVIRONMENTAL DESIGN (engineering), SOCIAL SCIENCE (anthropology, child psychology/development, economics, history, philosophy, political science/government, psychology, religion, sociology, and women's studies). Biology and engineering is the strongest academically. Psychology, biology, and English have the largest enrollments.

ACTIVITIES: There are no fraternities; 8% of women belong to 4 local and 4 national sororities. There are 60 groups on campus, including art, band, cheerleading, choir, chorus, communications, dance, drama, gay, honors, international, jazz band, literary magazine, musical theater, newspaper, political, religious, social, student government, and yearbook. Popular campus events include Founders Day, and Martin Luther King Jr.'s Birthday. **Sports:** There are 4 intercollegiate sports for women, and 6 intramural sports for women. Facilities include a gym, tennis courts, swimming pool, weight room, dance studios, and bowling lanes.

SERVICES: Counseling and information services are available, as is tutoring in every subject. **Library/Resources:** The library contains 500,000 volumes, 385,538 microform items, and subscribes to 1,439 periodicals including electronic. Special learning facilities include an art gallery, a language lab, a media center, and music and art studios. **Physically Challenged Students:** 25% of the campus is accessible. Facilities include wheelchair ramps, elevators, special parking, and specially equipped restrooms. **Special:** Students may cross-register with Atlanta University Center member institutions. Spelman offers internships, study abroad in several countries, student-designed majors, work-study programs at the school, B.A.-B.S. degrees, and dual majors, as well as a 3-2 engineering degree with Georgia Tech,

Rochester Institute of Technology, University of Alabama at Huntsville, Auburn and Boston Universities, and North Carolina Agricultural and Technical State University. The college grants credit for life experience and permits nondegree study. There are 9 national honor societies, including Phi Beta Kappa, and a freshman honors program. **Visiting:** There are regularly scheduled orientations for prospective students, including a general information session and a campus tour. There are also high school senior days and junior days. There are guides for informal visits. To schedule a visit, contact the Admissions Office. **Campus Safety and Security:** Measures include 24-hour foot and vehicle patrol, self-defense education, and security escort services. There are shuttle buses, emergency telephones, and lighted pathways/sidewalks.

REQUIREMENTS: The SAT or ACT is required. Applicants should be high school graduates or have a GED certificate. Students should have earned at least 12 academic credits, including 4 in English, 2 each in foreign language, math (algebra and geometry), social studies, and science (including a lab science). Students with additional years in math, science, and language and with AP and honors courses are considered more competitive. An essay is required. An audition or portfolio is recommended for art majors. A GPA of 2.0 is required. AP and CLEP credits are accepted. Important factors in the admissions decision are advanced placement or honors courses, leadership record, and recommendations by school officials. To graduate, students must complete 120 semester hours, including at least 30 or more in the major and maintain a GPA of 2.0. Core requirements include 8 credits of African studies, up to 8 of foreign language, 4 of international or women's studies, up to 4 each of English composition, computer literacy, and math, and 2 to 3 of phys ed, plus freshman orientation and sophmore assembly. Students also must complete 4 credits each of divisional requirements in social science, humanities, natural science, and fine arts. A reading course may be required, based on the placement test scores. **Procedure:** Freshmen are admitted fall. Entrance exams should be taken by December of the senior year. There are early decision, early admissions, and deferred admissions plans. Early decision applications should be filed by November 15; regular applications, by February 1 for fall entry, along with a $35 fee. Notification of early decision is sent December 31; regular decision, April 1. 297 early decision candidates were accepted for the 2014-2015 class. **Transfer Students:** 47 transfer students enrolled in 2013-2014. A 3.0 GPA is recommended, with a minimum 2.0 required. Applicants must submit high school and college transcripts, as well as 2 recommendations from instructors at the last school attended. Students with fewer than 30 semester hours of credit must also submit SAT or ACT scores. 30 of 120 credits required for the bachelor's degree must be completed at Spelman. **International Students:** The school actively recruits these students. They must take the TOEFL. They must also take the SAT or ACT.

ADMISSIONS: 39% of the 2014-2015 applicants were accepted. 71% of the current freshmen were in the top fifth of their class; 91% were in the top two fifths. **Admissions Contact:** Kristin Wyckoff, Assistant Director of Admissions. E-Mail: *admiss@spelman.edu* Web: *www.spelman.edu*

FINANCIAL AID: In 2014-2015, 82% of all full-time freshmen and continuing full-time students received some form of financial aid. 82% of all full-time freshmen and continuing full-time students received need-based aid. 20% of undergraduate students work part-time. Average annual earnings from campus work are $900. The average financial indebtedness of the 2014 graduate was $18,000. Spelman is a member of CSS. The FAFSA and the college's own financial statement are required. The deadline for filing freshman financial aid applications for fall entry is April 1.

THOMAS UNIVERSITY (*The complete profile is made available exclusively on our website, www.barronspac.com*)

TOCCOA FALLS COLLEGE (*The complete profile is made available exclusively on our website, www.barronspac.com*)

UNIVERSITY OF GEORGIA C-2
www.uga.edu

Athens, GA 30602	(706) 542-2112
	n/av
Fax: n/av	Email: nmcduff@uga.edu
Full-time: 10681 men, 14548 women	Faculty: I, av$
	Ph.D.s: 88%
Part-time: 834 men, 745 women	Student/Faculty: n/av
Graduate: 3406 men, 4866 women	Tuition: $10,836 ($29,046)
Year: semesters, summer session	Freshman Class: 20913
Room & Board: $9246	applied, 11652 accepted, 5243 enrolled
SAT or ACT: required	CEEB CODE: 5813
Application Deadline: January 15	VERY COMPETITIVE

The University of Georgia, chartered in 1785 and part of the University System of Georgia, offers degree programs in agricultural and environmental sciences, arts and sciences, business, ecology, education, engineering, environment and design, family and consumer sciences, forestry and natural resources, journalism and mass communication, law, pharmacy, public health, public and international affairs, social work and veterinary medicine. There are 17 undergraduate schools and 1 graduate school. In addition to regional accreditation, UGA has baccalaureate program accreditation with AACSB, ABET, ACEJMC, ACPE, ADA, ASLA, CSWE, NASAD, NASM, NCATE, NRPA, SAF, ALA/CoA, APA/CoA, ASHA, AVMA, AAMFT/COAMFTE, CFA, CADE-ADA, CACREP, CIDA, NASD, NASPAA-COPRA, and NAST. The 759-acre campus is in a small town 70 miles northeast of Atlanta. Including any residence halls, there are 463 buildings.

STUDENT LIFE: 89% of undergraduates are from Georgia. Others are from 50 states, 126 foreign countries, and Canada. 70% are White. 20% are Protestant. **Male To Female Ratio:** 1.4:1. The average age of freshmen is 18; all undergraduates, 20. 6% do not continue beyond their first year; 86% remain to graduate. **Housing:** 9983 students can be accommodated in college housing, which includes single-sex and coed dorms, on-campus apartments, and married student housing. In addition, there are honors houses, language houses, fraternity houses, sorority houses, learning communities within residence halls. On-campus housing is guaranteed for the freshman year only, is available on a first-come, and first-served basis. 7% of students commute. Alcohol is not permitted. All students may keep cars.

FACULTY/CLASSROOMS: 65% of faculty are male; 35% are female. No introductory courses are taught by graduate students.

PROGRAMS OF STUDY: UGA confers A.B., A.B.J., B.B.A., B.F.A., B.L.A., B.Mus., B.S., B.S.A., B.S.A.B., B.S.A.E., B.S.Bch.E., B.S.B.E., B.S.C.E., B.S.Chem., B.S.C.S.E., B.S.Ed., B.S.Env.E., B.S.E.H., B.S.Env., B.S.E.S., B.S.F.C.S., B.S.F.R., B.S.H.P., B.S.M.E. and B.S.W. degrees. Master's and Doctoral degrees are also awarded. Bachelor's degrees are awarded in AGRICULTURE (agricultural communications, agricultural economics, animal science, dairy science, fishing and fisheries, forestry and related sciences, horticulture, natural resource/environmental economics, natural resources, plant science, poultry science, soil science, and turfgrass and landscape management), BIOLOGICAL SCIENCE (biochemistry, bioinformatics, biology/biological science, biotechnology, ecology, entomology, genetics, marine science, microbiology, neurosciences, nutritional sciences, plant pathology, and toxicology), BUSINESS (accounting, accounting/CPA, business administration and management, business administration, mgmt, operations, fashion merchandising, finance, human resources, international business, management information systems, management science, marketing, nonprofit/public organization management, real estate, recreation and leisure services, and sports management), COMMUNICATIONS AND THE ARTS (advertising, Arabic, art history, art, art history and appreciation, broadcasting, Chinese, classical languages, communication studies, communication science, comparative literature, dance, English, French, German, Germanic languages and literature, Greek, historic preservation, Italian, Japanese, journalism, Latin, linguistics, media arts, music, music composition, music performance, music theory and composition, public relations, romance languages and literature, Russian, Spanish, studio art, and theatre arts), COMPUTER AND

PHYSICAL SCIENCE (astronomy and physics, chemistry, computer science, environmental chemistry, geology, mathematics, physics, and statistics), EDUCATION (agricultural education, art education, athletic training, early childhood education, education administration, elementary education, English education, health education, mathematics education, middle school education, music education, reading education, school psychology, science education, social studies education, special education, and teaching English as a second/foreign language (TESOL/TEFOL)), ENGINEERING AND ENVIRONMENTAL DESIGN (agricultural engineering, civil engineering, electrical/electronics engineering, engineering, environmental engineering, landscape architecture, and mechanical engineering), HEALTH PROFESSIONS (biology, biomedical science, environmental health science, exercise science, health promotion, kinesiology, music therapy, pharmaceutical science, pharmacy, public health, and veterinary science), SOCIAL SCIENCE (African American studies, anthropology, communication sciences and disorders, cognitive science, counseling/psychology, criminal justice, dietetics, economics, food production/management/services, food science, geography, history, home economics, human development, industrial and organizational psychology, interdisciplinary studies, Latin American studies, law, philosophy, political science/government, psychology, public administration, religion, social work, sociology, water resources, and women's studies). Biology, psychology, and finance have the largest enrollments.

ACTIVITIES: 22% of men belong to 36 national fraternities; 30% of women belong to 27 national sororities. There are 633 groups on campus, including art, band, cheerleading, chess, choir, chorale, chorus, computers, dance, debate, drama, drill team, environmental, ethnic, film, forensics, gay, honors, international, jazz band, literary magazine, marching band, musical theater, newspaper, orchestra, pep band, photography, political, professional, radio and TV, religious, social, social service, student government, symphony, and yearbook. Popular campus events include Dance Marathon, Relay for Life and Dawgs after Dark. **Sports:** There are 8 intercollegiate sports for men and 11 for women, and 24 intramural sports for men and 24 for women. Facilities include a 92,746-seat stadium, 12,000-seat basketball arena, 4,500-seat tennis stadium, 4 indoor tennis courts, 3,200-seat baseball field, complete football-training facilities, and a sports complex with a lake, a beach, playing fields, and trails. There is also the Ramsey Student Center with 5 gyms, 3 swimming pools, a strength/conditioning room, 10 racquetball courts, an indoor track, and a climbing wall. The Women's Athletic Complex hosts women's soccer and softball programs with 3,000-spectator capacity. **Graduates:** From July 1, 2013 to June 30, 2014, 7335 bachelor's degrees were awarded. The most popular majors were psychology (6%), biology (5%), and finance (5%). In an average class, 3% graduate in 3 years or less, 61% graduate in 4 years or less, 82% graduate in 5 years or less, and 85% graduate in 6 years or less. Of the 2013 graduating class, 15% were enrolled in graduate school within 6 months of graduation, and 62% were employed.

SERVICES: Counseling and information services are available, as is tutoring in every subject. There is a reader service for the blind, and remedial math, reading, and writing. Alternate format textbooks and class materials, note takers, modifications for tests and assignments, and counseling and advisement from learning disability specialists are available. There are also sign language interpreters, text type machines, FM/assistive listening devices, and a pilot closed-captioning program. **Library/Resources:** The 3 libraries contain 5.0 million volumes. Computerized library services include interlibrary loans, database searching, Internet access, and Wi-Fi capability. Special learning facilities include an art gallery, natural history museum, radio station, TV station, Bioscience Learning Center, Rare Book and Manuscript Library, Performing Arts Center, broadcast newsroom, State Botanical Garden of Georgia, Peabody Awards Archives, Cox Institute for Newspaper Management Studies, and Georgia Museum of Art. **Physically Challenged Students:** 90% of the campus is accessible. Facilities include wheelchair ramps, elevators, special parking, specially equipped restrooms, special class scheduling, lowered drinking fountains, lowered telephones, special housing. Wheelchair vans, auxiliary aides, residence hall accommodations, and an adaptive technology lab. **Special:** UGA offers cross-registration with University Center institutions in urban Atlanta. With the Governor's Intern Pro-

gram, students may serve a full-time 10-week internship in a state government agency; many other internships are available within the departments, as well as work-study programs within the university and with many area businesses. A Washington semester, an accelerated degree program in business, a general studies degree, student-designed majors, dual degrees and double majors, and nondegree study are also available. There are 25 national honor societies, including Phi Beta Kappa, and a freshman honors program. **Visiting:** There are regularly scheduled orientations for prospective students, including walking and driving tours of the campus and meetings with faculty, staff, and students. There are guides for informal visits, visitors may sit in on classes, and stay overnight. To schedule a visit, contact the Visitor Center at (706) 542-0842. **Campus Safety and Security:** Measures include 24-hour foot and vehicle patrol, emergency notification system, self-defense education, and security escort services. There are shuttle buses, emergency telephones, and lighted pathways/sidewalks.

REQUIREMENTS: The SAT or ACT is required. UGA admits freshmen primarily on the basis of high school curriculum, grades earned, and college admissions test scores. The university may consider qualitative information to determine a student's potential for success. Applicants should be high school graduates or present a GED certificate. Students should have taken 4 years of English, 4 each of math and science, 3 of social studies, and 2 of a foreign language. Satisfactory scores are required on the SAT or ACT. An audition is required for music majors. AP and CLEP credits are accepted. Students must have to a 2.0 GPA graduate, and must complete a minimum of 120 semester hours. A baccalaureate degree program must require at least 21 semester hours of upper division courses in the major field and at least 39 semester hours of upper division work overall. The core curriculum includes 9 credit hours of Foundation courses, 7-8 hours of Sciences, 3-4 hours of Quantitative Reasoning, 12 hours of World Languages and Culture, Humanities and the Arts, 9 hours of Social Sciences. Required specific disciplines are grammar, composition, literature, math, biological sciences, history, American government, and environmental literacy. Specific courses include basic phys ed and English 1101 and 1102. UGA also requires all students to pass the Regents Exit Exam, as well as exams on the federal and state constitutions. **Procedure:** Freshmen are admitted fall, spring, and summer. Entrance exams should be taken by January of the senior year. There is a deferred admissions plan. Early decision applications should be filed by October 15; regular applications, by January 15 for fall entry; October 1 for spring entry; and January 15 for summer entry, along with a $60 fee. Notification of early decision is sent December 1; regular decision, April 1. Applications are accepted on-line. **Transfer Students:** A transfer GPA of 3.2 is required of all sophomores (30-59 hrs) and 2.8 required with 60 hrs or more. These students are admitted based on space availability and there is no minimum GPA that guarantees admission. Students with fewer than 30 transferable hours are not eligible for transfer admission. 45 of 120 credits required for the bachelor's degree must be completed at UGA. **International Students:** There are 1184 international students enrolled. They must take the TOEFL with a minimum score of 550 on the paper-based TOEFL (PBT) or 80 on the Internet-based version (iBT). They must also take the SAT or ACT.

ADMISSIONS: 56% of the 2014-2015 applicants were accepted. There were 40 National Merit finalists. **Admissions Contact:** Nancy G. McDuff, VP of Admissions and Enrollment Management. E-Mail: nmcduff@uga.edu Web: www.uga.edu

FINANCIAL AID: UGA is a member of CSS. The FAFSA is required. The priority date for freshman financial aid applications for fall entry is March 1.

UNIVERSITY OF NORTH GEORGIA   C-1
www.ngcsu.edu

Dahlonega, GA 30597

	(706) 864-1754
	(800) 498-9581
Fax: (706) 864-1478	Email: rlaverriere@ngcsu.edu
Full-time: 1280 men, 1905 women	Faculty: IIA, --$
Part-time: 245 men, 575 women	Ph.D.s: n/av
Graduate: 150 men, 450 women	Student/Faculty: n/av
Year: semesters, summer session	Tuition: $4000 ($13,000)
Room & Board: $4500	Freshman Class: n/av
SAT: required	CEEB CODE: 5497
Application Deadline: n/av	COMPETITIVE

University of North Georgia, founded in 1873 as a military college, is today a liberal arts college that is part of the public University System of Georgia. One of 4 colleges in the United States classified as military colleges by the Department of the Army, the school requires all male resident students to join its Corps of Cadets; other students are given an option to join. The figures in the above capsule and in this profile are approximate. There are 4 undergraduate schools and one graduate school. In addition to regional accreditation, NGCSU has baccalaureate program accreditation with ACBSP, APTA, NCATE, and NLN. The 665-acre campus is in a small town 60 miles north of Atlanta. Including any residence halls, there are 25 buildings.

STUDENT LIFE: 95% of undergraduates are from Georgia. Others are from 33 states, 8 foreign countries, and Canada. 90% are from public schools. 93% are White. **Male To Female Ratio:** 1.7:1. The average age of freshmen is 19; all undergraduates, 22. **Housing:** 1200 students can be accommodated in college housing, which includes single-sex dorms and on-campus apartments. On-campus housing is available on a first-come and first-served basis. 69% of students commute. Alcohol is not permitted. All students may keep cars.

FACULTY/CLASSROOMS: 50% of faculty are male; 50% are female. All teach undergraduates. No introductory courses are taught by graduate students. The average class size in an introductory lecture is 30; in a laboratory is 30; and in a regular course is 30.

PROGRAMS OF STUDY: NGCSU confers A.B., B.S., B.B.A. and B.S.N. degrees. Associate and Master's degrees are also awarded. Bachelor's degrees are awarded in BIOLOGICAL SCIENCE (biology/biological science), BUSINESS (accounting, banking and finance, business administration and management, business economics, marketing/retailing/merchandising, and recreation and leisure services), COMMUNICATIONS AND THE ARTS (art, arts administration/management, English, French, music, and Spanish), COMPUTER AND PHYSICAL SCIENCE (chemistry, computer science, mathematics, and physics), EDUCATION (art education, early childhood education, elementary education, foreign languages education, mathematics education, middle school education, music education, physical education, science education, secondary education, social science education, and special education), ENGINEERING AND ENVIRONMENTAL DESIGN (preengineering), HEALTH PROFESSIONS (nursing, predentistry, premedicine, prepharmacy, and preveterinary science), SOCIAL SCIENCE (criminal justice, history, political science/government, prelaw, psychology, social science, and sociology). Education and premedicine is the strongest academically. Business and teacher education is the largest.

ACTIVITIES: 13% of men belong to 2 local and 4 national fraternities; 10% of women belong to 4 national sororities. There are 52 groups on campus, including band, cheerleading, choir, chorale, chorus, drama, drill team, ethnic, honors, jazz band, literary magazine, marching band, newspaper, pep band, political, professional, religious, student government, symphony, and yearbook. Popular campus events include Spring Jam, Frisbee Golf, and Military reviews. **Sports:** There are 5 intercollegiate sports for men and 6 for women, and 7 intramural sports for men and 7 for women. Facilities include a swimming pool, a track, a fully equipped exercise room, a rappeling tower, a confidence course, a picnic area, a 2000-seat gym, and a 250-seat arena.

SERVICES: Counseling and information services are available, as is tutoring in most subjects. There is a reader service for the blind, and remedial math, reading, and writing. **Library/Resources:** The 2 libraries contain 142,807 volumes, 774,482 microform items, 3,118 audio/video tapes/CDs/DVDs, and subscribe to 2,546 periodicals including electronic. Computerized library services include interlibrary loans, database searching, and Internet access. Special learning facilities include an art gallery, planetarium, a math lab, language lab, and writing center. **Physically Challenged Students:** 50% of the campus is accessible. Facilities include wheelchair ramps, elevators, special parking, specially equipped restrooms, and lowered drinking fountains. **Special:** Special academic programs include a co-op program in business, internships, a 3-2 engineering degree with Georgia Institute of Technology, study abroad in Europe, South America, and Canada, dual majors, and credit for life, military, or work experience. There are 9 national honor societies, including Phi Beta Kappa, a freshman honors program, and 8 departmental honors programs.

Visiting: There are regularly scheduled orientations for prospective students, including an admissions video, college overview, tour, and a meeting with an admissions counselor. There are guides for informal visits and visitors may stay overnight. To schedule a visit, contact the Admissions Office. **Campus Safety and Security:** Measures include 24-hour foot and vehicle patrol and security escort services. There are emergency telephones and lighted pathways/sidewalks.

REQUIREMENTS: The SAT is required. Students must have graduated from a secondary school with 4 years of English, 3 each of math, science, and social science, and 2 of a foreign language. The GED is accepted if granted at least 5 years later than expected high school graduation date. SAT II: Subject tests are required of home-schooled students. A GPA of 2.0 is required. AP and CLEP credits are accepted. Important factors in the admissions decision are leadership record, advanced placement or honors courses, and evidence of special talent. To graduate, students must complete 120 semester credit hours with a minimum GPA of 2.0. English, math, lab sciences, and social sciences are required. **Procedure:** Freshmen are admitted fall, spring, and summer. Entrance exams should be taken in the junior year. There are deferred admissions and rolling admissions plans. Applications should be filed by December 15 for spring entry; April 15 for summer entry, along with a $25 fee. applicants were on the 2014 waiting list; were admitted. Applications are accepted on-line. **Transfer Students:** Transfer students must have maintained a C average and a clear conduct record, and be in good academic standing. Those who have not completed 90 quarter hours of transferable credit must have completed the approved precollege curriculum and must submit high school transcripts and the SAT or ACT results. 45 of 120 credits required for the bachelor's degree must be completed at University of North Georgia. **International Students:** They must take the TOEFL. They must also take the SAT or ACT.

ADMISSIONS: **Admissions Contact:** Robert LaVerriere, Director of Undergraduate Admissions and Recruiting. E-Mail: *rlaverriere@ngcsu .edu* Web: *www.ngcsu.edu*

FINANCIAL AID: The FAFSA and the college's own financial statement are required. Check with the school for current application deadlines.

UNIVERSITY OF WEST GEORGIA (*The complete profile is made available exclusively on our website, www.barronspac.com*)

UNIVERSITY SYSTEM OF GEORGIA

The University System of Georgia, established in 1932, is a public system in Georgia. It is governed by an 18-member board of regents, whose chief administrator is the chancellor. The primary goal of the system is teaching, research, and public service. The main priorities are to provide broad access to undergraduate education with a high level of excellence, to provide sound programs of graduate education and research, addressing state and national problems and advancing the frontiers of knowledge, and to work cooperatively with all levels and sectors of education to improve the social, cultural, and economic welfare of the state's citizens. The total student enrollment for all 35 campuses is usually 314,000 with 17,767 faculty members. Altogether there are 1,007 baccalaureate, 645 master's, and 214 doctoral programs offered in the University System of Georgia. Profiles of the 4-year campuses are included in this section.

VALDOSTA STATE UNIVERSITY	C-5
www.valdosta.edu	

Valdosta, GA 31698

(229) 333-5791
(800) 618-1878

Fax: (229) 333-5482

Email: admissions@valdosta.edu

Full-time: 3739 men, 5280 women	Faculty: 416; IIA, --$
Part-time: 557 men, 792 women	Ph.D.s: 75%
Graduate: 518 men, 1545 women	Student/Faculty: 20 to 1
Year: semesters, summer session	Tuition: $4706 ($14,288)
Room & Board: $6480	Freshman Class: 6703 applied, 4744 accepted, 2467 enrolled
SAT CR/M/W: 503/492/482 ACT: 21	CEEB CODE: 5855
Application Deadline: July 1	COMPETITIVE

Valdosta State University, founded in 1906 and a unit of the University System of Georgia, is a public liberal arts institution offering degrees in arts and sciences, education, business administration, nursing, fine arts, social work, and library. Figures in the above capsule and in this profile are approximate. There are 5 undergraduate schools and 1 graduate school. In addition to regional accreditation, VSU has baccalaureate program accreditation with AACSB, NASAD, NASM, NCATE, CCNE, and NAST. The 172-acre campus is in a suburban area in southern Georgia, 3 1/2 hours from Atlanta and from Orlando, Florida. Including any residence halls, there are 94 buildings.

STUDENT LIFE: 96% of undergraduates are from Georgia. Others are from 45 states, 70 foreign countries, and Canada. 64% are White; 28% African American. **Male To Female Ratio:** 1.6:1. The average age of freshmen is 18; all undergraduates, 22. **Housing:** 2896 students can be accommodated in college housing, which includes coed dorms and on-campus apartments. In addition, there are honors houses, language houses, special-interest houses, honors, wellness, and many other living learning communities are available and 24-hour quiet wings in the dorms. On-campus housing is available on a first-come and first-served basis. 72% of students commute. All students may keep cars.

FACULTY/CLASSROOMS: 48% of faculty are male; 52% are female. 91% teach undergraduates. No introductory courses are taught by graduate students. The average class size in an introductory lecture is 30; in a laboratory is 23; and in a regular course is 18.

PROGRAMS OF STUDY: VSU confers B.A., B.S., B.B.A., B.G.S., B.M., B.S.Ed., B.S.E.P. and B.S.N. degrees. Associate degrees are also awarded. Bachelor's degrees are awarded in Biology, early childhood education, and nursing.

ACTIVITIES: 9% of women belong to 9 national sororities. There are 163 groups on campus, including art, band, cheerleading, chess, chorale, chorus, computers, dance, debate, drama, drum and bugle corps, environmental, ethnic, film, gay, honors, international, jazz band, literary magazine, marching band, musical theater, newspaper, orchestra, outdoor/recreation, pep band, political, professional, radio and TV, religious, social, social service, student government, and symphony. Popular campus events include Family Day, and the Happening. **Sports:** There are 6 intercollegiate sports for men and 5 for women, and 12 intramural sports for men and 12 for women. Facilities include a phys ed complex with a 5500-seat basketball arena, a health fitness center, a weight training room, and a human performance lab; and a gym with a weight room, training room, dance studio, auxiliary gym, outdoor pool, climbing wall, racketball courts, and a indoor track. **Graduates:** From July 1, 2013 to June 30, 2014, 1631 bachelor's degrees were awarded. The most popular majors were childhood education (11%), communication arts (6%), and nursing (6%). 110 companies recruited on campus in 2013-2014. In an average class, 16% graduate in 4 years or less, 37% graduate in 5 years or less, and 43% graduate in 6 years or less.

SERVICES: Counseling and information services are available, as is tutoring in some subjects, biology, chemistry, physics, math computer science, foreign langues, social science, and writing. There is a reader service for the blind. **Library/Resources:** The library contains 539,557 volumes, 1.1 million microform items, 27,582 audio/video tapes/CDs/DVDs, and subscribes to 2,732 periodicals including electronic. Computerized library services include interlibrary loans, database searching, Internet access, and Wi-Fi capability. Special learning facilities include an art gallery, planetarium, radio station, TV station, herbarium. **Physically Challenged Students:** All of the campus is accessible. Facilities include wheelchair ramps, elevators, special parking, specially equipped restrooms, special class scheduling, lowered drinking fountains, lowered telephones, special housing. Students registered with the Access Office are able to register for classes on the first day of registration regardless of classification. Also all campus transportation is accessible. **Special:** Valdosta offers co-op programs, internships, study abroad, accelerated degree program in RN to BSN/MSN Nursing program and 3-2 engineering degree with Georgia Institute of Technology. There are 28 national honor societies, including Phi Beta Kappa, and a freshman honors program. **Visiting:** There are regularly scheduled orientations for prospective students, including a tour of the campus, information sessions, advising, meal plan selection, fee payment. There are guides for informal

visits and visitors may sit in on classes. To schedule a visit, contact the Admissions Office. **Campus Safety and Security:** Measures include 24-hour foot and vehicle patrol, emergency notification system, self-defense education, and security escort services. There are shuttle buses, emergency telephones, lighted pathways/sidewalks, bicycle patrol, security cameras, and electronic key card access to residence halls.

REQUIREMENTS: The SAT or ACT is required. AP and CLEP credits are accepted. To graduate, all students must complete a minimum of 120 semester hours, including 60 in the core curriculum and 21 in a major, with a GPA of 2.0. Reseasonable proficiency in written and spoken English is also required. **Procedure:** There are deferred admissions and rolling admissions plans. Applications should be filed by July 1 for fall entry; December 1 for spring entry; and May 1 for summer entry. Notification is sent on a rolling basis. **Transfer Students:** 2094 transfer students enrolled in 2013-2014. 30 of 120 credits required for the bachelor's degree must be completed at VSU. **International Students:** There are 200 international students enrolled. They must take the TOEFL with a minimum score of 523 on the paper-based TOEFL (PBT) or 69 on the Internet-based version (iBT). TOEFL can be subsituted with SAT.

ADMISSIONS: 71% of the 2014-2015 applicants were accepted. The SAT scores for the 2014-2015 freshman class were: Critical Reading--51% below 500, 40% between 500 and 599, and 8% between 600 and 699; Math--58% below 500, 35% between 500 and 599, and 7% between 600 and 699; Writing--59% below 500, 35% between 500 and 599, and 6% between 600 and 699. **Admissions Contact:** Walter H. Peacock, Director of Admissions. E-Mail: *admissions@valdosta.edu* Web: *www.valdosta.edu*

FINANCIAL AID: In 2014-2015, 89% of all full-time freshmen and 83% of continuing full-time students received some form of financial aid. 56% of all full-time freshmen and 53% of continuing full-time students received need-based aid. The average freshman award was $14,351. Need-based scholarships or need-based grants averaged $4,044 ($6,700 maximum); need-based self-help aid (loans and jobs) averaged $2,840 ($7,000 maximum); non-need-based athletic scholarships averaged $3,339 ($12,176 maximum); and other non-need-based awards and non-need-based scholarships averaged $9,895 ($26,226 maximum). 6% of undergraduate students work part-time. Average annual earnings from campus work are $2150. The average financial indebtedness of the 2014 graduate was $21,117. VSU is a member of CSS. The priority date for freshman financial aid applications for fall entry is May 1. The deadline for filing freshman financial aid applications for fall entry is June 1.

WESLEYAN COLLEGE   C-3
www.wesleyancollege.edu

Macon, GA 31210	
	(912) 757-5206
	(800) 447-6610
Fax: (912) 757-4030	Email: admission@wesleyancollege.edu
Full-time: 379 women	Faculty: 50; IIB, --$
Part-time: 3 men, 210 women	Ph.D.s: 94%
Graduate: 13 men, 86 women	Student/Faculty: 10 to 1
Year: semesters, summer session	Tuition: $16,500
Room & Board: $7500	Freshman Class: 617 applied, 302 accepted, 135 enrolled
SAT: required ACT: 22	CEEB CODE: 5895
Application Deadline: February 1	COMPETITIVE

Wesleyan College, founded in 1836, is a private, liberal arts college for women, affiliated with the United Methodist Church. It is the world's first college chartered to grant degrees to women. Figures in the above capsule and in this profile are approximate. In addition to regional accreditation, Wesleyan has baccalaureate program accreditation with NASM. The 200-acre campus is in a suburban area 90 miles south of Atlanta. Including any residence halls, there are 19 buildings.

STUDENT LIFE: 74% of undergraduates are from Georgia. Others are from 25 states, and 16 foreign countries. 90% are from public schools. 48% are White; 23% Foreign; 22% African American. 53% are Protestant; 34% claim no religious affiliation. **Male To Female Ratio:** 42.2:1. The average age of freshmen is 18; all undergraduates, 22. 32% do not continue beyond their first year; 56% remain to graduate. **Housing:** 600 students can be accommodated in college housing, which includes single-sex dorms and on-campus apartments. On-campus housing is guaranteed for all 4 years. 76% of students live on campus; of those, 60% remain on campus on weekends. Alcohol is not permitted. All students may keep cars.

FACULTY/CLASSROOMS: 42% of faculty are male; 58% are female. All teach undergraduates, and 75% do both. No introductory courses are taught by graduate students. The average class size in an introductory lecture is 13; in a laboratory is 12; and in a regular course is 10.

PROGRAMS OF STUDY: Wesleyan confers A.B., and B.S.B.A. degrees. Master's degrees are also awarded. Bachelor's degrees are awarded in BIOLOGICAL SCIENCE (biology/biological science), BUSINESS (business administration and management and international business management), COMMUNICATIONS AND THE ARTS (advertising, art history and appreciation, communications, dramatic arts, English, French, music, Spanish, and studio art), COMPUTER AND PHYSICAL SCIENCE (chemistry, information sciences and systems, mathematics, physical sciences, and physics), EDUCATION (early childhood education and middle school education), ENGINEERING AND ENVIRONMENTAL DESIGN (environmental science), SOCIAL SCIENCE (American studies, economics, history, humanities, interdisciplinary studies, international relations, philosophy, political science/government, psychology, religion, and social science). Chemistry, biology, and philosophy are the strongest academically. Business, education, psychology, advertising and marketing have the largest enrollments.

ACTIVITIES: There are no fraternities or sororities. There are 51 groups on campus, including art, choir, chorus, computers, dance, debate, drama, ethnic, forensics, gay, honors, international, literary magazine, musical theater, newspaper, photography, political, professional, recreation, religious, social, social service, and student government. Popular campus events include Casino Night, Benefit Ball, and STUNT. **Sports:** There are 6 intercollegiate sports for women. Facilities include an equestrian arena, softball and soccer fields, an indoor pool, a gym, a dance studio, a weight room, a lake, a fitness trail, and a fitness center. **Graduates:** From July 1, 2013 to June 30, 2014, 92 bachelor's degrees were awarded. The most popular majors were business administration (28%), education (12%), and psychology (11%). In an average class, 41% graduate in 4 years or less, 44% graduate in 5 years or less, and 45% graduate in 6 years or less. Of the 2013 graduating class, 22% were enrolled in graduate school within 6 months of graduation, and 36% were employed.

SERVICES: Counseling and information services are available, as is tutoring in some subjects. There is remedial math and reading. Free tutors are available upon request, and the Academic Center is available for all students. **Library/Resources:** The library contains 143,071 volumes, 33,438 microform items, 4,267 audio/video tapes/CDs/DVDs, and subscribes to 615 periodicals including electronic. Computerized library services include interlibrary loans, database searching, and Internet access. Special learning facilities include an art gallery, a computerized teaching classroom, language and math labs, collaborative research science labs, and an arboretum. **Physically Challenged Students:** 65% of the campus is accessible. Facilities include wheelchair ramps, elevators, special parking, specially equipped restrooms, special class scheduling, lowered drinking fountains, and lowered telephones. **Special:** Wesleyan offers cross-registration with Mercer University and a 3-2 engineering degree with Georgia Institute of Technology and Auburn and Mercer Universities. More than 150 internships are available, as are interdisciplinary, student-designed, and dual majors, study abroad in 10 countries, a Washington semester, work-study programs, credit for life experience, nondegree study, and pass/fail options. There are 10 national honor societies and a freshman honors program. **Visiting:** There are

regularly scheduled orientations for prospective students, including a campus tour, parent/student panels, class visits, admission and financial aid sessions, and meals in the dining hall. There are guides for informal visits, visitors may sit in on classes, and stay overnight. To schedule a visit, contact the Admissions Office. **Campus Safety and Security:** Measures include 24-hour foot and vehicle patrol, self-defense education, and security escort services. There are emergency telephones, lighted pathways/sidewalks, dorm entrances are locked 24 hours a day, 7 days a week.

REQUIREMENTS: The SAT or ACT is required. The ACT Optional Writing test is also required. Each applicant for admission is reviewed on the following: performance in and quality of a college preparatory curriculum, standardized test score, counselor and teacher recommendation, writing ability, and cocurricular involvement. A minimum of 15 Carnegie units is required, including 4 units of English, 3 each of math, natural sciences, and social sciences, and 2 of foreign language. Admitted students must graduate from an accredited secondary school or have a GED certificate. The admission staff does not require but welcomes the opportunity to interview prospective students. Students who wish to be considered for a performance arts scholarship must submit a portfolio or audition. AP and CLEP credits are accepted. Important factors in the admissions decision are advanced placement and honors courses, evidence of special talent, and leadership record. To graduate, students must complete 120 credit hours with a minimum GPA of 2.0. Requirements include proficiency in writing, math, and modern foreign language, 10 courses distributed with 2 but no more than 3 from fine arts, humanities, science and math, and social sciences. A first-year seminar, a speech-intensive course, cross-cultural and workplace experience, and integrative experience in the major are also required. All classes are seminar based. **Procedure:** Freshmen are admitted fall and spring. Entrance exams should be taken by the fall of the senior year. There are early decision, early admissions, deferred admissions, and rolling admissions plans. Early decision applications should be filed by November 15; regular applications, by February 1 for fall entry; and December 1 for spring entry, along with a $30 fee. Notification of early decision is sent December 15; regular decision, 40 early decision candidates were accepted for the 2014-2015 class. Applications are accepted online. **Transfer Students:** 5 transfer students enrolled in 2013-2014. Applicants with fewer than 24 transferable semester hours must submit a final high school transcript and record of standardized test scores in addition to their college transcripts. 30 of 120 credits required for the bachelor's degree must be completed at Wesleyan. **International Students:** There are 79 international students enrolled. The school actively recruits these students. They must take the TOEFL. They must also take the SAT or ACT.

ADMISSIONS: 49% of the 2014-2015 applicants were accepted. The ACT scores were 36% below 21, 27% between 21 and 23, 25% between 24 and 26, 7% between 27 and 28, and 7% above 28. 49% of the current freshmen were in the top fifth of their class; 72% were in the top two fifths. 3 freshmen graduated first in their class. **Admissions Contact:** Patricia M. Gibbs, Vice President of Enrollment Services and Student Affairs. E-Mail: *admission@wesleyancollege.edu* Web: *www.wesleyancollege.edu*

FINANCIAL AID: In 2014-2015, 99% of all full-time freshmen and 96% of continuing full-time students received some form of financial aid. 71% of all full-time freshmen and 58% of continuing full-time students received need-based aid. The average freshman award was $13,842. Need-based scholarships or need-based grants averaged $10,116; need-based self-help aid (loans and jobs) averaged $3,064; and other non-need-based awards and non-need-based scholarships averaged $12,230. 40% of undergraduate students work part-time. Average annual earnings from campus work are $1000. The average financial indebtedness of the 2014 graduate was $21,872. The FAFSA and the college's own financial statement are required. The priority date for freshman financial aid applications for fall entry is March 1. The deadline for filing freshman financial aid applications for fall entry is May 1.

HAWAII

INSET 1

College Location

0 20 40 60 80 100
Miles

BRIGHAM YOUNG UNIVERSITY/HAWAII   C-2
www.byuh.edu

Laie, HI 96762	**(808) 675-3731**
	n/av
Fax: (808) 675-3741	Email: adm@byuh.edu
Full-time: 945 men, 1200 women	Faculty: 120
Part-time: 99 men, 153 women	Ph.D.s: 60%
Graduate: n/av	Student/Faculty: 18 to 1
Year: semesters, summer session	Tuition: $4940
Room & Board: $5746	Freshman Class: 1265 applied, 603 accepted, 297 enrolled
SAT: recommended ACT: 23	CEEB CODE: 4106
Application Deadline: February 15	VERY COMPETITIVE

BYU-Hawai'i is a private, comprehensive undergraduate institution that educates 2,400 students each year from 70 countries in Asia, the Pacific, the U.S., and other parts of the world. Figures in the above capsule and in this profile are approximate. There are 4 undergraduate schools. In addition to regional accreditation, BYU - Hawai'i has baccalaureate program accreditation with NCATE and CSWE. The 200-acre campus is in a rural area 38 miles from Honolulu. Including any residence halls, there are 42 buildings.

STUDENT LIFE: 83% of undergraduates are from out of state, mostly the West. Students are from 41 states, 75 foreign countries, and Canada. 44% are Foreign; 29% White; 22% Asian American. **Male To Female Ratio:** 1.3:1. The average age of freshmen is 21; all undergraduates, 23. 35% do not continue beyond their first year; 47% remain to graduate. **Housing:** 1635 students can be accommodated in college housing, which includes single-sex dorms, on-campus apartments, and married student housing. On-campus housing is guaranteed for the freshman year only, is available on a first-come, and first-served basis. 62% of students live on campus. Alcohol is not permitted. All students may keep cars.

FACULTY/CLASSROOMS: 80% of faculty are male; 20% are female. All teach undergraduates. No introductory courses are taught by graduate students. The average class size in an introductory lecture is 21; in a laboratory is 17; and in a regular course is 19.

PROGRAMS OF STUDY: BYU - Hawai'i confers B.A., B.S., B.F.A. and B.S.W. degrees. Bachelor's degrees are awarded in BIOLOGICAL SCIENCE (biology/biological science), BUSINESS (accounting, hospitality management services, international business management, and tourism), COMMUNICATIONS AND THE ARTS (art, English, fine arts, and music), COMPUTER AND PHYSICAL SCIENCE (computer science, information sciences and systems, and mathematics), EDUCATION (art education, business education, elementary education, English education, mathematics education, science education, social science education, special education, and teaching English

as a second/foreign language (TESOL/TEFOL)), HEALTH PROFESSIONS (predentistry and premedicine), SOCIAL SCIENCE (Hawaiian studies, history, interdisciplinary studies, international studies, Pacific area studies, physical fitness/movement, political science/government, psychology, and social work). International business management, accounting, hospitality and tourism management have the largest enrollments.

ACTIVITIES: There are no fraternities or sororities. There are 41 groups on campus, including art, band, cheerleading, chess, choir, chorale, communications, computers, dance, drama, ethnic, film, honors, international, jazz band, literary magazine, musical theater, newspaper, pep band, political, professional, religious, social, social service, and student government. Popular campus events include International Food Fest, International Cultural Night and Talent Show. **Sports:** There are 5 intercollegiate sports for men and 6 for women, and 10 intramural sports for men and 10 for women. Facilities include 3 softball fields, 2 soccer fields, a rugby field, 10 tennis and 4 racquetball courts, a swimming pool, a weight room, a bowling alley, a dance studio, pool tables, and 2 gyms. **Graduates:** From July 1, 2013 to June 30, 2014, 557 bachelor's degrees were awarded. The most popular majors were international business management (15%), information system (8%), and social work (6%). In an average class, 47% graduate in 6 years or less. Of the 2013 graduating class, 44% were enrolled in graduate school within 6 months of graduation, and 61% were employed.

SERVICES: Counseling and information services are available, as is tutoring in most subjects. There is remedial math, reading, and writing. **Library/Resources:** The library contains 21,004 volumes, 450,000 microform items, 9,538 audio/video tapes/CDs/DVDs, and subscribes to 17,000 periodicals including electronic. Computerized library services include interlibrary loans, database searching, Internet access, and Wi-Fi capability. Special learning facilities include an art gallery, natural history museum, the nearby Polynesian Cultural Center, which houses an art collection and an artifact collection, provides valuable research opportunities for students in related programs. **Physically Challenged Students:** 95% of the campus is accessible. Facilities include wheelchair ramps, elevators, special parking, specially equipped restrooms, lowered drinking fountains, and lowered telephones. **Special:** BYUH offers work-study programs with the Polynesian Cultural Center, internships, cooperative programs in most majors, non-degree study, student-designed majors in interdisciplinary studies, and pass/fail options. There are 5 national honor societies and a freshman honors program. **Visiting:** There are guides for informal visits. To schedule a visit, contact the University Advancement Office at magaleil@byuh.edu. **Campus Safety and Security:** Measures include 24-hour foot and vehicle patrol and security escort services. There are emergency telephones and lighted pathways/sidewalks.

REQUIREMENTS: The ACT is required. The SAT is recommended. Applicants should be high school graduates. Home-schooled and other non-traditional students should call for more information. A GPA of 2.0 is required. AP and CLEP credits are accepted. Important factors in the admissions decision are geographical diversity, recommendations by alumni, and personality/intangible qualities. Students must complete 31 to 43 credits in general education curriculum, as well as meet English proficiency, religious education, and exercise science requirements. A total of 120 credit hours, including 40 in the major, must be earned with a minimum GPA of 2.0 for graduation. A thesis is required in certain areas. **Procedure:** Freshmen are admitted to all sessions. Entrance exams should be taken prior to the application deadline. There is a deferred admissions plan. Applications should be filed by February 15 for fall entry; October 1 for winter entry; February 15 for spring entry; and February 15 for summer entry, along with a $35 fee. Notifications are sent April 1. Applications are accepted on-line. **Transfer Students:** 209 transfer students enrolled in 2013-2014. Applicants must have 30 hours of college credit, with a minimum GPA of 2.5. 30 of 120 credits required for the Bachelor's degree must be completed at BYU - Hawai'i. **International Students:** There are 942 international students enrolled. The school actively recruits these students. They must take the TOEFL with a minimum score of 500 on the paper-based TOEFL (PBT). They must also take the ACT.

ADMISSIONS: 48% of the 2014-2015 applicants were accepted. The ACT scores were 26% below 21, 22% between 21 and 23, 24% between 24 and 26, 16% between 27 and 28, and 12% above 28.
Admissions Contact: Arapata Meha, Dean of Admissions and Records. E-Mail: *adm@byuh.edu* Web: *www.byuh.edu*
FINANCIAL AID: The FAFSA is required. Check with the school for current application deadlines.

CHAMINADE UNIVERSITY OF HONOLULU *(The complete profile is made available exclusively on our website, www.barronspac.com)*

HAWAII PACIFIC UNIVERSITY	C-2
www.hpu.edu	

Honolulu, HI 96813	808-543-8088
	(866) 225-5478
Fax: (808) 543-8065	Email: admissions@hpu.edu
Full-time: 1566 men, 2378 women	Faculty: 235
Part-time: 1197 men, 1027 women	Ph.D.s: 64%
Graduate: 578 men, 717 women	Student/Faculty: 17 to 1
Year: semesters, summer session	Tuition: $21,030
Room & Board: $13,330	Freshman Class: 4129 applied, 2980 accepted, 492 enrolled
SAT CR/M/W: 480/490/470 ACT: 21	CEEB CODE: 4352
Application Deadline: n/av	COMPETITIVE

Hawaii Pacific University, founded in 1965, is a private (non-profit) coeducational institution offering 50 undergraduate and 14 graduate programs in liberal arts, business, natural sciences, nursing, international studies, and communication. Figures in the above capsule and in this profile are approximate. In addition to regional accreditation, HPU has baccalaureate program accreditation with CSWE, NLN, SATE, and WASC. The 135-acre campus is in an urban area in downtown Honolulu and suburban Kaneohe on the island of Oahu. Including any residence halls, there are 16 buildings.
STUDENT LIFE: 64% of undergraduates are from Hawaii. Others are from 50 states, 80 foreign countries, and Canada. 67% are from public schools. 29% are White; 19% Asian American; 13% Hispanic; 13% Foreign. **Male To Female Ratio:** 1.2:1. The average age of freshmen is 19; all undergraduates, 26. 34% do not continue beyond their first year; 39% remain to graduate. **Housing:** 200 students can be accommodated in college housing, which includes single-sex and coed dorms and off-campus apartments. There is also a homestay program. The housing office assists students in finding apartments and other living arrangements in Honolulu. On-campus housing is available on a first-come, first-served basis. Priority is given to out-of-town students. 97% of students commute. Alcohol is not permitted. All students may keep cars.
FACULTY/CLASSROOMS: 54% of faculty are male; 46% are female. 91% teach undergraduates, and 42% do both. No introductory courses are taught by graduate students. The average class size in an introductory lecture is 18; in a laboratory is 10; and in a regular course is 18.
PROGRAMS OF STUDY: HPU confers B.A., B.S., B.S.B.A., B.S.N., B.S.W., B.Ed. and B.S.H.S. degrees. Associate and Master's degrees are also awarded. Bachelor's degrees are awarded in AGRICULTURE (environmental studies), BIOLOGICAL SCIENCE (biochemistry, biology/biological science, marine biology, marine biology, marine biology, and marine science), BUSINESS (accounting, banking and finance, business administration and management, business economics, entrepreneurial studies, finance, finance, finance, human resources, international business management, management information systems, management information systems, management information systems, management science, marketing management, personnel management, small business management, and tourism), COMMUNICATIONS AND THE ARTS (advertising, communications, English, journalism, multimedia, and public relations), COMPUTER AND PHYSICAL SCIENCE (applied mathematics, chemistry, computer programming, computer science, mathematics, oceanography, and science), EDUCATION (elementary education

and teaching English as a second/foreign language (TESOL/TEFOL)), ENGINEERING AND ENVIRONMENTAL DESIGN (environmental science and military science), HEALTH PROFESSIONS (nursing, premedicine, and public health), SOCIAL SCIENCE (anthropology, classical/ancient civilization, criminal justice, economics, history, human services, humanities, international relations, international studies, Pacific area studies, political science/government, psychology, public administration, social science, social work, and sociology). Marine biology, nursing and computer science are the strongest academically. Nursing, computer science and management have the largest enrollments.
ACTIVITIES: There are no fraternities or sororities. There are 93 groups on campus, including art, band, cheerleading, chorale, computers, dance, debate, drama, environmental, ethnic, film, gay, honors, international, literary magazine, musical theater, newspaper, orchestra, pep band, political, professional, religious, social, social service, and student government. Popular campus events include Intercultural Day, Honors Banquet and Club Carnival. **Sports:** There are 6 intercollegiate sports for men and 6 for women, and 6 intramural sports for men and 6 for women. Facilities include an soccer and softball fields, tennis courts, and 2 regulation basketball courts, women's softball team, cheerleading squad and dance team. **Graduates:** From July 1, 2013 to June 30, 2014, 926 bachelor's degrees were awarded. The most popular majors were business administration (33%), nursing (28%), and psychology (7%). 133 companies recruited on campus in 2013-2014. In an average class, 4% graduate in 3 years or less, 23% graduate in 4 years or less, 36% graduate in 5 years or less, and 39% graduate in 6 years or less. Of the 2013 graduating class, 40% were enrolled in graduate school within 6 months of graduation, and 69% were employed.
SERVICES: Counseling and information services are available, as is tutoring in most subjects. There is remedial math, reading, and writing. **Library/Resources:** The 2 libraries contain 175,000 volumes, 415,000 microform items, 6,300 audio/video tapes/CDs/DVDs, and subscribe to 45,000 periodicals including electronic. Computerized library services include interlibrary loans, database searching, Internet access, and Wi-Fi capability. Special learning facilities include an art gallery, a research vessel. **Physically Challenged Students:** 75% of the campus is accessible. Facilities include wheelchair ramps, elevators, special parking, specially equipped restrooms, special class scheduling, lowered drinking fountains, and lowered telephones. **Special:** Upperclassmen may participate in internships and work-study programs with numerous companies and study abroad in 16 countries. HPU also offers accelerated degree and co-op programs in all majors, B.A.-B.S. degrees in most majors, student-designed majors, dual majors in all business subjects, a 3-2 engineering degree with Washington University in St. Louis and the University of Southern California, credit for military experience, nondegree study, and pass/fail options. There are 18 national honor societies, a freshman honors program, and 7 departmental honors programs. **Visiting:** There are regularly scheduled orientations for prospective students, during 9 a.m. daily, with an appointment required. There are guides for informal visits and visitors may sit in on classes. To schedule a visit, contact the Admissions Office. **Campus Safety and Security:** Measures include 24-hour foot and vehicle patrol, emergency notification system, and security escort services. There are shuttle buses, emergency telephones, and lighted pathways/sidewalks.
REQUIREMENTS: The SAT or ACT is required. Hawaii Pacific University prefers completion of 20 credits based on 4 years of English, 2 each of math and social studies, and 2 each of history and science. An essay and an interview are recommended. Certain programs, such as marine science and nursing, have more specific admission requirements. A GPA of 2.5 is required. AP and CLEP credits are accepted. Important factors in the admissions decision are recommendations by school officials, extracurricular activities record, and evidence of special talent. Seniors who have completed a minimum of 100 semester hours of credit toward their undergraduate degree program and have a cumulative GPA of at least 3.0 may enroll concurrently in certain graduate degree programs. Students enrolled in this program may earn a maximum of 12 semester hours of dual graduate and undergraduate credit while pursuing both degrees. (MA-TESL allows only 6 AL concurrent credits) **Procedure:** Freshmen are admitted to all sessions. Entrance exams should be taken during the spring or

summer of the junior year or the fall of the senior year. There are early admissions, deferred admissions, and rolling admissions plans. Application deadlines are open. Application fee is $50. Applications are accepted on-line. **Transfer Students:** 890 transfer students enrolled in 2013-2014. Applicants must have a GPA of 2.0 in a minimum of 24 credit hours. The SAT or ACT and an interview are recommended. 30 of 124 credits required for the Bachelor's degree must be completed at HPU. **International Students:** There are 632 international students enrolled. The school actively recruits these students. They must take the TOEFL with a minimum score of 550 on the paper-based TOEFL (PBT) or 80 on the Internet-based version (iBT) and the college's own test, or take the IELTS, scoring a minimum of 6, or the APIEL, scoring a minimum of 3.

ADMISSIONS: 72% of the 2014-2015 applicants were accepted. The SAT scores for the 2014-2015 freshman class were: Critical Reading--57% below 500, 35% between 500 and 599, 8% between 600 and 699, and 1% between 700 and 800; Math--52% below 500, 38% between 500 and 599, 9% between 600 and 699, and 1% between 700 and 800; Writing--63% below 500, 32% between 500 and 599, and 5% between 600 and 699. The ACT scores were 47% below 21, 30% between 21 and 23, 14% between 24 and 26, 5% between 27 and 28, and 5% above 28. 44% of the current freshmen were in the top fifth of their class; 76% were in the top two fifths. 18 freshmen graduated first in their class. **Admissions Contact:** Sara Sato, Asst. V.P. Enrollment Management. E-Mail: *admissions@hpu.edu* Web: *www.hpu.edu*

FINANCIAL AID: 36% of all full-time freshmen and % of continuing full-time students received need-based aid. The FAFSA is required. The priority date for freshman financial aid applications for fall entry is March 1.

UNIVERSITY OF HAWAII SYSTEM

The University of Hawaii System, established in 1907, is a public system in Hawaii. It is governed by a board of regents, whose chief administrators are the president and the chancellor. The primary goal of the system is to provide all qualified people in Hawaii an equal opportunity for quality college and university education, to create knowledge and gain insights through research and scholarship, to preserve and contribute to the artistic and cultural heritage of the community, and to provide other public service through the dissemination of current and new ideas and techniques. The main priorities are serving the state of Hawaii, achieving program quality, establishing Pacific/Asian focus, and adapting to scientific change. The total student enrollment of all 10 campuses is usually 58,941, with 3500 faculty members. Altogether there are 143 baccalaureate, 93 master's, and 54 doctoral programs offered in University of Hawaii System. 4-year campuses are located in Hilo, Manoa and West Oahu. Profiles of the 4-year campuses are included in this section.

UNIVERSITY OF HAWAII AT HILO	F-4
www.uhh.hawaii.edu	
Hilo, HI 96720	(808) 974-7414
	(800) 897-4456
Fax: (808) 933-0861	**Email:** uhhadm@hawaii.edu
Full-time: 880 men, 1335 women	**Faculty:** 162; IIB, +$
Part-time: 235 men, 400 women	**Ph.D.s:** 80%
Graduate: 30 men, 75 women	**Student/Faculty:** 14 to 1
Year: semesters, summer session	**Tuition:** $13,684 ($19,036)
Room & Board: $9382	**Freshman Class:** n/av
SAT or ACT: required	**CEEB CODE:** 4869
Application Deadline: n/av	**COMPETITIVE**

The University of Hawaii at Hilo, founded in 1970, is part of the public University of Hawaii and offers degree programs through its Colleges of Agriculture, Arts and Sciences, and Hawaiian language. It has a branch campus at Kealakekua, West Hawaii. Major programs include marine science, volcanology, and astronomy. Figures in the above capsule and in this profile are approximate. There are 3 undergraduate schools and 2 graduate schools. In addition to regional accreditation, UH Hilo has baccalaureate program accreditation with NLN. The 115-acre campus is in a small town 200 miles southeast of Honolulu. Including any residence halls, there are 54 buildings.

STUDENT LIFE: 69% of undergraduates are from Hawaii. Others are from 46 states, 32 foreign countries, and Canada. 76% are from public schools. 31% are White; 27% Asian American; 18% American Indian/Alaska Native. **Male To Female Ratio:** 1.6:1. The average age of all undergraduates is 27. 29% do not continue beyond their first year; 31% remain to graduate. **Housing:** 800 students can be accommodated in college housing, which includes coed dorms, on-campus apartments, off-campus apartments, and married student housing. In addition, there are honors houses, special-interest houses, There is an educational/recreational enrichment hall. On-campus housing is available on a first-come and first-served basis. Priority is given to out-of-town students. 79% of students commute. Alcohol is not permitted. All students may keep cars.

FACULTY/CLASSROOMS: 60% of faculty are male; 40% are female. All teach and do research. No introductory courses are taught by graduate students. The average class size in an introductory lecture is 25; in a laboratory is 25; and in a regular course is 17.

PROGRAMS OF STUDY: UH Hilo confers B.A., B.S., B.B.A. and B.S.N. degrees. Master's degrees are also awarded. Bachelor's degrees are awarded in AGRICULTURE (agriculture and environmental studies), BIOLOGICAL SCIENCE (biology/biological science and marine science), BUSINESS (business administration and management), COMMUNICATIONS AND THE ARTS (art, art/art studies, communications, English, Hawaiian, Japanese, linguistics, and music), COMPUTER AND PHYSICAL SCIENCE (astronomy, chemistry, computer science, geology, mathematics, natural sciences, and physics), ENGINEERING AND ENVIRONMENTAL DESIGN (environmental science), HEALTH PROFESSIONS (nursing), SOCIAL SCIENCE (administration of justice , anthropology, criminal justice, economics, geography, Hawaiian studies, history, Japanese studies, liberal arts/general studies, philosophy, political science/government, psychology, and sociology). Business, computer science, and biology are the strongest academically. Business, psychology, and marine science have the largest enrollments.

ACTIVITIES: There are no fraternities or sororities. There are 40 groups on campus, including art, band, cheerleading, chess, choir, chorale, chorus, computers, dance, drama, ethnic, gay, honors, international, jazz band, literary magazine, musical theater, newspaper, pep band, political, professional, religious, social, social service, and student government. Popular campus events include International Night, May Day, and Dances. **Sports:** There are 5 intercollegiate sports for men and 4 for women, and 10 intramural sports for men and 10 for women. Facilities include a student activities center with billiards and a game room, an athletic complex with basketball courts and a weight room, 8 tennis courts, and baseball, softball, and soccer fields. **Graduates:** From July 1, 2013 to June 30, 2014, 419 Bachelor's degrees were awarded. The most popular majors were psychology (15%), business administration (11%), and marine science (8%). 36 companies recruited on campus in 2013-2014. In an average class, 1% graduate in 3 years or less, 10% graduate in 4 years or less, 25% graduate in 5 years or less, and 31% graduate in 6 years or less.

SERVICES: Counseling and information services are available, as is tutoring in most subjects. There is remedial math, reading, and writing. **Library/Resources:** The library contains 240,000 volumes, 11,000 microform items, and subscribes to 1,200 periodicals including electronic. Computerized library services include interlibrary loans and database searching. Special learning facilities include an art gallery, a space science center and marine education center. **Physically Challenged Students:** 95% of the campus is accessible. Facilities include wheelchair ramps, elevators, special parking, specially equipped restrooms, special class scheduling, lowered drinking fountains, lowered telephones. **Special:** UH Hilo offers cross-registration with Hawaii Community College, a political science legislative internship and other internships in business and psychology, and many work-study programs. Students may study abroad through a variety of programs and other internships in business and psychology. The school permits a student-designed liberal studies major, dual degrees, a 3-2 engineering degree with the University of Hawaii at Manoa, nondegree study, pass/fail options, and credit for military experience. There are a freshman honors program and 1 departmental honors programs. **Visiting:** There are regularly scheduled orientations for prospective students, including a campus tour and a meeting with an admissions counselor. There are guides for informal visits and visitors may sit in on classes. To schedule a visit, contact the Admissions Office. **Campus Safety and Security:** Measures include 24-hour foot and vehicle patrol and self-defense education. There are emergency telephones and lighted pathways/sidewalks.

REQUIREMENTS: The SAT or ACT is required. Applicants should be high school graduates or present a GED certificate. Students should have earned 22 academic credits, including 4 units of English, 3 of math, 3 of life and physical sciences, and 7 of electives. A GPA of 2.5 is required. AP and CLEP credits are accepted. Important factors in the admissions decision are advanced placement or honors courses, recommendations by school officials, and evidence of special talent. To graduate, students must earn a minimum of 120 semester hours, including at least 30 in the college from which a degree is sought, with a 2.0 GPA overall and in the major. Students also must complete general education requirements, including 10 semester hours of natural sciences with 1 hour of lab, 9 each of humanities and social sciences, 6 of world cultures, and 3 each of English composition and quantitative reasoning. 3 writing-intensive sourses and 1 Hawaiian/Asian/Pacific course are also required. **Procedure:** Freshmen are admitted fall and spring. Entrance exams should be taken by November of the senior year. There are early admissions and rolling admissions plans. Applications should be filed by December 1 for spring entry, along with a $25 fee. Applications are accepted on-line.

Transfer Students: 577 transfer students enrolled in 2013-2014. Applicants must have a GPA of 2.0; those with fewer than 24 college credits must submit their high school transcript and SAT I or ACT results. 30 of 120 credits required for the bachelor's degree must be completed at UH Hilo. **International Students:** There are 311 international students enrolled. The school actively recruits these students. They must take the TOEFL and the college's own test. The SAT I or ACT is not required, but is recommended.

ADMISSIONS: 4 freshmen graduated first in their class. **Admissions Contact:** Admissions Office E-Mail: *uhhadm@hawaii.edu* Web: *www.uhh.hawaii.edu*

FINANCIAL AID: In 2014-2015, 55% of all full-time freshmen and 41% of continuing full-time students received some form of financial aid. 55% of all full-time freshmen and students received need-based aid. The average freshman award was $3,853. 70% of undergraduate students work part-time. Average annual earnings from campus work are $2600. The average financial indebtedness of the 2014 graduate was $10,698. UH Hilo is a member of CSS. The FAFSA and the college's own financial statement are required. The deadline for filing freshman financial aid applications for fall entry is March 1.

UNIVERSITY OF HAWAII AT MANOA   C-2
www.manoa@hawaii.edu

Honolulu, HI 96822

(808) 956-8975
(800) 823-9771

Fax: (808) 956-4148   **Email:** ar-info@hawaii.edu

Full-time: 5388 men, 6246 women   **Faculty:** 1306; I, av$

Part-time: 1261 men, 1507 women   **Ph.D.s:** 83%

Graduate: 2473 men, 3554 women   **Student/Faculty:** 16 to 1

Year: semesters, summer session   **Tuition:** $9100 ($23,932)

Room & Board: $10,279   **Freshman Class:** 6541 applied, 5130 accepted, 2010 enrolled

SAT CR/M/W: 530/560/520 **ACT:** 23   **CEEB CODE:** 4867

Application Deadline: May 1   **COMPETITIVE**

The University of Hawaii at Manoa, founded in 1907, is a public research institution in the University of Hawaii system. The undergraduate programs offered include liberal arts and sciences, business, education, engineering, nursing, tropical agriculture, architecture, travel industry management, physical science, technology, Hawaiian, Asian-Pacific studies, social work, and medicine. Figures in the above capsule and in this profile are approximate. There are 14 undergraduate schools and 15 graduate schools. In addition to regional accreditation, UHM has baccalaureate program accreditation with AACSB, ABET, ADA, CSWE, NAAB, NASM, NCATE, NLN, CODA, and NLNAC. The 320-acre campus is in a small town in Manoa, Valley, just outside downtown Honolulu.

STUDENT LIFE: 77% of undergraduates are from Hawaii. Others are from 50 states, 54 foreign countries, and Canada. 68% are from public schools. 45% are Asian American; 25% White. **Male To Female Ratio:** 1.2:1. The average age of freshmen is 18; all undergraduates, 22. 23% do not continue beyond their first year; 55% remain to graduate. **Housing:** 3696 students can be accommodated in college housing, which includes single-sex and coed dorms, on-campus apartments, and married student housing. In addition, there are honors houses, language houses, special-interest houses, Substance free/wellness, first-year experience, technology, and 24-hour quiet halls. On-campus housing is guaranteed for the freshman year only and is available on a lottery system for upperclassmen. Priority is given to out-of-town students. 81% of students commute. All students may keep cars.

FACULTY/CLASSROOMS: 56% of faculty are male; 44% are female. 81% teach undergraduates. Graduate students teach 20% of introductory courses. The average class size in an introductory lecture is 38; in a laboratory is 15; and in a regular course is 22.

PROGRAMS OF STUDY: UHM confers B.A., B.S., B.B.A., B.Ed., B.F.A., B.Mus. and B.S.W. degrees. Master's and Doctoral degrees are also awarded. Bachelor's degrees are awarded in AGRICULTURE (animal science, natural resource management, plant protection (pest management), plant science, and soil science), BIOLOGICAL SCIENCE (biology/biological science, botany, marine biology, microbiology, and zoology), BUSINESS (accounting, banking and finance, business administration and management, human resources, international business management, management information systems, management science, marketing/retailing/merchandising, recreation and leisure services, and tourism), COMMUNICATIONS AND THE ARTS (apparel design, art, Chinese, classics, communications, dance, dramatic arts, English, English as a second/foreign language, French, German, Hawaiian, Japanese, journalism, Korean, linguistics, music, Russian, Spanish, and speech/debate/rhetoric), COMPUTER AND PHYSICAL SCIENCE (atmospheric sciences and meteorology, chemistry, computer science, geology, geophysics and seismology, information sciences and systems, mathematics, and physics), EDUCATION (elementary education, physical education, and secondary education), ENGINEERING AND ENVIRONMENTAL DESIGN (bioengineering, civil engineering, electrical/electronics engineering, environmental science, and mechanical engineering), HEALTH PROFESSIONS (dental hygiene, exercise science, medical laboratory technology, medical technology, nursing, and speech pathology/audiology), SOCIAL SCIENCE (American studies, anthropology, Asian/Oriental studies, economics, ethnic studies, family/consumer resource management, food science, geography, Hawaiian studies, history, interdisciplinary studies, Pacific area studies, peace studies, philosophy, political science/government, psychology, religion, social work, sociology, and women's studies). Biology, art, and business have the largest enrollments.

ACTIVITIES: 1% of men belong to 1 local and 2 national fraternities; 1% of women belong to 1 local and 1 national sororities. There are 100 groups on campus, including art, band, cheerleading, chess, choir, chorale, chorus, dance, drama, drill team, ethnic, film, gay, honors, international, literary magazine, marching band, musical theater, newspaper, opera, pep band, photography, political, professional, radio and TV, religious, social, social service, student government, and symphony. Popular campus events include Live Band at Bale, Movie Nights, Sustainable UH, and Recreational Sports Events. **Sports:** There are 9 intercollegiate sports for men and 13 for women, and 24 intramural sports for men and 21 for women. Facilities include a 10,300-seat arena that houses men and women's basketball, and men and women's volleyball. In addition, the university has 2 gymnasiums, an over 10,000 square foot weight training and conditioning center, a 4312-seat baseball stadium, swimming facilities, 2 weight rooms, a turf field and rubberized track, a softball field, and 12 tennis courts, golf, sailing, water polo, cross country, cheerleading, football, and women's soccer. **Graduates:** From July 1, 2013 to June 30, 2014, 2957 Bachelor's degrees were awarded. The most popular majors were business/marketing (21%), social sciences (11%), and education (7%). 100 companies recruited on campus in 2013-2014. In an average class, 15% graduate in 4 years or less, 40% graduate in 5 years or less, and 51% graduate in 6 years or less.

SERVICES: Counseling and information services are available, as is tutoring in some subjects. There is a reader service for the blind.

Library/Resources: The 5 libraries contain 3.4 million volumes, 2.4 million microform items, and 73,000 audio/video tapes/CDs/DVDs, and subscribe to 59,000 periodicals including electronic. Computerized library services include interlibrary loans, database searching, Internet access, and Wi-Fi capability. Special learning facilities include an art gallery, radio station, and TV station. Hamilton houses research collections in: humanities, social sciences and technology, collections for Asia, Hawaii and the Pacific, archives manuscripts and other special collections. **Physically Challenged Students:** 40% of the campus is accessible. Facilities include wheelchair ramps, elevators, special parking, specially equipped restrooms, special class scheduling, lowered drinking fountains, lowered telephones. Disability access information is available on request, and auxiliary aids and program adjustments can be arranged on an individual basis. **Special:** Internships are available with a variety of employers, including the state legislature, and through 55 different offices as well as academic departments via career services. Co-op and work-study programs, and internships are also offered. Dual majors, non-degree study, and pass/fail options are available. The liberal studies program offers student-designed majors. Students may study abroad in any one of 20 countries for a summer, a semester, or a year. There are 9 national honor societies, including a Phi Beta Kappa chapter, a freshman honors program, and 45 departmental honors programs. **Visiting:** There are regularly scheduled orientations for prospective students. Visiting students can meet with an admissions representative and tour the campus with a current UH Manoa Student. To schedule a visit, contact the School and College Services at visituhm@hawaii.edu. **Campus Safety and Security:** Measures include 24-hour foot and vehicle patrol, emergency notification system, and security escort services. There are shuttle buses, emergency telephones, lighted pathways/sidewalks, crime alerts via campuswide e-mail, and a campus security web site.

REQUIREMENTS: The SAT or ACT is required. The ACT Optional Writing test is also required. Applicants must be graduates of an accredited secondary school, and have the minimum required score of 510 for each SAT section, or 22 on the ACT composite. The GED is also accepted. UHM requires 22 Carnegie units or 17 academic credits, including 4 units of English and 3 units each of math, science, and social studies, as well as 4 additional units of college preparatory courses and 5 electives. UHM requires applicants to be in the upper 40% of their class. A GPA of 2.8 is required. AP and CLEP credits are accepted. Important factors in the admissions decision are advanced placement or honors courses, recommendations by school officials, and leadership record. In most disciplines, a minimum GPA of 2.0

and a total of 124 credit hours are required for graduation. The total number of hours required in the major varies according to discipline. All students must fulfill general education core requirements. **Procedure:** Freshmen are admitted fall and spring. Entrance exams should be taken by December of the senior year for fall admission. There is a rolling admissions plan. Applications should be filed by May 1 for fall entry; October 1 for spring entry, along with a $70 fee. Notification is sent on a rolling basis. Applications are accepted on-line. **Transfer Students:** 1855 transfer students enrolled in 2013-2014. Applicants must have a total of 24 semester credits with a minimum GPA of 2.5. 30 of 124 credits required for the bachelor's degree must be completed at UHM. **International Students:** There are 628 international students enrolled. The school actively recruits these students. They must take the TOEFL with a minimum score of 500 on the paper-based TOEFL (PBT) or 100 on the Internet-based version (iBT). They must also take the SAT or ACT, scoring 510.

ADMISSIONS: 78% of the 2014-2015 applicants were accepted. The SAT scores for the 2014-2015 freshman class were: Critical Reading--34% below 500, 46% between 500 and 599, 18% between 600 and 699, and 2% between 700 and 800; Math--24% below 500, 47% between 500 and 599, 25% between 600 and 699, and 4% between 700 and 800; Writing--36% below 500, 49% between 500 and 599, 14% between 600 and 699, and 1% between 700 and 800. The ACT scores were 25% below 21, 32% between 21 and 23, 26% between 24 and 26, 10% between 27 and 28, and 7% above 28. 60% of the current freshmen were in the top fifth of their class; 82% were in the top two fifths. 24 freshmen graduated first in their class. **Admissions Contact:** Dr. Alan Yang, Interim Director of Admissions and Records. E-Mail: *ar-info@hawaii.edu* Web: *www.manoa@hawaii.edu*

FINANCIAL AID: In 2014-2015, 66% of all full-time freshmen and 59% of continuing full-time students received some form of financial aid. 38% of all full-time freshmen and 42% of continuing full-time students received need-based aid. The average freshman award was $11,914. Need-based scholarships or need-based grants averaged $9,133 ($14,050 maximum); need-based self-help aid (loans and jobs) averaged $3,246 ($7,700 maximum); non-need-based athletic scholarships averaged $10,460 ($16,900 maximum); and other non-need-based awards and non-need-based scholarships averaged $8,863 ($28,019 maximum). 27% of undergraduate students work part-time. Average annual earnings from campus work are $3211. The average financial indebtedness of the 2014 graduate was $17,447. The FAFSA and the college's own financial statement are required. The deadline for filing freshman financial aid applications for fall entry is March 1.

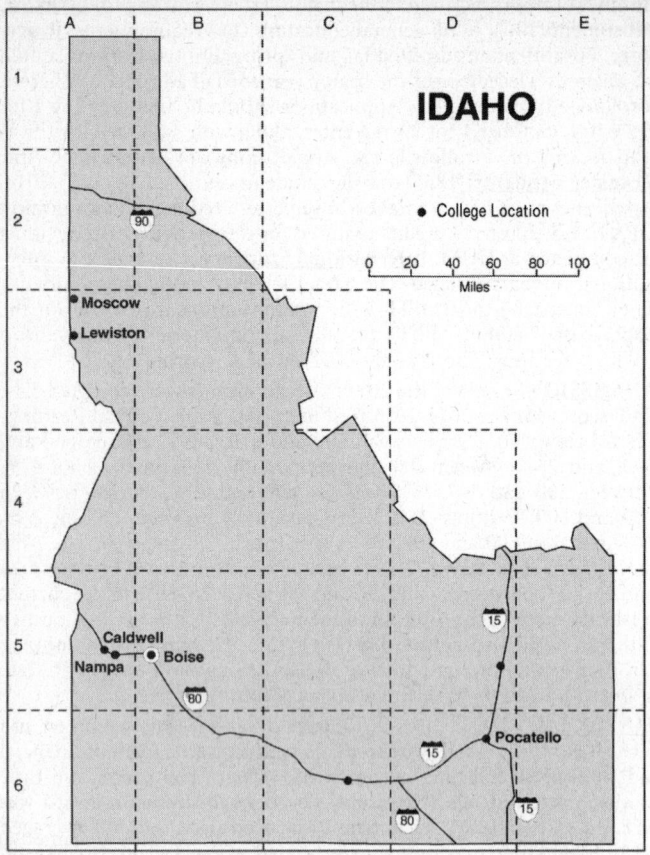

IDAHO

• College Location

0   20   40   60   80   100
            Miles

Moscow
Lewiston

Caldwell
Nampa   Boise

Pocatello

BOISE STATE UNIVERSITY (*The complete profile is made available exclusively on our website, www.barronspac.com*)

COLLEGE OF IDAHO   A-5
www.collegeofidaho.edu

Caldwell, ID 83605	
	(208) 459-5305
	(800) 224-3246
Fax: (208) 459-5757	Email: admissions@collegeofidaho.edu
Full-time: 418 men, 585 women	Faculty: 75; IIB, --$
Part-time: 20 men, 19 women	Ph.D.s: 85%
Graduate: 2 men, 15 women	Student/Faculty: 12 to 1
Year: other	Tuition: $19,750
Room & Board: $8252	Freshman Class: 1388 applied, 901 accepted, 292 enrolled
SAT CR/M/W: 545/540/525 ACT: 24	CEEB CODE: 4060
Application Deadline: July 15	COMPETITIVE+

The College of Idaho, founded in 1891, is a private institution offering degree programs in liberal arts education and the sciences. The college runs on a 13-4-13 calendar, with a 6-week intercession. Figures in the above capsule and in this profile are approximate. In addition to regional accreditation, C of I has baccalaureate program accreditation with NASDTEC. The 50-acre campus is in a small town 25 miles west of Boise. Including any residence halls, there are 21 buildings.

STUDENT LIFE: 83% of undergraduates are from Idaho. Others are from 28 states, 53 foreign countries, and Canada. 55% are White; 14% Hispanic; 11% Foreign. **Male To Female Ratio:** 1.4:1. The average age of freshmen is 18; all undergraduates, 20. 17% do not continue beyond their first year; 64% remain to graduate. **Housing:** 668 students can be accommodated in college housing, which includes single-sex and coed dorms, on-campus apartments, and off-campus apartments, an honors residence hall and special lifestyle floors (sub-

stance free, etc). On-campus housing is guaranteed for the freshman year only, is available on a first-come, first-served basis, and is available on a lottery system for upperclassmen. 62% of students live on campus; of those, 65% remain on campus on weekends. All students may keep cars.

FACULTY/CLASSROOMS: 55% of faculty are male; 45% are female. All teach undergraduates. No introductory courses are taught by graduate students.

PROGRAMS OF STUDY: C of I confers B.A., and B.S. degrees. Master's degrees are also awarded. Bachelor's degrees are awarded in AGRICULTURE (environmental studies), BIOLOGICAL SCIENCE (biology/biological science), BUSINESS (accounting, business administration and management, and international economics), COMMUNICATIONS AND THE ARTS (art, creative writing, literature, music, music theory and composition, Spanish, and theatre arts), COMPUTER AND PHYSICAL SCIENCE (chemistry and mathematics), EDUCATION (education, elementary education, and physical education), ENGINEERING AND ENVIRONMENTAL DESIGN (preengineering), HEALTH PROFESSIONS (clinical science, exercise science, health, nursing, pharmacy, and speech pathology/audiology), SOCIAL SCIENCE (anthropology, history, philosophy, political science/government, psychology, and religion). Biology, business, and psychology have the largest enrollments.

ACTIVITIES: 15% of men belong to 3 national fraternities; 22% of women belong to 1 local and 3 national sororities. There are 33 groups on campus, including international indoor soccer, math club and men's lacrosse, art, band, cheerleading, chess, choir, chorale, chorus, Coyote cinemas, dance, debate, drama, environmental, ethnic, forensics, gay, honors, international, jazz band, literary magazine, musical theater, newspaper, pep band, political, professional, religious, social, social service, student government, and yearbook. Popular campus events include Spring Fling, Coyote Connection, Taste of Harvest and Winterfest. **Sports:** There are 8 intercollegiate sports for men and 10 for women, and 7 intramural sports for men and 7 for women. Facilities include The J.A. Albertson Activities Center is the home of The College of Idaho athletics and the center for student recreation on campus. The Activities Center serves as the arena for all C of I's men's and women's basketball and volleyball home contests, and has been the host of numerous IDHSAA basketball tournaments. In addition to basketball and volleyball, the Activities Center has a full service weight room, athletic training facility, a 25-yard swimming pool, dance room, and a rock climbing wall. The College plays its home football and soccer games at 5,000 seat Simplot Stadium, two blocks from campus - a facility that is maintained by the City of Caldwell. The College has also partnered with the City of Caldwell on Wolfe Field, the only synthetic turf baseball field in Idaho. Home tennis matches are played on campus on the all-weather Laura Moore Cunningham Courts, while softball games are played at Symms Fields on the C of I campus. **Graduates:** The most popular majors were business (23%), biology (and related programs) (20%), and history (9%). 3 companies recruited on campus in 2013-2014. In an average class, 50% graduate in 4 years or less, 60% graduate in 5 years or less, and 64% graduate in 6 years or less.

SERVICES: Counseling and information services are available, as is tutoring in most subjects. **Library/Resources:** Computerized library services include interlibrary loans, database searching, Internet access, and Wi-Fi capability. Special learning facilities include an art gallery, natural history museum, planetarium, a rock and mineral collection, and the Robert E. Smylie Archives. **Physically Challenged Students:** 95% of the campus is accessible. Facilities include wheelchair ramps, elevators, special parking, specially equipped restrooms, lowered drinking fountains, special housing. **Special:** Co-op Programs: Idaho State University Dual Degree Doctoral Program in Pharmacy (BS/Pharm.D.), Idaho State University Dual Degree Program in Nursing (BS/BS), Idaho State University Dual Degree in Medical Laboratory Science (BS/BS), Idaho State University Speech-Language Pathology and Audiology (BS/BS), University of Idaho Juris Doctor (BA or BS/JD). In January 2013, faculty are leading month-long study courses in Australia, London, and Idaho's Sawtooth Mountains. The College of Idaho offers two types of off-campus study opportunities: C of I study programs led by faculty for our students. Foreign study opportunities for individual students offered by partner institutions. During the past few years, C of I faculty have led study tours to such places as Australia, China, Florida, France, Greece, Italy, London, Mexico, and Peru. C of I students also can study for a semester or more in more than 57 countries through our partner institutions. Approved Partner Programs for Study Abroad: Arcadia University-Center for Education Abroad, Brethren Colleges Abroad (BCA), Council Study Centers (CIEE), International Studies Abroad, Schiller International University, School for International Training (SIT), University Studies Abroad Consortium, University of Idaho. **Visiting:** There are regularly scheduled orientations for prospective students, student visits include an overnight stay with student hosts, class visitations, personal appointments with financial aid counselors, professors, and coaches, social events, and a campus tour. Individual tours can also be arranged. There are guides for informal visits, visitors may sit in on classes, and stay overnight. To schedule a visit, contact the Visit and Event Coordinator at visitcenter@collegeofidaho.com. **Campus Safety and Security:** Measures include 24-hour foot and vehicle patrol, emergency notification system, self-defense education, and security escort services. There are emergency telephones, lighted pathways/sidewalks, controlled access to dorms/residences, Electronic identification cards to all dorms and certain buildings throughout the campus.

REQUIREMENTS: The SAT or ACT is required. The ACT Optional Writing test is also required. Freshmen applicants who have graduated from high school, presented acceptable GED scores in lieu of a high school record, or met the college's home school policy (see section on home school applicants), and transfer applicants whose college record is of sufficient quality, may be admitted to the college in clear standing. Students not meeting the minimum standard for regular or conditional admission may be admitted to the college on a probational basis. Students may begin the application process any time after the last semester of their junior year in high school. In order to be considered for admission, students should submit the following materials to the Admission Office: An application for admission, official high school transcript, a transcript of any college work attempted, if you are considered for the Boone Program, you will need an on-campus interview with the Dean of Students and Dean of Enrollment, and an official ACT or SAT test scores. While there is no required pattern of high school study necessary for admission, the following combination is strongly recommended: English, 4 years, Language, 3 years, History and Social Science, 4 years, Laboratory Science, 3 years, and Mathematics, 4 years. AP credits are accepted. Important factors in the admissions decision are leadership record, advanced placement or honors courses, evidence of special talent, recommendations by school officials, personality/intangible qualities, extracurricular activities record, recommendations by alumni, geographical diversity, ability to finance college education, and parents or siblings attended your school.In order to earn the BA or BS degree, students must complete 124 credits, to include at least one major and three minors, covering all four PEAKs: Humanities and Fine Arts, Natural Sciences and Mathematics, Social Sciences and History, Professional Studies and Enhancement. Beyond the majors and minors chosen from the four PEAKs above, students must complete the following: The First-Year Seminar- This requirement covers the essential elements of academic inquiry: analytical reading, critical thinking, and well-reasoned writing Pre-modern Civilization- This requirement provides students with exposure to pre-1800 historical developments that form the foundation of modern systems of thought and ideals of education, thus conveying essential knowledge of the basic dimensions of Western or World intellectual cultures Liberal Arts Expectations- students are expected to engage in each of the areas listed below as part of their academic program: Writing, History, Mathematics, Natural Science, Foreign Language, Social Science, Literature, Philosophy/Religion, Fine Arts, and Cultural Diversity.GPA Requirements: A grade-point average of at least 2.00 (a) in The College of Idaho record and (b) in the entire undergraduate record. A grade-point average of at least 2.00 in the major field (a) in The College of Idaho record and (b) in the entire undergraduate record. A grade-point average of at least 2.00 in all minors. **Procedure:** Freshmen are admitted fall and spring. Entrance exams should be taken by the fall of the senior year. There are early admissions, deferred admissions, and rolling admissions plans. Early decision applications should be filed by November 15;

regular applications, by July 15 for fall entry; December 1 for winter entry; and January 15 for spring entry. Notification of early decision is sent December 15; regular decision, March 15. Applications are accepted on-line. **Transfer Students:** 52 transfer students enrolled in 2013-2014. Students who have already completed at least 28 semester credits or 42 quarter credits of continuous enrollment at accredited colleges or universities will be considered for admission on the basis of that academic record (rather than the secondary school record) provided they have a cumulative GPA of 2.0 or better. Transfer applicants should submit an application for admission and an official high school transcript, as well as official transcripts from all post-secondary institutions attended. A one to two page essay/personal statement and faculty evaluation is required. The transfer application deadline is August 1. Any applications submitted after this date will be considered by petition only. 30 of 124 credits required for the bachelor's degree must be completed at C of I. **International Students:** There are 107 international students enrolled. The school actively recruits these students. They must take the TOEFL with a minimum score of 550 on the paper-based TOEFL (PBT) or 79 on the Internet-based version (iBT), or take the IELTS language proficiency. They must also take the SAT or ACT.

ADMISSIONS: 65% of the 2014-2015 applicants were accepted. The SAT scores for the 2014-2015 freshman class were: Critical Reading--33% below 500, 30% between 500 and 599, 23% between 600 and 699, and 13% between 700 and 800; Math--33% below 500, 38% between 500 and 599, 27% between 600 and 699, and 3% between 700 and 800; Writing--39% below 500, 35% between 500 and 599, 24% between 600 and 699, and 2% between 700 and 800. The ACT scores were 20% below 21, 23% between 21 and 23, 27% between 24 and 26, 14% between 27 and 28, and 16% above 28. 46% of the current freshmen were in the top fifth of their class; 80% were in the top two fifths. **Admissions Contact:** Brian Bava, Dean of Enrollment Management. E-Mail: *admissions@collegeofidaho.edu* Web: *www.collegeofidaho.edu*

FINANCIAL AID: In 2014-2015, 98% of all full-time freshmen and 96% of continuing full-time students received some form of financial aid. 76% of all full-time freshmen and 71% of continuing full-time students received need-based aid. The average freshman award was $24,707. Need-based scholarships or need-based grants averaged $7,630; need-based self-help aid (loans and jobs) averaged $3,969; non-need-based athletic scholarships averaged $3,676; and other non-need-based awards and non-need-based scholarships averaged $13,304. 40% of undergraduate students work part-time. Average annual earnings from campus work are $792. The average financial indebtedness of the 2014 graduate was $27,000. The FAFSA and the college's own financial statement are required. The priority date for freshman financial aid applications for fall entry is February 15.

IDAHO STATE UNIVERSITY — D-6
www.isu.edu

Pocatello, ID 83209 — (208) 282-2475

Fax: (208) 282-4511

Full-time: 3657 men, 3784 women
Part-time: 1928 men, 2774 women
Graduate: 906 men, 1160 women
Year: semesters, summer session
Room & Board: $5838

Email: rosenico@isu.edu
Faculty: n/av
Ph.D.s: n/av
Student/Faculty: 16 to 1
Tuition: $6070 ($17,870)
Freshman Class: 3184 applied, 2925 accepted, 1705 enrolled

SAT CR/M/W: 528/530/515 ACT: 22
Application Deadline: August 1

CEEB CODE: 4355
COMPETITIVE

Idaho State University, founded in 1901, is a public institution offering programs in the liberal arts and sciences, business, education, engineering, and health professions. Figures in the above capsule and in this profile are approximate. There are 10 undergraduate schools and one graduate school. In addition to regional accreditation, ISU has baccalaureate program accreditation with AACSB, ABET, ACPE, ADA, CSWE, NASM, and NCATE. The 1100-acre campus is in an urban area 150 miles north of Salt Lake City. Including any residence halls, there are 100 buildings.

STUDENT LIFE: 90% of undergraduates are from Idaho. Others are from 48 states, 62 foreign countries, and Canada. 95% are from public schools. 77% are White. 53% claim no religious affiliation; 23% Latter-day Saints (Mormon). **Male To Female Ratio:** 1.2:1. The average age of freshmen is 20; all undergraduates, 25. **Housing:** 1214 students can be accommodated in college housing, which includes single-sex and coed dorms, on-campus apartments, and married student housing. In addition, there are special-interest houses, Graduate students housing, and a new apartment/classroom/meeting place/ food court complex. On-campus housing is available on a first-come and first-served basis. 92% of students commute. Alcohol is not permitted. All students may keep cars.

FACULTY/CLASSROOMS: 53% of faculty are male; 47% are female. No introductory courses are taught by graduate students. The average class size in an introductory lecture is 19 and in a laboratory is 14.

PROGRAMS OF STUDY: ISU confers B.A., B.S., B.A.G.S., B.A.S., B.A.T., B.B.A., B.F.A., B.M., B.M.E., B.U.S., H.B.A., H.B.B.A., H.B.F.A., B.S.H.S. and H.B.S. degrees. Associate, Master's, and Doctoral degrees are also awarded. Bachelor's degrees are awarded in BIOLOGICAL SCIENCE (biochemistry, biology/biological science, botany, ecology, microbiology, and zoology), BUSINESS (accounting, banking and finance, business administration and management, business data processing, human resources, insurance, management information systems, management science, and marketing/retailing/ merchandising), COMMUNICATIONS AND THE ARTS (art, communications, communication science, dramatic arts, English, French, German, music, music performance, and Spanish), COMPUTER AND PHYSICAL SCIENCE (chemistry, computer programming, computer science, geology, geoscience, information sciences and systems, mathematics, physics, statistics, and web services), EDUCATION (early childhood education, elementary education, health education, health information management, music education, physical education, secondary education, and specific learning disabilities), ENGINEERING AND ENVIRONMENTAL DESIGN (aircraft mechanics, automotive technology, civil engineering, civil engineering technology, computer technology, construction technology, electrical/electronics engineering, electromechanical technology, energy management technology, environmental science, graphic arts technology, laser electro-optics technology, manufacturing technology, mechanical engineering, nuclear engineering, and welding engineering), HEALTH PROFESSIONS (dental hygiene, emergency medical technologies, health, health care administration, health science, medical laboratory science, medical technology, nursing, physical therapy assistant, radiological science, and speech pathology/ audiology), SOCIAL SCIENCE (anthropology, culinary arts, dietetics, early childhood studies, economics, family/consumer studies, fire services administration, history, international studies, interpreter for the deaf, law enforcement and corrections, liberal arts/general studies, paralegal studies, philosophy, political science/government, psychology, social work, and sociology). Nursing, psychology and biology have the largest enrollments.

ACTIVITIES: 1% of men belong to 3 local and 3 national fraternities; 1% of women belong to 2 local and 3 national sororities. There are 156 groups on campus, including band, cheerleading, chess, choir, chorale, chorus, computers, dance, debate, drama, drill team, ethnic, gay, honors, international, jazz band, marching band, musical theater, newspaper, opera, pep band, photography, political, professional, radio and TV, religious, social, student government, symphony, and yearbook. Popular campus events include International Festivals, Tribal Events, Rodeo and Concerts. **Sports:** There are 5 intercollegiate sports for men and 8 for women, and 15 intramural sports for men and 14 for women. Facilities include playing fields, a field house, a gym, a recreation center, a swimming pool, tennis courts, an athletic arena, a fitness/wellness center, and facilities for bowling and billiards. **Graduates:** From July 1, 2013 to June 30, 2014, 1118 bachelor's degrees were awarded. The most popular majors were nursing (11%), elementary education (5%), and human resources (5%). 144 companies recruited on campus in 2013-2014.

SERVICES: Counseling and information services are available, as is tutoring in every subject. There is a reader service for the blind, and remedial math, reading, and writing. Sign language interpreters and special equipment are available for hearing-impaired students. **Library/Resources:** The library contains 6.0 million volumes, 2.0 million microform items, 6,170 audio/video tapes/CDs/DVDs, and subscribes to 113,787 periodicals including electronic. Computerized library services include interlibrary loans, database searching, Internet access, and Wi-Fi capability. Special learning facilities include an art gallery, natural history museum, radio station, TV station, an accelerator center, performing arts building, multi-use building (housing, classrooms, food service, shopping, study space, computer lab), RISE building used for special research. **Physically Challenged Students:** All of the campus is accessible. Facilities include wheelchair ramps, elevators, special parking, specially equipped restrooms, lowered drinking fountains, lowered telephones, special housing. **Special:** ISU participates in the Idaho Dental Education Program and several other medical co-op programs. Students may cross-register through the Western Undergraduate Exchange. ISU also offers on- and off-campus work-study, study abroad in over 50 countries, dual and student-designed majors, internships, credit by challenge exam or for life/military/work experience, nondegree study, and a general studies degree. As many as 16 credits of correspondence study may be applied toward the Bachelor's degree. ISU also offers 4 honor's Bachelor's degrees, a teacher certification program, as well as a joint MS/ BS degree in Chemistry. There are 10 national honor societies, a freshman honors program, and 4 departmental honors programs. **Visiting:** There are regularly scheduled orientations for prospective students, including a meeting with an administration specialist and a campus tour. After the tour, students meet with a faculty member from their desired program of study. There are guides for informal visits, visitors may sit in on classes, and stay overnight. To schedule a visit, contact the Admissions Office at (208) 282-2475. **Campus Safety and Security:** Measures include 24-hour foot and vehicle patrol, emergency notification system, self-defense education, and security escort services. There are shuttle buses, emergency telephones, lighted pathways/sidewalks, controlled access to dorms/ residences, An e-mail bulletin alert service, Reverse 911 available in Pocatello.

REQUIREMENTS: The ACT is required. The SAT is recommended. The SAT and ACT are accepted, but the ACT is preferred. Applicants must be graduates of an accredited secondary school or have a GED. They should prepare with 4 units of English, 3 each of math and science, 2.5 of social studies, 1.5 of health and humanities, and 1 of foreign language. A GPA of 2.3 is required. AP and CLEP credits are accepted. Students must satisfy general education requirements in the areas of written and spoken English, math, biological and physical sciences, fine arts, literature, philosophy, U.S. and non-U.S. history, government/economics, foreign language, psychology, anthropology, and sociology. General education courses that fulfill specific goals must be taken. To graduate, students must complete 120 credit hours, including 24 to 50 in the major, with a minimum GPA of 2.0. **Procedure:** Freshmen are admitted fall, spring, and summer. Entrance exams should be taken mid junior year or early in the senior year. There are deferred admissions and rolling admissions plans. Applications should be filed by August 1 for fall entry; December 1 for spring entry, along with a $40 fee. Applications are accepted on-line. **Transfer Students:** 500 transfer students enrolled in 2013-2014. Applicants must submit a final, official transcript from each college attended. At least 14 credit hours with a minimum GPA of 2.0 is required; students with fewer credit hours are subject to freshman admission requirements. Applicants with fewer than 25 credits must submit high school transcripts. 32 of 120 credits required for the bachelor's degree must be completed at ISU. **International Students:** There are 499 international students enrolled. The school actively recruits these students. They must take the TOEFL with a minimum score of 500 on the paper-based TOEFL (PBT) or 61 on the Internet-based version (iBT), or IELTS. U.S. graduates with A or B in English are exempt as students who complete ELS level 112.

ADMISSIONS: 92% of the 2014-2015 applicants were accepted. The SAT scores for the 2014-2015 freshman class were: Critical Reading--42% below 500, 32% between 500 and 599, 21% between 600 and 699, and 6% between 700 and 800; Math--36% below 500, 40% between 500 and 599, 21% between 600 and 699, and 3% between 700 and 800; Writing--40% below 500, 43% between 500 and 599, 14% between 600 and 699, and 3% between 700 and 800. The ACT scores were 44% below 21, 25% between 21 and 23, 18% between 24 and 26, 7% between 27 and 28, and 7% above 28. 23% of the current freshmen were in the top fifth of their class; 48% were in the top two fifths. 22 freshmen graduated first in their class. **Admissions Contact:** Matthew Kroeger, Director of Recruitment and Admissions. E-Mail: *admiss@isu.edu* Web: *www.isu.edu*

FINANCIAL AID: In 2014-2015, 64% of all full-time freshmen and 64% of continuing full-time students received some form of financial aid. 50% of all full-time freshmen and 48% of continuing full-time students received need-based aid. The average freshman award was $8,971. Need-based scholarships or need-based grants averaged $4,559; need-based self-help aid (loans and jobs) averaged $3,159; non-need-based athletic scholarships averaged $8,144; other non-need-based awards and non-need-based scholarships averaged $2,586; and $3,100 from other forms of aid. The average financial indebtedness of the 2014 graduate was $24,602. The FAFSA is required. The deadline for filing freshman financial aid applications for fall entry is February 20.

LEWIS-CLARK STATE COLLEGE   A-3
www.lcsc.edu

Lewiston, ID 83501	(208) 792-2210
	(800) 933-LCSC
Fax: (208) 792-2876	Email: admissions@lcsc.edu
Full-time: 960 men, 1315 women	Faculty: 134; IIB, --$
Part-time: 415 men, 805 women	Ph.D.s: 71%
Graduate: n/av	Student/Faculty: 17 to 1
Year: semesters, summer session	Tuition: $4092 ($11,382)
Room & Board: $3860	Freshman Class: n/av
SAT or ACT: required	CEEB CODE: 4385
Application Deadline: n/av	COMPETITIVE

Lewis-Clark State College, founded in 1893 and today part of the Idaho Higher Education System, offers programs in the arts and sciences, business, education, nursing, and preprofessional and technical training. It is named for the famed explorers, who once camped near what is now the campus. Figures in the above capsule and in this profile are approximate. There are 8 undergraduate schools. In addition to regional accreditation, Lewis-Clark has baccalaureate program accreditation with AACSB, NASDTEC, NCATE, and NLN. The 44-acre campus is in an urban area 100 miles southeast of Spokane. Including any residence halls, there are 29 buildings.

STUDENT LIFE: 86% of undergraduates are from Idaho. Others are from 20 states, 30 foreign countries, and Canada. 82% are White. **Male To Female Ratio:** 1.5:1. The average age of freshmen is 21; all undergraduates, 25. 46% do not continue beyond their first year; 28% remain to graduate. **Housing:** 300 students can be accommodated in college housing, which includes single-sex and coed dorms, off-campus apartments, and married student housing. In addition, there are honors houses and language houses. On-campus housing is available on a first-come and first-served basis. 91% of students commute. Alcohol is not permitted. All students may keep cars.

FACULTY/CLASSROOMS: 58% of faculty are male; 42% are female. All teach undergraduates. No introductory courses are taught by graduate students. The average class size in an introductory lecture is 33 and in a laboratory is 25.

PROGRAMS OF STUDY: Lewis-Clark confers B.A., B.S., B. Applied Sc., B. Applied Tech., B.S.N. and B.S.W. degrees. Associate degrees are also awarded. Bachelor's degrees are awarded in BIOLOGICAL SCIENCE (biology/biological science), BUSINESS (business administration and management), COMMUNICATIONS AND THE ARTS (communications and English), COMPUTER AND PHYSICAL SCIENCE (chemistry, computer science, geoscience, mathematics, and natural sciences), EDUCATION (elementary education and secondary education), HEALTH PROFESSIONS (nursing), SOCIAL SCIENCE (criminal justice, history, liberal arts/general studies, physical fitness/movement, psychology, social science, and social work). Education, business, and nursing are the strongest academically, and have the largest enrollments.

ACTIVITIES: There are no fraternities or sororities. There are 46 groups on campus, including and departmental., art, chess, choir, chorale, chorus, computers, dance, debate, drama, ethnic, honors,

international, jazz band, literary magazine, musical theater, newspaper, orchestra, political, professional, radio and TV, religious, social, and student government. Popular campus events include Artists Series and Dogwood Festival. **Sports:** There are 5 intercollegiate sports for men and 5 for women, and 8 intramural sports for men and 7 for women. Facilities include a gym, indoor tennis courts, and a baseball field. **Graduates:** From July 1, 2013 to June 30, 2014, 299 bachelor's degrees were awarded. The most popular majors were business (25%), justice studies (15%), and nursing (14%). Of the 2013 graduating class, 8% were enrolled in graduate school within 6 months of graduation.

SERVICES: Counseling and information services are available, as is tutoring in every subject. There is a reader service for the blind, and remedial math, reading, and writing. **Library/Resources:** The library contains 253,000 volumes, 53,000 microform items, 7,000 audio/video tapes/CDs/DVDs, and subscribes to 4,000 periodicals including electronic. Computerized library services include interlibrary loans and database searching. Special learning facilities include an art gallery, planetarium, radio station, TV station, an educational technology center. **Physically Challenged Students:** 99% of the campus is accessible. Facilities include wheelchair ramps, elevators, special parking, specially equipped restrooms, and special class scheduling. **Special:** Lewis-Clark offers cooperative programs and cross-registration with 3 Idaho universities, on-campus internships, work-study programs, student-designed majors, nondegree study, and pass/fail options. The college grants credit for military experience. There are also between-semester and weekend academic programs, and flexible scheduling in a variety of programs. A 3-2 engineering degree is available at Boise or Idaho State Universities. There are 1 national honor societies and a freshman honors program. **Visiting:** There are regularly scheduled orientations for prospective students, including STAR (Student Advising and Registration), and Warrior Discovery Day. There are guides for informal visits, visitors may sit in on classes, and stay overnight. To schedule a visit, contact the Office of Recruitment and Retention at (208) 792-2378. **Campus Safety and Security:** Measures include 24-hour foot and vehicle patrol, self-defense education, and security escort services. There are shuttle buses and lighted pathways/sidewalks.

REQUIREMENTS: The SAT or ACT is required. Lewis-Clark has a liberal admissions policy, but students must be high school graduates or present a GED certificate. They must have fulfilled requirements in English, math, social and natural sciences, fine arts, and speech, with a minimum GPA of 2.0. A GPA of 2.0 is required. AP and CLEP credits are accepted.Students must earn 128 credit hours, including 38 to 40 in the core curriculum and 48 in their major, with a minimum GPA of 2.0 to graduate. **Procedure:** Freshmen are admitted to all sessions. Entrance exams should be taken before registration. There are early admissions, deferred admissions, and rolling admissions plans. Application deadlines are open. Application fee is $35. Applications are accepted on-line. **Transfer Students:** 389 transfer students enrolled in 2013-2014. Applicants who do not have a minimum GPA of 2.0 must submit standardized test scores. 32 of 128 credits required for the bachelor's degree must be completed at Lewis-Clark. **International Students:** There are 94 international students enrolled. The school actively recruits these students. They must take the TOEFL.

ADMISSIONS: 5 freshmen graduated first in their class. **Admissions Contact:** Steven J. Bussolini, Director of Admission and Market Development. E-Mail: *admissions@lcsc.edu* Web: *www.lcsc.edu*

FINANCIAL AID: In 2014-2015, 68% of all full-time freshmen and 62% of continuing full-time students received some form of financial aid. 52% of all full-time freshmen and 50% of continuing full-time students received need-based aid. The average freshman award was $4,033. Need-based scholarships or need-based grants averaged $2,781 ($4,500 maximum); need-based self-help aid (loans and jobs) averaged $2,652 ($6,625 maximum); non-need-based athletic scholarships averaged $4,485 ($8,562 maximum); and other non-need-based awards and non-need-based scholarships averaged $2,873. 10% of undergraduate students work part-time. Average annual earnings from campus work are $1360. Lewis-Clark is a member of CSS. The FAFSA is required. The priority date for freshman financial aid applications for fall entry is March 1.

NORTHWEST NAZARENE UNIVERSITY   A-5
www.nnu.edu

Nampa, ID 83686	**(208) 467-8950**
	(877) NNU-4-YOU
Fax: (208) 467-8645	**Email:** admissions@nnu.edu
Full-time: n/av	**Faculty:** n/av
Part-time: n/av	**Ph.D.s:** 72%
Graduate: n/av	**Student/Faculty:** 13 to 1
Year: semesters, summer session	**Tuition:** $34,000
Room & Board: n/av	**Freshman Class:** 1099 applied, 1150 accepted, 271 enrolled
SAT CR/M/W: 510/540/510 **ACT:** 22	**CEEB CODE:** 4544
Application Deadline: August 15	**COMPETITIVE**

Northwest Nazarene University, founded in 1913, a comprehensive Christian university, offers over 60 areas of study, 19 master's degrees in seven different disciplines and one doctoral degree. The University also offers programs online as well as in Boise, Idaho Falls, McCall, Twin Falls and in cooperation with programs in 10 countries. Figures in the above capsule and in this profile are approximate. There is 1 undergraduate school and 1 graduate school. In addition to regional accreditation, NNU has baccalaureate program accreditation with ACBSP, CSWE, NASM, NCATE, CACREP, CCNE, and NACEP. The 90-acre campus is in a small town 20 miles west of Boise. Including any residence halls, there are 34 buildings.

STUDENT LIFE: 57% of undergraduates are from Idaho. Others are from 30 states, 28 foreign countries, and Canada. 73% are White. 66% are Protestant; 12% claim no religious affiliation. **Male To Female Ratio:** Is 1:1. The average age of freshmen is 19; all undergraduates, 22. 28% do not continue beyond their first year; 48% remain to graduate. **Housing:** College-sponsored housing includes single-sex dorms, on-campus apartments, and married student housing. On-campus housing is guaranteed for all 4 years. 51% of students live on campus; of those, 80% remain on campus on weekends. Alcohol is not permitted. All students may keep cars.

FACULTY/CLASSROOMS: 57% of faculty are male; 43% are female. No introductory courses are taught by graduate students.

PROGRAMS OF STUDY: NNU confers B.A., and B.S. degrees. Master's and doctoral degrees are also awarded. Bachelor's degrees are awarded in BIOLOGICAL SCIENCE (biochemistry and biology/biological science), BUSINESS (accounting, business administration and management, business administration, mgmt, operations, and recreation and leisure services), COMMUNICATIONS AND THE ARTS (art, communication, English, graphic design, music, and Spanish), COMPUTER AND PHYSICAL SCIENCE (chemistry, computer information systems, computer science, mathematics, and physics), EDUCATION (art education, Christian education, education of the exceptional child, elementary education, English education, mathematics education, music education, physical education, recreation education, and secondary education), ENGINEERING AND ENVIRONMENTAL DESIGN (computer graphics, engineering, and engineering physics), HEALTH PROFESSIONS (nursing), SOCIAL SCIENCE (biblical studies, criminal justice, cultural studies/critical theory and analysis, history, international studies, liberal arts/general studies, ministries, philosophy and religion, political science/government, psychology, social work, and youth ministry). Nursing, engineering, biology, chemistry, business and graphic design are the strongest academically. Nursing, engineering, biology/chemistry and business have the largest enrollments.

ACTIVITIES: There are no fraternities or sororities. There are 50 groups on campus, including American marketing association, art, band, cheerleading, choir, chorale, chorus, computers, debate, drama, environmental, ethnic, film, forensics, honors, international, jazz band, literary magazine, musical theater, newspaper, orchestra, pep band, photography, political, professional, radio and TV, religious, social, social service, student government, students in free enterprise/enactus, symphony, and yearbook. Popular campus events include Welcome Week, Week One and Spiritual Emphasis Week. **Sports:** There are 6 intercollegiate sports for men and 6 for women, and 7 intramural sports for men and 7 for women. Facilities include baseball field, 2 soccer fields, outdoor basketball, tennis, sand volleyball courts, track-and-field facility, golf, cross country, field house, park, and a softball field. **Graduates:** From July 1, 2013 to June 30, 2014, 280 bachelor's degrees were awarded. The most popular majors were business (19%), nursing (16%), and applied studies (9%). 100 companies recruited on campus in 2013-2014. In an average class, 49% graduate in 6 years or less.

SERVICES: Counseling and information services are available, as is tutoring in every subject. There is remedial math, reading, and writing. **Library/Resources:** Computerized library services include interlibrary loans, database searching, Internet access, and Wi-Fi capability. Special learning facilities include an art gallery, radio station, an educational media center. **Physically Challenged Students:** Facilities include wheelchair ramps, elevators, special parking, specially equipped restrooms, special class scheduling, lowered drinking fountains, lowered telephones, special housing, and alternate testing and evaluation methods. **Special:** NNU offers cross-registration with other Nazarene schools and study abroad in 14 countries. The university also offers internships, which are required in many majors, a work-study program, a general studies degree, dual and student-designed majors, and credit for military experience (Army ROTC program). Adult and Professional programs are offered in business, education and religion. There are 4 national honor societies, a freshman honors program, and 3 departmental honors programs. **Visiting:** There are regularly scheduled orientations for prospective students, including overnight stay in a dorm. campus tour, class attendance, financial and admission counseling, meetings with professor and coaches, and music and athletic try-outs. There are guides for informal visits, visitors may sit in on classes, and stay overnight. To schedule a visit, contact the Campus Visit Coordinator at (208) 467-8000. **Campus Safety and Security:** Measures include 24-hour foot and vehicle patrol, emergency notification system, and security escort services. There are emergency telephones, lighted pathways/sidewalks, controlled access to dorms/residences, a professional security company, student lock-up-unlock and walk-around-campus teams, and a city police substation.

REQUIREMENTS: The SAT or ACT is required. Applicants should be graduates of an accredited secondary school; the GED may also be accepted. For standard admission, students must fulfill 2 of the 3 following requirements: graduate with a 2.5 (or higher) GPA on a 4.0 scale, rank in the top 50% of their graduating class, or have an ACT composite score of 18 or a combined score of 870 on the Math and Critical Reasoning sections of the SAT. Provisional admission may be available for students who do not meet the above requirements. Applicants should prepare with 4 years of English, 3 each of math, science, and history or social science, and 2 of foreign language. NNU requires applicants to be in the upper 50% of their class. A GPA of 2.5 is required. AP and CLEP credits are accepted. All students must complete 124 semester credits, of which 43 must be upper division. Students must show competency in communication and language skills, have a 2.0 GPA, demonstrate math proficiency, complete a major field of study, and take a comprehensive exam. In addition, each student must complete general education requirements, which are divided into three categories: abilities (17 credits of English, communications, kinesiology, math, and humanities courses), contextual disciplines (15 credits of bible, theology, philosophy, and history courses as well as a cross-cultural experience), and explorations (23 credits of upper-division bible literature or theology, humanities, science, and social sciences electives). The number of hours required varies per major, as do senior internships and projects. **Procedure:** Freshmen are admitted fall, spring, and summer. Entrance exams should be taken early in the senior year. There are early admissions and rolling admissions plans. Early decision applications should be filed by December 15; regular applications, by August 15 for fall entry; and December 15 for winter entry, along with a $25 fee. Notification is sent on a rolling basis. Applications are accepted on-line. **Transfer Students:** 78 transfer students enrolled in 2013-2014. Students wishing to transfer to NNU must have completed 28 college or university semester credits and have a cumulative GPA of at least 2.0 and be in good academic standing at their previous institution. Students below the required GPA may be accepted provisionally at the discretion of the Admissions Committee. Students who have earned the equivalent of 12 semester credits may be admitted as transfer students. Official transcripts from all colleges previously attended must be submitted. 24 of 124 credits required for the bachelor's degree must be completed at NNU. **International Students:** There are 28 international students enrolled. The school actively recruits these students. They must take the TOEFL with a minimum score of 500 on the paper-based TOEFL (PBT) or 61 on the Internet-based version (iBT). They must also take the SAT or ACT, scoring 18.

ADMISSIONS: The SAT scores for the 2014-2015 freshman class were: Critical Reading--36% below 500, 38% between 500 and 599, 21% between 600 and 699, and 5% between 700 and 800; Math--32% below 500, 46% between 500 and 599, 20% between 600 and 699, and 2% between 700 and 800; Writing--45% below 500, 35% between 500 and 599, 18% between 600 and 699, and 2% between 700 and 800. The ACT scores were 36% below 21, 26% between 21 and 23, 22% between 24 and 26, 9% between 27 and 28, and 7% above 28. There were 43 National Merit finalists. 10 freshmen graduated first in their class. **Admissions Contact:** Shawn Blenker, Director of Admissions. E-Mail: *admissions@nnu.edu* Web: *www.nnu.edu*

FINANCIAL AID: In 2014-2015, 99% of all full-time freshmen students received some form of financial aid or need-based aid. The average freshman award was $17,934. Need-based scholarships or need-based grants averaged $3,990 ($8,100 maximum); need-based self-help aid (loans and jobs) averaged $3,872; and non-need-based athletic scholarships averaged $6,257 ($21,632 maximum). 66% of undergraduate students work part-time. Average annual earnings from campus work are $883. The average financial indebtedness of the 2014 graduate was $29,500. The FAFSA is required. The priority date for freshman financial aid applications for fall entry is March 1.

UNIVERSITY OF IDAHO   A-3
www.uidaho.edu

Moscow, ID 83844   (208) 885-6326
                                           (888) 884-3246
Fax: (208) 885-9119   **Email:** admappl@uidaho.edu
Full-time: 4260 men, 3667 women   **Faculty:** I, --$
Part-time: 717 men, 812 women   **Ph.D.s:** 74%
Graduate: 1349 men, 1029 women   **Student/Faculty:** n/av
Year: semesters, summer session   **Tuition:** $6524 ($20,662)
Room & Board: $8034   **Freshman Class:** 5614
                                      applied, 5172 accepted,
                                      1630 enrolled
SAT CR/M/W: 520/520/500 **ACT:** 22   **CEEB CODE:** 4843
Application Deadline: August 1   **COMPETITIVE**

The University of Idaho, founded in 1889 as a land-grant institution, offers programs in art, architecture, agriculture, business and economics, education, engineering, letters and science, and natural resources, forestry, wildlife, and range sciences. Figures in the above capsule and in this profile are approximate. There are 8 undergraduate schools and 1 graduate school. In addition to regional accreditation, U Idaho has baccalaureate program accreditation with AACSB, ABET, ADA, ASLA, CSAB, FIDER, NAAB, NASAD, NASM, NCATE, NRPA, SAF, and NWCCU. The 1585-acre campus is in a small town 90 miles southeast of Spokane, Washington. Including any residence halls, there are 146 buildings.

STUDENT LIFE: 74% of undergraduates are from Idaho. Others are from 47 states, 40 foreign countries, and Canada. 98% are from public schools. 79% are White. **Male To Female Ratio:** 0.9:1. The average age of freshmen is 18; all undergraduates, 22. 21% do not continue beyond their first year; 54% remain to graduate. **Housing:** 2246 students can be accommodated in college housing, which includes single-sex and coed dorms, on-campus apartments, and married student housing. In addition, there are honors houses, special-interest houses, fraternity houses, sorority houses, Alcohol-free, smoke-free, and living-learning communities. On-campus housing is guaranteed for all 4 years. 61% of students commute. Alcohol is not permitted. All students may keep cars.

FACULTY/CLASSROOMS: 65% of faculty are male; 35% are female. 90% teach undergraduates, 75% do research, and 95% do both. No introductory courses are taught by graduate students. The average class size in an introductory lecture is 30; in a laboratory is 17; and in a regular course is 24.

PROGRAMS OF STUDY: U Idaho confers B.A., B.F.A., B.G.S., B.I.D., B.Mus., B.S., B.S.A.L.S., B.S.A.V.S., B.S.Ag.Econ., B.S.Ag.Ed., B.S.Ag.L.S., B.S.Arch., B.S.Art.Ed., B.S.B.A.E., B.S.Biochem., B.S.Bus., B.S.C.E., B.S.C.S., B.S.Ch.E., B.S.Comp.E., B.S.Dan.,B.S.E.E., B.S.Ecol.Cons.Biol., B.S.Ed., B.S.Env.S., B.S.Early.Chdhd.Dev.Ed., B.S.F.C.S., B.S.F.S., B.S.Fire.Ecol.Mgmt., B.S.Fish.Res., B.S.For.Prod., B.S.For.Res., B.S.I.S., B.S.L.A., B.S.M.B.B., B.S.M.E., B.S.M.S.E., B.S.Microbiol., B.S.P.E., B.S.Rangeland Ecol.-Mgt., B.S.Rec., B.S.Res.Rc., B.S.Tech. and B.S.Wildl.Res. degrees. Master's and doctoral degrees are also awarded. Bachelor's degrees are awarded in AGRICULTURE (agricultural business management, agricultural communications, agricultural economics, agricultural mechanics, agricultural sciences, agriculture, animal science, conservation and regulation, dairy science, fishing and fisheries, forestry production and processing, forestry and related sciences, horticulture, natural resource management, plant science, range/farm management, soil science, and wildlife management), BIOLOGICAL SCIENCE (biochemistry, biology/biological science, botany, microbiology, and molecular biology), BUSINESS (accounting, business administration and management, business economics, human resources, management information systems, marketing management, marketing/retailing/merchandising, operations management, recreation and leisure services, and sports management), COMMUNICATIONS AND THE ARTS (advertising, animation, apparel design, applied art, applied music, art, broadcasting, creative writing, dance, design, digital communications, dramatic arts, English, English Writing, fine arts, French, journalism, music, music history and appreciation, music performance, music theory and composition, musical theater, public relations, Spanish, studio art, telecommunications, and theater management), COMPUTER AND PHYSICAL SCIENCE (applied mathematics, chemistry, computer science, digital arts/technology, geology, information sciences and systems, mathematics, and physics), EDUCATION (agricultural education, art education, athletic training, business education, education, education administration, elementary education, foreign languages education, general studies, industrial arts education, mathematics education, music education, physical education, recreation education, science education, secondary education, special education, and technical education), ENGINEERING AND ENVIRONMENTAL DESIGN (agricultural engineering, architecture, bioengineering, biomedical engineering, chemical engineering, civil engineering, computer engineering, electrical and computer engineering, electrical/electronics engineering, engineering, environmental engineering, environmental science, geological engineering, interior design, landscape architecture/design, materials engineering, and mechanical engineering), HEALTH PROFESSIONS (clinical science, exercise science, medical technology, movement science, and veterinary science), SOCIAL SCIENCE (American studies, anthropology, child care/child and family studies, counseling/psychology, criminal justice, economics, family/consumer studies, food science, geography, history, human development, interdisciplinary studies, international relations, international studies, Latin American studies, parks and recreation management, philosophy, political science/government, psychology, rural economics, sociology, and textiles and clothing). engineering, natural resources, and business are the strongest academically. Business, engineering, and psychology have the largest enrollments.

ACTIVITIES: 20% of men belong to 17 national fraternities; 20% of women belong to 10 national sororities. There are 191 groups on campus, including art, band, cheerleading, choir, chorale, chorus, computers, dance, drama, drill team, environmental, ethnic, film, gay, honors, international, jazz band, literary magazine, marching band, musical theater, newspaper, opera, orchestra, pep band, photography, political, professional, radio and TV, religious, social, social service, student government, and symphony. Popular campus events include Lionel Hampton Jazz Festival, the Borah Symposium, and Palouse fest, Homecoming, Mom's Weekend and Dad's Weekend. **Sports:** There are 6 intercollegiate sports for men and 8 for women, and 15 intramural sports for men and 16 for women. Facilities include an activity center, a 16,000-seat domed stadium for basketball and football games, indoor and outdoor tracks, a 2-pool swim center, 3 gyms, a 500-seat auditorium, an 18-hole championship golf course, tennis, racquetball, and handball courts, and a student recreation center with a 55-foot climbing wall. **Graduates:** From July 1, 2013 to June 30, 2014, 1981 bachelor's degrees were awarded. The most popular majors were business/marketing (10%), education (10%), and psychology (9%). 250 companies recruited on campus in 2013-2014. In an average class, 1% graduate in 3 years or less, 29% graduate in 4 years or less, 52% graduate in 5 years or less, and 54% graduate in 6 years or less.

SERVICES: Counseling and information services are available, as is tutoring in most subjects. There is a reader service for the blind, and remedial math and writing. There are centers for academic advising and counseling and testing. **Library/Resources:** The 2 libraries contain 1.4 million volumes, 2.6 million microform items, 11,329 audio/video tapes/CDs/DVDs, and subscribe to 25,475 periodicals including electronic. Computerized library services include interlibrary loans, database searching, Internet access, and Wi-Fi capability. Special learning facilities include an art gallery, radio station, TV station, an electron microscopy center, an IQ-Station (virtual reality tool) a lab animal facility, research institutes for water resources, geospacial lab, microelectronics, and aquaculture, university farms, experimental forests, and an arboretum and botanical garden. **Physically Challenged Students:** 87% of the campus is accessible. Facilities include wheelchair ramps, elevators, special parking, specially equipped restrooms, special class scheduling, lowered drinking fountains, lowered telephones, special housing. **Special:** UI offers cooperative programs and cross-registration with Washington State and Idaho State Universities, internships, extensive study-abroad programs, work-study programs, B.A.-B.S. degrees, dual and student-designed majors, a general studies degree, credit for life and work experience, nondegree study, and pass/fail options. There are 11 national honor societies and a freshman honors program. **Visiting:** There are regularly scheduled orientations for prospective students, including a visit with faculty and financial aid personnel, a tour of campus, and an overnight stay in the dorms or Greek houses and a visit to the Recreation Center. There are guides for informal visits, visitors may sit in on classes, and stay overnight. To schedule a visit, contact the Office of Admissions and Campus Visits. **Campus Safety and Security:** Measures include 24-hour foot and vehicle patrol, emergency notification system, and self-defense education. There are shuttle buses, emergency telephones, lighted pathways/sidewalks, controlled access to dorms/residences, the city police department has a campus division, and there is a violence prevention programs office.

REQUIREMENTS: Either the SAT or ACT test are required. Students from accredited high schools must have graduated and completed at least 8 credits in English, 6 each in math and natural science, 5 in social science, 3 in electives, and 2 in humanities/language. Homeschooled students, students from non-accredited high schools, and GED students will have their application for admission referred to a committee for a decision. A GPA of 2.5 is required. AP and CLEP credits are accepted. To graduate, students must complete at least 120 credit hours (128 for some majors), including 36 in upper-division courses and 40 in the major, with a minimum GPA of 2.0. The core curriculum requires a total of 33 to 36 credits in the following categories: communication, natural and applied science, mathematics, statistics, or computer science, humanities/social sciences, and an international course. **Procedure:** Freshmen are admitted to all sessions. Entrance exams should be taken during the junior or senior year of high school. There are deferred admissions and rolling admissions plans. Applications should be filed by August 1 for fall entry; December 15 for spring entry; and May 1 for summer entry, along with a $60 fee. Notification is sent on a rolling basis. Applications are accepted on-line. **Transfer Students:** 665 transfer students enrolled in 2013-2014. Applicants must have completed at least 14 credit hours with a cumulative GPA of at least 2.0. Students transferring from out-of-state schools into the College of Engineering must have a minimum cumulative GPA of 2.8. 32 of 120 credits required for the bachelor's degree must be completed at U Idaho. **International Students:** There are 320 international students enrolled. The school actively recruits these students. They must take the TOEFL with a minimum score of 550 on the paper-based TOEFL (PBT) or 79 on the Internet-based version (iBT). They must also take the SAT or ACT.

ADMISSIONS: 92% of the 2014-2015 applicants were accepted. The SAT scores for the 2014-2015 freshman class were: Critical Reading--40% below 500, 39% between 500 and 599, 17% between 600 and 699, and 4% between 700 and 800; Math--39% below 500, 36% between 500 and 599, 21% between 600 and 699, and 4% between 700 and 800; Writing--46% below 500, 39% between 500 and 599, 13% between 600 and 699, and 2% between 700 and 800. The ACT scores were 31% below 21, 27% between 21 and 23, 20% between 24 and 26, 11% between 27 and 28, and 12% above 28. 34% of the current freshmen were in the top fifth of their class; 61% were in the top two fifths. There were 25 National Merit finalists. 1 freshman graduated first in the class. **Admissions Contact:** Cezar Mesquita, Director, Admissions . E-Mail: *admappl@uidaho.edu* Web: *www.uidaho.edu/admissions*

FINANCIAL AID: In 2014-2015, 66% of all full-time freshmen and 65% of continuing full-time students received some form of financial aid. 53% of all full-time freshmen and 49% of continuing full-time students received need-based aid. The average freshman award was $13,670. Need-based scholarships or need-based grants averaged $4,575; need-based self-help aid (loans and jobs) averaged $5,971; non-need-based athletic scholarships averaged $18,220; and other non-need-based awards and non-need-based scholarships averaged $3,033. 88% of undergraduate students work part-time. The average financial indebtedness of the 2014 graduate was $25,691. U Idaho is a member of CSS. The FAFSA is required. The deadline for filing freshman financial aid applications for fall entry is February 15.

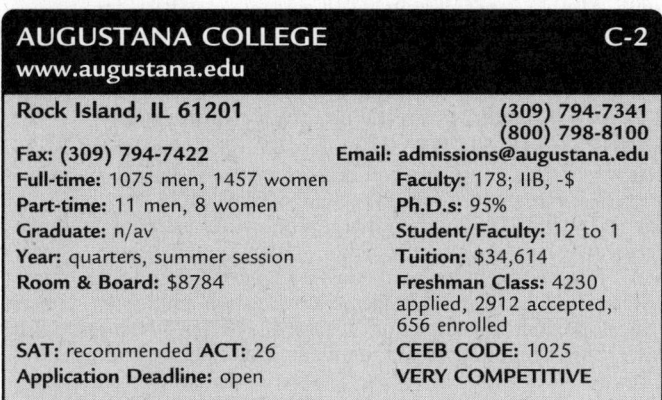

AUGUSTANA COLLEGE   C-2
www.augustana.edu

Rock Island, IL 61201	**(309) 794-7341**
	(800) 798-8100
Fax: (309) 794-7422	Email: admissions@augustana.edu
Full-time: 1075 men, 1457 women	**Faculty:** 178; IIB, -$
Part-time: 11 men, 8 women	**Ph.D.s:** 95%
Graduate: n/av	**Student/Faculty:** 12 to 1
Year: quarters, summer session	**Tuition:** $34,614
Room & Board: $8784	**Freshman Class:** 4230 applied, 2912 accepted, 656 enrolled
SAT: recommended **ACT:** 26	**CEEB CODE:** 1025
Application Deadline: open	**VERY COMPETITIVE**

Augustana College, founded in 1860, is a private liberal arts institution affiliated with the Evangelical Lutheran Church in America. Figures in the above capsule and in this profile are approximate. In addition to regional accreditation, Augustana has baccalaureate program accreditation with NASM and NCATE. The 115-acre campus is in a suburban area 165 miles west of Chicago. Including any residence halls, there are 47 buildings.

STUDENT LIFE: 85% of undergraduates are from Illinois. Others are from 31 states, 24 foreign countries, and Canada. 79% are White. 34% are Protestant; 33% Catholic; 11% unknown denominations. **Male To Female Ratio:** 1.3:1. The average age of freshmen is 18; all undergraduates, 20. 16% do not continue beyond their first year; 78% remain to graduate. **Housing:** 1786 students can be accommodated in college housing, which includes single-sex and coed dorms, on-campus apartments, and off-campus apartments. In addition, there are special-interest houses. On-campus housing is guaranteed for all 4 years. 73% of students live on campus; of those, 75% remain on campus on weekends. Alcohol is not permitted. All students may keep cars.

FACULTY/CLASSROOMS: 52% of faculty are male; 48% are female.

All teach undergraduates, and 60% do both. No introductory courses are taught by graduate students. The average class size in an introductory lecture is 21; in a laboratory is 17; and in a regular course is 20.

PROGRAMS OF STUDY: Augustana confers B.A. degrees. Bachelor's degrees are awarded in BIOLOGICAL SCIENCE (biochemistry and biology/biological science), BUSINESS (accounting, business administration and management, and international business management), COMMUNICATIONS AND THE ARTS (art, art history and appreciation, classics, communications, dramatic arts, English, French, German, music, music performance, Scandinavian languages, Spanish, speech/debate/rhetoric, and studio art), COMPUTER AND PHYSICAL SCIENCE (chemistry, computer science, earth science, geology, mathematics, and physics), EDUCATION (art education, elementary education, music education, physical education, and secondary education), ENGINEERING AND ENVIRONMENTAL DESIGN (engineering physics, landscape architecture/design, and preengineering), HEALTH PROFESSIONS (occupational therapy, premedicine, and speech pathology/audiology), SOCIAL SCIENCE (anthropology, Asian/Oriental studies, economics, geography, history, philosophy, political science/government, psychology, public administration, religion, social work, sociology, and women's studies). Premedicine, business/accounting, and biology have the largest enrollments.

ACTIVITIES: 23% of men belong to 7 local fraternities; 34% of women belong to 7 local sororities. There are 110 groups on campus, including and volunteer, alcohol responsibility, band, cheerleading, choir, chorale, chorus, computers, dance, debate, drama, environmental, ethnic, gay, honors, international, jazz band, literary magazine, musical theater, newspaper, opera, orchestra, pep band, political, professional, radio and TV, religious, social, social service, student government, and symphony. Popular campus events include Messiah performances, Greek Olympics and Humanities Festival. **Sports:** There are 11 intercollegiate sports for men and 10 for women, and 19 intramural sports for men and 18 for women. Facilities include a recreational center with an indoor 200-meter track, courts for basketball, volleyball, racquetball, and tennis, a weight room, and physical conditioning equipment. A phys ed center has courts for basketball, volleyball, racquetball, and badminton, weight and physical conditioning rooms, wrestling facilities, and a swimming pool. There is a lighted field and an all-weather track for football, soccer, and track and field, with stadium seating for 3,500. Facilities also include a baseball field, 10 outdoor tennis courts, and a dance studio. **Graduates:** From July 1, 2013 to June 30, 2014, 521 bachelor's degrees were awarded. The most popular majors were business/marketing (21%), biological/life science (18%), and psychology (8%). 238 companies recruited on campus in 2013-2014. In an average class, 70% graduate in 4 years or less, 76% graduate in 5 years or less, and 78% graduate in 6 years or less. Of the 2013 graduating class, 47% were enrolled in graduate school within 6 months of graduation, and 50% were employed.

SERVICES: Counseling and information services are available, as is tutoring in every subject. There is a reader service for the blind. **Library/Resources:** The 3 libraries contain 209,688 volumes, 78,666 microform items, 2,748 audio/video tapes/CDs/DVDs, and subscribe to 3,067 periodicals including electronic. Computerized library services include interlibrary loans, database searching, Internet access, and Wi-Fi capability. Special learning facilities include an art gallery, natural history museum, radio station, preschool, a center for communicative disorders, geology museum, planetarium/observatory, U.S. geological survey map repository, Swedish immigration research center, 3 outdoor environmental labs, and an educational technology building. **Physically Challenged Students:** 75% of the campus is accessible. Facilities include wheelchair ramps, elevators, special parking, specially equipped restrooms, lowered drinking fountains, lowered telephones, special housing. **Special:** Cooperative degree programs are offered in engineering, environmental management, forestry, landscape architecture, and occupational therapy with Duke, Iowa State, Northwestern, Purdue, and Washington (St. Louis) Universities and the University of Illinois (Urbana-Champaign). Domestic and international internships are offered. Study abroad is possible in 17 countries, including China, Peru, Sweden, Germany, and

France, as is fall term study in East Asia, Europe, and Latin America. Interdisciplinary majors are offered in earth science, teaching, Asian studies, and public administration. A B.A.-B.S. degree in occupational therapy is offered, as well as 3-2 engineering programs with the University of Illinois and Purdue, Washington (St. Louis), and Iowa State Universities. Work-study programs, double majors, phys ed credits, and pass/fail options are available. There are 13 national honor societies, including Phi Beta Kappa, a freshman honors program, and 12 departmental honors programs. **Visiting:** There are regularly scheduled orientations for prospective students, including information sessions with speakers, exhibits, campus tours, meetings with faculty, counselors, and students, and social activities. There are guides for informal visits, visitors may sit in on classes, and stay overnight. To schedule a visit, contact Vice President of Enrollment. **Campus Safety and Security:** Measures include 24-hour foot and vehicle patrol, emergency notification system, self-defense education, and security escort services. There are shuttle buses, lighted pathways/sidewalks, and controlled access to dorms/residences.

REQUIREMENTS: The SAT or ACT is recommended. Applicants should be graduates of an accredited secondary school with 16 academic credits, including 4 in English, 3 in math, 2 each in science and social studies, 1 in foreign language, and other science and math courses for appropriate majors. An audition for music majors and an interview are recommended. The GED is accepted. Students who choose not to submit ACT or SAT scores must interview and submit a photocopy of a graded high school paper. AP credits are accepted. Important factors in the admissions decision are advanced placement or honors courses, evidence of special talent, and recommendations by school officials. A total of 123 credits with a minimum GPA of 2.0 is required to graduate. Courses in foreign language, religion, writing, phys ed, fine arts, humanities, literature, and the sciences must be completed. **Procedure:** Freshmen are admitted fall, winter, and spring. Entrance exams should be taken by fall of the senior year. There are early admissions, deferred admissions, and rolling admissions plans. Application deadlines are open. The fall 2014 application fee was $35. Notification is sent on a rolling basis. applicants were on the 2014 waiting list; were admitted. Applications are accepted online. **Transfer Students:** 54 transfer students enrolled in 2013-2014. A minimum GPA of 2.0 is required. SAT or ACT scores and an interview are recommended. 60 of 123 credits required for the bachelor's degree must be completed at Augustana. **International Students:** There are 44 international students enrolled. The school actively recruits these students. They must take the TOEFL with a minimum score of 550 on the paper-based TOEFL (PBT) or 79 on the Internet-based version (iBT).

ADMISSIONS: 69% of the 2014-2015 applicants were accepted. The ACT scores were 8% below 21, 23% between 21 and 23, 28% between 24 and 26, 18% between 27 and 28, and 23% above 28. 58% of the current freshmen were in the top fifth of their class; 83% were in the top two fifths. **Admissions Contact:** Kent Brands, Vice President of Enrollment. E-Mail: *admissions@augustana.edu* Web: *www.augustana.edu*

FINANCIAL AID: In 2014-2015, 80% of all full-time freshmen and 75% of continuing full-time students received some form of financial aid. 79% of all full-time freshmen and 75% of continuing full-time students received need-based aid. The average freshman award was $24,505. Need-based scholarships or need-based grants averaged $15,396; need-based self-help aid (loans and jobs) averaged $6,572; and other non-need-based awards and non-need-based scholarships averaged $6,025. 80% of undergraduate students work part-time. Average annual earnings from campus work are $900. The average financial indebtedness of the 2014 graduate was $15,705. Augustana is a member of CSS. The FAFSA and the college's own financial statement are required. The deadline for filing freshman financial aid applications for fall entry is April 5.

AURORA UNIVERSITY — D-2
www.aurora.edu

Aurora, IL 60506

(630) 844-5533
(800) 742-5281

Fax: (630) 844-5535
Email: admission@aurora.edu
Full-time: 1081 men, 1771 women
Faculty: 110
Part-time: 114 men, 280 women
Ph.D.s: 84%
Graduate: 414 men, 1287 women
Student/Faculty: 18 to 1
Year: semesters, summer session
Tuition: $20,720
Room & Board: $8636
Freshman Class: 1872 applied, 1367 accepted, 501 enrolled
SAT CR/M: 470/470 ACT: 22
CEEB CODE: 1027
Application Deadline: June 20
COMPETITIVE

Aurora University, founded in 1893, is a private, independent institution that offers graduate and undergraduate degrees in arts and sciences, education, accounting, business, information technology, communication, criminal justice, nursing, health sciences, physical education, athletic training, recreation, special education, and social work. There are 4 undergraduate schools and 4 graduate schools. In addition to regional accreditation, AU has baccalaureate program accreditation with CSWE, NCATE, CCNE, and CAATE. The 35-acre campus is in a suburban area 40 miles west of Chicago. Including any residence halls, there are 28 buildings.

STUDENT LIFE: 90% of undergraduates are from Illinois. Others are from 40 states, 11 foreign countries, and Canada. 90% are from public schools. 61% are White; 20% Hispanic. 69% claim no religious affiliation; 15% Catholic; 15% Protestant. **Male To Female Ratio:** 2.1:1. The average age of freshmen is 18; all undergraduates, 24. 25% do not continue beyond their first year; 50% remain to graduate. **Housing:** 700 students can be accommodated in college housing, which includes single-sex and coed dorms. On-campus housing is available on a first-come and first-served basis. 75% of students commute. Alcohol is not permitted. All students may keep cars.

FACULTY/CLASSROOMS: 45% of faculty are male; 55% are female. 96% teach undergraduates. No introductory courses are taught by graduate students. The average class size in an introductory lecture is 24; in a laboratory is 16; and in a regular course is 22.

PROGRAMS OF STUDY: AU confers B.A., B.S., B.S.N. and B.S.W. degrees. Master's and Doctoral degrees are also awarded. Bachelor's degrees are awarded in BIOLOGICAL SCIENCE (biology/biological science), BUSINESS (accounting, business administration and management, management information systems, management science, marketing management, marketing/retailing/merchandising, organizational leadership and management, recreation and leisure services, and sustainable management), COMMUNICATIONS AND THE ARTS (art, communications, dramatic arts, English, and Spanish), COMPUTER AND PHYSICAL SCIENCE (actuarial science, computer science, and mathematics), EDUCATION (athletic training, bilingual/bicultural education, elementary education, physical education, secondary education, and special education), HEALTH PROFESSIONS (biology, health science, and nursing), SOCIAL SCIENCE (criminal justice, history, parks and recreation management, philosophy, political science/government, psychology, religion, social work, and sociology). Nursing, education, social work and business are the strongest academically. Nursing, education, and business have the largest enrollments.

ACTIVITIES: 1% of men belong to 1 local and 1 national fraternities; 1% of women belong to 1 local and 1 national sororities. There are 46 groups on campus, including art, cheerleading, chorale, computers, dance, drama, environmental, ethnic, honors, jazz band, literary magazine, newspaper, pep band, photography, political, professional, radio and TV, religious, social, social service, and student government. Popular campus events include Spring Fling, Arts and Ideas series. **Sports:** There are 10 intercollegiate sports for men and 10 for women, and 10 intramural sports for men and 10 for women. Facilities include a fitness center, a weight room, a 2,000-seat gym, football and soccer fields, theatre, voice and chorale facilities. **Graduates:** From July 1, 2013 to June 30, 2014, 551 bachelor's degrees were awarded. The most popular majors were education (22%), business

(19%), and health professions and related services (18%). 41 companies recruited on campus in 2013-2014. In an average class, 42% graduate in 4 years or less, 11% graduate in 5 years or less, and 1% graduate in 6 years or less. Of the 2013 graduating class, 20% were enrolled in graduate school within 6 months of graduation, and 80% were employed.

SERVICES: Counseling and information services are available, as is tutoring in most subjects. There is remedial math, reading, and writing. There are professional and peer tutors, workshops, and computer-based tutorials. **Library/Resources:** The library contains 83,589 volumes, 7,038 audio/video tapes/CDs/DVDs, and subscribes to 4,206 periodicals including electronic. Computerized library services include interlibrary loans, database searching, Internet access, and Wi-Fi capability. Special learning facilities include an art gallery, radio station, a Native American museum and a lakefront campus in southeastern Wisconsin. **Physically Challenged Students:** 98% of the campus is accessible. Facilities include wheelchair ramps, elevators, special parking, specially equipped restrooms, special class scheduling, and lowered drinking fountains. **Special:** AU offers cross-registration with North Central College and Benedictine University, field-related job experience, work-study programs, study abroad in a number of countries and travel programs during the May term. Internships, student-designed and dual majors, and dual-degree options such as B.A.-B.S. are available. There are 3 national honor societies and 9 departmental honors programs. **Visiting:** There are regularly scheduled orientations for prospective students, including meeting with an admission representative, a campus tour with students, and classroom visits if set up. There are guides for informal visits, visitors may sit in on classes, and stay overnight. To schedule a visit, contact the Office of Admission and Financial Aid. **Campus Safety and Security:** Measures include 24-hour foot and vehicle patrol, emergency notification system, self-defense education, and security escort services. There are emergency telephones and lighted pathways/sidewalks.

REQUIREMENTS: The ACT is required. The SAT is recommended. Applicants must be graduates of an accredited secondary school or have earned the GED. Secondary school academic units must include a minimum of 4 years of English and 3 years each of mathematics, social studies, science, and electives. An interview is recommended but not required. AU requires applicants to be in the upper 60% of their class. A GPA of 2.0 is required. AP and CLEP credits are accepted. Important factors in the admissions decision are advanced placement or honors courses, extracurricular activities record, and leadership record. To graduate, students must complete a minimum of 120 semester hours with a GPA of at least 2.0 on a 4.0 scale, including at least 52 semester hours at a senior college. General education distribution requirements include completion of a minimum of 38 semester hours in Aurora University's core sequences of Composition; Ways of Knowing (24 semester hours minimum), which includes Observation of Ourselves and Others, Observation of the Natural World, Aesthetic and Philosophical Expression, Mathematical and Technological Application, and a senior capstone in the major or equivalent cumulative senior year experience; and Ways of Living (8 semester hours minimum). Completion at Aurora University of at least 30 semester hours, including the last 24 semester hours in the degree, and including at least 18 semester hours in the major. A minimum of 30 semester hours numbered 3000 or above of which 15 semester hours must lie within the major and 15 semester hours must be completed at AU. Completion of the major requirements (with no grades lower than "C") for an approved major, including the senior capstone. Completion of writing intensive courses which include IDS1600, IDS2000 and the Writing for Success 3000-level requirement with no grades lower than "C." **Procedure:** Freshmen are admitted fall and spring. Entrance exams should be taken by late in the junior year or early in the senior year. There are deferred admissions and rolling admissions plans. Applications should be filed by June 20 for fall entry, along with a $25 fee. Notifications are sent September 1. Applications are accepted on-line. **Transfer Students:** 462 transfer students enrolled in 2013-2014. Applicants are required to have a minimum GPA of 2.0 and must have completed at least 15 semester hours at the post-secondary level. 30 of 120 credits required for the bachelor's degree must be completed at AU. **International Students:** There are 4 international students enrolled. They must take the TOEFL with a minimum score of 550 on the paper-based TOEFL (PBT) or 79 on the Internet-based version (iBT).

ADMISSIONS: 73% of the 2014-2015 applicants were accepted. The SAT scores for the 2014-2015 freshman class were: Critical Reading--69% below 500, 22% between 500 and 599, and 9% between 600 and 699; Math--69% below 500, 22% between 500 and 599, and 9% between 600 and 699. The ACT scores were 32% below 21, 37% between 21 and 23, 20% between 24 and 26, 7% between 27 and 28, and 4% above 28. 30% of the current freshmen were in the top fifth of their class; 65% were in the top two fifths. **Admissions Contact:** Linda Gebhard, Enrollment Information Manager. E-Mail: *admission@aurora.edu* Web: *www.aurora.edu*

FINANCIAL AID: In 2014-2015, 99% of all full-time freshmen and 97% of continuing full-time students received some form of financial aid. 86% of all full-time freshmen and 86% of continuing full-time students received need-based aid. The average freshman award was $18,208. Need-based scholarships or need-based grants averaged $7,628 ($15,466 maximum); need-based self-help aid (loans and jobs) averaged $4,279 ($6,500 maximum); and other non-need-based awards and non-need-based scholarships averaged $9,138 ($11,500 maximum). 100% of undergraduate students work part-time. Average annual earnings from campus work are $4500. The average financial indebtedness of the 2014 graduate was $24,083. The FAFSA is required. The priority date for freshman financial aid applications for fall entry is April 15.

BENEDICTINE UNIVERSITY   E-2
www.ben.edu

Lisle, IL 60532	(630) 829-6300
	n/av
Fax: (630) 829-6301	Email: admissions@ben.edu
Full-time: 1046 men, 1358 women	Faculty: IIA, -$
Part-time: 243 men, 293 women	Ph.D.s: 89%
Graduate: 655 men, 1711 women	Student/Faculty: 18 to 1
Year: semesters, summer session	Tuition: $29,340
Room & Board: $8480	Freshman Class: 2558 applied, 1974 accepted, 486 enrolled
ACT: 23	CEEB CODE: 1707
Application Deadline: n/av	COMPETITIVE

Benedictine University, founded in 1887, is a private, Roman Catholic liberal arts and sciences institution. There are 4 undergraduate schools and 4 graduate schools. In addition to regional accreditation, Benedictine has baccalaureate program accreditation with ADA and CCLN. The 108-acre campus is in a suburban area 25 miles west of Chicago. Including any residence halls, there are 11 buildings.

STUDENT LIFE: 94% of undergraduates are from Illinois. Others are from 50 states, 10 foreign countries, and Canada. 45% are White; 21% Asian American; 12% African American; 12% race unknown. **Male To Female Ratio:** 1.7:1. The average age of freshmen is 18; all undergraduates, 25. 27% do not continue beyond their first year; 52% remain to graduate. **Housing:** 756 students can be accommodated in college housing, which includes single-sex and coed dorms and on-campus apartments. On-campus housing is available on a first-come, first-served basis. All students may keep cars.

FACULTY/CLASSROOMS: 49% of faculty are male; 51% are female. All teach and do research. No introductory courses are taught by graduate students. The average class size in an introductory lecture is 21; in a laboratory is 17; and in a regular course is 19.

PROGRAMS OF STUDY: Benedictine confers B.A., B.S., B.B.A. and B.S.N. degrees. Associate, Master's, and Doctoral degrees are also awarded. Bachelor's degrees are awarded in BIOLOGICAL SCIENCE (biochemistry, biology/biological science, molecular biology, and nutrition), BUSINESS (accounting, banking and finance, business administration and management, business economics, international business management, management information systems, marketing management, marketing/retailing/merchandising, and organizational behavior), COMMUNICATIONS AND THE ARTS (arts administration/management, communications, creative writing, fine arts, literature, music, publishing, Spanish, and studio art), COMPUTER AND PHYSICAL SCIENCE (chemistry, computer science, mathematics, and physics), EDUCATION (elementary education and special education), ENGINEERING AND ENVIRONMENTAL DESIGN (engineering and applied science and environmental science), HEALTH PROFESSIONS (clinical science, health care administration, health science, nuclear medical technology, nursing, and radiation therapy), SOCIAL SCIENCE (economics, history, international studies, philosophy, political science/government, psychology, social science, sociology, and theological studies). Management, health science, and psychology have the largest enrollments.

ACTIVITIES: There are no fraternities or sororities. There are 46 groups on campus, including art, band, cheerleading, choir, chorus, computers, dance, debate, ethnic, honors, international, jazz band, literary magazine, musical theater, newspaper, pep band, political, professional, radio and TV, religious, social, social service, and student government. Popular campus events include Relay for Life, Quad Day, and Spring Ball. **Sports:** There are 8 intercollegiate sports for men and 9 for women, 11 intramural sports for men and 11 for women. Facilities include a recreation center housing a main arena, a weight room, a dance room, racquetball and tennis courts. A sports complex includes a football/soccer/track stadium, a baseball stadium, and a softball stadium. **Graduates:** From July 1, 2013 to June 30, 2014, 723 bachelor's degrees were awarded. The most popular majors were health science (12%), accounting (7%), and management (7%).

SERVICES: Counseling and information services are available, as is tutoring in most subjects. There is a reader service for the blind, and remedial math, reading, and writing. **Library/Resources:** The 4 libraries contain 274,635 volumes, 23,377 microform items, 51,032 audio/video tapes/CDs/DVDs, and subscribe to 66,295 periodicals including electronic. Computerized library services include interlibrary loans, database searching, Internet access, and Wi-Fi capability. Special learning facilities include an art gallery, natural history museum, radio station, and TV station. **Physically Challenged Students:** All of the campus is accessible. Facilities include wheelchair ramps, elevators, special parking, specially equipped restrooms, and lowered drinking fountains. **Special:** There is cross-registration with North Central College, Aurora University, and the Illinois Institute of Technology. Benedictine offers study abroad in 9 countries, and exchange programs can be arranged through other colleges. There are 3-2 pre-engineering degrees with Marquette University and the Universities of Illinois, Detroit, and Notre Dame, and an engineering degree with the Illinois Institute of Technology. Pre-professional programs including pre-podiatry, pre-physical therapy, and pre-nursing are offered. Work-study programs with a number of surrounding firms, internships, an accelerated degree program in management, credit for work and life experience, and dual majors are also offered. There are 11 national honor societies and a freshman honors program. **Visiting:** There are regularly scheduled orientations for prospective students, student visits include a regularly scheduled visit day and open houses each semester. There are guides for informal visits, visitors may sit in on classes, and stay overnight. To schedule a visit, contact the Enrollment Center. **Campus Safety and Security:** Measures include 24-hour foot and vehicle patrol, self-defense education, and security escort services. There are emergency telephones and lighted pathways/sidewalks.

REQUIREMENTS: The ACT is required. To be admitted, students must complete 4 years of English, 3 each of social studies, math, and lab science, and 2 of foreign language. The GED is accepted. Benedictine requires applicants to be in the upper 50% of their class. AP and CLEP credits are accepted. To graduate, students must complete 120 semester hours, including 36 in their majors, and maintain a minimum GPA of 2.0. They must complete 12 hours in the arts and humanities, 9 each in social sciences, natural sciences, and cultural heritage, 6 in rhetoric, and 3 each in speech, math, and freshman seminar. A thesis, capstone course or project, or comprehensive exam is required in specific departments. **Procedure:** Freshmen are admitted fall and spring. There is a rolling admissions plan. Application deadlines are open. Application fee is $40. Applications are accepted on-line. **Transfer Students:** 449 transfer students enrolled in 2013-2014. Applicants must have a C average. A minimum GPA of 2.0 is necessary, and an interview is required in some cases. Students who have completed fewer than 20 semester hours must submit ACT or

SAT scores. 30 of 120 credits required for the bachelor's degree must be completed at Benedictine. **International Students:** There are 50 international students enrolled. The school actively recruits these students. They must take the TOEFL with a minimum score of 550 on the paper-based TOEFL (PBT) or 79 on the Internet-based version (iBT).

ADMISSIONS: 77% of the 2014-2015 applicants were accepted. The ACT scores were 30% below 21, 27% between 21 and 23, 26% between 24 and 26, 9% between 27 and 28, and 8% above 28. 28% of the current freshmen were in the top fifth of their class; 59% were in the top two fifths. 3 freshmen graduated first in their class. **Admissions Contact:** Kari A. Gibbons, Director of Admissions. E-Mail: *admissions@ben.edu* Web: *www.ben.edu*

FINANCIAL AID: In 2014-2015, 98% of all full-time freshmen and 89% of continuing full-time students received some form of financial aid. 70% of all full-time freshmen and 62% of continuing full-time students received need-based aid. The average freshman award was $24,046. Need-based scholarships or need-based grants averaged $7,689 ($14,450 maximum); need-based self-help aid (loans and jobs) averaged $5,542 ($8,500 maximum); and other non-need-based awards and non-need-based scholarships averaged $16,585 ($36,600 maximum). 13% of undergraduate students work part-time. Average annual earnings from campus work are $1905. The average financial indebtedness of the 2014 graduate was $27,110. The FAFSA is required. The priority date for freshman financial aid applications for fall entry is March 1.

BLACKBURN COLLEGE   **C-4**
www.blackburn.edu

Carlinville, IL 62626	(217) 854-3231
	(800) 233-3550
Fax: (217) 854-3713	Email: alisha.kapp@blackburn.edu
Full-time: 242 men, 363 women	Faculty: 38
Part-time: 9 men, 13 women	Ph.D.s: 87%
Graduate: n/av	Student/Faculty: 14 to 1
Year: semesters, summer session	Tuition: $16,296
Room & Board: $5054	Freshman Class: 660 applied, 452 accepted, 142 enrolled
SAT: recommended ACT: 21	CEEB CODE: 1065
Application Deadline: July 31	COMPETITIVE

Blackburn College, founded in 1837, is a private liberal arts institution affiliated with the Presbyterian Church. The college is noted for its work program, which allows resident students to reduce their education costs and develop useful skills by managing and administering all essential campus jobs. Figures in the above capsule and in this profile are approximate. In addition to regional accreditation, Blackburn has baccalaureate program accreditation with NCA-HLC. The 80-acre campus is in a rural area 60 miles north of St. Louis, 45 miles south of Springfield, and 250 miles south of Chicago. Including any residence halls, there are 20 buildings.

STUDENT LIFE: 91% of undergraduates are from Illinois. Others are from 16 states, and 1 foreign countries. 85% are from public schools. 85% are White. 55% claim no religious affiliation; 25% Protestant; 12% Catholic. **Male To Female Ratio:** 1.5:1. The average age of freshmen is 18; all undergraduates, 21. 39% do not continue beyond their first year; 32% remain to graduate. **Housing:** 480 students can be accommodated in college housing, which includes single-sex and coed dorms. In addition, there are language houses, special-interest houses, A quiet residence hall. On-campus housing is guaranteed for all 4 years. 66% of students live on campus; of those, 60% remain on campus on weekends. All students may keep cars.

FACULTY/CLASSROOMS: 56% of faculty are male; 44% are female. All teach undergraduates, and 55% do research. No introductory courses are taught by graduate students. The average class size in an introductory lecture is 25; in a laboratory is 20; and in a regular course is 18.

PROGRAMS OF STUDY: Blackburn confers B.A. degrees. Bachelor's degrees are awarded in BIOLOGICAL SCIENCE (biochemistry, biology/biological science, and environmental biology), BUSINESS (accounting, business administration and management, marketing/retailing/merchandising, organizational leadership and management, and sports management), COMMUNICATIONS AND THE ARTS (art, arts administration/management, communications, creative writing, English literature, graphic design, music performance, musical theater, performing arts, and Spanish), COMPUTER AND PHYSICAL SCIENCE (chemistry, computer science, and mathematics), EDUCATION (art education, elementary education, English education, mathematics education, physical education, science education, secondary education, and social science education), HEALTH PROFESSIONS (medical laboratory technology and premedicine), SOCIAL SCIENCE (counseling/psychology, criminal justice, experimental psychology, history, interdisciplinary studies, political science/government, prelaw, psychology, and public administration). Elementary education, biology, and criminal justice are the strongest academically.

ACTIVITIES: There are no fraternities or sororities. There are 37 groups on campus, including art, band, cheerleading, chess, choir, chorale, chorus, dance, debate, drama, ethnic, gay, jazz band, literary magazine, musical theater, newspaper, political, religious, social, social service, student government, and yearbook. Popular campus events include Goodwill Games Residence Hall Events, and all College Convocations. **Sports:** There are 5 intercollegiate sports for men and 6 for women, and 15 intramural sports for men and 15 for women. Facilities include a gym, racquetball and tennis courts, weight rooms, an outdoor track, and playing fields for baseball, soccer, and softball. **Graduates:** From July 1, 2013 to June 30, 2014, 122 bachelor's degrees were awarded. The most popular majors were education (17%), criminal justice (15%), and business (8%). 17 companies recruited on campus in 2013-2014. In an average class, 32% graduate in 4 years or less, 44% graduate in 5 years or less, and 45% graduate in 6 years or less. Of the 2013 graduating class, 35% were enrolled in graduate school within 6 months of graduation, and 81% were employed.

SERVICES: Counseling and information services are available, as is tutoring in most subjects. **Library/Resources:** The library contains 65,500 volumes, 10,897 microform items, 1,299 audio/video tapes/CDs/DVDs, and subscribes to 85 periodicals including electronic. Computerized library services include interlibrary loans, database searching, Internet access, and Wi-Fi capability. Special learning facilities include an art gallery. **Physically Challenged Students:** 50% of the campus is accessible. Facilities include wheelchair ramps, elevators, special parking, specially equipped restrooms, special class scheduling, lowered drinking fountains, and lowered telephones. **Special:** Blackburn offers supervised off-campus internships related to student majors, co-op programs, work-study programs, and a semester in Ecuador, Wales, or Washington, D.C. A 3-2 engineering degree with Washington University in St. Louis or at the University of Missouri-Kansas City is offered. Students may design their own majors. There are 1 national honor societies. **Visiting:** There are regularly scheduled orientations for prospective students, including a campus tour and meetings with an admissions representative, the financial aid director, student life staff, a work program representative, and an academic faculty member. There are guides for informal visits, visitors may sit in on classes, and stay overnight. To schedule a visit, contact the Office of Admissions. **Campus Safety and Security:** Measures include emergency notification system, self-defense education, and security escort services. There are lighted pathways/sidewalks, Security service department through the work program.

REQUIREMENTS: The ACT is required. The SAT is recommended. Applicants should be graduates of an accredited secondary school or have a GED certificate. Blackburn recommends completion of 4 years of English, 2 to 4 of math, and 2 each of lab sciences, social sciences, and foreign language. A personal essay is required. Blackburn requires applicants to be in the upper 60% of their class. A GPA of 2.0 is required. AP and CLEP credits are accepted. Important factors in the admissions decision are leadership record, personality/intangible qualities, and recommendations by school officials. To graduate, students must complete 122 semester hours with a minimum 2.0 GPA. Requirements include intercultural courses in foreign languages or English, and foundation courses in writing, literature, math, social sciences, philosophy or religion, analysis, fine arts, and phys ed. Work program participation is required of resident students. All students must complete their last year in residence. **Procedure:** Freshmen are admitted fall, spring, and summer. Entrance exams should be taken in the junior year or early in the senior year. There is a rolling admissions plan. Applications should be filed by July 31 for fall entry; November 30 for spring entry, along with a $20 fee. Notification is sent on a rolling basis. Applications are accepted online. **Transfer Students:** 51 transfer students enrolled in 2013-2014. Applicants must submit official transcripts of college-level work and be in good standing at the previous institution attended. Students from accredited colleges may receive credit for grades of C or better; those with associate degrees may transfer some D grades. Credit for work at unaccredited institutions may be accepted provisionally. 30 of 122 credits required for the bachelor's degree must be completed at Blackburn. **International Students:** They must take the TOEFL with a minimum score of 550 on the paper-based TOEFL (PBT) or 80 on the Internet-based version (iBT). They must also take the SAT or ACT.

ADMISSIONS: 68% of the 2014-2015 applicants were accepted. The ACT scores were 48% below 21, 30% between 21 and 23, 12% between 24 and 26, 7% between 27 and 28, and 3% above 28. 30% of the current freshmen were in the top fifth of their class; 57% were in the top two fifths. 4 freshmen graduated first in their class. **Admissions Contact:** Alisha Kapp, Director of Admissions. E-Mail: *alisha.kapp@blackburn.edu* Web: *www.blackburn.edu*

FINANCIAL AID: In 2014-2015, 99% of all full-time freshmen and 98% of continuing full-time students received some form of financial aid. 97% of all full-time freshmen and 94% of continuing full-time students received need-based aid. The average freshman award was $15,401. Need-based scholarships or need-based grants averaged $7,414 ($22,650 maximum); need-based self-help aid (loans and jobs) averaged $4,181 ($6,140 maximum); and other non-need-based awards and non-need-based scholarships averaged $7,278 ($22,650 maximum). 108% of undergraduate students work part-time. Average annual earnings from campus work are $2738. The average financial indebtedness of the 2014 graduate was $16,456. Blackburn is a member of CSS. The FAFSA is required. The priority date for freshman financial aid applications for fall entry is March 1.

BRADLEY UNIVERSITY D-3
www.bradley.edu

Peoria, IL 61625	(309) 677-1000
	(800) 447-6460
Fax: (309) 677-2797	Email: admissions@bradley.edu
Full-time: 2210 men, 2591 women	Faculty: 345; IIA, +$
Part-time: 107 men, 153 women	Ph.D.s: 83%
Graduate: 372 men, 367 women	Student/Faculty: 13 to 1
Year: semesters, summer session	Tuition: $24,224
Room & Board: $7650	Freshman Class: 6221 applied, 4573 accepted, 1106 enrolled
SAT CR/M: 540/570 ACT: 25	CEEB CODE: 1070
Application Deadline: open	VERY COMPETITIVE

Bradley University, founded in 1897, is an independent, privately endowed institution offering a full range of baccalaureate and graduate-level programs. Figures in the above capsule and in this profile are approximate. There are 5 undergraduate schools and 1 graduate school. In addition to regional accreditation, Bradley has baccalaureate program accreditation with AACSB, ABET, ACCE, ADA, NASAD, NASM, NCATE, NLN, CACREP, CAPTE, and NAST. The 85-acre campus is in an urban area 160 miles southwest of Chicago. Including any residence halls, there are 44 buildings.

STUDENT LIFE: 88% of undergraduates are from Illinois. Others are from 39 states, 30 foreign countries, and Canada. 85% are from public schools. 80% are White. 42% are Protestant; 34% Catholic; 14% claim no religious affiliation. **Male To Female Ratio:** 1.2:1. The average age of freshmen is 18; all undergraduates, 20. 13% do not continue beyond their first year; 78% remain to graduate. **Housing:** 2200 students can be accommodated in college housing, which includes single-sex and coed dorms and on-campus apartments. In addition, there are fraternity houses and sorority houses. On-campus housing is guaranteed for all 4 years. 97% of students live on campus; of those, 99% remain on campus on weekends. Upperclassmen may keep cars.

FACULTY/CLASSROOMS: 62% of faculty are male; 38% are female. All teach and do research. No introductory courses are taught by graduate students. The average class size in a laboratory is 14 and in a regular course is 23.

PROGRAMS OF STUDY: Bradley confers B.A., B.F.A., B.M., B.S., B.S.C., B.S.C.E., B.S.E.E., B.S.I.E., B.S.M.E., B.S.M.F.E., B.S.M.F.E.T. and B.S.N. degrees. Master's and Doctoral degrees are also awarded. Bachelor's degrees are awarded in BIOLOGICAL SCIENCE (biochemistry, biology/biological science, and molecular biology), BUSINESS (accounting, banking and finance, business administration and management, entrepreneurial studies, international business management, management information systems, and marketing/retailing/merchandising), COMMUNICATIONS AND THE ARTS (art history and appreciation, communications, dramatic arts, English, French, German, graphic design, multimedia, music, music business management, music performance, music theory and composition, Spanish, and studio art), COMPUTER AND PHYSICAL SCIENCE (actuarial science, chemistry, computer science, information sciences and systems, mathematics, and physics), EDUCATION (art education, drama education, early childhood education, elementary education, music education, and special education), ENGINEERING AND ENVIRONMENTAL DESIGN (civil engineering, construction engineering, electrical/electronics engineering, engineering physics, environmental science, industrial engineering, manufacturing engineering, manufacturing technology, and mechanical engineering), HEALTH PROFESSIONS (health science, medical technology, and nursing), SOCIAL SCIENCE (criminal justice, dietetics, economics, family/consumer studies, history, international studies, liberal arts/general studies, philosophy, political science/government, psychology, religion, social work, and sociology). Business, engineering, and natural sciences are the strongest academically. Communication, elementary education, and psychology have the largest enrollments.

ACTIVITIES: 35% of men belong to 16 national fraternities; 27% of women belong to 12 national sororities. There are 250 groups on campus, including art, band, cheerleading, chess, choir, chorale, chorus, computers, dance, drama, environmental, ethnic, forensics, gay, honors, international, jazz band, literary magazine, musical theater, newspaper, orchestra, pep band, photography, political, professional, radio and TV, religious, social, social service, student government, and symphony. Popular campus events include Late Night BU, Founders Day, and Greek Week. **Sports:** There are 6 intercollegiate sports for men and 7 for women, and 24 intramural sports for men and 24 for women. Facilities include tennis courts, a civic center, playing fields, a field house, outdoor lighted basketball courts, and a 130,000-square-foot student recreation center with a pool, an indoor track, weights, cardio machines, spinning room, and a climbing wall. **Graduates:** From July 1, 2013 to June 30, 2014, 1169 bachelor's degrees were awarded. The most popular majors were nursing (6%), psychology (5%), and health science (5%). 403 companies recruited on campus in 2013-2014. In an average class, 54% graduate in 4 years or less, 76% graduate in 5 years or less, and 78% graduate in 6 years or less. Of the 2013 graduating class, 16% were enrolled in graduate school within 6 months of graduation, and 94% were employed.

SERVICES: Counseling and information services are available, as is tutoring in most subjects, introductory subjects and selected higher-level classes. There is remedial math and writing. **Library/Resources:** The library contains 511,000 volumes, 86,504 microform items, 13,774 audio/video tapes/CDs/DVDs, and subscribes to 41,689 periodicals including electronic. Computerized library services include interlibrary loans, database searching, Internet access, and Wi-Fi capability. Special learning facilities include an art gallery, radio station, and TV station. **Physically Challenged Students:** 80% of the campus is accessible. Facilities include wheelchair ramps, elevators, special parking, specially equipped restrooms, and lowered drinking fountains. **Special:** Special academic programs include an honors program, co-op programs, internships, a Washington semester, work-study programs, study abroad in 30 countries, B.A.-B.S. degrees in most majors, dual and student-designed majors, and leadership

fellowships. There are 31 national honor societies and a freshman honors program. **Visiting:** There are regularly scheduled orientations for prospective students, including class visits, campus tours, admissions information, financial assistance seminars, lunch, and student and parent meetings. There are guides for informal visits, visitors may sit in on classes, and stay overnight. To schedule a visit, contact the Office of Undergraduate Admissions. **Campus Safety and Security:** Measures include 24-hour foot and vehicle patrol, emergency notification system, self-defense education, and security escort services. There are emergency telephones, lighted pathways/sidewalks, Engravers for marking personal property, and a medical escort service.

REQUIREMENTS: The SAT or ACT is required. A GPA of 2.0 is required. AP and CLEP credits are accepted. Important factors in the admissions decision are advanced placement or honors courses, extracurricular activities record, and evidence of special talent. To graduate, the student must complete the school's basic skills and general education curriculum. Overall, the college requires 124 total credit hours, with 32 hours in the student's major and a minimum GPA of 2.0. **Procedure:** Freshmen are admitted to all sessions. Entrance exams should be taken in the spring of the junior year or the fall of the senior year. There is a rolling admissions plan. Application deadlines are open. Application fee is $35. Applications are accepted on-line. **Transfer Students:** 303 transfer students enrolled in 2013-2014. Transfer students must have a minimum GPA of 2.0. Those with fewer than 15 hours of college credit must submit their ACT or SAT scores and a high school transcript. 30 of 124 credits required for the bachelor's degree must be completed at Bradley. **International Students:** There are 40 international students enrolled. The school actively recruits these students. They must take the TOEFL with a minimum score of 550 on the paper-based TOEFL (PBT) or 79 on the Internet-based version (iBT). The SAT or ACT is recommended.

ADMISSIONS: 74% of the 2014-2015 applicants were accepted. The SAT scores for the 2014-2015 freshman class were: Critical Reading--27% below 500, 44% between 500 and 599, 23% between 600 and 699, and 6% between 700 and 800; Math--20% below 500, 38% between 500 and 599, 34% between 600 and 699, and 8% between 700 and 800. The ACT scores were 12% below 21, 23% between 21 and 23, 30% between 24 and 26, 17% between 27 and 28, and 17% above 28. 51% of the current freshmen were in the top fifth of their class; 83% were in the top two fifths. There were 5 National Merit finalists. 41 freshmen graduated first in their class. **Admissions Contact:** Angela Roberson, Associate Provost for Enrollment Management. E-Mail: *admissions@bradley.edu* Web: *www.bradley.edu*

FINANCIAL AID: 64% of all full-time freshmen and 57% of continuing full-time students received need-based aid. The average freshman award was $20,164. Need-based scholarships or need-based grants averaged $14,179 ($23,950 maximum); need-based self-help aid (loans and jobs) averaged $4,660 ($7,000 maximum); non-need-based athletic scholarships averaged $15,700 ($31,894 maximum); and other non-need-based awards and non-need-based scholarships averaged $8,388 ($23,950 maximum). 22% of undergraduate students work part-time. Average annual earnings from campus work are $1142. Bradley is a member of CSS. The FAFSA is required. The deadline for filing freshman financial aid applications for fall entry is March 1.

CHICAGO STATE UNIVERSITY   E-2
www.csu.edu

Chicago, IL 60628	(773) 995-2513
	(800) 278-3011
Fax: (773) 995-3820	Email: ug-admissions@csu.edu
Full-time: 917 men, 2092 women	Faculty: IIA, -$
Part-time: 392 men, 1211 women	Ph.D.s: 62%
Graduate: 467 men, 1022 women	Student/Faculty: n/av
Year: other, summer session	Tuition: $5482 ($9712)
Room & Board: n/av	Freshman Class: n/app
ACT: required	CEEB CODE: 1118
Application Deadline: July 15	COMPETITIVE

Chicago State University, founded in 1867, is a public commuter and residential institution controlled by the State of Illinois. It offers day and evening undergraduate programs through the Colleges of Arts and Sciences, Health Sciences, Business Administration, Education, and non traditional programs. Figures in the above capsule and in this profile are approximate. There are 5 undergraduate schools and 2 graduate schools. In addition to regional accreditation, Chicago State has baccalaureate program accreditation with AACSB, ACPE, ADA, CAHEA, NCATE, and NLN. The 161-acre campus is in an urban area 12 miles south of downtown Chicago. Including any residence halls, there are 13 buildings.

STUDENT LIFE: 98% of undergraduates are from Illinois. Others are from 24 states, 21 foreign countries, and Canada. 80% are African American. The average age of freshmen is 21; all undergraduates, 29. **Housing:** 360 students can be accommodated in college housing, which includes coed dorms. On-campus housing is available on a first-come, first-served basis. 97% of students commute. Alcohol is not permitted. All students may keep cars.

FACULTY/CLASSROOMS: 99% teach undergraduates. No introductory courses are taught by graduate students. The average class size in an introductory lecture is 60; in a laboratory is 26; and in a regular course is 35.

PROGRAMS OF STUDY: Chicago State confers B.A., B.S., B.M.E. and B.S.Ed. degrees. Master's and Doctoral degrees are also awarded. Bachelor's degrees are awarded in BIOLOGICAL SCIENCE (biochemistry and biology/biological science), BUSINESS (accounting, banking and finance, business administration and management, management science, marketing/retailing/merchandising, and recreation and leisure services), COMMUNICATIONS AND THE ARTS (art, broadcasting, English, music, Spanish, and speech/debate/rhetoric), COMPUTER AND PHYSICAL SCIENCE (chemistry, computer science, information sciences and systems, mathematics, and physics), EDUCATION (art education, bilingual/bicultural education, business education, early childhood education, elementary education, industrial arts education, music education, physical education, secondary education, and vocational education), HEALTH PROFESSIONS (health, health care administration, health science, nursing, predentistry, and premedicine), SOCIAL SCIENCE (African American studies, criminal justice, economics, geography, history, political science/government, prelaw, psychology, and sociology). Business administration and computer science is the strongest academically. Elementary education and nursing have the largest enrollments.

ACTIVITIES: 12% of men and 15% of women belong to 4 national fraternities; women belong to 4 national sororities. There are 72 groups on campus, including cheerleading, chess, choir, dance, honors, international, jazz band, literary magazine, newspaper, political, professional, radio and TV, religious, social, social service, and student government. Popular campus events include Welcome Week activities, Black Writers Conference and Hispanic Heritage Month. **Sports:** There are 6 intercollegiate sports for men and 6 for women, and 4 intramural sports for men and 2 for women. Facilities include tennis courts, indoor/outdoor tracks, an Olympic-size swimming pool, weight rooms, basketball courts, a fitness center, dance studio, a baseball field, and convocation center with 6300 seating capacity. **Graduates:** From July 1, 2013 to June 30, 2014, 839 bachelor's degrees were awarded. The most popular majors were general studies (26%), business administration (13%), and criminal justice (6%). In an average class, 7% graduate in 4 years or less and 22% graduate in 6 years or less.

SERVICES: Counseling and information services are available, as is tutoring in some subjects. There is remedial math, reading, and writing. Math, science and accounting. **Library/Resources:** The library contains 26,000 volumes, 388,028 microform items, and subscribes to 1,734 periodicals including electronic. Computerized library services include interlibrary loans, database searching, and Internet access. Special learning facilities include an art gallery, radio station, and a TV studio. **Physically Challenged Students:** All of the campus is accessible. Facilities include wheelchair ramps, elevators, special parking, specially equipped restrooms, lowered drinking fountains, and lowered telephones. **Special:** Chicago State offers a combined B.A.-B.S. degree, a board of governors degree program, a University Without Walls Program, and an individualized curriculum program.

Study abroad in Liberia and life experience credits are also provided. There are a freshman honors program. **Visiting:** There are regularly scheduled orientations for prospective students, including a tour of campus, admissions overview, and financial aid information. To schedule a visit, contact the Office of Admissions. **Campus Safety and Security:** Measures include 24-hour foot and vehicle patrol and security escort services. There are emergency telephones and lighted pathways/sidewalks.

REQUIREMENTS: The ACT is required, scores need not be submitted if the applicant is over 25 years of age. Graduation from an accredited secondary school is required; a GED will be accepted. Minimum credits submitted should include 4 units of English, 3 of math, 3 of science, and 3 of social sciences. A GPA of 2.5 is required. AP and CLEP credits are accepted. All students must complete 120 credit hours, including 40 hours in the major, maintain a 2.0 GPA, and fulfill foreign language requirement. They must complete a 39-hour core curriculum as well as examinations in English, math, reading, and the U.S. Constitution. **Procedure:** Freshmen are admitted to all sessions. There is a rolling admissions plan. Applications should be filed by July 15 for fall entry; November 15 for spring entry; and May 1 for summer entry, along with a $25 fee. Notification is sent on a rolling basis. Applications are accepted online. **Transfer Students:** Transfer students must have a minimum GPA of 2.0, and those with fewer than 24 hours must also meet freshman admission requirements. 30 of 120 credits required for the bachelor's degree must be completed at Chicago State. **International Students:** There are 26 international students enrolled. The school actively recruits these students. They must take the TOEFL with a minimum score of 525 on the paper-based TOEFL (PBT) or 69 on the Internet-based version (iBT) and the college's own test, or take the IETLS. They must also take the SAT or ACT.

ADMISSIONS: Matt Harrison, Director of Admissions. E-Mail: *ug-admissions@csu.edu* Web: *www.csu.edu*

FINANCIAL AID: In 2014-2015, 97% of all full-time freshmen and 97% of continuing full-time students received some form of financial aid, and need-based aid. The average freshman award was $16,154. Need-based scholarships or need-based grants averaged $7,263 ($9,540 maximum); need-based self-help aid (loans and jobs) averaged $3,473 ($7,000 maximum); non-need-based athletic scholarships averaged $10,575 ($17,010 maximum); and other non-need-based awards and non-need-based scholarships averaged $6,898 ($19,522 maximum). 5% of undergraduate students work part-time. Average annual earnings from campus work are $1918. The average financial indebtedness of the 2014 graduate was $28,955. The FAFSA is required. The priority date for freshman financial aid applications for fall entry is February 1. The deadline for filing freshman financial aid applications for fall entry is April 15.

COLUMBIA COLLEGE CHICAGO (*The complete profile is made available exclusively on our website, www.barronspac.com*)

CONCORDIA UNIVERSITY, RIVER FOREST E-2
www.curf.edu

River Forest, IL 60305	(708) 209-3101
	(866) GO-2-CURF
Fax: (708) 209-3473	Email: crfmalleyjp@curf.edu
Full-time: 351 men, 610 women	Faculty: 74
Part-time: 21 men, 50 women	Ph.D.s: 65%
Graduate: 428 men, 1323 women	Student/Faculty: 13 to 1
Year: semesters, summer session	Tuition: $20,000
Room & Board: $6300	Freshman Class: 680 applied, 628 accepted, 210 enrolled
ACT: required	CEEB CODE: 1140
Application Deadline:	COMPETITIVE

Concordia University, founded in 1864, is a private liberal arts institution affiliated with the Lutheran Church, Missouri Synod. Figures in the above capsule and in this profile are approximate. There are 4 undergraduate schools and one graduate school. In addition to regional accreditation, Concordia University has baccalaureate program accreditation with NCATE and NLN. The 40-acre campus is in a suburban area 10 miles west of downtown Chicago. Including any residence halls, there are 24 buildings.

STUDENT LIFE: 65% of undergraduates are from Illinois. Others are from 21 states, 1 foreign countries, and Canada. 66% are from public schools. 51% are White. 59% are undeclared denomination; 31% Protestant; 13% Catholic. **Male To Female Ratio:** 2.5:1. The average age of freshmen is 18; all undergraduates, 22. 27% do not continue beyond their first year; 53% remain to graduate. **Housing:** 775 students can be accommodated in college housing, which includes single-sex and coed dorms and married student housing. On-campus housing is guaranteed for all 4 years. 65% of students live on campus; of those, 75% remain on campus on weekends. Alcohol is not permitted. All students may keep cars.

FACULTY/CLASSROOMS: 50% of faculty are male; 50% are female. 82% teach undergraduates, and all teach and do research. No introductory courses are taught by graduate students. The average class size in an introductory lecture is 20; in a laboratory is 18; and in a regular course is 25.

PROGRAMS OF STUDY: Concordia University confers B.A., B.Mus. and B.Mus.Ed. degrees. Master's and Doctoral degrees are also awarded. Bachelor's degrees are awarded in BIOLOGICAL SCIENCE (biology/biological science), BUSINESS (accounting and business administration and management), COMMUNICATIONS AND THE ARTS (art, communications, English, and music), COMPUTER AND PHYSICAL SCIENCE (chemistry, computer programming, computer science, mathematics, natural sciences, and physical sciences), EDUCATION (computer education, early childhood education, elementary education, middle school education, music education, physical education, science education, and secondary education), HEALTH PROFESSIONS (premedicine), SOCIAL SCIENCE (geography, history, physical fitness/movement, political science/government, prelaw, psychology, religion, social science, social work, sociology, and theological studies). Elementary education, exercise science, and theology are the strongest academically. Elementary education, business, and psychology have the largest enrollments.

ACTIVITIES: There are no fraternities or sororities. There are 43 groups on campus, including band, cheerleading, choir, chorale, chorus, communications, dance, drama, ethnic, honors, jazz band, literary magazine, musical theater, newspaper, pep band, professional, religious, social, social service, student government, symphony, and yearbook. Popular campus events include Orientation Week, Campus Awareness Day and Family Weekend. **Sports:** There are 7 intercollegiate sports for men and 7 for women, and 12 intramural sports for men and 12 for women. Facilities include 2 gyms, an indoor swimming pool, weight training room, human performance lab, football and soccer fields, tennis courts, baseball and softball fields, track, first aid training room, table tennis, billiards, and table games. **Graduates:** From July 1, 2013 to June 30, 2014, 216 bachelor's degrees were awarded. The most popular majors were education (34%), business (8%), and sociology/social work (4%). In an average class, 36% graduate in 4 years or less, 41% graduate in 5 years or less, and 41% graduate in 6 years or less. Of the 2013 graduating class, 23% were enrolled in graduate school within 6 months of graduation, and 98% were employed.

SERVICES: Counseling and information services are available, as is tutoring in every subject. There is remedial math, reading, and writing. **Library/Resources:** The library contains 140,000 volumes, 480,000 microform items, 2,250 audio/video tapes/CDs/DVDs, and subscribes to 235 periodicals including electronic. Computerized library services include interlibrary loans, database searching, Internet access, and Wi-Fi capability. Special learning facilities include an art gallery, natural history museum, TV station, a early childhood resource center, human performance lab, language lab, computer center, and weather station. **Physically Challenged Students:** 74% of the campus is accessible. Facilities include wheelchair ramps, elevators, special parking, specially equipped restrooms, special class scheduling, lowered drinking fountains, and lowered telephones. **Special:** Cross-registration is possible with Dominican University and the Chicago Consortium of Colleges. Concordia also offers internships for liberal arts majors in the Chicago area, which provides numerous opportunities, study abroad in England, and pass/fail options. Work-study is possible, as is an accelerated degreee program in organiza-

tional management. There are 3 national honor societies, including Phi Beta Kappa, and a freshman honors program. **Visiting:** There are regularly scheduled orientations for prospective students, consisting of daily planned activities during orientation in the first week of the fall semester. There are guides for informal visits, visitors may sit in on classes, and stay overnight. To schedule a visit, contact the Office of Admission. **Campus Safety and Security:** Measures include 24-hour foot and vehicle patrol, self-defense education, and security escort services. There are shuttle buses, emergency telephones, and lighted pathways/sidewalks.

REQUIREMENTS: The ACT is required. Applicants should have 15 units of credit, with 11 units in college preparatory courses, including English, math, lab science, and social studies. A letter of recommendation is required, as is a minimum GPA of 2.0 in the college preparatory subjects and a ranking in the top half of their graduating class. Concordia University requires applicants to be in the upper 50% of their class. A GPA of 2.0 is required. AP and CLEP credits are accepted. Important factors in the admissions decision are advanced placement or honors courses, recommendations by school officials, and leadership record. All students are required to take 2 years of liberal arts, including humanities, English, science, religion, and social science, and 5 quarter hours of phys ed. A 2.0 to 2.25 GPA and a total of 128 to 150 quarter hours are required. The number of hours required for the major varies by program. **Procedure:** Freshmen are admitted to all sessions. Entrance exams should be taken in the spring of the junior year or fall of the senior year. There is a rolling admissions plan. Application deadlines are open. Applications are accepted on-line. **Transfer Students:** 90 transfer students enrolled in 2013-2014. A cumulative GPA of 2.0 or higher at all previous colleges plus a letter of recommendation are required. 48 of 128 credits required for the bachelor's degree must be completed at Concordia University. **International Students:** There are 5 international students enrolled. They must take the TOEFL or MELAB, or successfully complete Level 109 at an ELS language center.

ADMISSIONS: 92% of the 2014-2015 applicants were accepted. The ACT scores were 36% below 21, 23% between 21 and 23, 20% between 24 and 26, 9% between 27 and 28, and 12% above 28. 30% of the current freshmen were in the top fifth of their class; 41% were in the top two fifths. **Admissions Contact:** James P. Malley, Director of Admissions. E-Mail: *crfmalleyjp@curf.edu* Web: *www.curf.edu*

FINANCIAL AID: In 2014-2015, 93% of all full-time freshmen and 87% of continuing full-time students received some form of financial aid. 85% of all full-time freshmen and 67% of continuing full-time students received need-based aid. The average freshman award was $12,000. The average financial indebtedness of the 2014 graduate was $12,000. The FAFSA and the college's own financial statement, and student and parent 1040 U.S. tax forms are required. Check with the school for current application deadlines.

DEPAUL UNIVERSITY   E-2
www.depaul.edu

Chicago, IL 60604   (312) 362-8300
                                                     (800) 4-DEPAUL
Fax: (312) 362-5749   Email: admission@depaul.edu
Full-time: 6396 men, 7247 women   Faculty: 799; I, -$
Part-time: 1169 men, 1341 women   Ph.D.s: 86%
Graduate: 3584 men, 4062 women   Student/Faculty: n/av
Year: quarters, summer session   Tuition: $34,390
Room & Board: $12,552   Freshman Class: 19533
                                         applied, 13649 accepted,
                                         2544 enrolled
SAT CR/M: 586/569 ACT: 25   CEEB CODE: 1165
Application Deadline: February 1   VERY COMPETITIVE

DePaul University is the nation's largest Catholic university. Its partnerships throughout Chicago enable DePaul to provide an exceptional educational experience that is vibrant, pragmatic and socially engaged. Classes are small and taught by knowledgeable and experienced faculty members who take full advantage of Chicago's resources. DePaul's mission to provide a quality education to students from a broad range of backgrounds has resulted in one of the nation's most diverse student bodies. With ten colleges and schools, DePaul has campuses in Chicago's Loop and Lincoln Park neighborhoods and three suburban locations. There are 9 undergraduate schools and 10 graduate schools. In addition to regional accreditation, DePaul has baccalaureate program accreditation with AACSB and NASM. The 38-acre campus is in an urban area. Including any residence halls, there are 48 buildings.

STUDENT LIFE: 79% of undergraduates are from Illinois. Others are from 50 states, 86 foreign countries, and Canada. 78% are from public schools. 55% are White; 17% Hispanic. 34% are Catholic. **Male To Female Ratio:** 1.1:1. The average age of freshmen is 18; all undergraduates, 23. 13% do not continue beyond their first year; 71% remain to graduate. **Housing:** 2644 students can be accommodated in college housing, which includes coed dorms, on-campus apartments, and off-campus apartments. In addition, there are special-interest houses, Private studios and apartments, and traditional residence-style units. On-campus housing is available on a first-come, first-served basis, and is available on a lottery system for upperclassmen. Priority is given to out-of-town students. 84% of students commute. All students may keep cars.

FACULTY/CLASSROOMS: 53% of faculty are male; 47% are female. 80% do both. Graduate students teach 2% of introductory courses. The average class size in an introductory lecture is 25; in a laboratory is 19; and in a regular course is 29.

PROGRAMS OF STUDY: DePaul confers B.A., B.S., B.F.A., B.M., B.S.B. and B.S.P.E. degrees. Master's and Doctoral degrees are also awarded. Bachelor's degrees are awarded in BIOLOGICAL SCIENCE (biology/biological science), BUSINESS (accounting, banking and finance, business administration and management, business economics, finance, hospitality management services, human resources, management information systems, management science, marketing management, organizational behavior, and real estate), COMMUNICATIONS AND THE ARTS (animation, Arabic, art history, art, Chinese, communications, creative writing, dramatic arts, English, fine arts, French, German, graphic design, information technology, Italian, jazz, journalism, media arts, music, music business management, music performance, music theory and composition, performing arts, playwriting/screenwriting, public relations, Spanish, speech/debate/rhetoric, theatre arts, theater design, and theater management), COMPUTER AND PHYSICAL SCIENCE (applied mathematics, chemistry, computer programming, computer game design/development, computer science, computer security and information assurance, digital arts/technology, information sciences and systems, mathematics, physical sciences, and physics), EDUCATION (art education, early childhood education, education, education administration, elementary education, foreign languages education, health education, music education, physical education, secondary education, and special education), ENGINEERING AND ENVIRONMENTAL DESIGN (architectural history, computational sciences, computer graphics, computer technology, and environmental science), HEALTH PROFESSIONS (art therapy, clinical science, health science, and nursing), SOCIAL SCIENCE (African studies, American studies, anthropology, community services, East Asian studies, economics, geography, history, humanities, international studies, Islamic studies, Judaic studies, Latin American studies, peace studies, philosophy, political science/government, psychology, public administration, public affairs, religion, social science, social studies, sociology, urban studies, and women's studies). Accounting, finance, and psychology have the largest enrollments.

ACTIVITIES: 3% of men belong to 11 national fraternities; 8% of women belong to 16 national sororities. There are 317 groups on campus, including art, cheerleading, chess, choir, chorale, chorus, communications, computers, dance, debate, drama, environmental, ethnic, film, gay, honors, international, literary magazine, newspaper, pep band, photography, political, professional, radio and TV, religious, social, social service, and student government. Popular campus events include FEST (University Festival), Blue Demon Week, Blue Demon Dance, Welcome Week, Vincentian Service Day, New Student Service Day, and DemonTHON (DePaul's Dance Marathon). **Sports:** There are 6 intercollegiate sports for men and 7 for women, and 34 intramural sports for men and 34 for women. Facilities include The Ray Meyer Fitness and Recreation Center. The 123,000 square foot facility provides the DePaul community with a wide vari-

ety of fitness and recreation opportunities including a diverse offering of facility spaces, equipment, programs, and services. This state-of-the art facility offers: 12,000 square foot strength and conditioning area with more than 100 pieces of cardio equipment, selectorized equipment, and free weight area, 25-yard, six-lane swimming pool, 4 court gymnasium for basketball, volleyball, and badminton, 3 racquetball courtd, 1/8 mile banked jogging track, locker rooms, over 65 weekly Group Fitness classes, free to members, instructional classes including aquatics, yoga, dance, Pilates, marital arts, fitness training, and safety training. Personal training, massage therapy, intramural sports and club sports for students, faculty, and staff, outdoor equipment rentals, outdoor Adventure trips for students, faculty, and staff, and team challenge. **Graduates:** From July 1, 2013 to June 30, 2014, 3748 bachelor's degrees were awarded. The most popular majors were accountancy (7%), public relations and advertising (7%), and psychology (7%). 504 companies recruited on campus in 2013-2014. In an average class, 2% graduate in 3 years or less, 56% graduate in 4 years or less, 69% graduate in 5 years or less, and 71% graduate in 6 years or less.

SERVICES: There is a reader service for the blind, remedial reading and writing. The Center for Students with Disabilities offers clinician services which includes remediation of skills for time management, organizational skills, reading strategies and writing skills. The University provides free tutoring services across a range of departments and subjects area: University Writing Center, Quantitative Reasoning Lab, Math Department, College of Science/Health, computer software (Word, Excel, etc.), Computer Programming, and Accounting, amongst others. **Library/Resources:** The 6 libraries contain 1.1 million volumes, 241,432 microform items, 31,989 audio/video tapes/CDs/DVDs, and subscribe to 70,452 periodicals including electronic. Computerized library services include interlibrary loans, database searching, Internet access, and Wi-Fi capability. Special learning facilities include an art gallery, radio station, LEED-certified environmental science, and chemistry building with greenhouse and green roof, digital cinema laboratory with motion-capture system, green-screen studio, converged newsroom, 10 specialized computer research labs including artificial intelligence, biomedics informatics and mobile e-commerce, 1,300-seat theatre, art museum, and a fitness and recreational center with pool. **Physically Challenged Students:** Facilities include wheelchair ramps, elevators, special parking, specially equipped restrooms, special class scheduling, lowered drinking fountains, lowered telephones, special housing. The Center for Students with Disabilities coordinates DePaul University's provision of accommodations and other services to students with documented disabilities in accordance with the Americans with Disabilities Act and Section 504 of the Rehabilitation Act. All CSD programs and services are free of charge with the exception of a modest fee for students requesting weekly clinician services for academic support strategies. CSD works with the range of all documented disabilities, e.g., LD, AD/HD, medical conditions, chronic illness, psychiatric, physical/visual/hearing impaired, etc. Students may be full time, part-time, and undergraduate or graduate. CSD students are enrolled in university-wide colleges and schools such as Education, Business, Science and health, Cinema Digital Media (CDM), Communication, Law, Music, Theatre, Liberal Arts and social Sciences, and the School for New Learning (SNL) with declared majors across a wide spectrum of career tracks. **Special:** DePaul University is known and respected for its nearly 300 graduate and undergraduate programs and concentrations. The Irwin W. Steans Center for Community-based service learning (CbSL) and community service studies provides opportunities and experiences for students to develop social agency through CbSL courses, community internships, research, scholarships, placements, and community-based student employment. The University Internship Program assists students in finding an internship that fits their course of study and career goals. With several locations and programs available, the study abroad office is available to students who are looking for a variety of study abroad opportunities and programs. DePaul also offers accelerated degree programs, dual majors, certificate programs, pass/fail options, and concentrations within the theater major, including acting, costume design, general theater studies, lighting design, playwriting, production theater management, and theater technology. The School for New Learning provides evening and weekend degree programs for adult learners, with credit given for life and work experience. There are 19 national honor societies and a freshman honors program. **Visiting:** There are regularly scheduled orientations for prospective students, freshmen orientation, DePaul premiere, and transfer and adult student orientation, provide academic advising, assessment testing, and course registration, and information on social activities and residence life. There are guides for informal visits, visitors may sit in on classes, and stay overnight. To schedule a visit, contact the Office of Admission. **Campus Safety and Security:** Measures include 24-hour foot and vehicle patrol, emergency notification system, self-defense education, and security escort services. There are emergency telephones, lighted pathways/sidewalks, and controlled access to dorms/residences.

REQUIREMENTS: The SAT or ACT is recommended. Based on research and DePaul's student-centered approach to education, DePaul has adopted a test-optional alternative for freshman admission. Students applying for freshman admission can choose whether or not to submit ACT or SAT scores as part of the application. Students who do not submit test scores will be required to send responses to several short essay questions. Music School applicants and applicants for the Acting Program in the Theatre School are required to schedule an audition. An interview or portfolio review is required for Design, Technical, or Theatre Studies program applicants. A GPA of 2.0 is required. AP and CLEP credits are accepted. Important factors in the admissions decision are advanced placement or honors courses, leadership record, and personality/intangible qualities. At DePaul, our core curriculum   the Liberal Studies Program consists of two primary components: the Common Core and six distinct learning domains. All students (except School for New Learning) must complete general education requirements, including 4 courses in arts and literature, philosophical inquiry, religious dimensions, scientific inquiry self, society and the modern world, and understanding the past. These liberal studies vary by college. A total of 192 quarter hour credits, and a minimum GPA of 2.0 is required to graduate. **Procedure:** Freshmen are admitted to all sessions. Scores need to be submitted by February 1. There are early admissions, deferred admissions, and rolling admissions plans. Early decision applications should be filed by November 15; regular applications, by February 1 for fall entry; November 1 for winter entry; March 1 for spring entry; and May 1 for summer entry, along with a $25 fee. Notification of early decision is sent January 15; regular decision, March 15. applicants were on the 2014 waiting list; were admitted. Applications are accepted on-line. **Transfer Students:** 2574 transfer students enrolled in 2013-2014. A 2.0 GPA is required for most programs; a 2.5 for Driehaus College of Business, College of Education, and School of Music. Applicants with fewer than 30 semester hours or 44 quarter hours should submit high school transcripts and SAT or ACT scores. An audition is required for music and theater majors. 60 of 192 credits required for the bachelor's degree must be completed at DePaul. **International Students:** There are 466 international students enrolled. The school actively recruits these students. They must take the TOEFL with a minimum score of 550 on the paper-based TOEFL (PBT) or 80 on the Internet-based version (iBT), or take the International English Testing Systems. Based on research and DePaul's student-centered approach to education.

ADMISSIONS: 70% of the 2014-2015 applicants were accepted. The SAT scores for the 2014-2015 freshman class were: Critical Reading--13% below 500, 41% between 500 and 599, 37% between 600 and 699, and 8% between 700 and 800; Math--18% below 500, 43% between 500 and 599, 32% between 600 and 699, and 6% between 700 and 800. The ACT scores were 10% below 21, 22% between 21 and 23, 29% between 24 and 26, 17% between 27 and 28, and 22% above 28. 45% of the current freshmen were in the top fifth of their class; 75% were in the top two fifths. 8 freshmen graduated first in their class. **Admissions Contact:** Carlene Klaas-Kennelly, Dean of Undergraduate Admission. E-Mail: *admission@depaul.edu* Web: *http://www.depaul.edu/admission-and-aid/types-of-admission/Pages/default.aspx*

FINANCIAL AID: In 2014-2015, 73% of all full-time freshmen and 69% of continuing full-time students received some form of financial aid. 63% of all full-time freshmen and 59% of continuing full-time students received need-based aid. The average freshman award was $23,440. Need-based scholarships or need-based grants averaged $11,204 need-based self-help aid (loans and jobs) averaged $3,663;

non-need-based athletic scholarships averaged $19,759; and other non-need-based awards and non-need-based scholarships averaged $10,941. 17% of undergraduate students work part-time. The average financial indebtedness of the 2014 graduate was $24,292. The FAFSA is required. The priority date for freshman financial aid applications for fall entry is January 1. The deadline for filing freshman financial aid applications for fall entry is March 1.

DOMINICAN UNIVERSITY   E-2
www.dom.edu

River Forest, IL 60305   (708) 524-6795
                                          (800) 828-8475
Fax: (708) 524-6864   **Email:** domadmis@dom.edu
Full-time: 643 men, 1264 women   **Faculty:** 135; IIA, -$
Part-time: 56 men, 106 women   **Ph.D.s:** 63%
Graduate: 344 men, 1057 women   **Student/Faculty:** 11 to 1
Year: semesters, summer session   **Tuition:** $28,810
Room & Board: $8818   **Freshman Class:** 3502 applied, 2100 accepted, 497 enrolled
SAT CR/M/W: 520/548/527 **ACT:** 22   **CEEB CODE:** 1667
Application Deadline: July 1   **COMPETITIVE**

Dominican University, founded in 1901, is an independent liberal arts institution affiliated with the Roman Catholic Church and sponsored by the Sinsinawa Dominicans. Figures in the above capsule and in this profile are approximate. There are 3 undergraduate schools and 4 graduate schools. In addition to regional accreditation, Dominican University has baccalaureate program accreditation with ACBSP, ADA, CSWE, NCATE, and ALA. The 37-acre campus is in a suburban area 10 miles west of Chicago. Including any residence halls, there are 13 buildings.

STUDENT LIFE: 91% of undergraduates are from Illinois. Others are from 42 states, 17 foreign countries, and Canada. 66% are from public schools. 44% are White; 40% Hispanic. **Male To Female Ratio:** 2.3:1. The average age of freshmen is 19; all undergraduates, 21. 63% remain to graduate. **Housing:** 610 students can be accommodated in college housing, which includes single-sex and coed dorms, off-campus apartments, and married student housing. On-campus housing is available on a first-come and first-served basis. Priority is given to out-of-town students. 71% of students commute. All students may keep cars.

FACULTY/CLASSROOMS: 41% of faculty are male; 59% are female. 75% teach undergraduates, and 25% do both. No introductory courses are taught by graduate students. The average class size in an introductory lecture is 19; in a laboratory is 15; and in a regular course is 17.

PROGRAMS OF STUDY: Dominican University confers B.A., B.S. and B.M.S. degrees. Master's and Doctoral degrees are also awarded. Bachelor's degrees are awarded in BIOLOGICAL SCIENCE (biochemistry, biology/biological science, neurosciences, and nutrition), BUSINESS (accounting, apparel and accessories marketing, business administration and management, fashion merchandising, finance, international business management, and marketing management), COMMUNICATIONS AND THE ARTS (apparel design, art history, communications, dramatic arts, English, film arts, fine arts, French, graphic design, Italian, journalism, music, painting, performing arts, photography, Spanish, and theatre arts), COMPUTER AND PHYSICAL SCIENCE (chemistry, computer science, digital arts/technology, mathematics, and natural sciences), EDUCATION (early childhood education, education, elementary education, and secondary education), ENGINEERING AND ENVIRONMENTAL DESIGN (engineering and environmental science), HEALTH PROFESSIONS (nursing, predentistry, premedicine, and prepharmacy), SOCIAL SCIENCE (American studies, criminal justice, dietetics, economics, fashion design and technology, food production/management/services, food science, gender studies, history, international relations, legal studies, ministries, philosophy, political science/government, prelaw, psychology, religion, social science, sociology, theological studies, and women's studies). Business administration, health professions, and psychology are the strongest academically. Business administration, psychology, and biology have the largest enrollments.

ACTIVITIES: There are no fraternities or sororities. There are 31 groups on campus, including art, choir, communications, computers, dance, drama, environmental, ethnic, gay, honors, international, literary magazine, musical theater, newspaper, photography, political, professional, religious, social, social service, student government, and students for peace and justice. Popular campus events include Caritas Veritas. **Sports:** There are 7 intercollegiate sports for men and 6 for women, and 6 intramural sports for men and 6 for women. Facilities include a gym, an indoor running track, a weight room, a training room, a fitness center, a dance room, racquetball courts, and soccer fields. **Graduates:** From July 1, 2013 to June 30, 2014, 444 bachelor's degrees were awarded. The most popular majors were business (23%), health professions (14%), and social sciences (12%). 30 companies recruited on campus in 2013-2014. In an average class, 48% graduate in 4 years or less, 61% graduate in 5 years or less, and 63% graduate in 6 years or less. Of the 2013 graduating class, 32% were enrolled in graduate school within 6 months of graduation, and 53% were employed.

SERVICES: Counseling and information services are available, as is tutoring in most subjects. There is remedial math and writing. **Library/Resources:** The library contains 250,000 volumes, 50,000 microform items, and 5,000 audio/video tapes/CDs/DVDs, and subscribes to 35,000 periodicals including electronic. Computerized library services include interlibrary loans, database searching, Internet access, and Wi-Fi capability. Special learning facilities include an art gallery, a language lab, and a writing center. **Physically Challenged Students:** All of the campus is accessible. Facilities include wheelchair ramps, elevators, special parking, specially equipped restrooms, special class scheduling, lowered drinking fountains, and special housing. **Special:** Co-op programs in nursing with Rush University, cross-registration with Concordia University, internships, study abroad in 11 countries, and a Washington semester are offered. Student-designed majors and interdisciplinary majors, including computer information systems, math and computer science, and environmental science, credit for prior learning, and pass/fail options are possible. There is an accelerated degree program in organizational leadership, a joint B.A.-B.S. in engineering with the Illinois Institute of Technology, and a dual admission program with Midwestern University for pharmacy. There are 11 national honor societies and a freshman honors program. **Visiting:** There are regularly scheduled orientations for prospective students, including visiting day and open house programs, which consist of faculty and student presentations, tours, and an academic and co-curricular fair. Special events are also held during the summer. There are guides for informal visits, visitors may sit in on classes, and stay overnight. To schedule a visit, contact Office of Undergraduate Admissions. **Campus Safety and Security:** Measures include 24-hour foot and vehicle patrol, emergency notification system, self-defense education, and security escort services. There are shuttle buses, emergency telephones, lighted pathways/sidewalks, controlled access to dorms/residences, door alarms.

REQUIREMENTS: The SAT or ACT is required. Graduation from an accredited secondary school or satisfactory scores on the GED are required for admission. The school requires 14 academic credits or 16 Carnegie units. High school courses should include English, math, foreign language, social science, and lab science. An essay is required and an interview is recommended. AP and CLEP credits are accepted. Important factors in the admissions decision are advanced placement or honors courses, recommendations by school officials, and leadership record. To graduate, students must complete 124 credit hours with a minimum GPA of 2.0. A total of 30 to 56 hours is required in the major. All students must demonstrate proficiency, through a placement exam or the completion of specified courses, in English composition, math, computer competency, and library skills. In addition, students must take 1 interdisciplinary seminar at each academic level and 1 course each in natural sciences, history, fine arts and literature, social sciences, theology, and philosophy. 1 course must meet the multicultural requirement. **Procedure:** Freshmen are admitted fall and spring. Entrance exams should be taken in the junior year. There are deferred admissions and rolling admissions plans. Application deadlines are open. Application fee is $25. Notification is sent on a rolling basis. Applications are accepted on-line. **Transfer Students:** 125 transfer students enrolled in 2013-2014. A college transcript is required. Applicants must have a minimum of 12 credit

hours with a GPA of 2.5. An interview is recommended. The high school record will be evaluated if GPA is below 2.5 at the previous college. 34 of 124 credits required for the bachelor's degree must be completed at Dominican University. **International Students:** There are 57 international students enrolled. They must take the TOEFL with a minimum score of 550 on the paper-based TOEFL (PBT) or 79 on the Internet-based version (iBT). They must also take the SAT or ACT.

ADMISSIONS: 60% of the 2014-2015 applicants were accepted. The SAT scores for the 2014-2015 freshman class were: Critical Reading--38% below 500, 56% between 500 and 599,and 6% between 600 and 699; Math--38% below 500, 31% between 500 and 599, 25% between 600 and 699, and 6% between 700 and 800; Writing--31% below 500, 50% between 500 and 599, and 19% between 600 and 699. The ACT scores were 37% below 21, 34% between 21 and 23, 20% between 24 and 26, 4% between 27 and 28, and 5% above 28. 1 freshman graduated first in the class. **Admissions Contact:** Glenn Hamilton, Assistant Vice President for Enrollment . E-Mail: *domadmis@dom.edu* Web: *http://www.dom.edu/admission/index.html*

FINANCIAL AID: In 2014-2015, 95% of all full-time freshmen and 92% of continuing full-time students received some form of financial aid. 91% of all full-time freshmen and 87% of continuing full-time students received need-based aid. The average freshman award was $23,897. Need-based scholarships or need-based grants averaged $20,145; need-based self-help aid (loans and jobs) averaged $3,293; and other non-need-based awards and non-need-based scholarships averaged $6,222. 20% of undergraduate students work part-time. Average annual earnings from campus work are $2500. The average financial indebtedness of the 2014 graduate was $31,356. Dominican University is a member of CSS. The FAFSA is required. The priority date for freshman financial aid applications for fall entry is February 15.

EASTERN ILLINOIS UNIVERSITY   E-4
www.eiu.edu

Charleston, IL 61920	(217) 581-2223
Fax: (217) 581-7060	Email: admissions@eiu.edu
Full-time: 2727 men, 3949 women	Faculty: n/av
Part-time: 317 men, 647 women	Ph.D.s: n/av
Graduate: 490 men, 783 women	Student/Faculty: n/av
Year: semesters, summer session	Tuition: $11,108 ($28,088)
Room & Board: $9358	Freshman Class: 8918 applied, 4438 accepted, 1126 enrolled
SAT: required ACT: 22	CEEB CODE: 1199
Application Deadline: rolling	COMPETITIVE

Eastern Illinois University is a public comprehensive university that offers superior, accessible undergraduate and graduate education. Students learn the methods and results of free and rigorous inquiry in the arts, humanities, sciences, and professions, guided by a faculty known for its excellence in teaching, research, creative activity, and service. The University community is committed to diversity and inclusion and fosters opportunities for student-faculty scholarship and applied learning experiences within a student-centered campus culture. Throughout their education, students refine their abilities to reason and to communicate clearly so as to become responsible citizens and leaders. There are 5 undergraduate schools and 1 graduate school. In addition to regional accreditation, EIU has baccalaureate program accreditation with AACSB, ACEJMC, NASAD, NASM, NRPA, AAFCS, ACS, CAAHEP, ACTFL, NASPE, NCTM, NASP, CTTE, NAST, ASHA, ELCC, ACEI, NCTE, AAHE, NSTA, NAEYC, CACREP, ATMAE, CAA, CCNE, NCSS, CEC, HLC NCA, and ISBE. The 320-acre campus is in a small town 110 miles from Indianapolis, Indiana and 147 miles from St. Louis, Missouri. Including any residence halls, there are 80 buildings.

STUDENT LIFE: 96% of undergraduates are from Illinois. Others are from 36 states, 46 foreign countries, and Canada. 70% are White; 19% African American. **Male To Female Ratio:** 1.5:1. The average age of freshmen is 18; all undergraduates, 23. 24% do not continue beyond their first year; 59% remain to graduate. **Housing:** 5425 students can be accommodated in college housing, which includes single-sex and coed dorms, on-campus apartments, and married student housing. In addition, there are honors houses, special-interest houses, fraternity houses, and sorority houses. On-campus housing is guaranteed for the freshman year only, is available on a first-come, and first-served basis. 62% of students commute. All students may keep cars.

FACULTY/CLASSROOMS: No introductory courses are taught by graduate students. The average class size in a regular course is 16.

PROGRAMS OF STUDY: EIU confers B.A., B.F.A., B.Mus., B.S., B.S.Bus. and B.S.Ed. degrees. Master's degrees are also awarded. Bachelor's degrees are awarded in BIOLOGICAL SCIENCE (biology/biological science), BUSINESS (accounting, business administration and management, finance, management information systems, marketing, and organizational leadership and management), COMMUNICATIONS AND THE ARTS (art, communication studies, English, foreign language, journalism, music, recreation administration, and theatre arts), COMPUTER AND PHYSICAL SCIENCE (chemistry, clinical laboratory science, computer science, geology, mathematics, and physics), EDUCATION (athletic training, early childhood education, elementary education, general studies, middle school education, science education, social science education, special education, and technical education), ENGINEERING AND ENVIRONMENTAL DESIGN (engineering and industrial engineering technology), HEALTH PROFESSIONS (health, kinesiology, and nursing), SOCIAL SCIENCE (africana studies, communication sciences and disorders, economics, family/consumer studies, geography, history, philosophy, political science/government, psychology, and sociology). Communication disorders is the strongest academically. Kinesiology and sports studies, biological sciences and general studies have the largest enrollments.

ACTIVITIES: 20% of men belong to 14 national fraternities; 18% of women belong to 12 national sororities. There are 204 groups on campus, including art, band, cheerleading, choir, chorale, chorus, communications, dance, drama, drill team, environmental, ethnic, film, gay, honors, international, jazz band, literary magazine, marching band, musical theater, newspaper, opera, orchestra, pep band, political, professional, radio and TV, religious, social, social service, student government, symphony, and yearbook. Popular campus events include Celebration of the Arts, Homecoming, Family Weekend, Greek Week, PantherPalooza, Panther Service Day, Prowl, and Pizza with the Prez. **Sports:** There are 10 intercollegiate sports for men and 11 for women, and 30 intramural sports for men and 30 for women. Facilities include a swimming pool, gym, student recreation center, track, tennis courts, racquetball courts, jogging trail, baseball field, softball field, football field, basketball court, soccer field, and a rugby field. **Graduates:** From July 1, 2013 to June 30, 2014, 2138 bachelor's degrees were awarded. The most popular majors were kinesiology and sports studies (10%), communication studies (9%), and general studies (9%). 156 companies recruited on campus in 2013-2014. In an average class, 33% graduate in 4 years or less, 55% graduate in 5 years or less, and 59% graduate in 6 years or less.

SERVICES: Counseling and information services are available, as is tutoring in most subjects, biology, business, chemistry, writing (all subjects), economics, foreign language, geology/geography, history, mathematics, physics, political science, psychology and sociology. There is remedial math, reading, and writing. Student success center for help on study skills, test-taking and time management. **Library/Resources:** The library contains 1.8 million volumes, 577,061 microform items, 71,756 audio/video tapes/CDs/DVDs, and subscribes to 39,315 periodicals including electronic. Computerized library services include interlibrary loans, database searching, Internet access, and Wi-Fi capability. Special learning facilities include an art gallery, radio station, TV station, an observatory, scanning electron microscope, and an Thut greenhouse. **Physically Challenged Students:** 80% of the campus is accessible. Facilities include wheelchair ramps, elevators, special parking, specially equipped restrooms, special class scheduling, lowered drinking fountains, lowered telephones, and special housing. **Special:** EIU offers a B.S. in Engineering Cooperative with the University of Illinois at Champaign-Urbana or Southern Illinois University at Carbondale. Internships, study abroad, and double major options are available. Credit for life experience may be granted

through the General Studies program and the Organizational and Professional Development program. There are 44 national honor societies, a freshman honors program, and 24 departmental honors programs. **Visiting:** There are regularly scheduled orientations for prospective students, including a tour of the campus and residence halls, sessions on financial aid, housing, admission process, tips for academic success, steps to take after admission, transfer admission, academic and student services fair. There are guides for informal visits and visitors may sit in on classes. To schedule a visit, contact Stacy Smith at (217) 581-2223. **Campus Safety and Security:** Measures include 24-hour foot and vehicle patrol, emergency notification system, self-defense education, and security escort services. There are shuttle buses, emergency telephones, lighted pathways/sidewalks, controlled access to dorms/residences, student patrols, alert EIU, and warning sirens.

REQUIREMENTS: The SAT or ACT is required. All applicants must submit ACT or SAT scores and meet one of the following: rank in the top quarter of their high school class based on 6 or more semesters or have a GPA of 3.0 and have an ACT composite of at least 18 (SAT 860); rank in the top one half of their high school class based on 6 or more semesters or have a GPA of 2.5 and have an ACT composite score of at least 19 (SAT 910); rank in the top three quarters of their high school class based on 6 or more semesters or have a GPA of 2.25 and an ACT composite score of at least 22 (SAT 1020). Applicants must be graduates of an accredited secondary school or have passed the GED. 17 academic credits are required and should include 4 years of English and 3 years each of math, science, and social studies, including 2 years foreign language and 2 electives. EIU requires applicants to be in the upper 75% of their class. A GPA of 2.3 is required. AP and CLEP credits are accepted. A total of 120 credit hours, with a minimum of 40 hours in upper-division courses, must be completed for graduation. The minimum GPA required for graduation is 2.0 (2.65 in education). A core curriculum of 40 hours includes courses in language, humanities and fine arts, math, and social and behavioral science, scientific awareness, and senior seminar. **Procedure:** Freshmen are admitted fall, spring, and summer. Entrance exams should be taken EIU does not require entrance exams. There are deferred admissions and rolling admissions plans. Application deadlines are open. The fall 2014 application fee was $30. Notification is sent on a rolling basis. Applications are accepted online. **Transfer Students:** 888 transfer students enrolled in 2013-2014. Applicants with 30 or more college-level semester hours must have a cumulative grade point average of 2.0 on a 4.0 grading scale based on all college-level work attempted and a 2.0 cumulative grade point average on a 4.0 scale from the last institution attended. Applicants with 24 or more college-level semester hours must have a cumulative grade point average of 2.5 on a 4.0 grading scale based on all college-level work attempted and a 2.0 cumulative grade point average on a 4.0 scale from the last institution attended. Applicants with fewer than the required number of hours of earned credit must have at least a 2.0 grade point average on a 4.0 scale based on all college-level work attempted, a 2.0 grade point average on a 4.0 scale from the last institution attended and meet the freshman admission criteria. 42 of 120 credits required for the bachelor's degree must be completed at EIU. **International Students:** There are 72 international students enrolled. The school actively recruits these students. They must take the TOEFL with a minimum score of 500 on the paper-based TOEFL (PBT) or 61 on the Internet-based version (iBT) or take the MELAB, or the IELTS.

ADMISSIONS: 50% of the 2014-2015 applicants were accepted. The ACT scores were 41% below 21, 32% between 21 and 23, 16% between 24 and 26, 5% between 27 and 28, and 6% above 28. 25% of the current freshmen were in the top fifth of their class; 54% were in the top two fifths. **Admissions Contact:** Chris Dearth, Director of Admissions. E-Mail: *admissions@eiu.edu* Web: *http://www.eiu.edu*

FINANCIAL AID: In 2014-2015, 76% of all full-time freshmen and 69% of continuing full-time students received some form of financial aid. 59% of all full-time freshmen and 51% of continuing full-time students received need-based aid. The average freshman award was $12,129. Need-based scholarships or need-based grants averaged $3,431; need-based self-help aid (loans and jobs) averaged $3,014; non-need-based athletic scholarships averaged $6,703; and other non-need-based awards and non-need-based scholarships averaged

$3,286. The average financial indebtedness of the 2014 graduate was $31,219. The FAFSA is required. The priority date for freshman financial aid applications for fall entry is March 1.

ELMHURST COLLEGE — E-2
www.elmhurst.edu

Elmhurst, IL 60126	(630) 617-3400
	(800) 697-1871
Fax: (630) 617-5501	Email: admit@elmhurst.edu
Full-time: 1073 men, 1626 women	Faculty: 136; IIB, av$
Part-time: 71 men, 83 women	Ph.D.s: 79%
Graduate: 133 men, 271 women	Student/Faculty: 20 to 1
Year: 4-1-4, summer session	Tuition: $33,950
Room & Board: $9386	Freshman Class: 3193 applied, 2162 accepted, 510 enrolled
SAT CR/M/W: 540/550/530 ACT: 23	CEEB CODE: 1204
Application Deadline: n/av	COMPETITIVE

Elmhurst College is a premier, private, liberal arts college. Among Elmhurst's specialties is its synergy of two indispensable elements of a quality college experience: professional preparation and liberal learning. Elmhurst College has sought to prepare students superbly, both for their first jobs and for fulfilling lives. Elmhurst offers students of many backgrounds purposeful learning for the whole of life. There is one graduate school. In addition to regional accreditation, Elmhurst has baccalaureate program accreditation with CCNE. The 48-acre campus is in a suburban area 15 miles west of Chicago. Including any residence halls, there are 23 buildings.

STUDENT LIFE: 90% of undergraduates are from Illinois. Others are from 37 states, 31 foreign countries, and Canada. 89% are from public schools. 70% are White; 15% Hispanic. 36% are Catholic; 15% Protestant; 15% claim no religious affiliation. **Male To Female Ratio:** 1.6:1. The average age of freshmen is 18; all undergraduates, 22. 18% do not continue beyond their first year; 74% remain to graduate. **Housing:** 1112 students can be accommodated in college housing, which includes coed dorms, on-campus apartments, and off-campus apartments. 65% of students commute. Some may keep cars.

FACULTY/CLASSROOMS: 40% of faculty are male; 60% are female. All teach and do research. No introductory courses are taught by graduate students. The average class size in an introductory lecture is 19; in a laboratory is 15; and in a regular course is 16.

PROGRAMS OF STUDY: Elmhurst confers B.A., B.F.A, B.S., B.L.S. and B.Mus. degrees. Master's degrees are also awarded. Bachelor's degrees are awarded in BIOLOGICAL SCIENCE (biology/biological science and (Biological) Pre-Health Studies), BUSINESS (accounting, business administration and management, finance, international business management, management science, marketing/retailing/merchandising, sports management, and supply chain management), COMMUNICATIONS AND THE ARTS (art, arts administration/management, communications, communication science, English, French, German, graphic design, information technology, jazz, music, music business management, music performance, music theory and composition, Spanish, and theatre arts), COMPUTER AND PHYSICAL SCIENCE (chemistry, computer game design/development, computer science, information sciences and systems, mathematics, and physics), EDUCATION (art education, early childhood education, elementary education, mathematics education, music education, physical education, secondary education, and special education), ENGINEERING AND ENVIRONMENTAL DESIGN (environmental science and preengineering), HEALTH PROFESSIONS (exercise science, nursing, Pre-Health Studies, premedicine, prephysical therapy, preveterinary science, and speech pathology/audiology), SOCIAL SCIENCE (American studies, criminal justice, economics, geography, history, liberal arts/general studies, philosophy, political science/government, psychology, religion, sociology, theological studies, and urban studies). Biology, English, nursing and education are the strongest academically. Business, psychology, nursing and education-related programs have the largest enrollments.

ACTIVITIES: 9% of men belong to 3 national fraternities; 11% of women belong to 4 national sororities. There are 92 groups on campus, including art, band, cheerleading, chess, choir, chorale, chorus, communications, computers, dance, drama, environmental, ethnic, film, gay, honors, international, jazz band, literary magazine, musical theater, newspaper, orchestra, pep band, political, professional, radio and TV, religious, social, social service, student government, symphony, and yearbook. Popular campus events include Elmhurst College Jazz Festival, Lecture Series, Theater Performances, Summer Extravaganza, and the Performances by Elmhurst College Ensembles. **Sports:** There are 10 intercollegiate sports for men and 10 for women, and 7 intramural sports for men and 7 for women. Facilities include a phys ed center, weight rooms, courts for tennis, racquetball, and handball. Langhorst Athletic Field is home to the college's football, soccer, track and field teams. **Graduates:** From July 1, 2013 to June 30, 2014, 753 bachelor's degrees were awarded. The most popular majors were business (18%), health sciences (14%), and psychology (11%). 30 companies recruited on campus in 2013-2014. In an average class, 61% graduate in 4 years or less, 74% graduate in 5 years or less, and 74% graduate in 6 years or less. Of the 2013 graduating class, 33% were enrolled in graduate school within 6 months of graduation, and 78% were employed.

SERVICES: Counseling and information services are available, as is tutoring in most subjects. There is remedial math, reading, and writing. **Library/Resources:** The library contains 237,539 volumes, 49,798 microform items, 49,413 audio/video tapes/CDs/DVDs, and subscribes to 24,245 periodicals including electronic. Computerized library services include interlibrary loans, database searching, Internet access, and Wi-Fi capability. Special learning facilities include an art gallery, radio station, a recording studio that offers recording and control room spaces with grand piano and isolation booth and a digital 24-track hard drive Otari Radar system with automated status console; the SimBaby, a life-size, robotic model of an infant and SimMan, an adult patient simulator; an electron microscopy lab; an accelerator lab. **Physically Challenged Students:** 95% of the campus is accessible. Facilities include wheelchair ramps, elevators, special parking, specially equipped restrooms, lowered drinking fountains, and lowered telephones. **Special:** There are cooperative programs in all majors. In keeping with the hallmarks of the Elmhurst Experience, self-formation and early professional preparation, Career Education starts early-on in most students' academic experience. The Center for Professional Excellence provides experiential opportunities for career exploration to majors in 23 academic departments, e.g., internships, informational interviews, career shadowing, and connections to professional mentors. Internships varying from 1 month to one term are available in approximately 20 major fields. Students may study abroad in over 40 countries. Elmhurst also offers a Washington and Chicago Semester and a 3-2 engineering degree with the Illinois Institute of Technology, Washington University, and the Universities of Illinois and Southern California. There are accelerated degree programs in business administration, organizational leadership and communication, information technology, and pre-clinical psychology. Credit for life, military, and work experience, nondegree study and pass/fail options are possible. There are 23 national honor societies, a freshman honors program, and 25 departmental honors programs. **Visiting:** There are regularly scheduled orientations for prospective students, including an admissions interview, a campus tour, and faculty meetings if desired. There are guides for informal visits, visitors may sit in on classes, and stay overnight. To schedule a visit, contact Francesca Garza at (630) 617-3400. **Campus Safety and Security:** Measures include 24-hour foot and vehicle patrol, emergency notification system, and security escort services. There are shuttle buses, emergency telephones, lighted pathways/sidewalks, and controlled access to dorms/residences.

REQUIREMENTS: The SAT or ACT is required, with the ACT preferred. Candidates for admission must have completed 16 academic units of credit including at least 3 in English and 2 each of math, social science, and natural science lab courses. 2 years of a foreign language are recommended. AP and CLEP credits are accepted. Important factors in the admissions decision are advanced placement or honors courses, leadership record, and extracurricular activities record. Complete all aspects of the Integrated Curriculum or General Education program; complete all the requirements for a major; Earn a minimum of 32.00 course credits; Complete at least 10.00 course credits at the 300/400 level at a four-year institution; Achieve a minimum combined and institutional GPA of 2.0 (some majors require a higher GPA); earn one's final 8.00 course credits at Elmhurst College (residency requirement) **Procedure:** Freshmen are admitted fall and spring. Entrance exams should be taken by the spring of the senior year. There are early admissions, deferred admissions, and rolling admissions plans. Applications should be filed by January 15 for spring entry. Notification is sent on a rolling basis. Applications are accepted on-line. **Transfer Students:** 290 transfer students enrolled in 2013-2014. Qualified applicants should show evidence of their ability to successfully complete college-level work, based on their good standing at the last college or university attended. 32 of 128 credits required for the bachelor's degree must be completed at Elmhurst. **International Students:** There are 63 international students enrolled. The school actively recruits these students. They must take the TOEFL with a minimum score of 550 on the paper-based TOEFL (PBT) or 79 on the Internet-based version (iBT) or take the MELAB.

ADMISSIONS: 68% of the 2014-2015 applicants were accepted. The SAT scores for the 2014-2015 freshman class were: Critical Reading--39% below 500, 35% between 500 and 599, and 26% between 600 and 699; Math--39% below 500, 26% between 500 and 599, 30% between 600 and 699, and 4% between 700 and 800; Writing--48% below 500, 35% between 500 and 599, 13% between 600 and 699, and 4% between 700 and 800. The ACT scores were 23% below 21, 28% between 21 and 23, 27% between 24 and 26, 12% between 27 and 28, and 10% above 28. 38% of the current freshmen were in the top fifth of their class; 66% were in the top two fifths. 2 freshmen graduated first in their class. **Admissions Contact:** Stephanie Levenson, Director of Admissions. E-Mail: *admit@elmhurst.edu* Web: *www.elmhurst.edu*

FINANCIAL AID: The FAFSA is required. The priority date for freshman financial aid applications for fall entry is Februray 15.

EUREKA COLLEGE — D-3
www.eureka.edu

Eureka, IL 61530	
	(309) 467-6350
	(888) 4-EUREKA
Fax: (309) 467-6576	Email: admissions@eureka.edu
Full-time: n/av	Faculty: 44; IIB, --$
Part-time: n/av	Ph.D.s: 85%
Graduate: n/av	Student/Faculty: 12 to 1
Year: semesters, summer session	Tuition: $14,000
Room & Board: $5880	Freshman Class: 900 applied, 600 accepted, 140 enrolled
SAT: required ACT: 23	CEEB CODE: 1206
Application Deadline: August 1	COMPETITIVE

Eureka College, founded in 1855, is a small, private, liberal arts college affiliated with the Christian Church (Disciples of Christ). The figures in the above capsule and in this profile are approximate. There is one undergraduate school. In addition to regional accreditation, E.C. has baccalaureate program accreditation with NCATE. The 112-acre campus is in a small town 20 minutes east of Peoria, 20 minutes west of Bloomington, and 2 hours south of Chicago. Including any residence halls, there are 23 buildings.

STUDENT LIFE: 90% of undergraduates are from Illinois. Others are from 17 states, and 3 foreign countries. 80% are from public schools. 87% are White. 37% claim no religious affiliation; 31% Protestant; 28% Catholic. **Male To Female Ratio:** Is 1:1. The average age of freshmen is 18; all undergraduates, 21. 25% do not continue beyond their first year; 65% remain to graduate. **Housing:** 550 students can be accommodated in college housing, which includes single-sex and coed dorms. In addition, there are fraternity houses and sorority houses. On-campus housing is guaranteed for all 4 years. 80% of students live on campus; of those, 70% remain on campus on weekends. All students may keep cars.

FACULTY/CLASSROOMS: 64% of faculty are male; 36% are female. All teach undergraduates. No introductory courses are taught by graduate students. The average class size in an introductory lecture is 15; in a laboratory is 10; and in a regular course is 15.

PROGRAMS OF STUDY: E.C. confers B.A., and B.S. degrees. Bachelor's degrees are awarded in BIOLOGICAL SCIENCE (biology/biological science), BUSINESS (accounting, business administration and management, business economics, and management information systems), COMMUNICATIONS AND THE ARTS (communications, dramatic arts, English, fine arts, and music), COMPUTER AND PHYSICAL SCIENCE (chemistry, computer science, mathematics, and physical sciences), EDUCATION (athletic training, education, elementary education, music education, physical education, science education, and secondary education), HEALTH PROFESSIONS (medical laboratory technology), SOCIAL SCIENCE (child care/child and family studies, history, liberal arts/general studies, philosophy, physical fitness/movement, political science/government, psychology, religion, social science, and sociology). Chemistry, biology, and business administration are the strongest academically. Business administration, education, and psychology have the largest enrollments.

ACTIVITIES: 35% of men belong to 3 national fraternities; 35% of women belong to 1 local and 2 national sororities. There are 41 groups on campus, including art, band, cheerleading, choir, chorale, chorus, communications, computers, dance, drama, ethnic, honors, international, literary magazine, musical theater, newspaper, pep band, photography, political, professional, religious, social, social service, student government, and yearbook. Popular campus events include Pride Day, Tree Lighting Ceremony and Ivy Ceremony. **Sports:** There are 8 intercollegiate sports for men and 8 for women, and 6 intramural sports for men and 6 for women. Facilities include a gym, a pool, a weight room, tennis courts, and football, softball, and baseball fields and a wellness center. **Graduates:** From July 1, 2013 to June 30, 2014, 131 bachelor's degrees were awarded. The most popular majors were education (24%), business (23%), and psychology (15%). In an average class, 2% graduate in 3 years or less, 58% graduate in 4 years or less, and 5% graduate in 5 years or less. Of the 2013 graduating class, 20% were enrolled in graduate school within 6 months of graduation, and 75% were employed.

SERVICES: Counseling and information services are available, as is tutoring in most subjects. There is remedial reading and writing. There is a writing center and math lab located within the Learning Center. **Library/Resources:** The library contains 85,000 volumes, 4,989 microform items, 977 audio/video tapes/CDs/DVDs, and subscribes to 343 periodicals including electronic. Computerized library services include interlibrary loans, database searching, and Internet access. Special learning facilities include an art gallery, the Ronald Reagan Museum. **Physically Challenged Students:** 50% of the campus is accessible. Facilities include wheelchair ramps, elevators, special parking, and specially equipped restrooms. **Special:** Cooperative programs include a 3-2 engineering degree with Washington University in St. Louis and Illinois Institute of Technology, a 2-2 B.S.N. with Mennonite College of Nursing or St. Francis College of Nursing, and a 3-1 clinical lab science degree with St. Francis or St. John's School of Clinical Laboratory Science. Students may study abroad in most countries. Professional programs in arts management, art therapy, communications, prelaw, premedicine, preministry, and teacher education are offered. An interdisciplinary major in arts and letters combines visual, performing, and literary arts. Internships, student-designed, and dual majors are offered in various areas. A Washington semester is available. There are 7 national honor societies, a freshman honors program, and 100 departmental honors programs. **Visiting:** There are regularly scheduled orientations for prospective students, including visits with admissions and financial aid advisers, observing student panels, meetings with faculty and coaches, and campus tours. There are guides for informal visits, visitors may sit in on classes, and stay overnight. To schedule a visit, contact the Office of Admissions. **Campus Safety and Security:** There are lighted pathways/sidewalks, A city officer provides campus security in the evenings and on weekends.

REQUIREMENTS: The SAT or ACT is required. Applicants should be graduates of accredited secondary schools or have the GED. E.C. requires applicants to be in the upper 50% of their class. A GPA of 2.3 is required. AP and CLEP credits are accepted. Important factors in the admissions decision are recommendations by school officials, extracurricular activities record, and leadership record. All students must take English composition, biological and physical sciences, general studies, math, phys ed, Western civilization, 3 humanities courses, 3 social science courses, and a global awareness component. A total of at least 124 hours is required for graduation, including 32 hours in the major. A minimum GPA of 2.0 is required. **Procedure:** Freshmen are admitted to all sessions. Entrance exams should be taken by December of the senior year. There are deferred admissions and rolling admissions plans. Applications should be filed by August 1 for fall entry. Notification is sent on a rolling basis. Applications are accepted on-line. **Transfer Students:** 90 transfer students enrolled in 2013-2014. Applicants must have at least a 2.0 GPA in previous college work. Those with fewer than 30 hours of transferable credit must submit high school transcripts and ACT scores. Courses with grades below C are not accepted. 30 of 124 credits required for the bachelor's degree must be completed at E.C.. **International Students:** There are 12 international students enrolled. The school actively recruits these students. They must take the TOEFL.

ADMISSIONS: 67% of the 2014-2015 applicants were accepted. 35% of the current freshmen were in the top fifth of their class; 65% were in the top two fifths. **Admissions Contact:** Dr. Brian Sajko, Dean of Admissions and Financial Aid. E-Mail: *admissions@eureka.edu* Web: *www.eureka.edu*

FINANCIAL AID: In 2014-2015, 98% of all full-time freshmen and 98% of continuing full-time students received some form of financial aid. 30% of all full-time freshmen and 30% of continuing full-time students received need-based aid. The average freshman award was $4,000. 49% of undergraduate students work part-time. Average annual earnings from campus work are $1000. The average financial indebtedness of the 2014 graduate was $8,500. E.C. is a member of CSS. The FAFSA is required. The priority date for freshman financial aid applications for fall entry is April 1. The deadline for filing freshman financial aid applications for fall entry is August 1.

GREENVILLE COLLEGE   D-4
www.greenville.edu

Greenville, IL 62246

(618) 664-7100
(800) 345-4440

Fax: (618) 664-9841   Email: admissions@greenville.edu

Full-time: 606 men, 724 women	Faculty: 63; IIB, --$
Part-time: 21 men, 31 women	Ph.D.s: 66%
Graduate: 52 men, 142 women	Student/Faculty: 21 to 1
Year: 4-1-4, summer session	Tuition: $20,216
Room & Board: $6796	Freshman Class: 932 applied, 727 accepted, 252 enrolled
SAT CR/M/W: 480/490/470 **ACT:** 23	CEEB CODE: 1256
Application Deadline: August 1	COMPETITIVE

Greenville College, founded in 1892, is a private liberal arts institution affiliated with the Free Methodist Church. Greenville College seeks to transform students for lives of character and service through a Christ-centered education in the liberal arts and sciences. Figures in the above capsule and in this profile are approximate. There are 3 undergraduate schools. The 25-acre campus is in a small town 50 miles east of St. Louis. Including any residence halls, there are 48 buildings.

STUDENT LIFE: 72% of undergraduates are from Illinois. Others are from 42 states, 12 foreign countries,and Canada. The average age of freshmen is 18; all undergraduates, 24. 27% do not continue beyond their first year; 48% remain to graduate. **Housing:** 792 students can be accommodated in college housing, which includes single-sex dorms and on-campus apartments. On-campus housing is guaranteed for all 4 years. 54% of students live on campus; of those, 60% remain on campus on weekends. Alcohol is not permitted. All students may keep cars.

FACULTY/CLASSROOMS: 67% of faculty are male; 33% are female. 95% teach undergraduates. No introductory courses are taught by graduate students. The average class size in an introductory lecture is 20; in a laboratory is 16; and in a regular course is 19.

PROGRAMS OF STUDY: Greenville confers B.A., B.Mus.Ed. and B.S. degrees. Master's degrees are also awarded. Bachelor's degrees are awarded in BIOLOGICAL SCIENCE (biology/biological science and

environmental biology), BUSINESS (accounting, business administration and management, management information systems, marketing/retailing/merchandising, organizational leadership and management, and recreation and leisure services), COMMUNICATIONS AND THE ARTS (art, communications, contemporary Christian music, dramatic arts, English, media arts, music, music business management, public relations, Spanish, and speech/debate/rhetoric), COMPUTER AND PHYSICAL SCIENCE (chemistry, computer science, digital arts/technology, mathematics, and physics), EDUCATION (early childhood education, elementary education, English education, mathematics education, music education, physical education, science education, and special education), SOCIAL SCIENCE (criminal justice, history, international studies, liberal arts/general studies, ministries, pastoral studies, philosophy, psychology, religion, social work, sociology, and youth ministry). Biology, chemistry, and physics are the strongest academically. Education, music, and biology have the largest enrollments.

ACTIVITIES: There are no fraternities or sororities. There are 20 groups on campus, including art, band, cheerleading, choir, chorale, chorus, drama, ethnic, honors, jazz band, musical theater, newspaper, orchestra, pep band, professional, radio, religious, social, social service, and student government. Popular campus events include Agape Music Festival, All College Hike and Back to School Bash. **Sports:** There are 7 intercollegiate sports for men and 7 for women, and 6 intramural sports for men and 6 for women. Facilities include a gym, sports training annex, recreational center, 6 tennis courts, fitness pool, an all-weather track, softball, baseball, football, soccer, and practice fields. **Graduates:** From July 1, 2013 to June 30, 2014, 357 bachelor's degrees were awarded. The most popular majors were education (19%), biology (7%), and music (6%). In an average class, 1% graduate in 3 years or less, 39% graduate in 4 years or less, 49% graduate in 5 years or less, and 50% graduate in 6 years or less.

SERVICES: Counseling and information services are available, as is tutoring in some subjects, and lower-division general education courses. There is remedial math, reading, and writing. There is a program for at-risk freshmen. **Library/Resources:** The library contains 135,210 volumes, 17,384 microform items, 3,873 audio/video tapes/CDs/DVDs, and subscribes to 8,543 periodicals including electronic. Computerized library services include interlibrary loans, database searching, and Internet access. Special learning facilities include an art gallery, the bock museum. **Physically Challenged Students:** 25% of the campus is accessible. Facilities include wheelchair ramps, elevators, special parking, specially equipped restrooms, special class scheduling, and lowered drinking fountains. **Special:** The college provides opportunities for dual majors in such areas as psychology/religion, B.A.-B.S. degrees, student-designed programs in work-study programs, study abroad, credit by exam, internships, a general studies degree, pass/fail options, and nondegree study. A 3-2 engineering degree with the University of Illinois and Washington University, a 2-2 degree with St. John's College of Nursing, a 3-3 degree with Logan College of Chiropractic; an early acceptance program with Kirksville College of Osteopathic Medicine of A.T. Still University; and an American Studies program in Washington, D.C. are also available. Cross-registration is offered within the Wesleyan Urban Coalition, the Christian College Consortium, and the Council of Christian Colleges and Universities. There are 6 national honor societies and a freshman honors program. **Visiting:** There are regularly scheduled orientations for prospective students, including campus visits during scheduled preview days. There are guides for informal visits, visitors may sit in on classes, and stay overnight. To schedule a visit, contact the Admissions Office. **Campus Safety and Security:** Measures include self-defense education and security escort services. There are emergency telephones, lighted pathways/sidewalks, controlled access to dorms/residences, alarm systems in some buildings.

REQUIREMENTS: The SAT or ACT is required. The college recommends that applicants have 4 years of English, 2 years of foreign language, and 1 year each of algebra and geometry, laboratory science, and American history. Personal and academic references may also be considered in the application process. An essay is required. A GED certificate will be accepted. Greenville requires applicants to be in the upper 50% of their class. A GPA of 2.0 is required. AP and CLEP credits are accepted. Important factors in the admissions decision are leadership record, advanced placement or honors courses, and personality/intangible qualities. A minimum of 126 credits and a 2.0 GPA are required for graduation. All students must successfully complete the core requirements in addition to specific courses in communication, English, history, phys ed, and foreign language (B.A. only). Other degree requirements are fulfilled by in-depth study in biblical studies, cross-cultural experience, physical fitness activities, lab science, math, literature, philosophy, fine arts, psychology or sociology, and a writing-intensive course. **Procedure:** Freshmen are admitted to all sessions. Entrance exams should be taken in the spring of the junior year. There is a rolling admissions plan. Applications should be filed by August 1 for fall entry; December 1 for winter entry; and April 1 for summer entry, along with a $25 fee. Notification is sent on a rolling basis. Applications are accepted on-line. **Transfer Students:** 170 transfer students enrolled in 2013-2014. A minimum average grade of C or better is required. An associate degree will be accepted for transfer. 40 of 126 credits required for the bachelor's degree must be completed at Greenville. **International Students:** There are 26 international students enrolled. The school actively recruits these students. They must take the TOEFL with a minimum score of 500 on the paper-based TOEFL (PBT).

ADMISSIONS: 78% of the 2014-2015 applicants were accepted. The SAT scores for the 2014-2015 freshman class were: Critical Reading--56% below 500, 26% between 500 and 599, 17% between 600 and 699, and 1% between 700 and 800; Math--51% below 500, 36% between 500 and 599, and 13% between 600 and 699; Writing--60% below 500, 21% between 500 and 599, and 19% between 600 and 699. The ACT scores were 32% below 21, 20% between 21 and 23, 21% between 24 and 26, 13% between 27 and 28, and 14% above 28. 33% of the current freshmen were in the top fifth of their class; 62% were in the top two fifths. 7 freshmen graduated first in their class. **Admissions Contact:** Michael Ritter, Assistant VP for Enrollment. E-Mail: *admissions@greenville.edu* Web: *www.greenville.edu*

FINANCIAL AID: In 2014-2015, 92% of all full-time freshmen and 95% of continuing full-time students received some form of financial aid. 87% of all full-time freshmen and 66% of continuing full-time students received need-based aid. The average freshman award was $18,738. Need-based scholarships or need-based grants averaged $4,817; need-based self-help aid (loans and jobs) averaged $7,362; and other non-need-based awards and non-need-based scholarships averaged $6,971. 30% of undergraduate students work part-time. Average annual earnings from campus work are $996. The average financial indebtedness of the 2014 graduate was $25,000. Greenville is a member of CSS. The FAFSA is required. The priority date for freshman financial aid applications for fall entry is April 1. The deadline for filing freshman financial aid applications for fall entry is July 1.

uates, 20. 20% do not continue beyond their first year; 60% remain to graduate. **Housing:** 742 students can be accommodated in college housing, which includes single-sex and coed dorms and on-campus apartments. In addition, there are honors houses, language houses, and special-interest houses. On-campus housing is guaranteed for all 4 years. 67% of students live on campus; of those, 65% remain on campus on weekends. All students may keep cars.

FACULTY/CLASSROOMS: 57% of faculty are male; 43% are female. All teach undergraduates. No introductory courses are taught by graduate students. The average class size in an introductory lecture is 40; in a laboratory is 20; and in a regular course is 16.

PROGRAMS OF STUDY: IC confers B.A., and B.S. degrees. Bachelor's degrees are awarded in BIOLOGICAL SCIENCE (biochemistry and biology/biological science), BUSINESS (accounting and business administration and management), COMMUNICATIONS AND THE ARTS (communications, dramatic arts, English, fine arts, French, German, music, Spanish, and speech/debate/rhetoric), COMPUTER AND PHYSICAL SCIENCE (chemistry, computer science, information sciences and systems, mathematics, and physics), EDUCATION (elementary education, foreign languages education, science education, and secondary education), ENGINEERING AND ENVIRONMENTAL DESIGN (environmental science), HEALTH PROFESSIONS (exercise science and medical laboratory technology), SOCIAL SCIENCE (American studies, economics, history, international relations, philosophy, political science/government, prelaw, psychology, religion, and sociology). Life sciences is the strongest academically. Business management, education, and biology have the largest enrollments.

ACTIVITIES: There are no fraternities or sororities. There are 72 groups on campus, including art, band, cheerleading, chess, choir, chorale, communications, computers, dance, debate, drama, ethnic, forensics, gay, honors, international, literary magazine, music ensembles, newspaper, photography, political, professional, radio and TV, religious, social, social service, student government, and symphony. Popular campus events include Osage Orange Picnic, Honors Retreat and McGaw Fine Arts Series. **Sports:** There are 10 intercollegiate sports for men and 10 for women, and 7 intramural sports for men and 7 for women. Facilities include a fitness center with an olympic sized swimming pool, whirlpool and sauna, several gyms, and expansive weight and exercise room, and aerobics room, 7 basketball courts, volleyball courts, an indoor track, an outdoor track, and playing fields for soccer and football that have an artifical turf surface, a baseball field, an all-weather track, and 6 tennis courts. **Graduates:** From July 1, 2013 to June 30, 2014, 168 bachelor's degrees were awarded. The most popular majors were biological/life sciences (18%), intersidciplinary studies (16%), and education (13%). 6 companies recruited on campus in 2013-2014. In an average class, 1% graduate in 3 years or less, 50% graduate in 4 years or less, 62% graduate in 5 years or'less, and 62% graduate in 6 years or less. Of the 2013 graduating class, 20% were enrolled in graduate school within 6 months of graduation, and 80% were employed.

SERVICES: Counseling and information services are available, as is tutoring in every subject. There is a reader service for the blind. Note takers, scribes, and test readers are also available. **Library/Resources:** The library contains 183,172 volumes, 8,049 microform items, 4,041 audio/video tapes/CDs/DVDs, and subscribes to 631 periodicals including electronic. Computerized library services include interlibrary loans, database searching, Internet access, and Wi-Fi capability. Special learning facilities include an art gallery, radio station, theater, and observatory. **Physically Challenged Students:** 35% of the campus is accessible. Facilities include wheelchair ramps, elevators, special parking, specially equipped restrooms, special class scheduling, lowered drinking fountains, lowered telephones, and special housing. **Special:** The college offers study abroad in various countries, on- and off-campus work-study programs, and internships through the departments of communication, computer science and information systems, economics and business administration, English, and political science, and sociology. Also available are student-designed and dual majors, B.A.-B.S. degrees, a 3-2 engineering degree with the University of Illinois, Washington University, or Southern Illinois University-Edwardsville, and a 3-2 occupational therapy program with Washington University. A 3-1 cytotechnology program with Mayo School of Health-related Sciences, a 3-1 program in Medical

ILLINOIS COLLEGE	C-3
www.ic.edu	
Jacksonville, IL 62650	**(217) 245-3030**
	(866) 464-5265
Fax: (217) 245-3034	Email: Barb.Lundberg@ic.edu
Full-time: 487 men, 474 women	**Faculty:** 71; IIB, av$
Part-time: 5 men, 4 women	**Ph.D.s:** 80%
Graduate: 1 men, 16 women	**Student/Faculty:** 14 to 1
Year: semesters	**Tuition:** $18,800
Room & Board: $6970	**Freshman Class:** 2357 applied, 1370 accepted, 285 enrolled
SAT or ACT: required	**CEEB CODE:** 1315
Application Deadline: August 15	**VERY COMPETITIVE**

Illinois College, founded in 1829, is a private liberal arts institution with historical ties to the Presbyterian Church and the United Church of Christ. The figures in the above capsule are approximate. The 62-acre campus is in a small town 30 miles west of Springfield. Including any residence halls, there are 36 buildings.

STUDENT LIFE: 89% of undergraduates are from Illinois. Others are from 22 states, and 15 foreign countries. 91% are White. 62% are Protestant; 25% Catholic; 12% claim no religious affiliation. **Male To Female Ratio:** 1.0:1. The average age of freshmen is 18; all undergrad-

Technology with St. John's Hospital in Springfield, an Intercultural Exchange Program with Ritsumeikan University in Kyoto, Japan, Model United Nations simulations, and the Urban Studies Program of Associated Colleges of the Midwest in Chicago are offered. The College also offers opportunities for collaborative student/faculty research. There are 12 national honor societies, including Phi Beta Kappa, and 12 departmental honors programs. **Visiting:** There are regularly scheduled orientations for prospective students, including general information sessions with a member of the admissions staff, meeting with faculty, a campus tour, and lunch. There are guides for informal visits and visitors may sit in on classes. To schedule a visit, contact the Admissions Office. **Campus Safety and Security:** Measures include 24-hour foot and vehicle patrol, self-defense education, and security escort services. There are shuttle buses, emergency telephones, and lighted pathways/sidewalks.

REQUIREMENTS: The SAT or ACT is required. The ACT Optional Writing test is also required. Applicants must be graduates of an accredited secondary school or have a GED certificate. Students should have completed at least 15 academic credits, including 3 in English and 7 from the following: English, foreign language, history, lab science, math, and social studies. 1 recommendation and 1 essay or 2 letters recommendations are required. A GPA of 2.5 is required. AP and CLEP credits are accepted. Important factors in the admissions decision are advanced placement or honors courses, evidence of special talent, and ability to finance college education. To graduate, all students must fulfill general graduation and convocation requirements and complete at least 120 semester hours, including 24 hours of electives outside of the major discipline. Other requirements include 1 unit in public speaking, 1 unit in writing, 1 unit of library research methods, and a first-year seminar. To meet the convocation requirement, students must attend 30 cultural, artistic, or public affairs events. A 2.0 GPA is required. **Procedure:** Freshmen are admitted to all sessions. Entrance exams should be taken in the spring of the junior year or fall of the senior year of high school. There is a rolling admissions plan. Application deadlines are open. Notification is sent on a rolling basis. Applications are accepted on-line. **Transfer Students:** 44 transfer students enrolled in 2013-2014. Transfer students must have graduated from an accredited four year high school. A minimum of 2.0 for their most recent full-time semester of college level work and a minimum cumulative 2.0 GPA for all college work attempted. If 24 credits have not been completed, these student's high school record will be reviewed. 36 of 120 credits required for the bachelor's degree must be completed at IC. **International Students:** There are 24 international students enrolled. They must take the TOEFL.

ADMISSIONS: 58% of the 2014-2015 applicants were accepted. 13 freshmen graduated first in their class. **Admissions Contact:** Barbara J. Lundberg, Vice President for Enrollment. E-Mail: *Barb.Lundberg@ic.edu* Web: *www.ic.edu*

FINANCIAL AID: In 2014-2015, 99% of all full-time freshmen and 98% of continuing full-time students received some form of financial aid. 73% of all full-time freshmen and 67% of continuing full-time students received need-based aid. 55% of undergraduate students work part-time. Average annual earnings from campus work are $999. The average financial indebtedness of the 2014 graduate was $23,156. The FAFSA is required. The priority date for freshman financial aid applications for fall entry is March 1. The deadline for filing freshman financial aid applications for fall entry is May 1.

ILLINOIS INSTITUTE OF TECHNOLOGY   E-2
www.iit.edu

Chicago, IL 60616	(312) 567-3000
	(800) 448-2329
Fax: (312) 567-6939	Email: admission@iit.edu
Full-time: 1793 men, 817 women	Faculty: 250; I, +$
Part-time: 147 men, 44 women	Ph.D.s: 88%
Graduate: 2899 men, 1984 women	Student/Faculty: 9 to 1
Year: semesters, summer session	Tuition: $38,512
Room & Board: n/app	Freshman Class: 2597 applied, 1427 accepted, 408 enrolled
SAT CR/M/W: 600/660/590 ACT: 28	CEEB CODE: 1318
Application Deadline: open	HIGHLY COMPETITIVE+

Founded in 1890, IIT is a Ph.D.-granting university with students in engineering, sciences, architecture, psychology, design, humanities, business and law. IIT's interprofessional, technology-focused curriculum is designed to advance knowledge through research and scholarship, to cultivate invention improving the human condition, and to prepare students from throughout the world for a life of professional achievement, service to society, and individual fulfillment. Figures in the above capsule and in this profile are approximate. There are 6 undergraduate schools and 8 graduate schools. In addition to regional accreditation, IIT has baccalaureate program accreditation with ABET and NAAB. The 120-acre campus is in an urban area 3 miles south of downtown Chicago. Including any residence halls, there are 33 buildings.

STUDENT LIFE: 57% of undergraduates are from Illinois. Others are from 47 states, 83 foreign countries, and Canada. 83% are from public schools. 50% are White; 16% Foreign; 14% Asian American. The average age of freshmen is 18; all undergraduates, 22. 15% do not continue beyond their first year; 85% remain to graduate. **Housing:** 1184 students can be accommodated in college housing, which includes single-sex and coed dorms, on-campus apartments, and married student housing. In addition, there are fraternity houses and sorority houses. On-campus housing is guaranteed for all 4 years. 53% of students live on campus. All students may keep cars.

FACULTY/CLASSROOMS: 78% of faculty are male; 22% are female. No introductory courses are taught by graduate students. The average class size in an introductory lecture is 24; in a laboratory is 22; and in a regular course is 15.

PROGRAMS OF STUDY: IIT confers B.A., and B.S. degrees. Master's and Doctoral degrees are also awarded. Bachelor's degrees are awarded in BIOLOGICAL SCIENCE (biochemistry, biology/biological science, biophysics, and molecular biology), COMMUNICATIONS AND THE ARTS (technical and business writing), COMPUTER AND PHYSICAL SCIENCE (applied mathematics, chemistry, computer science, information sciences and systems, physics, and web technology), ENGINEERING AND ENVIRONMENTAL DESIGN (aeronautical engineering, architectural engineering, architecture, chemical engineering, civil engineering, computer engineering, electrical/electronics engineering, engineering management, industrial administration/management, manufacturing technology, materials science, mechanical engineering, and metallurgical engineering), SOCIAL SCIENCE (humanities, political science/government, and psychology). Architecture, engineering, and science and letters have the largest enrollments.

ACTIVITIES: 13% of men belong to 7 national fraternities; 15% of women belong to 2 local and 1 national sorority. There are 100 groups on campus, including and union, art, chess, choir, chorus, commuter, computers, dance, drama, environmental, ethnic, film, gay, honors, international, jazz band, musical theater, newspaper, photography, professional, radio and TV, religious, social, social service, student government, and yearbook. Popular campus events include International Fest, Greek Week and Spring Formal. **Sports:** There are 5 intercollegiate sports for men and 5 for women, and 10 intramural sports for men and 10 for women. Facilities include tennis, basketball, volleyball, racquetball, and squash courts, soccer and softball fields, a swimming pool, an exercise room, a weight room, a bowling alley, and a game room. **Graduates:** From July 1, 2013 to June 30, 2014, 518 bachelor's degrees were awarded. The most popular majors were engineering (49%), natural resources and conservation (20%), and computer and information sciences (9%). In an average class, 3% graduate in 3 years or less, 38% graduate in 4 years or less, 62% graduate in 5 years or less, and 67% graduate in 6 years or less.

SERVICES: Counseling and information services are available, as is tutoring in some subjects, math, electrical and computer engineering, chemistry, biology, mechanical, materials and aerospace engineering, physics, computer science and writing courses. There is a reader service for the blind. **Library/Resources:** The 3 libraries contain 1.3 million volumes, 4,256 audio/video tapes/CDs/DVDs, and subscribe to 24,596 periodicals including electronic. Computerized library services include interlibrary loans, database searching, Internet access, and Wi-Fi capability. Special learning facilities include an art gallery and radio station. **Physically Challenged Students:** 90% of the campus is accessible. Facilities include wheelchair ramps, elevators, special parking, specially equipped restrooms, lowered drinking fountains, special housing. **Special:** Co-op programs and internships are available to all majors. All countries are eligible for study abroad. Dual majors may include a variety of majors. Cross-registration available. There are 3 national honor societies. **Visiting:** There are regularly scheduled orientations for prospective students, including special events and open houses. Open houses include a brief welcome, tours of main campus, academic exploration sessions with faculty members, discussion panels with current students, and staff from numerous student service departments on hand to answer questions. There are guides for informal visits, visitors may sit in on classes, and stay overnight. To schedule a visit, contact the Office of Undergraduate Admission. **Campus Safety and Security:** Measures include 24-hour foot and vehicle patrol, emergency notification system, and security escort services. There are shuttle buses, emergency telephones, lighted pathways/sidewalks, and controlled access to dorms/residences.

REQUIREMENTS: Graduation from an accredited secondary school is required for admission. 17 academic credits are required for admission: 4 units of English; 4 units of math: 3 units of science, of these, 2 units must be laboratory science; 2 units of social studies and 2 units of history. In addition, 2 units of foreign language and 1 unit of computer science are recommended. AP credits are accepted. Important factors in the admissions decision are recommendations by school officials, leadership record, and advanced placement or honors courses. To graduate, all degree-seeking undergraduate students must complete: departmental curriculum, credit hour requirements as appropriate to the various curricula (a minimum of 126 hours total, a minimum of 45 hours taken at IIT), general education requirements and a minimum cumulative GPA of and a minimum major GPA of 2.00. General education requirements include 5 credit hours of mathematics, 2 credit hours in computer science, 21 credit hours in humanities and social or behavioral sciences, 11 credit hours in natural science or engineering, 2 credit hours of Introduction to the Profession and 6 credit hours of Interprofessional Projects (IPRO). **Procedure:** Freshmen are admitted fall, spring, and summer. There are deferred admissions and rolling admissions plans. Application deadlines are open. Notification is sent on a rolling basis. Applications are accepted on-line. **Transfer Students:** 277 transfer students enrolled in 2013-2014. Good academic standing at previous postsecondary institution, and a minimum 3.0 cumulative GPA 45 of 126 credits required for the bachelor's degree must be completed at IIT. **International Students:** There are 388 international students enrolled. The school actively recruits these students. They must take the TOEFL with a minimum score of 550 on the paper-based TOEFL (PBT) or 80 on the Internet-based version (iBT).

ADMISSIONS: 55% of the 2014-2015 applicants were accepted. The SAT scores for the 2014-2015 freshman class were: Critical Reading--14% below 500, 31% between 500 and 599, 44% between 600 and 699, and 11% between 700 and 800; Math--1% below 500, 17% between 500 and 599, 54% between 600 and 699, and 28% between 700 and 800; Writing--15% below 500, 40% between 500 and 599, 37% between 600 and 699, and 8% between 700 and 800. The ACT scores were 2% below 21, 10% between 21 and 23, 24% between 24 and 26, 24% between 27 and 28, and 40% above 28. 61% of the current freshmen were in the top fifth of their class; 87% were in the top two fifths. 2 freshmen graduated first in their class. **Admissions Contact:** Gerald Doyle, Associate Vice President, Undergraduate Admissions. E-Mail: *admission@iit.edu* Web: *www.iit.edu*

FINANCIAL AID: In 2014-2015, 100% of all full-time freshmen and 98% of continuing full-time students received some form of financial aid. 70% of all full-time freshmen and 58% of continuing full-time students received need-based aid. IIT is a member of CSS. The FAFSA is required. The priority date for freshman financial aid applications for fall entry is April 15.

ILLINOIS STATE UNIVERSITY   **D-3**
www.illinoisstate.edu

Normal, IL 61761	(309) 438-2181
	(800) 366-2478
Fax: (309) 438-3932	Email: admissions@ilstu.edu
Full-time: 7630 men, 9410 women	Faculty: 886; I, --$
Part-time: 549 men, 566 women	Ph.D.s: 83%
Graduate: 887 men, 1573 women	Student/Faculty: 19 to 1
Year: semesters, summer session	Tuition: $13,296 ($20,886)
Room & Board: $9814	Freshman Class: 15297 applied, 11301 accepted, 3589 enrolled
ACT: 24	CEEB CODE: 1319
Application Deadline: April 1	VERY COMPETITIVE

Illinois State University, founded in 1857, is a public institution offering instruction through schools of applied science and technology, arts and sciences, business, education, fine arts, and nursing. There are 6 undergraduate schools and 1 graduate school. In addition to regional accreditation, ISU has baccalaureate program accreditation with AACSB, ABET, ACCE, CSAB, CSWE, FIDER, NASAD, NASM, NCATE, and NRPA. The 1100-acre campus is in an urban area 125 miles south of Chicago and 180 miles north of St. Louis. Including any residence halls, there are 203 buildings.

STUDENT LIFE: 97% of undergraduates are from Illinois. Others are from 44 states, 38 foreign countries, and Canada. 78% are White. **Male To Female Ratio:** 1.3:1. The average age of freshmen is 18; all undergraduates, 21. 19% do not continue beyond their first year; 72% remain to graduate. **Housing:** 5844 students can be accommodated in college housing, which includes single-sex and coed dorms, on-campus apartments, and married student housing. In addition, there are honors houses and special-interest houses. On-campus housing is available on a first-come, first-served basis. 66% of students commute. Alcohol is not permitted. All students may keep cars.

FACULTY/CLASSROOMS: 46% of faculty are male; 54% are female. All teach undergraduates. Graduate students teach 37% of introductory courses. The average class size in an introductory lecture is 45 and in a laboratory is 25.

PROGRAMS OF STUDY: ISU confers B.S., B.A., B.S. Ed., B.S.W., B.S./M.P.A., B.F.A, B.M.E., B.M. and B.S.N. degrees. Master's and Doctoral degrees are also awarded. Bachelor's degrees are awarded in AGRICULTURE (agricultural business management and agriculture), BIOLOGICAL SCIENCE (biochemistry, biology/biological science, and molecular biology), BUSINESS (accounting, business administration and management, business information systems, finance, insurance, international business, and marketing), COMMUNICATIONS AND THE ARTS (art, communication studies, dramatic arts, English, French, German, graphic communications, journalism, media arts, music, music performance, public relations, Spanish, speech/debate/rhetoric, telecommunications, and theatre acting), COMPUTER AND PHYSICAL SCIENCE (chemistry, computer science, digital arts/technology, geology, information sciences and systems, mathematics, and physics), EDUCATION (business education, early childhood education, elementary education, health education, health information management, middle school education, music education, social science education, special education, and technical education), ENGINEERING AND ENVIRONMENTAL DESIGN (construction management, energy management technology, and industrial engineering technology), HEALTH PROFESSIONS (environmental health science, exercise science, health care administration, medical laboratory technology, nursing, and speech pathology/audiology), SOCIAL SCIENCE (anthropology, criminal justice, economics, family/consumer studies, fashion design and technology, geography, history, home economics, interdisciplinary studies, legal studies, parks and recreation management, philosophy, political science/government, psychology, safety management, social science, social work, and sociology). Elementary education, special education and business administration have the largest enrollments.

ACTIVITIES: 11% of men belong to 18 national fraternities; 14% of women belong to 15 national sororities. There are 365 groups on campus, including art, band, cheerleading, chess, choir, chorale, chorus, communications, computers, dance, debate, drama, drill team, ethnic, film, forensics, gay, honors, international, jazz band, literary magazine, marching band, musical theater, newspaper, opera, orchestra, pep band, photography, political, professional, radio and TV, religious, social, social service, student government, and symphony. Popular campus events include Festival ISU, International Fair, Madrigal Dinners, Family Weekend, and Homecoming. **Sports:** There are 7 intercollegiate sports for men and 10 for women, and 31 intramural sports for men and 31 for women. Facilities include a student recreational building, a basketball arena, a football stadium, a field house, baseball diamonds, tennis courts, olympic-size pools, an 18-hole golf course, a soccer and softball field, 18 acre field area that is devoted to intramurals and sport clubs, and a bowling and billiards center. **Graduates:** From July 1, 2013 to June 30, 2014, 4313 bachelor's degrees were awarded. The most popular majors were elementary education (5%), marketing (5%), and family and consumer sciences (4%). In an average class, 45% graduate in 4 years or less, 68% graduate in 5 years or less, and 72% graduate in 6 years or less.

SERVICES: Counseling and information services are available, as is tutoring in most subjects. There is a reader service for the blind. tutoring available for most 100 level courses. course materials are provided in an alternate format **Library/Resources:** The library contains 1.6 million volumes, 84,874 microform items, 38,032 audio/video tapes/CDs/DVDs, and subscribes to 79,903 periodicals including electronic. Computerized library services include interlibrary loans, database searching, Internet access, and Wi-Fi capability. Special learning facilities include an art gallery, planetarium, radio station, TV station, an distance-learning classrooms, a farm, and japanese gardens. **Physically Challenged Students:** All of the campus is accessible. Facilities include wheelchair ramps, elevators, special parking, specially equipped restrooms, special class scheduling, lowered drinking fountains, lowered telephones. **Special:** There are numerous cooperative programs and internships, dual majors, student-designed majors, and work-study programs both on campus and with nonprofit organizations. There is also a general studies degree, a 3-2 engineering program with the University of Illinois, a BS/MPA, and study abroad in 16 countries. Pass/fail options are available. Credit is given for military experience. ISU is part of the National Student Exchange, enabling qualifying juniors and seniors to study for up to 1 year at one of several hundred colleges around the country. There are 24 national honor societies, a freshman honors program, and 1 departmental honors program. **Visiting:** There are regularly scheduled orientations for prospective students, while attending Preview, students will have the opportunity to meet with their academic advisor, register for classes, meet current students and their future classmates, interact with faculty and staff from various academic departments. There are guides for informal visits, visitors may sit in on classes, and stay overnight. To schedule a visit, contact the Admissions Office. **Campus Safety and Security:** Measures include 24-hour foot and vehicle patrol, emergency notification system, self-defense education, and security escort services. There are shuttle buses, emergency telephones, lighted pathways/sidewalks, and controlled access to dorms/residences.

REQUIREMENTS: The ACT is required. Admission is based on a combination of factors including rigor of secondary school record, academic GPA, standardized test scores and application essay. AP and CLEP credits are accepted.Students must complete 39 hours of General Education and a total of 120 credit hours with a minimum GPA of 2.0. In addition, students must have senior college hours totaling 42 hours. Every student must have successfully completed a course designated as a course in the cultures and traditions of societies from Asia, the Middle East, Africa, Latin America, or Indigenous Peoples of the World. **Procedure:** Freshmen are admitted fall, spring, and summer. Entrance exams should be taken in the spring of junior year. There are deferred admissions and rolling admissions plans. Applications should be filed by April 1 for fall entry, along with a $40 fee. Notifications are sent September 1. 216 applicants were on the 2014 waiting list; 208 were admitted. Applications are accepted on-line. **Transfer Students:** 1801 transfer students enrolled in 2013-2014. Graduates of Illinois community colleges holding associate degrees are admitted pending receipt of transcripts. Other students must meet the requirements for beginning freshmen with a minimum 2.0

GPA. 30 of 120 credits required for the bachelor's degree must be completed at ISU. **International Students:** There are 138 international students enrolled. The school actively recruits these students. They must take the TOEFL with a minimum score of 550 on the paper-based TOEFL (PBT) or 79 on the Internet-based version (iBT). They must also take the SAT or ACT.

ADMISSIONS: 74% of the 2014-2015 applicants were accepted. The ACT scores were 16% below 21, 34% between 21 and 23, 32% between 24 and 26, 10% between 27 and 28, and 8% above 28. **Admissions Contact:** Jeff Mavros, Director of Admissions. E-Mail: *admissions@ilstu.edu* Web: *http://admissions.illinoisstate.edu/*

FINANCIAL AID: The FAFSA and CCS/Profile, or FAFSA, or FFS, or SFS are required. The deadline for filing freshman financial aid applications for fall entry is March 1.

ILLINOIS WESLEYAN UNIVERSITY D-3
www.iwu.edu

Bloomington, IL 61702

	(309) 556-3031
	(800) 332-2498
Fax: n/av	Email: iwuadmit@iwu.edu
Full-time: 882 men, 1119 women	Faculty: IIB, av$
Part-time: 4 men, 4 women	Ph.D.s: 92%
Graduate: n/av	Student/Faculty: 11 to 1
Year: other	Tuition: $39,316
Room & Board: $9136	Freshman Class: 3556 applied, 2076 accepted, 529 enrolled
SAT CR/M: 571/648 ACT: 27	CEEB CODE: 1320
Application Deadline: March 1	HIGHLY COMPETITIVE

Illinois Wesleyan University, founded in 1850, is a private institution offering major programs in liberal arts, fine arts, and nursing. The figures in the above capsule and in this profile are approximate. There are 5 undergraduate schools. In addition to regional accreditation, Illinois Wesleyan has baccalaureate program accreditation with NASM and CCNE. The 80-acre campus is in a suburban area 130 miles from Chicago and 160 miles from St. Louis, Missouri. Including any residence halls, there are 54 buildings.

STUDENT LIFE: 88% of undergraduates are from Illinois. Others are from 33 states, 23 foreign countries, and Canada. 80% are from public schools. 71% are White. **Male To Female Ratio:** 1.3:1. The average age of freshmen is 18; all undergraduates, 20. 78% remain to graduate. **Housing:** 1709 students can be accommodated in college housing, which includes coed dorms and on-campus apartments. In addition, there are honors houses, language houses, special-interest houses, fraternity houses, sorority houses, Internationalism, environmentalism, art and interfaith learning housing areas. 72% of students live on campus; of those, 75% remain on campus on weekends. All students may keep cars.

FACULTY/CLASSROOMS: 55% of faculty are male; 45% are female. All teach and do research. No introductory courses are taught by graduate students. The average class size in a laboratory is 13 and in a regular course is 17.

PROGRAMS OF STUDY: Illinois Wesleyan confers B.A., B.S., B.F.A., B.Mus., B.Mus.Ed. and B.S.N. degrees. Bachelor's degrees are awarded in AGRICULTURE (environmental studies), BIOLOGICAL SCIENCE (biology/biological science), BUSINESS (accounting, business administration and management, insurance and risk management, and international business management), COMMUNICATIONS AND THE ARTS (art, classics, English, French, German, guitar, music, music performance, music theory and composition, musical theater, performing arts, piano/organ, theater design, theater management, and voice), COMPUTER AND PHYSICAL SCIENCE (chemistry, computer science, and physics), EDUCATION (education and music education), HEALTH PROFESSIONS (nursing), SOCIAL SCIENCE (American studies, anthropology, economics, history, interdisciplinary studies, international studies, philosophy, political science/government, psychology, religion, sociology, and women and gender studies). Business administration/accounting, biology, and psychology have the largest enrollments.

ACTIVITIES: 32% of men belong to 6 national fraternities; 30% of women belong to 1 local and 4 national sororities. There are 185 groups on campus, including art, band, cheerleading, choir, chorale, chorus, computers, dance, drama, ethnic, film, gay, honors, international, jazz band, literary magazine, musical theater, newspaper, opera, orchestra, pep band, political, professional, radio and TV, religious, social, social service, student government, symphony, and yearbook. Popular campus events include Family Days, Comedy Clubs and International Festivals. **Sports:** There are 9 intercollegiate sports for men and 9 for women, and 15 intramural sports for men and 13 for women. Facilities include a fitness center with weight/exercise equipment and racquetball courts; a swimming pool with 1- and 3-meter diving boards; an activity center with a 200-meter, 6-lane indoor track and courts for tennis, recreational basketball, and volleyball; a separate gym for intercollegiate and other activities; an outdoor track; and softball, baseball, and soccer fields. **Graduates:** From July 1, 2013 to June 30, 2014, 482 bachelor's degrees were awarded. The most popular majors were business/marketing (21%), visual and performing arts (11%), and psychology (9%). 49 companies recruited on campus in 2013-2014. In an average class, 72% graduate in 4 years or less, 77% graduate in 5 years or less, and 78% graduate in 6 years or less.

SERVICES: Counseling and information services are available, as is tutoring in every subject. There is a reader service for the blind. Assistance in writing and study skills is also available but not at the remedial level. **Library/Resources:** The library contains 328,368 volumes, 443 microform items, 14,653 audio/video tapes/CDs/DVDs, and subscribes to 33,435 periodicals including electronic. Computerized library services include interlibrary loans, database searching, Internet access, and Wi-Fi capability. Special learning facilities include an art gallery, radio station, TV station, an observatory, a multicultural center, Action Research Center, Center for Human Rights, Peace Garden and a 20-acre tract of virgin timberland. **Physically Challenged Students:** 90% of the campus is accessible. Facilities include wheelchair ramps, elevators, special parking, specially equipped restrooms, special class scheduling, lowered drinking fountains, lowered telephones, and special housing. **Special:** There are several combined degree programs, including a 3-2 degree in forestry and environmental studies with Duke University and a 2-2 engineering degree with the University of Illinois. Students may study abroad in many locations throughout the world through the Institute for the International Education of Students (IES), Pembroke College, Keio University, University of Oxford, Arcadia University Center for Study Abroad, and other programs. Illinois Wesleyan also offers its own semester-long programs in London and Barcelona. The university also offers on-campus work-study, both credit and noncredit internships, Washington and United Nations semesters, B.A.-B.S. degrees, dual and student-designed majors, pass/fail options, and an honors research program for upperclass students. There are 25 national honor societies, including Phi Beta Kappa, and 44 departmental honors programs. **Visiting:** There are regularly scheduled orientations for prospective students, including a 1 to 1-1/2 hour guided tour in small groups, and with advance scheduling, interviews with an admissions counselor and faculty members in the fields of the student interest. Accepted applicants may visit classes or stay overnight. There are guides for informal visits, visitors may sit in on classes, and stay overnight. To schedule a visit, contact the Admissions Office. **Campus Safety and Security:** Measures include 24-hour foot and vehicle patrol, emergency notification system, self-defense education, and security escort services. There are shuttle buses, emergency telephones, lighted pathways/sidewalks, controlled access to dorms/residences, an emergency response team of key executives and staff members has developed policies and procedures for natural disasters and other crises.

REQUIREMENTS: The SAT or ACT is required. Applicants should graduate from an accredited secondary school; a GED may be accepted. 15 academic credits are required. It is strongly recommended that these units include 4 units of English, 3 each of natural science, math, and a foreign language, and 2 of social studies. An audition is required for theater and music majors and a portfolio for art majors. Illinois Wesleyan requires applicants to be in the upper 65% of their class. A GPA of 3.0 is required. AP credits are accepted. Important factors in the admissions decision are advanced placement

or honors courses, evidence of special talent, and personality/intangible qualities. For B.A., B.S., B.S.N., and B.F.A. degrees, a total of 32 course units (128 semester hours) is required for the bachelor's degree with a 2.0 GPA. General education requirements include 2 course units in natural sciences and 1 each in literature, English, intellectual traditions, formal reasoning, cultural and historical change, contemporary social institutions, the arts, history, humanities, math, and social science, analysis of values, and Gateway Colloquium, plus demonstrated proficiency in a foreign language. 2 additional writing-intensive courses are required, as is coursework focusing on U.S. and global diversity issues. 2 degree programs (B.M.Ed.and B.M.) require more than 32 course units due to additional requirements in the major. Phys ed is a noncredit graduation requirement. **Procedure:** Freshmen are admitted fall and spring. Entrance exams should be taken in the spring of the junior year. There are early admissions, deferred admissions, and rolling admissions plans. Early decision applications should be filed by November 1; regular applications, by March 1 for fall entry; and November 1 for spring entry. Notification is sent on a rolling basis. 149 applicants were on the 2014 waiting list; 2 were admitted. Applications are accepted on-line. **Transfer Students:** 32 transfer students enrolled in 2013-2014. Applicants must submit all high school and college transcripts. A GPA of at least 2.5 is required. An essay or personal statement is required. 16 of 32 credits required for the bachelor's degree must be completed at Illinois Wesleyan. **International Students:** There are 105 international students enrolled. The school actively recruits these students. They must take the TOEFL. They must also take the SAT or ACT.

ADMISSIONS: 58% of the 2014-2015 applicants were accepted. The SAT scores for the 2014-2015 freshman class were: Critical Reading--4% below 500, 35% between 500 and 599, 36% between 600 and 699, and 25% between 700 and 800; Math--5% below 500, 25% between 500 and 599, 44% between 600 and 699, and 25% between 700 and 800. There were 5 National Merit finalists. **Admissions Contact:** Tony Bankston, Dean of Admissions. E-Mail: *iwuadmit@iwu .edu* Web: *www.iwu.edu*

FINANCIAL AID: In 2014-2015, 71% of all full-time freshmen and 67% of continuing full-time students received some form of financial aid. 71% of all full-time freshmen and 67% of continuing full-time students received need-based aid. The average freshman award was $30,443. Need-based scholarships or need-based grants averaged $24,699; need-based self-help aid (loans and jobs) averaged $6,174; other non-need-based awards and non-need-based scholarships averaged $17,763; and $4,422 from other forms of aid. The average financial indebtedness of the 2014 graduate was $31,343. Illinois Wesleyan is a member of CSS. The FAFSA and the college's own financial statement are required. The deadline for filing freshman financial aid applications for fall entry is March 1.

JUDSON UNIVERSITY   E-1
www.judsoncollege.edu

Elgin, IL 60123-1498	(847) 628-2500
	(800) 879-5376
Fax: (847) 695-0216	Email: admissions@judsoncollege.edu
Full-time: 394 men, 521 women	Faculty: 54; IIB, -$
Part-time: 106 men, 174 women	Ph.D.s: 65%
Graduate: 27 men, 23 women	Student/Faculty: 17 to 1
Year: semesters	Tuition: $20,500
Room & Board: $7750	Freshman Class: 626 applied, 484 accepted, 221 enrolled
SAT or ACT: required	CEEB CODE: 1351
Application Deadline: open	COMPETITIVE

Judson University formerly Judson College, is an evangelical Christian college of the liberal arts, sciences, and professions. The figures in the above capsule and in this profile is approximate. There is one graduate school. In addition to regional accreditation, Judson has baccalaureate program accreditation with NAAB. The 90-acre campus is in a suburban area 45 miles northwest of Chicago. Including any residence halls, there are 15 buildings.

STUDENT LIFE: 65% of undergraduates are from Illinois. Others are from 21 states, 25 foreign countries, and Canada. 71% are white. 80% are Protestant. The average age of freshmen is 18; all undergraduates, 20. 22% do not continue beyond their first year; 50% remain to graduate.

FACULTY/CLASSROOMS: 66% of faculty are male; 34% are female. 80% teach undergraduates. No introductory courses are taught by graduate students. The average class size in an introductory lecture is 28; in a laboratory is 9; and in a regular course is 16.

PROGRAMS OF STUDY: Judson confers B.A. degrees. Master's degrees are also awarded. Bachelor's degrees are awarded in BIO-LOGICAL SCIENCE (biology/biological science), BUSINESS (accounting, business administration and management, international business management, and sports management), COMMUNICA-TIONS AND THE ARTS (communications, dramatic arts, English, fine arts, media arts, and music), COMPUTER AND PHYSICAL SCI-ENCE (chemistry, computer science, and mathematics), EDUCA-TION (early childhood education, elementary education, English education, mathematics education, music education, physical education, science education, and secondary education), ENGINEERING AND ENVIRONMENTAL DESIGN (preengineering), HEALTH PROFESSIONS (medical laboratory technology, nursing, predentistry, and premedicine), SOCIAL SCIENCE (anthropology, history, political science/government, prelaw, psychology, sociology, and youth ministry). Architecture, visual communications/graphic design, and education are the strongest academically. Business, youth ministry, worship arts, and psychology have the largest enrollments.

ACTIVITIES: There are no fraternities or sororities. There are 23 groups on campus, including art, band, business, cheerleading, choir, chorale, chorus, computers, drama, ethnic, honors, international, literary magazine, newspaper, orchestra, photography, political, radio and TV, religious, social, social service, and student government. Popular campus events include Spiritual Enrichment Week, Fall Orientation, and Christmas by Candlelight.

SERVICES: Counseling and information services are available, as is tutoring in some subjects. There is remedial math, reading, and writing. **Library/Resources:** The library contains 92,000 volumes, 27,000 microform items, 17,000 audio/video tapes/CDs/DVDs, and subscribes to 470 periodicals including electronic. Computerized library services include interlibrary loans, database searching, and Internet access. Special learning facilities include an art gallery and radio station. **Physically Challenged Students:** 80% of the campus is accessible. Facilities include wheelchair ramps, elevators, special parking, specially equipped restrooms, special class scheduling, lowered drinking fountains, lowered telephones, and special housing. **Special:** The college has co-op programs with North Park College, Rush University, and the Mennonite College of Nursing, cross-registration with the Christian College Coalition, and work-study programs with many businesses. Students may serve internships in art and business, take a Washington semester, a film studies semester in Hollywood, an ecology studies semester at Sable Institute in Michigan, or study abroad in numerous external programs recognized by Judson College. The college allows dual majors, student-designed majors, and accelerated degrees in business leadership and management, human services, human resource management, and criminal justice management. There is 1 national honor society, a freshman honors program, and 2 departmental honors programs. **Visiting:** There are regularly scheduled orientations for prospective students, including a tour, class visits, individual meetings with professors, coaches, choir and or band director, and other select campus administrators if requested. In addition, lunch or dinner in the cafeteria and the opportunity to meet with current students and the opportunity to stay a night in the dorms. There are guides for informal visits, visitors may sit in on classes, and stay overnight. To schedule a visit, contact the Enrollment Services Office at admission@judsoncollege.edu. **Campus Safety and Security:** Measures include 24-hour foot and vehicle patrol and security escort services. There are emergency telephones and lighted pathways/sidewalks.

REQUIREMENTS: The SAT or ACT is required with a minimum ACT score or a minimum SAT score. Judson requires applicants to be in the upper 50% of their class. A GPA of 2.0 is required. AP and CLEP credits are accepted.

FINANCIAL AID: In a recent year, 90% of all full-time freshmen and 90% of continuing full-time students received some form of financial aid. 90% of all full-time freshmen and 90% of continuing full-time students received need-based aid. Need-based scholarships or need-based grants averaged $7,212; need-based self-help aid (loans and jobs) averaged $8,568; and non-need-based athletic scholarships averaged $8,999. The FAFSA and the college's own financial statement are required. Check with the school for current application deadlines.

KENDALL COLLEGE (*The complete profile is made available exclusively on our website, www.barronspac.com*)

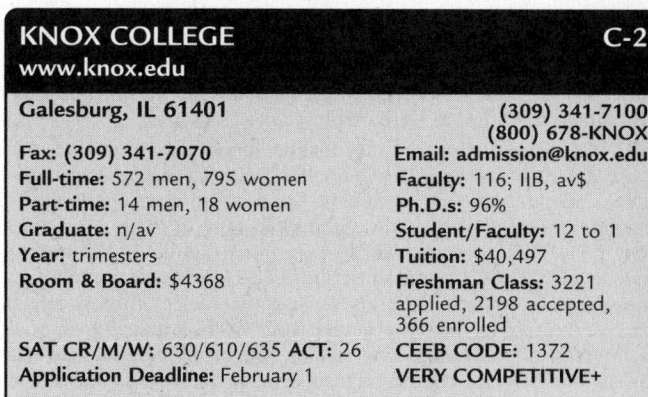

KNOX COLLEGE	C-2
www.knox.edu	
Galesburg, IL 61401	**(309) 341-7100**
	(800) 678-KNOX
Fax: (309) 341-7070	**Email:** admission@knox.edu
Full-time: 572 men, 795 women	**Faculty:** 116; IIB, av$
Part-time: 14 men, 18 women	**Ph.D.s:** 96%
Graduate: n/av	**Student/Faculty:** 12 to 1
Year: trimesters	**Tuition:** $40,497
Room & Board: $4368	**Freshman Class:** 3221 applied, 2198 accepted, 366 enrolled
SAT CR/M/W: 630/610/635 **ACT:** 26	**CEEB CODE:** 1372
Application Deadline: February 1	**VERY COMPETITIVE+**

Knox College, founded in 1837, is an independent liberal arts college. The 82-acre campus is in a small town 180 miles southwest of Chicago. Including any residence halls, there are 54 buildings.

STUDENT LIFE: 57% of undergraduates are from Illinois. Others are from 39 states, 45 foreign countries, and Canada. 73% are from public schools. 61% are White; 14% Hispanic; 13% Foreign. **Male To Female Ratio:** 1.4:1. The average age of freshmen is 18; all undergraduates, 20. 12% do not continue beyond their first year; 80% remain to graduate. **Housing:** 1210 students can be accommodated in college housing, which includes single-sex and coed dorms and on-campus apartments. In addition, there are language houses, special-interest houses, fraternity houses, and cultural centers (International House, Casa Latina, ABLE (Allied Blacks for Liberty and Equality House). On-campus housing is guaranteed for all 4 years and is available on a lottery system for upperclassmen. 80% of students live on campus; of those, 75% remain on campus on weekends. All students may keep cars.

FACULTY/CLASSROOMS: 55% of faculty are male; 45% are female. All teach undergraduates, all do research, and all teach and do research. No introductory courses are taught by graduate students. The average class size in an introductory lecture is 16; in a laboratory is 14; and in a regular course is 15.

PROGRAMS OF STUDY: Knox confers B.A. degrees. Bachelor's degrees are awarded in AGRICULTURE (environmental studies), BIOLOGICAL SCIENCE (biochemistry, biology/biological science, and neurosciences), COMMUNICATIONS AND THE ARTS (art history and appreciation, classics, creative writing, dramatic arts, English literature, French, German, Greek (classical), Latin, modern language, music, Spanish, and studio art), COMPUTER AND PHYS-ICAL SCIENCE (chemistry, computer science, mathematics, and physics), EDUCATION (elementary education, secondary education, and social studies education), SOCIAL SCIENCE (africana studies, American studies, anthropology, Asian/Oriental studies, economics, history, international relations, Latin American studies, philosophy, political science/government, psychology, sociology, and women's studies). Creative writing, computer science, psychology, and theatre are the strongest academically. Creative writing, economics, and psychology have the largest enrollments.

ACTIVITIES: 17% of men belong to 1 local and 5 national fraternities; 17% of women belong to 4 national sororities. There are 103 groups on campus, including band, chess, choir, communications, computers, dance, drama, environmental, ethnic, film, gay, international, jazz band, literary magazine, newspaper, orchestra, photography, political, professional, radio and TV, religious, social, social service, and student government. Popular campus events include International Fair (January), Rootabaga Jazz Festival (March) Lincoln Fest (Local Band All Day Festival). **Sports:** There are 11 intercollegiate sports for men and 10 for women, and 4 intramural sports for men and 4 for women. Facilities include a fitness center that includes cardio and selectorized equipment, fitness studio, and free weight area. Fieldhouse that includes an enclosed six-lane track and court space for various activities. Additionally Knox has a gymnasium, natatorium, football field, softball field, baseball field, outdoor track, tennis courts, and a soccer field. **Graduates:** From July 1, 2013 to June 30, 2014, 316 bachelor's degrees were awarded. The most popular majors were creative writing (11%), economics (9%), and educational studies (8%). 78 companies recruited on campus in 2013-2014. In an average class, 73% graduate in 4 years or less, 80% graduate in 5 years or less, and 80% graduate in 6 years or less. Of the 2013 graduating class, 16% were enrolled in graduate school within 6 months of graduation, and 61% were employed.

SERVICES: Counseling and information services are available, as is tutoring in most subjects. The Center for Teaching and Learning provides academic support to students in most subjects, particularly development of writing skills. **Library/Resources:** The 2 libraries contain 341,759 volumes, 98,748 microform items, 14,132 audio/video tapes/CDs/DVDs, and subscribe to 15,214 periodicals including electronic. Computerized library services include interlibrary loans, database searching, Internet access, and Wi-Fi capability. Special learning facilities include a radio station, 760–acre biological field station--is both a research and recreation area, Green Oaks Biological Field Station consists of forest, grassland, aquatic habitats and is the second site in the nation with a tall grass prairie restoration. The Knox Farm consisting of an acre of outdoor growing area and two season-extending "high tunnel" structures, the Knox Farm produces food for on-campus use and for sharing with the greater community. As one part of Knox's commitment to a transparent and more localized food chain, all of the food produced in the large high tunnel is served in Knox dining services, 110 yards east of the farm. The soil is amended with campus-generated compost, and no pesticides or artificial soil amendments are used within the farm. **Physically Challenged Students:** 75% of the campus is accessible. Facilities include wheelchair ramps, elevators, special parking, specially equipped restrooms, lowered drinking fountains, and special housing. **Special:** The normal academic load is 3 courses per term, with 3 terms per year. Cooperative programs are offered with Washington University in St. Louis in architecture and engineering; Columbia University in engineering and law; University of Illinois at Urbana-Champaign and Rensselaer Polytechnic Institute in engineering; Rush University in nursing and medical technology; Duke University in forestry and environmental management; and University of Chicago in law and social work. Study abroad is available in 30 countries. Other programs include a Washington semester, an urban studies semester, science and library research programs, work-study programs, and numerous internships. Dual majors, student-designed majors, and pass/fail options are available. Early admission to George Washington University Medical School is possible. Nondegree study is possible. Early admission program with Indiana University's Mauer School of Law. Knox College participates in the Kemper Scholars Program. There are 8 national honor societies, including Phi Beta Kappa, and 39 departmental honors programs. **Visiting:** There are regularly scheduled orientations for prospective students, Open houses for prospective students are offered in July, October, November, and January, and offer campus tours, class visits, lunch with students and professors, and informational sessions. Interviews are available on request. There are guides for informal visits, visitors may sit in on classes, and stay overnight. To schedule a visit, contact Beth Jonsberg at (800) 678-KNOX. **Campus Safety and Security:** Measures include 24-hour foot and vehicle patrol, emergency notification system, self-defense education, and security escort services. There are emergency telephones, lighted pathways/sidewalks, and controlled access to dorms/residences.

REQUIREMENTS: Successful applicants have excelled in a challenging college preparatory course of study, including at least 4 years of English; 3-4 years each of mathematics, science, and social studies; and 2-3 years of a second language. An essay is required and interview

strongly recommended. Submission of ACT or SAT scores is optional for most applicants; scores will be considered if submitted. Auditions or portfolio presentations are required for scholarship consideration only. AP credits are accepted. Important factors in the admissions decision are advanced placement or honors courses, recommendations by school officials, and personality/intangible qualities. Students must take a 1-term interdisciplinary preceptorial emphasizing writing and discussion skills. In addition to this, 2 writing intensive courses and 1 course emphasizing oral presentation are required. Two courses focusing on diversity are also required, as well as documentation of a significant experiential learning project outside the classroom. Breadth requirements include 1 course each in the 5 areas of arts, humanities, quantitative reasoning, natural and physical sciences, and social sciences. An additional minor or major, not in the department of the first major, is required. A 2.0 GPA is required, overall and in each major and minor. **Procedure:** Freshmen are admitted fall. Entrance exams should be taken by December 2015. There are early admissions and deferred admissions plans. Applications should be filed by February 1 for fall entry, along with a $40 fee. Notifications are sent March 30. 52 applicants were on the 2014 waiting list; 1 was admitted. Applications are accepted on-line. **Transfer Students:** 36 transfer students enrolled in 2013-2014. A 3.0 GPA is expected. An interview is recommended. 45 of 120 credits required for the bachelor's degree must be completed at Knox. **International Students:** There are 175 international students enrolled. The school actively recruits these students. They must take the TOEFL with a minimum score of 550 on the paper-based TOEFL (PBT) or 80 on the Internet-based version (iBT), or the IELTS is also acceptable.

ADMISSIONS: 68% of the 2014-2015 applicants were accepted. The SAT scores for the 2014-2015 freshman class were: Critical Reading--5% below 500, 28% between 500 and 599, 44% between 600 and 699, and 23% between 700 and 800; Math--4% below 500, 40% between 500 and 599, 39% between 600 and 699, and 17% between 700 and 800; Writing--4% below 500, 27% between 500 and 599, 55% between 600 and 699, and 14% between 700 and 800. The ACT scores were 10% below 21, 17% between 21 and 23, 26% between 24 and 26, 14% between 27 and 28, and 33% above 28. 47% of the current freshmen were in the top fifth of their class; 78% were in the top two fifths. There were 4 National Merit finalists. 11 freshmen graduated first in their class. **Admissions Contact:** Paul Steenis, Dean of Admission. E-Mail: *admission@knox.edu* Web: *www.knox.edu*

FINANCIAL AID: In 2014-2015, 99% of all full-time freshmen and 95% of continuing full-time students received some form of financial aid. 83% of all full-time freshmen and 74% of continuing full-time students received need-based aid. The average freshman award was $33,284. Need-based scholarships or need-based grants averaged $28,597; and need-based self-help aid (loans and jobs) averaged $4,639. 46% of undergraduate students work part-time. Average annual earnings from campus work are $1445. The average financial indebtedness of the 2014 graduate was $29,085. The FAFSA and the college's own financial statement are required. The priority date for freshman financial aid applications for fall entry is February 1.

LAKE FOREST COLLEGE   **E-1**
www.lakeforest.edu

Lake Forest, IL 60045	(847) 735-5000
	(800) 828-4751
Fax: (847) 735-6271	Email: admissions@lakeforest.edu
Full-time: 676 men, 916 women	Faculty: 100; IIB, +$
Part-time: 10 men, 5 women	Ph.D.s: 98%
Graduate: 4 men, 15 women	Student/Faculty: 15 to 1
Year: semesters, summer session	Tuition: $41,172
Room & Board: $9480	Freshman Class: 3479 applied, 1981 accepted, 416 enrolled
	CEEB CODE: 1392
Application Deadline: February 15	VERY COMPETITIVE

Lake Forest College, founded in 1857 is a private liberal arts institution located 30 miles north of Chicago and offers an innovative and challenging curriculum with abundant internship and research opportunities. There is one undergraduate school. In addition to regional accreditation, Lake Forest has baccalaureate program accreditation with HLC. The 107-acre campus is in a suburban area 30 miles north of Chicago. Including any residence halls, there are 43 buildings.

STUDENT LIFE: 54% of undergraduates are from Illinois. Others are from 43 states, 73 foreign countries, and Canada. 69% are from public schools. 57% are White; 15% Hispanic. The average age of freshmen is 18; all undergraduates, 20. 17% do not continue beyond their first year; 70% remain to graduate. **Housing:** 1245 students can be accommodated in college housing, which includes coed dorms and on-campus apartments. In addition, there are special-interest houses. On-campus housing is guaranteed for the freshman year only and is available on a lottery system for upperclassmen. Priority is given to out-of-town students. 75% of students live on campus; of those, 80% remain on campus on weekends. Upperclassmen may keep cars.

FACULTY/CLASSROOMS: 52% of faculty are male; 48% are female. All teach and do research. No introductory courses are taught by graduate students.

PROGRAMS OF STUDY: Lake Forest confers B.A. degrees. Master's degrees are also awarded. Bachelor's degrees are awarded in BIOLOGICAL SCIENCE (biology/biological science and neurosciences), BUSINESS (business economics and finance), COMMUNICATIONS AND THE ARTS (art, communications, English, French, music, Spanish, and theatre arts), COMPUTER AND PHYSICAL SCIENCE (chemistry, computer science, mathematics, and physics), EDUCATION (education and music education), ENGINEERING AND ENVIRONMENTAL DESIGN (environmental science), SOCIAL SCIENCE (American studies, anthropology, area studies, Asian/Oriental studies, economics, history, international relations, Latin American studies, philosophy, political science/government, psychology, religion, and sociology). Business, communication, and biology have the largest enrollments.

ACTIVITIES: 7% of men belong to 2 national fraternities; 11% of women belong to 5 national sororities. There are 51 groups on campus, including art, band, cheerleading, chess, choir, chorus, computers, dance, debate, drama, environmental, ethnic, film, gay, honors, international, jazz band, literary magazine, musical theater, newspaper, orchestra, pep band, photography, political, professional, radio and TV, religious, social, social service, and student government. Popular campus events include Homecoming, Global Fest, Gates Day of Service, and Spring Concert. **Sports:** There are 9 intercollegiate sports for men and 10 for women, and 16 intramural sports for men and 16 for women. Facilities include the Sports and Recreation Center houses a gymnasium, 1,200-square-foot training room, 9,600-square-foot weight room, 2,500-square-foot cardio suite, dance studio, basketball courts, racquetball and handball courts, three playing surfaces (wood court, tartan-surface, and artificial turf), batting/golf cages, suspended track, a pool, separate varsity locker rooms, and a cafe. Adjacent is an indoor hockey rink, outdoor sand volleyball courts, tennis courts, baseball, football, soccer, and intramural fields. **Graduates:** From July 1, 2013 to June 30, 2014, 320 bachelor's degrees were awarded. The most popular majors were communication (12%), economics (12%), and politics (10%). 694 companies recruited on campus in 2013-2014. In an average class, 62% graduate in 4 years or less, 70% graduate in 5 years or less, and 70% graduate in 6 years or less. Of the 2013 graduating class, 21% were enrolled in graduate school within 6 months of graduation, and 71% were employed.

SERVICES: Counseling and information services are available, as is tutoring in most subjects. **Library/Resources:** The library contains 298,000 volumes, 110,150 microform items, 12,635 audio/video tapes/CDs/DVDs, and subscribes to 16,980 periodicals including electronic. Computerized library services include interlibrary loans, database searching, Internet access, and Wi-Fi capability. Special learning facilities include an art gallery, radio station, a multimedia language lab, an electronic music studio with practice rooms, a technology resource center equipped with high-end computing hardware and software, a rhetoric and production room. **Physically Challenged Students:** 80% of the campus is accessible. Facilities include wheelchair ramps, elevators, special parking, specially equipped restrooms, special class scheduling, lowered drinking fountains, lowered telephones, and special housing. **Special:** Lake Forest offers cross-

registration with Associated Colleges of the Midwest, an extensive internship program, a student-designed Independent Scholar major, extensive off-campus study opportunities in over 15 countries with international internships available. Lake Forest has a number of accelerated and dual-degree programs including a 3-3 program in cooperation with a number of law schools whereby a student can earn a BA and JD in six years instead of seven. Students at Lake Forest can choose to earn a BA degree in communication or philosophy in just three years. The College also offers accelerated and dual degree programs in engineering, international studies, pharmacy, and nursing. There is a Phi Beta Kappa and a freshman honors program. **Visiting:** There are regularly scheduled orientations for prospective students, visits include class visitation, panel presentations, tours and individual appointments with faculty, coaches, and/or admission officers. There are guides for informal visits, visitors may sit in on classes, and stay overnight. To schedule a visit, contact the Admissions Office. **Campus Safety and Security:** Measures include 24-hour foot and vehicle patrol, emergency notification system, self-defense education, and security escort services. There are shuttle buses, emergency telephones, lighted pathways/sidewalks, and controlled access to dorms/residences.

REQUIREMENTS: Applicants are advised to complete a minimum of 16 academic credits, including 4 in English, 3 in math, 2 to 4 each in social and natural sciences, and study in 1 or more foreign languages. A GED is accepted. An interview is encouraged. AP credits are accepted. Important factors in the admissions decision are personality/intangible qualities, advanced placement or honors courses, and extracurricular activities record. All students are required to complete 32 courses with a minimum GPA of 2.0. General education requirements include 2 courses in natural science or math, 2 cultural diversity courses, and 1 course each in freshman studies, freshman writing, humanities, social science, and senior studies. **Procedure:** Freshmen are admitted fall and spring. Entrance exams should be taken in the junior or senior year. There are early decision and deferred admissions plans. Early decision applications should be filed by December 1; regular applications, by February 15 for fall entry; and December 1 for spring entry. Notification of early decision is sent December 20; regular decision, March 20. 45 early decision candidates were accepted for the 2014-2015 class. 30 applicants were on the 2014 waiting list; 15 were admitted. Applications are accepted on-line. **Transfer Students:** 68 transfer students enrolled in 2013-2014. Transfer applicants should have a minimum C average in all college work and should be in good standing with their previous institution. High school and college transcripts and a letter of recommendation from the academic dean or a teacher at the most recent college attended are required. 16 of 32 credits required for the bachelor's degree must be completed at Lake Forest. **International Students:** There are 171 international students enrolled. The school actively recruits these students. They must take the TOEFL with a minimum score of 550 on the paper-based TOEFL (PBT) or 83 on the Internet-based version (iBT). They must also take the SAT or ACT.

ADMISSIONS: 57% of the 2014-2015 applicants were accepted. 52% of the current freshmen were in the top fifth of their class; 76% were in the top two fifths. **Admissions Contact:** William G. Motzer, Vice President for Admissions and Career Services. E-Mail: *admissions@lakeforest.edu* Web: *www.lakeforest.edu*

FINANCIAL AID: In 2014-2015, 94% of all full-time freshmen and 91% of continuing full-time students received some form of financial aid. 80% of all full-time freshmen and 85% of continuing full-time students received need-based aid. The average freshman award was $30,300. Need-based scholarships or need-based grants averaged $27,875 ($49,000 maximum); need-based self-help aid (loans and jobs) averaged $4,700 ($10,000 maximum); and other non-need-based awards and non-need-based scholarships averaged $17,325 ($25,000 maximum). 140% of undergraduate students work part-time. Average annual earnings from campus work are $2000. The average financial indebtedness of the 2014 graduate was $26,899. Lake Forest is a member of CSS. The FAFSA is required. The priority date for freshman financial aid applications for fall entry is February 15. The deadline for filing freshman financial aid applications for fall entry is May 1.

LEWIS UNIVERSITY   E-2
www.lewisu.edu

Romeoville, IL 60446	**(815) 838-0500, ext. 5250**
	(800) 897-9000
Fax: (815) 836-5002	Email: admissions@lewisu.edu
Full-time: 1020 men, 1240 women	Faculty: 141; IIA, +$
Part-time: 320 men, 650 women	Ph.D.s: 57%
Graduate: 470 men, 795 women	Student/Faculty: 16 to 1
Year: semesters, summer session	Tuition: $17,000
Room & Board: $7050	Freshman Class: n/av
SAT or ACT: required	CEEB CODE: 1404
Application Deadline: open	**COMPETITIVE**

Lewis University, founded in 1932, is a private institution affiliated with the Roman Catholic Church and sponsored by the De La Salle Christian Brothers. A comprehensive liberal arts university, Lewis offers classes at its main campus and at more than 20 satellite locations in the Chicago metropolitan area. There are 4 undergraduate schools and 11 graduate schools. In addition to regional accreditation, Lewis has baccalaureate program accreditation with NCATE and NLN. The 350-acre campus is in a suburban area 30 miles southwest of downtown Chicago. Including any residence halls, there are 21 buildings.

STUDENT LIFE: 97% of undergraduates are from Illinois. Others are from 24 states, 30 foreign countries, and Canada. 75% are from public schools. 71% are White; 14% African American. 60% are Catholic. The average age of freshmen is 19; all undergraduates, 28. 19% do not continue beyond their first year. **Housing:** 900 students can be accommodated in college housing, which includes single-sex and coed dorms. On-campus housing is available on a first-come, first-served basis, and is available on a lottery system for upperclassmen. Priority is given to out-of-town students. 73% of students commute. All students may keep cars.

FACULTY/CLASSROOMS: 57% of faculty are male; 43% are female. All teach undergraduates. No introductory courses are taught by graduate students. The average class size in an introductory lecture is 14; in a laboratory is 11; and in a regular course is 13.

PROGRAMS OF STUDY: Lewis confers B.A., B.S., B.E.S. and B.S.N. degrees. Associate and Master's degrees are also awarded. Bachelor's degrees are awarded in BIOLOGICAL SCIENCE (biochemistry and biology/biological science), BUSINESS (accounting, banking and finance, business administration and management, human resources, management information systems, marketing/retailing/merchandising, and sports management), COMMUNICATIONS AND THE ARTS (broadcasting, communications, communications technology, dramatic arts, drawing, English, illustration, journalism, multimedia, music, music business management, painting, public relations, radio/television technology, and studio art), COMPUTER AND PHYSICAL SCIENCE (atmospheric sciences and meteorology, chemistry, computer science, mathematics, and physics), EDUCATION (athletic training, elementary education, secondary education, special education, and speech correction), ENGINEERING AND ENVIRONMENTAL DESIGN (aircraft mechanics, airline piloting and navigation, aviation administration/management, computer graphics, environmental science, and preengineering), HEALTH PROFESSIONS (community health work, health care administration, nursing, physical therapy, predentistry, premedicine, preoptometry, prepharmacy, and preveterinary science), SOCIAL SCIENCE (Christian studies, criminal justice, economics, history, liberal arts/general studies, philosophy, political science/government, prelaw, psychology, public administration, religion, safety and security technology, social work, and sociology). Aviation, criminal social justice, and nursing education are the strongest academically and have the largest enrollments.

ACTIVITIES: 3% of men belong to 4 local and 5 national fraternities; 2% of women belong to 3 national sororities. There are 27 groups on campus, including band, cheerleading, choir, chorale, chorus, dance, debate, drama, ethnic, flight team, forensics, honors, international, jazz band, literary magazine, musical theater, newspaper, orchestra, pep band, photography, political, professional, radio and TV, religious, social, social service, student government, symphony, and yearbook. Popular campus events include Fall and Spring Formals, Greek Stock and International Student Food Festival. **Sports:** There are 9 intercollegiate sports for men and 9 for women, and 10 intramural sports for men and 10 for women. Facilities include a recreation center containing a field house with 4 multipurpose courts, a fitness center, an aerobics studio, an 8-lane pool, and an indoor track, a tennis complex, an outdoor track, and baseball, softball, and soccer fields. **Graduates:** From July 1, 2013 to June 30, 2014, 816 bachelor's degrees were awarded. The most popular majors were nursing (12%), criminal and social justice (10%), and business administration (10%). In an average class, 24% graduate in 3 years or less, 42% graduate in 4 years or less, 45% graduate in 5 years or less, and 62% graduate in 6 years or less.

SERVICES: Counseling and information services are available, as is tutoring in most subjects. There is remedial math, reading, and writing. The University Success Program provides assistance to those students who do not meet the outright scholastic requirements. **Library/Resources:** The library contains 180,000 volumes, 13,100 microform items, 2,300 audio/video tapes/CDs/DVDs, and subscribes to 800 periodicals including electronic. Computerized library services include interlibrary loans, database searching, and Internet access. Special learning facilities include an art gallery, radio station, TV station, aviation building and airport. **Physically Challenged Students:** 95% of the campus is accessible. Facilities include wheelchair ramps, elevators, special parking, specially equipped restrooms, special class scheduling, lowered drinking fountains, and lowered telephones. **Special:** Lewis offers a general education degree, co-op programs with Chicago College of Pharmacy and Logan Chiropractic College, student-designed majors, B.A.-B.S. degrees in nursing, pass/fail options, dual majors, work-study programs, and nondegree study. Internships are required for some majors and optional for all others. There are accelerated-degree programs in business administration, computer network administration, health care leadership, RN-BSN, social and community studies, and nursing. The aviation program permits graduates to qualify for the FAA Airframe and Powerplant certificate. There are 10 national honor societies, a freshman honors program, and 10 departmental honors programs. **Visiting:** There are regularly scheduled orientations for prospective students, consisting of 1- or 2-day sessions (overnight optional) and parent orientation followed by a welcome weekend before the first class day in the fall. There are guides for informal visits, visitors may sit in on classes, and stay overnight. To schedule a visit, contact the Admissions Office. **Campus Safety and Security:** Measures include 24-hour foot and vehicle patrol and security escort services. There are emergency telephones and lighted pathways/sidewalks.

REQUIREMENTS: The SAT or ACT is required. The ACT is preferred, with a minimum composite score of 20. Applicants should be graduates of an accredited secondary school. The GED is accepted. Students should have 18 units consisting of 3 in English and 15 in other college preparatory subjects. A GPA of 2.0 is required. AP and CLEP credits are accepted. Important factors in the admissions decision are advanced placement or honors courses, leadership record, and extracurricular activities record. All students must earn 128 credit hours in courses acceptable for graduation, with one third of these courses in the core curriculum. Students must maintain a minimum GPA of 2.0. At least 4 upper-division courses must be taken in the major. Students must complete the Introduction to the College Experience course and pass a writing proficiency exam. **Procedure:** Freshmen are admitted to all sessions. Entrance exams should be taken prior to enrollment. There is a rolling admissions plan. Application deadlines are open. The fall 2014 application fee was $35. Notification is sent on a rolling basis. Applications are accepted on-line. **Transfer Students:** 487 transfer students enrolled in 2013-2014. Applicants must have a 2.0 GPA in transferable course work of at least 12 semester hours, submit official transcripts from all colleges attended, and be in good standing at the previous institution. 32 of 128 credits required for the bachelor's degree must be completed at Lewis. **International Students:** There are 73 international students enrolled. The school actively recruits these students. They must take the TOEFL. They must also take the SAT or ACT.

ADMISSIONS: Patrick Hughes, Dean of Admission. E-Mail: *admissions@lewisu.edu* Web: *www.lewisu.edu*

FINANCIAL AID: In 2014-2015, 67% of all full-time freshmen and

66% of continuing full-time students received some form of financial aid. 55% of all full-time freshmen and 48% of continuing full-time students received need-based aid. The average freshman award was $16,125. 12% of undergraduate students work part-time. Average annual earnings from campus work are $2400. The average financial indebtedness of the 2014 graduate was $15,621. Lewis is a member of CSS. The FAFSA is required. The deadline for filing freshman financial aid applications for fall entry is May 1.

LOYOLA UNIVERSITY CHICAGO — E-2
www.luc.edu

Chicago, IL 60660	(773) 508-3075
	(800) 262-2373
Fax: (773) 508-8926	Email: admission@luc.edu
Full-time: 3275 men, 6056 women	Faculty: I, av$
Part-time: 390 men, 601 women	Ph.D.s: 93%
Graduate: 2022 men, 3558 women	Student/Faculty: 14 to 1
Year: semesters, summer session	Tuition: $38,536
Room & Board: $13,110	Freshman Class: 20414 applied, 12931 accepted, 2292 enrolled
SAT CR/M/W: 580/580/580 ACT: 27	CEEB CODE: 1412
Application Deadline: April 1	VERY COMPETITIVE+

Loyola University of Chicago, founded in 1870, is a private Roman Catholic (Jesuit) university offering undergraduate curricula in the arts and sciences, business, communication, nursing, social work, and education. There are 8 undergraduate schools and 7 graduate schools. In addition to regional accreditation, Loyola has baccalaureate program accreditation with AACSB, ACPE, CSWE, NCATE, ACS, NAST, CCNE, and NCA-HLC. The 105-acre campus is in an urban area in Chicago. Including any residence halls, there are 74 buildings.

STUDENT LIFE: 65% of undergraduates are from Illinois. Others are from 50 states, 76 foreign countries, and Canada. 68% are from public schools. 60% are White; 13% Hispanic; 11% Asian American. 59% are Catholic; 23% Orthodox Hindu, Buddhist and Islam; 16% Protestant. **Male To Female Ratio:** 1.8:1. The average age of freshmen is 18; all undergraduates, 21. 15% do not continue beyond their first year; 73% remain to graduate. **Housing:** 4415 students can be accommodated in college housing, which includes single-sex and coed dorms and on-campus apartments. In addition, there are honors houses, fraternity houses, sorority houses, living-learning community floors. On-campus housing is available on a lottery system for upperclassmen. 56% of students commute. All students may keep cars.

FACULTY/CLASSROOMS: 49% of faculty are male; 51% are female. 92% teach undergraduates, and all do research. No introductory courses are taught by graduate students.

PROGRAMS OF STUDY: Loyola confers B.A., B.S., B.A.Classics., B.B.A., B.F.A., B.G., B.S.Ed., B.S.N and B.S.W. degrees. Master's and Doctoral degrees are also awarded. Bachelor's degrees are awarded in BIOLOGICAL SCIENCE (biochemistry, bioinformatics, biology/biological science, and biophysics), BUSINESS (accounting, business administration and management, business economics, entrepreneurial studies, finance, human resources, international business management, management information systems, marketing/retailing/merchandising, organizational leadership and management, and sports management), COMMUNICATIONS AND THE ARTS (advertising, art history, communications, dance, English, fine arts, French, Greek, Italian, journalism, Latin, media arts, music, Spanish, studio art, theatre arts, and visual design), COMPUTER AND PHYSICAL SCIENCE (chemistry, computer science, computer security and information assurance, information sciences and systems, mathematics, mathematics/computational, physics, software engineering, and statistics), EDUCATION (bilingual/bicultural education, early childhood education, elementary education, health information management, mathematics education, science education, secondary education, and special education), ENGINEERING AND ENVIRONMENTAL DESIGN (environmental science), HEALTH PROFESSIONS (clinical science, exercise science, and nursing), SOCIAL SCIENCE (African studies, African American studies, anthropology, applied psychology, classical/ancient civilization, criminal justice,

economics, forensic studies, history, human services, international studies, pastoral studies, philosophy, political science/government, psychology, religious education, social work, sociology, theological studies, and women's studies). Biology, psychology and nursing have the largest enrollments.

ACTIVITIES: 9% of men belong to 6 national fraternities; 10% of women belong to 9 national sororities. There are 185 groups on campus, including and fencing, ice hockey, lacrosse, quidditch, rugby, running club, soccer, softball, swim club, tennis, ultimate frisbee, volleyball, art, band, chess, choir, chorus, dance, debate, drama, environmental, ethnic, film, gay, honors, international, jazz band, literary magazine, newspaper, photography, political, professional, radio and TV, religious, social, social service, student government, and waterpolo. Popular campus events include New Year's Festival, President's Ball and Department of Programming Concert and Mainstage Events. **Sports:** There are 7 intercollegiate sports for men and 8 for women, and 20 intramural sports for men and 20 for women. Facilities include Loyola Soccer park with new seating capacity of 500 and state-of-the-art press box. Norville Center athletics complex includes a student-athlete academic center, a sports medicine facility, modern and fully furnished locker rooms, state-of-the-art strength and conditioning equipment, a Loyola athletics Wall of Fame, and other facilities that will transform the on-campus experience of all our students and help take Loyola's athletics to the next level.**Graduates:** From July 1, 2013 to June 30, 2014, 2287 bachelor's degrees were awarded. The most popular majors were biology (14%), nursing (12%), and psychology (11%). In an average class, 1% graduate in 3 years or less, 65% graduate in 4 years or less, 72% graduate in 5 years or less, and 73% graduate in 6 years or less.

SERVICES: Counseling and information services are available, as is tutoring in some subjects, general education courses. A writing center is also available for student use; small group tutoring; tutor-led study halls; academic skills workshop; and language learning center. **Library/Resources:** The 7 libraries contain 1.9 million volumes, 1.6 million microform items, and 13,833 audio/video tapes/CDs/DVDs, and subscribe to 56,112 periodicals including electronic. Computerized library services include interlibrary loans, database searching, Internet access, and Wi-Fi capability. Special learning facilities include an art gallery, radio station, theaters, art museums, digital media labs, convergence media studio, language learning resource center, neuroscience labs, clean energy lab, mock trial room, performance and specialized fine arts rooms, clinical simulation nursing laboratory, histology lab, geothermal system, ecodome greenhouse, aquaponics system showcase, artificial stream research facility, retreat and ecology campus. **Physically Challenged Students:** 90% of the campus is accessible. Facilities include wheelchair ramps, elevators, specially equipped restrooms, special class scheduling, lowered drinking fountains, lowered telephones. Selected dorms are wheelchair accessible. **Special:** There are study abroad service learning opportunities in Vietnam, Peru, El Salvador, South Africa, Chile, Spain, and India. Dual majors in math education/secondary education and physics/engineering, nondegree study, and pass/fail options are available. The school also offers a B.A.-B.S. degree in chemistry and a 3-2 engineering degree with Columbia and Washington Universities. There are 5-year programs and combination bachelor's/master's available. There are 9 national honor societies, including Phi Beta Kappa, and a freshman honors program. **Visiting:** There are regularly scheduled orientations for prospective students, including interviews and tours; students may attend classes if previous arrangements have been made. There are guides for informal visits and visitors may stay overnight. To schedule a visit, contact the Undergraduate Admissions Office. **Campus Safety and Security:** Measures include 24-hour foot and vehicle patrol, emergency notification system, self-defense education, and security escort services. There are shuttle buses, emergency telephones, lighted pathways/sidewalks, Hot spot tours, and bicycle safety U-lock program.

REQUIREMENTS: The SAT or ACT is required. Graduation from an accredited secondary school or satisfactory scores on the GED are required for admission. 15 academic credits are required. Secondary school courses should include 4 credits of English and 3 each of math, science, and social studies. AP and CLEP credits are accepted. Important factors in the admissions decision are advanced placement or honors courses, leadership record, and extracurricular activities record. To graduate, students must have a total of 120 credit hours with a minimum GPA of 2.0. There is a core requirement. The Core includes a total of 15 courses (45 credit hours of coursework), primarily from the arts and sciences, which develop important college-level skills and integrate an understanding of values through 10 required areas of knowledge. Important skills on which the Core focuses are communication, critical thinking, ethical awareness, information literacy, quantitativeand qualitative analysis, research methods, and technological literacy. The 10 required areas of knowledge include a college writing seminar, artistic knowledge and experience, historical knowledge, literary knowledge, quantitative analysis, scientific literacy, societal and cultural knowledge, philosophical knowledge, theological and religious studies, and ethics. For the core requirement, all students must take 9 hours each of theology, philosophy, and social sciences and 6 hours each of English composition and humanities. **Procedure:** Freshmen are admitted to all sessions. Entrance exams should be taken as early as possible, normally in the spring of the junior year. There is a rolling admissions plan. Applications should be filed by April 1 for fall entry. 684 applicants were on the 2014 waiting list; 99 were admitted. Applications are accepted on-line. Application fees are waived if application is completed on-line. **Transfer Students:** 597 transfer students enrolled in 2013-2014. Transfer students must have 20 transferable semester hours of credit, with a minimum GPA of 2.0 for the schools of arts and sciences and education. A minimum GPA of 2.5 is required for the schools of nursing and business administration. If transfers have fewer then 20 hours, students must meet the same requirements as entering freshmen. 45 of 120 credits required for the bachelor's degree must be completed at Loyola. **International Students:** There are 337 international students enrolled. The school actively recruits these students. They must take the TOEFL with a minimum score of 550 on the paper-based TOEFL (PBT) or 79 on the Internet-based version (iBT). They must also take the SAT or ACT.

ADMISSIONS: 63% of the 2014-2015 applicants were accepted. The SAT scores for the 2014-2015 freshman class were: Critical Reading--9% below 500, 49% between 500 and 599, 37% between 600 and 699, and 5% between 700 and 800; Math--11% below 500, 47% between 500 and 599, 36% between 600 and 699, and 6% between 700 and 800; Writing--10% below 500, 49% between 500 and 599, 36% between 600 and 699, and 6% between 700 and 800. The ACT scores were 2% below 21, 12% between 21 and 23, 34% between 24 and 26, 21% between 27 and 28, and 32% above 28. 63% of the current freshmen were in the top fifth of their class; 90% were in the top two fifths. 1 freshman graduated first in the class. **Admissions Contact:** Lori Greene, Director for Undergraduate Admissions. E-Mail: admission@luc.edu Web: www.luc.edu

FINANCIAL AID: In 2014-2015, 96% of all full-time freshmen and 93% of continuing full-time students received some form of financial aid. 70% of all full-time freshmen and 66% of continuing full-time students received need-based aid. The average freshman award was $30,750. Need-based scholarships or need-based grants averaged $19,482 ($57,347 maximum); need-based self-help aid (loans and jobs) averaged $12,810 ($37,000 maximum); non-need-based athletic scholarships averaged $25,991 ($50,400 maximum); and other non-need-based awards and non-need-based scholarships averaged $12,765 ($40,580 maximum). 30% of undergraduate students work part-time. Average annual earnings from campus work are $2404. The average financial indebtedness of the 2014 graduate was $34,404. The FAFSA is required. The deadline for filing freshman financial aid applications for fall entry is March 1.

MacMurray College, founded in 1846, is a private liberal arts institution affiliated with the United Methodist Church. The figures in the above capsule and in this profile are approximate. In addition to regional accreditation, MacMurray has baccalaureate program accreditation with CSWE and CCNE. The 60-acre campus is in a small town 30 miles west of Springfield. Including any residence halls, there are 17 buildings.

STUDENT LIFE: 88% of undergraduates are from Illinois. Others are from 17 states, 3 foreign countries, and Canada. 90% are from public schools. 79% are White; 11% African American. 78% are Protestant; 18% Catholic. The average age of freshmen is 19; all undergraduates, 22. 40% do not continue beyond their first year; 56% remain to graduate. **Housing:** 725 students can be accommodated in college housing, which includes single-sex and coed dorms. On-campus housing is guaranteed for all 4 years. 54% of students live on campus; of those, 70% remain on campus on weekends. All students may keep cars.

FACULTY/CLASSROOMS: 42% of faculty are male; 58% are female. All teach undergraduates. No introductory courses are taught by graduate students. The average class size in an introductory lecture is 41; in a laboratory is 14; and in a regular course is 17.

PROGRAMS OF STUDY: MacMurray confers B.A., B.S., B.S.N. and B.S.W. degrees. Associate degrees are also awarded. Bachelor's degrees are awarded in BIOLOGICAL SCIENCE (biology/biological science), BUSINESS (accounting, business administration and management, management information systems, marketing/retailing/merchandising, and sports management), COMMUNICATIONS AND THE ARTS (art, dramatic arts, English, music, and Spanish), COMPUTER AND PHYSICAL SCIENCE (chemistry, computer science, mathematics, and physics), EDUCATION (education of the deaf and hearing impaired, elementary education, music education, physical education, science education, secondary education, and special education), ENGINEERING AND ENVIRONMENTAL DESIGN (preengineering), HEALTH PROFESSIONS (nursing, predentistry, premedicine, and preveterinary science), SOCIAL SCIENCE (criminal justice, history, interpreter for the deaf, liberal arts/general studies, philosophy, political science/government, prelaw, psychology, religion, social work, and youth ministry). Education of the hearing impaired, and nursing are the strongest academically. Business, education, and criminal justice have the largest enrollments.

ACTIVITIES: 9% of men belong to 1 local and 2 national fraternities; 15% of women belong to 3 local sororities. There are 31 groups on campus, including art, bagpipe, band, cheerleading, choir, chorale, chorus, dance, drama, ethnic, gay, international, literary magazine, musical theater, newspaper, orchestra, pep band, photography, professional, religious, social, social service, student government, and yearbook. Popular campus events include Spring formal, Sigma Tau Gamma Day and Midnight Breakfasts. **Sports:** There are 9 intercollegiate sports for men and 8 for women, and 15 intramural sports for men and 15 for women. Facilities include a gym, 3 basketball courts, tennis and outdoor basketball courts, a competition-size swimming pool, a weight room, a wrestling room, dance studios, a game room and TV lounge. **Graduates:** From July 1, 2013 to June 30, 2014, 115 bachelor's degrees were awarded. The most popular majors were social work (12%), nursing (10%), and psychology (10%). 75 companies recruited on campus in 2013-2014. In an average class, 36% graduate in 4 years or less, 45% graduate in 5 years or less, and 52% graduate in 6 years or less. Of the 2013 graduating class, 15% were enrolled in graduate school within 6 months of graduation, and 90% were employed.

SERVICES: Counseling and information services are available, as is tutoring in every subject. There is remedial math, reading, and writing. The college provides services to visually and hearing impaired students through interpreters, readers, and note takers. **Library/Resources:** The library contains 1.8 million volumes, 28,093 microform items, 1,085 audio/video tapes/CDs/DVDs, and subscribes to 130 periodicals including electronic. Computerized library services include interlibrary loans, database searching, Internet access, and Wi-Fi capability. Special learning facilities include an art gallery. **Physically Challenged Students:** 90% of the campus is accessible. Facilities include wheelchair ramps, elevators, special parking, specially equipped restrooms, special class scheduling, and special housing. **Special:** The school has co-op programs in modern languages and international studies and cross-registration with 5 colleges

MACMURRAY COLLEGE	C-3
www.mac.edu	

Jacksonville, IL 62650	
	(217) 479-7056
	(800) 252-7485
Fax: (217) 291-0702	Email: admiss@mac.edu
Full-time: 267 men, 375 women	Faculty: 45; IIB, --$
Part-time: 15 men, 44 women	Ph.D.s: 62%
Graduate: n/av	Student/Faculty: 14 to 1
Year: semesters, summer session	Tuition: $16,000
Room & Board: $5505	Freshman Class: 1421 applied, 806 accepted, 186 enrolled
SAT: required ACT: 21	CEEB CODE: 1435
Application Deadline: n/av	COMPETITIVE

through the West Central Illinois Foreign Language Consortium. A 3-2 engineering degree with Washington and Columbia Universities a Washington semester, internships in all majors, work-study programs, dual majors, and pass/fail options are available. Students may study abroad in England, Germany, Japan, or Russia. There are 4 national honor societies, a freshman honors program, and 5 departmental honors programs. **Visiting:** There are regularly scheduled orientations for prospective students, including a financial aid conference, a tour, and faculty appointments. There are guides for informal visits, visitors may sit in on classes, and stay overnight. To schedule a visit, contact the Office of Admissions. **Campus Safety and Security:** Measures include security escort services. There are emergency telephones, lighted pathways/sidewalks, evening patrols, and evening sign-in at dorms.

REQUIREMENTS: The SAT or ACT is required. Applicants must be graduates of an accredited secondary school. The GED is accepted. Secondary school courses should include 4 years of English, 3 years of math, and 2 years each of science, foreign language, and social studies. MacMurray requires applicants to be in the upper 50% of their class. A GPA of 2.5 is required. AP and CLEP credits are accepted. Important factors in the admissions decision are advanced placement or honors courses, extracurricular activities record, and leadership record. To graduate, students must complete 120 semester hours with a minimum GPA of 2.0. All students must take 3 courses in rhetorical skills and a 3-course sequence on major ideas in Western civilization, a course in Diversity and the American Experience, and satisfy the requirements of the breadth component, a 16-hour distribution of non-major courses. They also must pass a proficiency exam in writing, given when students attain junior standing. **Procedure:** Freshmen are admitted to all sessions. Entrance exams should be taken in the spring of the junior year. There are deferred admissions and rolling admissions plans. Application deadlines are open. Notification is sent on a rolling basis. Applications are accepted on-line. **Transfer Students:** 101 transfer students enrolled in 2013-2014. Transfer students must have a minimum GPA of 2.0 in at least 28 transferable semester credits. Nursing applicants must have a GPA of 2.75 and a minimum score of 20 on the ACT. 30 of 120 credits required for the bachelor's degree must be completed at MacMurray. **International Students:** There are 8 international students enrolled. They must take the TOEFL. Some may be required to take the SAT or ACT with a minimum score of 950 (SAT) or 20 (ACT).

ADMISSIONS: 57% of the 2014-2015 applicants were accepted. The ACT scores were 50% below 21, 28% between 21 and 23, 15% between 24 and 26, 4% between 27 and 28, and 3% above 28. 28% of the current freshmen were in the top fifth of their class; 50% were in the top two fifths. 3 freshmen graduated first in their class. **Admissions Contact:** Robert La Verriere, Vice President for Enrollment. E-Mail: *admiss@mac.edu* Web: *www.mac.edu*

FINANCIAL AID: In 2014-2015, 99% of all full-time freshmen and 99% of continuing full-time students received some form of financial aid. 92% of all full-time freshmen and 80% of continuing full-time students received need-based aid. The average freshman award was $16,385. Need-based scholarships or need-based grants averaged $5,512 ($15,000 maximum); need-based self-help aid (loans and jobs) averaged $4,607 ($5,500 maximum); and other non-need-based awards and non-need-based scholarships averaged $11,279 ($15,300 maximum). 55% of undergraduate students work part-time. Average annual earnings from campus work are $1134. The average financial indebtedness of the 2014 graduate was $13,926. MacMurray is a member of CSS. The FAFSA is required. The deadline for filing freshman financial aid applications for fall entry is open.

MCKENDREE UNIVERSITY   C-5
www.mckendree.edu

Lebanon, IL 62254

Fax: (618) 537-6496
Full-time: 706 men, 823 women
Part-time: 289 men, 376 women
Graduate: 259 men, 754 women
Year: semesters, summer session
Room & Board: $7850

ACT: 24
Application Deadline: n/av

(618) 537-6833
(800) BEARCAT
Email: chall@mckendree.edu
Faculty: 94; IIA, --$
Ph.D.s: 90%
Student/Faculty: 16 to 1
Tuition: $22,070
Freshman Class: 1097 applied, 778 accepted, 304 enrolled
CEEB CODE: 1456
COMPETITIVE+

McKendree University, founded in 1828, is the oldest college in Illinois. It is a private liberal arts institution affiliated with the United Methodist Church. The figures in the above capsule and in this profile are approximate. There are 4 undergraduate schools and 4 graduate schools. In addition to regional accreditation, McKendree has baccalaureate program accreditation with NCATE, NLN, IACBE, and CAAHEP. The 115-acre campus is in a suburban area 23 miles east of St. Louis. Including any residence halls, there are 34 buildings.

STUDENT LIFE: 66% of undergraduates are from Illinois. Others are from 11 states, 13 foreign countries, and Canada. 92% are from public schools. 76% are White; 13% African American. 25% are Protestant; 23% Catholic. The average age of freshmen is 18; all undergraduates, 27. 22% do not continue beyond their first year; 70% remain to graduate. **Housing:** 692 students can be accommodated in college housing, which includes coed dorms and on-campus apartments. On-campus housing is guaranteed for all 4 years. 50% of students commute. Alcohol is not permitted. All students may keep cars.

FACULTY/CLASSROOMS: 48% of faculty are male; 52% are female. All teach and do research. No introductory courses are taught by graduate students. The average class size in an introductory lecture is 20; in a laboratory is 15; and in a regular course is 12.

PROGRAMS OF STUDY: McKendree confers B.A., B.S., B.B.A., B.F.A., B.S.Ed. and B.S.N. degrees. Master's degrees are also awarded. Bachelor's degrees are awarded in BIOLOGICAL SCIENCE (biology/biological science), BUSINESS (accounting, banking and finance, business administration and management, and marketing/retailing/merchandising), COMMUNICATIONS AND THE ARTS (art, dramatic arts, English, music, music business management, music history and appreciation, public relations, and speech/debate/rhetoric), COMPUTER AND PHYSICAL SCIENCE (chemistry, computer science, information sciences and systems, and mathematics), EDUCATION (art education, athletic training, business education, elementary education, music education, and physical education), HEALTH PROFESSIONS (health, medical laboratory technology, and nursing), SOCIAL SCIENCE (criminal justice, economics, gerontology, history, international relations, philosophy, political science/government, psychology, religion, religious music, social science, social work, and sociology). Business, math, and computer science are the strongest academically. Business, education, and nursing have the largest enrollments.

ACTIVITIES: 1% of men belong to 2 local and 3 national fraternities; 1% of women belong to 3 local sororities. There are 75 groups on campus, including art, band, cheerleading, choir, chorale, chorus, computers, dance, debate, drama, ethnic, film, forensics, gay, honors, international, jazz band, literary magazine, marching band, musical theater, newspaper, pep band, photography, political, professional, religious, social, social service, and student government. Popular campus events include Model United Nations, Family Festival and Midnight Breakfast. **Sports:** There are 10 intercollegiate sports for men and 10 for women, and 13 intramural sports for men and 13 for women. Facilities include a 1600-seat gym, an intramural gym, a fitness center, tennis courts, a student center with table tennis and billiards, an all-weather track, a 3000-seat football stadium, and playing fields for baseball, softball, and intramurals. **Graduates:** From July 1, 2013 to June 30, 2014, 516 bachelor's degrees were awarded. The most popular majors were business (37%), education (20%), and nursing (20%). 150 companies recruited on campus in 2013-2014. In an average class, 48% graduate in 4 years or less, 66% graduate in 5 years or less, and 70% graduate in 6 years or less. Of the 2013 graduating class, 29% were enrolled in graduate school within 6 months of graduation, and 90% were employed.

SERVICES: Counseling and information services are available, as is tutoring in every subject. There is a reader service for the blind, and remedial reading and writing. **Library/Resources:** The library contains 140,000 volumes, 40,000 microform items, 30,000 audio/video tapes/CDs/DVDs, and subscribes to 9,000 periodicals including electronic. Computerized library services include interlibrary loans, database searching, Internet access, and Wi-Fi capability. Special learning facilities include a **Physically Challenged Students:** 80% of the campus is accessible. Facilities include wheelchair ramps, elevators, special parking, specially equipped restrooms, special class scheduling, and lowered drinking fountains. **Special:** McKendree offers internships, work-study programs, study abroad in 11 countries, a

Washington semester, dual and student-designed majors, and nondegree study, as well as a 3-2 program in occupational therapy with Washington University in St. Louis. There are 12 national honor societies, a freshman honors program, and 1 departmental honors program. **Visiting:** There are regularly scheduled orientations for prospective students, consisting of Preview Days, where faculty members and personnel from several departments answer questions. Student-led tours of the campus and various other events are also available. There are guides for informal visits, visitors may sit in on classes, and stay overnight. **Campus Safety and Security:** Measures include 24-hour foot and vehicle patrol, emergency notification system, and security escort services. There are shuttle buses, emergency telephones, and lighted pathways/sidewalks.

REQUIREMENTS: The ACT is required. Students must be high school graduates or submit the GED certificate. Completion of at least 15 units of high school work is recommended. A recommendation from the secondary school counselor is required. McKendree requires applicants to be in the upper 50% of their class. A GPA of 2.5 is required. AP and CLEP credits are accepted. Important factors in the admissions decision are advanced placement or honors courses, leadership record, and evidence of special talent. To graduate, students must complete 128 semester hours, with a minimum GPA of 2.0. The 51-credit-hour core curriculum includes 9 credits of social science, 7 of science, 6 of freshman English, 3 each of speech, math, ethics, philosophy or religion, history, cross-cultural studies, literature, fine or performing arts, and computer competency, and 1 to 2 of phys ed. In addition, 2 writing-intensive courses and a writing proficiency exam must be taken. A thesis is required for biology majors seeking a B.S. degree. **Procedure:** Freshmen are admitted to all sessions. Entrance exams should be taken in the junior year. There is a rolling admissions plan. Application deadlines are open. Application fee is $40. Applications are accepted on-line. **Transfer Students:** 217 transfer students enrolled in 2013-2014. Applicants must have a minimum 2.25 GPA from all colleges previously attended. 64 of 128 credits required for the bachelor's degree must be completed at McKendree. **International Students:** There are 30 international students enrolled. The school actively recruits these students. They must take the TOEFL with a minimum score of 520 on the paper-based TOEFL (PBT) or 70 on the Internet-based version (iBT). They must also take the SAT or ACT, scoring 20.

ADMISSIONS: 71% of the 2014-2015 applicants were accepted. The ACT scores were 27% below 21, 34% between 21 and 23, 27% between 24 and 26, 4% between 27 and 28, and 7% above 28. 40% of the current freshmen were in the top fifth of their class; 70% were in the top two fifths. There were 96 National Merit finalists. 97 freshmen graduated first in their class. **Admissions Contact:** Chris Hall, Vice President for Admission and Financial Aid. E-Mail: *chall@ mckendree.edu* Web: *www.mckendree.edu*

FINANCIAL AID: In 2014-2015, 100% of all full-time freshmen and 96% of continuing full-time students received some form of financial aid. 94% of all full-time freshmen and 89% of continuing full-time students received need-based aid. The average freshman award was $20,472. Need-based scholarships or need-based grants averaged $17,039 ($29,920 maximum); need-based self-help aid (loans and jobs) averaged $4,093 ($11,500 maximum); and non-need-based athletic scholarships averaged $7,956 ($29,920 maximum). 22% of undergraduate students work part-time. Average annual earnings from campus work are $972. The average financial indebtedness of the 2014 graduate was $17,839. The FAFSA is required. Check with the school for current application deadlines.

Millikin is an independent, four-year university with students in traditional and non-traditional undergraduate and Masters degree programs. Millikin offers undergraduate programs in arts and sciences, fine arts, professional studies and business, graduate studies in business administration and nursing, and accelerated adult learning programs. There are 4 undergraduate schools and 2 graduate schools. In addition to regional accreditation, Millikin has baccalaureate program accreditation with ACBSP, NASM, NCATE, COA, CCNE, and CAATE. The 75-acre campus is in a suburban area 180 miles southwest of Chicago and 130 miles northeast of St. Louis. Including any residence halls, there are 33 buildings.

STUDENT LIFE: 87% of undergraduates are from Illinois. Others are from 34 states, 20 foreign countries, and Canada. 90% are from public schools. 73% are White; 14% African American. **Male To Female Ratio:** 1.5:1. The average age of freshmen is 18; all undergraduates, 21. 18% do not continue beyond their first year; 61% remain to graduate. **Housing:** 1387 students can be accommodated in college housing, which includes single-sex and coed dorms, on-campus apartments, and married student housing. In addition, there are special-interest houses, fraternity houses, sorority houses, living-learning communities. On-campus housing is available on a first-come, first-served basis, and is available on a lottery system for upperclassmen. 67% of students live on campus; of those, 75% remain on campus on weekends. Upperclassmen may keep cars.

FACULTY/CLASSROOMS: 43% of faculty are male; 57% are female. All teach undergraduates. No introductory courses are taught by graduate students. The average class size in an introductory lecture is 18; in a laboratory is 12; and in a regular course is 18.

PROGRAMS OF STUDY: Millikin confers B.A., B.S., B.F.A., B.M. and B.S.N. degrees. Master's and Doctoral degrees are also awarded. Bachelor's degrees are awarded in BIOLOGICAL SCIENCE (biochemistry, biology/adolescence education, biology/biological science, and molecular biology), BUSINESS (accounting, business administration and management, entrepreneurial studies, finance, international business management, management science, marketing/retailing/merchandising, organizational leadership and management, recreational facilities management, and sports management), COMMUNICATIONS AND THE ARTS (acting, art, communication, dramatic arts, English, journalism, music, music business management, music performance, musical theater, piano/organ, public relations, Spanish, studio art, theater design, visual and performing arts, and voice), COMPUTER AND PHYSICAL SCIENCE (actuarial science, chemistry, chemistry/adolescence education, information sciences and systems, mathematics, and physics), EDUCATION (art education, athletic training, early childhood education, education, elementary education, English education, mathematics education, music education, physical education, secondary education, and social science education), ENGINEERING AND ENVIRONMENTAL DESIGN (commercial art, computer graphics, and preengineering), HEALTH PROFESSIONS (allied health, art therapy, health and physical activity, nursing, predentistry, premedicine, preoptometry, prepharmacy, prephysical therapy, and preveterinary science), SOCIAL SCIENCE (ethics, politics, and social policy, history, human services, interdisciplinary studies, philosophy, political science/government, prelaw, psychology, and sociology). Music and theater is the strongest academically. Nursing, music, and theater have the largest enrollments.

ACTIVITIES: 20% of men belong to 5 national fraternities; 21% of women belong to 6 national sororities. There are 90 groups on campus, including art, band, cheerleading, chess, choir, chorale, chorus, computers, dance, debate, drama, drill team, environmental, ethnic, film, gay, honors, international, jazz band, literary magazine, musical theater, newspaper, opera, orchestra, pep band, photography, political, professional, radio and TV, religious, social, social service, student government, and symphony. Popular campus events include Homecoming, Fall Family Weekend, Millipalooza, and University Event. **Sports:** There are 8 intercollegiate sports for men and 9 for women, and 5 intramural sports for men and 5 for women. Facilities include 87,000-square feet indoor sports center with a 4-lane, 200-meter competitive-grade track, indoor soccer, 5 basketball/volleyball courts, batting cages, golf practice area, a climbing wall, aerobic and dance areas, and a fitness/wellness center; phys ed center with a 6-lane, 25-yard pool; a 3000-seat field house with 3 regulation-sized

---

MILLIKIN UNIVERSITY   D-3
www.millikin.edu

Decatur, IL 62522	
	(217) 424-6210
	(800) 373-7733
Fax: (217) 425-4669	Email: admis@millikin.edu
Full-time: 825 men, 1193 women	Faculty: 146; IIB, -$
Part-time: 35 men, 59 women	Ph.D.s: 80%
Graduate: 26 men, 51 women	Student/Faculty: 14 to 1
Year: semesters, summer session	Tuition: $29,620
Room & Board: $9320	Freshman Class: 3255 applied, 2042 accepted, 477 enrolled
SAT CR/M/W: 490/480/490 ACT: 22	CEEB CODE: 1470
Application Deadline: n/av	COMPETITIVE

basketball courts; a 4000-seat football field encircled by 8-lane all-weather track; 2 outdoor soccer fields; additional practice fields; and tennis courts. **Graduates:** From July 1, 2013 to June 30, 2014, 494 bachelor's degrees were awarded. The most popular majors were business/marketing (23%), visual and performing arts (17%), and health professions (12%). 30 companies recruited on campus in 2013-2014. In an average class, 51% graduate in 4 years or less, 61% graduate in 5 years or less, and 61% graduate in 6 years or less. Of the 2013 graduating class, 19% were enrolled in graduate school within 6 months of graduation, and 80% were employed.

SERVICES: Counseling and information services are available, as is tutoring in most subjects. There is a reader service for the blind. Math and writing centers, workshops on various topics are available. **Library/Resources:** The library contains 221,922 volumes, 21,000 microform items, 13,934 audio/video tapes/CDs/DVDs, and subscribes to 1,600 periodicals including electronic. Computerized library services include interlibrary loans, database searching, Internet access, and Wi-Fi capability. Special learning facilities include an art gallery, radio station, 32-track recording studio, computer imaging center, art museum and galleries, observatory with 20" reflecting telescope, 280-seat proscenium theater, 90-seat experimental space for student-directed productions, 3D arts building; student-owned and operated art gallery (Blue Connection), business incubator (The Hub), printing press (Carriage House Press), record label and music publishing company (First Step Records), publishing company (Bronze Man Books), and theatre company (Pipe Dreams Studio Theatre). **Physically Challenged Students:** 66% of the campus is accessible. Facilities include wheelchair ramps, elevators, special parking, specially equipped restrooms, special class scheduling, lowered drinking fountains, and special housing. **Special:** Millikin offers internships, a Washington semester through American University, study abroad in 28 countries, student-designed majors, a 3-2 engineering degree with Washington University, B.A.-B.S. degrees, credit by exam, and pass/fail options. Students may study multiple majors of their choice; Millikin also offers dual degree programs. There are preprofessional programs in engineering, law, optometry, dentistry, medicine, veterinary science, occupational therapy, medical technology, physical therapy, chiropractic, physician's assistant, and pharmacy. Students are also offered a United Nations semester at Drew University and can benefit from affiliate agreements with programs such as the Institute for the International Education of Students (IES), Ecole Superieure de Gestion et Commerce International (ESGCI), International Teacher-Scholars Program (ITSP), Tunghai University and the Chicago Center for Urban Life and Culture semester. There are 13 national honor societies, a freshman honors program, and 10 departmental honors programs. **Visiting:** There are regularly scheduled orientations for prospective students, consisting of meetings with students, faculty, coaches, and staff; a tour of the campus facilities; and curriculum, honors, housing, and financial aid presentations. There is also an opportunity for students to audition or have portfolios reviewed. There are guides for informal visits, visitors may sit in on classes, and stay overnight. To schedule a visit, contact the Office of Admission at admis@millikin.edu. **Campus Safety and Security:** Measures include 24-hour foot and vehicle patrol, emergency notification system, and security escort services. There are shuttle buses, emergency telephones, lighted pathways/sidewalks, and controlled access to dorms/residences.

REQUIREMENTS: The SAT or ACT is required. Applicants should be graduates of an accredited secondary school or have a GED. They should prepare with 4 units of English, 3 each of math and science, and 2 each of foreign language, social studies, and history. An audition is required for music-theater, music, or theater majors. A portfolio is required for art majors. Millikin requires applicants to be in the upper 50% of their class. A GPA of 2.5 is required. AP and CLEP credits are accepted. Important factors in the admissions decision are recommendations by school officials, advanced placement or honors courses, and leadership record.Requirements for graduation include courses in writing, math, fine arts, natural sciences, and oral communication. Sequential interdisciplinary requirements include first-year seminar, critical writing, reading, and research 1 and 2, U.S. culture studies, U.S. social structures, and global issues. Nonsequential requirements include quantitative reasoning, natural science with a lab, oral communication, and 2 courses in international cultures and

structures. The minimum GPA is 2.0 (higher for some programs); additional requirements for specific programs must be met. Students must complete a minimum of 124 credits (or more for some programs) with a minimum of 39 credits earned in courses numbered 300 or above; at least 12 credits must be in the major department or area. **Procedure:** Freshmen are admitted fall, spring, and summer. Entrance exams should be taken by May 1. There are deferred admissions and rolling admissions plans. Application deadlines are open. Notification is sent on a rolling basis. Applications are accepted online. **Transfer Students:** 104 transfer students enrolled in 2013-2014. Applicants are required to provide official transcripts from previous institutions and may submit ACT/SAT scores. Applicants who are in good standing at the previous institution and who have earned at least a C average in all college study previously attempted will be favorably considered for admission (additional requirements for specific programs). 33 of 124 credits required for the bachelor's degree must be completed at Millikin. **International Students:** There are 35 international students enrolled. The school actively recruits these students. They must take the TOEFL with a minimum score of 550 on the paper-based TOEFL (PBT) or 79 on the Internet-based version (iBT).

ADMISSIONS: 63% of the 2014-2015 applicants were accepted. The SAT scores for the 2014-2015 freshman class were: Critical Reading--52% below 500, 29% between 500 and 599, 14% between 600 and 699, and 5% between 700 and 800; Math--59% below 500, 12% between 500 and 599, 24% between 600 and 699, and 5% between 700 and 800; Writing--53% below 500, 26% between 500 and 599, 18% between 600 and 699, and 3% between 700 and 800. The ACT scores were 36% below 21, 24% between 21 and 23, 20% between 24 and 26, 10% between 27 and 28, and 10% above 28. 29% of the current freshmen were in the top fifth of their class; 59% were in the top two fifths. 13 freshmen graduated first in their class. **Admissions Contact:** Lin Stoner, Director, Office of Admission. E-Mail: *admis@ millikin.edu* Web: *www.millikin.edu*

FINANCIAL AID: In 2014-2015, 100% of all full-time freshmen and 98% of continuing full-time students received some form of financial aid. 86% of all full-time freshmen and 82% of continuing full-time students received need-based aid. The average freshman award was $24,333. Need-based scholarships or need-based grants averaged $9,369; need-based self-help aid (loans and jobs) averaged $4,025; and other non-need-based awards and non-need-based scholarships averaged $13,075. 44% of undergraduate students work part-time. Average annual earnings from campus work are $675. The average financial indebtedness of the 2014 graduate was $31,833. The FAFSA is required. The priority date for freshman financial aid applications for fall entry is March 1. The deadline for filing freshman financial aid applications for fall entry is May 1.

MONMOUTH COLLEGE C-2
www.monmouthcollege.edu

Monmouth, IL 61462	**309-457-2143**
	1-800-747-2687
Fax: 309-457-2141	**Email: admissions@monmouthcollege.edu**
Full-time: 581 men, 697 women	**Faculty:** 92; IIB, av$
Part-time: 11 men, 11 women	**Ph.D.s:** 85%
Graduate: n/av	**Student/Faculty:** 12 to 1
Year: semesters	**Tuition:** $33,200
Room & Board: $7650	**Freshman Class:** 2849 applied, 1969 accepted, 396 enrolled
SAT: required **ACT:** 23	**CEEB CODE:** 1484
Application Deadline: n/av	**COMPETITIVE**

Monmouth College, founded in 1853, is a selective, residential, private liberal arts and sciences college. In addition to regional accreditation, Monmouth College has baccalaureate program accreditation with ACS. The 112-acre campus is in a small town in west-central Illinois, 20 miles east of the Mississippi River, and 45 miles south of Rock Island and Moline. Including any residence halls, there are 39 buildings.

STUDENT LIFE: 92% of undergraduates are from Illinois. Others are from 29 states, 22 foreign countries, and Canada. 90% are from public schools. 64% are White, 13% Hispanic, 11% African American. 40% are Protestant; 30% claim no religious affiliation; 21% Catholic. The average age of freshmen is 18; all undergraduates, 20. 22% do not continue beyond their first year; 56% remain to graduate. **Housing:** 1435 students can be accommodated in college housing, which includes single-sex and coed dorms and on-campus apartments. In addition, there are honors houses, special-interest houses, fraternity houses, and sorority houses. On-campus housing is guaranteed for all 4 years. 92% of students live on campus; of those, 75% remain on campus on weekends. All students may keep cars.

FACULTY/CLASSROOMS: 55% of faculty are male; 45% are female. All teach undergraduates, all do research, and all teach and do research. No introductory courses are taught by graduate students. The average class size in an introductory lecture is 22; in a laboratory is 12; and in a regular course is 15.

PROGRAMS OF STUDY: Monmouth College confers B.A. degrees. Bachelor's degrees are awarded in BIOLOGICAL SCIENCE (biochemistry and biology/biological science), BUSINESS (accounting, business administration and management, and international business management), COMMUNICATIONS AND THE ARTS (art, classics, communications, dramatic arts, English, French, Greek, Latin, music, and Spanish), COMPUTER AND PHYSICAL SCIENCE (chemistry, computer programming, computer science, mathematics, and physics), EDUCATION (elementary education, physical education, and secondary education), ENGINEERING AND ENVIRONMENTAL DESIGN (environmental science), HEALTH PROFESSIONS (exercise science), SOCIAL SCIENCE (anthropology, biopsychology, economics, history, international studies, philosophy, political science/government, psychology, religion, and sociology). English, classics (Greek and Latin), history, chemistry and biochemistry are the strongest academically. Business, communications, and psychology have the largest enrollments.

ACTIVITIES: 22% of men and 18% of women belong to 4 national fraternities, and women belong to 3 national sororities. There are 69 groups on campus, including art, bagpipe, band, cheerleading, chess, choir, chorale, chorus, computers, dance, debate, drama, environmental, ethnic, film, forensics, gay, honors, international, jazz band, literary magazine, marching band, musical theater, newspaper, orchestra, pep band, photography, political, professional, radio and TV, religious, social, social service, and student government. Popular campus events include Homecoming, Scots Day (Founders Day) and Parents Weekend. **Sports:** There are 11 intercollegiate sports for men and 11 for women, and 14 intramural sports for men and 14 for women. Facilities include The Huff Athletic Center includes gym, indoor and outdoor track, all-purpose indoor courts, indoor batting cages, natatorium, 6-court tennis stadium, weight room, fitness/wellness center, dance studio, football, baseball, soccer, and softball fields, sand volleyball court, climbing wall, sauna, and steam room. **Graduates:** From July 1, 2013 to June 30, 2014, 258 bachelor's degrees were awarded. The most popular majors were business management (22%), communication/journalism (15%), and social sciences (11%). In an average class, 48% graduate in 4 years or less, 55% graduate in 5 years or less, and 56% graduate in 6 years or less. Of the 2013 graduating class, 26% were enrolled in graduate school within 6 months of graduation, and 74% were employed.

SERVICES: Counseling and information services are available, as is tutoring in most subjects, accounting, biology, chemistry, education, math/statistics, Spanish, French, business/economics, psychology, and sociolgy/anthropology. There is a reader service for the blind, remedial math, reading, and writing. Individualized academic-support services to students who seek , assistance including one-on-one tutoring and small-group and group tutoring **Library/Resources:** The library contains 342,938 volumes, 237,404 microform items, and 12,387 audio/video tapes/CDs/DVDs, and subscribes to 28,190 periodicals including electronic. Computerized library services include interlibrary loans, database searching, Internet access, and Wi-Fi capability. Special learning facilities include an art gallery, planetarium, radio station, TV station, Monmouth College has a prairie-habitat biology field station, Spring Grove Prairie, one of the finest virgin prairie plots in Illinois, a freshwater pond for field research on amphibians and reptiles, an educational garden, the 16.5-acre Le Suer Nature Preserve, the James Christie Shields Collection of Art and Antiquities collection housed in the Len G. Everett Galleries, the Lewis L. Gould U.S. First Ladies letter collection, and the region's largest collection of Western Illinois Native American artifacts and archeology lab. Hewes Library is a federal government documents repository. **Physically Challenged Students:** 98% of the campus is accessible. Facilities include wheelchair ramps, elevators, special parking, specially equipped restrooms, special class scheduling, lowered drinking fountains, lowered telephones, and special housing. **Special:** Monmouth has agreements with Rush University, Chicago, for nursing, occupational therapy, and medical technology; and 5- and 6-year coordinated degree partnerships (Masters) with Case Western Reserve (engineering), the University of Southern California (engineering) and Creighton University (atmospheric science). Students have the opportunity to study in more than 25 countries in Europe, Asia, Central and South America and Africa, as well as in programs within the United States. All Associated Colleges of the Midwest (ACM) programs, as well as internships, a Washington semester, and duel and student-designed majors are available. There are 13 national honor societies, a freshman honors program, and 20 departmental honors programs. **Visiting:** There are regularly scheduled orientations for prospective students, including tours, admissions and financial aid discussions, faculty appointments, lunch and entertainment, and a talk with the president. There are guides for informal visits, visitors may sit in on classes, and stay overnight. To schedule a visit, contact Angela Reimolds at admissions@monmouthcollege.edu. **Campus Safety and Security:** Measures include 24-hour foot and vehicle patrol, emergency notification system, self-defense education, and security escort services. There are shuttle buses, emergency telephones, lighted pathways/sidewalks, controlled access to dorms/residences, 24-hour foot and vehicle patrols, and key cards are required for entrance to all residence halls.

REQUIREMENTS: The SAT or ACT is required. A score of at least 22 on the ACT is highly recommended. Applicants must be graduates of accredited high schools with a GPA of 2.5. We strongly recommend that applicants have completed 4 years of English, 2 each of math, social studies, and science, including 1 of lab, 2 years of foreign language, and at least 1 of history. We accept the GED. A GPA of 2.5 is required. AP credits are accepted. Important factors in the admissions decision are advanced placement or honors courses, evidence of special talent, and extracurricular activities record.To graduate, all students must complete 32 course credits (equivalent to 128 credit hours) with a minimum GPA of 2.0. A major program must be completed with a minimum of C in all courses. Students must also fulfill 9 courses within the general education program, including an art course, science course with lab and language course(s). Students must successfully complete the integrated studies curriculum (one course per year) within the general education program. A topical major (of the student's design) is also possible. **Procedure:** Freshmen are admitted fall and spring. Entrance exams should be taken by the spring of the junior year. There are early admissions, deferred admissions, and rolling admissions plans. Application deadlines are open. Notification is sent on a rolling basis. Applications are accepted online. **Transfer Students:** Students must have a minimum GPA of 2.5. A satisfactory score of at least 19 on the ACT is recommended. 64 of 128 credits required for the bachelor's degree must be completed at Monmouth College. **International Students:** There are 49 international students enrolled. The school actively recruits these students. They must also take the SAT or ACT.

ADMISSIONS: 69% of the 2014-2015 applicants were accepted. The SAT scores for the 2014-2015 freshman class were: Critical Reading--34% below 500, 52% between 500 and 599, and 14% between 600 and 699; Math--24% below 500, 57% between 500 and 599, and 19% between 600 and 699; Writing--56% below 500, 29% between 500 and 599, and 5% between 600 and 699. The ACT scores were 34% below 21, 30% between 21 and 23, 20% between 24 and 26, 8% between 27 and 28, and 8% above 28. 25% of the current freshmen were in the top fifth of their class; 60% were in the top two fifths. **Admissions Contact:** Michael Blaesing, Director of Admissions. E-Mail: *admissions@monmouthcollege.edu* Web: *www.monmouthcollege.edu*

FINANCIAL AID: In 2014-2015, 100% of all full-time freshmen and continuing full-time students received some form of financial aid. 89% of all full-time freshmen and 87% of continuing full-time students received need-based aid. The average freshman award was $34,600. Need-based scholarships or need-based grants averaged $25,698; need-based self-help aid (loans and jobs) averaged $3,176; other non-need-based awards and non-need-based scholarships averaged $3,241; and $2,485 from other forms of aid. 51% of undergraduate students work part-time. Average annual earnings from campus work are $1400. The average financial indebtedness of the 2014 graduate was $26,193. The FAFSA, and International Certification of Finances and bank statements if applicable is required. The priority date for freshman financial aid applications for fall entry is February 1. The deadline for filing freshman financial aid applications for fall entry is May 1.

NATIONAL LOUIS UNIVERSITY (*The complete profile is made available exclusively on our website, www.barronspac.com*)

NORTH CENTRAL COLLEGE E-2
www.northcentralcollege.edu

Naperville, IL 60540	(630) 637-5800
	(800) 411-1861
Fax: (630) 637-5819	Email: admissions@noctrl.edu
Full-time: 1091 men, 1469 women	Faculty: 130; IIA, +$
Part-time: 90 men, 105 women	Ph.D.s: 89%
Graduate: 140 men, 147 women	Student/Faculty: 20 to 1
Year: quarters, summer session	Tuition: $29,733
Room & Board: $8610	Freshman Class: 3987 applied, 2401 accepted, 552 enrolled
ACT: 24	CEEB CODE: 1555
Application Deadline: n/av	VERY COMPETITIVE

North Central College, founded in 1861, is a private comprehensive liberal arts institution affiliated with the United Methodist Church. The college is highly selective, primarily residential, and primarily full-time undergraduate. There is 1 undergraduate school and 1 graduate school. In addition to regional accreditation, North Central has baccalaureate program accreditation with CAATE and ACS. The 64-acre campus is in a suburban area 30 miles west of Chicago. Including any residence halls, there are 42 buildings.

STUDENT LIFE: 93% of undergraduates are from Illinois. Others are from 30 states, 22 foreign countries, and Canada. 90% are from public schools. 79% are White. 56% are Protestant; 34% Catholic. The average age of freshmen is 18; all undergraduates, 21. 20% do not continue beyond their first year; 66% remain to graduate. **Housing:** 1537 students can be accommodated in college housing, which includes single-sex and coed dorms, on-campus apartments, and off-campus apartments. Substance free housing. On-campus housing is available on a lottery system for upperclassmen. 54% of students live on campus; of those, 90% remain on campus on weekends. All students may keep cars.

FACULTY/CLASSROOMS: 53% of faculty are male; 47% are female. All teach undergraduates. No introductory courses are taught by graduate students. The average class size in an introductory lecture is 24; in a laboratory is 20; and in a regular course is 22.

PROGRAMS OF STUDY: North Central confers B.A., and B.S. degrees. Master's degrees are also awarded. Bachelor's degrees are awarded in BIOLOGICAL SCIENCE (biochemistry and biology/biological science), BUSINESS (accounting, business administration and management, finance, human resources, international business management, marketing/retailing/merchandising, and sports management), COMMUNICATIONS AND THE ARTS (art history, art, broadcasting, Chinese, communications, English, English literature, English Writing, French, German, Japanese, jazz, journalism, music, Spanish, speech/debate/rhetoric, studio art, and theatre arts), COMPUTER AND PHYSICAL SCIENCE (actuarial science, applied mathematics, chemistry, computer science, mathematics, and physics), EDUCATION (art education, athletic training, elementary education, music education, and secondary education), ENGINEERING AND ENVIRONMENTAL DESIGN (graphic arts technology and preengineering), HEALTH PROFESSIONS (exercise science, nuclear medical technology, predentistry, premedicine, preveterinary science, and

radiation therapy), SOCIAL SCIENCE (anthropology, classical/ancient civilization, East Asian studies, economics, history, philosophy, political science/government, prelaw, psychology, religion, social science, and sociology). Business and education have the largest enrolllments.

ACTIVITIES: There are 60 groups on campus, including art, band, cheerleading, choir, chorale, chorus, dance, drama, environmental, ethnic, forensics, gay, honors, international, jazz band, literary magazine, musical theater, newspaper, pep band, photography, political, professional, radio and TV, religious, social, social service, and student government. Popular campus events include Springfest, Winter Comedy Series and Honors Day. **Sports:** There are 10 intercollegiate sports for men and 10 for women, and 12 intramural sports for men and 12 for women. Facilities include a indoor and outdoor tracks, recreation center, weight room, football and baseball stadiums, soccer fields, swimming pool, tennis courts, athletic training facility, and a human performance lab. **Graduates:** From July 1, 2013 to June 30, 2014, 582 bachelor's degrees were awarded. The most popular majors were psychology (7%), marketing (6%), and elementary education (6%). In an average class, 1% graduate in 3 years or less, 57% graduate in 4 years or less, 66% graduate in 5 years or less, and 68% graduate in 6 years or less.

SERVICES: Counseling and information services are available, as is tutoring in most subjects. There is a reader service for the blind, and remedial math. **Library/Resources:** The library contains 138,968 volumes, 105,494 microform items, 4,405 audio/video tapes/CDs/DVDs, and subscribes to 11,821 periodicals including electronic. Computerized library services include interlibrary loans, database searching, and Internet access. Special learning facilities include an art gallery, radio station, a foreign language lab, academic support services center, and a writing center. **Physically Challenged Students:** 90% of the campus is accessible. Facilities include wheelchair ramps, elevators, special parking, specially equipped restrooms, special class scheduling, lowered drinking fountains, lowered telephones, and special housing. **Special:** North Central offers co-op programs in radiation therapy, nuclear medicine technology, and chemical microscopy; cross-registration with Benedictine University and Aurora University; a Washington semester; and study abroad. Internships in most subject areas, a 3-2 engineering degree with the Universities of Minnesota and Illinios at Urbana-Champaign, experiential credit, and nondegree study are available. Dual majors, student-designed majors, and 5-year integrated Bachelor's/Master's degree programs are available. There are 18 national honor societies, a freshman honors program, and 14 departmental honors programs. **Visiting:** There are regularly scheduled orientations for prospective students, including the opportunity to hear a presentation about academic programs, student life, admission guidelines, and financial aid. Campus tours, faculty presentations, and coaches are also available. There are guides for informal visits, visitors may sit in on classes, and stay overnight. To schedule a visit, contact the Office of Admissions at admissions@noctrl.edu. **Campus Safety and Security:** Measures include 24-hour foot and vehicle patrol, emergency notification system, self-defense education, and security escort services. There are emergency telephones, lighted pathways/sidewalks, and controlled access to dorms/residences.

REQUIREMENTS: The ACT is required, with a minimum of 20 on the ACT or 940 on the SAT. Minimum requirements also include a GPA of at least 2.5 and involvement in school and/or community. An admission essay and/or admission interview may be recommended. The GED is accepted. The recommended secondary school courses are 4 years of English and 3 years each of math, science, social science, and foreign language. A GPA of 2.5 is required. AP and CLEP credits are accepted. All students must complete a general education core, including 9 hours in humanities and fine arts, 9 hours in social sciences, 6.5 hours in life and physical sciences, 3 to 6 hours in composition, and 3 hours each in speech communication and math. All freshman must complete an interdisciplinary course. In addition, all students take an intercultural seminar, a leadership, ethics, and values seminar, and a course in religion and ethics. A GPA of 2.0 and a total of 120 credit hours are required for graduation, with 27 to 51 credits taken in the major. Students in the College Scholars program must complete an Honor Thesis. **Procedure:** Freshmen are admitted to all sessions. Entrance exams should be taken in the spring of the junior year or the fall of the senior year. There are deferred admissions and rolling admissions plans. Application deadlines are open. Application fee is $25. Applications are accepted on-line. **Transfer Students:** 360 transfer students enrolled in 2013-2014. Applicants need a minimum 2.5 transferrable GPA or better and 27 transferrable semester hours. If they have not earned 27 transferrable hours, their high school transcripts and ACT/SAT scores are also considered. Students can be considered for admission with a college grade point average of 2.25 or above. 30 of 120 credits required for the bachelor's degree must be completed at North Central. **International Students:** There are 28 international students enrolled. The school actively recruits these students. They must take the TOEFL with a minimum score of 520 on the paper-based TOEFL (PBT) or 68 on the Internet-based version (iBT), or take the IELTS.

ADMISSIONS: 60% of the 2014-2015 applicants were accepted. The ACT scores were 11% below 21, 30% between 21 and 23, 31% between 24 and 26, 15% between 27 and 28, and 13% above 28. 47% of the current freshmen were in the top fifth of their class; 78% were in the top two fifths. 5 freshmen graduated first in their class. **Admissions Contact:** Dean of Admission and Financial Aid. E-Mail: *admissions@noctrl.edu* Web: *www.northcentralcollege.edu*

FINANCIAL AID: In 2014-2015, 99% of all full-time freshmen and 98% of continuing full-time students received some form of financial aid. 80% of all full-time freshmen and 76% of continuing full-time students received need-based aid. The average freshman award was $28,066. Need-based scholarships or need-based grants averaged $6,140; need-based self-help aid (loans and jobs) averaged $2,418; other non-need-based awards and non-need-based scholarships averaged $12,966; and $6,542 from other forms of aid. The average financial indebtedness of the 2014 graduate was $25,644. The FAFSA and the college's own financial statement are required. Check with the school for current application deadlines.

NORTH PARK UNIVERSITY   E-2
www.northpark.edu

Chicago, IL 60625	(773) 244-5500
	(800) 888-6728
	Email: molson@northpark.edu
Full-time: 699 men, 1070 women	**Faculty:** 108; IIA, -$
Part-time: 158 men, 297 women	**Ph.D.s:** 90%
Graduate: 322 men, 683 women	**Student/Faculty:** 18 to 1
Year: semesters, summer session	**Tuition:** $21,990
Room & Board: $8040	**Freshman Class:** 1864 applied, 1618 accepted, 425 enrolled
SAT CR/M: 530/500 **ACT:** 22	**CEEB CODE:** 1556
Application Deadline: April 1	**COMPETITIVE**

North Park University, founded in 1891, is a private comprehensive university affiliated with the Evangelical Covenant Church offering undergraduate and graduate education liberal arts and professional and theological programs. There are 6 undergraduate schools and 5 graduate schools. In addition to regional accreditation, North Park has baccalaureate program accreditation with NLN, ATS, CCNE, IACBE, and NASM. The 30-acre campus is in an urban area 10 miles northwest of downtown Chicago. Including any residence halls, there are 30 buildings.

STUDENT LIFE: 66% of undergraduates are from Illinois. Others are from 40 states, 28 foreign countries, and Canada. 58% are White; 11% Hispanic. 33% are Protestant; 20% Catholic; 20% claim no religious affiliation. The average age of freshmen is 18; all undergraduates, 21. 23% do not continue beyond their first year; 58% remain to graduate. **Housing:** 1130 students can be accommodated in college housing, which includes single-sex dorms, on-campus apartments, and off-campus apartments. In addition, there are special-interest houses. On-campus housing is guaranteed for all 4 years. Priority is given to out-of-town students. 50% of students commute. Alcohol is not permitted. Upperclassmen may keep cars.

FACULTY/CLASSROOMS: 47% of faculty are male; 53% are female. All teach undergraduates. No introductory courses are taught by graduate students. The average class size in an introductory lecture is 25; in a laboratory is 25; and in a regular course is 18.

PROGRAMS OF STUDY: North Park confers B.A., B.S., B.Mus., B.S.N., B.G.S. and B.M.E. degrees. Master's and Doctoral degrees are also awarded. Bachelor's degrees are awarded in BIOLOGICAL SCIENCE (biology/biological science), BUSINESS (accounting, banking and finance, business administration and management, international business management, and marketing/retailing/merchandising), COMMUNICATIONS AND THE ARTS (advertising, communications, English, French, music, music theory and composition, Scandinavian languages, and Spanish), COMPUTER AND PHYSICAL SCIENCE (chemistry, mathematics, and physics), EDUCATION (athletic training, early childhood education, elementary education, and secondary education), ENGINEERING AND ENVIRONMENTAL DESIGN (environmental science), HEALTH PROFESSIONS (exercise science, medical laboratory technology, nursing, physical therapy, predentistry, and premedicine), SOCIAL SCIENCE (African studies, anthropology, biblical studies, criminal justice, economics, French studies, history, international relations, philosophy, political science/government, prelaw, psychology, sociology, and youth ministry). Sciences, nursing, education, and liberal arts are the strongest academically. Business has the largest enrollments.

ACTIVITIES: There are no fraternities or sororities. There are 25 groups on campus, including art, band, cheerleading, choir, chorale, chorus, communications, computers, drama, environmental, ethnic, honors, international, jazz band, literary magazine, musical theater, newspaper, opera, orchestra, pep band, photography, political, professional, religious, social, social service, student government, symphony, and yearbook. Popular campus events include Dances, Concerts and Film Festivals. **Sports:** There are 7 intercollegiate sports for men and 8 for women, and 5 intramural sports for men and 5 for women. Facilities include football, baseball, track, and soccer fields, tennis courts, a weight room, a gym, and a fitness center. **Graduates:** From July 1, 2013 to June 30, 2014, 481 bachelor's degrees were awarded. The most popular majors were business and marketing (23%), health and related programs (22%), and communication (8%). In an average class, 39% graduate in 4 years or less, 52% graduate in 5 years or less, and 58% graduate in 6 years or less.

SERVICES: Counseling and information services are available, as is tutoring in every subject. There is a reader service for the blind, and remedial math, reading, and writing. An extended orientation program is available. **Library/Resources:** The library contains 225,000 volumes, 93,000 microform items, and 6,500 audio/video tapes/CDs/DVDs, and subscribes to 995 periodicals including electronic. Computerized library services include interlibrary loans, database searching, Internet access, and Wi-Fi capability. Special learning facilities include an art gallery. **Physically Challenged Students:** 90% of the campus is accessible. Facilities include wheelchair ramps, elevators, special parking, specially equipped restrooms, lowered drinking fountains, lowered telephones, and special housing. **Special:** Opportunities are provided for a co-op program in occupational therapy, internships, work-study, a Washington semester, 3-2 engineering degrees, accelerated degree programs in organization management and nursing, credit by examination, dual majors, student-designed majors, B.A.-B.S. degrees, pass/fail options, and study abroad. There are 6 national honor societies, a freshman honors program, and 5 departmental honors programs. **Visiting:** There are regularly scheduled orientations for prospective students. There are guides for informal visits, visitors may sit in on classes, and stay overnight. To schedule a visit, contact the Campus Visit Counselor at (773) 244-5511. **Campus Safety and Security:** Measures include 24-hour foot and vehicle patrol, emergency notification system, self-defense education, and security escort services. There are emergency telephones, lighted pathways/sidewalks, and controlled access to dorms/residences.

REQUIREMENTS: The SAT or ACT and ACT Writing Test are recommended. Graduation from an accredited secondary school is required; a GED will be accepted. Students should have completed course work in a foreign language, 4 years of English, and 3 years each of math, science, and social studies. A recommendations from a teacher is required. An essay is required. An interview is recommended and sometimes required. A GPA of 2.8 is required. AP and CLEP credits are accepted. Important factors in the admissions decision are evidence of special talent, personality/intangible qualities, and extracurricular activities record. Students must successfully complete 120 semester hours with a minimum 2.0 GPA. The required number of hours in the major varies. Students must meet a general education requirement of 46 semester hours. **Procedure:** Freshmen are admitted fall and winter. Entrance exams should be taken during spring of the junior year or fall of the senior year. There is a rolling admissions plan. Applications should be filed by April 1 for fall entry; December 15 for winter entry, along with a $40 fee. Applications are accepted on-line. **Transfer Students:** 300 transfer students enrolled in 2013-2014. To be eligible for transfer admission, students must submit 1 letter of recommendation and official transcripts from the previous college and must have maintained a minimum GPA of 2.5. An interview is also recommended. 30 of 120 credits required for the bachelor's degree must be completed at North Park. **International Students:** There are 100 international students enrolled. The school actively recruits these students. They must take the TOEFL with a minimum score of 550 on the paper-based TOEFL (PBT) or 80 on the Internet-based version (iBT) and the college's own test.

ADMISSIONS: 87% of the 2014-2015 applicants were accepted. The SAT scores for the 2014-2015 freshman class were: Critical Reading--33% below 500, 49% between 500 and 599, 17% between 600 and 699, and 1% between 700 and 800; Math--40% below 500, 43% between 500 and 599, 14% between 600 and 699, and 3% between 700 and 800. The ACT scores were 41% below 21, 25% between 21 and 23, 16% between 24 and 26, 9% between 27 and 28, and 9% above 28. 32% of the current freshmen were in the top fifth of their class; 61% were in the top two fifths. **Admissions Contact:** Director Undergraduate Admission. Web: *www.northpark.edu*

FINANCIAL AID: In 2014-2015, 98% of all full-time freshmen and 95% of continuing full-time students received some form of financial aid. 79% of all full-time freshmen and continuing full-time students received need-based aid. 20% of undergraduate students work part-time. Average annual earnings from campus work are $2000. The average financial indebtedness of the 2014 graduate was $28,467. The FAFSA is required. The priority date for freshman financial aid applications for fall entry is March 1. The deadline for filing freshman financial aid applications for fall entry is August 15.

NORTHEASTERN ILLINOIS UNIVERSITY *(The complete profile is made available exclusively on our website, www.barronspac.com)*

NORTHERN ILLINOIS UNIVERSITY — D-2
www.niu.edu

DeKalb, IL 60115	**(815) 753-0446**
Fax: (815) 753-1783	**Email:** admissions-info@niu.edu
Full-time: 8044 men, 8308 women	**Faculty:** 922; I, --$
Part-time: 900 men, 1025 women	**Ph.D.s:** 83%
Graduate: 2635 men, 3512 women	**Student/Faculty:** 18 to 1
Year: semesters, summer session	**Tuition:** $10,180 ($17,440)
Room & Board: $9588	**Freshman Class:** 17787 applied, 10409 accepted, 3033 enrolled
ACT: 22	**CEEB CODE:** 1559
Application Deadline: August 1	**COMPETITIVE**

Northern Illinois University, founded in 1895, is a publicly funded institution offering undergraduate and graduate programs in a comprehensive range of disciplines. There are 6 undergraduate schools and 2 graduate schools. In addition to regional accreditation, NIU has baccalaureate program accreditation with AACSB, ABET, ACEJMC, APTA, ASLA, CAHEA, NASAD, NASM, NCATE, and NLN. The 755-acre campus is in a small town 65 miles west of Chicago. Including any residence halls, there are 55 buildings.

STUDENT LIFE: 95% of undergraduates are from Illinois. Others are from 50 states, 95 foreign countries, and Canada. 84% are from public schools. 73% are White; 13% African American. The average age of freshmen is 18; all undergraduates, 22. 22% do not continue beyond their first year; 78% remain to graduate. **Housing:** 5800 students can be accommodated in college housing, which includes

single-sex and coed dorms, on-campus apartments, and married student housing. In addition, there are honors houses, language houses, special-interest houses, computer science, law, music, political science, and health professions. On-campus housing is guaranteed for the freshman year only, is available on a first-come, and first-served basis. 67% of students live on campus; of those, 60% remain on campus on weekends. All students may keep cars.

FACULTY/CLASSROOMS: 54% of faculty are male; 46% are female. Graduate students teach 20% of introductory courses. The average class size in an introductory lecture is 37; in a laboratory is 17; and in a regular course is 30.

PROGRAMS OF STUDY: NIU confers B.A., B.S., B.F.A., B.G.S., B.M. and B.S.Ed. degrees. Master's and Doctoral degrees are also awarded. Bachelor's degrees are awarded in BIOLOGICAL SCIENCE (biology/biological science and nutrition), BUSINESS (accounting, banking and finance, business administration and management, and marketing/retailing/merchandising), COMMUNICATIONS AND THE ARTS (art, art history and appreciation, communications, dramatic arts, English, French, German, journalism, music, Russian, Spanish, and studio art), COMPUTER AND PHYSICAL SCIENCE (atmospheric sciences and meteorology, chemistry, computer science, geology, geoscience, information sciences and systems, mathematics, and physics), EDUCATION (art education, early childhood education, elementary education, health education, music education, physical education, and special education), ENGINEERING AND ENVIRONMENTAL DESIGN (electrical/electronics engineering, industrial engineering, mechanical engineering, and technological management), HEALTH PROFESSIONS (clinical science, community health work, health science, nursing, and speech pathology/audiology), SOCIAL SCIENCE (anthropology, child care/child and family studies, dietetics, early childhood studies, economics, geography, history, liberal arts/general studies, philosophy, physical fitness/movement, political science/government, psychology, sociology, and textiles and clothing). Business, engineering, and sciences are the strongest academically. Business, education, and communications have the largest enrollments.

ACTIVITIES: 15% of men belong to 22 national fraternities; 11% of women belong to 15 national sororities. There are 200 groups on campus, including art, band, cheerleading, chess, choir, chorale, chorus, computers, dance, drama, drill team, ethnic, film, gay, honors, international, jazz band, literary magazine, marching band, musical theater, newspaper, orchestra, pep band, photography, political, professional, radio and TV, religious, social, social service, student government, and symphony. Popular campus events include Unity in Diversity Week, Greek Week, and Springfest. **Sports:** There are 8 intercollegiate sports for men and 8 for women, and 15 intramural sports for men and 15 for women. Facilities include a sports stadium, a recreation center and field house with facilities for basketball, volleyball, badminton, table tennis, tennis, racquetball/handball, and weight training, and 2 swimming pools. **Graduates:** From July 1, 2013 to June 30, 2014, 4027 bachelor's degrees were awarded. The most popular majors were teacher education (7%), communication studies (6%), and accountancy (6%). 800 companies recruited on campus in 2013-2014. In an average class, 47% graduate in 5 years or less and 48% graduate in 6 years or less. Of the 2013 graduating class, 19% were enrolled in graduate school within 6 months of graduation.

SERVICES: Formal tutoring is provided for eligible students. **Library/Resources:** The 4 libraries contain 2.2 million volumes, 3.6 million microform items, 59,076 audio/video tapes/CDs/DVDs, and subscribe to 32,722 periodicals including electronic. Computerized library services include interlibrary loans and database searching. Special learning facilities include an art gallery, radio station, TV station, an anthropology museum. **Physically Challenged Students:** 85% of the campus is accessible. Facilities include wheelchair ramps, elevators, special parking, specially equipped restrooms, special class scheduling, lowered drinking fountains, lowered telephones, special housing. **Special:** NIU offers internships in several areas. Students may study abroad in 30 countries. A physics/engineering degree is offered in cooperation with the University of Illinois. Either a B.A. or a B.S. may be obtained in the social science programs. Work-study programs, a general studies degree, co-op programs, pass/fail options, and student-designed majors are available. There are 5 national honor societies, a freshman honors program, and 18 departmental honors programs. **Visiting:** There are regularly scheduled orientations for prospective students, including open house programs, bus tours, faculty meetings, residence hall tours, and department receptions. There are guides for informal visits, visitors may sit in on classes, and stay overnight. To schedule a visit, contact the Office of Orientation and Student Assistance at (815) 753-1535. **Campus Safety and Security:** Measures include 24-hour foot and vehicle patrol, self-defense education, and security escort services. There are shuttle buses, emergency telephones, lighted pathways/sidewalks, a bicycle patrol.

REQUIREMENTS: The ACT is required. Students must have a minimum score of 19 on the ACT and be in the top half of their class, or have an ACT score of 23 and be in the upper two thirds of their class. Graduation from an accredited secondary school or satisfactory scores on the GED are required for admission. Secondary school courses must include 4 years of English and 2 to 3 years each of math, science, and social studies. In addition, students must have completed 1 to 2 years of art, film, foreign language, music, or theater. NIU requires applicants to be in the upper 50% of their class. AP and CLEP credits are accepted.To graduate, students must have a minimum of 124 credit hours and a minimum GPA of 2.0. All students must take English 103 and 104 and Communication Studies 100. In addition, students must take Math 101 or obtain at least a C in Math 155, 201, 206, 210, 211, or 229. The school also requires that students complete 29 hours in distributive studies areas, consisting of 9 to 12 hours in the humanities and arts, 7 to 11 hours in science and math, 6 to 9 hours in social science, and 3 to 6 hours in interdisciplinary studies. **Procedure:** Freshmen are admitted to all sessions. Entrance exams should be taken during the junior year. There is a rolling admissions plan. Applications should be filed by August 1 for fall entry. The fall 2014 application fee was $30. Applications are accepted on-line. **Transfer Students:** 2248 transfer students enrolled in 2013-2014. Transfer students with 24 or more credit hours must have a minimum GPA of 2.0. The core competency requirement in English, math, and speech must be satisfied by all transfer students. 30 of 124 credits required for the bachelor's degree must be completed at NIU. **International Students:** They must take the TOEFL with a minimum score of 527 on the paper-based TOEFL (PBT) or 71 on the Internet-based version (iBT).

ADMISSIONS: 59% of the 2014-2015 applicants were accepted. The ACT scores were 37% below 21, 30% between 21 and 23, 21% between 24 and 26, 7% between 27 and 28, and 5% above 28. 23% of the current freshmen were in the top fifth of their class; 54% were in the top two fifths. **Admissions Contact:** Director of Admissions. E-Mail: *admissions-info@niu.edu* Web: *www.niu.edu/*

FINANCIAL AID: In 2014-2015, 85% of all full-time freshmen and 75% of continuing full-time students received some form of financial aid. 67% of all full-time freshmen and 58% of continuing full-time students received need-based aid. 12% of undergraduate students work part-time. Average annual earnings from campus work are $1722. The average financial indebtedness of the 2014 graduate was $16,838. The FAFSA and the college's own financial statement are required. The priority date for freshman financial aid applications for fall entry is March 1.

NORTHWESTERN UNIVERSITY   E-2
www.northwestern.edu

Evanston, IL 60208	(847) 491-7271

Email: christopher-watson@northwestern.edu

Full-time: 4138 men, 4285 women	**Faculty:** 1409; I, ++$
Part-time: 152 men, 113 women	**Ph.D.s:** 100%
Graduate: 6971 men, 5338 women	**Student/Faculty:** 7 to 1
Year: trimesters, summer session	**Tuition:** $47,251
Room & Board: $14,389	**Freshman Class:** n/av
SAT or ACT: required	**CEEB CODE:** 1565
Application Deadline: January 1	**MOST COMPETITIVE**

Northwestern University, founded in 1851, is an independent, non-profit liberal arts institution. Northwestern University offers undergraduate study in the arts and sciences, education and social policy, journalism, music, communication, and engineering and applied science. There are 6 undergraduate schools and 7 graduate schools. In addition to regional accreditation, Northwestern has baccalaureate program accreditation with AACSB, ABET, ACEJMC, APTA, and NASM. The 240-acre campus is in a suburban area 12 miles north of Chicago on the shores of Lake Michigan. Including any residence halls, there are 180 buildings.

STUDENT LIFE: 72% of undergraduates are from out of state, mostly the Midwest. Students are from 50 states, 41 foreign countries, and Canada. 72% are from public schools. 53% are White; 16% Asian American; 13% race unknown. The average age of freshmen is 18; all undergraduates, 20. 3% do not continue beyond their first year; 93% remain to graduate. **Housing:** 4500 students can be accommodated in college housing, which includes single-sex and coed dorms. In addition, there are special-interest houses, fraternity houses, and sorority houses. On-campus housing is guaranteed for the freshman year only. 65% of students live on campus; of those, 95% remain on campus on weekends. Alcohol is not permitted. Upperclassmen may keep cars.

FACULTY/CLASSROOMS: 63% of faculty are male; 37% are female. All teach and do research. Graduate students teach 3% of introductory courses. The average class size in an introductory lecture is 35; in a laboratory is 14; and in a regular course is 22.

PROGRAMS OF STUDY: Northwestern confers B.A., B.S., B.A.C.M.N., B.A.Mus., B.M.E., B.Mus., B.Ph., B.P.H.C., B.S.A.M., B.S.B.M., B.S.C.H., B.S.C.I., B.S.C.M.N., B.S.C.O., B.S.C.S., B.S.Ed., B.S.E.E., B.S.E.N., B.S.E.S., B.S.G.E., B.S.G.S., B.S.I.E., B.S.J., B.S.M., B.S.M.D., B.S.M.E., B.S.M.F., B.S.M.T., B.S.S.E. and B.S.S.P. degrees. Master's and Doctoral degrees are also awarded. Bachelor's degrees are awarded in BIOLOGICAL SCIENCE (biology/biological science, ecology, molecular biology, and neurosciences), BUSINESS (organizational behavior), COMMUNICATIONS AND THE ARTS (art, art history and appreciation, classics, communications, communications technology, comparative literature, dance, dramatic arts, English, fine arts, French, German, Italian, jazz, journalism, linguistics, music, music performance, music technology, music theory and composition, percussion, performing arts, piano/organ, radio/television technology, Slavic languages, Spanish, strings, voice, and winds), COMPUTER AND PHYSICAL SCIENCE (applied mathematics, astronomy, chemistry, computer science, geology, information sciences and systems, mathematics, physics, and statistics), EDUCATION (education, mathematics education, music education, and secondary education), ENGINEERING AND ENVIRONMENTAL DESIGN (biomedical engineering, chemical engineering, civil engineering, computer engineering, electrical/electronics engineering, engineering, environmental engineering, environmental science, industrial engineering, manufacturing engineering, materials engineering, materials science, and mechanical engineering), HEALTH PROFESSIONS (premedicine and speech pathology/audiology), SOCIAL SCIENCE (African American studies, American studies, anthropology, cognitive science, economics, ethics, politics, and social policy, European studies, gender studies, geography, history, human development, international studies, philosophy, political science/government, psychology, religion, science and society, sociology, and urban studies). Journalism, communications, physical and life sciences are the strongest academically. Economics, political science, and engineering have the largest enrollments.

ACTIVITIES: 39% of men belong to 17 local fraternities; 45% of women belong to 12 local sororities. There are 400 groups on campus, including art, band, cheerleading, chess, choir, chorale, chorus, communications, dance, debate, drama, ethnic, film, gay, honors, international, jazz band, literary magazine, marching band, musical theater, newspaper, opera, orchestra, pep band, photography, political, professional, radio and TV, religious, social, social service, student government, symphony, and yearbook. Popular campus events include Dillo Day Music Festival, Dance Marathon, Wildcat Welcome, Family Weekend, and Homecoming. **Sports:** There are 8 intercollegiate sports for men and 11 for women, and 21 intramural sports for men and 19 for women. Facilities include a sailing center, sports pavilion, aquatics center, tennis center, and gymnasium. **Graduates:** From July 1, 2013 to June 30, 2014, 2797 bachelor's degrees were awarded. The most popular majors were social sciences (23%), communication/journalism (13%), and engineering (11%). 350 companies recruited on campus in 2013-2014. In an average class, 86% graduate in 4 years or less, 93% graduate in 5 years or less, and 94% graduate in 6 years or less.

SERVICES: Counseling and information services are available, as is tutoring in most subjects. One-on-one tutoring, peer mentoring, and study groups. **Library/Resources:** The 3 libraries contain 6.1 million volumes, 4.6 million microform items, 157,944 audio/video tapes/CDs/DVDs, and subscribe to 39,864 periodicals including electronic. Computerized library services include interlibrary loans, database searching, Internet access, and Wi-Fi capability. Special learning facilities include an art gallery, planetarium, radio station, TV station, and an observatory. **Physically Challenged Students:** All of the campus is accessible. Facilities include wheelchair ramps, elevators, special parking, specially equipped restrooms, special class scheduling, lowered drinking fountains, lowered telephones, and special housing. **Special:** The university offers cooperative engineering programs throughout the country, many off-campus field studies and research opportunities, internships in the arts, journalism, and teaching, study abroad in 50 countries, a Washington semester, and numerous work-study programs both on and off campus. There is an accelerated degree program in medical education, and B.A.-B.S. degrees in liberal arts and engineering, liberal arts and music, and music and engineering. An integrated science program, an interdisciplinary study in mathematical methods in social sciences and numerous other interdisciplinary majors, a variety of dual and student-designed majors, pass/fail options. Teaching media programs are also available. There are 23 national honor societies, including Phi Beta Kappa, a freshman honors program, and 40 departmental honors programs. **Visiting:** There are regularly scheduled orientations for prospective students, consisting of daily information sessions and campus tours Monday through Friday. There are guides for informal visits, visitors may sit in on classes, and stay overnight. To schedule a visit, contact Adam Logeman at admsac@northwestern.edu. **Campus Safety and Security:** Measures include 24-hour foot and vehicle patrol, emergency notification system, self-defense education, and security escort services. There are shuttle buses, emergency telephones, lighted pathways/sidewalks, controlled access to dorms/residences, A security keycard system in residence halls.

REQUIREMENTS: The SAT or ACT is required. Applicants must be graduates of an accredited secondary school or have a GED certificate, and have completed a minimum of 16 units, including 4 units of English, 3 of math, 2 or 3 each of a foreign language and history, and 2 of lab sciences. SAT II: Subject tests are required for the accelerated honors program in medical education and the integrated science program. Auditions are required for applicants to the Bienen School of Music. AP credits are accepted. Important factors in the admissions decision are leadership record, advanced placement or honors courses, evidence of special talent, personality/intangible qualities, recommendations by school officials, ability to finance college education, parents or siblings attended your school, extracurricular activities record, recommendations by alumni, and geographical diversity.Requirements for graduation vary by school and degree program. Students must maintain a minimum 2.0 GPA and complete a total of 45 to 48 quarter units (courses). **Procedure:** Freshmen are admitted to all sessions. Entrance exams should be taken by December of the senior year. There are early decision and deferred admissions plans. Early decision applications should be filed by November 1; regular applications, by January 1 for fall entry; October 1 for winter entry; and February 1 for spring entry, along with a $75 fee. Notification of early decision is sent December 15; regular decision, April 1. 936 early decision candidates were accepted for the 2014-2015 class. 3473 applicants were on the 2014 waiting list; 55 were admitted. Applications are accepted on-line. **Transfer Students:** 79 transfer students enrolled in 2013-2014. We require a minimum of one full year of college coursework for a student to be eligible to transfer. This is usually equivalent to 24 semester hours or 36 quarter hours. Our minimum GPA requirement is a 3.0, but most successful applicants have at least a 3.5. We do not have any course prerequisites for transfer applicants. 24 of 45 credits required for the bachelor's degree must be completed at Northwestern. **International Students:** There are 614 international students enrolled. The school actively recruits these students. They must take the TOEFL. They must also take the SAT or ACT.

ADMISSIONS: There were 136 National Merit finalists. 79 freshmen graduated first in their class. **Admissions Contact:** Christopher Watson, Dean of Undergraduate Admission. E-Mail: *christopher-watson@northwestern.edu* Web: *www.northwestern.edu*

FINANCIAL AID: In 2014-2015, 46% of all full-time freshmen and 47% of continuing full-time students received some form of financial aid. 44% of all full-time freshmen and 46% of continuing full-time students received need-based aid. The average freshman award was $40,597. Need-based scholarships or need-based grants averaged $38,027; need-based self-help aid (loans and jobs) averaged $4,951; non-need-based athletic scholarships averaged $36,229; and other non-need-based awards and non-need-based scholarships averaged $2,740. 29% of undergraduate students work part-time. Average annual earnings from campus work are $1790. The average financial indebtedness of the 2014 graduate was $18,623. Northwestern is a member of CSS. The CSS/Profile and FAFSA, and noncustodial profile, parent and student tax forms are required. The priority date for freshman financial aid applications for fall entry is March 5.

OLIVET NAZARENE UNIVERSITY — E-2
www.olivet.edu

Bourbonnais, IL 60914

(815) 939-5203
(800) 648-1463

Fax: (815) 935-4998
Email: admissions@olivet.edu

Full-time: 1086 men, 1532 women
Faculty: n/av

Part-time: 131 men, 438 women
Ph.D.s: 74%

Graduate: 449 men, 1046 women
Student/Faculty: n/av

Year: semesters, summer session
Tuition: $23,590

Room & Board: $6400
Freshman Class: 2893 applied, 2344 accepted, 773 enrolled

ACT: 23
CEEB CODE: 1596

Application Deadline: May 1
COMPETITIVE

Olivet Nazarene University, established in 1907, is a private, Christian, liberal arts institution affiliated with the Church of the Nazarene. Its undergraduate and graduate programs emphasize the liberal arts, business, communication, health science, art and fine arts, engineering, music, Bible and religious studies, and teacher preparation in an atmosphere of Christian culture. There are 4 undergraduate schools and one graduate school. In addition to regional accreditation, Olivet has baccalaureate program accreditation with ABET, ADA, CSWE, NASM, NCATE, CCNE, CAATE, and IACBE. The 250-acre campus is in a suburban area 50 miles south of Chicago. Including any residence halls, there are 53 buildings.

STUDENT LIFE: 64% of undergraduates are from Illinois. Others are from 45 states, 10 foreign countries, and Canada. 83% are White. 76% are Protestant; 14% Catholic. The average age of freshmen is 18; all undergraduates, 20. 27% do not continue beyond their first year; 55% remain to graduate. **Housing:** 2131 students can be accommodated in college housing, which includes single-sex dorms, on-campus apartments, and married student housing. In addition, there are honors houses. On-campus housing is guaranteed for all 4 years. 93% of students live on campus; of those, 80% remain on campus on weekends. Alcohol is not permitted. All students may keep cars.

FACULTY/CLASSROOMS: 57% of faculty are male; 43% are female. No introductory courses are taught by graduate students.

PROGRAMS OF STUDY: Olivet confers B.A., B.B.A., B.M., B.S., B.S.N. and B.S.W. degrees. Associate, Master's, and Doctoral degrees are also awarded. Bachelor's degrees are awarded in BIOLOGICAL SCIENCE (biology/biological science and zoology), BUSINESS (accounting, business administration and management, business communications, fashion merchandising, international business management, marketing/retailing/merchandising, recreation and leisure services, and sports management), COMMUNICATIONS AND THE ARTS (art, communications, digital communications, dramatic arts, drawing, English, journalism, media arts, music, music performance, music theory and composition, and Spanish), COMPUTER

AND PHYSICAL SCIENCE (actuarial science, chemistry, computer science, digital arts/technology, geoscience, information sciences and systems, mathematics, and physical sciences), EDUCATION (art education, athletic training, Christian education, early childhood education, elementary education, English education, mathematics education, music education, physical education, science education, and social science education), ENGINEERING AND ENVIRONMENTAL DESIGN (computer engineering, engineering, environmental design, environmental science, and geological engineering), HEALTH PROFESSIONS (exercise science and nursing), SOCIAL SCIENCE (biblical studies, child psychology/development, criminal justice, crosscultural studies, dietetics, economics, family/consumer studies, geography, history, ministries, missions, pastoral studies, philosophy, political science/government, psychology, public affairs, religion, religious music, social science, social work, sociology, Spanish studies, and youth ministry). Engineering and physical science is the strongest academically. Business administration and education have the largest enrollments.

ACTIVITIES: There are 79 groups on campus, including art, band, cheerleading, choir, chorale, chorus, computers, drama, ethnic, FCA, film, honors, international, jazz band, literary magazine, marching band, musical theater, newspaper, orchestra, pep band, photography, political, professional, radio and TV, religious, social, social service, student government, and yearbook. Popular campus events include Revival Services, Tiger Championship Wrestling, and Ollies Follies. **Sports:** There are 9 intercollegiate sports for men and 9 for women, and 19 intramural sports for men and 19 for women. Facilities include a 2,400-seat arena with basketball, volleyball, and racquetball courts; a separate gymnasium; a fitness center and a weight-lifting room; and an indoor track. There is a football field and an athletic park with softball, baseball, and soccer fields, a jogging track, track and field facilities, and tennis courts. **Graduates:** From July 1, 2013 to June 30, 2014, 647 bachelor's degrees were awarded. The most popular majors were elementary education (11%), business/marketing (8%), and nursing (5%). 65 companies recruited on campus in 2013-2014. In an average class, 1% graduate in 3 years or less, 44% graduate in 4 years or less, 56% graduate in 5 years or less, and 57% graduate in 6 years or less.

SERVICES: Counseling and information services are available, as is tutoring in every subject. There is remedial math, reading, and writing. **Library/Resources:** The library contains 529,092 volumes, 312,729 microform items, and 7,703 audio/video tapes/CDs/DVDs, and subscribes to 12,100 periodicals including electronic. Computerized library services include interlibrary loans, database searching, Internet access, and Wi-Fi capability. Special learning facilities include an art gallery, planetarium, radio station, TV station, smart board classrooms, a greenhouse, a solar telescope, a planetarium, and observation rooms. **Physically Challenged Students:** 95% of the campus is accessible. Facilities include wheelchair ramps, elevators, special parking, specially equipped restrooms, special class scheduling, lowered drinking fountains, lowered telephones, and special housing. **Special:** Special academic programs include a work-study program, which can be arranged with other institutions, and a general studies degree. A 4-year engineering program (ABET) is available. There are 6 national honor societies, a freshman honors program, and 5 departmental honors programs. **Visiting:** There are regularly scheduled orientations for prospective students, including class visits, financial aid appointments, an information tour, lunch, and personal professor meetings. There are guides for informal visits, visitors may sit in on classes, and stay overnight. To schedule a visit, contact the Campus Visit Coordinator. **Campus Safety and Security:** Measures include 24-hour foot and vehicle patrol, emergency notification system, self-defense education, and security escort services. There are emergency telephones and lighted pathways/sidewalks.

REQUIREMENTS: The ACT is required. The minimum ACT score required is 18. Olivet requires graduation from an accredited secondary school. Olivet does not have any specific high school course requirements, but there are some suggestions for high school courses. College preparatory courses completed with a C or above are recommended. In general, you should have 3 years of English and 2 years each of math, foreign language, and natural or social science. To enroll in the nursing program, you need a year of biology and a year of chemistry. In choosing high school courses, you should also take into consideration the career/major you intend to pursue. The GED is accepted. A GPA of 2.0 is required. AP and CLEP credits are accepted. To graduate, students must complete 128 semester hours of credit, with 32 to 70 in a major and a minimum of 40 hours of credit in upper-division courses, and maintain a minimum GPA of 2.0. The required general education studies, 50 to 61 hours, include 12 credit hours of Christianity, 9 to 10 of communication, 9 of natural science and math, 6 of social sciences, 6 to 8 of international culture, 6 of literature and the arts, and 3 of wellness/nutrition. **Procedure:** Freshmen are admitted to all sessions. Entrance exams should be taken during the spring of the junior year or during the fall of the senior year. There are deferred admissions and rolling admissions plans. Applications should be filed by May 1 for fall entry; December 1 for spring entry, along with a $25 fee. Applications are accepted on-line. **Transfer Students:** 268 transfer students enrolled in 2013-2014. Application and transcripts of all college work must be submitted. 30 of 128 credits required for the bachelor's degree must be completed at Olivet. **International Students:** There are 19 international students enrolled. They must take the TOEFL with a minimum score of 500 on the paper-based TOEFL (PBT) or 61 on the Internet-based version (iBT). They must also take the ACT, scoring 18.

ADMISSIONS: 81% of the 2014-2015 applicants were accepted. The ACT scores were 27% below 21, 25% between 21 and 23, 22% between 24 and 26, 12% between 27 and 28, and 15% above 28. 44% of the current freshmen were in the top fifth of their class; 67% were in the top two fifths. **Admissions Contact:** Director of Admissions. E-Mail: *admissions@olivet.edu* Web: *www.olivet.edu*

FINANCIAL AID: In 2014-2015, 99% of all full-time freshmen and 99% of continuing full-time students received some form of financial aid. 83% of all full-time freshmen and 74% of continuing full-time students received need-based aid. The average freshman award was $24,742. Need-based scholarships or need-based grants averaged $10,732 ($30,490 maximum); need-based self-help aid (loans and jobs) averaged $2,794 ($6,500 maximum); non-need-based athletic scholarships averaged $451 ($16,000 maximum); and other non-need-based awards and non-need-based scholarships averaged $14,016 ($30,490 maximum). 36% of undergraduate students work part-time. Average annual earnings from campus work are $1319. The average financial indebtedness of the 2014 graduate was $23,366. The FAFSA is required. The priority date for freshman financial aid applications for fall entry is March 1. The deadline for filing freshman financial aid applications for fall entry is August 1.

PRINCIPIA COLLEGE C-4
www.principiacollege.edu

Elsah, IL 62028	(618) 374-5181
	(800) 277-4648
Fax: (618) 374-4000	Email: brian.mccauley@principia.edu
Full-time: 221 men, 265 women	Faculty: n/av
Part-time: 2 men, 3 women	Ph.D.s: 45%
Graduate: n/av	Student/Faculty: 7 to 1
Year: semesters	Tuition: $25,640
Room & Board: $9500	Freshman Class: 228 applied, 213 accepted, 152 enrolled
SAT CR/M/W: 549/525/537 ACT: 24	CEEB CODE: 1630
Application Deadline: March 1	COMPETITIVE+

Principia College, founded in 1910, is a private liberal arts and sciences college for Christian Scientists. It is the only college in the world strictly for Christian Scientists. In addition to regional accreditation, Prin has baccalaureate program accreditation with NCATE. The 2600-acre campus is in a rural area 30 miles northeast of St. Louis. Including any residence halls, there are 33 buildings.

STUDENT LIFE: 90% of undergraduates are from out of state, mostly the Mid-West. Students are from 42 states, 23 foreign countries, and Canada. 61% are from public schools. 81% are White; 15% Foreign. The average age of freshmen is 18; all undergraduates, 20. 12% do not continue beyond their first year; 75% remain to graduate. **Housing:** 625 students can be accommodated in college housing, which includes single-sex and coed dorms, on-campus apartments, and married student housing. In addition, there are special-interest houses. On-campus housing is guaranteed for all 4 years. 99% of students live on campus; of those, 100% remain on campus on weekends. Alcohol is not permitted. All students may keep cars.

FACULTY/CLASSROOMS: 45% of faculty are male; 55% are female. All teach undergraduates, and 60% do research. No introductory courses are taught by graduate students. The average class size in an introductory lecture is 13; in a laboratory is 12; and in a regular course is 10.

PROGRAMS OF STUDY: Prin confers B.A., and B.S. degrees. Bachelor's degrees are awarded in BIOLOGICAL SCIENCE (biology/biological science), BUSINESS (business administration and management and sports management), COMMUNICATIONS AND THE ARTS (communications, dramatic arts, English, fine arts, French, languages, music, Spanish, and studio art), COMPUTER AND PHYSICAL SCIENCE (chemistry, computer science, mathematics, and physics), EDUCATION (elementary education), ENGINEERING AND ENVIRONMENTAL DESIGN (environmental science), SOCIAL SCIENCE (economics, history, international relations, philosophy, political science/government, religion, and sociology). Education, studio art, and biology are the strongest academically. Business administration, studio art, and education have the largest enrollments.

ACTIVITIES: There are no fraternities or sororities. There are 34 groups on campus, including art, cheerleading, choir, chorus, computers, dance, drama, ethnic, honors, international, jazz band, literary magazine, musical theater, newspaper, orchestra, photography, political, radio and TV, religious, social, social service, and student government. Popular campus events include Athletic Events, Dances, Drama and Dance Performances. **Sports:** There are 7 intercollegiate sports for men and 8 for women, and 3 intramural sports for men and 3 for women. Facilities include 2 gyms, a pool, indoor and outdoor tennis courts, a racquetball court, basketball/volleyball courts, a dance studio, a weight room, baseball, football, soccer, and practice fields, and a 6-lane track. **Graduates:** From July 1, 2013 to June 30, 2014, 134 bachelor's degrees were awarded. The most popular majors were business administration (17%), studio art (13%), and mass communication (7%). 20 companies recruited on campus in 2013-2014. In an average class, 74% graduate in 4 years or less, 72% graduate in 5 years or less, and 78% graduate in 6 years or less.

SERVICES: Counseling and information services are available, as is tutoring in most subjects. There is remedial reading and writing. Assistance in study skills is available. **Library/Resources:** The library contains 217,257 volumes, 115,665 microform items, 4,847 audio/video tapes/CDs/DVDs, and subscribes to 12,813 periodicals including electronic. Computerized library services include interlibrary loans, database searching, and Internet access. Special learning facilities include an art gallery, planetarium, radio station, and TV station. **Physically Challenged Students:** 85% of the campus is accessible. Facilities include wheelchair ramps, elevators, special parking, specially equipped restrooms, and lowered drinking fountains. **Special:** Students may design their own majors, study abroad, or pursue a B.A.-B.S. degree. Internships, student-planned with a professor, independent study, work-study, and an interdisciplinary major, global studies, are available. A 3-2 engineering program with Washington University in St. Louis, Southern Illinois University at Carbondale, the University of Southern California, or another university with approval is also possible. There are 1 national honor societies, a freshman honors program, and 3 departmental honors programs. **Visiting:** There are regularly scheduled orientations for prospective students, including a visit to classes, meeting professors, living in a dorm, and meeting students (3-day weekend). There are guides for informal visits, visitors may sit in on classes, and stay overnight. To schedule a visit, contact Amber McCartt at (618) 374-5175. **Campus Safety and Security:** Measures include 24-hour foot and vehicle patrol and emergency notification system. There are emergency telephones, lighted pathways/sidewalks, and controlled access to dorms/residences.

REQUIREMENTS: The SAT or ACT is required. An essay is required. SAT Subject Tests in foreign language and math are recommended. High school preparation should include 4 years of English, 3 of math (including algebra II), 2 to 3 of a foreign language, 2 to 3 of natural sciences, history or social sciences, and electives. A GPA of

2.3 is required. AP and CLEP credits are accepted. Important factors in the admissions decision are advanced placement or honors courses, recommendations by school officials, and recommendations by alumni.All students must complete a minimum of 180 quarter hours, with 45 to 93 quarter hours in the major (10 to 15 courses) and at least a 2.0 overall GPA. Courses in foreign language, literature, arts, religion and philosophy, history, social science, math, and natural sciences are required. In addition, students must be certified as proficient in written English, pass a moral reasoning seminar, and earn 4 credits in individual and team phys ed activities. **Procedure:** Freshmen are admitted fall and spring. Entrance exams should be taken in the spring of the junior year and again in the fall of the senior year. There are deferred admissions and rolling admissions plans. Applications should be filed by March 1 for fall entry; November 1 for winter entry. Notification of early decision is sent December 1; regular decision, March 15. Applications are accepted on-line. **Transfer Students:** 23 transfer students enrolled in 2013-2014. Applicants must be in good standing at their previous college or university and have a 2.3 GPA. 45 of 180 credits required for the bachelor's degree must be completed at Prin. **International Students:** There are 95 international students enrolled. The school actively recruits these students. They must take the TOEFL. They must also take the SAT or ACT.

ADMISSIONS: 93% of the 2014-2015 applicants were accepted. The SAT scores for the 2014-2015 freshman class were: Critical Reading--31% below 500, 37% between 500 and 599, 21% between 600 and 699, and 11% between 700 and 800; Math--40% below 500, 35% between 500 and 599, 18% between 600 and 699, and 7% between 700 and 800; Writing--39% below 500, 36% between 500 and 599, 15% between 600 and 699, and 10% between 700 and 800. The ACT scores were 12% below 21, 45% between 21 and 23, 15% between 24 and 26, 16% between 27 and 28, and 12% above 28. 28% of the current freshmen were in the top fifth of their class; 59% were in the top two fifths. There were 1 National Merit finalists. 2 freshmen graduated first in their class. **Admissions Contact:** Brian McCauley, Dean of Enrollment Management. E-Mail: *brian.mccauley@principia.edu* Web: *www.principiacollege.edu*

FINANCIAL AID: In 2014-2015, 95% of all full-time freshmen and 92% of continuing full-time students received some form of financial aid. 74% of all full-time freshmen and 76% of continuing full-time students received need-based aid. The average freshman award was $21,888. Need-based scholarships or need-based grants averaged $23,091 ($33,500 maximum); need-based self-help aid (loans and jobs) averaged $5,502 ($6,000 maximum); and other non-need-based awards and non-need-based scholarships averaged $20,642 ($25,500 maximum). 52% of undergraduate students work part-time. Average annual earnings from campus work are $1368. The average financial indebtedness of the 2014 graduate was $15,784. Prin is a member of CSS. The CSS/Profile is required. The priority date for freshman financial aid applications for fall entry is March 1. The deadline for filing freshman financial aid applications for fall entry is March 1.

QUINCY UNIVERSITY (*The complete profile is made available exclusively on our website, www.barronspac.com*)

ROCKFORD COLLEGE	D-1
www.rockford.edu	
Rockford, IL 61108	(815) 226-3383
	(800) 892-2984
Fax: (815) 226-2822	Email: jnordstrom@rockford.edu
Full-time: 299 men, 454 women	Faculty: 69
Part-time: 46 men, 70 women	Ph.D.s: 71%
Graduate: 176 men, 295 women	Student/Faculty: 11 to 1
Year: semesters, summer session	Tuition: $24,250
Room & Board: $6750	Freshman Class: n/av
ACT: 22	CEEB CODE: 1665
Application Deadline: August 15	COMPETITIVE

Rockford College, founded in 1847, is a private coeducational institution offering undergraduate and graduate instruction in liberal arts and professional programs. There is one undergraduate school and 2 graduate schools. In addition to regional accreditation, Rockford College has baccalaureate program accreditation with NLN, ACS, and IACBE. The 135-acre campus is in a suburban area 90 miles west of Chicago. Including any residence halls, there are 27 buildings.

STUDENT LIFE: 91% of undergraduates are from Illinois. Others are from 26 states, and 2 foreign countries. 73% are White. The average age of freshmen is 18; all undergraduates, 24. **Housing:** 356 students can be accommodated in college housing, which includes single-sex and coed dorms. In addition, there are special-interest houses, first-year student housing, substance-free, 24- hour quiet housing, and health and science major housing. On-campus housing is guaranteed for all 4 years. 65% of students commute. All students may keep cars.

FACULTY/CLASSROOMS: 56% of faculty are male; 44% are female. All teach undergraduates. No introductory courses are taught by graduate students. The average class size in an introductory lecture is 18; in a laboratory is 11; and in a regular course is 15.

PROGRAMS OF STUDY: Rockford College confers B.A., B.S., B.F.A. and B.S.N. degrees. Master's degrees are also awarded. Bachelor's degrees are awarded in BIOLOGICAL SCIENCE (biochemistry and biology/biological science), BUSINESS (accounting, business administration and management, and management information systems), COMMUNICATIONS AND THE ARTS (art, art history and appreciation, classics, dramatic arts, English, French, German, Latin, music, music performance, romance languages and literature, and Spanish), COMPUTER AND PHYSICAL SCIENCE (chemistry, computer science, mathematics, and science), EDUCATION (elementary education, physical education, and special education), HEALTH PROFESSIONS (nursing), SOCIAL SCIENCE (anthropology, economics, history, humanities, international studies, philosophy, political science/government, psychology, social science, and sociology). Business, education, nursing, and psychology have the largest enrollments.

ACTIVITIES: There are 21 groups on campus, including senior club, anime, black student union, bowling, mulicultural, nursing, poker, RAGE, Rockford paranormal society, Alpha Helix, art, band, cheerleading, chess, choir, chorale, dance, drama, environmental, ethnic, gay, honors, international, literary magazine, musical theater, opera, orchestra, pep band, political, professional, religious, social, social service, and student government. Popular campus events include Snowball Dance, International Food Fair, and Black History Month Events. **Sports:** There are 9 intercollegiate sports for men and 8 for women, and 7 intramural sports for men and 7 for women. Facilities include a swimming pool, athletic fields, tennis courts, and a fitness center. **Graduates:** From July 1, 2013 to June 30, 2014, 224 bachelor's degrees were awarded. The most popular majors were education (28%), business (22%), and nursing (10%). In an average class, 44% graduate in 5 years or less and 44% graduate in 6 years or less.

SERVICES: Counseling and information services are available, as is tutoring in most subjects. There is a reader service for the blind, remedial math and reading. Diagnostic testing is available. **Library/ Resources:** The library contains 146,829 volumes, 8,430 microform items, 2,819 audio/video tapes/CDs/DVDs, and subscribes to 389 periodicals including electronic. Computerized library services include interlibrary loans, database searching, and Internet access. Special learning facilities include an art gallery. **Physically Challenged Students:** Facilities include wheelchair ramps, elevators, special parking, specially equipped restrooms, special class scheduling, lowered drinking fountains, lowered telephones, and special housing. **Special:** Rockford College offers a variety of special academic opportunities including community-based learning, liberal arts honors program, internships, study abroad, and Washington semester. In addition to our traditional undergraduate programs, we offer English as a second language and an accelerated bachelor's degree in management studies. There are 6 national honor societies including Phi Beta Kappa. **Visiting:** There are regularly scheduled orientations for prospective students, consisting of an acedemic fair, opportunity to meet with social/athletic programs, and administrative offices, admission presentation, meal, tour, and meet with current students. There are guides for informal visits, visitors may sit in on classes, and stay overnight. To schedule a visit, contact the Admissions Office. **Campus Safety and Security:** Measures include 24-hour foot and vehicle patrol, emergency notification system, and security escort services. There are emergency telephones and lighted pathways/sidewalks.

REQUIREMENTS: The ACT is required. Admission to Rockford College is based primarily on high school GPA and test scores (GED also accepted). Prospective students are expected to have completed a college preparatory program of 15 units including 4 years of English; 3 years of mathematics (introductory through advanced algebra, geometry and trigonometry); 3 years of social sciences (emphasizing history and government); 3 years of laboratory science; and 2 years of electives chosen from music, art and/or foreign language at an accredited secondary school. Home schooled students also should meet the unit requirements. Auditions are required for performing arts students. Rockford College requires applicants to be in the upper 50% of their class. A GPA of 2.7 is required. AP and CLEP credits are accepted. To graduate, students must have a total of at least 124 credit hours and a minimum GPA of 2.0 (nursing 2.75). The required hours for each major varies. Students are required to take 12 hours of social sciences, 8 to 12 of science, mathematics, and computer science, 8 of language and literature, 11 of rhetoric, 6 of art, and 2 hours each of physical education. All students must complete a senior seminar or project. **Procedure:** Freshmen are admitted to all sessions. There are early admissions, deferred admissions, and rolling admissions plans. Application deadlines are open. Application fee is $35. Notifications are sent September 15. Applications are accepted on-line. **Transfer Students:** 164 transfer students enrolled in 2013-2014. In order to be considered for transfer admission, prospective students must have completed at least 12 credit hours of college-level work (at the 100-level or higher). Students transferring from other colleges must be in good academic standing in order to be considered for standard admission. High school transcripts and standardized test scores (ACT/SAT) also may be requested. 30 of 124 credits required for the bachelor's degree must be completed at Rockford College. **International Students:** There are 4 international students enrolled. The school actively recruits these students. They must take the TOEFL with a minimum score of 550 on the paper-based TOEFL (PBT) or 79 on the Internet-based version (iBT). Rockford College will also accept the IELTS test. They must also take the SAT or ACT, scoring 19.

ADMISSIONS: The ACT scores were 43% below 21, 26% between 21 and 23, 24% between 24 and 26, and 3% between 27 and 28. 28% of the current freshmen were in the top fifth of their class; 55% were in the top two fifths. **Admissions Contact:** Jennifer Nordstrom, Associate Vice President for Undergraduate Admissions and Strate. E-Mail: *jnordstrom@rockford.edu* Web: *www.rockford.edu*

FINANCIAL AID: In 2014-2015, 100% of all full-time freshmen and continuing full-time students received some form of financial aid. 81% of all full-time freshmen and 95% of continuing full-time students received need-based aid. The average freshman award was $24,895. Need-based scholarships or need-based grants averaged $8,332 ($13,468 maximum); need-based self-help aid (loans and jobs) averaged $3,768 ($11,600 maximum); and other non-need-based awards and non-need-based scholarships averaged $14,970 ($35,660 maximum). 24% of undergraduate students work part-time. Average annual earnings from campus work are $1355. The average financial indebtedness of the 2014 graduate was $26,000. The FAFSA is required. The priority date for freshman financial aid applications for fall entry is March 15.

ROOSEVELT UNIVERSITY   E-2
www.roosevelt.edu

Chicago, IL 60605	(847) 619-8620
	(877) APPLYRU
Fax: (847) 619-8636	Email: applyru@roosevelt.edu
Full-time: 680 men, 1180 women	Faculty: 190
Part-time: 745 men, 1695 women	Ph.D.s: 85%
Graduate: 1035 men, 2205 women	Student/Faculty: 10 to 1
Year: semesters, summer session	Tuition: $15,445
Room & Board: $7160	Freshman Class: n/av
SAT or ACT: required	CEEB CODE: 1666
Application Deadline:	VERY COMPETITIVE

Roosevelt University, founded in 1945, an independent, comprehensive university. The figures in the above capsule and in this profile are approximate. There are 5 undergraduate schools and 5 graduate schools. In addition to regional accreditation, Roosevelt has baccalaureate program accreditation with AACSB, NASM, and NCATE. The -acre campus is in an urban area downtown Chicago. Including any residence halls, there are 2 buildings.

STUDENT LIFE: 90% of undergraduates are from Illinois. Others are from 24 states, 70 foreign countries, and Canada. 44% are White; 27% African American; 12% Hispanic. **Male To Female Ratio:** 2.1:1. The average age of freshmen is 21; all undergraduates, 27. **Housing:** 300 students can be accommodated in college housing, which includes coed dorms. On-campus housing is available on a first-come and first-served basis. 94% of students commute.

FACULTY/CLASSROOMS: All teach undergraduates. No introductory courses are taught by graduate students.

PROGRAMS OF STUDY: Roosevelt confers B.A., B.S., B.A.Comp.Sci., B.A.Ed., B.F.A.Mus.Theater, B.G.S., B.M., B.S.B.A., B.S. in Hospitality Mgt. and B.S.Telecomm. degrees. Master's and doctoral degrees are also awarded. Bachelor's degrees are awarded in BIOLOGICAL SCIENCE (biology/biological science), BUSINESS (accounting, banking and finance, business administration and management, hotel/motel and restaurant management, insurance, insurance and risk management, management science, marketing/retailing/merchandising, and personnel management), COMMUNICATIONS AND THE ARTS (advertising, art history and appreciation, broadcasting, communications, dramatic arts, English, French, guitar, jazz, journalism, languages, literature, media arts, music, music history and appreciation, music performance, music theory and composition, musical theater, percussion, performing arts, piano/organ, public relations, Spanish, strings, telecommunications, theater design, theater management, voice, and winds), COMPUTER AND PHYSICAL SCIENCE (actuarial science, chemistry, computer science, information sciences and systems, mathematics, and statistics), EDUCATION (early childhood education, elementary education, music education, and secondary education), ENGINEERING AND ENVIRONMENTAL DESIGN (electrical/electronics engineering technology and environmental science), HEALTH PROFESSIONS (allied health, medical technology, nuclear medical technology, predentistry, premedicine, prepharmacy, and preveterinary science), SOCIAL SCIENCE (African American studies, American studies, economics, history, international studies, liberal arts/general studies, philosophy, political science/government, prelaw, psychology, public administration, social science, sociology, urban studies, and women's studies). Journalism, accounting, and psychology are the strongest academically.

ACTIVITIES: 1% of men belong to 1 local fraternity; 1% of women belong to 1 local sororities. There are 45 groups on campus, including model United Nations, band, choir, chorale, chorus, computers, cultural, drama, ethnic, honors, international, jazz band, literary magazine, musical theater, newspaper, opera, orchestra, political, professional, radio and TV, religious, social service, student government, and symphony. **Sports:** There are 1 intramural sports for men and 1 for women. Facilities include a fitness center and a recreational gym for basketball, volleyball, soccer, and intramural activities.

SERVICES: Counseling and information services are available, as is tutoring in most subjects. There is remedial math, reading, and writing. Arranged counseling, and testing. Emphasis is placed on individual program planning. **Library/Resources:** The 2 libraries contain 405,022 volumes, 130,233 microform items, and 10,000 audio/video tapes/CDs/DVDs, and subscribe to 1,601 periodicals including electronic. Computerized library services include interlibrary loans and database searching. Special learning facilities include a radio station. **Physically Challenged Students:** All of the campus is accessible. Facilities include wheelchair ramps, elevators, specially equipped restrooms, special class scheduling, lowered telephones. For special needs, contact the Disabled Student Services Office. **Special:** Roosevelt offers internships in approximately 20 subject areas, on-campus work-study, study abroad in 4 countries, dual and student-designed majors, pass/fail options, and noncredit courses. Adults older than 25 years of age may earn a Bachelor of General Studies through an accelerated degree program. Credit for life, military, and work experience is available in some majors through continuing education. The Roosevelt Scholars Program is offered. There are 4 national honor socie-

ties, a freshman honors program, and 20 departmental honors programs. **Visiting:** There are regularly scheduled orientations for prospective students, including open houses and Transfer Days. There are guides for informal visits and visitors may sit in on classes. To schedule a visit, contact the Undergraduate Admissions Office. **Campus Safety and Security:** There are shuttle buses and lighted pathways/sidewalks.

REQUIREMENTS: The SAT or ACT is required. In addition, Students must have completed 15 academic units, including 4 of English, 3 of math, 2 each of science, social studies, and foreign language, and 1 each of history and electives. An interview is recommended for all applicants, and an audition is required for music and theater candidates. A GPA of 2.3 is required. AP and CLEP credits are accepted. Important factors in the admissions decision are advanced placement or honors courses, evidence of special talent, and extracurricular activities record.For graduation, students must complete 120 credit hours, including 54 in the major, with a minimum GPA of 2.0, or 2.5 in the College of Education. The core curriculum consists of courses in the social sciences, natural sciences, and humanities, including English 101 and 102. The last 54 hours must be from a 4-year school. **Procedure:** Freshmen are admitted to all sessions. There are early decision, early admissions, deferred admissions, and rolling admissions plans. Application deadlines are open. The fall 2014 application fee was $25. Notifications are sent in ongoing. Applications are accepted on-line. **Transfer Students:** 732 transfer students enrolled in 2013-2014. Applicants must have earned a minimum GPA of 2.0 in all accredited college course work. Offical transcripts must be received from each college where course work was attempted. 30 of 120 credits required for the bachelor's degree must be completed at Roosevelt. **International Students:** The school actively recruits these students. They must take the college's own test.

ADMISSIONS: Gwen Kanelos, Assistant Vice President for Enrollment Services. E-Mail: *applyru@roosevelt.edu* Web: *www.roosevelt.edu*

FINANCIAL AID: In 2014-2015, 85% of all full-time freshmen and 65% of continuing full-time students received some form of financial aid. 75% of all full-time freshmen and 65% of continuing full-time students received need-based aid. The average freshman award was $10,500. Need-based scholarships or need-based grants averaged $7,725 ; need-based self-help aid (loans and jobs) averaged $7,170; and other non-need-based awards and non-need-based scholarships averaged $5,220. The FAFSA and the college's own financial statement are required. Check with the school for current application deadlines.

SAINT XAVIER UNIVERSITY

E-2

www.sxu.edu

Chicago, IL 60655	
	(773) 298-3050
	(800) 462-9288
Fax: (773) 298-3076	Email: admissions@sxu.edu
Full-time: 705 men, 1630 women	Faculty: IIA, av$
Part-time: 170 men, 565 women	Ph.D.s: 86%
Graduate: 510 men, 1995 women	Student/Faculty: n/av
Year: semesters, summer session	Tuition: $24,340
Room & Board: $8500	Freshman Class: n/av
ACT: required	CEEB CODE: 1708
Application Deadline:	COMPETITIVE

Saint Xavier University is a private institution founded by the Sisters of Mercy in 1846 and affiliated with the Roman Catholic Church. Figures in the above capsule and in this profile are approximate. There are 4 undergraduate schools and 4 graduate schools. In addition to regional accreditation, SXU has baccalaureate program accreditation with NASM and NLN. The 70-acre campus is in an urban area 15 miles southwest of Chicago's loop. Including any residence halls, there are 16 buildings.

STUDENT LIFE: 96% of undergraduates are from Illinois. Others are from 21 states, and 4 foreign countries. 50% are from public schools. 63% are White; 18% African American; 11% Hispanic. 80% are Catholic; 16% Protestant. **Male To Female Ratio:** 3.0:1. The average age of freshmen is 18; all undergraduates, 23. 24% do not continue beyond their first year. **Housing:** 630 students can be accommodated in college housing, which includes single-sex and coed dorms. On-campus housing is guaranteed for all 4 years. 81% of students commute. Alcohol is not permitted. All students may keep cars.

FACULTY/CLASSROOMS: 44% of faculty are male; 56% are female. All teach undergraduates. No introductory courses are taught by graduate students. The average class size in an introductory lecture is 20; in a laboratory is 15; and in a regular course is 16.

PROGRAMS OF STUDY: SXU confers B.A., B.S. and B.M. degrees. Master's degrees are also awarded. Bachelor's degrees are awarded in BIOLOGICAL SCIENCE (biology/biological science), BUSINESS (accounting, banking and finance, business administration and management, international business management, and marketing/retailing/merchandising), COMMUNICATIONS AND THE ARTS (communications, English, French, music, and Spanish), COMPUTER AND PHYSICAL SCIENCE (chemistry, computer science, and mathematics), EDUCATION (art education, early childhood education, elementary education, foreign languages education, middle school education, music education, science education, and secondary education), HEALTH PROFESSIONS (nursing, predentistry, premedicine, prepharmacy, and speech pathology/audiology), SOCIAL SCIENCE (criminal justice, history, philosophy, political science/government, prelaw, psychology, religion, social science, and sociology). Business, nursing, and education are the strongest academically and have the largest enrollments.

ACTIVITIES: There are 37 groups on campus, including art, band, cheerleading, choir, chorus, computers, drama, ethnic, honors, international, jazz band, literary magazine, marching band, musical theater, newspaper, pep band, political, professional, radio and TV, religious, social service, student government, and yearbook. Popular campus events include Xavierfest, Boat Bash, and Octoberfest. **Sports:** There are 4 intercollegiate sports for men and 5 for women, and 4 intramural sports for men and 4 for women. Facilities include baseball and softball diamonds, an outdoor sports facility, and a football field. The convocation and athletic center seats 2200 in the main arena with 4 additional competition courts. It also has racquetball courts, an indoor running track, training rooms, and a health and fitness center.

SERVICES: Counseling and information services are available, as is tutoring in every subject. There are reading and language clinics and a center for learning disabilities. **Library/Resources:** The library contains 172,104 volumes, 10,519 microform items, 2,282 audio/video tapes/CDs/DVDs, and subscribes to 798 periodicals including electronic. Computerized library services include interlibrary loans, database searching, and Internet access. Special learning facilities include an art gallery and radio station. **Physically Challenged Students:** 98% of the campus is accessible. Facilities include wheelchair ramps, elevators, special parking, specially equipped restrooms, special class scheduling, lowered drinking fountains, and lowered telephones. **Special:** The university offers internships and study abroad in England, Ireland, and Italy. There is a freshman honors program. **Visiting:** There are regularly scheduled orientations for prospective students. There are guides for informal visits, visitors may sit in on classes, and stay overnight. To schedule a visit, contact the Director of Admissions. **Campus Safety and Security:** Measures include 24-hour foot and vehicle patrol, self-defense education, and security escort services. There are shuttle buses, emergency telephones, and lighted pathways/sidewalks.

REQUIREMENTS: The ACT is required. Students must be graduates of an accredited secondary school and have earned 16 specific academic credits, including 4 years each of English and the natural and social sciences, 3 each of math and academic electives, and 2 years of a foreign language. The GED is accepted. AP and CLEP credits are accepted. To graduate, the student must complete 120 credit hours, including the school's 57-semester-hour core curriculum, and earn a GPA of 2.0. The credit hours required in the student's major vary by subject. **Procedure:** Freshmen are admitted fall and spring. Entrance exams should be taken during the spring of the junior year. There are deferred admissions and rolling admissions plans. Check with the school for current application deadlines. The application fee is $35. Notification is sent on a rolling basis. Applications are accepted on-line. **Transfer Students:** 471 transfer students enrolled in 2013-2014. Applicants must have completed 12 semester hours

with a GPA of 2.25. An interview is recommended. 30 of 120 credits required for the bachelor's degree must be completed at SXU. **International Students:** The school actively recruits these students. They must take the TOEFL.

ADMISSIONS: Director of Enrollment Services. E-Mail: *admissions@sxu.edu* Web: *www.sxu.edu*

FINANCIAL AID: The FAFSA is required. Check with the school for current application deadlines.

SCHOOL OF THE ART INSTITUTE OF CHICAGO *(The complete profile is made available exclusively on our website, www.barronspac.com)*

SHIMER COLLEGE	**C-1**
www.shimer.edu	
Chicago, IL 60616	**312-235-3504**
	n/av
Fax: (312) 235-3501	**Email:** admission@shimer.edu
Full-time: 36 men, 31 women	**Faculty:** 11
Part-time: 3 men, 4 women	**Ph.D.s:** 100%
Graduate: n/av	**Student/Faculty:** 7 to 1
Year: semesters, summer session	**Tuition:** $24,875
Room & Board: $8000	**Freshman Class:** 31 applied, 26 accepted, 12 enrolled
SAT CR/M/W: 690/570/560	**CEEB CODE:** 1717
Application Deadline: n/av	**VERY COMPETITIVE**

Shimer College, founded in 1853, is a private liberal arts institution that shares space on the campus of the Illinois Institute of Technology. Figures in the above capsule and in this profile are approximate. The College offers a curriculum based on original sources and a Socratic teaching method in discussion classes of 12 or fewer students. There is one undergraduate school. The 120-acre campus is in an urban area in Chicago, IL. Including any residence halls, there are 40 buildings.

STUDENT LIFE: 52% of undergraduates are from out of state. 77% are White. The average age of freshmen is 19; all undergraduates, 23. 16% do not continue beyond their first year; 63% remain to graduate. **Housing:** 76 students can be accommodated in college housing, which includes single-sex and coed dorms, on-campus apartments, and married student housing. Coed dorms, single students apartments, and theme housing. On-campus housing is guaranteed for all 4 years. 95% of students commute. All students may keep cars.

FACULTY/CLASSROOMS: 67% of faculty are male; 33% are female. All teach undergraduates. No introductory courses are taught by graduate students. The average class size in a regular course is 9.

PROGRAMS OF STUDY: Shimer confers B.A., and B.S. degrees. Bachelor's degrees are awarded in COMPUTER AND PHYSICAL SCIENCE (natural sciences), SOCIAL SCIENCE (humanities, liberal arts/general studies, and social science). Humanities and social science are the strongest academically. Humanities has the largest enrollment.

ACTIVITIES: There are 62 groups on campus, including art, band, chess, computers, dance, drama, ethnic, film, gay, international, jazz band, literary magazine, newspaper, orchestra, photography, political, radio and TV, religious, social, social service, and student government. Popular campus events include Community Lunch, Poetry Readings and a Talent Show. **Sports:** There is no sports program at Shimer. Facilities include students have use of a full service athletic facility and access to intramural sports. **Graduates:** From July 1, 2013 to June 30, 2014, 33 bachelor's degrees were awarded. The most popular majors were liberal arts/general studies (78%) and social sciences (22%). In an average class, 7% graduate in 3 years or less, 50% graduate in 4 years or less, 53% graduate in 5 years or less, and 58% graduate in 6 years or less. Of the 2013 graduating class, 20% were enrolled in graduate school within 6 months of graduation, and 70% were employed.

SERVICES: Counseling and information services are available, as is tutoring in every subject. **Library/Resources:** The 3 libraries contain

20,500 volumes, and 100 microform items. Computerized library services include interlibrary loans, database searching, and Internet access. Special learning facilities include a radio station. **Physically Challenged Students:** All of the campus is accessible. Facilities include wheelchair ramps, elevators, special parking, specially equipped restrooms, and special housing. **Special:** Shimer offers internships in all areas of study and study abroad at Oxford in England. There is an accelerated degree program, a B.A.-B.S. degree, dual majors in all areas, and a general studies degree. Nondegree study and pass/fail options are possible. **Visiting:** There are regularly scheduled orientations for prospective students, consisting of class visits, lunch, a tour, and an admission interview. There are guides for informal visits and visitors may sit in on classes. **Campus Safety and Security:** Measures include 24-hour foot and vehicle patrol, emergency notification system, and security escort services. There are shuttle buses, emergency telephones, lighted pathways/sidewalks, and controlled access to dorms/residences.

REQUIREMENTS: Applicants must submit essays, letters of recommendation, and an interview. The SAT or ACT required only of students who are applying for our Early Entrance program, a 55 year old program that offers full admission to high school age students - those who would be enrolling in their junior or senior years of high school, but prefer to matriculate early. Important factors in the admissions decision are evidence of special talent, personality/intangible qualities, and recommendations by school officials. To graduate, students must earn 125 credit hours with a GPA of at least 2.0, complete 2 comprehensive exams, and submit a thesis. The school requires 60 credit hours in the major for the B.S. degree, 40 for the B.A.; 65 in the core curriculum for the B.S., 85 for the B.A. **Procedure:** Freshmen are admitted fall, spring, and summer. There are deferred admissions and rolling admissions plans. Application deadlines are open. Application fee is $25. Applications are accepted on-line. **Transfer Students:** 7 transfer students enrolled in 2013-2014. Same as for all other applicants plus all post-secondary transcripts. 65 of 125 credits required for the bachelor's degree must be completed at Shimer. **International Students:** The school actively recruits these students. They must take the TOEFL with a minimum score of 590 on the paper-based TOEFL (PBT) or 97 on the Internet-based version (iBT).

ADMISSIONS: The SAT scores for the 2014-2015 freshman class were: Critical Reading--34% between 600 and 699, and 67% between 700 and 800; Math--67% between 500 and 599, and 34% between 600 and 699. **Admissions Contact:** Elaine Vincent, Director of Admissions. E-Mail: *admission@shimer.edu* Web: *www.shimer.edu*

FINANCIAL AID: In 2014-2015, 74% of all full-time freshmen and 84% of continuing full-time students received some form of financial aid, and need-based aid. The average freshman award was $17,741. Need-based scholarships or need-based grants averaged $13,902; need-based self-help aid (loans and jobs) averaged $13,789; other non-need-based awards and non-need-based scholarships averaged $5,120; and $3,150 from other forms of aid. 52% of undergraduate students work part-time. The average financial indebtedness of the 2014 graduate was $25,125. Shimer is a member of CSS. The FAFSA and the college's own financial statement are required. The priority date for freshman financial aid applications for fall entry is April 15. The deadline for filing freshman financial aid applications for fall entry is July 30.

SOUTHERN ILLINOIS UNIVERSITY SYSTEM

The Southern Illinois University System, established in 1965, is a public system in Illinois. It is governed by a board of trustees, whose chief administrator is the president. The primary goal of the system is to create and sustain the internal and external conditions that enable the campuses to fulfill their missions with excellence. The main priorities are to achieve and maintain excellence in teaching, research, and service; to achieve and maintain cultural diversity; and to provide educational opportunity to the disadvantaged. The total student enrollment is usually 35,500 with 2500 faculty members. Altogether there are approximately 128 baccalaureate, 112 master's, and 43 doctoral programs offered in the Southern Illinois University System. Profiles of the 4-year campuses are included in this section.

SOUTHERN ILLINOIS UNIVERSITY CARBONDALE D-5
www.siu.edu

Carbondale, IL 62901   **(618) 536-4405**

Fax: (618) 453-4609	Email: admissions@siu.edu
Full-time: 6407 men, 5466 women	Faculty: 829; I, --$
Part-time: 906 men, 682 women	Ph.D.s: 79%
Graduate: 2358 men, 2170 women	Student/Faculty: 15 to 1
Year: semesters, summer session	Tuition: $12,248 ($24,871)
Room & Board: $9694	Freshman Class: n/av
SAT CR/M: 553/565 ACT: 23	CEEB CODE: 1726
Application Deadline: May 1	COMPETITIVE

Southern Illinois University Carbondale, a public institution founded in 1869, is the flagship of the Southern Illinois University system. The multi-campus research university offers undergraduate programs in the Colleges of Agricultural Sciences, Applied Sciences and Arts, Business, Education and Human Services, Engineering, Liberal Arts, Mass Communication and Media Arts, and Science. The university also includes a School of Law, School of Medicine, Graduate School and University College. There are 8 undergraduate schools and 3 graduate schools. In addition to regional accreditation, has baccalaureate program accreditation with AACSB, ABET, ABFSE, ACEJMC, ADA, APTA, CAHEA, CSWE, FIDER, NAAB, NASAD, NCATE, NRPA, and SAF. The 1136-acre campus is in a small town 100 miles from St. Louis, MO. Including any residence halls, there are 246 buildings.

STUDENT LIFE: 85% of undergraduates are from Illinois. Others are from 48 states, 55 foreign countries, and Canada. 61% are White; 17% African American. The average age of freshmen is 19; all undergraduates, 23. 32% do not continue beyond their first year; 44% remain to graduate. **Housing:** 4681 students can be accommodated in college housing, which includes single-sex and coed dorms, on-campus apartments, and married student housing. In addition, there are honors houses, special-interest houses, family housing, Junior/Senior residence halls, and residence halls that stay open during breaks. On-campus housing is guaranteed for the freshman year only, is available on a first-come, and first-served basis. 69% of students commute. All students may keep cars.

FACULTY/CLASSROOMS: 62% of faculty are male; 38% are female. 84% teach undergraduates, 48% do research, and 48% do both. Graduate students teach 30% of introductory courses. The average class size in an introductory lecture is 130.

PROGRAMS OF STUDY: SIU confers B.A., B.S., B.F.A. and B.Mus. degrees. Associate, Master's, and Doctoral degrees are also awarded. Bachelor's degrees are awarded in AGRICULTURE (agricultural economics, agriculture, animal science, forestry and related sciences, and plant science), BIOLOGICAL SCIENCE (avian sciences, biology/biological science, botany, microbiology, physiology, and zoology), BUSINESS (accounting, banking and finance, business administration and management, business economics, fashion merchandising, funeral home services, management science, marketing/retailing/merchandising, and recreation and leisure services), COMMUNICATIONS AND THE ARTS (art, broadcasting, classics, design, dramatic arts, English, English literature, film arts, fine arts, foreign language, French, German, information technology, journalism, linguistics, music, musical theater, photography, radio/TV, radio/television technology, Russian, Spanish, speech/debate/rhetoric, and sports administration), COMPUTER AND PHYSICAL SCIENCE (chemistry, computer science, geology, information sciences and systems, mathematics, physics, and radiological technology), EDUCATION (athletic training, early childhood education, elementary education, health education, health information management, physical education, physical science secondary school education, special education, and vocational education), ENGINEERING AND ENVIRONMENTAL DESIGN (architecture, automotive technology, aviation administration/management, aviation computer technology, civil engineering, computer engineering, electrical/electronics engineering, electrical/electronics engineering technology, engineering technology, industrial engineering technology, interior design, mechanical engineering, and mining and mineral engineering),

HEALTH PROFESSIONS (dental hygiene, dental laboratory technology, health care administration, physician's assistant, rehabilitation therapy, respiratory therapy, and speech pathology/audiology), SOCIAL SCIENCE (africana studies, anthropology, architectural studies, clothing and textiles management/production/services, communication sciences and disorders, criminal justice, economics, family/consumer resource management, fire protection, food production/management/services, food science, geography, German area studies, history, international studies, law, liberal arts/general studies, paralegal studies, philosophy, political science/government, psychology, social science, social work, and sociology). Biological sciences, criminology and criminal justice, psychology, workforce education and development have the largest enrollments.

ACTIVITIES: 7% of men belong to 20 national fraternities; 6% of women belong to 12 national sororities. There are 473 groups on campus, including art, band, cheerleading, chess, choir, chorale, computers, dance, drama, drill team, environmental, ethnic, film, forensics, gay, honors, international, jazz band, literary magazine, marching band, musical theater, newspaper, opera, pep band, photography, political, professional, radio and TV, religious, social, social service, student government, symphony, and yearbook. Popular campus events include Cardboard Boat Regatta, International Festival, Heritage Celebration Months, and SpringFest. **Sports:** There are 10 intercollegiate sports for men and 10 for women, and 27 intramural sports for men and 27 for women. Facilities include 15,000 seat football stadium, 8,339 seat basketball arena, 502 seat softball stadium, volleyball, track, baseball, locker rooms and athletic training rooms, Troutt-Wittmann Academic and Training Center (Student-Athlete Academic Center and Weight Room), flag football fields, rugby fields, soccer fields, a lake with boat docks, tennis courts, ultimate frisbee fields, cross-country course. The Student Recreation Center houses an Olympic-size pool, indoor tracks, racquetball, squash, and tennis courts, aerobics equipment, a weight room, a Nautilus room, and numerous exercise stations. The center also offers volleyball, basketball, badminton, handball, indoor soccer, a climbing wall, a dance studio, a boxing practice room, and a martial arts practice room. **Graduates:** From July 1, 2013 to June 30, 2014, 3643 bachelor's degrees were awarded. The most popular majors were education (16%), engineering technologies/engineering (12%), and business/marketing (8%). 158 companies recruited on campus in 2013-2014. In an average class, 25% graduate in 4 years or less and 44% graduate in 6 years or less.

SERVICES: Counseling and information services are available, as is tutoring in most subjects. There is a reader service for the blind. Through SIUC's center for learning support services, students can receive one-on-one tutoring, group study sessions, math lab assistance, peer mentoring, and academic coaching. **Library/Resources:** The library contains 2.9 million volumes, 3.6 million microform items, 27,484 audio/video tapes/CDs/DVDs, and subscribes to 49,580 periodicals including electronic. Computerized library services include interlibrary loans, database searching, Internet access, and Wi-Fi capability. Special learning facilities include an art gallery, natural history museum, radio station, TV station, student-run newspaper, farms and timberlands, greenhouses, livestock facilities, archeological center, aviation program, crime study center, wildlife lab, international programs and services, broadcasting division that operates public television and radio stations, a dental lab, a child development lab, craft shop and museum. **Physically Challenged Students:** 98% of the campus is accessible. Facilities include wheelchair ramps, elevators, special parking, specially equipped restrooms, special class scheduling, lowered drinking fountains, lowered telephones, special housing. Classroom accommodations, and disability support services. **Special:** If you want to learn, we'll help take you as far as you want to go. Our academic offerings extend from the classroom and the lab to your residence hall and overseas. An honors program that will surprise high-achieving students. SIU's University Honors Program is an enriching, rewarding experience much like that of a private college. The UHP courses are more exclusive than others you will take at SIU small, limited to UHP students, and taught by our best faculty. Scholarship, leadership, mentorship, and other benefits are unlimited if you push yourself. Hands-on research opportunities for all students undergraduate and graduate. It's the exchange of ideas and thrill of discovery that define our culture.

REACH (Research-Enriched Academic Challenge) is just one program that offers undergraduates small grants and other opportunities to gain research expertise by working alongside faculty mentors. Study abroad fills student desires for a multidimensional education. Go beyond the classroom and see how the world works firsthand. We offer a variety of university-level, international study abroad experiences through semester- or year-abroad programs, short-term travel/study programs, and educational exchanges. Living/Learning Communities for those who want to live with like-minded students. You'll get to know professors and classmates betterÕ have greater access to academic resourcesÕ and find specialized programs right in your residence hall. Students who participate in a Living/Learning community often have higher GPAs, more positive campus experiences, and are more likely to graduate. At SIU, you also have access to The Saluki First Year, internships/co-ops, service learning, and writing in the disciplines. There are 23 national honor societies, a freshman honors program, and 9 departmental honors programs. **Visiting:** There are regularly scheduled orientations for prospective students, including new Student Orientation is a one-day program for new SIU students and their families. There are guides for informal visits, visitors may sit in on classes, and stay overnight. To schedule a visit, contact the Undergraduate Admissions. **Campus Safety and Security:** Measures include 24-hour foot and vehicle patrol, emergency notification system, self-defense education, and security escort services. There are shuttle buses, emergency telephones, lighted pathways/sidewalks, controlled access to dorms/residences, a student patrol program in addition to campus police officers.

REQUIREMENTS: The SAT or ACT is required. Freshmen applicants must: have graduated from high school before beginning classes at SIU. Exceptions are made for students participating in our High School Concurrent Enrollment program and for those who have earned the G.E.D. Meet high school course pattern requirements. Meet certain criteria based primarily on high school core grade point average, ACT or SAT score and course subject pattern. (The holistic review process also considers ACT or SAT subscores, high school rank, improvements in high school GPA from year to year, letters of recommendation, participation in service or extracurricular activities and extenuating circumstances.)" Meet transfer requirements if college-level work has been taken after high school graduation. An additional step or screening process is required for certain programs. Requirements for direct entry into some programs exceed university admission requirements. Please be sure to read the Special Conditions section. If you have completed less than 26 semester hours or 39 quarter hours of transferable college credit, you must apply as a freshman. Send, in addition to official college transcripts, your ACT or SAT scores and an official high school transcript that includes your class rank. You must, in this case, meet both freshman and transfer (2.0 GPA on 4.0 scale for all transferable work) requirements. AP and CLEP credits are accepted.I.Baccalaureate Degrees. Students must complete at least 120 semester hours of credit, which can include credit for work experience, College Level Examination Program (CLEP), Advance Placement Program (AP), military credit, and proficiency examination credit, with at least 42 semester hours (or equivalent number of quarter hours) in courses at the 300 level or above, earned at or awarded through proficiency examination from an accredited, senior-level institution. All credit granted may be applied toward the 42 hour requirement unless the credit has specifically been designated as being from a two-year college or credit has been awarded based on attendance at a two-year school. Meet the requirements of the academic unit, the major, and, when appropriate, the minor. Achieve at least a C average for all work taken at SIUC, and at least a C average for all major work taken at SIUC, with the exceptions granted by the forgiveness policy and the repeated grade policy. Students who do not meet the overall C average requirement may be graduated if he or she satisfies either of the following methods of computing their average: a. by excluding from calculation of the grade point average a maximum of ten semester hours of D or F grade earned outside the major which was taken prior to the last 60 semester hours of completed work at the university; or b. earning a grade point average of 2.10 or higher for the last 60 semester hours of work completed at the university. The repeat grade policy allows for only the last grade of a subsequently repeated course to be counted in the grade point average as approved by the chancellor, effective with courses taken Summer 1996 and beyond. Complete the last 30 semester hours or a total of 90 semester hours, in residence at SIUC. Residence credit is awarded for those courses for which the student has registered and earned a satisfactory grade at SIUC. Students enrolled in programs offered for the military will have completed the residence requirement for the university upon completion of all courses required by the program; Satisfactorily complete the university core curriculum requirements. **Procedure:** Freshmen are admitted fall, spring, and summer. Entrance exams should be taken during spring of the junior year. There is a deferred admissions plan. Applications should be filed by May 1 for fall entry, along with a $40 fee. Applications are accepted on-line. **Transfer Students:** 1784 transfer students enrolled in 2013-2014. All transfer students must have a minimum 2.0 GPA. Students are required to meet freshman admission requirements if they are under 21 years old and have fewer than 26 credit hours of acceptable transfer work. Some academic programs have higher admission requirements. 30 of 120 credits required for the bachelor's degree must be completed at SIUC. **International Students:** There are 676 international students enrolled. The school actively recruits these students. They must take the TOEFL with a minimum score of 520 on the paper-based TOEFL (PBT) or 68 on the Internet-based version (iBT). They must also take the SAT or ACT.

ADMISSIONS: 82% of the 2014-2015 applicants were accepted. The SAT scores for the 2014-2015 freshman class were: Critical Reading--32% below 500, 30% between 500 and 599, 30% between 600 and 699, and 8% between 700 and 800; Math--29% below 500, 33% between 500 and 599, 28% between 600 and 699, and 10% between 700 and 800. The ACT scores were 15% below 21, 46% between 21 and 23, 31% between 27 and 28, and 8% above 28. 24% of the current freshmen were in the top fifth of their class; 46% were in the top two fifths. 2 freshmen graduated first in their class. **Admissions Contact:** Harold Bardo, Interim Dir/Undergraduate Admissions. E-Mail: *admissions@siu.edu* Web: *http://admissions.siu.edu/*

FINANCIAL AID: In 2014-2015, 83% of all full-time freshmen and continuing full-time students received some form of financial aid. 55% of all full-time freshmen and continuing full-time students received need-based aid. The average freshman award was $16,057. Need-based scholarships or need-based grants averaged $8,592; need-based self-help aid (loans and jobs) averaged $4,787; non-need-based athletic scholarships averaged $18,774; other non-need-based awards and non-need-based scholarships averaged $6,455; and $3,351 from other forms of aid. The average financial indebtedness of the 2014 graduate was $30,138. The FAFSA is required. The priority date for freshman financial aid applications for fall entry is March 1.

SOUTHERN ILLINOIS UNIVERSITY EDWARDSVILLE   C-4
www.siue.edu

Edwardsville, IL 62026	
	(618) 650-3705
	(800) 447-SIUE
Fax: (618) 650-5013	**Email: admissions@siue.edu**
Full-time: 4496 men, 5152 women	**Faculty:** 556; IIA, av$
Part-time: 810 men, 883 women	**Ph.D.s:** 79%
Graduate: 1089 men, 1625 women	**Student/Faculty:** 15 to 1
Year: semesters, summer session	**Tuition:** $9251 ($19,673)
Room & Board: $8281	**Freshman Class:** 7660 applied, 6272 accepted, 2075 enrolled
ACT: 23	**CEEB CODE:** 1759
Application Deadline: May 1	**COMPETITIVE**

Southern Illinois University Edwardsville, founded in 1957, is part of the Southern Illinois University system and offers undergraduate programs in business, education, engineering, arts and sciences, and nursing. Graduate programs also are offered in 34 subject areas, including professional programs in pharmacy and dental medicine. There are 5 undergraduate schools and 1 graduate school. In addition to regional accreditation, SIUE has baccalaureate program accreditation with AACSB, ABET, ACCE, ACEJMC, CSWE, NASM, NCATE, CCNE, ASHA, and NAST. The 2660-acre campus is in a suburban area 18 miles northeast of downtown St. Louis, Missouri. Including any residence halls, there are 25 buildings.

STUDENT LIFE: 90% of undergraduates are from Illinois. Others are from 36 states, 40 foreign countries, and Canada. 74% are White; 13% African American. **Male To Female Ratio:** 1.2:1. The average age of all undergraduates is 21. 27% do not continue beyond their first year; 52% remain to graduate. **Housing:** 3524 students can be accommodated in college housing, which includes coed dorms, on-campus apartments, and married student housing. In addition, there are fraternity houses, honors wings and special-interest wings. On-campus housing is available on a first-come, first-served basis. Priority is given to out-of-town students. 71% of students commute. All students may keep cars.

FACULTY/CLASSROOMS: 51% of faculty are male; 49% are female. 84% teach undergraduates. Graduate students teach 4% of introductory courses.

PROGRAMS OF STUDY: SIUE confers B.A., B.S., B.F.A., B.L.S., B.M., B.S.A. and B.S.W. degrees. Master's degrees are also awarded. Bachelor's degrees are awarded in BIOLOGICAL SCIENCE (biochemistry, biology/biological science, ecology, and genetics), BUSINESS (accounting, business administration and management, business economics, entrepreneurial studies, human resources, international business management, management information systems, and marketing and distribution), COMMUNICATIONS AND THE ARTS (American literature, art, art history and appreciation, communications, dance, dramatic arts, English, French, German, journalism, languages, media arts, music, music business management, music history and appreciation, music performance, music theory and composition, musical theater, public relations, radio/television technology, Spanish, speech/debate/rhetoric, studio art, and theater design), COMPUTER AND PHYSICAL SCIENCE (actuarial science, applied mathematics, chemistry, computer management, computer science, earth science, mathematics, physics, and statistics), EDUCATION (art education, early childhood education, elementary education, health education, health information management, mathematics education, music education, physical education, science education, social science education, and special education), ENGINEERING AND ENVIRONMENTAL DESIGN (civil engineering, computer engineering, construction management, electrical/electronics engineering, industrial engineering, manufacturing engineering, and mechanical engineering), HEALTH PROFESSIONS (community health work, exercise science, medical technology, medical science, nursing, and speech pathology/audiology), SOCIAL SCIENCE (anthropology, criminal justice, economics, forensic studies, geography, gerontology, history, liberal arts/general studies, philosophy, political science/government, psychology, social work, and sociology). Nursing, biological sciences, and business administration have the largest enrollments.

ACTIVITIES: 7% of men belong to 9 national fraternities; 5% of women belong to 7 national sororities. There are 170 groups on campus, including academic and recreational, art, band, cheerleading, choir, chorale, chorus, dance, drama, environmental, ethnic, gay, honors, international, jazz band, literary magazine, musical theater, newspaper, opera, orchestra, pep band, photography, political, professional, radio and TV, religious, social, social service, student government, and symphony. Popular campus events include Welcome Week, Arts and Issues Series, International Week and Homecoming. **Sports:** There are 9 intercollegiate sports for men and 9 for women, and 17 intramural sports for men and 17 for women. Facilities include the Vadalabene Center and Student Fitness Center, which offer racquetball, basketball, aquatics, volleyball, indoor track, exercise, and weight training; the University Center, which features restaurants, a recreation center, billiards, and a bowling alley; an outdoor swimming pool; a lake for canoeing and sailing; an outdoor track-and-field and soccer stadium; baseball, softball, and soccer fields; extensive walking and biking trails; and a frisbee course. **Graduates:** From July 1, 2013 to June 30, 2014, 2223 bachelor's degrees were awarded. The most popular majors were business administration (20%), education (19%), and engineering (10%). 550 companies recruited on campus in 2013-2014. In an average class, 1% graduate in 3 years or less, 28% graduate in 4 years or less, 45% graduate in 5 years or less, and 50% graduate in 6 years or less.

SERVICES: Counseling and information services are available, as is

tutoring in most subjects. There is a reader service for the blind, remedial math, reading, and writing. **Library/Resources:** The library contains 810,537 volumes, 1.7 million microform items, 33,438 audio/video tapes/CDs/DVDs, and subscribes to 32,858 periodicals including electronic. Computerized library services include interlibrary loans, database searching, and Internet access. Special learning facilities include an art gallery, radio station, TV station, a recording studio, engineering labs, an anthropology museum, a greenhouse, an arboretum, and a nursing psychomotor skills lab. **Physically Challenged Students:** All of the campus is accessible. Facilities include wheelchair ramps, elevators, special parking, specially equipped restrooms, special class scheduling, lowered drinking fountains, lowered telephones. Visualtek large-screen TV, Kurzweil readers, test-taking facilities, accessible weight-training equipment, and a swimming pool. **Special:** SIUE offers cross-registration with the University of Missouri at St. Louis, co-op programs, internships, which are required by several majors, including mass communications and sociology, work-study programs, dual majors, B.A.-B.S. degrees, student-designed majors (available to specific honors students only), study abroad in 5 countries (England, France, Germany, the Netherlands, and Mexico), a liberal studies degree, and a 5-year (3+2) program in dental medicine. There are 20 national honor societies, a freshman honors program, and 15 departmental honors programs. **Visiting:** There are regularly scheduled orientations for prospective students, including visits before the semester starts. There are guides for informal visits and visitors may sit in on classes. To schedule a visit, contact the Office of Admissions at (618) 650-3705. **Campus Safety and Security:** Measures include 24-hour foot and vehicle patrol, emergency notification system, self-defense education, and security escort services. There are shuttle buses, emergency telephones, lighted pathways/sidewalks, emergency blue lights located throughout campus.

REQUIREMENTS: The ACT is required. Applicants must be graduates of an accredited secondary school or have a GED certificate. They must have completed 15 academic credits, based on 4 years of English, 3 each of math and lab science, 2 years of any combination of art, foreign language, music, and vocational education, at least 2 years of government and/or history, plus 1 more year of social studies. A GPA of 2.5 is required. AP and CLEP credits are accepted. To graduate, students must complete a total of 124 semester hours with a minimum GPA of 2.0. Students must fulfill general education requirements, including 9 hours of math/science, and complete a senior project. **Procedure:** Freshmen are admitted to all sessions. Entrance exams should be taken before high school graduation. There is a rolling admissions plan. Applications should be filed by May 1 for fall entry; December 15 for spring entry; and May 3 for summer entry, along with a $30 fee. Notification is sent on a rolling basis. Applications are accepted on-line. **Transfer Students:** 1242 transfer students enrolled in 2013-2014. Applicants must have a minimum 2.0 GPA in at least 30 semester hours earned. 30 of 124 credits required for the bachelor's degree must be completed at SIUE. **International Students:** There are 320 international students enrolled. The school actively recruits these students. They must take the TOEFL with a minimum score of 550 on the paper-based TOEFL (PBT) or 80 on the Internet-based version (iBT).

ADMISSIONS: 82% of the 2014-2015 applicants were accepted. The ACT scores were 31% below 21, 30% between 21 and 23, 22% between 24 and 26, 9% between 27 and 28, and 8% above 28. 33% of the current freshmen were in the top fifth of their class; 64% were in the top two fifths. **Admissions Contact:** Office of Admissions E-Mail: *admissions@siue.edu* Web: *www.siue.edu*

FINANCIAL AID: In 2014-2015, 75% of all full-time freshmen and 65% of continuing full-time students received some form of financial aid. 70% of all full-time freshmen and 65% of continuing full-time students received need-based aid. The average freshman award was $11,620. Need-based scholarships or need-based grants averaged $8,827; need-based self-help aid (loans and jobs) averaged $8,130; and non-need-based athletic scholarships averaged $10,660. 27% of undergraduate students work part-time. Average annual earnings from campus work are $7800. The average financial indebtedness of the 2014 graduate was $25,998. The FAFSA is required. The deadline for filing freshman financial aid applications for fall entry is March 1.

TRINITY CHRISTIAN COLLEGE E-2

www.trnty.edu

Palos Heights, IL 60463

(708) 597-3000
(800) 748-0085

Fax: (708) 385-5665
Email: admissions@trnty.edu

Full-time: 365 men, 716 women	Faculty: 79; IIB, -$
Part-time: 112 men, 257 women	Ph.D.s: 67%
Graduate: n/av	Student/Faculty: 14 to 1
Year: semesters, summer session	Tuition: $20,959
Room & Board: $7910	Freshman Class: 625 applied, 536 accepted, 201 enrolled

SAT CR/M: 543/552 ACT: 23
CEEB CODE: 1820

Application Deadline: August 15
COMPETITIVE

Trinity Christian College, founded in 1959, is a private college offering programs in arts and sciences, business, health science, liberal arts, music, religion, and teacher preparation. In addition to regional accreditation, Trinity has baccalaureate program accreditation with AACSB, CSWE, and CCNE. The 59-acre campus is in a suburban area 20 miles southwest of the Chicago Loop. Including any residence halls, there are 22 buildings.

STUDENT LIFE: 71% of undergraduates are from Illinois. Others are from 34 states, 3 foreign countries, and Canada. 52% are from public schools. 80% are White. 86% are Protestant; 14% Catholic. **Male To Female Ratio:** 2.0:1. The average age of freshmen is 18; all undergraduates, 21. 27% do not continue beyond their first year; 58% remain to graduate. **Housing:** 726 students can be accommodated in college housing, which includes coed dorms and off-campus apartments. On-campus housing is guaranteed for all 4 years. 61% of students live on campus; of those, 45% remain on campus on weekends. Alcohol is not permitted. All students may keep cars.

FACULTY/CLASSROOMS: 60% of faculty are male; 40% are female. All teach and do research. No introductory courses are taught by graduate students. The average class size in an introductory lecture is 25; in a laboratory is 18; and in a regular course is 18.

PROGRAMS OF STUDY: Trinity confers B.A. B.S., B.S.N. and B.S.W. degrees. Bachelor's degrees are awarded in BIOLOGICAL SCIENCE (biology/biological science), BUSINESS (accounting and business administration and management), COMMUNICATIONS AND THE ARTS (applied music, art, communications, English, music, music performance, Spanish, and studio art), COMPUTER AND PHYSICAL SCIENCE (chemistry, computer science, information sciences and systems, and mathematics), EDUCATION (art education, education, elementary education, music education, special education, and sports studies), HEALTH PROFESSIONS (nursing, predentistry, premedicine, and preoptometry), SOCIAL SCIENCE (biblical studies, criminal justice, history, ministries, philosophy, prelaw, psychology, social work, sociology, and theological studies). Business, education, and nursing are the strongest academically and have the largest enrollments.

ACTIVITIES: There are no fraternities or sororities. There are 18 groups on campus, including art, band, cheerleading, choir, chorale, chorus, dance, drama, ethnic, honors, jazz band, literary magazine, newspaper, pep band, photography, political, professional, religious, social, social service, student government, and yearbook. Popular campus events include the Opus Fine Arts Festival and the Trollstock Concert. **Sports:** There are 6 intercollegiate sports for men and 6 for women, and 7 intramural sports for men and 7 for women. Facilities include a gym, track, stadium, baseball diamond, and softball and soccer fields. **Graduates:** From July 1, 2013 to June 30, 2014, 303 bachelor's degrees were awarded. The most popular majors were elementary education (38%), business (17%), and nursing (13%). 10 companies recruited on campus in 2013-2014. In an average class, 54% graduate in 4 years or less, 58% graduate in 5 years or less, and 59% graduate in 6 years or less. Of the 2013 graduating class, 10% were enrolled in graduate school within 6 months of graduation, and 82% were employed.

SERVICES: Counseling and information services are available, as is tutoring in every subject. **Library/Resources:** The library contains 75,298 volumes, 54,158 microform items, 1,841 audio/video tapes/

CDs/DVDs, and subscribes to 16,711 periodicals including electronic. Computerized library services include interlibrary loans, database searching, Internet access, and Wi-Fi capability. Special learning facilities include an art gallery, a Dutch heritage collection. **Physically Challenged Students:** 95% of the campus is accessible. Facilities include wheelchair ramps, elevators, special parking, specially equipped restrooms, and lowered drinking fountains. **Special:** Students may have various part-time or full-time internships in their major field. There are study abroad programs in Spain, Nicaragua, Ecuador, and South Korea. Pass/fail options exist. Dual majors are offered. There are 1 national honor society and a freshman honors program. **Visiting:** There are regularly scheduled orientations for prospective students, including a tour, an interview, a seminar, and class visits. There are guides for informal visits, visitors may sit in on classes, and stay overnight. To schedule a visit, contact the Admissions Office at admissions@trnty.edu. **Campus Safety and Security:** Measures include 24-hour foot and vehicle patrol, self-defense education, and security escort services. There are emergency telephones and lighted pathways/sidewalks.

REQUIREMENTS: The ACT is recommended. Applicants should graduate from an accredited high school or have a GED. They should prepare with 3 or 4 years of high school English, 3 years of math, science, and social studies, or 2 years each of a combination of 2 subject areas chosen among foreign language, math, science, or social studies. An interview is required. A GPA of 2.0 is required. AP and CLEP credits are accepted. Important factors in the admissions decision are advanced placement or honors courses, leadership record, and recommendations by school officials. All students must take 9 credits in English, 6 each in philosophy, history, and theology, as well as distribution requirements in cross-cultural studies, natural sciences, social sciences, fine arts, math, and phys ed. Students must complete 125 credit hours and maintain a minimum GPA of 2.0 to graduate. **Procedure:** Freshmen are admitted fall and spring. Entrance exams should be taken during the last semester of the junior year. There is a rolling admissions plan. Applications should be filed by August 15 for fall entry; January 15 for spring entry. The fall 2014 application fee was $20. Notification is sent on a rolling basis. **Transfer Students:** 218 transfer students enrolled in 2013-2014. Applicants must have 24 hours of acceptable credits and a minimum 2.3 GPA. Associate degrees are recognized for transfer. 45 of 125 credits required for the bachelor's degree must be completed at Trinity. **International Students:** There are 36 international students enrolled. They must take the TOEFL. They must also take the SAT or ACT.

ADMISSIONS: 86% of the 2014-2015 applicants were accepted. The SAT scores for the 2014-2015 freshman class were: Critical Reading--32% below 500, 52% between 500 and 599, 11% between 600 and 699, and 5% between 700 and 800; Math--37% below 500, 47% between 500 and 599, and 16% between 600 and 699. The ACT scores were 35% below 21, 22% between 21 and 23, 14% between 24 and 26, 13% between 27 and 28, and 16% above 28. 36% of the current freshmen were in the top fifth of their class; 60% were in the top two fifths. 3 freshmen graduated first in their class. **Admissions Contact:** Admissions Office E-Mail: *admissions@trnty.edu* Web: *www.trnty.edu*

FINANCIAL AID: In 2014-2015, 96% of all full-time freshmen and 93% of continuing full-time students received some form of financial aid. 76% of all full-time freshmen and 71% of continuing full-time students received need-based aid. The average freshman award was $15,134. Need-based scholarships or need-based grants averaged $4,287 ($17,696 maximum); need-based self-help aid (loans and jobs) averaged $3,698 ($9,000 maximum); and non-need-based athletic scholarships averaged $3,710 ($11,000 maximum). Average annual earnings from campus work are $1600. The average financial indebtedness of the 2014 graduate was $32,847. The FAFSA is required. The deadline for filing freshman financial aid applications for fall entry is February 15.

TRINITY COLLEGE OF NURSING AND HEALTH SCIENCES
(The complete profile is made available exclusively on our website, www. barronspac.com)

TRINITY INTERNATIONAL UNIVERSITY   E-2
www.tiu.edu

Deerfield, IL 60015	(847) 317-7000
	(800) 822-3225
Fax: (847) 317-7081	Email: tcdadm@tiu.edu
Full-time: 445 men, 590 women	Faculty: IIA, --$
Part-time: 45 men, 185 women	Ph.D.s: 85%
Graduate: 1080 men, 550 women	Student/Faculty: n/av
Year: semesters, summer session	Tuition: $23,370
Room & Board: $7700	Freshman Class: n/av
SAT or ACT: required	CEEB CODE: 1810
Application Deadline: open	VERY COMPETITIVE

Trinity International University, established in 1897 by the Evangelical Free Church, is a Christian, liberal arts institution offering undergraduate, graduate, and doctoral programs. Figures in the above capsule and in this profile are approximate. There are 8 undergraduate schools and 3 graduate schools. In addition to regional accreditation, Trinity has baccalaureate program accreditation with ATS and CAAHEP. The 111-acre campus is in a suburban area 25 miles north of Chicago. Including any residence halls, there are 34 buildings.

STUDENT LIFE: 52% of undergraduates are from Illinois. Others are from 40 states, 45 foreign countries, and Canada. 69% are from public schools. 77% are White. 96% are Protestant. **Male To Female Ratio:** 0.8:1. The average age of freshmen is 18; all undergraduates, 21. 22% do not continue beyond their first year; 47% remain to graduate. **Housing:** 700 students can be accommodated in college housing, which includes single-sex dorms, on-campus apartments, and married student housing. On-campus housing is guaranteed for all 4 years. 58% of students live on campus; of those, 75% remain on campus on weekends. Alcohol is not permitted. Upperclassmen may keep cars.

FACULTY/CLASSROOMS: 68% of faculty are male; 32% are female. 56% teach undergraduates. No introductory courses are taught by graduate students. The average class size in an introductory lecture is 40; in a laboratory is 20; and in a regular course is 15.

PROGRAMS OF STUDY: Trinity confers B.A. degrees. Master's and Doctoral degrees are also awarded. Bachelor's degrees are awarded in BIOLOGICAL SCIENCE (biology/biological science), BUSINESS (accounting, business administration and management, human resources, international business management, marketing/retailing/merchandising, and sports management), COMMUNICATIONS AND THE ARTS (communications, English, and music), COMPUTER AND PHYSICAL SCIENCE (chemistry and mathematics), EDUCATION (athletic training, elementary education, physical education, and secondary education), HEALTH PROFESSIONS (physical therapy, premedicine, and sports medicine), SOCIAL SCIENCE (biblical studies, Christian studies, history, humanities, liberal arts/general studies, philosophy, psychology, social science, and youth ministry). Music, education, and biblical studies are the strongest academically. Business, Christian ministries, and education have the largest enrollments.

ACTIVITIES: There are no fraternities or sororities. There are 36 groups on campus, including art, band, cheerleading, choir, chorale, computers, debate, drama, ethnic, handbell choir and gospel choir, honors, international, jazz band, literary magazine, newspaper, orchestra, pep band, political, religious, social service, student government, and symphony. Popular campus events include Santa Lucia Festival, Fine Arts Series and Day of Prayer. **Sports:** There are 4 intercollegiate sports for men and 4 for women, and 6 intramural sports for men and 6 for women. Facilities include a student center, sports complex, and football and soccer fields. Students have access to a nearby indoor tennis and racquetball club. **Graduates:** From July 1, 2013 to June 30, 2014, 168 bachelor's degrees were awarded. The most popular majors were business (21%), Christian ministries (16%), and elementary education (12%). 24 companies recruited on campus in 2013-2014. In an average class, 33% graduate in 4 years or less, 9% graduate in 5 years or less, and 4% graduate in 6 years or less. Of the 2013 graduating class, 21% were enrolled in graduate school within 6 months of graduation, and 55% were employed.

SERVICES: Counseling and information services are available, as is

tutoring in every subject. There is a reader service for the blind, and remedial math, reading, and writing. **Library/Resources:** The library contains 247,650 volumes, 110,503 microform items, 6,741 audio/video tapes/CDs/DVDs, and subscribes to 1,091 periodicals including electronic. Computerized library services include interlibrary loans, database searching, and Internet access. **Physically Challenged Students:** 75% of the campus is accessible. Facilities include wheelchair ramps, elevators, special parking, specially equipped restrooms, and special class scheduling. **Special:** Students can cross-register with the Christian College Consortium and at Trinity Evangelical Divinity School. Trinity offers 3 levels of internships, study abroad in 7 countries, and an opportunity through the American Studies Program to spend a semester in Washington. Dual majors, a general studies degree, and nondegree study are offered. There are 2 national honor societies, a freshman honors program, and 15 departmental honors programs. **Visiting:** There are regularly scheduled orientations for prospective students, including class visits, meetings with professors and admission counselors, and a dorm visit. There are guides for informal visits, visitors may sit in on classes, and stay overnight. To schedule a visit, contact the Campus Visit Coordinator at visits@tiu .edu. **Campus Safety and Security:** Measures include 24-hour foot and vehicle patrol, self-defense education, and security escort services. There are emergency telephones and lighted pathways/sidewalks.

REQUIREMENTS: The SAT or ACT is required, the ACT is preferred. A satisfactory score on the SAT or ACT is required. Applicants should be graduates of an accredited high school and have completed 15 academic credits in art, a foreign language, math, music, science, social studies, and English. A GED is accepted. Recommendations from a pastor must be submitted. A GPA of 2.5 is required. AP and CLEP credits are accepted. Important factors in the admissions decision are personality/intangible qualities, leadership record, and advanced placement or honors courses. To graduate, all students must complete 126 semester hours, including 58 general education hours and a variable 36 to 54 hours in the major. A GPA of 2.0 is required. Chapel attendance, Christian service, Bible study, and science are also required. **Procedure:** Freshmen are admitted fall and spring. Entrance exams should be taken during spring of the junior year or fall of the senior year. There is a rolling admissions plan. Application deadlines are open. The fall 2014 application fee was $25. Applications are accepted on-line. **Transfer Students:** 90 transfer students enrolled in 2013-2014. Applicants must submit college transcripts and have a cumulative college GPA of 2.0 or higher. 30 of 126 credits required for the bachelor's degree must be completed at Trinity. **International Students:** They must take the TOEFL with a minimum score of 580 on the paper-based TOEFL (PBT). They must also take the SAT or ACT, scoring 19.

ADMISSIONS: 6 freshmen graduated first in their class. **Admissions Contact:** Aaron Mahl, Director of Undergraduate Admissions. E-Mail: *tcdadm@tiu.edu* Web: *www.tiu.edu*

FINANCIAL AID: In 2014-2015, 90% of all full-time freshmen and 86% of continuing full-time students received some form of financial aid. 63% of all full-time freshmen and 60% of continuing full-time students received need-based aid. The average freshman award was $17,895. Need-based scholarships or need-based grants averaged $8,442 ($12,000 maximum); need-based self-help aid (loans and jobs) averaged $5,513 ($5,625 maximum); and non-need-based athletic scholarships averaged $9,389 ($22,980 maximum). 53% of undergraduate students work part-time. Average annual earnings from campus work are $875. The average financial indebtedness of the 2014 graduate was $20,621. Trinity is a member of CSS. The FAFSA is required. Check with the school for current application deadlines.

UNIVERSITY OF CHICAGO   E-2
www.uchicago.edu

Chicago, IL 60637	**(773) 702-8650**
	n/av
Fax: (773) 702-4199	**Email:** jnondorf@uchicago.edu
Full-time: 2921 men, 2610 women	**Faculty:** 1261; I, ++$
Part-time: 31 men, 28 women	**Ph.D.s:** 100%
Graduate: 4301 men, 2617 women	**Student/Faculty:** 6 to 1
Year: quarters, summer session	**Tuition:** $42,783
Room & Board: $12,633	**Freshman Class:** 25273 applied, 3345 accepted, 1527 enrolled
SAT CR/M: 744/742 **ACT:** 33	**CEEB CODE:** 1832
Application Deadline: January 2	**MOST COMPETITIVE**

The University of Chicago, founded in 1890, is a private liberal arts institution offering undergraduate and graduate programs with emphases on the biological and physical sciences, the humanities, and the social sciences. There is 1 undergraduate school and 11 graduate schools. In addition to regional accreditation, Chicago has baccalaureate program accreditation with NCATE. The 215-acre campus is in an urban area in Chicago. Including any residence halls, there are 249 buildings.

STUDENT LIFE: 81% of undergraduates are from out of state, mostly the Midwest. Students are from 50 states, 103 foreign countries, and Canada. 46% are White; 18% Asian American. **Male To Female Ratio:** 0.7:1. The average age of freshmen is 18; all undergraduates, 19. 1% do not continue beyond their first year; 92% remain to graduate. **Housing:** 2992 students can be accommodated in college housing, which includes single-sex and coed dorms and on-campus apartments. International house. On-campus housing is guaranteed for all 4 years. 55% of students live on campus. Upperclassmen may keep cars.

FACULTY/CLASSROOMS: 68% of faculty are male; 32% are female. No introductory courses are taught by graduate students. The average class size in an introductory lecture is 22; in a laboratory is 14; and in a regular course is 25.

PROGRAMS OF STUDY: Chicago confers B.A., and B.S. degrees. Master's and Doctoral degrees are also awarded. Bachelor's degrees are awarded in BIOLOGICAL SCIENCE (biochemistry and biology/biological science), COMMUNICATIONS AND THE ARTS (art history and appreciation, classics, comparative literature, East Asian languages and literature, English, film arts, German, linguistics, media arts, music, romance languages and literature, Russian, Slavic languages, and visual and performing arts), COMPUTER AND PHYSICAL SCIENCE (applied mathematics, chemistry, computer science, geoscience, mathematics, physics, and statistics), ENGINEERING AND ENVIRONMENTAL DESIGN (environmental science), HEALTH PROFESSIONS (medical science), SOCIAL SCIENCE (African American studies, anthropology, classical/ancient civilization, economics, gender studies, geography, history, human development, humanities, interdisciplinary studies, international studies, Judaic studies, Latin American studies, law, medieval studies, Near Eastern studies, philosophy, political science/government, psychology, public affairs, religion, social science, sociology, South Asian studies, and theological studies). Social sciences, biological and biomedical science have the largest enrollments.

ACTIVITIES: There are 400 groups on campus, including and college bowl, improv groups, art, bagpipe, band, cheerleading, chess, choir, chorale, chorus, computers, dance, debate, drama, ethnic, film, gay, honors, international, jazz band, literary magazine, Model UN, musical theater, newspaper, orchestra, pep band, photography, political, professional, radio and TV, religious, social, social service, student government, and symphony. Popular campus events include Scavenger Hunt, Summer Breeze Festival, Kuviasungnerk Winter Festival and Festival of the Arts. **Sports:** There are 10 intercollegiate sports for men and 9 for women, and 32 intramural sports for men and 32 for women. The athletic facilities include a field house, a 1,500-seat stadium, outdoor 400m track, baseball and softball fields, a 1,500-seat arena, indoor basketball and squash courts, an indoor 200m track, weight and wrestling rooms, aerobic machines, and an indoor Olympic-sized pool. The University of Chicago also has a student activities center housing a movie theater, TV and pool rooms, and a pub. **Graduates:** From July 1, 2013 to June 30, 2014, 1242 bachelor's degrees were awarded. The most popular majors were economics (18%), biological sciences (10%), and political science (9%).

SERVICES: Counseling and information services are available, as is tutoring in some subjects, math, physics, chemistry, writing and biology. There is a reader service for the blind. **Library/Resources:** The 5 libraries contain 11.3 million volumes, 98,000 audio/video tapes/CDs/DVDs, and subscribe to 122,000 periodicals including electronic. Computerized library services include interlibrary loans, database searching, Internet access, and Wi-Fi capability. Special learning facilities include an art gallery, radio station, film studies center, language labs, museum of Near Eastern antiquities, and Renaissance Society (contemporary art). **Physically Challenged Students:** Facilities include wheelchair ramps, elevators, special parking, specially equipped restrooms, special class scheduling, lowered drinking fountains, lowered telephones, and special housing. **Special:** Special academic programs include cross-registration through the Committee on Institutional Cooperation, summer internship in Washington, and study abroad programs in 18 countries. B.A.-B.S. and general studies degrees are offered, as are student-designed majors. Bachelors-Masters joint programs are offered in many fields. Professional options in Public Policy Studies, Social Service Administration, and early admission to the University of Chicago Pritzker School of Medicine are available. Non-degree study and pass/fail options are possible. There is 1 national honor society including a chapter of Phi Beta Kappa. **Visiting:** There are regularly scheduled orientations for prospective students, including meeting with an admissions counselor and students, sitting in on classes, visiting faculty, and staying in a residence hall. There are guides for informal visits, visitors may sit in on classes, and stay overnight. To schedule a visit, contact the College Admissions at (773) 702-8650. **Campus Safety and Security:** Measures include 24-hour foot and vehicle patrol, emergency notification system, self-defense education, and security escort services. There are shuttle buses, emergency telephones, lighted pathways/sidewalks, and controlled access to dorms/residences.

REQUIREMENTS: The SAT or ACT is required. Other admissions criteria include a recommended secondary school curriculum of 4 years each of English, Mathematics, and Science, 3 years of foreign language, and 2 years each of history and social studies. The GED is accepted. An essay must be submitted, and an interview is recommended. AP credits are accepted. Important factors in the admissions decision are advanced placement or honors courses, personality/intangible qualities, and extracurricular activities record.To graduate, students must complete 42 quarter courses, including 9 to 13 courses in the major, with an overall GPA of at least 1.75 and at least 2.0 in the major. The core curriculum includes sequences in humanities, social sciences, biological and physical sciences, civilization studies, and foreign languages. Also required are 2 quarters of math and 1 of art, music, or drama. **Procedure:** Freshmen are admitted fall. Entrance exams should be taken during the junior or senior year. There are early admissions and deferred admissions plans. Early decision applications should be filed by November 1; regular applications, by January 2 for fall entry, along with a $75 fee. Notification of early decision is sent December 17; regular decision, April 1. Applications are accepted on-line. **Transfer Students:** 16 transfer students enrolled in 2013-2014. Proven ability and interest in liberal arts education is considered. Essay, broad course work, and solid performance at the home institution is considered critical. A recommendation is required from a secondary school, instructors, and dean of previous institution. 2-year residency is a requirement. 105 of 140 credits required for the bachelor's degree must be completed at Chicago. **International Students:** There are 522 international students enrolled. The school actively recruits these students. They must take the TOEFL with a minimum score of 104 on the Internet-based version (iBT), or take the IELTS, with a minimum overall score of 7. They must also take the SAT or ACT.

ADMISSIONS: 13% of the 2014-2015 applicants were accepted. The SAT scores for the 2014-2015 freshman class were: Critical Reading--16% between 600 and 699, and 84% between 700 and 800; Math--1% between 500 and 599, 18% between 600 and 699, and 81% between 700 and 800; Writing--1% between 500 and 599, 21%

between 600 and 699, and 78% between 700 and 800. 99% of the current freshmen were in the top fifth of their class. **Admissions Contact:** James Nondorf, Vice President and Dean, College Admissions and Financial Ai. E-Mail: *jnondorf@uchicago.edu* Web: *www.uchicago.edu*

FINANCIAL AID: In 2014-2015, 63% of all full-time freshmen and 56% of continuing full-time students received some form of financial aid. 45% of all full-time freshmen and 45% of continuing full-time students received need-based aid. The average freshman award was $42,128. Need-based scholarships or need-based grants averaged $39,904; need-based self-help aid (loans and jobs) averaged $3,476; and other non-need-based awards and non-need-based scholarships averaged $11,707. The average financial indebtedness of the 2014 graduate was $23,930. Chicago is a member of CSS. The CSS/Profile, FAFSA, and the college's own financial statement are required. The deadline for filing freshman financial aid applications for fall entry is February 1.

UNIVERSITY OF ILLINOIS SYSTEM

The University of Illinois System, established in 1867, is a public system in Illinois. It is governed by a board of trustees, whose chief administrator is the president. The primary goal of the system is to provide undergraduate, graduate and professional education, conduct research, public service and to promote economic development in the state. The main priorities are develop University of Illinois Urbana-Champaign (UIUC) into the nation's preeminent public research university, develop University of Illinois – Chicago (UIC) into the nation's premier urban public research university, position the University of Illinois Medical Center and health sciences colleges for the next quarter century, and develop University of Springfield (UIS) into one of the nation's top five small, public, liberal arts universities. The total student enrollment in a recent year for all 3 campuses was 78,117, there were 5879 faculty members. Altogether there are 224 baccalaureates, 220 masters, and 150 doctoral programs offered in the University of Illinois System. Profiles of the 4-year campuses are included in this section.

UNIVERSITY OF ILLINOIS AT CHICAGO E-2
www.uic.edu

Chicago, IL 60607 312-996-4366

Fax: 312-413-7628	Email: uicadmit@uic.edu
Full-time: 7662 men, 7797 women	Faculty: 1293
Part-time: 666 men, 582 women	Ph.D.s: 74%
Graduate: 4466 men, 6390 women	Student/Faculty: 17 to 1
Year: semesters, summer session	Tuition: $13,364 ($26,024)
Room & Board: $10,871	Freshman Class: 15914 applied, 11598 accepted, 3030 enrolled
SAT CR/M: 536/596 ACT: 24	CEEB CODE: 1851
Application Deadline: January 15	VERY COMPETITIVE

UIC provides undergraduate and graduate programs in liberal arts, fine arts, business, engineering, architecture, health sciences, music, teacher preparation, social work, and professional training in dentistry, medicine, and pharmacy. There are 10 undergraduate schools and 14 graduate schools. In addition to regional accreditation, UIC has baccalaureate program accreditation with AACSB, ABET, ACPE, CSWE, NAAB, NASAD, APA, CAPTE, and NASPAA. The 240-acre campus is in an urban area just west of downtown Chicago. Including any residence halls, there are 173 buildings.

STUDENT LIFE: 95% of undergraduates are from Illinois. Others are from 38 states, 58 foreign countries, and Canada. 90% are from public schools. 36% are White; 26% Hispanic; 23% Asian American. **Male To Female Ratio:** 1.2:1. The average age of freshmen is 18; all undergraduates, 21. 20% do not continue beyond their first year; 60% remain to graduate. **Housing:** 3718 students can be accommodated in college housing, which includes coed dorms and on-campus apartments. In addition, there are honors houses, special-interest houses, the President's Award House, and special-interest floors. On-campus housing is available on a first-come and first-served basis. 83% of students commute. All students may keep cars.

FACULTY/CLASSROOMS: 55% of faculty are male; 45% are female. 71% teach undergraduates, 19% do research, and 19% do both. Graduate students teach 39% of introductory courses. The average class size in an introductory lecture is 31; in a laboratory is 21; and in a regular course is 28.

PROGRAMS OF STUDY: UIC confers B.A., B.B.A., B.Des., B.Mus., B.S.N., B.S. and B.F.A. degrees. Master's and Doctoral degrees are also awarded. Bachelor's degrees are awarded in AGRICULTURE (environmental studies), BIOLOGICAL SCIENCE (biochemistry, biology/biological science, biophysics, forensic science, neurosciences, nutrition, and nutritional sciences), BUSINESS (accounting, banking and finance, business administration and management, business economics, business information systems, entrepreneurial studies, finance, management science, marketing/retailing/ merchandising, and real estate), COMMUNICATIONS AND THE ARTS (applied music, art history, art/art studies, art history and appreciation, communications, dramatic arts, English, English literature, film arts, film, television and digital media, fine arts, French, french and francophone studies, German, Germanic languages and literature, graphic design, graphic design & media, industrial design, Italian, music, music performance, painting, photography, Polish, Russian, Russian languages and literature, sculpture, Slavic languages, Spanish, studio art, theatre acting, theatre arts, theater design, theatre production, theatre studies, and visual and performing arts), COMPUTER AND PHYSICAL SCIENCE (chemistry, computer mathematics, computer science, digital arts/technology, earth science, environmental geology, geoenvironmental studies, information sciences and systems, mathematics, mathematics/computational, physics, science of earth systems, and statistics), EDUCATION (art education, childhood education: 1-6, early childhood education, elementary education, English education, health education, health information management, learner designed area of study, mathematics education, museum studies, nutrition education, physical education, secondary education, and sports and wellness studies), ENGINEERING AND ENVIRONMENTAL DESIGN (architecture, bioengineering, chemical engineering, civil engineering, computer engineering, electrical/electronics engineering, energy systems technology, engineering, engineering physics, history of architecture / urban development, industrial engineering technology, materials engineering, and mechanical engineering), HEALTH PROFESSIONS (allied health, dental hygiene, exercise science, nursing, occupational therapy, pharmacology, pharmacy, physical therapy, Pre-Health Studies, predentistry, premedicine, prepharmacy, and public health), SOCIAL SCIENCE (African American studies, anthropology, applied psychology, architectural studies, classical/ancient civilization, criminal justice, criminology, dietetics, economics, ethnic studies, forensic studies, French studies, gender studies, German area studies, history, humanities, Italian studies, Judaic studies, Latin American studies, law enforcement and corrections, philosophy, physical fitness/ movement, political science/government, psychology, public administration, public affairs, Russian and Slavic studies, sociology, Spanish studies, urban studies, and women & gender studies). Math, history, fine arts, nursing, and business are the strongest academically. Psychology, biological science, and accounting have the largest enrollments.

ACTIVITIES: 3% of men belong to 22 national fraternities; 2% of women belong to 21 national sororities. There are 285 groups on campus, including the American medical student association and the American student dental association, Indian graduate student association, Muslim student association, accounting club, art, band, cheerleading, chess, choir, chorus, communications, computers, dance, drama, environmental, ethnic, gay, honors, international, jazz band, literary magazine, musical theater, newspaper, political, professional, religious, social, social service, and student government. Popular campus events include Fun Fair, Meet the Greeks, New Student Convocation and Spark in the Park. **Sports:** There are 9 intercollegiate sports for men and 10 for women, and 52 intramural sports for men and 42 for women. Facilities include a 12,000-seat sports pavilion, 2 sports and fitness centers, a recreation center, a 1000-seat gym, 3 pools, racquetball and tennis courts, baseball, softball, and soccer fields, a bowling alley, indoor and outdoor tracks, and weight rooms.

Graduates: From July 1, 2013 to June 30, 2014, 3756 bachelor's degrees were awarded. The most popular majors were psychology (14%), biological sciences (11%), and nursing (6%). 300 companies recruited on campus in 2013-2014. In an average class, 30% graduate in 4 years or less, 51% graduate in 5 years or less, and 57% graduate in 6 years or less.

SERVICES: Counseling and information services are available, as is tutoring in most subjects. There is a reader service for the blind, and remedial math, reading, and writing. A writing center, and academic skills classes. **Library/Resources:** The 2 libraries contain 2.8 million volumes, 440,000 microform items, 24,940 audio/video tapes/CDs/ DVDs, and subscribe to 61,438 periodicals including electronic. Computerized library services include interlibrary loans, database searching, Internet access, and Wi-Fi capability. Special learning facilities include an art gallery, Jane Addams Hull House, which is a restored settlement house, and the James Woodworth Prairie Reserve. **Physically Challenged Students:** 80% of the campus is accessible. Facilities include wheelchair ramps, elevators, special parking, specially equipped restrooms, special class scheduling, lowered drinking fountains, and lowered telephones. **Special:** Special academic programs include a wide variety of co-op and program internships, work-study with some 70 on- and off-campus employers, and study abroad opportunities at accredited foreign universities, as well as special programs in France, Italy, Canada, Austria, Spain, and Mexico. Interdisciplinary majors are offered in architectural studies, communications and theater, math and computer science, bioengineering, and information and decision sciences. Up to 4 semester hours of credit may be granted for military experience. Dual and student-designed majors, nondegree study, and pass/fail options are available. There are 13 national honor societies, Phi Beta Kappa, a freshman honors program, and 90 departmental honors programs. **Visiting:** There are regularly scheduled orientations for prospective students, consisting of a general meeting, a college meeting, and campus tours. There are guides for informal visits, visitors may sit in on classes, and stay overnight. To schedule a visit, contact Robert M. Moranetz at (312) 413-7628. **Campus Safety and Security:** Measures include 24-hour foot and vehicle patrol, emergency notification system, self-defense education, and security escort services. There are shuttle buses, emergency telephones, lighted pathways/sidewalks, controlled access to dorms/residences, emergency call buttons across campus.

REQUIREMENTS: Either the ACT, SAT or SAT-I are required. Applicants should be graduates of an accredited secondary school the GED is accepted. The recommended secondary school curriculum varies according to the college program chosen, but 15 high school credits are required as follows: English 4; math 3; science 3; foreign language 2; and social studies. AP and CLEP credits are accepted. Students must demonstrate proficiency in written English through either course work or testing and complete 24 hours of general education, including at least 1 course in each of the general education categories: Analyzing the Natural World, Understanding the Individual and Society, Understanding the Past, Understanding the Creative Arts, Exploring the World Cultures, and Understanding U.S. Society. A minimum overall GPA of 2.0 is required. Total number of hours to graduate varies by major but is always at least 120. **Procedure:** Freshmen are admitted fall. Entrance exams should be taken in the spring of the junior year or the fall of the senior year. There are early decision and rolling admissions plans. Applications should be filed by January 15 for fall entry, along with a $50 fee. Notification is sent on a rolling basis. Applications are accepted on-line. **Transfer Students:** 2387 transfer students enrolled in 2013-2014. Transferable hours and minimum GPA vary according to program. 30 of 120 credits required for the bachelor's degree must be completed at UIC. **International Students:** There are 414 international students enrolled. The school actively recruits these students. They must take the TOEFL with a minimum score of 550 on the paper-based TOEFL (PBT) or 80 on the Internet-based version (iBT). They must also take the SAT or ACT. Freshmen minimum required scores depend on the specific college.

ADMISSIONS: 73% of the 2014-2015 applicants were accepted. The SAT scores for the 2014-2015 freshman class were: Critical Reading--36% below 500, 42% between 500 and 599, 11% between 600 and 699, and 10% between 700 and 800; Math--18% below 500, 30% between 500 and 599, 34% between 600 and 699, and 19% between

700 and 800. The ACT scores were 14% below 21, 29% between 21 and 23, 30% between 24 and 26, 13% between 27 and 28, and 14% above 28. 51% of the current freshmen were in the top fifth of their class; 85% were in the top two fifths. **Admissions Contact:** Malinda Lorkovich, Managing Director of Admissions. E-Mail: *uicadmit@uic .edu* Web: *http:/www.uic.edu/uic/admission/index.shtml*

FINANCIAL AID: In 2014-2015, 75% of all full-time freshmen and 74% of continuing full-time students received some form of financial aid. 65% of all full-time freshmen and 61% of continuing full-time students received need-based aid. The average freshman award was $14,420. Need-based scholarships or need-based grants averaged $13,768 need-based self-help aid (loans and jobs) averaged $3,744; non-need-based athletic scholarships averaged $21,860; and other non-need-based awards and non-need-based scholarships averaged $5,041. 18% of undergraduate students work part-time. Average annual earnings from campus work are $4881. The average financial indebtedness of the 2014 graduate was $23,158. UIC is a member of CSS. The FAFSA is required. The priority date for freshman financial aid applications for fall entry is March 1. The deadline for filing freshman financial aid applications for fall entry is March 1.

UNIVERSITY OF ILLINOIS AT URBANA-CHAMPAIGN   E-3
www.illinois.edu

Urbana, IL 61801	217-333-0302
	n/av
Fax: n/av	Email: admissions@illinois.edu
Full-time: 17685 men, 13831 women	Faculty: I, ++$
	Ph.D.s: 92%
Part-time: 770 men, 409 women	Student/Faculty: 19 to 1
Graduate: 6343 men, 5904 women	Tuition: $15,602 ($30,228)
Year: semesters, summer session	Freshman Class: n/av
Room & Board: $10,848	
SAT or ACT: required	CEEB CODE: 1836
Application Deadline: December 1	**HIGHLY COMPETITIVE**

The University of Illinois at Urbana-Champaign, founded in 1867, is the oldest and largest campus in the University of Illinois system, offering some 150 undergraduate and more than 100 graduate degree programs. There are 18 undergraduate schools. In addition to regional accreditation, Illinois has baccalaureate program accreditation with AACSB, AALE, ABET, ACEJMC, ADA, ASLA, CSAB, CSWE, NAAB, NASAD, NASM, NCATE, NRPA, SAF, ABA, ACS, APA, CAAHEP, CADE, NASD, and NAST. The 4938-acre campus is in a small town 140 miles south of Chicago, 125 miles west of Indianapolis, and 180 miles northeast of St. Louis. Including any residence halls, there are 705 buildings.

STUDENT LIFE: 76% of undergraduates are from Illinois. Others are from 50 states, 115 foreign countries, and Canada. 66% are White; 13% Asian American. The average age of freshmen is 18; all undergraduates, 20. 7% do not continue beyond their first year; 83% remain to graduate. **Housing:** 11034 students can be accommodated in college housing, which includes single-sex and coed dorms, on-campus apartments, and married student housing. In addition, there are language houses, special-interest houses, privately owned university-approved residence halls, fraternity and sorority houses. On-campus housing is guaranteed for all 4 years. 50% of students commute. All students may keep cars.

FACULTY/CLASSROOMS: 67% of faculty are male; 33% are female. 95% teach undergraduates, all do research, and 95% do both. Graduate students teach 38% of introductory courses. The average class size in an introductory lecture is 19; in a laboratory is 22; and in a regular course is 29.

PROGRAMS OF STUDY: Illinois confers A.B., B.S., B.A.U.P., B.F.A., B.Land.Arch., B.Mus., B.S.Ed., B.S.J., B.S.W. and B.V.M. degrees. Master's and Doctoral degrees are also awarded. Bachelor's degrees are awarded in AGRICULTURE (agricultural business management, agricultural communications, agricultural economics, agricultural mechanics, agronomy, animal science, forestry and related sciences, horticulture, natural resource management, range/farm manage-

ment, and wildlife management), BIOLOGICAL SCIENCE (biology/ biological science, biophysics, biotechnology, botany, cell biology, entomology, microbiology, molecular biology, nutrition, physiology, plant physiology, and wildlife biology), BUSINESS (accounting, banking and finance, entrepreneurial studies, hospitality management services, human resources, insurance, labor studies, logistics, management information systems, management science, marketing and distribution, marketing management, marketing/retailing/ merchandising, operations research, organizational behavior, personnel management, purchasing/inventory management, real estate, and recreation and leisure services), COMMUNICATIONS AND THE ARTS (advertising, art history and appreciation, broadcasting, classics, communications, comparative literature, crafts, dance, dramatic arts, East Asian languages and literature, English, English literature, film arts, fine arts, French, Germanic languages and literature, graphic design, Hebrew, industrial design, Italian, journalism, linguistics, media arts, music, music history and appreciation, music performance, music theory and composition, painting, photography, Portuguese, Russian languages and literature, sculpture, Spanish, speech/debate/rhetoric, and voice), COMPUTER AND PHYSICAL SCIENCE (actuarial science, astronomy, chemistry, computer management, computer mathematics, computer programming, geology, mathematics, physics, and statistics), EDUCATION (agricultural education, art education, athletic training, computer education, early childhood education, education, education of the multiply handicapped, elementary education, English education, foreign languages education, mathematics education, music education, physical education, science education, secondary education, and vocational education), ENGINEERING AND ENVIRONMENTAL DESIGN (aeronautical engineering, agricultural engineering, airline piloting and navigation, architectural engineering, architecture, aviation administration/management, bioengineering, ceramic engineering, chemical engineering, city/community/regional planning, civil engineering, computational sciences, computer engineering, computer technology, electrical/electronics engineering, engineering, engineering mechanics, engineering physics, geological engineering, industrial administration/management, industrial engineering, landscape architecture/design, materials engineering, materials science, mechanical engineering, metallurgical engineering, nuclear engineering, and plastics engineering), HEALTH PROFESSIONS (biomedical science, community health work, exercise science, health care administration, preveterinary science, public health, and rehabilitation therapy), SOCIAL SCIENCE (anthropology, child psychology/ development, dietetics, East Asian studies, economics, family/ consumer studies, food production/management/services, food science, geography, history, human development, humanities, international studies, Latin American studies, liberal arts/general studies, parks and recreation management, philosophy, political science/ government, prelaw, psychology, religion, Russian and Slavic studies, sociology, textiles and clothing, and women's studies). Engineering, and computer science, have the largest enrollments.

ACTIVITIES: 21% of men belong to 3 local and 59 national fraternities; 21% of women belong to 2 local and 34 national sororities. There are 1000 groups on campus, including art, band, cheerleading, chess, choir, chorale, chorus, computers, dance, debate, drama, drill team, environmental, ethnic, film, forensics, gay, honors, international, jazz band, literary magazine, marching band, musical theater, newspaper, opera, orchestra, pep band, photography, political, professional, radio and TV, religious, social, social service, student government, symphony, and yearbook. Popular campus events include Quad Day to introduce Campus Organizations, Homecoming, Dad's Weekend, and Mom's Weekend. **Sports:** There are 10 intercollegiate sports for men and 12 for women, and 21 intramural sports for men and 21 for women. Facilities include a 470,000-square-foot state-of-the-art indoor recreation space, along with 42 acres of outdoor recreation space for students' fitness and wellness needs, all major varsity sport facilities, and numerous student union facilities from bowling to exercise facilities. **Graduates:** The most popular majors were business, engineering, and social sciences/engineering technology. 6500 companies recruited on campus in 2013-2014.

SERVICES: Counseling and information services are available, as is tutoring in every subject. There is a reader service for the blind, remedial math, reading, and writing. Transportation and rehabilitation services are offered, as well as interpreters, note taking, taped lectures, and priority registration. **Library/Resources:** The 27 libraries contain 11.0 million volumes, and 1,000,000 audio/video tapes/CDs/DVDs. Computerized library services include interlibrary loans, database searching, Internet access, and Wi-Fi capability. Special learning facilities include an art gallery, natural history museum, planetarium, radio station, TV station, a language learning lab, performing arts center, a graphic technologies lab, world history and cultural museum, rehabilitation-education center, center for American music, Japan House and gardens, and rare books and special collections libraries. **Physically Challenged Students:** All of the campus is accessible. Facilities include wheelchair ramps, elevators, special parking, specially equipped restrooms, special class scheduling, lowered drinking fountains, lowered telephones, special housing. **Special:** Illinois offers numerous academic opportunities students outside of the classroom. Participate in research with a faculty member, work in Research Park, take a trip on one of our 400 study abroad programs taking you to every continent except Antarctica, and engage in a flexible curriculum that prepares you for life after Illinois. There are 89 national honor societies, including Phi Beta Kappa, a freshman honors program, and 99 departmental honors programs. **Visiting:** There are regularly scheduled orientations for prospective students, consisting of a university overview and admission presentation followed by student-led campus tour. There are guides for informal visits and visitors may sit in on classes. To schedule a visit, contact Campus Visits at (217) 333-0824. **Campus Safety and Security:** Measures include 24-hour foot and vehicle patrol, emergency notification system, self-defense education, and security escort services. There are shuttle buses, emergency telephones, lighted pathways/sidewalks, controlled access to dorms/residences, saferides program, safety presentations, and evaluations by campus police.

REQUIREMENTS: The SAT or ACT is required. The ACT Optional Writing test is also required. Applicants should be graduates of accredited secondary schools or have the GED. Advanced placement tests are encouraged and accepted. High school preparation must include 4 years of English, 3 or more of math, 2 each of lab science and social studies, 2 of the same foreign language, and 2 of flexible academic units. A personal and professional essay is required. Visual arts applicants must submit a portfolio; performing arts applicants are required to audition. AP credits are accepted. Important factors in the admissions decision are advanced placement or honors courses, evidence of special talent, and geographical diversity. All students must demonstrate satisfactory proficiency in the use of the English and 6 hours each in approved composition classes, Western/non-Western cultural studies, arts and humanities, social sciences/behavior, natural sciences/technology, and quantitative reasoning. Successful completion of either the third or fourth year (depending on college) of a language other than the student's primary language is required. Students must maintain a minimum GPA of 2.0 while completing 120 to 132 credit hours (depending on the major) in order to graduate. **Procedure:** Freshmen are admitted fall. Applications should be filed by December 1 for fall entry. The fall 2014 application fee was $50. Notifications are sent February 13. Applications are accepted on-line. **Transfer Students:** 1343 transfer students enrolled in 2013-2014. Transfer application requirements differ by degree program. Transfer requirements by program can be viewed in the Transfer Handbook on the Admissions website. Admission is also subject to the number of places available. 30 of 132 credits required for the bachelor's degree must be completed at Illinois. **International Students:** There are 5031 international students enrolled. The school actively recruits these students. They must take the TOEFL with a minimum score of 550 on the paper-based TOEFL (PBT) or 79 on the Internet-based version (iBT) They must also take the SAT and ACT, if the student has attended a U.S. institution for 2 or more years.

ADMISSIONS: There were 54 National Merit finalists. 9 freshmen graduated first in their class. **Admissions Contact:** Mike Drish, Director of Undergraduate Admissions. E-Mail: *admissions@illinois.edu* Web: *www.illinois.edu/admissions*

FINANCIAL AID: The FAFSA is required. Check with the school for current application deadlines.

UNIVERSITY OF ST. FRANCIS   E-2
www.stfrancis.edu

Joliet, IL 60435   (815) 740-3400
                                              (800) 735-7500

Fax: (815) 740-5032	Email: admissions@stfrancis.edu
Full-time: 474 men, 842 women	Faculty: 80
Part-time: 22 men, 41 women	Ph.D.s: 69%
Graduate: 217 men, 816 women	Student/Faculty: 14 to 1
Year: semesters, summer session	Tuition: $28,790
Room & Board: $8770	Freshman Class: 1509 applied, 763 accepted, 216 enrolled
ACT: 23	CEEB CODE: 1130
Application Deadline: August 1	COMPETITIVE

The University of St. Francis, founded as a college in 1920, is a private liberal arts and professional institution affiliated with the Roman Catholic Church. Figures in the above capsule and in this profile are approximate. There are 4 undergraduate schools and 4 graduate schools. In addition to regional accreditation, USF has baccalaureate program accreditation with ACBSP, CSWE, NCATE, NRPA, ARCPA, and CCNE. The 34-acre campus is in a suburban area 35 miles southwest of Chicago. Including any residence halls, there are 7 buildings.

STUDENT LIFE: 94% of undergraduates are from Illinois. Others are from 15 states, and 11 foreign countries. 92% are from public schools. 68% are White; 17% Hispanic. 53% are Catholic; 27% Protestant. **Male To Female Ratio:** 2.4:1. The average age of freshmen is 18; all undergraduates, 22. 19% do not continue beyond their first year; 56% remain to graduate. **Housing:** 411 students can be accommodated in college housing, which includes coed dorms and on-campus apartments. On-campus housing is guaranteed for the freshman year only, is available on a first-come, first-served basis, and is available on a lottery system for upperclassmen. 74% of students commute. All students may keep cars.

FACULTY/CLASSROOMS: 41% of faculty are male; 59% are female. 77% teach undergraduates. No introductory courses are taught by graduate students. The average class size in an introductory lecture is 20 and in a laboratory is 20.

PROGRAMS OF STUDY: USF confers B.A., B.S., B.B.A., B.S.N and B.S.W. degrees. Master's and doctoral degrees are also awarded. Bachelor's degrees are awarded in BIOLOGICAL SCIENCE (biology/biological science), BUSINESS (accounting, banking and finance, business administration and management, entrepreneurial studies, international business management, logistics, management science, marketing/retailing/merchandising, organizational leadership and management, and recreational facilities management), COMMUNICATIONS AND THE ARTS (art and design, communications, English, journalism, music, music performance, and visual and performing arts), COMPUTER AND PHYSICAL SCIENCE (computer programming, computer science, information sciences and systems, mathematics, and web technology), EDUCATION (art education, elementary education, music education, secondary education, and special education), ENGINEERING AND ENVIRONMENTAL DESIGN (computer technology and environmental science), HEALTH PROFESSIONS (allied health, health administration and policy, health care administration, medical technology, nuclear medical technology, nursing, predentistry, premedicine, preoptometry, prepharmacy, prephysical therapy, preveterinary science, radiation therapy, and radiograph medical technology), SOCIAL SCIENCE (counseling/psychology, criminal justice, history, liberal arts/general studies, political science/government, psychology, social work, and theological studies). Biology, education, and nursing are the strongest academically. Business, nursing, and biology have the largest enrollments.

ACTIVITIES: There are no fraternities; 2% of women belong to 1 national sorority. There are 56 groups on campus, including and saints ambassador corps, business, nursing, art, cheerleading, choir, chorale, chorus, communications, computers, dance, drama, education, environmental, ethnic, gay, honors, international, literary magazine, musical theater, newspaper, opera, orchestra, pep band, political, professional, radio and TV, religious, social, social service, student government, and symphony. Popular campus events include Exchanging Cultures, Spring Fling, Homecoming, Dogeball Tournament, and Talent Show. **Sports:** There are 9 intercollegiate sports for men and 9 for women, and 10 intramural sports for men and 10 for women. Facilities include a 10,000-seat football/soccer stadium with a Mondo-surface track around the turfed field and a 5,000-seat minor league baseball stadium are among the many off-campus facilities, as well as a six-field, lighted softball complex, three golf courses, two soccer fields and an indoor/outdoor tennis complex. On campus, a recreation center houses a 1,200-seat gymnasium, 1 racquetball court, a golf hitting studio, and a state-of-the-art fitness center. **Graduates:** From July 1, 2013 to June 30, 2014, 336 bachelor's degrees were awarded. The most popular majors were nursing (22%), education (16%), and business (14%). 94 companies recruited on campus in 2013-2014. In an average class, 38% graduate in 4 years or less, 55% graduate in 5 years or less, and 56% graduate in 6 years or less.

SERVICES: Counseling and information services are available, as is tutoring in most subjects. There is a reader service for the blind. **Library/Resources:** The library contains 143,421 volumes, 1,767 microform items, 9,026 audio/video tapes/CDs/DVDs, and subscribes to 20,711 periodicals including electronic. Computerized library services include interlibrary loans, database searching, Internet access, and Wi-Fi capability. Special learning facilities include an art gallery, radio station, TV station, a greenhouse, wireless education classroom, SimLab for nursing students, multimedia classrooms, mock trail courtroom in the mode building, and the Rialto square theater building. **Physically Challenged Students:** All of the campus is accessible. Facilities include wheelchair ramps, elevators, special parking, specially equipped restrooms, special class scheduling, lowered drinking fountains, and special housing. **Special:** Internships, on- and off-campus, paid and unpaid, are available in most majors. Dual and interdisciplinary majors, a pass/fail option, a Washington semester, study abroad, cross-registration with OCICU (Online Consortium of Independent Colleges and Universities), and credit for life, military, and work experience are available. There are 16 national honor societies and a freshman honors program. **Visiting:** There are regularly scheduled orientations for prospective students, visiting students can participate in an orientation, meet faculty, a tour, and student presentations. There are guides for informal visits, visitors may sit in on classes, and stay overnight. To schedule a visit, contact the USF Welcome Center at (815) 740-2270. **Campus Safety and Security:** Measures include 24-hour foot and vehicle patrol, emergency notification system, and security escort services. There are shuttle buses, emergency telephones, lighted pathways/sidewalks, controlled access to dorms/residences, routine fire inspection.

REQUIREMENTS: The ACT is required. Applicants must take 4 years of English, 3 of either art, music, foreign language, or computer science, and 3 math, including geometry, 2 science (1 lab), 2 social studies and 3 electives. USF requires applicants to be in the upper 50% of their class. A GPA of 2.5 is required. AP and CLEP credits are accepted. Important factors in the admissions decision are leadership record, advanced placement or honors courses, and personality/intangible qualities. Candidates for the bachelor's degree must complete the following: complete the Application for Graduation available in the Registrar's Office or through the MyUSF portal (Consult the Academic Calendar for specific deadlines), earn a minimum of 128 semester hours of college credit, complete the residency requirement of a minimum of 32 semester hours of approved undergraduate credit at USF. All students must complete a minimum of fifteen (15) hours of upper division (300-400) course work, in the major, in residence at USF. In addition, thirty (30) of the last thirty-six (36) hours taken before graduation must be USF courses. (Note: individual colleges may have additional residency requirements), complete all requirements with respect to the major program, support courses, liberal education, and electives, complete the writing intensive (WI) course requirements as listed below, achieve a cumulative grade point average of 2.0 or higher at USF, earn grades of "C" or higher in all courses required by the major and any minor programs, satisfy all financial requirements with the Business and Financial Aid Offices. It is the responsibility of the student to see that all graduation requirements are met. If a student withdraws for more than one semester, the catalog and regulations in effect at the time of their return will apply. Students completing a double major must select which degree

they wish to receive since the University only awards one degree at graduation (however, the second major will appear on the transcript). If a student returns to complete a second major, they may apply for a second degree only if the new major leads to a different degree and they have met the current general education requirements in place at the time of awarding. **Procedure:** Freshmen are admitted fall and spring. Entrance exams should be taken in the spring of the junior year or the fall of the senior year. There are deferred admissions and rolling admissions plans. Applications should be filed by August 1 for fall entry. Notifications are sent September 15. Applications are accepted on-line. **Transfer Students:** 174 transfer students enrolled in 2013-2014. Transfer students must have a GPA of 2.5 and must submit transcripts from colleges previously attended. Applicants with fewer than 30 semester hours must also submit high school transcripts. Applicants must have taken English at the college level, and math at the intermediate algebra level. 32 of 128 credits required for the bachelor's degree must be completed at USF. **International Students:** There are 25 international students enrolled. The school actively recruits these students. They must take the TOEFL with a minimum score of 550 on the paper-based TOEFL (PBT) or 79 on the Internet-based version (iBT). They must also take the SAT or ACT, scoring 20.

ADMISSIONS: 51% of the 2014-2015 applicants were accepted. The SAT scores for the 2014-2015 freshman class were: Critical Reading--50% below 500, 36% between 500 and 599, and 14% between 600 and 699; Math--50% below 500, 43% between 500 and 599, and 7% between 600 and 699; Writing--71% below 500, 22% between 500 and 599, and 7% between 700 and 800. The ACT scores were 24% below 21, 33% between 21 and 23, 27% between 24 and 26, 7% between 27 and 28, and 8% above 28. 32% of the current freshmen were in the top fifth of their class; 67% were in the top two fifths. **Admissions Contact:** Cynthia Lambert, Director of Undergraduate Admissions. E-Mail: *admissions@stfrancis.edu* Web: *www.stfrancis.edu*

FINANCIAL AID: In 2014-2015, 99% of all full-time freshmen and continuing full-time students received some form of financial aid. 84% of all full-time freshmen and continuing full-time students received need-based aid. The average freshman award was $25,881. Need-based scholarships or need-based grants averaged $9,629 need-based self-help aid (loans and jobs) averaged $5,546; non-need-based athletic scholarships averaged $12,575; and other non-need-based awards and non-need-based scholarships averaged $10,201. The average financial indebtedness of the 2014 graduate was $29,418. The FAFSA and the college's own financial statement are required. The priority date for freshman financial aid applications for fall entry is February 15.

VANDERCOOK COLLEGE OF MUSIC (*The complete profile is made available exclusively on our website, www.barronspac.com*)

WESTERN ILLINOIS UNIVERSITY   C-3
www.wiu.edu

Macomb, IL 61455	(309) 298-3157
	(877) PICK WIU
Fax: (309) 298-3111	Email: admissions@wiu.edu
Full-time: 4347 men, 4260 women	Faculty: 589; IIA, av$
Part-time: 544 men, 494 women	Ph.D.s: 68%
Graduate: 721 men, 1092 women	Student/Faculty: 15 to 1
Year: semesters, summer session	Tuition: $11,282 ($15,598)
Room & Board: $9450	Freshman Class: 10671 applied, 7431 accepted, 1605 enrolled
SAT: required ACT: 22	CEEB CODE: 1900
Application Deadline: May 15	COMPETITIVE

WIU-Macomb, founded in 1902, a traditional, residential four-year campus. WIU-Quad Cities, a metropolitan, non-residential campus and the only public university in the Quad Cities, has been providing educational opportunities to the region for more than 50 years. There are 5 undergraduate schools and one graduate school. In addition to regional accreditation, WIU has baccalaureate program accreditation with AACSB, ABET, ADA, ASLA, CSWE, NASAD, NASM, NCATE,

NRPA, ATMAE, ACCGC, and NAST. The 1050-acre campus is in a rural area 76 miles from Peoria, IL 83 miles from Springfield, IL and 151 miles from St. Louis, Missouri. Including any residence halls, there are 64 buildings.

STUDENT LIFE: 85% of undergraduates are from Illinois. Others are from 35 states, 55 foreign countries, and Canada. 81% are from public schools. 66% are White; 17% African American. **Male To Female Ratio:** 1.0:1. The average age of freshmen is 18; all undergraduates, 22. 28% do not continue beyond their first year; 54% remain to graduate. **Housing:** 4400 students can be accommodated in college housing, which includes single-sex and coed dorms, on-campus apartments, and married student housing. In addition, there are honors houses, special-interest houses, Academic majors, honors, and wellness floors in residence halls. On-campus housing is guaranteed for all 4 years. 59% of students commute. Alcohol is not permitted. All students may keep cars.

FACULTY/CLASSROOMS: 55% of faculty are male; 45% are female. 91% teach undergraduates, 90% do research, and 90% do both. Graduate students teach 3% of introductory courses. The average class size in an introductory lecture is 27; in a laboratory is 20; and in a regular course is 19.

PROGRAMS OF STUDY: WIU confers B.A., B.B., B.F.A, B.M., B.S., B.S.Ed. and B.S.W degrees. Master's and Doctoral degrees are also awarded. Bachelor's degrees are awarded in AGRICULTURE (agriculture and animal science), BIOLOGICAL SCIENCE (forensic science), BUSINESS (accounting, business administration and management, business administration marketing, finance, human resources/organizational mgmt, marketing, and supply chain management), COMMUNICATIONS AND THE ARTS (art, broadcasting, communication, English, foreign language, graphic communications, information technology, journalism, music, musical theater, Spanish, and theatre arts), COMPUTER AND PHYSICAL SCIENCE (chemistry, clinical laboratory science, computer science, geology, mathematics, and physics), EDUCATION (agricultural education, art education, bilingual/bicultural education, elementary education, museum studies, physical education, and special education), ENGINEERING AND ENVIRONMENTAL DESIGN (construction management, emergency/disaster science, engineering, engineering technology, and instructional design), HEALTH PROFESSIONS (biology, exercise science, health administration and policy, health science, nursing, and public health), SOCIAL SCIENCE (African American studies, anthropology, communication sciences and disorders, criminal justice, economics, family/consumer studies, fire protection, geography, history, history and political science, interdisciplinary studies, law enforcement and corrections, liberal arts, sciences, general studies, humanities, parks and recreation management, philosophy, psychology, religious studies, social work, sociology, and women's studies). Law enforcement, biology, agriculture, and elementary education are the strongest academically. Law enforcement, justice administration, general studies, and biology have the largest enrollments.

ACTIVITIES: 6% of men belong to 19 national fraternities; 6% of women belong to 10 national sororities. There are 270 groups on campus, including art, band, cheerleading, chess, choir, chorale, chorus, communications, computers, dance, drama, drill team, environmental, ethnic, gay, honors, international, jazz band, literary magazine, marching band, musical theater, newspaper, opera, orchestra, pep band, photography, political, professional, radio and TV, religious, social, social service, student government, and symphony. Popular campus events include Family Weekend, Homecoming Weekend, and International Bazaar. **Sports:** There are 10 intercollegiate sports for men and 10 for women, and 40 intramural sports for men and 40 for women. Facilities include an 18-hole golf course, tennis courts, basketball court, swimming pool, recreation center, softball, soccer, and football fields. **Graduates:** From July 1, 2013 to June 30, 2014, 2217 bachelor's degrees were awarded. The most popular majors were law enforcement and justice (17%), bachelor of general studies (12%), and agriculture (5%). 225 companies recruited on campus in 2013-2014. In an average class, 29% graduate in 4 years or less, 51% graduate in 5 years or less, and 56% graduate in 6 years or less.

SERVICES: Counseling and information services are available, as is tutoring in some subjects, business, art, English, math, computer science, science, social sciences, and humanities There is a reader service for the blind, and remedial math and writing. **Library/Resources:** The 5 libraries contain 1.0 million volumes, 112,108 microform items, 22,603 audio/video tapes/CDs/DVDs, and subscribe to 5,000 periodicals including electronic. Computerized library services include interlibrary loans, database searching, Internet access, and Wi-Fi capability. Special learning facilities include an art gallery, natural history museum, radio station, TV station, and international studies center. **Physically Challenged Students:** 95% of the campus is accessible. Facilities include wheelchair ramps, elevators, special parking, specially equipped restrooms, special class scheduling, lowered drinking fountains, and lowered telephones. **Special:** WIU offers internships in business, law enforcement, and physical training to name a few; study abroad group and exchange programs; and dual programs in engineering and clinical laboratory science. Student-designed majors and independent study are available through the General Studies and Interdisciplinary Studies programs. The General Studies degree program offers credit for work experience. Also available are a field campus and a life science station on the Mississippi River. There are 30 national honor societies, a freshman honors program, and 34 departmental honors programs. **Visiting:** There are regularly scheduled orientations for prospective students, consisting of registration, continental breakfast, university fair, program and Q/A, tours, meet with an advisor, lunch and residence hall tour, and financial aid session. There are guides for informal visits, visitors may sit in on classes, and stay overnight. To schedule a visit, contact the Admissions Office at admissions@wiu.edu. **Campus Safety and Security:** Measures include 24-hour foot and vehicle patrol, emergency notification system, self-defense education, and security escort services. There are shuttle buses, emergency telephones, lighted pathways/sidewalks, A beacon/call box system, and student patrols.

REQUIREMENTS: The SAT or ACT is required. Students must have 4 years of English, 3 years each of math, science, and social studies, and 2 electives in art, film, foreign language, music, speech, theater, journalism, religion, philosophy, or vocational education. Academic Services is a program for selected students who do not meet regular admission requirements. A GPA of 2.2 is required. AP and CLEP credits are accepted. To graduate, all students must complete at least 120 credit hours with at least 32 hours in the major and have a minimum 2.0 GPA. Students must take 43 hours in the fields of basic skills, well-being, natural science and math, historical and social foundations, and humanities. **Procedure:** Freshmen are admitted fall, spring, and summer. Entrance exams should be taken by April of the senior year. There are deferred admissions and rolling admissions plans. Applications should be filed by May 15 for fall entry, along with a $30 fee. Applications are accepted on-line. **Transfer Students:** 1243 transfer students enrolled in 2013-2014. Students transferring fewer than 24 semester credits or 36 quarter credits must meet freshman admissions standards, have a combined C average for all hours attempted, and be in good standing at their previous college. 30 of 120 credits required for the bachelor's degree must be completed at WIU. **International Students:** There are 212 international students enrolled. The school actively recruits these students. They must take the TOEFL with a minimum score of 550 on the paper-based TOEFL (PBT) or 79 on the Internet-based version (iBT), or successfully complete WIU's ESL program.

ADMISSIONS: 70% of the 2014-2015 applicants were accepted. The ACT scores were 54% below 21, 26% between 21 and 23, 13% between 24 and 26, 4% between 27 and 28, and 4% above 28. 21% of the current freshmen were in the top fifth of their class; 49% were in the top two fifths. **Admissions Contact:** Office of Admissions E-Mail: *admissions@wiu.edu* Web*http://www.wiu.edu/student_services/ undergraduate_admissions/*

FINANCIAL AID: In 2014-2015, 92% of all full-time freshmen and 87% of continuing full-time students received some form of financial aid. 72% of all full-time freshmen and 65% of continuing full-time students received need-based aid. The average freshman award was $15,030. Need-based scholarships or need-based grants averaged $5,826; need-based self-help aid (loans and jobs) averaged $3,005; non-need-based athletic scholarships averaged $312; other non-need-based awards and non-need-based scholarships averaged $1,900; and $3,987 from other forms of aid. 18% of undergraduate students work part-time. Average annual earnings from campus work are $1975.

The average financial indebtedness of the 2014 graduate was $25,000. The priority date for freshman financial aid applications for fall entry is February 15. The deadline for filing freshman financial aid applications for fall entry is open.

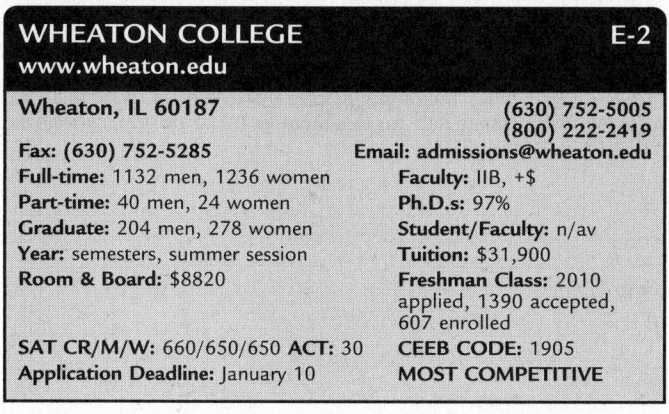

Wheaton College, founded in 1860, is a private nondenominational institution committed to providing students with a Christian education. A liberal arts school, it offers undergraduate programs in the sciences, business, the arts and fine arts, music, teacher preparation, and religious and Biblical studies. There is 1 undergraduate school and 1 graduate school. In addition to regional accreditation, Wheaton has baccalaureate program accreditation with NASM and NCATE. The 80-acre campus is in a suburban area 25 miles west of Chicago. Including any residence halls, there are 69 buildings.

STUDENT LIFE: 74% of undergraduates are from out of state, mostly the Midwest. Students are from 50 states, 39 foreign countries, and Canada. 49% are from public schools. 75% are White. 99% are Protestant. The average age of freshmen is 18; all undergraduates, 20. 7% do not continue beyond their first year; 89% remain to graduate.

Housing: 2148 students can be accommodated in college housing, which includes single-sex and coed dorms, on-campus apartments, off-campus apartments, and married student housing. In addition, the college owns and rents houses to groups of students. On-campus housing is guaranteed for all 4 years, is available on a first-come, first-served basis, and is available on a lottery system for upperclassmen. 90% of students live on campus; of those, 95% remain on campus on weekends. Alcohol is not permitted. Upperclassmen may keep cars.

FACULTY/CLASSROOMS: 62% of faculty are male; 38% are female. All teach and do research. No introductory courses are taught by graduate students. The average class size in an introductory lecture is 31; in a laboratory is 16; and in a regular course is 21.

PROGRAMS OF STUDY: Wheaton confers B.A., B.S., B.M. and B.M.E. degrees. Master's and Doctoral degrees are also awarded. Bachelor's degrees are awarded in BIOLOGICAL SCIENCE (biology/biological science), BUSINESS (business economics), COMMUNICATIONS AND THE ARTS (art, classical languages, communications, English, French, German, music, and Spanish), COMPUTER AND PHYSICAL SCIENCE (applied mathematics, chemistry, computer science, geology, mathematics, and physics), EDUCATION (Christian education, elementary education, music education, and secondary education), ENGINEERING AND ENVIRONMENTAL DESIGN (engineering and environmental science), HEALTH PROFESSIONS (health science and nursing), SOCIAL SCIENCE (anthropology, archeology, biblical studies, economics, history, interdisciplinary studies, international relations, philosophy, political science/government, psychology, social science, sociology, and urban studies). Business economics, and English have the largest enrollments.

ACTIVITIES: There are 94 groups on campus, including art, band, cheerleading, chess, choir, chorale, chorus, dance, debate, drama, environmental, ethnic, film, international, jazz band, literary magazine, musical theater, newspaper, opera, orchestra, pep band, political, professional, radio and TV, religious, social, social service, student government, symphony, and yearbook. Popular campus events include New Student Orientation, College Union Concerts and Talent Show. **Sports:** There are 11 intercollegiate sports for men and 10 for women, and 10 intramural sports for men and 9 for women. Facilities include A sports and recreation complex that features an 8,000-square-foot weight room, 3 student recreational gyms, an elevated jogging track, a climbing wall, recreation center, natatorium, and the King Arena. **Graduates:** From July 1, 2013 to June 30, 2014, 628 bachelor's degrees were awarded. The most popular majors were business economics (12%), English (7%), and biology (7%). 28 companies recruited on campus in 2013-2014. In an average class, 80% graduate in 4 years or less, 88% graduate in 5 years or less, and 89% graduate in 6 years or less. Of the 2013 graduating class, 32% were enrolled in graduate school within 6 months of graduation, and 70% were employed.

SERVICES: Counseling and information services are available, as is tutoring in most subjects. There is a reader service for the blind. Other services are provided as needed. **Library/Resources:** The library contains 476,521 volumes, 156,468 microform items, 35,029 audio/video tapes/CDs/DVDs, and subscribes to 6,251 periodicals including electronic. Computerized library services include interlibrary loans, database searching, Internet access, and Wi-Fi capability. Special learning facilities include an art gallery, radio station, TV station, a communications resource center with TV and audio studios, a special collection of British authors' books and papers, an evangelical museum with document archives, and the Center for Applied Christian Ethics. The Science Building includes A unique, interactive atrium museum featuring the Perry Mastodon, a geology exhibit, a natural history exhibit, a Foucault pendulum, and additional exhibits. **Physically Challenged Students:** 97% of the campus is accessible. Facilities include wheelchair ramps, elevators, special parking, specially equipped restrooms, lowered drinking fountains, lowered telephones. including housing for disabled students is provided as needed. **Special:** There are 12 national honor societies and 15 departmental honors programs. **Visiting:** There are regularly scheduled orientations for prospective students, consisting of presentations by faculty, administrators, students, and financial aid, and admissions staff, as well as social activities. There are guides for informal visits, visitors may sit in on classes, and stay overnight. To schedule a visit, contact the Admissions Office at admissions@wheaton.edu. **Campus Safety and Security:** Measures include 24-hour foot and vehicle patrol, emergency notification system, self-defense education, and security escort services. There are shuttle buses, emergency telephones, lighted pathways/sidewalks, and controlled access to dorms/residences.

REQUIREMENTS: The SAT or ACT is required. A high school diploma is required and the GED is accepted. Wheaton requires a general college preparatory program of 15 units, including 4 of English, 3 to 4 of math, science, and social studies, and 2 to 3 of a foreign language. AP credits are accepted. Important factors in the admissions decision are recommendations by school officials, advanced placement or honors courses, and personality/intangible qualities. To graduate, students must complete 124 semester hours, with 36 in upper-division courses and a minimum of 32 in a major, and maintain at least a 2.0 GPA. Students must satisfactorily meet all general education requirements in the areas of competency, Applied Health Science, and five learning clusters that include Studies in Faith and Reason, Nature, Society, Diversity, and Literature and the Arts; as well as a senior capstone course in the major. **Procedure:** Freshmen are admitted fall and spring. Entrance exams should be taken in October of senior year (early action) and December. There are early admissions and deferred admissions plans. Applications should be filed by January 10 for fall entry, along with a $50 fee. Notifications are sent April 1. 149 applicants were on the 2014 waiting list; 64 were admitted. Applications are accepted on-line. **Transfer Students:** 75 transfer students enrolled in 2013-2014. Applicants must have completed 15 semester hours with a 3.0 average and present a high school transcript, college transcript, and an essay or personal statement. 48 of 124 credits required for the bachelor's degree must be completed at Wheaton. **International Students:** There are 62 international students enrolled. The school actively recruits these students. They must take the TOEFL with a minimum score of 587 on the paper-based TOEFL (PBT) or 95 on the Internet-based version (iBT), and also take the TSE and TWE. They must also take the SAT or ACT.

ADMISSIONS: 69% of the 2014-2015 applicants were accepted. The

SAT scores for the 2014-2015 freshman class were: Critical Reading--2% below 500, 20% between 500 and 599, 43% between 600 and 699, and 34% between 700 and 800; Math--4% below 500, 23% between 500 and 599, 46% between 600 and 699, and 27% between 700 and 800; Writing--5% below 500, 17% between 500 and 599, 51% between 600 and 699, and 27% between 700 and 800. 68% of the current freshmen were in the top fifth of their class; 90% were in the top two fifths. There were 21 National Merit finalists. **Admissions Contact:** Ms. Shawn Leftwich, Director of Admissions. E-Mail: *admissions@wheaton.edu* Web: *www.wheaton.edu*

FINANCIAL AID: In 2014-2015, 84% of all full-time freshmen and 73% of continuing full-time students received some form of financial aid. 54% of all full-time freshmen and 51% of continuing full-time students received need-based aid. The average freshman award was $24,910. Need-based scholarships or need-based grants averaged $20,772 ($44,197 maximum); need-based self-help aid (loans and jobs) averaged $4,369 ($7,500 maximum); and other non-need-based awards and non-need-based scholarships averaged $5,668 ($43,929 maximum). 50% of undergraduate students work part-time. Average annual earnings from campus work are $1200. The average financial indebtedness of the 2014 graduate was $25,939. Wheaton is a member of CSS. The FAFSA and the college's own financial statement are required. The priority date for freshman financial aid applications for fall entry is February 15.

INDIANA

College Location

0   20   40   60   80   100
Miles

ANDERSON UNIVERSITY

www.anderson.edu

C-3

Anderson, IN 46012

(765) 641-4080
(800) 428-6414

Fax: (765) 641-4091
Full-time: 683 men, 991 women
Part-time: 104 men, 196 women
Graduate: 242 men, 181 women
Year: semesters, summer session
Room & Board: $9250

Email: info@anderson.edu
Faculty: 131; IIB, -$
Ph.D.s: 70%
Student/Faculty: 11 to 1
Tuition: $26,850
Freshman Class: 2659 applied, 1460 accepted, 441 enrolled

SAT CR/M: 515/514 **ACT:** 23
Application Deadline: open

CEEB CODE: 1016
COMPETITIVE

Anderson University, founded in 1917, is a private liberal arts institution affiliated with the Church of God. The university offers programs in theoretical and applied science, social and professional studies, the arts, culture, and religion. Figures in the above capsule and in this profile are approximate. There are 5 undergraduate schools and 4 graduate schools. In addition to regional accreditation, Anderson has baccalaureate program accreditation with ACBSP, CSWE, NASM, NCATE, and NLN. The 163-acre campus is in a suburban area 40 miles northeast of Indianapolis. Including any residence halls, there are 36 buildings.

STUDENT LIFE: 74% of undergraduates are from Indiana. Others are from 40 states, 20 foreign countries, and Canada. 97% are from public schools. 77% are White. 52% are Protestant; 45% claim no religious affiliation. **Male To Female Ratio:** 1.3:1. The average age of freshmen is 19; all undergraduates, 22. 27% do not continue beyond their first year; 57% remain to graduate. **Housing:** 1217 students can be accommodated in college housing, which includes single-sex dorms, on-campus apartments, off-campus apartments, and married student housing. On-campus housing is guaranteed for all 4 years. 60% of students live on campus; of those, 50% remain on campus on weekends. Alcohol is not permitted. All students may keep cars.

FACULTY/CLASSROOMS: 60% of faculty are male; 40% are female. 94% teach undergraduates. No introductory courses are taught by graduate students. The average class size in an introductory lecture is 24; in a laboratory is 17; and in a regular course is 17.

PROGRAMS OF STUDY: Anderson confers B.A., B.S., B.Mus., B.S.N. and B.S.E. degrees. Associate, Master's, and Doctoral degrees are also awarded. Bachelor's degrees are awarded in BIOLOGICAL SCIENCE (biology/biological science), BUSINESS (accounting, banking and finance, business administration and management, management science, marketing/retailing/merchandising, and sports management), COMMUNICATIONS AND THE ARTS (communications, dramatic arts, English, fine arts, French, graphic design, music business management, music performance, and Spanish), COMPUTER AND PHYSICAL SCIENCE (chemistry, computer science, mathematics, and physics), EDUCATION (art education, Christian education, elementary education, foreign languages education, health education, music education, physical education, science education, and social studies education), HEALTH PROFESSIONS (medical laboratory technology and nursing), SOCIAL SCIENCE (criminal justice, economics, family/consumer studies, history, philosophy, political science/government, psychology, religion, social work, and sociology). Physical sciences is the strongest academically. Business, education and nursing have the largest enrollments.

ACTIVITIES: There are no fraternities or sororities. There are 41 groups on campus, including art, band, cheerleading, choir, chorale, dance, debate, drama, ethnic, film, honors, international, jazz band, literary magazine, musical theater, newspaper, opera, orchestra, photography, political, professional, radio and TV, religious, social, social service, student government, and symphony. Popular campus events include Heritage Week, Spiritual Emphasis Week, Candles and Carols Christmas Performance. **Sports:** There are 8 intercollegiate sports for men and 8 for women, and 7 intramural sports for men and 7 for women. Facilities include 2 gyms, football, baseball/softball, and soccer fields, an 8-lane all-weather track, tennis courts, bowling alley, and a game room. The campus stadium seats 4200 and the indoor gym seats 2400. **Graduates:** From July 1, 2013 to June 30, 2014, 426 bachelor's degrees were awarded. The most popular majors were business/marketing (24%), education (13%), and health professions and related programs (10%). 35 companies recruited on campus in 2013-2014. In an average class, 46% graduate in 4 years or less, 56% graduate in 5 years or less, and 57% graduate in 6 years or less.

SERVICES: Counseling and information services are available, as is tutoring in most subjects. There is a reader service for the blind, and remedial math, reading, and writing. **Library/Resources:** The library contains 332,571 volumes, 38,706 microform items, 3,656 audio/video tapes/CDs/DVDs, and subscribes to 457 periodicals including electronic. Computerized library services include interlibrary loans and database searching. Special learning facilities include an art gallery, radio station, the Museum of the Bible and the Ancient Near East. **Physically Challenged Students:** 97% of the campus is accessible. Facilities include wheelchair ramps, elevators, special parking, specially equipped restrooms, special class scheduling, lowered drinking fountains, and lowered telephones. **Special:** Anderson offers co-op programs with Purdue University, internships, study abroad in 25 countries through the International Studies Program, and a Washington semester. Also available are credit for military experience and pass/fail options. Courses in electronic engineering may be taken through the Purdue Anderson campus. Preprofessional programs are offered in medical, podiatry, dentistry, law, engineering, seminary, and several allied health fields. There are 16 national honor societies, a freshman honors program, and 10 departmental honors programs. **Visiting:** There are regularly scheduled orientations for prospective students, including a campus tour, an academic overview, a financial aid and athletics overview, and appointments with professors and departmental chairs. There are guides for informal visits, visitors may sit in on classes, and stay overnight. To schedule a visit, contact the Admissions Office. **Campus Safety and Security:** Measures include 24-hour foot and vehicle patrol, emergency notification system, self-defense education, and security escort services. There are emergency telephones, lighted pathways/sidewalks, Indiana State police academy graduates are security officers.

REQUIREMENTS: The SAT or ACT is required. Applicants must be graduates of an accredited secondary school or have a GED certificate and submit a photograph, references, and a health form. A GPA of 2.0 is required. AP and CLEP credits are accepted. Important factors in the admissions decision are leadership record, recommendations by alumni, and personality/intangible qualities. Requirements for graduation include 120 credit hours with 40 to 58 hours in the general education core and at least 36 hours in the major. A minimum 2.0 GPA overall and in the major is required. All students must complete a liberal arts seminar. The last 24 credit hours must be taken in residence. **Procedure:** Freshmen are admitted fall and spring. Entrance exams should be taken in the fall of the junior year. There is a rolling admissions plan. Application deadlines are open. Application fee is $25. Applications are accepted online. **Transfer Students:** 98 transfer students enrolled in 2013-2014. Applicants must have a minimum 2.0 GPA, satisfactory SAT or ACT scores, and transcripts for all previously attended colleges. 24 of 120 credits required for the bachelor's degree must be completed at Anderson. **International Students:** There are 54 international students enrolled. They must take the TOEFL with a minimum score of 547 on the paper-based TOEFL (PBT) or 78 on the Internet-based version (iBT). They must also take the SAT.

ADMISSIONS: 55% of the 2014-2015 applicants were accepted. The SAT scores for the 2014-2015 freshman class were: Critical Reading--43% below 500, 39% between 500 and 599, 15% between 600 and 699, and 3% between 700 and 800; Math--41% below 500, 41% between 500 and 599, 16% between 600 and 699, and 2% between 700 and 800. The ACT scores were 23% below 21, 30% between 21 and 23, 27% between 24 and 26, 9% between 27 and 28, and 11% above 28. 44% of the current freshmen were in the top fifth of their class; 72% were in the top two fifths. 8 freshmen graduated first in their class. **Admissions Contact:** Admissions Counselor E-Mail: *info@anderson.edu* Web: *www.anderson.edu*

FINANCIAL AID: Anderson is a member of CSS. The FAFSA is required. Check with the school for current application deadlines.

BALL STATE UNIVERSITY D-3
www.bsu.edu

Muncie, IN 47306	(765) 285-8300
	(800) 482-4BSU
Fax: (765) 285-1632	Email: askus@.bsu.edu
Full-time: 6711 men, 8886 women	Faculty: 949; I
Part-time: 447 men, 608 women	Ph.Ds: 73%
Graduate: 1409 men, 2992 women	Student/Faculty: 16 to 1
Year: semesters, summer session	Tuition: $8980 ($23,650)
Room & Board: $8870	Freshman Class: 14302 applied, 9659 accepted, 3844 enrolled
SAT CR/M/W: 530/530/510 ACT: 22	CEEB CODE: 1051
Application Deadline: May 1	COMPETITIVE

Ball State University, founded in 1918, is a public university offering undergraduate and graduate programs through 7 academic colleges in applied sciences and technology, architecture and planning, business, communication, information, and media, fine arts, sciences and humanities, and teacher education. There are 7 undergraduate schools and 1 graduate school. In addition to regional accreditation, Ball State has baccalaureate program accreditation with AACSB, ABET, ACBSP, ACEJMC, ADA, AHEA, ASLA, CAHEA, CSAB, CSWE, NAAB, NASAD, NASM, NCATE, NLN, and TEAC. The 1140-acre campus is in a suburban area 56 miles northwest of Indianapolis. Including any residence halls, there are 106 buildings.

STUDENT LIFE: 90% of undergraduates are from Indiana. Others are from 50 states, 44 foreign countries, and Canada. 91% are from public schools. 85% are White. **Male To Female Ratio:** 1.5:1. The average age of freshmen is 18; all undergraduates, 20. **Housing:** 6906 students can be accommodated in college housing, which includes single-sex and coed dorms, on-campus apartments, and married student housing. In addition, there are honors houses, special-interest houses, living learning communities, wellness housing. On-campus housing is guaranteed for the freshman year only. 58% of students commute. Alcohol is not permitted. All students may keep cars.

FACULTY/CLASSROOMS: 53% of faculty are male; 47% are female. No introductory courses are taught by graduate students.

PROGRAMS OF STUDY: Ball State confers B.A., B.S., B.F.A., B.G.S., B.Mus. and B.S.W. degrees. Associate, Master's, and Doctoral degrees are also awarded. Bachelor's degrees are awarded in AGRICULTURE (natural resource management), BIOLOGICAL SCIENCE (biology/biological science), BUSINESS (accounting, banking and finance, business administration and management, business economics, entrepreneurial studies, human resources, marketing/retailing/merchandising, operations management, and personnel management), COMMUNICATIONS AND THE ARTS (art, classical languages, classics, dance, dramatic arts, English, French, German, Japanese, journalism, music, radio/television technology, Spanish, and speech/debate/rhetoric), COMPUTER AND PHYSICAL SCIENCE (actuarial science, chemistry, computer science, geology, mathematics, and physics), EDUCATION (business education, early childhood education, education of the multiply handicapped, elementary education, health education, industrial arts education, library science, physical education, and science education), ENGINEERING AND ENVIRONMENTAL DESIGN (architecture, engineering, environmental design, graphic arts technology, industrial engineering technology, landscape architecture/design, preengineering, and urban planning technology), HEALTH PROFESSIONS (medical laboratory technology, medical technology, nursing, predentistry, premedicine, preoptometry, prepharmacy, preveterinary science, respiratory therapy, and speech pathology/audiology), SOCIAL SCIENCE (anthropology, criminal justice, dietetics, economics, family/consumer studies, geography, history, Latin American studies, liberal arts/general studies, philosophy, political science/government, prelaw, psychology, religion, social work, sociology, urban studies, and women's studies). Architecture, business and education are the strongest academically. Elementary education, business, radio and television have the largest enrollments.

ACTIVITIES: 10% of men belong to 15 national fraternities; 11% of women belong to 1 local and 16 national sororities. There are 369 groups on campus, including art, band, cheerleading, chess, choir, chorale, chorus, computers, dance, debate, drama, drill team, ethnic, film, forensics, gay, honors, international, jazz band, literary magazine, marching band, musical theater, newspaper, opera, orchestra, pep band, photography, political, professional, radio and TV, religious, social, social service, student government, and symphony. Popular campus events include Late Night Carnival, Unity Week and Family Weekend. **Sports:** Facilities include the student recreation/wellness facility, which holds a 13,000-sq-ft fitness center with elevated jogging track, a 5-court basketball/volleyball gym, a 33-ft climbing wall, indoor turf field including 2 batting cages, an auxiliary gym, a game room, 9 racquetball/handball and 2 wallyball courts, a 6-lane, 25-yd competitive pool, and a field sports building. There is also a fitness center, an 11,500-seat arena and a 22,500-seat stadium. **Graduates:** From July 1, 2013 to June 30, 2014, 3299 bachelor's degrees were awarded. The most popular majors were general studies (12%), telecommunications (8%), and elementary education (6%).

SERVICES: Counseling and information services are available, as is tutoring in most subjects. There is a reader service for the blind. **Library/Resources:** The 3 libraries contain 1.1 million volumes, 1.1 million microform items, and 433,494 audio/video tapes/CDs/DVDs, and subscribe to 2,944 periodicals including electronic. Computerized library services include interlibrary loans, database searching, Internet access, and Wi-Fi capability. Special learning facilities include an art gallery, planetarium, radio station, TV station, research centers in solar energy, human performance, and international programs. **Physically Challenged Students:** 95% of the campus is accessible. Facilities include wheelchair ramps, elevators, special parking, specially equipped restrooms, special class scheduling, lowered drinking fountains, lowered telephones, special housing, A special resource guide, an accessibility map (including tactile), and text telephones (TDD) in all key offices are also available. **Special:** Nearly all undergraduate disciplines offer internships, and work study is available. Study abroad is possible at the university's London center and in 20 other programs; students may also spend a semester in Washington, D.C. Most disciplines offer dual majors, and accelerated degrees are available. There is a B.A.-B.S. degree in elementary/special education, 3-2 program in engineering, an award-winning program in entrepreneurship, a general studies degree, nondegree study, and pass/fail options. There are 33 national honor societies and a freshman honors program. **Visiting:** There are regularly scheduled orientations for prospective students, consisting of twice-a-day presentations and tours . There are guides for informal visits and visitors may sit in on classes. To schedule a visit, contact the Visitors Desk at (765) 285-5683. **Campus Safety and Security:** Measures include 24-hour foot and vehicle patrol, emergency notification system, self-defense education, and security escort services. There are shuttle buses, emergency telephones, lighted pathways/sidewalks, and controlled access to dorms/residences.

REQUIREMENTS: Admission is a holistic review based on strength of applicants' curriculum, grades in English, math, lab scienes, social sciences, and foreign language, curricula patterns and grade trends, and the SAT or ACT scores. AP and CLEP credits are accepted.All students must take at least 120 credits and maintain a 2.0 GPA for graduation; required hours in the major vary by program. Required courses are in English composition, math, speech, history, personal finance, physical sciences, social or behavioral sciences, humanities or fine arts, global studies, and 2 hours of phys ed. In addition, all juniors must pass a writing proficiency exam. **Procedure:** Freshmen are admitted fall, spring, and summer. Entrance exams should be taken during the spring of the junior year or early in the senior year. There are deferred admissions and rolling admissions plans. Applications should be filed by May 1 for fall entry; December 1 for spring entry; and April 1 for summer entry, along with a $55 fee. Notification is sent on a rolling basis. Applications are accepted on-line.

Transfer Students: 684 transfer students enrolled in 2013-2014. Transfer applicants should have earned a 2.0 GPA on a 4.0 scale (as computed by Ball State) to be considered for admission. An official high school transcript or GED score report and official transcripts from each post-secondary institution are required. 60 of 126 credits required for the bachelor's degree must be completed at Ball State. **International Students:** There are 369 international students enrolled. The school actively recruits these students. They must take the TOEFL with a minimum score of 550 on the paper-based TOEFL (PBT) or 79 on the Internet-based version (iBT). The SAT or ACT is recommended.

ADMISSIONS: 68% of the 2014-2015 applicants were accepted. The SAT scores for the 2014-2015 freshman class were: Critical Reading--34% below 500, 47% between 500 and 599, 17% between 600 and 699, and 2% between 700 and 800; Math--33% below 500, 47% between 500 and 599, 19% between 600 and 699, and 1% between 700 and 800; Writing--41% below 500, 46% between 500 and 599, 12% between 600 and 699, and 1% between 700 and 800. **Admissions Contact:** Chris Munchel, Director of Admissions. E-Mail: *askus@.bsu .edu* Web: *www.bsu.edu*

FINANCIAL AID: In 2014-2015, 76% of all full-time freshmen and 78% of continuing full-time students received some form of financial aid. 48% of all full-time freshmen and 47% of continuing full-time students received need-based aid. The average freshman award was $10,271. Need-based scholarships or need-based grants averaged $5,638; need-based self-help aid (loans and jobs) averaged $3,703; non-need-based athletic scholarships averaged $18,410; and other non-need-based awards and non-need-based scholarships averaged $7,514. The average financial indebtedness of the 2014 graduate was $27,373. Ball State is a member of CSS. The FAFSA is required. The priority date for freshman financial aid applications for fall entry is March 1.

BETHEL COLLEGE   C-1
www.bethelcollege.edu

Mishawaka, IN 46545   (574) 807-7600
     (800) 422-4101
Fax: (574) 807-7650   Email: Andrea.Helmuth@BethelCollege.edu

Full-time: 499 men, 916 women	**Faculty:** 82; IIB
Part-time: 95 men, 291 women	**Ph.D.s:** 61%
Graduate: 78 men, 84 women	**Student/Faculty:** 17 to 1
Year: semesters, summer session	**Tuition:** $24,280
Room & Board: $7280	**Freshman Class:** 721 applied, 702 accepted, 225 enrolled
SAT CR/M/W: 510/510/490 **ACT:** 23	**CEEB CODE:** 1079
Application Deadline: n/av	**COMPETITIVE**

Bethel College, founded in 1947, is a private institution affiliated with the Missionary Church, offering a liberal arts education with a Christian perspective. There are 3 undergraduate schools and 1 graduate school. In addition to regional accreditation, Bethel has baccalaureate program accreditation with NASM, NCATE, and NLN. The 80-acre campus is in a suburban area Northern Indiana, adjacent to South Bend, 90 miles east of Chicago. Including any residence halls, there are 52 buildings.

STUDENT LIFE: 76% of undergraduates are from Indiana. Others are from 31 states, 15 foreign countries, and Canada. 81% are from public schools. 79% are White; 12% African American. 74% are Protestant; 18% claim no religious affiliation. **Male To Female Ratio:** 1.9:1. The average age of freshmen is 19; all undergraduates, 27. 25% do not continue beyond their first year; 60% remain to graduate. **Housing:** 863 students can be accommodated in college housing, which includes single-sex dorms, on-campus apartments, off-campus apartments, and married student housing. In addition, there are special-interest houses, cultural awareness house, missions house, and urban ministries house. On-campus housing is guaranteed for all 4 years. 55% of students commute. Alcohol is not permitted. Upperclassmen may keep cars.

FACULTY/CLASSROOMS: 55% of faculty are male; 45% are female. All teach undergraduates. No introductory courses are taught by graduate students. The average class size in an introductory lecture is 30; in a laboratory is 10; and in a regular course is 17.

PROGRAMS OF STUDY: Bethel confers B.A., B.S. and B.S.N. degrees. Associate and Master's degrees are also awarded. Bachelor's degrees are awarded in BIOLOGICAL SCIENCE (biology/biological science, cell biology, environmental biology, and (Biological) Pre-Health Studies), BUSINESS (accounting, business administration and management, business economics, international business management, and sports management), COMMUNICATIONS AND THE ARTS (American Sign Language, art, communications, creative writing, dramatic arts, English, English Writing, graphic design, journalism, music performance, performing arts, Spanish, studio art, and theatre arts), COMPUTER AND PHYSICAL SCIENCE (chemistry, digital arts/technology, mathematics, and physical sciences), EDUCATION (art education, (Education) Childhood Education, early childhood education, education, elementary education, English education, mathematics education, music education, physical education, science education, secondary education, social studies education, and sports studies), ENGINEERING AND ENVIRONMENTAL DESIGN (chemical engineering, civil engineering, electrical/electronics engineering, engineering, engineering physics, environmental design, environmental science, mechanical engineering, and preengineering), HEALTH PROFESSIONS (art therapy, exercise science, nursing, Pre-Health Studies, predentistry, premedicine, preoptometry, and prephysical therapy), SOCIAL SCIENCE (biblical studies, Christian studies, criminal justice, economics, history, human services, interdisciplinary studies, international studies, interpreter for the deaf, liberal arts/general studies, ministries, missions, pastoral studies, philosophy, philosophy and religion, prelaw, psychology, religion, social science, sociology, and youth ministry). Psychology, religion/philosophy and nursing are the strongest academically. Nursing, business, and elementary education have the largest enrollments.

ACTIVITIES: There are no fraternities or sororities. There are 18 groups on campus, including art, band, cheerleading, choir, chorale, chorus, computers, drama, Fellowship of Christian Athletes, honors, international, jazz band, literary magazine, musical theater, newspaper, pep band, political, professional, radio and TV, religious, social, social service, student government, and yearbook. Popular campus events include Christmas Banquet, Junior-Senior Banquet, Spiritual Emphasis Week and Midnight Breakfast. **Sports:** There are 8 intercollegiate sports for men and 9 for women, and 10 intramural sports for men and 8 for women. Facilities include two gyms, two weight rooms, two exercise rooms, indoor baseball training facilities, baseball, softball, and soccer fields, tennis courts, and a practice track. **Graduates:** From July 1, 2013 to June 30, 2014, 397 bachelor's degrees were awarded. The most popular majors were business areas (39%), nursing (12%), and liberal studies (12%). 40 companies recruited on campus in 2013-2014. In an average class, 2% graduate in 3 years or less, 54% graduate in 4 years or less, 61% graduate in 5 years or less, and 62% graduate in 6 years or less. Of the 2013 graduating class, 11% were enrolled in graduate school within 6 months of graduation.

SERVICES: Counseling and information services are available, as is tutoring in every subject. There is remedial math, reading, and writing. **Library/Resources:** The library contains 156,326 volumes, 4,577 microform items, 2,844 audio/video tapes/CDs/DVDs, and subscribes to 3,219 periodicals including electronic. Computerized library services include interlibrary loans, database searching, Internet access, and Wi-Fi capability. Special learning facilities include an art gallery and radio station. **Physically Challenged Students:** 80% of the campus is accessible. Facilities include wheelchair ramps, elevators, special parking, specially equipped restrooms, lowered drinking fountains, and special housing. **Special:** Students may cross-register for courses at various local colleges including Northern Indiana Consortium for Education (NICE). Also available are a 3-2 engineering degree with the University of Notre Dame and Trine University (Angola), a liberal arts degree, degree programs for nontraditional students, and an online degree program in business. Bethel also offers a pass/fail option, student teaching, internships, and study abroad in 12 countries. There are 2 national honor societies, a freshman honors program, and 2 departmental honors programs. **Visiting:** There are regularly scheduled orientations for prospective students, including an interview, chapel visit, tour, lunch, and a class or professor visit as requested. There are guides for informal visits, visitors may sit in on classes, and stay overnight. To schedule a visit, contact the Office of Admission. **Campus Safety and Security:** Measures include 24-hour foot and vehicle patrol, emergency notification system, self-defense education, and security escort services. There are emergency telephones, lighted pathways/sidewalks, and controlled access to dorms/residences.

REQUIREMENTS: The SAT or ACT is required. Applicants should be graduates of a secondary school program or have the GED. Required secondary school credits include 8 units in English, 6 each in math, lab science, and social science, and 4 in a foreign language. Chemistry is required for nursing majors. An audition is required of music program applicants. A GPA of 2.0 is required. AP and CLEP credits are accepted. To graduate, students must complete 124 credits, including 24 to 52 in the major, with a minimum 2.0 GPA. Also required are 2 semesters of phys ed, 9 credits in Bible and religion, courses in communication skills, social science and history, fine arts and humanities, and natural sciences and math, and a Fitness/Wellness course. **Procedure:** Freshmen are admitted to all sessions. Entrance exams should be taken as early as possible in the junior or senior year. There are early admissions, deferred admissions, and rolling admissions plans. Application deadlines are open. Application fee is $25. Applications are accepted on-line. **Transfer Students:** 237 transfer students enrolled in 2013-2014. Grades of C or better are eligible for transfer; students without a minimum GPA of 2.0 may be admitted on probation. Other admission requirements are the same as for entering freshmen. 30 of 124 credits required for the bachelor's degree must be completed at Bethel. **International Students:** There are 35 international students enrolled. They must take the TOEFL with a minimum score of 540 on the paper-based TOEFL (PBT) or 76 on the Internet-based version (iBT), or take TJE or IELTS. They must also take the SAT or ACT.

ADMISSIONS: 97% of the 2014-2015 applicants were accepted. The SAT scores for the 2014-2015 freshman class were: Critical Reading--41% below 500, 39% between 500 and 599, 18% between 600 and 699, and 2% between 700 and 800; Math--40% below 500, 36% between 500 and 599, 22% between 600 and 699, and 2% between 700 and 800; Writing--52% below 500, 35% between 500 and 599, 12% between 600 and 699, and 1% between 700 and 800. The ACT scores were 31% below 21, 20% between 21 and 23, 25% between 24 and 26, 10% between 27 and 28, and 14% above 28. 42% of the current freshmen were in the top fifth of their class; 74% were in the top two fifths. There was 1 National Merit finalist. 8 freshmen graduated first in their class. **Admissions Contact:** Andrea Helmuth, Director of Admission. E-Mail: *Andrea.Helmuth@BethelCollege.edu* Web: *www.bethelcollege.edu*

FINANCIAL AID: In 2014-2015, 88% of all full-time freshmen and 87% of continuing full-time students received some form of financial aid. 78% of all full-time freshmen and 71% of continuing full-time students received need-based aid. The average freshman award was $20,242. Need-based scholarships or need-based grants averaged $8,680; need-based self-help aid (loans and jobs) averaged $3,626;

non-need-based athletic scholarships averaged $7,630; and other non-need-based awards and non-need-based scholarships averaged $8,338. 30% of undergraduate students work part-time. Average annual earnings from campus work are $1000. The average financial indebtedness of the 2014 graduate was $24,207. Bethel is a member of CSS. The FAFSA and the college's own financial statement are required. The priority date for freshman financial aid applications for fall entry is March 1. The deadline for filing freshman financial aid applications for fall entry is March 10.

BUTLER UNIVERSITY   C-3
www.butler.edu

Indianapolis, IN 46208	(317) 940-8100
	(888) 940-8100
Fax: (317) 940-8150	**Email:** admission@butler.edu
Full-time: 2 men, 2543 women	**Faculty:** IIA, av$
Part-time: 41 men, 41 women	**Ph.D.s:** 77%
Graduate: 244 men, 293 women	**Student/Faculty:** 13 to 1
Year: semesters, summer session	**Tuition:** $35,652
Room & Board: $11,920	**Freshman Class:** 10103 applied, 6917 accepted, 969 enrolled
SAT CR/M/W: 580/600/570 **ACT:** 28	**CEEB CODE:** 1073
Application Deadline: 2 1	**VERY COMPETITIVE+**

Butler University, founded in 1855, is an independent, private institution offering programs in liberal arts and sciences, business, communications, fine and performing arts, pharmacy and health sciences, and education. Butler emphasizes experiential learning (including internships, service learning, and research) and job placement outcomes. There are 6 undergraduate schools and 5 graduate schools. In addition to regional accreditation, Butler has baccalaureate program accreditation with AACSB, ACPE, NASAD, NASM, NCATE, ARCPA, ACS, CACREP, NASD, and NAST. The 290-acre campus is in a suburban area in the city of Indianapolis, approximately five miles north of downtown, near the Broad Ripple cultural district. Including any residence halls, there are 39 buildings.

STUDENT LIFE: 52% of undergraduates are from out of state, mostly the Mid-West. Students are from 46 states, 56 foreign countries, and Canada. 82% are White. 44% are Protestant; 31% Catholic; 12% claim no religious affiliation. **Male To Female Ratio:** 10.0:1. The average age of freshmen is 18; all undergraduates, 20. 10% do not continue beyond their first year; 79% remain to graduate. **Housing:** 2063 students can be accommodated in college housing, which includes single-sex and coed dorms and on-campus apartments. In addition, there are special-interest houses, fraternity houses, sorority houses, and special-interest units available in the residence halls. 68% of students live on campus. Alcohol is not permitted. All students may keep cars.

FACULTY/CLASSROOMS: 54% of faculty are male; 46% are female. No introductory courses are taught by graduate students. The average class size in an introductory lecture is 22; in a laboratory is 16; and in a regular course is 15.

PROGRAMS OF STUDY: Butler confers B.A., B.S., B.F.A., B.M., B.S.H.S. and B.S.E. degrees. Associate and Master's degrees are also awarded. Bachelor's degrees are awarded in BIOLOGICAL SCIENCE (biology/biological science), BUSINESS (accounting, banking and finance, international business management, management information systems, and marketing/retailing/merchandising), COMMUNICATIONS AND THE ARTS (advertising, art, arts administration/management, communications, dance, dramatic arts, English, French, German, Greek (classical), journalism, Latin, media arts, music, music performance, music theory and composition, performing arts, public relations, Spanish, speech/debate/rhetoric, theatre arts, and voice), COMPUTER AND PHYSICAL SCIENCE (actuarial science, chemistry, computer science, mathematics, physics, and software engineering), EDUCATION (elementary education, middle school education, music education, secondary education, and special education), ENGINEERING AND ENVIRONMENTAL DESIGN (biomedical engineering and engineering), HEALTH PROFESSIONS (health science, pharmacy, and speech pathology/audiology),

SOCIAL SCIENCE (anthropology, criminal justice, economics, gender studies, history, international studies, philosophy, political science/government, psychology, religion, science and society, and sociology). Pharmacy, physician assistant, dance, business, and engineering dual degree are the strongest academically. Pharmacy, biology, and marketing have the largest enrollments.

ACTIVITIES: 29% of men belong to 6 national fraternities; 37% of women belong to 9 national sororities. There are 153 groups on campus, including and veterans, mentoring, philanthropic, art, band, cheerleading, chess, choir, chorale, chorus, computers, dance, debate, drama, emerging leaders, environmental, ethnic, film, gay, honors, international, jazz band, literary magazine, marching band, newspaper, opera, orchestra, pep band, photography, political, professional, radio and TV, religious, social, social service, student government, symphony, and yearbook. Popular campus events include Bulldogs Into the Streets, Homecoming, Dance Marathon, ButlerPalooza, and Spring Sports Spectacular. **Sports:** There are 9 intercollegiate sports for men and 10 for women, and 16 intramural sports for men and 16 for women. Facilities include 9,000+-seat fieldhouse, a 20,000-seat football stadium, tennis courts, indoor and outdoor tracks, a weight-training room, an aerobics/exercise room, intramural fields, and baseball, softball, and soccer fields. Butler University's Health and Recreation Complex offers many new services to students, faculty, and staff, while expanding others presently available. In addition to being the main stomping ground for Butler's Department of Recreation, the HRC also houses Counseling and Consultation Services, Health Education and Health Services, making it a true wellness center on campus. **Graduates:** From July 1, 2013 to June 30, 2014, 756 bachelor's degrees were awarded. The most popular majors were marketing (7%), health sciences (7%), and biology (6%). In an average class, 63% graduate in 4 years or less, 77% graduate in 5 years or less, and 79% graduate in 6 years or less. Of the 2013 graduating class, 19% were enrolled in graduate school within 6 months of graduation, and 73% were employed.

SERVICES: Counseling and information services are available, as is tutoring in every subject. There is a reader service for the blind. A writer's studio offers assistance in all areas of the writing process. **Library/Resources:** The 2 libraries contain 221,109 volumes, 12,980 microform items, 16,898 audio/video tapes/CDs/DVDs, and subscribe to 33,276 periodicals including electronic. Computerized library services include interlibrary loans, database searching, Internet access, and Wi-Fi capability. Special learning facilities include a planetarium, radio station, TV station, and observatory. **Physically Challenged Students:** All of the campus is accessible. Facilities include wheelchair ramps, elevators, special parking, specially equipped restrooms, special class scheduling, and lowered drinking fountains. **Special:** Butler offers cross-registration with the 4 other members of the Consortium for Urban Education, co-op programs in business administration, and internships in pharmacy, arts administration, and business programs. A 3-2 degree program in engineering with Indiana University-Purdue University in Indianapolis, extensive study-abroad programs, and work-study programs are available. There are dual majors including French, German, and Spanish combined with business studies, student-designed majors, a general studies degree, pass/fail options, and nondegree study. There are 9 national honor societies, including Phi Beta Kappa, and a freshman honors program. **Visiting:** There are regularly scheduled orientations for prospective students. Traditional prospective student visits include an admission and financial aid presentation followed by a campus tour. There are guides for informal visits and visitors may sit in on classes. To schedule a visit, contact the Office of Admission at www.butler.edu/visit. **Campus Safety and Security:** Measures include 24-hour foot and vehicle patrol, emergency notification system, self-defense education, and security escort services. There are shuttle buses, emergency telephones, lighted pathways/sidewalks, and controlled access to dorms/residences.

REQUIREMENTS: The SAT or ACT is required. The ACT Optional Writing test is also required. Applicants must be slated to graduate from an accredited secondary school, and/or have demonstrated successful completion of all required academic units per the discretion of the Vice President of Enrollment Management or the Director of Admission. Applicants must be on track to earn at least 17 core academic units, including 4 years of English, 3 each of math and lab science, 2 each of the same foreign language, and 2 each of history/social science; the balance of coursework may include electives or advanced coursework in core academic courses. In addition to submitting the common application or Butler University Application, a separate application and audition or interview is required for all candidates applying for admission to the Jordan College of the Arts. Butler requires applicants to be in the upper 50% of their class. A GPA of 2.0 is required. AP and CLEP credits are accepted. Important factors in the admissions decision are advanced placement or honors courses, evidence of special talent, and leadership record. Our core curriculum is divided into two parts - a relatively structured set of common core elements and a more varied set of general core elements in which students have a broader choice of course within areas defined by specific learning objectives. In all of our core elements, we are committed to courses structured by learning objectives rather than disciplines. We seek to have core courses taught by the whole University community. **Procedure:** Freshmen are admitted to all sessions. Entrance exams should be taken during the junior year. There are early admissions and deferred admissions plans. Applications should be filed by February 1 for fall entry. Notifications are sent February 15. 587 applicants were on the 2014 waiting list; 175 were admitted. Applications are accepted on-line. **Transfer Students:** 80 transfer students enrolled in 2013-2014. Applicants who have completed more than 11 hours of college work following graduation from an accredited secondary school must present transcripts from all previous college attended, indicating good standing and a minimum GPA of 2.0, and an official high school transcript showing a posted date of graduation. Those students with fewer than 12 hours must also, submit SAT or ACT scores. Students wishing to transfer into pharmacy must apply through PharmCAS; Students applying to the professional phase of physician assistant program must apply through CASPA. No credits transfer for classes taken online. 45 of 126 credits required for the bachelor's degree must be completed at Butler. **International Students:** There are 117 international students enrolled. The school actively recruits these students. They must take the TOEFL with a minimum score of 550 on the paper-based TOEFL (PBT) or 79 on the Internet-based version (iBT), or complete level 5 at the American Language Academy on Butler's campus.

ADMISSIONS: 68% of the 2014-2015 applicants were accepted. The SAT scores for the 2014-2015 freshman class were: Critical Reading--9% below 500, 47% between 500 and 599, 37% between 600 and 699, and 7% between 700 and 800; Math--10% below 500, 38% between 500 and 599, 43% between 600 and 699, and 9% between 700 and 800; Writing--16% below 500, 47% between 500 and 599, 33% between 600 and 699, and 4% between 700 and 800. The ACT scores were 4% below 21, 8% between 21 and 23, 27% between 24 and 26, 20% between 27 and 28, and 41% above 28. 72% of the current freshmen were in the top fifth of their class; 92% were in the top two fifths. There were 5 National Merit finalists. 42 freshmen graduated first in their class. **Admissions Contact:** Aimee Rust-Scheuermann, Director of Admissions. E-Mail: *admission@butler.edu* Web: *www.butler.edu*

FINANCIAL AID: In 2014-2015, 95% of all full-time freshmen and 88% of continuing full-time students received some form of financial aid. 62% of all full-time freshmen and 62% of continuing full-time students received need-based aid. The average freshman award was $23,639. Need-based scholarships or need-based grants averaged $19,143; need-based self-help aid (loans and jobs) averaged $4,326; non-need-based athletic scholarships averaged $21,018; and other non-need-based awards and non-need-based scholarships averaged $13,157. 25% of undergraduate students work part-time. Average annual earnings from campus work are $1200. The average financial indebtedness of the 2014 graduate was $35,797. Butler is a member of CSS. The FAFSA and the college's own financial statement are required. The deadline for filing freshman financial aid applications for fall entry is March 1.

CALUMET COLLEGE OF ST. JOSEPH B-1
www.ccsj.edu

Whiting, IN 46394	(219) 473-4739
	(877) 700-9100
Fax: (219) 473-4259	
Full-time: 160 men, 310 women	Faculty: IIA, --$
Part-time: 345 men, 385 women	Ph.D.s: 50%
Graduate: 100 men, 40 women	Student/Faculty: n/av
Year: semesters, summer session	Tuition: $15,000
Room & Board: n/app	Freshman Class: n/av
SAT or ACT: recommended	CEEB CODE: 1776
Application Deadline: open	COMPETITIVE

Calumet College of St. Joseph, founded in 1951, is a private Catholic institution offering commuting students a liberal arts education in a Christian environment. The figures in the above capsule and in this profile are approximate. The 256-acre campus is in a small town 15 miles southeast of Chicago in northwest Indiana. Including any residence halls, there are 1 buildings.

STUDENT LIFE: 70% of undergraduates are from Indiana. Others are from 2 states. The average age of freshmen is 21; all undergraduates, 35. 42% do not continue beyond their first year; 58% remain to graduate. **Housing:** Alcohol is not permitted. All students commute. All students may keep cars.

FACULTY/CLASSROOMS: 75% of faculty are male; 25% are female. All teach undergraduates. No introductory courses are taught by graduate students. The average class size in an introductory lecture is 25; in a laboratory is 20; and in a regular course is 20.

PROGRAMS OF STUDY: CCSJ confers B.A., B.S., B.S.Ed. and B.S.M.T. degrees. Associate and Master's degrees are also awarded. Bachelor's degrees are awarded in BUSINESS (accounting, business administration and management, and institutional management), COMMUNICATIONS AND THE ARTS (English and media arts), COMPUTER AND PHYSICAL SCIENCE (information sciences and systems), EDUCATION (elementary education and secondary education), HEALTH PROFESSIONS (health care administration), SOCIAL SCIENCE (criminal justice, human services, law enforcement and corrections, liberal arts/general studies, paralegal studies, psychology, religion, theological studies, and urban studies). Management, accounting, and criminal justice are the strongest academically. Management, human services, and education have the largest enrollments.

ACTIVITIES: There are no fraternities or sororities. There are 15 groups on campus, including cheerleading, drama, ethnic, literary magazine, musical theater, newspaper, photography, professional, religious, social, social service, and student government. Popular campus events include Thanksgiving Ethnicfest and Student Appreciation Week. **Sports:** 1 intramural sports for men.

SERVICES: Counseling and information services are available, as is tutoring in most subjects. There is remedial math, reading, and writing. **Library/Resources:** The library contains 93,055 volumes, 3,035 microform items, 6,412 audio/video tapes/CDs/DVDs, and subscribes to 354 periodicals including electronic. Computerized library services include interlibrary loans and database searching. Special learning facilities include an art gallery. **Physically Challenged Students:** All of the campus is accessible. Facilities include wheelchair ramps, elevators, special parking, and specially equipped restrooms. **Special:** The college offers a cooperative 3-1 baccalaureate degree in medical technology with the schools of St. Margaret-Mercy Hospital in Indiana, where students complete their study and a clinical internship. Accelerated degree programs in organizational management, health-care management, and law enforcement management are possible. The LEAP program offers credit for life experience. Study abroad, internships, work-study programs, a general studies degree, pass/fail options, and nondegree study are possible. **Visiting:** There are regularly scheduled orientations for prospective students. There are guides for informal visits and visitors may sit in on classes. To schedule a visit, contact the Director of Admissions. **Campus Safety and Security:** There are emergency telephones and lighted pathways/sidewalks.

REQUIREMENTS: The SAT or ACT is recommended. Applicants should have completed 4 years of high school English, 3 to 4 of math, 2 to 3 of science, and 2 of social studies. The GED is accepted. An essay and an interview are recommended. The Vocabulary and Reading Assessment Test is required. A GPA of 2.0 is required. AP and CLEP credits are accepted. Important factors in the admissions decision are extracurricular activities record, leadership record, and evidence of special talent. All students must complete 42 semester hours of general education courses, including English composition, economics, speech, theology, philosophy, communication and fine arts, science and math, and social and behavioral science. A total of 124 semester hours with a minimum GPA of 2.0 is required to graduate. **Procedure:** Freshmen are admitted to all sessions. There are deferred admissions and rolling admissions plans. Application deadlines are open. Applications are accepted on-line. **Transfer Students:** A 2.0 GPA is required. An interview is recommended. The Vocabulary and Reading Assessment Test is required. 30 of 124 credits required for the bachelor's degree must be completed at CCSJ. **International Students:** They must take the TOEFL.

ADMISSIONS: Admissions Contact: Director of Admissions and Financial Aid Web: *www.ccsj.edu*

FINANCIAL AID: CCSJ is a member of CSS. The FAFSA and the college's own financial statement are required. Check with the school for current application deadlines.

DEPAUW UNIVERSITY B-3
www.depauw.edu

Greencastle, IN 46135	(765) 658-4006
	(800) 447-2495
Fax: (765) 658-4007	Email: admission@depauw.edu
Full-time: 1044 men, 1263 women	Faculty: 224; IIB, +$
Part-time: 14 men, 15 women	Ph.D.s: 91%
Graduate: n/av	Student/Faculty: 10 to 1
Year: 4-1-4	Tuition: $38,750
Room & Board: $10,200	Freshman Class: 4913 applied, 3023 accepted, 578 enrolled
SAT CR/M/W: 580/600/580 ACT: 27	CEEB CODE: 1166
Application Deadline: March 1	VERY COMPETITIVE+

DePauw University, founded in 1837, is a private institution affiliated with the United Methodist Church offering programs in the fields of liberal arts and music. Figures in the above capsule and in this profile are approximate. There are 2 undergraduate schools. In addition to regional accreditation, DePauw has baccalaureate program accreditation with NASM, NCATE, ACS, and CAAHEP. The 175-acre campus is in a small town 45 miles west of Indianapolis. Including any residence halls, there are 81 buildings.

STUDENT LIFE: 59% of undergraduates are from out of state, mostly the Mid-West. Students are from 41 states, and 19 foreign countries. 88% are from public schools. 75% are White. 45% are Protestant; 20% Catholic. The average age of freshmen is 19; all undergraduates, 20. 10% do not continue beyond their first year; 83% remain to graduate. **Housing:** 1490 students can be accommodated in college housing, which includes coed dorms, on-campus apartments, and off-campus apartments. In addition, there are special-interest houses, fraternity houses, sorority houses, international student housing. On-campus housing is guaranteed for all 4 years. 99% of students live on campus. All students may keep cars.

FACULTY/CLASSROOMS: 55% of faculty are male; 45% are female. All teach undergraduates, and 82% do research. No introductory courses are taught by graduate students. The average class size in an introductory lecture is 20; in a laboratory is 14; and in a regular course is 18.

PROGRAMS OF STUDY: DePauw confers B.A., B.M.A., B.M.E. and B.Mu. degrees. Bachelor's degrees are awarded in AGRICULTURE (natural resource management), BIOLOGICAL SCIENCE (biochemistry and biology/biological science), COMMUNICATIONS AND THE ARTS (art history and appreciation, classical languages, communications, English, English literature, French, German, Greek, Latin, linguistics, literature, music, music business management, music performance, music theory and composition, romance languages and literature, Spanish, and studio art), COMPUTER AND PHYSICAL SCIENCE (chemistry, computer science, earth science, geology, mathematics, and physics), EDUCATION (elementary education, foreign languages education, and music education), ENGINEERING AND ENVIRONMENTAL DESIGN (environmental science and preengineering), HEALTH PROFESSIONS (health), SOCIAL SCIENCE (African American studies, anthropology, classical/ancient civilization, East Asian studies, economics, gender studies, geography, history, interdisciplinary studies, peace studies, philosophy, physical fitness/movement, political science/government, psychology, religion, Russian and Slavic studies, sociology, and women's studies). English, economics, and communications have the largest enrollments.

ACTIVITIES: 78% of men belong to 12 national fraternities; 64% of women belong to 10 national sororities. There are 80 groups on campus, including art, band, cheerleading, chess, choir, chorale, chorus, computers, dance, debate, drama, ethnic, film, forensics, gay, honors, international, jazz band, literary magazine, musical theater, newspaper, opera, orchestra, pep band, political, professional, radio and TV, religious, social, social service, student government, and symphony. Popular campus events include Little 5 Track Meet, Monon Bell Football Game and Old Gold Day. **Sports:** There are 17 intercollegiate sports for men and 16 for women, and 14 intramural sports for men and 12 for women. Facilities include a recreation center, a 4000-seat stadium, baseball, soccer, and field hockey fields, 3 basketball courts, indoor/outdoor tennis courts and tracks, a pool, a fitness center, volleyball and badminton courts, and a 3200-seat indoor gym. **Graduates:** From July 1, 2013 to June 30, 2014, 499 bachelor's degrees were awarded. The most popular majors were English, communication/theatre, and music. In an average class, 79% graduate in 4 years or less and 81% graduate in 5 years or less.

SERVICES: Counseling and information services are available, as is tutoring in most subjects. There is a reader service for the blind. **Library/Resources:** The 3 libraries contain 818,618 volumes, 381,066 microform items, 34,325 audio/video tapes/CDs/DVDs, and subscribe to 29,188 periodicals including electronic. Computerized library services include interlibrary loans, database searching, and Internet access. Special learning facilities include an art gallery, natural history museum, radio station, TV station, an observatory, an arboretum, a digital video studio, and a digital media lab. **Physically Challenged Students:** 85% of the campus is accessible. Facilities include wheelchair ramps, elevators, special parking, specially equipped restrooms, special class scheduling, lowered drinking fountains, and lowered telephones. **Special:** DePauw offers dual majors in any 2 disciplines, student-designed majors, internships for honors programs and winter-term projects, unlimited study-abroad options through cooperative arrangements with other universities, a Washington semester, pass/fail options, and credit by departmental examination. Also available are 3-2 engineering degrees with Case Western Reserve, Columbia, and Washington Universities and a 3-2 nursing program with Rush University Hospital in Chicago. The Media Fellows, Management Fellows, and Science Research Fellows programs offer majors in any discipline, plus a semester-long internship. There are 13 national honor societies, including Phi Beta Kappa, a freshman honors program, and 12 departmental honors programs. **Visiting:** There are regularly scheduled orientations for prospective students, consisting of day-long student/parent programs that include campus tours, faculty viewpoints, conversations with students, admissions information, financial aid and career planning sessions, and a meal in a residence hall. There are guides for informal visits, visitors may sit in on classes, and stay overnight. To schedule a visit, contact the Admission Program and Visit Coordinator at (765) 658-4006. **Campus Safety and Security:** Measures include 24-hour foot and vehicle patrol, emergency notification system, self-defense education, and security escort services. There are shuttle buses, emergency telephones, and lighted pathways/sidewalks.

REQUIREMENTS: The SAT or ACT is required. Graduation from an accredited secondary school or a GED is required for admission. Course distribution should include 4 each in English and math, 3 to 4 each in social studies, and science (2 or more with lab), and 2 to 4 in a foreign language. An essay is required, and an interview is strongly recommended. Applicants for the School of Music must

audition. AP credits are accepted. Important factors in the admissions decision are advanced placement or honors courses, recommendations by school officials, and personality/intangible qualities. Students must demonstrate competence in oral communications, quantitative reasoning, and writing. Successful completion of 124 semester hours, including 32 to 40 in the major, is required for graduation. In addition, students must fulfill distribution requirements in natural sciences, social and behavioral sciences, literature and the arts, historical and philosophical understanding, foreign language, and self-expression. A comprehensive exam, thesis, or seminar is required for each major. **Procedure:** Freshmen are admitted fall and spring. Entrance exams should be taken as early as possible. There are early decision, early admissions, and deferred admissions plans. Early decision applications should be filed by November 1; regular applications, by March 1 for fall entry; and December 1 for spring entry, along with a $40 fee. Notification of early decision is sent January 1; regular decision, April 1. 50 early decision candidates were accepted for the 2014-2015 class. 216 applicants were on the 2014 waiting list; 112 were admitted. Applications are accepted on-line. **Transfer Students:** 21 transfer students enrolled in 2013-2014. Applicants must submit either SAT or ACT scores. High school and college transcripts are required, and a minimum GPA on previous college work of 3.0 is preferred. 60 of 124 credits required for the bachelor's degree must be completed at DePauw. **International Students:** There are 185 international students enrolled. The school actively recruits these students. They must take the TOEFL with a minimum score of 560 on the paper-based TOEFL (PBT) or 83 on the Internet-based version (iBT), or take the IELTS. They must also take the SAT or ACT.

ADMISSIONS: 62% of the 2014-2015 applicants were accepted. The SAT scores for the 2014-2015 freshman class were: Critical Reading -14% below 500, 40% between 500 and 599, 35% between 600 and 699, and 10% between 700 and 800; Math--8% below 500, 36% between 500 and 599, 41% between 600 and 699, and 14% between 700 and 800; Writing--13% below 500, 42% between 500 and 599, 37% between 600 and 699, and 7% between 700 and 800. **Admissions Contact:** Admission Officer E-Mail: *admission@depauw.edu* Web: *www.depauw.edu*

FINANCIAL AID: DePauw is a member of CSS. The CSS/Profile, FAFSA, and the college's own financial statement are required. The priority date for freshman financial aid applications for fall entry is February 15.

EARLHAM COLLEGE   D-3
www.earlham.edu

Richmond, IN 47374	(765) 983-1600
	(800) 327-5426
Fax: (765) 983-1560	**Email:** admission@earlham.edu
Full-time: 441 men, 540 women	**Faculty:** 101; IIB, av$
Part-time: 5 men, 7 women	**Ph.D.s:** 95%
Graduate: 33 men, 48 women	**Student/Faculty:** 10 to 1
Year: semesters	**Tuition:** $42,870
Room & Board: $8600	**Freshman Class:** 2001 applied, 1291 accepted, 270 enrolled
SAT CR/M/W: 650/620/620 **ACT:** 28	**CEEB CODE:** 1195
Application Deadline: February 15	**HIGHLY COMPETITIVE**

There is 1 undergraduate school and 2 graduate schools. In addition to regional accreditation, Earlham has baccalaureate program accreditation with ACS and ATS. The 800-acre campus is in a small town 70 miles east of Indianapolis and 40 miles west of Dayton. Including any residence halls, there are 64 buildings.

STUDENT LIFE: 84% of undergraduates are from out of state, mostly the Mid-West. Students are from 47 states, 62 foreign countries, and Canada. 65% are from public schools. 53% are White; 18% Foreign; 13% African American. 42% claim no religious affiliation; 40% Quaker, Christian, Buddhist, Hindu and Muslim; 11% Protestant. **Male To Female Ratio:** 1.2:1. The average age of freshmen is 18; all undergraduates, 20. 16% do not continue beyond their first year; 72% remain to graduate. **Housing:** 1004 students can be accommodated in college housing, which includes single-sex and coed dorms.

In addition, there are language houses, special-interest houses, service learning house, Jewish cultural center, an African American cultural center, International Cultural Center, LBGTQA. On-campus housing is guaranteed for all 4 years. 96% of students live on campus; of those, 84% remain on campus on weekends. All students may keep cars.

FACULTY/CLASSROOMS: 46% of faculty are male; 54% are female. All teach undergraduates. No introductory courses are taught by graduate students. The average class size in an introductory lecture is 45; in a laboratory is 18; and in a regular course is 12.

PROGRAMS OF STUDY: Earlham confers B.A. degrees. Master's degrees are also awarded. Bachelor's degrees are awarded in AGRICULTURE (environmental studies), BIOLOGICAL SCIENCE (biochemistry, biology/biological science, and neurosciences), BUSINESS (business administration and management), COMMUNICATIONS AND THE ARTS (art, dramatic arts, English, French, German, languages, linguistics, music, and Spanish), COMPUTER AND PHYSICAL SCIENCE (chemistry, computer science, geology, mathematics, and physics), ENGINEERING AND ENVIRONMENTAL DESIGN (environmental science), HEALTH PROFESSIONS (premedicine), SOCIAL SCIENCE (African American studies, anthropology, classical/ancient civilization, economics, history, human development, international studies, Japanese studies, Latin American studies, peace studies, philosophy, political science/government, psychology, religion, sociology, and women's studies). Life Sciences (pre-medical) and psychology are the strongest academically. Biology, psychology and business have the largest enrollments.

ACTIVITIES: There are no fraternities or sororities. There are 63 groups on campus, including art, cheerleading, choir, chorale, chorus, computers, dance, drama, environmental, ethnic, film, gay, honors, international, jazz band, literary magazine, newspaper, orchestra, photography, political, professional, radio and TV, religious, social, social service, student government, and symphony. Popular campus events include Research Conference, International Festival and Homecoming Dance. **Sports:** There are 8 intercollegiate sports for men and 8 for women, and 8 intramural sports for men and 8 for women. Facilities include an fitness center with cardiovascular equipment and weights, group fitness and dance rooms, a field house with 4 indoor courts for tennis, volleyball, and basketball, 2 racquetball courts, an indoor climbing wall, an indoor running track, a 25-meter pool, a performance gym, and a massage therapist. Outdoor facilities include a football field, 10 all-weather tennis courts, basketball courts, a trail for cross-country running and skiing, a new baseball field, and fields for softball, soccer, lacrosse, and field hockey. **Graduates:** From July 1, 2013 to June 30, 2014, 263 bachelor's degrees were awarded. The most popular majors were biology/life sciences (16%), interdisciplinary studies (16%), and social sciences (13%). In an average class, 62% graduate in 4 years or less, 67% graduate in 5 years or less, and 71% graduate in 6 years or less. Of the 2013 graduating class, 39% were enrolled in graduate school within 6 months of graduation, and 59% were employed.

SERVICES: Counseling and information services are available, as is tutoring in most subjects. A writing center is available. There is a reader service for the blind. **Library/Resources:** The 2 libraries contain 381,766 volumes, 159,946 microform items, 9,947 audio/video tapes/CDs/DVDs, and subscribe to 33,200 periodicals including electronic. Computerized library services include interlibrary loans, database searching, Internet access, and Wi-Fi capability. Special learning facilities include an art gallery, natural history museum, planetarium, radio station, an observatory, herbarium, greenhouse, equestrian facility (horse barn), and a center for the visual and performing arts. **Physically Challenged Students:** 72% of the campus is accessible. Facilities include wheelchair ramps, elevators, special parking, specially equipped restrooms, lowered drinking fountains, lowered telephones, and special housing. **Special:** Earlham's Center for Integrated Learning is a key feature for all Earlham students in developing what we call "the 10-Year Mindset." Features of this program include immersion experiences, career discernment, community based learning and learning in action. The Center helps students integrate their passions and their learning not only in the classroom, but also in off-campus study, internships, research and service. In addition, collaboration is the key to research and scholarly practice at Earlham. Students develop working relationships with faculty in the classroom, laboratory and in the field with many types of research opportunities.

Independent study, self-directed learning, internships and May Term intensive courses can also be important aspects of an Earlham education. However, the 10-Year Mindset is the guiding principle that helps students build a comprehensive and long-term plan of action. There are 2 national honor societies and a Phi Beta Kappa chapter. **Visiting:** There are regularly scheduled orientations for prospective students, including class visitation, an admissions interview, a tour, and special appointments with faculty. There are guides for informal visits, visitors may sit in on classes, and stay overnight. To schedule a visit, contact the Admissions Office at (765) 983-1600. **Campus Safety and Security:** Measures include 24-hour foot and vehicle patrol, emergency notification system, self-defense education, and security escort services. There are shuttle buses, emergency telephones, lighted pathways/sidewalks, and controlled access to dorms/residences.

REQUIREMENTS: In most cases, graduation from an accredited secondary school is required; a GED will be accepted. Students must have completed at least 15 academic credits, including 4 years of English, 3 of math, and 2 each of science, history or social studies, and a foreign language. Students are required to submit an essay and letters of recommendation from a teacher and guidance counselor. An interview is recommended. A GPA of 2.5 is required. AP credits are accepted. Important factors in the admissions decision are advanced placement or honors courses, evidence of special talent, and extracurricular activities record. To graduate, all students must complete the general education curriculum with courses that are devised to prepare students for a life of critical knowledge and informed action. Students must also maintain a minimum GPA of 2.0 and complete a total of 122 semester hours, including 32 semester hours in the major and at least 36-upper level semester hours and 40 outside the major division. A senior capstone experience is required. **Procedure:** Freshmen are admitted fall and spring. Entrance exams should be taken during the spring of the junior year or early fall of the senior year. There are early decision, early admissions, and deferred admissions plans. Early decision applications should be filed by November 1; regular applications, by February 15 for fall entry; November 1 for winter entry; and November 1 for spring entry. Notification of early decision is sent December 1; regular decision, February 15. 10 early decision candidates were accepted for the 2014-2015 class. 239 applicants were on the 2014 waiting list; 89 were admitted. Applications are accepted on-line. **Transfer Students:** 14 transfer students enrolled in 2013-2014. Applicants must have a minimum GPA of 2.5 in college course work. An interview is recommended. High school and college transcripts, an essay, and a statement of good standing from the prior institution are required. 62 of 122 credits required for the bachelor's degree must be completed at Earlham. **International Students:** There are 185 international students enrolled. The school actively recruits these students. They must take the TOEFL with a minimum score of 550 on the paper-based TOEFL (PBT) or 80 on the Internet-based version (iBT).

ADMISSIONS: 65% of the 2014-2015 applicants were accepted. The SAT scores for the 2014-2015 freshman class were: Critical Reading--2% below 500, 17% between 500 and 599, 56% between 600 and 699, and 24% between 700 and 800; Math--6% below 500, 31% between 500 and 599, 55% between 600 and 699, and 8% between 700 and 800; Writing--5% below 500, 34% between 500 and 599, 47% between 600 and 699, and 15% between 700 and 800. The ACT scores were 1% below 21, 7% between 21 and 23, 34% between 24 and 26, 17% between 27 and 28, and 41% above 28. 7 freshmen graduated first in their class. **Admissions Contact:** Jonathan Stroud, VP for Enrollment and Communications. E-Mail: *admission@earlham.edu* Web: *www.earlham.edu*

FINANCIAL AID: In 2014-2015, 98% of all full-time freshmen and 88% of continuing full-time students received some form of financial aid. 63% of all full-time freshmen and 45% of continuing full-time students received need-based aid. The average freshman award was $39,347. Need-based scholarships or need-based grants averaged $22,453 ($40,450 maximum); need-based self-help aid (loans and jobs) averaged $5,862 ($7,320 maximum); and other non-need-based awards and non-need-based scholarships averaged $18,501 ($53,480 maximum). 44% of undergraduate students work part-time. Average annual earnings from campus work are $1213. The average financial indebtedness of the 2014 graduate was $16,211. Earlham is a member of CSS. The FAFSA is required. The priority date for freshman financial aid applications for fall entry is March 1. The deadline for filing freshman financial aid applications for fall entry is March 1.

FRANKLIN COLLEGE — C-4
www.franklincollege.edu

Franklin, IN 46131   (317) 738-8758
       (800) 852-0232
Fax: (317) 738-8274   Email: admissions@franklincollege.edu
Full-time: 467 men, 541 women   Faculty: 74; IIB, -$
Part-time: 32 men, 35 women   Ph.D.s: 83%
Graduate: n/av   Student/Faculty: n/av
Year: 4-1-4, summer session   Tuition: $28,185
Room & Board: $8400   Freshman Class: 1772 applied, 1471 accepted, 364 enrolled
SAT CR/M/W: 500/510/480 ACT: 22   CEEB CODE: 1228
Application Deadline: open   COMPETITIVE

Franklin College, founded in 1834, is a private liberal arts college affiliated with the American Baptist Church. There is one undergraduate school. In addition to regional accreditation, Franklin College has baccalaureate program accreditation with NCATE and CAATE. The 207-acre campus is in a small town 20 miles south of Indianapolis. Including any residence halls, there are 23 buildings.

STUDENT LIFE: 91% of undergraduates are from Indiana. Others are from 19 states, and 16 foreign countries. 84% are White. 50% are Protestant; 27% claim no religious affiliation; 14% Catholic. **Male To Female Ratio:** 1.2:1. The average age of freshmen is 19; all undergraduates, 22. 21% do not continue beyond their first year; 62% remain to graduate. **Housing:** 724 students can be accommodated in college housing, which includes single-sex and coed dorms. In addition, there are special-interest houses, fraternity houses, a substance/alcohol-free residence hall living area. On-campus housing is available on a first-come, first-served basis, and is available on a lottery system for upperclassmen. 69% of students live on campus. All students may keep cars.

FACULTY/CLASSROOMS: 55% of faculty are male; 45% are female. All teach undergraduates. No introductory courses are taught by graduate students. The average class size in an introductory lecture is 18; in a laboratory is 15; and in a regular course is 16.

PROGRAMS OF STUDY: Franklin College confers B.A. degrees. Bachelor's degrees are awarded in BIOLOGICAL SCIENCE (biology ecology and field biology, biology/biological science, and life science secondary school education), BUSINESS (accounting, business administration and management, business administration - international, business administration, mgmt, operations, and business administration marketing), COMMUNICATIONS AND THE ARTS (art history, art, creative writing, English, French, journalism, multimedia, music, public relations, Spanish, studio art, studio art graphic design, studio art painting, and theatre arts), COMPUTER AND PHYSICAL SCIENCE (applied mathematics, chemistry, computer information systems, computer science, and mathematics), EDUCATION (athletic training, elementary education, English education, mathematics education, physical education, science education, secondary education, and social studies education), HEALTH PROFESSIONS (biology and exercise science), SOCIAL SCIENCE (economics, history, philosophy, political science/government, psychology, religion, and sociology). Biology, chemistry, journalism, public relations, business and education are the strongest academically. Biology, business, education, journalism, and exercise science have the largest enrollments.

ACTIVITIES: 49% of men belong to 5 national fraternities; 52% of women belong to 3 national sororities. There are 66 groups on campus, including art, band, cheerleading, choir, chorus, drama, environmental, ethnic, film, gay, honors, international, literary magazine, marching band, musical theater, newspaper, pep band, photography, political, professional, radio and TV, religious, social, social service, and student government. Popular campus events include Grizzly Grand Prix and Greek Week. **Sports:** There are 9 intercolle-

giate sports for men and 10 for women, and 6 intramural sports for men and 6 for women. Facilities include athletic and soccer fields, tennis courts, a phys ed center, and a fitness center. **Graduates:** From July 1, 2013 to June 30, 2014, 199 bachelor's degrees were awarded. The most popular majors were journalism (15%), biology (12%), and health sciences (9%). 45 companies recruited on campus in 2013-2014. In an average class, 54% graduate in 4 years or less, 60% graduate in 5 years or less, and 61% graduate in 6 years or less. Of the 2013 graduating class, 18% were enrolled in graduate school within 6 months of graduation.

SERVICES: Counseling and information services are available, as is tutoring in most subjects. There is a reader service for the blind, and remedial math, reading, and writing. **Library/Resources:** The library contains 132,248 volumes, 310,676 microform items, and 7,815 audio/video tapes/CDs/DVDs, and subscribes to 12,520 periodicals including electronic. Computerized library services include interlibrary loans, database searching, and Wi-Fi capability. Special learning facilities include a radio station and TV station. **Physically Challenged Students:** All of the campus is accessible. Facilities include wheelchair ramps, elevators, special parking, specially equipped restrooms, special class scheduling, lowered drinking fountains, and special housing. **Special:** Cooperative programs are available in Biology and Chemistry (health-related professions). A 3-2 engineering degree with Indiana University-Purdue University in Indianapolis is available, as are fall, winter, spring, and summer internships. Study abroad in various countries and cross-registration with 7 Indiana universities and colleges (Consortium for Urban Education) are available. There are 10 national honor societies, including a Phi Beta Kappa chapter. **Visiting:** There are regularly scheduled orientations for prospective students, including academic presentations, admissions and financial presentations, a student life presentation, campus tours, lunch, and opportunities to talk to professors . There are guides for informal visits, visitors may sit in on classes, and stay overnight. To schedule a visit, contact the Admissions Office at visits@franklincollege.edu. **Campus Safety and Security:** Measures include 24-hour foot and vehicle patrol, emergency notification system, and security escort services. There are emergency telephones, lighted pathways/sidewalks, and controlled access to dorms/residences.

REQUIREMENTS: The SAT or ACT is required. The ACT Optional Writing test is also required. Candidates for admission should have completed 4 years of English, 3 to 4 of math, 2 to 3 of science, 2 each of art and music, social studies, and a foreign language, and typing and basic computing skill courses. The GED is accepted and an essay is required. A GPA of 2.0 is required. AP and CLEP credits are accepted. Important factors in the admissions decision are leadership record, recommendations by school officials, and advanced placement or honors courses. Requirements for graduation include 80 hours outside the major, including general education, a minimum of 40 hours in the major, and 120 total credit hours. Each student must maintain a minimum GPA of 2.0 and must pass the Senior Competency Test, which is administered by the department in which the student completes a major. **Procedure:** Freshmen are admitted to all sessions. Entrance exams should be taken in spring of the junior year or fall of the senior year. There is a rolling admissions plan. Application deadlines are open. Application fee is $40. Notification is sent on a rolling basis. Applications are accepted on-line. Application fees are waived if application is completed on-line. **Transfer Students:** 18 transfer students enrolled in 2013-2014. Transfer students must have at least a 2.0 cumulative GPA and submit official transcripts from previously attended colleges. 48 of 120 credits required for the bachelor's degree must be completed at Franklin College. **International Students:** There are 20 international students enrolled. They must take the TOEFL with a minimum score of 550 on the paper-based TOEFL (PBT). Completion of level 109 in an English language service (ELS) center is necessary. They must also take the SAT or ACT.

ADMISSIONS: 83% of the 2014-2015 applicants were accepted. The SAT scores for the 2014-2015 freshman class were: Critical Reading--46% below 500, 42% between 500 and 599, and 11% between 600 and 699; Math--41% below 500, 43% between 500 and 599, and 15% between 600 and 699; Writing--55% below 500, and 36% between 500 and 599. The ACT scores were 12% below 21, 33% between 21 and 23, and 16% between 24 and 26. 35% of the current freshmen were in the top fifth of their class; 81% were in the top two fifths.

Admissions Contact: Jennifer Bostrom, Director of Admissions. E-Mail: *admissions@franklincollege.edu* Web: *www.franklincollege.edu*

FINANCIAL AID: In 2014-2015, 99% of all full-time freshmen and 100% of continuing full-time students received some form of financial aid. 83% of all full-time freshmen and 82% of continuing full-time students received need-based aid. The average freshman award was $22,416. Need-based scholarships or need-based grants averaged $18,389; and need-based self-help aid (loans and jobs) averaged $4,663 ($15,500 maximum). 34% of undergraduate students work part-time. Average annual earnings from campus work are $754. The average financial indebtedness of the 2014 graduate was $32,451. The FAFSA and the college's own financial statement are required. The priority date for freshman financial aid applications for fall entry is March 10.

GOSHEN COLLEGE
www.goshen.edu

C-1

Goshen, IN 46526

(574) 535-7535
(800) 348-7422

Fax: (574) 535-7609
Email: admission@goshen.edu

Full-time: 328 men, 443 women	**Faculty:** 76; IIB, -$
Part-time: 27 men, 81 women	**Ph.D.s:** 64%
Graduate: 10 men, 34 women	**Student/Faculty:** 12 to 1
Year: 4-1-4, summer session	**Tuition:** $26,900
Room & Board: $9000	**Freshman Class:** n/av
SAT or ACT: required	**CEEB CODE:** 1251
Application Deadline: n/av	**VERY COMPETITIVE**

Goshen College, founded in 1894, is a private, Christian, liberal arts institution affiliated with the Mennonite Church offering bachelor's and master's degrees in a variety of fields. The figures in the above capsule and in this profile are approximate. In addition to regional accreditation, Goshen College has baccalaureate program accreditation with CSWE and NCATE. The 135-acre campus is in a small town approximately 120 miles east of Chicago, and 30 miles southeast of South Bend, IN. Including any residence halls, there are 25 buildings.

STUDENT LIFE: 53% of undergraduates are from out of state, mostly the Mid-West. Students are from 33 states, 38 foreign countries, and Canada. 82% are White; 12% Hispanic. 87% are Protestant. **Male To Female Ratio:** 1.5:1. The average age of freshmen is 18; all undergraduates, 21. 15% do not continue beyond their first year; 69% remain to graduate. **Housing:** 700 students can be accommodated in college housing, which includes single-sex and coed dorms, on-campus apartments, off-campus apartments, and married student housing. In addition, there are special-interest houses. On-campus housing is guaranteed for all 4 years. 70% of students live on campus; of those, 85% remain on campus on weekends. Alcohol is not permitted. All students may keep cars.

FACULTY/CLASSROOMS: 50% of faculty are male; 50% are female. All teach undergraduates. No introductory courses are taught by graduate students. The average class size in an introductory lecture is 28; in a laboratory is 12; and in a regular course is 20.

PROGRAMS OF STUDY: Goshen College confers B.A., B.S. and B.S.N. degrees. Master's degrees are also awarded. Bachelor's degrees are awarded in AGRICULTURE (environmental studies), BIOLOGICAL SCIENCE (biochemistry, biology/biological science, ecology, and molecular biology), BUSINESS (accounting, business administration and management, and institutional management), COMMUNICATIONS AND THE ARTS (American Sign Language, art, broadcasting, communications, creative writing, dramatic arts, English, English Writing, graphic design, journalism, music, Spanish, and theatre arts), COMPUTER AND PHYSICAL SCIENCE (chemistry, computer programming, information sciences and systems, mathematics, and physics), EDUCATION (art education, business education, early childhood education, elementary education, English education, environmental education, foreign languages education, health education, mathematics education, middle school education, music education, physical education, science education, secondary education, and teaching English as a second/foreign language (TESOL/TEFOL)), ENGINEERING AND ENVIRONMENTAL

DESIGN (environmental science and preengineering), HEALTH PROFESSIONS (nursing, predentistry, premedicine, prepharmacy, and preveterinary science), SOCIAL SCIENCE (biblical studies, economics, history, interdisciplinary studies, peace studies, psychology, religion, social work, sociology, and youth ministry). Nursing, elementary education, and biology have the largest enrollments.

ACTIVITIES: There are 24 groups on campus, including art, choir, chorale, chorus, drama, environmental, ethnic, international, jazz band, literary magazine, musical theater, newspaper, opera, orchestra, photography, professional, radio and TV, religious, social, social service, student government, and yearbook. Popular campus events include Kick Off (student talent show), Martin Luther King Jr Day and Homecoming. **Sports:** There are 8 intercollegiate sports for men and 8 for women, and 3 intramural sports for men and 3 for women. Facilities include a fitness center with an indoor track, weight room, 3 basketball courts, 3 racquetball courts, and workout equipment. Athletic facilities include a soccer field, tennis courts, a sand volleyball court, a 400-meter all-weather track, and baseball and softball diamonds. **Graduates:** From July 1, 2013 to June 30, 2014, 221 bachelor's degrees were awarded. The most popular majors were nursing (19%), interdisciplinary (8%), and biology (6%). In an average class, 56% graduate in 4 years or less and 70% graduate in 6 years or less.

SERVICES: Counseling and information services are available, as is tutoring in every subject. There is a reader service for the blind, and remedial math, reading, and writing. **Library/Resources:** The library contains 120,000 volumes, 140,000 microform items, 1,500 audio/video tapes/CDs/DVDs, and subscribes to 900 periodicals including electronic. Computerized library services include interlibrary loans, database searching, Internet access, and Wi-Fi capability. Special learning facilities include an art gallery, radio station, and TV station. **Physically Challenged Students:** All of the campus is accessible. Facilities include wheelchair ramps, elevators, special parking, specially equipped restrooms, special class scheduling, lowered drinking fountains, and lowered telephones. **Special:** A semester-abroad in the required Study Service Term is possible in Cambodia, Morocco, Peru, Tanzania, Nicaragua, China and Senegal. **Visiting:** There are regularly scheduled orientations for prospective students, campus tour, a parents session, talks with professors, a financial aid session, visiting classes, an overnight stay in residence halls, a student panel, and a campus interview. There are guides for informal visits, visitors may sit in on classes, and stay overnight. To schedule a visit, contact the Admission Office. **Campus Safety and Security:** Measures include 24-hour foot and vehicle patrol, emergency notification system, and security escort services. There are lighted pathways/sidewalks and controlled access to dorms/residences.

REQUIREMENTS: The SAT or ACT is required. Applicants should be graduates of an accredited secondary school or have a GED equivalent, with 4 years of high school English, 2 to 4 years of math, and 2 years each of foreign language, science, history, and social studies. AP and CLEP credits are accepted. Important factors in the admissions decision are advanced placement or honors courses, leadership record, and recommendations by school officials. All students must complete the general education program, including courses in literature and communication, fine arts, Bible, religion, philosophy, natural science, math, social science, and history, and 12 hours of international education in the Study Service Term and 1 hour of phys ed. A total of 120 credit hours with a minimum GPA of 2.0 is required to graduate. **Procedure:** Freshmen are admitted to all sessions. Entrance exams should be taken by fall of the senior year. There are deferred admissions and rolling admissions plans. Application deadlines are open. Application fee is $25. Notification is sent on a rolling basis. Applications are accepted on-line. **Transfer Students:** A GPA of 2.0 or higher is required on previous college work. **International Students:** There are 82 international students enrolled. The school actively recruits these students. They must take the TOEFL. They must also take the SAT or ACT.

ADMISSIONS: Dan Koop Liechty, Director of Admissions. E-Mail: *admission@goshen.edu* Web: *www.goshen.edu*

FINANCIAL AID: Goshen College is a member of CSS. The FAFSA is required. Check with the school for current application deadlines.

GRACE COLLEGE AND SEMINARY C-2
www.grace.edu

Winona Lake, IN 46590	(574) 372-5100, ext. 6004
	(800) 54-GRACE
Fax: (574) 372-5120	Email: moyerkp@grace.edu
Full-time: 300 men, 465 women	Faculty: n/av
Part-time: 45 men, 60 women	Ph.D.s: 63%
Graduate: 15 men, 30 women	Student/Faculty: n/av
Year: semesters, summer session	Tuition: $21,700
Room & Board: $7100	Freshman Class: n/av
SAT or ACT: recommended	CEEB CODE: 1252
Application Deadline: n/av	VERY COMPETITIVE

Grace College, founded in 1948, is a Christian liberal arts institution affiliated with the Fellowship of Grace Brethren Churches. The figures in the above capsule and in this profile are approximate. There is 1 graduate school. In addition to regional accreditation, Grace has baccalaureate program accreditation with CSWE, NASM, and NCATE. The 150-acre campus is in a small town 40 miles west of Fort Wayne. Including any residence halls, there are 15 buildings.

STUDENT LIFE: 58% of undergraduates are from Indiana. Others are from 27 states, 5 foreign countries, and Canada. 74% are from public schools. 91% are White. 99% are Protestant. **Male To Female Ratio:** 1.5:1. The average age of freshmen is 18; all undergraduates, 23. 17% do not continue beyond their first year; 58% remain to graduate. **Housing:** 684 students can be accommodated in college housing, which includes single-sex dorms and on-campus apartments. On-campus housing is available on a first-come, first-served basis, and is available on a lottery system for upperclassmen. Priority is given to out-of-town students. 75% of students live on campus; of those, 80% remain on campus on weekends. Alcohol is not permitted. All students may keep cars.

FACULTY/CLASSROOMS: 72% of faculty are male; 23% are female. All teach undergraduates, and 10% do both. No introductory courses are taught by graduate students. The average class size in an introductory lecture is 48; in a laboratory is 14; and in a regular course is 17.

PROGRAMS OF STUDY: Grace confers B.A., B.S., B.M. and B.S.W. degrees. Associate and Master's degrees are also awarded. Bachelor's degrees are awarded in BIOLOGICAL SCIENCE (biology/biological science), BUSINESS (accounting, business administration and management, and management information systems), COMMUNICATIONS AND THE ARTS (art, communications, English, French, German, graphic design, journalism, music, and Spanish), COMPUTER AND PHYSICAL SCIENCE (mathematics and science), EDUCATION (art education, business education, elementary education, English education, foreign languages education, journalism education, mathematics education, music education, physical education, science education, and special education), HEALTH PROFESSIONS (predentistry and premedicine), SOCIAL SCIENCE (biblical studies, counseling/psychology, criminal justice, prelaw, psychology, religion, social work, sociology, and youth ministry). Biology, psychology, and business are the strongest academically. Psychology, elementary education, and biblical studies have the largest enrollments.

ACTIVITIES: There are 14 groups on campus, including band, cheerleading, choir, chorale, drama, honors, international, musical theater, newspaper, orchestra, pep band, religious, social, student government, and yearbook. Popular campus events include Fall Fest, Heart of the Holidays, and VIP Days. **Sports:** There are 8 intercollegiate sports for men and 8 for women, and 3 intramural sports for men and 3 for women. Facilities include a gym, soccer fields, tennis courts, softball and baseball diamonds, and a recreation center with basketball courts, indoor track, and weight and exercise rooms.

SERVICES: Counseling and information services are available, as is tutoring in most subjects. There is remedial math, reading, and writing. **Library/Resources:** The library contains 150,843 volumes, 26,000 microform items, 3,714 audio/video tapes/CDs/DVDs, and subscribes to 19,360 periodicals including electronic. Computerized library services include interlibrary loans, database searching, Internet access, and Wi-Fi capability. Special learning facilities include an art gallery. **Physically Challenged Students:** 80% of the campus is accessible. Facilities include wheelchair ramps, elevators, special parking, and specially equipped restrooms. **Special:** Students may study abroad in 5 countries. A B.A.-B.S. degree is available in all majors except languages, English, and biblical studies. Dual majors are offered in psychology, sociology, communication, business, accounting, youth ministries, and management information technology. There is 1 national honor society and a freshman honors program. **Visiting:** There are regularly scheduled orientations for prospective students, including tours, class visits, and meetings with professors. There are guides for informal visits, visitors may sit in on classes, and stay overnight. To schedule a visit, contact the Visitors Center at (574) 372-5100. **Campus Safety and Security:** Measures include 24-hour foot and vehicle patrol and security escort services. There are lighted pathways/sidewalks.

REQUIREMENTS: The SAT or ACT is recommended. Applicants must have completed 15 Carnegie units, including 4 of English, 3 each of math and science, 2 each of a foreign language and social studies, and 1 of history. A GED is accepted. Grace requires applicants to be in the upper 50% of their class. A GPA of 2.3 is required. AP and CLEP credits are accepted. Important factors in the admissions decision are advanced placement or honors courses, leadership record, and personality/intangible qualities. To graduate, students must complete 124 hours, including 36 to 54 in the major, and have a minimum GPA of 2.0. The required core curriculum of 56 hours consists of languages/literature, humanities, religion/philosophy, education, social sciences, and natural sciences. **Procedure:** Freshmen are admitted to all sessions. Entrance exams should be taken in October, December, or February. There are deferred admissions and rolling admissions plans. Check with the school for current application deadlines. The application fee is $30. Notification is sent on a rolling basis. Applications are accepted on-line. **Transfer Students:** Transfer applicants should have a minimum 2.0 GPA in addition to fulfilling freshman entrance requirements. 60 of 124 credits required for the bachelor's degree must be completed at Grace. **International Students:** They must take the TOEFL. They must also take the SAT or ACT.

ADMISSIONS: Ken Moyer, Dean of Enrollment Management. E-Mail: moyerkp@grace.edu Web: www.grace.edu

FINANCIAL AID: The FAFSA is required. Check with the school for current application deadlines.

HANOVER COLLEGE D-5
www.hanover.edu

Hanover, IN 47243	(812) 866-7022
	(800) 213-2178
Fax: (812) 866-7098	Email: admission@hanover.edu
Full-time: 475 men, 659 women	Faculty: 101; IIB, +$
Part-time: 7 men, 4 women	Ph.D.s: 98%
Graduate: n/av	Student/Faculty: 12 to 1
Year: 4-1-4	Tuition: $33,023
Room & Board: $10,050	Freshman Class: n/av
	CEEB CODE: 1290
Application Deadline: n/av	COMPETITIVE+

Hanover College, founded in 1827 and the oldest private college in Indiana, is a liberal arts school affiliated with the United Presbyterian Church. In addition to regional accreditation, Hanover has baccalaureate program accreditation with NCATE. The 650-acre campus is in a rural area 45 miles northeast of Louisville, Kentucky, 70 miles southwest of Cincinnati, and 90 miles south of Indianapolis. Including any residence halls, there are 36 buildings.

STUDENT LIFE: 67% of undergraduates are from Indiana. Others are from 23 states, and 25 foreign countries. 81% are from public schools. 81% are White. **Male To Female Ratio:** 1.4:1. The average age of freshmen is 18; all undergraduates, 19. 18% do not continue beyond their first year; 69% remain to graduate. **Housing:** 1150 students can be accommodated in college housing, which includes single-sex and coed dorms and on-campus apartments. In addition, there are honors houses, special-interest houses, fraternity houses, sorority houses, and a multicultural center. On-campus housing is guaranteed for all 4 years. 95% of students live on campus. All students may keep cars.

FACULTY/CLASSROOMS: 59% of faculty are male; 41% are female. All teach undergraduates. No introductory courses are taught by graduate students. The average class size in an introductory lecture is 14; in a laboratory is 15; and in a regular course is 14.

PROGRAMS OF STUDY: Hanover confers B.A. degrees. Bachelor's degrees are awarded in BIOLOGICAL SCIENCE (biochemistry, biology/biological science, and environmental biology), COMMUNICATIONS AND THE ARTS (art, art history and appreciation, classics, communications, dramatic arts, English, French, German, music, and Spanish), COMPUTER AND PHYSICAL SCIENCE (chemistry, computer science, environmental geology, geology, mathematics, and physics), EDUCATION (elementary education), ENGINEERING AND ENVIRONMENTAL DESIGN (environmental science), HEALTH PROFESSIONS (health and physical activity and kinesiology), SOCIAL SCIENCE (anthropology, economics, gender studies, history, international studies, medieval studies, philosophy, political science/government, psychology, sociology, and theological studies). Arts and sciences and interdisciplinary studies have the largest enrollments.

ACTIVITIES: 42% of men belong to 4 national fraternities; 32% of women belong to 4 national sororities. There are 60 groups on campus, including art, band, cheerleading, choir, chorus, computers, dance, debate, drama, environmental, ethnic, film, gay, honors, international, jazz band, literary magazine, marching band, musical theater, newspaper, orchestra, pep band, photography, political, professional, radio and TV, religious, social, social service, student government, and yearbook. Popular campus events include Community Artist Series, Wiffleball Tournament, and MLK Marade. **Sports:** There are 9 intercollegiate sports for men and 9 for women, and 10 intramural sports for men and 10 for women. Facilities include a health and recreation center consisting of a 2000-seat performance gym, a multisports forum, a suspended running track, racquetball and squash courts, a weight room, a training room, and a physiology lab. There also is an outdoor athletic complex consisting of a new 5000-seat football/track stadium, baseball, softball and soccer fields, new tennis courts, and a lacrosse field. **Graduates:** From July 1, 2013 to June 30, 2014, 228 bachelor's degrees were awarded. The most popular majors were psychology (10%), elementary education (9%), and biology (8%). 26 companies recruited on campus in 2013-2014. In an average class, 66% graduate in 4 years or less, 69% graduate in 5 years or less, and 69% graduate in 6 years or less. Of the 2013 graduating class, 25% were enrolled in graduate school within 6 months of graduation, and 68% were employed.

SERVICES: Counseling and information services are available, as is tutoring in most subjects. There is remedial writing. **Library/Resources:** The library contains 299,841 volumes, 53,006 microform items, and 7,501 audio/video tapes/CDs/DVDs, subscribes to 45,968 periodicals including electronic. Computerized library services include interlibrary loans, database searching, Internet access, and Wi-Fi capability. Special learning facilities include an art gallery, planetarium, radio station, TV station, a geology museum. **Physically Challenged Students:** 75% of the campus is accessible. Facilities include wheelchair ramps, elevators, special parking, specially equipped restrooms, special class scheduling, lowered drinking fountains, lowered telephones, and special housing. **Special:** Internships, study abroad in Australia, Belgium, France, Turkey, City Semester programs in Philadelphia, Washington, D.C., and Chicago, and self-designed majors including 2 or more disciplines, are offered. The Business Scholars Program provides preparation for a career in business, built on a liberal arts foundation, where everyone in the program completes a paid internship. There are 8 national honor societies and 8 departmental honors programs. **Visiting:** There are regularly scheduled orientations for prospective students. There are guides for informal visits, visitors may sit in on classes, and stay overnight. To schedule a visit, contact Lyn Lyon at (800) 213-2178. **Campus Safety and Security:** Measures include 24-hour foot and vehicle patrol, emergency notification system, self-defense education, and security escort services. There are shuttle buses, emergency telephones, lighted pathways/sidewalks, and controlled access to dorms/residences.

REQUIREMENTS: The SAT or ACT is required. Admission is competitive, based on the applicant pool. The college requires 18 academic credits, including 4 years of English and 2 each of a foreign language, math, science, and either history or social studies. The GED is accepted. The college also requires a foreign language achievement test for those who wish to meet their world language requirement in the language they studied in high school, as well as an essay; an interview is recommended. AP credits are accepted. Important factors in the admissions decision are recommendations by school officials, advanced placement or honors courses, and extracurricular activities record. To graduate, students must complete 36 units of credit, including 8 to 12 in the major, LADRs (12 to 13 units of general degree requirements), maintain a GPA of 2.0 overall, and in the major, pass a comprehensive exam and participate in a culminating experience. **Procedure:** Freshmen are admitted fall and winter. Entrance exams should be taken late in the spring of the junior year. There are deferred admissions and rolling admissions plans. Check with the school for current application deadlines. The application fee is $40. Applications are accepted on-line. Application fees are waived if application is completed on-line. **Transfer Students:** 10 transfer students enrolled in 2013-2014. Transfer students must submit transcripts from all colleges attended and must have performed successfully. SAT or ACT scores and high school record may also be taken into consideration. 17 of 36 credits required for the bachelor's degree must be completed at Hanover. **International Students:** There are 56 international students enrolled. The school actively recruits these students. They must take the TOEFL with a minimum score of 550 on the paper-based TOEFL (PBT) or 80 on the Internet-based version (iBT). They must also take the SAT or ACT.

ADMISSIONS: 53% of the current freshmen were in the top fifth of their class; 86% were in the top two fifths. 8 freshmen graduated first in their class. **Admissions Contact:** Chris Gage, Dean of Admission. E-Mail: *admission@hanover.edu* Web: *www.hanover.edu*

FINANCIAL AID: In 2014-2015, 99% of all full-time freshmen and 97% of continuing full-time students received some form of financial aid. 85% of all full-time freshmen and 83% of continuing full-time students received need-based aid. The average freshman award was $24,172. The average financial indebtedness of the 2014 graduate was $25,839. Hanover is a member of CSS. The FAFSA is required. The priority date for freshman financial aid applications for fall entry is March 1. The deadline for filing freshman financial aid applications for fall entry is March 1.

HUNTINGTON UNIVERSITY   **D-2**
www.huntington.edu

Huntington, IN 46750	**(260) 358-4000**
	(800) 642-6493
Fax: (260) 358-3699	**Email:** admissions@huntington.edu
Full-time: 406 men, 555 women	**Faculty:** 53
Part-time: 42 men, 50 women	**Ph.Ds:** 87%
Graduate: 32 men, 49 women	**Student/Faculty:** 13 to 1
Year: 4-1-4, summer session	**Tuition:** $24,040
Room & Board: $8180	**Freshman Class:** 780 applied, 759 accepted, 226 enrolled
SAT CR/M/W: 509/503/486 **ACT:** 24	**CEEB CODE:** 1304
Application Deadline: n/av	**COMPETITIVE+**

Huntington University is a comprehensive Christian college of the liberal arts offering graduate and undergraduate programs in more than 70 academic concentrations. Founded in 1897 by the Church of the United Brethren in Christ, Huntington University is located on a contemporary, lakeside campus in northeast Indiana. The university is a member of the Council for Christian Colleges and Universities (CCCU). Figures in the above capsule and in this profile are approximate. There is one graduate school. In addition to regional accreditation, Huntington has baccalaureate program accreditation with CSWE, NASM, NCATE, NCA-HLC, and CCNE. The 170-acre campus is in a small town 20 miles southwest of Fort Wayne. Including any residence halls, there are 25 buildings.

STUDENT LIFE: 64% of undergraduates are from Indiana. Others are from 31 states, 20 foreign countries, and Canada. 88% are White. 57% are Protestant; 38% Non-denominational. **Male To Female Ratio:** 1.4:1. The average age of freshmen is 18; all undergraduates,

20. 21% do not continue beyond their first year; 59% remain to graduate. **Housing:** 831 students can be accommodated in college housing, which includes single-sex dorms, off-campus apartments, and married student housing. On-campus housing is guaranteed for all 4 years. 74% of students live on campus; of those, 50% remain on campus on weekends. Alcohol is not permitted. All students may keep cars.

FACULTY/CLASSROOMS: 52% of faculty are male; 48% are female. 88% teach undergraduates. No introductory courses are taught by graduate students. The average class size in an introductory lecture is 25; in a laboratory is 19; and in a regular course is 19.

PROGRAMS OF STUDY: Huntington confers B.A., B.S., B.Mus., B.S.Sc. and B.S.N. degrees. Associate, Master's, and Doctoral degrees are also awarded. Bachelor's degrees are awarded in BIOLOGICAL SCIENCE (biology/biological science), BUSINESS (accounting, business administration and management, entrepreneurial studies, marketing management, nonprofit/public organization management, organizational behavior, small business management, and sports management), COMMUNICATIONS AND THE ARTS (animation, art, broadcasting, communications, creative writing, dramatic arts, English, English as a second/foreign language, English literature, film arts, fine arts, graphic design, journalism, media arts, music business management, music performance, music theory and composition, performing arts, public relations, studio art, theatre arts, and theater design), COMPUTER AND PHYSICAL SCIENCE (chemistry, computer science, information sciences and systems, mathematics, and physics), EDUCATION (art education, education, elementary education, English education, mathematics education, music education, physical education, science education, secondary education, social studies education, sports studies, and teaching English as a second/foreign language (TESOL/TEFOL)), HEALTH PROFESSIONS (exercise science, nursing, premedicine, prepharmacy, prephysical therapy, and recreation therapy), SOCIAL SCIENCE (area studies, biblical studies, counseling/psychology, criminal justice, economics, history, ministries, parks and recreation management, philosophy, prelaw, psychology, religion, religious music, social work, sociology, and youth ministry). Film, animation, exercise science, psychology, business and nursing are the strongest academically. Film and animation, exercise science and nursing have the largest enrollments.

ACTIVITIES: There are 35 groups on campus, including a service organization where students, faculty and staff volunteer more than 11, 000 hours each year, art, band, cheerleading, choir, chorale, chorus, communications, computers, dance, drama, environmental, ethnic, film, Friesen center for volunteer service, honors, international, jazz band, literary magazine, musical theater, newspaper, orchestra, pep band, political, professional, radio and TV, religious, social, social service, student government, and symphony. Popular campus events include Olympiad, Forester Night, Chapel series and Hoe Down. **Sports:** There are 8 intercollegiate sports for men and 8 for women, and 9 intramural sports for men and 9 for women. Facilities include a fieldhouse with an indoor running track, 3 basketball courts, one outdoor basketball court, indoor and outdoor tennis courts, softball and baseball diamonds, an outdoor track, soccer and intramural fields, weight room and aerobic facility, and a gym. **Graduates:** From July 1, 2013 to June 30, 2014, 252 bachelor's degrees were awarded. The most popular majors were business (19%), education (15%), and theology and religious vocations (13%). In an average class, 59% graduate in 6 years or less.

SERVICES: Counseling and information services are available, as is tutoring in some subjects. There is a reader service for the blind, and remedial math and writing. **Library/Resources:** The library contains 236,659 volumes, 11,803 microform items, 7,718 audio/video tapes/CDs/DVDs, and subscribes to 52,798 periodicals including electronic. Computerized library services include interlibrary loans, database searching, Internet access, and Wi-Fi capability. Special learning facilities include an art gallery, radio station, TV station, a writing center. Enterprise Resource Center which helps students with internships, resumes, job training and practicum, herbarium, nature preserve (Thornhill Nature Preserve), arboretum, greenhouse, studio theatre, exercise science training facilities (including a BODPOD), historical archives (United Brethren Historical Center). **Physically Challenged Students:** 64% of the campus is accessible. Facilities include wheelchair ramps, elevators, special parking, specially equipped restrooms,

lowered drinking fountains, and special housing. **Special:** Companies in the area offer a number of internships to students in concentrations such as business, sociology, social work, ministry and missions, education, graphic design, digital media arts, music business, and sport and recreation management. Students may study abroad in a number of countries. A Washington semester, a Hollywood semester, dual majors, correspondence courses with other schools, and an accelerated degree program in organizational management, business administration, accounting, nursing, marketing, human resource management, and organizational management are available. There are 11 national honor societies, a freshman honors program, and 6 departmental honors programs. **Visiting:** There are regularly scheduled orientations for prospective students, available on 3 days notice. There are guides for informal visits, visitors may sit in on classes, and stay overnight. To schedule a visit, contact Carlene Peters at (260) 359-4020. **Campus Safety and Security:** Measures include emergency notification system and security escort services. There are emergency telephones, lighted pathways/sidewalks, controlled access to dorms/residences, security on duty from 6 p.m. to 6 a.m.

REQUIREMENTS: The SAT or ACT is required. Applicants must have 4 years of English, 2 of college-preparatory math, and 3 of social studies. A GPA of 2.3 is required. AP and CLEP credits are accepted. Important factors in the admissions decision are recommendations by school officials, recommendations by alumni, and personality/intangible qualities. Students must complete a minimum of 128 credit hours including 36 in the major, and maintain a GPA of 2.0 overall and a major GPA of at least 2.0 (higher for some programs). Students must complete a program in general education, and take 36 hours in upper-division courses numbered 300 or above. 3 hours of math or computer science and religion courses are required. **Procedure:** Freshmen are admitted to all sessions. Entrance exams should be taken before or during the fall semester of the senior year. There are deferred admissions and rolling admissions plans. Application deadlines are open. Application fee is $20. Applications are accepted on-line. **Transfer Students:** 39 transfer students enrolled in 2013-2014. Transfer applicants should be in good standing at the college previously attended and have maintained a GPA of 2.0. Courses with a grade of C or better transfer. All transcripts and an essay are required. 90 of 128 credits required for the bachelor's degree must be completed at Huntington. **International Students:** There are 38 international students enrolled. The school actively recruits these students. They must take the TOEFL with a minimum score of 525 on the paper-based TOEFL (PBT) or 65 on the Internet-based version (iBT).

ADMISSIONS: 97% of the 2014-2015 applicants were accepted. The SAT scores for the 2014-2015 freshman class were: Critical Reading--43% below 500, 42% between 500 and 599, 12% between 600 and 699, and 3% between 700 and 800; Math--49% below 500, 36% between 500 and 599, 12% between 600 and 699, and 3% between 700 and 800; Writing--56% below 500, 33% between 500 and 599, 10% between 600 and 699, and 1% between 700 and 800. The ACT scores were 7% below 21, 42% between 21 and 23, 44% between 24 and 26, 30% between 27 and 28, and 8% above 28. 53% of the current freshmen were in the top fifth of their class; 79% were in the top two fifths. **Admissions Contact:** Jeff Berggren, Vice President for Enrollment Management & Marketing. E-Mail: *admissions@huntington.edu* Web: *www.huntington.edu*

FINANCIAL AID: In 2014-2015, 90% of all full-time freshmen and 90% of continuing full-time students received some form of financial aid. The average freshman award was $19,659. Need-based scholarships or need-based grants averaged $17,218; need-based self-help aid (loans and jobs) averaged $4,455; non-need-based athletic scholarships averaged $7,266; and other non-need-based awards and non-need-based scholarships averaged $12,362. 25% of undergraduate students work part-time. Average annual earnings from campus work are $3450. The average financial indebtedness of the 2014 graduate was $34,662. The FAFSA and the college's own financial statement are required. The priority date for freshman financial aid applications for fall entry is March 10.

INDIANA INSTITUTE OF TECHNOLOGY (*The complete profile is made available exclusively on our website, www.barronspac.com*)

INDIANA STATE UNIVERSITY   B-4
www.indiana.edu

Terre Haute, IN 47809

	(812) 237-2121
	(800) GO-2-ISU
Fax: (812) 237-8023	Email: admissions@indstate.edu
Full-time: 3700 men, 3625 women	Faculty: I, --$
Part-time: 520 men, 720 women	Ph.D.s: 80%
Graduate: 835 men, 1235 women	Student/Faculty: n/av
Year: semesters, summer session	Tuition: $8000 ($17,000)
Room & Board: $8000	Freshman Class: n/av
SAT or ACT: required	CEEB CODE: 1322
Application Deadline: n/av	COMPETITIVE

Indiana State University, founded in 1865, is a publicly supported institution offering undergraduate and graduate study in liberal arts and sciences, business, health, phys ed and recreation, education, nursing, and technology. The figures in the above capsule and in this profile are approximate. There are 6 undergraduate schools and 1 graduate school. In addition to regional accreditation, ISU has baccalaureate program accreditation with AACSB, ADA, AHEA, CAHEA, CSWE, FIDER, NASAD, NASM, NCATE, NLN, and NRPA. The 235-acre campus is in an urban area 75 miles west of Indianapolis. Including any residence halls, there are 55 buildings.

STUDENT LIFE: 86% of undergraduates are from Indiana. Others are from 50 states, 65 foreign countries, and Canada. 81% are White; 12% African American. **Male To Female Ratio:** 1.1:1. The average age of freshmen is 19; all undergraduates, 23. 31% do not continue beyond their first year; 45% remain to graduate. **Housing:** 3284 students can be accommodated in college housing, which includes single-sex and coed dorms and married student housing. In addition, there are honors houses, special-interest houses, Special freshman dorms. On-campus housing is guaranteed for all 4 years. 64% of students commute. Alcohol is not permitted. All students may keep cars.

FACULTY/CLASSROOMS: 56% of faculty are male; 44% are female. 86% teach undergraduates, 44% do research, and 39% do both. Graduate students teach 11% of introductory courses. The average class size in an introductory lecture is 31; in a laboratory is 22; and in a regular course is 25.

PROGRAMS OF STUDY: ISU confers B.A., B.S., B.F.A., B.M., B.M.E. and B.S.W. degrees. Associate, Master's, and Doctoral degrees are also awarded. Bachelor's degrees are awarded in BIOLOGICAL SCIENCE (biology/biological science), BUSINESS (accounting, banking and finance, business administration and management, insurance, management information systems, marketing and distribution, marketing/retailing/merchandising, recreation and leisure services, and sports management), COMMUNICATIONS AND THE ARTS (art history and appreciation, communications, dramatic arts, English, fine arts, French, German, journalism, music, Spanish, and studio art), COMPUTER AND PHYSICAL SCIENCE (chemistry, computer science, geology, mathematics, and physics), EDUCATION (art education, business education, early childhood education, elementary education, foreign languages education, health education, home economics education, industrial arts education, middle school education, music education, physical education, science education, secondary education, social studies education, and special education), ENGINEERING AND ENVIRONMENTAL DESIGN (aeronautical technology, airline piloting and navigation, computer technology, construction technology, electrical/electronics engineering technology, industrial engineering technology, interior design, manufacturing technology, and mechanical engineering technology), HEALTH PROFESSIONS (environmental health science, medical laboratory technology, nursing, and speech pathology/audiology), SOCIAL SCIENCE (African American studies, anthropology, child care/child and family studies, criminology, dietetics, economics, food science, geography, history, home economics, interdisciplinary studies, liberal arts/general studies, parks and recreation management, philosophy, political science/government, psychology, safety management, social work, sociology, and textiles and clothing). Financial services, teacher education, and aerospace technology are the strongest academically. Criminology, nursing, and elementary education are the largest.

ACTIVITIES: 10% of men belong to 19 national fraternities; 9% of women belong to 13 national sororities. There are 180 groups on campus, including art, band, cheerleading, choir, chorale, chorus, computers, dance, drama, drill team, ethnic, film, gay, honors, international, jazz band, literary magazine, marching band, musical theater, newspaper, orchestra, pep band, political, professional, radio and TV, religious, social, social service, student government, symphony, and yearbook. Popular campus events include Contemporary Music Festival, Theaterfest, and Black History Month. **Sports:** There are 6 intercollegiate sports for men and 8 for women, and 29 intramural sports for men and 29 for women. Facilities include a 20,000-seat football stadium, a 10,000-seat basketball arena, 2 softball diamonds, a baseball field, a soccer field, 2 indoor and outdoor tracks, 2 pools, indoor and outdoor basketball and tennis courts, racquetball, sand volleyball, and volleyball courts, a physical fitness center with weight-training facilities, a climbing wall, and fitness/wellness facilities located in 2 residence halls and the student union. **Graduates:** From July 1, 2013 to June 30, 2014, 1415 bachelor's degrees were awarded. The most popular majors were criminology (8%), elementary education (5%), and psychology (4%). 250 companies recruited on campus in 2013-2014. In an average class, 3% graduate in 3 years or less, 21% graduate in 4 years or less, 37% graduate in 5 years or less, and 42% graduate in 6 years or less.

SERVICES: Counseling and information services are available, as is tutoring in most subjects. There is a reader service for the blind. A learning skills center, an academic advisement center, a counseling center, student support services, a math lab, and a writing lab are available. **Library/Resources:** The library contains 1.3 million volumes, 961,984 microform items, 37,474 audio/video tapes/CDs/DVDs, and subscribes to 43,707 periodicals including electronic. Computerized library services include interlibrary loans, database searching, and Internet access. Special learning facilities include an art gallery, planetarium, radio station, an African American cultural center. **Physically Challenged Students:** 98% of the campus is accessible. Facilities include wheelchair ramps, elevators, special parking, specially equipped restrooms, special class scheduling, lowered drinking fountains, lowered telephones, special housing, and special dining hall facilities. **Special:** There is a freshman honors program. **Visiting:** There are regularly scheduled orientations for prospective students, consisting of Sycamore Preview Days, which include campus tours, opportunities to meet with academic advisers in the majors students are considering, and formal sessions with representatives from financial aid and the career center. There are guides for informal visits, visitors may sit in on classes, and stay overnight. To schedule a visit, contact the Admissions Office. **Campus Safety and Security:** Measures include 24-hour foot and vehicle patrol, emergency notification system, self-defense education, and security escort services. There are emergency telephones, lighted pathways/sidewalks, in-room safes, bicycle and car registration.

REQUIREMENTS: The SAT or ACT is required. The applicant must be a graduate of an accredited secondary school. The GED is accepted. An essay is not required. Applicants are reviewed based on a combination of class rank, GPA, strength of curriculum, academic progress, and standardized test scores. Those students who rank in the top 50% of their class are routinely admitted, whereas those in the bottom 50% of their class are reviewed on an individual basis. Routine admission does not guarantee admission to specific majors. A GPA of 2.5 is required. AP and CLEP credits are accepted. Important factors in the admissions decision are advanced placement or honors courses, leadership record, and extracurricular activities record. All students must complete the general education program, as well as a minimum of 50 hours of upper-division course work. Specific courses required include phys ed, English, speech, math, foreign language, and computer science. A minimum GPA of 2.0 (2.5 for education majors) and a total of 124 credit hours are required for graduation. The number of hours required in the major varies. **Procedure:** Freshmen are admitted fall, spring, and summer. Entrance exams should be taken before January 1. There are deferred admissions and rolling admissions plans. Check with the school for current application deadlines. The application fee is $25. Applications are accepted on-line. **Transfer Students:** 629 transfer students enrolled in 2013-2014. Transfer students must have a minimum GPA of 2.0. 30 of 124 credits required for the bachelor's degree must be completed at ISU. **International Students:** There are 136 international students enrolled. The school actively recruits these students. They must take the TOEFL with a minimum score of 500 on the paper-based TOEFL (PBT) or 61 on the Internet-based version (iBT). They must also take the SAT or ACT.

ADMISSIONS: 18 freshmen graduated first in their class. **Admissions Contact:** Richard Toomey, Director. E-Mail: *admissions@ indstate.edu* Web: *www.indiana.edu*

FINANCIAL AID: In 2014-2015, 68% of all full-time freshmen and 61% of continuing full-time students received some form of financial aid. 40% of all full-time freshmen and 39% of continuing full-time students received need-based aid. The average freshman award was $7,721. Need-based scholarships or need-based grants averaged $5,398; need-based self-help aid (loans and jobs) averaged $2,560; non-need-based athletic scholarships averaged $8,891; other non-need-based awards and non-need-based scholarships averaged $3,504; and $2,508 from other forms of aid. The average financial indebtedness of the 2014 graduate was $20,868. The FAFSA is required. Check with the school for current application deadlines.

INDIANA UNIVERSITY SYSTEM

The Indiana University System, established in 1820, is a public system in Indiana. It is governed by a board of trustees, whose chief administrator is the president. The primary goal of the system is research, teaching, and service. The main priorities are undergraduate education, research, graduate education, economical growth, and access to education. The total student enrollment is usually about 95,000 with 3800 faculty members. Altogether there are 313 baccalaureate, 207 master's, and 108 doctoral programs offered in Indiana University System. Profiles of the 4-year campuses are included in this section.

INDIANA UNIVERSITY BLOOMINGTON   C-4
www.iub.edu

Bloomington, IN 47405	(812) 855-0661
Fax: (812) 855-5102	Email: iuadmit@indiana.edu
Full-time: 15629 men, 15741 women	Faculty: I, av$
	Ph.D.s: 78%
Part-time: 2174 men, 2875 women	Student/Faculty: 17 to 1
Graduate: 5296 men, 4701 women	Tuition: $10,308 ($33,241)
Year: semesters, summer session	Freshman Class: 36362 applied, 27668 accepted, 7716 enrolled
Room & Board: $9493	
SAT CR/M/W: 575/600/565 ACT: 27	CEEB CODE: 1324
Application Deadline: February 1	VERY COMPETITIVE

IU Bloomington, founded in 1820, is the flagship campus of Indiana University's eight campuses statewide. Innovation, creativity, and academic freedom are hallmarks of IU Bloomington and its world-class contributions in research and the arts. Our school traditions include the world-famous Little 500 bicycle race, which furthur recognizes our commitment to emerging technologies. We nurture bright minds with an exceptional support network and breadth of programs. For technology infrastructure and support, our campus was named "most wired" among public universities. There are 17 undergraduate schools. In addition to regional accreditation, IU has baccalaureate program accreditation with AACSB, ACEJMC, CSWE, FIDER, NASAD, NASM, NLN, COAPRT, CCNE, and CAATE. The 1929-acre campus is in a small town 50 miles southwest of Indianapolis. Including any residence halls, there are 560 buildings.

STUDENT LIFE: 65% of undergraduates are from Indiana. Others are from 50 states, 148 foreign countries, and Canada. 69% are White; 14% Foreign. The average age of freshmen is 18; all undergraduates, 20. **Housing:** 12850 students can be accommodated in college housing, which includes single-sex and coed dorms, on-campus apartments, off-campus apartments, and married student housing. In addition, there are honors houses, language houses, special-interest houses, living-learning centers, an international center, a center for women, a wellness center, freshman interest groups (FIGs), and thematic communities. On-campus housing is guaranteed for the freshman year only, and is available on a first-come, first-served basis. 63% of students commute. Alcohol is not permitted. All students may keep cars.

FACULTY/CLASSROOMS: 59% of faculty are male; 41% are female. No introductory courses are taught by graduate students.

PROGRAMS OF STUDY: IU confers B.A., B.F.A., B.G.S., B.M., B.M.Ed., B.S., B.S.Ed., B.S.H.M.P., B.S.N., B.S.P.A., B.S.P.H. and B.S.W. degrees. Master's and Doctoral degrees are also awarded. Bachelor's degrees are awarded in AGRICULTURE (animal science and environmental studies), BIOLOGICAL SCIENCE (biochemistry, biology/adolescence education, biotechnology, human biology, health, and society, microbiology, and neurosciences), BUSINESS (accounting, apparel and accessories marketing, business administration and management, operations, entrepreneurial studies, finance, human resources/organizational mangement, international business, labor studies, nonprofit/public organization management, policy analysis and management, real estate, recreation and leisure services, sports management, supply chain management, and tourism), COMMUNICATIONS AND THE ARTS (arts administration/ management, ballet, communication studies, composition, comparative literature, dance, dramatic arts, dramatic arts, East Asian languages and literature, English, fine arts, folklore and mythology, French, German, Greek (classical), guitar, Italian, jazz, journalism, Latin, linguistics, music, music production/recording technology, music performance, musical theater, organ performance, percussion, piano/organ, Portuguese, Russian, sculpture, Slavic languages, Spanish, sports communication, studio art, telecommunications, theatre arts, visual and performing arts, and voice), COMPUTER AND PHYSICAL SCIENCE (astronomy, astrophysics, chemistry, chemistry/adolescence education, computer science, earth science / adolescence education, geology, informatics and computer science, mathematics, physics, and statistics), EDUCATION (art education, athletic training, early childhood education, elementary education, English education, general studies, health education, journalism education, mathematics education, music education, physical education / exercise science, secondary education, social studies education, Spanish education K-12, and special education), ENGINEERING AND ENVIRONMENTAL DESIGN (computational sciences, environmental science, interior design, and technological management), HEALTH PROFESSIONS (biology, community health work, exercise science, health administration and policy, health care administration, health science, kinesiology, nursing, nutrition and dietetics, optometry, public health, recreation therapy, and speech pathology/ audiology), SOCIAL SCIENCE (African American studies, American studies, anthropology, Asian/American studies, classical, cognitive science, criminal justice, cultural studies/critical theory and analysis, East Asian studies, Eastern European studies, economics, fashion design and technology, gender studies, geography, history, international studies, Judaic studies, legal studies, liberal arts/general studies, Near Eastern studies, philosophy, political science/government, psychology, public affairs, religious studies, Russian and Slavic studies, family studies/soc serv/marriage family, social work, sociology, and South Asian studies). Business, informatics, and biology have the largest enrollments.

ACTIVITIES: There are 650 groups on campus, including art, band, cheerleading, chess, choir, chorale, chorus, communications, computers, dance, debate, drama, drill team, environmental, ethnic, film, gay, honors, international, jazz band, literary magazine, marching band, musical theater, newspaper, opera, orchestra, photography, political, professional, radio and TV, religious, social, social service, student government, and symphony. Popular campus events include Little 500, Founder's Day, Homecoming Parade and IU Dance Marathon. **Sports:** There are 11 intercollegiate sports for men and 13 for women, and 27 intramural sports for men and 27 for women. Facilities include 204,000 square foot Student Recreational Sports Center (SRSC) which features three multi-sport gyms, a spacious strength and conditioning area with more than 400 pieces of cardiovascular and weight-training equipment, the Counsilman/Billingsley Aquatic Center, an elevated running track, and much more. Wildermuth Intramural Center (WIC) features 10 basketball/volleyball courts, a track, squash courts, strength and conditioning areas, and Royer pool (home training ground of legendary Olympian Mark Spitz). Facilities also include Woodlawn field (perfect for soccer, flag football, and more) and numerous tennis courts. IUB also has a track and field complex, softball field, a baseball complex with indoor and outdoor hitting cages, soccer, football, basketball, and a field hockey complex, a golf course, cross-country course and a rowing center. **Graduates:** From July 1, 2013 to June 30, 2014, 6815 bachelor's degrees were awarded. The most popular majors were business, management and marketing (17%), communication, journalist, and related programs (9%), and social sciences (9%). In an average class, 59% graduate in 4 years or less, 74% graduate in 5 years or less, and 78% graduate in 6 years or less.

SERVICES: Counseling and information services are available, as is tutoring in most subjects. There is a reader service for the blind, remedial math, reading, and writing. Skills workshops are also offered. **Library/Resources:** The 25 libraries contain 9.9 million volumes, 5.3 million microform items, and 309,524 audio/video tapes/CDs/DVDs. Computerized library services include interlibrary loans, database searching, Internet access, and Wi-Fi capability. Special learning facilities include an art gallery, natural history museum, radio station, TV station, an observatory, arboretum, museum of world cultures, garden and nature center, musical arts center, and more than 70 research centers. **Physically Challenged Students:** 95% of the campus is accessible. Facilities include wheelchair ramps, elevators, special parking, specially equipped restrooms, special class scheduling, lowered drinking fountains, lowered telephones, and scheduled transportation. **Special:** IU offers cooperative programs with universities in many countries, a variety of internships, and study abroad in more than 57 countries. A Washington semester, work-study programs, B.A.-B.S. degrees in the sciences and liberal arts, dual majors, online degrees and the general studies degree are available. Student-designed majors through the Individualized Major Program, credit for military experience, nondegree study and pass/fail options are also available. There are 10 national honor societies, including Phi Beta Kappa, and a freshman honors program. **Visiting:** There are regularly scheduled orientations for prospective students, including admissions counseling and answers to students' questions about the school. There are guides for informal visits, visitors may sit in on classes, and stay overnight. To schedule a visit, contact the Office of Admissions. **Campus Safety and Security:** Measures include 24-hour foot and vehicle patrol, emergency notification system, self-defense education, and security escort services. There are shuttle buses, emergency telephones, lighted pathways/sidewalks, controlled access to dorms/residences, and safety awareness education.

REQUIREMENTS: The SAT or ACT is required. Applicants must be graduates of an accredited secondary high school or have a GED certificate. Indiana residents must be on track to complete Core 40 curriculum, Core 40 academic curriculum, or the equivalent as a condition of offered admission. SAT: Subject tests are recommended for credit and placement. Auditions for music majors are required. An interview is recommended for information purposes. AP and CLEP credits are accepted. Important factors in the admissions decision are advanced placement or honors courses, parents or siblings attended your school, and recommendations by school officials. The general requirements for graduation include courses in English and writing, math, foreign language, arts and humanities, social and behavioral sciences, natural sciences, and culture studies. Students must complete 120 credit hours, with approximately 36 hours in the major. Many degrees have intensive writing requirements, and the minimum GPA requirement varies by department. Liberal arts requirements are common throughout all degree programs. **Procedure:** Freshmen are admitted to all sessions. Entrance exams should be taken Late in the junior year or early in the senior year. There are deferred admissions and rolling admissions plans. Applications should be filed by February 1 for fall entry; November 1 for spring entry; and February 1 for summer entry, along with a $60 fee. Applications are accepted on-line. **Transfer Students:** 912 transfer students enrolled in 2013-2014. Admission for transfers is selective. Decisions based on high school background, college curriculum, grade trends, choice of major, overall performance. If transferring with fewer than 26 credit hours, must also meet freshman guidelines. 2.3 GPA required for residents; 2.5 GPA for non-residents for consideration. 30 of 120 credits required for the bachelor's degree must be completed at IU. **International Students:** There are 3460 international students enrolled. The school actively recruits these students. They must take the TOEFL with a minimum score of 550 on the paper-

based TOEFL (PBT) or 79 on the Internet-based version (iBT). They must also take the SAT or ACT.

ADMISSIONS: 76% of the 2014-2015 applicants were accepted. The SAT scores for the 2014-2015 freshman class were: Critical Reading--17% below 500, 46% between 500 and 599, 30% between 600 and 699, and 7% between 700 and 800; Math--9% below 500, 39% between 500 and 599, 38% between 600 and 699, and 14% between 700 and 800; Writing--18% below 500, 47% between 500 and 599, 29% between 600 and 699, and 6% between 700 and 800. **Admissions Contact:** Sacha Thieme, Executive Director of Admissions. E-Mail: *iuadmit@indiana.edu* Web: *www.iub.edu*

FINANCIAL AID: In 2014-2015, 71% of all full-time freshmen and 78% of continuing full-time students received some form of financial aid. 43% of all full-time freshmen and 42% of continuing full-time students received need-based aid. The average freshman award was $13,237. Need-based scholarships or need-based grants averaged $11,965 ($45,974 maximum); need-based self-help aid (loans and jobs) averaged $3,253 ($6,133 maximum); non-need-based athletic scholarships averaged $25,854 ($45,988 maximum); and other non-need-based awards and non-need-based scholarships averaged $3,723 ($47,898 maximum). 20% of undergraduate students work part-time. Average annual earnings from campus work are $1690. IU is a member of CSS. The FAFSA is required. The priority date for freshman financial aid applications for fall entry is March 1. The deadline for filing freshman financial aid applications for fall entry is March 10.

INDIANA UNIVERSITY EAST — D-3
www.iue.edu/admissions

Richmond, IN 47374

(765) 973-8208
(800) 959-4485

Fax: (765) 973-8209
Email: applynow@iue.edu

Full-time: 712 men, 1303 women
Faculty: IIB, -$

Part-time: 921 men, 1494 women
Ph.D.s: 60%

Graduate: 39 men, 104 women
Student/Faculty: 15 to 1

Year: semesters, summer session
Tuition: $6783 ($18,081)

Room & Board: n/app
Freshman Class: 1388 applied, 885 accepted, 413 enrolled

SAT CR/M/W: 460/470/440 **ACT: 21**
CEEB CODE: 1194

Application Deadline: open
COMPETITIVE

Indiana University East, a regional campus of Indiana University, offers residents of eastern Indiana, western Ohio and beyond a broad range of bachelor's degrees and selected master's degrees and certificates through its traditional main campus in Richmond, off-campus sites, and online program options. Indiana University East challenges students to grow intellectually and personally in a supportive and scholarly environment where faculty teaching skills and participation in the creation and dissemination of new knowledge and artistic work enhance learning opportunities for all. Indiana University East values a diversity of backgrounds, experiences, and intellectual perspectives among its faculty, staff, and students and in its contributions to the cultural and economic development of the communities it serves. There are 8 undergraduate schools. In addition to regional accreditation, IU East has baccalaureate program accreditation with ACBSP, CSWE, ACEN, and CAEP. The 182-acre campus is in a small town 45 miles west of Dayton, Ohio. Including any residence halls, there are 10 buildings.

STUDENT LIFE: 75% of undergraduates are from Indiana. Others are from 41 states, 37 foreign countries, and Canada. 88% are White. The average age of freshmen is 19; all undergraduates, 26. **Housing:** Alcohol is not permitted. All students commute. All students may keep cars.

FACULTY/CLASSROOMS: 40% of faculty are male; 60% are female. No introductory courses are taught by graduate students.

PROGRAMS OF STUDY: IU East confers B.A., B.F.A., B.G.S., B.S., B.S.Ed., B.S.N and B.S.W. degrees. Associate and Master's degrees are also awarded. Bachelor's degrees are awarded in BIOLOGICAL SCIENCE (biochemistry, biotechnology, and life science), BUSINESS

(business administration and management), COMMUNICATIONS AND THE ARTS (communication studies, English, and fine arts), COMPUTER AND PHYSICAL SCIENCE (applied science, informatics and computer science, mathematics, and natural sciences/mathematics), EDUCATION (elementary education, general studies, and secondary education), HEALTH PROFESSIONS (biology and nursing), SOCIAL SCIENCE (criminal justice, history, humanities, humanities, political science/government, psychology, social work, and sociology). Business, nursing, and psychology have the largest enrollments.

ACTIVITIES: There are 30 groups on campus, including art, cheerleading, computers, dance, drama, environmental, ethnic, gay, honors, newspaper, pep band, political, professional, radio and TV, religious, social, social service, and student government. Popular campus events include Homecoming, and Spirit of Philanthropy. **Sports:** There are 5 intercollegiate sports for men and 6 for women. Facilities include Graf Recreation/Fitness Center, a softball field, tennis and sand volleyball courts, and a field house. **Graduates:** From July 1, 2013 to June 30, 2014, 549 bachelor's degrees were awarded. The most popular majors were business, management, marketing (27%), liberal arts and sciences, general studies and humanities (18%), and health professions and related programs (17%). In an average class, 9% graduate in 4 years or less, 22% graduate in 5 years or less, and 27% graduate in 6 years or less.

SERVICES: Counseling and information services are available, as is tutoring in some subjects, for several freshman-level courses. There is a reader service for the blind, and remedial math, reading, and writing. **Library/Resources:** The library contains 82,500 volumes, 489 microform items, and 1,300 audio/video tapes/CDs/DVDs. Computerized library services include interlibrary loans, database searching, Internet access, and Wi-Fi capability. Special learning facilities include an art gallery and radio station. **Physically Challenged Students:** 98% of the campus is accessible. Facilities include wheelchair ramps, elevators, special parking, lowered drinking fountains, lowered telephones. Special testing accommodations and note taking are available. **Special:** IU East offers a cooperative program in criminal justice with Indiana University-Purdue University and an organizational leadership program through Purdue's Statewide Technology program. IU East also offers online degrees, cross-registration with Earlham College, dual majors, independent study, an internship in social work, pass/fail options, study abroad through Indiana University Bloomington, and credit for life experience. Nondegree study is possible. There are 3 national honor societies and a freshman honors program. **Visiting:** There are regularly scheduled orientations for prospective students, Visits include tours, counseling, registration, and financial aid sessions. There are guides for informal visits and visitors may sit in on classes. To schedule a visit, contact the Admissions Office at (765) 973-8208. **Campus Safety and Security:** Measures include emergency notification system and security escort services. There are emergency telephones, lighted pathways/sidewalks, 14-hour foot and vehicle patrol.

REQUIREMENTS: The SAT is required. The ACT is recommended. Recent high school graduates from Indiana are expected to complete the Core 40 curriculum. Out-of-state students are expected to complete a minimum of 28 semester hours of college prep courses. The four units of academic electives include additional Math, Lab Science, Social Science, Computer Science, Foreign Language, or other college-prep courses. Recent high school graduates should rank in the upper half of their graduating class. AP and CLEP credits are accepted.To graduate, students must satisfactorily complete the General Education Curriculum (30 credit hours) which applies to all IU East students admitted effective summer 2013. Students must complete a minimum of 120 semester hours (30 hours taken at IU East) with a GPA of at least 2.0. **Procedure:** Freshmen are admitted to all sessions. Entrance exams should be taken during the junior or senior year. There are early admissions, deferred admissions, and rolling admissions plans. Application deadlines are open. Application fee is $35. Applications are accepted on-line. **Transfer Students:** 471 transfer students enrolled in 2013-2014. 30 of 120 credits required for the bachelor's degree must be completed at IU East. **International Students:** There are 9 international students enrolled. They must take the TOEFL with a minimum score of 550 on the paper-based TOEFL (PBT) or 79 on the Internet-based version (iBT).

ADMISSIONS: 64% of the 2014-2015 applicants were accepted. The SAT scores for the 2014-2015 freshman class were: Critical Reading--66% below 500, 28% between 500 and 599, 5% between 600 and 699, and 1% between 700 and 800; Math--64% below 500, 30% between 500 and 599, and 6% between 600 and 699; Writing--76% below 500, 21% between 500 and 599, and 3% between 600 and 699. **Admissions Contact:** Molly Vanderpool, Director of Admissions. E-Mail: *applynow@iue.edu* Web: *www.iue.edu/admissions*

FINANCIAL AID: In 2014-2015, 95% of all full-time freshmen and 89% of continuing full-time students received some form of financial aid. 79% of all full-time freshmen and 79% of continuing full-time students received need-based aid. The average freshman award was $8,983. Need-based scholarships or need-based grants averaged $7,823 ($18,981 maximum); need-based self-help aid (loans and jobs) averaged $2,792 ($5,484 maximum); non-need-based athletic scholarships averaged $1,228 ($7,000 maximum); and other non-need-based awards and non-need-based scholarships averaged $1,239 ($14,227 maximum). 7% of undergraduate students work part-time. Average annual earnings from campus work are $2358. The FAFSA and the college's own financial statement are required. The priority date for freshman financial aid applications for fall entry is March 1. The deadline for filing freshman financial aid applications for fall entry is March 10.

INDIANA UNIVERSITY KOKOMO *(The complete profile is made available exclusively on our website, www.barronspac.com)*

INDIANA UNIVERSITY NORTHWEST *(The complete profile is made available exclusively on our website, www.barronspac.com)*

INDIANA UNIVERSITY SOUTH BEND   C-1
www.iusb.edu

South Bend, IN 46634	(574) 520-4839
	(877) GO-2-IUSB
Fax: (574) 520-4834	Email: admissions@iusb.edu
Full-time: 1485 men, 2372 women	Faculty: IIA, --$
Part-time: 1332 men, 2104 women	Ph.D.s: 66%
Graduate: 187 men, 379 women	Student/Faculty: 13 to 1
Year: semesters, summer session	Tuition: $6905 ($18,081)
Room & Board: $8596	Freshman Class: 2456 applied, 1720 accepted, 921 enrolled
SAT CR/M/W: 480/480/450 ACT: 21	CEEB CODE: 1339
Application Deadline: July 31	COMPETITIVE

Indiana University South Bend is the only comprehensive public university in North Central Indiana and the third largest campus in the Indiana University system. There are 7 undergraduate schools. In addition to regional accreditation, IUSB has baccalaureate program accreditation with AACSB, NASM, CCNE, CODA, and CAEP. The 104-acre campus is in a suburban area 95 miles east of Chicago. Including any residence halls, there are 30 buildings.

STUDENT LIFE: 96% of undergraduates are from Indiana. Others are from 14 states, 76 foreign countries, and Canada. 76% are White. **Male To Female Ratio:** 1.6:1. The average age of freshmen is 19; all undergraduates, 23. **Housing:** 388 students can be accommodated in college housing, which includes single-sex and coed on-campus apartments and off-campus apartments. Special housing for international students. On-campus housing is available on a first-come, first-served basis. 91% of students commute. Alcohol is not permitted. All students may keep cars.

FACULTY/CLASSROOMS: 51% of faculty are male; 49% are female. No introductory courses are taught by graduate students.

PROGRAMS OF STUDY: IUSB confers B.A., B.S., B.F.A, B.G.S., B.M., B.S.Ed., B.S.N. and B.S.W. degrees. Associate and Master's degrees are also awarded. Bachelor's degrees are awarded in BIOLOGICAL SCIENCE (biochemistry, biology/adolescence education, and biology/biological science), BUSINESS (business administration and management and labor studies), COMMUNICATIONS AND THE ARTS (communication studies, communications, English, fine arts, French, German, journalism, music, Spanish, communication arts - speech, and theatre arts), COMPUTER AND PHYSICAL SCIENCE (actuarial science, applied mathematics, applied science, chemistry, chemistry/adolescence education, computer science, informatics and computer science, mathematics, and physics), EDUCATION (art education, elementary education, English education, general studies, mathematics education, music education, secondary education, social studies education, Spanish education K-12, and special education), HEALTH PROFESSIONS (dental education, dental hygiene, health care administration, medical imaging, medical technology, and nursing), SOCIAL SCIENCE (anthropology, criminal justice, economics, history, philosophy, political science/government, psychology, public affairs, social work, sociology, and women and gender studies). Business, nursing and elementary education have the largest enrollments.

ACTIVITIES: There are 90 groups on campus, including art, cheerleading, chess, chorus, debate, drama, ethnic, film, forensics, gay, honors, international, jazz band, literary magazine, musical theater, newspaper, opera, orchestra, pep band, photography, political, professional, religious, social, social service, student government, and symphony. Popular campus events include Titan Fest, Red and White Dance, Mini University Welcome Week and Alternative Spring Break Trips. **Sports:** There are 3 intercollegiate sports for men and 3 for women, and 7 intramural sports for men and 7 for women. Facilities include Student Activities Center features: courtside café, competition basketball / volleyball courts (3), racquetball / wallyball Courts (3), indoor running track (1/8 mile), group exercise / aerobic room, table tennis / billiards tables, locker rooms, athletic offices and a wellness center. The state-of- the-art fitness center features life fitness(-plate-loaded) equipment and hampton strength free-weight equipment, along with 23 pieces of cardiovascular machines and weight training machines.**Graduates:** From July 1, 2013 to June 30, 2014, 839 bachelor's degrees were awarded. The most popular majors were health professions (17%), business, management, marketing (17%), liberal arts and sciences, and general studies and humanities (14%). In an average class, 6% graduate in 4 years or less, 18% graduate in 5 years or less, and 26% graduate in 6 years or less.

SERVICES: Counseling and information services are available, as is tutoring in most subjects. There is remedial math, reading, and writing. Taped texts, note takers, and interpreters or transcription services are available. **Library/Resources:** The library contains 327,301 volumes, 177,374 microform items, and 31 audio/video tapes/CDs/DVDs. Computerized library services include interlibrary loans, database searching, Internet access, and Wi-Fi capability. Special learning facilities include an art gallery, science labs, studios for fine and performing arts, instructional media services, and an academic resource center. **Physically Challenged Students:** 95% of the campus is accessible. Facilities include wheelchair ramps, elevators, special parking, specially equipped restrooms, special class scheduling, lowered drinking fountains, and lowered telephones. **Special:** Cross-registration with Northern Indiana Consortium for education (NICE), internships, study abroad, accelerated degree programs, online degrees and dual majors are possible. There are 2 national honor societies and a freshman honors program. **Visiting:** There are regularly scheduled orientations for prospective students, including a visit to the admissions office, a campus tour, professor meetings, and information on financial aid. There are guides for informal visits, visitors may sit in on classes, and stay overnight. To schedule a visit, contact the Admissions Office. **Campus Safety and Security:** Measures include 24-hour foot and vehicle patrol, emergency notification system, and security escort services. There are emergency telephones and lighted pathways/sidewalks.

REQUIREMENTS: The SAT or ACT is required. Indiana high school graduates are expected to complete the Core 40 curriculum and are strongly encouraged to earn the Academic Honors Diploma. Out-of-state students are expected to complete a comparable college-prep curriculum. CLEP credits are accepted. Important factors in the admissions decision are advanced placement or honors courses, extracurricular activities record, and leadership record. All students must complete the campus-wide general education curriculum which is composed of three elements and requires a total of between 33 and 39 credit hours of course work. A total of 120 semester hours, with a minimum GPA of 2.0, is required to graduate. **Procedure:** Freshmen are admitted to all sessions. Entrance exams should be taken 1

year to 6 months before entering the university. There are deferred admissions and rolling admissions plans. Application deadlines are open. Application fee is $35. Applications are accepted on-line. **Transfer Students:** 407 transfer students enrolled in 2013-2014. A 2.0 GPA is required. College transcripts must be submitted. 30 of 120 credits required for the bachelor's degree must be completed at IUSB. **International Students:** There are 113 international students enrolled. The school actively recruits these students. They must take the TOEFL with a minimum score of 530 on the paper-based TOEFL (PBT) or 71 on the Internet-based version (iBT).

ADMISSIONS: 70% of the 2014-2015 applicants were accepted. The SAT scores for the 2014-2015 freshman class were: Critical Reading--61% below 500, 32% between 500 and 599, 6% between 600 and 699, and 1% between 700 and 800; Math--62% below 500, 31% between 500 and 599, 7% between 600 and 699, and 1% between 700 and 800; Writing--72% below 500, 24% between 500 and 599, and 4% between 600 and 699. **Admissions Contact:** Connie Peterson-Miller, Director of Admissions. E-Mail: *admissions@iusb.edu* Web: *www.iusb.edu*

FINANCIAL AID: In 2014-2015, 89% of all full-time freshmen and 87% of continuing full-time students received some form of financial aid. 72% of all full-time freshmen and 75% of continuing full-time students received need-based aid. The average freshman award was $8,231. Need-based scholarships or need-based grants averaged $6,541 ($24,127 maximum); need-based self-help aid (loans and jobs) averaged $2,891 ($6,281 maximum); non-need-based athletic scholarships averaged $570 ($4,000 maximum); and other non-need-based awards and non-need-based scholarships averaged $1,175 ($16,135 maximum). 8% of undergraduate students work part-time. Average annual earnings from campus work are $1763. The FAFSA is required. The priority date for freshman financial aid applications for fall entry is March 1. The deadline for filing freshman financial aid applications for fall entry is March 10.

INDIANA UNIVERSITY SOUTHEAST   C-5
www.ius.edu

New Albany, IN 47150	**(812) 941-2212**
Fax: (812) 941-2595	**Email:** admissions@ius.edu
Full-time: 1461 men, 2126 women	**Faculty:** IIA, -$
Part-time: 1007 men, 1395 women	**Ph.D.s:** 67%
Graduate: 161 men, 292 women	**Student/Faculty:** 14 to 1
Year: semesters, summer session	**Tuition:** $6827 ($18,081)
Room & Board: $9208	**Freshman Class:** 2038 applied, 1637 accepted, 983 enrolled
SAT CR/M/W: 480/470/460 **ACT:** 21	**CEEB CODE:** 1314
Application Deadline: August 17	**COMPETITIVE**

Indiana University Southeast is the regional campus of Indiana University that serves Southern Indiana and the Greater Louisville metropolitan area. There are 7 undergraduate schools. In addition to regional accreditation, IUS has baccalaureate program accreditation with AACSB, CCNE, and CAEP. The 179-acre campus is in a suburban area 10 miles northwest of Louisville, Kentucky, and 114 miles south of Indianapolis. Including any residence halls, there are 50 buildings.

STUDENT LIFE: 72% of undergraduates are from Indiana. Others are from 15 states, and 43 foreign countries. 84% are White. **Male To Female Ratio:** 1.5:1. The average age of freshmen is 19; all undergraduates, 24. **Housing:** 399 students can be accommodated in college housing, which includes single-sex on-campus apartments. On-campus housing is available on a first-come, first-served basis. 89% of students commute. Alcohol is not permitted. All students may keep cars.

FACULTY/CLASSROOMS: 44% of faculty are male; 56% are female. No introductory courses are taught by graduate students.

PROGRAMS OF STUDY: IUS confers B.A., B.F.A., B.G.S., B.S., B.S.Ed. and B.S.N. degrees. Associate and Master's degrees are also awarded. Bachelor's degrees are awarded in BIOLOGICAL SCIENCE (biochemistry), BUSINESS (business administration and management), COMMUNICATIONS AND THE ARTS (communication, English, fine arts, French, German, journalism, music, and Spanish), COMPUTER AND PHYSICAL SCIENCE (applied science, chemistry, clinical laboratory science, combined science, geoscience, informatics and computer science, and mathematics), EDUCATION (elementary education, English education, general studies, health information management, mathematics education, secondary education, social studies education, and special education), HEALTH PROFESSIONS (biology and nursing), SOCIAL SCIENCE (criminal justice, criminology, economics, history, international studies, philosophy, political science/government, psychology, and sociology). Business, nursing and general studies have the largest enrollments.

ACTIVITIES: There are 90 groups on campus, including art, band, cheerleading, choir, chorus, computers, dance, debate, drama, environmental, ethnic, film, gay, honors, international, literary magazine, newspaper, orchestra, pep band, political, professional, religious, social, social service, and student government. Popular campus events include International Festival, Wares of the World, Common Experience, and Hunger Banquet. **Sports:** There are 3 intercollegiate sports for men and 4 for women, and 11 intramural sports for men and 10 for women. Facilities include the campus fitness center, housed inside of the activities building, which has strength machines, a free weight area, plus a variety of cardiovascular exercise equipment that includes treadmills, bikes, elliptical, stairmaster and cross-strainers. In addition, SE has a basketball court, facilities for jogging, badminton, volleyball, gymnastics, 6 tennis courts, baseball and softball fields and playing fields. **Graduates:** From July 1, 2013 to June 30, 2014, 877 bachelor's degrees were awarded. The most popular majors were business, management, marketing (19%), education (14%), liberal arts and sciences, and general studies and humanities (12%). In an average class, 9% graduate in 4 years or less, 24% graduate in 5 years or less, and 32% graduate in 6 years or less.

SERVICES: Counseling and information services are available, as is tutoring in most subjects. There is a reader service for the blind, and remedial math, reading, and writing. The coordinator for services to students with disabilities provides information and coordination of needed services. **Library/Resources:** The library contains 366,009 volumes, 360,722 microform items, and 91,950 audio/video tapes/CDs/DVDs. Computerized library services include interlibrary loans, database searching, Internet access, and Wi-Fi capability. Special learning facilities include an art gallery. **Physically Challenged Students:** All of the campus is accessible. Facilities include wheelchair ramps, elevators, special parking, specially equipped restrooms, lowered drinking fountains, lowered telephones. Special accommodations as needed. **Special:** Cross-registration with Metroversity is possible, and opportunities are provided for study abroad, internships, work-study programs, dual majors, a general studies degree, credit by exam, nondegree study, online degree, accelerated degree programs, and pass/fail options. There are 18 national honor societies. **Visiting:** There are regularly scheduled orientations for prospective students, including an opportunity for students to apply for admission, financial aid, and scholarships, a faculty perspective, a student perspective, and a campus tour. There are guides for informal visits and visitors may sit in on classes. To schedule a visit, contact the Office of Admissions. **Campus Safety and Security:** Measures include 24-hour foot and vehicle patrol, emergency notification system, and self-defense education. There are emergency telephones and lighted pathways/sidewalks.

REQUIREMENTS: The SAT or ACT is required. High school graduates from Indiana are expected to complete the Core 40 curriculum. Out-of-state students are expected to complete a minimum of 28 semester hours of college preparatory courses. Scores from either the SAT or ACT are required for those applicants who graduated from high school within the past two years or who completed a GED and are 19 years of age or younger. Students who have been out of high school for over two years and do not meet the minimum requirements listed for traditional students may be asked to arrange for an interview with an admissions counselor to demonstrate intention through maturity and experience. AP and CLEP credits are accepted. Students must complete 120 credit hours, with 30 in upper-level courses and at least 25 in the major, and must maintain a minimum cumulative GPA of 2.0. **Procedure:** Freshmen are admitted to all sessions. Entrance exams should be taken late junior, early senior year.

There are early admissions, deferred admissions, and rolling admissions plans. Applications should be filed by August 17 for fall entry; December 31 for spring entry, along with a $35 fee. Notification is sent on a rolling basis. Applications are accepted on-line. **Transfer Students:** 507 transfer students enrolled in 2013-2014. A GPA of 2.0 is required for Indiana residents, 2.5 for out-of-state applicants. If the student has earned less than 26 hours of college transfer credit, high school transcripts or GED test scores are required as well as SAT or ACT scores if you have been out of high school less than 2 years. Transfer students are required to submit official transcripts from all previously attended colleges. 30 of 120 credits required for the bachelor's degree must be completed at IUS. **International Students:** There are 16 international students enrolled. They must take the TOEFL with a minimum score of 530 on the paper-based TOEFL (PBT) or 75 on the Internet-based version (iBT) and special tests as directed.

ADMISSIONS: 80% of the 2014-2015 applicants were accepted. The SAT scores for the 2014-2015 freshman class were: Critical Reading--59% below 500, 35% between 500 and 599, and 6% between 600 and 699; Math--62% below 500, 33% between 500 and 599, and 5% between 600 and 699; Writing--73% below 500, 22% between 500 and 599, and 5% between 600 and 699. **Admissions Contact:** Chris Crews, Interim Director of Admissions. E-Mail: *admissions@ius.edu* Web: *www.ius.edu*

FINANCIAL AID: In 2014-2015, 91% of all full-time freshmen and 83% of continuing full-time students received some form of financial aid. 69% of all full-time freshmen and 66% of continuing full-time students received need-based aid. The average freshman award was $7,372. Need-based scholarships or need-based grants averaged $5,967 ($19,201 maximum); need-based self-help aid (loans and jobs) averaged $2,990 ($6,672 maximum); non-need-based athletic scholarships averaged $1,158 ($3,000 maximum); and other non-need-based awards and non-need-based scholarships averaged $1,046 ($14,550 maximum). 9% of undergraduate students work part-time. Average annual earnings from campus work are $1570. The FAFSA is required. The priority date for freshman financial aid applications for fall entry is March 1. The deadline for filing freshman financial aid applications for fall entry is March 10.

INDIANA UNIVERSITY-PURDUE UNIVERSITY FORT WAYNE
D-2

www.ipfw.edu

Fort Wayne, IN 46805	(260) 481-6812
	(866) 597-0010
Fax: (260) 481-5450	Email: ASK@ipfw.edu
Full-time: 3195 men, 3776 women	Faculty: 408; IIA, -$
Part-time: 2468 men, 3235 women	Ph.D.s: 85%
Graduate: 217 men, 323 women	Student/Faculty: 17 to 1
Year: semesters, summer session	Tuition: $7949 ($19,092)
Room & Board: $7572	Freshman Class: 3386 applied, 3077 accepted, 1559 enrolled
SAT CR/M/W: 498/498/477 ACT: 22	CEEB CODE: 1336
Application Deadline: August 1	COMPETITIVE

Indiana University, founded in 1917, joined Purdue University at Fort Wayne, founded in 1944. The combined school, a state-controlled institution, offers programs in liberal arts, science, business, education, health sciences, engineering, technology, public affairs, and visual and performing arts. There are 8 undergraduate schools and 5 graduate schools. In addition to regional accreditation, IPFW has baccalaureate program accreditation with AACSB, ABET, ADA, NASM, NCATE, NLN, ACS, AMTA, CAC, CODA, EAC, NASPAA, TAC, and NAST. The 683-acre campus is in a suburban area 113 miles north of Indianapolis. Including any residence halls, there are 51 buildings.

STUDENT LIFE: 97% of undergraduates are from Indiana. Others are from 36 states, 46 foreign countries, and Canada. 80% are from public schools. 83% are White. The average age of freshmen is 21; all undergraduates, 22. 31% do not continue beyond their first year; 25% remain to graduate. **Housing:** 1204 students can be accommodated in college housing, which includes coed on-campus apartments. On-campus housing is available on a first-come, first-served basis. 94% of students commute. Alcohol is not permitted. All students may keep cars.

FACULTY/CLASSROOMS: 56% of faculty are male; 44% are female. All teach undergraduates, and 92% do research. Graduate students teach 3% of introductory courses. The average class size in an introductory lecture is 20; in a laboratory is 19; and in a regular course is 20.

PROGRAMS OF STUDY: IPFW confers B.A., B.S., B.F.A., B.G.S., B.Mus., B.Mus.Ed., B.S.B., B.S.C., B.S.C.E., B.S.Cp.E., B.S.Ed., B.S.E.E., B.S.G., B.S.M.E., B.S.P.A., B.S.L.S. and B.S.M.T. degrees. Associate and Master's degrees are also awarded. Bachelor's degrees are awarded in BIOLOGICAL SCIENCE (biochemistry and biology/ biological science), BUSINESS (accounting, banking and finance, business administration and management, business economics, hospitality management services, labor studies, management science, marketing/retailing/merchandising, and organizational leadership and management), COMMUNICATIONS AND THE ARTS (communications, crafts, dramatic arts, drawing, English, English literature, fine arts, French, German, graphic design, music, music performance, painting, percussion, photography, piano/organ, printmaking, sculpture, Spanish, speech/debate/rhetoric, strings, technical and business writing, telecommunications, visual design, and voice), COMPUTER AND PHYSICAL SCIENCE (actuarial science, chemistry, computer programming, computer science, earth science, geology, information sciences and systems, mathematics, physical sciences, physics, and statistics), EDUCATION (art education, computer education, early childhood education, elementary education, English education, foreign languages education, mathematics education, middle school education, music education, science education, and secondary education), ENGINEERING AND ENVIRONMENTAL DESIGN (civil engineering, computer engineering, computer graphics, electrical/electronics engineering, electrical/electronics engineering technology, engineering, engineering technology, industrial engineering technology, interior design, mechanical engineering, and mechanical engineering technology), HEALTH PROFESSIONS (health care administration, medical technology, music therapy, nursing, predentistry, premedicine, preoptometry, prepharmacy, preveterinary science, and speech pathology/audiology), SOCIAL SCIENCE (anthropology, criminal justice, economics, history, human services, liberal arts/general studies, philosophy, political science/ government, prelaw, psychology, public administration, public affairs, social science, sociology, and women's studies). Engineering and biology are the strongest academically. Business, education and engineering have the largest enrollments.

ACTIVITIES: There are 127 groups on campus, including art, band, cheerleading, chess, choir, chorus, dance, debate, drama, ethnic, film, forensics, gay, honors, international, jazz band, literary magazine, musical theater, newspaper, opera, orchestra, pep band, political, professional, radio and TV, religious, social, social service, student government, and symphony. Popular campus events include Mastodon Roast, and Freshmen Fest. **Sports:** There are 7 intercollegiate sports for men and 8 for women, and 19 intramural sports for men and 19 for women. Facilities include a physical fitness center with a gym, 3 basketball courts, an indoor track, a weight room, 4 racquetball courts, 1 wallyball court, a fencing and dance room, baseball and soccer fields, and an indoor soccer facility. **Graduates:** From July 1, 2013 to June 30, 2014, 1341 bachelor's degrees were awarded. The most popular majors were engineering (19%), general studies (15%), and health and human services (14%). 181 companies recruited on campus in 2013-2014. In an average class, 6% graduate in 4 years or less, 17% graduate in 5 years or less, and 25% graduate in 6 years or less.

SERVICES: Counseling and information services are available, as is tutoring in most subjects. There is a reader service for the blind, and remedial math, reading, and writing. **Library/Resources:** The library contains 366,918 volumes, 481,548 microform items, 4,634 audio/ video tapes/CDs/DVDs, and subscribes to 29,848 periodicals including electronic. Computerized library services include interlibrary loans, database searching, and Internet access. Special learning facilities include an art gallery, radio station, and TV station. **Physically Challenged Students:** All of the campus is accessible. Facilities include wheelchair ramps, elevators, special parking, specially equipped restrooms, special class scheduling, lowered drinking fountains, lowered telephones, and special housing. **Special:** There are continuing education, co-op, and work-study programs, as well as study abroad in 5 countries. An accelerated general studies degree, cross-registration with other Fort Wayne colleges, B.A.-B.S. degrees, dual majors, a Washington semester for public affairs students, internships, and credit for military experience are available. Nondegree study and pass/fail options are possible. An accelerated MBA degree is also offered. There are 16 national honor societies and a freshman honors program. **Visiting:** There are regularly scheduled orientations for prospective students. There are guides for informal visits and visitors may sit in on classes. To schedule a visit, contact the Admissions Office. **Campus Safety and Security:** Measures include 24-hour foot and vehicle patrol, emergency notification system, self-defense education, and security escort services. There are shuttle buses, emergency telephones, lighted pathways/sidewalks, and controlled access to dorms/residences.

REQUIREMENTS: The SAT or ACT is required, with a minimum composite score of 1420 on the SAT or a minimum composite score of 20 on the ACT. Indiana Core 40, Academic Honors, or Technical Honors Diploma are required for in-state students. Out-of-state students must complete a college prep curriculum IPFW requires applicants to be in the upper 50% of their class. A GPA of 2.8 is required. AP and CLEP credits are accepted. Important factors in the admissions decision are recommendations by school officials, evidence of special talent, and advanced placement or honors courses. All bachelor's degree students must complete 120 credits, including 33 general education hours, with a GPA of 2.0, and take English composition, speech communication, and math to graduate. Students must take 32 credit hours at the 200 level or above (including 15 credit hours at the 300 level or above) in their major. **Procedure:** Freshmen are admitted fall, spring, and summer. Entrance exams should be taken in the senior year of high school. There are deferred admissions and rolling admissions plans. Applications should be filed by August 1 for fall entry; December 15 for spring entry; and May 1 for summer entry, along with a $50 fee. Notification is sent on a rolling basis. Applications are accepted on-line. **Transfer Students:** 571 transfer students enrolled in 2013-2014. Transfer applicants must have a minimum GPA of 2.0. Grades of C or better transfer for credit. 32 of 120 credits required for the bachelor's degree must be completed at IPFW. **International Students:** There are 177 international students enrolled. The school actively recruits these students. They must take the TOEFL with a minimum score of 550 on the paper-based TOEFL (PBT) or 79 on the Internet-based version (iBT), or pass level 112 of an ESL program. They may also take the ACT or SAT.

ADMISSIONS: 91% of the 2014-2015 applicants were accepted. The SAT scores for the 2014-2015 freshman class were: Critical Reading--53% below 500, 35% between 500 and 599, 10% between 600 and 699, and 2% between 700 and 800; Math--52% below 500, 35% between 500 and 599, 12% between 600 and 699, and 1% between 700 and 800; Writing--63% below 500, 29% between 500 and 599, 6% between 600 and 699, and 1% between 700 and 800. The ACT scores were 39% below 21, 27% between 21 and 23, 17% between 24 and 26, 5% between 27 and 28, and 13% above 28. 29% of the current freshmen were in the top fifth of their class; 62% were in the top two fifths. 12 freshmen graduated first in their class. **Admissions Contact:** Tonishea Jackson, Director of Admissions. E-Mail: *ask@ipfw.edu* Web: *www.ipfw.edu*

FINANCIAL AID: In 2014-2015, 74% of all full-time freshmen and continuing full-time students received some form of financial aid. 51% of all full-time freshmen and continuing full-time students received need-based aid. The average freshman award was $9,274. Need-based scholarships or need-based grants averaged $5,601 ($13,021 maximum); need-based self-help aid (loans and jobs) averaged $3,176 ($26,398 maximum); non-need-based athletic scholarships averaged $12,779 ($39,791 maximum); and other non-need-based awards and non-need-based scholarships averaged $4,001 ($24,867 maximum). 1% of undergraduate students work part-time. Average annual earnings from campus work are $2000. The average financial indebtedness of the 2014 graduate was $28,930. IPFW is a member of CSS. The FAFSA is required. The priority date for freshman financial aid applications for fall entry is March 10.

INDIANA UNIVERSITY-PURDUE UNIVERSITY INDIANAPOLIS

C-3

www.iupui.edu

Indianapolis, IN 46202   (317) 274-4591

Fax: (317) 278-1862   Email: apply@iupui.edu
Full-time: 7434 men, 9828 women   Faculty: I, --$
Part-time: 2367 men, 2896 women   Ph.D.s: 85%
Graduate: 3654 men, 4511 women   Student/Faculty: 18 to 1
Year: semesters, summer session   Tuition: $8909 ($30,089)
Room & Board: $8702   Freshman Class: 12920 applied, 9107 accepted, 3949 enrolled
SAT CR/M/W: 495/505/480 ACT: 22   CEEB CODE: 1325
Application Deadline: May 1   COMPETITIVE

As Indiana's premier urban public research university, IUPUI believes in the power of transformation. We are committed to providing educational opportunities that transform the lives of our students, our community, and the changing world around us. There are 20 undergraduate schools. In addition to regional accreditation, IUPUI has baccalaureate program accreditation with AACSB, ABET, CSWE, NASAD, NASM, NLN, FEPAC, CAAHEP, and CODA. The 534-acre campus is in an urban area near downtown Indianapolis. Including any residence halls, there are 141 buildings.

STUDENT LIFE: 94% of undergraduates are from Indiana. Others are from 48 states, 149 foreign countries, and Canada. 70% are White. The average age of freshmen is 19; all undergraduates, 24. **Housing:** 1979 students can be accommodated in college housing, which includes coed dorms, on-campus apartments, off-campus apartments, and married student housing. In addition, there are honors houses, special-interest houses, International house, women in science house, sustainability house. On-campus housing is available on a first-come and first-served basis. 88% of students commute. Alcohol is not permitted. All students may keep cars.

FACULTY/CLASSROOMS: 55% of faculty are male; 45% are female. No introductory courses are taught by graduate students.

PROGRAMS OF STUDY: IUPUI confers B.A., B.S., B.S.B., B.A.E.D., B.F.A., B.G.S., B.S.B., B.S.C.E., B.S.E.D., B.S.E.E., B.S.H.S.M., B.S.K., B.S.M.E., B.S.M.T., B.S.P.A., B.S.P.E., B.S.P.H. and B.S.W. degrees. Associate, Master's, and Doctoral degrees are also awarded. Bachelor's degrees are awarded in AGRICULTURE (environmental studies), BIOLOGICAL SCIENCE (biology/adolescence education, biotechnology, forensic science, and neurosciences), BUSINESS (accounting, business administration and management, finance, human resources/organizational mgmt, labor studies, management science, marketing, marketing and distribution, organizational leadership and management, sports management, supply chain management, sustainable management, and tourism), COMMUNICATIONS AND THE ARTS (American Sign Language, art history, ceramic art and design, communication studies, English, English as a second/foreign language, fine arts, French, German, journalism, media arts, Technical Communication, music technology, painting, photography, printmaking, public relations, sculpture, and Spanish), COMPUTER AND PHYSICAL SCIENCE (actuarial science, chemistry, chemistry/adolescence education, clinical laboratory science, Computer Engineering Technology, computer information technology, computer science, earth science / adolescence education, energy science, geology, informatics and computer science, mathematics, and physics), EDUCATION (art education, early childhood education, elementary education, English education, general studies, health information management, health and education science, mathematics education, secondary education, social studies education, and Spanish education K-12), ENGINEERING AND ENVIRONMENTAL DESIGN (bioengineering, biomedical engineering, computer engineering, computer graphics, electrical/electronics engineering, electrical/electronics engineering technology, engineering management, environmental science, furniture design, interior design, manufacturing technology, mechanical engineering, mechanical engineering technology, and nuclear medicine technology), HEALTH PROFESSIONS (biology, cytotechnology, dental hygiene, environmental health science, exercise science, health administration and policy, health care administration, health science, medical imaging, kinesiology, medical technology, nursing, premedicine, preoccupational therapy, prepharmacy, pre-physician assistant, prephysical therapy, preveterinary science, public health, radiation therapy, and respiratory therapy), SOCIAL SCIENCE (africana studies, anthropology, criminal justice, economics, geography, history, interdisciplinary studies, international studies, philosophy, political science/government, prelaw, psychology, public affairs, religious studies, social work, and sociology). Nursing, general studies, and elementary education have the largest enrollments.

ACTIVITIES: 1% of men belong to 9 national fraternities; 2% of women belong to 10 national sororities. There are 350 groups on campus, including art, band, cheerleading, chess, computers, dance, debate, drama, environmental, ethnic, film, forensics, gay, honors, international, jazz band, literary magazine, newspaper, pep band, photography, political, professional, radio and TV, religious, social, social service, and student government. Popular campus events include Weeks of Welcome, Spring Dance, InternationalFest, Jag-A-Palooza, Cultural Heritage Months, IUPUI Regatta and FountainFest. **Sports:** There are 7 intercollegiate sports for men and 9 for women, and 11 intramural sports for men and 11 for women. Facilities include IUPUI Gymnasium (The Jungle), Michael A. Carroll Soccer Stadium, a competition pool, instructional pool and diving well, IUPUI Softball Complex, Michael A. Carroll Stadium, 12,000-seat track and field stadium, and the National Institute for Fitness and Sport: a 117,000-square foot facility with a 200-meter indoor track, free weights, Cybex and cardio equipment, pilates studio, indoor batting nets, and half-size basketball courts. **Graduates:** From July 1, 2013 to June 30, 2014, 3826 bachelor's degrees were awarded. The most popular majors were health professions (18%), business, management and marketing (16%), liberal arts and sciences and general studies and humanities (11%). In an average class, 18% graduate in 4 years or less, 36% graduate in 5 years or less, and 44% graduate in 6 years or less.

SERVICES: Counseling and information services are available, as is tutoring in most subjects. There is a reader service for the blind, and remedial math, reading, and writing. **Library/Resources:** The 5 libraries contain 2.1 million volumes, 457,716 microform items, and 1.5 million audio/video tapes/CDs/DVDs. Computerized library services include interlibrary loans, database searching, Internet access, and Wi-Fi capability. Special learning facilities include an art gallery, radio station, an 85-acre medical center, 100 research centers, 27 signature centers, the IU Research and Technology Corporation. **Physically Challenged Students:** All of the campus is accessible. Facilities include wheelchair ramps, elevators, special parking, specially equipped restrooms, special class scheduling, lowered drinking fountains, lowered telephones, classroom aids and sign language interpreters. **Special:** There is a metropolitan studies program for career work in the city and cross-registration with the Consortium for Urban Education. IUPUI also offers study abroad, combined B.A.-B.S. degree programs, internships, work-study programs, dual and student-designed majors, online degrees, nondegree study, nontraditional programs for adult learners, and interdisciplinary majors such as business economics and public policy, health occupations education, and interdisciplinary engineering. There are 10 national honor societies and a freshman honors program. **Visiting:** There are regularly scheduled orientations for prospective students, consisting of a campus tour and talks with students. There are guides for informal visits and visitors may sit in on classes. To schedule a visit, contact the Office of Admissions. **Campus Safety and Security:** Measures include 24-hour foot and vehicle patrol, emergency notification system, self-defense education, and security escort services. There are shuttle buses, emergency telephones, and lighted pathways/sidewalks.

REQUIREMENTS: The SAT or ACT is required. Indiana high school graduates are expected to complete the Core 40 curriculum, and are strongly encouraged to earn the Academic Honors Diploma. Out-of-state students are expected to complete a required core of classes. The units of academic electives can be a combination of additional mathematics, laboratory science, social science, computer science, foreign language, or other courses of college preparatory nature. Some IUPUI schools require additional courses, and that students rank in the upper half of high school class or score above average on the GED.

SAT or ACT scores for Indiana residents should be at or above the Indiana median. Student who have been out of high school for more than 1 year are not required to submit. AP and CLEP credits are accepted. All students must complete 120 to 126 credits required for the bachelor's degree. Most schools also require grades of C or higher in major courses. All beginning first-year students at Indiana University–Purdue University Indianapolis (IUPUI) will complete 30 hours of general education course work (the IUPUI General Education Core) prior to graduation with either an associate degree a baccalaureate degree. Course work is divided into the broad domains of Foundational Intellectual Skills (core communication, analytical reasoning, and cultural understanding) and course work that promotes Intellectual Breadth and Adaptiveness (life and physical sciences; and arts, humanities, and social sciences). **Procedure:** Freshmen are admitted to all sessions. Entrance exams should be taken by the end of junior year or fall of senior year. There are deferred admissions and rolling admissions plans. Application deadlines are open. Application fee is $50. Notification is sent on a rolling basis. Applications are accepted on-line. **Transfer Students:** 1717 transfer students enrolled in 2013-2014. Transfers who are Indiana residents must present a minimum GPA of 2.0 in all previous college work; out-of-state residents need a minimum 2.5. All applicants must be in good standing at their former schools. 30 of 120 credits required for the bachelor's degree must be completed at IUPUI. **International Students:** There are 764 international students enrolled. The school actively recruits these students. They must take the TOEFL with a minimum score of 550 on the paper-based TOEFL (PBT) or 79 on the Internet-based version (iBT).

ADMISSIONS: 70% of the 2014-2015 applicants were accepted. The SAT scores for the 2014-2015 freshman class were: Critical Reading--51% below 500, 36% between 500 and 599, 12% between 600 and 699, and 1% between 700 and 800; Math--47% below 500, 35% between 500 and 599, 16% between 600 and 699, and 2% between 700 and 800; Writing--59% below 500, 31% between 500 and 599, 9% between 600 and 699, and 1% between 700 and 800. **Admissions Contact:** Chris J. Foley, Director of Undergraduate Admissions. E-Mail: *apply@iupui.edu* Web: *www.iupui.edu*

FINANCIAL AID: In 2014-2015, 89% of all full-time freshmen and 86% of continuing full-time students received some form of financial aid. 69% of all full-time freshmen and 68% of continuing full-time students received need-based aid. The average freshman award was $11,272. Need-based scholarships or need-based grants averaged $8,561 ($43,731 maximum); need-based self-help aid (loans and jobs) averaged $3,520 ($9,724 maximum); non-need-based athletic scholarships averaged $8,689 ($24,000 maximum); and other non-need-based awards and non-need-based scholarships averaged $2,503 ($47,742 maximum). 11% of undergraduate students work part-time. Average annual earnings from campus work are $2448. The FAFSA is required. The priority date for freshman financial aid applications for fall entry is March 1. The deadline for filing freshman financial aid applications for fall entry is March 10.

INDIANA WESLEYAN UNIVERSITY   C-2
www.indwes.edu

Marion, IN 46953	765-677-1677
	1-866-GO-TO-IWU
Fax: 765-677-2333	Email: admissions@indwes.edu
Full-time: n/av	Faculty: n/av
Part-time: n/av	Ph.D.s: 67%
Graduate: n/av	Student/Faculty: 15 to 1
Year: semesters, summer session	Tuition: $24,102
Room & Board: $7713	Freshman Class: 2606 applied, 2521 accepted, 718 enrolled
SAT CR/M/W: 525/535/515 **ACT:** 24	CEEB CODE: 1446
Application Deadline: n/av	**VERY COMPETITIVE**

Indiana Wesleyan University, founded in 1920, is a private, evangelical Christian, liberal arts university. The University mission states: "Indiana Wesleyan University is a Christ-centered academic community committed to changing the world by developing students in

character, scholarship, and leadership." There are 6 undergraduate schools and 3 graduate schools. In addition to regional accreditation, IWU has baccalaureate program accreditation with CSWE, NASM, NCATE, CCNE, CACREP, and CAATE. The 320-acre campus is in a small town in north-central Indiana, 70 miles north of Indianapolis, 50 miles south of Fort Wayne. Including any residence halls, there are 64 buildings.

STUDENT LIFE: 53% of undergraduates are from Indiana. Others are from 46 states, 7 foreign countries, and Canada. 91% are White. 92% are Protestant. **Male To Female Ratio:** Is 1:1. The average age of freshmen is 18; all undergraduates, 20. 26% do not continue beyond their first year; 70% remain to graduate. **Housing:** 2801 students can be accommodated in college housing, which includes single-sex dorms, on-campus apartments, and married student housing. In addition, there are special-interest houses. On-campus housing is guaranteed for all 4 years, is available on a first-come, and first-served basis. 82% of students live on campus; of those, 75% remain on campus on weekends. Alcohol is not permitted. All students may keep cars.

FACULTY/CLASSROOMS: 60% of faculty are male; 40% are female. 98% teach undergraduates, 20% do research, and 20% do both. No introductory courses are taught by graduate students. The average class size in an introductory lecture is 50; in a laboratory is 15; and in a regular course is 18.

PROGRAMS OF STUDY: IWU confers A.B., B.A., B.S.N., B.S.M. and M.A. degrees. Associate, Master's, and Doctoral degrees are also awarded. Bachelor's degrees are awarded in BIOLOGICAL SCIENCE (biology/biological science), BUSINESS (accounting, banking and finance, business administration and management, management science, marketing/retailing/merchandising, and recreational facilities management), COMMUNICATIONS AND THE ARTS (applied music, art, ceramic art and design, communications, creative writing, English, illustration, music, music theory and composition, painting, photography, printmaking, Spanish, and studio art), COMPUTER AND PHYSICAL SCIENCE (chemistry, computer science, information sciences and systems, mathematics, and science), EDUCATION (art education, athletic training, elementary education, English education, mathematics education, music education, nursing education, physical education, science education, secondary education, social studies education, and special education), ENGINEERING AND ENVIRONMENTAL DESIGN (computer graphics and interior design), HEALTH PROFESSIONS (health, medical laboratory technology, nursing, and premedicine), SOCIAL SCIENCE (addiction studies, biblical studies, criminal justice, economics, history, law enforcement and corrections, liberal arts/general studies, ministries, political science/government, prelaw, psychology, religion, religious education, religious music, social studies, social work, and sociology). Nursing, education, pre-medicine, and religion are the strongest academically. Nursing, education, business, psychology, pre-medicine, and religion have the largest enrollments.

ACTIVITIES: There are no fraternities or sororities. There are 35 groups on campus, including art, band, cheerleading, choir, chorale, chorus, computers, drama, environmental, ethnic, film, honors, international, jazz band, literary magazine, musical theater, newspaper, opera, orchestra, pep band, photography, political, professional, radio and TV, religious, social, social service, student government, symphony, and yearbook. Popular campus events include Spotted Cow Music Festival, Friday Night Live and Taste of Marion. **Sports:** There are 9 intercollegiate sports for men and 9 for women, and 21 intramural sports for men and 21 for women. Facilities include a recreation and wellness center with fitness rooms, weight rooms, swimming pool, athletic training center, indoor track, practice/intramural gym, basketball gymnasium, locker rooms. Outdoor fields: soccer, baseball, softball, track and field, tennis courts. Indoor Sports Complex: long/triple jump pits, pole vault area, indoor weight throw, 8 lane 200 meter track, and a competition area. **Graduates:** From July 1, 2013 to June 30, 2014, 635 bachelor's degrees were awarded. The most popular majors were nursing (18%), elementary education (8%), and psychology (6%). In an average class, 56% graduate in 4 years or less, 68% graduate in 5 years or less, and 70% graduate in 6 years or less.

SERVICES: Counseling and information services are available, as is tutoring in most subjects. There is a reader service for the blind, and remedial math, reading, and writing. External testing, a note-taker service, and advocacy are available. **Library/Resources:** The library contains 276,070 volumes, 315,162 microform items, 11,479 audio/video tapes/CDs/DVDs, and subscribes to 106,118 periodicals including electronic. Computerized library services include interlibrary loans, database searching, Internet access, and Wi-Fi capability. Special learning facilities include an art gallery, radio station, TV station, a globe theatre, and the daily planet. **Physically Challenged Students:** 95% of the campus is accessible. Facilities include wheelchair ramps, elevators, special parking, specially equipped restrooms, special class scheduling, lowered drinking fountains, lowered telephones, special housing. **Special:** Students may study abroad in 20 countries. IWU also offers business, pastoral, nursing, and social work internships, cross-registration with CCCU, a Washington semester, work-study programs with the Economic Growth Council, pass/fail options, and nondegree study. Accelerated degree programs are available in accounting, business administration, business information, management, and nursing. Students may earn a B.A.-B.S. degree in management, business, and education. Dual majors and student-designed majors are available. Adult learners may earn credit for life experience toward bachelor's degrees in business. There are 6 national honor societies, a freshman honors program, and 12 departmental honors programs. **Visiting:** There are regularly scheduled orientations for prospective students, including appointments with admissions counselors and professors, campus tours, classroom visits, and meals. There are guides for informal visits, visitors may sit in on classes, and stay overnight. To schedule a visit, contact the Admissions Office. **Campus Safety and Security:** Measures include 24-hour foot and vehicle patrol, emergency notification system, and security escort services. There are emergency telephones, lighted pathways/sidewalks, and controlled access to dorms/residences.

REQUIREMENTS: The SAT or ACT is required. The completed application, high school transcript, test scores including an essay (SAT or ACT), recommendation, and a community values contract are necessary for an admission decision. A tuition deposit is required before registration and is fully refundable until May 1. The admission decision may be made with a high school transcript at the end of the junior year. It is to be followed later by the full four-year record and certification of graduation. A student should have a minimum of each of the following: 8 credits in language arts (equivalent to 4 years); 6-8 credits in mathematics (equivalent to 3-4 years); 6 credits in science (equivalent to 3 years); 6 credits in social studies (equivalent to 3 years); 4 credits in foreign language (equivalent to 2 years); 2 credits in health, physical education, safety (equivalent to 1 year); and 4-6 credits from other courses offered (equivalent to 2-3 years). Regular admission requires that applicants have at least a 2.6 cumulative high school GPA on a 4.0 scale and a 880 SAT (Math and Critical Reading) or 18 ACT score. Applicants who do not meet the requirements for regular admission may request special consideration. A GPA of 2.6 is required. AP and CLEP credits are accepted. Important factors in the admissions decision are ability to finance college education, advanced placement or honors courses, parents or siblings attended your school, evidence of special talent, personality/intangible qualities, extracurricular activities record, recommendations by alumni, recommendations by school officials, leadership record, and geographical diversity. A 52-credit general education core includes 12 credit hours of humanities, 10 of math and science, 9 each of English and history or social studies, 6 of biblical literature, and 3 each of intercultural experience and phys ed. Foreign language courses are required for the B.A., computer literacy courses for the B.S. To graduate, students must complete at least 124 semester hours, including 40 to 60 in a major field of study, with a minimum GPA of 2.0 overall and 2.25 in the major. A thesis is required for the honors college. **Procedure:** Freshmen are admitted to all sessions. Entrance exams should be taken during junior year, or early in their senior year. There are early decision, deferred admissions, and rolling admissions plans. Application deadlines are open. Application fee is $25. Applications are accepted on-line. **Transfer Students:** 106 transfer students enrolled in 2013-2014. In addition to standard admissions requirements, transfers must submit transcripts of all previous college work and be in good standing at their former school. 30 of 124 credits required for the bachelor's degree must be completed at IWU. **International Students:** There are 111 international students enrolled. The school actively recruits these students. They must take the TOEFL with a minimum score of 550 on the paper-based TOEFL (PBT) or 79 on the Internet-based version (iBT). They must also take the SAT or ACT, scoring 18.

ADMISSIONS: 97% of the 2014-2015 applicants were accepted. The SAT scores for the 2014-2015 freshman class were: Critical Reading--33% below 500, 45% between 500 and 599, 19% between 600 and 699, and 3% between 700 and 800; Math--32% below 500, 44% between 500 and 599, 22% between 600 and 699, and 2% between 700 and 800; Writing--43% below 500, 40% between 500 and 599, 15% between 600 and 699, and 2% between 700 and 800. The ACT scores were 5% below 21, 38% between 21 and 23, 47% between 24 and 26, and 10% above 28. 57% of the current freshmen were in the top fifth of their class; 85% were in the top two fifths. There were 10 National Merit finalists. 28 freshmen graduated first in their class. **Admissions Contact:** Tracy Curfman, Admissions Admistrative Assistant. E-Mail: *admissions@indwes.edu* Web: *http:/www.indwes.edu/Admissions/Undergraduate/*

FINANCIAL AID: In 2014-2015, 99% of all full-time freshmen and 94% of continuing full-time students received some form of financial aid. 73% of all full-time freshmen and 63% of continuing full-time students received need-based aid. The average freshman award was $21,377. Need-based scholarships or need-based grants averaged $13,847; need-based self-help aid (loans and jobs) averaged $7,446; non-need-based athletic scholarships averaged $6,994; and other non-need-based awards and non-need-based scholarships averaged $5,185. 51% of undergraduate students work part-time. The average financial indebtedness of the 2014 graduate was $31,482. The FAFSA and the college's own financial statement are required. The deadline for filing freshman financial aid applications for fall entry is March 1.

MANCHESTER UNIVERSITY C-2
www.manchester.edu

North Manchester, IN 46962	**(260) 982-5055**
	(800) 852-3648
Fax: (260) 982-5239	**Email:** admitinfo@manchester.edu
Full-time: 600 men, 600 women	**Faculty:** IIB, --$
Part-time: 5 men, 10 women	**Ph.D.s:** n/av
Graduate: n/av	**Student/Faculty:** n/av
Year: 4-1-4, summer session	**Tuition:** $25,970
Room & Board: $9100	**Freshman Class:** n/av
SAT or ACT: required	**CEEB CODE:** 1440
Application Deadline: open	**COMPETITIVE**

Manchester University, formerly Manchester College, established in 1889, is a private liberal arts college affiliated with the Church of the Brethren offering undergraduate programs in accounting, business and economics, premedicine, education, psychology, the social sciences, and the humanities. The figures in the above capsule and in this profile are approximate. There is 1 graduate school. In addition to regional accreditation, Manchester has baccalaureate program accreditation with CSWE and NCATE. The 124-acre campus is in a small town 35 miles west of Fort Wayne, Indiana. Including any residence halls, there are 44 buildings.

STUDENT LIFE: 90% of undergraduates are from Indiana. Others are from 21 states, 20 foreign countries, and Canada. 99% are from public schools. 89% are White. 36% are Protestant; 15% Catholic. **Male To Female Ratio:** 1.0:1. The average age of freshmen is 18; all undergraduates, 20. 30% do not continue beyond their first year; 55% remain to graduate. **Housing:** 995 students can be accommodated in college housing, which includes single-sex and coed dorms, on-campus apartments, off-campus apartments, and married student housing. In addition, there are special-interest houses. The Intercultural Center is a special interest facility providing social, cultural, and educational opportunities to students. Theme units for students interested in science, health, and international issues are located within the residence hall system. On-campus housing is guaranteed for all 4 years. 79% of students live on campus; of those, 50% remain on campus on weekends. Alcohol is not permitted. All students may keep cars.

FACULTY/CLASSROOMS: 53% of faculty are male; 47% are female. All teach undergraduates, 20% do research, and 20% do both. No introductory courses are taught by graduate students. The average class size in an introductory lecture is 30; in a laboratory is 15; and in a regular course is 20.

PROGRAMS OF STUDY: Manchester confers B.A., and B.S. degrees. Associate degrees are also awarded. Bachelor's degrees are awarded in AGRICULTURE (environmental studies), BIOLOGICAL SCIENCE (biochemistry and biology/biological science), BUSINESS (accounting, banking and finance, and business administration and management), COMMUNICATIONS AND THE ARTS (art, communications, English, French, German, music, and Spanish), COMPUTER AND PHYSICAL SCIENCE (chemistry, computer science, mathematics, and physics), EDUCATION (art education, elementary education, health education, middle school education, and secondary education), ENGINEERING AND ENVIRONMENTAL DESIGN (engineering), HEALTH PROFESSIONS (medical laboratory technology), SOCIAL SCIENCE (economics, history, interdisciplinary studies, peace studies, philosophy, political science/government, prelaw, psychology, religion, social work, and sociology). Education, accounting, and biology-chemistry are the strongest academically. Education, accounting, and communication studies have the largest enrollments.

ACTIVITIES: There are 53 groups on campus, including band, cheerleading, choir, chorale, chorus, computers, dance, drama, environmental, ethnic, gay, honors, international, jazz band, literary magazine, musical theater, newspaper, opera, orchestra, pep band, photography, political, professional, radio and TV, religious, social, social service, student government, symphony, and yearbook. Popular campus events include Parents Weekend, Sibling Weekend, International Fair, and May Day Weekend. **Sports:** There are 9 intercollegiate sports for men and 8 for women, and 13 intramural sports for men and 12 for women. Facilities include an 1800-seat gym, racquetball courts, a fitness center, tennis courts, cross-country and an all-weather track, and athletic fields for baseball, softball, soccer, and football. **Graduates:** From July 1, 2013 to June 30, 2014, 198 bachelor's degrees were awarded. The most popular majors were business (27%), education (17%), and health sciences (12%). 25 companies recruited on campus in 2013-2014. In an average class, 42% graduate in 4 years or less, 52% graduate in 5 years or less, and 52% graduate in 6 years or less. Of the 2013 graduating class, 18% were enrolled in graduate school within 6 months of graduation, and 75% were employed.

SERVICES: Counseling and information services are available, as is tutoring in every subject. There is a reader service for the blind. There is also a learning center with an academic assistance program, a seminar to enhance study and learning skills, and time and project management **Library/Resources:** The library contains 174,078 volumes, 23,014 microform items, 5,258 audio/video tapes/CDs/DVDs, and subscribes to 973 periodicals including electronic. Computerized library services include interlibrary loans, database searching, and Internet access. Special learning facilities include an art gallery, planetarium, radio station, a 100-acre nature preserve. **Physically Challenged Students:** 50% of the campus is accessible. Facilities include wheelchair ramps, elevators, special parking, specially equipped restrooms, special class scheduling, lowered drinking fountains, lowered telephones, and special housing. **Special:** The college offers cooperative programs in nursing and engineering science. The Brethren Colleges Abroad program allows study abroad in 13 countries, including Ecuador, China, England, France, Germany, Ireland, Japan, Mexico, and Spain. Manchester also offers B.A.-B.S. degrees, internships, work-study programs, dual majors, student-designed majors, a 3-2 engineering program, pass/fail options, and nondegree study. Other special academic features include independent study, required study in non-Western culture, and interdisciplinary programs in both peace studies and environmental studies. A January interterm permits internships, travel abroad, and concentrated classes on campus. There are 6 national honor societies, a freshman honors program, and 5 departmental honors programs. **Visiting:** There are regularly scheduled orientations for prospective students, student visits include meetings about financial aid, meetings with faculty and admissions, and campus tours. Visitors may also eat meals on campus, sit in on classes, and meet with current students. There are guides for informal visits, visitors may sit in on classes, and stay overnight. To schedule a visit, contact the Campus Visit Coordinator. **Campus Safety and Security:** Measures include 24-hour foot and vehicle patrol, emergency notification system, and security escort services. There are emergency telephones and lighted pathways/sidewalks.

REQUIREMENTS: The SAT or ACT is required. Applicants must have a minimum SAT I composite of 900, with 450 on each part, or an ACT composite of 18. Each application is reviewed on an individual basis. The GED is accepted. For high school students, the college recommends completion of 28 academic credits, based on 4 years each of English, math, and science, and 2 years each of foreign language, history, and social studies. A GPA of 2.3 is required. AP and CLEP credits are accepted. Important factors in the admissions decision are advanced placement or honors courses, leadership record, and recommendations by school officials. Students must complete a core curriculum, including requirements in humanities, social sciences, and natural sciences, as well as specific courses in English composition, public communication, Western civilization, and physical fitness. In order to graduate, students must complete a minimum of 128 semester hours, including 26 to 52 hours in a major field, with a GPA of at least 2.0 (2.5 for the education and athletic training majors). A comprehensive exam in the major is also required. A thesis for honors students is optional. **Procedure:** Freshmen are admitted to all sessions. Entrance exams should be taken by November of the senior year. There are deferred admissions and rolling admissions plans. Application deadlines are open. Application fee is $20. Notification is sent on a rolling basis. Applications are accepted on-line. **Transfer Students:** 29 transfer students enrolled in 2013-2014. Transfer students must present a minimum GPA of 2.0 in all previous college work. 96 of 128 credits required for the bachelor's degree must be completed at Manchester. **International Students:** There are 41 international students enrolled. The school actively recruits these students. They must take the TOEFL with a minimum score of 550 on the paper-based TOEFL (PBT).

ADMISSIONS: Adam Hohman, Associate Director of Admissions. E-Mail: *admitinfo@manchester.edu* Web: *www.manchester.edu*

FINANCIAL AID: In 2014-2015, 100% of all full-time freshmen and 96% of continuing full-time students received some form of financial aid. 84% of continuing full-time students received need-based aid. The average freshman award was $18,110. 40% of undergraduate students work part-time. The average financial indebtedness of the 2014 graduate was $16,333. The FAFSA is required. The deadline for filing freshman financial aid applications for fall entry is rolling.

MARIAN UNIVERSITY   C-3
www.marian.edu

Indianapolis, IN 46222   (317) 955-6300
                                                  (800) 772-7264
Fax: (317) 955-6401   Email: admissions@marian.edu
Full-time: 671 men, 1040 women   Faculty: 110
Part-time: 100 men, 339 women   Ph.D.s: 64%
Graduate: 256 men, 370 women   Student/Faculty: 16 to 1
Year: semesters, summer session   Tuition: $29,400
Room & Board: $9140   Freshman Class: 1825
                                        applied, 1377 accepted,
                                        321 enrolled
SAT CR/M/W: 500/510/460 ACT: 22   CEEB CODE: 1442
Application Deadline: August 1   COMPETITIVE

Marian University, is a private institution founded in 1851 by the Sisters of St. Francis and now affiliated with the Roman Catholic Church. The college offers undergraduate programs in the arts and sciences, business, education, fine arts, and the health professions. It also offers graduate programs in education as well as a doctorate in osteopathic medicine. There are 5 undergraduate schools and 1 graduate school. In addition to regional accreditation, Marian has baccalaureate program accreditation with AHEA, NCATE, NLN, CCNE, IACBE, and COCA. The 114-acre campus is in a suburban area 6 miles from downtown Indianapolis. Including any residence halls, there are 21 buildings.

STUDENT LIFE: 86% of undergraduates are from Indiana. Others are from 30 states, and 8 foreign countries. 80% are from public schools. 73% are White; 13% African American. 45% are Buddhism, Islam, Hinduism, Eastern Orthodox, and unknown; 38% Catholic; 15% Protestant. **Male To Female Ratio:** 1.7:1. The average age of freshmen is 19; all undergraduates, 25. 26% do not continue beyond their first year; 55% remain to graduate. **Housing:** 818 students can be accommodated in college housing, which includes coed dorms and on-campus apartments. In addition, there are special-interest houses. The Dorothy Day House for Peace and Justice is a special-interest house for those interested in living in community working for peace and justice. Marian also has the Bishop Brute House of Formation on-campus, where men studying for the priesthood live in community within a specific dormitory. On-campus housing is guaranteed for all 4 years. 66% of students commute. Alcohol is not permitted. All students may keep cars.

FACULTY/CLASSROOMS: 42% of faculty are male; 58% are female. 90% teach undergraduates. No introductory courses are taught by graduate students. The average class size in an introductory lecture is 22; in a laboratory is 18; and in a regular course is 16.

PROGRAMS OF STUDY: Marian confers B.A., B.S. and B.S.N. degrees. Associate, Master's, and Doctoral degrees are also awarded. Bachelor's degrees are awarded in BIOLOGICAL SCIENCE (biology/biological science), BUSINESS (accounting, banking and finance, business administration and management, and sports management), COMMUNICATIONS AND THE ARTS (art history and appreciation, communications, English, French, graphic design, music, Spanish, and studio art), COMPUTER AND PHYSICAL SCIENCE (chemistry and mathematics), EDUCATION (elementary education, physical education, and special education), ENGINEERING AND ENVIRONMENTAL DESIGN (environmental science), HEALTH PROFESSIONS (nursing), SOCIAL SCIENCE (economics, history, pastoral studies, philosophy, political science/government, psychology, religious education, sociology, and theological studies). Accounting, nursing, education, and biology are the strongest academically. Business administration, nursing and education have the largest enrollments.

ACTIVITIES: There are no fraternities or sororities. There are 42 groups on campus, including and departmental, art, band, cheerleading, choir, chorale, chorus, computers, dance, debate, drama, drill team, ethnic, forensics, honors, international, jazz band, literary magazine, marching band, musical theater, newspaper, pep band, photography, political, professional, religious, social, social service, student government, and yearbook. Popular campus events include Global Speaker Series, Field Day and Knightly Music Awards. **Sports:** There are 10 intercollegiate sports for men and 10 for women, and 4 intramural sports for men and 4 for women. Facilities include an varsity and intramural gyms, stadium, Velodrome and cycling center, racquetball courts, a fitness center, a weight-training room, and a phys ed assessment lab. **Graduates:** From July 1, 2013 to June 30, 2014, 550 bachelor's degrees were awarded. The most popular majors were nursing (47%), business/management/marketing/accounting/finance (24%), and education (5%). In an average class, 34% graduate in 4 years or less, 52% graduate in 5 years or less, and 53% graduate in 6 years or less. Of the 2013 graduating class, 13% were enrolled in graduate school within 6 months of graduation.

SERVICES: Counseling and information services are available, as is tutoring in most subjects. There is a reader service for the blind, and remedial math, reading, and writing. Study skills training and peer tutoring are available. **Library/Resources:** The library contains 113,000 volumes, 150 microform items, 2,200 audio/video tapes/CDs/DVDs, and subscribes to 230,000 periodicals including electronic. Computerized library services include interlibrary loans, database searching, Internet access, and Wi-Fi capability. Special learning facilities include an art gallery, and the 35-acre Wetlands Ecology Laboratory. **Physically Challenged Students:** 95% of the campus is accessible. Facilities include wheelchair ramps, elevators, special parking, specially equipped restrooms, and special class scheduling. **Special:** Co-op programs in accounting, finance, business administration, chemistry, management information systems, and sociology and cross-registration through the Consortium for Urban Education are offered. A dual degree program in math and computer science, a 3-2 engineering degree, and accelerated degrees in nursing and business administration are also offered. Internships, study

abroad, work-study, independent study, dual and student-designed majors, and pass/fail options are available. There are 10 national honor societies, a freshman honors program, and 7 departmental honors programs. **Visiting:** There are regularly scheduled orientations for prospective students, including a campus tour, visits with faculty and coaches, and financial aid information. There are guides for informal visits, visitors may sit in on classes, and stay overnight. To schedule a visit, contact the Office of Admissions. **Campus Safety and Security:** Measures include 24-hour foot and vehicle patrol, emergency notification system, self-defense education, and security escort services. There are shuttle buses, emergency telephones, lighted pathways/sidewalks, and controlled access to dorms/residences.

REQUIREMENTS: The SAT or ACT is required. The ACT Optional Writing test is also required. Applicants must be graduates of an accredited secondary school or have a GED. Marian requires 20 academic units, including 4 units in English, 2 units in math, of which algebra and geometry are recommended, and 2 units each in a lab science and social studies. A GPA of 2.3 is required. AP and CLEP credits are accepted. Important factors in the admissions decision are recommendations by school officials, recommendations by alumni, and leadership record.To graduate, students must complete 128 semester hours, including 30 to 40 in the major, with a minimum GPA of 2.0 overall and in the major. General education requirements include 14 semester hours in cultural awareness, 10 to 12 in scientific and quantitative reasoning, 9 to 17 in written and oral communication and foreign language, and 9 each in moral reasoning and individual and social awareness. **Procedure:** Freshmen are admitted to all sessions. Entrance exams should be taken at the end of the junior year or the beginning of the senior year. There are deferred admissions and rolling admissions plans. Applications should be filed by August 1 for fall entry; December 10 for spring entry; and April 15 for summer entry, along with a $35 fee. Notification is sent on a rolling basis. Applications are accepted on-line. Application fees are waived if application is completed on-line. **Transfer Students:** 95 transfer students enrolled in 2013-2014. In addition to meeting standard admissions requirements, applicants must submit transcripts of all college work and be in good standing at their former school. Students transferring must have a 2.0 GPA. 30 of 128 credits required for the bachelor's degree must be completed at Marian. **International Students:** There are 21 international students enrolled. The school actively recruits these students. They must take the TOEFL with a minimum score of 550 on the paper-based TOEFL (PBT) or 80 on the Internet-based version (iBT). They must also take the SAT or ACT.

ADMISSIONS: 75% of the 2014-2015 applicants were accepted. The SAT scores for the 2014-2015 freshman class were: Critical Reading--48% below 500, 39% between 500 and 599, 12% between 600 and 699, and 1% between 700 and 800; Math--39% below 500, 47% between 500 and 599, 13% between 600 and 699, and 1% between 700 and 800; Writing--64% below 500, 29% between 500 and 599, 6% between 600 and 699, and 1% between 700 and 800. The ACT scores were 32% below 21, 28% between 21 and 23, 20% between 24 and 26, 11% between 27 and 28, and 9% above 28. 34% of the current freshmen were in the top fifth of their class; 65% were in the top two fifths. 3 freshmen graduated first in their class. **Admissions Contact:** Luann Brames, Director of Enrollment. E-Mail: *admissions@marian.edu* Web: *www.marian.edu*

FINANCIAL AID: 11% of undergraduate students work part-time. Average annual earnings from campus work are $1300. The FAFSA and the college's own financial statement are required. The priority date for freshman financial aid applications for fall entry is March 10.

MARTIN UNIVERSITY (*The complete profile is made available exclusively on our website, www.barronspac.com*)

OAKLAND CITY UNIVERSITY (*The complete profile is made available exclusively on our website, www.barronspac.com*)

PURDUE UNIVERSITY SYSTEM

The Purdue University System, established in 1869, is a land-grant system in Indiana. It is governed by a board of trustees, whose chief administrator is the president. The primary goal of the system is to provide quality education to the citizens of Indiana. The main priorities are teaching, research, and public service. The total student enrollment is usually 75,000, with 4500 faculty members. Altogether there are approximately 375 baccalaureate, 88 master's, and 58 doctoral programs offered in the Purdue University System. Profiles of the 4-year campuses are included in this section.

PURDUE UNIVERSITY/CALUMET B-1
www.calumet.purdue.edu

Hammond, IN 46323	**(219) 989-2213**
	(800) HI PURDUE
Fax: (219) 989-2775	**Email:** adms.@calumet.purdue.edu
Full-time: 2210 men, 2840 women	**Faculty:** IIA, av$
Part-time: 1975 men, 1380 women	**Ph.D.s:** 90%
Graduate: 350 men, 615 women	**Student/Faculty:** n/av
Year: semesters, summer session	**Tuition:** $6821 ($14,798)
Room & Board: $7515	**Freshman Class:** n/av
SAT or ACT: required	**CEEB CODE:** 1638
Application Deadline: n/av	**COMPETITIVE**

Purdue University/Calumet, established in 1946, is a public commuter institution offering undergraduate degrees in general studies, liberal arts, and professional studies. Figures in the above capsule and in this profile are approximate. There are 7 undergraduate schools and 1 graduate school. In addition to regional accreditation, Purdue Cal has baccalaureate program accreditation with ABET, NCATE, and NLN. The 167-acre campus is in an urban area 25 miles southeast of Chicago. Including any residence halls, there are 21 buildings.

STUDENT LIFE: 91% of undergraduates are from Indiana. Others are from 30 states, and 27 foreign countries. 72% are from public schools. 68% are White; 15% African American; 14% Hispanic. **Male To Female Ratio:** 1.1:1. The average age of freshmen is 19; all undergraduates, 25. 64% do not continue beyond their first year; 24% remain to graduate. **Housing:** 376 students can be accommodated in college housing, which includes coed On-campus housing is available on a first-come, first-served basis. 97% of students commute. Alcohol is not permitted. All students may keep cars.

FACULTY/CLASSROOMS: 51% of faculty are male; 49% are female. No introductory courses are taught by graduate students. The average class size in an introductory lecture is 26; in a laboratory is 16; and in a regular course is 21.

PROGRAMS OF STUDY: Purdue Cal confers B.A., B.S., B.A.B., B.S.A., B.S.Chm., B.S.E. and B.S.I.M. degrees. Associate and Master's degrees are also awarded. Bachelor's degrees are awarded in BIOLOGICAL SCIENCE (biology/biological science, biotechnology, and microbiology), BUSINESS (accounting, banking and finance, business economics, hotel/motel and restaurant management, and marketing/retailing/merchandising), COMMUNICATIONS AND THE ARTS (broadcasting, communications, English, English literature, French, German, public relations, and Spanish), COMPUTER AND PHYSICAL SCIENCE (chemistry, computer programming, computer science, information sciences and systems, mathematics, and physics), EDUCATION (early childhood education, elementary education, foreign languages education, science education, and secondary education), ENGINEERING AND ENVIRONMENTAL DESIGN (computer engineering, computer graphics, computer technology, construction technology, electrical/electronics engineering, electrical/electronics engineering technology, engineering, engineering technology, industrial engineering technology, mechanical engineering, and mechanical engineering technology), HEALTH PROFESSIONS (medical laboratory technology, nursing, optometry, and physical therapy), SOCIAL SCIENCE (criminal justice, history, philosophy, political science/government, psychology, and sociology). Education, nursing, and foreign language are the strongest academically. Management, behavioral sciences, and manufacturing have the largest enrollments.

ACTIVITIES: There are 40 groups on campus, including art, cheerleading, chorus, computers, dance, drama, ethnic, film, gay, honors, international, literary magazine, musical theater, newspaper, political,

professional, religious, social, social service, special interest and student organization executive board, and student government. Popular campus events include Orientation, Latin Culture Month, and Black History Month. **Sports:** There are 2 intercollegiate sports for men and 2 for women, and 22 intramural sports for men and 22 for women. Facilities include a 1500-seat gym, racquetball courts, an outdoor volleyball court, a running track, a weight room, and a total fitness center.

SERVICES: Counseling and information services are available, as is tutoring in most subjects. There is a reader service for the blind, and remedial math, reading, and writing. **Library/Resources:** The library contains 269,648 volumes, 764,621 microform items, 998 audio/video tapes/CDs/DVDs, and subscribes to 228 periodicals including electronic. Computerized library services include interlibrary loans, database searching, and Internet access. Special learning facilities include an art gallery, a computer education building, and an educational media laboratory. **Physically Challenged Students:** All of the campus is accessible. Facilities include wheelchair ramps, elevators, special parking, specially equipped restrooms, special class scheduling, lowered drinking fountains, lowered telephones. There are electric door openers on all but 1 student building. **Special:** Some cooperative programs, internships, and work-study programs are available. Purdue Cal offers cross-registration in philosophy, study in Spain, and credit for military experience, as well as nondegree study and pass/fail options. There are 7 national honor societies, a freshman honors program, and 80 departmental honors programs. **Visiting:** There are regularly scheduled orientations for prospective students. There are guides for informal visits and visitors may sit in on classes. To schedule a visit, contact the Office of Admissions and Recruitment. **Campus Safety and Security:** Measures include 24-hour foot and vehicle patrol, self-defense education, and security escort services. There are emergency telephones, lighted pathways/sidewalks, and student patrols.

REQUIREMENTS: The SAT or ACT is required. The ACT Optional Writing test is also required. In addition, the SAT Subject test in math is required. Applicants must be graduates of an accredited secondary school. The GED is accepted. 33 Carnegie units are required for admission. Required courses vary, depending on the curriculum, and include 3 or 4 years of English, 2 or 3 years of math, 2 years of foreign language, and 1 year of history or social studies. A GPA of 2.0 is required. AP and CLEP credits are accepted. Important factors in the admissions decision are recommendations by school officials, advanced placement or honors courses, and personality/intangible qualities. Graduation requirements vary depending on the program. The total number of credit hours required for a degree varies from 126 to 136, with 24 to 73 in the major. All students must take English composition and 36 hours of general education courses and maintain a C average. **Procedure:** Freshmen are admitted to all sessions. SAT and ACT can be taken anytime during junior or senior year in high school. There are early admissions, deferred admissions, and rolling admissions plans. Check with the school for current application deadlines. Applications are accepted on-line. **Transfer Students:** Applicants must have a minimum GPA of 2.0. for transfer credit. 32 of 126 credits required for the bachelor's degree must be completed at Purdue Cal. **International Students:** The school actively recruits these students. They must take the TOEFL or MELAB. International students can take the SAT in place of the TOEFL.

ADMISSIONS: 3 freshmen graduated first in their class. **Admissions Contact:** Paul McGuinness, Admissions Director. E-Mail: *adms.@calumet.purdue.edu* Web: *www.calumet.purdue.edu*

FINANCIAL AID: Purdue Cal is a member of CSS. The CSS/Profile is required. Check with the school for current application deadlines.

PURDUE UNIVERSITY/WEST LAFAYETTE   B-3
www.purdue.edu

West Lafayette, IN 47907	(765) 494-1776

Fax: (765) 494-0544	Email: admissions@purdue.edu
Full-time: 16255 men, 11958 women	Faculty: n/av
	Ph.D.s: 98%
Part-time: 535 men, 507 women	Student/Faculty: 13 to 1
Graduate: 5614 men, 3901 women	Tuition: $9992 ($29,874)
Year: semesters, summer session	Freshman Class: 39706 applied, 23506 accepted, 6373 enrolled
Room & Board: $10,378	
SAT CR/M/W: 570/640/570 ACT: 28	CEEB CODE: 1631
Application Deadline: February 1	**HIGHLY COMPETITIVE**

Purdue University, founded in 1869, is a publicly supported institution offering degree programs with an emphasis on engineering, business, communications, arts, social sciences, allied health, and technology. There are 12 undergraduate schools and 1 graduate school. In addition to regional accreditation, Purdue University has baccalaureate program accreditation with AACSB, ABET, ACCE, ACPE, ADA, ASLA, FIDER, NASM, NCATE, NLN, SAF, ACS, APA, AVMA, CACREP, and CCNE. The 2595-acre campus is in a suburban area 65 miles northwest of Indianapolis. Including any residence halls, there are 376 buildings.

STUDENT LIFE: 55% of undergraduates are from Indiana. Others are from 50 states, 127 foreign countries, and Canada. 60% are White; 23% Foreign. **Male To Female Ratio:** 0.7:1. The average age of freshmen is 18; all undergraduates, 20. 7% do not continue beyond their first year; 74% remain to graduate. **Housing:** 11284 students can be accommodated in college housing, which includes single-sex and coed dorms, on-campus apartments, and married student housing. In addition, there are honors houses, fraternity houses, sorority houses, and 39 living learning communities. On-campus housing is guaranteed for all 4 years. 65% of students commute. Alcohol is not permitted. Upperclassmen may keep cars.

FACULTY/CLASSROOMS: 65% of faculty are male; 35% are female. No introductory courses are taught by graduate students. The average class size in an introductory lecture is 45; in a laboratory is 24; and in a regular course is 39.

PROGRAMS OF STUDY: Purdue University confers B.A., B.S., B.S.A.A.E., B.S.A.B.E., B.S.B.M.E., B.S.C.E., B.S.Ch., B.S.Ch.E., B.S.C.M.P.E., B.S.C.N.E., B.S.E., B.S.E.E., B.S.E.H., B.S.F.O.R., B.S.I.E., B.S.I.M., B.S.L.A., B.S.L.S.G.E., B.S.M.E., B.S.M.S.E. and B.S.N.E. degrees. Associate, Master's, and Doctoral degrees are also awarded. Bachelor's degrees are awarded in AGRICULTURE (agricultural business management, agricultural communications, agricultural economics, agriculture, agronomy, animal science, fishing and fisheries, forestry and related sciences, horticulture, natural resource management, plant protection (pest management), plant science, soil science, and wood science), BIOLOGICAL SCIENCE (biochemistry, biology/biological science, cell biology, ecology, entomology, genetics, microbiology, molecular biology, nutrition, plant genetics, plant physiology, and wildlife biology), BUSINESS (accounting, banking and finance, entrepreneurial studies, fashion merchandising, hospitality management services, human resources, marketing management, marketing/retailing/merchandising, organizational leadership and management, retailing, and tourism), COMMUNICATIONS AND THE ARTS (advertising, apparel design, art history and appreciation, audio technology, broadcasting, classics, communications, comparative literature, creative writing, dramatic arts, English, film arts, fine arts, French, German, graphic design, industrial design, Japanese, journalism, Latin, Latin, linguistics, photography, public relations, Russian, Spanish, and visual and performing arts), COMPUTER AND PHYSICAL SCIENCE (actuarial science, applied mathematics, applied physics, atmospheric sciences and meteorology, chemistry, computer science, earth science, geology, information sciences and systems, mathematics, physics, radiological technology, science, software engineering, and statistics), EDUCATION (agricultural education, art education, athletic training, early childhood education, education, elementary education, English education, foreign languages education, health education, mathematics educa-

tion, science education, secondary education, social studies education, special education, and technical education), ENGINEERING AND ENVIRONMENTAL DESIGN (aeronautical engineering, aeronautical technology, agricultural engineering, air traffic control, airline piloting and navigation, aviation administration/management, aviation computer technology, bioengineering, biomedical engineering, chemical engineering, chemical engineering technology, civil engineering, computational sciences, computer engineering, computer graphics, computer technology, construction engineering, construction management, construction technology, electrical/electronics engineering, electrical/electronics engineering technology, engineering management, environmental science, food services technology, industrial administration/management, industrial engineering, industrial engineering technology, interior design, landscape architecture/design, manufacturing engineering, manufacturing technology, materials science, mechanical engineering, mechanical engineering technology, nuclear engineering, occupational safety and health, and surveying engineering), HEALTH PROFESSIONS (clinical science, environmental health science, exercise science, health science, medical laboratory technology, nursing, pharmaceutical science, radiological science, and speech pathology/audiology), SOCIAL SCIENCE (African American studies, anthropology, Asian/American studies, Asian/Oriental studies, behavioral science, criminal justice, dietetics, economics, family and community services, family/consumer studies, fashion design and technology, food production/management/services, food science, French studies, history, Italian studies, Japanese studies, Judaic studies, liberal arts/general studies, medieval studies, philosophy, physical fitness/movement, political science/government, psychology, religion, Russian and Slavic studies, social studies, social work, sociology, Spanish studies, and women's studies). Engineering, actuarial science, and industrial management are the strongest academically. Management, preengineering, and mechanical engineering have the largest enrollments.

ACTIVITIES: 19% of men belong to 5 local and 51 national fraternities; 23% of women belong to 7 local and 31 national sororities. There are 983 groups on campus, including band, cheerleading, chess, choir, chorale, chorus, computers, dance, debate, drama, ethnic, film, forensics, gay, honors, international, jazz band, literary magazine, marching band, newspaper, orchestra, pep band, photography, political, professional, radio and TV, religious, social, social service, student government, and symphony. Popular campus events include Grand Prix Race, Old Masters, Gala week, Mortar Board Leadership Conference, Purdue University Dance Marathon, Martin Luther King Day of Service, Industrial Round Table, Big Man on Campus, Diwali, Relay for Life, B-Involved Fair, Starry Night. **Sports:** There are 10 intercollegiate sports for men and 10 for women, and 41 intramural sports for men and 41 for women. Facilities include varsity 14,000-seat arena, 62,000-seat stadium, an intercollegiate athletic facility, recreational gym, field house, an athletic center, intramural playing fields, 2 golf courses, baseball, softball, track, and women's soccer, recreational sports gym, recreational turf facility, 8 lane x 50-meter competition pool and 6 lane 25-yard dive pool, 125 acre outdoor recreation playing fields, 6 outdoor tennis courts, 4 outdoor sand volleyball courts, 2 outdoor basketball courts, 18-hole disc golf, trap and skeet range, and crew boathouse. **Graduates:** From July 1, 2013 to June 30, 2014, 6834 bachelor's degrees were awarded. The most popular majors were management (6%), mechanical engineering (5%), and accounting (3%). 1345 companies recruited on campus in 2013-2014. In an average class, 1% graduate in 3 years or less, 49% graduate in 4 years or less, 71% graduate in 5 years or less, and 74% graduate in 6 years or less. Of the 2013 graduating class, 63% were employed within 6 months of graduation.

SERVICES: Counseling and information services are available, as is tutoring in every subject. There is a reader service for the blind, and remedial math, reading, and writing. **Library/Resources:** The 13 libraries contain 2.6 million volumes, 3.0 million microform items, 7,708 audio/video tapes/CDs/DVDs, and subscribe to 130,085 periodicals including electronic. Computerized library services include interlibrary loans, database searching, Internet access, and Wi-Fi capability. Special learning facilities include an art gallery and radio station. **Physically Challenged Students:** 90% of the campus is accessible. Facilities include wheelchair ramps, elevators, special parking, specially equipped restrooms, special class scheduling, lowered drinking fountains, lowered telephones, special housing. Lab with assistive technology and special computers. **Special:** Cooperative programs are available in engineering, technology, agriculture, science, and health and human sciences. Cross-registration with Purdue's regional campuses, numerous internships, study abroad in 44 countries, dual majors, student-designed majors, nondegree study, and pass/fail options are also offered. There are 33 national honor societies, including Phi Beta Kappa, a freshman honors program, and 10 departmental honors programs. **Visiting:** There are regularly scheduled orientations for prospective students, including fall and spring preview days, which consist of admission, financial aid, housing, and school sessions, a campus tour, and dormitory visits. The Summer Visit Program consists of a counselors' orientation and campus and residence hall visits. There are guides for informal visits and visitors may sit in on classes. To schedule a visit, contact the Office of Admissions. **Campus Safety and Security:** Measures include 24-hour foot and vehicle patrol, emergency notification system, self-defense education, and security escort services. There are shuttle buses, emergency telephones, lighted pathways/sidewalks, and public transportation routes throughout campus.

REQUIREMENTS: The SAT or ACT is required. The ACT Optional Writing test is also required. Purdue requires that most students have 4 years of English, 3-4 years of math, 3 to 4 years of lab sciences, 3 to 4 years of social sciences, and 2 years of foreign language. The GED is also accepted. AP and CLEP credits are accepted. Important factors in the admissions decision are advanced placement or honors courses, extracurricular activities record, and geographical diversity. To graduate, students must be enrolled for at least 2 semesters and complete 32 semester hours of course work, complete approximately 128 hours and earn a minimum GPA of 2.0. In most majors, students must take courses in English, math, science, computer science, and social sciences. **Procedure:** Freshmen are admitted to all sessions. Entrance exams should be taken at the end of the junior year. There is a rolling admissions plan. Applications should be filed by February 1 for fall entry, along with a $60 fee. Applications are accepted online. **Transfer Students:** 586 transfer students enrolled in 2013-2014. Requirements for transfer students vary greatly depending on each students unique situation, including academic background and intended major. For this reason, we encourage prospective students to visit our website and read in depth about the requirements that pertain to your specific situation. 32 of 120 credits required for the bachelor's degree must be completed at Purdue University. **International Students:** There are 5282 international students enrolled. The school actively recruits these students. They must take the TOEFL with a minimum score of 570 on the paper-based TOEFL (PBT) or 88 on the Internet-based version (iBT), or take the IELTS, SAT, or the ACT.

ADMISSIONS: 59% of the 2014-2015 applicants were accepted. The SAT scores for the 2014-2015 freshman class were: Critical Reading--16% below 500, 44% between 500 and 599, 32% between 600 and 699, and 9% between 700 and 800; Math--7% below 500, 27% between 500 and 599, 37% between 600 and 699, and 28% between 700 and 800; Writing--16% below 500, 43% between 500 and 599, 33% between 600 and 699, and 7% between 700 and 800. The ACT scores were 8% below 21, 16% between 21 and 23, 23% between 24 and 26, 13% between 27 and 28, and 41% above 28. 70% of the current freshmen were in the top fifth of their class; 94% were in the top two fifths. 101 freshmen graduated first in their class. **Admissions Contact:** Pamela Horne, Dean of Admissions/Assistant VP for Enrollment. E-Mail: *admissions@purdue.edu* Web: *www.purdue.edu*

FINANCIAL AID: In 2014-2015, 76% of all full-time freshmen and 73% of continuing full-time students received some form of financial aid. 67% of all full-time freshmen and 56% of continuing full-time students received need-based aid. The average freshman award was $11,675. Need-based scholarships or need-based grants averaged $3,627; need-based self-help aid (loans and jobs) averaged $4,596; non-need-based athletic scholarships averaged $381; and other non-need-based awards and non-need-based scholarships averaged $3,071. 29% of undergraduate students work part-time. Average annual earnings from campus work are $1941. The average financial indebtedness of the 2014 graduate was $28,343. The FAFSA is required. The priority date for freshman financial aid applications for fall entry is March 1. The deadline for filing freshman financial aid applications for fall entry is March 1.

ROSE-HULMAN INSTITUTE OF TECHNOLOGY   B-4
www.rose-hulman.edu

Terre Haute, IN 47803   (812) 877-8892
                                             (800) 248-7448
Fax: (812) 877-8941   Email: admissions@rose-hulman.edu
Full-time: 1762 men, 496 women   Faculty: 182; IIB, ++$
Part-time: 13 men, 9 women   Ph.D.s: 99%
Graduate: 76 men, 32 women   Student/Faculty: 13 to 1
Year: quarters, summer session   Tuition: $41,283
Room & Board: $12,057   Freshman Class: 4404
                                  applied, 2589 accepted,
                                  582 enrolled
SAT CR/M/W: 610/670/590 ACT: 30   CEEB CODE: 1668
Application Deadline: March 1   MOST COMPETITIVE

Rose-Hulman Institute of Technology, founded in 1874, is a private college emphasizing engineering, science, and math. In addition to regional accreditation, Rose-Hulman has baccalaureate program accreditation with ABET. The 200-acre campus is in a suburban area on the east side of Terre Haute. Including any residence halls, there are 37 buildings.

STUDENT LIFE: 66% of undergraduates are from out of state, mostly the Mid-West. Students are from 47 states, 15 foreign countries, and Canada. 76% are White; 11% Foreign. **Male To Female Ratio:** 0.3:1. The average age of freshmen is 18; all undergraduates, 20. 6% do not continue beyond their first year; 94% remain to graduate. **Housing:** 1284 students can be accommodated in college housing, which includes single-sex and coed dorms and on-campus apartments. In addition, there are fraternity houses, sorority houses, sophomore residence hall. On-campus housing is guaranteed for the freshman year only, is available on a first-come, first-served basis, and is available on a lottery system for upperclassmen. 59% of students live on campus; of those, 60% remain on campus on weekends. All students may keep cars.

FACULTY/CLASSROOMS: 78% of faculty are male; 22% are female. All teach undergraduates, and 20% do research. No introductory courses are taught by graduate students. The average class size in an introductory lecture is 20; in a laboratory is 22; and in a regular course is 20.

PROGRAMS OF STUDY: Rose-Hulman confers B.S. degrees. Master's degrees are also awarded. Bachelor's degrees are awarded in BIOLOGICAL SCIENCE (biochemistry and biology/biological science), COMPUTER AND PHYSICAL SCIENCE (chemistry, computer science, mathematics, physics, and software engineering), ENGINEERING AND ENVIRONMENTAL DESIGN (biomedical engineering, chemical engineering, civil engineering, computer engineering, electrical/electronics engineering, engineering physics, mechanical engineering, and optical engineering), SOCIAL SCIENCE (economics). Engineering, science, and mathematics are the strongest academically. Mechanical engineering, chemical engineering, and electrical engineering have the largest enrollments.

ACTIVITIES: 26% of men belong to 8 national fraternities; 26% of women belong to 3 national sororities. There are 111 groups on campus, including art, band, cheerleading, chess, chorale, chorus, computers, dance, debate, drama, drill team, ethnic, film, gay, honors, international, jazz band, literary magazine, musical theater, newspaper, pep band, photography, political, professional, radio and TV, religious, social, social service, and student government. Popular campus events include Art Shows, Concerts and Plays. **Sports:** There are 11 intercollegiate sports for men and 11 for women, and 22 intramural sports for men and 22 for women. Facilities include a field house, recreational center, swimming pool, tennis courts, and intramural fields. **Graduates:** From July 1, 2013 to June 30, 2014, 459 bachelor's degrees were awarded. The most popular majors were mechanical engineering (34%), chemical engineering (14%), and electrical engineering (10%). 338 companies recruited on campus in

2013-2014. In an average class, 3% graduate in 3 years or less, 62% graduate in 4 years or less, 77% graduate in 5 years or less, and 78% graduate in 6 years or less. Of the 2013 graduating class, 20% were enrolled in graduate school within 6 months of graduation, and 78% were employed.

SERVICES: Counseling and information services are available, as is tutoring in most subjects. **Library/Resources:** The library contains 42,355 volumes, 810 audio/video tapes/CDs/DVDs, and subscribes to 9,114 periodicals including electronic. Computerized library services include interlibrary loans, database searching, and Internet access. Special learning facilities include an art gallery, planetarium, and radio station. **Physically Challenged Students:** 95% of the campus is accessible. Facilities include wheelchair ramps, elevators, special parking, specially equipped restrooms, special class scheduling, and lowered drinking fountains. **Special:** The institute offers co-op programs, independent study, cross-registration with Indiana State University and Saint Mary-of-the-Woods College, summer industrial internships, study abroad, and dual majors. Pass/fail options also are available. There are 7 national honor societies and 3 departmental honors programs. **Visiting:** There are regularly scheduled orientations for prospective students, including interviews, campus tours, and academic meetings. There are guides for informal visits, visitors may sit in on classes, and stay overnight. To schedule a visit, contact Nancy Apple at (800) 248-7448. **Campus Safety and Security:** Measures include 24-hour foot and vehicle patrol, emergency notification system, and security escort services. There are emergency telephones, lighted pathways/sidewalks, medical transports, and free traffic assistance.

REQUIREMENTS: The SAT or ACT is required. Candidates should have at least 16 units of credit, including 4 in English, 2 in social sciences, and 1 each in math, chemistry, physics, and electives. An essay and interview are recommended. Rose-Hulman requires applicants to be in the upper 25% of their class. AP credits are accepted. Important factors in the admissions decision are advanced placement or honors courses, recommendations by school officials, and extracurricular activities record. All students must complete at least 192 to 195 quarter hours with a minimum GPA of 2.0 and 36 hours in the humanities and social sciences. Freshmen are required to take math, biology, chemistry, or physics. The total number of hours required in the major varies. **Procedure:** Freshmen are admitted fall. Entrance exams should be taken in the fall of the senior year or spring of the junior year. There is a deferred admissions plan. Early decision applications should be filed by November 1; regular applications, by March 1 for fall entry, along with a $40 fee. Notification of early decision is sent December 15; regular decision, March 15. 379 applicants were on the 2014 waiting list; 2 were admitted. Applications are accepted on-line. Application fees are waived if application is completed on-line. **Transfer Students:** 10 transfer students enrolled in 2013-2014. Applicants need 1 year each of calculus, physics, and chemistry and a minimum GPA of 3.0. An interview is recommended. **International Students:** There are 236 international students enrolled. The school actively recruits these students. They must take the TOEFL with a minimum score of 550 on the paper-based TOEFL (PBT) or 80 on the Internet-based version (iBT). They must also take the SAT or ACT, scoring 550.

ADMISSIONS: 59% of the 2014-2015 applicants were accepted. The SAT scores for the 2014-2015 freshman class were: Critical Reading--2% below 500, 40% between 500 and 599, 43% between 600 and 699, and 14% between 700 and 800; Math--13% between 500 and 599, 55% between 600 and 699, and 32% between 700 and 800; Writing--11% below 500, 42% between 500 and 599, 39% between 600 and 699, and 8% between 700 and 800. The ACT scores were 3% between 21 and 23, 19% between 24 and 26, 17% between 27 and 28, and 61% above 28. 88% of the current freshmen were in the top fifth of their class; 99% were in the top two fifths. There were 12 National Merit finalists. 42 freshmen graduated first in their class. **Admissions Contact:** Lisa Norton, Dean of Admissions. E-Mail: *admissions@ rose-hulman.edu* Web: *www.rose-hulman.edu*

FINANCIAL AID: In 2014-2015, 99% of all full-time freshmen and 96% of continuing full-time students received some form of financial aid. 65% of all full-time freshmen and 61% of continuing full-time students received need-based aid. The average freshman award was $26,595. Need-based scholarships or need-based grants averaged $25,240 ($57,442 maximum); need-based self-help aid (loans and jobs) averaged $6,751 ($38,800 maximum); and other non-need-based awards and non-need-based scholarships averaged $9,932 ($56,342 maximum). 43% of undergraduate students work part-time. Average annual earnings from campus work are $1288. The average financial indebtedness of the 2014 graduate was $35,224. Rose-Hulman is a member of CSS. The FAFSA is required. The priority date for freshman financial aid applications for fall entry is March 1.

SAINT JOSEPH'S COLLEGE   B-2
www.saintjoe.edu

Rensselaer, IN 47978

(219) 866-6170
(800) 447-8781

Fax: (219) 866-6122
Full-time: 421 men, 591 women
Part-time: 37 men, 93 women
Graduate: 12 men, 12 women
Year: semesters, summer session
Room & Board: $8610

Email: admissions@saintjoe.edu
Faculty: 79; IIB
Ph.D.s: 75%
Student/Faculty: 13 to 1
Tuition: $27,890
Freshman Class: 1572 applied, 1044 accepted, 216 enrolled

SAT CR/M: 505/505 **ACT:** 22
Application Deadline: open

CEEB CODE: 1697
COMPETITIVE

Saint Joseph's College, founded in 1889, is a private Catholic institution providing a liberal arts core curriculum with an interdisciplinary approach and practical, career-oriented experiences. There is 1 undergraduate school and 1 graduate school. In addition to regional accreditation, SJC has baccalaureate program accreditation with NCATE, IACBE, CCNE, and NCATE. The 180-acre campus is in a small town 80 miles south of Chicago and 90 miles north of Indianapolis. Including any residence halls, there are 26 buildings.

STUDENT LIFE: 78% of undergraduates are from Indiana. Others are from 19 states, 5 foreign countries, and Canada. 76% are from public schools. 80% are White. 53% are Protestant; 40% Catholic. **Male To Female Ratio:** 1.5:1. The average age of freshmen is 19; all undergraduates, 22. 26% do not continue beyond their first year; 45% remain to graduate. **Housing:** 782 students can be accommodated in college housing, which includes single-sex and coed dorms and on-campus apartments. housing for nontraditional or adult students and special-interest floors. On-campus housing is guaranteed for all 4 years. 60% of students live on campus; of those, 60% remain on campus on weekends. All students may keep cars.

FACULTY/CLASSROOMS: 49% of faculty are male; 51% are female. All teach undergraduates. No introductory courses are taught by graduate students. The average class size in an introductory lecture is 17; in a laboratory is 18; and in a regular course is 14.

PROGRAMS OF STUDY: SJC confers B.A., B.S. and B.S.N. degrees. Associate and Master's degrees are also awarded. Bachelor's degrees are awarded in BIOLOGICAL SCIENCE (biology/biological science), BUSINESS (accounting, business administration and management, and sports management), COMMUNICATIONS AND THE ARTS (art, communications, creative writing, dramatic arts, English, music, music business management, and theatre arts), COMPUTER AND PHYSICAL SCIENCE (chemistry, computer science, and mathematics), EDUCATION (athletic training, elementary education, middle school education, physical education, and secondary education), HEALTH PROFESSIONS (medical technology, nursing, predentistry, and premedicine), SOCIAL SCIENCE (criminal justice, economics, history, international studies, ministries, philosophy, political science/government, prelaw, psychology, religion, and sociology). Accounting, biology-chemistry, and education are the strongest academically. Business administration, biological sciences, and nursing have the largest enrollments.

ACTIVITIES: There are no fraternities or sororities. There are 35 groups on campus, including art, band, cheerleading, chess, choir, chorale, chorus, computers, dance, debate, drama, environmental, ethnic, film, forensics, honors, jazz band, literary magazine, marching band, musical theater, newspaper, orchestra, pep band, photography, political, professional, radio and TV, religious, social, social service, and student government. Popular campus events include Little 500 Go-Kart Race, Little Siblings Weekend and Science Olympiad Regional Tournament. **Sports:** There are 9 intercollegiate sports for men and 9 for women, and 8 intramural sports for men and 8 for women. Facilities include a field house, 2500-seat gym, recreation center, baseball complex, softball complex, lighted soccer field, football facility, an outdoor track and field facility, and a lake with a sand beach. **Graduates:** From July 1, 2013 to June 30, 2014, 206 bachelor's degrees were awarded. The most popular majors were nursing (23%), business administration (12%), and biological sciences (11%). 4 companies recruited on campus in 2013-2014. In an average class, 1% graduate in 3 years or less, 39% graduate in 4 years or less, 45% graduate in 5 years or less, and 45% graduate in 6 years or less. Of the 2013 graduating class, 16% were enrolled in graduate school within 6 months of graduation, and 67% were employed.

SERVICES: Counseling and information services are available, as is tutoring in every subject. There is a reader service for the blind, and remedial math, reading, and writing. **Library/Resources:** The library contains 127,757 volumes, 67,764 microform items, 16,716 audio/video tapes/CDs/DVDs, and subscribes to 13,262 periodicals including electronic. Computerized library services include interlibrary loans, database searching, Internet access, and Wi-Fi capability. Special learning facilities include a radio station and TV station. **Physically Challenged Students:** 74% of the campus is accessible. Facilities include wheelchair ramps, elevators, special parking, specially equipped restrooms, special class scheduling, lowered drinking fountains, and lowered telephones. **Special:** Cross-registration with Saint Elizabeth's School of Nursing is offered. Internships in all fields, a Washington semester, accelerated degree programs, and study abroad throughout Europe and Latin America are available. Dual majors are offered in biology/chemistry and music/business administration. Credit for life, military, and work experience, nondegree study, student-designed majors, and pass/fail options are offered. The Core program consists of lectures and discussions over a 4-year period. There are 4 national honor societies and a freshman honors program. **Visiting:** There are regularly scheduled orientations for prospective students, consisting of discover days, special interest days, early registration, and freshman orientation. There are guides for informal visits, visitors may sit in on classes, and stay overnight. To schedule a visit, contact the Admissions Office at (800) 447-8781. **Campus Safety and Security:** Measures include 24-hour foot and vehicle patrol, emergency notification system, and security escort services. There are lighted pathways/sidewalks and controlled access to dorms/residences.

REQUIREMENTS: The SAT or ACT is required. Applicants should be graduates of an accredited secondary school or have earned the GED. They should have completed 15 academic credits, 10 of which must be from the following academic fields: English, foreign language, social studies, math, and natural sciences. Acceptance is based on high school GPA and SAT or ACT scores. A GPA of 2.0 is required. AP and CLEP credits are accepted. Important factors in the admissions decision are advanced placement or honors courses, extracurricular activities record, and leadership record. Students must complete 45 hours in the general education program and 36 hours in the major. A total of 120 credit hours with a minimum GPA of 2.0 is required to graduate. **Procedure:** Freshmen are admitted fall and spring. Entrance exams should be taken by January of the senior year. There are deferred admissions and rolling admissions plans. Application deadlines are open. Application fee is $25. Notifications are sent December 15. Applications are accepted on-line. Application fees are waived if application is completed on-line. **Transfer Students:** 31 transfer students enrolled in 2013-2014. Applicants must have a GPA of 2.0. Grades of C or better transfer for credit. 30 of 120 credits required for the bachelor's degree must be completed at SJC. **International Students:** There are 7 international students enrolled. They must take the TOEFL with a minimum score of 550 on the paper-based TOEFL (PBT) or 80 on the Internet-based version (iBT). **ADMISSIONS:** 66% of the 2014-2015 applicants were accepted. The SAT scores for the 2014-2015 freshman class were: Critical Reading--47% below 500, 43% between 500 and 599, and 10% between 600 and 699; Math--47% below 500, 36% between 500 and 599, 16% between 600 and 699, and 1% between 700 and 800. The ACT scores were 43% below 21, 31% between 21 and 23, 16% between 24 and

26, 5% between 27 and 28, and 5% above 28. 25% of the current freshmen were in the top fifth of their class; 57% were in the top two fifths. 3 freshmen graduated first in their class. **Admissions Contact:** Mike Ramian, Director of Admissions. E-Mail: *admissions@saintjoe.edu* Web: *www.saintjoe.edu*

FINANCIAL AID: In 2014-2015, 99% of all full-time freshmen and 99% of continuing full-time students received some form of financial aid. 92% of all full-time freshmen and 85% of continuing full-time students received need-based aid. The average freshman award was $28,097. Need-based scholarships or need-based grants averaged $11,500 ($36,500 maximum); need-based self-help aid (loans and jobs) averaged $2,203 ($36,500 maximum); non-need-based athletic scholarships averaged $4,068 ($35,410 maximum); and other non-need-based awards and non-need-based scholarships averaged $9,270 ($36,500 maximum). 32% of undergraduate students work part-time. Average annual earnings from campus work are $1500. The average financial indebtedness of the 2014 graduate was $30,899. SJC is a member of CSS. The FAFSA, and the combined admission and financial aid application is required. The deadline for filing freshman financial aid applications for fall entry is March 1.

SAINT MARY-OF-THE-WOODS COLLEGE (*The complete profile is made available exclusively on our website, www.barronspac.com*)

SAINT MARY'S COLLEGE	C-1
www.saintmarys.edu	
Notre Dame, IN 46556	**(574) 284-4587**
	(800) 551-7621
Fax: (574) 284-4716	**Email: admission@saintmarys.edu**
Full-time: 1469 women	**Faculty:** 133; IIB, av$
Part-time: 10 women	**Ph.D.s:** 83%
Graduate: n/av	**Student/Faculty:** 11 to 1
Year: semesters, summer session	**Tuition:** $34,600
Room & Board: $10,560	**Freshman Class:** 1529 applied, 1310 accepted, 437 enrolled
SAT CR/M/W: 560/540/550 **ACT:** 25	**CEEB CODE:** 1702
Application Deadline: February 15	**COMPETITIVE+**

Saint Mary's College, established in 1844, was founded and sponsored by the Congregation of the Sisters of the Holy Cross. It continues to be a Catholic comprehensive college for women in the liberal arts tradition. Figures in the above capsule and in this profile are approximate. There is 1 undergraduate school. In addition to regional accreditation, Saint Mary's has baccalaureate program accreditation with CSWE, NASAD, NASM, NCATE, and CCNE. The 100-acre campus is in a suburban area in South Bend, IN and 90 miles east of Chicago. Including any residence halls, there are 20 buildings.

STUDENT LIFE: 75% of undergraduates are from out of state, mostly the Mid-West. Students are from 40 states, 17 foreign countries, and Canada. 55% are from public schools. 77% are White; 12% Hispanic. 87% are Catholic; 11% Protestant. The student base is all female. The average age of freshmen is 18; all undergraduates, 20. 13% do not continue beyond their first year; 71% remain to graduate. **Housing:** 1350 students can be accommodated in college housing, which includes single-sex dorms and on-campus apartments. On-campus housing is guaranteed for all 4 years, is available on a first-come, first-served basis. 91% of students live on campus; of those, 75% remain on campus on weekends. All students may keep cars.

FACULTY/CLASSROOMS: 31% of faculty are male; 69% are female. All teach undergraduates, all do research, and all teach and do research. No introductory courses are taught by graduate students. The average class size in an introductory lecture is 20; in a laboratory is 15; and in a regular course is 15.

PROGRAMS OF STUDY: Saint Mary's confers B.A., B.S., B.B.A., B.F.A. and B.Mus. degrees. Bachelor's degrees are awarded in BIOLOGICAL SCIENCE (biology/biological science), BUSINESS (accounting, business administration and management, and management information systems), COMMUNICATIONS AND THE ARTS (art, communications, creative writing, English literature, fine arts,

French, Italian, music, Spanish, and visual and performing arts), COMPUTER AND PHYSICAL SCIENCE (chemistry, mathematics, and statistics), EDUCATION (elementary education), HEALTH PROFESSIONS (nursing and speech pathology/audiology), SOCIAL SCIENCE (economics, history, humanities, international studies, philosophy, political science/government, psychology, religion, social work, and sociology). Nursing, communication studies and psychology have the largest enrollments.

ACTIVITIES: There are no fraternities or sororities. There are 75 groups on campus, including art, band, cheerleading, choir, chorale, chorus, dance, drama, environmental, ethnic, gay, honors, international, literary magazine, marching band, musical theater, newspaper, opera, orchestra, pep band, photography, political, professional, radio and TV, religious, social, social service, student government, and yearbook. Popular campus events include Back to School Dance, School Formal and Dance Marathon. **Sports:** There are 8 intercollegiate sports for women, and 8 intramural sports for women. Facilities include an athletic facility, outdoor tennis and volleyball courts, and soccer and softball fields. **Graduates:** From July 1, 2013 to June 30, 2014, 373 bachelor's degrees were awarded. The most popular majors were nursing (14%), elementary education (11%), and biology (9%). 30 companies recruited on campus in 2013-2014. In an average class, 68% graduate in 4 years or less, 70% graduate in 5 years or less, and 71% graduate in 6 years or less. Of the 2013 graduating class, 31% were enrolled in graduate school within 6 months of graduation, and 77% were employed.

SERVICES: Counseling and information services are available, as is tutoring in most subjects. **Library/Resources:** The library contains 244,651 volumes, 18,729 microform items, 3,539 audio/video tapes/CDs/DVDs, and subscribes to 30,704 periodicals including electronic. Computerized library services include interlibrary loans, database searching, Internet access, and Wi-Fi capability. Special learning facilities include an art gallery, radio station, and TV station. **Physically Challenged Students:** All of the campus is accessible. Facilities include wheelchair ramps, elevators, special parking, specially equipped restrooms, lowered drinking fountains, and special housing. **Special:** Cross-registration is permitted with the University of Notre Dame and a consortium of 6 northern Indiana colleges. Opportunities are provided for internships, a Washington semester, dual and student-designed majors, a 3-2 engineering degree with the University of Notre Dame, non-degree study, pass/fail options, and study abroad in more than 20 countries. All students must complete a senior comprehensive project or exam and demonstrate proficiency in writing before graduating. There are 14 national honor societies. **Visiting:** There are regularly scheduled orientations for prospective students, including campus tours and visits with admissions and financial aid counselors and faculty and athletic staff. There are guides for informal visits, visitors may sit in on classes, and stay overnight. To schedule a visit, contact Wanda Dudley at (800) 551-7621. **Campus Safety and Security:** Measures include 24-hour foot and vehicle patrol, emergency notification system, self-defense education, and security escort services. There are shuttle buses, emergency telephones, lighted pathways/sidewalks, controlled access to dorms/residences, key cards for controlled residence hall entry.

REQUIREMENTS: The SAT or ACT is required. Graduation from an accredited secondary school is required; a GED will be accepted. Applicants must have completed 16 academic credits, including 4 in English, 3 in math, and 2 in a foreign language, history or social studies, and lab science with the remainder from college preparatory electives in the above areas. An essay is required. AP and CLEP credits are accepted. Important factors in the admissions decision are extracurricular activities record, advanced placement or honors courses, and recommendations by school officials. Students must successfully complete 128 credits, with at least 24 in the major, and must maintain a minimum GPA of 2.0. Students must complete the Sophia Program, a learning outcomes based general education curriculum promoting integration with majors and minors. Advanced proficiency in composition within the student's major must also be demonstrated, and a comprehensive exam in the major area is required by the end of the senior year. **Procedure:** Freshmen are admitted fall and spring. Entrance exams should be taken between March of the junior year and December of senior year. There are early decision, deferred admissions, and rolling admissions plans. Early decision applications

should be filed by November 15; regular applications, by February 15 for fall entry; and November 15 for spring entry. Notification of early decision is sent December 15; regular decision, January 15. 72 early decision candidates were accepted for the 2014-2015 class. Applications are accepted on-line. **Transfer Students:** 18 transfer students enrolled in 2013-2014. Students must submit a transcript from high school and each previous college attended, along with an essay, a recommendation from a college adviser, and SAT or ACT test scores if the student has fewer than 30 semester hours of transferable credit. All transfer applicants must have maintained a minimum GPA of 3.0. An interview is recommended. Syllabi or course description required for credit evaluation. 60 of 128 credits required for the bachelor's degree must be completed at Saint Mary's. **International Students:** There are 31 international students enrolled. The school actively recruits these students. They must take the TOEFL with a minimum score of 500 on the paper-based TOEFL (PBT) or 80 on the Internet-based version (iBT), or take the IELTS. They must also take the SAT or ACT.

ADMISSIONS: 86% of the 2014-2015 applicants were accepted. The SAT scores for the 2014-2015 freshman class were: Critical Reading--23% below 500, 46% between 500 and 599, 26% between 600 and 699, and 6% between 700 and 800; Math--28% below 500, 46% between 500 and 599, 22% between 600 and 699, and 5% between 700 and 800; Writing--23% below 500, 49% between 500 and 599, 21% between 600 and 699, and 6% between 700 and 800. The ACT scores were 12% below 21, 21% between 21 and 23, 29% between 24 and 26, 18% between 27 and 28, and 20% above 28. 48% of the current freshmen were in the top fifth of their class; 82% were in the top two fifths. 6 freshmen graduated first in their class. **Admissions Contact:** Kristin McAndrew, Director of Admissions. E-Mail: *admission@ saintmarys.edu* Web: *www.saintmarys.edu*

FINANCIAL AID: In 2014-2015, 99% of all full-time freshmen and 97% of continuing full-time students received some form of financial aid. 69% of all full-time freshmen and 56% of continuing full-time students received need-based aid. The average freshman award was $29,550. Need-based scholarships or need-based grants averaged $24,872; need-based self-help aid (loans and jobs) averaged $4,457; and other non-need-based awards and non-need-based scholarships averaged $13,429. 83% of undergraduate students work part-time. Average annual earnings from campus work are $1800. The average financial indebtedness of the 2014 graduate was $31,986. Saint Mary's is a member of CSS. The CSS/Profile and FAFSA are required. The priority date for freshman financial aid applications for fall entry is March 1.

TAYLOR UNIVERSITY   D-3
www.taylor.edu

Upland, IN 46989	**(765) 998-5565**
	(800) 882-3456
Fax: (765) 998-4925	**Email:** admissions@taylor.edu
Full-time: 826 men, 999 women	**Faculty:** 126; IIB, av$
Part-time: 93 men, 186 women	**Ph.D.s:** 90%
Graduate: 37 men, 76 women	**Student/Faculty:** 14 to 1
Year: 4-1-4, summer session	**Tuition:** $29,538
Room & Board: $8283	**Freshman Class:** 1496 applied, 1317 accepted, 435 enrolled
SAT CR/M/W: 560/570/545 **ACT:** 27	**CEEB CODE:** 1802
Application Deadline: December 1	**VERY COMPETITIVE+**

Taylor University, founded in 1846, is a private Christian interdenominational liberal arts institution. The figures in the above capsule and in this profile are approximate. There are 3 undergraduate schools and 1 graduate school. In addition to regional accreditation, Taylor has baccalaureate program accreditation with ABET, CSWE, NASM, NCATE, and CELP. The 952-acre campus is in a rural area 70 miles north of Indianapolis and 45 miles south of Fort Wayne. Including any residence halls, there are 43 buildings.

STUDENT LIFE: 61% of undergraduates are from out of state, mostly the Mid-West. Students are from 42 states, 30 foreign countries, and Canada. 86% are White. 98% are Protestant. **Male To**

Female Ratio: 1.3:1. The average age of freshmen is 19; all undergraduates, 20.5. 12% do not continue beyond their first year; 74% remain to graduate. **Housing:** 1772 students can be accommodated in college housing, which includes single-sex dorms, on-campus apartments, off-campus apartments, and married student housing. On-campus housing is guaranteed for all 4 years. 88% of students live on campus; of those, 83% remain on campus on weekends. Alcohol is not permitted. Upperclassmen may keep cars.

FACULTY/CLASSROOMS: 74% of faculty are male; 26% are female. 98% teach undergraduates. No introductory courses are taught by graduate students. The average class size in an introductory lecture is 26; in a laboratory is 10; and in a regular course is 20.

PROGRAMS OF STUDY: Taylor confers B.A., B.B.A., B.Mus. and B.S. degrees. Associate and Master's degrees are also awarded. Bachelor's degrees are awarded in AGRICULTURE (environmental studies), BIOLOGICAL SCIENCE (biology/biological science), BUSINESS (accounting, banking and finance, business administration and management, business administration marketing, finance, international business, international business management, marketing, and sports management), COMMUNICATIONS AND THE ARTS (art, communications, communications technology, dramatic arts, English, English as a second/foreign language, English literature, English Writing, film arts, film, television and digital media, fine arts, journalism, media arts, English and Professional Communication, music, music performance, music theory and composition, public relations, Spanish, technical and business writing, theatre arts, visual and performing arts, vocal performance, and writing), COMPUTER AND PHYSICAL SCIENCE (chemistry, Computer Engineering Technology, computer science, mathematics, natural sciences, physics, and web services), EDUCATION (art education, (Education) Childhood Education, Christian education, early childhood education, education, elementary education, English education, foreign languages education, health education, mathematics education, music education, physical education, science education, secondary education, social studies education, social studies secondary school education, and teaching English as a second/foreign language (TESOL/TEFOL)), ENGINEERING AND ENVIRONMENTAL DESIGN (computer engineering, computer graphics, engineering physics, environmental science, and systems engineering), HEALTH PROFESSIONS (biology, exercise science, health science, kinesiology, premedicine, and public health), SOCIAL SCIENCE (biblical studies, Christian studies, development economics, economics, geography, history, humanities, interdisciplinary studies, international relations, international studies, liberal arts/general studies, liberal arts, sciences, general studies, humanities, ministries, philosophy, philosophy and religion, political science/government, psychology, social work, and sociology). Engineering, physics, and biology are the strongest academically. Business, education and kinesiology have the largest enrollments.

ACTIVITIES: There are no fraternities or sororities. There are 65 groups on campus, including art, band, choir, chorale, chorus, computers, debate, drama, ethnic, film, honors, international, jazz band, literary magazine, musical theater, newspaper, opera, orchestra, pep band, photography, political, professional, radio and TV, religious, social, social service, student government, and symphony. Popular campus events include Taylathon, AirBand, Silent Night and Spiritual Renewal and Emphasis Weeks. **Sports:** There are 8 intercollegiate sports for men and 8 for women, and 9 intramural sports for men and 9 for women. Facilities include Odle Arena and Kesler Student Activities Center, which house an indoor track, multi-purpose athletic courts and fitness center with swimming/lap pool, a field house, an Wheeler football stadium and practice fields with artificial turf, tennis and racquetball courts, outdoor track, multiple baseball and softball fields, soccer field and a lake for swimming and ice skating. **Graduates:** From July 1, 2013 to June 30, 2014, 414 bachelor's degrees were awarded. The most popular majors were elementary education (11%), business administration (8%), and psychology (7%). 100 companies recruited on campus in 2013-2014. In an average class, 2% graduate in 3 years or less, 66% graduate in 4 years or less, 76% graduate in 5 years or less, and 74% graduate in 6 years or less. Of the 2013 graduating class, 15% were enrolled in graduate school within 6 months of graduation, and 64% were employed. **SERVICES:** Counseling and information services are available, as is

tutoring in most subjects. There is a reader service for the blind, and remedial math, reading, and writing. **Library/Resources:** The library contains 201,738 volumes, 14,661 microform items, 15,841 audio/video tapes/CDs/DVDs, and subscribes to 41,429 periodicals including electronic. Computerized library services include interlibrary loans, database searching, Internet access, and Wi-Fi capability. Special learning facilities include an art gallery, radio station, TV station, environmental study laboratory, NASA-approved clean room, particle accelerator, NASA project space research equipment, 65-acre arboretum, C. S. Lewis Collection, observatory room, 10 kW photovoltaic solar array and two 50 kW wind turbines available for student data collection. **Physically Challenged Students:** 95% of the campus is accessible. Facilities include wheelchair ramps, elevators, special parking, specially equipped restrooms, special class scheduling, lowered drinking fountains, and lowered telephones. **Special:** Opportunities are provided for internships, cooperative programs, a Washington semester, very active study abroad program in over 35 countries, work-study programs, dual majors, student-designed majors, and B.A.-B.S. degrees. There is cross-registration with the other members of the Council for Christian Colleges and Universities, and the Christian College Consortium. There are 7 national honor societies, Phi Beta Kappa, a freshman honors program, and 23 departmental honors programs. **Visiting:** There are regularly scheduled orientations for prospective students, including a campus tour, lunch, class meetings, faculty meetings, a financial aid session, and an admissions interview. There are guides for informal visits, visitors may sit in on classes, and stay overnight. To schedule a visit, contact Amy Barnett at (765) 998-5134. **Campus Safety and Security:** Measures include 24-hour foot and vehicle patrol, emergency notification system, self-defense education, and security escort services. There are lighted pathways/sidewalks.

REQUIREMENTS: The SAT or ACT and ACT Writing Test are recommended. Graduation from an accredited secondary school is required; a GED will be accepted. It is recommended that applicants complete 4 years of English, 3 to 4 each of math and lab science, 2 each of social studies and a foreign language, and course work in computing, typing/keyboarding, and the arts. The application includes 1 essay. Either ACT or SAT scores are required. High school transcripts and recommendation forms from a guidance counselor and pastor are also required. An interview is recommended for all students, and an audition is required for music majors. Taylor requires applicants to be in the upper 40% of their class. A GPA of 2.8 is required. AP and CLEP credits are accepted. Important factors in the admissions decision are recommendations by school officials, extracurricular activities record, and leadership record. Students must complete at least 128 total hours of which at least 42 must be upper division (300/400). To graduate, students must have a minimum cumulative GPA of 2.0 and a 2.3 GPA (2.5 in social work) in all majors and minors and demonstrate proficiency in writing, math, science, and reading. Students must also complete a senior paper, exam, or project in their major(s). General education requirements include courses in spiritual formation, speech, expository writing, fine arts, computer science, literature, science, history, math, social science, and a course designated as cross-cultural. The B.A. degree requires the equivalency of 2 years of 1 foreign language. Most B.S. degrees must be combined with systems analysis curriculum. **Procedure:** Freshmen are admitted fall, winter, and spring. Entrance exams should be taken during the spring of the junior year or fall of the senior year. There are early admissions and deferred admissions plans. Early decision applications should be filed by November 1; regular applications, by December 1 for fall entry; February 1 for winter entry; and April 1 for spring entry, along with a $25 fee. Notification of early decision is sent November 20. Applications are accepted online. **Transfer Students:** 58 transfer students enrolled in 2013-2014. Applicants must have maintained a minimum GPA of 2.5 and have completed at least 12 credit hours at the previous college. An interview is recommended. 64 of 128 credits required for the bachelor's degree must be completed at Taylor. **International Students:** There are 97 international students enrolled. The school actively recruits these students. They must take the TOEFL with a minimum score of 550 on the paper-based TOEFL (PBT). The school will accept the TOEFL in lieu of the SAT or the ACT.

ADMISSIONS: 88% of the 2014-2015 applicants were accepted. The

SAT scores for the 2014-2015 freshman class were: Critical Reading--26% below 500, 33% between 500 and 599, 29% between 600 and 699, and 12% between 700 and 800; Math--24% below 500, 33% between 500 and 599, 37% between 600 and 699, and 6% between 700 and 800; Writing--30% below 500, 41% between 500 and 599, 25% between 600 and 699, and 4% between 700 and 800. The ACT scores were 9% below 21, 16% between 21 and 23, 24% between 24 and 26, 20% between 27 and 28, and 31% above 28. 60% of the current freshmen were in the top fifth of their class; 85% were in the top two fifths. **Admissions Contact:** Amy Barnett, Executive Director of Admissions. E-Mail: *admissions@taylor.edu* Web: *www.taylor.edu*

FINANCIAL AID: In 2014-2015, 99% of all full-time freshmen and 97% of continuing full-time students received some form of financial aid. 68% of all full-time freshmen and 58% of continuing full-time students received need-based aid. The average freshman award was $19,455. Need-based scholarships or need-based grants averaged $2,723 ($14,000 maximum); need-based self-help aid (loans and jobs) averaged $3,713 ($7,400 maximum); non-need-based athletic scholarships averaged $1,302 ($29,298 maximum); and other non-need-based awards and non-need-based scholarships averaged $11,717 ($30,482 maximum). 64% of undergraduate students work part-time. Average annual earnings from campus work are $1326. The average financial indebtedness of the 2014 graduate was $25,125. Taylor is a member of CSS. The FAFSA is required. The priority date for freshman financial aid applications for fall entry is March 10. The deadline for filing freshman financial aid applications for fall entry is March 10.

TRINE UNIVERSITY   D-1
www.trine.edu

Angola, IN 46703	(260) 665-4365
	(800) 347-4878
Fax: (260) 665-4578	Email: admit@trine.edu
Full-time: 1141 men, 456 women	Faculty: 87; IIB, av$
Part-time: 43 men, 15 women	Ph.D.s: 61%
Graduate: 18 men, 23 women	Student/Faculty: 18 to 1
Year: semesters, summer session	Tuition: $29,600
Room & Board: $9800	Freshman Class: n/av
SAT CR/M: 510/546 ACT: 30	CEEB CODE: 1811
Application Deadline: August 1	HIGHLY COMPETITIVE+

Trine University, formerly Tri-State University, was founded in 1884 and is a private, independent university. Figures in the above capsule and in this profile are approximate. There are 5 undergraduate schools and 1 graduate school. In addition to regional accreditation, has baccalaureate program accreditation with ABET, ACBSP, and NCATE. The 400-acre campus is in a small town 40 miles north of Ft. Wayne. Including any residence halls, there are 22 buildings.

STUDENT LIFE: 78% of undergraduates are from Indiana. Others are from 30 states, 16 foreign countries, and Canada. 80% are from public schools. 84% are White. **Male To Female Ratio:** 0.4:1. The average age of freshmen is 18; all undergraduates, 21. 28% do not continue beyond their first year; 51% remain to graduate. **Housing:** 1186 students can be accommodated in college housing, which includes single-sex and coed dorms and on-campus apartments. In addition, there are honors houses. On-campus housing is guaranteed for all 4 years. 85% of students live on campus; of those, 65% remain on campus on weekends. Alcohol is not permitted. All students may keep cars.

FACULTY/CLASSROOMS: 67% of faculty are male; 33% are female. All teach undergraduates, 10% do research, and 10% do both. No introductory courses are taught by graduate students. The average class size in an introductory lecture is 30; in a laboratory is 16; and in a regular course is 18.

PROGRAMS OF STUDY: confers B.A., and B.S. degrees. Associate, Master's, and Doctoral degrees are also awarded. Bachelor's degrees are awarded in BIOLOGICAL SCIENCE (biology/biological science), BUSINESS (accounting, banking and finance, business administration and management, management information systems, management science, marketing/retailing/merchandising, recreation and leisure services, recreational facilities management, and sports management), COMMUNICATIONS AND THE ARTS (communications), COMPUTER AND PHYSICAL SCIENCE (chemistry, computer science, cyber intelligence/security studies, information sciences and systems, mathematics, and physical sciences), EDUCATION (elementary education, English education, mathematics education, physical education, science education, secondary education, and social science education), ENGINEERING AND ENVIRONMENTAL DESIGN (chemical engineering, civil engineering, computer engineering, drafting and design technology, electrical/electronics engineering, engineering management, environmental science, industrial administration/management, and mechanical engineering), HEALTH PROFESSIONS (physical therapy and pre-medicine), SOCIAL SCIENCE (criminal justice, forensic studies, psychology, and social science). Engineering, math/computer science, and science are the strongest academically. Engineering, psychology, and business have the largest enrollments.

ACTIVITIES: 26% of men belong to 8 national fraternities; 20% of women belong to 5 local sororities. There are 35 groups on campus, including band, cheerleading, choir, chorus, computers, dance, drama, environmental, ethnic, forensics, honors, international, jazz band, marching band, newspaper, pep band, professional, radio and TV, religious, social service, student government, and yearbook. Popular campus events include Homecoming, Bingo for Bucks and Moonlight Breakfast. **Sports:** There are 10 intercollegiate sports for men and 10 for women, and 6 intramural sports for men and 5 for women. Facilities include a gym, basketball and racquetball courts, an 18-hole golf course, a tennis court, a football stadium, and practice and playing fields for soccer, lacrosse, baseball, and softball. **Graduates:** From July 1, 2013 to June 30, 2014, 295 bachelor's degrees were awarded. The most popular majors were engineering (33%), business (19%), and education (9%). 80 companies recruited on campus in 2013-2014. In an average class, 35% graduate in 4 years or less, 50% graduate in 5 years or less, and 51% graduate in 6 years or less. Of the 2013 graduating class, 25% were enrolled in graduate school within 6 months of graduation, and 97% were employed.

SERVICES: Counseling and information services are available, as is tutoring in some subjects. There is remedial math. **Library/Resources:** The library contains 154,527 volumes, 668 microform items, 19,216 audio/video tapes/CDs/DVDs, and subscribes to 31,993 periodicals including electronic. Computerized library services include interlibrary loans, database searching, Internet access, and Wi-Fi capability. Special learning facilities include a radio station. **Physically Challenged Students:** 98% of the campus is accessible. Facilities include wheelchair ramps, elevators, special parking, specially equipped restrooms, special class scheduling, lowered drinking fountains, lowered telephones, and special housing. **Special:** Cooperative education programs are available in engineering and business. Opportunities exist for internships and work-study programs with the university and many companies. Study abroad is offered in more than 31 countries. There are 12 national honor societies and a freshman honors program. **Visiting:** There are regularly scheduled orientations for prospective students, including meetings with faculty, administrators, financial aid personnel, and a coach (if the student is an athlete), and a campus tour. There are guides for informal visits, visitors may sit in on classes, and stay overnight. To schedule a visit, contact the Admissions Office. **Campus Safety and Security:** Measures include 24-hour foot and vehicle patrol, emergency notification system, self-defense education, and security escort services. There are emergency telephones and lighted pathways/sidewalks.

REQUIREMENTS: The SAT or ACT is required. Candidates for admission should be graduates of accredited secondary schools. The GED is accepted. Most students should have 4 years of English and 3 years each of science, social studies, and math. A GPA of 2.5 is required. AP and CLEP credits are accepted. Important factors in the admissions decision are advanced placement or honors courses, recommendations by school officials, and leadership record. Candidates for graduation must complete 120 to 132 semester hours, satisfying the general education program and major requirements and maintaining a minimum overall GPA of 2.0. Required courses vary by degree sought. All students must complete a general education curriculum including science, math, American studies, social science, global studies, English composition, humanistics, computer literacy, and oral communication course work. Some majors have senior design projects. The number of hours in the major varies from 40 to 60. **Procedure:** Freshmen are admitted to all sessions. Entrance exams should be taken in the junior or senior year. There are deferred admissions and rolling admissions plans. Applications should be filed by August 1 for fall entry. Notifications are sent August 15. Applications are accepted on-line. **Transfer Students:** 27 transfer students enrolled in 2013-2014. In addition, to meeting the university's requirements for freshmen, applicants must have satisfactory records from previous institutions. 30 of 120 credits required for the bachelor's degree must be completed at Trine. **International Students:** There are 150 international students enrolled. The school actively recruits these students. They must take the TOEFL with a minimum score of 550 on the paper-based TOEFL (PBT) or 79 on the Internet-based version (iBT). Applicants not transferring credits in math or English must be tested in those subjects.

ADMISSIONS: The SAT scores for the 2014-2015 freshman class were: Critical Reading--46% below 500, 41% between 500 and 599, 12% between 600 and 699, and 1% between 700 and 800; Math--28% below 500, 43% between 500 and 599, 25% between 600 and 699, and 4% between 700 and 800. 50% of the current freshmen were in the top fifth of their class; 76% were in the top two fifths. 12 freshmen graduated first in their class. **Admissions Contact:** Dr. Stuart Jones, Dean of Admissions. E-Mail: *admit@trine.edu* Web: *www.trine.edu*

FINANCIAL AID: In 2014-2015, 92% of all full-time freshmen and 81% of continuing full-time students received some form of financial aid. 79% of all full-time freshmen and 86% of continuing full-time students received need-based aid. The average freshman award was $24,825. Need-based scholarships or need-based grants averaged $4,351 ($7,000 maximum); need-based self-help aid (loans and jobs) averaged $5,407 ($5,500 maximum); and other non-need-based awards and non-need-based scholarships averaged $13,050 ($17,000 maximum). 56% of undergraduate students work part-time. Average annual earnings from campus work are $774. The average financial indebtedness of the 2014 graduate was $28,742. The FAFSA is required. The priority date for freshman financial aid applications for fall entry is March 1.

UNIVERSITY OF EVANSVILLE A-5
www.evansville.edu

Evansville, IN 47722	(812) 488-2468
	(800) 423-8633
Fax: (812) 488-4076	Email: admission@evansville.edu
Full-time: 1021 men, 1244 women	Faculty: 176; IIA, -$
Part-time: 60 men, 95 women	Ph.D.s: 86%
Graduate: 40 men, 107 women	Student/Faculty: 13 to 1
Year: semesters, summer session	Tuition: $31,776
Room & Board: $10,880	Freshman Class: 2762 applied, 2291 accepted, 532 enrolled
SAT CR/M/W: 560/560/530 ACT: 26	CEEB CODE: 1208
Application Deadline: n/av	VERY COMPETITIVE+

The University of Evansville, founded in 1854, is a private institution affiliated with the United Methodist Church. The University offers undergraduate degree programs in arts and sciences, business administration, education and health sciences, and engineering and computer science. There are 4 undergraduate schools and 4 graduate schools. In addition to regional accreditation, UE has baccalaureate program accreditation with AACSB, ABET, APTA, NASM, NCATE, NLN, and CAATE. The 75-acre campus is in an urban area 180 miles southwest of Indianapolis, 170 miles east of St. Louis, and 120 miles west of Louisville. Including any residence halls, there are 54 buildings.

STUDENT LIFE: 59% of undergraduates are from Indiana. Others are from 41 states, 52 foreign countries, and Canada. 73% are White; 14% Foreign. 61% are Protestant; 33% Catholic. **Male To Female Ratio:** 1.3:1. The average age of freshmen is 18; all undergraduates, 20. 15% do not continue beyond their first year; 64% remain to graduate. **Housing:** 1919 students can be accommodated in college housing, which includes single-sex and coed dorms and on-campus

apartments. In addition, there are honors houses, fraternity houses, international connection, students in math and sciences. On-campus housing is guaranteed for the freshman year only, is available on a first-come, first-served basis, and is available on a lottery system for upperclassmen. Priority is given to out-of-town students. 64% of students live on campus; of those, 85% remain on campus on weekends. Alcohol is not permitted. All students may keep cars.

FACULTY/CLASSROOMS: 55% of faculty are male; 45% are female. All teach undergraduates. No introductory courses are taught by graduate students.

PROGRAMS OF STUDY: UE confers B.A., B.S., B.F.A. and B.M. degrees. Associate, Master's, and Doctoral degrees are also awarded. Bachelor's degrees are awarded in AGRICULTURE (environmental studies), BIOLOGICAL SCIENCE (biochemistry, biology/biological science, and neurosciences), BUSINESS (accounting, business administration and management, finance, international business, marketing, and sports management), COMMUNICATIONS AND THE ARTS (art history, art, communications, creative writing, dramatic arts, French, German, graphic design, literature, music, music business management, music performance, Spanish, and theater management), COMPUTER AND PHYSICAL SCIENCE (chemistry, clinical laboratory science, computer science, mathematics, and physics), EDUCATION (art education, athletic training, drama education, elementary education, English education, foreign languages education, mathematics education, music education, science education, social studies education, and special education), ENGINEERING AND ENVIRONMENTAL DESIGN (civil engineering, computer engineering, electrical/electronics engineering, environmental science, and mechanical engineering), HEALTH PROFESSIONS (exercise science, health care administration, music therapy, nursing, predentistry, premedicine, preoptometry, prepharmacy, preveterinary science, and public health), SOCIAL SCIENCE (archeology, biblical studies, classical/ancient civilization, cognitive science, criminal justice, economics, history, interdisciplinary studies, international studies, liberal arts/general studies, philosophy, political science/government, prelaw, psychology, sociology, and theological studies). Theater, engineering and physical therapy are the strongest academically. Exercise science, mechanical engineering, and nursing have the largest enrollments.

ACTIVITIES: 29% of men belong to 6 national fraternities; 27% of women belong to 1 local and 4 national sororities. There are 144 groups on campus, including art, band, cheerleading, choir, chorale, chorus, computers, dance, drama, environmental, ethnic, film, gay, honors, international, jazz band, literary magazine, musical theater, newspaper, opera, orchestra, pep band, political, professional, radio and TV, religious, social, social service, student government, symphony, and yearbook. Popular campus events include Labor Day Picnic and Student Organization Fair, Bike Race and Sunset Concert. **Sports:** There are 6 intercollegiate sports for men and 8 for women, and 17 intramural sports for men and 17 for women. Facilities include a 2500-seat soccer stadium, 650-seat softball stadium, 1200-seat baseball stadium, a 25-yard pool, a conditioning room, an aerobics room, three free weight rooms, an indoor track, eight outdoor tennis courts, a 1/2-mile security lighted jogging trail, basketball, racquetball, and volleyball courts. **Graduates:** From July 1, 2013 to June 30, 2014, 554 bachelor's degrees were awarded. The most popular majors were health professions and related programs (13%), business/marketing (12%), and visual and performing arts (10%). In an average class, 53% graduate in 4 years or less, 64% graduate in 5 years or less, and 64% graduate in 6 years or less.

SERVICES: Counseling and information services are available, as is tutoring in some subjects, especially science, math, and foreign language. Special requests in most subjects are accommodated. There is remedial writing. **Library/Resources:** The library contains 282,262 volumes, 474,391 microform items, 14,597 audio/video tapes/CDs/DVDs, and subscribes to 50 periodicals including electronic. Computerized library services include interlibrary loans, database searching, Internet access, and Wi-Fi capability. Special learning facilities include an art gallery and radio station. **Physically Challenged Students:** 87% of the campus is accessible. Facilities include wheelchair ramps, elevators, special parking, specially equipped restrooms, special class scheduling, lowered drinking fountains, and special housing. **Special:** Students may study abroad at the University of Evansville

British campus, Harlaxton College, and many places throughout the world. There is also an Israeli archeological excavation program, an accelerated bachelor of science in global leadership degree, combined bachelor's/graduate degrees, cooperative education (business administration, chemistry, engineering, environmental studies), dual enrollment of high school students, ESL, and teacher certification, as well as honors, independent study programs, internships, and student-designed majors. There are 15 national honor societies and a freshman honors program. **Visiting:** There are regularly scheduled orientations for prospective students, including a campus tour, faculty academic sessions, financial aid and admission appointments, and study abroad and honors program sessions. There are guides for informal visits, visitors may sit in on classes, and stay overnight. To schedule a visit, contact Brittany Chidester at (800) 423-8633. **Campus Safety and Security:** Measures include 24-hour foot and vehicle patrol, emergency notification system, self-defense education, and security escort services. There are emergency telephones and lighted pathways/sidewalks.

REQUIREMENTS: The SAT or ACT is required. The ACT Optional Writing test is also required. To be competitive for admission, students should submit a minimum SAT composite score of 1500 (math, critical reading, and writing) or ACT composite of 21. Applicants must be graduates of accredited secondary schools; applicants who have been homeschooled are also considered. The University requires completion of 4 years of college preparatory English, 3 years of math, 3 years of science, and 3 years of social studies. Two years of a foreign language are recommended. An interview is recommended but not required. AP and CLEP credits are accepted. Important factors in the admissions decision are extracurricular activities record, personality/intangible qualities, and advanced placement or honors courses. To graduate, students must complete at least 120 semester hours with a minimum GPA of 2.0 cumulative and in their major. All students must complete a 41-hour general education program. A demonstration of writing proficiency, a capstone course in the major, and a demonstration of foreign language proficiency are required for graduation. Students must complete at least 39 credit hours in courses numbered 300 or above, at least 48 credit hours in residence at UE, and at least 51 percent of course work in their major at UE. **Procedure:** Freshmen are admitted fall and spring. Entrance exams should be taken by fall of senior year. There is a deferred admissions plan. Early decision applications should be filed by December 2. Notification of early decision is sent December 16. Applications are accepted on-line. Application fees are waived if application is completed on-line. **Transfer Students:** 74 transfer students enrolled in 2013-2014. Applicants must submit official transcripts from each college from which they earned credit and must have a minimum GPA of 2.0 in all previous college work. High school transcripts, standardized test scores, and comments from the Dean of Students Recommendation Form are optional but considered if submitted with the application. 48 of 120 credits required for the bachelor's degree must be completed at UE. **International Students:** There are 305 international students enrolled. The school actively recruits these students. They must take the TOEFL with a minimum score of 61 on the Internet-based version (iBT).

ADMISSIONS: 83% of the 2014-2015 applicants were accepted. The SAT scores for the 2014-2015 freshman class were: Critical Reading--20% below 500, 50% between 500 and 599, 23% between 600 and 699, and 7% between 700 and 800; Math--18% below 500, 45% between 500 and 599, 31% between 600 and 699, and 6% between 700 and 800; Writing--33% below 500, 42% between 500 and 599, 22% between 600 and 699, and 3% between 700 and 800. The ACT scores were 10% below 21, 20% between 21 and 23, 25% between 24 and 26, 20% between 27 and 28, and 25% above 28. 52% of the current freshmen were in the top fifth of their class; 84% were in the top two fifths. There was 1 National Merit finalist. 25 freshmen graduated first in their class. **Admissions Contact:** Scott Henne, Dean of Admission. E-Mail: *admission@evansville.edu* Web: *www.evansville.edu*

FINANCIAL AID: In 2014-2015, 95% of all full-time freshmen and 94% of continuing full-time students received some form of financial aid. 70% of all full-time freshmen and 65% of continuing full-time students received need-based aid. The average freshman award was $27,844. Need-based scholarships or need-based grants averaged $24,598 ($25,284 maximum); need-based self-help aid (loans and

jobs) averaged $4,356 ($9,025 maximum); and non-need-based athletic scholarships averaged $29,802 ($43,456 maximum). 18% of undergraduate students work part-time. Average annual earnings from campus work are $1525. The average financial indebtedness of the 2014 graduate was $25,731. UE is a member of CSS. The FAFSA is required. The deadline for filing freshman financial aid applications for fall entry is March 10.

UNIVERSITY OF INDIANAPOLIS *(The complete profile is made available exclusively on our website, www.barronspac.com)*

UNIVERSITY OF NOTRE DAME C-1
www.nd.edu

Notre Dame, IN 46556	**(574) 631-7505**
Fax: (574) 631-8865	**Email:** admissions@nd.edu
Full-time: 4452 men, 4007 women	**Faculty:** I, +$
Part-time: 13 men, 5 women	**Ph.D.s:** 90%
Graduate: 2185 men, 1462 women	**Student/Faculty:** 11 to 1
Year: semesters, summer session	**Tuition:** $44,605
Room & Board: $12,512	**Freshman Class:** 17647 applied, 3936 accepted, 2070 enrolled
SAT CR/M/W: 710/720/700 **ACT:** 33	**CEEB CODE:** 1841
Application Deadline: January 1	**MOST COMPETITIVE**

The University of Notre Dame, founded in 1842, is a comprehensive Catholic research university. Programs are offered through the Colleges of Arts and Letters, Mendoza College of Business, Engineering, Science and the School of Architecture. Figures in the above capsule and in this profile are approximate. There are 5 undergraduate schools and 6 graduate schools. In addition to regional accreditation, Notre Dame has baccalaureate program accreditation with AACSB, ABET, and NAAB. The 1250-acre campus is in a suburban area 90 miles east of Chicago. Including any residence halls, there are 159 buildings.

STUDENT LIFE: 92% of undergraduates are from out of state, mostly the Mid-West. Students are from 50 states, 87 foreign countries, and Canada. 42% are from public schools. 71% are White. **Male To Female Ratio:** 0.8:1. The average age of freshmen is 18; all undergraduates, 20. 1% do not continue beyond their first year; 99% remain to graduate. **Housing:** 7121 students can be accommodated in college housing, which includes single-sex dorms. On-campus housing is guaranteed for the freshman year only, and is available on a first-come, first-served basis. 80% of students live on campus; of those, 95% remain on campus on weekends. Upperclassmen may keep cars.

FACULTY/CLASSROOMS: 69% of faculty are male; 31% are female. No introductory courses are taught by graduate students. The average class size in an introductory lecture is 38; in a laboratory is 21; and in a regular course is 30.

PROGRAMS OF STUDY: Notre Dame confers B.A., B.S., B.Arch., B.B.A. and B.F.A. degrees. Master's and Doctoral degrees are also awarded. Bachelor's degrees are awarded in BIOLOGICAL SCIENCE (biochemistry and biology/biological science), BUSINESS (accounting, banking and finance, management information systems, management science, and marketing/retailing/merchandising), COMMUNICATIONS AND THE ARTS (Arabic, art history and appreciation, Chinese, design, English, film arts, French, German, Greek, Italian, Japanese, music, romance languages and literature, Russian, Spanish, and studio art), COMPUTER AND PHYSICAL SCIENCE (applied physics, chemistry, computer science, geoenvironmental studies, mathematics, medical physics, and physics), EDUCATION (science education), ENGINEERING AND ENVIRONMENTAL DESIGN (aeronautical engineering, architecture, chemical engineering, civil engineering, computer engineering, electrical/electronics engineering, environmental science, and mechanical engineering), HEALTH PROFESSIONS (predentistry and premedicine), SOCIAL SCIENCE (African studies, American studies, anthropology, classical/ancient civilization, economics, history, liberal arts/general studies, medieval studies, philosophy, philosophy and religion, political science/government, psychology, sociology, and theological studies). Engineering, theology and business are the strongest academically. Finance, psychology, and economics have the largest enrollments.

ACTIVITIES: There are no fraternities or sororities. There are 400 groups on campus, including art, bagpipe, band, cheerleading, chess, choir, chorale, chorus, computers, dance, debate, drama, drill team, ethnic, film, forensics, honors, international, jazz band, literary magazine, marching band, musical theater, newspaper, orchestra, pep band, photography, political, professional, radio, religious, social, social service, student government, symphony, and yearbook. Popular campus events include Spring Festival, Home Football Weekends and Collegiate Jazz Festival. **Sports:** There are 13 intercollegiate sports for men and 13 for women, and 16 intramural sports for men and 13 for women. Facilities include indoor and outdoor tennis, swimming pools, golf courses, several outdoor general use recreational fields, indoor 100-yard general use facility with track, 2 full-service fitness and rec centers, lake and beach, boat house on river, varsity softball/baseball stadiums, football stadium, basketball/volleyball arena, a track, soccer stadium, lacrosse stadium, hockey arena, fencing gym, volleyball practice area, varsity rowing, gym and varsity football practice fields. **Graduates:** From July 1, 2013 to June 30, 2014, 2173 bachelor's degrees were awarded. The most popular majors were finance (11%), accountancy (8%), and political science (7%). 576 companies recruited on campus in 2013-2014. In an average class, 89% graduate in 4 years or less, 94% graduate in 5 years or less, and 95% graduate in 6 years or less. Of the 2013 graduating class, 29% were enrolled in graduate school within 6 months of graduation, and 55% were employed.

SERVICES: There is a reader service for the blind. **Library/Resources:** The 10 libraries contain 3.5 million volumes, 4.2 million microform items, 290,052 audio/video tapes/CDs/DVDs, and subscribe to 7,687 periodicals including electronic. Computerized library services include interlibrary loans, database searching, Internet access, and Wi-Fi capability. Special learning facilities include an art gallery, art museum and performing arts center. **Physically Challenged Students:** 95% of the campus is accessible. Facilities include wheelchair ramps, elevators, special parking, specially equipped restrooms, special class scheduling, lowered drinking fountains, lowered telephones, and special housing. **Special:** Cross-registration is offered with Saint Mary's College. Study abroad is possible in 20 countries. A 5-year arts and letters/engineering B.A.-B.S. degree is offered. There is a program of liberal studies, centered on the discussion of great books. Internships, an accelerated degree program, a Washington semester, dual majors, 3-2 engineering degrees, and pass/fail options are available. There are 16 national honor societies, including Phi Beta Kappa, and 24 departmental honors programs. **Visiting:** There are regularly scheduled orientations for prospective students, including small group sessions for students, larger sessions for parents, and tours for all. Visitors may sit in on classes and stay overnight. To schedule a visit, contact the Admissions Office at (574) 631-7505. **Campus Safety and Security:** Measures include 24-hour foot and vehicle patrol, emergency notification system, self-defense education, and security escort services. There are shuttle buses, emergency telephones, lighted pathways/sidewalks, controlled access to dorms/residences. Vehicle access is controlled, pedestrian access is not.

REQUIREMENTS: The SAT or ACT is required. Applicants should be graduates of an accredited secondary school with 16 Carnegie credits completed, including 4 years of English, 3 of math, and 2 each of science, foreign language, and history. The SAT subject test in a foreign language is recommended. An essay is required. An audition or a portfolio is recommended for some majors. AP credits are accepted. All students must complete courses in English, philosophy, science, history, theology, math, social science, and phys ed. A total of 125 semester hours with a minimum GPA of 2.0 is required to graduate. **Procedure:** Freshmen are admitted in fall. Entrance exams should be taken by fall of the senior year. There is a deferred admissions plan. Applications should be filed by January 1 for fall entry, along with a $75 fee. Notification of early decision is sent December 21; regular decision, April 10. 1521 applicants were on the 2014 waiting list. Applications are accepted on-line. **Transfer Students:** 127 transfer students enrolled in 2013-2014. Applicants should have completed at least 27 semester hours of transferable credit and maintained

a 3.3 GPA in all courses. Admission depends on openings in each undergraduate college. 60 of 125 credits required for the bachelor's degree must be completed at Notre Dame. **International Students:** There are 354 international students enrolled. The school actively recruits these students. They must take the TOEFL with a minimum score of 560 on the paper-based TOEFL (PBT) or 100 on the Internet-based version (iBT). They must also take the SAT or ACT.

ADMISSIONS: 22% of the 2014-2015 applicants were accepted. The SAT scores for the 2014-2015 freshman class were: Critical Reading--1% below 500, 8% between 500 and 599, 33% between 600 and 699, and 58% between 700 and 800; Math--4% between 500 and 599, 27% between 600 and 699, and 69% between 700 and 800; Writing--2% below 500, 9% between 500 and 599, 37% between 600 and 699, and 52% between 700 and 800. The ACT scores were 10% between 27 and 28, and 90% above 28. **Admissions Contact:** Donald Bishop, AVP for Undergraduate Enrollment. E-Mail: *admissions@nd.edu* Web: *www.nd.edu*

FINANCIAL AID: In 2014-2015, 73% of all full-time freshmen and 82% of continuing full-time students received some form of financial aid. 95% of all full-time freshmen and 95% of continuing full-time students received need-based aid. The average freshman award was $38,664. Need-based scholarships or need-based grants averaged $30,722; need-based self-help aid (loans and jobs) averaged $5,483; non-need-based athletic scholarships averaged $31,019; and other non-need-based awards and non-need-based scholarships averaged $14,793. 27% of undergraduate students work part-time. Average annual earnings from campus work are $1948. The average financial indebtedness of the 2014 graduate was $29,480. Notre Dame is a member of CSS. The CSS/Profile FAFSA, and Federal Tax form(s) and W-2 forms are required. The priority date for freshman financial aid applications for fall entry is February 15. The deadline for filing freshman financial aid applications for fall entry is February 15.

UNIVERSITY OF SAINT FRANCIS   **D-2**
www.stfrancis.edu

Fort Wayne, IN 46808   **(260) 434-7426**
     (800) 729-4732
Fax: (260) 434-7590   Email: jroth@sf.edu
Full-time: 510 men, 965 women   Faculty: n/av
Part-time: 60 men, 315 women   Ph.D.s: 46%
Graduate: 65 men, 240 women   Student/Faculty: n/av
Year: semesters, summer session   Tuition: $22,810
Room & Board: $7000   Freshman Class: n/av
SAT or ACT: required   CEEB CODE: 1693
Application Deadline: open   **COMPETITIVE**

University of Saint Francis is a private Roman Catholic liberal arts college founded in 1890 by the Sisters of Saint Francis. The figures in the above capsule and in this profile are approximate. There are 5 undergraduate schools and 1 graduate school. In addition to regional accreditation, USF has baccalaureate program accreditation with CAHEA, CSWE, NCATE, and NLN. The 108-acre campus is in a suburban area on the west side of Fort Wayne. Including any residence halls, there are 22 buildings.

STUDENT LIFE: 91% of undergraduates are from Indiana. Others are from 13 states, and 2 foreign countries. 75% are White. 40% are Protestant; 30% claim no religious affiliation; 28% Catholic. **Male To Female Ratio:** 2.4:1. The average age of freshmen is 24; all undergraduates, 25. 33% do not continue beyond their first year; 54% remain to graduate. **Housing:** 377 students can be accommodated in college housing, which includes coed dorms and on-campus apartments. On-campus housing is guaranteed for the freshman year only, and is available on a first-come, first-served basis. 80% of students commute. Alcohol is not permitted. All students may keep cars.

FACULTY/CLASSROOMS: 39% of faculty are male; 61% are female. 94% teach undergraduates. No introductory courses are taught by graduate students. The average class size in an introductory lecture is 30; in a laboratory is 11; and in a regular course is 20.

PROGRAMS OF STUDY: USF confers B.A., B.S., B.B.A., B.L.S., B.S.Ed., B.S.N. and B.S.W. degrees. Associate and Master's degrees are also awarded. Bachelor's degrees are awarded in BIOLOGICAL SCIENCE (biology/biological science), BUSINESS (accounting and business administration and management), COMMUNICATIONS AND THE ARTS (communications, English, fine arts, music technology, and studio art), COMPUTER AND PHYSICAL SCIENCE (chemistry, mathematics, and science), EDUCATION (art education, business education, elementary education, English education, health education, mathematics education, science education, secondary education, social studies education, and special education), ENGINEERING AND ENVIRONMENTAL DESIGN (environmental science), HEALTH PROFESSIONS (exercise science, medical laboratory technology, nursing, predentistry, and premedicine), SOCIAL SCIENCE (American studies, history, liberal arts/general studies, ministries, philosophy, psychology, religion, social work, and sociology). Nursing, education, and history are the strongest academically. Business, art, and nursing have the largest enrollments.

ACTIVITIES: There are no fraternities or sororities. There are 30 groups on campus, including art, cheerleading, choir, dance, drama, ethnic, film, honors, jazz band, musical theater, newspaper, pep band, photography, professional, radio and TV, religious, social, social service, and student government. Popular campus events include Little Regatta and Spring Fling. **Sports:** There are 7 intercollegiate sports for men and 8 for women, and 4 intramural sports for men and 4 for women. Facilities include a gym with 2 basketball courts or 3 volleyball courts, a weight room, a baseball diamond, a beach volleyball pit, a football stadium, and soccer, baseball, and softball fields. **Graduates:** From July 1, 2013 to June 30, 2014, 192 bachelor's degrees were awarded. In an average class, 3% graduate in 3 years or less, 33% graduate in 4 years or less, 39% graduate in 5 years or less, and 51% graduate in 6 years or less. Of the 2013 graduating class, 4% were enrolled in graduate school within 6 months of graduation, and 95% were employed.

SERVICES: Counseling and information services are available, as is tutoring in most subjects. There is remedial math, reading, and writing, as well as help for the learning disabled, individual counseling, and peer tutoring. **Library/Resources:** The 2 libraries contain 85,544 volumes, 618,843 microform items, 1,487 audio/video tapes/CDs/DVDs, and subscribe to 520 periodicals including electronic. Computerized library services include interlibrary loans, database searching, and Internet access. Special learning facilities include an art gallery, planetarium, and radio station. **Physically Challenged Students:** 95% of the campus is accessible. Facilities include wheelchair ramps, elevators, special parking, specially equipped restrooms, and lowered drinking fountains. **Special:** Internships in art, business, and communication are available, as well as nondegree study. Students also can receive credit for life experience. Cross-registration with the Fort Wayne Higher Education Consortium is available, as well as dual and student-designed majors. There is 1 national honor society, a freshman honors program, and 1 departmental honors program. **Visiting:** There are regularly scheduled orientations for prospective students, including meetings with faculty and staff and student tours. There are guides for informal visits, visitors may sit in on classes, and stay overnight. To schedule a visit, contact the Admissions Office. **Campus Safety and Security:** Measures include 24-hour foot and vehicle patrol and security escort services. There are emergency telephones and lighted pathways/sidewalks.

REQUIREMENTS: The SAT or ACT is required. A GPA of 2.3 is required. AP and CLEP credits are accepted. Important factors in the admissions decision are recommendations by school officials, advanced placement or honors courses, and extracurricular activities record. All students must complete courses in humanities, social and behavioral science, religious studies, life and physical sciences, oral and written communication, phys ed, computer science, and math. 128 semester hours with a minimum GPA of 2.0 and at least 30 hours in the major are required to graduate. A comprehensive exam is required in biology and business administration, and a thesis is required in history. **Procedure:** Freshmen are admitted to all sessions. Entrance exams should be taken in the spring of the junior year or fall of the senior year. There are deferred admissions and rolling admissions plans. Application deadlines are open. Application fee is $20. Notification is sent on a rolling basis. **Transfer Students:** 286 transfer students enrolled in 2013-2014. Applicants need a minimum cumulative GPA of 2.3 and must submit all college transcripts. 32 of

128 credits required for the bachelor's degree must be completed at USF. **International Students:** They must take the TOEFL.

ADMISSIONS: 5 freshmen graduated first in their class. **Admissions Contact:** Judy Roth, Director of Admissions. E-Mail: *jroth@sf.edu* Web: *www.stfrancis.edu*

FINANCIAL AID: In 2014-2015, 90% of all full-time freshmen and 95% of continuing full-time students received some form of financial aid. 90% of all full-time freshmen and 95% of continuing full-time students received need-based aid. The average freshman award was $13,228. Need-based scholarships or need-based grants averaged $2,163 ($5,000 maximum); need-based self-help aid (loans and jobs) averaged $3,460 ($2,625 maximum); non-need-based athletic scholarships averaged $4,401 ($20,938 maximum); and other non-need-based awards and non-need-based scholarships averaged $2,613 ($7,000 maximum). 9% of undergraduate students work part-time. Average annual earnings from campus work are $877. USF is a member of CSS. The FAFSA is required. Check with the school for current application deadlines.

UNIVERSITY OF SOUTHERN INDIANA   A-5
www.usi.edu

Evansville, IN 47712

Fax: (812) 465-7154

(812) 464-1765
(800) 467-1965
Email: mrusk@usi.edu

Full-time: 2848 men, 4132 women	**Faculty:** 352; IIA
Part-time: 492 men, 942 women	**Ph.Ds:** 69%
Graduate: 199 men, 751 women	**Student/Faculty:** 17 to 1
Year: semesters, summer session	**Tuition:** $6957 ($16,297)
Room & Board: $7928	**Freshman Class:** 5831 applied, 3756 accepted, 1613 enrolled
SAT CR/M/W: 499/503/476 **ACT:** 22	**CEEB CODE:** 1335
Application Deadline: August 15	**COMPETITIVE**

The University of Southern Indiana, founded in 1965, is a public institution offering undergraduate programs in business, liberal arts, nursing and health professions, and science, engineering and education. There are 4 undergraduate schools and 1 graduate school. In addition to regional accreditation, USI has baccalaureate program accreditation with AACSB, ABET, ACEJMC, CSWE, NASAD, and NCATE. The 1400-acre campus is in a suburban area in Evansville, Indiana and is within 150 miles of Indianapolis, IN, St. Louis, MO and Nashville, TN. Including any residence halls, there are 86 buildings.

STUDENT LIFE: 87% of undergraduates are from Indiana. Others are from 33 states, 32 foreign countries, and Canada. 86% are White. **Male To Female Ratio:** 1.6:1. The average age of freshmen is 18; all undergraduates, 22. 28% do not continue beyond their first year; 39% remain to graduate. **Housing:** 2808 students can be accommodated in college housing, which includes coed dorms, on-campus apartments, off-campus apartments, and married student housing. In addition, there are honors houses, special-interest houses, fraternity houses, sorority houses, International student housing. On-campus housing is available on a first-come, first-served basis. Priority is given to out-of-town students. 70% of students commute. Alcohol is not permitted. All students may keep cars.

FACULTY/CLASSROOMS: 42% of faculty are male; 58% are female. All teach undergraduates. No introductory courses are taught by graduate students. The average class size in an introductory lecture is 52; in a laboratory is 24; and in a regular course is 24.

PROGRAMS OF STUDY: USI confers B.A., B.S., B.G.S., B.S.E., B.S.N. and B.S.W. degrees. Associate, Master's, and Doctoral degrees are also awarded. Bachelor's degrees are awarded in BIOLOGICAL SCIENCE (biology/biological science, biophysics, and nutrition), BUSINESS (accounting, business administration and management, business communications, electronic business, finance, management information systems, marketing/retailing/merchandising, and sports management), COMMUNICATIONS AND THE ARTS (advertising, art, broadcasting, communications, English, French, German, journalism, performing arts, public relations, radio/television technology,

Spanish, speech/debate/rhetoric, and theatre arts), COMPUTER AND PHYSICAL SCIENCE (chemistry, computer science, geology, and mathematics), EDUCATION (art education, business education, early childhood education, elementary education, English education, mathematics education, middle school education, physical education, science education, secondary education, social science education, and special education), ENGINEERING AND ENVIRONMENTAL DESIGN (engineering, environmental science, industrial administration/management, and manufacturing technology), HEALTH PROFESSIONS (dental hygiene, exercise science, health care administration, nursing, occupational therapy, and radiological science), SOCIAL SCIENCE (anthropology, criminal justice, economics, history, international studies, philosophy, political science/government, psychology, social work, and sociology). Nursing is the strongest academically. Nursing, business administration, and biology have the largest enrollments.

ACTIVITIES: 8% of men belong to 7 national fraternities; 11% of women belong to 7 national sororities. There are 143 groups on campus, including art, cheerleading, chess, choir, chorus, communications, computers, dance, drama, environmental, ethnic, film, gay, honors, international, jazz band, literary magazine, musical theater, newspaper, pep band, photography, political, professional, radio and TV, religious, social, social service, and student government. Popular campus events include Welcome Week, Welcome Fun Fest, Midnight Madness and International Food Festival. **Sports:** There are 7 intercollegiate sports for men and 8 for women, and 21 intramural sports for men and 21 for women. Facilities include RFWC which offers almost 100,000 square feet of recreational space. RFWC includes the following facilities: cardio and weight machine area, including treadmills, elliptical machines, stationary bikes, Nu-step, and 16 pieces with personal entertainment monitors; 12 large screen plasma TVs, stretching and ab area, free weight room, 3 multipurpose courts, men's and women's locker rooms with showers, indoor track, climbing center, equipment checkout, group exercise rooms, lounge with computers and printer, and wireless access, game room, lactation room, and computer lab. **Graduates:** From July 1, 2013 to June 30, 2014, 1575 bachelor's degrees were awarded. The most popular majors were nursing (12%), health services (10%), and business (7%). 239 companies recruited on campus in 2013-2014. In an average class, 17% graduate in 4 years or less, 34% graduate in 5 years or less, and 39% graduate in 6 years or less. Of the 2013 graduating class, 13% were enrolled in graduate school within 6 months of graduation, and 83% were employed.

SERVICES: Counseling and information services are available, as is tutoring in most subjects. There is a reader service for the blind, and remedial math, reading, and writing. **Library/Resources:** The library contains 260,344 volumes, 539,660 microform items, 3,039 audio/video tapes/CDs/DVDs, and subscribes to 60,575 periodicals including electronic. Computerized library services include interlibrary loans, database searching, Internet access, and Wi-Fi capability. Special learning facilities include an art gallery, radio station, and TV station. **Physically Challenged Students:** 95% of the campus is accessible. Facilities include wheelchair ramps, elevators, special parking, specially equipped restrooms, special class scheduling, lowered drinking fountains, lowered telephones. **Special:** Students may participate in cooperative programs, internships and work-study programs. Study abroad, dual majors, pass/fail options, and B.A.-B.S. degrees are possible. There are 5 national honor societies and a freshman honors program. **Visiting:** There are regularly scheduled orientations for prospective students, including meetings with counselors and faculty and campus tours. There are guides for informal visits, visitors may sit in on classes, and stay overnight. To schedule a visit, contact the Office of Admission at (800) 467-1965. **Campus Safety and Security:** Measures include 24-hour foot and vehicle patrol, emergency notification system, self-defense education, and security escort services. There are shuttle buses, emergency telephones, and lighted pathways/sidewalks.

REQUIREMENTS: The SAT or ACT is required. Applicants must be graduates of an accredited secondary school, with a minimum GPA of 2.0. The GED is accepted. An interview is recommended if the student is below admissions standards. A GPA of 2.0 is required. AP and CLEP credits are accepted. Important factors in the admissions decision are advanced placement or honors courses, evidence of special

talent, and leadership record. **Procedure:** Freshmen are admitted fall, spring, and summer. Entrance exams should be taken in the spring term of the junior year. There is a rolling admissions plan. Applications should be filed by August 15 for fall entry, along with a $40 fee. Applications are accepted on-line. **Transfer Students:** 570 transfer students enrolled in 2013-2014. Grades of C- and above will transfer for credit. 30 of 120 credits required for the bachelor's degree must be completed at USI. **International Students:** There are 225 international students enrolled. The school actively recruits these students. They must take the TOEFL with a minimum score of 525 on the paper-based TOEFL (PBT) or 71 on the Internet-based version (iBT). They must also take the SAT or ACT.

ADMISSIONS: 64% of the 2014-2015 applicants were accepted. The SAT scores for the 2014-2015 freshman class were: Critical Reading--51% below 500, 39% between 500 and 599, 10% between 600 and 699, and 1% between 700 and 800; Math--49% below 500, 38% between 500 and 599, 12% between 600 and 699, and 1% between 700 and 800; Writing--63% below 500, 30% between 500 and 599, 6% between 600 and 699, and 1% between 700 and 800. The ACT scores were 41% below 21, 30% between 21 and 23, 19% between 24 and 26, 7% between 27 and 28, and 3% above 28. 29% of the current freshmen were in the top fifth of their class; 60% were in the top two fifths. 34 freshmen graduated first in their class. **Admissions Contact:** Mark Rusk, Interim Director of Admissions. E-Mail: *mrusk@usi.edu* Web: *www.usi.edu*

FINANCIAL AID: In 2014-2015, 69% of all full-time freshmen and 63% of continuing full-time students received some form of financial aid. 89% of all full-time freshmen and 91% of continuing full-time students received need-based aid. The average freshman award was $4,084. Need-based scholarships or need-based grants averaged $7,595 ($13,606 maximum); need-based self-help aid (loans and jobs) averaged $3,280 ($5,500 maximum); non-need-based athletic scholarships averaged $2,834 ($16,463 maximum); and other non-need-based awards and non-need-based scholarships averaged $2,625 ($18,397 maximum). 22% of undergraduate students work part-time. Average annual earnings from campus work are $1210. The average financial indebtedness of the 2014 graduate was $25,443. The FAFSA and the college's own financial statement are required. The deadline for filing freshman financial aid applications for fall entry is March 1.

VALPARAISO UNIVERSITY B-1
www.valpo.edu

Valparaiso, IN 46383
(219) 464-5011
(888) GO-VALPO

Fax: (219) 464-6898 **Email:** undergrad.admission@valpo.edu

Full-time: 1520 men, 1639 women	**Faculty:** 248; IIA, av$
Part-time: 53 men, 48 women	**Ph.D.s:** 85%
Graduate: 621 men, 635 women	**Student/Faculty:** 13 to 1
Year: semesters, summer session	**Tuition:** $34,760
Room & Board: $10,180	**Freshman Class:** n/av
	CEEB CODE: 1874
Application Deadline: rolling	**VERY COMPETITIVE+**

Valparaiso University, founded in 1859, is an independent institution affiliated with the Lutheran Church and offering degree programs in arts and sciences, business, engineering, nursing and health professions, and law. Figures in the above capsule and in this profile are approximate. There are 5 undergraduate schools and 4 graduate schools. In addition to regional accreditation, Valpo has baccalaureate program accreditation with AACSB, ABET, CSWE, NASM, NCATE, ABA, AALS, CCNE, and ACS. The 350-acre campus is in a small town 55 miles southeast of Chicago. Including any residence halls, there are 60 buildings.

STUDENT LIFE: 59% of undergraduates are from out of state, mostly the Mid-West. Students are from 42 states, 33 foreign countries, and Canada. 73% are White. 57% are Protestant; 26% Catholic. **Male To Female Ratio:** 1.1:1. The average age of freshmen is 18; all undergraduates, 21. 16% do not continue beyond their first year; 71% remain to graduate. **Housing:** 2315 students can be accommodated in college housing, which includes single-sex and coed dorms and on-campus apartments. In addition, there are language houses and fraternity houses. On-campus housing is guaranteed for all 4 years. 65% of students live on campus. Alcohol is not permitted. Upperclassmen may keep cars.

FACULTY/CLASSROOMS: 55% of faculty are male; 45% are female. 87% teach undergraduates. No introductory courses are taught by graduate students. The average class size in an introductory lecture is 25; in a laboratory is 22; and in a regular course is 21.

PROGRAMS OF STUDY: Valpo confers B.A., B.L.P.S., B.Mus., B.Mus.Ed., B.S., B.S.Acc., B.S.Bus.Adm., B.S.C.E., B.S.Comp.Eng., B.S.Ed., B.S.E.E., B.S.H.C.L., B.S.M.E., B.S.N., B.S.P.E. and B.S.W. degrees. Associate, Master's, and Doctoral degrees are also awarded. Bachelor's degrees are awarded in BIOLOGICAL SCIENCE (biochemistry and biology/biological science), BUSINESS (accounting, banking and finance, business administration and management, business intelligence and analytics, finance, international economics, management science, marketing/retailing/merchandising, and sports management), COMMUNICATIONS AND THE ARTS (art, classics, communications, creative writing, digital communications, dramatic arts, English, English Writing, French, German, music, music performance, music theory and composition, Spanish, technical and business writing, theatre arts, and voice), COMPUTER AND PHYSICAL SCIENCE (actuarial science, astronomy, atmospheric sciences and meteorology, chemistry, computer science, geology, mathematics, and physics), EDUCATION (art education, elementary education, English education, foreign languages education, mathematics education, music education, physical education, psychology education, science education, secondary education, social science education, and social studies education), ENGINEERING AND ENVIRONMENTAL DESIGN (civil engineering, computer engineering, computer technology, electrical/electronics engineering, environmental science, and mechanical engineering), HEALTH PROFESSIONS (exercise science, health care administration, nursing, Pre-Health Studies, and pre-medicine), SOCIAL SCIENCE (American studies, criminology, East Asian studies, economics, geography, history, humanities, interdisciplinary studies, international public service, international relations, ministries, philosophy, political science/government, prelaw, psychology, religion, religious music, social science, social work, sociology, and theological studies). Nursing, business, and engineering have the largest enrollments.

ACTIVITIES: 20% of men belong to 8 national fraternities; 20% of women belong to 5 national sororities. There are 118 groups on campus, including art, band, cheerleading, choir, chorale, chorus, dance, debate, drama, environmental, ethnic, film, gay, honors, international, jazz band, literary magazine, musical theater, newspaper, orchestra, pep band, photography, political, professional, radio and TV, religious, social, social service, student government, symphony, and yearbook. Popular campus events include Christmas Concert, Martin Luther King Day Celebration and Jazz Festival. **Sports:** There are 9 intercollegiate sports for men and 10 for women, and 20 intramural sports for men and 20 for women. Facilities include a 5,100-seat arena, swimming pool, 7 additional playing floors, a track and field facility, racquetball/handball courts, a fitness center, a football stadium, a tennis complex, soccer, softball, and baseball fields, and indoor batting facilities. **Graduates:** From July 1, 2013 to June 30, 2014, 617 bachelor's degrees were awarded. The most popular majors were nursing (22%), English (5%), and biology (5%). 160 companies recruited on campus in 2013-2014. In an average class, 1% graduate in 3 years or less, 58% graduate in 4 years or less, 69% graduate in 5 years or less, and 71% graduate in 6 years or less. Of the 2013 graduating class, 18% were enrolled in graduate school within 6 months of graduation, and 73% were employed.

SERVICES: Counseling and information services are available, as is tutoring in most subjects. There is a reader service for the blind. A writing center provides assistance. The Academic Success Center coordinates all academic support services and resources, including tutoring, advising, and support groups. **Library/Resources:** The 2 libraries contain 576,342 volumes, 1.8 million microform items, 9,906 audio/video tapes/CDs/DVDs, and subscribe to 54,570 periodicals including electronic. Computerized library services include interlibrary loans, database searching, Internet access, and Wi-Fi capability. Special learning facilities include an art gallery, planetarium, radio station, observatory, weather station, center for visual and performing arts, virtual nursing learning center, solar energy research facility, and scientific visualization laboratory. **Physically Challenged Students:** 59% of the campus is accessible. Facilities include wheelchair ramps, elevators, special parking, specially equipped restrooms, lowered drinking fountains, and special housing. **Special:** There is cross-registration with Indiana University Northwest at the undergraduate level in geology. Off-campus study programs in the United States include a Washington semester programs, a Chicago urban semester, a Chicago arts semester, and a Chicago Business, Entrepreneurship, and Society program. Students may also study abroad in 19 countries including Greece, England, Spain, China, Japan, Namibia, France, Germany, Mexico, India, Thailand, Costa Rica, Chile, Israel, Ireland, Hungary, Nicaragua, Chile and Italy. Co-op programs, internships, the B.A.-B.S. degree, work-study programs, dual and student-designed majors, an accelerated degree program in numerous majors, pass/fail options, and non-degree study are also available. Other special academic features include Christ College, which is the honors college. There are 8 national honor societies, including Phi Beta Kappa, a freshman honors program, and 26 departmental honors programs. **Visiting:** There are regularly scheduled orientations for prospective students, includes a campus tour conducted by a current student, an interview with a counselor, the option to meet with professors, attend a class, and meet with a coach. There are guides for informal visits, visitors may sit in on classes, and stay overnight. To schedule a visit, contact the Office of Admission. **Campus Safety and Security:** Measures include 24-hour foot and vehicle patrol, emergency notification system, and security escort services. There are shuttle buses, emergency telephones, lighted pathways/sidewalks, and controlled access to dorms/residences.

REQUIREMENTS: The SAT or ACT is required. Valparaiso University requires completion of 4 years of English, 3 to 4 years of math, 2 to 3 years of lab science, 2 years each of history and foreign language, and 3 years of additional academic courses. An application essay is required and an interview is recommended for all applicants; an audition is required for music majors. AP and CLEP credits are accepted. Important factors in the admissions decision are advanced placement or honors courses, extracurricular activities record, and evidence of special talent. General education requirements include the 10-credit Valpo core plus 2 courses in theology, courses in natural sciences, humanities, cultural diversity, and social sciences, 1 course in quantitative analysis, and 1 credit hour in physical education. Requirements may vary by degree program, particularly in the professional colleges. To graduate, students must complete at least 124 credit hours, including a minimum of 27 in the major, with a GPA of at least 2.0. **Procedure:** Freshmen are admitted fall, spring, and summer. Entrance exams should be taken prior to the senior year. There are deferred admissions and rolling admissions plans. Application deadlines are open. Notifications are sent October 1. Applications are accepted on-line. **Transfer Students:** 192 transfer students enrolled in 2013-2014. Applicants must submit official transcripts from all colleges attended. To be considered for admission, a minimum 2.0 cumulative grade point average in college coursework is required for most programs. However, some programs require a minimum 3.0 grade point average for transfer students. If the applicant has completed fewer than 24 credit hours, entrance exam scores and a high school transcript are required. A completed transfer evaluation form from the Dean of Students of the current institution must also be submitted. An interview is recommended. 30 of 124 credits required for the bachelor's degree must be completed at Valpo. **International Students:** There are 261 international students enrolled. The school actively recruits these students. They must take the TOEFL with a minimum score of 550 on the paper-based TOEFL (PBT) or 80 on the Internet-based version (iBT) or take the IELTS, GCE, or GCSE English Exam, IB Higher Level English Exam, or SAT or ACT exams. They must also take the SAT or ACT.

ADMISSIONS: 57% of the current freshmen were in the top fifth of their class; 86% were in the top two fifths. There were 4 National Merit finalists. 11 freshmen graduated first in their class. **Admissions Contact:** David Fevig, Asst. Vice President, Enrollment Mgt.. E-Mail: *undergrad.admission@valpo.edu* Web: *www.valpo.edu*

FINANCIAL AID: In 2014-2015, 95% of all full-time freshmen and 92% of continuing full-time students received some form of financial aid. 79% of all full-time freshmen and 72% of continuing full-time

students received need-based aid. The average freshman award was $28,945. Need-based scholarships or need-based grants averaged $25,054; need-based self-help aid (loans and jobs) averaged $5,815; non-need-based athletic scholarships averaged $14,608; and other non-need-based awards and non-need-based scholarships averaged $16,187. 35% of undergraduate students work part-time. Average annual earnings from campus work are $1740. The average financial indebtedness of the 2014 graduate was $35,449. The FAFSA is required. The priority date for freshman financial aid applications for fall entry is March 1.

WABASH COLLEGE   B-3
www.wabash.edu

Crawfordsville, IN 47933

                                                    (765) 361-6254
                                                    (800) 345-5385
Fax: (765) 361-6437   Email: admissions@wabash.edu
Full-time: 924 men, no women   Faculty: 83; IIB, +$
Part-time: 2 men   Ph.D.s: 94%
Graduate: n/av   Student/Faculty: 11 to 1
Year: semesters   Tuition: $37,750
Room & Board: $9130   Freshman Class: 1117
                                applied, 881 accepted, 256
                                enrolled
SAT CR/M/W: 550/570/510 ACT: 25   CEEB CODE: 1895
Application Deadline: December 1 COMPETITIVE+

Wabash College, founded in 1832, is a private liberal arts college that educates men to think critically, act responsibly, lead effectively, and live humanely. There is one undergraduate school. In addition to regional accreditation, Wabash has baccalaureate program accreditation with NCATE. The 60-acre campus is in a small town 45 miles northwest of Indianapolis. Including any residence halls, there are 66 buildings.

STUDENT LIFE: 75% of undergraduates are from Indiana. Others are from 33 states, and 12 foreign countries. 83% are from public schools. 75% are White. The student base is all male. The average age of freshmen is 18; all undergraduates, 20. 11% do not continue beyond their first year; 72% remain to graduate. **Housing:** 887 students can be accommodated in college housing, which includes single-sex dorms and on-campus apartments. In addition, there are fraternity houses. On-campus housing is guaranteed for the freshman year only, and is available on a first-come, first-served basis. 86% of students live on campus. All students may keep cars.

FACULTY/CLASSROOMS: 64% of faculty are male; 36% are female. All teach undergraduates, 75% do research, and 75% do both. No introductory courses are taught by graduate students. The average class size in an introductory lecture is 23 and in a laboratory is 17.

PROGRAMS OF STUDY: Wabash confers A.B. degrees. Bachelor's degrees are awarded in BIOLOGICAL SCIENCE (biochemistry and biology/biological science), BUSINESS (finance), COMMUNICATIONS AND THE ARTS (art, classics, dramatic arts, English, French, German, Greek, Latin, music, Spanish, and speech/debate/rhetoric), COMPUTER AND PHYSICAL SCIENCE (chemistry, mathematics, and physics), SOCIAL SCIENCE (economics, Hispanic American studies, history, philosophy, political science/government, psychology, and religion). Chemistry, economics, and religion are the strongest academically. History, economics, and political science have the largest enrollments.

ACTIVITIES: 53% of men belong to 9 national fraternities. There are no sororities. There are 60 groups on campus, including art, band, chess, choir, chorale, chorus, communications, computers, dance, debate, drama, environmental, ethnic, film, forensics, gay, honors, international, jazz band, literary magazine, musical theater, newspaper, orchestra, pep band, photography, political, professional, radio and TV, religious, social, social service, student government, symphony, and yearbook. Popular campus events include Homecoming, Pan-Hel Weekend, Monon Bell, Honor Scholars Weekend, National Act, Oktoberfest, and Chapel Sing. **Sports:** There are 12 intercollegiate sports for men, and 20 intramural sports for men. Facilities include a 4500-seat football stadium with FieldTurf Dura-spine Pro

surface, indoor and outdoor tennis courts, baseball stadium, soccer stadium, natatorium, indoor track, all-weather outdoor track, wrestling practice facility, 1800-seat basketball arena, racquetball courts, aerobics room, wellness center. **Graduates:** From July 1, 2013 to June 30, 2014, 172 bachelor's degrees were awarded. The most popular majors were psychology (14%), history (12%), and biology (11%). 45 companies recruited on campus in 2013-2014. In an average class, 1% graduate in 3 years or less, 68% graduate in 4 years or less, 72% graduate in 5 years or less, and 73% graduate in 6 years or less. Of the 2013 graduating class, 24% were enrolled in graduate school within 6 months of graduation, and 53% were employed.

SERVICES: Counseling and information services are available, as is tutoring in some subjects, including economics, math, physics, biology, chemistry, and Spanish. There is a reader service for the blind. There is a quantitative skills center as well as a writing center where, under professional supervision, students help each other. **Library/Resources:** The library contains 276,184 volumes, 18,418 microform items, 17,064 audio/video tapes/CDs/DVDs, and subscribes to 19,782 periodicals including electronic. Computerized library services include interlibrary loans, database searching, Internet access, and Wi-Fi capability. Special learning facilities include an art gallery, radio station, an archival center, Wabash Center for the teaching of theology and religion, center of inquiry in the liberal arts, two biological field stations. **Physically Challenged Students:** 60% of the campus is accessible. Facilities include wheelchair ramps, elevators, special parking, specially equipped restrooms, special class scheduling, lowered drinking fountains, special housing. Braille signage in some buildings. Theater equipped for hearing-impared patrons. Some laboratory rooms with lowered work stations. **Special:** Wabash offers internships with off-campus organizations, study abroad in approximately 40 countries, a Washington semester with American University, dual majors, a B.A.-B.S. degree in engineering, and a 3-2 engineering program with Purdue University, Columbia University and Washington University in St. Louis. A tuition-free Ninth Semester Teacher Education Program is also available. Wabash also has a 4-1 program with the Indiana University Kelley School of Business that leads to a BA-MS (in accounting). Wabash has a new major in financial economics, and interdisciplinary minors in Hispanic studies, Asian studies, multicultural American studies, international studies, and gender studies. There are 9 national honor societies and Phi Beta Kappa. **Visiting:** There are regularly scheduled orientations for prospective students, consisting of a tour, lunch, opportunity to meet faculty, coaches, and alumni, and panel discussions on academics, extracurricular activities, and financial aid. There are guides for informal visits, visitors may sit in on classes, and stay overnight. To schedule a visit, contact Mary Towell at (800) 345-5385. **Campus Safety and Security:** Measures include 24-hour foot and vehicle patrol, emergency notification system, and security escort services. There are lighted pathways/sidewalks and controlled access to dorms/residences.

REQUIREMENTS: The SAT or ACT is required. Wabash recommends applicants have 4 high school courses in English, 3 to 4 in math, and 2 each in foreign language, lab science, and social studies. An essay is required, and an interview is recommended. AP credits are accepted. Important factors in the admissions decision are advanced placement or honors courses, leadership record, and extracurricular activities record. All students must complete at least 3 courses each in literature/fine arts, behavioral science, and natural science/math, 2 in history, philosophy, or religion, and 1 in quantitative skills. To graduate, students must maintain a minimum 2.0 GPA for 136 credit hours (34 courses), which include a freshman tutorial and the all-freshmen course Enduring Questions. The student must pass a written comprehensive exam in the major as well as a senior oral exam and must demonstrate proficiency in English and proficiency in a foreign language at a level equivalent to 2 college courses. **Procedure:** Freshmen are admitted fall and spring. Entrance exams should be taken by the spring of the junior year or fall of the senior year. There are early decision, early admissions, deferred admissions, and rolling admissions plans. Early decision applications should be filed by November 15 and regular applications, and December 1 for spring entry, along with a $40 fee. Notification of early decision is sent December 1; regular decision, on a rolling basis. 38 early decision candidates were accepted for the 2014-2015 class. 38 applicants were on the 2014 waiting list; 2 were admitted. Applications are accepted on-line. **Transfer Students:** 4 transfer students enrolled in 2013-2014. Applicants must submit official transcripts of all college courses attended. Wabash strongly considers the overall high school and college background of applicants. Courses must be liberal arts in nature with a minimum GPA of 2.0 to transfer. Recommendations from the college adviser and dean of students at the previous college attended and a personal written statement are required, with an interview strongly recommended. 24 of 34 credits required for the bachelor's degree must be completed at Wabash. **International Students:** There are 65 international students enrolled. The school actively recruits these students. They must take the TOEFL with a minimum score of 550 on the paper-based TOEFL (PBT) or 80 on the Internet-based version (iBT). They must also take the SAT or ACT.

ADMISSIONS: 79% of the 2014-2015 applicants were accepted. The SAT scores for the 2014-2015 freshman class were: Critical Reading--24% below 500, 47% between 500 and 599, 25% between 600 and 699, and 4% between 700 and 800; Math--18% below 500, 41% between 500 and 599, 35% between 600 and 699, and 6% between 700 and 800; Writing--39% below 500, 39% between 500 and 599, 20% between 600 and 699, and 2% between 700 and 800. The ACT scores were 14% below 21, 23% between 21 and 23, 31% between 24 and 26, 16% between 27 and 28, and 16% above 28. 56% of the current freshmen were in the top fifth of their class; 84% were in the top two fifths. 7 freshmen graduated first in their class. **Admissions Contact:** Charles Timmons, Senior Associate Director of Admissions. E-Mail: *admissions@wabash.edu* Web: *www.wabash.edu*

FINANCIAL AID: In 2014-2015, 82% of all full-time freshmen and 79% of continuing full-time students received some form of financial aid. 81% of all full-time freshmen and 78% of continuing full-time students received need-based aid. The average freshman award was $32,745. Need-based scholarships or need-based grants averaged $25,485; need-based self-help aid (loans and jobs) averaged $6,039; and other non-need-based awards and non-need-based scholarships averaged $1,221. 52% of undergraduate students work part-time. Average annual earnings from campus work are $2650. The average financial indebtedness of the 2014 graduate was $30,734. Wabash is a member of CSS. The CSS/Profile, FAFSA, and Federal tax transcript with W-2 statements are required. The priority date for freshman financial aid applications for fall entry is February 15. The deadline for filing freshman financial aid applications for fall entry is March 1.

IOWA

0 20 40 60 80 100
Miles

● College Location

ALLEN COLLEGE *(The complete profile is made available exclusively on our website, www.barronspac.com)*

ASHFORD UNIVERSITY   F-3
www.ashford.edu

Clinton, IA 52733-2967	(563) 243-6102
	(800) 242-4153
Fax: (563) 242-2003	Email: admissions@ashford.edu
Full-time: 2210 men, 7525women	Faculty: n/av
Part-time: 25men, 45women	Ph.D.s: n/av
Graduate: 210 men, 410 women	Student/Faculty: n/av
Year: semesters, summer session	Tuition: $16,500
Room & Board: $6500	Freshman Class: n/av
SAT or ACT: required	CEEB CODE: 6418
Application Deadline: see profile	COMPETITIVE

Ashford University is a private liberal arts college founded in 1918. Figures in the above capsule and in this profile are approximate. The library contains 80,759 volumes, 73,405 microform items, and 2,458 audio/video tapes/CDs/DVDs, and subscribes to 645 periodicals including electronic. Computerized library services include interlibrary loans, database searching, Internet access, and laptop Internet portals. Special learning facilities include a learning resource center, art gallery, and a living lab adjacent to the campus. The 25-acre campus is in a small town 135 miles west of Chicago, Illinois. Including any residence halls, there are 6 buildings.

STUDENT LIFE: 55% of undergraduates are from Iowa. Others are from 49 states, 8 foreign countries, and Canada. 62% are white; 23% African American. The average age of freshmen is 33; all undergraduates, 34.

FACULTY/CLASSROOMS: All teach undergraduates. No introductory courses are taught by graduate students.

PROGRAMS OF STUDY: AU confers B.A., B.S., B.A.S., and B.G.S degrees. Associate and master's degrees are also awarded. Bachelor's degrees are awarded in BIOLOGICAL SCIENCE (biology/biological science), BUSINESS (accounting, business administration and management, management information systems, and sports management), COMMUNICATIONS AND THE ARTS (English, public relations, and visual and performing arts), COMPUTER AND PHYSICAL SCIENCE (computer mathematics, computer science, and natural sciences), EDUCATION (business education, elementary education, physical education, and science education), ENGINEERING AND ENVIRONMENTAL DESIGN (computer graphics), HEALTH PROFESSIONS (clinical science, cytotechnology, health care administration, health science, and nuclear medical technology), SOCIAL SCIENCE (criminal justice, environmental studies, history, psychology, social science, and sociology). Accounting, business

---

administration, and elementary education are the strongest academically. Liberal arts, elementary education, and business administration have the largest enrollments.

ACTIVITIES: There are no fraternities or sororities. There are 20 groups on campus, including band, choir, computers, drama, ethnic, gay, honors, international, musical theater, newspaper, professional, religious, SISEA (Iowa State Education Association), social, social service, and student government. Popular campus events include Family Weekend, Matriculation Ceremony, and Earth Day.

SERVICES: Counseling and information services are available, as is tutoring in most subjects. There is a reader service for the blind, and remedial math, reading, and writing. There is also voice-activated computer software, proctoring exams, and prep courses for the GRE and MCAT.

REQUIREMENTS: The ACT is required and preferred, but the SAT is accepted. Applicants must be graduates of an accredited secondary school, have completed secondary-level home schooling as defined by state law, or have earned a GED. In addition, they must meet 2 of the following requirements: a GPA of 2.0 in college preparatory or regular high school courses, rank in the upper half of the graduating class, or a minimum ACT or SAT score. AP and CLEP credits are accepted.

FINANCIAL AID: AU is a member of CSS. The FAFSA and parents' and student's income tax forms are required. Check with the school for current deadlines.

BRIAR CLIFF UNIVERSITY   B-2
www.briarcliff.edu

Sioux City, IA 51104	(712) 279-5200
	(800) 662-3303
Fax: (712) 279-1632	Email: Sharisue.Wilcoxon@briarcliff.edu
Full-time: 417 men, 476 women	Faculty: 61; IIB, --$
Part-time: 54 men, 132 women	Ph.D.s: 75%
Graduate: 13 men, 66 women	Student/Faculty: 13 to 1
Year: trimesters, summer session	Tuition: $22,536
Room & Board: $6978	Freshman Class: 1774 applied, 1035 accepted, 237 enrolled
ACT: 21	CEEB CODE: 6046
Application Deadline: open	COMPETITIVE

Briar Cliff University, founded in 1930, is a private Roman Catholic-Franciscan liberal arts institution. Figures in the above capsule and in this profile are approximate. There are 2 undergraduate schools and 1 graduate school. In addition to regional accreditation, Briar Cliff University has baccalaureate program accreditation with AACSB, CSWE, and NLN. The 70-acre campus is in a suburban area minutes from downtown Sioux City. Including any residence halls, there are 13 buildings.

STUDENT LIFE: 65% of undergraduates are from Iowa. Others are from 26 states, 2 foreign countries, and Canada. 82% are from public schools. 82% are White. 55% are Catholic; 26% claim no religious affiliation; 23% Protestant. **Male To Female Ratio:** 1.4:1. The average age of freshmen is 18; all undergraduates, 23. 34% do not continue beyond their first year; 41% remain to graduate. **Housing:** 577 students can be accommodated in college housing, which includes coed dorms. In addition, there are special-interest houses. On-campus housing is guaranteed for the freshman year only. 63% of students live on campus. All students may keep cars.

FACULTY/CLASSROOMS: 48% of faculty are male; 52% are female. All teach undergraduates. No introductory courses are taught by graduate students. The average class size in an introductory lecture is 20; in a laboratory is 18; and in a regular course is 20.

PROGRAMS OF STUDY: Briar Cliff University confers B.A., B.S., B.S.N. and B.S.W. degrees. Associate and Master's degrees are also awarded. Bachelor's degrees are awarded in BIOLOGICAL SCIENCE (biology/biological science), BUSINESS (accounting, business administration and management, and human resources), COMMUNICATIONS AND THE ARTS (art, communications, dramatic arts,

---

622   www.barronspac.com

English, graphic design, journalism, media arts, music, and Spanish), COMPUTER AND PHYSICAL SCIENCE (chemistry, computer science, information sciences and systems, mathematics, and radiological technology), EDUCATION (elementary education, health education, and secondary education), ENGINEERING AND ENVIRONMENTAL DESIGN (environmental science), HEALTH PROFESSIONS (medical technology, nursing, and sports medicine), SOCIAL SCIENCE (criminal justice, history, political science/government, psychology, social work, sociology, and theological studies). Biology, business administration, and education are the strongest academically. Nursing has the largest enrollment.

ACTIVITIES: There are no fraternities or sororities. There are 44 groups on campus, including art, cheerleading, choir, chorale, chorus, computers, dance, drama, ethnic, film, honors, jazz band, literary magazine, musical theater, newspaper, pep band, photography, professional, radio and TV, religious, social, social service, and student government. Popular campus events include Texas Hold 'em Tournaments, Welcome Week, and Theater Productions. **Sports:** There are 9 intercollegiate sports for men and 10 for women, and 9 intramural sports for men and 9 for women. Facilities include baseball, softball, and soccer fields, recreation center with 2 racquetball courts, running track, tennis courts, 2 basketball/volleyball courts, and a weight-lifting facilities. **Graduates:** From July 1, 2013 to June 30, 2014, 204 bachelor's degrees were awarded. The most popular majors were business/ marketing (33%), health professions and related sciences (11%), and biological/ life sciences (8%). 46 companies recruited on campus in 2013-2014. In an average class, 43% graduate in 4 years or less, 53% graduate in 5 years or less, and 55% graduate in 6 years or less. Of the 2013 graduating class, 37% were enrolled in graduate school within 6 months of graduation.

SERVICES: Counseling and information services are available, as is tutoring in most subjects. There is remedial math, reading, and writing. **Library/Resources:** The library contains 82,007 volumes, 21,664 microform items, 1,244 audio/video tapes/CDs/DVDs. Computerized library services include interlibrary loans, database searching, Internet access, and Wi-Fi capability. Special learning facilities include an art gallery, radio station, TV station, an integrated multimedia center, a nursing simulation lab, a human anatomy/cadaver lab, and an entrepreneurship lab. **Physically Challenged Students:** 90% of the campus is accessible. Facilities include wheelchair ramps, elevators, special parking, specially equipped restrooms, lowered drinking fountains, and lowered telephones. **Special:** Internships, study abroad, dual majors, work-study programs, accelerated degree programs in business administration, human resource management, and professional studies, student-designed interdisciplinary majors, and pass/fail options are available. Students may earn a 3-2 engineering degree with Iowa State University. There are 4 national honor societies, a freshman honors program, and 3 departmental honors programs. **Visiting:** There are regularly scheduled orientations for prospective students, including a presidential welcome, a meeting with faculty and student panels, a luncheon, campus tours, a slide show, and financial aid information. There are guides for informal visits, visitors may sit in on classes, and stay overnight. To schedule a visit, contact the Admissions Office. **Campus Safety and Security:** Measures include 24-hour foot and vehicle patrol, emergency notification system, and security escort services. There are emergency telephones, lighted pathways/sidewalks, and controlled access to dorms/residences.

REQUIREMENTS: The ACT is required. SAT is accepted but the ACT is preferred, and a score of 18 qualifies for automatic acceptance review. Applicants need not be graduates of an accredited secondary school. The GED is accepted. Admission to freshman standing requires 4 years each of English and math, 3 of science, 2 of history, and 1 of social studies. Two years of foreign language is recommended A GPA of 2.0 is required. AP and CLEP credits are accepted. Important factors in the admissions decision are leadership record, extracurricular activities record, and advanced placement or honors courses.To graduate, students must complete a minimum of 124 semester hours, maintain a GPA of 2.0 with no more than 1 D in the major, complete the three components of Briar Cliff's general educational program, and complete a major field of concentration. **Procedure:** Freshmen are admitted to all sessions. Entrance exams should be taken by October for scholarship consideration, and by April for

admission. There is a rolling admissions plan. Application deadlines are open. Application fee is $20. Notification is sent on a rolling basis. Applications are accepted on-line. **Transfer Students:** 37 transfer students enrolled in 2013-2014. Applicants must have a minimum GPA of 2.0 with at least 10 credit hours earned and satisfactory dismissal from the previous institution. Grades of D or better transfer for credit. 31 of 124 credits required for the bachelor's degree must be completed at Briar Cliff University. **International Students:** There are 6 international students enrolled. They must take the TOEFL or MELAB. Students may be required to have a telephone interview with an ESL advisor.

ADMISSIONS: 58% of the 2014-2015 applicants were accepted. The ACT scores were 40% below 21, 28% between 21 and 23, 20% between 24 and 26, 9% between 27 and 28, and 3% above 28. 25% of the current freshmen were in the top fifth of their class; 50% were in the top two fifths. 2 freshmen graduated first in their class. **Admissions Contact:** Sharisue Wilcoxon, Vice President/Enrollment Management. E-Mail: *Sharisue.Wilcoxon@briarcliff.edu* Web: *www.briarcliff.edu*

FINANCIAL AID: In 2014-2015, 100% of all full-time freshmen and 98% of continuing full-time students received some form of financial aid. 73% of all full-time freshmen and 64% of continuing full-time students received need-based aid. The average freshman award was $12,250. Need-based scholarships or need-based grants averaged $3,900; need-based self-help aid (loans and jobs) averaged $7,255; and non-need-based athletic scholarships averaged $5,109. 23% of undergraduate students work part-time. Average annual earnings from campus work are $750. The average financial indebtedness of the 2014 graduate was $30,100. The FAFSA is required. The priority date for freshman financial aid applications for fall entry is March 1.

BUENA VISTA UNIVERSITY	B-2
www.bvu.edu	
Storm Lake, IA 50588	**(712) 749-2235**
	(800) 383-9600
Fax: (712) 749-2035	Email: admissions@bvu.edu
Full-time: 412 men, 432 women	Faculty: 84; IIB, -$
Part-time: 12 men, 5 women	Ph.D.s: 83%
Graduate: 5 men, 46 women	Student/Faculty: 10 to 1
Year: 4-1-4, summer session	Tuition: $30,406
Room & Board: $8782	Freshman Class: 1227 applied, 833 accepted, 201 enrolled
ACT: 22	CEEB CODE: 6047
Application Deadline: open	COMPETITIVE

Buena Vista University, founded in 1891, is a private institution affiliated with the Presbyterian Church. The university offers undergraduate degree programs in business, education, communication and arts, science, social science, philosophy, and religion, and an accredited master's program in education. Programs emphasize career education with a liberal arts foundation. There are 5 undergraduate schools and 1 graduate school. In addition to regional accreditation, Buena Vista has baccalaureate program accreditation with CSWE and CAATE. The 60-acre campus is in a small town 65 miles east of Sioux City. Including any residence halls, there are 16 buildings.

STUDENT LIFE: 76% of undergraduates are from Iowa. Others are from 25 states, and 11 foreign countries. 90% are from public schools. 74% are White. 43% are Protestant; 29% Catholic; 18% claim no religious affiliation. **Male To Female Ratio:** 1.1:1. The average age of freshmen is 18; all undergraduates, 20. 27% do not continue beyond their first year; 54% remain to graduate. **Housing:** 870 students can be accommodated in college housing, which includes single-sex and coed dorms. In addition, there are honors houses and special-interest houses. On-campus housing is guaranteed for all 4 years. 85% of students live on campus; of those, 60% remain on campus on weekends. All students may keep cars.

FACULTY/CLASSROOMS: 54% of faculty are male; 46% are female. All teach undergraduates. No introductory courses are taught by graduate students. The average class size in an introductory lecture is 25; in a laboratory is 20; and in a regular course is 14.

PROGRAMS OF STUDY: Buena Vista confers B.A., B.S., B.A.S. and B.A.Sc. degrees. Master's degrees are also awarded. Bachelor's degrees are awarded in BIOLOGICAL SCIENCE (biology/biological science), BUSINESS (accounting, banking and finance, business administration and management, business economics, international business management, marketing/retailing/merchandising, and sports management), COMMUNICATIONS AND THE ARTS (art, arts administration/management, communications, English, graphic design, music, Spanish, and theatre arts), COMPUTER AND PHYSICAL SCIENCE (chemistry, computer science, mathematics, physics, and science), EDUCATION (art education, business education, elementary education, music education, science education, secondary education, and special education), ENGINEERING AND ENVIRONMENTAL DESIGN (environmental science), SOCIAL SCIENCE (criminal justice, economics, history, philosophy, physical fitness/movement, political science/government, psychology, public administration, religion, social science, and social work). Biology, mathematics, and business are the strongest academically. Biology, education, and business have the largest enrollments.

ACTIVITIES: There are no fraternities or sororities. There are 60 groups on campus, including art, band, cheerleading, choir, chorale, chorus, communications, computers, dance, debate, drama, drill team, environmental, ethnic, gay, honors, international, jazz band, musical theater, newspaper, pep band, photography, political, professional, radio and TV, religious, social, social service, and student government. Popular campus events include Academic and Cultural Events Series, Buenafication Day, American Heritage Lecture Series, and Scholars Day. **Sports:** There are 9 intercollegiate sports for men and 8 for women, and 10 intramural sports for men and 10 for women. Facilities include a 380-seat auditorium, a 1000-seat auditorium, a 4000-seat stadium, a field house with a 4000-seat gym, basketball, volleyball, racquetball, and tennis courts, football, softball, and baseball fields, a track, facilities for weight training and other recreational activities, an Olympic-size indoor pool, and a game room. **Graduates:** From July 1, 2013 to June 30, 2014, 195 bachelor's degrees were awarded. The most popular majors were management (8%), elementary education (8%), and biology (8%). 40 companies recruited on campus in 2013-2014.

SERVICES: Counseling and information services are available, as is tutoring in most subjects. There is a reader service for the blind, and remedial math, reading, and writing. **Library/Resources:** The library contains 5,000 volumes, 41,372 microform items, 6,000 audio/video tapes/CDs/DVDs, and subscribes to 639 periodicals including electronic. Computerized library services include interlibrary loans, database searching, Internet access, and Wi-Fi capability. Special learning facilities include an art gallery, radio station, TV station, a student newspaper desktop production lab. **Physically Challenged Students:** Facilities include wheelchair ramps, elevators, special parking, specially equipped restrooms, special class scheduling, lowered drinking fountains, lowered telephones. **Special:** Special academic offerings include 3-2 engineering degree programs with Washington University School of Engineering and Applied Science in St. Louis and the University of Minnesota College of Science and Engineering. Buena Vista has also partnered with the University of Iowa College of Law and the Creighton University School of Law in a 3+3 Accelerated Law School Entry Program. Students may study abroad in Japan, Taiwan, Australia, and Europe. Buena Vista offers dual and student-designed majors, credit for life experience, and pass/fail options in courses outside the major field. Nondegree study is possible. Internships are required in many majors and encouraged in most. The J. Leslie Rollins Fellowship allows 1 or 2 students each year to design an internship anywhere in the world. There are 5 national honor societies and a freshman honors program. **Visiting:** There are regularly scheduled orientations for prospective students, campus tour and meetings with an admissions counselor, faculty representatives, coaches, and activity representatives in the student's areas of interest. There are guides for informal visits, visitors may sit in on classes, and stay overnight. To schedule a visit, contact Bridget Kurkowski at (712) 749-2078. **Campus Safety and Security:** Measures include 24-hour foot and vehicle patrol, emergency notification system, self-defense education, and security escort services. There are shuttle buses, emergency telephones, lighted pathways/sidewalks, controlled access to dorms/residences, An enhanced 911 system on campus.

REQUIREMENTS: The ACT is required. SAT scores may be submitted instead. Applicants must be graduates of an accredited secondary school or have earned a GED. The college requires 13 academic credits, including 4 of English and 3 each of math, social studies, and science. Campus visits and an interview are recommended. AP and CLEP credits are accepted. Important factors in the admissions decision are advanced placement or honors courses, leadership record, and recommendations by school officials. All students must complete 9 semester hours each of natural sciences, humanities, social sciences, and 3 semester hours of fine arts. In addition, students must successfully complete requirements in intellectual foundation courses in mathematics and communication. Students must also participate in the Academic and Cultural Events Series, through which they attend lectures and performances by national and world leaders. The bachelor's degree requires a minimum of 128 semester hours, including 32 to 64 hours in the major, with a GPA of at least 2.0, or higher for some majors. **Procedure:** Freshmen are admitted fall, winter, and spring. Entrance exams should be taken during the spring of the junior year or October of the senior year. There are deferred admissions and rolling admissions plans. Application deadlines are open. Notification is sent on a rolling basis. Applications are accepted online. Application fees are waived if application is completed on-line. **Transfer Students:** 40 transfer students enrolled in 2013-2014. A high school diploma and a minimum GPA of 2.5 from the applicant's college are required. 30 of 128 credits required for the bachelor's degree must be completed at Buena Vista. **International Students:** There are 62 international students enrolled. The school actively recruits these students. They must take the TOEFL with a minimum score of 500 on the paper-based TOEFL (PBT) or 59 on the Internet-based version (iBT) and the college's own test.

ADMISSIONS: 68% of the 2014-2015 applicants were accepted. The ACT scores were 31% below 21, 29% between 21 and 23, 26% between 24 and 26, 7% between 27 and 28, and 7% above 28. 41% of the current freshmen were in the top fifth of their class; 70% were in the top two fifths. 12 freshmen graduated first in their class. **Admissions Contact:** Bridget Kurkowski, Director of Admissions. E-Mail: *admissions@bvu.edu* Web: *www.bvu.edu*

FINANCIAL AID: In 2014-2015, 99% of all full-time freshmen and 98% of continuing full-time students received some form of financial aid. The FAFSA and the college's own financial statement are required. The deadline for filing freshman financial aid applications for fall entry is June 1.

CENTRAL COLLEGE D-3
www.central.edu

Pella, IA 50219

(641) 628-7637
(877) 462-3687

Fax: (641) 628-5316
Full-time: 634 men, 648 women
Part-time: 9 men, 17 women
Graduate: n/av
Year: semesters, summer session
Room & Board: $9980

Application Deadline: March 1

Email: admission@central.edu
Faculty: 96; IIB, av$
Ph.D.s: 88%
Student/Faculty: 13 to 1
Tuition: $32,124
Freshman Class: 2216 applied, 2024 accepted, 429 enrolled
CEEB CODE: 6087
COMPETITIVE+

Central College, founded in 1853, offers more than 70 academic programs in a residential, liberal arts environment. Central is dedicated to student success and the formation of lifelong connections. There is one undergraduate school. In addition to regional accreditation, Central College has baccalaureate program accreditation with NASM, NCATE, CAATE, and ACS. The 169-acre campus is in a small town 45 miles southeast of Des Moines. Including any residence halls, there are 50 buildings.

STUDENT LIFE: 80% of undergraduates are from Iowa. Others are from 30 states, and 11 foreign countries. 96% are from public schools. 90% are White. 59% are Protestant; 23% Unknown denominations; 17% Catholic. **Male To Female Ratio:** 1.0:1. The average age of freshmen is 18; all undergraduates, 20. 19% do not continue beyond their first year; 67% remain to graduate. **Housing:** 1383 students can be accommodated in college housing, which includes single-sex and coed dorms and on-campus apartments. In addition, there are language houses, special-interest houses, fraternity houses, and sorority houses. On-campus housing is guaranteed for all 4 years. 94% of students live on campus; of those, 71% remain on campus on weekends. Alcohol is not permitted. All students may keep cars.

FACULTY/CLASSROOMS: 55% of faculty are male; 45% are female. All teach and do research. No introductory courses are taught by graduate students. The average class size in an introductory lecture is 22; in a laboratory is 18; and in a regular course is 22.

PROGRAMS OF STUDY: Central College confers B.A. degrees. Bachelor's degrees are awarded in BIOLOGICAL SCIENCE (biochemistry and biology/biological science), BUSINESS (accounting and business administration and management), COMMUNICATIONS AND THE ARTS (art, communications, dramatic arts, English, French, German, linguistics, music, and Spanish), COMPUTER AND PHYSICAL SCIENCE (actuarial science, chemistry, computer science, mathematics, natural sciences, and physics), EDUCATION (athletic training, elementary education, and music education), ENGINEERING AND ENVIRONMENTAL DESIGN (environmental science), HEALTH PROFESSIONS (exercise science), SOCIAL SCIENCE (anthropology, economics, history, international studies, philosophy, political science/government, psychology, religion, and sociology). Exercise science, business management, and biology have the largest enrollments.

ACTIVITIES: 4% of men belong to 5 local fraternities; 3% of women belong to 2 local sororities. There are 80 groups on campus, including and mock trial, entrepreneurship, art, band, cheerleading, choir, chorus, communications, drama, drill team, environmental, ethnic, gay, honors, international, jazz band, literary magazine, musical theater, newspaper, orchestra, pep band, photography, political, professional, religious, social, social service, student government, and sustainability. Popular campus events include Lemming Race, Breakfast of Champions, and Candle Light Christmas Concert. **Sports:** There are 10 intercollegiate sports for men and 9 for women, and 6 intramural sports for men and 7 for women. Facilities include A gymnasium and fieldhouse with indoor track, tennis, fitness center for strength/conditioning, football/track stadium, competition and practice soccer fields, golf practice facility, cross country course, baseball and softball fields, plus a new fitness center for general student use. **Graduates:** From July 1, 2013 to June 30, 2014, 304 bachelor's degrees were awarded. The most popular majors were exercise science (16%), business management (11%), and biology (10%). 19 companies recruited on campus in 2013-2014. In an average class, 58% graduate in 4 years or less, 67% graduate in 5 years or less, and 68% graduate in 6 years or less. Of the 2013 graduating class, 20% were enrolled in graduate school within 6 months of graduation, and 69% were employed.

SERVICES: Counseling and information services are available, as is tutoring in every subject. **Library/Resources:** The 3 libraries contain 158,193 volumes, 2,085 microform items, 7,741 audio/video tapes/CDs/DVDs, and subscribe to 345 periodicals including electronic. Computerized library services include interlibrary loans, database searching, Internet access, and Wi-Fi capability. Special learning facilities include an art gallery. **Physically Challenged Students:** 90% of the campus is accessible. Facilities include wheelchair ramps, elevators, special parking, specially equipped restrooms, special class scheduling, lowered drinking fountains, lowered telephones, and special housing. **Special:** Nearly half the students participate in study abroad programs in London, Paris, Vienna, Mexico, Spain, Wales, Peru, Belize, Costa Rica, Turkey, and Ghana. Central also offers internship opportunities in Washington, D.C., Chicago, and New York. 76% of Central student complete internships before graduation. Individualized interdisciplinary majors are also available. There is a freshman honors program. **Visiting:** There are regularly scheduled orientations for prospective students, consisting of registration session with academic advisor, and presentations by the academic dean, student life dean, financial aid director, registrar and admission staff. There are guides for informal visits, visitors may sit in on classes, and stay overnight. To schedule a visit, contact the Admission Office at admission@central.edu. **Campus Safety and Security:** Measures include 24-hour foot and vehicle patrol, emergency notification system, self-defense education, and security escort services. There are

emergency telephones, lighted pathways/sidewalks, and controlled access to dorms/residences.

REQUIREMENTS: The ACT is required. All applicants must be graduates of an accredited secondary school or have earned a GED. Candidates who have an ACT composite score of 20 or above (940-970 SAT critical reading and mathematics combined), have a 2.70 cumulative high school GPA, rank in the top half of their secondary school graduating class and have met the recommended college-preparatory curriculum are typically admitted. Central College requires applicants to be in the upper 50% of their class. A GPA of 2.7 is required. AP and CLEP credits are accepted. Important factors in the admissions decision are advanced placement or honors courses, extracurricular activities record, and leadership record.Students are required to complete 120 semester hours, including at least 20 hours of 300-level or above, with a minimum 2.0 cumulative and major GPA. Core requirements include courses in integrative studies, disciplinary studies, global sustainability, global perspective, and writing intensive. **Procedure:** Freshmen are admitted fall, spring, and summer. Entrance exams should be taken spring of the junior year of high school. There are deferred admissions and rolling admissions plans. Applications should be filed by March 1 for fall entry; November 1 for spring entry; and May 1 for summer entry, along with a $25 fee. Notification is sent on a rolling basis. Applications are accepted on-line. **Transfer Students:** 128 transfer students enrolled in 2013-2014. Each transfer student is considered individually. Interviews are encouraged. 45 of 120 credits required for the bachelor's degree must be completed at Central College. **International Students:** There are 19 international students enrolled. The school actively recruits these students. They must take the TOEFL with a minimum score of 530 on the paper-based TOEFL (PBT) or 71 on the Internet-based version (iBT). They must also take the SAT or ACT.

ADMISSIONS: 91% of the 2014-2015 applicants were accepted. 40% of the current freshmen were in the top fifth of their class; 73% were in the top two fifths. 35 freshmen graduated first in their class. **Admissions Contact:** Chevy Frieburger, Director of Admission. E-Mail: *admission@central.edu* Web: *www.central.edu*

FINANCIAL AID: In 2014-2015, 100% of all full-time freshmen and 99% of continuing full-time students received some form of financial aid. 85% of all full-time freshmen and 80% of continuing full-time students received need-based aid. The average freshman award was $30,539. Need-based scholarships or need-based grants averaged $20,893 ($32,124 maximum); need-based self-help aid (loans and jobs) averaged $2,991 ($7,500 maximum); other non-need-based awards and non-need-based scholarships averaged $4,136 ($24,880 maximum); and $2,519 from other forms of aid. 67% of undergraduate students work part-time. Average annual earnings from campus work are $865. The average financial indebtedness of the 2014 graduate was $31,304. Central College is a member of CSS. The FAFSA is required. The priority date for freshman financial aid applications for fall entry is March 15.

CLARKE UNIVERSITY   E-2
www.clarke.edu

Dubuque, IA 52001	(563) 588-6436
	(800) 383-2345
Fax: (563) 588-6789	Email: Emily.kruse@clarke.edu
Full-time: 259 men, 576 women	Faculty: 83; IIB, --$
Part-time: 45 men, 69 women	Ph.D.s: 69%
Graduate: 60 men, 191 women	Student/Faculty: 10 to 1
Year: semesters, summer session	Tuition: $28,900
Room & Board: $8700	Freshman Class: 1381 applied, 968 accepted, 183 enrolled
SAT CR/M: 473/506 ACT: 23	CEEB CODE: 6099
Application Deadline: open	COMPETITIVE

Clarke University, established in 1843, is a private Catholic institution. A strong liberal arts core is integrated into all majors and pre-professional programs. In addition to regional accreditation, Clarke has baccalaureate program accreditation with APTA, CSWE, NASM,

NCATE, and NLN. The 55-acre campus is in a small town 150 miles west of Chicago. Including any residence halls, there are 14 buildings.

STUDENT LIFE: 62% of undergraduates are from Iowa. Others are from 28 states, and 7 foreign countries. 80% are from public schools. 89% are White. 41% are Catholic; 12% Protestant. **Male To Female Ratio:** 2.3:1. The average age of freshmen is 18; all undergraduates, 24. 27% do not continue beyond their first year; 68% remain to graduate. **Housing:** 577 students can be accommodated in college housing, which includes single-sex and coed dorms and on-campus apartments. Residence hall reserved for upperclassmen, and an apartment residence building reserved for juniors and seniors. On-campus housing is guaranteed for all 4 years. 60% of students live on campus; of those, 33% remain on campus on weekends. All students may keep cars.

FACULTY/CLASSROOMS: 34% of faculty are male; 66% are female. All teach and do research. No introductory courses are taught by graduate students. The average class size in an introductory lecture is 24; in a laboratory is 11; and in a regular course is 14.

PROGRAMS OF STUDY: Clarke confers B.A., B.S., B.A.S., B.F.A. and B.S.N. degrees. Associate, Master's, and Doctoral degrees are also awarded. Bachelor's degrees are awarded in BIOLOGICAL SCIENCE (biochemistry, bioinformatics, and biology/biological science), BUSINESS (accounting, business administration and management, entrepreneurial studies, marketing management, and sports management), COMMUNICATIONS AND THE ARTS (advertising, art, art history and appreciation, communications, dramatic arts, English, music, musical theater, Spanish, and studio art), COMPUTER AND PHYSICAL SCIENCE (chemistry, computer science, computer security and information assurance, information sciences and systems, and mathematics), EDUCATION (art education, athletic training, elementary education, music education, secondary education, and special education), HEALTH PROFESSIONS (nursing and physical therapy), SOCIAL SCIENCE (criminology, food science, history, liberal arts/general studies, philosophy, physical fitness/movement, political science/government, psychology, religion, social work, and sociology). Physical therapy, biology, chemistry and math are the strongest academically. Business administration, nursing and education have the largest enrollments.

ACTIVITIES: There are no fraternities or sororities. There are 50 groups on campus, including art, cheerleading, choir, chorus, computers, drama, environmental, ethnic, gay, honors, international, jazz band, literary magazine, newspaper, pep band, photography, political, professional, religious, social, social service, and student government. Popular campus events include Family Weekend, New Year's Dance and Midnight Pancake Breakfast. **Sports:** There are 8 intercollegiate sports for men and 8 for women, and 15 intramural sports for men and 13 for women. Facilities include a 1000-seat gym, a 700-seat arena, an indoor track, a soccer field, basketball, volleyball, tennis, and racquetball courts, a fitness trail, weight and aerobics rooms, and an indoor batting cage/pitching mound area. There are baseball/softball fields and 2 alpine ski courses nearby, plus a municipal golf course adjacent to the campus. **Graduates:** From July 1, 2013 to June 30, 2014, 203 bachelor's degrees were awarded. The most popular majors were nursing (30%), philosophy (14%), and education (9%). 50 companies recruited on campus in 2013-2014. In an average class, 49% graduate in 4 years or less, 66% graduate in 5 years or less, and 68% graduate in 6 years or less. Of the 2013 graduating class, 22% were enrolled in graduate school within 6 months of graduation, and 68% were employed.

SERVICES: Counseling and information services are available, as is tutoring in most subjects. There is remedial math, reading, and writing. **Library/Resources:** The library contains 97,891 volumes, 7,912 microform items, and 1,753 audio/video tapes/CDs/DVDs, and subscribes to 60,529 periodicals including electronic. Computerized library services include interlibrary loans, database searching, Internet access, and Wi-Fi capability. Special learning facilities include an art gallery, planetarium, an art slide library, electronic music studio, and several computer-integrated specialized departmental labs. **Physically Challenged Students:** 90% of the campus is accessible. Facilities include wheelchair ramps, elevators, special parking, specially equipped restrooms, special class scheduling, lowered drinking fountains, and lowered telephones. **Special:** There are 4 national honor societies, a freshman honors program, and 3 departmental honors

programs. **Visiting:** There are guides for informal visits, visitors may sit in on classes, and stay overnight. To schedule a visit, contact the Admissions Office. **Campus Safety and Security:** Measures include 24-hour foot and vehicle patrol, emergency notification system, and security escort services. There are emergency telephones, lighted pathways/sidewalks, and controlled access to dorms/residences.

REQUIREMENTS: The SAT or ACT is required. The high school transcript should include 4 years of English, 3 each of math, history/social science, and science (4 for human biology and physical therapy majors), 2 of the same foreign language, and 5 of electives. A GPA of 2.0 is required. AP and CLEP credits are accepted. Important factors in the admissions decision are advanced placement or honors courses. To graduate, all students must complete 124 semester hours, with 30 to 70 in the major, and maintain a GPA of 2.0 (2.5 for education majors or 3.25 for physical therapy majors). Students must complete Cornerstone I and II, a Capstone course, and 6 hours each in religious studies, philosophy, fine arts, humanities, math, and natural sciences, and social sciences **Procedure:** Freshmen are admitted to all sessions. Entrance exams should be taken in the spring of the junior year or the fall of the senior year. There are deferred admissions and rolling admissions plans. Application deadlines are open. Application fee is $25. Applications are accepted on-line. **Transfer Students:** 58 transfer students enrolled in 2013-2014. Applicants must submit a transcript and a recommendation from the dean of students for each college attended. Students with fewer than 24 completed semester hours must also submit a high school transcript and SAT or ACT scores. 30 of 124 credits required for the bachelor's degree must be completed at Clarke. **International Students:** There are 7 international students enrolled. The school actively recruits these students. They must take the TOEFL with a minimum score of 527 on the paper-based TOEFL (PBT) or 71 on the Internet-based version (iBT). They must also take the SAT or ACT.

ADMISSIONS: 70% of the 2014-2015 applicants were accepted. The SAT scores for the 2014-2015 freshman class were: Critical Reading--75% below 500, and 25% between 500 and 599; Math--37% below 500, and 63% between 500 and 599. The ACT scores were 24% below 21, 23% between 21 and 23, 23% between 24 and 26, 10% between 27 and 28, and 8% above 28. 34% of the current freshmen were in the top fifth of their class; 71% were in the top two fifths. **Admissions Contact:** Emily Kruse, Assistant Director of Admissions. E-Mail: *Emily.kruse@clarke.edu* Web: *www.clarke.edu*

FINANCIAL AID: In 2014-2015, 100% of all full-time freshmen and 99% of continuing full-time students received some form of financial aid. 84% of all full-time freshmen and 84% of continuing full-time students received need-based aid. The average freshman award was $27,301. Need-based scholarships or need-based grants averaged $6,157; need-based self-help aid (loans and jobs) averaged $3,648; non-need-based athletic scholarships averaged $2,513; and other non-need-based awards and non-need-based scholarships averaged $12,582. 35% of undergraduate students work part-time. Average annual earnings from campus work are $964. The average financial indebtedness of the 2014 graduate was $30,594. The FAFSA is required. The priority date for freshman financial aid applications for fall entry is April 15. The deadline for filing freshman financial aid applications for fall entry is rolling.

COE COLLEGE   E-3
www.coe.edu

Cedar Rapids, IA 52402	**(319) 399-8046**
	(877) CALL-COE
Fax: (319) 399-8816	**Email:** jstaker@coe.edu
Full-time: 595 men, 765 women	**Faculty:** 95; IIB, -$
Part-time: 36 men, 39 women	**Ph.D.s:** 90%
Graduate: 1 women	**Student/Faculty:** 14 to 1
Year: semesters, summer session	**Tuition:** $37,320
Room & Board: $8230	**Freshman Class:** 3403 applied, 1882 accepted, 376 enrolled
SAT CR/M/W: 570/570/530 **ACT:** 25	**CEEB CODE:** 6101
Application Deadline: March 1	**VERY COMPETITIVE**

Coe College, founded in 1851, Coe has a distinctive reputation for quality, offers superb academic and exciting social opportunities in a thriving urban setting that allows students to grow and succeed. In addition to regional accreditation, Coe has baccalaureate program accreditation with NASM, CAAHEP, CCNE, CAATE, and ACS. The 53-acre campus is in an urban area in the heart of the Cedar Rapids community, 225 miles west of Chicago. Including any residence halls, there are 32 buildings.

STUDENT LIFE: 51% of undergraduates are from Iowa. Others are from 38 states, 20 foreign countries, and Canada. 73% are White. **Male To Female Ratio:** 1.3:1. The average age of freshmen is 19; all undergraduates, 20. 22% do not continue beyond their first year; 67% remain to graduate. **Housing:** 1150 students can be accommodated in college housing, which includes single-sex and coed dorms and on-campus apartments. In addition, there are honors houses, special-interest houses, living learning community. On-campus housing is guaranteed for all 4 years. 89% of students live on campus; of those, 75% remain on campus on weekends. All students may keep cars.

FACULTY/CLASSROOMS: 50% of faculty are male; 49% are female. All teach undergraduates. No introductory courses are taught by graduate students. The average class size in an introductory lecture is 13; in a laboratory is 14; and in a regular course is 16.

PROGRAMS OF STUDY: Coe confers B.A., B.M. and B.S.N. degrees. Bachelor's degrees are awarded in AGRICULTURE (environmental studies), BIOLOGICAL SCIENCE (biochemistry, biology/biological science, molecular biology, and neurosciences), BUSINESS (accounting, business administration and management, and organizational behavior), COMMUNICATIONS AND THE ARTS (art, art history and appreciation, communications, creative writing, English, film arts, French, German, literature, music, public relations, Spanish, theatre arts, and writing), COMPUTER AND PHYSICAL SCIENCE (chemistry, computer science, mathematics, physics, and science), EDUCATION (athletic training, elementary education, music education, physical education, and secondary education), ENGINEERING AND ENVIRONMENTAL DESIGN (environmental science and pre-engineering), HEALTH PROFESSIONS (nursing, physical therapy, predentistry, premedicine, prephysical therapy, and preveterinary science), SOCIAL SCIENCE (African American studies, American studies, Asian/Oriental studies, economics, French studies, gender studies, German area studies, history, industrial and organizational psychology, interdisciplinary studies, philosophy, political science/government, prelaw, psychology, religion, sociology, Spanish studies, and women's studies). Chemistry, physics, and psychology are the strongest academically. Business administration and biology has the largest enrollments.

ACTIVITIES: 30% of men belong to 5 national fraternities; 26% of women belong to 3 national sororities. There are 80 groups on campus, including student activities committee, student alumni association, student athletic advisory committee, art, band, cheerleading, choir, chorale, chorus, communications, computers, dance, drama, environmental, ethnic, film, gay, honors, international, jazz band, literary magazine, musical theater, newspaper, orchestra, pep band, photography, political, professional, radio and TV, religious, social, social service, student government, Student Senate, and symphony. Popular campus events include Coe Olympics, International Student Banquet and Cultural Show, Flunk Day, and Prez Ball. **Sports:** There are 11 intercollegiate sports for men and 10 for women. Facilities include a racquet center with 4 indoor and 6 outdoor tennis courts, 4 racquetball courts, 2 squash courts, and a 200-meter indoor track and a field house with an indoor natatorium, a wrestling room, a fitness center, a rock-climbing wall, courts for basketball and volleyball, and batting cages for baseball and softball. There also are a 400-meter outdoor track, softball diamond, and 2000-seat football/soccer stadium, baseball field and soccer practice field. **Graduates:** From July 1, 2013 to June 30, 2014, 284 bachelor's degrees were awarded. The most popular majors were business administration (15%), psychology (10%), and biology (8%). In an average class, 61% graduate in 4 years or less, 68% graduate in 5 years or less, and 70% graduate in 6 years or less. Of the 2013 graduating class, 28% were enrolled in graduate school within 6 months of graduation, and 70% were employed.

SERVICES: Counseling and information services are available, as is tutoring in most subjects, sciences, math, business, and foreign languages. There is a reader service for the blind, and remedial math, reading, and writing. A writing center and an academic achievement program are available. **Library/Resources:** The library contains 521,630 volumes, 521,630 microform items, and 12,152 audio/video tapes/CDs/DVDs, and subscribes to 3,641 periodicals including electronic. Computerized library services include interlibrary loans, database searching, Internet access, and Wi-Fi capability. Special learning facilities include an art gallery, radio station, an ornithological wing. **Physically Challenged Students:** 80% of the campus is accessible. Facilities include wheelchair ramps, elevators, special parking, specially equipped restrooms, special class scheduling, lowered drinking fountains, lowered telephones, and special housing. **Special:** Coe offers cross-registration with nearby Mount Mercy University and the University of Iowa. 31 Off-campus programs are offered; 8 domestic and 23 international in 19 countries. Nondegree study, dual majors and student-designed majors also are possible. Practicum experience is required for graduation. Core course instructors serve as students' academic advisors. There are 8 national honor societies, including Phi Beta Kappa, and a freshman honors program. **Visiting:** There are regularly scheduled orientations for prospective students, consisting of tours, a luncheon, and informational sessions on admission, financial aid, and student life. There are guides for informal visits, visitors may sit in on classes, and stay overnight. To schedule a visit, contact Sharon Fair at (319) 399-8500. **Campus Safety and Security:** Measures include 24-hour foot and vehicle patrol, emergency notification system, and security escort services. There are emergency telephones, lighted pathways/sidewalks, and controlled access to dorms/residences.

REQUIREMENTS: The SAT or ACT is required. Coe recommends that applicants have 4 years in English, 3 each in math, history, science, and social studies, and 2 in foreign language. All students must submit an essay. Coe requires ACT or SAT scores for admittance. The GED is accepted. A GPA of 3.0 is required. AP credits are accepted. Important factors in the admissions decision are advanced placement or honors courses, recommendations by school officials, and extracurricular activities record.All students must take 5 writing-emphasis courses, a first-year seminar, and a distribution of courses in fine arts, humanities, natural sciences and mathematics, social sciences, and diverse cultural perspectives. A minimum of 32 course credits, including 9 to 12 in the major, and a 2.0 GPA are required for graduation. All students are required to do a practicum experience including an internship, independent research project, or off-campus study program. Students in the honors program must submit a thesis. **Procedure:** Freshmen are admitted fall and spring. Entrance exams should be taken in the spring of the junior year or the fall of the senior year. There are deferred admissions and rolling admissions plans. Applications should be filed by March 1 for fall entry, along with a $30 fee. Notification is sent on a rolling basis. Applications are accepted on-line. **Transfer Students:** 29 transfer students enrolled in 2013-2014. Applicants must be high school graduates, have a minimum GPA of 2.5, and submit either SAT or ACT scores. An associate degree and an interview also are recommended. 8 of 32 credits required for the bachelor's degree must be completed at Coe. **International Students:** There are 50 international students enrolled. The school actively recruits these students. They must take the TOEFL with a minimum score of 520 on the paper-based TOEFL (PBT) or 68 on the Internet-based version (iBT), or take the IELTS. They must also take the SAT or ACT.

ADMISSIONS: 55% of the 2014-2015 applicants were accepted. The SAT scores for the 2014-2015 freshman class were: Critical Reading--20% below 500, 41% between 500 and 599, 34% between 600 and 699, and 5% between 700 and 800; Math--12% below 500, 46% between 500 and 599, 32% between 600 and 699, and 10% between 700 and 800; Writing--32% below 500, 38% between 500 and 599, 27% between 600 and 699, and 3% between 700 and 800. The ACT scores were 12% below 21, 23% between 21 and 23, 27% between 24 and 26, 15% between 27 and 28, and 23% above 28. 56% of the current freshmen were in the top fifth of their class; 81% were in the top two fifths. 14 freshmen graduated first in their class. **Admissions Contact:** Julie Staker, Dean of Admission. E-Mail: *jstaker@coe.edu* Web: *www.coe.edu*

FINANCIAL AID: In 2014-2015, 99% of all full-time freshmen and continuing full-time students received some form of financial aid.

87% of all full-time freshmen and 84% of continuing full-time students received need-based aid. The average freshman award was $35,550. 51% of undergraduate students work part-time. Average annual earnings from campus work are $1132. The average financial indebtedness of the 2014 graduate was $31,992. The FAFSA is required. The priority date for freshman financial aid applications for fall entry is March 1.

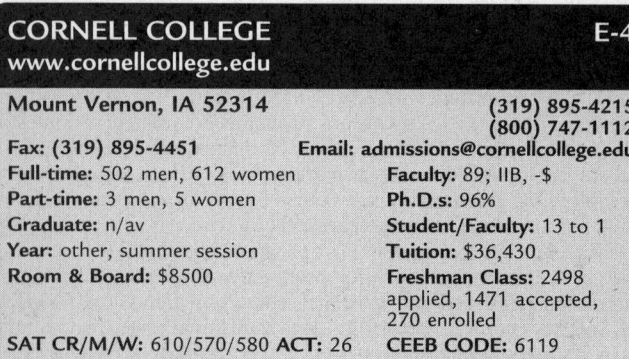

CORNELL COLLEGE E-4
www.cornellcollege.edu

Mount Vernon, IA 52314	(319) 895-4215
	(800) 747-1112
Fax: (319) 895-4451	Email: admissions@cornellcollege.edu
Full-time: 502 men, 612 women	Faculty: 89; IIB, -$
Part-time: 3 men, 5 women	Ph.D.s: 96%
Graduate: n/av	Student/Faculty: 13 to 1
Year: other, summer session	Tuition: $36,430
Room & Board: $8500	Freshman Class: 2498 applied, 1471 accepted, 270 enrolled
SAT CR/M/W: 610/570/580 ACT: 26	CEEB CODE: 6119
Application Deadline: March 1	**VERY COMPETITIVE**

Cornell College, founded in 1853, is private institution affiliated with the United Methodist Church. Its emphases are on the liberal arts and on student service and leadership. Cornell has a one-course-at-a-time calendar in which the year is divided into eight 3 1/2 week terms. In addition to regional accreditation, Cornell has baccalaureate program accreditation with ACS. The 129-acre campus is in a small town 15 miles east of Cedar Rapids and 3 hours west of Chicago. Including any residence halls, there are 44 buildings.

STUDENT LIFE: 83% of undergraduates are from out of state, mostly the Mid-West. Students are from 46 states, and 17 foreign countries. 68% are from public schools. 65% are White; 13% Hispanic. **Male To Female Ratio:** 1.2:1. The average age of freshmen is 18; all undergraduates, 20. 17% do not continue beyond their first year; 66% remain to graduate. **Housing:** 1124 students can be accommodated in college housing, which includes single-sex and coed dorms and on-campus apartments. In addition, there are special-interest houses, living and learning communities and connect floors. On-campus housing is guaranteed for all 4 years, is available on a first-come, first-served basis, and is available on a lottery system for upperclassmen. 91% of students live on campus; of those, 66% remain on campus on weekends. All students may keep cars.

FACULTY/CLASSROOMS: 56% of faculty are male; 54% are female. All teach undergraduates, 80% do research, and 80% do both. No introductory courses are taught by graduate students. The average class size in an introductory lecture is 18; in a laboratory is 18; and in a regular course is 16.

PROGRAMS OF STUDY: Cornell confers B.A., B.Mus. and B.S.S. degrees. Bachelor's degrees are awarded in BIOLOGICAL SCIENCE (biochemistry and biology/biological science), BUSINESS (business economics), COMMUNICATIONS AND THE ARTS (art history and appreciation, dramatic arts, English, fine arts, French, German, languages, music, Russian, Spanish, and studio art), COMPUTER AND PHYSICAL SCIENCE (chemistry, computer science, geology, mathematics, and physics), EDUCATION (art education, elementary education, foreign languages education, music education, science education, and secondary education), ENGINEERING AND ENVIRONMENTAL DESIGN (environmental science), SOCIAL SCIENCE (archeology, classical/ancient civilization, economics, ethnic studies, history, international relations, Latin American studies, medieval studies, philosophy, political science/government, psychology, religion, Russian and Slavic studies, sociology, and women's studies). Art, English, and theatre are the strongest academically. Psychology; economics and business, biochemistry and molecular biology have the largest enrollments.

ACTIVITIES: 16% of men belong to 8 local fraternities; 22% of women belong to 8 local sororities. There are 175 groups on campus, including mock trial, performing arts, steel drum band., art, band,

cheerleading, chess, choir, chorale, chorus, communications, computers, dance, debate, drama, environmental, ethnic, gay, honors, international, jazz band, leadership development, literary magazine, musical theater, newspaper, opera, orchestra, pep band, photography, political, professional, radio and TV, religious, social, social service, student government, and yearbook. Popular campus events include Knock Your Block Off and Music Mondays. **Sports:** There are 8 intercollegiate sports for men and 7 for women, and 12 intramural sports for men and 12 for women. Facilities include a multisport center, including a 2000-seat basketball and volleyball arena, sports fitness and training facilities, 200 meter indoor track, a wrestling room, 4 multipurpose courts for tennis, basketball, and volleyball, batting cages, golf hitting nets; a 2500-seat football and track stadium; and baseball, soccer, softball, and football practice fields and 6 outdoor tennis courts. **Graduates:** From July 1, 2013 to June 30, 2014, 275 bachelor's degrees were awarded. The most popular majors were psychology (14%), biochemistry and molecular biology (13%), and art/art history (10%). 15 companies recruited on campus in 2013-2014. In an average class, 1% graduate in 3 years or less, 64% graduate in 4 years or less, 66% graduate in 5 years or less, and 68% graduate in 6 years or less.

SERVICES: Counseling and information services are available, as is tutoring in most subjects. **Library/Resources:** The library contains 232,914 volumes, 69,348 microform items, 9,467 audio/video tapes/CDs/DVDs, and subscribes to 491 periodicals including electronic. Computerized library services include interlibrary loans, database searching, Internet access, and Wi-Fi capability. Special learning facilities include an art gallery, natural history museum, and radio station. **Physically Challenged Students:** 50% of the campus is accessible. Facilities include wheelchair ramps, elevators, special parking, specially equipped restrooms, special class scheduling, lowered drinking fountains, and lowered telephones. **Special:** Special academic programs include study abroad in 25 to 30 countries, internships including a Washington semester, double majors, student-designed majors, and interdisciplinary majors in biochemistry and molecular biology, environmental studies, classical studies, ethnic studies, Latin American studies, Russian studies, anthropolgy and sociology, international relations, and women's studies. A cooperative degree program in Medical Technology with St. Luke's Methodist Hospital, a degree program in Nursing and Allied Health Science with Rush University, a 3-2 engineering program with the University of Minnesota, and a 3-4 architecture program with Washington University, and a 3-2 forestry or environmental management program with Duke University are also available. There are 16 national honor societies and Phi Beta Kappa. **Visiting:** There are regularly scheduled orientations for prospective students, including campus tours and meetings with an informational panel, a student panel, financial aid staff, and faculty and coaches as requested. There are guides for informal visits, visitors may sit in on classes, and stay overnight. To schedule a visit, contact the Visit Coordinator at (800) 747-1112. **Campus Safety and Security:** Measures include 24-hour foot and vehicle patrol, emergency notification system, self-defense education, and security escort services. There are emergency telephones and lighted pathways/sidewalks.

REQUIREMENTS: The SAT or ACT is required. Applicants should be graduates of an accredited secondary school, with a recommended 4 years each of English, 3 or more years of math and science, and social studies, 2 or more years of a foreign language. An essay and a secondary school report are required, and an interview is advised. The GED is accepted. AP credits are accepted. Important factors in the admissions decision are advanced placement or honors courses, evidence of special talent, and leadership record.Students choosing the BA degree must complete 31 course credits (124 semester hours), with at least a 2.0 cumulative GPA. B.A. candidates must complete the requirements of a faculty approved major usually 8 to 15 courses in the major and distribution requirements including: a first year seminar, a first year writing course, 2 courses in humanities, 1 courses in the natural sciences, 1 course in social sciences, 1 course each in fine arts and math, 1 interdisciplinary thinking experience, and 1 to 4 courses in a foreign language. **Procedure:** Freshmen are admitted fall. There are early decision, early admissions, and deferred admissions plans. Early decision applications should be filed by November 1; regular applications, by March 1 for fall entry, along with a $30 fee.

Notification of early decision is sent December 15; regular decision, April 1. 7 early decision candidates were accepted for the 2014-2015 class. 81 applicants were on the 2014 waiting list; 33 were admitted. Applications are accepted on-line. **Transfer Students:** 45 transfer students enrolled in 2013-2014. Applicants must provide all items required of traditional students; in addition, they must submit official college transcripts from all other institutions they have attended. 15 of 31 credits required for the bachelor's degree must be completed at Cornell. **International Students:** There are 64 international students enrolled. The school actively recruits these students. They must take the TOEFL with a minimum score of 550 on the paper-based TOEFL (PBT) or 79 on the Internet-based version (iBT), or take the IELTS or STEP, SAT or ACT exams may also be submitted.

ADMISSIONS: 59% of the 2014-2015 applicants were accepted. The SAT scores for the 2014-2015 freshman class were: Critical Reading--13% below 500, 33% between 500 and 599, 35% between 600 and 699, and 19% between 700 and 800; Math--19% below 500, 37% between 500 and 599, 34% between 600 and 699, and 10% between 700 and 800; Writing--18% below 500, 42% between 500 and 599, 33% between 600 and 699, and 7% between 700 and 800. The ACT scores were 5% below 21, 17% between 21 and 23, 29% between 24 and 26, 17% between 27 and 28, and 32% above 28. 62% of the current freshmen were in the top fifth of their class; 84% were in the top two fifths. 13 freshmen graduated first in their class. **Admissions Contact:** Colleen Murphy, Vice President of Enrollment. E-Mail: *admissions@cornellcollege.edu* Web: *www.cornellcollege.edu*

FINANCIAL AID: In 2014-2015, 99% of all full-time freshmen and 97% of continuing full-time students received some form of financial aid. 80% of all full-time freshmen and 77% of continuing full-time students received need-based aid. The average freshman award was $33,552. Need-based scholarships or need-based grants averaged $10,000 ($41,219 maximum); need-based self-help aid (loans and jobs) averaged $250 ($8,500 maximum); and other non-need-based awards and non-need-based scholarships averaged $6,000 ($30,000 maximum). 63% of undergraduate students work part-time. Average annual earnings from campus work are $1900. The average financial indebtedness of the 2014 graduate was $27,342. Cornell is a member of CSS. The FAFSA is required. The priority date for freshman financial aid applications for fall entry is March 1. The deadline for filing freshman financial aid applications for fall entry is March 1.

DORDT COLLEGE   **B-2**
www.dordt.edu

Sioux Center, IA 51250	(712) 722-6080
	(800) 34-DORDT
Fax: (712) 722-1967	Email: admissions@dordt.edu
Full-time: 728 men, 658 women	Faculty: 80; IIB, -$
Part-time: 44 men, 41 women	Ph.D.s: 85%
Graduate: 25 men, 29 women	Student/Faculty: 15 to 1
Year: semesters	Tuition: $26,540
Room & Board: $7620	Freshman Class: 1355 applied, 1022 accepted, 381 enrolled
SAT: required ACT: 25	CEEB CODE: 6171
Application Deadline: August 1	COMPETITIVE+

Dordt College, founded in 1955, is a private institution affiliated with the Christian Reformed Church. The curriculum, which is designed to reflect the principles of the Christian faith, leads to degrees in liberal arts, agriculture, art, music, business, engineering, and teaching preparation. The figures in the above capsule and in this profile are approximate. In addition to regional accreditation, Dordt has baccalaureate program accreditation with ABET and CSWE. The 120-acre campus is in a rural area 42 miles north of Sioux City. Including any residence halls, there are 25 buildings.

STUDENT LIFE: 60% of undergraduates are from out of state, mostly the Mid-West. Students are from 34 states, 26 foreign countries, and Canada. 40% are from public schools. 88% are White. 99% are Protestant. **Male To Female Ratio:** 0.9:1. The average age of freshmen is 18; all undergraduates, 21. 15% do not continue beyond their first year; 68% remain to graduate. **Housing:** 1300 students can be

accommodated in college housing, which includes single-sex dorms, on-campus apartments, and off-campus apartments. On-campus housing is guaranteed for all 4 years. 90% of students live on campus; of those, 80% remain on campus on weekends. Alcohol is not permitted. All students may keep cars.

FACULTY/CLASSROOMS: 85% of faculty are male; 15% are female. All teach undergraduates. No introductory courses are taught by graduate students. The average class size in an introductory lecture is 30; in a laboratory is 20; and in a regular course is 25.

PROGRAMS OF STUDY: Dordt confers B.A., B.S., B.S.N. and B.S.W. degrees. Associate and master's degrees are also awarded. Bachelor's degrees are awarded in AGRICULTURE (agricultural business management, agriculture, and animal science), BIOLOGICAL SCIENCE (biology/biological science), BUSINESS (accounting, banking and finance, business administration and management, business economics, management information systems, marketing management, recreational facilities management, secretarial studies/office management, and sports management), COMMUNICATIONS AND THE ARTS (advertising, art history, art, broadcasting, church music, communication, communications, dramatic arts, Dutch, English, English as a second/foreign language, film, television and digital media, fine arts, German, graphic design, journalism, languages, literature, music, music performance, music theory and composition, Spanish, speech/debate/rhetoric, theatre acting, theatre arts, visual and performing arts, and vocal music education), COMPUTER AND PHYSICAL SCIENCE (actuarial science, chemistry, computer programming, computer science, information sciences and systems, mathematics, physical sciences, and physics), EDUCATION (agricultural education, art education, athletic training, business education, (Education) Childhood Education, early childhood education, education, elementary education, English education, foreign languages education, mathematics education, middle school education, music education, physical education, physical science secondary school education, science education, secondary education, social science education, and special education), ENGINEERING AND ENVIRONMENTAL DESIGN (architectural engineering, bioengineering, chemical engineering, civil engineering, computer engineering, construction management, electrical/electronics engineering, engineering, environmental science, and mechanical engineering), HEALTH PROFESSIONS (exercise science, health science, medical laboratory technology, nursing, predentistry, premedicine, preoptometry, prepharmacy, prephysical therapy, and preveterinary science), SOCIAL SCIENCE (criminal justice, economics, history, ministries, missions, philosophy, philosophy and religion, political science/government, prelaw, psychology, public administration, religion, religious studies, social science, social work, sociology, and youth ministry). Engineering, business administration, and social work are the strongest academically. Education has the largest enrollment.

ACTIVITIES: There are no fraternities or sororities. There are 25 groups on campus, including band, choir, chorale, chorus, computers, dance, debate, drama, drill team, environmental, film, forensics, international, jazz band, literary magazine, newspaper, opera, orchestra, pep band, photography, PLIA (Putting Love into Action), political, professional, radio and TV, religious, social, social service, student government, symphony, and yearbook. Popular campus events include Parents Day in October. **Sports:** There are 7 intercollegiate sports for men and 7 for women, and 10 intramural sports for men and 10 for women. Facilities include a 2500-seat gym with 2 courts; an 85,000-square-foot recreation center, which includes a 200-meter indoor track, 3 courts adaptable for basketball, volleyball, and tennis, 3 racquetball courts, weight-lifting and exercise equipment rooms, and a golf simulation room; an outdoor track; tennis courts; soccer, softball, and baseball fields; and an indoor pool and ice arena adjacent to the campus. **Graduates:** From July 1, 2013 to June 30, 2014, 290 bachelor's degrees were awarded. The most popular majors were business, education, and engineering. 40 companies recruited on campus in 2013-2014. In an average class, 68% graduate in 4 years or less. Of the 2013 graduating class, 15% were enrolled in graduate school within 6 months of graduation, and 96% were employed.

SERVICES: Counseling and information services are available, as is tutoring in every subject. There is a reader service for the blind, and remedial math, reading, and writing. **Library/Resources:** The library contains 185,000 volumes, 14,819 microform items, 5,000 audio/video tapes/CDs/DVDs, and subscribes to 700 periodicals including electronic. Computerized library services include interlibrary loans. Special learning facilities include a planetarium, radio station, and 2 observatories, as well as a 160-acre agriculture stewardship center just north of the campus. **Physically Challenged Students:** All of the campus is accessible. Facilities include wheelchair ramps, elevators, special parking, specially equipped restrooms, special class scheduling, lowered drinking fountains, lowered telephones, and special housing. **Special:** Students may study abroad in 10 countries. Dordt also offers a Washington semester, a Chicago Metro semester, a joint nursing degree program with St. Luke's School of Nursing, a B.S.N. with Briar Cliff University, B.A.-B.S. degrees in engineering and agriculture, and numerous internships in all majors. Dual majors, student-designed majors, and pass/fail options are available. There is a freshman honors program. **Visiting:** There are regularly scheduled orientations for prospective students, including tours, class visits, personal visits with professors and coaches, and a financial aid session. There are guides for informal visits, visitors may sit in on classes, and stay overnight. To schedule a visit, contact the Admissions Office. **Campus Safety and Security:** Measures include 24-hour foot and vehicle patrol. There are lighted pathways/sidewalks.

REQUIREMENTS: The SAT or ACT is required. Applicants must be graduates of accredited secondary schools or have earned a GED. The college requires 18 academic credits, including 4 in English and 2 each in foreign language, math, science, and social studies. A GPA of 2.3 is required. AP and CLEP credits are accepted. Important factors in the admissions decision are advanced placement or honors courses, evidence of special talent, and leadership record. All students must complete a college introductory course and a distribution of 14 other courses in the various academic disciplines, including General Education 300. Proficiency requirements must be met in English, math, and phys ed. To graduate, students must complete a minimum of 126 credits with a 2.0 GPA. **Procedure:** Freshmen are admitted fall and spring. Entrance exams should be taken by October of the senior year and no later than April. There is a rolling admissions plan. Applications should be filed by August 1 for fall entry; December 1 for spring entry. Applications are accepted on-line. **Transfer Students:** 60 transfer students enrolled in 2013-2014. Transfer students must have a GPA of 2.0. 62 of 126 credits required for the bachelor's degree must be completed at Dordt. **International Students:** There are 60 international students enrolled. The school actively recruits these students. They must take the TOEFL with a minimum score of 72 on the Internet-based version (iBT). They must also take the SAT or ACT.

ADMISSIONS: 75% of the 2014-2015 applicants were accepted. The SAT scores for the 2014-2015 freshman class were: Critical Reading--47% below 500, 29% between 500 and 599, 21% between 600 and 699, and 3% between 700 and 800; Math--22% below 500, 45% between 500 and 599, 30% between 600 and 699, and 3% between 700 and 800; Writing--43% below 500, 40% between 500 and 599, and 17% between 600 and 699. The ACT scores were 15% below 21, 25% between 21 and 23, 36% between 24 and 26, 20% between 27 and 28, and 15% above 28. 62% of the current freshmen were in the top fifth of their class; 75% were in the top two fifths. **Admissions Contact:** Quentin Van Essen, Executive Director of Admissions. E-Mail: *admissions@dordt.edu* Web: *www.dordt.edu*

FINANCIAL AID: In 2014-2015, 98% of all full-time freshmen and 95% of continuing full-time students received some form of financial aid. 85% of all full-time freshmen and 85% of continuing full-time students received need-based aid. The average freshman award was $21,900. Need-based scholarships or need-based grants averaged $4,000 ($6,000 maximum); need-based self-help aid (loans and jobs) averaged $8,000 ($12,000 maximum); non-need-based athletic scholarships averaged $6,000 ($9,000 maximum); and other non-need-based awards and non-need-based scholarships averaged $7,000 ($12,500 maximum). 70% of undergraduate students work part-time. Average annual earnings from campus work are $1500. The average financial indebtedness of the 2014 graduate was $22,400. Dordt is a member of CSS. The FAFSA and the college's own financial statement are required. Check with the school for current application deadlines.

DRAKE UNIVERSITY   C-3
www.drake.edu

Des Moines, IA 50311

(515) 271-3181
(800) 44-DRAKE

Fax: (515) 271-2831
Full-time: 1371 men, 1806 women
Part-time: 94 men, 93 women
Graduate: 623 men, 1075 women
Year: semesters, summer session
Room & Board: $9270

Email: admission@drake.edu
Faculty: 246; IIA, av$
Ph.D.s: 91%
Student/Faculty: 11 to 1
Tuition: $32,246
Freshman Class: 5930 applied, 3911 accepted, 850 enrolled

SAT: required ACT: 27
Application Deadline:

CEEB CODE: 6168
VERY COMPETITIVE+

Drake University, founded in 1881, is a private institution offering undergraduate and graduate programs in arts and sciences, business and public administration, pharmacy and health sciences, journalism and mass communication, education, fine arts, and law. Figures in the above capsule and in this profile are approximate. There are 5 undergraduate schools and 4 graduate schools. In addition to regional accreditation, Drake has baccalaureate program accreditation with ACEJMC, ACPE, NASAD, and NASM. The 120-acre campus is in an urban area in Des Moines. Including any residence halls, there are 49 buildings.

STUDENT LIFE: 70% of undergraduates are from out of state, mostly the Mid-West. Students are from 38 states, 34 foreign countries, and Canada. 89% are from public schools. 79% are White. **Male To Female Ratio:** 1.4:1. The average age of freshmen is 18; all undergraduates, 21. 11% do not continue beyond their first year; 78% remain to graduate. **Housing:** 1787 students can be accommodated in college housing, which includes coed dorms and off-campus apartments. In addition, there are fraternity houses and sorority houses. On-campus housing is guaranteed for the freshman year only, is available on a first-come, first-served basis, and is available on a lottery system for upperclassmen. 75% of students live on campus; of those, 80% remain on campus on weekends. All students may keep cars.

FACULTY/CLASSROOMS: 56% of faculty are male; 64% are female. 84% teach undergraduates. No introductory courses are taught by graduate students. The average class size in an introductory lecture is 29; in a laboratory is 14; and in a regular course is 27.

PROGRAMS OF STUDY: Drake confers B.A., B.S., B.A.Journ. and Mass Comm., B.F.A., B.Mus., B.Mus.Ed., B.S.B.A. and B.S.Ed. degrees. Master's and doctoral degrees are also awarded. Bachelor's degrees are awarded in BIOLOGICAL SCIENCE (biology/biological science and neurosciences), BUSINESS (accounting, banking and finance, business administration and management, international business management, management science, and marketing management), COMMUNICATIONS AND THE ARTS (advertising, art history and appreciation, broadcasting, communications, dramatic arts, English, graphic design, journalism, music, music business management, music performance, printmaking, public relations, speech/debate/rhetoric, and studio art), COMPUTER AND PHYSICAL SCIENCE (actuarial science, chemistry, computer science, information sciences and systems, mathematics, and physics), EDUCATION (elementary education, mathematics education, music education, and secondary education), ENGINEERING AND ENVIRONMENTAL DESIGN (environmental science), HEALTH PROFESSIONS (pharmacy), SOCIAL SCIENCE (economics, ethics, politics, and social policy, history, international relations, philosophy, political science/government, psychology, religion, and sociology). Actuarial science, pharmacy, and physics/astronomy are the strongest academically. Pharmacy, marketing, and actuarial science have the largest enrollments.

ACTIVITIES: 34% of men belong to 9 national fraternities; 28% of women belong to 5 national sororities. There are 160 groups on campus, including art, band, cheerleading, chess, choir, chorale, chorus, computers, dance, drama, drill team, ethnic, film, gay, honors, international, jazz band, literary magazine, marching band, musical theater, newspaper, opera, orchestra, pep band, photography, political, professional, radio and TV, religious, social, social service, student government, and symphony. Popular campus events include Drake Relays, Supreme Court Days and Iowa Caucuses. **Sports:** There are 8 intercollegiate sports for men and 10 for women, and 24 intramural sports for men and 24 for women. Facilities include a football stadium, an indoor swimming pool, an aerobics room, 2 weight rooms, basketball, volleyball, and badminton courts, 2 indoor tracks and 1 outdoor track, 4 racquetball courts, and 6 indoor and 6 outdoor tennis courts. A recreation and sports facility seats 7000. **Graduates:** From July 1, 2013 to June 30, 2014, 938 bachelor's degrees were awarded. The most popular majors were business/marketing (36%), communication/journalism (12%), and social sciences (7%). In an average class, 66% graduate in 4 years or less, 72% graduate in 5 years or less, and 73% graduate in 6 years or less.

SERVICES: There is a reader service for the blind. The Student Disability Service works with recordings for blind, and dyslexic students. **Library/Resources:** The 2 libraries contain 558,044 volumes, 936,863 microform items, 3,609 audio/video tapes/CDs/DVDs, and subscribe to 74,473 periodicals including electronic. Computerized library services include interlibrary loans, database searching, Internet access, and Wi-Fi capability. Special learning facilities include an art gallery, radio station, TV station, an observatory, and the Henry G. Harmon Fine Arts Center. **Physically Challenged Students:** 90% of the campus is accessible. Facilities include wheelchair ramps, elevators, special parking, specially equipped restrooms, special class scheduling, lowered drinking fountains, lowered telephones, an IBM-compatible computer and scanner that includes a voice and screen enlargement program, closed-caption television, and TDD at multiple locations. **Special:** Study abroad is available in 60 countries and at sea. The university offers cross-registration with Des Moines area colleges, including Grand View, internships, a Washington semester, cooperative programs in computer science, and work-study programs. Dual majors, B.A.-B.S. degrees, a 3-2 engineering degree with Washington University, student-designed majors, credit for military experience, and nondegree study are possible. Students may take a maximum of 12 hours of course work on a credit/no credit basis. There are 25 national honor societies, including Phi Beta Kappa, a freshman honors program, and 19 departmental honors programs. **Visiting:** There are regularly scheduled orientations for prospective students, including an opportunity for students and parents to confer with professors, meet with current students, and attend information sessions on academic programs, financial aid, housing, and the Drake campus. Also included are a walking tour and lunch. There are guides for informal visits, visitors may sit in on classes, and stay overnight. To schedule a visit, contact the Office of Admission. **Campus Safety and Security:** Measures include 24-hour foot and vehicle patrol, emergency notification system, self-defense education, and security escort services. There are shuttle buses, emergency telephones, and lighted pathways/sidewalks.

REQUIREMENTS: The SAT or ACT is required. Applicants must be graduates of an accredited secondary school. The GED is accepted. Students should have completed 4 years of English, 3 years of math, and 9 other units to be selected from English, foreign languages, social studies, math, lab sciences, and others. A portfolio is required for art majors and for those seeking scholarship consideration. An audition is necessary for admission to the music and theatre programs. Tapes are accepted. A GPA of 3.3 is required. AP and CLEP credits are accepted. Important factors in the admissions decision are advanced placement or honors courses, recommendations by school officials, and extracurricular activities record. Undergraduates must take a first-year seminar and general education courses and satisfy 11 areas of inquiry requirements that include writing, critical thinking, artistic experience, historical consciousness, information and technical literacy, multicultural experience, scientific and quantitative literacy, values and ethics, and the engaged citizen. A capstone demonstration is required. For graduation, 124 credit hours are required with 27 to 36 hours in the major. The minimum GPA is 2.0. **Procedure:** Freshmen are admitted to all sessions. Entrance exams should be taken during the spring of the junior year or early fall of the senior year. There are deferred admissions and rolling admissions plans. Check with the school for current application deadlines. The application fee is $25. Application fees are waived if application is completed on-line. **Transfer Students:** Applicants must have a mini-

mum GPA of 2.0 and have completed 24 credit hours for evaluation. Grades of C or better transfer for credit. There is no assurance that all courses transferred will apply toward the major requirement. The final 30 hours must be completed in residence. Transfer students are admitted in the fall, spring, and summer. 30 of 124 credits required for the bachelor's degree must be completed at Drake. **International Students:** There are 265 international students enrolled. The school actively recruits these students. They must take the TOEFL with a minimum score of 550 on the paper-based TOEFL (PBT) or 79 on the Internet-based version (iBT). They must also take the SAT or ACT.

ADMISSIONS: 66% of the 2014-2015 applicants were accepted. The SAT scores for the 2014-2015 freshman class were: Critical Reading--14% below 500, 42% between 500 and 599, 31% between 600 and 699, and 13% between 700 and 800; Math--10% below 500, 36% between 500 and 599, 36% between 600 and 699, and 19% between 700 and 800. The ACT scores were 16% between 24 and 26, 57% between 27 and 28, and 26% above 28. **Admissions Contact:** Laura Linn, Director of Admissions. E-Mail: *admission@drake.edu* Web: *www.drake.edu*

FINANCIAL AID: 76% of all full-time freshmen and continuing full-time students received need-based aid. The average freshman award was $22,999. Need-based scholarships or need-based grants averaged $17,454; need-based self-help aid (loans and jobs) averaged $4,733; and non-need-based athletic scholarships averaged $18,692. The average financial indebtedness of the 2014 graduate was $25,633. Drake is a member of CSS. The FAFSA is required. Check with the school for current application deadlines.

GRACELAND UNIVERSITY   C-4
www.graceland.edu

Lamoni, IA 50140   (641) 784-5119
                                         (866) 893-6882
Fax: (641) 784-5480   Email: sshields@graceland.edu
Full-time: 575 men, 775 women   Faculty: IIB
Part-time: 135 men, 560 women   Ph.D.s: 47%
Graduate: 75 men, 265 women   Student/Faculty: n/av
Year: 4-1-4, summer session   Tuition: $20,980
Room & Board: $7040   Freshman Class: n/av
SAT or ACT: required   CEEB CODE: 6249
Application Deadline: n/av   **COMPETITIVE**

Graceland University, established in 1895, is a private liberal arts college sponsored by the Community of Christ. Graceland also maintains a campus in Independence, Missouri. The figures in the above capsule and in this profile are approximate. There are 4 undergraduate schools and 4 graduate schools. In addition to regional accreditation, Graceland has baccalaureate program accreditation with NCATE, NLN, and CCNE. The 167-acre campus is in a small town 80 miles south of Des Moines. Including any residence halls, there are 28 buildings.

STUDENT LIFE: 60% of undergraduates are from out of state, mostly the Mid-West. Students are from 49 states, 35 foreign countries, and Canada. 64% are White. 16% are Protestant. **Male To Female Ratio:** 2.0:1. The average age of freshmen is 18; all undergraduates, 20. 30% do not continue beyond their first year; 47% remain to graduate. **Housing:** 715 students can be accommodated in college housing, which includes single-sex dorms and married student housing. On-campus housing is guaranteed for all 4 years. 64% of students live on campus; of those, 68% remain on campus on weekends. Alcohol is not permitted. All students may keep cars.

FACULTY/CLASSROOMS: 47% of faculty are male; 53% are female. 93% teach undergraduates, and 10% do research. No introductory courses are taught by graduate students. The average class size in an introductory lecture is 24; in a laboratory is 24; and in a regular course is 11.

PROGRAMS OF STUDY: Graceland confers B.A., B.S. and B.S.N. degrees. Master's degrees are also awarded. Bachelor's degrees are awarded in BIOLOGICAL SCIENCE (biology/biological science), BUSINESS (accounting, business administration and management, international business management, recreation and leisure services, and recreational facilities management), COMMUNICATIONS AND THE ARTS (communications, dramatic arts, English, German, graphic design, literature, modern language, music, Spanish, speech/debate/rhetoric, and studio art), COMPUTER AND PHYSICAL SCIENCE (chemistry, computer science, information sciences and systems, mathematics, and science), EDUCATION (athletic training, elementary education, music education, and physical education), ENGINEERING AND ENVIRONMENTAL DESIGN (commercial art), HEALTH PROFESSIONS (health, medical laboratory technology, nursing, predentistry, premedicine, and preveterinary science), SOCIAL SCIENCE (addiction studies, criminal justice, economics, history, human services, international studies, liberal arts/general studies, philosophy, psychology, religion, social science, and sociology). Business administration, education, and nursing have the largest enrollments.

ACTIVITIES: There are no fraternities or sororities. There are 54 groups on campus, including environmental, art, band, cheerleading, chess, choir, chorale, chorus, computers, dance, drama, drill team, entrepreneurial, ethnic, gay, honors, international, jazz band, musical theater, newspaper, orchestra, pep band, political, professional, radio and TV, religious, social, social service, student government, symphony, and yearbook. Popular campus events include Renaissance Week, Multicultural Week, and New Year's in November. **Sports:** There are 9 intercollegiate sports for men and 8 for women, and 17 intramural sports for men and 17 for women. Facilities include a sports complex with an all-weather track and lighted soccer and football fields; a phys ed center with an indoor junior Olympic-size pool, a 5-court gym, an indoor track, a weight room, and courts for racquetball, basketball, volleyball, and tennis; an intramural sports complex; 8 lighted tennis courts; an 18-hole disc golf course; and 2 small lakes.

SERVICES: Counseling and information services are available, as is tutoring in most subjects. There is a reader service for the blind, remedial math, reading, and writing. **Library/Resources:** The library contains 199,447 volumes, 914 microform items, 3,658 audio/video tapes/CDs/DVDs, and subscribes to 624 periodicals including electronic. Computerized library services include interlibrary loans, database searching, and Internet access. Special learning facilities include an art gallery, radio station, a center for the study of the Korean War. **Physically Challenged Students:** 86% of the campus is accessible. Facilities include wheelchair ramps, elevators, special parking, specially equipped restrooms, special class scheduling, lowered drinking fountains, lowered telephones. **Special:** Internships are required in business, education, recreation, communications, and publication design. Graceland offers study abroad, cross-registration, B.A.-B.S. degrees, work-study, dual and student-designed majors, and a general studies degree. Credit for life, military, or work experience is possible. A pass/fail option is available for 2 courses each semester. The university also offers nondegree study, home study in addiction studies and nursing, a program for students with learning disabilities, an accelerated degree program in nursing, and a 3-2 engineering degree with the University of Iowa and the University of Missouri-Rolla. There are 3 national honor societies, a freshman honors program, and 6 departmental honors programs. **Visiting:** There are regularly scheduled orientations for prospective students, including a campus tour and opportunities to meet students, faculty, and campus personnel. There are guides for informal visits, visitors may sit in on classes, and stay overnight. **Campus Safety and Security:** Measures include 24-hour foot and vehicle patrol and security escort services. There are emergency telephones, lighted pathways/sidewalks, night security personnel.

REQUIREMENTS: The SAT or ACT is required. Graceland requires applicants to meet 2 of the following 3 criteria: rank in the upper 50% of their class, a GPA of 2.5, or a minimum score on the SAT or ACT. Applicants must be graduates of an accredited secondary school. The GED is accepted. An interview is recommended. A GPA of 2.5 is required. AP and CLEP credits are accepted. Important factors in the admissions decision are advanced placement or honors courses, evidence of special talent, and leadership record. To graduate, students must complete 128 credit hours, including 39 in upper-division courses and an average of 40 in the major, and maintain a minimum GPA of 2.0 overall and in the major. General education requirements

include studies in humanities, social sciences, natural sciences, behavioral sciences, ethics, math, computer science, leadership, thinking skills, human diversity, and the arts. **Procedure:** Freshmen are admitted to all sessions. Entrance exams should be taken in the junior or senior year. There is a rolling admissions plan. Check with the school for current application deadlines. The application fee is $50. Applications are accepted on-line. **Transfer Students:** Applicants must submit official transcripts from all colleges attended and from high school. The required GPA varies by the number of hours of college study completed. Transfer students are admitted every term. 32 of 128 credits required for the bachelor's degree must be completed at Graceland. **International Students:** The school actively recruits these students. They must take the TOEFL.

ADMISSIONS: Admissions Contact: Stephaine Shields, Admissions. E-Mail: *sshields@graceland.edu* Web: *www.graceland.edu*

FINANCIAL AID: The FAFSA is required. Check with the school for current application deadlines.

GRAND VIEW UNIVERSITY C-3
www.grandview.edu

Des Moines, IA 50316

(515) 263-2810
(800) 444-6083

Fax: (515) 263-2974   Email: djohnson@grandview.edu
Full-time: 766 men, 962 women   **Faculty:** 95
Part-time: 117 men, 251 women   **Ph.D.s:** 68%
Graduate: 11 men, 22 women   **Student/Faculty:** 18 to 1
Year: semesters, summer session   **Tuition:** $23,496
Room & Board: $7554   **Freshman Class:** n/av
SAT: recommended   **CEEB CODE:** 6251
Application Deadline: open   **COMPETITIVE**

Grand View University, formerly Grand View College, founded in 1896, is a private liberal arts college affiliated with the Evangelical Lutheran Church in America, that focuses on connecting liberal arts with career preparation. There is one graduate school. In addition to regional accreditation, Grand View has baccalaureate program accreditation with NLN. The 25-acre campus is in an urban area in Des Moines. Including any residence halls, there are 27 buildings.

STUDENT LIFE: 87% of undergraduates are from Iowa. Others are from 34 states, 16 foreign countries, and Canada. 80% are White. 15% are Catholic; 13% Protestant. **Male To Female Ratio:** 1.4:1. The average age of freshmen is 18; all undergraduates, 22. 31% do not continue beyond their first year; 49% remain to graduate. **Housing:** 900 students can be accommodated in college housing, which includes coed dorms and on-campus apartments. In addition, there are special-interest houses. On-campus housing is available on a first-come, first-served basis, and is available on a lottery system for upperclassmen. Priority is given to out-of-town students. 63% of students commute. All students may keep cars.

FACULTY/CLASSROOMS: 39% of faculty are male; 61% are female. All teach undergraduates. No introductory courses are taught by graduate students. The average class size in an introductory lecture is 20; in a laboratory is 10; and in a regular course is 15.

PROGRAMS OF STUDY: Grand View confers B.A., and B.S.N. degrees. Master's degrees are also awarded. Bachelor's degrees are awarded in BIOLOGICAL SCIENCE (biochemistry, biology/biological science, and biotechnology), BUSINESS (accounting, business administration and management, management information systems, and sports management), COMMUNICATIONS AND THE ARTS (broadcasting, communications, English, graphic design, journalism, music, and visual and performing arts), COMPUTER AND PHYSICAL SCIENCE (computer science and mathematics), EDUCATION (art education, elementary education, music education, physical education, and secondary education), HEALTH PROFESSIONS (nursing), SOCIAL SCIENCE (criminal justice, human services, political science/government, and psychology). Art, nursing and education are the strongest academically. Business, nursing, biology and education have the largest enrollments.

ACTIVITIES: There are no fraternities or sororities. There are 43 groups on campus, including art, band, cheerleading, choir, chorale, chorus, computers, dance, departmental, drama, drill team, ethnic, gay, honors, international, jazz band, literary magazine, newspaper, pep band, political, professional, radio and TV, religious, social service, student government, and yearbook. **Sports:** There are 12 intercollegiate sports for men and 12 for women, and 8 intramural sports for men and 8 for women. Facilities include a 1200-seat wellness with facilities for varsity athletics and recreation programs and an athletic field. **Graduates:** From July 1, 2013 to June 30, 2014, 460 bachelor's degrees were awarded. The most popular majors were business administration (23%), nursing (14%), and education (10%). 70 companies recruited on campus in 2013-2014. In an average class, 39% graduate in 4 years or less, 47% graduate in 5 years or less, and 49% graduate in 6 years or less. Of the 2013 graduating class, 8% were enrolled in graduate school within 6 months of graduation, and 90% were employed.

SERVICES: Counseling and information services are available, as is tutoring in every subject. There is a reader service for the blind, and remedial math, reading, and writing. **Library/Resources:** The library contains 135,448 volumes, 11,334 microform items, 3,801 audio/video tapes/CDs/DVDs, and subscribes to 27,077 periodicals including electronic. Computerized library services include interlibrary loans, database searching, and Internet access. Special learning facilities include an art gallery, radio station, and TV station. **Physically Challenged Students:** 90% of the campus is accessible. Facilities include wheelchair ramps, elevators, special parking, specially equipped restrooms, special class scheduling, lowered drinking fountains, lowered telephones. Support services for the disabled. **Special:** Co-op programs, cross-registration with Drake University and Des Moines Area Community College, student-designed majors, study abroad, and internships for most majors are available. Dual majors, a B.A.-B.S. degree, a Washington semester, work-study programs, and an accelerated degree program in business administration are offered. Nondegree study, a liberal arts degree, a certificate in art therapy, and pass/fail options are possible. There are 10 national honor societies, a freshman honors program, and 1 departmental honors program. **Visiting:** There are regularly scheduled orientations for prospective students, including placement tests, a financial aid session, lunch, advisor meetings, and a registration session. There are guides for informal visits, visitors may sit in on classes, and stay overnight. To schedule a visit, contact the Admissions Office at (515) 263-2810. **Campus Safety and Security:** Measures include 24-hour foot and vehicle patrol, emergency notification system, and security escort services. There are emergency telephones, lighted pathways/sidewalks, and controlled access to dorms/residences.

REQUIREMENTS: The ACT is required. The SAT and ACT Writing Test are recommended, with a minimum recommended score of 18 on the ACT or the equivalent on the SAT. Students must be graduates of an accredited secondary school. The GED is also accepted. Grand View recommends that students should have completed 4 courses in English, 3 courses each in math, science, and social science, and 2 courses in a foreign language. A GPA of 2.0 is required. AP and CLEP credits are accepted. Students must complete core requirements, including courses in English, public speaking, liberal arts, integrating seminar, other culture encounter, religion or philosophy, history or other humanities, lab science, and social science. Students must complete at least 124 hours of work, including 60 hours in courses other than the major and 24 hours in the major. Students must maintain an overall GPA of 2.0 and a 2.2 GPA in the major. Students must also demonstrate computer proficiency. **Procedure:** Freshmen are admitted fall, spring, and summer. Entrance exams should be taken during the second semester of the junior year. There are deferred admissions and rolling admissions plans. Application deadlines are open. Applications are accepted on-line. **Transfer Students:** 303 transfer students enrolled in 2013-2014. Applicants must submit transcripts from each college attended. Students who are not transferring with an associate or bachelor's degree must submit a high school transcript. Those with less than 24 college credits must also submit ACT or SAT test results. 30 of 124 credits required for the bachelor's degree must be completed at Grand View. **International Students:** There are 35 international students enrolled. They must take the TOEFL with a minimum score of 550 on the paper-based TOEFL (PBT) or 77 on the Internet-based version (iBT). They must also take the SAT or ACT, scoring 18.

ADMISSIONS: 8 freshmen graduated first in their class. **Admissions**

Contact: Diane Schafer Johnson, Director of Admissions. E-Mail: *djohnson@grandview.edu* Web: *www.grandview.edu*

FINANCIAL AID: In 2014-2015, 99% of all full-time freshmen and 98% of continuing full-time students received some form of financial aid. 90% of all full-time freshmen and 86% of continuing full-time students received need-based aid. Average annual earnings from campus work are $1500. The average financial indebtedness of the 2014 graduate was $36,794. The FAFSA is required. The deadline for filing freshman financial aid applications for fall entry is April 15.

GRINNELL COLLEGE	D-3
www.grinnell.edu	

Grinnell, IA 50112	(641) 269-3600
	(800) 247-0113
Fax: (641) 269-4800	Email: askgrin@grinnell.edu
Full-time: 751 men, 913 women	Faculty: 160; IIB, ++$
Part-time: 40 men, 17 women	Ph.D.s: 100%
Graduate: n/av	Student/Faculty: 10 to 1
Year: semesters	Tuition: $43,656
Room & Board: $9998	Freshman Class: 3979 applied, 1395 accepted, 423 enrolled
SAT or ACT: required	CEEB CODE: 6252
Application Deadline: April 1	HIGHLY COMPETITIVE

Grinnell College, founded in 1846, is a private institution that offers undergraduate degree programs in the arts and sciences. The 120-acre campus is in a small town 55 miles east of Des Moines. Including any residence halls, there are 64 buildings.

STUDENT LIFE: 88% of undergraduates are from out of state, mostly the Mid-West. Students are from 50 states, 51 foreign countries, and Canada. 70% are from public schools. 57% are White; 12% Foreign. 41% claim no religious affiliation; 21% Protestant; 18% includes Muslim, Hindu and Buddhist; 14% Catholic. **Male To Female Ratio:** 1.2:1. The average age of freshmen is 18; all undergraduates, 20. 7% do not continue beyond their first year; 86% remain to graduate. **Housing:** 1340 students can be accommodated in college housing, which includes single-sex and coed dorms and on-campus apartments. In addition, there are language houses and special-interest houses. On-campus housing is guaranteed for all 4 years. 88% of students live on campus; of those, 95% remain on campus on weekends. All students may keep cars.

FACULTY/CLASSROOMS: 54% of faculty are male; 46% are female. All teach and do research. No introductory courses are taught by graduate students. The average class size in an introductory lecture is 20; in a laboratory is 13; and in a regular course is 17.

PROGRAMS OF STUDY: Grinnell confers B.A. degrees. Bachelor's degrees are awarded in BIOLOGICAL SCIENCE (biochemistry and biology/biological science), COMMUNICATIONS AND THE ARTS (art, Chinese, classics, dramatic arts, English, French, German, music, Russian, and Spanish), COMPUTER AND PHYSICAL SCIENCE (chemistry, computer science, mathematics, physics, and science), SOCIAL SCIENCE (anthropology, economics, history, philosophy, political science/government, psychology, religion, sociology, and women's studies). Economics, psychology and political science have the largest enrollments.

ACTIVITIES: There are no fraternities or sororities. There are 250 groups on campus, including art, chess, choir, chorale, chorus, computers, dance, debate, drama, environmental, ethnic, film, forensics, gay, honors, international, jazz band, literary magazine, musical theater, newspaper, orchestra, photography, political, radio and TV, religious, social, social service, student government, and yearbook. Popular campus events include Titular Head Student Film Festival and Grinnell Relays. **Sports:** There are 10 intercollegiate sports for men and 10 for women, and 16 intramural sports for men and 16 for women. Facilities include a phys ed complex, a gym, a fitness center, 5 sports fields, a track, a pool, and 3 intramural fields. **Graduates:** From July 1, 2013 to June 30, 2014, 334 bachelor's degrees were awarded. The most popular majors were economics (9%), political science (8%), and history (8%). 19 companies recruited on campus in 2013-2014. In an average class, 81% graduate in 4 years or less, 86% graduate in 5 years or less, and 86% graduate in 6 years or less. Of the 2013 graduating class, 33% were enrolled in graduate school within 6 months of graduation, and 50% were employed.

SERVICES: Counseling and information services are available, as is tutoring in every subject. There is a reader service for the blind. There are reading, writing, math, and science labs. **Library/Resources:** The 3 libraries contain 649,916 volumes, 416,593 microform items, and 34,144 audio/video tapes/CDs/DVDs, and subscribe to 22,059 periodicals including electronic. Computerized library services include interlibrary loans, database searching, Internet access, and Wi-Fi capability. Special learning facilities include an art gallery, radio station, an observatory, physics museum, a print and drawing study room. **Physically Challenged Students:** 80% of the campus is accessible. Facilities include wheelchair ramps, elevators, special parking, specially equipped restrooms, special class scheduling, lowered drinking fountains, lowered telephones, and special housing. **Special:** Students may participate in 63 study-abroad programs in 33 countries or in off-campus study at selected locations in the United States. Grinnell offers cooperative programs in architecture with Washington University in St. Louis and a 3-2 engineering program with California Institute of Technology, Columbia University, Washington University, and Rensselaer Polytechnic Institute. There is also an extensive internship program, a Washington semester, a general studies degree in science, student-designed majors, and S/D/F grading options in selected courses. Grinnell's special "plus-2" option permits students to add 2 credits to a regular course through independent study. Students may pursue one of 11 interdisciplinary concentrations in addition to their major. Accelerated degree programs of 6 to 7 semesters may be approved on an individual basis. There are 2 national honor societies including Phi Beta Kappa. **Visiting:** There are regularly scheduled orientations for prospective students, including a campus tour, an interview with a member of the admissions staff, an opportunity to attend classes, presentations/discussions with students and faculty from a number of academic departments, and complimentary meals. There are guides for informal visits, visitors may sit in on classes, and stay overnight. To schedule a visit, contact the Admissions Office. **Campus Safety and Security:** Measures include 24-hour foot and vehicle patrol, emergency notification system, self-defense education, and security escort services. There are emergency telephones, lighted pathways/sidewalks, controlled access to dorms/residences, fire drills, and a committee on personal safety education.

REQUIREMENTS: The SAT or ACT is required. Applicants must be graduates of accredited secondary schools. The college recommends 20 Carnegie units, 4 each in English and math and 3 to 4 each in lab science, social studies or history, and a foreign language. An essay is required and an interview is recommended. AP credits are accepted. Important factors in the admissions decision are advanced placement or honors courses, extracurricular activities record, and leadership record. All students are required to take a tutorial in the first semester focusing on writing. All students must also complete a major field, which includes between 32 and 48 credits in most departments. Of the total 124 credits needed for the bachelor's degree, no more than 48 may be earned in any one department or 92 in any one division, and a minimum 2.0 GPA must be maintained. **Procedure:** Freshmen are admitted fall. Entrance exams should be taken during the second semester of the junior year or early in the fall semester of the senior year. There are early decision, early admissions, and deferred admissions plans. Early decision applications should be filed by November 15; regular applications, by April 1 for fall entry; and November 1 for spring entry, along with a $30 fee. Notification of early decision is sent December 15; regular decision, May 15. 137 early decision candidates were accepted for the 2014-2015 class. 1266 applicants were on the 2014 waiting list; 8 were admitted. Applications are accepted online. **Transfer Students:** 14 transfer students enrolled in 2013-2014. Students must have a 3.0 GPA and submit all high school transcripts, college transcripts, an essay or personal statement, standardized test scores, and a statement of good standing from prior institutions. 62 of 124 credits required for the bachelor's degree must be completed at Grinnell. **International Students:** There are 210 international students enrolled. The school actively recruits these students. They must take the TOEFL with a minimum score of 550 on the paper-based

TOEFL (PBT) or 80 on the Internet-based version (iBT). They must also take the SAT or ACT.

ADMISSIONS: 35% of the 2014-2015 applicants were accepted. The SAT scores for the 2014-2015 freshman class were: Critical Reading--1% below 500, 17% between 500 and 599, 46% between 600 and 699, and 36% between 700 and 800; Math--1% below 500, 13% between 500 and 599, 37% between 600 and 699, and 49% between 700 and 800. 70% of the current freshmen were in the top fifth of their class; 92% were in the top two fifths. **Admissions Contact:** Joseph P. Bagnoli Jr., Vice President for Enrollment, Dean of A. E-Mail: *askgrin@grinnell.edu* Web: *www.grinnell.edu*

FINANCIAL AID: In 2014-2015, 89% of all full-time freshmen and 87% of continuing full-time students received some form of financial aid. 73% of all full-time freshmen and 71% of continuing full-time students received need-based aid. The average freshman award was $42,392. Need-based scholarships or need-based grants averaged $36,762; need-based self-help aid (loans and jobs) averaged $4,974; and other non-need-based awards and non-need-based scholarships averaged $656. The average financial indebtedness of the 2014 graduate was $16,570. Grinnell is a member of CSS. The CSS/Profile and FAFSA, and a noncustodial profile are required. The priority date for freshman financial aid applications for fall entry is February 1. The deadline for filing freshman financial aid applications for fall entry is February 1.

IOWA BOARD OF REGENTS

The Iowa Board of Regents, established in 1909, is a public system in Iowa. It is governed by the Iowa State board of regents, whose chief administrator is the governor. The primary goal of the system is teaching, research, and public service. The total student enrollment is usually about 67,500 with 4500 faculty members. Altogether there are 276 baccalaureate, 290 master's, and 183 doctoral programs offered in the Iowa Board of Regents. Profiles of the 4-year campuses are included in this section.

IOWA STATE UNIVERSITY   C-3
www.iastate.edu

Ames, IA 50011	(515) 294-5836
	(800) 262-3810
Fax: (515) 294-2592	Email: admissions@iastate.edu
Full-time: 11100 men, 9500 women	Faculty: I, av$
Part-time: 775 men, 610 women	Ph.D.s: 88%
Graduate: 2825 men, 2240 women	Student/Faculty: n/av
Year: semesters, summer session	Tuition: $8508 ($20,224)
Room & Board: $7895	Freshman Class: n/av
SAT or ACT: required	CEEB CODE: 6306
Application Deadline: n/av	COMPETITIVE

Iowa State University, established in 1858, is a public land-grant institution offering undergraduate and graduate programs in agriculture, business, design, engineering, human sciences, liberal arts and sciences, and veterinary medicine. The figures in the above capsule and in this profile are approximate. There are 7 undergraduate schools and 1 graduate school. In addition to regional accreditation, Iowa State has baccalaureate program accreditation with AACSB, ABET, ACEJMC, ADA, AHEA, ASLA, CSAB, FIDER, NAAB, NASM, SAF, ACS, and APA. The 1788-acre campus is in an urban area 30 miles north of Des Moines. Including any residence halls, there are 284 buildings.

STUDENT LIFE: 77% of undergraduates are from Iowa. Others are from 50 states, 115 foreign countries, and Canada. 94% are from public schools. 84% are White. **Male To Female Ratio:** 0.8:1. The average age of freshmen is 18; all undergraduates, 21. 14% do not continue beyond their first year; 68% remain to graduate. **Housing:** 10000 students can be accommodated in college housing, which includes single-sex and coed dorms, on-campus apartments, and married student housing. In addition, there are honors houses, special-interest houses, fraternity houses, sorority houses, nonalcoholic houses, cross-cultural houses, nonsmoking houses, quiet houses, academic learning communities, and adult undergraduate housing. On-campus housing is guaranteed for all 4 years. 52% of students live on campus. All students may keep cars.

FACULTY/CLASSROOMS: 66% of faculty are male; 34% are female. 98% teach undergraduates, 95% do research, and 98% do both. Graduate students teach 15% of introductory courses. The average class size in a laboratory is 18 and in a regular course is 31.

PROGRAMS OF STUDY: Iowa State confers B.A, B.S., B.Arch., B.B.A., B.F.A., B.L.A., B.L.S. and B.Mus. degrees. Master's and Doctoral degrees are also awarded. Bachelor's degrees are awarded in AGRICULTURE (agricultural business management, agriculture, agronomy, animal science, dairy science, forestry and related sciences, horticulture, international agriculture, plant protection (pest management), and plant science), BIOLOGICAL SCIENCE (biochemistry, biology/biological science, biophysics, entomology, genetics, microbiology, nutrition, and plant pathology), BUSINESS (accounting, banking and finance, business administration and management, fashion merchandising, hotel/motel and restaurant management, international business management, management science, marketing/retailing/merchandising, and transportation management), COMMUNICATIONS AND THE ARTS (advertising, communications, creative writing, design, English, fine arts, French, German, graphic design, journalism, linguistics, music, Russian, Spanish, and speech/debate/rhetoric), COMPUTER AND PHYSICAL SCIENCE (atmospheric sciences and meteorology, chemistry, computer science, earth science, geology, mathematics, physics, and statistics), EDUCATION (agricultural education, early childhood education, elementary education, health education, industrial arts education, music education, physical education, and secondary education), ENGINEERING AND ENVIRONMENTAL DESIGN (aeronautical engineering, agricultural engineering, architecture, chemical engineering, city/community/regional planning, civil engineering, computer engineering, construction engineering, electrical/electronics engineering, engineering, engineering technology, environmental science, industrial engineering technology, interior design, landscape architecture/design, materials engineering, and mechanical engineering), SOCIAL SCIENCE (anthropology, child care/child and family studies, child psychology/development, dietetics, economics, family/consumer resource management, family/consumer studies, fashion design and technology, food science, history, international relations, liberal arts/general studies, philosophy, political science/government, psychology, religion, sociology, and textiles and clothing). Engineering, agriculture, and statistics are the strongest academically. Engineering, business, and agriculture have the largest enrollments.

ACTIVITIES: 13% of men belong to 1 local and 29 national fraternities; 12% of women belong to 1 local and 17 national sororities. There are 687 groups on campus, including recreation/sports, art, band, cheerleading, chess, choir, chorale, chorus, computers, dance, debate, drama, drum and bugle corps, ethnic, film, forensics, gay, honoraries, honors, international, jazz band, literary magazine, marching band, musical theater, newspaper, opera, orchestra, pep band, photography, political, professional, radio and TV, religious, social, social service, student government, and symphony. Popular campus events include VEISHEA, Spring Festival, and Honors Week. **Sports:** There are 7 intercollegiate sports for men and 12 for women, and 43 intramural sports for men and 43 for women. Facilities include a coliseum, a stadium/field, a baseball and softball complex, a track complex, a tennis complex, multipurpose gyms, swimming pools, an ice center, a phys ed building, recreation centers, multipurpose intramural-recreation fields, and a competitive soccer site.

SERVICES: Counseling and information services are available, as is tutoring in most subjects. There is a reader service for the blind, and remedial math and writing. A Kurzweil and Arkanstone reader, enlargement services, talking and braille text from the Iowa Commission for the Blind, a braille printer, loaner computers, steno-captioning service, a TTY telecommunications device, FM listeners, and sign interpreters are also available. **Library/Resources:** The library contains 2.4 million volumes, 3.4 million microform items, 64,524 audio/video tapes/CDs/DVDs, and subscribes to 29,850 periodicals including electronic. Computerized library services include interlibrary loans and database searching. Special learning facilities include an art gallery, natural history museum, planetarium, radio

station, and TV station. **Physically Challenged Students:** 95% of the campus is accessible. Facilities include wheelchair ramps, elevators, special parking, specially equipped restrooms, special class scheduling, lowered drinking fountains, lowered telephones. **Special:** Iowa State offers cooperative programs in engineering, forestry, agronomy, chemistry, computer science, economics, agricultural systems technology, business administration, industrial technology, and performing arts and cross-registration with the Universities of Iowa and Northern Iowa. Internships, study abroad in 38 countries, dual majors, the B.A.-B.S. degree, student-designed majors, and accelerated degree programs are available. Interdisciplinary studies include agricultural biochemistry, agricultural systems technology, animal ecology, public service and administration in agriculture, and engineering operations. There are work-study programs, a Washington semester, nondegree study, and pass/no pass options. There are 16 national honor societies, including Phi Beta Kappa, and a freshman honors program. **Visiting:** There are regularly scheduled orientations for prospective students, including presentations on academics, admissions, residence hall living, fraternity and sorority life, and financial aid. There is also a group session with an adviser and a tour of the campus. There are guides for informal visits, visitors may sit in on classes, and stay overnight. To schedule a visit, contact The Admissions Office. **Campus Safety and Security:** Measures include 24-hour foot and vehicle patrol, self-defense education, and security escort services. There are shuttle buses, emergency telephones, lighted pathways/sidewalks, a help van for motorists.

REQUIREMENTS: The SAT or ACT is required. Applicants must graduate from an accredited secondary school. The GED is accepted. For admission to freshman standing, students must have completed 4 years of English, 3 each of math and science, and 2 to 3 of social studies. For the College of Liberal Arts and Sciences, 2 years of a single foreign language are also required. Iowa State requires applicants to be in the upper 50% of their class. AP and CLEP credits are accepted. A minimum of 120 1/2 to 169 1/2 credit hours, depending on the major, and a GPA of 2.0 are required for graduation. The total number of credits required in the major varies. All students must take freshman English, library instruction, 3 credits in U.S. diversity, and 3 credits in internationalization. **Procedure:** Freshmen are admitted to all sessions. Entrance exams should be taken during the spring of the junior year or the fall of the senior year. There are deferred admissions and rolling admissions plans. Check with the school for current application deadlines. The fall 2014 application fee was $30. Applications are accepted on-line. **Transfer Students:** Applicants must have a minimum GPA of 2.0 and at least 24 semester credits of acceptable transfer course work. They must also submit standardized test scores and provide a statement of good standing from prior institutions. 32 of 125 credits required for the bachelor's degree must be completed at Iowa State. **International Students:** The school actively recruits these students. They must take the TOEFL and the college's own test.

ADMISSIONS: **Admissions Contact:** Phil Caffrey, Associate Director of Admissions. E-Mail: *admissions@iastate.edu* Web: *www.iastate.edu*

FINANCIAL AID: The FAFSA is required. Check with the school for current application deadlines.

IOWA WESLEYAN COLLEGE (*The complete profile is made available exclusively on our website, www.barronspac.com*)

LORAS COLLEGE	E-2
www.loras.edu	
Dubuque, IA 52004	(563) 588-7236
	(800) 245-6727
Fax: (563) 588-7119	Email: adms@loras.edu
Full-time: 765 men, 705 women	Faculty: IIB, --$
Part-time: 25 men, 40 women	Ph.D.s: 89%
Graduate: 30 men, 75 women	Student/Faculty: n/av
Year: semesters, summer session	Tuition: $29,908
Room & Board: $7524	Freshman Class: n/av
SAT or ACT: required	CEEB CODE: 0670
Application Deadline: open	VERY COMPETITIVE

Loras College, founded in 1839, is a private Roman Catholic liberal arts institution offering degree programs in humanities, social and behavioral studies, natural sciences, philosophy and religious studies, and professional studies. The figures in the above capsule and in this profile are approximate. In addition to regional accreditation, Loras has baccalaureate program accreditation with NCATE and ACS. The 60-acre campus is in a small town 180 miles west of Chicago and 250 miles south of Minneapolis. Including any residence halls, there are 18 buildings.

STUDENT LIFE: 54% of undergraduates are from Iowa. Others are from 21 states, and 7 foreign countries. 64% are from public schools. 93% are White. 64% are Catholic; 24% claim no religious affiliation. **Male To Female Ratio:** Is 1:1. The average age of freshmen is 18; all undergraduates, 20. 21% do not continue beyond their first year; 65% remain to graduate. **Housing:** 1027 students can be accommodated in college housing, which includes single-sex and coed dorms, on-campus apartments, and off-campus apartments. In addition, there are honors houses. On-campus housing is guaranteed for all 4 years and is available on a lottery system for upperclassmen. 66% of students live on campus; of those, 65% remain on campus on weekends. All students may keep cars.

FACULTY/CLASSROOMS: 56% of faculty are male; 44% are female. All teach undergraduates. No introductory courses are taught by graduate students. The average class size in an introductory lecture is 18; in a laboratory is 15; and in a regular course is 17.

PROGRAMS OF STUDY: Loras confers B.A., B.S. and B.M. degrees. Associate and Master's degrees are also awarded. Bachelor's degrees are awarded in BIOLOGICAL SCIENCE (biochemistry and biology/biological science), BUSINESS (banking and finance, business administration and management, management information systems, and marketing/retailing/merchandising), COMMUNICATIONS AND THE ARTS (broadcasting, creative writing, English literature, journalism, media arts, music, public relations, Spanish, studio art, and visual and performing arts), COMPUTER AND PHYSICAL SCIENCE (chemistry, computer science, mathematics, and science), EDUCATION (athletic training, early childhood education, education, elementary education, physical education, and special education), ENGINEERING AND ENVIRONMENTAL DESIGN (electrical/electronics engineering), HEALTH PROFESSIONS (exercise science), SOCIAL SCIENCE (criminal justice, economics, history, international studies, philosophy, political science/government, psychology, religion, social work, and sociology). Accounting and business, education, and social sciences have the largest enrollments.

ACTIVITIES: There are no fraternities; 3% of women belong to 1 national sorority. There are 150 groups on campus, including band, cheerleading, choir, chorus, computers, dance, debate, drama, ethnic, film, forensics, gay, honors, international, jazz band, literary magazine, musical theater, newspaper, photography, political, professional, programming board, radio and TV, religious, social, social service, student government, and yearbook. Popular campus events include Family Weekend, Tri-College Free Day, and Awareness Week. **Sports:** There are 11 intercollegiate sports for men and 10 for women. Facilities include a 74,000-square-foot athletic wellness facility, a sports center with 3 gym floors, a swimming pool, 4 racquetball courts, and an 8-lane Olympic indoor/outdoor track. There are also 5 outdoor tennis courts, a field house for basketball games, a football field, a soccer field, and a softball field. The campus stadium seats 3500.

SERVICES: Counseling and information services are available, as is tutoring in every subject. There is a reader service for the blind, remedial math and writing. **Library/Resources:** The library contains 374,740 volumes, 10,322 microform items, 2,175 audio/video tapes/CDs/DVDs, and subscribes to 16,169 periodicals including electronic. Computerized library services include interlibrary loans, database searching, Internet access, and Wi-Fi capability. Special learning facilities include an art gallery, planetarium, radio station, TV station, the center for Dubuque History. **Physically Challenged Students:** 65% of the campus is accessible. Facilities include wheelchair ramps, elevators, special parking, specially equipped restrooms, special class scheduling, lowered drinking fountains, lowered telephones, special housing. An LD program is designed for helping physically disabled students. **Special:** The college offers cross-registration with Clarke College and the University of Dubuque and study abroad in 10 countries. Also available are various internships, on-campus work-study programs, a 3-2 engineering degree, a Washington semester, pass/fail options, combined liberal arts and preprofessional programs, dual and student-designed majors, and adult degree programs offering a B.A.-B.S. degree. There are 3 national honor societies and a freshman honors program. **Visiting:** There are regularly scheduled orientations for prospective students, consisting of 5 fall visitation days for all students and 7 programs for specific geographic locations. There are guides for informal visits, visitors may sit in on classes, and stay overnight. To schedule a visit, contact the Office of Admissions. **Campus Safety and Security:** Measures include 24-hour foot and vehicle patrol and security escort services. There are lighted pathways/sidewalks.

REQUIREMENTS: The SAT or ACT is required. Applicants must be graduates of an accredited secondary school or have a GED certificate and have completed 4 units of English and 3 each of math, science, social studies, and history. An essay and an interview are recommended. A GPA of 2.5 is required. AP and CLEP credits are accepted. Important factors in the admissions decision are evidence of special talent, advanced placement or honors courses, and leadership record.To earn any degree students must complete a total of 120 hours with a minimum GPA of 2.0 and 36 to 37 hours of general education. There are additional requirements for a bachelor of music degree. All students must complete and present 2 1-credit student portfolios for review. A thesis and/or comprehensive exam is required for some majors. **Procedure:** Freshmen are admitted fall and spring. Entrance exams should be taken in April or June before the senior year or October of the senior year. There is a rolling admissions plan. Application deadlines are open. Application fee is $25. Notification is sent on a rolling basis. Applications are accepted on-line. **Transfer Students:** Transfer students must have a minimum 2.0 GPA and submit transcripts of previous college work. 30 of 120 credits required for the bachelor's degree must be completed at Loras. **International Students:** The school actively recruits these students. They must take the TOEFL.

ADMISSIONS: 46 freshmen graduated first in their class. **Admissions Contact:** Sharon Lyons, Director of Admissions. E-Mail: *adms@loras.edu* Web: *www.loras.edu*

FINANCIAL AID: The FAFSA is required. Check with the school for current application deadlines.

LUTHER COLLEGE E-1
www.luther.edu

Decorah, IA 52101

(563) 387-1287
(800) 458-8437

Fax: (563) 387-2159

Email: admissions@luther.edu

Full-time: 1022 men, 1317 women
Part-time: 23 men, 23 women
Graduate: n/av
Year: 4-1-4, summer session
Room & Board: $7350

Faculty: 179; IIB, av$
Ph.D.s: 93%
Student/Faculty: 13 to 1
Tuition: $38,370
Freshman Class: 3440 applied, 2448 accepted, 559 enrolled

SAT CR/M/W: 520/560/520 ACT: 26
Application Deadline: n/av

CEEB CODE: 0675
COMPETITIVE+

Founded in 1861, Luther College is a residential, liberal arts institution affiliated with the Evangelical Lutheran Church. One of the outstanding undergraduate institutions in the Midwest, Luther offers more than 60 majors, minors, pre-professional and special programs leading to the bachelor of arts degree. In addition to regional accreditation, Luther has baccalaureate program accreditation with CSWE, NASM, NCATE, and NLN. The 200-acre campus is in a small town in Northeast Iowa at the intersection of State Highway 9 and U.S. Route 52, and is 70 miles southeast of Rochester, Minnesota, and 56 miles southwest of La Crosse, Wisconsin. Including any residence halls, there are 35 buildings.

STUDENT LIFE: 69% of undergraduates are from out of state, mostly the Mid-West. Students are from 40 states, 61 foreign countries, and Canada. 90% are from public schools. 84% are White. 58%

are Protestant; 17% Catholic. **Male To Female Ratio:** 1.3:1. The average age of freshmen is 18; all undergraduates, 20. 15% do not continue beyond their first year; 81% remain to graduate. **Housing:** 2138 students can be accommodated in college housing, which includes coed dorms, on-campus apartments, off-campus apartments, and married student housing. In addition, there are special-interest houses, sustainability house, dialogue floors, and wellness floors. On-campus housing is guaranteed for all 4 years and is available on a lottery system for upperclassmen. 85% of students live on campus; of those, 90% remain on campus on weekends. All students may keep cars.

FACULTY/CLASSROOMS: 51% of faculty are male; 49% are female. All teach undergraduates. No introductory courses are taught by graduate students. The average class size in an introductory lecture is 19; in a laboratory is 12; and in a regular course is 19.

PROGRAMS OF STUDY: Luther confers B.A. degrees. Bachelor's degrees are awarded in AGRICULTURE (environmental studies), BIOLOGICAL SCIENCE (biology/biological science), BUSINESS (accounting and management science), COMMUNICATIONS AND THE ARTS (art, classical languages, communications, dance, English, French, German, music, Russian, Spanish, and theatre arts), COMPUTER AND PHYSICAL SCIENCE (chemistry, computer science, mathematics, physics, and statistics), EDUCATION (athletic training, elementary education, and physical education), HEALTH PROFESSIONS (health and nursing), SOCIAL SCIENCE (African American studies, anthropology, biblical languages, economics, history, international studies, philosophy, political science/government, psychology, religion, social work, sociology, and women's studies). Biology, music and English are the strongest academically. Biology, music, and management, have the largest enrollments.

ACTIVITIES: 3% of men belong to 3 local fraternities; 5% of women belong to 3 local sororities. There are 99 groups on campus, including art, band, cheerleading, choir, chorale, chorus, communications, computers, dance, debate, drama, drill team, environmental, ethnic, forensics, gay, honors, international, jazz band, literary magazine, musical theater, newspaper, opera, orchestra, pep band, photography, political, professional, radio and TV, religious, social, social service, student government, symphony, and yearbook. Popular campus events include Christmas at Luther, Ethnic Arts Fair and Parents Weekend. **Sports:** There are 10 intercollegiate sports for men and 9 for women, and 45 intramural sports for men and 45 for women. Facilities include 5 hardwood basketball courts, six-lane pool with a seating capacity of 600, 4 batting cages, a fitness center, climbing wall, 3 soccer fields, golf driving range, dance studio, 4000-seat stadium and 3500-seat gym, 6 indoor tennis courts, 3 racquetball courts, an indoor 6-lane 200-meter track, outdoor 8-lane polyurethane 400-meter track, 12 outdoor tennis courts, and a new aquatic center. **Graduates:** From July 1, 2013 to June 30, 2014, 530 bachelor's degrees were awarded. The most popular majors were management (12%), music (12%), and biology (11%). 207 companies recruited on campus in 2013-2014. In an average class, 74% graduate in 4 years or less, 81% graduate in 5 years or less, and 81% graduate in 6 years or less. Of the 2013 graduating class, 16% were enrolled in graduate school within 6 months of graduation, and 68% were employed.

SERVICES: Counseling and information services are available, as is tutoring in every subject. There is a reader service for the blind, remedial reading and writing. Drop-in tutoring available in mathematics, writing, speech/debate, accounting, chemistry, music theory, modern languages, and physics. Reading machines, tape recorders, note taking, and a learning center are available **Library/Resources:** The library contains 471,826 volumes, 24,839 microform items, 14,264 audio/video tapes/CDs/DVDs, and subscribes to 30,000 periodicals including electronic. Computerized library services include interlibrary loans, database searching, and Internet access. Special learning facilities include an art gallery, natural history museum, planetarium, and radio station. **Physically Challenged Students:** 95% of the campus is accessible. Facilities include wheelchair ramps, elevators, special parking, specially equipped restrooms, special class scheduling, lowered drinking fountains, lowered telephones, and special housing. **Special:** Internships in most disciplines, study away opportunities both domestically and in many countries (e.g. Malta, Germany, England, Italy, South Africa, Tanzania, China, Ecuador, Switzerland, Austria, Ireland, Norway, Netherlands, Belgium, Den-

mark, Sweden, Jamaica, Chile, Cambodia, Czech Republic, Poland, Japan,Belize, Peru), a Washington semester, student-designed and dual majors, and 3-2 engineering degrees with Washington University in St. Louis and the University of Minnesota are available, as are on-campus work-study programs. There are 17 national honor societies, including Phi Beta Kappa, and a freshman honors program. **Visiting:** There are regularly scheduled orientations for prospective students. There are guides for informal visits, visitors may sit in on classes, and stay overnight. To schedule a visit, contact the Admissions Office. **Campus Safety and Security:** Measures include 24-hour foot and vehicle patrol, emergency notification system, self-defense education, and security escort services. There are shuttle buses, emergency telephones, lighted pathways/sidewalks, controlled access to dorms/residences, personal safety education; safety alerts, security cameras, shelter areas in residence halls known as SHIP (Shelter Here Inside Phone) areas.

REQUIREMENTS: The SAT or ACT is required. In order to be considered for admission, the applicant should be within 2 semesters of graduation from an accredited high school and should complete the following college preparatory coursework: 4 years of English, which may include 1 year of speech, communications, or journalism; 3 years of math; 3 years of social science; 2 years of natural science, including 1 year of lab science; and 2 years of a foreign language study are recommended. Applicants who do not meet these standards will be considered for admission if they submit above-average ACT or SAT scores. A GPA of 2.5 is required. AP and CLEP credits are accepted. Important factors in the admissions decision are advanced placement or honors courses, evidence of special talent, and extracurricular activities record. Students must complete 128 credit hours for a B.A. with a cumulative grade-point average of 2.0 (C) or higher. The 128 hours must include the following: 30 fall/spring full courses or their equivalents. A full course is equivalent to 4 credit hours; other courses offered are equivalent to 2 credit hours or 1 credit hour, and 2 January terms. These 2 month-long terms must include a first-year seminar, and one of the following types of experiences: study away, directed readings, student-initiated project. At least 20 course equivalents outside the student's major discipline. 64 credit hours completed in residence. All-college requirements: Common ground; Fields of inquiry; Integrative understanding; Perspectives and skills. **Procedure:** Freshmen are admitted fall, winter, and spring. Entrance exams should be taken by the fall of the senior year. There are deferred admissions and rolling admissions plans. Application deadlines are open. Notifications are sent November 1. Applications are accepted on-line. Application fees are waived if application is completed on-line. **Transfer Students:** 36 transfer students enrolled in 2013-2014. Applicants must meet the same high school standards and the SAT or ACT requirements as entering freshmen, with a minimum GPA of 2.5 in parallel college course work. 64 of 128 credits required for the bachelor's degree must be completed at Luther. **International Students:** There are 146 international students enrolled. The school actively recruits these students. They must take the TOEFL with a minimum score of 550 on the paper-based TOEFL (PBT) or 80 on the Internet-based version (iBT), or take the IELTS.

ADMISSIONS: 71% of the 2014-2015 applicants were accepted. The SAT scores for the 2014-2015 freshman class were: Critical Reading-38% below 500, 31% between 500 and 599, 22% between 600 and 699, and 9% between 700 and 800; Math--20% below 500, 37% between 500 and 599, 32% between 600 and 699, and 11% between 700 and 800; Writing--42% below 500, 32% between 500 and 599, 17% between 600 and 699, and 9% between 700 and 800. The ACT scores were 9% below 21, 19% between 21 and 23, 34% between 24 and 26, 22% between 27 and 28, and 16% above 28. 52% of the current freshmen were in the top fifth of their class; 85% were in the top two fifths. There were 8 National Merit finalists. 22 freshmen graduated first in their class. **Admissions Contact:** Scot Schaeffer, Vice President for Enrollment Management. E-Mail: *admissions@luther .edu* Web: *www.luther.edu*

FINANCIAL AID: In 2014-2015, 100% of all full-time freshmen and 100% of continuing full-time students received some form of financial aid. 76% of all full-time freshmen and 69% of continuing full-time students received need-based aid. The average freshman award was $33,020. Need-based scholarships or need-based grants averaged $24,622; and need-based self-help aid (loans and jobs) averaged

$6,636. 77% of undergraduate students work part-time. Average annual earnings from campus work are $1208. The average financial indebtedness of the 2014 graduate was $27,172. Luther is a member of CSS. The FAFSA and the college's own financial statement, and a family tax return are required. The priority date for freshman financial aid applications for fall entry is March 1.

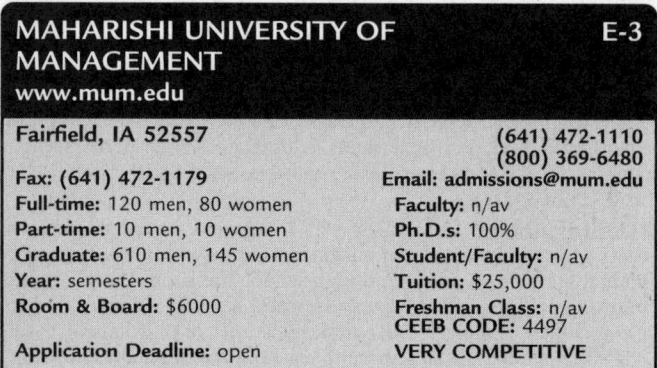

MAHARISHI UNIVERSITY OF MANAGEMENT	E-3
www.mum.edu	
Fairfield, IA 52557	**(641) 472-1110**
	(800) 369-6480
Fax: (641) 472-1179	Email: admissions@mum.edu
Full-time: 120 men, 80 women	Faculty: n/av
Part-time: 10 men, 10 women	Ph.D.s: 100%
Graduate: 610 men, 145 women	Student/Faculty: n/av
Year: semesters	Tuition: $25,000
Room & Board: $6000	Freshman Class: n/av
	CEEB CODE: 4497
Application Deadline: open	VERY COMPETITIVE

Maharishi University of Management, established in 1971, is a private institution offering undergraduate and graduate programs in a broad range of disciplines. The University provides consciousness-based education and incorporates the group practice of the Maharishi Transcendental Meditation technique into a traditional academic program. The figures in the above capsule and in this profile are approximate. There are 5 undergraduate schools and 5 graduate schools. The 272-acre campus is in a small town 114 miles southeast of Des Moines and 60 miles southwest of Iowa City. Including any residence halls, there are 50 buildings.

STUDENT LIFE: 61% of undergraduates are from out of state, mostly the Mid-West. Students are from 21 states, 29 foreign countries, and Canada. 74% are White; 17% Foreign. **Male To Female Ratio:** 0.3:1. 39% do not continue beyond their first year; 46% remain to graduate. **Housing:** 350 students can be accommodated in college housing, which includes single-sex dorms, on-campus apartments, and married student housing. In addition, there are special-interest houses, privately owned, on-campus family housing for students with families. On-campus housing is guaranteed for all 4 years. 70% of students live on campus; of those, 90% remain on campus on weekends. Alcohol is not permitted. All students may keep cars.

FACULTY/CLASSROOMS: 80% of faculty are male; 20% are female. All teach undergraduates, 20% do research, and 20% do both. No introductory courses are taught by graduate students. The average class size in an introductory lecture is 35 and in a regular course is 10.

PROGRAMS OF STUDY: confers B.A., B.S. and B.F.A. degrees. Master's and doctoral degrees are also awarded. Bachelor's degrees are awarded in BUSINESS (management science), COMMUNICATIONS AND THE ARTS (dramatic arts, fine arts, and literature), COMPUTER AND PHYSICAL SCIENCE (computer science and mathematics), EDUCATION (education). Sustainable living, Maharishi Vedic science, and business have the largest enrollments.

ACTIVITIES: There are no fraternities or sororities. There are 15 groups on campus, including and permaculture, entrepreneurial, international, art, chess, chorale, chorus, dance, drama, ecology, environmental, ethnic, international, musical theater, newspaper, photography, political, professional, radio and TV, religious, social, social service, student government, and yearbook. Popular campus events include Sports Festivals, Seasonal Celebrations, and International Cultural Exchange Festival. **Sports:** There are 2 intercollegiate sports for men and 1 for women, and 5 intramural sports for men and 5 for women. Facilities include outdoor and indoor tennis, basketball, and volleyball courts, a gym, a weight-training room, a field house, a swimming pool, a table tennis room, batting and golf driving cages, a golf putting range, an indoor 4-lane jogging track, a dance studio, and a rock-climbing wall.

SERVICES: Counseling and information services are available, as is tutoring in every subject. There is remedial math, reading, and writ-

Library/Resources: The library contains 150,294 volumes, 59,851 microform items, 21,291 audio/video tapes/CDs/DVDs, and subscribes to 23,345 periodicals including electronic. Computerized library services include interlibrary loans, database searching, and Internet access. Special learning facilities include an art gallery, radio station, a psycho-physiology, electronic engineering, visual technology, and physics labs, a scanning electron microscope, and domes for practicing the Transcendental Meditation Sidhi program. **Physically Challenged Students:** 95% of the campus is accessible. Facilities include wheelchair ramps, special parking, specially equipped restrooms, and lowered telephones. **Special:** Opportunities are provided for internships, study abroad, and nondegree study. Systematic programs are offered in the Science of Creative Intelligence, by which students apply knowledge to practical professional values. There are several 1-month blocks a year during which students may study, for example, art in Italy, literature in Switzerland, or business In China. There is a freshman honors program. **Visiting:** There are regularly scheduled orientations for prospective students, including campus tours, visits to classes, interviews, student panels, and informal dinners. There are guides for informal visits, visitors may sit in on classes, and stay overnight. To schedule a visit, contact the Admissions Office. **Campus Safety and Security:** Measures include 24-hour foot and vehicle patrol and security escort services. There are emergency telephones and lighted pathways/sidewalks.

REQUIREMENTS: Applicants must graduate from an accredited secondary school or have a GED. An essay and 2 personal recommendations are required. An interview is recommended. A GPA of 2.5 is required. AP and CLEP credits are accepted. Important factors in the admissions decision are personality/intangible qualities, recommendations by school officials, and leadership record. Students must complete 166 credit units with a minimum of 60 credits in the major and must also complete the core curriculum of 18 units as well as 20 units in a distribution of academic fields. All students must maintain a minimum GPA of 2.0. Requirements include health and fitness courses, the Science of Creative Intelligence course with its applied aspect, the Transcendental Meditation program, and courses in math and writing. The 42-week school year and block scheduling system allow students to take 1 course at a time. **Procedure:** Freshmen are admitted fall and spring. Entrance exams should be taken in the fall of the senior year or spring of the junior year. There are early admissions, deferred admissions, and rolling admissions plans. Application deadlines are open. Application fee is $15. Applications are accepted on-line. **Transfer Students:** Students must have a 2.5 GPA and acceptable recommendations as well as meet all standards set by the university. 66 of 166 credits required for the bachelor's degree must be completed at Maharishi University. **International Students:** The school actively recruits these students. They must take the TOEFL and the college's own test.

ADMISSIONS: There was 1 National Merit finalist. **Admissions Contact:** Barbara Rainbow, Associate Dean of Admissions. E-Mail: *admissions@mum.edu* Web: *www.mum.edu*

FINANCIAL AID: The FAFSA is required. Check with the school for current application deadlines.

MERCY COLLEGE OF HEALTH SCIENCES	C-3
www.mchs.edu	
Des Moines, IA 50309	**(515) 643-6604**
	(800) 637-2994
Fax: (515) 643-6698	Email: admissions@mchs.edu
Full-time: 55 men, 335 women	Faculty: 51
Part-time: 46 men, 410 women	Ph.D.s: 22%
Graduate: n/av	Student/Faculty: 7 to 1
Year: semesters, summer session	Tuition: $14,460
Room & Board: n/app	Freshman Class: 111 applied, 93 accepted, 43 enrolled
ACT: required	CEEB CODE: 2803
Application Deadline: June 15	VERY COMPETITIVE

Mercy College of Health Sciences was founded in 1995 and is a private school affiliated with the Religious Sisters of Mercy, a religious order of Roman Catholic Women. There are 3 undergraduate schools. In addition to regional accreditation, Mercy College has baccalaureate program accreditation with CCNE. The 5-acre campus is in an urban area in downtown Des Moines, Iowa. Including any residence halls, there are 5 buildings.

STUDENT LIFE: 98% of undergraduates are from Iowa. Others are from 13 states. 85% are White. **Male To Female Ratio:** 7.4:1. The average age of freshmen is 26; all undergraduates, 26. Alcohol is not permitted. All students may keep cars.

FACULTY/CLASSROOMS: 17% of faculty are male; 83% are female. All teach undergraduates. No introductory courses are taught by graduate students.

PROGRAMS OF STUDY: Mercy College confers B.S. degrees. Associate degrees are also awarded. Bachelor's degrees are awarded in HEALTH PROFESSIONS (health care administration, health science, nursing, and premedicine). Nursing, nuclear medicine, radiologic technology and surgical technology are the strongest academically. Nursing has the largest enrollment.

ACTIVITIES: There are no fraternities or sororities. Groups on campus include association of nursing students, Alpha Beta Kappa, national honor society, Sigma Theta Tau International Honor Society of Nursing, honors, professional, science club, and student government. Popular campus events include Cultural Fair, and Community Service Opportunities. **Sports:** There is no sports program at Mercy College. **Graduates:** From July 1, 2013 to June 30, 2014, 70 bachelor's degrees were awarded. The most popular majors were associate of science in nursing (49%), bachelors of science in nursing (17%), and associate of science radiologic technology (4%).

SERVICES: Counseling and information services are available, as is tutoring in most subjects. **Library/Resources:** The 5 libraries contain 12,188 volumes, and 796 audio/video tapes/CDs/DVDs, and subscribe to 7,000 periodicals including electronic. Computerized library services include interlibrary loans, database searching, Internet access, and Wi-Fi capability. Special learning facilities include a **Physically Challenged Students:** All of the campus is accessible. Facilities include wheelchair ramps, elevators, special parking, specially equipped restrooms, and lowered drinking fountains. **Special:** Clinical experience are an integral components for most academic programs. Bachelor of Science degrees in Nursing, Health Care Administration, Health Sciences (Pre-Medicine). There are 2 national honor societies and 2 departmental honors programs. **Visiting:** There are regularly scheduled orientations for prospective students. There are guides for informal visits. To schedule a visit, contact the Admissions Office at (515) 643-6715. **Campus Safety and Security:** Measures include security escort services. There are shuttle buses and lighted pathways/sidewalks.

REQUIREMENTS: The ACT is required. A GPA of 2.3 is required. AP and CLEP credits are accepted. Graduation requirements: service learning, critical thinking, communication. Critical thinking and caring courses, and a minimum GPA is also required. **Procedure:** Freshmen are admitted fall, spring, and summer. There is a rolling admissions plan. Applications should be filed by June 15 for fall entry; October 15 for spring entry; and March 15 for summer entry. Applications are accepted on-line. **Transfer Students:** Requirements vary by program. 30 credits required for the bachelor's degree must be completed at Mercy College.

ADMISSIONS: 84% of the 2014-2015 applicants were accepted. **Admissions Contact:** Kara Donovan, Director of Admissions. E-Mail: *admissions@mchs.edu* Web: *www.mchs.edu*

FINANCIAL AID: In 2014-2015, 91% of all full-time freshmen and 92% of continuing full-time students received some form of financial aid. 88% of all full-time freshmen and 89% of continuing full-time students received need-based aid. The average freshman award was $8,291. Need-based scholarships or need-based grants averaged $5,739 ($16,413 maximum); and need-based self-help aid (loans and jobs) averaged $6,869 ($20,886 maximum). 1% of undergraduate students work part-time. Average annual earnings from campus work are $2125. The average financial indebtedness of the 2014 graduate was $29,111. The FAFSA is required. The priority date for freshman financial aid applications for fall entry is April 1. The deadline for filing freshman financial aid applications for fall entry is July 1.

MORNINGSIDE COLLEGE   B-2
www.morningside.edu

Sioux City, IA 51106

(712) 274-5111
(800) 831-0806

Fax: (712) 274-5101

Email: mscadm@morningside.edu

Full-time: 610 men, 669 women

Faculty: 81; IIB, --$

Part-time: 21 men, 21 women

Ph.D.s: 73%

Graduate: 260 men, 1243 women

Student/Faculty: 15 to 1

Year: semesters, summer session

Tuition: $27,180

Room & Board: $8250

Freshman Class: 4150 applied, 2358 accepted, 353 enrolled

ACT: 23

CEEB CODE: 6415

Application Deadline: open

COMPETITIVE

Morningside College, founded in 1894, is a private college affiliated with the United Methodist Church. Its curriculum includes the liberal arts and pre-professional and professional programs of study. There is 1 undergraduate school and 1 graduate school. In addition to regional accreditation, Morningside has baccalaureate program accreditation with NASM, NCATE, NLN, and HLC. The 69-acre campus is in a suburban area 100 miles north of Omaha at the convergence of the states of South Dakota, Iowa, and Nebraska. Including any residence halls, there are 25 buildings.

STUDENT LIFE: 64% of undergraduates are from Iowa. Others are from 26 states, and 8 foreign countries. 82% are White. 69% claim no religious affiliation; 25% Protestant. **Male To Female Ratio:** 2.2:1. The average age of freshmen is 18; all undergraduates, 21. 25% do not continue beyond their first year; 46% remain to graduate. **Housing:** 912 students can be accommodated in college housing, which includes coed dorms, on-campus apartments, and married student housing. In addition, there are fraternity houses, sorority houses, freshman halls, upperclassman leadership-themed, and apartment-style residence hall. On-campus housing is guaranteed for all 4 years. 60% of students live on campus; of those, 75% remain on campus on weekends. All students may keep cars.

FACULTY/CLASSROOMS: 49% of faculty are male; 51% are female. All teach undergraduates. No introductory courses are taught by graduate students. The average class size in an introductory lecture is 27; in a laboratory is 17; and in a regular course is 21.

PROGRAMS OF STUDY: Morningside confers B.A., B.S., B.Mus., B.Mus.Ed. and B.S.N. degrees. Master's degrees are also awarded. Bachelor's degrees are awarded in AGRICULTURE (agricultural business management and agricultural sciences), BIOLOGICAL SCIENCE (biology/biological science), BUSINESS (business administration and management and management information systems), COMMUNICATIONS AND THE ARTS (advertising, art, communications, dramatic arts, English, graphic design, music, photography, and Spanish), COMPUTER AND PHYSICAL SCIENCE (chemistry, computer science, mathematics, and physics), EDUCATION (art education, education, elementary education, English education, mathematics education, music education, science education, social studies education, and special education), HEALTH PROFESSIONS (medical technology and nursing), SOCIAL SCIENCE (history, international relations, philosophy, political science/government, psychology, and religion). Business administration, biology, and education have the largest enrollments.

ACTIVITIES: 4% of men belong to 2 national fraternities; 2% of women belong to 1 national sorority. There are 41 groups on campus, including art, band, cheerleading, choir, chorale, chorus, computers, dance, drama, drill team, environmental, ethnic, honors, international, jazz band, literary magazine, newspaper, orchestra, pep band, photography, political, professional, radio and TV, religious, social, and student government. Popular campus events include Friday is Writing Day, Campus Event Series and Christmas at Morningside. **Sports:** There are 11 intercollegiate sports for men and 10 for women, and 13 intramural sports for men and 13 for women. Facilities include an 8000-seat stadium, a football field, a campus recreation center with basketball, volleyball, and racquetball/handball courts, an elevated track, a weight room, and a 6-lane, 25-yard pool. **Graduates:** From July 1, 2013 to June 30, 2014, 274 bachelor's degrees were awarded. The most popular majors were business (27%), education (16%), and biology (11%). In an average class, 3% graduate in 3 years or less, 46% graduate in 4 years or less, 54% graduate in 5 years or less, and 54% graduate in 6 years or less. Of the 2013 graduating class, 17% were enrolled in graduate school within 6 months of graduation. **SERVICES:** Counseling and information services are available, as is tutoring in most subjects. There is a reader service for the blind, remedial math, reading, and writing. **Library/Resources:** The library contains 51,948 volumes, 3,763 microform items, 1,377 audio/video tapes/CDs/DVDs, and subscribes to 148 periodicals including electronic. Computerized library services include interlibrary loans, database searching, and Internet access. Special learning facilities include an art gallery, radio station, TV station, a theater. **Physically Challenged Students:** 80% of the campus is accessible. Facilities include wheelchair ramps, elevators, special parking, specially equipped restrooms, special class scheduling, lowered drinking fountains, and lowered telephones. **Special:** There is a co-op program in medical technology. Internships are available in all departments. Study abroad in 11 countries, a Washington semester, work-study programs, both on campus and with 20 nonprofit agencies, and student-designed majors are available. There are 15 national honor societies and a freshman honors program. **Visiting:** There are regularly scheduled orientations for prospective students, consists of a campus tour, appointments with faculty and financial aid, and an interview with an admissions counselor. There are guides for informal visits, visitors may sit in on classes, and stay overnight. To schedule a visit, contact the Office of Admissions. **Campus Safety and Security:** Measures include emergency notification system, self-defense education, and security escort services. There are emergency telephones, lighted pathways/sidewalks, and controlled access to dorms/residences.

REQUIREMENTS: The ACT is required. Applicants must be graduates of an accredited secondary school. The GED is accepted. A portfolio is required for all studio art majors and an audition for performing music majors. Applicants graduating from high school 5 years or more prior to entering college are exempted from submitting the ACT scores. Those entering from a home-schooled environment must submit a completed Home School Credit Evaluation form, which may be obtained in the Office of Admissions. Morningside requires applicants to be in the upper 50% of their class. A GPA of 2.5 is required. AP and CLEP credits are accepted. Important factors in the admissions decision are recommendations by school officials, evidence of special talent, and advanced placement or honors courses. The total number of credit hours required for graduation is 124 with 44 hours of core curriculum in liberal arts and 30 hours minimum in the major. Students must have a minimum GPA of 2.0 to graduate. **Procedure:** Freshmen are admitted to all sessions. Entrance exams should be taken in the junior year. There is a rolling admissions plan. Application deadlines are open. Applications are accepted on-line. **Transfer Students:** 76 transfer students enrolled in 2013-2014. Transfer applicants must take the ACT and have an interview. They must have 24 semester hours with a 2.25 or above cumulative GPA. They must present official transcripts of previous collegiate records. 30 of 124 credits required for the bachelor's degree must be completed at Morningside. **International Students:** There are 23 international students enrolled. The school actively recruits these students. They must take the TOEFL with a minimum score of 500 on the paper-based TOEFL (PBT) or 61 on the Internet-based version (iBT). They must also take the ACT.

ADMISSIONS: 57% of the 2014-2015 applicants were accepted. The ACT scores were 26% below 21, 30% between 21 and 23, 25% between 24 and 26, 10% between 27 and 28, and 9% above 28. 33% of the current freshmen were in the top fifth of their class; 61% were in the top two fifths. 5 freshmen graduated first in their class. **Admissions Contact:** Terri Curry, VP Admissions. E-Mail: *mscadm@morningside.edu* Web: *www.morningside.edu*

FINANCIAL AID: The FAFSA is required. The priority date for freshman financial aid applications for fall entry is March 1.

MOUNT MERCY UNIVERSITY	E-3
www.mtmercy.edu	

Cedar Rapids, IA 52402

	(319) 368-6460
	(800) 248-4504
Fax: (319) 363-5270	Email: admission@.mtmercy.edu
Full-time: 254 men, 604 women	Faculty: 75
Part-time: 172 men, 414 women	Ph.D.s: 63%
Graduate: 90 men, 228 women	Student/Faculty: 14 to 1
Year: 4-1-4, summer session	Tuition: $27,010
Room & Board: $8310	Freshman Class: 695 applied, 395 accepted, 134 enrolled
SAT: reccomended ACT: 22	CEEB CODE: 6417
Application Deadline: n/av	COMPETITIVE

The men and women who make up our student body come from all over Iowa and the world. They choose Mount Mercy for our small, hands-on classes, meaningful faculty interaction, vibrant student life and our commitment to leadership and compassionate service. There are 5 graduate schools. In addition to regional accreditation, Mount Mercy has baccalaureate program accreditation with CSWE and NLN. The 40-acre campus is in an urban area in Cedar Rapids in eastern Iowa. Including any residence halls, there are 19 buildings. **STUDENT LIFE:** 91% of undergraduates are from Iowa. Others are from 19 states, 27 foreign countries, and Canada. 85% are White. 25% are Catholic; 25% Protestant; 25% claim no religious affiliation. **Male To Female Ratio:** 2.4:1. The average age of freshmen is 18; all undergraduates, 26. 19% do not continue beyond their first year; 72% remain to graduate. **Housing:** 476 students can be accommodated in college housing, which includes single-sex and coed dorms and on-campus apartments. In addition, there are special-interest houses, and themed living learning communities. On-campus housing is guaranteed for all 4 years. 64% of students commute. All students may keep cars.

FACULTY/CLASSROOMS: 35% of faculty are male; 65% are female. 93% teach undergraduates, and 2% do both. No introductory courses are taught by graduate students. The average class size in an introductory lecture is 25; in a laboratory is 14; and in a regular course is 25.

PROGRAMS OF STUDY: Mount Mercy confers B.A., B.A.A., B.A.S., B.B.A., B.S. and B.S.N. degrees. Master's degrees are also awarded. Bachelor's degrees are awarded in AGRICULTURE (conservation and regulation), BIOLOGICAL SCIENCE (biology/biological science), BUSINESS (accounting, business administration and management, finance, human resources, management information systems, and marketing/retailing/merchandising), COMMUNICATIONS AND THE ARTS (art, communications, English, graphic design, journalism, and music), COMPUTER AND PHYSICAL SCIENCE (actuarial science, computer science, and mathematics), EDUCATION (early childhood education, elementary education, middle school education, and secondary education), HEALTH PROFESSIONS (health care administration, medical laboratory technology, and nursing), SOCIAL SCIENCE (criminal justice, history, international studies, philosophy, political science/government, psychology, religion, social work, and sociology). Business, nursing, education, and criminal justice have the largest enrollments.

ACTIVITIES: There are no fraternities or sororities. There are 34 groups on campus, including academic club, art, cheerleading, choir, chorale, chorus, computers, dance, drama, drill team, environmental, ethnic, film, honors, international, jazz band, literary magazine, musical theater, newspaper, political, professional, religious, social, social service, and student government. Popular campus events include Octoberfest, Bingo Nights, and Vegas Night. **Sports:** There are 7 intercollegiate sports for men and 8 for women, and 17 intramural sports for men and 17 for women. The recreation center offers practice facilities, a weight room, fully-equipped training room, and separate locker rooms for general use and those designated for the student-athletes in men's and women's sports, a cardio and weight area, plus a large group exercise rooms where classes are offered each semester. Including equipment and spaces for a variety of cardiovascular and muscle-building workout routines. **Graduates:** From July 1, 2013 to June 30, 2014, 407 bachelor's degrees were awarded. The most popular majors were nursing (24%), business (10%), and accounting (9%). 47 companies recruited on campus in 2013-2014. In an average class, 1% graduate in 3 years or less, 64% graduate in 4 years or less, 70% graduate in 5 years or less, and 72% graduate in 6 years or less. Of the 2013 graduating class, 17% were enrolled in graduate school within 6 months of graduation, and 92% were employed.

SERVICES: Counseling and information services are available, as is tutoring in most subjects. There is a reader service for the blind, and remedial math, reading, and writing. **Library/Resources:** The library contains 129,268 volumes, 54,937 microform items, and 9,336 audio/video tapes/CDs/DVDs, and subscribes to 3,526 periodicals including electronic. Computerized library services include interlibrary loans, database searching, Internet access, and Wi-Fi capability. Special learning facilities include an art gallery, all of the classrooms are "smart" technology classrooms. **Physically Challenged Students:** 95% of the campus is accessible. Facilities include wheelchair ramps, elevators, special parking, specially equipped restrooms, special class scheduling, and lowered drinking fountains. **Special:** Mount Mercy offers internships in most majors, study abroad opportunities, work-study programs on campus, several adult accelerated business majors, an accelerated degree completion program for RNs, and student-designed, interdisciplinary majors. Credit for prior experiential learning may be granted, and pass/fail options are available. There are 3 national honor societies, a freshman honors program, and 10 departmental honors programs. **Visiting:** There are regularly scheduled orientations for prospective students, consisting of a presidential welcome, campus tour, student panel, faculty academic fair, presentations on college selection and admission requirements, and student evaluation. There are guides for informal visits, visitors may sit in on classes, and stay overnight. To schedule a visit, contact the Admissions Office at admission@mtmercy.edu . **Campus Safety and Security:** Measures include 24-hour foot and vehicle patrol, emergency notification system, self-defense education, and security escort services. There are emergency telephones, lighted pathways/sidewalks, controlled access to dorms/residences, safety personnel who are on duty 24-hours-a-day, 365-days-a-year, with regularly scheduled patrols, extensive video monitoring of building entrances building exits, and most parking facilities. Surveillance is monitored and recorded. After hours, use of residence elevators and entry to student room corridors require a resident-only passkey.

REQUIREMENTS: The SAT or ACT is recommended. The Admissions Committee evaluates all applications on an individual basis. Strong consideration will be given to applicants with the following: Cumulative grade point average of 2.75 (on a 4.0 scale), composite ACT score of 20 (940 SAT) with sub-scores of 17 or higher, class rank in the top half of their graduating class. While specific courses are not required for admission, students applying to Mount Mercy are encouraged to complete the following high school coursework: 4 years of English, 3 years of Mathematics, 3 years of Social Studies, and 3 years of Science A GPA of 2.5 is required. AP and CLEP credits are accepted. Important factors in the admissions decision are leadership record, extracurricular activities record, and geographical diversity. To graduate, students must complete 123 semester hours; have a minimum cumulative GPA of at least 2.00; a minimum cumulative GPA in all credits taken at MMU; completion of the core curriculum requirements; completions of a major program of study; at least 12 semester hours, above course number 200, completed in the major; a minimum of 30 semester hours completed at MMU; a minimum of 30 consecutive semester hours completed at MMU immediately preceding graduation. **Procedure:** Freshmen are admitted to all sessions. Entrance exams should be taken in the junior year or the fall of the senior year. There are deferred admissions and rolling admissions plans. Check with the school for current application deadlines. Notification is sent on a rolling basis. Applications are accepted online. Application fees are waived if application is completed on-line. **Transfer Students:** 177 transfer students enrolled in 2013-2014. Mount Mercy evaluates all files on an individual basis. While specific courses are not required for admission, the transcripts will be evaluated to ensure that strong college curriculum has been successfully completed. Strong consideration will be given to applicants who have the following: Cumulative transfer grade point average of 2.50 (on a 4.0 scale). Students looking to transfer with two semesters or less will

be reviewed by the Admission Committee. A complete admission file includes: Application for admission, official high school transcripts. For applicants who have not earned an associates degree or higher from an accredited college or university official transcripts from all previous colleges attended are required. For applicants who have earned an associates degree or higher from an accredited college or university, updated copies of college transcripts will need to be sent prior to enrollment for students who apply for admission while enrolled at another college. 30 of 123 credits required for the bachelor's degree must be completed at Mount Mercy. **International Students:** There are 50 international students enrolled. The school actively recruits these students. They must take the TOEFL with a minimum score of 550 on the paper-based TOEFL (PBT) or 79 on the Internet-based version (iBT), or take the ICHS 6.5; Step EIKEN Grade 1; IELTS (6.5); ACT (20); SAT (940). They must also take the SAT or ACT, scoring 20.

ADMISSIONS: 57% of the 2014-2015 applicants were accepted. The ACT scores were 40% below 21, 27% between 21 and 23, 20% between 24 and 26, 9% between 27 and 28, and 4% above 28. 30% of the current freshmen were in the top fifth of their class; 62% were in the top two fifths. 1 freshman graduated first in the class. **Admissions Contact:** Terri Crumley, Dean of Admissions. E-Mail: *admission@.mtmercy.edu* Web: *www.mtmercy.edu*

FINANCIAL AID: In 2014-2015, 100% of all full-time freshmen and 97% of continuing full-time students received some form of financial aid. 81% of all full-time freshmen and 90% of continuing full-time students received need-based aid. The average freshman award was $19,799. 41% of undergraduate students work part-time. Average annual earnings from campus work are $1570. The average financial indebtedness of the 2014 graduate was $27,279. The FAFSA is required. The priority date for freshman financial aid applications for fall entry is March 1.

NORTHWESTERN COLLEGE OF IOWA   B-2
www.nwciowa.edu

Orange City, IA 51041	(712) 707-7130
	(800) 747-4757
Fax: (712) 707-7164	Email: admissions@nwciowa.edu
Full-time: 475 men, 625 women	Faculty: 84; IIB, --$
Part-time: 21 men, 84 women	Ph.D.s: 83%
Graduate: n/av	Student/Faculty: 13 to 1
Year: semesters, summer session	Tuition: $27,830
Room & Board: $8410	Freshman Class: 1254 applied, 976 accepted, 315 enrolled
SAT CR/M/W: 520/580/520 ACT: 24	CEEB CODE: 6490
Application Deadline: n/av	VERY COMPETITIVE

Northwestern College of Iowa is a Christian college engaging students in courageous and faithful learning and living that empowers them to follow Christ and pursue God's redeeming work in the world. In addition to regional accreditation, Northwestern has baccalaureate program accreditation with CSWE, NCATE, CAATE, IACBE, and CCNE. The 100-acre campus is in a small town 40 miles northeast of Sioux City, and 75 miles southeast of Sioux Falls, South Dakota. Including any residence halls, there are 30 buildings.

STUDENT LIFE: 54% of undergraduates are from Iowa. Others are from 34 states, 24 foreign countries, and Canada. 80% are from public schools. 83% are White. 78% are Protestant; 14% claim no religious affiliation. **Male To Female Ratio:** 1.4:1. The average age of freshmen is 18; all undergraduates, 21. 22% do not continue beyond their first year; 63% remain to graduate. **Housing:** 1055 students can be accommodated in college housing, which includes single-sex dorms, on-campus apartments, and married student housing. On-campus housing is guaranteed for all 4 years. 82% of students live on campus; of those, 80% remain on campus on weekends. Alcohol is not permitted. All students may keep cars.

FACULTY/CLASSROOMS: 61% of faculty are male; 39% are female. All teach undergraduates, 75% do research, and 75% do both. No introductory courses are taught by graduate students. The average

class size in an introductory lecture is 22; in a laboratory is 11; and in a regular course is 15.

PROGRAMS OF STUDY: Northwestern confers B.A., B.A.A.T. and B.S.N. degrees. Bachelor's degrees are awarded in AGRICULTURE (agricultural business management), BIOLOGICAL SCIENCE (biology/biological science), BUSINESS (accounting, business administration and management, and business economics), COMMUNICATIONS AND THE ARTS (dramatic arts, graphic design, journalism, literature, music, public relations, and Spanish), COMPUTER AND PHYSICAL SCIENCE (actuarial science, chemistry, computer science, information sciences and systems, and mathematics), EDUCATION (art education, athletic training, business education, Christian education, early childhood education, elementary education, foreign languages education, middle school education, music education, physical education, science education, secondary education, and special education), HEALTH PROFESSIONS (medical laboratory technology, nursing, predentistry, and premedicine), SOCIAL SCIENCE (criminal justice, economics, history, philosophy, physical fitness/movement, political science/government, prelaw, psychology, religion, religious music, social work, sociology, and youth ministry). Biology, education, and religion are the strongest academically. Business, education, and kinesiology have the largest enrollments.

ACTIVITIES: There are no fraternities or sororities. There are 35 groups on campus, including art, band, cheerleading, choir, chorus, communications, computers, dance, drama, drill team, environmental, ethnic, film, honors, international, jazz band, literary magazine, musical theater, newspaper, orchestra, photography, political, professional, radio and TV, religious, social, social service, student government, symphony, and yearbook. Popular campus events include Clash of the Classes, Airband, Coly Christmas Bash, Homecoming, NC/DC singing competition, RUSH Student Dance Exhibition, and Winter Formal. **Sports:** There are 8 intercollegiate sports for men and 8 for women, and 19 intramural sports for men and 19 for women. Facilities include a wood-floored gymnasium for basketball and volleyball that seats 2200, a turf football field surrounded by an eight-lane polyurethane track with 2200-seat stadium seating, 2 full-sized practice football fields, 2 soccer fields, a football/track locker room, a one-tenth-mile/six-lane indoor track, 3 handball/racquetball courts, 4 basketball and volleyball courts for recreational use, 2 indoor tennis courts, gymnastics/wrestling rooms, athletes' weight room and training room, student and community fitness center with free weights and fitness equipment. **Graduates:** From July 1, 2013 to June 30, 2014, 268 bachelor's degrees were awarded. The most popular majors were business administration (16%), elementary education (15%), and nursing (9%). In an average class, 2% graduate in 3 years or less, 56% graduate in 4 years or less, 65% graduate in 5 years or less, and 66% graduate in 6 years or less. Of the 2013 graduating class, 14% were enrolled in graduate school within 6 months of graduation, and 81% were employed.

SERVICES: Counseling and information services are available, as is tutoring in most subjects. There is remedial math, reading, and writing. **Library/Resources:** The library contains 120,000 volumes, 110,000 microform items, 6,000 audio/video tapes/CDs/DVDs, and subscribes to 840 periodicals including electronic. Computerized library services include interlibrary loans, database searching, Internet access, and Wi-Fi capability. Special learning facilities include an art gallery and radio station. **Physically Challenged Students:** 90% of the campus is accessible. Facilities include wheelchair ramps, elevators, special parking, specially equipped restrooms, lowered drinking fountains, and special housing. **Special:** Northwestern offers cross-registration with Dordt College, student-designed majors, numerous internships, semester programs in Chicago, Washington, D.C., and Denver, and study abroad in over 20 countries, including China, Oman, Romania, Egypt, Spain, France, and the Netherlands. There are 2 national honor societies, a freshman honors program, and 23 departmental honors programs. **Visiting:** There are regularly scheduled orientations for prospective students, campus tour, meet with financial aid and admissions personnel, attend chapel, meet with a faculty member and attend a class in the student's area of interest. There are guides for informal visits, visitors may sit in on classes, and stay overnight. To schedule a visit, contact Laura De Boer at (712) 707-7142 . **Campus Safety and Security:** Measures include emergency notification system. There are emergency telephones, lighted pathways/sidewalks, and controlled access to dorms/residences.

REQUIREMENTS: The ACT is required. Applicants with a minimum ACT composite of 19, in the top half of their high school class, and with a 2.4 GPA are generally accepted. Applicants should be graduates of an accredited secondary school. The suggested distribution of high school courses is 4 years of English, 3 years each of math, foreign language, and social studies, and 2 of natural science. The GED is accepted. A GPA of 2.0 is required. AP and CLEP credits are accepted. Important factors in the admissions decision are personality/intangible qualities, leadership record, and evidence of special talent. All students are required to take an integrated general education core curriculum, including a first-year seminar, eight credits of Christian story and tradition courses, between 31 and 44 credits in a variety of disciplines, and a senior seminar. Students must maintain a 2.0 GPA for 124 total credits and pass both writing and math competency levels. **Procedure:** Freshmen are admitted to all sessions. Entrance exams should be taken Spring semester of the junior year of high school. There is a rolling admissions plan. Application deadlines are open. Notifications are sent November 1. Applications are accepted on-line. Application fees are waived if application is completed online. **Transfer Students:** 49 transfer students enrolled in 2013-2014. Transfer applicants must submit a transcript and letter of recommendation. A minimum college GPA of 2.0 is required. 30 of 124 credits required for the bachelor's degree must be completed at Northwestern. **International Students:** There are 40 international students enrolled. The school actively recruits these students. They must take the TOEFL with a minimum score of 475 on the paper-based TOEFL (PBT) or 53 on the Internet-based version (iBT).

ADMISSIONS: 78% of the 2014-2015 applicants were accepted. The SAT scores for the 2014-2015 freshman class were: Critical Reading--32% below 500, 39% between 500 and 599, 16% between 600 and 699, and 13% between 700 and 800; Math--26% below 500, 29% between 500 and 599, 42% between 600 and 699, and 3% between 700 and 800; Writing--48% below 500, 26% between 500 and 599, and 26% between 600 and 699. The ACT scores were 17% below 21, 29% between 21 and 23, 24% between 24 and 26, 13% between 27 and 28, and 17% above 28. 46% of the current freshmen were in the top fifth of their class; 76% were in the top two fifths. 24 freshmen graduated first in their class. **Admissions Contact:** Kenton Pauls, Dean of Enrollment Management. E-Mail: *admissions@nwciowa.edu* Web: *www.nwciowa.edu*

FINANCIAL AID: In 2014-2015, 100% of all full-time freshmen and 100% of continuing full-time students received some form of financial aid. 98% of all full-time freshmen and 93% of continuing full-time students received need-based aid. The average freshman award was $27,960. Need-based scholarships or need-based grants averaged $6,592 ($19,880 maximum); need-based self-help aid (loans and jobs) averaged $4,706 ($10,140 maximum); non-need-based athletic scholarships averaged $5,442 ($17,500 maximum); and other non-need-based awards and non-need-based scholarships averaged $13,094 ($37,850 maximum). 84% of undergraduate students work part-time. Average annual earnings from campus work are $980. The average financial indebtedness of the 2014 graduate was $28,660. The FAFSA is required. The priority date for freshman financial aid applications for fall entry is April 1. The deadline for filing freshman financial aid applications for fall entry is June 30.

SIMPSON COLLEGE   C-3
www.simpson.edu

Indianola, IA 50125	**(515) 961-1624**
	(800) 362-2454, ext. 1624
Fax: (515) 961-1870	**Email:** admiss@simpson.edu
Full-time: 618 men, 777 women	**Faculty:** 98
Part-time: 187 men, 235 women	**Ph.D.s:** 84%
Graduate: 19 men, 30 women	**Student/Faculty:** 15 to 1
Year: other, summer session	**Tuition:** $28,123
Room & Board: $7963	**Freshman Class:** 1343 applied, 1145 accepted, 332 enrolled
SAT: required **ACT:** 24	**CEEB CODE:** 6650
Application Deadline: n/av	**COMPETITIVE+**

Simpson College, founded in 1860 is a private liberal arts college affiliated with the United Methodist Church. Simpson combines the best of a liberal arts education with outstanding career preparation and extracurricular programs. More than 40 majors, minors, and pre-professional programs are offered. Extra-curricular activities at Simpson are designed to supplement and reinforce the academic program and contribute toward a total learning experience. Activities range from award-winning fine arts programs to nationally recognized NCAA Division III teams. In addition to regional accreditation, Simpson has baccalaureate program accreditation with NASM and CAATE. The 80-acre campus is in a small town 12 miles south of Des Moines, Iowa's capital city. Including any residence halls, there are 45 buildings.

STUDENT LIFE: 89% of undergraduates are from Iowa. Others are from 24 states, and 7 foreign countries. 98% are from public schools. 88% are White. 32% are Buddhist and unknown; 29% Protestant; 18% Catholic. **Male To Female Ratio:** 1.3:1. The average age of freshmen is 18; all undergraduates, 23. 23% do not continue beyond their first year; 70% remain to graduate. **Housing:** 1268 students can be accommodated in college housing, which includes single-sex and coed dorms and on-campus apartments. In addition, there are special-interest houses, fraternity houses, sorority houses, theme houses. On-campus housing is guaranteed for all 4 years. 83% of students live on campus; of those, 80% remain on campus on weekends. All students may keep cars.

FACULTY/CLASSROOMS: 56% of faculty are male; 44% are female. All teach undergraduates. No introductory courses are taught by graduate students. The average class size in an introductory lecture is 26; in a laboratory is 22; and in a regular course is 22.

PROGRAMS OF STUDY: Simpson confers B.A., and B.Mus. degrees. Master's degrees are also awarded. Bachelor's degrees are awarded in BIOLOGICAL SCIENCE (biochemistry and biology/biological science), BUSINESS (accounting, business administration and management, international business management, marketing management, and sports management), COMMUNICATIONS AND THE ARTS (art, communications, dramatic arts, English, French, German, graphic design, journalism, multimedia, music, music performance, and Spanish), COMPUTER AND PHYSICAL SCIENCE (actuarial science, chemistry, computer science, information sciences and systems, mathematics, and physics), EDUCATION (athletic training, elementary education, music education, physical education, and secondary education), ENGINEERING AND ENVIRONMENTAL DESIGN (environmental science and preengineering), HEALTH PROFESSIONS (exercise science, predentistry, premedicine, preoptometry, prepharmacy, prephysical therapy, and preveterinary science), SOCIAL SCIENCE (criminal justice, economics, forensic studies, history, interdisciplinary studies, international relations, philosophy, political science/government, prelaw, psychology, religion, and sociology). Management, communication studies, and marketing have the largest enrollments.

ACTIVITIES: 18% of men belong to 1 local and 3 national fraternities; 20% of women belong to 3 national sororities.There are 75 groups on campus, including art, band, campus activities board, cheerleading, choir, chorale, computers, drama, drill team, environmental, ethnic, gay, honors, international, jazz band, literary magazine, musical theater, newspaper, opera, pep band, political, professional, radio and TV, religious, social, social service, student government, and yearbook. Popular campus events include Back to School Stand-Around, Homecoming Yell Like Hell Pep Rally, and Lessons and Carols Christmas Concert. **Sports:** There are 10 intercollegiate sports for men and 9 for women, and 50 intramural sports for men and 50 for women. Facilities include an athletic center with a gym, a wrestling practice room, a weight room/workout facility, a training facility, 2 racquetball courts, a 25-meter swimming pool, a sauna, and classrooms; a field house for volleyball, basketball, and wrestling; a football and soccer stadium with artificial turf and an 8-lane all-weather track; a tennis center with 6 all-weather courts; a baseball field and a softball complex; practice and intramural fields; and outdoor basketball and sand volleyball courts. **Graduates:** From July 1, 2013 to June 30, 2014, 431 bachelor's degrees were awarded. The most popular majors were management (12%), communication studies (9%), and marketing (8%). 72 companies recruited on campus in 2013-2014. In an average class, 57% graduate in 4 years

or less, 66% graduate in 5 years or less, and 68% graduate in 6 years or less. Of the 2013 graduating class, 15% were enrolled in graduate school within 6 months of graduation, and 78% were employed.

SERVICES: Counseling and information services are available, as is tutoring in every subject. There is a reader service for the blind. **Library/Resources:** The library contains 160,044 volumes, 9,894 microform items, 4,422 audio/video tapes/CDs/DVDs, and subscribes to 26,749 periodicals including electronic. Computerized library services include interlibrary loans, database searching, Internet access, and Wi-Fi capability. Special learning facilities include an art gallery, radio station, Avery O. Craven antebellum period collection, the George Washington Carver papers, the Iowa History Center, the John C. Culver Center for Public Policy Studies, an education lab, and a cadaver lab. **Physically Challenged Students:** All of the campus is accessible. Facilities include wheelchair ramps, elevators, special parking, specially equipped restrooms, special class scheduling, lowered drinking fountains, and special housing. **Special:** Internships, study abroad, a Washington semester, and work-study are all available. Dual and student-designed majors are possible. There is a pre-professional program in ministry, and 3-2 engineering degrees are offered with Washington University at St. Louis, Iowa State University, and Institute of Technology (University of Minnesota). There are 10 national honor societies, a freshman honors program, and 8 departmental honors programs. **Visiting:** There are regularly scheduled orientations for prospective students, Orientation is scheduled 4 times throughout the summer to allow incoming students to meet with an academic advisor, register for classes, and participate in activity information sessions. Parents are encouraged to attend. There are guides for informal visits, visitors may sit in on classes, and stay overnight. To schedule a visit, contact the Visit Coordinator. **Campus Safety and Security:** Measures include 24-hour foot and vehicle patrol, emergency notification system, and security escort services. There are emergency telephones, lighted pathways/sidewalks, and controlled access to dorms/residences.

REQUIREMENTS: The SAT or ACT is required. Applicants must be graduates of an accredited secondary school; however, the GED is accepted. ACT or SAT test scores, counselor recommendations, GPA, college prep course grades, and class rank are all considered in a selective admissions process. The college strongly recommends that applicants complete 4 years of English and 3 each of math, lab science, social science, and a foreign language. A visit to campus to speak with an admissions representative is also recommended. AP and CLEP credits are accepted. Important factors in the admissions decision are recommendations by school officials, advanced placement or honors courses, and extracurricular activities record. Students must satisfactorily complete the Engaged Citizenship curriculum including a first-year colloquium; a senior capstone course; complete two May term courses; and complete a major course load. **Procedure:** Freshmen are admitted to all sessions. Entrance exams should be taken during the junior or senior year. There are deferred admissions and rolling admissions plans. Application deadlines are open. Notification is sent on a rolling basis. Applications are accepted on-line. **Transfer Students:** 79 transfer students enrolled in 2013-2014. In addition to freshman requirements, transfer applicants are considered on the basis of college work taken and grades received. It is recommended that applicants take either the SAT or ACT. The recommended GPA is 2.5, and grades of 2.0 and above transfer for credit. 32 of 128 credits required for the bachelor's degree must be completed at Simpson. **International Students:** There are 13 international students enrolled. The school actively recruits these students. They must take the TOEFL with a minimum score of 550 on the paper-based TOEFL (PBT) or 79 on the Internet-based version (iBT), SAT or ACT scores are also recommended.

ADMISSIONS: 85% of the 2014-2015 applicants were accepted. The ACT scores were 20% below 21, 33% between 21 and 23, 22% between 24 and 26, 14% between 27 and 28, and 11% above 28. 42% of the current freshmen were in the top fifth of their class; 75% were in the top two fifths. 18 freshmen graduated first in their class. **Admissions Contact:** Deborah Tierney, Vice President for Enrollment. E-Mail: *admiss@simpson.edu* Web: *www.simpson.edu*

FINANCIAL AID: In 2014-2015, 100% of all full-time freshmen and 99% of continuing full-time students received some form of financial aid. 88% of all full-time freshmen and 86% of continuing full-time

students received need-based aid. The average freshman award was $30,412. Need-based scholarships or need-based grants averaged $8,227; need-based self-help aid (loans and jobs) averaged $3,458; and other non-need-based awards and non-need-based scholarships averaged $18,727. 44% of undergraduate students work part-time. Average annual earnings from campus work are $1000. The average financial indebtedness of the 2014 graduate was $34,055. The FAFSA is required. The priority date for freshman financial aid applications for fall entry is April 1. The deadline for filing freshman financial aid applications for fall entry is July 1.

ST. AMBROSE UNIVERSITY   E-3
www.sau.edu

Davenport, IA 52803   (563) 333-6300
                                             (800) 383-2627
Fax: (563) 333-6038   Email: HalliganMegFf@sau.edu
Full-time: 995 men, 1419 women   Faculty: 163
Part-time: 140 men, 333 women   Ph.D.s: 74%
Graduate: 287 men, 555 women   Student/Faculty: 11 to 1
Year: semesters, summer session   Tuition: $22,590
Room & Board: $8255   Freshman Class: 2075
                                  applied, 1702 accepted,
                                  577 enrolled
ACT: 23   CEEB CODE: 6617
Application Deadline: open   COMPETITIVE

St. Ambrose University, a private institution founded in 1882 in affiliation with the Roman Catholic Church, offers degree programs through the colleges of arts and sciences, business, education, health sciences, and professional studies. There is a college-level seminary. There are 4 undergraduate schools and 15 graduate schools. In addition to regional accreditation, St. Ambrose has baccalaureate program accreditation with ABET, ACBSP, CSWE, ACOTE, CCNE, and CAPTE. The 123-acre campus is in an urban area 180 miles west of Chicago. Including any residence halls, there are 29 buildings.

STUDENT LIFE: 56% of undergraduates are from out of state, mostly the Mid-West. Students are from 26 states, 12 foreign countries, and Canada. 70% are from public schools. 81% are White. 64% are Catholic; 36% Protestant. **Male To Female Ratio:** 1.6:1. The average age of freshmen is 18; all undergraduates, 23. 26% do not continue beyond their first year; 65% remain to graduate. **Housing:** 1507 students can be accommodated in college housing, which includes single-sex and coed dorms, on-campus apartments, and off-campus apartments. There are townhouse residences for upper-division students. On-campus housing is guaranteed for all 4 years. 52% of students live on campus; of those, 60% remain on campus on weekends. All students may keep cars.

FACULTY/CLASSROOMS: 52% of faculty are male; 48% are female. 88% teach undergraduates. No introductory courses are taught by graduate students. The average class size in an introductory lecture is 17; in a laboratory is 14; and in a regular course is 17.

PROGRAMS OF STUDY: St. Ambrose confers B.A., B.S., B.A.M.T., B.B.A., B.B.A.A., B.E.D., B.E.S., B.M.E., B.S.I.E., B.S.N. and B.S.S. degrees. Master's and doctoral degrees are also awarded. Bachelor's degrees are awarded in BIOLOGICAL SCIENCE (biology/biological science), BUSINESS (accounting, business administration and management, business economics, international business management, management science, marketing/retailing/merchandising, and sports management), COMMUNICATIONS AND THE ARTS (communications, English, fine arts, French, German, graphic design, music, Spanish, and speech/debate/rhetoric), COMPUTER AND PHYSICAL SCIENCE (chemistry, computer science, mathematics, and physics), EDUCATION (art education, early childhood education, elementary education, music education, physical education, and secondary education), ENGINEERING AND ENVIRONMENTAL DESIGN (engineering physics and industrial engineering), HEALTH PROFESSIONS (health science), SOCIAL SCIENCE (criminal justice, criminology, economics, forensic studies, history, philosophy, political science/government, psychology, public administration, sociology, and theological studies). Biology, chemistry, and engineering physics are the strongest academically. Business, psychology, and elementary education have the largest enrollments.

ACTIVITIES: There are no fraternities or sororities. There are 45 groups on campus, including art, band, cheerleading, choir, chorale, chorus, computers, dance, debate, drama, ethnic, gay, honors, international, jazz band, literary magazine, musical theater, newspaper, opera, orchestra, pep band, photography, political, professional, radio and TV, religious, social, social service, student government, and symphony. Popular campus events include Multicultural Weeks and Brother/Sister Weekend. **Sports:** There are 11 intercollegiate sports for men and 11 for women, and 63 intramural sports for men and 63 for women. Facilities include tennis, handball/racquetball, and volleyball courts, a golf room, an archery range, a gym, a weight-lifting room, and a jogging track. **Graduates:** From July 1, 2013 to June 30, 2014, 647 bachelor's degrees were awarded. The most popular majors were business (28%), education (11%), and nursing (10%). 130 companies recruited on campus in 2013-2014. In an average class, 2% graduate in 3 years or less, 53% graduate in 4 years or less, 64% graduate in 5 years or less, and 65% graduate in 6 years or less. Of the 2013 graduating class, 18% were enrolled in graduate school within 6 months of graduation, and 98% were employed.

SERVICES: Counseling and information services are available, as is tutoring in most subjects. There is a reader service for the blind, and remedial math, reading, and writing. **Library/Resources:** The library contains 156,303 volumes, 7,066 microform items, and 3,606 audio/video tapes/CDs/DVDs, and subscribes to 15,552 periodicals including electronic. Computerized library services include interlibrary loans, database searching, Internet access, and Wi-Fi capability. Special learning facilities include an art gallery, radio station, TV station, an observatory. **Physically Challenged Students:** 96% of the campus is accessible. Facilities include wheelchair ramps, elevators, special parking, specially equipped restrooms, special class scheduling, lowered drinking fountains, and special housing. **Special:** The university offers co-op and work-study programs, study abroad in England, Ireland, Ecuador, Italy, Spain, Austria, and Germany, internships, a 3-2 engineering degree with the University of Iowa and Iowa State University, accelerated degree programs, and student-designed majors. Credit for life, military, and work experience, nondegree study, and pass/fail options also are available. There are 12 national honor societies and 7 departmental honors programs. **Visiting:** There are regularly scheduled orientations for prospective students, including breakfast, welcome, testing, panel given by current students, student and parent meeting with faculty mentor, and evening meeting and activity; on the next day, there is advising and registration. Parents follow their own agenda (with panels and tours). There are guides for informal visits, visitors may sit in on classes, and stay overnight. To schedule a visit, contact the Admissions Office. **Campus Safety and Security:** Measures include 24-hour foot and vehicle patrol, emergency notification system, self-defense education, and security escort services. There are emergency telephones, lighted pathways/sidewalks, controlled access to residence halls from 7 p.m. to 7 a.m.

REQUIREMENTS: The ACT is required. The ACT Optional Writing test is also required. The SAT, with a satisfactory score, may be substituted. Applicants must be graduates of an accredited secondary school; the GED is accepted. An interview is recommended. St. Ambrose requires applicants to be in the upper 50% of their class. AP and CLEP credits are accepted. Important factors in the admissions decision are recommendations by school officials, leadership record, and parents or siblings attended your school.To graduate, all students must complete at least 120 credit hours, including 45 outside the major and 30 in upper-level courses. A minimum GPA of 2.0 is required. Students must also demonstrate proficiency in English composition, math, public speaking, and library skills, among other requirements. Selections of courses must include those that provide an opportunity to develop specific skills, content knowledge, and exposure to attitude and value development. **Procedure:** Freshmen are admitted to all sessions. Entrance exams should be taken in the spring of the junior year. There is a rolling admissions plan. Application deadlines are open. Application fee is $25. Applications are accepted on-line. **Transfer Students:** 284 transfer students enrolled in 2013-2014. Applicants must have a college GPA of 2.0. 30 of 120 credits required for the Bachelor's degree must be completed at St. Ambrose. **International Students:** There are 14 international students enrolled. They must take the TOEFL with a minimum score of 500 on the paper-based TOEFL (PBT) or 61 on the Internet-based version (iBT). They must also take the SAT or ACT.

ADMISSIONS: 82% of the 2014-2015 applicants were accepted. The ACT scores were 28% below 21, 35% between 21 and 23, 19% between 24 and 26, 9% between 27 and 28, and 9% above 28. 28% of the current freshmen were in the top fifth of their class; 54% were in the top two fifths. 36 freshmen graduated first in their class. **Admissions Contact:** Meg Halligan, Director of Admissions. E-Mail: *HalliganMegFf@sau.edu* Web: *www.sau.edu*

FINANCIAL AID: In 2014-2015, 99% of all full-time freshmen and 98% of continuing full-time students received some form of financial aid. 75% of all full-time freshmen and 72% of continuing full-time students received need-based aid. The average freshman award was $21,901. Need-based scholarships or need-based grants averaged $5,997 ($13,350 maximum); need-based self-help aid (loans and jobs) averaged $4,254 ($8,048 maximum); non-need-based athletic scholarships averaged $4,689 ($17,500 maximum); and other non-need-based awards and non-need-based scholarships averaged $8,472 ($22,590 maximum). 100% of undergraduate students work part-time. Average annual earnings from campus work are $1392. The average financial indebtedness of the 2014 graduate was $30,013. St. Ambrose is a member of CSS. The FAFSA is required. The priority date for freshman financial aid applications for fall entry is March 15.

UNIVERSITY OF DUBUQUE   E-2
www.dbq.edu

Dubuque, IA 52001	(563) 589-3214
	(800) 722-5583
Fax: (563) 589-3690	Email: jjames@dbq.edu
Full-time: 710 men, 410 women	Faculty: n/av
Part-time: 30 men, 35 women	Ph.D.s: 80%
Graduate: 170 men, 110 women	Student/Faculty: n/av
Year: semesters, summer session	Tuition: $22,620
Room & Board: $7580	Freshman Class: n/av
SAT or ACT: required	CEEB CODE: 6869
Application Deadline: n/av	COMPETITIVE

The University of Dubuque, established in 1852, is a private, liberal arts institution affiliated with the Presbyterian Church. Strengths in the undergraduate curriculum include environmental science, business, aviation, education, and computer graphics/interactive media. The figures in the above capsule and in this profile are approximate. There are 3 undergraduate schools and 2 graduate schools. The 56-acre campus is in a suburban area 180 miles northwest of Chicago. Including any residence halls, there are 24 buildings.

STUDENT LIFE: 60% of undergraduates are from out of state, mostly the Mid-West. Students are from 35 states, and 21 foreign countries. 90% are from public schools. 79% are White; 12% African American. 50% are Catholic; 40% Protestant. **Male To Female Ratio:** 0.6:1. The average age of freshmen is 18; all undergraduates, 22. 12% do not continue beyond their first year; 59% remain to graduate. **Housing:** 600 students can be accommodated in college housing, which includes coed dorms, on-campus apartments, and married student housing. In addition, there are special-interest houses. On-campus housing is guaranteed for all 4 years. 30% of students commute. Alcohol is not permitted. All students may keep cars.

FACULTY/CLASSROOMS: 55% of faculty are male; 45% are female. All teach undergraduates. No introductory courses are taught by graduate students. The average class size in an introductory lecture is 25; in a laboratory is 16; and in a regular course is 17.

PROGRAMS OF STUDY: UD confers B.A., B.S. and B.B.A. degrees. Associate, Master's, and Doctoral degrees are also awarded. Bachelor's degrees are awarded in BIOLOGICAL SCIENCE (biology/biological science), BUSINESS (accounting and business administration and management), COMMUNICATIONS AND THE ARTS (English and speech/debate/rhetoric), COMPUTER AND PHYSICAL SCIENCE (computer science), EDUCATION (education and physical education), ENGINEERING AND ENVIRONMENTAL DESIGN (aviation administration/management, computer graphics, and environmental science), HEALTH PROFESSIONS (nursing), SOCIAL SCIENCE (philosophy, psychology, religion, and sociology). Nursing, computer graphics, and business are the strongest academically. Busi-

ness, aviation management/flight operations, and computer graphics have the largest enrollments.

ACTIVITIES: 11% of men belong to 5 local fraternities; 10% of women belong to 3 local sororities. There are 50 groups on campus, including art, cheerleading, choir, chorale, chorus, computers, dance, drama, ecology, ethnic, honors, international, musical theater, newspaper, pep band, political, professional, religious, social, social service, and student government. Popular campus events include Founder's Day Ball, Annual Gala, and Family Weekend. **Sports:** There are 10 intercollegiate sports for men and 9 for women, and 13 intramural sports for men and 13 for women. Facilities include a sports center with basketball and volleyball courts, 2 racquetball courts, a wrestling room, an athletic training room, a football field and track, baseball and softball fields, a practice football/intramural field, and a cardiovascular workout center.

SERVICES: Counseling and information services are available, as is tutoring in some subjects, such as English, math, economics, accounting, and computer literacy. There is remedial math, reading, and writing. **Library/Resources:** The library contains 164,859 volumes, 20,739 microform items, and 2,180 audio/video tapes/CDs/DVDs, and subscribes to 801 periodicals including electronic. Computerized library services include interlibrary loans, database searching, and Internet access. Special learning facilities include an art gallery and planetarium. **Physically Challenged Students:** 50% of the campus is accessible. Facilities include wheelchair ramps, elevators, special parking, specially equipped restrooms, special class scheduling, and lowered drinking fountains. **Special:** UD offers cross-registration with Loras and Clarke Colleges, internships, study abroad through the Maastricht Center for Transatlantic Studies, work-study programs, accelerated degree programs, B.A.-B.S. degrees, dual and student-designed majors, credit for life, military, and work experience, nondegree study, and pass/fail options. B.A.-M.A. programs are offered in conjunction with the university's theological seminary. Adult degree programs and an environmental field trip to Colorado and New Mexico are available. There are 8 national honor societies and 2 departmental honors programs. **Visiting:** There are regularly scheduled orientations for prospective students, including a campus tour and visits with coaches, faculty, admissions, and financial aid advisers. There are guides for informal visits, visitors may sit in on classes, and stay overnight. To schedule a visit, contact the Admission Director. **Campus Safety and Security:** Measures include 24-hour foot and vehicle patrol, self-defense education, and security escort services. There are shuttle buses, emergency telephones, lighted pathways/sidewalks, security-locked residence halls.

REQUIREMENTS: The SAT or ACT is required. Applicants must graduate from an accredited secondary school with a minimum of 4 years in English and 3 each in math, social sciences, and natural sciences. Other academic areas, such as foreign languages, business courses, computer programming, and the fine and performing arts, are also considered. The GED is accepted. Essays and recommendations are required. Auditions are required for music scholarship candidates. AP and CLEP credits are accepted. Important factors in the admissions decision are leadership record, recommendations by school officials, and extracurricular activities record. As part of our mission, the University aims to prepare students for successful, professional careers and fulfilling lives by providing them with an education that encourages their growth as whole persons. A total of 120 credits must be earned, with a minimum GPA of 2.0 (2.5 for education majors) for graduation. At UD, we combine professional preparation and the liberal arts to create programs that serve our students. **Procedure:** Freshmen are admitted fall and spring. Entrance exams should be taken before the senior year. There are deferred admissions and rolling admissions plans. Check with the school for current application deadlines. The fall 2014 application fee was $25. Applications are accepted on-line. **Transfer Students:** A minimum GPA of 2.0 is required. The applicant must be in good standing at all previously attended institutions. 30 of 120 credits required for the bachelor's degree must be completed at UD. **International Students:** The school actively recruits these students. They must take the TOEFL and the college's own test.

ADMISSIONS: 10 freshmen graduated first in their class. **Admissions Contact:** Jesse L. James, Admission Director. E-Mail: *jjames@dbq.edu* Web: *www.dbq.edu*

FINANCIAL AID: The FAFSA is required. Check with the school for current application deadlines.

UNIVERSITY OF IOWA E-3
www.uiowa.edu

Iowa City, IA 52242	(319) 335-3847
	n/av
Fax: (319) 335-1535	Email: admissions@uiowa.edu
Full-time: 9384 men, 10162 women	Faculty: 1484; I, av$
Part-time: 1410 men, 1398 women	Ph.D.s: 97%
Graduate: 4546 men, 4487 women	Student/Faculty: 16 to 1
Year: semesters, summer session	Tuition: $8079 ($27,409)
Room & Board: $9614	Freshman Class: 24097 applied, 19506 accepted, 4666 enrolled
SAT CR/M: 540/620 ACT: 25	CEEB CODE: 6681
Application Deadline: April 1	VERY COMPETITIVE

Home to more than 30,000 students and some of the nation's top scholars and researchers, the University of Iowa offers more than 200 areas of study on a vibrant and diverse campus. The University delivers the energy and opportunity of a leading university, but remains one of the smallest and most affordable universities among its peer institutions. There are 6 undergraduate schools and 10 graduate schools. In addition to regional accreditation, Iowa has baccalaureate program accreditation with AACSB, ABET, ACEJMC, ACPE, ADA, APTA, CSWE, NASM, NRPA, CACREP, ISBE, and ACEJ. The 1700-acre campus is in a small town 110 miles east of Des Moines and 220 miles west of Chicago. Including any residence halls, there are 264 buildings.

STUDENT LIFE: 55% of undergraduates are from Iowa. Others are from 50 states, 61 foreign countries, and Canada. 92% are from public schools. 65% are White; and 12% Foreign. **Male To Female Ratio:** 1.0:1. The average age of freshmen is 18; all undergraduates, 21. 14% do not continue beyond their first year; 70% remain to graduate. **Housing:** 5897 students can be accommodated in college housing, which includes coed dorms, on-campus apartments, off-campus apartments, and married student housing. In addition, there are honors houses, special-interest houses, Living-Learning Communities: Arts, Business, Education, Global Village, Healthy Living, Honors, Chemistry, Journalism, Leadership, Engineering, Pre-Med, Sustainability, and Iowa Writers. On-campus housing is available on a first-come and first-served basis. 75% of students commute. Alcohol is not permitted. All students may keep cars.

FACULTY/CLASSROOMS: 67% of faculty are male; 33% are female. Graduate students teach 20% of introductory courses. The average class size in an introductory lecture is 103; in a laboratory is 17; and in a regular course is 18.

PROGRAMS OF STUDY: Iowa confers B.A., B.S., B.A.S., B.B.A., B.F.A., B.L.S., B.M., B.S.E. and B.S.N. degrees. Master's and Doctoral degrees are also awarded. Bachelor's degrees are awarded in BIOLOGICAL SCIENCE (biochemistry, biology/biological science, and microbiology), BUSINESS (accounting, banking and finance, business administration and management, business economics, management science, marketing management, recreation and leisure services, and recreational facilities management), COMMUNICATIONS AND THE ARTS (Arabic, art, art history and appreciation, ceramic art and design, Chinese, classics, communications, comparative literature, dance, dramatic arts, drawing, English, film arts, fine arts, French, German, graphic design, Greek, Italian, Japanese, jazz, journalism, Latin, linguistics, metal/jewelry, music, painting, percussion, performing arts, photography, piano/organ, Portuguese, printmaking, Russian, sculpture, Spanish, speech/debate/rhetoric, strings, theatre arts, and voice), COMPUTER AND PHYSICAL SCIENCE (actuarial science, applied physics, astronomy, chemistry, computer science, geology, information sciences and systems, mathematics, physics, and statistics), EDUCATION (art education, athletic training, elementary education, foreign languages education, health education, mathematics education, middle school education, music education, science education, secondary education, and sports studies), ENGINEERING AND ENVIRONMENTAL DESIGN (biomedical engineering, chemical engineering, civil engineering, electrical/electronics engineering, engineering, environmental science, industrial administration/management, industrial engineering, and mechanical engineering), HEALTH PROFESSIONS (medical laboratory science, medical laboratory technology, music therapy, nuclear medical technology, nursing, pharmacy, predentistry, premedicine, preoptometry, prepharmacy, prephysical therapy, prepodiatry, preveterinary science, radiological science, recreation therapy, and speech pathology/audiology), SOCIAL SCIENCE (African American studies, American studies, anthropology, Asian/Oriental studies, classical/ancient civilization, economics, gender studies, geography, history, international studies, liberal arts/general studies, parks and recreation management, philosophy, political science/government, prelaw, psychology, religion, Russian and Slavic studies, Sanskrit and Indian studies, social science, social work, sociology, and women's studies). Business, engineering, creative writing, speech language pathology/audiology, and social psychology are the strongest academically. Business, engineering, nursing, pre-medicine, pharmacy, and psychology have the largest enrollments.

ACTIVITIES: 14% of men belong to 27 national fraternities; 19% of women belong to 23 national sororities. There are 500 groups on campus, including art, bagpipe, band, cheerleading, chess, choir, chorale, chorus, computers, dance, debate, drama, drill team, environmental, ethnic, film, forensics, gay, honors, international, jazz band, literary magazine, marching band, musical theater, newspaper, opera, orchestra, pep band, photography, political, professional, radio and TV, religious, social, social service, student government, and symphony. Popular campus events include Dance Marathon, Riverfest, RiverRun and Cultural Diversity Festival. **Sports:** There are 10 intercollegiate sports for men and 12 for women, and 36 intramural sports for men and 32 for women. Facilities include a campus recreation and wellness center which includes: a climbing wall, competitive swimming pool, lazy river, deep diving well, leisure pool, jogging track, two basketball/volleyball courts, a multi-activity gym, a cafe, locker rooms, and fitness rooms. Iowa has a 70,585-seat stadium for Hawkeye football, a 15,500-seat arena, softball and baseball stadiums, an 18-hole golf course, a pool, basketball, racquetball, and handball courts, outdoor and indoor tennis courts and running tracks, weight and fitness rooms, a 1000-seat field hockey stadium, a field campus for hiking (Lake Macbride), cross-country skiing, canoeing, and a soccer field. **Graduates:** From July 1, 2013 to June 30, 2014, 5339 bachelor's degrees were awarded. The most popular majors were business (19%), engineering (6%), and psychology (6%). 679 companies recruited on campus in 2013-2014. In an average class, 1% graduate in 3 years or less, 47% graduate in 4 years or less, 68% graduate in 5 years or less, and 70% graduate in 6 years or less.

SERVICES: Counseling and information services are available, as is tutoring in most subjects. There is a reader service for the blind, and remedial math, reading, and writing. **Library/Resources:** The 8 libraries contain 7.4 million volumes. Computerized library services include interlibrary loans, database searching, Internet access, and Wi-Fi capability. Special learning facilities include an art gallery, natural history museum, radio station, TV station, UI hospitals and clinics, the Iowa Center for the Arts, Oakdale Research Center, Macbride Raptor Project, Iowa Lakeside lab, and a driving simulator. **Physically Challenged Students:** 98% of the campus is accessible. Facilities include wheelchair ramps, elevators, special parking, specially equipped restrooms, special class scheduling, lowered drinking fountains, lowered telephones, special housing. **Special:** The University offers a wide array of internships and experience-based learning opportunities, combined degree programs, 3+3 program with College of Law, joint bachelors/master programs, 3+2 program with College of Public Health, 22 certificate programs including Aging Studies, American Indian & Native Studies, American Sign Language and Deaf Studies, Critical Cultural Competence, Disability Studies, Entrepreneurial Management, Fundraising and Philanthropy Communication, Global Health Studies, Human Rights, International Business, Latin American Studies, Leadership Studies, Medieval Studies, Museum Studies, Nonprofit Management, Performing Arts Entrepreneurship, Public Health, Risk Management and Insurance, Sustainability, Technological Entrepreneurship, Writing, and Wind Energy. There are 18 national honor societies, including Phi Beta Kappa, a freshman honors program, and 52 departmental honors programs. **Visiting:** There are regularly scheduled orientations for prospective students, including information sessions, campus tours, lunch, and visits to departments and residence halls. There are guides for informal visits and visitors may sit in on classes. To schedule a visit, contact the Admission Visitors Center at (319) 335-1569. **Campus Safety and Security:** Measures include 24-hour foot and vehicle patrol, emergency notification system, self-defense education, and security escort services. There are shuttle buses, emergency telephones, lighted pathways/sidewalks, controlled access to dorms/residences, code blue phones, defense courses, and WhistleSAFE program.

REQUIREMENTS: The SAT or ACT is required. Applicants must have completed 4 years of high school English, 3 each of social studies, science, and math (including 2 years of algebra and 1 of geometry), and 2 years of a single world language. Music and dance students must audition. AP and CLEP credits are accepted.To graduate, students must complete at least 120 semester hours, with a GPA of 2.0. The general education program includes rhetoric, historical perspectives, world language, quantitative and formal reasoning, international and global issues, values, society and diversity, and natural and social sciences. **Procedure:** Freshmen are admitted to all sessions. Entrance exams should be taken in the junior year. There are deferred admissions and rolling admissions plans. Applications should be filed by April 1 for fall entry; November 15 for spring entry; and April 1 for summer entry, along with a $40 fee. Notification is sent on a rolling basis. Applications are accepted on-line. **Transfer Students:** 1172 transfer students enrolled in 2013-2014. For the College of Liberal Arts, a GPA of at least 2.5 is required for applicants with 24 or more semester hours of credit. Those with fewer credits are considered on the same criteria as freshmen. Other colleges have different requirements. 30 of 120 credits required for the bachelor's degree must be completed at Iowa. **International Students:** There are 2117 international students enrolled. The school actively recruits these students. They must take the TOEFL with a minimum score of 530 on the paper-based TOEFL (PBT) or 80 on the Internet-based version (iBT), International students must submit TOEFL for admission purposes and may be asked to take a proficiency exam after arriving on campus.

ADMISSIONS: 81% of the 2014-2015 applicants were accepted. The SAT scores for the 2014-2015 freshman class were: Critical Reading--35% below 500, 31% between 500 and 599, 25% between 600 and 699, and 9% between 700 and 800; Math--14% below 500, 26% between 500 and 599, 34% between 600 and 699, and 26% between 700 and 800. The ACT scores were 10% below 21, 23% between 21 and 23, 29% between 24 and 26, 17% between 27 and 28, and 21% above 28. 48% of the current freshmen were in the top fifth of their class; 80% were in the top two fifths. There were 26 National Merit finalists. 56 freshmen graduated first in their class. **Admissions Contact:** E-Mail: *admissions@uiowa.edu* Web: *www.uiowa.edu*

FINANCIAL AID: In 2014-2015, 80% of all full-time freshmen and 80% of continuing full-time students received some form of financial aid. 46% of all full-time freshmen and 46% of continuing full-time students received need-based aid. The average freshman award was $12,603. Need-based scholarships or need-based grants averaged $6,824 ($17,000 maximum); need-based self-help aid (loans and jobs) averaged $5,857 ($12,000 maximum); non-need-based athletic scholarships averaged $20,455 ($26,000 maximum); and other non-need-based awards and non-need-based scholarships averaged $1,800 ($12,500 maximum). 80% of undergraduate students work part-time. Average annual earnings from campus work are $5220. The average financial indebtedness of the 2014 graduate was $26,296. The FAFSA and the college's own financial statement are required. Check with the school for current application deadlines.

UNIVERSITY OF NORTHERN IOWA D-2
www.uni.edu

Cedar Falls, IA 50614	(319) 273-2281
	(800) 772-2037
Fax: (319) 273-2885	Email: admissions@uni.edu
Full-time: 3895 men, 5227 women	Faculty: 490; IIA, av$
Part-time: 539 men, 481 women	Ph.D.s: 75%
Graduate: 549 men, 1237 women	Student/Faculty: 16 to 1
Year: semesters, summer session	Tuition: $7749 ($17,647)
Room & Board: $8046	Freshman Class: 3354 applied, 4069 accepted, 1797 enrolled
ACT: 23	CEEB CODE: 6307
Application Deadline: August 15	COMPETITIVE

The University of Northern Iowa, established in 1876, is a public institution offering degree programs in business administration, education, humanities, arts, sciences, and social and behavioral sciences. There are 4 undergraduate schools and 1 graduate school. In addition to regional accreditation, UNI has baccalaureate program accreditation with AACSB, ABET, CSWE, NASM, NRPA, ACS, CAAHEP, CACREP, ASHA, NAIT, NCFR, and NASP. The 910-acre campus is in a small town in Cedar Falls, Iowa, about 60 miles northwest of Cedar Rapids. Including any residence halls, there are 64 buildings.

STUDENT LIFE: 89% of undergraduates are from Iowa. Others are from 46 states, 64 foreign countries, and Canada. 93% are from public schools. 84% are White. **Male To Female Ratio:** 1.4:1. The average age of freshmen is 18; all undergraduates, 21. 15% do not continue beyond their first year; 67% remain to graduate. **Housing:** 5198 students can be accommodated in college housing, which includes single-sex and coed dorms, on-campus apartments, and married student housing. In addition, there are honors houses and special-interest houses. On-campus housing is guaranteed for all 4 years, is available on a first-come, first-served basis, and is available on a lottery system for upperclassmen. 60% of students commute. All students may keep cars.

FACULTY/CLASSROOMS: 48% of faculty are male; 52% are female. 85% teach undergraduates. Graduate students teach 4% of introductory courses. The average class size in an introductory lecture is 29; in a laboratory is 20; and in a regular course is 21.

PROGRAMS OF STUDY: UNI confers B.A., B.S., B.A.T., B.F.A., B.L.S. and B.Mus. degrees. Master's and Doctoral degrees are also awarded. Bachelor's degrees are awarded in BIOLOGICAL SCIENCE (biochemistry, bioinformatics, biology/biological science, biotechnology, microbiology, and nutrition), BUSINESS (accounting, banking and finance, management information systems, management science, marketing/retailing/merchandising, real estate, and recreation and leisure services), COMMUNICATIONS AND THE ARTS (art history and appreciation, broadcasting, communications, dramatic arts, English, fine arts, graphic design, music, music performance, music theory and composition, public relations, Spanish, speech/debate/rhetoric, studio art, and theater design), COMPUTER AND PHYSICAL SCIENCE (chemistry, computer management, computer science, earth science, geology, information sciences and systems, mathematics, physics, and science), EDUCATION (art education, athletic training, business education, early childhood education, elementary education, foreign languages education, health education, middle school education, music education, physical education, science education, special education, teaching English as a second/foreign language (TESOL/TEFOL), and technical education), ENGINEERING AND ENVIRONMENTAL DESIGN (computer technology, construction management, electromechanical technology, energy management technology, environmental science, industrial engineering technology, and manufacturing technology), HEALTH PROFESSIONS (speech pathology/audiology), SOCIAL SCIENCE (anthropology, clothing and textiles management/production/services, criminology, economics, family and community services, geography, gerontology, history, humanities, liberal arts/general studies, philosophy, political science/government, psychology, public administration, religion, Russian and Slavic studies, social science, social work, and sociology). Teaching majors, biology, communication, and accounting are the strongest academically. Elementary education, communication and accounting have the largest enrollments.

ACTIVITIES: 4% of men belong to 4 national fraternities; 6% of women belong to 4 national sororities. There are 249 groups on campus, including University Ambassadors, alumni, art, band, cheerleading, chess, choir, chorale, chorus, communications, computers, dance, debate, drama, drill team, environmental, ethnic, film, forensics, gay, honors, international, jazz band, literary magazine, marching band, musical theater, newspaper, opera, orchestra, pep band, political, professional, radio and TV, religious, social, social service, student government, and symphony. Popular campus events include Welcome Week, Relay for Life, Dance Marathon and Homecoming. **Sports:** There are 7 intercollegiate sports for men and 10 for women, and 23 intramural sports for men and 25 for women. Facilities include a domed stadium, field house, basketball facility, wellness and recreation center with an 8-lane swimming pool, 6 handball/racquetball courts, climbing wall, weight rooms, basketball courts, fitness center in the union, and exercise rooms in several of the residence halls on campus. **Graduates:** From July 1, 2013 to June 30, 2014, 2357 bachelor's degrees were awarded. The most popular majors were elementary education (12%), communication (7%), and biology (6%). 394 companies recruited on campus in 2013-2014. In an average class, 2% graduate in 3 years or less, 38% graduate in 4 years or less, 61% graduate in 5 years or less, and 64% graduate in 6 years or less. Of the 2013 graduating class, 15% were enrolled in graduate school within 6 months of graduation, and 78% were employed.

SERVICES: Counseling and information services are available, as is tutoring in some subjects, liberal arts core and major courses in science, math, humanities, biology, chemistry, physics, earth science, economics, calculus, statistics, research methods, music, management, finance, accounting, plus writing and reading assistance. There is a reader service for the blind, remedial math, reading, and writing. Supplemental Instruction in Cal.I &II, Humanities, Stats., A&P I, Org. Chem.; College Success Workshops; Supportive Seminars in Humanities. **Library/Resources:** The library contains 946,670 volumes, 1.1 million microform items, 30,359 audio/video tapes/CDs/DVDs, and subscribes to 61,043 periodicals including electronic. Computerized library services include interlibrary loans, database searching, Internet access, and Wi-Fi capability. Special learning facilities include an art gallery, natural history museum, planetarium, radio station, the university sponsors the Native Roadside Vegetation Center, the Iowa Center for Immigrant Leadership and Integration, a waste reduction center, a performing arts center, and several research institutes. **Physically Challenged Students:** 95% of the campus is accessible. Facilities include wheelchair ramps, elevators, special parking, specially equipped restrooms, special class scheduling, lowered drinking fountains, lowered telephones, and special housing. **Special:** Internships and co-op programs are offered through all colleges of the university. Students may study abroad in 28 countries and may participate in a Washington semester. Interdisciplinary majors include safety education, chemistry/marketing, design/human environment, and natural history interpretation. Cross-registration, work-study programs, a general studies degree, dual and student-designed majors, nondegree study, and pass/fail options are also available. There are 25 national honor societies and a freshman honors program. **Visiting:** There are regularly scheduled orientations for prospective students, including a student panel, lunch, a campus tour, and presentations by admissions, financial aid, housing, and academic departments. There are guides for informal visits and visitors may sit in on classes. To schedule a visit, contact Jenny Connolly at admissions@uni.edu. **Campus Safety and Security:** Measures include 24-hour foot and vehicle patrol, emergency notification system, self-defense education, and security escort services. There are shuttle buses, emergency telephones, lighted pathways/sidewalks, and controlled access to dorms/residences.

REQUIREMENTS: The ACT is required. A regents admissions index (RAI) score of 245 guarantees admission. High school requirements include 4 years of English, 3 each of math, social studies, and science, and 2 or more of electives, which may include foreign language and fine arts. The GED, with a minimum standard score average of 57, and no single score below 500, is accepted. AP and CLEP credits are accepted. Important factors in the admissions decision are advanced placement or honors courses, evidence of special talent, and recommendations by school officials. Degree requirements include completion of 120 to 130 credits, with 30 to 60 in the major. Liberal arts majors must maintain a minimum GPA of 2.0 (2.5 for business, communication, and education majors). Liberal arts core requirements include 11 hours of civilizations and cultures, 9 each of natural science/technology, social science, and communication, 6 of arts/literature/philosophy/religion, and 3 of personal wellness. Students must meet requirements in foreign language and complete a capstone course. Education students must complete a 32-credit professional sequence. **Procedure:** Freshmen are admitted to all sessions. Entrance exams should be taken by October of the senior year. There is a rolling admissions plan. Applications should be filed by August 15 for fall entry; December 31 for spring entry; and May 15 for summer entry, along with a $40 fee. Applications are accepted on-line. **Transfer Students:** 904 transfer students enrolled in 2013-2014. Applicants must have a minimum GPA of 2.0 to 2.5, depending on the number

of credits they wish to transfer. A small number of applicants may be admitted on academic probation. 32 of 120 credits required for the bachelor's degree must be completed at UNI. **International Students:** There are 338 international students enrolled. The school actively recruits these students. They must take the TOEFL with a minimum score of 550 on the paper-based TOEFL (PBT) or 79 on the Internet-based version (iBT) or take the MELAB, the Comprehensive English Language Test, and the college's own test.

ADMISSIONS: The ACT scores were 30% below 21, 33% between 21 and 23, 22% between 24 and 26, 8% between 27 and 28, and 7% above 28. 36% of the current freshmen were in the top fifth of their class; 71% were in the top two fifths. 68 freshmen graduated first in their class. **Admissions Contact:** Scott Ketelsen, Interim Director of Admissions. E-Mail: *admissions@uni.edu* Web: *www.uni.edu*

FINANCIAL AID: In 2014-2015, 91% of all full-time freshmen and 90% of continuing full-time students received some form of financial aid. 57% of all full-time freshmen and 49% of continuing full-time students received need-based aid. The average freshman award was $11,620. Need-based scholarships or need-based grants averaged $4,513 ($9,486 maximum); need-based self-help aid (loans and jobs) averaged $2,742 ($5,500 maximum); non-need-based athletic scholarships averaged $6,868 ($25,001 maximum); and other non-need-based awards and non-need-based scholarships averaged $1,561 ($22,394 maximum). 33% of undergraduate students work part-time. Average annual earnings from campus work are $2243. The average financial indebtedness of the 2014 graduate was $23,163. The FAFSA is required. The deadline for filing freshman financial aid applications for fall entry is open.

UPPER IOWA UNIVERSITY *(The complete profile is made available exclusively on our website, www.barronspac.com)*

WARTBURG COLLEGE   **D-2**
www.wartburg.edu

Waverly, IA 50677	**(319) 352-8264**
	(800) 772-2085
Fax: (319) 352-8579	**Email:** admissions@wartburg.edu
Full-time: 788 men, 885 women	**Faculty:** n/av
Part-time: 34 men, 40 women	**Ph.D.s:** 83%
Graduate: n/av	**Student/Faculty:** 11 to 1
Year: other, summer session	**Tuition:** $32,740
Room & Board: $8315	**Freshman Class:** n/av
SAT or ACT: required	**CEEB CODE:** 6926
Application Deadline: n/av	**VERY COMPETITIVE**

Wartburg College is a selective liberal arts college of the ELCA, internationally recognized for community engagement. Wartburg is dedicated to challenging and nurturing students for lives of leadership and service as a spirited expression of their faith and learning. Opportunities for service-learning, leadership, undergraduate research, global and multicultural studies, and participation in co-curricular activities enrich the academic experience. Wartburg helps students discover their life's purpose through meaning and vocal discernment. In addition to regional accreditation, Wartburg has baccalaureate program accreditation with CSWE, NASM, and NCATE. The 118-acre campus is in a small town 15 miles north of Waterloo/Cedar Falls, Iowa. Including any residence halls, there are 37 buildings.

STUDENT LIFE: 68% of undergraduates are from Iowa. Others are from 29 states, 53 foreign countries, and Canada. 84% are White. 70% are Protestant; 22% Catholic. **Male To Female Ratio:** 1.1:1. The average age of freshmen is 18; all undergraduates, 20. 24% do not continue beyond their first year; 65% remain to graduate. **Housing:** 1443 students can be accommodated in college housing, which includes single-sex and coed dorms and on-campus apartments. In addition, there are honors houses, language houses, and special-interest houses. On-campus housing is guaranteed for all 4 years. 83% of students live on campus; of those, 75% remain on campus on weekends. All students may keep cars.

FACULTY/CLASSROOMS: 52% of faculty are male; 48% are female. All teach undergraduates, and 42% do research. No introductory courses are taught by graduate students. The average class size in a laboratory is 20 and in a regular course is 20.

PROGRAMS OF STUDY: Wartburg confers B.A., B.A.A., B.A.S., B.M. and B.M.E. degrees. Bachelor's degrees are awarded in BIOLOGICAL SCIENCE (biochemistry and biology/biological science), BUSINESS (accounting, banking and finance, business administration and management, international business management, marketing/retailing/merchandising, and recreation and leisure services), COMMUNICATIONS AND THE ARTS (applied music, art, arts administration/management, broadcasting, communications, creative writing, dramatic arts, English, French, German, graphic design, journalism, music, music performance, music theory and composition, public relations, and Spanish), COMPUTER AND PHYSICAL SCIENCE (chemistry, computer science, information sciences and systems, mathematics, and physics), EDUCATION (art education, elementary education, English education, foreign languages education, journalism education, mathematics education, music education, physical education, science education, secondary education, and social studies education), ENGINEERING AND ENVIRONMENTAL DESIGN (engineering and applied science), HEALTH PROFESSIONS (medical laboratory technology, music therapy, and occupational therapy), SOCIAL SCIENCE (economics, French studies, German area studies, history, international relations, peace studies, philosophy, political science/government, psychology, religion, religious music, social work, and sociology). Biology, music, mathematics, chemistry, biochemistry, and engineering are the strongest academically. Business, biology and communication arts have the largest enrollments.

ACTIVITIES: There are no fraternities or sororities. There are 100 groups on campus, including art, band, cheerleading, chess, choir, chorale, chorus, communications, computers, dance, debate, drama, drum and bugle corps, environmental, ethnic, forensics, gay, honors, international, jazz band, literary magazine, musical theater, newspaper, opera, orchestra, pep band, political, professional, radio and TV, religious, social, social service, student government, and symphony. Popular campus events include Artist Series, Convocations, Family Weekend, Homecoming, Culture Week, Martin Luther King Week and Outfly. **Sports:** There are 10 intercollegiate sports for men and 9 for women, and 8 intramural sports for men and 8 for women. Facilities include a 200,000 square-foot sports and wellness center that includes an indoor pool, 200-meter track, racquetball courts, batting cages, golf hitting area, tennis/badminton/volleyball courts, weight rooms, a fitness area, and an aerobics and wrestling room, a 5000-seat stadium with a football field and all-weather track, a 2000-seat gym, a lighted baseball park, football, soccer, and softball fields, and outdoor tennis courts. **Graduates:** From July 1, 2013 to June 30, 2014, 402 bachelor's degrees were awarded. The most popular majors were biology (15%), business administration (13%), and communication arts (9%). In an average class, 3% graduate in 3 years or less, 64% graduate in 4 years or less, 65% graduate in 5 years or less. Of the 2013 graduating class, 24% were enrolled in graduate school within 6 months of graduation, and 64% were employed.

SERVICES: Counseling and information services are available, as is tutoring in most subjects. There is remedial math. There is a comprehensive academic support center, a supplemental instruction program, and assistance with mathematics, and speech writing and delivery. A writing and reading center is also available. Academic support services are also delivered in the residence halls. **Library/Resources:** The library contains 367,895 volumes, 8,611 microform items, 5,983 audio/video tapes/CDs/DVDs, and subscribes to 83,318 periodicals including electronic. Computerized library services include interlibrary loans, database searching, Internet access, and Wi-Fi capability. Special learning facilities include an art gallery, radio station, TV station, a business center, classroom technology center, fine arts center, journalism lab, symbolic computation lab, music computer lab, Center for Community Engagement, Institute for Leadership Education, 6 acres of native grasses and prairie plants, and more than 100 acres of native timber used for field trips and research. **Physically Challenged Students:** 85% of the campus is accessible. Facilities include wheelchair ramps, elevators, special parking, specially equipped restrooms, special class scheduling, lowered drinking fountains, lowered telephones, and special housing. **Special:** Special academic programs at Wartburg include those in leadership education and global and multicultural studies. Internships are available in all majors and there are internship programs in Denver, Washington, D.C., and abroad. Study abroad in 65 countries, on and off campus work-study, dual majors in any combination, and individualized majors are possible. 3-1 degrees are possible in clinical laboratory science and occupational therapy, as well as 3-1 and 2-2 degrees in nursing. A deferred admit program with the University of Iowa College of Dentistry is offered, as is an array of experiential learning opportunities. There are 11 national honor societies and a freshman honors program. **Visiting:** There are regularly scheduled orientations for prospective students, including an introduction to academic and student life conducted by administrators, faculty, and students. There are guides for informal visits, visitors may sit in on classes, and stay overnight. To schedule a visit, contact the Admissions Office. **Campus Safety and Security:** Measures include 24-hour foot and vehicle patrol, emergency notification system, and security escort services. There are emergency telephones, lighted pathways/sidewalks, controlled access to dorms/residences, 24-hour patrol, and student escort service.

REQUIREMENTS: The SAT or ACT is required, with a minimum score of 910 on the SAT or 19 on the ACT expected. Candidates for admission must be graduates of an accredited secondary school, having completed 4 years of English, 3 each of math and science, 2 each of social studies and foreign language, and 1 of introduction to computers. The GED is accepted, with an average of 50 or above. A GPA of 2.2 is required. AP and CLEP credits are accepted. Important factors in the admissions decision are advanced placement or honors courses, recommendations by school officials, and leadership record. Degree requirements include a minimum cumulative and major GPA of 2.0 and completion of 36 course credits (128 semester hours), including 4 May term course credits. All students must complete the Wartburg Plan of Essential Education, an integrative and interdisciplinary program of study, based on course work in thinking strategies, reasoning skills, faith and reflection, health and wellness, and literacy in writing, diversity, and a foreign langauage. Students must also demonstrate proficiency in information systems and in oral communication and must complete a Capstone course. Inquiry Studies 101/201 are required of all students. **Procedure:** Freshmen are admitted fall and winter. Entrance exams should be taken before the senior year. There are early admissions and rolling admissions plans. Check with the school for current application deadlines. Notification is sent on a rolling basis. Applications are accepted on-line. **Transfer Students:** Applicants must have earned an associate degree or have maintained a minimum GPA of 2.0 in previous college work for 1 year. The ACT or the SAT must be taken; the minimum acceptable ACT score is 19. Students must submit official transcripts from all colleges attended. 7 of 36 credits required for the bachelor's degree must be completed at Wartburg. **International Students:** There are 141 international students enrolled. The school actively recruits these students. They must take the TOEFL with a minimum score of 480 on the paper-based TOEFL (PBT) or 55 on the Internet-based version (iBT). SAT or ACT scores are not required but are useful in admissions decisions and for placement.

ADMISSIONS: There was 1 National Merit finalist. 32 freshmen graduated first in their class. **Admissions Contact:** Todd Coleman, Assistant Vice President for Admissions. E-Mail: *admissions@wartburg.edu* Web: *www.wartburg.edu*

FINANCIAL AID: In 2014-2015, 99% of all full-time freshmen and 99% of continuing full-time students received some form of financial aid. 91% of all full-time freshmen and 88% of continuing full-time students received need-based aid. The average freshman award was $28,965. Need-based scholarships or need-based grants averaged $9,527 ($29,050 maximum); need-based self-help aid (loans and jobs) averaged $5,442 ($8,000 maximum); and other non-need-based awards and non-need-based scholarships averaged $20,676 ($43,707 maximum). 60% of undergraduate students work part-time. Average annual earnings from campus work are $2500. The average financial indebtedness of the 2014 graduate was $36,567. The FAFSA is required. The priority date for freshman financial aid applications for fall entry is March 1.

WILLIAM PENN UNIVERSITY   D-3
www.wmpenn.edu

Oskaloosa, IA 52577   (641) 673-1012
                                            (800) 779-7366
Fax: (641) 673-2113   Email: admissions@wmpenn.edu
Full-time: 900 men, 750 women   Faculty: n/av
Part-time: 70 men, 115 women   Ph.D.s: n/av
Graduate: 40 men, 45 women   Student/Faculty: n/av
Year: varies, summer session   Tuition: $20,000
Room & Board: $6000   Freshman Class: n/av
ACT: required   CEEB CODE: 6943
Application Deadline: open   **COMPETITIVE**

William Penn University, founded in 1873, is a private liberal arts institution affiliated with the Society of Friends (Quakers). The figures in the above capsule and in this profile are approximate. There are 2 undergraduate schools and 1 graduate school. In addition to regional accreditation, William Penn has baccalaureate program accreditation with NCATE. The 53-acre campus is in a rural area 58 miles southeast of Des Moines. Including any residence halls, there are 13 buildings.

STUDENT LIFE: 73% of undergraduates are from Iowa. Others are from 41 states, 10 foreign countries, and Canada. 90% are from public schools. 83% are White. 44% are Protestant; 39% claim no religious affiliation; 13% Catholic. **Male To Female Ratio:** 0.9:1. The average age of freshmen is 19; all undergraduates, 25. 35% do not continue beyond their first year; 35% remain to graduate. **Housing:** 500 students can be accommodated in college housing, which includes single-sex and coed dorms, on-campus apartments, and married student housing. On-campus housing is guaranteed for all 4 years. 55% of students commute. Alcohol is not permitted. All students may keep cars.

FACULTY/CLASSROOMS: 57% of faculty are male; 43% are female. All teach undergraduates. No introductory courses are taught by graduate students. The average class size in an introductory lecture is 25.

PROGRAMS OF STUDY: William Penn confers B.A., B.S., and B.S.N. degrees. Associate and master's degrees are also awarded. Bachelor's degrees are awarded in BIOLOGICAL SCIENCE (biology/biological science and biotechnology), BUSINESS (accounting, business administration and management, recreation and leisure services, and sports management), COMMUNICATIONS AND THE ARTS (communications, digital communications, English, fine arts, journalism, and public relations), COMPUTER AND PHYSICAL SCIENCE (computer science), EDUCATION (elementary education, health education, physical education, science education, secondary education, and special education), ENGINEERING AND ENVIRONMENTAL DESIGN (environmental science, industrial administration/management, and industrial engineering technology), SOCIAL SCIENCE (criminology, history, human services, political science/government, psychology, and sociology). Elementary and secondary education, industrial technology, and business are the strongest academically. Education and business has the largest enrollments.

ACTIVITIES: 5% of men belong to 2 local fraternities; 5% of women belong to 2 local and 1 national sororities. There are 25 groups on campus, including art, band, cheerleading, choir, chorale, chorus, computers, dance, drama, drum and bugle corps, ethnic, honors, international, jazz band, literary magazine, marching band, musical theater, newspaper, pep band, photography, political, professional, radio and TV, religious, social, social service, student government, and yearbook. Popular campus events include Multicultural Day and Campus Beautification Day. **Sports:** There are 8 intercollegiate sports for men and 7 for women, and 6 intramural sports for men and 6 for women. Facilities include a gym with 2 regulation-size basketball courts and wrestling and weight training rooms, baseball and softball fields, 3 tennis courts, and football and soccer practice fields. Penn Activity Center houses a 300 meter walking/jogging track, 2 full-sized basketball/volleyball courts, an aerobic fitness area, and 40 yards of artificial turf. **Graduates:** From July 1, 2013 to June 30, 2014, 220 bachelor's degrees were awarded. The most popular majors were business management (61%), elementary education (9%), and psychology (5%). 160 companies recruited on campus in 2013-2014. In an average class, 56% graduate in 4 years or less, 90% graduate in 5 years or less, and 98% graduate in 6 years or less. Of the 2013 graduating class, 15% were enrolled in graduate school within 6 months of graduation, and 75% were employed.

SERVICES: Counseling and information services are available, as is tutoring in most subjects. There is remedial math, reading, and writing. **Library/Resources:** The library contains 64,974 volumes, 1,733 audio/video tapes/CDs/DVDs, and subscribes to 31,974 periodicals including electronic. Computerized library services include interlibrary loans, database searching, Internet access, and Wi-Fi capability. Special learning facilities include an art gallery, radio station, and Mideast collection. **Physically Challenged Students:** 70% of the campus is accessible. Facilities include wheelchair ramps, elevators, special parking, specially equipped restrooms, special class scheduling, and lowered drinking fountains. **Special:** William Penn offers internships, work-study programs with local businesses, dual majors, nondegree study, pass/fail options, and 3-2 engineering degree programs with Iowa State and Washington Universities. Preprofessional studies, driver and safety education, and endorsements in numerous secondary education subjects are also offered. There are 2 national honor societies including Phi Beta Kappa. **Visiting:** There are regularly scheduled orientations for prospective students, including a 1-day visit comprised of meetings with faculty, student services, financial aid, personnel, and people who share students' interests. There are guides for informal visits, visitors may sit in on classes, and stay overnight. To schedule a visit, contact the Visitor Coordinator. **Campus Safety and Security:** Measures include 24-hour foot and vehicle patrol, emergency notification system, and self-defense education. There are emergency telephones, lighted pathways/sidewalks, and controlled access to dorms/residences.

REQUIREMENTS: The ACT is required. Applicants must be graduates of an accredited secondary school and should have completed 15 high school units. The GED is accepted. ACT is required of traditional undergraduates only. Our college for working adults does not require ACT scores. AP and CLEP credits are accepted. Important factors in the admissions decision are evidence of special talent, extracurricular activities record, and leadership record.To graduate, students must complete 124 hours, with 30 to 75 hours in the major. A GPA of 2.0 overall and in major and minor courses is required. Leadership core requirements total 47 hours in English/communications, math, natural science, social science, religion, fine arts, and philosophy. **Procedure:** Freshmen are admitted to all sessions. Entrance exams should be taken late in the junior year or early in the senior year. There are early admissions, deferred admissions, and rolling admissions plans. Application deadlines are open. Application fee is $20. Applications are accepted on-line. **Transfer Students:** 189 transfer students enrolled in 2013-2014. Applicants must be in good standing at their previous institution and submit official transcripts from previously attended schools. 30 of 124 credits required for the bachelor's degree must be completed at William Penn. **International Students:** There are 20 international students enrolled. The school actively recruits these students. They must take the TOEFL with a minimum score of 500 on the paper-based TOEFL (PBT).

ADMISSIONS: 2 freshmen graduated first in their class. **Admissions Contact:** Kerra Strong, Director of Admissions. E-Mail: *admissions@wmpenn.edu* Web: *www.wmpenn.edu*

FINANCIAL AID: In 2014-2015, 99% of all full-time freshmen and continuing full-time students received some form of financial aid. 96% of all full-time freshmen and 96% of continuing full-time students received need-based aid. The average freshman award was $18,373. 70% of undergraduate students work part-time. Average annual earnings from campus work are $1600. The average financial indebtedness of the 2014 graduate was $18,600. The FAFSA is required. Check with the school for current application deadlines.

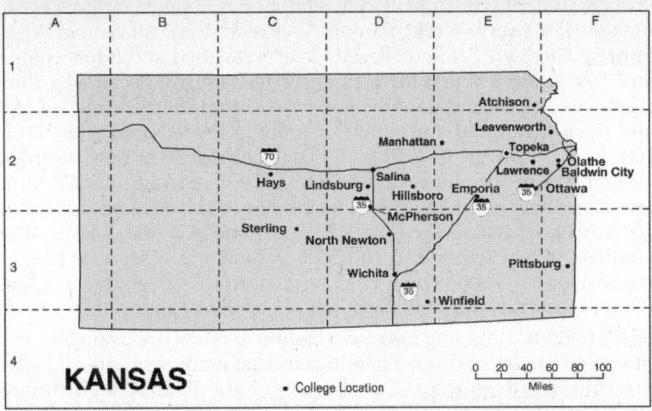

KANSAS

A B C D E F

Atchison

Leavenworth

Manhattan   Topeka
Hays   Lindsburg   Salina   Lawrence   Olathe
                Baldwin City
        Hillsboro   Emporia   Ottawa
            McPherson
Sterling   North Newton

            Wichita   Pittsburg

                Winfield

0 20 40 60 80 100
Miles

● College Location

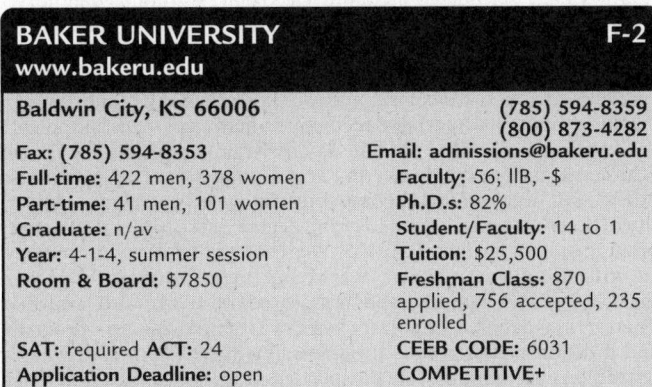

BAKER UNIVERSITY   F-2
www.bakeru.edu

Baldwin City, KS 66006   (785) 594-8359
                            (800) 873-4282

Fax: (785) 594-8353   Email: admissions@bakeru.edu
Full-time: 422 men, 378 women   Faculty: 56; IIB, -$
Part-time: 41 men, 101 women   Ph.D.s: 82%
Graduate: n/av   Student/Faculty: 14 to 1
Year: 4-1-4, summer session   Tuition: $25,500
Room & Board: $7850   Freshman Class: 870
                        applied, 756 accepted, 235
                        enrolled
SAT: required ACT: 24   CEEB CODE: 6031
Application Deadline: open   COMPETITIVE+

Baker University, founded in 1858, is a private liberal arts institution affiliated with the United Methodist Church. There are 4 undergraduate schools and 2 graduate schools. In addition to regional accreditation, Baker has baccalaureate program accreditation with ACBSP, NASM, NCATE, and CCNE. The 26-acre campus is in a rural area 50 miles southwest of Kansas City and 15 miles south of Lawrence. Including any residence halls, there are 26 buildings.

STUDENT LIFE: 74% of undergraduates are from Kansas. Others are from 24 states, 8 foreign countries, and Canada. 95% are from public schools. 76% are White. **Male To Female Ratio:** 1.0:1. The average age of freshmen is 19; all undergraduates, 20. 24% do not continue beyond their first year; 58% remain to graduate. **Housing:** 588 students can be accommodated in college housing, which includes single-sex and coed dorms and on-campus apartments. In addition, there are fraternity houses and sorority houses. On-campus housing is guaranteed for all 4 years. 74% of students live on campus; of those, 50% remain on campus on weekends. Alcohol is not permitted. All students may keep cars.

FACULTY/CLASSROOMS: 51% of faculty are male; 49% are female. All teach undergraduates. No introductory courses are taught by graduate students. The average class size in an introductory lecture is 25; in a laboratory is 15; and in a regular course is 16.

PROGRAMS OF STUDY: Baker confers B.A., B.M.E. and B.S. degrees. Bachelor's degrees are awarded in BIOLOGICAL SCIENCE (biology/biological science), BUSINESS (accounting, business administration and management, international business management, and sports management), COMMUNICATIONS AND THE ARTS (art history and appreciation, communications, dramatic arts, English, French, German, media arts, music, Spanish, and studio art), COMPUTER AND PHYSICAL SCIENCE (chemistry, computer science, mathematics, and physics), EDUCATION (art education, elementary education, English education, mathematics education, music education, physical education, science education, and secondary education), HEALTH PROFESSIONS (exercise science and nursing), SOCIAL SCIENCE (economics, history, international studies, philosophy, psychology, religion, and sociology). Business, exercise science, and elementary education have the largest enrollments.

ACTIVITIES: 27% of men belong to 1 local and 4 national fraterni-

ties; 42% of women belong to 3 national sororities. There are 55 groups on campus, including art, band, cheerleading, choir, chorale, chorus, communications, computers, dance, drama, drill team, environmental, ethnic, gay, honors, international, jazz band, literary magazine, newspaper, orchestra, pep band, photography, professional, radio and TV, religious, social, social service, and student government. Popular campus events include Maple Leaf Festival, International Education Week and Springfest Week. **Sports:** There are 10 intercollegiate sports for men and 10 for women, and 5 intramural sports for men and 5 for women. Facilities include a 3,500-seat football/track stadium, a 2,500-seat gym, a 500-seat baseball stadium, practice and varsity fields for football, track, soccer, softball and baseball, 2 basketball courts, 4 racquetball courts, 4 tennis courts, a jogging track, a wellness facility, and a weight room. **Graduates:** From July 1, 2013 to June 30, 2014, 185 bachelor's degrees were awarded. The most popular majors were business (16%), exercise science (9%), and elematry education (8%). In an average class, 2% graduate in 3 years or less, 40% graduate in 4 years or less, 56% graduate in 5 years or less, and 58% graduate in 6 years or less.

SERVICES: Counseling and information services are available, as is tutoring in most subjects. There is a reader service for the blind, and remedial math, reading, and writing. **Library/Resources:** The library contains 106,549 volumes, 160,000 microform items, 6,366 audio/video tapes/CDs/DVDs, and subscribes to 160 periodicals including electronic. Computerized library services include interlibrary loans, database searching, and Internet access. Special learning facilities include an art gallery, natural history museum, radio station, TV station, a greenhouse, and wetlands. **Physically Challenged Students:** 90% of the campus is accessible. Facilities include wheelchair ramps, elevators, special parking, specially equipped restrooms, special class scheduling, lowered drinking fountains, lowered telephones, and special housing. **Special:** Internships are encouraged for students in most majors. Baker also offers study abroad, work-study, B.A.-B.S. degrees, accelerated degrees, and dual and student-designed majors. A 3-2 engineering degree may be earned in conjunction with Washington University in St. Louis, the University of Kansas, and University of Missouri in Kansas City. Interdisciplinary majors are offered in international studies. There are 21 national honor societies, a freshman honors program, and 1 departmental honors program. **Visiting:** There are regularly scheduled orientations for prospective students, including Preview Days scheduled for both freshman and transfers in spring and fall. Individual visits are scheduled daily. There are guides for informal visits, visitors may sit in on classes, and stay overnight. To schedule a visit, contact the Admissions Office. **Campus Safety and Security:** Measures include 24-hour foot and vehicle patrol, emergency notification system, and security escort services. There are lighted pathways/sidewalks.

REQUIREMENTS: The SAT or ACT is required. Candidates for admission must graduate from an accredited secondary school or earn a GED. High school course work in English, a foreign language, social studies, math, and natural science is recommended. Applications of students not meeting these requirements will be reviewed, and students may be invited for an on-campus interview, as necessary. AP and CLEP credits are accepted.To graduate, all students must complete 128 credit hours, including 24 to 36 hours in the major, a cornerstone liberal arts core, 6 core liberal studies courses and 4 linked courses in disciplines, and a minimal level of proficiency in written and oral communication and math. A minimum GPA of 2.0 is required. **Procedure:** Freshmen are admitted to all sessions. Entrance exams should be taken in the fall of the senior year. There is a rolling admissions plan. Application deadlines are open. Applications are accepted on-line. **Transfer Students:** 67 transfer students enrolled in 2013-2014. Transfer applicants must supply a recommendation form, available from the Baker Admissions Office. The ACT or the SAT score, official high school transcript, and official transcripts of all college courses are required. The minimum GPA is 2.3. 31 of 132 credits required for the bachelor's degree must be completed at Baker. **International Students:** There are 12 international students enrolled. The school actively recruits these students. They must take the TOEFL with a minimum score of 525 on the paper-based TOEFL (PBT) or 69 on the Internet-based version (iBT). They must also take the SAT or ACT.

ADMISSIONS: 87% of the 2014-2015 applicants were accepted. The ACT scores were 24% below 21, 26% between 21 and 23, 31% between 24 and 26, 9% between 27 and 28, and 11% above 28. 29% of the current freshmen were in the top fifth of their class; 64% were in the top two fifths. 8 freshmen graduated first in their class. **Admissions Contact:** Kevin Kropf, Director of Enrollemtn Management. E-Mail: *admissions@bakeru.edu* Web: *www.bakeru.edu*

FINANCIAL AID: The FAFSA and the college's own financial statement are required. The priority date for freshman financial aid applications for fall entry is March 1. The deadline for filing freshman financial aid applications for fall entry is rolling.

BENEDICTINE COLLEGE E-1
www.benedictine.edu

Atchison, KS 66002

(913) 367-5340
(800) 467-5340

Fax: (913) 367-6102 **Email:** phelgesen@benedictine.edu

Full-time: 766 men, 899 women **Faculty:** 95

Part-time: 158 men, 170 women **Ph.D.s:** 76%

Graduate: 33 men, 44 women **Student/Faculty:** 14 to 1

Year: semesters, summer session **Tuition:** $21,475

Room & Board: $7705 **Freshman Class:** 3538 applied, 2081 accepted, 470 enrolled

ACT: required **CEEB CODE:** 6056

Application Deadline: n/av **VERY COMPETITIVE**

Benedictine College, established in 1971 by a merger of St. Benedict's College and Mount Saint Scholastics College, is a liberal arts, Catholic, Benedictine institution. Figures in the above capsule and in this profile are approximate. There is 1 undergraduate school and 2 graduate schools. In addition to regional accreditation, Benedictine has baccalaureate program accreditation with NASM, NCATE, CAATE, and CCNE. The 225-acre campus is in a small town 45 miles north of Kansas City. Including any residence halls, there are 27 buildings.

STUDENT LIFE: 60% of undergraduates are from out of state, mostly the Mid-West. Students are from 44 states, 12 foreign countries, and Canada. 55% are from public schools. 84% are White. 76% are Catholic. **Male To Female Ratio:** 1.2:1. The average age of freshmen is 18; all undergraduates, 20. 20% do not continue beyond their first year; 55% remain to graduate. **Housing:** 1240 students can be accommodated in college housing, which includes single-sex and coed dorms. On-campus housing is guaranteed for all 4 years. 77% of students live on campus; of those, 70% remain on campus on weekends. All students may keep cars.

FACULTY/CLASSROOMS: 66% of faculty are male; 34% are female. All teach undergraduates. No introductory courses are taught by graduate students. The average class size in an introductory lecture is 25; in a laboratory is 20; and in a regular course is 20.

PROGRAMS OF STUDY: Benedictine confers B.A., B.S. and B.Mus.Ed degrees. Associate and Master's degrees are also awarded. Bachelor's degrees are awarded in BIOLOGICAL SCIENCE (biochemistry and biology/biological science), BUSINESS (accounting and business administration and management), COMMUNICATIONS AND THE ARTS (art, dramatic arts, English, French, journalism, music, Spanish, and theater management), COMPUTER AND PHYSICAL SCIENCE (astronomy, chemistry, computer science, mathematics, natural sciences, and physics), EDUCATION (athletic training, elementary education, music education, physical education, secondary education, and special education), ENGINEERING AND ENVIRONMENTAL DESIGN (engineering), HEALTH PROFESSIONS (nursing), SOCIAL SCIENCE (economics, history, liberal arts/general studies, philosophy, political science/government, psychology, religion, social science, sociology, and youth ministry). Biology, engineering, and education are the strongest academically. Business, and theology have the largest enrollments.

ACTIVITIES: There are no fraternities or sororities. There are 35 groups on campus, including band, cheerleading, choir, chorale, computers, dance, drama, drill team, ethnic, honors, international, jazz band, literary magazine, musical theater, newspaper, orchestra, pep band, photography, political, professional, religious, social, social service, student government, and symphony. Popular campus events include Discovery Week, Parents Weekend, and All School Mass. **Sports:** There are 7 intercollegiate sports for men and 8 for women, and 7 intramural sports for men and 7 for women. Facilities include a gym, weight rooms, a football and track stadium, baseball, softball, and track fields, and an isometrics training room. **Graduates:** From July 1, 2013 to June 30, 2014, 336 bachelor's degrees were awarded. The most popular majors were business (20%), education (10%), and theology/youth ministry (6%). 26 companies recruited on campus in 2013-2014. In an average class, 42% graduate in 4 years or less, 46% graduate in 5 years or less, and 53% graduate in 6 years or less. Of the 2013 graduating class, 15% were enrolled in graduate school within 6 months of graduation, and 75% were employed.

SERVICES: Counseling and information services are available, as is tutoring in most subjects. There is remedial math, reading, and writing. **Library/Resources:** The library contains 231,796 volumes, 10,803 microform items, 737 audio/video tapes/CDs/DVDs, and subscribes to 425 periodicals including electronic. Computerized library services include interlibrary loans, database searching, and Internet access. **Physically Challenged Students:** 80% of the campus is accessible. Facilities include wheelchair ramps, elevators, special parking, specially equipped restrooms, special class scheduling, and lowered drinking fountains. **Special:** Benedictine offers cross-registration with the 14 other members of the Kansas City Regional Council for Higher Education and study abroad in several countries. The school also offers a 3-2 occupational therapy program with Washington University of St. Louis and a 3-2 engineering degree. Internships, work-study programs, dual majors, B.A.-B.S. degrees in chemistry and biology, an interdisciplinary music marketing major, student-designed majors, pass/fail options, and nondegree study are also available. There are 4 national honor societies, a freshman honors program, and 4 departmental honors programs. **Visiting:** There are regularly scheduled orientations for prospective students, consisting of an advanced placement exam, preregistration, meetings with the dean, student affairs, and business office and financial aid representatives, and campus tours. The orientations are scheduled for April, June, and July. There are guides for informal visits, visitors may sit in on classes, and stay overnight. To schedule a visit, contact the Admissions Office. **Campus Safety and Security:** Measures include 24-hour foot and vehicle patrol, emergency notification system, and security escort services. There are lighted pathways/sidewalks and controlled access to dorms/residences.

REQUIREMENTS: The ACT is required. Applicants should graduate in the upper 50% of their class at an accredited secondary school. Students should have 16 academic units, including 4 in English, 3 to 4 in math, 2 to 4 in foreign language and science, 2 in social science, and 1 in history. An interview is recommended. Counselor recommendations are required. A GPA of 2.0 is required. AP and CLEP credits are accepted. Important factors in the admissions decision are advanced placement or honors courses, recommendations by school officials, and recommendations by alumni. To graduate, students must complete 128 semester hours, pass a comprehensive exam in their major, and earn a minimum GPA of 2.0 overall and in the major. Curriculum requirements include 9 hours each in philosophy and religious studies, 8 hours each in English, natural science, and foreign language, 6 each in Western civilization and social science, 4 in math, 3 in fine arts, and 2 each in speech communication and phys. ed. A dean's colloquium and a comprehensive exam are also required. **Procedure:** Freshmen are admitted to all sessions. Entrance exams should be taken before the July following graduation from high school. There are deferred admissions and rolling admissions plans. Application deadlines are open. Application fee is $25. Notification is sent on a rolling basis. Applications are accepted on-line. **Transfer Students:** 78 transfer students enrolled in 2013-2014. Applicants must submit transcripts from all colleges attended, a statement of courses in progress, and, if transferring with less than 60 hours, a high school transcript and ACT score. A minimum GPA of 2.0 is required. 30 of 128 credits required for the bachelor's degree must be completed at Benedictine. **International Students:** There are 21 international students enrolled. The school actively recruits these students. They must take the TOEFL with a minimum score of 533 on the paper-based TOEFL (PBT) or 72 on the Internet-based version (iBT) or take the MELAB. They must also take the SAT or ACT, scoring 18.

ADMISSIONS: 59% of the 2014-2015 applicants were accepted. 47% of the current freshmen were in the top fifth of their class; 70% were in the top two fifths. **Admissions Contact:** Pete Helgesen, Dean of Enrollment Management. E-Mail: *phelgesen@benedictine.edu* Web: *www.benedictine.edu*

FINANCIAL AID: In 2014-2015, 100% of all full-time freshmen and 99% of continuing full-time students received some form of financial aid. 64% of all full-time freshmen and 64% of continuing full-time students received need-based aid. The average freshman award was $21,132. Need-based scholarships or need-based grants averaged $4,015 ($8,550 maximum); need-based self-help aid (loans and jobs) averaged $3,880 ($5,234 maximum); non-need-based athletic scholarships averaged $14,444 ($28,900 maximum); other non-need-based awards and non-need-based scholarships averaged $12,426 ($20,000 maximum); and $2,828 from other forms of aid. 28% of undergraduate students work part-time. Average annual earnings from campus work are $778. The average financial indebtedness of the 2014 graduate was $27,303. Benedictine is a member of CSS. The FAFSA and the college's own financial statement are required. The priority date for freshman financial aid applications for fall entry is April 1. The deadline for filing freshman financial aid applications for fall entry is August 1.

BETHANY COLLEGE (*The complete profile is made available exclusively on our website, www.barronspac.com*)

BETHEL COLLEGE	D-3
www.bethel-college.edu	

North Newton, KS 67117	(316) 284-5230
	(800) 522-1887, ext. 230
Fax: (316) 284-5870	Email: admissions@bethelks.edu
Full-time: 228 men, 240 women	Faculty: 38
Part-time: 9 men, 6 women	Ph.D.s: 66%
Graduate: n/av	Student/Faculty: 10 to 1
Year: 4-1-4	Tuition: $24,400
Room & Board: $7760	Freshman Class: 833 applied, 409 accepted, 110 enrolled
SAT: required ACT: 22	CEEB CODE: 6037
Application Deadline: n/av	COMPETITIVE

Bethel College, established in 1887, is a private liberal arts institution affiliated with the Mennonite Church. There is one undergraduate school. In addition to regional accreditation, Bethel has baccalaureate program accreditation with CSWE, NCATE, CCNE, and CAATE. The 90-acre campus is in a suburban area 25 miles north of Wichita. Including any residence halls, there are 21 buildings.

STUDENT LIFE: 62% of undergraduates are from Kansas. Others are from 30 states, 8 foreign countries, and Canada. 71% are White; 15% African American. **Male To Female Ratio:** 1.0:1. The average age of freshmen is 18; all undergraduates, 21. 23% do not continue beyond their first year; 52% remain to graduate. **Housing:** 434 students can be accommodated in college housing, which includes coed dorms, and special housing for international students and disabled students. On-campus housing is guaranteed for all 4 years. 71% of students live on campus; of those, 98% remain on campus on weekends. Alcohol is not permitted. All students may keep cars.

FACULTY/CLASSROOMS: 42% of faculty are male; 58% are female. All teach undergraduates, 50% do research, and 50% do both. No introductory courses are taught by graduate students. The average class size in an introductory lecture is 21; in a laboratory is 11; and in a regular course is 18.

PROGRAMS OF STUDY: Bethel confers B.A., B.S. and B.S.N. degrees. Bachelor's degrees are awarded in BIOLOGICAL SCIENCE (biology/biological science), BUSINESS (business administration and management), COMMUNICATIONS AND THE ARTS (art, communications, English, graphic design, and music), COMPUTER AND PHYSICAL SCIENCE (chemistry, mathematics, and natural sciences), EDUCATION (athletic training, elementary education, and health and physical education), HEALTH PROFESSIONS (nursing),

SOCIAL SCIENCE (history, psychology, religion, and social work). English, biology, and psychology are the strongest academically. Nursing and elementary education have the largest enrollments.

ACTIVITIES: There are no fraternities or sororities. There are 30 groups on campus, including choral groups, theater and music ensembles, band, campus ministries, cheerleading, chess, choir, chorale, chorus, computers, debate, drama, environmental, ethnic, forensics, gay, international, jazz band, literary magazine, newspaper, orchestra, political, professional, radio and TV, religious, social, social service, student government, symphony, and yearbook. Popular campus events include Fall Festival, Christmas Gala and Spring Fling. **Sports:** There are 7 intercollegiate sports for men and 7 for women, and 18 intramural sports for men and 18 for women. Facilities include including indoor gyms, weight rooms, cardio-exercise room, tennis courts, soccer practice fields, all-weather track, outdoor stadium complex for football, soccer, track with an 8-lane track, artificial field turf, football practice field, outdoor basketball court, and an outdoor sand volleyball court. **Graduates:** From July 1, 2013 to June 30, 2014, 106 bachelor's degrees were awarded. The most popular majors were health professions/related programs (19%), business/marketing and visual and performing arts (13%), and communications/journalism (9%). In an average class, 35% graduate in 4 years or less and 15% graduate in 5 years or less.

SERVICES: Counseling and information services are available, as is tutoring in most subjects. There is a reader service for the blind, and remedial math, reading, and writing. **Library/Resources:** The 2 libraries contain 147,965 volumes, 14,377 microform items, 7,113 audio/video tapes/CDs/DVDs, and subscribe to 32,765 periodicals including electronic. Computerized library services include interlibrary loans, database searching, Internet access, and Wi-Fi capability. Special learning facilities include an art gallery, natural history museum, radio station, TV station, an observatory. **Physically Challenged Students:** 75% of the campus is accessible. Facilities include wheelchair ramps, elevators, special parking, specially equipped restrooms, special class scheduling, lowered drinking fountains, and special housing. **Special:** Students may cross-register with Associated Colleges of Central Kansas (ACCK) institutions and Hesston College. Internships are required in many majors. Work-study programs, study abroad, dual majors, and a Washington semester are available. The college offers a 3-2 engineering degree with University of Kansas, Kansas State University, and Wichita State University. **Visiting:** There are regularly scheduled orientations for prospective students, including a campus tour, classroom observations, visits with faculty, an interview with an admissions counselor, and lunch, and overnight residence hall lodging. There are guides for informal visits, visitors may sit in on classes, and stay overnight. To schedule a visit, contact the Admissions Office. **Campus Safety and Security:** There are emergency telephones and lighted pathways/sidewalks.

REQUIREMENTS: The SAT or ACT is required. Applicants should present a satisfactory score for SAT and ACT, with a minimum GPA of 2.5 for automatic admission. The GED is accepted. Auditions are required of candidates applying for some scholarships, and interviews are recommended for all applicants. Specific departmental requirements may vary. CLEP, AP, and International Baccalaureate credit may be awarded. A GPA of 2.0 is required. AP and CLEP credits are accepted. Important factors in the admissions decision are evidence of special talent, recommendations by alumni, and parents or siblings attended your school. To graduate, students must earn a total of 124 credits, including 24 to 50 in the major, 12 to 50 of those in upper-level courses, with a GPA of 2.0. Students must also meet general education requirements that include demonstrating competency in writing, math, speech, and foreign language. Additional core requirements include convocation, religious studies, cross-cultural learning, and peace, justice, and conflict studies. Distribution requirements include at least six hours in each division: arts and humanities, science and mathematics, and social sciences. **Procedure:** Freshmen are admitted to all sessions. Entrance exams should be taken by the fall of the senior year. There is a rolling admissions plan. Application deadlines are open. Application fee is $20. Notification is sent on a rolling basis. Applications are accepted on-line. **Transfer Students:** 63 transfer students enrolled in 2013-2014. A high school transcript (or GED), or official college transcript (minimum 2.0 GPA), ACT or SAT scores (waived if the student has more than 24 hours accepted in transfer to Bethel College), and a transfer recommendation are required. Automatic admission requires a cumulative GPA of 2.0 and satisfactory ACT or SAT scores. 30 of 30 credits required for the bachelor's degree must be completed at Bethel. **International Students:** There are 11 international students enrolled. They must take the TOEFL with a minimum score of 540 on the paper-based TOEFL (PBT) or 76 on the Internet-based version (iBT). They must also take the SAT or ACT.

ADMISSIONS: 49% of the 2014-2015 applicants were accepted. The SAT scores for the 2014-2015 freshman class were: Critical Reading--95% below 500, 5% between 500 and 599; Math--90% below 500, 10% between 500 and 599; Writing--100% below 500. The ACT scores were 91% below 21, and 37% above 28. **Admissions Contact:** Todd H. Moore, Vice President for Amisssions. E-Mail: *admissions@ bethelks.edu* Web: *www.bethel-college.edu*

FINANCIAL AID: In 2014-2015, 100% of all full-time freshmen and 78% of continuing full-time students received some form of financial aid. 87% of all full-time freshmen and 78% of continuing full-time students received need-based aid. The average freshman award was $24,117. Need-based scholarships or need-based grants averaged $4,910; need-based self-help aid (loans and jobs) averaged $7,083; non-need-based athletic scholarships averaged $5,125; other non-need-based awards and non-need-based scholarships averaged $5,933; and $9,631 from other forms of aid. 42% of undergraduate students work part-time. Average annual earnings from campus work are $1384. The average financial indebtedness of the 2014 graduate was $24,132. The FAFSA is required. The priority date for freshman financial aid applications for fall entry is August 15.

EMPORIA STATE UNIVERSITY   E-2
www.emporia.edu

Emporia, KS 66801	**(620) 341-5465**
	(877) GO-TO-ESU
Fax: (620) 341-5599	**Email:** go2esu@emporia.edu
Full-time: 1353 men, 2092 women	**Faculty:** 250; IIA, --$
Part-time: 179 men, 249 women	**Ph.D.s:** 78%
Graduate: 703 men, 1457 women	**Student/Faculty:** 17 to 1
Year: semesters, summer session	**Tuition:** $5614 ($17,388)
Room & Board: $7283	**Freshman Class:** 2452 applied, 1488 accepted, 696 enrolled
ACT: 22	**CEEB CODE:** 6335
Application Deadline: open	**COMPETITIVE**

Emporia State University is a premier comprehensive university focused on academic excellence, student success, leadership, and community and global engagement. Emporia State University is a dynamic and progressive student-centered learning community that fosters student success through engagement in academic excellence, community and global involvement, and the pursuit of personal and professional fulfillment. Figures in the above capsule and in this profile are approximate. There are 3 undergraduate schools and 1 graduate school. In addition to regional accreditation, ESU has baccalaureate program accreditation with AACSB, NASAD, NASM, NCATE, NLN, CAAHEP, and ACS. The 207-acre campus is in a small town 110 miles from Kansas City. Including any residence halls, there are 20 buildings.

STUDENT LIFE: 92% of undergraduates are from Kansas. Others are from 46 states and 45 foreign countries. 74% are White. The average age of freshmen is 18; all undergraduates, 22. 27% do not continue beyond their first year; 42% remain to graduate. **Housing:** 792 students can be accommodated in college housing, which includes single-sex and coed dorms and on-campus apartments. In addition, there are honors houses, special-interest houses, fraternity houses, and sorority houses. On-campus housing is guaranteed for the freshman year only, and is available on a first-come, first-served basis. Priority is given to out-of-town students. 74% of students commute. All students may keep cars.

FACULTY/CLASSROOMS: 53% of faculty are male; 47% are female. All teach undergraduates. Graduate students teach 9% of introductory courses. The average class size in an introductory lecture is 20; in a laboratory is 10; and in a regular course is 23.

PROGRAMS OF STUDY: ESU confers B.A., B.S., B.F.A., B.I.S., B Mus., B.Mus.Ed., B.S.Bus., B.S.Ed. and B.S.N. degrees. Master's and Doctoral degrees are also awarded. Bachelor's degrees are awarded in BIOLOGICAL SCIENCE (biochemistry and biology/biological science), BUSINESS (accounting, business administration and management, marketing/retailing/merchandising, and recreation and leisure services), COMMUNICATIONS AND THE ARTS (art, communications, dramatic arts, English, modern language, music, and theatre arts), COMPUTER AND PHYSICAL SCIENCE (chemistry, computer science, earth science, information sciences and systems, mathematics, physical sciences, and physics), EDUCATION (art education, athletic training, business education, elementary education, foreign languages education, health education, music education, physical education, and secondary education), HEALTH PROFESSIONS (health care administration, health science, nursing, and rehabilitation therapy), SOCIAL SCIENCE (criminal justice, economics, history, liberal arts/general studies, political science/government, psychology, social science, and sociology). Teacher education, both elementary and secondary are the strongest academically. Elementary education, business administration, and biology have the largest enrollments.

ACTIVITIES: 16% of men belong to 8 national fraternities; 12% of women belong to 6 national sororities. There are 130 groups on campus, including art, band, cheerleading, choir, chorale, chorus, computers, debate, drama, drill team, environmental, ethnic, film, gay, honors, international, jazz band, literary magazine, marching band, musical theater, newspaper, opera, orchestra, pep band, political, professional, religious, social, social service, student government, symphony, and yearbook. Popular campus events include Family Day, International Student Festival, and Homecoming. **Sports:** There are 7 intercollegiate sports for men and 8 for women, and 12 intramural sports for men and 12 for women. Facilities include a 7000-seat stadium, a student recreation center, an Olympic-size pool, 5 gyms, 6 handball courts, exercise, physical therapy, and dance rooms, a sports complex with 3 softball fields and 1 baseball diamond, an all-weather 8-lane track, and 3 additional softball fields separate from the sports complex. **Graduates:** From July 1, 2013 to June 30, 2014, 713 bachelor's degrees were awarded. The most popular majors were education (22%), business administration (15%), and health fields (10%). 185 companies recruited on campus in 2013-2014. In an average class, 20% graduate in 4 years or less, 35% graduate in 5 years or less, and 41% graduate in 6 years or less. Of the 2013 graduating class, 20% were enrolled in graduate school within 6 months of graduation, and 22% were employed.

SERVICES: There is a reader service for the blind, and remedial math, reading, and writing. **Library/Resources:** The library contains 826,379 volumes, 60,262 microform items, 2,998 audio/video tapes/CDs/DVDs, and subscribes to 41,417 periodicals including electronic. Computerized library services include interlibrary loans, database searching, Internet access, and Wi-Fi capability. Special learning facilities include an art gallery, natural history museum, planetarium, theaters, geology museum, and Great Plains study center. **Physically Challenged Students:** All of the campus is accessible. Facilities include wheelchair ramps, elevators, special parking, specially equipped restrooms, special class scheduling, lowered drinking fountains, lowered telephones, and special housing. **Special:** ESU offers internships in many majors, study abroad in 34 countries, work-study programs, on-campus and on-line general studies degrees, B.A.-B.S. degrees, dual and student-designed majors, 3-2 engineering degrees with Kansas State University, Wichita State University, and the University of Kansas, credit for military experience, non-degree study, independent study, evening and Saturday classes, and pass/no credit options. There are 22 national honor societies and a freshman honors program. **Visiting:** There are regularly scheduled orientations for prospective students, visits include campus and residence hall tours, meetings with admissions and financial aid personnel, and appointments with academic and extracurricular personnel. There are guides for informal visits, and visitors may sit in on classes, and stay overnight. To schedule a visit, contact Lyndel Landgren at (877) 468-6378. **Campus Safety and Security:** Measures include 24-hour foot and vehicle patrol, emergency notification system, self-defense education, and security escort services. There are emergency telephones, lighted pathways/sidewalks, motorist-assist programs, safety and self-awareness programs for students and parents, 24-hour residence hall monitoring, and smoke detectors in residence halls.

REQUIREMENTS: The ACT is required. Applicants must meet 1 of these 3 criteria: an ACT score of 21 or above, class rank in the top third, or a 2.0 GPA in the Kansas core curriculum in-state and a 2.5 for out-of-state applicants. Students should have completed 4 units of English, 3 each of natural science, math, and social science, and 1 of computer technology. Applicants may also be admitted through an exceptions window and are encouraged to apply. A GPA of 2.0 is required. AP and CLEP credits are accepted. To graduate, all students must complete at least 124 credit hours, including 40 in upper-division courses, with a minimum GPA of 2.0. Students must also pass competency exams in reading, math, and writing and complete the general education program for their field of study, which includes courses in math, physical and applied science, humanities, history, speech, cultural diversity, and fitness and phys ed. **Procedure:** Freshmen are admitted to all sessions. Entrance exams should be taken during October or December of the senior year. There are deferred admissions and rolling admissions plans. Application deadlines are open. Application fee is $30. Applications are accepted on-line. **Transfer Students:** 387 transfer students enrolled in 2013-2014. Applicants must submit official transcripts of all previous college work. The minimum GPA depends on the number of semester hours earned. Physical activity requirements must be met. 30 of 124 credits required for the bachelor's degree must be completed at ESU. **International Students:** There are 519 international students enrolled. The school actively recruits these students. They must take the TOEFL with a minimum score of 520 on the paper-based TOEFL (PBT) or 68 on the Internet-based version (iBT). They must also take the ACT.

ADMISSIONS: 61% of the 2014-2015 applicants were accepted. The ACT scores were 35% below 21, 31% between 21 and 23, 19% between 24 and 26, 9% between 27 and 28, and 8% above 28. 2% of the current freshmen were in the top fifth of their class. 31 freshmen graduated first in their class. **Admissions Contact:** Laura Eddy, Director of Admissions. E-Mail: *go2esu@emporia.edu* Web: *www.emporia.edu*

FINANCIAL AID: In 2014-2015, 95% of all full-time freshmen and 88% of continuing full-time students received some form of financial aid. 67% of all full-time freshmen and 66% of continuing full-time students received need-based aid. The average freshman award was $11,730. Need-based scholarships or need-based grants averaged $5,696 ($27,136 maximum); need-based self-help aid (loans and jobs) averaged $5,464 ($12,216 maximum); non-need-based athletic scholarships averaged $2,719 ($23,287 maximum); and other non-need-based awards and non-need-based scholarships averaged $7,743 ($19,271 maximum). 15% of undergraduate students work part-time. Average annual earnings from campus work are $3300. The average financial indebtedness of the 2014 graduate was $23,538. The FAFSA and the state aid form are required. The priority date for freshman financial aid applications for fall entry is February 2.

FORT HAYS STATE UNIVERSITY C-2
www.fhsu.edu

Hays, KS 67601	(785) 628-5666
	(800) 628-FHSU
Fax: (785) 628-4014	Email: tigers@fhsu.edu
Full-time: 2010 men, 2310 women	Faculty: IIA
Part-time: 1550 men, 2000 women	Ph.D.s: 77%
Graduate: 510 men, 870 women	Student/Faculty: n/av
Year: semesters, summer session	Tuition: $4354 ($15,320)
Room & Board: $7000	Freshman Class: n/av
ACT: recommended	CEEB CODE: 6218
Application Deadline: open	COMPETITIVE

Fort Hays State University, established in 1902, is a public liberal arts institution offering programs in arts and sciences, business and entrepreneurship, education, health and life sciences, and pre-professional study. The figures in the above capsule and in this profile are approxi-

mate. There are 4 undergraduate schools and 1 graduate school. In addition to regional accreditation, FHSU has baccalaureate program accreditation with AACSB, NASM, NCATE, and NLN. The 200-acre campus is in a small town 180 miles northwest of Wichita. Including any residence halls, there are 44 buildings.

STUDENT LIFE: 93% of undergraduates are from Kansas. Others are from 36 states, 32 foreign countries, and Canada. 95% are from public schools. 87% are White. **Male To Female Ratio:** 1.3:1. The average age of freshmen is 18; all undergraduates, 23. 61% do not continue beyond their first year; 40% remain to graduate. **Housing:** 1000 students can be accommodated in college housing, which includes single-sex and coed dorms, on-campus apartments, and married student housing. In addition, there are fraternity houses, sorority houses, apartments for students with families, and apartments for nontraditional-age students. 82% of students commute. All students may keep cars.

FACULTY/CLASSROOMS: 59% of faculty are male; 41% are female. All teach undergraduates. No introductory courses are taught by graduate students. The average class size in an introductory lecture is 17; in a laboratory is 17; and in a regular course is 18.

PROGRAMS OF STUDY: FHSU confers B.A., B.S., B.B.A., B.F.A., B.G.S., B.M. and B.S.W. degrees. Associate and Master's degrees are also awarded. Bachelor's degrees are awarded in AGRICULTURE (agricultural business management and agriculture), BIOLOGICAL SCIENCE (biology/biological science), BUSINESS (accounting, banking and finance, business administration and management, management information systems, marketing/retailing/merchandising, and office supervision and management), COMMUNICATIONS AND THE ARTS (art, communications, English, fine arts, French, German, modern language, music, music performance, music theory and composition, Spanish, and telecommunications), COMPUTER AND PHYSICAL SCIENCE (chemistry, computer science, geology, information sciences and systems, mathematics, physical sciences, physics, radiological technology, and science), EDUCATION (art education, elementary education, music education, physical education, and technical education), HEALTH PROFESSIONS (nursing and speech pathology/audiology), SOCIAL SCIENCE (criminal justice, economics, history, liberal arts/general studies, philosophy, political science/government, psychology, social work, and sociology). Speech pathology is the strongest academically. Interdisciplinary studies, teacher education, and business administration have the largest enrollments.

ACTIVITIES: 1% of men belong to 3 national fraternities; 1% of women belong to 3 national sororities. There are 85 groups on campus, including art, band, cheerleading, choir, chorale, chorus, computers, dance, debate, drama, drill team, ethnic, film, gay, honors, international, jazz band, literary magazine, marching band, musical theater, newspaper, opera, orchestra, pep band, photography, political, professional, radio and TV, religious, social, social service, student government, symphony, and yearbook. Popular campus events include Octoberfest and Parents Day. **Sports:** There are 8 intercollegiate sports for men and 7 for women, and 40 intramural sports for men and 40 for women. Facilities include a 6300-seat stadium, tennis courts, and a coliseum containing a 6800-seat basketball arena, a track, and wrestling and training rooms.

SERVICES: Counseling and information services are available, as is tutoring in most subjects. There is remedial math and reading. **Library/Resources:** The library contains 300,000 volumes, 500,000 microform items, 1,480 audio/video tapes/CDs/DVDs, and subscribes to 3,100 periodicals including electronic. Computerized library services include interlibrary loans, database searching, Internet access, and Wi-Fi capability. Special learning facilities include an art gallery, radio station, TV station, an English lab. **Physically Challenged Students:** 95% of the campus is accessible. Facilities include wheelchair ramps, elevators, special parking, specially equipped restrooms, special class scheduling, lowered drinking fountains, lowered telephones. **Special:** Students may, with approval, earn their degrees through a cooperative program with FHSU and another accredited institution, or a correspondence or extension school. Cross-registration with several community colleges, internships, study abroad, work-study programs, a 3-2 engineering degree with Kansas State University, B.A.-B.S. degrees, a general studies degree, and pass/fail options are available. There are 21 national honor societies and a freshman honors program. <u>Visiting:</u> There are regularly scheduled orientations for prospective students. There are guides for informal visits, and visitors may sit in on classes, and stay overnight. To schedule a visit, contact Tina Schiel at tlschiel@fhsu.edu. <u>Campus Safety and Security:</u> Measures include 24-hour foot and vehicle patrol and security escort services. There are emergency telephones and lighted pathways/sidewalks.

<u>REQUIREMENTS:</u> The ACT is recommended. A GPA of 2.0 is required. AP and CLEP credits are accepted. To graduate, students must earn an overall minimum GPA of 2.0 or higher in some departments for 124 credit hours, including 40 hours in upper-level study, and 30 hours minimum in the major. The 55-hour liberal arts general education curriculum includes courses addressing personal wellness, analysis and communication, international studies, humanities, math, and natural, social, and behavioral sciences. <u>Procedure:</u> Freshmen are admitted fall, spring, and summer. Entrance exams should be taken in the senior year. There is a rolling admissions plan. Application deadlines are open. Application fee is $30. Applications are accepted on-line. <u>Transfer Students:</u> Applicants must have a minimum college GPA of 2.0 and submit official college transcripts from all institutions previously attended. 30 of 124 credits required for the bachelor's degree must be completed at FHSU. <u>International Students:</u> The school actively recruits these students. They must take the TOEFL.

<u>ADMISSIONS:</u> Roger Schieferecke, Director of Admissions. E-Mail: *tigers@fhsu.edu* Web: *www.fhsu.edu*

<u>FINANCIAL AID:</u> The FFS and the college's own financial statement are required. Check with the school for current application deadlines.

FRIENDS UNIVERSITY   D-3
www.friends.edu

Wichita, KS 67213 (316) 295-5000
(800) 794-6945
Fax: (316) 295-5101

Full-time: 640 men, 788 women	Faculty: IIA, --$
Part-time: 142 men, 199 women	Ph.D.s: n/av
Graduate: 257 men, 476 women	Student/Faculty: n/av
Year: semesters, summer session	Tuition: $22,500
Room & Board: $6600	Freshman Class: 786 applied, 456 accepted, 196 enrolled
	CEEB CODE: 6224
Application Deadline: open	COMPETITIVE

Friends University, established in 1898, is a nondenominational, independent Christian University that incorporates liberal arts instruction and professional studies into a high-quality undergraduate and graduate education. Figures in the above capsule and in this profile are approximate. There are 2 undergraduate schools and 1 graduate school. In addition to regional accreditation, Friends has baccalaureate program accreditation with NASM and NCATE. The 54-acre campus is in an urban area in the heart of Wichita, Kansas adjacent to highway 54, approximately 200 miles southwest of Kansas City. Including any residence halls, there are 19 buildings.

<u>STUDENT LIFE:</u> 81% of undergraduates are from Kansas. Others are from 18 states, 11 foreign countries, and Canada. 81% are from public schools. 70% are White; 11% African American; 11% Hispanic. 66% are Protestant; 37% claim no religious affiliation; 13% Catholic. <u>Male To Female Ratio:</u> 1.4:1. The average age of freshmen is 18; all undergraduates, 21. 40% do not continue beyond their first year; 60% remain to graduate. <u>Housing:</u> 423 students can be accommodated in college housing, which includes coed dorms, on-campus apartments, and off-campus apartments. a limited number of university-owned houses are available. On-campus housing is available on a first-come and first-served basis. 56% of students commute. Alcohol is not permitted. All students may keep cars.

<u>FACULTY/CLASSROOMS:</u> 92% teach undergraduates. No introductory courses are taught by graduate students. The average class size in an introductory lecture is 35; in a laboratory is 18; and in a regular course is 25.

<u>PROGRAMS OF STUDY:</u> Friends confers B.A., B.S., B.B.A., B.F.A.

and B.Mus. degrees. Associate and Master's degrees are also awarded. Bachelor's degrees are awarded in BIOLOGICAL SCIENCE (biology/biological science, wildlife biology, and zoology), BUSINESS (accounting, banking and finance, business administration and management, business economics, human resources, international business management, and management information systems), COMMUNICATIONS AND THE ARTS (art, ballet, communications, English, fine arts, music, music performance, musical theater, performing arts, and Spanish), COMPUTER AND PHYSICAL SCIENCE (chemistry, computer science, information sciences and systems, mathematics, and radiological technology), EDUCATION (art education, business education, drama education, education, elementary education, English education, foreign languages education, health education, music education, recreation education, science education, secondary education, and social science education), ENGINEERING AND ENVIRONMENTAL DESIGN (environmental science), HEALTH PROFESSIONS (health science, premedicine, and radiological science), SOCIAL SCIENCE (Christian studies, counseling/psychology, criminal justice, forensic studies, history, human services, liberal arts/general studies, philosophy and religion, political science/government, psychology, and religion). Science is the strongest academically. Business and education has the largest enrollments.

<u>ACTIVITIES:</u> There are no fraternities or sororities. There are 24 groups on campus, including Psychology Club, Spanish Club, Zoo Science, art, band, cheerleading, choir, chorale, chorus, communications, computers, dance, drama, ethnic, honors, international, jazz band, literary magazine, musical theater, newspaper, orchestra, pep band, photography, political, professional, religious, Singing Quakers, social, social service, student government, symphony, and yearbook. Popular campus events include Homecoming Week, Cherry Carnival and Chili Cookoff. <u>Sports:</u> There are 9 intercollegiate sports for men and 8 for women, and 8 intramural sports for men and 8 for women. Facilities include Friends University is home to Adair-Austin Stadium includes a 2600-seat stadium with Sportexe Momentum 46 brand turf for football and soccer, "Eurotan S" Sandwich Track surface system, Forrest C. Lattner Tennis Courts, and Garvey PE Center with 2,300 capcity gymnasium for basketball and volleyball games. The center also includes an auxillary indoor practic facility for baseball, softball, and track programs as well as spacious lockers rooms, racquetball courts, two weight rooms, and the athletic training and sports medicine facilities.

<u>SERVICES:</u> Counseling and information services are available, as is tutoring in most subjects. There is a reader service for the blind. <u>Library/Resources:</u> Computerized library services include interlibrary loans, database searching, and Internet access. Special learning facilities include an art gallery, an observatory. <u>Physically Challenged Students:</u> 95% of the campus is accessible. Facilities include wheelchair ramps, elevators, special parking, specially equipped restrooms, special class scheduling, lowered drinking fountains, and lowered telephones. <u>Special:</u> Students may cross-register with Newman University at no additional charge. Oportunity to participate in a long-standing study-abroad program is available in Cancun, Mexico; several other study-abroad programs of both shorter and longer duration have occurred in London, Paris, Italy, Cuba, Germany, Scotland, to name a few. Friends University offers several accelerated degree completion programs for the adult student in the College of Adult and Professional Studies. Friends also offers credit for life, military, and work experience. There is 1 national honor society, a freshman honors program, and 1 departmental honors program. <u>Visiting:</u> There are regularly scheduled orientations for prospective students, including half-day classroom visits, individual instructor visits, discussion with current students, a tour, lunch, and a financial aid session. There are guides for informal visits, and visitors may sit in on classes and stay overnight. To schedule a visit, contact the Admissions Office. <u>Campus Safety and Security:</u> Measures include 24-hour foot and vehicle patrol, emergency notification system, and security escort services. There are lighted pathways/sidewalks and controlled access to dorms/residences.

<u>REQUIREMENTS:</u> Candidates for admission must graduate from an accredited secondary school or earn a GED, having completed 4 courses in English, 2 each in history and math, and 1 each in science and social studies. The composite ACT score or converted SAT score

is multiplied by the high school GPA. A result of 45 is the minimum for full admission; students scoring lower may be admitted provisionally. Transfer students with at least 15 transferrable hours and adult students aged 23 or older are not required to submit test scores. A GPA of 2.0 is required. AP and CLEP credits are accepted. To graduate, students must complete 124 credit hours, including 33 to 54 in general education (varies by degree sought) and 24 to 45 in the major, with a minimum GPA of 2.0. Distribution requirements include course work in humanities, fine arts, religion and philosophy, behavioral science, and natural science. **Procedure:** Freshmen are admitted fall and spring. Entrance exams should be taken in the spring of the junior year or fall of the senior year. There is a rolling admissions plan. Application deadlines are open. Application fee is $35. Notification is sent on a rolling basis. **Transfer Students:** Applicants with fewer than 15 semester hours must submit ACT or SAT I scores and high school and college transcripts. 30 of 124 credits required for the bachelor's degree must be completed at Friends. **International Students:** The school actively recruits these students. They must take the TOEFL, unless they are either native speakers of English or non-native speakers who attended an English-speaking high school. SAT or ACT scores may be submitted in place of TOEFL scores.

ADMISSIONS: 58% of the 2014-2015 applicants were accepted. The SAT scores for the 2014-2015 freshman class were: Critical Reading--67% below 500, 21% between 500 and 599, and 12% between 600 and 699; Math--63% below 500, 25% between 500 and 599, and 12% between 600 and 699. **Admissions Contact:** Tony Myers, Director of Admissions. Web: *www.friends.edu*

FINANCIAL AID: The FAFSA is required. Check with the school for current application deadlines.

KANSAS STATE UNIVERSITY — E-2
www.k-state.edu

Manhattan, KS 66506   (785) 532-6250

Fax: (785) 532-6393	Email: k-state@k-state.edu
Full-time: 9496 men, 8614 women	Faculty: I, --$
Part-time: 1007 men, 1052 women	Ph.D.s: 82%
Graduate: 1956 men, 2456 women	Student/Faculty: n/av
Year: semesters, summer session	Tuition: $8585 ($21,530)
Room & Board: $7710	Freshman Class: 9839 applied, 9437 accepted, 3821 enrolled
ACT: 24	CEEB CODE: 6334
Application Deadline: open	VERY COMPETITIVE

Kansas State University, established in 1863, is a land-grant institution offering degree programs in agriculture, arts and sciences, business, engineering, human ecology, architecture, education, veterinary medicine, technology and aviation. Figures in the above capsule and in this profile are approximate. There are 9 undergraduate schools and 1 graduate school. In addition to regional accreditation, K-State has baccalaureate program accreditation with AACSB, ABET, ACCE, ACEJMC, AHEA, CSWE, FIDER, NAAB, NASAD, NASM, NCATE, NRPA, LAAB, CEA, CIDA, CAATE, CAA, CADE, NASPAA, CADE, NAEYC, ACPHA, AVMA, AABI, and NAST. The 668-acre campus is in a suburban area 125 miles west of Kansas City. Including any residence halls, there are 96 buildings.

STUDENT LIFE: 78% of undergraduates are from Kansas. Others are from 50 states, 112 foreign countries, and Canada. 76% are White. **Male To Female Ratio:** 1.0:1. The average age of freshmen is 18; all undergraduates, 20. 18% do not continue beyond their first year; 60% remain to graduate. **Housing:** 4580 students can be accommodated in college housing, which includes single-sex and coed dorms, on-campus apartments, off-campus apartments, and married student housing. In addition, there are honors houses, special-interest houses, fraternity houses, and sorority houses. On-campus housing is available on a first-come and first-served basis. 75% of students commute. All students may keep cars.

FACULTY/CLASSROOMS: 61% of faculty are male; 39% are female. No introductory courses are taught by graduate students. The average class size in a regular course is 30.

PROGRAMS OF STUDY: K-State confers B.A., B.S., B.F.A., B.M. and B.M.E. degrees. Associate, Master's, and Doctoral degrees are also awarded. Bachelor's degrees are awarded in AGRICULTURE (agricultural business management, agricultural communications, agricultural economics, agronomy, animal science, animal feed science, bakery science, fish and game management, horticulture, milling science, and wildlife management), BIOLOGICAL SCIENCE (biochemistry, biology/biological science, life science, microbiology, nutrition, and wildlife biology), BUSINESS (accounting, apparel and accessories marketing, banking and finance, business administration and management, entrepreneurial studies, hotel/motel and restaurant management, management information systems, marketing/retailing/merchandising, and personal financial planning), COMMUNICATIONS AND THE ARTS (apparel design, applied music, art, communications, dramatic arts, English, journalism, modern language, and music), COMPUTER AND PHYSICAL SCIENCE (chemistry, computer science, geology, information sciences and systems, mathematics, physical sciences, physics, and statistics), EDUCATION (agricultural education, art education, athletic training, early childhood education, elementary education, music education, and secondary education), ENGINEERING AND ENVIRONMENTAL DESIGN (aeronautical technology, agricultural engineering, agricultural engineering technology, airline piloting and navigation, architectural engineering, architecture, chemical engineering, civil engineering, computer engineering, construction management, electrical/electronics engineering, electrical/electronics engineering technology, engineering management, engineering technology, industrial engineering, interior design, landscape architecture/design, manufacturing engineering, and mechanical engineering), HEALTH PROFESSIONS (exercise science, medical technology, preveterinary science, and speech pathology/audiology), SOCIAL SCIENCE (anthropology, child care/child and family studies, dietetics, economics, ethnic studies, family and community services, family/consumer studies, food science, geography, history, human ecology, humanities, parks and recreation management, philosophy, physical fitness/movement, political science/government, psychology, social science, social work, sociology, textiles and clothing, and women's studies). Architecture, engineering, and accounting are the strongest academically. Business administration, mechanical engineering and animal sciences have the largest enrollments.

ACTIVITIES: 14% of men belong to 28 national fraternities; 20% of women belong to 18 national sororities. There are 478 groups on campus, including band, cheerleading, chess, choir, chorale, chorus, computers, dance, debate, drama, drill team, ethnic, film, gay, honors, international, jazz band, literary magazine, marching band, musical theater, newspaper, orchestra, pep band, photography, political, professional, radio and TV, religious, social, social service, student government, symphony, and yearbook. Popular campus events include Family Weekend and K-State Open House. **Sports:** There are 6 intercollegiate sports for men and 8 for women, and 49 intramural sports for men and 49 for women. Facilities include indoor and outdoor tracks, baseball fields, tennis courts, basketball courts, swimming pools, a football stadium, and an indoor practice field. A multipurpose recreation facility is open 16 hours a day. **Graduates:** From July 1, 2013 to June 30, 2014, 3677 bachelor's degrees were awarded. The most popular majors were business administration (11%), animal sciences (5%), and family studies and human services (5%). In an average class, 26% graduate in 4 years or less, 53% graduate in 5 years or less, and 60% graduate in 6 years or less. Of the 2013 graduating class, 21% were enrolled in graduate school within 6 months of graduation, and 71% were employed.

SERVICES: Counseling and information services are available, as is tutoring in every subject. There is a reader service for the blind, and remedial math, reading, and writing. **Library/Resources:** The 5 libraries contain 3.0 million volumes, 1.6 million microform items, 148,382 audio/video tapes/CDs/DVDs, and subscribe to 81,942 periodicals including electronic. Computerized library services include interlibrary loans, database searching, and Internet access. Special learning facilities include an art gallery, planetarium, radio station, TV station, a nuclear reactor, laser center, a cancer research center, and telecommunications satellite teaching. **Physically Challenged Students:** 90% of the campus is accessible. Facilities include wheelchair ramps, elevators, special parking, specially equipped restrooms, special class scheduling, lowered drinking fountains, lowered telephones, a campus shuttle service. **Special:** K-State offers co-op programs, internships, and dual degrees and majors through most of its colleges. Study abroad is available in more than 100 countries. Concurrent bachelor's/master's degree programs are available in 11 major areas. There are 78 national honor societies, including Phi Beta Kappa, a freshman honors program, and 7 departmental honors programs. **Visiting:** There are regularly scheduled orientations for prospective students, including campus tours and visits with academic advisers and admissions representatives. There are guides for informal visits, and visitors may sit in on classes and stay overnight. To schedule a visit, contact the Office of Admissions. **Campus Safety and Security:** Measures include 24-hour foot and vehicle patrol, emergency notification system, self-defense education, and security escort services. There are shuttle buses, emergency telephones, lighted pathways/sidewalks, televised monitors in parking lots, CPR classes, and vehicle assistance devices.

REQUIREMENTS: Applicants must meet 1 of these 3 criteria: an ACT score of 21 or above, class rank in the top third, or a 2.0 GPA in the Kansas core curriculum. It is recommended that students complete 4 units of English, 3 each of natural science, math, and social studies, and 1 of computer technology. The GED is accepted. AP and CLEP credits are accepted. Bachelor's degree programs require a minimum of 120 or more semester credit hours for completion. All undergraduates must complete 6 credit hours of expository writing and 2 credit hours of public speaking. Other requirements vary by college and program. **Procedure:** Freshmen are admitted to all sessions. Entrance exams should be taken in the junior and senior years. There is a rolling admissions plan. Application deadlines are open. The fall 2014 application fee was $30. Notification is sent on a rolling basis. Applications are accepted on-line. **Transfer Students:** 1509 transfer students enrolled in 2013-2014. Applicants must have a minimum of 24 transfer credit hours and a college GPA of 2.0 or otherwise must meet freshman requirements. Students must submit official transcripts from previous colleges attended. 30 of 120 credits required for the bachelor's degree must be completed at K-State. **International Students:** There are 1376 international students enrolled. The school actively recruits these students. They must take the TOEFL with a minimum score of 550 on the paper-based TOEFL (PBT) or 79 on the Internet-based version (iBT), or present acceptable scores on the SAT or the ACT. An English proficiency test is given at the university.

ADMISSIONS: 96% of the 2014-2015 applicants were accepted. The ACT scores were 17% below 21, 27% between 21 and 23, 26% between 24 and 26, 12% between 27 and 28, and 18% above 28. **Admissions Contact:** Larry Moeder, Asst VP for Student Life/Dir Adm & FA. E-Mail: *k-state@k-state.edu* Web: *www.k-state.edu*

FINANCIAL AID: In 2014-2015, 83% of all full-time freshmen and 70% of continuing full-time students received some form of financial aid. 43% of all full-time freshmen and 45% of continuing full-time students received need-based aid. The average freshman award was $12,619. Need-based scholarships or need-based grants averaged $4,140; need-based self-help aid (loans and jobs) averaged $3,855; non-need-based athletic scholarships averaged $12,762; and other non-need-based awards and non-need-based scholarships averaged $6,568. K-State is a member of CSS. The FAFSA is required. The priority date for freshman financial aid applications for fall entry is March 1.

Kansas Wesleyan, founded in 1886, is affiliated with the United Methodist Church. The college offers undergraduate programs in the arts and sciences, business, and education. The figures in the above capsule and in this profile are approximate. There is one graduate school. In addition to regional accreditation, Kansas Wesleyan has baccalaureate program accreditation with NCATE and NLN. The 25-acre campus is in an urban area 85 miles north of Wichita. Including any residence halls, there are 12 buildings.

STUDENT LIFE: 75% of undergraduates are from Kansas. Others are from 14 states, 12 foreign countries, and Canada. 92% are from public schools. 85% are White. 48% are Protestant; 39% claim no religious affiliation; 13% Catholic. The average age of freshmen is 20; all undergraduates, 24. 33% do not continue beyond their first year. **Housing:** 450 students can be accommodated in college housing, which includes single-sex dorms, on-campus apartments, and married student housing. On-campus housing is guaranteed for all 4 years. 55% of students live on campus; of those, 45% remain on campus on weekends. Alcohol is not permitted. All students may keep cars.

FACULTY/CLASSROOMS: All teach undergraduates. No introductory courses are taught by graduate students. The average class size in an introductory lecture is 24; in a laboratory is 7; and in a regular course is 13.

PROGRAMS OF STUDY: Kansas Wesleyan confers B.A., B.S. and B.S.N. degrees. Associate and Master's degrees are also awarded. Bachelor's degrees are awarded in BIOLOGICAL SCIENCE (biology/biological science), BUSINESS (accounting and business economics), COMMUNICATIONS AND THE ARTS (communications, dramatic arts, English, music, Spanish, speech/debate/rhetoric, and studio art), COMPUTER AND PHYSICAL SCIENCE (chemistry, computer science, mathematics, and physics), EDUCATION (art education, music education, physical education, secondary education, and special education), HEALTH PROFESSIONS (nursing), SOCIAL SCIENCE (addiction studies, criminal justice, history, prelaw, psychology, religion, religious education, and sociology). Premedicine, nursing, and preengineering are the strongest academically. Education, nursing, and business have the largest enrollments.

ACTIVITIES: There are no fraternities or sororities. There are 38 groups on campus, including art, band, cheerleading, choir, chorale, chorus, computers, dance, departmental, drama, ethnic, film, honors, international, literary magazine, musical theater, newspaper, pep band, photography, professional, radio and TV, religious, social, social service, student government, and yearbook. Popular campus events include Lilac Fete, Sweetheart Dance, and Family Weekend. **Sports:** There are 7 intercollegiate sports for men and 7 for women, and 8 intramural sports for men and 6 for women. Facilities include a student activities center, a gym, a sand volleyball court, football practice and game fields, a multipurpose courtyard, a track, and a weight room.

SERVICES: Counseling and information services are available, as is tutoring in most subjects. There is remedial reading and writing. **Library/Resources:** The library contains 82,000 volumes, 33,505 microform items, 984 audio/video tapes/CDs/DVDs, and subscribes to 421 periodicals including electronic. Computerized library services include interlibrary loans, database searching, and Internet access. Special learning facilities include an art gallery, planetarium, radio station, and TV station. **Physically Challenged Students:** 90% of the campus is accessible. Facilities include wheelchair ramps, elevators, special parking, specially equipped restrooms, special class scheduling, lowered drinking fountains, and lowered telephones. **Special:** Cross-registration is available with other members of the Associated Colleges of Central Kansas and the Salina College Consortium. Cooperative degree programs are offered in agriculture, cytotechnology, engineering, environmental studies, and medical technology. Kansas Wesleyan also offers January interterm study trips throughout the United States and abroad, Washington, D.C., and UN semesters, internships, dual majors, student designed majors, credit for life experience, and nondegree study. A 3-2 engineering degree is offered with Columbia University and Washington University at St. Louis. There are 4 national honor societies and a freshman honors program. **Visiting:** There are regularly scheduled orientations for prospective students. There are guides for informal visits, and visitors may sit in on classes and stay overnight. To schedule a visit, contact the Admis-

---

KANSAS WESLEYAN UNIVERSITY   **D-2**
www.kwu.edu

Salina, KS 67401	(785) 827-5541, ext. 1285
	(800) 874-1154
Fax: (785) 827-0927	**Email:** admissions@kwu.edu
Full-time: 310 men, 380 women	**Faculty:** n/av
Part-time: 40 men, 70 women	**Ph.D.s:** n/av
Graduate: 45 men, 30 women	**Student/Faculty:** n/av
Year: semesters, summer session	**Tuition:** $25,000
Room & Board: $7000	**Freshman Class:** n/av
SAT or ACT: required	**CEEB CODE:** 6337
Application Deadline: open	**COMPETITIVE**

sions Office. **Campus Safety and Security:** Measures include self-defense education and security escort services. There are lighted pathways/sidewalks, random security checks and private service security guards.

REQUIREMENTS: The SAT or ACT is required. Applicants must be graduates of accredited secondary schools or have earned a GED. An interview is recommended. A GPA of 2.5 is required. AP and CLEP credits are accepted. Students must demonstrate proficiency in English and math and must fulfill distribution requirements in 15 liberal arts components, including environmental awareness, biblical heritage, and lifetime recreation. Courses in phys ed and computers are required. To graduate, students must complete at least 126 credit hours, including 30 to 40 in a major field of study, with a minimum GPA of 2.0. **Procedure:** Freshmen are admitted to all sessions. Entrance exams should be taken as early as possible. There are deferred admissions and rolling admissions plans. Application deadlines are open. The fall 2014 application fee was $20. Notification is sent on a rolling basis. **Transfer Students:** Transfers must submit transcripts from all colleges previously attended. Those students transferring fewer than 15 credit hours must submit ACT scores and a high school transcript. A minimum GPA of 2.0 is recommended. 63 of 126 credits required for the bachelor's degree must be completed at Kansas Wesleyan. **International Students:** The school actively recruits these students. They must take the TOEFL.

ADMISSIONS: Admissions Office E-Mail: *admissions@kwu.edu* Web: *www.kwu.edu*

FINANCIAL AID: The FAFSA, and tax forms are required. Check with the school for current application deadlines.

MCPHERSON COLLEGE   D-2
www.mcpherson.edu

McPherson, KS 67460

(620) 241-0731
(800) 365-7402

Fax: (620) 241-8443   Email: admiss@mcpherson.edu

Full-time: 365 men, 234 women	Faculty: n/av
Part-time: 18 men, 15 women	Ph.D.s: 72%
Graduate: 5 men, 7 women	Student/Faculty: 15 to 1
Year: 4-1-4, summer session	Tuition: $20,600
Room & Board: $7538	Freshman Class: n/av
SAT or ACT: required	CEEB CODE: 6404
Application Deadline: n/av	**COMPETITIVE**

McPherson College, founded in 1887 and affiliated with the Church of the Brethren, is a private institution offering undergraduate programs in the arts and sciences, business, and education. The figures in the above capsule and in this profile are approximate. There is 1 undergraduate school and 1 graduate school. In addition to regional accreditation, McPherson has baccalaureate program accreditation with NCATE. The 23-acre campus is in a small town 60 miles north of Wichita. Including any residence halls, there are 16 buildings.

STUDENT LIFE: 53% of undergraduates are from Kansas. Others are from 29 states, and 2 foreign countries. 99% are from public schools. 80% are White; 13% African American. 43% claim no religious affiliation; 13% Catholic. The average age of freshmen is 18; all undergraduates, 21. **Housing:** 392 students can be accommodated in college housing, which includes single-sex and coed dorms and on-campus apartments. On-campus housing is guaranteed for all 4 years. 79% of students live on campus; of those, 65% remain on campus on weekends. Alcohol is not permitted. All students may keep cars.

FACULTY/CLASSROOMS: 72% of faculty are male; 28% are female. All teach undergraduates. No introductory courses are taught by graduate students. The average class size in an introductory lecture is 30; in a laboratory is 12; and in a regular course is 15.

PROGRAMS OF STUDY: McPherson confers B.A., and B.S. degrees. Master's degrees are also awarded. Bachelor's degrees are awarded in BIOLOGICAL SCIENCE (biology/biological science), BUSINESS (business administration and management), COMMUNICATIONS AND THE ARTS (art, communications, dramatic arts, English, music, Spanish, and speech/debate/rhetoric), COMPUTER AND PHYSICAL SCIENCE (chemistry and mathematics), EDUCATION

(elementary education, physical education, secondary education, and special education), SOCIAL SCIENCE (history, philosophy, psychology, religion, and sociology). Business, education and technology have the largest enrollments.

ACTIVITIES: There are no fraternities or sororities. There are 18 groups on campus, including art, band, cheerleading, choir, chorus, computers, drama, ethnic, gay, honors, international, musical theater, newspaper, orchestra, pep band, professional, religious, social service, and student government. Popular campus events include Family Weekend. **Sports:** There are 5 intercollegiate sports for men and 6 for women, and 6 intramural sports for men and 6 for women. Facilities include a sports center with 2 full-size basketball/volleyball courts, a racquetball court, and a fitness center with an open weight-training room, football/track stadium, practice fields, and tennis courts. **Graduates:** From July 1, 2013 to June 30, 2014, 105 bachelor's degrees were awarded.

SERVICES: Counseling and information services are available, as is tutoring in most subjects. There is remedial reading and writing. **Library/Resources:** The library contains 98,214 volumes, 60,799 microform items, 4,626 audio/video tapes/CDs/DVDs, and subscribes to 26,828 periodicals including electronic. Computerized library services include interlibrary loans, database searching, Internet access, and Wi-Fi capability. Special learning facilities include an art gallery, natural history museum, an automobile restoration center. **Physically Challenged Students:** 95% of the campus is accessible. Facilities include wheelchair ramps, elevators, special parking, specially equipped restrooms, special class scheduling, lowered drinking fountains, and special housing. **Special:** Cross-registration with other colleges is available through the Associated Colleges of Central Kansas. McPherson also offers internships, study abroad in 10 countries, co-op programs, credit by exam, a general studies degree, student-designed majors, and pass/fail options. There are preprofessional programs in health, engineering, law, forestry, veterinary medicine, nursing and medicine, optometry, and dentistry. There are 3 national honor societies, including Phi Beta Kappa, and 3 departmental honors programs. **Visiting:** There are regularly scheduled orientations for prospective students, consisting of campus tours, meetings with admissions personnel, and class attendance. There are guides for informal visits, and visitors may sit in on classes and stay overnight. To schedule a visit, contact the Admissions Office at pfannenm@mcpherson.edu. **Campus Safety and Security:** Measures include emergency notification system. There are emergency telephones and lighted pathways/sidewalks.

REQUIREMENTS: The SAT or ACT is required. The GED is accepted. A GPA of 2.0 is required. AP and CLEP credits are accepted. Important factors in the admissions decision are recommendations by school officials, evidence of special talent, and parents or siblings attended your school. To graduate, students must complete 124 credits, including 32 in the major, with a GPA of 2.0. All students must fulfill general education requirements in the following areas: written and oral communication, aesthetics, history, society, natural sciences, technology and culture, and religion/beliefs/values. Students must also participate in an integrative seminar and a service experience, and must complete a global/intercultural experience, which may include intercultural studies courses or modern language courses. **Procedure:** Freshmen are admitted fall, winter, and spring. Entrance exams should be taken in the junior year of high school. There are deferred admissions and rolling admissions plans. Application deadlines are open. Application fee is $25. Notification is sent on a rolling basis. Applications are accepted on-line. **Transfer Students:** 288 transfer students enrolled in 2013-2014. Applicants must have satisfactorily completed 12 credit hours of college course work covering 3 academic areas with a 2.0 GPA. 32 of 124 credits required for the bachelor's degree must be completed at McPherson. **International Students:** There are 12 international students enrolled. They must take the TOEFL. They must also take the ACT, scoring 18.

ADMISSIONS: **Admissions Contact:** Carol Williams, Director of Admissions and Financial Aid. E-Mail: *admiss@mcpherson.edu* Web: *www.mcpherson.edu*

FINANCIAL AID: The FAFSA is required. Check with the school for current application deadlines.

MIDAMERICA NAZARENE UNIVERSITY   F-2
www.mnu.edu

Olathe, KS 66062	**(913) 791-3380**
	(800) 800-8887
Fax: (913) 791-3487	Email: admissions@mnu.edu
Full-time: 550 men, 620 women	Faculty: n/av
Part-time: 45 men, 105 women	Ph.D.s: n/av
Graduate: 120 men, 325 women	Student/Faculty: n/av
Year: semesters, summer session	Tuition: $21,250
Room & Board: $6750	Freshman Class: n/av
SAT or ACT: required	CEEB CODE: 6437
Application Deadline: n/av	**COMPETITIVE**

MidAmerica Nazarene University was founded in 1966 as a private liberal arts institution affiliated with the Church of the Nazarene. The figures in the above capsule and in this profile are approximate. There are 4 graduate schools. In addition to regional accreditation, MNU has baccalaureate program accreditation with ACBSP, NASM, and NLN. The 105-acre campus is in a suburban area 19 miles southwest of downtown Kansas City, Missouri. Including any residence halls, there are 22 buildings.

STUDENT LIFE: 66% of undergraduates are from Kansas. Others are from 38 states, and 10 foreign countries. 88% are from public schools. 81% are White. 74% are Protestant; 15% claim no religious affiliation. The average age of freshmen is 18; all undergraduates, 24. 33% do not continue beyond their first year; 55% remain to graduate. **Housing:** 699 students can be accommodated in college housing, which includes single-sex dorms, on-campus apartments, and off-campus apartments. On-campus housing is guaranteed for all 4 years. 55% of students live on campus; of those, 75% remain on campus on weekends. Alcohol is not permitted. All students may keep cars.

FACULTY/CLASSROOMS: 64% of faculty are male; 36% are female. All teach undergraduates. No introductory courses are taught by graduate students. The average class size in an introductory lecture is 15; in a laboratory is 33; and in a regular course is 17.

PROGRAMS OF STUDY: MNU confers B.A., B.M.Ed. and B.S.N. degrees. Associate and Master's degrees are also awarded. Bachelor's degrees are awarded in AGRICULTURE (international agriculture), BIOLOGICAL SCIENCE (biology/biological science), BUSINESS (accounting, business administration and management, international business management, marketing/retailing/merchandising, and sports management), COMMUNICATIONS AND THE ARTS (communications, dramatic arts, English, graphic design, modern language, music, music performance, and Spanish), COMPUTER AND PHYSICAL SCIENCE (chemistry, computer science, mathematics, and physics), EDUCATION (athletic training, business education, Christian education, elementary education, English education, health education, mathematics education, music education, physical education, science education, social studies education, and speech correction), HEALTH PROFESSIONS (nursing), SOCIAL SCIENCE (criminal justice, history, ministries, missions, psychology, sociology, urban studies, and youth ministry). Management and human relations, nursing, and elementary education have the largest enrollments.

ACTIVITIES: There are no fraternities or sororities. There are 43 groups on campus, including psychology, writers, agriculture, cheerleading, choir, chorus, computers, drama, ethnic, honors, international, jazz band, newspaper, orchestra, pep band, political, professional, radio and TV, religious, student government, and yearbook. Popular campus events include Mr. MNU and Welcome Week. **Sports:** There are 6 intercollegiate sports for men and 6 for women, and 6 intramural sports for men and 6 for women. Facilities include a weight room, a football stadium, basketball/volleyball arena, a gym, a track, tennis and sand volleyball courts, and softball, baseball, and soccer fields.

SERVICES: Counseling and information services are available, as is tutoring in most subjects. There is a reader service for the blind, and remedial math, reading, and writing. There are also test-taking accommodations, interpreters for the hearing impaired, and note takers for the blind, hearing impaired, and learning disabled. **Library/Resources:** The library contains 120,520 volumes, 354,309 microform items, 4,640 audio/video tapes/CDs/DVDs, and subscribes to 225 periodicals including electronic. Computerized library services include interlibrary loans, database searching, Internet access, and Wi-Fi capability. Special learning facilities include a radio station and TV station. **Physically Challenged Students:** 90% of the campus is accessible. Facilities include wheelchair ramps, elevators, special parking, specially equipped restrooms, special class scheduling, and lowered drinking fountains. **Special:** MidAmerica Nazarene University offers nondegree study, cross-registration with the Christian College Coalition, study abroad in 4 countries, internships, and a Washington semester. There are accelerated degree programs in management and human relations and in nursing. There are 1 national honor society and 4 departmental honors programs. **Visiting:** There are regularly scheduled orientations for prospective students, including an academic fair, advising, class visitation, informational meetings, social activities, and experiencing residential life. There are guides for informal visits, and visitors may sit in on classes, and stay overnight. To schedule a visit, contact the Office of Admissions. **Campus Safety and Security:** Measures include 24-hour foot and vehicle patrol, self-defense education, and security escort services. There are emergency telephones and lighted pathways/sidewalks.

REQUIREMENTS: The SAT or ACT is required. Recommended composite score of 18 on the ACT or a satisfactory score on the SAT. Candidates for admission should be graduates of an accredited secondary school. The GED is accepted. Students should have completed 15 units of study, including 4 units of English and 3 each of natural science, social studies, and math. An essay is optional. AP and CLEP credits are accepted. All students must meet core curriculum requirements in humanities-communications, natural sciences-math, social sciences, religion-philosophy, and phys ed. Students must maintain a minimum GPA of 2.0 and complete 126 semester hours to graduate. **Procedure:** Freshmen are admitted to all sessions. Entrance exams should be taken during the senior year. There is a rolling admissions plan. Check with the school for current application deadlines. The application fee is $25. **Transfer Students:** 116 transfer students enrolled in 2013-2014. Transfer applicants should have earned 24 or more hours at an accredited institution and not be on academic or disciplinary probation. ACT or SAT scores are required. 30 of 126 credits required for the bachelor's degree must be completed at MNU. **International Students:** They must take the TOEFL, ACT, and/or SAT where English is the official first language. They must also take the SAT or ACT, and placement tests for incoming freshmen.

ADMISSIONS: 15 freshmen graduated first in their class. **Admissions Contact:** Brigit Mattox, Associate Director. E-Mail: admissions@mnu.edu Web: www.mnu.edu

FINANCIAL AID: The FAFSA and the college's own financial statement are required. Check with the school for current application deadlines.

NEWMAN UNIVERSITY   D-3
www.newmanu.edu

Wichita, KS 67213	**(316) 942-4291, ext. 2144**
	(877) NEWMANU
Fax: (316) 942-4483	Email: admissions@newmanu.edu
Full-time: 394 men, 727 women	Faculty: 74; IIB, --$
Part-time: 668 men, 1006 women	Ph.D.s: 61%
Graduate: 219 men, 722 women	Student/Faculty: 17 to 1
Year: semesters, summer session	Tuition: $23,580
Room & Board: $6800	Freshman Class: n/av
	CEEB CODE: 6615
Application Deadline: open	**COMPETITIVE+**

Newman University established in 1933, is a private liberal arts institution affiliated with the Roman Catholic Church, named for John Henry Cardinal Newman and founded by the Adorers of the Blood of Christ for the purpose of empowering graduates to transform society. Figures in the above capsule and in this profile are approximate. There are 3 undergraduate schools and 3 graduate schools. In addition to regional accreditation, NU has baccalaureate program accreditation with CSWE, NCATE, ACOTE, CoARC, ARRT, KS Dept of Ed, CCNE, and COA. The 61-acre campus is in an urban area in Wichita west of downtown. Including any residence halls, there are 12 buildings.

STUDENT LIFE: 91% of undergraduates are from Kansas. Others are from 28 states, 30 foreign countries, and Canada. 54% are from public schools. 74% are White. 59% are Catholic. **Male To Female Ratio:** 1.9:1. The average age of freshmen is 18; all undergraduates, 21. 24% do not continue beyond their first year; 52% remain to graduate. **Housing:** 406 students can be accommodated in college housing, which includes single-sex and coed dorms, on-campus apartments, and married student housing. In addition, there are special-interest houses. On-campus housing is guaranteed for the freshman year only, is available on a first-come, and first-served basis. 75% of students commute. Alcohol is not permitted. All students may keep cars.

FACULTY/CLASSROOMS: 33% of faculty are male; 67% are female. 94% teach undergraduates, 25% do research, and 25% do both. No introductory courses are taught by graduate students. The average class size in an introductory lecture is 22; in a laboratory is 16; and in a regular course is 19.

PROGRAMS OF STUDY: NU confers B.A., B.B.A., B.S. and B.S.N. degrees. Associate and Master's degrees are also awarded. Bachelor's degrees are awarded in BIOLOGICAL SCIENCE (biochemistry and biology/biological science), BUSINESS (accounting, business administration and management, and management information systems), COMMUNICATIONS AND THE ARTS (art, communications, English, and sports media), COMPUTER AND PHYSICAL SCIENCE (chemistry, information sciences and systems, and mathematics), EDUCATION (early childhood education, elementary education, and secondary education), HEALTH PROFESSIONS (health science, nursing, and ultrasound technology), SOCIAL SCIENCE (counseling/psychology, criminal justice, forensic studies, history, interdisciplinary studies, liberal arts/general studies, pastoral studies, philosophy, psychology, sociology, and theological studies). Nursing,allied health and pre-med, biology, and chemistry are the strongest academically. Nursing, biology and education have the largest enrollments.

ACTIVITIES: There are no fraternities or sororities. There are 26 groups on campus, including art, cheerleading, choir, chorale, chorus, communications, computers, dance, drama, environmental, ethnic, honors, international, literary magazine, musical theater, newspaper, pep band, photography, political, professional, religious, social, social service, and student government. Popular campus events include Family Weekend, Newman Week, Homecoming, Weeks of Welcome/Welcome Back Bash, and Gerber Institute Activities. **Sports:** There are 8 intercollegiate sports for men and 9 for women, and 10 intramural sports for men and 9 for women. Facilities include baseball and softball fields, soccer fields, and a gym with 1 main basketball court, 2 side-by-side courts, 6 locker rooms, weight room, aerobics room, and wrestling room. **Graduates:** From July 1, 2013 to June 30, 2014, 266 bachelor's degrees were awarded. The most popular majors were nursing (18%), education (14%), and biology (11%). 48 companies recruited on campus in 2013-2014. In an average class, 36% graduate in 4 years or less and 52% graduate in 6 years or less. Of the 2013 graduating class, 17% were enrolled in graduate school within 6 months of graduation, and 76% were employed.

SERVICES: Counseling and information services are available, as is tutoring in most subjects. There is a reader service for the blind, and remedial math and writing. **Library/Resources:** The library contains 90,129 volumes, 143,723 microform items, 2,300 audio/video tapes/CDs/DVDs, and subscribes to 7,015 periodicals including electronic. Computerized library services include interlibrary loans, database searching, Internet access, and Wi-Fi capability. Special learning facilities include an art gallery, allied health and nursing labs, and ITV studio facilities. **Physically Challenged Students:** All of the campus is accessible. Facilities include wheelchair ramps, elevators, special parking, specially equipped restrooms, special class scheduling, and lowered drinking fountains. **Special:** Newman University offers co-op placements in most majors, internships, dual majors, and study abroad in England, Europe, and Latin America. Majors in counseling, business studies, education, RN to BSN, and interdisciplinary studies can be satisfied through evening, weekend and online classes. There are 11 national honor societies and a freshman honors program. **Vis-**

iting: There are regularly scheduled orientations for prospective students, include meetings with faculty, athletic coaches, co-curricular sponsors, financial aid counselors, admissions counselors, and a campus tour. There are guides for informal visits, and visitors may sit in on classes, and stay overnight. To schedule a visit, contact Jann Reusser at (316) 942-4291 ext. 2144. **Campus Safety and Security:** Measures include 24-hour foot and vehicle patrol, emergency notification system, self-defense education, and security escort services. There are emergency telephones, lighted pathways/sidewalks, and controlled access to dorms/residences.

REQUIREMENTS: Criteria: cumulative grade point average of at least 2.0 on a 4.0 scale or an average GED score of 450 with no individual score below 410, ACT composite score of 18 or a combined verbal, math and writing SAT score of 1290. The recommended high school curriculum is 4 units English, 3 unit math, 3 units science and 3 units social science. A GPA of 2.0 is required. AP and CLEP credits are accepted. Important factors in the admissions decision are leadership record, advanced placement or honors courses, evidence of special talent, personality/intangible qualities, recommendations by alumni, recommendations by school officials, ability to finance college education, parents or siblings attended your school, extracurricular activities record, and geographical diversity.Degree requirements include completion of 124 credit hours. The number of credits required in the major varies. A minimum GPA of 2.0 is required for graduation, and students must fulfill the university's Newman Studies Program requirements which include skills, general education and core courses. **Procedure:** Freshmen are admitted fall, spring, and summer. Entrance exams should be taken during the spring of the junior year or fall of the senior year. There are deferred admissions and rolling admissions plans. Application deadlines are open. Application fee is $20. Notification is sent on a rolling basis. Applications are accepted on-line. Application fees are waived if application is completed on-line. **Transfer Students:** 309 transfer students enrolled in 2013-2014. A minimum GPA of 2.0 is required. 30 of 124 credits required for the bachelor's degree must be completed at NU. **International Students:** There are 73 international students enrolled. They must take the TOEFL with a minimum score of 530 on the paperbased TOEFL (PBT) or 74 on the Internet-based version (iBT).

ADMISSIONS: 45% of the current freshmen were in the top fifth of their class; 68% were in the top two fifths. 10 freshmen graduated first in their class. **Admissions Contact:** Jann Reusser, Admissions Secretary/Receptionist. E-Mail: *admissions@newmanu.edu* Web: *www.newmanu.edu*

FINANCIAL AID: In 2014-2015, 99% of all full-time freshmen and 94% of continuing full-time students received some form of financial aid. 68% of all full-time freshmen and 68% of continuing full-time students received need-based aid. The average freshman award was $11,344. Need-based scholarships or need-based grants averaged $2,777 ($6,448 maximum); need-based self-help aid (loans and jobs) averaged $1,574 ($2,750 maximum); non-need-based athletic scholarships averaged $3,870 ($10,714 maximum); and other non-need-based awards and non-need-based scholarships averaged $9,641 ($17,863 maximum). 10% of undergraduate students work part-time. Average annual earnings from campus work are $1748. The average financial indebtedness of the 2014 graduate was $25,936. The FAFSA is required. The priority date for freshman financial aid applications for fall entry is March 1.

OTTAWA UNIVERSITY · E-2
www.ottawa.edu

Ottawa, KS 66067	**(785) 242-5200, ext. 5555**
	(800) 755-5200,
Fax: (785) 229-1008	**Email: admiss@ottawa.edu**
Full-time: 350 men, 200 women	**Faculty:** IIB
Part-time: 15 men, 20 women	**Ph.D.s:** n/av
Graduate: n/av	**Student/Faculty:** n/av
Year: semesters, summer session	**Tuition:** $15,000
Room & Board: n/app	**Freshman Class:** n/av
ACT: required	**CEEB CODE:** 6547
Application Deadline: open	**VERY COMPETITIVE**

Ottawa University, founded in 1865 and affiliated with the American Baptist Churches, is a private institution offering programs through the divisions of arts and humanities, natural sciences, and social and behavioral sciences. The figures in the above capsule and in this profile are approximate. The 64-acre campus is in a small town 45 miles southwest of Kansas City. Including any residence halls, there are 15 buildings.

STUDENT LIFE: 55% of undergraduates are from Kansas. Others are from 18 states, 5 foreign countries, and Canada. 99% are from public schools. 77% are White; 11% African American. 64% are Protestant; 20% claim no religious affiliation; 13% Catholic. The average age of freshmen is 19; all undergraduates, 22. 25% do not continue beyond their first year; 30% remain to graduate. **Housing:** 428 students can be accommodated in college housing, which includes single-sex dorms, on-campus apartments, and married student housing. On-campus housing is guaranteed for all 4 years. 58% of students live on campus; of those, 65% remain on campus on weekends. Alcohol is not permitted. All students may keep cars.

FACULTY/CLASSROOMS: 60% of faculty are male; 40% are female. All teach undergraduates. No introductory courses are taught by graduate students. The average class size in a laboratory is 12.

PROGRAMS OF STUDY: OU confers B.A. degrees. Bachelor's degrees are awarded in BIOLOGICAL SCIENCE (biology/biological science), BUSINESS (accounting, business administration and management, and management information systems), COMMUNICATIONS AND THE ARTS (art, communications, dramatic arts, English, and music), COMPUTER AND PHYSICAL SCIENCE (chemistry, information sciences and systems, and mathematics), EDUCATION (elementary education and physical education), SOCIAL SCIENCE (history, human services, political science/government, psychology, religion, and sociology). English, business, and math are the strongest academically. Business, teacher education, and human services have the largest enrollments.

ACTIVITIES: There are no fraternities or sororities. There are 35 groups on campus, including cheerleading, choir, chorale, chorus, computers, dance, debate, drama, ethnic, forensics, honors, international, jazz band, musical theater, newspaper, orchestra, pep band, photography, professional, radio and TV, religious, social, social service, student government, and yearbook. Popular campus events include Family Day, Charter Day, and Christmas Feast. **Sports:** There are 7 intercollegiate sports for men and 7 for women, and 12 intramural sports for men and 12 for women. Facilities include a field, a sports complex, an athletic center, and a gym with a wellness center.

SERVICES: Counseling and information services are available, as is tutoring in most subjects. There is remedial math, reading, and writing. **Library/Resources:** The library contains 90,000 volumes, and subscribes to 400 periodicals including electronic. Computerized library services include interlibrary loans and database searching. Special learning facilities include an art gallery and radio station. **Physically Challenged Students:** 50% of the campus is accessible. Facilities include wheelchair ramps, elevators, special parking, specially equipped restrooms, and special class scheduling. **Special:** Internships are available, especially in business, human services, and teacher education. Student-designed majors are an option. 3/2 engineering degrees with Kansas state and the University of Kansas, 3 +1 degree in medical technology, and preprofessional programs in premedicine, predentistry, prelaw, and preministry are available. Work-study programs are also offered. There are 2 national honor societies. **Visiting:** There are regularly scheduled orientations for prospective students, including discovery day in the early spring, which gives prospective students a chance to meet faculty, students, and staff and to learn more about Ottawa University, the admissions process, and financial aid. There are guides for informal visits, and visitors may sit in on classes and stay overnight. To schedule a visit, contact the Admissions Office. **Campus Safety and Security:** Measures include self-defense education and security escort services. There are lighted pathways/sidewalks, night security guard. In addition, students are issued individual residence hall security and room keys.

REQUIREMENTS: The ACT is required. The GED is accepted. There are no specific high school courses required, but a sound college preparatory curriculum is highly recommended. A GPA of 2.5 is required. AP and CLEP credits are accepted. Important factors in the admissions decision are parents or siblings attended your school, recommendations by alumni, and recommendations by school officials. To graduate, students must complete 9 courses in 8 academic areas with a minimum GPA of 2.0. The university requires students to complete 124 semester hours, with 24 to 40 in the major. Three interdisciplinary general education seminars must be completed. In addition, students must attend 10 University Program events each semester for 6 semesters. **Procedure:** Freshmen are admitted to all sessions. Entrance exams should be taken as early as possible. There is a rolling admissions plan. Application deadlines are open. The fall 2014 application fee was $15. **Transfer Students:** Transfer applicants must submit transcripts from all colleges attended and must have a 2.0 GPA and 12 hours of college credit, or else they must meet freshman requirements. 30 of 124 credits required for the bachelor's degree must be completed at OU. **International Students:** The school actively recruits these students. They must take the TOEFL or MELAB.

ADMISSIONS: Tim Albers, Director of Admissions. E-Mail: *admiss@ottawa.edu* Web: *www.ottawa.edu*

FINANCIAL AID: The FAFSA and the college's own financial statement are required. Check with the school for current application deadlines.

PITTSBURG STATE UNIVERSITY   F-3
www.pittstate.edu

Pittsburg, KS 66762	(620) 235-4251
	(800) 854-PITT
Fax: (620) 235-6003	Email: psuadmit@pittstate.edu
Full-time: 3005 men, 2729 women	Faculty: 316; IIA, --$
Part-time: 214 men, 218 women	Ph.D.s: 77%
Graduate: 426 men, 697 women	Student/Faculty: 19 to 1
Year: semesters, summer session	Tuition: $5494 ($15,050)
Room & Board: $6538	Freshman Class: 2876 applied, 2280 accepted, 1116 enrolled
ACT: 22	CEEB CODE: 6336
Application Deadline: open	COMPETITIVE

Pittsburg State University, founded in 1903, is a state-supported institution offering programs in arts and sciences, business, education, and technology. There are 4 undergraduate schools and 1 graduate school. In addition to regional accreditation, Pitt State has baccalaureate program accreditation with AACSB, ABET, CSWE, NASM, NCATE, NRPA, CACREP, CCNE, ACS, AWI, FEF, HRDAA, and MPAC. The 630-acre campus is in a small town 120 miles south of Kansas City. Including any residence halls, there are 54 buildings.

STUDENT LIFE: 74% of undergraduates are from Kansas. Others are from 39 states, and 41 foreign countries. 82% are White. The average age of freshmen is 19; all undergraduates, 22. 27% do not continue beyond their first year; 47% remain to graduate. **Housing:** 1192 students can be accommodated in college housing, which includes coed dorms and married student housing, substance free, and academic excellence floors. On-campus housing is available on a first-come and first-served basis. 80% of students commute. Alcohol is not permitted. All students may keep cars.

FACULTY/CLASSROOMS: 54% of faculty are male; 46% are female. 94% teach undergraduates. Graduate students teach 10% of introductory courses. The average class size in an introductory lecture is 33; in a laboratory is 21; and in a regular course is 22.

PROGRAMS OF STUDY: Pitt State confers B.B.A., B.F.A., B.A.S., B.S.T., B.A., B.M.T., B.S., B.S.E., B.S.E.T., B.M., B.M.E., B.S.N. and B.S.V.T.E., B.I.S. and B.G.S. degrees. Associate and Master's degrees are also awarded. Bachelor's degrees are awarded in AGRICULTURE (environmental studies, plant science, and wood science), BIOLOGICAL SCIENCE (biochemistry, biology/biological science, cell biology, environmental biology, molecular biology, plant physiology, and wildlife biology), BUSINESS (accounting, banking and finance, business administration and management, business economics, fashion merchandising, international business management, marketing management, recreation and leisure services, and recreational facilities management), COMMUNICATIONS AND THE ARTS (advertising, art, broadcasting, ceramic art and design, communications, creative writing, dramatic arts, English, French, journalism, literature, metal/jewelry, music, music performance, painting, public relations, Spanish, and technical and business writing), COMPUTER AND PHYSICAL SCIENCE (actuarial science, chemistry, computer security and information assurance, environmental chemistry, information sciences and systems, mathematics, physics, and polymer science), EDUCATION (art education, early childhood education, education, elementary education, English education, home economics education, mathematics education, music education, physical education, psychology education, secondary education, social studies education, technical education, and vocational education), ENGINEERING AND ENVIRONMENTAL DESIGN (automotive technology, commercial art, construction management, construction technology, electrical/electronics engineering technology, graphic arts technology, graphic and printing production, interior design, manufacturing technology, mechanical engineering technology, plastics technology, preengineering, technological management, and woodworking), HEALTH PROFESSIONS (medical technology, nursing, pharmaceutical chemistry, predentistry, premedicine, preoptometry, prepharmacy, prephysical therapy, preveterinary science, and recreation therapy), SOCIAL SCIENCE (counseling/psychology, criminal justice, early childhood studies, family/consumer resource management, family/consumer studies, geography, history, international studies, liberal arts/general studies, political science/government, prelaw, psychology, safety management, social work, and sociology). Education, nursing, business, and technology have the largest enrollments.

ACTIVITIES: 7% of men belong to 6 national fraternities; 8% of women belong to 3 national sororities. There are 150 groups on campus, including recreational and special interest, art, band, cheerleading, chess, choir, chorale, chorus, computers, dance, debate, drama, drill team, environmental, ethnic, film, forensics, gay, honors, housing, international, jazz band, literary magazine, marching band, newspaper, opera, orchestra, pep band, photography, political, professional, radio and TV, religious, social, social service, student government, symphony, and yearbook. Popular campus events include Greek Week, Multicultural Month, Homecoming and Apple Day. **Sports:** There are 7 intercollegiate sports for men and 6 for women, and 24 intramural sports for men and 24 for women. Facilities include a football stadium, indoor and outdoor tracks, a basketball arena, softball diamonds, a baseball field, a weight room, an Olympic-size pool, volleyball, racquetball, and badminton courts, indoor and outdoor tennis courts, outdoor basketball courts and sand volleyball courts, a 50,000-square-foot recreation center, 4 gyms, a cardio and strength fitness center with a 1/10-mile track, and a dance studio. **Graduates:** From July 1, 2013 to June 30, 2014, 1131 bachelor's degrees were awarded. The most popular majors were engineering technology (17%), business/marketing (15%), and education (13%). 423 companies recruited on campus in 2013-2014. In an average class, 4% graduate in 3 years or less, 26% graduate in 4 years or less, 48% graduate in 5 years or less, and 50% graduate in 6 years or less. Of the 2013 graduating class, 76% were employed within 6 months of graduation. **SERVICES:** Counseling and information services are available, as is tutoring in most subjects, accounting, biology, chemistry, elementary education, English, modern language/Spanish, math, music, computers, physics, psychology, reading/study, art, sociology, and writing. There is a reader service for the blind. There are also counseling services, a center for student accommodations, and a writing center. **Library/Resources:** The 2 libraries contain 712,681 volumes, 100,614 microform items, 10,151 audio/video tapes/CDs/DVDs, and subscribe to 35,360 periodicals including electronic. Computerized library services include interlibrary loans, database searching, Internet access, and Wi-Fi capability. Special learning facilities include an art gallery, planetarium, radio station, TV station, a dedicated channel on local cable TV, a nature reach, an herbarium, an observatory, a field biology reserve, a technology center, a mammal collection, a greenhouse, a polymer research lab, a broadcasting lab, and a cadaver lab. **Physically Challenged Students:** 70% of the campus is accessible. Facilities include wheelchair ramps, elevators, special parking, specially equipped restrooms, special class scheduling, lowered drinking fountains, and lowered telephones. **Special:** Co-op and work-study programs by arrangement, internships in psychology, technology, social work, and by arrangement elsewhere, a general studies degree, B.A.-B.S. degrees, dual majors, credit by exam, non-degree study, student-designed majors, and pass/fail options are available. Pitt State has student exchange programs with 20 countries. There are 9 national honor societies, a freshman honors program, and 26 departmental honors programs. **Visiting:** There are regularly scheduled orientations for prospective students, meet with current students, other offices on campus, tours. There are guides for informal visits and visitors may sit in on classes. To schedule a visit, contact the Admission Office. **Campus Safety and Security:** Measures include 24-hour foot and vehicle patrol, emergency notification system, self-defense education, and security escort services. There are emergency telephones, lighted pathways/sidewalks, controlled access to dorms/residences, crime prevention programs, an engraving program for valuables, a crisis management plan and procedures, and e-mail, text, and phone alerts.

REQUIREMENTS: The ACT is required. Applicants must meet 1 of these 4 criteria: an ACT score of 21 or above, class rank in the top third, a 2.0 GPA in the Kansas core curriculum (2.5 GPA for out-of-state students), or have 24 or more transferable college credit hours with at least a 2.0 GPA. Candidates may also be accepted through an exceptions window. The GED is accepted. Pitt State requires applicants to be in the upper 33% of their class. A GPA of 2.0 is required. AP and CLEP credits are accepted. To graduate, students must complete at least 124 semester hours, including 36 to 60 hours in the major, with a minimum GPA of 2.0. General education requirements total 46 to 54 hours (up to 54 for education majors) and include courses in English, speech, math, humanities, social and behavioral sciences, natural and physical sciences, producing and consuming, nutrition, and health/well-being. **Procedure:** Freshmen are admitted to all sessions. Entrance exams should be taken before the first semester of the freshman year of college. There is a rolling admissions plan. Application deadlines are open. Application fee is $30. Applications are accepted on-line. **Transfer Students:** 530 transfer students enrolled in 2013-2014. Applicants must have 24 credit hours and a college GPA of 2.0 or else meet freshman admissions requirements. 30 of 124 credits required for the bachelor's degree must be completed at Pitt State. **International Students:** There are 289 international students enrolled. The school actively recruits these students. They must take the TOEFL with a minimum score of 520 on the paper-based TOEFL (PBT) or 68 on the Internet-based version (iBT), or take the IELTS.

ADMISSIONS: 79% of the 2014-2015 applicants were accepted. The ACT scores were 40% below 21, 32% between 21 and 23, 16% between 24 and 26, 6% between 27 and 28, and 6% above 28. 28% of the current freshmen were in the top fifth of their class; 55% were in the top two fifths. 53 freshmen graduated first in their class. **Admissions Contact:** Melinda Roelfs, Director of Admission. E-Mail: *psuadmit@pittstate.edu* Web: *www.pittstate.edu*

FINANCIAL AID: The FAFSA is required. The priority date for freshman financial aid applications for fall entry is March 1.

SOUTHWESTERN COLLEGE D-3
www.sckans.edu

Winfield, KS 67156

(620) 229-6364
(800) 846-1543 x6236

Fax: (620) 229-6344	Email: marla.sexson@sckans.edu
Full-time: 247 men, 256 women	Faculty: 45; IIB, --$
Part-time: 13 men, 6 women	Ph.D.s: 71%
Graduate: 25 men, 35 women	Student/Faculty: 12 to 1
Year: semesters, summer session	Tuition: $22,756
Room & Board: $6514	Freshman Class: 339 applied, 298 accepted, 148 enrolled
SAT CR/M/W: 455/486/433 ACT: 22	CEEB CODE: 6670
Application Deadline: August 1	COMPETITIVE

Southwestern College, established in 1885, is a private institution affiliated with the Kansas West Conference of the United Methodist Church. Figures in the above capsule and in this profile are approximate. In addition to regional accreditation, Southwestern has baccalaureate program accreditation with CSWE, NASM, NCATE, CAATE, CCNE, and NAEYC. The 82-acre campus is in a small town 45 miles southeast of Wichita. Including any residence halls, there are 20 buildings.

STUDENT LIFE: 59% of undergraduates are from Kansas. Others are from 20 states, and 9 foreign countries. 66% are White. 36% claim no religious affiliation; 31% Protestant; 11% Catholic. **Male To Female Ratio:** 1.0:1. The average age of freshmen is 19; all undergraduates, 21. 40% do not continue beyond their first year; 51% remain to graduate. **Housing:** 625 students can be accommodated in college housing, which includes single-sex and coed dorms, on-campus apartments, and married student housing. In addition, there are honors houses. On-campus housing is guaranteed for the freshman year only, and is available on a first-come and first-served basis. 71% of students live on campus; of those, 42% remain on campus on weekends. Alcohol is not permitted. All students may keep cars.

FACULTY/CLASSROOMS: 51% of faculty are male; 49% are female. All teach undergraduates. No introductory courses are taught by graduate students. The average class size in an introductory lecture is 16; in a laboratory is 10; and in a regular course is 7.

PROGRAMS OF STUDY: Southwestern confers B.A., B.S., B.G.S., B.Mus. and B.Ph. degrees. Master's and Doctoral degrees are also awarded. Bachelor's degrees are awarded in BIOLOGICAL SCIENCE (biochemistry, biology/biological science, and marine biology), BUSINESS (accounting, business administration and management, business communications, and sports management), COMMUNICATIONS AND THE ARTS (communications, dramatic arts, English, music, and music performance), COMPUTER AND PHYSICAL SCIENCE (chemistry, computer science, digital arts/technology, and mathematics), EDUCATION (athletic training, drama education, early childhood education, elementary education, mathematics education, music education, physical education, and sports and wellness studies), SOCIAL SCIENCE (history, interdisciplinary studies, liberal arts/general studies, philosophy and religion, and psychology). Biology, business administration, and education have the largest enrollments.

ACTIVITIES: There are no sororities. There are 33 groups on campus, including discipleship, green team, band, cheerleading, choir, chorus, computers, dance, drama, environmental, ethnic, film, honors, international, jazz band, leadership, literary magazine, musical theater, newspaper, orchestra, pep band, photography, political, professional, radio and TV, religious, social, student government, symphony, and yearbook. Popular campus events include Movie Nights, Spring Formal and Stau Bau. **Sports:** There are 7 intercollegiate sports for men and 8 for women, and 4 intramural sports for men and 4 for women. Facilities include a 2400-seat stadium, tennis and basketball courts, playing floors, exercise rooms, a gym, an indoor swimming pool, a running track, a soccer field, a weight room, and a frisbee golf course. **Graduates:** From July 1, 2013 to June 30, 2014, 137 bachelor's degrees were awarded. The most popular majors were nursing (10%), biology (8%), and psychology (7%). In an average class, 1% graduate in 3 years or less, 41% graduate in 4 years or less, 50% graduate in 5 years or less, and 51% graduate in 6 years or less. Of the 2013 graduating class, 39% were enrolled in graduate school within 6 months of graduation, and 39% were employed.

SERVICES: Counseling and information services are available, as is tutoring in every subject. There is remedial math, reading, and writing. A reader service is available for dyslexic students. **Library/Resources:** The library contains 68,081 volumes, 192 microform items, 9,758 audio/video tapes/CDs/DVDs, and subscribes to 26,372 periodicals including electronic. Computerized library services include interlibrary loans, database searching, Internet access, and Wi-Fi capability. Special learning facilities include an art gallery, radio station, TV station, a biological field station. **Physically Challenged Students:** 80% of the campus is accessible. Facilities include wheelchair ramps, elevators, special parking, specially equipped restrooms, special class scheduling, lowered drinking fountains, and lowered telephones. **Special:** Southwestern offers internships in industry and social and civic agencies and a Washington semester through The Institute for Experiential Learning. Exchange programs are available. Combinations or degrees are possible with approval from the Academic Affairs Committee. Work-study programs, nondegree study, and pass/fail options are also available. There are 3 national honor societies, a freshman honors program, and 2 departmental honors programs. **Visiting:** There are regularly scheduled orientations for prospective students, including 4 Explore More events. There are guides for informal visits, visitors may sit in on classes, and stay overnight. To schedule a visit, contact the Admissions Office. **Campus Safety and Security:** Measures include 24-hour foot and vehicle patrol, emergency notification system, self-defense education, and security escort services. There are lighted pathways/sidewalks and controlled access to dorms/residences.

REQUIREMENTS: The ACT is required. The SAT is recommended. All candidates for admission must graduate from an accredited secondary school with a specified college-bound curriculum. The GED is accepted and an essay is required. Interviews are recommended. A GPA of 2.5 is required. AP and CLEP credits are accepted. To graduate, students must earn 124 credits, fulfill all requirements of the major, and maintain a GPA of 2.0. Students must complete the general education requirements. **Procedure:** Freshmen are admitted fall, spring, and summer. There is a rolling admissions plan. Applications should be filed by August 1 for fall entry; January 1 for spring entry, along with a $25 fee. Applications are accepted on-line. **Transfer Students:** 79 transfer students enrolled in 2013-2014. Applicants must have a college GPA of 2.0 and must submit an essay. 30 of 124 credits required for the bachelor's degree must be completed at Southwestern. **International Students:** There are 31 international students enrolled. The school actively recruits these students. They must take the TOEFL with a minimum score of 550 on the paper-based TOEFL (PBT) or 80 on the Internet-based version (iBT).

ADMISSIONS: 88% of the 2014-2015 applicants were accepted. The SAT scores for the 2014-2015 freshman class were: Critical Reading--69% below 500, 25% between 500 and 599, 3% between 600 and 699, and 3% between 700 and 800; Math--61% below 500, 29% between 500 and 599, 7% between 600 and 699, and 3% between 700 and 800; Writing--75% below 500, 22% between 500 and 599, and 3% between 600 and 699. The ACT scores were 31% below 21, 29% between 21 and 23, 27% between 24 and 26, 9% between 27 and 28, and 4% above 28. 34% of the current freshmen were in the top fifth of their class; 70% were in the top two fifths. 8 freshmen graduated first in their class. **Admissions Contact:** Marla Sexson, Vice President for Enrollment Management. E-Mail: *marla.sexson@sckans.edu* Web: *www.sckans.edu*

FINANCIAL AID: In 2014-2015, 100% of all full-time freshmen and 98% of continuing full-time students received some form of financial aid. 74% of all full-time freshmen and 75% of continuing full-time students received need-based aid. The average freshman award was $25,059. Need-based scholarships or need-based grants averaged $5,809 ($9,550 maximum); need-based self-help aid (loans and jobs) averaged $4,894 ($9,000 maximum); non-need-based athletic scholarships averaged $4,000 ($4,000 maximum); and other non-need-based awards and non-need-based scholarships averaged $8,124 ($13,500 maximum). Average annual earnings from campus work are $1400. The average financial indebtedness of the 2014 graduate was $34,056. The FAFSA and the college's own financial statement are required. Check with the school for current application deadlines.

STERLING COLLEGE   C-3
www.sterling.edu

Sterling, KS 67579   (620) 278-4275
(800) 346-1017
Fax: (620) 278-4416   Email: admissions@sterling.edu
Full-time: 327 men, 310 women   Faculty: 38
Part-time: 40 men, 59 women   Ph.D.s: 53%
Graduate: n/av   Student/Faculty: 14 to 1
Year: 4-1-4, summer session   Tuition: $20,050
Room & Board: $7166   Freshman Class: 821 applied, 414 accepted, 149 enrolled
SAT CR/M/W: 460/470/460 ACT: 21   CEEB CODE: 6684
Application Deadline: n/av   COMPETITIVE

Sterling College, established in 1887, is a private liberal arts institution affiliated with the Presbyterian Church, offering undergraduate curricula in 17 majors plus teacher preparation. Figures in the above capsule and in this profile are approximate. In addition to regional accreditation, Sterling has baccalaureate program accreditation with NCATE, CAATE, and NCATE. The 43-acre campus is in a rural area 70 miles northwest of Wichita. Including any residence halls, there are 19 buildings.

STUDENT LIFE: 51% of undergraduates are from Kansas. Others are from 32 states, and 6 foreign countries. 85% are from public schools. 79% are White. 54% are Protestant; 31% claim no religious affiliation; 15% Catholic. **Male To Female Ratio:** 1.0:1. The average age of freshmen is 18; all undergraduates, 20. 35% do not continue beyond their first year; 46% remain to graduate. **Housing:** 589 students can be accommodated in college housing, which includes single-sex dorms. On-campus housing is guaranteed for all 4 years. 73% of students live on campus; of those, 70% remain on campus on weekends. Alcohol is not permitted. All students may keep cars.

FACULTY/CLASSROOMS: 71% of faculty are male; 29% are female. All teach undergraduates, and 30% do both. No introductory courses are taught by graduate students. The average class size in an introductory lecture is 40; in a laboratory is 25; and in a regular course is 20.

PROGRAMS OF STUDY: Sterling confers B.A., and B.S. degrees. Bachelor's degrees are awarded in BIOLOGICAL SCIENCE (biology/biological science), BUSINESS (business administration and management and sports management), COMMUNICATIONS AND THE ARTS (art, communications, dramatic arts, English, and music), COMPUTER AND PHYSICAL SCIENCE (chemistry and mathematics), EDUCATION (athletic training, elementary education, and music education), HEALTH PROFESSIONS (exercise science), SOCIAL SCIENCE (behavioral science, history, religious education, and theological studies). All programs have a strong academic core. Most have required or optional concentrations. Business administration, education, exercise science, and sports management have the largest enrollments.

ACTIVITIES: There are no fraternities or sororities. There are 23 groups on campus, including art, band, cheerleading, choir, chorale, dance, debate, drama, ethnic, forensics, honors, jazz band, literary magazine, musical theater, newspaper, photography, political, professional, radio and TV, religious, social, social service, student government, and yearbook. Popular campus events include Mission Trips, Last Blast (end of year party), and Fall Musical and Theater Productions. **Sports:** There are 6 intercollegiate sports for men and 6 for women, and 6 intramural sports for men and 6 for women. Facilities include a weight-training facility, exercise deck, swimming pool, track, football field and stadium, baseball diamond, soccer field, practice fields, basketball and tennis courts, sand volleyball, outdoor basketball, and horseshoe pits. **Graduates:** In an average class, 42% graduate in 4 years or less, 48% graduate in 5 years or less, and 49% graduate in 6 years or less.

SERVICES: Counseling and information services are available, as is tutoring in most subjects. There is remedial writing. Special accommodations are provided on an as-needed basis. **Library/Resources:** The library contains 61,430 volumes, 2,120 microform items, 2,125 audio/video tapes/CDs/DVDs, and subscribes to 846 periodicals including electronic. Computerized library services include interlibrary loans, database searching, and Internet access. Special learning facilities include an art gallery, radio station, a museum, and a theater. **Physically Challenged Students:** 88% of the campus is accessible. Facilities include wheelchair ramps, elevators, special parking, specially equipped restrooms, and special class scheduling. **Special:** Sterling offers cross-registration with the Associated Colleges of Central Kansas and the Council of Christian Colleges and Universities. Internships are available in most majors, as is study abroad in 7 countries. A Washington semester and work-study programs are offered. Student-designed majors and a dual degree program in biology and medical technology with Wichita State University are possible. There are 3 national honor societies. **Visiting:** There are regularly scheduled orientations for prospective students, including visits with admissions, financial aid, current students, and faculty and campus and housing tours. There are guides for informal visits, visitors may sit in on classes, and stay overnight. To schedule a visit, contact the Admissions Office. **Campus Safety and Security:** Measures include emergency notification system. There are lighted pathways/sidewalks, controlled access to dorms/residences, evening foot and vehicle patrol.

REQUIREMENTS: The SAT or ACT is required. Applicants must graduate from an accredited secondary school or have a GED. An interview is recommended. A GPA of 2.2 is required. AP and CLEP credits are accepted. Important factors in the admissions decision are personality/intangible qualities, extracurricular activities record, and leadership record. To graduate, students must complete 52 to 57 credits in a general education curriculum, including writing, math, science, social science, philosophy, fine arts, and religion. They must have an overall GPA of 2.0, with 2.5 in the major. (Higher for Education Licensure students.) A total of 124 credits must be earned, with 45 to 60 in the major. Chapel/convocation requirements must also be met. **Procedure:** Freshmen are admitted fall and spring. Entrance exams should be taken in the spring of the junior year. There are early admissions, deferred admissions, and rolling admissions plans. Application deadlines are open. Application fee is $25. Notification is sent on a rolling basis. Applications are accepted on-line. **Transfer Students:** 77 transfer students enrolled in 2013-2014. Transfer students must have a minimum composite ACT score of 18 or a satisfactory SAT score if they have fewer than 12 hours of college credit; and a 2.2 GPA. 24 of 124 credits required for the bachelor's degree must be completed at Sterling. **International Students:** There are 6 international students enrolled. They must take the TOEFL with a minimum score of 525 on the paper-based TOEFL (PBT) or 70 on the Internet-based version (iBT), or ACT or SAT. They must also take the SAT or ACT, scoring 18.

ADMISSIONS: 50% of the 2014-2015 applicants were accepted. The SAT scores for the 2014-2015 freshman class were: Critical Reading--73% below 500, 23% between 500 and 599, and 4% between 600 and 699; Math--65% below 500, 31% between 500 and 599, and 4% between 600 and 699; Writing--77% below 500, 15% between 500 and 599, and 8% between 600 and 699. The ACT scores were 37% below 21, 31% between 21 and 23, 20% between 24 and 26, 5% between 27 and 28, and 7% above 28. 19% of the current freshmen were in the top fifth of their class; 49% were in the top two fifths. 4 freshmen graduated first in their class. **Admissions Contact:** Dennis Dutton, VP for Enrollment Services. E-Mail: *admissions@sterling.edu* Web: *www.sterling.edu*

FINANCIAL AID: Average annual earnings from campus work are $1200. The FAFSA is required. The deadline for filing freshman financial aid applications for fall entry is April 1.

TABOR COLLEGE   D-2
www.tabor.edu

Hillsboro, KS 67063

(620) 947-3121
(800) TABOR-99

Fax: (620) 947-6276   Email: admissions@tabor.edu
Full-time: 350 men, 250 women   **Faculty:** IIB
Part-time: 40 men, 100 women   **Ph.D.s:** n/av
Graduate: 5 men, 10 women   **Student/Faculty:** n/av
Year: 4-1-4   **Tuition:** $21,560
Room & Board: $7450   **Freshman Class:** n/av
ACT: required   **CEEB CODE:** 6815
Application Deadline: n/av   **COMPETITIVE**

Tabor College, established in 1908, is a private liberal arts facility affiliated with the Mennonite Brethren Church. The figures in the above capsule and in this profile are approximate. There are 2 undergraduate schools. In addition to regional accreditation, Tabor has baccalaureate program accreditation with CSWE and NASM. The 26-acre campus is in a rural area 50 miles north of Wichita. Including any residence halls, there are 28 buildings.

STUDENT LIFE: 68% of undergraduates are from Kansas. Others are from 23 states, 5 foreign countries, and Canada. 90% are from public schools. 89% are White. 89% are Protestant. The average age of freshmen is 18; all undergraduates, 20. 10% do not continue beyond their first year; 87% remain to graduate. **Housing:** 210 students can be accommodated in college housing, which includes single-sex dorms and off-campus apartments. On-campus housing is guaranteed for all 4 years. 78% of students live on campus; of those, 85% remain on campus on weekends. Alcohol is not permitted. All students may keep cars.

FACULTY/CLASSROOMS: 65% of faculty are male; 35% are female. All teach undergraduates. No introductory courses are taught by graduate students. The average class size in an introductory lecture is 32; in a laboratory is 12; and in a regular course is 20.

PROGRAMS OF STUDY: Tabor confers B.A., and B.S. degrees. Associate degrees are also awarded. Bachelor's degrees are awarded in BIOLOGICAL SCIENCE (biology/biological science), BUSINESS (accounting, business administration and management, marketing/retailing/merchandising, and office supervision and management), COMMUNICATIONS AND THE ARTS (applied art, communications, English, graphic design, and music), COMPUTER AND PHYSICAL SCIENCE (chemistry, computer science, mathematics, and natural sciences), EDUCATION (athletic training, business education, elementary education, health education, middle school education, music education, physical education, science education, secondary education, and special education), SOCIAL SCIENCE (biblical studies, history, humanities, international studies, ministries, philosophy, psychology, religion, social science, and sociology). Science is the strongest academically. Business and education have the largest enrollments.

ACTIVITIES: There are no fraternities or sororities. There are 18 groups on campus, including art, band, cheerleading, choir, chorale, chorus, computers, drama, drill team, ethnic, honors, international, jazz band, musical theater, newspaper, pep band, photography, political, religious, social service, student government, and yearbook. Popular campus events include Service Emphasis Week and Mission Emphasis Week. **Sports:** There are 8 intercollegiate sports for men and 8 for women, and 10 intramural sports for men and 10 for women. Facilities include 4 lighted tennis courts, 2 racquetball courts, lighted football and baseball fields, several practice fields, a soccer field, a curbed metric all-weather track, a gym with 2 playing floors, a practice/intramural gym, an indoor soccer court, and aerobic exercise, athletic training, and weight rooms.

SERVICES: Counseling and information services are available, as is tutoring in most subjects. Tutoring is available for most learning disabled students and for those on academic probation. **Library/Resources:** The library contains 80,099 volumes, 435 microform items, 1,640 audio/video tapes/CDs/DVDs, and subscribes to 265 periodicals including electronic. Computerized library services include interlibrary loans, database searching, and Internet access. **Physically Challenged Students:** 75% of the campus is accessible. Facilities include wheelchair ramps, elevators, special parking, specially equipped restrooms, special class scheduling, lowered drinking fountains, and lowered telephones. **Special:** Cross-registration is offered with the Association of Colleges of Central Kansas. Study abroad in 5 countries is possible. Dual majors, student-designed majors, internships, a Washington semester for juniors or seniors, and pass/fail options are available, as is a 3-2 engineering degree with Wichita State University. An accelerated degree program in management organizational development and preprofessional curricula in allied health, law, and medicine are also offered. There is a freshman honors program and 1 departmental honors program. **Visiting:** There are regularly scheduled orientations for prospective students, including a tour, admissions interview, and faculty, class, and financial aid visits. If requested, an audition or tryout will be scheduled. There are guides for informal visits, and visitors may sit in on classes and stay overnight. To schedule a visit, contact the Admissions Counselors. **Campus Safety and Security:** There are lighted pathways/sidewalks.

REQUIREMENTS: The ACT is required. An essay is required and an interview is recommended. A GPA of 2.0 is required. AP and CLEP credits are accepted. All students must complete 47 to 59 hours of general education courses including biblical and religious studies, history of diverse cultures, creative expression, natural and mathematical systems, values, social sciences, language, communication, computer literacy, physical fitness, and a college success seminar. A total of 124 credits, 16 of which must be in the major, with a minimum GPA of 2.0, is required in order to graduate. **Procedure:** Freshmen are admitted to all sessions. Entrance exams should be taken in October of the senior year. There is a rolling admissions plan. Check with the school for current application deadlines. Applications are accepted on-line. **Transfer Students:** A minimum 2.0 GPA is required and an interview is recommended. 33 of 124 credits required for the bachelor's degree must be completed at Tabor. **International Students:** They must take the TOEFL. They must also take the SAT or ACT.

ADMISSIONS: **Admissions Contact:** Rusty Allen, Director of Admissions. E-Mail: *admissions@tabor.edu* Web: *www.tabor.edu*

FINANCIAL AID: The FAFSA, and a federal income tax form, and W-2 forms are required. Check with the school for current application deadlines.

UNIVERSITY OF KANSAS   E-2
www.ku.edu

Lawrence, KS 66045   **(785) 864-3911**

Fax: (785) 864-5017	Email: adm@ku.edu
Full-time: 8671 men, 8664 women	Faculty: 1338; I, av$
Part-time: 1012 men, 996 women	Ph.D.s: 91%
Graduate: 3547 men, 4290 women	Student/Faculty: 18 to 1
Year: semesters, summer session	Tuition: $9707 ($23,847)
Room & Board: $7896	Freshman Class: 15767 applied, 14414 accepted, 4084 enrolled
SAT: required ACT: 25	CEEB CODE: 6871
Application Deadline: n/av	COMPETITIVE+

The University of Kansas, founded in 1866, is a public, comprehensive research institution. Its undergraduate and graduate programs emphasize the liberal arts, architecture, business, engineering, fine arts, health professions, journalism, law, medicine, music, nursing, pharmacy, social welfare, and teacher preparation. There are 11 undergraduate schools and 3 graduate schools. In addition to regional accreditation, KU has baccalaureate program accreditation with AACSB, ABET, ACEJMC, ACPE, CSWE, NAAB, NASAD, NASM, NCATE, CAAHEP, CAHIIM, CoARC, CCNE, NAACLS, ACOTE, AMTA, caATe, and CEA. The 1000-acre campus is in a suburban area 30 miles west of Kansas City. Including any residence halls, there are 220 buildings.

STUDENT LIFE: 69% of undergraduates are from Kansas. Others are from 49 states, 73 foreign countries, and Canada. 72% are White. **Male To Female Ratio:** 1.1:1. The average age of freshmen is 18; all undergraduates, 21. 20% do not continue beyond their first year; 62% remain to graduate. **Housing:** 5239 students can be accommodated in college housing, which includes single-sex and coed dorms, on-campus apartments, and married student housing. In addition, there are honors houses, special-interest floors, and 1 residence hall with a fine arts emphasis. On-campus housing is available on a first-come and first-served basis. 75% of students commute. Alcohol is not permitted. All students may keep cars.

FACULTY/CLASSROOMS: 58% of faculty are male; 42% are female. 98% teach undergraduates, all do research, and 98% do both. Graduate students teach 18% of introductory courses. The average class size in a laboratory is 15 and in a regular course is 25.

PROGRAMS OF STUDY: KU confers B.A., B.S., B.A.E., B.B.A., B.F.A., B.G.S., B.M., B.M.E., B.S.B., B.S.E., B.S.J., B.S.N. and B.S.W. degrees. Master's and Doctoral degrees are also awarded. Bachelor's degrees are awarded in AGRICULTURE (environmental studies), BIOLOGICAL SCIENCE (biochemistry, biology/biological science, microbiology, and molecular biology), BUSINESS (accounting, business administration and management, finance, management information systems, marketing/retailing/merchandising, sports management, and supply chain management), COMMUNICATIONS AND THE ARTS (art, art history and appreciation, ceramic art and design, choral music, classical languages, dance, design, dramatic arts, East Asian languages and literature, English, fiber/textiles/weaving, film arts, fine arts, French, German, Germanic languages and literature, graphic design, illustration, industrial design, information technology, journalism, linguistics, metal/jewelry, music, music history and appreciation, music performance, music theory and composition, musicology/ethnomusicology, painting, percussion, piano/organ, printmaking, sculpture, Slavic languages, Spanish, speech/debate/rhetoric, strings, theater design, voice, and winds), COMPUTER AND PHYSICAL SCIENCE (astronomy, atmospheric sciences and meteorology, chemistry, computer science, geology, information sciences and systems, mathematics, and physics), EDUCATION (art education, athletic training, early childhood education, elementary education, health education, health information management, middle school education, music education, physical education, secondary education, and sports studies), ENGINEERING AND ENVIRONMENTAL DESIGN (aeronautical engineering, architectural engineering, architectural history, architecture, chemical engineering, civil engineering, computer engineering, electrical/electronics engineering, engineering physics, interior design, mechanical engineering, and petroleum/natural gas engineering), HEALTH PROFESSIONS (community health work, cytotechnology, medical laboratory technology, music therapy, nursing, occupational therapy, pharmacy, respiratory therapy, and sports medicine), SOCIAL SCIENCE (African studies, African American studies, American studies, anthropology, archeology, behavioral science, classical/ancient civilization, developmental psychology, economics, European studies, geography, history, humanities, international studies, Latin American studies, liberal arts/general studies, philosophy, political science/government, psychology, public administration, religion, Russian and Slavic studies, social work, sociology, and women's studies). Pharmacy and engineering is the strongest academically. Engineering, biological sciences, and business have the largest enrollments.

ACTIVITIES: 16% of men belong to 29 national fraternities; 21% of women belong to 16 national sororities. There are 532 groups on campus, including art, band, cheerleading, chess, choir, chorale, chorus, communications, computers, dance, debate, drama, environmental, ethnic, film, gay, honors, international, jazz band, literary magazine, marching band, musical theater, newspaper, opera, orchestra, pep band, photography, political, professional, radio and TV, religious, social, social service, student government, and symphony. Popular campus events include Late Night in the Phog (basketball season kickoff), Homecoming, Rock Chalk Revue, Hawk Week, Basketball and Football Games. **Sports:** There are 7 intercollegiate sports for men and 11 for women, and 31 intramural sports for men and 31 for women. Facilities include a 16,300-seat basketball arena; a 50,100-seat football stadium; a sports pavilion with an indoor football field and indoor track; a health and phys ed center with 2 indoor pools, handball and racquetball courts, and gyms; lacrosse, ultimate, cricket, and rugby fields; tennis center; a bowling alley; a student recreation center containing an indoor climbing wall, a suspended jogging track, 4 racquetball courts, a free weight/cardiovascular area, aerobic and martial arts studios, multipurpose courts, and golf simulator; a rowing boathouse; an athletic center with volleyball and basketball courts; a football complex; a 1,500 seat softball stadium; a baseball park with clubhouse; a 2,500 seat soccer stadium; a 7,000 seat track and field stadium; a strength center; a golf training center; and an outdoor education center/challenge course. **Graduates:** From July 1, 2013 to June 30, 2014, 4091 bachelor's degrees were awarded. The most popular majors were business (16%), engineering (8%), and social sciences (7%). 500 companies recruited on campus in 2013-2014. In an average class, 1% graduate in 3 years or less, 36% graduate in 4 years or less, 56% graduate in 5 years or less, and 62% graduate in 6 years or less. Of the 2013 graduating class, 26% were enrolled in graduate school within 6 months of graduation, and 70% were employed.

SERVICES: Counseling and information services are available, as is tutoring in most subjects, including how-to sessions on study and organizational skills and a workshop. There is a reader service for the blind, and remedial math. A writing center is available to students. **Library/Resources:** The 12 libraries contain 4.6 million volumes. Computerized library services include interlibrary loans, database searching, Internet access, and Wi-Fi capability. Special learning facilities include a natural history museum, radio station, TV station, art museum, classics museum, entomology museum, film studio, space technology center, state-of-the-art performing arts center, organ recital hall, Robert J.Dole Institute of Politics, and Hall Center for the Humanities. **Physically Challenged Students:** 95% of the campus is

accessible. Facilities include wheelchair ramps, elevators, special parking, specially equipped restrooms, special class scheduling, lowered drinking fountains, and lowered telephones. **Special:** Special academic programs include Honors program, internships, study abroad in over 70 countries, a Washington semester, and work-study programs with the university. A cooperative program in engineering is offered, as are B.A.-B.S. degrees in many combinations, interdisciplinary majors, and dual majors in any approved combination. General studies degrees are available in many areas, and student-designed majors are possible. Nondegree study and pass/fail options are offered. There are 21 national honor societies, including Phi Beta Kappa, and a freshman honors program. **Visiting:** There are regularly scheduled orientations for prospective students, consisting of a summer orientation program that includes a 1-day campus visit. There are guides for informal visits, and visitors may sit in on classes, and stay overnight. To schedule a visit, contact the KU Visitor Center at (785) 864-3911. **Campus Safety and Security:** Measures include 24-hour foot and vehicle patrol, emergency notification system, and security escort services. There are shuttle buses, emergency telephones, lighted pathways/sidewalks, and controlled access to dorms/residences.

REQUIREMENTS: The SAT or ACT is required. In addition, for Fall 2015, Kansas resident applicants must have a minimum 2.0 GPA in the qualified admissions college preparatory curriculum; and have an ACT composite score of 21 or SAT combined score (math and critical reading) of 980; or rank in the top third of their high school class. College preparatory curriculum includes 4 units of English, 3 of college preparatory math, 3 of natural science (1 must be chemistry or physics), 3 of social sciences (includes history), and 3 electives. Nonresidents have the same curriculum requirements, but they must have a minimum GPA of 2.5; and an ACT composite score of 24 or SAT combined score of 1090; or be in the top third of their high school class. FALL 2016 new admissions standards. Kansas residents must complete the Kansas Qualified Admissions Curriculum with 2.0 GPA, have an overall 3.0 GPA and 24+ ACT (1090 SAT), or 3.25 overall GPA and 21+ ACT (980 SAT). Nonresidents must meet the above criteria with a 2.5+ GPA, have an overall 3.0 GPA and 24+ ACT (1090 SAT), or 3.25 overall GPA and 21+ ACT (980 SAT). Students who don't meet these criteria will have their application reviewed on a case-by-case basis. A GPA of 2.0 is required. AP and CLEP credits are accepted.To graduate with a B.A., B.S., or B.G.S. degree, all students must complete at least 120 credit hours, including 30 to 50 credit hours in the major, and maintain a GPA of at least 2.0. These, as well as curricula and distribution requirements, vary according to the school and the major. **Procedure:** Freshmen are admitted to all sessions. Entrance exams should be taken by the end of the junior year. There is a rolling admissions plan. Application deadlines are open. Application fee is $30. Applications are accepted on-line. **Transfer Students:** 1204 transfer students enrolled in 2013-2014. For entrance to the College of Liberal Arts and Sciences, transfer students must meet minimum GPA of 2.0 in-state or 2.5 out-of-state and freshman admissions requirements, if the student is transferring with less than 24 credit hours. The criteria vary widely within the other KU schools, some of which may also consider the ACT score and course work. 30 of 120 credits required for the bachelor's degree must be completed at KU. **International Students:** There are 1092 international students enrolled. The school actively recruits these students. They must take the TOEFL or take the IELTS.

ADMISSIONS: 91% of the 2014-2015 applicants were accepted. The ACT scores were 14% below 21, 22% between 21 and 23, 27% between 24 and 26, 15% between 27 and 28, and 22% above 28. There were 28 National Merit finalists. **Admissions Contact:** Lisa Pinamonti Kress, Director of Admissions. E-Mail: *adm@ku.edu* Web: *www.ku.edu*

FINANCIAL AID: In 2014-2015, 73% of all full-time freshmen and 62% of continuing full-time students received some form of financial aid. 29% of all full-time freshmen and 29% of continuing full-time students received need-based aid. The average freshman award was $9,160. Need-based scholarships or need-based grants averaged $5,529; need-based self-help aid (loans and jobs) averaged $3,305; non-need-based athletic scholarships averaged $21,053; and other non-need-based awards and non-need-based scholarships averaged $3,327. 15% of undergraduate students work part-time. Average annual earnings from campus work are $4800. The average financial indebtedness of the 2014 graduate was $25,268. The FAFSA is required. The priority date for freshman financial aid applications for fall entry is November 1. The deadline for filing freshman financial aid applications for fall entry is March 1.

UNIVERSITY OF SAINT MARY   F-2
www.stmary.edu

Leavenworth, KS 66048	(913) 682-5151
	(800) 752-7043
Fax: (913) 758-6140	Email: admissions@stmary.edu
Full-time: 250 men; 300 women	Faculty: n/av
Part-time: 60 men, 215 women	Ph.D.s: n/av
Graduate: 95 men, 220 women	Student/Faculty: n/av
Year: semesters, summer session	Tuition: $20,750
Room & Board: $7650	Freshman Class: n/av
SAT or ACT: required	CEEB CODE: 6630
Application Deadline: n/av	COMPETITIVE+

The University of Saint Mary, founded in 1923, is a private liberal arts institution affiliated with the Roman Catholic Church and sponsored by the Sisters of Charity of Leavenworth. The figures in the above capsule and in this profile are approximate. There is 1 undergraduate school and 1 graduate school. In addition to regional accreditation, USM has baccalaureate program accreditation with NCATE and IACBE. The 240-acre campus is in a small town 25 miles northwest of Kansas City, Missouri. Including any residence halls, there are 10 buildings.

STUDENT LIFE: 65% of undergraduates are from Kansas. Others are from 39 states, and 4 foreign countries. 74% are White. 34% are Catholic; 34% claim no religious affiliation; 32% Protestant. The average age of freshmen is 18; all undergraduates, 26. 40% do not continue beyond their first year; 44% remain to graduate. **Housing:** 333 students can be accommodated in college housing, which includes single-sex and coed dorms. On-campus housing is guaranteed for all 4 years. 56% of students commute. All students may keep cars.

FACULTY/CLASSROOMS: 43% of faculty are male; 57% are female. All teach undergraduates. No introductory courses are taught by graduate students. The average class size in an introductory lecture is 25 and in a laboratory is 12.

PROGRAMS OF STUDY: USM confers B.A., and B.S. degrees. Associate and Master's degrees are also awarded. Bachelor's degrees are awarded in BIOLOGICAL SCIENCE (biology/biological science), BUSINESS (accounting, business administration and management, and sports management), COMMUNICATIONS AND THE ARTS (art, dramatic arts, and English), COMPUTER AND PHYSICAL SCIENCE (chemistry, information sciences and systems, and mathematics), EDUCATION (elementary education), HEALTH PROFESSIONS (biomedical science, clinical science, and nursing), SOCIAL SCIENCE (applied psychology, child psychology/development, criminology, history, interdisciplinary studies, international studies, liberal arts/general studies, pastoral studies, political science/government, psychology, sociology, and theological studies). Elementry education, business administration, and psychology are the strongest academically.

ACTIVITIES: There are no fraternities or sororities. There are 25 groups on campus, including art, cheerleading, choir, chorale, chorus, computers, dance, drama, honors, literary magazine, musical theater, newspaper, opera, political, professional, religious, social, social service, and student government. Popular campus events include Fall Convocation, Founders Day, and Family Weekend. **Sports:** There are 4 intercollegiate sports for men and 4 for women, and 8 intramural sports for men and 8 for women. Facilities include a 500-seat sports center, soccer and softball fields, a multipurpose field, 3 tennis courts, a sandlot volleyball court, 2 racquetball courts, a weight and exercise room, a swimming pool, a dance and aerobics space, a walking trail, and an indoor jogging track.

SERVICES: Counseling and information services are available, as is tutoring in most subjects. **Library/Resources:** The library contains 120,000 volumes, 1,675 microform items, and subscribes to 301 periodicals including electronic. Computerized library services include interlibrary loans, database searching, and Internet access. Special learning facilities include an art gallery, and several special library collections. **Physically Challenged Students:** 90% of the campus is accessible. Facilities include wheelchair ramps, elevators, special parking, and specially equipped restrooms. **Special:** The university offers study abroad at various locations in Europe, Latin America, or Australia. CLEP and credit for life experience, internships in most major programs, evening and weekend study programs, pass/fail option, and dual majors are also available. There are 2 national honor societies. **Visiting:** There are regularly scheduled orientations for prospective students, visits include interviews with faculty and financial aid representatives, and touring the campus. There are guides for informal visits and visitors may sit in on classes. To schedule a visit, contact the Admissions Office. **Campus Safety and Security:** Measures include self-defense education. There are lighted pathways/sidewalks, 14-hour foot and vehicle patrols, and controlled access to residence halls.

REQUIREMENTS: The SAT or ACT is required. Applicants should be graduates of an accredited secondary school. The GED is accepted. A GPA of 2.5 is required. AP and CLEP credits are accepted. Important factors in the admissions decision are parents or siblings attended your school, recommendations by alumni, and recommendations by school officials. To graduate, students must complete all general education requirements and earn at least 128 credits, including 30 to 60 in the major, with a minimum GPA of 2.0. The core curriculum includes freshman humanities and a senior integration project. Distribution requirements include courses in English, math, natural science, social and behavioral sciences, philosophy, history, and foreign language, plus an additional literature course, a fine arts course, and 2 courses in theology. Students must also fulfill cultural literacy and lifetime physical wellness requirements. **Procedure:** Freshmen are admitted fall and spring. Entrance exams should be taken in the spring of the junior year and fall of the senior year. There are early decision, early admissions, and rolling admissions plans. Application deadlines are open. Application fee is $25. Notification is sent on a rolling basis. **Transfer Students:** A college GPA of 2.0 is required. 30 of 128 credits required for the bachelor's degree must be completed at USM. **International Students:** The school actively recruits these students. They must take the TOEFL with a minimum score of 500 on the paper-based TOEFL (PBT) or 61 on the Internet-based version (iBT).

ADMISSIONS: Admissions Contact: Brandon Johnson, Director of Admissions. E-Mail: *admissions@stmary.edu* Web: *www.stmary.edu*

FINANCIAL AID: USM is a member of CSS. The FAFSA is required. Check with the school for current application deadlines.

WASHBURN UNIVERSITY   E-2
www.washburn.edu

Topeka, KS 66621	(785) 670-1030
	1-877-281-2637
Fax: (785) 670-1113	Email: admissions@washburn.edu
Full-time: 1636 men, 2267 women	Faculty: 252; IIA, av$
Part-time: 786 men, 1212 women	Ph.D.s: 87%
Graduate: 343 men, 478 women	Student/Faculty: 14 to 1
Year: semesters, summer session	Tuition: $6038 ($13,526)
Room & Board: $6541	Freshman Class: 1416 applied, 1390 accepted, 801 enrolled
ACT: 22	CEEB CODE: 6928
Application Deadline: August 1	COMPETITIVE

Washburn is a publicly funded, independently governed, state-coordinated university. Established in 1865, the school offers more than 200 programs leading to certification, associate, bachelor, master, professional, and juris doctor degrees through the College of Arts and Sciences and the Schools of Law, Business, Nursing, and Applied Studies. There are 4 undergraduate schools and 5 graduate schools. In addition to regional accreditation, Washburn has baccalaureate program accreditation with AACSB, CAHEA, CSWE,

NASAD, NASM, NCATE, ACS, CAAHEP, and CAATE. The 160-acre campus is in an urban area 60 miles west of Kansas City. Including any residence halls, there are 29 buildings.

STUDENT LIFE: 91% of undergraduates are from Kansas. Others are from 37 states, 38 foreign countries, and Canada. 92% are from public schools. The average age of freshmen is 19; all undergraduates, 24. 34% do not continue beyond their first year; 37% remain to graduate. **Housing:** 674 students can be accommodated in college housing, which includes coed dorms and on-campus apartments. In addition, there are special-interest houses, fraternity houses, and sorority houses. On-campus housing is available on a first-come and first-served basis. Priority is given to out-of-town students. 85% of students commute. Alcohol is not permitted. All students may keep cars.

FACULTY/CLASSROOMS: 44% of faculty are male; 56% are female. 92% teach undergraduates. No introductory courses are taught by graduate students. The average class size in an introductory lecture is 24; in a laboratory is 18; and in a regular course is 19.

PROGRAMS OF STUDY: Washburn confers B.A., B.A.S., B.B.A., B.Ed., B.F.A., B.H.S., B.I.S., B.L.S., B.M., B.P.A., B.S., B.S.C.J., B.S.N. and B.S.W. degrees. Associate, Master's, and Doctoral degrees are also awarded. Bachelor's degrees are awarded in BIOLOGICAL SCIENCE (biochemistry, biology/biological science, and molecular biology), BUSINESS (accounting, banking and finance, business administration and management, business economics, and marketing/retailing/merchandising), COMMUNICATIONS AND THE ARTS (art, art history and appreciation, communications, dramatic arts, English, French, German, media arts, music, music performance, Spanish, speech/debate/rhetoric, and theater design), COMPUTER AND PHYSICAL SCIENCE (chemistry, computer science, mathematics, physics, and science), EDUCATION (art education, athletic training, early childhood education, education, elementary education, music education, physical education, and secondary education), ENGINEERING AND ENVIRONMENTAL DESIGN (technological management), HEALTH PROFESSIONS (clinical science, health care administration, nursing, prepharmacy, and ultrasound technology), SOCIAL SCIENCE (anthropology, corrections, criminal justice, economics, forensic studies, history, human services, interdisciplinary studies, law enforcement and corrections, liberal arts/general studies, paralegal studies, philosophy, political science/government, psychology, public administration, religion, social work, and sociology). Natural sciences, art, and music are the strongest academically. Business administration, criminal justice, and nursing have the largest enrollments.

ACTIVITIES: 7% of men belong to 1 local and 5 national fraternities; 7% of women belong to 4 national sororities. There are 150 groups on campus, including art, band, campus activities board and peer educators, cheerleading, chess, choir, chorus, computers, dance, debate, drama, drill team, drum and bugle corps, environmental, ethnic, forensics, gay, honors, international, jazz band, literary magazine, marching band, musical theater, newspaper, orchestra, pep band, political, professional, radio and TV, religious, social, social service, student government, symphony, and yearbook. Popular campus events include Greek Week, Student Activities Fair and the Annual Sunflower Music Festival. **Sports:** There are 5 intercollegiate sports for men and 5 for women, and 20 intramural sports for men and 20 for women. Facilities include a recreation and wellness center with rock-climbing wall, indoor track, gym, cardiovascular and resistance training area, and wellness suite; a 2,700-seat field house for indoor sports; a 7,200-seat stadium for intercollegiate football; and a health center with a 6-lane swimming pool. **Graduates:** From July 1, 2013 to June 30, 2014, 819 bachelor's degrees were awarded. The most popular majors were nursing/health professions (26%), business (14%), and education (8%). 181 companies recruited on campus in 2013-2014. In an average class, 37% graduate in 6 years or less. Of the 2013 graduating class, 22% were enrolled in graduate school within 6 months of graduation, and 69% were employed.

SERVICES: Counseling and information services are available, as is tutoring in most subjects. There is a reader service for the blind, and remedial math and writing. **Library/Resources:** The 2 libraries contain 451,534 volumes, 88,198 microform items, 4,612 audio/video tapes/CDs/DVDs, and subscribe to 87,358 periodicals including electronic. Computerized library services include interlibrary loans, data-base searching, Internet access, and Wi-Fi capability. Special learning facilities include an art gallery, planetarium, radio station, and TV station. **Physically Challenged Students:** 95% of the campus is accessible. Facilities include wheelchair ramps, elevators, special parking, specially equipped restrooms, special class scheduling, lowered drinking fountains, lowered telephones, special housing. Note takers, readers, library assistance, recorders, reading machines, videotaped classes, oral tests, learning center, tutors, and extended time for tests are also available. **Special:** Washburn offers a co-op program in computer information science, engineering, social/behavioral science, education, and health profession; internships in numerous departments; and study abroad in 20 countries. Dual and student-designed majors, B.A.-B.S. degrees, an integrated studies degree, credit by examination, nondegree study, and pass/fail options are also available. A 3-2 engineering degree is possible in conjunction with the University of Kansas and Kansas State University. There are 11 national honor societies and a freshman honors program. **Visiting:** There are regularly scheduled orientations for prospective students, consisting of a campus visit program Monday through Friday at 9:00 a.m. and 2:00 p.m. that includes a tour, visits with faculty, financial aid information, and the opportunity to have all questions answered. There are guides for informal visits, visitors may sit in on classes, and stay overnight. To schedule a visit, contact the Admissions Office. **Campus Safety and Security:** Measures include 24-hour foot and vehicle patrol, emergency notification system, self-defense education, and security escort services. There are emergency telephones, lighted pathways/sidewalks, Whistle campaign, operation ID, textbook ID program, bicycle patrol, and fire safety programs for residential living facilities.

REQUIREMENTS: The ACT is required. Applicants should be graduates of an accredited secondary school or have the GED. AP and CLEP credits are accepted. **Procedure:** Freshmen are admitted to all sessions. Entrance exams should be taken during the junior year. There is a rolling admissions plan. Applications should be filed by August 1 for fall entry; January 2 for spring entry; and May 12 for summer entry. The fall 2014 application fee was $20. Applications are accepted on-line. **Transfer Students:** 514 transfer students enrolled in 2013-2014. Applicants must meet the same requirements as incoming freshmen. 30 of 120 credits required for the bachelor's degree must be completed at Washburn. **International Students:** There are 220 international students enrolled. The school actively recruits these students. They must take the TOEFL with a minimum score of 523 on the paper-based TOEFL (PBT) or 72 on the Internet-based version (iBT).

ADMISSIONS: 98% of the 2014-2015 applicants were accepted. The ACT scores were 35% below 21, 29% between 21 and 23, 20% between 24 and 26, 9% between 27 and 28, and 7% above 28. 27 freshmen graduated first in their class. **Admissions Contact:** Kris Klima, Director, Admissions. E-Mail: *admissions@washburn.edu* Web: *www.washburn.edu*

FINANCIAL AID: In 2014-2015, 64% of all full-time freshmen and 63% of continuing full-time students received some form of financial aid. 41% of all full-time freshmen and 41% of continuing full-time students received need-based aid. The average freshman award was $8,785. Need-based scholarships or need-based grants averaged $4,779; need-based self-help aid (loans and jobs) averaged $3,615; non-need-based athletic scholarships averaged $7,595; and other non-need-based awards and non-need-based scholarships averaged $3,064. 14% of undergraduate students work part-time. Average annual earnings from campus work are $2400. The average financial indebtedness of the 2014 graduate was $27,328. Washburn is a member of CSS. The FAFSA, and admission/scholarship application is required. The priority date for freshman financial aid applications for fall entry is February 15.

WICHITA STATE UNIVERSITY D-3
www.wichita.edu

Wichita, KS 67260	**(316) 978-3456**
	(316) 978-3085
Fax: (316) 978-3174	**Email: admissions@wichita.edu**
Full-time: 4208 men, 4482 women	**Faculty:** n/av
Part-time: 1184 men, 1425 women	**Ph.D.s:** 80%
Graduate: 1484 men, 1540 women	**Student/Faculty:** 18 to 1
Year: semesters, summer session	**Tuition:** $7557 ($16,113)
Room & Board: $7050	**Freshman Class:** 4517 applied, 4315 accepted, 1584 enrolled
SAT CR/M: 550/560 **ACT:** 24	**CEEB CODE:** 6884
Application Deadline: n/av	**COMPETITIVE+**

Wichita State University, established in 1895, is a public institution offering programs in the liberal arts and sciences, business, engineering, education, and health professions. Figures in the above capsule and in this profile are approximate. There are 6 undergraduate schools and 1 graduate school. In addition to regional accreditation, WSU has baccalaureate program accreditation with AACSB, ABET, ADA, APTA, CAHEA, CSWE, NASM, NCATE, and NLN. The 330-acre campus is in an urban area in the metropolitan Wichita area. Including any residence halls, there are 61 buildings.
STUDENT LIFE: 96% of undergraduates are from Kansas. Others are from 49 states, 88 foreign countries, and Canada. 64% are White. **Female To Male Ratio:** 1.1:1. The average age of freshmen is 19; all undergraduates, 23. 27% do not continue beyond their first year; 43% remain to graduate. **Housing:** 1453 students can be accommodated in college housing, which includes coed dorms, on-campus apartments, and married student housing. In addition, there are honors houses, fraternity houses, sorority houses, theme housing, and coed dorms. On-campus housing is available on a first-come, first-served basis. 92% of students commute. All students may keep cars.
FACULTY/CLASSROOMS: 51% of faculty are male; 49% are female. No introductory courses are taught by graduate students. The average class size in an introductory lecture is 23; in a laboratory is 20; and in a regular course is 15.
PROGRAMS OF STUDY: WSU confers A.A.,B.A., B.A.Ed., BAES., BASM., B.B.A, B.F.A., B.G.S., B.M., B.M.E., B.S., BSASE., B.S.CPE., B.S.E.E., B.S.H.S., B.S.I.E., B.S.M.E., B.S.M.F.E. and B.S.N. degrees. Associate, master's, and doctoral degrees are also awarded. Bachelor's degrees are awarded in BIOLOGICAL SCIENCE (biology/biological science), BUSINESS (accounting, banking and finance, business administration and management, entrepreneurial studies, human resources, international business management, management science, marketing/retailing/merchandising, and sports management), COMMUNICATIONS AND THE ARTS (art, art history and appreciation, communications, English, French, graphic design, Latin, music, Spanish, studio art, and visual and performing arts), COMPUTER AND PHYSICAL SCIENCE (chemistry, computer science, geology, mathematics, and physics), EDUCATION (art education, elementary education, music education, physical education, secondary education, and special education), ENGINEERING AND ENVIRONMENTAL DESIGN (aeronautical engineering, computer engineering, electrical/electronics engineering, industrial engineering, manufacturing engineering, and mechanical engineering), HEALTH PROFESSIONS (health care administration, medical laboratory technology, nursing, physician's assistant, and speech pathology/audiology), SOCIAL SCIENCE (anthropology, criminal justice, economics, ethnic studies, gerontology, history, liberal arts/general studies, philosophy, political science/government, psychology, social work, sociology, and women's studies). Engineering programs, physics and chemistry are the strongest academically. Psychology, nursing, elementary education and business administration have the largest enrollments.
ACTIVITIES: 4% of men belong to 10 national fraternities; 5% of women belong to 8 national sororities. There are 200 groups on campus, including TV station, art, band, cheerleading, chess, choir, chorus, computers, dance, debate, drama, environmental, ethnic, film, gay, honors, international, jazz band, literary magazine, Model

UN, musical theater, newspaper, opera, orchestra, pep band, photography, political, professional, religious, social, social service, student government, and symphony. Popular campus events include Hippodrome, International Week and ShocktoberFest. **Sports:** There are 14 intercollegiate sports for men and 12 for women, and 30 intramural sports for men and 30 for women. Facilities include a 10,656-seat arena, 2 stadiums, an 18-hole golf course, a baseball field, a tennis complex, and a recreation and sports center. **Graduates:** From July 1, 2013 to June 30, 2014, 2124 bachelor's degrees were awarded. The most popular majors were business/marketing (17%), health professions and related programs (17%), and engineering (11%). 75 companies recruited on campus in 2013-2014. In an average class, 44% graduate in 6 years or less.
SERVICES: Counseling and information services are available, as is tutoring in most subjects. There is a reader service for the blind, remedial math, reading, and writing. Group and individual psychological services are available for students and their families. **Library/Resources:** The library contains 1.9 million volumes, 1.2 million microform items, 200,973 audio/video tapes/CDs/DVDs, and subscribes to 61,010 periodicals including electronic. Computerized library services include interlibrary loans, database searching, Internet access, and Wi-Fi capability. Special learning facilities include an art gallery, natural history museum, TV station, electronic classroom, telecourses, the National Institute for Aviation Research, museum of art, and public observatory. **Physically Challenged Students:** 98% of the campus is accessible. Facilities include wheelchair ramps, elevators, special parking, specially equipped restrooms, special class scheduling, lowered drinking fountains, lowered telephones. wheelchairs, and braille typewriters. Interpreters for the hearing impaired, note taking, and typing services are also offered. **Special:** WSU offers co-op programs, internships, study abroad, work-study programs, and a Washington semester. Dual and student-designed majors, a general studies degree, credit by exam, nondegree study, and pass/fail options are also available. There are 14 national honor societies and a freshman honors program. **Visiting:** There are regularly scheduled orientations for prospective students, students may schedule their visit online through the school's web site. There are guides for informal visits, visitors may sit in on classes, and stay overnight. To schedule a visit, contact the Admissions Office. **Campus Safety and Security:** Measures include 24-hour foot and vehicle patrol, self-defense education, and security escort services. There are shuttle buses, emergency telephones, lighted pathways/sidewalks, and bicycle patrol.
REQUIREMENTS: The SAT or ACT is required. Applicants must submit a minimum composite ACT score of 21 or a satisfactory SAT score. Requirements include 4 years of English, 3 each of math, natural and social sciences, (one of these units must be lab), social studies, and academic electives. AP and CLEP credits are accepted. Important factors in the admissions decision are leadership record, evidence of special talent, and extracurricular activities record. To graduate, students need at least 124 credit hours, with a GPA of 2.0 to 2.5, depending on the major. Specific distribution requirements, as well as department requirements, must also be met. The core curriculum consists of 14 courses (42 hours) in general education. Students must have a minimum of 45 credit hours in courses numbered 300 or above. **Procedure:** Freshmen are admitted to all sessions. There are deferred admissions and rolling admissions plans. Application deadlines are open. The fall 2014 application fee was $30. Applications are accepted on-line. **Transfer Students:** 1478 transfer students enrolled in 2013-2014. Applicants must have a minimum GPA of 2.0 to 2.5, depending on the WSU college they wish to enter. 30 of 124 credits required for the bachelor's degree must be completed at WSU. **International Students:** The school actively recruits these students. They must take the TOEFL with a minimum score of 530 on the paper-based TOEFL (PBT) or 72 on the Internet-based version (iBT).
ADMISSIONS: 96% of the 2014-2015 applicants were accepted. The SAT scores for the 2014-2015 freshman class were: Critical Reading-- 34% below 500, 32% between 500 and 599, 28% between 600 and 699, and 6% between 700 and 800. Math-- 19% below 500, 49% between 500 and 599, 28% between 600 and 699, and 4% between 700 and 800. The ACT scores were 8% below 21, 48% between 21 and 23, and 43% above 28. 20% of the current freshmen were in the top fifth of their class; 80% were in the top two fifths. **Admissions Contact:** E-Mail: *admissions@wichita.edu* Web: *www.wichita.edu*

FINANCIAL AID: In 2014-2015, 72% of all full-time freshmen and 73% of continuing full-time students received some form of financial aid. 37% of all full-time freshmen and 34% of continuing full-time students received need-based aid. The average freshman award was $5,812. Need-based scholarships or need-based grants averaged $4,400; need-based self-help aid (loans and jobs) averaged $3,332; non-need-based athletic scholarships averaged $7,618; other non-need-based awards and non-need-based scholarships averaged $3,267; and $2,430 from other forms of aid. The average financial indebtedness of the 2014 graduate was $23,534. The FAFSA is required. The deadline for filing freshman financial aid applications for fall entry is March 15.

KENTUCKY

KENTUCKY

1 College Location

0 20 40 60 80 100
Miles

Highland Heights
Crestview Hills
Louisville
Georgetown
Frankfort
Midway
Lexington
Grayson
Morehead
Owensboro
Wilmore
Danville
Richmond
Berea
Pikeville
Campbellsville
Columbia
Pippa Passes
Bowling Green
Barbourville
Murray
Williamsburg

ALICE LLOYD COLLEGE *(The complete profile is made available exclusively on our website, www.barronspac.com)*

ASBURY UNIVERSITY   D-3
www.asbury.edu

Wilmore, KY 40390   (859) 858-3511
                                        (800) 888-1818
Fax: (859) 858-3921   **Email:** admissions@asbury.edu
Full-time: 517 men, 809 women   **Faculty:** 87
Part-time: 90 men, 116 women   **Ph.D.s:** 74%
Graduate: 54 men, 196 women   **Student/Faculty:** 12 to 1
Year: semesters, summer session   **Tuition:** $26,076
Room & Board: $5962   **Freshman Class:** 1211 applied, 796 accepted, 322 enrolled
SAT CR/M: 568/558 **ACT:** 24   **CEEB CODE:** 1019
Application Deadline: n/av   **VERY COMPETITIVE**

Asbury University is an independent liberal arts university, providing undergraduate and graduate educational programs guided by the classical tradition of orthodox Christian thought. On this foundation, we seek to provide an excellent integrated educational experience that appreciates truth in all areas of life and develops whole persons for achievement and service. Figures in the above capsule and in this profile are approximate. There are 3 undergraduate schools and 3 graduate schools. In addition to regional accreditation, Asbury has baccalaureate program accreditation with CSWE, NASM, and NCATE. The 65-acre campus is in a small town 20 minutes south of Lexington, KY. Including any residence halls, there are 30 buildings. **STUDENT LIFE:** 51% of undergraduates are from out of state, mostly the South. Students are from 42 states, 17 foreign countries, and Canada. 67% are from public schools. 87% are White. 83% are Protestant; 15% unknown denominations. **Male To Female Ratio:** 1.7:1. The average age of freshmen is 18; all undergraduates, 20. 17% do not continue beyond their first year; 68% remain to graduate. **Housing:** 1168 students can be accommodated in college housing, which includes single-sex dorms, on-campus apartments, off-campus apartments, and married student housing. In addition, there are language houses. On-campus housing is guaranteed for all 4 years. 85% of students live on campus; of those, 70% remain on campus on weekends. Alcohol is not permitted. Upperclassmen may keep cars. **FACULTY/CLASSROOMS:** 51% of faculty are male; 49% are female.

94% teach undergraduates, and 1% do both. No introductory courses are taught by graduate students. The average class size in an introductory lecture is 20; in a laboratory is 16; and in a regular course is 18. **PROGRAMS OF STUDY:** Asbury confers B.A. and B.S. degrees. Associate and Master's degrees are also awarded. Bachelor's degrees are awarded in AGRICULTURE (equine science), BIOLOGICAL SCIENCE (biochemistry and biology/biological science), BUSINESS (accounting, business administration and management, recreation and leisure services, and sports management), COMMUNICATIONS AND THE ARTS (art, classical languages, communications, creative writing, dramatic arts, English, film, television and digital media, French, journalism, music, Spanish, and theatre acting), COMPUTER AND PHYSICAL SCIENCE (actuarial mathematics, applied mathematics, chemistry, mathematics, and physical sciences), EDUCATION (art education, Christian education, elementary education, English education, foreign languages education, mathematics education, middle school education, music education, physical education, science education, secondary education, and social studies education), ENGINEERING AND ENVIRONMENTAL DESIGN (preengineering), HEALTH PROFESSIONS (exercise science, health science, Pre-Health Studies, and prephysical therapy), SOCIAL SCIENCE (biblical languages, biblical studies, criminal justice, history, ministries, missions, philosophy, political science/government, psychology, religion, social work, sociology, and youth ministry). Media communications and communication arts, teacher education, business, social work, and Christian studies have the largest enrollments. **ACTIVITIES:** There are no fraternities or sororities. There are 45 groups on campus, including art, band, cheerleading, choir, chorale, chorus, computers, debate, drama, ethnic, film, forensics, honors, international, jazz band, literary magazine, missionary, musical theater, newspaper, opera, orchestra, photography, political, professional, radio and TV, religious, social service, student government, and yearbook. Popular campus events include High Bridge Film Festival, Homecoming, Fall Revival, and Missions Conference. **Sports:** There are 8 intercollegiate sports for men and 9 for women, and 7 intramural sports for men and 7 for women. Facilities include a 1,500-seat gym, athletic fields, tennis courts, an indoor swimming pool, indoor/outdoor basketball courts, indoor horseback riding arena, and student center. **Graduates:** From July 1, 2013 to June 30, 2014, 323 bachelor's degrees were awarded. The most popular majors were media communication (16%), education (13%), and business management (9%). In an average class, 2% graduate in 3 years or less, 56% graduate in 4 years or less, 63% graduate in 5 years or less, and 64% graduate in 6 years or less. **SERVICES:** Counseling and information services are available, as is tutoring in most subjects. There is remedial writing. For students on academic probation, there are special classes and mentors who provide help in such areas as time management and test-taking skills. There is some help available for the visually impaired, such as tapes and agencies that offer aid. **Library/Resources:** The library contains 184,084 volumes, 13,238 microform items, 7,188 audio/video tapes/ CDs/DVDs, and subscribes to 299 periodicals including electronic. Computerized library services include interlibrary loans, database searching, Internet access, and Wi-Fi capability. Special learning facilities include an art gallery, radio station, TV station, Miller Center for Communication Arts, and blackbox theatre, and equine center houses classrooms, stables, and riding arena. **Physically Challenged Students:** 80% of the campus is accessible. Facilities include wheelchair ramps, elevators, special parking, specially equipped restrooms, special class scheduling, lowered drinking fountains, and lowered telephones. **Special:** For-credit internships are available in several academic areas as are opportunities for study abroad in 14 countries. 3-2 engineering degrees are offered with the University of Kentucky. There are 6 national honor societies. **Visiting:** There are regularly scheduled orientations for prospective students, including visits, scheduled individually or during planned visitation weekends, in which students stay overnight in dorms, visit classes, attend departmental open houses and financial aid sessions, and participate in chapel and campus events. There are guides for informal visits, visitors may sit in on classes, and stay overnight. To schedule a visit, contact the Admissions Visit Coordinators at visit@asbury.edu. **Campus Safety and Security:** Measures include 24-hour foot and vehicle patrol, emergency notification system, and security escort services. There are lighted pathways/sidewalks. There are planning forums and a student parking and safety committee.

REQUIREMENTS: The SAT or ACT is required. An official high school transcript or the GED is required for all new students and for transfer students with fewer than 30 college credit hours. Applicants should have completed 15 high school academic credits, including 4 units of English, 3 of math, and 2 each of lab science, social studies, and a foreign language. A GPA of 2.5 is required. AP and CLEP credits are accepted.To graduate with a bachelor's degree, students must complete a minimum of 124 cumulative semester hours, fulfill any liberal arts core requirements, and meet all requirements for at least one chosen major (50% of which must be completed at Asbury University), plus maintain a minimum GPA of 2.0. Traditional undergraduates earning a Bachelor of Arts degree must demonstrate proficiency in foreign language through the third semester college level. Students must complete 12 of their final 21 credit hours with Asbury University. **Procedure:** Freshmen are admitted to all sessions. Entrance exams should be taken in the junior year or in the first semester of the senior year. There are early admissions, deferred admissions, and rolling admissions plans. Application deadlines are open. Notification is sent on a rolling basis. Applications are accepted on-line. **Transfer Students:** 52 transfer students enrolled in 2013-2014. Applicants with 18 quarter hours or 12 semester hours of college work or more are considered transfers. They must have an overall minimum GPA of 2.5 and be in good standing at each previous institution attended. Transfers with fewer than 30 semester hours of college work must submit a high school transcript. 49 of 124 credits required for the bachelor's degree must be completed at Asbury. **International Students:** There are 25 international students enrolled. They must take the TOEFL with a minimum score of 550 on the paper-based TOEFL (PBT) or 80 on the Internet-based version (iBT). **ADMISSIONS:** 66% of the 2014-2015 applicants were accepted. The SAT scores for the 2014-2015 freshman class were: Critical Reading--21% below 500, 41% between 500 and 599, 33% between 600 and 699, and 5% between 700 and 800; Math--24% below 500, 40% between 500 and 599, 32% between 600 and 699, and 4% between 700 and 800. The ACT scores were 17% below 21, 27% between 21 and 23, 26% between 24 and 26, 11% between 27 and 28, and 19% above 28. 47% of the current freshmen were in the top fifth of their class; 75% were in the top two fifths. 9 freshmen graduated first in their class. **Admissions Contact:** Lisa Harper, Director of Admissions. E-Mail: *admissions@asbury.edu* Web: *www.asbury.edu*

FINANCIAL AID: In 2014-2015, 79% of all full-time freshmen and 79% of continuing full-time students received some form of financial aid. 79% of all full-time freshmen and 77% of continuing full-time

students received need-based aid. The average freshman award was $19,835. Need-based scholarships or need-based grants averaged $14,781; need-based self-help aid (loans and jobs) averaged $4,117; non-need-based athletic scholarships averaged $5,261; and other non-need-based awards and non-need-based scholarships averaged $13,764. The average financial indebtedness of the 2014 graduate was $27,916. The FAFSA and the college's own financial statement are required. The priority date for freshman financial aid applications for fall entry is March 1. The deadline for filing freshman financial aid applications for fall entry is May 1.

BELLARMINE UNIVERSITY D-2
www.bellarmine.edu

Louisville, KY 40205

(502) 272-8131
(800) 274-4723

Fax: (502) 272-8002 — Email: admissions@bellarmine.edu

Full-time: 869 men, 1475 women	**Faculty:** 129; IIA, av$
Part-time: 90 men, 296 women	**Ph.D.s:** 82%
Graduate: 275 men, 597 women	**Student/Faculty:** 17 to 1
Year: semesters, summer session	**Tuition:** $33,180
Room & Board: $9770	**Freshman Class:** 4317 applied, 3716 accepted, 607 enrolled
SAT CR/M: 546/551 **ACT:** 24	**CEEB CODE:** 1056
Application Deadline: February 1	**VERY COMPETITIVE**

Bellarmine University, founded in 1950, is an independent Catholic university offering undergraduate and graduate programs in the liberal arts and professional studies. Figures in the above capsule and in this profile are approximate. There are 6 undergraduate schools and 6 graduate schools. In addition to regional accreditation, Bellarmine has baccalaureate program accreditation with AACSB, NCATE, CAAHEP, CAPTE, CCNE, CoARC, and NAACLS. The 144-acre campus is in a suburban area in Louisville, Kentucky. Including any residence halls, there are 42 buildings.

STUDENT LIFE: 68% of undergraduates are from Kentucky. Others are from 29 states, 20 foreign countries, and Canada. 63% are from public schools. 81% are White. 49% are Catholic; 25% Protestant. **Male To Female Ratio:** 1.9:1. The average age of freshmen is 18; all undergraduates, 21. 22% do not continue beyond their first year; 63% remain to graduate. **Housing:** 1127 students can be accommodated in college housing, which includes single-sex and coed dorms and on-campus apartments. In addition, there are honors houses and special-interest houses. On-campus housing is available on a first-come, first-served basis, and is available on a lottery system for upperclassmen. Priority is given to out-of-town students. 53% of students commute. Alcohol is not permitted. All students may keep cars.

FACULTY/CLASSROOMS: 48% of faculty are male; 52% are female. 85% teach undergraduates, and 75% do both. No introductory courses are taught by graduate students. The average class size in an introductory lecture is 21; in a laboratory is 17; and in a regular course is 21.

PROGRAMS OF STUDY: Bellarmine confers B.A., B.S., B.S.H.S. and B.S.N. degrees. Master's and Doctoral degrees are also awarded. Bachelor's degrees are awarded in BIOLOGICAL SCIENCE (biochemistry, biology/biological science, biophysics, and molecular biology), BUSINESS (accounting, banking and finance, and business administration and management), COMMUNICATIONS AND THE ARTS (arts administration/management, communications, English, fine arts, languages, music, music technology, Spanish, speech/ debate/rhetoric, and studio art), COMPUTER AND PHYSICAL SCIENCE (actuarial science, chemistry, computer science, mathematics, and physics), EDUCATION (elementary education, middle school education, and special education), ENGINEERING AND ENVIRONMENTAL DESIGN (computer engineering, computer technology, and preengineering), HEALTH PROFESSIONS (clinical science, exercise science, medical technology, nursing, predentistry, premedicine, prephysical therapy, preveterinary science, and respiratory therapy), SOCIAL SCIENCE (criminal justice, economics, history, interdisciplinary studies, international studies, liberal arts/general studies, philosophy, political science/government, psychology, sociology, and theological studies). Preprofessional programs, nursing, and accounting are the strongest academically.

ACTIVITIES: 1% of men and 3 of women belong to 3 national fraternities; 1% of women belong to 1 national sorority. There are 50 groups on campus, including and wind ensemble, art, band, cheerleading, chess, choir, chorale, chorus, computers, dance, debate, drama, ethnic, gay, honors, international, jazz band, literary magazine, mock trial team, musical theater, newspaper, opera, pep band, photography, political, professional, radio and TV, religious, social, social service, and student government. Popular campus events include Hillside Concerts, Midnight Breakfast, and Ball on the Belle (Halloween Cruise). **Sports:** There are 9 intercollegiate sports for men and 10 for women, and 8 intramural sports for men and 8 for women. Facilities include a 3000-seat basketball and volleyball arena and a fully lit, 2000-seat soccer, field hockey, lacrosse, and track stadium with an artificial turf field and an 8-lane dual-durometer polyurethane poured surface. **Graduates:** From July 1, 2013 to June 30, 2014, 607 bachelor's degrees were awarded. The most popular majors were health professions and related sciences (32%), business/marketing (16%), and psychology (9%). In an average class, 1% graduate in 3 years or less, 51% graduate in 4 years or less, 65% graduate in 5 years or less, and 66% graduate in 6 years or less. Of the 2013 graduating class, 23% were enrolled in graduate school within 6 months of graduation, and 90% were employed.

SERVICES: Counseling and information services are available, as is tutoring in every subject. The Academic Resource Center provides one-on-one or group tutoring for all 100- and 200-level courses. Disability Services provides note takers, distraction-reduced testing environments, extended time, books on tape, and scribe services. **Library/Resources:** The library contains 128,772 volumes, 316,810 microform items, and 4,964 audio/video tapes/CDs/DVDs, and subscribes to 105,441 periodicals including electronic. Computerized library services include interlibrary loans, database searching, Internet access, and Wi-Fi capability. Special learning facilities include an art gallery, radio station, the Thomas Merton Center. **Physically Challenged Students:** 85% of the campus is accessible. Facilities include wheelchair ramps, elevators, special parking, specially equipped restrooms, special class scheduling, lowered drinking fountains, lowered telephones, and special housing. **Special:** Cross-registration may be arranged through Kentuckiana Metroversity, a consortium of colleges in Kentucky and southern Indiana. Bellarmine also offers study abroad in more than 50 countries, internships in most majors, a Washington semester, a liberal studies degree, dual majors, accelerated degree programs, credit for life experience, pass/fail options during the junior and senior years, and a marine biology program in the Bahamas. There is also an honors program and the Brown Leadership Program. There are 5 national honor societies and a freshman honors program. **Visiting:** There are regularly scheduled orientations for prospective students, including an admissions and financial aid session, a campus tour, interviews with faculty, and participation in a student panel. There are guides for informal visits, visitors may sit in on classes, and stay overnight. To schedule a visit, contact the Office of Admission. **Campus Safety and Security:** Measures include 24-hour foot and vehicle patrol, self-defense education, and security escort services. There are shuttle buses, emergency telephones, lighted pathways/sidewalks, controlled access to dorms/residences, security alert bulletins, CPR-certified security, and security cameras in residence halls and in the parking lot.

REQUIREMENTS: The SAT or ACT is required. High school courses should include 4 years of English, 3 years of math, and 2 years each of science and social studies. 2 years of foreign language is recommended. The GED is accepted. An essay may be requested. A GPA of 2.5 is required. AP and CLEP credits are accepted. Important factors in the admissions decision are recommendations by school officials, advanced placement or honors courses, and extracurricular activities record. In order to graduate, students must complete a minimum of 126 credit hours with a minimum GPA of 2.0. Between 24 and 52 hours are required in the major. All students must fulfill 49 credit hours of core requirements, including English, philosophy, theology, math, social sciences, natural sciences, fine arts, and Western civilization. Required freshman, sophomore, junior, and senior seminars focus on the American experience, transcultural experience, and Catholic social justice. Students in the honors program must

complete a senior honors thesis. **Procedure:** Freshmen are admitted fall, spring, and summer. Entrance exams should be taken by December of the senior year. There is a deferred admissions plan. Applications should be filed by February 1 for fall entry, along with a $25 fee. Applications are accepted on-line. **Transfer Students:** 78 transfer students enrolled in 2013-2014. Applicants should have a minimum college GPA of 2.0 and submit transcripts from all postsecondary schools attended. 36 of 126 credits required for the bachelor's degree must be completed at Bellarmine. **International Students:** There are 51 international students enrolled. The school actively recruits these students. They must take the TOEFL with a minimum score of 550 on the paper-based TOEFL (PBT) or 80 on the Internet-based version (iBT), or take the MELAB. The SAT or ACT be used in lieu of the TOEFL.

ADMISSIONS: 86% of the 2014-2015 applicants were accepted. The SAT scores for the 2014-2015 freshman class were: Critical Reading--28% below 500, 46% between 500 and 599, 25% between 600 and 699, and 1% between 700 and 800; Math--24% below 500, 48% between 500 and 599, 24% between 600 and 699, and 4% between 700 and 800. The ACT scores were 12% below 21, 33% between 21 and 23, 30% between 24 and 26, 12% between 27 and 28, and 11% above 28. 50% of the current freshmen were in the top fifth of their class; 80% were in the top two fifths. 10 freshmen graduated first in their class. **Admissions Contact:** Timothy Sturgeon, Dean of Admissions. E-Mail: *admissions@bellarmine.edu* Web: *www.bellarmine.edu*

FINANCIAL AID: In 2014-2015, 100% of all full-time freshmen and 97% of continuing full-time students received some form of financial aid. 77% of all full-time freshmen and 71% of continuing full-time students received need-based aid. The average freshman award was $27,350. Need-based scholarships or need-based grants averaged $20,704; need-based self-help aid (loans and jobs) averaged $5,923; non-need-based athletic scholarships averaged $6,000; other non-need-based awards and non-need-based scholarships averaged $20,404; and $3,391 from other forms of aid. 65% of undergraduate students work part-time. Average annual earnings from campus work are $1000. The average financial indebtedness of the 2014 graduate was $23,925. The FAFSA is required. The priority date for freshman financial aid applications for fall entry is March 1. The deadline for filing freshman financial aid applications for fall entry is May 1.

BEREA COLLEGE   E-3
www.berea.edu

Berea, KY 40404   (859) 985-3500
              (800) 326-5948

Fax: (859) 985-3512	Email: hodsonl@berea.edu
Full-time: 686 men, 892 women	Faculty: 132; IIB, av$
Part-time: 26 men, 17 women	Ph.D.s: 989%
Graduate: n/av	Student/Faculty: 10 to 1
Year: semesters, summer session	Tuition: $870
Room & Board: $6322	Freshman Class: 1649 applied, 555 accepted, 416 enrolled
SAT CR/M/W: 545/570/540 ACT: 24	CEEB CODE: 1060
Application Deadline: n/av	COMPETITIVE

Berea College, founded in 1855, is a private liberal arts institution. Berea combines college, federal, and state grants, as well as outside scholarships earned by students, to provide every admitted student with a 4-year, full-tuition scholarship. The college provides a laptop for every student. As part of these scholarship agreements, each student is required to work on campus at least 10 hours weekly while carrying a normal academic load. There is 1 undergraduate school. In addition to regional accreditation, Berea has baccalaureate program accreditation with NCATE and CCNE. The 140-acre campus is in a suburban area 40 miles south of Lexington, KY. Including any residence halls, there are 47 buildings.

STUDENT LIFE: 53% of undergraduates are from out of state, mostly the South. Students are from 43 states, and 62 foreign countries. 66% are White; 16% African American. **Male To Female Ratio:** 1.3:1. The average age of freshmen is 18; all undergraduates, 21. 16% do not continue beyond their first year; 62% remain to graduate.

Housing: 1389 students can be accommodated in college housing, which includes single-sex dorms, on-campus apartments, and married student housing. In addition, there are special-interest houses, Ecovillage and a Deep Green Residence Hall (sustainable living). On-campus housing is guaranteed for all 4 years. 82% of students live on campus. Alcohol is not permitted. Some may keep cars.

FACULTY/CLASSROOMS: 55% of faculty are male; 45% are female. All teach undergraduates. No introductory courses are taught by graduate students. The average class size in a laboratory is 20 and in a regular course is 20.

PROGRAMS OF STUDY: Berea confers B.A. and B.S. degrees. Bachelor's degrees are awarded in AGRICULTURE (agriculture), BIOLOGICAL SCIENCE (biology/biological science), BUSINESS (business administration and management), COMMUNICATIONS AND THE ARTS (art, communications, dramatic arts, English, French, German, music, Spanish, and theatre arts), COMPUTER AND PHYSICAL SCIENCE (applied mathematics, chemistry, computer science, mathematics, and physics), EDUCATION (education, elementary education, and physical education), ENGINEERING AND ENVIRONMENTAL DESIGN (industrial engineering technology), HEALTH PROFESSIONS (nursing), SOCIAL SCIENCE (African studies, African American studies, Asian/Oriental studies, child care/child and family studies, economics, history, philosophy, political science/government, psychology, religion, sociology, and women's studies). Business administration, technology and applied design, child and family studies have the largest enrollments.

ACTIVITIES: There are no fraternities or sororities. There are 75 groups on campus, including art, band, cheerleading, chess, choir, chorus, communications, dance, debate, drama, environmental, ethnic, gay, honors, international, jazz band, literary magazine, newspaper, orchestra, pep band, photography, political, professional, religious, social, social service, and student government. Popular campus events include Mountain Day and Labor Day. **Sports:** There are 9 intercollegiate sports for men and 9 for women, and 4 intramural sports for men and 4 for women. Facilities include an indoor swimming pool, 5 racquetball courts, 15 tennis courts, playing fields, a dance studio, a 3-lane indoor walking track, an 8-lane all-weather track, and weight training and cardiovascular exercise rooms. **Graduates:** From July 1, 2013 to June 30, 2014, 337 bachelor's degrees were awarded. The most popular majors were biology (9%), child and family studies (8%), and agriculture and natural resources (6%). 110 companies recruited on campus in 2013-2014. In an average class, 48% graduate in 4 years or less, 62% graduate in 5 years or less, and 62% graduate in 6 years or less.

SERVICES: Counseling and information services are available, as is tutoring in some subjects. There is a reader service for the blind, and remedial math, reading, and writing. The Center for Transformative Learning supports research, writing, and public speaking across the curriculum. **Library/Resources:** The library contains 374,320 volumes, 149,517 microform items, 11,900 audio/video tapes/CDs/DVDs, and subscribes to 535 periodicals including electronic. Computerized library services include interlibrary loans, database searching, Internet access, and Wi-Fi capability. Special learning facilities include an art gallery, planetarium, a geology museum. **Physically Challenged Students:** 53% of the campus is accessible. Facilities include wheelchair ramps, elevators, special parking, specially equipped restrooms, special class scheduling, lowered drinking fountains, lowered telephones, electronic doors, and a lift chair for the indoor pool. **Special:** Students may study abroad in many countries. They can also participate in internships, and independent and team-initiated studies. Student-designed majors are available. A 3-2 engineering degree is offered with the University of Kentucky. All students must participate in an on-campus work program 10 to 15 hours per week. There are 19 national honor societies. **Visiting:** There are regularly scheduled orientations for prospective students. Student visits consist of an introductory session and a tour of campus and residence halls. For applicants, the visit includes a private interview and/or conversation with an admissions representative. There are guides for informal visits, visitors may sit in on classes, and stay overnight. To schedule a visit, contact the Campus Visit Reservation Center at (800) 326-5948 or (859) 985-3500. **Campus Safety and Security:** Measures include 24-hour foot and vehicle patrol, emergency notification system, self-defense education, and security escort services.

There are emergency telephones, lighted pathways/sidewalks, ongoing programs on campus safety, theft prevention, assault and rape prevention, fire prevention, defensive driving, and occupational safety, including work with hazardous materials.

REQUIREMENTS: Either the ACT or SAT is required. Applicants should be graduates of an accredited secondary school. The GED is accepted. Home-schooled students are also encouraged to apply. Financial need is a requirement for admission. Berea recommends 4 units in English, 3 in math, and 2 each in foreign language, science, and social studies. AP and CLEP credits are accepted. Important factors in the admissions decision are ability to finance college education, geographical diversity, and advanced placement or honors courses. Berea's curriculum offers the advantage of interdisciplinary general study coupled with intensive study in 31 major fields (some of which have multiple concentrations) and 32 minor fields of study. In all academic disciplines, students acquire knowledge and deepen their understanding of the subject area, while gaining competency in applying the content and methods of inquiry to daily life. A degree is conferred upon the completion of both the General Education curriculum and the curriculum of a selected major, provided the student has earned the minimum number of credits (including 20 outside the major), and has earned a cumulative grade point average (GPA) of 2.0 or higher in all courses, as well as in the major course work. (Please be aware that some academic programs require a GPA higher than the College requirement of 2.0.) A minimum of 32 earned course credits (typically 34 in Nursing) is required for graduation, with at least 20 courses taken outside the major discipline. **Procedure:** Freshmen are admitted fall. Entrance exams should be taken during the junior year or early in the senior year. There is a rolling admissions plan. Application deadlines are open. Applications are accepted on-line. **Transfer Students:** 46 transfer students enrolled in 2013-2014. Applicants must be in good standing at the last college attended, and have a minimum GPA of 2.0. 8 of 33 credits required for the bachelor's degree must be completed at Berea. **International Students:** There are 120 international students enrolled. They must take the TOEFL with a minimum score of 500 on the paper-based TOEFL (PBT) or 61 on the Internet-based version (iBT), IELTS, scoring 5 overall and 5 in each exam area, or SAT, scoring 1210 (430 Critical Reading), or ACT.

ADMISSIONS: 34% of the 2014-2015 applicants were accepted. The SAT scores for the 2014-2015 freshman class were: Critical Reading--20% below 500, 52% between 500 and 599, 23% between 600 and 699, and 5% between 700 and 800; Math--20% below 500, 38% between 500 and 599, 36% between 600 and 699, and 7% between 700 and 800; Writing--21% below 500, 54% between 500 and 599, 20% between 600 and 699, and 5% between 700 and 800. The ACT scores were 13% below 21, 31% between 21 and 23, 28% between 24 and 26, 12% between 27 and 28, and 16% above 28. 58% of the current freshmen were in the top fifth of their class; 89% were in the top two fifths. 12 freshmen graduated first in their class. **Admissions Contact:** Luke Hodson, Director of Admissions . E-Mail: *hodsonl@berea.edu* Web: *www.berea.edu*

FINANCIAL AID: In 2014-2015, 100% of all full-time freshmen and 100% of continuing full-time students received some form of financial aid. 100% of all full-time freshmen and 100% of continuing full-time students received need-based aid. The average freshman award was $31,547. 100% of undergraduate students work part-time. The FAFSA is required. The priority date for freshman financial aid applications for fall entry is January 31. The deadline for filing freshman financial aid applications for fall entry is March 1.

BRESCIA UNIVERSITY B-3
www.brescia.edu

Owensboro, KY 42301

(270) 685-3131
(877) BRESCIA

Fax: n/av

Email: admissions@brescia.edu

Full-time: 199 men, 443 women

Faculty: 38

Part-time: 23 men, 136 women

Ph.D.s: 70%

Graduate: 6 men, 11 women

Student/Faculty: 13 to 1

Year: semesters, summer session

Tuition: $18,140

Room & Board: $8000

Freshman Class: 5798 applied, 1189 accepted, 163 enrolled

SAT or ACT: required

CEEB CODE: 1071

Application Deadline: open

VERY COMPETITIVE+

Brescia University, founded in 1925 as a women's junior college, became a 4-year, coeducational liberal arts institution in 1950. It is a private school affiliated with the Roman Catholic Church. The university offers certificates, associate, baccalaureate, and master's degrees through on-ground and online classes. Figures in the above capsule and in this profile are approximate. There are 6 undergraduate schools and 2 graduate schools. In addition to regional accreditation, Brescia has baccalaureate program accreditation with CSWE and NCATE. The 6-acre campus is in an urban area 32 miles southeast of Evansville, Indiana, and 125 miles from both Louisville and Nashville. Including any residence halls, there are 19 buildings.

STUDENT LIFE: 78% of undergraduates are from Kentucky. Others are from 42 states, 8 foreign countries, and Canada. 89% are White. 39% are Catholic; 32% Protestant; 27% claim no religious affiliation. **Male To Female Ratio:** 2.6:1. The average age of freshmen is 19; all undergraduates, 26. 33% do not continue beyond their first year. **Housing:** 224 students can be accommodated in college housing, which includes single-sex and coed dorms and on-campus apartments. In addition, there are honors houses and special-interest houses. On-campus housing is available on a first-come, first-served basis, and is available on a lottery system for upperclassmen. 60% of students commute. Alcohol is not permitted. All students may keep cars.

FACULTY/CLASSROOMS: 47% of faculty are male; 53% are female. All teach undergraduates. No introductory courses are taught by graduate students. The average class size in an introductory lecture is 14; in a laboratory is 10; and in a regular course is 12.

PROGRAMS OF STUDY: Brescia confers B.A., B.S., and B.S.W. degrees. Associate and Masters degrees are also awarded. Bachelor's degrees are awarded in BIOLOGICAL SCIENCE (biochemistry and biology/biological science), BUSINESS (accounting, banking and finance, business administration and management, business economics, and human resources), COMMUNICATIONS AND THE ARTS (art, English, graphic design, Spanish, and theatre arts), COMPUTER AND PHYSICAL SCIENCE (chemistry, computer science, mathematics, and physical sciences), EDUCATION (art education, early childhood education, education of the mentally handicapped, elementary education, and special education), HEALTH PROFESSIONS (medical laboratory technology, medical technology, and speech pathology/audiology), SOCIAL SCIENCE (addiction studies, history, liberal arts/general studies, pastoral studies, psychology, religion, social studies, and social work). Education, business, and English are the strongest academically. Business, social work, and education have the largest enrollments.

ACTIVITIES: There are no fraternities or sororities. There are 25 groups on campus, including philosophy, art, choir, chorus, communications, computers, creative writing, drama, honors, international, literary magazine, musical theater, newspaper, pep band, political, professional, religious, social, social service, and student government. Popular campus events include Homecoming, Opening Year Mass, Founders Convocation and Inaugural Ball. **Sports:** There are 7 intercollegiate sports for men and 8 for women, and 5 intramural sports for men and 5 for women. Facilities include a gym, two tennis courts, weight room, game room, cardiovascular workout room, racquetball court, batting cage, baseball field and soccer field. **Graduates:** From July 1, 2013 to June 30, 2014, 87 bachelor's degrees were awarded. The most popular majors were social work (25%), business (16%), and communication sciences and disorders (10%). In an average class, 17% graduate in 4 years or less, 26% graduate in 5 years or less, and 32% graduate in 6 years or less.

SERVICES: Counseling and information services are available, as is tutoring in most subjects. There is remedial math, reading, and writing. **Library/Resources:** The library contains 156,380 volumes, 55,283 microform items, 3,709 audio/video tapes/CDs/DVDs, and subscribes to 27,527 periodicals including electronic. Computerized library services include interlibrary loans and database searching. Special learning facilities include an art gallery. **Physically Challenged Students:** 95% of the campus is accessible. Facilities include wheelchair ramps, elevators, special parking, specially equipped restrooms, lowered drinking fountains, and lowered telephones. **Special:** Brescia offers a combined engineering degree with the University of Kentucky and the University of Louisville. Work-study programs, student-designed majors, nondegree study, dual majors, study abroad

in Mexico, an internship in professional writing, pass/fail options and cross-registration with Kentucky Wesleyan are available. The Weekend College offers four 9-week modules of study. There are 2 national honor societies and a freshman honors program. **Visiting:** There are regularly scheduled orientations for prospective students, including spring and fall open houses for freshmen and a spring transfer open house. There are guides for informal visits, visitors may sit in on classes, and stay overnight. To schedule a visit, contact The Office of Admissions. **Campus Safety and Security:** Measures include emergency notification system and security escort services. There are emergency telephones, lighted pathways/sidewalks, and night security.

REQUIREMENTS: The SAT or ACT is required. Essays and recommendations are helpful. High school units should include 4 of English, 3 of math, and 2 each in social studies, science, foreign language, fine arts, and computer science. AP and CLEP credits are accepted. Important factors in the admissions decision are advanced placement or honors courses and recommendations by school officials. All students must earn 128 credit hours, including 42 upper-division hours, and 30 or more hours in the major, while maintaining an overall GPA of 2.0 and 2.5 in the major. Distribution requirements include 18 hours in aesthetics, language, and literature, 12 in social science, 9 each in fine arts, science, and math, 6 in religious studies, and 3 in philosophy. Students must also demonstrate computer competency. **Procedure:** Freshmen are admitted to all sessions. Entrance exams should be taken at the end of the junior year. There is a rolling admissions plan. Application deadlines are open. The fall 2014 application fee was $25. Applications are accepted on-line. **Transfer Students:** 120 transfer students enrolled in 2013-2014. Transfer students must have a minimum GPA of 2.0. 42 of 128 credits required for the bachelor's degree must be completed at Brescia. **International Students:** The school actively recruits these students. They must take the TOEFL. They must also take the SAT or ACT.

ADMISSIONS: 21% of the 2014-2015 applicants were accepted. The SAT scores for the 2014-2015 freshman class were: Math--53% below 500, and 47% between 500 and 599. The ACT scores were 20% below 21, 45% between 21 and 23, 17% between 24 and 26, 15% between 27 and 28, and 3% above 28. **Admissions Contact:** Christy Rohner, Director of Admissions. E-Mail: *admissions@brescia.edu* Web: *www.brescia.edu*

FINANCIAL AID: 100% of undergraduate students work part-time. Brescia is a member of CSS. The FAFSA is required. The deadline for filing freshman financial aid applications for fall entry is March 1.

CAMPBELLSVILLE UNIVERSITY   D-3
www.campbellsville.edu

Campbellsville, KY 42718	(270) 789-5220
	(800) 264-6014
Fax: (270) 789-5071	Email: admissions@campbellsville.edu
Full-time: 875 men, 954 women	Faculty: 146
Part-time: 392 men, 757 women	Ph.D.s: 67%
Graduate: 182 men, 271 women	Student/Faculty: 14 to 1
Year: semesters, summer session	Tuition: $21,600
Room & Board: $7120	Freshman Class: 2477 applied, 1651 accepted, 579 enrolled
SAT: recommended ACT: 21	CEEB CODE: 1097
Application Deadline: n/av	COMPETITIVE

Campbellsville University, founded in 1906, is a private, comprehensive institution affiliated with the Kentucky Baptist Convention. Figures in the above capsule and in this profile are approximate. There are 7 undergraduate schools and 8 graduate schools. In addition to regional accreditation, Campbellsville has baccalaureate program accreditation with NASM. The 90-acre campus is in a small town 85 miles southwest of Lexington and 85 miles southeast of Louisville. Including any residence halls, there are 56 buildings.

STUDENT LIFE: 84% of undergraduates are from Kentucky. Others are from 33 states, 36 foreign countries, and Canada. 95% are from public schools. 80% are White; 11% African American. 60% are Protestant; 12% claim no religious affiliation. **Male To Female Ratio:** 1.4:1. The average age of freshmen is 19; all undergraduates, 25. 30% do not continue beyond their first year; 42% remain to graduate. **Housing:** 1044 students can be accommodated in college housing, which includes single-sex dorms, on-campus apartments, and married student housing. In addition, there are honors houses and special-interest houses. On-campus housing is guaranteed for all 4 years. 64% of students commute. Alcohol is not permitted. All students may keep cars.

FACULTY/CLASSROOMS: 51% of faculty are male; 49% are female. All teach undergraduates. No introductory courses are taught by graduate students. The average class size in an introductory lecture is 24; in a laboratory is 12; and in a regular course is 17.

PROGRAMS OF STUDY: Campbellsville confers B.A., B.S., B.M., B.S.B.A., B.S.Med.Tech. and B.S.W. degrees. Associate and Master's degrees are also awarded. Bachelor's degrees are awarded in BIOLOGICAL SCIENCE (biology/biological science), BUSINESS (accounting, business administration and management, business economics, marketing management, office supervision and management, and sports management), COMMUNICATIONS AND THE ARTS (art, communications, English, music, music performance, theatre arts, and voice), COMPUTER AND PHYSICAL SCIENCE (chemistry, computer science, information sciences and systems, and mathematics), EDUCATION (athletic training, early childhood education, elementary education, health education, middle school education, music education, physical education, recreation education, social science education, and teaching English as a second/foreign language (TESOL/TEFOL)), ENGINEERING AND ENVIRONMENTAL DESIGN (preengineering), HEALTH PROFESSIONS (exercise science, medical laboratory technology, nursing, predentistry, premedicine, prepharmacy, and sports medicine), SOCIAL SCIENCE (biblical studies, Christian studies, criminal justice, economics, history, political science/government, prelaw, psychology, religious education, religious music, social work, sociology, and youth ministry). Biology, chemistry, and music are the strongest academically. Elementary education, business administration, and social work have the largest enrollments.

ACTIVITIES: There are no fraternities or sororities. There are 45 groups on campus, including art, band, cheerleading, choir, chorale, chorus, computers, dance, drama, environmental, ethnic, honors, international, jazz band, literary magazine, marching band, musical theater, newspaper, opera, orchestra, pep band, photography, political, professional, radio and TV, religious, social, social service, student government, and symphony. Popular campus events include Valentine Banquet, a Christmas Celebration, and Heritage Day. **Sports:** There are 9 intercollegiate sports for men and 9 for women, and 10 intramural sports for men and 10 for women. Facilities include a swimming pool, a 1700-seat gym, a football stadium, a baseball field, an intramural activities center with skating facilities and large game rooms, and softball and soccer fields, and an indoor practice field. **Graduates:** From July 1, 2013 to June 30, 2014, 325 bachelor's degrees were awarded. The most popular majors were education (18%), business (16%), and religion (16%). In an average class, 42% graduate in 6 years or less.

SERVICES: Counseling and information services are available, as is tutoring in most subjects. There is remedial math, reading, and writing. There is also an AIDS education program and a study skills program. **Library/Resources:** The 2 libraries contain 108,000 volumes, 24,000 microform items, and 8,000 audio/video tapes/CDs/DVDs, and subscribe to 360 periodicals including electronic. Computerized library services include interlibrary loans, database searching, and Internet access. Special learning facilities include an art gallery, radio station, TV station, a teacher resource center, the Kentuckiana Collection, Clay Hill Memorial Forest, and the American Civil War Institute. **Physically Challenged Students:** 85% of the campus is accessible. Facilities include wheelchair ramps, elevators, special parking, specially equipped restrooms, special class scheduling, lowered drinking fountains, lowered telephones. **Special:** Legislative and public administration internships, a Washington semester, and federal work-study programs are available. The university also offers a semester in London program, a 3-2 engineering degree with the University of Kentucky, dual majors, credit by exam, credit for life, military, and work experience, non-degree study, and pass/fail options.

There is a freshman honors program. **Visiting:** There are regularly scheduled orientations for prospective students, consisting of visitation days held in October, February and April. There are guides for informal visits, visitors may sit in on classes, and stay overnight. To schedule a visit, contact the Admissions Office. **Campus Safety and Security:** Measures include 24-hour foot and vehicle patrol, emergency notification system, self-defense education, and security escort services. There are emergency telephones, lighted pathways/sidewalks, and controlled access to dorms/residences.

REQUIREMENTS: The ACT is required. The SAT is recommended. The SAT may be substituted for the ACT. Applicants must be graduates of an accredited secondary school with a GPA of 2.0. The GED is accepted. An interview is recommended. A GPA of 2.0 is required. AP and CLEP credits are accepted. Important factors in the admissions decision are evidence of special talent, leadership record, and advanced placement or honors courses. All candidates must be of good moral character. All students must complete a minimum of 128 semester hours, including 30 in the major, 21 in the minor, and 51 in general education courses. The minimum GPA is 2.5 for education majors, 2.1 for all others. All students must fulfill an English composition requirement. **Procedure:** Freshmen are admitted to all sessions. Entrance exams should be taken no later than February of the senior year. There are deferred admissions and rolling admissions plans. Check with the school for current application deadlines. The fall 2014 application fee was $20. Applications are accepted on-line. **Transfer Students:** 239 transfer students enrolled in 2013-2014. Of the 128 credits needed to graduate, all students must complete one third of the credits required for the major and the minor at the university. The last year must be completed in residence. 30 of 120 credits required for the bachelor's degree must be completed at Campbellsville. **International Students:** There are 159 international students enrolled. The school actively recruits these students. They must take the TOEFL. They must also take the SAT or ACT.

ADMISSIONS: 67% of the 2014-2015 applicants were accepted. The ACT scores were 46% below 21, 27% between 21 and 23, 15% between 24 and 26, 6% between 27 and 28, and 6% above 28. 46% of the current freshmen were in the top fifth of their class; 74% were in the top two fifths. **Admissions Contact:** David Walters, Vice President for Admissions. E-Mail: *admissions@campbellsville.edu* Web: *www.campbellsville.edu*

FINANCIAL AID: In 2014-2015, 95% of all full-time freshmen and 94% of continuing full-time students received some form of financial aid. 87% of all full-time freshmen and 83% of continuing full-time students received need-based aid. 44% of undergraduate students work part-time. The FAFSA is required. The priority date for freshman financial aid applications for fall entry is February 20. The deadline for filing freshman financial aid applications for fall entry is July 31.

CENTRE COLLEGE

D-3

www.centre.edu

Danville, KY 40422	**(859) 238-5350**
	(800) 423-6236
Fax: (859) 238-5373	Email: admission@centre.edu
Full-time: 539 men, 647 women	Faculty: 102; IIB, av$
Part-time: 1 men, 2 women	Ph.D.s: 98%
Graduate: n/av	Student/Faculty: 12 to 1
Year: 4-1-4	Tuition: $28,000
Room & Board: $7000	Freshman Class: 2159 applied, 1312 accepted, 316 enrolled
SAT CR/M: 625/615 ACT: 28	CEEB CODE: 1109
Application Deadline: February 1	HIGHLY COMPETITIVE+

Centre College, founded in 1819 by the Presbyterian Church, is a private liberal arts and sciences institution. The figures in the above capsule and in this profile are approximate. The 150-acre campus is in a small town 35 miles southwest of Lexington and 80 miles southeast of Louisville. Including any residence halls, there are 67 buildings. **STUDENT LIFE:** 56% of undergraduates are from Kentucky. Others are from 40 states, 11 foreign countries, and Canada. 64% are from public schools. 90% are White. 52% are Protestant; 23% Catholic; 23% claim no religious affiliation. **Male To Female Ratio:** 1.2:1. The average age of freshmen is 18; all undergraduates, 20. 5% do not continue beyond their first year; 80% remain to graduate. **Housing:** 1050 students can be accommodated in college housing, which includes single-sex and coed dorms and on-campus apartments. In addition, there are special-interest houses, fraternity houses, sorority houses, an international student house. On-campus housing is guaranteed for all 4 years. 95% of students live on campus; of those, 90% remain on campus on weekends. All students may keep cars.

FACULTY/CLASSROOMS: 64% of faculty are male; 37% are female. All teach and do research. No introductory courses are taught by graduate students. The average class size in an introductory lecture is 25; in a laboratory is 15; and in a regular course is 19.

PROGRAMS OF STUDY: Centre confers B.A. and B.S. degrees. Bachelor's degrees are awarded in BIOLOGICAL SCIENCE (biochemistry, biology/biological science, and molecular biology), COMMUNICATIONS AND THE ARTS (art history and appreciation, dramatic arts, English, fine arts, French, German, music, and Spanish), COMPUTER AND PHYSICAL SCIENCE (chemical physics, chemistry, computer science, mathematics, physical chemistry, and physics), EDUCATION (elementary education), SOCIAL SCIENCE (anthropology, classical/ancient civilization, economics, history, international relations, philosophy, political science/government, psychobiology, psychology, religion, and sociology). Biology, history, and psychology are the strongest academically and have the largest enrollments.

ACTIVITIES: 46% of men belong to 4 national fraternities; 52% of women belong to 4 national sororities. There are 105 groups on campus, including art, band, cheerleading, choir, chorale, chorus, computers, dance, debate, drama, environmental, ethnic, film, forensics, gay, honors, international, jazz band, literary magazine, musical theater, newspaper, orchestra, pep band, photography, political, professional, radio and TV, religious, social, social service, student government, and yearbook. Popular campus events include Carnival, Honors Convocation, and Honor Walk. **Sports:** There are 9 intercollegiate sports for men and 10 for women, and 8 intramural sports for men and 8 for women. Facilities include a complex with a 1500-seat gym, 3 basketball courts, 2 volleyball courts, training room, game room, sauna, weight room, fitness center, and racquetball/handball courts. There is also a 2500-seat stadium, tennis courts, and playing fields for football, track, baseball, softball, soccer, field hockey, and other sports. The natatorium has a 25-yard, 6-lane swimming pool. Golf teams compete at the local country club. **Graduates:** From July 1, 2013 to June 30, 2014, 270 bachelor's degrees were awarded. The most popular majors were English (13%), anthropology/sociology (13%), and Spanish (12%). 21 companies recruited on campus in 2013-2014. In an average class, 80% graduate in 4 years or less, 80% graduate in 5 years or less, and 80% graduate in 6 years or less. Of the 2013 graduating class, 30% were enrolled in graduate school within 6 months of graduation, and 63% were employed.

SERVICES: Counseling and information services are available, as is tutoring in most subjects. There is a reader service for the blind. **Library/Resources:** The library contains 361,512 volumes, 56,755 microform items, and 4,357 audio/video tapes/CDs/DVDs, and subscribes to 19,397 periodicals including electronic. Computerized library services include interlibrary loans, database searching, Internet access, and Wi-Fi capability. Special learning facilities include an art gallery, natural history museum, radio station, TV station, a performing arts center. **Physically Challenged Students:** 70% of the campus is accessible. Facilities include wheelchair ramps, elevators, special parking, specially equipped restrooms, special class scheduling, lowered drinking fountains, lowered telephones, special housing. **Special:** Centre offers internships, study abroad in 12 countries, a Washington semester through American University, work-study, and a 3-2 engineering degree with Vanderbilt University, Washington University at St. Louis, Columbia University, and the University of Kentucky. Student-designed majors, interdisciplinary majors including chemical physics, secondary education certification, and pre-law, pre-business, and pre-medicine programs are available. Pass/fail options also are available. There are 8 national honor societies including Phi Beta Kappa. **Visiting:** There are regularly scheduled orienta-

tions for prospective students, including a campus tour, an interview, pre-tour, and faculty appointments. There are guides for informal visits, visitors may sit in on classes, and stay overnight. To schedule a visit, contact the Office of Admission. **Campus Safety and Security:** Measures include 24-hour foot and vehicle patrol, emergency notification system, self-defense education, and security escort services. There are emergency telephones, lighted pathways/sidewalks, controlled access to dorms/residences, a working relationship with outside agencies.

REQUIREMENTS: The SAT or ACT and ACT Writing Test are recommended. No minimum test scores are required. Students should have completed a minimum of 15 academic credits, including 4 years each in English and math, 3 years each in science and social studies, 2 years in foreign language, and 1 year in an art- or music-related course. An essay is required, and an interview is strongly recommended. AP credits are accepted. Important factors in the admissions decision are advanced placement or honors courses, extracurricular activities record, and recommendations by school officials. All students must earn an overall GPA of 2.0 and complete a minimum of 111 credit hours. Students also must demonstrate competency in writing, foreign language, and math plus 1 course beyond basic skills in math, foreign language, or computer science. A freshman humanities program and a freshman seminar must be completed. Core curriculum requirements include 2 courses each in the humanities or art from the aesthetic context, the scientific/technological context; the social context, and the fundamental questions context. 2 phys ed courses must be completed by the end of sophomore year. **Procedure:** Freshmen are admitted in fall. Entrance exams should be taken by February of the senior year. There is a deferred admissions plan. Applications should be filed by February 1 for fall entry. The fall 2014 application fee was $40. Notification of early decision is sent January 15; regular decision, March 15. 186 applicants were on the 2014 waiting list; 19 were admitted. Applications are accepted on-line. **Transfer Students:** 6 transfer students enrolled in 2013-2014. Applicants for transfer must have all previous college transcripts on file and a recommendation from the dean of the most recent college attended. If the student has completed fewer than 2 years of college work, high school records must also be submitted. 45 of 111 credits required for the bachelor's degree must be completed at Centre. **International Students:** There are 25 international students enrolled. They must take the TOEFL, or may submit SAT or ACT scores.

ADMISSIONS: 61% of the 2014-2015 applicants were accepted. The SAT scores for the 2014-2015 freshman class were: Critical Reading--6% below 500, 31% between 500 and 599, 38% between 600 and 699, and 25% between 700 and 800; Math--6% below 500, 28% between 500 and 599, 56% between 600 and 699, and 10% between 700 and 800. The ACT scores were 2% below 21, 6% between 21 and 23, 25% between 24 and 26, 22% between 27 and 28, and 45% above 28. 79% of the current freshmen were in the top fifth of their class; 95% were in the top two fifths. There were 8 National Merit finalists. 29 freshmen graduated first in their class. **Admissions Contact:** Bob Nesmith, Director of Admissions. E-Mail: *admission@centre.edu* Web: *www.centre.edu*

FINANCIAL AID: In 2014-2015, 95% of all full-time freshmen and 96% of continuing full-time students received some form of financial aid. 58% of all full-time freshmen and 56% of continuing full-time students received need-based aid. The average freshman award was $22,193. Need-based scholarships or need-based grants averaged $19,673 ($28,000 maximum); and need-based self-help aid (loans and jobs) averaged $4,599 ($5,300 maximum). 24% of undergraduate students work part-time. Average annual earnings from campus work are $1750. The average financial indebtedness of the 2014 graduate was $15,700. Centre is a member of CSS. The FAFSA and the college's own financial statement are required. The priority date for freshman financial aid applications for fall entry is February 15. The deadline for filing freshman financial aid applications for fall entry is March 1.

EASTERN KENTUCKY UNIVERSITY E-3
www.eku.edu

Richmond, KY 40475	**(859) 622-2106**
	(800) 465-9191
Fax: (859) 622-3024	Email: admissions@eku.edu
Full-time: 4653 men, 6345 women	Faculty: 584; IIA, --$
Part-time: 898 men, 1763 women	Ph.D.s: 66%
Graduate: 691 men, 1489 women	Student/Faculty: 19 to 1
Year: semesters, summer session	Tuition: $5682 ($15,382)
Room & Board: $5479	Freshman Class: n/av
ACT: required	CEEB CODE: 1200
Application Deadline: August 1	**COMPETITIVE**

Eastern Kentucky University, established in 1906, is a public, state-supported institution offering degree programs in the arts and sciences, business, environmental studies, health fields, education, and public service occupations. The figures in the above capsule and in this profile are approximate. There are 5 undergraduate schools and 1 graduate school. In addition to regional accreditation, EKU has baccalaureate program accreditation with AACSB, ADA, AHEA, CSWE, FIDER, NASM, NCATE, NLN, and NRPA. The 628-acre campus is in a small town 20 miles south of Lexington. Including any residence halls, there are 98 buildings.

STUDENT LIFE: 87% of undergraduates are from Kentucky. Others are from 43 states, 32 foreign countries, and Canada. 90% are from public schools. 91% are White. **Male To Female Ratio:** 1.5:1. The average age of freshmen is 19; all undergraduates, 23. 35% do not continue beyond their first year; 37% remain to graduate. **Housing:** 5260 students can be accommodated in college housing, which includes single-sex and coed dorms, on-campus apartments, and married student housing. In addition, there are honors houses, special-interest houses, special accommodations for senior home economics students. On-campus housing is guaranteed for all 4 years. 71% of students commute. Alcohol is not permitted. All students may keep cars.

FACULTY/CLASSROOMS: 49% of faculty are male; 51% are female. 98% teach undergraduates, and 25% do both. No introductory courses are taught by graduate students. The average class size in an introductory lecture is 30; in a laboratory is 15; and in a regular course is 25.

PROGRAMS OF STUDY: EKU confers B.A., B.S., B.B.A., B.F.A., B.I.S., B.M., B.M.Ed., B.S.N. and B.S.W. degrees. Associate and Master's degrees are also awarded. Bachelor's degrees are awarded in AGRICULTURE (agriculture, horticulture, and wildlife management), BIOLOGICAL SCIENCE (biology/biological science and microbiology), BUSINESS (accounting, banking and finance, business administration and management, and marketing/retailing/merchandising), COMMUNICATIONS AND THE ARTS (art, broadcasting, dramatic arts, English, French, journalism, music, performing arts, public relations, Spanish, and speech/debate/rhetoric), COMPUTER AND PHYSICAL SCIENCE (chemistry, computer programming, computer science, geology, mathematics, and statistics), EDUCATION (art education, business education, education of the deaf and hearing impaired, elementary education, foreign languages education, health education, home economics education, industrial arts education, middle school education, music education, physical education, secondary education, special education, and technical education), ENGINEERING AND ENVIRONMENTAL DESIGN (airline piloting and navigation, construction technology, environmental science, interior design, and manufacturing technology), HEALTH PROFESSIONS (environmental health science, health care administration, nursing, and occupational therapy), SOCIAL SCIENCE (anthropology, child care/child and family studies, corrections, dietetics, economics, fire protection, forensic studies, geography, history, paralegal studies, philosophy, political science/government, psychology, social work, and sociology). Occupational therapy, psychology, and nursing are the strongest academically. Education, nursing, and law enforcement have the largest enrollments.

ACTIVITIES: There are 140 groups on campus, including art, band, cheerleading, choir, chorale, chorus, computers, dance, debate, drama, drill team, ethnic, film, gay, honors, international, jazz band, marching band, musical theater, newspaper, orchestra, pep band, photography, political, professional, radio and TV, religious, social service, student government, and symphony. Popular campus events include Hanging of the Greens at Christmas, International Month, and Fraternity/Sorority Competitions. **Sports:** There are 8 intercollegiate sports for men and 8 for women, and 12 intramural sports for men and 12 for women. Facilities include a dance studio, 5 gyms, 1 outdoor and 2 indoor swimming pools, 19 outdoor hard-court and 4 indoor tennis courts, handball and racquetball courts, training rooms, a martial arts room, a wellness center, a 7000-seat basketball arena, a 20,000-seat stadium, an 8-lane outdoor track, a field hockey area, an 18-hole golf course, fields for baseball, softball, soccer, weight facilities, and a conditioning center. **Graduates:** From July 1, 2013 to June 30, 2014, 1979 bachelor's degrees were awarded. The most popular majors were criminal justice and police studies (9%), nursing (9%), and curriculum and instruction (9%).

SERVICES: Counseling and information services are available, as is tutoring in some subjects. There is a reader service for the blind, and remedial math, reading, and writing. Tutoring is available in other fields upon request. **Library/Resources:** The 3 libraries contain 764,662 volumes, 1.3 million microform items, and 12,209 audio/video tapes/CDs/DVDs, and subscribe to 19,033 periodicals including electronic. Computerized library services include interlibrary loans, database searching, and Internet access. Special learning facilities include an art gallery, natural history museum, planetarium, radio station, TV station, a law enforcement complex that includes a training tank for underwater rescue and recovery. **Physically Challenged Students:** 85% of the campus is accessible. Facilities include wheelchair ramps, elevators, special parking, specially equipped restrooms, special class scheduling, lowered drinking fountains, and lowered telephones. **Special:** EKU offers cooperative programs with all academic colleges, internships, study abroad in various European countries, and a 3-2 engineering degree with The University of Kentucky or Auburn University. Students may opt for credit by exam, non-degree study, pass/fail options, student-designed and dual majors, and a general studies degree. There are 23 national honor societies, including Phi Beta Kappa, a freshman honors program, and 1 departmental honors program. **Visiting:** There are regularly scheduled orientations for prospective students, consisting of a 1-day program during the summer prior to fall enrollment. There are guides for informal visits, visitors may sit in on classes, and stay overnight. To schedule a visit, contact the Admissions Office. **Campus Safety and Security:** Measures include 24-hour foot and vehicle patrol, emergency notification system, self-defense education, and security escort services. There are shuttle buses, emergency telephones, lighted pathways/sidewalks, 16 crime-prevention programs.

REQUIREMENTS: The ACT is required. A GPA of 2.0 is required. AP and CLEP credits are accepted. Important factors in the admissions decision are evidence of special talent, extracurricular activities record, and leadership record. All students must complete 51 credit hours of general education requirements, including courses in phys ed, health, English, natural science, social science, math, and the humanities. Students must complete a total of 128 credit hours, including 45 to 60 credits in the major, with a minimum GPA of 2.0. **Procedure:** Freshmen are admitted to all sessions. Entrance exams should be taken prior to enrollment. There is a rolling admissions plan. Applications should be filed by August 1 for fall entry, along with a $30 fee. Applications are accepted on-line. **Transfer Students:** 952 transfer students enrolled in 2013-2014. Applicants must have a 2.0 cumulative GPA from all accredited institutions previously attended and must not have been dismissed. 30 of 128 credits required for the bachelor's degree must be completed at EKU. **International Students:** There are 159 international students enrolled. The school actively recruits these students. They must take the TOEFL. They must also take the ACT, scoring 21, or the SAT for those applicants from states where the SAT is dominant.

ADMISSIONS: Stephen A. Byrn, Director of Admissions. E-Mail: *admissions@eku.edu* Web: *www.eku.edu*

FINANCIAL AID: EKU is a member of CSS. The CSS/Profile and the college's own financial statement are required. The deadline for filing freshman financial aid applications for fall entry is April 15.

GEORGETOWN COLLEGE D-2
www.georgetowncollege.edu

Georgetown, KY 40324	**(502) 863-8009** **(800) 788-9985**
Fax: (502) 868-7733	Email: admissions@georgetowncollege.edu
Full-time: 441 men, 509 women	**Faculty:** 90; IIB, --$
Part-time: 11 men, 18 women	**Ph.D.s:** 95%
Graduate: 58 men, 225 women	**Student/Faculty:** 9 to 1
Year: semesters, summer session	**Tuition:** $32,960
Room & Board: $8480	**Freshman Class:** 2089 applied, 1837 accepted, 273 enrolled
SAT CR/M: 520/524 **ACT:** 24	**CEEB CODE:** 1249
Application Deadline: August 1	**COMPETITIVE+**

Georgetown College, dating back to 1787 and chartered in 1829, is a small residential liberal arts college distinguished by a combination of respected, rigorous undergraduate and graduate programs, an array of opportunities for involvement and leadership, a commitment to Christian values and its distinctive heritage. There is 1 undergraduate school and 1 graduate school. In addition to regional accreditation, Georgetown has baccalaureate program accreditation with NCATE, ACS, and CAATE. The 104-acre campus is in a suburban area 12 miles north of Lexington just off I-75, about an hour from Louisville and Cincinnati. Including any residence halls, there are 42 buildings.

STUDENT LIFE: 74% of undergraduates are from Kentucky. Others are from 30 states, and 12 foreign countries. 85% are from public schools. 79% are White. 81% are Protestant; 11% Catholic. **Male To Female Ratio:** 1.5:1. The average age of freshmen is 18; all undergraduates, 20. 28% do not continue beyond their first year; 55% remain to graduate. **Housing:** 1325 students can be accommodated in college housing, which includes single-sex dorms, on-campus apartments, and married student housing. In addition, there are fraternity houses and sorority houses. On-campus housing is guaranteed for all 4 years. 91% of students live on campus; of those, 50% remain on campus on weekends. Alcohol is not permitted. All students may keep cars.

FACULTY/CLASSROOMS: 50% of faculty are male; 50% are female. 92% teach undergraduates. No introductory courses are taught by graduate students. The average class size in an introductory lecture is 14 and in a regular course is 12.

PROGRAMS OF STUDY: Georgetown confers B.A. and B.S. degrees. Master's degrees are also awarded. Bachelor's degrees are awarded in BIOLOGICAL SCIENCE (biochemistry and biology/biological science), BUSINESS (accounting, banking and finance, business administration and management, business economics, international business management, management information systems, marketing/retailing/merchandising, and sports management), COMMUNICATIONS AND THE ARTS (art, communications, creative writing, dramatic arts, English, fine/studio arts, general, French, music, performing arts, and Spanish), COMPUTER AND PHYSICAL SCIENCE (chemistry, mathematics, and physics), EDUCATION (athletic training, elementary education, English education, foreign languages education, history education, mathematics education, middle school education, secondary education, and social studies secondary school education), ENGINEERING AND ENVIRONMENTAL DESIGN (environmental science and preengineering), HEALTH PROFESSIONS (exercise science, predentistry, premedicine, prepharmacy, and prephysical therapy), SOCIAL SCIENCE (American studies, economics, European studies, family/juvenile justice, history, interdisciplinary studies, justice and society, liberal arts/general studies, philosophy, political science/government, prelaw, psychology, religion, safety and security technology, and sociology). Biology, chemistry, psychology, education, and English are the strongest academically. Kinesiology, psychology, education, business, and communication/media studies have the largest enrollments.

ACTIVITIES: 27% of men belong to 1 local and 4 national fraternities; 35% of women belong to 4 national sororities. There are 80 groups on campus, including and equine scholars, Christian leadership scholars, art, band, cheerleading, choir, chorale, chorus, communications, computers, dance, dance team, drama, environmental,

ethnic, forensics, honors, international, jazz band, literary magazine, musical theater, newspaper, pep band, photography, political, professional, radio and TV, religious, social, social service, and student government. Popular campus events include Songfest, Chapel Day/Bid Day, Belle of the Blue, Midnight Brunch, Grubfest, Family Weekend, and Hanging of the Green. **Sports:** There are 8 intercollegiate sports for men and 11 for women, and 11 intramural sports for men and 11 for women. Facilities include a 3000-seat stadium, 8 tennis courts, soccer, baseball, football, softball and intramural fields, 1550-seat gym, racquetball courts, training room, and a fitness center housing a Nautilus area, a weight-lifting area, basketball courts, recreation room, and dressing rooms. **Graduates:** From July 1, 2013 to June 30, 2014, 224 bachelor's degrees were awarded. The most popular majors were psychology (15%), communication and media studies (13%), and biology (10%). 80 companies recruited on campus in 2013-2014. In an average class, 51% graduate in 4 years or less, 60% graduate in 5 years or less, and 60% graduate in 6 years or less.

SERVICES: Counseling and information services are available, as is tutoring in every subject. **Library/Resources:** The library contains 185,592 volumes, 189,600 microform items, and 10,465 audio/video tapes/CDs/DVDs, and subscribes to 42,015 periodicals including electronic. Computerized library services include interlibrary loans, database searching, Internet access, and Wi-Fi capability. Special learning facilities include an art gallery, planetarium, radio station, center for civic engagement, center for solids alalysis and a writing lab. **Physically Challenged Students:** 70% of the campus is accessible. Facilities include wheelchair ramps, elevators, special parking, specially equipped restrooms, special class scheduling, and lowered drinking fountains. **Special:** Georgetown offers an innovative Spanish Immersion program; and cross-registration with the University of Kentucky for Army and Air Force ROTC for aerospace studies. A 3-2 engineering degree and nursing degree are available with the University of Kentucky. Internships, co-op programs in math, political science and other areas; study abroad in 28 countries, including a dual degree at Oxford University, work-study programs, student-designed majors, and pass/fail options are available. Interdisciplinary majors of all kinds, frequently including business administration, communication arts, psychology and religion combinations among others, are designed by students. A dual BA/BTh degree is offered in religion with Regents Park College of Oxford University. There are 20 national honor societies and a freshman honors program. **Visiting:** There are regularly scheduled orientations for prospective students, consisting of campus tours and information on admissions, financial assistance, student life, academic programs, and meetings with faculty. There are guides for informal visits, visitors may sit in on classes, and stay overnight. To schedule a visit, contact Terri Hulette at (800) 788-9985. **Campus Safety and Security:** Measures include 24-hour foot and vehicle patrol, emergency notification system, self-defense education, and security escort services. There are shuttle buses, emergency telephones, lighted pathways/sidewalks, and controlled access to dorms/residences.

REQUIREMENTS: ACT or SAT required. Applicants should have completed 4 high school credits in English, 3 each in math and science, 2 in a foreign language, and 1 each in social studies and history, with additional credits in electives strongly encouraged. A student essay is required; Kentucky high school applicants may substitute a writing portfolio entry. AP and CLEP credits are accepted. Important factors in the admissions decision are advanced placement or honors courses, evidence of special talent, extracurricular activities record, and leadership record. All students are required to complete the Foundations and Core curriculum, a general education program including courses from several disciplines across campus emphasizing writing, quantitative skills, world languages, wellness, science and inquiry, religion, and culture. A minimum of 120 semester hours, including 24 to 42 in the major, with a minimum GPA of 2.0, is required to graduate, as is successful completion of a comprehensive exam in the major. **Procedure:** Freshmen are admitted to all sessions. Entrance exams should be taken from December of the junior year through October of the senior year. There are early decision, early admissions, deferred admissions, and rolling admissions plans. Early decision applications should be filed by October 15; regular applications, by August 1 for fall entry, along with a $30 fee. Notification is sent on a rolling basis. Applications are accepted on-line. **Transfer**

Students: 52 transfer students enrolled in 2013-2014. Applicants must be in good standing at the school most recently attended and must submit official college and sometimes high school transcripts. 30 of 120 credits required for the bachelor's degree must be completed at Georgetown. **International Students:** There are 18 international students enrolled. The school actively recruits these students. They must take the TOEFL with a minimum score of 520 on the paper-based TOEFL (PBT) or 68 on the Internet-based version (iBT).

ADMISSIONS: 88% of the 2014-2015 applicants were accepted. The SAT scores for the 2014-2015 freshman class were: Critical Reading--37% below 500, 40% between 500 and 599, and 23% between 600 and 699; Math--23% below 500, 69% between 500 and 599, and 8% between 600 and 699. The ACT scores were 21% below 21, 27% between 21 and 23, 26% between 24 and 26, 12% between 27 and 28, and 14% above 28. 40% of the current freshmen were in the top fifth of their class; 69% were in the top two fifths. 15 freshmen graduated first in their class. **Admissions Contact:** Michelle Lynch, V.P. for Enrollment Management. E-Mail: *admissions@georgetowncollege.edu* Web: *http://www.georgetowncollege.edu/admissions/*

FINANCIAL AID: In 2014-2015, 99% of all full-time freshmen and 96% of continuing full-time students received some form of financial aid. 86% of all full-time freshmen and 85% of continuing full-time students received need-based aid. The average freshman award was $30,405. Need-based scholarships or need-based grants averaged $21,767 ($39,690 maximum); need-based self-help aid (loans and jobs) averaged $4,375 ($8,500 maximum); non-need-based athletic scholarships averaged $7,089 ($29,147 maximum); and other non-need-based awards and non-need-based scholarships averaged $17,169 ($38,690 maximum). 61% of undergraduate students work part-time. Average annual earnings from campus work are $937. The average financial indebtedness of the 2014 graduate was $26,730. The FAFSA is required. The priority date for freshman financial aid applications for fall entry is February 1.

KENTUCKY CHRISTIAN UNIVERSITY *(The complete profile is made available exclusively on our website, www.barronspac.com)*

KENTUCKY STATE UNIVERSITY *(The complete profile is made available exclusively on our website, www.barronspac.com)*

KENTUCKY WESLEYAN COLLEGE   B-3
www.kwc.edu

Owensboro, KY 42301	**(270) 852-3120** **(800) 999-0592**
Fax: (270) 852-3133	**Email:** rsmith@kwc.edu
Full-time: 326 men, 315 women	**Faculty:** 48; IIB
Part-time: 19 men, 18 women	**Ph.D.s:** 84%
Graduate: n/av	**Student/Faculty:** 12 to 1
Year: semesters, summer session	**Tuition:** $20,240
Room & Board: $7200	**Freshman Class:** 910 applied, 193 accepted, 158 enrolled
SAT CR/M/W: 470/490/460 **ACT:** 22	**CEEB CODE:** 1369
Application Deadline: open	**COMPETITIVE**

Kentucky Wesleyan College, founded in 1858, is a private liberal arts institution affiliated with the United Methodist Church. KWC offers undergraduate programs in natural sciences, humanities and fine arts, and social sciences. Figures in the above capsule and in this profile are approximate. In addition to regional accreditation, KWC has baccalaureate program accreditation with IACBE. The 52-acre campus is in a suburban area 95 miles southwest of Louisville and 120 miles north of Nashville. Including any residence halls, there are 15 buildings.

STUDENT LIFE: 72% of undergraduates are from Kentucky. Others are from 22 states, 6 foreign countries, and Canada. 90% are from public schools. 74% are White. 60% are Protestant; 25% claim no religious affiliation; 12% Catholic. **Male To Female Ratio:** 1.0:1. The average age of freshmen is 18; all undergraduates, 22. 30% do not continue beyond their first year; 44% remain to graduate. **Housing:**

520 students can be accommodated in college housing, which includes single-sex and coed dorms, on-campus apartments, and off-campus apartments. On-campus housing is guaranteed for all 4 years. 55% of students commute. Alcohol is not permitted. All students may keep cars.

FACULTY/CLASSROOMS: 50% of faculty are male; 50% are female. All teach undergraduates. No introductory courses are taught by graduate students. The average class size in an introductory lecture is 20; in a laboratory is 15; and in a regular course is 15.

PROGRAMS OF STUDY: KWC confers B.A., B.S., B.M. and B.M.E. degrees. Bachelor's degrees are awarded in BIOLOGICAL SCIENCE (biology/biological science and zoology), BUSINESS (accounting, business administration and management, business economics, human resources, and sports management), COMMUNICATIONS AND THE ARTS (art, communications, English, fine arts, music, music business management, and Spanish), COMPUTER AND PHYSICAL SCIENCE (chemistry, computer science, and physics), EDUCATION (art education, elementary education, middle school education, music education, physical education, and secondary education), ENGINEERING AND ENVIRONMENTAL DESIGN (pre-engineering), HEALTH PROFESSIONS (health, predentistry, and premedicine), SOCIAL SCIENCE (criminal justice, history, political science/government, prelaw, psychology, and sociology). Natural sciences, education and business are the strongest academically. Business administration, biology and education have the largest enrollments.

ACTIVITIES: 11% of men belong to 3 national fraternities; 11% of women belong to 2 national sororities. There are 48 groups on campus, including art, band, cheerleading, choir, chorale, chorus, computers, dance, drama, ethnic, literary magazine, marching band, musical theater, newspaper, pep band, photography, political, professional, radio and TV, religious, social, social service, student government, symphony, and yearbook. Popular campus events include Family Weekend, Theater Productions and Lessons in Carols. **Sports:** There are 6 intercollegiate sports for men and 7 for women, and 7 intramural sports for men and 7 for women. Facilities include a health and recreation center, which houses an 800-seat gym, a fully equipped weight-training center, racquetball courts, indoor batting and pitching facilities for softball and baseball, and a multipurpose auxiliary gym. Outdoor facilities include a baseball park, a softball park, a soccer field, a football field, and additional practice fields for football and soccer, and varsity basketball games are played in the Owensboro Sports Center. **Graduates:** From July 1, 2013 to June 30, 2014, 155 bachelor's degrees were awarded. The most popular majors were business (22%), education (12%), and biology (9%). 20 companies recruited on campus in 2013-2014. In an average class, 30% graduate in 4 years or less, 40% graduate in 5 years or less, and 44% graduate in 6 years or less. Of the 2013 graduating class, 21% were enrolled in graduate school within 6 months of graduation, and 21% were employed.

SERVICES: Counseling and information services are available, as is tutoring in most subjects. There is a reader service for the blind, and remedial math, reading, and writing. **Library/Resources:** The library contains 99,795 volumes, and 144,661 microform items, 2,027 audio/video tapes/CDs/DVDs, and subscribes to 145 periodicals including electronic. Computerized library services include interlibrary loans, database searching, Internet access, and Wi-Fi capability. Special learning facilities include an art gallery and radio station. **Physically Challenged Students:** 95% of the campus is accessible. Facilities include wheelchair ramps, elevators, special parking, specially equipped restrooms, special class scheduling, and lowered drinking fountains. **Special:** Internships, dual majors, and student-designed majors are available in many programs and are established on an individual basis. A 3-2 degree in engineering is offered with Auburn University and the University of Kentucky. A Washington semester and study abroad in 5 countries are also available. There are 8 national honor societies and 7 departmental honors programs. **Visiting:** There are regularly scheduled orientations for prospective students, including a campus tour, meetings with faculty and students, and dining on campus. There are guides for informal visits, visitors may sit in on classes, and stay overnight. To schedule a visit, contact the Admissions Office. **Campus Safety and Security:** Measures include 24-hour foot and vehicle patrol, emergency notification system, and security escort services. There are lighted pathways/sidewalks and controlled access to dorms/residences.

REQUIREMENTS: The SAT or ACT is required. Applicants should have completed 13 high school units in college preparatory English, math, science, social studies, and a foreign language, or the GED equivalent. Applicants are considered individually. AP and CLEP credits are accepted. All students are required to complete the following general education program of skills and content requirements: 9 hours each in humanities, 6 hours each in aesthetics and social sciences, 3 hours each in math, religion, multicultural studies, and communication skills, 7 in natural science. Students must demonstrate proficiency in math, computing, and oral and written communication. To graduate, students must complete a total of 128 credit hours, including 36 in the major, with a 2.0 GPA. **Procedure:** Freshmen are admitted to all sessions. Entrance exams should be taken during the spring of the junior year or the fall of the senior year. There are deferred admissions and rolling admissions plans. Application deadlines are open. Notification is sent on a rolling basis. Applications are accepted on-line. **Transfer Students:** 95 transfer students enrolled in 2013-2014. Transfer applicants should have a minimum GPA of 2.0 in all course work and be in good standing at the previously attended institution. 30 of 120 credits required for the bachelor's degree must be completed at KWC. **International Students:** There are 10 international students enrolled. The school actively recruits these students. They must take the TOEFL with a minimum score of 500 on the paper-based TOEFL (PBT) or 70 on the Internet-based version (iBT). SAT or ACT scores are required of international students who do not have a TOEFL score or who want to play NCAA sports.

ADMISSIONS: 21% of the 2014-2015 applicants were accepted. The SAT scores for the 2014-2015 freshman class were: Critical Reading--58% below 500, 36% between 500 and 599, and 6% between 600 and 699; Math--55% below 500, 36% between 500 and 599, and 9% between 600 and 699; Writing--61% below 500, 36% between 500 and 599, and 3% between 600 and 699. The ACT scores were 38% below 21, 29% between 21 and 23, 16% between 24 and 26, 7% between 27 and 28, and 10% above 28. 1 freshman graduated first in the class. **Admissions Contact:** Rahad Smith, Director of Admissions. E-Mail: *rsmith@kwc.edu* Web: *www.kwc.edu*

FINANCIAL AID: In 2014-2015, 100% of all full-time freshmen and 95% of continuing full-time students received some form of financial aid. 100% of all full-time freshmen and 95% of continuing full-time students received need-based aid. 50% of undergraduate students work part-time. The FAFSA is required. The priority date for freshman financial aid applications for fall entry is March 15. The deadline for filing freshman financial aid applications for fall entry is August 1.

LINDSEY WILSON COLLEGE   D-3
www.lindsey.edu

Columbia, KY 42728

	(270) 384-8100
	(800) 264-0138
Fax: (270) 384-8591	Email: fergusonc@lindsey.edu
Full-time: 875 men, 1204 women	Faculty: 95
Part-time: 43 men, 83 women	Ph.D.s: 72%
Graduate: 103 men, 333 women	Student/Faculty: 19 to 1
Year: semesters, summer session	Tuition: $22,550
Room & Board: $8670	Freshman Class: n/av
SAT CR/M/W: 480/500/395 ACT: 21	CEEB CODE: 1409
Application Deadline: open	COMPETITIVE

Lindsey Wilson College, founded in 1903, is a private liberal arts college affiliated with the United Methodist Church, offering undergraduate programs in arts and sciences, business administration, education, human services, and pre-health. There is 1 graduate school. In addition to regional accreditation, Lindsey has baccalaureate program accreditation with NCATE. The 45-acre campus is in a small town 100 miles southeast of Louisville. Including any residence halls, there are 45 buildings.

STUDENT LIFE: 81% of undergraduates are from Kentucky. Others are from 30 states, 28 foreign countries, and Canada. 64% are White;

21% race unknown. 75% are Protestant. **Male To Female Ratio:** 1.6:1. The average age of freshmen is 19; all undergraduates, 23. 38% do not continue beyond their first year; 34% remain to graduate. **Housing:** 1150 students can be accommodated in college housing, which includes single-sex dorms and on-campus apartments. In addition, there are honors houses. On-campus housing is guaranteed for all 4 years, is available on a first-come, first-served basis, and is available on a lottery system for upperclassmen. 50% of students commute. Alcohol is not permitted. All students may keep cars.

FACULTY/CLASSROOMS: 43% of faculty are male; 57% are female. All teach undergraduates. No introductory courses are taught by graduate students. The average class size in an introductory lecture is 20; in a laboratory is 20; and in a regular course is 20.

PROGRAMS OF STUDY: Lindsey confers B.A., B.S.N. and B.S. degrees. Associate, Master's, and Doctoral degrees are also awarded. Bachelor's degrees are awarded in BIOLOGICAL SCIENCE (biology/biological science), BUSINESS (accounting, business administration and management, and recreation and leisure services), COMMUNICATIONS AND THE ARTS (art, communications, English, media arts, and theatre studies), COMPUTER AND PHYSICAL SCIENCE (mathematics), EDUCATION (art education, elementary education, music education, and secondary education), HEALTH PROFESSIONS (nursing), SOCIAL SCIENCE (American studies, criminal justice, history, human services, liberal arts/general studies, ministries, psychobiology, psychology, and social science). Human services and biology are the strongest academically. Human services, business, and education have the largest enrollments.

ACTIVITIES: There are no fraternities or sororities. There are 40 groups on campus, including art, band, cheerleading, choir, chorale, chorus, computers, dance, drama, environmental, film, honors, international, jazz band, literary magazine, marching band, musical theater, newspaper, pep band, photography, political, professional, religious, social, social service, and student government. Popular campus events include Founders Day and Malvina Farkle Day (community service). **Sports:** There are 10 intercollegiate sports for men and 13 for women, and 10 intramural sports for men and 10 for women. Facilities include a sports center with a 1000-seat gym and a 72000 sq ft health and wellness center with a weight-training room, competition swimming pool and many other amenities, a sand volleyball court, and the student union building. **Graduates:** From July 1, 2013 to June 30, 2014, 436 bachelor's degrees were awarded. The most popular majors were human services and counseling (51%), business administration (9%), and criminal justice (6%). In an average class, 2% graduate in 3 years or less, 25% graduate in 4 years or less, 33% graduate in 5 years or less, and 34% graduate in 6 years or less.

SERVICES: Counseling and information services are available, as is tutoring in every subject. There is remedial math, reading, and writing. **Library/Resources:** The library contains 105,000 volumes, 16,000 microform items, and 5,250 audio/video tapes/CDs/DVDs, and subscribes to 16,000 periodicals including electronic. Computerized library services include interlibrary loans, database searching, Internet access, and Wi-Fi capability. Special learning facilities include an art gallery. **Physically Challenged Students:** 95% of the campus is accessible. Facilities include wheelchair ramps, elevators, special parking, specially equipped restrooms, special class scheduling, lowered drinking fountains, and special housing. **Special:** Human services majors are offered a social services practicum in their field of study. Internships, work-study programs, a Washington semester, a general studies degree, student-designed majors, and pass/fail options in some courses are available. Study abroad is possible through Lindsey in London and the Northern Ireland Exchange. There are 3 national honor societies and a freshman honors program. **Visiting:** There are regularly scheduled orientations for prospective students. There are guides for informal visits, visitors may sit in on classes, and stay overnight. To schedule a visit, contact the Admissions Office at admissions@lindsey.edu. **Campus Safety and Security:** Measures include 24-hour foot and vehicle patrol, emergency notification system, and security escort services. There are lighted pathways/sidewalks and controlled access to dorms/residences.

REQUIREMENTS: The ACT is required. Applicants should have completed 20 academic high school credits or the GED equivalent. A GPA of 2.5 is required. AP and CLEP credits are accepted. Important factors in the admissions decision are geographical diversity, recommendations by alumni, and recommendations by school officials. All students must complete 45 hours of general education core requirements, including courses in communication of ideas, math, natural science, religion, humanities, fine arts, social behavioral science, and phys ed as well as a 1-hour personal development career seminar. A total of 120 semester hours, with a minimum GPA of 2.0, is required to graduate. **Procedure:** Freshmen are admitted to all sessions. Entrance exams should be taken during the junior year. There is a rolling admissions plan. Application deadlines are open. Applications are accepted on-line. **Transfer Students:** 96 transfer students enrolled in 2013-2014. Transfer applicants are required to submit an official transcript from schools previously attended. An interview is recommended. 120 of 120 credits required for the bachelor's degree must be completed at Lindsey. **International Students:** There are 96 international students enrolled. The school actively recruits these students. They must take the TOEFL with a minimum score of 450 on the paper-based TOEFL (PBT) or 45 on the Internet-based version (iBT). They must also take the SAT or ACT.

ADMISSIONS: The SAT scores for the 2014-2015 freshman class were: Critical Reading--62% below 500, 30% between 500 and 599, and 8% between 600 and 699; Math--46% below 500, and 54% between 500 and 599; Writing--100% below 500. The ACT scores were 46% below 21, 28% between 21 and 23, 18% between 24 and 26, 5% between 27 and 28, and 3% above 28. 29% of the current freshmen were in the top fifth of their class; 55% were in the top two fifths. 7 freshmen graduated first in their class. **Admissions Contact:** Charity Fergurson, Director of Admissions. E-Mail: *fergusonc@lindsey .edu* Web: *www.lindsey.edu*

FINANCIAL AID: In 2014-2015, 95% of all full-time freshmen and 74% of continuing full-time students received some form of financial aid. 95% of all full-time freshmen and 74% of continuing full-time students received need-based aid. The average freshman award was $21,685. Need-based scholarships or need-based grants averaged $17,242 ($34,270 maximum); and need-based self-help aid (loans and jobs) averaged $4,443 ($27,228 maximum). Lindsey is a member of CSS. The FAFSA is required. The priority date for freshman financial aid applications for fall entry is February 1.

MIDWAY COLLEGE (*The complete profile is made available exclusively on our website, www.barronspac.com*)

MOREHEAD STATE UNIVERSITY E-2
www.moreheadstate.edu

Morehead, KY 40351	(606) 783-2000
	(800) 585-6781
Fax: (606) 783-5038	Email: admissions@moreheadstate.edu
Full-time: 2565 men, 3644 women	Faculty: IIA, --$
Part-time: 1400 men, 2467 women	Ph.D.s: 68%
Graduate: 482 men, 800 women	Student/Faculty: n/av
Year: semesters, summer session	Tuition: $5280 ($13,340)
Room & Board: $5620	Freshman Class: 5241 applied, 4364 accepted, 1685 enrolled
ACT: 22 SAT: required	CEEB CODE: 1487
Application Deadline: open	COMPETITIVE

Morehead State University, founded in 1887, is a public institution offering degree programs in applied science and technology, humanities, educational and behavioral sciences, and business. The figures in the above capsule and in this profile are approximate. There are 4 undergraduate schools and 1 graduate school. In addition to regional accreditation, MSU has baccalaureate program accreditation with AACSB, ACBSP, CSWE, NASM, NCATE, and NLN. The 1016-acre campus is in a small town 60 miles east of Lexington. Including any residence halls, there are 140 buildings.

STUDENT LIFE: 86% of undergraduates are from Kentucky. Others are from 37 states, 22 foreign countries, and Canada. 95% are from public schools. 96% are White. **Male To Female Ratio:** 1.6:1. The average age of freshmen is 18; all undergraduates, 23. 39% do not continue beyond their first year. **Housing:** 3250 students can be accommodated in college housing, which includes coed dorms, on-campus apartments, and married student housing. In addition, there are honors houses, language houses, fraternity houses, sorority houses, cross-cultural house, and housing for farm students, handicapped housing, some private rooms. On-campus housing is guaranteed for all 4 years. 70% of students commute. Alcohol is not permitted. All students may keep cars.

FACULTY/CLASSROOMS: 55% of faculty are male; 45% are female. All teach undergraduates. No introductory courses are taught by graduate students. The average class size in a regular course is 19.

PROGRAMS OF STUDY: MSU confers A.B., B.S., B.B.A., B.M., B.M.Ed., B.S.N., B.S.W. and B.U.S. degrees. Associate, Master's, and Doctoral degrees are also awarded. Bachelor's degrees are awarded in AGRICULTURE (agriculture), BIOLOGICAL SCIENCE (biology/biological science and ecology), BUSINESS (accounting, banking and finance, business economics, management information systems, management science, marketing management, and real estate), COMMUNICATIONS AND THE ARTS (communications, dramatic arts, English, music, and speech/debate/rhetoric), COMPUTER AND PHYSICAL SCIENCE (chemistry, computer science, earth science, geology, mathematics, and physics), EDUCATION (agricultural education, business education, elementary education, health education, industrial arts education, middle school education, physical education, and special education), ENGINEERING AND ENVIRONMENTAL DESIGN (industrial engineering technology), HEALTH PROFESSIONS (medical technology and nursing), SOCIAL SCIENCE (geography, history, liberal arts/general studies, paralegal studies, philosophy, political science/government, psychology, social science, social work, and sociology). Biology, music, and nursing are the strongest academically. Elementary education has the largest enrollment.

ACTIVITIES: 27% of men and 20% of women belong to 12 national fraternities; 21% of women belong to 9 national sororities. There are 95 groups on campus, including art, band, cheerleading, choir, chorale, chorus, computers, dance, drama, drill team, drum and bugle corps, environmental, ethnic, gay, honors, international, jazz band, marching band, musical theater, newspaper, orchestra, pep band, photography, political, professional, radio and TV, religious, social, social service, student government, symphony, and yearbook. Popular campus events include Greek Week, Black History Month, and Welcome Week. **Sports:** There are 9 intercollegiate sports for men and 9 for women, and 24 intramural sports for men and 24 for women. Facilities include an athletic complex, a 6500-seat gym, a 10000-seat stadium, a pool, bowling lanes, and a wellness/fitness center. **Graduates:** From July 1, 2013 to June 30, 2014, 1116 bachelor's degrees were awarded. The most popular majors were education (13%), liberal arts/general studies and business/marketing (12%), and health professions and related programs (9%). 70 companies recruited on campus in 2013-2014. In an average class, 40% graduate in 6 years or less.

SERVICES: Counseling and information services are available, as is tutoring in most subjects. There is a reader service for the blind, and remedial math, reading, and writing. **Library/Resources:** The library contains 522,673 volumes, 819,736 microform items, 22,194 audio/video tapes/CDs/DVDs, and subscribes to 3,046 periodicals including electronic. Computerized library services include interlibrary loans, database searching, Internet access, and Wi-Fi capability. Special learning facilities include an art gallery, planetarium, radio station, TV station, a 320-acre farm complex, space science center, and robotics lab. **Physically Challenged Students:** 85% of the campus is accessible. Facilities include wheelchair ramps, elevators, special parking, specially equipped restrooms, special class scheduling, lowered drinking fountains, lowered telephones, and special housing. **Special:** Cross-registration is offered with the University of Kentucky. Students may earn specialist certification in education, co-op programs. Internships, study abroad in 3 countries, a Washington semester, a 3-2 engineering degree, dual and student-designed majors, a general studies degree, credit for life experience, pass/fail options, and non-degree study are available. There are 12 national honor societies and a freshman honors program. **Visiting:** There are regularly scheduled orientations for prospective students, consisting of registration for classes, advisement, and an overview of MSU. There are guides for informal visits and visitors may sit in on classes. To schedule a visit, contact the Enrollment Services. **Campus Safety and Security:** Measures include 24-hour foot and vehicle patrol, emergency notification system, self-defense education, and security escort services. There are shuttle buses, emergency telephones, and lighted pathways/sidewalks.

REQUIREMENTS: The SAT or ACT is required. Applicants should have completed the Kentucky Pre-College Curriculum requirement. An interview is recommended. A GPA of 2.0 is required. AP and CLEP credits are accepted. All students must complete 42 semester hours (45 for teacher certification) of general education courses, including 15 hours in communications and humanities, 12 in natural and mathematical sciences, 12 in social and behavioral sciences, and 3 in health or phys ed. A total of 128 semester hours, with a minimum GPA of 2.0, is required to graduate. **Procedure:** Freshmen are admitted fall, spring, and summer. Entrance exams should be taken in the spring of the junior year. There is a rolling admissions plan. Application deadlines are open. Application fee is $30. Notification is sent on a rolling basis. Applications are accepted on-line. **Transfer Students:** 501 transfer students enrolled in 2013-2014. Applicants should have a minimum GPA of 2.0 with at least 12 credit hours earned and be in good standing at their previous institution. They must have completed a pre-college curriculum or meet any deficiencies. 32 of 128 credits required for the bachelor's degree must be completed at MSU. **International Students:** There are 44 international students enrolled. The school actively recruits these students. They must take the TOEFL with a minimum score of 500 on the paper-based TOEFL (PBT) or 61 on the Internet-based version (iBT). They must also take the SAT or ACT, with the ACT preferred.

ADMISSIONS: 83% of the 2014-2015 applicants were accepted. The ACT scores were 10% below 21, and 55% between 21 and 23, and 35% above 28. 33% of the current freshmen were in the top fifth of their class; 58% were in the top two fifths. **Admissions Contact:** Erin Wright, Director of Institutional Research. E-Mail: *admissions@ moreheadstate.edu* Web: *www.moreheadstate.edu*

FINANCIAL AID: In 2014-2015, 98% of all full-time freshmen received some form of financial aid. 60% of all full-time freshmen received need-based aid. The average freshman award was $7,778. Need-based scholarships or need-based grants averaged $2,174 ($4,050 maximum); need-based self-help aid (loans and jobs) averaged $1,985 ($2,625 maximum); non-need-based athletic scholarships averaged $3,645 ($9,688 maximum); and other non-need-based awards and non-need-based scholarships averaged $2,095 ($6,000 maximum). 16% of undergraduate students work part-time. Average annual earnings from campus work are $1496. The average financial indebtedness of the 2014 graduate was $16,431. The FAFSA and the college's own financial statement are required. The deadline for filing freshman financial aid applications for fall entry is April 1.

MURRAY STATE UNIVERSITY — B-4
www.murraystate.edu

Murray, KY 42071

(270) 809-3750
(800) 272-4678 ext. 1

Fax: (270) 809-3780

Email: lharris@murraystate.edu

Full-time: 3106 men, 4264 women
Part-time: 832 men, 1242 women
Graduate: 698 men, 1065 women
Year: semesters, summer session
Room & Board: $7912

Faculty: 429; IIA, -$
Ph.Ds: 77%
Student/Faculty: 17 to 1
Tuition: $7392 ($20,112)
Freshman Class: 4760 applied, 3806 accepted, 1508 enrolled

ACT: 24
Application Deadline: August 1

CEEB CODE: 1494
COMPETITIVE

Murray State University, founded in 1922, is a public institution offering degree programs in business, education, health professions, human services, humanities, fine arts, engineering, technology, science, nursing, and agriculture. There are 7 undergraduate schools and 6 graduate schools. In addition to regional accreditation, MSU has baccalaureate program accreditation with AACSB, ABET, ACEJMC, CSWE, NASAD, NASM, NCATE, ACEND, ACS, AVMA, CAATE, CCNE, CACREP, COA, MPAC, NAST, and NKBA. The 253-acre campus is in a small town 115 miles northwest of Nashville in Murray, Kentucky. Including any residence halls, there are 88 buildings.

STUDENT LIFE: 69% of undergraduates are from Kentucky. Others are from 43 states, 50 foreign countries, and Canada. 80% are White. **Male To Female Ratio:** 1.4:1. The average age of freshmen is 18; all undergraduates, 23. 28% do not continue beyond their first year; 53% remain to graduate. **Housing:** 3200 students can be accommodated in college housing, which includes single-sex and coed dorms, on-campus apartments, and married student housing. We have a residential college system, with a faculty member serving as a college head in each building. On-campus housing is guaranteed for all 4 years, and is available on a first-come, first-served basis. 70% of students commute. Alcohol is not permitted. All students may keep cars.

FACULTY/CLASSROOMS: 59% of faculty are male; 41% are female. 96% teach undergraduates, all do research, and 96% do both. No introductory courses are taught by graduate students.

PROGRAMS OF STUDY: MSU confers B.A., B.S., B.A.B., B.S.B., B.F.A., B.I.S., B.M., B.S.A., B.S.N., B.S.E. and B.S.W. degrees. Associate, Master's, and Doctoral degrees are also awarded. Bachelor's degrees are awarded in AGRICULTURE (agricultural business management, agricultural mechanics, agricultural sciences, agri hortiulture, agr agronomy, and equine science), BIOLOGICAL SCIENCE (biology/adolescence education, biology/biological science, biology (pre-physician assistant), forensic science, marine biology, molecular biology, nutrition, and wildlife biology), BUSINESS (accounting, accounting (finance), accounting (financial planning), accounting (information systems), business administration and management, business communications, business intelligence and analytics, entrepreneurial studies, finance, finance (financial planning), human resources/organizational management, international business, integrative studies, management science, marketing, nonprofit/public organization management, recreation and leisure services, recreation/leisure (adventure leadership), recreation/leisure (community recreation), and supply chain management), COMMUNICATIONS AND THE ARTS (advertising, art history, creative writing, English literature, French, German, graphic design and media, instrumental music education, Japanese, journalism, keyboard - piano concentration, music, music business management, music composition, music performance, public relations, radio/television technology, Spanish, studio art, telecommunications systems management, theatre arts, and vocal music education), COMPUTER AND PHYSICAL SCIENCE (applied mathematics, applied physics, applied physics (pre-MBA), chemistry, chemistry/adolescence education, chemistry / chemical biology, chemistry (pre-MBA), computer information systems, computer science, earth science, earth science / adolescence education, environmental geology, mathematics, mathematics - actuarial concentration, physics, and polymer science), EDUCATION (agricultural education, art education, athletic training, early childhood education, elementary education, English education, foreign languages education, health information management, health and physical education, history education, home economics education, industrial arts education, marketing and distribution education, mathematics education, middle school education, physical science secondary school education, social studies secondary school education, Spanish education K-12, specific learning disabilities, teaching English as a second/foreign language (TESOL/TEFOL), and technical education), ENGINEERING AND ENVIRONMENTAL DESIGN (agricultural engineering technology, architectural technology, civil engineering technology, construction technology, electrical/electronics engineering technology, engineering graphics and design, engineering physics, environmental engineering technology, interior design, manufacturing technology, and occupational safety and health), HEALTH PROFESSIONS (biomedical science, community health work, exercise science, nursing, nutrition and dietetics, Pre-Health Studies, predentistry, premedicine, preoptometry, preoccupational therapy, prepharmacy, prephysician assistant, prephysical therapy, preveterinary science, speech pathology/audiology, and veterinary technology), SOCIAL SCIENCE (archeology, criminal justice, economics, food production/management/services, geography information science, history, international studies, liberal arts, sciences, general studies, humanities, philosophy, philosophy (aesthetics/media writing), philosophy (history/contemporary thought), philosophy (political thought), philosophy and religion, political science/government, psychology, public administration, social work, and sociology). Telecommunications systems management, occupational safety and health, and accounting are the strongest academically. Nursing, animal health technology, and business administration have the largest enrollments.

ACTIVITIES: 14% of men belong to 12 national fraternities; 15% of women belong to 9 national sororities. There are 153 groups on campus, including art, band, cheerleading, chess, choir, chorale, chorus, communications, computers, dance, debate, drama, drill team, environmental, ethnic, film, forensics, gay, honors, international, jazz band, literary magazine, marching band, musical theater, newspaper, opera, orchestra, pep band, photography, political, professional, radio and TV, religious, social, social service, student government, and symphony. Popular campus events include All-Campus Sing, Campus Lights, Alpha Phi Alpha Step-Off, Mr. MSU, Miss MSU, Homecoming and Related Festivities, Take Back the Night, Alliance Drag Show, Rock-a-Thon, Watermelon Bust, NPHC Step Show, Diwali Festival of Lights, Annual Hypnotist Show. **Sports:** There are 7 intercollegiate sports for men and 10 for women, and 10 intramural sports for men and 10 for women. Facilities include a 73,000-square-foot recreation and wellness center with 2 pools, 3 gyms, racquetball courts, indoor track, cardio and weight areas, an Internet lounge, aerobic studios, and a fitness assessment center. An additional gym, with swimming pool, basketball court, dance/aerobic studio, and racquetball courts, is also available for student use. Athletic and recreation sports facilities include a 16,500-seat stadium, 8500-seat sports arena and special events center, golf course, soccer fields, baseball fields, rifle range, volleyball courts, basketball courts, tennis courts, and a fitness trail. **Graduates:** From July 1, 2013 to June 30, 2014, 1469 bachelor's degrees were awarded. The most popular majors were integrated studies (9%), nursing (7%), and animal health technology (6%). 286 companies recruited on campus in 2013-2014. In an average class, 29% graduate in 4 years or less, 48% graduate in 5 years or less, and 53% graduate in 6 years or less.

SERVICES: Counseling and information services are available, as is tutoring in most subjects. There is a reader service for the blind, and remedial math, reading, and writing. **Library/Resources:** The 2 libraries contain 399,387 volumes, 203,544 microform items, and 34,388 audio/video tapes/CDs/DVDs, and subscribe to 924 periodicals including electronic. Computerized library services include interlibrary loans, database searching, Internet access, and Wi-Fi capability. Special learning facilities include an art gallery, radio station, TV station, Writing Center, Oral Communications Center, Ross Mathematics Studies and Career Center, Speech and Hearing Clinic, Arboretum, Biological Research Station, Watershed Studies Institute, Mid-America Remote Sensing Center, Wrather Museum (history museum and cultural events center), Lovett Auditorium and CFSB Center (used for musical and theater productions, concerts, and lectures), Price Doyle Fine Arts Center (for performances and exhibitions), State Farm Financial Services Center (applied learning for students in Finance and Economics), 4 agricultural research farms, Breathitt Veterinary Center, Cherry Agricultural Exposition Center. **Physically Challenged Students:** Facilities include wheelchair ramps, elevators, special parking, specially equipped restrooms, special class scheduling, lowered drinking fountains, lowered telephones, and special housing. **Special:** MSU offers BA/BS degrees in several fields, and students can pursue double majors in any degree program. Students can design interdisciplinary majors in the Liberal Arts and Integrated Studies degree programs. Co-op programs, internships, and work-study are available in several degree programs. Cross-registration is available through the National Student Exchange. There are 16 national honor societies and a freshman honors program. **Visiting:** There are regularly scheduled orientations for prospective students. Students are invited to attend sessions planned before all academic terms for which they are first enrolling. These sessions contain both academic and social orientation. There are guides for informal visits and visitors may sit in on classes. To schedule a visit, contact Shawn Smee at ssmee@murraystate.edu. **Campus Safety and Security:** Measures include 24-hour foot and vehicle patrol, emergency notification system, self-defense education, and security escort services. There are shuttle buses, emergency telephones, lighted pathways/sidewalks, and controlled access to dorms/residences.

REQUIREMENTS: The ACT is required. Students must have a mini-mum composite score of 18 on the ACT. Applicants must rank in the top half of their class or have a 3.0 GPA. Applicants should have successfully completed 22 high school academic credits, which includes 4 units in English, 3 in math, 3 in science with at least 1 lab science, 3 in social studies, 2 years in a foreign language, 1 in visual/performing arts and 5 in electives; in addition, MSU strongly recommends a fourth year of math. Social sciences must include U. S. history and world civilization. Math must include 3 algebra I and above courses. Sciences must include biology and chemistry or physics. A portfolio or audition is required for art and music majors. AP and CLEP credits are accepted. All students must complete University Studies (general education) requirements, including courses in communications, sciences, math, philosophy, history, social sciences, and, for the BA degree, foreign language. A total of 120 semester hours with a minimum of 40 hours earned in residence. 42 of the 120 hours must be earned in 300-level or above courses. **Procedure:** Freshmen are admitted to all sessions. Entrance exams should be taken before January of the enrollment year. There is a rolling admissions plan. Applications should be filed by August 1 for fall entry; December 1 for spring entry; and May 1 for summer entry, along with a $40 fee. Applications are accepted on-line. **Transfer Students:** 981 transfer students enrolled in 2013-2014. A student who has 24 semester hours or more of transferable degree credit, with a minimum of a 2.0 cumulative grade point average on all previous courses, is eligible for admission. Applicants must be in good standing academically and financially at all previous schools attended. Students who have less than 24 hours of credit must present official copies of high school transcript and either the ACT or SAT. 40 of 120 credits required for the bachelor's degree must be completed at MSU. **International Students:** There are 460 international students enrolled. The school actively recruits these students. They must take the TOEFL with a minimum score of 527 on the paper-based TOEFL (PBT) or 71 on the Internet-based version (iBT), or take the IELTS.

ADMISSIONS: 80% of the 2014-2015 applicants were accepted. The ACT scores were 25% below 21, 29% between 21 and 23, 23% between 24 and 26, 11% between 27 and 28, and 12% above 28. 34% of the current freshmen were in the top fifth of their class; 65% were in the top two fifths. 49 freshmen graduated first in their class. **Admissions Contact:** Lesa Harris, Director of Undergraduate Admissions. E-Mail: lharris@murraystate.edu Web: http://www.murraystate.edu/admissions.htm

FINANCIAL AID: In 2014-2015, 85% of all full-time freshmen and 86% of continuing full-time students received some form of financial aid. 60% of all full-time freshmen and 60% of continuing full-time students received need-based aid. The average freshman award was $12,630. Need-based scholarships or need-based grants averaged $5,894 ($23,439 maximum); need-based self-help aid (loans and jobs) averaged $5,844 ($23,597 maximum); non-need-based athletic scholarships averaged $9,423 ($28,931 maximum); other non-need-based awards and non-need-based scholarships averaged $7,456 ($39,308 maximum); and $7,405 from other forms of aid. 22% of undergraduate students work part-time. Average annual earnings from campus work are $2310. The average financial indebtedness of the 2014 graduate was $24,554. The FAFSA and the college's own financial statement, are required. The priority date for freshman financial aid applications for fall entry is February 1. The deadline for filing freshman financial aid applications for fall entry is September 1.

NORTHERN KENTUCKY UNIVERSITY   **D-1**
www.nku.edu

Highland Heights, KY 41099   (859) 572-5220, ext. 5744
                                                        (800) 637-9948
Fax: (859) 572-6665
Full-time: 4478 men, 5258 women   Email: gorbrandt@nku.edu
Part-time: 1334 men, 1724 women   Faculty: IIA, -$
Graduate: 901 men, 1568 women   Ph.D.s: 72%
Year: semesters, summer session   Student/Faculty: 19 to 1
Room & Board: $7750   Tuition: $8376 ($16,464)
                                        Freshman Class: 8724
                                        applied, 5105 accepted,
                                        2225 enrolled
SAT CR/M/W: 500/510/490 ACT: 22   CEEB CODE: 1574
Application Deadline: August 1   COMPETITIVE

Northern Kentucky University, founded in 1968, is a publicly controlled institution offering undergraduate and graduate programs in arts and sciences, business, health professions, informatics, and education and human services. There are 5 undergraduate schools and 6 graduate schools. In addition to regional accreditation, NKU has baccalaureate program accreditation with AACSB, ABET, ACCE, CSWE, NASM, NCATE, NLN, NASPAA, CAATE, and JRCERT. The 424-acre campus is in a suburban area in Highland Heights, Kentucky, 7 miles southeast of Cincinnati, Ohio. Including any residence halls, there are 41 buildings.

STUDENT LIFE: 69% of undergraduates are from Kentucky. Others are from 45 states, 59 foreign countries, and Canada. 82% are White. **Male To Female Ratio:** 1.3:1. The average age of freshmen is 19; all undergraduates, 24. 33% do not continue beyond their first year. **Housing:** 1820 students can be accommodated in college housing, which includes single-sex and coed dorms and on-campus apartments. In addition, there are honors houses. On-campus housing is available on a first-come, first-served basis. Priority is given to out-of-town students. 87% of students commute. Alcohol is not permitted. All students may keep cars.

FACULTY/CLASSROOMS: 54% of faculty are male; 46% are female. No introductory courses are taught by graduate students.

PROGRAMS OF STUDY: NKU confers B.A., B.S., B.M., B.S.N., B.F.A , B.H.S. and B.S.W. degrees. Associate, Master's, and Doctoral degrees are also awarded. Bachelor's degrees are awarded in BIOLOGICAL SCIENCE (biology/adolescence education and biology/biological science), BUSINESS (accounting, business administration and management, business information systems, entrepreneurial studies, finance, human resources, labor studies, marketing and distribution, organizational leadership and management, and sports management), COMMUNICATIONS AND THE ARTS (communications, dramatic arts, English, fine arts, French, German, Japanese, journalism, music, music composition, music performance, public relations, radio/television technology, Spanish, adolescence education, speech/debate/rhetoric, studio art, and theatre arts), COMPUTER AND PHYSICAL SCIENCE (chemistry, chemistry/adolescence education, computer engineering technology, computer information technology, computer science, geology, information sciences and systems, mathematics, physics, radiological technology, science, and statistics), EDUCATION (athletic training, business education, early childhood education, elementary education, English education, industrial arts education, mathematics education, middle school education, music education, physical education, secondary education, and special education), ENGINEERING AND ENVIRONMENTAL DESIGN (architectural engineering, construction management, construction technology, electrical/electronics engineering technology, environmental science, manufacturing engineering, manufacturing technology, and mechanical engineering technology), HEALTH PROFESSIONS (exercise science, health science, medical technology, mental health/human services, nursing, predentistry, premedicine, preoptometry, prepharmacy, prephysical therapy, and preveterinary science), SOCIAL SCIENCE (anthropology, criminal justice, economics, forensic studies, geography, history, liberal arts/general studies, philosophy, political science/government, prelaw, psychology, public administration, public history/archives, social science, social studies, social work, sociology, and women's studies). Organizational leadership, computer information technology and nursing have the largest enrollments.

ACTIVITIES: 8% of men belong to 7 national fraternities; 8% of women belong to 7 national sororities. There are 221 groups on campus, including a mock trial, leadership, recreational, special interest, art, cheerleading, choir, chorale, chorus, computers, cultural, dance, drama, drill team, environmental, ethnic, film, gay, honors, international, jazz band, literary magazine, musical theater, newspaper, pep band, photography, political, professional, radio and TV, religious, social, social service, and student government. Popular campus events include Welcome Week, Freshfusion, Pumpkin Bust, Feast4Finals and Homecoming. **Sports:** There are 8 intercollegiate sports for men and 9 for women, and 12 intramural sports for men and 13 for women. Facilities include a 2000-seat gym, baseball and soccer fields, tennis and racquetball courts, a track, weight room, and swimming pool. **Graduates:** From July 1, 2013 to June 30, 2014, 2109 bachelor's degrees were awarded. The most popular majors were

business/marketing (27%), health professions (12%), and education (10%). 225 companies recruited on campus in 2013-2014. In an average class, 14% graduate in 4 years or less, 31% graduate in 5 years or less, and 38% graduate in 6 years or less.

SERVICES: Counseling and information services are available, as is tutoring in most subjects. There is a reader service for the blind, and remedial math, reading, and writing. There are also developmental education courses. **Library/Resources:** The 2 libraries contain 925,652 volumes, 620,179 microform items, and 20,088 audio/video tapes/CDs/DVDs, and subscribe to 51,986 periodicals including electronic. Computerized library services include interlibrary loans, database searching, Internet access, and Wi-Fi capability. Special learning facilities include an art gallery, planetarium, radio station, TV station, digitorium, herbarium, and the anthropology museum. **Physically Challenged Students:** All of the campus is accessible. Facilities include wheelchair ramps, elevators, special parking, specially equipped restrooms, special class scheduling, lowered drinking fountains, lowered telephones, and special housing. **Special:** A 3-2 engineering degree is offered with the University of Kentucky. Cross-registration is possible through the Greater Cincinnati Area Consortium of colleges and universities. Study abroad in 34 countries, a Washington semester, on-campus work-study programs, an accelerated degree program, an interdisciplinary honors program, B.A.-B.S. degrees, dual majors, and pass/fail options are offered. There are co-op programs in most majors. Student-designed majors and credit for work experience are available. Non-degree study is possible. There are 14 national honor societies, a freshman honors program, and 9 departmental honors programs. **Visiting:** There are regularly scheduled orientations for prospective students, consisting of a 1-day program with sessions on student services and financial aid, activities, a campus tour, and academic information, advising, and registration. There are guides for informal visits, visitors may sit in on classes, and stay overnight. To schedule a visit, contact the Office of Admissions at (859) 572-5220. **Campus Safety and Security:** Measures include 24-hour foot and vehicle patrol, emergency notification system, and security escort services. There are shuttle buses, emergency telephones, lighted pathways/sidewalks, controlled access to dorms/residences, ALICE training.

REQUIREMENTS: The SAT or ACT is required. A GPA of 2.0 is required. AP and CLEP credits are accepted. All students must complete 37 semester hours of general studies, including communication written and oral, mathematics/statistics, natural sciences, culture, self and society, global viewpoints, along with major and minor requirements. A total of 120 semester hours, with a minimum GPA of 2.0, is required to graduate. **Procedure:** Freshmen are admitted fall, spring, and summer. Entrance exams should be taken prior to enrollment. There are deferred admissions and rolling admissions plans. Early decision applications should be filed by February 1; regular applications, by August 1 for fall entry; December 1 for winter entry; December 1 for spring entry; and May 1 for summer entry, along with a $40 fee. Applications are accepted on-line. **Transfer Students:** 886 transfer students enrolled in 2013-2014. Students must be eligible to return to their previous institution. College transcripts from previous institutions are required. 30 of 120 credits required for the bachelor's degree must be completed at NKU. **International Students:** There are 504 international students enrolled. The school actively recruits these students. They must take the TOEFL with a minimum score of 86 on the Internet-based version (iBT).

ADMISSIONS: 59% of the 2014-2015 applicants were accepted. The SAT scores for the 2014-2015 freshman class were: Critical Reading--46% below 500, 38% between 500 and 599, 13% between 600 and 699, and 2% between 700 and 800; Math--55% below 500, 31% between 500 and 599, 12% between 600 and 699, and 2% between 700 and 800. The ACT scores were 37% below 21, 29% between 21 and 23, 20% between 24 and 26, 7% between 27 and 28, and 7% above 28. **Admissions Contact:** Melissa Gorbrandt, Director of Admissions. E-Mail: *gorbrandt@nku.edu* Web: *www.nku.edu*

FINANCIAL AID: 61% of all full-time freshmen and 53% of continuing full-time students received need-based aid. The FAFSA and the college's own financial statement are required. The priority date for freshman financial aid applications for fall entry is March 1. The deadline for filing freshman financial aid applications for fall entry is April 1.

SPALDING UNIVERSITY (*The complete profile is made available exclusively on our website, www.barronspac.com*)

THOMAS MORE COLLEGE D-2
www.thomasmore.edu

Crestview Hills, KY 41017	(859) 344-3514
	(800) 825-4557
Fax: (859) 344-3444	Email: lehmerk@thomasmore.edu
Full-time: 579 men, 561 women	Faculty: 72
Part-time: 223 men, 139 women	Ph.D.s: 75%
Graduate: 56 men, 42 women	Student/Faculty: 16 to 1
Year: semesters, summer session	Tuition: $27,220
Room & Board: $7540	Freshman Class: n/av
SAT CR/M: 480/490 ACT: 22	CEEB CODE: 1876
Application Deadline: August 1	COMPETITIVE

Thomas More College, founded in 1921 as Villa Madonna College, is a private Catholic institution offering undergraduate programs in liberal arts and sciences, plus graduate degrees in business administration and education. Figures in the above capsule and in this profile are approximate. There is 1 undergraduate school and 2 graduate schools. In addition to regional accreditation, Thomas More has baccalaureate program accreditation with NLN. The 100-acre campus is in a suburban area 8 miles south of Cincinnati. Including any residence halls, there are 10 buildings.

STUDENT LIFE: 53% of undergraduates are from out of state, mostly the Mid-West. Students are from 17 states, and 3 foreign countries. 65% are from public schools. 78% are White. 46% claim no religious affiliation; 28% Catholic; 22% Protestant. **Male To Female Ratio:** 0.9:1. The average age of freshmen is 18; all undergraduates, 23. 39% do not continue beyond their first year; 50% remain to graduate. **Housing:** 400 students can be accommodated in college housing, which includes single-sex and coed dorms. On-campus housing is available on a first-come, first-served basis. Priority is given to out-of-town students. 68% of students commute. All students may keep cars.

FACULTY/CLASSROOMS: 59% of faculty are male; 41% are female. All teach undergraduates. No introductory courses are taught by graduate students. The average class size in an introductory lecture is 14; in a laboratory is 11; and in a regular course is 14.

PROGRAMS OF STUDY: Thomas More confers B.A., B.S., B.B.A., B.E.S. and B.S.N. degrees. Associate and Master's degrees are also awarded. Bachelor's degrees are awarded in BIOLOGICAL SCIENCE (biology/biological science), BUSINESS (accounting, business administration and management, and sports marketing), COMMUNICATIONS AND THE ARTS (art, communications, dramatic arts, English, and Spanish), COMPUTER AND PHYSICAL SCIENCE (chemistry, computer science, mathematics, and physics), EDUCATION (art education, business education, elementary education, middle school education, secondary education, and social studies education), ENGINEERING AND ENVIRONMENTAL DESIGN (environmental science), HEALTH PROFESSIONS (health care administration, medical laboratory technology, and nursing), SOCIAL SCIENCE (criminal justice, economics, forensic studies, history, humanities, international studies, liberal arts/general studies, philosophy, political science/government, psychology, sociology, and theological studies). Business, biology and nursing have the largest enrollments.

ACTIVITIES: 2% of men belong to 1 national fraternity; 2% of women belong to 1 national sorority. There are 35 groups on campus, including art, cheerleading, chorus, computers, drama, environmental, ethnic, honors, international, literary magazine, marching band, political, professional, religious, social, social service, student government, and yearbook. Popular campus events include Spring Pig Roast, Welcome Carnival, and Presidential Inauguration Ball. **Sports:** There are 8 intercollegiate sports for men and 8 for women, and 5 intramural sports for men and 5 for women. Facilities include an athletic/convocation center with a 1500-seat indoor gym, a football/soccer complex plus baseball and softball fields, 16 tennis courts (8 indoor), 4 racquetball courts, an indoor pool, a track, and weight and exercise rooms. **Graduates:** From July 1, 2013 to June 30, 2014, 254 bachelor's degrees were awarded. The most popular majors were business (42%), nursing (10%), and education (8%). 46 companies recruited on campus in 2013-2014. In an average class, 35% graduate

in 4 years or less, 46% graduate in 5 years or less, and 49% graduate in 6 years or less. Of the 2013 graduating class, 27% were enrolled in graduate school within 6 months of graduation, and 95% were employed.

SERVICES: Counseling and information services are available, as is tutoring in every subject. There is a reader service for the blind, and remedial math, reading, and writing. Signing for the hearing impaired is available. **Library/Resources:** The library contains 114,230 volumes, 28,429 microform items, 2,386 audio/video tapes/CDs/DVDs, and subscribes to 368 periodicals including electronic. Computerized library services include interlibrary loans, database searching, and Internet access. Special learning facilities include an art gallery, observatory, and biology field station on the Ohio River. **Physically Challenged Students:** 90% of the campus is accessible. Facilities include wheelchair ramps, elevators, special parking, and specially equipped restrooms. **Special:** There are co-op programs in all majors except nursing. The 3-2 engineering degree is available from the accredited engineering school of the student's choice. Cross-registration is possible through the Greater Cincinnati Consortium. There are also internships, study abroad in many countries. B.A. and B.S. degrees, student-designed majors, work-study programs, credit for life experience, and pass/fail options. The Bachelor of Elected Studies and Bachelor of Arts-Student Initiated degrees provide students with an individualized program. Nondegree study is possible. There are 9 national honor societies and 9 departmental honors programs. **Visiting:** There are regularly scheduled orientations for prospective students, including a campus tour and meetings with an admissions counselor, a professor in one's major field (if decided), and financial aid staff. There are guides for informal visits, visitors may sit in on classes, and stay overnight. To schedule a visit, contact the Admissions Office. **Campus Safety and Security:** Measures include 24-hour foot and vehicle patrol, emergency notification system, self-defense education, and security escort services. There are lighted pathways/sidewalks and controlled access to dorms/residences.

REQUIREMENTS: The SAT or ACT is required, with a minimum composite score of 20 on the ACT (20 on the English section) or 1010 on the SAT (480 on the verbal section). Applicants should have completed 17 high school academic units, including 4 of English, 3 each of math, science, and social studies, 2 of non-native language, and 1 each of arts appreciation and computer literacy. Thomas More requires applicants to be in the upper 50% of their class. A GPA of 2.0 is required. AP and CLEP credits are accepted. Important factors in the admissions decision are advanced placement or honors courses, leadership record, and personality/intangible qualities. All students must complete 56 to 61 hours of core requirements, including 9 credits in theology, 6 each in English, social sciences, global history, fine arts, foreign language, philosophy, and natural sciences, and 3 each in communication and math. A total of 128 credit hours, including 36 to 76 in the major, with a minimum GPA of 2.0 is required to graduate. **Procedure:** Freshmen are admitted to all sessions. Entrance exams should be taken in the spring of the junior year or in the fall of the senior year. There are deferred admissions and rolling admissions plans. Applications should be filed by August 1 for fall entry; January 2 for spring entry, along with a $25 fee. Applications are accepted on-line. **Transfer Students:** 65 transfer students enrolled in 2013-2014. Applicants should be in good academic standing and have a minimum GPA of 2.0 in 24 semester hours earned. 38 of 128 credits required for the bachelor's degree must be completed at Thomas More. **International Students:** There are 8 international students enrolled. The school actively recruits these students. They must take the TOEFL with a minimum score of 515 on the paper-based TOEFL (PBT) or 66 on the Internet-based version (iBT). They must also take the SAT or ACT, scoring 20.

ADMISSIONS: The SAT scores for the 2014-2015 freshman class were: Critical Reading--55% below 500, 36% between 500 and 599, and 9% between 600 and 699; Math--51% below 500, 31% between 500 and 599, 13% between 600 and 699, and 5% between 700 and 800. The ACT scores were 28% below 21, 35% between 21 and 23, 24% between 24 and 26, 5% between 27 and 28, and 8% above 28. 23% of the current freshmen were in the top fifth of their class; 52% were in the top two fifths. **Admissions Contact:** Kristi Lehmer, Executive Dir. of Enrollment Management. E-Mail: lehmerk@thomasmore.edu Web: www.thomasmore.edu

FINANCIAL AID: In 2014-2015, 100% of all full-time freshmen and

86% of continuing full-time students received some form of financial aid. 82% of all full-time freshmen and 63% of continuing full-time students received need-based aid. The average freshman award was $21,063. Need-based scholarships or need-based grants averaged $16,356; need-based self-help aid (loans and jobs) averaged $4,458; and other non-need-based awards and non-need-based scholarships averaged $15,861. Average annual earnings from campus work are $2100. The average financial indebtedness of the 2014 graduate was $32,601. Thomas More is a member of CSS. The FAFSA and the college's own financial statement are required. The deadline for filing freshman financial aid applications for fall entry is January 15.

TRANSYLVANIA UNIVERSITY   D-3
www.transy.edu

Lexington, KY 40508	(859) 233-8242
	(800) 872-6798
Fax: (859) 233-8797	**Email:** bgoan@transy.edu
Full-time: 419 men, 592 women	**Faculty:** 87; IIB, +$
Part-time: 4 men	**Ph.D.s:** 96%
Graduate: n/av	**Student/Faculty:** 11 to 1
Year: 4-1-4, summer session	**Tuition:** $33,360
Room & Board: $9300	**Freshman Class:** 1250 applied, 1193 accepted, 262 enrolled
SAT CR/M: 590/580 **ACT:** 27	**CEEB CODE:** 1808
Application Deadline: February 1	**VERY COMPETITIVE+**

Transylvania University, founded in 1780, is an independent liberal arts institution affiliated with the Christian Church (Disciples of Christ). Through an engagement with the liberal arts, Transylvania prepares its students for a humane and fulfilling personal and public life by cultivating independent thinking, open-mindedness, creative expression, and commitment to lifelong learning and social responsibility in a diverse world. There is 1 undergraduate school. In addition to regional accreditation, Transy has baccalaureate program accreditation with NCATE. The 48-acre campus is in an urban area in an historic district of downtown Lexington. Including any residence halls, there are 24 buildings.

STUDENT LIFE: 73% of undergraduates are from Kentucky. Others are from 25 states, and 7 foreign countries. 85% are from public schools. 80% are White. 34% are Mormon, Muslim, Orthodox and Buddhist; 30% Protestant; 18% Catholic; 17% claim no religious affiliation. **Male To Female Ratio:** 1.4:1. The average age of freshmen is 18; all undergraduates, 20. 15% do not continue beyond their first year; 72% remain to graduate. **Housing:** 900 students can be accommodated in college housing, which includes single-sex and coed dorms and on-campus apartments. In addition, there are language houses. On-campus housing is guaranteed for all 4 years. 76% of students live on campus; of those, 80% remain on campus on weekends. All students may keep cars.

FACULTY/CLASSROOMS: 55% of faculty are male; 45% are female. All teach undergraduates. No introductory courses are taught by graduate students. The average class size in an introductory lecture is 18; in a laboratory is 14; and in a regular course is 18.

PROGRAMS OF STUDY: Transy confers B.A. degrees. Bachelor's degrees are awarded in BIOLOGICAL SCIENCE (biochemistry, biology/biological science, and neurosciences), BUSINESS (accounting and business administration and management), COMMUNICATIONS AND THE ARTS (art history, art, classics, dramatic arts, English, French, Germanic languages and literature, music, Spanish, studio art, and theatre arts), COMPUTER AND PHYSICAL SCIENCE (chemistry, computer science, mathematics, and physics), EDUCATION (education, elementary education, and middle school education), HEALTH PROFESSIONS (exercise science), SOCIAL SCIENCE (anthropology, economics, history, philosophy, political science/government, psychology, religion, and sociology). Business, biology, and psychology have the largest enrollments.

ACTIVITIES: 45% of men belong to 4 national fraternities; 60% of women belong to 4 national sororities. There are 65 groups on campus, including art, band, cheerleading, choir, chorale, chorus, computers, dance, debate, drama, environmental, ethnic, forensics, gay, honors, international, jazz band, literary magazine, musical theater, newspaper, opera, orchestra, pep band, political, professional, radio and TV, religious, social, social service, student government, and yearbook. **Sports:** There are 10 intercollegiate sports for men and 12 for women, and 18 intramural sports for men and 18 for women. Facilities include a 1300-seat performance gym, a fitness center with an indoor jogging track, swimming pool, basketball and racquetball/handball courts, 6 tennis courts, and 3 athletic fields (baseball, men's soccer/field hockey, and women's soccer/softball). **Graduates:** From July 1, 2013 to June 30, 2014, 238 bachelor's degrees were awarded. The most popular majors were biology (11%), psychology (11%), and exercise science (11%). 13 companies recruited on campus in 2013-2014. In an average class, 1% graduate in 3 years or less, 70% graduate in 4 years or less, 70% graduate in 5 years or less, and 72% graduate in 6 years or less. Of the 2013 graduating class, 40% were enrolled in graduate school within 6 months of graduation, and 41% were employed.

SERVICES: Counseling and information services are available, as is tutoring in every subject. The Academic Center for Excellence (ACE) provides additional help **Library/Resources:** The library contains 276,000 volumes, 60 microform items, 4,483 audio/video tapes/CDs/DVDs, and subscribes to 19,000 periodicals including electronic. Computerized library services include interlibrary loans, database searching, Internet access, and Wi-Fi capability. Special learning facilities include an art gallery, natural history museum, and radio station. **Physically Challenged Students:** 90% of the campus is accessible. Facilities include wheelchair ramps, elevators, special parking, specially equipped restrooms, special class scheduling, lowered drinking fountains. Arrangements are made according to individual needs. **Special:** 3-2 engineering degrees with the University of Kentucky and Vanderbilt University are offered. Cross-registration with May Term Consortium schools, internships, study abroad in 17 countries, work-study programs, a Washington semester, dual majors, and student-designed majors are available. There are 9 national honor societies. **Visiting:** There are regularly scheduled orientations for prospective students, consisting of campus open houses in fall and winter for high school juniors and seniors, including a welcome program, an academic information fair, campus tours, a luncheon, a financial aid session, and a faculty session. There are guides for informal visits, visitors may sit in on classes, and stay overnight. To schedule a visit, contact the Office of Admissions. **Campus Safety and Security:** Measures include 24-hour foot and vehicle patrol, emergency notification system, self-defense education, and security escort services. There are shuttle buses, emergency telephones, lighted pathways/sidewalks, and controlled access to dorms/residences.

REQUIREMENTS: The SAT or ACT is required. One essay and 2 recommendations are required. An interview is strongly recommended. Transy requires applicants to be in the upper 50% of their class. A GPA of 2.0 is required. AP credits are accepted. Important factors in the admissions decision are advanced placement or honors courses, recommendations by school officials, and extracurricular activities record. Students must fulfill requirements in five general areas: Area I Introduction to Critical Skills, Area II Approaches to Learning, Area III Cultural Traditions, Area IV Upper-level Liberal Arts (2+2), and Area V Writing Intensive Courses. **Procedure:** Freshmen are admitted fall and winter. Entrance exams should be taken during the junior year and no later than December of the senior year for scholarship consideration or February for general admission. There is a deferred admissions plan. Early decision applications should be filed by December 1; regular applications, by February 1 for fall entry; and December 5 for winter entry. Notification of early decision is sent January 15; regular decision, March 15. Applications are accepted on-line. **Transfer Students:** 8 transfer students enrolled in 2013-2014. Applicants must have a minimum college GPA of 2.75 and should submit official copies of all college transcripts, 2 recommendations, and 1 essay. A high school transcript or GED is required. 18 of 36 credits required for the bachelor's degree must be completed at Transy. **International Students:** There are 36 international students enrolled. The school actively recruits these students. They must take the TOEFL. They must also take the ACT or SAT, scoring 1030.

ADMISSIONS: 95% of the 2014-2015 applicants were accepted. The SAT scores for the 2014-2015 freshman class were: Critical Reading-

-22% below 500, 33% between 500 and 599, 35% between 600 and 699, and 10% between 700 and 800; Math--14% below 500, 40% between 500 and 599, 28% between 600 and 699, and 19% between 700 and 800. The ACT scores were 4% below 21, 10% between 21 and 23, 28% between 24 and 26, 15% between 27 and 28, and 43% above 28. 70% of the current freshmen were in the top fifth of their class; 89% were in the top two fifths. There were 7 National Merit finalists.

Admissions Contact: Brad Goan, VP for Enrollment and Dean of Admissions. E-Mail: *bgoan@transy.edu* Web: *www.transy.edu*

FINANCIAL AID: In 2014-2015, 99% of all full-time freshmen and 98% of continuing full-time students received some form of financial aid. 66% of all full-time freshmen and 67% of continuing full-time students received need-based aid. The average freshman award was $27,367. Need-based scholarships or need-based grants averaged $23,628 ($45,760 maximum); need-based self-help aid (loans and jobs) averaged $5,063 ($9,300 maximum); and other non-need-based awards and non-need-based scholarships averaged $16,172 ($45,760 maximum). 51% of undergraduate students work part-time. Average annual earnings from campus work are $1568. The average financial indebtedness of the 2014 graduate was $28,079. Transy is a member of CSS. The FAFSA is required. The priority date for freshman financial aid applications for fall entry is January 1. The deadline for filing freshman financial aid applications for fall entry is March 1.

UNION COLLEGE   E-4
www.unionky.edu

Barbourville, KY 40906

	(606) 546-1612
	(800) 489-8646
Fax: (606) 546-1667	**Email: enrollme@unionky.edu**
Full-time: 423 men, 359 women	**Faculty:** 52; IIB
Part-time: 28 men, 60 women	**Ph.D.s:** 52%
Graduate: 101 men, 168 women	**Student/Faculty:** 13 to 1
Year: semesters, summer session	**Tuition:** $22,980
Room & Board: $6700	**Freshman Class:** 1385 applied, 1042 accepted, 240 enrolled
SAT CR/M: 469/506 **ACT:** 22	**CEEB CODE:** 1825
Application Deadline: open	**COMPETITIVE**

Union College, founded in 1879, is a private liberal arts institution affiliated with the United Methodist Church. Figures in the above capsule and in this profile are approximate. There is 1 graduate school. The 100-acre campus is in a small town 95 miles south of Lexington, Kentucky and 85 miles north of Knoxville, Tennessee. Including any residence halls, there are 20 buildings.

STUDENT LIFE: 67% of undergraduates are from Kentucky. Others are from 27 states, 14 foreign countries, and Canada. 77% are White. 41% claim no religious affiliation; 32% Baptist, Pentecostal, Church of Christ, and Unknown; 19% Protestant. **Male To Female Ratio:** 1.1:1. The average age of freshmen is 19; all undergraduates, 22. 38% do not continue beyond their first year; 32% remain to graduate. **Housing:** 472 students can be accommodated in college housing, which includes single-sex dorms, on-campus apartments, off-campus apartments, and married student housing. On-campus housing is guaranteed for all 4 years, and is available on a first-come, first-served basis. 52% of students live on campus. Alcohol is not permitted. All students may keep cars.

FACULTY/CLASSROOMS: 52% of faculty are male; 48% are female. 84% teach undergraduates. No introductory courses are taught by graduate students. The average class size in an introductory lecture is 25 and in a regular course is 20.

PROGRAMS OF STUDY: Union confers B.A. and B.S. degrees. Master's degrees are also awarded. Bachelor's degrees are awarded in BIOLOGICAL SCIENCE (biology/biological science), BUSINESS (accounting, business administration and management, international business management, marketing management, organizational leadership and management, recreational facilities management, and sports management), COMMUNICATIONS AND THE ARTS (communications, dramatic arts, English, and fine arts), COMPUTER AND PHYSICAL SCIENCE (chemistry and mathematics), EDUCA-

TION (athletic training, education, elementary education, middle school education, physical education, science education, secondary education, social studies education, and special education), ENGINEERING AND ENVIRONMENTAL DESIGN (computer technology), HEALTH PROFESSIONS (exercise science, health, and nursing), SOCIAL SCIENCE (criminal justice, history, Latin American studies, ministries, psychology, religion, social work, and sociology). Education, business, and nursing are the strongest academically. Business, education, and nursing have the largest enrollments.

ACTIVITIES: There are no fraternities or sororities. There are 31 groups on campus, including cheerleading, choir, chorale, chorus, computers, drama, ethnic, gay, honors, international, literary magazine, pep band, professional, radio and TV, religious, social, social service, student government, and yearbook. Popular campus events include Springfest, Student Holiday Dinner, and CIRCLES Ceremony. **Sports:** There are 12 intercollegiate sports for men and 13 for women, and 5 intramural sports for men and 3 for women. Facilities include a 3,000-seat campus stadium, an 1,800-seat gym, an indoor pool with bleachers for 300, 6 tennis courts, a weight-training center, an athletic training center, a 500-seat baseball stadium with 3 batting cages and a practice infield, a soccer field with stands for 250, a softball field with stands for 150, and practice fields for football and soccer. **Graduates:** From July 1, 2013 to June 30, 2014, 112 bachelor's degrees were awarded. The most popular majors were education (21%), business/marketing (19%), and health professions/related programs (10%). In an average class, 17% graduate in 4 years or less, 30% graduate in 5 years or less, and 32% graduate in 6 years or less.

SERVICES: Counseling and information services are available, as is tutoring in most subjects. There is a reader service for the blind, and remedial math, reading, and writing. There is a tutoring lab with computer support. **Library/Resources:** The library contains 230,938 volumes, 453,787 microform items, 4,686 audio/video tapes/CDs/DVDs, and subscribes to 114,865 periodicals including electronic. Computerized library services include interlibrary loans, database searching, Internet access, and Wi-Fi capability. Special learning facilities include a radio station. **Physically Challenged Students:** 85% of the campus is accessible. Facilities include wheelchair ramps, elevators, special parking, specially equipped restrooms, special class scheduling, and lowered drinking fountains. **Special:** Work-study programs, study abroad in 7 countries, an accelerated business degree completion program, and internships in business, sociology, psychology, recreational management, and mass communications are available. There are 2 national honor societies and a freshman honors program. **Visiting:** There are regularly scheduled orientations for prospective students, consisting of advising and registration, parent sessions, and break-out sessions. There are guides for informal visits, visitors may sit in on classes, and stay overnight. To schedule a visit, contact Sam Lee at slee@unionky.edu. **Campus Safety and Security:** Measures include 24-hour foot and vehicle patrol, emergency notification system, self-defense education, and security escort services. There are emergency telephones, lighted pathways/sidewalks, controlled access to dorms/residences. The campus web site has a notification system (alert system) that provides information about recent crimes on campus.

REQUIREMENTS: The SAT or ACT is required. Standardized test scores are not required for students 25 of older. All first-year students should have completed a pre-college high school curriculum that includes 4 units of English, 3 of math, 2 each of lab science and social science, and the study of a foreign language. An official, sealed high school transcript or an official GED score report is also required. A GPA of 2.0 is required. AP and CLEP credits are accepted. Important factors in the admissions decision are evidence of special talent, geographical diversity, and advanced placement or honors courses.All students are required to complete 43 credits in a liberal education core, including 21 hours in humanities, 7 to 8 of general science, 6 of social science, and 3 each of wellness, math, and cultural studies. **Procedure:** Freshmen are admitted to all sessions. Entrance exams should be taken by January of the senior year. There are deferred admissions and rolling admissions plans. Application deadlines are open. Application fee is $10. Notification is sent on a rolling basis. Applications are accepted on-line. **Transfer Students:** 75 transfer students enrolled in 2013-2014. Applicants should have a minimum GPA of 2.0. 32 of 120 credits required for the bachelor's degree must be completed at Union. **International Students:** There are 51 international students enrolled. The school actively recruits these students. They must take the TOEFL with a minimum score of 550 on the paper-based TOEFL (PBT) and the college's own test, and also complete an ELS program at level 109. They must also take the SAT or ACT, scoring 18.

ADMISSIONS: 75% of the 2014-2015 applicants were accepted. The ACT scores were 50% below 21, 29% between 21 and 23, 14% between 24 and 26, 6% between 27 and 28, and 1% above 28. **Admissions Contact:** Sam Lee, Director: Undergraduate Enrollment. E-Mail: *enrollme@unionky.edu* Web: *www.unionky.edu*

FINANCIAL AID: In 2014-2015, 100% of all full-time freshmen and 100% of continuing full-time students received some form of financial aid. 83% of all full-time freshmen and 78% of continuing full-time students received need-based aid. The average freshman award was $24,687. Need-based scholarships or need-based grants averaged $18,482; need-based self-help aid (loans and jobs) averaged $3,552; and other non-need-based awards and non-need-based scholarships averaged $6,687. Average annual earnings from campus work are $1500. The average financial indebtedness of the 2014 graduate was $24,948. Union is a member of CSS. The CSS/Profile and FAFSA are required. The priority date for freshman financial aid applications for fall entry is February 15.

UNIVERSITY OF KENTUCKY   D-3
www.uky.edu

Lexington, KY 40506	(859) 257-2000
Fax: (859) 257-3823	Email: admissions@uky.edu
Full-time: 9445 men, 9733 women	Faculty: 1207; I, av$
Part-time: 878 men, 771 women	Ph.D.s: 93%
Graduate: 3152 men, 4055 women	Student/Faculty: n/av
Year: semesters, summer session	Tuition: $9676 ($19,864)
Room & Board: $10,192	Freshman Class: n/av
SAT or ACT: required	CEEB CODE: 1837
Application Deadline: n/av	**COMPETITIVE**

The University of Kentucky, founded in 1865, is a public land-grant institution offering undergraduate and graduate programs in a variety of areas. Figures in the above capsule and in this profile are approximate. There are 13 undergraduate schools and 1 graduate school. In addition to regional accreditation, UK has baccalaureate program accreditation with AACSB, ABET, ACEJMC, ACPE, ADA, AHEA, APTA, ASLA, CAHEA, CSWE, FIDER, NAAB, NASAD, NASM, NCATE, NLN, NRPA, and SAF. The 764-acre campus is in a suburban area 75 miles south of Cincinnati. Including any residence halls, there are 335 buildings.

STUDENT LIFE: 79% of undergraduates are from Kentucky. Others are from 49 states, 114 foreign countries, and Canada. 79% are White. **Male To Female Ratio:** 1.1:1. The average age of freshmen is 18; all undergraduates, 21. 19% do not continue beyond their first year; 58% remain to graduate. **Housing:** 6166 students can be accommodated in college housing, which includes single-sex and coed dorms, on-campus apartments, and married student housing. In addition, there are honors houses, language houses, special-interest houses, fraternity houses, and sorority houses. On-campus housing is available on a first-come, first-served basis. 74% of students commute. Alcohol is not permitted. All students may keep cars.

FACULTY/CLASSROOMS: 64% of faculty are male; 36% are female. No introductory courses are taught by graduate students.

PROGRAMS OF STUDY: UK confers B.A., B.S., B.Arch., B.B.A., B.F.A., B.H.S. and B.M. degrees. Master's and Doctoral degrees are also awarded. Bachelor's degrees are awarded in AGRICULTURE (agricultural economics, agriculture, animal science, and forestry and related sciences), BIOLOGICAL SCIENCE (biology/biological science, botany, and zoology), BUSINESS (accounting, banking and finance, business economics, hotel/motel and restaurant management, and marketing/retailing/merchandising), COMMUNICATIONS AND THE ARTS (advertising, art history and appreciation, arts administration/management, communications, dramatic arts,

English, French, German, Italian, journalism, linguistics, music, music performance, Russian, Spanish, and telecommunications), COMPUTER AND PHYSICAL SCIENCE (chemistry, computer science, geology, mathematics, and physics), EDUCATION (agricultural education, art education, business education, early childhood education, elementary education, foreign languages education, health education, mathematics education, middle school education, music education, physical education, science education, secondary education, social studies education, and special education), ENGINEERING AND ENVIRONMENTAL DESIGN (chemical engineering, civil engineering, electrical/electronics engineering, landscape architecture/design, materials engineering, mechanical engineering, and mining and mineral engineering), HEALTH PROFESSIONS (nursing, physical therapy, and physician's assistant), SOCIAL SCIENCE (anthropology, economics, food science, geography, history, Latin American studies, philosophy, political science/government, psychology, social work, sociology, and textiles and clothing). Pharmacy, architecture, and allied health are the strongest academically. Finance, accounting, and marketing have the largest enrollments.

ACTIVITIES: 16% of men belong to 24 national fraternities; 25% of women belong to 19 national sororities. There are 272 groups on campus, including band, cheerleading, chess, choir, chorale, chorus, computers, dance, debate, drama, drill team, environmental, ethnic, gay, honors, international, jazz band, literary magazine, marching band, musical theater, newspaper, orchestra, pep band, photography, political, professional, radio and TV, religious, social, social service, student government, symphony, and yearbook. Popular campus events include Little Kentucky Derby, Cultural Diversity Week, and Spotlight Jazz Series. **Sports:** There are 11 intercollegiate sports for men and 12 for women, and 22 intramural sports for men and 22 for women. Facilities include a 67600-seat football stadium, a 24500-seat arena for basketball and other activities, an aquatic center and swimming pool, baseball fields, a training center, indoor tennis courts, and a field house. **Graduates:** From July 1, 2013 to June 30, 2014, 3285 bachelor's degrees were awarded. The most popular majors were business (20%), engineering (10%), and health professions (9%). In an average class, 21% graduate in 4 years or less, 43% graduate in 5 years or less, and 51% graduate in 6 years or less.

SERVICES: There is a reader service for the blind and remedial math. **Library/Resources:** The 13 libraries contain 2.8 million volumes, 5.9 million microform items, 73,600 audio/video tapes/CDs/DVDs, and subscribe to 26,539 periodicals including electronic. Computerized library services include database searching. Special learning facilities include an art gallery, natural history museum, radio station, and TV station. **Physically Challenged Students:** 90% of the campus is accessible. Facilities include wheelchair ramps, elevators, special parking, specially equipped restrooms, special class scheduling, lowered drinking fountains, and lowered telephones. **Special:** Co-op programs are offered in engineering, business, computer science, math, and agriculture. The Academic Common Market allows students in 14 southern states to study outside the university. Internships in a variety of fields, study abroad in 36 countries, work-study programs with the university and local businesses, and credit for life experience are also available. An accelerated degree program, B.A.-B.S. degrees, dual and double majors, a general studies degree, student-designed majors, a 3-2 engineering degree with several smaller schools in Kentucky, non-degree study, and pass/fail options are also offered. There are 12 national honor societies, including Phi Beta Kappa, and a freshman honors program. **Visiting:** There are regularly scheduled orientations for prospective students, including a campus tour and information on admissions, housing, financial aid, and campus activities. There are guides for informal visits and visitors may sit in on classes. **Campus Safety and Security:** Measures include 24-hour foot and vehicle patrol, emergency notification system, self-defense education, and security escort services. There are shuttle buses, emergency telephones, lighted pathways/sidewalks, and controlled access to dorms/residences.

REQUIREMENTS: The SAT or ACT is required. Minimum scores vary with the GPA. Applicants must complete 20 Carnegie units, including 4 years of English, 3 of math, and 2 each of science and social studies. A fourth year of math, 2 years of foreign language, and 1 year of fine arts also are recommended. A portfolio is required for art studio courses, and an audition is required for music performance. AP and CLEP credits are accepted. All students must maintain a minimum 2.0 GPA and complete at least 120 credit hours. Students must demonstrate competency in math, foreign language, writing, and oral communications. Required studies include courses in basic skills, inference, and communicative skills, along with disciplinary and cross-disciplinary studies. **Procedure:** Freshmen are admitted to all sessions. Entrance exams should be taken before Christmas of the senior year. There is a rolling admissions plan. Applications should be filed by October 15 for spring entry; April 15 for summer entry, along with a $20 fee. **Transfer Students:** 1443 transfer students enrolled in 2013-2014. Transfer students need a minimum GPA of 2.0. If they have fewer than 24 credit hours, they must meet freshmen admission standards. With 24 credits or more, the SAT I or ACT is not required. 30 of 120 credits required for the bachelor's degree must be completed at UK. **International Students:** There are 366 international students enrolled. The school actively recruits these students. They must take the TOEFL.

ADMISSIONS: Randy Mills, Associate Director for Recruitment. E-Mail: *admissions@uky.edu* Web: *www.uky.edu*

FINANCIAL AID: 32% of all full-time freshmen and 34% of continuing full-time students received need-based aid. The average freshman award was $6,007. UK is a member of CSS. The FAFSA is required. The deadline for filing freshman financial aid applications for fall entry is February 15.

UNIVERSITY OF LOUISVILLE　　　D-2
www.louisville.edu

Louisville, KY 40292	(502) 852-6531
	(800) 334-8635
Fax: (502) 852-4476	Email: admitme@louisville.edu
Full-time: 6036 men, 6516 women	Faculty: I, -$
Part-time: 1750 men, 1561 women	Ph.D.s: 86%
Graduate: 2714 men, 2954 women	Student/Faculty: 18 to 1
Year: semesters, summer session	Tuition: $10,236 ($24,124)
Room & Board: $7710	Freshman Class: 10606 applied, 7832 accepted, 2888 enrolled
SAT CR/M: 550/530 ACT: 25	CEEB CODE: 1838
Application Deadline: August 19	COMPETITIVE

The University of Louisville, founded in 1798, is a public institution offering a wide range of undergraduate and graduate academic programs. There are 9 undergraduate schools and 12 graduate schools. In addition to regional accreditation, U of L has baccalaureate program accreditation with AACSB, ABET, ACCE, ADA, CSAB, CSWE, NASM, NCATE, ABA, CCNE, CEPH, CIDA, COAES, COSMA, and NAST. The 640-acre campus is in an urban area in Louisville, KY. Including any residence halls, there are 205 buildings.

STUDENT LIFE: 82% of undergraduates are from Kentucky. Others are from 50 states, 83 foreign countries, and Canada. 74% are White. **Male To Female Ratio:** 1.1:1. The average age of freshmen is 18; all undergraduates, 23. 19% do not continue beyond their first year; 54% remain to graduate. **Housing:** 5154 students can be accommodated in college housing, which includes coed dorms, on-campus apartments, off-campus apartments, and married student housing. In addition, there are honors houses, special-interest houses, fraternity houses, sorority houses, living learning communities, theme communities. On-campus housing is guaranteed for the freshman year only, and is available on a first-come, first-served basis. Priority is given to out-of-town students. 64% of students commute. All students may keep cars.

FACULTY/CLASSROOMS: 58% of faculty are male; 42% are female. No introductory courses are taught by graduate students.

PROGRAMS OF STUDY: U of L confers B.A., B.B.E., B.C.C., B.C.E., B.C.H., B.E.E., B.F.A., B.I.E., B.M., B.M.C., B.M.E., B.S., B.S.B.A., B.S.E., B.S.N., B.S.R. and B.S.W. degrees. Associate, Master's, and Doctoral degrees are also awarded. Bachelor's degrees are awarded in AGRICULTURE (equine science), BIOLOGICAL SCIENCE (biology/biological science), BUSINESS (accounting, banking and finance, business administration and management, business econom-

ics, management science, marketing/retailing/merchandising, and sports management), COMMUNICATIONS AND THE ARTS (American Sign Language, art history, art, art history and appreciation, communications, dramatic arts, English, French, linguistics, music, and Spanish), COMPUTER AND PHYSICAL SCIENCE (atmospheric sciences and meteorology, chemistry, computer science, information sciences and systems, mathematics, and physics), EDUCATION (art education, business education, early childhood education, elementary education, foreign languages education, middle school education, music education, physical education, science education, secondary education, and teaching English as a second/foreign language (TESOL/TEFOL)), ENGINEERING AND ENVIRONMENTAL DESIGN (bioengineering, chemical engineering, civil engineering, computer engineering, electrical/electronics engineering, engineering, engineering management, industrial engineering, and mechanical engineering), HEALTH PROFESSIONS (dental hygiene, health, medical laboratory technology, medical science, music therapy, nursing, and public health), SOCIAL SCIENCE (administration of justice , anthropology, criminal justice, geography, history, humanities, liberal arts/general studies, paralegal studies, philosophy, political science/government, psychology, social work, sociology, and women's studies). Engineering, health professional, and business management are the strongest academically. Arts and sciences, education and human development have the largest enrollments.

ACTIVITIES: 10% of men belong to 19 national fraternities; 9% of women belong to 14 national sororities. There are 388 groups on campus, including art, band, cheerleading, chess, choir, chorale, chorus, computers, dance, debate, ethnic, gay, honors, international, jazz band, literary magazine, marching band, newspaper, opera, orchestra, pep band, photography, political, professional, radio and TV, religious, social, social service, student government, and symphony. Popular campus events include Homecoming, Welcome Week, International Fashion Show and Fryberger Greek Sing. **Sports:** There are 10 intercollegiate sports for men and 13 for women, and 37 intramural sports for men and 37 for women. Facilities include 22,000-seat downtown multipurpose arena, 55,000-seat football stadium, indoor and outdoor tennis courts, golf course, track, soccer field, baseball stadium, field hockey, lacrosse, softball, volleyball courts, a natorium, 128-000 square foot student recreation center that includes exercise and weight facility, six basketball courts, a multiactivity court, jogging track, aerobics studio, fitness labs, boathouse for rowing, a gaming area and classrooms. **Graduates:** From July 1, 2013 to June 30, 2014, 2821 bachelor's degrees were awarded. The most popular majors were communications (8%), psychology (8%), and health and human performance (7%). In an average class, 25% graduate in 4 years or less, 47% graduate in 5 years or less, and 54% graduate in 6 years or less.

SERVICES: Counseling and information services are available, as is tutoring in most subjects. There is a reader service for the blind. **Library/Resources:** The 6 libraries contain 2.3 million volumes, 2.3 million microform items, and 59,378 audio/video tapes/CDs/DVDs, and subscribe to 90,591 periodicals including electronic. Computerized library services include interlibrary loans, database searching, Internet access, and Wi-Fi capability. Special learning facilities include an art gallery, planetarium, and radio station. **Physically Challenged Students:** 90% of the campus is accessible. Facilities include wheelchair ramps, elevators, special parking, specially equipped restrooms, special class scheduling, lowered drinking fountains, lowered telephones, and special housing. **Special:** Cross-registration with other schools, study abroad in 5 countries (China, Panama, Portugal, Trinidad, Canada), work-study programs, and B.A.-B.S. degrees are offered. A general studies degree, nondegree study, and pass/fail options are available. Co-op programs in engineering and business and internships are also possible. There are 16 national honor societies, a freshman honors program, and 1 departmental honors programs. **Visiting:** There are regularly scheduled orientations for prospective students, including admissions presentation, campus tour, and optional faculty appointments. There are guides for informal visits. To schedule a visit, contact Kristen Ellis at Kristen.ellis@louisville.edu **Campus Safety and Security:** Measures include 24-hour foot and vehicle patrol, emergency notification system, self-defense education, and security escort services. There are shuttle buses, emergency telephones, lighted pathways/sidewalks, and controlled access to dorms/residences.

REQUIREMENTS: The SAT or ACT is required. Applicants must be graduates from an accredited high school or have received a GED, must have completed a precollege curriculum with a GPA of 2.5, and must have at least 1 of the following: a composite ACT score of 20 or a satisfactory SAT score; completion of the U of L enhanced precollege curriculum (PCC) with a minimum GPA of 2.5; or a rank in the top 15% of the high school graduating class. AP and CLEP credits are accepted. Distribution requirements include at least 6 hours each in social sciences, natural sciences, the history of world civilizations, and humanities. Freshmen are required to take college writing or advanced composition and 2 phys ed courses. A total of 123 semester hours, including 46 to 60 hours in the major, with a minimum GPA of 2.5 (2.0 in education, 2.75 in engineering) is required to graduate. **Procedure:** Freshmen are admitted fall, spring, and summer. Entrance exams should be taken in the spring or the summer of the junior year. There is a rolling admissions plan. Applications should be filed by August 19 for fall entry, along with a $50 fee. Applications are accepted on-line. **Transfer Students:** 1082 transfer students enrolled in 2013-2014. Transfer students must have a minimum GPA of 2.0. 30 of 123 credits required for the bachelor's degree must be completed at U of L. **International Students:** There are 255 international students enrolled. They must take the TOEFL with a minimum score of 550 on the paper-based TOEFL (PBT) or 79 on the Internet-based version (iBT), or take the IELTS. Some programs may require proof of calculus readiness.

ADMISSIONS: 74% of the 2014-2015 applicants were accepted. The SAT scores for the 2014-2015 freshman class were: Critical Reading--25% below 500, 45% between 500 and 599, 25% between 600 and 699, and 5% between 700 and 800; Math--39% below 500, 37% between 500 and 599, 20% between 600 and 699, and 4% between 700 and 800. The ACT scores were 11% below 21, 27% between 21 and 23, 27% between 24 and 26, 15% between 27 and 28, and 20% above 28. There were 24 National Merit finalists. **Admissions Contact:** Jenny Sawyer, Executive Director of Admissions. E-Mail: *admitme@louisville.edu* Web: *www.louisville.edu*

FINANCIAL AID: In 2014-2015, 73% of all full-time freshmen and 14% of continuing full-time students received some form of financial aid. 26% of all full-time freshmen and 8% of continuing full-time students received need-based aid. The average freshman award was $7,098. Need-based scholarships or need-based grants averaged $1,515 ($5,761 maximum); need-based self-help aid (loans and jobs) averaged $1,628 ($2,750 maximum); non-need-based athletic scholarships averaged $2,249 ($14,054 maximum); other non-need-based awards and non-need-based scholarships averaged $2,093 ($12,062 maximum); and $2,510 from other forms of aid. The average financial indebtedness of the 2014 graduate was $26,063. The FAFSA is required. The priority date for freshman financial aid applications for fall entry is February 15.

UNIVERSITY OF PIKEVILLE (*The complete profile is made available exclusively on our website, www.barronspac.com*)

UNIVERSITY OF THE CUMBERLANDS   E-4
www.ucumberlands.edu

Williamsburg, KY 40769	(606) 539-4241
	(800) 343-1609
Fax: (606) 539-4303	Email: admiss@ucumberlands.edu
Full-time: 809 men, 888 women	Faculty: 122
Part-time: 387 men, 571 women	Ph.D.s: 74%
Graduate: 873 men, 2209 women	Student/Faculty: 16 to 1
Year: semesters, summer session	Tuition: $20,000
Room & Board: $7500	Freshman Class: 1616 applied, 1539 accepted, 405 enrolled
SAT CR/M: 480/500 ACT: 22	CEEB CODE: 1145
Application Deadline: open	COMPETITIVE

University of the Cumberlands, founded in 1888, is a private liberal arts institution affiliated with the Kentucky Baptist Convention. The

school is committed to challenging students with an innovative education while remaining keenly aware of the importance of traditional liberal arts education. Our commitment to traditional values is reflected by our undergraduate curriculum which provides the foundation for a deeper understanding of advanced studies. The figures in the above capsule and in this profile are approximate. There is 1 undergraduate school and 9 graduate schools. In addition to regional accreditation, Patriots has baccalaureate program accreditation with SACSCOC. The 100-acre campus is in a small town 100 miles south of Lexington and 65 miles north of Knoxville. Including any residence halls, there are 38 buildings.

STUDENT LIFE: 68% of undergraduates are from Kentucky. Others are from 38 states, 26 foreign countries, and Canada. 95% are from public schools. 74% are White. 79% are Protestant; 11% claim no religious affiliation. **Male To Female Ratio:** 1.8:1. The average age of freshmen is 18; all undergraduates, 21. 37% do not continue beyond their first year; 40% remain to graduate. **Housing:** 1213 students can be accommodated in college housing, which includes single-sex dorms. On-campus housing is guaranteed for all 4 years. 75% of students live on campus; of those, 42% remain on campus on weekends. Alcohol is not permitted. All students may keep cars.

FACULTY/CLASSROOMS: 49% of faculty are male; 51% are female. 85% teach undergraduates. No introductory courses are taught by graduate students. The average class size in an introductory lecture is 36; in a laboratory is 10; and in a regular course is 14.

PROGRAMS OF STUDY: Patriots confers B.A., B.S., B.G.S. and B.M. degrees. Associate, Master's, and Doctoral degrees are also awarded. Bachelor's degrees are awarded in BIOLOGICAL SCIENCE (biology/biological science), BUSINESS (accounting, business administration and management, office supervision and management, and sports management), COMMUNICATIONS AND THE ARTS (art, church music, communications, dramatic arts, English, journalism, music, and Spanish), COMPUTER AND PHYSICAL SCIENCE (chemistry, information sciences and systems, mathematics, and physics), EDUCATION (art education, elementary education, English education, health education, mathematics education, middle school education, music education, physical education, science education, social studies education, Spanish education K-12, and special education), ENGINEERING AND ENVIRONMENTAL DESIGN (preengineering), HEALTH PROFESSIONS (exercise science, health, predentistry, premedicine, prepharmacy, prephysical therapy, preveterinary science, and public health), SOCIAL SCIENCE (criminal justice, history, missions, political science/government, prelaw, psychology, religion, religious music, and social work). Biology, business, and education are the strongest academically and have the largest enrollments.

ACTIVITIES: There are no fraternities or sororities. There are 49 groups on campus, including art, band, cheerleading, choir, chorale, chorus, dance, debate, drama, drill team, environmental, forensics, honors, international, jazz band, literary magazine, marching band, musical theater, newspaper, outdoor adventure club, pep band, political, professional, radio and TV, religious, social, social service, and student government. Popular campus events include Madrigal Dinner, Hanging of the Greens, and Homecoming. **Sports:** There are 15 intercollegiate sports for men and 15 for women, and 12 intramural sports for men and 12 for women. Facilities include a gym for intramurals and recreation; an athletic complex with facilities for men's and women's basketball and volleyball, a weight room, and a swimming pool; a game room; tennis courts; baseball and softball fields; a practice football field, a football field, a soccer practice field, a soccer field, and a wrestling gym. Lacrosse fields will be ready next year. **Graduates:** From July 1, 2013 to June 30, 2014, 279 bachelor's degrees were awarded. The most popular majors were business administration (15%), exercise and sports science (11%), and psychology (10%). 30 companies recruited on campus in 2013-2014. In an average class, 1% graduate in 3 years or less, 24% graduate in 4 years or less, 40% graduate in 5 years or less, and 43% graduate in 6 years or less. Of the 2013 graduating class, 20% were enrolled in graduate school within 6 months of graduation, and 75% were employed.

SERVICES: Counseling and information services are available, as is tutoring in every subject. **Library/Resources:** The library contains 137,244 volumes, 806,000 microform items, 3,719 audio/video tapes/CDs/DVDs, and subscribes to 58,720 periodicals including electronic.

Computerized library services include interlibrary loans, database searching, Internet access, and Wi-Fi capability. Special learning facilities include an art gallery, natural history museum, radio station, TV station, a distance learning lab. **Physically Challenged Students:** 75% of the campus is accessible. Facilities include wheelchair ramps, elevators, special parking, specially equipped restrooms, special class scheduling, lowered drinking fountains, and lowered telephones. **Special:** Internships, study abroad in England, China, Spain, France, and Thailand, and work-study programs with the university, local businesses, and other educational institutions are available. The university offers B.A.-B.S. degrees in all majors except music, dual majors in all major fields, a general studies degree, nondegree study, and a 3-2 engineering degree with University of Kentucky. There are 13 national honor societies, a freshman honors program, and 13 departmental honors programs. **Visiting:** There are regularly scheduled orientations for prospective students, consisting of a tour, a departmental conference, an advising session, adjustment information, general information, and first college class. There are guides for informal visits, visitors may sit in on classes, and stay overnight. To schedule a visit, contact Shelleigh Moses at shelleigh.moses@ ucumberlands.edu. **Campus Safety and Security:** Measures include 24-hour foot and vehicle patrol, emergency notification system, self-defense education, and security escort services. There are lighted pathways/sidewalks and controlled access to dorms/residences.

REQUIREMENTS: The SAT or ACT is required, with composite scores of better than 17 for the ACT or 780 for the SAT required. Consideration is given to those with ACT scores of 16 and 17, provided the high school GPA is 2.5 or above in college prep classes. Although each application is considered individually, students must have fulfilled general high school requirements of 4 years of English, 3 each of math and science, and 2 of social studies. AP and CLEP credits are accepted. Important factors in the admissions decision are advanced placement or honors courses, leadership record, and recommendations by school officials. All students must complete 128 semester hours, including 40 hours of liberal arts courses and an average of 36 hours in a major, while maintaining an overall GPA of 2.0 (2.5 for those seeking teacher certification). General education requirements include courses from the areas of art, music, theater, speech, religion, English composition, literature, history, math, natural and social sciences, community service, and fine arts or philosophy. A comprehensive exam may be required. Programs presented for graduation must include 2 majors, 1 major and 1 minor, 1 major with 15 hours of restricted electives, or 3 minors, or 1 concentration. **Procedure:** Freshmen are admitted to all sessions. Entrance exams should be taken prior to admission consideration. There is a rolling admissions plan. Application deadlines are open. Application fee is $30. Applications are accepted on-line. Application fees are waived if application is completed on-line. **Transfer Students:** 113 transfer students enrolled in 2013-2014. Applicants must have verification from their previous school that they are eligible to return. Students with fewer than 30 semester or 45 quarter hours must meet freshman admissions requirements. 30 of 128 credits required for the bachelor's degree must be completed at Cumberlands. **International Students:** There are 110 international students enrolled. The school actively recruits these students. They must take the college's own test.

ADMISSIONS: 95% of the 2014-2015 applicants were accepted. The SAT scores for the 2014-2015 freshman class were: Critical Reading--59% below 500, 29% between 500 and 599, 10% between 600 and 699, and 2% between 700 and 800; Math--48% below 500, 39% between 500 and 599, and 13% between 600 and 699. The ACT scores were 37% below 21, 29% between 21 and 23, 16% between 24 and 26, 8% between 27 and 28, and 10% above 28. 34% of the current freshmen were in the top fifth of their class; 61% were in the top two fifths. 5 freshmen graduated first in their class. **Admissions Contact:** Erica Harris, Director of Admissions. E-Mail: *admiss@ucumberlands .edu* Web: *www.ucumberlands.edu*

FINANCIAL AID: In 2014-2015, 99% of all full-time freshmen and 99% of continuing full-time students received some form of financial aid. 87% of all full-time freshmen and 85% of continuing full-time students received need-based aid. The average freshman award was $24,910. Need-based scholarships or need-based grants averaged $5,819 ($23,645 maximum); need-based self-help aid (loans and jobs) averaged $3,588 ($8,000 maximum); non-need-based athletic scholarships averaged $2,540 ($28,000 maximum); other non-need-based awards and non-need-based scholarships averaged $10,269 ($28,000 maximum); and $2,694 from other forms of aid. 68% of undergraduate students work part-time. Average annual earnings from campus work are $2131. The average financial indebtedness of the 2014 graduate was $18,954. The FAFSA is required. The priority date for freshman financial aid applications for fall entry is February 1.

WESTERN KENTUCKY UNIVERSITY (*The complete profile is made available exclusively on our website, www.barronspac.com*)

LOUISIANA

• College Location

0   20   40   60   80   100
Miles

CENTENARY COLLEGE OF LOUISIANA   A-1

www.centenary.edu

Shreveport, LA 71104

Fax: (318) 869-5005
Full-time: 248 men, 323 women
Part-time: 10 men, 5 women
Graduate: 29 men, 46 women
Year: semesters, summer session
Room & Board: $12,150

(318) 869-5131
(800) 234-4448
Email: admission@centenary.edu
Faculty: 54; IIB, av$
Ph.D.s: 100%
Student/Faculty: 9 to 1
Tuition: $33,500
Freshman Class: 670
applied, 442 accepted, 128
enrolled
CEEB CODE: 6082

Application Deadline: August 1   **COMPETITIVE+**

Centenary College of Louisiana is a private, four-year arts and sciences college affiliated with the United Methodist Church. Founded in 1825, it is the oldest chartered liberal arts college west of the Mississippi River. There are 2 graduate schools. In addition to regional accreditation, Centenary College has baccalaureate program accreditation with NASM and ACS. The 65-acre campus is in an urban area in the Shreveport/Bossier City located in the northwest corner of Louisiana near the Texas and Arkansas borders. Including any residence halls, there are 23 buildings.

STUDENT LIFE: 64% of undergraduates are from Louisiana. Others are from 28 states and 7 foreign countries. **Male To Female Ratio:** 1.3:1. The average age of freshmen is 18; all undergraduates, 20. **Housing:** College-sponsored housing includes single-sex and coed dorms. In addition, there are fraternity houses, sorority houses, Including theme housing. On-campus housing is guaranteed for all 4 years, and is available on a first-come, first-served basis. 60% of students live on campus. Alcohol is not permitted. All students may keep cars.

FACULTY/CLASSROOMS: 61% of faculty are male; 39% are female. No introductory courses are taught by graduate students. The average class size in an introductory lecture is 12 and in a laboratory is 11.

PROGRAMS OF STUDY: Centenary College confers B.A. and B.S.

degrees. Master's degrees are also awarded. Bachelor's degrees are awarded in BIOLOGICAL SCIENCE (biochemistry, biology/biological science, biophysics, and neurosciences), BUSINESS (business administration and management and business economics), COMMUNICATIONS AND THE ARTS (art, communications, dance, dramatic arts, English, French, German, Latin, music, music performance, Spanish, and studio art), COMPUTER AND PHYSICAL SCIENCE (chemistry, geology, mathematics, and physics), ENGINEERING AND ENVIRONMENTAL DESIGN (environmental science), SOCIAL SCIENCE (economics, history, interdisciplinary studies, liberal arts/general studies, philosophy, political science/government, psychology, religion, religious music, and sociology). Biological/life sciences, business and marketing, visual and performing arts have the largest enrollments.

ACTIVITIES: There are 60 groups on campus, including cheerleading, choir, chorale, communications, dance, drama, environmental club, film, gay, honors, international, jazz band, musical theater, newspaper, opera, photography, political, professional, radio and TV, religious, social, social service, student government, symphony, and yearbook. Popular campus events include Spring Fling, President's Convocation and Freak Week. **Sports:** There are 8 intercollegiate sports for men and 9 for women. Facilities include a 3000-seat gym, 2 weight rooms, basketball, racquetball, volleyball, and tennis courts, baseball, soccer, and softball fields, a fitness center with aerobic exercise and strengthening equipment, and a natatorium. **Graduates:** From July 1, 2013 to June 30, 2014, 198 bachelor's degrees were awarded. The most popular majors were biological/life sciences (18%), business and marketing (17%), and visual and performing arts (16%). In an average class, 1% graduate in 3 years or less and 59% graduate in 4 years or less.

SERVICES: Counseling and information services are available, as is tutoring in most subjects. **Library/Resources:** The 2 libraries contain 180,000 volumes, 310,671 microform items, 425 audio/video tapes/CDs/DVDs, and subscribe to 942 periodicals including electronic. Computerized library services include interlibrary loans, database searching, and Internet access. Special learning facilities include an art gallery, radio station, a theater, and an art museum. **Physically Challenged Students:** 95% of the campus is accessible. Facilities include wheelchair ramps, elevators, special parking, specially equipped restrooms, special class scheduling, lowered drinking fountains, lowered telephones. **Special:** Centenary offers study abroad in 7 countries, cross-registration with Associated Colleges of the South, internships in all majors, a Washington semester, and a work-study program within the college. A 3-1 communications disorders degree with Louisiana State University Medical Center is possible, as is a 3-2 engineering degree with Washington University in St. Louis, University of Southern California, Columbia University, Texas A&M University, and Case Western Reserve Universities. A 3-2 applied science preprofessional degree combine with health administration or medical school is available. Pre-veterinary studies, general studies and interdisciplinary degrees, and student-designed majors are available. There are 7 national honor societies and 15 departmental honors programs. **Visiting:** There are regularly scheduled orientations for prospective students, consisting of information sessions with a counselor, tour of the campus, visit to a class or with faculty, and lunch. There are guides for informal visits, visitors may sit in on classes, and stay overnight. To schedule a visit, contact Nora Fradin at nfradin@centenary.edu. **Campus Safety and Security:** Measures include 24-hour foot and vehicle patrol and security escort services. There are emergency telephones and lighted pathways/sidewalks.

REQUIREMENTS: The SAT or ACT is required. Applicants should be high school graduates with a minimum composite score of 950 on the SAT or 20 on the ACT, although accepted students average 1145 and 26 respectively. Secondary school preparation should include 15 academic credits, including 4 of English, 3 each of math and science, 2 each of a foreign language and history, 1 of social studies, and electives. Music students must audition; art students are advised to present a portfolio. AP credits are accepted. Important factors in the admissions decision are advanced placement or honors courses, extracurricular activities record, and personality/intangible qualities.To graduate, all students must complete 124 semester hours, with

694

a maximum of 45 in a non-interdisciplinary major and a minimum of 30 at the upper-division level, including a writing and speaking class in the major at the junior level, and maintain a minimum GPA of 2.0. There are 48 to 52 hours of distribution requirements. Core curriculum requirements include courses in the humanities, social sciences, hard sciences, and math. In addition, freshmen must take a first year experience course. All students must complete a Trek component, study or live in a different culture, or study abroad, and fulfill career explorations. **Procedure:** Freshmen are admitted fall, spring, and summer. Entrance exams should be taken by the fall of the senior year. There are early decision, early admissions, and rolling admissions plans. Early decision applications should be filed by December 15; regular applications, by August 1 for fall entry, along with a $30 fee. Notifications are sent September 1. Applications are accepted on-line. **Transfer Students:** 19 transfer students enrolled in 2013-2014. Transfer applicants must have a minimum GPA of 2.0 and demonstrate good performance in a liberal arts curriculum. 45 credits required for the bachelor's degree must be completed at Centenary College. **International Students:** There are 16 international students enrolled. The school actively recruits these students. They must take the TOEFL with a minimum score of 550 on the paper-based TOEFL (PBT) or 79 on the Internet-based version (iBT).

ADMISSIONS: 66% of the 2014-2015 applicants were accepted. **Admissions Contact:** Thomas Newton, Director of Admissions. E-Mail: *admission@centenary.edu* Web: *www.centenary.edu*

FINANCIAL AID: In 2014-2015, 99% of all full-time freshmen and 99% of continuing full-time students received some form of financial aid. 77% of all full-time freshmen and 75% of continuing full-time students received need-based aid. The average freshman award was $27,911. Need-based scholarships or need-based grants averaged $25,646 ($35,740 maximum); need-based self-help aid (loans and jobs) averaged $6,723 ($14,200 maximum); and other non-need-based awards and non-need-based scholarships averaged $14,369 ($36,126 maximum). 32% of undergraduate students work part-time. The average financial indebtedness of the 2014 graduate was $23,760. The FAFSA is required. The priority date for freshman financial aid applications for fall entry is February 15.

DILLARD UNIVERSITY
www.dillard.edu

D-4

New Orleans, LA 70122

(504) 816-4951
(800) 216-6637

Fax: 504-816-4895
Email: tsteffen@dillard.edu

Full-time: n/av	Faculty: 82
Part-time: n/av	Ph.D.s: 56%
Graduate: n/av	Student/Faculty: n/av
Year: semesters, summer session	Tuition: $15,250
Room & Board: $5690	Freshman Class: n/av
SAT or ACT: recommended	CEEB CODE: 6164
Application Deadline: n/av	**VERY COMPETITIVE**

Dillard University, established in 1869, is an independent, nonsectarian, liberal arts institution, affiliated with the United Church of Christ and the United Methodist Church. It offers undergraduate programs 19 baccalaureate degrees in the colleges of arts of sciences, professional studies, and general studies. There are 3 undergraduate schools. In addition to regional accreditation, Dillard has baccalaureate program accreditation with NLN. The 55-acre campus is in an urban area in New Orleans. Including any residence halls, there are 21 buildings.

STUDENT LIFE: 67% of undergraduates are from Louisiana. Others are from 29 states, 12 foreign countries, and Canada. 98% are African American. **Male To Female Ratio:** Is 1:1. 28% do not continue beyond their first year. **Housing:** College-sponsored housing includes single-sex dorms, on-campus apartments, and off-campus apartments. On-campus housing is guaranteed for the freshman year only, is available on a first-come, first-served basis, and is available on a lottery system for upperclassmen. Priority is given to out-of-town students. 30% of students commute. Alcohol is not permitted. All students may keep cars.

FACULTY/CLASSROOMS: 43% of faculty are male; 57% are female.

All teach undergraduates. No introductory courses are taught by graduate students. The average class size in an introductory lecture is 30.

PROGRAMS OF STUDY: Dillard confers B.A., B.S. and B.S.N. degrees. Bachelor's degrees are awarded in BIOLOGICAL SCIENCE (biology/biological science), BUSINESS (accounting and business administration and management), COMMUNICATIONS AND THE ARTS (art, communications, English, music, music business management, and music performance), COMPUTER AND PHYSICAL SCIENCE (chemistry, computer science, and physics), HEALTH PROFESSIONS (nursing and public health), SOCIAL SCIENCE (economics, history, political science/government, psychology, sociology, and urban studies). Biological sciences has the largest enrollment.

ACTIVITIES: 4% of men belong to 4 national fraternities; 11% of women belong to 4 national sororities. There are 64 groups on campus, including art, cheerleading, chess, choir, chorus, dance, drama, ethnic, honors, professional, religious, social service, student government, and yearbook. Popular campus events include Coronation, Avenue of the Oaks Gala, and Founder's Day. **Sports:** There are 3 intercollegiate sports for men and 3 for women. Facilities include a gym, swimming pool, nautilus room, tennis courts, dance facility, and game room. **Graduates:** From July 1, 2013 to June 30, 2014, 278 bachelor's degrees were awarded. The most popular majors were public health (16%), biology (13%), and mass communications (9%). Of the 2013 graduating class, 45% were enrolled in graduate school within 6 months of graduation, and 45% were employed.

SERVICES: Counseling and information services are available, as is tutoring in every subject. There is remedial math, reading, and writing. **Library/Resources:** The library contains 104,615 volumes, 21,638 microform items, 426 audio/video tapes/CDs/DVDs, and subscribes to 295 periodicals including electronic. Computerized library services include interlibrary loans and database searching. Special learning facilities include an art gallery. **Physically Challenged Students:** 70% of the campus is accessible. Facilities include wheelchair ramps, elevators, special parking, specially equipped restrooms, and special class scheduling. **Special:** Opportunities are provided for internships, work-study programs, credit by exam, nondegree study, and pass/fail options. All social science majors are encouraged to pursue a double major. There is a 4-year co-op degree in music therapy with Loyola University, a clinical public health curriculum with Howard University, a 5-year joint degree in urban studies with Columbia University, and preengineering dual degree programs with the Georgia Institute of Technology and Auburn and Columbia Universities. There are 3 national honor societies. **Visiting:** There are regularly scheduled orientations for prospective students, scheduled on individual basis. There are guides for informal visits, visitors may sit in on classes, and stay overnight. To schedule a visit, contact Coordinator of Campus Tours and Special Events at (504) 816-4670. **Campus Safety and Security:** Measures include 24-hour foot and vehicle patrol. There are shuttle buses and lighted pathways/sidewalks.

REQUIREMENTS: The SAT or ACT is recommended. Graduation from an accredited secondary school is required; a GED will be accepted. Applicants must submit an academic record of 20 units, distributed as follows: 4 units in English, 3 each in math and natural sciences, 2 in social studies, and 8 in other academic electives. Recommendations from a high school teacher and the principal or a student counselor are required. A GPA of 2.2 is required. AP credits are accepted. Important factors in the admissions decision are recommendations by school officials, leadership record, and personality/intangible qualities. Students must successfully complete 125 semester hours and maintain a minimum overall GPA of 2.0 or better in all courses in the major. In addition, all students must complete 35 semester hours in the core curriculum, which includes courses in English composition, world literature, English literature, math, natural sciences, world history, political science, economics, university assembly, phys ed, and academic orientation. Additionally, each student must engage in a minimum of 120 clock hours of volunteer service in the community. **Procedure:** Freshmen are admitted spring. Entrance exams should be taken between April of the junior year and December of the senior year. There are early admissions, deferred admissions, and rolling admissions plans. Applications should be filed by December 1 for spring entry, along with a $30 fee. Notification is sent on a rolling basis. Applications are accepted on-line. **Transfer Students:** 46 transfer students enrolled in 2013-2014. Applicants for transfer must submit a secondary school record or equivalent, transcripts from previous colleges showing an average grade of C, and personal recommendations. No more than 60 semester hours may be submitted for transfer credit. 65 of 125 credits required for the bachelor's degree must be completed at Dillard. **International Students:** There are 12 international students enrolled. They must take the TOEFL with a minimum score of 550 on the paper-based TOEFL (PBT). They must also take the SAT or ACT, scoring 18.

ADMISSIONS: Thomas Steffen, Director of Recruitment. E-Mail: *tsteffen@dillard.edu* Web: *www.dillard.edu*

FINANCIAL AID: In 2014-2015, 99% of all full-time freshmen and continuing full-time students received some form of financial aid. 93% of all full-time freshmen and continuing full-time students received need-based aid. 25% of undergraduate students work part-time. Average annual earnings from campus work are $2000. The average financial indebtedness of the 2014 graduate was $26,250. Dillard is a member of CSS. The FAFSA and the college's own financial statement are required. The deadline for filing freshman financial aid applications for fall entry is March 1.

GRAMBLING STATE UNIVERSITY *(The complete profile is made available exclusively on our website, www.barronspac.com)*

LOUISIANA COLLEGE www.lacollege.edu	**B-3**
Pineville, LA 71359	(318) 487-7259 (800) 487-1906
Fax: (318) 487-7550	**Email:** melder@lacollege.edu
Full-time: 436 men, 420 women	**Faculty:** 60
Part-time: 67 men, 133 women	**Ph.D.s:** 60%
Graduate: n/av	**Student/Faculty:** 14 to 1
Year: semesters, summer session	**Tuition:** $11,490
Room & Board: $4256	**Freshman Class:** 549 applied, 429 accepted, 246 enrolled
SAT: required **ACT:** 22	**CEEB CODE:** 6371
Application Deadline: n/av	**COMPETITIVE**

Louisiana College, founded in 1906, is a private liberal arts college affiliated with the Southern Baptist Churches of Louisiana. LC offers more than 80 majors, minors, and pre-professional programs of study. The college is one of the most recognized colleges in the South. Figures in the above capsule and in this profile are approximate. In addition to regional accreditation, LC has baccalaureate program accreditation with AACSB, ACBSP, CSWE, NASM, and NLN. The 81-acre campus is in a small town in the heart of Louisiana, 1 mile northeast of Alexandria. Including any residence halls, there are 25 buildings.

STUDENT LIFE: 92% of undergraduates are from Louisiana. Others are from 16 states, 5 foreign countries, and Canada. 88% are White. 66% are Protestant; 18% claim no religious affiliation; 13% Catholic. **Male To Female Ratio:** 1.1:1. The average age of freshmen is 18; all undergraduates, 22. 36% do not continue beyond their first year; 43% remain to graduate. **Housing:** 726 students can be accommodated in college housing, which includes single-sex dorms, on-campus apartments, and married student housing. On-campus housing is guaranteed for all 4 years. 54% of students live on campus. Alcohol is not permitted. All students may keep cars.

FACULTY/CLASSROOMS: 57% of faculty are male; 43% are female. All teach undergraduates. No introductory courses are taught by graduate students. The average class size in an introductory lecture is 30; in a laboratory is 20; and in a regular course is 18.

PROGRAMS OF STUDY: LC confers B.A., B.S., B.G.S., B.M., B.S.N. and B.S.W. degrees. Associate degrees are also awarded. Bachelor's degrees are awarded in BIOLOGICAL SCIENCE (biology/biological science), BUSINESS (business administration and management), COMMUNICATIONS AND THE ARTS (communications, dramatic arts, English, French, graphic design, journalism, languages, multi-

media, music, speech/debate/rhetoric, and studio art), COMPUTER AND PHYSICAL SCIENCE (chemistry and mathematics), EDUCATION (art education, athletic training, business education, elementary education, English education, health education, mathematics education, music education, science education, secondary education, social studies education, and special education), HEALTH PROFESSIONS (exercise science, medical laboratory technology, music therapy, nursing, predentistry, premedicine, preoptometry, and preveterinary science), SOCIAL SCIENCE (criminal justice, economics, history, philosophy, prelaw, psychology, public administration, religion, religious education, religious music, social work, and sociology). Education, biology, and business have the largest enrollments.

ACTIVITIES: 5% of men belong to 4 local fraternities; 15% of women belong to 4 local sororities. There are 57 groups on campus, including a Union Board (campus programming), art, band, Breaking All Barriers (Diversity), cheerleading, choir, chorale, chorus, communications, debate, drama, honors, international, jazz band, literary magazine, marching band, musical theater, newspaper, opera, pep band, political, professional, radio and TV, religious, social, social service, student government, symphony, and yearbook. Popular campus events include Gala Christmas, Sanders Lecture Series, and Miss LC Pageant. **Sports:** There are 5 intercollegiate sports for men and 5 for women, and 11 intramural sports for men and 11 for women. Facilities include a field house for basketball, a baseball field, a fitness/wellness center, a jogging trail, tennis courts, an intramural/soccer/football field, an outdoor beach volleyball court, softball field, and a practice football field. **Graduates:** From July 1, 2013 to June 30, 2014, 159 bachelor's degrees were awarded. The most popular majors were nursing (9%), biology (9%), and social work (8%). 65 companies recruited on campus in 2013-2014. In an average class, 24% graduate in 4 years or less, 41% graduate in 5 years or less, and 45% graduate in 6 years or less.

SERVICES: Counseling and information services are available, as is tutoring in most subjects. There is a reader service for the blind, and remedial math and writing. PASS (Program to Assist Student Success) offers services for students with documented learning disabilities. **Library/Resources:** The library contains 138,985 volumes, 126,266 microform items, 2,500 audio/video tapes/CDs/DVDs, and subscribes to 19,993 periodicals including electronic. Computerized library services include interlibrary loans, database searching, and Internet access. Special learning facilities include an art gallery, radio station, a performing arts center. **Physically Challenged Students:** 95% of the campus is accessible. Facilities include wheelchair ramps, elevators, special parking, specially equipped restrooms, and lowered telephones. **Special:** Study abroad in London and Hong Kong, interdisciplinary studies, work-study programs, non-degree study, internships, dual majors, and pass/fail options are offered. There are 13 national honor societies and a freshman honors program. **Visiting:** There are regularly scheduled orientations for prospective students, consisting of spring and fall campus preview days and a 2-day orientation and pre-registration in June. There are guides for informal visits, visitors may sit in on classes, and stay overnight. To schedule a visit, contact the Office of Admissions at admissions@lacollege.edu. **Campus Safety and Security:** Measures include 24-hour foot and vehicle patrol, self-defense education, and security escort services. There are lighted pathways/sidewalks.

REQUIREMENTS: The SAT or ACT is required. Candidates for admission must have completed 17 units, which must include 4 of English, 3 of math (algebra I, II, and geometry), 3 of social studies, and 3 of science (2 with lab). Graduates of accredited high school's must meet one of the following requirements for unconditional admission: (1) score at least 20 composite on ACT or satisfactorily on the SAT and possess a GPA of 2.0 on a 4.0 scale; or (2) possess an academic GPA of 2.0 on a 4.0 scale and rank in the upper 50% of their graduating class with an acceptable ACT or SAT score. AP and CLEP credits are accepted. Important factors in the admissions decision are extracurricular activities record, leadership record, and advanced placement or honors courses. To graduate, students must complete 127 total credit hours, 42 of which must be junior-senior level, including a central core of 56 hours in all degree programs, and maintain a minimum GPA of 2.0, 2.25 in the major. They must also complete cultural/intellectual and spiritual enrichment requirements and earn at least 25% of credit applied toward degree through instruction offered by LC. They must complete the last 30 hours of course work at LC, and take 3 hours each of phys ed and computer applications. **Procedure:** Freshmen are admitted fall, spring, and summer. Entrance exams should be taken during the junior or senior year. There is a rolling admissions plan. Application deadlines are open. Application fee is $25. Notification is sent on a rolling basis. Applications are accepted on-line. **Transfer Students:** Applicants must have an overall minimum GPA of 2.0 and finish all remedial course work prior to transfer. 30 of 127 credits required for the bachelor's degree must be completed at LC. **International Students:** They must take the TOEFL, which is waived for students taking the SAT who earn 480 on the verbal section. They must also take the SAT or ACT.

ADMISSIONS: 78% of the 2014-2015 applicants were accepted. The ACT scores were 38% below 21, 29% between 21 and 23, 16% between 24 and 26, 9% between 27 and 28, and 8% above 28. **Admissions Contact:** Renee Melder, Director of Admissions. E-Mail: *melder@lacollege.edu* Web: *www.lacollege.edu*

FINANCIAL AID: 19% of undergraduate students work part-time. The FAFSA, FFS, and the college's own financial statement are required. The priority date for freshman financial aid applications for fall entry is March 15. The deadline for filing freshman financial aid applications for fall entry is October 1.

LOUISIANA STATE UNIVERSITY SYSTEM

The Louisiana State University System, established in 1860, is a public system in Louisiana. It is governed by a board of supervisors, whose chief administrator is the president. The primary goal of the system is to foster excellence in teaching, research, and public service. The main priorities are undergraduate education, graduate education, and economic development. The total student enrollment is usually about 90,000, with 3500 faculty members. Altogether there are approximately 228 baccalaureate, 220 master's, and 86 doctoral programs offered in the Louisiana State University System. Profiles of the 4-year campuses are included in this section.

LOUISIANA STATE UNIVERSITY   C-4
www.lsu.edu

Baton Rouge, LA 70803   **(225) 578-1175**

Fax: (225) 578-4433
Full-time: 10979 men, 11832 women
Part-time: 1101 men, 1011 women
Graduate: 2713 men, 2842 women
Year: semesters, summer session
Room & Board: $10,804

SAT CR/M: 559/577 **ACT:** 26
Application Deadline: April 15

Email: admissions@lsu.edu
Faculty: 1053
Ph.D.s: 89%
Student/Faculty: 22 to 1
Tuition: $7873 ($25,790)
Freshman Class: 16005 applied, 12002 accepted, 5501 enrolled
CEEB CODE: 6373
COMPETITIVE+

Louisiana State University in Baton Rouge, a public institution founded in 1860, and part of the Louisiana State University System, offers programs in the colleges of agriculture, humanities and social sciences, business administration, coast and environment, art and design, human sciences and education, engineering, music and dramatic arts, mass communication, and science. Figures in the above capsule and in this profile are approximate. There are 11 undergraduate schools and 2 graduate schools. In addition to regional accreditation, LSU has baccalaureate program accreditation with AACSB, ABET, ACCE, ACEJMC, ASLA, CSWE, FIDER, NAAB, NASAD, NASM, NCATE, SAF, and ADA. The 2000-acre campus is in an urban area in Baton Rouge, Louisiana. Including any residence halls, there are 250 buildings.
STUDENT LIFE: 80% of undergraduates are from Louisiana. Others are from 49 states, 81 foreign countries, and Canada. 52% are from public schools. 76% are White; 11% African American. 40% are Catholic; 33% Protestant; 23% claim no religious affiliation. **Male To Female Ratio:** 1.1:1. The average age of freshmen is 19; all undergraduates, 21. 18% do not continue beyond their first year; 69% remain

to graduate. **Housing:** 7450 students can be accommodated in college housing, which includes single-sex and coed dorms, on-campus apartments, and married student housing. In addition, there are honors houses, special-interest houses, fraternity houses, and sorority houses. 75% of students commute. All students may keep cars.
FACULTY/CLASSROOMS: 64% of faculty are male; 36% are female. 89% teach undergraduates, 75% do research, and 73% do both. Graduate students teach 17% of introductory courses. The average class size in an introductory lecture is 52; in a laboratory is 25; and in a regular course is 38.
PROGRAMS OF STUDY: LSU confers B.A., B.S., B.A.M.C., B.Arch., B.F.A., B.I.S., B.I.D., B.L.A., B.M., B.M.Ed., B.S.B.E., B.S.C.E., B.S.Ch.E., B.S.E.E., B.S.Env.E., B.S.C.M., B.S.F., B.S.I.E., B.S. in Coastal Environmental Science, B.S. in Geol., B.S.M.E. and B.S.P.E. degrees. Master's and Doctoral degrees are also awarded. Bachelor's degrees are awarded in AGRICULTURE (agricultural business management, animal science, environmental studies, forestry and related sciences, natural resource management, and plant science), BIOLOGICAL SCIENCE (biochemistry, biology/biological science, microbiology, and nutrition), BUSINESS (accounting, banking and finance, business administration and management, human resources, international economics, management science, marketing/retailing/merchandising, and sports management), COMMUNICATIONS AND THE ARTS (communications, dramatic arts, English, French, journalism, music, Spanish, and studio art), COMPUTER AND PHYSICAL SCIENCE (chemistry, computer science, geology, information sciences and systems, mathematics, and physics), EDUCATION (agricultural education, athletic training, early childhood education, elementary education, music education, and special education), ENGINEERING AND ENVIRONMENTAL DESIGN (architecture, bioengineering, chemical engineering, civil engineering, computer engineering, construction management, electrical/electronics engineering, environmental engineering, environmental science, industrial engineering, interior design, landscape architecture/design, mechanical engineering, and petroleum/natural gas engineering), HEALTH PROFESSIONS (speech pathology/audiology), SOCIAL SCIENCE (anthropology, child care/child and family studies, economics, geography, history, interdisciplinary studies, international studies, liberal arts/general studies, philosophy, physical fitness/movement, political science/government, psychology, sociology, and textiles and clothing). Biological sciences, chemistry, civil and environmental engineering, English and French studies are the strongest academically. Biological sciences, mass communication and kinesiology have the largest enrollments.
ACTIVITIES: 17% of men belong to 23 national fraternities; 26% of women belong to 16 national sororities. There are 300 groups on campus, including art, band, cheerleading, choir, chorus, communications, computers, dance, debate, drama, environmental, ethnic, film, gay, honors, international, jazz band, literary magazine, marching band, musical theater, newspaper, opera, orchestra, pep band, political, professional, radio and TV, religious, social, social service, student government, symphony, and yearbook. Popular campus events include Fall Fest, Home Football Games, and Groovin on the Grounds. **Sports:** There are 9 intercollegiate sports for men and 11 for women, and 23 intramural sports for men and 23 for women. Facilities include a 92,300-seat football stadium, a 13,500-seat domed sports center, a 9,200-seat baseball stadium, a 400-meter track with seating for 5,600, a natatorium with an 8-lane Olympic pool and diving well, an indoor track, and courts for handball, badminton, volleyball, and tennis. The campus recreation facility provides a multifaceted program that includes aquatics, sports clubs, informal recreation, fitness classes, instructional sports, personal training, intramural sports, outdoor recreation, challenge course, climbing wall, and special-events activities. There is also an indoor practice facility for football, a soccer field that seats 1,200, and a softball stadium that seats 1,200. **Graduates:** From July 1, 2013 to June 30, 2014, 4529 bachelor's degrees were awarded. The most popular majors were biological sciences (7%), kinesiology (6%), and mass communication (6%). 527 companies recruited on campus in 2013-2014. In an average class, 40% graduate in 4 years or less, 65% graduate in 5 years or less, and 69% graduate in 6 years or less. Of the 2013 graduating class, 22% were enrolled in graduate school within 6 months of graduation, and 58% were employed.
SERVICES: Counseling and information services are available, as is

tutoring in some subjects, including English, math, foreign languages, and sciences. There is remedial reading and writing. **Library/ Resources:** The 5 libraries contain 3.8 million volumes, 2.3 million microform items, and 26,938 audio/video tapes/CDs/DVDs, and subscribe to 337,837 periodicals including electronic. Computerized library services include interlibrary loans, database searching, Internet access, and Wi-Fi capability. Special learning facilities include an art gallery, natural history museum, radio station, TV station, 3 herbaria, and museums of natural science, natural history, geoscience, rural life, and art. **Physically Challenged Students:** 85% of the campus is accessible. Facilities include wheelchair ramps, elevators, special parking, specially equipped restrooms, special class scheduling, lowered drinking fountains, lowered telephones, special housing. **Special:** Co-op programs in all areas of engineering and landscape architecture, cross-registration with Southern University and Baton Rouge Community College, study abroad, and work-study programs are offered. B.A.-B.S. degrees, dual majors, a general studies degree, non-degree study, an evening school, a program of study for adult learners, and pass/fail options are available. There are 23 national honor societies, including Phi Beta Kappa, and a freshman honors program. **Visiting:** There are regularly scheduled orientations for prospective students, including an information session and a tour of campus. Department appointments can be arranged. There are guides for informal visits. To schedule a visit, contact the Office of Enrollment Management at (225) 578-6908. **Campus Safety and Security:** Measures include 24-hour foot and vehicle patrol, emergency notification system, self-defense education, and security escort services. There are shuttle buses, emergency telephones, lighted pathways/ sidewalks, controlled access to dorms/residences, and specialized crime prevention programs.

REQUIREMENTS: The SAT or ACT is required. Applicants must be graduates of an accredited secondary school. GED certificates may be accepted in unusual circumstances. Students must have completed 19 units, including 4 credits in English, 4 each in specific math, science, and social studies courses, 2 credits in a foreign language, and one additional credit from certain courses in the visual and performing arts. A GPA of 3.0 is required. AP and CLEP credits are accepted. Important factors in the admissions decision are advanced placement or honors courses, extracurricular activities record, and evidence of special talent. To graduate, all students must have a minimum overall 2.0 GPA in 120 to 162 credit hours. They must complete a general education component of 39 semester hours in approved courses in 6 major areas, including humanities, natural sciences, English composition, analytical reasoning, social sciences, and the arts. Students must earn at least 25% of required hours for their degree at LSU and meet college residency requirements. **Procedure:** Freshmen are admitted to all sessions. Entrance exams should be taken in spring of the junior year or fall of the senior year. There are early admissions, deferred admissions, and rolling admissions plans. Applications should be filed by April 15 for fall entry; December 1 for spring entry; and April 15 for summer entry, along with a $40 fee. Notification is sent on a rolling basis. Applications are accepted on-line. **Transfer Students:** 866 transfer students enrolled in 2013-2014. Transfer students must submit an official transcript from each previously attended school. Requirements are 30 or more semester hours with a minimum 2.5 GPA, and college level English and math courses. 30 of 120 credits required for the bachelor's degree must be completed at LSU. **International Students:** There are 442 international students enrolled. The school actively recruits these students. They must take the TOEFL with a minimum score of 550 on the paper-based TOEFL (PBT) or 79 on the Internet-based version (iBT), or take the IELTS (minimum score of 6.5). They must also take the SAT or ACT.

ADMISSIONS: 75% of the 2014-2015 applicants were accepted. The SAT scores for the 2014-2015 freshman class were: Critical Reading--22% below 500, 51% between 500 and 599, 24% between 600 and 699, and 4% between 700 and 800; Math--15% below 500, 44% between 500 and 599, 35% between 600 and 699, and 6% between 700 and 800. The ACT scores were 5% below 21, 27% between 21 and 23, 31% between 24 and 26, 17% between 27 and 28, and 21% above 28. 44% of the current freshmen were in the top fifth of their class; 73% were in the top two fifths. There were 43 National Merit finalists. 355 freshmen graduated first in their class. **Admissions Contact:** David Kurpius, Associate VC Enrollment Management. E-Mail: *admissions@lsu.edu* Web: *www.lsu.edu*

FINANCIAL AID: In 2014-2015, 93% of all full-time freshmen and 84% of continuing full-time students received some form of financial aid. 38% of all full-time freshmen and 35% of continuing full-time students received need-based aid. The average freshman award was $12,800. Need-based scholarships or need-based grants averaged $7,300; need-based self-help aid (loans and jobs) averaged $3,400; non-need-based athletic scholarships averaged $19,500; and other non-need-based awards and non-need-based scholarships averaged $6,600. 27% of undergraduate students work part-time. Average annual earnings from campus work are $2500. The average financial indebtedness of the 2014 graduate was $21,613. The FAFSA and the college's own financial statement are required. The priority date for freshman financial aid applications for fall entry is April 1.

LOUISIANA STATE UNIVERSITY IN SHREVEPORT   A-1
www.lsus.edu

Shreveport, LA 71115	(318) 797-5061
Fax: (318) 797-5286	Email: kimberly.thornton@lsus.edu
Full-time: 776 men, 1084 women	Faculty: 127
Part-time: 719 men, 1076 women	Ph.D.s: 79%
Graduate: 551 men, 774 women	Student/Faculty: 20 to 1
Year: semesters, summer session	Tuition: $5606 ($15,020)
Room & Board: n/app	Freshman Class: 695 applied, 621 accepted, 345 enrolled
SAT CR/M: 500/530 ACT: 22	CEEB CODE: 6355
Application Deadline: July 15	COMPETITIVE

Louisiana State University in Shreveport, established in 1965, is a state-supported, primarily commuter institution offering undergraduate and graduate programs through the colleges of liberal arts, business, education, and sciences. Figures in the above capsule and in this profile are approximate. There are 4 undergraduate schools and 4 graduate schools. In addition to regional accreditation, LSUS has baccalaureate program accreditation with AACSB, ABET, NCATE, and ACS. The 258-acre campus is in an urban area 7 miles south of downtown Shreveport. Including any residence halls, there are 18 buildings.

STUDENT LIFE: 92% of undergraduates are from Louisiana. Others are from 40 states, 25 foreign countries, and Canada. 95% are from public schools. 63% are White; 20% African American. **Male To Female Ratio:** 1.4:1. The average age of freshmen is 18; all undergraduates, 23. 35% do not continue beyond their first year; 30% remain to graduate. **Housing:** 480 students can be accommodated in college housing, which includes single-sex and coed on-campus apartments. On-campus housing is guaranteed for all 4 years, and is available on a first-come, first-served basis. All students may keep cars.

FACULTY/CLASSROOMS: 59% of faculty are male; 41% are female. 80% teach undergraduates, 70% do research, and 70% do both. No introductory courses are taught by graduate students. The average class size in an introductory lecture is 30; in a laboratory is 18; and in a regular course is 19.

PROGRAMS OF STUDY: LSUS confers B.A., B.S., B.C.J. and B.G.S. degrees. Master's degrees are also awarded. Bachelor's degrees are awarded in BIOLOGICAL SCIENCE (biochemistry and biology/ biological science), BUSINESS (accounting, banking and finance, business administration and management, management science, and marketing/retailing/merchandising), COMMUNICATIONS AND THE ARTS (communications, English, and fine arts), COMPUTER AND PHYSICAL SCIENCE (chemistry, computer science, mathematics, and physics), EDUCATION (elementary education and secondary education), HEALTH PROFESSIONS (community health work), SOCIAL SCIENCE (history, liberal arts/general studies, psychology, and sociology). Biology, computer science, chemistry, and business administration are the strongest academically. Psychology, and biology have the largest enrollments.

ACTIVITIES: 5% of men belong to 6 national fraternities; 2% of women belong to 4 national sororities. There are 70 groups on campus, including cheerleading, computers, dance, debate, drama, ethnic, film, forensics, honors, international, literary magazine, photography, political, professional, religious, social, social service, student activities board, student government, and yearbook. Popular campus events include Fall Fest, Spring Fling and Welcome Back Bash. **Sports:** There are 3 intercollegiate sports for men and 3 for women. Facilities include tennis and racquetball courts, sand or volleyball courts, a swimming pool, gym, weight room, dance studio, football fields, softball diamonds, and a soccer field. **Graduates:** From July 1, 2013 to June 30, 2014, 639 bachelor's degrees were awarded. The most popular majors were business/marketing (23%), general studies (14%), and biology (11%). In an average class, 30% graduate in 6 years or less.

SERVICES: Counseling and information services are available, as is tutoring in some subjects. There is remedial math and writing. **Library/Resources:** The library contains 915,751 volumes, 396,114 microform items, 4,508 audio/video tapes/CDs/DVDs, and subscribes to 2,000 periodicals including electronic. Computerized library services include interlibrary loans, database searching, and Internet access. Special learning facilities include an art gallery, natural history museum, a pioneer heritage center, and a museum of life sciences. **Physically Challenged Students:** All of the campus is accessible. Facilities include wheelchair ramps, elevators, special parking, specially equipped restrooms, special class scheduling, lowered drinking fountains, lowered telephones, special housing. **Special:** Opportunities are provided for internships, a Washington semester, a general studies degree, credit for military service schools, non-degree study, and pass/fail options. There are 12 national honor societies and a freshman honors program. **Visiting:** There are regularly scheduled orientations for prospective students, including a preview program during the spring semester for high school juniors and seniors. Students may stay overnight for this scheduled visit. There are guides for informal visits. To schedule a visit, contact Kimberly Thornton at kimberly.thornton@lsus.edu. **Campus Safety and Security:** Measures include 24-hour foot and vehicle patrol, self-defense education, and security escort services. There are emergency telephones, lighted pathways/sidewalks, commissioned university police officers.

REQUIREMENTS: The ACT is required. Students must have a minimum composite score of 20. Graduation from an accredited secondary school is required, with the 19 State approved core courses. AP and CLEP credits are accepted. A minimum of 120 semester hours, with a minimum GPA of 2.0, is required for the bachelor's degree. **Procedure:** Freshmen are admitted to all sessions. Entrance exams should be taken at least 2 months before start of the current semester. There is a rolling admissions plan. Applications should be filed by July 15 for fall entry; December 1 for spring entry; and May 1 for summer entry, along with a $10 fee. Notification is sent on a rolling basis. **Transfer Students:** Transfers must be in good academic standing, with 18 transferable hours and a GPA of 2.0. They must be eligible to continue at the last institution attended. 30 of 120 credits required for the bachelor's degree must be completed at LSUS. **International Students:** There are 43 international students enrolled. They must take the TOEFL with a minimum score on the paper-based TOEFL (PBT) or 61 on the Internet-based version (iBT). They must also take the SAT or ACT, scoring 20.

ADMISSIONS: 89% of the 2014-2015 applicants were accepted. The SAT scores for the 2014-2015 freshman class were: Critical Reading--40% below 500, and 60% between 500 and 599; Math--17% below 500, and 83% between 500 and 599. The ACT scores were 30% below 21, 32% between 21 and 23, 24% between 24 and 26, 6% between 27 and 28, and 5% above 28. **Admissions Contact:** Kimberly.thornton@lsus.edu, Director of Admissions. E-Mail: *kimberly.thornton@lsus.edu* Web: *www.lsus.edu*

FINANCIAL AID: 90% of undergraduate students work part-time. Average annual earnings from campus work are $3200. The FAFSA is required. The deadline for filing freshman financial aid applications for fall entry is June 1.

LOUISIANA TECH UNIVERSITY B-1
www.latech.edu

Ruston, LA 71272

(318) 257-3036
(800) LATECH-1

Fax: (318) 257-2499   Email: bulldog@latech.edu
Full-time: n/av   Faculty: 397; I
Part-time: 800 men, 1000 women   Ph.D.s: 80%
Graduate: 820 men, 1410 women   Student/Faculty: 23 to 1
Year: trimesters, summer session   Tuition: $7302 ($18,411)
Room & Board: $4000   Freshman Class: n/av
ACT: 24   CEEB CODE: 4633
Application Deadline: n/av   **COMPETITIVE**

Louisiana Tech University, founded in 1894, is a public institution offering programs in arts and sciences, business, agriculture, engineering, health science, education, fine and liberal arts, and human ecology. There are 5 undergraduate schools and 5 graduate schools. In addition to regional accreditation, Tech has baccalaureate program accreditation with AACSB, ABET, ADA, AHEA, ASLA, CAHEA, FIDER, NAAB, NASAD, NASM, NCATE, NLN, SAF, CIDA, CAA, CAHIIM, and NAEYC. The 260-acre campus is in a small town 30 miles west of Monroe and 90 miles east of Shreveport, Louisiana. Including any residence halls, there are 146 buildings.

STUDENT LIFE: 85% of undergraduates are from Louisiana. Others are from 44 states, 65 foreign countries, and Canada. 70% are White; 16% African American. 51% are Protestant; 12% Catholic. **Male To Female Ratio:** 1.5:1. The average age of freshmen is 19; all undergraduates, 20. 22% do not continue beyond their first year; 49% remain to graduate. **Housing:** 3067 students can be accommodated in college housing, which includes single-sex and coed dorms and married student housing. In addition, there are honors houses. On-campus housing is guaranteed for all 4 years. 74% of students commute. Alcohol is not permitted. All students may keep cars.

FACULTY/CLASSROOMS: 65% of faculty are male; 35% are female. 95% teach undergraduates. Graduate students teach 2% of introductory courses. The average class size in an introductory lecture is 40; in a laboratory is 20; and in a regular course is 26.

PROGRAMS OF STUDY: Tech confers B.A., B.S., B. Arch., B.F.A. and B.G.S. degrees. Associate, Master's, and Doctoral degrees are also awarded. Bachelor's degrees are awarded in AGRICULTURE (agricultural business management, animal science, forestry and related sciences, and wildlife management), BIOLOGICAL SCIENCE (biology/biological science), BUSINESS (accounting, banking and finance, business administration and management, business economics, business systems analysis, management science, marketing/retailing/merchandising, and personnel management), COMMUNICATIONS AND THE ARTS (English, fine arts, French, journalism, music, music performance, Spanish, and speech/debate/rhetoric), COMPUTER AND PHYSICAL SCIENCE (chemistry, computer science, geology, mathematics, and physics), EDUCATION (art education, early childhood education, elementary education, foreign languages education, music education, physical education, secondary education, and special education), ENGINEERING AND ENVIRONMENTAL DESIGN (airline piloting and navigation, architecture, aviation administration/management, biomedical engineering, chemical engineering, civil engineering, construction engineering, electrical/electronics engineering technology, environmental science, industrial engineering, and mechanical engineering), HEALTH PROFESSIONS (medical laboratory technology, medical records administration/services, and speech pathology/audiology), SOCIAL SCIENCE (dietetics, geography, history, liberal arts/general studies, political science/government, psychology, and sociology). Business and engineering are the strongest academically and have the largest enrollments.

ACTIVITIES: 7% of men belong to 9 national fraternities; 11% of women belong to 5 national sororities. There are 121 groups on campus, including art, band, cheerleading, choir, chorale, chorus, computers, dance, debate, drama, drill team, drum and bugle corps, ethnic, film, honors, international, jazz band, marching band, musical theater, newspaper, opera, orchestra, pep band, photography, political, professional, radio and TV, religious, social, social service, student government, symphony, and yearbook. Popular campus events include International Student Festival, Spring Fling, and Little Theater Concerts. **Sports:** There are 5 intercollegiate sports for men and 5 for women, and 10 intramural sports for men and 10 for women. Facilities include a football stadium, a coliseum, an intramural complex, natatorium, 9-hole golf course, and 10 lighted tennis courts. **Graduates:** From July 1, 2013 to June 30, 2014, 1401 bachelor's degrees were awarded. The most popular majors were business (22%), engineering (17%), and education (11%). 632 companies recruited on campus in 2013-2014. In an average class, 29% graduate in 4 years or less, 49% graduate in 5 years or less, and 55% graduate in 6 years or less.

SERVICES: Counseling and information services are available, as is tutoring in some subjects. There is a reader service for the blind, and remedial math, reading, and writing. **Library/Resources:** The library contains 1.1 million volumes, 2.1 million microform items, 511 audio/video tapes/CDs/DVDs, and subscribes to 2,932 periodicals including electronic. Computerized library services include interlibrary loans and database searching. Special learning facilities include an art gallery, natural history museum, planetarium, and radio station. **Physically Challenged Students:** 95% of the campus is accessible. Facilities include wheelchair ramps, elevators, special parking, specially equipped restrooms, lowered drinking fountains, and lowered telephones. **Special:** Co-op programs are available in engineering and applied and natural sciences, and cross-registration with Grambling State University is offered. Internships in agriculture, engineering, dietetics, and human ecology are offered. Study abroad, work-study programs, dual majors, a general studies degree, nondegree study, and pass/fail options are available. There is a Phi Beta Kappa chapter, a freshman honors program, and 20 departmental honors programs. **Visiting:** There are regularly scheduled orientations for prospective students. There are guides for informal visits and visitors may stay overnight. To schedule a visit, contact the Admissions Office. **Campus Safety and Security:** Measures include 24-hour foot and vehicle patrol, self-defense education, and security escort services. There are emergency telephones and lighted pathways/sidewalks.

REQUIREMENTS: The ACT is required. Applicants must be graduates of an accredited secondary school or have a GED. Students must have graduated in the upper half of their class. A GPA of 2.3 is required. AP credits are accepted. All students must complete 45 quarter hours of general education courses, including 12 hours in humanities, 9 each in natural and social sciences, 6 each in English and math, and 3 in arts or computer literacy. A total of 120 to 142 quarter hours, with a minimum GPA of 2.0, is required to graduate. **Procedure:** Freshmen are admitted to all sessions. There is a rolling admissions plan. Applications should be filed by October 24 for winter entry; January 30 for spring entry; and May 9 for summer entry. The fall 2014 application fee was $20. **Transfer Students:** 526 transfer students enrolled in 2013-2014. Transfer applicants should have a 2.0 GPA and be eligible to enroll in the school from which they are transferring. 30 of 120 credits required for the bachelor's degree must be completed at Tech. **International Students:** There are 139 international students enrolled. The school actively recruits these students. They must take the TOEFL.

ADMISSIONS: There were 5 National Merit finalists. **Admissions Contact:** Jan Albritton, Admissions Office. E-Mail: *bulldog@latech .edu* Web: *www.latech.edu*

FINANCIAL AID: In 2014-2015, 71% of all full-time freshmen students received some form of financial aid. 71% of all full-time freshmen students received need-based aid. 27% of undergraduate students work part-time. The FAFSA is required. The deadline for filing freshman financial aid applications for fall entry is July 16.

LOYOLA UNIVERSITY NEW ORLEANS   D-4

www.loyno.edu

New Orleans, LA 70118

Fax: (504) 865-3383

Full-time: 1242 men, 1744 women
Part-time: 91 men, 123 women
Graduate: 597 men, 1136 women
Year: semesters, summer session
Room & Board: $11,629

SAT or ACT: required
Application Deadline: n/av

(504) 865-3240
(800) 4-LOYOLA
Email: admit@loyno.edu

Faculty: 266; IIA, +$
Ph.Ds: 75%
Student/Faculty: 10 to 1
Tuition: $34,592
Freshman Class: 6486 applied, 4257 accepted, 877 enrolled

CEEB CODE: 6374

VERY COMPETITIVE

Loyola University New Orleans, founded in 1912, is a private institution operated by the Society of Jesus and affiliated with the Roman Catholic Church. Figures in the above capsule and in this profile are approximate. There are 4 undergraduate schools and 6 graduate schools. In addition to regional accreditation, Loyola has baccalaureate program accreditation with AACSB, NASM, NLN, AALS, ABA, ACS, CACREP, NASM, and NLNAC. The 26-acre campus is in a suburban area 5 miles from downtown New Orleans. Including any residence halls, there are 29 buildings.

STUDENT LIFE: 58% of undergraduates are from out of state, mostly the South. Students are from 53 states, 48 foreign countries, and Canada. 47% are from public schools. 52% are White; 15% African American; 15% Hispanic. 41% are Catholic; 17% Protestant. **Male To Female Ratio:** 1.6:1. The average age of freshmen is 18; all undergraduates, 20. 33% do not continue beyond their first year; 67% remain to graduate. **Housing:** 1350 students can be accommodated in college housing, which includes single-sex and coed dorms and on-campus apartments. In addition, there are special-interest houses, an honors floor. On-campus housing is available on a first-come, first-served basis. Priority is given to out-of-town students. 65% of students live on campus; of those, 75% remain on campus on weekends. Upperclassmen may keep cars.

FACULTY/CLASSROOMS: 55% of faculty are male; 45% are female. 84% teach undergraduates, and 90% do research. No introductory courses are taught by graduate students. The average class size in an introductory lecture is 26; in a laboratory is 26; and in a regular course is 18.

PROGRAMS OF STUDY: Loyola confers B.A., B.S., B.Acc., B.B.A., B.C.J., B.F.A., B.L.S., B.Mus., B.Mus.Ed., B.Mus. Therapy, B.S.N., B.A. Music, B.S. Mus. Industry, and B.A.Mus. degrees. Master's and Doctoral degrees are also awarded. Bachelor's degrees are awarded in AGRICULTURE (environmental studies), BIOLOGICAL SCIENCE (biology/biological science), BUSINESS (accounting, banking and finance, business administration and management, international business management, management science, and marketing/retailing/merchandising), COMMUNICATIONS AND THE ARTS (communications, creative writing, dramatic arts, English literature, fine arts, French, graphic design, guitar, jazz, music, music business management, music performance, music theory and composition, piano/organ, Spanish, studio art, visual and performing arts, and voice), COMPUTER AND PHYSICAL SCIENCE (chemistry, mathematics, and physics), EDUCATION (music education), ENGINEERING AND ENVIRONMENTAL DESIGN (preengineering), HEALTH PROFESSIONS (music therapy, nursing, predentistry, premedicine, and preveterinary science), SOCIAL SCIENCE (anthropology, classical/ancient civilization, criminal justice, economics, forensic studies, history, Latin American studies, liberal arts/general studies, philosophy, political science/government, psychology, religion, religious education, social science, and sociology). Mass communication, psychology, and marketing (business) have the largest enrollments.

ACTIVITIES: Men belong to 2 local and 2 national fraternities; 6% of women belong to 4 national sororities. There are 85 groups on campus, including art, band, cheerleading, choir, chorale, chorus, computers, dance, drama, environmental, ethnic, film, forensics, gay, honors, international, jazz band, literary magazine, musical theater, newspaper, opera, orchestra, photography, political, professional, radio and TV, religious, social, social service, student government, symphony, and yearbook. Popular campus events include Loyola Week, Wolves on the Prowl Community Service Day, and Loyola-palooza Spring Music Festival. **Sports:** There are 6 intercollegiate sports for men and 7 for women, and 7 intramural sports for men and 7 for women. Facilities include a sports complex with an arena, 6 multipurpose courts for basketball, tennis, volleyball, badminton, and floor hockey, 2 racquetball courts, an Olympic-style natatorium, a jogging track, and a weight-lifting and conditioning area. **Graduates:** From July 1, 2013 to June 30, 2014, 546 bachelor's degrees were awarded. The most popular majors were psychology (10%), communications (10%), and music business (7%). 320 companies recruited on campus in 2013-2014. In an average class, 47% graduate in 4 years or less, 58% graduate in 5 years or less, and 58% graduate in 6 years or less.

SERVICES: Counseling and information services are available, as is tutoring in most subjects. There is remedial math and writing. Peer tutoring is available in all introductory common curriculum courses. A reader service for the blind is provided for all exams and for course work if books on tape are not sufficient. **Library/Resources:** The 2 libraries contain 584,939 volumes, 1.4 million microform items, 17,352 audio/video tapes/CDs/DVDs, and subscribe to 169,032 periodicals including electronic. Computerized library services include interlibrary loans, database searching, and Internet access. Special learning facilities include an art gallery, radio station, TV station, humanities lab with Perseus Project and TLG TV, multimedia classrooms graphic lab, visual arts lab, communications lab, business computer lab, multimedia training center, and center for non-profit communication. **Physically Challenged Students:** 99% of the campus is accessible. Facilities include wheelchair ramps, elevators, special parking, specially equipped restrooms, lowered drinking fountains, lowered telephones, special housing. Special class relocation to provide accessibility. **Special:** Cross-registration is available with, our Lady of Holy Cross, Xavier University, Notre Dame Seminary, the University of New Orleans, Tulane University, and Southern University of New Orleans. Internships with the New Orleans business community are also available. Study abroad in 8 countries, dual and student-designed majors, nondegree studies, an accelerated R.N. to M.S.N. program, and a general studies degree are offered. A Washington semester through American University and a 3-2 engineering degree with Tulane University and the University of New Orleans is also available. There are 7 national honor societies, a freshman honors program, and 8 departmental honors programs. **Visiting:** There are regularly scheduled orientations for prospective students, including class and department visits, a student panel, a tour, a financial aid session, a campus support panel, and meetings with faculty members. There are guides for informal visits, visitors may sit in on classes, and stay overnight. To schedule a visit, contact the Admissions Office. **Campus Safety and Security:** Measures include 24-hour foot and vehicle patrol, emergency notification system, self-defense education, and security escort services. There are shuttle buses, emergency telephones, lighted pathways/sidewalks, controlled access to dorms/residences, CCTV coverage, card access control, intrusion alarm monitoring, first aid medical assistance, motor vehicle assistance, bicycle registration, fingerprinting services, and crime prevention services.

REQUIREMENTS: The SAT or ACT is required. Candidates for admission must be graduates of an accredited secondary school or have a GED. They should have completed 4 units in high school English and 3 each in math, science, and social sciences, along with 4 academic electives; 2 units in a foreign language are recommended. A portfolio is required for fine arts students; an audition for music majors. An interview is recommended for scholarship consideration. AP and CLEP credits are accepted. Important factors in the admissions decision are advanced placement or honors courses, evidence of special talent, extracurricular activities record, recommendations by school officials, parents or siblings attended your school, personality/intangible qualities, recommendations by alumni, and geographical diversity. All students must complete a core curriculum that includes courses in English composition and literature, math, philosophy, science, world civilization, social science and religious studies; the number of credit hours varies by college. At least 120 credit hours, with at least 30 in the major, and a minimum GPA of

2.0 are required to graduate. **Procedure:** Freshmen are admitted to all sessions. Entrance exams should be taken during the junior or senior year. There is a rolling admissions plan. Application deadlines are open. Application fee is $20. Applications are accepted on-line. **Transfer Students:** 150 transfer students enrolled in 2013-2014. Applicants must have a minimum 2.25 GPA on all attempted college-level work; 12 credit hours are needed for consideration. 30 of 120 credits required for the bachelor's degree must be completed at Loyola. **International Students:** There are 123 international students enrolled. The school actively recruits these students. They must take the TOEFL with a minimum score of 550 on the paper-based TOEFL (PBT) or 79 on the Internet-based version (iBT) and the college's own test, Scores are minimum score for a student to be admitted through the LIEP Pilot Program. They must also take the SAT or ACT.

ADMISSIONS: 66% of the 2014-2015 applicants were accepted. **Admissions Contact:** Salvadore A. Liberto, VP for Enrollment Managementent. E-Mail: *admit@loyno.edu* Web: *www.loyno.edu*

FINANCIAL AID: In 2014-2015, 86% of all full-time freshmen and 88% of continuing full-time students received some form of financial aid. 86% of all full-time freshmen and 88% of continuing full-time students received need-based aid. The average freshman award was $30,148. Need-based scholarships or need-based grants averaged $26,199; need-based self-help aid (loans and jobs) averaged $4,682; non-need-based athletic scholarships averaged $11,094; and other non-need-based awards and non-need-based scholarships averaged $14,633. 33% of undergraduate students work part-time. Average annual earnings from campus work are $1920. The average financial indebtedness of the 2014 graduate was $23,178. The FAFSA is required. The priority date for freshman financial aid applications for fall entry is March 1. The deadline for filing freshman financial aid applications for fall entry is May 1.

MCNEESE STATE UNIVERSITY B-4
www.mcneese.edu

Lake Charles, LA 70609	(337) 475-5504
	(800) 622-3352
Fax: (337) 475-5151	Email: admissions@mcneese.edu
Full-time: 2300 men, 3659 women	Faculty: IIA, --$
Part-time: 582 men, 960 women	Ph.D.s: 66%
Graduate: 270 men, 578 women	Student/Faculty: 21 to 1
Year: semesters, summer session	Tuition: $2649 ($5161)
Room & Board: n/app	Freshman Class: n/av
	CEEB CODE: 6403
Application Deadline: n/av	COMPETITIVE

McNeese State University, founded in 1939, and part of the University of Louisiana System, is a public institution offering programs in business, engineering, education, science, liberal arts, and nursing. Figures in the above capsule and in this profile are approximate. There are 7 undergraduate schools and 1 graduate school. In addition to regional accreditation, MSU has baccalaureate program accreditation with AACSB, ADA, CAHEA, CSAB, NASAD, NASM, NCATE, AAFCS, ACS, EAC/ABET, CAATE, CADE, CCNE, CAC/ABET, NAACLS, NLNAC, JRCET, and TAC/ABET. The 121-acre campus is in a suburban area 130 miles west of Baton Rouge and 150 miles east of Houston, Texas. Including any residence halls, there are 88 buildings.

STUDENT LIFE: 90% of undergraduates are from Louisiana. Others are from 34 states, 49 foreign countries, and Canada. 73% are White; 18% African American. **Male To Female Ratio:** 1.6:1. The average age of freshmen is 20; all undergraduates, 23. 31% do not continue beyond their first year. **Housing:** 975 students can be accommodated in college housing, which includes coed dorms and on-campus apartments. On-campus housing is guaranteed for all 4 years, and is available on a first-come, first-served basis. Alcohol is not permitted. All students may keep cars.

FACULTY/CLASSROOMS: 48% of faculty are male; 52% are female. No introductory courses are taught by graduate students.
PROGRAMS OF STUDY: MSU confers B.A., B.S., B.S.N. and B.G.S.

degrees. Associate and Master's degrees are also awarded. Bachelor's degrees are awarded in AGRICULTURE (agriculture and natural resource management), BIOLOGICAL SCIENCE (biology/biological science and nutritional sciences), BUSINESS (accounting, business administration and management, marketing, and organizational leadership and management), COMMUNICATIONS AND THE ARTS (art, communication, English, languages, and music), COMPUTER AND PHYSICAL SCIENCE (chemistry, computer science, mathematics, and radiological technology), EDUCATION (athletic training, early childhood education, elementary education, and health education), ENGINEERING AND ENVIRONMENTAL DESIGN (engineering and engineering technology), HEALTH PROFESSIONS (clinical science and nursing), SOCIAL SCIENCE (criminal justice, gender studies, history, liberal arts/general studies, political science/government, psychology, and sociology). Nursing, engineering, and education have the largest enrollments.

ACTIVITIES: Groups on campus include art, band, cheerleading, choir, chorale, chorus, computers, dance, debate, drama, drill team, ethnic, honors, international, jazz band, marching band, musical theater, newspaper, orchestra, pep band, political, professional, religious, social, social service, student government, symphony, and yearbook. Popular campus events include Homecoming, and Spring Fling. **Sports:** Facilities include a football stadium, softball and intramural fields, an indoor/outdoor track, a 50-meter pool, baseball complex, outdoor tennis courts, weight room, racquetball courts, and 3 regulation basketball courts, golf, cross country, volleyball and soccer. **Graduates:** From July 1, 2013 to June 30, 2014, 1177 bachelor's degrees were awarded. The most popular majors were general studies (15%), nursing (14%), and engineering (6%).

SERVICES: Counseling and information services are available, as is tutoring in some subjects. **Library/Resources:** Computerized library services include interlibrary loans, database searching, Internet access, and Wi-Fi capability. Special learning facilities include an art gallery, planetarium, a 503- acre farm, a vertebrate museum, a community health care clinic, meat processing plant, Southwest Louisiana Entrepreneurial and Economic Development Center. **Physically Challenged Students:** Facilities include wheelchair ramps, elevators, special parking, specially equipped restrooms, lowered drinking fountains. Academic planning and registration assistance, and classroom and testing accommodations. **Special:** MSU offers co-op programs in engineering, internships in clinical lab sciences, radiologic science, business and education, dual majors, a general studies degree, nondegree study, and credit for military experience. Innovation program available. There is a freshman honors program. **Visiting:** There are regularly scheduled orientations for prospective students. There are guides for informal visits, visitors may sit in on classes, and stay overnight.. **Campus Safety and Security:** Measures include 24-hour foot and vehicle patrol, emergency notification system, and security escort services. There are emergency telephones and lighted pathways/sidewalks.

REQUIREMENTS: First-time freshmen who are graduates of state-approved Louisiana high schools must meet the following admission criteria: completion of the Regents' high school core 4 curriculum; need no developmental courses; and have a minimum high school overall GPA of 2.35; and one of the following: Minimum high school core GPA of 2.0 on a 4.0 scale as reported by the Department of Education OR ACT composite score of 20 or greater (SAT combined mathematics and critical reading score of 940). AP and CLEP credits are accepted. McNeese State University's general education curriculum consists of coursework from six, broad disciplinary areas: writing (6 hours), mathematics (6 hours), natural sciences (9 hours), humanities (9 hours), social and behavioral sciences (6 hours), and fine arts (3 hours). The mission of this core curriculum is to provide students with a foundation of knowledge, skills, and methods of inquiry that support advanced study in their chosen degree program and constitute the characteristics of an informed, college-educated citizen. **Procedure:** Freshmen are admitted to all sessions. There are early admissions and rolling admissions plans. Application deadlines are open. Application fee is $20. Applications are accepted on-line. **Transfer Students:** Transfer students who have earned 18 or more college-level academic credit hours must either have earned a transferable associate degree or higher from a regionally accredited institution or meet the following admission standards: cumulative GPA of at least 2.0 on all college-level academic courses; be eligible to return to the institution from which they are transferring; completed a college-level English and mathematics course designed to fulfill general education requirements. Transfer students who have a cumulative GPA of at least 2.0 on all college-level academic courses, but who have earned less than 18 college-level academic hours, must meet first-time freshman admission standards. 30 of 120 credits required for the bachelor's degree must be completed at MSU. **International Students:** There are 292 international students enrolled. The school actively recruits these students. They must take the TOEFL with a minimum score of 500 on the paper-based TOEFL (PBT). They must also take the SAT or ACT.

ADMISSIONS: The ACT scores were 36% below 21, 37% between 21 and 23, 17% between 24 and 26, 5% between 27 and 28, and 5% above 28. **Admissions Contact:** Kara Smith, Director of Admissions and Recruiting. E-Mail: *admissions@mcneese.edu* Web: *www.mcneese .edu*

FINANCIAL AID: The FAFSA, FFS, and the college's own financial statement are required. Check with the school for current application deadlines.

NICHOLLS STATE UNIVERSITY   D-4
www.nicholls.edu

Thibodaux, LA 70310   (985) 448-4507
                                                (877) 642-4655
Fax: (985) 448-4929   Email: nicholls@nicholls.edu
Full-time: 1956 men, 3021 women   Faculty: 283
Part-time: 385 men, 839 women   Ph.Ds: 56%
Graduate: 145 men, 536 women   Student/Faculty: 18 to 1
Year: semesters, summer session   Tuition: $3595 ($8109)
Room & Board: $3500   Freshman Class: 2129
                                              applied, 1787 accepted,
                                              1202 enrolled
ACT: 21   CEEB CODE: 6221
Application Deadline: August 15   COMPETITIVE

Nicholls State University, established in 1948, and part of the University of Louisiana System, is a public liberal arts institution offering instruction in health sciences, fine arts, business, teacher preparation, and agricultural and technical disciplines. Figures in the above capsule and in this profile are approximate. There are 6 undergraduate schools and 4 graduate schools. In addition to regional accreditation, Nicholls has baccalaureate program accreditation with AACSB, ACEJMC, ADA, CSAB, NASAD, NASM, NCATE, NLN, AAFCS, CAAHEP, and CCNE. The 210-acre campus is in a small town 50 miles southwest of New Orleans and 60 miles southeast of Baton Rouge. Including any residence halls, there are 48 buildings.

STUDENT LIFE: 96% of undergraduates are from Louisiana. Others are from 32 states, 45 foreign countries, and Canada. 69% are from public schools. 75% are White; 18% African American. 37% are Catholic; 18% Protestant. **Male To Female Ratio:** 1.8:1. The average age of freshmen is 20; all undergraduates, 23. 34% do not continue beyond their first year; 26% remain to graduate. **Housing:** 1503 students can be accommodated in college housing, which includes single-sex and coed dorms, on-campus apartments, and married student housing. On-campus housing is guaranteed for the freshman year only, and is available on a first-come, first-served basis. 83% of students commute. Alcohol is not permitted. All students may keep cars.

FACULTY/CLASSROOMS: 51% of faculty are male; 49% are female. Graduate students teach 1% of introductory courses.

PROGRAMS OF STUDY: Nicholls confers B.A., B.S., B.G.S., B.M.E. and B.S.N. degrees. Associate and Master's degrees are also awarded. Bachelor's degrees are awarded in AGRICULTURE (agricultural business management), BIOLOGICAL SCIENCE (biology/biological science), BUSINESS (accounting, banking and finance, business administration and management, marketing/retailing/ merchandising, and personnel management), COMMUNICATIONS AND THE ARTS (art, communications, English, French, journalism, and music), COMPUTER AND PHYSICAL SCIENCE (chemistry, computer science, information sciences and systems, and mathematics), EDUCATION (business education, elementary education, music education, secondary education, and special education), ENGINEERING AND ENVIRONMENTAL DESIGN (manufacturing technology and petroleum/natural gas engineering), HEALTH PROFESSIONS (health science, nursing, and speech pathology/audiology), SOCIAL SCIENCE (dietetics, family/consumer studies, food production/management/services, history, political science/government, psychology, and sociology). Languages, literature, biological sciences, accounting, and business law are the strongest academically. Nursing, general studies, and teacher education have the largest enrollments.

ACTIVITIES: 10% of men belong to 7 national fraternities; 5% of women belong to 7 national sororities. Groups on campus include art, band, cheerleading, choir, chorale, chorus, computers, dance, debate, drama, drill team, ethnic, gay, honors, international, jazz band, literary magazine, marching band, musical theater, newspaper, pep band, photography, political, professional, radio and TV, religious, social, social service, student government, symphony, and yearbook. Popular campus events include Midterm Exam Week Breakfast, Family Day, and Crawfish Boil. **Sports:** There are 6 intercollegiate sports for men and 8 for women, and 4 intramural sports for men and 4 for women. Facilities include a stadium, 2 gyms, tennis and racquetball courts, a soccer field, a swimming pool, baseball and softball fields, and a weight room. **Graduates:** From July 1, 2013 to June 30, 2014, 724 bachelor's degrees were awarded. The most popular majors were nursing (11%), general studies (10%), and accounting (5%). 196 companies recruited on campus in 2013-2014. In an average class, 9% graduate in 4 years or less, 20% graduate in 5 years or less, and 26% graduate in 6 years or less.

SERVICES: Counseling and information services are available, as is tutoring in most subjects. There is a reader service for the blind, and remedial math and writing. Tutoring is available in math, English, computer science, biology, chemistry, physics, and foreign languages. **Library/Resources:** Computerized library services include interlibrary loans, database searching, and Internet access. Special learning facilities include an art gallery, radio station, TV station, a culinary institute, a rural development institute, and centers for the study of dyslexia, women and government, and economic education. **Physically Challenged Students:** Facilities include wheelchair ramps, elevators, special parking, specially equipped restrooms, special class scheduling, lowered drinking fountains, and lowered telephones. **Special:** Internships are offered in business areas, government, home economics, computer science, and psychology. A Washington semester congressional internship and dual majors in education are available. Cross-registration with Fletcher Community College and River Parishes Community College and study abroad in 5 countries are offered. There are 12 national honor societies, a freshman honors program, and 1 departmental honors program. **Visiting:** There are regularly scheduled orientations for prospective students, consisting of general information, advising, and registration. There are guides for informal visits, visitors may sit in on classes, and stay overnight. **Campus Safety and Security:** Measures include 24-hour foot and vehicle patrol, emergency notification system, self-defense education, and security escort services. There are emergency telephones and lighted pathways/sidewalks.

REQUIREMENTS: The ACT is recommended. Applicants must be graduates of an accredited secondary school or have the GED. Institutional placement tests are given for English, math, and reading. Nicholls requires applicants to be in the upper 50% of their class. AP and CLEP credits are accepted. All students must complete general education requirements, including 9 hours each in English, natural sciences, and humanities, 6 hours each in social sciences and math, 3 hours in the arts, and student development, freshman and computer science course. At least 120 total credit hours, plus a minimum of 24 hours in the major, with a minimum GPA of 2.0, are required to graduate. Students also take a general education competency test before graduation. **Procedure:** Freshmen are admitted to all sessions. Entrance exams should be taken as early as possible. There are deferred admissions and rolling admissions plans. Application deadlines are open. The fall 2014 application fee was $20. Notification is sent on a rolling basis. Applications are accepted on-line. **Transfer Students:** 240 transfer students enrolled in 2013-2014. Transfer applicants must be eligible to return to the institution from which

they are transferring, must have earned a minimum of 12 college-level hours, have a GPA of 2.0 on college-level courses, and require not more than 1 developmental course. 30 of 120 credits required for the bachelor's degree must be completed at Nicholls. **International Students:** There are 42 international students enrolled. The school actively recruits these students. They must take the TOEFL with a minimum score of 500 on the paper-based TOEFL (PBT) or 61 on the Internet-based version (iBT).

ADMISSIONS: 84% of the 2014-2015 applicants were accepted. The ACT scores were 47% below 21, 33% between 21 and 23, 15% between 24 and 26, 3% between 27 and 28, and 2% above 28. 31% of the current freshmen were in the top fifth of their class; 58% were in the top two fifths. 43 freshmen graduated first in their class. **Admissions Contact:** Becky L. Durocher, Director of Admissions. E-Mail: *nicholls@nicholls.edu* Web: *www.nicholls.edu*

FINANCIAL AID: In 2014-2015, 84% of all full-time freshmen and 74% of continuing full-time students received some form of financial aid. 46% of all full-time freshmen and 48% of continuing full-time students received need-based aid. The average freshman award was $5,534. Need-based scholarships or need-based grants averaged $2,160 ($7,257 maximum); need-based self-help aid (loans and jobs) averaged $2,187 ($5,797 maximum); non-need-based athletic scholarships averaged $4,763 ($7,751 maximum); and other non-need-based awards and non-need-based scholarships averaged $2,238 ($6,039 maximum). 9% of undergraduate students work part-time. Average annual earnings from campus work are $1696. The average financial indebtedness of the 2014 graduate was $16,710. The FAFSA is required. The priority date for freshman financial aid applications for fall entry is April 15. The deadline for filing freshman financial aid applications for fall entry is November 1.

NORTHWESTERN STATE UNIVERSITY OF LOUISIANA   B-2
www.nsula.edu

Natchitoches, LA 71497	(318) 357-4503 (800) 327-1903
Fax: (318) 357-5567	Email: recruiting@nsula.edu
Full-time: 1767 men, 6579 women	Faculty: 248; IIA
Part-time: 746 men, 2077 women	Ph.D.s: 61%
Graduate: 236 men, 872 women	Student/Faculty: 20 to 1
Year: semesters, summer session	Tuition: $6246 ($16,366)
Room & Board: $8122	Freshman Class: 4127 applied, 2371 accepted, 1169 enrolled
SAT CR/M: 480/500 ACT: 21	CEEB CODE: 6492
Application Deadline: July 6	COMPETITIVE

Northwestern State University is a responsive, student-oriented institution that is committed to the creation, dissemination, and acquisition of knowledge through teaching, research, and service. The University maintains as its highest priority excellence in teaching in graduate and undergraduate programs. Northwestern State University will prepare its students to become productive members of society and will promote economic development and improvements in the quality of life of the citizens in its region. There are 4 undergraduate schools and 1 graduate school. In addition to regional accreditation, NSU has baccalaureate program accreditation with AACSB, ABET, CSWE, NASAD, NASM, NCATE, NLN, AAFCS, CCNE, JRCERT, and NAST. The 916-acre campus is in a small town in central Louisiana, 60 miles south of Shreveport. Including any residence halls, there are 56 buildings.

STUDENT LIFE: 87% of undergraduates are from Louisiana. Others are from 46 states, 34 foreign countries, and Canada. 59% are White; 26% African American. **Male To Female Ratio:** 3.5:1. The average age of freshmen is 19; all undergraduates, 24. 27% do not continue beyond their first year; 40% remain to graduate. **Housing:** 1517 students can be accommodated in college housing, which includes coed dorms and on-campus apartments. In addition, there are honors houses and special-interest houses. On-campus housing is available on a first-come, first-served basis. 81% of students commute. Alcohol is not permitted. All students may keep cars.

FACULTY/CLASSROOMS: 41% of faculty are male; 59% are female. 90% teach undergraduates. Graduate students teach 1% of introductory courses. The average class size in an introductory lecture is 30; in a laboratory is 19; and in a regular course is 29.

PROGRAMS OF STUDY: NSU confers B.A., B.A.S., B.S., B.F.A., B.G.S., B.M., B.M.Ed., B.S.N. and B.S.W. degrees. Associate, Master's, and Doctoral degrees are also awarded. Bachelor's degrees are awarded in BIOLOGICAL SCIENCE (biology/biological science), BUSINESS (accounting, business administration and management, hospitality management services, and organizational leadership and management), COMMUNICATIONS AND THE ARTS (communications, dramatic arts, English, fine arts, foreign language, music, music business management, and musical theater), COMPUTER AND PHYSICAL SCIENCE (information sciences and systems, mathematics, and physical sciences), EDUCATION (early childhood education, elementary education, health education, music education, and secondary education), ENGINEERING AND ENVIRONMENTAL DESIGN (electrical/electronics engineering technology, industrial engineering, and industrial engineering technology), HEALTH PROFESSIONS (allied health, biology, exercise science, nursing, and radiological science), SOCIAL SCIENCE (addiction studies, criminal justice, family/consumer studies, geography, history, humanities, humanities and social science, international relations, liberal arts/general studies, psychology, public administration, and social work). Liberal arts (Scholars' College), creative and performing arts, and computer information systems are the strongest academically. Nursing, liberal arts/general studies, and business administration, education/teaching and learning have the largest enrollments.

ACTIVITIES: 10% of men belong to 7 national fraternities; 6% of women belong to 8 national sororities. There are 103 groups on campus, including art, band, cheerleading, choir, chorale, chorus, communications, computers, dance, debate, drama, drill team, ethnic, gay, honors, international, jazz band, literary magazine, marching band, musical theater, newspaper, opera, orchestra, pep band, photography, political, professional, radio and TV, religious, social, social service, student government, symphony, and yearbook. Popular campus events include Spring Fling Weeks, Greek Week and Welcome Week. **Sports:** There are 5 intercollegiate sports for men and 5 for women, and 18 intramural sports for men and 18 for women. Facilities include a 16,000-seat football stadium, a 5000-seat indoor gym, sports training and basketball centers, a track, and a coliseum. The largest auditorium/arena seats 1500. NSU also has a wellness, recreation, and activity center that contains 2 gyms with 4 basketball courts, a 3000-square foot free weights area, a 2800-square foot strength machine weight area, a 2800-square foot cardio-equipment area, a group exercise studio, a spin cycle class studio, a fitness assessment lab, 2 game rooms, 3 racquetball courts, men's and women's locker areas, steam rooms, a massage room, an equipment service center, a student café, meeting rooms, and an indoor track.

Graduates: From July 1, 2013 to June 30, 2014, 1119 bachelor's degrees were awarded. The most popular majors were nursing/health professions (21%), general studies/liberal arts (12%), and business administration (8%). 271 companies recruited on campus in 2013-2014. In an average class, 1% graduate in 3 years or less, 21% graduate in 4 years or less, 37% graduate in 5 years or less, and 42% graduate in 6 years or less.

SERVICES: Counseling and information services are available, as is tutoring in most subjects. There is a reader service for the blind and remedial math. **Library/Resources:** The library contains 331,637 volumes, 632,689 microform items, 5,514 audio/video tapes/CDs/DVDs, and subscribes to 700 periodicals including electronic. Computerized library services include interlibrary loans, database searching, Internet access, and Wi-Fi capability. Special learning facilities include an art gallery, natural history museum, radio station, TV station, Cammie G. Henry Research Center, and the Creole Heritage Center. **Physically Challenged Students:** 96% of the campus is accessible. Facilities include wheelchair ramps, elevators, special parking, specially equipped restrooms, special class scheduling, lowered drinking fountains, lowered telephones, and special housing. **Special:** NSU offers cooperative programs with local businesses, internships, an exchange program in education with South Korea, and work-study programs. A general studies degree, credit for experience, nondegree study, dual majors, and pass/fail options are available. There are 9

national honor societies, a freshman honors program, and 5 departmental honors programs. **Visiting:** There are regularly scheduled orientations for prospective students, consisting of a campus tour, with special focus on financial aid, housing and board, academic requirements, selecting a major, registration, campus organizations, and adapting to the college. There are guides for informal visits and visitors may sit in on classes. To schedule a visit, contact Jana Lucky at (318) 357-4503. **Campus Safety and Security:** Measures include 24-hour foot and vehicle patrol, emergency notification system, self-defense education, and security escort services. There are shuttle buses, emergency telephones, and lighted pathways/sidewalks.

REQUIREMENTS: The ACT is required. Applicants must complete 4 units of English, math, science, and social studies, 2 units of foreign language, and 1 unit of fine arts. Students must have a score of 21 on the ACT (or SAT equivalent) or have a 2.35 high school GPA in the above classes and they must need no more than 1 development course. A minimum 2.0 high school GPA is required. Different admission standards apply for students who are out of state, home schooled, over 24, or foreign. Certain GED students can be admitted. Developmental needs can be met by taking the COMPASS. Exceptions are available for some students. The Louisiana Scholars' College has more stringent admission criteria. A GPA of 2.0 is required. AP and CLEP credits are accepted. To graduate, all students must complete their senior year in residence, plus an approved 39-hour core curriculum, the university education requirement, and a minimum of 120 semester hours, with at least 30 semester hours in the major field. Distribution requirements include 9 credits each of humanities and natural sciences; 6 each of English, mathematics, and social/behavioral sciences; as well as 3 of fine arts. A minimum 2.0 GPA is needed for all hours taken at NSU. **Procedure:** Freshmen are admitted fall, spring, and summer. Entrance exams should be taken before the semester begins. There are deferred admissions and rolling admissions plans. Applications should be filed by July 6 for fall entry; November 2 for spring entry; and April 5 for summer entry, along with a $20 fee. Applications are accepted on-line. **Transfer Students:** 606 transfer students enrolled in 2013-2014. Transfer students must be eligible for readmission to their former university or college in order to enter NSU, and they must submit college transcripts and a statement of good standing. Students also must have completed a college-level English and a college-level math course and must have a 2.0 non-developmental college GPA. Students with less than 18 hours of non-developmental classes must also meet the freshman admission standards. 30 of 120 credits required for the bachelor's degree must be completed at NSU. **International Students:** There are 59 international students enrolled. The school actively recruits these students. They must take the TOEFL with a minimum score of 500 on the paper-based TOEFL (PBT) or 61 on the Internet-based version (iBT). They must also take the SAT or ACT, scoring 21.

ADMISSIONS: 57% of the 2014-2015 applicants were accepted. The SAT scores for the 2014-2015 freshman class were: Critical Reading--68% below 500, 28% between 500 and 599, 3% between 600 and 699, and 1% between 700 and 800; Math--51% below 500, 40% between 500 and 599, 7% between 600 and 699, and 1% between 700 and 800. The ACT scores were 42% below 21, 30% between 21 and 23, 17% between 24 and 26, 7% between 27 and 28, and 4% above 28. 35% of the current freshmen were in the top fifth of their class; 64% were in the top two fifths. 45 freshmen graduated first in their class. **Admissions Contact:** Jana Lucky, Director of University Recruiting. E-Mail: recruiting@nsula.edu Web: www.nsula.edu

FINANCIAL AID: In 2014-2015, 93% of all full-time freshmen and 86% of continuing full-time students received some form of financial aid. 68% of all full-time freshmen and 65% of continuing full-time students received need-based aid. The average freshman award was $9,142. Need-based scholarships or need-based grants averaged $4,518 ($6,550 maximum); need-based self-help aid (loans and jobs) averaged $5,254 ($15,613 maximum); non-need-based athletic scholarships averaged $8,021 ($19,820 maximum); other non-need-based awards and non-need-based scholarships averaged $3,453 ($17,792 maximum); and $959 from other forms of aid. 5% of undergraduate students work part-time. The average financial indebtedness of the 2014 graduate was $23,710. The FAFSA and the college's own financial statement are required. The priority date for freshman financial aid applications for fall entry is May 1.

OUR LADY OF HOLY CROSS COLLEGE D-4
www.olhcc.edu

New Orleans, LA 70131	(504) 394-7744
Fax: (504) 391-2421	Email: kkopecky@olhcc.edu
Full-time: n/av	Faculty: n/av
Part-time: n/av	Ph.D.s: n/av
Graduate: n/av	Student/Faculty: n/av
Year: semesters, summer session	Tuition: $8090
Room & Board: n/app	Freshman Class: 250 applied, 231 accepted, 158 enrolled
ACT: required	CEEB CODE: 6002
Application Deadline: July 20	COMPETITIVE

Our Lady of Holy Cross College, founded in 1916, is a private commuter college affiliated with the Roman Catholic Church. Figures in the above capsule and in this capsule are approximate. In addition to regional accreditation, OLHCC has baccalaureate program accreditation with NLN, CACREP, JRCERT, and IACBE. The 15-acre campus is in an urban area in New Orleans. Including any residence halls, there are 2 buildings.

STUDENT LIFE: 99% of undergraduates are from Louisiana. Others are from 4 states. 39% are from public schools. 74% are White; 15% African American. 74% are Catholic; 14% Protestant. **Male To Female Ratio:** Is 1:1. The average age of freshmen is 18; all undergraduates, 25. 10% do not continue beyond their first year; 70% remain to graduate. **Housing:** College-sponsored housing includes off-campus apartments. Alcohol is not permitted. All students may keep cars.

FACULTY/CLASSROOMS: 20% of faculty are male; 80% are female. 98% teach undergraduates, and 2% do research. No introductory courses are taught by graduate students. The average class size in an introductory lecture is 25; in a laboratory is 24; and in a regular course is 20.

PROGRAMS OF STUDY: OLHCC confers B.A., and B.S. degrees. Associate and Master's degrees are also awarded. Bachelor's degrees are awarded in BIOLOGICAL SCIENCE (biology/biological science), BUSINESS (accounting, business administration and management, and marketing and distribution), COMMUNICATIONS AND THE ARTS (English), EDUCATION (elementary education and secondary education), HEALTH PROFESSIONS (health science and nursing), SOCIAL SCIENCE (behavioral science, history, liberal arts/general studies, social psychology, and social science). Nursing is the strongest academically. Nursing, business, and education have the largest enrollments.

ACTIVITIES: There are no fraternities or sororities. There are 11 groups on campus, including choir, chorus, computers, drama, ethnic, honors, international, literary magazine, professional, social, social service, and student government. Popular campus events include Fall Fest, Crawfish Boil, and Christmas dances. **Sports:** There are 5 intramural sports for men and 4 for women.

SERVICES: There is remedial math, reading, and writing. **Library/Resources:** The library contains 56,700 volumes, 136,015 microform items, 13,598 audio/video tapes/CDs/DVDs, and subscribes to 601 periodicals including electronic. Computerized library services include interlibrary loans and database searching. **Physically Challenged Students:** All of the campus is accessible. Facilities include wheelchair ramps, elevators, special parking, specially equipped restrooms, lowered drinking fountains, and lowered telephones. **Special:** Co-op programs in business, internships with the Navy Civilian Personnel Office, study abroad in France, and credit for life, military, and work experience are offered. **Visiting:** There are regularly scheduled orientations for prospective students. There are guides for informal visits and visitors may sit in on classes. **Campus Safety and Security:** Measures include self-defense education and security escort services. There are emergency telephones, and lighted pathways/sidewalks. There is a foot patrol inside and outside of the building from 7:30 a.m. to 10 p.m.

REQUIREMENTS: The ACT is required. The GED is accepted. A GPA of 2.0 is required. AP and CLEP credits are accepted. Important

factors in the admissions decision are leadership record, recommendations by school officials, and recommendations by alumni. A total of 128 credit hours, with 33 to 36 hours in the major, and a minimum GPA of 2.0 are required to graduate. All students must take courses in theology, philosophy, literature, English composition, math, natural sciences, library orientation, social sciences, speech, fine arts, and computer science. **Procedure:** Freshmen are admitted to all sessions. Entrance exams should be taken a week before registration. Applications should be filed by July 20 for fall entry; December 20 for spring entry; and May 1 for summer entry. The fall 2014 application fee was $15. **Transfer Students:** Transfer applicants must have an overall 2.0 GPA for unconditional admission. 30 of 128 credits required for the bachelor's degree must be completed at OLHCC. **International Students:** They must take the TOEFL.

ADMISSIONS: 92% of the 2014-2015 applicants were accepted. **Admissions Contact:** Kristine H. Kopecky, VP for Student Affairs. E-Mail: *kkopecky@olhcc.edu* Web: *www.olhcc.edu*

FINANCIAL AID: 3% of undergraduate students work part-time. Average annual earnings from campus work are $1000. The FAFSA and the college's own financial statement are required. The deadline for filing freshman financial aid applications for fall entry is April 15.

SOUTHEASTERN LOUISIANA UNIVERSITY D-3
www.southeastern.edu

Hammond, LA 70402	(985) 549-5910
	(800) 222-7358
Fax: (985) 549-5632	Email: admissions@selu.edu
Full-time: 3934 men, 6065 women	Faculty: 510; IIA, --$
Part-time: 1552 men, 2193 women	Ph.D.s: 65%
Graduate: 270 men, 935 women	Student/Faculty: 23 to 1
Year: semesters, summer session	Tuition: $5715 ($17,734)
Room & Board: $7610	Freshman Class: 3665 applied, 3263 accepted, 2438 enrolled
ACT: 21	CEEB CODE: 6656
Application Deadline: July 15	COMPETITIVE

Southeastern Louisiana University, founded in 1925, is a public university offering more than 70 undergraduate and graduate degree programs. Figures in the above capsule and in this profile are approximate. There are 5 undergraduate schools. In addition to regional accreditation, Southeastern has baccalaureate program accreditation with AACSB, ABET, CSWE, NASAD, NASM, NCATE, ACS, CCNE, AAFCS, CAA, CACREP, and ATMAE. The 365-acre campus is in a small town 60 miles northwest of New Orleans and 50 miles east of Baton Rouge. Including any residence halls, there are 102 buildings.

STUDENT LIFE: 95% of undergraduates are from Louisiana. Others are from 39 states, 40 foreign countries, and Canada. 67% are White; 15% African American. **Male To Female Ratio:** 1.6:1. The average age of freshmen is 18.2; all undergraduates, 21.7. 32% do not continue beyond their first year; 33% remain to graduate. **Housing:** 2387 students can be accommodated in college housing, which includes single-sex and coed dorms and on-campus apartments. In addition, there are honors houses, fraternity houses, and sorority houses. On-campus housing is guaranteed for the freshman year only, and is available on a first-come, first-served basis. Priority is given to out-of-town students. 83% of students commute. All students may keep cars.

FACULTY/CLASSROOMS: 45% of faculty are male; 55% are female. 97% teach undergraduates. Graduate students teach 1% of introductory courses. The average class size in an introductory lecture is 37; in a laboratory is 20; and in a regular course is 29.

PROGRAMS OF STUDY: Southeastern confers B.A., B.S., B.B.A., B.G.S. and B.M. degrees. Associate, master's, and doctoral degrees are also awarded. Bachelor's degrees are awarded in BIOLOGICAL SCIENCE (biology/biological science), BUSINESS (accounting, business administration and management, marketing/retailing/merchandising, sports management, and supply chain management), COMMUNICATIONS AND THE ARTS (art, communications, English, music, and Spanish), COMPUTER AND PHYSICAL SCIENCE (chemistry, computer science, mathematics, and physics),

EDUCATION (athletic training, early childhood education, elementary education, English education, health education, middle school education, physical education, social science education, and special education), ENGINEERING AND ENVIRONMENTAL DESIGN (engineering technology, industrial engineering technology, and occupational safety and health), HEALTH PROFESSIONS (health and nursing), SOCIAL SCIENCE (criminal justice, family/consumer studies, history, liberal arts/general studies, political science/government, psychology, social work, and sociology). Nursing, general studies, and biological sciences have the largest enrollments.

ACTIVITIES: 5% of men belong to 13 local and 13 national fraternities; 5% of women belong to 8 local and 8 national sororities. There are 131 groups on campus, including art, band, cheerleading, choir, computers, dance, environmental, ethnic, film, gay, honors, international, jazz band, marching band, musical theater, newspaper, orchestra, photography, political, professional, radio and TV, religious, social, social service, student government, and yearbook. Popular campus events include Fanfare (cultural events month), Strawberry Jubilee, and Gumbo Ya Ya. **Sports:** There are 7 intercollegiate sports for men and 8 for women. Facilities include a weight, fitness, and aerobics rooms, an indoor elevated track, basketball, volleyball, badminton, tennis, and racquetball courts, multipurpose fields, a pool, gym, a football stadium, and baseball and soccer fields. **Graduates:** From July 1, 2013 to June 30, 2014, 1967 bachelor's degrees were awarded. The most popular majors were general studies (12%), management (10%), and nursing (8%). In an average class, 12% graduate in 4 years or less, 27% graduate in 5 years or less, and 33% graduate in 6 years or less.

SERVICES: Counseling and information services are available, as is tutoring in some subjects, math, including English, biology, physics, chemistry, foreign languages, accounting, economics, and computer science. There is remedial math and reading. **Library/Resources:** The library contains 494,881 volumes, 513,432 microform items, 35,208 audio/video tapes/CDs/DVDs, and subscribes to 1,539 periodicals including electronic. Computerized library services include interlibrary loans, database searching, Internet access, and Wi-Fi capability. Special learning facilities include an art gallery, radio station, and TV station. **Physically Challenged Students:** 90% of the campus is accessible. Facilities include wheelchair ramps, elevators, special parking, specially equipped restrooms, special class scheduling, special housing. **Special:** Through a special adult learning initiative known as CALL (Center for Adult Learning in Louisiana), Southeastern is now offering registered nurses who are graduates of associate or diploma programs the opportunity to earn their bachelor of science degree in nursing completely online. The Turtle Cove Environmental Research Station is the environmental research, education, outreach, and restoration facility for Southeastern Louisiana University. The Institute for Biodiversity and Interdisciplinary Studies (IBIS) increases our understanding of the ecosystems of the Gulf Coast and the Lake Pontchartrain drainage basin in particular with an emphasis on fostering interdisciplinary understanding for students and other participants that will allow a generation to address environmental and biodiversity issues in a more comprehensive and inclusive manner. The university also offers summer abroad programs. There are 16 national honor societies, a freshman honors program, and 20 departmental honors programs. **Visiting:** There are regularly scheduled orientations for prospective students, including a 2-day program of credit exams, academic advising, class registration, social programs, and session presentations. There are guides for informal visits, visitors may sit in on classes, and stay overnight. To schedule a visit, contact Mr. Richard Beaugh at admission@selu.edu. **Campus Safety and Security:** Measures include 24-hour foot and vehicle patrol, emergency notification system, self-defense education, and security escort services. There are shuttle buses, emergency telephones, lighted pathways/sidewalks, controlled access to dorms/residences, community policing, bicycle patrols, and video cameras.

REQUIREMENTS: The ACT is required. Applicants should have completed the Louisiana Regents High School core curriculum, meet developmental course requirements, have a minimum high school GPA of 2.0 and ACT score of 21. AP and CLEP credits are accepted. To graduate, students must complete one of the curricula, including demonstrated proficency in English and math and have a cumulative degree GPA of 2.0 (2.5 in some majors). **Procedure:** Freshmen are

admitted fall, spring, and summer. Entrance exams should be taken prior to registering for classes. There are deferred admissions and rolling admissions plans. Applications should be filed by July 15 for fall entry; December 1 for spring entry; and May 1 for summer entry, along with a $20 fee. Applications are accepted on-line. **Transfer Students:** 599 transfer students enrolled in 2013-2014. 30 of 120 credits required for the bachelor's degree must be completed at Southeastern. **International Students:** There are 181 international students enrolled. They must take the TOEFL with a minimum score of 500 on the paper-based TOEFL (PBT) or 61 on the Internet-based version (iBT). They must also take the ACT, scoring 21.

ADMISSIONS: 89% of the 2014-2015 applicants were accepted. The ACT scores were 35% below 21, 37% between 21 and 23, 18% between 24 and 26, 6% between 27 and 28, and 4% above 28. 17% of the current freshmen were in the top fifth of their class; 32% were in the top two fifths. 57 freshmen graduated first in their class. **Admissions Contact:** Mr. Richard Beaugh, Director of Admissions. E-Mail: *admissions@selu.edu* Web: *http://www.southeastern.edu/admin/admissions/index.html*

FINANCIAL AID: The average financial indebtedness of the 2014 graduate was $20,044. Southeastern is a member of CSS. The FAFSA is required. The priority date for freshman financial aid applications for fall entry is May 1.

SOUTHERN UNIVERSITY SYSTEM

The Southern University System, established in 1880, is a public system in Louisiana. It is governed by the Southern University board of supervisors and the Louisiana Board of Regents, whose chief administrator is the president. The primary goal of the system is teaching. The main priorities are teaching, public service, and research. The total student enrollment is usually about 14,000 with 650 faculty members. Altogether there are 144 baccalaureate, 42 master's, and 1 doctoral program offered by the Southern University System. Profiles of the 4-year campuses are included in this section.

SOUTHERN UNIVERSITY AND A&M COLLEGE (*The complete profile is made available exclusively on our website, www. barronspac.com*)

SOUTHERN UNIVERSITY AT NEW ORLEANS (*The complete profile is made available exclusively on our website, www.barronspac.com*)

TULANE UNIVERSITY	D-4
www.tulane.edu	
New Orleans, LA 70118	**(504) 865-5731**
	(800) 873-9283
Fax: (504) 862-8715	Email: undergrad.admission@tulane.edu
Full-time: 2752 men, 3854 women	Faculty: 634; I, av$
Part-time: 717 men, 1030 women	Ph.D.s: 95%
Graduate: 2430 men, 2748 women	Student/Faculty: 10 to 1
Year: semesters, summer session	Tuition: $48,305
Room & Board: $12,556	Freshman Class: 28901 applied, 8078 accepted, 1647 enrolled
SAT CR/M/W: 660/660/680 ACT: 31	CEEB CODE: 6832
Application Deadline: January 15	MOST COMPETITIVE

Tulane University is one of the country's most respected universities. With top-ranked programs in the academic and professional schools, research and educational partnerships that span the globe, and its location in historic New Orleans, Tulane University offers an unparalleled educational experience. Founded in 1834, Tulane is home to schools and colleges offering undergraduate, graduate, and professional degrees in architecture, business, science and engineering, law, liberal arts, medicine, public health and tropical medicine, and social work. There are 6 undergraduate schools and 8 graduate schools. In addition to regional accreditation, Tulane University has baccalaureate program accreditation with AACSB, ABET, CSAB, CSWE, NAAB, TEAC, and ACS. The 110-acre campus is in an urban area in New

Orleans (uptown). Including any residence halls, there are 92 buildings.

STUDENT LIFE: 74% of undergraduates are from out of state, mostly the Northeast. Students are from 50 states, 100 foreign countries, and Canada. 74% are White. **Male To Female Ratio:** 1.3:1. The average age of freshmen is 18; all undergraduates, 22. **Housing:** 4056 students can be accommodated in college housing, which includes single-sex and coed dorms, on-campus apartments, and married student housing. In addition, there are honors houses, fraternity houses, sorority houses, and special-interest floors. On-campus housing is available on a lottery system for upperclassmen. 56% of students commute. Upperclassmen may keep cars.

FACULTY/CLASSROOMS: 60% of faculty are male; 40% are female. No introductory courses are taught by graduate students.

PROGRAMS OF STUDY: Tulane University confers B.A., B.A.R., B.B.S., B.F.A., B.G.S., B.M.T., B.P.A., B.P.E., B.P.H., B.S., B.S.E., B.S.M., B.S.W. and M.Arch degrees. Associate, Master's, and Doctoral degrees are also awarded. Bachelor's degrees are awarded in BIOLOGICAL SCIENCE (biochemistry, cell biology, ecology, environmental biology, evolutionary biology, molecular biology, and neurosciences), BUSINESS (accounting, banking and finance, business administration and management, entrepreneurial studies, finance, management science, and marketing management), COMMUNICATIONS AND THE ARTS (art history and appreciation, classics, communications, dance, dramatic arts, English, film arts, French, German, Greek (modern), Italian, jazz, journalism, linguistics, media arts, music, music composition, Portuguese, Russian, Spanish, studio art, and theater design), COMPUTER AND PHYSICAL SCIENCE (chemistry, digital arts/technology, earth science, geology, information sciences and systems, mathematics, physics, science, and web technology), EDUCATION (early childhood education, health education, and psychology education), ENGINEERING AND ENVIRONMENTAL DESIGN (architecture, biomedical engineering, chemical engineering, computer technology, engineering physics, and environmental science), HEALTH PROFESSIONS (community health work and public health), SOCIAL SCIENCE (African studies, American studies, anthropology, Asian/Oriental studies, cognitive science, economics, gender studies, (Social Science) Global Studies, history, homeland security/emergency preparedness, humanities, Judaic studies, Latin American studies, legal studies, liberal arts/general studies, medieval studies, paralegal studies, philosophy, political science/government, psychology, religion, Russian and Slavic studies, social science, social studies, social work, sociology, and women's studies). Environmental sciences, political economy, and preprofessional programs are the strongest academically. Liberal arts, business, science and engineering have the largest enrollments.

ACTIVITIES: 30% of men belong to 12 national fraternities; 50% of women belong to 12 national sororities. There are 344 groups on campus, including art, band, cheerleading, chess, choir, chorale, chorus, communications, computers, dance, debate, drama, drill team, drum and bugle corps, environmental, ethnic, film, gay, honors, international, jazz band, literary magazine, marching band, musical theater, newspaper, orchestra, pep band, photography, political, professional, radio and TV, religious, social, social service, student government, symphony, and yearbook. Popular campus events include Crawfest, Wave Good-Bye, and Technology Expo, and Homecoming. **Sports:** There are 6 intercollegiate sports for men and 7 for women, and 24 intramural sports for men and 24 for women. Facilities include a baseball diamond, a track complex, tennis facility, a recreation center with indoor and outdoor pools, indoor track, squash and racquetball courts, gymnastics area, weight room, exercise rooms and equipment, and basketball and volleyball facilities. Yulman Stadium is the on-campus venue for football. **Graduates:** From July 1, 2013 to June 30, 2014, 1712 bachelor's degrees were awarded. The most popular majors were business (25%), social science (16%), and biological/life science (10%). 141 companies recruited on campus in 2013-2014.

SERVICES: Counseling and information services are available, as is tutoring in most subjects, high-demand math and science classes, and some languages. There is a reader service for the blind. **Library/ Resources:** The 8 libraries contain 4.5 million volumes, 2.5 million microform items, 155,896 audio/video tapes/CDs/DVDs, and subscribe to 132,499 periodicals including electronic. Computerized

library services include interlibrary loans, database searching, Internet access, and Wi-Fi capability. Special learning facilities include an art gallery, natural history museum, radio station, TV station, an observatory, Middle American Research Institute, Amistad Research Center, Tulane Jazz Archives, Latin American Library, Tulane Center for Research on Women, Koch Herbarium, Tulane Museum of Natural History, and the Newcomb Art Gallery. **Physically Challenged Students:** 60% of the campus is accessible. Facilities include wheelchair ramps, elevators, special parking, specially equipped restrooms, lowered drinking fountains, lowered telephones, and special housing. **Special:** Students may pursue cross-registration with Loyola and Xavier Universities, numerous internships, study abroad in 23 countries, work-study programs, a Washington semester, and B.A.-B.S. degrees in liberal arts, engineering, and architecture. Tulane also offers accelerated joint degrees with its schools of medicine, law, business, and public health, student-designed, dual, and interdisciplinary majors, including art and biology, Greek and Latin, mathematical economics, political economy, and cognitive studies, a 3-2 engineering degree with Xavier University of Louisiana, joint graduate/ professional programs, and 4+1 programs. There are 37 national honor societies, including Phi Beta Kappa, a freshman honors program, and 37 departmental honors programs. **Visiting:** There are regularly scheduled orientations for prospective students, including 3 on-campus Saturday programs in the fall, daily information sessions, and tours Monday through Friday and Saturday mornings during the academic year. Also, selected classes are open to visitors. In the spring semester, more structured programs are available daily. There are guides for informal visits, visitors may sit in on classes, and stay overnight. To schedule a visit, contact the Office of Undergraduate Admissions. **Campus Safety and Security:** Measures include 24-hour foot and vehicle patrol, emergency notification system, self-defense education, and security escort services. There are shuttle buses, emergency telephones, lighted pathways/sidewalks, controlled access to dorms/residences, trained student patrols, and programs about living safely off campus. Victim resources include academic assistance, legal counseling, emergency housing, and security review of home and personal security habits. In addition, there are bike patrols, limited dorm access, smoke detectors in dorms, and surveillance cameras.

REQUIREMENTS: The SAT or ACT is required. A GPA of 3.5 is required. AP credits are accepted. Important factors in the admissions decision are advanced placement or honors courses, recommendations by school officials, and extracurricular activities record. All students in the liberal arts and sciences must meet proficiency requirements in English, foreign language, and math. They must take a distribution component including courses in humanities and fine arts, social sciences, and sciences and math. A total of 120 credits, including at least 24 in the major, with a minimum cumulative GPA of 2.0, is required to graduate. **Procedure:** Freshmen are admitted fall and spring. Entrance exams should be taken during spring of the junior year or fall of the senior year. There is a deferred admissions plan. Applications should be filed by January 15 for fall entry; November 1 for spring entry. Notifications are sent April 1. Applications are accepted on-line. **Transfer Students:** 116 transfer students enrolled in 2013-2014. Applicants must submit SAT or ACT scores, high school transcripts, proof of good standing at previously attended institutions, and transcripts (with course descriptions) from all colleges or universities attended. A minimum 3.0 GPA is recommended. 60 of 120 credits required for the bachelor's degree must be completed at Tulane University. **International Students:** There are 251 international students enrolled. The school actively recruits these students. They must take the TOEFL with a minimum score of 550 on the paper-based TOEFL (PBT) or 88 on the Internet-based version (iBT). They must also take the SAT or ACT.

ADMISSIONS: 28% of the 2014-2015 applicants were accepted. The SAT scores for the 2014-2015 freshman class were: Critical Reading--2% below 500, 15% between 500 and 599, 53% between 600 and 699, and 30% between 700 and 800; Math--1% below 500, 11% between 500 and 599, 58% between 600 and 699, and 30% between 700 and 800; Writing--2% below 500, 8% between 500 and 599, 58% between 600 and 699, and 38% between 700 and 800. **Admissions Contact:** Earl Retif, VP for Enrollment Management. E-Mail: *undergrad.admission@tulane.edu* Web: *www.tulane.edu*

FINANCIAL AID: In 2014-2015, 45% of all full-time freshmen and

continuing full-time students received some form of financial aid. 44% of all full-time freshmen and continuing full-time students received need-based aid. 55% of undergraduate students work part-time. Average annual earnings from campus work are $2500. The average financial indebtedness of the 2014 graduate was $31,653. Tulane University is a member of CSS. The CSS/Profile FAFSA, and the Noncustodial Profile and the Business/Farm Supplement (as applicable) are required. The priority date for freshman financial aid applications for fall entry is February 15.

UNIVERSITY OF LOUISIANA AT LAFAYETTE   C-4
www.louisiana.edu

Lafayette, LA 70504   (337) 482-6473

Fax: (337) 482-6195   Email: admissions@louisiana.edu
Full-time: 5000 men, 7000 women   Faculty: 666
Part-time: 920 men, 1640 women   Ph.D.s: 79%
Graduate: 700 men, 930 women   Student/Faculty: 18 to 1
Year: semesters, summer session   Tuition: $3000 ($9000)
Room & Board: $3130   Freshman Class: n/av
SAT or ACT: required   CEEB CODE: 6672
Application Deadline: open   COMPETITIVE

University of Louisiana at Lafayette founded in 1898, is a public institution offering degree programs in liberal arts, fine arts, business, agriculture, technical disciplines, health science, engineering, and teacher preparation. Figures in the above capsule and in this profile are approximate. There are 9 undergraduate schools and 1 graduate school. In addition to regional accreditation, UL Lafayette has baccalaureate program accreditation with AACSB, ABET, ACEJMC, ADA, AHEA, ASLA, CAHEA, CSAB, FIDER, NAAB, NASM, NCATE, and NLN. The 1375-acre campus is in an urban area 129 miles west of New Orleans. Including any residence halls, there are 239 buildings.
STUDENT LIFE: 95% of undergraduates are from Louisiana. Others are from 48 states, 102 foreign countries, and Canada. 74% are White; 17% African American. 50% are Catholic; 31% claim no religious affiliation; 12% Protestant. **Male To Female Ratio:** 1.4:1. The average age of freshmen is 19; all undergraduates, 24. 28% do not continue beyond their first year; 30% remain to graduate. **Housing:** 1860 students can be accommodated in college housing, which includes single-sex dorms, on-campus apartments, and married student housing. There are residence halls for athletes and for pan-Hellenic groups. On-campus housing is guaranteed for all 4 years. 89% of students commute. All students may keep cars.
FACULTY/CLASSROOMS: 59% of faculty are male; 41% are female. No introductory courses are taught by graduate students.
PROGRAMS OF STUDY: UL Lafayette confers B.A., B.S., B.A.M., B.F.A., B.G.S., B.M.E., B.M.P., B.M.P.P., B.S.A., B.S.A.E., B.S.B.A., B.S.C.E., B.S.C.I.E., B.S.E.E., B.S.I.T., B.S.M.E., B.S.N. and B.S.P.E. degrees. Master's and Doctoral degrees are also awarded. Bachelor's degrees are awarded in BUSINESS (accounting, banking and finance, business administration and management, fashion merchandising, hotel/motel and restaurant management, management science, marketing/retailing/merchandising, and personnel management), COMMUNICATIONS AND THE ARTS (advertising, broadcasting, communications, dance, dramatic arts, English, fine arts, French, music, public relations, Spanish, and telecommunications), COMPUTER AND PHYSICAL SCIENCE (chemistry, computer science, geology, mathematics, physics, and statistics), EDUCATION (agricultural education, art education, elementary education, English education, foreign languages education, health education, home economics education, industrial arts education, mathematics education, music education, science education, secondary education, social studies education, and special education), ENGINEERING AND ENVIRONMENTAL DESIGN (chemical engineering, civil engineering, computer engineering, electrical/electronics engineering, industrial engineering, interior design, land use management and reclamation, mechanical engineering, and petroleum/natural gas engineering), HEALTH PROFESSIONS (nursing and speech

pathology/audiology), SOCIAL SCIENCE (anthropology, criminal justice, dietetics, economics, history, philosophy, political science/government, psychology, and sociology). Computer science, engineering, math, statistics, and physical sciences are the strongest academically. Nursing, elementary education, and business administration have the largest enrollments.
ACTIVITIES: 3% of men and 3 of women belong to 14 national fraternities; 5% of women belong to 8 national sororities. There are 200 groups on campus, including band, cheerleading, choir, chorus, computers, dance, debate, drama, drum and bugle corps, ethnic, forensics, gay, honors, international, jazz band, marching band, musical theater, newspaper, opera, orchestra, photography, political, professional, radio and TV, religious, social, social service, student government, and yearbook. Popular campus events include Rajun Roar, Black Expo Week, and Entertainment Week. **Sports:** There are 8 intercollegiate sports for men and 7 for women, and 16 intramural sports for men and 16 for women. Facilities include a 31,000-seat stadium, 12,000-seat basketball arena, gym, track, a softball park, tennis courts, various playing fields, and a health and phys ed complex.
Graduates: From July 1, 2013 to June 30, 2014, 2025 bachelor's degrees were awarded. The most popular majors were business (20%), general studies (14%), and education (14%). 114 companies recruited on campus in 2013-2014. In an average class, 7% graduate in 4 years or less, 21% graduate in 5 years or less, and 29% graduate in 6 years or less.
SERVICES: Counseling and information services are available, as is tutoring in most subjects. There is remedial math, reading, and writing. Entering freshman can only be in 1 remedial course. **Library/Resources:** The library contains 873,173 volumes, 1.8 million microform items, 255,992 audio/video tapes/CDs/DVDs, and subscribes to 4,965 periodicals including electronic. Computerized library services include interlibrary loans and database searching. Special learning facilities include an art gallery, radio station, a numerous research centers for environmental, business, science, computer, and business studies. **Physically Challenged Students:** 90% of the campus is accessible. Facilities include wheelchair ramps, elevators, special parking, specially equipped restrooms, special class scheduling. **Special:** Various internships are available, including a Washington semester. Students may study in France, Canada, Belgium, Japan, and Mexico. UL Lafayette also offers an accelerated degree program in nursing, B.A.-B.S. degrees, and dual majors. There are 6 national honor societies and a freshman honors program. **Visiting:** There are regularly scheduled orientations for prospective students, including campus tours. There are guides for informal visits.. **Campus Safety and Security:** Measures include 24-hour foot and vehicle patrol and security escort services. There are shuttle buses, emergency telephones, and lighted pathways/sidewalks.
REQUIREMENTS: The SAT or ACT is required. Admissions criteria are based on a sliding scale of standardized test scores and GPA. Students should be graduates of accredited secondary schools or have the GED. UL Lafayette requires that students have at least 4 units in English, 3 each in math, science, and social studies, and 4 1/2 in electives, recommended to include 2 in foreign language, 1 each in fine arts and speech, and 1/2 in computer studies. A GPA of 2.0 is required. AP and CLEP credits are accepted. Students are required to complete 42 semester hours of general education courses in the arts, literature, history, math, sciences, behavioral sciences, and composition. Phys ed is required in all but engineering and nursing programs. A minimum of 124 semester hours, with at least 33 in the major, is required for graduation. A minimum GPA of 2.0 is needed; some majors require higher GPAs. **Procedure:** Freshmen are admitted to all sessions. There are early admissions, deferred admissions, and rolling admissions plans. Application deadlines are open. Application fee is $20. **Transfer Students:** 740 transfer students enrolled in 2013-2014. A cumulative GPA of 2.0 is required. 30 of 124 credits required for the bachelor's degree must be completed at UL Lafayette. **International Students:** There are 259 international students enrolled. The school actively recruits these students. They must take the TOEFL. They must also take the SAT or ACT, scoring 18.
ADMISSIONS: Leroy Broussard, Director of Admissions. E-Mail: *admissions@louisiana.edu* Web: *www.louisiana.edu*
FINANCIAL AID: 30% of undergraduate students work part-time. Average annual earnings from campus work are $1250. UL Lafayette

is a member of CSS. The FAFSA is required. The deadline for filing freshman financial aid applications for fall entry is March 1.

UNIVERSITY OF LOUISIANA AT MONROE   C-1
www.ulm.edu

Monroe, LA 71209 (318) 342-5430
 n/av
Fax: (318) 342-1915 Email: schmeer@ulm.edu
Full-time: 1785 men, 3109 women Faculty: IIA, --$
Part-time: 942 men, 1440 women Ph.D.s: 50%
Graduate: 481 men, 888 women Student/Faculty: n/av
Year: semesters, summer session Tuition: $6318 ($16,890)
Room & Board: $6680 Freshman Class: 3454 applied, 2668 accepted, 1325 enrolled
SAT CR/M: 500/540 ACT: 22 CEEB CODE: 6482
Application Deadline: open **COMPETITIVE**

The University of Louisiana at Monroe, founded in 1931, is a public institution offering programs in business, education, liberal arts, pharmacy and health sciences, and pure and applied science. There are 3 undergraduate schools and 1 graduate school. In addition to regional accreditation, ULM has baccalaureate program accreditation with AACSB, ABET, ACCE, ACEJMC, ACPE, ADA, CSWE, NASM, NCATE, AAFCS, AOTA, ASLHA, CACREP, CCNE, and NASPE. The 238-acre campus is in an urban area in Northeast Louisiana, 90 miles east of Shreveport on I-20. Including any residence halls, there are 75 buildings.

STUDENT LIFE: 91% of undergraduates are from Louisiana. Others are from 45 states, 64 foreign countries, and Canada. 64% are White; 24% African American. **Male To Female Ratio:** 1.7:1. The average age of freshmen is 18.1; all undergraduates, 21.2. **Housing:** 1862 students can be accommodated in college housing, which includes single-sex and coed dorms and on-campus apartments. a scholastic residence hall. On-campus housing and is available on a first-come, first-served basis. 76% of students commute. Alcohol is not permitted. All students may keep cars.

FACULTY/CLASSROOMS: 45% of faculty are male; 55% are female. No introductory courses are taught by graduate students. The average class size in an introductory lecture is 24; in a laboratory is 5; and in a regular course is 24.

PROGRAMS OF STUDY: ULM confers B.A., B.S., B.B.A., B.F.A., B.G.S., B.M. and B.M.E. degrees. Associate, Master's, and Doctoral degrees are also awarded. Bachelor's degrees are awarded in AGRICULTURE (agricultural business management), BIOLOGICAL SCIENCE (biology/biological science, forensic psychology, and toxicology), BUSINESS (accounting, business administration and management, finance, insurance, insurance and risk management, management information systems, management science, marketing, marketing/retailing/merchandising, organizational leadership and management, and professional program in accounting), COMMUNICATIONS AND THE ARTS (art, communication, communication studies, communications, English, foreign language, French, modern language, music, and Spanish), COMPUTER AND PHYSICAL SCIENCE (atmospheric sciences and meteorology, computer information systems, computer science, information sciences and systems, mathematics, and radiological technology), EDUCATION (childhood education: 1-6, education administration, elementary education, English education, foreign languages education, health education, mathematics education, middle school education, music education, secondary education, social studies education, and special education), ENGINEERING AND ENVIRONMENTAL DESIGN (aviation administration/management, construction, and construction management), HEALTH PROFESSIONS (biology, clinical science, dental hygiene, dental laboratory technology, exercise science, health, medical imaging, kinesiology, medical laboratory science, nursing, nursing home administration, occupational therapy, pharmaceutical science, pharmacology, pharmacy, and speech pathology/audiology), SOCIAL SCIENCE (clinical psychology, communication sciences & disorders, counseling/psychology, criminal justice, economics, experimental psychology, gerontology, history, liberal arts/

general studies, political science/government, psychology, social work, and sociology). Pharmacy, health sciences, business, and education are the strongest academically. Pharmacy, nursing, and general studies have the largest enrollments.

ACTIVITIES: 4% of men belong to 1 local and 6 national fraternities; 4% of women belong to 7 national sororities. There are 118 groups on campus, including art, band, cheerleading, choir, chorale, chorus, computers, dance, debate, drama, drill team, drum and bugle corps, ethnic, film, honors, international, jazz band, literary magazine, marching band, musical theater, newspaper, opera, orchestra, pep band, political, professional, radio and TV, religious, social, social service, student government, symphony, and yearbook. Popular campus events include Week of Welcome, Lyceum Series, Spring Fever, Athletics Events, and Casino Night. **Sports:** There are 7 intercollegiate sports for men and 9 for women, and 44 intramural sports for men and 31 for women. Facilities include a coliseum, 2 stadiums, a natatorium, tennis courts, a softball complex, an activity center, a baseball complex, outdoor volleyball courts, and a bayou. **Graduates:** From July 1, 2013 to June 30, 2014, 1025 bachelor's degrees were awarded. The most popular majors were general studies (10%), nursing (5%), and psychology (5%).

SERVICES: Counseling and information services are available, as is tutoring in most subjects. There is remedial math, reading, and writing. **Library/Resources:** The library contains 1.2 million volumes, 579,146 microform items, 87 audio/video tapes/CDs/DVDs, and subscribes to 579,146 periodicals including electronic. Computerized library services include interlibrary loans, database searching, Internet access, and Wi-Fi capability. Special learning facilities include an art gallery, natural history museum, planetarium, radio station, a herbarium, state poison control center, and state tumor registry. **Physically Challenged Students:** 98% of the campus is accessible. Facilities include wheelchair ramps, elevators, special parking, specially equipped restrooms, special class scheduling, lowered drinking fountains, and specially equipped dorm rooms. **Special:** ULM offers cross-registration with Grambling State University and Louisiana Tech University. Internships are available in accounting, information sciences, pharmacy, nursing, clinical laboratory science, radiological technology, dental hygiene, occupational therapy, and communication disorders. In addition, students may participate in the accelerated degree programs in speech language and nursing. There are 22 national honor societies, a freshman honors program, and 2 departmental honors programs. **Visiting:** There are regularly scheduled orientations for prospective students. Visiting students may participate in the mandatory PREP program, which includes campus tours, meetings with deans/advisers, class registration, and placement examinations. There are guides for informal visits and visitors may sit in on classes. To schedule a visit, contact the Office of Recruitment and Admissions at (318) 342-5435. **Campus Safety and Security:** Measures include 24-hour foot and vehicle patrol, emergency notification system, self-defense education, and security escort services. There are emergency telephones, lighted pathways/sidewalks, and controlled access to dorms/residences.

REQUIREMENTS: The ACT is required. Applicants must be graduates of an accredited high school or have a GED. CLEP credits are accepted. Students are required to take the freshmen year seminar, 9 hours each of natural/physical sciences and humanities, 6 each of English, social sciences, and math, and 3 of the arts. An overall minimum GPA of 2.0 is required for graduation along with a total number of credits that varies by degree. **Procedure:** Freshmen are admitted to all sessions. Entrance exams should be taken by April 1. There is a rolling admissions plan. Application deadlines are open. The fall 2014 application fee was $20. Applications are accepted on-line. **Transfer Students:** Applicants must have a minimum overall GPA of 2.0 from a regionally accredited institution and at least 12 semester hours of college-level credit above the remedial level, including a math and an English course. Students who have completed fewer than 12 semester hours of college credit must meet ULM freshman admission requirements. 30 credits required for the bachelor's degree must be completed at ULM. **International Students:** There are 153 international students enrolled. The school actively recruits these students. They must take the TOEFL with a minimum score of 500 on the paper-based TOEFL (PBT). Only athletes are required to submit ACT/SAT scores due to NCAA requirements.

ADMISSIONS: 77% of the 2014-2015 applicants were accepted. The

SAT scores for the 2014-2015 freshman class were: Critical Reading--45% below 500, 32% between 500 and 599, 22% between 600 and 699, and 1% between 700 and 800; Math--37% below 500, 37% between 500 and 599, 22% between 600 and 699, and 4% between 700 and 800. The ACT scores were 34% below 21, 30% between 21 and 23, 22% between 24 and 26, 6% between 27 and 28, and 7% above 28. **Admissions Contact:** Mary Schmeer, Associate Director of Admissions. E-Mail: *schmeer@ulm.edu* Web: *www.ulm.edu*

FINANCIAL AID: The FAFSA is required. Check with the school for current application deadlines.

UNIVERSITY OF NEW ORLEANS — D-4
www.uno.edu

New Orleans, LA 70148	**(504) 280-6595**
Fax: (504) 280-5522	Email: admissions@uno.edu
Full-time: 3104 men, 3400 women	Faculty: 326; I
Part-time: 974 men, 1175 women	Ph.D.s: 67%
Graduate: 1116 men, 1594 women	Student/Faculty: 20 to 1
Year: semesters, summer session	Tuition: $3984 ($11,028)
Room & Board: $5240	Freshman Class: 1767 applied, 1430 accepted, 1119 enrolled
SAT CR/M/W: 550/550/540 ACT: 21	CEEB CODE: 6379
Application Deadline: n/av	COMPETITIVE

University of New Orleans, founded in 1958, is a public liberal arts institution. Figures in the above capsule and in this profile are approxiate. There are 6 undergraduate schools. In addition to regional accreditation, UNO has baccalaureate program accreditation with AACSB, ABET, NASM, NCATE, NAST, CACREP, and NLN. The 395-acre campus is in an urban area in New Orleans. Including any residence halls, there are 34 buildings.

STUDENT LIFE: 70% of undergraduates are from Louisiana. Others are from 50 states, 85 foreign countries, and Canada. 62% are from public schools. 60% are White; 19% African American. 67% claim no religious affiliation; 19% Catholic. **Male To Female Ratio:** 1.2:1. The average age of freshmen is 19; all undergraduates, 24. 31% do not continue beyond their first year. **Housing:** 1426 students can be accommodated in college housing, which includes coed dorms and married student housing. On-campus housing is available on a first-come, first-served basis. 95% of students commute. All students may keep cars.

FACULTY/CLASSROOMS: 59% of faculty are male; 41% are female. No introductory courses are taught by graduate students.

PROGRAMS OF STUDY: UNO confers B.A., B.S. and B.G.S. degrees. Master's and Doctoral degrees are also awarded. Bachelor's degrees are awarded in BIOLOGICAL SCIENCE (biology/biological science), BUSINESS (accounting, banking and finance, business administration and management, hotel/motel and restaurant management, marketing/retailing/merchandising, and tourism), COMMUNICATIONS AND THE ARTS (art, art history and appreciation, communications, dramatic arts, English, fine arts, French, music, Spanish, and studio art), COMPUTER AND PHYSICAL SCIENCE (chemistry, computer science, earth science, geology, geophysics and seismology, mathematics, and physics), EDUCATION (early childhood education, elementary education, English education, foreign languages education, mathematics education, music education, physical education, and secondary education), ENGINEERING AND ENVIRONMENTAL DESIGN (civil engineering, electrical/electronics engineering, environmental science, marine engineering, mechanical engineering, and naval architecture and marine engineering), HEALTH PROFESSIONS (health, medical technology, premedicine, and preveterinary science), SOCIAL SCIENCE (anthropology, economics, geography, history, international studies, philosophy, political science/government, psychology, sociology, and urban studies). Business administration, general studies, film, theater, and communication arts have the largest enrollments.

ACTIVITIES: 1% of men belong to 8 national fraternities; 1% of women belong to 8 national sororities. There are 108 groups on campus, including art, band, choir, chorale, chorus, computers, dance, drama, ethnic, film, gay, honors, international, jazz band, literary magazine, newspaper, opera, orchestra, pep band, political, professional, radio and TV, religious, social, social service, and student government. Popular campus events include International Night, Cultural Tea Hour, and Swamp Ball. **Sports:** There are 3 intercollegiate sports for men and 3 for women, and 10 intramural sports for men and 10 for women. Facilities include a lakefront arena, an privateer park, 1/10 mile indoor jogging/walking track; various group exercise classes such as indoor cycling, yoga and step aerobics, 2 dry saunas, 2 racquetball courts, 3 basketball courts, snack bar, outdoor deck adjacent to pool, and natatorium (25-yard/4-lane lap pool) for water group exercise and lap/recreational swimming. **Graduates:** From July 1, 2013 to June 30, 2014, 1368 bachelor's degrees were awarded. The most popular majors were business (16%), psychology (5%), film, theater, and communication arts (5%). 284 companies recruited on campus in 2013-2014. In an average class, 47% graduate in 4 years or less, 17% graduate in 5 years or less, and 24% graduate in 6 years or less.

SERVICES: Counseling and information services are available, as is tutoring in most subjects. There is a reader service for the blind, and remedial math, reading, and writing. **Library/Resources:** The library contains 896,000 volumes, 12.4 million microform items, 22,775 audio/video tapes/CDs/DVDs, and subscribes to 4,950 periodicals including electronic. Computerized library services include interlibrary loans, database searching, and Internet access. Special learning facilities include an art gallery and radio station. **Physically Challenged Students:** 80% of the campus is accessible. Facilities include wheelchair ramps, elevators, special parking, specially equipped restrooms, lowered drinking fountains, lowered telephones, and special housing. **Special:** Students may participate in co-op programs and may cross-register with Southern University in New Orleans, Elaine P. Nunez Community College, and Delgado Community College. Internships are available, and work-study programs are available with various federal agencies and private companies. Students may study abroad in 14 countries or participate in a Washington semester. UNO also offers dual majors, B.A.-B.S. degrees, pre-professional programs in cardiopulmonary science, dental hygiene, dentistry, medical technology, medicine, nursing, occupational therapy, opthalmic medical technology, pharmacy, physical therapy, physician's assistant, rehabilitation counseling, and veterinary medicine. 3-2 engineering degrees with Xavier University, Southern University in New Orleans, Loyola University New Orleans, and Dillard University are offered. There are 12 national honor societies, and a freshman honors program. **Campus Safety and Security:** Measures include 24-hour foot and vehicle patrol, emergency notification system, self-defense education, and security escort services. There are emergency telephones, lighted pathways/sidewalks, monitored parking.

REQUIREMENTS: The SAT or ACT is required. Students who graduate from state-approved high schools must complete the Louisiana Board of Regents Core Curriculum require no more than one developmental/remedial cours, and one of the following: ACT composite score of 23 or greater (SAT 1060) or high school cumulative GPA of 2.5 or greater with an ACT (SAT equivalent) of 18 or greater on the English and or Math sub scores or high school graduation rank in the top 25% of class. AP and CLEP credits are accepted. Important factors in the admissions decision are advanced placement or honors courses, recommendations by school officials, and evidence of special talent Requirements for graduation include completion of courses in English, literature, math, humanities and art, science, social science, and computer literacy. Students must complete 120 hours with a minimum GPA of 2.0. **Procedure:** Freshmen are admitted to all sessions. Entrance exams should be taken at least 6 months prior to enrollment. There are early admissions, deferred admissions, and rolling admissions plans. Applications should be filed by November 15 for spring entry; May 1 for summer entry. The fall 2014 application fee was $40. Applications are accepted on-line. **Transfer Students:** A student must have completed at least 18 hours of non-remedial course work, have a 2.25 GPA from an accredited college or university, and have completed all developmental course work before transferring. Students who have not earned at least 18 hours of non-remedial course work are required to submit an official high school transcript and official ACT or SAT test scores. 30 of 120 credits required for the bachelor's degree must be completed at UNO. **International Students:** There are 267 international students enrolled. The school actively recruits these students. They must take the TOEFL with a minimum score of 525 on the paper-based TOEFL (PBT) or 71 on the Internet-based version (iBT), If they, do not have the TOEFL, they must submit the ACT or SAT.

ADMISSIONS: 81% of the 2014-2015 applicants were accepted. The SAT scores for the 2014-2015 freshman class were: Critical Reading--35% below 500, 31% between 500 and 599, 30% between 600 and 699, and 4% between 700 and 800; Math--32% below 500, 34% between 500 and 599, 29% between 600 and 699, and 5% between 700 and 800; Writing--35% below 500, 40% between 500 and 599, 22% between 600 and 699, and 3% between 700 and 800. The ACT scores were 37% below 21, 35% between 21 and 23, 18% between 24 and 26, 6% between 27 and 28, and 4% above 28. **Admissions Contact:** Office of Admissions E-Mail: *admissions@uno.edu* Web: *www.uno.edu*

FINANCIAL AID: In 2014-2015, 71% of all full-time freshmen and 67% of continuing full-time students received some form of financial aid. 46% of all full-time freshmen and 45% of continuing full-time students received need-based aid. The average freshman award was $6,830. UNO is a member of CSS. The FAFSA is required. The deadline for filing freshman financial aid applications for fall entry is May 15.

XAVIER UNIVERSITY OF LOUISIANA   D-4
www.xula.edu

New Orleans, LA 70125	(504) 520-7388
	877-XAVIERU
Fax: (504) 520-7941	Email: apply@xula.edu
Full-time: 751 men, 1884 women	Faculty: 161
Part-time: 39 men, 76 women	Ph.D.s: 84%
Graduate: 185 men, 464 women	Student/Faculty: 13 to 1
Year: semesters, summer session	Tuition: $17,900
Room & Board: $7400	Freshman Class: 4463 applied, 2860 accepted, 786 enrolled
SAT CR/M/W: 480/480/470 ACT: 22	CEEB CODE: 6975
Application Deadline: July 1	COMPETITIVE

Xavier University of Louisiana, founded by Saint Katharine Drexel and the Sisters of the Blessed Sacrament, is Catholic and historically Black. The ultimate purpose of the University is to contribute to the promotion of a more just and humane society by preparing its students to assume roles of leadership and service in a global society. This preparation takes place in a diverse learning and teaching environment that incorporates all relevant educational means, including research and community service. There is 1 undergraduate school and 1 graduate school. In addition to regional accreditation, Xavier has baccalaureate program accreditation with ACBSP, ACPE, NASM, and NCATE. The 29-acre campus is in an urban area 2 miles from downtown New Orleans. Including any residence halls, there are 65 buildings.

STUDENT LIFE: 58% of undergraduates are from Louisiana. Others are from 34 states, and 5 foreign countries. 20% are from public schools. 75% are African American; 11% Asian American. 26% are Catholic; 24% Baptist. **Male To Female Ratio:** 2.5:1. The average age of freshmen is 18; all undergraduates, 20. 30% do not continue beyond their first year; 46% remain to graduate. **Housing:** 1433 students can be accommodated in college housing, which includes single-sex and coed dorms and on-campus apartments. In addition, there are honors houses. On-campus housing and is available on a first-come, first-served basis. Priority is given to out-of-town students. 53% of students commute. Alcohol is not permitted. All students may keep cars.

FACULTY/CLASSROOMS: 50% of faculty are male; 50% are female. No introductory courses are taught by graduate students. The average class size in an introductory lecture is 25; in a laboratory is 21; and in a regular course is 21.

PROGRAMS OF STUDY: Xavier confers B.A., B.S. and B.M. degrees.

Master's and Doctoral degrees are also awarded. Bachelor's degrees are awarded in BIOLOGICAL SCIENCE (biochemistry and biology/biological science), BUSINESS (accounting, business administration and management, and business economics), COMMUNICATIONS AND THE ARTS (communications, English, fine arts, French, languages, music, music performance, and Spanish), COMPUTER AND PHYSICAL SCIENCE (chemistry, computer science, mathematics, physics, and statistics), EDUCATION (art education, elementary education, English education, mathematics education, middle school education, music education, science education, and social studies education), HEALTH PROFESSIONS (premedicine and speech pathology/audiology), SOCIAL SCIENCE (history, philosophy, political science/government, psychology, sociology, and theological studies). Science, education, and English are the strongest academically. Pharmacy, biology, and business have the largest enrollments.

ACTIVITIES: 5% of men belong to 4 national fraternities; 1% of women belong to 4 national sororities. There are 80 groups on campus, including art, band, cheerleading, chess, choir, chorus, computers, dance, drill team, ethnic, honors, international, jazz band, literary magazine, newspaper, opera, pep band, political, professional, radio and TV, religious, social, social service, student government, and symphony. Popular campus events include Wellness Week, Octoberfest, and Culturefest. **Sports:** There are 4 intercollegiate sports for men and 3 for women, and 12 intramural sports for men and 12 for women. Facilities include a recreation room. **Graduates:** From July 1, 2013 to June 30, 2014, 280 bachelor's degrees were awarded. The most popular majors were biological/life sciences (38%), physical sciences (17%), and psychology (10%). 25 companies recruited on campus in 2013-2014. In an average class, 29% graduate in 4 years or less, 40% graduate in 5 years or less, and 42% graduate in 6 years or less. Of the 2013 graduating class, 31% were enrolled in graduate school within 6 months of graduation, and 14% were employed.

SERVICES: Counseling and information services are available, as is tutoring in every subject. There is a reader service for the blind, and remedial math, reading, and writing. **Library/Resources:** The library contains 261,000 volumes, 779,654 microform items, 6,074 audio/video tapes/CDs/DVDs, and subscribes to 1,624 periodicals including electronic. Computerized library services include interlibrary loans, database searching, Internet access, and Wi-Fi capability. Special learning facilities include a radio station, TV station, Xavier University of Louisiana Confucius Institute, (partnering with Hebei University in China), is the first Confucius Institute among the nation's HBCUs and in the State of Louisiana. **Physically Challenged Students:** 99% of the campus is accessible. Facilities include wheelchair ramps, elevators, special parking, specially equipped restrooms, special class scheduling, lowered drinking fountains, lowered telephones, and special housing. **Special:** The university offers cooperative programs in any major and 3-2 engineering degrees with Tulane, Louisiana State, Morgan State, and Southern Universities as well as the Universities of Wisconsin, Maryland, New Orleans, and Detroit, and Georgia Institute of Technology. In addition, students may cross-register at colleges of the New Orleans Consortium. Internships are available in legal, political, and pharmaceutical areas. Students may earn an accelerated degree in biology, chemistry, psychology, or political science, pursue dual majors in engineering and biostatistics, opt for non-degree study, and earn a B.A.-B.S. degree in almost any combination. Students may study abroad in 6 countries or participate in an exchange program with Notre Dame University. There are 7 national honor societies, a freshman honors program, and 7 departmental honors programs. **Visiting:** There are guides for informal visits, visitors may sit in on classes, and stay overnight. To schedule a visit, contact the Admissions Office. **Campus Safety and Security:** Measures include 24-hour foot and vehicle patrol and security escort services. There are shuttle buses, emergency telephones, and lighted pathways/sidewalks.

REQUIREMENTS: The SAT or ACT is required. Applicants must have earned a high school diploma or the GED. Candidates must also have completed 4 units of English, 2 of math, 1 each of science and social studies, and 8 of academic electives. A GPA of 2.0 is required. AP and CLEP credits are accepted. Important factors in the admissions decision are advanced placement or honors courses, recommendations by school officials, and evidence of special talent.

Requirements for graduation include 9 semester hours in English, 6 each in history, social science, language, theology, philosophy, and natural sciences, 3 each in speech, math, and the arts, and 1 in health and phys ed. Students must complete 128 to 132 total credit hours, including 24 to 54 total hours in the major. Students must maintain a minimum GPA of 2.0, take Introduction to African American History/Culture, pass a comprehensive exam, and by the beginning of the junior year declare a minor in an academic discipline other than the major. **Procedure:** Freshmen are admitted fall, spring, and summer. Entrance exams should be taken in the spring of the junior year or the fall of the senior year. Early decision applications should be filed by March 1; regular applications, by July 1 for fall entry, along with a $25 fee. Notification of early decision is sent October 15; regular decision, April 15. Applications are accepted on-line. **Transfer Students:** 122 transfer students enrolled in 2013-2014. Applicants must submit college transcripts. High school transcripts are required of applicants with fewer than 30 transferable credits. 30 of 128 credits required for the bachelor's degree must be completed at Xavier. **International Students:** There are 33 international students enrolled. They must take the TOEFL. They must also take the SAT or ACT.

ADMISSIONS: 64% of the 2014-2015 applicants were accepted. The SAT scores for the 2014-2015 freshman class were: Critical Reading--55% below 500, 35% between 500 and 599, 9% between 600 and 699, and 1% between 700 and 800; Math--57% below 500, 32% between 500 and 599, and 11% between 600 and 699; Writing--63% below 500, 31% between 500 and 599, ND 6% between 600 and 699. The ACT scores were 14% below 21, 56% between 21 and 23, 29% between 24 and 26, 29% between 27 and 28, and 1% above 28. 29% of the current freshmen were in the top fifth of their class; 55% were in the top two fifths. **Admissions Contact:** Winston D. Brown, Dean of Admissions. E-Mail: *apply@xula.edu* Web: *www.xula.edu*

FINANCIAL AID: In 2014-2015, 93% of all full-time freshmen and 90% of continuing full-time students received some form of financial aid. 86% of all full-time freshmen and 82% of continuing full-time students received need-based aid. The average freshman award was $17,144. Need-based scholarships or need-based grants averaged $5,701; need-based self-help aid (loans and jobs) averaged $5,222; and non-need-based athletic scholarships averaged $16,360. The average financial indebtedness of the 2014 graduate was $26,106. Xavier is a member of CSS. The FAFSA is required. The priority date for freshman financial aid applications for fall entry is January 1. The deadline for filing freshman financial aid applications for fall entry is rolling.

MAINE

A map showing College Locations with a scale of 0 to 80 Miles.

Cities labeled: Fort Kent, Presque Isle, Orono, Farmington, Bangor, Waterville, Unity, Machias, Castine, Augusta, Bar Harbor, Lewiston, Brunswick, Standish, Gorham, Portland, Biddeford. Interstate 95 is shown.

• College Location

BATES COLLEGE   B-5
www.bates.edu

Lewiston, ME 04240	(207) 786-6000
	1-855-228-3755
Fax: (207) 786-6025	Email: admission@bates.edu
Full-time: 879 men, 894 women	Faculty: 155; IIB, ++$
Part-time: n/av	Ph.D.s: 90%
Graduate: n/av	Student/Faculty: 10 to 1
Year: n/av	Tuition: $47,030
Room & Board: $13,690	Freshman Class: 5044 applied, 1282 accepted, 495 enrolled
SAT CR/M/W: 680/680/680 ACT: 31	CEEB CODE: 3076
Application Deadline: January 1	MOST COMPETITIVE

Bates College, is a private, highly selective, residential college devoted to undergraduate study in the liberal arts. Bates has always stood firmly for the ideals of academic rigor, intellectual curiosity, egalitarianism, social justice and freedom. Bates is recognized for its inclusive social character and progressive tradition, and is rightly celebrated as one of the first U.S. institutions of higher learning to admit women and people of color. A Bates education fosters intellectual inquiry and reflection, personal growth, and a commitment to the world beyond oneself. There is 1 undergraduate school. In addition to regional accreditation, Bates has baccalaureate program accreditation with CFAT and ACS. The 133-acre campus is in a small town 35 miles north of Portland. Including any residence halls, there are 170 buildings.

STUDENT LIFE: 90% of undergraduates are from out of state, mostly the Northeast. Students are from 45 states, 60 foreign countries, and Canada. 56% are from public schools. 72% are White. **Male To Female Ratio:** 1.0:1. The average age of freshmen is 19; all undergraduates, 20. 5% do not continue beyond their first year; 88% remain to graduate. **Housing:** 1614 students can be accommodated in college housing, which includes single-sex and coed dorms. In addition, there is special-interest house, chemical-free housing, quiet/study housing, and themed-based housing. On-campus housing is guaranteed for all 4 years. 91% of students live on campus; of those, 100% remain on campus on weekends. All students may keep cars.

FACULTY/CLASSROOMS: 50% of faculty are male; 50% are female. All teach and do research. No introductory courses are taught by graduate students. The average class size in an introductory lecture is 26; in a laboratory is 24; and in a regular course is 24.

PROGRAMS OF STUDY: Bates confers B.A. and B.S. degrees. Bachelor's degrees are awarded in AGRICULTURE (environmental studies), BIOLOGICAL SCIENCE (biochemistry, biology/biological science, and neurosciences), COMMUNICATIONS AND THE ARTS (art/visual culture, Chinese, English, french and francophone studies, German, Japanese, music, Russian, Spanish, speech/debate/rhetoric, and theatre acting), COMPUTER AND PHYSICAL SCIENCE (chemistry, geology, mathematics, and physics), SOCIAL SCIENCE (African American studies, American studies, anthropology, asian studies, classical/ancient civilization, East Asian studies, economics, European studies, history, interdisciplinary studies, Latin American studies, medieval studies, philosophy, political science/government, psychology, religious studies, sociology, and women and gender studies). Psychology, economics, and history have the largest enrollments.

ACTIVITIES: There are no fraternities or sororities. There are 110 groups on campus, including art, chess, choir, chorale, chorus, computers, dance, debate, drama, environmental, ethnic, film, gay, honors, international, jazz band, literary magazine, musical theater, newspaper, orchestra, pep band, photography, political, professional, radio and TV, religious, social, social service, student government, symphony, and yearbook. Popular campus events include Parents and Family Weekend, Homecoming, Mount David Summit, Winter Carnival, Reunion Weekend, International Dinners, and Ocean Clambakes. **Sports:** There are 16 intercollegiate sports for men and 17 for women, and 12 intramural sports for men and 12 for women. Facilities include a pool, a field house, indoor and outdoor tracks, indoor and outdoor tennis courts, 3 basketball courts, 3 volleyball courts, dance and fencing space, squash and racquetball courts, training rooms, a rock-climbing wall, a boat house, a winter sports arena, a weight room and football, soccer, baseball, softball, and lacrosse fields. **Graduates:** From July 1, 2013 to June 30, 2014, 448 bachelor's degrees were awarded. The most popular majors were economics (13%), psychology (12%), and politics (11%). In an average class, 83% graduate in 4 years or less, 88% graduate in 5 years or less, and 93% graduate in 6 years or less.

SERVICES: Counseling and information services are available, as is tutoring in every subject. There is a reader service for the blind, and remedial math and writing. **Library/Resources:** The library contains 600,000 volumes, 183,300 microform items, 38,000 audio/video tapes/CDs/DVDs, and subscribes to 73,000 periodicals including electronic. Computerized library services include interlibrary loans, database searching, Internet access, and Wi-Fi capability. Special learning facilities include an art gallery, planetarium, radio station, TV station, a learning research center, art gallery, planetarium, radio station, television studio, a 654-acre mountain conservation area, an observatory, a language resource center, and the Edmund S. Muskie archives. **Physically Challenged Students:** 80% of the campus is accessible. Facilities include wheelchair ramps, elevators, special parking, specially equipped restrooms, special class scheduling, lowered drinking fountains, and lowered telephones. **Special:** Bates College offers Co-op programs in engineering, internships, research apprenticeships, work-study programs, study abroad, and a Washington semester. Student-designed, and interdisciplinary majors, and a dual-degree 3-2 engineering degree with Columbia University, Dartmouth College, Case Western Reserve University, Rensselaer Polytechnic Institute, and Washington University in St. Louis are available. Students in any major may graduate in 3 years. Students may also participate in the Williams-Mystic Seaport program in marine biology and maritime history, and exchanges with Spelman College, Morehouse College, Washington and Lee University, and McGill University are possible. There are 2 national honor societies, including Phi Beta Kappa, and 32 departmental honors programs. **Visiting:** There are guides for informal visits, visitors may sit in on classes, and stay overnight. To schedule a visit, contact the Office of Admission. **Campus Safety and Security:** Measures include 24-hour foot and vehicle patrol, emergency notification system, self-defense education, and security escort services. There are shuttle buses, emergency telephones, lighted pathways/sidewalks, controlled access to dorms/residences, electronic access control in residence halls and all major buildings on campus, automated 911 telephone system and emergency public address system.

REQUIREMENTS: Candidates for admission should have completed at least 4 years of English, 3 each of math, social science, and a foreign language, and 2 of lab science. Essays are required and an interview on or off campus is strongly recommended. The submission of test scores is optional. AP credits are accepted. Important factors in the admissions decision are advanced placement or honors courses, evidence of special talent, and leadership record. Requirements for graduation include one major plus two general education concentrations (which are comprised of four courses and may alternatively be satisfied by another major(s) or minor(s) or a combination thereof); three writing attentive courses; and three courses focused on scientific reasoning, laboratory experience, and quantitative literacy. The total number of hours in the major varies by department, but students should take at least 32 courses, plus 2 short terms, and maintain a minimum GPA of 2.0. All majors require a senior thesis or capstone project. **Procedure:** Freshmen are admitted fall and winter. There are early decision and deferred admissions plans. Early decision applications should be filed by November 15; regular applications, by January 1 for fall entry; and November 1 for winter entry, along with a $60 fee. Notification of early decision is sent December 20; regular decision, April 1. 284 early decision candidates were accepted for the 2014-2015 class. Applications are accepted on-line. **Transfer Students:** 3 transfer students enrolled in 2013-2014. More weight is given to the student's college record than to high school credentials. Applicants must submit official college and final high school transcripts, a statement of good standing, 3 letters of recommendation, and an essay. An interview is strongly recommended. 16 of 32 credits required for the bachelor's degree must be completed at Bates. **International Students:** There are 122 international students enrolled. The school actively recruits these students.

ADMISSIONS: 25% of the 2014-2015 applicants were accepted. The SAT scores for the 2014-2015 freshman class were: Critical Reading--4% between 500 and 599, 63% between 600 and 699, and 33% between 700 and 800; Math--1% below 500, 7% between 500 and 599, 60% between 600 and 699, and 32% between 700 and 800; Writing--9% between 500 and 599, 48% between 600 and 699, and 43% between 700 and 800. The ACT scores were 2% between 24 and 26, 14% between 27 and 28, and 83% above 28. 81% of the current freshmen were in the top fifth of their class; 96% were in the top two fifths. **Admissions Contact:** Leigh Weisenburger, Dean of Admission and Financial Aid. E-Mail: *admission@bates.edu* Web: *www.bates.edu*

FINANCIAL AID: In 2014-2015, 47% of all full-time freshmen and 46% of continuing full-time students received some form of financial aid. 47% of all full-time freshmen and 45% of continuing full-time students received need-based aid. Bates is a member of CSS. The CSS/Profile, FAFSA, and parent and student tax returns and W-2 forms are required. The deadline for filing freshman financial aid applications for fall entry is February 15.

Bowdoin College, established in 1794, is a private liberal arts institution. In addition to regional accreditation, Bowdoin has baccalaureate program accreditation with ACS. The 207-acre campus is in a small town 25 miles northeast of Portland. Including any residence halls, there are 120 buildings.

STUDENT LIFE: 89% of undergraduates are from out of state, mostly the Northeast. Students are from 47 states, 28 foreign countries, and Canada. 53% are from public schools. 63% are White; 13% Hispanic. 38% claim no religious affiliation; 25% Protestant; 23% Catholic. **Male To Female Ratio:** 1.0:1. The average age of freshmen is 18; all undergraduates, 20. 2% do not continue beyond their first year; 93% remain to graduate. **Housing:** 1770 students can be accommodated in college housing, which includes coed dorms, on-campus apartments, and off-campus apartments. All first-year students participate in the College House System; their residence floor is affiliated with 1 of 8 College Houses. All upperclass students are also eligible to participate. Housing is guaranteed for first-year and sophomore students; historically we have also accommodated any junior or senior who desired on-campus housing. On-campus housing is available on a lottery system for upperclassmen. 92% of students live on campus; of those, 95% remain on campus on weekends. Upperclassmen may keep cars.

FACULTY/CLASSROOMS: 51% of faculty are male; 49% are female. All teach and do research. No introductory courses are taught by graduate students. The average class size in an introductory lecture is 28; in a laboratory is 14; and in a regular course is 16.

PROGRAMS OF STUDY: Bowdoin confers A.B. degrees. Bachelor's degrees are awarded in AGRICULTURE (environmental studies), BIOLOGICAL SCIENCE (biochemistry, biology/biological science, and neurosciences), COMMUNICATIONS AND THE ARTS (art history, classics, English, French, German, music, romance languages and literature, Russian, Spanish, studio art, and theatre arts), COMPUTER AND PHYSICAL SCIENCE (chemical physics, chemistry, computer mathematics, computer science, earth science, mathematics, mathematics – economics, oceanography, and physics), EDUCATION (mathematics education), SOCIAL SCIENCE (africana studies, anthropology, asian studies, classical/ancient civilization, Eastern European studies, economics, gender studies, history, interdisciplinary studies, Latin American studies, philosophy, political science/government, psychology, religion, sociology, and women's studies). Biology, economics, and government and legal studies are the strongest academically. Government and legal studies, economics, and mathematics have the largest enrollments.

ACTIVITIES: There are no fraternities or sororities. There are 110 groups on campus, including art, band, cheerleading, chess, choir, chorale, chorus, communications, computers, dance, debate, drama, drill team, environmental, ethnic, film, gay, honors, Improvisational comedy, international, jazz band, literary magazine, musical theater, newspaper, orchestra, photography, political, professional, radio and TV, religious, social, social service, and student government. Popular campus events include Common Good Day, Ivies Weekend, Winter Weekend, Asia Week, Museum Receptions, Junior/Senior Ball, Common Hour, Spring Gala, and Bowdoin-Colby Ice Hockey Games. **Sports:** There are 16 intercollegiate sports for men and 17 for women, and 5 intramural sports for men and 5 for women. Facilities include an ice arena, a field house, a swimming pool, 2 gyms, indoor and outdoor track facilities, tennis and squash courts, a climbing wall, a boathouse, outdoor leadership center, and cross-country ski trails. The fitness center offers cardiovascular fitness equipment, weight machines, free weights, and rowing machines along with a variety of fitness classes. There are 60 acres of playing fields for football, baseball, softball, lacrosse, field hockey, soccer, rugby, and ultimate frisbee. **Graduates:** From July 1, 2013 to June 30, 2014, 491 bachelor's degrees were awarded. The most popular majors were government and legal studies (16%), economics (12%), and mathematics (9%). 120 companies recruited on campus in 2013-2014. In an average class, 86% graduate in 4 years or less, 92% graduate in 5 years or less, and 93% graduate in 6 years or less. Of the 2013 graduating class, 15% were enrolled in graduate school within 6 months of graduation, and 71% were employed.

SERVICES: Counseling and information services are available, as is tutoring in most subjects. There is a reader service for the blind. A counselor is available to assist students with accommodations as

---

BOWDOIN COLLEGE   B-5
www.bowdoin.edu

Brunswick, ME 04011   **(207) 725-3100**

Fax: (207) 725-3101	Email: admissions@bowdoin.edu
Full-time: 901 men, 901 women	Faculty: 189; IIB, ++$
Part-time: 1 men, 2 women	Ph.D.s: 99%
Graduate: n/av	Student/Faculty: 9 to 1
Year: semesters	Tuition: $46,808
Room & Board: $12,760	Freshman Class: 6935 applied, 1034 accepted, 503 enrolled
SAT CR/M/W: 720/720/720 ACT: 33	CEEB CODE: 3089
Application Deadline: January 1	MOST COMPETITIVE

needed. Tutoring is available through the Quantitative Reasoning Program and the Writing Project. **Library/Resources:** The 5 libraries contain 1.4 million volumes, 76,463 microform items, and 28,938 audio/video tapes/CDs/DVDs, and subscribe to 59,927 periodicals including electronic. Computerized library services include interlibrary loans, database searching, Internet access, and Wi-Fi capability. Special learning facilities include an art gallery, radio station, TV station, a museum of art, arctic museum, language media center, women's resource center, electronic classroom, coastal studies center, African American center, crafts center, ceramics studio, photography darkroom, printmaking studio, woodworking studio, digital media lab, sculpture studio, dance studio, scientific station located in the Bay of Fundy, educational research and development program, theaters, music halls, recording studio, community service resource center, environmental studies center, and visual arts center. **Physically Challenged Students:** 72% of the campus is accessible. Facilities include wheelchair ramps, elevators, special parking, specially equipped restrooms, special class scheduling, lowered drinking fountains, lowered telephones, special housing. All new buildings and renovations to old buildings are built to ADA compliance standards. **Special:** A.B. degrees in 42 majors (including 9 interdisciplinary majors), with single, coordinate, double and self-designed major options. Plus (+) and minus (-) grading system, with credit/D/fail option. Dean's list, Latin Honors and departmental honors awarded. First-year seminars, intermediate and advanced independent study, student research and close work with faculty advisors strongly emphasized. Study abroad during the junior year encouraged. Washington semester. Academic support programs include the Baldwin Program for Academic Development, Quantitative Reasoning Program, Writing Project, Office of Student Fellowships and Research, Health Professions Advising. Dual-degree programs offered in Engineering (3-2 with California Inst of Tech, Columbia University, Dartmouth College,and University of Maine, Orono) and Law (3-3 with Columbia University). Teacher Certification program. There is 1 national honor society including Phi Beta Kappa. **Visiting:** There are regularly scheduled orientations for prospective students, the Admissions Office offers student-led campus tours, one-hour information sessions with an admissions representative, and personal interviews. There are guides for informal visits, visitors may sit in on classes, and stay overnight. To schedule a visit, contact the Admissions Office. **Campus Safety and Security:** Measures include 24-hour foot and vehicle patrol, emergency notification system, self-defense education, and security escort services. There are shuttle buses, emergency telephones, lighted pathways/sidewalks, controlled access to dorms/residences, Residences are locked 24 hours a day, and a staffed communications center is available around the clock.

REQUIREMENTS: Typical applicants for admission will have had 4 years each of English, social studies, foreign language, and math; 3 to 4 years of laboratory sciences; and one course each in art, music, and history. A high school record, 2 teacher recommendations, an advisor's estimate of the applicant's character and accomplishments, and an essay are required. Applicants must submit the Common Application as well as the Bowdoin Supplement to be considered for admission. AP credits are accepted. Important factors in the admissions decision are advanced placement or honors courses, recommendations by school officials, and extracurricular activities record. To qualify for the bachelor of arts degree, a student must have: successfully passed thirty-two full-credit courses (or the equivalent); completed a first-year seminar; completed at least one full-credit course (or the equivalent) in each of the following five distribution areas mathematical, computational, or statistical reasoning; inquiry in the natural sciences; exploring social differences; international perspectives; and visual and performing arts; completed at least one full-credit course (or the equivalent) in natural sciences and mathematics, social and behavioral sciences, and humanities (in addition to the required course in the visual and performing arts); and completed an approved major. **Procedure:** Freshmen are admitted fall. Entrance exams should be taken by the late summer before the freshman year. There are early decision and deferred admissions plans. Early decision applications should be filed by November 15; regular applications, by January 1 for fall entry, along with a $60 fee. Notification of early decision is sent December 15; regular decision, April 5. 237 early decision candidates were accepted for the 2014-2015 class. Applications are accepted on-line. **Transfer Students:** 5 transfer students enrolled in 2013-2014. College grades of B or better are required to transfer. Applicants should submit high school and college transcripts, a dean's or advisor's statement from the most recent college attended, and 2 recommendations from recent professors. Transfer applicants must submit the Common Application, transfer essay and Bowdoin Supplement to be considered for admission. 16 of 32 credits required for the bachelor's degree must be completed at Bowdoin. **International Students:** There are 93 international students enrolled. The school actively recruits these students. They must take the TOEFL with a minimum score of 600 on the paper-based TOEFL (PBT) or 100 on the Internet-based version (iBT). SAT scores are not required for admission but must be submitted at matriculation for counseling and placement.

ADMISSIONS: 15% of the 2014-2015 applicants were accepted. The SAT scores for the 2014-2015 freshman class were: Critical Reading--3% between 500 and 599, 27% between 600 and 699, and 70% between 700 and 800; Math--1% between 500 and 599, 32% between 600 and 699, and 67% between 700 and 800; Writing--3% between 500 and 599, 29% between 600 and 699, and 68% between 700 and 800. The ACT scores were 6% between 27 and 28, and 94% above 28. 96% of the current freshmen were in the top fifth of their class; 99% were in the top two fifths. There were 30 National Merit finalists. 26 freshmen graduated first in their class. **Admissions Contact:** Scott A. Meiklejohn, Dean of Admissions and Financial Aid. E-Mail: *admissions@bowdoin.edu* Web: *www.bowdoin.edu*

FINANCIAL AID: In 2014-2015, 51% of all full-time freshmen and 49% of continuing full-time students received some form of financial aid. 44% of all full-time freshmen and 45% of continuing full-time students received need-based aid. The average freshman award was $43,080. Need-based scholarships or need-based grants averaged $41,180 ($59,750 maximum); need-based self-help aid (loans and jobs) averaged $1,871 ($1,900 maximum); and other non-need-based awards and non-need-based scholarships averaged $1,000 ($1,000 maximum). 65% of undergraduate students work part-time. Average annual earnings from campus work are $1637. The average financial indebtedness of the 2014 graduate was $25,503. Bowdoin is a member of CSS. The CSS/Profile and FAFSA, and noncustodial profile and business/farm supplement are required. The deadline for filing freshman financial aid applications for fall entry is February 15.

COLBY COLLEGE B-4
www.colby.edu

Waterville, ME 04901

(207) 859-4818
(800) 723-3032

Fax: (207) 859-4828
Email: admissions@colby.edu
Full-time: 874 men, 946 women
Faculty: 173; IIB, ++$
Part-time: n/av
Ph.D.s: 98%
Graduate: n/av
Student/Faculty: 10 to 1
Year: 4-1-4
Tuition: $45,760
Room & Board: $11,750
Freshman Class: 5407 applied, 1408 accepted, 483 enrolled
SAT CR/M/W: 660/680/670 ACT: 30
CEEB CODE: 3280
Application Deadline: January 1
MOST COMPETITIVE

Colby College, founded in 1813, is a private liberal arts college. Figures in the above capsule and in this profile are approximate. There is 1 undergraduate school. In addition to regional accreditation, Colby has baccalaureate program accreditation with ACS. The 714-acre campus is in a small town 75 miles north of Portland. Including any residence halls, there are 60 buildings.

STUDENT LIFE: 88% of undergraduates are from out of state, mostly the Northeast. Students are from 42 states, 76 foreign countries, and Canada. 51% are from public schools. 60% are White; 11% race unknown. **Male To Female Ratio:** 1.1:1. The average age of freshmen is 18; all undergraduates, 20. 7% do not continue beyond their first year; 90% remain to graduate. **Housing:** 1779 students can be accommodated in college housing, which includes coed dorms and on-campus apartments. In addition, there are special-interest houses, substance-free halls, quiet residence halls and apartments for seniors.

On-campus housing is guaranteed for all 4 years. 96% of students live on campus; of those, 95% remain on campus on weekends. All students may keep cars.

FACULTY/CLASSROOMS: 58% of faculty are male; 42% are female. All teach undergraduates and do research. No introductory courses are taught by graduate students. The average class size in an introductory lecture is 27; in a laboratory is 16; and in a regular course is 16.

PROGRAMS OF STUDY: Colby confers B.A. degrees. Bachelor's degrees are awarded in AGRICULTURE (environmental studies), BIOLOGICAL SCIENCE (biochemistry, biology/biological science, environmental biology, and neurosciences), COMMUNICATIONS AND THE ARTS (art history, classics, creative writing, English, Germanic languages and literature, music, Russian languages and literature, Spanish, studio art, and theatre arts), COMPUTER AND PHYSICAL SCIENCE (applied mathematics, chemistry, computer science, geology, geoscience, mathematics, physics, and science technology), SOCIAL SCIENCE (African American studies, American studies, anthropology, classical/ancient civilization, East Asian studies, economics, French studies, (Social Science) Global Studies, history, Latin American studies, philosophy, political science/government, psychology, religion, sociology, and women's studies). Economics, biology and global studies have the largest enrollments.

ACTIVITIES: There are no fraternities or sororities. There are 107 groups on campus, including outdoor, women's and coed woodsmen's team, art, band, choir, chorale, chorus, communications, computers, dance, debate, drama, environmental, ethnic, film, gay, honors, human rights, international, jazz band, literary magazine, musical theater, newspaper, orchestra, photography, political, professional, radio and TV, religious, social, social service, student government, symphony, and yearbook. Popular campus events include Winter Carnival, Foss Arts Festival and International Extravaganza. **Sports:** There are 16 intercollegiate sports for men and 17 for women, and 8 intramural sports for men and 8 for women. Facilities include an athletic center with fitness, weight training, yoga and exercise areas, a gym with badminton, volleyball, and basketball courts, a hockey and skating rink, a field house for track and field, climbing wall, soccer, baseball, softball, tennis, lacrosse, and golf, a swimming pool and saunas; physical therapy and athletic training center, squash and handball courts, outdoor playing fields including two artificial-turf fields, tennis courts, an all-weather track, cross-country skiing and running trails, and an FIS-certified Nordic ski race course adjacent to campus and woodsmen's area for lumberjack events and competition. **Graduates:** From July 1, 2013 to June 30, 2014, 510 bachelor's degrees were awarded. The most popular majors were economics (15%), biology (12%), and global studies (10%). 46 companies recruited on campus in 2013-2014. In an average class, 86% graduate in 4 years or less, 90% graduate in 5 years or less, and 90% graduate in 6 years or less. Of the 2013 graduating class, 24% were enrolled in graduate school within 6 months of graduation, and 87% were employed.

SERVICES: Counseling and information services are available, as is tutoring in every subject. There is a reader service for the blind. There is also a writing center and a support program for learning-disabled students. **Library/Resources:** The 3 libraries contain 1.6 million volumes, 300,500 microform items, 26,052 audio/video tapes/CDs/DVDs, and subscribe to 19,877 periodicals including electronic. Computerized library services include interlibrary loans, database searching, Internet access, and Wi-Fi capability. Special learning facilities include an art gallery, radio station, an astronomy observatory and classroom, 128-acre arboretum, electronic-research classroom, MIDI studio/electronic-music lab, language resource center, proscenium-style theater, research greenhouses, Maine's largest art museum. **Physically Challenged Students:** 93% of the campus is accessible. Facilities include wheelchair ramps, elevators, special parking, specially equipped restrooms, special class scheduling, lowered drinking fountains, and lowered telephones. **Special:** Colby incorporates research in majors across the curriculum and showcases research results at its annual Colby Liberal Arts Symposium. Study abroad is accessible through more than 200 programs in more than 60 countries, and two thirds of students participate during their time at Colby. Colby offers opportunities to study or intern in Washington, D.C, on-campus work-study, exchange programs with the Claremont Colleges and Howard University, 3-2 engineering degree

programs with Dartmouth College and Columbia University, and a semester-in-residence program working with research scientists at the Bigelow Laboratory for Ocean Sciences. Students, with approval, may pursue independent majors. Colby offers combined and interdisciplinary majors including four that combine interdisciplinary computation with biology, environmental studies, music, and theater and dance. The Jan Plan, pioneered by Colby in 1962, offers a month-long term for internships or focused study on or off campus. There are 9 national honor societies, including Phi Beta Kappa, and 26 departmental honors programs. **Visiting:** There are regularly scheduled orientations for prospective students, including panel discussions, tours, class visits, complimentary meals, interviews, and information sessions. There are guides for informal visits, visitors may sit in on classes, and stay overnight. To schedule a visit, contact the Admissions Office. **Campus Safety and Security:** Measures include 24-hour foot and vehicle patrol, emergency notification system, self-defense education, and security escort services. There are shuttle buses, emergency telephones, lighted pathways/sidewalks, controlled access to dorms/residences, radical attack defense classes for women, fire safety with drills and inspections, ID program for bikes, computers, party checks, and alcohol education.

REQUIREMENTS: The SAT or ACT is required. Candidates should be high school graduates with a recommended academic program of 4 years of English, 3 each of foreign language and math, and 2 each of science (including lab work), social studies/history, and other college-preparatory courses. AP credits are accepted. Important factors in the admissions decision are recommendations by school officials, extracurricular activities record, and personality/intangible qualities. To graduate, all students must take English composition and fulfill a three-semester foreign language requirement. They must also take 2 courses in the natural sciences and 1 course each in the arts, historical studies, literature, quantitative reasoning, the social sciences, and human or cultural diversity, and meet Colby's wellness requirement by attending 8 lectures. Students must complete a total of 128 credit hours, including 3 January term courses, and maintain a GPA of 2.0. **Procedure:** Freshmen are admitted fall and spring. Entrance exams should be taken by January of the senior year. There are early decision and deferred admissions plans. Early decision applications should be filed by November 15; regular applications, by January 1 for fall entry; and January 1 for winter entry. Notification of early decision is sent December 15; regular decision, April 1. 259 early decision candidates were accepted for the 2014-2015 class. 637 applicants were on the 2014 waiting list; 3 were admitted. Applications are accepted on-line. Application fees are waived if application is completed on-line. **Transfer Students:** 9 transfer students enrolled in 2013-2014. Applicants must have a minimum GPA of 3.0 and, as a rule, have earned enough credit hours to qualify for at least sophomore standing. They must be in good academic and social standing and should submit references from a faculty member and a dean of their current school. If the SAT or ACT has been taken, the results may be submitted as well. 64 of 128 credits required for the bachelor's degree must be completed at Colby. **International Students:** There are 153 international students enrolled. The school actively recruits these students. They must take the TOEFL, or IELTS if English is not the first language nor the current language of instruction. They must also submit the SAT or ACT or three SAT Subject Tests of their choice sent by the testing agency.

ADMISSIONS: 26% of the 2014-2015 applicants were accepted. The SAT scores for the 2014-2015 freshman class were: Critical Reading--2% below 500, 15% between 500 and 599, 51% between 600 and 699, and 31% between 700 and 800; Math--12% between 500 and 599, 49% between 600 and 699, and 39% between 700 and 800; Writing--1% below 500, 14% between 500 and 599, 48% between 600 and 699, and 36% between 700 and 800. The ACT scores were 1% between 21 and 23, 8% between 24 and 26, 16% between 27 and 28, and 74% above 28. 84% of the current freshmen were in the top fifth of their class; 98% were in the top two fifths. There were 2 National Merit finalists. 4 freshmen graduated first in their class. **Admissions Contact:** Steve Thomas, Director of Admissions. E-Mail: *admissions@colby.edu* Web: *www.colby.edu/admissions*

FINANCIAL AID: In 2014-2015, 48% of all full-time freshmen and 49% of continuing full-time students received some form of financial aid. 42% of all full-time freshmen and 42% of continuing full-time

students received need-based aid. The average freshman award was $40,541. Need-based scholarships or need-based grants averaged $43,302 ($60,190 maximum); need-based self-help aid (loans and jobs) averaged $1,635 ($1,800 maximum); and other non-need-based awards and non-need-based scholarships averaged $4,085 ($21,345 maximum). 67% of undergraduate students work part-time. Average annual earnings from campus work are $1325. Colby is a member of CSS. The CSS/Profile, FAFSA, the college's own financial statement, and tax returns (to finalize awards) are required. The deadline for filing freshman financial aid applications for fall entry is February 1.

COLLEGE OF THE ATLANTIC   D-5
www.coa.edu

Bar Harbor, ME 04609	(207) 288-5015
	(800) 528-0025
Fax: (207) 288-4126	Email: inquiry@coa.edu
Full-time: 112 men, 232 women	Faculty: 29
Part-time: 2 men, 10 women	Ph.D.s: 90%
Graduate: 1 men, 7 women	Student/Faculty: 10 to 1
Year: trimesters	Tuition: $38,952
Room & Board: $9258	Freshman Class: 455 applied, 333 accepted, 104 enrolled
SAT CR/M/W: 640/610/610 ACT: 28	CEEB CODE: 3305
Application Deadline: February 15	HIGHLY COMPETITIVE+

College of the Atlantic was founded in 1969 on the premise that education should go beyond understanding the world as it is, to enabling students to actively shape its future. A leader in experiential education and environmental stewardship, COA has pioneered a distinctive interdisciplinary approach to learning human ecology that develops the kinds of creative thinkers and doers needed by all sectors of society in addressing the compelling and growing needs of our world. Figures in the above capsule and in this profile are approximate. There is 1 undergraduate school and 1 graduate school. In addition to regional accreditation, COA has baccalaureate program accreditation with NEASC. The 35-acre campus is in a small town 45 miles southeast of Bangor, along the Atlantic Ocean shoreline. Including any residence halls, there are 20 buildings.

STUDENT LIFE: 82% of undergraduates are from out of state, mostly the Northeast. Students are from 38 states, 36 foreign countries, and Canada. 73% are from public schools. 70% are White; 16% Foreign. **Male To Female Ratio:** 2.2:1. The average age of freshmen is 19; all undergraduates, 21. 19% do not continue beyond their first year; 69% remain to graduate. **Housing:** 153 students can be accommodated in college housing, which includes coed dorms and substance-free houses. On-campus housing is guaranteed for the freshman year only, is available on a first-come, first-served basis, and is available on a lottery system for upperclassmen. Priority is given to out-of-town students. 58% of students commute. Alcohol is not permitted. All students may keep cars.

FACULTY/CLASSROOMS: 56% of faculty are male; 44% are female. All teach undergraduates, 80% do research, and 80% do both. No introductory courses are taught by graduate students. The average class size in an introductory lecture is 12; in a laboratory is 12; and in a regular course is 12.

PROGRAMS OF STUDY: COA confers B.A. degrees. Master's degrees are also awarded. Bachelor's degrees are awarded in SOCIAL SCIENCE (human ecology). Human ecology is the strongest academically and has the largest enrollment are the strongest academically.

ACTIVITIES: There are no fraternities or sororities. There are 20 groups on campus, including botany club, fiber club, international student club, taxidermy club and gentleman's club, art, campus committee on sustainability, chess, chorus, computers, dance, drama, environmental, film, gay, international, jazz band, literary magazine, newspaper, orchestra, photography, political, social, social service, student government, and yearbook. Popular campus events include Bar Island Swim, Fandango Talent Show, Earth Day, and Aurora Ballealis (winter dance), Spanish Festival, Human Ecology Forums, Fall Community Show. **Sports:** There is no sports program at COA. Facil-

ities include pool, Nautilus equipment, and volleyball and basketball court, as well as nearby tennis courts. Acadia National Park offers seasonal outdoor activities - hiking, biking, cross-country skiing. The college has an active outdoor program, with camping and outdoor equipment and canoes, sea kayaks, and sailboats for student use; it also offers a sailing class, sea kayaking class, and wilderness first responder class. There are yoga and martial arts classes on campus, as well as a bouldering wall and an ice-skating rink in winter. SCUBA instruction is offered. Dance instruction is also available. **Graduates:** From July 1, 2013 to June 30, 2014, 75 bachelor's degrees were awarded. The most popular majors were human ecology (100%). 15 companies recruited on campus in 2013-2014. In an average class, 59% graduate in 4 years or less, 68% graduate in 5 years or less, and 69% graduate in 6 years or less. Of the 2013 graduating class, 3% were enrolled in graduate school within 6 months of graduation, and 80% were employed.

SERVICES: Counseling and information services are available, as is tutoring in some subjects. There is remedial math and writing. **Library/Resources:** The library contains 60,000 volumes, 37,000 microform items, and 3,300 audio/video tapes/CDs/DVDs, and subscribes to 30,000 periodicals including electronic. Computerized library services include interlibrary loans, database searching, Internet access, and Wi-Fi capability. Special learning facilities include an art gallery, natural history museum, writing center, taxidermy lab, sculpture, painting, animation and ceramics studios, marine mammal research center, 2 greenhouses, community garden on campus, 2 organic farms (a few miles off campus), sustainable enterprise hatchery, ocean-going vessels and 2 offshore island research centers. **Physically Challenged Students:** 80% of the campus is accessible. Facilities include wheelchair ramps, elevators, special parking, specially equipped restrooms, lowered drinking fountains, lowered telephones. **Special:** Students may cross-register with the University of Maine. There are Eco League exchanges are available with Alaska Pacific University, and Green Mountain, Northland, and Prescott colleges. COA offers study abroad programs in Mexico, Guatemala, and France, and study abroad programs as well as independent residencies abroad. A 10-week internship is a requirement of graduation; students are assisted in finding internships in the U.S. and abroad in an area of interest. All students design their own path to completion of their B.A. in human ecology. **Visiting:** There are regularly scheduled orientations for prospective students. There is an annual fall tour for high school seniors on Columbus day. Students attend classes, stay in student housing, and are invited to join outings at Acadia National Park. There is also a weekend for transfer students. There are guides for informal visits, visitors may sit in on classes, and stay overnight. To schedule a visit, contact Donna McFarland at (207) 288-5015. **Campus Safety and Security:** Measures include 24-hour foot and vehicle patrol and security escort services. There are shuttle buses, emergency telephones, and lighted pathways/sidewalks.

REQUIREMENTS: Candidates for admission must be high school graduates who have completed 4 years of English, 3-4 years of math, 2-3 years of science, 2 years of a foreign language, and 1 year of history. AP credits are accepted. Important factors in the admissions decision are personality/intangible qualities, extracurricular activities record, and recommendations by school officials. All students major in human ecology, which serves as a focus for a self-designed pathway to understanding the relationships between humans and environment. Students complete a total of 36 COA credits, including an interdisciplinary core course, two courses each in environmental science, human studies, and arts and design, along with a history, writing, and quantitative reasoning course. Also required are a 3-credit internship (taking students off-campus either for a term or during the summer), human ecology essay, community service and a culminating 3-credit senior, or capstone, project, which can be accomplished either in one term, or spread out throughout the senior year. **Procedure:** Freshmen are admitted fall, winter, and spring. Entrance exams should be taken in the junior or senior year. There are early decision and deferred admissions plans. Early decision applications should be filed by December 1; regular applications, by February 15 for fall entry; November 15 for winter entry; and February 15 for spring entry, along with a $50 fee. Notification of early decision is sent December 15; regular decision, April 1. 37 early decision candidates were accepted for the 2014-2015 class. Applications are accepted on-line. **Transfer Students:** 43 transfer students enrolled in 2013-2014. Only coursework for which the student has received a grade of "C" (2.0) or better will be accepted for transfer credit. Students need to apply and send a transcript. COA credits refer to one COA course (one trimester course). 18 of 36 credits required for the bachelor's degree must be completed at COA. **International Students:** There are 56 international students enrolled. The school actively recruits these students. They must take the TOEFL, submit SAT scores, or the IB English exam score.

ADMISSIONS: 73% of the 2014-2015 applicants were accepted. The SAT scores for the 2014-2015 freshman class were: Critical Reading--2% below 500, 23% between 500 and 599, 54% between 600 and 699, and 21% between 700 and 800; Math--5% below 500, 42% between 500 and 599, and 53% between 600 and 699; Writing--7% below 500, 33% between 500 and 599, 58% between 600 and 699, and 2% between 700 and 800. The ACT scores were 50% between 21 and 23, 30% between 24 and 26, 20% between 27 and 28, and 50% above 28. 69% of the current freshmen were in the top fifth of their class; 97% were in the top two fifths. **Admissions Contact:** Heather Albert-Knopp, Dean. E-Mail: *inquiry@coa.edu* Web: *www.coa.edu*

FINANCIAL AID: In 2014-2015, 97% of all full-time freshmen and 93% of continuing full-time students received some form of financial aid. 90% of all full-time freshmen and 81% of continuing full-time students received need-based aid. The average freshman award was $38,035. Need-based scholarships or need-based grants averaged $35,233 ($49,890 maximum); need-based self-help aid (loans and jobs) averaged $5,767 ($8,000 maximum); and other non-need-based awards and non-need-based scholarships averaged $9,213 ($10,000 maximum). 74% of undergraduate students work part-time. Average annual earnings from campus work are $2500. The average financial indebtedness of the 2014 graduate was $19,285. COA is a member of CSS. The FAFSA and the college's own financial statement are required. The deadline for filing freshman financial aid applications for fall entry is February 15.

HUSSON UNIVERSITY (*The complete profile is made available exclusively on our website, www.barronspac.com*)

MAINE COLLEGE OF ART (*The complete profile is made available exclusively on our website, www.barronspac.com*)

MAINE MARITIME ACADEMY　　　　C-5
www.mainemaritime.edu

Castine, ME 04420	(207) 326-2215
	(800) 227-8465
Fax: (207) 326-2515	Email: jeff.wright@mma.edu
Full-time: 750 men, 175 women	Faculty: n/av
Part-time: 5 men, 5 women	Ph.Ds: n/av
Graduate: 10 men, 10 women	Student/Faculty: n/av
Year: semesters	Tuition: $11,525 ($21,525)
Room & Board: $9548	Freshman Class: n/av
SAT or ACT: required	CEEB CODE: 3505
Application Deadline: May 1	COMPETITIVE

Maine Maritime Academy, founded in 1941, is a public institution offering degree programs in ocean and marine-oriented studies with emphasis on engineering, transportation, business management, and ocean sciences, to prepare graduates for private and public sector careers and the uniformed services of the United States. The academic calendar consists of 2 semesters plus a 2- to 3- month annual training cruise for the USCG. The figures given in the above capsule and in this profile are approximate. There are 4 undergraduate schools and 1 graduate school. In addition to regional accreditation, MMA has baccalaureate program accreditation with ABET. The 50-acre campus is in a small town 38 miles south of Bangor on the east coast of Penobscot Bay. Including any residence halls, there are 14 buildings. **STUDENT LIFE:** 69% of undergraduates are from Maine. Others are from 40 states, 7 foreign countries, and Canada. 90% are from public schools. 98% are White. **Male To Female Ratio:** 0.2:1. The average age of freshmen is 19; all undergraduates, 24. 12% do not continue

beyond their first year; 75% remain to graduate. **Housing:** 625 students can be accommodated in college housing, which includes single-sex and coed dorms and on-campus apartments. On-campus housing is guaranteed for all 4 years. 85% of students live on campus; of those, 40% remain on campus on weekends. Alcohol is not permitted. All students may keep cars.

FACULTY/CLASSROOMS: 75% of faculty are male; 25% are female. All teach undergraduates. No introductory courses are taught by graduate students. The average class size in an introductory lecture is 30; in a laboratory is 15; and in a regular course is 25.

PROGRAMS OF STUDY: MMA confers B.S. degrees. Associate and master's degrees are also awarded. Bachelor's degrees are awarded in BUSINESS (international business management), COMPUTER AND PHYSICAL SCIENCE (oceanography), ENGINEERING AND ENVIRONMENTAL DESIGN (engineering, engineering technology, marine engineering, maritime science, and transportation technology). Marine systems engineering is the strongest academically. Marine transportation and marine engineering have the largest enrollments.

ACTIVITIES: 10% of men and 10% of women belong to 1 national fraternity. There are no sororities. There are 30 groups on campus, including billiards, chess, engineering, hockey, marshal arts, outing, rugby, sailing, scuba, social, amateur radio, bagpipe, band, chess, chorale, drama, drill team, drum and bugle corps, environmental, ethnic, international, newspaper, pep band, photography, professional, social, social service, student government, and yearbook. Popular campus events include GSA Weekend, BSA Klondike Derby and Veterans Day. **Sports:** There are 6 intercollegiate sports for men and 6 for women, and 10 intramural sports for men and 10 for women. Facilities include Olympic pool, two weight rooms, field house with 3 climbing walls, gym, racquetball/squash courts, aerobics room, weight/workout room on training ship, and synthetic multisport athletic field. **Graduates:** From July 1, 2013 to June 30, 2014, 160 bachelor's degrees were awarded. The most popular majors were marine engineering (30%), marine transportation (30%), and power engineering (15%).

SERVICES: Counseling and information services are available, as is tutoring in most subjects. There is a reader service for the blind, and remedial math, reading, and writing. **Library/Resources:** The library contains 88,490 volumes, 5,000 microform items, 808 audio/video tapes/CDs/DVDs, and subscribes to 1,311 periodicals including electronic. Computerized library services include interlibrary loans, database searching, Internet access, and Wi-Fi capability. Special learning facilities include a natural history museum, planetarium, more than 60 vessels, bridge simulator, radar sims, power plant sims, and cargo system simulators. **Physically Challenged Students:** All of the campus is accessible. Facilities include wheelchair ramps, elevators, special parking, specially equipped restrooms, and special housing. **Special:** The 2-month freshman and junior year training cruises give students practical experience aboard the academy's 500-foot ship. There are cadet shipping co-ops on assigned merchant ships for 65 to 90 days. Co-op programs and internships for all programs are offered, as is study abroad through special agreements with other maritime colleges worldwide. Dual and student-designed majors are possible. **Visiting:** There are regularly scheduled orientations for prospective students, consisting of 3 open houses per year. Campus visits are available weekdays throughout the year. Visitors may sit in on classes and stay overnight. To schedule a visit, contact Admissions office at admissions@mma.edu. **Campus Safety and Security:** Measures include 24-hour foot and vehicle patrol and self-defense education. There are emergency telephones, lighted pathways/sidewalks, controlled access to dorms/residences, on-campus medical and counseling services, and locked dorm.

REQUIREMENTS: The SAT or ACT is required. Candidates for admission must have completed 4 years of English, 3 years of math, and 2 years of lab science. Courses must include algebra I, algebra II, trigonometry, geometry, and either chemistry or physics with a lab. A GPA of 2.0 is required. AP and CLEP credits are accepted. Important factors in the admissions decision are advanced placement or honors courses, evidence of special talent, and leadership record. A minimum GPA of 2.0 in an average of 140 total credit hours is required for graduation. GPA in the major must be at least 2.25. A senior thesis is required for some majors and a comprehensive exam is required for USCG license candidates. **Procedure:** Freshmen are admitted fall and spring. Entrance exams should be taken as early as possible in the senior year. There are early decision, deferred admissions, and rolling admissions plans. Early decision applications should be filed by December 31; regular applications, by May 1 for fall entry; and November 1 for spring entry. The fall 2014 application fee was $15. Applications are accepted on-line. **Transfer Students:** 16 transfer students enrolled in 2013-2014. Applicants must have a minimum 2.0 GPA in previous college work and meet the same prerequisites as entering freshmen. **International Students:** They must take the TOEFL.

ADMISSIONS: Jeff Wright, Director of Admissions. E-Mail: *jeff.wright@mma.edu* Web: *www.mainemaritime.edu*

FINANCIAL AID: The FAFSA, a student and parent tax returns, and a verification worksheet are required. Check with the school for current application deadlines.

SAINT JOSEPH'S COLLEGE OF MAINE — A-5
www.sjcme.edu

Standish, ME 04084	
	(207) 893-7746
	(800) 338-7057
Fax: (207) 893-7862	Email: admission@sjcme.edu
Full-time: 300 men, 600 women	Faculty: 63; IIB, --$
Part-time: 9 men, 21 women	Ph.D.s: 98%
Graduate: n/av	Student/Faculty: 15 to 1
Year: semesters, summer session	Tuition: $27,000
Room & Board: $10,700	Freshman Class: n/av
SAT: required ACT: 21	CEEB CODE: 3755
Application Deadline: open	COMPETITIVE

Saint Joseph's College of Maine, founded in 1912, is a private, Roman Catholic institution offering liberal arts and pre-professional programs. Figures in the above capsule and in this profile are approximate. In addition to regional accreditation, Saint Joseph's College of Maine has baccalaureate program accreditation with CCNE. The 350-acre campus is in a rural area 18 miles west of Portland. Including any residence halls, there are 20 buildings.

STUDENT LIFE: 60% of undergraduates are from Maine. Others are from 15 states, 3 foreign countries, and Canada. 82% are White. **Male To Female Ratio:** 2.0:1. The average age of freshmen is 18; all undergraduates, 20. 18% do not continue beyond their first year; 59% remain to graduate. **Housing:** 829 students can be accommodated in college housing, which includes single-sex, coed dorms, and substance free housing. On-campus housing is guaranteed for all 4 years. 83% of students live on campus; of those, 65% remain on campus on weekends. All students may keep cars.

FACULTY/CLASSROOMS: 48% of faculty are male; 52% are female. All teach undergraduates, 39% do research, and 38% do both. No introductory courses are taught by graduate students. The average class size in an introductory lecture is 25; in a laboratory is 12; and in a regular course is 18.

PROGRAMS OF STUDY: Saint Joseph's College of Maine confers B.A., B.S., B.S.B.A. and B.S.N. degrees. Associate degrees are also awarded. Bachelor's degrees are awarded in BIOLOGICAL SCIENCE (biology/biological science), BUSINESS (business administration and management), COMMUNICATIONS AND THE ARTS (communications and English), COMPUTER AND PHYSICAL SCIENCE (chemistry and mathematics), EDUCATION (elementary education and physical education), ENGINEERING AND ENVIRONMENTAL DESIGN (environmental science), HEALTH PROFESSIONS (nursing and prepharmacy), SOCIAL SCIENCE (criminal justice, history, philosophy, psychology, sociology, and theological studies). Business, nursing, and biology are the strongest academically. Elementary education, business, and nursing have the largest enrollments.

ACTIVITIES: There are no fraternities or sororities. There are 28 groups on campus, including campus activities board, campus ministry, high adventure club, superKids, cheerleading, choir, chorale, computers, dance, drama, ethnic, habitat for humanity, honors, international, literary magazine, musical theater, newspaper, pep band, photography, political, professional, radio and TV, religious,

social, social service, student government, and yearbook. Popular campus events include Family Weekend, Christmas Benefit Concert, and Spring Fling. **Sports:** There are 5 intercollegiate sports for men and 6 for women, and 12 intramural sports for men and 12 for women. Facilities include a multipurpose facility housing a gym, workout room with free weights, Nautilus and other weight-training equipment, a cardiovascular workout room, dance aerobics rooms, climbing wall, 25-meter pool, saunas, and an elevated jogging track. There are also soccer and field hockey fields, a private beach on a lake, lighted athletic fields for baseball and softball, cross-country running and ski trails, and a low ropes course. **Graduates:** From July 1, 2013 to June 30, 2014, 213 bachelor's degrees were awarded. The most popular majors were education (20%), business (20%), and nursing (12%). 43 companies recruited on campus in 2013-2014. In an average class, 54% graduate in 4 years or less, 60% graduate in 5 years or less, and 61% graduate in 6 years or less. Of the 2013 graduating class, 15% were enrolled in graduate school within 6 months of graduation, and 89% were employed.

SERVICES: Counseling and information services are available, as is tutoring in every subject. There is a reader service for the blind. **Library/Resources:** The library contains 98,626 volumes, 29,010 microform items, 1,000 audio/video tapes/CDs/DVDs, and subscribes to 11,461 periodicals including electronic. Computerized library services include interlibrary loans, database searching, and Internet access. Special learning facilities include a radio station, and a telescope observatory. **Physically Challenged Students:** 75% of the campus is accessible. Facilities include wheelchair ramps, elevators, special parking, specially equipped restrooms, special class scheduling, and lowered drinking fountains. **Special:** Saint Joseph's offers internships, cross-registration with 4 southern Maine colleges, study abroad in 5 countries, a semester at sea, dual majors, work-study programs, and non-degree study. There are 2 national honor societies, a freshman honors program, and 6 departmental honors programs. **Visiting:** There are regularly scheduled orientations for prospective students, including application and acceptance day programs, visits on 5 fall Saturdays, and summer visits. There are guides for informal visits, visitors may sit in on classes, and stay overnight. **Campus Safety and Security:** Measures include 24-hour foot and vehicle patrol, self-defense education, and security escort services. There are emergency telephones, lighted pathways/sidewalks, round-the-clock security officers.

REQUIREMENTS: The SAT or ACT is required. Candidates for admission must be high school graduates who have completed a college preparatory curriculum with a recommended 4 units in English, 3 to 4 in math, 2 in foreign language, and 1 to 3 each in history, science, and social studies. A GPA of 2.0 is required. AP and CLEP credits are accepted. Important factors in the admissions decision are advanced placement or honors courses, recommendations by school officials, and extracurricular activities record. To graduate, students must complete 128 credit hours with a minimum GPA of 2.0, including 8 hours of English, history, theology, and a foreign language, 4 each of science and math, and 8 of electives. **Procedure:** Freshmen are admitted fall and spring. Entrance exams should be taken by January of the senior year. There are early admissions, deferred admissions, and rolling admissions plans. Application deadlines are open. The fall 2014 application fee was $40. Notifications are sent December 18. 45 applicants were on the 2014 waiting list; 25 were admitted. Applications are accepted on-line. **Transfer Students:** 40 transfer students enrolled in 2013-2014. Transfer students should have a minimum GPA of 2.0. 32 of 128 credits required for the bachelor's degree must be completed at Saint Joseph's College of Maine. **International Students:** There are 3 international students enrolled. They must take the TOEFL. They must also take the SAT or ACT.

ADMISSIONS: 2 freshmen graduated first in their class. **Admissions Contact:** Vincent Kloskowski, Dean of Admissions. E-Mail: *admission@sjcme.edu* Web: *www.sjcme.edu*

FINANCIAL AID: In 2014-2015, 99% of all full-time freshmen and continuing full-time students received some form of financial aid. 80% of all full-time freshmen and 81% of continuing full-time students received need-based aid. The average freshman award was $17,086. Need-based scholarships or need-based grants averaged $12,302 ($25,700 maximum); need-based self-help aid (loans and jobs) averaged $5,772 ($6,625 maximum); and other non-need-based awards and non-need-based scholarships averaged $13,398 ($20,390 maximum). 35% of undergraduate students work part-time. Average annual earnings from campus work are $896. The average financial indebtedness of the 2014 graduate was $16,020. Saint Joseph's College of Maine is a member of CSS. The FAFSA and the college's own financial statement are required. The priority date for freshman financial aid applications for fall entry is March 1.

THOMAS COLLEGE (*The complete profile is made available exclusively on our website, www.barronspac.com*)

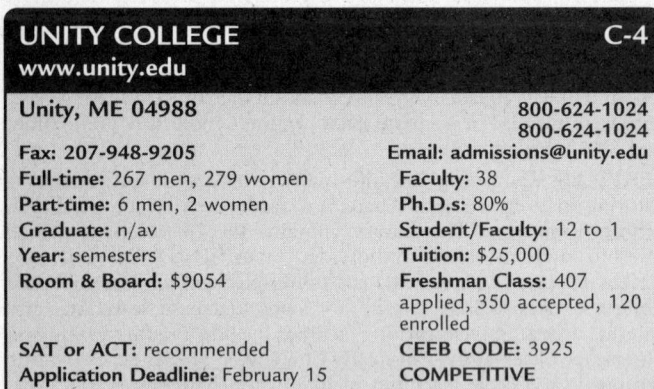

UNITY COLLEGE	C-4
www.unity.edu	
Unity, ME 04988	800-624-1024
	800-624-1024
Fax: 207-948-9205	Email: admissions@unity.edu
Full-time: 267 men, 279 women	**Faculty:** 38
Part-time: 6 men, 2 women	**Ph.D.s:** 80%
Graduate: n/av	**Student/Faculty:** 12 to 1
Year: semesters	**Tuition:** $25,000
Room & Board: $9054	**Freshman Class:** 407 applied, 350 accepted, 120 enrolled
SAT or ACT: recommended	**CEEB CODE:** 3925
Application Deadline: February 15	**COMPETITIVE**

Unity College is a small, private college in rural Maine that provides dedicated, engaged students with a liberal arts education that emphasizes the environment and natural resources. Unity College graduates are prepared to be environmental stewards, effective leaders, and responsible citizens through active learning experiences within a supportive community. There is 1 undergraduate school. In addition to regional accreditation, Unity has baccalaureate program accreditation with SMTC. The 225-acre campus is in a small town in mid-coast Maine. Including any residence halls, there are 30 buildings.

STUDENT LIFE: 74% of undergraduates are from out of state, mostly the Northeast. Students are from 40 states and 1 foreign country. 97% are from public schools. 92% are White. **Male To Female Ratio:** 1.0:1. The average age of freshmen is 18; all undergraduates, 20. 23% do not continue beyond their first year; 53% remain to graduate. **Housing:** 360 students can be accommodated in college housing, which includes single-sex and coed dorms and on-campus apartments. On-campus housing is guaranteed for all 4 years and is available on a lottery system for upperclassmen. 71% of students live on campus; of those, 89% remain on campus on weekends. All students may keep cars.

FACULTY/CLASSROOMS: 54% of faculty are male; 46% are female. All teach undergraduates and do research. No introductory courses are taught by graduate students. The average class size in an introductory lecture is 19; in a laboratory is 14; and in a regular course is 18.

PROGRAMS OF STUDY: Unity confers B.A., and B.S. degrees. Associate degrees are also awarded. Bachelor's degrees are awarded in AGRICULTURE (agriculture, animal science, conservation and regulation, environmental studies, natural resource management, range/farm management, and wildlife management), BIOLOGICAL SCIENCE (biology/biological science, ecology, marine biology, and wildlife biology), BUSINESS (recreation and leisure services), COMMUNICATIONS AND THE ARTS (art and English), COMPUTER AND PHYSICAL SCIENCE (geology and natural sciences), EDUCATION (education and secondary education), ENGINEERING AND ENVIRONMENTAL DESIGN (environmental science and land use management and reclamation), HEALTH PROFESSIONS (recreation therapy), SOCIAL SCIENCE (ethics, politics, and social policy, law enforcement and corrections, and parks and recreation management). Biology, earth and environmental science, and sustainable agriculture are the strongest academically. Conservation law enforcement, captive wildlife care and education, and wildlife biology have the largest enrollment.

ACTIVITIES: There are no fraternities or sororities. There are 36 groups on campus, including art, band, chorus, drama, environmen-

tal, gay, honors, literary magazine, outdoor and environmental clubs, photography, and student government. Popular campus events include Regional Woodsman's Meet in October, Empty Bowls Community Service and Earth Day Activities. **Sports:** There are 3 intercollegiate sports for men and 4 for women, and 10 intramural sports for men and 10 for women. Facilities include a gym, a weight training room, playing fields, a nature trail, and game rooms. **Graduates:** From July 1, 2013 to June 30, 2014, 138 bachelor's degrees were awarded. The most popular majors were conservation law enforcement (20%), captive wildlife care and education (17%), and wildlife biology/management (16%). 76 companies recruited on campus in 2013-2014. In an average class, 10% graduate in 3 years or less, 45% graduate in 4 years or less, 53% graduate in 5 years or less, and 53% graduate in 6 years or less. Of the 2013 graduating class, 13% were enrolled in graduate school within 6 months of graduation, and 90% were employed.

SERVICES: Counseling and information services are available, as is tutoring in most subjects. There is a reader service for the blind, and remedial math, reading, and writing. A full-time learning disability specialist is on staff. **Library/Resources:** The library contains 52,467 volumes, 2,625 audio/video tapes/CDs/DVDs, and subscribes to 1,748 periodicals including electronic. Computerized library services include interlibrary loans, database searching, Internet access, and Wi-Fi capability. Special learning facilities include an art gallery, organic gardens, greenhouse, and performing art center. **Physically Challenged Students:** Facilities include wheelchair ramps, special parking, specially equipped restrooms, and special housing. **Special:** The college offers credit-bearing internships, study abroad, a Washington semester, work-study programs, accelerated degree programs, dual majors, and an honors program. There is a freshman honors program. **Visiting:** There are regularly scheduled orientations for prospective students. There are guides for informal visits, visitors may sit in on classes, and stay overnight. To schedule a visit, contact the Admissions Office. **Campus Safety and Security:** Measures include 24-hour foot and vehicle patrol and emergency notification system. There are emergency telephones, lighted pathways/sidewalks, and controlled access to dorms/residences.

REQUIREMENTS: The SAT or ACT and ACT Writing Test are recommended. Applicants must be graduates of an accredited secondary school with a minimum GPA of 2.3. The GED is accepted. Five short answer essays are required and an interview is recommended. AP and CLEP credits are accepted. Important factors in the admissions decision are extracurricular activities record, advanced placement or honors courses, and leadership record. General education requirements include 38 credits. Included are Composition and Communication, math, computer science proficiency, life science, physical science, humanities, art, community-based learning, and environmental studies. Students must complete 120 credit hours with a minimum GPA of 2.0. An capstone course is required in all bachelor's degree programs. A minimum of 30 credits must be taken at the junior and senior level. **Procedure:** Freshmen are admitted fall and spring. Entrance exams should be taken in the junior or senior year. There are early decision, early admissions, and deferred admissions plans. Early decision applications should be filed by December 15; regular applications, by February 15 for fall entry; and November 1 for spring entry, along with a $25 fee. Notification of early decision is sent January 2; regular decision, March 1. Applications are accepted on-line. **Transfer Students:** 34 transfer students enrolled in 2013-2014. Applicants must present a minimum college GPA of 2.4 and are encouraged to submit SAT scores. 30 of 120 credits required for the bachelor's degree must be completed at Unity. **International Students:** The school actively recruits these students. They must take the TOEFL.

ADMISSIONS: 86% of the 2014-2015 applicants were accepted. 20% of the current freshmen were in the top fifth of their class; 55% were in the top two fifths. **Admissions Contact:** Joe Saltalamachia, Director of Admission. E-Mail: *admissions@unity.edu* Web: *www.unity.edu*

FINANCIAL AID: In 2014-2015, 99% of all full-time freshmen and 97% of continuing full-time students received some form of financial aid. 91% of all full-time freshmen and 86% of continuing full-time students received need-based aid. The average freshman award was $27,943. Need-based scholarships or need-based grants averaged $15,799 ($24,405 maximum); need-based self-help aid (loans and jobs) averaged $5,390 ($6,700 maximum); and other non-need-based awards and non-need-based scholarships averaged $6,754 ($22,659 maximum). 59% of undergraduate students work part-time. Average annual earnings from campus work are $1062. The average financial indebtedness of the 2014 graduate was $40,320. The FAFSA is required. The priority date for freshman financial aid applications for fall entry is March.

UNIVERSITY OF MAINE SYSTEM

The University of Maine System, established in 1968, is a private system in Maine. It is governed by a board of trustees, whose chief administrator is the chancellor. The primary goal of the system is teaching, research, and public service. The main priorities are to strengthen human services through programs in education, health, and social services; to provide international exchange and foreign language programs; and to conduct science and technology education and basic and applied research. The total student enrollment is usually about 40,000 for all 7 campuses. Profiles of the 4-year campuses are included in this section.

UNIVERSITY OF MAINE   C-4
www.umaine.edu

Orono, ME 04469	**(207) 581-1598**
	(877) 486-2364
Fax: (207) 581-1213	Email: umaineadmissions@maine.edu
Full-time: 4276 men, 3853 women	Faculty: n/av
Part-time: 579 men, 631 women	Ph.D.s: 85%
Graduate: 677 men, 1270 women	Student/Faculty: n/av
Year: semesters, summer session	Tuition: $10,606 ($28,486)
Room & Board: $9296	Freshman Class: 11552 applied, 9539 accepted, 2068 enrolled
SAT CR/M/W: 530/540/510 **ACT:** 24	CEEB CODE: 3916
Application Deadline: open	COMPETITIVE+

The University of Maine, established in 1865, is a publicly funded land-grant institution in the University of Maine System. The university offers degree programs in the arts and sciences, business, public policy, health fields, engineering, education, forestry and agriculture. There are 6 undergraduate schools and 1 graduate school. In addition to regional accreditation, UMaine has baccalaureate program accreditation with AACSB, ABET, ADA, AHEA, CSAB, CSWE, NASM, NCATE, NLN, SAF, ACS, APA, ASLHA, CCNE, and NASPAA. The 660-acre campus is in a small town 8 miles north of Bangor. Including any residence halls, there are 202 buildings.

STUDENT LIFE: 76% of undergraduates are from Maine. Others are from 44 states, 65 foreign countries, and Canada. 78% are White. **Male To Female Ratio:** 1.0:1. The average age of freshmen is 18; all undergraduates, 21. 23% do not continue beyond their first year. **Housing:** 3494 students can be accommodated in college housing, which includes coed dorms, on-campus apartments, off-campus apartments, and married student housing. In addition, there are honors houses, language houses, special-interest houses, substance-free housing, and quiet sections. On-campus housing is guaranteed for the freshman year only, and is available on a first-come, first-served basis. 62% of students commute. All students may keep cars. **FACULTY/CLASSROOMS:** 55% of faculty are male; 45% are female. Graduate students teach 12% of introductory courses. The average class size in an introductory lecture is 48; in a laboratory is 19; and in a regular course is 40.

PROGRAMS OF STUDY: UMaine confers B.A., B.S., B.F.A. and B.M.E. degrees. Master's and doctoral degrees are also awarded. Bachelor's degrees are awarded in AGRICULTURE (agriculture, animal science, forest engineering, forestry and related sciences, horticulture, wildlife management, and wood science), BIOLOGICAL SCIENCE (biochemistry, biology/biological science, botany, marine science, microbiology, molecular biology, nutrition, and zoology), BUSINESS (accounting, business administration and management, business administration marketing, business economics, and finance), COMMUNICATIONS AND THE ARTS (art history, com-

munication, communications, dramatic arts, English, French, journalism, media arts, modern language, music, music performance, romance languages and literature, Spanish, and studio art), COMPUTER AND PHYSICAL SCIENCE (chemistry, computer science, earth science, mathematics, and physics), EDUCATION (art education, athletic training, elementary education, music education, physical education, secondary education, and university studies), ENGINEERING AND ENVIRONMENTAL DESIGN (bioengineering, chemical engineering, civil engineering, computer engineering, construction technology, electrical/electronics engineering, electrical/electronics engineering technology, engineering physics, environmental science, mechanical engineering, mechanical engineering technology, paper and pulp science, and surveying engineering), HEALTH PROFESSIONS (kinesiology, medical laboratory technology, nursing, speech pathology/audiology, and veterinary science), SOCIAL SCIENCE (anthropology, child care/child and family studies, economics, food science, history, interdisciplinary studies, international studies, parks and recreation management, philosophy, political science/government, psychology, social work, sociology, and women and gender studies). Psychology, nursing and mechanical engineering have the largest enrollments.

ACTIVITIES: Men belong to 2 local and 15 national fraternities; and women belong to 8 national sororities. There are 212 groups on campus, including art, band, cheerleading, chess, choir, chorale, chorus, computers, dance, debate, drama, drill team, environmental, ethnic, film, forensics, gay, honors, international, jazz band, literary magazine, marching band, musical theater, newspaper, opera, orchestra, pep band, photography, political, professional, radio and TV, religious, social, social service, student government, symphony, and yearbook. Popular campus events include Maine Day, Homecoming, Family and Friends Weekend, and International Culturefest. **Sports:** There are 8 intercollegiate sports for men and 9 for women, and 26 intramural sports for men and 26 for women. Facilities include on- and off-campus sports arenas for hockey and basketball, a field house, swimming and diving center, an indoor climbing center, a student recreation center, a recreation swimming pool, weight room, indoor track, dance studio, basketball, volleyball, badminton, squash, tennis, racquetball courts, baseball, softball, soccer, field hockey, football fields, sports dome, and a year-round maintained forest trail system. **Graduates:** From July 1, 2013 to June 30, 2014, 1540 bachelor's degrees were awarded. The most popular majors were business/marketing (13%), engineering (11%), and education (10%). 191 companies recruited on campus in 2013-2014. In an average class, 37% graduate in 4 years or less, 56% graduate in 5 years or less, and 60% graduate in 6 years or less.

SERVICES: Counseling and information services are available, as is tutoring in some subjects. There is a reader service for the blind. Developmental courses are offered in remedial math, reading and writing. **Library/Resources:** The library contains 2.0 million volumes, 2.4 million microform items, and 144,166 audio/video tapes/CDs/DVDs, and subscribes to 99,000 periodicals including electronic. Computerized library services include interlibrary loans, database searching, Internet access, and Wi-Fi capability. Special learning facilities include an art gallery, planetarium, radio station, a concert hall and four other performance spaces, music facilities, a digital media lab, prototyping facilities, 3-D printers, an anthropology museum, a laboratory for surface science and technology, and an advanced structures and composites center. **Physically Challenged Students:** 90% of the campus is accessible. Facilities include wheelchair ramps, elevators, special parking, specially equipped restrooms, special class scheduling, lowered drinking fountains, lowered telephones, a transport van. **Special:** Cross-registration at other University of Maine campuses, internships at the upper level, a Washington semester, work-study programs both on- and off-campus, dual majors, a general studies degree, and pass/fail options are available. Students may study abroad in more than 40 countries. Cooperative programs are available in most majors, and accelerated degrees may be arranged. There are 20 national honor societies, including Phi Beta Kappa, and a freshman honors program. **Visiting:** There are regularly scheduled orientations for prospective students, includes an opening welcome, campus tours, registration, department tours, a student panel, admissions, financial aid and student life sessions, a performing arts presentation, and music auditions. There are guides for informal visits and visitors may sit in on classes. To schedule a visit, contact Silverio Barrera at silverio.barrerajr@maine.edu. **Campus Safety and Security:** Measures include 24-hour foot and vehicle patrol, emergency notification system, self-defense education, and security escort services. There are emergency telephones, lighted pathways/sidewalks, text and email emergency communication system.

REQUIREMENTS: The SAT or ACT is required. The GED is accepted. The number of academic or Carnegie credits required varies according to the program. The required secondary school courses also vary with each program but should include 4 credits of English, 3 of math, 2 of lab science, 2 of social studies, 2 in a foreign language, and 3 of electives. Guidance counselor recommendation is required for high school students. An essay is required. An audition is required for music majors. AP and CLEP credits are accepted. Important factors in the admissions decision are advanced placement or honors courses, leadership record, extracurricular activities record, recommendations by school officials, and evidence of special talent. To graduate, students must complete a minimum of 120 credit hours, including at least 48 in the major, with a GPA of 2.0 or higher. 40 credits in approved courses must be taken. General education requirements include 18 credits in human values and social context, six credits in math/statistics/computer science, two courses in science, and at least one course in ethics. English composition is required. Students must demonstrate writing competency and complete a capstone. **Procedure:** Freshmen are admitted fall and spring. Entrance exams should be taken by January of the senior year. There are deferred admissions and rolling admissions plans. Application deadlines are open. The fall 2014 application fee was $40. Notifications are sent February 1. Applications are accepted on-line. **Transfer Students:** 469 transfer students enrolled in 2013-2014. Applicants must submit transcripts of all college and high school records. A minimum GPA of 2.0 is required. Some majors specify a higher cumulative GPA. 30 of 120 credits required for the bachelor's degree must be completed at UMaine. **International Students:** There are 321 international students enrolled. The school actively recruits these students. They must take the TOEFL with a minimum score of 550 on the paper-based TOEFL (PBT) or 79 on the Internet-based version (iBT). They must also take the SAT or ACT.

ADMISSIONS: 83% of the 2014-2015 applicants were accepted. The SAT scores for the 2014-2015 freshman class were: Critical Reading--32% below 500, 44% between 500 and 599, 21% between 600 and 699, and 3% between 700 and 800; Math--28% below 500, 44% between 500 and 599, 24% between 600 and 699, and 4% between 700 and 800; Writing--41% below 500, 42% between 500 and 599, 16% between 600 and 699, and 2% between 700 and 800. The ACT scores were 20% below 21, 27% between 21 and 23, 24% between 24 and 26, 17% between 27 and 28, and 13% above 28. 39% of the current freshmen were in the top fifth of their class; 68% were in the top two fifths. There were 2 National Merit finalists. **Admissions Contact:** Brian M. Manter, Director of Recruitment. E-Mail: umaineadmissions@maine.edu Web: www.umaine.edu

FINANCIAL AID: In 2014-2015, 97% of all full-time freshmen and 91% of continuing full-time students received some form of financial aid. 79% of all full-time freshmen and 77% of continuing full-time students received need-based aid. The average freshman award was $17,923. Need-based scholarships or need-based grants averaged $7,892; need-based self-help aid (loans and jobs) averaged $5,308; non-need-based athletic scholarships averaged $435; and other non-need-based awards and non-need-based scholarships averaged $4,287. 35% of undergraduate students work part-time. Average annual earnings from campus work are $2214. The average financial indebtedness of the 2014 graduate was $33,875. The FAFSA is required. The priority date for freshman financial aid applications for fall entry is March 1.

UNIVERSITY OF MAINE AT AUGUSTA B-5

www.uma.edu

Augusta, ME 04430 (207) 621-3465

Fax: (207) 621-3333	Email: jhenry@maine.edu
Full-time: 639 men, 1260 women	Faculty: 104; IIB, -$
Part-time: 772 men, 2319 women	Ph.D.s: 54%
Graduate: n/av	Student/Faculty: 15 to 1
Year: semesters, summer session	Tuition: $6855 ($15,375)
Room & Board: n/a	Freshman Class: 875 applied, 817 accepted, 512 enrolled
	CEEB CODE: 3929
Application Deadline: June 15	COMPETITIVE

The University of Maine at Augusta, founded in 1965, offers both associate and baccalaureate degrees and is part of the University of Maine System. Figures in the above capsule and in this profile are approximate. There are 3 undergraduate schools. In addition to regional accreditation, UMA has baccalaureate program accreditation with ADA, NLN, and NEASC. The 159-acre campus is in a small town 50 miles north of Portland. Including any residence halls, there are 15 buildings.

STUDENT LIFE: 97% of undergraduates are from Maine. Others are from 35 states, 3 foreign countries, and Canada. 99% are from public schools. 73% are White. **Male To Female Ratio:** 2.5:1. The average age of freshmen is 27; all undergraduates, 32. 46% do not continue beyond their first year; 30% remain to graduate. **Housing:** Alcohol is not permitted. All students commute. All students may keep cars.

FACULTY/CLASSROOMS: 43% of faculty are male; 47% are female. All teach undergraduates. No introductory courses are taught by graduate students. The average class size in an introductory lecture is 20; in a laboratory is 16; and in a regular course is 18.

PROGRAMS OF STUDY: UMA confers B.A., B.A.S., B. Mus. and B.S. degrees. Associate degrees are also awarded. Bachelor's degrees are awarded in BIOLOGICAL SCIENCE (biology/biological science), BUSINESS (accounting and business administration and management), COMMUNICATIONS AND THE ARTS (art, English, and jazz), COMPUTER AND PHYSICAL SCIENCE (applied science and information sciences and systems), EDUCATION (library science), ENGINEERING AND ENVIRONMENTAL DESIGN (architecture), HEALTH PROFESSIONS (dental hygiene, mental health/human services, and nursing), SOCIAL SCIENCE (interdisciplinary studies, law enforcement and corrections, liberal arts/general studies, public administration, and social science). Mental health and human services have the largest enrollments.

ACTIVITIES: There are no fraternities or sororities. There are 17 groups on campus, including and music ensembles, art, drama, gay, honors, international, jazz band, literary magazine, newspaper, pep band, professional, religious, social, social service, student government, and theater. Popular campus events include Mile of Art, Jazz Week and Plunkett Poetry Festival. **Sports:** There are 2 intercollegiate sports for men and 3 for women, and 4 intramural sports for men and 4 for women. Facilities include the UMA Community Outdoor Leisure Center, which is also open to the public. Facilities provide for seasonal activities and feature a running and cross-country skiing trail, tennis courts, a soccer field, and a softball field. Indoor facilities include a small gym, a racquetball court, and a small fitness center. **Graduates:** From July 1, 2013 to June 30, 2014, 362 bachelor's degrees were awarded. The most popular majors were health professions (29%), liberal arts/general studies (20%), and business/marketing (17%). 10 companies recruited on campus in 2013-2014.

SERVICES: Counseling and information services are available, as is tutoring in some subjects. There is remedial math and writing. There are workshops on a variety of student success skills, such as effective learning and reducing test anxiety **Library/Resources:** The 2 libraries contain 93,897 volumes, 4,676 microform items, 4,783 audio/video tapes/CDs/DVDs, and subscribe to 493 periodicals including electronic. Computerized library services include interlibrary loans, database searching, Internet access, and Wi-Fi capability. Special learning facilities include an art gallery, an interactive television system. **Physi-**

cally Challenged Students: 95% of the campus is accessible. Facilities include wheelchair ramps, elevators, special parking, specially equipped restrooms, special class scheduling, lowered drinking fountains, and lowered telephones. Special: Work-study and internship programs with local employers, study abroad in Germany, and a student-designed interdisciplinary studies major are available. Cross-registration is offered with University of Maine system campuses. There is 1 national honor society. Visiting: There are regularly scheduled orientations for prospective students, during the month before the beginning of a semester. There are guides for informal visits and visitors may sit in on classes. Campus Safety and Security: Measures include emergency notification system and security escort services. There are emergency telephones and lighted pathways/sidewalks.

REQUIREMENTS: Students are encouraged to submit SAT scores for placement only. Applicants should have a high school diploma or the GED. Recommended secondary preparation varies according to the degree program. Applicants for the B.M. program must audition. UMA requires applicants to be in the upper 25% of their class. A GPA of 2.0 is required. AP and CLEP credits are accepted. All students must complete at least 120 hours, including 30 to 40 in the major, with a minimum GPA of 2.0. All degree programs require courses in communications, humanities, college writing, and fine arts. 6 credits of writing-intensive course work is required. Procedure: Freshmen are admitted fall, spring, and summer. There are deferred admissions and rolling admissions plans. Applications should be filed by June 15 for fall entry; October 15 for spring entry, along with a $40 fee. Notification is sent on a rolling basis. Applications are accepted on-line. Transfer Students: 625 transfer students enrolled in 2013-2014. High school/college transcripts and a statement of good standing from prior institutions are required. Standardized test scores are required for some students, and an interview is recommended. 30 of 120 credits required for the bachelor's degree must be completed at UMA. International Students: There are 42 international students enrolled. They must take the TOEFL with a minimum score of 500 on the paper-based TOEFL (PBT).

ADMISSIONS: 93% of the 2014-2015 applicants were accepted. 12% of the current freshmen were in the top fifth of their class; 63% were in the top two fifths. Admissions Contact: Jonathan Henry, Dean of Enrollment Services. E-Mail: jhenry@maine.edu Web: www.uma.edu

FINANCIAL AID: In 2014-2015, 90% of all full-time freshmen and 99% of continuing full-time students received some form of financial aid. 84% of all full-time freshmen and 90% of continuing full-time students received need-based aid. The average freshman award was $8,026. Need-based scholarships or need-based grants averaged $5,816 ($6,640 maximum); need-based self-help aid (loans and jobs) averaged $6,164 ($7,500 maximum); non-need-based athletic scholarships averaged $2,850; and other non-need-based awards and non-need-based scholarships averaged $6,156 ($2,600 maximum). 5% of undergraduate students work part-time. Average annual earnings from campus work are $1757. The average financial indebtedness of the 2014 graduate was $24,353. The FAFSA is required. The priority date for freshman financial aid applications for fall entry is March 1.

UNIVERSITY OF MAINE AT FARMINGTON (*The complete profile is made available exclusively on our website, www.barronspac.com*)

UNIVERSITY OF MAINE AT FORT KENT (*The complete profile is made available exclusively on our website, www.barronspac.com*)

UNIVERSITY OF MAINE AT MACHIAS   E-4
www.umm.maine.edu

Machias, ME 04654	
	(207) 255-1318
	(888) 468-6866
Fax: (207) 255-1363	Email: ummadmissions@maine.edu
Full-time: 200 men, 300 women	Faculty: 31; IIB, --$
Part-time: 145 men, 542 women	Ph.D.s: 71%
Graduate: n/av	Student/Faculty: 15 to 1
Year: semesters, summer session	Tuition: $5000 ($12,195)
Room & Board: $5678	Freshman Class: 374 applied, 312 accepted, 120 enrolled
SAT required ACT: 22	CEEB CODE: 3956
Application Deadline: open	COMPETITIVE

The University of Maine at Machias, founded in 1909, is a publicly funded liberal arts institution in the University of Maine system. Figures in the above capsule and in this profile are approximate. In addition to regional accreditation, UMM has baccalaureate program accreditation with NRPA. The 42-acre campus is in a rural area 85 miles east of Bangor. Including any residence halls, there are 8 buildings.

STUDENT LIFE: 82% of undergraduates are from Maine. Others are from 26 states, 16 foreign countries, and Canada. 98% are from public schools. 90% are White. Male To Female Ratio: 2.4:1. The average age of freshmen is 20; all undergraduates, 29. 28% do not continue beyond their first year; 45% remain to graduate. Housing: 353 students can be accommodated in college housing, which includes single-sex and coed dorms. On-campus housing is guaranteed for all 4 years. 76% of students commute. All students may keep cars.

FACULTY/CLASSROOMS: 54% of faculty are male; 46% are female. All teach undergraduates. No introductory courses are taught by graduate students. The average class size in an introductory lecture is 21; in a laboratory is 16; and in a regular course is 17.

PROGRAMS OF STUDY: UMM confers B.A., B.S. and B.C.S. degrees. Bachelor's degrees are awarded in BIOLOGICAL SCIENCE (biology/biological science and marine biology), BUSINESS (accounting, business administration and management, marketing/retailing/merchandising, and recreation and leisure services), COMMUNICATIONS AND THE ARTS (English and fine arts), EDUCATION (business education and elementary education), ENGINEERING AND ENVIRONMENTAL DESIGN (environmental science), SOCIAL SCIENCE (behavioral science, history, human services, and liberal arts/general studies). Elementary education, marine biology, and environmental studies are the strongest academically. Elementary education, business administration, and behavioral science have the largest enrollments.

ACTIVITIES: 7% of men belong to 2 local and 2 national fraternities; 3% of women belong to 1 local and 3 national sororities. There are 34 groups on campus, including and pop band, art, cheerleading, chorale, chorus, communications, computers, dance, drama, gay, honors, international, literary magazine, musical theater, outing club, pep band, photography, professional, radio and TV, religious, social service, and student government. Popular campus events include Winter Carnival, Spring Weekend, and Family Weekend. Sports: There are 3 intercollegiate sports for men and 4 for women, and 10 intramural sports for men and 10 for women. Facilities include 2 gyms, weight/exercise rooms, handball/raquetball courts, a pool, and a 64-acre recreational center with a lodge and cabins on the lake. Graduates: From July 1, 2013 to June 30, 2014, 100 bachelor's degrees were awarded. The most popular majors were behavioral science (15%), business administration (13%), and recreation management (13%). 10 companies recruited on campus in 2013-2014. In an average class, 19% graduate in 4 years or less, 42% graduate in 5 years or less, and 46% graduate in 6 years or less.

SERVICES: Counseling and information services are available, as is tutoring in every subject. There is remedial math, reading, and writing. The Student Resource Coordinator provides one-on-one services, including learning strategies, study skills, and assistance with papers and learning styles. Library/Resources: The library contains 82,000 volumes, 5,000 microform items, 3,000 audio/video tapes/CDs/DVDs, and subscribes to 320 periodicals including electronic. Computerized library services include interlibrary loans, database searching, and Internet access. Special learning facilities include an art gallery, radio station, aquariums for marine and aquaculture studies. Physically Challenged Students: 85% of the campus is accessible. Facilities include wheelchair ramps, elevators, special parking, specially equipped restrooms, lowered drinking fountains, and automatic doors. Special: Co-op programs in all majors except education, cross-registration, internships, work-study programs, a B.A.-B.S. degree, study abroad in England and Wales, and a student designed concentration in environmental science are available. UMM also offers a Bachelor of College Studies program, credit for prior learning, nondegree study, and a pass/fail option in certain courses. There is a freshman honors program. Visiting: There are regularly scheduled orientations for prospective students, consisting of traditional orientations prior to the fall and spring semesters, which include programming to guide students in all aspects of starting college. UMM also offers two summer student orientations, which include aspects of the fall orientations plus a parent orientation. There are guides for informal visits and visitors may sit in on classes. **Campus Safety and Security:** Measures include self-defense education and security escort services. There are lighted pathways/sidewalks, a keyless entry system for residence halls, and security patrol from 5 p.m. to 5 a.m. daily.

REQUIREMENTS: The SAT or ACT is required. All candidates must be graduates of an accredited secondary school, although the GED is accepted. UMM also recommends completion of 4 units of English, 3 of math, 2 each of lab science, social science/history, and fine arts or foreign language, and 3 of electives. An essay is required and an interview is strongly recommended. UMM requires applicants to be in the upper 50% of their class. A GPA of 2.0 is required. AP and CLEP credits are accepted. Important factors in the admissions decision are extracurricular activities record, leadership record, and recommendations by school officials.To graduate, students must complete a minimum of 120 credit hours with a GPA of 2.0. The core curriculum consists of 40-43 hours in the areas of communication skills, science and math, humans in social context, fine arts, historical and cultural perspectives, and lifetime fitness. **Procedure:** Freshmen are admitted fall, spring, and summer. There are early admissions, deferred admissions, and rolling admissions plans. Application deadlines are open. Application fee is $40. Notification is sent on a rolling basis. Applications are accepted on-line. **Transfer Students:** 36 transfer students enrolled in 2013-2014. A minimum college GPA of 2.0 and evidence of good standing are required of transfer applicants. 30 of 120 credits required for the bachelor's degree must be completed at UMM. **International Students:** There are 50 international students enrolled. The school actively recruits these students. They must take the TOEFL. They must also take the SAT or ACT.

ADMISSIONS: 83% of the 2014-2015 applicants were accepted. The ACT scores were 43% below 21, 14% between 21 and 23, 29% between 24 and 26, 7% between 27 and 28, and 7% above 28. 23% of the current freshmen were in the top fifth of their class; 53% were in the top two fifths. **Admissions Contact:** Sarah Guancial, Admissions Counselor. E-Mail: *ummadmissions@maine.edu* Web: *www. umm.maine.edu*

FINANCIAL AID: In 2014-2015, 88% of all full-time freshmen and 80% of continuing full-time students received some form of financial aid. 78% of all full-time freshmen and 82% of continuing full-time students received need-based aid. The average freshman award was $8,488. Need-based scholarships or need-based grants averaged $5,884; need-based self-help aid (loans and jobs) averaged $3,439; and other non-need-based awards and non-need-based scholarships averaged $6,420. The FAFSA is required. The deadline for filing freshman financial aid applications for fall entry is March 1.

UNIVERSITY OF MAINE AT PRESQUE ISLE *(The complete profile is made available exclusively on our website, www.barronspac.com)*

UNIVERSITY OF NEW ENGLAND	B-6
www.une.edu	

Biddeford, ME 04005	1-800-477-4863
	(800) 477-4863
Fax: 207-602-4900	Email: admissions@une.edu
Full-time: 642 men, 1543 women	Faculty: 137
Part-time: 8 men, 19 women	Ph.D.s: 78%
Graduate: 1042 men, 2605 women	Student/Faculty: 16 to 1
Year: semesters, summer session	Tuition: $34,080
Room & Board: $12,670	Freshman Class: 4317 applied, 3699 accepted, 576 enrolled
SAT CR/M: 531/540 ACT: 23	CEEB CODE: 3751
Application Deadline: February 15	COMPETITIVE

The University of New England (UNE) is an innovative health sciences university grounded in the liberal arts, with 2 coastal Maine campuses and study abroad opportunities. UNE has internationally recognized scholars in the sciences, health, medicine and humanities; offers more than 40 undergraduate, graduate and professional degree programs; and is home to Maine's only medical school. It is one of a handful of private universities with a comprehensive health education mission including medicine, pharmacy, dental medicine, nursing and an array of allied health professions. UNE's interprofessional education initiatives prepare future healthcare professionals to practice comprehensive and collaborative team-based care. Both graduate and undergraduate students engage in research and scholarship alongside dedicated faculty who are committed to their academic and professional success. There are 2 undergraduate schools and 6 graduate schools. In addition to regional accreditation, UNE has baccalaureate program accreditation with ACBSP, ADA, APTA, CSWE, NLN, CAAHEP, AOA, CAATE, and NLNAC. The 623-acre campus is in a small town in a residential area outside of Portland, Maine. The Biddeford campus is on the banks of the Saco River and the shore of the Atlantic Ocean in Biddeford, ME. Including any residence halls, there are 51 buildings.

STUDENT LIFE: 67% of undergraduates are from out of state, mostly the Northeast. Students are from 35 states, 14 foreign countries, and Canada. 70% are White; 14% race unknown. **Male To Female Ratio:** 2.5:1. The average age of freshmen is 18; all undergraduates, 20. 20% do not continue beyond their first year; 80% remain to graduate. **Housing:** 1619 students can be accommodated in college housing, which includes single-sex and coed dorms. On-campus housing is guaranteed for the freshman year only. 63% of students live on campus. All students may keep cars.

FACULTY/CLASSROOMS: 42% of faculty are male; 58% are female. 45% teach undergraduates. No introductory courses are taught by graduate students. The average class size in a laboratory is 20 and in a regular course is 25.

PROGRAMS OF STUDY: UNE confers B.A., B.S. and B.S.N. degrees. Master's and Doctoral degrees are also awarded. Bachelor's degrees are awarded in AGRICULTURE (animal science and environmental studies), BIOLOGICAL SCIENCE (biochemistry, biology/biological science, marine biology, and marine science), BUSINESS (business administration and management and sports management), COMMUNICATIONS AND THE ARTS (communications and English), COMPUTER AND PHYSICAL SCIENCE (chemistry and mathematics), EDUCATION (art education, athletic training, education, elementary education, and secondary education), ENGINEERING AND ENVIRONMENTAL DESIGN (environmental science), HEALTH PROFESSIONS (biomedical science, dental hygiene, exercise science, health care administration, health science, nursing, occupational therapy, premedicine, prepharmacy, and preventive/wellness health care), SOCIAL SCIENCE (history, liberal arts/general studies, philosophy, political science/government, psychobiology, psychology, social science, and sociology). Medical biology, nursing and health have the largest enrollments.

ACTIVITIES: There are no fraternities or sororities. There are 63 groups on campus, including and skiing, surfing, art, communications, dance, drama, environmental, ethnic, gay, honors, international, literary magazine, musical theater, newspaper, pep band, professional, religious, sailing, social, social service, student government, and yearbook. Popular campus events include Welcome Week, Family and Friends Weekend and Full Leadership Retreat. **Sports:** There are 6 intercollegiate sports for men and 9 for women, and 8 intramural sports for men and 8 for women. Facilities include the Harold Alfond Forum, which is a 106,500-square foot state-of-the-art facility that includes an ice hockey arena, a performance court, and a multi-purpose indoor fields. Additionally, there is a fitness center, team/locker rooms, two athletic training rooms, administrators/ coaches' offices, academic offices, classroom space, meeting space, and a dining area. The Big Blue Turf is a synthetic turf field, which includes bleacher seating for 550 spectators, competition lighting, a press box, and state-of-the-art scoreboard. The Campus Center houses a gym, indoor track, fitness center, six-lane pool, lockers rooms, hot tub, saunas, campus bookstore, a racquetball court, snack shop, and three multipurpose rooms.**Graduates:** From July 1, 2013 to June 30, 2014, 466 bachelor's degrees were awarded. The most popular majors were medical biology (18%), nursing (13%), and applied exercise science (10%). In an average class, 53% graduate in 4 years or less, 64% graduate in 5 years or less, and 61% graduate in 6 years or less.

SERVICES: Counseling and information services are available, as is

tutoring in most subjects. There is a reader service for the blind, and remedial math, reading, and writing. **Library/Resources:** The 2 libraries contain 135,000 volumes, 536 microform items, 2,573 audio/video tapes/CDs/DVDs, and subscribe to 85,000 periodicals including electronic. Computerized library services include interlibrary loans, database searching, Internet access, and Wi-Fi capability. Special learning facilities include an art gallery, and a marine science and education center. **Physically Challenged Students:** 85% of the campus is accessible. Facilities include wheelchair ramps, elevators, special parking, specially equipped restrooms, special class scheduling, lowered drinking fountains, lowered telephones, special housing. **Special:** UNE offers cross-registration with the Greater Portland Alliance of Colleges and Universities, internships in all majors, work-study programs, study abroad, dual majors in all departments, a 3-2 pre-physician assistant program, a 2-4 pre-pharm/pharm-D program and 3-2 pre-occupational therapy program. There are 2 national honor societies. **Visiting:** There are regularly scheduled orientations for prospective students, including a tour and information session. There are guides for informal visits and visitors may sit in on classes. To schedule a visit, contact the Office of Undergraduate Admissions. **Campus Safety and Security:** Measures include 24-hour foot and vehicle patrol, emergency notification system, self-defense education, and security escort services. There are shuttle buses, emergency telephones, lighted pathways/sidewalks, controlled access to dorms/residences. A safe-ride program provides drivers for students.

REQUIREMENTS: The SAT or ACT is required. Applicants should be high school graduates with 4 years of English, 3 years each of math and science, and 2 years each of history and social studies. The GED is accepted. AP and CLEP credits are accepted. Important factors in the admissions decision are advanced placement or honors courses, recommendations by school officials, and leadership record. A total of at least 120 credits with a minimum GPA of 2.0 is required for graduation. Some programs require more than 120 credits. Students must take 43 credits in a liberal arts core curriculum of humanities, sciences, and social sciences. Most majors require 1-semester internships. Courses in English composition, human traditions, environmental studies, lab science, creative arts, and math are required. **Procedure:** Freshmen are admitted fall and spring. Entrance exams should be taken in the spring of the junior year or the fall of the senior year. There are early decision and deferred admissions plans. Early decision applications should be filed by December 1; regular applications, by February 15 for fall entry; and December 1 for spring entry, along with a $40 fee. Notification is sent on a rolling basis. Applications are accepted on-line. **Transfer Students:** 121 transfer students enrolled in 2013-2014. Transfer applicants should present a GPA of at least 2.5 in prior college work. 30 of 120 credits required for the bachelor's degree must be completed at UNE. **International Students:** There are 13 international students enrolled. They must take the TOEFL with a minimum score of 550 on the paper-based TOEFL (PBT) or 79 on the Internet-based version (iBT).

ADMISSIONS: 86% of the 2014-2015 applicants were accepted. The SAT scores for the 2014-2015 freshman class were: Critical Reading--32% below 500, 49% between 500 and 599, 17% between 600 and 699, and 2% between 700 and 800; Math--25% below 500, 53% between 500 and 599, 19% between 600 and 699, and 2% between 700 and 800. The ACT scores were 22% below 21, 38% between 21 and 23, 19% between 24 and 26, 6% between 27 and 28, and 16% above 28. **Admissions Contact:** Scott Steinberg, Dean of University Admission. E-Mail: *admissions@une.edu* Web: *www.une.edu*

FINANCIAL AID: In 2014-2015, 100% of all full-time freshmen and 99% of continuing full-time students received some form of financial aid. 72% of all full-time freshmen and 66% of continuing full-time students received need-based aid. The FAFSA is required. The deadline for filing freshman financial aid applications for fall entry is May 1.

UNIVERSITY OF SOUTHERN MAINE — A-5
www.usm.maine.edu

Gorham, ME 04038
(207) 780-5670
(800) 800-4876

Fax: (207) 780-5640
Email: usmadm@maine.maine.edu

Full-time: 2166 men, 2665 women
Part-time: 1128 men, 1659 women
Graduate: 686 men, 1351 women
Year: semesters, summer session
Room & Board: $8762

Faculty: IIA, +$
Ph.D.s: 74%
Student/Faculty: n/av
Tuition: $7814 ($20,024)
Freshman Class: 3676 applied, 3819 accepted, 924 enrolled

SAT CR/M/W: 500/500/490 **ACT:** 21
Application Deadline: February 15

CEEB CODE: 3691
COMPETITIVE

The University of Southern Maine, founded in 1878, is a publicly funded, multicampus, comprehensive, residential, liberal arts institution serving the University of Maine system. Figures in the above capsule and in this profile are approximate. There are 5 undergraduate schools and 8 graduate schools. In addition to regional accreditation, USM has baccalaureate program accreditation with AACSB, ABET, CSAB, CSWE, NASM, NCATE, NLN, and NRPA. The 144-acre campus is in an urban area 110 miles north of Boston, MA. Including any residence halls, there are 66 buildings.

STUDENT LIFE: 90% of undergraduates are from Maine. Others are from 35 states, 27 foreign countries, and Canada. 97% are White. **Male To Female Ratio:** 1.4:1. The average age of freshmen is 19; all undergraduates, 25. **Housing:** 1835 students can be accommodated in college housing, which includes coed dorms, on-campus apartments, and married student housing. In addition, there are honors houses, special-interest houses, a fine arts house. On-campus housing is guaranteed for all 4 years. 81% of students commute. All students may keep cars.

FACULTY/CLASSROOMS: 53% of faculty are male; 47% are female. 80% teach undergraduates, all do research, and 80% do both. No introductory courses are taught by graduate students. The average class size in an introductory lecture is 50; in a laboratory is 20; and in a regular course is 22.

PROGRAMS OF STUDY: USM confers B.A., B.S., B.F.A. and B.M. degrees. Associate, Master's, and Doctoral degrees are also awarded. Bachelor's degrees are awarded in BIOLOGICAL SCIENCE (biology/biological science), BUSINESS (accounting and business administration and management), COMMUNICATIONS AND THE ARTS (communications, dramatic arts, English, fine arts, French, music, and music performance), COMPUTER AND PHYSICAL SCIENCE (chemistry, computer science, geology, geoscience, mathematics, and physics), EDUCATION (music education and technical education), ENGINEERING AND ENVIRONMENTAL DESIGN (electrical/electronics engineering, environmental science, and industrial engineering technology), HEALTH PROFESSIONS (environmental health science, health science, nursing, recreation therapy, and sports medicine), SOCIAL SCIENCE (anthropology, economics, geography, history, philosophy, political science/government, psychology, social work, sociology, and women's studies). Electrical engineering, computer science, and nursing are the strongest academically. Business administration, nursing, and psychology have the largest enrollments.

ACTIVITIES: 2% of men belong to 1 local and 3 national fraternities; 2% of women belong to 2 local and 2 national sororities. There are 100 groups on campus, including ski, commuter, environmental, art, band, cheerleading, chess, choir, chorale, chorus, computers, dance, drama, ethnic, gay, honors, international, jazz band, literary magazine, musical theater, opera, orchestra, outing, photography, political, professional, religious, social, social service, and student government. Popular campus events include Winter Weekend, Spring Fling, and Comedy Nights. **Sports:** There are 12 intercollegiate sports for men and 13 for women, and 14 intramural sports for men and 14 for women. Facilities include gyms, tennis courts, athletic fields, racquetball and squash courts, cross-country ski trails, two weight-training and fitness facilities, an ice arena, a field house, and an indoor track. **Graduates:** From July 1, 2013 to June 30, 2014, 1101 bachelor's degrees were awarded. The most popular majors were health professions (20%), social sciences (19%), and business (13%).

SERVICES: Counseling and information services are available, as is tutoring in most subjects. There is a reader service for the blind, and remedial math, reading, and writing. **Library/Resources:** The 3 libraries contain 455,129 volumes, 731,755 microform items, 5,288 audio/video tapes/CDs/DVDs, and subscribe to 3,249 periodicals including electronic. Computerized library services include interlibrary loans and database searching. Special learning facilities include an art gallery, planetarium, TV station, cartography collections. **Physically Challenged Students:** All of the campus is accessible. Facilities include wheelchair ramps, elevators, special parking, specially equipped restrooms, special class scheduling, lowered drinking fountains, and lowered telephones. **Special:** Cross-registration within the University of Maine system and 4 Greater Portland colleges, a Washington semester, and study abroad in more than 12 countries are offered. Internships, co-op and work-study programs, a B.A.-B.S. degree, dual and student-designed majors, a 2-2 engineering program with the University of Maine, credit for life experience, nondegree study, and pass/fail options are also available. There is a January intersession. There are 2 national honor societies, a freshman honors program, and 1 departmental honors program. **Visiting:** There are regularly scheduled orientations for prospective students, including regularly scheduled campus tours and group information sessions, as well as special events such as fall open houses. Interviews are also available on request. There are guides for informal visits and visitors may sit in on classes. **Campus Safety and Security:** Measures include 24-hour foot and vehicle patrol, self-defense education, and security escort services. There are shuttle buses, emergency telephones, lighted pathways/sidewalks, and preventive programs within residence halls.

REQUIREMENTS: The SAT or ACT is required. Applicants must be graduates of an accredited secondary school. The GED is accepted. Either 41 academic credits or 20 1/2 Carnegie units are required. Secondary school courses should include 4 years of English, 3 of math, 2 each of a foreign language and lab science, and 1 each of history and social studies. An essay is required, as are auditions for music applicants and interviews for applicants to the School of Applied Science. Guidance counselor recommendations are required for those students applying during their senior year. A GPA of 2.0 is required. AP and CLEP credits are accepted. Important factors in the admissions decision are advanced placement or honors courses, recommendations by school officials, and extracurricular activities record. A total of 120 hours, of which 36 to 94 are in the major, and a minimum GPA of 2.0 are required for graduation. All students must fulfill the distribution requirements of the 3-part core curriculum: basic competence, methods of inquiry/ways of knowing, and interdisciplinary studies. **Procedure:** Freshmen are admitted fall and spring. Entrance exams should be taken by May of the junior year or January of the senior year. There are deferred admissions and rolling admissions plans. Applications should be filed by February 15 for fall entry; December 1 for spring entry. The fall 2014 application fee was $40. Applications are accepted on-line. **Transfer Students:** 848 transfer students enrolled in 2013-2014. Applicants must have a minimum GPA of 2.0 or 2.75 for those from non-regionally accredited institutions. Students who have been out of high school for less than 3 years must submit SAT scores. 30 of 120 credits required for the bachelor's degree must be completed at USM. **International Students:** They must take the TOEFL.

ADMISSIONS: The SAT scores for the 2014-2015 freshman class were: Critical Reading--47% below 500, 39% between 500 and 599, 12% between 600 and 699, and 2% between 700 and 800; Math--50% below 500, 40% between 500 and 599, 9% between 600 and 699, and 1% between 700 and 800; Writing--51% below 500, 37% between 500 and 599, 11% between 600 and 699, and 1% between 700 and 800. The ACT scores were 45% below 21, 32% between 21 and 23, 15% between 24 and 26, 3% between 27 and 28, and 5% above 28. 22% of the current freshmen were in the top fifth of their class; 51% were in the top two fifths. **Admissions Contact:** Scott Steinberg, Dean of Undergraduate Admission. E-Mail: *usmadm@maine.maine.edu* Web: *www.usm.maine.edu*

FINANCIAL AID: The FAFSA is required. The deadline for filing freshman financial aid applications for fall entry is February 15.

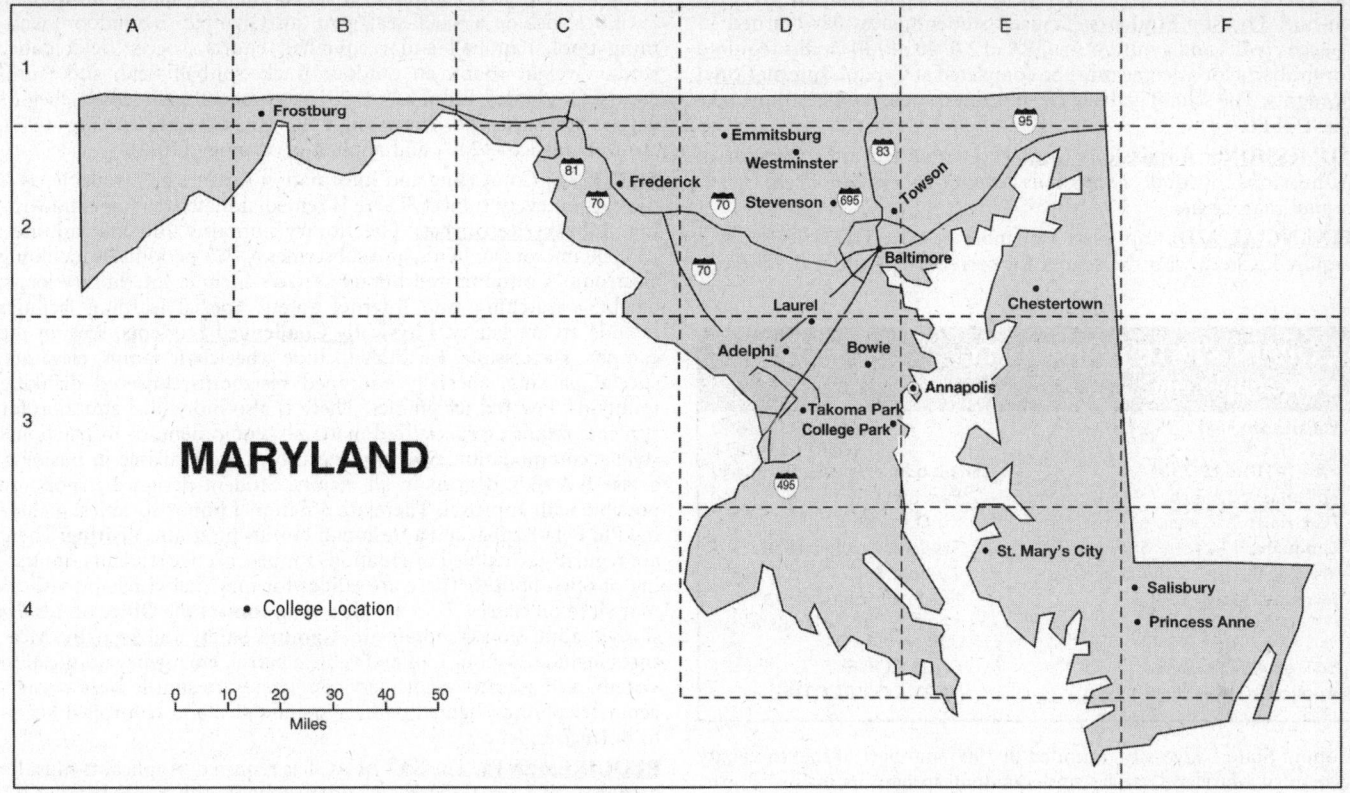

MARYLAND

- College Location

0 10 20 30 40 50
Miles

BOWIE STATE UNIVERSITY (*The complete profile is made available exclusively on our website, www.barronspac.com*)

CAPITOL COLLEGE   D-3
www.capitol-college.edu

Laurel, MD 20708   (301) 369-2800
                                              (800) 950-1992
Fax: (301) 953-1442   Email: admissions@capitol-college.edu

Full-time: 100 men, 40 women	**Faculty:** n/av
Part-time: 130 men, 30 women	**Ph.D.s:** n/av
Graduate: 340 men, 130 women	**Student/Faculty:** n/av
Year: semesters, summer session	**Tuition:** $18,000
Room & Board: $3850	**Freshman Class:** n/av
SAT: required	**CEEB CODE:** 5101
Application Deadline: open	**COMPETITIVE**

Capitol College was founded in 1927 as the Capitol Radio Engineering Institute, a correspondence school. Today it is a private college offering undergraduate programs in engineering and computer technology, as well as graduate programs in management and electronic commerce. There is 1 graduate school. In addition to regional accreditation, Capitol has baccalaureate program accreditation with ABET. The 52-acre campus is in a rural area 19 miles north of Washington, D.C. Including any residence halls, there are 9 buildings.

STUDENT LIFE: 72% of undergraduates are from Maryland. Others are from 16 states, and 21 foreign countries. 43% are White; 39% African American. The average age of freshmen is 23; all undergraduates, 28. 41% do not continue beyond their first year. **Housing:** 100 students can be accommodated in college housing, which includes coed on-campus apartments. On-campus housing is available on a first-come, first-served basis. Priority is given to out-of-town students. 87% of students commute. All students may keep cars.

FACULTY/CLASSROOMS: All teach undergraduates. No introductory courses are taught by graduate students. The average class size in an introductory lecture is 20 and in a regular course is 22.

PROGRAMS OF STUDY: Capitol confers B.S. degrees. Associate and

master's degrees are also awarded. Bachelor's degrees are awarded in COMMUNICATIONS AND THE ARTS (telecommunications), COMPUTER AND PHYSICAL SCIENCE (optics), ENGINEERING AND ENVIRONMENTAL DESIGN (computer engineering, electrical/electronics engineering, and engineering technology). Electrical/electronics engineering is the strongest academically and have the largest enrollments.

ACTIVITIES: There are no fraternities or sororities. There are 17 groups on campus, including chess, computers, literary magazine, newspaper, professional, and student government. Popular campus events include Octoberfest and Spring Bash. **Sports:** Facilities include an off-campus gym, a basketball court, a student center, and an athletic field.

SERVICES: Counseling and information services are available, as is tutoring in most subjects. **Library/Resources:** The library contains 10,000 volumes, and subscribes to 100 periodicals including electronic. Computerized library services include interlibrary loans and database searching. **Physically Challenged Students:** All of the campus is accessible. Facilities include wheelchair ramps, elevators, special parking, specially equipped restrooms, and lowered drinking fountains. **Special:** Internships and work-study programs are offered through the school's cooperative education program. There are 2 national honor societies. **Visiting:** There are regularly scheduled orientations for prospective students. There are guides for informal visits, visitors may sit in on classes, and stay overnight. To schedule a visit, contact the Admissions Office. **Campus Safety and Security:** There are lighted pathways/sidewalks.

REQUIREMENTS: The SAT is required, with a minimum composite score of 860. Applicants should be graduates of an accredited secondary school. The GED is accepted. 20 academic credits or 20 Carnegie units are required. Secondary school courses must include 4 units of English, 3 of math, and 2 each of science and social studies. An essay and an interview are recommended. A GPA of 2.8 is required. AP and CLEP credits are accepted. Important factors in the admissions decision are advanced placement or honors courses, recommendations by school officials, and extracurricular activities record. A minimum GPA of 2.0 and 130 to 137 credit hours are required for graduation. Additional curriculum requirements vary with the major. **Procedure:** Freshmen are admitted to all sessions. Entrance exams should be taken by March 1. There is a rolling admissions plan. Application deadlines are open. Application fee is $25. Applications are accepted on-line. **Transfer Students:** Transfer students must have earned 15 college credits and a minimum GPA of 2.0. 40 of 130 credits required for the bachelor's degree must be completed at Capitol. **International Students:** The school actively recruits these students. They must take the TOEFL.

ADMISSIONS: **Admissions Contact:** Darnell Edwards, Director of Admissions. E-Mail: *admissions@capitol-college.edu* Web: *www.capitol-college.edu*

FINANCIAL AID: Capitol is a member of CSS. The CSS/Profile is required. Check with the school for current application deadlines.

COPPIN STATE UNIVERSITY   D-2
www.coppin.edu

Baltimore, MD 21216	**(410) 951-3600**
	(800) 635-3674
Fax: (410) 523-7351	Email: admissions@coppin.edu
Full-time: 554 men, 1935 women	**Faculty:** 143; IIA, -$
Part-time: 137 men, 616 women	**Ph.D.s:** 55%
Graduate: 174 men, 516 women	**Student/Faculty:** 17 to 1
Year: semesters, summer session	**Tuition:** $6624 ($11,885)
Room & Board: $9603	**Freshman Class:** 5593 applied, 1988 accepted, 632 enrolled
SAT or ACT: required	**CEEB CODE:** 5122
Application Deadline: June 15	**VERY COMPETITIVE**

Coppin State University, founded in 1900 and part of the university system of Maryland, offers undergraduate programs in liberal arts, teacher education, and nursing. There are 5 undergraduate schools and 1 graduate school. In addition to regional accreditation, Coppin has baccalaureate program accreditation with NCATE, NLN, and NCSWE. The 65-acre campus is in an urban area in Baltimore, Maryland. Including any residence halls, there are 13 buildings.

STUDENT LIFE: 90% of undergraduates are from Maryland. Others are from 10 states, 5 foreign countries, and Canada. 90% are from public schools. 86% are African American. The average age of freshmen is 19; all undergraduates, 23. **Housing:** 600 students can be accommodated in college housing, which includes coed dorms. The housing office maintains lists of community housing available. On-campus housing is available on a first-come, first-served basis. 79% of students commute. Alcohol is not permitted. Upperclassmen may keep cars.

FACULTY/CLASSROOMS: 55% of faculty are male; 45% are female. No introductory courses are taught by graduate students. The average class size in a regular course is 25.

PROGRAMS OF STUDY: Coppin confers B.A., B.S. and B.S.N. degrees. Master's degrees are also awarded. Bachelor's degrees are awarded in BIOLOGICAL SCIENCE (biology/biological science), BUSINESS (accounting, business administration and management, management science, and sports management), COMMUNICATIONS AND THE ARTS (English and visual and performing arts), COMPUTER AND PHYSICAL SCIENCE (chemistry, computer science, and mathematics), EDUCATION (elementary education, health information management, and special education), HEALTH PROFESSIONS (health, nursing, and rehabilitation therapy), SOCIAL SCIENCE (applied psychology, criminal justice, history, interdisciplinary studies, international studies, liberal arts/general studies, political science/government, psychology, social science, social work, and urban studies). Business, psychology, criminal justice and nursing are the strongest academically and have the largest enrollments.

ACTIVITIES: 20% of men and 30 of women belong to 5 national fraternities; 27% of women belong to 4 national sororities. There are 35 groups on campus, including art, cheerleading, choir, chorus, computers, dance, drama, ethnic, film, honors, international, marching band, musical theater, newspaper, political, professional, religious, social, social service, and student government. Popular campus events include The Lyceum Series, Honors Program, and Black His-

tory Month. **Sports:** There are 7 intercollegiate sports for men and 7 for women, and 5 intramural sports for men and 5 for women. Facilities include a 4,000-seat gym, an Olympic-size indoor swimming pool, handball and racquetball courts, soccer field, dance studio, weight room, an outdoor track, softball field, and tennis courts. **Graduates:** From July 1, 2013 to June 30, 2014, 484 bachelor's degrees were awarded. The most popular majors were nursing (16%), criminal justice (12%), and applied psychology (10%).

SERVICES: Counseling and information services are available, as is tutoring in every subject. There is remedial math, reading, and writing. **Library/Resources:** The library contains 200,000 volumes, 233,000 microform items, and subscribes to 715 periodicals including electronic. Computerized library services include interlibrary loans, database searching, and Internet access. Special learning facilities include an art gallery. **Physically Challenged Students:** 95% of the campus is accessible. Facilities include wheelchair ramps, elevators, special parking, specially equipped restrooms, lowered drinking fountains, lowered telephones. There is also individual attention for students requiring specialized materials, equipment, or instructional style accommodation. **Special:** Internships are available in business, as are B.A.-B.S. degrees in all majors. Student-designed majors are possible with approval. There are 3 national honor societies, including Phi Beta Kappa, and a freshman honors program. **Visiting:** There are regularly scheduled orientations for prospective students, consisting of open houses. There are guides for informal visits and visitors may sit in on classes. To schedule a visit, contact the Office of Admissions at admissions@coppin.edu. **Campus Safety and Security:** Measures include 24-hour foot and vehicle patrol, emergency notification system, and security escort services. There are shuttle buses, emergency telephones, lighted pathways/sidewalks, and controlled access to dorms/residences.

REQUIREMENTS: The SAT or ACT is required. Applicants must be graduates of an accredited secondary school with a minimum GPA of 2.0 or have a GED certificate. Students must have completed 4 courses in English, 2 courses each in history, math, science, and social studies, and 1 course in foreign language. Up to 15% of a freshman class may be admitted conditionally without these requirements, and those students who graduated high school more than 5 years ago will be reviewed individually. A GPA of 2.5 is required. AP and CLEP credits are accepted. Important factors in the admissions decision are advanced placement or honors courses, extracurricular activities record, and evidence of special talent.To graduate, all students must have a minimum 2.0 GPA and complete a minimum of 120 credit hours (varies by program of study), with 36 to 40 hours in the major. Students must complete about 50 hours of liberal arts courses in English, math, speech, history, health, physical education, natural and social sciences, and philosophy. All seniors must take a standardized exit exam relevant to their major. **Procedure:** Freshmen are admitted to all sessions. There is a rolling admissions plan. Applications should be filed by June 15 for fall entry; December 15 for spring entry. The fall 2014 application fee was $50. Applications are accepted on-line. **Transfer Students:** Transfer students must have a minimum 2.0 GPA and be in good academic standing at their former institutions. Applicants with fewer than 25 credits must meet freshman requirements. 30 of 120 credits required for the bachelor's degree must be completed at Coppin. **International Students:** They must take the TOEFL with a minimum score of 500 on the paper-based TOEFL (PBT). They must also take the SAT or ACT.

ADMISSIONS: 36% of the 2014-2015 applicants were accepted. **Admissions Contact:** Michelle Gross, Director of Admissions. E-Mail: *admissions@coppin.edu* Web: *www.coppin.edu*

FINANCIAL AID: Coppin is a member of CSS. The FAFSA and the college's own financial statement are required. The priority date for freshman financial aid applications for fall entry is March 1.

FROSTBURG STATE UNIVERSITY (*The complete profile is made available exclusively on our website, www.barronspac.com*)

GOUCHER COLLEGE D-2
www.goucher.edu

Baltimore, MD 21204

(410) 337-6100
(800) 468-2437

Fax: (410) 337-6354   Email: admissions@goucher.edu

Full-time: 478 men, 969 women   **Faculty:** 136; IIB, av$

Part-time: 5 men, 19 women   **Ph.D.s:** 89%

Graduate: 135 men, 508 women   **Student/Faculty:** 11 to 1

Year: semesters   **Tuition:** $40,558

Room & Board: $11,482   **Freshman Class:** 3340 applied, 2528 accepted, 403 enrolled

SAT CR/M/W: 590/570/560 **ACT:** 26   **CEEB CODE:** 5257

Application Deadline: February 1   **VERY COMPETITIVE+**

Goucher has been a small college, since 1885, with a big view of the world. The college offers 33 majors and six interdisciplinary areas for undergraduates and nine graduate programs. There is 1 undergraduate school and 1 graduate school. The 287-acre campus is in a suburban area 8 miles north of downtown Baltimore. Including any residence halls, there are 20 buildings.

STUDENT LIFE: 74% of undergraduates are from out of state, mostly the Middle Atlantic. Students are from 47 states, 30 foreign countries, and Canada. 62% are from public schools. 67% are White. The average age of freshmen is 18; all undergraduates, 20. 23% do not continue beyond their first year; 77% remain to graduate. **Housing:** 1227 students can be accommodated in college housing, which includes single-sex and coed dorms and on-campus apartments. In addition, there are language houses, special-interest houses, healthy living house, language house, peace house, art house, and gaming house. On-campus housing is available on a first-come, first-served basis, and is available on a lottery system for upperclassmen. 88% of students live on campus; of those, 80% remain on campus on weekends. All students may keep cars.

FACULTY/CLASSROOMS: 42% of faculty are male; 58% are female. All teach undergraduates. No introductory courses are taught by graduate students. The average class size in an introductory lecture is 18 and in a laboratory is 18.

PROGRAMS OF STUDY: Goucher confers B.A. degrees. Master's degrees are also awarded. Bachelor's degrees are awarded in AGRICULTURE (environmental studies), BIOLOGICAL SCIENCE (biochemistry and biology/biological science), BUSINESS (business administration and management), COMMUNICATIONS AND THE ARTS (art history, art, communications, dance, English, French, music, Russian, Spanish, and theatre arts), COMPUTER AND PHYSICAL SCIENCE (chemistry, computer science, mathematics, and physics), EDUCATION (education and special education), SOCIAL SCIENCE (American studies, anthropology, economics, history, interdisciplinary studies, international relations, peace studies, philosophy, political science/government, psychology, religion, sociology, and women's studies). Biology, chemistry, and history are the strongest academically. Psychology, English, and business management have the largest enrollments.

ACTIVITIES: There are no fraternities or sororities. There are 65 groups on campus, including art, campus agricultural co-op, chorale, chorus, communications, computers, dance, debate, drama, environmental, ethnic, film, gay, honors, international, jazz band, literary magazine, musical theater, newspaper, opera, orchestra, political, professional, radio and TV, religious, social, social service, student government, symphony, and yearbook. Popular campus events include Get into Goucher Day, Spring Gala, Opening Celebration, African-American Heritage Month Programs, Hispanic Heritage Month Programs, **Sports:** There are 9 intercollegiate sports for men and 11 for women, and 4 intramural sports for men and 4 for women. Facilities include 2 gyms, an indoor swimming pool, weight room, training room, cardio fitness center, racquetball, squash, and tennis courts, indoor-outdoor equestrian facilities, an outdoor track, outdoor volleyball court, outdoor basketball court, a disc golf course, nature trails. **Graduates:** From July 1, 2013 to June 30, 2014, 273 bachelor's degrees were awarded. The most popular majors were psychology (12%), communications (10%), and business management

(9%). 67 companies recruited on campus in 2013-2014. In an average class, 51% graduate in 4 years or less, 61% graduate in 5 years or less, and 63% graduate in 6 years or less.

SERVICES: Many academic support options are available through the college's Academic Center for Excellence (ACE). **Library/Resources:** The library contains 362,685 volumes, 22,268 microform items, 18,708 audio/video tapes/CDs/DVDs, and subscribes to 28,000 periodicals including electronic. Computerized library services include interlibrary loans, database searching, Internet access, and Wi-Fi capability. Special learning facilities include an art gallery, radio station, three multi-purpose performance spaces ranging in size from a few hundred to 1,000 seats, a robotics lab, a rooftop observatory providing public observing, advanced teaching labs for physics and computer science, research labs for math, physics, and psychology, a technology/learning center, international technology and media center, and centers for writing, math, and politics. **Physically Challenged Students:** All of the campus is accessible. Facilities include wheelchair ramps, elevators, special parking, specially equipped restrooms, special class scheduling, lowered drinking fountains, special housing. **Special:** Goucher offers internships in Baltimore and Washington D.C., study abroad in 28 countries, and other off-campus experiences. The college also collaborates with many of the 14 other colleges in the Baltimore Collegetown Network. Students may cross-register with Johns Hopkins, Towson University, Peabody Institute, Stevenson University, Coppin State College, University of Maryland Baltimore, University of Maryland Baltimore County, Loyola College, and Maryland Institute College of Art. 3-2 engineering degrees with Johns Hopkins University and Columbia University are offered. Dual majors and student-designed, interdisciplinary majors are an option. There is 1 national honor society, including Phi Beta Kappa. **Visiting:** There are regularly scheduled orientations for prospective students, a multi-day experience introducing students to Goucher, academic life, the campus community, and the Baltimore area. There are guides for informal visits, visitors may sit in on classes, and stay overnight. To schedule a visit, contact the Office of Admissions at admissions@goucher.edu. **Campus Safety and Security:** Measures include 24-hour foot and vehicle patrol, emergency notification system, self-defense education, and security escort services. There are shuttle buses, emergency telephones, lighted pathways/sidewalks, controlled access to dorms/residences, An officer-manned gatehouse during evening and overnight hours, green dot program.

REQUIREMENTS: Applicants should be graduates of an accredited high school or have earned the GED. A personal essay is required, and an interview is recommended. Prospective performing or visual arts majors are urged to seek an audition or submit a portfolio. As an alternative to the traditional Common Application or Universal Application, Goucher has created the Goucher Video Application. AP credits are accepted. Important factors in the admissions decision are extracurricular activities record, recommendations by school officials, and advanced placement or honors courses.To graduate, all students must complete 120 credit hours, with a minimum GPA of 2.00. The number of required hours for each major varies by major. Requirements include; 1 lab-related course in the natural sciences; 1 course each in social sciences, mathematical reasoning, artistic/creative expression, textual analysis/critical perspectives, understanding diverse perspectives, environmental sustainability, and a physical education activity course. Students are also required to demonstrate proficiency in college writing and a foreign language. Other requirements include a study abroad experience, for which students receive a voucher to help offset the cost. First year students attending college full-time for the first time must also complete a transitions course and a Frontiers course. **Procedure:** Freshmen are admitted fall and spring. Entrance exams should be taken in spring of the junior year or fall of the senior year. There are early decision, early admissions, and deferred admissions plans. Early decision applications should be filed by November 15; regular applications, by February 1 for fall entry; and December 1 for spring entry, along with a $55 fee. Notification of early decision is sent December 15; regular decision, April 1. 50 early decision candidates were accepted for the 2014-2015 class. 64 applicants were on the 2014 waiting list; 8 were admitted. Applications are accepted on-line. **Transfer Students:** 38 transfer students enrolled in 2013-2014. An interview, a personal essay, and recommendations from college teachers or counselors are also required, as is a graded paper. 60 of 120 credits required for the bachelor's degree must be completed at Goucher. **International Students:** There are 38 international students enrolled. The school actively recruits these students. They must take the TOEFL with a minimum score of 550 on the paper-based TOEFL (PBT) or 79 on the Internet-based version (iBT).

ADMISSIONS: 76% of the 2014-2015 applicants were accepted. The SAT scores for the 2014-2015 freshman class were: Critical Reading--17% below 500, 36% between 500 and 599, 34% between 600 and 699, and 14% between 700 and 800; Math--23% below 500, 41% between 500 and 599, 30% between 600 and 699, and 6% between 700 and 800; Writing--21% below 500, 42% between 500 and 599, 28% between 600 and 699, and 9% between 700 and 800. The ACT scores were 11% below 21, 13% between 21 and 23, 30% between 24 and 26, 17% between 27 and 28, and 29% above 28. 42% of the current freshmen were in the top fifth of their class; 76% were in the top two fifths. 3 freshmen graduated first in their class. **Admissions Contact:** Carlton E. Surbeck, Director of Admissions. E-Mail: *admissions@goucher.edu* Web: *www.goucher.edu*

FINANCIAL AID: In 2014-2015, 71% of all full-time freshmen and 93% of continuing full-time students received some form of financial aid. 71% of all full-time freshmen and 92% of continuing full-time students received need-based aid. The average freshman award was $26,444. Need-based scholarships or need-based grants averaged $28,191; need-based self-help aid (loans and jobs) averaged $4,667; and other non-need-based awards and non-need-based scholarships averaged $16,099. 63% of undergraduate students work part-time. Average annual earnings from campus work are $2100. The average financial indebtedness of the 2014 graduate was $25,580. Goucher is a member of CSS. The CSS/Profile, FAFSA, and the college's own financial statement are required. The priority date for freshman financial aid applications for fall entry is February 1. The deadline for filing freshman financial aid applications for fall entry is April 1.

HOOD COLLEGE C-2
www.hood.edu/admission

Frederick, MD 21701	(301) 696-3400
	(800) 922-1599
Fax: (301) 696-3819	Email: admission@hood.edu
Full-time: 442 men, 823 women	Faculty: 81; IIA, --$
Part-time: 36 men, 86 women	Ph.D.s: 96%
Graduate: 347 men, 659 women	Student/Faculty: 12 to 1
Year: semesters, summer session	Tuition: $33,280
Room & Board: $11,350	Freshman Class: 1686 applied, 1366 accepted, 281 enrolled
SAT CR/M/W: 520/530/510 ACT: 21	CEEB CODE: 5296
Application Deadline: June 15	COMPETITIVE

Hood College, founded in 1893, is an independent, comprehensive college that offers an integration of the liberal arts and professional preparation, as well as undergraduate majors in the natural sciences. Figures in the above capsule and in this profile are approximate. There is 1 graduate school. In addition to regional accreditation, Hood has baccalaureate program accreditation with AACSB, CSWE, and NCATE. The 50-acre campus is in a suburban area 45 miles northwest of Washington, D.C. and 45 miles west of Baltimore. Including any residence halls, there are 34 buildings.

STUDENT LIFE: 76% of undergraduates are from Maryland. Others are from 30 states, 20 foreign countries, and Canada. 82% are from public schools. 65% are White; 12% African American. 53% claim no religious affiliation; 30% Protestant. **Male To Female Ratio:** 1.9:1. The average age of freshmen is 18; all undergraduates, 22. 22% do not continue beyond their first year; 68% remain to graduate. **Housing:** 828 students can be accommodated in college housing, which includes single-sex and coed dorms and off-campus apartments. In addition, there are honors houses, language houses, special-interest floors in the residence halls include living/learning communities and a community service floor. On-campus housing is guaranteed for all 4 years, is available on a first-come, first-served basis, and is available on a lottery system for upperclassmen. 56% of students live on campus; of those, 65% remain on campus on weekends. All students may keep cars.

FACULTY/CLASSROOMS: 43% of faculty are male; 57% are female. All teach and do research. No introductory courses are taught by graduate students. The average class size in an introductory lecture is 16; in a laboratory is 13; and in a regular course is 14.

PROGRAMS OF STUDY: Hood confers B.A., B.S. and B.S.N degrees. Master's degrees are also awarded. Bachelor's degrees are awarded in BIOLOGICAL SCIENCE (biochemistry and biology/biological science), BUSINESS (business administration and management, management science, and marketing), COMMUNICATIONS AND THE ARTS (art, communications, English, French, German, music, and Spanish), COMPUTER AND PHYSICAL SCIENCE (chemistry, computer science, and mathematics), EDUCATION (early childhood education, elementary education, English education, foreign languages education, mathematics education, science education, secondary education, and special education), ENGINEERING AND ENVIRONMENTAL DESIGN (computational sciences and environmental science), HEALTH PROFESSIONS (nursing), SOCIAL SCIENCE (archeology, economics, history, Latin American studies, law, Middle Eastern studies, philosophy, political science/government, psychology, religion, social work, and sociology). Chemistry, social work and psychology are the strongest academically. Management, psychology, and biology have the largest enrollments.

ACTIVITIES: There are no fraternities or sororities. There are 79 groups on campus, including art, band, cheerleading, choir, chorale, chorus, computers, dance, drama, environmental, ethnic, film, gay, honors, international, jazz band, literary magazine, musical theater, newspaper, orchestra, political, professional, radio and TV, religious, social, social service, and student government. Popular campus events include Ring Formal, Liberation of the Black Mind Weekend, and Crab Fest. **Sports:** There are 8 intercollegiate sports for men and 10 for women, and 4 intramural sports for men and 5 for women. Facilities include an athletic center for intercollegiate, recreational and intramural activites, including men's and women's basketball and volleyball, with two-level fitness center and cardio room, full-service athletic training room, locker rooms, swimming pool and multiuse turf fields (field hockey, soccer, and lacrosse). **Graduates:** From July 1, 2013 to June 30, 2014, 317 bachelor's degrees were awarded. The most popular majors were education (14%), psychology (13%), and biology (10%). 110 companies recruited on campus in 2013-2014. In an average class, 2% graduate in 3 years or less, 54% graduate in 4 years or less, 66% graduate in 5 years or less, and 68% graduate in 6 years or less. Of the 2013 graduating class, 45% were enrolled in graduate school within 6 months of graduation, and 84% were employed.

SERVICES: Counseling and information services are available, as is tutoring in some subjects. There are readers for the blind and interpreters for the hearing impaired. There is remedial math and writing. There are also services for students with learning disabilities, a language lab, and courses in time management and study skills. **Library/Resources:** The library contains 214,180 volumes, 734,910 microform items, 7,726 audio/video tapes/CDs/DVDs, and subscribes to 24,926 periodicals including electronic. Computerized library services include interlibrary loans, database searching, Internet access, and Wi-Fi capability. Special learning facilities include an art gallery, radio station, aquatic center, a child development lab, an observatory, and information technology center. **Physically Challenged Students:** 50% of the campus is accessible. Facilities include wheelchair ramps, elevators, special parking, specially equipped restrooms, special class scheduling, and special housing. **Special:** The college offers a Washington semester with American University, dual majors, student-designed majors, a B.A.-B.S. degree in engineering/math, credit for life experience, nondegree study, pass/fail options, and cross-registration with area colleges and the Duke University Marine Sciences Education Consortium. Internships of up to 15 credits are available in all majors at more than 100 sites throughout the United States and abroad. Students may study abroad in the Dominican Republic, Japan, Spain, France, and other countries. There is a 4-year honors program featuring 1 interdisciplinary course per semester and special co-curricular activities. There are 16 national honor societies, a freshman honors program, and 8 departmental honors programs. **Visiting:** There are regularly scheduled orientations for prospective students, including tours and meetings with faculty, students, and administrators; and admissions interviews. There are guides for informal visits, visitors may sit in on classes, and stay overnight. To schedule a visit, contact Lisa Troth at admission@hood.edu. **Campus Safety and Security:** Measures include 24-hour foot and vehicle patrol, emergency notification system, self-defense education, and security escort services. There are emergency telephones, lighted pathways/sidewalks, and controlled access to dorms/residences.

REQUIREMENTS: The SAT or ACT is required. Applicants should be graduates of an accredited secondary school. The GED is accepted. Hood recommends the completion of at least 16 academic credits in high school, including courses in English, social sciences, natural sciences, foreign languages, and math. Hood College is SAT Optional for students with a high school GPA of 3.25 or higher on a 4.0 scale. A GPA of 2.5 is required. AP and CLEP credits are accepted. Important factors in the admissions decision are advanced placement or honors courses, leadership record, and extracurricular activities record. To graduate, students must complete a total of 124 credit hours, with a minimum GPA of 2.0, and a 2.0 GPA in the major. 24 to 52 credits are required in a student's major. All students must complete 42 to 48 credits in the core curriculum, which includes English, math, and language courses, courses in methods of inquiry, and interdisciplinary courses in Western civilization, non-Western civilization and society, science, and technology. Phys ed courses are also required. Enrollment in the final 30 credits must be on the Hood Campus as a degree candidate. **Procedure:** Freshmen are admitted fall and spring. Entrance exams should be taken in spring of the junior year or fall of the senior year. There are early decision, early admissions, deferred admissions, and rolling admissions plans. Early decision applications should be filed by November 1; regular applications, by June 15 for fall entry; and December 31 for spring entry, along with a $35 fee. Notification of early decision is sent November 15; regular decision, March 1. 15 early decision candidates were accepted for the 2014-2015 class. Applications are accepted on-line. Application fees are waived if application is completed on-line. **Transfer Students:** 119 transfer students enrolled in 2013-2014. Applicants must have at least 12 college credits and a minimum GPA of 2.5. A total of 70 credits may be transferred. 30 of 124 credits required for the bachelor's degree must be completed at Hood. **International Students:** There are 36 international students enrolled. The school actively recruits these students. They must take the TOEFL with a minimum score of 550 on the paper-based TOEFL (PBT) or 79 on the Internet-based version (iBT), or take the IELTS. They must also take the SAT or ACT. SAT scores may be substituted for the TOEFL.

ADMISSIONS: 81% of the 2014-2015 applicants were accepted. The SAT scores for the 2014-2015 freshman class were: Critical Reading--39% below 500, 40% between 500 and 599, 19% between 600 and 699, and 2% between 700 and 800; Math--38% below 500, 40% between 500 and 599, 21% between 600 and 699, and 2% between 700 and 800; Writing--43% below 500, 43% between 500 and 599, 13% between 600 and 699, and 1% between 700 and 800. The ACT scores were 48% below 21, 19% between 21 and 23, 22% between 24 and 26, 7% between 27 and 28, and 4% above 28. 35% of the current freshmen were in the top fifth of their class; 66% were in the top two fifths. 1 freshman graduated first in the class. **Admissions Contact:** Terry Whittum, Vice President for Enrollment Management. E-Mail: *admission@hood.edu* Web: *www.hood.edu/admission*

FINANCIAL AID: In 2014-2015, 99% of all full-time freshmen and 98% of continuing full-time students received some form of financial aid. 85% of all full-time freshmen and 85% of continuing full-time students received need-based aid. The average freshman award was $26,703. Need-based scholarships or need-based grants averaged $23,480; need-based self-help aid (loans and jobs) averaged $6,202; and other non-need-based awards and non-need-based scholarships averaged $18,539. 24% of undergraduate students work part-time. Average annual earnings from campus work are $2000. The average financial indebtedness of the 2014 graduate was $26,890. Hood is a member of CSS. The FAFSA is required. The priority date for freshman financial aid applications for fall entry is February 15.

JOHNS HOPKINS UNIVERSITY   D-2
www.jhu.edu

Baltimore, MD 21218   (410) 516-8341

Fax: (410) 516-6025   Email: gotojhu@jhu.edu
Full-time: 2388 men, 2173 women   **Faculty:** 447
Part-time: 25 men, 5 women   **Ph.D.s:** 92%
Graduate: 1022 men, 644 women   **Student/Faculty:** 10 to 1
Year: 4-1-4, summer session   **Tuition:** $36,400
Room & Board: $11,092   **Freshman Class:** 14848
                                        applied, 3603 accepted,
                                        1206 enrolled
SAT CR/M/W: 680/710/680 **ACT:** 31 **CEEB CODE:** 5532
Application Deadline: January 1   **MOST COMPETITIVE**

Johns Hopkins University, founded in 1876, is a private multicampus institution offering undergraduate degrees at the Homewood campus through the Zanvyl Krieger School of Arts and Sciences, the Whiting School of Engineering, and the Peabody Institute (music). There are 5 undergraduate schools and 8 graduate schools. In addition to regional accreditation, Johns Hopkins has baccalaureate program accreditation with ABET. The 140-acre campus is in a suburban area in a residential setting in northern Baltimore. Including any residence halls, there are 40 buildings.

STUDENT LIFE: 85% of undergraduates are from out of state, mostly the Middle Atlantic. Students are from 50 states, 49 foreign countries, and Canada. 60% are from public schools. 46% are White; 24% Asian American. The average age of freshmen is 18; all undergraduates, 20. 3% do not continue beyond their first year; 93% remain to graduate. **Housing:** 2700 students can be accommodated in college housing, which includes single-sex and coed dorms, on-campus apartments, and off-campus apartments. In addition, there are special-interest houses, Non-university-sponsored fraternity and sorority houses. On-campus housing is available on a lottery system for upperclassmen. 61% of students live on campus. Upperclassmen may keep cars.

FACULTY/CLASSROOMS: 72% of faculty are male; 28% are female. No introductory courses are taught by graduate students.

PROGRAMS OF STUDY: Johns Hopkins confers B.A. and B.S. degrees. Master's and Doctoral degrees are also awarded. Bachelor's degrees are awarded in BIOLOGICAL SCIENCE (biology/biological science, biophysics, cell biology, molecular biology, and neurosciences), COMMUNICATIONS AND THE ARTS (art history and appreciation, classics, creative writing, English, French, German, Italian, media arts, romance languages and literature, and Spanish), COMPUTER AND PHYSICAL SCIENCE (applied mathematics, chemistry, computer science, earth science, mathematics, natural sciences, and physics), ENGINEERING AND ENVIRONMENTAL DESIGN (biomedical engineering, chemical engineering, civil engineering, computer engineering, electrical/electronics engineering, engineering, engineering mechanics, environmental engineering, environmental science, materials engineering, materials science, and mechanical engineering), SOCIAL SCIENCE (African studies, anthropology, cognitive science, East Asian studies, economics, history, history of science, humanities, interdisciplinary studies, international studies, Latin American studies, Near Eastern studies, philosophy, political science/government, psychology, social science, and sociology). International studies, public health studies, and biomedical engineering have the largest enrollments.

ACTIVITIES: 24% of men belong to 11 national fraternities; 23% of women belong to 7 national sororities. There are 250 groups on campus, including art, band, cheerleading, chess, choir, chorale, chorus, computers, dance, debate, drama, ethnic, film, forensics, gay, honors, international, jazz band, literary magazine, marching band, musical theater, newspaper, opera, orchestra, pep band, photography, political, professional, radio and TV, religious, social, social service, student government, symphony, and volunteer organizations. Popular campus events include Culturefest, Fall Fest, and Spring Fair. **Sports:** There are 14 intercollegiate sports for men and 12 for women, and 20 intramural sports for men and 20 for women. Facilities include a recreation center with a swimming pool and diving pool, wrestling and fencing rooms, varsity weight room, fitness center, saunas, climbing wall, an indoor jogging track, and courts for basketball, badminton, squash, volleyball and handball. There is also a 4000-seat stadium, outdoor playing fields, and tennis courts. **Graduates:** From July 1, 2013 to June 30, 2014, 1004 bachelor's degrees were awarded. The most popular majors were biomedical engineering (11%), international studies (10%), and public health studies (9%). 224 companies recruited on campus in 2013-2014. In an average class, 3% graduate in 3 years or less, 83% graduate in 4 years or less, 91% graduate in 5 years or less, and 92% graduate in 6 years or less. Of the 2013 graduating class, 38% were enrolled in graduate school within 6 months of graduation, and 47% were employed.

SERVICES: Counseling and information services are available, as is tutoring in most subjects. There is a reader service for the blind. **Library/Resources:** The 4 libraries contain 2.6 million volumes, 4.1 million microform items, 9,707 audio/video tapes/CDs/DVDs, and subscribe to 30,120 periodicals including electronic. Computerized library services include interlibrary loans, database searching, Internet access, and Wi-Fi capability. Special learning facilities include an art gallery, radio station, and a space telescope science institute. **Physically Challenged Students:** Facilities include wheelchair ramps, elevators, special parking, specially equipped restrooms, special class scheduling, lowered drinking fountains, lowered telephones. JHU works with all individuals to ensure access to all programs. Also, existing housing is accommodated as needed. **Special:** Internships, dual majors in music and arts and sciences/engineering, cross-registration with Baltimore-area colleges and Johns Hopkins divisions, a cooperative double degree with Peabody Conservatory of Music, a student-designed semester at the Johns Hopkins School of International Studies in Washington, D.C., and various multidisciplinary programs are offered. Students may enroll at Johns Hopkins in Bologna, Italy, or Nanjing, China, or arrange programs in Europe, South America, the Far East, or Australia. Students may earn combined B.A.-B.S. degrees in physics, computer science, applied math, and statistics. There are 4 national honor societies, including Phi Beta Kappa, and 25 departmental honors programs. **Visiting:** There are regularly scheduled orientations for prospective students, including scheduled open house programs, campus tours and group information sessions offered weekday mornings and afternoons, and individual day visits with a current student. There are guides for informal visits, visitors may sit in on classes, and stay overnight. To schedule a visit, contact the Office of Undergraduate Admissions. **Campus Safety and Security:** Measures include 24-hour foot and vehicle patrol, emergency notification system, self-defense education, and security escort services. There are shuttle buses, emergency telephones, and lighted pathways/sidewalks.

REQUIREMENTS: The SAT or ACT is required. Freshman applicants must take either the SAT or the ACT with Writing. For those submitting SAT scores, Johns Hopkins recommends that applicants also submit 3 SAT subject trests. In addition, applicants should be graduates of an accredited secondary school or have the GED. The university recommends that secondary preparation include 4 years each of English and math, 2 (prefer 3) of social science or history and lab science, and 3 to 4 of a foreign language (2 for engineering majors). 2 personal essays are required, and an interview is recommended. AP credits are accepted. Important factors in the admissions decision are advanced placement or honors courses, extracurricular activities record, and personality/intangible qualities. Although there is no required core curriculum, all students must take 40 hours in the major and 30 hours outside their major field. The B.A. requires a total of 120 hours; the B.S. in engineering requires 120 to 128 hours, depending on the major. A GPA of at least 2.0 is required for graduation. All students must take at least 4 courses (2 for engineers) with a writing-intensive component to graduate. **Procedure:** Freshmen are admitted fall. Entrance exams should be taken by December for regular decision, or November for early decision. There are early decision and deferred admissions plans. Early decision applications should be filed by November 1; regular applications, by January 1 for fall entry, along with a $70 fee. Notification of early decision is sent December 15; regular decision, April 1. 447 early decision candidates were accepted for the 2014-2015 class. 1319 applicants were on the 2014 waiting list; 446 were admitted. Applications are accepted on-line. **Transfer Students:** 36 transfer students enrolled in 2013-2014. Appli-

cants should have sophomore or junior standing and at least a B average in previous college work. Applications must include a written essay and at least 1 letter of recommendation. High school records are also required. 60 of 120 credits required for the bachelor's degree must be completed at Johns Hopkins. **International Students:** There are 290 international students enrolled. The school actively recruits these students. They must take the TOEFL with a minimum score of 600 on the paper-based TOEFL (PBT). They must also take the SAT or ACT.

ADMISSIONS: 24% of the 2014-2015 applicants were accepted. The SAT scores for the 2014-2015 freshman class were: Critical Reading--1% below 500, 11% between 500 and 599, 51% between 600 and 699, and 37% between 700 and 800; Math--7% between 500 and 599, 39% between 600 and 699, and 53% between 700 and 800; Writing--13% between 500 and 599, 51% between 600 and 699, and 35% between 700 and 800. The ACT scores were 2% between 21 and 23, 13% between 24 and 26, 11% between 27 and 28, and 74% above 28. 92% of the current freshmen were in the top fifth of their class; 98% were in the top two fifths. 81 freshmen graduated first in their class. **Admissions Contact:** Dr. John Latting, Director of Undergraduate Admissions. E-Mail: *gotojhu@jhu.edu* Web: *www.jhu.edu*

FINANCIAL AID: Johns Hopkins is a member of CSS. The CSS/Profile and FAFSA are required. The deadline for filing freshman financial aid applications for fall entry is March 1.

LOYOLA UNIVERSITY MARYLAND   D-2
www.loyola.edu

Baltimore, MD 21210   (410) 617-5012
                                 (800) 221-9107

Fax: n/av	Email: admission@loyola.edu
Full-time: 1691 men, 2344 women	Faculty: n/av
Part-time: 21 men, 28 women	Ph.Ds: n/av
Graduate: 589 men, 1294 women	Student/Faculty: 12 to 1
Year: semesters, summer session	Tuition: $44,090
Room & Board: $12,790	Freshman Class: 13863 applied, 8266 accepted, 1137 enrolled
SAT CR/M: 591/599 ACT: 27	CEEB CODE: 5379
Application Deadline: January 15	VERY COMPETITIVE+

A Catholic, Jesuit comprehensive university in Baltimore, Loyola University Maryland is committed to the ideals of liberal education and the development of the whole person, a university dedicated to inspiring its students to learn, lead and serve in a diverse and changing world. There are 3 undergraduate schools and 3 graduate schools. In addition to regional accreditation, has baccalaureate program accreditation with AACSB, ABET, CSAB, NASDTEC, NCATE, and MSHEC. The 89-acre campus is in an urban area 3 miles from downtown Baltimore. Including any residence halls, there are 51 buildings.

STUDENT LIFE: 83% of undergraduates are from out of state, mostly the Middle Atlantic. 78% are White. **Housing:** 3291 students can be accommodated in college housing, which includes single-sex and coed dorms and on-campus apartments. In addition, there are honors houses and special-interest houses. On-campus housing is guaranteed for the freshman year only, is available on a first-come, first-served basis, and is available on a lottery system for upperclassmen. Upperclassmen may keep cars.

FACULTY/CLASSROOMS: 51% of faculty are male; 49% are female. All teach undergraduates. No introductory courses are taught by graduate students.

PROGRAMS OF STUDY: confers B.A., B.S., B.B.A. and B.S.E. degrees. Master's and Doctoral degrees are also awarded. Bachelor's degrees are awarded in BIOLOGICAL SCIENCE (biology/biological science), BUSINESS (accounting and business administration and management), COMMUNICATIONS AND THE ARTS (communications, creative writing, English, fine arts, French, German, Latin, and Spanish), COMPUTER AND PHYSICAL SCIENCE (chemistry, computer science, mathematics, and physics), EDUCATION (elementary education), ENGINEERING AND ENVIRONMENTAL DESIGN (engineering), HEALTH PROFESSIONS (speech pathology/

audiology), SOCIAL SCIENCE (classical/ancient civilization, economics, history, philosophy, political science/government, psychology, sociology, and theological studies). General business, communication and social sciences have the largest enrollments.

ACTIVITIES: There are no fraternities or sororities. There are 194 groups on campus, including art, band, cheerleading, chess, choir, chorale, chorus, computers, dance, drama, ethnic, film, gay, honors, international, jazz band, literary magazine, musical theater, newspaper, orchestra, pep band, photography, political, professional, radio and TV, religious, social, social service, student government, symphony, and yearbook. Popular campus events include Modern Masters Series, Humanities Symposium, Loyolapalooza, International Festival, Evergreen Players, ChordBusters, Luna Fest, Poisened Cup Players, Bull and Oyster Roast. **Sports:** There are 8 intercollegiate sports for men and 9 for women, and 8 intramural sports for men and 8 for women. Facilities include the Ridley Athletic Complex which is home of Loyola's NCAA Division I men's and women's lacrosse and soccer teams. It features a 6,000-seat grandstand, Sportexe Momentum field, a video scoreboard, practice field, training facilities, and locker rooms. FAC's signature natatorium, Mangione aquatic center, stretches eight lanes across its 25-yard length and 75-foot width. Other FAC highlights include a 30-foot indoor climbing wall, a 6,000-square foot fitness center with more than 70 pieces of fitness machinery, an elevated indoor track, four racquetball and two squash courts, two areobic/martial arts studios, a three-court gymnasium and a multi-activity court with rounded corners and plexi-glass walls for indoor soccer and floor hockey. **Graduates:** From July 1, 2013 to June 30, 2014, 903 bachelor's degrees were awarded. The most popular majors were business/marketing (32%), communications/journalism (12%), and psychology (9%). 94 companies recruited on campus in 2013-2014. In an average class, 79% graduate in 4 years or less, 5% graduate in 5 years or less, and 84% graduate in 6 years or less. Of the 2013 graduating class, 25% were enrolled in graduate school within 6 months of graduation, and 26% were employed.

SERVICES: Counseling and information services are available, as is tutoring in most subjects. There is a reader service for the blind, and remedial math. **Library/Resources:** The library contains 1.1 million volumes, 691 microform items, 19,086 audio/video tapes/CDs/DVDs, and subscribes to 56,888 periodicals including electronic. Computerized library services include interlibrary loans, database searching, and Internet access. Special learning facilities include an art gallery, radio station, and TV station. **Physically Challenged Students:** 99% of the campus is accessible. Facilities include wheelchair ramps, elevators, special parking, specially equipped restrooms, special class scheduling, lowered drinking fountains, and lowered telephones. **Special:** Loyola offers cross-registration with Johns Hopkins, Towson, and Morgan State Universities, Goucher College, the College of Notre Dame, Maryland Art Institute, and Peabody Conservatory. Credit-bearing internships are available in most majors and study abroad is possible in 27 countries. Work-study programs and dual majors are also offered. **Visiting:** There are regularly scheduled orientations for prospective students. We offer daily visits on most weekdays, Monday through Friday. Reservations are required. The visit lasts approximately 2.5 to 3 hours and includes a group information session, a campus tour, and an interview (optional). There are guides for informal visits and visitors may sit in on classes. To schedule a visit, contact the Admission Office. **Campus Safety and Security:** Measures include 24-hour foot and vehicle patrol, emergency notification system, self-defense education, and security escort services. There are shuttle buses, emergency telephones, lighted pathways/sidewalks, and controlled access to dorms/residences.

REQUIREMENTS: Loyola University is test optional. SAT and ACT are considered if submitted. All applicants should have graduated from an accredited secondary school or have earned the GED. Secondary preparation should include 4 years of English, 4 each of math, foreign language, and natural science, and 2 to 3 of history. AP and CLEP credits are accepted. Important factors in the admissions decision are advanced placement or honors courses, recommendations by school officials, and extracurricular activities record. All students must complete 120 hours, including 36 in the major, with at least a 2.0 GPA. The required core curriculum includes 2 courses each in history, language (at the second-year level), literature, philosophy,

social sciences, and theology; 1 course each in composition, ethics, fine arts, math, humanities, and natural sciences; and 1 additional course in math, natural science, or computer science. **Procedure:** Freshmen are admitted fall, spring, and summer. Entrance exams should be taken by December of the senior year. There are early admissions, deferred admissions, and rolling admissions plans. Early decision applications should be filed by November 1; regular applications, by January 15 for fall entry, along with a $50 fee. Notification of early decision is sent January 15; regular decision, March 15. Applications are accepted on-line. **Transfer Students:** 60 of 120 credits required for the bachelor's degree must be completed at Loyola. **International Students:** There are 22 international students enrolled. The school actively recruits these students. They must take the TOEFL with a minimum score of 550 on the paper-based TOEFL (PBT) or 79 on the Internet-based version (iBT).

ADMISSIONS: 60% of the 2014-2015 applicants were accepted. The SAT scores for the 2014-2015 freshman class were: Critical Reading--4% below 500, 51% between 500 and 599, 39% between 600 and 699, and 6% between 700 and 800; Math--6% below 500, 40% between 500 and 599, 48% between 600 and 699, and 6% between 700 and 800. **Admissions Contact:** Office of Admission E-Mail: *admission@loyola.edu* Web: *www.loyola.edu*

FINANCIAL AID: The CSS/Profile, FAFSA, and if applicable, a non-custodial parent's profile are required. The priority date for freshman financial aid applications for fall entry is February 15. The deadline for filing freshman financial aid applications for fall entry is February 15.

MARYLAND INSTITUTE COLLEGE OF ART *(The complete profile is made available exclusively on our website, www.barronspac.com)*

MCDANIEL COLLEGE   D-2
www.mcdaniel.edu/undergraduate

Westminster, MD 21157	(410) 857-2230
	(800) 638-5005
Fax: 410857-2757	Email: admissions@mcdaniel.edu
Full-time: 777 men, 881 women	Faculty: 107; IIB, av$
Part-time: 16 men, 18 women	Ph.D.s: 99%
Graduate: 373 men, 1191 women	Student/Faculty: 11 to 1
Year: 4-1-4, summer session	Tuition: $36,960
Room & Board: $8640	Freshman Class: 2942 applied, 2232 accepted, 453 enrolled
SAT CR/M: 550/555 ACT: 24	CEEB CODE: 5898
Application Deadline: February 15	VERY COMPETITIVE

McDaniel College, founded in 1867, is a four-year private college of the liberal arts and sciences offering more than 70 undergraduate programs of study, including dual and student-designed majors, plus highly regarded graduate and professional studies programs. McDaniel is the only American university with a European campus in Budapest, Hungary. The figures in the above capsule and in this profile are approximate. There is 1 undergraduate school and 1 graduate school. In addition to regional accreditation, McDaniel has baccalaureate program accreditation with CSWE and NCATE. The 160-acre campus is in a suburban area 30 miles from Baltimore's Inner Harbor and 60 miles from Washington, D.C. Including any residence halls, there are 73 buildings.

STUDENT LIFE: 64% of undergraduates are from Maryland. Others are from 39 states, 25 foreign countries, and Canada. 80% are from public schools. 74% are White; 13% African American. The average age of freshmen is 18; all undergraduates, 20. 16% do not continue beyond their first year; 72% remain to graduate.

FACULTY/CLASSROOMS: 44% of faculty are male; 56% are female. All teach undergraduates, and 50% do both. No introductory courses are taught by graduate students. The average class size in an introductory lecture is 18; in a laboratory is 17; and in a regular course is 15.

PROGRAMS OF STUDY: McDaniel confers B.A. degrees. Master's degrees are also awarded. Bachelor's degrees are awarded in BIOLOGICAL SCIENCE (biology/biological science), BUSINESS (business administration and management), COMMUNICATIONS AND THE ARTS (art history and appreciation, communications, dramatic arts, English, fine arts, French, German, music, and Spanish), COMPUTER AND PHYSICAL SCIENCE (chemistry, computer science, mathematics, and physics), EDUCATION (physical education), ENGINEERING AND ENVIRONMENTAL DESIGN (environmental science), SOCIAL SCIENCE (asian studies, economics, history, Middle Eastern studies, philosophy, political science/government, psychology, religion, social work, and sociology). Psychology, health and physical education/fitness, business administration, and biology have the largest enrollments.

ACTIVITIES: 17% of men belong to 1 local and 3 national fraternities; 18% of women belong to 1 local and 5 national sororities. There are 100 groups on campus, including Green Terror Productions, Heroes Helping Hopkins, Outdoors Club, Ultimate Frisbee, various ethnic and cultural student organizations, art, band, Canine Companions for Independence, cheerleading, choir, chorale, chorus, computers, dance, drama, environmental, ethnic, film, forensics, gay, honors, international, jazz band, literary magazine, musical theater, newspaper, opera, orchestra, pep band, photography, political, professional, radio and TV, religious, social, social service, student government, symphony, and yearbook. Popular campus events include Homecoming, Late Night Carnival, Fall Fest, Midnight Madness, Cultural Dinners, Spring Fling, Relay for Life, and Improv performances.

SERVICES: Counseling and information services are available, as is tutoring in most subjects. There is a reader service for the blind, and remedial math, reading, and writing. The library contains 222,268 volumes, 1.4 million microform items, 24,477 audio/video tapes/CDs/DVDs, and subscribes to 717 periodicals including electronic. Computerized library services include interlibrary loans, database searching, Internet access, and Wi-Fi capability. Special learning facilities include an art gallery, radio station, TV station, Observatory, Human Performance Lab, Video Production Lab, Photography Studio, Graphics Lab, and student research science labs.

REQUIREMENTS: The SAT or ACT is required. Applicants must be graduates of an accredited secondary school or have a GED. A minimum of 16 academic credits are required, including 4 years of English, 3 each of foreign language, math, and social studies, and 3 of a lab science. SAT Subject Tests and an interview are recommended. An essay and academic recommendations are required. McDaniel requires applicants to be in the upper 50% of their class. A GPA of 2.5 is required. AP and CLEP credits are accepted. Important factors in the admissions decision are advanced placement or honors courses, leadership record, and evidence of special talent.

ADMISSIONS: 76% of the 2013-2014 applicants were accepted. The SAT scores for the 2013-2014 freshman class were: Critical Reading--25% below 500, 48% between 500 and 599, 22% between 600 and 699, and 5% between 700 and 800; Math--25% below 500, 44% between 500 and 599, 28% between 600 and 699, and 3% between 700 and 800. The ACT scores were 3% below 21, 38% between 21 and 23, and 13% above 28. There were 1 National Merit finalists. 18 freshmen graduated first in their class.

FINANCIAL AID: In 2013-2014, 76% of all full-time freshmen and 73% of continuing full-time students received some form of financial aid. 76% of all full-time freshmen and 72% of continuing full-time students received need-based aid. The average freshman award was $30,159. Need-based scholarships or need-based grants averaged $26,171; need-based self-help aid (loans and jobs) averaged $4,209; other non-need-based awards and non-need-based scholarships averaged $17,064; and $3,351 from other forms of aid. 18% of undergraduate students work part-time. Average annual earnings from campus work are $768. The average financial indebtedness of the 2013 graduate was $29,554. The FAFSA and the college's own financial statement are required. The priority date for freshman financial aid applications for fall entry is March 1.

MORGAN STATE UNIVERSITY   D-2
www.morgan.edu

Baltimore, MD 21251	**(443) 885-3000**
	(800) 332-6674
Fax: (443) 319-3684	**Email:** Admissions@morgan.edu
Full-time: 2522 men, 3272 women	**Faculty:** n/av
Part-time: 341 men, 456 women	**Ph.D.s:** 80%
Graduate: 516 men, 845 women	**Student/Faculty:** n/av
Year: semesters, summer session	**Tuition:** $6500 ($14,500)
Room & Board: $8000	**Freshman Class:** 5644 applied, 3252 accepted, 1037 enrolled
SAT or ACT: required	**CEEB CODE:** 5416
Application Deadline: n/av	**VERY COMPETITIVE**

Morgan State University, founded in 1867, is a comprehensive public institution offering undergraduate and graduate programs leading to liberal arts, preprofessional, and professional degrees. Figures in the above capsule and in this profile are approximate. There are 6 undergraduate schools and 4 graduate schools. In addition to regional accreditation, Morgan State has baccalaureate program accreditation with AACSB, ABET, ADA, ASLA, CSWE, NAAB, NASAD, NASM, and NCATE. The 140-acre campus is in a suburban area in the northeast corner of Baltimore. Including any residence halls, there are 41 buildings.

STUDENT LIFE: 60% of undergraduates are from Maryland. Others are from 40 states, 20 foreign countries, and Canada. 91% are from public schools. 92% are African American. The average age of freshmen is 18; all undergraduates, 21. 24% do not continue beyond their first year; 45% remain to graduate. **Housing:** 1800 students can be accommodated in college housing, which includes single-sex dorms and on-campus apartments. In addition, there are honors houses. On-campus housing is guaranteed for the freshman year only, is available on a first-come, first-served basis. 70% of students commute. Alcohol is not permitted. All students may keep cars.

FACULTY/CLASSROOMS: 60% of faculty are male; 40% are female. All teach undergraduates, 76% do research, and 76% do both. No introductory courses are taught by graduate students. The average class size in an introductory lecture is 25; in a laboratory is 26; and in a regular course is 21.

PROGRAMS OF STUDY: Morgan State confers B.A., B.S., A.B. and B.S.Ed. degrees. Master's and Doctoral degrees are also awarded. Bachelor's degrees are awarded in BIOLOGICAL SCIENCE (biology/biological science), BUSINESS (accounting, business administration and management, hospitality management services, and marketing/retailing/merchandising), COMMUNICATIONS AND THE ARTS (dramatic arts, English, fine arts, music, speech/debate/rhetoric, and telecommunications), COMPUTER AND PHYSICAL SCIENCE (chemistry, computer science, information sciences and systems, mathematics, and physics), EDUCATION (elementary education, health education, and physical education), ENGINEERING AND ENVIRONMENTAL DESIGN (civil engineering, electrical/electronics engineering, engineering physics, and industrial engineering technology), HEALTH PROFESSIONS (medical laboratory technology and mental health/human services), SOCIAL SCIENCE (African American studies, economics, history, home economics, philosophy, political science/government, psychology, religion, social work, and sociology). Engineering, chemistry and social work are the strongest academically. Business administration, accounting and electrical engineering have the largest enrollments.

ACTIVITIES: 4% of men belong to 2 local and 4 national fraternities; 3% of women belong to 3 local and 4 national sororities. There are 150 groups on campus, including art, band, cheerleading, chess, choir, chorale, chorus, computers, dance, debate, drama, drill team, drum and bugle corps, ethnic, film, forensics, gay, honors, international, jazz band, literary magazine, marching band, musical theater, newspaper, opera, orchestra, pep band, photography, political, professional, radio and TV, religious, social, social service, student government, symphony, and yearbook. Popular campus events include Kwanzaa and I Love Morgan Day. **Sports:** There are 6 intercollegiate sports for men and 6 for women, and 17 intramural sports for men and 16 for women. Facilities include a field house, gym, weight room, swimming pool, tennis and racquetball courts, and various playing fields. **Graduates:** From July 1, 2013 to June 30, 2014, 899 bachelor's degrees were awarded. The most popular majors were business/marketing (23%), communication/journalism (12%), and engineering (10%). 79 companies recruited on campus in 2013-2014. In an average class, 12% graduate in 4 years or less, 34% graduate in 5 years or less, and 41% graduate in 6 years or less. Of the 2013 graduating class, 47% were enrolled in graduate school within 6 months of graduation, and 89% were employed.

SERVICES: Counseling and information services are available, as is tutoring in every subject. There is a reader service for the blind, and remedial math, reading, and writing. There are also note takers and sign language interpreters for disabled students. **Library/Resources:** The library contains 389,516 volumes, 738,311 microform items, 45,855 audio/video tapes/CDs/DVDs, and subscribes to 3,011 periodicals including electronic. Computerized library services include interlibrary loans and database searching. Special learning facilities include an art gallery, radio station, and TV station. **Physically Challenged Students:** 90% of the campus is accessible. Facilities include wheelchair ramps, elevators, special parking, specially equipped restrooms, special class scheduling, and lowered drinking fountains. **Special:** Co-op programs in public and private institutions may be arranged for pharmacy honors, predentistry, premedicine, and special education students. The university also offers internships for juniors and seniors, study abroad in 3 countries, work-study programs, and preprofessional physical therapy and prelaw programs. Dual majors may be pursued but do not lead to a dual degree. There are 28 national honor societies and a freshman honors program. **Visiting:** There are regularly scheduled orientations for prospective students, including placement testing and academic advising. There are guides for informal visits, visitors may sit in on classes, and stay overnight.. **Campus Safety and Security:** Measures include 24-hour foot and vehicle patrol, self-defense education, and security escort services. There are shuttle buses, emergency telephones, and lighted pathways/sidewalks.

REQUIREMENTS: The SAT or ACT is required. Applicants should be high school graduates or have earned the GED, and are encouraged to have 4 years of English, 3 of math, 2 each of science, social studies, and history, and 1 of a foreign language. A personal essay is recommended and, when appropriate, an audition. A GPA of 2.5 is required. AP and CLEP credits are accepted. Important factors in the admissions decision are recommendations by school officials, evidence of special talent, and parents or siblings attended your school. To graduate, students must complete at least 120 credit hours, including 74 in the major, with a 2.0 GPA. All students must pass speech and writing proficiency exams prior to their senior year. The 46-credit general education requirement includes courses in English, humanities, logic, history, behavioral science, science, math, African American history, and health and phys ed. Seniors must pass a proficiency exam in their major. **Procedure:** Freshmen are admitted fall and spring. Entrance exams should be taken during the fall semester of the junior or senior year. There is a rolling admissions plan. Check with the school for current application deadlines. The application fee is $45. **Transfer Students:** 482 transfer students enrolled in 2013-2014. Applicants with fewer than 24 credits must submit high school transcripts; those with fewer than 12 credits must also submit SAT scores. Applicants are expected to have at least a 2.0 GPA in all college work attempted and be in good standing at the last institution attended. 30 of 120 credits required for the bachelor's degree must be completed at Morgan State. **International Students:** They must take the TOEFL or ALIGU. They must also take the SAT or ACT. Students who have not attended any school during the preceding 3 years are not required to submit standardized test scores.

ADMISSIONS: 58% of the 2014-2015 applicants were accepted. **Admissions Contact:** Edwin T. Johnson, Director of Admission and Recruitment. E-Mail: *Admissions@morgan.edu* Web: *www.morgan.edu*

FINANCIAL AID: Morgan State is a member of CSS. The FAFSA and the college's own financial statement are required. Check with the school for current application deadlines.

MOUNT SAINT MARY'S UNIVERSITY   D-2
www.msmary.edu

Emmitsburg, MD 21727	(301) 447-5214
	(800) 448-4347
Fax: (301) 447-5860	Email: admissions@msmary.edu
Full-time: 763 men, 960 women	Faculty: 108; IIA, -$
Part-time: 36 men, 51 women	Ph.D.s: 92%
Graduate: 317 men, 178 women	Student/Faculty: 13 to 1
Year: semesters, summer session	Tuition: $36,021
Room & Board: $11,975	Freshman Class: 6142 applied, 4107 accepted, 510 enrolled
SAT CR/M/W: 520/530/510 ACT: 22	CEEB CODE: 5421
Application Deadline: March 1	COMPETITIVE

Mount St. Mary's University, founded in 1808, is a private liberal arts institution affiliated with the Roman Catholic Church. There are 4 undergraduate schools and 5 graduate schools. In addition to regional accreditation, The Mount has baccalaureate program accreditation with NASDTEC, NCATE, and IACBE. The 1400-acre campus is in a rural area 60 miles northwest of Washington, D.C., and 50 miles west of Baltimore. Including any residence halls, there are 32 buildings.

STUDENT LIFE: 53% of undergraduates are from Maryland. Others are from 35 states, 13 foreign countries, and Canada. 64% are from public schools. 71% are White; 11% African American. 72% are Catholic; 16% Protestant. **Male To Female Ratio:** 1.1:1. The average age of freshmen is 18; all undergraduates, 21. 21% do not continue beyond their first year; 66% remain to graduate. **Housing:** 1448 students can be accommodated in college housing, which includes coed dorms and on-campus apartments. In addition, there are special-interest houses, wellness floors, and quiet floors. On-campus housing is guaranteed for all 4 years. 83% of students live on campus; of those, 80% remain on campus on weekends. All students may keep cars.

FACULTY/CLASSROOMS: 60% of faculty are male; 40% are female. 87% teach undergraduates, 49% do research, and 49% do both. No introductory courses are taught by graduate students. The average class size in an introductory lecture is 22; in a laboratory is 14; and in a regular course is 20.

PROGRAMS OF STUDY: The Mount confers B.A., and B.S. degrees. Master's degrees are also awarded. Bachelor's degrees are awarded in BIOLOGICAL SCIENCE (biochemistry and biology/biological science), BUSINESS (accounting, business administration and management, and sports management), COMMUNICATIONS AND THE ARTS (communications, English, fine arts, French, German, and Spanish), COMPUTER AND PHYSICAL SCIENCE (chemistry, computer science, information sciences and systems, and mathematics), EDUCATION (elementary education), ENGINEERING AND ENVIRONMENTAL DESIGN (environmental science), HEALTH PROFESSIONS (health science), SOCIAL SCIENCE (criminal justice, economics, history, human services, interdisciplinary studies, international studies, philosophy, political science/government, psychology, social studies, sociology, and theological studies). Business, criminal justice and elementary education have the largest enrollments.

ACTIVITIES: There are no fraternities or sororities. There are 70 groups on campus, including art, band, cheerleading, chess, choir, chorale, computers, dance, debate, drama, environmental, ethnic, honors, international, literary magazine, musical theater, newspaper, pep band, political, professional, radio and TV, religious, social, social service, student government, and yearbook. Popular campus events include Acoustic Battle, Christmas Dance, Crab Feast, Homecoming and Special Olympics. **Sports:** There are 7 intercollegiate sports for men and 9 for women, and 24 intramural sports for men and 22 for women. Facilities include an multipurpose indoor courts, a track, pool, aerobics facilities, sauna, weight room, basketball arena, lighted tennis courts, and playing fields. **Graduates:** From July 1, 2013 to June 30, 2014, 378 bachelor's degrees were awarded. The most popular majors were business (21%), elementary education (10%), and accounting (8%). 26 companies recruited on campus in 2013-2014. In an average class, 1% graduate in 3 years or less, 58% graduate in 4 years or less, 63% graduate in 5 years or less, and 64% graduate in

6 years or less. Of the 2013 graduating class, 33% were enrolled in graduate school within 6 months of graduation, and 65% were employed.

SERVICES: Counseling and information services are available, as is tutoring in every subject. There is a reader service for the blind, and remedial math. There is a study skills and language lab, and a writing center. Closed-caption TV and software for sight-impaired students are also available. **Library/Resources:** The library contains 147,503 volumes, 2,321 audio/video tapes/CDs/DVDs, and subscribes to 16,148 periodicals including electronic. Computerized library services include interlibrary loans, database searching, Internet access, and Wi-Fi capability. Special learning facilities include an art gallery, radio station, TV station, archives. **Physically Challenged Students:** 85% of the campus is accessible. Facilities include wheelchair ramps, elevators, special parking, specially equipped restrooms, special class scheduling, lowered drinking fountains, and lowered telephones. **Special:** Mount Saint Mary's offers cross-registration with an area community college, study abroad in the U.K., Europe, and South America, and secondary teacher certification in English, foreign languages, math, and social studies. Dual majors, interdisciplinary majors in biopsychology, American culture, and classical studies, a general studies degree, 3 dual degree programs, and nondegree and accelerated study are possible. A number of independently designed internships, work-study programs, and pass/fail options are available. The Veritas Program is a common 4 year curriculum integrated with every academic major. It includes leadership development and cultural components. There are 20 national honor societies and a freshman honors program. **Visiting:** There are regularly scheduled orientations for prospective students, including campus tours and information sessions on academic programs, community life, admissions, and financial aid. There are guides for informal visits, visitors may sit in on classes, and stay overnight. To schedule a visit, contact the Admissions Office. **Campus Safety and Security:** Measures include 24-hour foot and vehicle patrol, emergency notification system, and security escort services. There are emergency telephones, lighted pathways/sidewalks, and controlled access to dorms/residences.

REQUIREMENTS: The SAT is required. Applicants should be graduates of an accredited secondary school or hold the GED. Secondary preparation should include 4 years of English, 3 each of math, history, natural science, and social sciences, and 2 of a foreign language. An interview is recommended. AP and CLEP credits are accepted. Important factors in the admissions decision are recommendations by school officials, advanced placement or honors courses, and extracurricular activities record. Students are required to take a 4-year, 33 credit core curriculum in liberal arts (with an additional 24 credits in domain areas, some of which overlap in the major area). The common educational experience includes a liberal arts symposium, a Western civilization sequence including art and literature, and courses in philosophy, theology, foreign language, math, American culture, and ethics. Graduation requirements include 120 credits, with most majors requiring 36 credits (30 to 36 in the major) and a minimum GPA of 2.0. **Procedure:** Freshmen are admitted fall and spring. Entrance exams should be taken by January of the senior year. There are early admissions, deferred admissions, and rolling admissions plans. Application deadlines are open. Application fee is $45. Applications are accepted on-line. **Transfer Students:** 40 transfer students enrolled in 2013-2014. Transfer applicants should have at least a 2.0 GPA in previous college work, be in good academic and disciplinary standing, and account for all time elapsed since graduation from high school. 30 of 120 credits required for the bachelor's degree must be completed at The Mount. **International Students:** There are 17 international students enrolled. They must take the TOEFL with a minimum score of 550 on the paper-based TOEFL (PBT) or 83 on the Internet-based version (iBT). They must also take the SAT or ACT.

ADMISSIONS: 67% of the 2014-2015 applicants were accepted. The SAT scores for the 2014-2015 freshman class were: Critical Reading--34% below 500, 45% between 500 and 599, 18% between 600 and 699, and 3% between 700 and 800; Math--34% below 500, 50% between 500 and 599, 14% between 600 and 699, and 2% between 700 and 800; Writing--42% below 500, 43% between 500 and 599, 13% between 600 and 699, and 2% between 700 and 800. The ACT scores were 34% below 21, 39% between 21 and 23, 18% between 24 and 26, 5% between 27 and 28, and 4% above 28. 30% of the current freshmen were in the top fifth of their class; 60% were in the top two fifths. 3 freshmen graduated first in their class. **Admissions Contact:** Michael Post, Dean of Admissions and Enrollment Management. E-Mail: *admissions@msmary.edu* Web: *www.msmary.edu*

FINANCIAL AID: In 2014-2015, 99% of all full-time freshmen and 98% of continuing full-time students received some form of financial aid. 76% of all full-time freshmen and 69% of continuing full-time students received need-based aid. The average freshman award was $26,271. Need-based scholarships or need-based grants averaged $2,850 ($17,510 maximum); need-based self-help aid (loans and jobs) averaged $5,570 ($7,030 maximum); non-need-based athletic scholarships averaged $15,584 ($47,996 maximum); and other non-need-based awards and non-need-based scholarships averaged $18,406 ($35,021 maximum). 42% of undergraduate students work part-time. Average annual earnings from campus work are $1184. The average financial indebtedness of the 2014 graduate was $36,130. The FAFSA is required. The deadline for filing freshman financial aid applications for fall entry is March 1.

NOTRE DAME OF MARYLAND UNIVERSITY D-2
www.ndm.edu

Baltimore, MD 21210

(410) 532-5330
(800) 435-0200

Fax: (410) 532-6287

Email: admiss@ndm.edu

Full-time: 650 women	Faculty: 74; IIB, av$
Part-time: 90 men, 880 women	Ph.Ds: 65%
Graduate: 270 men, 1190 women	Student/Faculty: 8 to 1
Year: 4-1-4, summer session	Tuition: $24,100
Room & Board: $7400	Freshman Class: n/av
SAT or ACT: required	CEEB CODE: 5114
Application Deadline: open	**VERY COMPETITIVE**

The College of Notre Dame of Maryland, founded in 1873, is a private liberal arts institution primarily for women and affiliated with the Catholic Church. The figures in the above capsule and in this profile are approximate. There is 1 graduate school. In addition to regional accreditation, Notre Dame has baccalaureate program accreditation with NLN. The 58-acre campus is in a suburban area 10 miles north of Baltimore. Including any residence halls, there are 11 buildings.

STUDENT LIFE: 70% of undergraduates are from Maryland. Others are from 21 states. **Male To Female Ratio:** 7.6:1. **Housing:** 450 students can be accommodated in college housing, which includes single-sex dorms. On-campus housing is guaranteed for all 4 years. 65% of students live on campus; of those, 60% remain on campus on weekends. Alcohol is not permitted. All students may keep cars.

FACULTY/CLASSROOMS: 30% of faculty are male; 70% are female. All teach undergraduates. No introductory courses are taught by graduate students. The average class size in an introductory lecture is 30; in a laboratory is 20; and in a regular course is 20.

PROGRAMS OF STUDY: Notre Dame confers B.A., and B.S. degrees. Master's degrees are also awarded. Bachelor's degrees are awarded in BIOLOGICAL SCIENCE (biology/biological science), BUSINESS (accounting, banking and finance, business administration and management, international business management, and marketing/retailing/merchandising), COMMUNICATIONS AND THE ARTS (art history and appreciation, classics, communications, English, graphic design, modern language, music, photography, and studio art), COMPUTER AND PHYSICAL SCIENCE (chemistry, computer science, information sciences and systems, mathematics, and physics), EDUCATION (art education, early childhood education, elementary education, foreign languages education, music education, science education, secondary education, and special education), ENGINEERING AND ENVIRONMENTAL DESIGN (preengineering), HEALTH PROFESSIONS (nursing, predentistry, premedicine, and prepharmacy), SOCIAL SCIENCE (economics, history, interdisciplinary studies, international relations, liberal arts/

general studies, political science/government, prelaw, psychology, and religion). Business, education, and communication arts are the strongest academically.

ACTIVITIES: There are no fraternities or sororities. There are 24 groups on campus, including art, choir, dance, drama, ethnic, honors, international, literary magazine, newspaper, political, professional, radio and TV, religious, social, social service, student government, and yearbook. Popular campus events include Honors Convocation, Antostal Day, and Multicultural Awareness Week. **Sports:** Facilities include a sports/activities complex that houses racquetball courts, a dance studio, a fitness center, an indoor walking track, a game room, an activities resource center, and a basketball court.

SERVICES: Counseling and information services are available, as is tutoring in most subjects. **Library/Resources:** The library contains 290,000 volumes, 378,138 microform items, 24,000 audio/video tapes/CDs/DVDs, and subscribes to 2,000 periodicals including electronic. Computerized library services include database searching. Special learning facilities include an art gallery, planetarium, radio station, TV station, graphic arts studio, roof-top greenhouse, and cultural center. **Physically Challenged Students:** 98% of the campus is accessible. Facilities include wheelchair ramps, elevators, special parking, specially equipped restrooms, and lowered drinking fountains. **Special:** The college offers cross-registration with Johns Hopkins, Townson State, and Morgan State Universities; Coppin State, Goucher, and Loyola Colleges; and the Maryland Institute College of Art. Study abroad, internships, dual bachelor's degrees in nursing and engineering, 3-2 engineering degrees with Johns Hopkins University and the University of Maryland, and pass/fail options are available. Notre Dame's Weekend College offers bachelor's degree programs for employed adults. There are 8 national honor societies, a freshman honors program, and 4 departmental honors programs. **Visiting:** There are regularly scheduled orientations for prospective students, consisting of programs in June and January, each of which includes a stay in the dormitory, registration, and advisement. There are guides for informal visits and visitors may sit in on classes. To schedule a visit, contact the Office of Admissions. **Campus Safety and Security:** Measures include 24-hour foot and vehicle patrol, self-defense education, and security escort services. There are lighted pathways/sidewalks.

REQUIREMENTS: The SAT or ACT is required. For scholarship purposes, applicants should be graduates of an accredited secondary school. 18 academic credits are required, including 4 units of English, 3 each of math and a foreign language, and 2 each of history and science, plus 4 electives. An essay is required and an interview is recommended. AP credits are accepted. Important factors in the admissions decision are recommendations by school officials, advanced placement or honors courses, and leadership record. To graduate, students must complete a total of 128 credit hours with a minimum GPA of 2.0 (2.5 in many majors). All students must fulfill the distribution requirements in the general education core, the major, and electives, and must demonstrate proficiency in writing, public speaking, computer literacy, and library research. In most majors, a minimum of 42 hours is required. All students must take a speech course and 2 courses in phys ed, and some majors require senior practicums. **Procedure:** Freshmen are admitted fall and spring. Entrance exams should be taken no later than January of the senior year. There are early decision, early admissions, deferred admissions, and rolling admissions plans. Application deadlines are open. Notifications are sent in starting. Applications are accepted on-line. **Transfer Students:** Notre Dame requires a minimum GPA of 2.5 for transfer students but recommends a GPA of 3.0. A combined score of 800 is required for the SAT I and 18 for the ACT. Students must also submit a letter of recommendation and an essay. 60 of 128 credits required for the bachelor's degree must be completed at Notre Dame. **International Students:** The school actively recruits these students. They must take the TOEFL.

ADMISSIONS: Sharon Bogdan, Director of Admissions. E-Mail: *admiss@ndm.edu* Web: *www.ndm.edu*

FINANCIAL AID: In 2014-2015, 85% of all full-time freshmen and 89% of continuing full-time students received some form of financial aid. 80% of all full-time freshmen and 75% of continuing full-time students received need-based aid. The average freshman award was $20,796. Need-based scholarships or need-based grants averaged $15,600 ($22,750 maximum); need-based self-help aid (loans and jobs) averaged $4,011 ($6,125 maximum); and other non-need-based awards and non-need-based scholarships averaged $9,202 ($18,700 maximum). Notre Dame is a member of CSS. The CSS/Profile and FAFSA are required. Check with the school for current application deadlines.

SALISBURY UNIVERSITY — F-4
www.salisbury.edu

Salisbury, MD 21801	(410) 543-6161
	n/av
Fax: (410) 546-6016	Email: easkoglund@salisbury.edu
Full-time: 3190 men, 4215 women	Faculty: 410
Part-time: 289 men, 310 women	Ph.D.s: 83%
Graduate: 168 men, 471 women	Student/Faculty: 18 to 1
Year: 4-1-4, summer session	Tuition: $8128 ($16,474)
Room & Board: $10,240	Freshman Class: 8905 applied, 4895 accepted, 1246 enrolled
SAT CR/M/W: 575/580/570 ACT: 24	CEEB CODE: 5403
Application Deadline: January 15	VERY COMPETITIVE

Salisbury University, founded in 1925, is a public comprehensive university providing undergraduate programs in the liberal arts, sciences, preprofessional and professional programs, and select, mostly applied, graduate programs in business, education, nursing, psychology, English, and history. There are 4 undergraduate schools and 1 graduate school. In addition to regional accreditation, SU has baccalaureate program accreditation with AACSB, CSWE, NASM, and NCATE. The 182-acre campus is in a rural area 30 miles from Ocean City, 120 miles from Baltimore and 120 miles from Washington, D.C. Including any residence halls, there are 66 buildings.

STUDENT LIFE: 85% of undergraduates are from Maryland. Others are from 29 states, 69 foreign countries, and Canada. 80% are from public schools. 74% are White; 12% African American. The average age of freshmen is 18; all undergraduates, 21. 19% do not continue beyond their first year; 67% remain to graduate.

FACULTY/CLASSROOMS: 43% of faculty are male; 57% are female. All teach undergraduates, 6% do research, and 6% do both. Graduate students teach 4% of introductory courses. The average class size in an introductory lecture is 29; in a laboratory is 21; and in a regular course is 25.

PROGRAMS OF STUDY: SU confers B.A., B.S., B.A.S.W. and B.F.A. degrees. Master's and Doctoral degrees are also awarded. Bachelor's degrees are awarded in AGRICULTURE (environmental studies), BIOLOGICAL SCIENCE (biology/biological science), BUSINESS (accounting, banking and finance, business administration and management, management information systems, and marketing/retailing/merchandising), COMMUNICATIONS AND THE ARTS (art, communications, English, English as a second/foreign language, fine arts, French, music, Spanish, and theater management), COMPUTER AND PHYSICAL SCIENCE (chemistry, computer science, earth science, information sciences and systems, mathematics, physical sciences, and physics), EDUCATION (athletic training, early childhood education, education, education administration, elementary education, health education, mathematics education, physical education, reading education, and teaching English as a second/foreign language (TESOL/TEFOL)), HEALTH PROFESSIONS (environmental health science, exercise science, health care administration, medical technology, nursing, and respiratory therapy), SOCIAL SCIENCE (economics, geography, history, interdisciplinary studies, international studies, peace studies, philosophy, political science/government, psychology, social science, social work, and sociology). Nursing, education, and business are the strongest academically. Biology, nursing, and elementary education have the largest enrollments.

ACTIVITIES: 6% of men belong to 10 national fraternities; 4% of women belong to 5 national sororities. There are 132 groups on campus, including art, cheerleading, choir, chorale, chorus, computers, dance, debate, drama, ethnic, film, gay, honors, international, jazz band, literary magazine, musical theater, newspaper, opera, orchestra, pep band, photography, political, professional, radio and TV, religious, social, social service, student government, and symphony. Popular campus events include Oktoberfest, Gullfest, Homecoming Week, Big Event (Community Service), Relay for Life, Multicultural Festival.

SERVICES: Counseling and information services are available, as is tutoring in most subjects. There is a reader service for the blind, and remedial math and reading. The 2 libraries contain 287,318 volumes, 756,650 microform items, 1,798 audio/video tapes/CDs/DVDs, and subscribe to 1,035 periodicals including electronic. Computerized library services include interlibrary loans, database searching, and Internet access. Special learning facilities include an art gallery, radio station, TV station, Nabb Research Center for Delmarva History and Culture, Scarborough Student Leadership Center, Center for Conflict Resolution, Richard A Henson Medical Simulation Center.

REQUIREMENTS: Applicants must be graduates of accredited secondary schools or have earned a GED. The university requires 15 academic credits, including 4 in English, 3 each in math and social studies, 3 in science (2 with labs), and 2 in foreign language. Auditions are required for admission into the music and B.F.A. programs once admission to the university is granted. Essays are recommended but not required. A campus visit is recommended for all students. The SAT is not required for any enrolling student with a 3.5 or greater GPA. A GPA of 2.0 is required. AP and CLEP credits are accepted. Important factors in the admissions decision are advanced placement or honors courses, leadership record, and extracurricular activities record.

ADMISSIONS: 55% of the 2013-2014 applicants were accepted. The SAT scores for the 2013-2014 freshman class were: Critical Reading--6% below 500, 62% between 500 and 599, 29% between 600 and 699, and 3% between 700 and 800; Math--4% below 500, 54% between 500 and 599, 39% between 600 and 699, and 3% between 700 and 800; Writing--7% below 500, 60% between 500 and 599, 31% between 600 and 699, and 2% between 700 and 800. The ACT scores were 3% below 21, 43% between 21 and 23, % between 24 and 26, 53% between 27 and 28, and 1% above 28. 59% of the current freshmen were in the top fifth of their class; 93% were in the top two fifths. There were 3 National Merit finalists. 2 freshmen graduated first in their class.

FINANCIAL AID: In 2013-2014, 88% of all full-time freshmen and 75% of continuing full-time students received some form of financial aid. 61% of all full-time freshmen and 66% of continuing full-time students received need-based aid. The average freshman award was $10,768. Need-based scholarships or need-based grants averaged $5,460; need-based self-help aid (loans and jobs) averaged $3,118; and other non-need-based awards and non-need-based scholarships averaged $2,698. 18% of undergraduate students work part-time. Average annual earnings from campus work are $3000. The average financial indebtedness of the 2013 graduate was $23,545. SU is a member of CSS. The FAFSA is required. The priority date for freshman financial aid applications for fall entry is March 1. The deadline for filing freshman financial aid applications for fall entry is December 31.

SOJOURNER-DOUGLASS COLLEGE (*The complete profile is made available exclusively on our website, www.barronspac.com*)

ST. JOHN'S COLLEGE-ANNAPOLIS	E-3
www.stjohnscollege.edu	

Annapolis, MD 21404	(410) 626-2522
	(800) 727-9238
Fax: (410) 269-7916	Email: admissions@sjca.edu
Full-time: 247 men, 215 women	Faculty: 73
Part-time: 1 men	Ph.D.s: 78%
Graduate: 46 men, 29 women	Student/Faculty: 8 to 1
Year: semesters	Tuition: $43,256
Room & Board: $10,334	Freshman Class: 357 applied, 289 accepted, 136 enrolled
SAT CR/M: 640/570 ACT: 27	CEEB CODE: 5598
Application Deadline: open	**HIGHLY COMPETITIVE**

St. John's College, founded as King William's School in 1696 and chartered as St. John's in 1784, is a private institution that offers a single all-required curriculum sometimes called the Great Books Program. Students and faculty work together in small discussion classes without lecture courses, written finals, or emphasis on grades. The program is a rigorous interdisciplinary curriculum based on the great works of literature, math, philosophy, theology, sciences, political theory, music, history, and economics. There is also a campus in Santa Fe, New Mexico. The figures in the above capsule and in this profile are approximate. There is 1 undergraduate school and 1 graduate school. The 36-acre campus is in a small town 35 miles east of Washington, D.C., and 32 miles south of Baltimore. Including any residence halls, there are 18 buildings.

STUDENT LIFE: 83% of undergraduates are from out of state, mostly the South. Students are from 43 states, 12 foreign countries, and Canada. 60% are from public schools. 90% are White. 58% claim no religious affiliation; 22% Protestant. The average age of freshmen is 19; all undergraduates, 20. 20% do not continue beyond their first year; 76% remain to graduate. **Housing:** 375 students can be accommodated in college housing, which includes single-sex and coed dorms. On-campus housing is guaranteed for the freshman year only and is available on a lottery system for upperclassmen. 75% of students live on campus; of those, 95% remain on campus on weekends. Upperclassmen may keep cars.

FACULTY/CLASSROOMS: 73% of faculty are male; 27% are female. All teach undergraduates. No introductory courses are taught by graduate students. The average class size in a laboratory is 15 and in a regular course is 15.

PROGRAMS OF STUDY: St. John's confers B.A. degrees. Master's degrees are also awarded. Bachelor's degrees are awarded in SOCIAL SCIENCE (liberal arts/general studies, Western European studies, and Western civilization/culture).

ACTIVITIES: There are no fraternities or sororities. There are 49 groups on campus, including Christian fellowship, community garden, fencing, Jewish fellowship, vegetarian, waltz and swing, woodshop, chorus, dance, drama, film, international, literary magazine, newspaper, orchestra, photography, poetry, and student government. Popular campus events include Reality Weekend, Senior Prank, and College Navy Croquet Match. **Sports:** There are 4 intercollegiate sports for men and 4 for women, and 19 intramural sports for men and 19 for women. Facilities include a gym with a weight room, cardio room, and indoor running track, tennis courts, a boathouse for sailing and crew, a pier with floating docks, and playing fields. **Graduates:** From July 1, 2013 to June 30, 2014, 104 bachelor's degrees were awarded. The most popular majors were liberal arts (100%). 7 companies recruited on campus in 2013-2014. In an average class, 63% graduate in 4 years or less, 71% graduate in 5 years or less, and 76% graduate in 6 years or less. Of the 2013 graduating class, 13% were enrolled in graduate school within 6 months of graduation, and 60% were employed.

SERVICES: Counseling and information services are available, as is tutoring in some subjects. There is remedial math and writing. **Library/Resources:** The 2 libraries contain 133,000 volumes, 2,000 microform items, 5,000 audio/video tapes/CDs/DVDs, and subscribe to 240 periodicals including electronic. Computerized library services include interlibrary loans, database searching, Internet access, and Wi-Fi capability. Special learning facilities include an art gallery and planetarium. **Physically Challenged Students:** 70% of the campus is accessible. Facilities include wheelchair ramps, elevators, special parking, specially equipped restrooms, special class scheduling, lowered drinking fountains, lowered telephones, and special housing. **Special:** St. John's offers summer internships and an informal study-abroad program. **Visiting:** There are regularly scheduled orientations for prospective students, consisting of an overnight stay on campus, class visits, and a tour. There are guides for informal visits, visitors may sit in on classes, and stay overnight. To schedule a visit, contact the Admission Office. **Campus Safety and Security:** Measures include 24-hour foot and vehicle patrol, emergency notification system, self-defense education, and security escort services. There are emergency telephones, lighted pathways/sidewalks, and controlled access to dorms/residences.

REQUIREMENTS: Applicants need not be high school graduates;

some students are admitted before they complete high school. Test scores may be submitted but are not required. Secondary preparation should include 4 years of English, 3 years of math, and 2 years each of foreign language, science, and history. Applicants must submit written essays, which are critical to the admissions decision, and are strongly urged to visit. Important factors in the admissions decision are recommendations by school officials, advanced placement or honors courses, and personality/intangible qualities.The common curriculum, equivalent to 132 credits, covers a range of classic to modern works. Students attend small seminars; 9-week preceptorials on specific works or topics; language, music, and math tutorials; and a 3-year natural sciences lab. Active learning occurs through discussion, translations, writing, experiment, mathematical demonstration, and musical analysis. Students take oral exams each semester and submit annual essays. Sophomores also take a math exam and seniors an oral exam that admits them to degree candidacy. Seniors also present a final essay to the faculty and take a 1-hour public oral exam. **Procedure:** Freshmen are admitted fall. There are early admissions, deferred admissions, and rolling admissions plans. Application deadlines are open. Notification is sent on a rolling basis. Applications are accepted on-line. **Transfer Students:** 16 transfer students enrolled in 2013-2014. Transfer students may enter only as freshmen and must complete the entire program at St. John's. The admissions criteria are the same as for regular students. Students in good academic standing may transfer to the Santa Fe campus at the beginning of any academic year. 132 of 132 credits required for the bachelor's degree must be completed at St. John's. **International Students:** There are 12 international students enrolled. The school actively recruits these students. They must take the TOEFL. They must also take the SAT.

ADMISSIONS: 81% of the 2014-2015 applicants were accepted. The SAT scores for the 2014-2015 freshman class were: Critical Reading--2% below 500, 10% between 500 and 599, 40% between 600 and 699, and 48% between 700 and 800; Math--4% below 500, 29% between 500 and 599, 44% between 600 and 699, and 23% between 700 and 800. The ACT scores were 12% between 24 and 26, 46% between 27 and 28, and 42% above 28. There were 4 National Merit finalists. **Admissions Contact:** John Christensen, Director of Admissions. E-Mail: *admissions@sjca.edu* Web: *www.stjohnscollege.edu*

FINANCIAL AID: In 2014-2015, 61% of all full-time freshmen and 68% of continuing full-time students received some form of financial aid. 57% of all full-time freshmen and 65% of continuing full-time students received need-based aid. The average freshman award was $30,545. Need-based scholarships or need-based grants averaged $23,445; and need-based self-help aid (loans and jobs) averaged $7,100. 75% of undergraduate students work part-time. Average annual earnings from campus work are $2700. The average financial indebtedness of the 2014 graduate was $23,760. St. John's is a member of CSS. The CSS/Profile, FAFSA, and parent and student federal tax returns are required. Check with the school for current application deadlines.

ST. MARY'S COLLEGE OF MARYLAND E-4
www.smcm.edu

St. Marys City, MD 20686	(240) 895-5000
	(800) 492-7181
Fax: (240) 895-5001	Email: admissions@smcm.edu
Full-time: 726 men, 983 women	Faculty: 142; IIB, +$
Part-time: 35 men, 27 women	Ph.D.s: 97%
Graduate: 4 men, 29 women	Student/Faculty: 12 to 1
Year: semesters, summer session	Tuition: $13,824 ($28,674)
Room & Board: $11,930	Freshman Class: 1874 applied, 1478 accepted, 379 enrolled
SAT CR/M/W: 590/580/580 ACT: 26	CEEB CODE: 5601
Application Deadline: February 15	VERY COMPETITIVE

St. Mary's College of Maryland, founded in 1840, is a small public liberal arts college designated by law as a Maryland honors college in 1992. There is 1 graduate school. In addition to regional accreditation, SMCM has baccalaureate program accreditation with ACS. The 319-acre campus is in a rural area 70 miles southeast of Washington, D.C. Including any residence halls, there are 58 buildings.

STUDENT LIFE: 90% of undergraduates are from Maryland. Others are from 29 states, 12 foreign countries, and Canada. 80% are from public schools. 73% are White. **Male To Female Ratio:** 1.4:1. The average age of freshmen is 18; all undergraduates, 20. 14% do not continue beyond their first year; 81% remain to graduate. **Housing:** 1571 students can be accommodated in college housing, which includes single-sex and coed dorms and on-campus apartments. In addition, there are language houses and special-interest houses. On-campus housing is guaranteed for all 4 years, is available on a first-come, first-served basis. 83% of students live on campus; of those, 80% remain on campus on weekends. All students may keep cars.

FACULTY/CLASSROOMS: 56% of faculty are male; 44% are female. All teach and do research. No introductory courses are taught by graduate students.

PROGRAMS OF STUDY: SMCM confers B.A. degrees. Master's degrees are also awarded. Bachelor's degrees are awarded in BIOLOGICAL SCIENCE (biochemistry and biology/biological science), COMMUNICATIONS AND THE ARTS (art, art history and appreciation, dramatic arts, English, film arts, languages, music, and visual and performing arts), COMPUTER AND PHYSICAL SCIENCE (chemistry, computer science, mathematics, natural sciences, and physics), SOCIAL SCIENCE (anthropology, Asian/Oriental studies, economics, history, philosophy, political science/government, psychology, public affairs, religion, and sociology). Biology, psychology, and economics have the largest enrollments.

ACTIVITIES: There are no fraternities or sororities. There are 92 groups on campus, including academic, and sports, art, cheerleading, choir, chorale, chorus, dance, drama, drum and bugle corps, environmental, ethnic, gay, honors, international, jazz band, literary magazine, musical theater, newspaper, orchestra, outdoors, political, professional, radio and TV, religious, social, student government, symphony, and yearbook. Popular campus events include World Carnival, River Concert Series, the Great Cardboard-Boat Race, Dance Club Shows, Burlesque Club Shows, Acapella Group Shows. **Sports:** There are 8 intercollegiate sports for men and 9 for women, and 10 intramural sports for men and 10 for women. Facilities include an Olympic-size 50 meter pool, 25-yard swimming pool, 1,200-seat basketball and volleyball arena, an expanded health and fitness center, weight room, training room, exercise room, 2 gymnasiums, and locker and team rooms. Physical education, athletics, and recreation facilities also include 5 varsity practice fields, a track, 6 lighted tennis courts, an outdoor stadium, rowing center, and baseball facilities. **Graduates:** From July 1, 2013 to June 30, 2014, 450 bachelor's degrees were awarded. The most popular majors were psychology (18%), economics (11%), and biology (11%). 32 companies recruited on campus in 2013-2014. In an average class, 65% graduate in 4 years or less and 81% graduate in 6 years or less.

SERVICES: Counseling and information services are available, as is tutoring in some subjects. There is a reader service for the blind. **Library/Resources:** The library contains 172,545 volumes, 18,832 microform items, 7,284 audio/video tapes/CDs/DVDs, and subscribes to 514 periodicals including electronic. Computerized library services include interlibrary loans, database searching, Internet access, and Wi-Fi capability. Special learning facilities include an art gallery, radio station, TV station, historic archeological site, and estuarine research facilities. **Physically Challenged Students:** 95% of the campus is accessible. Facilities include wheelchair ramps, elevators, special parking, specially equipped restrooms, special class scheduling, lowered drinking fountains, lowered telephones, special housing. Living suites that meet ADA standards are also available. **Special:** St. Mary's offers internships, study abroad, national and international exchange programs, work-study, and both dual and student-designed majors. Credit bearing internships offered by St. Mary's include a computer science co-op program and the Washington program in political science. St. Mary's has an MOU with the George Washington University's Semester in Washington program. Non-degree study and pass/fail options are possible. There are 8 national honor societies including Phi Beta Kappa. **Visiting:** There are regularly scheduled orientations for prospective students. Student visits include personal interviews, group presentations, open house programs, meetings with faculty and students, and campus tours. There are guides for informal visits and visitors may sit in on classes. To schedule a visit, contact Lindsey Siferd at (800) 492-7181. **Campus Safety and Security:** Measures include 24-hour foot and vehicle patrol, emergency notification system, self-defense education, and security escort services. There are emergency telephones, lighted pathways/sidewalks, controlled access to dorms/residences, student security-assistant foot patrols, and nighthawk program from 8 p.m. until midnight.

REQUIREMENTS: The SAT or ACT is required. A student's high school record is most important to us, with careful attention paid to co-curricular activities (including work and family responsibilities), essays, letters of recommendation, and standardized test scores (either SAT Reasoning or ACT required). A competitive candidate pursues a rigorous high school curriculum which includes four years of English, three years of social science, three years of mathematics, three years of science, and a range of academic electives. Study of a foreign language is strongly recommended. Advanced Placement, International Baccalaureate, and honors courses are highly valued. First-year applicants must possess an earned high school diploma or a satisfactory score on the GED. AP credits are accepted. Students must complete complete core curriculum requirements, which include a liberal arts seminar, a foreign language course, six breadth categories, and an academic experience that takes students outside the classroom (e.g., study abroad, internships, service-learning). There is also a St. Mary's Project or a senior capstone experience. Students must meet additional requirements in their major fields and complete at least 128 semester hours, with at least 44 upper division credits and at least a 2.0 GPA. **Procedure:** Freshmen are admitted fall and spring. Entrance exams should be taken by January of the senior year. There are early decision and deferred admissions plans. Early decision applications should be filed by November 1; regular applications, by February 15 for fall entry; and November 1 for spring entry, along with a $50 fee. Notification of early decision is sent December 15; regular decision, March 15. 124 early decision candidates were accepted for the 2014-2015 class. 168 applicants were on the 2014 waiting list; 18 were admitted. Applications are accepted on-line. **Transfer Students:** 133 transfer students enrolled in 2013-2014. A competitive candidate has completed at least 12 hours of credit with a minimum grade point average of 2.75 in all college courses and has earned a high school diploma or satisfactory score on the General Education Development (GED) examination. 58 of 128 credits required for the bachelor's degree must be completed at SMCM. **International Students:** There are 27 international students enrolled. The school actively recruits these students. They must take the TOEFL with a minimum score of 550 on the paper-based TOEFL (PBT) or 90 on the Internet-based version (iBT). They must also take the SAT or ACT.

ADMISSIONS: 79% of the 2014-2015 applicants were accepted. The SAT scores for the 2014-2015 freshman class were: Critical Reading--12% below 500, 40% between 500 and 599, 37% between 600 and 699, and 10% between 700 and 800; Math--14% below 500, 43% between 500 and 599, 38% between 600 and 699, and 5% between 700 and 800; Writing--18% below 500, 42% between 500 and 599, 34% between 600 and 699, and 6% between 700 and 800. The ACT scores were 11% below 21, 19% between 21 and 23, 29% between 24 and 26, 17% between 27 and 28, and 24% above 28. 54% of the current freshmen were in the top fifth of their class; 81% were in the top two fifths. 3 freshmen graduated first in their class. **Admissions Contact:** Gary Sherman, Vice President of Enrollment Management. E-Mail: *admissions@smcm.edu* Web: *www.smcm.edu*

FINANCIAL AID: In 2014-2015, 84% of all full-time freshmen and 73% of continuing full-time students received some form of financial aid. 50% of all full-time freshmen and 44% of continuing full-time students received need-based aid. The average freshman award was $6,507. Need-based scholarships or need-based grants averaged $7,531 ($22,353 maximum); need-based self-help aid (loans and jobs) averaged $5,123 ($1,074 maximum); and other non-need-based awards and non-need-based scholarships averaged $3,109 ($20,324 maximum). 55% of undergraduate students work part-time. Average annual earnings from campus work are $1593. The average financial indebtedness of the 2014 graduate was $19,420. The FAFSA is required. The priority date for freshman financial aid applications for fall entry is February 15. The deadline for filing freshman financial aid applications for fall entry is February 28.

STEVENSON UNIVERSITY — D-2
www.stevenson.edu

Stevenson, MD 21153

410-486-7001
1-877-468-6852

Fax: 443-352-4440
Email: admissions@stevenson.edu

Full-time: 1172 men, 2031 women	Faculty: 126; IIB, +$
Part-time: 156 men, 449 women	Ph.D.s: 74%
Graduate: 124 men, 390 women	Student/Faculty: 24 to 1
Year: semesters, summer session	Tuition: $28,980
Room & Board: $12,490	Freshman Class: n/av
SAT or ACT: required	CEEB CODE: 5856
Application Deadline: n/av	COMPETITIVE

Stevenson University, founded as Villa Julie College in 1947, is the third-largest independent university in Maryland and offers more than 25 undergraduate degree programs. Figures in the above capsule and in this profile are approximate. There are 5 undergraduate schools and 1 graduate school. In addition to regional accreditation, Stevenson has baccalaureate program accreditation with NCATE, NLN, ABA, CCNE, and CSHSE. The 168-acre campus is in a suburban area 10 miles northwest of Baltimore. Including any residence halls, there are 31 buildings.

STUDENT LIFE: 82% of undergraduates are from Maryland. Others are from 36 states, and 2 foreign countries. 75% are from public schools. 56% are White; 28% African American. The average age of freshmen is 19; all undergraduates, 23. 21% do not continue beyond their first year; 63% remain to graduate. **Housing:** 1845 students can be accommodated in college housing, which includes single-sex and coed dorms and on-campus apartments. In addition, there are special-interest houses. On-campus housing is available on a first-come, first-served basis, and is available on a lottery system for upperclassmen. 52% of students commute. All students may keep cars.

FACULTY/CLASSROOMS: 44% of faculty are male; 56% are female. 96% teach undergraduates. No introductory courses are taught by graduate students. The average class size in an introductory lecture is 19; in a laboratory is 15; and in a regular course is 15.

PROGRAMS OF STUDY: confers B.A., and B.S. degrees. Master's degrees are also awarded. Bachelor's degrees are awarded in BIOLOGICAL SCIENCE (biology/biological science and biotechnology), BUSINESS (accounting, business administration and management, business communications, business systems analysis, fashion merchandising, and marketing management), COMMUNICATIONS AND THE ARTS (art, dramatic arts, English literature, film arts, video, and visual design), COMPUTER AND PHYSICAL SCIENCE (applied mathematics, chemistry, computer security and information assurance, information sciences and systems, and mathematics), EDUCATION (early childhood education, elementary education, and middle school education), HEALTH PROFESSIONS (medical laboratory technology and nursing), SOCIAL SCIENCE (fashion design and technology, history, human services, interdisciplinary studies, paralegal studies, psychology, and public affairs). Sciences and education are the strongest academically. Nursing and business have the largest enrollments.

ACTIVITIES: There are no fraternities; 3% of women belong to 2 national sororities. There are 45 groups on campus, including art, band, cheerleading, chess, choir, computers, dance, drama, environmental, ethnic, film, forensics, gay, honors, international, jazz band, literary magazine, marching band, musical theater, mustang activities and programming board, newspaper, orchestra, pep band, photography, political, professional, radio and TV, religious, social, social service, and student government. Popular campus events include Welcome Picnic, Founder's Day, Homecoming, and LOL Stevenson Comedy. **Sports:** There are 11 intercollegiate sports for men and 12 for women, and 7 intramural sports for men and 7 for women. Facilities include stadium, a gymnasium, tennis courts, softball, and golf facilities. **Graduates:** From July 1, 2013 to June 30, 2014, 977 bachelor's degrees were awarded. The most popular majors were health professions and related program (24%), business/marketing (16%), and criminal justice/law enforcement administration (10%). 80 companies recruited on campus in 2013-2014. In an average class, 48% graduate in 4 years or less, 59% graduate in 5 years or less, and 63%

graduate in 6 years or less. Of the 2013 graduating class, 4% were enrolled in graduate school within 6 months of graduation, and 81% were employed.

SERVICES: Counseling and information services are available, as is tutoring in most subjects. There is remedial math, reading, and writing. Free individual tutoring as well as study groups led by a tutor, peer tutoring, paraprofessional tutoring, and faculty tutoring are available. **Library/Resources:** The 2 libraries contain 358,990 volumes, 199,324 microform items, 22,781 audio/video tapes/CDs/DVDs, and subscribe to 72,659 periodicals including electronic. Computerized library services include interlibrary loans, database searching, Internet access, and Wi-Fi capability. Special learning facilities include an art gallery, radio station, a theater, and a video studio. **Physically Challenged Students:** All of the campus is accessible. Facilities include wheelchair ramps, elevators, special parking, specially equipped restrooms, special class scheduling, lowered drinking fountains, lowered telephones, and special housing. **Special:** Co-op programs and internships are available. In addition, study abroad, service learning, field placements, independent study and research, and other experiential learning opportunities are offered as part of classes. Cross-registration, work study, accelerated degree programs, and student-designed majors are possible. There are 10 national honor societies, a freshman honors program, and 1 departmental honors programs. **Visiting:** There are regularly scheduled orientations for prospective students, including a general overview, information on how to apply and how to finance a college education, special academic presentations, tours, meetings with faculty and students, and lunch. There are guides for informal visits, visitors may sit in on classes, and stay overnight. To schedule a visit, contact the Admissions Office at admissions@stevenson.edu. **Campus Safety and Security:** Measures include 24-hour foot and vehicle patrol, emergency notification system, self-defense education, and security escort services. There are shuttle buses, emergency telephones, lighted pathways/sidewalks, and controlled access to dorms/residences.

REQUIREMENTS: The SAT or ACT is required. Applicants must be graduates of an accredited secondary school. Although a secondary transcript is required, particular secondary preparation is not stipulated for all programs. Some degree programs do require specific high school courses, however. An essay is required and an interview is recommended. A GPA of 2.0 is required. AP and CLEP credits are accepted.The core curriculum includes courses in writing, communication, fine arts, social sciences, math, natural science, humanities, and phys ed. Courses in computer information systems are also required. Students must complete a minimum of 120 hours, including 45 hours in upper-level courses, with at least a 2.0 overall GPA. The number of hours required per major varies. Many majors require a capstone course or an internship. **Procedure:** Freshmen are admitted fall, spring, and summer. Entrance exams should be taken between September and November of the senior year. There are deferred admissions and rolling admissions plans. Application deadlines are open. Application fee is $40. Applications are accepted online. **Transfer Students:** Transfer applicants must provide both college and high school transcripts and have a minimum 2.5 GPA. Transfer students with a 2.0 cumulative GPA and other accomplishments or experience may be granted conditional admission to the college. 30 of 120 credits required for the bachelor's degree must be completed at Stevenson. **International Students:** There is 1 international student enrolled. They must take the TOEFL with a minimum score of 550 on the paper-based TOEFL (PBT) or 80 on the Internet-based version (iBT).

ADMISSIONS: The SAT scores for the 2014-2015 freshman class were: Critical Reading--49% below 500, 42% between 500 and 599, 8% between 600 and 699, and 1% between 700 and 800; Math--47% below 500, 40% between 500 and 599, 12% between 600 and 699, and 1% between 700 and 800; Writing--51% below 500, 40% between 500 and 599, 8% between 600 and 699, and 1% between 700 and 800. 42% of the current freshmen were in the top fifth of their class; 56% were in the top two fifths. **Admissions Contact:** Mark J. Hergan, Vice President for Enrollment Management. E-Mail: *admissions@stevenson.edu* Web: *www.stevenson.edu*

FINANCIAL AID: In 2014-2015, 99% of all full-time freshmen and 96% of continuing full-time students received some form of financial aid. 75% of all full-time freshmen and 68% of continuing full-time students received need-based aid. The average freshman award was $42,756. Need-based scholarships or need-based grants averaged $5,916 ($12,000 maximum); need-based self-help aid (loans and jobs) averaged $3,376 ($3,500 maximum); other non-need-based awards and non-need-based scholarships averaged $4,510 ($26,976 maximum); and $3,456 from other forms of aid. 24% of undergraduate students work part-time. Average annual earnings from campus work are $1910. The average financial indebtedness of the 2014 graduate was $30,203. is a member of CSS. The FAFSA is required. The priority date for freshman financial aid applications for fall entry is February 15.

TOWSON UNIVERSITY   D-2
www.towson.edu

Towson, MD 21252

Fax: (410) 704-3030

Full-time: 5540 men, 8645 women
Part-time: 940 men, 1105 women
Graduate: 890 men, 2655 women
Year: semesters, summer session
Room & Board: $8000
SAT or ACT: required
Application Deadline:

(410) 704-2113
(888) 4-TOWSON
Email: admissions@towson.edu
Faculty: IIA, -$
Ph.D.s: 52%
Student/Faculty: n/av
Tuition: $8000 ($17,500)
Freshman Class: n/av
CEEB CODE: 5404
VERY COMPETITIVE

Towson University, founded in 1866, is part of the university system of Maryland and offers undergraduate and graduate programs in liberal arts and sciences, allied health sciences, education, fine arts, communication, and business and economics. Figures in the above capsule and in this profile are approximate. There are 7 undergraduate schools and 1 graduate school. In addition to regional accreditation, Towson has baccalaureate program accreditation with AACSB, CAHEA, NASDTEC, NASM, NCATE, NLN, ACOTE, AOTA, CAAHEP, and NCATE. The 328-acre campus is in a suburban area 8 miles north of Baltimore City's Inner Harbor. Including any residence halls, there are 44 buildings.

STUDENT LIFE: 80% of undergraduates are from Maryland. Others are from 28 states, 12 foreign countries, and Canada. 69% are White; 12% African American. The average age of freshmen is 19; all undergraduates, 22. **Housing:** 3518 students can be accommodated in college housing, which includes coed dorms and on-campus apartments. In addition, there are honors houses, special-interest houses, separate floors that are alcohol-free, smoke-free, and substance-free, leadership and quiet floors, and an international house. On-campus housing is available on a first come, first served basis, and is available on a lottery system for upperclassmen. Priority is given to out-of-town students. 78% of students commute. Upperclassmen may keep cars.

FACULTY/CLASSROOMS: 50% of faculty are male; 50% are female. No introductory courses are taught by graduate students. The average class size in an introductory lecture is 25; in a laboratory is 24; and in a regular course is 25.

PROGRAMS OF STUDY: Towson confers B.A., B.S., B.F.A. and B.M. degrees. Master's and Doctoral degrees are also awarded. Bachelor's degrees are awarded in BIOLOGICAL SCIENCE (biology/biological science and molecular biology), BUSINESS (accounting, business administration and management, and sports management), COMMUNICATIONS AND THE ARTS (art, communications, dance, English, French, German, media arts, music, Spanish, and theater design), COMPUTER AND PHYSICAL SCIENCE (chemistry, computer science, earth science, geology, geoscience, information sciences and systems, mathematics, and physics), EDUCATION (art education, athletic training, dance education, early childhood education, education, education of the deaf and hearing impaired, elementary education, music education, physical education, and special education), ENGINEERING AND ENVIRONMENTAL DESIGN (environmental science), HEALTH PROFESSIONS (exercise science, health care administration, health science, medical laboratory technology, nursing, occupational therapy, speech pathology/audiology, and sports medicine), SOCIAL SCIENCE (anthropology, crosscultural studies, economics, family/consumer studies, geography, gerontology, history, interdisciplinary studies, international studies, law, philosophy, political science/government, psychology, religion, social science, sociology, and women's studies). Fine arts, business, and education are the strongest academically. Business disciplines, mass communications, and psychology have the largest enrollments.

ACTIVITIES: 8% of men belong to 13 national fraternities; 6% of women belong to 11 national sororities. Groups on campus include art, band, cheerleading, choir, chorale, chorus, computers, dance, drama, drill team, environmental, ethnic, forensics, gay, honors, international, jazz band, literary magazine, marching band, musical theater, orchestra, pep band, photography, political, professional, religious, social, social service, student government, and symphony. Popular campus events include Fraternity and Sorority Dances, Ethics Forum, and Tiger Fest. **Sports:** There are 7 intercollegiate sports for men and 12 for women. Facilities include an athletic center, a stadium, baseball and softball fields, tennis courts, a pool, a soccer field, and 3 practice fields. Recreation facilities include 3 gyms, a weight room, a pool, lighted playing fields, and an indoor climbing wall. **Graduates:** From July 1, 2013 to June 30, 2014, 3120 bachelor's degrees were awarded. The most popular majors were business administration (16%), psychology (8%), and mass communication (7%). 115 companies recruited on campus in 2013-2014.

SERVICES: Counseling and information services are available, as is tutoring in most subjects. There is a reader service for the blind, and remedial math, reading, and writing. There are also note takers, English language and tutorial services centers, a writing lab, and signers for the hearing impaired. **Library/Resources:** The library contains 364,468 volumes, 830,286 microform items, 14,174 audio/video tapes/CDs/DVDs, and subscribes to 2,164 periodicals including electronic. Computerized library services include interlibrary loans, database searching, and Internet access. Special learning facilities include an art gallery, planetarium, TV station, a curriculum center, a herbarium, animal museum, observatory, and greenhouse. **Physically Challenged Students:** 85% of the campus is accessible. Facilities include wheelchair ramps, elevators, special parking, specially equipped restrooms, special class scheduling, lowered drinking fountains, lowered telephones, special housing, automatic doors, assistive listening devices in theaters and concert halls, and interior and exterior signage. **Special:** Towson University offers cooperative programs with other institutions in the University System of Maryland and at Loyola College, the College of Notre Dame, and Johns Hopkins University, cross-registration at more than 80 colleges through the National Student Exchange, and study abroad. Students may pursue a dual major in physics and engineering, an interdisciplinary studies degree, which allows them to design their own majors, a 3-2 engineering program with the University of Maryland at College Park and Penn State, or nondegree study. There are pass/fail options, extensive evening offerings, and opportunities to earn credits between semesters. Internships are available in most majors, and work-study programs are offered both on and off campus. There are 20 national honor societies, a freshman honors program, and 12 departmental honors programs. **Visiting:** There are regularly scheduled orientations for prospective students, including campus tours, a session for parents, a session on the admissions process for transfers and freshmen, and a roundtable discussion. There are guides for informal visits. To schedule a visit, contact the Admissions Office. **Campus Safety and Security:** Measures include 24-hour foot and vehicle patrol, emergency notification system, self-defense education, and security escort services. There are shuttle buses, emergency telephones, lighted pathways/sidewalks, controlled access to dorms/residences, operation ID, and a police dog on campus.

REQUIREMENTS: The SAT or ACT is required. The ACT Optional Writing test is also required. Applicants should have graduated from an accredited secondary school or earned the GED. Secondary preparation should include 4 years of English, 3 each of math, lab science, and social studies, and 2 of foreign language. Prospective music and dance majors must audition. A GPA of 3.1 is required. AP and CLEP credits are accepted. Important factors in the admissions decision are advanced placement or honors courses, recommendations by school officials, and leadership record. Students must complete course work in the arts, English, humanities, math, biological or physical science, social science, information technology, and global awareness. **Procedure:** Freshmen are admitted fall and spring. Entrance exams should

be taken in the junior or senior year. There are deferred admissions and rolling admissions plans. Check with the school for current application deadlines. The fall 2014 application fee was $45. Notification is sent on a rolling basis. Applications are accepted on-line. **Transfer Students:** 2500 transfer students enrolled in 2013-2014. Transfer applicants should have earned at least 30 academic credits. For those with fewer than 30 attempted, freshmen requirements must be met. Minimum GPA requirements range from 2.0 to 2.5, depending on the number of credits completed. Transcripts are required. 30 of 120 credits required for the bachelor's degree must be completed at Towson. **International Students:** The school actively recruits these students. They must take the TOEFL and the college's own test, The TOEFL is required at preadmission; a college test is required at postadmission. They must also take the SAT or ACT, scoring 550. but the school accepts the TOEFL as a substitute for the verbal SAT.

ADMISSIONS: 9 freshmen graduated first in their class. **Admissions Contact:** Louise Shulack, Director of Admissions. E-Mail: *admissions@towson.edu* Web: *www.towson.edu*

FINANCIAL AID: In 2014-2015, 70% of all full-time freshmen and 62% of continuing full-time students received some form of financial aid. 43% of all full-time freshmen and 39% of continuing full-time students received need-based aid. The average freshman award was $12,131. Need-based scholarships or need-based grants averaged $7,019; need-based self-help aid (loans and jobs) averaged $3,503; non-need-based athletic scholarships averaged $9,663; and other non-need-based awards and non-need-based scholarships averaged $3,502. 72% of undergraduate students work part-time. Average annual earnings from campus work are $1185. The average financial indebtedness of the 2014 graduate was $14,085. The FAFSA is required. Check with the school for current application deadlines.

UNITED STATES NAVAL ACADEMY	E-3
www.usna.edu	

Annapolis, MD 21402	(410) 293-4361
	(888) 249-7707
Fax: (410) 293-1815	Email: webmail@usna.edu
Full-time: 3479 men, 1032 women	Faculty: 549; IIB, ++$
Part-time: n/av	Ph.D.s: 64%
Graduate: n/av	Student/Faculty: 8 to 1
Year: semesters	Tuition: see profile
Room & Board: n/app	Freshman Class: 18457 applied, 1398 accepted, 1191 enrolled
SAT CR/M: 661/679 **ACT:** required	CEEB CODE: 5809
Application Deadline: January 31	MOST COMPETITIVE

The United States Naval Academy, founded in 1845, is a national military service college offering undergraduate degree programs and professional training in aviation, surface ships, submarines, and various military, maritime, and technical fields. The U.S. Navy pays tuition, room and board, medical and dental care, and a monthly stipend to all Naval Academy students. Graduates earn a Bachelor of Science degree and a commission in the United States Navy or the United States Marine Corps and have a five year obligation of active military service. There is 1 undergraduate school. In addition to regional accreditation, Annapolis has baccalaureate program accreditation with ABET, CSAB, and ACS. The 338-acre campus is in a small town on the Chesapeake Bay 30 miles southeast of Baltimore, Maryland and 32 miles east of Washington, D.C. Including any residence halls, there are 75 buildings.

STUDENT LIFE: 96% of undergraduates are from out of state. Students are from 50 states, and 30 foreign countries. 65% are White; 11% Hispanic. **Male To Female Ratio:** 0.3:1. The average age of freshmen is 18; all undergraduates, 20. 6% do not continue beyond their first year; 89% remain to graduate. **Housing:** 4700 students can be accommodated in college housing, which includes coed dorms. On-campus housing is guaranteed for all 4 years. Some may keep cars.

FACULTY/CLASSROOMS: 72% of faculty are male; 28% are female. All teach undergraduates, 80% do research, and 80% do both. No introductory courses are taught by graduate students. The average

class size in an introductory lecture is 20; in a laboratory is 18; and in a regular course is 18.

PROGRAMS OF STUDY: Annapolis confers B.S. degrees. Bachelor's degrees are awarded in BUSINESS (operations research), COMMUNICATIONS AND THE ARTS (Arabic, Chinese, and English), COMPUTER AND PHYSICAL SCIENCE (chemistry, computer science, information sciences and systems, mathematics, oceanography, physics, and science), ENGINEERING AND ENVIRONMENTAL DESIGN (aeronautical engineering, computer engineering, electrical/electronics engineering technology, engineering, marine engineering, mechanical engineering, naval architecture and marine engineering, nuclear engineering, ocean engineering, and systems engineering), HEALTH PROFESSIONS (cytotechnology), SOCIAL SCIENCE (economics, history, and political science/government).

ACTIVITIES: There are no fraternities or sororities. There are 109 groups on campus, including bagpipe, cheerleading, chess, choir, chorus, computers, debate, drama, drill team, drum and bugle corps, ethnic, honors, international, jazz band, literary magazine, marching band, Military Professional, musical theater, orchestra, pep band, photography, professional, radio and TV, religious, social, social service, student government, and yearbook. Popular campus events include Commissioning Week, which includes the Plebe Recognition Ceremony, Ring Dance, and Graduation. **Sports:** There are 21 intercollegiate sports for men and 13 for women, and 23 intramural sports for men and 23 for women. Facilities include a 34,000-seat stadium, a 5700-seat basketball arena, Olympic pool with a diving well for 10-meter diving boards, wrestling arena, 200-meter indoor track, 400-meter outdoor track, indoor ice rink, 6 Nautilus and weight rooms, facilities for gymnastics, boxing, volleyball, swimming, water polo, racquetball, basketball and personal conditioning, squash courts, climbing wall, baseball stadium, crew house, 18 hole golf course, soccer facility, a sailing center, indoor and outdoor tennis courts, and 2 athletic field houses. **Graduates:** From July 1, 2013 to June 30, 2014, 1082 bachelor's degrees were awarded. The most popular majors were political science (10%), oceanography (10%), and economics (9%). 2 companies recruited on campus in 2013-2014. In an average class, 87% graduate in 4 years or less. Of the 2013 graduating class, 6% were enrolled in graduate school within 6 months of graduation, and 100% were employed.

SERVICES: Counseling and information services are available, as is tutoring in most subjects. There is remedial math, reading, and writing. **Library/Resources:** The library contains 1.1 million volumes, 185,010 microform items, 7,664 audio/video tapes/CDs/DVDs, and subscribes to 70,911 periodicals including electronic. Computerized library services include interlibrary loans, database searching, Internet access, and Wi-Fi capability. Special learning facilities include a planetarium, radio station, propulsion lab, wind tunnels, an oceanographic research vessel, field laboratory, weather station, towing tanks, a flight simulator, a naval history museum, chamber facilities, environmental chamber facilities, 16-inch Cassegrain reflector telescope, and a 12-meter satellite earth station. **Physically Challenged Students:** All of the campus is accessible. Facilities include wheelchair ramps, elevators, special parking, and specially equipped restrooms. **Special:** A voluntary graduate program is available for those midshipmen who complete academic graduation requirements by the end of their seventh semester and are selected to begin master's work at nearby universities. Midshipmen selected as Trident Scholars spend their senior year in independent research at the Naval Academy. Study abroad for one semester is available in countries around the world. Honors programs are available in selected majors. There are 9 national honor societies and 9 departmental honors programs. **Visiting:** There are regularly scheduled orientations for prospective students, visitation weekends for highly competitive candidates for admission, and summer seminar weeks for rising high school seniors. There are guides for informal visits, visitors may sit in on classes, and stay overnight. To schedule a visit, contact USNA Admissions. **Campus Safety and Security:** Measures include 24-hour foot and vehicle patrol, emergency notification system, and self-defense education. There are emergency telephones, lighted pathways/sidewalks, controlled access to dorms/residences, in-room safes, and gate guards.

REQUIREMENTS: The SAT or ACT is required. Candidates must be unmarried with no dependents, U.S. citizens of good moral character, and between 17 and 22 years of age. Candidates should have a solid secondary school background, including 4 years each of English and math, 2 years of a foreign language, and 1 year each of U.S. history, world or European history, chemistry, physics, and computer literacy. Candidates must obtain an official nomination from congressional or military sources. An interview is conducted, and medical and physical aptitude exams must be passed to qualify for admission. AP credits are accepted. Students must complete approximately 140 semester hours, including core requirements in mathematics, engineering, natural sciences, humanities, and social sciences. Professional development courses and physical education are required during all 4 years. Physical readiness test must be passed semi-annually. During required summer training sessions, students train aboard U.S. Navy ships, submarines, and aircraft and with units of the U.S. Marine Corps. Graduates serve at least 5 years on active duty as commissioned officers of the United States Navy or United States Marine Corps. **Procedure:** Freshmen are admitted summer. Entrance exams should be taken during December of the junior year in high school. There are early admissions and rolling admissions plans. Applications should be filed by January 31 for fall entry. Notifications are sent April 15. Applications are accepted on-line. **Transfer Students:** All students enter as freshmen/plebes and must complete the entire 47 month program. 140 of 140 credits required for the bachelor's degree must be completed at Annapolis. **International Students:** There are 59 international students enrolled. The school actively recruits these students. They must take the TOEFL. They must also take the SAT or ACT.

ADMISSIONS: 8% of the 2014-2015 applicants were accepted. The SAT scores for the 2014-2015 freshman class were: Critical Reading--5% below 500, 32% between 500 and 599, 44% between 600 and 699, and 19% between 700 and 800; Math--1% below 500, 19% between 500 and 599, 51% between 600 and 699, and 29% between 700 and 800. 76% of the current freshmen were in the top fifth of their class; 91% were in the top two fifths. 168 freshmen graduated first in their class. **Admissions Contact:** Candidate Guidance Office E-Mail: *webmail@usna.edu* Web: *www.usna.edu*

FINANCIAL AID: Check with the school for current application deadlines.

UNIVERSITY OF MARYLAND/BALTIMORE COUNTY   D-2
www.umbc.edu

Baltimore, MD 21250	(410) 455-2291
Fax: (410) 455-1094	Email: admissions@umbc.edu
Full-time: 4365 men, 3610 women	Faculty: I, -$
Part-time: 765 men, 750 women	Ph.D.s: 85%
Graduate: 1165 men, 1425 women	Student/Faculty: n/av
Year: semesters, summer session	Tuition: $9967 ($20,370)
Room & Board: $10,521	Freshman Class: n/av
SAT or ACT: required	CEEB CODE: 5835
Application Deadline: see profile	VERY COMPETITIVE

UMBC, founded in 1966, is a public research university offering programs in liberal arts and sciences and engineering. There are 4 undergraduate schools and 3 graduate schools. The figures in the above capsule and this profile are approximate. In addition to regional accreditation, UMBC has baccalaureate program accreditation with ABET, CSWE, and NCATE. The library contains 1.0 million volumes, 1.1 million microform items, 1.9 million audio/video tapes/CDs/DVDs, and subscribes to 4138 periodicals including electronic. Computerized library services include interlibrary loans, database searching, and Internet access. Special learning facilities include a learning resource center, an art gallery, a radio station, the Imaging Research Center, the Howard Hughes Medical Institute, and a telescope. The 530-acre campus is in a suburban area 5 miles southwest of Baltimore and 35 miles north of Washington, D.C. Including any residence halls, there are 50 buildings.

STUDENT LIFE: 89% of undergraduates are from Maryland. Others are from 43 states, 95 foreign countries, and Canada. 52% are white;

18% Asian American; 15% African American. The average age of freshmen is 18; all undergraduates, 22. 15% do not continue beyond their first year; 56% remain to graduate.

FACULTY/CLASSROOMS: 61% of faculty are male; 39% are female. No introductory courses are taught by graduate students. The average class size in an introductory lecture is 41; in a laboratory, 28; and in a regular course, 30.

PROGRAMS OF STUDY: UMBC confers B.A., B.S., B.F.A., and B.S.E. degrees. Master's and doctoral degrees are also awarded. Bachelor's degrees are awarded in AGRICULTURE (environmental studies), BIOLOGICAL SCIENCE (biochemistry, bioinformatics, and biology/biological science), COMMUNICATIONS AND THE ARTS (communications, dance, dramatic arts, English, fine arts, French, German, linguistics, modern language, music, Russian, Spanish, theater design, and visual and performing arts), COMPUTER AND PHYSICAL SCIENCE (chemistry, computer science, information sciences and systems, mathematics, physics, and statistics), ENGINEERING AND ENVIRONMENTAL DESIGN (chemical engineering, computer engineering, environmental science, and mechanical engineering), HEALTH PROFESSIONS (emergency medical technologies and health science), SOCIAL SCIENCE (African American studies, American studies, anthropology, classical/ancient civilization, economics, gender studies, geography, history, interdisciplinary studies, philosophy, political science/government, psychology, social work, sociology, and women's studies). Information systems, computer science, and biological sciences have the largest enrollments.

ACTIVITIES: 4% of men belong to 11 national fraternities; 4% of women belong to 8 national sororities. There are 180 groups on campus, including art, band, cheerleading, chess, choir, chorus, computers, Council of Majors, dance, debate, drama, ethnic, film, gay, honors, Intellectual Sports Council, international, jazz band, literary magazine, Model United Nations, musical threater, newspaper, opera, orchestra, pep band, political, professional, radio and TV, religious, social, social service, student government, and symphony. Popular campus events include Quadmania, Welcome Week, and Family Weekend.

SERVICES: Counseling and information services are available, as is tutoring in most subjects. There is a reader service for the blind and remedial math, reading, and writing. Other services include notetakers, readers, mobility training, American Sign Language interpreters, and scribes for students who have a need based on a manual or learning disability.

REQUIREMENTS: The SAT or ACT is required. Minimum high school preparation should include 4 years of English, 3 years each of social science/history and math, including algebra I and II and geometry, 3 years of lab sciences and 2 of a foreign language. An essay is required of all freshman applicants. A GPA of 3.0 is required. AP and CLEP credits are accepted. Important factors in the admissions decision are advanced placement or honors courses, recommendations by school officials, and leadership record.

FINANCIAL AID: The FAFSA is required. Check with the school for current application deadlines.

UNIVERSITY OF MARYLAND/COLLEGE PARK   D-3
www.umd.edu

College Park, MD 20742	(301) 314-8385
	(800) 422-5867
Fax: (301) 314-9693	Email: ApplyMaryland@umd.edu
Full-time: 13270 men, 11757 women	Faculty: 1756; I, +$
	Ph.D.s: 88%
Part-time: 1207 men, 822 women	Student/Faculty: 15 to 1
Graduate: 5553 men, 5001 women	Tuition: $9427 ($29,720)
Year: semesters, summer session	Freshman Class: 26205 applied, 12293 accepted, 4129 enrolled
Room & Board: $10,633	
SAT or ACT: required	CEEB CODE: 5814
Application Deadline: January 20	HIGHLY COMPETITIVE

University of Maryland/College Park, founded in 1856, is a land-

---

grant institution, the flagship campus of the state's university system, offering undergraduate and graduate degrees. There are 11 undergraduate schools and 13 graduate schools. In addition to regional accreditation, Maryland has baccalaureate program accreditation with AACSB, ABET, ACEJMC, ASLA, NASM, NCATE, and CADE. The 1250-acre campus is in a suburban area 3 miles northeast of Washington, D.C., and 35 miles south of Baltimore. Including any residence halls, there are 259 buildings.

STUDENT LIFE: 77% of undergraduates are from Maryland. Others are from 49 states, 76 foreign countries, and Canada. 52% are White; 16% Asian American; 13% African American. **Male To Female Ratio:** 1.1:1. The average age of freshmen is 18; all undergraduates, 21. 4% do not continue beyond their first year; 85% remain to graduate. **Housing:** 12439 students can be accommodated in college housing, which includes single-sex and coed dorms and on-campus apartments. In addition, there are honors houses, language houses, special-interest houses, fraternity houses, and sorority houses. On-campus housing is guaranteed for the freshman year only and is available on a lottery system for upperclassmen. 56% of students commute. All students may keep cars.

FACULTY/CLASSROOMS: 61% of faculty are male; 39% are female. 58% teach undergraduates, and 42% do research. Graduate students teach 12% of introductory courses. The average class size in an introductory lecture is 35; in a laboratory is 21; and in a regular course is 34.

PROGRAMS OF STUDY: Maryland confers B.A., B.S., B.L.A., B.M. and B.M.E. degrees. Master's and doctoral degrees are also awarded. Bachelor's degrees are awarded in AGRICULTURE (agricultural business management, agricultural economics, agriculture, animal science, natural resource management, and plant science), BIOLOGICAL SCIENCE (biochemistry, biology/biological science, microbiology, and nutrition), BUSINESS (accounting, business administration and management, finance, international business management, logistics, management information systems, marketing, operations management, and supply chain management), COMMUNICATIONS AND THE ARTS (Arabic, art history and appreciation, Chinese, classics, communications, dance, dramatic arts, English, English literature, film arts, foreign language, French, Germanic languages and literature, Japanese, journalism, linguistics, music, music performance, music theory and composition, romance languages and literature, Russian, Spanish, studio art, and theatre arts), COMPUTER AND PHYSICAL SCIENCE (astronomy, atmospheric sciences and meteorology, chemistry, computer science, geology, information sciences and systems, mathematics, physical sciences, and physics), EDUCATION (art education, drama education, early childhood education, education, elementary education, middle school education, music education, physical education, secondary education, and special education), ENGINEERING AND ENVIRONMENTAL DESIGN (aerospace engineering, architecture, bioengineering, chemical engineering, civil engineering, computer engineering, electrical/electronics engineering, engineering, environmental science, fire protection engineering, landscape architecture/design, materials engineering, and mechanical engineering), HEALTH PROFESSIONS (community health work, predentistry, preveterinary science, public health, speech pathology/audiology, and veterinary science), SOCIAL SCIENCE (African American studies, American studies, anthropology, criminal justice, criminology, economics, family/consumer studies, geography, history, interdisciplinary studies, Italian studies, Judaic studies, philosophy, political science/government, prelaw, psychology, Russian and Slavic studies, sociology, and women's studies). Engineering, computer science, and business are the strongest academically. Biological sciences, economics, psychology are the largest.

ACTIVITIES: 13% of men belong to 32 national fraternities; 14% of women belong to 24 national sororities. There are 675 groups on campus, including art, band, cheerleading, chess, choir, chorale, chorus, computers, dance, debate, drama, drill team, environmental, ethnic, film, forensics, gay, honors, international, jazz band, literary magazine, marching band, musical theater, newspaper, opera, orchestra, pep band, photography, political, professional, radio and TV, religious, social, social service, student government, symphony, and yearbook. Popular campus events include Art Attack, Union All-Niter and Maryland Day. **Sports:** There are 8 intercollegiate sports for men and 11 for women, and 17 intramural sports for men and 17 for women. Facilities include 2 indoor and 2 outdoor swimming pools, intramural fields, tennis, squash, racquetball, volleyball, and basketball courts, a fitness center including weight rooms, aerobic rooms, martial arts rooms, saunas, and an indoor track, a bowling alley, golf course, an outdoor artificial turf field. Athletic facilities include a 51,000-seat stadium, a 17,950-seat gym, and indoor and outdoor artificial turf practice fields. **Graduates:** From July 1, 2013 to June 30, 2014, 7044 bachelor's degrees were awarded. The most popular majors were engineering (12%), biological sciences (7%), and criminology and crinimal justice (5%). In an average class, 67% graduate in 4 years or less, 82% graduate in 5 years or less, and 85% graduate in 6 years or less.

SERVICES: Counseling and information services are available, as is tutoring in most subjects, including all 100- and 200-level courses. There is a reader service for the blind, and remedial math. **Library/ Resources:** The 7 libraries contain 4.3 million volumes, 508,530 microform items, and 402,053 audio/video tapes/CDs/DVDs, and subscribe to 146,645 periodicals including electronic. Computerized library services include interlibrary loans, database searching, Internet access, and Wi-Fi capability. Special learning facilities include an art gallery, radio station, TV station, an observatory. **Physically Challenged Students:** 95% of the campus is accessible. Facilities include wheelchair ramps, elevators, special parking, specially equipped restrooms, special class scheduling, lowered drinking fountains, lowered telephones, special shuttle service, and electronic doors. **Special:** Each of the 11 undergraduate schools offers special programs, and there is a campus-wide co-op education program offering engineering and other majors. In addition, the university offers cross-registration with other colleges in the Consortium of Universities of the Washington Metropolitan area, several living-learning programs for undergraduates, the B.A./B.S. degree in most majors, dual and student-designed majors, non-degree study, an accelerated veterinary medicine program, varied study abroad opportunities, work-study programs with government and nonprofit organizations, and internship opportunities with federal and state legislators, the local media, and various federal agencies. There are 49 national honor societies, including Phi Beta Kappa, a freshman honors program, and 39 departmental honors programs. **Visiting:** There are regularly scheduled orientations for prospective students, consisting of 3 fall and 4 spring open house programs for admitted students, as well as regularly scheduled information sessions followed by a campus tour. There are guides for informal visits, visitors may sit in on classes, and stay overnight. To schedule a visit, contact the Office of Undergraduate Admissions. **Campus Safety and Security:** Measures include 24-hour foot and vehicle patrol, emergency notification system, self-defense education, and security escort services. There are shuttle buses, emergency telephones, lighted pathways/sidewalks, controlled access to dorms/ residences, Video surveillance.

REQUIREMENTS: The SAT or ACT is required. The ACT Optional Writing test is also required. In addition, The university evaluates exam scores along with GPA, curriculum, and other criteria. Applicants should be graduates of accredited secondary schools or have the GED. Secondary preparation should include 4 years of English, 3 of history or social sciences, 2 of algebra and 1 of plane geometry, and 2 of lab sciences. An essay and counselor recommendation are required. Music majors must also audition. Applicants who submit the ACT rather than the SAT must submit the ACT Writing Test. AP and CLEP credits are accepted. Important factors in the admissions decision are advanced placement or honors courses, recommendations by school officials, parents or siblings attended your school, evidence of special talent, extracurricular activities record, and geographical diversity. Most programs require a minimum of 120 credits for graduation; the number of hours required in the major varies. All students are required to complete a set of General Education courses. **Procedure:** Freshmen are admitted fall, spring, and summer. Entrance exams should be taken at the end of the junior year or the beginning of the senior year. There are deferred admissions and rolling admissions plans. Early decision applications should be filed by November 1; regular applications, by January 20 for fall entry; and December 1 for spring entry, along with a $65 fee. Notification of early decision is sent February 15; regular decision, April 1. Applications are accepted on-line. **Transfer Students:** 1854 transfer students enrolled in 2013-2014. Transfer applicants from regionally accredited institutions should have attempted at least 12 credits and have earned at least a 2.5 GPA, although this requirement varies depending on space available. Applicants from Maryland community colleges may be given special consideration. 30 of 120 credits required for the bachelor's degree must be completed at Maryland. **International Students:** There are 1022 international students enrolled. They must take the TOEFL with a minimum score of 100 on the Internet-based version (iBT), or take the IELTS. They must also take the SAT or ACT.

ADMISSIONS: 47% of the 2014-2015 applicants were accepted. The SAT scores for the 2014-2015 freshman class were: Critical Reading--6% below 500, 23% between 500 and 599, 49% between 600 and 699, and 22% between 700 and 800; Math--3% below 500, 15% between 500 and 599, 42% between 600 and 699, and 40% between 700 and 800. **Admissions Contact:** Admissions Officer E-Mail: *ApplyMaryland@umd.edu* Web: *www.umd.edu*

FINANCIAL AID: 37% of all full-time freshmen and 34% of continuing full-time students received need-based aid. The average freshman award was $12,986. Need-based scholarships or need-based grants averaged $9,100; need-based self-help aid (loans and jobs) averaged $5,553; non-need-based athletic scholarships averaged $17,485; and other non-need-based awards and non-need-based scholarships averaged $6,451. 19% of undergraduate students work part-time. Average annual earnings from campus work are $5000. The average financial indebtedness of the 2014 graduate was $25,254. The FAFSA is required. The priority date for freshman financial aid applications for fall entry is February 15.

UNIVERSITY OF MARYLAND/EASTERN SHORE
F-4

www.umes.edu

Princess Anne, MD 21853	(410) 651-6410
Fax: (410) 651-7922	Email: ccmills@mail.umes.edu
Full-time: 1225 men, 1810 women	Faculty: IIA, av$
Part-time: 125 men, 175 women	Ph.D.s: 80%
Graduate: 190 men, 255 women	Student/Faculty: n/av
Year: semesters, summer session	Tuition: $7000 ($14,000)
Room & Board: $7000	Freshman Class: n/av
SAT: required	CEEB CODE: 5400
Application Deadline: n/av	VERY COMPETITIVE

The University of Maryland/Eastern Shore, founded in 1886, is a public university and part of the University of Maryland System offering undergraduate and graduate programs in the arts and sciences, professional studies, and agricultural sciences. The figures in the above capsule and in this profile are approximate. There are 3 undergraduate schools and 1 graduate school. The 700-acre campus is in a rural area 15 miles south of Salisbury. Including any residence halls, there are 40 buildings.

STUDENT LIFE: 71% of undergraduates are from Maryland. Others are from 32 states, 48 foreign countries, and Canada. 85% are from public schools. 76% are African American; 18% White. 90% are Protestant. The average age of freshmen is 18; all undergraduates, 24. 25% do not continue beyond their first year; 36% remain to graduate. **Housing:** 1530 students can be accommodated in college housing, which includes single-sex dorms, on-campus apartments, and off-campus apartments. In addition, there are honors houses, fraternity houses, and a residential complex. On-campus housing is available on a first-come, first-served basis, and is available on a lottery system for upperclassmen. 50% of students commute. All students may keep cars.

FACULTY/CLASSROOMS: 45% of faculty are male; 55% are female. 85% teach undergraduates, and 15% do research. Graduate students teach 1% of introductory courses. The average class size in an introductory lecture is 75; in a laboratory is 18; and in a regular course is 30.

PROGRAMS OF STUDY: UMES confers B.A., B.S., B.G.S. and B.M. degrees. Master's and Doctoral degrees are also awarded. Bachelor's degrees are awarded in AGRICULTURE (agriculture and poultry science), BIOLOGICAL SCIENCE (biology/biological science), BUSINESS (accounting, business administration and management, and hotel/motel and restaurant management), COMMUNICATIONS AND THE ARTS (English), COMPUTER AND PHYSICAL SCIENCE (chemistry, computer science, and mathematics), EDUCATION (agricultural education, art education, business education, elementary education, health education, home economics education, industrial arts education, mathematics education, music education, physical education, science education, secondary education, and social science education), ENGINEERING AND ENVIRONMENTAL DESIGN (aeronautical science, construction technology, engineering technology, and environmental science), HEALTH PROFESSIONS (physical therapy and rehabilitation therapy), SOCIAL SCIENCE (criminal justice, history, home economics, liberal arts/general studies, and sociology). Physical therapy, engineering, and environmental science are the strongest academically. Business, hotel/restaurant management, and biology have the largest enrollments.

ACTIVITIES: 20% of men belong to 4 national fraternities; 20% of women belong to 4 national sororities. There are 25 groups on campus, including art, band, cheerleading, choir, chorale, chorus, computers, dance, drama, drill team, ethnic, honors, international, jazz band, literary magazine, musical theater, newspaper, pep band, photography, political, professional, radio and TV, religious, social, social service, student government, and yearbook. Popular campus events include Parents Day, Spring Festival, and Ethnic Festival. **Sports:** There are 5 intercollegiate sports for men and 5 for women, and 4 intramural sports for men and 4 for women. Facilities include an indoor swimming pool and a 3000-seat stadium.

SERVICES: Counseling and information services are available, as is tutoring in every subject. There is remedial math, reading, and writing. **Library/Resources:** The library contains 150,000 volumes. Computerized library services include interlibrary loans and database searching. Special learning facilities include an art gallery and radio station. **Physically Challenged Students:** 20% of the campus is accessible. Facilities include wheelchair ramps, elevators, special parking, specially equipped restrooms, special class scheduling, lowered drinking fountains, and lowered telephones. **Special:** Students may cross-register at Salisbury State University. A cooperative education program, internships, a winter term, work-study programs, a general studies degree, and dual and student-designed majors are offered. Also available are an accelerated degree program and a 3-2 engineering degree with the University of Maryland/College Park. There are pass/fail options. There is 1 national honor society, a freshman honors program, and 10 departmental honors programs. **Visiting:** There are regularly scheduled orientations for prospective students, including 2 formal orientation sessions and 9 visitation/open house days. There are guides for informal visits and visitors may sit in on classes. To schedule a visit, contact the Office of Recruitment at (410) 651-6178. **Campus Safety and Security:** Measures include 24-hour foot and vehicle patrol and security escort services. There are shuttle buses, emergency telephones, lighted pathways/sidewalks, and a student security team.

REQUIREMENTS: The SAT is required. Applicants should be graduates of accredited secondary schools or have the GED. High school preparation should include 4 years of English, 3 each of social science or history and math, including 2 of algebra and 1 of geometry, and 2 of lab science. An essay and interview are recommended. UMES recommends that prospective art education majors submit a portfolio. A GPA of 2.5 is required. AP and CLEP credits are accepted. Important factors in the admissions decision are advanced placement or honors courses, leadership record, and recommendations by school officials. Students must complete 122 hours, including 36 hours in the major, 15 in communicative and quantitative skills, 9 in humanities, 7 in natural sciences, 6 in social sciences, and 4 in health and phys ed. A minimum 2.0 overall GPA is required. **Procedure:** Freshmen are admitted to all sessions. Entrance exams should be taken in April. There are early decision, early admissions, deferred admissions, and rolling admissions plans. Check with the school for current application deadlines. The fall 2014 application fee was $25. **Transfer Students:** Transfer applicants must have attempted at least 9 credits at another institution and have at least a cumulative GPA of 2.0 or have earned an associate degree or completed 56 hours of

community college work. 75 of 122 credits required for the bachelor's degree must be completed at UMES. **International Students:** They must take the TOEFL. They must also take the SAT, scoring 800.

ADMISSIONS: Cheryll Collier-Mills, Director of Admissions and Recruitment. E-Mail: *ccmills@mail.umes.edu* Web: *www.umes.edu*

FINANCIAL AID: UMES is a member of CSS. The the college's own financial statement is required. Check with the school for current application deadlines.

UNIVERSITY OF MARYLAND/UNIVERSITY COLLEGE (*The complete profile is made available exclusively on our website, www. barronspac.com*)

UNIVERSITY SYSTEM OF MARYLAND

The University System of Maryland, established in 1856, is a public system in Maryland. It is governed by a board of regents, whose chief administrator is chancellor. The primary goal of the system is research, teaching, and public service. The total student enrollment for all eleven campuses is usually 105,000 with 8,000 faculty members. Altogether there are 347 baccalaureate, 212 master's and 115 doctoral programs offered in the University System of Maryland. Profiles of the 4-year campuses are included in this section.

WASHINGTON ADVENTIST UNIVERSITY (*The complete profile is made available exclusively on our website, www.barronspac.com*)

WASHINGTON COLLEGE	E-2
www.washcoll.edu	

Chestertown, MD 21620	(410) 778-7700
	(800) 422-1782
Fax: (410) 778-7287	Email: wc_admissions@washcoll.edu
Full-time: 600 men, 817 women	**Faculty:** 91; IIB, +$
Part-time: 19 men, 18 women	**Ph.D.s:** 95%
Graduate: 9 men, 9 women	**Student/Faculty:** 12 to 1
Year: semesters	**Tuition:** $42,592
Room & Board: $10,010	**Freshman Class:** 5318 applied, 2960 accepted, 388 enrolled
SAT CR/M: 585/570	**CEEB CODE:** 5888
Application Deadline: February 15	**VERY COMPETITIVE**

Washington College, founded in 1782, is an independent college offering programs in the liberal arts and sciences, business management, and teacher preparation. There is 1 graduate school. The 112-acre campus is in a small town 75 miles from Baltimore. Including any residence halls, there are 71 buildings.

STUDENT LIFE: 55% of undergraduates are from out of state, mostly the Middle Atlantic. Students are from 30 states, 34 foreign countries, and Canada. 68% are from public schools. 73% are White. The average age of freshmen is 18; all undergraduates, 20. 18% do not continue beyond their first year; 74% remain to graduate. **Housing:** 1226 students can be accommodated in college housing, which includes single-sex and coed dorms and on-campus apartments. In addition, there are special-interest houses, fraternity houses, International house, a science house, and substance-free housing, theme housing and wellness housing. On-campus housing is guaranteed for the freshman year only and is available on a lottery system for upperclassmen. 85% of students live on campus; of those, 65% remain on campus on weekends. All students may keep cars.

FACULTY/CLASSROOMS: 54% of faculty are male; 46% are female. All teach undergraduates. No introductory courses are taught by graduate students. The average class size in an introductory lecture is 15; in a laboratory is 16; and in a regular course is 15.

PROGRAMS OF STUDY: WC confers B.A., and B.S. degrees. Master's degrees are also awarded. Bachelor's degrees are awarded in AGRICULTURE (environmental studies), BIOLOGICAL SCIENCE (biology/biological science), BUSINESS (business administration and management), COMMUNICATIONS AND THE ARTS (art, dramatic arts, English, fine arts, French, German, music, and Spanish),

COMPUTER AND PHYSICAL SCIENCE (chemistry, computer science, mathematics, and physics), ENGINEERING AND ENVIRONMENTAL DESIGN (environmental science), SOCIAL SCIENCE (American studies, anthropology, economics, history, humanities, interdisciplinary studies, international studies, liberal arts, sciences, general studies, humanities, philosophy, political science/government, psychology, and sociology). Biology, business management, and psychology have the largest enrollments.

ACTIVITIES: 8% of men belong to 3 national fraternities; 14% of women belong to 3 national sororities. There are 100 groups on campus, including and education and leadership, band, chorale, chorus, computers, dance, debate, drama, environmental, ethnic, gay, honors, international, jazz band, literary magazine, minority and human rights, newspaper, orchestra, photography, political, professional, radio and TV, religious, social, social service, student government, and yearbook. Popular campus events include Fall and Spring Convocations, George Washington Birthday Ball, War on the Shore, and May Day. **Sports:** There are 8 intercollegiate sports for men and 10 for women, and 12 intramural sports for men and 11 for women. Facilities include a stadium, swim center, gym, field house, squash and racquetball courts, fitness center, playing and practice fields, and a boathouse. There are riding facilities nearby. **Graduates:** From July 1, 2013 to June 30, 2014, 325 bachelor's degrees were awarded. The most popular majors were social sciences (20%), business and marketing (15%), and biological and life sciences (11%). 75 companies recruited on campus in 2013-2014. In an average class, 2% graduate in 3 years or less, 75% graduate in 4 years or less, 77% graduate in 5 years or less, and 80% graduate in 6 years or less. Of the 2013 graduating class, 15% were enrolled in graduate school within 6 months of graduation, and 75% were employed.

SERVICES: Counseling and information services are available, as is tutoring in every subject. There is remedial math and writing. **Library/Resources:** The library contains 219,461 volumes, 100,635 microform items, 8,701 audio/video tapes/CDs/DVDs, and subscribes to 28,222 periodicals including electronic. Computerized library services include interlibrary loans, database searching, Internet access, and Wi-Fi capability. Special learning facilities include an art gallery, radio station, the center for the American Experience, the center for Environment and Society, the Kohl Gallery, and the Rose O'Neill Literary House. **Physically Challenged Students:** 95% of the campus is accessible. Facilities include wheelchair ramps, elevators, special parking, specially equipped restrooms, special class scheduling, lowered drinking fountains, lowered telephones. **Special:** A program that provides internships, externships, and job shadowing during all four years is available in all majors. There is study abroad in 26 countries and a Washington, D.C. semester. The college offers a 3-2 nursing program with Johns Hopkins University and a 3-2 pharmacology program, along with an option for a student-designed interdisciplinary major. There are 19 national honor societies including Phi Beta Kappa. **Visiting:** There are regularly scheduled orientations for prospective students, consisting of weekday visits. There are guides for informal visits and visitors may sit in on classes. To schedule a visit, contact the Admissions Office at ADM_OFF@washcoll.edu. **Campus Safety and Security:** Measures include 24-hour foot and vehicle patrol, emergency notification system, and security escort services. There are emergency telephones, lighted pathways/sidewalks, controlled access to dorms/residences, including peer education through student groups.

REQUIREMENTS: The SAT is required. Applicants must be graduates of an accredited secondary school or have a GED. 16 Carnegie units are required; 20 are recommended. Applicants should take high school courses in English, foreign language, history, math, science, and social studies. An essay is required, and an interview is recommended. A GPA of 2.4 is required. AP and CLEP credits are accepted. Important factors in the admissions decision are advanced placement or honors courses, recommendations by school officials, and leadership record. All students are required to take a freshman Global Perspective seminar and courses distributed among the social sciences, natural sciences, humanities, quantitative studies, foreign languages, and a writing requirement. The Senior Capstone Experience consists of a comprehensive exam, thesis, or independent project. Students must complete 128 credit hours, including at least 32 in the major, to graduate. A minimum GPA of 2.0 is required. **Procedure:** Freshmen are admitted fall and spring. Entrance exams should be taken in the spring of the junior year or fall of the senior year. There are early decision, deferred admissions, and rolling admissions plans. Early decision applications should be filed by November 1; regular applications, by February 15 for fall entry; and December 1 for spring entry, along with a $50 fee. Notification is sent on a rolling basis. 51 early decision candidates were accepted for the 2014-2015 class. 426 applicants were on the 2014 waiting list; 22 were admitted. Applications are accepted on-line. **Transfer Students:** 27 transfer students enrolled in 2013-2014. Requirements for students are a minimum GPA of 2.3, a high school transcript, college transcript(s) and essay or personal statement. An interview and standardized test scores are recommended. 56 of 128 credits required for the bachelor's degree must be completed at WC. **International Students:** There are 73 international students enrolled. The school actively recruits these students. They must take the TOEFL with a minimum score of 550 on the paper-based TOEFL (PBT) or 79 on the Internet-based version (iBT). They must also take the SAT or ACT.

ADMISSIONS: 56% of the 2014-2015 applicants were accepted. The SAT scores for the 2014-2015 freshman class were: Critical Reading--8% below 500, 46% between 500 and 599, 40% between 600 and 699, and 6% between 700 and 800; Math--13% below 500, 42% between 500 and 599, 41% between 600 and 699, and 4% between 700 and 800. 55% of the current freshmen were in the top fifth of their class; 82% were in the top two fifths. There were 3 National Merit finalists. 3 freshmen graduated first in their class. **Admissions Contact:** Kevin Coveney, Vice President of Admissions. E-Mail: *wc_admissions@washcoll.edu* Web: *http://www.washcoll.edu/admissions/*

FINANCIAL AID: In 2014-2015, 92% of all full-time freshmen and 90% of continuing full-time students received some form of financial aid. 100% of all full-time freshmen and 98% of continuing full-time students received need-based aid. The average freshman award was $31,111. Need-based scholarships or need-based grants averaged $25,047; need-based self-help aid (loans and jobs) averaged $3,834; other non-need-based awards and non-need-based scholarships averaged $15,782; and $3,413 from other forms of aid. 40% of undergraduate students work part-time. Average annual earnings from campus work are $1000. The average financial indebtedness of the 2014 graduate was $34,208. WC is a member of CSS. The FAFSA the college's own financial statement, and signed copies of the student's and parents' federal tax returns and W2s are required. The deadline for filing freshman financial aid applications for fall entry is February 15.

MASSACHUSETTS

College Location

0 10 20 30 40
Miles

AMERICAN INTERNATIONAL COLLEGE (*The complete profile is made available exclusively on our website, www.barronspac.com*)

AMHERST COLLEGE   B-2
www.amherst.edu

Amherst, MA 01002	**(413) 542-2321**
Fax: (413) 542-2527	Email: prooney@amherst.edu
Full-time: 900 men, 885 women	Faculty: 220; IIB, ++$
Part-time: n/av	Ph.D.s: 97%
Graduate: n/av	Student/Faculty: 8 to 1
Year: semesters	Tuition: $46,574
Room & Board: $12,170	Freshman Class: n/av
SAT or ACT: required	CEEB CODE: 3003
Application Deadline: January 1	**MOST COMPETITIVE**

Amherst College, founded in 1821, is a private liberal arts institution. The 1015-acre campus is in a small town 90 miles west of Boston. Including any residence halls, there are 75 buildings. **STUDENT LIFE:** 88% of undergraduates are from out of state, mostly the Middle Atlantic. Students are from 46 states, 31 foreign countries, and Canada. 59% are from public schools. 42% are White; 13% Asian American; 13% Hispanic; 11% African American. **Male To Female Ratio:** 1.0:1. The average age of freshmen is 18; all undergraduates, 20. 2% do not continue beyond their first year; 96% remain to graduate. **Housing:** College-sponsored housing includes coed dorms. In addition, there are language houses, special-interest houses, 1 cooperative house. On-campus housing is guaranteed for all 4 years. 99% of students live on campus; of those, 95% remain on campus on weekends. Upperclassmen may keep cars. **FACULTY/CLASSROOMS:** 53% of faculty are male; 47% are female. All teach and do research. No introductory courses are taught by graduate students. The average class size in a regular course is 16. **PROGRAMS OF STUDY:** Amherst confers B.A. degrees. Bachelor's degrees are awarded in AGRICULTURE (environmental studies), BIOLOGICAL SCIENCE (biochemistry, biology/biological science, biophysics, and neurosciences), COMMUNICATIONS AND THE ARTS (art history, classics, dance, English, film, television and digital media, fine arts, French, German, music, Russian, Spanish, and theatre studies), COMPUTER AND PHYSICAL SCIENCE (astronomy, chemistry, computer science, geology, mathematics, and physics), SOCIAL SCIENCE (African American studies, American studies, anthropology, architectural studies, asian studies, economics, European studies, history, interdisciplinary studies, law, philosophy, political science/government, psychology, religion, sociology, and women & gender studies). Economics, political science, and history have the largest enrollments. **ACTIVITIES:** There are no fraternities or sororities. There are 110 groups on campus, including art, band, chess, choir, chorale, chorus, communications, computers, dance, debate, drama, environmental, ethnic, film, gay, honors, international, jazz band, literary magazine, musical theater, newspaper, opera, orchestra, photography, political, professional, radio and TV, religious, social, social service, student government, symphony, and yearbook. Popular campus events include Fall Festival, Harlem Renaissance, and Spring Weekend Concert. **Sports:** There are 13 intercollegiate sports for men and 14 for women, and 6 intramural sports for men and 6 for women. Facilities include 2 gyms, a pool, a field house, a hockey rink, an outdoor track, a fitness center, 10 international squash courts, an indoor jogging track, 3 indoor and 30 outdoor tennis courts, baseball and softball diamonds, a 9-hole golf course, and playing fields. **Graduates:** From July 1, 2013 to June 30, 2014, 464 bachelor's degrees were awarded. The most popular majors were economics (15%), political science (14%), and history (11%). 46 companies recruited on campus in 2013-2014. In an average class, 89% graduate in 4 years or less, 95% graduate in 5 years or less, and 96% graduate in 6 years or less. Of the 2013 graduating class, 16% were enrolled in graduate school within 6 months of graduation, and 69% were employed. **SERVICES:** Counseling and information services are available, as is tutoring in every subject. There is a reader service for the blind. A quantitative skills center and a writing center are also available. **Library/Resources:** The 5 libraries contain 1.5 million volumes, 544,991 microform items, 59,039 audio/video tapes/CDs/DVDs, and subscribe to 15,780 periodicals including electronic. Computerized library services include interlibrary loans, database searching, Internet access, and Wi-Fi capability. Special learning facilities include an art gallery, natural history museum, planetarium, radio station, an observatory, the Emily Dickinson Museum, and the Amherst Center for Russian Culture. **Physically Challenged Students:** Facilities include wheelchair ramps, elevators, special parking, specially equipped restrooms, special class scheduling, lowered drinking fountains, and lowered telephones. **Special:** Students may cross-register through the Five College Consortium, the other members of which are all within 10 miles of Amherst, or through the Twelve College Exchange Program. A number of Interterm and summer internships are available, as is study-abroad in 40 countries. Dual majors, triple majors, student-designed interdisciplinary majors based on independent study as of junior or senior year, and work-study programs are possible. There are limited pass/fail options. There are 2 national honor societies, including Phi Beta Kappa, and 37 departmental honors programs. **Visiting:** There are regularly scheduled orientations for prospective students, dean-led information sessions and student-led tours. There are guides for informal visits, visitors may sit in on classes, and stay overnight. To schedule a visit, contact the Admission Office. **Campus Safety and Security:** Measures include 24-hour foot and vehicle patrol, emergency notification system, self-defense education, and security escort services. There are emergency telephones, lighted pathways/sidewalks, controlled access to dorms/residences, ACEMS (Amherst College Emergency Medical Service), and access code pad security to dorms. **REQUIREMENTS:** The SAT or ACT is required, plus 2 SAT: Subject tests are required for admission. Amherst strongly recommends that applicants take 4 years of English, math through calculus, 3 or 4 years of a foreign language, 2 years of history and social science, and at least 2 years of natural science, including a lab science. 2 essays are required. Important factors in the admissions decision are advanced placement or honors courses, recommendations by school officials, and evidence of special talent. To earn the B.A., all students must complete 32 courses, equivalent to 128 credits, 8 to 14 of which are in the major, with at least a C average. Other than a 1-semester freshman seminar in liberal studies, there are no specific course requirements. A thesis or comparable work is required for honors candidates. **Procedure:** Freshmen are admitted fall. Entrance exams should be taken no later than December of the senior year. There are early decision and deferred admissions plans. Early decision applications should be filed by November 15; regular applications, by January 1 for fall entry, along with a $60 fee. Notification of early decision is sent December 15; regular decision, April 1. 182 early decision candidates were accepted for the 2014-2015 class. Applications are accepted on-line. **Transfer Students:** 13 transfer students enrolled in 2013-2014. Applicants must have full sophomore standing prior to applying and a minimum 3.0 GPA in previous college work. Transfers are accepted for the sophomore and junior classes only, and Amherst recommends that they submit SAT or ACT scores, plus high school and college transcripts, and seek a personal interview. 64 of 128 credits required for the bachelor's degree must be completed at Amherst. **International Students:** There are 171 international students enrolled. The school actively recruits these students. They must take the TOEFL with a minimum score of 600 on the paper-based TOEFL (PBT) or 100 on the Internet-based version (iBT) or take the MELAB, or the SAT: ELAP if English is not the applicant's first language. They must also take the SAT or ACT.

ADMISSIONS: The SAT scores for the 2014-2015 freshman class were: Critical Reading--4% between 500 and 599, 30% between 600 and 699, and 66% between 700 and 800; Math--4% between 500 and 599, 31% between 600 and 699, and 65% between 700 and 800; Writing--4% between 500 and 599, 32% between 600 and 699, and 63% between 700 and 800; 100% were in the top two fifths. **Admissions Contact:** Peter Rooney, Director of Public Affairs. E-Mail: *prooney@ amherst.edu* Web: *www.amherst.edu*

FINANCIAL AID: In 2014-2015, 58% of all full-time freshmen and 61% of continuing full-time students received some form of financial aid. 57% of all full-time freshmen and 61% of continuing full-time students received need-based aid. The average freshman award was $48,528. Need-based scholarships or need-based grants averaged $47,553; and need-based self-help aid (loans and jobs) averaged $1,697. 60% of undergraduate students work part-time. Average annual earnings from campus work are $1250. The CSS/Profile and FAFSA are required. The deadline for filing freshman financial aid applications for fall entry is February 15.

ANNA MARIA COLLEGE   C-2
www.annamaria.edu

Paxton, MA 01612	(508) 849-3360
	(800) 344-4586
Fax: (508) 849-3362	Email: admission@annamaria.edu
Full-time: 310 men, 400 women	Faculty: n/av
Part-time: 100 men, 120 women	Ph.D.s: 50%
Graduate: 125 men, 210 women	Student/Faculty: n/av
Year: semesters, summer session	Tuition: $25,000
Room & Board: $9600	Freshman Class: n/app
SAT or ACT: required	CEEB CODE: 3005
Application Deadline: n/av	**COMPETITIVE**

Anna Maria College, founded in 1946, is a small, comprehensive Catholic college offering career-oriented programs in liberal and fine arts, business, and teacher preparation. The figures in the above capsule and in this profile are approximate. There are 5 undergraduate schools and 1 graduate school. In addition to regional accreditation, AMC has baccalaureate program accreditation with CSWE and NLN. The 180-acre campus is in a rural area 8 miles northwest of Worcester. Including any residence halls, there are 13 buildings.

STUDENT LIFE: 84% of undergraduates are from Massachusetts. Others are from 14 states, 2 foreign countries, and Canada. 78% are White. **Male To Female Ratio:** 1.4:1. The average age of freshmen is 19; all undergraduates, 20. 36% do not continue beyond their first year; 49% remain to graduate. **Housing:** 459 students can be accommodated in college housing, which includes coed dorms and substance-free housing. On-campus housing is guaranteed for the freshman year only, is available on a first-come, first-served basis, and is available on a lottery system for upperclassmen. Priority is given to out-of-town students. 54% of students commute. All students may keep cars.

FACULTY/CLASSROOMS: 53% of faculty are male; 47% are female. All teach undergraduates. No introductory courses are taught by graduate students. The average class size in an introductory lecture is 20; in a laboratory is 20; and in a regular course is 13.

PROGRAMS OF STUDY: AMC confers B.A., B.S., B.M. and B.S.N. degrees. Associate and Master's degrees are also awarded. Bachelor's degrees are awarded in BUSINESS (business administration and management and sports management), COMMUNICATIONS AND THE ARTS (art, English, graphic design, media arts, modern language, music, music performance, studio art, and visual and performing arts), COMPUTER AND PHYSICAL SCIENCE (computer science), EDUCATION (early childhood education, elementary education, and music education), ENGINEERING AND ENVIRONMENTAL DESIGN (environmental science), HEALTH PROFESSIONS (art therapy, music therapy, and nursing), SOCIAL SCIENCE (criminal justice, fire science, history, human development, humanities, liberal arts/general studies, paralegal studies, political science/government, psychology, religion, social science, social work, and sociology). Criminal justice, fire science, and business have the largest enrollments.

ACTIVITIES: There are no fraternities or sororities. There are 25 groups on campus, including art, cheerleading, choir, chorus, computers, dance, drama, ethnic, gay, honors, international, jazz band, musical theater, newspaper, political, professional, religious, social, social service, student government, and yearbook. Popular campus events include Harvest Weekend, Mr. AMC, and Trick or Treating for Children. **Sports:** There are 5 intercollegiate sports for men and 5 for women, and 3 intramural sports for men and 2 for women. Facilities include an activities center with a basketball court, locker rooms, and weight and fitness equipment, soccer, baseball, and softball fields, an outdoor basketball court, and a fitness trail. **Graduates:** From July 1, 2013 to June 30, 2014, 157 bachelor's degrees were awarded. The most popular majors were criminal justice (18%), social work and psychology (15%), and fire science (14%). 9 companies recruited on campus in 2013-2014. In an average class, 49% graduate in 4 years or less and 55% graduate in 6 years or less.

SERVICES: Counseling and information services are available, as is tutoring in every subject. There is a reader service for the blind, and remedial math, reading, and writing. **Library/Resources:** The library contains 75,789 volumes, 1,702 microform items, 6,095 audio/video tapes/CDs/DVDs, and subscribes to 291 periodicals including electronic. Computerized library services include interlibrary loans, database searching, and Internet access. Special learning facilities include an art gallery, an audiovisual center, and a nature trail. **Physically Challenged Students:** 80% of the campus is accessible. Facilities include wheelchair ramps, elevators, special parking, specially equipped restrooms, special class scheduling, lowered drinking fountains, and special housing. **Special:** Cross-registration with the Colleges of the Worcester Consortium and internships in all majors are available. The college offers study abroad, a Washington semester, student-designed majors, accelerated degree programs, a general studies degree, credit by exam, work-study programs, and 5-year advanced degree programs in business, counseling psychology, criminal justice, education, visual art, and fire science. There are 6 national honor societies. **Visiting:** There are regularly scheduled orientations for prospective students, including on-campus interviews, campus tours, day visitation program by appointment, and a fall open house. There are guides for informal visits, visitors may sit in on classes, and stay overnight. To schedule a visit, contact the Undergraduate Admission Office. **Campus Safety and Security:** Measures include 24-hour foot and vehicle patrol and security escort services. There are shuttle buses, emergency telephones, and lighted pathways/sidewalks.

REQUIREMENTS: The SAT or ACT is required. A GED is accepted. 16 academic units are recommended, including 4 years of English, 2 years each of foreign language, history, math, and sciences, and 1 year of social studies. An interview is recommended. When applicable, an audition and portfolio are required. Students who have been out of high school for 3 or more years, or transfer students with 10 or more college-level courses, do not need to submit standardized test scores. An essay is required. A GPA of 2.0 is required. AP and CLEP credits are accepted. Important factors in the admissions decision are advanced placement or honors courses, extracurricular activities record, and leadership record. The 60-credit core curriculum consists of classes in English, literature, math, computers, natural science, foreign language, fine arts, history, philosophy, social/behavioral sciences, and religious studies. A total of 120 credits is required for graduation, with a minimum of 30 in the major and a 2.0 GPA. **Procedure:** Freshmen are admitted fall and spring. Entrance exams should be taken in spring of the junior year or fall of the senior year.

There are deferred admissions and rolling admissions plans. Application deadlines are open. The fall 2014 application fee was $40. Notification is sent on a rolling basis. Applications are accepted on-line. **Transfer Students:** 34 transfer students enrolled in 2013-2014. Transfers with a minimum GPA of 2.0 are accepted for upper-division work. High school and college transcripts are required. An essay or personal statement and a statement of good standing from prior institutions are also required. 60 of 120 credits required for the bachelor's degree must be completed at AMC. **International Students:** There are 2 international students enrolled. The school actively recruits these students. They must take the TOEFL with a minimum score of 470 on the paper-based TOEFL (PBT). They must also take the SAT or ACT.

ADMISSIONS: Timothy Donahue, Director of Admissions. E-Mail: *admission@annamaria.edu* Web: *www.annamaria.edu*

FINANCIAL AID: In 2014-2015, 93% of all full-time freshmen and 85% of continuing full-time students received some form of financial aid. 77% of all full-time freshmen and 70% of continuing full-time students received need-based aid. The average freshman award was $15,703. Need-based scholarships or need-based grants averaged $6,256; need-based self-help aid (loans and jobs) averaged $4,539; and other non-need-based awards and non-need-based scholarships averaged $6,707. 19% of undergraduate students work part-time. Average annual earnings from campus work are $1200. The average financial indebtedness of the 2014 graduate was $30,000. The FAFSA and the state aid form are required. Check with the school for current application deadlines.

ASSUMPTION COLLEGE — C-2
www.assumption.edu

Worcester, MA 01609	**(508) 767-7285**
	(866) 477-7776
Fax: (508) 799-4412	**Email: admiss@assumption.edu**
Full-time: 832 men, 1159 women	**Faculty:** 142; IIB, av$
Part-time: 5 men	**Ph.D.s:** 93%
Graduate: 137 men, 357 women	**Student/Faculty:** 12 to 1
Year: semesters, summer session	**Tuition:** $36,160
Room & Board: $10,962	**Freshman Class:** 4402 applied, 3579 accepted, 571 enrolled
SAT CR/M: 550/560 **ACT:** 25	**CEEB CODE:** 3009
Application Deadline: February 15	**COMPETITIVE+**

Assumption College, founded in 1904 by Augustinians of the Assumption, offers a Catholic, liberal arts and sciences education to undergraduates, along with programs for graduate and continuing education students. There is 1 undergraduate school and 1 graduate school. In addition to regional accreditation, Assumption has baccalaureate program accreditation with CRE and ACS. The 180-acre campus is in a suburban area 45 miles west of Boston in New England's 2nd largest city, Worcester, MA. Including any residence halls, there are 48 buildings.

STUDENT LIFE: 66% of undergraduates are from Massachusetts. Others are from 25 states, 23 foreign countries, and Canada. 68% are from public schools. 74% are White. **Male To Female Ratio:** 1.6:1. The average age of freshmen is 18; all undergraduates, 20. 17% do not continue beyond their first year; 71% remain to graduate. **Housing:** 1907 students can be accommodated in college housing, which includes single-sex dorms and on-campus apartments. In addition, there are special-interest houses, freshman dorms, substance-free dorms, first-year experience dorm, and a living/learning center. On-campus housing is guaranteed for all 4 years. 87% of students live on campus; of those, 80% remain on campus on weekends. Upperclassmen may keep cars.

FACULTY/CLASSROOMS: 56% of faculty are male; 44% are female. All teach undergraduates. No introductory courses are taught by graduate students. The average class size in a laboratory is 17 and in a regular course is 21.

PROGRAMS OF STUDY: Assumption confers B.A. degrees. Master's degrees are also awarded. Bachelor's degrees are awarded in BIO-LOGICAL SCIENCE (biology/biological science, biotechnology, and molecular biology), BUSINESS (accounting, business administration and management, international business management, marketing management, and organizational behavior), COMMUNICATIONS AND THE ARTS (art history, classics, English, French, graphic design, languages, music, Spanish, and studio art), COMPUTER AND PHYSICAL SCIENCE (chemistry, computer science, and mathematics), EDUCATION (education), ENGINEERING AND ENVIRONMENTAL DESIGN (environmental science), HEALTH PROFESSIONS (rehabilitation therapy), SOCIAL SCIENCE (criminology, economics, history, human services, international studies, Italian studies, Latin American studies, philosophy, political science/government, psychology, sociology, and theological studies). Natural sciences, psychology, and business studies are the strongest academically. Business studies, natural sciences, human services and rehabilitation studies have the largest enrollments.

ACTIVITIES: There are no fraternities or sororities. There are 60 groups on campus, including art, band, cheerleading, choir, chorale, chorus, computers, dance, drama, environmental, ethnic, film, honors, international, jazz band, literary magazine, musical theater, newspaper, orchestra, pep band, photography, political, professional, radio and TV, religious, social, social service, student government, and yearbook. Popular campus events include Midnight Madness Baketball Kickoff, Campus Concert and Duck Day. **Sports:** There are 10 intercollegiate sports for men and 11 for women. Facilities include a 1,200-seat multisports stadium, a 3,000-seat gym, baseball and softball diamonds, a field hockey area, a soccer field, and tennis courts. A recreation center houses a 6-lane swimming pool, a jogging/walking track, 2 racquetball courts, an aerobics/dance studio, a multipurpose room with TRX equipment, fully equipped Bodymaster and free-weight rooms, a fitness center, a varsity weight room, and a field house with 3 multipurpose courts for basketball, volleyball, and floor hockey. **Graduates:** From July 1, 2013 to June 30, 2014, 485 bachelor's degrees were awarded. The most popular majors were human services and rehabilitation studies (12%), psychology (11%), and accounting (10%). 416 companies recruited on campus in 2013-2014. In an average class, 66% graduate in 4 years or less, 70% graduate in 5 years or less, and 71% graduate in 6 years or less. Of the 2013 graduating class, 19% were enrolled in graduate school within 6 months of graduation, and 76% were employed.

SERVICES: Counseling and information services are available, as is tutoring in most subjects. There is a reader service for the blind. Signing for the deaf, and technology services for the disabled. **Library/Resources:** The library contains 227,234 volumes, 27,485 microform items, 2,885 audio/video tapes/CDs/DVDs, and subscribes to 1,791 periodicals including electronic. Computerized library services include interlibrary loans, database searching, Internet access, and Wi-Fi capability. Special learning facilities include a radio station and TV station. **Physically Challenged Students:** 71% of the campus is accessible. Facilities include wheelchair ramps, elevators, special parking, specially equipped restrooms, special class scheduling, lowered drinking fountains, lowered telephones, and special housing. **Special:** Co-op program in marine studies. Cross-registration with the Colleges of Worcester Consortium is offered. The college has its own study abroad campus in Rome, and study abroad is available through other providers as well. The college offers internships, a Washington semester, student-designed and dual majors, credit by exam, and credit for military experience. The college offers 6-in-5 programs in accounting (BA/MBA), special education(BA/MA), school counseling (BA/MA), and rehabilitation counseling (BA/MA); a 3/-2 program in engineering with the University of Notre Dame; and multiple combined degree programs with other institutions; see undergraduate catalog for details. There are 11 national honor societies and a freshman honors program. **Visiting:** There are regularly scheduled orientations for prospective students, consisting of new student orientation, meetings with future classmates, choosing roommates, registration, testing, conferences with academic advisers, and discussions of aspects of college life. There are guides for informal visits and visitors may sit in on classes. To schedule a visit, contact the Office of Admissions. **Campus Safety and Security:** Measures include 24-hour foot and vehicle patrol, emergency notification system, self-defense education, and security escort services. There are shuttle buses, emergency telephones, lighted pathways/sidewalks, and controlled access to dorms/residences.

REQUIREMENTS: Applicants must graduate from an accredited secondary school or have a GED. 18 academic units are required, including 4 years of English, 3 of math, and 2 each of history, science, and foreign language. An essay and an interview are recommended. AP and CLEP credits are accepted. Important factors in the admissions decision are advanced placement or honors courses, leadership record, and recommendations by school officials.Students must complete a core curriculum of 3 courses from different disciplines in social science: 2 courses in 1 and 1 course in another of the 3 areas of math, natural science, and foreign languages; 2 courses each of English composition, philosophy, and theology; 1 each of literature, history, and either art, music, or theater arts, and 1 additional course in 2 of the 3 areas of philosophy and theology, literature, and history. A minimum of 120 semester credit hours, with a minimum of 38 semester courses, must be completed; 8 to 14 courses must be in the upper division of the major. A minimum 2.0 GPA is required. **Procedure:** Freshmen are admitted fall and spring. Entrance exams should be taken in May of the junior year or November of the senior year. There are early admissions and deferred admissions plans. Applications should be filed by February 15 for fall entry; December 15 for spring entry, along with a $50 fee. Notifications are sent March 15. 68 applicants were on the 2014 waiting list; 3 were admitted. Applications are accepted on-line. **Transfer Students:** 57 transfer students enrolled in 2013-2014. Transfer students must have maintained a minimum 2.5 GPA at their previous college. SAT scores and high school and college transcripts are required. 60 of 120 credits required for the bachelor's degree must be completed at Assumption. **International Students:** There are 35 international students enrolled. The school actively recruits these students. They must take the TOEFL with a minimum score of 550 on the paper-based TOEFL (PBT) or 80 on the Internet-based version (iBT).

ADMISSIONS: 81% of the 2014-2015 applicants were accepted. The SAT scores for the 2014-2015 freshman class were: Critical Reading--18% below 500, 54% between 500 and 599, 23% between 600 and 699, and 5% between 700 and 800; Math--17% below 500, 55% between 500 and 599, 25% between 600 and 699, and 3% between 700 and 800. The ACT scores were 11% below 21, 22% between 21 and 23, 43% between 24 and 26, 13% between 27 and 28, and 11% above 28. 34% of the current freshmen were in the top fifth of their class; 67% were in the top two fifths. 5 freshmen graduated first in their class. **Admissions Contact:** Evan E. Lipp, Vice President for Enrollment Management. E-Mail: *admiss@assumption.edu* Web: *www.assumption.edu/admissions/undergraduate/*

FINANCIAL AID: In 2014-2015, 98% of all full-time freshmen and 98% of continuing full-time students received some form of financial aid. 80% of all full-time freshmen and 77% of continuing full-time students received need-based aid. The average freshman award was $24,098. Need-based scholarships or need-based grants averaged $21,215 ($45,968 maximum); need-based self-help aid (loans and jobs) averaged $4,252 ($10,500 maximum); non-need-based athletic scholarships averaged $9,658 ($46,872 maximum); and other non-need-based awards and non-need-based scholarships averaged $14,741 ($24,500 maximum). The average financial indebtedness of the 2014 graduate was $34,417. The FAFSA is required. The deadline for filing freshman financial aid applications for fall entry is February 15.

ATLANTIC UNION COLLEGE   D-2
www.atlanticuc.edu

South Lancaster, MA 01561	(978) 368-2239
	(800) 282-2030
Fax: (978) 368-2517	Email: enroll@atlanticuc.edu
Full-time: 150 men, 250 women	Faculty: n/av
Part-time: 20 men, 30 women	Ph.D.s: 42%
Graduate: 5 men, 10 women	Student/Faculty: n/av
Year: semesters, summer session	Tuition: $17,000
Room & Board: $7600	Freshman Class: n/av
SAT or ACT: required	CEEB CODE: 3010
Application Deadline: n/av	COMPETITIVE

Atlantic Union College, established in 1882, is a private liberal arts institution associated with the Seventh-Day Adventist church and offers professional and preprofessional programs. The figures in the above capsule and in this profile are approximate. There are no undergraduate schools. In addition to regional accreditation, AUC has baccalaureate program accreditation with CSWE, NASM, and NLN. The 135-acre campus is in a small town 50 miles west of Boston. Including any residence halls, there are 54 buildings.

STUDENT LIFE: 55% of undergraduates are from out of state, mostly the Northeast. Students are from 14 states, 21 foreign countries, and Canada. 53% are African American; 22% Hispanic; 20% White; 15% Foreign. The average age of freshmen is 21; all undergraduates, 23. 27% do not continue beyond their first year. **Housing:** 469 students can be accommodated in college housing, which includes single-sex dorms, on-campus apartments, and married student housing. On-campus housing is guaranteed for all 4 years. 56% of students live on campus; of those, 85% remain on campus on weekends. Alcohol is not permitted. All students may keep cars.

FACULTY/CLASSROOMS: 45% of faculty are male; 55% are female. All teach undergraduates. No introductory courses are taught by graduate students. The average class size in an introductory lecture is 18; in a laboratory is 30; and in a regular course is 16.

PROGRAMS OF STUDY: AUC confers B.A., B.S. and B.M. degrees. Associate and master's degrees are also awarded. Bachelor's degrees are awarded in BIOLOGICAL SCIENCE (biology/biological science and life science), BUSINESS (accounting and business administration and management), COMMUNICATIONS AND THE ARTS (art, English, and music), COMPUTER AND PHYSICAL SCIENCE (computer science, information sciences and systems, and mathematics), EDUCATION (early childhood education, elementary education, and music education), HEALTH PROFESSIONS (nursing), SOCIAL SCIENCE (culinary arts, history, liberal arts/general studies, ministries, psychology, religion, social work, and theological studies). Nursing, business, and psychology are the strongest academically. Nursing, business, and education have the largest enrollments.

ACTIVITIES: There are 13 groups on campus, including art, band, choir, chorale, drama, ethnic, honors, newspaper, orchestra, religious, social, student government, and yearbook. Popular campus events include Fall Picnic, Cultural Heritage Weeks, and Fine Arts Week. **Sports:** There are 7 intramural sports for men and 7 for women. Facilities include a gym and field house with a weight room and tennis/volleyball/badminton, racquetball/handball, and basketball courts, a swimming pool, and athletic fields for flag football, soccer, softball, and baseball.

SERVICES: Counseling and information services are available, as is tutoring in most subjects. There is remedial math, reading, and writing. Additional services are provided upon request **Library/Resources:** The library contains 139,000 volumes, 17,336 microform items, 4,754 audio/video tapes/CDs/DVDs, and subscribes to 469 periodicals including electronic. Computerized library services include interlibrary loans, database searching, and Internet access. Special learning facilities include an art gallery, model elementary and secondary schools, and music conservatory. **Physically Challenged Students:** 73% of the campus is accessible. Facilities include wheelchair ramps, elevators, special parking, specially equipped restrooms, special class scheduling, and lowered drinking fountains. **Special:** There is cross-registration with Mount Wachusett Community College and the Colleges of Worcester Consortium. Students may study abroad in 6 countries. AUC also offers newspaper and biology research internships, cooperative programs in several majors, pass/fail options, and nondegree study. The Summer Advantage in New England program offers precollege credit to high school honor students. There is also an adult degree program, in which most study is done at home and in which student-designed majors are permitted. Dual majors, an accelerated degree in management and professional studies, a 1-3 engineering degree with Walla Walla College, and preprofessional curricula in dentistry, dental hygiene, medicine, respiratory therapy, radiologic technology, and veterinary medicine in conjunction with Loma Linda University are offered. There are 3 national honor societies, a freshman honors program, and 4 departmental honors programs. **Visiting:** There are regularly scheduled orientations for prospective students, including campus tours, class visits, and financial aid and admissions information sessions. There are guides for informal visits, visitors may sit in on classes, and stay overnight. **Campus Safety and Security:** Measures include self-defense education and security escort services. There are lighted pathways/sidewalks.

REQUIREMENTS: The SAT or ACT is required. Applicants should be graduates of an accredited secondary school. The GED is accepted with a minimum score of 250. Required academic credits include 4 years of high school English and 2 years each of a foreign language, math, history, and science. A GPA of 2.2 is required. AP and CLEP credits are accepted. Important factors in the admissions decision are recommendations by school officials, recommendations by alumni, and personality/intangible qualities. Students must complete 9 hours each in humanities, science, and social science and 12 hours in religion/ethics. Foreign language proficiency, a phys ed requirement, 40 hours of community service, and a course in college writing must also be completed. AUC requires 128 to 143 credit hours for the bachelor's degree, with 30 to 60 in the major, and a 2.0 GPA. **Procedure:** Freshmen are admitted fall and spring. Entrance exams should be taken during the senior year of high school. There is a rolling admissions plan. Check with the school for current application deadlines. The fall 2014 application fee was $25. Notification is sent on a rolling basis. Applications are accepted on-line. **Transfer Students:** Applicants who have completed at least 24 semester hours are not required to submit SAT or ACT scores. Applicants from junior colleges may receive credit for up to 72 semester hours. Only a grade of C or better transfers for credit. 30 of 128 credits required for the bachelor's degree must be completed at AUC. **International Students:** The school actively recruits these students. They must take the TOEFL. They must also take the ACT.

ADMISSIONS: Rosita Lashley, Director of Admissions. E-Mail: *enroll@atlanticuc.edu* Web: *www.atlanticuc.edu*

FINANCIAL AID: AUC is a member of CSS. The FAFSA is required. Check with the school for current application deadlines.

BABSON COLLEGE   D-2
www.babson.edu

Babson Park, MA 02457	(781) 239-5522
	(800) 488-3696
Fax: (781) 239-4135	Email: ugradadmission@babson.edu
Full-time: 1070 men, 730 women	Faculty: IIB
Part-time: n/av	Ph.D.s: 72%
Graduate: 1200 men, 440 women	Student/Faculty: n/av
Year: semesters, summer session	Tuition: $39,040
Room & Board: $12,900	Freshman Class: n/av
SAT or ACT: required	CEEB CODE: 3075
Application Deadline:	HIGHLY COMPETITIVE

Babson College, founded in 1919, is a private business school. All students start their own businesses during their freshman year with money loaned by the college. The figures in the above capsule and in this profile are approximate. There is 1 graduate school. In addition to regional accreditation, Babson has baccalaureate program accreditation with AACSB. The 370-acre campus is in a suburban area 14 miles west of Boston. Including any residence halls, there are 53 buildings.

STUDENT LIFE: 70% of undergraduates are from out of state, mostly the Northeast. Students are from 47 states, 60 foreign countries, and Canada. 50% are from public schools. 44% are White; 18% Foreign; 11% Asian American. **Male To Female Ratio:** 0.5:1. The average age of freshmen is 18; all undergraduates, 20. 5% do not continue beyond their first year; 85% remain to graduate. **Housing:** 1441 students can be accommodated in college housing, which includes single-sex and coed dorms, on-campus apartments, and married student housing. In addition, there are special-interest houses, substance-free living, fraternity and sorority towers, and a cultural house. On-campus housing is guaranteed for all 4 years. 85% of students live on campus; of those, 80% remain on campus on weekends. All students may keep cars.

FACULTY/CLASSROOMS: 69% of faculty are male; 31% are female. No introductory courses are taught by graduate students. The average

class size in an introductory lecture is 34; in a laboratory is 20; and in a regular course is 27.

PROGRAMS OF STUDY: Babson confers B.S.M. degrees. Master's degrees are also awarded. Bachelor's degrees are awarded in BUSINESS (business administration and management).

ACTIVITIES: 10% of men belong to 7 national fraternities; 12% of women belong to 3 national sororities. There are 60 groups on campus, including art, band, cappella, cheerleading, choir, chorus, dance, drama, ethnic, gay, honors, international, jazz band, literary magazine, musical theater, newspaper, photography, political, professional, radio and TV, religious, social, social service, student government, and yearbook. Popular campus events include Multicultural Week. **Sports:** There are 11 intercollegiate sports for men and 11 for women, and 11 intramural sports for men and 11 for women. Facilities include a sports complex with an indoor pool, a 200-meter, 6-lane indoor track, a 1500-square-foot field house, a 600-seat gym with 3 basketball courts, 5 squash and 2 racquetball courts, a fitness center, a dance aerobics studio, locker rooms with saunas, and a sports medicine facility. **Graduates:** From July 1, 2013 to June 30, 2014, 424 bachelor's degrees were awarded. 301 companies recruited on campus in 2013-2014. In an average class, 80% graduate in 4 years or less, 85% graduate in 5 years or less, and 85% graduate in 6 years or less. Of the 2013 graduating class, 3% were enrolled in graduate school within 6 months of graduation, and 92% were employed.

SERVICES: Counseling and information services are available, as is tutoring in most subjects. There are writing/speech skills and math/science skills centers. **Library/Resources:** The library contains 132,024 volumes, 346,941 microform items, 4,645 audio/video tapes/CDs/DVDs, and subscribes to 511 periodicals including electronic. Computerized library services include interlibrary loans, database searching, and Internet access. Special learning facilities include an art gallery, radio station, performing arts theater, and centers for entrepreneurial studies, management, language and culture, writing, math, visual arts, executive education, and women's leadership. **Physically Challenged Students:** 75% of the campus is accessible. Facilities include wheelchair ramps, elevators, special parking, specially equipped restrooms, special class scheduling, lowered drinking fountains, and special housing. **Special:** There is cross-registration with Brandeis University, Wellesley College, and F.W. Olin College of Engineering. Internships and study abroad in 27 countries are available. There is a freshman honors program and 10 departmental honors programs. **Visiting:** There are regularly scheduled orientations for prospective students, including an open house each year, personal interviews, campus tours, group information sessions and Fall Preview Days (select Saturdays-. There are guides for informal visits. To schedule a visit, contact the Admission Office. **Campus Safety and Security:** Measures include 24-hour foot and vehicle patrol, self-defense education, and security escort services. There are shuttle buses, emergency telephones, lighted pathways/sidewalks, a motorist assist program, a transportation service for the cross-registration program, vans available to students for school activities, and crime prevention programs.

REQUIREMENTS: The SAT or ACT is required. Applicants must be graduates of an accredited secondary school or have a GED. 16 academic courses are required, including 4 credits of English, 3 of math, 2 of social studies, and 1 of science. A fourth year of math is strongly recommended. Essays are required. SAT Subject tests in math are recommended. AP credits are accepted. Important factors in the admissions decision are advanced placement or honors courses, evidence of special talent, and leadership record. Students must complete a curriculum of general management and liberal arts, with 50% in management and 50% in liberal arts. A total of 128 semester hours is required for graduation. A minimum GPA of 2.0 is required. **Procedure:** Freshmen are admitted fall. Entrance exams should be taken prior to application (SAT or ACT). There are early decision, early admissions, and deferred admissions plans. Check with the school for current application deadlines. The fall 2014 application fee was $60. Applications are accepted on-line. **Transfer Students:** Transfer applicants are expected to demonstrate solid academic performance at their prior institution and must submit 1 essay and 1 recommendation from a college teacher or administrator, in addition to a high school transcript and SAT scores. They must also submit course descriptions and syllabi for any courses they have taken. 64 of 128 credits required for the bachelor's degree must be completed at Babson. **International Students:** There are 318 international students enrolled. The school actively recruits these students. They must take the TOEFL with a minimum score of 600 on the paper-based TOEFL (PBT) or 100 on the Internet-based version (iBT), English Language Proficiency Test. They must also take the SAT or ACT.

ADMISSIONS: Grant Gosselin, Dean of Undergraduate Admission. E-Mail: ugradadmission@babson.edu Web: www.babson.edu

FINANCIAL AID: In 2014-2015, 4% of all full-time freshmen and 41% of continuing full-time students received some form of financial aid. 45% of all full-time freshmen and 41% of continuing full-time students received need-based aid. The average freshman award was $26,171. Need-based scholarships or need-based grants averaged $29,787; and need-based self-help aid (loans and jobs) averaged $5,013. 32% of undergraduate students work part-time. Average annual earnings from campus work are $1580. The average financial indebtedness of the 2014 graduate was $24,900. The CSS/Profile and FAFSA, and tax returns are required. Check with the school for current application deadlines.

BARD COLLEGE AT SIMON'S ROCK   A-2
www.simons-rock.edu

Great Barrington, MA 01230

	n/av
	(800) 235-7186
Fax: (413) 541-0081	Email: admit@simons-rock.edu
Full-time: 141 men, 200 women	Faculty: 48
Part-time: 6 men, 3 women	Ph.D.s: 89%
Graduate: n/av	Student/Faculty: 6 to 1
Year: semesters	Tuition: $46,703
Room & Board: $12,690	Freshman Class: 218 applied, 201 accepted, 145 enrolled
SAT CR/M/W: 690/650/640 ACT: 27	CEEB CODE: 3795
Application Deadline: May 1	HIGHLY COMPETITIVE+

Bard College at Simon's Rock is the world's only four-year college of the liberal arts and sciences specifically designed for bright, highly motivated students ready to begin college after the tenth or eleventh grade. Students are taught exclusively in small seminars by a supportive, highly-trained faculty. Degrees are granted in over 40 areas of study. Most graduates proceed to earn graduate and professional degrees at highly selective universities. Simon's Rock was founded in 1964 and joined the Bard College network in 1979. There is one undergraduate school. The library contains 83,690 volumes, 3,896 microform items, 5,817 audio/video tapes/CDs/DVDs, and subscribes to 978 periodicals including electronic. Computerized library services include interlibrary loans, database searching, Internet access, and Wi-Fi capability. Special learning facilities include an art gallery. The 210-acre campus is in a small town in the Berkshire Hills of Western MA, approximately 2 hours from New York City and Boston. Including any residence halls, there are 47 buildings.

STUDENT LIFE: 86% of undergraduates are from out of state, mostly the Middle Atlantic. Students are from 35 states, and 18 foreign countries. 72% are from public schools. 57% are White. The average age of freshmen is 16; all undergraduates, 17. 30% do not continue beyond their first year; 73% remain to graduate.

FACULTY/CLASSROOMS: 45% of faculty are male; 54% are female. All teach and do research. No introductory courses are taught by graduate students. The average class size in an introductory lecture is 14; in a laboratory is 10; and in a regular course is 12.

PROGRAMS OF STUDY: Simon's Rock confers B.A. degrees. Associate degrees are also awarded. Bachelor's degrees are awarded in AGRICULTURE (environmental studies), BIOLOGICAL SCIENCE (biology/biological science and ecology), COMMUNICATIONS AND THE ARTS (art/art studies, art history and appreciation, ceramic art and design, creative writing, dance, dramatic arts, drawing, intermedia/multimedia, linguistics, literature, music, painting, and photography), COMPUTER AND PHYSICAL SCIENCE (chemistry, computer science, mathematics, natural sciences, physics, and quantitative methods), ENGINEERING AND ENVIRONMENTAL

DESIGN (preengineering), HEALTH PROFESSIONS (premedicine), SOCIAL SCIENCE (African American studies, American studies, Asian/Oriental studies, crosscultural studies, cultural studies/critical theory & analysis, French studies, gender studies, geography, German area studies, history, philosophy, political science/government, psychology, Russian and Slavic studies, and Spanish studies). Preengineering, theater, and psychology have the largest enrollments.

ACTIVITIES: There are no fraternities or sororities. There are 20 groups on campus, including boffing, QueerSA, student action service learning, USO, art, black student union, chess, choir, chorus, computers, dance, debate, drama, environmental, ethnic, film, gay, international, jazz band, literary magazine, musical theater, newspaper, opera, orchestra, photography, political, professional, religious, social, social service, student government, and yearbook. Popular campus events include May Fest, Prom and Dance Concert.

SERVICES: Counseling and information services are available, as is tutoring in every subject. There is a reader service for the blind. Study skills instruction is available.

REQUIREMENTS: Applicants are required to submit application form, parent statement, 3 letters of recommendation, personal interview, high school transcript and school report, and application essays. Test scores are optional, but will be considered if submitted. Important factors in the admissions decision are personality/intangible qualities, recommendations by school officials, advanced placement or honors courses, evidence of special talent, recommendations by alumni, ability to finance college education, leadership record, parents or siblings attended your school, extracurricular activities record, and geographical diversity.

ADMISSIONS: 92% of the 2013-2014 applicants were accepted. The SAT scores for the 2013-2014 freshman class were: Critical Reading--9% below 500, 9% between 500 and 599, 27% between 600 and 699, and 55% between 700 and 800; Math--9% below 500, 18% between 500 and 599, 46% between 600 and 699, and 27% between 700 and 800; Writing--9% between 500 and 599, 45% between 600 and 699, and 46% between 700 and 800. The ACT scores were 10% below 21, 10% between 21 and 23, 30% between 24 and 26, 30% between 27 and 28, and 20% above 28. 61% of the current freshmen were in the top fifth of their class; 81% were in the top two fifths.

FINANCIAL AID: In 2013-2014, 87% of all full-time freshmen and 76% of continuing full-time students received some form of financial aid. 82% of all full-time freshmen and 72% of continuing full-time students received need-based aid. The average freshman award was $37,292. Need-based scholarships or need-based grants averaged $34,864; need-based self-help aid (loans and jobs) averaged $5,207; and other non-need-based awards and non-need-based scholarships averaged $21,108. The average financial indebtedness of the 2013 graduate was $28,175. Simon's Rock is a member of CSS. The CSS/Profile and FAFSA are required. The priority date for freshman financial aid applications for fall entry is February 1. The deadline for filing freshman financial aid applications for fall entry is May 1.

BAY PATH COLLEGE   B-3
www.baypath.edu

Longmeadow, MA 01106

	(413) 565-1331
	(800) 782-7284
Fax: (413) 565-1105	Email: admiss@baypath.edu
Full-time: 1110 women	Faculty: 36
Part-time: 250 women	Ph.D.s: 54%
Graduate: 30 men, 95 women	Student/Faculty: 31 to 1
Year: semesters	Tuition: $25,030
Room & Board: $13,830	Freshman Class: n/av
SAT or ACT: required	CEEB CODE: 3078
Application Deadline: n/av	COMPETITIVE

Bay Path College, founded in 1897, is a comprehensive, private college offering innovative undergraduate programs for women only and graduate programs for men and women. The figures in the above capsule and in this profile are approximate. There is 1 graduate school. In addition to regional accreditation, Bay Path has baccalaureate program accreditation with ABA and AOTA. The 48-acre campus is in a suburban area 3 miles south of Springfield. Including any residence halls, there are 17 buildings.

STUDENT LIFE: 59% of undergraduates are from Massachusetts. Others are from 15 states, and 6 foreign countries. 93% are from public schools. 79% are White; 11% African American. **Male To Female Ratio:** 48.5:1. The average age of freshmen is 18; all undergraduates, 35. **Housing:** 376 students can be accommodated in college housing, which includes single-sex dorms. On-campus housing is guaranteed for all 4 years. 66% of students live on campus; of those, 60% remain on campus on weekends. Alcohol is not permitted. All students may keep cars.

FACULTY/CLASSROOMS: 40% of faculty are male; 60% are female. All teach undergraduates. No introductory courses are taught by graduate students.

PROGRAMS OF STUDY: Bay Path confers B.A., and B.S. degrees. Associate and Master's degrees are also awarded. Bachelor's degrees are awarded in BIOLOGICAL SCIENCE (biology/biological science), BUSINESS (business administration and management, international business management, and marketing/retailing/merchandising), COMMUNICATIONS AND THE ARTS (communications), EDUCATION (early childhood education and elementary education), ENGINEERING AND ENVIRONMENTAL DESIGN (interior design), HEALTH PROFESSIONS (occupational therapy), SOCIAL SCIENCE (child psychology/development, criminal justice, forensic studies, law, liberal arts/general studies, and psychology).

ACTIVITIES: There are 39 groups on campus, including habitat for humanity, winter guard, cheerleading, choir, chorale, computers, dance, drama, ethnic, forensics, gay, honors, international, literary magazine, musical theater, newspaper, political, political awareness, professional, radio and TV, religious, social, social service, student government, and yearbook. Popular campus events include Father/Daughter and Mother/Daughter Banquets, Karaoke Unplugged, and Dinner with the President. **Sports:** There are 5 intercollegiate sports for women. Facilities include a fitness center that houses a weight-training room, a dance studio, and an aerobics room and a nearby 12-acre playing field with soccer and softball fields, a walking/jogging track, and a field house.

SERVICES: Counseling and information services are available, as is tutoring in every subject. **Library/Resources:** The library contains 47,415 volumes, 4,326 microform items, 3,632 audio/video tapes/CDs/DVDs, and subscribes to 156 periodicals including electronic. Computerized library services include interlibrary loans, database searching, and Internet access. Special learning facilities include a radio station and TV station. **Physically Challenged Students:** 50% of the campus is accessible. Facilities include wheelchair ramps, elevators, special parking, and specially equipped restrooms. **Special:** Cross-registration is possible with other member schools of the Cooperating Colleges of Greater Springfield Consortium. Bay Path's capital of the world program allows students to visit a different world center during each spring break. **Visiting:** There are regularly scheduled orientations for prospective students. There are guides for informal visits, visitors may sit in on classes, and stay overnight. To schedule a visit, contact the Director of Admissions. **Campus Safety and Security:** Measures include 24-hour foot and vehicle patrol, self-defense education, and security escort services. There are emergency telephones, lighted pathways/sidewalks, fire, vehicle, and driving safety education programs.

REQUIREMENTS: The SAT or ACT is required. Applicants should have completed at least 4 academic courses each year, including 4 years of English, 3 of math, at least 2 each of social studies and lab sciences, and 2 of a foreign language. An essay is required, as are letters of recommendation from a guidance counselor and a teacher. An interview is strongly recommended. A GPA of 2.0 is required. AP and CLEP credits are accepted.To graduate, students must complete at least 120 credits with a minimum GPA of 2.0. The 46-hour core curriculum includes course work in communication, science, social science, math, and fine and performing arts. **Procedure:** Freshmen are admitted fall and spring. Entrance exams should be taken in the spring of the junior year or by December of the senior year. There are deferred admissions and rolling admissions plans. Application deadlines are open. The fall 2014 application fee was $25. Applications are accepted on-line. **Transfer Students:** 35 transfer students

enrolled in 2013-2014. Applicants must be in good standing at their previous school and are encouraged to arrange for an interview at Bay Path. Students who have earned fewer than 12 credits must submit SAT or ACT scores. 30 of 120 credits required for the bachelor's degree must be completed at Bay Path. **International Students:** The school actively recruits these students. They must take the TOEFL. They must also take the SAT or ACT.

ADMISSIONS: Lisa Casassa, Director of Admissions. E-Mail: *admiss@baypath.edu* Web: *www.baypath.edu*

FINANCIAL AID: In 2014-2015, 78% of all full-time freshmen and 69% of continuing full-time students received some form of financial aid. The average freshman award was $12,570. Need-based scholarships or need-based grants averaged $7,247 ($16,550 maximum); need-based self-help aid (loans and jobs) averaged $5,322 ($8,625 maximum); and other non-need-based awards and non-need-based scholarships averaged $11,498 ($13,550 maximum). 39% of undergraduate students work part-time. Average annual earnings from campus work are $400. The average financial indebtedness of the 2014 graduate was $21,312. Bay Path is a member of CSS. The FAFSA and the college's own financial statement, and and parent and student income tax forms are required. Check with the school for current application deadlines.

BECKER COLLEGE   C-2
www.becker.edu

Worcester, MA 01609

508-373-9400
1.877.523.2537

Fax: (508) 890-1500
Email: admissions@becker.edu

Full-time: 670 men, 733 women	Faculty: 193
Part-time: 98 men, 325 women	Ph.D.s: 61%
Graduate: n/av	Student/Faculty: n/av
Year: semesters, summer session	Tuition: $30,340
Room & Board: $11,080	Freshman Class: 3350 applied, 2088 accepted, 381 enrolled
	CEEB CODE: 3079
Application Deadline: open	COMPETITIVE

Becker College, founded in 1784, baccalaureate degree programs are offered on the College's two distinctive campuses, located in Worcester and Leicester, Massachusetts. Both undergraduate and adult learning programs make Becker a place where students gain the experience they need to contribute to a global society and rise to the top of their chosen professions. Figures in the above capsule and in this profile are approximate. There are 4 undergraduate schools. In addition to regional accreditation, has baccalaureate program accreditation with NLN and AVMA-Vet Tech. The campus is in an urban area about 40 miles west of Boston in Worcester. Including any residence halls, there are 49 buildings.

STUDENT LIFE: 69% of undergraduates are from Massachusetts. Others are from 33 states and 13 foreign countries. 67% are from public schools. 76% are White. **Male To Female Ratio:** 1.4:1. The average age of freshmen is 18; all undergraduates, 24. 35% do not continue beyond their first year; 30% remain to graduate. **Housing:** 700 students can be accommodated in college housing, which includes single-sex and coed dorms. In addition, there are special-interest houses, and living learning communities. On-campus housing is available on a first-come, first-served basis. 61% of students commute. All students may keep cars.

FACULTY/CLASSROOMS: 40% of faculty are male; 60% are female. 77% teach undergraduates. No introductory courses are taught by graduate students. The average class size in an introductory lecture is 17; in a laboratory is 12; and in a regular course is 17.

PROGRAMS OF STUDY: Becker confers B.A., and B.S. degrees. Associate degrees are also awarded. Bachelor's degrees are awarded in AGRICULTURE (animal science), BIOLOGICAL SCIENCE (biology/biological science), BUSINESS (business administration and management, marketing and distribution, and sports management), COMMUNICATIONS AND THE ARTS (communications, design, and graphic design), COMPUTER AND PHYSICAL SCIENCE (computer game design/development), EDUCATION (early childhood education and elementary education), HEALTH PROFESSIONS (exercise science, nursing, preveterinary science, and veterinary science), SOCIAL SCIENCE (criminal justice, early childhood studies, forensic studies, liberal arts/general studies, and psychology). Interactive media (game design), veterinary science are the strongest academically. Interactive media (game design) has the largest enrollment.

ACTIVITIES: There are 22 groups on campus, including art, cheerleading, chorale, chorus, communications, dance, drama, ethnic, gay, honors, international, musical theater, newspaper, professional, religious, social, social service, student government, and yearbook. **Sports:** There are 8 intercollegiate sports for men and 8 for women, and 5 intramural sports for men and 5 for women. **Graduates:** From July 1, 2013 to June 30, 2014, 347 bachelor's degrees were awarded. The most popular majors were business (28%), animal studies (including pre-veterinary science) (26%), and nursing (17%). In an average class, 31% graduate in 6 years or less. Of the 2013 graduating class, 15% were enrolled in graduate school within 6 months of graduation, and 79% were employed.

SERVICES: Counseling and information services are available, as is tutoring in most subjects. There is remedial math and writing. There is also an academic support center for students. **Library/Resources:** Computerized library services include interlibrary loans, database searching, Internet access, and Wi-Fi capability. **Physically Challenged Students:** Facilities include wheelchair ramps, elevators, special parking, specially equipped restrooms, lowered drinking fountains, lowered telephones, special housing. All classes are accessible. **Special:** Cross-registration is offered through the Worcester Consortium of Higher Education. There are co-op programs, internships, study abroad, work-study programs. There are 3 national honor societies and a freshman honors program. **Visiting:** There are regularly scheduled orientations for prospective students, fall and spring on campus events. There are guides for informal visits, visitors may sit in on classes, and stay overnight. To schedule a visit, contact the Admissions Receptionist at admissions@becker.edu. **Campus Safety and Security:** Measures include 24-hour foot and vehicle patrol, self-defense education, and security escort services. There are shuttle buses, emergency telephones, and lighted pathways/sidewalks.

REQUIREMENTS: The SAT or ACT is required. The ACT is recommended. In addition, a high school transcript is required. A GPA of 2.0 is required. AP and CLEP credits are accepted.To graduate, baccalaureate students must complete at least 122 semester hours and maintain a 2.0 minimum GPA. Distribution requirements vary with the program of study. **Procedure:** Freshmen are admitted fall and spring. Entrance exams should be taken before submitting the application. There are early admissions, deferred admissions, and rolling admissions plans. Application deadlines are open. Notifications are sent November 15. Applications are accepted on-line. **Transfer Students:** 207 transfer students enrolled in 2013-2014. Requirements for transfer students depend on the program. Must have at least a 2.0 GPA from prior institution. 30 of 15 credits required for the bachelor's degree must be completed at Becker. **International Students:** There are 11 international students enrolled. The school actively recruits these students. They must take the TOEFL with a minimum score of 550 on the paper-based TOEFL (PBT) or 80 on the Internet-based version (iBT). They must also take the SAT or ACT.

ADMISSIONS: 62% of the 2014-2015 applicants were accepted. 17% of the current freshmen were in the top fifth of their class; 48% were in the top two fifths. **Admissions Contact:** Debbie Gallo, Associate Director of Admissions. E-Mail: *admissions@becker.edu* Web: *www. becker.edu*

FINANCIAL AID: In 2014-2015, 100% of all full-time freshmen and 93% of continuing full-time students received some form of financial aid. 57% of all full-time freshmen and 61% of continuing full-time students received need-based aid. Average annual earnings from campus work are $993. The average financial indebtedness of the 2014 graduate was $41,666. The FAFSA, the state aid form, and the college's own financial statement are required. The priority date for freshman financial aid applications for fall entry is March 15.

BENJAMIN FRANKLIN INSTITUTE OF TECHNOLOGY (*The complete profile is made available exclusively on our website, www. barronspac.com*)

BENTLEY UNIVERSITY   D-2
www.bentley.edu

Waltham, MA 02452   (781) 891-2244
                                              (800) 523-2354
Fax: (781) 891-3414   Email: ugadmission@bentley.edu
Full-time: 2499 men, 1671 women   **Faculty:** 229; IIA, ++$
Part-time: 57 men, 37 women   **Ph.D.s:** 77%
Graduate: 625 men, 679 women   **Student/Faculty:** 14 to 1
Year: semesters, summer session   **Tuition:** $42,511
Room & Board: $13,949   **Freshman Class:** 7477
                                       applied, 3448 accepted,
                                       978 enrolled

SAT CR/M/W: 590/650/600 **ACT:** 28   **CEEB CODE:** 3096
Application Deadline: January 7   **HIGHLY COMPETITIVE+**

Bentley University is an internationally recognized business university, dedicated to preparing the next generation of smart, nimble and compassionate leaders. Bentley combines an advanced business curriculum with the best of the arts and sciences, taught using the latest technology by a faculty that collaborates across disciplines. Bentley offers a wide variety of majors and minors, as well as optional Liberal Studies and Business Studies majors designed to create a modern intersection of the arts and sciences and business that's unique in higher education. Bentley students are highly sought after by today's leading organizations because of their professionalism, exposure to state-of-the-art research tools, and diverse, real-world experience. There is 1 graduate school. In addition to regional accreditation, Bentley has baccalaureate program accreditation with AACSB and EQUIS. The 163-acre campus is in a suburban area in Waltham, Massachusetts. Including any residence halls, there are 45 buildings.

STUDENT LIFE: 55% of undergraduates are from out of state, mostly the Northeast. Students are from 45 states, 80 foreign countries, and Canada. 70% are from public schools. 60% are White; 16% Foreign. **Male To Female Ratio:** 0.8:1. The average age of freshmen is 18; all undergraduates, 20. 6% do not continue beyond their first year; 88% remain to graduate. **Housing:** College-sponsored housing includes coed dorms, on-campus apartments, and off-campus apartments. In addition, there are special-interest houses, and honors housing available for first-year students. Special interest buildings exist for upperclass students. On-campus housing is guaranteed for all 4 years. 85% of students live on campus; of those, 85% remain on campus on weekends. Upperclassmen may keep cars.

FACULTY/CLASSROOMS: 61% of faculty are male; 39% are female. 84% teach undergraduates, and 64% do research. No introductory courses are taught by graduate students. The average class size in an introductory lecture is 28; in a laboratory is 18; and in a regular course is 28.

PROGRAMS OF STUDY: Bentley confers B.A., and B.S. degrees. Master's and Doctoral degrees are also awarded. Bachelor's degrees are awarded in BUSINESS (accounting, business administration and management, business (dual major program), business administration marketing, business communications, business economics, business information systems, business systems analysis, and finance), COMMUNICATIONS AND THE ARTS (media arts), COMPUTER AND PHYSICAL SCIENCE (actuarial science, computer information systems, information sciences and systems, and mathematics), ENGINEERING AND ENVIRONMENTAL DESIGN (environmental science), HEALTH PROFESSIONS (health), SOCIAL SCIENCE (economics, history, interdisciplinary studies, international studies, liberal arts/general studies, philosophy, public administration, and Spanish studies). Accounting, management, finance, and marketing are the strongest academically. Finance, economics-finance, and marketing are the largest.

ACTIVITIES: 11% of men belong to 2 local and 10 national fraternities; 16% of women belong to 3 national sororities. There are 106 groups on campus, including art, band, cheerleading, chess, choir, chorus, computers, dance, debate, drama, environmental, ethnic, film, gay, honors, international, jazz band, literary magazine, musical theater, newspaper, orchestra, photography, political, professional, radio and TV, religious, social, social service, student government, and yearbook. Popular campus events include Groove Boston, Halloween Party, Culture Fest, Festival of Colors, Spring Day and Fashion Shows. **Sports:** There are 12 intercollegiate sports for men and 11 for women, and 7 intramural sports for men and 7 for women. Facilities include a 118,000-square foot multipurpose facility, features a field house, two-story fitness center, fitness center for varsity athletes, athletic team and general locker rooms, a competition-sized swimming pool, athletic training room and rehabilitation area, and 24 athletic offices. **Graduates:** From July 1, 2013 to June 30, 2014, 1070 bachelor's degrees were awarded. The most popular majors were marketing (16%), economics-finance (14%), and corporate finance and accounting (13%). 290 companies recruited on campus in 2013-2014. In an average class, 83% graduate in 4 years or less, 87% graduate in 5 years or less, and 88% graduate in 6 years or less. Of the 2013 graduating class, 24% were enrolled in graduate school within 6 months of graduation, and 79% were employed.

SERVICES: Counseling and information services are available, as is tutoring in most subjects. There is a reader service for the blind, and remedial math, reading, and writing. There is a natural reader, and additional assistive programs available upon request. **Library/ Resources:** The library contains 182,399 volumes, 9,001 microform items, 25,395 audio/video tapes/CDs/DVDs, and subscribes to 76,596 periodicals including electronic. Computerized library services include interlibrary loans, database searching, Internet access, and Wi-Fi capability. Special learning facilities include an art gallery, radio station, TV station, Academic Technology Center; Winer Accounting Center for Electronic Learning and Business Measurement (ACELAB); The Bentley Library; The Center for Languages and International Collaboration (CLIC); The Center for Marketing Technology (CMT); The Computer Information Systems (CIS) Sandbox; The Design and Usability Center (DUC); Media and Culture Labs and Studio; Trading Room (Hughey Center for Financial Services); Center for Arts and Sciences (Valente Center); Center for Business Ethics (CBE); Service-Learning Center; Center for Women in Business; The Center for Quantitative Analysis; Center for International Students and Scholars; The Multicultural Center; The Writing Center; Spiritual Life Center; The Cronin Office of International Education; Bentley Global Cyberlaw Center (BGCC); Center for Integration of Science and Industry. **Physically Challenged Students:** 80% of the campus is accessible. Facilities include wheelchair ramps, elevators, special parking, specially equipped restrooms, special class scheduling, special housing. All other items available upon request. **Special:** Bentley offers a cross registration with Brandeis University and Regis College. Many students have been offered permanent, professional positions as a result of the participation in the internship program. Both for-credit and not-for-credit internships are available to students looking for valuable career-related work experience. Study abroad programs are offered in 29 countries as well as Semester at Sea. Work-study is offered through various departments throughout campus. Students can access available openings through an on-campus employment website. B.S. available in Accountancy; Actuarial Science; Computer Information Systems; Corporate Finance and Accounting; Creative Industries; Economics-Finance; Finance; Information Design and Corporate Communication; Information Systems Audit and Control; Management; Managerial Economics; Marketing; Mathematical Sciences; Professional Sales B.A. available in Global Studies; Health Studies; History; Liberal Arts (single or interdisciplinary); Media and Culture; Philosophy; Public Policy; Spanish Studies; Sustainability Sciences. The optional Liberal Studies double major allows business majors to make meaningful connections across and within disciplines, and to develop valuable skills in critical thinking, creative analysis and communication - skills that are vital to succeed both professionally and personally. In addition, Bentley offers several 5-year programs through which students earn a bachelor's and master's degree. There are 5 national honor societies, a freshman honors program, and 17 departmental honors programs. **Visiting:** There are regularly scheduled orientations for prospective students, fall, spring, and summer open house programs; Interviews are arranged by appointment; Campus tours and group information sessions take place regularly throughout the year; Visits are available during the week and some selected Saturdays. There are guides for informal visits. To schedule a visit, contact the Office of Undergraduate Admission at (781) 891-2244. **Campus Safety and Security:** Measures include 24-hour foot and vehicle patrol, emergency notification system, self-defense education, and security escort services. There are shuttle buses, emergency telephones, lighted pathways/sidewalks, controlled access to dorms/residences, new student and parent orientation safety presentations; anonymous crime reporting tip line on web; community policing programs; CCTV cameras throughout campus.

REQUIREMENTS: The SAT or ACT is required. The ACT Optional Writing test is also required. The SAT or ACT with writing component is required. Applicants must be graduates of an accredited high school or have a GED. Recommended high school preparation is 4 units each in English and math, geometry, and a senior-year math course; 3 units science; 3 units in a foreign language; 3 units in history; and 2 additional units in English, math, social science or lab science, foreign language, or speech. AP and CLEP credits are accepted. Important factors in the admissions decision are advanced placement or honors courses, extracurricular activities record, and recommendations by school officials. All undergraduate students complete general education courses in areas such as IT, writing and literature, mathematics, economics, history and social science. Students in B.S. programs take a common core of nine courses covering areas such as business ethics, accounting, finance, business statistics, and strategic management. All students take elective courses that fulfill diversity, international and communication-intensive requirements. A total of 122 credit hours for students beginning as freshmen, 121 for transfer students with a minimum GPA of 2.0 overall and 2.0 in the major are required for graduation. All first year students must take a first-year seminar. **Procedure:** Freshmen are admitted fall and spring. Entrance exams should be taken scores must be received by January 7. There are early decision, early admissions, and deferred admissions plans. Early decision applications should be filed by November 1; regular applications, by January 7 for fall entry, along with a $50 fee. Notification of early decision is sent December 21; regular decision, March 31. 112 early decision candidates were accepted for the 2014-2015 class. Applications are accepted on-line. **Transfer Students:** 125 transfer students enrolled in 2013-2014. Transfer application, personal statement, official transcripts, mid-year progress report and two letters of recommendation 60 of 122 credits required for the bachelor's degree must be completed at Bentley. **International Students:** There are 665 international students enrolled. The school actively recruits these students. They must take the TOEFL with a minimum score of 577 on the paper-based TOEFL (PBT) or 90 on the Internet-based version (iBT) and the Comprehensive English Language Test, or take the Pearson's, or the IELTS. They must also take the SAT or ACT.

ADMISSIONS: 46% of the 2014-2015 applicants were accepted. The SAT scores for the 2014-2015 freshman class were: Critical Reading--9% below 500, 43% between 500 and 599, 43% between 600 and 699, and 5% between 700 and 800; Math--2% below 500, 19% between 500 and 599, 56% between 600 and 699, and 24% between 700 and 800; Writing--7% below 500, 39% between 500 and 599, 45% between 600 and 699, and 9% between 700 and 800. The ACT scores were 1% below 21, 7% between 21 and 23, 24% between 24 and 26, 27% between 27 and 28, and 41% above 28. 66% of the current freshmen were in the top fifth of their class; 90% were in the top two fifths. 15 freshmen graduated first in their class. **Admissions Contact:** Erik Vardaro, Director of Undergraduate Admission. E-Mail: ugadmission@bentley.edu Web: www.bentley.edu

FINANCIAL AID: In 2014-2015, 76% of all full-time freshmen and 73% of continuing full-time students received some form of financial aid. 46% of all full-time freshmen and 45% of continuing full-time students received need-based aid. The average freshman award was $33,890. Need-based scholarships or need-based grants averaged $30,000 ($44,400 maximum); need-based self-help aid (loans and jobs) averaged $4,695 ($7,500 maximum); non-need-based athletic scholarships averaged $30,520 ($55,620 maximum); and other non-need-based awards and non-need-based scholarships averaged $16,917 ($39,600 maximum). 24% of undergraduate students work part-time. Average annual earnings from campus work are $1045. The average financial indebtedness of the 2014 graduate was $30,602. Bentley is a member of CSS. The CSS/Profile and FAFSA, and Federal tax returns, including all schedules for parents and student are required. The deadline for filing freshman financial aid applications for fall entry is February 1.

BERKLEE COLLEGE OF MUSIC (*The complete profile is made available exclusively on our website, www.barronspac.com*)

BOSTON ARCHITECTURAL COLLEGE (*The complete profile is made available exclusively on our website, www.barronspac.com*)

BOSTON COLLEGE   E-2
www.bc.edu

| Chestnut Hill, MA 02467 | (617) 552-3100 |
| | (800) 360-2522 |

Fax: (617) 552-0798

Full-time: 4189 men, 4965 women	Faculty: I, +$
Part-time: n/av	Ph.Ds: 95%
Graduate: 1911 men, 2510 women	Student/Faculty: n/av
Year: semesters, summer session	Tuition: $47,436
Room & Board: $13,186	Freshman Class: 23223 applied, 7875 accepted, 2288 enrolled
SAT CR/M/W: 665/695/685 ACT: 30	CEEB CODE: 3083
Application Deadline: January 1	MOST COMPETITIVE

Boston College, founded in 1863, is an independent institution affiliated with the Roman Catholic Church and the Jesuit Order. It offers undergraduate programs in the arts and sciences, business, nursing, and education, and graduate and professional programs. There are 4 undergraduate schools and 7 graduate schools. In addition to regional accreditation, BC has baccalaureate program accreditation with AACSB, CSWE, NCATE, and NLN. The 338-acre campus is in a suburban area 6 miles west of Boston. Including any residence halls, there are 147 buildings.

STUDENT LIFE: 78% of undergraduates are from out of state, mostly the Northeast. Students are from 49 states, 59 foreign countries, and Canada. 49% are from public schools. 62% are White. **Male To Female Ratio:** 1.2:1. The average age of freshmen is 18; all undergraduates, 21. 5% do not continue beyond their first year; 91% remain to graduate. **Housing:** 7309 students can be accommodated in college housing, which includes single-sex and coed dorms and on-campus apartments. In addition, there are honors houses, special-interest houses, community and multicultural housing, quiet residences, single-sex freshman halls, perspectives academic program housing, and a substance-free residence. On-campus housing is guaranteed for the freshman year only and is available on a lottery system for upperclassmen. 85% of students live on campus; of those, 90% remain on campus on weekends. Upperclassmen may keep cars.

FACULTY/CLASSROOMS: 53% of faculty are male; 47% are female. All teach and do research. Graduate students teach 14% of introductory courses. The average class size in a laboratory is 15 and in a regular course is 30.

PROGRAMS OF STUDY: BC confers B.A., and B.S. degrees. Master's and Doctoral degrees are also awarded. Bachelor's degrees are awarded in BIOLOGICAL SCIENCE (biochemistry and biology/biological science), BUSINESS (accounting, banking and finance, business administration and management, business economics, human resources, management science, marketing/retailing/merchandising, and operations research), COMMUNICATIONS AND THE ARTS (art history and appreciation, classics, communications, dramatic arts, English, film arts, French, Italian, linguistics, music, romance languages and literature, and studio art), COMPUTER AND PHYSICAL SCIENCE (chemistry, computer science, geology, geophysics and seismology, information sciences and systems, mathematics, and physics), EDUCATION (early childhood education, elementary education, secondary education, and special education), ENGINEERING AND ENVIRONMENTAL DESIGN (environmental science), HEALTH PROFESSIONS (nursing), SOCIAL SCIENCE (applied psychology, classical/ancient civilization, developmental psychology, economics, German area studies, Hispanic American studies, history, human development, philosophy, political science/government, psychology, Russian and Slavic studies, sociology, and theological studies). Finance, economics, chemistry and biology are the strongest academically. Communications, finance and economics have the largest enrollments.

ACTIVITIES: There are no fraternities or sororities. There are 230 groups on campus, including art, band, cheerleading, chess, choir, chorale, chorus, communications, computers, dance, debate, drama, environmental, ethnic, film, gay, honors, international, jazz band, literary magazine, marching band, musical theater, newspaper, orchestra, pep band, photography, political, professional, radio and TV, religious, social, social service, student government, symphony, and yearbook. Popular campus events include Middlemarch Ball, Christmas Chorale and Senior Week. **Sports:** There are 12 intercollegiate sports for men and 15 for women, and 38 intramural sports for men and 30 for women. Facilities include a 44,500-seat stadium, a forum that seats 8500 for basketball and 7600 for ice hockey, soccer fields, baseball fields, and a track. BC also has a student recreation complex with: equipment for cardio, weight, strength training, dozens of group exercise class options including spinning, yoga, pilates, an indoor pool diving, swimming, and dedicated indoor courts for basketball, racquetball, squash, tennis and volleyball. **Graduates:** From July 1, 2013 to June 30, 2014, 2305 bachelor's degrees were awarded. The most popular majors were finance (10%), economics (9%), and communication (8%). 300 companies recruited on campus in 2013-2014. In an average class, 89% graduate in 4 years or less and 91% graduate in 6 years or less. Of the 2013 graduating class, 20% were enrolled in graduate school within 6 months of graduation, and 63% were employed.

SERVICES: Counseling and information services are available, as is tutoring in most subjects. There is a reader service for the blind. Academic development center serves all students. **Library/Resources:** The 8 libraries contain 2.9 million volumes, 4.3 million microform items, 2,099 audio/video tapes/CDs/DVDs, and subscribe to 44,110 periodicals including electronic. Computerized library services include interlibrary loans, database searching, and Internet access. Special learning facilities include an art gallery, radio station, and TV station. **Physically Challenged Students:** 95% of the campus is accessible. Facilities include wheelchair ramps, elevators, special parking, specially equipped restrooms, special class scheduling, lowered drinking fountains, lowered telephones, and special housing. **Special:** There are internship programs in management and in arts and sciences. Students may cross-register with Boston University, Brandeis University, Hebrew College, Pine Manor College, Regis College, and Tufts University. BC also offers a Washington semester in cooperation with American University, work-study programs with nonprofit agencies, study abroad, and dual and student-designed majors. Students may pursue a 3-2 engineering program with Boston University and accelerated 5-year programs in social work and education. There are 12 national honor societies, including Phi Beta Kappa, a freshman honors program, and 4 departmental honors programs. **Visiting:** There are regularly scheduled orientations for prospective students, group information sessions and campus tours Monday through Friday. There are guides for informal visits and visitors may sit in on classes. To schedule a visit, contact the Office of Undergraduate Admission. **Campus Safety and Security:** Measures include 24-hour foot and vehicle patrol, emergency notification system, self-defense education, and security escort services. There are shuttle buses, emergency telephones, lighted pathways/sidewalks, controlled access to dorms/residences. Safety seminars and safety walking tours are offered for incoming students during orientation. A fire safety awareness week is held every year with a mock dorm room burning demonstration, distribution of fire safety education materials, and drills. Students and faculty/staff members can also opt into an emergency alert system that can send emergency messages from the university to cell phones.

REQUIREMENTS: The SAT or ACT is required. The ACT Optional Writing test is also required. Students may take either the SAT test with Writing or the ACT test with Writing. Applicants must be graduates of an accredited high school completing 4 units each of English, foreign language, science, and math. Those students applying to the school of nursing must complete at least 2 years of a lab science including 1 unit of chemistry. Applicants to the school of management are strongly encouraged to take 4 years of college preparatory math. An essay is required. AP credits are accepted. Core requirements include 2 courses each in natural science, social science, history, philosophy, and theology; 1 course each in literature, writing, math, and cultural diversity; and proficiency in a foreign language for College of Arts and Science students. To graduate, students must complete 120 credits (or 117 for nursing majors) including at least

30 in the major with a minimum 1.667 GPA (1.5 in management). Computer science is required for management majors, and a freshman writing seminar for all students except honors and AP students. Students in the honors program may elect to take courses in lieu of a thesis. Scholars of the college must complete a scholar's project before graduation. **Procedure:** Freshmen are admitted fall and spring. Entrance exams should be taken no later than January of the senior year. There are early admissions and deferred admissions plans. Early decision applications should be filed by November 1; regular applications, by January 1 for fall entry; and November 1 for spring entry, along with a $70 fee. Notification of early decision is sent December 25; regular decision, April 15. 6000 applicants were on the 2014 waiting list; 280 were admitted. Applications are accepted on-line. **Transfer Students:** 166 transfer students enrolled in 2013-2014. Applicants must have a current GPA of at least 3.0 and must have earned a minimum of 9 semester hours. High school transcripts, letters of recommendation, and SAT or ACT scores are required. 60 of 120 credits required for the bachelor's degree must be completed at BC. **International Students:** There are 639 international students enrolled. The school actively recruits these students. They must take the TOEFL with a minimum score of 600 on the paper-based TOEFL (PBT) or 100 on the Internet-based version (iBT), TOEFL requirement will be waived if student scores 600+ on SAT Critical Reading or 27+ on ACT English. They must also take the SAT or ACT. SAT Subject Tests will be considered if submitted, but are not required.

ADMISSIONS: 34% of the 2014-2015 applicants were accepted. The SAT scores for the 2014-2015 freshman class were: Critical Reading--2% below 500, 14% between 500 and 599, 51% between 600 and 699, and 33% between 700 and 800; Math--2% below 500, 9% between 500 and 599, 43% between 600 and 699, and 46% between 700 and 800; Writing--2% below 500, 9% between 500 and 599, 46% between 600 and 699, and 43% between 700 and 800. 96% of the current freshmen were in the top fifth of their class; 99% were in the top two fifths. **Admissions Contact:** John L. Mahoney Jr., Director Undergraduate Admission. Web: *www.bc.edu*

FINANCIAL AID: 42% of all full-time freshmen and 43% of continuing full-time students received need-based aid. The average freshman award was $35,378. Need-based scholarships or need-based grants averaged $32,146; need-based self-help aid (loans and jobs) averaged $6,023; non-need-based athletic scholarships averaged $48,574; and other non-need-based awards and non-need-based scholarships averaged $19,222. 26% of undergraduate students work part-time. Average annual earnings from campus work are $2500. The average financial indebtedness of the 2014 graduate was $21,139. BC is a member of CSS. The CSS/Profile and FAFSA, and the federal IRS income tax form, W-2s, Divorced/Separated Statement (when applicable) are required. The deadline for filing freshman financial aid applications for fall entry is February 1.

BOSTON CONSERVATORY E-2
www.bostonconservatory.edu

Boston, MA 02215	(617) 912-9153
Fax: n/av	
Full-time: 217 men, 286 women	Faculty: n/av
Part-time: 2 men, 7 women	Ph.D.s: n/av
Graduate: 100 men, 107 women	Student/Faculty: 5 to 1
Year: semesters	Tuition: $37,300
Room & Board: $17,080	Freshman Class: n/av
	CEEB CODE: 3084
Application Deadline: December 1	VERY COMPETITIVE

Boston Conservatory, founded in 1867, is a private college providing degree programs in music, musical theater, and dance. Figures in this profile are approximate. There are 3 graduate schools. In addition to regional accreditation, BC has baccalaureate program accreditation with NASM. The campus is in an urban area in Boston's Back Bay. Including any residence halls, there are 9 buildings.

STUDENT LIFE: 80% of undergraduates are from out of state, mostly the Northeast. Students are from 40 states, 24 foreign countries, and Canada. **Male To Female Ratio:** 1.3:1. The average age of freshmen is 18. 19% do not continue beyond their first year. **Housing:** 182 students can be accommodated in college housing, which includes coed dorms. On-campus housing is guaranteed for the freshman year only and is available on a lottery system for upperclassmen. 72% of students commute. Alcohol is not permitted. No one may keep cars.

FACULTY/CLASSROOMS: All teach undergraduates. No introductory courses are taught by graduate students. The average class size in an introductory lecture is 15; in a laboratory is 5; and in a regular course is 15.

PROGRAMS OF STUDY: confers B.F.A., and B.M. degrees. Master's degrees are also awarded. Bachelor's degrees are awarded in COMMUNICATIONS AND THE ARTS (dance, guitar, music, music performance, music theory and composition, musical theater, opera, and piano/organ), EDUCATION (music education). Music has the largest enrollment.

ACTIVITIES: Men belong to 1 national fraternity; and women belong to 2 national sororities. There are 19 groups on campus, including band, choir, chorale, chorus, dance, drama, gay, international, musical theater, newspaper, opera, orchestra, political, professional, religious, social service, student government, and yearbook. Popular campus events include Parents Weekend, Off the Block Program, Drag Show, and Thanksgiving Dinner. **Sports:** There is no sports program at BC . **Graduates:** From July 1, 2013 to June 30, 2014, 117 bachelor's degrees were awarded. The most popular majors were musical theater (46%), music (40%), and dance (14%).

SERVICES: Counseling and information services are available, as is tutoring in some subjects. Writing, music theory, music history **Library/Resources:** The library contains 40,000 volumes, and subscribes to 120 periodicals including electronic. Computerized library services include interlibrary loans and database searching. **Physically Challenged Students:** 20% of the campus is accessible. Facilities include elevators. **Special:** There are 3 national honor societies and 1 departmental honors program. **Visiting:** Visitors may sit in on classes. To schedule a visit, contact the Admissions Office at (617) 912-9153. **Campus Safety and Security:** Measures include 24-hour foot and vehicle patrol. There are emergency telephones and controlled access to dorms/residences.

REQUIREMENTS: SAT or the ACT is required for undergraduate admission. An audition is the most important factor for acceptance and merit scholarship. GPA and standardized test scores are considered in concert with each other to determine ability to undertake the academic, liberal arts component of the undergraduate degree. A GPA of 2.7 is required. AP and CLEP credits are accepted. Important factors in the admissions decision are evidence of special talent, extracurricular activities record, and personality/intangible qualities. **Procedure:** Freshmen are admitted fall. Entrance exams should be taken as early as possible. There is a deferred admissions plan. Applications should be filed by December 1 for fall entry, along with a $110 fee. Notifications are sent April 1. 30 applicants were on the 2014 waiting list. Applications are accepted on-line. **Transfer Students:** 15 transfer students enrolled in 2013-2014. A successful audition and a 3.0 GPA are required. Transfer credits are determined through transcript review conducted by the dean and Registrar. The high school transcript is required if fewer than 2 semesters worth of college-level work have been undertaken/earned. **International Students:** There are 62 international students enrolled. The school actively recruits these students. They must take the TOEFL or MELAB. They must also take the SAT or ACT. An audition also is required.

ADMISSIONS: Meghan Cadwallader, Director of Admissions. Web: *www.bostonconservatory.edu*

FINANCIAL AID: BC is a member of CSS. The FAFSA is required. Check with the school for current application deadlines.

BOSTON UNIVERSITY
www.bu.edu

E-2

Boston, MA 02215	(617) 353-2300 n/av
Fax: (617) 353-9695	Email: admissions@bu.edu, or intadmis@bu.edu

Full-time: 6454 men, 10165 women
Part-time: 709 men, 689 women
Graduate: 6184 men, 7911 women
Year: semesters, summer session
Room & Board: $14,030

Faculty: 1129; I, +$
Ph.D.s: 89%
Student/Faculty: 13 to 1
Tuition: $46,664
Freshman Class: 54190 applied, 18701 accepted, 3915 enrolled

SAT CR/M/W: 640/660/660 **ACT:** 30
Application Deadline: January 1
CEEB CODE: 3087
MOST COMPETITIVE

Boston University is a private teaching and research university committed to excellence in undergraduate education. Students study with world-renowned faculty that include Fulbright Scholars, Pulitzer Prize winners, MacArthur Fellows, Nobel Prize winners, and a former Poet Laureate. In nine undergraduate schools and colleges, BU offers students more than 250 programs of study, internships in the US and abroad, one of the nations's most extensive study abroad programs, and cutting-edge research with faculty mentors. Housing is guaranteed for four years in a variety of on-campus residences including high-rise buildings and historic brownstones. BU students engage with their campus community through nearly 500 student organizations, club and intramural sports, and 24 NCAA Division-I varsity sports teams. Students experience the city of Boston as an extension of the campus for study, internships, employment, and cultural and recreational activities. There are 9 undergraduate schools and 13 graduate schools. In addition to regional accreditation, BU has baccalaureate program accreditation with AACSB, ABET, and NASM. The 135-acre campus is in an urban area on the Charles River in Boston's Back Bay. Including any residence halls, there are 324 buildings.

STUDENT LIFE: 78% of undergraduates are from out of state, mostly the Middle Atlantic. Students are from 50 states, 134 foreign countries, and Canada. 67% are from public schools. 46% are White; 19% Foreign; 14% Asian American. 31% claim no religious affiliation; 28% Protestant; 20% Catholic; 12% Buddhist, Hindu, Islamic, and Eastern Rite Orthodox. **Male To Female Ratio:** 1.4:1. The average age of freshmen is 18; all undergraduates, 20. 7% do not continue beyond their first year; 84% remain to graduate. **Housing:** 11,350 students can be accommodated in college housing, which includes single-sex and coed dorms, on-campus apartments, off-campus apartments, and married student housing. In addition, there are honors houses, language houses, special-interest houses, International floors. On-campus housing is guaranteed for all 4 years. 75% of students live on campus; of those, 80% remain on campus on weekends. All students may keep cars.

FACULTY/CLASSROOMS: 60% of faculty are male; 40% are female. 62% teach undergraduates. No introductory courses are taught by graduate students. The average class size in an introductory lecture is 70; in a laboratory is 18; and in a regular course is 17.

PROGRAMS OF STUDY: BU confers B.A., B.S., B.F.A., B.L.S., Mus.B. and B.S.B.A. degrees. Master's and Doctoral degrees are also awarded. Bachelor's degrees are awarded in AGRICULTURE (environmental studies), BIOLOGICAL SCIENCE (biochemistry, biology/biological science, ecology, environmental biology, marine biology, neurosciences, nutrition, and physiology), BUSINESS (business administration and management and hotel/motel and restaurant management), COMMUNICATIONS AND THE ARTS (art history and appreciation, Chinese, classical languages, classics, communications, dramatic arts, English, film arts, French, Germanic languages and literature, graphic design, Greek (classical), journalism, Latin, linguistics, music, music history and appreciation, music performance, music theory and composition, painting, performing arts, Russian languages and literature, scenic and lighting design, sculpture, Spanish, theatre arts, theater design, and theater management), COMPUTER AND PHYSICAL SCIENCE (astronomy, astronomy and physics, astrophysics, chemistry, chemistry education, computer science, earth science, geophysics and seismology, mathematics, phys-

ics, and planetary and space science), EDUCATION (art education, athletic training, bilingual/bicultural education, early childhood education, education, education of the deaf and hearing impaired, elementary education, English education, foreign languages education, mathematics education, music education, physical education, science education, social studies education, and special education), ENGINEERING AND ENVIRONMENTAL DESIGN (biomedical engineering, computer engineering, electrical/electronics engineering, engineering, manufacturing engineering, and mechanical engineering), HEALTH PROFESSIONS (biomedical science, health science, occupational therapy, physical therapy, and speech pathology/audiology), SOCIAL SCIENCE (American studies, anthropology, archeology, architectural studies, asian studies, classical/ancient civilization, criminal justice, economics, European studies, French studies, geography, Hispanic American studies, history, interdisciplinary studies, international relations, Italian studies, Japanese studies, Latin American studies, Middle Eastern studies, philosophy, political science/government, psychology, religion, sociology, and urban studies). The Kilachand Honors College and the accelerated medical and dental programs, are the strongest academically. Communications, business, and engineering have the largest enrollments.

ACTIVITIES: 3% of men belong to 1 local and 8 national fraternities; 5% of women belong to 9 national sororities. There are 500 groups on campus, including and sports, art, band, cheerleading, chess, choir, chorale, chorus, communications, computers, dance, debate, drama, environmental, ethnic, film, gay, honors, international, jazz band, literary magazine, marching band, multicultural, musical theater, newspaper, opera, orchestra, pep band, photography, political, professional, radio and TV, religious, social, social service, student government, symphony, and yearbook. Popular campus events include Fall Welcome (Splash), World Fair and Culture Fest, and Head of the Charles River Regatta. **Sports:** There are 10 intercollegiate sports for men and 14 for women, and 17 intramural sports for men and 17 for women. Facilities include 2 multipurpose fields, softball field, indoor track and tennis center, 3 outdoor tennis courts, two ice rinks, competition pool, 2 recreational pools, rock wall, 3-court multipurpose gymnasium, 4-court wood gymnasium, 6 squash/racquetball courts, dance studio, fitness center, boathouse, and sailing pavilion. **Graduates:** From July 1, 2013 to June 30, 2014, 4426 bachelor's degrees were awarded. The most popular majors were management (20%), communications (16%), and engineering (8%). 600 companies recruited on campus in 2013-2014. In an average class, 4% graduate in 3 years or less, 81% graduate in 4 years or less, 84% graduate in 5 years or less, and 84% graduate in 6 years or less.

SERVICES: Counseling and information services are available, as is tutoring in most subjects, such as liberal arts, science, engineering, management, and writing. There is a reader service for the blind. Comprehensive learning strategy for learning disabled is available. **Library/Resources:** The 23 libraries contain 3.7 million volumes, 4.9 million microform items, 181,869 audio/video tapes/CDs/DVDs, and subscribe to 98,765 periodicals including electronic. Computerized library services include interlibrary loans, database searching, Internet access, and Wi-Fi capability. Special learning facilities include an art gallery, planetarium, radio station, TV station. BU has over 2,000 research laboratories on campus, 3 supercomputers that are available for student use, and four specialized high-performance computer labs. BU also has an astronomy observatory, 20th-century archives, a theater company in residence, the Geddes language lab, a speech, language, and hearing clinic; a performance center; a multi-media center; the Life Sciences and Engineering building; the Engineering Product Innovation Center; and the Photonics Center which houses state-of-the-art laboratories for developing new light-based technologies. **Physically Challenged Students:** 90% of the campus is accessible. Facilities include wheelchair ramps, elevators, special parking, specially equipped restrooms, special class scheduling, lowered drinking fountains, lowered telephones, special housing. on-campus transportation, relocation of classes/events for access, tactile and access maps, visual fire alarms for the deaf, adaptive computers, and readers, notetakers and ASL interpreters. **Special:** Boston University offers many opportunities for students to excel, including: Kilachand Honors College - a university-wide honors program, BU's Seven-Year Accelerated Medical and Dental Programs, which allow hight motivated students to complete their bachelor's degree and medical or dental doctorate in seven years, and the MMEDIC/ENGMEDIC integrated curriculums where students begin their medical studies as undergraduates. BU's Dual Degree program enables students to earn two degrees simultaneously. Combined bachelors and masters programs are also available in many disciplines. Students conduct research with faculty or independently though our Undergraduate Research Opportunities Progam and Work for Distinction. Students have many opportunities to intern in the US and abroad, and participate in more than 70 BU study abroad programs around the world. There are 16 national honor societies, including Phi Beta Kappa, a freshman honors program, and 6 departmental honors programs. **Visiting:** There are regularly scheduled orientations for prospective students, admissions at the Alan and Sherry Leventhal center is open Mon.-Fri. and some Saturdays during the academic year. Appointments can be made for class visits or lunch with current students. Campus tours and information sessions are also offered. There are guides for informal visits, visitors may sit in on classes, and stay overnight. To schedule a visit, contact the Admissions Reception Center at the Alan and Sherry Leventhal Center at (617) 353-2318. **Campus Safety and Security:** Measures include 24-hour foot and vehicle patrol, emergency notification system, self-defense education, and security escort services. There are shuttle buses, emergency telephones, lighted pathways/sidewalks, mountain bicycle patrol system. There is a uniformed safety/security assistant on duty 24 hours a day in large residence halls and there are 60 academy-trained officers in the university police department.

REQUIREMENTS: The SAT or ACT is required. The ACT Optional Writing test is also required. Applicants are evaluated on an individual basis. For most BU programs, the recommended curriculum includes four years of English, three to four years of math (pre-calculus/calculus recommended), three to four years of lab sciences, three to four years of history/social science, and two to four years of a foreign language. Students may submit the ACT (with Writing) in place of the SAT. Students applying to the Accelerated Medical or Dental Programs are required to submit Subject Tests in chemistry, math (level 2), and a foreign language (recommended). Candidates for the College of Fine Arts must present a portfolio or participate in an audition. AP and CLEP credits are accepted. Important factors in the admissions decision are advanced placement or honors courses, leadership record, and ability to finance college education. All students are required to complete at least 128 credit hours to qualify for graduation from Boston University. The individual schools and colleges within BU have specific academic requirements and standards for determining satisfactory completion of a program of study such as grades, majors, concentrations, divisional studies, or internships. **Procedure:** Freshmen are admitted fall and spring. Entrance exams should be taken in the junior year or early in the senior year. There are early decision, early admissions, and deferred admissions plans. Early decision applications should be filed by November 1; regular applications, by January 1 for fall entry, along with a $85 fee. Notification of early decision is sent December 15; regular decision, April 1. 727 early decision candidates were accepted for the 2014-2015 class. 3503 applicants were on the 2014 waiting list; 2 were admitted. Applications are accepted on-line. **Transfer Students:** 478 transfer students enrolled in 2013-2014. College transcript and a complete high school transcript (or GED) must be submitted. Recommendations and an essay are also required. **International Students:** There are 3039 international students enrolled. The school actively recruits these students. They must take the TOEFL with a minimum score of 550 on the paper-based TOEFL (PBT) or 84 on the Internet-based version (iBT), or take the IELTS. They must also take the SAT or ACT.

ADMISSIONS: 35% of the 2014-2015 applicants were accepted. The SAT scores for the 2014-2015 freshman class were: Critical Reading--1% below 500, 21% between 500 and 599, 59% between 600 and 699, and 19% between 700 and 800; Math--1% below 500, 18% between 500 and 599, 58% between 600 and 699, and 24% between 700 and 800; Writing--1% below 500, 16% between 500 and 599, 59% between 600 and 699, and 25% between 700 and 800. The ACT scores were 2% between 21 and 23, 14% between 24 and 26, 22% between 27 and 28, and 63% above 28. 82% of the current freshmen were in the top fifth of their class; 98% were in the top two fifths. 58 freshmen graduated first in their class. **Admissions Contact:** Kelly Walter,

Assoc VP & Exec Dir of Undergraduate Adm. E-Mail: *admissions@bu .edu, or intadmis@bu.edu* Web: *www.bu.edu*

FINANCIAL AID: In 2014-2015, 55% of all full-time freshmen and 56% of continuing full-time students received some form of financial aid. 38% of all full-time freshmen and 39% of continuing full-time students received need-based aid. The average freshman award was $33,841. Need-based scholarships or need-based grants averaged $33,797 ($64,816 maximum); need-based self-help aid (loans and jobs) averaged $6,236 ($9,500 maximum); non-need-based athletic scholarships averaged $40,066 ($63,180 maximum); and other non-need-based awards and non-need-based scholarships averaged $17,409 ($56,919 maximum). 32% of undergraduate students work part-time. Average annual earnings from campus work are $1625. The average financial indebtedness of the 2014 graduate was $39,167. BU is a member of CSS. The CSS/Profile and FAFSA are required. The deadline for filing freshman financial aid applications for fall entry is February 15.

BRANDEIS UNIVERSITY   D-2
www.brandeis.edu

Waltham, MA 02454

Fax: (781) 736-3536
Full-time: 1593 men, 2118 women
Part-time: 8 men, 10 women
Graduate: 1116 men, 1100 women
Year: semesters, summer session
Room & Board: n/app

(781) 736-3500
(800) 622-0622
Email: admissions@brandeis.edu
Faculty: n/av
Ph.D.s: 95%
Student/Faculty: n/av
Tuition: n/av
Freshman Class: 10004 applied, 3523 accepted, 859 enrolled

SAT CR/M/W: 680/690/690 **ACT:** 31
Application Deadline: January 1
CEEB CODE: 3092
MOST COMPETITIVE

Brandeis University, founded in 1948 is a private research university with a liberal arts focus. The residential campus is a dynamic and diverse learning community known for its vibrant, free thinking intellectual atmosphere and offers easy access to Boston and its many attractions. The University is named for the late Louis Dembitz Brandeis, the distinguished associate justice of the United States Supreme Court, and reflects the values of academic excellence, commitment to social justice, respect for creativity and diversity, and concern for the world that he personified. There is 1 undergraduate school and 4 graduate schools. The 235-acre campus is in a suburban area 10 miles west of Boston. Including any residence halls, there are 97 buildings.

STUDENT LIFE: 76% of undergraduates are from out of state, mostly the Northeast. Students are from 47 states, 61 foreign countries, and Canada. 48% are White; 18% Foreign; 13% Asian American. **Male To Female Ratio:** 1.2:1. The average age of freshmen is 18; all undergraduates, 20. **Housing:** College-sponsored housing includes coed On-campus housing is guaranteed for the freshman year only, is available on a first-come, first-served basis, and is available on a lottery system for upperclassmen. 77% of students live on campus. Upperclassmen may keep cars.

FACULTY/CLASSROOMS: No introductory courses are taught by graduate students.

PROGRAMS OF STUDY: Brandeis confers B.A., and B.S. degrees. Master's and Doctoral degrees are also awarded. Bachelor's degrees are awarded in AGRICULTURE (environmental studies), BIOLOGICAL SCIENCE (biochemistry, biology/biological science, biophysics, and neurosciences), BUSINESS (business administration and management), COMMUNICATIONS AND THE ARTS (art history and appreciation, classics, comparative literature, creative writing, English, film arts, French, German, linguistics, music, Russian languages and literature, Spanish, studio art, and theatre arts), COMPUTER AND PHYSICAL SCIENCE (chemistry, computer science, mathematics, and physics), HEALTH PROFESSIONS (health science), SOCIAL SCIENCE (African American studies, American studies, anthropology, East Asian studies, economics, European studies, history, interdisciplinary studies, international studies,

Islamic studies, Judaic studies, Latin American studies, Middle Eastern studies, Near Eastern studies, philosophy, political science/government, psychology, sociology, and women's studies).

ACTIVITIES: There are no fraternities or sororities. **Sports:** Facilities include a 70,000 square foot field house including a 1800 seat basketball arena, 3 indoor tennis courts, 3 indoor basketball courts, 7 squash courts, 6 lane indoor track, several multipurpose rooms for aerobics, dance, group fitness, sauna in men's and women's locker rooms, fencing room, weight room, turf soccer field, grass club field, baseball and softball diamonds, 12 outdoor tennis courts, 6 lane indoor pool, and 8 lane outdoor track. **Graduates:** From July 1, 2013 to June 30, 2014, 833 bachelor's degrees were awarded. The most popular majors were biology (11%), economics (10%), and psychology (7%).

SERVICES: **Library/Resources:** The 2 libraries contain 1.7 million volumes, 960,389 microform items, 43,766 audio/video tapes/CDs/DVDs, and subscribe to 104,329 periodicals including electronic. Computerized library services include interlibrary loans, database searching, Internet access, and Wi-Fi capability. Special learning facilities include an art gallery, TV station, a spatial orientation laboratory, an astronomical observatory, an emotion laboratory, a cultural center, a treasure hall, an art museum, and an audiovisual center. **Physically Challenged Students:** Facilities include wheelchair ramps, elevators, special parking, specially equipped restrooms, special class scheduling, lowered drinking fountains, lowered telephones. Libraries, student centers, several other buildings, sports facilities, and the majority of residence halls are fully accessible. **Special:** Students may pursue interdepartmental programs in 18 different fields. Students may cross-register with Boston, Wellesley, Babson, Bentley and Olin Colleges and Boston and Tufts Universities. Beginning Fall 2013 eligible upperclassmen may also enroll in one online consortium class through Semester Online. Study abroad is possible in 69 countries. Internships are available in virtually every field, and work-study is also available. Dual and student-designed majors can be arranged. The university also offers credit by exam, nondegree study, and pass/fail options. Opportunities for early acceptance to area medical schools are offered to Brandeis students. There is a chapter of Phi Beta Kappa. **Visiting:** There are regularly scheduled orientations for prospective students, including most weekdays we offer morning and afternoon information sessions led by admissions counselors and followed by student-led tours. Information sessions are typically held Mon-Fri at 10:15 a.m., 2:15 p.m.; tours at 9am, 11am, 1pm and 3pm. There are guides for informal visits and visitors may sit in on classes. To schedule a visit, contact the Office of Admissions at admissions@brandeis.edu.

REQUIREMENTS: Eligible applicants can choose one of the following three submission options: Option 1: Submit SAT with writing or ACT with writing Option 2: Submit a combination of three SAT Subject Tests and/or AP tests (or IB exams) Option 3: Submit an academic portfolio through the Common Application including: One graded analytical paper from 11th or 12th grade and a second academic Teacher Evaluation *Home-schooled applicants and candidates applying from secondary schools that provide written evaluations rather than grades are required to submit the SAT or the ACT test with the writing section. *All international applicants must submit either the SAT or the ACT test with the writing section. AP credits are accepted. Important factors in the admissions decision are advanced placement or honors courses, recommendations by school officials, and geographical diversity. All candidates for a bachelor's degree must satisfactorily complete a major, a writing requirement, a foreign language requirement, a group of courses designed to provide a strong foundation in general education, and the phys ed requirement. Oral communication, quantitative reasoning, and non-Western and comparative studies requirements also must be met. No courses used to fulfill any general university requirement may be taken on the pass/fail grading option. **Procedure:** Freshmen are admitted fall, spring, and summer. Entrance exams should be taken by January of the senior year. There are early decision and deferred admissions plans. Early decision applications should be filed by November 1; regular applications, by January 1 for fall entry; and November 1 for spring entry, along with a $75 fee. Notification of early decision is sent December 1; regular decision, April 1. 287 early decision candidates were accepted for the 2014-2015 class. 1405

applicants were on the 2014 waiting list; 3 were admitted. Applications are accepted on-line. **Transfer Students:** 60 transfer students enrolled in 2013-2014. Major consideration is given to the quality of college-level work completed, the secondary school record, professors' and deans' evaluations as well as the students fit for our institution. Because there is a 2-year residence requirement, students should apply before entering their junior year. 64 of 128 credits required for the bachelor's degree must be completed at Brandeis. **International Students:** There are 666 international students enrolled. The school actively recruits these students. They must take the TOEFL with a minimum score of 600 on the paper-based TOEFL (PBT) or 100 on the Internet-based version (iBT), or take the IELTS. They must also take the SAT or ACT.

ADMISSIONS: 35% of the 2014-2015 applicants were accepted. The SAT scores for the 2014-2015 freshman class were: Critical Reading--1% below 500, 9% between 500 and 599, 45% between 600 and 699, and 44% between 700 and 800; Math--1% below 500, 8% between 500 and 599, 44% between 600 and 699, and 47% between 700 and 800; Writing--1% below 500, 8% between 500 and 599, 44% between 600 and 699, and 47% between 700 and 800. The ACT scores were 2% between 21 and 23, 5% between 24 and 26, 14% between 27 and 28, and 78% above 28. 89% of the current freshmen were in the top fifth of their class; 98% were in the top two fifths. There were 14 National Merit finalists. 28 freshmen graduated first in their class. **Admissions Contact:** Jennifer Walker, Executive Director of Admissions. E-Mail: *admissions@brandeis.edu* Web: *www.brandeis.edu*

FINANCIAL AID: Brandeis is a member of CSS. Check with the school for current application deadlines.

BRIDGEWATER STATE UNIVERSITY   E-3
www.bridgew.edu

Bridgewater, MA 02325	**(508) 531-1237**

Fax: (508) 531-1746	Email: admissions@bridgew.edu
Full-time: 3337 men, 4695 women	Faculty: 321
Part-time: 712 men, 940 women	Ph.D.s: 92%
Graduate: 474 men, 1259 women	Student/Faculty: 25 to 1
Year: semesters, summer session	Tuition: $8052 ($14,192)
Room & Board: $10,700	Freshman Class: 6170 applied, 4525 accepted, 1454 enrolled
SAT CR/M: 499/511 ACT: 21	CEEB CODE: 3517
Application Deadline: February 15	COMPETITIVE

As the comprehensive public university of Southeastern Massachusetts, Bridgewater State University has a responsibility to educate the residents of Southeastern Massachusetts and the commonwealth, and to use its intellectual, scientific and technological resources to support and advance the economic and cultural life of the region and the state. Bridgewater's growing number of innovative academic programs helps to ensure that Bridgewater State University students are prepared to think critically, communicate effectively and act responsibly within a context of personal and professional ethics. For example, BSU's Academic Achievement Center, and particularly its first-year advising program, is often cited as a model for other institutions to follow. At the same time, the Adrian Tinsley Program for Undergraduate Research represents an unparalleled opportunity for students to work closely with faculty mentors and to present research and creative work at regional and national conferences. While maintaining its historic focus on the preparation of teachers, Bridgewater State University provides a broad range of baccalaureate degree programs through its College of Humanities and Social Sciences, Bartlett College of Science and Mathematics, College of Education and Allied Studies and its Ricciardi College of Business. Bridgewater State University offers 32 undergraduate academic programs with 90 different areas of concentration as well as internships, research programs, study abroad and honors programs. Bridgewater is a leader in the adoption of technology for instruction and administration. Through its extensive information technology resources, the college makes technology an integral component of teaching and learning and serves as a regional resource on technology in higher education, K-12, and government and business settings. In addition to enjoying a fully wireless campus, our students and faculty benefit from having cutting edge educational technology in all classrooms, and from extensive computer support services. There are three sororities, four fraternities and one co-educational fraternity offered at BSU. Bridgewater State's Student Government Association (SGA) is an organization of students which represent the Bridgewater State community. Through SGA, the student body can express their academic and social wants and needs. There are 5 undergraduate schools and 1 graduate school. In addition to regional accreditation, BSU has baccalaureate program accreditation with CSWE, NASAD, NASDTEC, NASM, NCATE, ACS, FAA, CAATE, NASPAA, and CACREP. The 278-acre campus is in a suburban area 28 miles from Boston. Including any residence halls, there are 38 buildings.

STUDENT LIFE: 96% of undergraduates are from Massachusetts. Others are from 27 states, 22 foreign countries, and Canada. 83% are White. **Male To Female Ratio:** 1.5:1. The average age of freshmen is 18; all undergraduates, 22. 19% do not continue beyond their first year; 54% remain to graduate. **Housing:** 2781 students can be accommodated in college housing, which includes coed dorms and on-campus apartments. Break housing for athletes, student teachers, visiting lecturers, international students and special housing for disabled students. On-campus housing is available on a first-come, first-served basis. 65% of students commute. Alcohol is not permitted. Upperclassmen may keep cars.

FACULTY/CLASSROOMS: 50% of faculty are male; 50% are female. All teach undergraduates. No introductory courses are taught by graduate students. The average class size in an introductory lecture is 23; in a laboratory is 17; and in a regular course is 19.

PROGRAMS OF STUDY: BSU confers B.A., B.S. and B.S.Ed. degrees. Master's degrees are also awarded. Bachelor's degrees are awarded in BIOLOGICAL SCIENCE (biology/biological science), BUSINESS (accounting, finance, and management science), COMMUNICATIONS AND THE ARTS (art, art history and appreciation, English, fine arts, music, Spanish, and speech/debate/rhetoric), COMPUTER AND PHYSICAL SCIENCE (chemistry, computer science, earth science, geochemistry, mathematics, and physics), EDUCATION (art education, athletic training, dance education, drama education, early childhood education, elementary education, health education, music education, physical education, and special education), ENGINEERING AND ENVIRONMENTAL DESIGN (aeronautical science), SOCIAL SCIENCE (anthropology, criminal justice, economics, geography, philosophy, political science/government, psychology, social work, and sociology). Geography, anthropology, and political science are the strongest academically. Education, business/management, and psychology have the largest enrollments.

ACTIVITIES: 7% of men belong to 4 national fraternities; 6% of women belong to 3 national sororities. There are 90 groups on campus, including art, band, chorale, communications, computers, dance, drama, environmental, ethnic, forensics, gay, honors, international, jazz band, musical theater, newspaper, political, professional, religious, social, social service, student government, and yearbook. Popular campus events include Homecoming, Springfest and Campus Movie Fest. **Sports:** There are 9 intercollegiate sports for men and 10 for women, and 15 intramural sports for men and 16 for women. Facilities include the Adrian Tinsley Center which has a Competition Court with NCAA regulation basketball and volleyball venue that seats 1000 spectators. This center also has Synthetic Multipurpose Courts which are lined for basketball, volleyball, badminton, and tennis. The Adrian Tinsley Center also houses a Walking/Jogging Track which is a 1/8 mile three lane track that encircles the 32,000 square foot gymnasium area. This center also houses the 9,000 square foot Thornburg Fitness Center which is equipped with some of the most current equipment on the market including cardiovascular machines, selectorized weight machines, plate-loaded equipment, free-weights, and Olympic lifting platforms. BSU also has the John J. Kelly Gymnasium which houses a large and small gym, the Dr. Mary Jo Moriarty Pool, weight room, classrooms and offices. Bridgewater State University also has the Edward C. Swenson Athletic Complex where the BSU Bears compete in football and soccer, Alumni Park where our baseball and softball players compete, and Dr. Henry Rosen Memorial Tennis Courts. **Graduates:** From July 1, 2013 to June 30, 2014, 1747 bachelor's degrees were awarded. The most pop-

ular majors were education (19%), business/marketing (17%), and psychology (13%). 21 companies recruited on campus in 2013-2014. In an average class, 1% graduate in 3 years or less, 28% graduate in 4 years or less, 50% graduate in 5 years or less, and 54% graduate in 6 years or less. Of the 2013 graduating class, 17% were enrolled in graduate school within 6 months of graduation, and 79% were employed.

SERVICES: Counseling and information services are available, as is tutoring in most subjects. There is a reader service for the blind, and remedial math, reading, and writing. There are recorded texts, classroom interpreters, scribes and note takers, testing accommodations, and a speech/hearing/language center. **Library/Resources:** The library contains 352,584 volumes, 715,736 microform items, and 7,613 audio/video tapes/CDs/DVDs, subscribes to 55,658 periodicals including electronic. Computerized library services include interlibrary loans, database searching, and Internet access. Special learning facilities include an art gallery, observatory, and a greenhouse. **Physically Challenged Students:** All of the campus is accessible. Facilities include wheelchair ramps, elevators, special parking, specially equipped restrooms, special class scheduling, lowered drinking fountains, lowered telephones, special housing. **Special:** Opportunities are provided for cross-registration with other Massachusetts Colleges and Universities, internships available in most majors, double majors, joint/dual degree in B.S. and M.S. in Criminal Justice and B.S.Ed. in Elementary Education and M.Ed. in Special Education, core curriculum requirements, non-degree study, and study abroad programs. Bridgewater State University participates in The Washington Center Internship Program, National Student Exchange, Southeastern Association for Cooperation in Higher Education, and the College Academic Program Sharing. There are 13 national honor societies, including Phi Beta Kappa, a freshman honors program, and 28 departmental honors programs. **Visiting:** There are regularly scheduled orientations for prospective students, campus tours for prospective students Monday through Thursday at 11 a.m. and 3 p.m. when college is in session and 10 a.m. and 2 p.m. during summer months. BSU also offers prospective students and their families to participate in an interactive open. There are guides for informal visits and visitors may sit in on classes. To schedule a visit, contact the Admissions Office at (508) 531-1237. **Campus Safety and Security:** Measures include 24-hour foot and vehicle patrol, emergency notification system, and security escort services. There are shuttle buses, emergency telephones, lighted pathways/sidewalks, controlled access to dorms/residences, Bridgewater State University Police Department, University-operated transit system that runs from 7:15 a.m. to 8:00 p.m., Monday through Friday, and a safety-escort van that runs from 7 p.m. to 3 a.m, 7 days a week.

REQUIREMENTS: Graduation from an accredited secondary school is required; SAT or ACT scores required, a GED will be accepted. Applicants must have successfully completed 16 Carnegie units, including 4 units of English, 3 units of Mathematics, 3 units of Science with 2 lab units, 2 units of a foreign language, 2 units of Social Studies, and 2 in other college preparatory electives. An essay is recommended. A GPA of 2.0 is required. AP and CLEP credits are accepted. Important factors in the admissions decision are advanced placement or honors courses, leadership record, parents or siblings attended your school, evidence of special talent, extracurricular activities record, recommendations by alumni, recommendations by school officials, ability to finance college education, personality/intangible qualities, and geographical diversity. Students are required to complete a minimum of 120 semester hours, with 30 to 36 hours in the major and 52 to 55 hours in core curriculum courses. Students must maintain a minimum GPA of 2.0. **Procedure:** Freshmen are admitted fall and spring. There are early admissions and deferred admissions plans. Applications should be filed by February 15 for fall entry; November 1 for spring entry, along with a $40 fee. Notifications are sent April 15. 445 applicants were on the 2014 waiting list; 126 were admitted. Applications are accepted on-line. **Transfer Students:** 1044 transfer students enrolled in 2013-2014. Transfer students must have maintained a minimum GPA of 2.5 from 12 to 24 credits or 2.0 from more than 24 credits at a previous institution. College transcripts and an essay are required of all transfer students; some students must submit high school transcripts and standardized test scores. 30 of 120 credits required for the bachelor's degree must be completed at BSU. **International Students:** There are 53 international students enrolled. They must take the TOEFL with a minimum score of 500 on the paper-based TOEFL (PBT) or 61 on the Internet-based version (iBT), or take the IELTS-International English Language Testing System. They must also take the SAT or ACT.

ADMISSIONS: 73% of the 2014-2015 applicants were accepted. The SAT scores for the 2014-2015 freshman class were: Critical Reading--48% below 500, 41% between 500 and 599, 10% between 600 and 699, and 1% between 700 and 800; Math--40% below 500, 47% between 500 and 599, 12% between 600 and 699, and 1% between 700 and 800. The ACT scores were 46% below 21, 43% between 21 and 23, 7% between 24 and 26, 2% between 27 and 28, and 2% above 28. **Admissions Contact:** Gregg A. Meyer, Dean of University Admissions. E-Mail: *admissions@bridgew.edu* Web: *www2.bridgew.edu*

FINANCIAL AID: 13% of undergraduate students work part-time. Average annual earnings from campus work are $3570. The average financial indebtedness of the 2014 graduate was $30,189. The FAFSA is required. The deadline for filing freshman financial aid applications for fall entry is March 1.

CAMBRIDGE COLLEGE (*The complete profile is made available exclusively on our website, www.barronspac.com*)

CLARK UNIVERSITY — C-2
www.clarku.edu

Worcester, MA 01610	(508) 793-7431
	(800) 462-5275
Fax: (508) 793-8821	Email: admissions@clarku.edu
Full-time: 949 men, 1321 women	Faculty: 197; IIA, ++$
Part-time: 48 men, 62 women	Ph.D.s: 96%
Graduate: 511 men, 660 women	Student/Faculty: 9 to 1
Year: semesters, summer session	Tuition: $39,550
Room & Board: $7470	Freshman Class: 5551 applied, 3416 accepted, 621 enrolled
SAT CR/M/W: 620/600/620 ACT: 28	CEEB CODE: 3279
Application Deadline: January 15	HIGHLY COMPETITIVE+

Clark University, founded in 1887, is an independent liberal arts and research institution. Figures in the above capsule and in this profile are approximate. There are 2 undergraduate schools and 3 graduate schools. In addition to regional accreditation, Clark has baccalaureate program accreditation with AACSB and NASDTEC. The 50-acre campus is in an urban area 50 miles west of Boston. Including any residence halls, there are 69 buildings.

STUDENT LIFE: 63% of undergraduates are from out of state, mostly the Northeast. Students are from 41 states, 62 foreign countries, and Canada. 75% are from public schools. 61% are White; 12% Foreign. 42% claim no religious affiliation; 18% Protestant; 15% Catholic; 12% Jewish. **Male To Female Ratio:** 1.4:1. The average age of freshmen is 19; all undergraduates, 20. 10% do not continue beyond their first year; 81% remain to graduate. **Housing:** 1745 students can be accommodated in college housing, which includes single-sex and coed dorms, on-campus apartments, and off-campus apartments. In addition, there are special-interest houses, wellness and quiet houses. On-campus housing is guaranteed for the freshman year only and is available on a lottery system for upperclassmen. 70% of students live on campus. All students may keep cars.

FACULTY/CLASSROOMS: 56% of faculty are male; 44% are female. All teach and do research. No introductory courses are taught by graduate students. The average class size in an introductory lecture is 25; in a laboratory is 17; and in a regular course is 21.

PROGRAMS OF STUDY: Clark confers B.A., and B.S. degrees. Master's and Doctoral degrees are also awarded. Bachelor's degrees are awarded in BIOLOGICAL SCIENCE (biochemistry and biology/biological science), BUSINESS (business administration and management), COMMUNICATIONS AND THE ARTS (art history and appreciation, communications, comparative literature, dramatic arts, English, film arts, fine arts, French, languages, music, romance languages and literature, Spanish, studio art, and visual and performing arts), COMPUTER AND PHYSICAL SCIENCE (chemistry, computer science, mathematics, and physics), ENGINEERING AND ENVIRONMENTAL DESIGN (environmental science), HEALTH PROFESSIONS (predentistry and premedicine), SOCIAL SCIENCE (Asian/Oriental studies, classical/ancient civilization, economics, geography, history, international relations, international studies, philosophy, political science/government, prelaw, psychology, sociology, and women's studies). Psychology, political science, and biology/biochemistry have the largest enrollments.

ACTIVITIES: There are no fraternities or sororities. There are 120 groups on campus, including art, band, chess, choir, chorale, chorus, computers, dance, debate, drama, environmental, ethnic, film, gay, honors, international, jazz band, literary magazine, musical theater, newspaper, orchestra, pep band, photography, political, professional, radio and TV, religious, social, social service, student government, symphony, and yearbook. Popular campus events include Gryphon and Pleiades Honor Society Variety Show, International Gala, and Speaker's Forum. **Sports:** There are 8 intercollegiate sports for men and 9 for women, and 14 intramural sports for men and 14 for women. Facilities include an athletic center with a 2000-seat gym, a pool, a fitness center, tennis courts, outdoor fields, and baseball and softball diamonds. **Graduates:** From July 1, 2013 to June 30, 2014, 519 bachelor's degrees were awarded. The most popular majors were psychology (17%), political science (9%), and biology and biochemistry (8%). 80 companies recruited on campus in 2013-2014. In an average class, 1% graduate in 3 years or less, 77% graduate in 4 years or less, 80% graduate in 5 years or less, and 81% graduate in 6 years or less. Of the 2013 graduating class, 40% were enrolled in graduate school within 6 months of graduation, and 30% were employed.

SERVICES: Counseling and information services are available, as is tutoring in some subjects, math, biology, chemistry, economics, and psychology. For learning-disabled students, the university provides early orientation, alternative test-taking accommodations, and a learning specialist. **Library/Resources:** The 6 libraries contain 650,601 volumes, 61,262 microform items, 2,390 audio/video tapes/CDs/DVDs, and subscribe to 2,133 periodicals including electronic. Computerized library services include interlibrary loans, database searching, Internet access, and Wi-Fi capability. Special learning facilities include an art gallery, radio station, a TV studio, campus cable network, center for music with 2 studios for electronic music, 2 theaters, and magnetic resonance imaging facility. **Physically Challenged Students:** 95% of the campus is accessible. Facilities include wheelchair ramps, elevators, special parking, specially equipped restrooms, special class scheduling, lowered drinking fountains, lowered telephones, and special housing. **Special:** For-credit internships are available in all disciplines with private corporations and small businesses, medical centers, and government agencies. There is cross-registration with members of the Worcester Consortium, including 9 other colleges and universities. Clark also offers study abroad in 16 countries, a Washington semester with American University, work-study programs, accelerated degree programs, dual and student-designed majors, pass/no record options, and a 3-2 engineering degree with Columbia University. A gerontology certificate is offered with the Worcester Consortium for Higher Education. There are 10 national honor societies, including Phi Beta Kappa, and 21 departmental honors programs. **Visiting:** There are regularly scheduled orientations for prospective students, consisting of open houses during fall and spring semesters, which include tours, information sessions, and talks with faculty, administration, and coaches. There are guides for informal visits and visitors may sit in on classes. To schedule a visit, contact the Admissions Office at admissions@clarku.edu. **Campus Safety and Security:** Measures include 24-hour foot and vehicle patrol, emergency notification system, self-defense education, and security escort services. There are shuttle buses, emergency telephones, lighted pathways/sidewalks, and controlled access to dorms/residences.

REQUIREMENTS: SAT or ACT are optional. Applicants must graduate from an accredited secondary school or have a GED. 16 Carnegie units are required, including 4 years of English, 3 each of math and science, and 2 each of foreign languages and social studies, including history. AP credits are accepted. Each student is required to complete 2 critical thinking courses in 2 categories of verbal expression and formal analysis, and 6 perspectives courses, representing the categories of aesthetics, comparative, historical, language and culture, science, and values. A student must receive passing grades in a minimum of 32 full courses, with a C- or better in at least 24 of these courses, and maintain a minimum 2.0 GPA to graduate. **Procedure:** Freshmen are admitted fall and spring. Entrance exams should be taken by November of the senior year. There are early admissions and deferred admissions plans. Applications should be filed by January 15 for fall entry; November 15 for spring entry, along with a $55 fee. Notifications are sent April 1. 226 applicants were on the 2014 waiting list; 6 were admitted. Applications are accepted on-line. **Transfer Students:** 42 transfer students enrolled in 2013-2014. Applicants should have a minimum GPA of about 2.8. At least one full semester of college course work is required. High school and college transcripts, recent SAT or ACT test scores, a statement of good standing from previous institutions attended, and a transfer statement are required. Grades of C or better in comparable course work transfer for credit. 16 of 32 credits required for the bachelor's degree must be completed at Clark. **International Students:** There are 280 international students enrolled. The school actively recruits these students. They must take the TOEFL with a minimum score of 550 on the paper-based TOEFL (PBT) or 80 on the Internet-based version (iBT), or take the IELTS, scoring 6.5.

ADMISSIONS: 62% of the 2014-2015 applicants were accepted. The SAT scores for the 2014-2015 freshman class were: Critical Reading--6% below 500, 28% between 500 and 599, 47% between 600 and 699, and 19% between 700 and 800; Math--7% below 500, 42% between 500 and 599, 43% between 600 and 699, and 8% between 700 and 800; Writing--6% below 500, 31% between 500 and 599, 46% between 600 and 699, and 17% between 700 and 800. The ACT scores were 7% between 21 and 23, 25% between 24 and 26, 24% between 27 and 28, and 44% above 28. 65% of the current freshmen were in the top fifth of their class; 93% were in the top two fifths. 8 freshmen graduated first in their class. **Admissions Contact:** Donald Honeman, Dean of Admissions. E-Mail: *admissions@clarku.edu* Web: *www.clarku.edu*

FINANCIAL AID: In 2014-2015, 92% of all full-time freshmen and continuing full-time students received some form of financial aid. 62% of all full-time freshmen and continuing full-time students received need-based aid. The average freshman award was $28,417. Need-based scholarships or need-based grants averaged $26,375; and need-based self-help aid (loans and jobs) averaged $4,993. 75% of undergraduate students work part-time. Average annual earnings from campus work are $2000. The average financial indebtedness of the 2014 graduate was $24,990. Clark is a member of CSS. The CSS/Profile and FAFSA are required. The deadline for filing freshman financial aid applications for fall entry is February 1.

COLLEGE OF ART AND DESIGN AT LESLEY UNIVERSITY (*The complete profile is made available exclusively on our website, www.barronspac.com*)

COLLEGE OF THE HOLY CROSS   C-2
www.holycross.edu

Worcester, MA 01610	**(508) 793-2443**
	(800) 442-2421
Fax: (508) 793-3888	**Email:** admissions@holycross.edu
Full-time: 1467 men, 1437 women	**Faculty:** 287; IIB, ++$
Part-time: 12 men, 21 women	**Ph.D.s:** 96%
Graduate: n/av	**Student/Faculty:** 10 to 1
Year: semesters	**Tuition:** $45,692
Room & Board: $12,350	**Freshman Class:** 5302 applied, 2298 accepted, 774 enrolled
SAT CR/M/W: 648/655/658 **ACT:** 29	**CEEB CODE:** 3282
Application Deadline: January 15	**MOST COMPETITIVE**

The College of the Holy Cross is the only liberal arts college that embraces a Catholic, Jesuit identity. And of the 28 Jesuit colleges and universities in the United States, Holy Cross stands alone in its exclusive commitment to undergraduate education. Students enjoy a full array of athletic facilities, fitness and wellness centers, and outstand-

ing arts spaces. There is one undergraduate school. In addition to regional accreditation, Holy Cross has baccalaureate program accreditation with NAST. The 174-acre campus is in a suburban area 45 miles west of Boston. Including any residence halls, there are 35 buildings.

STUDENT LIFE: 63% of undergraduates are from out of state, mostly the Northeast. Students are from 46 states, 16 foreign countries, and Canada. 49% are from public schools. 70% are White; 11% Hispanic. 72% are Catholic; 14% Unknown denominations. **Male To Female Ratio:** 1.0:1. The average age of freshmen is 18; all undergraduates, 20. 6% do not continue beyond their first year; 92% remain to graduate. **Housing:** 2503 students can be accommodated in college housing, which includes coed dorms and on-campus apartments. In addition, there are special-interest houses, substance-free housing, and first-year living and learning housing. On-campus housing is guaranteed for all 4 years. 91% of students live on campus; of those, 90% remain on campus on weekends. Upperclassmen may keep cars.

FACULTY/CLASSROOMS: 53% of faculty are male; 47% are female. All teach and do research. No introductory courses are taught by graduate students. The average class size in a regular course is 19.

PROGRAMS OF STUDY: Holy Cross confers A.B. degrees. Bachelor's degrees are awarded in AGRICULTURE (environmental studies), BIOLOGICAL SCIENCE (biology/biological science), BUSINESS (accounting), COMMUNICATIONS AND THE ARTS (art history and appreciation, Chinese, classics, dramatic arts, English, French, German, Italian, literature, music, Russian, Spanish, and studio art), COMPUTER AND PHYSICAL SCIENCE (chemistry, computer science, mathematics, and physics), ENGINEERING AND ENVIRONMENTAL DESIGN (architecture), SOCIAL SCIENCE (anthropology, Asian/Oriental studies, economics, German area studies, history, Italian studies, medieval studies, Middle Eastern studies, philosophy, political science/government, psychology, religion, and sociology). Economics, political science, and English have the largest enrollments.

ACTIVITIES: There are no fraternities or sororities. There are 100 groups on campus, including art, band, cheerleading, choir, chorale, chorus, computers, dance, debate, drama, environmental, ethnic, film, gay, honors, international, investing club, jazz band, literary magazine, marching band, musical theater, newspaper, orchestra, pep band, photography, political, professional, religious, social, social service, student government, symphony, and yearbook. Popular campus events include Family Weekend, Purple Pride Day, Winter Homecoming, Spring Weekend. **Sports:** There are 13 intercollegiate sports for men and 14 for women, and 11 intramural sports for men and 10 for women. Facilities include baseball, football, soccer fields and stadiums, indoor and outdoor running tracks, swimming pool, ice rink, indoor crew tanks, basketball arena, weight and exercise rooms, wellness centers, tennis, squash, and racquetball courts. **Graduates:** From July 1, 2013 to June 30, 2014, 679 bachelor's degrees were awarded. The most popular majors were economics (14%), political science (11%), and English (11%). 116 companies recruited on campus in 2013-2014. In an average class, 90% graduate in 4 years or less, 92% graduate in 5 years or less, and 92% graduate in 6 years or less. Of the 2013 graduating class, 13% were enrolled in graduate school within 6 months of graduation, and 61% were employed.

SERVICES: Counseling and information services are available, as is tutoring in calculus, biology, chemistry, physics, economics, accounting, classics, Spanish, writing and psychology statistics. **Library/Resources:** The 7 libraries contain 639,721 volumes, 16,587 microform items, 36,898 audio/video tapes/CDs/DVDs, and subscribe to 8,264 periodicals including electronic. Computerized library services include interlibrary loans, database searching, Internet access, and Wi-Fi capability. Special learning facilities include an art gallery, greenhouses, research-level laboratories and equipment, and a multimedia resource center. **Physically Challenged Students:** 85% of the campus is accessible. Facilities include wheelchair ramps, elevators, special parking, specially equipped restrooms, special class scheduling, lowered drinking fountains, lowered telephones, special housing. **Special:** Academic internships are available through the Center for Interdisciplinary Studies. Student-designed majors, dual majors including economics-accounting major, a Washington semester, and study abroad in approximately 15 countries are possible. The College also offers several 4- to 6-week programs in locations such as Jerusalem, London, Moscow, Paris and Rome. There is a 3-2 engineering program with Columbia University, internships, and an accelerated degree program. Students may cross-register with other universities in a local consortium. There are 2 national honor societies, including Phi Beta Kappa, and 5 departmental honors programs. **Visiting:** There are regularly scheduled orientations for prospective students, open houses in October and November consist of informational panels on academics, admissions, financial aid, and student life, as well as tours of the facilities. There are guides for informal visits, visitors may sit in on classes, and stay overnight. To schedule a visit, contact the Admissions Office. **Campus Safety and Security:** Measures include 24-hour foot and vehicle patrol, emergency notification system, self-defense education, and security escort services. There are shuttle buses, emergency telephones, lighted pathways/sidewalks, controlled access to dorms/residences, and card access control system.

REQUIREMENTS: Applicants should be graduates of an accredited secondary school or hold the GED. Recommended preparatory courses include English, foreign language, history, math, and science. An essay is required. Students have the option to submit standardized test scores if they believe the results represent a fuller picture of their achievements and potential; students who opt not to submit scores will not be at any disadvantage in admissions decisions. An interview is recommended. AP credits are accepted. Important factors in the admissions decision are extracurricular activities record, recommendations by school officials, and advanced placement or honors courses. Distribution requirements include social science, natural and mathematical science, cross-cultural studies, religious and philosophical studies, historical studies and the arts, and literature. In addition, students must demonstrate competence in a classical or modern language or American sign language. A total of 32 courses worth at least 1 unit each is required for graduation, with 10 to 14 courses in the major. The minimum GPA for graduation is 2.0. **Procedure:** Freshmen are admitted fall. Entrance exams should be taken no later than January 15th of the senior year. There are early decision and deferred admissions plans. Early decision applications should be filed by December 15; regular applications, by January 15 for fall entry, along with a $60 fee. Notification of early decision is sent January 15; regular decision, April 1. 340 early decision candidates were accepted for the 2014-2015 class. 343 applicants were on the 2014 waiting list. Applications are accepted on-line. **Transfer Students:** 16 transfer students enrolled in 2013-2014. Standardized test scores are not required but applicants must provide transcripts and 2 professor recommendations. Personal interviews are highly recommended. 64 of 128 credits required for the bachelor's degree must be completed at Holy Cross. **International Students:** There are 42 international students enrolled. The school actively recruits these students. They must take the TOEFL with a minimum score of 600 on the paper-based TOEFL (PBT) or 100 on the Internet-based version (iBT).

ADMISSIONS: 43% of the 2014-2015 applicants were accepted. The SAT scores for the 2014-2015 freshman class were: Critical Reading--1% below 500, 19% between 500 and 599, 58% between 600 and 699, and 22% between 700 and 800; Math--1% below 500, 13% between 500 and 599, 62% between 600 and 699, and 24% between 700 and 800; Writing--2% below 500, 14% between 500 and 599, 54% between 600 and 699, and 30% between 700 and 800. 13 freshmen graduated first in their class. **Admissions Contact:** Ann McDermott, Director. E-Mail: *admissions@holycross.edu* Web: *www.holycross.edu*

FINANCIAL AID: In 2014-2015, 61% of all full-time freshmen and 60% of continuing full-time students received some form of financial aid. 55% of all full-time freshmen and 55% of continuing full-time students received need-based aid. The average freshman award was $33,293. Need-based scholarships or need-based grants averaged $33,991; need-based self-help aid (loans and jobs) averaged $5,911; non-need-based athletic scholarships averaged $41,168; and other non-need-based awards and non-need-based scholarships averaged $45,080. 51% of undergraduate students work part-time. Average annual earnings from campus work are $1810. The average financial indebtedness of the 2014 graduate was $28,354. Holy Cross is a member of CSS. The CSS/Profile and FAFSA, and student and parent federal tax returns; business and farm supplement, if applicable are required. The deadline for filing freshman financial aid applications for fall entry is February 1.

CURRY COLLEGE (*The complete profile is made available exclusively on our website, www.barronspac.com*)

EASTERN NAZARENE COLLEGE · E-2

www.enc.edu

Quincy, MA 02170	**(617) 745-3711**
	(800) 883-6288
Fax: (617) 745-3980	Email: admissio@enc.edu
Full-time: 245 men, 355 women	Faculty: n/av
Part-time: 15 men, 25 women	Ph.D.s: 57%
Graduate: 30 men, 140 women	Student/Faculty: n/av
Year: 4-1-4, summer session	Tuition: $24,860
Room & Board: $8600	Freshman Class: n/av
SAT or ACT: required	CEEB CODE: 3365
Application Deadline: n/av	COMPETITIVE

Eastern Nazarene College, founded in 1918, is a private college affiliated with the Church of the Nazarene. It offers a program in the liberal arts. The figures in the above capsule and in this profile are approximate. There is one graduate school. In addition to regional accreditation, ENC has baccalaureate program accreditation with CSWE. The 15-acre campus is in a suburban area 6 miles south of Boston. Including any residence halls, there are 16 buildings.

STUDENT LIFE: 55% of undergraduates are from out of state, mostly the Northeast. Students are from 27 states, 24 foreign countries, and Canada. 88% are White. 88% are Protestant. The average age of freshmen is 18; all undergraduates, 20. 25% do not continue beyond their first year; 60% remain to graduate. **Housing:** 638 students can be accommodated in college housing, which includes single-sex dorms and married student housing. On-campus housing is guaranteed for all 4 years. 75% of students live on campus; of those, 75% remain on campus on weekends. Alcohol is not permitted. All students may keep cars.

FACULTY/CLASSROOMS: 72% of faculty are male; 28% are female. 83% teach undergraduates. No introductory courses are taught by graduate students. The average class size in an introductory lecture is 75; in a laboratory is 20; and in a regular course is 22.

PROGRAMS OF STUDY: ENC confers B.A., and B.S. degrees. Associate and Master's degrees are also awarded. Bachelor's degrees are awarded in BIOLOGICAL SCIENCE (biology/biological science and marine biology), BUSINESS (accounting and business administration and management), COMMUNICATIONS AND THE ARTS (advertising, broadcasting, communications, dramatic arts, English, French, journalism, literature, music, music performance, Spanish, and speech/debate/rhetoric), COMPUTER AND PHYSICAL SCIENCE (chemistry, computer science, mathematics, physics, and science), EDUCATION (athletic training, education, elementary education, music education, science education, and social science education), ENGINEERING AND ENVIRONMENTAL DESIGN (computer engineering, engineering physics, and environmental science), HEALTH PROFESSIONS (sports medicine), SOCIAL SCIENCE (child psychology/development, Christian studies, clinical psychology, history, ministries, physical fitness/movement, psychology, religion, religious music, social studies, social work, and sociology). Chemistry, physics, and history are the strongest academically. Education, business, and psychology have the largest enrollments.

ACTIVITIES: There are 34 groups on campus, including band, cheerleading, choir, chorale, chorus, drama, jazz band, literary magazine, musical theater, newspaper, pep band, photography, professional, radio and TV, religious, social service, student government, and yearbook. Popular campus events include Freshmen Breakout, All-School Outing, and Junior/Senior Banquet. **Sports:** There are 5 intercollegiate sports for men and 5 for women, and 4 intramural sports for men and 5 for women. Facilities include a phys ed center equipped with a basketball area, batting cage, and playing courts.

SERVICES: Counseling and information services are available, as is tutoring in most subjects. There is remedial math, reading, and writing. **Library/Resources:** The library contains 115,000 volumes, and subscribes to 600 periodicals including electronic. Computerized library services include interlibrary loans and database searching. Special learning facilities include a radio station. **Physically Challenged Students:** 65% of the campus is accessible. Facilities include wheelchair ramps, elevators, special parking, and specially equipped restrooms. **Special:** Internships are available in the metropolitan

Boston area. Study abroad in Costa Rica, a Washington semester, a 3-2 engineering degree with Boston University, and a cooperative program with the Massachusetts College of Pharmacy are offered. Work-study programs, dual majors, credit for life, military, and work experience, and pass/fail options are available. An off-campus degree-completion program for adults in business administration is offered. There is 1 national honor society. **Visiting:** There are regularly scheduled orientations for prospective students. There are guides for informal visits, visitors may sit in on classes, and stay overnight. To schedule a visit, contact the Office of Admissions. **Campus Safety and Security:** Measures include 24-hour foot and vehicle patrol, self-defense education, and security escort services. There are emergency telephones and lighted pathways/sidewalks.

REQUIREMENTS: The SAT or ACT is required. Applicants must be graduates of an accredited secondary school or have a GED. They must have a minimum of 16 academic credits, including 4 of English, 2 to 4 each of math and foreign language, 1 to 4 of science, and 1 to 2 each of history and social studies. Music students must audition. An essay and interview are recommended. A GPA of 2.3 is required. AP and CLEP credits are accepted. Important factors in the admissions decision are advanced placement or honors courses, recommendations by school officials, and leadership record. All students must complete the core curriculum of writing and rhetoric, biblical history, social science, science or math, symbolic systems and intercultural awareness, philosophy and religion, and phys ed. A total of 130 credits is required for the B.A. or B.S., with 32 to 40 in the major. Minimum GPA for graduation is 2.0. **Procedure:** Freshmen are admitted to all sessions. Entrance exams should be taken in the spring of the junior year. There are deferred admissions and rolling admissions plans. Check with the school for current application deadlines. The fall 2014 application fee was $25. **Transfer Students:** A minimum 2.0 GPA is required. An interview is recommended. 60 of 130 credits required for the bachelor's degree must be completed at ENC. **International Students:** They must take the TOEFL.

ADMISSIONS: Rodney Rogers, Director of Admissions. E-Mail: *admissio@enc.edu* Web: *www.enc.edu*

FINANCIAL AID: ENC is a member of CSS. The FAFSA and the college's own financial statement are required. Check with the school for current application deadlines.

ELMS COLLEGE
www.elms.edu

Chicopee, MA 01013

B-3

(413) 592-3189
(800) 255-ELMS

Fax: (413) 594-2781
Email: admissions@elms.edu

Full-time: 65 men, 360 women
Part-time: 25 men, 190 women
Graduate: 20 men, 80 women
Year: semesters
Room & Board: $9800
SAT or ACT: required
Application Deadline: open

Faculty: IIA, --$
Ph.D.s: 76%
Student/Faculty: n/av
Tuition: $14,100
Freshman Class: n/av
CEEB CODE: 3283

VERY COMPETITIVE

Elms College, founded in 1928 as College of Our Lady of the Elms, is a Roman Catholic institution offering undergraduate degrees in liberal arts and sciences and graduate degrees in liberal arts, education, and theology. The figures in the above capsule and in this profile are approximate. In addition to regional accreditation, College of Our Lady of the Elms has baccalaureate program accreditation with CSWE and NLN. The 32-acre campus is in a suburban area 2 miles north of Springfield and 90 miles west of Boston. Including any residence halls, there are 11 buildings.

STUDENT LIFE: 85% of undergraduates are from Massachusetts. Others are from 9 states, and 10 foreign countries. 74% are from public schools. 80% are White. 60% are Catholic. **Female To Male Ratio:** 5.7:1. The average age of freshmen is 20; all undergraduates, 22. 11% do not continue beyond their first year. **Housing:** 315 students can be accommodated in college housing, which includes single-sex and coed dorms. On-campus housing is guaranteed for all 4 years. 60% of students commute. All students may keep cars.

FACULTY/CLASSROOMS: 35% of faculty are male; 65% are female.

90% teach undergraduates, 93% do research, and 92% do both. No introductory courses are taught by graduate students. The average class size in an introductory lecture is 13; in a laboratory is 8; and in a regular course is 11.

PROGRAMS OF STUDY: Elms confers B.A., and B.S. degrees. Associate and master's degrees are also awarded. Bachelor's degrees are awarded in BIOLOGICAL SCIENCE (biology/biological science), BUSINESS (accounting, business administration and management, international business management, and marketing/retailing/merchandising), COMMUNICATIONS AND THE ARTS (English, fine arts, and Spanish), COMPUTER AND PHYSICAL SCIENCE (chemistry, computer science, mathematics, and natural sciences), EDUCATION (bilingual/bicultural education, early childhood education, elementary education, foreign languages education, middle school education, science education, secondary education, special education, and teaching English as a second/foreign language (TESOL/TEFOL)), HEALTH PROFESSIONS (health science, medical laboratory technology, nursing, predentistry, premedicine, and speech pathology/audiology), SOCIAL SCIENCE (American studies, international studies, paralegal studies, prelaw, psychology, religion, social work, and sociology). Nursing, education, and biology are the strongest academically. Education, business, and nursing are the largest.

ACTIVITIES: There are no fraternities or sororities. There are 41 groups on campus, including art, choir, chorale, chorus, computers, dance, drama, ethnic, honors, international, literary magazine, musical theater, newspaper, photography, professional, radio and TV, religious, social, social service, student government, and yearbook. Popular campus events include Soph Show, Cap and Gown, and Ring Ceremony. **Sports:** There are 6 intercollegiate sports for men and 9 for women, and 6 intramural sports for men and 6 for women. Facilities include fitness and athletic center housing a suspended indoor track, a 25-meter, 6-lane pool, a weight and aerobics room, a multipurpose arena, a basketball court, and a volleyball court.

SERVICES: Counseling and information services are available, as is tutoring in every subject. There is a reader service for the blind, and remedial math, reading, and writing. There also is an academic advising and resource center, a counseling service office, career services, wellness services, student activities, a campus ministry office, and resident advisers. **Library/Resources:** The library contains 103,136 volumes, 77,784 microform items, and 2,208 audio/video tapes/CDs/DVDs, and subscribes to 695 periodicals including electronic. Computerized library services include interlibrary loans and database searching. Special learning facilities include an art gallery, radio station, TV station, and rare books collection. **Physically Challenged Students:** 40% of the campus is accessible. Facilities include wheelchair ramps, elevators, special parking, specially equipped restrooms, special class scheduling, lowered drinking fountains, lowered telephones. **Special:** Students may cross-register at any of the Cooperating Colleges of Greater Springfield or Consortium of Sisters of St. Joseph Colleges. Internships are available with local hospitals, businesses, and schools. Study abroad, student-designed interdepartmental majors, accelerated degree programs, work-study, dual majors, nondegree study, and pass/fail options are offered. There are 5 national honor societies, including Phi Beta Kappa, and a freshman honors program. **Visiting:** There are regularly scheduled orientations for prospective students, including tours and interviews scheduled weekdays between 9 a.m. and 4 p.m. as well as 2 open houses in the fall and 1 in the spring. There are guides for informal visits, visitors may sit in on classes, and stay overnight. To schedule a visit, contact the Admission Office. **Campus Safety and Security:** Measures include 24-hour foot and vehicle patrol, self-defense education, and security escort services. There are emergency telephones, lighted pathways/sidewalks, A safety and security manual is published each year, and there is a safety and security committee of administrators, students, faculty, and staff.

REQUIREMENTS: The SAT or ACT is required. Applicants should be graduates of accredited high schools or have earned the GED. Secondary preparation should include 4 units of English, 3 each of math and science, and 2 each of foreign language, history, and social studies. A personal essay is required; an interview is recommended. A GPA of 2.5 is required. AP and CLEP credits are accepted. Important factors in the admissions decision are advanced placement or honors courses, recommendations by school officials, and extracurricular activities record. To graduate, all students must complete 120 hours with a 2.0 GPA. 54 hours are required in courses in rhetoric, computer science, history, religion, phys ed, philosophy, sociology, fine arts, humanities, foreign language, math, senior seminar, and service learning experience. **Procedure:** Freshmen are admitted fall and spring. Entrance exams should be taken no later than November of the senior year. There are early admissions, deferred admissions, and rolling admissions plans. Application deadlines are open. The fall 2014 application fee was $30. Applications are accepted on-line. **Transfer Students:** Applicants must have a minimum 2.0 GPA. 45 of 120 credits required for the Bachelor's degree must be completed at Elms. **International Students:** The school actively recruits these students.

ADMISSIONS: Joseph P. Wagner, Director of Admission. E-Mail: *admissions@elms.edu* Web: *www.elms.edu*

FINANCIAL AID: Elms is a member of CSS. The FAFSA and the college's own financial statement are required. Check with the school for current application deadlines.

EMERSON COLLEGE — E-2
www.emerson.edu

Boston, MA 02116   (617) 824-8600
    n/av

Fax: (617) 824-8609   Email: admission@emerson.edu
Full-time: 1439 men, 2268 women   Faculty: 197; IIA, +$
Part-time: 20 men, 38 women   Ph.D.s: 144%
Graduate: 182 men, 586 women   Student/Faculty: 13 to 1
Year: semesters, summer session   Tuition: $37,350
Room & Board: $15,096   Freshman Class: 8710 applied, 4283 accepted, 857 enrolled
SAT CR/M/W: 632/606/625 ACT: 28   CEEB CODE: 3367
Application Deadline: January 15   HIGHLY COMPETITIVE+

Emerson College, founded in 1880, is the premier college in the United States for the study of communication and the arts. There are 2 undergraduate schools and 2 graduate schools. The 8-acre campus is in an urban area on Boston Common in the Theater District. Including any residence halls, there are 10 buildings.

STUDENT LIFE: 76% of undergraduates are from out of state, mostly the Middle Atlantic. Students are from 47 states, 30 foreign countries, and Canada. 75% are from public schools. 68% are White; 11% Hispanic. **Male To Female Ratio:** 1.8:1. The average age of freshmen is 18; all undergraduates, 20. 12% do not continue beyond their first year; 82% remain to graduate. **Housing:** 2086 students can be accommodated in college housing, which includes coed dorms. Living and learning communities such as a writers' block and digital culture floors. On-campus housing is guaranteed for the freshman year only, is available on a first-come, first-served basis, and is available on a lottery system for upperclassmen. 58% of students live on campus; of those, 75% remain on campus on weekends. No one may keep cars.

FACULTY/CLASSROOMS: 53% of faculty are male; 47% are female. All teach undergraduates. Graduate students teach 4% of introductory courses. The average class size in an introductory lecture is 35; in a laboratory is 18; and in a regular course is 24.

PROGRAMS OF STUDY: Emerson confers B.A., B.S. and B.F.A. degrees. Master's and Doctoral degrees are also awarded. Bachelor's degrees are awarded in BUSINESS (marketing management), COMMUNICATIONS AND THE ARTS (advertising, broadcasting, communications, creative writing, dramatic arts, film arts, journalism, media arts, musical theater, performing arts, public relations, publishing, radio/television technology, speech/debate/rhetoric, theater design, and theater management), HEALTH PROFESSIONS (speech pathology/audiology), SOCIAL SCIENCE (interdisciplinary studies). Visual and media arts, writing, and literature and publishing are the strongest academically. Visual and media arts, performing arts, and communication have the largest enrollments.

ACTIVITIES: 3% of men belong to 2 local and 1 national fraternities; 3% of women belong to 2 local and 1 national sororities. There are 80 groups on campus, including digital media, marketing/PR clubs, radio stations, chorale, computers, dance, debate, drama, environmental, ethnic, film, forensics, gay, honors, international, literary magazine, musical theater, newspaper, photography, political, professional, radio and TV, religious, social, social service, student government, theatre troupes, and yearbook. Popular campus events include Evvy's Award Show, and Emerson Recognition and Achievement Awards. **Sports:** There are 7 intercollegiate sports for men and 8 for women. Facilities include a gymnasium, 10,000-square-foot fitness center, and lighted athletic field. **Graduates:** From July 1, 2013 to June 30, 2014, 922 bachelor's degrees were awarded. The most popular majors were visual and performing arts (22%), communication/journalism (20%), and business/marketing (15%). In an average class, 80% graduate in 6 years or less. Of the 2013 graduating class, 8% were enrolled in graduate school within 6 months of graduation, and 81% were employed.

SERVICES: Counseling and information services are available, as is tutoring in most subjects. There is remedial math, reading, and writing. **Library/Resources:** The library contains 163,314 volumes, 9,414 microform items, 16,574 audio/video tapes/CDs/DVDs, and subscribes to 57,169 periodicals including electronic. Computerized library services include interlibrary loans, database searching, Internet access, and Wi-Fi capability. Special learning facilities include an art gallery, radio station, TV station, sound-treated television studios, film production facilities and digital production labs, speech-language-hearing clinics, several theaters, 2 radio stations, marketing research suite, and digital newsroom. **Physically Challenged Students:** 85% of the campus is accessible. Facilities include wheelchair ramps, elevators, specially equipped restrooms, special class scheduling, and special housing. **Special:** Student-designed, interdisciplinary, and dual majors are available. Cross-registration is offered with the 6-member Boston ProArts consortium. Nearly 800 internships are possible, 600 in Boston and 200 in Los Angeles. Internships bear credit and are graded. Emerson has nondegree study as well as study abroad in the Netherlands, China, and a summer film program in Prague. There is 1 national honor society and a freshman honors program. **Visiting:** There are regularly scheduled orientations for prospective students, including an information session with an admission representative and a tour lead by a current student. There are guides for informal visits and visitors may sit in on classes. **Campus Safety and Security:** Measures include 24-hour foot and vehicle patrol, emergency notification system, self-defense education, and security escort services. There are shuttle buses, emergency telephones, lighted pathways/sidewalks, and controlled access to dorms/residences.

REQUIREMENTS: The SAT or ACT is required. The ACT Optional Writing test is also required. Emerson is a member of the Common Application and requires an Application Supplement. Candidates must have graduated from high school (or have a GED) and present 4 years of English and 3 years each in science, social studies, foreign language, and math. Candidates for performing arts programs are required to submit a theatre-related resume and either audition or interview, or submit a portfolio or an essay. Candidates for film are required to submit either a 5-8 minute video sample and statement, or a 5-10 page script. AP and CLEP credits are accepted. Important factors in the admissions decision are advanced placement or honors courses, evidence of special talent, and recommendations by school officials. All students must complete 128 credit hours, with 40 to 64 in their major and a minimum GPA of 2.0. The general education curriculum consists of 4 foundations courses (oral and written communication and quantitative reasoning), 7 perspectives courses (liberal arts humanities), and 2 global/U.S. diversity courses. **Procedure:** Freshmen are admitted fall and spring. Entrance exams should be taken before December of the senior year. There are early decision and deferred admissions plans. Early decision applications should be filed by November 1; regular applications, by January 15 for fall entry; and November 1 for spring entry, along with a $65 fee. Notification of early decision is sent December 15; regular decision, April 1. 1711 applicants were on the 2014 waiting list; 272 were admitted. Applications are accepted on-line. **Transfer Students:** 221 transfer students enrolled in 2013-2014. Requirements for transfer students are the same as for all students. Note that BFA Performance degrees do not accept transfer applicants. 48 of 128 credits required for the bachelor's degree must be completed at Emerson. **International Students:** There are 204 international students enrolled. The school actively recruits these students. They must take the TOEFL with a minimum score of 550 on the paper-based TOEFL (PBT) or 80 on the Internet-based version (iBT). Students must take the IELTS. They must also take the SAT or ACT.

ADMISSIONS: 49% of the 2014-2015 applicants were accepted. The SAT scores for the 2014-2015 freshman class were: Critical Reading--2% below 500, 27% between 500 and 599, 53% between 600 and 699, and 18% between 700 and 800; Math--5% below 500, 37% between 500 and 599, 49% between 600 and 699, and 9% between 700 and 800; Writing--3% below 500, 28% between 500 and 599, 54% between 600 and 699, and 15% between 700 and 800. The ACT scores were 2% below 21, 7% between 21 and 23, 24% between 24 and 26, 28% between 27 and 28, and 39% above 28. 60% of the current freshmen were in the top fifth of their class; 89% were in the top two fifths. 8 freshmen graduated first in their class. **Admissions Contact:** Christopher Wright, Director of Undergraduate Admission. E-Mail: *admission@emerson.edu* Web: *www.emerson.edu*

FINANCIAL AID: In 2014-2015, 72% of all full-time freshmen and 69% of continuing full-time students received some form of financial aid. 64% of all full-time freshmen and 62% of continuing full-time students received need-based aid. The average freshman award was $29,847. Need-based scholarships or need-based grants averaged $18,996 ($52,726 maximum); need-based self-help aid (loans and jobs) averaged $4,357 ($9,000 maximum); and other non-need-based awards and non-need-based scholarships averaged $16,191 ($52,946 maximum). 61% of undergraduate students work part-time. Average annual earnings from campus work are $2008. The average financial indebtedness of the 2014 graduate was $23,606. The CSS/Profile and FAFSA are required. The priority date for freshman financial aid applications for fall entry is March 1.

EMMANUEL COLLEGE   E-2
www.emmanuel.edu

Boston, MA 02115	(617) 735-9715
Fax: (617) 735-9801	Email: enroll@emmanuel.edu
Full-time: 533 men, 1324 women	Faculty: 97; IIB, av$
Part-time: 47 men, 272 women	Ph.D.s: 82%
Graduate: 50 men, 210 women	Student/Faculty: 14 to 1
Year: semesters, summer session	Tuition: $34,670
Room & Board: $13,315	Freshman Class: 6623 applied, 4006 accepted, 515 enrolled
SAT CR/M/W: 550/540/550 ACT: 23	CEEB CODE: 3368
Application Deadline: February 15	VERY COMPETITIVE

Emmanuel College, founded by the Sisters of Notre Dame de Namur in 1919, is a coed, residential, Catholic liberal arts and sciences college. The College's beautiful campus is neighbored by a world-class medical center, two major art museums and Fenway Park. Its unique location gives students the opportunity to explore real-world experiences through internships, research and strategic partnerships within the Longwood Medical and Academic Area and the city of Boston. There is 1 graduate school. The library contains 185,400 volumes, 1,883 audio/video tapes/CDs/DVDs, and subscribes to 2,100 periodicals including electronic. Computerized library services include interlibrary loans, database searching, Internet access, and Wi-Fi capability. Special learning facilities include an art gallery and radio station. The 17-acre campus is in an urban area in Boston. Including any residence halls, there are 10 buildings.

STUDENT LIFE: 58% of undergraduates are from Massachusetts. Others are from 29 states, 44 foreign countries, and Canada. 71% are White; 11% race unknown. The average age of freshmen is 18; all undergraduates, 20. 19% do not continue beyond their first year; 58% remain to graduate.

FACULTY/CLASSROOMS: 40% of faculty are male; 60% are female. All teach undergraduates. No introductory courses are taught by graduate students. The average class size in an introductory lecture is 22; in a laboratory is 18; and in a regular course is 20.

PROGRAMS OF STUDY: Emmanuel confers B.A., B.F.A. and B.S. degrees. Master's degrees are also awarded. Bachelor's degrees are awarded in AGRICULTURE (environmental studies), BIOLOGICAL SCIENCE (biochemistry, biology/biological science, biomathematics, and neurosciences), BUSINESS (accounting, business administration and management, and sports management), COMMUNICATIONS AND THE ARTS (communications, English, English literature, Spanish, and studio art), COMPUTER AND PHYSICAL SCIENCE (chemistry and mathematics), EDUCATION (elementary education and secondary education), ENGINEERING AND ENVIRONMENTAL DESIGN (graphic arts technology), HEALTH PROFESSIONS (art therapy and nursing), SOCIAL SCIENCE (American studies, counseling/psychology, developmental psychology, forensic studies, history, interdisciplinary studies, international studies, liberal arts/general studies, philosophy, political science/government, psychology, religion, and sociology). English and communication, management, psychology, and the sciences have the largest enrollments.

ACTIVITIES: There are 48 groups on campus, including art, band, cheerleading, chess, choir, chorus, dance, debate, drama, ethnic, gay, honors, international, jazz band, literary magazine, musical theater, newspaper, orchestra, pep band, photography, political, professional, radio and TV, religious, social, social service, student government, and yearbook. Popular campus events include Moonlight Breakfast, Student Leadership Reception, Latin Explosion, Midnight Madness, and Family Weekend.

SERVICES: Counseling and information services are available, as is tutoring in every subject. There is a reader service for the blind, and remedial math and writing.

REQUIREMENTS: The SAT or ACT is required. Applicants must be graduates of an accredited secondary school or have a GED. 16 academic credits are required, including 4 years of English, 3 years of math and social studies, 2 years of the same foreign language, and 2 years of lab science. An essay and an interview are encouraged but not required. AP credits are accepted. Important factors in the admissions decision are advanced placement or honors courses, recommendations by school officials, leadership record, parents or siblings attended your school, evidence of special talent, personality/intangible qualities, extracurricular activities record, recommendations by alumni, geographical diversity, and ability to finance college education.

ADMISSIONS: 60% of a recent year applicants were accepted. The SAT scores for the recent year freshman class were: Critical Reading--20% below 500, 57% between 500 and 599, 21% between 600 and 699, and 2% between 700 and 800; Math--24% below 500, 54% between 500 and 599, 20% between 600 and 699, and 2% between 700 and 800; Writing--19% below 500, 55% between 500 and 599, 24% between 600 and 699, and 2% between 700 and 800. The ACT scores were 10% below 21, 43% between 21 and 23, 26% between 24 and 26, 12% between 27 and 28, and 9% above 28. 43% of the current freshmen were in the top fifth of their class; 75% were in the top two fifths.

FINANCIAL AID: In a recent year 99% of all full-time freshmen and 95% of continuing full-time students received some form of financial aid. 84% of all full-time freshmen and 80% of continuing full-time students received need-based aid. The average freshman award was $26,601. 38% of undergraduate students work part-time. Average annual earnings from campus work are $1800. The FAFSA and the college's own financial statement are required. The priority date for freshman financial aid applications for fall entry is February 15.

ENDICOTT COLLEGE   E-2
www.endicott.edu

Beverly, MA 01915	(978) 921-1000 (800) 325-1114
Fax: (978) 232-2520	Email: admissio@endicott.edu
Full-time: 1023 men, 1590 women	Faculty: 91; IIB, +$
Part-time: 104 men, 238 women	Ph.D.s: 70%
Graduate: 368 men, 917 women	Student/Faculty: 27 to 1
Year: 4-1-4, summer session	Tuition: $29,494
Room & Board: $13,734	Freshman Class: 3842 applied, 2809 accepted, 765 enrolled
SAT CR/M/W: 532/543/530 ACT: 27	CEEB CODE: 3369
Application Deadline: February 15	VERY COMPETITIVE+

Endicott College offers Doctoral, Master's, Bachelor and Associate degree programs in the professional and liberal arts. Founded in 1939, Endicott provides an education built upon a combination of theory and practice, which is tested through internships and work experience. There are 8 undergraduate schools and 1 graduate school. In addition to regional accreditation, Endicott has baccalaureate program accreditation with NASAD, NCATE, NLN, NASAD, CIDA, and AHPCA. The 235-acre campus is in a suburban area 20 miles north of Boston. Including any residence halls, there are 53 buildings.

STUDENT LIFE: 52% of undergraduates are from out of state, mostly the Northeast. Students are from 30 states, and 29 foreign countries. 79% are from public schools. 86% are White. **Male To Female Ratio:** 1.8:1. The average age of freshmen is 18; all undergraduates, 19. 17% do not continue beyond their first year; 73% remain to graduate. **Housing:** 2130 students can be accommodated in college housing, which includes single-sex and coed dorms, on-campus apartments, and off-campus apartments. In addition, there are honors houses, special-interest houses, single-parent, international, academic themed, healthy living and oceanfront housing available. On-campus housing is guaranteed for the freshman year only, is available on a first-come, first-served basis, and is available on a lottery system for upperclassmen. 86% of students live on campus; of those, 85% remain on campus on weekends. Upperclassmen may keep cars.

FACULTY/CLASSROOMS: 44% of faculty are male; 56% are female. No introductory courses are taught by graduate students. The average class size in an introductory lecture is 18 and in a laboratory is 10.

PROGRAMS OF STUDY: Endicott confers B.A., B.S. and B.F.A. degrees. Associate, Master's, and Doctoral degrees are also awarded. Bachelor's degrees are awarded in BIOLOGICAL SCIENCE (biotechnology), BUSINESS (accounting, business administration and management, entrepreneurial studies, finance, hospitality management services, hotel/motel and restaurant management, international business management, marketing management, and sports management), COMMUNICATIONS AND THE ARTS (communications, digital communications, English, fine arts, graphic design, photography, and studio art), COMPUTER AND PHYSICAL SCIENCE (applied mathematics, computer science, and mathematics), EDUCATION (athletic training, education, and physical education), ENGINEERING AND ENVIRONMENTAL DESIGN (bioengineering, environmental science, and interior design), HEALTH PROFESSIONS (art therapy, exercise science, and nursing), SOCIAL SCIENCE (criminal justice, history, international studies, liberal arts/general studies, political science/government, and psychology). Business management, nursing, and sport management have the largest enrollments.

ACTIVITIES: There are no fraternities or sororities. There are 60 groups on campus, including Crew, Outdoor Adventure and Fitness, art, band, cheerleading, chorale, chorus, computers, dance, debate, drama, environmental, ethnic, film, gay, honors, international, jazz band, literary magazine, musical theater, newspaper, pep band, photography, political, professional, radio and TV, religious, Sailing, social, social service, student government, and yearbook. Popular campus events include Family/Homecoming Weekend, Annual Regatta, Festival of Lights, Performing Arts Events and Ice Skating on campus ponds. **Sports:** There are 10 intercollegiate sports for men and 9 for women, and 9 intramural sports for men and 9 for women. Facilities include a 2,200-seat multi-purpose turf stadium with an athletic support building, a new turf baseball/soccer field, 6 outdoor tennis courts, a separate softball stadium, and sailing/kayaking, and cross country courses (5k and 8k). Indoor facilities include a 1400-seat gym with a racquetball, indoor tennis, and basketball courts, weight, fitness, and group fitness rooms, indoor track, rock climbing wall, and a field house. **Graduates:** From July 1, 2013 to June 30, 2014, 633 bachelor's degrees were awarded. The most popular majors were business administration (17%), sport management (12%), and nursing (9%). 98 companies recruited on campus in 2013-2014. In an average class, 71% graduate in 4 years or less, 73% graduate in 5 years or less, and 73% graduate in 6 years or less. Of the 2013 graduating class, 21% were enrolled in graduate school within 6 months of graduation, and 75% were employed.

SERVICES: Counseling and information services are available, as is tutoring in every subject. There is a reader service for the blind. **Library/Resources:** The library contains 120,600 volumes, 6,987 microform items, 1,975 audio/video tapes/CDs/DVDs, and subscribes to 80,316 periodicals including electronic. Computerized library services include interlibrary loans, database searching, Internet access, and Wi-Fi capability. Special learning facilities include an art gallery, radio station, TV station, state-of-the-art nursing and science labs, several fine art studios (interior design, graphic design, photography, painting, ceramics, etc.) recital hall, black box theater, nature trails, private beaches and marshland, a student-run restaurant, and an archives museum. **Physically Challenged Students:** 95% of the campus is accessible. Facilities include wheelchair ramps, elevators, special parking, specially equipped restrooms, special class scheduling, and lowered drinking fountains. **Special:** Three internships are required of most undergraduates. Students may study abroad. There are accelerated degree programs in Business Administration, Hospitality Management, Liberal Studies, Liberal Studies/Education, Nursing and Psychology. Cross-registration available through NECCUM. Five-year bachelor/master's programs available. There are 14 national honor societies, a freshman honors program, and 1 departmental honors program. **Visiting:** There are regularly scheduled orientations for prospective students, includes testing, preregistration, and an introduction to general student life. There are guides for informal visits, visitors may sit in on classes, and stay overnight. To schedule a visit, contact the Office of Admission. **Campus Safety and Security:** Measures include 24-hour foot and vehicle patrol, emergency notification system, self-defense education, and security escort services. There are shuttle buses, emergency telephones, lighted pathways/sidewalks, controlled access to dorms/residences, license plate recognition system, security cameras, property identification, crime prevention workshops, and alcohol safety programs.

REQUIREMENTS: The SAT or ACT is recommended. Essays and two science and math recommendations are required for Nursing (including chemistry) and Athletic Training majors. AP and CLEP credits are accepted. All undergraduates complete a senior thesis and multiple internships. Core requirements for undergraduate students include the areas of writing and academic inquiry. General education requirements include completing at least 3 credits in each of the College's eight thematic categories. **Procedure:** Freshmen are admitted fall and spring. Entrance exams should be taken in fall of the senior year. Applications should be filed by February 15 for fall entry; December 15 for spring entry, along with a $50 fee. 42 applicants were on the 2014 waiting list. Applications are accepted on-line. **Transfer Students:** 99 transfer students enrolled in 2013-2014. Official high school and college transcripts and a letter of recommendation are required. 24 of 124 credits required for the bachelor's degree must be completed at Endicott. **International Students:** There are 43 international students enrolled. The school actively recruits these students. They must take the TOEFL with a minimum score of 550 on the paper-based TOEFL (PBT) or 79 on the Internet-based version (iBT). They must also take the SAT or ACT.

ADMISSIONS: 73% of the 2014-2015 applicants were accepted. The SAT scores for the 2014-2015 freshman class were: Critical Reading--29% below 500, 53% between 500 and 599, 17% between 600 and 699, and 1% between 700 and 800; Math--23% below 500, 53% between 500 and 599, 22% between 600 and 699, and 2% between 700 and 800; Writing--31% below 500, 51% between 500 and 599, 17% between 600 and 699, and 1% between 700 and 800. **Admissions Contact:** Thomas J. Redman, Vice President Admissions. E-Mail: *admissio@endicott.edu* Web: *www.endicott.edu*

FINANCIAL AID: In 2014-2015, 91% of all full-time freshmen and 88% of continuing full-time students received some form of financial aid. 64% of all full-time freshmen and 63% of continuing full-time students received need-based aid. The average freshman award was $21,354.. 36% of undergraduate students work part-time. Average annual earnings from campus work are $1500. The average financial indebtedness of the 2014 graduate was $39,178. Endicott is a member of CSS. The FAFSA and the college's own financial statement are required. The priority date for freshman financial aid applications for fall entry is March 15.

FITCHBURG STATE UNIVERSITY   C-2
www.fitchburgstate.edu

Fitchburg, MA 01420	(978) 665-3140
	(800) 705-9692
Fax: (978) 665-4540	Email: admissions@fitchburgstate.edu
Full-time: 1529 men, 1909 women	Faculty: 194
Part-time: 372 men, 429 women	Ph.D.s: 91%
Graduate: 578 men, 1846 women	Student/Faculty: 15 to 1
Year: semesters	Tuition: $8985 ($15,065)
Room & Board: $8256	Freshman Class: 3819 applied, 2835 accepted, 801 enrolled
SAT CR/M/W: 490/450/480 ACT: 21	CEEB CODE: 3519
Application Deadline: March 1	COMPETITIVE

Fitchburg State University, founded in 1894, is a comprehensive public university offering undergraduate, graduate and continuing education programs. In addition to regional accreditation, Fitchburg State has baccalaureate program accreditation with ABET and NCATE. The library contains 208,450 volumes, 125,344 microform items, 2,774 audio/video tapes/CDs/DVDs, and subscribes to 757 periodicals including electronic. Computerized library services include interlibrary loans, database searching, Internet access, and Wi-Fi capability. Special learning facilities include an art gallery and radio station. The 78-acre campus is in a suburban area 45 miles west of Boston. Including any residence halls, there are 35 buildings.

STUDENT LIFE: 92% of undergraduates are from Massachusetts. Others are from 26 states, and 4 foreign countries. 80% are from public schools. 85% are White. The average age of freshmen is 18; all undergraduates, 22. 27% do not continue beyond their first year; 50% remain to graduate.

FACULTY/CLASSROOMS: 52% of faculty are male; 48% are female. All teach undergraduates. No introductory courses are taught by graduate students. The average class size in an introductory lecture is 27; in a laboratory is 15; and in a regular course is 24.

PROGRAMS OF STUDY: Fitchburg State confers B.A., B.S., B.S.N. and B.S.Ed. degrees. Master's degrees are also awarded. Bachelor's degrees are awarded in BIOLOGICAL SCIENCE (biology/biological science, biotechnology, environmental biology, and neurosciences), BUSINESS (accounting, business administration and management, international business management, international economics, management science, and marketing management), COMMUNICATIONS AND THE ARTS (communications, dramatic arts, English, graphic design, literature, photography, theater management, and video), COMPUTER AND PHYSICAL SCIENCE (applied mathematics, chemistry, computer science, earth science, and mathematics), EDUCATION (early childhood education, education, elementary education, industrial arts education, middle school education, secondary education, special education, technical education, and vocational education), ENGINEERING AND ENVIRONMENTAL DESIGN (architectural technology, construction technology, electrical/electronics engineering technology, energy management technology, industrial engineering technology, and manufacturing technology), HEALTH PROFESSIONS (exercise science, health science, and nursing), SOCIAL SCIENCE (cognitive science, criminal justice, developmental psychology, economics, geography, history, human services, industrial and organizational psychology, interdisciplinary studies, political science/government, prelaw, psychology, and sociology). Business administration, and nursing have the largest enrollments.

ACTIVITIES: 1% of men belong to 2 national fraternities; 3% of women belong to 3 national sororities. There are 60 groups on campus, including band, cheerleading, choir, chorus, computers, dance, drama, environmental, ethnic, film, gay, honors, international, jazz band, literary magazine, newspaper, photography, political, professional, radio and TV, religious, social, social service, and student government. Popular campus events include Falcon Fest, Rock the Block, and Center Stage Performing Arts Series.

SERVICES: Counseling and information services are available, as is tutoring in most subjects. There is a reader service for the blind, and remedial math, reading, and writing.

REQUIREMENTS: The SAT or ACT is required. Applicants should be graduates of accredited high schools or have the GED. Secondary preparation should include 4 years of English, 3 years each of math and liberal arts or phys ed, and 2 years each of a foreign language, social studies, including U.S. history, and science. A GPA of 2.0 is required. AP and CLEP credits are accepted. Important factors in the admissions decision are advanced placement or honors courses, leadership record, and extracurricular activities record.

ADMISSIONS: 74% of the 2013-2014 applicants were accepted. The SAT scores for the 2013-2014 freshman class were: Critical Reading--48% below 500, 40% between 500 and 599, 11% between 600 and 699, and 1% between 700 and 800; Math--40% below 500, 46% between 500 and 599, 14% between 600 and 699, and 1% between 700 and 800; Writing--51% below 500, 39% between 500 and 599, 9% between 600 and 699, and 1% between 700 and 800. The ACT scores were 41% below 21, 37% between 21 and 23, 11% between 24 and 26, 7% between 27 and 28, and 4% above 28.

FINANCIAL AID: The FAFSA is required. The deadline for filing freshman financial aid applications for fall entry is March 1.

FRAMINGHAM STATE UNIVERSITY   D-2
www.framingham.edu

Framingham, MA 01701	(508) 626-4500
Fax: (508) 626-4017	Email: admissions@framingham.edu
Full-time: 1418 men, 2507 women	Faculty: 187
Part-time: 278 men, 406 women	Ph.D.s: 89%
Graduate: 405 men, 1485 women	Student/Faculty: 16 to 1
Year: semesters, summer session	Tuition: $8320 ($14,400)
Room & Board: $10,534	Freshman Class: 5207 applied, 3242 accepted, 808 enrolled
SAT CR/M/W: 506/508/495 ACT: 22	CEEB CODE: 3518
Application Deadline: February 15	COMPETITIVE

Framingham State University, founded in 1839, is a comprehensive public institution offering degree programs based on a liberal arts foundation that includes unique career programs. There is 1 graduate school. In addition to regional accreditation, FSU has baccalaureate program accreditation with ADA and NLN. The 73-acre campus is in a suburban area 20 miles west of Boston. Including any residence halls, there are 22 buildings.

STUDENT LIFE: 95% of undergraduates are from Massachusetts. Others are from states, 21 foreign countries, and Canada. 76% are White. **Male To Female Ratio:** 2.1:1. The average age of freshmen is 18; all undergraduates, 22. 25% do not continue beyond their first year; 51% remain to graduate. **Housing:** 1931 students can be accommodated in college housing, which includes single-sex and coed dorms. On-campus housing is available on a first-come and first-served basis. 52% of students live on campus; of those, 67% remain on campus on weekends. Alcohol is not permitted. Upperclassmen may keep cars.

FACULTY/CLASSROOMS: 42% of faculty are male; 58% are female. All teach undergraduates. No introductory courses are taught by graduate students. The average class size in an introductory lecture is 22; in a laboratory is 16; and in a regular course is 22.

PROGRAMS OF STUDY: FSU confers B.A., B.S. and B.S.Ed. degrees. Master's degrees are also awarded. Bachelor's degrees are awarded in BIOLOGICAL SCIENCE (biology/biological science and nutrition), BUSINESS (accounting, business administration and management, fashion merchandising, finance, and marketing), COMMUNICATIONS AND THE ARTS (American Sign Language, art history and appreciation, communications, English, modern language, and studio art), COMPUTER AND PHYSICAL SCIENCE (chemistry, computer science, and mathematics), EDUCATION (business education, early childhood education, elementary education, and global studies), ENGINEERING AND ENVIRONMENTAL DESIGN (environmental science), HEALTH PROFESSIONS (nursing), SOCIAL SCIENCE (criminology, economics, family/consumer studies, fashion design and technology, food science, geography, history, interdisciplinary studies, political science/government, psychology, sociology, and textiles and clothing). Psychology, business administration, food and nutrition have the largest enrollments.

ACTIVITIES: There are no fraternities or sororities. There are 50 groups on campus, including art, cheerleading, chorale, chorus, computers, dance, drama, ethnic, gay, honors, international, literary magazine, musical theater, newspaper, political, professional, radio and TV, religious, social, social service, and student government. Popular campus events include Sandbox Festival, Super Weekends and Semi-Formal Dance. **Sports:** There are 6 intercollegiate sports for men and 7 for women, and 9 intramural sports for men and 9 for women. Facilities include an athletic and recreation center, gym, and a student center. In addition, there are two all-weather turf fields for soccer, football, field hockey, softball, women's lacrosse and intramural sports available on lower campus fields. **Graduates:** From July 1, 2013 to June 30, 2014, 795 bachelor's degrees were awarded. The most popular majors were business administration (15%), psychology (13%), and communication arts (8%). 150 companies recruited on campus in 2013-2014. Of the 2013 graduating class, 20% were enrolled in graduate school within 6 months of graduation, and 93% were employed.

SERVICES: Counseling and information services are available, as is tutoring in most subjects. There is a reader service for the blind, and remedial math, reading, and writing. The Center for Academic Support and Advising (CASA) offers free tutoring in writing, math, and reading. Subject tutoring may be arranged for an hourly fee. FSU also offers supplemental instruction attached to a variety of courses. **Library/Resources:** The library contains 216,902 volumes, 4,288 audio/video tapes/CDs/DVDs, and subscribes to 163 periodicals including electronic. Computerized library services include interlibrary loans, database searching, Internet access, and Wi-Fi capability. Special learning facilities include an art gallery, planetarium, radio station, Center for Global Education, Center for Social Research, Metrowest Economic Research Center, McAuliffe Center for Education and Teaching Excellence, Challenger Learning Center, NASA Educator Resource Center, Metrowest STEM Education Network, Child Development Laboratory, Education Curriculum Library, Entrepreneur Innovation Center, John C. Stalker Institute for Food and Nutrition, Framingham State/Boston Children's Hospital Food Study, Greenhouse, and a Planetarium. **Physically Challenged Students:** 95% of the campus is accessible. Facilities include wheelchair ramps, elevators, special parking, specially equipped restrooms, special class scheduling, lowered drinking fountains, and lowered telephones. **Special:** The university offers a 2-3 preengineering program in cooperation with the University of Massachusetts at Amherst, Lowell, and Dartmouth. Study abroad in 8 countries, a Washington semester, and various internships are available. Pass/fail options are limited to 2 courses. There are 11 national honor societies, a freshman honors program, and 8 departmental honors programs. **Visiting:** There are regularly scheduled orientations for prospective students, include campus tours, advising, and information sessions (majors, computing, campus life and resources). There are guides for informal visits and visitors may sit in on classes. To schedule a visit, contact the Office of Undergraduate Admissions. **Campus Safety and Security:** Measures include 24-hour foot and vehicle patrol, emergency notification system, self-defense education, and security escort services. There are shuttle buses, emergency telephones, lighted pathways/sidewalks, security cameras, residence hall security and card access.

REQUIREMENTS: The SAT is required. Applicants must have a high school diploma or the GED. Secondary preparation must total 16 college-preparatory credits, including 4 years of English, 3 each of math and science (2 with lab), and 2 each of foreign language and social science. The required 2 years of electives may include additional academic subjects or art, music, or computer courses. Prospective studio art majors must submit a portfolio. AP and CLEP credits are accepted. Important factors in the admissions decision are advanced placement or honors courses, leadership record, and recommendations by school officials. The university's goal-based general education model includes writing, math, language, literature or philosophy, visual or performing arts, physical science, life science, historical studies, social and behavioral sciences, forces in the United States, study of Constitutions, gender, class, and race; and non-Western studies. Every student must take 12 general education courses and

fulfill all required goals. A total of 128 credits (32 courses), including 40 to 68 credits in the major, and a 2.0 GPA are required to graduate. **Procedure:** Freshmen are admitted fall and spring. Entrance exams should be taken in the spring of the junior year or fall of the senior year. There are early admissions, deferred admissions, and rolling admissions plans. Applications should be filed by February 15 for fall entry; December 1 for spring entry, along with a $45 fee. Notification is sent on a rolling basis. Applications are accepted on-line. **Transfer Students:** 414 transfer students enrolled in 2013-2014. Applicants with more than 24 transferable college credits must present a college GPA between 2.00-2.50 for admission consideration; those with fewer than 24 transferable credits must also meet freshman admission requirements. Official transcripts must be submitted from all colleges previously attended at the time of application. 32 of 128 credits required for the bachelor's degree must be completed at FSU. **International Students:** They must take the TOEFL with a minimum score of 550 on the paper-based TOEFL (PBT) or 79 on the Internet-based version (iBT). They must also take the SAT or ACT.

ADMISSIONS: 62% of the 2014-2015 applicants were accepted. The SAT scores for the 2014-2015 freshman class were: Critical Reading--46% below 500, 43% between 500 and 599, 11% between 600 and 699, and 1% between 700 and 800; Math--66% below 500, 48% between 500 and 599, 10% between 600 and 699, and 1% between 700 and 800; Writing--50% below 500, 41% between 500 and 599, and 8% between 600 and 699. The ACT scores were 36% below 21, 34% between 21 and 23, 18% between 24 and 26, and 11% between 27 and 28. **Admissions Contact:** Shayna Eddy, Director of Undergraduate Admissions. E-Mail: *admissions@framingham.edu* Web: *www.framingham.edu*

FINANCIAL AID: In 2014-2015, 88% of all full-time freshmen and 78% of continuing full-time students received some form of financial aid. 71% of all full-time freshmen and 63% of continuing full-time students received need-based aid. The average freshman award was $9,911. Need-based scholarships or need-based grants averaged $3,229 ; need-based self-help aid (loans and jobs) averaged $5,254; and other non-need-based awards and non-need-based scholarships averaged $1,428. 60% of undergraduate students work part-time. Average annual earnings from campus work are $1050. The average financial indebtedness of the 2014 graduate was $19,300. FSU is a member of CSS. The FAFSA is required. The priority date for freshman financial aid applications for fall entry is March 1.

FRANKLIN W. OLIN COLLEGE OF ENGINEERING *(The complete profile is made available exclusively on our website, www. barronspac.com)*

GORDON COLLEGE   E-1
www.gordon.edu/admissions

Wenham, MA 01984	**(978) 867-4218**
	(866) 464-6736
Fax: (978) 867-4682	Email: admissions@gordon.edu
Full-time: 654 men, 1043 women	Faculty: 97; IIB, +$
Part-time: 11 men, 28 women	Ph.D.s: 88%
Graduate: 53 men, 290 women	Student/Faculty: 13 to 1
Year: semesters, summer session	Tuition: $34,390
Room & Board: $9930	Freshman Class: n/av
SAT CR/M/W: 582/575/575 ACT: 26	CEEB CODE: 3417
Application Deadline: August 1	**VERY COMPETITIVE**

Gordon College, is a distinctive blend an evangelical Christian liberal arts institution. It has a strong heritage of community service and a long tradition of international education. The College offers 38 majors and 41 concentrations in the arts and sciences, with graduate programs in education and music education. As a Christian institution whose students, faculty and staff represent over 40 denominations, Gordon retains a commitment to integrating faith and learning, a heritage once embraced by many esteemed New England institutions. This commitment is exemplified by Gordon's Center for Faith and Inquiry. Consistent with its founding vision, Gordon's identity and reach are worldwide. The College also has a long history of humanitarian service both domestically and abroad, which is evident in high student participation in spring, summer and winter break service trips, and in service-learning and internship programs. Along with its affiliations with the Christian College Consortium, the council for Christian Colleges and Universities, and the Council of Independent Colleges, Gordon is actively involved with the Annapolis Group, an alliance of 130 of the nation's leading independent liberal arts colleges including Cornell, Wellesley, Williams, Pomona, Claremont and Scripps. There is 1 undergraduate school and 2 graduate schools. In addition to regional accreditation, Gordon has baccalaureate program accreditation with CSWE, NASDTEC, NASM, DECM, MBHE, and NEASC. The 480-acre campus is in a suburban area 25 miles north of Boston. Including any residence halls, there are 40 buildings.

STUDENT LIFE: 68% of undergraduates are from out of state, mostly the Northeast. Students are from 41 states, 39 foreign countries, and Canada. 61% are from public schools. 74% are White. 95% are Protestant. **Male To Female Ratio:** 1.9:1. The average age of freshmen is 18; all undergraduates, 20. 19% do not continue beyond their first year; 72% remain to graduate. **Housing:** 1428 students can be accommodated in college housing, which includes single-sex and coed dorms, on-campus apartments, and married student housing. In addition, there are special-interest houses, and vocation exploration. On-campus housing is guaranteed for all 4 years. 86% of students live on campus; of those, 70% remain on campus on weekends. Alcohol is not permitted. All students may keep cars.

FACULTY/CLASSROOMS: 50% of faculty are male; 50% are female. All teach and do research. No introductory courses are taught by graduate students. The average class size in an introductory lecture is 39; in a laboratory is 14; and in a regular course is 14.

PROGRAMS OF STUDY: Gordon confers B.A., B.S. and B.Mu. degrees. Master's degrees are also awarded. Bachelor's degrees are awarded in BIOLOGICAL SCIENCE (biology/biological science), BUSINESS (accounting, banking and finance, business administration and management, finance, and recreation and leisure services), COMMUNICATIONS AND THE ARTS (art, communications, dramatic arts, English, French, German, languages, linguistics, music, music performance, and Spanish), COMPUTER AND PHYSICAL SCIENCE (chemistry, computer science, mathematics, and physics), EDUCATION (early childhood education, elementary education, middle school education, music education, secondary education, and special education), HEALTH PROFESSIONS (physical therapy), SOCIAL SCIENCE (biblical studies, economics, history, international studies, philosophy, political science/government, psychology, social work, sociology, and youth ministry). Biology, physics, Christian Ministries, education, economics, and music are the strongest academically. Psychology, business administration, and biology have the largest enrollments.

ACTIVITIES: There are no fraternities or sororities. There are 115 groups on campus, including art, band, cheerleading, choir, chorale, chorus, dance, debate, drama, environmental, ethnic, extensive options for student outreaches and off-campus ministries, film, honors, international, jazz band, literary magazine, musical theater, newspaper, opera, orchestra, photography, political, professional, radio and TV, religious, social, social service, student government, and symphony. Popular campus events include Golden Goose, Gordon Globes, Senior Formal, Gordon Has Talent, and Christmas at Gordon. **Sports:** There are 9 intercollegiate sports for men and 11 for women, and 15 intramural sports for men and 15 for women. Facilities include a gym, weight rooms, tennis courts, athletic fields, training room, indoor swimming pool, climbing wall, racquetball courts, aerobics room, ski/running trails, outdoor ropes course, sauna, indoor walking track, outdoor track and field facilities. **Graduates:** From July 1, 2013 to June 30, 2014, 386 bachelor's degrees were awarded. The most popular majors were business administration (13%), social sciences (10%), and education (9%). 120 companies recruited on campus in 2013-2014. In an average class, 61% graduate in 4 years or less and 71% graduate in 6 years or less. Of the 2013 graduating class, 16% were enrolled in graduate school within 6 months of graduation, and 68% were employed.

SERVICES: Counseling and information services are available, as is tutoring in most subjects including math, writing, and core science. There is a reader service for the blind, and writing and academic support centers. **Library/Resources:** The library contains 151,750 volumes, 154 microform items, 5,503 audio/video tapes/CDs/DVDs, and subscribes to 1,521 periodicals including electronic. Computerized library services include interlibrary loans, database searching, Internet access, and Wi-Fi capability. Special learning facilities include an art gallery and radio station. **Physically Challenged Students:** 80% of the campus is accessible. Facilities include wheelchair ramps, elevators, special parking, specially equipped restrooms, special class scheduling, lowered drinking fountains, lowered telephones, and special housing. **Special:** Gordon offers cooperative education, internships, and cross-registration with other institutions in the Northeast Consortium of Colleges and Universities in Massachusetts. There is a 3-2 engineering program with the University of Southern California. B.A.- B.S. degrees, dual majors, student-designed majors, nondegree study, and pass/fail options are available. Off-campus study opportunities include a Washington semester, the Christian College Consortium Visitor Program, the LaVida Wilderness Expedition, and study abroad in Europe, the Middle East and China. There are 8 national honor societies, a freshman honors program, and 13 departmental honors programs. **Visiting:** There are regularly scheduled orientations for prospective students, consisting of numerous open house programs throughout the fall, winter, and spring. There are guides for informal visits, visitors may sit in on classes, and stay overnight. To schedule a visit, contact Leah LaPalombara at (866) 464-6736. **Campus Safety and Security:** Measures include 24-hour foot and vehicle patrol, emergency notification system, self-defense education, and security escort services. There are shuttle buses, emergency telephones, lighted pathways/sidewalks, controlled access to dorms/residences, and a gated entrance.

REQUIREMENTS: The SAT or ACT is required. The ACT Optional Writing test is also required. Applicants must graduate from an accredited secondary school or have a GED. A minimum of 17 Carnegie units is required, including 4 English courses and 2 courses each in math, science, and social studies. Foreign language is a recommended elective. A personal statement, a personal reference, and an interview are required. Music majors must audition. Art majors must submit a portfolio for acceptance to the program. AP credits are accepted. Important factors in the admissions decision are advanced placement or honors courses, evidence of special talent, personality/intangible qualities, extracurricular activities record, leadership record, recommendations by alumni, and geographical diversity. All students must demonstrate competency in writing, and foreign language. The core curriculum consists of 36 credits, 8 credits in biblical studies, 4 in social science, 4 in natural sciences, math and computer science, 8 in humanities, 8 in language studies, and 4 in freshman seminar. 3 Physical and outdoor education courses and 20 credits in thematic courses. A total of 124 credits is required for graduation, with 20 or more in a major and a minimum GPA of 2.0. **Procedure:** Freshmen are admitted fall and spring. Entrance exams should be taken spring of the junior year and the fall of the senior year. There are early decision, early admissions, deferred admissions, and rolling admissions plans. Early decision applications should be filed by November 1; regular applications, by August 1 for fall entry; and November 1 for spring entry, along with a $50 fee. Notification of early decision is sent December 1; regular decision, January 1. 20 early decision candidates were accepted for the 2014-2015 class. 50 applicants were on the 2014 waiting list; 49 were admitted. Applications are accepted on-line. **Transfer Students:** 60 transfer students enrolled in 2013-2014. Applicants must have a minimum GPA of 2.00. College transcripts, high school transcripts, and SAT or ACT scores if the applicant has completed less than 1 year of full-time study, an interview, and personal and academic references are required. 32 of 124 credits required for the bachelor's degree must be completed at Gordon. **International Students:** There are 117 international students enrolled. The school actively recruits these students. They must take the TOEFL with a minimum score of 85 on the Internet-based version (iBT). They must also take the SAT or ACT.

ADMISSIONS: The SAT scores for the 2014-2015 freshman class were: Critical Reading--17% below 500, 38% between 500 and 599, 36% between 600 and 699, and 9% between 700 and 800; Math--18% below 500, 40% between 500 and 599, 32% between 600 and 699, and 9% between 700 and 800; Writing--18% below 500, 42% between 500 and 599, 33% between 600 and 699, and 8% between 700 and 800.

The ACT scores were 11% below 21, 20% between 21 and 23, 22% between 24 and 26, 20% between 27 and 28, and 27% above 28. 59% of the current freshmen were in the top fifth of their class; 86% were in the top two fifths. 15 freshmen graduated first in their class.

Admissions Contact: June Bodoni, Executive Director of Admissions. E-Mail: *admissions@gordon.edu* Web: *www.gordon.edu/admissions*

FINANCIAL AID: In 2014-2015, 100% of all full-time freshmen and 97% of continuing full-time students received some form of financial aid. 68% of all full-time freshmen and 74% of continuing full-time students received need-based aid. The average freshman award was $23,567. Need-based scholarships or need-based grants averaged $19,684; need-based self-help aid (loans and jobs) averaged $4,834; and other non-need-based awards and non-need-based scholarships averaged $13,349. 61% of undergraduate students work part-time. Average annual earnings from campus work are $887. The average financial indebtedness of the 2014 graduate was $37,410. Gordon is a member of CSS. The FAFSA is required. The priority date for freshman financial aid applications for fall entry is March 1. The deadline for filing freshman financial aid applications for fall entry is March 1.

HAMPSHIRE COLLEGE   **B-2**
www.hampshire.edu

Amherst, MA 01002	(413) 559-5471
Fax: (413) 559-5631	Email: admissions@hampshire.edu
Full-time: 645 men, 846 women	Faculty: 121; IIB, +$
Part-time: n/av	Ph.D.s: 93%
Graduate: n/av	Student/Faculty: 12 to 1
Year: 4-1-4	Tuition: $46,290
Room & Board: $12,030	Freshman Class: n/av
	CEEB CODE: 3447
Application Deadline: n/av	MOST COMPETITIVE

Hampshire College, founded in 1965, is a private institution offering a liberal arts education with an emphasis on independent research, creative work, and multidisciplinary study. Figures in the above capsule and in this profile are approximate. The 800-acre campus is in a rural area in Amherst, Massachusetts. Including any residence halls, there are 28 buildings.

STUDENT LIFE: 80% of undergraduates are from out of state, mostly the Northeast. Students are from 46 states, and Canada. 65% are from public schools. 66% are White. **Male To Female Ratio:** 1.3:1. The average age of freshmen is 18; all undergraduates, 20. 19% do not continue beyond their first year; 66% remain to graduate. **Housing:** 1400 students can be accommodated in college housing, which includes single-sex and coed dorms and on-campus apartments. In addition, there are special-interest houses. We have 3 living and learning communities plus various themed housing options. On-campus housing is guaranteed for all 4 years. All students may keep cars.

FACULTY/CLASSROOMS: 46% of faculty are male; 54% are female. All teach undergraduates. No introductory courses are taught by graduate students. The average class size in a regular course is 14.

PROGRAMS OF STUDY: Hampshire confers B.A. degrees. Bachelor's degrees are awarded in AGRICULTURE (agriculture and animal science), BIOLOGICAL SCIENCE (biology/biological science, botany, ecology, marine biology, nutrition, and physiology), COMMUNICATIONS AND THE ARTS (art history and appreciation, communications, comparative literature, creative writing, dance, dramatic arts, film arts, fine arts, journalism, linguistics, literature, media arts, music, performing arts, photography, and video), COMPUTER AND PHYSICAL SCIENCE (chemistry, computer science, geology, mathematics, physics, and science), EDUCATION (education), ENGINEERING AND ENVIRONMENTAL DESIGN (architecture, environmental design, and environmental science), HEALTH PROFESSIONS (health science and premedicine), SOCIAL SCIENCE (African studies, African American studies, American studies, anthropology, Asian/Oriental studies, cognitive science, crosscultural studies, economics, family/consumer studies, geography, history, humanities, international relations, international studies, Judaic studies, Latin American studies, law, Middle Eastern studies, peace studies, philosophy, political science/government, psychology, religion, sociology, urban studies, and women's studies). Film, photography, and video are the strongest academically. Social sciences has the largest enrollment.

ACTIVITIES: There are no fraternities or sororities. There are 80 groups on campus, including art, chorus, computers, dance, drama, environmental, ethnic, film, gay, international, literary magazine, musical theater, newspaper, orchestra, photography, political, radio and TV, religious, social, social service, and student government. Popular campus events include Hampshire Halloween, and Spring Jam,. **Sports:** There are 3 intercollegiate sports for men and 3 for women, and 18 intramural sports for men and 18 for women. Facilities include 2 multipurpose sports centers housing a glass-enclosed swimming pool, a 12,000-square-foot playing floor, a 30-foot climbing wall, a weight-lifting area, 4 indoor tennis courts, and a jogging track. Other facilities include soccer fields, 10 outdoor tennis courts, 2 softball diamonds, and a 2-mile nature trail.

SERVICES: Counseling and information services are available, as is tutoring in most subjects. There is a reader service for the blind. Advising center, a writing and reading program, and a lab quantitative skills program. **Library/Resources:** The library contains 124,710 volumes, 4,534 microform items, 8,727 audio/video tapes/CDs/DVDs, and subscribes to 731 periodicals including electronic. Computerized library services include interlibrary loans, database searching, Internet access, and Wi-Fi capability. Special learning facilities include an art gallery, radio station, multimedia center, farm center, music and dance studios, optics lab, electronics shop, integrated greenhouse and aquaculture facility, fabrication shop, and performing arts center. **Physically Challenged Students:** 90% of the campus is accessible. Facilities include wheelchair ramps, elevators, special parking, specially equipped restrooms, special class scheduling, lowered drinking fountains, lowered telephones. The college provides a variety of support services to meet individual special needs. **Special:** Cross-registration is possible with other members of the Five College Consortium (Amherst College, the University of Massachusetts, Smith College, and Mount Holyoke). Internships, multidisciplinary dual majors, and study abroad (in the ISEP program, Tibetan Center, or a Costa Rica semester) are offered. All majors are student-designed. Students may complete their programs in fewer than 4 years. **Visiting:** There are regularly scheduled orientations for prospective students, including interviews, information sessions, campus tours, Discover Hampshire Days, Campus Visitation Days, and an overnight program. There are guides for informal visits, visitors may sit in on classes, and stay overnight. To schedule a visit, contact the Admissions Office at admissions@hampshire.edu. **Campus Safety and Security:** Measures include 24-hour foot and vehicle patrol and security escort services. There are lighted pathways/sidewalks, EMT on-call program, and dorm doors accessible by students only.

REQUIREMENTS: Applicants must submit all transcripts from 9th grade on or GED/state equivalency exam results. Students are required to submit a personal statement and an analytic essay or academic paper. An interview is recommended. AP credits are accepted. Important factors in the admissions decision are personality/intangible qualities, evidence of special talent, and extracurricular activities record.All students must complete 3 divisions of study. In Division I: Basic Studies, students complete courses in cognitive science, humanities, arts and cultural studies, natural science, interdisciplinary arts, and social science and must complete 2 courses or the Division I exam project. In Division II: Concentration, students explore their field or fields of emphasis through individually designed internships or field studies. In Division III: Advanced Studies, students complete a major independent study project centered on a specific topic, question, or idea. Students must also partcipate in service to the college or the surrounding community and consider some aspect of their work from a non-Western perspective. **Procedure:** Freshmen are admitted fall and spring. There are early decision, early admissions, and deferred admissions plans. Check with the school for current application deadlines. The fall 2014 application fee was $55. Applications are accepted on-line. **Transfer Students:** 62 transfer students enrolled in 2013-2014. A proposed program of study, high school and college transcripts, and 1 recommendation must be submitted. **International Students:** The school actively recruits these students. They must take the TOEFL.

ADMISSIONS: The SAT scores for the 2014-2015 freshman class were: Critical Reading--5% below 500, 20% between 500 and 599, 47% between 600 and 699, and 27% between 700 and 800; Math--14% below 500, 35% between 500 and 599, 41% between 600 and 699, and 10% between 700 and 800; Writing--8% below 500, 27% between 500 and 599, 46% between 600 and 699, and 19% between 700 and 800. **Admissions Contact:** Barbara L. Maryak, Acting Dean of Admissions. E-Mail: *admissions@hampshire.edu* Web: *www.hampshire.edu*

FINANCIAL AID: In 2014-2015, 61% of all full-time freshmen and continuing full-time students received some form of financial aid. 61% of all full-time freshmen and continuing full-time students received need-based aid. The average freshman award was $35,100. Need-based scholarships or need-based grants averaged $30,700; need-based self-help aid (loans and jobs) averaged $4,700; and other non-need-based awards and non-need-based scholarships averaged $12,400. The average financial indebtedness of the 2014 graduate was $20,085. Hampshire is a member of CSS. The CSS/Profile, FAFSA, and the college's own financial statement, and noncustodial parent statement are required. Check with the school for current application deadlines.

HARVARD COLLEGE/HARVARD UNIVERSITY   D-2
www.college.harvard.edu

Cambridge, MA 02138   (617) 495-1551

Fax: (617) 495-8821	Email: college@harvard.edu
Full-time: 3510 men, 3140 women	Faculty: I, ++$
Part-time: 10 men, 10 women	Ph.D.s: n/av
Graduate: 5565 men, 5350 women	Student/Faculty: n/av
Year: semesters, summer session	Tuition: $38,500
Room & Board: $14,870	Freshman Class: n/av
SAT or ACT: required	CEEB CODE: 3434
Application Deadline: n/av	**MOST COMPETITIVE**

Harvard College is the undergraduate college of Harvard University. Harvard College was founded in 1636. Harvard University also has 10 graduate schools. The figures in the above capsule and in this profile are approximate. In addition to regional accreditation, Harvard has baccalaureate program accreditation with ABET. The 380-acre campus is in an urban area across the Charles River from Boston. Including any residence halls, there are 400 buildings.

STUDENT LIFE: 81% of undergraduates are from out of state, mostly the Middle Atlantic. Students are from 50 states, 118 foreign countries, and Canada. 67% are from public schools. 43% are White; 17% Asian American. **Male To Female Ratio:** 0.9:1. The average age of freshmen is 18; all undergraduates, 20. 96% remain to graduate.

Housing: 6325 students can be accommodated in college housing, which includes coed dorms and on-campus apartments. On-campus housing is guaranteed for all 4 years. 97% of students live on campus. All students may keep cars.

FACULTY/CLASSROOMS: 98% teach undergraduates, 97% do research, and 95% do both. No introductory courses are taught by graduate students. The average class size in a regular course is 25.

PROGRAMS OF STUDY: Harvard confers A.B., and S.B. degrees. Master's and Doctoral degrees are also awarded. Bachelor's degrees are awarded in BIOLOGICAL SCIENCE (biochemistry, biology/biological science, and biophysics), COMMUNICATIONS AND THE ARTS (art history and appreciation, Chinese, classics, creative writing, English, fine arts, folklore and mythology, French, German, Greek, Hebrew, Italian, Japanese, Latin, linguistics, literature, music, Portuguese, Russian, and Spanish), COMPUTER AND PHYSICAL SCIENCE (applied mathematics, astronomy, chemistry, computer science, geology, geophysics and seismology, mathematics, physical sciences, physics, and statistics), ENGINEERING AND ENVIRONMENTAL DESIGN (engineering, environmental design, environ-

mental science, and preengineering), SOCIAL SCIENCE (African American studies, American studies, anthropology, Asian/Oriental studies, economics, European studies, history, humanities, Middle Eastern studies, philosophy, political science/government, psychology, religion, Russian and Slavic studies, Sanskrit and Indian studies, social science, social studies, sociology, and women's studies). Economics, government, and biology have the largest enrollments.

ACTIVITIES: There are no fraternities or sororities. There are 250 groups on campus, including art, band, cheerleading, chess, choir, chorale, chorus, computers, dance, debate, drama, ethnic, film, gay, honors, international, jazz band, literary magazine, marching band, musical theater, newspaper, opera, orchestra, pep band, photography, political, professional, radio and TV, religious, social, social service, student government, symphony, and yearbook. Popular campus events include Harvard/Yale football, Head of the Charles Crew Regatta, and Cultural Rhythms Festival. **Sports:** There are 21 intercollegiate sports for men and 20 for women, and 16 intramural sports for men and 16 for women. Facilities include several gyms and athletic centers, pools, a track, boat houses, a sailing center, a hockey rink, and various courts and playing fields.

SERVICES: Counseling and information services are available, as is tutoring in every subject. There is a reader service for the blind. **Library/Resources:** The 97 libraries contain 15.0 million volumes, and subscribe to 100,000 periodicals including electronic. Computerized library services include interlibrary loans and database searching. Special learning facilities include an art gallery, natural history museum, planetarium, and radio station. **Physically Challenged Students:** Facilities include wheelchair ramps, elevators, special parking, specially equipped restrooms, special class scheduling, lowered drinking fountains, lowered telephones. **Special:** Students may cross-register with MIT and with other schools within the university and may design their own concentrations or enroll for nondegree study. Internships and study abroad may be arranged. Accelerated degree programs, dual majors, a 3-2 engineering degree, and a combined A.B.-S.B. in engineering are offered. There are pass/fail options. There is a Phi Beta Kappa chapter. **Visiting:** There are regularly scheduled orientations for prospective students, consisting of group information sessions and tours. There are guides for informal visits, visitors may sit in on classes, and stay overnight. To schedule a visit, contact the Undergraduate Admissions Office. **Campus Safety and Security:** Measures include 24-hour foot and vehicle patrol, self-defense education, and security escort services. There are shuttle buses, emergency telephones, and lighted pathways/sidewalks.

REQUIREMENTS: The SAT or ACT is required, as well as 3 SAT Subject tests. Applicants need not be high school graduates but are expected to be well prepared academically. An essay and an interview are required, in addition to a transcript, a counselor report, and 2 teacher recommendations from academic disciplines. AP credits are accepted. Important factors in the admissions decision are evidence of special talent, personality/intangible qualities, and recommendations by school officials. In 8 semesters, students must pass a minimum of 32 1-semester courses. The average course load is 4 courses per semester, but the course rate may be varied for special reasons. A typical balanced program devotes about one-fourth of its courses to core curriculum requirements, one-half to the concentration (or major field), and the remaining one-fourth to electives. **Procedure:** Freshmen are admitted fall. Entrance exams should be taken by January of the senior year. There is a deferred admissions plan. Check with the school for current application deadlines. The fall 2014 application fee was $65. Applications are accepted on-line. **Transfer Students:** Transfer applicants must have completed at least 1 full year of daytime study in a degree-granting program at 1 institution. Students are required to submit the SAT or ACT, 2 letters of recommendation, high school and college transcripts with a dean's report, and several essays. 16 of 32 credits required for the bachelor's degree must be completed at Harvard. **International Students:** The school actively recruits these students. They must also take the SAT or ACT.

ADMISSIONS: Marlyn McGrath, Director of Admissions. E-Mail: *college@harvard.edu* Web: *www.college.harvard.edu*

FINANCIAL AID: Harvard is a member of CSS. The CSS/Profile, FAFSA, the college's own financial statement, and federal tax forms are required. Check with the school for current application deadlines.

HELLENIC COLLEGE/HOLY CROSS GREEK D-2
ORTHODOX SCHOOL OF THEOLOGY
www.hchc.edu

Brookline, MA 02445	**(617) 850-1285**
	866-424-2338
Fax: (617) 850-1460	**Email:** gfloor@hchc.edu
Full-time: 61 men, 38 women	**Faculty:** 13
Part-time: n/av	**Ph.D.s:** 90%
Graduate: 125 men, 16 women	**Student/Faculty:** 9 to 1
Year: semesters	**Tuition:** $2545
Room & Board: $13,240	**Freshman Class:** 64 applied, 52 accepted, 38 enrolled
SAT CR/M/W: 550/450/460 **ACT:** 22	**CEEB CODE:** 3449
Application Deadline: May 1	**COMPETITIVE**

Hellenic College, founded in 1968, is a private college affiliated with the Greek Orthodox Church. It offers programs in the classics, elementary education, religious studies, human development, management and leadership, and literature and history. Figures in the above capsule and in this profile are approximate. There is 1 undergraduate school and 1 graduate school. In addition to regional accreditation, HCHC has baccalaureate program accreditation with NASDTEC. The 59-acre campus is in an urban area 4 miles southwest of Boston. Including any residence halls, there are 7 buildings.

STUDENT LIFE: 90% of undergraduates are from out of state, mostly the Mid-West. Students are from 25 states, 9 foreign countries, and Canada. 90% are from public schools. 95% are White; 13% Foreign. 95% are Eastern Orthodox.. **Male To Female Ratio:** 0.3:1. The average age of freshmen is 20; all undergraduates, 22. 5% do not continue beyond their first year; 95% remain to graduate. **Housing:** 220 students can be accommodated in college housing, which includes coed dorms, on-campus apartments, and married student housing. On-campus housing is available on a first-come and first-served basis. 90% of students live on campus; of those, 90% remain on campus on weekends. Alcohol is not permitted. All students may keep cars.

FACULTY/CLASSROOMS: 70% of faculty are male; 30% are female. No introductory courses are taught by graduate students. The average class size in an introductory lecture is 20; in a laboratory is 20; and in a regular course is 15.

PROGRAMS OF STUDY: HCHC confers B.A. degrees. Master's degrees are also awarded. Bachelor's degrees are awarded in BUSINESS (business administration and management), COMMUNICATIONS AND THE ARTS (classics and literature), EDUCATION (elementary education), SOCIAL SCIENCE (history, human development, and religion). Religious studies and elementary education is the strongest academically. Religious studies and human development have the largest enrollments.

ACTIVITIES: There are no fraternities or sororities. Groups on campus include choir, ethnic, religious, social, social service, and student government. Popular campus events include Feast of the Holy Cross, Matriculation Day, and Campus Christmas Party. **Sports:** There are 4 intramural sports for men and 3 for women. Facilities include a gym, tennis, basketball, and racquetball courts, and a soccer field. **Graduates:** From July 1, 2013 to June 30, 2014, 12 bachelor's degrees were awarded. The most popular majors were religious studies (50%), management and leadership (25%), and human development (25%). In an average class, 97% graduate in 4 years or less. Of the 2013 graduating class, 60% were enrolled in graduate school within 6 months of graduation, and 30% were employed.

SERVICES: Counseling and information services are available, as is tutoring in some subjects. Greek and music writing and composition are avaliable. There is remedial math, reading, and writing. **Library/Resources:** The library contains 63,374 volumes, 883 microform items, 3,015 audio/video tapes/CDs/DVDs, and subscribes to 720 periodicals including electronic. Computerized library services include interlibrary loans, database searching, and Internet access. **Physically Challenged Students:** 10% of the campus is accessible. Facilities include wheelchair ramps, elevators, special parking, specially equipped restrooms, and lowered drinking fountains. **Special:**

The college offers cross-registration with Boston Theological Institute, Newbury College, and Boston College, credit by examination, and study abroad in Greece. There are a freshman honors program. **Visiting:** There are regularly scheduled orientations for prospective students, including observation of classroom and student life. There are guides for informal visits, visitors may sit in on classes, and stay overnight. To schedule a visit, contact the Office of Admissions at admissions@hchc.edu. **Campus Safety and Security:** There are shuttle buses, lighted pathways/sidewalks, a 16-hour security patrol.

REQUIREMENTS: The SAT or ACT is required. Applicants should graduate from an accredited secondary school or have a GED. 15 academic credits are required, including 4 units of English, 2 each of math, foreign language, and social studies, and 1 of science. An essay is required. AP and CLEP credits are accepted. Important factors in the admissions decision are recommendations by school officials, advanced placement or honors courses, and recommendations by alumni. To graduate, students must complete 129 credits, with 39 in the major, and maintain a minimum overall GPA of 2.0. General education requirements include 72 credits, with courses in English language and literature, music, history, science, philosophy, and social science. **Procedure:** Freshmen are admitted fall and spring. There are deferred admissions and rolling admissions plans. Early decision applications should be filed by December 1; regular applications, by May 1 for fall entry; and December 1 for spring entry. The fall 2014 application fee was $50. Notification of early decision is sent February 1; regular decision, June 15. **Transfer Students:** 11 transfer students enrolled in 2013-2014. An essay, college transcripts, recommendation letters, an interview, and a health certificate are required. SAT or ACT scores and high school transcripts are waived if the student has 24 or more college credit hours. 60 of 129 credits required for the bachelor's degree must be completed at HCHC. **International Students:** There are 5 international students enrolled. They must take the TOEFL with a minimum score of 500 on the paper-based TOEFL (PBT) or 61 on the Internet-based version (iBT).

ADMISSIONS: 81% of the 2014-2015 applicants were accepted. The SAT scores for the 2014-2015 freshman class were: Critical Reading--30% below 500, 35% between 500 and 599, 30% between 600 and 699, and 5% between 700 and 800; Math--55% below 500, 35% between 500 and 599, 5% between 600 and 699, and 5% between 700 and 800; Writing--45% below 500, 35% between 500 and 599, and 20% between 600 and 699. The ACT scores were 20% below 21, 60% between 21 and 23, and 20% between 24 and 26. **Admissions Contact:** Gregory Floor, Director for Admissions. E-Mail: *gfloor@hchc.edu* Web: *www.hchc.edu*

FINANCIAL AID: In 2014-2015, 95% of all full-time freshmen and continuing full-time students received some form of financial aid. 95% of all full-time freshmen and continuing full-time students received need-based aid. 36% of undergraduate students work part-time. Average annual earnings from campus work are $1600. The average financial indebtedness of the 2014 graduate was $31,000. The FAFSA and the college's own financial statement are required. Check with the school for current application deadlines.

LASELL COLLEGE (*The complete profile is made available exclusively on our website, www.barronspac.com*)

LESLEY UNIVERSITY D-2
www.hchc.edu

Cambridge, MA 02138	**(617) 349-8800**
	(800) 999-1959
Fax: (617) 349-8810	**Email:** lcadmission@lesley.edu
Full-time: 323 men, 1075 women	**Faculty:** IIA, av$
Part-time: 45 men, 155 women	**Ph.D.s:** 85%
Graduate: 481 men, 2766 women	**Student/Faculty:** 20 to 1
Year: semesters, summer session	**Tuition:** $32,250
Room & Board: $14,100	**Freshman Class:** n/av
SAT or ACT: required	**CEEB CODE:** 3483
Application Deadline: n/av	**COMPETITIVE**

Lesley University, founded in 1909, is a private undergraduate institution, offering degree programs in education, human services, and the arts. Expanded resources, course work, and opportunities are available to students through the larger coeducational Lesley University system, including cross-registration with the Lesley University College of Art and Design. Figures in the above capsule and in this profile are approximate. There are 2 undergraduate schools and 2 graduate schools. In addition to regional accreditation, Lesley has baccalaureate program accreditation with NASAD, TEAC, AACTE, and CACREP. The 5-acre campus is in an urban area outside of Harvard Square in Cambridge, MA. Including any residence halls, there are 53 buildings.

STUDENT LIFE: 58% of undergraduates are from Massachusetts. Others are from 33 states, 24 foreign countries, and Canada. 84% are from public schools. 71% are White; 12% race unknown. **Male To Female Ratio:** 4.7:1. The average age of freshmen is 18; all undergraduates, 20. 27% do not continue beyond their first year; 73% remain to graduate. **Housing:** 803 students can be accommodated in college housing, which includes single-sex and coed dorms. In addition, there are special-interest houses, Social interest and themed housing. On-campus housing is available on a first-come and first-served basis. All students may keep cars.

FACULTY/CLASSROOMS: 44% of faculty are male; 56% are female. All teach and do research. No introductory courses are taught by graduate students. The average class size in an introductory lecture is 20; in a laboratory is 14; and in a regular course is 14.

PROGRAMS OF STUDY: Lesley confers B.S., and B.F.A. degrees. Associate, Master's, and Doctoral degrees are also awarded. Bachelor's degrees are awarded in BUSINESS (management science), COMMUNICATIONS AND THE ARTS (creative writing and visual and performing arts), COMPUTER AND PHYSICAL SCIENCE (natural sciences), EDUCATION (early childhood education, elementary education, middle school education, and special education), SOCIAL SCIENCE (human services, humanities, psychology, and social science). Education, counseling, photography and art therapy have the largest enrollments.

ACTIVITIES: There are no fraternities or sororities. There are 25 groups on campus, including Third Wave (a women's group), student athlete advisory committee, choir, chorus, dance, drama, ethnic, gay, international, literary magazine, musical theater, photography, political, professional, religious, Second Start, social, social service, and student government. Popular campus events include Family and Friends Weekend, Quad Fest, and World Fest. **Sports:** There are 7 intercollegiate sports for men and 7 for women, and 3 intramural sports for men and 5 for women. Facilities include outdoor tennis courts, and a fitness center with nautilus circuit, free weights, and cardiovascular equipment. Students may also use an Olympic-size swimming pool at a nearby school as well as the indoor and outdoor facilities at a nearby school, including two full size basketball courts, two racquetball courts, a rowing tank, a softball court, an indoor track and a lighted outdoor soccer field. **Graduates:** From July 1, 2013 to June 30, 2014, 426 bachelor's degrees were awarded. The most popular majors were liberal studies (18%), visual and performing arts (7%), and psychology (7%). 100 companies recruited on campus in 2013-2014. In an average class, 33% graduate in 4 years or less, 10% graduate in 5 years or less, and 3% graduate in 6 years or less.

SERVICES: Counseling and information services are available, as is tutoring in most subjects. There is a reader service for the blind, and remedial math. Study skills and interpreter services are available. **Library/Resources:** The 2 libraries contain 124,022 volumes, 878,938 microform items, 42,680 audio/video tapes/CDs/DVDs, and subscribe to 861 periodicals including electronic. Computerized library services include interlibrary loans, database searching, Internet access, and Wi-Fi capability. Special learning facilities include an art gallery, center for teaching resources, media production facility, and instructional computing and math achievement center. **Physically Challenged Students:** 85% of the campus is accessible. Facilities include wheelchair ramps, elevators, special parking, specially equipped restrooms, special class scheduling, lowered drinking fountains. The Disability Services Office provides document review and arranges for reasonable accommodations for special needs students. **Special:** Study abroad in Cuba, England, and Sweden, and 6 others by arrangement, a Washington Justice semester, and on-campus

work-study programs are offered. All students participate in at least 3 field placement experiences, beginning in their freshman year. There are combined accelerated degree programs in management, counseling, and education majors. Dual majors and student-designed majors are also available. Accelerated and weekend course programs as well as cross-registration with AIB are offered for Adult Baccalaureate College and School of Education. There is a freshman honors program and 2 departmental honors programs. **Visiting:** There are regularly scheduled orientations for prospective students, includes personal interviews with professional staff, student campus tours, information sessions, class visits, and meetings with financial aid. There are guides for informal visits, visitors may sit in on classes, and stay overnight. To schedule a visit, contact Lesley College Admissions. **Campus Safety and Security:** Measures include 24-hour foot and vehicle patrol, self-defense education, and security escort services. There are shuttle buses, emergency telephones, lighted pathways/sidewalks, including watch tours.

REQUIREMENTS: The SAT or ACT is required. It is recommended that students complete 20 academic units in high school, including 4 in English, 3 in science, 3 in math, and 2 in U.S. history. SAT or ACT scores, a writing sample, and 2 recommendations are also required as part of the application; a personal interview is recommended. Applicants must have a high school diploma from an accredited secondary school or a GED. AP and CLEP credits are accepted. Important factors in the admissions decision are evidence of special talent, personality/intangible qualities, and advanced placement or honors courses. Students must complete 45 hours of general education requirements, including 15 of humanities, 12 of natural science, 9 of social science, 6 of multicultural perspectives, and 3 of first-year seminar; emphasis is given to cross-curriculum components in writing, critical and quantitative reasoning, global perspectives, and leadership and ethics. Art Institute of Boston Students must also complete a Foundation year. To graduate, students need 128 total credit hours, including 30 to 33 in the liberal arts majors or 41 to 43 in professional majors. **Procedure:** Freshmen are admitted fall and spring. Entrance exams should be taken by February 15. There are deferred admissions and rolling admissions plans. Early decision applications should be filed by December 1; regular applications, by November 15 for spring entry, along with a $50 fee. Notification of early decision is sent January 1; regular decision, on a rolling basis. 2 applicants were on the 2014 waiting list. Applications are accepted on-line. **Transfer Students:** 108 transfer students enrolled in 2013-2014. Applicants must have a minimum 2.5 GPA. They must provide high school and college transcripts, complete an essay or personal statement, and have a statement of good standing from prior institution. An interview is recommended for all Lesley College students and required of all Art Institute of Boston Students. 45 of 124 credits required for the bachelor's degree must be completed at Lesley. **International Students:** There are 32 international students enrolled. The school actively recruits these students. They must take the TOEFL with a minimum score of 500 on the paper-based TOEFL (PBT).

ADMISSIONS: The SAT scores for the 2014-2015 freshman class were: Critical Reading--23% below 500, 48% between 500 and 599, 24% between 600 and 699, and 5% between 700 and 800; Math--40% below 500, 40% between 500 and 599, 19% between 600 and 699, and 1% between 700 and 800; Writing--28% below 500, 50% between 500 and 599, 21% between 600 and 699, and 1% between 700 and 800. The ACT scores were 3% below 21, 59% between 21 and 23, 16% between 24 and 26, 20% between 27 and 28, and 2% above 28. 40% of the current freshmen were in the top fifth of their class; 75% were in the top two fifths. **Admissions Contact:** Deb Kocar, Director of Admissions. E-Mail: *lcadmission@lesley.edu* Web: *www.hchc.edu*

FINANCIAL AID: In 2014-2015, 75% of all full-time freshmen and 70% of continuing full-time students received some form of financial aid. 79% of all full-time freshmen and 71% of continuing full-time students received need-based aid. The average freshman award was $15,652. Need-based scholarships or need-based grants averaged $14,331; need-based self-help aid (loans and jobs) averaged $5,938; and other non-need-based awards and non-need-based scholarships averaged $12,667. 25% of undergraduate students work part-time. Average annual earnings from campus work are $1400. The average financial indebtedness of the 2014 graduate was $18,000. The FAFSA and the college's own financial statement, and parent and student federal tax returns are required. The priority date for freshman financial aid applications for fall entry is March 1. The deadline for filing freshman financial aid applications for fall entry is February 15.

MASSACHUSETTS BOARD OF HIGHER EDUCATION

The Massachusetts Board of Higher Education, established in 1980, is a public system in Massachusetts. It is governed by a 13-member Board of Regents appointed by the governor, whose chief administrator is the chancellor. The primary goal of the system is to govern the state's public higher education system. The total student enrollment is usually about 260,000. Profiles of the 4-year campuses are included in this section.

MASSACHUSETTS COLLEGE OF LIBERAL ARTS   A-1
www.mcla.edu

North Adams, MA 01247	(413) 662-5410
Fax: (413) 662-5179	Email: admissions@mcla.edu
Full-time: 518 men, 852 women	Faculty: 87
Part-time: 58 men, 126 women	Ph.D.s: 80%
Graduate: 74 men, 129 women	Student/Faculty: 13 to 1
Year: semesters, summer session	Tuition: $8975 ($17,920)
Room & Board: $9638	Freshman Class: n/av
	CEEB CODE: 3521
Application Deadline: open	COMPETITIVE

Massachusetts College of Liberal Arts (MCLA) delivers a high-quality, affordable education that provides students with the critical thinking and communication skills of greatest value to their development, their community and their future employers. As the public liberal arts college of the Commonwealth, MCLA is committed to preparing students for success at work and in life. MCLA provides unmatched, hands-on growth opportunities early, and often, in an inspiring, creative community. In addition to regional accreditation, MCLA has baccalaureate program accreditation with CAATE. The 80-acre campus is in a rural area 45 miles east of Albany, NY. Including any residence halls, there are 20 buildings. **STUDENT LIFE:** 75% of undergraduates are from Massachusetts. Others are from 21 states and 1 foreign country. 75% are White. **Male To Female Ratio:** 1.7:1. The average age of freshmen is 18; all undergraduates, 22. 22% do not continue beyond their first year; 52% remain to graduate. **Housing:** 1020 students can be accommodated in college housing, which includes single-sex and coed dorms and on-campus apartments. In addition, there are special-interest houses. On-campus housing is guaranteed for all 4 years. 61% of students live on campus. All students may keep cars. **FACULTY/CLASSROOMS:** 51% of faculty are male; 49% are female. No introductory courses are taught by graduate students. **PROGRAMS OF STUDY:** MCLA confers B.A., and B.S. degrees. Master's degrees are also awarded. Bachelor's degrees are awarded in AGRICULTURE (environmental studies), BIOLOGICAL SCIENCE (biology/biological science), BUSINESS (accounting and business administration and management), COMMUNICATIONS AND THE ARTS (art, arts administration/management, communications, English, English literature, English Writing, fine arts, performing arts, and visual and performing arts), COMPUTER AND PHYSICAL SCIENCE (chemistry, computer science, mathematics, and physics), EDUCATION (athletic training, education, childhood education, education, mathematics education, middle school education, and secondary education), HEALTH PROFESSIONS (allied health, cyto-technology, and pre-health studies), SOCIAL SCIENCE (history, interdisciplinary studies, liberal arts/general studies, philosophy, philosophy and religion, political science/government, psychology, public administration, and sociology). **ACTIVITIES:** There are 50 groups on campus, including band, cheerleading, choir, chorale, chorus, computers, dance, drama, environmental, ethnic, gay, honors, international, jazz band, literary magazine, musical theater, newspaper, photography, political,

professional, radio and TV, religious, social, social service, student government, and yearbook. **Sports:** There are 6 intercollegiate sports for men and 7 for women. Facilities include a campus center with a swimming pool, weight rooms, a fitness center, and handball, squash, and racquetball courts. The campus also features an outdoor complex with tennis courts and soccer, baseball, and softball fields, a 1,750-seat gym, and a 5-mile cross-country running trail. **Graduates:** From July 1, 2013 to June 30, 2014, 374 bachelor's degrees were awarded. The most popular majors were business (18%), English (15%), and psychology (13%). In an average class, 34% graduate in 4 years or less, 47% graduate in 5 years or less, and 52% graduate in 6 years or less.

SERVICES: Counseling and information services are available, as is tutoring in some subjects. There is remedial math, reading, and writing. **Library/Resources:** The library contains 170,000 volumes, 290,000 microform items, 6,300 audio/video tapes/CDs/DVDs, and subscribes to 70 periodicals including electronic. Computerized library services include interlibrary loans, database searching, and Internet access. Special learning facilities include an art gallery, radio station, and TV station. **Physically Challenged Students:** 95% of the campus is accessible. Facilities include wheelchair ramps, elevators, special parking, specially equipped restrooms, and special class scheduling. **Special:** There are 8 national honor societies, a freshman honors program, and 7 departmental honors programs. **Visiting:** There are regularly scheduled orientations for prospective students. There are guides for informal visits and visitors may sit in on classes. To schedule a visit, contact the Admissions Office. **Campus Safety and Security:** Measures include 24-hour foot and vehicle patrol, emergency notification system, self-defense education, and security escort services. There are emergency telephones and lighted pathways/sidewalks.

REQUIREMENTS: The SAT or ACT is required. MCLA's admission criteria can be described as moderately selective with a strong emphasis placed on a student's academic performance in high school. Successful candidates for admission should meet MCLA's sliding scale which correlates high school grade point average with SAT or ACT scores. Secondly, applicants should demonstrate completion of 16 Carnegie units, including 4 courses in English, 3 each in science and math, and 2 each in foreign language, history/social science, and electives. The GED is also accepted. AP and CLEP credits are accepted. All students must complete at least 120 credits, including 40 in the core curriculum, and maintain a GPA of at least 2.0. **Procedure:** Freshmen are admitted fall and spring. Entrance exams should be taken by January of the senior year. There are early decision, early admissions, deferred admissions, and rolling admissions plans. Application deadlines are open. The fall 2014 application fee was $40. Notification is sent on a rolling basis. Applications are accepted on-line. **Transfer Students:** 164 transfer students enrolled in 2013-2014. MCLA's transfer policy is highly dependent on a student's performance at their previous college(s). A minimum grade point average is expected to be a 2.5 to be considered for admission. Students applying without an earned Associate's degree must submit official high school transcript and standardized test scores. 45 of 120 credits required for the bachelor's degree must be completed at MCLA. **International Students:** There are 10 international students enrolled. The school actively recruits these students. They must take the TOEFL with a minimum score of 550 on the paper-based TOEFL (PBT). They must also take the SAT.

ADMISSIONS: Gina Puc, Director of Admissions. E-Mail: *admissions@mcla.edu* Web: *www.mcla.edu*

FINANCIAL AID: In 2014-2015, 79% of all full-time freshmen and 80% of continuing full-time students received some form of financial aid. 78% of all full-time freshmen and 78% of continuing full-time students received need-based aid. The average freshman award was $13,990. Need-based scholarships or need-based grants averaged $6,704; and need-based self-help aid (loans and jobs) averaged $3,736. MCLA is a member of CSS. The FAFSA is required. The priority date for freshman financial aid applications for fall entry is March 1.

MASSACHUSETTS COLLEGE OF PHARMACY AND HEALTH SCIENCES *(The complete profile is made available exclusively on our website, www.barronspac.com)*

MASSACHUSETTS INSTITUTE OF TECHNOLOGY
D-2

web.mit.edu

Cambridge, MA 02139	(617) 253-3400
	n/av
Fax: (617) 258-8304	Email: admissions@mit.edu
Full-time: 2449 men, 2031 women	Faculty: 1011; I, ++$
Part-time: 16 men, 7 women	Ph.D.s: 98%
Graduate: 4602 men, 2084 women	Student/Faculty: 4 to 1
Year: 4-1-4, summer session	Tuition: $45,016
Room & Board: $13,224	Freshman Class: 18109 applied, 1620 accepted, 1135 enrolled
SAT CR/M/W: 730/780/740 ACT: 34	CEEB CODE: 3514
Application Deadline: January 1	MOST COMPETITIVE

Massachusetts Institute of Technology, founded in 1861, is a private, independent, institution offering programs in architecture and planning, engineering, humanities, arts, and social sciences, management, science, and health sciences, and technology. Figures in the above capsule and in this profile are approximate. There are 5 undergraduate schools and 5 graduate schools. In addition to regional accreditation, MIT has baccalaureate program accreditation with AACSB, ABET, CSAB, and ACS. The 168-acre campus is in an urban area 1 mile north of Boston. Including any residence halls, there are 151 buildings.

STUDENT LIFE: 91% of undergraduates are from out of state, mostly the Middle Atlantic. Students are from 50 states, 92 foreign countries, and Canada. 37% are White; 24% Asian American; 15% Hispanic. **Male To Female Ratio:** 0.6:1. The average age of freshmen is 19; all undergraduates, 20. 3% do not continue beyond their first year; 97% remain to graduate. **Housing:** 3570 students can be accommodated in college housing, which includes single-sex and coed dorms, on-campus apartments, and married student housing. In addition, there are language houses, special-interest houses, fraternity houses, sorority houses, Off-campus independent living groups, and non-Greek cooperative houses. On-campus housing is guaranteed for all 4 years. 75% of students live on campus. Some may keep cars.

FACULTY/CLASSROOMS: 79% of faculty are male; 21% are female. All teach and do research. No introductory courses are taught by graduate students.

PROGRAMS OF STUDY: MIT confers B.S. degrees. Master's and Doctoral degrees are also awarded. Bachelor's degrees are awarded in BIOLOGICAL SCIENCE (biology/biological science and neurosciences), BUSINESS (management science), COMMUNICATIONS AND THE ARTS (creative writing, digital communications, linguistics, literature, media arts, and music), COMPUTER AND PHYSICAL SCIENCE (chemistry, computer science, earth science, mathematics, physics, and science technology), ENGINEERING AND ENVIRONMENTAL DESIGN (aeronautical engineering, aerospace studies, architecture, bioengineering, biomedical engineering, chemical engineering, civil engineering, electrical/electronics engineering, engineering, environmental engineering, materials engineering, materials science, mechanical engineering, nuclear engineering, and ocean engineering), SOCIAL SCIENCE (anthropology, archeology, cognitive science, economics, history, humanities, interdisciplinary studies, philosophy, political science/government, and urban studies). Engineering, science, management and social science programs are the strongest academically. Engineering has the largest enrollment.

ACTIVITIES: 42% of men belong to 2 local and 25 national fraternities; 31% of women belong to 6 national sororities. Groups on campus include art, band, cheerleading, chess, choir, chorale, chorus, computers, dance, debate, drama, environmental, ethnic, film, gay, honors, international, jazz band, literary magazine, marching band, musical theater, newspaper, orchestra, over 400 recognized organizations on campus, photography, political, professional, radio and TV, religious, social, social service, student government, symphony, and yearbook. Popular campus events include Independent Activities Period and Spring Weekend. **Sports:** There are 16 intercollegiate sports for men and 15 for women, and 20 intramural sports for men

and 20 for women. Facilities include an athletic complex with 10 buildings and 26 acres of playing fields. **Graduates:** From July 1, 2013 to June 30, 2014, 1011 bachelor's degrees were awarded. The most popular majors were computer science and engineering (9%), engineering (mechanical engineering 2-A) (7%), and electrical engineering/computer science (7%). 307 companies recruited on campus in 2013-2014. In an average class, 84% graduate in 4 years or less, 91% graduate in 5 years or less, and 93% graduate in 6 years or less. Of the 2013 graduating class, 39% were enrolled in graduate school within 6 months of graduation, and 52% were employed.

SERVICES: Counseling and information services are available, as is tutoring in most subjects. There is a reader service for the blind. Accommodations for students with documented disabilities are determined on an individual basis. **Library/Resources:** The 5 libraries contain 3.6 million volumes, 2.4 million microform items, and 47,457 audio/video tapes/CDs/DVDs. Computerized library services include interlibrary loans, database searching, Internet access, and Wi-Fi capability. Special learning facilities include an art gallery, radio station, TV station, numerous labs and centers. **Physically Challenged Students:** Facilities include wheelchair ramps, elevators, special parking, specially equipped restrooms, special class scheduling, lowered drinking fountains, lowered telephones. Wheelchair lifts, and automatic doors. An assistive technology lab and assistance with library services are available, upon determination of need. **Special:** MIT offers cross-registration with Harvard, Wellesley, the Massachusetts College of Art and Design, and the School of the Museum of Fine Arts. Internships are offered in a number of programs. Short and long-term study abroad options are offered. The Undergraduate Research Opportunities Program (UROP) cultivates and supports research partnerships between MIT undergraduates and faculty. There are 10 national honor societies and including Phi Beta Kappa. **Visiting:** There are regularly scheduled orientations for prospective students, including daily tours (Monday through Friday) preceded by an information session with admissions staff. Visitors may sit in on classes and stay overnight. To schedule a visit, contact the Office of Admissions. **Campus Safety and Security:** Measures include 24-hour foot and vehicle patrol, emergency notification system, self-defense education, and security escort services. There are shuttle buses, emergency telephones, lighted pathways/sidewalks, and automated external defibrillators (AEDs) are stationed across campus.

REQUIREMENTS: The SAT or ACT is required. The ACT Optional Writing test is also required. 2 SAT Subject Tests, including 1 each of math and science, are required. 14 academic units are recommended, including 4 each of English, math, and science, 2 of social studies, and a foreign language. The GED is accepted. Essays, 2 teacher evaluations, an official transcript, and a guidance counselor report are required. An interview is strongly recommended. AP credits are accepted. To graduate, students must fulfill the General Institute Requirements, as well as communication and physical education requirements, and fulfill departmental program requirements. The General Institute Requirements consist of 6 courses in science, 1 in lab science, 2 in restricted science and technology electives, and 8 in humanities, arts, and social sciences for a total of 17 courses. **Procedure:** Freshmen are admitted fall. Entrance exams should be taken by the January test date. There are early admissions and deferred admissions plans. Applications should be filed by January 1 for fall entry, along with a $75 fee. Notifications are sent March 20. 849 applicants were on the 2014 waiting list. Applications are accepted on-line. **Transfer Students:** 23 transfer students enrolled in 2013-2014. In order to apply, applicant must have minimum of 2 semesters of college, but not more than 5 semesters, at the time they would enroll. Transfer credit is assessed by each academic department on a course by course basis. Enrolling transfer students are required to complete at least 3 semesters at MIT to earn a bachelors degree. For entry in the Spring semester, only U.S. Citizens and Permanent Residents may apply. Applicants who are not US Citizens or Permanent Residents must apply for entry in the Fall semester. **International Students:** There are 468 international students enrolled. The school actively recruits these students. They must also take the SAT or ACT. Non-English speakers may substitute the TOEFL for the SAT or ACT.

ADMISSIONS: 9% of the 2014-2015 applicants were accepted. The SAT scores for the 2014-2015 freshman class were: Critical Reading--4% between 500 and 599, 32% between 600 and 699, and 65%

between 700 and 800; Math--10% between 600 and 699, and 90% between 700 and 800; Writing--3% between 500 and 599, 28% between 600 and 699, and 69% between 700 and 800. The ACT scores were 2% between 27 and 28, and 98% above 28. 100% of the current freshmen were in the top fifth of their class; 100% were in the top two fifths. 203 freshmen graduated first in their class. **Admissions Contact:** Stuart Schmill, Dean of Admissions. E-Mail: *admissions@ mit.edu* Web: *web.mit.edu*

FINANCIAL AID: In 2014-2015, 86% of all full-time freshmen and 74% of continuing full-time students received some form of financial aid. 62% of all full-time freshmen and 62% of continuing full-time students received need-based aid. The average freshman award was $32,749. Need-based scholarships or need-based grants averaged $36,162 ($61,889 maximum); and need-based self-help aid (loans and jobs) averaged $4,438 ($6,000 maximum). 63% of undergraduate students work part-time. Average annual earnings from campus work are $2971. The average financial indebtedness of the 2014 graduate was $20,794. MIT is a member of CSS. The CSS/Profile and FAFSA, and parent W-2s, 1040s, and the business tax form are required. The deadline for filing freshman financial aid applications for fall entry is February 15.

MASSACHUSETTS MARITIME ACADEMY E-4
www.maritime.edu

Buzzards Bay, MA 02532
(508) 830-5000
(800) 544-3411

Fax: (508) 830-5077 **Email: admissions@maritime.edu**

Full-time: 820 men, 105 women **Faculty:** n/av

Part-time: 40 men, 10 women **Ph.D.s:** n/av

Graduate: 40 men, 5 women **Student/Faculty:** n/av

Year: semesters **Tuition:** $6340 ($20,000)

Room & Board: $9000 **Freshman Class:** n/av

SAT or ACT: required **CEEB CODE:** 3515

Application Deadline: n/av **COMPETITIVE**

Massachusetts Maritime Academy, founded in 1891, is the oldest continuously operating maritime academy in the country. Cooperative educational learning and leadership training opportunities prepare graduates for professional positions within private industry or, if opted, military commissions. Figures in the above capsule and in this profile are approximate. The 55-acre campus is in a small town 60 miles south of Boston. Including any residence halls, there are 9 buildings.

STUDENT LIFE: 70% of undergraduates are from Massachusetts. Others are from 26 states, and 11 foreign countries. 73% are from public schools. 90% are White. **Male To Female Ratio:** 0.1:1. The average age of freshmen is 18; all undergraduates, 21. 15% do not continue beyond their first year; 70% remain to graduate. **Housing:** 800 students can be accommodated in college housing, which includes coed dorms. On-campus housing is guaranteed for all 4 years. 97% of students live on campus; of those, 35% remain on campus on weekends. Alcohol is not permitted. All students may keep cars.

FACULTY/CLASSROOMS: 96% of faculty are male; 4% are female. All teach undergraduates, and 3% do research. No introductory courses are taught by graduate students. The average class size in an introductory lecture is 25; in a laboratory is 12; and in a regular course is 22.

PROGRAMS OF STUDY: MMA confers B.S. degrees. Master's degrees are also awarded. Bachelor's degrees are awarded in BUSINESS (international business management and transportation management), ENGINEERING AND ENVIRONMENTAL DESIGN (environmental engineering, industrial engineering, and marine engineering). Marine engineering is the strongest academically and has the largest enrollment.

ACTIVITIES: There are no fraternities or sororities. There are 15 groups on campus, including band, choir, chorus, computers, drill team, jazz band, marching band, newspaper, photography, professional, religious, scuba, social service, student government, and yearbook. Popular campus events include Ring Dance, Emory Rice Day,

and Recognition. **Sports:** There are 8 intercollegiate sports for men and 6 for women, and 13 intramural sports for men and 5 for women. Facilities include football and baseball fields, a pistol range, outdoor tennis and basketball courts, a sailing center, an Olympic-size swimming pool, 2 weight rooms, 3 multipurpose handball courts, and wrestling courts and fitness rooms. An indoor gym/auditorium seats 2500.

SERVICES: Counseling and information services are available, as is tutoring in most subjects. **Library/Resources:** The library contains 40,171 volumes, 11,674 microform items, 1,113 audio/video tapes/ CDs/DVDs, and subscribes to 505 periodicals including electronic. Computerized library services include interlibrary loans, database searching, Internet access, and Wi-Fi capability. Special learning facilities include a planetarium, full bridge-training simulator, oil-spill management simulator, liquid cargo-handling simulator, and computer-aided design lab. **Physically Challenged Students:** 90% of the campus is accessible. Facilities include wheelchair ramps, elevators, special parking, and specially equipped restrooms. **Special:** MMA offers a junior-year internship in a commercial shipping program. Educational experience includes a minimum of 120 days aboard a training ship, with visits to foreign ports. There are cooperative programs in facilities and environmental engineering and in marine safety and environmental protection. A dual major is available in marine engineering and marine transportation. A concentration is available in emergency management. **Visiting:** There are regularly scheduled orientations for prospective students, including a campus tour and an admissions interview. An optional overnight visit can be arranged. There are open house programs. There are guides for informal visits, visitors may sit in on classes, and stay overnight. To schedule a visit, contact the Admission Office. **Campus Safety and Security:** Measures include 24-hour foot and vehicle patrol. There are lighted pathways/sidewalks.

REQUIREMENTS: The SAT or ACT is required. Applicants must have graduated from an accredited secondary school or hold a GED certificate. They should have completed 16 Carnegie units, including 4 in English, 3 in math, and 2 each in a foreign language, science, and social science. An essay is required, and an interview is strongly recommended. AP and CLEP credits are accepted. Important factors in the admissions decision are advanced placement or honors courses, leadership record, and extracurricular activities record. All students must complete 164 credit hours with a minimum of 60 hours in the major and a GPA of 2.0. Requirements include 4 courses in phys ed, 2 each in chemistry and naval science, and 1 each in algebra/ trigonometry, introduction to computers, English composition, American literature, Western civilization, economics, analysis, American government, first aid, admiralty law, introduction to marine transportation, introduction to marine engineering, and calculus. All students must complete at least 1 sea term. **Procedure:** Freshmen are admitted fall. There are early decision, deferred admissions, and rolling admissions plans. Application deadlines are open. The fall 2014 application fee was $50. Applications are accepted on-line. **Transfer Students:** Students must have a minimum GPA of 2.0. 30 of 164 credits required for the bachelor's degree must be completed at MMA. **International Students:** They must take the TOEFL. They must also take the SAT or ACT.

ADMISSIONS: Francis McDonald, Dean of Enrollment Services. E-Mail: *admissions@maritime.edu* Web: *www.maritime.edu*

FINANCIAL AID: MMA is a member of CSS. The CSS/Profile, FAFSA, and the college's own financial statement are required. Check with the school for current application deadlines.

MERRIMACK COLLEGE D-1
www.merrimack.edu

North Andover, MA 01845
(978) 837-5100
n/av

Fax: (978) 837-5133 **Email: admissions@merrimack.edu**

Full-time: 1135 men, 1035 women **Faculty:** IIB, +$

Part-time: 76 men, 73 women **Ph.D.s:** 84%

Graduate: 18 men, 116 women **Student/Faculty:** n/av

Year: semesters, summer session **Tuition:** $32,865

Room & Board: $11,350 **Freshman Class:** 3869 applied, 3400 accepted, 610 enrolled
CEEB CODE: 3525

Application Deadline: February 15 **COMPETITIVE**

Merrimack College, founded in 1947 by the order of St. Augustine, is a private, selective college. The College offers over 40 undergraduate majors. Merrimack also offers graduate programs in education and part-time degree completion and certificate programs. Figures in the above capsule and in this profile are approximate. There are 4 undergraduate schools and 1 graduate school. In addition to regional accreditation, Merrimack has baccalaureate program accreditation with ABET, CAATE, and ACS. The 220-acre campus is in a suburban area 25 miles north of Boston. Including any residence halls, there are 34 buildings.

STUDENT LIFE: 74% of undergraduates are from Massachusetts. Others are from 20 states, 22 foreign countries, and Canada. 73% are White. **Male To Female Ratio:** 1.0:1. The average age of freshmen is 18; all undergraduates, 20. 13% do not continue beyond their first year; 69% remain to graduate. **Housing:** 1634 students can be accommodated in college housing, which includes single-sex and coed dorms and on-campus apartments. In addition, there are special-interest houses, international houses, a wellness house, and theme housing, including Austin Scholars housing. On-campus housing is guaranteed for all 4 years. 81% of students live on campus; of those, 81% remain on campus on weekends. Upperclassmen may keep cars.

FACULTY/CLASSROOMS: 53% of faculty are male; 47% are female. No introductory courses are taught by graduate students. The average class size in an introductory lecture is 25; in a laboratory is 15; and in a regular course is 15.

PROGRAMS OF STUDY: Merrimack confers B.A., and B.S. degrees. Associate and Master's degrees are also awarded. Bachelor's degrees are awarded in BIOLOGICAL SCIENCE (biochemistry and biology/biological science), BUSINESS (accounting, business administration and management, business economics, international business management, and marketing/retailing/merchandising), COMMUNICATIONS AND THE ARTS (communications, English, and modern language), COMPUTER AND PHYSICAL SCIENCE (chemistry, computer science, mathematics, and physics), EDUCATION (elementary education and secondary education), ENGINEERING AND ENVIRONMENTAL DESIGN (civil engineering, electrical/electronics engineering, and environmental science), HEALTH PROFESSIONS (allied health, predentistry, premedicine, and sports medicine), SOCIAL SCIENCE (economics, history, philosophy, political science/government, prelaw, psychology, religion, and sociology). Science, engineering, and business are the strongest academically. Biology, business administration, and sports medicine have the largest enrollments.

ACTIVITIES: 3% of men belong to 2 national fraternities; 9% of women belong to 3 national sororities. There are 57 groups on campus, including art, cheerleading, choir, chorale, chorus, communications, computers, dance, drama, environmental, ethnic, film, gay, honors, international, jazz band, literary magazine, musical theater, newspaper, pep band, photography, political, professional, radio and TV, religious, social, social service, student government, and yearbook. Popular campus events include Spring Weekend, Mr. Merrimack, Cram Jam, Merrimack Survivor, and Relay for Life. **Sports:** There are 10 intercollegiate sports for men and 12 for women, and 6 intramural sports for men and 5 for women. Facilities include an athletic complex, including an ice rink, a basketball court, an aerobics studio, and a well-equipped exercise room, and outdoor facilities including 2 sets of tennis courts, baseball, football, softball, soccer, lacrosse, and field hockey fields, and a turf field. **Graduates:** From July 1, 2013 to June 30, 2014, 402 bachelor's degrees were awarded. The most popular majors were business administration (11%), finance (8%), and marketing (8%). 100 companies recruited on campus in 2013-2014. In an average class, 51% graduate in 4 years or less, 62% graduate in 5 years or less, and 69% graduate in 6 years or less.

SERVICES: Counseling and information services are available, as is tutoring in every subject. There is a reader service for the blind. Math and writing resource centers are available to all students. **Library/Resources:** The library contains 176,908 volumes, and 2,672 audio/video tapes/CDs/DVDs, and subscribes to 4,800 periodicals including electronic. Computerized library services include interlibrary loans, database searching, Internet access, and Wi-Fi capability. Special learning facilities include an art gallery, planetarium, radio station, TV station, astronomy dome and telescope; Rogers Center for the

Arts; Diversity Education Center; Center for Augustinian Study & Legacy; Center for Biotechnology and Biomedical Sciences; Center for the Study of Jewish-Christian-Muslim Relations; RFID (Radio Frequency Identification) technology lab. **Physically Challenged Students:** 95% of the campus is accessible. Facilities include wheelchair ramps, elevators, special parking, specially equipped restrooms, special class scheduling, lowered drinking fountains, lowered telephones, and special housing. **Special:** Merrimack offers cooperative programs in business, engineering, liberal arts, and computer science, cross-registration through the Northeast Consortium, internships in all arts and science programs, study abroad in 9 countries, and a Washington semester at American University. Work-study programs, a 5-year combined B.A.-B.S. degree in many major fields, and dual and self-designed majors are available. General studies, nondegree study, and pass/fail options are possible. There are 7 national honor societies and 3 departmental honors programs. **Visiting:** There are regularly scheduled orientations for prospective students, including campus open houses (total of 4) and several Saturday information sessions for prospective freshman candidates during the fall months. Transfer students have 2 fall semester open house/information session and 2 during the winter/spring month. Visitors may sit in on classes. To schedule a visit, contact the Office of Admissions. **Campus Safety and Security:** Measures include 24-hour foot and vehicle patrol, emergency notification system, self-defense education, and security escort services. There are shuttle buses, emergency telephones, lighted pathways/sidewalks, controlled access to dorms/residences, and rape aggressive defense is available through police services.

REQUIREMENTS: For business administration, humanities, and social science majors, Merrimack recommends that applicants complete 4 units of English, 3 math and 2 science, 3 of social studies, and 2 foreign language. For other majors, an additional math course and 1 additional course in science are needed. An essay is required, and an interview is recommended. Applicants should have completed 19 Carnegie units. AP and CLEP credits are accepted. **Procedure:** Freshmen are admitted fall and spring. Entrance exams should be taken during the spring of the junior year and the fall of the senior year. There are early decision, early admissions, and deferred admissions plans. Early decision applications should be filed by November 15; regular applications, by February 15 for fall entry. Notification of early decision is sent January 1; regular decision, March 15. Applications are accepted on-line. **Transfer Students:** 72 transfer students enrolled in 2013-2014. Applicants must have maintained a minimum 2.5 GPA; some programs require a higher GPA. Transfer students must complete the transfer application and essay and must submit official college/university transcript (from each college/university attended), course descriptions of all courses completed from each college/university (needed for evaluation and determination of transfer credit), and a letter of recommendation. Student must not be under disciplinary censure and must be eligible to return to previous institution. A high school transcript is required if the student has less than 30 semester hours of college-level credit completed at the time of application. 48 of 124 credits required for the bachelor's degree must be completed at Merrimack. **International Students:** There are 55 international students enrolled. The school actively recruits these students. They must take the TOEFL with a minimum score of 550 on the paper-based TOEFL (PBT) or 75 on the Internet-based version (iBT).

ADMISSIONS: 88% of the 2014-2015 applicants were accepted. 16% of the current freshmen were in the top fifth of their class; 44% were in the top two fifths. 1 freshman graduated first in the class. **Admissions Contact:** Mark Barrett, Dean, Undergraduate Admissions. E-Mail: *admissions@merrimack.edu* Web: *www.merrimack.edu*

FINANCIAL AID: Merrimack is a member of CSS. The FAFSA, Noncustodial profile, Business/Farm Supplement, Sibling verification are required. The deadline for filing freshman financial aid applications for fall entry is February 1.

MONTSERRAT COLLEGE OF ART (*The complete profile is made available exclusively on our website, www.barronspac.com*)

MOUNT HOLYOKE COLLEGE — B-2
www.mtholyoke.edu

South Hadley, MA 01075	**(413) 538-2023** n/av
Fax: (413) 538-2409	**Email:** admission@mtholyoke.edu
Full-time: no men, 2161 women	**Faculty:** 208; IIB, ++$
Part-time: 1 men, 27 women	**Ph.D.s:** 94%
Graduate: 9 men, 57 women	**Student/Faculty:** 10 to 1
Year: semesters	**Tuition:** $42,656
Room & Board: $12,490	**Freshman Class:** 3201 applied, 1751 accepted, 547 enrolled
	CEEB CODE: 3529
Application Deadline: January 15	**MOST COMPETITIVE**

Mount Holyoke College, founded in 1837, is an independent, liberal arts college and the oldest institution of higher learning for women in the United States. The 800-acre campus is in a small town 90 miles west of Boston and 160 miles north of New York City. Including any residence halls, there are 68 buildings.

STUDENT LIFE: 77% of undergraduates are from out of state, mostly the Middle Atlantic. Students are from 45 states, 74 foreign countries, and Canada. 60% are from public schools. 46% are White; 25% Foreign. **Male To Female Ratio:** 224.5:1. The average age of freshmen is 18; all undergraduates, 20. 9% do not continue beyond their first year; 80% remain to graduate. **Housing:** 2136 students can be accommodated in college housing, which includes single-sex dorms and on-campus apartments. Special accommodations are available by need. On-campus housing is guaranteed for all 4 years. 95% of students live on campus; of those, 70% remain on campus on weekends. All students may keep cars.

FACULTY/CLASSROOMS: 42% of faculty are male; 58% are female. All teach and do research. No introductory courses are taught by graduate students. The average class size in an introductory lecture is 27; in a laboratory is 12; and in a regular course is 16.

PROGRAMS OF STUDY: Mount Holyoke confers A.B. degrees. Master's degrees are also awarded. Bachelor's degrees are awarded in AGRICULTURE (environmental studies), BIOLOGICAL SCIENCE (biochemistry, biology/biological science, and neurosciences), COMMUNICATIONS AND THE ARTS (art history and appreciation, classics, dance, dramatic arts, English, film arts, French, Greek, Italian, Latin, music, romance languages and literature, Spanish, and studio art), COMPUTER AND PHYSICAL SCIENCE (astronomy, chemistry, computer science, geology, mathematics, physics, and statistics), EDUCATION (psychology education), ENGINEERING AND ENVIRONMENTAL DESIGN (architecture), SOCIAL SCIENCE (africana studies, anthropology, Asian/Oriental studies, classical/ancient civilization, East Asian studies, economics, gender studies, geography, German area studies, history, international relations, Latin American studies, medieval studies, Middle Eastern studies, philosophy, political science/government, psychology, religion, Russian and Slavic studies, sociology, and South Asian studies). Sciences, social sciences, and international relations are the strongest academically. Psychology, international relations, and economics have the largest enrollments.

ACTIVITIES: There are no fraternities or sororities. There are 130 groups on campus, including art, band, cheerleading, choir, chorale, chorus, computers, dance, debate, drama, environmental, ethnic, film, gay, honors, international, jazz band, literary magazine, newspaper, orchestra, photography, political, professional, radio and TV, religious, social, social service, student government, and symphony. Popular campus events include NightFest!, Mountain Day, No Study Zone, Capella Jams, Pangy Day, and Cultural Nights. **Sports:** There are 14 intercollegiate sports for women. Facilities include indoor athletic and recreational facilities. Inside the building, include a fitness center, a gymnasium, a natatorium, a field house and dance studios, turf and track complex, soccer field, activity field, and tennis courts. Also in close proximity are the college's canoe house and a scenic one-mile loop around upper lake for running, walking or riding a horse. Mount Holyoke College Equestrian Center is considered to be one of the finest facilities for educational and competitive riding available to students anywhere. Its stable provides over 69 spacious,

airy, rubber-matted stalls, a large outdoor all-weather footing show arena, a permanent dressage arena, two indoor arenas, all-weather turnout paddocks, hunt field and a cross-country course through 120 acres of woods, fields, and streams. **Graduates:** From July 1, 2013 to June 30, 2014, 578 bachelor's degrees were awarded. The most popular majors were economics (10%), international relations (9%), and English (9%). 69 companies recruited on campus in 2013-2014. In an average class, 76% graduate in 4 years or less, 80% graduate in 5 years or less, and 80% graduate in 6 years or less. Of the 2013 graduating class, 19% were enrolled in graduate school within 6 months of graduation, and 91% were employed.

SERVICES: Counseling and information services are available, as is tutoring in every subject, writing center is available to all students at all levels. There is a reader service for the blind. Special testing accommodations, diagnostic testing services, note-taking services, as well as readers and tutors, are available. There is also an adaptive technology lab. **Library/Resources:** The 2 libraries contain 1.3 million volumes, 24,430 microform items, and 11,884 audio/video tapes/CDs/DVDs, and subscribe to 7,111 periodicals including electronic. Computerized library services include interlibrary loans, database searching, Internet access, and Wi-Fi capability. Special learning facilities include an art gallery, radio station, an observatory, a child study center, a botanical garden and greenhouse, an equestrian center, a conference center, and centers for global initiatives, leadership, and the environment. **Physically Challenged Students:** Facilities include wheelchair ramps, elevators, special parking, specially equipped restrooms, special class scheduling, lowered drinking fountains, and special housing. **Special:** Mount Holyoke offers students cross-registration through the Five-College Consortium. Other opportunities include the 12-College Exchange Program, science and international studies internships, study abroad in over 50 countries (semester or full-year), a Washington semester, work-study, student-designed majors, dual majors, accelerated degrees, nondegree study, and pass/fail options. A teacher licensure program is available. Mount Holyoke's "The Lynk" program enables students to meaningfully link their liberal arts education with their career goals through internships, research projects, and summer employment. There are 5 national honor societies and Phi Beta Kappa. **Visiting:** There are regularly scheduled orientations for prospective students, including tours, on-campus interviews, overnight stays, and meetings with professors and coaches. There are guides for informal visits, visitors may sit in on classes, and stay overnight. To schedule a visit, contact the Admission Office. **Campus Safety and Security:** Measures include 24-hour foot and vehicle patrol, emergency notification system, self-defense education, and security escort services. There are shuttle buses, emergency telephones, lighted pathways/sidewalks, and controlled access to dorms/residences.

REQUIREMENTS: The school recommends that applicants have 4 years each of English and foreign language, 3 each of math and science, and 2 of social studies. An essay is required and an interview is strongly recommended. AP credits are accepted. Important factors in the admissions decision are advanced placement or honors courses, leadership record, and recommendations by school officials. Students must complete 128 total credits with a final GPA of 2.0. Students must complete a first-year seminar and a major (generally 32-56 credits). At least 68 credits must be earned from course work outside the major department. Students must complete one course each in the humanities, science/math, and social sciences. Students must also complete a foreign language course, a multicultural perspectives course, and 4 units (2 semesters) of physical education courses. While not required, students may also elect to complete any number (or none) of the following: a second major, a minor (but not both a second major and a minor), a Five College certificate, or a Nexus program. At least 64 of the student's 128 credits must be earned at Mount Holyoke over a minimum of 4 semesters during the student's sophomore, junior and senior years. **Procedure:** Freshmen are admitted fall and spring. Entrance exams should be taken before the application deadline. There are early decision and deferred admissions plans. Early decision applications should be filed by November 15; regular applications, by January 15 for fall entry, along with a $60 fee. Notification of early decision is sent January 1; regular decision, April 1. 154 early decision candidates were accepted for the 2014-2015 class. 268 applicants were on the 2014 waiting list; 4 were admitted. Applications are accepted on-line. Application fees are waived if application is completed on-line. **Transfer Students:** 62 transfer students enrolled in 2013-2014. A statement of good standing, transcripts of secondary school or college-level work, and an essay are required of transfer applicants. An interview is recommended. SAT scores will be considered if submitted but are not required. 64 of 128 credits required for the bachelor's degree must be completed at Mount Holyoke. **International Students:** There are 551 international students enrolled. The school actively recruits these students. They must take the TOEFL with a minimum score of 100 on the Internet-based version (iBT).

ADMISSIONS: 55% of the 2014-2015 applicants were accepted. 80% of the current freshmen were in the top fifth of their class; 91% were in the top two fifths. 19 freshmen graduated first in their class. **Admissions Contact:** Diane C. Anci, VP of Enrollment and Dean of Admissions. E-Mail: *admission@mtholyoke.edu* Web: *www.mtholyoke.edu*

FINANCIAL AID: In 2014-2015, 80% of all full-time freshmen and continuing full-time students received some form of financial aid. 68% of all full-time freshmen and 67% of continuing full-time students received need-based aid. The average freshman award was $36,827. Need-based scholarships or need-based grants averaged $32,155; need-based self-help aid (loans and jobs) averaged $5,620; and other non-need-based awards and non-need-based scholarships averaged $17,727. 67% of undergraduate students work part-time. Average annual earnings from campus work are $1140. Mount Holyoke is a member of CSS. The CSS/Profile and FAFSA, and parent and student tax returns and noncustodial parent form are required. The priority date for freshman financial aid applications for fall entry is February 15. The deadline for filing freshman financial aid applications for fall entry is March 1.

MOUNT IDA COLLEGE *(The complete profile is made available exclusively on our website, www.barronspac.com)*

NEW ENGLAND CONSERVATORY OF MUSIC *(The complete profile is made available exclusively on our website, www.barronspac.com)*

NEWBURY COLLEGE *(The complete profile is made available exclusively on our website, www.barronspac.com)*

NICHOLS COLLEGE *(The complete profile is made available exclusively on our website, www.barronspac.com)*

NORTHEASTERN UNIVERSITY	E-2
www.northeastern.edu	
Boston, MA 02115	**(617) 373-2200**
Fax: (617) 373-8780	Email: admissions@neu.edu
Full-time: 8466 men, 8461 women	Faculty: I, +$
Part-time: n/av	Ph.D.s: 95%
Graduate: 4128 men, 3510 women	Student/Faculty: 13 to 1
Year: semesters, summer session	Tuition: $41,686
Room & Board: $13,610	Freshman Class: n/av
	CEEB CODE: 3667
Application Deadline: January 1	**MOST COMPETITIVE**

Northeastern University, founded in 1898, is a private research university. Northeastern is the leader in worldwide experiential learning, urban engagement, and interdisciplinary research that meets global and societal needs. Our broad mix of experience-based education programs our signature cooperative education program, as well as student research, service learning, and global learning build the connections that enable students to transform their lives. The University offers a comprehensive range of undergraduate and graduate programs leading to degrees through the doctorate in nine colleges and schools. There are 7 undergraduate schools and 8 graduate schools. In addition to regional accreditation, Northeastern has baccalaureate program accreditation with AACSB, ABET, ACPE, NAAB, CAATE, CCNE, and ACS. The 73-acre campus is in an urban area in the heart

of Boston, on Huntington Avenue, also known as the Avenue of the Arts. Including any residence halls, there are 88 buildings.

STUDENT LIFE: 67% of undergraduates are from out of state, mostly the Northeast. Students are from 48 states, 119 foreign countries, and Canada. **Male To Female Ratio:** 1.0:1. The average age of freshmen is 18; all undergraduates, 20. **Housing:** 8354 students can be accommodated in college housing, which includes single-sex and coed dorms, on-campus apartments, and off-campus apartments. In addition, there are honors houses, special-interest houses, academic/college-based, innovation, global perspective, leadership, creative expression, green living, community service. On-campus housing is guaranteed for the freshman year only, is available on a first-come, first-served basis, and is available on a lottery system for upperclassmen. Upperclassmen may keep cars.

FACULTY/CLASSROOMS: 57% of faculty are male; 43% are female. No introductory courses are taught by graduate students.

PROGRAMS OF STUDY: Northeastern confers B.A., B.S., B.F.A. and B.L.A. degrees. Master's and Doctoral degrees are also awarded. Bachelor's degrees are awarded in AGRICULTURE (environmental studies), BIOLOGICAL SCIENCE (biochemistry, biology/biological science, marine biology, and neurosciences), BUSINESS (accounting, business administration and management, international business management, and management information systems), COMMUNICATIONS AND THE ARTS (American Sign Language, art, communications, dramatic arts, English, film arts, graphic design, journalism, languages, linguistics, multimedia, music, music technology, studio art, and theatre arts), COMPUTER AND PHYSICAL SCIENCE (applied physics, chemistry, computer programming, computer science, digital arts/technology, earth science, information sciences and systems, mathematics, and physics), ENGINEERING AND ENVIRONMENTAL DESIGN (architecture, chemical engineering, civil engineering, computer engineering, electrical/electronics engineering, environmental science, industrial engineering, landscape architecture/design, and mechanical engineering), HEALTH PROFESSIONS (health science, nursing, pharmaceutical science, pharmacy, physical therapy, and speech pathology/audiology), SOCIAL SCIENCE (African American studies, anthropology, Asian/Oriental studies, criminal justice, economics, history, interdisciplinary studies, Judaic studies, philosophy, philosophy and religion, political science/government, psychology, religion, and sociology). Business administration, engineering, and sciences have the largest enrollments.

ACTIVITIES: 8% of men belong to 18 national fraternities; 12% of women belong to 11 national sororities. There are 331 groups on campus, including art, band, cheerleading, chess, chorale, chorus, computers, dance, debate, drama, environmental, ethnic, film, gay, honors, international, jazz band, literary magazine, musical theater, newspaper, orchestra, pep band, political, professional, radio and TV, religious, resident student association, social, social service, student government, symphony, and yearbook. Popular campus events include Springfest, Senior Week, Welcome Week and Carnevale. **Sports:** There are 7 intercollegiate sports for men and 9 for women, and 31 intramural sports for men and 31 for women. Facilities include an outdoor and indoor tracks, a indoor hockey arena, swimming pool, indoor and outdoor tennis courts, racquetball, squash, volleyball, basketball courts and three fitness centers. **Graduates:** From July 1, 2013 to June 30, 2014, 3368 bachelor's degrees were awarded. The most popular majors were business (20%), health professions (13%), and engineering (12%). 500 companies recruited on campus in 2013-2014. In an average class, 82% graduate in 6 years or less.

SERVICES: Counseling and information services are available, as is tutoring in most subjects. There is remedial math, reading, and writing. **Library/Resources:** The 3 libraries contain 896,213 volumes, 1.3 million microform items, 18,210 audio/video tapes/CDs/DVDs, and subscribe to 128,027 periodicals including electronic. Computerized library services include interlibrary loans, database searching, Internet access, and Wi-Fi capability. Special learning facilities include an art gallery, radio station, architecture studio, TV production suite, and various research labs. **Physically Challenged Students:** 95% of the campus is accessible. Facilities include wheelchair ramps, elevators, special parking, specially equipped restrooms, special class scheduling, lowered drinking fountains, lowered telephones, special housing. There are specially equipped labs and a tunnel system connecting the major administrative and academic buildings. **Special:** Northeastern offers a variety of experiential learning opportunities; co-op, research, global experience, and service -learning in Boston, throughout the U.S., and around the world to integrate classroom instruction with professional experience. Northeastern takes a flexible student-centered approach to academics that allows you to create the education that best suits your goals and aspirations. We offer four- and five-year programs, combined degree programs, interdisciplinary study options, study abroad in dozens of countries, undergraduate research opportunities, an Honors Program, work-study through the university and in neighboring public and private agencies, and student-designed majors. There are 14 national honor societies and a freshman honors program. **Visiting:** There are regularly scheduled orientations for prospective students. There are guides for informal visits. To schedule a visit, contact the Office of Undergraduate Admissions. **Campus Safety and Security:** Measures include 24-hour foot and vehicle patrol, emergency notification system, self-defense education, and security escort services. There are shuttle buses, emergency telephones, lighted pathways/sidewalks, controlled access to dorms/residences, and in-room safes.

REQUIREMENTS: The SAT or ACT is required. The ACT Optional Writing test is also required. Northeastern requires that applicants have 17 academic units, including 4 in English, 3 each in math, science, and social studies, and 2 each in foreign language and history. Recommended are 4 units in math and science, and a foreign language. An essay is required. AP credits are accepted. Important factors in the admissions decision are advanced placement or honors courses, leadership record, evidence of special talent, extracurricular activities record, geographical diversity, and recommendations by school officials. Although each college has its own requirements, students must generally complete at least 128 semester hours with a minimum GPA of 2.0. Students must also fulfill the university-wide general education requirement. **Procedure:** Freshmen are admitted fall. Entrance exams should be taken from May of the junior year through December of the senior year. There are early admissions and deferred admissions plans. Early decision applications should be filed by November 1; regular applications, by January 1 for fall entry, along with a $75 fee. Notification of early decision is sent December 31; regular decision, April 1. Applications are accepted on-line. **Transfer Students:** 683 transfer students enrolled in 2013-2014. The most successful transfer students have earned a cumulative GPA of 3.3. Students have also completed the introductory-level courses for their intended majors. Transfer students with less than 24 semester hours of college-level credit must also submit their high school transcripts and SAT or ACT scores. **International Students:** There are 2881 international students enrolled. The school actively recruits these students. They must take the TOEFL with a minimum score of 92 on the Internet-based version (iBT).

ADMISSIONS: 86% of the current freshmen were in the top fifth of their class; 97% were in the top two fifths. **Admissions Contact:** Ronne Patrick Turner, Associate VP, Enrollment/Dean, Admission. E-Mail: *admissions@neu.edu* Web: *www.northeastern.edu/admissions*

FINANCIAL AID: The CSS/Profile and FAFSA are required. The priority date for freshman financial aid applications for fall entry is February 15.

PINE MANOR COLLEGE *(The complete profile is made available exclusively on our website, www.barronspac.com)*

REGIS COLLEGE *(The complete profile is made available exclusively on our website, www.barronspac.com)*

SALEM STATE UNIVERSITY *(The complete profile is made available exclusively on our website, www.barronspac.com)*

SIMMONS COLLEGE	E-2
www.simmons.edu	

Boston, MA 02115	(617) 521-2515
	(800) 345-8468
Fax: (617) 521-3190	Email: ugadm@simmons.edu
Full-time: 1484 women	Faculty: 143
Part-time: 35 men, 190 women	Ph.D.s: n/av
Graduate: 331 men, 2313 women	Student/Faculty: 7 to 1
Year: semesters, summer session	Tuition: $36,230
Room & Board: $13,736	Freshman Class: 3999 applied, 2086 accepted, 306 enrolled
SAT CR/M/W: 594/580/597 ACT: 26	CEEB CODE: 3761
Application Deadline: February 1	VERY COMPETITIVE

Simmons College, founded in 1899, is a private institution with an undergraduate college for women that offers a comprehensive education combining the arts, sciences, and humanities with preprofessional training. All graduate programs are co-ed, with the exception of the women-only MBA program. There are 5 undergraduate schools and 5 graduate schools. In addition to regional accreditation, Simmons has baccalaureate program accreditation with AACSB, APTA, CSWE, ACS, CCNE, and ACEND. The 12-acre campus is in an urban area in Boston. Including any residence halls, there are 17 buildings.

STUDENT LIFE: 71% of undergraduates are from Massachusetts. Others are from 51 states, 65 foreign countries, and Canada. 68% are White. **Male To Female Ratio:** 10.9:1. The average age of freshmen is 20; all undergraduates, 22. 14% do not continue beyond their first year; 68% remain to graduate. **Housing:** 1015 students can be accommodated in college housing, which includes single-sex and coed dorms and off-campus apartments. In addition, there are special-interest houses, theme housing, wellness housing, cooperative housing, women's dorms, and non-trad students with dependents. On-campus housing is guaranteed for the freshman year only, is available on a first-come, first-served basis, and is available on a lottery system for upperclassmen. 59% of students live on campus; of those, 70% remain on campus on weekends. No one may keep cars.

FACULTY/CLASSROOMS: 28% of faculty are male; 72% are female. No introductory courses are taught by graduate students. The average class size in an introductory lecture is 11 and in a laboratory is 19.

PROGRAMS OF STUDY: Simmons confers B.A., B.S. and B.S.W. degrees. Master's and Doctoral degrees are also awarded. Bachelor's degrees are awarded in AGRICULTURE (environmental studies), BIOLOGICAL SCIENCE (biochemistry, biology/biological science, and biometrics and biostatistics), BUSINESS (business administration and management, finance, management information systems, marketing and distribution, and retailing), COMMUNICATIONS AND THE ARTS (arts administration/management, communications, English, French, information technology, music, and Spanish), COMPUTER AND PHYSICAL SCIENCE (chemistry, computer science, mathematics, and physics), EDUCATION (education, elementary education, health information management, secondary education, special education, and teaching English as a second/foreign language (TESOL/TEFOL)), HEALTH PROFESSIONS (exercise science, nursing, physical therapy, and public health), SOCIAL SCIENCE (African American studies, biopsychology, dietetics, East Asian studies, economics, food production/management/services, food science, history, interdisciplinary studies, international relations, philosophy, political science/government, psychobiology, psychology, social work, sociology, and women's studies). Nursing has the largest enrollment.

ACTIVITIES: There are no fraternities or sororities. There are 66 groups on campus, including Model UN, art, campus ministries, choir, chorale, chorus, communications, dance, drama, ethnic, film, gay, honors, international, jazz band, literary magazine, newspaper, orchestra, political, professional, radio and TV, religious, social service, student government, symphony, and yearbook. Popular campus events include Connections Carnival - the Simmons Student Organization and Involvement Fair, Winter Wonderland, and Almost Midnight Breakfast. **Sports:** Facilities include an 8-lane pool, a spa and sauna, 1 racquetball and 2 squash courts, 2 rowing tanks, 3 fitness rooms, a dance studio, an indoor running area, 2 volleyball courts, and a basketball court. **Graduates:** From July 1, 2013 to June 30, 2014, 477 bachelor's degrees were awarded. The most popular majors were health professions and related programs (42%), social sciences (22%), business, management, and marketing and related support services (7%). 160 companies recruited on campus in 2013-2014. In an average class, 68% graduate in 6 years or less. Of the 2013 graduating class, 18% were enrolled in graduate school within 6 months of graduation, and 58% were employed.

SERVICES: Counseling and information services are available, as is tutoring in every subject. There is a reader service for the blind, and remedial writing. **Library/Resources:** The library contains 291,528 volumes, 13,580 microform items, 3,013 audio/video tapes/CDs/DVDs, and subscribes to 3,935 periodicals including electronic. Computerized library services include interlibrary loans, database searching, Internet access, and Wi-Fi capability. Special learning facilities include an art gallery, radio station, writing center, tutoring, and disability services. **Physically Challenged Students:** Facilities include wheelchair ramps, elevators, special parking, specially equipped restrooms, special class scheduling, and lowered drinking fountains. **Special:** Cross-registration is available with the New England Conservatory of Music, Hebrew, Emmanuel, and Wheelock Colleges, Massachusetts College of Art, Massachusetts College of Pharmacy and Health Sciences, and Wentworth Institute of Technology. Simmons offers study abroad in Europe through the Institute of European studies. A Washington semester at American University, accelerated degree programs, profit and nonprofit internship programs, a B.A.-B.S. degree, dual majors, interdisciplinary majors, student-designed majors, work-study programs, and pass/fail options are also offered. There is a dual-degree program in chemistry, pharmacy, and physician's assistant with Massachusetts College of Pharmacy. There are 6 national honor societies, a freshman honors program, and 12 departmental honors programs. **Visiting:** There are regularly scheduled orientations for prospective students. There are guides for informal visits, visitors may sit in on classes, and stay overnight. To schedule a visit, contact Stephanie Charles, Admissions Office. **Campus Safety and Security:** Measures include 24-hour foot and vehicle patrol, emergency notification system, self-defense education, and security escort services. There are emergency telephones, lighted pathways/sidewalks, and controlled access to dorms/residences.

REQUIREMENTS: The SAT or ACT is required. The ACT Optional Writing test is also required. Simmons recommends that applicants have 4 years of English, math, foreign language, and social studies, as well as 3 years of science and history. An essay is required, and an interview is strongly recommended. AP and CLEP credits are accepted. Important factors in the admissions decision are advanced placement or honors courses, leadership record, parents or siblings attended your school, evidence of special talent, personality/intangible qualities, extracurricular activities record, ability to finance college education, recommendations by alumni, geographical diversity, and recommendations by school officials. To graduate, students must complete 128 semester hours, including 24 to 48 in the major, and maintain a minimum GPA of 2.0. Eight semester hours in a supervised independent learning experience or an internship are also required. Students must also fulfill foreign language, math competency, and technology competency requirements. In addition to completing the multidisciplinary core courses, students must complete 1 course from each of the following 6 modes of inquiry categories: creative and performing arts; language, literature, and culture; quantitative analysis and reasoning; scientific inquiry; social and historical perspectives; and psychological and ethical development. A thesis is optional. **Procedure:** Freshmen are admitted fall and spring. There are early admissions and deferred admissions plans. February 1 for fall entry; December 1 for spring entry, along with a $55 fee. Notifications are sent March 15. 69 applicants were on the 2014 waiting list; 34 were admitted. Applications are accepted on-line. Application fees are waived if application is completed on-line. **Transfer Students:** 33 transfer students enrolled in 2013-2014. Applicants should have a GPA of 2.8, at least 17 college-level credit hours, official transcripts from all colleges attended, and a faculty recommendation and dean's report from the previous college attended. 48 of 128 credits required

for the bachelor's degree must be completed at Simmons. **International Students:** There are 111 international students enrolled. The school actively recruits these students. They must take the TOEFL with a minimum score of 83 on the Internet-based version (iBT), or take the IELTS. They must also take the SAT or ACT.

ADMISSIONS: 52% of the 2014-2015 applicants were accepted. The SAT scores for the 2014-2015 freshman class were: Critical Reading--7% below 500, 48% between 500 and 599, 35% between 600 and 699, and 10% between 700 and 800; Math--6% below 500, 53% between 500 and 599, 37% between 600 and 699, and 4% between 700 and 800; Writing--9% below 500, 41% between 500 and 599, 42% between 600 and 699, and 8% between 700 and 800. The ACT scores were 7% below 21, 20% between 21 and 23, 31% between 24 and 26, 16% between 27 and 28, and 26% above 28. 72% of the current freshmen were in the top fifth of their class; 96% were in the top two fifths. 4 freshmen graduated first in their class. **Admissions Contact:** Ellen Johnson, Director. E-Mail: *ugadm@simmons.edu* Web: *www.simmons.edu*

FINANCIAL AID: In 2014-2015, 99% of all full-time freshmen and 94% of continuing full-time students received some form of financial aid. 83% of all full-time freshmen and 77% of continuing full-time students received need-based aid. The average freshman award was $28,269. Need-based scholarships or need-based grants averaged $20,907 ($54,546 maximum); need-based self-help aid (loans and jobs) averaged $4,038 ($10,000 maximum); and other non-need-based awards and non-need-based scholarships averaged $3,325 ($54,559 maximum). 35% of undergraduate students work part-time. Average annual earnings from campus work are $1253. Simmons is a member of CSS. The FAFSA and the college's own financial statement, and federal tax returns, institutional form are required. The priority date for freshman financial aid applications for fall entry is March 1.

SMITH COLLEGE B-2
www.smith.edu

Northampton, MA 01063 (413) 585-2500
n/av

Fax: (413) 585-2527	Email: admission@smith.edu
Full-time: 2544 women	Faculty: 275; IIB, ++$
Part-time: 19 women	Ph.D.s: 99%
Graduate: 26 men, 154 women	Student/Faculty: 9 to 1
Year: semesters	Tuition: $44,724
Room & Board: $14,950	Freshman Class: 4466 applied, 1885 accepted, 617 enrolled
SAT CR/M/W: 675/680/675 ACT: 30	CEEB CODE: 3762
Application Deadline: January 15	MOST COMPETITIVE

Smith College, founded in 1871, is the largest independent Women's College in the United States and offers a liberal arts education. Figures in the above capsule and in this profile are approximate. There is 1 undergraduate school and 1 graduate school. In addition to regional accreditation, Smith has baccalaureate program accreditation with ABET. The 156-acre campus is in a small town 90 miles west of Boston. Including any residence halls, there are 118 buildings.

STUDENT LIFE: 77% of undergraduates are from out of state, mostly the Northeast. Students are from 48 states, 72 foreign countries, and Canada. 64% are from public schools. 46% are White; 13% Asian American; 13% Foreign. 40% are Hindu, Buddhist, Muslim, Unitarian, and Christian Scientists; 20% Protestant; 18% claim no religious affiliation; 14% Catholic. **Male To Female Ratio:** 104.5:1. The average age of freshmen is 18; all undergraduates, 20. 9% do not continue beyond their first year; 86% remain to graduate. **Housing:** 2440 students can be accommodated in college housing, which includes single-sex dorms and on-campus apartments. In addition, there are language houses, special-interest houses, non-smoking houses, 2 cooperative houses, housing for non-traditional-age students, an apartment complex for a limited number of juniors and seniors, and a non-trad students with dependents. On-campus housing is guaranteed for all 4 years. 100% of students live on campus; of those, 95% remain on campus on weekends. Upperclassmen may keep cars.

FACULTY/CLASSROOMS: 45% of faculty are male; 55% are female. All teach and do research. No introductory courses are taught by graduate students. The average class size in an introductory lecture is 25; in a laboratory is 13; and in a regular course is 20.

PROGRAMS OF STUDY: Smith confers A.B., and B.S.Eng. degrees. Master's and Doctoral degrees are also awarded. Bachelor's degrees are awarded in BIOLOGICAL SCIENCE (biochemistry, biology/biological science, and neurosciences), COMMUNICATIONS AND THE ARTS (art history and appreciation, classics, comparative literature, creative writing, dance, dramatic arts, East Asian languages and literature, English, film arts, French, German languages and literature, Greek, Italian, Latin, music, Russian, Spanish, and studio art), COMPUTER AND PHYSICAL SCIENCE (astronomy, chemistry, computer science, geology, mathematics, and physics), EDUCATION (early childhood education, education, and elementary education), ENGINEERING AND ENVIRONMENTAL DESIGN (architecture, engineering, and environmental science), HEALTH PROFESSIONS (exercise science), SOCIAL SCIENCE (African studies, African American studies, American studies, anthropology, classical/ancient civilization, cognitive science, economics, ethics, politics, social policy, European and French studies, history, international relations, Japanese studies, Judaic studies, Latin American, Luso-Brazilian studies, medieval studies, Middle Eastern studies, philosophy, political science/government, psychology, religion, Russian and Slavic studies, sociology, urban studies, and women's studies). Art, economics, government and psychology have the largest enrollments.

ACTIVITIES: There are no fraternities or sororities. There are 127 groups on campus, including art, cheerleading, chess, chorus, computers, dance, debate, drama, environmental, ethnic, gay, honors, international, jazz band, literary magazine, musical theater, newspaper, orchestra, photography, political, professional, radio and TV, religious, social, social service, student government, symphony, and yearbook. Popular campus events include International Student Day, Spring and Winter Weekends and Rally Day. **Sports:** There are 14 intercollegiate sports for women, and 4 intramural sports for women. Facilities include indoor and outdoor tracks and tennis courts, riding rings, 2 gyms, a climbing wall, an indoor swimming pool with 1- and 3-meter diving boards, 2 weight-training rooms, a dance studio, 2 athletic training rooms, a human performance lab, squash courts, and field hockey, soccer, lacrosse, and softball fields. There is a performing arts center and a concert hall. **Graduates:** From July 1, 2013 to June 30, 2014, 670 bachelor's degrees were awarded. The most popular majors were social sciences (23%), foreign languages, literatures, and linguistics/psychology/visual and performing arts (10%), area, ethnic, and and gender studies (9%). 71 companies recruited on campus in 2013-2014. In an average class, 82% graduate in 4 years or less, 85% graduate in 5 years or less, and 86% graduate in 6 years or less.

SERVICES: Counseling and information services are available, as is tutoring in every subject. There is a reader service for the blind. Numerous services are provided for learning-disabled students, including note taking, oral tests, readers, tutors, books on tape, reading software, voice recognition, tape recorders, extended-timed tests, and writing counselors. **Library/Resources:** The 4 libraries contain 1.5 million volumes, 149,402 microform items, and 76,662 audio/video tapes/CDs/DVDs, and subscribe to 60,916 periodicals including electronic. Computerized library services include interlibrary loans, database searching, Internet access, and Wi-Fi capability. Special learning facilities include an art gallery, radio station, TV station, astronomy observatories, center for foreign languages and culture, digital design studio, plant and horticultural labs, art studios with casting, printmaking, and darkroom facilities, and specialized libraries for science, music, and art, and the Quantitative Learning Center, and the Jacobson Center for writing, teaching and learning. **Physically Challenged Students:** 85% of the campus is accessible. Facilities include wheelchair ramps, elevators, special parking, specially equipped restrooms, special class scheduling, lowered drinking fountains, lowered telephones. **Special:** Smith offers study abroad in more than 50 countries including the Smith College programs in Italy, France, Germany, and Switzerland, affiliated programs in India, Japan, Russia, China, South Africa, Peru, Brazil, and Spain, and many others. Other opportunities include cross-registration with 5 area colleges, a Washington semester, Smithsonian internships, exchanges

with historically Black colleges and other liberal arts colleges, and at BioSphere2. A 3-2 engineering degree is offered with Dartmouth College. Support for nontraditional-age students and for international students is provided, and funding for a summer internship is available for every undergraduate. Accelerated degree programs, student-designed majors, dual majors, and non-degree study are offered. There are 3 national honor societies and Phi Beta Kappa. **Visiting:** There are regularly scheduled orientations for prospective students, including student-guided tours available 4 times a day, Monday through Friday, when school is in full session and on Saturday mornings from September to January. Interviews may also be scheduled during these times. Information sessions are offered twice daily most of the year. There are guides for informal visits, visitors may sit in on classes, and stay overnight. To schedule a visit, contact the Office of Admissions. **Campus Safety and Security:** Measures include 24-hour foot and vehicle patrol, emergency notification system, self-defense education, and security escort services. There are shuttle buses, emergency telephones, lighted pathways/sidewalks, first-year students are required to attend panel discussions on campus safety. Specialized personal safety presentations, including self defense and sexual assault information, are provided to various houses and organizations. There are crime prevention programs including bicycle registration.

REQUIREMENTS: Smith highly recommends that applicants have 4 years of English, 3 years each of math, science, and a foreign language, and 2 years of history, and 1 year of academic electives. SAT and ACT are considered but not required. Interviews are recommended. The GED is accepted. AP credits are accepted. All students plan individual programs in consultation with faculty advisers and take 64 credits outside their major and 36 to 64 credits in the major. Students must maintain a minimum 2.0 GPA in all academic work and during the senior year. A total of 128 credits is needed to graduate. A writing-intensive course is required for first-year students. A thesis is required for departmental honors programs. Distribution requirements are necessary for Latin honors eligibility. **Procedure:** Freshmen are admitted fall. Entrance exams should be taken before January of the senior year. There are early decision, early admissions, and deferred admissions plans. Early decision applications should be filed by November 15; regular applications, by January 15 for fall entry, along with a $60 fee. Notification of early decision is sent December 15; regular decision, April 1. 158 early decision candidates were accepted for the 2014-2015 class. 289 applicants were on the 2014 waiting list; 44 were admitted. Applications are accepted online. **Transfer Students:** 45 transfer students enrolled in 2013-2014. Criteria for transfer students are similar to those for entering freshmen, with more emphasis on the college record. 64 of 64 credits required for the bachelor's degree must be completed at Smith. **International Students:** The school actively recruits these students. They must take the TOEFL with a minimum score of 600 on the paper-based TOEFL (PBT) or 95 on the Internet-based version (iBT). They must also take the SAT or ACT if the language of instruction is English.

ADMISSIONS: 42% of the 2014-2015 applicants were accepted. The SAT scores for the 2014-2015 freshman class were: Critical Reading--1% below 500, 15% between 500 and 599, 49% between 600 and 699, and 34% between 700 and 800; Math--1% below 500, 13% between 500 and 599, 47% between 600 and 699, and 37% between 700 and 800; Writing--12% between 500 and 599, 46% between 600 and 699, and 41% between 700 and 800. The ACT scores were 4% between 21 and 23, 36% between 27 and 28, and 59% above 28. **Admissions Contact:** Debra Shaver, Director of Admissions. E-Mail: *admission@smith.edu* Web: *www.smith.edu*

FINANCIAL AID: In 2014-2015, 67% of all full-time freshmen and 69% of continuing full-time students received some form of financial aid. 58% of all full-time freshmen and 63% of continuing full-time students received need-based aid. The average freshman award was $42,427. Need-based scholarships or need-based grants averaged $40,117; need-based self-help aid (loans and jobs) averaged $4,523; other non-need-based awards and non-need-based scholarships averaged $11,812; and $3,202 from other forms of aid. The average financial indebtedness of the 2014 graduate was $24,758. Smith is a member of CSS. The CSS/Profile, FAFSA, and the college's own financial statement are required. The deadline for filing freshman financial aid applications for fall entry is February 15.

SPRINGFIELD COLLEGE — B-3
www.springfieldcollege.edu

Springfield, MA 01109	(413) 748-3136
	(800) 343-1257
Fax: (413) 748-3694	Email: admissions@spfldcol.edu
Full-time: n/av	Faculty: 210; IIA, av$
Part-time: n/av	Ph.D.s: 62%
Graduate: n/av	Student/Faculty: 10 to 1
Year: semesters, summer session	Tuition: $25,500
Room & Board: $10,500	Freshman Class: n/av
SAT or ACT: required	CEEB CODE: 3763
Application Deadline: n/av	COMPETITIVE

Springfield College, established in 1885, is a private liberal arts and sciences institution. Figures in the above capsule and in this profile are approximate. There are 3 undergraduate schools and one graduate school. In addition to regional accreditation, S.C. has baccalaureate program accreditation with APTA, CAHEA, and NRPA. The 160-acre campus is in a suburban area 26 miles north of Hartford, Connecticut. Including any residence halls, there are 38 buildings.

STUDENT LIFE: Students are from 30 states, 12 foreign countries, and Canada. 83% are from public schools. 93% are White. The average age of freshmen is 18; all undergraduates, 21. 12% do not continue beyond their first year. **Housing:** 1980 students can be accommodated in college housing, which includes single-sex and coed dorms, on-campus apartments, off-campus apartments, and married student housing. In addition, there are special-interest houses and a wellness dorm. On-campus housing is guaranteed for all 4 years. 85% of students live on campus; of those, 70% remain on campus on weekends. Alcohol is not permitted. Upperclassmen may keep cars.

FACULTY/CLASSROOMS: 52% of faculty are male; 48% are female. No introductory courses are taught by graduate students. The average class size in an introductory lecture is 125; in a laboratory is 20; and in a regular course is 30.

PROGRAMS OF STUDY: S.C. confers B.A., and B.S. degrees. Master's and Doctoral degrees are also awarded. Bachelor's degrees are awarded in BIOLOGICAL SCIENCE (biochemistry, biology/ biological science, and biotechnology), BUSINESS (business administration and management and sports management), COMMUNICATIONS AND THE ARTS (English and fine arts), COMPUTER AND PHYSICAL SCIENCE (chemistry, information sciences and systems, and mathematics), EDUCATION (early childhood education, elementary education, health education, middle school education, physical education, science education, and secondary education), ENGINEERING AND ENVIRONMENTAL DESIGN (computer graphics), HEALTH PROFESSIONS (art therapy, emergency medical technologies, environmental health science, health care administration, predentistry, premedicine, recreation therapy, and rehabilitation therapy), SOCIAL SCIENCE (gerontology, history, human services, parks and recreation management, physical fitness/ movement, political science/government, prelaw, psychology, and sociology). Physical therapy and athletic training is the strongest academically. Physical education has the largest enrollment.

ACTIVITIES: There are no fraternities or sororities. There are 58 groups on campus, including art, band, cheerleading, choir, chorus, club sports, communications, computers, dance, drama, ethnic, film, gay, honors, international, jazz band, literary magazine, musical theater, newspaper, pep band, professional, radio and TV, religious, social, social service, student government, and yearbook. Popular campus events include Parents Weekend and Stepping Up Day. **Sports:** There are 13 intercollegiate sports for men and 11 for women, and 10 intramural sports for men and 10 for women. Facilities include a 2000-seat stadium, a 2000-seat gym, a superturf football/ soccer/lacrosse/field hockey field, 8 tennis courts, baseball and softball fields, and free weight and Nautilus rooms. **Graduates:** Of the 2013 graduating class, 19% were enrolled in graduate school within 6 months of graduation, and 78% were employed.

SERVICES: Counseling and information services are available, as is tutoring in every subject. There is remedial math and writing. **Library/Resources:** The library contains 168,332 volumes, 736,056 microform items, 3,200 audio/video tapes/CDs/DVDs, and subscribes to 831 periodicals including electronic. Computerized library services include interlibrary loans and database searching. Special learning facilities include an art gallery, radio station, an outdoor center. **Physically Challenged Students:** 75% of the campus is accessible. Facilities include wheelchair ramps, elevators, special parking, specially equipped restrooms, special class scheduling, and lowered drinking fountains. **Special:** There is a co-op program and cross-registration with cooperating colleges in the greater Springfield area. Internships are required in most majors, and there is limited study abroad. There are 2 national honor societies. **Visiting:** There are guides for informal visits, visitors may sit in on classes, and stay overnight. To schedule a visit, contact the Admissions Office. **Campus Safety and Security:** Measures include 24-hour foot and vehicle patrol, self-defense education, and security escort services. There are shuttle buses, emergency telephones, and lighted pathways/sidewalks.

REQUIREMENTS: The SAT or ACT is required. Applicants must be graduates of an accredited secondary school and have completed 4 years of English and 3 years each of history, math, and science. The school accepts the GED. An essay is required and an interview is recommended. Applications are accepted on-line. AP and CLEP credits are accepted. Important factors in the admissions decision are advanced placement or honors courses, leadership record, and extra-curricular activities record.To graduate, students must complete a total of 130 credits with a 2.0 GPA. Core requirements include 50 semester hours in English, social and natural sciences, health, religion, philosophy, and art, and 4 credits in phys ed. **Procedure:** Freshmen are admitted fall and spring. Entrance exams should be taken by November of the senior year. There are early decision, early admissions, deferred admissions, and rolling admissions plans. Early decision applications should be filed by December 1, along with a $40 fee. Notification of early decision is sent February 1; regular decision, March 15. Applications are accepted on-line. **Transfer Students:** Grades of 2.0 transfer for credit. Transfer students are admitted in the fall and spring. **International Students:** There are 20 international students enrolled. The school actively recruits these students. They must take the TOEFL. They must also take the SAT or ACT.

ADMISSIONS: Mary N. DeAngelo, Director of Admissions. E-Mail: *admissions@spfldcol.edu* Web: *www.springfieldcollege.edu*

FINANCIAL AID: The CSS/Profile and FAFSA, and tax returns for parents and the student are required. The deadline for filing freshman financial aid applications for fall entry is March 15.

STONEHILL COLLEGE — E-3
www.stonehill.edu

Easton, MA 02357	(508) 565-1373
	n/av
Fax: (508) 565-1545	Email: admissions@stonehill.edu
Full-time: 984 men, 1575 women	Faculty: 156; IIB, +$
Part-time: 9 men, 14 women	Ph.D.s: 85%
Graduate: n/av	Student/Faculty: 16 to 1
Year: semesters, summer session	Tuition: $33,920
Room & Board: $12,860	Freshman Class: 7052 applied, 4500 accepted, 728 enrolled
SAT CR/M: 590/600 ACT: 26	CEEB CODE: 3770
Application Deadline: January 15	HIGHLY COMPETITIVE

Stonehill is a selective Catholic college with a welcoming community and beautiful campus. Dedicated, supportive faculty mentor students in over 80 academic programs in the liberal arts, sciences, and business. Nearly 90% of students participate in internships, study abroad, research, practicum, and field work. Our location offers easy access to jobs, museums, sports games, and more. Stonehill is a vibrant community where students learn to live lives that make a difference. Figures in the above capsule and in this profile are approximate. In addition to regional accreditation, Stonehill has baccalaureate program accreditation with ACS and AUPHA. The 384-acre campus is in a suburban area 22 miles south of Boston. Including any residence halls, there are 65 buildings.

STUDENT LIFE: 53% of undergraduates are from Massachusetts.

Others are from 29 states, and 10 foreign countries. 90% are White. 71% are Catholic; 13% claim no religious affiliation. **Male To Female Ratio:** 1.6:1. The average age of freshmen is 18; all undergraduates, 19. 8% do not continue beyond their first year; 85% remain to graduate. **Housing:** 2199 students can be accommodated in college housing, which includes single-sex and coed dorms. In addition, there are special-interest houses, Substance-free/wellness housing, and community service housing. On-campus housing is guaranteed for all 4 years. 92% of students live on campus; of those, 85% remain on campus on weekends. Upperclassmen may keep cars.

FACULTY/CLASSROOMS: 58% of faculty are male; 42% are female. All teach and do research. No introductory courses are taught by graduate students. The average class size in an introductory lecture is 21.

PROGRAMS OF STUDY: Stonehill confers B.A., B.S. and B.S.B.A. degrees. Bachelor's degrees are awarded in AGRICULTURE (environmental studies), BIOLOGICAL SCIENCE (biochemistry, biology/biological science, and neurosciences), BUSINESS (accounting, banking and finance, business administration and management, international business management, and marketing/retailing/merchandising), COMMUNICATIONS AND THE ARTS (art history and appreciation, communications, English, fine arts, French, music, and Spanish), COMPUTER AND PHYSICAL SCIENCE (chemistry, computer science, mathematics, and physics), EDUCATION (education), HEALTH PROFESSIONS (health care administration), SOCIAL SCIENCE (American studies, Christian studies, criminology, economics, gender studies, history, interdisciplinary studies, international studies, philosophy, political science/government, psychology, public administration, religion, and sociology). Business, biology, and psychology have the largest enrollments.

ACTIVITIES: There are no fraternities or sororities. There are 77 groups on campus, including art, band, cheerleading, choir, chorale, chorus, computers, dance, drama, environmental, ethnic, film, gay, honors, international, literary magazine, musical theater, newspaper, pep band, photography, political, professional, radio and TV, religious, social, social service, student government, and yearbook. Popular campus events include Skyhawk Weekend, Spring Weekend, and Halloween Mixer. **Sports:** There are 9 intercollegiate sports for men and 11 for women, and 20 intramural sports for men and 20 for women. Facilities include a 2400-seat stadium for football, field hockey, soccer, and lacrosse, a 500-seat field for men's and women's soccer, a 2000-seat gym with basketball and volleyball courts, 5000 square feet of weight and cardiovascular fitness areas, a recreational and intramural sports complex, tennis courts, baseball, softball, and field hockey fields, a regulation beach volleyball court, and 3 recreational fields for intramural and club sports. **Graduates:** From July 1, 2013 to June 30, 2014, 573 bachelor's degrees were awarded. The most popular majors were business (25%), psychology (8%), and English (7%). 356 companies recruited on campus in 2013-2014. In an average class, 80% graduate in 4 years or less, 84% graduate in 5 years or less, and 85% graduate in 6 years or less. Of the 2013 graduating class, 41% were enrolled in graduate school within 6 months of graduation, and 71% were employed.

SERVICES: Counseling and information services are available, as is tutoring in most subjects, a learning disabilities specialist and free diagnostic testing are also available as are auxiliary aids for hearing impaired students, note takers, and other resources based on need. There is a reader service for the blind, and remedial writing. **Library/Resources:** The library contains 243,500 volumes, 150,431 microform items, 9,593 audio/video tapes/CDs/DVDs, and subscribes to 13,111 periodicals including electronic. Computerized library services include interlibrary loans, database searching, Internet access, and Wi-Fi capability. Special learning facilities include an art gallery, radio station, an observatory, an institute for the study of law and society, and several archives and special collections. **Physically Challenged Students:** All of the campus is accessible. Facilities include wheelchair ramps, elevators, special parking, specially equipped restrooms, special class scheduling, lowered drinking fountains, lowered telephones, special housing. **Special:** There are 20 national honor societies and a freshman honors program. **Visiting:** There are regularly scheduled orientations for prospective students, consisting of group information sessions and guided campus tours available by appointment throughout the year. Visitors may sit in on classes. To

schedule a visit, contact the Admissions Office. **Campus Safety and Security:** Measures include 24-hour foot and vehicle patrol, emergency notification system, self-defense education, and security escort services. There are emergency telephones, lighted pathways/sidewalks, controlled access to dorms/residences, bicycle patrols, and a weekend guest sign-in policy.

REQUIREMENTS: Applicants should be graduates of an accredited high school or have earned the GED. Secondary preparation should include 4 units of English, 3 units of foreign language, 3 units of science, 4 units of math, and 3 combined units of history, political science, and social sciences plus 3 elective subjects. An essay, school report, 2 teacher evaluations, and a completed common application sent with a Stonehill Supplemental Information Form are required. AP credits are accepted. Important factors in the admissions decision are advanced placement or honors courses, leadership record, and extracurricular activities record. All students must complete a cornerstone program, which consists of 4 common courses within history/literature and philosophy/religious studies; a learning community consisting of 2 linked courses and a 3rd integrated course; a moral inquiry course; and a senior capstone experience within the major. Distribution requirements include 2 semesters of a foreign language and 1 course each in in natural scientific inquiry, social scientific inquiry, and statistical reasoning. Students must complete 120 hours 40 3- to 4-credit courses while maintaining a minimum GPA of 2.0. **Procedure:** Freshmen are admitted fall and spring. There are early decision, early admissions, and deferred admissions plans. Early decision applications should be filed by November 1; regular applications, by January 15 for fall entry; and November 1 for spring entry, along with a $60 fee. Notification of early decision is sent December 25; regular decision, March 15. 44 early decision candidates were accepted for the 2014-2015 class. 67 applicants were on the 2014 waiting list; 33 were admitted. Applications are accepted on-line. **Transfer Students:** 26 transfer students enrolled in 2013-2014. Applicants must have a minimum GPA of 2.0. Official high school transcripts and college transcripts along with catalogs with course descriptions from all colleges attended are required. An essay and 2 recommendations are required, and an interview is recommended. 60 of 120 credits required for the bachelor's degree must be completed at Stonehill. **International Students:** There are 12 international students enrolled. The school actively recruits these students. They must take the TOEFL.

ADMISSIONS: 64% of the 2014-2015 applicants were accepted. The SAT scores for the 2014-2015 freshman class were: Critical Reading--4% below 500, 43% between 500 and 599, 47% between 600 and 699, and 6% between 700 and 800; Math--4% below 500, 37% between 500 and 599, 52% between 600 and 699, and 7% between 700 and 800. The ACT scores were 1% below 21, 10% between 21 and 23, 32% between 24 and 26, 33% between 27 and 28, and 24% above 28. 65% of the current freshmen were in the top fifth of their class; 92% were in the top two fifths. 7 freshmen graduated first in their class. **Admissions Contact:** Daniel Monahan, Dean of Admissions. E-Mail: *admissions@stonehill.edu* Web: *www.stonehill.edu*

FINANCIAL AID: In 2014-2015, 97% of all full-time freshmen and 88% of continuing full-time students received some form of financial aid. 60% of all full-time freshmen and 57% of continuing full-time students received need-based aid. The average freshman award was $24,000. Need-based scholarships or need-based grants averaged $18,000 ($43,000 maximum); need-based self-help aid (loans and jobs) averaged $7,700 ($9,000 maximum); non-need-based athletic scholarships averaged $9,000 ($48,000 maximum); and other non-need-based awards and non-need-based scholarships averaged $9,000 ($34,000 maximum). 47% of undergraduate students work part-time. Stonehill is a member of CSS. The CSS/Profile and FAFSA, and non-custodial profile and business/farm supplement are required. The deadline for filing freshman financial aid applications for fall entry is February 1.

SUFFOLK UNIVERSITY   E-2
www.suffolk.edu

Boston, MA 02108

(617) 573-8460
(800) 6SUFFOL

Fax: (617) 742-4291

Email: admission@suffolk.edu

Full-time: 2262 men, 2868 women

Faculty: 449; IIA, ++$

Part-time: 185 men, 181 women

Ph.D.s: 86%

Graduate: 1170 men, 1655 women

Student/Faculty: 10 to 1

Year: semesters, summer session

Tuition: $32,660

Room & Board: $14,638

Freshman Class: 8786
applied, 7372 accepted,
1085 enrolled

SAT CR/M/W: 510/509/506 ACT: 22

CEEB CODE: 3771

Application Deadline: March 1

COMPETITIVE

Suffolk University gives its students unparalleled access to the city and the wealth of opportunities it offers. Yet we are also a personal, student-centered school, where faculty and administrators know students by name. As we have done for 107 years, we strive for one thing: give students the tools they need to be successful, smart, and satisfied at whatever they choose to do. There are 2 undergraduate schools and 3 graduate schools. In addition to regional accreditation, Suffolk has baccalaureate program accreditation with AACSB, ABET, FIDER, and NASAD. The 2-acre campus is in an urban area in the heart of downtown Boston. Including any residence halls, there are 13 buildings.

STUDENT LIFE: 67% of undergraduates are from Massachusetts. Others are from 45 states, 108 foreign countries, and Canada. 60% are from public schools. 39% are White; 22% Foreign; 12% race unknown; 11% Hispanic. **Male To Female Ratio:** 1.3:1. The average age of freshmen is 18; all undergraduates, 21. 25% do not continue beyond their first year; 55% remain to graduate. **Housing:** 1249 students can be accommodated in college housing, which includes coed dorms. On-campus housing is available on a first-come, first-served basis, and is available on a lottery system for upperclassmen. Alcohol is not permitted. No one may keep cars.

FACULTY/CLASSROOMS: 60% of faculty are male; 40% are female. All teach undergraduates. No introductory courses are taught by graduate students. The average class size in an introductory lecture is 20 and in a laboratory is 15.

PROGRAMS OF STUDY: Suffolk confers B.A., B.S., B.F.A., B.S.B.A., B.S.G.S. and B.S.J. degrees. Associate, master's, and doctoral degrees are also awarded. Bachelor's degrees are awarded in AGRICULTURE (environmental studies), BIOLOGICAL SCIENCE (biochemistry, biology/biological science, biotechnology, life science, and marine science), BUSINESS (accounting, banking and finance, entrepreneurial studies, international business management, international economics, management science, and marketing/retailing/merchandising), COMMUNICATIONS AND THE ARTS (advertising, art history and appreciation, broadcasting, communications, creative writing, dramatic arts, English, film arts, fine arts, French, graphic design, journalism, media arts, music history and appreciation, performing arts, public relations, Spanish, and speech/debate/rhetoric), COMPUTER AND PHYSICAL SCIENCE (chemistry, computer programming, computer science, information sciences and systems, mathematics, and physics), EDUCATION (business education, English education, mathematics education, and science education), ENGINEERING AND ENVIRONMENTAL DESIGN (computer engineering, electrical/electronics engineering, environmental engineering, environmental science, and interior design), HEALTH PROFESSIONS (medical laboratory technology and radiological science), SOCIAL SCIENCE (African American studies, American studies, criminal justice, economics, European studies, German area studies, history, human development, human services, humanities, international relations, paralegal studies, philosophy, political science/government, psychology, social science, sociology, and women's studies). Business, sociology, and communications are the strongest academically. Communications and journalism, management, and marketing have the largest enrollments.

ACTIVITIES: There are 75 groups on campus, including evening students, recycling, transfer students, art, choir, chorale, chorus, com-

puters, dance, debate, drama, ethnic, film, forensics, gay, honors, international, jazz band, literary magazine, musical theater, newspaper, orientation, photography, political, professional, radio and TV, religious, social, social service, and student government. Popular campus events include Hispanic Fiesta, Fallfest Talent Show, and Temple Street Fair. **Sports:** There are 7 intercollegiate sports for men and 6 for women, and 2 intramural sports for men and 2 for women. Facilities include a basketball, volleyball, and aerobics facility, intramurals, and indoor baseball/softball practice and a fully equipped fitness center. **Graduates:** From July 1, 2013 to June 30, 2014, 1313 bachelor's degrees were awarded. The most popular majors were communications (16%), finance (8%), and management (8%). 121 companies recruited on campus in 2013-2014. In an average class, 1% graduate in 3 years or less, 45% graduate in 4 years or less, 51% graduate in 5 years or less, and 55% graduate in 6 years or less. Of the 2013 graduating class, 17% were enrolled in graduate school within 6 months of graduation, and 22% were employed.

SERVICES: Counseling and information services are available, as is tutoring in every subject. There is a reader service for the blind, and remedial math, reading, and writing. **Library/Resources:** The 3 libraries contain 155,248 volumes, 144,091 microform items, 1,973 audio/video tapes/CDs/DVDs, and subscribe to 23,949 periodicals including electronic. Computerized library services include interlibrary loans, database searching, Internet access, and Wi-Fi capability. Special learning facilities include an art gallery, radio station, and TV station. **Physically Challenged Students:** Facilities include wheelchair ramps, elevators, specially equipped restrooms, special class scheduling, lowered drinking fountains, and lowered telephones. **Special:** There are 15 national honor societies, a freshman honors program, and 11 departmental honors programs. **Visiting:** There are regularly scheduled orientations for prospective students, students visits include a general presentation and an overview panel presentation of student life, career and co-op opportunities, learning center services, and athletics and academic department meetings, and campus tours. There are guides for informal visits and visitors may sit in on classes. To schedule a visit, contact the Admissions Office at admission@suffolk.edu. **Campus Safety and Security:** Measures include 24-hour foot and vehicle patrol, emergency notification system, self-defense education, and security escort services. There are emergency telephones and lighted pathways/sidewalks.

REQUIREMENTS: The SAT or ACT is required. The ACT Optional Writing test is also required. Applicants should have a high school diploma or the GED. Recommended secondary preparation includes 4 years of English, 3 of math, 2 each of a foreign language and science, and 1 of American history. Exact requirements differ by degree program. A personal essay is required, and an interview is recommended. A GPA of 2.0 is required. AP and CLEP credits are accepted. Important factors in the admissions decision are advanced placement or honors courses, recommendations by school officials, and leadership record. All students must complete their semester hours with at least a 2.0 GPA. Distribution requirements vary by degree program. **Procedure:** Freshmen are admitted fall, spring, and summer. Entrance exams should be taken by December of the senior year. There are early admissions and deferred admissions plans. Early decision applications should be filed by November 15; regular applications, by March 1 for fall entry; and December 15 for spring entry, along with a $50 fee. Notification of early decision is sent December 20; regular decision, January 15. 423 applicants were on the 2014 waiting list; 99 were admitted. Applications are accepted on-line. **Transfer Students:** 448 transfer students enrolled in 2013-2014. Applicants should have a minimum 2.5 GPA from an accredited college. Those with fewer than 15 college credits must submit a high school transcript. 30 of 120 credits required for the bachelor's degree must be completed at Suffolk. **International Students:** There are 1219 international students enrolled. The school actively recruits these students. They must take the TOEFL with a minimum score of 550 on the paper-based TOEFL (PBT) or 80 on the Internet-based version (iBT). They must also take the SAT or ACT and the college's own entrance exam.

ADMISSIONS: 84% of the 2014-2015 applicants were accepted. The SAT scores for the 2014-2015 freshman class were: Critical Reading--47% below 500, 38% between 500 and 599, 14% between 600 and 699, and 1% between 700 and 800; Math--41% below 500, 42% between 500 and 599, 15% between 600 and 699, and 2% between

700 and 800; Writing--44% below 500, 40% between 500 and 599, 14% between 600 and 699, and 1% between 700 and 800. The ACT scores were 33% below 21, 31% between 21 and 23, 23% between 24 and 26, 6% between 27 and 28, and 4% above 28. 30% of the current freshmen were in the top fifth of their class; 60% were in the top two fifths. 4 freshmen graduated first in their class. **Admissions Contact:** John Hamel, Director of Undergraduate Admissions. E-Mail: *admission@suffolk.edu* Web: *www.suffolk.edu*

FINANCIAL AID: In 2014-2015, 93% of all full-time freshmen and 70% of continuing full-time students received some form of financial aid. 72% of all full-time freshmen and 69% of continuing full-time students received need-based aid. The average freshman award was $22,253. Need-based scholarships or need-based grants averaged $3,458 ($32,660 maximum); need-based self-help aid (loans and jobs) averaged $2,917 ($3,500 maximum); and other non-need-based awards and non-need-based scholarships averaged $9,654 ($32,660 maximum). 15% of undergraduate students work part-time. Average annual earnings from campus work are $1653. The FAFSA and the college's own financial statement, and verification of income are required. The deadline for filing freshman financial aid applications for fall entry is February 15.

TUFTS UNIVERSITY   D-2
www.tufts.edu

Medford, MA 02155   (617) 627-3170
n/av

Fax: (617) 627-3860	Email: admissions.inquiry@ase.tufts.edu
Full-time: 2541 men, 2603 women	Faculty: 480; I, +$
Part-time: 36 men, 52 women	Ph.D.s: 93%
Graduate: 2368 men, 3283 women	Student/Faculty: 9 to 1
Year: semesters, summer session	Tuition: $46,598
Room & Board: $12,182	Freshman Class: 16389 applied, 3503 accepted, 1309 enrolled
SAT CR/M/W: 715/720/720 ACT: 32	CEEB CODE: 3901
Application Deadline: January 1	MOST COMPETITIVE

Tufts University, founded in 1852, is a private institution offering undergraduate programs in liberal arts and sciences and engineering. Figures in the above capsule and in this profile are approximate and apply to the Medford/Somerville campus resources unless otherwise noted. There are 2 undergraduate schools and 8 graduate schools. In addition to regional accreditation, Tufts has baccalaureate program accreditation with ABET, ADA, and CAHEA. The 150-acre campus is in a suburban area 5 miles northwest of Boston. Including any residence halls, there are 135 buildings.

STUDENT LIFE: 77% of undergraduates are from out of state, mostly the Northeast. Students are from 50 states, 56 foreign countries, and Canada. 64% are from public schools. 56% are White; 11% Asian American. **Male To Female Ratio:** 1.2:1. The average age of freshmen is 18; all undergraduates, 20. 3% do not continue beyond their first year; 92% remain to graduate. **Housing:** 3372 students can be accommodated in college housing, which includes single-sex and coed dorms and on-campus apartments. In addition, there are language houses, special-interest houses, fraternity houses and cooperative houses. On-campus housing is available on a lottery system for upperclassmen. 63% of students live on campus. Upperclassmen may keep cars.

FACULTY/CLASSROOMS: 58% of faculty are male; 42% are female. All teach and do research. No introductory courses are taught by graduate students. The average class size in a regular course is 20.

PROGRAMS OF STUDY: Tufts confers B.A., B.S., B.F.A., B.S.C.E., B.S.Ch.E., B.S. Comp. Eng., B.S.E., B.S.E.E., B.S.E.S., B.S. Environmental Eng., B.S.M.E., B.S.B.M.E. and B.S.C.S degrees. Master's and Doctoral degrees are also awarded. Bachelor's degrees are awarded in BIOLOGICAL SCIENCE (biochemistry, biology/biological science, biophysics, and biotechnology), COMMUNICATIONS AND THE ARTS (Arabic, art history and appreciation, Chinese, classics, dramatic arts, English, French, German, Greek, Italian, Japanese, Latin, music, Russian, and Spanish), COMPUTER AND PHYSICAL SCIENCE (applied mathematics, applied physics, astrophysics, chemical physics, chemistry, computer science, geology, mathematics, and physics), ENGINEERING AND ENVIRONMENTAL DESIGN (architecture, biomedical engineering, chemical engineering, civil engineering, computer engineering, electrical/electronics engineering, engineering, engineering and applied science, engineering physics, environmental engineering, environmental science, and mechanical engineering), HEALTH PROFESSIONS (community health work), SOCIAL SCIENCE (African studies, American studies, anthropology, archeology, Asian/Oriental studies, biopsychology, child psychology/development, cognitive science, economics, German area studies, history, international relations, Judaic studies, Latin American studies, Middle Eastern studies, peace studies, philosophy, political science/government, psychology, religion, Russian and Slavic studies, sociology, urban studies, and women's studies). International relations, engineering, philosophy, biology, cognitive and brain science are the strongest academically. International relations, economics, and political science have the largest enrollments.

ACTIVITIES: 14% of men belong to 1 local and 9 national fraternities; 11% of women belong to 4 national sororities. There are 285 groups on campus, including Leonard Carmichael Society (community service), art, band, cheerleading, chess, choir, chorale, chorus, communications, computers, dance, debate, drama, environmental, ethnic, film, forensics, gay, honors, international, jazz band, literary magazine, marching band, musical theater, newspaper, opera, orchestra, pep band, photography, political, professional, radio and TV, religious, social, social service, student government, symphony, Tufts Mountain Club (outdoors), and yearbook. Popular campus events include Tuftonia's Day, Fan the Fire Athletics Event, student and faculty directed arts performances, and EPIIC International Symposium.

Sports: There are 14 intercollegiate sports for men and 15 for women, and 17 intramural sports for men and 18 for women. Facilities include Steve Tisch Sports and Fitness Center, football stadium, 2 gyms, an 8-lane all-weather track, 9 tennis courts, a field house, an indoor cage, an indoor track, 7 squash courts, a swimming pool, a dance room, a weight room, spin studio, yoga studio, a sauna, a sailing center, an exercise center, film room, and baseball, softball, soccer, lacrosse, and playing fields. **Graduates:** From July 1, 2013 to June 30, 2014, 1396 bachelor's degrees were awarded. The most popular majors were international relations (13%), economics (6%), and biology (6%). 150 companies recruited on campus in 2013-2014. In an average class, 87% graduate in 4 years or less and 92% graduate in 6 years or less. Of the 2013 graduating class, 18% were enrolled in graduate school within 6 months of graduation, and 58% were employed.

SERVICES: Counseling and information services are available, as is tutoring in every subject, as needed through the Academic Resources Center. There is a reader service for the blind. Services are also available through other campus offices, groups, classes, and offices.

Library/Resources: The 2 libraries contain 1.1 million volumes, 1.2 million microform items, 62,320 audio/video tapes/CDs/DVDs, and subscribe to 63,462 periodicals including electronic. Computerized library services include interlibrary loans, database searching, Internet access, and Wi-Fi capability. Special learning facilities include an art gallery, radio station, TV station, a 300 seat recital hall, theater in the round, center for scientific visualization (ultra high resolution display wall w/HD capability). **Physically Challenged Students:** 90% of the campus is accessible. Facilities include wheelchair ramps, elevators, special parking, specially equipped restrooms, special class scheduling, lowered drinking fountains, lowered telephones. **Special:** The university offers cross-registration at Boston University, Boston College, and Brandeis University, a Washington semester, domestic exchanges with Swarthmore College or Spellman College, and study abroad in England, Spain, France, Chile, Japan, Ghana, China, Hong Kong, and Germany. Many internships are available. Double majors in the liberal arts are common; student-designed majors are possible. There is a 5-year B.A./M.A. or B.S./M.S. program in liberal arts or engineering, a B.A.-B.F.A. program with the Museum School of Fine Arts, and a B.A.-B.M. program with the New England Conservatory of Music. There are 4 national honor societies and Phi Beta Kappa.

Visiting: There are regularly scheduled orientations for prospective students. There are guides for informal visits and visitors may sit in on classes. To schedule a visit, contact the Admissions Office.

Campus Safety and Security: Measures include 24-hour foot and vehicle patrol, emergency notification system, self-defense education, and security escort services. There are shuttle buses, emergency telephones, lighted pathways/sidewalks, and controlled access to dorms/residences.

REQUIREMENTS: The SAT or ACT is required. The ACT Optional Writing test is also required. The university accepts either the SAT Reasoning Test and the results of 2 SAT: Subject tests or the ACT with Writing Section. Liberal arts applicants should take the 2 SAT: Subject test of their choice; engineering applicants should take a math level I or II, and either physics or chemistry. In addition, all applicants should be high school graduates or hold the GED. Academic preparation is expected to include 4 years each of English, foreign language, social studies, math, and natural sciences. AP credits are accepted. Important factors in the admissions decision are advanced placement or honors courses, recommendations by school officials, and personality/intangible qualities. Liberal arts students must complete 34 courses, 10 of them in the area of concentration. Requirements include foundation courses in writing, quantitative reasoning, and foreign language or culture and courses in humanities, arts, social sciences, math, and natural sciences. Requirements for engineering students include a total of 38 courses, 10 are engineering introduction courses, 8 are engineering foundation courses, 12 of them in the area of concentration, and distribution requirements in English, humanities, arts, and social sciences. **Procedure:** Freshmen are admitted fall. Entrance exams should be taken by January of the senior year. There are early decision and deferred admissions plans. Early decision applications should be filed by November 1; regular applications, by January 1 for fall entry, along with a $70 fee. Notification of early decision is sent December 15; regular decision, April 1. 546 early decision candidates were accepted for the 2014-2015 class. Applications are accepted on-line. **Transfer Students:** 50 transfer students enrolled in 2013-2014. Admission is competitive. Primary consideration is given to college and secondary school achievement and record of personal involvement. Transfer students must submit the Common Application for Transfer Students, the Tufts Supplement, transcripts from both high school and college, a college official's report, letters of recommendation, as well as either the SAT or the ACT with Writing. 17 of 34 credits required for the bachelor's degree must be completed at Tufts. **International Students:** There are 334 international students enrolled. The school actively recruits these students. They must take the TOEFL with a minimum score of 650 on the paper-based TOEFL (PBT) or 100 on the Internet-based version (iBT), IELTS exam is also accepted. They must also take the SAT or ACT. The student must also take the ACT with Writing or the SAT Reasoning Test and 2 SAT subject tests.

ADMISSIONS: 21% of the 2014-2015 applicants were accepted. The SAT scores for the 2014-2015 freshman class were: Critical Reading--6% between 500 and 599, 30% between 600 and 699, and 64% between 700 and 800; Math--3% between 500 and 599, 28% between 600 and 699, and 69% between 700 and 800; Writing--4% between 500 and 599, 32% between 600 and 699, and 64% between 700 and 800. 99% of the current freshmen were in the top fifth of their class; 100% were in the top two fifths. There were 76 National Merit finalists. **Admissions Contact:** Lee A. Coffin, Dean of Admissions. E-Mail: *admissions.inquiry@ase.tufts.edu* Web: *www.tufts.edu*

FINANCIAL AID: In 2014-2015, 38% of all full-time freshmen and 39% of continuing full-time students received some form of financial aid. 38% of all full-time freshmen and 39% of continuing full-time students received need-based aid. The average freshman award was $35,839. Need-based scholarships or need-based grants averaged $34,098; and need-based self-help aid (loans and jobs) averaged $3,909. Tufts is a member of CSS. The CSS/Profile and FAFSA, and parent and student federal income tax forms are required. The deadline for filing freshman financial aid applications for fall entry is February 15.

UNIVERSITY OF MASSACHUSETTS AMHERST   **B-2**

www.umass.edu

Amherst, MA 01003   (413) 545-0222
    n/av

Fax: (413) 545-4312	Email: mail@admissions.umass.edu
Full-time: 10704 men, 9980 women	Faculty: 1232; I, +$
Part-time: 639 men, 929 women	Ph.D.s: 94%
Graduate: 3144 men, 3239 women	Student/Faculty: 17 to 1
Year: semesters, summer session	Tuition: $13,258 ($28,813)
Room & Board: $10,957	Freshman Class: 35868 applied, 22556 accepted, 4621 enrolled
SAT CR/M: 590/620 ACT: 27	CEEB CODE: 0917
Application Deadline: January 15	VERY COMPETITIVE+

Established in 1863, University of Massachusetts Amherst is a public research, land-grant institution offering over 100 academic majors. There are 8 undergraduate schools and 8 graduate schools. In addition to regional accreditation, UMass Amherst has baccalaureate program accreditation with AACSB, ABET, ASLA, FIDER, NASM, NCATE, NLN, SAF, ACBSP, ACPHA, ACS, APA, ASLHA, CCNE, and CEPH. The 1463-acre campus is in a small town 90 miles west of Boston and 60 miles north of Hartford, Connecticut. Including any residence halls, there are 318 buildings.

STUDENT LIFE: 77% of undergraduates are from Massachusetts. Others are from 49 states, 71 foreign countries, and Canada. 68% are White. **Male To Female Ratio:** 1.0:1. The average age of freshmen is 18; all undergraduates, 21. 10% do not continue beyond their first year; 76% remain to graduate. **Housing:** 13,436 students can be accommodated in college housing, which includes single-sex and coed dorms, on-campus apartments, and married student housing. In addition, there are honors houses, language houses, special-interest houses, fraternity houses, sorority houses, and first-year housing. On-campus housing is guaranteed for the freshman year only and is available on a lottery system for upperclassmen. 65% of students live on campus. All students may keep cars.

FACULTY/CLASSROOMS: 57% of faculty are male; 43% are female. All teach and do research. No introductory courses are taught by graduate students.

PROGRAMS OF STUDY: UMass Amherst confers B.A., B.S., B.B.A., B.F.A., B.G.S. and B.Mus. degrees. Associate, Master's, and Doctoral degrees are also awarded. Bachelor's degrees are awarded in AGRICULTURE (agricultural economics, animal science, natural resource management, plant science, soil science, and wood science), BIOLOGICAL SCIENCE (biochemistry, biology/biological science, microbiology, and nutrition), BUSINESS (accounting, banking and finance, business administration and management, hospitality management services, marketing management, operations management, and sports management), COMMUNICATIONS AND THE ARTS (art history and appreciation, Chinese, classics, communications, comparative literature, dance, dramatic arts, English, Germanic languages and literature, Japanese, journalism, linguistics, music, music performance, Portuguese, Spanish, and studio art), COMPUTER AND PHYSICAL SCIENCE (astronomy, chemistry, computer science, earth science, geology, mathematics, physics, and science), EDUCATION (education), ENGINEERING AND ENVIRONMENTAL DESIGN (architecture, chemical engineering, civil engineering, computer engineering, construction technology, electrical/electronics engineering, environmental design, environmental science, industrial engineering, landscape architecture/design, and mechanical engineering), HEALTH PROFESSIONS (exercise science, nursing, predentistry, premedicine, preveterinary science, public health, and speech pathology/audiology), SOCIAL SCIENCE (African American studies, anthropology, economics, food science, French studies, gender studies, geography, history, interdisciplinary studies, Italian studies, Judaic studies, law, liberal arts/general studies, Middle Eastern studies, philosophy, political science/government, psychology, Russian and Slavic studies, sociology, and women's studies). Psychology, biology, and management have the largest enrollments.

ACTIVITIES: 8% of men belong to 1 local and 19 national fraterni-

ties; 6% of women belong to 2 local and 15 national sororities. There are 365 groups on campus, including art, band, cheerleading, chess, choir, chorale, chorus, communications, computers, dance, debate, drama, environmental, ethnic, film, gay, honors, international, jazz band, literary magazine, marching band, musical theater, newspaper, opera, orchestra, pep band, photography, political, professional, radio and TV, religious, social, social service, student government, student-owned businesses, and symphony. Popular campus events include First Week, Festival of the Arts, Multicultural Film Festival, Cultural Night, Jazz in July, and Center Series Events. **Sports:** There are 9 intercollegiate sports for men and 10 for women, and 21 intramural sports for men and 22 for women. Facilities include 120 acres of multipurpose fields, softball and soccer fields, a 20,000-seat football stadium, a track, and 22 tennis courts. Indoor facilities include a 120,000-sq-ft recreation center with weight and fitness equipment, a 3-court gym, a wellness center, and an elevated jogging track. Other facilities include 3 pools, 3 handball/squash, racquetball courts, 2 gyms, a wrestling room, 2 dance studios, weight-training rooms, fitness centers, basketball/volleyball/badminton courts, and an indoor track. The indoor sports arena has 10,500 seats and 2 Olympic-sized ice sheets. Body shops are also available in residential areas. **Graduates:** From July 1, 2013 to June 30, 2014, 5737 bachelor's degrees were awarded. The most popular majors were psychology (9%), communication (6%), and biology (4%). 312 companies recruited on campus in 2013-2014. In an average class, 63% graduate in 4 years or less, 72% graduate in 5 years or less, and 76% graduate in 6 years or less. Of the 2013 graduating class, 21% were enrolled in graduate school within 6 months of graduation, and 73% were employed.

SERVICES: Counseling and information services are available, as is tutoring in most subjects. There is a reader service for the blind. **Library/Resources:** The 2 libraries contain 4.4 million volumes, 2.0 million microform items, 46,814 audio/video tapes/CDs/DVDs, and subscribe to 236,676 periodicals including electronic. Computerized library services include interlibrary loans, database searching, Internet access, and Wi-Fi capability. Special learning facilities include an art gallery, radio station, TV station, including botanical gardens, a astronomical observatory, and learning commons. **Physically Challenged Students:** All of the campus is accessible. Facilities include wheelchair ramps, elevators, special parking, specially equipped restrooms, special class scheduling, lowered drinking fountains, lowered telephones, special housing. All programs are made accessible through accommodations. **Special:** Cross-registration is possible with Smith, Mount Holyoke, Hampshire, and Amherst Colleges. Co-op programs, internships in every major, study abroad in more than 70 countries, domestic exchange, a Washington semester, work-study programs, dual majors, and B.A.-B.S. degrees are available. Accelerated degrees are currently offered in economics, communication, and environmental design and are being planned for other programs, including management. The Bachelor's Degree with Individual Concentration (BDIC) is also available. The Commonwealth Honors College welcomes honor students who meet entrance requirements. There are also teacher certification, distance learning, independent study, and ESL programs. There are 46 national honor societies, including Phi Beta Kappa, a freshman honors program, and 75 departmental honors programs. **Visiting:** There are regularly scheduled orientations for prospective students, including 3 guided tours daily weekdays, 2 tours daily on weekends and twice-daily information sessions. There are guides for informal visits and visitors may sit in on classes.. **Campus Safety and Security:** Measures include 24-hour foot and vehicle patrol, emergency notification system, self-defense education, and security escort services. There are shuttle buses, emergency telephones, lighted pathways/sidewalks, and controlled access to dorms/residences.

REQUIREMENTS: The SAT is required. Applicants must be graduates of an accredited secondary school or have the GED. The university recommends that students complete 16 Carnegie units including 4 years of English, 3 years each of math, and science (including 2 years lab), and 2 years each of electives, foreign language, and social studies. 4 years of math are required for business, computer science, and engineering majors. Students must present a portfolio for admission to the art program and must audition for admission to music and dance. AP and CLEP credits are accepted. Important factors in the admissions decision are advanced placement or honors courses, extracur-

ricular activities record, and recommendations by school officials. Students must complete 120 credit hours and maintain a minimum GPA of 2.0 overall and in the major. For the general education requirement, students must take 4 courses in Social World, 2 courses in Social and Cultural Diversity, 2 courses in Biological and Physical World, 2 courses in Writing, and 1 each in Basic Math Skills, Integrative Experience, and Analytic Reasoning. There is an Interdisciplinary option. **Procedure:** Freshmen are admitted fall and spring. Entrance exams should be taken as soon as possible after admissions deadline. There are early admissions, deferred admissions, and rolling admissions plans. Applications should be filed by January 15 for fall entry; October 1 for spring entry, along with a $75 fee. Notifications are sent in March. 1403 applicants were on the 2014 waiting list; 26 were admitted. Applications are accepted on-line. **Transfer Students:** 1158 transfer students enrolled in 2013-2014. Transfer applicants must submit transcripts from all colleges or universities attended and an essay. Those with fewer than 27 credits must submit high school transcripts and SAT scores. Priority is given to students with an associate degree. Grades of C- or better in comparable coursework transfer for credit. 45 of 120 credits required for the bachelor's degree must be completed at UMass Amherst. **International Students:** There are 681 international students enrolled. The school actively recruits these students. They must take the TOEFL with a minimum score of 80 on the Internet-based version (iBT). They must also take the SAT or ACT.

ADMISSIONS: 63% of the 2014-2015 applicants were accepted. The SAT scores for the 2014-2015 freshman class were: Critical Reading--8% below 500, 44% between 500 and 599, 39% between 600 and 699, and 9% between 700 and 800; Math--3% below 500, 33% between 500 and 599, 49% between 600 and 699, and 16% between 700 and 800. The ACT scores were 2% below 21, 10% between 21 and 23, 31% between 24 and 26, 21% between 27 and 28, and 36% above 28. 57% of the current freshmen were in the top fifth of their class; 92% were in the top two fifths. **Admissions Contact:** Kevin Kelly, Director of Admissions. E-Mail: *mail@admissions.umass.edu* Web: *www.umass.edu*

FINANCIAL AID: In 2014-2015, 57% of all full-time freshmen and 60% of continuing full-time students received some form of financial aid. 51% of all full-time freshmen and 50% of continuing full-time students received need-based aid. The average freshman award was $14,197. Need-based scholarships or need-based grants averaged $8,971; need-based self-help aid (loans and jobs) averaged $3,766; non-need-based athletic scholarships averaged $22,784; and other non-need-based awards and non-need-based scholarships averaged $4,386. The average financial indebtedness of the 2014 graduate was $28,999. UMass Amherst is a member of CSS. The FAFSA is required. The priority date for freshman financial aid applications for fall entry is March 1.

UNIVERSITY OF MASSACHUSETTS BOSTON   E-2

www.umb.edu

Boston, MA 02125	(617) 287-6000 n/av
Fax: (617) 287-5999	Email: enrollment.info@umb.edu
Full-time: 4169 men, 4890 women	Faculty: 602; I, av$
Part-time: 1240 men, 1809 women	Ph.D.s: 96%
Graduate: 746 men, 1431 women	Student/Faculty: 15 to 1
Year: semesters, summer session	Tuition: $11,966 ($28,390)
Room & Board: $11,100	Freshman Class: 8453 applied, 5981 accepted, 1542 enrolled
SAT CR/M: 515/535 ACT: required	CEEB CODE: 3924
Application Deadline: April 1	VERY COMPETITIVE

The University of Massachusetts Boston, established in 1964, is a public research institution offering undergraduate studies in arts and sciences and in preprofessional training. There are 8 undergraduate schools and 10 graduate schools. In addition to regional accreditation, UMass Boston has baccalaureate program accreditation with AACSB, ABET, AACTE, ACS, APA, CCNE, and AACSB. The 187-

acre campus is in an urban area 5 miles south of downtown Boston. Including any residence halls, there are 8 buildings.

STUDENT LIFE: 95% of undergraduates are from Massachusetts. Others are from 40 states, 151 foreign countries, and Canada. 45% are White; 13% African American. **Male To Female Ratio:** 1.3:1. The average age of freshmen is 19; all undergraduates, 25. 21% do not continue beyond their first year; 38% remain to graduate. Alcohol is not permitted. All students commute. All students may keep cars.

FACULTY/CLASSROOMS: 51% of faculty are male; 49% are female. All teach undergraduates. No introductory courses are taught by graduate students. The average class size in an introductory lecture is 27; in a laboratory is 16; and in a regular course is 27.

PROGRAMS OF STUDY: UMass Boston confers B.A., and B.S. degrees. Master's and Doctoral degrees are also awarded. Bachelor's degrees are awarded in BIOLOGICAL SCIENCE (biochemistry and biology/biological science), BUSINESS (labor studies and management science), COMMUNICATIONS AND THE ARTS (art, classical languages, classics, communications, dramatic arts, English, French, information technology, Italian, music, and Spanish), COMPUTER AND PHYSICAL SCIENCE (chemistry, computer science, earth science, information sciences and systems, mathematics, and physics), EDUCATION (early childhood education), ENGINEERING AND ENVIRONMENTAL DESIGN (electrical and computer engineering, engineering, and engineering physics), HEALTH PROFESSIONS (exercise science, medical technology, and nursing), SOCIAL SCIENCE (African American studies, American studies, anthropology, asian studies, community services, criminal justice, economics, ethics, politics, and social policy, geography, gerontology, Hispanic American studies, history, human services, paralegal studies, philosophy, physical fitness/movement, political science/government, psychology, sociology, and women's studies). Management, nursing, and psychology have the largest enrollments.

ACTIVITIES: There are no fraternities or sororities. There are 100 groups on campus, including radio, concert band, model UN, music ensembles, art, band, campus ministries, cheerleading, chess, choir, chorale, chorus, computers, dance, drama, ethnic, film, gay, honors, international, jazz band, literary magazine, musical theater, newspaper, orchestra, photography, political, professional, religious, social, social service, and student government. Popular campus events include Convocation Day, Seasonal Festivals and Lecture Series. **Sports:** There are 8 intercollegiate sports for men and 8 for women, and 12 intramural sports for men and 12 for women. Facilities include an athletic center with a 3500-seat gym with 4 basketball and 2 volleyball courts, an ice rink that seats 1000, a Olympic-size swimming pool with high-dive area, a multipurpose weight room, a sports medicine area; an 8-lane, 400-meter track; 8 tennis courts; a softball diamond, 3 multipurpose fields primarily used for soccer and lacrosse, and other recreational fields; a boat house, dock, and fleet of sailboats and rowing dories; and a fitness center with strength-training equipment. **Graduates:** From July 1, 2013 to June 30, 2014, 2366 bachelor's degrees were awarded. The most popular majors were business/marketing (20%), health professions and related programs (18%), and social sciences (12%). In an average class, 13% graduate in 4 years or less, 32% graduate in 5 years or less, and 38% graduate in 6 years or less.

SERVICES: Counseling and information services are available, as is tutoring in every subject. There is a reader service for the blind, and remedial math, reading, and writing. There are also reading study skills workshops and a math resource center available. **Library/Resources:** The library contains 985,400 volumes, 803,284 microform items, and subscribes to 411,534 periodicals including electronic. Computerized library services include interlibrary loans, database searching, Internet access, and Wi-Fi capability. Special learning facilities include an art gallery, planetarium, tropical greenhouse, observatory, adaptive computer lab, languages lab, and applied language and math center. **Physically Challenged Students:** All of the campus is accessible. Facilities include wheelchair ramps, elevators, special parking, specially equipped restrooms, special class scheduling, lowered drinking fountains, lowered telephones, amplified phones, powered doors, indoor-connected building access, an accessible shuttle bus, an adaptive computer lab, and a center for students with disabilities. **Special:** Students may cross-register with Boston Public Colleges, Massachusetts College of Art, Bunker Hill Community College, Rox-

bury Community College, and Hebrew College. UMass Boston also offers cooperative programs, internships, study abroad, work-study programs, student-designed majors, B.A.-B.S. degrees, nondegree study, pass/fail options, and dual and interdisciplinary majors, including anthropology/history, biology/medical technology, philosophy/public policy, and psychology/sociology. Also available are 3-1 and 2-2 engineering programs with various area institutions. The College of Public and Community Service provides social-oriented education, There are 3 national honor societies and a freshman honors program. **Visiting:** There are regularly scheduled orientations for prospective students, including general information sessions about the university and the admissions process and a tour of the campus. There are guides for informal visits and visitors may sit in on classes. To schedule a visit, contact the Enrollment Information Services at (617) 287-6000. **Campus Safety and Security:** Measures include 24-hour foot and vehicle patrol, emergency notification system, self-defense education, and security escort services. There are shuttle buses, emergency telephones, lighted pathways/sidewalks, Operation ID, motorist assistance, and crime prevention programs.

REQUIREMENTS: The SAT or ACT is required. Applicants should be graduates of an accredited secondary school. The GED is accepted. The university requires the completion of 16 Carnegie units, including 4 years of English, 3 of college preparatory math and science, 2 each of a foreign language and social studies, and 2 electives in the above academic areas or in humanities, arts, or computer science. A GPA of 3.0 is required. AP and CLEP credits are accepted. For graduation, students must complete 120 credit hours (123 hours in the College of Nursing) and maintain a minimum GPA of 2.0. Distribution requirements vary by college. All students must demonstrate writing proficiency. **Procedure:** Freshmen are admitted fall and spring. Entrance exams should be taken by the fall of the senior year. There are deferred admissions and rolling admissions plans. Applications should be filed by April 1 for fall entry, along with a $60 fee. Notification is sent on a rolling basis. Applications are accepted on-line. **Transfer Students:** 1677 transfer students enrolled in 2013-2014. Applicants with fewer than 24 credits must meet freshman requirements. To transfer, students must have a minimum college GPA of 2.5. Grades of C- or better transfer for credit. 30 of 120 credits required for the bachelor's degree must be completed at UMass Boston. **International Students:** The school actively recruits these students. They must take the TOEFL with a minimum score of 550 on the paper-based TOEFL (PBT) or 79 on the Internet-based version (iBT). They must also take the SAT or ACT if the language of instruction is English.

ADMISSIONS: 71% of the 2014-2015 applicants were accepted. The SAT scores for the 2014-2015 freshman class were: Critical Reading--43% below 500, 39% between 500 and 599, 15% between 600 and 699, and 3% between 700 and 800; Math--29% below 500, 49% between 500 and 599, 19% between 600 and 699, and 3% between 700 and 800. **Admissions Contact:** John Drew, Director of Undergraduate Admissions. E-Mail: *enrollment.info@umb.edu* Web: *www.umb.edu*

FINANCIAL AID: The FAFSA is required. The priority date for freshman financial aid applications for fall entry is March 1.

UNIVERSITY OF MASSACHUSETTS DARTMOUTH   D-4
www.umassd.edu

North Dartmouth, MA 02747   (508) 999-8605
    n/av

Fax: (508) 999-8755   Email: admissions@umassd.edu
Full-time: 3430 men, 2943 women   Faculty: 378; IIA, ++$
Part-time: 455 men, 609 women   Ph.D.s: 89%
Graduate: 753 men, 863 women   Student/Faculty: 17 to 1
Year: semesters, summer session   Tuition: $11,681 ($24,156)
Room & Board: $10,542   Freshman Class: 8119 applied, 6094 accepted, 1435 enrolled

SAT CR/M/W: 510/530/510 **ACT:** 23   CEEB CODE: 3786
Application Deadline: open   COMPETITIVE

University of Massachusetts Dartmouth, founded in 1895, is a public institution that provides undergraduate and graduate programs in the liberal and creative arts and sciences and in professional training. There are 5 undergraduate schools and 3 graduate schools. In addition to regional accreditation, UMass Dartmouth has baccalaureate program accreditation with AACSB, ABET, NASAD, NASDTEC, ACS, NAACLS, and CCNE. The 710-acre campus is in a suburban area approximately 60 miles south of Boston and 28 miles east of Providence, Rhode Island. Including any residence halls, there are 35 buildings.

STUDENT LIFE: 94% of undergraduates are from Massachusetts. Others are from 42 states, 55 foreign countries, and Canada. 88% are from public schools. 66% are White. **Male To Female Ratio:** 1.0:1. The average age of freshmen is 19; all undergraduates, 23. 26% do not continue beyond their first year; 50% remain to graduate. **Housing:** 4494 students can be accommodated in college housing, which includes coed dorms and on-campus apartments. In addition, there are honors houses, special-interest houses, quiet housing, substance awareness housing, apartments and townhouses for upperclassmen. On-campus housing is guaranteed for the freshman year only, is available on a first-come, first-served basis, and is available on a lottery system for upperclassmen. Priority is given to out-of-town students. 54% of students live on campus; of those, 35% remain on campus on weekends. All students may keep cars.

FACULTY/CLASSROOMS: 52% of faculty are male; 48% are female. All teach undergraduates. Graduate students teach 1% of introductory courses. The average class size in an introductory lecture is 33; in a laboratory is 23; and in a regular course is 14.

PROGRAMS OF STUDY: UMass Dartmouth confers B.A., B.S. and B.F.A. degrees. Master's and Doctoral degrees are also awarded. Bachelor's degrees are awarded in BIOLOGICAL SCIENCE (biochemistry, biology/biological science, biotechnology, and marine biology), BUSINESS (accounting, business administration and management, finance, management information systems, marketing/retailing/merchandising, and operations management), COMMUNICATIONS AND THE ARTS (art history and appreciation, ceramic art and design, English, English literature, English Writing, fiber/textiles/weaving, French, graphic design, illustration, metal/jewelry, music, painting, photography, Portuguese, sculpture, Spanish, and visual design), COMPUTER AND PHYSICAL SCIENCE (astronomy and physics, chemistry, computer science, mathematics, physics, and software engineering), EDUCATION (art education), ENGINEERING AND ENVIRONMENTAL DESIGN (bioengineering, civil engineering, computer engineering, electrical/electronics engineering, manufacturing engineering, materials science, and mechanical engineering), HEALTH PROFESSIONS (clinical science, cytotechnology, health science, medical laboratory science, and nursing), SOCIAL SCIENCE (anthropology, criminal justice, economics, history, interdisciplinary studies, liberal arts/general studies, philosophy, political science/government, psychology, sociology, and women and gender studies). Engineering, physical/life sciences and design/fine arts are the strongest academically. nursing, psychology and liberal arts have the largest enrollments.

ACTIVITIES: 1% of men belong to 5 local and 1 national fraternities; 1% of women belong to 3 local and 3 national sororities. There are 128 groups on campus, including art, band, cheerleading, choir, chorale, chorus, computers, dance, drama, ethnic, gay, honors, international, jazz band, literary magazine, musical theater, newspaper, orchestra, political, professional, radio and TV, religious, social, social service, student government, symphony, and yearbook. Popular campus events include Welcome Back Week, Homecoming Weekend and Family Fall Weekend. **Sports:** There are 11 intercollegiate sports for men and 12 for women, and 10 intramural sports for men and 7 for women. Facilities include a 1650-seat gym, an 1250-seat football stadium, an aquatic sports center, 10 tennis courts, a 10,000-sq-ft fitness center, a running track, and soccer, softball, and intramural fields. **Graduates:** From July 1, 2013 to June 30, 2014, 1241 bachelor's degrees were awarded. The most popular majors were marketing (8%), nursing (8%), and accounting (8%).

SERVICES: Counseling and information services are available, as is tutoring in most subjects, through the writing/reading, science/engineering, math/business, and academic resource centers There is a reader service for the blind, and remedial math. **Library/Resources:**

The 2 libraries contain 438,887 volumes, 69,407 microform items, and 7,913 audio/video tapes/CDs/DVDs, and subscribe to 2,783 periodicals including electronic. Computerized library services include interlibrary loans, database searching, Internet access, and Wi-Fi capability. Special learning facilities include an art gallery, radio station, an observatory, marine research vessels, and a number of cultural and research centers. **Physically Challenged Students:** 97% of the campus is accessible. Facilities include wheelchair ramps, elevators, special parking, specially equipped restrooms, special class scheduling, lowered drinking fountains, lowered telephones, special housing. **Special:** The university permits cross-registration through the SACHEM Consortium of 9 schools in Massachusetts. Study abroad in 9 countries, an engineering or business co-op program, a Washington semester, internships, numerous work-study programs, dual majors, service learning opportunities and student-designed majors are available. Non-degree study, pass/fail options, B.S. to M.S. degrees in chemistry, nursing, computer science, electrical engineering, civil engineering, computer engineering, and mechanical engineering, a B.A.-M.A. in psychology, a English B.A. to Professional Writing Master's, a BA - MAT in several fields, along with MPP-JD and MBA - JD programs. There is a freshman honors program. **Visiting:** There are regularly scheduled orientations for prospective students, including scheduled campus tours Monday through Friday and most Saturdays. There are guides for informal visits and visitors may sit in on classes. **Campus Safety and Security:** Measures include 24-hour foot and vehicle patrol, emergency notification system, self-defense education, and security escort services. There are shuttle buses, emergency telephones, lighted pathways/sidewalks, controlled access to dorms/residences, and bicycle patrol.

REQUIREMENTS: The SAT is required. Applicants should have 4 years of English, 3 each of science and math, 2 of the same foreign language, 1 each of social studies and U.S. history, and 2 of college-preparatory electives. The GED is accepted. An audition is necessary for music majors, and a portfolio is recommended for studio arts and design applicants. All applicants must submit an essay. A GPA of 3.0 is required. AP and CLEP credits are accepted. Important factors in the admissions decision are recommendations by school officials, advanced placement or honors courses, and evidence of special talent. Each student must complete the requirements of the 5 clusters that comprise the University Studies curriculum: Cluster 1 Foundations for Engagement, Cluster 2 the Natural World, Cluster 3 the Cultural World, Cluster 4 the Social World and Cluster 5 the Educated and Engaged Citizen. A freshman English composition course is required. Colleges set some additional distribution course requirements. The B.A. requires foreign language study. To graduate, students must complete 120 to 132 credit hours and maintain a 2.0 GPA. **Procedure:** Freshmen are admitted fall and spring. Entrance exams should be taken spring of the junior year or early fall of the senior year. There are deferred admissions and rolling admissions plans. Application deadlines are open. Application fee is $60. Notification of early decision is sent December 15; regular decision, on a rolling basis. Applications are accepted on-line. **Transfer Students:** 475 transfer students enrolled in 2013-2014. Applicants must submit all official college transcripts and must take the SAT unless they graduated from high school more than 3 years prior to applying. Those with fewer than 24 transferable credits may need to submit high school records. 45 of 120 credits required for the bachelor's degree must be completed at UMass Dartmouth. **International Students:** There are 100 international students enrolled. They must take the TOEFL with a minimum score of 520 on the paper-based TOEFL (PBT) or 68 on the Internet-based version (iBT). They must also take the SAT or ACT.

ADMISSIONS: 75% of the 2014-2015 applicants were accepted. The SAT scores for the 2014-2015 freshman class were: Critical Reading--41% below 500, 41% between 500 and 599, 16% between 600 and 699, and 2% between 700 and 800; Math--30% below 500, 47% between 500 and 599, 21% between 600 and 699, and 2% between 700 and 800; Writing--45% below 500, 41% between 500 and 599, 13% between 600 and 699, and 2% between 700 and 800. The ACT scores were 25% below 21, 30% between 21 and 23, 25% between 24 and 26, 6% between 27 and 28, and 14% above 28. 36% of the current freshmen were in the top fifth of their class; 66% were in the top two fifths. 5 freshmen graduated first in their class. **Admissions Contact:** Michael Lynch, Director of Admissions. E-Mail: *admissions@umassd.edu* Web: *www.umassd.edu/undergraduate*

FINANCIAL AID: The FAFSA is required. The priority date for freshman financial aid applications for fall entry is March 1.

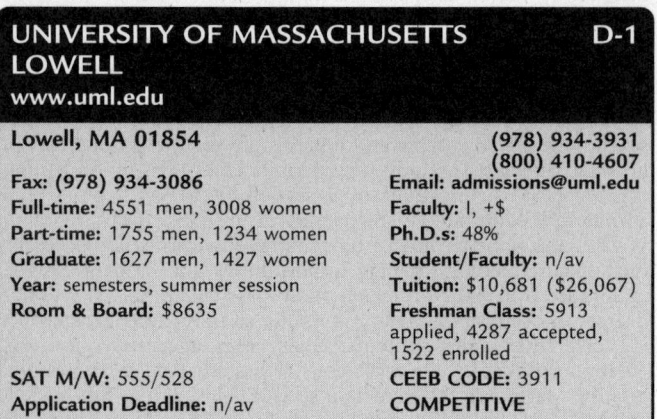

UNIVERSITY OF MASSACHUSETTS LOWELL   **D-1**
www.uml.edu

Lowell, MA 01854   **(978) 934-3931**
   (800) 410-4607

Fax: (978) 934-3086   **Email: admissions@uml.edu**
Full-time: 4551 men, 3008 women   **Faculty:** I, +$
Part-time: 1755 men, 1234 women   **Ph.D.s:** 48%
Graduate: 1627 men, 1427 women   **Student/Faculty:** n/av
Year: semesters, summer session   **Tuition:** $10,681 ($26,067)
Room & Board: $8635   **Freshman Class:** 5913 applied, 4287 accepted, 1522 enrolled

SAT M/W: 555/528
Application Deadline: n/av   **CEEB CODE:** 3911
   COMPETITIVE

The University of Massachussetts Lowell, founded in 1895, is a public institution offering undergraduate programs through the schools of arts and sciences, engineering, health professions, management science, music, and graduate programs in education. The figures in the above capsule and in this profile are approximate. There are 5 undergraduate schools and 1 graduate school. In addition to regional accreditation, UMass Lowell has baccalaureate program accreditation with AACSB, ABET, APTA, CAHEA, CSAB, NASAD, NASM, NCATE, and NLN. The 100-acre campus is in an urban area 30 miles northwest of Boston. Including any residence halls, there are 37 buildings.

STUDENT LIFE: 85% of undergraduates are from Massachusetts. Others are from 43 states, 28 foreign countries, and Canada. 72% are White. **Male To Female Ratio:** 0.7:1. The average age of freshmen is 18; all undergraduates, 23. 21% do not continue beyond their first year; 79% remain to graduate. **Housing:** 3081 students can be accommodated in college housing, which includes single-sex and coed dorms, off-campus apartments, and married student housing. In addition, there are special-interest houses. On-campus housing is guaranteed for the freshman year only, is available on a first-come, and first-served basis. 64% of students commute. All students may keep cars.

FACULTY/CLASSROOMS: 61% of faculty are male; 39% are female. No introductory courses are taught by graduate students.

PROGRAMS OF STUDY: UMass Lowell confers B.A., B.F.A., B.L.A., B.M., B.S., B.S.B.A., B.S.E., B.S.E.T., B.S.I.M. and B.S.I.T. degrees. Associate, Master's, and Doctoral degrees are also awarded. Bachelor's degrees are awarded in BIOLOGICAL SCIENCE (biology/biological science), BUSINESS (business administration and management), COMMUNICATIONS AND THE ARTS (English, fine arts, modern language, and music performance), COMPUTER AND PHYSICAL SCIENCE (applied mathematics, chemistry, computer science, information sciences and systems, mathematics, and physics), ENGINEERING AND ENVIRONMENTAL DESIGN (chemical engineering, civil engineering, electrical/electronics engineering, engineering technology, environmental science, industrial administration/management, industrial engineering technology, mechanical engineering, and plastics engineering), HEALTH PROFESSIONS (clinical science, community health work, exercise science, and nursing), SOCIAL SCIENCE (American studies, criminal justice, economics, history, liberal arts/general studies, philosophy, political science/government, psychology, and sociology). Engineering and management have the largest enrollments.

ACTIVITIES: There are no fraternities or sororities. There are 100 groups on campus, including art, band, cheerleading, computers, drama, ethnic, gay, honors, international, marching band, musical theater, newspaper, pep band, photography, political, professional, radio and TV, religious, social, social service, and student government. **Sports:** There are 15 intercollegiate sports for men and 10 for women, and 34 intramural sports for men and 34 for women. Facilities include a 2,000-seat gym, a pool, weight-training facilities, and

areas for gymnastics, wrestling, and judo. There are also courts for handball, squash, and tennis and various playing fields. **Graduates:** From July 1, 2013 to June 30, 2014, 1337 bachelor's degrees were awarded. The most popular majors were business administration (16%), engineering (11%), and criminal justice (7%). In an average class, 22% graduate in 4 years or less, 44% graduate in 5 years or less, and 46% graduate in 6 years or less.

SERVICES: Counseling and information services are available, as is tutoring in most subjects. There is a reader service for the blind, and remedial writing. **Library/Resources:** The 3 libraries contain 382,599 volumes, 91,022 microform items, 14,353 audio/video tapes/CDs/DVDs, and subscribe to 32,744 periodicals including electronic. Computerized library services include interlibrary loans, database searching, Internet access, and Wi-Fi capability. Special learning facilities include an art gallery, natural history museum, radio station, many experimental and investigative labs, and the Research Foundation, which includes a materials testing division and centers for atmospheric research and tropical disease. **Physically Challenged Students:** 70% of the campus is accessible. Facilities include wheelchair ramps, elevators, special parking, specially equipped restrooms, special class scheduling, lowered drinking fountains, and lowered telephones. **Special:** Cross-registration, co-op, and work-study programs are available, as are opportunities for study abroad. The university offers a combined B.A.-B.S. degree in engineering, dual majors, nondegree study, and pass/fail options. There are 2 national honor societies, a freshman honors program, and 100 departmental honors programs. **Visiting:** There are regularly scheduled orientations for prospective students. To schedule a visit, contact the Office of Student Services at (978) 934-2105. **Campus Safety and Security:** Measures include 24-hour foot and vehicle patrol, self-defense education, and security escort services. There are shuttle buses, emergency telephones, and lighted pathways/sidewalks.

REQUIREMENTS: The SAT or ACT is required, but the SAT is preferred. In addition, applicants should have a high school diploma or the GED. The university recommends that secondary preparation include 4 courses in English, 3 each in social science/history and math, 2 each in science and a foreign language, and 2 academic electives. Prospective music majors must audition, and an interview is recommended for all students. AP and CLEP credits are accepted. All students must complete a minimum of 120 credits with a 2.0 GPA. Core requirements include 6 credits of English composition, 3 credits of human values, and an area distribution requirement of 27 to 29 credits outside the major in behavioral and social science, fine arts and the humanities, and math and the sciences. **Procedure:** Freshmen are admitted fall and spring. Entrance exams should be taken by January of the senior year. There are deferred admissions and rolling admissions plans. Application deadlines are open. Application fee is $40. 89 applicants were on the 2014 waiting list; 27 were admitted. Applications are accepted on-line. **Transfer Students:** 935 transfer students enrolled in 2013-2014. Transfer applicants must present at least a 2.0 GPA in previous college work. Those with fewer than 30 credits must meet freshman admission requirements. 30 of 120 credits required for the bachelor's degree must be completed at UMass Lowell. **International Students:** There are 55 international students enrolled. They must take the TOEFL with a minimum score of 550 on the paper-based TOEFL (PBT) or 79 on the Internet-based version (iBT). They must also take the SAT or ACT.

ADMISSIONS: 73% of the 2014-2015 applicants were accepted. The SAT scores for the 2014-2015 freshman class were: Critical Reading--34% below 500, 48% between 500 and 599, 16% between 600 and 699, and 2% between 700 and 800; Math--23% below 500, 47% between 500 and 599, 27% between 600 and 699, and 3% between 700 and 800. 15% of the current freshmen were in the top fifth of their class; 58% were in the top two fifths. 8 freshmen graduated first in their class. **Admissions Contact:** Kerrie Johnston, Director of Admissions. E-Mail: *admissions@uml.edu* Web: *www.uml.edu*

FINANCIAL AID: In 2014-2015, 94% of all full-time freshmen and continuing full-time students received some form of financial aid. 94% of all full-time freshmen and continuing full-time students received need-based aid. The average freshman award was $12,705. Need-based scholarships or need-based grants averaged $6,805; need-based self-help aid (loans and jobs) averaged $6,593; non-need-based athletic scholarships averaged $4,834; and other non-need-based awards and non-need-based scholarships averaged $2,435. 16% of undergraduate students work part-time. Average annual earnings from campus work are $3090. The average financial indebtedness of the 2014 graduate was $21,542. The FAFSA is required. The priority date for freshman financial aid applications for fall entry is March 1.

WELLESLEY COLLEGE — D-2
www.wellesley.edu

Wellesley, MA 02481	**(781) 283-2270**
	n/av
Fax: (781) 283-3678	Email: admission@wellesley.edu
Full-time: 2160 women	Faculty: 346; IIB, ++$
Part-time: 12 women	Ph.D.s: 94%
Graduate: n/av	Student/Faculty: 7 to 1
Year: semesters, summer session	Tuition: $45,078
Room & Board: $13,960	Freshman Class: 4667 applied, 1418 accepted, 593 enrolled
SAT CR/M/W: 692/686/699 ACT: 30	CEEB CODE: 3957
Application Deadline: January 15	MOST COMPETITIVE

Wellesley College, founded in 1870, ranked among the United States' top liberal arts and sciences colleges. Wellesley has a deep tradition of educating women who will make a difference in the world. Living and learning on a campus, just outside of Boston, full of self-directed and intellectually curious women helps students develop the skills needed to succeed in all professional fields, including those traditionally dominated by men. Every resource at the College is devoted to undergraduate women. Students have extraordinary opportunities to cultivate their leadership abilities and gain lifelong access to a legendary network of accomplished Wellesley alumnae. There is 1 undergraduate school. The 500-acre campus is in a suburban area 12 miles west of Boston. Including any residence halls, there are 64 buildings.

STUDENT LIFE: 84% of undergraduates are from out of state, mostly the Middle Atlantic. Students are from 50 states, 93 foreign countries, and Canada. 59% are from public schools. 40% are White; 23% Asian American; 12% Foreign. The student base is all female. The average age of freshmen is 18; all undergraduates, 20. 6% do not continue beyond their first year; 94% remain to graduate. **Housing:** 2211 students can be accommodated in college housing, which includes single-sex dorms. In addition, there are language houses, special-interest houses, language corridors, and co-ops. On-campus housing is guaranteed for all 4 years. 97% of students live on campus; of those, 97% remain on campus on weekends. Upperclassmen may keep cars.

FACULTY/CLASSROOMS: 44% of faculty are male; 56% are female. All teach and do research. No introductory courses are taught by graduate students. The average class size in an introductory lecture is 30 and in a regular course is 19.

PROGRAMS OF STUDY: Wellesley confers B.A. degrees. Bachelor's degrees are awarded in AGRICULTURE (environmental studies), BIOLOGICAL SCIENCE (biochemistry, biology/biological science, and neurosciences), COMMUNICATIONS AND THE ARTS (art history and appreciation, Chinese, comparative literature, dramatic arts, English, film arts, French, German, Greek, Japanese, Latin, music, Russian, Russian languages and literature, Spanish, and studio art), COMPUTER AND PHYSICAL SCIENCE (astronomy, astrophysics, chemistry, computer science, geology, mathematics, and physics), ENGINEERING AND ENVIRONMENTAL DESIGN (architecture), SOCIAL SCIENCE (African American studies, American studies, anthropology, archeology, Asian/Oriental studies, classical/ancient civilization, cognitive science, economics, French studies, German area studies, history, international relations, Italian studies, Japanese studies, Judaic studies, Latin American studies, medieval studies, Middle Eastern studies, peace studies, philosophy, political science/government, psychology, religion, sociology, and women's studies). Psychology, English, economics, political science, and biological sciences have the largest enrollments.

ACTIVITIES: There are no fraternities or sororities. There are 160 groups on campus, including art, cheerleading, chess, choir, chorale, chorus, communications, computers, dance, debate, drama, environmental, ethnic, film, gay, honors, international, jazz band, literary magazine, musical theater, newspaper, orchestra, photography, political, professional, radio and TV, religious, social, social service, student government, symphony, and yearbook. Popular campus events include Lake Day, Marathon Monday/Scream Tunnel, and Spring Concert. **Sports:** There are 13 intercollegiate sports for women, and 21 intramural sports for women. Facilities include an indoor pool, dance studios, a weight room, an indoor track, golf course, courts for racquetball, squash, tennis, and volleyball. **Graduates:** From July 1, 2013 to June 30, 2014, 597 bachelor's degrees were awarded. The most popular majors were economics (16%), psychology (9%), and English (7%). 80 companies recruited on campus in 2013-2014. In an average class, 82% graduate in 4 years or less, 85% graduate in 5 years or less, and 91% graduate in 6 years or less. Of the 2013 graduating class, 18% were enrolled in graduate school within 6 months of graduation, and 65% were employed.

SERVICES: Counseling and information services are available, as is tutoring in every subject. There is a reader service for the blind. **Library/Resources:** The 5 libraries contain 944,870 volumes, 313 microform items, 34,947 audio/video tapes/CDs/DVDs, and subscribe to 90,845 periodicals including electronic. Computerized library services include interlibrary loans, database searching, Internet access, and Wi-Fi capability. Special learning facilities include an art gallery, radio station, a science center, a botanic greenhouse, an observatory, a center for child developmental studies, centers for research on women, and a media and technology center. **Physically Challenged Students:** All of the campus is accessible. Facilities include wheelchair ramps, elevators, special parking, specially equipped restrooms, special class scheduling, lowered drinking fountains, lowered telephones, special housing, signage in braille. **Special:** Students may cross-register at MIT, Brandeis University, or Babson College. Exchange programs are available with Spelman College in Georgia and Mills College in California, with members of the Twelve College Exchange Program, with Williams College's maritime studies program, and with Connecticut College's National Theater Institute. Study abroad is possible through Wellesley-administered programs in France and Germany, exchange programs in Argentina, Japan, Korea, and the United Kingdom, and other programs in Italy, Japan, Spain, South Africa, and China. There are more than 150 approved study abroad programs available. There are summer internship programs in Boston and Washington, D.C. Dual majors, student-designed majors, non-degree study, and pass/fail options are possible. A 3-2 program with MIT, Dartmouth, and Columbia awards a B.A.-B.S. degree. There are 2 national honor societies, including Phi Beta Kappa, and 51 departmental honors programs. **Visiting:** There are regularly scheduled orientations for prospective students. There are guides for informal visits, visitors may sit in on classes, and stay overnight. To schedule a visit, contact the Admission Office at admission@wellesley.edu. **Campus Safety and Security:** Measures include 24-hour foot and vehicle patrol, emergency notification system, self-defense education, and security escort services. There are shuttle buses, emergency telephones, lighted pathways/sidewalks, and controlled access to dorms/residences.

REQUIREMENTS: The SAT or ACT is required. The SAT Reasoning Test and 2 SAT subject tests, or the ACT with Writing are required. Wellesley College does not require a fixed plan of secondary school course preparation. Entering students normally have completed 4 years of college preparatory studies in secondary school that include training in clear and coherent writing and interpreting literature; history; principles of math (typically 4 years); competence in at least 1 foreign language, ancient or modern (usually 4 years of study); and experience in at least 2 lab sciences. An essay is required, and an interview is recommended. AP credits are accepted. Important factors in the admissions decision are advanced placement or honors courses, extracurricular activities record, and leadership record. All students must complete 32 units, at least 8 of which are in the major field, with a minimum 2.0 GPA. Requirements include 3 courses each in humanities, social science, and natural science and math, 1 multicultural course, 1 semester of expository writing in any department, and 2 credits in phys ed. Students must also possess proficiency in a modern or ancient foreign language. A thesis is required for departmental honors. A quantitative reasoning requirement must be satisfied by all students. **Procedure:** Freshmen are admitted fall. Entrance exams should be taken during the spring of the junior year or fall of the senior year . There are early decision and deferred admissions plans. Early decision applications should be filed by November 1; regular applications, by January 15 for fall entry. Notification of early decision is sent December 15; regular decision, April 1. 147 early decision candidates were accepted for the 2014-2015 class. 687 applicants were on the 2014 waiting list; 85 were admitted. Applications are accepted on-line. Application fees are waived if application is completed on-line. **Transfer Students:** 19 transfer students enrolled in 2013-2014. Applicants must provide high school and college transcripts, SAT or ACT scores if they submitted them to their current institution, a personal statement, and a statement of good standing from institutions previously attended. 16 of 32 credits required for the bachelor's degree must be completed at Wellesley. **International Students:** There are 280 international students enrolled. The school actively recruits these students. They must also take the SAT or ACT.

ADMISSIONS: 30% of the 2014-2015 applicants were accepted. The SAT scores for the 2014-2015 freshman class were: Critical Reading--6% between 500 and 599, 40% between 600 and 699, and 55% between 700 and 800; Math--9% between 500 and 599, 42% between 600 and 699, and 48% between 700 and 800; Writing--3% between 500 and 599, 38% between 600 and 699, and 59% between 700 and 800. 97% of the current freshmen were in the top fifth of their class; 100% were in the top two fifths. **Admissions Contact:** Board of Admission E-Mail: *admission@wellesley.edu* Web: *www.wellesley.edu*

FINANCIAL AID: In 2014-2015, 61% of all full-time freshmen and continuing full-time students received some form of financial aid. 61% of all full-time freshmen and continuing full-time students received need-based aid. The average freshman award was $39,988. Need-based scholarships or need-based grants averaged $39,988; and need-based self-help aid (loans and jobs) averaged $4,232. 61% of undergraduate students work part-time. Average annual earnings from campus work are $2000. The average financial indebtedness of the 2014 graduate was $14,030. Wellesley is a member of CSS. The CSS/Profile and FAFSA, and and the most recent income tax returns of parents and student. are required. The priority date for freshman financial aid applications for fall entry is March 1.

WENTWORTH INSTITUTE OF TECHNOLOGY
E-2

www.wit.edu

Boston, MA 02115	(617) 989-4000
	(800) 556-0610
Fax: (617) 989-4010	Email: admissions@wit.edu
Full-time: 2653 men, 680 women	Faculty: 135
Part-time: 343 men, 52 women	Ph.D.s: 50%
Graduate: n/av	Student/Faculty: 25 to 1
Year: semesters, summer session	Tuition: $20,150
Room & Board: $9650	Freshman Class: 2329 applied, 1867 accepted, 859 enrolled
SAT: required ACT: 23	CEEB CODE: 3958
Application Deadline: n/av	COMPETITIVE

Wentworth Institute of Technology, founded in 1904, is a private college specializing in architecture, design, engineering, technology, and management. The figures in the above capsule and in this profile are approximate. In addition to regional accreditation, Wentworth has baccalaureate program accreditation with ABET, ACCE, FIDER, NAAB, and IACBE. The 35-acre campus is in an urban area in Boston. Including any residence halls, there are 27 buildings.

STUDENT LIFE: 60% of undergraduates are from Massachusetts. Others are from 39 states, 51 foreign countries, and Canada. 72% are White. The average age of freshmen is 19; all undergraduates, 22. 31% do not continue beyond their first year; 52% remain to graduate. **Housing:** 1665 students can be accommodated in college housing, which includes coed dorms and on-campus apartments. On-campus housing is guaranteed for all 4 years and is guaranteed for the freshman year only. 60% of students live on campus. Alcohol is not permitted. Upperclassmen may keep cars.

FACULTY/CLASSROOMS: 76% of faculty are male; 24% are female. All teach undergraduates. No introductory courses are taught by graduate students. The average class size in an introductory lecture is 25; in a laboratory is 25; and in a regular course is 21.

PROGRAMS OF STUDY: Wentworth confers B.S., and B.Arch. degrees. Associate degrees are also awarded. Bachelor's degrees are awarded in COMMUNICATIONS AND THE ARTS (industrial design), COMPUTER AND PHYSICAL SCIENCE (computer science and information sciences and systems), ENGINEERING AND ENVIRONMENTAL DESIGN (architecture, biomedical engineering, civil engineering technology, computer technology, construction management, construction technology, electrical/electronics engineering technology, electromechanical technology, environmental science, industrial administration/management, interior design, mechanical engineering technology, and technological management). Architecture, computer science, and electronic engineering technology have the larges enrollments.

ACTIVITIES: There are no fraternities or sororities. There are 50 groups on campus, including communications, computers, dance, drama, ethnic, gay, honors, international, literary magazine, musical theater, newspaper, orchestra, professional, radio and TV, religious, social, social service, student government, and yearbook. Popular campus events include Design Lecture Series, Beaux Arts Ball, and Women's History Month. **Sports:** There are 9 intercollegiate sports for men and 6 for women, and 5 intramural sports for men and 5 for women. Facilities include gyms, tennis courts, a riflery range, a fitness center, an outdoor basketball court, and softball, soccer, and lacrosse playing fields.

SERVICES: Counseling and information services are available, as is tutoring in every subject. There is remedial math and writing. Free tutoring is available to all students through the learning center. **Library/Resources:** The library contains 77,000 volumes, 90 microform items, 750 audio/video tapes/CDs/DVDs, and subscribes to 500 periodicals including electronic. Computerized library services include interlibrary loans, database searching, and Internet access. Special learning facilities include a radio station, printed-circuit lab, CAD/CAM/CAE labs, design studios, and numerically controlled manufacturing systems. **Physically Challenged Students:** 30% of the campus is accessible. Facilities include wheelchair ramps, elevators, special parking, specially equipped restrooms, special class scheduling, lowered drinking fountains, and lowered telephones. **Special:** Wentworth offers extensive cooperative programs; cross-registration with other members of the Colleges of the Fenway Consortium; study abroad, including study in France for third-year architecture students; interdisciplinary majors, including engineering technology and facilities planning and management; a dual major in technical management; and nondegree study. Most students at the bachelor's level attend school in the summer, as most cooperative work occurs during the academic year. There is 1 national honor society. **Visiting:** There are regularly scheduled orientations for prospective students, including daily tours and information programs, Monday to Friday. There are guides for informal visits and visitors may sit in on classes. To schedule a visit, contact the Admissions Office. **Campus Safety and Security:** Measures include 24-hour foot and vehicle patrol, self-defense education, and security escort services. There are shuttle buses, emergency telephones, lighted pathways/sidewalks, all campus police officers have emergency medical training.

REQUIREMENTS: The SAT or ACT is required. Applicants must be graduates of an accredited secondary school or have the GED. High school course requirements vary by major. AP and CLEP credits are accepted. Important factors in the admissions decision are advanced placement or honors courses, leadership record, and extracurricular activities record. For a bachelor's degree, students must complete a total of 136 to 176 hours, depending on the major, with a minimum GPA of 2.0 overall and 2.5 in the major. An introductory computer course is required of all students. All full-time bachelor's degree candidates must complete 2 semesters of co-op, beginning after the first 2 years of study. A writing competency assessment is required at the end of the sophomore year. **Procedure:** Freshmen are admitted fall and spring. Entrance exams should be taken in the spring of the junior year or the fall of the senior year. There are deferred admissions and rolling admissions plans. Check with the school for current application deadlines. Notification is sent on a rolling basis. Applications are accepted on-line. **Transfer Students:** 197 transfer students enrolled in 2013-2014. Requirements for transfer students vary by program. All applicants must submit official college and high school transcripts. Portfolios and faculty reviews are recommended of applicants to industrial design, interior design, and architecture programs. Grades of C or better transfer for credit. Transfer students must take 50% of the course work in their degree program at Wentworth to graduate. **International Students:** There are 120 international students enrolled. The school actively recruits these students. They must also take the SAT or ACT.

ADMISSIONS: 80% of the 2014-2015 applicants were accepted. **Admissions Contact:** Office of Admissions E-Mail: *admissions@wit .edu* Web: *www.wit.edu*

FINANCIAL AID: In 2014-2015, 80% of all full-time freshmen and 80% of continuing full-time students received some form of financial aid. 60% of all full-time freshmen and 65% of continuing full-time students received need-based aid. 29% of undergraduate students work part-time. The FAFSA is required. The priority date for freshman financial aid applications for fall entry is March 1. The deadline for filing freshman financial aid applications for fall entry is June 1.

WESTERN NEW ENGLAND UNIVERSITY   B-3
www.wne.edu

Springfield, MA 01119	
	(413) 782-1321
	(800) 325-1122 ext. 1321
Fax: (413) 782-1777	Email: learn@wne.edu
Full-time: 1565 men, 1011 women	Faculty: 165; IIA, +$
Part-time: 78 men, 78 women	Ph.D.s: 90%
Graduate: 525 men, 709 women	Student/Faculty: 13 to 1
Year: semesters, summer session	Tuition: $33,466
Room & Board: $12,688	Freshman Class: 6216 applied, 4982 accepted, 758 enrolled
SAT CR/M: 520/550 ACT: 24	CEEB CODE: 3962
Application Deadline: open	COMPETITIVE+

Western New England University, founded in 1919, is a private non-sectarian institution offering undergraduate programs in business, engineering and arts and sciences. There are 3 undergraduate schools and 5 graduate schools. In addition to regional accreditation, WNE has baccalaureate program accreditation with AACSB, ABET, CSWE, and ABA. The 215-acre campus is in a suburban area 90 miles west of Boston, MA, 30 miles from Hartford, CT, and 150 miles from New York City. Including any residence halls, there are 26 buildings.

STUDENT LIFE: 54% of undergraduates are from out of state, mostly the Northeast. Students are from 30 states, 20 foreign countries, and Canada. 75% are White. 97% claim no religious affiliation. **Male To Female Ratio:** 0.8:1. The average age of freshmen is 18; all undergraduates, 20. 24% do not continue beyond their first year; 60% remain to graduate. **Housing:** 2000 students can be accommodated in college housing, which includes coed dorms, on-campus apartments, and married student housing. Freshmen are grouped by academic interest areas or theme housing. On-campus housing is guaranteed for all 4 years. 69% of students live on campus. All students may keep cars.

FACULTY/CLASSROOMS: No introductory courses are taught by graduate students. The average class size in an introductory lecture is 20; in a laboratory is 17; and in a regular course is 19.

PROGRAMS OF STUDY: WNE confers B.A., B.S., B.B.A., B.A.L.S., B.S.B.A., B.S.B.E., B.S.C.J., B.S.E.E., B.S.H.S., B.S.I.E., B.S.M.E., B.S.W., B.S.B.M.E. and B.S.C.E. degrees. Associate, Master's, and Doctoral degrees are also awarded. Bachelor's degrees are awarded in BIOLOGICAL SCIENCE (biology/biological science and neurosciences), BUSINESS (accounting, business administration and management, finance, management science, marketing/retailing/merchandising, and sports management), COMMUNICATIONS AND THE ARTS (advertising, communications, creative writing, English, and public relations), COMPUTER AND PHYSICAL SCIENCE (chemistry, computer science, information sciences and systems, and mathematics), EDUCATION (elementary education and

secondary education), ENGINEERING AND ENVIRONMENTAL DESIGN (bioengineering, biomedical engineering, civil engineering, computer engineering, electrical/electronics engineering, industrial engineering, mechanical engineering, and preengineering), HEALTH PROFESSIONS (health science), SOCIAL SCIENCE (criminal justice, economics, forensic studies, history, Iberian studies, international studies, law, liberal arts/general studies, parks and recreation management, philosophy, political science/government, psychology, social work, and sociology). Engineering is the strongest academically. Psychology, accounting and mechanical engineering have the largest enrollments.

ACTIVITIES: There are no fraternities or sororities. There are 60 groups on campus, including art, band, cheerleading, chorus, computers, dance, drama, environmental, ethnic, film, forensics, gay, honors, international, jazz band, literary magazine, musical theater, newspaper, pep band, photography, political, professional, radio and TV, religious, social, social service, student government, and yearbook. Popular campus events include Spring Week, Family and Friends Weekend, Midnight Madness and Mr. University. **Sports:** There are 10 intercollegiate sports for men and 9 for women, and 13 intramural sports for men and 13 for women. Facilities include a healthful living center equipped for basketball (2,000 seats), wrestling, racquetball, squash, aerobics, fitness, and volleyball, as well as a weight room, an 8-lane pool, and a track. The 1,200-seat Golden Bear Stadium serves multiple varsity sports including football, field hockey, and men's and women's lacrosse, tennis courts and baseball and softball fields. Suprenant Field is home to the Golden Bear men's and women's soccer teams. **Graduates:** From July 1, 2013 to June 30, 2014, 538 bachelor's degrees were awarded. The most popular majors were psychology (11%), accounting (10%), and mechanical engineering (8%). 40 companies recruited on campus in 2013-2014. In an average class, 1% graduate in 3 years or less, 50% graduate in 4 years or less, 59% graduate in 5 years or less, and 60% graduate in 6 years or less.

SERVICES: Counseling and information services are available, as is tutoring in most subjects. There is a reader service for the blind. **Library/Resources:** The 2 libraries contain 156,431 volumes, 194,418 microform items, 6,731 audio/video tapes/CDs/DVDs, and subscribe to 46,285 periodicals including electronic. Computerized library services include interlibrary loans, database searching, Internet access, and Wi-Fi capability. Special learning facilities include an art gallery, radio station, TV station, a math, writing and science centers. **Physically Challenged Students:** Facilities include wheelchair ramps, elevators, special parking, specially equipped restrooms, special class scheduling, lowered drinking fountains, lowered telephones, and special housing. **Special:** Students may cross-register with cooperating colleges of Greater Springfield. The college offers internships, study abroad, a Washington semester, work-study programs, B.A.-B.S. degrees, an accelerated degree program, and dual and student-designed majors. The 3+3 law program offers qualified students the opportunity to earn a J.D. in 6 years. There is also a 6-year biomedical engineering/law program, a 5-year Bachelor/M.B.A., a 5-year accounting/M.S.A., a 5-year B.S./M.S. in Engineering Management and Electrical Engineering and Mechanical Engineering. There are 14 national honor societies and a freshman honors program. **Visiting:** There are regularly scheduled orientations for prospective students, including multiple open houses. There are guides for informal visits, visitors may sit in on classes, and stay overnight. To schedule a visit, contact the Undergraduate Admissions Office. **Campus Safety and Security:** Measures include 24-hour foot and vehicle patrol, emergency notification system, self-defense education, and security escort services. There are emergency telephones, lighted pathways/sidewalks, controlled access to dorms/residences, security cameras, medical response, fire response, and a comprehensive public safety awareness program.

REQUIREMENTS: The SAT is required. Applicants must be graduates of an approved secondary school and must have completed 4 years of high school English, 2 or more years of math, 1 or more years of science, and 1 year of history and social science. An interview is recommended. ACT is accepted in lieu of SAT. AP and CLEP credits are accepted. Important factors in the admissions decision are advanced placement or honors courses, extracurricular activities record, and recommendations by school officials. To graduate, students must complete 122 credit hours, with a minimum GPA of 2.0. Requirements include 2 courses each in English, math, lab science, and phys ed, and 1 course each in history, culture, and computers. A first-year seminar is also required for freshmen. Other requirements vary according to the major. **Procedure:** Freshmen are admitted fall and spring. Entrance exams should be taken in the spring of the junior year or fall of the senior year. There are early admissions, deferred admissions, and rolling admissions plans. Application deadlines are open. Application fee is $40. Notification is sent on a rolling basis. Applications are accepted on-line. **Transfer Students:** 131 transfer students enrolled in 2013-2014. Applicants must have a minimum GPA of 2.3. Grades of C- or better transfer for credit. The university admits transfer students in the fall and spring. 30 of 122 credits required for the bachelor's degree must be completed at WNE. **International Students:** There are 74 international students enrolled. The school actively recruits these students. They must take the TOEFL with a minimum score of 550 on the paper-based TOEFL (PBT) or 79 on the Internet-based version (iBT). They must also take the SAT or ACT.

ADMISSIONS: 80% of the 2014-2015 applicants were accepted. The SAT scores for the 2014-2015 freshman class were: Critical Reading--38% below 500, 46% between 500 and 599, 15% between 600 and 699, and 1% between 700 and 800; Math--25% below 500, 49% between 500 and 599, 24% between 600 and 699, and 2% between 700 and 800. The ACT scores were 15% below 21, 27% between 21 and 23, 37% between 24 and 26, 12% between 27 and 28, and 9% above 28. 34% of the current freshmen were in the top fifth of their class; 67% were in the top two fifths. 1 freshman graduated first in the class. **Admissions Contact:** Bryan Gross, Vice President for Enrollment Management. E-Mail: *learn@wne.edu* Web: *www.wne.edu*

FINANCIAL AID: In 2014-2015, 98% of all full-time freshmen and 96% of continuing full-time students received some form of financial aid. The average freshman award was $28,860. Need-based scholarships or need-based grants averaged $17,100; need-based self-help aid (loans and jobs) averaged $11,265; and other non-need-based awards and non-need-based scholarships averaged $495. 40% of undergraduate students work part-time. Average annual earnings from campus work are $1800. The FAFSA, and IRS Data Retrieval is required. The priority date for freshman financial aid applications for fall entry is rolling. The deadline for filing freshman financial aid applications for fall entry is rolling.

WESTFIELD STATE UNIVERSITY B-3
www.westfield.ma.edu

Westfield, MA 01086 (413) 572-5218 n/av

Fax: (413) 572-0520 Email: admissions@westfield.ma.edu
Full-time: 2300 men, 2610 women Faculty: 231; IIA, av$
Part-time: 344 men, 353 women Ph.D.s: 90%
Graduate: 201 men, 530 women Student/Faculty: 21 to 1
Year: semesters, summer session Tuition: $8682 ($14,762)
Room & Board: $9615 Freshman Class: 5152 applied, 3839 accepted, 1224 enrolled
SAT CR/M: 500/510 ACT: 20 CEEB CODE: 3523
Application Deadline: March 1 COMPETITIVE

Westfield State University, founded in 1838, is a public university with liberal arts and sciences, teacher preparation programs and professional training in business, nursing, and allied health fields. There is 1 undergraduate school and 1 graduate school. In addition to regional accreditation, Westfield State has baccalaureate program accreditation with ABET, CSWE, NASM, NCATE, CAAHEP, and CCNE. The 256-acre campus is in a suburban area in western Massachusetts, 15 miles west of Springfield, 100 miles west of Boston. Including any residence halls, there are 25 buildings.

STUDENT LIFE: 93% of undergraduates are from Massachusetts. Others are from 25 states, 7 foreign countries, and Canada. 79% are White. **Male To Female Ratio:** 1.2:1. The average age of freshmen is 18; all undergraduates, 21. 21% do not continue beyond their first year; 59% remain to graduate. **Housing:** 3059 students can be accom-

modated in college housing, which includes coed dorms, on-campus apartments, and off-campus apartments. In addition, there are special-interest houses, special housing for disabilities students, and special housing for international students. On-campus housing is guaranteed for all 4 years. 54% of students live on campus. Upperclassmen may keep cars.

FACULTY/CLASSROOMS: 49% of faculty are male; 51% are female. All teach undergraduates. No introductory courses are taught by graduate students. The average class size in an introductory lecture is 21; in a laboratory is 16; and in a regular course is 21.

PROGRAMS OF STUDY: Westfield State confers B.A., B.S., B.S.E., B.S.N. and B.S.W. degrees. Master's degrees are also awarded. Bachelor's degrees are awarded in BIOLOGICAL SCIENCE (biology/biological science), BUSINESS (business administration and management), COMMUNICATIONS AND THE ARTS (art, communications, English, music, Spanish, and theatre arts), COMPUTER AND PHYSICAL SCIENCE (chemistry, computer science, information sciences and systems, mathematics, and science), EDUCATION (athletic training, early childhood education, elementary education, and special education), ENGINEERING AND ENVIRONMENTAL DESIGN (city/community/regional planning and environmental science), HEALTH PROFESSIONS (nursing), SOCIAL SCIENCE (criminal justice, economics, ethnic studies, history, liberal arts/general studies, physical fitness/movement, political science/government, psychology, social work, and sociology). Business managment, education, and criminal justice are the largest.

ACTIVITIES: There are 82 groups on campus, including art, band, cheerleading, chess, choir, chorale, chorus, communications, computers, dance, drama, environmental, ethnic, gay, honors, international, jazz band, literary magazine, musical theater, newspaper, orchestra, pep band, photography, political, professional, radio and TV, religious, social, social service, student government, and symphony. Popular campus events include Homecoming, Spring Weekend, and Comedy Night. **Sports:** There are 8 intercollegiate sports for men and 10 for women, and 8 intramural sports for men and 5 for women. Facilities include a track, baseball and softball fields, a 400-seat gym, and a 5,000-seat stadium. **Graduates:** From July 1, 2013 to June 30, 2014, 1373 bachelor's degrees were awarded. The most popular majors were business management (18%), liberal studies (17%), and criminal justice (15%). 220 companies recruited on campus in 2013-2014. In an average class, 44% graduate in 4 years or less, 57% graduate in 5 years or less, and 59% graduate in 6 years or less.

SERVICES: Counseling and information services are available, as is tutoring in every subject. There is a reader service for the blind. **Library/Resources:** The library contains 160,284 volumes, 481,151 microform items, 5,064 audio/video tapes/CDs/DVDs, and subscribes to 1,933 periodicals including electronic. Computerized library services include interlibrary loans, database searching, Internet access, and Wi-Fi capability. Special learning facilities include an art gallery, natural history museum, radio station, TV station, a geology museum, and a greenhouse. **Physically Challenged Students:** 75% of the campus is accessible. Facilities include wheelchair ramps, elevators, special parking, specially equipped restrooms, special class scheduling, lowered telephones, and special housing. **Special:** Students may cross-register through College Academic Program Sharing, National Student Exchange, and Cooperating Colleges of Greater Springfield. Internships are for credit only in conjunction with all major programs. The University offers international exchange programs in China, Ireland, and Poland and hundreds of study abroad programs in over 35 countries, a Washington semester for political science, criminal justice, and psychology majors, an internship program with Walt Disney World, dual majors, student-designed majors, some credit for military experience and has a multi-department Honors Program. There are 16 national honor societies and a freshman honors program. **Visiting:** There are regularly scheduled orientations for prospective students, including a campus tour, classroom observation, academic department presentations, lunch with faculty, staff, and students, and a question-and-answer session moderated by a panel of administrators. There are guides for informal visits. To schedule a visit, contact the Admissions Office. **Campus Safety and Security:** Measures include 24-hour foot and vehicle patrol, emergency notification system, self-defense education, and security escort services. There are shuttle buses, emergency telephones, lighted pathways/sidewalks, and controlled access to dorms/residences.

REQUIREMENTS: The SAT or ACT is required. Applicants must achieve a minimum 3.0 cumulative average in academic subjects. Students who have between a 2.0 and a 3.0 GPA may be accepted via a sliding scale, contingent upon the SAT or ACT scores. They must be graduates of an accredited secondary school and must have completed 4 years of college preparatory level English, 3 years of math (algebra I and II and geometry), 2 years of social sciences (including 1 year of U.S history), 3 years of sciences, including 2 with lab, 2 foreign language, and 2 years of electives. The GED is accepted. A portfolio is required for admission to the art program, and an audition is necessary for admission to the music program. All applicants must submit either SAT or ACT scores unless they have a documented learning disability. AP and CLEP credits are accepted.Students must complete a total of 120 credit hours, with 43 or more credits in 9 specified areas and 30 to 40 hours in the major. The college requires a 2.0 GPA overall and 2.0 in major courses. U.S. history or government and diversity awareness courses are required. **Procedure:** Freshmen are admitted fall and spring. Entrance exams should be taken in the spring of the junior year and fall of the senior year. There are deferred admissions and rolling admissions plans. Applications should be filed by March 1 for fall entry; December 1 for spring entry, along with a $50 fee. Notifications are sent March 15. Applications are accepted on-line. **Transfer Students:** 439 transfer students enrolled in 2013-2014. Transfer students must have 24 transferable credits with a minimum cumulative GPA of 2.0 (higher for some majors). A grade of C- or better with a 2.0 GPA will transfer for credit. Transfer students are admitted in the fall and spring. For students transferring from a Massachusetts Community College, a D may be transferred for credit. 30 of 120 credits required for the bachelor's degree must be completed at Westfield State. **International Students:** There are 25 international students enrolled. The school actively recruits these students. They must take the TOEFL with a minimum score of 550 on the paper-based TOEFL (PBT) or 79 on the Internet-based version (iBT), or take the IELTS. They must also take the SAT or ACT.

ADMISSIONS: 75% of the 2014-2015 applicants were accepted. The SAT scores for the 2014-2015 freshman class were: Critical Reading--46% below 500, 44% between 500 and 599, 9% between 600 and 699, and 1% between 700 and 800; Math--37% below 500, 50% between 500 and 599, 12% between 600 and 699, and 1% between 700 and 800. The ACT scores were 50% below 21, 28% between 21 and 23, and 22% between 24 and 26. 21% of the current freshmen were in the top fifth of their class; 52% were in the top two fifths. 1 freshman graduated first in the class. **Admissions Contact:** Kelly Hart, Director of Admissions. E-Mail: *admissions@westfield.ma.edu* Web: *www.westfield.ma.edu*

FINANCIAL AID: Westfield State is a member of CSS. The FAFSA is required. The deadline for filing freshman financial aid applications for fall entry is March 1.

WHEATON COLLEGE   D-3

wheatoncollege.edu

Norton, MA 02766	**(508) 286-8251**
	(800) 394-6003
Fax: (508) 286-8271	**Email:** admission@wheatoncollege.edu
Full-time: 591 men, 1030 women	**Faculty:** 139; IIB, +$
Part-time: 1 women	**Ph.D.s:** 88%
Graduate: n/av	**Student/Faculty:** 11 to 1
Year: semesters	**Tuition:** $43,774
Room & Board: $11,160	**Freshman Class:** 3448 applied, 2075 accepted, 437 enrolled
SAT CR/M: 625/620 **ACT:** 29	**CEEB CODE:** 3963
Application Deadline: January 15	**HIGHLY COMPETITIVE+**

Wheaton College, established in 1834, is an independent liberal arts institution. Figures in the above capsule and in this profile are approximate. The 400-acre campus is in a suburban area 35 miles south of Boston and 20 miles north of Providence. Including any residence halls, there are 81 buildings.

STUDENT LIFE: 67% of undergraduates are from out of state, mostly the Northeast. Students are from 39 states, 68 foreign countries, and Canada. 62% are from public schools. 74% are White. **Male To Female Ratio:** 1.7:1. The average age of freshmen is 18; all undergraduates, 20. 14% do not continue beyond their first year; 77% remain to graduate. **Housing:** 1525 students can be accommodated in college housing, which includes single-sex and coed dorms. In addition, there are language houses, and special-interest houses, which include, among others, house of living arts, women of color/social responsibility, global awareness, and outdoors education. On-campus housing is guaranteed for all 4 years and is available on a lottery system for upperclassmen. 95% of students live on campus; of those, 60% remain on campus on weekends. Some may keep cars.

FACULTY/CLASSROOMS: 49% of faculty are male; 51% are female. All teach and do research. No introductory courses are taught by graduate students. The average class size in an introductory lecture is 40; in a laboratory is 20; and in a regular course is 35.

PROGRAMS OF STUDY: Wheaton confers A.B. degrees. Bachelor's degrees are awarded in BIOLOGICAL SCIENCE (biochemistry, bioinformatics, biology/biological science, and neurosciences), COMMUNICATIONS AND THE ARTS (art history and appreciation, classics, creative writing, dance, dramatic arts, English, film arts, fine arts, German, Greek, Latin, literature, music, Russian, and studio art), COMPUTER AND PHYSICAL SCIENCE (chemistry, computer mathematics, computer science, mathematics, mathematics – economics, and physics), ENGINEERING AND ENVIRONMENTAL DESIGN (environmental science), SOCIAL SCIENCE (African studies, African American studies, American studies, anthropology, Asian/Oriental studies, economics, French studies, Hispanic American studies, history, international relations, Italian studies, philosophy, political science/government, psychology, religion, Russian and Slavic studies, sociology, and women's studies). Arts and sciences is the strongest academically. Psychology, economics, and English have the largest enrollments.

ACTIVITIES: There are no fraternities or sororities. There are 90 groups on campus, including Zen meditation group, habitat for humanity, voices united to jam (gospel choir), art, BACCHUS, band, choir, chorale, chorus, dance, debate, drama, environmental, ethnic, film, gay, honors, international, jazz band, literary magazine, musical theater, newspaper, orchestra, pep band, photography, political, professional, radio and TV, religious, social, social service, student government, symphony, and yearbook. Popular campus events include Otis Social Justice Symposium and Award, Spring Weekend, and Season of Service. **Sports:** There are 9 intercollegiate sports for men and 12 for women, and 9 intramural sports for men and 9 for women. Facilities include an 8-lane stretch pool, a field house with 5 tennis courts, 1 outdoor and 5 indoor basketball courts, a 200-meter track, a golf/archery range and batting cage, an 850-seat gym, 7 lighted outdoor tennis courts, a running course, a baseball stadium, 2 athletic fields, a softball field, an aerobics/dance studio, and a fitness center. **Graduates:** From July 1, 2013 to June 30, 2014, 428 bachelor's degrees were awarded. The most popular majors were psychology (15%), English (9%), and economics (8%). 17 companies recruited on campus in 2013-2014. In an average class, 73% graduate in 4 years or less, 76% graduate in 5 years or less, and 77% graduate in 6 years or less. Of the 2013 graduating class, 19% were enrolled in graduate school within 6 months of graduation, and 37% were employed.

SERVICES: Counseling and information services are available, as is tutoring in most subjects. There is a reader service for the blind, and remedial writing. Peer tutoring and note takers for hearing-impaired students are available. **Library/Resources:** The library contains 364,628 volumes, 56,204 microform items, 17,605 audio/video tapes/CDs/DVDs, and subscribes to 26,713 periodicals including electronic. Computerized library services include interlibrary loans, database searching, Internet access, and Wi-Fi capability. Special learning facilities include an art gallery, planetarium, radio station, a greenhouse, and an observatory. **Physically Challenged Students:** 50% of the campus is accessible. Facilities include wheelchair ramps, elevators, special parking, specially equipped restrooms, special class scheduling, and lowered telephones. **Special:** Students may cross-register with Brown University as well as with colleges in the Southeastern Association for Cooperation in Higher Education in Massachusetts and with schools participating in the 12 College Exchange Program. Wheaton offers study abroad in 90 countries, internship programs, nondegree study, dual majors, student-designed majors, a Washington semester at American University, and interdisciplinary majors, including math and economics, math and computer science, physics and astronomy, and theater and English dramatic literature. Dual-degree programs exist with the following institutions: Thayer School of Engineering, Dartmouth College (B.S. Engineering); Emerson College (M.A. Integrated Marketing Communication); Graduate School of Management, University of Rochester (M.B.A.); George Washington University (B.S. Engineering); School of the Museum of Fine Arts (B.F.A.); Andover-Newton Theological School (M.A. Religion); and New England School of Optometry (Doctor of Optometry). There are 8 national honor societies, including Phi Beta Kappa, a freshman honors program, and 100 departmental honors programs. <u>Visiting:</u> There are regularly scheduled orientations for prospective students, including class visits, tours, panels on financial aid, student life, and athletics, lunch with faculty, and department open houses. There are guides for informal visits, visitors may sit in on classes, and stay overnight. To schedule a visit, contact the Admission Office. <u>Campus Safety and Security:</u> Measures include 24-hour foot and vehicle patrol, emergency notification system, self-defense education, and security escort services. There are emergency telephones, lighted pathways/sidewalks, and controlled access to dorms/residences.

<u>REQUIREMENTS:</u> Applicants must be graduates of an accredited secondary school. Recommended courses include English with emphasis on composition skills, 4 years; foreign language and math, 4 years each; social studies, 3 years; history, 2 years, and 3 years science, 2 of which lab. Wheaton requires an essay and strongly recommends an interview. AP credits are accepted. Important factors in the admissions decision are advanced placement or honors courses, extracurricular activities record, and personality/intangible qualities. Among the requirements for graduation are 32 course credits (4 semester hours each), with a minimum of 10 courses in the major. The requirements for each major are determined by the department. The core classes consist of First-year Seminar, English, quantitative skills, foreign language, and non-Western history. Students must maintain a minimum GPA of 2.0 (C-) in all courses to remain in good academic standing. <u>Procedure:</u> Freshmen are admitted fall and spring. Entrance exams should be taken in October and/or November. There are early decision, early admissions, and deferred admissions plans. Early decision applications should be filed by November 15; regular applications, by January 15 for fall entry; and November 1 for spring entry, along with a $55 fee. Notification of early decision is sent December 15; regular decision, April 1. 108 early decision candidates were accepted for the 2014-2015 class. 198 applicants were on the 2014 waiting list; 38 were admitted. Applications are accepted online. <u>Transfer Students:</u> 14 transfer students enrolled in 2013-2014. Transfer students are encouraged to present a strong B average in their college work to date. Preference will be given to college over high school work. The college transcript is evaluated. High school and college transcripts, an essay or personal statement, a statement of good standing, 2 instructor recommendations, and a midterm evaluation are required. 16 of 32 credits required for the bachelor's degree must be completed at Wheaton. <u>International Students:</u> There are 125 international students enrolled. The school actively recruits these students. They must take the TOEFL with a minimum score of 580 on the paper-based TOEFL (PBT) or 90 on the Internet-based version (iBT).

<u>ADMISSIONS:</u> 60% of the 2014-2015 applicants were accepted. The SAT scores for the 2014-2015 freshman class were: Critical Reading--6% below 500, 26% between 500 and 599, 50% between 600 and 699, and 17% between 700 and 800; Math--6% below 500, 26% between 500 and 599, 52% between 600 and 699, and 16% between 700 and 800. The ACT scores were 21 and 23, 27% between 24 and 26, 19% between 27 and 28, and 54% above 28. 62% of the current freshmen were in the top fifth of their class; 88% were in the top two fifths. 184 freshmen graduated first in their class. <u>Admissions Contact:</u> Gail Berson, VP for Enr and Dean of Adm & Student Aid. E-Mail: *admission@wheatoncollege.edu* Web: *wheatoncollege.edu*

<u>FINANCIAL AID:</u> In 2014-2015, 83% of all full-time freshmen and 80% of continuing full-time students received some form of financial aid. 67% of all full-time freshmen and 60% of continuing full-time students received need-based aid. The average freshman award was $30,463. Need-based scholarships or need-based grants averaged

$29,534 ($49,760 maximum); need-based self-help aid (loans and jobs) averaged $5,278 ($7,000 maximum); and other non-need-based awards and non-need-based scholarships averaged $12,753 ($17,500 maximum). 55% of undergraduate students work part-time. Average annual earnings from campus work are $1115. The average financial indebtedness of the 2014 graduate was $25,778. Wheaton is a member of CSS. The CSS/Profile and FAFSA, and parents' and student's federal tax returns, and if applicable, noncustodial profile and business/farm supplement are required. The deadline for filing freshman financial aid applications for fall entry is February 1.

WHEELOCK COLLEGE E-2
www.wheelock.edu

Boston, MA 02215	**(617) 879-2206**
	(800) 734-5212
Fax: (617) 879-2449	**Email: undergrad@wheelock.edu**
Full-time: 40 men, 600 women	**Faculty:** 65; IIA, av$
Part-time: 3 men, 37 women	**Ph.D.s:** 89%
Graduate: 23 men, 330 women	**Student/Faculty:** 10 to 1
Year: semesters	**Tuition:** $23,625
Room & Board: $9450	**Freshman Class:** 703 applied, 535 accepted, 181 enrolled
SAT: required	**CEEB CODE:** 3964
Application Deadline: March 1	**COMPETITIVE**

Wheelock College, established in 1888, is a private institution with programs in education, child life and family studies, social work, juvenile justice and youth advocacy, and human services. The figures in the above capsule and in this capsule are approximate. There is 1 graduate school. In addition to regional accreditation, has baccalaureate program accreditation with CSWE and NCATE. The 7-acre campus is in an urban area in Boston. Including any residence halls, there are 12 buildings.

<u>STUDENT LIFE:</u> 63% of undergraduates are from Massachusetts. Others are from 22 states, and 2 foreign countries. 90% are from public schools. 85% are White. <u>Male To Female Ratio:</u> 14.7:1. The average age of freshmen is 18; all undergraduates, 20. 29% do not continue beyond their first year; 73% remain to graduate. <u>Housing:</u> 500 students can be accommodated in college housing, which includes single-sex and coed dorms, cooperative living house, nonsmoking floors, and a wellness floor. On-campus housing is guaranteed for all 4 years. 73% of students live on campus; of those, 50% remain on campus on weekends. Upperclassmen may keep cars.

<u>FACULTY/CLASSROOMS:</u> 13% of faculty are male; 87% are female. 70% teach undergraduates. No introductory courses are taught by graduate students. The average class size in an introductory lecture is 20; in a laboratory is 17; and in a regular course is 15.

<u>PROGRAMS OF STUDY:</u> Wheelock confers B.A., B.S. and B.S.W. degrees. Associate and Master's degrees are also awarded. Bachelor's degrees are awarded in EDUCATION (early childhood education, elementary education, and special education), SOCIAL SCIENCE (child care/child and family studies, human development, and social work). Teaching, social work, and child life are the strongest academically and have the largest enrollments.

<u>ACTIVITIES:</u> There are no fraternities or sororities. There are 25 groups on campus, including sign choir, women's center, best buddies, choir, chorale, chorus, dance, drama, ethnic, gay, honors, international, professional, religious, social, social service, and student government. Popular campus events include Kids Day, Family Weekend, and COF Concerts and carnivals. <u>Sports:</u> There are 5 intercollegiate sports for women, and 9 intramural sports for men and 9 for women. Facilities include a sports complex at a neighboring college with a pool and diving board, racquetball courts, a weight room, an indoor track, a basketball court, crew tanks, and cardiovascular equipment. <u>Graduates:</u> From July 1, 2013 to June 30, 2014, 81 bachelor's degrees were awarded. The most popular majors were teacher education (68%), child life (16%), and social work (16%). 35 companies recruited on campus in 2013-2014. In an average class, 48% graduate in 4 years or less, 52% graduate in 5 years or less, and 53%

graduate in 6 years or less. Of the 2013 graduating class, 22% were enrolled in graduate school within 6 months of graduation, and 95% were employed.

SERVICES: Counseling and information services are available, as is tutoring in every subject. There is a reader service for the blind, and remedial math, reading, and writing. Academic support services provide individualized assistance upon request. **Library/Resources:** The library contains 83,573 volumes, 483,257 microform items, 3,633 audio/video tapes/CDs/DVDs, and subscribes to 12,629 periodicals including electronic. Computerized library services include interlibrary loans, database searching, Internet access, and Wi-Fi capability. Special learning facilities include an art gallery, the Wheelock family theater. **Physically Challenged Students:** 67% of the campus is accessible. Facilities include wheelchair ramps, elevators, special parking, specially equipped restrooms, special class scheduling, lowered drinking fountains, lowered telephones. Assistive technology available in the learning center. **Special:** Wheelock offers cross-registration with all colleges in the Colleges of the Fenway and internships that include student teaching and social work practice. Dual majors, study-abroad programs, and pass/fail options are available. Students may receive credit for life and work experience. Students begin practical fieldwork their freshman year and continue for all 4 years. There is 1 national honor society. **Visiting:** There are regularly scheduled orientations for prospective students and information sessions are held on select Saturdays in the fall and spring. Students hear a presentation from a counselor, have a tour, and may speak to a counselor individually. There are guides for informal visits, visitors may sit in on classes, and stay overnight. To schedule a visit, contact the Undergraduate Admissions Office. **Campus Safety and Security:** Measures include 24-hour foot and vehicle patrol and security escort services. There are emergency telephones and lighted pathways/sidewalks.

REQUIREMENTS: The SAT is required. Applicants must be graduates of an accredited secondary school and must have completed 4 years of English, 3 years of math, and 2 years each of science and history. The GED is accepted. The college requires a graded writing sample and recommends an interview. AP and CLEP credits are accepted. Important factors in the admissions decision are advanced placement or honors courses, evidence of special talent, and personality/intangible qualities. To graduate, students must complete between 134 and 140 credit hours, with a minimum GPA of 2.0. Wheelock requires at least a 32-credit major combined with a 36-credit professional studies program. Students must earn 26 credits in English composition, math, human growth and development, children and their environments, first-year seminar, visual and performing arts, and 1 course in first aid. **Procedure:** Freshmen are admitted fall and spring. Entrance exams should be taken in the spring of the junior year and/or fall of the senior year. There are early decision, deferred admissions, and rolling admissions plans. Early decision applications should be filed by December 1; regular applications, by March 1 for fall entry; and December 1 for spring entry, along with a $35 fee. Notification of early decision is sent December 15; regular decision, on a rolling basis. 41 early decision candidates were accepted for the 2014-2015 class. Applications are accepted on-line. **Transfer Students:** 75 transfer students enrolled in 2013-2014. Transfer students must have a minimum GPA of 2.0 and must present 1 letter of recommendation. Grades of C- or better transfer for credit. Applicants must submit all official high school and college transcripts. 67 of 134 credits required for the bachelor's degree must be completed at Wheelock. **International Students:** There are 5 international students enrolled. They must take the TOEFL. They must also take the SAT or ACT. Applicants should submit SAT or ACT scores or TOEFL scores if English is not their official language. **ADMISSIONS:** 76% of the 2014-2015 applicants were accepted. The ACT scores were 56% below 21, 11% between 21 and 23, and 33% between 24 and 26. 28% of the current freshmen were in the top fifth of their class; 54% were in the top two fifths. **Admissions Contact:** Lynne Harding, Dean of Admissions. E-Mail: *undergrad@wheelock .edu* Web: *www.wheelock.edu*

FINANCIAL AID: In 2014-2015, 94% of all full-time freshmen and 82% of continuing full-time students received some form of financial aid. 63% of all full-time freshmen and 70% of continuing full-time students received need-based aid. The average freshman award was $23,709. Need-based scholarships or need-based grants averaged $6,821 ($19,200 maximum); need-based self-help aid (loans and jobs) averaged $4,425 ($8,425 maximum); and other non-need-based awards and non-need-based scholarships averaged $18,026 ($23,600 maximum). 33% of undergraduate students work part-time. Average annual earnings from campus work are $1800. The average financial indebtedness of the 2014 graduate was $21,125. The FAFSA is required. The priority date for freshman financial aid applications for fall entry is February 15.

WILLIAMS COLLEGE   A-1
www.williams.edu

Williamstown, MA 01267

(413) 597-2211
n/av

Fax: n/av   **Email:** admission@williams.edu

Full-time: 992 men, 1023 women	**Faculty:** 274; IIB, ++$
Part-time: 15 men, 15 women	**Ph.D.s:** 97%
Graduate: 25 men, 29 women	**Student/Faculty:** 7 to 1
Year: 4-1-4	**Tuition:** $48,310
Room & Board: $12,760	**Freshman Class:** 6316 applied, 1220 accepted, 546 enrolled
SAT CR/M/W: 740/720/740 **ACT:** 33	**CEEB CODE:** 3965
Application Deadline: January 1	**MOST COMPETITIVE**

Williams College, founded in 1793, is a private institution offering undergraduate degrees in liberal arts and graduate degrees in art history and development economics. There are 2 graduate schools. The 450-acre campus is in a small town 150 miles north of New York City and west of Boston. Including any residence halls, there are 97 buildings.

STUDENT LIFE: 88% of undergraduates are from out of state, mostly the Northeast. Students are from 47 states, 54 foreign countries, and Canada. 56% are White; 12% Hispanic; 11% Asian American. **Male To Female Ratio:** 1.0:1. The average age of freshmen is 19; all undergraduates, 20. 2% do not continue beyond their first year; 95% remain to graduate. **Housing:** College-sponsored housing includes coed dorms and on-campus apartments as well as cooperative housing, in which students prepare their own meals. On-campus housing is guaranteed for all 4 years. Upperclassmen may keep cars.

FACULTY/CLASSROOMS: 57% of faculty are male; 43% are female. No introductory courses are taught by graduate students.

PROGRAMS OF STUDY: Williams confers B.A. degrees. Master's degrees are also awarded. Bachelor's degrees are awarded in BIOLOGICAL SCIENCE (biology/biological science), COMMUNICATIONS AND THE ARTS (Arabic, art, art history and appreciation, classics, dramatic arts, English, fine arts, French, German, literature, music, Russian, and Spanish), COMPUTER AND PHYSICAL SCIENCE (astronomy, astrophysics, chemistry, computer science, geology, mathematics, physics, and statistics), SOCIAL SCIENCE (American studies, anthropology, Asian/Oriental studies, economics, history, philosophy, political science/government, psychology, religion, sociology, and women's studies).

ACTIVITIES: Groups on campus include a capella singing groups, handbell choir, art, band, chess, choir, chorale, chorus, comedy group, communications, computers, dance, debate, drama, environmental, ethnic, film, gay, honors, international, jazz band, literary magazine, marching band, musical theater, newspaper, opera, orchestra, pep band, photography, political, professional, radio and TV, religious, social, social service, student government, symphony, and yearbook. Popular campus events include Winter Carnival, Mountain Day, and Claiming Williams. **Sports:** There are 16 intercollegiate sports for men and 15 for women, and 17 intramural sports for men and 17 for women. Facilities include 2 gyms, a 50-meter pool, a dance studio, a weight room, rowing tanks, a boathouse, a golf course, playing fields, artificial turf field, indoor and outdoor tracks, and courts for tennis, squash, and paddle tennis. **Graduates:** From July 1, 2013 to June 30, 2014, 523 bachelor's degrees were awarded. The most popular majors were economics (16%), psychology (13%), and history (13%). In an average class, 88% graduate in 4 years or less, 94% graduate in 5 years or less, and 95% graduate in 6 years or less.
SERVICES: Counseling and information services are available, as is

tutoring in every subject. There is a reader service for the blind, and remedial math, reading, and writing. Services include a peer health program, rape and sexual assault hotline, and 10-1 counseling service. **Library/Resources:** Computerized library services include interlibrary loans, database searching, Internet access, and Wi-Fi capability. Special learning facilities include an art gallery, planetarium, radio station, a 2500-acre experimental forest, an environmental studies center, a center for foreign languages, literatures, and cultures, a rare book library, a studio art center, and a three-stage center for the performing arts. **Physically Challenged Students:** Facilities include wheelchair ramps, elevators, special parking, specially equipped restrooms, special class scheduling, lowered drinking fountains, lowered telephones, special housing. **Special:** Students may cross-register at Bennington or Massachusetts College of Liberal Arts and study abroad in Madrid, Oxford, Cairo, Beijing, and Kyoto, or any approved program with another college or university. Teaching and medical field experiences, dual and student-designed majors, internships, and a 3-2 engineering program with Columbia University is offered. There are pass/fail options during the winter term. Each department offers Oxford-style tutorials where students meet with the professor weekly in groups of 2-3. There are 2 national honor societies, including Phi Beta Kappa. **Visiting:** There are regularly scheduled orientations for prospective students, including panels, forums, class visits, and campus tours. There are guides for informal visits, visitors may sit in on classes, and stay overnight. To schedule a visit, contact the Admission Office at (413) 597-2211. **Campus Safety and Security:** Measures include 24-hour foot and vehicle patrol, emergency notification system, self-defense education, and security escort services. There are emergency telephones, lighted pathways/sidewalks, and controlled access to dorms/residences.

REQUIREMENTS: The SAT or ACT is required. In addition, Williams requires the following standardized tests: - SAT or ACT with Writing - Two SAT Subject Tests. Applicants to Williams should pursue the strongest program of study offered by their secondary schools. While there are no absolute requirements for admission, competitive candidates typically study English, math, natural science, foreign language and social studies in four-year sequences and present a distinguished record throughout their secondary school career. AP credits are accepted. All students must complete 4 winter study courses and 32 courses regular semester courses, 9 of which are in the major field, with a C- or higher. Requirements include 3 semester-long courses in each of 3 academic divisions: languages and arts, social sciences, and science and math. **Procedure:** Freshmen are admitted fall. There are early decision and deferred admissions plans. Early decision applications should be filed by November 15; regular applications, by January 1 for fall entry. The fall 2014 application fee was $65. Notification of early decision is sent 12 15; regular decision, 236 early decision candidates were accepted for the 2014-2015 class. 594 applicants were on the 2014 waiting list; 70 were admitted. Applications are accepted on-line. **Transfer Students:** Transfer applicants should present a 3.5 GPA in previous college work and must submit either SAT or ACT scores. 16 of 32 credits required for the bachelor's degree must be completed at Williams. **International Students:** There are 144 international students enrolled. The school actively recruits these students. They must take the TOEFL if English is not the applicant's first language. They must also take the SAT or ACT.

ADMISSIONS: 19% of the 2014-2015 applicants were accepted. The SAT scores for the 2014-2015 freshman class were: Critical Reading--5% between 500 and 599, 26% between 600 and 699, and 69% between 700 and 800; Math--5% between 500 and 599, 30% between 600 and 699, and 65% between 700 and 800; Writing--3% between 500 and 599, 24% between 600 and 699, and 73% between 700 and 800. **Admissions Contact:** Richard Nesbitt, Director of Admissions. E-Mail: *admission@williams.edu* Web: *www.williams,edu*

FINANCIAL AID: 48% of all full-time freshmen and 50% of continuing full-time students received need-based aid. The average freshman award was $47,675. Need-based scholarships or need-based grants averaged $43,460; and need-based self-help aid (loans and jobs) averaged $4,215. The average financial indebtedness of the 2014 graduate was $12,627. The CSS/Profile and FAFSA are required. The deadline for filing freshman financial aid applications for fall entry is February 1.

WORCESTER POLYTECHNIC INSTITUTE C-2
www.wpi.edu

Worcester, MA 01609	**(508) 831-5286**
	n/av
Fax: (508) 831-5875	Email: admissions@wpi.edu
Full-time: 2762 men, 1334 women	Faculty: 331; IIA, ++$
Part-time: 100 men, 39 women	Ph.D.s: 91%
Graduate: 1530 men, 616 women	Student/Faculty: 14 to 1
Year: quarters, summer session	Tuition: $42,778
Room & Board: $13,082	Freshman Class: 10233 applied, 4480 accepted, 1062 enrolled
SAT CR/M/W: 620/700/620 ACT: 30	CEEB CODE: 3969
Application Deadline: February 1	MOST COMPETITIVE

Worcester Polytechnic Institute, founded in 1865, is a private technological university offering degrees in the sciences, engineering, computer science, business management, and the liberal arts. The academic program emphasizes professional-level project work. There is 1 graduate school. In addition to regional accreditation, WPI has baccalaureate program accreditation with AACSB, ABET, and NEASC. The 90-acre campus is in a suburban area 40 miles west of Boston. Including any residence halls, there are 49 buildings.

STUDENT LIFE: 62% of undergraduates are from out of state, mostly the Northeast. Students are from 48 states, 68 foreign countries, and Canada. 74% are from public schools. 64% are White; 12% Foreign. The average age of freshmen is 18; all undergraduates, 20. 3% do not continue beyond their first year; 81% remain to graduate. **Housing:** 1676 students can be accommodated in college housing, which includes coed dorms, on-campus apartments, and off-campus apartments. In addition, there are special-interest houses, fraternity houses, and sorority houses. On-campus housing is guaranteed for the freshman year only and is available on a lottery system for upperclassmen. 62% of students live on campus; of those, 75% remain on campus on weekends. Upperclassmen may keep cars.

FACULTY/CLASSROOMS: 75% of faculty are male; 25% are female. All teach undergraduates. No introductory courses are taught by graduate students. The average class size in an introductory lecture is 100; in a laboratory is 20; and in a regular course is 20.

PROGRAMS OF STUDY: WPI confers B.A., and B.S. degrees. Master's and Doctoral degrees are also awarded. Bachelor's degrees are awarded in AGRICULTURE (environmental studies), BIOLOGICAL SCIENCE (biochemistry and biotechnology), BUSINESS (business administration and management, management engineering, and management information systems), COMMUNICATIONS AND THE ARTS (technical and business writing), COMPUTER AND PHYSICAL SCIENCE (actuarial science, chemistry, computer science, digital arts/technology, mathematics, and physics), ENGINEERING AND ENVIRONMENTAL DESIGN (aeronautical engineering, architectural engineering, biomedical engineering, chemical engineering, civil engineering, computer graphics, electrical/electronics engineering, engineering physics, environmental engineering, industrial engineering, materials engineering, mechanical engineering, and technology and public affairs), SOCIAL SCIENCE (economics, fire protection, humanities, interdisciplinary studies, social science, and systems science). Engineering, biology, and computer science have the largest enrollments.

ACTIVITIES: 30% of men belong to 14 national fraternities; 41% of women belong to 1 local and 5 national sororities. There are 220 groups on campus, including art, band, cheerleading, chess, choir, chorale, chorus, computers, dance, debate, drama, environmental, ethnic, forensics, gay, honors, international, jazz band, literary magazine, marching band, musical theater, newspaper, orchestra, pep band, photography, political, professional, radio and TV, religious, social, social service, student government, symphony, and yearbook. Popular campus events include Traditions Day, New Voices Festival, and Quad Fest. **Sports:** There are 10 intercollegiate sports for men and 10 for women, and 7 intramural sports for men and 7 for women. Facilities include an aerobics area, softball fields, an 8-lane synthetic surface track, a fitness center, a crew center, a playing field with artificial turf, a pool, basketball, tennis, racquetball and squash courts, and a 2800-seat gym. The sports and recreation center holds a 4-court gym, an indoor track, 14,000-sq-ft of fitness space, a rowing tank, and a 25-meter competition pool. **Graduates:** From July 1, 2013 to June 30, 2014, 884 bachelor's degrees were awarded. The most popular majors were mechanical engineering (24%), biomedical engineering (10%), and electrical and computer engineering (9%). 206 companies recruited on campus in 2013-2014. In an average class, 76% graduate in 4 years or less, 83% graduate in 5 years or less, and 81% graduate in 6 years or less. Of the 2013 graduating class, 22% were enrolled in graduate school within 6 months of graduation, and 68% were employed.

SERVICES: Counseling and information services are available, as is tutoring in every subject. **Library/Resources:** The library contains 563,590 volumes, 112,960 microform items, 2,772 audio/video tapes/CDs/DVDs, and subscribes to 84,460 periodicals including electronic. Computerized library services include interlibrary loans, database searching, Internet access, and Wi-Fi capability. Special learning facilities include an art gallery, radio station, a robotics lab, a wind tunnel, and a greenhouse. **Physically Challenged Students:** 96% of the campus is accessible. Facilities include wheelchair ramps, elevators, special parking, specially equipped restrooms, special class scheduling, and lowered drinking fountains. **Special:** Students may cross-register with 9 other colleges in the Colleges of Worcester Consortium. Co-op programs in all majors, internships, work-study programs, dual majors in every subject, student-designed majors, non-degree study, and pass/fail options are all available. There is an accelerated degree program in fire protection engineering and math. There are 44 special project centers in 25 countries. There are 21 national honor societies. **Visiting:** There are regularly scheduled orientations for prospective students, consisting of meetings and presentations from various academic and extracurricular groups. There are guides for informal visits, visitors may sit in on classes, and stay overnight. To schedule a visit, contact Barbara Hassett at admissions@wpi.edu. **Campus Safety and Security:** Measures include 24-hour foot and vehicle patrol, emergency notification system, self-defense education, and security escort services. There are shuttle buses, emergency telephones, lighted pathways/sidewalks, and a student-run emergency medical service supervised by the campus police department.

REQUIREMENTS: Applicants must have completed 4 years of math, including precalculus, 4 years of English, and 2 lab sciences. An essay is required and a letter of recommendation, is needed from either a math or science teacher and the guidance counselor. Those opting for Flex Path will submit academic work in place of the SAT or ACT. AP credits are accepted. Important factors in the admissions decision are advanced placement or honors courses, recommendations by school officials, and extracurricular activities record. For a B.S. degree, WPI requires that students in science and engineering complete an individual project in the humanities. Students must also complete 2 major team projects. Distribution requirements vary according to the major, and all students must take courses in social sciences and phys ed. **Procedure:** Freshmen are admitted fall. Entrance exams should be taken between April and January. There are early admissions and deferred admissions plans. Applications should be filed by February 1 for fall entry; November 15 for spring entry, along with a $65 fee. Notifications are sent April 1. 3023 applicants were on the 2014 waiting list; 203 were admitted. Applications are accepted on-line. **Transfer Students:** 50 transfer students enrolled in 2013-2014. Grades of C or better transfer for credit. A high school transcript or GED is required. Students who have been out of school for a year or more must present a resume or personal biography, and 2 academic recommendations. Also they must have completed a calculus course and 2 lab sciences courses. 75 of 135 credits required for the bachelor's degree must be completed at WPI. **International Students:** There are 507 international students enrolled. The school actively recruits these students. They must take the TOEFL with a minimum score of 550 on the paper-based TOEFL (PBT) or 80 on the Internet-based version (iBT) or take the MELAB and the college's own test, or take the IELTS. They must also take the SAT or ACT or a Flex Path Supplement.

ADMISSIONS: 44% of the 2014-2015 applicants were accepted. The SAT scores for the 2014-2015 freshman class were: Critical Reading--8% below 500, 30% between 500 and 599, 44% between 600 and 699, and 19% between 700 and 800; Math--9% between 500 and 599, 43% between 600 and 699, and 48% between 700 and 800; Writing--6% below 500, 31% between 500 and 599, 48% between 600 and 699, and 16% between 700 and 800. The ACT scores were 0% below 21, 2% between 21 and 23, 12% between 24 and 26, 21% between 27 and 28, and 65% above 28. 88% of the current freshmen were in the top fifth of their class; 99% were in the top two fifths. There were 9 National Merit finalists. 48 freshmen graduated first in their class. **Admissions Contact:** Edward J. Connor, Dean of Admissions. E-Mail: *admissions@wpi.edu* Web: *www.wpi.edu*

FINANCIAL AID: In 2014-2015, 68% of all full-time freshmen and 68% of continuing full-time students received some form of financial aid. 68% of all full-time freshmen and 68% of continuing full-time students received need-based aid. The average freshman award was $31,426. Need-based scholarships or need-based grants averaged $21,380; and need-based self-help aid (loans and jobs) averaged $3,324. 25% of undergraduate students work part-time. Average annual earnings from campus work are $2640. WPI is a member of CSS. The CSS/Profile and FAFSA, and CSS Noncustodial Profile, and WPI Upper-Class Application are required. The deadline for filing freshman financial aid applications for fall entry is February 1.

WORCESTER STATE UNIVERSITY C-2
www.worcester.edu

Worcester, MA 01602	(508) 929-8040
	(866) 972-2255
Fax: (508) 929-8183	Email: admissions@worcester.edu
Full-time: 1692 men, 2465 women	Faculty: 206; IIA, +$
Part-time: 538 men, 868 women	Ph.D.s: 82%
Graduate: 200 men, 587 women	Student/Faculty: 20 to 1
Year: semesters, summer session	Tuition: $8557 ($14,637)
Room & Board: $11,255	Freshman Class: 4158 applied, 2549 accepted, 794 enrolled
SAT CR/M: 490/500 ACT: 22	CEEB CODE: 3524
Application Deadline: May 1	COMPETITIVE

Worcester State University, established in 1874, is part of the Massachusetts public higher education system and offer undergraduate and graduate programs. A liberal arts core is emphasized, as are selected areas of science, the health professions, education, business, and management. There are 2 undergraduate schools and 1 graduate school. In addition to regional accreditation, WSU has baccalaureate program accreditation with ASHA, ACOTE, JRCEP, NASP, CAEP, CCNE, and MACN. The 58-acre campus is in an urban area on the west side of Worcester, Massachusetts, 45 miles west of Boston. Including any residence halls, there are 13 buildings.

STUDENT LIFE: 96% of undergraduates are from Massachusetts. Others are from 25 states, 25 foreign countries, and Canada. 70% are White. The average age of freshmen is 18; all undergraduates, 24. **Housing:** 1577 students can be accommodated in college housing, which includes single-sex and coed dorms and on-campus apartments. On-campus housing is available on a first-come and first-served basis. Priority is given to out-of-town students. 75% of students commute. Alcohol is not permitted. All students may keep cars.

FACULTY/CLASSROOMS: 43% of faculty are male; 57% are female. No introductory courses are taught by graduate students.

PROGRAMS OF STUDY: WSU confers B.A., and B.S. degrees. Master's degrees are also awarded. Bachelor's degrees are awarded in BIOLOGICAL SCIENCE (biology/biological science and biotechnology), BUSINESS (business administration and management), COMMUNICATIONS AND THE ARTS (communications, English, Spanish, and visual and performing arts), COMPUTER AND PHYSICAL SCIENCE (chemistry, computer science, mathematics, and natural sciences), EDUCATION (early childhood education, elementary education, and health education), HEALTH PROFESSIONS (nursing, occupational therapy, and speech pathology/audiology), SOCIAL SCIENCE (criminal justice, economics, geography, history, psychology, sociology, and urban studies). Occupational therapy and nursing is the strongest academically. Business administration, psychology, and criminal justice have the largest enrollments.

ACTIVITIES: There are no fraternities or sororities. There are 40

groups on campus, including cheerleading, chess, chorale, computers, dance, drama, environmental, ethnic, gay, honors, newspaper, political, professional, radio and TV, religious, social, social service, student government, and yearbook. Popular campus events include Multicultural Festival, Homecoming, SGA Auction to Benefit Homeless and Lecture Series. **Sports:** There are 9 intercollegiate sports for men and 11 for women, and 10 intramural sports for men and 10 for women. Facilities include a weight room, John Coughlin stadium, softball and baseball, and ice rink. **Graduates:** From July 1, 2013 to June 30, 2014, 986 bachelor's degrees were awarded. The most popular majors were business administration (18%), psychology (12%), and criminal justice (11%).

SERVICES: Counseling and information services are available, as is tutoring in most subjects. There is a reader service for the blind, and remedial math, reading, and writing. **Library/Resources:** The library contains 133,645 volumes, 16,500 microform items, 3,976 audio/video tapes/CDs/DVDs, and subscribes to 57,292 periodicals including electronic. Computerized library services include interlibrary loans, database searching, Internet access, and Wi-Fi capability. Special learning facilities include a radio station, including photographic labs, an audiovisual center, multimedia classrooms with satellite connectivity, discipline-specific computer labs, and a speech, language, and hearing clinic. **Physically Challenged Students:** All of the campus is accessible. Facilities include wheelchair ramps, elevators, special parking, specially equipped restrooms, lowered drinking fountains, lowered telephones, and special housing. **Special:** Cross-registration with the Worcester Consortium for Higher Education is available, as are internships, study abroad (more than 60 countries), a Washington semester, work-study, non-degree study, and a pass/fail option. There are 20 national honor societies, a freshman honors program, and 16 departmental honors programs. **Visiting:** There are regularly scheduled orientations for prospective students, including a campus tour and review of campus life and organizations, success in college, special opportunities, and available services. To schedule a visit, contact the Admissions Office. **Campus Safety and Security:** Measures include 24-hour foot and vehicle patrol, emergency notification system, self-defense education, and security escort services. There are shuttle buses, emergency telephones, lighted pathways/sidewalks, controlled access to dorms/residences, crime prevention programs offered throughout the year to both students and faculty/staff.

REQUIREMENTS: The SAT or ACT is required. For students with a GPA of 2.9 or above, a minimum SAT or ACT score may be required. For students whose GPA is below 2.9, a minimum SAT or ACT score is applied according to a scale established by WSC. Applicants must graduate from an accredited secondary school. They should have completed 4 years of English, 3 of math, 2 each of a foreign language, a lab science, and social studies, including 1 year of U.S. history and government, and 2 electives. The College Board Student Descriptive questionnaire must be submitted. AP and CLEP credits are accepted. A GPA of 2.0 is required. AP and CLEP credits are accepted. Candidates for a baccalaureate degree must complete 120 semester-hour credits with a 2.0 cumulative grade point average (GPA) and a minimum of 2.0 GPA or higher in the departmental and ancillary courses of the major field of concentration. To receive a baccalaureate degree from Worcester State University, a student must complete 30 of the last 40 credits at Worcester State University, earn a majority of credits in the major at Worcester State University and earn a majority of credits in the minor (if elected) at the University. **Procedure:** Freshmen are admitted fall, spring, and summer. Entrance exams should be taken in spring of the junior year or fall of the senior year. There is a rolling admissions plan. Applications should be filed by May 1 for fall entry, along with a $50 fee. Notifications are sent in rolling. Applications are accepted on-line. **Transfer Students:** 575 transfer students enrolled in 2013-2014. Transfer applicants must have earned a minimum of 12 college credits with a minimum 2.5 GPA or 13 to 23 credits with a minimum 2.0 GPA. Students with fewer than 24 transfer credits may be admitted under the same criteria as first-time freshmen. 30 of 120 credits required for the bachelor's degree must be completed at WSU. **International Students:** There are 36 international students enrolled. They must take the TOEFL with a minimum score of 79 on the Internet-based version (iBT). They must also take the SAT.

ADMISSIONS: 61% of the 2014-2015 applicants were accepted. The SAT scores for the 2014-2015 freshman class were: Critical Reading--52% below 500, 39% between 500 and 599, 8% between 600 and 699, and 1% between 700 and 800; Math--44% below 500, 45% between 500 and 599, 10% between 600 and 699, and 1% between 700 and 800. The ACT scores were 33% below 21, 27% between 21 and 23, 22% between 24 and 26, 13% between 27 and 28, and 5% above 28. **Admissions Contact:** Joseph DiCarlo, Director of Admissions. E-Mail: *admissions@worcester.edu* Web: *www.worcester.edu*

FINANCIAL AID: WSU is a member of CSS. The FAFSA and the college's own financial statement are required. The priority date for freshman financial aid applications for fall entry is March 1. The deadline for filing freshman financial aid applications for fall entry is May 1.

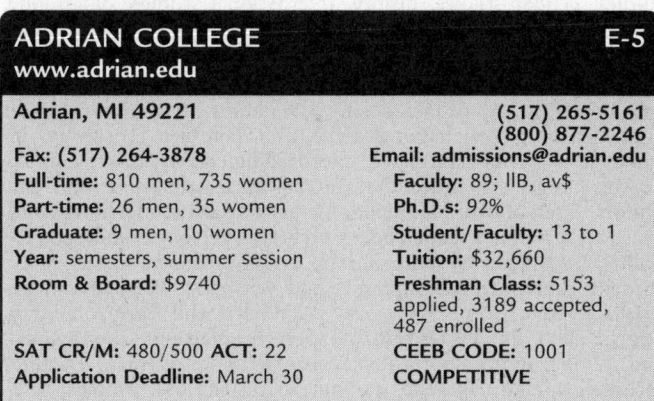

MICHIGAN

• College Location

0 20 40 60 80 100
Miles

ADRIAN COLLEGE
www.adrian.edu

E-5

Adrian, MI 49221	**(517) 265-5161**
	(800) 877-2246
Fax: (517) 264-3878	Email: admissions@adrian.edu
Full-time: 810 men, 735 women	Faculty: 89; IIB, av$
Part-time: 26 men, 35 women	Ph.D.s: 92%
Graduate: 9 men, 10 women	Student/Faculty: 13 to 1
Year: semesters, summer session	Tuition: $32,660
Room & Board: $9740	Freshman Class: 5153 applied, 3189 accepted, 487 enrolled
SAT CR/M: 480/500 ACT: 22	CEEB CODE: 1001
Application Deadline: March 30	COMPETITIVE

Adrian College, founded in 1859, is a private liberal arts institution affiliated with the United Methodist Church. There is 1 undergraduate school and 4 graduate schools. In addition to regional accreditation, Adrian has baccalaureate program accreditation with CSWE, NCATE, TEAC, and CAATE. The 132-acre campus is in a small town 35 miles southwest of Ann Arbor. Including any residence halls, there are 41 buildings.

STUDENT LIFE: 75% of undergraduates are from Michigan. 80% are White. 48% claim no religious affiliation; 23% Protestant; 18% Catholic. 46% remain to graduate. **Housing:** 1600 students can be accommodated in college housing, which includes single-sex and coed dorms, on-campus apartments, and off-campus apartments. In addition, there are honors houses, special-interest houses, fraternity houses, substance-free, smoke-free, extended quiet hours, upperclassmen only residence halls, and theme housing. On-campus housing is guaranteed for all 4 years. All students may keep cars.

FACULTY/CLASSROOMS: 52% of faculty are male; 48% are female. All teach undergraduates. No introductory courses are taught by graduate students. The average class size in an introductory lecture is 19; in a laboratory is 15; and in a regular course is 12.

PROGRAMS OF STUDY: Adrian confers B.A., B.S., B.B.A., B.F.A.,

B.M., B.M.E. and B.S.W. degrees. Associate and Master's degrees are also awarded. Bachelor's degrees are awarded in AGRICULTURE (environmental studies), BIOLOGICAL SCIENCE (biology/biological science), BUSINESS (accounting, business administration and management, international business management, marketing management, and sports management), COMMUNICATIONS AND THE ARTS (arts administration/management, communications, dramatic arts, English, French, German, journalism, literature, music, music performance, musical theater, Spanish, and studio art), COMPUTER AND PHYSICAL SCIENCE (chemistry, earth science, mathematics, and physics), EDUCATION (elementary education, physical education, and secondary education), ENGINEERING AND ENVIRONMENTAL DESIGN (environmental science and interior design), HEALTH PROFESSIONS (exercise science), SOCIAL SCIENCE (criminal justice, economics, history, international studies, Japanese studies, philosophy, political science/government, psychology, religion, social work, and sociology). Accounting and business administration, and exercise science have the largest enrollments.

ACTIVITIES: 18% of men belong to 4 national fraternities; 19% of women belong to 3 national sororities. There are 79 groups on campus, including and exercise groups, equestrian team, gamers council, sports, various outdoors, art, band, cheerleading, choir, chorale, chorus, computers, dance, drama, environmental, ethnic, feminist empowerment movement, gay, honors, international, jazz band, literary magazine, marching band, musical theater, newspaper, orchestra, pep band, photography, political, professional, radio and TV, religious, social, social service, student government, symphony, and yearbook. Popular campus events include Family Weekend, International Week, Dance Marathon, One-Act Plays, Sadie Hawkins Dance, Sibs 'n' Kids Weekend. **Sports:** There are 13 intercollegiate sports for men and 18 for women, and 6 intramural sports for men and 6 for women. Facilities include a sport and fitness center featuring a multipurpose forum with 3 courts for basketball, volleyball, and tennis, an indoor track, racquetball courts, a weight room, a 1,350-seat performance gym; a 5,000-seat football stadium, baseball and softball fields; 2 soccer fields, 6 tennis courts, a 400-meter track, and numerous intramural fields. **Graduates:** From July 1, 2013 to June 30, 2014, 314 bachelor's degrees were awarded. The most popular majors were business and accounting (22%), exercise science and athletic training (11%), and biology (10%). 22 companies recruited on campus in 2013-2014. In an average class, 54% graduate in 6 years or less. Of the 2013 graduating class, 20% were enrolled in graduate school within 6 months of graduation, and 22% were employed.

SERVICES: Counseling and information services are available, as is tutoring in most subjects. There is a reader service for the blind, remedial math, reading, and writing. **Library/Resources:** The library contains 163,727 volumes, 51,188 microform items, 4,032 audio/video tapes/CDs/DVDs, and subscribes to 10,373 periodicals including electronic. Computerized library services include interlibrary loans, database searching, Internet access, and Wi-Fi capability. Special learning facilities include an art gallery, planetarium, radio station, a solar greenhouse, palatinate lab, and an observatory. **Physically Challenged Students:** Facilities include wheelchair ramps, elevators, special parking, specially equipped restrooms, lowered drinking fountains, lowered telephones, special housing. Diagnostic testing, learning services, note-taking services, oral testing, extended time, priority seating, readers, tape recording, texts on tape, tutors, student and psychological support groups. **Special:** Adrian offers pre-professional programs in architectture, engineering, health sciences, law, ministry, medical technology, and art therapy; study abroad in 16 countries and a Washington Semester; student-designed majors and internships in more than 450 locations, and a 3-2 engineering degree with Washington University in St. Louis and the University of Detroit Mercy. There are 15 national honor societies and a freshman honors program. **Visiting:** There are regularly scheduled orientations for prospective students, including a student-guided campus tour and visits with an admissions counselor, professors from the student's area of interest, and an athletics coach. There are guides for informal visits, visitors may sit in on classes, and stay overnight. To schedule a visit, contact the Office of Admissions at visitac@adrian.edu. **Campus Safety and Security:** Measures include 24-hour foot and vehicle patrol, self-defense education, and security escort services. There are emergency telephones and lighted pathways/sidewalks.

REQUIREMENTS: The SAT or ACT is required. Applicants must be graduates of an accredited secondary school. The GED is accepted. Each student is reviewed individually based on GPA and test scores. Adrian requires applicants to be in the upper 50% of their class. AP and CLEP credits are accepted. Important factors in the admissions decision are advanced placement or honors courses, leadership record, and extracurricular activities record. To graduate, students must maintain a 2.0 average over 124 credit hours, 30 of which must be in upper-division courses. 22 hours of distribution requirements and 21 of basic educational proficiency are required, including 2 semesters of foreign language and 1 each of communication, English, fine arts, fitness, humanities, math, natural or physical science, religion or philosophy, and social science. **Procedure:** Freshmen are admitted fall and spring. Entrance exams should be taken during the spring of the junior year or fall of the senior year. There are deferred admissions and rolling admissions plans. Application deadlines are open. Applications are accepted on-line. **Transfer Students:** 65 transfer students enrolled in 2013-2014. Applicants must have an above-average GPA and provide final high school transcripts. If the student has completed fewer than 24 semester hours, ACT or SAT test scores are also required. Grades of 2.0 and above transfer for credit. The college admits transfer students every semester. 34 of 124 credits required for the bachelor's degree must be completed at Adrian. **International Students:** There are 69 international students enrolled. The school actively recruits these students. They must take the TOEFL with a minimum score of 500 on the paper-based TOEFL (PBT) or 73 on the Internet-based version (iBT). They must also take the SAT or ACT.

ADMISSIONS: 62% of the 2014-2015 applicants were accepted. The SAT scores for the 2014-2015 freshman class were: Critical Reading--55% below 500, and 45% between 500 and 599; Math--41% below 500, 52% between 500 and 599, and 7% between 600 and 699. The ACT scores were 38% below 21, 34% between 21 and 23, 16% between 24 and 26, 6% between 27 and 28, and 6% above 28. 11 freshmen graduated first in their class. **Admissions Contact:** Erin DeSmet, Director of Admissions. E-Mail: *edesmet@adrian.edu* Web: *www.adrian.edu*

FINANCIAL AID: In 2014-2015, 99% of all full-time freshmen and 99% of continuing full-time students received some form of financial aid. 83% of all full-time freshmen and 86% of continuing full-time students received need-based aid. The average freshman award was $33,831. Need-based scholarships or need-based grants averaged $22,666 ($38,806 maximum); need-based self-help aid (loans and jobs) averaged $12,008 ($45,500 maximum); and other non-need-based awards and non-need-based scholarships averaged $15,472 ($31,870 maximum). 39% of undergraduate students work part-time. Average annual earnings from campus work are $1500. The average financial indebtedness of the 2014 graduate was $41,000. Adrian is a member of CSS. The FAFSA is required. The priority date for freshman financial aid applications for fall entry is March 1.

ALBION COLLEGE   **D-5**
www.albion.edu

Albion, MI 49224	**(517) 629-0321**
	(800) 858-6770
Fax: (517) 629-0569	Email: admission@albion.edu
Full-time: 643 men, 625 women	Faculty: 101; IIB, -$
Part-time: 9 men, 7 women	Ph.D.s: 96%
Graduate: n/av	Student/Faculty: 11 to 1
Year: semesters, summer session	Tuition: $35,866
Room & Board: $10,144	Freshman Class: 4430 applied, 2498 accepted, 346 enrolled
SAT CR/M: 540/540 ACT: 24	CEEB CODE: 1007
Application Deadline: open	COMPETITIVE

Albion College, established in 1835, is a private institution affiliated with the United Methodist Church and offering undergraduate

degrees in liberal arts curricula. In addition to regional accreditation, Albion has baccalaureate program accreditation with NASM, TEAC, ACS, and CAATE. The 574-acre campus is in a small town in south central Michigan, 65 miles from Detroit. Including any residence halls, there are 94 buildings.

STUDENT LIFE: 91% of undergraduates are from Michigan. Others are from 23 states, 20 foreign countries, and Canada. 82% are White. 49% claim no religious affiliation; 26% Catholic; 20% Protestant. The average age of freshmen is 18; all undergraduates, 20. 19% do not continue beyond their first year; 65% remain to graduate. **Housing:** 1755 students can be accommodated in college housing, which includes single-sex and coed dorms, on-campus apartments, and married student housing. In addition, there are special-interest houses, fraternity houses, and special interest annexes. On-campus housing is guaranteed for all 4 years. 89% of students live on campus. All students may keep cars.

FACULTY/CLASSROOMS: 56% of faculty are male; 44% are female. All teach undergraduates, 89% do research. No introductory courses are taught by graduate students. The average class size in an introductory lecture is 21; in a laboratory is 14; and in a regular course is 16.

PROGRAMS OF STUDY: Albion confers B.A., and B.F.A. degrees. Bachelor's degrees are awarded in AGRICULTURE (environmental studies and forestry and related sciences), BIOLOGICAL SCIENCE (biochemistry and biology/biological science), BUSINESS (accounting, accounting/CPA, business administration and management, and finance), COMMUNICATIONS AND THE ARTS (art, art history and appreciation, communication studies, creative writing, English, French, German, music, music performance, Spanish, theatre arts, and visual and performing arts), COMPUTER AND PHYSICAL SCIENCE (actuarial mathematics, chemistry, earth science, geology, mathematics, and physics), EDUCATION (athletic training, English education, and music education), ENGINEERING AND ENVIRONMENTAL DESIGN (engineering and environmental science), HEALTH PROFESSIONS (exercise science, predentistry, and premedicine), SOCIAL SCIENCE (anthropology, economics, ethnic studies, gender studies, history, international studies, philosophy, political science/government, psychology, public affairs, religion, sociology, and women's studies). Economics, biology, and psychology have the largest enrollments.

ACTIVITIES: 53% of men belong to 6 national fraternities; 42% of women belong to 7 national sororities. There are 110 groups on campus, including art, band, cheerleading, chess, choir, chorale, chorus, computers, dance, drama, environmental, ethnic, film, gay, honors, international, jazz band, literary magazine, marching band, musical theater, newspaper, opera, orchestra, pep band, photography, political, professional, radio and TV, religious, social, social service, student government, symphony, and yearbook. Popular campus events include Briton Bash, Day of Woden and Party on Perry. **Sports:** There are 12 intercollegiate sports for men and 11 for women, and 10 intramural sports for men and 10 for women. Facilities include a sprankle/sprandel stadium, soccer/lacrosse complex, baseball complex, softball complex, alumni field entrance and outdoor plaza a Dean aquatic center a cardiovascular fitness room and a held questrian center. The Dow Recreation and Wellness Center, located adjacent to Sprankle-Sprandel Stadium, is devoted to educational and recreational purposes, including individual and group sports activities, physical conditioning, and health and wellness programs. The Lomas Fieldhouse includes court space for intramural sports, 1/9-mile track, 2 racquetball courts, weight room, classroom, locker rooms. The Ungrodt Tennis Center offers a state-of-the-art, 4-court indoor facility. **Graduates:** From July 1, 2013 to June 30, 2014, 321 bachelor's degrees were awarded. The most popular majors were economics and management (16%), psychological science (15%), and biology (12%). 53 companies recruited on campus in 2013-2014. In an average class, 65% graduate in 4 years or less, 73% graduate in 5 years or less, and 74% graduate in 6 years or less. Of the 2013 graduating class, 42% were enrolled in graduate school within 6 months of graduation, and 37% were employed.

SERVICES: Counseling and information services are available, as is tutoring in most subjects. There is a reader service for the blind. The Academic Skills center includes the Learning Support center, Disability services, the Quantitative Studies center, and the Writing center. **Library/Resources:** The library contains 350,709 volumes, 51,080 microform items, 12,876 audio/video tapes/CDs/DVDs, and subscribes to 68,616 periodicals including electronic. Computerized library services include interlibrary loans, database searching, and Internet access. Special learning facilities include an art gallery, planetarium, radio station, a nature center a equestrian center, and a Dow analytical science laboratory. **Physically Challenged Students:** 90% of the campus is accessible. Facilities include wheelchair ramps, elevators, special parking, specially equipped restrooms, special class scheduling, lowered drinking fountains, and lowered telephones. **Special:** Albion offers study abroad in 40 countries, and study/internship programs in New York City, Philadelphia, Washington, D.C., Oak Ridge, and Chicago. Students may earn a dual engineering degree in conjunction with Columbia University, Michigan Technological University, or the University of Michigan. Student-designed majors and interdisciplinary majors in fields including environmental science, ethnic studies, international studies, and women's and gender studies are available. There are 6 national honor societies, including Phi Beta Kappa, a freshman honors program, and 13 departmental honors programs. **Visiting:** There are regularly scheduled orientations for prospective students, consisting of 4 programs held in early June and 1 in August for students and parents. There are guides for informal visits, visitors may sit in on classes, and stay overnight. To schedule a visit, contact Martha Bunde at (517) 629-0769. **Campus Safety and Security:** Measures include 24-hour foot and vehicle patrol, emergency notification system, self-defense education, and security escort services. There are shuttle buses, emergency telephones, lighted pathways/sidewalks, and controlled access to dorms/residences.

REQUIREMENTS: The SAT or ACT is required. Applicants must graduate from an accredited secondary school or earn a GED. Completion of 15 Carnegie credits is required. A strong background in English, math, and the lab and social sciences is recommended as the best preparation for academic success. The Admission Committee will consider courses taken, grades earned, the academic rigor of the program and SAT/ACT scores as corroborative evidence. Applications are accepted on-line at the Albion web site and through the Common App. AP and CLEP credits are accepted. Important factors in the admissions decision are advanced placement or honors courses, extracurricular activities record, and personality/intangible qualities. Requirements for graduation: 32 units (128 semester hours) – a minimum of the last 12 units must be taken at Albion College, a minimum of one major, completion of the core (see below), pass the Writing Competence Exam and have a minimum of 2.0 cum GPA, and submission of an Application for Degree. CORE REQUIREMENT: at Albion, the general education requirement is referred to as "the core." Students begin to fulfill the core in their first semester with Liberal Arts 101; some will be able to complete much of the core requirement by the end of their first year. Liberal Arts 101 (First-Year Seminar; 1 unit), Modes of Inquiry (1 unit in each) - Textual Analysis; Artistic Creation and Analysis; Scientific Analysis; Modeling and Analysis; Historical and Cultural Analysis. Category Requirements (1 unit in each) - Environmental Studies; Ethnicity Studies; Gender Studies; and Global Studies. Distribution Requirement: one unit in fine arts (art and art history, music, theatre, honors); 2 units in humanities (English, foreign languages, philosophy, religious studies, honors); 2 units in mathematics or natural sciences (biology, chemistry, computer science, geological sciences, mathematics, physics, honors); two units in social science (anthropology and sociology, economics and management, history, political science, psychology, speech communication, honors). **Procedure:** Freshmen are admitted fall and spring. Entrance exams should be taken in April or June of the junior year. There are early admissions, deferred admissions, and rolling admissions plans. Application deadlines are open. Application fee is $40. Notification is sent on a rolling basis. Application fees are waived if application is completed on-line. **Transfer Students:** 27 transfer students enrolled in 2013-2014. Transfer applicants must submit official college transcripts. Grades of 2.0 or better are considered for transfer credit. Albion evaluates the applicant's course work before conferring transfer credit. 48 of 128 credits required for the bachelor's degree must be completed at Albion. **International Students:** There are 42 international students enrolled. The school actively recruits these students. They must take the TOEFL with a minimum score of 550 on the paper-based TOEFL (PBT) or 79 on the Internet-based version (iBT). They must also take the SAT or ACT.

ADMISSIONS: 56% of the 2014-2015 applicants were accepted. The SAT scores for the 2014-2015 freshman class were: Critical Reading--24% below 500, 58% between 500 and 599, and 18% between 600 and 699; Math--12% below 500, 70% between 500 and 599, 12% between 600 and 699, and 6% between 700 and 800. The ACT scores were 21% below 21, 29% between 21 and 23, 25% between 24 and 26, 17% between 27 and 28, and 17% above 28. **Admissions Contact:** Mandy Dubiel, Director of Admissions. E-Mail: *admission@albion .edu* Web: *www.albion.edu*

FINANCIAL AID: In 2014-2015, 99% of all full-time freshmen and continuing full-time students received some form of financial aid. 78% of all full-time freshmen and continuing full-time students received need-based aid. The average freshman award was $29,246. Need-based scholarships or need-based grants averaged $24,012; need-based self-help aid (loans and jobs) averaged $6,271; other non-need-based awards and non-need-based scholarships averaged $5,380; and $16,943 from other forms of aid. 54% of undergraduate students work part-time. Average annual earnings from campus work are $1094. The average financial indebtedness of the 2014 graduate was $37,191. The FAFSA is required. The priority date for freshman financial aid applications for fall entry is February 1.

ALMA COLLEGE — D-4
www.alma.edu

Alma, MI 48801-1599	**(989) 463-7139**
	(800) 321-ALMA
Fax: (989) 463-7057	**Email:** admissions@alma.edu
Full-time: 613 men, 740 women	**Faculty:** 96; IIB, av$
Part-time: 19 men, 24 women	**Ph.D.s:** 84%
Graduate: n/av	**Student/Faculty:** 12 to 1
Year: n/av	**Tuition:** $34,585
Room & Board: $9490	**Freshman Class:** 2338 applied, 1683 accepted, 357 enrolled
SAT CR/M/W: 518/546/496 **ACT:** 24	**CEEB CODE:** 1010
Application Deadline: open	**COMPETITIVE**

Alma College, offers a personalized education with multiple paths and experiences leading to success. Strong academic programs and a deep regard for students as individuals are fundamental to an Alma education, with small classes and many opportunities for one-on-one collaboration with dedicated faculty. In addition to regional accreditation, Alma has baccalaureate program accreditation with NASM, TEAC, ACS, and CAAHEP. The 128-acre campus is in a small town 50 miles north of Lansing, Alma, MI, located in the middle of Michigan's Lower Peninsula. Including any residence halls, there are 28 buildings.

STUDENT LIFE: 91% of undergraduates are from Michigan. Others are from 32 states, 9 foreign countries, and Canada. 91% are from public schools. 87% are White. 40% are Protestant; 35% claim no religious affiliation; 21% Catholic. The average age of freshmen is 18; all undergraduates, 20. 22% do not continue beyond their first year; 78% remain to graduate. **Housing:** 1322 students can be accommodated in college housing, which includes coed dorms and on-campus apartments. In addition, there are special-interest houses, fraternity houses, sorority houses, and international house. On-campus housing is guaranteed for all 4 years. 93% of students live on campus; of those, 65% remain on campus on weekends. All students may keep cars.

FACULTY/CLASSROOMS: 56% of faculty are male; 44% are female. All teach undergraduates, and all do research. No introductory courses are taught by graduate students. The average class size in an introductory lecture is 18; in a laboratory is 12; and in a regular course is 16.

PROGRAMS OF STUDY: Alma confers B.A., B.S., B.M., B.S.N. and B.F.A. degrees. Bachelor's degrees are awarded in AGRICULTURE (environmental studies), BIOLOGICAL SCIENCE (biochemistry, biology/biological science, and biotechnology), BUSINESS (accounting, accounting/CPA, business administration and management, finance, international business management, and marketing), COM-

MUNICATIONS AND THE ARTS (art, communications, dance, English, French, German, music, Spanish, and theatre arts), COMPUTER AND PHYSICAL SCIENCE (chemistry, computer science, mathematics, and physics), EDUCATION (athletic training, early childhood education, educational studies, elementary education, secondary education, and special education), HEALTH PROFESSIONS (exercise science, health care administration, health science, and nursing), SOCIAL SCIENCE (anthropology, economics, history, philosophy, political science/government, psychology, religion, and sociology). Integrative physiology and health science, biology, business administration, education, and English are the strongest academically. Business, integrative physiology, health science, and biology have the largest enrollments.

ACTIVITIES: 25% of men belong to 2 local and 4 national fraternities; 32% of women belong to 1 local and 4 national sororities. There are 80 groups on campus, including art, bagpipe, band, cheerleading, chess, choir, chorale, chorus, computers, dance, drama, environmental, ethnic, gay, honors, international, jazz band, literary magazine, marching band, newspaper, orchestra, political, professional, radio and TV, religious, social, social service, student government, symphony, and yearbook. Popular campus events include Song Fest, and Highland Festival. **Sports:** There are 11 intercollegiate sports for men and 11 for women, and 13 intramural sports for men and 13 for women. Facilities include a recreation center with a climbing wall, fitness center, 4 courts, and suspended 3-lane track, an indoor gym and pool, an outdoor sports complex with an artificial turf playing field, an 8-lane track, baseball, soccer, and softball fields, a weight training room, and racquetball and tennis courts. **Graduates:** From July 1, 2013 to June 30, 2014, 283 bachelor's degrees were awarded. The most popular majors were business administration (19%), integrative physiology and health science (11%), and biology (8%). In an average class, 1% graduate in 3 years or less, 47% graduate in 4 years or less, 60% graduate in 5 years or less, and 61% graduate in 6 years or less. Of the 2013 graduating class, 22% were enrolled in graduate school within 6 months of graduation, and 63% were employed.

SERVICES: Counseling and information services are available, as is tutoring in every subject, both individual and group tutoring are available. There is a reader service for the blind. **Library/Resources:** The library contains 265,000 volumes, 247,000 microform items, 13,500 audio/video tapes/CDs/DVDs, and subscribes to 1,500 periodicals including electronic. Computerized library services include interlibrary loans, database searching, Internet access, and Wi-Fi capability. Special learning facilities include an art gallery, planetarium, radio station, a writing lab, and digital media commons. **Physically Challenged Students:** 75% of the campus is accessible. Facilities include wheelchair ramps, elevators, special parking, specially equipped restrooms, special class scheduling, lowered drinking fountains. 2 residence halls with private baths, and several small housing units. **Special:** Alma offers internships in many fields, study abroad in 18 countries, experiential learning program at the Philadelphia Center, and a Washington semester at American University. There are work-study programs, dual majors, B.A.-B.S. degrees, and student-designed majors in a wide variety of subjects. The college confers 3-2 engineering degrees in conjunction with the University of Michigan and Kettering University. Non-degree study may be pursued, and students have a pass/fail grading option. A 4-week spring term provides intensive study in 1 course, often combined with travel. There are 3 national honor societies, including Phi Beta Kappa, a freshman honors program, and 17 departmental honors programs. **Visiting:** There are regularly scheduled orientations for prospective students, consisting of faculty talks, tours, a meal on campus, financial aid information, and admissions sessions. There are guides for informal visits, visitors may sit in on classes, and stay overnight. To schedule a visit, contact the Admissions Office. **Campus Safety and Security:** Measures include emergency notification system and security escort services. There are emergency telephones, lighted pathways/sidewalks, controlled access to dorms/residences, 24-hour foot patrol, and ID card access to residence halls.

REQUIREMENTS: The SAT or ACT is required. The ACT is preferred. Applicants must have graduated from an accredited secondary school and have earned 16 Carnegie units, including 4 years of English and 3 each of math, science, and social studies, with 2 of a foreign language recommended. Alma prefers applicants in the upper

25% of their class. Portfolio and audition are required for performing arts scholarships. A GPA of 3.0 is required. AP credits are accepted. Important factors in the admissions decision are advanced placement or honors courses, leadership record, and recommendations by school officials. Degree requirements include completion of a minimum of 136 credit hours; 148 hours are required for the B.F.A. degree, 136 to 156 for the B.M. degree. Students must attain a minimum GPA of 2.0, or 3.0 for fine arts majors. All students must demonstrate proficiency in English, second language/international awareness, communication, and computation, and they must complete distribution requirements, which include 12 fine arts and humanities credits and 12 each of social science and natural science credits. The total number of program credits is 36 for a departmental major, 56 for an interdepartmental major, and 56 to 68 for self-directed majors. **Procedure:** Freshmen are admitted fall and winter. Entrance exams should be taken in the spring of the junior year or as late as the winter of the senior year. There are deferred admissions and rolling admissions plans. Application deadlines are open. Application fee is $25. Notification is sent on a rolling basis. Applications are accepted on-line. Application fees are waived if application is completed on-line. **Transfer Students:** 44 transfer students enrolled in 2013-2014. Students wishing to transfer to Alma must have a minimum GPA of 2.0 from other colleges attended. 34 of 136 credits required for the bachelor's degree must be completed at Alma. **International Students:** There are 14 international students enrolled. The school actively recruits these students. They must take the TOEFL with a minimum score of 550 on the paper-based TOEFL (PBT) or 79 on the Internet-based version (iBT). The SAT or ACT is required if the TOEFL is not submitted.

ADMISSIONS: 72% of the 2014-2015 applicants were accepted. The SAT scores for the 2014-2015 freshman class were: Critical Reading--39% below 500, 39% between 500 and 599, and 22% between 600 and 699; Math--56% below 500, 33% between 500 and 599, and 11% between 600 and 699; Writing--56% below 500, 39% between 500 and 599, and 11% between 600 and 699. The ACT scores were 22% below 21, 25% between 21 and 23, 27% between 24 and 26, 16% between 27 and 28, and 10% above 28. 45% of the current freshmen were in the top fifth of their class; 75% were in the top two fifths. 14 freshmen graduated first in their class. **Admissions Contact:** Amanda Slenski, Director of Admissions. E-Mail: *admissions@alma.edu* Web: *www.alma.edu*

FINANCIAL AID: In 2014-2015, 100% of all full-time freshmen and continuing full-time students received some form of financial aid. 90% of all full-time freshmen and 90% of continuing full-time students received need-based aid. The average freshman award was $18,916. Need-based scholarships or need-based grants averaged $24,110; and need-based self-help aid (loans and jobs) averaged $3,848. 41% of undergraduate students work part-time. Average annual earnings from campus work are $1818. The FAFSA is required. The priority date for freshman financial aid applications for fall entry is March 1.

ANDREWS UNIVERSITY   C-5
www.andrews.edu

Berrien Springs, MI 49104   (616) 471-6343
  (800) 253-2874
Fax: (616) 471-3228   Email: undergraduate@andrews.edu
Full-time: 783 men, 931 women   Faculty: 148
Part-time: 107 men, 143 women   Ph.D.s: 72%
Graduate: 1097 men, 528 women   Student/Faculty: 12 to 1
Year: semesters, summer session   Tuition: $21,170
Room & Board: $6860   Freshman Class: 1809 applied, 879 accepted, 377 enrolled
SAT: required ACT: 23   CEEB CODE: 1030
Application Deadline: open   COMPETITIVE+

Andrews University, established in 1874, is a private institution affiliated with the Seventh-day Adventist Church that offers undergraduate degrees in business, education, arts and sciences, architecture, and technology. There are 5 undergraduate schools and 6 graduate schools. In addition to regional accreditation, Andrews has baccalaureate program accreditation with AACSB, ABET, ADA, AHEA, APTA, CAHEA, CSWE, NAAB, NASM, NCATE, NLN, and IACBE. The 1600-acre campus is in a rural area 10 miles south of Benton Harbor. Including any residence halls, there are 51 buildings.

STUDENT LIFE: 56% of undergraduates are from out of state, mostly the Middle Atlantic. Students are from 46 states, 51 foreign countries, and Canada. 23% are from public schools. 42% are White; 25% African American; 12% Foreign. 89% are Protestant; 12% unknown denominations. The average age of freshmen is 18; all undergraduates, 22. 21% do not continue beyond their first year; 58% remain to graduate. **Housing:** 1500 students can be accommodated in college housing, which includes single-sex dorms, on-campus apartments, and married student housing. On-campus housing is available on a first-come, first-served basis. 54% of students live on campus. Alcohol is not permitted. All students may keep cars.

FACULTY/CLASSROOMS: 64% of faculty are male; 36% are female. No introductory courses are taught by graduate students. The average class size in a laboratory is 16 and in a regular course is 18.

PROGRAMS OF STUDY: Andrews confers B.A., B.S., B.B.A., B.F.A., B.Mus., B.S.D., B.S.Educ., B.S.El.Ed., B.S.Eng., B.S.W. and B.T. degrees. Associate, Master's, and Doctoral degrees are also awarded. Bachelor's degrees are awarded in AGRICULTURE (agriculture, animal science, and horticulture), BIOLOGICAL SCIENCE (anatomy, biochemistry, biology/biological science, biophysics, botany, molecular biology, nutrition, and zoology), BUSINESS (accounting, banking and finance, business administration and management, business economics, management information systems, and marketing/retailing/merchandising), COMMUNICATIONS AND THE ARTS (art, ceramic art and design, communications, creative writing, design, English, French, graphic design, journalism, literature, music, music performance, painting, photography, public relations, Spanish, and visual and performing arts), COMPUTER AND PHYSICAL SCIENCE (applied mathematics, chemistry, computer science, information sciences and systems, mathematics, and physics), EDUCATION (art education, elementary education, English education, mathematics education, music education, science education, secondary education, social studies education, and teaching English as a second/foreign language (TESOL/TEFOL)), ENGINEERING AND ENVIRONMENTAL DESIGN (aeronautical technology, aircraft mechanics, architecture, aviation administration/management, aviation computer technology, biomedical equipment technology, computer graphics, computer technology, electrical/electronics engineering, engineering, environmental science, graphic arts technology, and landscape architecture/design), HEALTH PROFESSIONS (allied health, art therapy, biomedical science, medical laboratory technology, nursing, preveterinary science, public health, and speech pathology/audiology), SOCIAL SCIENCE (anthropology, behavioral science, crosscultural studies, dietetics, economics, family/consumer studies, history, human development, interdisciplinary studies, pastoral studies, political science/government, psychology, religion, religious education, social studies, social work, sociology, theological studies, and youth ministry). Health sciences, business, and architecture have the largest enrollments.

ACTIVITIES: There are 30 groups on campus, including band, choir, chorale, chorus, computers, drama, ethnic, honors, international, newspaper, professional, religious, social, social service, and student government. Popular campus events include Alumni Weekend and International Food Fair. **Sports:** There are 6 intramural sports for men and 4 for women. Facilities include a gym, pool, racquetball courts, and health clubs in 2 of 3 dorms. **Graduates:** From July 1, 2013 to June 30, 2014, 341 bachelor's degrees were awarded. The most popular majors were health professions (20%), business (10%), and biology/life science (8%). In an average class, 34% graduate in 4 years or less, 51% graduate in 5 years or less, and 58% graduate in 6 years or less.

SERVICES: Counseling and information services are available, as is tutoring in most subjects. There are math, writing, and reading, learning, and assessment centers. **Library/Resources:** The library contains 747,764 volumes, 83,520 microform items, 48,447 audio/video tapes/CDs/DVDs, and subscribes to 2,874 periodicals including electronic. Computerized library services include interlibrary loans, database searching, and Internet access. Special learning facilities include an art gallery, natural history museum, an archeological museum. **Physically Challenged Students:** 50% of the campus is accessible. Facilities include wheelchair ramps, elevators, special parking, specially equipped restrooms, special class scheduling, lowered drinking fountains, lowered telephones, special housing, A special committee handles needs as they arise. **Special:** Students may pursue a second major in business administration. Study abroad, student-designed majors, nondegree study, and pass/fail options are available. There are a freshman honors program. **Visiting:** There are regularly scheduled orientations for prospective students, consisting of tours, meetings with faculty, and social activities. There are guides for informal visits, visitors may sit in on classes, and stay overnight. To schedule a visit, contact the Admissions Office. **Campus Safety and Security:** Measures include 24-hour foot and vehicle patrol and security escort services. There are lighted pathways/sidewalks, and CPR training.

REQUIREMENTS: The SAT or ACT is required. Candidates for admission must graduate from an accredited secondary school or earn a GED. 10 Carnegie units are required, and students must have completed 4 courses in English and 2 courses each in history, math, and science. Interviews are recommended for all applicants. A GPA of 2.3 is required. CLEP credits are accepted. Important factors in the admissions decision are advanced placement or honors courses, recommendations by school officials, and evidence of special talent. Students must complete a minimum of 124 semester credits. Specific course requirements include religion, English, behavioral sciences, fine arts, and phys ed. **Procedure:** Freshmen are admitted fall, spring, and summer. Entrance exams should be taken as early as possible. There are deferred admissions and rolling admissions plans. Application deadlines are open. Application fee is $30. **Transfer Students:** 131 transfer students enrolled in 2013-2014. Transfer applicants must submit a high school transcript and transcripts from all colleges attended. A maximum of 70 semester credits from a 2-year school or 90 semester credits from a 4-year school may be transferred toward a bachelor's degree. Credits should be relevant to the student's major at Andrews University. The minimum GPA is 2.25, and the ACT is preferred. Students must meet freshman entrance requirements if they are transferring with less than sophomore standing from an accredited college. 30 of 124 credits required for the bachelor's degree must be completed at Andrews. **International Students:** There are 230 international students enrolled. The school actively recruits these students. They must take the TOEFL with a minimum score of 550 on the paper-based TOEFL (PBT). They must also take the SAT or ACT.

ADMISSIONS: 49% of the 2014-2015 applicants were accepted. The ACT scores were 34% below 21, 26% between 21 and 23, 21% between 24 and 26, 11% between 27 and 28, and 8% above 28. 32% of the current freshmen were in the top fifth of their class; 55% were in the top two fifths. There were 2 National Merit finalists. **Admissions Contact:** Shanna Leak, Undergraduate Admissions Supervisor. E-Mail: *undergraduate@andrews.edu* Web: *www.andrews.edu*

FINANCIAL AID: The FAFSA is required. The priority date for freshman financial aid applications for fall entry is open.

AQUINAS COLLEGE   D-4
www.aquinas.edu

Grand Rapids, MI 49506	(616) 632-2860
	(800) 678-9593
Fax: (616) 732-4469	Email: admissions@aquinas.edu
Full-time: 667 men, 1029 women	Faculty: 88; IIB, --$
Part-time: 101 men, 125 women	Ph.D.s: 80%
Graduate: 52 men, 119 women	Student/Faculty: 13 to 1
Year: semesters, summer session	Tuition: $25,250
Room & Board: $7810	Freshman Class: n/av
SAT: recommended ACT: 23	CEEB CODE: 5750
Application Deadline: open	COMPETITIVE

Aquinas College, established in 1866, is a private liberal arts institution affiliated with the Roman Catholic Church and offers undergraduate and graduate degrees through day and evening programs.

Figures in the above capsule and in this profile are approximate. There is 1 undergraduate school and 2 graduate schools. In addition to regional accreditation, Aquinas has baccalaureate program accreditation with TEAC. The 107-acre campus is in a suburban area east of downtown Grand Rapids, MI. Including any residence halls, there are 30 buildings.

STUDENT LIFE: 95% of undergraduates are from Michigan. Others are from 22 states, 5 foreign countries, and Canada. 86% are White. 53% are Catholic; 18% claim no religious affiliation; 15% Non-denominational and unknown; 14% Protestant. The average age of freshmen is 18; all undergraduates, 22. 23% do not continue beyond their first year; 61% remain to graduate. **Housing:** 862 students can be accommodated in college housing, which includes single-sex and coed dorms and on-campus apartments. In addition, there are special-interest houses, and service learning houses. On-campus housing is guaranteed for the freshman year only, is available on a first-come, first-served basis, and is available on a lottery system for upperclassmen. Priority is given to out-of-town students. 71% of students live on campus; of those, 68% remain on campus on weekends. All students may keep cars.

FACULTY/CLASSROOMS: 54% of faculty are male; 46% are female. All teach undergraduates. No introductory courses are taught by graduate students. The average class size in an introductory lecture is 20; in a laboratory is 20; and in a regular course is 17.

PROGRAMS OF STUDY: Aquinas confers B.A., B.S., B.A.G.E., B.F.A., B.S.B.A. and B.S.I.B. degrees. Associate and Master's degrees are also awarded. Bachelor's degrees are awarded in AGRICULTURE (environmental studies), BIOLOGICAL SCIENCE (biology/biological science and environmental biology), BUSINESS (accounting, business administration and management, business communications, business economics, human resources, information and communication technology, international business management, management information systems, marketing and distribution, marketing management, nonprofit/public organization management, recreation and leisure services, recreational facilities management, and sports management), COMMUNICATIONS AND THE ARTS (art history, art, art history and appreciation, arts administration/management, ceramic art and design, communications, drawing, English, English literature, English Writing, fine arts, French, German, jazz, journalism, language arts, literature, modern language, music, music business management, music history and appreciation, music performance, music theory and composition, musical theater, painting, performing arts, photography, printmaking, sculpture, Spanish, theater management, and visual and performing arts), COMPUTER AND PHYSICAL SCIENCE (chemistry, information sciences and systems, mathematics, mathematics/computational, and mathematics/theoretical), EDUCATION (art education, athletic training, (Education) Childhood Education, early childhood education, education, education of the multiply handicapped, education of the physically handicapped, elementary education, English education, health education, mathematics education, music education, physical education, science education, secondary education, social science education, special education, specific learning disabilities, sports and wellness studies, and teaching English as a second/foreign language (TESOL/TEFOL)), ENGINEERING AND ENVIRONMENTAL DESIGN (environmental science and preengineering), HEALTH PROFESSIONS (health, premedicine, and sports medicine), SOCIAL SCIENCE (Christian studies, community services, economics, French studies, geography, (Social Science) Global Studies, history, human services, interdisciplinary studies, international relations, international studies, liberal arts/general studies, philosophy, political science/government, prelaw, psychology, public administration, religion, religious music, social science, social studies, sociology, and theological studies). Business administration, English and biology have the largest enrollments.

ACTIVITIES: There are no fraternities or sororities. There are 55 groups on campus, including art, band, cheerleading, choir, chorale, chorus, computers, dance, drama, environmental, ethnic, honors, international, jazz band, literary magazine, musical theater, newspaper, pep band, photography, political, professional, radio and TV, religious, social, social service, and student government. Popular campus events include Spring Fling, Moose Cafe and a Jazz Festival. **Sports:** There are 10 intercollegiate sports for men and 12 for women,

and 4 intramural sports for men and 4 for women. Facilities include Health and fitness center with volleyball and basketball competition courts, classrooms, athletic training lab and state of the art work out equipment. Artificial turf soccer and lacrosse field. **Graduates:** From July 1, 2013 to June 30, 2014, 381 bachelor's degrees were awarded. The most popular majors were business administration, education, and social science. 50 companies recruited on campus in 2013-2014. In an average class, 34% graduate in 4 years or less, 51% graduate in 5 years or less, and 52% graduate in 6 years or less. Of the 2013 graduating class, 22% were enrolled in graduate school within 6 months of graduation, and 73% were employed.

SERVICES: Counseling and information services are available, as is tutoring in most subjects. There is a reader service for the blind, remedial math, reading, and writing. **Library/Resources:** The library contains 100,014 volumes, 227,444 microform items, 41,050 audio/video tapes/CDs/DVDs, and subscribes to 558 periodicals including electronic. Computerized library services include interlibrary loans, database searching, Internet access, and Wi-Fi capability. Special learning facilities include an art gallery, radio station, greenhouses, observatory, and nature trails. **Physically Challenged Students:** 95% of the campus is accessible. Facilities include wheelchair ramps, elevators, special parking, specially equipped restrooms, special class scheduling, lowered drinking fountains, and lowered telephones. **Special:** Students may cross-register with the Dominican Consortium and may study abroad in Ireland, Germany, France, Spain, Costa Rica, Italy, or Japan. Co-op programs and internships are available in all majors, and work-study programs are also available. Students may pursue dual majors in business administration and accounting, sports management, communication arts, or art and B.A.-B.S. degrees in business, geography, or psychology. Student-designed majors can be arranged. Aquinas offers a general studies degree and may confer credit for life, military experience. A pass/fail grading option is available. Preengineering, prehealth, and teacher certification programs are all available in conjunction with majors offered at Aquinas. There are 5 national honor societies, a freshman honors program, and 5 departmental honors programs. **Visiting:** There are regularly scheduled orientations for prospective students, consisting of a tour of the campus and presentations by financial aid personnel, program directors, coaches, and faculty. There are guides for informal visits, visitors may sit in on classes, and stay overnight. To schedule a visit, contact the Admissions Office. **Campus Safety and Security:** Measures include 24-hour foot and vehicle patrol, emergency notification system, self-defense education, and security escort services. There are emergency telephones, lighted pathways/sidewalks, and controlled access to dorms/residences.

REQUIREMENTS: The ACT is required. The SAT and ACT Writing Test are recommended. Candidates for admission must graduate from an accredited secondary school. Students must have completed 15 Carnegie units and 4 years of English and social studies and 3 to 4 years each of math and science. AP and CLEP credits are accepted. Important factors in the admissions decision are advanced placement or honors courses, leadership record, and extracurricular activities record. To graduate, students must complete 124 semester hours, with 30 to 48 in the major, and maintain a minimum GPA of 2.0. The general education program consists of a core of 18 to 30 hours, which includes, from the first to the fourth year, foreign language and a yearlong integrated skills course, and courses in the humanities, religion, and global perspectives; and distribution requirements of 30 to 33 hours, which include courses in cultural diversity, mythology and spirituality, natural sciences, the fine arts, and quantitative reasoning and technology. **Procedure:** Freshmen are admitted fall and winter. Entrance exams should be taken during the spring of the junior year. There is a rolling admissions plan. Application deadlines are open. Applications are accepted on-line. **Transfer Students:** 74 transfer students enrolled in 2013-2014. Transfer applicants must have earned at least 12 credits in academic course work from an accredited junior or 4-year college with a minimum GPA of 2.0. Interviews are recommended. 30 of 124 credits required for the bachelor's degree must be completed at Aquinas. **International Students:** There are 5 international students enrolled. They must take the TOEFL with a minimum score of 550 on the paper-based TOEFL (PBT). They must also take the ACT.

ADMISSIONS: The ACT scores were 28% below 21, 25% between

21 and 23, 28% between 24 and 26, 14% between 27 and 28, and 5% above 28. 25% of the current freshmen were in the top fifth of their class; 78% were in the top two fifths. **Admissions Contact:** Angela Schlosser Bacon, Director of Admissions. E-Mail: *schloang@aquinas .edu* Web: *www.aquinas.edu*

FINANCIAL AID: In 2014-2015, 98% of all full-time freshmen and 90% of continuing full-time students received some form of financial aid. 90% of all full-time freshmen and 88% of continuing full-time students received need-based aid. The average freshman award was $20,873. Need-based scholarships or need-based grants averaged $18,711; need-based self-help aid (loans and jobs) averaged $3,200; non-need-based athletic scholarships averaged $3,212; and other non-need-based awards and non-need-based scholarships averaged $12,033. 26% of undergraduate students work part-time. Average annual earnings from campus work are $1632. The average financial indebtedness of the 2014 graduate was $14,983. The FAFSA is required. The deadline for filing freshman financial aid applications for fall entry is June 1.

BAKER COLLEGE OF FLINT *(The complete profile is made available exclusively on our website, www.barronspac.com)*

CALVIN COLLEGE D-4
www.calvin.edu

Grand Rapids, MI 49546	(616) 526-6106
	(800) 688-0122
Fax: (616) 526-6777	**Email: admissions@calvin.edu**
Full-time: 1687 men, 2073 women	**Faculty:** 275; IIB, +$
Part-time: 74 men, 60 women	**Ph.D.s:** 85%
Graduate: 21 men, 78 women	**Student/Faculty:** 14 to 1
Year: 4-1-4, summer session	**Tuition:** $29,635
Room & Board: $9485	**Freshman Class:** 3679 applied, 2691 accepted, 951 enrolled
SAT CR/M: 590/600 **ACT:** 26	**CEEB CODE:** 1095
Application Deadline: August 15	**VERY COMPETITIVE**

Calvin College, established in 1876, is a private institution affiliated with the Christian Reformed Church, offering undergraduate and graduate degrees in liberal arts and in some professional programs. Calvin is perhaps best known for the integration of learning and Christian faith. In every aspect of college life   teaching and learning, athletics and the arts, campus life and community activities   Calvin offers an outstanding education of the mind and heart. There is 1 undergraduate school and 2 graduate schools. In addition to regional accreditation, Calvin has baccalaureate program accreditation with ABET, CSWE, NASM, NCATE, ACS, and CCNE. The 390-acre campus is in a suburban area 7 miles southeast of downtown Grand Rapids. Including any residence halls, there are 40 buildings.

STUDENT LIFE: 51% of undergraduates are from Michigan. Others are from 47 states, 55 foreign countries, and Canada. 44% are from public schools. 75% are White. 54% are Protestant. The average age of freshmen is 18; all undergraduates, 20. 13% do not continue beyond their first year; 74% remain to graduate. **Housing:** 2400 students can be accommodated in college housing, which includes single-sex dorms, on-campus apartments, and off-campus apartments. In addition, there are language houses, special-interest houses, The college offers residence halls with living-learning floors that are focused on outdoor recreation, environmental care, race and ethnicity and honors living. The college also offers an intentional living-learning community for athletes and students who are seeking to live an active lifestyle. There are also five off-campus urban houses with a community/urban focus. On-campus housing is available on a lottery system for upperclassmen. 60% of students live on campus; of those, 90% remain on campus on weekends. Alcohol is not permitted. All students may keep cars.

FACULTY/CLASSROOMS: 58% of faculty are male; 42% are female. All teach undergraduates, all do research. No introductory courses are taught by graduate students. The average class size in an introductory lecture is 28; in a laboratory is 20; and in a regular course is 24.

PROGRAMS OF STUDY: Calvin confers B.A., B.S., B.A.S.P.A., B.C.S., B.F.A., B.M.E., B.S.A., B.S.E., B.S.N., B.S.P.A., B.S.R. and B.S.W. degrees. Master's degrees are also awarded. Bachelor's degrees are awarded in AGRICULTURE (environmental studies), BIOLOGICAL SCIENCE (biochemistry, biology/biological science, and biotechnology), BUSINESS (accounting, accounting/CPA, business administration and management, business communications, recreation and leisure services, and sports management), COMMUNICATIONS AND THE ARTS (American literature, art history, art/art studies, art and design, art history and appreciation, art/visual culture, Chinese, classical languages, classics, communications, creative writing, digital communications, dramatic arts, Dutch, English, English literature, film arts, film, television and digital media, fine arts, French, German, graphic design, Greek, information technology, Japanese, language arts, Latin, linguistics, literature, media arts, music, music history and appreciation, music performance, music theory and composition, piano/organ, Spanish, strategic communication, theatre arts, video, voice, vocal music education, and writing), COMPUTER AND PHYSICAL SCIENCE (chemistry, computer programming, computer science, digital arts/technology, earth science, environmental geology, geology, information sciences and systems, mathematics, natural sciences, and physics), EDUCATION (art education, early childhood education, education, elementary education, English education, mathematics education, music education, physical education, science education, secondary education, and special education), ENGINEERING AND ENVIRONMENTAL DESIGN (chemical engineering, civil engineering, computer engineering, electrical/electronics engineering, engineering, environmental science, and mechanical engineering), HEALTH PROFESSIONS (biology, exercise science, nursing, occupational therapy, predentistry, premedicine, preoptometry, prepharmacy, prephysical therapy, preveterinary science, public health, recreation therapy, and speech pathology/audiology), SOCIAL SCIENCE (area studies, Asian/Oriental studies, asian studies, classical and near eastern civilization, development economics, economics, geography, history, interdisciplinary studies, international relations, international studies, philosophy, political science/government, prelaw, psychology, public administration, religion, religious music, social work, sociology, theology, and theological studies). Biology, accounting, and English are the strongest academically. Education, business and engineering have the largest enrollments.

ACTIVITIES: There are no fraternities or sororities. There are 40 groups on campus, including art, band, chess, choir, chorale, chorus, computers, dance, drama, environmental, ethnic, film, honors, international, jazz band, literary magazine, musical theater, newspaper, orchestra, pep band, political, professional, radio and TV, religious, social, social service, student government, symphony, and yearbook. Popular campus events include Festival of Faith and Writing, Festival of Faith and Music, Sem Pond Jump, Rangeela, The January Series, Dance Guild, and Cardboard Canoe Contest. **Sports:** There are 9 intercollegiate sports for men and 10 for women, and 18 intramural sports for men and 14 for women. Facilities include Calvin's state-of-the-art athletic facilities include a 5,000-seat arena, a 10,000-square-foot fitness center, a 40-foot climbing wall, an Olympic-size pool, an additional three full-size basketball courts, a dance studio, an indoor track and tennis center with a 200-meter track and four full-size indoor tennis courts, a soccer facility, baseball and softball diamonds, an 8K cross-country course, an eight-lane, 400-meter polyurethane track, a weight-training/exercise room, six outdoor tennis courts, two sand beach volleyball courts, an ice skating rink and a paved recreational trail around campus. **Graduates:** From July 1, 2013 to June 30, 2014, 852 bachelor's degrees were awarded. The most popular majors were business administration and management general (10%), nursing (8%), and engineering (7%). 109 companies recruited on campus in 2013-2014. In an average class, 1% graduate in 3 years or less, 58% graduate in 4 years or less, 72% graduate in 5 years or less, and 74% graduate in 6 years or less. Of the 2013 graduating class, 25% were enrolled in graduate school within 6 months of graduation, and 72% were employed.

SERVICES: Counseling and information services are available, as is tutoring in most subjects. There is a reader service for the blind, remedial math, reading, and writing. There is a braille print service for the blind, books on tape, note taking, interpreting, diagnostic testing, special advising, and early registration. **Library/Resources:** The library contains 1.3 million volumes, 809,332 microform items, 26,107 audio/video tapes/CDs/DVDs, and subscribes to 37,319 periodicals including electronic. Computerized library services include interlibrary loans, database searching, Internet access, and Wi-Fi capability. Special learning facilities include an art gallery, radio station, the college has a TV studio, an ecosystem preserve, an interpretive center, an integrated scientific research experimental laboratory, an observatory with a 16-inch telescope, a greenhouse, a human performance lab, a community garden and an audiology and speech pathology clinic. **Physically Challenged Students:** 95% of the campus is accessible. Facilities include wheelchair ramps, elevators, special parking, specially equipped restrooms, special class scheduling, lowered drinking fountains, lowered telephones and special housing. **Special:** Dual and student-designed majors are available. Students may study off-campus in semester-long programs in China, Hungary, Britain, France, Ghana, Honduras, Peru, Spain, Washington, D.C. and New Mexico. In addition, Calvin's January Interim takes students to more than 30 countries. The college also offers cooperative programs in a variety of majors and locations around the world. Calvin also offers a master's degree in speech pathology and audiology (SPAUD) and education. Experiential learning opportunities are a staple at Calvin as well. In the college's most recent Career Outcomes Report, 82-percent of 2013 grads reported completing at least one internship/practicum while at Calvin. There are 6 national honor societies, a freshman honors program, and 25 departmental honors programs. **Visiting:** There are regularly scheduled orientations for prospective students, prospective students and their families are invited to explore Calvin firsthand by scheduling an individual visit through the admissions office or through participating in a regularly scheduled Fridays at Calvin visit. There are guides for informal visits, visitors may sit in on classes, and stay overnight. To schedule a visit, contact the Admissions Office. **Campus Safety and Security:** Measures include 24-hour foot and vehicle patrol, emergency notification system, self-defense education, and security escort services. There are emergency telephones, lighted pathways/sidewalks, controlled access to dorms/residences, a crime alert bulletin, and reports in the school newspaper.

REQUIREMENTS: The ACT is required. In selecting students for admission, Calvin College looks for evidence of a student's Christian commitment and his or her capacity and desire to learn. Students who are interested in the Christian perspective and curriculum of Calvin, and who show interest in its aims, are eligible for consideration. Although the prospect of academic success is of primary consideration, the aspirations of the applicant, the recommendation of a high school teacher, and the ability of Calvin to be of service, will also be considered. A GPA of 2.5 is required. AP and CLEP credits are accepted. Important factors in the admissions decision are recommendations by school officials, leadership record, and extracurricular activities record. Degree requirements include completion of 124 credit hours, with 28 credits in the major. All students must complete specific course work in English, religion, history, science, math, communication, fine arts, psychology or sociology, economics or political science, philosophy, kinesiology, research and information technology, foreign language and cross-cultural engagement. A minimum GPA of 2.0 is required. **Procedure:** Freshmen are admitted fall and spring. Entrance exams should be taken during the spring of the junior year or fall of the senior year. There are deferred admissions and rolling admissions plans. Applications should be filed by August 15 for fall entry; January 15 for spring entry, along with a $35 fee. Applications are accepted on-line. **Transfer Students:** 75 transfer students enrolled in 2013-2014. Applicants from 4-year colleges are required to have a minimum GPA of 2.0; from 2-year colleges, 2.5. The SAT minimum requirements are 390 on the critical reading section and 420 on the math section. A minimum score of 20 is required on the ACT. 32 of 124 credits required for the bachelor's degree must be completed at Calvin. **International Students:** There are 379 international students enrolled. The school actively recruits these students. They must take the TOEFL with a minimum score of 550 on the paper-based TOEFL (PBT) or 80 on the Internet-based version (iBT), or take the MELAB if they scored low on the TOEFL. They must also take the SAT or ACT, scoring 20. Exceptions are made for strong students without access to standardized exams.

ADMISSIONS: 73% of the 2014-2015 applicants were accepted. The SAT scores for the 2014-2015 freshman class were: Critical Reading- -19% below 500, 36% between 500 and 599, 36% between 600 and 699, and 10% between 700 and 800; Math--13% below 500, 34% between 500 and 599, 40% between 600 and 699, and 13% between 700 and 800. The ACT scores were 10% below 21, 19% between 21 and 23, 24% between 24 and 26, 17% between 27 and 28, and 30% above 28. 55% of the current freshmen were in the top fifth of their class; 78% were in the top two fifths. There were 9 National Merit finalists. 30 freshmen graduated first in their class. **Admissions Contact:** Ben Arendt, Director of Admissions. E-Mail: *admissions@calvin .edu* Web: *www.calvin.edu*

FINANCIAL AID: In 2014-2015, 98% of all full-time freshmen and 95% of continuing full-time students received some form of financial aid. 67% of all full-time freshmen and 62% of continuing full-time students received need-based aid. The average freshman award was $19,000. Need-based scholarships or need-based grants averaged $17,000 ($20,000 maximum); need-based self-help aid (loans and jobs) averaged $5,400 ($7,500 maximum); and other non-need-based awards and non-need-based scholarships averaged $8,500 ($15,000 maximum). 50% of undergraduate students work part-time. Average annual earnings from campus work are $2000. The average financial indebtedness of the 2014 graduate was $29,400. Calvin is a member of CSS. The FAFSA and the college's own financial statement are required. The priority date for freshman financial aid applications for fall entry is February 15. The deadline for filing freshman financial aid applications for fall entry is August 1.

CENTRAL MICHIGAN UNIVERSITY   D-4
www.cmich.edu

Mount Pleasant, MI 48859

(989) 774-3076
(888) 292-5366

Fax: (989) 774-7267	Email: cmuadmit@cmich.edu
Full-time: 8465 men, 10946 women	Faculty: 629; I, --$
Part-time: 1159 men, 1669 women	Ph.D.s: 81%
Graduate: 2568 men, 3767 women	Student/Faculty: 21 to 1
Year: semesters, summer session	Tuition: $11,550 ($23,670)
Room & Board: $8780	Freshman Class: 18025 applied, 12565 accepted, 3733 enrolled ACT: 23
	CEEB CODE: 1106
Application Deadline: open	COMPETITIVE

Central Michigan University, founded in 1892, is a public university offering programs in liberal arts, business, and health, education, and human services. There are 8 undergraduate schools and 1 graduate school. In addition to regional accreditation, CMU has baccalaureate program accreditation with AACSB, ABET, ACEJMC, CSWE, NASAD, NASM, NCATE, NRPA, and CADE. The 480-acre campus is in a small town 70 miles north of Lansing, MI. Including any residence halls, there are 56 buildings.

STUDENT LIFE: 93% of undergraduates are from Michigan. Others are from 50 states, 71 foreign countries, and Canada. 70% are from public schools. 73% are white; 12% African American. **Male To Female Ratio:** 1.3:1. The average age of freshmen is 19; all undergraduates, 23. 23% do not continue beyond their first year; 60% remain to graduate. **Housing:** 7529 students can be accommodated in college housing, which includes single-sex and coed dorms, on-campus apartments, and married student housing. In addition, there are honors houses, residential colleges for business, education, and human services, health professions, science and technology, and music. On-campus housing is guaranteed for all 4 years. 67% of students commute. Alcohol is not permitted. All students may keep cars.

FACULTY/CLASSROOMS: 56% of faculty are male; 44% are female. All teach undergraduates. Graduate students teach 2% of introductory courses. The average class size in an introductory lecture is 39 and in a laboratory is 22.

PROGRAMS OF STUDY: CMU confers B.A., B.S., B.A.A., B.F.A., B.Indiv.S., B.Mus., B.S.B.A., B.S.E., and B.S.E.T. degrees. Master's and doctoral degrees are also awarded. Bachelor's degrees are awarded in AGRICULTURE (environmental studies and natural resource management), BIOLOGICAL SCIENCE (biochemistry, biology/biological science, and neurosciences), BUSINESS (accounting, banking and finance, business administration and management, entrepreneurial studies, hospitality management services, human resources, international business management, logistics, management information systems, management science, marketing and distribution, marketing management, marketing/retailing/merchandising, purchasing/inventory management, real estate, recreational facilities management, and retailing), COMMUNICATIONS AND THE ARTS (apparel design, art, broadcasting, communications, design, dramatic arts, English, French, German, graphic design, journalism, language arts, music, music history and appreciation, music performance, music theory and composition, musical theater, photography, piano/organ, public relations, Spanish, speech/debate/rhetoric, theater design, visual and performing arts, and voice), COMPUTER AND PHYSICAL SCIENCE (actuarial science, chemistry, computer science, earth science, geology, information sciences and systems, mathematics, oceanography, physical sciences, physics, science, and statistics), EDUCATION (athletic training, business education, education, elementary education, foreign languages education, music education, and physical education), ENGINEERING AND ENVIRONMENTAL DESIGN (computer technology, electrical/electronics engineering, engineering technology, environmental science, industrial administration/management, interior design, manufacturing technology, mechanical engineering, and mechanical engineering technology), HEALTH PROFESSIONS (biomedical science, health, health care administration, public health, recreation therapy, rehabilitation therapy, speech pathology/audiology, and sports medicine), SOCIAL SCIENCE (anthropology, child psychology/development, cognitive science, community services, criminal justice, dietetics, early childhood studies, economics, European studies, family/consumer studies, food production/management/services, geography, history, interdisciplinary studies, law, parks and recreation management, philosophy, psychology, religion, social science, social studies, social work, sociology, and women's studies). Psychology, marketing, and accounting have the largest enrollments.

ACTIVITIES: 5% of men belong to 14 national fraternities; 10% of women belong to 14 national sororities. There are 400 groups on campus, including art, band, cheerleading, choir, chorus, communications, computers, dance, drama, environmental, ethnic, forensics, gay, honors, international, jazz band, literary magazine, marching band, musical theater, orchestra, pep band, photography, political, professional, religious, social, social service, student government, and symphony. Popular campus events include Homecoming, Michigan Story Festival, and Native American Pow Wow. **Sports:** There are 6 intercollegiate sports for men and 10 for women, and 21 intramural sports for men and 21 for women. Facilities include a football stadium, softball fields, field hockey complex, an indoor athletic complex, indoor and outdoor track, soccer field, baseball stadium, arena, and student activity center. **Graduates:** From July 1, 2013 to June 30, 2014, 4063 bachelor's degrees were awarded. The most popular majors were business (23%), teaching education (11%), and fitness and exercise science (9%). 400 companies recruited on campus in 2013-2014. In an average class, 1% graduate in 3 years or less, 18% graduate in 4 years or less, 45% graduate in 5 years or less, and 57% graduate in 6 years or less. Of a recent year's graduating class, 15% were enrolled in graduate school within 6 months of graduation, and 80% were employed.

SERVICES: Counseling and information services are available, as is tutoring in most subjects. There is a reader service for the blind, and remedial math, reading, and writing. **Library/Resources:** The library contains 1.5 million volumes, 1.4 million microform items, 23,061 audio/video tapes/CDs/DVDs, and subscribes to 2,731 periodicals including electronic. Computerized library services include interlibrary loans, database searching, and Internet access, and Wi-Fi capability. Special learning facilities include an art gallery, natural history museum, TV station, Museum of Cultural and Natural History, Clarke Historical Library, Gerald L. Poor School Museum, Brooks Astronomical Observatory, leadership institute, and a multicultural education center. **Physically Challenged Students:** 95% of the campus is accessible. Facilities include wheelchair ramps, elevators, special parking, special parking, specially equipped restrooms, special class scheduling, lowered drinking fountains, lowered telephones, special housing. There is also a Student Disability Services office. **Spe-**

cial: CMU offers internships in business administration, study abroad in 43 countries, and dual majors in chemistry/physics and computer science/math. Student-designed majors are available for a bachelor of indvidualized studies, and there is credit for life, military, and work experience. Students may take up to 25 hours for pass/fail grades. CMU off-campus programs offers external degree programs in which students can get degrees without attending classes on campus. There are 13 national honor societies, a freshman honors program, and 21 departmental honors programs. **Visiting:** There are guides for informal visits, visitors may sit in on classes, and stay overnight. To schedule a visit, contact the Admissions Office. **Campus Safety and Security:** Measures include emergency notification system and security escort services. There are shuttle buses, emergency telephones, lighted pathways/sidewalks, and blue light phone system.

REQUIREMENTS: The ACT is required. Applicants must be high school graduates or hold a GED. The university strongly recommends 4 years each of English and math, 3 each of science and social studies, and 2 of foreign language, as well as 1 course each in computer science and fine arts. AP and CLEP credits are accepted. Students must complete 124 credit hours, including 30 in the major, with a GPA of 2.0. They must fulfill the requirements in the University Program (27-30 semester hours of coursework in humanities, natural science, and social science, an integrative and area studies), and fulfill University competency requirements in written English (Freshman and Advanced Composition), oral English, and math. **Procedure:** Freshmen are admitted to all sessions. Entrance exams should be taken during junior or senior year of high school. There are deferred admissions and rolling admissions plans. Application deadlines are open. Application fee is $35. Applications are accepted on-line. **Transfer Students:** 1091 transfer students enrolled in 2013-2014. Transfer students must have a GPA of 2.0. 30 of 124 credits required for the bachelor's degree must be completed at CMU. **International Students:** There are 527 international students enrolled. The school actively recruits these students. They must take the TOEFL with a minimum score of 550 on the paper-based TOEFL (PBT) or 79 on the Internet-based version (iBT).

ADMISSIONS: 70% of the 2014-2015 applicants were accepted. The ACT scores were 29% below 21, 34% between 21 and 23, 22% between 24 and 26, 9% between 27 and 28, and 6% above 28. 33% of the current freshmen were in the top fifth of their class; 62% were in the top two fifths. 59 freshman graduated first in their class. **Admissions Contact:** Krista Casey, Assistant Director of Admissions. E-Mail: *cmuadmit@cmich.edu* Web: *www.cmich.edu*

FINANCIAL AID: In 2014-2015, 66% of all full-time freshmen and 62% of continuing full-time students received some form of financial aid. 56% of all full-time freshmen and 57% of continuing full-time students received need-based aid. The average freshman award was $13,814. Need-based scholarships or need-based grants averaged $8,069; need-based self-help aid (loans and jobs) averaged $6,249; non-need-based athletic scholarships averaged $15,110; and other non-need based awards and non-need-based scholarships averaged $4,161. 25% of undergraduate students work part-time. Average annual earnings from campus work is $3500. The average financial indebtedness of the 2014 graduate was $33,545. The FAFSA is required. The priority date for freshman financial aid applications for fall entry is March 1.

COLLEGE FOR CREATIVE STUDIES   E-5
www.collegeforcreativestudies.edu

Detroit, MI 48202   (313) 664-7425
                                         (800) 952-ARTS
Fax: (313) 872-2739   Email: admissions@collegeforcreativestudies.edu

Full-time: 568 men, 514 women	**Faculty:** 51
Part-time: 133 men, 148 women	**Ph.D.s:** 76%
Graduate: 38 men, 22 women	**Student/Faculty:** 11 to 1
Year: semesters, summer session	**Tuition:** $37,090
Room & Board: $8250	**Freshman Class:** 1284 applied, 624 accepted, 242 enrolled
SAT: required **ACT:** 22	**CEEB CODE:** 1035
Application Deadline: August 1	**COMPETITIVE**

The College for Creative Studies, established in 1906, is a private, independent institution offering comprehensive 4-year B.F.A programs in animation and digital media, crafts, fine arts, communication design, industrial design, interior design, and photography, as well as teacher certification in art education. Figures in the above capsule and in this profile are approximate. In addition to regional accreditation, CCS has baccalaureate program accreditation with NASAD. The 11-acre campus is in an urban area 3 miles from downtown Detroit. Including any residence halls, there are 6 buildings.

STUDENT LIFE: 83% of undergraduates are from Michigan. Others are from 35 states, 18 foreign countries, and Canada. 71% are White. The average age of freshmen is 22; all undergraduates, 22. 27% do not continue beyond their first year; 56% remain to graduate. **Housing:** 263 students can be accommodated in college housing, which includes coed dorms. Coed dorms. On-campus housing is available on a first-come and first-served basis. Priority is given to out-of-town students. 72% of students commute. Alcohol is not permitted. All students may keep cars.

FACULTY/CLASSROOMS: 60% of faculty are male; 40% are female. All teach undergraduates. No introductory courses are taught by graduate students. The average class size in an introductory lecture is 20; in a laboratory is 15; and in a regular course is 18.

PROGRAMS OF STUDY: CCS confers B.F.A degrees. Bachelor's degrees are awarded in COMMUNICATIONS AND THE ARTS (advertising, animation, ceramic art and design, fine arts, glass, graphic design, illustration, industrial design, metal/jewelry, painting, photography, printmaking, and sculpture), COMPUTER AND PHYSICAL SCIENCE (digital arts/technology), EDUCATION (art education), ENGINEERING AND ENVIRONMENTAL DESIGN (interior design), SOCIAL SCIENCE (textiles and clothing). Industrial design and communication design is the strongest academically. Animation and digital media have the largest enrollments.

ACTIVITIES: There are 6 groups on campus, including ethnic, professional, and student government. Popular campus events include Student Exhibition, Noel Night, and Detroit Festival of the Arts. **Sports:** There is no sports program at CCS. **Graduates:** From July 1, 2013 to June 30, 2014, 248 bachelor's degrees were awarded. The most popular majors were visual and performing arts (100%). 35 companies recruited on campus in 2013-2014.

SERVICES: Counseling and information services are available, as is tutoring in every subject. There is remedial reading and writing. **Library/Resources:** The library contains 21,000 volumes, and subscribes to 100 periodicals including electronic. Special learning facilities include an art gallery. **Physically Challenged Students:** All of the campus is accessible. Facilities include wheelchair ramps, elevators, special parking, specially equipped restrooms, and lowered telephones. **Special:** Internships are available within the student's departmental major. Credit for internships and dual majors are available. Study abroad is possible. **Visiting:** There are regularly scheduled orientations for prospective students, including an introduction to the college by an admission professional, a digital presentation of student work, application/financial aid information, and a campus tour. The orientations are scheduled every other week from September through April. There are guides for informal visits and visitors may sit in on classes. To schedule a visit, contact the Admission Office. **Campus Safety and Security:** Measures include 24-hour foot and vehicle patrol and security escort services. There are lighted pathways/sidewalks.

REQUIREMENTS: The SAT or ACT is required. Applicants must graduate from an accredited secondary school or earn a GED. A portfolio of representative work and an essay are required. A general college preparatory program is recommended. AP and CLEP credits are accepted. Important factors in the admissions decision are advanced placement or honors courses and evidence of special talent. Degree requirements include work in English, computer literacy, sciences, behavioral science, art, history, speech, philosophy, and art and design. Students must complete 42 credits in liberal arts. A minimum GPA of 2.0 is required, and students must complete 126 credits with 63 in the major, to graduate. **Procedure:** Freshmen are admitted fall and winter. There are deferred admissions and rolling admissions plans. Applications should be filed by August 1 for fall entry, along with a $35 fee. Notifications are sent September 15. Applications are accepted on-line. **Transfer Students:** 148 transfer students enrolled in 2013-2014. Transfer applicants should submit a portfolio that includes artwork done at the previous college. Transcripts and portfolio review will determine how many credits may transfer. The approval of the chairperson of the department to which the student is applying is required for transfer of studio credit. High school and college transcripts are required. 33 of 126 credits required for the bachelor's degree must be completed at CCS. **International Students:** The school actively recruits these students. They must take the TOEFL. They must also take the SAT or ACT.

ADMISSIONS: 49% of the 2014-2015 applicants were accepted. **Admissions Contact:** Admissions Officer E-Mail: *admissions@ collegeforcreativestudies.edu* Web: *www.collegeforcreativestudies.edu*

FINANCIAL AID: The average financial indebtedness of the 2014 graduate was $54,000. The FAFSA is required. The priority date for freshman financial aid applications for fall entry is July 1.

CONCORDIA UNIVERSITY, ANN ARBOR   E-5
www.cuaa.edu

Ann Arbor, MI 48105

	(734) 995-7311
	(800) 253-0680
Fax: (734) 995-4610	Email: admission@cuaa.edu
Full-time: 186 men, 242 women	Faculty: 39
Part-time: 53 men, 40 women	Ph.D.s: 60%
Graduate: 154 men, 400 women	Student/Faculty: 11 to 1
Year: semesters, summer session	Tuition: $19,870
Room & Board: $7350	Freshman Class: 429 applied, 281 accepted, 94 enrolled
SAT CR/M/W: 575/550/560 ACT: 22	CEEB CODE: 1094
Application Deadline: open	VERY COMPETITIVE

Concordia University, established in 1963, is a private institution affiliated with the Missouri Synod of the Lutheran Church, offering undergraduate and graduate degrees in the arts and sciences, business, education, and human services. The figures in the above capsule and in this profile are approximate. There are 4 undergraduate schools and 2 graduate schools. In addition to regional accreditation, Concordia has baccalaureate program accreditation with NCATE. The 187-acre campus is in a suburban area 40 miles west of Detroit. Including any residence halls, there are 30 buildings.

STUDENT LIFE: 83% of undergraduates are from Michigan. Others are from 20 states, 6 foreign countries, and Canada. 85% are White. 30% are Protestant. The average age of freshmen is 18; all undergraduates, 23. 31% do not continue beyond their first year; 47% remain to graduate. **Housing:** 436 students can be accommodated in college housing, which includes single-sex dorms and married student housing. On-campus housing is guaranteed for all 4 years. 57% of students live on campus; of those, 60% remain on campus on weekends. Alcohol is not permitted. All students may keep cars.

FACULTY/CLASSROOMS: 47% of faculty are male; 53% are female. All teach undergraduates. No introductory courses are taught by graduate students. The average class size in an introductory lecture is 24; in a laboratory is 12; and in a regular course is 11.

PROGRAMS OF STUDY: Concordia confers B.A. degrees. Associate and Master's degrees are also awarded. Bachelor's degrees are awarded in BIOLOGICAL SCIENCE (biology/biological science), BUSINESS (business administration and management and hospitality management services), COMMUNICATIONS AND THE ARTS (art, communications, dramatic arts, English, Greek, journalism, language arts, music, and Spanish), COMPUTER AND PHYSICAL SCIENCE (chemistry, mathematics, physical sciences, physics, and science), EDUCATION (early childhood education, elementary education, health education, physical education, and secondary education), ENGINEERING AND ENVIRONMENTAL DESIGN (preengineering), HEALTH PROFESSIONS (predentistry and premedicine), SOCIAL SCIENCE (biblical languages, criminal justice, family/consumer studies, history, philosophy, psychology, religion, religious music, safety management, social studies, and sociology). Education, business, and family life are the strongest academically.

Business administration, teacher education, and English have the largest enrollments.

ACTIVITIES: There are 21 groups on campus, including band, choir, chorale, communications, computers, dance, debate, drama, ethnic, jazz band, musical theater, newspaper, pep band, religious, social, social service, student government, and yearbook. Popular campus events include Boar's Head Festival, Servant Events, and a Fall Carnival. **Sports:** There are 5 intercollegiate sports for men and 5 for women, and 10 intramural sports for men and 10 for women. Facilities include a soccer field, baseball and softball diamonds, sand volleyball courts, a phys ed building (gym), and an open field for intramurals. **Graduates:** From July 1, 2013 to June 30, 2014, 112 bachelor's degrees were awarded. The most popular majors were teacher education (21%), business (21%), and criminal justice (10%). In an average class, 1% graduate in 3 years or less, 19% graduate in 4 years or less, 35% graduate in 5 years or less, and 37% graduate in 6 years or less.

SERVICES: Counseling and information services are available, as is tutoring in every subject. There is remedial math. There is also a writing lab with consultants. **Library/Resources:** The library contains 117,000 volumes, 300,000 microform items, 1,400 audio/video tapes/CDs/DVDs, and subscribes to 660 periodicals including electronic. Computerized library services include interlibrary loans, database searching, Internet access, and Wi-Fi capability. Special learning facilities include an art gallery. **Physically Challenged Students:** 90% of the campus is accessible. Facilities include wheelchair ramps, elevators, special parking, specially equipped restrooms, and lowered drinking fountains. **Special:** Internships are available in most academic majors. Cross-registration is available with Eastern Michigan and Kettering Universities, Schoolcraft College, Henry Ford Community College, Michigan State Police Training Division, and Michigan Academy of Emergency Services. Students may study abroad in 6 countries. Accelerated degree programs are available in business administration, criminal justice administration, communication, hospitality management, and public safety. The college confers credit for life, military, and work experience through the School of Adult and Continuing Education. Nondegree study, dual majors in many combinations, student-designed majors, a 3-2 engineering degree with Kettering University, and a pass/fail grading option are available. **Visiting:** There are regularly scheduled orientations for prospective students, including several preview days, Senior Day, Junior Day, Art Day, Music Day, and Theatre Day. Individual tours are arranged by appointment. There are guides for informal visits, visitors may sit in on classes, and stay overnight. To schedule a visit, contact the Admissions Office. **Campus Safety and Security:** Measures include 24-hour foot and vehicle patrol and security escort services. There are lighted pathways/sidewalks and controlled access to dorms/residences.

REQUIREMENTS: The SAT or ACT is required. The ACT is preferred. Applicants must graduate from an accredited secondary school or have the GED. 20 Carnegie units are recommended, including 4 units in English, 3 in math, and 2 each in science, social studies, and foreign language. AP and CLEP credits are accepted. Important factors in the admissions decision are leadership record, advanced placement or honors courses, and evidence of special talent. Degree requirements include completion of 128 credit hours, with at least 30 in the major, and up to 49 credit hours of general studies, and a minimum GPA of 2.0. The student must also demonstrate proficiency in foreign language, writing, speech, and math. Required courses include upper-level general studies, writing-intensive courses, a freshman seminar, physical activities, computer applications, religion, humanities, social science, language/communication, and science. A senior project is required. Education students must take the Michigan Test for Teacher Certification. **Procedure:** Freshmen are admitted fall and spring. There are deferred admissions and rolling admissions plans. Application deadlines are open. The fall 2014 application fee was $25. Notification is sent on a rolling basis. Applications are accepted on-line. **Transfer Students:** 91 transfer students enrolled in 2013-2014. A GPA of 2.0 is required for transfer students; a GPA of 2.5 is required for admittance to the teacher education program. Transfer students who have earned 12 or more credits are not required to take the ACT. Interviews are recommended. 30 of 128 credits required for the bachelor's degree must be completed at Concordia. **International Students:** There are 7 international students

enrolled. They must take the TOEFL with a minimum score of 520 on the paper-based TOEFL (PBT) or 68 on the Internet-based version (iBT) or take the MELAB. They must also take the SAT or ACT.

ADMISSIONS: 66% of the 2014-2015 applicants were accepted. The SAT scores for the 2014-2015 freshman class were: Critical Reading--36% below 500, 21% between 500 and 599, 21% between 600 and 699, and 22% between 700 and 800; Math--28% below 500, 43% between 500 and 599, and 29% between 600 and 699; Writing--43% below 500, 7% between 500 and 599, 29% between 600 and 699, and 21% between 700 and 800. The ACT scores were 36% below 21, 20% between 21 and 23, 27% between 24 and 26, 11% between 27 and 28, and 6% above 28. **Admissions Contact:** Amy Becher, Executive Director of Enrollment Services. E-Mail: *bechea@cuaa.edu* Web: *www.cuaa.edu*

FINANCIAL AID: In 2014-2015, 100% of all full-time freshmen and 100% of continuing full-time students received some form of financial aid. 65% of all full-time freshmen and 69% of continuing full-time students received need-based aid. The average freshman award was $18,392. Need-based scholarships or need-based grants averaged $5,047 ($13,505 maximum); need-based self-help aid (loans and jobs) averaged $7,766 ($9,000 maximum); non-need-based athletic scholarships averaged $8,274 ($17,500 maximum); and other non-need-based awards and non-need-based scholarships averaged $6,500 ($19,700 maximum). 42% of undergraduate students work part-time. Average annual earnings from campus work are $1781. The average financial indebtedness of the 2014 graduate was $25,000. The FAFSA and the college's own financial statement are required. The deadline for filing freshman financial aid applications for fall entry is March 1.

CORNERSTONE UNIVERSITY AND GRAND RAPIDS THEOLOGICAL SEMINARY   D-4

www.cornerstone.edu

Grand Rapids, MI 49525	**(616) 222-1426** **(800) 787-9778**
Fax: (616) 222-1418	Email: admissions@cornerstone.edu
Full-time: 600 men, 881 women	Faculty: 55
Part-time: 251 men, 420 women	Ph.D.s: 40%
Graduate: 327 men, 291 women	Student/Faculty: 21 to 1
Year: semesters, summer session	Tuition: $25,112
Room & Board: $8226	Freshman Class: 1962 applied, 1648 accepted, 303 enrolled
SAT CR/M/W: 544/529/504 ACT: 23	CEEB CODE: 1253
Application Deadline: August 15	COMPETITIVE

Cornerstone University and Grand Rapids Theological Seminary, founded in 1941, is a private liberal arts college and graduate seminary educating students from a Christian perspective. Major undergraduate programs include business, media studies, teacher education and religion. There are 3 undergraduate schools and 2 graduate schools. In addition to regional accreditation, Cornerstone University has baccalaureate program accreditation with CSWE, NASM, ATS, NASM, and CSWE. The 132-acre campus is in a suburban area on the northeast side of Grand Rapids, MI. Including any residence halls, there are 37 buildings.

STUDENT LIFE: 85% of undergraduates are from Michigan. Others are from 37 states, 30 foreign countries, and Canada. 62% are from public schools. 84% are White. 66% are Protestant. The average age of freshmen is 18; all undergraduates, 24. 22% do not continue beyond their first year; 48% remain to graduate. **Housing:** 880 students can be accommodated in college housing, which includes single-sex dorms, on-campus apartments, and married student housing. In addition, there are honors houses. On-campus housing is guaranteed for the freshman year only, is available on a first-come, first-served basis. Priority is given to out-of-town students. 65% of students live on campus; of those, 50% remain on campus on weekends. Alcohol is not permitted. All students may keep cars.

FACULTY/CLASSROOMS: 67% of faculty are male; 33% are female. All teach undergraduates, 50% do research, and 50% do both. No introductory courses are taught by graduate students. The average class size in an introductory lecture is 60; in a laboratory is 24; and in a regular course is 21.

PROGRAMS OF STUDY: Cornerstone University confers B.A., B.Mus. and B.S. degrees. Associate and Master's degrees are also awarded. Bachelor's degrees are awarded in BIOLOGICAL SCIENCE (biology/biological science), BUSINESS (accounting, business administration and management, international business management, international economics, marketing/retailing/merchandising, and sports management), COMMUNICATIONS AND THE ARTS (advertising, applied music, audio technology, communications, English, English Writing, fine arts, graphic design, literature, media arts, music, music performance, musical theater, speech/debate/rhetoric, and video), COMPUTER AND PHYSICAL SCIENCE (chemistry), EDUCATION (education, elementary education, English education, middle school education, music education, physical education, science education, and secondary education), HEALTH PROFESSIONS (exercise science, Pre-Health Studies, predentistry, premedicine, and preveterinary science), SOCIAL SCIENCE (biblical studies, Christian studies, family/consumer studies, history, humanities, interdisciplinary studies, liberal arts/general studies, philosophy, psychology, religion, religious education, social work, and youth ministry). English, music and education are the strongest academically. Education, business, psychology, and media/film have the largest enrollments.

ACTIVITIES: There are 22 groups on campus, including band, cheerleading, choir, chorale, chorus, dance, drama, environmental, ethnic, film, honors, international, jazz band, musical theater, newspaper, orchestra, pep band, photography, political, professional, radio and TV, religious, social, social service, student government, and symphony. Popular campus events include Sibling Weekends, Friends Weekend and Variety Show. **Sports:** There are 5 intercollegiate sports for men and 5 for women, and 4 intramural sports for men and 4 for women. Facilities include a 2,700-seat basketball/volleyball arena, a field house servicing tennis, volleyball, basketball, soccer, and softball, a baseball diamond, 2 soccer fields/intramural fields, a softball field, a sand volleyball court, a fitness center, human performance labs, 6 locker rooms, a training room, and racquetball courts. **Graduates:** From July 1, 2013 to June 30, 2014, 461 bachelor's degrees were awarded. The most popular majors were business (45%), psychology (12%), and education (8%). 30 companies recruited on campus in 2013-2014. In an average class, 30% graduate in 4 years or less, 43% graduate in 5 years or less, and 48% graduate in 6 years or less. Of the 2013 graduating class, 8% were enrolled in graduate school within 6 months of graduation, and 91% were employed.

SERVICES: Counseling and information services are available, as is tutoring in every subject, a learning center with a computer lab and special adaptive software that specialize in writing and math, tutoring by appointment in the residence halls, test-taking assistance, and readers and typists as needed. There is a reader service for the blind, and remedial math and writing. **Library/Resources:** The library contains 375,000 volumes, 276,107 microform items, 5,226 audio/video tapes/CDs/DVDs, and subscribes to 39,500 periodicals including electronic. Computerized library services include interlibrary loans, database searching, Internet access, and Wi-Fi capability. Special learning facilities include a radio station, the Center for Excellence in Teaching and Learning, and the Cornerstone University Learning Center. **Physically Challenged Students:** All of the campus is accessible. Facilities include wheelchair ramps, elevators, special parking, specially equipped restrooms, special class scheduling, special housing. large computer monitors for the visually impaired, and soundproof rooms for using tape recorders that read books-on-tape. **Special:** All students choose a student-ministries assignment each semester. Cornerstone requires internships in many areas of study. Study abroad programs, accelerated degrees in organizational leadership, management, business administration, ministry leadership, and education, and a Washington semester are available. There are 3 national honor societies, including Phi Beta Kappa, a freshman honors program, and 3 departmental honors programs. **Visiting:** There are regularly scheduled orientations for prospective students, Admissions and financial aid presentations, class visits, meeting with a faculty member, and course preregistration. There are guides for informal visits, visitors

may sit in on classes, and stay overnight. To schedule a visit, contact Kayleigh Boston, Admissions Office. **Campus Safety and Security:** Measures include 24-hour foot and vehicle patrol, emergency notification system, self-defense education, and security escort services. There are emergency telephones, lighted pathways/sidewalks, and controlled access to dorms/residences.

REQUIREMENTS: The college requires an official high school transcript or GED certificate with a minimum 2.5 high school GPA. Either an ACT or SAT score must be submitted, with a minimum score of 19 for the ACT and a minimum score of 1350 (total) for the SAT. A reference from a pastor or other Christian leader is required. Auditions are required for music scholarships. In addition, the following program is recommended for college preparation: 14 Carnegie units (including 4 years of English, 3 each of math and social sciences, 2 each of science and foreign language), as well as 8 semesters of academic electives. AP and CLEP credits are accepted. Important factors in the admissions decision are personality/intangible qualities, advanced placement or honors courses, and extracurricular activities record. To graduate, students must complete 120 to 129 credit hours depending on the degree, including 46 in the liberal arts core. The number of hours in the major varies. The student must have an overall GPA of 2.0, 2.5 in the major, 2.0 in the minor, and pass a comprehensive exam in his or her field. **Procedure:** Freshmen are admitted to all sessions. Entrance exams should be taken during the junior or senior year of high school. There are deferred admissions and rolling admissions plans. Applications should be filed by August 15 for fall entry; January 15 for spring entry, along with a $25 fee. Applications are accepted on-line. Application fees are waived if application is completed on-line. **Transfer Students:** 37 transfer students enrolled in 2013-2014. The college requires official college transcript(s) from students (minimum college GPA of 2.0), as well as a reference from a pastor or other Christian leader. In addition, if the applicant has fewer than 24 hours of college credit, an official high school transcript is required (minimum high school GPA of 2.5) and official ACT or SAT scores (minimum ACT score of 19, SAT score of 1350). 32 of 120 credits required for the bachelor's degree must be completed at Cornerstone University. **International Students:** There are 49 international students enrolled. The school actively recruits these students. They must take the TOEFL with a minimum score of 500 on the paper-based TOEFL (PBT) or 61 on the Internet-based version (iBT). They must also take the SAT or ACT, scoring 900.

ADMISSIONS: 84% of the 2014-2015 applicants were accepted. The SAT scores for the 2014-2015 freshman class were: Critical Reading--31% below 500, 34% between 500 and 599, 31% between 600 and 699, and 3% between 700 and 800; Math--34% below 500, 46% between 500 and 599, 17% between 600 and 699, and 3% between 700 and 800; Writing--20% below 500, 23% between 500 and 599, and 6% between 600 and 699. The ACT scores were 27% below 21, 30% between 21 and 23, 26% between 24 and 26, 9% between 27 and 28, and 8% above 28. 31% of the current freshmen were in the top fifth of their class; 64% were in the top two fifths. 5 freshmen graduated first in their class. **Admissions Contact:** Lisa Link, Director of Admissions. E-Mail: *admissions@cornerstone.edu* Web: *www.cornerstone.edu*

FINANCIAL AID: In 2014-2015, 100% of all full-time freshmen and 98% of continuing full-time students received some form of financial aid. 85% of all full-time freshmen and 81% of continuing full-time students received need-based aid. The average freshman award was $23,811. Need-based scholarships or need-based grants averaged $15,028 ($36,098 maximum); need-based self-help aid (loans and jobs) averaged $2,366 ($5,500 maximum); non-need-based athletic scholarships averaged $1,069 ($15,000 maximum); and other non-need-based awards and non-need-based scholarships averaged $5,348 ($20,306 maximum). 34% of undergraduate students work part-time. Average annual earnings from campus work are $1011. The average financial indebtedness of the 2014 graduate was $27,919. The FAFSA is required. The priority date for freshman financial aid applications for fall entry is March 1.

DAVENPORT UNIVERSITY (*The complete profile is made available exclusively on our website, www.barronspac.com*)

EASTERN MICHIGAN UNIVERSITY   D-5
www.emich.edu

Ypsilanti, MI 48197

(734) 487-3060
(800) GO TO EMU

Fax: (734) 487-6559   Email: undergraduate.admissions@emich.edu

Full-time: 5326 men, 7725 women

Part-time: 2187 men, 2970 women

Graduate: 1458 men, 2595 women

Year: semesters, summer session

Room & Board: $8941

Faculty: 775; IIA, +$

Ph.D.s: 75%

Student/Faculty: 17 to 1

Tuition: $9663 ($25,706)

Freshman Class: 12353 applied, 8500 accepted, 2630 enrolled

SAT CR/M/W: 483/509/486 **ACT:** 22

Application Deadline: August 30

CEEB CODE: 1201

COMPETITIVE

Eastern Michigan University, founded in 1849, is a public institution offering programs in arts and sciences, business, education, health and human services, and technology. There are 6 undergraduate schools and 1 graduate school. In addition to regional accreditation, EMU has baccalaureate program accreditation with AACSB, ACCE, CSWE, NASM, NCATE, ACPHA, ACOTE, ABA, ACS, APA, ASHA, CCNE, CADE, CAAHEP, CAAT, CIDA, HLC, MDOE, NAACLS, NASPAA, CNSS, and PAB. The 460-acre campus is in a suburban area 8 miles east of Ann Arbor. Including any residence halls, there are 120 buildings.

STUDENT LIFE: 92% of undergraduates are from Michigan. Others are from 49 states, 55 foreign countries, and Canada. 90% are from public schools. 66% are White; 18% African American. The average age of freshmen is 18; all undergraduates, 22. 28% do not continue beyond their first year; 42% remain to graduate. **Housing:** 3688 students can be accommodated in college housing, which includes coed dorms, on-campus apartments, and married student housing. In addition, there are honors houses, special-interest houses, sorority houses, Special housing known as community of scholars, upper-class halls, and a first-year center. On-campus housing is available on a first-come, first-served basis. 71% of students commute. All students may keep cars.

FACULTY/CLASSROOMS: 46% of faculty are male; 54% are female. 95% teach undergraduates. Graduate students teach 2% of introductory courses.

PROGRAMS OF STUDY: EMU confers B.A., B.S., B.A.E., B.A. in Language and World Business, B.B.A., B.B.E., B.F.A., B.M.E., B.M.T., B.M.U., B.S.N. and B.S.W. degrees. Master's and Doctoral degrees are also awarded. Bachelor's degrees are awarded in BIOLOGICAL SCIENCE (biochemistry, biology/biological science, and nutrition), BUSINESS (accounting, apparel and accessories marketing, banking and finance, business administration and management, business data processing, business economics, business systems analysis, entrepreneurial studies, fashion merchandising, hospitality management services, hotel/motel and restaurant management, international business management, labor studies, management information systems, management science, marketing management, marketing/retailing/merchandising, office supervision and management, personnel management, supply chain management, tourism, and trade and industrial supervision and management), COMMUNICATIONS AND THE ARTS (advertising, American literature, animation, applied music, art, art history and appreciation, arts administration/management, classical languages, communications, communications technology, creative writing, dance, design, dramatic arts, English, English literature, film arts, fine arts, French, German, graphic design, historic preservation, Japanese, journalism, language arts, linguistics, literature, media arts, music, music performance, percussion, performing arts, piano/organ, public relations, Spanish, speech/debate/rhetoric, strings, technical and business writing, telecommunications, visual and performing arts, voice, and winds), COMPUTER AND PHYSICAL SCIENCE (actuarial science, applied mathematics, astronomy, chemistry, computer programming, computer science, computer security and information assurance, earth science, geology, hydrogeology, information sciences and systems, mathematics, physics, polymer science, science, and statistics), EDUCATION (art education, athletic training, bilingual/bicultural education, business education, computer education, drama education, early childhood

education, education, education of the deaf and hearing impaired, education of the emotionally handicapped, education of the mentally handicapped, education of the multiply handicapped, education of the physically handicapped, education of the visually handicapped, educational media, elementary education, English education, foreign languages education, health education, industrial arts education, mathematics education, middle school education, music education, physical education, psychology education, reading education, school psychology, science education, secondary education, social foundations, social studies education, special education, technical education, and trade and industrial education), ENGINEERING AND ENVIRONMENTAL DESIGN (airline piloting and navigation, applied aviation, aviation administration/management, city/community/regional planning, computer engineering, computer graphics, computer technology, construction management, electrical/electronics engineering technology, engineering physics, engineering technology, interior design, land use management and reclamation, manufacturing engineering, manufacturing technology, mechanical engineering technology, military science, plastics technology, and urban planning technology), HEALTH PROFESSIONS (allied health, exercise science, health care administration, medical laboratory science, medical laboratory technology, music therapy, nursing, occupational therapy, recreation therapy, speech pathology/audiology, and sports medicine), SOCIAL SCIENCE (African studies, African American studies, anthropology, area studies, Asian/Oriental studies, child care/child and family studies, clothing and textiles management/production/services, counseling/psychology, criminal justice, dietetics, economics, gender studies, geography, gerontology, history, interdisciplinary studies, international relations, Latin American studies, Middle Eastern studies, paralegal studies, philosophy, political science/government, psychology, public administration, Russian and Slavic studies, social studies, social work, sociology, textiles and clothing, urban studies, and women's studies). Education, business, and health/nursing are the strongest academically. Elementary education, arts/sciences, and business have the largest enrollments.

ACTIVITIES: 4% of men belong to 1 local and 10 national fraternities; 4% of women belong to 1 local and 11 national sororities. There are 300 groups on campus, including art, band, cheerleading, chess, choir, chorale, chorus, computers, dance, debate, drama, drill team, environmental, ethnic, film, forensics, gay, honors, international, jazz band, literary magazine, marching band, musical theater, newspaper, opera, orchestra, pep band, photography, political, professional, radio and TV, religious, social, social service, student government, and symphony. Popular campus events include Martin Luther King Birthday Celebration and Family Weekend. **Sports:** There are 12 intercollegiate sports for men and 15 for women, and 20 intramural sports for men and 20 for women. Facilities include a 30,000-seat stadium, outdoor playing fields, a field house, a student recreation and intramural center, and an outdoor park including a lake, amphitheater, lighted basketball courts, volleyball courts, and lake house. There are 2 pools, a whirlpool/sauna, softball and soccer fields, 4 weight rooms, an aerobic studio, and a pro shop. **Graduates:** From July 1, 2013 to June 30, 2014, 3249 bachelor's degrees were awarded. The most popular majors were psychology (7%), social work (5%), and liberal arts elementary teaching (5%). 600 companies recruited on campus in 2013-2014. In an average class, 1% graduate in 3 years or less, 13% graduate in 4 years or less, 27% graduate in 5 years or less, and 37% graduate in 6 years or less.

SERVICES: Counseling and information services are available, as is tutoring in every subject. There is a reader service for the blind, and remedial math, reading, and writing. Notetakers and interpreters are provided for the handicapped. **Library/Resources:** The library contains 1.1 million volumes, 993,806 microform items, 20,726 audio/video tapes/CDs/DVDs, and subscribes to 25,522 periodicals including electronic. Computerized library services include interlibrary loans, database searching, Internet access, and Wi-Fi capability. Special learning facilities include an art gallery, radio station, and TV station. **Physically Challenged Students:** 93% of the campus is accessible. Facilities include wheelchair ramps, elevators, special parking, specially equipped restrooms, special class scheduling, lowered drinking fountains, lowered telephones, and special housing. **Special:** EMU offers internships, work-study programs, a Washington semester in public administration, and co-op programs and cross-registration with the University of Michigan at Ann Arbor, Concordia College, and Washtenaw Community College. Students may study abroad in more than 23 countries. EMU allows dual majors, nondegree study, B.A.-B.S. degrees in all majors, student-designed majors, and accelerated degree programs, and confers a general studies degree, as well as a B.A.-B.B.A. degree in language and world business. Students may receive credit for life, military, and work experience, and pass/fail options are open. There are 9 national honor societies, a freshman honors program, and 36 departmental honors programs. <u>Visiting:</u> There are regularly scheduled orientations for prospective students, including tours scheduled every morning and afternoon, as well as Saturday morning, with trained student tour guides. There are guides for informal visits, visitors may sit in on classes, and stay overnight. To schedule a visit, contact the Admissions On-Campus Programs. <u>Campus Safety and Security:</u> Measures include 24-hour foot and vehicle patrol, emergency notification system, self-defense education, and security escort services. There are shuttle buses, emergency telephones, lighted pathways/sidewalks, controlled access to dorms/residences, Bicycle patrols, a crime prevention officer, area police officers in dorms, an anonymous tip line, operation identification, vehicle glass etching, a bike lock lease program, and surveillance cameras.

<u>REQUIREMENTS:</u> The SAT or ACT is required. A minimum composite of 17 on the ACT, or a satisfactory score on the SAT is required. Applicants should be high school graduates or hold a GED. The university recommends that students complete 21 academic credits in high school, consisting of 4 each in English, math, and science, 2 each in foreign language and social studies, 1 in history, and 4 in other traditional college-preparatory courses. A portfolio is required for applicants to the art program, and an audition is required for music students. AP and CLEP credits are accepted.To graduate, students must have a GPA of 2.0, and complete a minimum of 124 semester hours, including usually 30 in the major, 20 in the minor (or 50 in a comprehensive major), and 40 in General Education. In addition to distribution requirements, students must have a course in global awareness, a course in U.S. diversity, and satisfy requirements for learning beyond the classroom <u>Procedure:</u> Freshmen are admitted to all sessions. Entrance exams should be taken by November of the senior year of high school. There are early admissions and rolling admissions plans. Applications should be filed by August 30 for fall entry; January 2 for winter entry; April 25 for spring entry; and June 21 for summer entry. The fall 2014 application fee was $35. Notification is sent on a rolling basis. Applications are accepted on-line. <u>Transfer Students:</u> 1769 transfer students enrolled in 2013-2014. Transfer students must have at least 12 semester hours of college credit, with a GPA of 2.0. 30 of 124 credits required for the bachelor's degree must be completed at EMU. <u>International Students:</u> There are 353 international students enrolled. The school actively recruits these students. They must take the TOEFL with a minimum score of 500 on the paper-based TOEFL (PBT) or 61 on the Internet-based version (iBT) or take the MELAB, or take the IELTS.

<u>ADMISSIONS:</u> 69% of the 2014-2015 applicants were accepted. The SAT scores for the 2014-2015 freshman class were: Critical Reading--40% below 500, 33% between 500 and 599, 17% between 600 and 699, and 2% between 700 and 800; Math--35% below 500, 37% between 500 and 599, 17% between 600 and 699, and 3% between 700 and 800; Writing--37% below 500, 37% between 500 and 599, 8% between 600 and 699, and 2% between 700 and 800. The ACT scores were 36% below 21, 29% between 21 and 23, 21% between 24 and 26, 8% between 27 and 28, and 6% above 28. 22 freshmen graduated first in their class. <u>Admissions Contact:</u> Brian Selfridge, Freshmen Admissions. E-Mail: *undergraduate.admissions@emich.edu* Web: *www.emich.edu*

<u>FINANCIAL AID:</u> In 2014-2015, 97% of all full-time freshmen and 75% of continuing full-time students received some form of financial aid. 61% of all full-time freshmen and 62% of continuing full-time students received need-based aid. The average freshman award was $13,104. Need-based scholarships or need-based grants averaged $6,283 ($9,061 maximum); need-based self-help aid (loans and jobs) averaged $3,533 ($5,500 maximum); non-need-based athletic scholarships averaged $17,719 ($34,795 maximum); and other non-need-based awards and non-need-based scholarships averaged $7,919

($28,128 maximum). 16% of undergraduate students work part-time. Average annual earnings from campus work are $3400. The average financial indebtedness of the 2014 graduate was $24,402. The FAFSA is required. The priority date for freshman financial aid applications for fall entry is February 1. The deadline for filing freshman financial aid applications for fall entry is December 19.

FERRIS STATE UNIVERSITY   D-4
www.ferris.edu

Big Rapids, MI 49307	(231) 591-2100
Fax: (231) 591-3944	Email: admissions@ferris.edu
Full-time: 4636 men, 4469 women	Faculty: IIA, +$
Part-time: 1688 men, 2564 women	Ph.D.s: 35%
Graduate: 532 men, 711 women	Student/Faculty: 16 to 1
Year: semesters, summer session	Tuition: $10,839 ($16,629)
Room & Board: $9208	Freshman Class: 10486 applied, 8176 accepted, 1926 enrolled
SAT: required ACT: 22	CEEB CODE: 1222
Application Deadline: August 1	COMPETITIVE

Ferris State University, established in 1884, is a public institution offering day and evening courses through its Schools of Arts and Sciences, Education and Human Services, Health Professions, Engineering Technology, Business, and Pharmacy, MI College of Optometry, and Kendall College of Art and Design. There are 6 undergraduate schools and 5 graduate schools. In addition to regional accreditation, Ferris State has baccalaureate program accreditation with ABET, ACBSP, ACCE, ACPE, CSWE, and NLN. The 941-acre campus is in a small town 55 miles north of Grand Rapids. Including any residence halls, there are 110 buildings.

<u>STUDENT LIFE:</u> 92% of undergraduates are from Michigan. Others are from 47 states, 40 foreign countries, and Canada. 78% are White. The average age of freshmen is 18; all undergraduates, 22. 29% do not continue beyond their first year. <u>Housing:</u> 3893 students can be accommodated in college housing, which includes single-sex and coed dorms, on-campus apartments, and married student housing. In addition, there are honors houses, language houses, special-interest houses, Honors, substance free, 1st year experience, quiet house, graphic design and sophomore leadership. On-campus housing is guaranteed for all 4 years. 61% of students commute. All students may keep cars.

<u>FACULTY/CLASSROOMS:</u> 53% of faculty are male; 47% are female. All teach undergraduates. No introductory courses are taught by graduate students. The average class size in an introductory lecture is 24; in a laboratory is 14; and in a regular course is 17.

<u>PROGRAMS OF STUDY:</u> Ferris State confers B.A., B.S., B.F.A., B.S.N., B.S.W., B.B. and B.I.S. degrees. Associate, Master's, and doctoral degrees are also awarded. Bachelor's degrees are awarded in BIOLOGICAL SCIENCE (biochemistry, biology/adolescence education, biology/biological science, and biotechnology), BUSINESS (accounting, banking and finance, business administration w/legal studies, business administration and management, business administration/aviation, business data processing, collaborative design, facilities management, finance, hospitality management services, hotel and restaurant administration, hotel/motel and restaurant management, human resources, insurance, insurance and risk management, integrative studies, marketing, marketing/retailing/merchandising, operations management, recreation and leisure services, resort management, professional golf management, and professional tennis management), COMMUNICATIONS AND THE ARTS (advertising, applied speech communication, art history and appreciation, communication, communications, digital media, digital media software engineering, drawing, drawing with printmaking focus, English, fashion studies, fine arts, graphic communications management, graphic design, illustration, industrial design, journalism and technical communications, metal/jewelry, music industry, Technical Communication, painting, photography, printmaking, printing management, public relations, sculpture, sports communication, and television and digital media production), COMPUTER AND PHYSICAL

SCIENCE (actuarial science, applied mathematics, chemistry, chemistry education, computer networks and systems, computer programming, computer information systems, digital animation, game design, and industrial technology), EDUCATION (business education, early childhood education, elementary education, English education, health information management, history education, mathematics education, pro-mo-ted-technical education, social studies education, and technical education), ENGINEERING AND ENVIRONMENTAL DESIGN (architecture and sustainability, automotive technology, construction management, construction mgmt/commercial/industrial, construction mgmt/highway/bridge, electrical/electronics engineering technology, engineering technology, furniture design, HVACR eng tech & energy management, HVACR engineering technology, heavy equip service engineering, manufacturing engineering, mechanical engineering technology, plastics engineering, preengineering, product design engineering technology, surveying engineering, and welding engineering), HEALTH PROFESSIONS (allied health, biology, dental hygiene, health care administration, healthcare marketing, medical records administration/services, molecular diagnostics, nuclear medical technology, nursing, optometry, Pre-Health Studies, prephysical therapy, and public health), SOCIAL SCIENCE (criminal justice, history, political science/government, psychology, social studies, social work, and sociology). Pharmacy and optometry are the strongest academically. Pharmacy/pre pharmacy, nursing and criminal justice have the largest enrollments.

ACTIVITIES: 4% of men belong to 30 national fraternities; 1% of women belong to 11 national sororities. There are 244 groups on campus, including art, band, cheerleading, choir, chorus, communications, dance, drama, drill team, ethnic, film, gay, honors, international, jazz band, musical theater, newspaper, orchestra, pep band, political, professional, radio and TV, religious, social, social service, student government, and symphony. Popular campus events include Ferris Fest and Autumn a LIVE Concert. **Sports:** There are 7 intercollegiate sports for men and 8 for women, and 14 intramural sports for men and 13 for women. Facilities include a golf course, racquetball and fitness club, an ice arena, 10,000-seat stadium, student recreation center with a pool, and tennis courts. **Graduates:** From July 1, 2013 to June 30, 2014, 2412 bachelor's degrees were awarded. The most popular majors were criminal justice (18%), nursing (10%), and pharmacy (6%). 280 companies recruited on campus in 2013-2014. In an average class, 13% graduate in 3 years or less, 29% graduate in 4 years or less, 42% graduate in 5 years or less, and 49% graduate in 6 years or less.

SERVICES: Counseling and information services are available, as is tutoring in most subjects. There is a reader service for the blind, remedial math, reading, and writing. **Library/Resources:** The library contains 265,596 volumes, 3.6 million microform items, 6,811 audio/video tapes/CDs/DVDs, and subscribes to 77,625 periodicals including electronic. Computerized library services include interlibrary loans, database searching, Internet access, and Wi-Fi capability. Special learning facilities include an art gallery, natural history museum, radio station, and TV station. **Physically Challenged Students:** 98% of the campus is accessible. Facilities include wheelchair ramps, elevators, special parking, specially equipped restrooms, special class scheduling, lowered drinking fountains, lowered telephones, and special housing. **Special:** Ferris State offers co-op programs in automotive service technology, internships, study abroad, work-study programs, accelerated degrees, dual and student-designed majors, credit for life, military, and work experience. There are 11 national honor societies and a freshman honors program. **Visiting:** There are regularly scheduled orientations for prospective students, consisting of an admission's presentation, lunch and campus tour. There are guides for informal visits. To schedule a visit, contact the Admissions Office. **Campus Safety and Security:** Measures include 24-hour foot and vehicle patrol, emergency notification system, self-defense education, and security escort services. There are emergency telephones, lighted pathways/sidewalks, and controlled access to dorms/residences.

REQUIREMENTS: The SAT or ACT is required. Applicants must graduate from an accredited secondary school or earn a GED. 4 years each of English and math. 3 years of science (2 lab) and 3 social studies. 2 years of foreign language, and 1 computer science are

advised. AP and CLEP credits are accepted. Important factors in the admissions decision are personality/intangible qualities, leadership record, and advanced placement or honors courses. Degree requirements include a minimum 2.0 GPA. The total number of credit hours required varies. General education courses required include English, speech, math, humanities, social science, cultural enrichment, and natural science subjects. **Procedure:** Freshmen are admitted fall, spring, and summer. Entrance exams should be taken before course registration. There is a rolling admissions plan. Applications should be filed by August 1 for fall entry, along with a $30 fee. Applications are accepted on-line. Application fees are waived if application is completed on-line. **Transfer Students:** 2251 transfer students enrolled in 2013-2014. A GPA of at least 2.0 is required, as are college transcripts, and a statement of good standing from previously attended institutions. Some students may need to submit high school transcripts and test scores. 30 of 120 credits required for the bachelor's degree must be completed at Ferris State. **International Students:** There are 351 international students enrolled. The school actively recruits these students. They must take the TOEFL with a minimum score of 500 on the paper-based TOEFL (PBT) or 61 on the Internet-based version (iBT). They must also take the SAT or ACT, scoring 17 and a supplemental math exam.

ADMISSIONS: 78% of the 2014-2015 applicants were accepted. The ACT scores were 41% below 21, 27% between 21 and 23, 19% between 24 and 26, 7% between 27 and 28, and 6% above 28. **Admissions Contact:** Admissions Officer E-Mail: *admissions@ferris.edu* Web: *www.ferris.edu*

FINANCIAL AID: In 2014-2015, 94% of all full-time freshmen and 89% of continuing full-time students received some form of financial aid. 69% of all full-time freshmen and 66% of continuing full-time students received need-based aid. The average freshman award was $15,850. Need-based scholarships or need-based grants averaged $2,855; need-based self-help aid (loans and jobs) averaged $2,375; non-need-based athletic scholarships averaged $255; and other non-need-based awards and non-need-based scholarships averaged $10,365. 17% of undergraduate students work part-time. Average annual earnings from campus work are $2509. The average financial indebtedness of the 2014 graduate was $35,739. Ferris State is a member of CSS. The FAFSA is required. The priority date for freshman financial aid applications for fall entry is February 15. The deadline for filing freshman financial aid applications for fall entry is rolling.

GRACE BIBLE COLLEGE   **D-4**
www.gbcol.edu

Grand Rapids, MI 49509	(616) 538-2330
	(800) 968-1887
Fax: (616) 538-2330	Email: enrollment@gbcol.edu
Full-time: 101 men, 80 women	Faculty: 7
Part-time: 6 men, 7 women	Ph.D.s: 43%
Graduate: n/av	Student/Faculty: 26 to 1
Year: semesters	Tuition: $13,920
Room & Board: $6850	Freshman Class: 141 applied, 84 accepted, 48 enrolled
SAT CR/M/W: 560/540/500 ACT: 21	CEEB CODE: 0809
Application Deadline: n/av	COMPETITIVE

Grace Bible College, founded in 1939, is a private institution affiliated with the Grace Gospel Fellowship. It's mission is to provide a curriculum that integrates general education and biblical studies and prepares students for service in their career, church, and society. Figures in the above capsule and in this profile are approximate. In addition to regional accreditation, GBC has baccalaureate program accreditation with AABC. The 21-acre campus is in a suburban area on the southwest side of Grand Rapids. Including any residence halls, there are 12 buildings.

STUDENT LIFE: 80% of undergraduates are from Michigan. Others are from 15 states, and 2 foreign countries. 93% are White. 97% are Protestant. The average age of freshmen is 19; all undergraduates, 21. 21% do not continue beyond their first year; 75% remain to graduate.

Housing: 110 students can be accommodated in college housing, which includes single-sex dorms, on-campus apartments, off-campus apartments, and married student housing. On-campus housing is guaranteed for all 4 years. 52% of students live on campus; of those, 75% remain on campus on weekends. Alcohol is not permitted. All students may keep cars.

FACULTY/CLASSROOMS: 72% of faculty are male; 28% are female. All teach undergraduates. No introductory courses are taught by graduate students. The average class size in an introductory lecture is 60 and in a regular course is 16.

PROGRAMS OF STUDY: GBC confers B.S., B.Mus., B.R.E. and B.Th. degrees. Associate degrees are also awarded. Bachelor's degrees are awarded in BUSINESS (business administration and management), COMMUNICATIONS AND THE ARTS (music), COMPUTER AND PHYSICAL SCIENCE (digital arts/technology), EDUCATION (elementary education and secondary education), SOCIAL SCIENCE (biblical studies, early childhood studies, human services, interdisciplinary studies, missions, pastoral studies, religious education, and youth ministry). Elementary/secondary education, youth ministry, and human services have the largest enrollments.

ACTIVITIES: Groups on campus include cheerleading, choir, drama, jazz band, musical theater, religious, and student government. Popular campus events include Winter Formal, Missions Conference, and Campus Service Days. **Sports:** There are 2 intercollegiate sports for men and 2 for women. Facilities include a 300-seat soccer field and an athletic center with a 500-seat gym for basketball and volleyball, a racquetball court, and an exercise and weight room. **Graduates:** From July 1, 2013 to June 30, 2014, 31 bachelor's degrees were awarded. The most popular majors were education (33%), youth and pastoral ministries (17%), and visual performing arts and digital media (17%). In an average class, 20% graduate in 3 years or less, 46% graduate in 4 years or less, 62% graduate in 5 years or less, and 75% graduate in 6 years or less.

SERVICES: Counseling and information services are available, as is tutoring in most subjects. **Library/Resources:** The library contains 42,867 volumes, 53 microform items, 2,582 audio/video tapes/CDs/DVDs, and subscribes to 54,292 periodicals including electronic. Computerized library services include interlibrary loans, database searching, Internet access, and Wi-Fi capability. **Physically Challenged Students:** 85% of the campus is accessible. Facilities include wheelchair ramps, elevators, special parking, specially equipped restrooms, and lowered drinking fountains. **Special:** Cross-registration is available with Cornerstone and Davenport Universities. GBC offers 6-month internships for theology majors. Most 4-year degree programs require a semester practicum. **Visiting:** There are regularly scheduled orientations for prospective students, consisting of 7 Friday programs a year that include workshops, class visits, and campus tours. There are guides for informal visits, visitors may sit in on classes, and stay overnight. To schedule a visit, contact the Director of Enrollment. **Campus Safety and Security:** There are lighted pathways/sidewalks, an evening and overnight foot patrol.

REQUIREMENTS: The ACT is required. The ACT is preferred. Applicants must be graduates of accredited secondary schools or have earned a GED. The application must show involvement in Christian activities and personal salvation through Jesus Christ. GBC requires applicants to be in the upper 50% of their class. AP and CLEP credits are accepted. To graduate, students must complete 126 to 158 credits, depending on the major, with a minimum GPA of 2.0 and must be considered worthy in character and conduct by the faculty. Course work is required in arts and sciences, ministry studies, Bible/theology, math/computer science, lab science, and phys ed. Attendance is expected at worship services twice a week. **Procedure:** Freshmen are admitted fall and spring. There is a rolling admissions plan. Application deadlines are open. **Transfer Students:** 20 transfer students enrolled in 2013-2014. Applicants must present a GPA of 2.0 and be in good standing at their previous school. Those with fewer than 24 college credit hours must submit high school records. 63 of 126 credits required for the bachelor's degree must be completed at GBC. **International Students:** They must take the TOEFL.

ADMISSIONS: 60% of the 2014-2015 applicants were accepted. The SAT scores for the 2014-2015 freshman class were: Critical Reading--35% below 500, and 66% between 500 and 599; Math--34% below 500, and 66% between 500 and 599; Writing--34% below 500, 33% between 500 and 599, and 33% between 600 and 699. The ACT scores were 45% below 21, 26% between 21 and 23, 19% between 24 and 26, 7% between 27 and 28, and 3% above 28. 32% of the current freshmen were in the top fifth of their class; 41% were in the top two fifths. **Admissions Contact:** Kevin Gilliam, Director of Enrollment. E-Mail: *enrollment@gbcol.edu* Web: *www.gbcol.edu*

FINANCIAL AID: In 2014-2015, 98% of all full-time freshmen and 97% of continuing full-time students received some form of financial aid. 74% of all full-time freshmen and 81% of continuing full-time students received need-based aid. The average freshman award was $7,780. Need-based scholarships or need-based grants averaged $3,383 ($5,350 maximum); need-based self-help aid (loans and jobs) averaged $2,063 ($3,500 maximum); and other non-need-based awards and non-need-based scholarships averaged $3,946 ($4,500 maximum). 43% of undergraduate students work part-time. Average annual earnings from campus work are $2300. The average financial indebtedness of the 2014 graduate was $16,689. The FAFSA is required. The priority date for freshman financial aid applications for fall entry is March 1.

GRAND VALLEY STATE UNIVERSITY   D-4
www.gvsu.edu

Allendale, MI 49401

(616) 331-5000
(800) 748-0246

Fax: (616) 331-2000
Full-time: 7699 men, 10964 women
Part-time: 1136 men, 1432 women
Graduate: 1102 men, 2235 women
Year: semesters, summer session
Room & Board: $7920

Email: admissions@gvsu.edu
Faculty: 1069; IIA, av$
Ph.D.s: 78%
Student/Faculty: 17 to 1
Tuition: $10,078 ($14,568)
Freshman Class: 17880 applied, 14596 accepted, 3966 enrolled

ACT: 24 SAT: required
Application Deadline: July 23

CEEB CODE: 1258
COMPETITIVE+

Grand Valley State University, founded in 1960, is a comprehensive public institution offering graduate and undergraduate liberal arts and professional education. Figures in the above capsule and in this profile are approximate. There are 8 undergraduate schools and 7 graduate schools. In addition to regional accreditation, GVSU has baccalaureate program accreditation with AACSB, ABET, APTA, CSWE, NASAD, NASM, NCATE, and NLN. The 1342-acre campus is in a small town 12 miles west of Grand Rapids. Including any residence halls, there are 72 buildings.

STUDENT LIFE: 95% of undergraduates are from Michigan. Others are from 40 states, 73 foreign countries, and Canada. 75% are from public schools. 91% are White. The average age of freshmen is 18; all undergraduates, 21. 18% do not continue beyond their first year; 56% remain to graduate. **Housing:** 5820 students can be accommodated in college housing, which includes single-sex and coed dorms, on-campus apartments, off-campus apartments, and married student housing. In addition, there are honors houses, language houses, special-interest houses, fraternity houses, and sorority houses. On-campus housing is guaranteed for the freshman year only, is available on a first-come, first-served basis, and is available on a lottery system for upperclassmen. Priority is given to out-of-town students. 73% of students commute. Alcohol is not permitted. All students may keep cars.

FACULTY/CLASSROOMS: 51% of faculty are male; 49% are female. 97% teach undergraduates. No introductory courses are taught by graduate students. The average class size in an introductory lecture is 37; in a laboratory is 21; and in a regular course is 27.

PROGRAMS OF STUDY: GVSU confers B.A., B.S., B.B.A., B.F.A., B.M., B.M.E., B.S.E., B.S.N. and B.S.W. degrees. Master's and Doctoral degrees are also awarded. Bachelor's degrees are awarded in AGRICULTURE (natural resource management), BIOLOGICAL SCIENCE (biology/biological science and cell biology), BUSINESS (accounting, banking and finance, business administration and management, business economics, hotel/motel and restaurant management, international business management, management science, marketing/retailing/merchandising, and personnel management), COMMUNICATIONS AND THE ARTS (advertising, art, art history and appreciation, broadcasting, Chinese, classics, communications, creative writing, dance, design, dramatic arts, English, film arts, fine arts, French, German, journalism, languages, music, photography, and Spanish), COMPUTER AND PHYSICAL SCIENCE (chemistry, computer science, earth science, geochemistry, geology, information sciences and systems, mathematics, physics, science, and statistics), EDUCATION (art education, athletic training, elementary education, foreign languages education, middle school education, music education, science education, secondary education, and special education), ENGINEERING AND ENVIRONMENTAL DESIGN (engineering, industrial engineering technology, and occupational safety and health), HEALTH PROFESSIONS (biomedical science, clinical science, exercise science, health science, medical laboratory technology, nursing, physical therapy, physician's assistant, predentistry, premedicine, and recreation therapy), SOCIAL SCIENCE (anthropology, behavioral science, biopsychology, criminal justice, economics, geography, history, international relations, law, liberal arts/general studies, philosophy, political science/government, prelaw, psychology, public administration, Russian and Slavic studies, social science, social work, and sociology). Health sciences, English, and psychology have the largest enrollments.

ACTIVITIES: 5% of women belong to 10 national sororities. There are 250 groups on campus, including art, band, cheerleading, chess, choir, chorale, chorus, computers, dance, drama, environmental, ethnic, film, gay, honors, international, jazz band, literary magazine, marching band, musical theater, newspaper, opera, orchestra, pep band, photography, political, professional, radio and TV, religious, social, social service, student government, and symphony. Popular campus events include Family Day, Hispanic Awareness Week and Black History Month. **Sports:** There are 9 intercollegiate sports for men and 10 for women, and 26 intramural sports for men and 26 for women. Facilities include a football stadium, a baseball field, a basketball arena, swimming and diving pools, an indoor track, a weight room, a fitness building/intramural center, an outdoor cross-country track, and an outdoor soccer field. **Graduates:** From July 1, 2013 to June 30, 2014, 4301 bachelor's degrees were awarded. The most popular majors were business/marketing (16%), biological/life sciences (9%), and health sciences (8%). 192 companies recruited on campus in 2013-2014. In an average class, 30% graduate in 4 years or less, 56% graduate in 5 years or less, and 63% graduate in 6 years or less. Of the 2013 graduating class, 25% were enrolled in graduate school within 6 months of graduation, and 79% were employed.

SERVICES: Counseling and information services are available, as is tutoring in most subjects. There is a reader service for the blind, remedial math, reading, and writing. **Library/Resources:** The 2 libraries contain 708,000 volumes, 868,850 microform items, 19,804 audio/video tapes/CDs/DVDs, and subscribe to 73,759 periodicals including electronic. Computerized library services include interlibrary loans, database searching, Internet access, and Wi-Fi capability. Special learning facilities include an art gallery, radio station, TV station, a cadaver lab, 2 Great Lakes research vessels, a performance auditorium, and dance studios. **Physically Challenged Students:** 98% of the campus is accessible. Facilities include wheelchair ramps, elevators, special parking, specially equipped restrooms, special class scheduling, lowered drinking fountains, and lowered telephones. **Special:** Many programs offer dual majors and internships, and most majors qualify for B.A.-B.S. degrees. There is an engineering cooperative program, a student-designed major in liberal studies, and many work-study programs. Outside opportunities include study abroad in 10 countries and a Washington semester. There are 14 national honor societies, a freshman honors program, and 12 departmental honors programs. **Visiting:** There are regularly scheduled orientations for prospective students, including registration activities. There are guides for informal visits, visitors may sit in on classes, and stay overnight. To schedule a visit, contact the Admissions Office. **Campus Safety and Security:** Measures include 24-hour foot and vehicle patrol, emergency notification system, self-defense education, and security escort services. There are shuttle buses, emergency telephones, and lighted pathways/sidewalks.

REQUIREMENTS: The SAT or ACT is required. Michigan residents must submit ACT test scores, nonresidents either ACT or SAT scores. In addition, high school transcripts should indicate 4 years of English with 1 composition course, 3 each of math (including 2 years of algebra), science (including 1 lab), and social studies, and 2 of a foreign language. Applicants who graduated from high school more than 3 years ago need not show test results. The GED is accepted. A GPA of 3.0 is required. AP and CLEP credits are accepted. Important factors in the admissions decision are extracurricular activities record, recommendations by school officials, and advanced placement or honors courses. To graduate, students must have earned 30 credits in general education, composed of 10 courses selected from specific groups, and have completed the university's required courses in English and math, as well as the upper-division writing course. A total of 120 credits, with 36 to 60 in the major, and a GPA of 2.0, are required to graduate. **Procedure:** Freshmen are admitted to all sessions. Entrance exams should be taken during the junior year. There is a rolling admissions plan. Applications should be filed by July 23 for fall entry, along with a $30 fee. Notification is sent on a rolling basis. Applications are accepted on-line. **Transfer Students:** 1800 transfer students enrolled in 2013-2014. Transfer students must have a minimum of 30 college credits with a 2.0 GPA. They must submit previous college transcripts and a statement of good standing from prior institutions. 30 of 120 credits required for the bachelor's degree must be completed at GVSU. **International Students:** There are 272 international students enrolled. The school actively recruits these students. They must take the TOEFL with a minimum score of 550 on the paper-based TOEFL (PBT) or 80 on the Internet-based version (iBT) or take the MELAB and the Comprehensive English Language Test. They must also take the SAT or ACT.

ADMISSIONS: 82% of the 2014-2015 applicants were accepted. The ACT scores were 19% below 21, 31% between 21 and 23, 28% between 24 and 26, 12% between 27 and 28, and 10% above 28. 45% of the current freshmen were in the top fifth of their class; 80% were in the top two fifths. 18 freshmen graduated first in their class. **Admissions Contact:** Jodi Chycinski, Director of Admissions. E-Mail: *admissions@gvsu.edu* Web: *www.gvsu.edu*

FINANCIAL AID: In 2014-2015, 67% of all full-time freshmen and 65% of continuing full-time students received some form of financial aid. 60% of all full-time freshmen and 59% of continuing full-time students received need-based aid. The average freshman award was $10,949. Need-based scholarships or need-based grants averaged $7,469; and need-based self-help aid (loans and jobs) averaged $4,937. 12% of undergraduate students work part-time. Average annual earnings from campus work are $3330. The average financial indebtedness of the 2014 graduate was $24,876. GVSU is a member of CSS. The FAFSA is required. The deadline for filing freshman financial aid applications for fall entry is February 15.

HILLSDALE COLLEGE D-5
www.hillsdale.edu

Hillsdale, MI 49242   (517) 437-7341

Fax: (517) 607-2223	**Email:** admissions@hillsdale.edu
Full-time: 688 men, 749 women	**Faculty:** 133
Part-time: 21 men, 14 women	**Ph.D.s:** 88%
Graduate: 22 men, 10 women	**Student/Faculty:** 11 to 1
Year: semesters, summer session	**Tuition:** $23,616
Room & Board: $9250	**Freshman Class:** 1833 applied, 972 accepted, 359 enrolled
SAT CR/M/W: 680/620/650 **ACT:** 29	**CEEB CODE:** 1295
Application Deadline: February 15	**MOST COMPETITIVE**

Hillsdale College, founded in 1844, is a private liberal arts college, emphasizing classical liberal arts, pre-professional, business, education, science and humanities. There is 1 undergraduate school and 1 graduate school. The 400-acre campus is in a small town 120 miles southwest of Detroit. Including any residence halls, there are 81 buildings.

STUDENT LIFE: 65% of undergraduates are from out of state, mostly the Midwest. Students are from 49 states, 9 foreign countries, and Canada. 51% are from public schools. The average age of freshmen is 20; all undergraduates, 20. 6% do not continue beyond their first year; 82% remain to graduate. **Housing:** 1100 students can be accommodated in college housing, which includes single-sex dorms and on-campus apartments. In addition, there are honors houses, fraternity houses, and sorority houses. On-campus housing is guaranteed for all 4 years. 74% of students live on campus; of those, 90% remain on campus on weekends. Alcohol is not permitted. All students may keep cars.

FACULTY/CLASSROOMS: 72% of faculty are male; 28% are female. All teach undergraduates, all do research. No introductory courses are taught by graduate students. The average class size in an introductory lecture is 30; in a laboratory is 15; and in a regular course is 18.

PROGRAMS OF STUDY: Hillsdale confers B.A., and B.S. degrees. Master's and Doctoral degrees are also awarded. Bachelor's degrees are awarded in BIOLOGICAL SCIENCE (biochemistry and biology/biological science), BUSINESS (accounting, finance, international business management, marketing/retailing/merchandising, and sports management), COMMUNICATIONS AND THE ARTS (art, classical languages, classics, comparative literature, English, French, German, music, Spanish, speech/debate/rhetoric, and theatre arts), COMPUTER AND PHYSICAL SCIENCE (chemistry, mathematics, mathematics/computational, and physics), EDUCATION (physical education), HEALTH PROFESSIONS (exercise science and sports psychology), SOCIAL SCIENCE (American studies, Christian studies, economics, European studies, history, philosophy, philosophy and religion, political science/government, psychology, religion, and sociology). Biology, classical studies, and economics are the strongest academically. English, history, and economics have the largest enrollments.

ACTIVITIES: 26% of men belong to 4 national fraternities; 37% of women belong to 3 national sororities. There are 48 groups on campus, including art, bagpipe, band, cheerleading, chess, choir, chorale, chorus, communications, computers, dance, debate, drama, ethnic, film, forensics, honors, international, jazz band, literary magazine, musical theater, newspaper, opera, orchestra, pep band, photography, political, professional, religious, social, social service, student government, symphony, and yearbook. Popular campus events include Welcome Party, Parents Weekend, President's Ball, Greek Week, Homecoming, Garden Party, Convocation, and Centralhallapalooza. **Sports:** There are 9 intercollegiate sports for men and 11 for women, and 14 intramural sports for men and 12 for women. Facilities include an athletic complex with a ProGrass artificial turf football field, a swimming pool, a 200-meter Mondo indoor track and tennis facility, a basketball arena, weight room, a Mondo outdoor Olympic track, an exercise/physiology room, and volleyball, handball, racquetball, wallyball courts. The campus stadium seats 5000; the gym 1750.

Graduates: From July 1, 2013 to June 30, 2014, 336 bachelor's degrees were awarded. The most popular majors were English (14%), history (12%), and economics (12%). 115 companies recruited on campus in 2013-2014. In an average class, 1% graduate in 3 years or less, 70% graduate in 4 years or less, 81% graduate in 5 years or less, and 82% graduate in 6 years or less. Of the 2013 graduating class, 19% were enrolled in graduate school within 6 months of graduation, and 74% were employed.

SERVICES: Counseling and information services are available, as is tutoring in every subject. A writing center on campus and a peer tutoring program are administered by current students. **Library/Resources:** The library contains 903,154 volumes, 92,863 microform items, 31,084 audio/video tapes/CDs/DVDs, and subscribes to 570 periodicals including electronic. Computerized library services include interlibrary loans, database searching, Internet access, and Wi-Fi capability. Special learning facilities include an art gallery, natural history museum, Greenhouse, Sage Center for the Arts, Howard Music Hall, media center, K-8 private academy, Slayton Arboretum, rare books library, shooting range, Herbert Henry Dow Science Building, Strosaker Science Center, Mary Randall Preschool. **Physically Challenged Students:** 85% of the campus is accessible. Facilities include wheelchair ramps, elevators, special parking, specially equipped restrooms, lowered drinking fountains. Special accommodations according to individual needs. **Special:** Special academic programs include the Washington Journalism Internship at the National Journalism Center and the Washington-Hillsdale Intern Program (WHIP), which places students in congressional or government offices. Students may study abroad in France, Germany, or Spain, and qualified students are chosen to attend Oxford University for a year. A business internship is offered in London at Regents College. The college offers an accelerated degree; interdisciplinary majors, including political economy combining economics, history, and political science; 3-2 and 2-2 engineering degrees; and work-study programs at the city radio station WCSR and the city newspaper, the Hillsdale Daily News. There are 21 national honor societies, a freshman honors program, and 15 departmental honors programs. **Visiting:** There are regularly scheduled orientations for prospective students, agenda is customized based on visitor request; almost all visits include a campus tour and meeting with an Admissions Representative. Visitors may sit in on classes and stay overnight. To schedule a visit, contact Margaret Braman at admissions@hillsdale.edu. **Campus Safety and Security:** Measures include 24-hour foot and vehicle patrol, emergency notification system, self-defense education, and security escort services. There are shuttle buses, emergency telephones, lighted pathways/sidewalks, and controlled access to dorms/residences.

REQUIREMENTS: The SAT or ACT is required. The student must be a high school graduate or have earned a GED, and must have completed 4 years of English, 3 each of math and science, and 2 each of history, social studies, and foreign language. The college requires 2 letters of recommendation and an essay. An interview is also recommended. For music majors, an audition is required for a scholarship. The school recommends taking SAT: Subject tests. AP and CLEP credits are accepted. Important factors in the admissions decision are advanced placement or honors courses, leadership record, and extracurricular activities record. The completion of the bachelor's degree requires 124 semester hours of college work with an accumulative grade-point average of 2.0 ("C"). No fewer than two, nor more than four, of the 124 hours are to be taken in physical education activity courses. Not more than 48 hours may be presented from any one discipline. The required Core Curriculum includes courses in English, the Fine Arts, Philosophy/Religion, Mathematics, the Physical Sciences, History, Politics, the Social Sciences, and Classical/Modern Languages. Students transferring to Hillsdale must earn an accumulative grade-point average of 2.0 ("C") in all work taken at Hillsdale. A grade of "C–" or higher must be obtained in each of the courses counted toward a field of concentration. Course options must be selected and completed according to the divisional requirements, generally during the first two years. Exceptions may be made for transfer students and for those enrolled in pre-professional programs. Each student is required to enroll in two CCA seminars, one of which must be taken during the freshman or sophomore year and one in the junior or senior year. A satisfactory command of English must be consistently demonstrated. **Procedure:** Freshmen are admitted fall, spring, and summer. Entrance exams should be taken in the spring of the junior year and/or the fall of the senior year. There is a early decision plan. Early decision applications should be filed by November 15; regular applications, by February 15 for fall entry; and December 15 for spring entry, along with a $35 fee. Notification of early decision is sent December 1; regular decision, April 1. 86 early decision candidates were accepted for the 2014-2015 class. 38 applicants were on the 2014 waiting list; 2 were admitted. Applications are accepted on-line. Application fees are waived if application is completed on-line. **Transfer Students:** 23 transfer students enrolled in 2013-2014. Transfer students must have a GPA of 3.35, and have a transfer evaluation form completed by the dean of students of their school. Hillsdale also requires high school and college transcripts. **International Students:** There are 19 international students enrolled. The school actively recruits these students.

ADMISSIONS: 53% of the 2014-2015 applicants were accepted. The SAT scores for the 2014-2015 freshman class were: Critical Reading--3% below 500, 17% between 500 and 599, 37% between 600 and 699, and 43% between 700 and 800; Math--3% below 500, 27% between 500 and 599, 47% between 600 and 699, and 23% between 700 and 800; Writing--3% below 500, 20% between 500 and 599, 50% between 600 and 699, and 27% between 700 and 800. The ACT scores were 1% below 21, 3% between 21 and 23, 17% between 24 and 26, 18% between 27 and 28, and 61% above 28. 22% of the current freshmen were in the top fifth of their class; 26% were in the top two fifths. There were 13 National Merit finalists. 11 freshmen graduated first in their class. **Admissions Contact:** Doug Banbury , Associate VP of Admissions. E-Mail: *admissions@hillsdale.edu* Web: *http:/www.hillsdale.edu/admissions*

FINANCIAL AID: In 2014-2015, 92% of all full-time freshmen and 96% of continuing full-time students received some form of financial aid. 44% of all full-time freshmen and 43% of continuing full-time students received need-based aid. The average freshman award was $12,377. Need-based scholarships or need-based grants averaged $8,774 ($17,190 maximum); need-based self-help aid (loans and jobs) averaged $5,761 ($10,000 maximum); non-need-based athletic scholarships averaged $13,270 ($34,066 maximum); and other non-need-based awards and non-need-based scholarships averaged $10,326 ($22,920 maximum). 66% of undergraduate students work part-time. Average annual earnings from campus work are $2080. The average financial indebtedness of the 2014 graduate was $25,502. Hillsdale is a member of CSS. The CSS/Profile and FFS are required. The priority date for freshman financial aid applications for fall entry is May 1.

HOPE COLLEGE   C-4
www.hope.edu

Holland, MI 49422	(616) 395-7850
	(800) 968-7850
Fax: (616) 395-7130	Email: admissions@hope.edu
Full-time: 1296 men, 1981 women	Faculty: 249; IIB, av$
Part-time: 68 men, 87 women	Ph.D.s: 76%
Graduate: n/av	Student/Faculty: 12 to 1
Year: semesters, summer session	Tuition: $29,560
Room & Board: $9090	Freshman Class: 4158 applied, 2931 accepted, 832 enrolled
SAT CR/M: 590/590 ACT: 26	CEEB CODE: 1301
Application Deadline: open	VERY COMPETITIVE

Hope College, founded by Dutch pioneers in 1866, is a private liberal arts institution affiliated with the Reformed Church in America. In addition to regional accreditation, Hope has baccalaureate program accreditation with ABET, CSWE, NASAD, NASM, TEAC, ACS, CCNE, NASD, NAST, and CAATE. The 120-acre campus is in an urban area 26 miles southwest of Grand Rapids and 5 miles east of Lake Michigan. Including any residence halls, there are 130 buildings.

STUDENT LIFE: 65% of undergraduates are from Michigan. Others are from 40 states, 23 foreign countries, and Canada. 88% are from public schools. 85% are White. 66% are Protestant; 19% Catholic; 15% unknown denominations. The average age of freshmen is 18; all undergraduates, 20. 11% do not continue beyond their first year; 78% remain to graduate. **Housing:** 2633 students can be accommodated in college housing, which includes single-sex and coed dorms, on-campus apartments, and married student housing. In addition, there are language houses, special-interest houses, fraternity houses, sorority houses, student cottages. On-campus housing is guaranteed for all 4 years. 78% of students live on campus; of those, 75% remain on campus on weekends. Alcohol is not permitted. All students may keep cars.

FACULTY/CLASSROOMS: 56% of faculty are male; 44% are female. All teach undergraduates. No introductory courses are taught by graduate students. The average class size in an introductory lecture is 21; in a laboratory is 17; and in a regular course is 19.

PROGRAMS OF STUDY: Hope confers B.A., B.S., B.Mus. and B.S.N. degrees. Bachelor's degrees are awarded in BIOLOGICAL SCIENCE (biochemistry, biology/adolescence education, biology/biological science, and cell biology), BUSINESS (accounting, accounting/CPA, and business administration and management), COMMUNICATIONS AND THE ARTS (art, art history and appreciation, classical languages, communications, creative writing, dance, dramatic arts, English, fine arts, French, German, language arts, Latin, music, music performance, piano/organ, piano performance, Spanish, theatre arts, and vocal music education), COMPUTER AND PHYSICAL SCIENCE (chemistry, chemistry education, computer science, geology, mathematics, and physics), EDUCATION (art edu-

cation, athletic training, dance education, elementary education, English education, foreign languages education, history education, music education, science education, secondary education, and special education), ENGINEERING AND ENVIRONMENTAL DESIGN (engineering), HEALTH PROFESSIONS (exercise science and nursing), SOCIAL SCIENCE (economics, history, international studies, Japanese studies, philosophy, physical fitness/movement, political science/government, psychology, religion, social work, sociology, and women's studies). Chemistry, biological sciences and psychology are the strongest academically. Management, psychology and biology have the largest enrollments.

ACTIVITIES: 12% of men belong to 7 local and 1 national fraternity; 14% of women belong to 7 local and 1 national sorority. There are 78 groups on campus, including art, band, cheerleading, chess, choir, chorale, chorus, computers, dance, drama, environmental, ethnic, honors, international, jazz band, literary magazine, musical theater, newspaper, orchestra, pep band, political, professional, radio and TV, religious, social, social service, student government, symphony, and yearbook. Popular campus events include The Pull, Spring Festival, and Nykerk Cup Competition. **Sports:** There are 11 intercollegiate sports for men and 11 for women, and 14 intramural sports for men and 15 for women. Facilities include athletic fields include 4 full-size soccer fields, softball and baseball stadium, and an outdoor track and field area. The fieldhouse/arena seats 3200 and hosts basketball and volleyball. There is also a 6-court indoor tennis center, a health and phys ed center that contains 3 basketball/volleyball courts, a running track, a swimming and diving pool, exercise rooms, 3 dance studios, 3 racquetball courts, weight training and cardiovascular equipment. **Graduates:** From July 1, 2013 to June 30, 2014, 693 bachelor's degrees were awarded. The most popular majors were psychology (10%), management (10%), and biology (7%). 36 companies recruited on campus in 2013-2014. In an average class, 1% graduate in 3 years or less, 68% graduate in 4 years or less, 76% graduate in 5 years or less, and 78% graduate in 6 years or less. Of the 2013 graduating class, 28% were enrolled in graduate school within 6 months of graduation, and 75% were employed.

SERVICES: Counseling and information services are available, as is tutoring in most subjects. There is a reader service for the blind. **Library/Resources:** The 2 libraries contain 368,869 volumes, 382,734 microform items, 17,879 audio/video tapes/CDs/DVDs, and subscribe to 7,329 periodicals including electronic. Computerized library services include interlibrary loans, database searching, Internet access, and Wi-Fi capability. Special learning facilities include an art gallery, planetarium, radio station, TV station, an academic support center, and a modern and classical language lab. **Physically Challenged Students:** 95% of the campus is accessible. Facilities include wheelchair ramps, elevators, special parking, specially equipped restrooms, special class scheduling, lowered drinking fountains, special housing. **Special:** The college offers internships in all academic areas as well as on-campus work-study programs, student-designed majors, study abroad in more than 57 countries, and Washington, Chicago, New York, and Philadelphia semesters. Students may have dual majors. There are 20 national honor societies, including Phi Beta Kappa, and 1 departmental honors program. **Visiting:** There are regularly scheduled orientations for prospective students, including tours, classes, lunch with a current student, and appointments with professors. There are guides for informal visits, visitors may sit in on classes, and stay overnight. To schedule a visit, contact the Admissions Office. **Campus Safety and Security:** Measures include 24-hour foot and vehicle patrol and security escort services. There are shuttle buses, emergency telephones, and lighted pathways/sidewalks.

REQUIREMENTS: All applicants must submit either an ACT or SAT score. The college requires a high school transcript, which must include 4 years of English, 2 each of math, a foreign language, and social science, and 1 year of a lab science, as well as 5 other academic courses. The college requires submission of an essay and recommends an interview. A portfolio or audition is required for certain majors. The GED is considered. AP and CLEP credits are accepted. Important factors in the admissions decision are advanced placement or honors courses, evidence of special talent, and leadership record. To graduate with a B.A. or B.S. degree, students must complete 126 semester hours with a 2.0 GPA. All students must take 56 hours of the general education program, including a first-year seminar, 10 hours of math and natural science, 8 of cultural heritage, 6 each of social science, performing and fine arts, and religion, 4 each of a language and writing, 4 in a senior seminar, 4 credits of cultural diversity courses, and 2 hours of health dynamics. **Procedure:** Freshmen are admitted fall and spring. Entrance exams should be taken during spring of the junior year or fall of the senior year. There are deferred admissions and rolling admissions plans. Application deadlines are open. The fall 2014 application fee was $35. 629 applicants were on the 2014 waiting list; 95 were admitted. Applications are accepted on-line. **Transfer Students:** 50 transfer students enrolled in 2013-2014. Transfer students must have a GPA of 2.0 in at least 1 year of liberal arts courses. 30 of 126 credits required for the bachelor's degree must be completed at Hope. **International Students:** There are 86 international students enrolled. The school actively recruits these students. They must take the TOEFL with a minimum score of 79 on the Internet-based version (iBT). They must also take the SAT or ACT.

ADMISSIONS: 70% of the 2014-2015 applicants were accepted. The SAT scores for the 2014-2015 freshman class were: Critical Reading--14% below 500, 37% between 500 and 599, 38% between 600 and 699, and 12% between 700 and 800; Math--12% below 500, 39% between 500 and 599, 39% between 600 and 699, and 9% between 700 and 800. The ACT scores were 8% below 21, 19% between 21 and 23, 27% between 24 and 26, 17% between 27 and 28, and 29% above 28. 51% of the current freshmen were in the top fifth of their class; 83% were in the top two fifths. **Admissions Contact:** William C. Vanderbilt, Vice President for Admissions. E-Mail: *admissions@hope.edu* Web: *www.hope.edu*

FINANCIAL AID: In 2014-2015, 93% of all full-time freshmen and 85% of continuing full-time students received some form of financial aid. 58% of all full-time freshmen and 51% of continuing full-time students received need-based aid. The average freshman award was $18,126. Need-based scholarships or need-based grants averaged $11,088; need-based self-help aid (loans and jobs) averaged $4,890; and other non-need-based awards and non-need-based scholarships averaged $2,148. The average financial indebtedness of the 2014 graduate was $19,982. Hope is a member of CSS. The FAFSA and the college's own financial statement are required. The priority date for freshman financial aid applications for fall entry is March 1.

KALAMAZOO COLLEGE D-5
www.kzoo.edu

Kalamazoo, MI 49006	**(269) 337-7000**
	(800) 253-3602
Fax: (269) 337-7390	**Email:** admissions@kzoo.edu
Full-time: 630 men, 818 women	**Faculty:** 102; IIB, +$
Part-time: 4 men, 9 women	**Ph.D.s:** 92%
Graduate: n/av	**Student/Faculty:** 12 to 1
Year: quarters	**Tuition:** $40,728
Room & Board: $8679	**Freshman Class:** 2366 applied, 1648 accepted, 359 enrolled
SAT CR/M/W: 600/632/606 **ACT:** 27	**CEEB CODE:** 1365
Application Deadline: January 15	**HIGHLY COMPETITIVE**

As a highly selective, nationally renowned, and internationally oriented four-year college of arts and sciences, Kalamazoo College has developed a tradition of excellence in the fulfillment of this mission. Founded in 1833, "K" College is among the 100 oldest colleges and universities in the nation. The 60-acre campus is in a suburban area 140 miles from the Detroit and Chicago area. Including any residence halls, there are 30 buildings.

STUDENT LIFE: 31% of undergraduates are from out of state, mostly the Midwest. The average age of freshmen is 18; all undergraduates, 20. **Housing:** 875 students can be accommodated in college housing, which includes single-sex and coed dorms. In addition, there are special-interest houses, including a wellness house. On-campus housing is available on a lottery system for upperclassmen. 66% of students live on campus; of those, 75% remain on campus on weekends. Upperclassmen may keep cars.

FACULTY/CLASSROOMS: 48% of faculty are male; 52% are female.

All teach undergraduates. No introductory courses are taught by graduate students. The average class size in an introductory lecture is 26; in a laboratory is 14; and in a regular course is 22.

PROGRAMS OF STUDY: Kalamazoo confers B.A. degrees. Bachelor's degrees are awarded in BIOLOGICAL SCIENCE (biology/biological science), BUSINESS (business economics), COMMUNICATIONS AND THE ARTS (art, art history and appreciation, dramatic arts, English, French, German, music, and Spanish), COMPUTER AND PHYSICAL SCIENCE (chemistry, computer science, mathematics, and physics), HEALTH PROFESSIONS (health science), SOCIAL SCIENCE (anthropology, classical/ancient civilization, economics, history, human development, interdisciplinary studies, international studies, philosophy, political science/government, psychology, religion, and sociology). Foreign languages, international studies and commerce, and health sciences are the strongest academically. Economics business pyschology and biology have the largest enrollments.

ACTIVITIES: There are 70 groups on campus, including art, cheerleading, chess, choir, chorus, computers, dance, drama, environmental, ethnic, film, gay, honors, international, jazz band, literary magazine, musical theater, newspaper, orchestra, photography, political, professional, radio and TV, religious, social, social service, student government, and symphony. Popular campus events include Homecoming – dance, pep rally, Monte Carlo Casino night games and dancing, K-Fest - student involvement, outdoor movies (spring/fall). **Sports:** There are 8 intercollegiate sports for men and 9 for women, and 8 intramural sports for men and 7 for women. Facilities include a field house that houses a 2000-seat gym, basketball and volleyball courts, weight-training rooms, and a dance studio; a 1500-seat, 11-court tennis stadium; a racquet center with 4 tennis courts and 3 racquetball courts; a natatorium, an athletic field complex and field house, turf football and soccer/lacrosse fields as well as natural turf baseball and softball fields. A intramural/recreation field was also installed. Each of the athletic fields have bleachers, scoreboards, and press boxes. A stadium services building houses the football press box, restrooms, and a concession stand. The Kalamazoo College Field House has five team locker rooms, common meeting areas, a state-of-the-art athletic training facility, and the Hornets Suite used for larger gatherings and meetings. **Graduates:** From July 1, 2013 to June 30, 2014, 287 bachelor's degrees were awarded. The most popular majors were social sciences (17%), biological/life sciences (12%), and physical sciences (12%). In an average class, 72% graduate in 4 years or less, 77% graduate in 5 years or less, and 77% graduate in 6 years or less.

SERVICES: Counseling and information services are available, as is tutoring in most subjects. writing center, language labs, and supplemental instruction **Library/Resources:** The library contains 397,384 volumes, 15,025 microform items, 7,523 audio/video tapes/CDs/DVDs, and subscribes to 1,364 periodicals including electronic. Computerized library services include interlibrary loans, database searching, Internet access, and Wi-Fi capability. Special learning facilities include an art gallery, radio station, and TV station. **Physically Challenged Students:** 25% of the campus is accessible. Facilities include wheelchair ramps, elevators, special parking, specially equipped restrooms, special class scheduling, and special housing. **Special:** Kalamazoo College through the Center for International Programs currently sends students to 59 programs in 25 countries on 6 continents. Over the past four years, the K-College graduate participation rate in our study abroad programs is 80% to 85% and the school allows dual and interdisciplinary majors, and has Inter-Institutional enrollment with Western Michigan University. A 3-2 engineering degree is offered with Washington University and the University of Michigan. There are 3 national honor societies and a Phi Beta Kappa chapter. **Visiting:** There are regularly scheduled orientations for prospective students, including interviews, tours, overnight and class visits as requested. Special preview events include formal presentation of the unique curriculum and financial aid seminars. There are guides for informal visits, visitors may sit in on classes, and stay overnight. To schedule a visit, contact the Visit Coordinator. **Campus Safety and Security:** Measures include 24-hour foot and vehicle patrol, emergency notification system, self-defense education, and security escort services. There are emergency telephones, lighted pathways/sidewalks, and controlled access to dorms/residences.

REQUIREMENTS: The SAT or ACT is required. The ACT Optional

Writing test is also required. The college requires a high school transcript, an essay, supplement and teacher and counselor recommendations; an interview is recommended. Applications are online only. The College is a Common Application exclusive member. AP credits are accepted. Important factors in the admissions decision are recommendations by school officials, leadership record, and advanced placement or honors courses. To graduate, students must complete 36 academic units, including a minimum of 8 units in the major, with a minimum 2.0 GPA. The college requires sophomore and senior seminars and completion of a senior individualized project. The student must also take 5 noncredit courses in phys ed and show proficiency in writing as well as in a foreign language. **Procedure:** Freshmen are admitted fall. Entrance exams should be taken by December of the senior year. There are early decision, early admissions, and deferred admissions plans. Early decision applications should be filed by November 15; regular applications, by January 15 for fall entry. The fall 2014 application fee was $40. Notification of early decision is sent December 1; regular decision, April 1. 28 early decision candidates were accepted for the 2014-2015 class. 365 applicants were on the 2014 waiting list; 61 were admitted. Applications are accepted on-line. Application fees are waived if application is completed on-line. **Transfer Students:** 16 transfer students enrolled in 2013-2014. In addition to the Transfer Application, we require the College Official's Report, Instructor Evaluation, official high school and college transcripts. While an interview is not required, it is strongly recommended. And most cases, successful transfer applicants present grades of a B average or better in their current courses. 18 of 36 credits required for the bachelor's degree must be completed at Kalamazoo. **International Students:** There are 88 international students enrolled. The school actively recruits these students. They must take the TOEFL with a minimum score of 550 on the paper-based TOEFL (PBT) or 80 on the Internet-based version (iBT), or take the SAT, IELTS, or IB programs. They must also take the SAT or ACT.

ADMISSIONS: 70% of the 2014-2015 applicants were accepted. The SAT scores for the 2014-2015 freshman class were: Critical Reading--13% below 500, 35% between 500 and 599, 37% between 600 and 699, and 15% between 700 and 800; Math--6% below 500, 34% between 500 and 599, 33% between 600 and 699, and 27% between 700 and 800; Writing--11% below 500, 33% between 500 and 599, 39% between 600 and 699, and 17% between 700 and 800. The ACT scores were 3% below 21, 10% between 21 and 23, 26% between 24 and 26, 21% between 27 and 28, and 40% above 28. 4 freshmen graduated first in their class. **Admissions Contact:** Eric P. Staab, Dean of Admission. E-Mail: *admissions@kzoo.edu* Web: *www.kzoo.edu*

FINANCIAL AID: In 2014-2015, 98% of all full-time freshmen and 98% of continuing full-time students received some form of financial aid. 74% of all full-time freshmen and 67% of continuing full-time students received need-based aid. The average freshman award was $36,012. Need-based scholarships or need-based grants averaged $28,977; need-based self-help aid (loans and jobs) averaged $6,405; and other non-need-based awards and non-need-based scholarships averaged $630. The average financial indebtedness of the 2014 graduate was $28,405. The FAFSA and the college's own financial statement are required. The priority date for freshman financial aid applications for fall entry is February 15.

KETTERING UNIVERSITY

E-4

www.kettering.edu

Flint, MI 48504	(810) 762-7865
	(800) 955-4464
Fax: (810) 762-9837	Email: admissions@kettering.edu
Full-time: 1853 men, 325 women	Faculty: 125
Part-time: n/av	Ph.D.s: 93%
Graduate: 352 men, 145 women	Student/Faculty: 17 to 1
Year: semesters, summer session	Tuition: $25,658
Room & Board: $5798	Freshman Class: n/av
	CEEB CODE: 1246
Application Deadline: n/av	HIGHLY COMPETITIVE

Kettering University is a private college founded in 1919. In the 4.5-

year undergraduate program students alternate 11-week terms of full-time classes with 12-week terms of full-time paid professional cooperative education (co-op) work experience in industry. Students typically begin co-op during their freshman year and co-op in 43 states and several countries. The figures in the above capsule and in this profile are approximate. There are 3 undergraduate schools and 1 graduate school. In addition to regional accreditation, Kettering has baccalaureate program accreditation with ABET and ACBSP. The 85-acre campus is in a suburban area 60 miles north of Detroit. Including any residence halls, there are 10 buildings.

STUDENT LIFE: 66% of undergraduates are from Michigan. Others are from 49 states, 18 foreign countries, and Canada. 85% are from public schools. 75% are White. The average age of freshmen is 18; all undergraduates, 21. 86% do not continue beyond their first year; 64% remain to graduate. **Housing:** 623 students can be accommodated in college housing, which includes single-sex and coed dorms and on-campus apartments. In addition, there are fraternity houses and sorority houses. On-campus housing is guaranteed for the freshman year only and is available on a lottery system for upperclassmen. Priority is given to out-of-town students. 79% of students commute. Alcohol is not permitted. All students may keep cars.

FACULTY/CLASSROOMS: 80% of faculty are male; 20% are female. All teach undergraduates, 16% do research. No introductory courses are taught by graduate students. The average class size in an introductory lecture is 40; in a laboratory is 14; and in a regular course is 20.

PROGRAMS OF STUDY: Kettering confers B.S. degrees. Master's degrees are also awarded. Bachelor's degrees are awarded in BIOLOGICAL SCIENCE (biochemistry), COMPUTER AND PHYSICAL SCIENCE (applied mathematics, applied physics, chemistry, and computer science), ENGINEERING AND ENVIRONMENTAL DESIGN (computer engineering, electrical/electronics engineering, engineering physics, industrial engineering, and mechanical engineering). Mechanical, electrical, and computer engineering have the largest enrollments.

ACTIVITIES: 37% of men belong to 13 national fraternities; 31% of women belong to 6 national sororities. There are 43 groups on campus, including art, band, computers, dance, drama, environmental, ethnic, gay, honors, international, literary magazine, newspaper, photography, political, professional, radio and TV, religious, social, social service, student government, and yearbook. Popular campus events include Greek Week, Diversity Week, and Student and Alumni Industry Speaker Series. **Sports:** There is no sports program at Kettering. Facilities include a recreation center with 2 basketball/volleyball and 2 tennis/basketball/volleyball courts; 3 racquetball and squash courts; a one-eighth mile track; an Olympic-size pool, free weight, Nautilus, fitness room with comprehensive assortment of fitness machines and group exercise room. A 5 acre sports and recreation complex includes 4 softball and 2 multipurpose fields, a golf green, 1 km outdoor track, 2 sand volleyball courts, and a picnic pavilion. **Graduates:** From July 1, 2013 to June 30, 2014, 395 bachelor's degrees were awarded. The most popular majors were mechanical engineering (57%), electrical engineering (17%), and computer engineering (8%). 303 companies recruited on campus in 2013-2014. In an average class, 5% graduate in 4 years or less, 52% graduate in 5 years or less, and 61% graduate in 6 years or less. Of the 2013 graduating class, 40% were enrolled in graduate school within 6 months of graduation, and 96% were employed.

SERVICES: Counseling and information services are available, as is tutoring in most subjects. Tutoring is routinely available for most subjects in the Academic Support Center, in the residence hall, and with faculty. Supplemental tutoring is coordinated through the Academic Services Department. Math and writing labs are available. **Library/Resources:** The library contains 133,210 volumes, 35,000 microform items, 800 audio/video tapes/CDs/DVDs, and subscribes to 400 periodicals including electronic. Computerized library services include interlibrary loans, database searching, and Internet access. Special learning facilities include an art gallery, radio station, and industrial history archives. **Physically Challenged Students:** All of the campus is accessible. Facilities include wheelchair ramps, elevators, special parking, specially equipped restrooms, special class scheduling, lowered drinking fountains, and lowered telephones. **Special:** All undergraduate students participate in paid professional cooperative education work experience. Students may pursue a dual major in any degree combination. Accelerated degree programs in engineering are available in most majors, as is study abroad in 3 countries. There are 8 national honor societies. **Visiting:** There are regularly scheduled orientations for prospective students, including 2 open house programs for prospective students. There are guides for informal visits, visitors may sit in on classes, and stay overnight. To schedule a visit, contact the Admissions Office. **Campus Safety and Security:** Measures include 24-hour foot and vehicle patrol, self-defense education, and security escort services. There are emergency telephones, lighted pathways/sidewalks, controlled access to dorms/residences, after-hours access (e.g., to the academic building) is secure via the tunnel from the residence hall and campus center.

REQUIREMENTS: The SAT or ACT is required. Applicants must graduate from an accredited secondary school with a minimum of 16 academic credits. Applicants must have completed 3 years of English, 3 1/2 years of math, including trigonometry, and 2 years of lab science, 1 of which must be chemistry or physics (both are strongly recommended). AP credits are accepted. Important factors in the admissions decision are leadership record, advanced placement or honors courses, and extracurricular activities record. Degree requirements include completion of 160 credit hours, with 60 in the major. All students must take specific courses in math, chemistry, physics, written and oral communication, humanities, and economics, and complete at least 5 terms of co-op experience in industry plus 2 work terms designated for a senior thesis project. A minimum grade average of 80 on a scale of 100 is required for graduation. The GPA is determined by a formula combining the numerical grades achieved and the number of credits attempted. Students must complete a thesis. **Procedure:** Freshmen are admitted fall, winter, and summer. Entrance exams should be taken during the spring of the junior year and fall of the senior year. There are deferred admissions and rolling admissions plans. Application deadlines are open. Application fee is $35. Applications are accepted on-line. **Transfer Students:** 40 transfer students enrolled in 2013-2014. Transfer applicants must present the same minimum preparation as freshmen in math and science and must submit both high school and college transcripts and SAT or ACT scores. Required courses can be taken in high school or college. A minimum GPA of 3.0 in English, math, and science is expected. Transfers who present less than 30 credits of full-time study will be judged on both their college and high school record and test scores. 88 of 160 credits required for the bachelor's degree must be completed at Kettering. **International Students:** There are 33 international students enrolled. The school actively recruits these students. They must take the TOEFL or MELAB.

ADMISSIONS: The SAT scores for the 2014-2015 freshman class were: Critical Reading--17% below 500, 47% between 500 and 599, 27% between 600 and 699, and 9% between 700 and 800; Math--6% below 500, 25% between 500 and 599, 51% between 600 and 699, and 18% between 700 and 800. The ACT scores were 3% below 21, 12% between 21 and 23, 40% between 24 and 26, 17% between 27 and 28, and 28% above 28. 64% of the current freshmen were in the top fifth of their class; 94% were in the top two fifths. 18 freshmen graduated first in their class. **Admissions Contact:** Barbara Sosin, Director of Admissions. E-Mail: *admissions@kettering.edu* Web: *www.kettering.edu*

FINANCIAL AID: In 2014-2015, 89% of all full-time freshmen and 84% of continuing full-time students received some form of financial aid. 79% of all full-time freshmen and 67% of continuing full-time students received need-based aid. The average freshman award was $18,078. Need-based scholarships or need-based grants averaged $2,309; need-based self-help aid (loans and jobs) averaged $3,672 ($4,700 maximum); and other non-need-based awards and non-need-based scholarships averaged $13,567. 18% of undergraduate students work part-time. Average annual earnings from campus work are $820. The average financial indebtedness of the 2014 graduate was $30,903. The FAFSA and the college's own financial statement are required. The priority date for freshman financial aid applications for fall entry is February 14.

LAKE SUPERIOR STATE UNIVERSITY D-2
www.lssu.edu

Sault Sainte Marie, MI 49783

(906) 635-2693
(888) 800-5778

Fax: (906) 635-6669
Full-time: 1082 men, 1022 women
Part-time: 180 men, 237 women
Graduate: 1 men, 7 women
Year: semesters, summer session
Room & Board: $8481

Email: admissions@lssu.edu
Faculty: 114
Ph.D.s: 60%
Student/Faculty: 17 to 1
Tuition: $9640 ($14,510)
Freshman Class: 1425 applied, 1278 accepted, 429 enrolled

ACT: 21
Application Deadline: open

CEEB CODE: 1421
COMPETITIVE

Lake Superior State University, founded in 1946, is a public university that provides a blend of liberal and technical studies, offering undergraduate degrees in 45 areas of study. Figures in the above capsule and in this profile are approximate. There are 12 undergraduate schools and 1 graduate school. In addition to regional accreditation, Lake State has baccalaureate program accreditation with ABET, NLN, CAAHEP, CAATE, HEHPAC, ABA, and AAMC. The 115-acre campus is in a small town in Michigan's Upper Peninsula, 45 minutes north of the Mackinac Bridge. Including any residence halls, there are 37 buildings.

STUDENT LIFE: 90% of undergraduates are from Michigan. 79% are White. The average age of freshmen is 18; all undergraduates, 23. 30% do not continue beyond their first year; 70% remain to graduate. **Housing:** 900 students can be accommodated in college housing, which includes single-sex and coed dorms, on-campus apartments, and married student housing. In addition, there are honors houses, fraternity houses, and sorority houses. On-campus housing is guaranteed for the freshman year only, is available on a first-come, first-served basis, and is available on a lottery system for upperclassmen. 66% of students commute. All students may keep cars.

FACULTY/CLASSROOMS: 43% of faculty are male; 47% are female. All teach undergraduates. No introductory courses are taught by graduate students. The average class size in an introductory lecture is 25; in a laboratory is 15; and in a regular course is 30.

PROGRAMS OF STUDY: Lake State confers B.A., and B.S. degrees. Associate and Master's degrees are also awarded. Bachelor's degrees are awarded in AGRICULTURE (fish and game management and wildlife management), BIOLOGICAL SCIENCE (biology/biological science), BUSINESS (accounting, banking and finance, business administration and management, international business management, and marketing/retailing/merchandising), COMMUNICATIONS AND THE ARTS (communications, English, fine arts, and Spanish), COMPUTER AND PHYSICAL SCIENCE (chemistry, computer management, computer science, geology, information sciences and systems, and mathematics), EDUCATION (athletic training, early childhood education, elementary education, and secondary education), ENGINEERING AND ENVIRONMENTAL DESIGN (computer engineering, electrical/electronics engineering, engineering, engineering management, engineering technology, environmental engineering technology, environmental science, manufacturing technology, and mechanical engineering), HEALTH PROFESSIONS (clinical science, environmental health science, exercise science, medical laboratory technology, nursing, predentistry, premedicine, and recreation therapy), SOCIAL SCIENCE (criminal justice, economics, fire science, forensic studies, French studies, history, human services, paralegal studies, parks and recreation management, political science/government, prelaw, psychology, social science, and sociology). Engineering technology, nursing, and natural sciences are the strongest academically. Business and criminal justice have the largest enrollments.

ACTIVITIES: There are 60 groups on campus, including band, cheerleading, chess, chorale, computers, dance, drama, ethnic, film, gay, honors, jazz band, newspaper, pep band, political, professional, radio and TV, religious, social, social service, and student government. Popular campus events include Winter Carnival, Spring Fling and Great Lake State Weekend. **Sports:** There are 5 intercollegiate sports for men and 6 for women. Facilities include a 4000-seat ice arena, a 2500-seat gym with a new hardwood floor, swimming and diving pools, 4 handball/squash courts, a weight-training and isometric room, a dance studio, a training room, a firing range, and offices. **Graduates:** From July 1, 2013 to June 30, 2014, 427 bachelor's degrees were awarded. The most popular majors were protective services (18%), business (17%), and health professions (12%). In an average class, 40% graduate in 6 years or less.

SERVICES: Counseling and information services are available, as is tutoring in most subjects, on request and free of charge. There is a reader service for the blind, and remedial math, reading, and writing. There are also math, reading, and writing labs. **Library/Resources:** The library contains 106,618 volumes, 810 audio/video tapes/CDs/DVDs, and subscribes to 950 periodicals including electronic. Computerized library services include interlibrary loans and database searching. Special learning facilities include a natural history museum, planetarium, radio station, fish hatchery and aquatics lab, and interactive television for distance education. **Physically Challenged Students:** Facilities include wheelchair ramps, elevators, special parking, specially equipped restrooms, special class scheduling, lowered drinking fountains, and lowered telephones. **Special:** Lake State offers internships in criminal justice, medical technology, human services, legal assistance studies, and natural resources technology, work-study programs, co-op programs in engineering technology, and cross-registration with the Canadian Colleges of Sault and Algoma and Bridge International Consortium. Study abroad and student-designed majors are available, as are B.A.-B.S. degrees and dual majors. Distance learning and weekend college study formats are offered. There is a freshman honors program. **Visiting:** There are regularly scheduled orientations for prospective students. There are guides for informal visits and visitors may sit in on classes. To schedule a visit, contact the Admissions Office. **Campus Safety and Security:** Measures include 24-hour foot and vehicle patrol, self-defense education, and security escort services. There are lighted pathways/sidewalks.

REQUIREMENTS: The ACT is required. Applicants should be high school graduates with 4 years of English, 3 each of math and science, 2 each of a foreign language and social studies, and 1 of history and should have a GPA of 2.0. The GED is accepted. AP and CLEP credits are accepted. Important factors in the admissions decision are advanced placement or honors courses, recommendations by school officials, and recommendations by alumni.To graduate, students must complete 124 semester hours with a GPA of 2.0. The core curriculum includes course work in computer literacy, English, oral communications, aesthetics, critical thinking, humanities, math, science, social science, ethics, and cultural diversity. At least 32 of the final credits, and 50% of all upper-level courses, must be taken in residence at Lake State. Math and English competency must be met. **Procedure:** Freshmen are admitted to all sessions. There are deferred admissions and rolling admissions plans. Application deadlines are open. The fall 2014 application fee was $35. Applications are accepted on-line. **Transfer Students:** 186 transfer students enrolled in 2013-2014. Applicants must be eligible to return to the last institution attended and must have an overall college GPA of 2.0. High school transcripts, ACT scores, and/or GED scores are required if transferring with fewer than 19 semester hours of credit. 32 of 124 credits required for the bachelor's degree must be completed at Lake State. **International Students:** The school actively recruits these students. They must take the TOEFL.

ADMISSIONS: 90% of the 2014-2015 applicants were accepted. The ACT scores were 35% below 21, 29% between 21 and 23, 21% between 24 and 26, 9% between 27 and 28, and 6% above 28. **Admissions Contact:** Allan Case, Director of Admissions. E-Mail: *admissions@lssu.edu* Web: *www.lssu.edu*

FINANCIAL AID: In 2014-2015, 73% of all full-time freshmen and 69% of continuing full-time students received some form of financial aid. 61% of all full-time freshmen and 62% of continuing full-time students received need-based aid. The average freshman award was $10,306. Average annual earnings from campus work are $2500. The average financial indebtedness of the 2014 graduate was $22,896. The FAFSA, and OSAP is required. The priority date for freshman financial aid applications for fall entry is February 21.

LAWRENCE TECHNOLOGICAL UNIVERSITY
E-5

www.ltu.edu

Southfield, MI 48075

(248) 204-3160
(800) CALL-LTU

Fax: (248) 204-3188
Full-time: 1148 men, 448 women
Part-time: 981 men, 220 women
Graduate: 863 men, 354 women
Year: semesters, summer session
Room & Board: $8682

Email: admissions@ltu.edu
Faculty: 122
Ph.D.s: 67%
Student/Faculty: 11 to 1
Tuition: $28,948
Freshman Class: 2285 applied, 1312 accepted, 337 enrolled

SAT CR/M/W: 540/600/520 **ACT:** 25
Application Deadline: n/av

CEEB CODE: 1399
VERY COMPETITIVE

Lawrence Technological University, founded in 1932 as Lawrence Institute of Technology, is a private institution housing colleges of engineering, management, arts and sciences, and architecture and design. There are 4 undergraduate schools and 4 graduate schools. In addition to regional accreditation, Lawrence Tech has baccalaureate program accreditation with ABET, ACBSP, FIDER, NAAB, NASAD, CIDA, ASC, and IACBE. The 102-acre campus is in a suburban area 30 minutes north of downtown Detroit. Including any residence halls, there are 11 buildings.

STUDENT LIFE: 96% of undergraduates are from Michigan. Others are from 24 states, 43 foreign countries, and Canada. 49% are White; 20% race unknown; 17% Asian American. The average age of freshmen is 18; all undergraduates, 21. 18% do not continue beyond their first year; 45% remain to graduate. **Housing:** 595 students can be accommodated in college housing, which includes coed on-campus apartments and off-campus apartments. Arbor Lofts a private apartment complex for student use. On-campus housing is available on a first-come and first-served basis. 76% of students commute. All students may keep cars.

FACULTY/CLASSROOMS: 70% of faculty are male; 30% are female. 90% teach undergraduates. No introductory courses are taught by graduate students. The average class size in an introductory lecture is 17; in a laboratory is 12; and in a regular course is 15.

PROGRAMS OF STUDY: Lawrence Tech confers B.A., B.S., B.F.A. and B.F.M. degrees. Associate, Master's, and Doctoral degrees are also awarded. Bachelor's degrees are awarded in BIOLOGICAL SCIENCE (biochemistry, biotechnology, and molecular biology), BUSINESS (business administration and management and international business management), COMMUNICATIONS AND THE ARTS (animation, audio technology, communications, English, game design and development, illustration, industrial design, information technology, media arts, and technical and business writing), COMPUTER AND PHYSICAL SCIENCE (chemistry, computer science, environmental chemistry, information sciences and systems, mathematics, mathematics/computational, and physics), ENGINEERING AND ENVIRONMENTAL DESIGN (architectural engineering, architecture, biomedical engineering, civil engineering, computer engineering, computer graphics, construction management, electrical/electronics engineering, engineering, engineering technology, industrial administration/management, industrial engineering, interior architecture, interior design, mechanical engineering, technological management, and transportation engineering), SOCIAL SCIENCE (architectural studies, humanities, and psychology). Mathematics, computer science, and engineering are the strongest academically. Engineering and architecture have the largest enrollments.

ACTIVITIES: 10% of men belong to 1 local and 5 national fraternities; 15% of women belong to 2 local and 1 national sororities. There are 70 groups on campus, including chess, chorus, communications, computers, dance, gay, international, literary magazine, newspaper, pep band, photography, religious, robotics, social, social service, and student government. Popular campus events include Discovery Days, New Student Convocation, and Welcome Back Picnic, Homecoming, Winterfest, Chinese New Year, International Fest, and Greek Week. **Sports:** There are 8 intercollegiate sports for men and 8 for women, and 13 intramural sports for men and 13 for women. Facilities include a field house with 4 racquetball courts, weight room, track, sauna, and a gym. The gym seats 1,500; an arena 350, soccer field, and disc golf course. <u>Graduates:</u> From July 1, 2013 to June 30, 2014, 340 bachelor's degrees were awarded. The most popular majors were engineering (37%), architecture (35%), and computer science (9%). 180 companies recruited on campus in 2013-2014. In an average class, 35% graduate in 4 years or less, 42% graduate in 5 years or less, and 45% graduate in 6 years or less. Of the 2013 graduating class, 83% were employed within 6 months of graduation.

SERVICES: Counseling and information services are available, as is tutoring in most subjects. There is a reader service for the blind, remedial math, reading, and writing. There is also an Academic Achievement Center <u>Library/Resources:</u> The library contains 232,876 volumes, 30,464 microform items, 1,381 audio/video tapes/CDs/DVDs, and subscribes to 110,395 periodicals including electronic. Computerized library services include interlibrary loans, database searching, Internet access, and Wi-Fi capability. <u>Physically Challenged Students:</u> 97% of the campus is accessible. Facilities include wheelchair ramps, elevators, special parking, specially equipped restrooms, special class scheduling, lowered drinking fountains, lowered telephones, and special housing. <u>Special:</u> There are co-op programs in a number of majors, internships, study abroad in 8 countries and dual majors available. There is 1 national honor society and 2 departmental honors programs. <u>Visiting:</u> There are regularly scheduled orientations for prospective students. There are guides for informal visits, visitors may sit in on classes, and stay overnight. To schedule a visit, contact the Admissions Office. <u>Campus Safety and Security:</u> Measures include 24-hour foot and vehicle patrol, emergency notification system, and security escort services. There are emergency telephones, lighted pathways/sidewalks, and closed-circuit camera monitoring.

REQUIREMENTS: The ACT is required. The SAT is recommended. Students must have a high school diploma and a GPA of no lower than 2.5, at least 2.0 in each subject area pertaining to their major. Applicants should have taken 4 years each of math, science, and English, and 3 years of social science. The GED is accepted. An interview is recommended. A GPA of 2.5 is required. AP and CLEP credits are accepted. Important factors in the admissions decision are advanced placement or honors courses, personality/intangible qualities, and leadership record. Senior projects are required in most degree programs. <u>Procedure:</u> Freshmen are admitted to all sessions. Entrance exams should be taken in the semester preceding entry. There are deferred admissions and rolling admissions plans. Application deadlines are open. Application fee is $30. Notification is sent on a rolling basis. Applications are accepted on-line. <u>Transfer Students:</u> 166 transfer students enrolled in 2013-2014. Admission is based on the college GPA, which must be 2.0 or higher, with 30 or more semester hours. If less than 30 hours have been completed, admission is based on high school transcripts. 30 of 120 credits required for the bachelor's degree must be completed at Lawrence Tech. <u>International Students:</u> There are 155 international students enrolled. The school actively recruits these students. They must take the TOEFL with a minimum score of 550 on the paper-based TOEFL (PBT) or 79 on the Internet-based version (iBT) or take the MELAB and the Comprehensive English Language Test. There are placement exams for incoming freshman only.

ADMISSIONS: 57% of the 2014-2015 applicants were accepted. The SAT scores for the 2014-2015 freshman class were: Critical Reading--25% below 500, 58% between 500 and 599, 10% between 600 and 699, and 8% between 700 and 800; Math--17% below 500, 27% between 500 and 599, 50% between 600 and 699, and 6% between 700 and 800; Writing--38% below 500, 44% between 500 and 599, and 15% between 600 and 699. The ACT scores were 24% below 21, 10% between 21 and 23, 24% between 24 and 26, 19% between 27 and 28, and 23% above 28. 42% of the current freshmen were in the top fifth of their class; 73% were in the top two fifths. 3 freshmen graduated first in their class. <u>Admissions Contact:</u> Jane Rohrback, Admissions Director. E-Mail: *admissions@ltu.edu* Web: *www.ltu.edu*

FINANCIAL AID: In 2014-2015, 94% of all full-time freshmen and 77% of continuing full-time students received some form of financial aid. 58% of all full-time freshmen and 52% of continuing full-time students received need-based aid. The average freshman award was $16,910. Need-based scholarships or need-based grants averaged

$5,282 ($37,955 maximum); need-based self-help aid (loans and jobs) averaged $7,324 ($16,500 maximum); non-need-based athletic scholarships averaged $15,134 ($30,000 maximum); and other non-need-based awards and non-need-based scholarships averaged $16,866 ($34,500 maximum). 94% of undergraduate students work part-time. Average annual earnings from campus work are $2277. The average financial indebtedness of the 2014 graduate was $38,966. Lawrence Tech is a member of CSS. The FAFSA is required. The deadline for filing freshman financial aid applications for fall entry is April 1.

MADONNA UNIVERSITY   E-5
www.madonna.edu

Livonia, MI 48150	**(734) 432-5341**
	(800) 852-4951
Fax: (734) 432-5424	Email: mquattro@madonna.edu
Full-time: 502 men, 1165 women	**Faculty:** 95; IIB, av$
Part-time: 600 men, 1101 women	**Ph.D.s:** 54%
Graduate: 235 men, 824 women	**Student/Faculty:** 15 to 1
Year: semesters, summer session	**Tuition:** $16,340
Room & Board: $8200	**Freshman Class:** 1071 applied, 665 accepted, 208 enrolled
SAT CR/M/W: 630/580/560 **ACT:** 23	**CEEB CODE:** 1437
Application Deadline: open	**VERY COMPETITIVE**

Madonna University is an independent Catholic university, founded in 1947 by the Felician Sisters with the values of St. Francis of Assisi, where students receive a quality liberal arts education combined with career preparation and community service. Students enjoy personal instruction from skilled professors dedicated to student success. Madonna boasts more than 100 undergraduate and 35 graduate programs. Madonna's teacher education program, once again, received exemplary status from the Michigan Dept. of Education. Madonna courses also are offered in centers in Orchard Lake, Gaylord, Southwest Detroit, and Macomb, Michigan. The first-year experience eases the transition from high school to college and introduces students to service learning. Students also participate in Alternative Spring Break service projects. There are 7 undergraduate schools and 1 graduate school. In addition to regional accreditation, MU has baccalaureate program accreditation with CSWE, NCATE, ACEND, CCNE, and ABA. The 82-acre campus is in a suburban area 25 miles west of Detroit. Including any residence halls, there are 5 buildings.

STUDENT LIFE: 99% of undergraduates are from Michigan. Others are from 6 states, 7 foreign countries, and Canada. 76% are from public schools. 61% are White; 16% Foreign; 12% African American. 36% are Catholic; 34% Hindu, Islam/Muslim, and Undeclared; 21% Protestant. The average age of freshmen is 19; all undergraduates, 27. 18% do not continue beyond their first year; 57% remain to graduate. **Housing:** 272 students can be accommodated in college housing, which includes single-sex dorms. On-campus housing is guaranteed for all 4 years. 92% of students commute. Alcohol is not permitted. All students may keep cars.

FACULTY/CLASSROOMS: 42% of faculty are male; 58% are female. 99% teach undergraduates. No introductory courses are taught by graduate students. The average class size in an introductory lecture is 18; in a laboratory is 15; and in a regular course is 18.

PROGRAMS OF STUDY: MU confers B.A., B.S., B.A.S., B.Mus, B.S.N., B.S.W., B.A.P.M. and B.A.P.T. degrees. Associate, Master's, and Doctoral degrees are also awarded. Bachelor's degrees are awarded in BIOLOGICAL SCIENCE (biochemistry, biology/biological science, and nutrition), BUSINESS (accounting, business administration and management, hospitality management services, international business management, management science, marketing/retailing/merchandising, and sports management), COMMUNICATIONS AND THE ARTS (art, broadcasting, communications, English, fine arts, graphic design, journalism, language arts, music, Spanish, speech/debate/rhetoric, technical and business writing, and video), COMPUTER AND PHYSICAL SCIENCE (applied science, chemistry, computer science, information sciences and systems, mathematics, natural sciences, and science), EDUCATION (art education, music education, and secondary education), ENGINEER-ING AND ENVIRONMENTAL DESIGN (commercial art, environmental science, and occupational safety and health), HEALTH PROFESSIONS (allied health, hospice care, medical laboratory technology, and nursing), SOCIAL SCIENCE (child psychology/development, criminal justice, dietetics, family/consumer studies, fire science, food science, gerontology, history, interpreter for the deaf, Japanese studies, liberal arts/general studies, pastoral studies, psychology, religion, religious music, safety and security technology, social science, social work, and sociology). Nursing is the strongest academically. Nursing and criminal justice have the largest enrollments.

ACTIVITIES: There are 40 groups on campus, including future alumni network, art, choir, chorale, computers, dance, environmental, ethnic, film, honors, international, literary magazine, musical theater, newspaper, peace and justice, photography, professional, radio and TV, religious, social, social service, and student government. Popular campus events include Peace and Justice Week, Alternative Spring Breaks, Retreats, Recitals, Art Gallery Exhibits, Musical Theater events, Blood Drives, Welcome Events, 5K, Madonna Mile and International Festival. **Sports:** There are 5 intercollegiate sports for men and 6 for women. Facilities include Madonna athletic facilities include the Livonia campus Activities Center, where basketball and volleyball are played, as well as Ilitch Ballpark (baseball) Madonna University Field (softball), and a new synthetic turf soccer field. In addition, the golf teams use several area golf courses, and cross-country calls Cass Benton Park home. The activities center includes a weight training room, and a 1500 700-seat gym. **Graduates:** From July 1, 2013 to June 30, 2014, 710 bachelor's degrees were awarded. The most popular majors were nursing (19%), criminal justice (10%), and international business (4%). 22 companies recruited on campus in 2013-2014. In an average class, 21% graduate in 4 years or less, 46% graduate in 5 years or less, and 56% graduate in 6 years or less. Of the 2013 graduating class, 21% were enrolled in graduate school within 6 months of graduation, and 88% were employed.

SERVICES: Counseling and information services are available, as is tutoring in most subjects. There is a reader service for the blind, remedial math, reading, and writing. Interpreters and note takers for hearing-impaired and visually impaired students. **Library/Resources:** The library contains 191,242 volumes, 453,260 microform items, 938 audio/video tapes/CDs/DVDs, and subscribes to 64,451 periodicals including electronic. Computerized library services include interlibrary loans, database searching, Internet access, and Wi-Fi capability. Special learning facilities include an art gallery, radio station, TV station, a writing lab, and the center for Personalized Instruction, Office of Disability Resources, and Office of Service Learning, Sign Language Studies Lab, Franciscan Center for Science and Media, Nursing Simulation Labs. **Physically Challenged Students:** All of the campus is accessible. Facilities include wheelchair ramps, elevators, special parking, specially equipped restrooms, special class scheduling, lowered drinking fountains, lowered telephones. Telecommunication devices and visible fire alarms for hearing-impaired students, talking books, tape recorders, diagnostic testing service, early syllabus, recorded exams, a Learning Center, oral exams, proofreading service, reading machine, take-home exams, software for vision impaired students, and adjustable computer monitors. **Special:** Madonna University participates in a Metro Detroit Catholic College Consortium with Marygrove College, Sacred Heart Seminary, and the University of Detroit Mercy. Students may pursue co-op programs in 30 majors, internships, and may receive prior learning for life, military, or work experience. Work-study positions are available at Madonna University. Study abroad in 17 countries is also possible. There are 11 national honor societies. **Visiting:** There are regularly scheduled orientations for prospective students, includes an interview and a tour of the campus. Provides an opportunity to learn about academic and support services, opportunities, and programs for a successful college experience. There are guides for informal visits, visitors may sit in on classes, and stay overnight. To schedule a visit, contact Office of Undergraduate Admissions at admissions@madonna.edu. **Campus Safety and Security:** Measures include 24-hour foot and vehicle patrol, emergency notification system, and security escort services. There are emergency telephones, lighted pathways/sidewalks, controlled access to dorms/residences, an emergency car service.

REQUIREMENTS: The ACT is required. In addition, should have completed 4 years of English, 3 of math, 2 of science, and 1 of history. The school accepts the GED. An essay is required. For some majors, students are asked to submit a portfolio or to appear for an interview or audition. AP and CLEP credits are accepted. Important factors in the admissions decision are advanced placement or honors courses, recommendations by school officials, and leadership record. To graduate, students must complete at least 120 semester hours with a 2.0 GPA; required hours in the major vary from 30 to 65, including a capstone senior seminar. A minimum of 52 hours of general education courses are required, including a writing assessment unless waived per ACT writing subscore. There is a residency requirement that the last 15 (associates) or 30 (baccalaureate) semester hours must be completed at Madonna. **Procedure:** Freshmen are admitted to all sessions. Entrance exams should be taken during either the junior or senior year. There is a rolling admissions plan. Application deadlines are open. Application fee is $25. Notification is sent on a rolling basis. Applications are accepted on-line. **Transfer Students:** 504 transfer students enrolled in 2013-2014. Applicants must be in good academic and personal standing at their previous colleges and must submit official transcripts of college and high school work. Courses completed at an accredited institution with a grade of C or better will be considered for transfer credit. 30 of 120 credits required for the bachelor's degree must be completed at MU. **International Students:** There are 93 international students enrolled. The school actively recruits these students.

ADMISSIONS: 62% of the 2014-2015 applicants were accepted. The SAT scores for the 2014-2015 freshman class were: Critical Reading--20% below 500, 60% between 600 and 699, and 20% between 700 and 800; Math--20% below 500, 40% between 500 and 599, 20% between 600 and 699, and 20% between 700 and 800; Writing--20% below 500, 60% between 500 and 599, and 20% between 700 and 800. The ACT scores were 27% below 21, 29% between 21 and 23, 25% between 24 and 26, 11% between 27 and 28, and 8% above 28. 36% of the current freshmen were in the top fifth of their class. 1 freshman graduated first in the class. **Admissions Contact:** Michael Quattro, Director of Undergraduate Admissions. E-Mail: *mquattro@madonna .edu* Web: *www.madonna.edu*

FINANCIAL AID: 15% of undergraduate students work part-time. Average annual earnings from campus work are $1216. The average financial indebtedness of the 2014 graduate was $26,510. The FAFSA is required. The priority date for freshman financial aid applications for fall entry is March 1.

MARYGROVE COLLEGE — E-5
www.marygrove.edu

Detroit, MI 48221	**(313) 927-1240**
	(866) 313-1927
Fax: (313) 927-1345	Email: anash5086@marygrove.edu
Full-time: 119 men, 339 women	**Faculty:** 55; IIA, --$
Part-time: 56 men, 274 women	**Ph.Ds:** 85%
Graduate: 410 men, 1558 women	**Student/Faculty:** 8 to 1
Year: semesters, summer session	**Tuition:** $14,690
Room & Board: $6600	**Freshman Class:** 802 applied, 353 accepted, 127 enrolled
ACT: 17	**CEEB CODE:** 1452
Application Deadline: August 15	**COMPETITIVE**

Founded in 1927 and grounded in the liberal arts, Marygrove College is a private comprehensive institution affiliated with the Catholic Church. In addition to regional accreditation, has baccalaureate program accreditation with CSWE. The library contains 76,689 volumes, 68,750 microform items, and 2,834 audio/video tapes/CDs/DVDs, and subscribes to 447 periodicals including electronic. Computerized library services include interlibrary loans and database searching. Special learning facilities include an art gallery, a writing center, a learning clinic, and a theater. The 50-acre campus is in an urban area 11 miles from downtown Detroit. Including any residence halls, there are 4 buildings.

STUDENT LIFE: 99% of undergraduates are from Michigan. Others 9 foreign countries. 63% are African American. The average age of freshmen is 20; all undergraduates, 30.

FACULTY/CLASSROOMS: 43% of faculty are male; 57% are female. All teach undergraduates. No introductory courses are taught by graduate students.

PROGRAMS OF STUDY: confers B.A., B.S., B.A.S., B.B.A., B.F.A., B.M. and B.S.W. degrees. Associate and master's degrees are also awarded. Bachelor's degrees are awarded in BIOLOGICAL SCIENCE (biology/biological science), BUSINESS (business administration and management), COMMUNICATIONS AND THE ARTS (art, dance, English, language arts, and music), COMPUTER AND PHYSICAL SCIENCE (chemistry, computer science, mathematics, and science), EDUCATION (early childhood education, social studies education, and special education), ENGINEERING AND ENVIRONMENTAL DESIGN (environmental science), HEALTH PROFESSIONS (art therapy), SOCIAL SCIENCE (child psychology/development, criminal justice, forensic studies, history, political science/government, psychology, religion, social science, and social work). Business, English, and education are the strongest academically. Business, English, forensic science, and education have the largest enrollments.

ACTIVITIES: 1% of men belong to 4 local and 4 national fraternities; 10% of women belong to 2 local and 2 national sororities. There are 12 groups on campus, including art, choir, chorale, computers, dance, honors, religious, social service, and student government. Popular campus events include Spirit Week, and Martin Luther King Week, and Contemporary American Authors Lecture Series.

SERVICES: Counseling and information services are available, as is tutoring in most subjects. There is remedial math, reading, and writing.

REQUIREMENTS: The ACT is required. The applicant must be a graduate of an accredited high school. An interview is recommended. The student's average, class rank, recommendations, and special talents are important factors in admission. Entering students must take the College Placement Examinations. A GPA of 2.0 is required. AP and CLEP credits are accepted. Important factors in the admissions decision are recommendations by school officials, evidence of special talent, and advanced placement or honors courses.

ADMISSIONS: 44% of the 2013-2014 applicants were accepted.

FINANCIAL AID: In 2013-2014, 98% of continuing full-time students received some form of financial aid. 90% of all full-time freshmen and 98% of continuing full-time students received need-based aid. Marygrove is a member of CSS. The CSS/Profile, FAFSA, and the college's own financial statement are required. The deadline for filing freshman financial aid applications for fall entry is March 15.

MICHIGAN STATE UNIVERSITY D-4
www.beaspartan.msu.edu

East Lansing, MI 48824	**(517) 355-8332**
	n/av
Fax: (517) 353-1647	Email: admis@msu.edu
Full-time: 17112 men, 17602 women	Faculty: 2411; I, +$
	Ph.D.s: 93%
Part-time: 1642 men, 1405 women	Student/Faculty: 17 to 1
Graduate: 4966 men, 6389 women	Tuition: $13,246 ($35,026)
Year: semesters, summer session	Freshman Class: 33216
Room & Board: $9204	applied, 21950 accepted, 7850 enrolled
SAT: required ACT: 26	
Application Deadline: July 25	**VERY COMPETITIVE**

Michigan State University Spartans work to advance the common good in uncommon ways. The nation's pioneer land-grant university, MSU began as a bold experiment that democratized higher education and helped bring science and innovation into everyday life. Today, MSU is one of the top research universities in the world on one of the biggest, greenest campuses in the nation and is home to a diverse community of dedicated students and scholars, athletes and artists, scientists and leaders. There are 14 undergraduate schools and 14 graduate schools. In addition to regional accreditation, MSU has baccalaureate program accreditation with AACSB, ABET, ACEJMC, ADA, ASLA, CAHEA, CSWE, FIDER, NASM, NCATE, NLN, and SAF. The 5239-acre campus is in a suburban area 80 miles northwest of Detroit. Including any residence halls, there are 538 buildings.

STUDENT LIFE: 75% of undergraduates are from Michigan. Others are from 50 states, 130 foreign countries, and Canada. 72% are White. **Male To Female Ratio:** 1.1:1. The average age of freshmen is 18; all undergraduates, 20. 9% do not continue beyond their first year; 71% remain to graduate. **Housing:** 16000 students can be accommodated in college housing, which includes single-sex and coed dorms, on-campus apartments, and married student housing. In addition, there are honors houses, special-interest houses, Residential colleges, living-learning communities, quiet floors, and substance-free environments. On-campus housing is guaranteed for all 4 years. 60% of students commute. Upperclassmen may keep cars.

FACULTY/CLASSROOMS: 58% of faculty are male; 42% are female. No introductory courses are taught by graduate students. The average class size in an introductory lecture is 100; in a laboratory is 30; and in a regular course is 30.

PROGRAMS OF STUDY: MSU confers B.A., B.S., B.F.A., B.Land.Arch., B.Mus. and B.S. in Nursing degrees. Master's and Doctoral degrees are also awarded. Bachelor's degrees are awarded in AGRICULTURE (agriculture, animal science, environmental studies, fishing and fisheries, forestry and related sciences, horticulture, natural resource management, soil science, and wildlife management), BIOLOGICAL SCIENCE (biochemistry, bioinformatics, biology/biological science, biotechnology, botany, entomology, environmental biology, microbiology, nutrition, physiology, plant pathology, and zoology), BUSINESS (accounting, banking and finance, business administration and management, hospitality management services, human resources, marketing management, marketing/retailing/merchandising, personnel management, and tourism), COMMUNICATIONS AND THE ARTS (advertising, art history and appreciation, communications, dramatic arts, East Asian languages and literature, English, French, German, jazz, journalism, Latin, linguistics, music, music performance, music theory and composition, Russian, Spanish, studio art, and telecommunications), COMPUTER AND PHYSICAL SCIENCE (astrophysics, chemical physics, chemistry, computer science, earth science, geology, geophysics and seismology, geoscience, information sciences and systems, mathematics, physical sciences, physics, and statistics), EDUCATION (agricultural education, art education, education, music education, physical education, and special education), ENGINEERING AND ENVIRONMENTAL DESIGN (chemical engineering, city/community/regional planning, civil engineering, computational sciences, computer engineering, construction management, electrical/electronics engineering, engineering, engineering mechanics, interior design, landscape architecture/design, manufacturing engineering, materials engineering, mechanical engineering, textile technology, and urban planning technology), HEALTH PROFESSIONS (clinical science, medical laboratory technology, music therapy, nursing, speech pathology/audiology, and veterinary science), SOCIAL SCIENCE (American studies, anthropology, child psychology/development, classical/ancient civilization, criminal justice, dietetics, economics, family and community services, family/consumer resource management, family/consumer studies, food production/management/services, food science, geography, history, humanities, interdisciplinary studies, parks and recreation management, philosophy, political science/government, prelaw, psychology, public administration, religion, social science, social work, sociology, and women's studies). Education, business, and physics are the strongest academically. Business, communications, and social science have the largest enrollments.

ACTIVITIES: There are 630 groups on campus, including art, band, cheerleading, chess, choir, chorale, chorus, communications, computers, dance, debate, drama, drill team, environmental, ethnic, film, forensics, gay, honors, international, jazz band, literary magazine, marching band, musical theater, newspaper, opera, orchestra, pep band, photography, political, professional, radio and TV, religious, social, social service, student government, symphony, and yearbook. Popular campus events include Athletic Events (football, basketball, hockey in particular), Welcome Week, and Homecoming. **Sports:** There are 12 intercollegiate sports for men and 13 for women, and 22 intramural sports for men and 22 for women. Facilities include a 76,000-seat stadium, a 4000-seat gym and field house, an ice arena, and a multipurpose 15,500-seat student events center. The university also has an indoor football practice facility, 3 intramural facilities, indoor and outdoor tennis courts, ball fields, a running track, 2 golf courses, and 4 swimming pools, including 1 Olympic-size outdoor pool. **Graduates:** From July 1, 2013 to June 30, 2014, 7976 bachelor's degrees were awarded. The most popular majors were business (19%), communications (14%), and social science (10%). In an average class, 36% graduate in 4 years or less, 66% graduate in 5 years or less, and 71% graduate in 6 years or less.

SERVICES: Counseling and information services are available, as is tutoring in most subjects. There is a reader service for the blind, remedial math, reading, and writing. **Library/Resources:** The 11 libraries contain 4.5 million volumes, 5.6 million microform items, 299,287 audio/video tapes/CDs/DVDs, and subscribe to 34,500 periodicals including electronic. Computerized library services include interlibrary loans, database searching, Internet access, and Wi-Fi capability. Special learning facilities include an art gallery, natural history museum, planetarium, radio station, TV station, a botanical garden, a superconducting cyclotron lab, environmental toxicology center, pesticide research center, a center for computer-aided and engineering and manufacturing. **Physically Challenged Students:** 75% of the campus is accessible. Facilities include wheelchair ramps, elevators, special parking, specially equipped restrooms, special class scheduling, lowered drinking fountains, lowered telephones, special housing. Tape recorders, videotaped classes, reading machines, readers, and note takers. **Special:** Special academic programs include an engineering co-op program with business and industry; internships in business, education, political science, agriculture, and communication arts; study abroad in more than 62 countries; on-campus work-study programs; and a sea semester. An accelerated degree program in all majors and student-designed majors are offered at the Honors College. Non-degree study, pass/fail options in some courses, and dual majors are possible. Educationally disadvantaged students may avail themselves of the College Achievement Admissions Program (CAAP). Cross-registration with the Committee on Institutional Cooperation schools is available. There are 48 national honor societies, including Phi Beta Kappa, and a freshman honors program. **Visiting:** There are regularly scheduled orientations for prospective students, including a presentation and a tour of the campus. There are guides for informal visits, visitors may sit in on classes, and stay overnight. To schedule a visit, contact the Office of Admissions at admis@msu.edu. **Campus Safety and Security:** Measures include 24-hour foot and vehicle patrol, emergency notification system, self-defense education, and security escort services. There are shuttle buses, emergency telephones, lighted pathways/sidewalks, controlled access to dorms/residences, regional/campus bus service.

REQUIREMENTS: The SAT or ACT is required. The ACT Optional Writing test is also required. Applicants must be graduates of an accredited secondary school and have completed 4 years of English, 3 years each of math and social studies, 2 years of science, and 2 years of a single foreign language. A personal statement is strongly recommended. The GED is accepted. Music majors must audition. AP and CLEP credits are accepted. Important factors in the admissions decision are recommendations by school officials, advanced placement or honors courses, and evidence of special talent. To graduate, students must complete a freshman writing course and a writing course specified by the major and degree program. Students must complete the 26-credit University Integrative Studies requirement consisting of 8 credits of arts and humanities, 8 of social, behavioral, and economic sciences, 8 of general science, and 3 of a transcollegiate course. Students must also complete a math requirement determined by each undergraduate college (minimum of college algebra plus trigonometry/finite math/statistics.) A minimum 2.0 GPA and 120 semester hours are required. **Procedure:** Freshmen are admitted fall, spring, and summer. Entrance exams should be taken during the junior year of high school. There are deferred admissions and rolling admissions plans. Applications should be filed by July 25 for fall entry; December 1 for spring entry; and April 15 for summer entry, along with a $50 fee. Applications are accepted on-line. **Transfer Students:** 1513 transfer students enrolled in 2013-2014. To transfer, a minimum GPA of 2.0 is required, (prefer 3.0 overall GPA). MSU Integrative Studies requirement should be fulfilled (28 general graduation credits), and college algebra completed. 30 of 120 credits required for the bachelor's degree must be completed at MSU. **International Students:** There are 4519 international students enrolled. The school actively recruits these students. They must take the

TOEFL with a minimum score of 550 on the paper-based TOEFL (PBT) or 79 on the Internet-based version (iBT) or take the MELAB and the college's own test, MSUELT.

ADMISSIONS: 66% of the 2014-2015 applicants were accepted. The SAT scores for the 2014-2015 freshman class were: Critical Reading--40% below 500, 30% between 500 and 599, 15% between 600 and 699, and 5% between 700 and 800; Math--11% below 500, 27% between 500 and 599, 40% between 600 and 699, and 24% between 700 and 800; Writing--37% below 500, 43% between 500 and 599, 15% between 600 and 699, and 4% between 700 and 800. The ACT scores were 5% below 21, 21% between 21 and 23, 30% between 24 and 26, 28% between 27 and 28, and 16% above 28. 66% of the current freshmen were in the top fifth of their class; 94% were in the top two fifths. **Admissions Contact:** James Cotter, Director of Admissions. E-Mail: *admis@msu.edu* Web: *www.beaspartan.msu.edu*

FINANCIAL AID: In 2014-2015, 93% of all full-time freshmen and 68% of continuing full-time students received some form of financial aid. 28% of all full-time freshmen and 22% of continuing full-time students received need-based aid. The average freshman award was $9,324.. The FAFSA is required. The priority date for freshman financial aid applications for fall entry is March 1. The deadline for filing freshman financial aid applications for fall entry is June 30.

MICHIGAN TECHNOLOGICAL UNIVERSITY
B-2

www.mtu.edu

Houghton, MI 49931	906-487-2335 / 888-688-1885
Fax: 906-487-2125	Email: mtu4u@mtu.edu
Full-time: 3912 men, 1334 women	Faculty: 402; I, -$
Part-time: 301 men, 111 women	Ph.D.s: 87%
Graduate: 1019 men, 423 women	Student/Faculty: 13 to 1
Year: semesters, summer session	Tuition: $14,040 ($29,520)
Room & Board: $9516	Freshman Class: 5111 applied, 3859 accepted, 1199 enrolled
SAT CR/M/W: 600/650/595 **ACT:** 27	CEEB CODE: 1464
Application Deadline:	HIGHLY COMPETITIVE

Michigan Technological University, founded in 1885, is a state-supported institution offering degrees in engineering, liberal arts, sciences, forestry, business, and technology. There are 5 undergraduate schools and 1 graduate school. In addition to regional accreditation, Michigan Tech has baccalaureate program accreditation with AACSB, ABET, ACCE, SAF, TEAC, and NAACLS. The 925-acre campus is in a small town 325 miles north of Milwaukee, Wisconsin. Including any residence halls, there are 33 buildings.

STUDENT LIFE: 74% of undergraduates are from Michigan. Others are from 44 states, 33 foreign countries, and Canada. 85% are White. **Male To Female Ratio:** 0.4:1. The average age of freshmen is 18; all undergraduates, 21. 15% do not continue beyond their first year; 85% remain to graduate. **Housing:** 2959 students can be accommodated in college housing, which includes coed dorms, on-campus apartments, married student housing, and honors houses. On-campus housing is guaranteed for the freshman year only, is available on a first-come, and first-served basis. 53% of students commute. All students may keep cars.

FACULTY/CLASSROOMS: 70% of faculty are male; 30% are female. All teach undergraduates, 75% do research, and 74% do both. Graduate students teach 9% of introductory courses. The average class size in an introductory lecture is 34; in a laboratory is 17; and in a regular course is 25.

PROGRAMS OF STUDY: Michigan Tech confers B.A., and B.S. degrees. Associate, Master's, and Doctoral degrees are also awarded. Bachelor's degrees are awarded in AGRICULTURE (forestry and related sciences and wildlife management), BIOLOGICAL SCIENCE (biochemistry, bioinformatics, biology/biological science, and ecology), BUSINESS (accounting, finance, management engineering, management information systems, management science, marketing, and sports management), COMMUNICATIONS AND THE ARTS (audio technology, communications, English, technical and business writing, theater design, and theatre studies), COMPUTER AND PHYSICAL SCIENCE (applied physics, chemistry, computer information systems, computer science, geology, geophysics and seismology, mathematics, physics, software engineering, and statistics), EDUCATION (secondary education), ENGINEERING AND ENVIRONMENTAL DESIGN (biomedical engineering, chemical engineering, civil engineering, computer engineering, construction management, electrical/electronics engineering, electrical/electronics engineering technology, engineering, environmental engineering, geological engineering, materials engineering, mechanical engineering, mechanical engineering technology, and surveying engineering), HEALTH PROFESSIONS (exercise science, medical laboratory science, pharmaceutical chemistry, predentistry, premedicine, prepharmacy, and prephysical therapy), SOCIAL SCIENCE (anthropology, economics, history, liberal arts/general studies, psychology, and social science). Engineering and sciences is the strongest academically. Mechanical engineering, chemical engineering, and civil engineering have the largest enrollments.

ACTIVITIES: There are 233 groups on campus, including art, band, cheerleading, chess, choir, chorale, chorus, computers, dance, drama, ethnic, film, gay, honors, international, jazz band, literary magazine, musical theater, newspaper, orchestra, pep band, photography, political, professional, radio and TV, religious, social, social service, student government, and symphony. Popular campus events include Winter Carnival, K-Day, Homecoming, Spring Fling, Spirit of the Harvest Powwow, Make a Difference Day, International Night, Parade of Nations, Safe House Halloween, Division I Hockey, Undergraduate Research Expo, and LeaderShape Institute. **Sports:** There are 7 intercollegiate sports for men and 7 for women, and 15 intramural sports for men and 15 for women. Facilities include Student Development Complex with facilities like: John J. MacInnes Student Ice Arena, with a seating capacity of 4,200 and fourteen rentable luxury suites/skyboxes, fitness center, swimming pool, multipurpose room, climbing wall, varsity gym with a seating capacity of 3200, a studio, shooting range, outdoor softball fields and sand volleyball courts, Sherman field, upper and lower soccer fields and Hubbell field, tech trails, and Peter J. Grant hockey education center. **Graduates:** From July 1, 2013 to June 30, 2014, 1084 bachelor's degrees were awarded. The most popular majors were mechanical engineering (17%), civil engineering (10%), and electrical engineering (10%). 439 companies recruited on campus in 2013-2014. In an average class, 25% graduate in 4 years or less, 58% graduate in 5 years or less, and 64% graduate in 6 years or less.

SERVICES: Counseling and information services are available, as is tutoring in most subjects. There is a reader service for the blind. Biological Sciences Learning Center; Business and Economics Tidwell Learning Center; Chemistry Learning Center; Civil and Environmental Engineering Learning Center; Computer Science Learning Center; Electrical and Computer Engineering Learning Center; Engineering Learning Center; First-Year Engineering Learning Center; Forestry Learning Center; Mathematics Learning Center; Multiliteracies Center **Library/Resources:** The library contains 536,742 volumes, 312,101 microform items, 1,496 audio/video tapes/CDs/DVDs, and subscribes to 125,399 periodicals including electronic. Computerized library services include interlibrary loans, database searching, Internet access, and Wi-Fi capability. Special learning facilities include an art gallery, radio station, the A.E. Seaman Mineral Museum, which is the official mineral museum of Michigan; the Rozsa Center for the Performing Arts, State-of-the-art theater; Ford Center with 4,000-acre Ford Forest; Cosmic Ray Observatory; X-ray Fluorescence Spectrometer; Process Simulation and Control Center; Remote Sensing Institute; Computer-aided Engineering Lab; Micro Fabrication Lab; Subsurface Visualization Lab; and the Great Lakes Research Center on the waterfront. **Physically Challenged Students:** 90% of the campus is accessible. Facilities include wheelchair ramps, elevators, special parking, specially equipped restrooms, special class scheduling, lowered drinking fountains, and special housing. **Special:** Michigan Technological University is a leading public research university developing new technologies and preparing students to create the future for a prosperous and sustainable world. Michigan Tech offers more than 130 undergraduate and graduate degree programs in engineering; forest resources; computing; technology; business; econom-

ics; natural, physical and environmental sciences; arts; humanities; and social sciences. Accelerated Master's Degrees are available in nearly 20 areas. Over 400 companies visit campus annually to recruit students for co-ops, internships, and full-time jobs. The Pavlis Honors College provides opportunities for students to participate in the Enterprise Program--teams of students working on large-scale government- and industry-sponsored projects--the Honors Institute, Pavlis Institute for Global Technological Leadership, Research Scholars Program, and more. Students may also participate in industry-sponsored senior design or international senior design. Study abroad opportunities exist in over 40 countries. Undergraduate research is also available last year, students spent over 126,000 hours working on paid undergraduate research. Michigan Tech offers dual degrees, double majors, minors, and certificate programs. Students looking to enroll in professional health programs will find an early assurance program with Michigan State University for medical school and Central Michigan University for physical therapy (DPT). Agreements for 3+2 programs with many institutions in the Midwest are in place. There are 12 national honor societies and 23 departmental honors programs. **Visiting:** There are regularly scheduled orientations for prospective students. There are guides for informal visits, visitors may sit in on classes, and stay overnight. To schedule a visit, contact the Admissions Office at mtu4u@mtu.edu. **Campus Safety and Security:** Measures include 24-hour foot and vehicle patrol, emergency notification system, self-defense education, and security escort services. There are shuttle buses, emergency telephones, lighted pathways/sidewalks, and controlled access to dorms/residences.

REQUIREMENTS: First-year applicants are required to submit an official high school transcript with grades through at least the junior year and official ACT or SAT scores. Scores may be sent directly from the testing agency, or reported on the official high school transcript or on Michigan Tech's Counselor Information Page. Transfer student applicants are required to submit official college transcripts from all institutions previously attended. An official high school transcript is required for transfer applicants who have not earned an Associate's degree or higher at time of application to Michigan Tech. Applicants to programs in the Visual and Performing Arts Department must provide essay responses; select majors must submit examples of creative work. We encourage GED and home school applicants to apply. AP and CLEP credits are accepted. To graduate, students must complete 120 to 145 credit hours and maintain a minimum GPA (both cumulative and in the major department) of 2.0. The general education curriculum, required for all baccalaureate students and included in the 120-145 credits, consists of 4 core courses, a 12 credit hour distribution requirement, physical education, and a 16 credit hour science/math requirement. Students must take 30 credit hours of upper-level courses at MTU that apply to the degree requirements, and 30 of the last 36 credit hours, regardless of level, must be completed at MTU. **Procedure:** Freshmen are admitted to all sessions. Entrance exams should be taken scores will be accepted until time of enrollment. There are deferred admissions and rolling admissions plans. Application deadlines are open. Notifications are sent June 20. Applications are accepted on-line. Application fees are waived if application is completed on-line. **Transfer Students:** 207 transfer students enrolled in 2013-2014. Transfer students must have a minimum GPA of 2.75 on a 4.0 scale; grades of B or better are expected in math and science courses. Some selected programs require a 2.5 cumulative transfer GPA. 30 of 120 credits required for the bachelor's degree must be completed at Michigan Tech. **International Students:** There are 248 international students enrolled. The school actively recruits these students. They must take the TOEFL with a minimum score of 550 on the paper-based TOEFL (PBT) or 79 on the Internet-based version (iBT) or take the MELAB, or take the IELTS or TOEIC or Pearson Test of English or Eiken STEP.

ADMISSIONS: 76% of the 2014-2015 applicants were accepted. The SAT scores for the 2014-2015 freshman class were: Critical Reading--9% below 500, 36% between 500 and 599, 37% between 600 and 699, and 18% between 700 and 800; Math--1% below 500, 28% between 500 and 599, 49% between 600 and 699, and 22% between 700 and 800; Writing--20% below 500, 30% between 500 and 599, 43% between 600 and 699, and 7% between 700 and 800. The ACT scores were 2% below 21, 14% between 21 and 23, 28% between 24 and 26, 22% between 27 and 28, and 34% above 28. 55% of the current freshmen were in the top fifth of their class; 84% were in the top two fifths. 44 freshmen graduated first in their class. **Admissions Contact:** Allison Carter, Director of Admissions. E-Mail: *mtu4u@mtu.edu* Web: *http://www.mtu.edu/admissions/*

FINANCIAL AID: Michigan Tech is a member of CSS. Check with the school for current application deadlines.

NORTHERN MICHIGAN UNIVERSITY   C-2
www.nmu.edu

Marquette, MI 49855

(906) 227-2650
(800) 682-9797

Fax: (906) 227-1747   Email: admiss@nmu.edu
Full-time: 3170 men, 3844 women   Faculty: 330; IIA, av$
Part-time: 339 men, 488 women   Ph.D.s: 75%
Graduate: 264 men, 487 women   Student/Faculty: 22 to 1
Year: semesters, summer session   Tuition: $9324 ($14,556)
Room & Board: $8954   Freshman Class: 6841 applied, 4940 accepted, 1663 enrolled
ACT: 22   CEEB CODE: 1560
Application Deadline: open   **COMPETITIVE**

Northern Michigan University, founded in 1899, is a public institution offering undergraduate programs in the arts and sciences, business, education, health science, human services, nursing, and technology. There are 4 undergraduate schools and 1 graduate school. In addition to regional accreditation, NMU has baccalaureate program accreditation with AACSB, ADA, CSWE, NASM, NCATE, and NLN. The 359-acre campus is in an urban area on the southern shores of Lake Superior. Including any residence halls, there are 55 buildings.

STUDENT LIFE: 80% of undergraduates are from Michigan. Others are from 48 states, 39 foreign countries, and Canada. 79% are White. **Male To Female Ratio:** 1.3:1. The average age of freshmen is 18.5; all undergraduates, 23. 28% do not continue beyond their first year; 49% remain to graduate. **Housing:** 3250 students can be accommodated in college housing, which includes coed dorms, on-campus apartments, and married student housing. In addition, there are honors houses, special-interest houses, Smoke-free and chemical-free houses. On-campus housing is guaranteed for all 4 years. 58% of students commute. All students may keep cars.

FACULTY/CLASSROOMS: 56% of faculty are male; 44% are female. All teach undergraduates. Graduate students teach 1% of introductory courses. The average class size in an introductory lecture is 30; in a laboratory is 17; and in a regular course is 23.

PROGRAMS OF STUDY: NMU confers B.A., B.S., B.F.A., B.M.Ed., B.S.N. and B.S.W. degrees. Associate, Master's, and Doctoral degrees are also awarded. Bachelor's degrees are awarded in BIOLOGICAL SCIENCE (biochemistry, biology/biological science, botany, ecology, microbiology, physiology, and zoology), BUSINESS (accounting, banking and finance, business administration and management, entrepreneurial studies, and marketing/retailing/merchandising), COMMUNICATIONS AND THE ARTS (broadcasting, communications, design, dramatic arts, English, fine arts, French, language arts, music, public relations, Spanish, and speech/debate/rhetoric), COMPUTER AND PHYSICAL SCIENCE (chemistry, computer programming, computer science, earth science, information sciences and systems, mathematics, and physics), EDUCATION (art education, business education, computer education, education of the mentally handicapped, elementary education, health education, industrial arts education, music education, physical education, science education, and secondary education), ENGINEERING AND ENVIRONMENTAL DESIGN (architecture, construction management, electrical/electronics engineering technology, industrial engineering technology, and manufacturing technology), HEALTH PROFESSIONS (chiropractic, clinical science, cytotechnology, medical laboratory technology, nursing, physician's assistant, predentistry, premedicine, preveterinary science, and speech pathology/audiology), SOCIAL SCIENCE (criminal justice, economics, geography, history, international studies, parks and recreation management, philosophy, physi-

cal fitness/movement, political science/government, prelaw, psychology, public administration, social work, sociology, and water resources). Nursing, chemistry, and education are the strongest academically. Art and design, nursing, and criminal justice have the largest enrollments.

ACTIVITIES: 1% of men belong to 2 national fraternities; 1% of women belong to 1 local and 2 national sororities. There are 271 groups on campus, including and health, philosophy, art, band, cheerleading, chess, choir, chorale, chorus, communications, computers, dance, drama, drill team, environmental, ethnic, film, gay, honors, international, international dance club, jazz band, literary magazine, marching band, musical theater, newspaper, orchestra, pep band, photography, political, professional, radio and TV, religious, social, social service, student government, and symphony. Popular campus events include Winterfest, Be a Part from the Start, and U.P. 200 Dog Sled Race. **Sports:** There are 5 intercollegiate sports for men and 8 for women, and 12 intramural sports for men and 12 for women. Facilities include indoor and outdoor playing fields, an aerobic and fitness training area, an ice rink, swimming pool, diving tank, field house, an 8000-seat stadium, 4000-seat basketball and hockey arena, rock-climbing wall, racquetball courts. **Graduates:** From July 1, 2013 to June 30, 2014, 1299 bachelor's degrees were awarded. The most popular majors were art and design (8%), criminal justice (7%), and nursing (7%). In an average class, 2% graduate in 3 years or less, 22% graduate in 4 years or less, 43% graduate in 5 years or less, and 49% graduate in 6 years or less.

SERVICES: Counseling and information services are available, as is tutoring in most subjects. There is a reader service for the blind, remedial math, reading, and writing. **Library/Resources:** The library contains 540,830 volumes, 131,919 microform items, 5,641 audio/video tapes/CDs/DVDs, and subscribes to 35,686 periodicals including electronic. Computerized library services include interlibrary loans, database searching, Internet access, and Wi-Fi capability. Special learning facilities include an art gallery, radio station, TV station, a learning resource center, computing help desk, regional heritage center, and an observatory. **Physically Challenged Students:** All of the campus is accessible. Facilities include wheelchair ramps, elevators, special parking, specially equipped restrooms, lowered drinking fountains, lowered telephones, and special housing. **Special:** NMU offers internships, a co-op program in business, study abroad in a number of countries, a Washington semester, dual majors in computer information and accounting, and student-designed majors in individual studies and liberal arts. There are 7 national honor societies, a freshman honors program, and 1 departmental honors program. **Visiting:** There are regularly scheduled orientations for prospective students, including an admissions interview, a tour, and a faculty visit. Visitors may sit in on classes and stay overnight. To schedule a visit, contact the Campus Visit Office. **Campus Safety and Security:** Measures include 24-hour foot and vehicle patrol, emergency notification system, self-defense education, and security escort services. There are shuttle buses, emergency telephones, lighted pathways/sidewalks, and a crime prevention program with a full-time staff.

REQUIREMENTS: The ACT is required, with a GPA of 2.25 and a minimum composite score of 900 for the SAT l and 19 for the ACT. Applicants must be graduates of accredited secondary schools or have earned a GED. NMU requires 12 to 16 Carnegie units; recommended secondary school preparation includes 4 years of English, 3 each of math, history, social studies, foreign language, and science, 2 of fine arts or performing arts, and 1 of computer instruction. Students seeking art scholarships must submit a portfolio; those seeking music and theater scholarships must audition. A GPA of 2.3 is required. AP and CLEP credits are accepted. Students must earn 40 semester credits in liberal studies, including courses in humanities, composition, natural sciences/math, social sciences, communications, and visual and performing arts. Graduation requirements vary by degree program; at the minimum, students must earn 124 semester credits, including 32 in a major field, with a GPA of 2.0. Courses in phys ed/health and world culture are also required. **Procedure:** Freshmen are admitted to all sessions. Entrance exams should be taken during the year prior to enrollment. There are deferred admissions and rolling admissions plans. Application deadlines are open. The fall 2014 application fee was $35. Notification is sent on a rolling basis. Applications are accepted on-line. **Transfer Students:** 510 transfer students enrolled in 2013-2014. Applicants must present a minimum GPA of 2.0 in at least 12 semester credits of college-level work. 32 of 124 credits required for the bachelor's degree must be completed at NMU. **International Students:** There are 86 international students enrolled. The school actively recruits these students. They must take the TOEFL with a minimum score of 500 on the paper-based TOEFL (PBT) or 61 on the Internet-based version (iBT). They must also take the SAT or ACT, scoring 19. Canadian students must take the SAT or ACT.

ADMISSIONS: 72% of the 2014-2015 applicants were accepted. The ACT scores were 41% below 21, 27% between 21 and 23, 19% between 24 and 26, 6% between 27 and 28, and 6% above 28. **Admissions Contact:** Gerri Daniels, Director of Admissions. E-Mail: *admiss@nmu.edu* Web: *www.nmu.edu*

FINANCIAL AID: In 2014-2015, 94% of all full-time freshmen and 88% of continuing full-time students received some form of financial aid. 59% of all full-time freshmen and 58% of continuing full-time students received need-based aid. The average freshman award was $12,830. Need-based scholarships or need-based grants averaged $5,282 ($10,000 maximum); need-based self-help aid (loans and jobs) averaged $4,195 ($9,500 maximum); non-need-based athletic scholarships averaged $9,240 ($26,363 maximum); and other non-need-based awards and non-need-based scholarships averaged $7,597 ($26,463 maximum). 31% of undergraduate students work part-time. Average annual earnings from campus work are $2179. The average financial indebtedness of the 2014 graduate was $25,500. The FAFSA is required. The priority date for freshman financial aid applications for fall entry is March 1.

NORTHWOOD UNIVERSITY *(The complete profile is made available exclusively on our website, www.barronspac.com)*

OAKLAND UNIVERSITY   E-4
www.oakland.edu

Rochester, MI 48309

	(248) 370-3360
	(800) OAK-UNIV
Fax: n/av	Email: ouinfo@oakland.edu
Full-time: 4719 men, 7161 women	Faculty: I, --$
Part-time: 1741 men, 2569 women	Ph.D.s: n/av
Graduate: 1339 men, 2211 women	Student/Faculty: n/av
Year: semesters, summer session	Tuition: $11,183 ($25,598)
Room & Board: $8208	Freshman Class: 12152 applied, 7551 accepted, 2464 enrolled
ACT: 22	CEEB CODE: 1497
Application Deadline: n/av	COMPETITIVE

Oakland University, established in 1957, is a comprehensive state-supported institution serving a primarily commuter student body. Figures in the above capsule and in this profile are approximate. There are 7 undergraduate schools and 7 graduate schools. In addition to regional accreditation, Oakland has baccalaureate program accreditation with AACSB, ABET, CSWE, NASM, TEAC, NASPAA, NAST, NASD, ACS, CCNE, CACREP, and CAPTE. The 1444-acre campus is in a suburban area 25 miles north of Detroit. Including any residence halls, there are 46 buildings.

STUDENT LIFE: Most undergraduates are from out of state, including the Midwest. 77% are White. **Male To Female Ratio:** 1.5:1. The average age of freshmen is 18; all undergraduates, 23. **Housing:** College-sponsored housing includes single-sex and coed dorms, on-campus apartments, and married student housing. In addition, there are honors houses, special-interest houses, fraternity houses, sorority houses, living learning communities, international village, and Eco interest, pre-business, pre-nursing, scholars tower. On-campus housing is guaranteed for all 4 years. All students may keep cars.

FACULTY/CLASSROOMS: 54% of faculty are male; 46% are female. No introductory courses are taught by graduate students.

PROGRAMS OF STUDY: Oakland confers B.A., B.S., B.F.A., B.I.S., B.Mus., B.S.E., B.S.N. and B.S.W. degrees. Master's and Doctoral degrees are also awarded. Bachelor's degrees are awarded in BIO-LOGICAL SCIENCE (biochemistry and biology/biological science), BUSINESS (accounting, banking and finance, business administration and management, business economics, human resources, management information systems, marketing/retailing/merchandising, operations management, and personnel management), COMMUNICATIONS AND THE ARTS (art history and appreciation, Chinese, communications, dance, dramatic arts, English, film arts, French, German, Japanese, journalism, linguistics, music, performing arts, Spanish, and studio art), COMPUTER AND PHYSICAL SCIENCE (chemistry, computer science, information sciences and systems, mathematics, medical physics, physics, and statistics), EDUCATION (elementary education and music education), ENGINEERING AND ENVIRONMENTAL DESIGN (computer engineering, electrical/electronics engineering, engineering chemistry, engineering physics, environmental science, industrial engineering, mechanical engineering, and occupational safety and health), HEALTH PROFESSIONS (allied health, health science, medical laboratory science, nursing, and preventive/wellness health care), SOCIAL SCIENCE (African American studies, anthropology, East Asian studies, economics, history, international relations, Latin American studies, liberal arts/general studies, philosophy, political science/government, psychology, public administration, Russian and Slavic studies, social work, sociology, South Asian studies, and women's studies). Arts, health science are the strongest academically. Health science, elementary education, and nursing have the largest enrollments.

ACTIVITIES: 2% of men belong to 6 national fraternities; 2% of women belong to 6 national sororities. There are 190 groups on campus, including art, band, cheerleading, choir, chorale, chorus, computers, dance, drama, environmental, ethnic, film, forensics, gay, honors, international, jazz band, musical theater, newspaper, orchestra, pep band, political, professional, radio and TV, religious, social, social service, student government, and symphony. Popular campus events include Welcome Week, Hispanic Celebration, and Week of Champions at OU. **Sports:** There are 7 intercollegiate sports for men and 9 for women, and 18 intramural sports for men and 18 for women. Facilities include a 250,000-square-foot student recreation and athletic center that includes softball and baseball diamonds, an indoor track, soccer and touch football fields, and facilities for swimming, basketball, weight training, dance, fencing, handball, squash, racquetball, and golf. **Graduates:** From July 1, 2013 to June 30, 2014, 2345 bachelor's degrees were awarded. The most popular majors were nursing (14%), business (13%), and education (8%). 190 companies recruited on campus in 2013-2014.

SERVICES: Counseling and information services are available, as is tutoring in most subjects. There is a reader service for the blind, remedial math, reading, and writing. There is a mentorship program. **Library/Resources:** The 2 libraries contain 851,190 volumes, 1.2 million microform items, 29,868 audio/video tapes/CDs/DVDs, and subscribe to 43,501 periodicals including electronic. Computerized library services include interlibrary loans, database searching, Internet access, and Wi-Fi capability. Special learning facilities include an art gallery, radio station, TV station, the Product Development and Manufacturing Center, the Historical House Museum, and the Lean-Learning Institute. **Physically Challenged Students:** 99% of the campus is accessible. Facilities include wheelchair ramps, elevators, special parking, specially equipped restrooms, special class scheduling, lowered drinking fountains, lowered telephones, special housing. Automatic door openers. **Special:** Special academic programs include internships, cooperative programs for most disciplines, and many work-study opportunities. There are organized programs for study abroad in 8 countries; independent programs can be arranged. Oakland also offers a B.A. or B.S. degree in biology and economics, a general studies program, dual majors, a student-designed major, cross-registration with Macomb Community College, and preprofessional studies in medicine, dentistry, optometry, and veterinary medicine. There are 12 national honor societies and a freshman honors program. **Visiting:** There are regularly scheduled orientations for prospective students, including a review of services, academic advising, and course registration. There are guides for informal visits, visitors may sit in on classes, and stay overnight. To schedule a visit, contact the Admissions Office at visit@oakland.edu. **Campus Safety and Security:** Measures include 24-hour foot and vehicle patrol, emergency notification system, self-defense education, and security escort services. There are shuttle buses, emergency telephones, lighted pathways/sidewalks, controlled access to dorms/residences and text alert.

REQUIREMENTS: The ACT is required. Admissions requirements include graduation from an accredited secondary school and high school level college preparatory work, including 4 years of English and 3 years each of math, science, and social studies. 2 years of foreign language is recommended as well. Music and dance majors must audition. AP and CLEP credits are accepted.To graduate, students must complete 124 credit hours (153 to 161 for the B.Mus. or 128 for the B.S.Env.Health). All students must complete 40 credits of general education requirements, including at least 1 course (3 or more credits) from the list of approved courses in each of the 10 knowledge areas: writing, formal reasoning, arts, foreign language and culture, global perspective, literature, natural science and technology, social science, Western civilization, and knowledge application. A GPA of 2.0 is required. **Procedure:** Freshmen are admitted to all sessions. Entrance exams should be taken during the spring of the junior year or early fall of the senior year. There are deferred admissions and rolling admissions plans. Check with the school for current application deadlines. Notification is sent on a rolling basis. Applications are accepted on-line. **Transfer Students:** 1891 transfer students enrolled in 2013-2014. Applicants must have at least a 2.5 GPA; a higher GPA is required in some majors. 32 of 124 credits required for the bachelor's degree must be completed at Oakland. **International Students:** They must take the TOEFL with a minimum score of 550 on the paper-based TOEFL (PBT) or 79 on the Internet-based version (iBT) or take the MELAB. They must also take the ACT.

ADMISSIONS: 62% of the 2014-2015 applicants were accepted. **Admissions Contact:** Eleanor Reynolds, Assistant Vice President Student Affairs Admissions. E-Mail: *ouinfo@oakland.edu* Web: *www. oakland.edu*

FINANCIAL AID: The average freshman award was $12,885. Need-based scholarships or need-based grants averaged $5,645; need-based self-help aid (loans and jobs) averaged $3,173; and non-need-based athletic scholarships averaged $11,515. The FAFSA is required. The deadline for filing freshman financial aid applications for fall entry is April 1.

OLIVET COLLEGE *(The complete profile is made available exclusively on our website, www.barronspac.com)*

ROCHESTER COLLEGE *(The complete profile is made available exclusively on our website, www.barronspac.com)*

SAGINAW VALLEY STATE UNIVERSITY   D-4
www.svsu.edu

University Center, MI 48710	(989) 964-4200
	(800) 968-9500
Fax: (989) 790-0180	Email: admissions@svsu.edu
Full-time: 3098 men, 4313 women	Faculty: n/av
Part-time: 640 men, 746 women	Ph.D.s: n/av
Graduate: 287 men, 745 women	Student/Faculty: n/av
Year: semesters, summer session	Tuition: $8691 ($20,409)
Room & Board: $8678	Freshman Class: 6275 applied, 4965 accepted, 1507 enrolled
ACT: 22	CEEB CODE: 1766
Application Deadline: n/av	COMPETITIVE

Saginaw Valley State University, founded in 1963, is a state-supported institution offering undergraduate and graduate degrees in arts and behavioral sciences, business and management, education, nursing and health sciences, and science, engineering, and technology. Figures in the above capsule and in this profile are approximate. There are 5 undergraduate schools and 5 graduate schools. In addition to regional accreditation, SVSU has baccalaureate program accreditation with AACSB, ABET, CSWE, NASM, NCATE, ACS, NAACLS, ACOTE, CCNE, and CAATE. The 782-acre campus is in a suburban area 5 miles north of Saginaw. Including any residence halls, there are 90 buildings.

STUDENT LIFE: 92% of undergraduates are from Michigan. Others are from 23 states, 35 foreign countries, and Canada. 95% are from public schools. 72% are White. **Male To Female Ratio:** 1.4:1. The average age of freshmen is 18; all undergraduates, 22. 29% do not continue beyond their first year; 40% remain to graduate. **Housing:** 2736 students can be accommodated in college housing, which includes coed dorms and on-campus apartments, including healthy life-style floors and buildings, and first-year suites. On-campus housing is available on a first come, first served basis. 69% of students commute. All students may keep cars.

FACULTY/CLASSROOMS: No introductory courses are taught by graduate students. The average class size in an introductory lecture is 25 and in a laboratory is 17.

PROGRAMS OF STUDY: SVSU confers B.A., B.S., B.A.S., B.B.A., B.F.A., B.P.A., B.S.E.E., B.S.M.E., B.S.N. and B.S.W. degrees. Master's and Doctoral degrees are also awarded. Bachelor's degrees are awarded in BIOLOGICAL SCIENCE (biochemistry and biology/biological science), BUSINESS (accounting, banking and finance, business administration and management, business economics, finance, international business management, and marketing management), COMMUNICATIONS AND THE ARTS (art, communications, creative writing, design, dramatic arts, English, fine arts, French, music, Spanish, and technical and business writing), COMPUTER AND PHYSICAL SCIENCE (applied mathematics, applied science, chemical physics, chemistry, computer science, information sciences and systems, mathematics, optics, and physics), EDUCATION (art education, athletic training, drama education, elementary education, English education, foreign languages education, mathematics education, music education, physical education, science education, social studies education, and special education), ENGINEERING AND ENVIRONMENTAL DESIGN (electrical/electronics engineering, engineering technology, industrial administration/management, mechanical engineering, and preengineering), HEALTH PROFESSIONS (exercise science, health science, medical laboratory science, medical technology, nursing, predentistry, premedicine, and prephysical therapy), SOCIAL SCIENCE (criminal justice, economics, history, interdisciplinary studies, international studies, political science/government, prelaw, psychology, public administration, social work, and sociology). Nursing, social work, and criminal justice have the largest enrollments.

ACTIVITIES: 3% of men belong to 7 national fraternities; 3% of women belong to 1 local and 3 national sororities. There are 165 groups on campus, including art, band, cheerleading, chess, choir, chorus, computers, dance, drama, environmental, ethnic, film, gay, honors, international, jazz band, literary magazine, marching band, musical theater, newspaper, orchestra, pep band, photography, political, professional, radio and TV, religious, social, social service, and student government. Popular campus events include Battle of the Valleys, Cards Party and International Food Festival. **Sports:** There are 8 intercollegiate sports for men and 8 for women, and 16 intramural sports for men and 16 for women. Facilities include a health and phys ed complex with an Olympic-size pool, indoor track, basketball courts, badminton courts, volleyball courts, racquetball courts, fitness center, tennis courts, intramural, baseball, softball, soccer fields, archery range, fitness trail, football stadium, golf driving range, putting green, and horse shoe pits. **Graduates:** From July 1, 2013 to June 30, 2014, 1265 bachelor's degrees were awarded. The most popular majors were nursing (10%), criminal justice (7%), and social work (7%). 370 companies recruited on campus in 2013-2014. In an average class, 9% graduate in 4 years or less, 30% graduate in 5 years or less, and 40% graduate in 6 years or less. Of the 2013 graduating class, 20% were enrolled in graduate school within 6 months of graduation, and 86% were employed.

SERVICES: Counseling and information services are available, as is tutoring in most subjects. There is a reader service for the blind, and remedial math, reading, and writing. **Library/Resources:** The library contains 364,160 volumes, 354,265 microform items, 27,070 audio/video tapes/CDs/DVDs, and subscribes to 48,336 periodicals including electronic. Computerized library services include interlibrary loans, database searching, Internet access, and Wi-Fi capability. Special learning facilities include an art gallery, radio station, an observatory. **Physically Challenged Students:** 99% of the campus is accessible. Facilities include wheelchair ramps, elevators, special parking, specially equipped restrooms, special class scheduling, lowered drinking fountains, lowered telephones, special housing. Electronically opened doors, and special access to the library. All buildings are interconnected on the second floor. **Special:** Study abroad in 53 countries, internships, and Michigan Work Study and Federal College Work Study job opportunities within several on-campus departments. There are 4 national honor societies. **Visiting:** There are regularly scheduled orientations for prospective students, including tours, help with schedules, basic information and counseling. There are guides for informal visits. To schedule a visit, contact the Office of Admissions at tours@svsu.edu. **Campus Safety and Security:** Measures include 24-hour foot and vehicle patrol, emergency notification system, self-defense education, and security escort services. There are emergency telephones, lighted pathways/sidewalks, The SVSU public safety department has commissioned police officers providing police services.

REQUIREMENTS: The ACT is required. Applicants must submit a completed undergraduate application for admission, an official high school transcript or GED, and ACT results. SVSU recommends high school students take a rigorous college preparatory curriculum prior to enrolling at SVSU: four years of English, three years of math, three years of natural sciences, three years of social sciences, and two years of the same foreign language. AP and CLEP credits are accepted. Students must complete a minimum of 124 credits, satisfy basic skills and general education requirements, and maintain a minimum GPA of 2.0. The General Education Program consists of 35 credit hours in 10 categories. **Procedure:** Freshmen are admitted to all sessions. There are deferred admissions and rolling admissions plans. Application deadlines are open. Application fee is $30. Applications are accepted on-line. **Transfer Students:** 595 transfer students enrolled in 2013-2014. Transfer students with fewer than 24 credits from a previous college must submit high school and college transcripts. ACT or SAT scores must be submitted. A minimum GPA of 2.0 is needed. An interview may be required. 31 of 124 credits required for the bachelor's degree must be completed at SVSU. **International Students:** There are 505 international students enrolled. The school actively recruits these students. They must take the TOEFL with a minimum score of 500 on the paper-based TOEFL (PBT) or 61 on the Internet-based version (iBT).

ADMISSIONS: 79% of the 2014-2015 applicants were accepted. The ACT scores were 45% below 21, 25% between 21 and 23, 19% between 24 and 26, 7% between 27 and 28, and 5% above 28. 36% of the current freshmen were in the top fifth of their class; 62% were in the top two fifths. 52 freshmen graduated first in their class. **Admissions Contact:** Jennifer Pahl, Director of Admissions. E-Mail: *admissions@svsu.edu* Web: *www.svsu.edu*

FINANCIAL AID: In 2014-2015, 94% of all full-time freshmen and 91% of continuing full-time students received some form of financial aid. 65% of all full-time freshmen and 64% of continuing full-time students received need-based aid. Average annual earnings from campus work are $1500. The FAFSA is required. Check with the school for current application deadlines.

SIENA HEIGHTS UNIVERSITY	E-5
www.sienaheights.edu	

Adrian, MI 49221	(517) 264-7185
	(800) 521-0009
Fax: (517) 264-7745	Email: admissions@sienahts.edu
Full-time: 606 men, 639 women	**Faculty:** 76
Part-time: 442 men, 715 women	**Ph.D.s:** 66%
Graduate: 80 men, 160 women	**Student/Faculty:** 12 to 1
Year: semesters, summer session	**Tuition:** $22,740
Room & Board: $9300	**Freshman Class:** 1422 applied, 962 accepted, 300 enrolled
ACT: 21	**CEEB CODE:** 1719
Application Deadline: August 1	**COMPETITIVE**

Siena Heights University is a Catholic university founded in 1919 and sponsored by the Adrian Dominican Sisters. Enrolling a diverse community of traditional-age and working adult students, Siena Heights

is a coeducational North Central accredited institution founded in the liberal arts tradition, offering associate's, bachelor's, master's and specialist's degrees. The University is headquartered in Adrian, MI, where it offers a traditional undergraduate experience, and degree completion centers are located in Dearborn, Southfield, Benton Harbor, Monroe, Battle Creek, Lansing, Jackson and Online. There are 2 undergraduate schools and one graduate school. In addition to regional accreditation, Siena has baccalaureate program accreditation with CSWE, NASAD, TEAC, and CCNE. The 140-acre campus is in a small town 75 miles southwest of Detroit. Including any residence halls, there are 14 buildings.

STUDENT LIFE: 89% of undergraduates are from Michigan. Others are from 37 states, 12 foreign countries, and Canada. 67% are White; 12% African American; 12% race unknown. 35% are Protestant; 26% claim no religious affiliation; 21% Catholic. **Male To Female Ratio:** 1.3:1. The average age of freshmen is 18; all undergraduates, 29. 43% do not continue beyond their first year; 53% remain to graduate.

Housing: 605 students can be accommodated in college housing, which includes single-sex and coed dorms, on-campus apartments, and married student housing. Special housing for international students; coed dorms and dorm floors exclusively for men and women. On-campus housing is available on a first-come, first-served basis, and is available on a lottery system for upperclassmen. 71% of students commute. All students may keep cars.

FACULTY/CLASSROOMS: 46% of faculty are male; 54% are female. All teach undergraduates. No introductory courses are taught by graduate students.

PROGRAMS OF STUDY: Siena confers B.A., B.S., B.A.S. and B.F.A. degrees. Associate and Master's degrees are also awarded. Bachelor's degrees are awarded in BIOLOGICAL SCIENCE (biology/biological science), BUSINESS (accounting and business administration and management), COMMUNICATIONS AND THE ARTS (art history and appreciation, communications, English, fine arts, graphic design, music, Spanish, studio art, theatre arts, and visual and performing arts), COMPUTER AND PHYSICAL SCIENCE (chemistry, computer information systems, information sciences and systems, mathematics, and natural sciences), EDUCATION (art education, elementary education, music education, science education, special education, and trade and industrial education), HEALTH PROFESSIONS (Pre-Health Studies and premedicine), SOCIAL SCIENCE (child psychology/development, criminal justice, history, human services, humanities, liberal arts/general studies, philosophy, psychology, public administration, religion, social science, and social work). Business administration, nursing, and biology have the largest enrollments.

ACTIVITIES: 2% of men belong to 1 national fraternity; 2% of women belong to 1 national sorority. There are 30 groups on campus, including art, band, cheerleading, choir, chorus, computers, dance, drama, environmental, ethnic, gay, international, jazz band, literary magazine, marching band, musical theater, newspaper, pep band, photography, professional, religious, social, social service, student government, and symphony. Popular campus events include Alumni/Family Weekend, International Dinner, Athletic Banquets, Homecoming, and Common Dialog Day. **Sports:** There are 10 intercollegiate sports for men and 11 for women. Facilities include The Mary and Sash Spencer Complex and O'Laughlin Stadium are, state of the art facilities hosting 7 teams' home events, including football, soccer, track, and lacrosse, and much of the Athletics Department administration and staff. The Siena Heights Field House houses basketball and volleyball teams, and it also features 3 practice courts, a 200-meter track, and seating for over 2000. Baseball Diamond has chairback and lawn seating with a pressbox and offices. The field has a turf infield and natural grass outfield with a red clay mount. Additional structures include The Christensen Memorial Softball Field and additional track and field facilities. **Graduates:** From July 1, 2013 to June 30, 2014, 849 bachelor's degrees were awarded. The most popular majors were health professions and related programs (24%), business (22%), and law enforcement and related programs (11%). In an average class, 43% graduate in 6 years or less.

SERVICES: Counseling and information services are available, as is tutoring in most subjects. There is remedial math, reading, and writing. **Library/Resources:** The library contains 206,966 volumes, 3,134 microform items, and 1,543 audio/video tapes/CDs/DVDs, and subscribes to 47,565 periodicals including electronic. Computerized library services include interlibrary loans, database searching, Internet access, and Wi-Fi capability. Special learning facilities include an art gallery. **Physically Challenged Students:** 90% of the campus is accessible. Facilities include wheelchair ramps, elevators, special parking, specially equipped restrooms, special class scheduling, lowered drinking fountains. We have an Office of Disability Resources and have long been a Student Support Services grant recipient. **Special:** The most unique program is the Bachelors in Applied Science for adult learners looking to complete their degree. SHU also offers Completely Online Programs and many additional distance learning opportunities. There is a Liberal Arts core curriculum that includes traditional general studies groupings of courses as well as Liberal Arts Studies courses that reflect Dominican and University values. SHU also offers dual enrollment credit for high school students and a variety of study abroad opportunities. There is 1 national honor society. **Visiting:** There are regularly scheduled orientations for prospective students. There are guides for informal visits, visitors may sit in on classes, and stay overnight. To schedule a visit, contact Trudy Mohre at tmohre@sienaheights.edu. **Campus Safety and Security:** Measures include 24-hour foot and vehicle patrol, emergency notification system, self-defense education, and security escort services. There are lighted pathways/sidewalks, StormReady Community - National Weather Service.

REQUIREMENTS: The ACT is required, with a minimum score of 17. Admissions requirements include graduation from an accredited secondary school. The GED is accepted. Applications are accepted on-line. A GPA of 2.5 is required. AP and CLEP credits are accepted. Degree requirements may vary according to which college you attend and which major you select. Generally, the following requirement apply: 120 semester hours with a minimum of a 2.0 GPA. **Procedure:** Freshmen are admitted fall and spring. There are deferred admissions and rolling admissions plans. Applications should be filed by August 1 for fall entry. Notifications are sent July 1. Application fees are waived if application is completed on-line. **Transfer Students:** 474 transfer students enrolled in 2013-2014. **International Students:** There are 25 international students enrolled. The school actively recruits these students. They must take the TOEFL. They must also take the ACT, scoring 18.

ADMISSIONS: 68% of the 2014-2015 applicants were accepted. **Admissions Contact:** Trudy Mohre, Director of Admissions. E-Mail: *tmohre@sienahieghts.edu or admissions@sienahts.edu* Web: *www.sienaheights.edu*

FINANCIAL AID: In 2014-2015, 96% of all full-time freshmen and 80% of continuing full-time students received some form of financial aid. 73% of all full-time freshmen and 69% of continuing full-time students received need-based aid. Siena is a member of CSS. The FAFSA is required. The deadline for filing freshman financial aid applications for fall entry is August 1.

SPRING ARBOR UNIVERSITY D-5
www.arbor.edu

Spring Arbor, MI 49283	(517) 750-6468
	(800) 968-0011
Fax: (517) 750-6620	Email: admissions@arbor.edu
Full-time: 555 men, 815 women	Faculty: IIA
Part-time: 65 men, 120 women	Ph.D.s: 61%
Graduate: 290 men, 950 women	Student/Faculty: n/av
Year: semesters, summer session	Tuition: $19,790
Room & Board: $6950	Freshman Class: n/av
ACT: recommended	CEEB CODE: 1732
Application Deadline: open	COMPETITIVE

Founded in 1873 by leaders of the Free Methodist Church, Spring Arbor University offers a Christ-centered, liberal arts education with more than 50 undergraduate programs, 7 degree-completion programs, and 7 graduate programs. The figures in the above capsule are approximate. There are 3 undergraduate schools and 7 graduate schools. In addition to regional accreditation, SAU has baccalaureate program accreditation with CSWE, NCATE, and CCNE. The 123-acre campus is in a small town 8 miles southwest of Jackson. Including any residence halls, there are 36 buildings.

STUDENT LIFE: 85% of undergraduates are from Michigan. Others are from 30 states, 6 foreign countries, and Canada. 90% are White. 67% are Protestant; 20% unknown nondenominations; 11% claim no religious affiliation. **Male To Female Ratio:** 2.1:1. 28% do not continue beyond their first year; 59% remain to graduate. **Housing:** 1060 students can be accommodated in college housing, which includes single-sex dorms, on-campus apartments, and married student housing. On-campus housing is guaranteed for all 4 years. 68% of students live on campus; of those, 60% remain on campus on weekends. Alcohol is not permitted. Upperclassmen may keep cars.

FACULTY/CLASSROOMS: 60% of faculty are male; 40% are female. 94% teach undergraduates. No introductory courses are taught by graduate students. The average class size in a regular course is 18.

PROGRAMS OF STUDY: SAU confers B.A., and B.S.W. degrees. Associate Master's degrees are also awarded. Bachelor's degrees are awarded in BIOLOGICAL SCIENCE (biochemistry and biology/biological science), BUSINESS (accounting, business administration and management, and management information systems), COMMUNICATIONS AND THE ARTS (advertising, art, broadcasting, communications, English, film arts, language arts, music, Spanish, video, and visual and performing arts), COMPUTER AND PHYSICAL SCIENCE (chemistry, computer science, mathematics, and physics), EDUCATION (Christian education, music education, and special education), HEALTH PROFESSIONS (exercise science and nursing), SOCIAL SCIENCE (biblical studies, history, missions, philosophy, philosophy and religion, physical fitness/movement, psychology, social science, social studies, social work, sociology, theological studies, and youth ministry). Business, teacher education, and English are the strongest academically. Teacher education, business, and philosophy/religion have the largest enrollments.

ACTIVITIES: There are 41 groups on campus, including art, band, choir, chorale, drama, ethnic, film, honors, international, jazz band, literary magazine, musical theater, newspaper, pep band, radio and TV, religious, social, social service, student government, symphony, and yearbook. Popular campus events include Porchfest, Arbor Games, and Midnight Breakfast. **Sports:** There are 7 intercollegiate sports for men and 7 for women, and 7 intramural sports for men and 6 for women. Facilities include a weight room, basketball courts and volleyball courts, a 4-lane indoor track, an Olympic-sized swimming pool with sauna, an exercise lab, varsity and general locker rooms, and a training room. Other facilities include 3 batting cages, a cougar clubhouse (professional style locker rooms with separate wings for baseball, softball, and men's and women's soccer,including laundry and shower facilities), a 500-seat baseball stadium, softball diamonds, a soccer field, an 8-lane outdoor track (with long jump pit, high jump area, steeplechase hurdle, and throwing area), and 8 tennis courts (2 lighted). **Graduates:** From July 1, 2013 to June 30, 2014, 684 bachelor's degrees were awarded. The most popular majors were business (36%), family life (17%), and teacher education (16%). In an average class, 1% graduate in 3 years or less, 38% graduate in 4 years or less, 54% graduate in 5 years or less, and 59% graduate in 6 years or less. Of the 2013 graduating class, 25% were enrolled in graduate school within 6 months of graduation, and 63% were employed.

SERVICES: Counseling and information services are available, as is tutoring in most subjects. There is a reader service for the blind, remedial math, reading, and writing. Religious counseling and health services are also available. **Library/Resources:** The library contains 112,811 volumes, 576,594 microform items, 3,943 audio/video tapes/CDs/DVDs, and subscribes to 587 periodicals including electronic. Computerized library services include interlibrary loans, database searching, and Internet access. Special learning facilities include an art gallery, radio station, TV production facilities and equipment. **Physically Challenged Students:** 80% of the campus is accessible. Facilities include wheelchair ramps, elevators, special parking, specially equipped restrooms, lowered drinking fountains, lowered telephones, and special housing. **Special:** Study abroad is available in more than 12 countries. A Washington semester is available through the American Studies Program. The university also offers cross-registration with Jackson Community College, work-study, a dual major in physics/math, student-designed majors, pass/fail options, and nondegree study. Alternative programs for adult learners provide field-based study and assign credit for life experience. An accelerated B.A. program for such students is offered. A 3-2 engineering degree is offered with the University of Michigan, Western Michigan University, and Tri-State University. There are 3 national honor societies and a freshman honors program. **Visiting:** There are regularly scheduled orientations for prospective students, including a tour, class and chapel attendance, lunch, and a student panel discussion. There are guides for informal visits, visitors may sit in on classes, and stay overnight. To schedule a visit, contact the Admissions Office. **Campus Safety and Security:** Measures include 24-hour foot and vehicle patrol, emergency notification system, self-defense education, and security escort services. There are lighted pathways/sidewalks, controlled access to dorms/residences, key card entry to some dorms.

REQUIREMENTS: Applicants must be graduates of accredited secondary schools or have a GED. ACT or SAT test scores are required, with the ACT recommended. An interview is advised for those who do not meet the requirements. Home-schooled applicants must take the ACT or the SAT, provide transcripts of course work, and submit a 2- to 3-page paper. AP and CLEP credits are accepted. Important factors in the admissions decision are personality/intangible qualities, parents or siblings attended your school, and leadership record. Students must complete 4 Christian perspective courses plus cross-cultural studies, writing skills, speech, and physical fitness. Liberal arts requirements are in fine arts, humanities, natural science/math, philosophy/religion, and social science. To graduate, at least 124 semester hours, with 40 hours in upper-division courses and including 30 to 60 in the major, are needed. A minimum GPA of 2.0 overall and 2.2 in the major is also required. Students must also complete the University CORE, which includes communication skills, physical fitness, and liberal arts requirements. **Procedure:** Freshmen are admitted to all sessions. Entrance exams should be taken in the spring of the junior year or fall of the senior year. There are deferred admissions and rolling admissions plans. Application deadlines are open. The fall 2014 application fee was $30. Notification is sent on a rolling basis. Applications are accepted on-line. **Transfer Students:** 102 transfer students enrolled in 2013-2014. Applicants should have a minimum GPA of 2.0 and are encouraged to arrange an interview. A release of information form is required from the previous college attended. 30 of 124 credits required for the bachelor's degree must be completed at SAU. **International Students:** There are 20 international students enrolled. They must take the TOEFL with a minimum score of 525 on the paper-based TOEFL (PBT), the SAT or ACT may be required for some students.

ADMISSIONS: 8 freshmen graduated first in their class. **Admissions Contact:** Randy Comfort, Director of Admissions. E-Mail: *admissions@arbor.edu* Web: *www.arbor.edu*

FINANCIAL AID: In 2014-2015, 100% of all full-time freshmen and 87% of continuing full-time students received some form of financial aid. 84% of all full-time freshmen and 83% of continuing full-time students received need-based aid. The average freshman award was $19,168. Need-based scholarships or need-based grants averaged $9,643; need-based self-help aid (loans and jobs) averaged $3,699; and non-need-based athletic scholarships averaged $3,677. 32% of undergraduate students work part-time. Average annual earnings from campus work are $1250. The average financial indebtedness of the 2014 graduate was $13,834. The FAFSA is required. Check with the school for current application deadlines.

UNIVERSITY OF DETROIT MERCY	E-5
www.udmercy.edu	

Detroit, MI 48221	(313) 993-1245
	(800) 635-5020
Fax: (313) 993-3317	Email: admissions@udmercy.edu
Full-time: 800 men, 1100 women	Faculty: n/av
Part-time: 400 men, 1100 women	Ph.D.s: 85%
Graduate: 1105 men, 1095 women	Student/Faculty: n/av
Year: semesters, summer session	Tuition: $32,550
Room & Board: $9590	Freshman Class: n/av
SAT or ACT: required	CEEB CODE: 1835
Application Deadline: n/av	VERY COMPETITIVE

University of Detroit Mercy, founded in 1877, is a private, independent institution affiliated with the Jesuits and Sisters of Mercy. It offers undergraduate programs in liberal arts, education and human services, business administration, engineering and science, architecture, and nursing and health sciences. The figures in the above capsule and in this profile are approximate. There are 6 undergraduate schools and 7 graduate schools. In addition to regional accreditation, UDM has baccalaureate program accreditation with AACSB, ABET, ADA, CSWE, NAAB, and NLN. The 70-acre campus is in an urban area 7 miles north of downtown Detroit.

STUDENT LIFE: 93% of undergraduates are from Michigan. Others are from 27 states, 19 foreign countries, and Canada. 50% are White; 33% African American. 32% are Catholic; 32% unknown denominations and religions; 26% claim no religious affiliation; 11% Protestant. **Male To Female Ratio:** 1.4:1. The average age of freshmen is 18; all undergraduates, 29. 12% do not continue beyond their first year. **Housing:** 955 students can be accommodated in college housing, which includes coed dorms and married student housing. Freshman residence program, honors floors, and peace and justice floor. On-campus housing is guaranteed for all 4 years. 79% of students commute. All students may keep cars.

FACULTY/CLASSROOMS: No introductory courses are taught by graduate students.

PROGRAMS OF STUDY: UDM confers B.A., B.S., B.Arch., B.B.A., B.C.E., B.E.E., B.En., B.F.A., B.M.E., B.S.C.S., B.S.Ed., B.S.N. and B.S.W. degrees. Master's and Doctoral degrees are also awarded. Bachelor's degrees are awarded in BIOLOGICAL SCIENCE (biochemistry and biology/biological science), BUSINESS (accounting and business administration and management), COMMUNICATIONS AND THE ARTS (communications, dramatic arts, and English), COMPUTER AND PHYSICAL SCIENCE (chemistry, computer science, information sciences and systems, and mathematics), EDUCATION (early childhood education, elementary education, middle school education, secondary education, and special education), ENGINEERING AND ENVIRONMENTAL DESIGN (architecture, civil engineering, electrical/electronics engineering, engineering, manufacturing engineering, and mechanical engineering), HEALTH PROFESSIONS (dental hygiene, health care administration, nursing, predentistry, premedicine, and sports medicine), SOCIAL SCIENCE (addiction studies, criminal justice, economics, history, human services, liberal arts/general studies, paralegal studies, philosophy, political science/government, prelaw, psychology, religion, social work, and sociology). Nursing, biology, and engineering are the strongest academically. Nursing, and biology (pre-med, predent), have the largest enrollments.

ACTIVITIES: There are 50 groups on campus, including cheerleading, drama, ethnic, honors, international, literary magazine, newspaper, pep band, political, professional, radio and TV, religious, social, social service, and student government. Popular campus events include Engineering and Architecture Week, Ethics Bowl, and Alternative Spring Break. **Sports:** There are 7 intercollegiate sports for men and 8 for women, and 7 intramural sports for men and 7 for women. Facilities include a fitness center, a gym, racquetball/handball courts, an indoor track, a game room in the Student Union, and soccer and softball field, an outdoor track.

SERVICES: Counseling and information services are available, as is tutoring in most subjects, all freshman courses and many other courses There is remedial math, reading, and writing. **Library/Resources:** The 3 libraries contain 733,000 volumes, 1.0 million microform items, 33,153 audio/video tapes/CDs/DVDs, and subscribe to 4,049 periodicals including electronic. Computerized library services include interlibrary loans, database searching, and Internet access. Special learning facilities include a radio station. **Physically Challenged Students:** 80% of the campus is accessible. Facilities include wheelchair ramps, elevators, special parking, and special class scheduling. **Special:** Cooperative education is mandatory for engineering, architecture, and nursing majors and is optional for others. Cross-registration is available with a consortium of Catholic colleges in the Detroit area. There are internships, and a B.A.-B.S. degree is available for math, chemistry, and biology majors. An accelerated 6-year degree program in dentistry is provided. Study abroad is available in Italy, and Poland. Academic exploration courses are provided to help students who are undecided about a future vocation. There are 3 national honor societies and a freshman honors program. **Visiting:** There are regularly scheduled orientations for prospective students, including a look at student life, testing and advising, and registration. There are guides for informal visits, visitors may sit in on classes, and stay overnight. To schedule a visit, contact the Admissions Office. **Campus Safety and Security:** Measures include 24-hour foot and vehicle patrol, self-defense education, and security escort services. There are emergency telephones and lighted pathways/sidewalks.

REQUIREMENTS: The SAT or ACT is required. Graduation from an accredited secondary school is required; a GED will be accepted. Students must submit 16 academic credits, which should include, as a minimum, 4 units of English, 3 of math, and 2 each of history or social studies and natural science, including a lab course. Remaining credits should be distributed in a foreign language, speech, music, art, and other college preparatory electives. An interview is recommended. AP and CLEP credits are accepted. Important factors in the admissions decision are advanced placement or honors courses.Students must successfully complete at least 126 credit hours, including a core curriculum, and maintain a minimum GPA of 2.0. Required courses include English composition, religion, philosophy, speech fundamentals, math, and a computer course. **Procedure:** Freshmen are admitted to all sessions. Entrance exams should be taken during the junior or senior year. There are early admissions and rolling admissions plans. Check with the school for current application deadlines. The fall 2014 application fee was $25. Applications are accepted on-line. **Transfer Students:** Transfer applicants with fewer than 24 semester hours of credit at an accredited institution must submit SAT or ACT scores and must have maintained a minimum GPA of 2.0. If the student is older than 23 years of age, SAT /ACT scores need not be submitted. 32 of 126 credits required for the bachelor's degree must be completed at UDM. **International Students:** The school actively recruits these students. They must take the college's own test.

ADMISSIONS: Admissions Counselors. E-Mail: *admissions@udmercy.edu* Web: *www.udmercy.edu*

FINANCIAL AID: UDM is a member of CSS. The FAFSA is required. Check with the school for current application deadlines.

UNIVERSITY OF MICHIGAN/ANN ARBOR   E-5
www.umich.edu

Ann Arbor, MI 48109	(734) 764-7433
Fax: (734) 936-0740	Email: info@umich.edu
Full-time: 13478 men, 13019 women	Faculty: 2174; I, +$
	Ph.D.s: 91%
Part-time: 504 men, 365 women	Student/Faculty: 12 to 1
Graduate: 8863 men, 6946 women	Tuition: $12,634 ($37,782)
Year: trimesters, summer session	Freshman Class: 31613
Room & Board: $9468	applied, 16006 accepted, 6496 enrolled
SAT CR/M/W: 640/690/660 ACT: 30	CEEB CODE: 1839
Application Deadline: February 1	MOST COMPETITIVE

The University of Michigan/Ann Arbor, founded in 1817, is the main campus of the University of Michigan. The public institution offers undergraduate programs in the arts and sciences, architecture, business administration, education, engineering, fine arts, kinesiology, natural resources, nursing, and professional studies, as well as a wide range of graduate and professional programs. Figures in the above capsule and in this profile are approximate. There are 12 undergraduate schools and 18 graduate schools. In addition to regional accreditation, UM has baccalaureate program accreditation with AACSB, ABET, ACEJMC, ACPE, ADA, ASLA, CSWE, NAAB, NASAD, NASM, NCATE, NLN, and SAF. The 3177-acre campus is in a suburban area 38 miles west of Detroit. Including any residence halls, there are 538 buildings.

STUDENT LIFE: 64% of undergraduates are from Michigan. Others are from 50 states, 86 foreign countries, and Canada. 66% are White; 11% Asian American. **Male To Female Ratio:** 0.9:1. The average age

of freshmen is 18; all undergraduates, 20. 4% do not continue beyond their first year; 90% remain to graduate. **Housing:** 11,664 students can be accommodated in college housing, which includes single-sex and coed dorms, on-campus apartments, and married student housing. In addition, there are honors houses, language houses, special-interest houses, fraternity houses, sorority houses, substance-free dorm rooms, women-in-science housing, and cooperative housing. On-campus housing is guaranteed for the freshman year only, is available on a first-come, first-served basis, and is available on a lottery system for upperclassmen. 63% of students commute. All students may keep cars.

FACULTY/CLASSROOMS: 60% of faculty are male; 40% are female. All teach and do research. No introductory courses are taught by graduate students. The average class size in an introductory lecture is 70; in a laboratory is 18; and in a regular course is 31.

PROGRAMS OF STUDY: UM confers B.A., B.S., A.B.Ed., B.B.A., B.D.A., B.F.A., B.G.S., B.Mus., B.Mus.A., B.S.Chem., B.S.E., B.S.Ed. and B.S.N. degrees. Master's and Doctoral degrees are also awarded. Bachelor's degrees are awarded in AGRICULTURE (environmental studies), BIOLOGICAL SCIENCE (biochemistry, biology/biological science, biophysics, botany, cell biology, ecology, evolutionary biology, microbiology, molecular biology, and neurosciences), BUSINESS (business administration and management, organizational behavior, and sports management), COMMUNICATIONS AND THE ARTS (Arabic, art, art history and appreciation, audio technology, ceramic art and design, classical languages, classics, communications, comparative literature, creative writing, dance, design, dramatic arts, drawing, English, English literature, fiber/textiles/weaving, film arts, French, German, Germanic languages and literature, graphic design, Greek, Greek (modern), Hebrew, historic preservation, illustration, industrial design, Italian, jazz, Latin, linguistics, literature, metal/jewelry, music, music history and appreciation, music performance, music technology, music theory and composition, musical theater, painting, performing arts, photography, printmaking, Russian, Russian languages and literature, sculpture, Spanish, speech/debate/rhetoric, theater design, video, and winds), COMPUTER AND PHYSICAL SCIENCE (astronomy, astrophysics, atmospheric sciences and meteorology, chemistry, computer science, earth science, environmental geology, geology, geoscience, mathematics, oceanography, physics, and statistics), EDUCATION (athletic training, elementary education, music education, and physical education), ENGINEERING AND ENVIRONMENTAL DESIGN (aeronautical engineering, aerospace studies, architecture, biomedical engineering, chemical engineering, civil engineering, computer engineering, electrical/electronics engineering, engineering, engineering physics, environmental engineering, geological engineering, geophysical engineering, industrial engineering, materials engineering, materials science, mechanical engineering, naval architecture and marine engineering, and nuclear engineering), HEALTH PROFESSIONS (dental hygiene, exercise science, nursing, pharmaceutical chemistry, pharmaceutical science, pharmacy, and radiological science), SOCIAL SCIENCE (African studies, African American studies, American studies, anthropology, archeology, Asian/Oriental studies, behavioral science, biblical studies, Caribbean studies, classical/ancient civilization, cognitive science, Eastern European studies, economics, European studies, Hispanic American studies, history, humanities, interdisciplinary studies, international studies, Islamic studies, Judaic studies, Latin American studies, liberal arts/general studies, medieval studies, Mexican-American/Chicano studies, Middle Eastern studies, Near Eastern studies, philosophy, physical fitness/movement, political science/government, psychology, public affairs, Puerto Rican studies, religion, Russian and Slavic studies, social science, sociology, Western European studies, and women's studies). Psychology, engineering, and business administration have the largest enrollments.

ACTIVITIES: 16% of men belong to 40 national fraternities; 20% of women belong to 1 local and 27 national sororities. There are 1303 groups on campus, including art, band, cheerleading, chess, choir, chorale, chorus, computers, dance, debate, drama, environmental, ethnic, film, forensics, gay, honors, international, jazz band, literary magazine, marching band, musical theater, newspaper, opera, orchestra, pep band, photography, political, professional, radio and TV, religious, social, social service, student government, symphony, and yearbook. Popular campus events include Martin Luther King Day, Native American PowWow, and FestiFall. <u>Sports:</u> There are 14 intercollegiate sports for men and 14 for women, and 23 intramural sports for men and 23 for women. Facilities include a 107,501-seat stadium, a 1000-seat gym, an indoor track and tennis complex, an indoor practice center, 3 recreational buildings, 2 golf courses, a natatorium and separate swimming pools, an ice arena, soccer and field hockey fields, and several other athletic arenas, the largest of which seats 13,000. <u>Graduates:</u> From July 1, 2013 to June 30, 2014, 6457 bachelor's degrees were awarded. The most popular majors were engineering (18%), psychology (10%), and economics (6%). In an average class, 70% graduate in 4 years or less, 86% graduate in 5 years or less, and 88% graduate in 6 years or less.

<u>SERVICES:</u> Counseling and information services are available, as is tutoring in some subjects, introductory English and math There is a reader service for the blind. <u>Library/Resources:</u> The 27 libraries contain 10.6 million volumes, 10.6 million microform items, 126,011 audio/video tapes/CDs/DVDs, and subscribe to 83,062 periodicals including electronic. Computerized library services include interlibrary loans, database searching, Internet access, and Wi-Fi capability. Special learning facilities include an art gallery, natural history museum, planetarium, radio station, TV station, archeology museum, botanical gardens, two historical museums, electronics music studio, and digital media commons. <u>Physically Challenged Students:</u> 99% of the campus is accessible. Facilities include wheelchair ramps, elevators, special parking, specially equipped restrooms, special class scheduling, lowered drinking fountains, lowered telephones, special housing. para-transit service, specially equipped vans, talking calculators, telecommunication devices for the deaf, and an adaptive technology computing site that includes a high-speed scanner, voice input and voice output, braille display and large-print screens, and a braille printer. <u>Special:</u> There are 22 national honor societies, including Phi Beta Kappa, and a freshman honors program. <u>Visiting:</u> There are regularly scheduled orientations for prospective students, Students visits include placement testing, academic advising, course registration, social activities, and informational programs on student life, computing resources, campus safety, and career planning. There are guides for informal visits and visitors may sit in on classes. To schedule a visit, contact the Office of Undergraduate Admissions. <u>Campus Safety and Security:</u> Measures include 24-hour foot and vehicle patrol, emergency notification system, self-defense education, and security escort services. There are shuttle buses, emergency telephones, lighted pathways/sidewalks, controlled access to dorms/residences, a nite-owl bus service, officer bicycle patrols, and a taxi service.

<u>REQUIREMENTS:</u> Applicants must submit either SAT or ACT scores. Applicants must be graduates of accredited secondary schools or have earned a GED. The university requires 16 Carnegie units, including 4 in English, 3 in math (4 for engineering majors), 3 in history and social studies, 2 in foreign language, and 3 in science. The following are recommended electives: 1 unit of hands-on computer study and 2 units of fine or performing arts. An essay is required for all applicants. Students applying to the School of Art must submit a portfolio; those applying to the School of Music must present an audition. AP and CLEP credits are accepted. Important factors in the admissions decision are advanced placement or honors courses, evidence of special talent, and geographical diversity. Academic requirements vary by program. For the College of Literature, Science, and the Arts, most students must fulfill requirements in English, race and ethnicity, and foreign language. Students must also complete 9 semester hours each of humanities, social science, and natural science/math. Students must meet the quantitative reasoning requirement, designed to ensure proficiency in using and analyzing quantitative information. To graduate, students must complete 120 to 128 semester hours, including 24 to 30 in a major field, with a minimum GPA of 2.0. <u>Procedure:</u> Freshmen are admitted to all sessions. Entrance exams should be taken by the end of the junior year or the beginning of the senior. There are deferred admissions and rolling admissions plans. Applications should be filed by February 1 for fall entry; October 1 for winter entry; February 1 for spring entry; and February 1 for summer entry. The fall 2014 application fee was $65. 9409 applicants were on the 2014 waiting list; 3724 were admitted. Applications are accepted on-line. <u>Transfer Students:</u> 1032 transfer

students enrolled in 2013-2014. A minimum college GPA of 3.0 is required for junior-level transfers. 60 of 120 credits required for the bachelor's degree must be completed at UM. <u>International Students:</u> There are 1644 international students enrolled. They must take the TOEFL with a minimum score of 570 on the paper-based TOEFL (PBT) or 88 on the Internet-based version (iBT) or take the MELAB. They must also take the SAT or ACT.

<u>ADMISSIONS:</u> 51% of the 2014-2015 applicants were accepted. 95% of the current freshmen were in the top fifth of their class; 99% were in the top two fifths. There were 83 National Merit finalists. <u>Admissions Contact:</u> Web: *www.admissions.umich.edu*

<u>FINANCIAL AID:</u> In 2014-2015, 47% of all full-time freshmen and 48% of continuing full-time students received some form of financial aid. 48% of all full-time freshmen and continuing full-time students received need-based aid. Need-based scholarships or need-based grants averaged $11,656; need-based self-help aid (loans and jobs) averaged $7,640; non-need-based athletic scholarships averaged $29,281; and other non-need-based awards and non-need-based scholarships averaged $5,450. UM is a member of CSS. The FAFSA, and noncustodial profile and tax returns is required. The priority date for freshman financial aid applications for fall entry is April 29. The deadline for filing freshman financial aid applications for fall entry is May 30.

UNIVERSITY OF MICHIGAN/DEARBORN   E-5
www.umdearborn.edu

Dearborn, MI 48128	(313) 593-5100
	(313) 593-5000
Fax: (313) 436-9167	Email: admissions@umd.umich.edu
Full-time: 2441 men, 2428 women	Faculty: IIA, ++$
Part-time: 1168 men, 1291 women	Ph.D.s: 80%
Graduate: 861 men, 600 women	Student/Faculty: n/av
Year: semesters, summer session	Tuition: $9885 ($21,862)
Room & Board: n/app	Freshman Class: 4807 applied, 2908 accepted, 889 enrolled
	CEEB CODE: 1861
Application Deadline: open	VERY COMPETITIVE

The University of Michigan/Dearborn, founded in 1959, is a public, comprehensive commuter institution that is part of the University of Michigan system. The emphasis of its degree programs is on the liberal arts, management, engineering, and education. There are 4 undergraduate schools and 4 graduate schools. In addition to regional accreditation, UM - Dearborn has baccalaureate program accreditation with AACSB, ABET, and NCATE. The 196-acre campus is in a suburban area 10 miles from Detroit. Including any residence halls, there are 20 buildings.

<u>STUDENT LIFE:</u> 95% of undergraduates are from Michigan. Others are from 33 states, 76 foreign countries, and Canada. 68% are White; 11% African American. <u>Male To Female Ratio:</u> 1.0:1. The average age of freshmen is 18; all undergraduates, 25. <u>Housing:</u> College-sponsored housing includes Alcohol is not permitted. All students commute. All students may keep cars.

<u>FACULTY/CLASSROOMS:</u> No introductory courses are taught by graduate students. The average class size in a regular course is 29.

<u>PROGRAMS OF STUDY:</u> UM - Dearborn confers B.A., B.S., B.B.A., B.G.S., B.S.A. and B.S.E. degrees. Master's degrees are also awarded. Bachelor's degrees are awarded in AGRICULTURE (environmental studies), BIOLOGICAL SCIENCE (biochemistry, biology/biological science, and microbiology), BUSINESS (accounting, business administration and management, management information systems, management science, marketing management, and supply chain management), COMMUNICATIONS AND THE ARTS (art history and appreciation, arts administration/management, communications, English, French, language arts, and music history and appreciation), COMPUTER AND PHYSICAL SCIENCE (chemistry, computer science, geology, mathematics, physics, science, and software engineering), EDUCATION (early childhood education, education, elementary education, mathematics education, science

education, secondary education, social studies education, and special education), ENGINEERING AND ENVIRONMENTAL DESIGN (bioengineering, computer engineering, electrical/electronics engineering technology, engineering, environmental science, industrial engineering technology, manufacturing engineering, and mechanical engineering), HEALTH PROFESSIONS (biology and health), SOCIAL SCIENCE (African American studies, American studies, anthropology, behavioral science, criminal justice, economics, Hispanic American studies, history, humanities, international studies, liberal arts/general studies, philosophy, political science/government, psychology, social studies, sociology, urban studies, women and gender studies, and women's studies). Electrical engineering and business administration is the strongest academically. Mechanical engineering, prebusiness, and business administration have the largest enrollments.

ACTIVITIES: 2% of men and 1% of women belong to 7 national fraternities; 2% of women belong to 4 national sororities. There are 129 groups on campus, including art, cheerleading, chess, chorale, computers, dance, debate, drama, environmental, ethnic, film, gay, honors, international, jazz band, literary magazine, newspaper, pep band, photography, political, professional, radio and TV, religious, social, social service, and student government. Popular campus events include Martin Luther King Diversity Celebration, Native American Pow Wow and Fall Fest. **Sports:** There are 1 intercollegiate sports for men and 2 for women, and 21 intramural sports for men and 20 for women. Facilities include a 1200-seat gym, an ice rink, an indoor/outdoor track, a playing field, sand volleyball courts, weight and exercise rooms, outdoor tennis courts, and river rouge trail. **Graduates:** From July 1, 2013 to June 30, 2014, 1227 bachelor's degrees were awarded. The most popular majors were psychology (8%), business/marketing (7%), and communication/journalism (5%). In an average class, 14% graduate in 4 years or less, 41% graduate in 5 years or less, and 50% graduate in 6 years or less.

SERVICES: Counseling and information services are available, as is tutoring in most subjects, science, computer classes, composition, and math There is a reader service for the blind, and remedial math, reading, and writing. **Library/Resources:** The library contains 382,065 volumes, 544,977 microform items, 6,070 audio/video tapes/CDs/DVDs, and subscribes to 16,828 periodicals including electronic. Computerized library services include interlibrary loans, database searching, and Internet access. Special learning facilities include an art gallery, natural history museum, radio station, TV station, a nature preserve, an Armenian research center, Early Childhood Education Center, an engineering education and practice center, a National Historic Landmark, and an astronomy dome. **Physically Challenged Students:** All of the campus is accessible. Facilities include wheelchair ramps, elevators, special parking, specially equipped restrooms, lowered drinking fountains, and lowered telephones. **Special:** UM-Dearborn offers internships, study abroad, work-study and accelerated degree programs, a general studies degree, a dual major in engineering math, student-designed majors, and co-op programs in engineering, business administration, and arts and sciences. Nondegree study and pass/fail options are possible. There are 1 national honor societies, a freshman honors program, and 2 departmental honors programs. **Visiting:** There are regularly scheduled orientations for prospective students, consisting of a tour, a student panel, academic unit introduction, and campus life sessions. There are guides for informal visits and visitors may sit in on classes. To schedule a visit, contact the Admissions Office. **Campus Safety and Security:** Measures include 24-hour foot and vehicle patrol, self-defense education, and security escort services. There are emergency telephones, lighted pathways/sidewalks, vehicle etching, crime prevention day, CPR training, and a rape awareness seminar.

REQUIREMENTS: Other admissions requirements normally include graduation from an accredited secondary school; recommended high school units include 4 years each in math, English, and history, 3 each in science and foreign language, and 1 each in art and information technology. The GED is accepted with a minimum score of 55. An essay and interview are recommended. A GPA of 3.0 is required. AP credits are accepted. Important factors in the admissions decision are advanced placement or honors courses, recommendations by school officials, and leadership record. Each college within the university has its own requirements. To graduate, students must complete 120 to

128 credit hours. **Procedure:** Freshmen are admitted to all sessions. Entrance exams should be taken in the spring of the junior year or the fall of the senior year. There are deferred admissions and rolling admissions plans. Check with the school for current application deadlines. The fall 2014 application fee was $30. Notification is sent on a rolling basis. Applications are accepted on-line. **Transfer Students:** 843 transfer students enrolled in 2013-2014. Applicants are required to have 25 to 30 transferable semester/credit hours; if they have fewer than 25, the SAT or ACT is mandatory. The required minimum GPA ranges from 2.5 to 3.0, depending on major. 60 of 128 credits required for the bachelor's degree must be completed at UM - Dearborn. **International Students:** There are 75 international students enrolled. They must take the TOEFL with a minimum score of 550 on the paper-based TOEFL (PBT) or 80 on the Internet-based version (iBT) or take the MELAB, or the APIEL exam. They must also take the SAT or ACT, scoring 22.

ADMISSIONS: 60% of the 2014-2015 applicants were accepted. The ACT scores were 29% between 21 and 23, 28% between 24 and 26, 13% between 27 and 28, and 12% above 28. 14 freshmen graduated first in their class. **Admissions Contact:** Deb Peffer, Director of Admissions and Orientation. E-Mail: *admissions@umd.umich.edu* Web: *www.umd.umich.edu*

FINANCIAL AID: The average freshman award was $10,662. Need-based scholarships or need-based grants averaged $5,644 need-based self-help aid (loans and jobs) averaged $4,199; and $3,368 from other forms of aid. The average financial indebtedness of the 2014 graduate was $23,437. The FAFSA is required. Check with the school for current application deadlines.

UNIVERSITY OF MICHIGAN-FLINT   E-4
www.umflint.edu

Flint, MI 48502   **(810) 762-3300**

Fax: (810) 762-3272	**Email:** admissions@unflint.edu
Full-time: 1960 men, 2530 women	**Faculty:** 287; IIA, av$
Part-time: 889 men, 1764 women	**Ph.D.s:** 69%
Graduate: 556 men, 856 women	**Student/Faculty:** 15 to 1
Year: semesters, summer session	**Tuition:** $9844 ($18,796)
Room & Board: $7703	**Freshman Class:** 3003 applied, 2345 accepted, 724 enrolled
SAT CR/M/W: 610/595/580 **ACT:** 21	**CEEB CODE:** 1853
Application Deadline: August 20	**COMPETITIVE+**

The University of Michigan-Flint, established in 1956, is a public institution offering programs in the liberal arts and sciences, education, health professions, and business. Figures in the above capsule and in this profile are approximate. There are 4 undergraduate schools and 6 graduate schools. In addition to regional accreditation, UM-Flint has baccalaureate program accreditation with AACSB, APTA, CSWE, NASM, NCATE, NLN, AACN, ACS, CCNE, and JRCERT. The 73-acre campus is in an urban area 60 miles northwest of Detroit, 50 miles east of Lansing, and 55 miles north of Ann Arbor. Including any residence halls, there are 9 buildings.

STUDENT LIFE: 92% of undergraduates are from Michigan. Others are from 37 states, 34 foreign countries, and Canada. 97% are from public schools. 68% are White; 11% African American. **Male To Female Ratio:** 1.5:1. The average age of freshmen is 19; all undergraduates, 26. 20% do not continue beyond their first year; 40% remain to graduate. **Housing:** 310 students can be accommodated in college housing, which includes coed dorms and off-campus apartments. On-campus housing is available on a first-come and first-served basis. 96% of students commute. Alcohol is not permitted. All students may keep cars.

FACULTY/CLASSROOMS: 42% of faculty are male; 58% are female. All teach and do research. No introductory courses are taught by graduate students. The average class size in an introductory lecture is 24; in a laboratory is 17; and in a regular course is 20.

PROGRAMS OF STUDY: UM-Flint confers B.A., B.S., B.A.S., B.B.A., B.F.A., B.S.E., B.S.N., B.S.W. , B.M., B.M.E. and B.I.S. degrees.

Master's and Doctoral degrees are also awarded. Bachelor's degrees are awarded in BIOLOGICAL SCIENCE (biology/biological science and ecology), BUSINESS (accounting, banking and finance, business administration and management, human resources, and marketing/retailing/merchandising), COMMUNICATIONS AND THE ARTS (art, communications, dramatic arts, English, French, music, and Spanish), COMPUTER AND PHYSICAL SCIENCE (applied science, chemistry, computer science, mathematics, physical sciences, physics, and science), EDUCATION (early childhood education, education, elementary education, foreign languages education, music education, and secondary education), ENGINEERING AND ENVIRONMENTAL DESIGN (engineering), HEALTH PROFESSIONS (environmental health science, health care administration, health science, medical laboratory technology, nursing, physical therapy, and radiation therapy), SOCIAL SCIENCE (anthropology, applied psychology, community psychology, criminal justice, economics, geography, history, philosophy, political science/government, psychology, public administration, social science, social work, sociology, and urban studies). Business and Nursing is the strongest academically. Business, education, and health sciences have the largest enrollments.

ACTIVITIES: 5% of men belong to 6 national fraternities; 4% of women belong to 7 national sororities. There are 103 groups on campus, including art, band, cheerleading, choir, chorale, chorus, computers, dance, debate, drama, ethnic, gay, honors, jazz band, literary magazine, musical theater, newspaper, political, professional, radio and TV, religious, social, social service, and student government. Popular campus events include Welcome Back Week, Winter Block Party and Presidents Ball. **Sports:** There are 13 intramural sports for men and 12 for women. Facilities include a recreation building housing a multipurpose gym, racquetball courts, a weight training area, and a swimming pool. **Graduates:** From July 1, 2013 to June 30, 2014, 1102 bachelor's degrees were awarded. The most popular majors were registered nursing (18%), health care administration / management (7%), and business administration / management (5%). 179 companies recruited on campus in 2013-2014. In an average class, 11% graduate in 4 years or less, 31% graduate in 5 years or less, and 39% graduate in 6 years or less.

SERVICES: Counseling and information services are available, as is tutoring in every subject. There is a reader service for the blind, remedial math, reading, and writing. There are sign language interpreters, note takers, and testing accomodations **Library/Resources:** The library contains 353,617 volumes, 600,610 microform items, 10,581 audio/video tapes/CDs/DVDs, and subscribes to 559 periodicals including electronic. Computerized library services include interlibrary loans, database searching, and Internet access. Special learning facilities include an art gallery and radio station. **Physically Challenged Students:** 97% of the campus is accessible. Facilities include wheelchair ramps, elevators, special parking, specially equipped restrooms, special class scheduling, lowered drinking fountains, lowered telephones. Telephone for the hearing impaired. Reasonable accommodations may be made for students with documented disabilities. **Special:** Special arrangements include co-op programs and dual majors, student-designed majors, cross-registration with Mott Community College, internships, study abroad, work-study, a 3-2 engineering program, an accelerated business degree, a general studies degree, nondegree study, and pass/fail options. There are 5 national honor societies, including Phi Beta Kappa, a freshman honors program, and 47 departmental honors programs. **Visiting:** There are regularly scheduled orientations for prospective students. There are guides for informal visits and visitors may sit in on classes. To schedule a visit, contact the Admissions Office. **Campus Safety and Security:** Measures include 24-hour foot and vehicle patrol, emergency notification system, self-defense education, and security escort services. There are shuttle buses, emergency telephones, and lighted pathways/sidewalks.

REQUIREMENTS: The SAT or ACT is required, with the ACT preferred. Graduation from secondary school is required, with 4 years of English, 3 each of math and social studies, and 2 of science. The GED is accepted. SAT: Subject tests and an interview are recommended. Applied music students must audition. A GPA of 2.7 is required. AP and CLEP credits are accepted. Important factors in the admissions decision are advanced placement or honors courses, evidence of special talent, and leadership record. To graduate, all stu-

dents must complete at least 120 credits, including 30 to 70 in the major along with satisfying all major requirements, and maintain a GPA of 2.0. Distribution requirements total 50 credits in English composition, humanities, fine arts, social science, and natural science. **Procedure:** Freshmen are admitted to all sessions. Entrance exams should be taken in the spring of the junior year or fall of the senior year. There are deferred admissions and rolling admissions plans. Applications should be filed by August 20 for fall entry; December 1 for winter entry. The fall 2014 application fee was $30. Notification is sent on a rolling basis. Applications are accepted on-line. **Transfer Students:** 857 transfer students enrolled in 2013-2014. Applicants must have at least 12 college credits and a minimum GPA of 2.0 in transferable courses. An associate degree and an interview are recommended. 45 of 120 credits required for the bachelor's degree must be completed at UM-Flint. **International Students:** There are 425 international students enrolled. The school actively recruits these students. They must take the TOEFL with a minimum score of 500 on the paper-based TOEFL (PBT) or 61 on the Internet-based version (iBT). Students must take the MELAB, or IELTS. They must also take the SAT or ACT.

ADMISSIONS: 78% of the 2014-2015 applicants were accepted. The SAT scores for the 2014-2015 freshman class were: Critical Reading--30% below 500, 10% between 500 and 599, 40% between 600 and 699, and 20% between 700 and 800; Math--20% below 500, 30% between 500 and 599, 30% between 600 and 699, and 20% between 700 and 800; Writing--20% below 500, 50% between 500 and 599, and 30% between 700 and 800. The ACT scores were 45% below 21, 25% between 21 and 23, 16% between 24 and 26, 7% between 27 and 28, and 7% above 28. 34% of the current freshmen were in the top fifth of their class; 63% were in the top two fifths. 7 freshmen graduated first in their class. **Admissions Contact:** Jon Davidson, Director of Admissions. E-Mail: *admissions@list.umich.edu* Web: *www.umflint.edu*

FINANCIAL AID: In 2014-2015, 61% of all full-time freshmen and 73% of continuing full-time students received some form of financial aid. 41% of all full-time freshmen and 54% of continuing full-time students received need-based aid. The average freshman award was $10,259. Need-based scholarships or need-based grants averaged $5,897; need-based self-help aid (loans and jobs) averaged $3,699; and other non-need-based awards and non-need-based scholarships averaged $4,246. Average annual earnings from campus work are $2398. The average financial indebtedness of the 2014 graduate was $27,336. The FAFSA, and Institution's own financial form spring/summer sessions only is required. The deadline for filing freshman financial aid applications for fall entry is March 1.

WAYNE STATE UNIVERSITY   E-5
wayne.edu

Detroit, MI 48202   (313) 577-2424

Fax: (313) 577-7536	Email: admissions@wayne.edu
Full-time: 5367 men, 6663 women	Faculty: I, -$
Part-time: 2837 men, 3480 women	Ph.D.s: n/av
Graduate: 3965 men, 5266 women	Student/Faculty: 15 to 1
Year: semesters, summer session	Tuition: $12,350 ($26,592)
Room & Board: $9713	Freshman Class: 12199 applied, 9433 accepted, 2195 enrolled
ACT: 23	CEEB CODE: 1898
Application Deadline: August 1	COMPETITIVE

Wayne State University, founded in 1868, is a nationally recognized research institution dedicated to preparing students to excel in an increasingly fast-paced and interconnected global society. As Michigan's only urban research university, WSU occupies a unique niche as a catalyst for investigating and helping to resolve the myriad issues facing residents of the contemporary urban environment. WSU prides itself on providing world-class education in the real world on six campuses throughout metro Detroit. There are 9 undergraduate schools and 11 graduate schools. In addition to regional accreditation, Wayne State; WSU has baccalaureate program accreditation with AACSB, ABET, ABFSE, ACPE, CSWE, NASM, ACS, CAA. CCNE, IAA, MDE, ABFSE, JRCERT, ACEND, NAACLS, NASD, NAST, and NASM. The 192-acre campus is in an urban area 2 miles north of downtown Detroit in the New Center area. Including any residence halls, there are 90 buildings.

STUDENT LIFE: 98% of undergraduates are from Michigan. Others are from 40 states, 43 foreign countries, and Canada. 54% are White; 20% African American. **Male To Female Ratio:** 1.3:1. The average age of freshmen is 18; all undergraduates, 24. 25% do not continue beyond their first year; 75% remain to graduate. **Housing:** 3070 students can be accommodated in college housing, which includes single-sex and coed dorms and on-campus apartments. Special Interest living communities are available in the dormitories. On-campus housing is available on a first-come and first-served basis. 88% of students commute. All students may keep cars.

FACULTY/CLASSROOMS: 55% of faculty are male; 45% are female. No introductory courses are taught by graduate students.

PROGRAMS OF STUDY: Master's and Doctoral degrees are also awarded. Bachelor's degrees are awarded in BIOLOGICAL SCIENCE (biochemistry, biology/biological science, biophysics, and nutrition), BUSINESS (accounting, banking and finance, business administration and management, funeral home services, labor studies, management information systems, marketing/retailing/merchandising, organizational leadership and management, and supply chain management), COMMUNICATIONS AND THE ARTS (art, art history and appreciation, classics, communications, communication science, dance, design, dramatic arts, English, film arts, fine arts, German, information technology, journalism, language arts, linguistics, media arts, music, public relations, romance languages and literature, Russian, Slavic languages, and theatre arts), COMPUTER AND PHYSICAL SCIENCE (astronomy, chemistry, computer science, geology, information sciences and systems, mathematics, physics, and radiological technology), EDUCATION (art education, elementary education, English education, health education, mathematics education, physical education, recreation education, science education, social studies education, special education, and technical education), ENGINEERING AND ENVIRONMENTAL DESIGN (biomedical engineering, chemical engineering, civil engineering, computer technology, construction management, electrical and computer engineering, electrical/electronics engineering, electrical/electronics engineering technology, electromechanical technology, environmental science, industrial engineering, industrial engineering technology, manufacturing technology, mechanical engineering, and mechanical engineering technology), HEALTH PROFESSIONS (biology, clinical science, exercise science, health science, kinesiology, nursing, public health, radiation therapy, and speech pathology/audiology), SOCIAL SCIENCE (African studies, anthropology, Asian/Oriental studies, communication sciences & disorders, criminal justice, dietetics, economics, food science, history, liberal arts/general studies, Near Eastern studies, philosophy, political science/government, psychology, public affairs, social work, sociology, urban studies, and women's studies). Medical school, engineering, and social work are the strongest academically. Biology, psychology, and engineering have the largest enrollments.

ACTIVITIES: There are 395 groups on campus, including art, band, cheerleading, chess, choir, chorale, chorus, communications, computers, dance, debate, drama, drill team, environmental, ethnic, film, forensics, gay, honors, international, jazz band, literary magazine, marching band, musical theater, newspaper, orchestra, pep band, photography, political, professional, radio and TV, religious, social, social service, student government, and symphony. Popular campus events include Student Organization Day, International Fair, and Detroit Festival of the Arts, and Alternatce Spring Break Detroit.

Sports: There are 8 intercollegiate sports for men and 8 for women, and 10 intramural sports for men and 10 for women. Facilities include WSU's athletic complex houses two full gymnasiums, a weight room, racquetball and squash courts, a competition swimming pool, an outdoor track, tennis courts, baseball fields, softball, and football fields and a football stadium. The recreation center includes weight rooms, exercise equipment, indoor basketball courts, an indoor track, climbing wall and ropes course, massage studios, women's only workout area, indoor putting greens, and much more.

Graduates: From July 1, 2013 to June 30, 2014, 3047 bachelor's degrees were awarded. The most popular majors were business, management, marketing, and related support services (17%), psychology (14%), and health professions and related programs (8%). 6054 companies recruited on campus in 2013-2014. In an average class, 13% graduate in 4 years or less, 25% graduate in 5 years or less, and 34% graduate in 6 years or less.

SERVICES: Counseling and information services are available, as is tutoring in every subject. There is a reader service for the blind, and remedial math, reading, and writing. Tutorial services are available through centralized counseling or academic departments. **Library/Resources:** The 6 libraries contain 2.8 million volumes. Computerized library services include interlibrary loans, database searching, Internet access, and Wi-Fi capability. Special learning facilities include an art gallery, natural history museum, planetarium, and radio station. **Physically Challenged Students:** All of the campus is accessible. Facilities include wheelchair ramps, elevators, special parking, specially equipped restrooms, lowered drinking fountains, lowered telephones, special housing. Educational accessibility services. **Special:** Special academic programs include internships, study abroad, on-campus work-study programs, accelerated degree programs in liberal arts and science, engineering, and nursing, co-op programs, non-degree study, double majors,l 3-2 engineering and computer science programs There are including Phi Beta Kappa, a freshman honors program, and 49 departmental honors programs. **Visiting:** There are regularly scheduled orientations for prospective students, including meeting with advisors, registering for classes, meeting upperclassmen, and touring the campus. There are guides for informal visits, visitors may sit in on classes, and stay overnight. To schedule a visit, contact the Office of Undergraduate Admissions. **Campus Safety and Security:** Measures include 24-hour foot and vehicle patrol, emergency notification system, self-defense education, and security escort services. There are shuttle buses, emergency telephones, lighted pathways/sidewalks, and controlled access to dorms/residences.

REQUIREMENTS: The ACT is required. At Wayne State, we know that students come from different backgrounds and experiences, which are things that make our students so great! That's why we look at each individual applicant as that - an individual. The Office of Undergraduate Admissions will review your grade-point average, ACT or SAT score and any other supporting documentation you provide us or we request from you. AP and CLEP credits are accepted. To graduate, students must complete at least 120 credit hours and have a minimum GPA of 2.0 for all WSU course work. Students must complete general education requirements, all school/college, departmental and program requirements, and complete at least thirty credits at Wayne State. **Procedure:** Freshmen are admitted to all sessions. Entrance exams should be taken the ACT or SAT should be taken in the junior year. There are deferred admissions and rolling admissions plans. Applications should be filed by August 1 for fall entry; January 1 for winter entry; May 1 for spring entry; and May 1 for summer entry, along with a $25 fee. Applications are accepted on-line. **Transfer Students:** 2775 transfer students enrolled in 2013-2014. You can be admitted to Wayne State as a transfer student if you have at least 24 transferable credits of previous college work and a minimum 2.5 cumulative grade-point average from all higher education institutions you've attended. Students who have completed an Associate Degree may be admitted with a grade point average of a 2.0 or better. 30 of 120 credits required for the bachelor's degree must be completed at Wayne State; WSU. **International Students:** There are 538 international students enrolled. The school actively recruits these students. They must take the TOEFL with a minimum score of 550 on the paper-based TOEFL (PBT) or 79 on the Internet-based version (iBT) or take the MELAB. They must also take the SAT or ACT.

ADMISSIONS: 77% of the 2014-2015 applicants were accepted. The ACT scores were 25% below 21, 28% between 21 and 23, 24% between 24 and 26, 11% between 27 and 28, and 13% above 28. 42% of the current freshmen were in the top fifth of their class; 72% were in the top two fifths. **Admissions Contact:** La Joyce Brown, Sr Director, Undergraduate Admissions. E-Mail: *admissions@wayne.edu* Web: *http://wayne.edu/admissions/undergrad/*

FINANCIAL AID: In 2014-2015, 92% of all full-time freshmen and 85% of continuing full-time students received some form of financial aid. 68% of all full-time freshmen and 67% of continuing full-time

students received need-based aid. WSU is a member of CSS. The FAFSA is required. The priority date for freshman financial aid applications for fall entry is March 31. The deadline for filing freshman financial aid applications for fall entry is March 31.

WESTERN MICHIGAN UNIVERSITY   D-5
www.wmich.edu

Kalamazoo, MI 49008	**(269) 387-1000**
	(269) 387-2000
Fax: (269) 387-2096	Email: ask-wmu@wmich.edu
Full-time: 7957 men, 7756 women	Faculty: 713; I, -$
Part-time: 1565 men, 1611 women	Ph.D.s: 79%
Graduate: 2178 men, 2847 women	Student/Faculty: 22 to 1
Year: semesters, summer session	Tuition: $10,685 ($24,917)
Room & Board: $8943	Freshman Class: 14008 applied, 11775 accepted, 3012 enrolled
ACT: 22	CEEB CODE: 1902
Application Deadline: open	**COMPETITIVE**

Western Michigan University is a dynamic, globally engaged institution that combines the resources of a national research university with the support and personal attention often found at a small college. There are 7 undergraduate schools and 1 graduate school. In addition to regional accreditation, WMU has baccalaureate program accreditation with AACSB, ABET, ADA, CSWE, FIDER, NASAD, NASM, NCATE, AABI, ACOTE, ACCGC, CAATE, CCNE, NASD, and NAST. The 1200-acre campus is in an urban area 140 miles west of Detroit and 140 miles east of Chicago. Including any residence halls, there are 151 buildings.

STUDENT LIFE: 89% of undergraduates are from Michigan. Others are from 41 states, 64 foreign countries, and Canada. 70% are White; 11% African American. **Male To Female Ratio:** 1.0:1. The average age of freshmen is 18; all undergraduates, 22. 22% do not continue beyond their first year; 78% remain to graduate. **Housing:** 5825 students can be accommodated in college housing, which includes single-sex and coed dorms, on-campus apartments, off-campus apartments, and married student housing. In addition, there are honors houses, special-interest houses, fraternity houses, sorority houses, Second year experience, and transfer student communities. On-campus housing is guaranteed for all 4 years, is available on a first-come, and first-served basis. 72% of students commute. All students may keep cars.

FACULTY/CLASSROOMS: 50% of faculty are male; 50% are female. Graduate students teach 24% of introductory courses. The average class size in an introductory lecture is 94; in a laboratory is 23; and in a regular course is 33.

PROGRAMS OF STUDY: WMU confers B.A., B.S., B.B.A., B.F.A., B.Mus., B.S.E., B.S.N. and B.S.W. degrees. Master's and Doctoral degrees are also awarded. Bachelor's degrees are awarded in AGRICULTURE (environmental studies), BIOLOGICAL SCIENCE (biochemistry and biology/biological science), BUSINESS (accounting, banking and finance, business administration and management, business economics, entrepreneurial studies, fashion merchandising, finance, human resources, management information systems, marketing/retailing/merchandising, personal financial planning, recreation and leisure services, supply chain management, and tourism), COMMUNICATIONS AND THE ARTS (advertising, art history, art, communications, creative writing, dance, dramatic arts, English, film, television and digital media, French, German, graphic design, jazz, journalism, Latin, music, music performance, music theory and composition, musical theater, performing arts, public relations, Spanish, telecommunications, theater design, and theatre studies), COMPUTER AND PHYSICAL SCIENCE (applied mathematics, chemistry, computer information systems, computer science, earth science, geochemistry, geology, geophysics and seismology, hydrogeology, mathematics, physics, and statistics), EDUCATION (art education, athletic training, business education, early childhood education, education, education of the emotionally handicapped, education of the mentally handicapped, elementary education, foreign languages education, health education, health information management, middle

school education, music education, physical education, secondary education, and special education), ENGINEERING AND ENVIRONMENTAL DESIGN (aerospace engineering, aircraft mechanics, airline piloting and navigation, aviation administration/management, chemical engineering, city/community/regional planning, civil engineering, computer engineering, construction engineering, drafting and design technology, electrical/electronics engineering, engineering management, graphic and printing production, industrial engineering, interior design, manufacturing engineering, manufacturing technology, mechanical engineering, paper and pulp science, and paper engineering), HEALTH PROFESSIONS (biomedical science, community health work, exercise science, music therapy, nursing, occupational therapy, and speech pathology/audiology), SOCIAL SCIENCE (African studies, anthropology, behavioral science, child care/child and family studies, clothing and textiles management/production/services, criminal justice, dietetics, economics, family/consumer studies, food production/management/services, gender studies, geography, history, interdisciplinary studies, international studies, philosophy, political science/government, psychology, public history/archives, religion, social work, sociology, textiles and clothing, and women's studies). Business, nursing, and biomedical sciences have the largest enrollments.

ACTIVITIES: 5% of men belong to 16 national fraternities; 6% of women belong to 12 national sororities. There are 327 groups on campus, including art, band, cheerleading, chess, choir, chorale, chorus, computers, dance, drama, environmental, ethnic, film, gay, honors, international, jazz band, literary magazine, marching band, musical theater, newspaper, opera, orchestra, pep band, photography, political, professional, radio and TV, religious, social, social service, student government, and symphony. Popular campus events include Campus Classic, CommUniversity, Bronco Bash and Family Weekend. **Sports:** There are 6 intercollegiate sports for men and 9 for women, and 11 intramural sports for men and 11 for women. Facilities include an 240,000 sq ft recreation center designed as a sports village, which includes a recreational swimming pool, a swirl pool, weight and fitness room with more than 100 stations, facilities for basketball, floor hockey, and indoor soccer, a climbing wall, an elevated track for jogging, facilities for aerobics, indoor cycling, badminton, tennis, and volleyball. The field house includes a 5800-seat arena for basketball and volleyball competition and facilities for gymnasts. There is also a 400-meter Olympic model Martin-surface track, a cross-country course, tennis courts, a 30,000-seat stadium, competition swimming pool, and an ice arena. **Graduates:** From July 1, 2013 to June 30, 2014, 3887 bachelor's degrees were awarded. The most popular majors were business/marketing (20%), health professions and related programs (10%), and education (9%). 442 companies recruited on campus in 2013-2014. In an average class, 23% graduate in 4 years or less, 46% graduate in 5 years or less, and 54% graduate in 6 years or less.

SERVICES: Counseling and information services are available, as is tutoring in most subjects. There is a reader service for the blind, remedial math, reading, and writing. **Library/Resources:** The 4 libraries contain 2.0 million volumes, 2.1 million microform items, 26,191 audio/video tapes/CDs/DVDs, and subscribe to 108,885 periodicals including electronic. Computerized library services include interlibrary loans, database searching, Internet access, and Wi-Fi capability. Special learning facilities include an art gallery, radio station, aviation flight simulators, electron microscope, particle accelerator, a paper manufacturing and fiber recovery pilot plant, a business technology and research park, health education facility, and numerous specialized labs in the academic departments. **Physically Challenged Students:** 85% of the campus is accessible. Facilities include wheelchair ramps, elevators, special parking, specially equipped restrooms, special class scheduling, lowered drinking fountains, lowered telephones, special housing. The University contracts with Metro to provide door-to-door services with a lift as requested, and adaptive computer equipment are also available. **Special:** Cross-registration is available through the Kalamazoo Consortium. Opportunities are provided for internships in occupational and music therapy, teaching, business, history, and engineering and an accelerated degree programs in engineering, communication, music, Spanish, statistics, orientation and mobility and vision rehabilitation therapy. Also available are work-study programs, student-designed majors, pass/fail options, and credit by exam. WMU offers students study abroad programs in 35 countries, and access to foreign study opportunities in almost every country in the world through linkages with other universities and organizations. There are 19 national honor societies, including Phi Beta Kappa, a freshman honors program, and 32 departmental honors programs. **Visiting:** There are regularly scheduled orientations for prospective students, visiting students can participate in an admission presentation, departmental advising, lunch, and a campus tour. There are guides for informal visits and visitors may sit in on classes. To schedule a visit, contact the Campus Visit Center at (269) 387-2289. **Campus Safety and Security:** Measures include 24-hour foot and vehicle patrol, emergency notification system, self-defense education, and security escort services. There are shuttle buses, emergency telephones, lighted pathways/sidewalks, controlled access to dorms/residences, There is also a student watch program, operation identification, an enhanced telephone system, and a residence hall security system.

REQUIREMENTS: The ACT is required. Applicants must submit an official high school transcript. An audition is required for music majors. An interview may be recommended. The College of Fine Arts requires an audition, portfolio, or interview of all applicants. A GPA of 2.5 is required. AP and CLEP credits are accepted. Important factors in the admissions decision are advanced placement or honors courses, extracurricular activities record, and recommendations by school officials.Students must complete 122 semester hours, including 37 of general education courses and a minimum of 24 in the major. A minimum GPA of 2.0 is required. Students must complete courses in fine arts, humanities, US culture, non-Western world, social science, natural science with lab, science and technology, and health and well-being. Comprehensive exams are required in some departments. All students must demonstrate computer literacy. **Procedure:** Freshmen are admitted to all sessions. Entrance exams should be taken during the junior year or early in the senior year. There is a rolling admissions plan. Application deadlines are open. Applica-tion fee is $40. Notification is sent on a rolling basis. Applications are accepted on-line. **Transfer Students:** 2884 transfer students enrolled in 2013-2014. Minimum 60 hours from a 4-year accredited institution for a bachelors degree at WMU. While students may transfer in unlimited number of hours, 60 hours must be completed at a four year institution and at least 30 hours at WMU. 30 of 122 credits required for the bachelor's degree must be completed at WMU. **International Students:** There are 695 international students enrolled. The school actively recruits these students. They must take the TOEFL with a minimum score of 550 on the paper-based TOEFL (PBT) or 80 on the Internet-based version (iBT).

ADMISSIONS: 84% of the 2014-2015 applicants were accepted. The ACT scores were 35% below 21, 29% between 21 and 23, 21% between 24 and 26, 8% between 27 and 28, and 7% above 28. 26% of the current freshmen were in the top fifth of their class; 57% were in the top two fifths. There were 2 National Merit finalists. 25 freshmen graduated first in their class. **Admissions Contact:** Christopher Tremblay, Interim Director of Admissions. E-Mail: *ask-wmu@wmich .edu* Web: *www.wmich.edu*

FINANCIAL AID: In 2014-2015, 67% of all full-time freshmen and 61% of continuing full-time students received some form of financial aid. 46% of all full-time freshmen and 42% of continuing full-time students received need-based aid. The average freshman award was $11,423. Need-based scholarships or need-based grants averaged $5,962 ($25,000 maximum); need-based self-help aid (loans and jobs) averaged $5,851 ($6,000 maximum); non-need-based athletic scholarships averaged $25,002 ($28,692 maximum); and other non-need-based awards and non-need-based scholarships averaged $5,689 ($18,400 maximum). 18% of undergraduate students work part-time. Average annual earnings from campus work are $4962. The average financial indebtedness of the 2014 graduate was $26,916. The FAFSA is required. The priority date for freshman financial aid applications for fall entry is March 1.

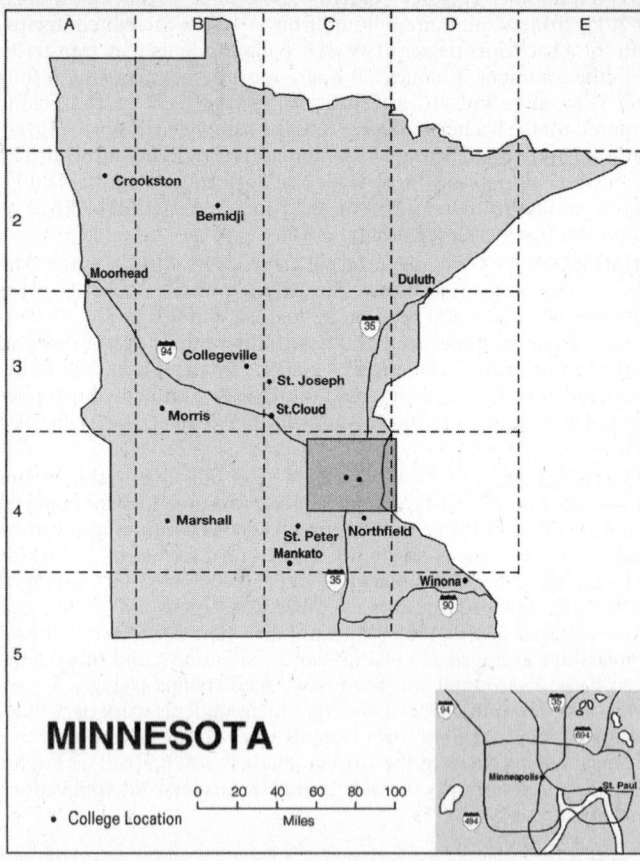

MINNESOTA

```
        0  20  40  60  80  100
                Miles
```

- College Location

AUGSBURG COLLEGE   C-4
www.augsburg.edu

Minneapolis, MN 55454	**(612) 330-1001**
	(800) 788-5678
Fax: (612) 330-1581	Email: admissions@augsburg.edu
Full-time: 1231 men, 1343 women	Faculty: 195; IIB, -$
Part-time: 197 men, 353 women	Ph.D.s: 85%
Graduate: 286 men, 606 women	Student/Faculty: 13 to 1
Year: varies, summer session	Tuition: $27,628
Room & Board: $7514	Freshman Class: 2346 applied, 1217 accepted, 449 enrolled
SAT CR/M: 505/565 ACT: 22	CEEB CODE: 6014
Application Deadline: May 1	COMPETITIVE

Augsburg College, established in 1869, is a private liberal arts institution affiliated with the Evangelical Lutheran Church. Figures in the above capsule and in this profile are approximate. There is 1 undergraduate school and 1 graduate school. In addition to regional accreditation, Augsburg has baccalaureate program accreditation with CSWE, NASM, NCATE, and NLN. The 23-acre campus is in an urban area in Minneapolis. Including any residence halls, there are 26 buildings.

STUDENT LIFE: 89% of undergraduates are from Minnesota. Others are from 41 states, 20 foreign countries, and Canada. 71% are White. 51% are Protestant; 30% claim no religious affiliation; 16% Catholic. **Male To Female Ratio:** 1.3:1. The average age of freshmen is 19; all undergraduates, 26. 19% do not continue beyond their first year; 60% remain to graduate. **Housing:** 1150 students can be accommodated in college housing, which includes coed dorms, on-campus apartments, and married student housing. In addition, there are special-interest houses. On-campus housing is guaranteed for the freshman year only, is available on a first-come, first-served basis, and is available on a lottery system for upperclassmen. Priority is given to out-of-town students. 54% of students live on campus; of those, 50% remain on campus on weekends. All students may keep cars.

FACULTY/CLASSROOMS: 49% of faculty are male; 51% are female. 99% teach undergraduates. No introductory courses are taught by graduate students. The average class size in an introductory lecture is 20; in a laboratory is 16; and in a regular course is 16.

PROGRAMS OF STUDY: Augsburg confers B.A., B.S., B.M. and B.S.N. degrees. Master's degrees are also awarded. Bachelor's degrees are awarded in BIOLOGICAL SCIENCE (biology/biological science), BUSINESS (accounting, business administration and management, international business management, management information systems, and marketing/retailing/merchandising), COMMUNICATIONS AND THE ARTS (art history and appreciation, communications, dramatic arts, English, French, German, music, Scandinavian languages, Spanish, speech/debate/rhetoric, and studio art), COMPUTER AND PHYSICAL SCIENCE (chemistry, computer science, mathematics, and physics), EDUCATION (elementary education, health education, music education, physical education, and secondary education), HEALTH PROFESSIONS (music therapy), SOCIAL SCIENCE (East Asian studies, economics, history, international relations, philosophy, political science/government, psychology, religion, Russian and Slavic studies, Scandinavian studies, social work, sociology, urban studies, and women's studies). Physics, chemistry, and English are the strongest academically. Business, communication, and education have the largest enrollments.

ACTIVITIES: There are no fraternities or sororities. There are 40 groups on campus, including art, band, cheerleading, choir, chorus, dance, drama, ethnic, gay, honors, international, jazz band, literary magazine, newspaper, orchestra, pep band, political, professional, radio and TV, religious, social, social service, and student government. Popular campus events include Days in May, Spring Affair, and Advent Vespers. **Sports:** There are 9 intercollegiate sports for men and 7 for women, and 4 intramural sports for men and 4 for women. Facilities include a 1500-seat sports field, a 2800-seat gym, tennis courts, a double-rink ice arena, and a domed field facility for winter. **Graduates:** From July 1, 2013 to June 30, 2014, 539 bachelor's degrees were awarded. The most popular majors were business management (10%), accounting/public accounting (6%), and elementary education (6%). 66 companies recruited on campus in 2013-2014. In an average class, 7% graduate in 3 years or less, 38% graduate in 4 years or less, 53% graduate in 5 years or less, and 55% graduate in 6 years or less. Of the 2013 graduating class, 24% were enrolled in graduate school within 6 months of graduation, and 85% were employed.

SERVICES: Counseling and information services are available, as is tutoring in every subject. There is a reader service for the blind, and remedial math and writing. Taped textbooks and adaptive computer technology, including a text scanner, speaking software, a touch tablet, and text magnification software, are available. **Library/Resources:** The library contains 182,289 volumes, 21,355 microform items, 3,477 audio/video tapes/CDs/DVDs, and subscribes to 686 periodicals including electronic. Computerized library services include interlibrary loans, database searching, Internet access, and Wi-Fi capability. Special learning facilities include an art gallery, planetarium, and radio station. **Physically Challenged Students:** 95% of the campus is accessible. Facilities include wheelchair ramps, elevators, special parking, specially equipped restrooms, special class scheduling, lowered drinking fountains, lowered telephones, and special housing. **Special:** Special academic programs include internships and co-op programs in business, government, and nonprofit and community-based organizations, a Washington semester, and study abroad in Europe, Latin America, and Africa. There are student-designed majors, cross-registration through the Associated Colleges of the Twin Cities (ACTC), dual and 3-2 engineering degrees with Washington University, Michigan Technological University, and the University of Minnesota, and preprofessional programs in dentistry, law, medicine, physical therapy, pharmacy, theology, and veterinary medicine. Credit for previous learning experience may be granted, and pass/fail options are possible. There is 1 national honor society, a freshman honors program, and 1 departmental honors program. **Visiting:** There are regularly scheduled orientations for prospective students, including admissions interviews and campus tours. Students may also arrange to meet with professors and coaches and to attend lectures. There are guides for informal visits, visitors may sit in on classes, and stay overnight. To schedule a visit, contact the Admissions Office. **Campus Safety and Security:** Measures include 24-hour foot and vehicle patrol, self-defense education, and security escort services. There are emergency telephones, lighted pathways/sidewalks, and controlled access to dorms/residences.

REQUIREMENTS: The ACT is required, with a minimum score of 22. Admissions requirements include graduation from an accredited secondary school with 4 years of English. The GED is also accepted. An essay is required, and an interview is recommended. AP and CLEP credits are accepted. Important factors in the admissions decision are advanced placement or honors courses, leadership record, and recommendations by school officials.To graduate, all students must have a minimum GPA of 2.0 and a total of 32 courses, with 10 to 15 in the major. They must complete 15 courses from 8 perspective areas and a first-year fall orientation and seminar. Students must also satisfy entry-level and graduation skills requirements in writing, critical thinking, math, quantitative reasoning, and speaking and demonstrate proficiency in 2 sports. **Procedure:** Freshmen are admitted fall and spring. Entrance exams should be taken during the fall of the senior year in high school. There are deferred admissions and rolling admissions plans. Applications should be filed by May 1 for fall entry; December 1 for spring entry, along with a $25 fee. Notification is sent on a rolling basis. Applications are accepted on-line. **Transfer Students:** 282 transfer students enrolled in 2013-2014. Applicants must have a minimum GPA of 2.2 in college course work. 9 of 32 credits required for the bachelor's degree must be completed at Augsburg. **International Students:** There are 44 international students enrolled. The school actively recruits these students. They must take the TOEFL with a minimum score of 550 on the paper-based TOEFL (PBT) or 80 on the Internet-based version (iBT). They must also take the SAT or ACT, scoring 22.

ADMISSIONS: 52% of the 2014-2015 applicants were accepted. The SAT scores for the 2014-2015 freshman class were: Critical Reading--50% below 500, 25% between 500 and 599, 21% between 600 and 699, and 4% between 700 and 800; Math--21% below 500, 33% between 500 and 599, 38% between 600 and 699, and 8% between 700 and 800. The ACT scores were 38% below 21, 27% between 21 and 23, 23% between 24 and 26, 8% between 27 and 28, and 4% above 28. 28% of the current freshmen were in the top fifth of their class; 55% were in the top two fifths. 5 freshmen graduated first in their class. **Admissions Contact:** Carola Thorson, Director of Admissions. E-Mail: *admissions@augsburg.edu* Web: *www.augsburg.edu*

FINANCIAL AID: In 2014-2015, 97% of all full-time freshmen and 87% of continuing full-time students received some form of financial aid. 77% of all full-time freshmen and 64% of continuing full-time students received need-based aid. Need-based scholarships or need-based grants averaged $11,308 ($27,892 maximum); and $1,631 from other forms of aid. 44% of undergraduate students work part-time. The FAFSA and the college's own financial statement are required. The priority date for freshman financial aid applications for fall entry is April 15. The deadline for filing freshman financial aid applications for fall entry is August 1.

BEMIDJI STATE UNIVERSITY   B-2
www.bemidjistate.edu

Bemidji, MN 56601	
	(218) 755-2040
	(877) 236-4354
Fax: (218) 755-2074	Email: admissions@bemidjistate.edu
Full-time: 1701 men, 1823 women	Faculty: IIB, av$
Part-time: 419 men, 801 women	Ph.D.s: 79%
Graduate: 79 men, 194 women	Student/Faculty: n/av
Year: semesters, summer session	Tuition: $7500
Room & Board: $6000	Freshman Class: 3343 applied, 1317 accepted, 743 enrolled
ACT: required	CEEB CODE: 6676
Application Deadline: open	**VERY COMPETITIVE**

Bemidji State University, founded in 1919, is a public liberal arts university. Figures in the above capsule and in this profile are approximate. There are 3 undergraduate schools and 1 graduate school. In

addition to regional accreditation, has baccalaureate program accreditation with CSWE, NASM, and NLN. The 89-acre campus is in a small town 220 miles northwest of Minneapolis. Including any residence halls, there are 21 buildings.

STUDENT LIFE: 87% of undergraduates are from Minnesota. Others are from 46 states, 34 foreign countries, and Canada. 95% are from public schools. 89% are White. **Male To Female Ratio:** 1.3:1. The average age of freshmen is 18; all undergraduates, 24. 28% do not continue beyond their first year; 44% remain to graduate. **Housing:** 1700 students can be accommodated in college housing, which includes single-sex and coed dorms and on-campus apartments. In addition, there are special-interest houses, fraternity houses, single-parent apartments. On-campus housing is available on a first-come, first-served basis. 68% of students commute. Alcohol is not permitted. All students may keep cars.

FACULTY/CLASSROOMS: 59% of faculty are male; 41% are female. 99% teach undergraduates, and 15% do research. Graduate students teach 1% of introductory courses. The average class size in an introductory lecture is 35; in a laboratory is 20; and in a regular course is 23.

PROGRAMS OF STUDY: confers B.A., B.S. and B.F.A. degrees. Associate and master's degrees are also awarded. Bachelor's degrees are awarded in AGRICULTURE (environmental studies), BIOLOGICAL SCIENCE (biology/biological science), BUSINESS (accounting and business administration and management), COMMUNICATIONS AND THE ARTS (broadcasting, communications, English, fine arts, German, journalism, languages, music, and Spanish), COMPUTER AND PHYSICAL SCIENCE (chemistry, computer science, earth science, geology, mathematics, and physics), EDUCATION (art education, early childhood education, elementary education, foreign languages education, health education, industrial arts education, middle school education, science education, and secondary education), ENGINEERING AND ENVIRONMENTAL DESIGN (industrial engineering technology), HEALTH PROFESSIONS (medical laboratory technology, nursing, predentistry, and premedicine), SOCIAL SCIENCE (community services, criminal justice, economics, geography, history, parks and recreation management, philosophy, political science/government, prelaw, psychology, social science, social work, and sociology). Nursing, accounting, and engineering are the strongest academically. Business administration, and elementary and secondary education have the largest enrollments.

ACTIVITIES: 1% of men belong to 2 national fraternities; 1% of women belong to 1 national sorority. There are 80 groups on campus, including art, band, cheerleading, choir, chorus, computers, dance, drama, environmental, ethnic, gay, honors, international, jazz band, literary magazine, musical theater, newspaper, opera, orchestra, pep band, political, professional, radio and TV, religious, social, social service, and student government. Popular campus events include Funtastic Dance Follies, Madrigal Music, Plays and Concerts. **Sports:** There are 7 intercollegiate sports for men and 7 for women, and 7 intramural sports for men and 4 for women. Facilities include a basketball gym, an Olympic-size pool, a hockey arena, a football stadium, indoor and outdoor tracks, baseball and softball fields, tennis, racquetball, and handball courts, weight rooms, and a dance studio. **Graduates:** From July 1, 2013 to June 30, 2014, 888 bachelor's degrees were awarded. The most popular majors were business/marketing (18%), education (16%), and health professions and related programs (11%). 45 companies recruited on campus in 2013-2014. In an average class, 42% graduate in 6 years or less. Of the 2013 graduating class, 14% were enrolled in graduate school within 6 months of graduation, and 90% were employed.

SERVICES: Counseling and information services are available, as is tutoring in every subject. There is a reader service for the blind, and remedial math, reading, and writing. **Library/Resources:** The library contains 190,000 volumes, 721,255 microform items, 2,500 audio/video tapes/CDs/DVDs, and subscribes to 907 periodicals including electronic. Computerized library services include interlibrary loans and database searching. Special learning facilities include an art gallery, radio station, and TV station. **Physically Challenged Students:** 95% of the campus is accessible. Facilities include wheelchair ramps, elevators, special parking, specially equipped restrooms, lowered drinking fountains, and lowered telephones. **Special:** Students may attend other schools within the Minnesota State University system and study abroad in 10 countries. Paid internships and work-study programs are available in many fields. Students may receive credit for life, military, and work experience. Student-designed dual majors, nondegree study, and pass/fail options are offered. There are 2 national honor societies and a freshman honors program. **Visiting:** There are regularly scheduled orientations for prospective students, including an interview with an admissions counselor, a tour of the campus, and visits with faculty. There are guides for informal visits, visitors may sit in on classes, and stay overnight. To schedule a visit, contact the Admissions Office. **Campus Safety and Security:** Measures include 24-hour foot and vehicle patrol, emergency notification system, self-defense education, and security escort services. There are shuttle buses, emergency telephones, lighted pathways/sidewalks, controlled access to dorms/residences, in-room safes, locked buildings overnight, controlled sportsman's weapons storage, 24/7 campus security team.

REQUIREMENTS: The ACT is required. Applicants must have a minimum high school rank of 50% or a composite score of 21 on the ACT. They should have had 4 years of English and 3 years each of math, science, and social studies. A GPA of 2.0 is required. AP and CLEP credits are accepted. Important factors in the admissions decision are recommendations by school officials, advanced placement or honors courses, and extracurricular activities record. All students must complete at least 128 semester hours, of which 42 are general education, including courses in freshman English, the humanities, social science, physical science, liberal education activities, and phys ed. Students must maintain a minimum GPA of 2.0; a 2.3 GPA is required in the major (2.5 for education majors). **Procedure:** Freshmen are admitted to all sessions. Entrance exams should be taken during the junior year. There are deferred admissions and rolling admissions plans. Application deadlines are open. The fall 2014 application fee was $20. Applications are accepted on-line. **Transfer Students:** 349 transfer students enrolled in 2013-2014. Applicants must have a minimum GPA of 2.0. 32 of 128 credits required for the bachelor's degree must be completed at Bemidji. **International Students:** There are 150 international students enrolled. The school actively recruits these students. They must take the TOEFL.

ADMISSIONS: 39% of the 2014-2015 applicants were accepted. **Admissions Contact:** Russ Kreager, Associate Director for Admissions. E-Mail: *admissions@bemidjistate.edu* Web: *www.bemidjistate.edu*

FINANCIAL AID: In 2014-2015, 83% of all full-time freshmen and 78% of continuing full-time students received some form of financial aid. 78% of all full-time freshmen and 78% of continuing full-time students received need-based aid. The average freshman award was $9,457. Need-based scholarships or need-based grants averaged $6,030; need-based self-help aid (loans and jobs) averaged $4,436; non-need-based athletic scholarships averaged $4,080; other non-need-based awards and non-need-based scholarships averaged $3,598; and $9,967 from other forms of aid. 25% of undergraduate students work part-time. Average annual earnings from campus work are $1490. The average financial indebtedness of the 2014 graduate was $20,470. The FAFSA and the college's own financial statement are required. Check with the school for current application deadlines.

sity affiliated with the Converge Worldwide (Baptist General Conference). The figures in the above capsule and in this profile are approximate. There are 2 undergraduate schools and 2 graduate schools. In addition to regional accreditation, Bethel has baccalaureate program accreditation with CSWE, TEAC, CAATE, and CCNE. The 247-acre campus is in a suburban area 10 miles north of Minneapolis/St. Paul. Including any residence halls, there are 39 buildings.

STUDENT LIFE: 78% of undergraduates are from Minnesota. Others are from 43 states, 22 foreign countries, and Canada. 80% are from public schools. 90% are White. 97% are Protestant. **Male To Female Ratio:** 1.3:1. The average age of freshmen is 18; all undergraduates, 20. 15% do not continue beyond their first year; 75% remain to graduate. **Housing:** 2076 students can be accommodated in college housing, which includes coed dorms, on-campus apartments, and off-campus apartments. On-campus housing is available on a first-come, first-served basis and is available on a lottery system for upperclassmen. 70% of students live on campus; of those, 60% remain on campus on weekends. Alcohol is not permitted. Upperclassmen may keep cars.

FACULTY/CLASSROOMS: 51% of faculty are male; 49% are female. All teach undergraduates. No introductory courses are taught by graduate students. The average class size in a laboratory is 20 and in a regular course is 22.

PROGRAMS OF STUDY: Bethel confers B.A., B.S., B.Mus. and B.Mus.Ed degrees. Associate, Master's, and Doctoral degrees are also awarded. Bachelor's degrees are awarded in AGRICULTURE (environmental studies), BIOLOGICAL SCIENCE (biochemistry, biology/biological science, and molecular biology), BUSINESS (accounting, banking and finance, and business administration and management), COMMUNICATIONS AND THE ARTS (art, communications, dramatic arts, English, English literature, French, journalism, multimedia, music, music performance, Spanish, and visual and performing arts), COMPUTER AND PHYSICAL SCIENCE (applied physics, chemistry, computer science, mathematics, and physics), EDUCATION (athletic training, business education, early childhood education, education, elementary education, English education, foreign languages education, health education, mathematics education, middle school education, music education, physical education, science education, secondary education, social studies education, and teaching English as a second/foreign language (TESOL/TEFOL)), ENGINEERING AND ENVIRONMENTAL DESIGN (engineering and applied science and environmental science), HEALTH PROFESSIONS (community health work, exercise science, and nursing), SOCIAL SCIENCE (biblical studies, economics, history, international relations, philosophy, political science/government, psychology, religious music, social studies, social work, theological studies, Third World studies, and youth ministry). Physics, chemistry, and nursing are the strongest academically. Business, education, and nursing have the largest enrollments.

ACTIVITIES: There are no fraternities or sororities. There are 74 groups on campus, including art, band, choir, chorale, chorus, dance, debate, drama, drill team, environmental, ethnic, film, forensics, honors, international, jazz band, literary magazine, musical theater, newspaper, orchestra, pep band, political, professional, radio and TV, religious, social, social service, student government, and symphony. Popular campus events include Nikdg and Gadkin and Festival of Christmas. **Sports:** There are 9 intercollegiate sports for men and 9 for women, and 6 intramural sports for men and 6 for women. Facilities include a gym; an indoor recreation center, with 1/8-mile track and 4 multipurpose courts, weight room, and racquetball courts; soccer fields; tennis courts; and a football, baseball, and softball stadium. **Graduates:** From July 1, 2013 to June 30, 2014, 756 bachelor's degrees were awarded. The most popular majors were education (16%), business/marketing (14%), and health professions and related (11%). 125 companies recruited on campus in 2013-2014. In an average class, 63% graduate in 4 years or less, 73% graduate in 5 years or less, and 75% graduate in 6 years or less. Of the 2013 graduating class, 22% were enrolled in graduate school within 6 months of graduation, and 74% were employed.

SERVICES: Counseling and information services are available, as is tutoring in every subject. There is a reader service for the blind. The Academic Enrichment and Support Center offers individual peer tutoring, student-led help sessions, a writing lab, and consultation on

---

BETHEL UNIVERSITY   C-4
www.bethel.edu

St. Paul, MN 55112	(651) 638-6242
	(800) 255-8706
Fax: (651) 635-1490	Email: buadmissions-cas@bethel.edu
Full-time: 1131 men, 1642 women	Faculty: 188, IIA, -$
Part-time: 191 men, 457 women	Ph.D.s: 78%
Graduate: 994 men, 1023 women	Student/Faculty: 15 to 1
Year: 4-1-4, summer session	Tuition: $27,020
Room & Board: $7920	Freshman Class: 2179 applied, 1734 accepted, 727 enrolled
SAT CR/M: 590/580 ACT: 25	CEEB CODE: 6038
Application Deadline: n/av	VERY COMPETITIVE

Bethel University, established in 1871, is a private liberal arts univera variety of topics **Library/Resources:** The library contains 194,196 volumes, 195,650 microform items, 15,503 audio/video tapes/CDs/DVDs, and subscribes to 38,080 periodicals including electronic. Computerized library services include interlibrary loans, database searching, Internet access, and Wi-Fi capability. Special learning facilities include an art gallery and radio station. **Physically Challenged Students:** 99% of the campus is accessible. Facilities include wheelchair ramps, elevators, special parking, specially equipped restrooms, special class scheduling, lowered drinking fountains, lowered telephones, and special housing. **Special:** Cross-registration is available through the Council for Christian Colleges and Universities. Students may arrange internships and study abroad in various countries. Students may design their own major and earn a 3-2 engineering degree. An adult degree completion program is offered. There are 6 national honor societies, a freshman honors program, and 6 departmental honors programs. **Visiting:** There are regularly scheduled orientations for prospective students, consisting of a campus tour, visits with advisors, faculty, coaches, chapel and class visits, and meals in the dining center. There are guides for informal visits, visitors may sit in on classes, and stay overnight. To schedule a visit, contact the Admissions Office. **Campus Safety and Security:** Measures include 24-hour foot and vehicle patrol, emergency notification system, self-defense education, and security escort services. There are shuttle buses, emergency telephones, lighted pathways/sidewalks, controlled access to dorms/residences, camera systems (parking lots and buildings).

REQUIREMENTS: The SAT or ACT is required. The PSAT is accepted. An interview is recommended. Requirements include a personal statement, contact information for an academic or spiritual reference, and an official transcript and class ranking from an accredited secondary school (GED is accepted). Bethel requires applicants to be in the upper 50% of their class. A GPA of 2.5 is required. AP and CLEP credits are accepted. Important factors in the admissions decision are advanced placement or honors courses, extracurricular activities record, and personality/intangible qualities. Students must complete a minimum of 122 semester credit hours, with 30 to 60 in the major and 51 to 52 in general education. Specific general education courses include Introduction to the Bible, Christianity and Western Culture, College Writing, Creativity in Fine Arts, and Physical Wellness. An overall GPA of 2.0 and a GPA of 2.25 in the major are needed. **Procedure:** Freshmen are admitted fall and spring. Entrance exams should be taken spring of junior year. There is a rolling admissions plan. Application deadlines are open. Notifications are sent October 1. 43 applicants were on the 2014 waiting list; 10 were admitted. Applications are accepted on-line. **Transfer Students:** 164 transfer students enrolled in 2013-2014. Applicants must have a minimum GPA of 2.5 and must submit all college transcripts. 28 of 122 credits required for the bachelor's degree must be completed at Bethel. **International Students:** There are 8 international students enrolled. They must take the TOEFL with a minimum score of 525 on the paper-based TOEFL (PBT) or 70 on the Internet-based version (iBT).

ADMISSIONS: 80% of the 2014-2015 applicants were accepted. The SAT scores for the 2014-2015 freshman class were: Critical Reading--20% below 500, 31% between 500 and 599, 30% between 600 and 699, and 19% between 700 and 800; Math--20% below 500, 39% between 500 and 599, 28% between 600 and 699, and 14% between 700 and 800. The ACT scores were 17% below 21, 23% between 21 and 23, 26% between 24 and 26, 14% between 27 and 28, and 21% above 28. 45% of the current freshmen were in the top fifth of their class; 74% were in the top two fifths. 31 freshmen graduated first in their class. **Admissions Contact:** Jay Fedje, Director of Admissions. E-Mail: *buadmissions-cas@bethel.edu* Web: *www.bethel.edu*

FINANCIAL AID: In 2014-2015, 99% of all full-time freshmen and 94% of continuing full-time students received some form of financial aid. 71% of all full-time freshmen and 68% of continuing full-time students received need-based aid. The average freshman award was $19,129. Need-based scholarships or need-based grants averaged $7,041 ($27,794 maximum); need-based self-help aid (loans and jobs) averaged $3,753 ($8,700 maximum); and other non-need-based awards and non-need-based scholarships averaged $8,335 ($31,020 maximum). 56% of undergraduate students work part-time. Average annual earnings from campus work are $1500. The average financial indebtedness of the 2014 graduate was $30,496. Bethel is a member of CSS. The FAFSA and the college's own financial statement are required. The priority date for freshman financial aid applications for fall entry is April 15.

CARLETON COLLEGE C-4
www.carleton.edu

Northfield, MN 55057	(507) 222-4190
	(800) 995-CARL
Fax: (507) 222-4526	Email: admissions@carleton.edu
Full-time: 968 men, 1074 women	Faculty: 247; IIB, ++$
Part-time: 3 men, 12 women	Ph.D.s: 95%
Graduate: n/av	Student/Faculty: 9 to 1
Year: trimesters	Tuition: $47,736
Room & Board: $12,366	Freshman Class: 6297 applied, 1434 accepted, 521 enrolled
SAT or ACT: required	CEEB CODE: 6081
Application Deadline: January 15	MOST COMPETITIVE

Carleton College, founded in 1866, is a private liberal arts college. The 1040-acre campus is in a small town 35 miles south of Minneapolis-St. Paul. Including any residence halls, there are 49 buildings.

STUDENT LIFE: 82% of undergraduates are from out of state, mostly the Mid-West. Students are from 49 states, 31 foreign countries, and Canada. 60% are from public schools. 65% are White. 44% claim no religious affiliation; 23% Protestant; 12% Buddhist, Hindu, Muslim, Taoist, and Unitarian Universalist. **Male To Female Ratio:** 1.1:1. The average age of freshmen is 18; all undergraduates, 20. 4% do not continue beyond their first year; 96% remain to graduate. **Housing:** 1858 students can be accommodated in college housing, which includes single-sex and coed dorms, on-campus apartments, and off-campus apartments. In addition, there are language houses and special-interest houses. On-campus housing is guaranteed for all 4 years. 96% of students live on campus; of those, 97% remain on campus on weekends. No one may keep cars.

FACULTY/CLASSROOMS: 52% of faculty are male; 48% are female. All teach and do research. No introductory courses are taught by graduate students. The average class size in an introductory lecture is 20; in a laboratory is 16; and in a regular course is 17.

PROGRAMS OF STUDY: Carleton confers B.A. degrees. Bachelor's degrees are awarded in AGRICULTURE (environmental studies), BIOLOGICAL SCIENCE (biology/biological science), COMMUNICATIONS AND THE ARTS (art history and appreciation, classics, English, French, German, Greek, Latin, linguistics, media arts, music, romance languages and literature, Russian, Spanish, and studio art), COMPUTER AND PHYSICAL SCIENCE (chemistry, computer science, geology, mathematics, and physics), SOCIAL SCIENCE (African studies, African American studies, American studies, anthropology, Asian/Oriental studies, classical/ancient civilization, economics, history, international relations, Latin American studies, philosophy, political science/government, psychology, religion, sociology, and women's studies). Sciences, biological, history, psychology, English and languages, political science and economics are the strongest academically. Social sciences, history, sciences, have the largest enrollments.

ACTIVITIES: There are no fraternities or sororities. There are 200 groups on campus, including hobby club, art, band, chess, choir, chorale, chorus, computers, dance, debate, drama, educational, environmental, ethnic, film, gay, honors, international, jazz band, literary magazine, musical theater, newspaper, orchestra, photography, political, professional, radio and TV, religious, social, social service, student government, and symphony. Popular campus events include Mai Fete, Spring Concert, Mid-Winter Ball, Ebony, and Golden Shillers Film Festival. **Sports:** There are 23 intercollegiate sports for men and 23 for women, and 8 intramural sports for men and 8 for women. Facilities include a gym with a 1220-seat arena, 6-lane swimming pool, and wrestling room, a recreation center with a gym, dance studio, indoor tennis court, sauna, 5-lane swimming pool, 7000-seat stadium complex with handball and racquetball courts, 200-meter indoor track, baseball batting cage, weight room, and an additional recreation center with a 200-meter indoor track, sport courts, weight room, dance studio, and climbing wall. In addition, there are fields for baseball, softball, soccer, ultimate Frisbee, lacrosse, rugby, field hockey, 12 outdoor tennis courts, and 16 miles of running, biking, hiking, and cross-country skiing trails in Carleton's 880-acre arboretum. **Graduates:** From July 1, 2013 to June 30, 2014, 496 bachelor's degrees were awarded. The most popular majors were biology (14%), political science/international relations (11%), and mathematics and statistics (10%). In an average class, 91% graduate in 4 years or less, 93% graduate in 5 years or less, and 93% graduate in 6 years or less.

SERVICES: Counseling and information services are available, as is tutoring in every subject. There is a reader service for the blind. **Library/Resources:** The library contains 1.1 million volumes, 351,524 microform items, 24,642 audio/video tapes/CDs/DVDs, and subscribes to 74,435 periodicals including electronic. Computerized library services include interlibrary loans, database searching, Internet access, and Wi-Fi capability. Special learning facilities include an art gallery, radio station, an observatory, an 880-acre arboretum, and Weitz Center for Creativity. **Physically Challenged Students:** 39% of the campus is accessible. Facilities include wheelchair ramps, elevators, special parking, specially equipped restrooms, special class scheduling, lowered drinking fountains, lowered telephones, and special housing. **Special:** Students may cross-register with St. Olaf College and pursue a variety of internships. The college offers study abroad in over 50 countries. Dual majors in all areas and student designed majors are available. Students may earn a 3-2 engineering degree with Washington or Columbia Universities. There are 3 national honor societies and Phi Beta Kappa. **Visiting:** There are regularly scheduled orientations for prospective student. Prospective students can attend an information session, take a tour, have an interview, sit in on classes, have a meal in the dining halls, and attend panels on particular topics pertinent to study abroad, financial aid or other topics. There are guides for informal visits, visitors may sit in on classes, and stay overnight. To schedule a visit, contact the Admissions Office. **Campus Safety and Security:** Measures include 24-hour foot and vehicle patrol, emergency notification system, self-defense education, and security escort services. There are emergency telephones, lighted pathways/sidewalks, controlled access to dorms/residences, and nighttime transport service.

REQUIREMENTS: The SAT or ACT is required. The ACT Optional Writing test is also required. There are no secondary school requirements, but it is recommended that applicants have completed 4 years of English, 3 years each of math and a foreign language, 2 years each of history and science, and 1 year of social studies. An essay and 2 teacher recommendations are required. AP credits are accepted. Important factors in the admissions decision are advanced placement or honors courses, personality/intangible qualities, and evidence of special talent. To graduate, a student must complete 210 credits and maintain a 2.0 cumulative GPA. A normal course load is 18 credits per term (there are 3 terms). Students also explore an integrated exercise in their major in the form of a comprehensive exam, an extensive research project, paper or public presentation. The goal is to demonstrate proficiency within their major. A first-year seminar and course work in Quantitative Reasoning and Global Citizenship are also required. **Procedure:** Freshmen are admitted fall. Entrance exams should be taken before February 15. There are early decision and deferred admissions plans. Early decision applications should be filed by November 15; regular applications, by January 15 for fall entry, along with a $30 fee. Notification of early decision is sent December 15; regular decision, April 15. 218 early decision candidates were accepted for the 2014-2015 class. 385 applicants were on the 2014 waiting list; 9 were admitted. Applications are accepted on-line. Application fees are waived if application is completed on-line. **Transfer Students:** 2 transfer students enrolled in 2013-2014. Transfers are usually accepted for sophomore and junior classes. A 3.0 GPA is recommended. 108 of 210 credits required for the bachelor's degree must be completed at Carleton. **International Students:** There are 189 international students enrolled. The school actively recruits these students. They must take the TOEFL with a minimum score of 600 on the paper-based TOEFL (PBT) or 100 on the Internet-based version (iBT). They must also take the SAT or ACT.

ADMISSIONS: 23% of the 2014-2015 applicants were accepted. 91% of the current freshmen were in the top fifth of their class; 100% were in the top two fifths. **Admissions Contact:** Paul Thiboutot, VP &

Dean of Admissions & Financial Aid. E-Mail: *admissions@carleton .edu* Web: *www.carleton.edu*

FINANCIAL AID: In 2014-2015, 75% of all full-time freshmen and 87% of continuing full-time students received some form of financial aid. 53% of all full-time freshmen and 55% of continuing full-time students received need-based aid. The average freshman award was $39,757. Need-based scholarships or need-based grants averaged $36,030; need-based self-help aid (loans and jobs) averaged $5,511; and other non-need-based awards and non-need-based scholarships averaged $2,000. 82% of undergraduate students work part-time. Average annual earnings from campus work are $1737. The average financial indebtedness of the 2014 graduate was $18,302. Carleton is a member of CSS. The CSS/Profile and FAFSA are required. The deadline for filing freshman financial aid applications for fall entry is February 15.

COLLEGE OF SAINT BENEDICT   C-3
www.csbsju.edu

St. Joseph, MN 56374	(320) 363-5060
	(800) 544-1489
Fax: (320) 363-3206	Email: admissions@csbsju.edu
Full-time: 1992 women	Faculty: 144; IIB, +$
Part-time: 28 women	Ph.D.s: 92%
Graduate: n/av	Student/Faculty: 12 to 1
Year: semesters	Tuition: $39,402
Room & Board: $9957	Freshman Class: 1768 applied, 1453 accepted, 542 enrolled
SAT or ACT: required	CEEB CODE: 6104
Application Deadline: January 15	VERY COMPETITIVE

The College of Saint Benedict (CSB) and Saint John's University (SJU) are nationally-leading liberal arts colleges whose unique partnership offers students the educational choices of a large university and the individual attention of a premier small college. In addition to regional accreditation, Saint Ben's has baccalaureate program accreditation with ADA, NASM, NCATE, ACS, and CCNE. The 600-acre campus is in a small town 70 miles northwest of Minneapolis and 10 miles west of St. Cloud. Including any residence halls, there are 51 buildings.

STUDENT LIFE: 79% of undergraduates are from Minnesota. Others are from 32 states, and 16 foreign countries. 77% are from public schools. 80% are White. 59% are Catholic; 26% Protestant; 14% claim no religious affiliation. The student base is all female. The average age of freshmen is 18; all undergraduates, 20. 12% do not continue beyond their first year; 81% remain to graduate. **Housing:** 1665 students can be accommodated in college housing, which includes single-sex dorms and on-campus apartments. In addition, there are special-interest houses, wellness communities and eco/environmental houses. On-campus housing is guaranteed for the freshman year only, is available on a first-come, first-served basis, and is available on a lottery system for upperclassmen. 89% of students live on campus. All students may keep cars.

FACULTY/CLASSROOMS: 47% of faculty are male; 53% are female. All teach and do research. No introductory courses are taught by graduate students. The average class size in an introductory lecture is 21; in a laboratory is 13; and in a regular course is 17.

PROGRAMS OF STUDY: Saint Ben's confers B.A., and B.S.N. degrees. Bachelor's degrees are awarded in AGRICULTURE (environmental studies), BIOLOGICAL SCIENCE (biochemistry, biology/biological science, and nutrition), BUSINESS (accounting and management science), COMMUNICATIONS AND THE ARTS (art, classics, communications, English, French, German, music, Spanish, and theatre arts), COMPUTER AND PHYSICAL SCIENCE (chemistry, computer science, mathematics, natural sciences, and physics), EDUCATION (elementary education), ENGINEERING AND ENVIRONMENTAL DESIGN (preengineering), HEALTH PROFESSIONS (nursing, occupational therapy, predentistry, premedicine, preoptometry, prepharmacy, prephysical therapy, and preveterinary science), SOCIAL SCIENCE (Asian/Oriental studies, economics, gender studies, Hispanic American studies, history, humanities, liberal arts/general studies, peace studies, philosophy, political science/government, prelaw, psychology, social science, sociology, and theological studies). Nursing, biology, and psychology have the largest enrollments.

ACTIVITIES: There are no fraternities or sororities. There are 120 groups on campus, including academic clubs, art, band, choir, chorale, chorus, computers, dance, debate, drama, environmental, ethnic, film, gay, honors, international, jazz band, literary magazine, musical theater, newspaper, opera, orchestra, outdoor leadership center, pep band, political, professional, radio and TV, religious, social, social service, student government, and symphony. Popular campus events include Pines Spring Concert, Asian New Year, Festival of Culture, Community Barbecue, Club Involvement Fair, Johnnie Bennie Live Fall Concert, Maple Syrup Festival, and Homecoming. **Sports:** There are 11 intercollegiate sports for women. Facilities include a 1000-seat volleyball and basketball arena, racquetball and indoor and outdoor tennis courts, an indoor pool, a field house with an indoor running track, an aerobics studio, a fitness center with exercise and weight-training equipment, a softball diamond, and soccer fields. Students have access to St. John's University facilities as well, where they can also access lakes for canoeing, fishing, swimming, rowing, and kayaking and 20 miles of on-campus wooded hiking and jogging trails along with a climbing wall. **Graduates:** From July 1, 2013 to June 30, 2014, 495 bachelor's degrees were awarded. The most popular majors were psychology (12%), biology (10%), communication, and and nursing (9%). 126 companies recruited on campus in 2013-2014. In an average class, 1% graduate in 3 years or less, 74% graduate in 4 years or less, 79% graduate in 5 years or less, and 81% graduate in 6 years or less. Of the 2013 graduating class, 17% were enrolled in graduate school within 6 months of graduation, and 81% were employed.

SERVICES: Counseling and information services are available, as is tutoring in most subjects, a writing center, and a math skills center. The College of Saint Benedict and Saint John's University established a Disability Services Office. Individual tutoring is available as needed. Academic and psychological counseling are available on an unlimited basis. **Library/Resources:** The 2 libraries contain 715,683 volumes, 25,308 microform items, 63,384 audio/video tapes/CDs/DVDs, and subscribe to 97,011 periodicals including electronic. Computerized library services include interlibrary loans, database searching, Internet access, and Wi-Fi capability. Special learning facilities include an art gallery, radio station, TV station, a pottery studio and kiln, a labyrinth, dance studio, green house and Saint Benedict's Monastery Heritage Museum. At Saint John's University there is Saint John's Outdoor University, an observatory, a greenhouse, an herbarium, natural history museum, and the Hill Museum and Manuscript library. **Physically Challenged Students:** 97% of the campus is accessible. Facilities include wheelchair ramps, elevators, special parking, specially equipped restrooms, special class scheduling, lowered drinking fountains, special housing, exterior power assist doors, and accessible busing options. **Special:** Students may cross-register with St. Cloud State University. There are study-abroad programs in Australia, Austria, Chile, China, Coventry-England, France, Germany, Guatemala, Greece, Ireland (Cork and Galway), Italy, India, Japan, London-England, Northern Ireland, South Africa, and Spain. Many short-term study abroad opportunities are also offered. Internships, dual and student-designed majors, preprofessional programs, and liberal studies degrees may be pursued. A 3-2 engineering program is offered through the University of Minnesota, as is a 3-1 program in dentistry. Nondegree study and a pass/fail grading option are also available. There are 4 national honor societies, including Phi Beta Kappa, and a freshman honors program. **Visiting:** There are regularly scheduled orientations for prospective students. Programs include admissions and financial aid presentations, campus tours and student panels. There are guides for informal visits, visitors may sit in on classes, and stay overnight. To schedule a visit, contact the CSB/SJU Admissions Office. **Campus Safety and Security:** Measures include 24-hour foot and vehicle patrol, emergency notification system, self-defense education, and security escort services. There are shuttle buses, emergency telephones, lighted pathways/sidewalks, and controlled access to dorms/residences.

REQUIREMENTS: The SAT or ACT is required. Students should be graduates of an accredited secondary school. Academic preparation should include 17 units, including 4 of English, 3 of math, 2 each of a lab science and social studies, and 4 electives. A foreign language is recommended. The GED is accepted. An essay is required. Home-schooled applicants are not required to have a high school diploma but are required to provide appropriate documentation of college preparatory curriculum. Saint Ben's requires applicants to be in the upper 50% of their class. A GPA of 3.0 is required. AP and CLEP credits are accepted. Important factors in the admissions decision are advanced placement or honors courses, leadership record, and extra-curricular activities record.To graduate students must complete a first-year seminar and a junior-senior ethics seminar intended as a capstone for the liberal arts experience, and fulfill gender, intercultural, experiential learning, and fine arts requirements. Distribution requirements include 4 credits in fine arts, 2 courses each in humanities and theology, and 1 course each in math, natural science, and social science. All students must prove math and foreign language proficiency. A total of 124 credits must be earned, with a minimum GPA of 2.0. Attendance at 8 fine arts experiences is also required. **Procedure:** Freshmen are admitted fall and spring. Entrance exams should be taken during the spring of the junior year or fall of the senior year. There are early admissions and deferred admissions plans. Application deadlines are open. Notification of early decision is sent December 15; regular decision, April 1. Applications are accepted on-line. **Transfer Students:** 23 transfer students enrolled in 2013-2014. Transfer applicants must have a minimum college GPA of 2.75. An essay or personal statement, high school and college transcripts, and a transfer student evaluation form are required. Standardized test scores may be required of some. 45 of 124 credits required for the bachelor's degree must be completed at Saint Ben's. **International Students:** There are 92 international students enrolled. The school actively recruits these students. They must take the TOEFL with a minimum score of 550 on the paper-based TOEFL (PBT) or 80 on the Internet-based version (iBT). IELTS also accepted with minimum score of 6.5. They must also take the SAT or ACT, scoring 21. In certain cases, the SAT or ACT may replace TOEFL.

ADMISSIONS: 82% of the 2014-2015 applicants were accepted. The SAT scores for the 2014-2015 freshman class were: Critical Reading--20% below 500, 53% between 500 and 599, 21% between 600 and 699, and 6% between 700 and 800; Math--28% below 500, 41% between 500 and 599, 23% between 600 and 699, and 8% between 700 and 800; Writing--30% below 500, 40% between 500 and 599, 26% between 600 and 699, and 4% between 700 and 800. The ACT scores were 10% below 21, 19% between 21 and 23, 29% between 24 and 26, 16% between 27 and 28, and 26% above 28. 61% of the current freshmen were in the top fifth of their class; 90% were in the top two fifths. There was 1 National Merit finalist. 40 freshmen graduated first in their class. **Admissions Contact:** Dr. Calvin Mosley, Vice President for Admission & Financial. E-Mail: *admissions@csbsju.edu* Web: *www.csbsju.edu*

FINANCIAL AID: In 2014-2015, 97% of all full-time freshmen and 95% of continuing full-time students received some form of financial aid. 74% of all full-time freshmen and 69% of continuing full-time students received need-based aid. The average freshman award was $33,343. Need-based scholarships or need-based grants averaged $27,478; need-based self-help aid (loans and jobs) averaged $6,335; and other non-need-based awards and non-need-based scholarships averaged $17,962. 75% of undergraduate students work part-time. Average annual earnings from campus work are $3150. The average financial indebtedness of the 2014 graduate was $39,437. Saint Ben's is a member of CSS. The FAFSA and the college's own financial statement are required. The priority date for freshman financial aid applications for fall entry is March 15.

COLLEGE OF SAINT SCHOLASTICA   D-2
www.css.edu

Duluth, MN 55811	(218) 723-6046
	(800) 447-5444
Fax: (218) 723-5991	Email: eberg@css.edu
Full-time: 737 men, 1581 women	Faculty: 181; IIB, -$
Part-time: 123 men, 418 women	Ph.D.s: 56%
Graduate: 339 men, 1039 women	Student/Faculty: 14 to 1
Year: semesters, summer session	Tuition: $32,842
Room & Board: $8598	Freshman Class: 1809 applied, 1315 accepted, 432 enrolled
SAT CR/M/W: 470/480/470 ACT: 24	CEEB CODE: 6107
Application Deadline: n/av	COMPETITIVE

The College of St. Scholastica, founded in 1912, is an independent private college that provides intellectual and moral preparation for responsible living and meaningful work. Saint Scholastica has extended campuses in St. Paul, Brainerd, Rochester, and St. Cloud, MN. The college is guided by the Benedictine values of community, hospitality, respect, stewardship, and love of learning. Figures in the above capsule and in this profile are approximate. There are 6 undergraduate schools and 1 graduate school. In addition to regional accreditation, Saints has baccalaureate program accreditation with APTA, CSWE, TEAC, ACOTE, CAHIIM, and CAATE. The 186-acre campus is in a suburban area 150 miles north of Minneapolis and St. Paul, MN. Including any residence halls, there are 18 buildings.

STUDENT LIFE: 84% of undergraduates are from Minnesota. Others are from 49 states, 38 foreign countries, and Canada. 83% are White. 37% claim no religious affiliation; 27% Protestant; 24% Catholic. **Female To Male Ratio:** 2.5:1. The average age of freshmen is 18; all undergraduates, 25. 16% do not continue beyond their first year; 61% remain to graduate. **Housing:** 1075 students can be accommodated in college housing, which includes single-sex and coed dorms and on-campus apartments. On-campus housing is available on a first-come, first-served basis, and is available on a lottery system for upperclassmen. 53% of students live on campus; of those, 75% remain on campus on weekends. All students may keep cars.

FACULTY/CLASSROOMS: 40% of faculty are male; 59% are female. All teach undergraduates. No introductory courses are taught by graduate students. The average class size in an introductory lecture is 24; in a laboratory is 16; and in a regular course is 21.

PROGRAMS OF STUDY: Saints confers B.A., and B.S. degrees. Master's and Doctoral degrees are also awarded. Bachelor's degrees are awarded in BIOLOGICAL SCIENCE (biochemistry and biology/biological science), BUSINESS (accounting, business administration and management, finance, management science, marketing management, and organizational behavior), COMMUNICATIONS AND THE ARTS (advertising, communications, English, journalism, languages, and music), COMPUTER AND PHYSICAL SCIENCE (chemistry, computer science, mathematics, and natural sciences), EDUCATION (education and social science education), HEALTH PROFESSIONS (exercise science, health care administration, health science, and nursing), SOCIAL SCIENCE (behavioral science, economics, history, humanities, Native American studies, peace studies, philosophy, psychology, religion, and social work). Nursing, management, and biological sciences have the largest enrollments.

ACTIVITIES: There are no fraternities or sororities. There are 68 groups on campus, including band, cheerleading, choir, chorale, chorus, computers, dance, drama, ethnic, gay, honors, international, jazz band, literary magazine, newspaper, pep band, photography, political, professional, radio and TV, religious, social, social service, and student government. Popular campus events include Mayfest Week, Fall Fest and International Week. **Sports:** There are 9 intercollegiate sports for men and 9 for women, and 14 intramural sports for men and 14 for women. Facilities include a 63,000-square-foot wellness center, which includes a 6-lane 200 meter track, aerobic studio, free weight room, complete machine fitness space, athletic trainer's room, and climbing wall. **Graduates:** From July 1, 2013 to June 30, 2014, 841 bachelor's degrees were awarded. The most popular majors were nursing (45%), management (20%), and biological sciences

(12%). In an average class, 55% graduate in 4 years or less, 60% graduate in 5 years or less, and 61% graduate in 6 years or less. Of the 2013 graduating class, 29% were enrolled in graduate school within 6 months of graduation, and 63% were employed.

SERVICES: There are no fraternities or sororities. There are 68 groups on campus, including band, cheerleading, choir, chorale, chorus, computers, dance, drama, ethnic, gay, honors, international, jazz band, literary magazine, newspaper, pep band, photography, political, professional, radio and TV, religious, social, social service, and student government. Popular campus events include Mayfest Week, Fall Fest and International Week. **Sports:** There are 9 intercollegiate sports for men and 9 for women, and 14 intramural sports for men and 14 for women. Facilities include a 63,000-square-foot wellness center, which includes a 6-lane 200 meter track, aerobic studio, free weight room, complete machine fitness space, athletic trainer's room, and climbing wall. **Graduates:** From July 1, 2013 to June 30, 2014, 841 bachelor's degrees were awarded. The most popular majors were nursing (45%), management (20%), and biological sciences (12%). In an average class, 55% graduate in 4 years or less, 60% graduate in 5 years or less, and 61% graduate in 6 years or less. Of the 2013 graduating class, 29% were enrolled in graduate school within 6 months of graduation, and 63% were employed.

REQUIREMENTS: The SAT or ACT is required. Students are also required to send official high school transcripts. AP and CLEP credits are accepted.To graduate, students must complete 128 semester credits, with a 2.0 GPA. Approximately 52 credits of general education courses are required. The hours required in the major vary. Some majors require an internship for graduation. A senior project may be required. **Procedure:** Freshmen are admitted to all sessions. Entrance exams should be taken by January of the senior year of high school. There are deferred admissions and rolling admissions plans. Application deadlines are open. Notification is sent on a rolling basis. Applications are accepted on-line. **Transfer Students:** 404 transfer students enrolled in 2013-2014. Applicants must have a GPA of 2.0. 32 of 128 credits required for the bachelor's degree must be completed at Saints. **International Students:** There are 117 international students enrolled. The school actively recruits these students. They must take the TOEFL with a minimum score of 550 on the paper-based TOEFL (PBT) or 79 on the Internet-based version (iBT).

ADMISSIONS: 73% of the 2014-2015 applicants were accepted. The SAT scores for the 2014-2015 freshman class were: Critical Reading-- 67% below 500, 20% between 500 and 599, and 13% between 600 and 699. Math-- 67% below 500, 20% between 500 and 599, and 13% between 600 and 699. Writing-- 60% below 500 and 40% between 500 and 599. The ACT scores were 29% below 21, 22% between 21 and 23, 19% between 24 and 26, 17% between 27 and 28, and 13% above 28. 44% of the current freshmen were in the top fifth of their class; 76% were in the top two fifths. 11 freshmen graduated first in their class. **Admissions Contact:** Eric Berg, Vice President for Enrollment Management. E-Mail: *eberg@css.edu* Web: *www.css.edu*

FINANCIAL AID: In 2014-2015, 83% of all full-time freshmen and 80% of continuing full-time students received some form of financial aid. 83% of all full-time freshmen and 80% of continuing full-time students received need-based aid. The average freshman award was $24,921. Need-based scholarships or need-based grants averaged $8,126; need-based self-help aid (loans and jobs) averaged $4,260; and other non-need-based awards and non-need-based scholarships averaged $14,622. 29% of undergraduate students work part-time. Average annual earnings from campus work are $1970. The average financial indebtedness of the 2014 graduate was $43,113. The FAFSA is required. The priority date for freshman financial aid applications for fall entry is March 1.

CONCORDIA COLLEGE - MOORHEAD   A-2
www.concordiacollege.edu

Moorhead, MN 56562	(218) 299-3004
	(800) 699-9897
Fax: (218) 299-4720	Email: admissions@cord.edu
Full-time: 952 men, 1536 women	Faculty: 181
Part-time: 16 men, 27 women	Ph.D.s: 85%
Graduate: 4 men, 23 women	Student/Faculty: 14 to 1
Year: semesters, summer session	Tuition: $32,814
Room & Board: $7160	Freshman Class: 2493 applied, 1944 accepted, 684 enrolled
SAT CR/M: 570/550 ACT: 25	CEEB CODE: 6113
Application Deadline: open	VERY COMPETITIVE

Concordia College, founded in 1891, is a private, liberal arts institution affiliated with the Evangelical Lutheran Church in America. Figures in the above capsule and in this profile are approximate. There are 2 undergraduate schools and 1 graduate school. In addition to regional accreditation, Concordia has baccalaureate program accreditation with CSWE, NASM, CCNE, ACEND, and MN Board of Examiners for Nursing Home Administration. The 113-acre campus is in a suburban area 230 miles northwest of Minneapolis and St. Paul. Including any residence halls, there are 42 buildings.

STUDENT LIFE: 67% of undergraduates are from Minnesota. Others are from 33 states, 31 foreign countries, and Canada. 94% are from public schools. 83% are White. 43% are Protestant; 36% unknown religion; 17% Catholic. **Male To Female Ratio:** 1.6:1. The average age of freshmen is 18; all undergraduates, 20. 16% do not continue beyond their first year; 71% remain to graduate. **Housing:** 1792 students can be accommodated in college housing, which includes single-sex and coed dorms and on-campus apartments. In addition, there are language houses, special-interest houses, and townhouses. On-campus housing is guaranteed for the freshman year only, is available on a first-come, first-served basis, and is available on a lottery system for upperclassmen. 64% of students live on campus. Alcohol is not permitted. All students may keep cars.

FACULTY/CLASSROOMS: 51% of faculty are male; 49% are female. All teach and do research. No introductory courses are taught by graduate students. The average class size in an introductory lecture is 23; in a laboratory is 17; and in a regular course is 19.

PROGRAMS OF STUDY: Concordia confers B.A., and B.M. degrees. Master's degrees are also awarded. Bachelor's degrees are awarded in BIOLOGICAL SCIENCE (biology/biological science and nutrition), BUSINESS (accounting, business administration and management, and international business management), COMMUNICATIONS AND THE ARTS (art, Chinese, classical languages, classics, communications, dramatic arts, English, French, German, journalism, Latin, music, music performance, music theory and composition, and Spanish), COMPUTER AND PHYSICAL SCIENCE (applied science, chemistry, mathematics, and physics), EDUCATION (art education, business education, elementary education, foreign languages education, health education, mathematics education, music education, physical education, secondary education, and social studies education), ENGINEERING AND ENVIRONMENTAL DESIGN (environmental science), HEALTH PROFESSIONS (clinical science, exercise science, health, and nursing), SOCIAL SCIENCE (history, humanities, international studies, philosophy, political science/government, psychology, religion, Scandinavian studies, social work, and sociology). Natural sciences is the strongest academically. Education, business, and biology have the largest enrollments.

ACTIVITIES: There are no fraternities or sororities. There are 106 groups on campus, including art, band, cheerleading, choir, chorale, chorus, communications, dance, debate, drama, environmental, ethnic, forensics, gay, honors, international, jazz band, literary magazine, musical theater, newspaper, orchestra, pep band, photography, political, professional, radio and TV, religious, social, social service, student government, and symphony. Popular campus events include Christmas Concert, Martin Luther King Jr. Day, and National Book Award Celebration. **Sports:** There are 11 intercollegiate sports for men and 11 for women, and 6 intramural sports for men and 5 for women. Facilities include a 200-meter indoor track with 4 multipurpose volleyball/basketball/tennis courts, an indoor swimming pool and sauna, a 7,000-seat stadium with an all-weather track, a field house with a 4,500-seat auditorium that features 2 basketball courts, an auxiliary gym, a weight room, 6 outdoor tennis courts, softball and soccer competition fields, a baseball complex, and soccer practice fields. **Graduates:** From July 1, 2013 to June 30, 2014, 540 bachelor's degrees were awarded. The most popular majors were business (17%), education (15%), and biology (12%). In an average class, 65% graduate in 4 years or less, 71% graduate in 5 years or less, and 71% graduate in 6 years or less. Of the 2013 graduating class, 32% were enrolled in graduate school within 6 months of graduation, and 82% were employed.

SERVICES: Counseling and information services are available, as is tutoring in most subjects. There is a reader service for the blind, and an interpreter service for the deaf. **Library/Resources:** The library contains 346,744 volumes, 44,055 microform items, 26,572 audio/video tapes/CDs/DVDs, and subscribes to 4,342 periodicals including electronic. Computerized library services include interlibrary loans, database searching, Internet access, and Wi-Fi capability. Special learning facilities include an art gallery, radio station, TV station, an observatory, a field biology research facility, a laser facility; a nursing simulation lab, and a 2MeV hypervelocity dust particle accelerator. **Physically Challenged Students:** 95% of the campus is accessible. Facilities include wheelchair ramps, elevators, special parking, specially equipped restrooms, special class scheduling, lowered drinking fountains, special housing. **Special:** Co-op programs and internships are available in most majors, and dual majors are available in all majors. There is a Washington semester and an urban studies semester in Chicago. Study abroad in 26 countries, on- and off-campus work-study, a B.A.-B.M. degree in music, and a 3-2 engineering degree with the University of Minnesota are available. Nondegree study for special students and pass/fail options also are possible. Cross-registration is offered through the Tri-College University Consortium. There are 18 national honor societies, a freshman honors program, and 16 departmental honors programs. **Visiting:** There are regularly scheduled orientations for prospective students, including an extensive campus tour and meetings with admissions counselors and faculty members. There are guides for informal visits, visitors may sit in on classes, and stay overnight. To schedule a visit, contact the Office of Admissions. **Campus Safety and Security:** Measures include 24-hour foot and vehicle patrol, emergency notification system, and security escort services. There are emergency telephones, lighted pathways/sidewalks, and controlled access to dorms/residences.

REQUIREMENTS: The SAT or ACT is required. Two character references are required, and an interview is recommended. The GED is accepted. Academic performance and preparation, as evidenced in a high school transcript, are the most important factors in the admissions decision. AP and CLEP credits are accepted. Important factors in the admissions decision are advanced placement or honors courses, recommendations by school officials, and leadership record. All students must maintain a minimum GPA of 2.0 while taking 126 semester hours, including at least 32 in the major. Required courses include written communication, oral communication, an introduction to liberal arts, and 2 courses each in physical education and religion. Exploration requirements include 7 courses taken from 6 areas: science and math, social science, world language, humanities and arts plus 2 perspectives courses to include 1 U.S. cultural diversity course and 1 international and global perspectives course. The final course in the Core Curriculum is a writing-intensive capstone course. **Procedure:** Freshmen are admitted to all sessions. Entrance exams should be taken by the first semester of the senior year. There are early admissions, deferred admissions, and rolling admissions plans. Application deadlines are open. Application fee is $20. Notification is sent on a rolling basis. Applications are accepted on-line. **Transfer Students:** 42 transfer students enrolled in 2013-2014. Transfer applicants must have a minimum 2.0 GPA and provide official transcripts from previously attended schools. 28 of 126 credits required for the bachelor's degree must be completed at Concordia. **International Students:** There are 102 international students enrolled. The school actively recruits these students. They must take the TOEFL with a minimum score of 73 on the Internet-based version (iBT).

ADMISSIONS: 78% of the 2014-2015 applicants were accepted. The

SAT scores for the 2014-2015 freshman class were: Critical Reading--23% below 500, 33% between 500 and 599, 35% between 600 and 699, and 10% between 700 and 800; Math--33% below 500, 29% between 500 and 599, 23% between 600 and 699, and 15% between 700 and 800; Writing--31% below 500, 37% between 500 and 599, 23% between 600 and 699, and 10% between 700 and 800. The ACT scores were 13% below 21, 22% between 21 and 23, 29% between 24 and 26, 16% between 27 and 28, and 20% above 28. 53% of the current freshmen were in the top fifth of their class; 81% were in the top two fifths. There were 4 National Merit finalists. **Admissions Contact:** Office of Admissions E-Mail: *admissions@cord.edu* Web: *www.concordiacollege.edu*

FINANCIAL AID: In 2014-2015, 99% of all full-time freshmen and 97% of continuing full-time students received some form of financial aid. 77% of all full-time freshmen and 73% of continuing full-time students received need-based aid. The average freshman award was $27,769. Need-based scholarships or need-based grants averaged $21,188; and need-based self-help aid (loans and jobs) averaged $7,676. 52% of undergraduate students work part-time. Average annual earnings from campus work are $1405. Concordia is a member of CSS. The FAFSA is required. The deadline for filing freshman financial aid applications for fall entry is rolling.

CONCORDIA UNIVERSITY SAINT PAUL   C-4
www.csp.edu

St. Paul, MN 55104	
	(651) 641-8230
	(800) 333-4705
Fax: (651) 603-6320	Email: admissions@csp.edu
Full-time: 600 men, 774 women	Faculty: 73
Part-time: 402 men, 644 women	Ph.D.s: 73%
Graduate: 488 men, 1149 women	Student/Faculty: 18 to 1
Year: semesters, summer session	Tuition: $20,250
Room & Board: $8000	Freshman Class: 1435 applied, 764 accepted, 242 enrolled
ACT: 21	CEEB CODE: 6114
Application Deadline: August 1	COMPETITIVE

Concordia University, founded in 1893 and a member of the Concordia University System, is a private institution affiliated with the Lutheran Church Missouri Synod and offering programs in teacher education, business, church vocations, and the liberal arts. Master's programs and bachelor's degree completion programs for adult learners are also offered. There are 3 undergraduate schools and 1 graduate school. In addition to regional accreditation, CSP has baccalaureate program accreditation with ACBSP and NCATE. The 37-acre campus is in an urban area in the Midway area of the Twin Cities, between Minneapolis and St. Paul. Including any residence halls, there are 24 buildings.

STUDENT LIFE: 77% of undergraduates are from Minnesota. Others are from 45 states, 9 foreign countries, and Canada. 69% are White. 47% are Protestant. **Male To Female Ratio:** 1.7:1. The average age of freshmen is 18; all undergraduates, 26. 29% do not continue beyond their first year; 47% remain to graduate. **Housing:** 514 students can be accommodated in college housing, which includes single-sex and coed dorms, on-campus apartments, and married student housing. On-campus housing is guaranteed for the freshman year only, and is available on a first-come, first-served basis. Priority is given to out-of-town students. 77% of students commute. All students may keep cars.

FACULTY/CLASSROOMS: 46% of faculty are male; 54% are female. 85% teach undergraduates. No introductory courses are taught by graduate students. The average class size in an introductory lecture is 15; in a laboratory is 19; and in a regular course is 15.

PROGRAMS OF STUDY: CSP confers B.A., B.S. and B.B.A. degrees. Associate, Master's, and Doctoral degrees are also awarded. Bachelor's degrees are awarded in BIOLOGICAL SCIENCE (biology/biological science), BUSINESS (accounting, banking and finance, business administration and management, marketing management, organizational leadership and management, and sports manage-

ment), COMMUNICATIONS AND THE ARTS (art, choral music, church music, communications, creative writing, design, dramatic arts, English, English Writing, graphic design, instrumental music education, music, music business management, strategic communication, studio art, theatre arts, and vocal music education), COMPUTER AND PHYSICAL SCIENCE (information sciences and systems and mathematics), EDUCATION (art education, childhood education: 1-6, Christian education, early childhood education, education of the emotionally handicapped, elementary education, English education, mathematics education, middle school education, music education, physical education, science education, secondary education, social studies education, social studies secondary school education, and special education), HEALTH PROFESSIONS (community health work and radiological science), SOCIAL SCIENCE (child care/child and family studies, criminal justice, food production/management/services, history, physical fitness/movement, psychology, religion, religious education, religious music, sociology, and theological studies). Business, teacher education, and church worker programs have the largest enrollments.

ACTIVITIES: There are no fraternities or sororities. There are 40 groups on campus, including art, band, cheerleading, choir, chorus, dance, drama, ethnic, honors, international, jazz band, musical theater, newspaper, pep band, political, professional, religious, social, social service, and student government. Popular campus events include Fine Arts Christmas Concert, and Spring Honors Convocation. **Sports:** There are 6 intercollegiate sports for men and 7 for women, and 8 intramural sports for men and 8 for women. Facilities include a 1200-seat gym, health and wellness center, a stadium for football, soccer, track and field, and baseball and softball playing fields. **Graduates:** From July 1, 2013 to June 30, 2014, 436 bachelor's degrees were awarded. The most popular majors were organizational leadership (16%), marketing (11%), and teacher education (8%). 60 companies recruited on campus in 2013-2014. In an average class, 1% graduate in 3 years or less, 27% graduate in 4 years or less, 43% graduate in 5 years or less, and 46% graduate in 6 years or less. Of the 2013 graduating class, 10% were enrolled in graduate school within 6 months of graduation, and 81% were employed.

SERVICES: Counseling and information services are available, as is tutoring in every subject. There is a reader service for the blind, and remedial math, reading, and writing. **Library/Resources:** The library contains 161,959 volumes, 11,516 microform items, 3,128 audio/video tapes/CDs/DVDs, and subscribes to 297 periodicals including electronic. Computerized library services include interlibrary loans, database searching, Internet access, and Wi-Fi capability. Special learning facilities include an art gallery. **Physically Challenged Students:** 90% of the campus is accessible. Facilities include wheelchair ramps, elevators, special parking, specially equipped restrooms, special class scheduling, lowered drinking fountains, lowered telephones. **Special:** Concordia, St. Paul offers cross-registration with other members of the Concordia University System, internships in many programs, and study-abroad opportunities. Accelerated degree programs and interdisciplinary majors are also available. Credit for life experience, nondegree study, and pass/fail options are possible. Degree completion programs designed for working adults are offered in cohort-delivered format via face-to-face or on-line learning. There is 1 national honor society, a freshman honors program, and 1 departmental honors program. **Visiting:** There are regularly scheduled orientations for prospective students, including a campus tour, class visits, and a meeting with professors. There are guides for informal visits, visitors may sit in on classes, and stay overnight. To schedule a visit, contact the Office of Undergraduate Admission. **Campus Safety and Security:** Measures include 24-hour foot and vehicle patrol, emergency notification system, self-defense education, and security escort services. There are emergency telephones, lighted pathways/sidewalks, and controlled access to dorms/residences.

REQUIREMENTS: The ACT is required. Applicants are normally expected to have 4 years of English, 2 each of math, science, fine arts, and history/social studies, and 1 of health or phys ed. An interview is recommended. 2 letters of recommendation are required. The GED is accepted. A GPA of 2.0 is required. AP and CLEP credits are accepted. To graduate, students must complete 128 credit hours in the form of 1 major or 2 minors, GPA varies from 2.0 to 2.75, and required hours in the major vary from 32 to 44, depending on the program.

The core curriculum consists of 48 hours of liberal arts courses. **Procedure:** Freshmen are admitted fall and spring. Entrance exams should be taken during the senior year. There are deferred admissions and rolling admissions plans. Applications should be filed by August 1 for fall entry; December 1 for spring entry, along with a $30 fee. Applications are accepted on-line. **Transfer Students:** 940 transfer students enrolled in 2013-2014. Applicants must have a 2.0 GPA and submit 2 letters of recommendation. Students with fewer than 1 year of college credits must also submit ACT scores and an official high school transcript. 32 of 128 credits required for the bachelor's degree must be completed at CSP. **International Students:** There are 91 international students enrolled. The school actively recruits these students. They must take the TOEFL with a minimum score of 513 on the paper-based TOEFL (PBT) or 65 on the Internet-based version (iBT) or take the MELAB.

ADMISSIONS: 53% of the 2014-2015 applicants were accepted. The ACT scores were 47% below 21, 25% between 21 and 23, 18% between 24 and 26, 7% between 27 and 28, and 3% above 28. 22% of the current freshmen were in the top fifth of their class; 53% were in the top two fifths. 2 freshmen graduated first in their class. **Admissions Contact:** Kristin Vogel, Assoc VP for Traditional Enrollment. E-Mail: *admissions@csp.edu* Web: *www.csp.edu*

FINANCIAL AID: In 2014-2015, 79% of all full-time freshmen and 76% of continuing full-time students received some form of financial aid. 79% of all full-time freshmen and 73% of continuing full-time students received need-based aid. The average freshman award was $15,620. Need-based scholarships or need-based grants averaged $11,556; need-based self-help aid (loans and jobs) averaged $3,397; and other non-need-based awards and non-need-based scholarships averaged $4,896. 12% of undergraduate students work part-time. Average annual earnings from campus work are $1453. The average financial indebtedness of the 2014 graduate was $25,084. The FAFSA, the college's own financial statement, and federal tax return are required. The priority date for freshman financial aid applications for fall entry is March 1.

GUSTAVUS ADOLPHUS COLLEGE　　C-4
www.gustavus.edu

St. Peter, MN 56082　　(507) 933-7676
　　(800) GUSTAVU
Fax: (507) 933-6270　　Email: admission@gustavus.edu
Full-time: 1117 men, 1306 women　　Faculty: 201; IIB, av$
Part-time: 21 men, 11 women　　Ph.D.s: 85%
Graduate: n/av　　Student/Faculty: 12 to 1
Year: 4-1-4　　Tuition: $39,120
Room & Board: $9050　　Freshman Class: 4804 applied, 3037 accepted, 610 enrolled
ACT: 27　　CEEB CODE: 6253
Application Deadline: November 1　　HIGHLY COMPETITIVE

Gustavus Adolphus College, founded in 1862, is a private liberal arts college affiliated with the Evangelical Luteran Church in America. Figures in the above capsule and in this profile are approximate. In addition to regional accreditation, Gustavus has baccalaureate program accreditation with NASM, NCATE, NLN, CCNE, and NASPE. The 340-acre campus is in a small town 65 miles southwest of Minneapolis. Including any residence halls, there are 56 buildings. **STUDENT LIFE:** 81% of undergraduates are from Minnesota. Others are from 43 states, 15 foreign countries, and Canada. 94% are from public schools. 85% are White. 72% are Protestant; 21% Catholic. **Male To Female Ratio:** 1.2:1. The average age of freshmen is 18; all undergraduates, 20. 9% do not continue beyond their first year; 80% remain to graduate. **Housing:** 2103 students can be accommodated in college housing, which includes coed dorms and on-campus apartments. In addition, there are language houses and special-interest houses. On-campus housing is guaranteed for all 4 years and is available on a lottery system for upperclassmen. 85% of students live on campus; of those, 75% remain on campus on weekends. All students may keep cars.
FACULTY/CLASSROOMS: 52% of faculty are male; 48% are female.

All teach and do research. No introductory courses are taught by graduate students. The average class size in an introductory lecture is 25; in a laboratory is 15; and in a regular course is 15.
PROGRAMS OF STUDY: Gustavus confers B.A. degrees. Bachelor's degrees are awarded in AGRICULTURE (environmental studies), BIOLOGICAL SCIENCE (biochemistry and biology/biological science), BUSINESS (accounting, business administration and management, business economics, and international business management), COMMUNICATIONS AND THE ARTS (classics, communications, dance, dramatic arts, English, fine arts, French, music, Russian, Scandinavian languages, Spanish, and speech/debate/rhetoric), COMPUTER AND PHYSICAL SCIENCE (chemistry, computer science, geology, mathematics, and physics), EDUCATION (art education, business education, elementary education, foreign languages education, health education, middle school education, music education, science education, and secondary education), HEALTH PROFESSIONS (nursing, physical therapy, predentistry, and premedicine), SOCIAL SCIENCE (anthropology, economics, geography, history, philosophy, political science/government, prelaw, psychology, religion, social science, sociology, and women's studies). Physical science and social science are the strongest academically. Business, biology, and communication studies have the largest enrollments.

ACTIVITIES: 14% of men belong to 6 local and 1 national fraternities; 14% of women belong to 5 local and 1 national sororities. There are 125 groups on campus, including art, band, cheerleading, choir, chorus, computers, dance, debate, drama, environmental, ethnic, film, forensics, gay, honors, international, jazz band, literary magazine, musical theater, newspaper, orchestra, pep band, political, professional, radio and TV, religious, social, social service, student government, symphony, and yearbook. Popular campus events include Christmas in Christ Chapel, Earth Jam All-Day Music Festival, and Building Bridges Diversity Conference. **Sports:** There are 12 intercollegiate sports for men and 13 for women, and 17 intramural sports for men and 10 for women. Facilities include an ice arena, an Olympic-size pool, a gymnastics area, an indoor tennis center, an arena, playing fields, artificial turf football field, racquetball and tennis courts, a weight room, an indoor and an outdoor running track, and varsity and intramural fields for soccer, softball, baseball, lacrosse, rugby, and ultimate Frisbee. **Graduates:** From July 1, 2013 to June 30, 2014, 603 bachelor's degrees were awarded. The most popular majors were biology (9%), economics/management (6%), and psychology (5%). 40 companies recruited on campus in 2013-2014. In an average class, 2% graduate in 3 years or less, 80% graduate in 4 years or less, 82% graduate in 5 years or less, and 82% graduate in 6 years or less. Of the 2013 graduating class, 34% were enrolled in graduate school within 6 months of graduation, and 66% were employed.

SERVICES: Counseling and information services are available, as is tutoring in most subjects. A writing lab is available; ESL services are available; and disability services are also available. **Library/Resources:** The library contains 311,480 volumes, 43,075 microform items, 105,799 audio/video tapes/CDs/DVDs, and subscribes to 32,340 periodicals including electronic. Computerized library services include interlibrary loans, database searching, Internet access, and Wi-Fi capability. Special learning facilities include an art gallery, radio station, an arboretum, observatory, greenhouses, bronze-casting facility, geology museum, and many specialized laboratories. **Physically Challenged Students:** All of the campus is accessible. Facilities include wheelchair ramps, elevators, special parking, specially equipped restrooms, special class scheduling, lowered drinking fountains, lowered telephones, and special housing. **Special:** Co-op programs in nursing with St. Olaf College and cross-registration with Minnesota State University are available. The college offers internships, a Washington semester, study abroad in 22 countries, student-designed majors, nondegree study, work-study, and pass/fail options for some courses. A 3-2 engineering degree program with the University of Minnesota and Minnesota State University, Mankato is offered. The Curriculum II core offers a 12-course interdisciplinary program. There are 16 national honor societies, including Phi Beta Kappa, and 12 departmental honors programs. **Visiting:** There are regularly scheduled orientations for prospective students, consisting of an interview, a tour, and meetings with faculty and students. There are guides for informal visits, visitors may sit in on classes, and stay overnight. To schedule a visit, contact the Admissions Office. **Campus Safety and Security:** Measures include 24-hour foot and vehicle patrol, emergency notification system, and security escort services. There are shuttle buses, emergency telephones, lighted pathways/sidewalks, and controlled access to dorms/residences.

REQUIREMENTS: Applicants must have completed 4 years of English, 3 each of math and science, and 2 each of a foreign language, history, and social studies. AP credits are accepted. Important factors in the admissions decision are advanced placement or honors courses and evidence of special talent. All students are required to complete 32 courses plus 2 January interim courses and two-half courses in personal fitness and lifetime activity. Nine courses must be in the following areas (1 each): the arts, biblical, and theological studies, literary and rhetorical studies, historical and philosophical studies, mathematical and logical reasoning, natural science perspective, human behavior and social institutions, and non-western cultures. A minimum GPA of 2.0 is necessary for graduation. A total of 7 to 11 courses is required in the major. **Procedure:** Freshmen are admitted fall, winter, and spring. Entrance exams should be taken in the fall of the senior year. There are deferred admissions and rolling admissions plans. Applications should be filed by November 1 for fall entry; December 1 for winter entry; and January 1 for spring entry. Notifications are sent in November. Applications are accepted on-line. **Transfer Students:** 32 transfer students enrolled in 2013-2014. Transfer applicants must have earned a 2.4 GPA at their previous college. 72 of 140 credits required for the bachelor's degree must be completed at Gustavus. **International Students:** There are 58 international students enrolled. The school actively recruits these students. They must take the TOEFL.

ADMISSIONS: 63% of the 2014-2015 applicants were accepted. The ACT scores were 2% below 21, 13% between 21 and 23, 31% between 24 and 26, 20% between 27 and 28, and 34% above 28. 56% of the current freshmen were in the top fifth of their class; 88% were in the top two fifths. There were 4 National Merit finalists. 23 freshmen graduated first in their class. **Admissions Contact:** Dr. Thomas Crady, Dean of Admissions. E-Mail: *admission@gustavus.edu* Web: *www.gustavus.edu*

FINANCIAL AID: In 2014-2015, 93% of all full-time freshmen and 92% of continuing full-time students received some form of financial aid. 69% of all full-time freshmen and 65% of continuing full-time students received need-based aid. The average freshman award was $31,279. Need-based scholarships or need-based grants averaged $26,732; and need-based self-help aid (loans and jobs) averaged $9,317. 71% of undergraduate students work part-time. Average annual earnings from campus work are $1600. The average financial indebtedness of the 2014 graduate was $33,523. Gustavus is a member of CSS. The CSS/Profile, FAFSA, and the college's own financial statement are required. The priority date for freshman financial aid applications for fall entry is January 1. The deadline for filing freshman financial aid applications for fall entry is April 15.

HAMLINE UNIVERSITY   C-4
www.hamline.edu

St. Paul, MN 55104

(651) 523-2207
(800) 753-9753

Fax: (651) 523-2458 Email: admission@.hamline.edu

Full-time: 903 men, 1259 women	Faculty: n/av
Part-time: 30 men, 50 women	Ph.D.s: 88%
Graduate: 766 men, 1461 women	Student/Faculty: 13 to 1
Year: 4-1-4, summer session	Tuition: $36,286
Room & Board: $9392	Freshman Class: 3417 applied, 2378 accepted, 521 enrolled
SAT CR/M/W: 550/540/540 ACT: 24	CEEB CODE: 6265
Application Deadline: n/av	**VERY COMPETITIVE**

Hamline University, founded in 1854, is a private liberal arts and sciences university affiliated with the United Methodist Church. There are 3 undergraduate schools and 4 graduate schools. In addition to regional accreditation, Hamline has baccalaureate program accreditation with NASM, NCATE, ABA, and ACS. The 60-acre campus is in an urban area between the downtowns of Minneapolis and St. Paul.

STUDENT LIFE: 78% of undergraduates are from Minnesota. Others are from 44 states, 34 foreign countries, and Canada. 72% are White. 28% are Lutheran, Buddhist and unknown; 19% Catholic; 17% claim no religious affiliation. **Male To Female Ratio:** 1.6:1. The average age of freshmen is 18; all undergraduates, 20. 17% do not continue beyond their first year; 65% remain to graduate. **Housing:** 955 students can be accommodated in college housing, which includes coed dorms, on-campus apartments, and married student housing. In addition, there are language houses, special-interest houses, fraternity houses, PRIDE black student alliance house, Hmong student asociation house, and Amity Scholar house. On-campus housing is guaranteed for all 4 years. 58% of students commute. All students may keep cars.

FACULTY/CLASSROOMS: 43% of faculty are male; 57% are female. No introductory courses are taught by graduate students.

PROGRAMS OF STUDY: Hamline confers B.A., B.S., B.B.A. and B.F.A degrees. Master's and Doctoral degrees are also awarded. Bachelor's degrees are awarded in AGRICULTURE (environmental studies), BIOLOGICAL SCIENCE (biochemistry and biology/biological science), BUSINESS (accounting, business administration and management, global/general management, and international business management), COMMUNICATIONS AND THE ARTS (art history, art, communications, creative writing, dramatic arts, English, fine arts, French, German, music, music performance, Spanish, and theatre arts), COMPUTER AND PHYSICAL SCIENCE (chemistry, digital arts/technology, mathematics, and physics), EDUCATION (athletic training, education, elementary education, foreign languages education, music education, science education, and secondary education), HEALTH PROFESSIONS (exercise science and premedicine), SOCIAL SCIENCE (anthropology, criminal justice, East Asian studies, economics, forensic studies, history, Latin American studies, paralegal studies, peace studies, philosophy, political science/government, prelaw, psychology, religion, social science, social studies, sociology, urban studies, and women's studies). social sciences, business, and psychology have the largest enrollments.

ACTIVITIES: There are 60 groups on campus, including art, band, cheerleading, chess, choir, chorale, chorus, computers, dance, drama, environmental, ethnic, film, forensics, gay, honors, international, jazz band, literary magazine, musical theater, newspaper, orchestra, pep band, photography, political, professional, radio and TV, religious, social, social service, student government, and symphony. Popular campus events include World Fest, Fall Organization Fair, and Women's Leadership Retreat. **Sports:** There are 9 intercollegiate sports for men and 10 for women, and 11 intramural sports for men and 11 for women. Facilities include a stadium, field house, swimming pool, playing field, and an athletic center. **Graduates:** From July 1, 2013 to June 30, 2014, 428 bachelor's degrees were awarded. The most popular majors were social sciences (15%), psychology (13%), and business (5%). 85 companies recruited on campus in 2013-2014. In an average class, 56% graduate in 4 years or less, 6% graduate in 5 years or less, and 2% graduate in 6 years or less.

SERVICES: Counseling and information services are available, as is tutoring in every subject. There is a reader service for the blind, and remedial math, reading, and writing. **Library/Resources:** Computerized library services include interlibrary loans, database searching, Internet access, and Wi-Fi capability. Special learning facilities include an art gallery, radio station, centers for global and environmental education, and for excellence in urban teaching. There are also centers for writing and quantitative reasoning. **Physically Challenged Students:** Facilities include wheelchair ramps, elevators, special parking, specially equipped restrooms, special class scheduling, lowered drinking fountains, lowered telephones, and special housing. **Special:** Cross-registration with Augsburg, Macalester, Saint Catherine Colleges and the University of Saint Thomas is possible. Students may select cooperative programs, study abroad, a Washington semester with American University, dual majors, student-designed majors, and pass/fail options. Students may earn a 3-2 or 4-2 engineering degree at the University of Minnesota or Washington University. On-campus work-study is available, as are extensive internship opportunities on and off campus. There is a Phi Beta Kappa and a freshman honors program. **Visiting:** There are guides for informal visits, visitors may sit in on classes, and stay overnight. To schedule a visit, contact the Admissions Office at (651) 523-2014. **Campus Safety and**

Security: Measures include 24-hour foot and vehicle patrol, emergency notification system, self-defense education, and security escort services. There are emergency telephones, lighted pathways/ sidewalks, and controlled access to dorms/residences.

REQUIREMENTS: The SAT or ACT is required. It is recommended that candidates for admission complete 4 years of English with 1 year of college preparatory writing, 4 years of social studies, 4 years of academic electives, 4 years each of math, 3 years of lab science, 4 years of social science, and 2 years of a foreign language. The GED is accepted. AP and CLEP credits are accepted.To graduate, students must complete a minimum of 32 course credits within their field of concentration with a minimum overall GPA of 2.0. 63 course credits must be outside the major. In their first year, all students are required to take a freshman seminar and freshman English and demonstrate computer literacy. All students must also take a variety of general education courses to apply toward the "Hamline Plan." An independent study project and an internship are also required. **Procedure:** Freshmen are admitted to all sessions. There are early decision, early admissions, deferred admissions, and rolling admissions plans. Application deadlines are open. Notification of early decision is sent December 20; regular decision. Applications are accepted on-line. **Transfer Students:** 140 transfer students enrolled in 2013-2014. Transfer applicants must submit the application form, transcript copies, teacher/advisor recommendation, and a secondary school transcript, if fewer than 32 semester hours have been competed. Applicants must submit an essay or personal statement. A minimum college GPA of 2.0 is required. 56 of 128 credits required for the bachelor's degree must be completed at Hamline. **International Students:** There are 30 international students enrolled. The school actively recruits these students. They must take the TOEFL with a minimum score of 550 on the paper-based TOEFL (PBT) or 80 on the Internet-based version (iBT). They must also take the SAT or ACT.

ADMISSIONS: 70% of the 2014-2015 applicants were accepted. The SAT scores for the 2014-2015 freshman class were: Critical Reading--36% below 500, 32% between 500 and 599, 22% between 600 and 699, and 10% between 700 and 800; Math--27% below 500, 51% between 500 and 599, 19% between 600 and 699, and 3% between 700 and 800; Writing--31% below 500, 36% between 500 and 599, 31% between 600 and 699, and 3% between 700 and 800. The ACT scores were 20% below 21, 24% between 21 and 23, 21% between 24 and 26, 11% between 27 and 28, and 19% above 28. **Admissions Contact:** Undergraduate Admission E-Mail: *admission@.hamline.edu* Web: *www.hamline.edu*

FINANCIAL AID: In 2014-2015, 99% of all full-time freshmen and 98% of continuing full-time students received some form of financial aid. 89% of all full-time freshmen and 84% of continuing full-time students received need-based aid. The average freshman award was $31,477. The average financial indebtedness of the 2014 graduate was $36,006. The FAFSA is required. The priority date for freshman financial aid applications for fall entry is March 15.

MACALESTER COLLEGE C-4
www.macalester.edu

St. Paul, MN 55105

	(651) 696-6357
	(800) 231-7974
Fax: (651) 696-6724	Email: admissions@macalester.edu
Full-time: 810 men, 1235 women	Faculty: 248; IIB, +$
Part-time: 8 men, 20 women	Ph.Ds: 94%
Graduate: n/av	Student/Faculty: 10 to 1
Year: semesters	Tuition: $47,195
Room & Board: $10,496	Freshman Class: 6463 applied, 2349 accepted, 541 enrolled
SAT CR/M/W: 700/660/680 ACT: 30	CEEB CODE: 6390
Application Deadline: January 15	MOST COMPETITIVE

Macalester College, founded in 1874, is a nonsectarian liberal arts and sciences institution. In addition to regional accreditation, Macalester has baccalaureate program accreditation with NASM. The 53-acre campus is in an urban area midway between downtown St. Paul and Minneapolis. Including any residence halls, there are 65 buildings. **STUDENT LIFE:** 82% of undergraduates are from out of state,

mostly the Mid-West. Students are from 48 states, 90 foreign countries, and Canada. 66% are from public schools. 66% are White; 14% Foreign. **Female To Male Ratio:** 1.5:1. The average age of freshmen is 18; all undergraduates, 20. 6% do not continue beyond their first year; 90% remain to graduate. **Housing:** 1296 students can be accommodated in college housing, which includes single-sex and coed dorms and on-campus apartments. In addition, there are language houses, special-interest houses, Vegetarian co-op, a cultural house, interfaith house, and gender neutral section. On-campus housing is available on a lottery system for upperclassmen. 66% of students live on campus; of those, 90% remain on campus on weekends. Upperclassmen may keep cars.

FACULTY/CLASSROOMS: 46% of faculty are male; 54% are female. All teach undergraduates, and 80% do both. No introductory courses are taught by graduate students. The average class size in an introductory lecture is 20; in a laboratory is 11; and in a regular course is 17.

PROGRAMS OF STUDY: Macalester confers B.A. degrees. Bachelor's degrees are awarded in AGRICULTURE (environmental studies), BIOLOGICAL SCIENCE (biology/biological science and neurosciences), COMMUNICATIONS AND THE ARTS (art, Chinese, classics, dramatic arts, English, French, Japanese, linguistics, media arts, music, Russian, and Spanish), COMPUTER AND PHYSICAL SCIENCE (chemistry, computer science, geology, mathematics, and physics), EDUCATION (education), SOCIAL SCIENCE (American studies, anthropology, Asian/Oriental studies, economics, geography, German area studies, history, humanities, international studies, Latin American studies, philosophy, political science/ government, psychology, religion, sociology, and women's studies). International studies, economics, biology, chemistry, and political science are the strongest academically. Math, computer science, psychology, and economics are the largest.

ACTIVITIES: There are no fraternities or sororities. There are 121 groups on campus, including social justice organizations, art, bagpipe, band, chess, choir, chorale, chorus, computers, dance, debate, drama, environmental, ethnic, forensics, gay, honors, international, jazz band, literary magazine, multi faith council, newspaper, orchestra, photography, political, professional, radio and TV, religious, social, social service, student government, and symphony. Popular campus events include Midnight Breakfast, Mac Idol, Spring Fest and Founders Day. **Sports:** There are 10 intercollegiate sports for men and 11 for women, and 12 intramural sports for men and 12 for women. Facilities include a field house, a 1200-seat gym, 10-lane swimming pool, 4000-seat stadium for football, soccer, and outdoor track, 2 racquetball courts, 6 tennis courts, an indoor track and field facility, weight room, 2 racquetball/squash courts and baseball and softball diamonds. **Graduates:** From July 1, 2013 to June 30, 2014, 605 bachelor's degrees were awarded. The most popular majors were biology (10%), political science (8%), and economics (7%). 54 companies recruited on campus in 2013-2014. In an average class, 85% graduate in 4 years or less, 89% graduate in 5 years or less, and 90% graduate in 6 years or less. Of the 2013 graduating class, 11% were enrolled in graduate school within 6 months of graduation, and 60% were employed.

SERVICES: Counseling and information services are available, as is tutoring in some subjects, math, chemistry, physics, and writing There is a reader service for the blind. **Library/Resources:** The library contains 433,498 volumes, 87,004 microform items, and 42,018 audio/video tapes/CDs/DVDs, and subscribes to 5,492 periodicals including electronic. Computerized library services include interlibrary loans, database searching, Internet access, and Wi-Fi capability. Special learning facilities include an art gallery, radio station, an academic support center, a 280-acre natural history study area 25 miles from campus. **Physically Challenged Students:** 90% of the campus is accessible. Facilities include wheelchair ramps, elevators, special parking, specially equipped restrooms, special class scheduling, lowered drinking fountains, lowered telephones, and special housing. **Special:** Cross-registration at Minneapolis College of Art and Design is offered; in addition, the college belongs to several consortiums, including the Associated Colleges of the Twin Cities. There also are cooperative programs in liberal arts and architecture with Washington University in St. Louis, engineering with the same school and the University of Minnesota. Internships are available in government, financial services, law, medicine, research, the arts, and other fields.

Students study abroad in more than 68 countries. Student-designed majors and pass/fail options for no more than 1 course per semester also are available. There are 16 national honor societies, including Phi Beta Kappa, and 30 departmental honors programs. **Visiting:** There are regularly scheduled orientations for prospective students, including interviews, information sessions, a class visit, and a tour of campus. There are guides for informal visits, visitors may sit in on classes, and stay overnight. To schedule a visit, contact the Admissions Office at (800) 231-7974. **Campus Safety and Security:** Measures include 24-hour foot and vehicle patrol, emergency notification system, self-defense education, and security escort services. There are emergency telephones, lighted pathways/sidewalks, controlled access to dorms/residences, Security site on the school's web site.

REQUIREMENTS: The SAT or ACT is required. In addition, Applicants should have earned at least 16 academic credits, including 4 years of English and 3 each in math, laboratory science, foreign language, and social studies/history. The college also expects applicants to have taken honors, AP, or IB courses where available. An essay is required, and an interview is recommended. AP credits are accepted. Important factors in the admissions decision are advanced placement or honors courses, extracurricular activities record, and recommendations by school officials. All students are required to complete 128 semester hours, with 32 to 44 in the major, and an overall minimum GPA of 2.0. Required courses include 12 hours in humanities and fine arts, 8 hours in natural science and/or math, 8 hours in social science, 4 hours each in US multiculturalism, internationalism and writing, 4 to 12 hours in quantitative reasoning, and a first-year course. Second language proficiency equivalent to 2 years of college-level language must be shown, and every major requires a capstone experience. **Procedure:** Freshmen are admitted fall. Entrance exams should be taken in the fall of the senior year or before. There are early decision and deferred admissions plans. Early decision applications should be filed by November 15; regular applications, by January 15 for fall entry, along with a $40 fee. Notification of early decision is sent December 15; regular decision, March 30. 120 early decision candidates were accepted for the 2014-2015 class. 510 applicants were on the 2014 waiting list; 215 were admitted. Applications are accepted on-line. **Transfer Students:** 19 transfer students enrolled in 2013-2014. Transfer students should follow the application instructions found on the Admissions website for U.S. Transfer Students and for International Transfer Students. Transfer applicants should usually present a cumulative grade point average of "B+" (or 3.33 average) or better. The application fee for transfer students is $40. Students considering transferring to Macalester may have their transcripts evaluated for the transfer of course credits prior to applying by sending an official transcript and specifically requesting this service from the Registrar's Office. This evaluation is only preliminary, but is complete enough to be helpful in planning for transfer. 64 of 128 credits required for the bachelor's degree must be completed at Macalester. **International Students:** There are 278 international students enrolled. The school actively recruits these students. They must take the TOEFL with a minimum score of 600 on the paper-based TOEFL (PBT) or 100 on the Internet-based version (iBT), or take the IELTS 7.0 minimum. They must also take the SAT or ACT.

ADMISSIONS: 36% of the 2014-2015 applicants were accepted. The SAT scores for the 2014-2015 freshman class were: Critical Reading--4% between 500 and 599, 45% between 600 and 699, and 50% between 700 and 800. Math-- 16% between 500 and 599, 56% between 600 and 699, and 29% between 700 and 800. Writing-- 9% between 500 and 599, 50% between 600 and 699, and 41% between 700 and 800. The ACT scores were % below 21, 1% between 21 and 23, 7% between 24 and 26, 20% between 27 and 28, and 72% above 28. 87% of the current freshmen were in the top fifth of their class; 99% were in the top two fifths. There were 20 National Merit finalists. 29 freshmen graduated first in their class. **Admissions Contact:** Lorne T. Robinson, Dean of Admissions and Financial Aid. E-Mail: *admissions@macalester.edu* Web: *www.macalester.edu*

FINANCIAL AID: In 2014-2015, 84% of all full-time freshmen and 76% of continuing full-time students received some form of financial aid. 73% of all full-time freshmen and 68% of continuing full-time students received need-based aid. The average freshman award was $40,994. Need-based scholarships or need-based grants averaged $35,594; and need-based self-help aid (loans and jobs) averaged

$5,400. 70% of undergraduate students work part-time. Average annual earnings from campus work are $1800. The average financial indebtedness of the 2014 graduate was $24,156. Macalester is a member of CSS. The CSS/Profile and FAFSA, and parent's W-2 and tax forms are required. The priority date for freshman financial aid applications for fall entry is February 8. The deadline for filing freshman financial aid applications for fall entry is March 1.

METROPOLITAN STATE UNIVERSITY *(The complete profile is made available exclusively on our website, www.barronspac.com)*

MINNEAPOLIS COLLEGE OF ART AND DESIGN *(The complete profile is made available exclusively on our website, www. barronspac.com)*

MINNESOTA STATE UNIVERSITY, MANKATO — C-4
www.mnsu.edu

Mankato, MN 56001

(507) 389-1822
(800) 722-0544

Fax: (507) 389-1511
Email: admissions@mnsu.edu

Full-time: 5554 men, 5588 women
Faculty: IIA, av$

Part-time: 871 men, 1321 women
Ph.D.s: 80%

Graduate: 746 men, 1235 women
Student/Faculty: 20 to 1

Year: semesters, summer session
Tuition: $7574 ($15,052)

Room & Board: $8042
Freshman Class: 5605 applied, 5292 accepted, 2215 enrolled

ACT: 23
CEEB CODE: 6677

Application Deadline: n/av
COMPETITIVE

Minnesota State University, Mankato, founded in 1868 and a unit of Minnesota State Colleges and Universities, offers programs in the liberal arts and sciences, as well as business, education, engineering and technology, and nursing. The figures in the above capsule and in this profile are approximate. There are 6 undergraduate schools and 1 graduate school. In addition to regional accreditation, Minnesota State or MSU has baccalaureate program accreditation with AACSB, ABET, ADA, CSWE, NASAD, NASM, NCATE, NLN, and NRPA. The 354-acre campus is in a rural area 85 miles southwest of Minneapolis-St. Paul. Including any residence halls, there are 25 buildings.

STUDENT LIFE: 83% of undergraduates are from Minnesota. Others are from 48 states, 68 foreign countries, and Canada. 94% are from public schools. 76% are White. **Male To Female Ratio:** 1.1:1. The average age of freshmen is 19; all undergraduates, 22. 26% do not continue beyond their first year; 49% remain to graduate. **Housing:** 3100 students can be accommodated in college housing, which includes single-sex and coed dorms, on-campus apartments, and special-interest floors, including freshman quiet-study floors, upperclass floors, engineering floors, and computer science floors. On-campus housing is guaranteed for the freshman year only, and is available on a first-come, first-served basis. 82% of students commute. Alcohol is not permitted. All students may keep cars.

FACULTY/CLASSROOMS: 51% of faculty are male; 49% are female. 96% teach undergraduates, and 51% do research. Graduate students teach 4% of introductory courses. The average class size in an introductory lecture is 43; in a laboratory is 11; and in a regular course is 21.

PROGRAMS OF STUDY: Minnesota State or MSU confers B.A., B.S., B.F.A., B.Mus., B.S.E.E. and B.S.M.E. degrees. Associate, Master's, and Doctoral degrees are also awarded. Bachelor's degrees are awarded in BIOLOGICAL SCIENCE (biochemistry, biology/biological science, biotechnology, life science, and life science secondary school education), BUSINESS (accounting, banking and finance, business administration and management, finance, international business, international business management, management science, marketing, recreation and leisure services, and sports management), COMMUNICATIONS AND THE ARTS (art, communication studies, communications, dance, dramatic arts, English, English as a second/foreign language, French, German, journalism, media management, music, music business management, music industry, Technical Communication, Spanish, speech/debate/rhetoric, and theatre studies), COMPUTER AND PHYSICAL SCIENCE (chemistry, chemistry/adolescence education, Computer Engineering Technology, computer information technology, computer security and information assurance, earth science, information sciences and systems, mathematics, and physics), EDUCATION (art education, dance education, early childhood education, education, elementary education, foreign languages education, general studies, health education, mathematics education, middle school education, music education, physical education, science education, secondary education, social studies education, and special education), ENGINEERING AND ENVIRONMENTAL DESIGN (automotive technology, aviation administration/management, civil engineering, computer engineering, construction management, electrical/electronics engineering, electrical/electronics engineering technology, engineering technology, environmental science, food services technology, manufacturing engineering, manufacturing technology, mechanical engineering, military science, and preengineering), HEALTH PROFESSIONS (allied health, clinical science, community health work, dental hygiene, exercise science, health science, medical laboratory science, nursing, predentistry, premedicine, prepharmacy, preveterinary science, public health, and speech pathology/audiology), SOCIAL SCIENCE (American Indian studies, anthropology, communication sciences & disorders, cognitive science, corrections, criminal justice, dietetics, economics, ethnic studies, family/consumer studies, geography, history, human development, humanities, international relations, law enforcement and corrections, parks and recreation management, philosophy, political science/government, prelaw, psychology, Scandinavian studies, social studies, social work, sociology, urban studies, and women's studies). Engineering, nursing, and sciences are the strongest academically. Business, nursing, and education have the largest enrollments.

ACTIVITIES: 4% of men belong to 7 national fraternities; 3% of women belong to 4 national sororities. There are 250 groups on campus, including art, band, cheerleading, choir, chorale, chorus, computers, dance, drama, ethnic, film, forensics, gay, honors, international, jazz band, literary magazine, musical theater, newspaper, opera, orchestra, pep band, photography, political, professional, radio and TV, religious, social, social service, and student government. Popular campus events include multicultural activities, celebrations, Greek Week, and the Big Event. **Sports:** There are 11 intercollegiate sports for men and 11 for women, and 55 intramural sports for men and 55 for women. Facilities include a 7000-seat stadium; a field house; a recreation center including an indoor swimming pool, racquetball courts, a walking/jogging track, multipurpose rooms, weights, and workout machines; 2 gyms; an indoor track; tennis courts; and a 5000-seat ice hockey arena (city owned). **Graduates:** From July 1, 2013 to June 30, 2014, 2414 bachelor's degrees were awarded. The most popular majors were nursing (9%), management (5%), and psychology (5%). 238 companies recruited on campus in 2013-2014. In an average class, 2% graduate in 3 years or less, 18% graduate in 4 years or less, 42% graduate in 5 years or less, and 49% graduate in 6 years or less.

SERVICES: Counseling and information services are available, as is tutoring in most subjects. There is a reader service for the blind, and remedial math, reading, and writing. Also available are alternative testing accommodations, note taking, sign language interpreting, and taped texts. **Library/Resources:** The library contains 1.2 million volumes, 253,560 microform items, and 30,686 audio/video tapes/CDs/DVDs, and subscribes to 3,126 periodicals including electronic. Computerized library services include interlibrary loans, database searching, Internet access, and Wi-Fi capability. Special learning facilities include an art gallery, radio station, 2 observatories, and high ropes course . **Physically Challenged Students:** All of the campus is accessible. Facilities include wheelchair ramps, elevators, special parking, specially equipped restrooms, special class scheduling, lowered drinking fountains, lowered telephones, special housing. **Special:** The university offers cross-registration within the Minnesota State University System and with Bethany Lutheran College and Gustavus Adolphus College. Students may serve internships, study abroad, or participate in an accelerated degree program. B.A.-B.S. degrees, dual and student-designed majors, nondegree study, and pass/fail options also are available. There are 25 national honor societies and a freshman honors program. **Visiting:** There are regularly scheduled orientations for prospective students, consisting of overview presentations, campus tours, and academic information fairs. There are guides for informal visits and visitors may sit in on classes. To schedule a visit, contact the Office of Admission. **Campus Safety and Security:** Measures include 24-hour foot and vehicle patrol, emergency notification system, self-defense education, and security escort services. There are shuttle buses, emergency telephones, lighted pathways/sidewalks, controlled access to dorms/residences, closed-circuit parking lot cameras, and motion-sensitive lights in low traffic areas. $

REQUIREMENTS: The ACT is required. Applicants must be graduates of an accredited secondary school and rank in the top 50% of their high school class or have an ACT composite score of 21 or higher along with a satisfactory class rank. AP and CLEP credits are accepted. To graduate, students must complete 128 semester hours of credit, with a minimum GPA of 2.0 and at least 45 hours in the major. Most programs require 44 hours of general education, including courses in English, speech, science, math, social/behavioral science, arts and humanities, cultural diversity, global perspective, ethnic/civic responsibility, and people and the environment. **Procedure:** Freshmen are admitted to all sessions. Entrance exams should be taken in the spring of the junior year or the fall of the senior year. There are deferred admissions and rolling admissions plans. Check with the school for current application deadlines. The application fee is $20. Notification is sent on a rolling basis. Applications are accepted on-line. **Transfer Students:** 1014 transfer students enrolled in 2013-2014. Transfer applicants must have a minimum GPA of 2.0 and have completed at least 67% of all college-level courses attempted. 30 of 128 credits required for the bachelor's degree must be completed at Minnesota State or MSU. **International Students:** There are 1040 international students enrolled. The school actively recruits these students. They must take the TOEFL with a minimum score of 500 on the paper-based TOEFL (PBT) or 61 on the Internet-based version (iBT), or an English placement test at matriculation.

ADMISSIONS: 94% of the 2014-2015 applicants were accepted. The ACT scores were 9% below 21, 62% between 21 and 23, 16% between 24 and 26, 12% between 27 and 28, and 1% above 28. 20% of the current freshmen were in the top fifth of their class; 55% were in the top two fifths. 20 freshmen graduated first in their class. **Admissions Contact:** Admissions Officer. E-Mail: *admissions@mnsu.edu* Web: *www.mnsu.edu*

FINANCIAL AID: In 2014-2015, 80% of all full-time freshmen and 80% of continuing full-time students received some form of financial aid. 80% of all full-time freshmen and 80% of continuing full-time students received need-based aid. The average freshman award was $6,134. Need-based scholarships or need-based grants averaged $5,290 ; need-based self-help aid (loans and jobs) averaged $4,409; non-need-based athletic scholarships averaged $5,827; and other non-need-based awards and non-need-based scholarships averaged $2,271. 21% of undergraduate students work part-time. Average annual earnings from campus work are $1960. The FAFSA is required. The priority date for freshman financial aid applications for fall entry is March 15.

MINNESOTA STATE UNIVERSITY, MOORHEAD   A-2
www.mnstate.edu

Moorhead, MN 56563	(218)477-2161
	n/av
Fax: (218) 477-4374	Email: dragon@mnstate.edu
Full-time: 2526 men, 3304 women	Faculty: IIA, -$
Part-time: 484 men, 698 women	Ph.D.s: n/av
Graduate: 106 men, 379 women	Student/Faculty: n/av
Year: semesters, summer session	Tuition: $6924
Room & Board: $6468	Freshman Class: 3393 applied, 2489 accepted, 2238 enrolled
ACT: required	CEEB CODE: 6678
Application Deadline: n/av	VERY COMPETITIVE

Minnesota State University Moorhead, founded in 1887, is a public comprehensive institution. There are 4 undergraduate schools and 1 graduate school. In addition to regional accreditation, MSU Moorhead has baccalaureate program accreditation with ACCE, CSWE, NASAD, NASM, NCATE, ABA, ACS, and ASLH. The 119-acre campus is in a suburban area 240 miles northwest of Minneapolis-St. Paul and across the river from Fargo, North Dakota. Including any residence halls, there are 28 buildings.

STUDENT LIFE: 83% are White. **Male To Female Ratio:** 1.4:1. The average age of freshmen is 19; all undergraduates, 23. **Housing:** 1844 students can be accommodated in college housing, which includes single-sex and coed dorms and on-campus apartments. In addition, there are sorority houses, and living learning communities. On-campus housing is available on a first-come, first-served basis. 81% of students commute. Alcohol is not permitted. All students may keep cars.

FACULTY/CLASSROOMS: 61% of faculty are male; 39% are female. No introductory courses are taught by graduate students.

PROGRAMS OF STUDY: MSU Moorhead confers B.A., B.S., B.F.A., B.M., B.S.N., and B.S.W. degrees. Associate, Master's, and Doctoral degrees are also awarded. Bachelor's degrees are awarded in BIOLOGICAL SCIENCE (biology/biological science), BUSINESS (accounting, banking and finance, business administration and management, international business management, management science, marketing/retailing/merchandising, and operations management), COMMUNICATIONS AND THE ARTS (broadcasting, communications, dramatic arts, English, film arts, fine arts, journalism, music, music technology, public relations, Spanish, and speech/debate/rhetoric), COMPUTER AND PHYSICAL SCIENCE (chemistry, computer science, computer security and information assurance, earth science, geoscience, mathematics, and physics), EDUCATION (art education, athletic training, early childhood education, elementary education, English education, foreign languages education, health education, mathematics education, music education, physical education, science education, social studies education, and special education), ENGINEERING AND ENVIRONMENTAL DESIGN (construction management, graphic arts technology, and industrial engineering technology), HEALTH PROFESSIONS (community health work, exercise science, health care administration, medical laboratory technology, nursing, predentistry, premedicine, prepharmacy, preveterinary science, and speech pathology/audiology), SOCIAL SCIENCE (anthropology, criminal justice, East Asian studies, economics, gerontology, history, international studies, law, paralegal studies, philosophy, political science/government, prelaw, psychology, social work, sociology, Spanish studies, and women's studies).

ACTIVITIES: 2% of men belong to 1% of women belong to 2 local and 2 national sororities. There are 150 groups on campus, including art, band, cheerleading, choir, chorus, computers, dance, drama, drill team, ethnic, film, gay, honors, international, jazz band, literary magazine, musical theater, newspaper, orchestra, pep band, photography, political, professional, radio and TV, religious, social, social service, and student government. Popular campus events include Celebrations of Nations, Straw Hat Summer Theatre, and Dragon Frost. **Sports:** There are 5 intercollegiate sports for men and 9 for women, and 14 intramural sports for men and 14 for women. Facilities include a 40,000 square foot Dragon Wellness Center. This facility has 2 full basketball or volleyball courts, exercise room with cardio and strength training equipment, rock climing wall and an elevated indoor running track. Comstock Memorial Union provides meeting rooms, programming areas, TV lounges, and informal general lounges. **Graduates:** From July 1, 2013 to June 30, 2014, 1229 bachelor's degrees were awarded. The most popular majors were mass communication (8%), elementary education (5%), and social work (5%).

SERVICES: Counseling and information services are available, as is tutoring in every subject. There is a reader service for the blind, and remedial math, reading, and writing. **Library/Resources:** The library contains 656,104 volumes, 872,378 microform items, 25,290 audio/video tapes/CDs/DVDs, and subscribes to 2,245 periodicals including electronic. Computerized library services include interlibrary loans and database searching. Special learning facilities include an art gallery, planetarium, radio station, TV station and a regional science center. **Physically Challenged Students:** Facilities include wheelchair ramps, elevators, special parking, specially equipped restrooms, lowered drinking fountains, and lowered telephones. **Special:** Internships are available in most disciplines. The university offers cross-registration with North Dakota State University and Concordia College and is a member of the National Student Exchange. Study abroad program allows students to study at any of 125 member universities. A variety of internships are available at local, state and federal government agencies, service organizations and in the private sector. There are 7 national honor societies, a freshman honors program, and 1 departmental honors program. **Visiting:** There are regularly scheduled orientations for prospective students, including a campus tour, lunch, and meetings with faculty and an admissions officer. There are guides for informal visits. To schedule a visit, contact Admissions Office. **Campus Safety and Security:** Measures include 24-hour foot and vehicle patrol, emergency notification system, self-defense education, and security escort services. There are emergency telephones, lighted pathways/sidewalks, and in-room safes.

REQUIREMENTS: The ACT is required. A high school diploma is required, and the GED is accepted. A SAT satisfactory score or ACT score of 21 is required for applicants whose high school rank is below the top half. MSU Moorhead requires applicants to be in the upper 50% of their class. AP and CLEP credits are accepted.To graduate students must have a 2.0 GPA and complete 120 semester hours, including a liberal arts core of 45 credits and 43 semester hours in upper-division courses. Required courses include 2 in English, 6 credits each of natural science, social science, humanities, and communication systems, and 5 credits in cultural diversity. All students must complete an upper-level writing requirement. **Procedure:** Freshmen are admitted fall, spring, and summer. Entrance exams should be taken in the junior or senior year of high school. There is a rolling admissions plan. Check with the school for current application deadlines. The fall 2014 application fee was $20. Applications are accepted online. **Transfer Students:** 659 transfer students enrolled in 2013-2014. Applicants must submit a high school transcript or GED score and all other transcripts for post-secondary schools attended. A minimum GPA of 2.0 (higher for entry in some departments) is necessary for transfer credit. 30 of 120 credits required for the bachelor's degree must be completed at MSU Moorhead. **International Students:** There are 320 international students enrolled. The school actively recruits these students. They must take the TOEFL with a minimum score of 500 on the paper-based TOEFL (PBT) or 61 on the Internet-based version (iBT).

ADMISSIONS: 73% of the 2014-2015 applicants were accepted. **Admissions Contact:** Jeremy Johnson, Interim Director of Admissions. E-Mail: *dragon@mnstate.edu* Web: *www.mnstate.edu*

FINANCIAL AID: The FAFSA is required. Check with the school for current application deadlines.

NORTH CENTRAL UNIVERSITY   C-4
www.northcentral.edu

Minneapolis, MN 55404	(612) 343-4469
	800-289-6222
Fax: (612) 343-4146	Email: jdmartin@northcentral.edu
Full-time: 587 men, 718 women	Faculty: 60
Part-time: n/av	Ph.D.s: 50%
Graduate: n/av	Student/Faculty: 18 to 1
Year: semesters, summer session	Tuition: $23,050
Room & Board: $3350	Freshman Class: n/av
SAT: required ACT: 21	CEEB CODE: 0051
Application Deadline: June 1	COMPETITIVE

North Central University, founded in 1930 and affiliated with the Assemblies of God, is a Christian University that emphasizes rigorous academic training and spiritual passion. There are 5 undergraduate schools. The 12-acre campus is in an urban area in downtown Minneapolis. Including any residence halls, there are 24 buildings.

STUDENT LIFE: 54% of undergraduates are from Minnesota. Others are from 40 states, 11 foreign countries, and Canada. 88% are from public schools. 82% are White. 99% are Protestant. **Male To**

Female Ratio: 1.2:1. The average age of freshmen is 18; all undergraduates, 20. 25% do not continue beyond their first year; 40% remain to graduate. **Housing:** 950 students can be accommodated in college housing, which includes single-sex dorms, on-campus apartments, and married student housing. On-campus housing is available on a first-come, first-served basis. 80% of students live on campus; of those, 80% remain on campus on weekends. Alcohol is not permitted. All students may keep cars.

FACULTY/CLASSROOMS: 63% of faculty are male; 37% are female. All teach undergraduates. No introductory courses are taught by graduate students. The average class size in an introductory lecture is 80; in a laboratory is 15; and in a regular course is 25.

PROGRAMS OF STUDY: NCU confers B.A. and B.S. degrees. Associate degrees are also awarded. Bachelor's degrees are awarded in COMMUNICATIONS AND THE ARTS (communications), EDUCATION (elementary education), SOCIAL SCIENCE (behavioral science, biblical languages, ministries, pastoral studies, religion, religious education, and religious music). Pastoral studies, youth ministry, and psychology are the strongest academically. Pastoral Studies, youth ministry, and business administration have the largest enrollments.

ACTIVITIES: There are no fraternities or sororities. There are 28 groups on campus, including art, band, choir, chorale, chorus, drama, jazz band, literary magazine, musical theater, newspaper, orchestra, photography, political, professional, radio and TV, religious, social, and student government. Popular campus events include All-College Picnic, Community Outreach Day, and Spring Banquet. **Sports:** There are 6 intercollegiate sports for men and 6 for women, and 4 intramural sports for men and 4 for women. Facilities include Elliot Park, the Clark-Danielson College Life Center Gym, and the National Sports Complex.

SERVICES: Counseling and information services are available, as is tutoring in every subject. **Library/Resources:** The library contains 70,041 volumes, 29 microform items, 200 audio/video tapes/CDs/DVDs, and subscribes to 325 periodicals including electronic. Computerized library services include interlibrary loans, database searching, and Internet access. Special learning facilities include a radio station. **Physically Challenged Students:** All of the campus is accessible. Facilities include wheelchair ramps, elevators, special parking, specially equipped restrooms, special class scheduling, lowered drinking fountains, and lowered telephones. **Special:** Students may pursue co-op programs in nursing or secondary education, study abroad in 6 countries, and nondegree study. Credit for life, military, or work experience is possible. Work-study, dual majors, and student-designed majors are available. There is 1 national honor society and 1 departmental honors program. **Visiting:** There are regularly scheduled orientations for prospective students. There are guides for informal visits, visitors may sit in on classes, and stay overnight. To schedule a visit, contact the Admissions Office. **Campus Safety and Security:** Measures include 24-hour foot and vehicle patrol, emergency notification system, self-defense education, and security escort services. There are shuttle buses, lighted pathways/sidewalks, and controlled access to dorms/residences.

REQUIREMENTS: The SAT or ACT is required. The college requires a minimum ACT score of 18, high school transcripts, and academic and pastoral references. A GPA of 2.2 is required. AP and CLEP credits are accepted. Students must complete 129 to 144 credits for their particular bachelor's degree. Each program has specific requirements, including general education and Biblical studies core classes. Internships are required for all programs. Students must take 60 or more total hours in their major, with a minimum overall GPA of 2.0 (2.2 for teacher education). **Procedure:** Freshmen are admitted fall and spring. Entrance exams should be taken during junior or senior year of high school. There is a rolling admissions plan. Applications should be filed by June 1 for fall entry; December 31 for spring entry, along with a $25 fee. Notification is sent on a rolling basis. **Transfer Students:** Transfer applicants must submit a completed application, a pastor's reference, a high school transcript or the GED, and college transcripts. Applicants with less than a year of college credit must also submit ACT or SAT scores and academic references. 27 of 129 credits required for the bachelor's degree must be completed at NCU. **International Students:** They must take the TOEFL. They must also take the SAT and ACT, scoring 18.

ADMISSIONS: Joshua Martin, Admissions Director. E-Mail: *jdmartin@northcentral.edu* Web: *www.northcentral.edu*

FINANCIAL AID: 100% of undergraduate students work part-time. The FAFSA, FFS, and the college's own financial statement are required. Check with the school for current application deadlines.

NORTHWESTERN COLLEGE　C-4
www.nwc.edu

St. Paul, MN 55113	(651) 631-5209
	(800) 827-6827
Fax: (651) 631-5680	Email: kkfaffler@nwc.edu
Full-time: 770 men, 1040 women	Faculty: n/av
Part-time: 25 men, 30 women	Ph.D.s: n/av
Graduate: 52 men, 42 women	Student/Faculty: n/av
Year: semesters, summer session	Tuition: $25,700
Room & Board: $8000	Freshman Class: n/av
ACT: required	CEEB CODE: 6489
Application Deadline: August 1	COMPETITIVE

Northwestern College, founded in 1902, is a Christian college offering traditional undergraduate programs in liberal arts and professional studies with emphasis on a biblical worldview and providing nontraditional educational opportunities through its Graduate and Continuing Education Division. The figures in the above capsule and in this profile are approximate. In addition to regional accreditation, Northwestern has baccalaureate program accreditation with NASM. The 107-acre campus is in a suburban area 3 miles from St. Paul and 5 miles from Minneapolis. Including any residence halls, there are 17 buildings.

STUDENT LIFE: 68% of undergraduates are from Minnesota. Others are from 31 states, and 25 foreign countries. 68% are from public schools. 90% are White. 99% are Protestant. **Male To Female Ratio:** 1.3:1. The average age of freshmen is 18; all undergraduates, 20. 21% do not continue beyond their first year; 61% remain to graduate. **Housing:** 1335 students can be accommodated in college housing, which includes single-sex dorms, on-campus apartments, and married student housing. In addition, there are special-interest houses. On-campus housing is guaranteed for the freshman year only, and is available on a first-come, first-served basis. Priority is given to out-of-town students. 67% of students live on campus; of those, 70% remain on campus on weekends. Alcohol is not permitted. Upperclassmen may keep cars.

FACULTY/CLASSROOMS: 56% of faculty are male; 44% are female. All teach undergraduates. No introductory courses are taught by graduate students. The average class size in an introductory lecture is 39; in a laboratory is 17; and in a regular course is 22.

PROGRAMS OF STUDY: Northwestern confers B.A., B.S., B.M.E. and B.Mus. degrees. Associate degrees are also awarded. Bachelor's degrees are awarded in BIOLOGICAL SCIENCE (biochemistry and biology/biological science), BUSINESS (accounting, banking and finance, business administration and management, international business management, management information systems, and marketing management), COMMUNICATIONS AND THE ARTS (animation, broadcasting, communications, dramatic arts, English, English as a second/foreign language, graphic design, journalism, music, music performance, music theory and composition, piano/organ, public relations, Spanish, strings, studio art, and voice), COMPUTER AND PHYSICAL SCIENCE (mathematics), EDUCATION (art education, early childhood education, elementary education, English education, mathematics education, music education, physical education, and social studies education), HEALTH PROFESSIONS (exercise science), SOCIAL SCIENCE (biblical studies, criminal justice, crosscultural studies, history, interdisciplinary studies, ministries, pastoral studies, psychology, religious education, urban studies, and youth ministry). Education, music, communication, biology, and business are the strongest academically. Education, business, and Christian ministries have the largest enrollments.

ACTIVITIES: There are no fraternities or sororities. There are 30 groups on campus, including band, cheerleading, chess, choir, chorale, chorus, computers, drama, ethnic, forensics, honors, international, jazz band, literary magazine, musical theater, newspaper, opera, orchestra, pep band, political, professional, radio and TV, religious, social, social service, student government, and yearbook. Popular campus events include Spring Variety Shows, Christmas at Northwestern, and Day of Prayer and Service. **Sports:** There are 8 intercollegiate sports for men and 8 for women, and 8 intramural sports for men and 8 for women. Facilities include softball, baseball, soccer, and football fields, outdoor tennis courts, and a waterfront for aquatic sports in summer and broomball in winter. There is a health and physical education center, with a full basketball court, 2 racquetball courts, an elevated jogging surface, a fitness center, and an athletic training room. The student center and 1 apartment residence have small swimming pools. **Graduates:** From July 1, 2013 to June 30, 2014, 433 bachelor's degrees were awarded. The most popular majors were education (19%), Christian ministries/biblical studies (19%), and business (15%). 150 companies recruited on campus in 2013-2014. In an average class, 8% graduate in 3 years or less, 45% graduate in 4 years or less, 59% graduate in 5 years or less, and 61% graduate in 6 years or less. Of the 2013 graduating class, 6% were enrolled in graduate school within 6 months of graduation, and 89% were employed.

SERVICES: Counseling and information services are available, as is tutoring in some subjects. There is remedial math, reading, and writing. **Library/Resources:** The library contains 124,574 volumes, 70,350 microform items, 5,092 audio/video tapes/CDs/DVDs, and subscribes to 1,263 periodicals including electronic. Computerized library services include interlibrary loans, database searching, Internet access, and Wi-Fi capability. Special learning facilities include an art gallery, radio station, and TV station. **Physically Challenged Students:** 70% of the campus is accessible. Facilities include wheelchair ramps, elevators, special parking, specially equipped restrooms, special class scheduling, lowered drinking fountains, and special housing. **Special:** The college offers 8 study-abroad programs and 4 U.S. off-campus programs through the Council for Christian Colleges and Universities. International business majors are placed in overseas internships. A 3-2 engineering degree with the University of Minnesota-Twin Cities is offered. There are 6 national honor societies, a freshman honors program, and 11 departmental honors programs. **Visiting:** There are regularly scheduled orientations for prospective students. There are guides for informal visits, visitors may sit in on classes, and stay overnight. To schedule a visit, contact the Admissions Office. **Campus Safety and Security:** Measures include 24-hour foot and vehicle patrol, emergency notification system, self-defense education, and security escort services. There are shuttle buses, emergency telephones, lighted pathways/sidewalks, controlled access to dorms/residences. The campus has limited accessibility due to being surrounded on 3 sides by Lake Johanna, and the main entrance to the campus is gated.

REQUIREMENTS: The ACT is preferred but the SAT is accepted. A high school diploma is required; the GED is accepted. The minimum high school GPA is 2.0, but a 3.0 or higher is recommended. Applicants are expected to have completed the following Carnegie units: 4 in English, 3 each in math, science, and social studies, and 2 others. 2 in foreign language are recommended. A statement of Christian faith and an assent to a lifestyle agreement are required. 2 letters of reference must be submitted, including 1 from the applicant's pastor. A personal interview is required for some students. Northwestern requires applicants to be in the upper 50% of their class. A GPA of 2.0 is required. AP and CLEP credits are accepted. Important factors in the admissions decision are personality/intangible qualities, recommendations by school officials, and leadership record. To graduate, students must complete 125 to 166 semester credits (depends on specific major) with a 2.0 GPA. The number of credits required in the major varies from 36 to 100 (average of 58). A core curriculum of 64 to 68 credits is built around a biblical worldview theme, thoroughly integrating general education and biblical worldview studies. **Procedure:** Freshmen are admitted to all sessions. Entrance exams should be taken during the fall of the senior year of high school. There are deferred admissions and rolling admissions plans. Applications should be filed by August 1 for fall entry; December 15 for spring entry; and May 1 for summer entry, along with a $30 fee. Notification is sent on a rolling basis. Applications are accepted on-line. **Transfer Students:** 108 transfer students enrolled in 2013-2014. Applicants must have an average of C or better from an accredited institution. 30 of 125 credits required for the bachelor's degree must be com-

pleted at Northwestern. **International Students:** There are 9 international students enrolled. They must take the TOEFL or MELAB, or take the ACT or SAT.

ADMISSIONS: Kenneth K. Faffler, Director of Admissions. E-Mail: *kkfaffler@nwc.edu* Web: *www.nwc.edu*

FINANCIAL AID: In 2014-2015, 98% of all full-time freshmen and 94% of continuing full-time students received some form of financial aid. 80% of all full-time freshmen and 81% of continuing full-time students received need-based aid. The average freshman award was $15,864. Need-based scholarships or need-based grants averaged $11,949; need-based self-help aid (loans and jobs) averaged $4,302; and other non-need-based awards and non-need-based scholarships averaged $6,150. 10% of undergraduate students work part-time. Average annual earnings from campus work are $2516. The average financial indebtedness of the 2014 graduate was $25,162. The FAFSA and the college's own financial statement are required. Check with the school for current application deadlines.

SAINT JOHN'S UNIVERSITY B-3
www.csbsju.edu

Collegeville, MN 56321

(320) 363-5060
(800) 544-1489

Fax: (320) 363-3206
Full-time: 1758 men
Part-time: 31 men
Graduate: 53 men, 53 women
Year: semesters
Room & Board: $9280

Email: admissions@csbsju.edu
Faculty: 133; IIB, +$
Ph.D.s: 88%
Student/Faculty: 12 to 1
Tuition: $38,704
Freshman Class: 1461 applied, 1157 accepted, 450 enrolled

SAT or ACT: required
Application Deadline: January 15

CEEB CODE: 6624
COMPETITIVE

Saint John's University (SJU) and The College of Saint Benedict (CSB) are nationally-leading liberal arts colleges whose unique partnership offers students the educational choices of a large university and the individual attention of a premier small college. There is 1 graduate school. In addition to regional accreditation, St. John's has baccalaureate program accreditation with ADA, NASM, NCATE, ACS, ATS, and CCNE. The 2500-acre campus is in a rural area 15 miles west of St. Cloud and 75 miles northwest of Minneapolis and St. Paul. Including any residence halls, there are 61 buildings.

STUDENT LIFE: 74% of undergraduates are from Minnesota. Others are from 40 states, 22 foreign countries, and Canada. 70% are from public schools. 81% are White. 55% are Catholic; 28% Protestant; 16% claim no religious affiliation. **Male To Female Ratio:** 0.0:1. The average age of freshmen is 18; all undergraduates, 20. 12% do not continue beyond their first year; 81% remain to graduate. **Housing:** 1584 students can be accommodated in college housing, which includes single-sex dorms and on-campus apartments. In addition, there are special-interest houses, eco houses, and a Benedictine living community. On-campus housing is guaranteed for the freshman year only, is available on a first-come, first-served basis, and is available on a lottery system for upperclassmen. 87% of students live on campus. All students may keep cars.

FACULTY/CLASSROOMS: 47% of faculty are male; 53% are female. All teach and do research. No introductory courses are taught by graduate students. The average class size in an introductory lecture is 21; in a laboratory is 13; and in a regular course is 17.

PROGRAMS OF STUDY: St. John's confers B.A. and B.S.N. degrees. Master's degrees are also awarded. Bachelor's degrees are awarded in AGRICULTURE (environmental studies), BIOLOGICAL SCIENCE (biochemistry, biology/biological science, and nutrition), BUSINESS (accounting and management science), COMMUNICATIONS AND THE ARTS (art, classics, communications, English, French, German, music, Spanish, and theatre arts), COMPUTER AND PHYSICAL SCIENCE (chemistry, computer science, mathematics, natural sciences, and physics), EDUCATION (elementary education), ENGINEERING AND ENVIRONMENTAL DESIGN (preengineering), HEALTH PROFESSIONS (nursing, occupational therapy, predentistry, premedicine, preoptometry, prepharmacy, prephysical therapy, and preveterinary science), SOCIAL SCIENCE (Asian/Oriental studies, economics, gender studies, Hispanic American studies, history, humanities, liberal arts/general studies, peace studies, philosophy, political science/government, prelaw, psychology, social science, sociology, and theological studies). Global business leadership, accounting, and biology have the largest enrollments.

ACTIVITIES: There are no fraternities or sororities. There are 120 groups on campus, including an outdoor leadership center, academic, art, band, choir, chorale, chorus, computers, dance, debate, drama, environmental, ethnic, film, gay, honors, international, jazz band, literary magazine, musical theater, newspaper, opera, orchestra, pep band, political, professional, radio and TV, religious, social, social service, student government, and symphony. Popular campus events include Pines Spring Concert, Asian New Year, Festival of Culture, Community Barbecue, Club Involvement Fair, Johnnie Bennie Live Fall Concert, Maple Syrup Festival, and Homecoming. **Sports:** There are 12 intercollegiate sports for men. Facilities include an artificial turf football field (and 7,800-seat stadium), 3,000-seat basketball arena, hardwood racquetball courts, soccer, baseball, lacrosse, and rugby fields, indoor and outdoor tennis courts, indoor and outdoor tracks, a complete fitness center, a swimming pool, a climbing wall, a wrestling room, a training room, locker facilities for 12 intercollegiate teams, an outdoor intramural hockey rink, 5 lakes for canoeing, fishing, swimming, rowing, and kayaking, 20 miles of on-campus wooded hiking and jogging trails, and access to all athletic facilities at the College of Saint Benedict. **Graduates:** From July 1, 2013 to June 30, 2014, 444 bachelor's degrees were awarded. The most popular majors were business management (21%), accounting (11%), and biology (11%). 126 companies recruited on campus in 2013-2014. In an average class, 1% graduate in 3 years or less, 72% graduate in 4 years or less, 79% graduate in 5 years or less, and 81% graduate in 6 years or less. Of the 2013 graduating class, 15% were enrolled in graduate school within 6 months of graduation, and 84% were employed.

SERVICES: Counseling and information services are available, as is tutoring in most subjects. There is a writing center and math skills center. The College of Saint Benedict and Saint John's University established a Disability Services Office. Accomodations are provided on a case by case basis for enrolled students who provide adequate documentation of a disability. Individual tutoring is available as needed. Academic and psychological counseling are available on an unlimited basis. **Library/Resources:** The 2 libraries contain 715,683 volumes, 25,308 microform items, 63,384 audio/video tapes/CDs/DVDs, and subscribe to 97,011 periodicals including electronic. Computerized library services include interlibrary loans, database searching, Internet access, and Wi-Fi capability. Special learning facilities include an art gallery, natural history museum, radio station, TV station, a pottery studio and kiln, Saint John's Outdoor University, an observatory, a greenhouse, an herbarium, and the Hill Museum and Manuscript Library, and Saint Benedict's Monastery Heritage Museum at the College of Saint Benedict. **Physically Challenged Students:** 90% of the campus is accessible. Facilities include wheelchair ramps, elevators, special parking, specially equipped restrooms, special class scheduling, lowered drinking fountains, special housing. **Special:** Students may cross-register with St. Cloud State University. There are study-abroad programs in Australia, Austria, Chile, China, Coventry-England, France, Germany, Guatemala, Greece, Ireland (Cork and Galway), Italy, India, Japan, London-England, Northern Ireland, South Africa, and Spain. Many short term study abroad opportunities are also offered. Internships, dual and student-designed majors, preprofessional programs, and liberal studies degrees may be pursued. A 3-2 engineering program is offered through the University of Minnesota, as is a 3-1 program in dentistry. Nondegree study and a pass/fail grading option are also available. There are 3 national honor societies, including Phi Beta Kappa, and a freshman honors program. **Visiting:** There are regularly scheduled orientations for prospective students. Programs include admissions and financial aid presentations, campus tours and student panels. There are guides for informal visits, visitors may sit in on classes, and stay overnight. To schedule a visit, contact the CSB/SJU Admissions Office at (800) 544-1489. **Campus Safety and Security:** Measures include 24-hour foot and vehicle patrol, emergency notification

system, self-defense education, and security escort services. There are shuttle buses, emergency telephones, lighted pathways/sidewalks, and controlled access to dorms/residences.

REQUIREMENTS: The SAT or ACT is required. Students should be graduates of an accredited secondary school. Academic preparation should include 17 units, including 4 of English, 3 of math, 2 each of a lab science and social studies, and 4 electives. A foreign language is recommended. The GED is accepted. An essay is required. Home-schooled applicants are not required to have a high school diploma but are required to provide appropriate documentation of college preparatory curriculum and standardized test scores. St. John's requires applicants to be in the upper 50% of their class. A GPA of 3.0 is required. AP and CLEP credits are accepted. Important factors in the admissions decision are advanced placement or honors courses, leadership record, and extracurricular activities record. To graduate students must complete a first-year seminar and a junior-senior ethics seminar intended as a capstone for the liberal arts experience, and fulfill gender, intercultural, experiential learning, and fine arts requirements. Distribution requirements include 4 credits in fine arts, 2 courses each in humanities and theology, and 1 course each in math, natural science, and social science. All students must prove math and foreign language proficiency. A total of 124 credits must be earned, with a minimum GPA of 2.0. Attendance at 8 fine arts experiences is also required. **Procedure:** Freshmen are admitted fall and spring. Entrance exams should be taken during the spring of the junior year or fall of the senior year. There are early admissions and deferred admissions plans. Application deadlines are open. Notification of early decision is sent December 15; regular decision, April 1. Applications are accepted on-line. **Transfer Students:** 24 transfer students enrolled in 2013-2014. Transfer applicants must have a minimum college GPA of 2.75. An essay or personal statement, high school and college transcripts, and a transfer student evaluation form are required. Standardized test scores and an interview may be required of some. 45 of 124 credits required for the bachelor's degree must be completed at St. John's. **International Students:** There are 98 international students enrolled. The school actively recruits these students. They must take the TOEFL with a minimum score of 550 on the paper-based TOEFL (PBT) or 80 on the Internet-based version (iBT), IELTS also accepted with minimum score of 6.5. They must also take the SAT or ACT.

ADMISSIONS: 79% of the 2014-2015 applicants were accepted. The SAT scores for the 2014-2015 freshman class were: Critical Reading--33% below 500, 40% between 500 and 599, 21% between 600 and 699, and 6% between 700 and 800; Math--26% below 500, 49% between 500 and 599, 14% between 600 and 699, and 11% between 700 and 800; Writing--34% below 500, 46% between 500 and 599, 15% between 600 and 699, and 5% between 700 and 800. The ACT scores were 11% below 21, 22% between 21 and 23, 29% between 24 and 26, 16% between 27 and 28, and 22% above 28. 37% of the current freshmen were in the top fifth of their class; 74% were in the top two fifths. There were 3 National Merit finalists. **Admissions Contact:** Dr. Calvin Mosley, Vice President Admission and Financial Aid. E-Mail: *admissions@csbsju.edu* Web: *www.csbsju.edu*

FINANCIAL AID: In 2014-2015, 94% of all full-time freshmen and 93% of continuing full-time students received some form of financial aid. 73% of all full-time freshmen and 66% of continuing full-time students received need-based aid. The average freshman award was $32,415. Need-based scholarships or need-based grants averaged $28,121; need-based self-help aid (loans and jobs) averaged $6,051; and other non-need-based awards and non-need-based scholarships averaged $16,482. 50% of undergraduate students work part-time. Average annual earnings from campus work are $3150. The average financial indebtedness of the 2014 graduate was $38,089. St. John's is a member of CSS. The FAFSA and the college's own financial statement are required. The priority date for freshman financial aid applications for fall entry is March 15.

SAINT MARY'S UNIVERSITY OF MINNESOTA
D-5

www.smumn.edu

Winona, MN 55987

(507) 457-1700
(800) 635-5987

Fax: (507) 457-1722   Email: admission@smumn.edu

Full-time: 631 men, 667 women	Faculty: 86; IIA, --$
Part-time: 256 men, 350 women	Ph.D.s: 88%
Graduate: 1145 men, 2776 women	Student/Faculty: 14 to 1
Year: semesters	Tuition: $30,315
Room & Board: $7965	Freshman Class: 1743 applied, 1294 accepted, 334 enrolled

SAT CR/M/W: 516/520/512 **ACT: 23**   CEEB CODE: 6632

Application Deadline: May 1   **COMPETITIVE**

Saint Mary's, founded in 1912, is a private, Lasallian Catholic, comprehensive institution, guided by the De La Salle Christian Brothers since 1933. At the coeducational, residential Winona campus, the undergraduate College combines traditional liberal arts and sciences with career preparation in a student-centered environment. The Schools of Graduate and Professional Programs (SGPP) is one of the largest graduate schools in Minnesota. A pioneer in outreach education since 1984, SGPP offers certificate, bachelor completion, master's, specialist, and doctoral programs at the university's Twin Cities and Winona campuses, and centers in Rochester, Apple Valley, and Oakdale. Courses are also offered in greater Minnesota and Wisconsin, Kenya and Jamaica. There are 4 undergraduate schools and 3 graduate schools. In addition to regional accreditation, SMU has baccalaureate program accreditation with NASM, IACBE, and JRCNMT. The 350-acre campus is in a small town 110 miles southeast of Twin Cities and 275 miles northwest of Chicago. Including any residence halls, there are 47 buildings.

STUDENT LIFE: 54% of undergraduates are from Minnesota. Others are from 32 states, 15 foreign countries, and Canada. 70% are from public schools. 60% are White; 20% race unknown. 52% are Catholic; 15% Protestant. **Male To Female Ratio:** 1.9:1. The average age of freshmen is 19; all undergraduates, 20. 22% do not continue beyond their first year; 65% remain to graduate. **Housing:** 1113 students can be accommodated in college housing, which includes single-sex and coed dorms and on-campus apartments. In addition, there are special-interest houses, living learning communities, first-year residence halls, and substance-free residence halls. On-campus housing is guaranteed for all 4 years. 93% of students live on campus; of those, 75% remain on campus on weekends. All students may keep cars.

FACULTY/CLASSROOMS: 65% of faculty are male; 35% are female. All teach and do research. No introductory courses are taught by graduate students. The average class size in an introductory lecture is 16; in a laboratory is 14; and in a regular course is 15.

PROGRAMS OF STUDY: SMU confers B.A. and B.S. degrees. Master's and Doctoral degrees are also awarded. Bachelor's degrees are awarded in BIOLOGICAL SCIENCE (biochemistry, biology/biological science, biophysics, environmental biology, and life science secondary school education), BUSINESS (accounting, business administration and management, business intelligence and analytics, entrepreneurial studies, finance, international business, marketing, and sports management), COMMUNICATIONS AND THE ARTS (art, graphic design, journalism, literature, music industry, music performance, public relations, Spanish, Spanish / adolescence education, studio art, and theatre arts), COMPUTER AND PHYSICAL SCIENCE (actuarial science, chemistry, chemistry/adolescence education, computer science, mathematics, and physics), EDUCATION (elementary education, English education, mathematics education, music education, secondary education, and social studies education), ENGINEERING AND ENVIRONMENTAL DESIGN (engineering physics and nuclear medicine technology), HEALTH PROFESSIONS (cardiac sonography, cytotechnology, medical laboratory science, and prephysical therapy), SOCIAL SCIENCE (criminal justice, (Social Science) Global Studies, history, human services, pastoral studies, philosophy, political science/government, psychology, social science,

sociology, theology, and youth ministry). Biology, biochemistry, and theology are the strongest academically. Marketing, biology, and accounting have the largest enrollments.

ACTIVITIES: 4% of men belong to 2 national fraternities; 3% of women belong to 1 national sorority. There are 85 groups on campus, including art, band, cheerleading, choir, chorale, chorus, dance, drama, environmental, ethnic, gay, honors, international, jazz band, literary magazine, musical theater, newspaper, political, professional, radio and TV, religious, social, social service, student government, and yearbook. Popular campus events include Cardinal Days, Taylor Richmond Benefit Dance and Finals Breakfast. **Sports:** There are 10 intercollegiate sports for men and 11 for women. Facilities include basketball, indoor tennis, and racquetball courts, an indoor ice arena, exercise and weight rooms, baseball, softball, and soccer fields, Nordic ski and running trails, an indoor track, an indoor swimming pool, a dance studio, a Frisbee disc course, an outdoor track, and a high ropes course. **Graduates:** From July 1, 2013 to June 30, 2014, 257 bachelor's degrees were awarded. The most popular majors were marketing (9%), biology (7%), and public relations (6%). 8 companies recruited on campus in 2013-2014. In an average class, 1% graduate in 3 years or less, 55% graduate in 4 years or less, 63% graduate in 5 years or less, and 65% graduate in 6 years or less.

SERVICES: Counseling and information services are available, as is tutoring in most subjects. There is a reader service for the blind, and remedial math, reading, and writing. **Library/Resources:** The library contains 209,807 volumes, 200,692 microform items, and 9,789 audio/video tapes/CDs/DVDs, and subscribes to 40,015 periodicals including electronic. Computerized library services include interlibrary loans, database searching, Internet access, and Wi-Fi capability. Special learning facilities include an art gallery, radio station, an observatory. **Physically Challenged Students:** 93% of the campus is accessible. Facilities include wheelchair ramps, elevators, special parking, specially equipped restrooms, lowered drinking fountains, lowered telephones, special housing. **Special:** Students may cross-register with Winona State University. Internships, co-op programs, student teaching and study abroad, work-study programs, and a Washington semester are available. The university also offers dual and student-designed majors, non-degree study, pass/fail options, credit for life, military, and work experience, and an honors program that also serves as an alternative general education program. There are 14 national honor societies. **Visiting:** There are regularly scheduled orientations for prospective students, including an interview, a tour, class visits, and lunch. There are guides for informal visits, visitors may sit in on classes, and stay overnight. To schedule a visit, contact the Office of Admissions. **Campus Safety and Security:** Measures include 24-hour foot and vehicle patrol, emergency notification system, and security escort services. There are emergency telephones, lighted pathways/sidewalks, and controlled access to dorms/residences.

REQUIREMENTS: The SAT or ACT is required. Candidates for admission should have completed 4 units of English, 3 each of math and natural science, 2 of social studies, and 6 academic electives. Completion of 2 units of foreign language is recommended. A GPA of 2.5 is required. AP and CLEP credits are accepted. Important factors in the admissions decision are advanced placement or honors courses, leadership record, and extracurricular activities record. Students must have a 2.0 cumulative major GPA and complete a minimum of 122 semester credits, including at least 45 at the upper-division level. Students must complete a major program and the general education program. **Procedure:** Freshmen are admitted fall and spring. Entrance exams should be taken by the fall of the senior year. There are early admissions, deferred admissions, and rolling admissions plans. Applications should be filed by May 1 for fall entry; December 1 for spring entry, along with a $25 fee. Notification is sent on a rolling basis. Applications are accepted on-line. **Transfer Students:** 47 transfer students enrolled in 2013-2014. Applicants must have a 2.0 GPA with at least 12 credits. 60 of 122 credits required for the bachelor's degree must be completed at SMU. **International Students:** There are 37 international students enrolled. The school actively recruits these students. They must take the TOEFL with a minimum score of 550 on the paper-based TOEFL (PBT) or 79 on the Internet-based version (iBT).

ADMISSIONS: 74% of the 2014-2015 applicants were accepted. The

SAT scores for the 2014-2015 freshman class were: Critical Reading--44% below 500, 31% between 500 and 599, 22% between 600 and 699, and 3% between 700 and 800; Math--38% below 500, 50% between 500 and 599, 9% between 600 and 699, and 3% between 700 and 800; Writing--47% below 500, 41% between 500 and 599, 9% between 600 and 699, and 3% between 700 and 800. The ACT scores were 31% below 21, 22% between 21 and 23, 26% between 24 and 26, 10% between 27 and 28, and 10% above 28. **Admissions Contact:** Nathan Ament, Director of Admission. E-Mail: *admission@smumn .edu* Web: *www.smumn.edu*

FINANCIAL AID: In 2014-2015, 99% of all full-time freshmen and 96% of continuing full-time students received some form of financial aid. 79% of all full-time freshmen and 74% of continuing full-time students received need-based aid. 30% of undergraduate students work part-time. Average annual earnings from campus work are $1776. The average financial indebtedness of the 2014 graduate was $33,216. The FAFSA and the college's own financial statement are required. The priority date for freshman financial aid applications for fall entry is March 15. The deadline for filing freshman financial aid applications for fall entry is open.

SOUTHWEST MINNESOTA STATE UNIVERSITY
B-4

www.southwestmsu.edu

Marshall, MN 56258	(507) 537-6286
	(800) 642-0684
Fax: (507) 537-7154	Email: shearerr@southwestmsu.edu
Full-time: 1075 men, 1250 women	Faculty: IIB, +$
Part-time: 150 men, 235 women	Ph.D.s: 76%
Graduate: 155 men, 370 women	Student/Faculty: n/av
Year: semesters, summer session	Tuition: $9000
Room & Board: $7500	Freshman Class: n/av
SAT: recommended ACT: required	CEEB CODE: 6703
Application Deadline: n/av	COMPETITIVE

Southwest Minnesota State University, founded in 1963, is a public institution offering programs in liberal arts, technology, and pre-professional training. The figures in the above capsule and in this profile are approximate. In addition to regional accreditation, SMSU has baccalaureate program accreditation with CSWE and ACS. The 216-acre campus is in a rural area 150 miles southwest of Minneapolis. Including any residence halls, there are 24 buildings.

STUDENT LIFE: 75% of undergraduates are from Minnesota. Others are from 29 states, 33 foreign countries, and Canada. 95% are from public schools. 85% are White. **Male To Female Ratio:** 1.3:1. The average age of freshmen is 19; all undergraduates, 22. 25% do not continue beyond their first year; 35% remain to graduate. **Housing:** 1182 students can be accommodated in college housing, which includes single-sex and coed dorms and on-campus apartments. In addition, there are special-interest houses, a quiet house, and a weekend programming house. On-campus housing is guaranteed for the freshman year only. Alcohol is not permitted. All students may keep cars.

FACULTY/CLASSROOMS: 56% of faculty are male; 44% are female. All teach undergraduates. No introductory courses are taught by graduate students. The average class size in an introductory lecture is 26; in a laboratory is 19; and in a regular course is 21.

PROGRAMS OF STUDY: SMSU confers B.A., B.S. and B.A.S. degrees. Associate and Master's degrees are also awarded. Bachelor's degrees are awarded in AGRICULTURE (agricultural business management), BIOLOGICAL SCIENCE (biology/biological science), BUSINESS (accounting, business administration and management, hotel/motel and restaurant management, and marketing/retailing/merchandising), COMMUNICATIONS AND THE ARTS (art, communications, creative writing, dramatic arts, literature, music, and Spanish), COMPUTER AND PHYSICAL SCIENCE (applied science, chemistry, computer science, and mathematics), EDUCATION (art education, early childhood education, elementary education, foreign languages education, health education, mathematics education, music education, physical education, and science education), ENGI-

NEERING AND ENVIRONMENTAL DESIGN (environmental science), HEALTH PROFESSIONS (dental laboratory technology and medical technology), SOCIAL SCIENCE (history, interdisciplinary studies, law enforcement and corrections, political science/government, psychology, public administration, social work, and sociology). Education, business administration, and psychology have the largest enrollments.

ACTIVITIES: There are no fraternities or sororities. There are 100 groups on campus, including art, band, cheerleading, chess, choir, chorus, computers, dance, debate, drama, ethnic, forensics, honors, international, jazz band, literary magazine, marching band, musical theater, newspaper, orchestra, pep band, political, professional, radio and TV, religious, social, social service, student government, and symphony. Popular campus events include Martin Luther King Celebration, Cinco de Mayo, and Dakota Indigenous Nations Studies Conference. **Sports:** There are 5 intercollegiate sports for men and 6 for women, and 14 intramural sports for men and 13 for women. Facilities include a 2000-seat gym, a baseball complex, softball facilities, racquetball courts, a football stadium, wrestling rooms, a weight room, an Olympic-size pool, a 3800-seat mulitipurpose facility, a soccer field, and a fitness center.

SERVICES: Counseling and information services are available, as is tutoring in most subjects. There is a reader service for the blind, and remedial math, reading, and writing. **Library/Resources:** The library contains 168,000 volumes, 228,000 microform items, and 12,000 audio/video tapes/CDs/DVDs, and subscribes to 950 periodicals including electronic. Computerized library services include interlibrary loans, database searching, Internet access, and Wi-Fi capability. Special learning facilities include an art gallery, natural history museum, planetarium, radio station, and TV station. **Physically Challenged Students:** 98% of the campus is accessible. Facilities include wheelchair ramps, elevators, special parking, specially equipped restrooms, special class scheduling, lowered drinking fountains, lowered telephones, and special housing. **Special:** SMSU has cooperative programs with various local colleges, cross-registration with several state universities, and an accelerated degree. SMSU also offers internships in every discipline, work-study programs, student-designed and interdisciplinary majors including speech communication and theater arts, nondegree study, pass/fail options, and credit for life, military, and work experience. There are 2 national honor societies and a freshman honors program. **Visiting:** There are regularly scheduled orientations for prospective students. There are guides for informal visits, visitors may sit in on classes, and stay overnight. To schedule a visit, contact the Admissions Office. **Campus Safety and Security:** Measures include 24-hour foot and vehicle patrol, self-defense education, and security escort services. There are emergency telephones and lighted pathways/sidewalks.

REQUIREMENTS: The ACT or SAT is required. Admission is based on class rank or ACT/SAT composite. Students should be graduates of an accredited secondary school or have a GED certificate. An interview is recommended. SMSU requires applicants to be in the upper 50% of their class. AP and CLEP credits are accepted. Important factors in the admissions decision are recommendations by school officials, leadership record, and personality/intangible qualities.To graduate, students must complete at least 128 semester credit hours, a minimum of 27 of which must be at the 300 or 400 level, and a liberal arts core curriculum, with a minimum GPA of 2.0. **Procedure:** Freshmen are admitted to all sessions. Entrance exams should be taken during the junior or senior year. There are deferred admissions and rolling admissions plans. Check with the school for current application deadlines. The fall 2014 application fee was $20. Notification is sent on a rolling basis. Applications are accepted on-line. **Transfer Students:** Applicants need a minimum GPA of 2.0 in previous college-level work at an accredited institution. High school transcripts are required if students are transferring with fewer than 24 semester credits. 48 of 128 credits required for the bachelor's degree must be completed at SMSU. **International Students:** The school actively recruits these students. They must take the TOEFL.

ADMISSIONS: Richard Shearer, Director of Enrollment. E-Mail: *shearerr@southwestmsu.edu* Web: *www.southwestmsu.edu*

FINANCIAL AID: The FAFSA and the college's own financial statement are required. Check with the school for current application deadlines.

ST. CATHERINE UNIVERSITY   C-4
www.stkate.edu

St. Paul, MN 55105

(651) 690-8850
(800) 656-KATE

Fax: (651) 690-8824
Email: admissions@stkate.edu

Full-time: 20 men, 2168 women
Part-time: 103 men, 1268 women
Graduate: 150 men, 1308 women
Year: 4-1-4, summer session
Room & Board: $8002

Faculty: 292; IIA, --$
Ph.D.s: 55%
Student/Faculty: 12 to 1
Tuition: $29,780
Freshman Class: 2375 applied, 1473 accepted, 682 enrolled

SAT CR/M: 560/525 ACT: 24
Application Deadline: open

CEEB CODE: 6105
COMPETITIVE+

A dynamic university educating students to lead and influence, St. Catherine prepares students to make a difference in their professions, their communities and the world. At the University's heart is the largest, most innovative college for women in the nation. St. Catherine also offers a range of graduate and associate programs for women and men. The figures in the above capsule and in this profile are approximate. There are 4 undergraduate schools and 1 graduate school. In addition to regional accreditation, SCU has baccalaureate program accreditation with ADA, APTA, CSWE, NASM, NLN, and NAACLS. The 110-acre campus is in an urban area 6 miles southwest of downtown St. Paul, MN. Including any residence halls, there are 22 buildings.

STUDENT LIFE: 89% of undergraduates are from Minnesota. Others are from 30 states, 34 foreign countries, and Canada. 86% are from public schools. 68% are White; 11% African American. 50% are Catholic; 20% Protestant. **Male To Female Ratio:** 17.4:1. The average age of freshmen is 18; all undergraduates, 22. 16% do not continue beyond their first year; 67% remain to graduate. **Housing:** 900 students can be accommodated in college housing, which includes single-sex dorms and on-campus apartments. apartments for student-parents, and theme housing. On-campus housing is available on a first-come, first-served basis, and is available on a lottery system for upperclassmen. 56% of students commute. All students may keep cars.

FACULTY/CLASSROOMS: 21% of faculty are male; 79% are female. All teach undergraduates. No introductory courses are taught by graduate students. The average class size in an introductory lecture is 19; in a laboratory is 14; and in a regular course is 13.

PROGRAMS OF STUDY: SCU confers B.A. and B.S. degrees. Associate, Master's, and Doctoral degrees are also awarded. Bachelor's degrees are awarded in BIOLOGICAL SCIENCE (biochemistry, biology/biological science, and nutrition), BUSINESS (accounting, business administration and management, fashion merchandising, international business management, international economics, management information systems, and marketing/retailing/merchandising), COMMUNICATIONS AND THE ARTS (American Sign Language, art, classics, communications, dramatic arts, English, fine arts, French, Latin, media arts, music, musical theater, Spanish, and speech/debate/rhetoric), COMPUTER AND PHYSICAL SCIENCE (chemistry, information sciences and systems, and mathematics), EDUCATION (art education, early childhood education, elementary education, home economics education, music education, physical education, and secondary education), ENGINEERING AND ENVIRONMENTAL DESIGN (food services technology), HEALTH PROFESSIONS (exercise science, health care administration, medical records administration/services, nursing, occupational therapy, rehabilitation therapy, and respiratory therapy), SOCIAL SCIENCE (dietetics, economics, ethnic studies, family/consumer studies, fashion design and technology, history, international relations, interpreter for the deaf, philosophy, political science/government, psychology, social studies, social work, sociology, theological studies, and women's studies). Biology, chemistry, and psychology are the strongest academically. Nursing, social work, and accounting have the largest enrollments.

ACTIVITIES: There are no fraternities or sororities. There are 42 groups on campus, including art, band, cheerleading, choir, chorale, chorus, dance, drama, ethnic, gay, honors, international, literary magazine, musical theater, newspaper, photography, political, professional, radio and TV, religious, social, social service, and student government. Popular campus events include Winter Charity Ball, Dew Drop Bop, and KatWalk Fashion Show. **Sports:** There are 11 intercollegiate sports for women and 8 intramural sports for women. Facilities include a fitness facility, a gym, a weight room, a swimming pool, an outdoor fitness course, tennis courts, a soccer field, and a softball field. **Graduates:** From July 1, 2013 to June 30, 2014, 534 bachelor's degrees were awarded. The most popular majors were health professions and related programs (32%), business/marketing (14%), and public administration and social service/education (7%). 13 companies recruited on campus in 2013-2014. In an average class, 45% graduate in 4 years or less, 63% graduate in 5 years or less, and 67% graduate in 6 years or less. Of the 2013 graduating class, 22% were enrolled in graduate school within 6 months of graduation, and 84% were employed.

SERVICES: Counseling and information services are available, as is tutoring in most subjects. There is a reader service for the blind, and remedial math, reading, and writing. **Library/Resources:** The 2 libraries contain 250,865 volumes, 180,946 microform items, and 7,844 audio/video tapes/CDs/DVDs, and subscribe to 2,763 periodicals including electronic. Computerized library services include interlibrary loans, database searching, Internet access, and Wi-Fi capability. Special learning facilities include an art gallery, radio station, an observatory, and anatomy lab. **Physically Challenged Students:** 90% of the campus is accessible. Facilities include wheelchair ramps, elevators, special parking, specially equipped restrooms, special class scheduling, lowered drinking fountains, and lowered telephones. **Special:** SCU offers co-op programs with Carondolet College, the University of Minnesota, and George Washington University, and cross-registration with the Associated Colleges of the Twin Cities and other colleges sponsored by the Sisters of St. Joseph. Students may arrange internships, a Washington semester, and study abroad. Dual majors are available in the sciences and engineering. Students may receive credit for life, military, or work experience. Student-designed majors, non-degree study, and pass/fail options are available. The Weekend College offers a B.A. degree. There are 24 national honor societies, including Phi Beta Kappa, and a freshman honors program. **Visiting:** There are regularly scheduled orientations for prospective students, including a tour, an admissions interview, and an appointment with a faculty member. There are guides for informal visits, visitors may sit in on classes, and stay overnight. To schedule a visit, contact the Admissions Office. **Campus Safety and Security:** Measures include 24-hour foot and vehicle patrol, emergency notification system, self-defense education, and security escort services. There are emergency telephones, lighted pathways/sidewalks, and controlled access to dorms/residences.

REQUIREMENTS: The SAT or ACT is required. Applicants must have completed a college preparatory program including 4 courses in English, 3 in math, and 2 each in a foreign language, science, and social studies. SCU requires applicants to be in the upper 50% of their class. A GPA of 2.5 is required. AP and CLEP credits are accepted. Important factors in the admissions decision are advanced placement or honors courses, recommendations by school officials, and extracurricular activities record. To graduate, students must complete 130 semester credits, including a liberal arts core with courses in history, foreign language, philosophy, math, fine arts, literature, and theology, and 80 credits outside the major. Required courses are the Reflective Woman and the Global Search for Justice. At least 36 hours are required in the major. Students must have a minimum 2.0 GPA and demonstrate proficiency in composition, math, and computer literacy. **Procedure:** Freshmen are admitted fall and winter. Entrance exams should be taken during the senior year. There are deferred admissions and rolling admissions plans. Application deadlines are open. Notification is sent on a open basis. Applications are accepted on-line. **Transfer Students:** 354 transfer students enrolled in 2013-2014. Transfer applicants must submit high school and college transcripts. 48 of 130 credits required for the bachelor's degree must be completed at SCU. **International Students:** There are 48 international students enrolled. The school actively recruits these students. They must take the TOEFL with a minimum score of 500 on the paper-based TOEFL (PBT) or 61 on the Internet-based version (iBT) or take the MELAB and the college's own test. The SAT is required only if the student attended a U.S. high school, whether in this country or overseas.

ADMISSIONS: 62% of the 2014-2015 applicants were accepted. The SAT scores for the 2014-2015 freshman class were: Critical Reading--27% below 500, 39% between 500 and 599, 17% between 600 and 699, and 17% between 700 and 800; Math--27% below 500, 56% between 500 and 599, and 17% between 600 and 699. The ACT scores were 1% below 21, 48% between 24 and 26, 44% between 27 and 28, and 7% above 28. 53% of the current freshmen were in the top fifth of their class; 85% were in the top two fifths. 11 freshmen graduated first in their class. **Admissions Contact:** Marlene Mohs, Associate Dean of Admissions. E-Mail: *admissions@stkate.edu* Web: *www.stkate .edu*

FINANCIAL AID: In 2014-2015, 99% of all full-time freshmen and 91% of continuing full-time students received some form of financial aid. 63% of all full-time freshmen and 60% of continuing full-time students received need-based aid. The average freshman award was $30,592. Need-based scholarships or need-based grants averaged $10,581; need-based self-help aid (loans and jobs) averaged $5,504; other non-need-based awards and non-need-based scholarships averaged $11,278; and $5,215 from other forms of aid. 100% of undergraduate students work part-time. Average annual earnings from campus work are $3200. The average financial indebtedness of the 2014 graduate was $39,607. SCU is a member of CSS. The FAFSA and the college's own financial statement are required. The priority date for freshman financial aid applications for fall entry is April 15.

ST. CLOUD STATE UNIVERSITY   C-3
www.stcloudstate.edu

St. Cloud, MN 56301	(320) 308-2244
	(800) 369-4260
Fax: (320) 308-2243	**Email:** scsu4u@stcloud.state.edu
Full-time: 5400 men, 6250 women	**Faculty:** IIA, av$
Part-time: 1190 men, 1685 women	**Ph.D.s:** n/av
Graduate: 555 men, 925 women	**Student/Faculty:** n/av
Year: semesters, summer session	**Tuition:** $6100 ($12,700)
Room & Board: $4500	**Freshman Class:** n/av
ACT: required	**CEEB CODE:** 6679
Application Deadline: n/av	**COMPETITIVE**

St. Cloud State University, founded in 1869, is a comprehensive university offering programs that include the liberal arts and career preparation with emphasis on diversity, hands-on learning, and service to the community. There are 6 undergraduate schools and 1 graduate school. In addition to regional accreditation, SCSU has baccalaureate program accreditation with AACSB, ABET, ACEJMC, ASLA, CSWE, NASAD, NASM, and NCATE. The 100-acre campus is in a suburban area 60 miles northwest of Minneapolis. Including any residence halls, there are 50 buildings.

STUDENT LIFE: 92% of undergraduates are from Minnesota. Others are from 50 states, 85 foreign countries, and Canada. 77% are White. **Male To Female Ratio:** 1.2:1. The average age of freshmen is 19; all undergraduates, 22. 29% do not continue beyond their first year. **Housing:** 3000 students can be accommodated in college housing, which includes single-sex and coed dorms. Special housing for international students. 82% of students commute. Alcohol is not permitted. All students may keep cars.

FACULTY/CLASSROOMS: 56% of faculty are male; 44% are female. All teach undergraduates. No introductory courses are taught by graduate students.

PROGRAMS OF STUDY: SCSU confers B.A., B.S., B.E.S., B.F.A. and B.Mus. degrees. Associate, Master's, and Doctoral degrees are also awarded. Bachelor's degrees are awarded in BIOLOGICAL SCIENCE (biology/biological science), BUSINESS (accounting, banking and finance, business administration and management, business economics, international business management, marketing/retailing/merchandising, and personnel management), COMMUNICATIONS AND THE ARTS (advertising, broadcasting, communications, dramatic arts, English, fine arts, journalism, languages, music, and speech/debate/rhetoric), COMPUTER AND PHYSICAL SCIENCE (atmospheric sciences and meteorology, chemistry, computer science, earth science, geology, mathematics, physics, and statistics), EDUCATION (art education, early childhood education, elementary education, foreign languages education, guidance education, health education, industrial arts education, music education, science education, and secondary education), ENGINEERING AND ENVIRONMENTAL DESIGN (aviation administration/management, electrical/electronics engineering, engineering technology, and manufacturing engineering), HEALTH PROFESSIONS (predentistry, premedicine, public health, and speech pathology/audiology), SOCIAL SCIENCE (anthropology, criminal justice, economics, geography, history, international relations, philosophy, political science/government, prelaw, psychology, public administration, social science, social work, sociology, and urban studies). Mass communication, elementary education, and special education have the largest enrollments.

ACTIVITIES: There are 240 groups on campus, including hobby, entrepreneurial, travel, art, band, cheerleading, chess, choir, chorale, chorus, computers, dance, drama, ethnic, film, gay, honors, international, jazz band, literary magazine, marching band, musical theater, opera, orchestra, pep band, photography, political, professional, radio and TV, religious, social, social service, sports, student government, symphony, and yearbook. Popular campus events include Music Festival, Ethnic Awareness Week, and major speakers and workshops.

SERVICES: Counseling and information services are available, as is tutoring in every subject. There is a reader service for the blind, and remedial math, reading, and writing. **Library/Resources:** The library contains 887,462 volumes, 1.8 million microform items, 24,244 audio/video tapes/CDs/DVDs, and subscribes to 1,762 periodicals including electronic. Computerized library services include interlibrary loans, database searching, Internet access, and Wi-Fi capability. Special learning facilities include an art gallery, natural history museum, planetarium, radio station, TV station, Herb Brooks National Hockey and Events Center. **Physically Challenged Students:** 86% of the campus is accessible. Facilities include wheelchair ramps, elevators, special parking, specially equipped restrooms, special class scheduling, lowered drinking fountains, and lowered telephones. **Special:** The university offers cross-registration, internships in almost all majors, work-study programs, and study abroad in 25 countries. Students may take dual majors, design their own majors for a Bachelor of Elective Studies degree, and earn a general degree or a B.A.-B.S. degree in all majors, including meteorology and photographic technology. The university gives credit for military experience and allows nondegree study and pass/fail options. There are 4 national honor societies and a freshman honors program. **Visiting:** There are regularly scheduled orientations for prospective students. There are guides for informal visits and visitors may sit in on classes. To schedule a visit, contact the Admissions Office. **Campus Safety and Security:** Measures include 24-hour foot and vehicle patrol and security escort services. There are shuttle buses, emergency telephones, lighted pathways/sidewalks, required short safety course.

REQUIREMENTS: The ACT is required. SCSU requires applicants to be in the upper 50% of their class. AP and CLEP credits are accepted. Students must complete a minimum of 120 semester credit hours, including 40 hours of general education requirements and 60 to 180 hours in the major, and maintain at least a 2.0 GPA (higher for many majors). Students must complete English 191, English 192, Speech 192, 2 credits in phys ed, and 24 credits in philosophy/humanities/fine arts, natural science and math, social and behavioral science, and diversity courses. **Procedure:** Freshmen are admitted fall, spring, and summer. Entrance exams should be taken in the junior or senior year. Application deadlines are open. The fall 2014 application fee was $20. Notification is sent on a rolling basis. **Transfer Students:** Applicants must have a minimum 2.0 GPA from their previous college if they transfer with 12 or more credits. If they have fewer than 12 credits, they are treated as entering freshmen. 30 of 120 credits required for the bachelor's degree must be completed at SCSU. **International Students:** The school actively recruits these students. They must take the TOEFL.

ADMISSIONS: Pat Krueger, Associate Director of Admissions. E-Mail: *scsu4u@stcloud.state.edu* Web: *www.stcloudstate.edu*

FINANCIAL AID: The FAFSA and the college's own financial statement are required. Check with the school for current application deadlines.

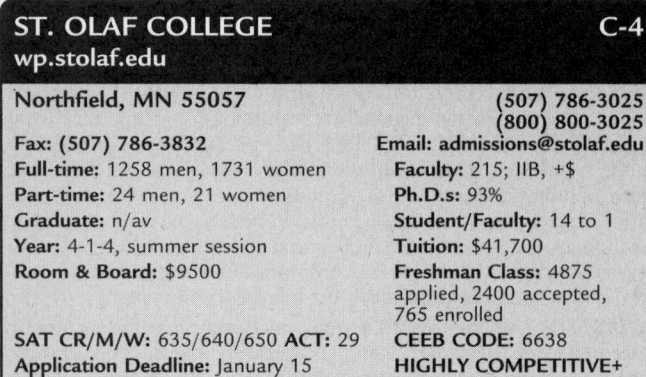

ST. OLAF COLLEGE   C-4
wp.stolaf.edu

Northfield, MN 55057	(507) 786-3025
	(800) 800-3025
Fax: (507) 786-3832	Email: admissions@stolaf.edu
Full-time: 1258 men, 1731 women	Faculty: 215; IIB, +$
Part-time: 24 men, 21 women	Ph.D.s: 93%
Graduate: n/av	Student/Faculty: 14 to 1
Year: 4-1-4, summer session	Tuition: $41,700
Room & Board: $9500	Freshman Class: 4875 applied, 2400 accepted, 765 enrolled
SAT CR/M/W: 635/640/650 ACT: 29	CEEB CODE: 6638
Application Deadline: January 15	HIGHLY COMPETITIVE+

One of the nation's leading liberal arts colleges, St. Olaf College offers a distinctive education grounded in academic rigor, residential learning, global engagement, and a vibrant Lutheran faith tradition. St. Olaf provides an uncommon educational experience that fully prepares students to make a meaningful difference in our changing world. There is 1 undergraduate school. In addition to regional accreditation, St. Olaf has baccalaureate program accreditation with CSWE, NASM, NCATE, CCNE, NASD, and NAST. The 300-acre campus is in a small town 35 miles south of Minneapolis/St. Paul. Including any residence halls, there are 55 buildings.

STUDENT LIFE: 52% of undergraduates are from out of state, mostly the Mid-West. Students are from 49 states, 73 foreign countries, and Canada. 76% are White. 43% are Protestant; 16% Catholic; 16% claim no religious affiliation; 13% Christian, and unkown. **Male To Female Ratio:** 1.4:1. The average age of freshmen is 18; all undergraduates, 20. 7% do not continue beyond their first year; 89% remain to graduate. **Housing:** 2970 students can be accommodated in college housing, which includes coed dorms. In addition, there are honors houses, language houses, and special-interest houses. On-campus housing is guaranteed for all 4 years. 93% of students live on campus. Alcohol is not permitted. Some may keep cars.

FACULTY/CLASSROOMS: 54% of faculty are male; 46% are female. All teach and do research. No introductory courses are taught by graduate students. The average class size in an introductory lecture is 24; in a laboratory is 21; and in a regular course is 23.

PROGRAMS OF STUDY: St. Olaf confers B.A. and B.Mus. degrees. Bachelor's degrees are awarded in AGRICULTURE (environmental studies), BIOLOGICAL SCIENCE (biology/biological science), COMMUNICATIONS AND THE ARTS (art history and appreciation, classics, dance, English, French, German, Greek, Latin, music, music performance, music theory and composition, Norwegian, Russian, Spanish, studio art, and theatre arts), COMPUTER AND PHYSICAL SCIENCE (chemistry, computer science, mathematics, and physics), EDUCATION (music education and social studies education), HEALTH PROFESSIONS (exercise science and nursing), SOCIAL SCIENCE (American studies, Asian/American studies, classical/ancient civilization, economics, ethnic studies, Hispanic American studies, history, interdisciplinary studies, medieval studies, philosophy, political science/government, psychology, religion, religious music, Russian and Slavic studies, social work, sociology, and women's studies). Biology, mathematics, and economics have the largest enrollments.

ACTIVITIES: There are no fraternities or sororities. There are 257 groups on campus, including art, band, chess, choir, chorus, computers, dance, drama, drill team, ethnic, film, gay, honors, international, jazz band, literary magazine, musical theater, newspaper, opera, orchestra, pep band, photography, political, professional, radio and TV, religious, social, social service, student government, and symphony. Popular campus events include Christmas Festival and President's Ball. **Sports:** There are 22 intercollegiate sports for men and 19 for women, and 35 intramural sports for men and 32 for women. Facilities include 2 athletic complexes, a field house with batting

cages, a long-jump pit, 5 indoor tennis courts, and a 6-lane indoor track, plus an upper level walking/running track, a fitness center, 45-foot climbing wall, a soccer pitch, baseball diamonds, 2 weight rooms, a football field, an 8-lane all-weather track and field, a 9-hole Frisbee golf course, and practice and recreation space. **Graduates:** From July 1, 2013 to June 30, 2014, 780 bachelor's degrees were awarded. The most popular majors were biology (12%), mathematics (10%), and economics (9%). 183 companies recruited on campus in 2013-2014. In an average class, 86% graduate in 4 years or less, 88% graduate in 5 years or less, and 89% graduate in 6 years or less.

SERVICES: Counseling and information services are available, as is tutoring in every subject. There is a reader service for the blind. Study sessions are available. **Library/Resources:** The 4 libraries contain 729,470 volumes, 13,107 microform items, 690,167 audio/video tapes/CDs/DVDs, and subscribe to 76,530 periodicals including electronic. Computerized library services include interlibrary loans, database searching, Internet access, and Wi-Fi capability. Special learning facilities include an art gallery, radio station, TV station, 700 acres of land dedicated to natural habitat, sustainable agriculture, and conventional agriculture. **Physically Challenged Students:** 76% of the campus is accessible. Facilities include wheelchair ramps, elevators, special parking, specially equipped restrooms, special class scheduling, lowered drinking fountains, lowered telephones, special housing, electric door openers, curb cuts, and a sling for swimming pool entry. **Special:** St. Olaf offers cross-registration with Carleton College, study abroad in more than 50 countries, a dozen domestic off-campus programs, pre-professional programs, internships, and a 3-2 B.A.-B.S.E. degree in engineering with Washington University in St. Louis or the University of Minnesota. There are dual majors, non-degree study, on-campus work study, and pass/fail options. The Center for Integrative Studies allows students to design individual majors with an emphasis on tutorials and seminars. St. Olaf's Conversation programs, focusing on the great books, American studies, Asian studies, environmental studies, and scientific inquiry, foster intimate learning communities that engage students in interdisciplinary study, critical thinking, and thoughtful discussion of major issues that transcend disciplinary borders and historical, cultural, and social contexts. There are 22 national honor societies, including Phi Beta Kappa. **Visiting:** There are regularly scheduled orientations for prospective students. Offerings include: tours, class visits, information sessions, interviews and more. There are guides for informal visits, visitors may sit in on classes, and stay overnight. **Campus Safety and Security:** Measures include 24-hour foot and vehicle patrol, emergency notification system, self-defense education, and security escort services. There are emergency telephones, lighted pathways/sidewalks, and controlled access to dorms/residences.

REQUIREMENTS: The SAT or ACT is required. It is recommended that applicants complete 4 years of English, 4 of math and social studies/history, 4 of science (2 labs), and 4 of a foreign language. AP credits are accepted. In addition to the distribution requirements, students are required to demonstrate skills at an intermediate level in a foreign language, proficiency in English composition, to complete the phys ed requirement and to have taken a 1/4-credit oral communication course and a 1-credit mathematical reasoning course. A first-year writing course is also required. Distribution requirements include courses in history, literature, art, science, human behavior, Bible and theology, multicultural studies, and ethical issues. A minimum of 24 full-course credits out of 35 must be graded, 18 must be upper-division. A minimum of 8 full-credit courses in a disciplinary or interdisciplinary major are required. All majors include writing requirements. Students must complete 35 credits and maintain a minimum GPA of 2.0. **Procedure:** Freshmen are admitted fall, winter, and spring. Entrance exams should be taken in the spring of the junior year or the fall of the senior year. There are early decision and deferred admissions plans. Early decision applications should be filed by November 15; regular applications, by January 15 for fall entry. Notification of early decision is sent December 15; regular decision, March 15. 202 early decision candidates were accepted for the 2014-2015 class. 562 applicants were on the 2014 waiting list; 75 were admitted. Applications are accepted on-line. **Transfer Students:** 26 transfer students enrolled in 2013-2014. 17 of 35 credits required for the bachelor's degree must be completed at St. Olaf. **International Students:** There are 217 international students enrolled. The school actively recruits these students. They must take the TOEFL with a minimum score of 90 on the Internet-based version (iBT), or take the IELTS. They must also take the SAT or ACT.

ADMISSIONS: 49% of the 2014-2015 applicants were accepted. The SAT scores for the 2014-2015 freshman class were: Critical Reading--10% below 500, 24% between 500 and 599, 39% between 600 and 699, and 27% between 700 and 800; Math--7% below 500, 25% between 500 and 599, 43% between 600 and 699, and 25% between 700 and 800. The ACT scores were 2% below 21, 6% between 21 and 23, 19% between 24 and 26, 13% between 27 and 28, and 60% above 28. 75% of the current freshmen were in the top fifth of their class; 93% were in the top two fifths. There were 30 National Merit finalists. 32 freshmen graduated first in their class. **Admissions Contact:** David Wagner, Director of Admissions. E-Mail: *admissions@stolaf .edu* Web: *wp.stolaf.edu*

FINANCIAL AID: In 2014-2015, 93% of all full-time freshmen and 91% of continuing full-time students received some form of financial aid. 70% of all full-time freshmen and 65% of continuing full-time students received need-based aid. The average freshman award was $32,220. Need-based scholarships or need-based grants averaged $29,948; need-based self-help aid (loans and jobs) averaged $4,898; and other non-need-based awards and non-need-based scholarships averaged $15,130. 67% of undergraduate students work part-time. Average annual earnings from campus work are $1182. The average financial indebtedness of the 2014 graduate was $28,396. St. Olaf is a member of CSS. The CSS/Profile and FAFSA are required. The priority date for freshman financial aid applications for fall entry is February 1. The deadline for filing freshman financial aid applications for fall entry is February 1.

UNIVERSITY OF MINNESOTA SYSTEM

The University of Minnesota System, established in 1851, is a public system in Minnesota. It is governed by a board of trustees, whose chief administrator is the president. The primary goal of the system is teaching, research, and public service. The main priorities are undergraduate education, basic and applied research, and graduate education. The total student enrollment for all five campuses is usually 75,000 with 3500 faculty members. Altogether there are 236 baccalaureate, 191 master's, 123 doctoral programs offered in the University Minnesota System. Profiles of the 4-year campuses are included in this section.

UNIVERSITY OF MINNESOTA CROOKSTON	A-2
www.umcrookston.edu	

Crookston, MN 56716	(218) 281-8569
	(800) 232-6466
Fax: (218) 281-8575	Email: Info@UMCrookston.edu
Full-time: 724 men, 669 women	Faculty: 73; IIB, -$
Part-time: 590 men, 781 women	Ph.D.s: 40%
Graduate: n/av	Student/Faculty: 20 to 1
Year: semesters, summer session	Tuition: $11,456
Room & Board: $6378	Freshman Class: 670 applied, 472 accepted, 121 enrolled
SAT CR/M/W: 480/520/490 ACT: 22	CEEB CODE: 6893
Application Deadline: n/av	COMPETITIVE

The University of Minnesota/Crookston, founded in 1965, is a public institution offering applied bachelor degree programs, including online opportunities, in agriculture, arts, humanities, and social sciences, business, math, science, technology and natural resources. There are 4 undergraduate schools. The 108-acre campus is in a small town 290 miles northwest of Minneapolis, and 25 miles southeast of Grand Forks, North Dakota. Including any residence halls, there are 35 buildings.

STUDENT LIFE: 67% of undergraduates are from Minnesota. Others are from 42 states, 16 foreign countries, and Canada. 76% are White. **Male To Female Ratio:** 1.1:1. The average age of freshmen is

19; all undergraduates, 26. 24% do not continue beyond their first year; 51% remain to graduate. **Housing:** 563 students can be accommodated in college housing, which includes coed dorms and on-campus apartments. On-campus housing is available on a first-come, first-served basis. Priority is given to out-of-town students. 20% of students commute. Alcohol is not permitted. All students may keep cars.

FACULTY/CLASSROOMS: 558% of faculty are male; 48% are female. All teach undergraduates, 40% do research, and 40% do both. No introductory courses are taught by graduate students. The average class size in an introductory lecture is 25; in a laboratory is 18; and in a regular course is 25.

PROGRAMS OF STUDY: UMC confers B.S., B.A.H. and B.M.M. degrees. Bachelor's degrees are awarded in AGRICULTURE (agricultural business management, agronomy, animal science, equine science, horticulture, and natural resource management), BIOLOGICAL SCIENCE (biology/biological science), BUSINESS (accounting, business administration and management, marketing management, organizational behavior, and sports management), COMMUNICATIONS AND THE ARTS (communications), COMPUTER AND PHYSICAL SCIENCE (information sciences and systems and software engineering), EDUCATION (early childhood education and elementary education), ENGINEERING AND ENVIRONMENTAL DESIGN (agricultural engineering technology, airline piloting and navigation, applied aviation, computer technology, environmental science, and industrial administration/management), HEALTH PROFESSIONS (health, health care administration, and health science), SOCIAL SCIENCE (criminal justice). Business management, natural resources, and equine science have the largest enrollments.

ACTIVITIES: 1% of men and 1 of women belong to 1 national fraternity; 1% of women belong to 1 national sorority. There are 39 groups on campus, including cheerleading, chess, choir, chorale, chorus, computers, drama, environmental, ethnic, gay, honors, international, pep band, political, professional, religious, social, social service, and student government. Popular campus events include What's on Wednesday (WOW), Ag-Arama and Winter Wonderland. **Sports:** There are 4 intercollegiate sports for men and 7 for women, and 10 intramural sports for men and 10 for women. Facilities include a 3200-seat gym; an indoor complex with basketball/volleyball and racquetball courts, a training room with a sauna, and a fitness center; a lit football field surrounded by an all-weather track; tennis courts; and soccer, baseball, and softball fields. **Graduates:** From July 1, 2013 to June 30, 2014, 314 bachelor's degrees were awarded. The most popular majors were business management (18%), natural resources (15%), and applied studies (7%). 30 companies recruited on campus in 2013-2014. In an average class, 11% graduate in 3 years or less, 36% graduate in 4 years or less, 42% graduate in 5 years or less, and 53% graduate in 6 years or less. Of the 2013 graduating class, 8% were enrolled in graduate school within 6 months of graduation, and 92% were employed.

SERVICES: Counseling and information services are available, as is tutoring in most subjects. There is a reader service for the blind, and remedial math and writing. The Academic Assistance Center also provides help with study strategies and English as a second language, and federally funded student support services are available to those who are eligible. **Library/Resources:** The library contains 244,686 volumes, 26,204 microform items, 2,222 audio/video tapes/CDs/DVDs. Computerized library services include interlibrary loans, database searching, Internet access, and Wi-Fi capability. **Physically Challenged Students:** 95% of the campus is accessible. Facilities include wheelchair ramps, elevators, special parking, specially equipped restrooms, special class scheduling, lowered drinking fountains, lowered telephones, and special housing. **Special:** UMC offers cross-registration with the University of North Dakota (Air Force ROTC). The internship or field experience requirement may be completed through on-the-job experience in the private sector, with a government agency, or through other appropriate work experience; a minimum of 450 hours of employment or volunteer assignments is usually required for satisfactory evaluation of the student's progress. Study abroad in more than 200 locations and student-designed majors are available. There is 1 national honor society, a freshman honors program, and 1 departmental honors program. **Visiting:**

There are regularly scheduled orientations for prospective students. There are guides for informal visits, visitors may sit in on classes, and stay overnight. To schedule a visit, contact the Admissions Office at umcinfo@umc.edu. **Campus Safety and Security:** Measures include emergency notification system, self-defense education, and security escort services. There are shuttle buses, emergency telephones, and lighted pathways/sidewalks.

REQUIREMENTS: The ACT is recommended, with a minimum score of 21 on the ACT or 980 on the SAT. Applicants must have successfully completed a high school or college preparatory program; the GED is accepted. A minimum 2.0 GPA is required. The strength of the high school curriculum is considered. Students failing to meet minimum requirements of GPA and ACT or SAT scores will be referred to the admissions committee for an admission decision. AP and CLEP credits are accepted.To graduate, students must complete 120 credit hours, including 40 credits of liberal education and 40 upper-division credits, with a minimum GPA of 2.0. 3 credits of technology are required. **Procedure:** Freshmen are admitted fall and spring. Entrance exams should be taken by May 1. There are deferred admissions and rolling admissions plans. Application deadlines are open. Application fee is $30. Notification is sent on a rolling basis. Applications are accepted on-line. **Transfer Students:** 240 transfer students enrolled in 2013-2014. Transfer students with fewer than 24 earned college credits need to submit an official high school transcript, ACT or SAT scores, and official transcripts from previous colleges. Transfer students with 24 or more semester credits need to submit only official transcripts from previous colleges. A minimum 2.0 college GPA is required. 30 of 120 credits required for the bachelor's degree must be completed at UMC. **International Students:** There are 145 international students enrolled. The school actively recruits these students. They must take the TOEFL with a minimum score of 520 on the paper-based TOEFL (PBT) or 68 on the Internet-based version (iBT), or take the MELAB or the IELTS. Native English-speaking students are not required to submit TOEFL scores but are required to submit ACT, SAT, or other standardized college entrance.

ADMISSIONS: 70% of the 2014-2015 applicants were accepted. The SAT scores for the 2014-2015 freshman class were: Critical Reading--53% below 500, 27% between 500 and 599, and 13% between 600 and 699; Math--20% below 500, 53% between 500 and 599, 7% between 600 and 699, and 7% between 700 and 800; Writing--57% below 500, and 43% between 500 and 599. The ACT scores were 41% below 21, 29% between 21 and 23, 19% between 24 and 26, 9% between 27 and 28, and 2% above 28. 37% of the current freshmen were in the top fifth of their class; 60% were in the top two fifths. 3 freshmen graduated first in their class. **Admissions Contact:** Peter Phaiah, Vice Chancellor of Student Affairs. E-Mail: *Info@UMCrookston.edu* Web: *www.umcrookston.edu*

FINANCIAL AID: In 2014-2015, 74% of all full-time freshmen and 70% of continuing full-time students received some form of financial aid. 71% of all full-time freshmen and 64% of continuing full-time students received need-based aid. The average freshman award was $13,370. Need-based scholarships or need-based grants averaged $9,574 need-based self-help aid (loans and jobs) averaged $4,780; and other non-need-based awards and non-need-based scholarships averaged $3,640. Average annual earnings from campus work are $1200. The average financial indebtedness of the 2014 graduate was $27,608. The FAFSA is required. The priority date for freshman financial aid applications for fall entry is March 1.

The University of Minnesota Duluth, founded in 1895, is a liberal arts institution offering undergraduate and graduate programs as a campus of the University of Minnesota. There are 5 undergraduate schools and 1 graduate school. In addition to regional accreditation, UMD has baccalaureate program accreditation with AACSB, ABET, ACPE, ASLA, CSAB, CSWE, NASM, NCATE, ASLHA, CAA, NASM, and NRPA. The 250-acre campus is in an urban area 150 miles north of Minneapolis and St. Paul. Including any residence halls, there are 58 buildings.

STUDENT LIFE: 82% of undergraduates are from Minnesota. Others are from 42 states, 64 foreign countries, and Canada. 95% are from public schools. 83% are White. **Male To Female Ratio:** 0.9:1. The average age of freshmen is 18; all undergraduates, 20. 19% do not continue beyond their first year; 53% remain to graduate. **Housing:** 3081 students can be accommodated in college housing, which includes single-sex and coed dorms and on-campus apartments. In addition, there are honors houses. On-campus housing is available on a first-come, first-served basis. 72% of students commute. Alcohol is not permitted. All students may keep cars.

FACULTY/CLASSROOMS: 55% of faculty are male; 45% are female. All teach undergraduates, and 75% do both. No introductory courses are taught by graduate students. The average class size in an introductory lecture is 60; in a laboratory is 20; and in a regular course is 30.

PROGRAMS OF STUDY: UMD confers B.A., B.S., B.A.A., B.Acc., B.A.Sc., B.B.A., B.F.A., B.Mus., B.S.Ch.E., B.S.C.E., B.S.E.C.E. and B.S.M.E. degrees. Master's and Doctoral degrees are also awarded. Bachelor's degrees are awarded in AGRICULTURE (environmental studies), BIOLOGICAL SCIENCE (biochemistry, biology/biological science, cell biology, and molecular biology), BUSINESS (accounting, business administration and management, management information systems, and organizational leadership and management), COMMUNICATIONS AND THE ARTS (art, art history and appreciation, communications, dramatic arts, English, graphic design, jazz, music, music performance, Spanish, and studio art), COMPUTER AND PHYSICAL SCIENCE (actuarial science, applied physics, chemistry, computer science, geology, information sciences and systems, mathematics, physics, and statistics), EDUCATION (art education, athletic training, elementary education, foreign languages education, health education, mathematics education, middle school education, music education, physical education, recreation education, science education, secondary education, and social studies education), ENGINEERING AND ENVIRONMENTAL DESIGN (chemical engineering, civil engineering, computer engineering, electrical/electronics engineering, environmental science, industrial engineering, and mechanical engineering), HEALTH PROFESSIONS (hospital administration), SOCIAL SCIENCE (anthropology, criminology, early childhood studies, economics, geography, German area studies, history, interdisciplinary studies, international studies, Native American studies, philosophy, political science/government, prelaw, psychology, sociology, urban studies, and women's studies). Business, sciences, and engineering are the strongest academically. Business administration, biology, and psychology have the largest enrollments.

ACTIVITIES: 1% of men belong to 1 local and 3 national fraternities; 1% of women belong to 1 local and 2 national sororities. There are 231 groups on campus, including jazz choir, wind ensemble, art, band, chamber orchestra, cheerleading, chess, choir, chorale, chorus, computers, dance, drama, environmental, ethnic, film, gay, honors, international, jazz band, literary magazine, marching band, musical theater, newspaper, opera, orchestra, pep band, photography, political, professional, radio and TV, religious, social, social service, and student government. Popular campus events include Out Cold Winter Festival, Black History Month, and Hispanic Heritage Month. **Sports:** There are 6 intercollegiate sports for men and 8 for women, and 26 intramural sports for men and 26 for women. Facilities include 2 rock-climbing walls, a multipurpose ice center, a football and track-and-field stadium, a baseball park, softball and soccer fields, a field house for track and tennis, a gym for basketball and volleyball, a nearby country club for cross-country and golf, and a cardio and weight facility. **Graduates:** From July 1, 2013 to June 30, 2014, 2168 bachelor's degrees were awarded. The most popular majors were psychology (7%), communication (5%), and finance (5%). 126 companies recruited on campus in 2013-2014. In an average class, 1% graduate in 3 years or less, 28% graduate in 4 years or less, 49% grad-

---

UNIVERSITY OF MINNESOTA/DULUTH   D-2
www.d.umn.edu

Duluth, MN 55812	
	(218) 726-7171
	(800) 232-1339
Fax: (218) 726-6394	Email: **umdadmis@d.umn.edu**
Full-time: 5350 men, 4568 women	**Faculty:** 454; IIA, av$
Part-time: n/av	**Ph.D.s:** 63%
Graduate: 199 men, 264 women	**Student/Faculty:** 20 to 1
Year: semesters, summer session	**Tuition:** $12,802 ($16,468)
Room & Board: $7004	**Freshman Class:** 7456 applied, 5694 accepted, 2105 enrolled
SAT CR/M/W: 510/540/530 **ACT:** 24	**CEEB CODE:** 6873
Application Deadline: February 1	**COMPETITIVE**

uate in 5 years or less, and 54% graduate in 6 years or less. Of the 2013 graduating class, 12% were enrolled in graduate school within 6 months of graduation, and 75% were employed.

SERVICES: Counseling and information services are available, as is tutoring in some subjects. There is a reader service for the blind, and remedial math and writing. Workshops and seminars are also offered on study skills, note taking, time management, test-taking strategies, and goal setting. **Library/Resources:** The library contains 738,103 volumes, 756,339 microform items, 19,443 audio/video tapes/CDs/DVDs, and subscribes to 65,521 periodicals including electronic. Computerized library services include interlibrary loans, database searching, Internet access, and Wi-Fi capability. Special learning facilities include an art gallery, planetarium, radio station, Glensheen historic mansion, child care center, speech and hearing clinic, performing arts centers (theatre and music), and a visual imaging lab. **Physically Challenged Students:** All of the campus is accessible. Facilities include wheelchair ramps, elevators, special parking, specially equipped restrooms, lowered drinking fountains, lowered telephones, and special housing. **Special:** Students may study abroad in England, Sweden, Finland, and Australia. UMD also offers cross-registration with the College of St. Scholastica and the University of Wisconsin/Superior, internships, work-study programs, a B.A.-B.S. degree in several fields, student-designed majors, and nondegree study. There is 1 national honor society, including Phi Beta Kappa, a freshman honors program, and 28 departmental honors programs. **Visiting:** There are regularly scheduled orientations for prospective students, including an information session, a campus tour, and a chance to meet with admissions counselors, faculty, or coaches and representatives from the five collegiate units. There are guides for informal visits and visitors may sit in on classes. To schedule a visit, contact Office of Admissions. **Campus Safety and Security:** Measures include 24-hour foot and vehicle patrol, emergency notification system, self-defense education, and security escort services. There are emergency telephones and lighted pathways/sidewalks.

REQUIREMENTS: The ACT is required. The ACT Optional Writing test is also required. Applicants must have completed 4 years in English, 3 each in math and sciences, and 2 each in a single second language and social studies. Course work in the visual and performing arts and computer skills is recommended. Students with a GED certificate will be admitted selectively as space permits. AP and CLEP credits are accepted. To graduate, students must complete 120 to 136 semester credits, including 2 courses in college writing, and a liberal education distribution of at least 35 credits in 10 academic areas. At least 4 credits of course work must emphasize cultural diversity, and 4 should emphasize an international perspective. **Procedure:** Freshmen are admitted fall and spring. Entrance exams should be taken at the end of junior year or the beginning of senior year. There is a rolling admissions plan. Applications should be filed by February 1 for fall entry; November 15 for spring entry, along with a $35 fee. Notification is sent on a rolling basis. Applications are accepted on-line. **Transfer Students:** 544 transfer students enrolled in 2013-2014. Applicants who have completed 26 or more semester credits must have a minimum 2.0 GPA and a 75% completion ratio; applicants who have attempted fewer than 26 semester credits must have a high school rank at or above the 50th percentile, a 1.8 GPA in their previous college work, and a 75% completion ratio. **International Students:** There are 172 international students enrolled. The school actively recruits these students. They must take the TOEFL with a minimum score of 550 on the paper-based TOEFL (PBT) or 80 on the Internet-based version (iBT).

ADMISSIONS: 76% of the 2014-2015 applicants were accepted. The SAT scores for the 2014-2015 freshman class were: Critical Reading--40% below 500, 34% between 500 and 599, 23% between 600 and 699, and 3% between 700 and 800; Math--28% below 500, 46% between 500 and 599, 21% between 600 and 699, and 5% between 700 and 800; Writing--36% below 500, 41% between 500 and 599, 21% between 600 and 699, and 2% between 700 and 800. The ACT scores were 15% below 21, 33% between 21 and 23, 33% between 24 and 26, 11% between 27 and 28, and 8% above 28. 33% of the current freshmen were in the top fifth of their class; 71% were in the top two fifths. **Admissions Contact:** Beth Esselstrom, Director of Admissions. E-Mail: *umdadmis@d.umn.edu* Web: *www.d.umn.edu*

FINANCIAL AID: In 2014-2015, 63% of all full-time freshmen and 61% of continuing full-time students received some form of financial aid. 63% of all full-time freshmen and 60% of continuing full-time students received need-based aid. The average freshman award was $10,478. Need-based scholarships or need-based grants averaged $7,658; need-based self-help aid (loans and jobs) averaged $3,740; and other non-need-based awards and non-need-based scholarships averaged $3,391. 14% of undergraduate students work part-time. The average financial indebtedness of the 2014 graduate was $18,214. The FAFSA is required. The priority date for freshman financial aid applications for fall entry is February 15.

UNIVERSITY OF MINNESOTA/MORRIS   B-3
www.morris.umn.edu

Morris, MN 56267	(320) 589-6035
	(888) UMM-EDUC
Fax: (320) 589-1673	Email: admissions@morris.umn.edu
Full-time: 725 men, 1125 women	Faculty: IIB, -$
Part-time: n/av	Ph.D.s: 97%
Graduate: n/av	Student/Faculty: n/av
Year: semesters, summer session	Tuition: $11,822
Room & Board: $7620	Freshman Class: n/app
SAT or ACT: required	CEEB CODE: 6890
Application Deadline: n/av	VERY COMPETITIVE

The University of Minnesota/Morris, founded in 1959, is a public liberal arts institution within the University of Minnesota system. The figures in the above capsule and in this profile are approximate. There is 1 undergraduate school. In addition to regional accreditation, UMM has baccalaureate program accreditation with NCATE. The 130-acre campus is in a small town 150 miles northwest of Minneapolis. Including any residence halls, there are 36 buildings.

STUDENT LIFE: 86% of undergraduates are from Minnesota. Others are from 27 states, 17 foreign countries, and Canada. 95% are from public schools. 79% are White. **Male To Female Ratio:** 1.6:1. The average age of freshmen is 18; all undergraduates, 21. 18% do not continue beyond their first year; 60% remain to graduate. **Housing:** 1032 students can be accommodated in college housing, which includes coed dorms and on-campus apartments. On-campus housing is guaranteed for all 4 years, is available on a first-come, first-served basis, and is available on a lottery system for upperclassmen. 60% of students live on campus; of those, 80% remain on campus on weekends. Alcohol is not permitted. All students may keep cars.

FACULTY/CLASSROOMS: 58% of faculty are male; 42% are female. All teach undergraduates, and 89% do both. No introductory courses are taught by graduate students. The average class size in an introductory lecture is 16; in a laboratory is 16; and in a regular course is 16.

PROGRAMS OF STUDY: UMM confers B.A. degrees. Bachelor's degrees are awarded in BIOLOGICAL SCIENCE (biology/biological science), BUSINESS (management science), COMMUNICATIONS AND THE ARTS (art history and appreciation, dramatic arts, English, French, German, music, Spanish, speech/debate/rhetoric, and studio art), COMPUTER AND PHYSICAL SCIENCE (chemistry, computer science, geology, mathematics, physics, and statistics), EDUCATION (elementary education and secondary education), HEALTH PROFESSIONS (premedicine), SOCIAL SCIENCE (anthropology, economics, European studies, history, Latin American studies, liberal arts/general studies, philosophy, political science/government, prelaw, psychology, social science, sociology, and women's studies). Psychology and sciences are the strongest academically. Education, English, and biology have the largest enrollments.

ACTIVITIES: There are no fraternities or sororities. There are 100 groups on campus, including riding, campus activities, reading instruction, swing dancing, art, band, cheerleading, chess, choir, chorus, computers, dance, debate, drama, ethnic, forensics, gay, honors, international, jazz band, literary magazine, mentoring, musical theater, newspaper, orchestra, photography, political, professional, radio and TV, religious, social, social service, student government, and yearbook. Popular campus events include Cultural Heritage Week, Diversity Jam, and Jazz Fest. **Sports:** There are 6 intercollegiate sports for men and 10 for women, and 12 intramural sports for men and 12 for women. Facilities include a 4500-seat stadium, a phys ed center, 5 gyms, wrestling, exercise, and weight rooms, an Olympic-size pool, handball and racquetball courts, a track, fields for softball, baseball, soccer, and football, a diving well, a warm-water pool and slide, an indoor track, and a cardiovascular fitness room. **SERVICES:** Counseling and information services are available, as is tutoring in every subject. There is a reader service for the blind, and remedial math, reading, and writing. **Library/Resources:** The library contains 197,220 volumes, 221,216 microform items, 2,140 audio/video tapes/CDs/DVDs, and subscribes to 885 periodicals including electronic. Computerized library services include interlibrary loans and database searching. Special learning facilities include an art gallery, radio station, TV station, a language lab, an observatory, and an agricultural experiment station. **Physically Challenged Students:** 70% of the campus is accessible. Facilities include wheelchair ramps, elevators, special parking, specially equipped restrooms, special class scheduling, lowered drinking fountains, and a disability services coordinator. Special learning equipment and services are available through the academic assistance center. **Special:** UMM offers work-study programs, internships, study abroad, dual majors, student-designed majors, nondegree study, pass/fail options, and credit for life, military, and work experience. There is a 3-2 engineering degree with the University of Minnesota at Twin Cities. A competitive, merit-based program that pairs students and professors to undertake creative projects is available. There is a freshman honors program and 100 departmental honors programs. **Visiting:** There are regularly scheduled orientations for prospective students, including a campus tour, lunch with faculty, a session with admissions staff, and a student panel. There are guides for informal visits, visitors may sit in on classes, and stay overnight. To schedule a visit, contact the Admissions Office. **Campus Safety and Security:** Measures include 24-hour foot and vehicle patrol, self-defense education, and security escort services. There are shuttle buses, emergency telephones, and lighted pathways/sidewalks.

REQUIREMENTS: The SAT or ACT is required. The ACT Optional Writing test is also required. In addition, applicants should be graduates of an accredited secondary school or have a GED certificate. They must have completed 4 years of English, 3 each of math and science, 2 of a single foreign language, and 1 each of social studies and American history. A GPA of 3.0 is required. AP and CLEP credits are accepted. Important factors in the admissions decision are leadership record, extracurricular activities record, and advanced placement or honors courses. In addition to 40 semester hours in the major, students are required to complete 60 credits of a general education curriculum, including courses in writing, computing, foreign language or equivalent, and advanced study, as well as courses focusing on the arts, the physical and abstract worlds, and the self and others. All first-year students participate in a freshman seminar, and the cumulative of their major work is presented in the senior seminar, which is a requirement for all seniors. **Procedure:** Freshmen are admitted fall and spring. Entrance exams should be taken before December 1 of the senior year. There are deferred admissions and rolling admissions plans. Check with the school for current application deadlines. The fall 2014 application fee was $35. Applications are accepted on-line. **Transfer Students:** Applicants must complete the application for admission, submit all college transcripts, and have maintained a minimum GPA of 2.5. 30 of 120 credits required for the bachelor's degree must be completed at UMM.

ADMISSIONS: Jaime Moquin, Director of Admissions. E-Mail: *admissions@morris.umn.edu* Web: *www.morris.umn.edu*

FINANCIAL AID: The FAFSA is required. Check with the school for current application deadlines.

UNIVERSITY OF MINNESOTA/TWIN CITIES	C-4
www.umn.edu	

Minneapolis, MN 55455	(612) 625-2008
	(800) 752-1000
Fax: (612) 625-1693	Email: admissions@tc.umn.edu.
Full-time: 14125 men, 14779 women	Faculty: 1, av$
	Ph.D.s: n/av
Part-time: 2609 men, 2838 women	Student/Faculty: n/av
Graduate: 7989 men, 8807 women	Tuition: $13,626 (2,876)
Year: semesters, summer session	Freshman Class: n/av
Room & Board: $8554	CEEB CODE: 6874
Application Deadline: n/av	HIGHLY COMPETITIVE

University of Minnesota/Twin Cities, founded in 1851, is a land-grant institution offering programs in liberal and fine arts, physical and biological sciences, health sciences, education, natural resources, human ecology, business, agriculture, and engineering and professional training in law, medicine, dentistry, pharmacy, and veterinary medicine. There are 11 undergraduate schools and 16 graduate schools. In addition to regional accreditation, The U has baccalaureate program accreditation with AACSB, ABET, ABFSE, ACEJMC, ADA, APTA, ASLA, CSWE, FIDER, NAAB, NASM, NCATE, NLN, and SAF. The 2000-acre campus is in an urban area within both Minneapolis and St. Paul. Including any residence halls, there are 205 buildings.

STUDENT LIFE: 75% of undergraduates are from Minnesota. Others are from 50 states, 141 foreign countries, and Canada. 85% are from public schools. 66% are White; 12% Foreign. **Male To Female Ratio:** 1.1:1. The average age of freshmen is 18; all undergraduates, 21. 8% do not continue beyond their first year; 75% remain to graduate. **Housing:** 6952 students can be accommodated in college housing, which includes single-sex and coed dorms, on-campus apartments, off-campus apartments, and married student housing. In addition, there are honors houses, special-interest houses, fraternity houses, sorority houses, cooperative housing. On-campus housing is guaranteed for the freshman year only, is available on a first-come, first-served basis, and is available on a lottery system for upperclassmen. 77% of students commute. Alcohol is not permitted. All students may keep cars.

FACULTY/CLASSROOMS: 56% of faculty are male; 44% are female. All teach and do research. No introductory courses are taught by graduate students.

PROGRAMS OF STUDY: The U confers B.A., B.S., B.A.E.M., B.C.E., B.S.Ch., B.Ch.E., B.Comp.Sci., B.E.E., B.F.A., B.G.E., B.I.S., B.Materials Sci.E., B.S. Mathematics, B.M.E., B.S.Bus., B.S.G., B.S. in Astrophysics, B.S. in Geophysics, B.S.N., B.S. Statistics., B.A.S., B.A.Sc., B.B.A.E., B.B.P.E., B.Bm.E., B.Comp.E., B.D.A., B.E.D., B.Mus. and B.S.Phys. degrees. Master's and doctoral degrees are also awarded. Bachelor's degrees are awarded in AGRICULTURE (agricultural business management, agricultural economics, animal science, fishing and fisheries, forestry production and processing, forestry and related sciences, and natural resource management), BIOLOGICAL SCIENCE (biochemistry, biology/biological science, botany, cell biology, ecology, evolutionary biology, genetics, microbiology, nutrition, physiology, and wildlife biology), BUSINESS (accounting, business administration and management, management science, marketing/retailing/merchandising, recreation and leisure services, recreational facilities management, and retailing), COMMUNICATIONS AND THE ARTS (apparel design, art, art history and appreciation, Chinese, classical languages, dance, English, film arts, French, German, Greek, Hebrew, Italian, Japanese, languages, Latin, linguistics, music, Russian, Scandinavian languages, Spanish, speech/debate/rhetoric, and studio art), COMPUTER AND PHYSICAL SCIENCE (actuarial science, astrophysics, chemistry, computer science, geology, geophysics and seismology, mathematics, physics, and statistics), EDUCATION (agricultural education, art education, bilingual/bicultural education, business education, early childhood education, elementary education, English education, home economics education, industrial arts education, mathematics education, music education, physical education, science education, social studies education, and teaching English as a second/foreign language (TESOL/TEFOL)), ENGINEERING AND ENVIRONMENTAL DESIGN (aerospace studies, architecture, bioengineering, chemical engineering, civil engineering, electrical/electronics engineering, environmental design, geological engineering, industrial engineering, interior design, landscape architecture/design, materials engineering, materials science, mechanical engineering, and metallurgical engineering), HEALTH PROFESSIONS (dental hygiene, medical laboratory technology, music therapy, nursing, occupational therapy, pharmacy, physical therapy, predentistry, premedicine, prepharmacy, preveterinary science, and speech pathology/audiology), SOCIAL SCIENCE (African studies, African American studies, American Indian studies, American studies, anthropology, Asian/Oriental studies, child psychology/development, East Asian studies, economics, food science, geography, history, humanities, international relations, Mexican-American/Chicano studies, Middle Eastern studies, philosophy, political science/government, prelaw, psychology, Russian and Slavic studies, sociology, South Asian studies, textiles and clothing, urban studies, and women's studies). Engineering, psychology, and economics are the strongest academically and have the largest enrollments.

ACTIVITIES: There are 600 groups on campus, including art, band, cheerleading, chess, choir, chorale, chorus, computers, dance, debate, drama, drill team, environmental, ethnic, film, gay, honors, international, jazz band, literary magazine, marching band, musical theater, newspaper, orchestra, pep band, photography, political, professional, radio and TV, religious, social, social service, student government, and symphony. Popular campus events include homecoming. **Sports:** There are 12 intercollegiate sports for men and 11 for women, and 16 intramural sports for men and 16 for women. Facilities include an outdoor stadium, 3 gyms, 2 field houses, a hockey rink, an Olympic-size aquatic center, and a student recreation center. **Graduates:** From July 1, 2013 to June 30, 2014, 7594 bachelor's degrees were awarded. The most popular majors were psychology (4%), communication studies (3%), and journalism (3%). In an average class, 5% graduate in 3 years or less, 59% graduate in 4 years or less, 76% graduate in 5 years or less, and 76% graduate in 6 years or less.

SERVICES: Counseling and information services are available, as is tutoring in every subject. There is a reader service for the blind, and remedial math, reading, and writing. There is test proctoring and sign language interpreters. **Library/Resources:** The 14 libraries contain 6.2 million volumes, 5.4 million microform items, 500,000 audio/video tapes/CDs/DVDs, and subscribe to 48,105 periodicals including electronic. Computerized library services include interlibrary loans, database searching, and Internet access. Special learning facilities include an art gallery, natural history museum, planetarium, radio station, and TV station. **Physically Challenged Students:** Facilities include wheelchair ramps, elevators, special parking, specially equipped restrooms, special class scheduling, lowered drinking fountains, lowered telephones, special housing, listening devices, TTY and volume-control phones, print enlargers, and adaptive computers. In addition, support groups and counselors provide assistance with all areas of university life and career planning. **Special:** The university offers cooperative programs, cross-registration with the Minnesota Community College system, internships, study abroad in 65 countries, work-study programs both on and off campus, a B.A.-B.S. degree in all majors, a general studies degree, and dual and student-designed majors. Pass/fail options and credit for life, military, or work experience are available. There are 21 national honor societies, including Phi Beta Kappa, a freshman honors program, and 8 departmental honors programs. **Visiting:** There are regularly scheduled orientations for prospective students. There are guides for informal visits, visitors may sit in on classes, and stay overnight. To schedule a visit, contact the Visit Line at (612) 625-0000. **Campus Safety and Security:** Measures include 24-hour foot and vehicle patrol, emergency notification system, self-defense education, and security escort services. There are shuttle buses, emergency telephones, lighted pathways/sidewalks, a 20-member university police force, and blue-light phone centers.

REQUIREMENTS: The SAT or ACT is required. The university uses a formula index in evaluating high school rank and ACT test scores. A portfolio is required for studio arts and architecture, an audition for music, and an interview for architecture and education. A high school diploma is required; the GED is accepted. AP and CLEP credits are accepted. Important factors in the admissions decision are advanced placement or honors courses, evidence of special talent, and leadership record. To graduate, students must complete 120 to 130 semester credits, including 45 in the major, with a minimum GPA of 2.0. Distribution requirements include course work in the 4 areas of communication, language, and symbolic systems, physical and biological sciences, the individual and society, and artistic expression. Other requirements vary by program. **Procedure:** Freshmen are admitted to all sessions. Entrance exams should be taken by the end of the junior year or October/November/December of the senior year. There are early admissions, deferred admissions, and rolling admissions plans. Application deadlines are open. Application fee is $55. Notification is sent on a rolling basis. Applications are accepted on-line. **Transfer Students:** Admission requirements vary by major/program, with a minimum 2.2 GPA needed for consideration. Col-

lege transcripts are required. 30 of 120 credits required for the bachelor's degree must be completed at The U. **International Students:** They must take the TOEFL or MELAB and the college's own test. They must also take the SAT or ACT. ACT for residents of Minnesota and neighboring states, SAT for residents of other states.

ADMISSIONS: 77% of the current freshmen were in the top fifth of their class; 98% were in the top two fifths. **Admissions Contact:** Rachelle Hernandez, Director of Admissions. E-Mail: *admissions@ tc.umn.edu.* Web: *www.umn.edu*

FINANCIAL AID: In 2014-2015, 50% of all full-time freshmen students received some form of financial aid. The average freshman award was $14,017. Need-based scholarships or need-based grants averaged $10,349; and need-based self-help aid (loans and jobs) averaged $6,213. The FAFSA and the college's own financial statement are required. Check with the school for current application deadlines.

UNIVERSITY OF SAINT THOMAS   C-4
www.stthomas.edu

St. Paul, MN 55105	(651) 962-6150
	(800) 328-6819, ext. 2-6150
Fax: (651) 962-6160	Email: admissions@stthomas.edu
Full-time: 3217 men, 2877 women	Faculty: I, av$
Part-time: 137 men, 119 women	Ph.Ds: n/av
Graduate: 1896 men, 1973 women	Student/Faculty: 15 to 1
Year: 4-1-4, summer session	Tuition: $35,305
Room & Board: $8986	Freshman Class: 5540 applied, 4774 accepted, 1368 enrolled
SAT CR/M: 580/590 ACT: 25	CEEB CODE: 6110
Application Deadline: n/av	COMPETITIVE+

The University of Saint Thomas, founded in 1885, is a private liberal arts institution affiliated with the Roman Catholic Church. Figures in the above capsule and in this profile are approximate. There are 4 undergraduate schools and 8 graduate schools. In addition to regional accreditation, Saint Thomas has baccalaureate program accreditation with AACSB, ABET, CSWE, NASM, NCATE, and ACS. The 78-acre campus is in an urban area 5 miles west of St. Paul and 5 miles east of Minneapolis.

STUDENT LIFE: 78% of undergraduates are from Minnesota. **Male To Female Ratio:** 0.9:1. The average age of freshmen is 18; all undergraduates, 21. 12% do not continue beyond their first year; 88% remain to graduate. **Housing:** College-sponsored housing includes single-sex dorms, on-campus apartments, and off-campus apartments. In addition, there are special-interest houses, chemical-free houses, first-year experience houses, women in science housing, special housing for disabled students, theme housing, wellness housing, and housing options for Catholic women and Catholic men. On-campus housing is available on a first-come, first-served basis, and is available on a lottery system for upperclassmen. 61% of students commute. All students may keep cars.

FACULTY/CLASSROOMS: No introductory courses are taught by graduate students.

PROGRAMS OF STUDY: Saint Thomas confers B.A., B.S., B.S.M.E., B.S.E.E. and B.M. degrees. Master's and doctoral degrees are also awarded. Business has the largest enrollment.

ACTIVITIES: There are no fraternities or sororities. There are 140 groups on campus, including band, choir, chorus, computers, dance, drama, ethnic, gay, honors, international, jazz band, literary magazine, newspaper, pep band, political, professional, radio and TV, religious, social, social service, student government, and yearbook. **Sports:** There are 10 intercollegiate sports for men and 10 for women. Facilities include 180,000 square foot, a 2,000-seat basketball and volleyball arena, aquatic center containing an eight-lane swimming pool, diving area, field house with 200-meter, six-lane track. Beneath the field house are locker rooms, meeting rooms, training rooms and other support facilities. The west wing contains a fitness center, weight room and aerobics rooms on the first floor, and offices, classrooms and labs on the second and third floors. **Graduates:** From July 1, 2013 to June 30, 2014, 1283 bachelor's degrees were awarded.

SERVICES: **Library/Resources:** The 5 libraries contain 695,137 volumes, 1.1 million microform items, and 76,383 audio/video tapes/CDs/DVDs, and subscribe to 193,510 periodicals including electronic. Computerized library services include interlibrary loans, database searching, and Wi-Fi capability. Special learning facilities include an art gallery, radio station, and TV station. **Special:** There is a freshman honors program. **Visiting:** There are regularly scheduled orientations for prospective students. There are guides for informal visits, visitors may sit in on classes, and stay overnight. To schedule a visit, contact the Visit Coordinator. **Campus Safety and Security:** Measures include 24-hour foot and vehicle patrol, emergency notification system, and security escort services. There are shuttle buses, emergency telephones, lighted pathways/sidewalks, and controlled access to dorms/residences.

REQUIREMENTS: The SAT is recommended. AP and CLEP credits are accepted. **Procedure:** Freshmen are admitted fall and spring. Entrance exams should be taken by the fall of the senior year. There are deferred admissions and rolling admissions plans. Application deadlines are open. Applications are accepted on-line. **Transfer Students:** 271 transfer students enrolled in 2013-2014. Transfer applicants must have a minimum GPA of 2.3 in transferable college credits. 32 of 132 credits required for the bachelor's degree must be completed at Saint Thomas. **International Students:** They must take the TOEFL or MELAB. They must also take the SAT or ACT.

ADMISSIONS: 86% of the 2014-2015 applicants were accepted. **Admissions Contact:** Marla Friederichs, Associate Vice President for Enrollment Management. E-Mail: *admissions@stthomas.edu* Web: *www.stthomas.edu*

FINANCIAL AID: The FAFSA is required. Check with the school for current application deadlines.

WINONA STATE UNIVERSITY   D-5
www.winona.edu

Winona, MN 55987	**(507) 457-5100**
	(800) DIAL-WSU
Fax: (507) 457-5620	Email: admissions@winona.edu
Full-time: 2802 men, 4400 women	Faculty: IIA, -$
Part-time: 292 men, 615 women	Ph.D.s: 59%
Graduate: 146 men, 400 women	Student/Faculty: 24 to 1
Year: semesters, summer session	Tuition: $8750 ($14,250)
Room & Board: $7890	Freshman Class: 7099 applied, 4475 accepted, 1648 enrolled
ACT: 23	CEEB CODE: 6680
Application Deadline: July 12	COMPETITIVE

Winona State University, founded in 1858, is a mid-sized comprehensive regional university that is part of the Minnesota State Colleges and Universities system. There are 5 undergraduate schools and 1 graduate school. In addition to regional accreditation, WSU has baccalaureate program accreditation with AACSB, ABET, CSWE, NASM, NCATE, CCNE, CAAT, and CACREP. The 125-acre campus is in an urban area 120 miles southeast of Minneapolis and St. Paul. Including any residence halls, there are 35 buildings.

STUDENT LIFE: 69% of undergraduates are from Minnesota. 86% are White. **Male To Female Ratio:** 1.7:1. The average age of freshmen is 18; all undergraduates, 22. 24% do not continue beyond their first year; 57% remain to graduate. **Housing:** 2722 students can be accommodated in college housing, which includes single-sex and coed dorms and on-campus apartments. In addition, there are special-interest houses. On-campus housing is guaranteed for the freshman year only, and is available on a first-come, first-served basis. 72% of students commute. Alcohol is not permitted. All students may keep cars.

FACULTY/CLASSROOMS: 39% of faculty are male; 61% are female. No introductory courses are taught by graduate students. The average class size in a regular course is 30.

PROGRAMS OF STUDY: WSU confers B.A., B.S., B.S.E., B.S.N., B.S.W., B.A.S. and B.M. degrees. Associate, Master's, and Doctoral degrees are also awarded. Bachelor's degrees are awarded in BIOLOGICAL SCIENCE (biology/biological science), BUSINESS (accounting, banking and finance, business administration and management, business economics, human resources/organizational mgmt, management information systems, marketing, and recreation and leisure services), COMMUNICATIONS AND THE ARTS (broadcasting, communication studies, dramatic arts, English, fine arts, graphic design, journalism, music, music performance, Spanish, and speech/debate/rhetoric), COMPUTER AND PHYSICAL SCIENCE (applied science, chemistry, computer science, earth science, earth science / adolescence education, geology, mathematics, physics, and statistics), EDUCATION (art education, athletic training, business education, early childhood education, elementary education, foreign languages education, health education, mathematics education, music education, physical education, science education, secondary education, social studies education, special education, specific learning disabilities, and teaching English as a second/foreign language (TESOL/TEFOL)), ENGINEERING AND ENVIRONMENTAL DESIGN (materials engineering and preengineering), HEALTH PROFESSIONS (community health work, cytotechnology, exercise science, health care administration, movement science, nursing, predentistry, premedicine, preoptometry, prepharmacy, prephysical therapy, prepodiatry, preveterinary science, and public health), SOCIAL SCIENCE (criminal justice, economics, (Social Science) Global Studies, history, paralegal studies, physical fitness/movement, political science/government, prelaw, psychology, public administration, social work, sociology, and women and gender studies). Nursing, education, and engineering are the strongest academically. Nursing, elementary education, and business administration have the largest enrollments.

ACTIVITIES: There are 155 groups on campus, including art, band, cheerleading, chess, choir, chorale, chorus, computers, dance, debate, drama, environmental, ethnic, film, forensics, gay, honors, international, jazz band, literary magazine, musical theater, newspaper, orchestra, pep band, photography, political, professional, radio and TV, religious, social, social service, student government, and symphony. Popular campus events include homecoming. **Sports:** There are 5 intercollegiate sports for men and 10 for women, and 16 intramural sports for men and 16 for women. Facilities include a 4000-seat stadium, baseball field, softball field, 8 gyms in multiples buildings, weight room, gymnastic practice area, a swimming pool, 5 handball/racquetball courts, cardio-fitness center with 60 machines, and a walking/jogging inside track. **Graduates:** From July 1, 2013 to June 30, 2014, 1672 bachelor's degrees were awarded. The most popular majors were nursing (15%), business administration (9%), and elementary education (8%). In an average class, 34% graduate in 4 years or less, 54% graduate in 5 years or less, and 57% graduate in 6 years or less.

SERVICES: Counseling and information services are available, as is tutoring in most subjects. **Library/Resources:** The library contains 479,521 volumes, 27,501 microform items, 21,446 audio/video tapes/CDs/DVDs, and subscribes to 34,393 periodicals including electronic. Computerized library services include interlibrary loans, database searching, and Wi-Fi capability. Special learning facilities include an art gallery and radio station. **Physically Challenged Students:** 3% of the campus is accessible. Facilities include wheelchair ramps, elevators, special parking, specially equipped restrooms, special class scheduling, lowered drinking fountains, lowered telephones, and special housing. **Special:** WSU offers cross-registration with St. Mary's University, study abroad in 12 countries, internships, work-study programs, student-designed majors, dual majors, pass/fail options, and credit for life, military, and work experience. Students may earn accelerated degrees in all majors and a general studies degree. There are 9 national honor societies and 6 departmental honors programs. **Visiting:** There are regularly scheduled orientations for prospective students, including daily tours and admissions visits from October through January on select Saturday mornings. There are guides for informal visits and visitors may sit in on classes. To schedule a visit, contact the Office of Admissions at admissions@winona.edu. **Campus Safety and Security:** Measures include 24-hour foot and vehicle patrol, emergency notification system, self-defense education, and security escort services. There are shuttle buses, emergency telephones, lighted pathways/sidewalks, and controlled access to dorms/residences.

REQUIREMENTS: The ACT is required. Candidates should have completed 4 units of English, 1 of which may be speech; 3 each of math and science; 2 each of a foreign language and social studies; 1 of history; and 1 elective, preferably in world culture, the arts, or computer science. AP and CLEP credits are accepted.To graduate, students must complete 120 credit hours with a minimum GPA of 2.0. General education requirements include 3 credits in public speaking, 3 credits in English, 7 credits in natural sciences, 3 in math and logical reasoning, 9 in history and social sciences, 9 in humanities and fine arts, and 2 in phys ed. Majors average 46 credits, and some require a capstone experience. **Procedure:** Freshmen are admitted fall, spring, and summer. Entrance exams should be taken in the junior year. There is a rolling admissions plan. Applications should be filed by July 12 for fall entry; November 22 for spring entry. The fall 2014 application fee was $20. Applications are accepted on-line. **Transfer Students:** 632 transfer students enrolled in 2013-2014. Applicants must have completed 24 semester hours of credit with a minimum GPA of 2.4. 30 of 120 credits required for the bachelor's degree must be completed at WSU. **International Students:** There are 273 international students enrolled. The school actively recruits these students. They must take the TOEFL with a minimum score of 520 on the paper-based TOEFL (PBT) or 68 on the Internet-based version (iBT).

ADMISSIONS: 63% of the 2014-2015 applicants were accepted. **Admissions Contact:** Carl Stange, Director of Admissions. E-Mail: *admissions@winona.edu* Web: *www.winona.edu*

FINANCIAL AID: In 2014-2015, 60% of all full-time freshmen and 60% of continuing full-time students received some form of financial aid. 43% of all full-time freshmen and 41% of continuing full-time students received need-based aid. The average freshman award was $6,680. Need-based scholarships or need-based grants averaged $4,697; need-based self-help aid (loans and jobs) averaged $3,479; non-need-based athletic scholarships averaged $1,867; and other non-need-based awards and non-need-based scholarships averaged $2,065. The average financial indebtedness of the 2014 graduate was $35,087. The FAFSA is required. The priority date for freshman financial aid applications for fall entry is May 1.

MISSISSIPPI

A   B   C   D   E

- Holly Springs
- Blue Mountain
- University
- Cleveland
- Itta Bena
- Columbus
- Mississippi State
- Clinton
- Tougaloo
- Jackson
- Alcorn State
- Hattiesburg

• College Location

0 20 40 60 80 100
Miles

ALCORN STATE UNIVERSITY   B-4
www.alcorn.edu

Alcorn State, MS 39096   (601) 877-6147
    n/av

Fax: (601) 877-6347	Email: ebarnes@.alcorn.edu
Full-time: 980 men, 1725 women	Faculty: IIB, -$
Part-time: 60 men, 245 women	Ph.D.s: 64%
Graduate: 165 men, 505 women	Student/Faculty: 17 to 1
Year: semesters, summer session	Tuition: $4500 ($10,000)
Room & Board: $5000	Freshman Class: n/av
SAT: recommended ACT: required	CEEB CODE: 1008
Application Deadline: open	COMPETITIVE

Alcorn State University, founded in 1871, is a public institution offering programs in agriculture, the arts and sciences, business, engineering, and nursing. The figures in the above capsule and in this profile are approximate. There are 6 undergraduate schools and 1 graduate school. In addition to regional accreditation, has baccalaureate program accreditation with AACSB, ADA, AHEA, NASM, NCATE, NLN, AAFCS, and NAIT. The 1756-acre campus is in a rural area 45 miles south of Vicksburg and 7 miles west of Lorman. Including any residence halls, there are 128 buildings.

STUDENT LIFE: 81% of undergraduates are from Mississippi. Others are from 32 states, 13 foreign countries, and Canada. 95% are from public schools. 91% are African American. **Male To Female Ratio:** 2.1:1. The average age of freshmen is 24; all undergraduates, 25. 28% do not continue beyond their first year; 45% remain to graduate. **Housing:** 2495 students can be accommodated in college housing, which includes single-sex dorms. In addition, there are honors houses. On-campus housing is guaranteed for all 4 years. 56% of students commute. Alcohol is not permitted. All students may keep cars.

FACULTY/CLASSROOMS: 55% of faculty are male; 45% are female. 92% teach undergraduates. No introductory courses are taught by graduate students.

PROGRAMS OF STUDY: confers B.A., B.S., B.M., B.M.E. and B.S.N.

---

degrees. Associate and Master's degrees are also awarded. Bachelor's degrees are awarded in AGRICULTURE (agricultural business management and agricultural economics), BIOLOGICAL SCIENCE (biology/biological science and nutrition), BUSINESS (accounting, business administration and management, and recreation and leisure services), COMMUNICATIONS AND THE ARTS (communications, English, and music), COMPUTER AND PHYSICAL SCIENCE (applied science, chemistry, computer science, and mathematics), EDUCATION (elementary education and special education), ENGINEERING AND ENVIRONMENTAL DESIGN (computer technology), HEALTH PROFESSIONS (health science, nursing, and sports medicine), SOCIAL SCIENCE (child psychology/development, criminal justice, economics, history, political science/government, psychology, social work, and sociology). Business administration, biology, and elementary education have the largest enrollments.

ACTIVITIES: 7% of men belong to 4 local and 4 national fraternities; 10% of women belong to 4 local and 4 national sororities. There are 79 groups on campus, including band, cheerleading, choir, chorus, dance, drama, honors, jazz band, marching band, newspaper, photography, radio and TV, religious, student government, and yearbook. Popular campus events include High School Day and Career Development Day. **Sports:** There are 8 intercollegiate sports for men and 10 for women, and 9 intramural sports for men and 9 for women. Facilities include a 10,000-seat stadium and a 5000-seat gym. **Graduates:** From July 1, 2013 to June 30, 2014, 399 bachelor's degrees were awarded. The most popular majors were general studies (20%), biology (12%), and nursing (9%). 214 companies recruited on campus in 2013-2014. In an average class, 45% graduate in 6 years or less. Of the 2013 graduating class, 38% were enrolled in graduate school within 6 months of graduation, and 99% were employed.

SERVICES: Counseling and information services are available, as is tutoring in most subjects. There is remedial math, reading, and writing. Remedial English **Library/Resources:** The library contains 225,423 volumes, 581,883 microform items, 17,200 audio/video tapes/CDs/DVDs, and subscribes to 40,741 periodicals including electronic. Computerized library services include interlibrary loans, database searching, Internet access, and Wi-Fi capability. Special learning facilities include a radio station. **Physically Challenged Students:** 15% of the campus is accessible. Facilities include wheelchair ramps, elevators, special parking, specially equipped restrooms, and lowered drinking fountains. **Special:** The university offers internships and work-study programs. There is 1 national honor society, including Phi Beta Kappa, a freshman honors program, and 5 departmental honors programs. **Visiting:** There are regularly scheduled orientations for prospective students. There are guides for informal visits, visitors may sit in on classes, and stay overnight.. **Campus Safety and Security:** Measures include 24-hour foot and vehicle patrol. There are lighted pathways/sidewalks.

REQUIREMENTS: The ACT is required. The SAT is recommended. In addition, students must have graduated from an accredited high school with at least a C average and have completed 15 1/2 units of a college prep curriculum. A GPA of 2.0 is required. AP and CLEP credits are accepted.To graduate, students must complete at least 128 semester hours with a minimum GPA of 2.0. Core requirements include 12 hours of social science, 9 each of natural science and creative arts, 6 of English, 4 of phys ed or military science, and 3 each of math and oral communications, as well as 1 of student adjustment. **Procedure:** Freshmen are admitted to all sessions. Entrance exams should be taken so that scores may be submitted at the time application is made. There are early decision, deferred admissions, and rolling admissions plans. Application deadlines are open. Notification is sent on a rolling basis. **Transfer Students:** 286 transfer students enrolled in 2013-2014. Applicants must have at least 6 hours each of composition and lab sciences, 3 hours of college algebra or above, and 9 other transferable elective hours and must have maintained an overall minimum GPA of 2.0. 104 of 128 credits required for the bachelor's degree must be completed at Alcorn. **International Students:** There are 30 international students enrolled. The school actively recruits these students. They must take the TOEFL with a minimum score of 525 on the paper-based TOEFL (PBT). They must also take the SAT or ACT, scoring 21.

ADMISSIONS: Emanuel F. Barnes, Director of Admissions. E-Mail: *ebarnes@alcorn.edu* Web: *www.alcorn.edu*

FINANCIAL AID: In 2014-2015, 42% of all full-time freshmen and continuing full-time students received some form of financial aid. 31% of all full-time freshmen and continuing full-time students received need-based aid. The average freshman award was $6,199. Need-based scholarships or need-based grants averaged $3,974 ($4,310 maximum); need-based self-help aid (loans and jobs) averaged $3,308 ($3,500 maximum); non-need-based athletic scholarships averaged $9,192 ($14,696 maximum); and other non-need-based awards and non-need-based scholarships averaged $5,162 ($9,550 maximum). 27% of undergraduate students work part-time. Average annual earnings from campus work are $1700. The average financial indebtedness of the 2014 graduate was $22,842. is a member of CSS. The FAFSA and the college's own financial statement are required. Check with the school for current application deadlines.

BELHAVEN UNIVERSITY C-4
www.belhaven.edu

Jackson, MS 39202	(601) 968-5940
	(800) 960-5940
Fax: (601) 968-8946	Email: admission@belhaven.edu
Full-time: 556 men, 685 women	Faculty: n/av
Part-time: 425 men, 910 women	Ph.D.s: 55%
Graduate: 376 men, 897 women	Student/Faculty: 13 to 1
Year: semesters, summer session	Tuition: $19,970
Room & Board: $7200	Freshman Class: 2280 applied, 1074 accepted, 324 enrolled
SAT CR/M: 530/500 ACT: 22	CEEB CODE: 1055
Application Deadline: n/av	COMPETITIVE

Belhaven University, formerly Belhaven College, was founded in 1883 and is a private liberal arts institution with a Presbyterian heritage. Figures in the above capsule and in this profile are approximate. There is 1 graduate school. In addition to regional accreditation, Belhaven has baccalaureate program accreditation with NASAD and NASM. The 42-acre campus is in an urban area in Jackson, MS. Including any residence halls, there are 17 buildings.

STUDENT LIFE: 70% of undergraduates are from Mississippi. Others are from 29 states, and 28 foreign countries. 44% are African American; 38% White. 87% are Protestant. **Male To Female Ratio:** 1.8:1. The average age of freshmen is 28; all undergraduates, 31. 28% do not continue beyond their first year; 57% remain to graduate. **Housing:** 556 students can be accommodated in college housing, which includes single-sex dorms. On-campus housing is guaranteed for all 4 years, and is available on a first-come, first-served basis. 75% of students commute. Alcohol is not permitted. All students may keep cars.

FACULTY/CLASSROOMS: 58% of faculty are male; 32% are female. All teach undergraduates. No introductory courses are taught by graduate students. The average class size in a regular course is 18.

PROGRAMS OF STUDY: Belhaven confers B.A., B.S., B.A.A., B.B.A., B.F.A., B.H.A. and B.S.M. degrees. Associate and Master's degrees are also awarded. Bachelor's degrees are awarded in BIOLOGICAL SCIENCE (biology/biological science), BUSINESS (accounting and business administration and management), COMMUNICATIONS AND THE ARTS (art, arts administration/management, ballet, broadcasting, communications, creative writing, dance, dramatic arts, English, and music), COMPUTER AND PHYSICAL SCIENCE (chemistry, computer science, information sciences and systems, and mathematics), EDUCATION (athletic training and elementary education), HEALTH PROFESSIONS (exercise science and sports medicine), SOCIAL SCIENCE (biblical studies, history, humanities, interdisciplinary studies, international studies, philosophy, political science/government, psychology, religious music, and social work). Biology and chemistry are the strongest academically. Business administration and education have the largest enrollments.

ACTIVITIES: There are no fraternities or sororities. There are 24 groups on campus, including art, band, cheerleading, choir, chorus, dance, drama, ethnic, honors, jazz band, literary magazine, marching band, musical theater, newspaper, orchestra, political, professional,

religious, social service, student government, and yearbook. Popular campus events include Singing Christmas Tree, Concert and Lecture Series and Lake Day. **Sports:** There are 8 intercollegiate sports for men and 7 for women, and 6 intramural sports for men and 6 for women. Facilities include a gym, 5 tennis courts, a lake, intramural and soccer field, baseball field, football/soccer practice field, an athletic training facility, and an exercise, weight, and conditioning complex. **Graduates:** From July 1, 2013 to June 30, 2014, 475 bachelor's degrees were awarded. The most popular majors were business administration (37%), social sciences (11%), and healthcare administration and management (8%). In an average class, 32% graduate in 4 years or less, 47% graduate in 5 years or less, and 49% graduate in 6 years or less.

SERVICES: There is remedial math, reading, and writing. **Library/Resources:** The library contains 118,374 volumes, 11,867 microform items, 3,815 audio/video tapes/CDs/DVDs, and subscribes to 15,117 periodicals including electronic. Computerized library services include interlibrary loans, database searching, Internet access, and Wi-Fi capability. Special learning facilities include an art gallery. **Physically Challenged Students:** 25% of the campus is accessible. Facilities include wheelchair ramps, elevators, special parking, specially equipped restrooms, special class scheduling, lowered drinking fountains, and special housing. **Special:** Students may participate in various internships, including one in Washington, D.C., or in 6 countries through the study-travel program. Belhaven also offers accelerated degree programs, dual majors, student-designed majors, nondegree study, pass/fail options, a 3-2 engineering degree with Mississippi State University, and work-study. 2 1-month summer sessions and 2 2-week minisessions offer additional opportunities for credit. There are 7 national honor societies, a freshman honors program, and 17 departmental honors programs. **Visiting:** There are regularly scheduled orientations for prospective students, including Preview Days, which allow students to see the campus, meet students, interview with faculty and admissions, and attend classes. There are guides for informal visits, visitors may sit in on classes, and stay overnight. To schedule a visit, contact the Admissions Office. **Campus Safety and Security:** Measures include 24-hour foot and vehicle patrol and security escort services. There are lighted pathways/sidewalks and controlled access to dorms/residences.

REQUIREMENTS: The SAT or ACT is recommended. Applicants should be graduates of an accredited secondary school, with 16 academic units, including 4 of English, 2 of math, 1 each of history and natural science, a recommended 2 of a foreign language, and 6 of electives. A personal recommendation and essay are also required. A GPA of 2.0 is required. AP and CLEP credits are accepted. Requirements for graduation vary by degree, but students must complete at least 124 semester hours, including 25 hours of World View Curriculum courses, with a minimum 2.0 GPA. **Procedure:** Freshmen are admitted to all sessions. Entrance exams should be taken in the junior year. There is a rolling admissions plan. Check with the school for current application deadlines. The application fee is $25. Applications are accepted on-line. **Transfer Students:** Transfer applicants must have a minimum 2.0 GPA and submit all college transcripts. 31 of 124 credits required for the bachelor's degree must be completed at Belhaven. **International Students:** There are 82 international students enrolled. They must take the TOEFL. They must also take the SAT or ACT.

ADMISSIONS: 47% of the 2014-2015 applicants were accepted. The SAT scores for the 2014-2015 freshman class were: Critical Reading--39% below 500, 31% between 500 and 599, 27% between 600 and 699, and 3% between 700 and 800; Math--45% below 500, 44% between 500 and 599, and 11% between 600 and 699. The ACT scores were 42% below 21, 28% between 21 and 23, 16% between 24 and 26, 7% between 27 and 28, and 7% above 28. **Admissions Contact:** Suzanne Sullivan, Assistant VP for University Advancement. E-Mail: *admission@belhaven.edu* Web: *www.belhaven.edu*

FINANCIAL AID: In 2014-2015, 57% of all full-time freshmen and continuing full-time students received some form of financial aid. 56% of all full-time freshmen and continuing full-time students received need-based aid. The average freshman award was $12,563. Need-based scholarships or need-based grants averaged $4,587; need-based self-help aid (loans and jobs) averaged $4,730; non-need-based athletic scholarships averaged $13,656; and other non-need-based awards and non-need-based scholarships averaged $11,436. Average annual earnings from campus work are $2031. The average financial indebtedness of the 2014 graduate was $31,000. The FAFSA is required. Check with the school for current application deadlines.

BLUE MOUNTAIN COLLEGE (*The complete profile is made available exclusively on our website, www.barronspac.com*)

DELTA STATE UNIVERSITY (*The complete profile is made available exclusively on our website, www.barronspac.com*)

JACKSON STATE UNIVERSITY (*The complete profile is made available exclusively on our website, www.barronspac.com*)

MILLSAPS COLLEGE	C-4
www.millsaps.edu	

Jackson, MS 39210	(601) 974-1050
	(800) 352-1050
Fax: (601) 974-1059	Email: admissions@millsaps.edu
Full-time: 384 men, 346 women	Faculty: 86; IIB, av$
Part-time: 5 men, 9 women	Ph.D.s: 95%
Graduate: 41 men, 19 women	Student/Faculty: 8 to 1
Year: semesters, summer session	Tuition: $32,520
Room & Board: $11,368	Freshman Class: 1901 applied, 902 accepted, 171 enrolled
SAT CR/M: 540/560 ACT: 26	CEEB CODE: 1471
Application Deadline: rolling	VERY COMPETITIVE+

Millsaps College, founded in 1890, is an independent liberal arts institution affiliated with the United Methodist Church. Millsaps College is known for its academic strength, national-caliber faculty, small class size, and spirit of community service. Figures in the above capsule and in this profile are approximate. There is 1 graduate school. In addition to regional accreditation, Millsaps has baccalaureate program accreditation with AACSB, NCATE, and ACS. The 100-acre campus is in an urban area in the capital city of Jackson. Including any residence halls, there are 33 buildings.

STUDENT LIFE: 58% of undergraduates are from out of state, mostly the South. Students are from 25 states, 14 foreign countries, and Canada. 61% are from public schools. 76% are White. 51% claim no religious affiliation; 33% Protestant; 14% Catholic. **Male To Female Ratio:** 0.9:1. The average age of freshmen is 18; all undergraduates, 20. 21% do not continue beyond their first year; 67% remain to graduate. **Housing:** 950 students can be accommodated in college housing, which includes single-sex and coed dorms. In addition, there are special-interest houses, fraternity houses, designated housing for freshmen, special housing for disabled students, and a service learning residence hall dedicated to community service and leadership. On-campus housing is available on a first-come, first-served basis and is available on a lottery system for upperclassmen. 88% of students live on campus; of those, 75% remain on campus on weekends. All students may keep cars.

FACULTY/CLASSROOMS: 50% of faculty are male; 50% are female. All teach undergraduates, and 90% do both. No introductory courses are taught by graduate students. The average class size in an introductory lecture is 20; in a laboratory is 20; and in a regular course is 13.

PROGRAMS OF STUDY: Millsaps confers B.A., B.S. and B.B.A. degrees. Master's degrees are also awarded. Bachelor's degrees are awarded in BIOLOGICAL SCIENCE (biochemistry, biology/biological science, and neurosciences), BUSINESS (accounting and business administration and management), COMMUNICATIONS AND THE ARTS (art history and appreciation, classics, communications, creative writing, English, music, Spanish, and studio art), COMPUTER AND PHYSICAL SCIENCE (applied mathematics, chemistry, geology, mathematics, and physics), EDUCATION (education), SOCIAL SCIENCE (anthropology, economics, European studies, history, Latin American studies, philosophy, political science/government, psychology, public administration, religion, and sociology). Biology, chemistry and premed are the strongest academically.

Business administration, biology and psychology have the largest enrollments.

ACTIVITIES: 60% of men belong to 6 national fraternities; 64% of women belong to 4 national sororities. There are 80 groups on campus, including art, cheerleading, choir, chorale, chorus, computers, dance, debate, drama, environmental, ethnic, gay, honors, international, literary magazine, musical theater, newspaper, pep band, photography, political, professional, religious, social, social service, student government, and yearbook. Popular campus events include Major Madness, Project Midtown, and Homecoming. **Sports:** There are 9 intercollegiate sports for men and 9 for women, and 9 intramural sports for men and 9 for women. Facilities include a 63,300-square-foot activities center containing a fitness center with basketball and volleyball courts, a cardio theater, an aerobics room, fitness and weight-training equipment, a free-weight room, an outdoor pool, racquetball and handball courts, and a squash court. Outdoor areas include 6 tennis courts, a sand volleyball court, and softball, baseball, football, soccer, and multipurpose fields. **Graduates:** From July 1, 2013 to June 30, 2014, 202 bachelor's degrees were awarded. The most popular majors were biology (13%), accounting (13%), and business administration (12%). 276 companies recruited on campus in 2013-2014. In an average class, 1% graduate in 3 years or less, 62% graduate in 4 years or less, 66% graduate in 5 years or less, and 67% graduate in 6 years or less. Of the 2013 graduating class, 40% were enrolled in graduate school within 6 months of graduation, and 33% were employed.

SERVICES: Counseling and information services are available, as is tutoring in most subjects. A writing center, a language lab, and a math lab are available. **Library/Resources:** The library contains 200,396 volumes, 35,525 microform items, 8,984 audio/video tapes/CDs/DVDs, and subscribes to 38,588 periodicals including electronic. Computerized library services include interlibrary loans, database searching, Internet access, and Wi-Fi capability. Special learning facilities include an art gallery, an observatory, a multidisciplinary laboratory, and a molecular biology/functional genomics research lab. **Physically Challenged Students:** 90% of the campus is accessible. Facilities include wheelchair ramps, elevators, special parking, specially equipped restrooms, special class scheduling, lowered drinking fountains, lowered telephones, special housing. Other needs can be addressed through the ADA coordinator on an individual basis. **Special:** Millsaps sponsors international studies programs in Africa, Asia, Europe, and Latin America. Direct exchange options are offered in Japan and Ireland. Students may also participate in a wide variety of field research, honors, internship, fellowships, and service learning programs. There are 28 national honor societies, including Phi Beta Kappa, and 19 departmental honors programs. **Visiting:** There are regularly scheduled orientations for prospective students, including meetings with faculty and student services personnel and tours of the campus. There are guides for informal visits, visitors may sit in on classes, and stay overnight. To schedule a visit, contact the Admissions Office. **Campus Safety and Security:** Measures include 24-hour foot and vehicle patrol, emergency notification system, self-defense education, and security escort services. There are emergency telephones, lighted pathways/sidewalks, controlled access to dorms/residences, controlled access to all buildings during specified hours, gated entrances to campus.

REQUIREMENTS: The SAT or ACT is required. Applicants should be graduates of an accredited secondary school or have a GED certificate, and have completed at least 14 academic units, including 4 in English, 3 in math, 2 in social studies, and 2 in history. An essay is required. A GPA of 2.5 is required. AP and CLEP credits are accepted. Important factors in the admissions decision are advanced placement or honors courses, extracurricular activities record, and recommendations by school officials. To graduate, students must complete 128 credit hours with 32 to 48 hours in the major and a minimum GPA of 2.0. The core curriculum includes 4 interdisciplinary courses in humanities and 4 in the sciences and math. Students must also take Introduction to Liberal Studies during the freshman year and reflections on Liberal Studies during the senior year. Other requirements include satisfactory completion of a 7-paper writing proficiency portfolio and a comprehensive exam in the specific field of study. **Procedure:** Freshmen are admitted fall and spring. Entrance exams should be taken in the spring of the junior year or fall of the senior year.

There are early admissions, deferred admissions, and rolling admissions plans. Early decision applications should be filed by January 12. Notification is sent on a rolling basis. Applications are accepted online. **Transfer Students:** 36 transfer students enrolled in 2013-2014. Applicants must have a minimum GPA of 2.75 and be in good standing at their previous school. Requirements include high school and college transcripts, an essay or personal statement, and ACT or SAT scores. 32 of 128 credits required for the bachelor's degree must be completed at Millsaps. **International Students:** There are 23 international students enrolled. The school actively recruits these students. They must take the TOEFL with a minimum score of 550 on the paper-based TOEFL (PBT) or 80 on the Internet-based version (iBT), or take the IELTS. They must also take the SAT or ACT, scoring 21.

ADMISSIONS: 47% of the 2014-2015 applicants were accepted. The SAT scores for the 2014-2015 freshman class were: Critical Reading--25% below 500, 39% between 500 and 599, 28% between 600 and 699, and 8% between 700 and 800; Math--17% below 500, 47% between 500 and 599, 33% between 600 and 699, and 3% between 700 and 800. The ACT scores were 9% below 21, 23% between 21 and 23, 27% between 24 and 26, 18% between 27 and 28, and 23% above 28. 48% of the current freshmen were in the top fifth of their class; 79% were in the top two fifths. 6 freshmen graduated first in their class. **Admissions Contact:** Tammy Teixeira, Director of Admissions Operations. E-Mail: *admissions@millsaps.edu* Web: *www.millsaps.edu*

FINANCIAL AID: In 2014-2015, 99% of all full-time freshmen and 98% of continuing full-time students received some form of financial aid. 67% of all full-time freshmen and 57% of continuing full-time students received need-based aid. The average freshman award was $30,461. Need-based scholarships or need-based grants averaged $24,248 ($44,890 maximum); need-based self-help aid (loans and jobs) averaged $8,358 ($28,790 maximum); and other non-need-based awards and non-need-based scholarships averaged $20,865 ($44,890 maximum). 76% of undergraduate students work part-time. Average annual earnings from campus work are $175. The average financial indebtedness of the 2014 graduate was $27,926. The FAFSA is required. The priority date for freshman financial aid applications for fall entry is March 1.

MISSISSIPPI COLLEGE C-4
www.mc.edu

Clinton, MS 39058	(601) 925-3800
	(800) 738-1236
Fax: (601) 925-3950	Email: enrollment-services@mc.edu
Full-time: n/av	Faculty: n/av
Part-time: n/av	Ph.D.s: n/av
Graduate: n/av	Student/Faculty: n/av
Year: semesters, summer session	Tuition: $14,848
Room & Board: $7150	Freshman Class: 1763 applied, 1080 accepted, 466 enrolled
SAT CR/M: 550/520 ACT: 23	CEEB CODE: 1477
Application Deadline: open	COMPETITIVE

Mississippi College, founded in 1826 and affiliated with the Southern Baptist Church, is a private institution offering degrees in liberal arts, business, education, and health sciences. The figures in the above capsule and in this profile are approximate. There are 6 undergraduate schools and 2 graduate schools. In addition to regional accreditation, MC has baccalaureate program accreditation with ACBSP, CSWE, NASM, and NCATE. The 320-acre campus is in a suburban area 5 miles west of Jackson. Including any residence halls, there are 30 buildings.

STUDENT LIFE: 60% of undergraduates are from Mississippi. Others are from 39 states and 29 foreign countries. 94% are Protestant. The average age of freshmen is 18; all undergraduates, 24. **Housing:** 1800 students can be accommodated in college housing, which includes single-sex dorms, on-campus apartments, and off-campus apartments. On-campus housing is available on a first-come, first-served basis. 55% of students live on campus. Alcohol is not permitted. All students may keep cars.

FACULTY/CLASSROOMS: No introductory courses are taught by graduate students. The average class size in an introductory lecture is 30; in a laboratory is 25; and in a regular course is 25.

PROGRAMS OF STUDY: MC confers B.A., B.S., B.M., B.M.Ed., B.S.B.A., B.S.Ed., B.S.N. and B.S.W. degrees. Master's and Doctoral degrees are also awarded. Bachelor's degrees are awarded in BIOLOGICAL SCIENCE (biochemistry and biology/biological science), BUSINESS (accounting, business administration and management, and marketing/retailing/merchandising), COMMUNICATIONS AND THE ARTS (applied music, art, communications, English, French, graphic design, languages, modern language, music, music theory and composition, piano/organ, Spanish, voice, and winds), COMPUTER AND PHYSICAL SCIENCE (chemistry, computer science, mathematics, and physics), EDUCATION (art education, business education, elementary education, music education, and special education), ENGINEERING AND ENVIRONMENTAL DESIGN (engineering physics and interior design), HEALTH PROFESSIONS (nursing), SOCIAL SCIENCE (American studies, Christian studies, criminal justice, family/consumer studies, history, paralegal studies, political science/government, psychology, religious music, social studies, social work, and sociology). Biology and chemistry are the strongest academically. Business, nursing, and education have the largest enrollments.

ACTIVITIES: There are 70 groups on campus, including art, band, cheerleading, chess, choir, chorale, chorus, computers, dance, debate, drama, environmental, ethnic, forensics, honors, international, jazz band, literary magazine, marching band, musical theater, newspaper, opera, pep band, political, professional, radio and TV, religious, social, social service, student government, symphony, and yearbook. Popular campus events include I Love America Day, Derby Day, and Spring Fever Week. **Sports:** There are 9 intercollegiate sports for men and 8 for women, and 8 intramural sports for men and 8 for women. Facilities include a coliseum, an 8300-seat stadium, tennis courts, soccer and softball fields, a swimming pool, 4000-seat gym, a fitness facility, and a campus weight-training facility. **Graduates:** From July 1, 2013 to June 30, 2014, 522 bachelor's degrees were awarded. The most popular majors were business administration (15%), nursing (11%), and biology (10%). In an average class, 36% graduate in 4 years or less, 50% graduate in 5 years or less, and 52% graduate in 6 years or less.

SERVICES: Counseling and information services are available, as is tutoring in most subjects. There is remedial math, reading, and writing. **Library/Resources:** The 2 libraries contain 370,404 volumes, 540,471 microform items, 18,348 audio/video tapes/CDs/DVDs, and subscribe to 4,742 periodicals including electronic. Computerized library services include interlibrary loans, database searching, Internet access, and Wi-Fi capability. Special learning facilities include an art gallery, radio station, and TV station. **Physically Challenged Students:** Facilities include wheelchair ramps, elevators, special parking, specially equipped restrooms, special class scheduling, lowered drinking fountains, lowered telephones, special housing, wide doors and special dorm rooms equipped for the physically disabled. **Special:** Cooperative programs, including a 3-2 engineering degree and a program in agriculture, are offered with the University of Mississippi, Mississippi State University, and Auburn University. MC also offers study abroad in up to 10 countries, a 3-3 program with the School of Law, work-study programs, internships, B.A.-B.S. degrees, and credit for military experience and by exam. There are 25 national honor societies and a freshman honors program. **Visiting:** There are regularly scheduled orientations for prospective students, including attending classes, touring the campus, and meeting with administrators and departmental advisers. There are guides for informal visits, visitors may sit in on classes, and stay overnight. To schedule a visit, contact the Director of Admissions. **Campus Safety and Security:** Measures include 24-hour foot and vehicle patrol, emergency notification system, self-defense education, and security escort services. There are shuttle buses, emergency telephones, lighted pathways/sidewalks, and controlled access to dorms/residences.

REQUIREMENTS: In addition to the application for admission, students must submit a 250-word essay, at least 1 letter of recommendation (3 are recommended for scholarship consideration), and a transcript from all schools previously attended. For freshmen, SAT or ACT scores must be submitted (ACT is preferred). A well-rounded high school program is advisable. An interview is recommended, as is a portfolio or audition for some majors. A GPA of 2.0 is required. AP and CLEP credits are accepted. Important factors in the admissions decision are personality/intangible qualities, extracurricular activities record, and leadership record. To graduate, students must complete 130 credit hours, with an average of C or better in the major. The core curriculum includes English, history, economics, computer science, religion, math, art, social science, phys ed, and chapel. 30 hours are usually required in the major; some majors require 36 to 45. Students must pass a writing proficiency exam. B.A. candidates and English majors must take 12 hours of a foreign language. **Procedure:** Freshmen are admitted fall, spring, and summer. Entrance exams should be taken by December of the senior year. There are early decision, deferred admissions, and rolling admissions plans. Application deadlines are open. Notification is sent on a rolling basis. Applications are accepted on-line. **Transfer Students:** 440 transfer students enrolled in 2013-2014. Applicants must be junior college graduates or students in good academic standing with the college they last attended. They must have a minimum GPA of 2.0. Transfer students will be considered as freshmen if fewer than 12 semester hours or 16 quarter hours have been completed. Applicants must submit transcripts from all schools previously attended. 33 of 130 credits required for the bachelor's degree must be completed at MC. **International Students:** There are 76 international students enrolled. The school actively recruits these students. They must take the TOEFL and the college's own test.

ADMISSIONS: 61% of the 2014-2015 applicants were accepted. The SAT scores for the 2014-2015 freshman class were: Critical Reading-43% below 500, 30% between 500 and 599, 24% between 600 and 699, and 4% between 700 and 800; Math--41% below 500, 33% between 500 and 599, 19% between 600 and 699, and 7% between 700 and 800. The ACT scores were 30% below 21, 23% between 21 and 23, 20% between 24 and 26, 12% between 27 and 28, and 16% above 28. 4 freshmen graduated first in their class. **Admissions Contact:** Chad Phillips, Director of Admissions. E-Mail: *enrollment-services@mc.edu* Web: *www.mc.edu*

FINANCIAL AID: In 2014-2015, 96% of all full-time freshmen and 95% of continuing full-time students received some form of financial aid. 56% of all full-time freshmen and 60% of continuing full-time students received need-based aid. The average freshman award was $12,363. Need-based scholarships or need-based grants averaged $4,118; need-based self-help aid (loans and jobs) averaged $1,774; and other non-need-based awards and non-need-based scholarships averaged $6,471. The average financial indebtedness of the 2014 graduate was $26,323. The FAFSA is required. The priority date for freshman financial aid applications for fall entry is March 1.

MISSISSIPPI STATE UNIVERSITY E-3
www.msstate.edu

Mississippi State, MS 39762	(662) 325-2224
Fax: (662) 325-7360	Email: admit@msstate.edu
Full-time: 7830 men, 7174 women	Faculty: 882; I, --$
Part-time: 696 men, 690 women	Ph.D.s: 76%
Graduate: 1966 men, 2009 women	Student/Faculty: 19 to 1
Year: semesters, summer session	Tuition: $6264 ($15,828)
Room & Board: $8486	Freshman Class: 10449 applied, 7245 accepted, 2894 enrolled
SAT: required ACT: 23	CEEB CODE: 1480
Application Deadline: August 1	COMPETITIVE

Mississippi State University, founded in 1878, is a land-grant and sea-grant institution, a Carnegie doctoral/research-extensive institution, and the largest university in Mississippi. The university offers over 180 bachelor's, master's, specialist, and doctoral degrees in over 90 academic programs through colleges of Agriculture and Life Sciences, Arts and Sciences, Architecture, Business and Industry, Education, Engineering, Forest Resources, and Veterinary Medicine. There are 9 undergraduate schools and 1 graduate school. In addition to regional accreditation, MSU has baccalaureate program accreditation with AACSB, ABET, ACCE, AHEA, ASLA, CSWE, FIDER, NAAB,

NASAD, NASM, NCATE, SAF, ACS, CACREP, NASPAA, and APA. The 4200-acre campus is in a small town 125 miles northeast of Jackson, MS.

STUDENT LIFE: 76% of undergraduates are from Mississippi. Others are from 50 states, 83 foreign countries, and Canada. 70% are White; 20% African American. **Male To Female Ratio:** 0.9:1. The average age of freshmen is 18; all undergraduates, 21. 18% do not continue beyond their first year; 82% remain to graduate. **Housing:** College-sponsored housing includes single-sex and coed dorms, on-campus apartments, and married student housing. In addition, there are honors houses, special-interest houses, fraternity houses, and sorority houses. On-campus housing is available on a first-come, first-served basis. 73% of students commute. Alcohol is not permitted. All students may keep cars.

FACULTY/CLASSROOMS: 60% of faculty are male; 41% are female. 81% teach undergraduates, and 9% do research. No introductory courses are taught by graduate students.

PROGRAMS OF STUDY: MSU confers B.A., B.S., B.Accy., B.Arch., B.B.A., B.F.A., B.G.S., B.Land.Arch., B.Mus.Ed. and B.S.W. degrees. Master's and Doctoral degrees are also awarded. Bachelor's degrees are awarded in AGRICULTURE (agricultural business management, agricultural economics, agriculture, agronomy, animal science, fishing and fisheries, forestry production and processing, horticulture, plant protection (pest management), poultry science, and wildlife management), BIOLOGICAL SCIENCE (biochemistry, biology/biological science, and microbiology), BUSINESS (accounting, banking and finance, business administration and management, insurance, marketing/retailing/merchandising, real estate, and trade and industrial supervision and management), COMMUNICATIONS AND THE ARTS (art, communications, English, and languages), COMPUTER AND PHYSICAL SCIENCE (chemistry, computer science, geoscience, information sciences and systems, mathematics, physics, and science), EDUCATION (agricultural education, business education, education, elementary education, music education, physical education, secondary education, special education, and technical education), ENGINEERING AND ENVIRONMENTAL DESIGN (aerospace studies, agricultural engineering technology, architecture, bioengineering, chemical engineering, civil engineering, computer engineering, electrical/electronics engineering, industrial engineering, industrial engineering technology, landscape architecture/design, and mechanical engineering), HEALTH PROFESSIONS (medical technology), SOCIAL SCIENCE (anthropology, economics, food science, history, interdisciplinary studies, liberal arts/general studies, philosophy, political science/government, psychology, social work, and sociology). Accounting, biochemistry, and physics are the strongest academically. General business administration, elementary education, and biology have the largest enrollments.

ACTIVITIES: 16% of men belong to 17 national fraternities; 21% of women belong to 1 local and 12 national sororities. There are 400 groups on campus, including art, band, cheerleading, chess, choir, chorale, chorus, communications, computers, dance, debate, drama, drill team, ethnic, film, gay, honors, international, jazz band, literary magazine, marching band, musical theater, newspaper, opera, orchestra, pep band, photography, political, professional, radio and TV, religious, social, social service, student government, symphony, and yearbook. Popular campus events include pep rallies, concerts and lyceum series. **Sports:** Facilities include a 52,000-seat football stadium, a 6,700-seat baseball park, a 9,200-seat multipurpose coliseum, a physical fitness complex, an all-weather track, 4 practice football fields, a 6-court tennis complex, an 18-hole golf course, 5 lighted tennis courts, the Sanderson Center, which consists of 7 basketball courts, 6 volleyball courts, 8 racquetball courts, 10000 square feet for strength and aerobic conditioning, 3 full size dance studios, an indoor rock climbing wall, a 1/8 mile walking track, and RecPlex, which is a multipurpose field complex with 4 softball, 2 soccer, and 6 flag football fields. **Graduates:** From July 1, 2013 to June 30, 2014, 2922 bachelor's degrees were awarded. The most popular majors were business/marketing (19%), education (18%), and engineering (13%). In an average class, 30% graduate in 4 years or less, 54% graduate in 5 years or less, and 60% graduate in 6 years or less.

SERVICES: Counseling and information services are available, as is tutoring in every subject. There is a reader service for the blind, and remedial math, reading, and writing. Writing effectiveness, study assistance, preparation for professional exams and credit courses in reading and study skills are available. **Library/Resources:** The 2 libraries contain 2.4 million volumes, 3.5 million microform items, 29,796 audio/video tapes/CDs/DVDs, and subscribe to 115,841 periodicals including electronic. Computerized library services include interlibrary loans, database searching, Internet access, and Wi-Fi capability. Special learning facilities include an art gallery, natural history museum, planetarium, radio station, TV station, Cullis and Gladys Wade Clock Museum, Dunn-Seiler Museum, Giles Hall Gallery, Lois Dowdle Cobb Museum, Mississippi Entomological Museum, and many others. **Physically Challenged Students:** 90% of the campus is accessible. Facilities include wheelchair ramps, elevators, special parking, specially equipped restrooms, special class scheduling, lowered drinking fountains, lowered telephones, special housing, phones equipped with TTY in the union and library. **Special:** Cooperative education, cross-registration with the Academic Common Market, internships, and study abroad in 15 countries are offered. Work-study programs, a Washington semester, accelerated degree programs, a general studies degree, nondegree study, student-designed majors, B.A.-B.S. degrees, and pass/fail options for some courses are available. There are 40 national honor societies, a freshman honors program, and 14 departmental honors programs. **Visiting:** There are regularly scheduled orientations for prospective students, including 2 day sessions for freshmen, and 1-day session for transfers. There are guides for informal visits, visitors may sit in on classes, and stay overnight. To schedule a visit, contact Recruitment and Campus Visit Program. **Campus Safety and Security:** Measures include 24-hour foot and vehicle patrol, emergency notification system, self-defense education, and security escort services. There are shuttle buses, emergency telephones, and lighted pathways/sidewalks.

REQUIREMENTS: The SAT or ACT is required. Applicants should have completed 15 1/2 high school academic credits, including 4 in English, 3 each in math, science, and social science, 2 advanced electives (foreign language, world geography, 4th year lab-based science, or 4th year math), and 1/2 credit in the computer as a productivity tool (not keyboarding). Full admission is granted with all of the above and one of the following: minimum 3.2 GPA on required high school courses; 2.5 GPA on required high school classes or class standing in top 50% with ACT score of 16 or higher/SAT I combined score of 750 or higher; 2.0 GPA on required high school classes with ACT score of 18 or higher/SAT I combined 840 or higher; or National Collegiate Athletic Association standards for student-athletes who are full qualifiers under Division I guidelines. Students with a GED are accepted with the required ACT/SAT I score. AP and CLEP credits are accepted. The core curriculum includes 6 to 9 hours of math and natural science, 6 each of humanities, English composition, and social behavior, and 3 each of public speaking, computer literacy, and fine arts, and junior/senior-level writing. The total number of hours required for graduation and in the major varies. A minimum GPA of 2.0 must be maintained. **Procedure:** Freshmen are admitted fall, spring, and summer. Entrance exams should be taken in the spring of junior year or fall semester of senior year. There are deferred admissions and rolling admissions plans. Applications should be filed by August 1 for fall entry; November 15 for spring entry; and May 15 for summer entry. The fall 2014 application fee was $35. Notification is sent on a rolling basis. Applications are accepted on-line. **Transfer Students:** 1754 transfer students enrolled in 2013-2014. Applicants must submit an official college transcript from each college attended, indicating a minimum GPA of 2.0 (some departments require 2.5), and must be in good standing at their previous school. 31 of 124 credits required for the bachelor's degree must be completed at MSU. **International Students:** There are 237 international students enrolled. The school actively recruits these students. They must take the TOEFL with a minimum score of 525 on the paper-based TOEFL (PBT) or 71 on the Internet-based version (iBT). They must also take the SAT.

ADMISSIONS: 69% of the 2014-2015 applicants were accepted. The SAT scores for the 2014-2015 freshman class were: Critical Reading--32% below 500, 38% between 500 and 599, 24% between 600 and 699, and 5% between 700 and 800; Math--27% below 500, 36% between 500 and 599, 30% between 600 and 699, and 7% between 700 and 800. The ACT scores were 31% below 21, 20% between 21 and 23, 21% between 24 and 26, 12% between 27 and 28, and 17%

above 28. 27% of the current freshmen were in the top fifth of their class; 27% were in the top two fifths. There were 17 National Merit finalists. **Admissions Contact:** Dr. Phil Bonfanti, Executive Director, Enrollment. E-Mail: *admit@msstate.edu* Web: *www.msstate.edu*

FINANCIAL AID: 63% of all full-time freshmen and 62% of continuing full-time students received need-based aid. The average freshman award was $13,045. Need-based scholarships or need-based grants averaged $5,440 ; need-based self-help aid (loans and jobs) averaged $3,316; non-need-based athletic scholarships averaged $12,426; and other non-need-based awards and non-need-based scholarships averaged $3,161. The average financial indebtedness of the 2014 graduate was $24,535. The FAFSA and State Grant/ Scholarship Application is required. The deadline for filing freshman financial aid applications for fall entry is April 1.

MISSISSIPPI UNIVERSITY FOR WOMEN E-2
www.muw.edu

Columbus, MS 39701

	(662) 329-7106
	(877) 462-8439
Fax: (662) 241-7481	Email: admissions@muw.edu
Full-time: 300 men, 1600 women	Faculty: IIA
Part-time: 300 men, 1000 women	Ph.D.s: 68%
Graduate: 20 men, 100 women	Student/Faculty: n/av
Year: semesters, summer session	Tuition: $4400 ($7600)
Room & Board: $3000	Freshman Class: n/av
SAT or ACT: recommended	CEEB CODE: 1481
Application Deadline: open	COMPETITIVE

Mississippi University for Women, founded in 1884, is a public institution offering degrees in liberal arts, education, business and communications, nursing, human sciences, science and math, health and kinesiology, and culinary arts. Figures in the above capsule and in this profile are approximate. There are 4 undergraduate schools and 4 graduate schools. In addition to regional accreditation, MUW has baccalaureate program accreditation with ACBSP, NASAD, NASM, NCATE, and NLN. The 110-acre campus is in a small town 120 miles west of Birmingham, Alabama. Including any residence halls, there are 53 buildings.

STUDENT LIFE: 89% of undergraduates are from Mississippi. Others are from 20 states, 25 foreign countries, and Canada. 84% are from public schools. 70% are White; 27% African American. **Male To Female Ratio:** 4.4:1. The average age of freshmen is 19; all undergraduates, 29. 30% do not continue beyond their first year; 43% remain to graduate. **Housing:** 1100 students can be accommodated in college housing, which includes single-sex dorms, on-campus apartments, and married student housing. On-campus housing is available on a first-come, first-served basis. 77% of students commute. Alcohol is not permitted. All students may keep cars.

FACULTY/CLASSROOMS: 39% of faculty are male; 61% are female. 94% teach undergraduates. No introductory courses are taught by graduate students. The average class size in an introductory lecture is 35; in a laboratory is 23; and in a regular course is 25.

PROGRAMS OF STUDY: MUW confers B.A., B.S., B.F.A., B.M. and B.S.N. degrees. Associate, Master's, and Doctoral degrees are also awarded. Bachelor's degrees are awarded in BIOLOGICAL SCIENCE (biology/biological science and microbiology), BUSINESS (accounting, business administration and management, and sports management), COMMUNICATIONS AND THE ARTS (communications, English, fine arts, music, and Spanish), COMPUTER AND PHYSICAL SCIENCE (chemistry, mathematics, and physical sciences), EDUCATION (art education, elementary education, and music education), HEALTH PROFESSIONS (nursing, public health, and speech pathology/audiology), SOCIAL SCIENCE (culinary arts, food production/management/services, history, paralegal studies, physical fitness/movement, political science/government, psychology, and social science). Biology, chemistry, and English are the strongest academically. Business, nursing, and elementary education have the largest enrollments.

ACTIVITIES: 10% of men belong to 2 local and 1 national fraternities; 20% of women belong to 12 local and 3 national sororities. There are 84 groups on campus, including art, band, choir, chorale, chorus, computers, dance, drama, ethnic, film, honors, international, jazz band, literary magazine, musical theater, newspaper, orchestra, photography, political, professional, radio and TV, religious, social, social service, student government, and yearbook. Popular campus events include Mardi Gras and Oktoberfest. **Sports:** There are 5 intramural sports for men and 5 for women. Facilities include a gym, tennis and racquetball courts, indoor swimming pool, a gymnastics room, a weight room, a dance studio, a 3-hole pitch-and-putt golf course, a soccer and flag football field. **Graduates:** From July 1, 2013 to June 30, 2014, 617 bachelor's degrees were awarded. The most popular majors were nursing (40%), elementary education (7%), and general studies (7%).

SERVICES: Counseling and information services are available, as is tutoring in most subjects. There is remedial math, reading, and writing. **Library/Resources:** The library contains 232,638 volumes, 569,448 microform items, and 98 audio/video tapes/CDs/DVDs, and subscribes to 1,620 periodicals including electronic. Computerized library services include interlibrary loans and database searching. Special learning facilities include an art gallery, radio station, a distance learning studio. **Physically Challenged Students:** 95% of the campus is accessible. Facilities include wheelchair ramps, elevators, special parking, specially equipped restrooms, special class scheduling, lowered drinking fountains, and lowered telephones. **Special:** Cross-registration and a 3-2 engineering degree are available with Mississippi State University. MUW also offers internships in all colleges, co-op and work-study programs, several combinations of dual majors, study abroad in 5 countries, credit for experience, nondegree study, and a pass/fail option. There are 15 national honor societies, a freshman honors program, and 3 departmental honors programs. **Visiting:** There are regularly scheduled orientations for prospective students, including talks with various student services officers and preregistration. There are guides for informal visits, visitors may sit in on classes, and stay overnight. To schedule a visit, contact the Director of Admissions. **Campus Safety and Security:** Measures include 24-hour foot and vehicle patrol and security escort services. There are lighted pathways/sidewalks, controlled access to dorms/ residences, guard gates, and freshman orientation class.

REQUIREMENTS: The SAT or ACT is recommended. Prospective students should have completed 4 units of English; 3 each of math, science, and social studies courses in U.S. history, world history, government, and economics or geography; 2 of advanced electives, including foreign language or geography; and a course in computer applications. A GPA of 2.0 is required. AP and CLEP credits are accepted. Important factors in the admissions decision are recommendations by school officials, leadership record, and advanced placement or honors courses. To graduate, students must complete 124 credit hours, including 30 to 39 in a major, with a minimum GPA of 2.0. The core curriculum requires 12 hours of English, 8 of lab-based science, 6 each of history and social sciences, 3 each of speech or philosophy, fine arts, and math, 1 of phys ed, and 1 of a freshman seminar. **Procedure:** Freshmen are admitted to all sessions. Entrance exams should be taken as early as possible. There are early decision, early admissions, and rolling admissions plans. Application deadlines are open. The fall 2014 application fee was $25. **Transfer Students:** Applicants must have a GPA of 2.0 in 6 semester hours of both English composition and a lab science, 3 of college algebra or above, and 9 of transferable electives. High school and college transcripts are required. 32 of 128 credits required for the bachelor's degree must be completed at MUW. **International Students:** The school actively recruits these students. They must take the TOEFL. They must also take the SAT or ACT, scoring 16.

ADMISSIONS: Shelley Moss, Interim Director of Admissions. E-Mail: *admissions@muw.edu* Web: *www.muw.edu*

FINANCIAL AID: MUW is a member of CSS. The FAFSA is required. Check with the school for current application deadlines.

MISSISSIPPI VALLEY STATE UNIVERSITY (*The complete profile is made available exclusively on our website, www.barronspac.com*)

RUST COLLEGE   D-1
www.rustcollege.edu

Holly Springs, MS 38635	(662) 252-8000, ext. 4059
	(888) 886-8492, ext. 4059
Fax: (662) 252-8895	**Email:** jbmcdonald@rustcollege.edu
Full-time: 300 men, 550 women	**Faculty:** n/av
Part-time: 60 men, 105 women	**Ph.D.s:** 47%
Graduate: n/av	**Student/Faculty:** n/av
Year: semesters, summer session	**Tuition:** $7400
Room & Board: $3200	**Freshman Class:** n/av
SAT or ACT: required	**CEEB CODE:** 1669
Application Deadline: n/av	**COMPETITIVE**

Rust College, founded in 1866, is a private liberal arts college affiliated with the United Methodist Church. The academic year consists of semesters, each divided into two 8-week modules, plus a summer term. Figures in the above capsule and in this profile are approximate. The 126-acre campus is in a small town 35 miles southeast of Memphis, Tennessee. Including any residence halls, there are 23 buildings.

STUDENT LIFE: 55% of undergraduates are from Mississippi. Others are from 24 states and 6 foreign countries. 90% are from public schools. 93% are African American. 60% are Protestant; 29% claim no religious affiliation. **Male To Female Ratio:** 1.8:1. The average age of freshmen is 19; all undergraduates, 22. 57% do not continue beyond their first year. **Housing:** 856 students can be accommodated in college housing, which includes single-sex dorms. In addition, there are honors houses. On-campus housing is guaranteed for all 4 years. 65% of students live on campus; of those, 50% remain on campus on weekends. Alcohol is not permitted. All students may keep cars.

FACULTY/CLASSROOMS: 67% of faculty are male; 33% are female. All teach undergraduates. No introductory courses are taught by graduate students. The average class size in an introductory lecture is 10; in a laboratory is 10; and in a regular course is 25.

PROGRAMS OF STUDY: Rust confers B.A., B.S. and B.S.W. degrees. Associate degrees are also awarded. Bachelor's degrees are awarded in BIOLOGICAL SCIENCE (biology/biological science), BUSINESS (business administration and management), COMMUNICATIONS AND THE ARTS (communications, English, journalism, and music), COMPUTER AND PHYSICAL SCIENCE (chemistry, computer science, and mathematics), EDUCATION (business education, elementary education, English education, mathematics education, science education, secondary education, and social science education), HEALTH PROFESSIONS (health), SOCIAL SCIENCE (political science/government, social work, and sociology). Business administration and management are the strongest academically. Biology, computer science, and social work have the largest enrollments.

ACTIVITIES: 2% of men belong to 3 local and 3 national fraternities; 6% of women belong to 4 local and 4 national sororities. There are 32 groups on campus, including band, cheerleading, choir, chorale, computers, drama, ethnic, honors, international, marching band, newspaper, political, radio and TV, religious, social, social service, and student government. Popular campus events include Career Day, Religious Emphasis Week, and African American Student Leadership Conference. **Sports:** There are 7 intercollegiate sports for men and 7 for women. Facilities include a 2500-seat gym, swimming pool, tennis courts, a track, 2000-seat stadium, bowling alley, pool tables, and the Magic Johnson Sports Arena.

SERVICES: Counseling and information services are available, as is tutoring in most subjects. There is remedial math, reading, and writing. **Library/Resources:** The library contains 123,055 volumes, and 106 audio/video tapes/CDs/DVDs, and subscribes to 340 periodicals including electronic. Computerized library services include interlibrary loans, database searching, and Internet access. Special learning facilities include a radio station, TV station, the Dr. Ron Trojak collection of African tribal art. **Physically Challenged Students:** All of the campus is accessible. Facilities include wheelchair ramps, elevators, special parking, specially equipped restrooms, and lowered drinking fountains. **Special:** Internships are available in all areas and may be required for some majors. On-campus work-study, study abroad, credit by examination, independent study, B.A.-B.S. degrees, and dual majors in a variety of programs are available. There are 3-2 degrees in preprofessional programs and medical technology and a 3-2 engineering degree with the student's school of choice. There are 3 national honor societies, a freshman honors program, and 5 departmental honors programs. **Visiting:** There are regularly scheduled orientations for prospective students, including a campus tour, departmental visits, introduction to the application process, financial aid orientation, and question-and-answer session. There are guides for informal visits, visitors may sit in on classes, and stay overnight. To schedule a visit, contact Enrollment Services. **Campus Safety and Security:** Measures include 24-hour foot and vehicle patrol and security escort services. There are lighted pathways/sidewalks.

REQUIREMENTS: The SAT or ACT is required. Students must submit 19 academic credits, including 4 in English, 3 each in math, science, and social studies, and 6 electives. An audition, an interview, and 2 letters of recommendation are required. The GED is accepted. An essay and portfolio are recommended. A GPA of 2.0 is required. AP and CLEP credits are accepted. Important factors in the admissions decision are evidence of special talent, extracurricular activities record, and recommendations by school officials. All students must earn a minimum of 124 semester hours while maintaining a cumulative GPA of 2.0. Distribution requirements include 59 1/2 general education credits in the fields of education, humanities, science, math and a required freshman program. A minimum of 50 credits constitutes a major, and comprehensive exams are given in all programs. Required courses in addition to the freshman program include math, biology, physical science, computer science, English, foreign language, literature, speech, social science, and history. **Procedure:** Freshmen are admitted fall, spring, and summer. Entrance exams should be taken prior to the first semester of the freshman year. There is a rolling admissions plan. Check with the school for current application deadlines. The fall 2014 application fee was $10. Applications are accepted on-line. **Transfer Students:** Transfer applicants with at least 15 semester hours of credit need not take the ACT or SAT. No credits for courses with a grade below C and no credits for any course that is not in keeping with the college's catalog will be accepted. 30 of 124 credits required for the bachelor's degree must be completed at Rust. **International Students:** They must take the TOEFL. They must also take the SAT or ACT.

ADMISSIONS: Johnny McDonald, Director Enrollment Services. E-Mail: *jbmcdonald@rustcollege.edu* Web: *www.rustcollege.edu*

FINANCIAL AID: The FFS and the college's own financial statement are required. Check with the school for current application deadlines.

TOUGALOO COLLEGE (*The complete profile is made available exclusively on our website, www.barronspac.com*)

UNIVERSITY OF MISSISSIPPI   D-2
www.olemiss.edu

University, MS 38677	(662) 915-7226
	(800) OLE-MISS
Fax: (662) 915-1831	Email: admissions@olemiss.edu
Full-time: 7285 men, 8999 women	Faculty: n/av
Part-time: 532 men, 544 women	Ph.D.s: 84%
Graduate: 1292 men, 1460 women	Student/Faculty: n/av
Year: semesters, summer session	Tuition: $6796 ($19,144)
Room & Board: $9908	Freshman Class: 16102 applied, 13078 accepted, 3810 enrolled
SAT CR/M: 540/540 ACT: 24	CEEB CODE: 1840
Application Deadline: July 1	COMPETITIVE+

The University of Mississippi, the flagship university for the state of Mississippi, opened in 1848. It offers nationally recognized programs across a broad range of undergraduate and graduate studies, from medicine and law to creative writing and accountancy. Ole Miss is the state's largest university, and was named as the nation's 13th-fastest growing university. There are 8 undergraduate schools and 3 graduate schools. In addition to regional accreditation, Ole Miss has baccalaureate program accreditation with ABET, ACEJMC, ASLA, CSWE,

NASAD, NASM, NCATE, NRPA, ACS, FSE, and NAST. The 3391-acre campus is in a small town 70 miles southeast of Memphis, Tennessee. Including any residence halls, there are 192 buildings.

STUDENT LIFE: 57% of undergraduates are from Mississippi. Others are from 50 states, 92 foreign countries, and Canada. 75% are White; 14% African American. **Male To Female Ratio:** 1.2:1. The average age of freshmen is 19; all undergraduates, 22. 14% do not continue beyond their first year; 58% remain to graduate. **Housing:** 5341 students can be accommodated in college housing, which includes single-sex dorms, on-campus apartments, off-campus apartments, and married student housing. In addition, there are honors houses, special-interest houses, fraternity houses, sorority houses, living-learning communities and freshman interest groups. On-campus housing is guaranteed for the freshman year only, is available on a first-come, first-served basis, and is available on a lottery system for upperclassmen. Alcohol is not permitted. All students may keep cars.

FACULTY/CLASSROOMS: 54% of faculty are male; 46% are female. No introductory courses are taught by graduate students.

PROGRAMS OF STUDY: Ole Miss confers B.A., B.A.Ed., B.A.J., B.A.P.R.M., B.Accy., B.B.A., B.F.A., B.G.S., B.M., B.P.S., B.S., B.S.C.E., B.S.C.J., B.S.Ch.E., B.S.C.S., B.S.E.E., B.S.E.S., B.S.F.C.S., B.S.G.E., B.S.J., B.S.M.E. and B.S.W. degrees. Master's and Doctoral degrees are also awarded. Bachelor's degrees are awarded in BIOLOGICAL SCIENCE (biochemistry and biology/biological science), BUSINESS (accounting, banking and finance, business administration and management, business economics, finance, hospitality management services, insurance, management information systems, management science, marketing/retailing/merchandising, and real estate), COMMUNICATIONS AND THE ARTS (art, art history and appreciation, Chinese, communication science, creative writing, English, French, German, journalism, linguistics, music, Spanish, and theatre arts), COMPUTER AND PHYSICAL SCIENCE (chemistry, computer science, geology, mathematics, and physics), EDUCATION (elementary education, English education, mathematics education, science education, social science education, and special education), ENGINEERING AND ENVIRONMENTAL DESIGN (chemical engineering, civil engineering, electrical/electronics engineering, geological engineering, and mechanical engineering), HEALTH PROFESSIONS (exercise science, medical technology, pharmaceutical science, speech pathology/audiology, and speech therapy), SOCIAL SCIENCE (African American studies, anthropology, area studies, classical/ancient civilization, dietetics, economics, family/consumer studies, forensic studies, history, international studies, liberal arts/general studies, paralegal studies, parks and recreation management, philosophy, political science/government, psychology, public administration, religion, social work, and sociology). Accountancy, pharmacy, and creative writing are the strongest academically. Business, engineering and education have the largest enrollments.

ACTIVITIES: Groups on campus include art, band, cheerleading, chess, choir, chorale, chorus, computers, dance, drama, drill team, ethnic, gay, honors, international, jazz band, literary magazine, marching band, musical theater, newspaper, orchestra, pep band, political, professional, radio and TV, religious, social, social service, student government, symphony, and yearbook. Popular campus events include Welcome Week, Red and Blue Week, The Big Event, Faulkner and Yoknapatawpha Conference and Oxford Conference for the Book. **Sports:** There are 6 intercollegiate sports for men and 8 for women. Facilities include a 60,580-seat football stadium, 8700-seat basketball coliseum, baseball stadium, intramural fields, women's soccer complex, softball complex, volleyball courts, an indoor tennis facility, golf course, track and field complex, athletics training center, fitness center with indoor pool, racquetball courts and basketball courts, and equipment rental and guides for high-adventure outdoor activities, including camping, skiing, scuba, canoeing, kayaking and backpacking. **Graduates:** From July 1, 2013 to June 30, 2014, 2661 bachelor's degrees were awarded. The most popular majors were teacher education (13%), marketing (7%), and psychology (6%). In an average class, 37% graduate in 4 years or less, 55% graduate in 5 years or less, and 58% graduate in 6 years or less.

SERVICES: Counseling and information services are available, as is tutoring in every subject. There is a reader service for the blind, and remedial math and reading. **Library/Resources:** The 2 libraries contain 2.3 million volumes, 2.8 million microform items, and 107,010 audio/video tapes/CDs/DVDs, and subscribe to 195,484 periodicals including electronic. Computerized library services include interlibrary loans, database searching, Internet access, and Wi-Fi capability. Special learning facilities include an art gallery, radio station, TV station, Mary Buie Museum, the Center for the Study of Southern Culture, the National Center for Physical Acoustics, Rowan Oak, the home of William Faulkner, the National Center for Natural Products Research, the National Food Service Management Institute, the Croft Institute for International Studies, the Sally McDonnell Barksdale Honors College, and the Center for Intelligence and Security Studies. **Physically Challenged Students:** Facilities include wheelchair ramps, elevators, special parking, specially equipped restrooms, special class scheduling, lowered drinking fountains, lowered telephones. Handicap accessible dorm rooms are available. **Special:** Study abroad in numerous countries, internships and work-study programs within the college are offered. Online programs, dual majors, a general studies degree, credit by exam, special testing in music and languages, credit for military experience, and limited pass/fail options also are available. U.S. internships in Washington, D.C. and New York. International internships in Sydney, London, Dublin, Scottish Parliament, and South Africa. There is a Phi Beta Kappa chapter and a freshman honors program. **Visiting:** There are regularly scheduled orientations for prospective students. There are guides for informal visits, visitors may sit in on classes, and stay overnight. To schedule a visit, contact the Office of Admissions. **Campus Safety and Security:** Measures include 24-hour foot and vehicle patrol, emergency notification system, self-defense education, and security escort services. There are shuttle buses, emergency telephones, lighted pathways/sidewalks, and controlled access to dorms/residences.

REQUIREMENTS: Applicants need 15 academic credits, including 4 units in English, 3 each in math (4th recommended), 3 sciences with lab (4th recommended), and 3 social studies, 1 in foreign language, and 1/2 in computer applications. Electives should include 2nd year foreign language or world geography. A portfolio for art majors and an audition for theater and music majors are required. A GPA of 2.0 is required. AP and CLEP credits are accepted.The core curriculum includes the following courses required for all entering freshmen students: six hours of English composition; three hours of college algebra or quantitative reasoning or statistics (taken from a department of mathematics) or a more advanced mathematics course; six hours of laboratory science; and fifteen hours of humanities, social/behavioral sciences, and fine arts (to include at least three hours of course work from each area). For the award of a bachelor's degree from any school or college of the University of Mississippi, a student must earn a GPA of at least 2.0 on all course work submitted in fulfillment of the course requirements for the degree. In addition, the student must earn a minimum GPA of 2.0 on all course work attempted at the University of Mississippi. Finally, the student must have a minimum 2.0 GPA on all college work attempted at any institution of higher learning. There may be additional grade requirements for the College of Liberal Arts or the professional schools. It is the student's responsibility to check on the requirements applicable to the specific degree for which he or she is a candidate. **Procedure:** Freshmen are admitted to all sessions. There are early admissions, deferred admissions, and rolling admissions plans. Applications should be filed by July 1 for fall entry, along with a $40 fee. **Transfer Students:** Transfer students must have earned a minimum 2.0 GPA on previous college work. The SAT or ACT may be required depending on credits earned. 30 of 126 credits required for the bachelor's degree must be completed at Ole Miss. **International Students:** The school actively recruits these students. They must take the TOEFL and the college's own test. They must also take the SAT or ACT.

ADMISSIONS: 81% of the 2014-2015 applicants were accepted. The SAT scores for the 2014-2015 freshman class were: Critical Reading--32% below 500, 45% between 500 and 599, 19% between 600 and 699, and 4% between 700 and 800; Math--30% below 500, 46% between 500 and 599, 20% between 600 and 699, and 4% between 700 and 800. The ACT scores were 21% below 21, 24% between 21 and 23, 24% between 24 and 26, 12% between 27 and 28, and 19% above 28. 39% of the current freshmen were in the top fifth of their class; 66% were in the top two fifths. There were 22 National Merit finalists. 57 freshmen graduated first in their class. **Admissions Con-**

tact: Whitman Smith, Director of Enrollment Services. E-Mail: *admissions@olemiss.edu* Web: *www.olemiss.edu*

FINANCIAL AID: In 2014-2015, 87% of all full-time freshmen and 79% of continuing full-time students received some form of financial aid. 74% of all full-time freshmen and 52% of continuing full-time students received need-based aid. The average freshman award was $13,838. Need-based scholarships or need-based grants averaged $8,329 ($43,638 maximum); need-based self-help aid (loans and jobs) averaged $3,585 ($10,000 maximum); non-need-based athletic scholarships averaged $13,562 ($36,756 maximum); and other non-need-based awards and non-need-based scholarships averaged $6,973 ($39,619 maximum). 16% of undergraduate students work part-time. Average annual earnings from campus work are $2361. The average financial indebtedness of the 2014 graduate was $26,443. Ole Miss is a member of CSS. The FAFSA is required. The priority date for freshman financial aid applications for fall entry is March 1. The deadline for filing freshman financial aid applications for fall entry is February 15.

UNIVERSITY OF SOUTHERN MISSISSIPPI D-5
www.usm.edu

Hattiesburg, MS 39406 (601) 266-5000 / n/av

Fax: (601) 266-5148	Email: admissions@usm.edu
Full-time: 4250 men, 7143 women	Faculty: 687; I
Part-time: 967 men, 1298 women	Ph.D.s: 76%
Graduate: 1039 men, 1771 women	Student/Faculty: 18 to 1
Year: semesters, summer session	Tuition: $6336 ($14,448)
Room & Board: $6834	Freshman Class: 4436 applied, 2473 accepted, 1787 enrolled
ACT: 22	CEEB CODE: 1479
Application Deadline: June 30	COMPETITIVE

The University of Southern Mississippi, founded in 1910, is a public institution offering comprehensive undergraduate and graduate programs. Figures in the above capsule and in this profile are approximate. There are 6 undergraduate schools and 1 graduate school. In addition to regional accreditation, Southern Miss has baccalaureate program accreditation with AACSB, ABET, ACEJMC, ADA, AHEA, ASLA, CAHEA, CSAB, CSWE, FIDER, NASAD, NASM, NCATE, NLN, and NRPA. The 1090-acre campus is in a suburban area 90 miles southeast of Jackson, and 105 miles north of New Orleans. Including any residence halls, there are 176 buildings.

STUDENT LIFE: 88% of undergraduates are from Mississippi. Others are from 50 states, 57 foreign countries, and Canada. 65% are White; 29% African American. **Male To Female Ratio:** 1.6:1. The average age of freshmen is 18; all undergraduates, 23. 25% do not continue beyond their first year; 50% remain to graduate. **Housing:** 3400 students can be accommodated in college housing, which includes single-sex dorms and married student housing. In addition, there are special-interest houses, fraternity houses, sorority houses, a section in 1 dorm is reserved for honor students. Freshmen are housed together. On-campus housing is available on a first-come, first-served basis. 72% of students commute. Alcohol is not permitted. All students may keep cars.

FACULTY/CLASSROOMS: 49% of faculty are male; 51% are female. 64% do both. No introductory courses are taught by graduate students.

PROGRAMS OF STUDY: Southern Miss confers B.A., B.S., B.F.A., B.M., B.M.E. and B.S.B.A degrees. Master's and Doctoral degrees are also awarded. Bachelor's degrees are awarded in BIOLOGICAL SCIENCE (biology/biological science), BUSINESS (accounting, banking and finance, business administration and management, business economics, hotel/motel and restaurant management, international business management, marketing/retailing/merchandising, and personnel management), COMMUNICATIONS AND THE ARTS (advertising, communications, dance, design, dramatic arts, English, fine arts, journalism, languages, music, radio/television technology, and speech/debate/rhetoric), COMPUTER AND PHYSICAL SCIENCE (chemistry, computer science, geology, information sciences and systems, mathematics, physics, polymer science, and statistics), EDUCATION (art education, business education, early childhood education, elementary education, foreign languages education, guidance education, health education, home economics education, industrial arts education, middle school education, music education, science education, and secondary education), ENGINEERING AND ENVIRONMENTAL DESIGN (architectural technology, computer technology, construction technology, electrical/electronics engineering technology, engineering technology, and mechanical engineering technology), HEALTH PROFESSIONS (medical laboratory technology, nursing, predentistry, premedicine, and speech pathology/audiology), SOCIAL SCIENCE (anthropology, criminal justice, economics, geography, history, international studies, parks and recreation management, philosophy, political science/government, prelaw, psychology, social science, social work, and sociology). Curriculum instruction, special education, human performance, management, and international business have the largest enrollments.

ACTIVITIES: 15% of men belong to 14 national fraternities; 17% of women belong to 11 national sororities. There are 239 groups on campus, including art, band, cheerleading, choir, chorale, chorus, computers, dance, drama, drum and bugle corps, ethnic, film, gay, honors, international, jazz band, literary magazine, marching band, musical theater, newspaper, opera, orchestra, pep band, photography, political, professional, radio and TV, religious, social, social service, student government, and symphony. **Sports:** There are 6 intercollegiate sports for men and 6 for women, and 36 intramural sports for men and 36 for women. Facilities include a recreational lake, a football stadium, a basketball coliseum, a baseball park, a softball stadium, a track and field stadium, a fitness institute, a natatorium, volleyball courts, and playing fields for softball, flag football, and soccer. **Graduates:** From July 1, 2013 to June 30, 2014, 2520 bachelor's degrees were awarded. The most popular majors were nursing (9%), elementary education (6%), and psychology (6%). 918 companies recruited on campus in 2013-2014. In an average class, 8% graduate in 4 years or less, 43% graduate in 5 years or less, and 49% graduate in 6 years or less.

SERVICES: Counseling and information services are available, as is tutoring in most subjects. There is a reader service for the blind, and remedial math, reading, and writing. **Library/Resources:** The 2 libraries contain 122,428 volumes, 4.9 million microform items, 33,189 audio/video tapes/CDs/DVDs, and subscribe to 24,369 periodicals including electronic. Computerized library services include interlibrary loans, database searching, and Internet access. Special learning facilities include an art gallery, natural history museum, radio station, TV station, TV production studios, the Museum of Natural Science, and a music resource center. **Physically Challenged Students:** 80% of the campus is accessible. Facilities include wheelchair ramps, elevators, special parking, specially equipped restrooms, special class scheduling, lowered drinking fountains, lowered telephones, special housing. **Special:** USM offers many cooperative programs, internships, dual majors, nondegree study, limited pass/fail options, credit for life experience, and study abroad in 12 countries. The university also participates in the Title IV College Work-Study Program. Accelerated degrees, distance learning, ESL, independent study, and a teacher certification program are also available. There are 27 national honor societies and a freshman honors program. **Visiting:** There are regularly scheduled orientations for prospective students, including campus tours and general session orientations. There are guides for informal visits and visitors may sit in on classes. To schedule a visit, contact Office of Admissions at (601) 266-5000. **Campus Safety and Security:** Measures include 24-hour foot and vehicle patrol, emergency notification system, self-defense education, and security escort services. There are shuttle buses, emergency telephones, lighted pathways/sidewalks, and controlled access to dorms/residences.

REQUIREMENTS: The ACT is required. Full admission will be granted to the following: all students completing the College Preparatory Curriculum (CPC) with a minimum of a 3.2 high school GPA on the CPC and a submitted ACT (composite) or SAT score. All students completing the College Preparatory Curriculum (CPC) with a minimum of a 2.5 high school GPA on the CPC or a class rank in the top 50 percent, as well as a score of 16 or higher on the ACT (composite) or a combined SAT score of 760, all students completing the College Preparatory Curriculum (CPC) with a minimum of 2.0 high school GPA on the CPC and a score of 18 or higher on the ACT (composite) or a combined SAT score of 860, and students who satisfy the National Collegiate Athletic Association (NCAA) standards for student-athletes who are full qualifiers under Division I guidelines. AP and CLEP credits are accepted. To graduate, students must complete at least 128 semester hours, including 64 at the senior college level, with a minimum GPA of 2.0. Core requirements include courses in reasoning and communication skills, English, including composition, history, humanities and fine arts, social and behavioral sciences, human wellness, and natural and applied sciences. **Procedure:** Freshmen are admitted fall, spring, and summer. Entrance exams should be taken in the fall of the senior year. Applications should be filed by June 30 for fall entry; January 1 for spring entry; and May 1 for summer entry, along with a $35 fee. Notification is sent on a rolling basis. Applications are accepted on-line. **Transfer Students:** 1787 transfer students enrolled in 2013-2014. Students must have either an associate degree intended for transfer from a regionally accredited institution or have completed the 30 semester hours of designated coursework outlined below with a minimum 2.0 cumulative grade point average for admission. Students must complete 6 semester hours of English Composition (English Composition I and II), 3 semester hours of mathematics (college algebra, quantitative reasoning, or higher mathematics) 6 semester hours of natural science (courses must be laboratory-based, with the lecture courses accompanied by the respective lab course), 9 semester hours of humanities and fine arts (common examples of acceptable coursework are history, philosophy, religion, world literature, art, music), 6 semester hours of social or behavioral sciences (common examples of acceptable coursework are anthropology, geography, sociology, psychology, and social work). 32 of 128 credits required for the bachelor's degree must be completed at Southern Miss. **International Students:** The school actively recruits these students. They must take the TOEFL with a minimum score of 525 on the paper-based TOEFL (PBT). They must also take the SAT or ACT, scoring 18.

ADMISSIONS: 56% of the 2014-2015 applicants were accepted. The SAT scores for the 2014-2015 freshman class were: Critical Reading--35% below 500, 43% between 500 and 599, 18% between 600 and 699, and 4% between 700 and 800; Math--42% below 500, 40% between 500 and 599, and 18% between 600 and 699. The ACT scores were 41% below 21, 24% between 21 and 23, 19% between 24 and 26, 7% between 27 and 28, and 9% above 28. There were 6 National Merit finalists. **Admissions Contact:** Amanda King, Admissions Office. E-Mail: *admissions@usm.edu* Web: *www.usm.edu*

FINANCIAL AID: In 2014-2015, 66% of all full-time freshmen and 64% of continuing full-time students received some form of financial aid. 75% of all full-time freshmen and 70% of continuing full-time students received need-based aid. Need-based scholarships or need-based grants averaged $4,505; need-based self-help aid (loans and jobs) averaged $3,552; non-need-based athletic scholarships averaged $7,396; and other non-need-based awards and non-need-based scholarships averaged $5,568. The college's own financial statement is required. Check with the school for current application deadlines.

WILLIAM CAREY UNIVERSITY (*The complete profile is made available exclusively on our website, www.barronspac.com*)

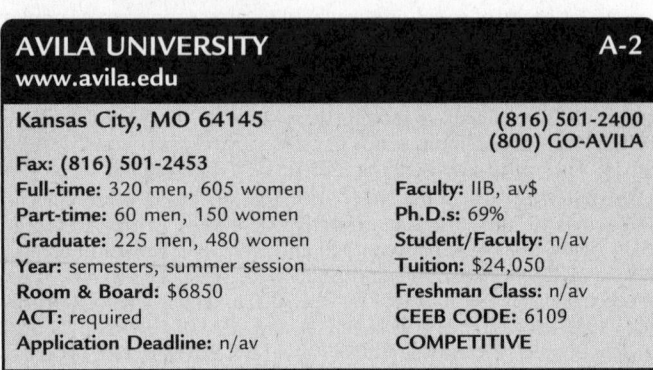

MISSOURI

• College Location

0   20   40   60   80   100
Miles

AVILA UNIVERSITY
www.avila.edu

A-2

Kansas City, MO 64145

(816) 501-2400
(800) GO-AVILA

Fax: (816) 501-2453

Full-time: 320 men, 605 women	Faculty: IIB, av$
Part-time: 60 men, 150 women	Ph.D.s: 69%
Graduate: 225 men, 480 women	Student/Faculty: n/av
Year: semesters, summer session	Tuition: $24,050
Room & Board: $6850	Freshman Class: n/av
ACT: required	CEEB CODE: 6109
Application Deadline: n/av	COMPETITIVE

Avila University, founded in 1916, is a comprehensive liberal arts institution sponsored by the Sisters of St. Joseph of Carondelet. The figures in the above capsule and in this profile are approximate. There are 7 undergraduate schools and 3 graduate schools. In addition to regional accreditation, Avila has baccalaureate program accreditation with CAHEA, CSWE, and CCNE. The 48-acre campus is in a suburban area in Kansas City, MO. Including any residence halls, there are 11 buildings.

STUDENT LIFE: 55% of undergraduates are from Missouri. Others are from 21 states, 34 foreign countries, and Canada. 87% are from public schools. 66% are White; 14% African American. 26% are Catholic. **Male To Female Ratio:** 2.0:1. The average age of freshmen is 18; all undergraduates, 23. 33% do not continue beyond their first year; 51% remain to graduate. **Housing:** 310 students can be accommodated in college housing, which includes single-sex and coed dorms and on-campus apartments. On-campus housing is guaranteed for the freshman year only, is available on a first-come, first-served basis, and is available on a lottery system for upperclassmen. Priority is given to out-of-town students. 71% of students commute. All students may keep cars.

FACULTY/CLASSROOMS: 33% of faculty are male; 67% are female. All teach and do research. No introductory courses are taught by graduate students. The average class size in an introductory lecture is 22; in a laboratory is 25; and in a regular course is 14.

PROGRAMS OF STUDY: Avila confers B.A., B.S., B.F.A., B.S.B.A., B.S.N. and B.S.W. degrees. Master's degrees are also awarded. Bachelor's degrees are awarded in BIOLOGICAL SCIENCE (biology/biological science), BUSINESS (accounting, banking and finance, business administration and management, international business management, management science, and marketing/retailing/merchandising), COMMUNICATIONS AND THE ARTS (art, communications, dramatic arts, English, and music), COMPUTER AND PHYSICAL SCIENCE (chemistry, computer science, information sciences and systems, mathematics, and radiological technology), EDUCATION (business education, elementary education, middle school education, and special education), HEALTH PROFESSIONS (medical laboratory technology, nursing, premedicine, and sports medicine), SOCIAL SCIENCE (history, paralegal studies, political science/government, psychology, social work, sociology, and theological studies). Nursing, education, and communications are the strongest academically. Nursing, education, and radiologic technology have the largest enrollments.

ACTIVITIES: There are 37 groups on campus, including art, cheerleading, choir, chorale, chorus, computers, dance, drama, ethnic, film, gay, honors, international, literary magazine, mock trial, musical theater, newspaper, photography, political, professional, radio and TV, religious, social, social service, and student government. Popular campus events include Student Appreciation Day, Organization Fair, and International Festival. **Sports:** There are 4 intercollegiate sports for men and 7 for women. Facilities include a field house with basketball and volleyball courts, a training room, and weight and fitness equipment. There is also an athletic complex with baseball, softball, and soccer fields, tennis courts, and practice fields. **Graduates:** From July 1, 2013 to June 30, 2014, 222 bachelor's degrees were awarded. The most popular majors were business (18%), nursing (15%), and radiologic science (12%). In an average class, 32% graduate in 4 years or less, 35% graduate in 5 years or less, and 46% graduate in 6 years or less. Of the 2013 graduating class, 29% were enrolled in graduate school within 6 months of graduation, and 90% were employed.

SERVICES: Counseling and information services are available, as is tutoring in most subjects. There is a reader service for the blind, and remedial math, reading, and writing. **Library/Resources:** The library contains 81,755 volumes, 493,760 microform items, 2,910 audio/video tapes/CDs/DVDs, and subscribes to 550 periodicals including electronic. Computerized library services include interlibrary loans, database searching, Internet access, and Wi-Fi capability. Special learning facilities include an art gallery, radio station, TV station, a 500-seat theater, an interactive video library, video production facilities, a Nursing Education and Resource Center, and a dance studio. **Physically Challenged Students:** 95% of the campus is accessible. Facilities include wheelchair ramps, elevators, special parking, specially equipped restrooms, special class scheduling, lowered drinking fountains, and lowered telephones. **Special:** Students may cross-register with the Kansas City Area Student Exchange, the Sisters of Saint Joseph College Consortium, and the Council of Independent Colleges Student Exchange. Avila also offers internships in business, communication, graphic design, paralegal, and other majors, work-study, a Washington center program, dual majors in science, math, and health professions, and accelerated degree programs in business administration and psychology. There are 6 national honor societies and 4 departmental honors programs. **Visiting:** There are regularly scheduled orientations for prospective students, including a visit with admissions and a faculty member a campus tour, and an appointment with the athletics or performance grant manager. There are guides for informal visits, visitors may sit in on classes, and stay overnight. To schedule a visit, contact the Campus Visit Coordinator. **Campus Safety and Security:** Measures include 24-hour foot and vehicle patrol and security escort services. There are emergency telephones, lighted pathways/sidewalks, controlled access to dorms/residences, There are evening and night security patrols and 24-hour closed-circuit television in residence hall entryways, computer labs, and the student lounge. Another closed circuit system monitors gym areas. In addition, all University parking lot entrances are monitored by closed circuit system.

REQUIREMENTS: The ACT is required. Applicants must be graduates of an accredited secondary school or have a GED certificate. They should have completed 16 academic units, including 4 in English, 3 in math, 2 to 4 in foreign language, 2 to 3 in natural and social sciences, and 1 to 2 in fine arts. A GPA of 2.5 is required. AP and CLEP credits are accepted. Important factors in the admissions decision are recommendations by school officials, extracurricular activities record, and leadership record. To graduate, students must complete at least 128 semester hours with a minimum 2.0 GPA. The 41- to 46-hour core curriculum consists of courses in composition, communication, math, history, literature, theology, philosophy, the arts, the sciences, and social institutions. The average hours in a major range from 36 to 60. **Procedure:** Freshmen are admitted to all sessions. Entrance exams should be taken in the spring or summer of the junior year. There is a rolling admissions plan. Application deadlines are open. Application fee is $25. Notification is sent on a rolling basis. Applications are accepted on-line. **Transfer Students:** 194 transfer students enrolled in 2013-2014. Applicants must have a minimum GPA of 2.0. 30 of 128 credits required for the bachelor's degree must be completed at Avila. **International Students:** There are 94 international students enrolled. The school actively recruits these students. They must take the TOEFL with a minimum score of 500 on the paper-based TOEFL (PBT) or 61 on the Internet-based version (iBT).

ADMISSIONS: 1 freshman graduated first in the class. **Admissions Contact:** Patti Harper, Director of Admissions. Web: *www.avila.edu*

FINANCIAL AID: In 2014-2015, 97% of all full-time freshmen and 87% of continuing full-time students received some form of financial aid. 76% of all full-time freshmen and 74% of continuing full-time students received need-based aid. The average freshman award was $8,550. Need-based scholarships or need-based grants averaged $6,393 ($6,638 maximum); need-based self-help aid (loans and jobs) averaged $3,353 ($4,957 maximum); non-need-based athletic scholarships averaged $3,212 ($3,260 maximum); and $3,417 from other forms of aid. 92% of undergraduate students work part-time. Average annual earnings from campus work are $1200. The average financial indebtedness of the 2014 graduate was $16,625. The FAFSA is required. Check with the school for current application deadlines.

CENTRAL METHODIST UNIVERSITY   C-2
www.centralmethodist.edu

Fayette, MO 65248	**(660) 248-6251**
	(877) CMU-1854
Fax: (660) 248-1872	**Email: admissions@centralmethodist.edu**
Full-time: 575 men, 583 women	**Faculty:** 63
Part-time: 5 men, 10 women	**Ph.D.s:** 83%
Graduate: n/av	**Student/Faculty:** 16 to 1
Year: semesters, summer session	**Tuition:** $21,320
Room & Board: $6920	**Freshman Class:** 1344 applied, 897 accepted, 302 enrolled
ACT: required	**CEEB CODE:** 6089
Application Deadline: n/av	**VERY COMPETITIVE**

Central Methodist University, founded in 1854, is a private liberal arts institution affiliated with the Methodist Church. In addition to regional accreditation, CMU has baccalaureate program accreditation with NASM and CCNE. The 83-acre campus is in a small town 30 miles northwest of Columbia. Including any residence halls, there are 16 buildings.

STUDENT LIFE: 90% of undergraduates are from Missouri. Others are from 23 states, 8 foreign countries, and Canada. 96% are from public schools. 85% are White. 86% are Protestant; 14% Catholic. **Male To Female Ratio:** 1.0:1. The average age of freshmen is 18; all undergraduates, 21. 35% do not continue beyond their first year; 43% remain to graduate. **Housing:** 700 students can be accommodated in college housing, which includes single-sex and coed dorms, off-campus apartments, and married student housing. On-campus housing is guaranteed for all 4 years. 59% of students live on campus. Alcohol is not permitted. All students may keep cars.

FACULTY/CLASSROOMS: 60% of faculty are male; 63% are female. All teach undergraduates. No introductory courses are taught by graduate students. The average class size in an introductory lecture is 30; in a laboratory is 24; and in a regular course is 12.

PROGRAMS OF STUDY: CMU confers B.A., B.S., B.M., B.M.E., B.S.E. and B.S.N., B.G.S., B.A.S.M. and B.ACC. degrees. Associate and Master's degrees are also awarded. Bachelor's degrees are awarded in BIOLOGICAL SCIENCE (biology/biological science and marine biology), BUSINESS (accounting, business administration and management, recreational facilities management, and sports management), COMMUNICATIONS AND THE ARTS (broadcasting, communications, dramatic arts, English, music, and Spanish), COMPUTER AND PHYSICAL SCIENCE (chemistry, computer science, mathematics, and physics), EDUCATION (athletic training, early childhood education, elementary education, middle school education, music education, physical education, social science education, and special education), ENGINEERING AND ENVIRONMENTAL DESIGN (environmental science), HEALTH PROFESSIONS (nursing), SOCIAL SCIENCE (criminal justice, history, interdisciplinary studies, philosophy, political science/government, psychology, religion, and sociology). Sciences, music, and preprofessional programs are the strongest academically. Business, education, and nursing have the largest enrollments.

ACTIVITIES: 21% of men belong to 3 local and 2 national fraternities; 24% of women belong to 4 local sororities. There are 37 groups on campus, including premed and criminal justice, band, cheerleading, choir, chorale, chorus, computers, dance, debate, drama, drill team, honors, jazz band, literary magazine, marching band, newspaper, opera, photography, political, prelaw, professional, radio and TV, religious, social, social service, and student government. Popular campus events include Music Festival. **Sports:** There are 5 intercollegiate sports for men and 4 for women, and 10 intramural sports for men and 10 for women. Facilities include a field house with a 2000-seat gym, playing fields, and a recreation center. **Graduates:** From July 1, 2013 to June 30, 2014, 149 bachelor's degrees were awarded. The most popular majors were health professions/related programs (19%), education (19%), and social sciences (15%). In an average class, 30% graduate in 4 years or less, 38% graduate in 5 years or less, and 42% graduate in 6 years or less.

SERVICES: Counseling and information services are available, as is tutoring in some subjects. There is remedial reading. **Library/Resources:** The library contains 102,695 volumes, 140,812 microform items, 3,736 audio/video tapes/CDs/DVDs, and subscribes to 447 periodicals including electronic. Computerized library services include interlibrary loans, database searching, Internet access, and Wi-Fi capability. Special learning facilities include an art gallery, natural history museum, radio station, TV station, an observatory. **Physically Challenged Students:** 65% of the campus is accessible. Facilities include wheelchair ramps, elevators, special parking, specially equipped restrooms, special class scheduling, and lowered drinking fountains. **Special:** CMU offers cooperative programs in medical technology and physical therapy and 3-2 engineering degrees with the University of Missouri at Rolla, the University of Evansville, Stanford University, and Washington University in St. Louis. Work-study programs, internships, study abroad, dual majors, a general studies degree, and nondegree study are also available. There are 14 national honor societies and a freshman honors program. **Visiting:** There are regularly scheduled orientations for prospective students, including meeting with admissions and financial assistance staff, a campus tour, and visits with faculty members. There are guides for informal visits, visitors may sit in on classes, and stay overnight. To schedule a visit, contact the Admissions Office. **Campus Safety and Security:** Measures include 24-hour foot and vehicle patrol, emergency notification system, and security escort services. There are emergency telephones, lighted pathways/sidewalks, controlled access to dorms/residences, key-card access to student housing.

REQUIREMENTS: The ACT is required. A minimum score of 21 on the ACT is required. Those students with a GPA lower than 2.5 may request conditional admission. Applicants should be graduates of an accredited secondary school or have a GED certificate. Recommended preparatory courses include 4 units of English, 3 of math, and 2 each of science, social studies, and humanities. A GPA of 2.5 is required. AP and CLEP credits are accepted. Important factors in the admissions decision are advanced placement or honors courses, evidence of special talent, and extracurricular activities record.To graduate, students must complete 124 to 131 credit hours, including at least 24 in the major, depending on the degree. A minimum GPA of 2.0 is required for all but the athletic training and education programs, which require a 2.5. Students must complete 53 hours of a distribution curriculum, including computer literacy, computer science, phys ed, religion, philosophy, freshman orientation to college life, and a senior capstone. **Procedure:** Freshmen are admitted to all sessions. There is a rolling admissions plan. Application deadlines are open. The fall 2014 application fee was $20. Applications are accepted on-line. **Transfer Students:** 105 transfer students enrolled in 2013-2014. Transfer applicants must be in good academic standing at their previous college and have a 2.0 cumulative GPA. 30 of 124 credits required for the bachelor's degree must be completed at CMU. **International Students:** There are 11 international students enrolled. They must take the TOEFL with a minimum score of 550 on the paper-based TOEFL (PBT).

ADMISSIONS: 67% of the 2014-2015 applicants were accepted. 4 freshmen graduated first in their class. **Admissions Contact:** Office of Admissions E-Mail: *admissions@centralmethodist.edu* Web: *www.centralmethodist.edu*

FINANCIAL AID: In 2014-2015, 100% of all full-time freshmen and 96% of continuing full-time students received some form of financial aid. 89% of all full-time freshmen and 81% of continuing full-time students received need-based aid. The average freshman award was $17,813. Need-based scholarships or need-based grants averaged $5,030; need-based self-help aid (loans and jobs) averaged $3,187; non-need-based athletic scholarships averaged $4,725; other non-need-based awards and non-need-based scholarships averaged $8,871; and $3,467 from other forms of aid. 27% of undergraduate students work part-time. Average annual earnings from campus work are $1045. The average financial indebtedness of the 2014 graduate was $21,828. The FAFSA is required. Check with the school for current application deadlines.

COLLEGE OF THE OZARKS B-4
www.cofo.edu

Point Lookout, MO 65726	**(417) 334-6411, ext. 4219**
	(800) 222-0525
Fax: (417) 335-2618	**Email: admiss4@cofo.edu**
Full-time: 697 men, 731 women	**Faculty:** 83
Part-time: 14 men, 13 women	**Ph.D.s:** 54%
Graduate: 1 men, no women	**Student/Faculty:** 15 to 1
Year: semesters	**Tuition:** see profile
Room & Board: n/app	**Freshman Class:** 1337 applied, 284 accepted, 256 enrolled
SAT CR/M/W: 600/560/600 **ACT:** 23	**CEEB CODE:** 6713
Application Deadline: February 15	**VERY COMPETITIVE**

College of the Ozarks, founded in 1906, is a private liberal arts college affiliated with the Presbyterian Church. The College of the Ozarks is tuition-free. The cost to the College for providing an education is approximately $18,100 (2014-2015) per year per student. Most colleges and universities pass along part of this cost as tuition. This is not the case at College of the Ozarks. The College guarantees to meet all of this cost for each full-time student by using earnings from its endowment, operating its own mandatory student Work Education Program, accepting student aid grants, gifts, and other sources. As a result, each full-time student's Cost of Education is met 100% by participating in the Work Education Program and a combination of private, institutional, and federal/state student aid-but without loans of any kind. Debt is openly discouraged. C of O is a liberal arts based college, founded more than a century ago with deep roots in the Christian tradition. The College seeks students who are of good character, bright, willing to work and would have a difficult time paying to attend another college. The five aims of the College are to encourage academic, Christian, patriotic, cultural and vocational growth in its students. There is 1 undergraduate school. In addition to regional accreditation, C of O has baccalaureate program accreditation with ADA. The 1000-acre campus is in a small town 40 miles south of Springfield, adjacent to the resort town of Branson. Including any residence halls, there are 96 buildings.

STUDENT LIFE: 79% of undergraduates are from Missouri. Others are from 26 states, and 16 foreign countries. 76% are from public schools. 94% are White. 86% are Protestant; 11% Morman, and unknown denomination. **Male To Female Ratio:** 1.0:1. The average age of freshmen is 18; all undergraduates, 21. 14% do not continue beyond their first year; 64% remain to graduate. **Housing:** 1054 students can be accommodated in college housing, which includes single-sex dorms. Student members of the volunteer fire department have living facilities at the fire department. On-campus housing is guaranteed for all 4 years. 81% of students live on campus; of those, 70% remain on campus on weekends. Alcohol is not permitted. All students may keep cars.

FACULTY/CLASSROOMS: 51% of faculty are male; 49% are female. All teach undergraduates. No introductory courses are taught by graduate students. The average class size in an introductory lecture is 35; in a laboratory is 15; and in a regular course is 20.

PROGRAMS OF STUDY: C of O confers B.A., and B.S. degrees. Bachelor's degrees are awarded in AGRICULTURE (agricultural business management, agricultural sciences, agriculture, agri hortiulture, agronomy, agr agronomy, animal science, conservation and regulation, and horticulture), BIOLOGICAL SCIENCE (biology ecology and field biology, biology/adolescence education, and biology/biological science), BUSINESS (accounting, business administration and management, business administration - international, business administration, mgmt, operations, business administration marketing, business economics, hotel/motel and restaurant management, international business management, marketing management, and meeting / special event mgmt), COMMUNICATIONS AND THE ARTS (art, communication, communications, communications technology, dramatic arts, English, journalism, media arts, music, music business management, music ministry, music theatre accompanying, music theory and composition, musical theater, performing arts, public relations, Spanish, communication arts - speech, speech and theatre education, studio art, studio art ceramics, studio art computer art, studio art fibers, studio art graphic design, studio art painting, theater design, theatre studies, and theatre ministry), COMPUTER AND PHYSICAL SCIENCE (chemistry, chemistry/adolescence education, computer science, information sciences and systems, and mathematics), EDUCATION (agricultural education, art education, business education, early childhood education, elementary education, English education, mathematics education, music education, physical education, physical education / exercise science, recreation education, secondary education, social studies education, Spanish education K-12, and vocational education), ENGINEERING AND ENVIRONMENTAL DESIGN (graphic arts technology and preengineering), HEALTH PROFESSIONS (allied health, health, medical technology, nursing, premedicine, prepharmacy, and preveterinary science), SOCIAL SCIENCE (biblical studies, child care/child and family studies, Christian studies, clothing and textiles management/production/services, corrections, criminal justice, criminology, culinary arts, dietetics, family/consumer studies, food science, history, home economics, interdisciplinary studies, law enforcement and corrections, ministries, philosophy, prelaw, psychology, religion, religious music, social science, family studies/soc serv/marriage family, social work, and sociology). Nursing, business, agriculture, and education are the strongest academically. Education, business, and agriculture have the largest enrollments.

ACTIVITIES: There are 40 groups on campus, including art, band, cheerleading, choir, chorale, computers, dance, drama, honors, international, jazz band, musical theater, newspaper, orchestra, pep band, photography, political, professional, religious, social service, student government, and yearbook. Popular campus events include Honor America, 9/11 Remembrance Ceremony, Convocation Speakers, Spring Fest, Mud Fest, Lip Sync, Homecoming, NAIA Division II Men's Championship Tournament. **Sports:** There are 3 intercollegiate sports for men and 3 for women, and 17 intramural sports for men and 17 for women. Facilities include The Howell W. Keeter Athletic Complex features a main gym with a seating capacity of 4,500 and also houses a training room, swimming pool, dance studio, racquetball courts, weight room, seven locker rooms, four classrooms, faculty offices and an additional basketball court. The Garrison Athletic Complex, an addition to the Keeter Athletic Complex, includes a state-of-the art fitness center, indoor running track, and gymnasium. Located to the north of the complex are all-weather track, lighted baseball and intramural fields, and tennis courts. **Graduates:** From July 1, 2013 to June 30, 2014, 317 bachelor's degrees were awarded. The most popular majors were education (15%), business (14%), and agriculture (9%). 197 companies recruited on campus in 2013-2014. In an average class, 50% graduate in 4 years or less, 64% graduate in 5 years or less, and 65% graduate in 6 years or less. Of the 2013 graduating class, 15% were enrolled in graduate school within 6 months of graduation, and 90% were employed.

SERVICES: Counseling and information services are available, as is tutoring in some subjects. Services are provided on an individual basis. There is remedial math and writing. **Library/Resources:** The library contains 265,081 volumes, 30,715 microform items, 4,487 audio/video tapes/CDs/DVDs, and subscribes to 200,000 periodicals including electronic. Computerized library services include interlibrary loans, database searching, Internet access, and Wi-Fi capability. Special learning facilities include an art gallery, the Ralph Foster Museum, Edwards Mill (working grist mill) and weaving studio, fire department, print shop, greenhouses, fruitcake and jelly kitchen, day care center, farm operations, farmers market, Gaetz tractor museum and the Ozarkiana room, containing historical periodicals and pictures of the Ozarks. **Physically Challenged Students:** 80% of the campus is accessible. Facilities include wheelchair ramps, elevators, special parking, specially equipped restrooms, and special housing. **Special:** Medical Tech. program with Cox Health System for 35 hours. AuSable Institute of Environmental Studies Program (M.I.) and The Keeter for Character Education Patriotic Travel Program. There are 8 national honor societies, a freshman honors program, and 7 departmental honors programs. **Visiting:** There are regularly scheduled orientations for prospective students Monday through Friday. There are guides for informal visits and visitors may sit in on classes. To schedule a visit, contact the Admissions Office at admiss4@cofo.edu. **Campus Safety and Security:** Measures include 24-hour foot and vehicle patrol, emergency notification system, and security escort services. There are emergency telephones, lighted pathways/sidewalks, controlled access to dorms/residences, fire department on campus, and security cameras.

REQUIREMENTS: The ACT is required. The ACT Optional Writing test is also required. Students should be in the top half of their graduating class and score at least a 20 on the ACT (950 SAT). Students should have a 3.00 grade point average. Students who have taken the college preparatory curriculum in high school are more competitive in the admission process than those who have not. Current college preparatory courses include four units of English, three units of mathematics, three units of social studies, and three units of science. The College is most concerned with the core courses of English, history/social science, mathematics, and science. Because the College's mission focuses on serving students with financial need, students must demonstrate a significant level of financial need. C of O requires applicants to be in the upper 50% of their class. A GPA of 3.0 is required. AP and CLEP credits are accepted. Important factors in the admissions decision are ability to finance college education, leadership record, and advanced placement or honors courses.Graduation Requirements; Completion of a minimum of 125 semester hours of credit with a 2.00 or higher cumulative grade point average (GPA). Remedial classes, including all College of the Ozarks classes beginning with a zero (0) do not count toward graduation. Completion of at least one major with a minimum of a 2.00 GPA for the major. Some majors have higher GPA requirements. A major must include at least 30 required hours (major/collateral) with at least 15 hours upper division (300-400 level) courses. Completion of all general education courses with a minimum of a 2.00 GPA. Completion of at least 36 credit hours of upper division courses. No more than six of those hours may be in internship. Students with transfer hours must complete a minimum of 45 credit hours at the College of the Ozarks. At least 12 credit hours must be in the major field including nine upper division hours. Exceptions may be made with the approval of the Dean of the College. Participation in the College Work Education Program as a full-time student for at least one semester is required for completion of degree. The last 30 hours of credit must be completed at the College of the Ozarks unless a waiver

is granted in writing from the Dean of the College. The faculty and the Board of Trustees vote on all graduates. To be approved for graduation, all students must have satisfied all current degree and instructional requirements, as well as be in compliance with all College regulations at time of graduation. Students will graduate with either a Bachelor of Arts degree, Bachelor of Science degree, or a Bachelor of Science in Nursing degree. **Procedure:** Freshmen are admitted fall and spring. Entrance exams should be taken during October or December of the senior year. There is a rolling admissions plan. Applications should be filed by February 15 for fall entry. Notifications are sent March 1. 1026 applicants were on the 2014 waiting list; 2 were admitted. Applications are accepted on-line. **Transfer Students:** 52 transfer students enrolled in 2013-2014. Transfer Student Admissions: Students with fewer than 24 transferable college semester hours completed elsewhere should submit the materials listed above plus the transfer student documents that are noted. This includes a college transcript (from all institutions attended) and a transfer student form. The transfer student form attests to the positive character of the student and must be completed by the dean of students at the institution from which the student is transferring. Transfer students with 24 or more transferable college semester hours need not submit ACT scores and high school transcripts, but they are required to submit college transcripts and the transfer student form. Reference forms for transfer students should be submitted by college academic personnel. Transfer applicants with over 60 hours may be ineligible for admission. 45 of 125 credits required for the bachelor's degree must be completed at C of O . **International Students:** There are 29 international students enrolled. They must take the TOEFL with a minimum score of 550 on the paper-based TOEFL (PBT) or 79 on the Internet-based version (iBT), also take the ACT or the SAT. They must also take the SAT or ACT.

ADMISSIONS: 21% of the 2014-2015 applicants were accepted. The SAT scores for the 2014-2015 freshman class were: Critical Reading--33% between 500 and 599, and 67% between 600 and 699; Math--22% below 500, 44% between 500 and 599, 23% between 600 and 699, and 11% between 700 and 800; Writing--44% between 500 and 599, 45% between 600 and 699, and 11% between 700 and 800. The ACT scores were 24% below 21, 37% between 21 and 23, 23% between 24 and 26, 8% between 27 and 28, and 8% above 28. 45% of the current freshmen were in the top fifth of their class; 80% were in the top two fifths. 11 freshmen graduated first in their class. **Admissions Contact:** Dr. Marci Linson, Dean of Admissions. E-Mail: admiss4@cofo.edu Web: www.cofo.edu

FINANCIAL AID: In 2014-2015, 100% of all full-time freshmen and continuing full-time students received some form of financial aid. 93% of all full-time freshmen and 94% of continuing full-time students received need-based aid. The average freshman award was $15,961. Need-based scholarships or need-based grants averaged $12,866 ($14,706 maximum); need-based self-help aid (loans and jobs) averaged $3,402 ($4,158 maximum); and non-need-based athletic scholarships averaged $2,439 ($5,900 maximum). 100% of undergraduate students work part-time. Average annual earnings from campus work are $4200. The average financial indebtedness of the 2014 graduate was $6,424. The FAFSA is required. The priority date for freshman financial aid applications for fall entry is February 15. The deadline for filing freshman financial aid applications for fall entry is February 15.

COLUMBIA COLLEGE   C-2
www.ccis.edu

Columbia, MO 65216

(573) 875-7352
(800) 231-7352

Fax: (573) 875-7506

Email: admissions@ccis.edu

Full-time: 329 men, 418 women

Faculty: 69; av$

Part-time: 41 men, 66 women

Ph.D.s: 90%

Graduate: 75 men, 153 women

Student/Faculty: 9 to 1

Year: semesters, summer session

Tuition: $19,386

Room & Board: $6440

Freshman Class: 616 applied, 119 accepted, 116 enrolled

SAT CR/M: 495/525 **ACT:** 24

CEEB CODE: 6095

Application Deadline: August 13

COMPETITIVE

Columbia College, a private, coeducational institution, offers associate baccalaureate and master's degrees that prepare students of differing backgrounds for entry level or advanced positions in various occupations and professions. Founded in 1851 by charter of the Missouri legislature and then named Christian Female College, Columbia College assumed its current name and became coeducational in 1970. Although it retains a covenant with the Christian Church (Disciples of Christ), Columbia College is a nonsectarian institution. Students may enroll in day, evening or online education classes at the home campus in Columbia, Missouri, or in its Adult Higher Education Division at one of the many Nationwide campuses. There is 1 undergraduate school and 1 graduate school. In addition to regional accreditation, Columbia has baccalaureate program accreditation with CSWE and NCACS. The 36-acre campus is in an urban area 120 miles east of Kansas City and 120 miles west of St. Louis. Including any residence halls, there are 28 buildings.

STUDENT LIFE: 87% of undergraduates are from Missouri. 74% are White. **Male To Female Ratio:** 1.4:1. The average age of freshmen is 18; all undergraduates, 22. 30% do not continue beyond their first year; 70% remain to graduate. **Housing:** 395 students can be accommodated in college housing, which includes single-sex, coed dorms, on-campus apartments, and living learning communities. On-campus housing is guaranteed for all 4 years, is available on a first-come, and first-served basis. 62% of students commute. Alcohol is not permitted. All students may keep cars.

FACULTY/CLASSROOMS: 48% of faculty are male; 52% are female. 92% teach undergraduates. No introductory courses are taught by graduate students.

PROGRAMS OF STUDY: Columbia confers B.A., B.S., B.G.S. and B.F.A. degrees. Associate and Master's degrees are also awarded. Bachelor's degrees are awarded in AGRICULTURE (environmental studies), BIOLOGICAL SCIENCE (biology/biological science), BUSINESS (accounting, banking and finance, business administration and management, entrepreneurial studies, finance, human resources, international business management, marketing/retailing/merchandising, and sports management), COMMUNICATIONS AND THE ARTS (art, ceramic art and design, communications, English, fine arts, graphic design, painting, photography, printmaking, and public relations), COMPUTER AND PHYSICAL SCIENCE (chemistry, computer science, information sciences and systems, and mathematics), EDUCATION (education, education administration, elementary education, middle school education, and secondary education), ENGINEERING AND ENVIRONMENTAL DESIGN (military science), HEALTH PROFESSIONS (health administration and policy, health care administration, and nursing), SOCIAL SCIENCE (American studies, criminal justice, fire services administration, forensic studies, history, human services, interdisciplinary studies, liberal arts/general studies, philosophy, political science/government, psychology, social work, and sociology). Psychology, chemisty, computer science, forensic science, mathmatics, and computer information systems are the strongest academically. Business administration has the largest enrollment.

ACTIVITIES: Groups on campus include Model UN and student government, art, choir, chorale, dance, drama, drum and bugle corps, environmental, ethnic, forensics, gay, honors, international, international student, orchestra, photography, political, professional, religious, social, social service, and student government. Popular campus events include Ivy Chain, Holiday Lighting Ceremony and Schiffman Ethics. **Sports:** There are 4 intercollegiate sports for men and 6 for women, and 16 intramural sports for men and 16 for women. Facilities include softball and soccer fields, a dance studio, indoor tennis courts, an exercise/weight room, and a gym and sports complex. **Graduates:** From July 1, 2013 to June 30, 2014, 170 bachelor's degrees were awarded. The most popular majors were management (20%), general studies (15%), and biology (12%). 135 companies recruited on campus in 2013-2014. In an average class, 38% graduate in 6 years or less.

SERVICES: Counseling and information services are available, as is tutoring in some subjects, American or world history, speech, intro to computer information systems and ethics. **Library/Resources:** The library contains 63,273 volumes, 1,761 audio/video tapes/CDs/DVDs, and subscribes to 199 periodicals including electronic. Computerized library services include interlibrary loans, database searching, and

Internet access. Special learning facilities include an art gallery. **Physically Challenged Students:** All of the campus is accessible. Facilities include wheelchair ramps, elevators, special parking, specially equipped restrooms, special class scheduling, lowered drinking fountains, lowered telephones, and special housing. **Special:** Columbia offers cross-registration with the University of Missouri/Columbia and Stephens College, internships, study abroad in more than 20 countries, B.A.-B.S. degrees in most disciplines, an interdisciplinary studies degree, student-designed and dual majors, nondegree study, and pass/fail options. Select students who complete a special 2-semester project earn a bachelor's degree with distinction (B.A.D.). There are 16 national honor societies, a freshman honors program, and 1 departmental honors programs. **Visiting:** There are regularly scheduled orientations for prospective students, including a campus tour, a workshop in financial aid, an academic/organization fair, and a luncheon. There are guides for informal visits and visitors may sit in on classes. To schedule a visit, contact the Admissions Office. **Campus Safety and Security:** Measures include 24-hour foot and vehicle patrol, emergency notification system, and security escort services. There are emergency telephones, lighted pathways/sidewalks, and controlled access to dorms/residences.

REQUIREMENTS: The SAT or ACT and ACT Writing Test are recommended. Applicants must be graduates of an accredited secondary school or have a GED certificate. Students should have completed 4 units of English, 3 of math including 2 of algebra and 1 of geometry, and 3 each of natural science and social studies, and 2 of foreign language. A GPA of 2.5 is required. AP and CLEP credits are accepted. To graduate, students must complete 60 credit hours for an Associate's degree or 120 credit hours for a Bachelors degree with a minimum GPA of 2.0. Distribution requirements include 12 hours in basic skills (English Composition, Speech, Computer Information Systems and Math); six hours in humanities, history, social and behavioral science; 5-6 hours in math/science and three hours in ethics. Bachelor of Art degrees require six hours of a foreign language or culture and society courses, ethics course, and 39 hours of upper-level course work. Most majors require students to complete a capstone course with the exception of Bachelors in General Studies and Associates degrees. **Procedure:** Freshmen are admitted to all sessions. Entrance exams should be taken in spring of the junior year or fall of the senior year. There are deferred admissions and rolling admissions plans. Applications should be filed by August 13 for fall entry; January 1 for spring entry, along with a $35 fee. Applications are accepted on-line. **Transfer Students:** Applicants must have a minimum GPA of 2.0 in the last semester attended and must submit a high school transcript with SAT or ACT scores. 24 of 120 credits required for the bachelor's degree must be completed at Columbia. **International Students:** There are 76 international students enrolled. The school actively recruits these students. They must take the TOEFL with a minimum score of 500 on the paper-based TOEFL (PBT) or 61 on the Internet-based version (iBT). They must also take the ACT.

ADMISSIONS: 19% of the 2014-2015 applicants were accepted. The SAT scores for the 2014-2015 freshman class were: Critical Reading-30% below 500, 20% between 500 and 599, 40% between 600 and 699, and 10% between 700 and 800; Math--20% below 500, 40% between 500 and 599, 20% between 600 and 699, and 20% between 700 and 800. **Admissions Contact:** Stephanie Johnson, Director of Admissions. E-Mail: *admissions@ccis.edu* Web: *www.ccis.edu*

FINANCIAL AID: In 2014-2015, 62% of all full-time freshmen and 56% of continuing full-time students received some form of financial aid. 62% of all full-time freshmen and 56% of continuing full-time students received need-based aid. The average freshman award was $16,198. Need-based scholarships or need-based grants averaged $5,342; need-based self-help aid (loans and jobs) averaged $2,607; non-need-based athletic scholarships averaged $11,840; and other non-need-based awards and non-need-based scholarships averaged $9,385. Columbia is a member of CSS. The FAFSA and the college's own financial statement are required. The priority date for freshman financial aid applications for fall entry is March 1. The deadline for filing freshman financial aid applications for fall entry is April 30.

COX COLLEGE *(The complete profile is made available exclusively on our website, www.barronspac.com)*

CULVER-STOCKTON COLLEGE C-1
www.culver.edu

Canton, MO 63435

(573) 288-6331
(800) 537-1883

Fax: (573) 288-6618

Email: admissions@culver.edu

Full-time: 401 men, 371 women

Faculty: 49

Part-time: 12 men, 46 women

Ph.D.s: 71%

Graduate: 7 men, 6 women

Student/Faculty: 13 to 1

Year: semesters, summer session

Tuition: $23,300

Room & Board: $7600

Freshman Class: 2040 applied, 1209 accepted, 220 enrolled

SAT: recommended ACT: 21

CEEB CODE: 6123

Application Deadline: n/av

COMPETITIVE

Culver-Stockton College, established in 1853, is a private liberal arts institution affiliated with the Christian Church (Disciples of Christ). Figures in the above capsule and in this profile are approximate. In addition to regional accreditation, C-SC has baccalaureate program accreditation with NASM, NLN, IACBE, and CAATE. The 143-acre campus is in a small town 125 miles north of St. Louis. Including any residence halls, there are 21 buildings.

STUDENT LIFE: 52% of undergraduates are from Missouri. Others are from 28 states, 13 foreign countries, and Canada. 95% are from public schools. 78% are White; 12% African American. 87% are Protestant; 45% Catholic; 27% claim no religious affiliation. **Male To Female Ratio:** 1.0:1. The average age of freshmen is 18; all undergraduates, 20. 32% do not continue beyond their first year; 49% remain to graduate. **Housing:** 719 students can be accommodated in college housing, which includes single-sex and coed dorms. In addition, there are fraternity houses and sorority houses. On-campus housing is guaranteed for all 4 years. 74% of students live on campus; of those, 50% remain on campus on weekends. All students may keep cars.

FACULTY/CLASSROOMS: 52% of faculty are male; 48% are female. All teach undergraduates. No introductory courses are taught by graduate students. The average class size in an introductory lecture is 20; in a laboratory is 17; and in a regular course is 16.

PROGRAMS OF STUDY: C-SC confers B.A., B.S., B.F.A., B.M.E. and B.S.N. degrees. Master's degrees are also awarded. Bachelor's degrees are awarded in BIOLOGICAL SCIENCE (biochemistry and biology/biological science), BUSINESS (accounting, business administration and management, finance, and sports management), COMMUNICATIONS AND THE ARTS (art, arts administration/management, communications, dramatic arts, English, fine arts, graphic design, music, and musical theater), COMPUTER AND PHYSICAL SCIENCE (mathematics), EDUCATION (art education, athletic training, drama education, education, elementary education, music education, and physical education), HEALTH PROFESSIONS (nursing), SOCIAL SCIENCE (criminal justice, history, legal studies, political science/government, psychology, and religion). Accounting, education and nursing are the strongest academically. Business, nursing and psychology have the largest enrollments.

ACTIVITIES: 36% of men belong to 5 national fraternities; 39% of women belong to 3 national sororities. There are 38 groups on campus, including art, band, cheerleading, choir, chorus, communications, dance, drama, environmental, ethnic, gay, honors, international, jazz band, literary magazine, musical theater, newspaper, orchestra, photography, political, professional, radio and TV, religious, social, social service, student government, and symphony. Popular campus events include National Collegiate Alcohol Awareness Week, Honors Day, Hillstock, Up 'til Dawn, Wildcat Welcome and Greek Week. **Sports:** There are 8 intercollegiate sports for men and 8 for women, and 8 intramural sports for men and 8 for women. Facilities include a 2,000-seat football stadium, a soccer field, a baseball field, softball field,intramural fields, a dance studio, a weight room, exercise equipment, and a field house with basketball, volleyball, tennis, and racquetball courts. There is also a golf course, bowling alley, and swimming pool available off-campus for students. **Graduates:** From July 1, 2013 to June 30, 2014, 124 bachelor's degrees were awarded. The most popular majors were business (12%), sport management (10%), and nursing (8%). 29 companies recruited on

campus in 2013-2014. In an average class, 41% graduate in 4 years or less, 46% graduate in 5 years or less, and 46% graduate in 6 years or less. Of the 2013 graduating class, 23% were enrolled in graduate school within 6 months of graduation, and 74% were employed.

SERVICES: Counseling and information services are available, as is tutoring in most subjects. There is remedial math and writing. **Library/Resources:** The library contains 211,393 volumes, 156 microform items, 6,000 audio/video tapes/CDs/DVDs, and subscribes to 25,561 periodicals including electronic. Computerized library services include interlibrary loans, database searching, Internet access, and Wi-Fi capability. Special learning facilities include an art gallery, planetarium, radio station, TV station, a phage genomics research facility with DNA sequencer, astronomy observation deck, biological research station, collegiate teaching greenhouse, rare books collection, a performing arts center with a multi-media editing suite and recording studio, a publications lab, a photography studio, a simulated classroom, mock trial courtroom with legal research library, 17 computer labs and a tutoring center. **Physically Challenged Students:** 40% of the campus is accessible. Facilities include wheelchair ramps, elevators, special parking, specially equipped restrooms, and lowered drinking fountains. **Special:** Culver-Stockton offers a joint-degree program in nursing in conjunction with Blessing-Rieman College of Nursing and a 3-2 occupational therapy degree with Washington University in St. Louis. Study abroad, internships, and individualized majors are also available. There are 11 national honor societies, a freshman honors program, and 9 departmental honors programs. **Visiting:** There are regularly scheduled orientations for prospective students, includes meetings with professors, students, coaches,financial aid and extracurricular advisers, financial aid information, a student life panel, and campus tours. There are guides for informal visits, visitors may sit in on classes, and stay overnight. To schedule a visit, contact Gaye Redd at (800) 537-1883. **Campus Safety and Security:** Measures include 24-hour foot and vehicle patrol, emergency notification system, self-defense education, and security escort services. There are emergency telephones, lighted pathways/sidewalks, and controlled access to dorms/residences.

REQUIREMENTS: The SAT or ACT is recommended. Requirements include secondary school records with GPA and SAT or ACT (preferred) scores. Recommended is a college preparatory program including 4 years of English, 2 to 4 of science, 3 years of social studies, and 2 of math. The GED is accepted. A GPA of 2.0 is required. AP and CLEP credits are accepted.To graduate, students must complete 120 credit hours, including 30 to 72 in the major, with a minimum GPA of 2.0. Distribution requirements include 1 course each in western culture, creativity and arts, diverse populations, individual and society, natural science, and quantitative literacy. English composition, speech, religion, phys ed, and Academic and Cultural Events are also required. **Procedure:** Freshmen are admitted fall and spring. Entrance exams should be taken by April of the entering school year. There are deferred admissions and rolling admissions plans. Application deadlines are open. Applications are accepted on-line. **Transfer Students:** 80 transfer students enrolled in 2013-2014. Transfer applicants must submit college transcripts and must have a minimum college GPA of 2.0. 30 of 120 credits required for the bachelor's degree must be completed at C-SC. **International Students:** There are 14 international students enrolled. The school actively recruits these students. They must take the TOEFL with a minimum score of 550 on the paper-based TOEFL (PBT) or 79 on the Internet-based version (iBT), International students are not required to take the TOEFL if they have resided in this country for 1 semester or submit SAT or ACT scores. They must also take the SAT or ACT.

ADMISSIONS: 59% of the 2014-2015 applicants were accepted. The SAT scores for the 2014-2015 freshman class were: Critical Reading--53% below 500, 40% between 500 and 599, and 7% between 600 and 699; Math--33% below 500, and 67% between 500 and 599. The ACT scores were 51% below 21, 26% between 21 and 23, 15% between 24 and 26, 5% between 27 and 28, and 3% above 28. 20% of the current freshmen were in the top fifth of their class; 50% were in the top two fifths. 4 freshmen graduated first in their class. **Admissions Contact:** Misty McBee, Director of Admission. E-Mail: admissions@culver.edu Web: www.culver.edu

FINANCIAL AID: In 2014-2015, 100% of all full-time freshmen and continuing full-time students received some form of financial aid.

95% of all full-time freshmen and 89% of continuing full-time students received need-based aid. The average freshman award was $20,644. Need-based scholarships or need-based grants averaged $17,372 ($30,900 maximum); need-based self-help aid (loans and jobs) averaged $3,678 ($34,952 maximum); non-need-based athletic scholarships averaged $5,239 ($9,000 maximum); and other non-need-based awards and non-need-based scholarships averaged $8,845 ($30,900 maximum). 45% of undergraduate students work part-time. Average annual earnings from campus work are $1295. The average financial indebtedness of the 2014 graduate was $22,975. C-SC is a member of CSS. The FAFSA is required. The priority date for freshman financial aid applications for fall entry is March 1. The deadline for filing freshman financial aid applications for fall entry is June 1.

DRURY UNIVERSITY B-3
www.drury.edu

Springfield, MO 65802

(417) 873-7205
(800) 922-2274

Fax: (417) 866-3873
Email: druryad@drury.edu

Full-time: 681 men, 744 women
Faculty: 140; IIB, -$

Part-time: 19 men, 10 women
Ph.D.s: 90%

Graduate: 92 men, 205 women
Student/Faculty: 10 to 1

Year: semesters, summer session
Tuition: $23,885

Room & Board: $8024
Freshman Class: 1106 applied, 823 accepted, 272 enrolled

ACT: 25
CEEB CODE: 6169

Application Deadline: May 1
VERY COMPETITIVE

Drury is a small, liberal arts university that has held to its core values since its establishment in 1873. These values find their origins in Drury's unique church affiliation, and they are responsible for an academic and spiritual environment that provides students with unique opportunities and advantages. Drury's tradition encourages students to explore ethics and spirituality in a non-judgmental, tolerant atmosphere that cherishes diversity. This atmosphere is described quite well in early 20th century college literature: "Nothing is more important than that individuals work out for themselves a satisfactory philosophy of life while avoiding the offenses of sectarianism, the church-related college is able to give its students definite help in arriving at adequate standards of value in relation to religion and the spiritual life. The need for a satisfactory philosophy of life has not been diminished in the complex global community that characterizes the twenty-first century. Drury has, for more than 135 years, maintained a commitment to small classes and personal interactions among students, staff, faculty, and administration that will serve today's students quite well. Early 1900s college literature emphasized small size as a means to maintain an intimate personal relationship between student(s) and teachers, as well as among the students themselves. This affords a distinct advantage (for) youth seeking to find (their) proper place in life and to develop the latent resources of character and personality. There are 3 undergraduate schools and 7 graduate schools. In addition to regional accreditation, Drury has baccalaureate program accreditation with AACSB, ACBSP, NAAB, NASM, NCATE, AMTS, and ACS. The 80-acre campus is in an urban area 200 miles southwest of St. Louis and 150 miles southeast of Kansas City Including any residence halls, there are 44 buildings.
STUDENT LIFE: 83% of undergraduates are from Missouri. Others are from 31 states, 38 foreign countries, and Canada. 85% are from public schools. 77% are White; 12% Foreign. 70% are Protestant; 16% Catholic. **Male To Female Ratio:** 1.2:1. The average age of freshmen is 18; all undergraduates, 21. 16% do not continue beyond their first year; 64% remain to graduate. **Housing:** 1022 students can be accommodated in college housing, which includes coed dorms, on-campus apartments, off-campus apartments, and married student housing. In addition, there are honors houses, fraternity houses, and leadership, and living-learning communities. On-campus housing is guaranteed for all 4 years. 59% of students live on campus; of those, 80% remain on campus on weekends. All students may keep cars.
FACULTY/CLASSROOMS: 57% of faculty are male; 43% are female. All teach undergraduates, and 40% do both. No introductory courses

are taught by graduate students. The average class size in an introductory lecture is 21; in a laboratory is 21; and in a regular course is 18.
PROGRAMS OF STUDY: Drury confers B.A., B.Arch., B.M.E., B.M.T., B.B.A., M.ED., A.S., B.M. and B.S.Ed. degrees. Master's degrees are also awarded. Bachelor's degrees are awarded in AGRICULTURE (environmental studies and natural resource management), BIOLOGICAL SCIENCE (biology/biological science), BUSINESS (accounting, banking and finance, business administration and management, management information systems, marketing management, organizational leadership and management, and sports management), COMMUNICATIONS AND THE ARTS (advertising, art history and appreciation, arts administration/management, communications, design, dramatic arts, English, fine arts, French, German, media arts, music, public relations, radio/television technology, Spanish, and visual design), COMPUTER AND PHYSICAL SCIENCE (chemistry, computer science, mathematics, and physics), EDUCATION (elementary education, music education, physical education, and secondary education), ENGINEERING AND ENVIRONMENTAL DESIGN (architecture and environmental science), HEALTH PROFESSIONS (environmental health science, exercise science, health science, music therapy, predentistry, premedicine, preoptometry, preosteopathy, prepharmacy, prephysical therapy, preveterinary science, and respiratory therapy), SOCIAL SCIENCE (American studies, criminal justice, criminology, economics, history, human services, international studies, philosophy, political science/government, prelaw, psychology, religion, sociology, and Spanish studies). Premedicine, business and architecture are the strongest academically. Psychology, business/marketing, and biology have the largest enrollments.
ACTIVITIES: 23% of men belong to 4 national fraternities; 28% of women belong to 4 national sororities. There are 100 groups on campus, including and academic interests., environment, leadership, student life, art, band, cheerleading, chess, choir, chorale, chorus, computers, dance, debate, drama, environmental, ethnic, film, forensics, gay, honors, international, jazz band, literary magazine, minority students, musical theater, newspaper, opera, orchestra, pep band, photography, political, professional, radio and TV, religious, social, social service, student government, and symphony. Popular campus events include Homecoming, Fireworks on Sunderland Field, Fall Festival, Earth Day and Christmas Vespers. **Sports:** There are 9 intercollegiate sports for men and 10 for women, and 5 intramural sports for men and 5 for women. Facilities include An Gold LEED certified 3100-seat event center, a gym, lighted tennis court, racquetball courts, a soccer stadium also used for intramurals, a practice field for soccer, a baseball training center, baseball field (off-campus), a tennis stadium (off-campus), an Olympic-size pool, a fitness center, a running track, a Wellness Program with free massages and exercise classes. **Graduates:** From July 1, 2013 to June 30, 2014, 373 bachelor's degrees were awarded. The most popular majors were psychology (21%), business/marketing (17%), and biological/life sciences (12%). 50 companies recruited on campus in 2013-2014. In an average class, 1% graduate in 3 years or less, 47% graduate in 4 years or less, 63% graduate in 5 years or less, and 66% graduate in 6 years or less. Of the 2013 graduating class, 39% were enrolled in graduate school within 6 months of graduation.
SERVICES: Counseling and information services are available, as is tutoring in every subject. There is a reader service for the blind, and remedial writing. There is a math and reading learning center, a writing center, and a communications center. **Library/Resources:** The library contains 194,988 volumes, 13,565 microform items, 5,344 audio/video tapes/CDs/DVDs, and subscribes to 469 periodicals including electronic. Computerized library services include interlibrary loans, database searching, Internet access, and Wi-Fi capability. Special learning facilities include an art gallery, radio station, TV station, astronomical observatory, greenhouse, teleconference facility, art and architecture slide collection, speech communication center, and writing center. **Physically Challenged Students:** 95% of the campus is accessible. Facilities include wheelchair ramps, elevators, special parking, specially equipped restrooms, special class scheduling, lowered drinking fountains, and lowered telephones. **Special:** Drury offers study abroad in Aigina, Greece and 19 other countries as well as cross-registration with colleges in 8 countries; nearly 50% of students study abroad. Premedical early admission arrangements

with St. Louis University, the University of Missouri, and Kirksville College of Osteopathic Medicine and a 3-2 engineering dual-degree program in conjunction with the University of Missouri and Washington University are available. Co-op programs include computer information systems and arts administration. 75% of students complete a professional internship; options include public and private sectors and a Washington semester. Work study, credit by exam, non-degree study, dual majors in most majors, and satisfactory/unsatisfactory options are also possible. There are 11 national honor societies, including Phi Beta Kappa, a freshman honors program, and 8 departmental honors programs. **Visiting:** There are regularly scheduled orientations for prospective students, including visit days for all students as well as visit days specialized for premed, architecture, pre-engineering, math, physics, computer sciences, arts and sciences, and social sciences students. There are guides for informal visits, visitors may sit in on classes, and stay overnight. To schedule a visit, contact Kim Atkison at (417) 873-7205. **Campus Safety and Security:** Measures include 24-hour foot and vehicle patrol, emergency notification system, self-defense education, and security escort services. There are shuttle buses, emergency telephones, lighted pathways/sidewalks, controlled access to dorms/residences, lighted parking lots with security cameras.

REQUIREMENTS: The ACT is required. Applicants must be graduates of an accredited secondary school or have a GED certificate. Recommended high school credits include 4 units of English and at least 3 each of math through algebra II, natural science, and social studies. An essay and a reference from the high school counselor or principal are required. A GPA of 3.0 is required. AP and CLEP credits are accepted. Important factors in the admissions decision are ability to finance college education, recommendations by school officials, and personality/intangible qualities. To graduate, students must complete 124 credit hours (150 for accounting and 170 for B.Arch.). They must also maintain a minimum GPA of 2.0 and complete 26 to 32 credit hours in the major (99 for architecture). Students pursue a broad curriculum called CORE that includes requirements in science, math, humanities, fine arts, fitness, foreign language, and social science, **Procedure:** Freshmen are admitted to all sessions. Entrance exams should be taken in the spring of the junior year or fall of the senior year. There are deferred admissions and rolling admissions plans. Applications should be filed by May 1 for fall entry; January 10 for spring entry, along with a $50 fee. Notifications are sent October 1. Applications are accepted on-line. **Transfer Students:** 78 transfer students enrolled in 2013-2014. Applicants must have a minimum GPA of 2.0 in all college work completed and supply an essay or writing sample. 30 of 124 credits required for the bachelor's degree must be completed at Drury. **International Students:** There are 164 international students enrolled. The school actively recruits these students. They must take the TOEFL with a minimum score of 530 on the paper-based TOEFL (PBT) or 71 on the Internet-based version (iBT), or take the TOEFL, or IELTS. They must also take the SAT or ACT.

ADMISSIONS: 74% of the 2014-2015 applicants were accepted. The SAT scores for the 2014-2015 freshman class were: Critical Reading--17% below 500, 39% between 500 and 599, 22% between 600 and 699, and 22% between 700 and 800; Math--13% below 500, 52% between 500 and 599, 30% between 600 and 699, and 5% between 700 and 800; Writing--43% below 500, 26% between 500 and 599, 22% between 600 and 699, and 9% between 700 and 800. The ACT scores were 10% below 21, 21% between 21 and 23, 35% between 24 and 26, 12% between 27 and 28, and 22% above 28. 61% of the current freshmen were in the top fifth of their class; 84% were in the top two fifths. **Admissions Contact:** Jay Fedje, Dean of Admission. E-Mail: *druryad@drury.edu* Web: *www.drury.edu*

FINANCIAL AID: In 2014-2015, 81% of all full-time freshmen and 87% of continuing full-time students received some form of financial aid. 81% of all full-time freshmen and 86% of continuing full-time students received need-based aid. The average freshman award was $20,111. Need-based scholarships or need-based grants averaged $15,621; need-based self-help aid (loans and jobs) averaged $5,842; non-need-based athletic scholarships averaged $13,389; and other non-need-based awards and non-need-based scholarships averaged $8,404. 74% of undergraduate students work part-time. Average annual earnings from campus work are $2000. The average financial indebtedness of the 2014 graduate was $25,336. Drury is a member

of CSS. The FAFSA and the college's own financial statement are required. The priority date for freshman financial aid applications for fall entry is January 10. The deadline for filing freshman financial aid applications for fall entry is May 1.

EVANGEL UNIVERSITY	B-3
www.evangel.edu	
Springfield, MO 65802	(417) 865-2811 x7205
	(800) EVANGEL
Fax: (417) 865-9599	Email: admissions@evangel.edu
Full-time: 726 men, 978 women	**Faculty:** n/av
Part-time: 90 men, 85 women	**Ph.D.s:** 63%
Graduate: 66 men, 134 women	**Student/Faculty:** n/av
Year: semesters, summer session	**Tuition:** $19,520
Room & Board: $3570	**Freshman Class:** 1163 applied, 857 accepted, 432 enrolled
SAT or ACT: recommended	**CEEB CODE:** 6198
Application Deadline: n/av	**COMPETITIVE**

Evangel University, established in 1955, is a private facility affiliated with the Assemblies of God. Figures in the above capsule and in this profile are approximate. There is one graduate school. In addition to regional accreditation, Evangel has baccalaureate program accreditation with CSWE, NASM, and NCATE. The 80-acre campus is in an urban area 225 miles west of St. Louis. Including any residence halls, there are 21 buildings.

STUDENT LIFE: 55% of undergraduates are from Missouri. Others are from 51 states, 61 foreign countries, and Canada. 79% are from public schools. 74% claim no religious affiliation; 12% Protestant. **Male To Female Ratio:** 1.4:1. The average age of freshmen is 18; all undergraduates, 21. 31% do not continue beyond their first year. **Housing:** 1460 students can be accommodated in college housing, which includes single-sex and coed dorms and married student housing. Including honors communities. On-campus housing is guaranteed for all 4 years. 75% of students live on campus; of those, 100% remain on campus on weekends. Alcohol is not permitted. All students may keep cars.

FACULTY/CLASSROOMS: All teach undergraduates. No introductory courses are taught by graduate students. The average class size in an introductory lecture is 40 and in a regular course is 20.

PROGRAMS OF STUDY: Evangel confers B.A., B.S., B.B.A., B.F.A., B.M. and B.S.W. degrees. Associate and Master's degrees are also awarded. Bachelor's degrees are awarded in BIOLOGICAL SCIENCE (biology/biological science), BUSINESS (accounting, management science, and marketing/retailing/merchandising), COMMUNICATIONS AND THE ARTS (art, broadcasting, communications, design, dramatic arts, English, journalism, music, music performance, Spanish, and speech/debate/rhetoric), COMPUTER AND PHYSICAL SCIENCE (chemistry, computer science, and mathematics), EDUCATION (business education, early childhood education, elementary education, foreign languages education, music education, physical education, science education, secondary education, and special education), HEALTH PROFESSIONS (medical laboratory technology), SOCIAL SCIENCE (biblical studies, criminal justice, history, international studies, missions, parks and recreation management, political science/government, psychology, public administration, religion, religious music, social science, social work, and sociology). Science and technology and behavioral science is the strongest academically. Business has the largest enrollment.

ACTIVITIES: There are 19 groups on campus, including band, cheerleading, choir, chorale, chorus, drama, forensics, honors, jazz band, marching band, musical theater, newspaper, orchestra, pep band, photography, political, professional, radio and TV, religious, student government, symphony, and yearbook. Popular campus events include College Weekend. **Sports:** There are 5 intercollegiate sports for men and 6 for women, and 4 intramural sports for men and 4 for women. Facilities include a student activities center and a 2,000-seat gym. **Graduates:** From July 1, 2013 to June 30, 2014, 322 bachelor's degrees were awarded. The most popular majors were business/marketing (23%), education (13%), and communications/journalism (10%). 88 companies recruited on campus in 2013-2014. In an average class, 25% graduate in 4 years or less, 36% graduate in 5 years or less, and 37% graduate in 6 years or less.

SERVICES: Counseling and information services are available, as is tutoring in every subject. There is a reader service for the blind, and remedial math, reading, and writing. **Library/Resources:** The library contains 96,487 volumes, 11,386 microform items, 6,801 audio/video tapes/CDs/DVDs, and subscribes to 748 periodicals including electronic. Computerized library services include interlibrary loans, database searching, Internet access, and Wi-Fi capability. Special learning facilities include an art gallery, radio station, and TV station. **Physically Challenged Students:** All of the campus is accessible. Facilities include wheelchair ramps, elevators, special parking, specially equipped restrooms, lowered drinking fountains, and lowered telephones. **Special:** There are 3-2 engineering degrees available in conjunction with the University of Missouri at Columbia. Other options include work-study, credit by exam, and a Washington semester. There are 9 national honor societies and 8 departmental honors programs. **Visiting:** There are regularly scheduled orientations for prospective students, consisting of scheduled visits every Friday and by appointment. There are guides for informal visits, visitors may sit in on classes, and stay overnight. To schedule a visit, contact the Office of Admissions. **Campus Safety and Security:** Measures include 24-hour foot and vehicle patrol, emergency notification system, and security escort services. There are emergency telephones, lighted pathways/sidewalks, and controlled access to dorms/residences.

REQUIREMENTS: The SAT or ACT is recommended. The recommended preparatory curriculum includes 3 credits in English, 2 each in math and social studies, and 1 in lab science. The GED is accepted. A GPA of 2.0 is required. AP and CLEP credits are accepted. All students must complete 50 to 53 general education hours, including courses in phys ed, computer literacy, English composition, English literature, and Bible study. A minimum GPA of 2.0 is required for graduation. Students must complete 124 credit hours, 36 of which are upper division level, with approximately 30 credit hours in the major. **Procedure:** Freshmen are admitted to all sessions. Entrance exams should be taken before high school graduation. There is a rolling admissions plan. Application deadlines are open. Application fee is $25. Applications are accepted on-line. **Transfer Students:** 134 transfer students enrolled in 2013-2014. Transfer applicants must be in good standing with their previous institutions and have a cumulative GPA of 2.0. 30 of 124 credits required for the bachelor's degree must be completed at Evangel. **International Students:** There are 9 international students enrolled. They must take the TOEFL. They must also take the SAT or ACT.

ADMISSIONS: 74% of the 2014-2015 applicants were accepted. **Admissions Contact:** Cheir Meyer, Director of Admissions. E-Mail: *admissions@evangel.edu* Web: *www.evangel.edu*

FINANCIAL AID: In 2014-2015, 84% of all full-time freshmen and 99% of continuing full-time students received some form of financial aid. 47% of all full-time freshmen and 58% of continuing full-time students received need-based aid. The average freshman award was $11,729. Need-based scholarships or need-based grants averaged $15,263; need-based self-help aid (loans and jobs) averaged $10,468; non-need-based athletic scholarships averaged $5,477; other non-need-based awards and non-need-based scholarships averaged $4,155; and $3,933 from other forms of aid. 21% of undergraduate students work part-time. Average annual earnings from campus work are $1100. The average financial indebtedness of the 2014 graduate was $34,434. The FAFSA is required. Check with the school for current application deadlines.

Fontbonne University, a Catholic coeducational institution of higher learning sponsored by the Sisters of St. Joseph of Carondelet, is rooted in the Judeo-Christian tradition. The university is dedicated to the discovery, understanding, preservation and dissemination of truth. Undergraduate and graduate programs are offered in an atmosphere characterized by a commitment to open communication, personal concern and diversity. Fontbonne University seeks to educate students to think critically, to act ethically and to assume responsibility as citizens and leaders. Figures in the above capsule and in this profile are approximate. There are 2 undergraduate schools and 19 graduate schools. In addition to regional accreditation, Fontbonne has baccalaureate program accreditation with ACBSP, ADA, CSWE, NCATE, CAA of ASHA, CED, and ACEND. The 16-acre campus is in a suburban area in Clayton, Missouri, 1 mile west of St. Louis city limits. Including any residence halls, there are 10 buildings.

STUDENT LIFE: 88% of undergraduates are from Missouri. Others are from 21 states, and 19 foreign countries. 55% are from public schools. 63% are White; 33% African American. 55% are Catholic; 23% Protestant. **Male To Female Ratio:** 2.4:1. The average age of freshmen is 19; all undergraduates, 29. 42% do not continue beyond their first year; 51% remain to graduate. **Housing:** 270 students can be accommodated in college housing, which includes coed dorms, on-campus apartments, and off-campus apartments. On-campus housing is available on a first-come and first-served basis. Priority is given to out-of-town students. 90% of students commute. All students may keep cars.

FACULTY/CLASSROOMS: No introductory courses are taught by graduate students. The average class size in an introductory lecture is 12; in a laboratory is 13; and in a regular course is 12.

PROGRAMS OF STUDY: Fontbonne confers B.A., B.S., B.B.A. and B.F.A. degrees. Master's degrees are also awarded. Bachelor's degrees are awarded in BIOLOGICAL SCIENCE (biology/biological science and nutritional sciences), BUSINESS (accounting, apparel and accessories marketing, business administration and management, fashion merchandising, marketing management, marketing/retailing/merchandising, sports management, and supply chain management), COMMUNICATIONS AND THE ARTS (advertising, art, communications, dramatic arts, English, English literature, English Writing, fine arts, performing arts, theatre acting, theatre arts, theatre production, theater management, and writing), COMPUTER AND PHYSICAL SCIENCE (computer science, computer security and information assurance, information sciences and systems, and mathematics), EDUCATION (childhood education: 1-6, drama education, early childhood education, education, education of the deaf and hearing impaired, elementary education, English education, general studies, mathematics education, middle school education, secondary education, and special education), HEALTH PROFESSIONS (predentistry, premedicine, prephysical therapy, and speech pathology/audiology), SOCIAL SCIENCE (behavioral science, child care/child and family studies, communication sciences and disorders, dietetics, family/consumer studies, history, human services, liberal arts/general studies, prelaw, psychology, religion, religious studies, social work, and sociology). Education, computer science, and math are the strongest academically. Business administration, organizational studies, and education have the largest enrollments.

ACTIVITIES: There are 32 groups on campus, including Griffn Gang (athletic support club), computers, dance, drama, environmental, ethnic, Fontbonne activities board (planning of on campus activites, gay, honors, international, literary magazine, musical theater, newspaper, photography, political, professional, religious, social, social service, and student government. Popular campus events include Spring Fest, Art Shows, International Bazaar, Lip Sync Contest, Comedy Nights and Musical Performances. **Sports:** There are 9 intercollegiate sports for men and 9 for women. Facilities include a student activity center that houses a 1000-seat gym, weight room, track, aerobics room, and cafe. **Graduates:** From July 1, 2013 to June 30, 2014, 466 bachelor's degrees were awarded. The most popular majors were business administration (37%), special education (10%), and organizational behavior studies (10%). 25 companies recruited on campus in 2013-2014. In an average class, 33% graduate in 4 years or less, 51% graduate in 5 years or less, and 54% graduate in 6 years or less.

SERVICES: Counseling and information services are available, as is tutoring in every subject. There is remedial math, reading, and writ-

---

FONTBONNE UNIVERSITY   D-3
www.fontbonne.edu

St. Louis, MO 63105

(314) 889-1413
(800) 205-5862

Fax: (314) 889-1451   Email: kquigley@fontbonne.edu

Full-time: 460 men, 1075 women	Faculty: n/av
Part-time: 160 men, 390 women	Ph.D.s: 69%
Graduate: 250 men, 645 women	Student/Faculty: n/av
Year: semesters, summer session	Tuition: $22,684
Room & Board: $8700	Freshman Class: n/av
SAT or ACT: required	CEEB CODE: 6216
Application Deadline: n/av	**COMPETITIVE**

ing. **Library/Resources:** The library contains 91,172 volumes, 3,564 audio/video tapes/CDs/DVDs, and subscribes to 23,463 periodicals including electronic. Computerized library services include interlibrary loans, database searching, Internet access, and Wi-Fi capability. Special learning facilities include an art gallery, a biological greenhouse, test and demo kitchens for dietetics, speech-language and audiology clinics. **Physically Challenged Students:** All of the campus is accessible. Facilities include wheelchair ramps, elevators, special parking, specially equipped restrooms, special class scheduling, lowered drinking fountains, and special housing. **Special:** Fontbonne offers cross-registration with several area colleges and a student exchange program with the Sisters of St. Joseph Consortium. There are also cooperative programs in all majors except education, internships with major companies, study abroad in 2 countries, work-study programs, student-designed and dual majors, credit by exam, nondegree study, pass/fail options, and B.A.-B.S. degrees. In addition, an accelerated degree program in business is available, as are 3-2 degrees in engineering and social work with Washington University. There is 1 national honor society and a freshman honors program. **Visiting:** There are regularly scheduled orientations for prospective students, including a campus tour, a financial aid presentation, and visits with faculty and current students. There are guides for informal visits, visitors may sit in on classes, and stay overnight. To schedule a visit, contact the Admissions Office. **Campus Safety and Security:** Measures include 24-hour foot and vehicle patrol, emergency notification system, and security escort services. There are shuttle buses and controlled access to dorms/residences.

REQUIREMENTS: The SAT or ACT is required, with a satisfactory SAT or ACT score. Applicants must be graduates of an accredited secondary school or have a GED certificate. They must have completed 16 academic credits, including 4 in English, 3 in math, 2 each in science and social studies, and 1 in history. An audition or portfolio may be required. Fontbonne requires applicants to be in the upper 50% of their class. A GPA of 2.5 is required. AP and CLEP credits are accepted. Important factors in the admissions decision are advanced placement or honors courses, extracurricular activities record, and leadership record. To graduate, students must complete 128 credit hours, including 44 in general education requirements, with a minimum GPA of 2.0. The number of hours required for the major varies. **Procedure:** Freshmen are admitted to all sessions. Entrance exams should be taken prior to registration. There are deferred admissions and rolling admissions plans. Check with the school for current application deadlines. The application fee is $25. Applications are accepted on-line. **Transfer Students:** 233 transfer students enrolled in 2013-2014. Applicants must have a minimum GPA of 2.0 and either submit ACT or the SAT scores or take a placement test. Students with fewer than 30 credits must submit a high school transcript. An interview is recommended. 32 of 128 credits required for the bachelor's degree must be completed at Fontbonne. **International Students:** There are 26 international students enrolled. The school actively recruits these students. They must take the TOEFL.

ADMISSIONS: 1 freshman graduated first in the class. **Admissions Contact:** Keith Quigley, Director of Freshman Recruitment. E-Mail: *kquigley@fontbonne.edu* Web: *www.fontbonne.edu*

FINANCIAL AID: The CSS/Profile, FAFSA, FFS, and the college's own financial statement are required. Check with the school for current application deadlines.

HANNIBAL-LAGRANGE UNIVERSITY   D-2
www.hlg.edu

Hannibal, MO 63401   **(800) HLG-1119**

Fax: (573) 221-6594	**Email:** Ray.Summerlin@hlg.edu
Full-time: n/av	**Faculty:** 65
Part-time: n/av	**Ph.D.s:** n/av
Graduate: n/av	**Student/Faculty:** 12 to 1
Year: semesters, summer session	**Tuition:** $17,920
Room & Board: $6570	**Freshman Class:** 696 applied, 448 accepted, 184 enrolled
ACT: required	**CEEB CODE:** 6266
Application Deadline: August 29	**COMPETITIVE**

Hannibal-LaGrange University, founded in 1858, is a private facility affiliated with the Southern Baptist Church. There is one graduate school. In addition to regional accreditation, HLGU has baccalaureate program accreditation with NLN. The 165-acre campus is in a small town 100 miles north of St. Louis. Including any residence halls, there are 22 buildings.

STUDENT LIFE: 80% of undergraduates are from Missouri. Others are from 29 states, and 27 foreign countries. 83% are White. 80% are Protestant. 37% do not continue beyond their first year; 54% remain to graduate. **Housing:** 550 students can be accommodated in college housing, which includes single-sex dorms and on-campus apartments. On-campus housing is available on a first-come and first-served basis. 53% of students commute. Alcohol is not permitted. All students may keep cars.

FACULTY/CLASSROOMS: All teach undergraduates. No introductory courses are taught by graduate students. The average class size in an introductory lecture is 25 and in a laboratory is 15.

PROGRAMS OF STUDY: HLGU confers B.A., B.S., B.A.S., B.S.E. and B.S.N. degrees. Associate and Master's degrees are also awarded. Bachelor's degrees are awarded in BIOLOGICAL SCIENCE (biology/biological science), BUSINESS (accounting, business administration and management, organizational behavior, and recreation and leisure services), COMMUNICATIONS AND THE ARTS (art, communications, dramatic arts, English, music, music performance, and speech/debate/rhetoric), COMPUTER AND PHYSICAL SCIENCE (computer programming, information sciences and systems, and mathematics), EDUCATION (Christian education, early childhood education, elementary education, and secondary education), HEALTH PROFESSIONS (exercise science and nursing), SOCIAL SCIENCE (biblical studies, criminal justice, history, liberal arts/general studies, missions, psychology, religious music, social work, and sociology). Nursing, and education are the strongest academically. Education, criminal justice, nursing, business, and organizational management have the largest enrollments.

ACTIVITIES: There are 24 groups on campus, including Alpha Tau Beta, Fellowship of Christian Athletes, Gatekeepers, Lambda Alpha Epsilon, Naturea Investigato Circulus, Phi Beta Lambda (Future Business Leaders), Pi Gamam Mu, Alpha Chi, art, cheerleading, choir, chorus, drama, ethnic, honors, international, musical theater, newspaper, professional, radio and TV, religious, social, social service, student government, and yearbook. Popular campus events include Campus Visitation Days, Experience HLGU Day, Trojan Turkey Trek, Homecoming and Booster Banquet. **Sports:** There are 8 intercollegiate sports for men and 8 for women, and 7 intramural sports for men and 7 for women. Facilities include baseball, softball, and soccer fields and a 41,000-square-foot sports complex that contains a gym, weight and aerobics rooms, and volleyball, tennis, and racquetball courts. **Graduates:** From July 1, 2013 to June 30, 2014, 257 bachelor's degrees were awarded. The most popular majors were education, nursing, and organizational management. In an average class, 39% graduate in 6 years or less. Of the 2013 graduating class, 33% were enrolled in graduate school within 6 months of graduation, and 55% were employed.

SERVICES: Counseling and information services are available, as is tutoring in some subjects, Based on available tutors, math, english, writing, literature, science, behavioral science, accounting and business, history, Bible There is remedial math and writing. **Library/Resources:** The library contains 121,840 volumes, 22,152 microform items, 6,702 audio/video tapes/CDs/DVDs, and subscribes to 266 periodicals including electronic. Computerized library services include interlibrary loans, database searching, and Internet access. Special learning facilities include an art gallery, radio station, a theatre, mission center, sports complex, nature trail and testing lab. **Physically Challenged Students:** 70% of the campus is accessible. Facilities include wheelchair ramps, elevators, special parking, specially equipped restrooms, special class scheduling, special housing. **Special:** Credit by examination, prior learning assessment, online courses, adult programs, and self-designed liberal arts degree There are 2 national honor societies, a freshman honors program, and 2 departmental honors programs. **Visiting:** There are regularly scheduled orientations for prospective students, consisting of Encounter Days, which are organized tours of the campus covering financial aid, student affairs, and academic areas, and which include lunch in the cafeteria. There are guides for informal visits, visitors may sit in on classes, and stay overnight. To schedule a visit, contact Ray Summerlin at ray.summerlin@hlg.edu. **Campus Safety and Security:** Measures include 24-hour foot and vehicle patrol, emergency notification system, self-defense education, and security escort services. There are emergency telephones, lighted pathways/sidewalks, and controlled access to dorms/residences.

REQUIREMENTS: The ACT is required. Applicants must be graduates of an accredited secondary school or have the GED. AP and CLEP credits are accepted. All students must complete a minimum of 124 credit hours with a 2.0 GPA to graduate. The major usually requires 36 or more credit hours of study. General education requirements include 8 hours in natural science; 6 hours each in Bible, composition, literature, foreign language, history, fine arts, and social science; 3 hours each in speech and algebra; 2 hours in phys ed; and 1 hour in Success in Education. Different core requirements pertain to education and nursing students. **Procedure:** Freshmen are admitted to all sessions. Entrance exams should be taken before registration. There is a rolling admissions plan. Applications should be filed by August 29 for fall entry; January 8 for spring entry. The fall 2014 application fee was $25. Applications are accepted on-line. **Transfer Students:** 187 transfer students enrolled in 2013-2014. Applicants must submit transcripts from all colleges attended. Students applying with fewer than 30 credit hours must also submit a high school transcript along with ACT or SAT scores. 32 of 124 credits required for the bachelor's degree must be completed at HLGU. **International Students:** There are 115 international students enrolled. The school actively recruits these students. They must take the TOEFL with a minimum score of 520 on the paper-based TOEFL (PBT) or 68 on the Internet-based version (iBT). They must also take the SAT or ACT, scoring 20.

ADMISSIONS: 64% of the 2014-2015 applicants were accepted. 21% of the current freshmen were in the top fifth of their class; 52% were in the top two fifths. **Admissions Contact:** Dr. Ray Summerlin, Vice President of Enrollment Management. E-Mail: *Ray.Summerlin@hlg.edu* Web: *www.hlg.edu*

FINANCIAL AID: In 2014-2015, 88% of all full-time freshmen and 90% of continuing full-time students received some form of financial aid. 55% of all full-time freshmen and 71% of continuing full-time students received need-based aid. The average freshman award was $18,397. Need-based scholarships or need-based grants averaged $1,299 ($5,645 maximum); need-based self-help aid (loans and jobs) averaged $1,753 ($4,454 maximum); non-need-based athletic scholarships averaged $2,418 ($11,500 maximum); and other non-need-based awards and non-need-based scholarships averaged $12,928 ($17,960 maximum). 70% of undergraduate students work part-time. Average annual earnings from campus work are $1500. The FAFSA is required. Check with the school for current application deadlines.

HARRIS-STOWE STATE UNIVERSITY *(The complete profile is made available exclusively on our website, www.barronspac.com)*

KANSAS CITY ART INSTITUTE *(The complete profile is made available exclusively on our website, www.barronspac.com)*

LINCOLN UNIVERSITY *(The complete profile is made available exclusively on our website, www.barronspac.com)*

LINDENWOOD UNIVERSITY	**D-2**
www.lindenwood.edu	

St. Charles, MO 63301	**(636) 949-4949**
Fax: (636) 949-4989	Email: admissions@lindenwood.edu
Full-time: 2460 men, 3185 women	Faculty: IIA, -$
Part-time: 100 men, 160 women	Ph.D.s: 60%
Graduate: 1065 men, 2680 women	Student/Faculty: 29 to 1
Year: 4-1-4, summer session	Tuition: $14,380
Room & Board: $7500	Freshman Class: n/av
SAT or ACT: required	CEEB CODE: 6367
Application Deadline:	COMPETITIVE

Lindenwood University, founded in 1827, is a private institution offering undergraduate and graduate degree programs in the arts and sciences, business, education, and preprofessional fields. The figures in the above capsule and in this profile are approximate. There are 8 undergraduate schools and 5 graduate schools. In addition to regional accreditation, Lindenwood has baccalaureate program accreditation with TEAC and CAAHEP. The 500-acre campus is in a suburban area 25 miles west of St. Louis. Including any residence halls, there are 37 buildings.

STUDENT LIFE: 73% of undergraduates are from Missouri. Others are from 43 states, 63 foreign countries, and Canada. 76% are White; 12% African American. **Male To Female Ratio:** 1.7:1. The average age of freshmen is 19; all undergraduates, 25. 38% do not continue beyond their first year; 40% remain to graduate. **Housing:** 3500 students can be accommodated in college housing, which includes single-sex dorms, on-campus apartments, and married student housing. In addition, there are sorority houses. On-campus housing is guaranteed for all 4 years. 68% of students live on campus; of those, 67% remain on campus on weekends. Alcohol is not permitted. All students may keep cars.

FACULTY/CLASSROOMS: 49% of faculty are male; 51% are female. 99% teach undergraduates. No introductory courses are taught by graduate students. The average class size in an introductory lecture is 30; in a laboratory is 25; and in a regular course is 25.

PROGRAMS OF STUDY: Lindenwood confers B.A., B.S. and B.F.A. degrees. Master's and Doctoral degrees are also awarded. Bachelor's degrees are awarded in BIOLOGICAL SCIENCE (biology/biological science), BUSINESS (accounting, banking and finance, business administration and management, human resources, management information systems, marketing/retailing/merchandising, and sports management), COMMUNICATIONS AND THE ARTS (art history and appreciation, communications, creative writing, dance, dramatic arts, English, French, music, performing arts, Spanish, and studio art), COMPUTER AND PHYSICAL SCIENCE (chemistry, computer science, and mathematics), EDUCATION (athletic training, business education, early childhood education, elementary education, music education, physical education, science education, and secondary education), ENGINEERING AND ENVIRONMENTAL DESIGN (engineering), HEALTH PROFESSIONS (medical technology), SOCIAL SCIENCE (criminal justice, fashion design and technology, history, human services, international studies, liberal arts/general studies, ministries, political science/government, prelaw, psychology, public administration, religion, social work, and sociology). Biology, education, and mass communications, are the strongest academically and have the largest enrollments.

ACTIVITIES: 1% of men belong to 1 local and 2 national fraternities; 1% of women belong to 1 national sorority. There are 71 groups on campus, including art, band, cheerleading, chess, choir, chorale, chorus, computers, dance, debate, drama, drill team, ethnic, film, forensics, honors, international, jazz band, literary magazine, marching band, musical theater, newspaper, pep band, photography, political, professional, radio and TV, religious, social, social service, and student government. Popular campus events include Spring Fling, Alumni Weekend, and Christmas Walk. **Sports:** There are 20 intercollegiate sports for men and 19 for women, and 9 intramural sports for men and 9 for women. Facilities include an indoor pool, a gym, weight rooms, a 5000-seat stadium, a 3000-seat performance arena, a sand volleyball court, tennis courts, softball, baseball, and soccer fields, a state-of-the art all-weather track, and an 800-seat dual ice rink. Students may use the local golf course and bowling alley for a discounted fee. **Graduates:** From July 1, 2013 to June 30, 2014, 1010 bachelor's degrees were awarded. The most popular majors were business administration (24%), elementary education (7%), and criminology (6%). 84 companies recruited on campus in 2013-2014. In an average class, 26% graduate in 4 years or less, 38% graduate in 5 years or less, and 40% graduate in 6 years or less. Of the 2013 graduating class, 14% were enrolled in graduate school within 6 months of graduation, and 94% were employed.

SERVICES: Counseling and information services are available, as is tutoring in every subject. There is a reader service for the blind, and remedial math, reading, and writing. **Library/Resources:** The library contains 171,562 volumes, 26,128 microform items, 1,763 audio/video tapes/CDs/DVDs, and subscribes to 793 periodicals including electronic. Computerized library services include interlibrary loans, database searching, Internet access, and Wi-Fi capability. Special learning facilities include an art gallery, radio station, TV station, a greenhouse, a wetlands program facility, a success center, and the Boone Home historic site. **Physically Challenged Students:** 50% of the campus is accessible. Facilities include wheelchair ramps, elevators, special parking, specially equipped restrooms, special class scheduling, lowered drinking fountains, lowered telephones. **Special:** The university offers internships in most majors, a co-op program in computer science, study abroad and a Washington semester for juniors, and cross-registration through a consortium of Greater St. Louis College and Universities. Dual and student-designed majors, accelerated degree programs, 3-2 degrees in engineering with Washington University in St. Louis and the University of Missouri-Columbia, work-study programs, and nondegree study are also available. There are evening and weekend classes for working adults and 5-year bachelor's programs. There are 9 national honor societies, a freshman honors program, and 6 departmental honors programs. **Visiting:** There are regularly scheduled orientations for prospective students, including an admissions interview, a campus tour and advising. There are guides for informal visits, visitors may sit in on classes, and stay overnight. To schedule a visit, contact the Office of Undergraduate Admissions. **Campus Safety and Security:** Measures include 24-hour foot and vehicle patrol, emergency notification system, self-defense education, and security escort services. There are emergency telephones and lighted pathways/sidewalks.

REQUIREMENTS: The SAT or ACT is required. Applicants must be graduates of an accredited secondary school or have a GED. High school preparation should include at least 16 academic units, including 4 years of English, 2 to 3 each of math, science, and social studies, 2 of a foreign language, and some study of fine or performing arts. An essay and an interview are recommended. Lindenwood requires applicants to be in the upper 50% of their class. A GPA of 2.5 is required. AP and CLEP credits are accepted. Important factors in the admissions decision are leadership record, evidence of special talent, and advanced placement or honors courses. In order to graduate, students must complete a minimum of 128 credit hours, including at least 36 in the major and 42 in upper-division courses, with a minimum GPA of 2.0. Core curriculum courses include 10 hours of math and science, 9 each of social sciences, humanities, and civilization, 6 of English, and 3 each of fine arts and communications. They must score at proficiency level on a writing assessment. **Procedure:** Freshmen are admitted to all sessions. There are deferred admissions and rolling admissions plans. Application deadlines are open. Application fee is $30. **Transfer Students:** 803 transfer students enrolled in 2013-2014. Applicants must have a minimum GPA of 2.0 and should submit official college transcripts in order to transfer credits. 38 of 128 credits required for the bachelor's degree must be completed at Lindenwood. **International Students:** There are 557 international students enrolled. The school actively recruits these students. They must take the TOEFL with a minimum score of 500 on the paper-based TOEFL (PBT) or 61 on the Internet-based version (iBT). They must also take the SAT or ACT.

ADMISSIONS: 3 freshmen graduated first in their class. **Admissions Contact:** Joe Parisi, Associate Dean of Admissions. E-Mail: *admissions@lindenwood.edu* Web: *www.lindenwood.edu*

FINANCIAL AID: In 2014-2015, 98% of all full-time freshmen and continuing full-time students received some form of financial aid. 66% of all full-time freshmen and continuing full-time students received need-based aid. 72% of undergraduate students work part-time. Average annual earnings from campus work are $2400. The average financial indebtedness of the 2014 graduate was $15,500. The FAFSA is required. Check with the school for current application deadlines.

MARYVILLE UNIVERSITY OF SAINT LOUIS   D-3
www.maryville.edu

St. Louis, MO 63141

Fax: (314) 529-9927
Full-time: 623 men, 1229 women
Part-time: 201 men, 765 women
Graduate: 419 men, 2694 women
Year: semesters, summer session
Room & Board: $9972

ACT: 25
Application Deadline: n/av

(314) 529-9350
(800) 627-9855
Email: admissions@maryville.edu
Faculty: IIA, -$
Ph.D.s: 80%
Student/Faculty: n/av
Tuition: $25,884
Freshman Class: 1576 applied, 1134 accepted, 412 enrolled
CEEB CODE: 6399
VERY COMPETITIVE

Maryville University, founded in 1872, is a selective, comprehensive and nationally ranked private institution. Maryville offers more than 75 degrees at the undergraduate, masters and doctoral levels to students from 50 states and 30 countries. Maryville's athletics teams compete at the Division II level in the Great Lakes Valley Conference. There are 4 undergraduate schools and 5 graduate schools. In addition to regional accreditation, Maryville has baccalaureate program accreditation with ACBSP, FIDER, NASAD, NASM, NCATE, AOTA, CAPTE, and CCNE. The 130-acre campus is in a suburban area 20 miles west of downtown St. Louis. Including any residence halls, there are 30 buildings.

STUDENT LIFE: 80% of undergraduates are from Missouri. Others are from 50 states, and 30 foreign countries. 91% are from public schools. 75% are White. 63% claim no religious affiliation; 12% Catholic. **Male To Female Ratio:** 3.8:1. The average age of freshmen is 18; all undergraduates, 25. 13% do not continue beyond their first year; 67% remain to graduate. **Housing:** 675 students can be accommodated in college housing, which includes single-sex and coed dorms and on-campus apartments. On-campus housing is available on a first-come, first-served basis, and is available on a lottery system for upperclassmen. 76% of students commute. All students may keep cars.

FACULTY/CLASSROOMS: 32% of faculty are male; 68% are female. No introductory courses are taught by graduate students. The average class size in an introductory lecture is 16 and in a laboratory is 14.

PROGRAMS OF STUDY: Maryville confers B.A., B.S., B.F.A., B.S.C.L.S., B.S.M.T. and B.S.N. degrees. Master's and Doctoral degrees are also awarded. Bachelor's degrees are awarded in AGRICULTURE (environmental studies), BIOLOGICAL SCIENCE (biochemistry and biology/biological science), BUSINESS (accounting, business administration and management, international business management, marketing management, organizational leadership and management, and sports management), COMMUNICATIONS AND THE ARTS (communications, English, graphic design, and studio art), COMPUTER AND PHYSICAL SCIENCE (actuarial science, chemistry, information sciences and systems, mathematics, and science), EDUCATION (art education, early childhood education, elementary education, middle school education, and secondary education), ENGINEERING AND ENVIRONMENTAL DESIGN (engineering, environmental science, and interior design), HEALTH PROFESSIONS (clinical science, health science, music therapy, nursing, occupational therapy, physical therapy, and rehabilitation therapy), SOCIAL SCIENCE (criminology, forensic studies, history, international studies, liberal arts/general studies, paralegal studies, psychology, and sociology). Actuarial science, education and physical therapy are the strongest academically. Nursing, business administration, and psychology have the largest enrollments.

ACTIVITIES: There are 75 groups on campus, including art, cheerleading, chorale, dance, environmental, ethnic, forensics, gay, honors, international, jazz band, literary magazine, newspaper, orchestra, pep band, political, professional, religious, social, social service, and student government. Popular campus events include Saturday Night Live Comedy Series, Fall Festival, and Bingo and Brew. **Sports:** There are 7 intercollegiate sports for men and 9 for women, and 5 intramural sports for men and 5 for women. Facilities include soccer, softball, and baseball fields, wrestling facility, a gym, outdoor and indoor basketball hoops, an expanded fitness center, table tennis and billiards, and outdoor walking and hiking trails. **Graduates:** From July 1, 2013 to June 30, 2014, 656 bachelor's degrees were awarded. The most popular majors were nursing/health professions (51%), business administration (16%), and psychology (8%). 60 companies recruited on campus in 2013-2014. In an average class, 67% graduate in 6 years or less.

SERVICES: Counseling and information services are available, as is tutoring in every subject. There is a reader service for the blind. There also is a writing center, learning styles inventory, and help with time management and test-taking skills, study skills materials, workshops, and individual consultations. **Library/Resources:** The library contains 67,249 volumes, 443,597 microform items, and 4,603 audio/video tapes/CDs/DVDs, and subscribes to 85,674 periodicals including electronic. Computerized library services include interlibrary loans, database searching, Internet access, and Wi-Fi capability. Special learning facilities include an art gallery, an observatory, a teaching lab, art and design labs, clinical labs for nursing, occupational therapy, and physical therapy, a communications lab, video conferencing facilities on all campuses, 50 multimedia-ready classrooms, and residence hall computer labs. **Physically Challenged Students:** All of the campus is accessible. Facilities include wheelchair ramps, elevators, special parking, specially equipped restrooms, special class scheduling, lowered drinking fountains, lowered telephones. **Special:** There is cross-registration with Missouri Baptist College and Fontbonne, Webster, and Lindenwood Universities. Students may choose internships in various fields, and cooperative programs are available with various employers Other options include dual and student-designed majors, study abroad in China, England, France, Italy, Japan, Spain, and other countries, a 3-2 engineering degree with Washington University, and a Washington semester. Accelerated degree programs are offered in actuarial science and nursing. A 3+4 B.S./O.D. optometry degree with the University of Missouri-St. Louis and a B.A. criminal justice/criminology degree in association with St. Louis County and Municipal Police Academy are possible. There are 6 national honor societies and a freshman honors program. **Visiting:** There are regularly scheduled orientations for prospective students, including visiting the campus and arranging a personal interview with an admissions counselor. There are guides for informal visits, visitors may sit in on classes, and stay overnight. To schedule a visit, contact the Admissions Office at (800) 627-9855 . **Campus Safety and Security:** Measures include 24-hour foot and vehicle patrol, emergency notification system, self-defense education, and security escort services. There are emergency telephones, lighted pathways/sidewalks, video security systems in residence halls, and security key operated dorm entrances.

REQUIREMENTS: The ACT is required. Students must have graduated from an accredited secondary school with 22 academic credits or have the GED. Expected preparatory courses include 4 units of English, 3 of math, and 2 each of science and social studies, plus 3 additional units in any of the preceding areas or in a foreign language. Some majors have additional admission requirements. A GPA of 2.5 is required. AP and CLEP credits are accepted. Important factors in the admissions decision are recommendations by school officials, advanced placement or honors courses, and leadership record. To graduate, all students must complete a minimum of 128 credit hours, with a minimum GPA of 2.0. The core curriculum consists of 12 credit hours each of humanities, math and science, and social and behavioral science, and 8 credit hours each of communication skills and fine arts. 48 upper-division credits must be completed. **Procedure:** Freshmen are admitted to all sessions. Entrance exams should be taken during the junior year. There is a rolling admissions plan. Check with the school for current application deadlines. The fall 2014 application fee was $30. Notification is sent on a rolling basis. Applications are accepted on-line. **Transfer Students:** 336 transfer students enrolled in 2013-2014. A minimum GPA of 2.0, or higher for some majors, is required. Some majors may require ACT or SAT. 30 of 128 credits required for the bachelor's degree must be completed at Maryville. **International Students:** There are 67 international students enrolled. The school actively recruits these students. They must take the TOEFL with a minimum score of 500 on the paper-based TOEFL (PBT) or 61 on the Internet-based version (iBT).

ADMISSIONS: 72% of the 2014-2015 applicants were accepted. The ACT scores were 6% below 21, 21% between 21 and 23, 33% between 24 and 26, 19% between 27 and 28, and 15% above 28. 51% of the current freshmen were in the top fifth of their class; 84% were in the top two fifths. 7 freshmen graduated first in their class. **Admissions Contact:** Shani Lenore-Jenkins, Associate Vice President of Enrollment. E-Mail: *admissions@maryville.edu* Web: *www.maryville.edu*

FINANCIAL AID: 12% of undergraduate students work part-time. Average annual earnings from campus work are $2200. The FAFSA is required. The priority date for freshman financial aid applications for fall entry is March 1. The deadline for filing freshman financial aid applications for fall entry is April 1.

MISSOURI BAPTIST UNIVERSITY   D-3
www.mobap.edu

St. Louis, MO 63141	(314) 392-2296
	(877) 434-1115
Fax: (314) 434-7596	Email: admissions@mobap.edu
Full-time: 690 men, 699 women	Faculty: IIB
Part-time: 952 men, 1750 women	Ph.D.s: 59%
Graduate: 312 men, 918 women	Student/Faculty: 20 to 1
Year: semesters, summer session	Tuition: $22,760
Room & Board: $9070	Freshman Class: n/av
ACT: 22	CEEB CODE: 2258
Application Deadline: open	COMPETITIVE

Missouri Baptist University, established in 1964, is a private liberal arts institution. There is 1 undergraduate school and 1 graduate school. In addition to regional accreditation, MBU has baccalaureate program accreditation with NASM and NCATE. The 65-acre campus is in a suburban area 15 miles west of St. Louis. Including any residence halls, there are 15 buildings.

STUDENT LIFE: 88% of undergraduates are from Missouri. Others are from 36 states, 21 foreign countries, and Canada. 58% are White; 30% race unknown. 51% are Protestant; 12% Catholic. **Male To Female Ratio:** 1.7:1. The average age of freshmen is 19; all undergraduates, 19. **Housing:** 346 students can be accommodated in college housing, which includes single-sex dorms, on-campus apartments, and off-campus apartments. On-campus housing is available on a first-come and first-served basis. 80% of students commute. Alcohol is not permitted. All students may keep cars.

FACULTY/CLASSROOMS: 52% of faculty are male; 48% are female. No introductory courses are taught by graduate students. The average class size in an introductory lecture is 30; in a laboratory is 20; and in a regular course is 25.

PROGRAMS OF STUDY: MBU confers B.A., B.S., B.M., B.M.E., B.P.S. and B.S.E. degrees. Associate, Master's, and Doctoral degrees are also awarded. Bachelor's degrees are awarded in BIOLOGICAL SCIENCE (biochemistry, biology/biological science, and biotechnology), BUSINESS (accounting, applied management, business administration and management, management science, marketing management, and sports management), COMMUNICATIONS AND THE ARTS (communications, English, journalism, music, music ministry, music performance, musical theater, public relations, and theatre arts), COMPUTER AND PHYSICAL SCIENCE (chemistry, information sciences and systems, and mathematics), EDUCATION (business education, early childhood education, elementary education, health education, middle school education, music education, physical education, and secondary education), HEALTH PROFESSIONS (exercise science, health care administration, and health science), SOCIAL SCIENCE (behavioral science, child psychology/development, Christian studies, criminal justice, history, human services, liberal arts/general studies, ministries, psychology, religious music, and social science). Business administration, elementary education, and criminal justice have the largest enrollments.

ACTIVITIES: There are 24 groups on campus, including band, business, cheerleading, choir, chorale, chorus, communications, computers, dance, drama, film, honors, international, jazz band, literary magazine, musical theater, opera, orchestra, photography, political, professional, radio and TV, religious, social service, and student government. Popular campus events include Spring Musical, Christmas

Concert, and Hanging of the Green. <u>Sports:</u> There are 13 intercollegiate sports for men and 13 for women, and 6 intramural sports for men and 6 for women. Facilities include Our 47,000-square-foot Carl and Deloris Petty Sports and Recreation Complex includes a 1,000-seat gymnasium, a suspended indoor track, locker rooms, a concession area in Spartan Hall, state-of-the-art training and fitness centers. In addition the campus also has baseball, softball, and soccer fields. <u>Graduates:</u> From July 1, 2013 to June 30, 2014, 384 bachelor's degrees were awarded.

<u>SERVICES:</u> Counseling and information services are available, as is tutoring in some subjects, by appointment: accounting, economics, grammar, Greek, music appreciation, old and new testament history, psychology, and Spanish. There is a reader service for the blind, and remedial math and writing. Walk-in tutoring in math, biology and chemistry <u>Library/Resources:</u> The library contains 20,064 volumes, 3,708 microform items, 2,847 audio/video tapes/CDs/DVDs, and subscribes to 3,000 periodicals including electronic. Computerized library services include interlibrary loans, database searching, Internet access, and Wi-Fi capability. Special learning facilities include a radio station, an audiovisual production lab. <u>Physically Challenged Students:</u> 80% of the campus is accessible. Facilities include wheelchair ramps, elevators, special parking, specially equipped restrooms, special class scheduling, lowered drinking fountains, and special housing. <u>Special:</u> There is cross-registration with Fontbonne, and Maryville, Lindenwood, and Webster Universities. Students may opt for credit by examination, non-degree study, and student-designed majors. A 3-2 engineering degree with the University of Missouri/Columbia or a 2-2 engineering degree with the Missouri University of Science and Technology is available. Study abroad is possible at Harlaxton College in England, Hong Kong Baptist University, or through Webster University, Best Semester, Consortium for Global Education, or the Center for Cross Cultural Study . MBU also offers internships in various disciplines and dual majors in some fields. There are 3 national honor societies and a freshman honors program. <u>Visiting:</u> There are regularly scheduled orientations for prospective students, student visits include a welcome weekend, open houses, and campus tours. There are guides for informal visits, visitors may sit in on classes, and stay overnight. To schedule a visit, contact the Admissions Office. <u>Campus Safety and Security:</u> Measures include 24-hour foot and vehicle patrol, emergency notification system, self-defense education, and security escort services. There are shuttle buses, emergency telephones, lighted pathways/sidewalks, and controlled access to dorms/residences.

<u>REQUIREMENTS:</u> The ACT is required. Applicants must have a minimum score of 20 on the ACT or a satisfactory score on the SAT. Applicants must be graduates of an accredited secondary school. GED and home-schooled students are accepted. MBU requires applicants to be in the upper 50% of their class. A GPA of 2.0 is required. AP and CLEP credits are accepted. Important factors in the admissions decision are advanced placement or honors courses, leadership record, and evidence of special talent.All students must take courses in the humanities/fine arts, social and behavioral sciences, natural sciences, phys ed, computer literacy, and old and new testament history. A minimum GPA of 2.0 is required (some majors require a GPA of 2.5 or better). To graduate, students must complete at least 128 credit hours, with a minimum of 30 hours in the major and 45 hours of upper-division courses; pass a general education exam and an exit exam or other assessment in the major; and complete a capstone project. <u>Procedure:</u> Freshmen are admitted to all sessions. Entrance exams should be taken during the junior year. There is a rolling admissions plan. Application deadlines are open. Application fee is $35. Applications are accepted on-line. Application fees are waived if application is completed on-line. <u>Transfer Students:</u> 451 transfer students enrolled in 2013-2014. Applicants must have a 2.0 GPA, with some programs requiring 2.5 or better. Students must submit official transcripts from all previous colleges attended, along with a character reference. 24 of 128 credits required for the bachelor's degree must be completed at MBU. <u>International Students:</u> There are 28 international students enrolled. The school actively recruits these students. They must take the TOEFL with a minimum score of 550 on the paper-based TOEFL (PBT) or 80 on the Internet-based version (iBT). They must also take the ACT, scoring 20.

<u>ADMISSIONS:</u> Cynthia Sutton, Director of Admissions. E-Mail: *admissions@mobap.edu* Web: *www.mobap.edu*

<u>FINANCIAL AID:</u> In 2014-2015, 100% of all full-time freshmen and continuing full-time students received some form of financial aid. The FAFSA and the college's own financial statement are required. Check with the school for current application deadlines.

MISSOURI SOUTHERN STATE UNIVERSITY   A-4
www.mssu.edu

Joplin, MO 64801	(417) 625-9379
	(866) 818-6778
Fax: (417) 659-4429	Email: admissions@mssu.edu
Full-time: 1792 men, 2348 women	Faculty: 197; IIB, -$
Part-time: 580 men, 841 women	Ph.D.s: 62%
Graduate: 8 men, 44 women	Student/Faculty: 19 to 1
Year: semesters, summer session	Tuition: $5762 ($11,156)
Room & Board: $6299	Freshman Class: 2002 applied, 1922 accepted, 856 enrolled
ACT: 21	CEEB CODE: 6322
Application Deadline: September 1	COMPETITIVE

Missouri Southern State University, founded in 1937, is a public, primarily commuter institution offering undergraduate degree programs in the arts and sciences, business, education, psychology, and technology. There are 4 undergraduate schools and 1 graduate school. In addition to regional accreditation, Missouri Southern has baccalaureate program accreditation with ABET, ACBSP, ADA, NCATE, NLN, and NAACLS. The 365-acre campus is in a small town in the southwest corner of the state, 138 miles south of Kansas City. Including any residence halls, there are 41 buildings.

<u>STUDENT LIFE:</u> 80% of undergraduates are from Missouri. Others are from 46 states, 30 foreign countries, and Canada. 77% are White. <u>Male To Female Ratio:</u> 1.4:1. The average age of freshmen is 20; all undergraduates, 25. 35% do not continue beyond their first year; 36% remain to graduate. <u>Housing:</u> 722 students can be accommodated in college housing, which includes single-sex dorms and on-campus apartments. On-campus housing is available on a first-come and first-served basis. 87% of students commute. Alcohol is not permitted. All students may keep cars.

<u>FACULTY/CLASSROOMS:</u> 52% of faculty are male; 48% are female. All teach undergraduates. No introductory courses are taught by graduate students.

<u>PROGRAMS OF STUDY:</u> Missouri Southern confers B.A., B.S., B.G.S., B.S.B.A. and B.S.E. degrees. Associate and Master's degrees are also awarded. Bachelor's degrees are awarded in AGRICULTURE (conservation and regulation), BIOLOGICAL SCIENCE (biochemistry, bioinformatics, biology/adolescence education, ecology, forensic science, life science, marine biology, microbiology, and physiology), BUSINESS (accounting, business administration and management, finance, financial services, human resources/organizational mgmt, international business, international business information systems, logistics, management information systems, marketing, and marketing management), COMMUNICATIONS AND THE ARTS (art, art and design, art/visual culture, choral music, communications, English/literature/Writing, fine arts/studio arts, general, French, German, graphic design, instrumental music education, language arts, literature, music, music industry, piano performance, public relations, speech and theatre education, studio art, studio art painting, theatre arts, theatre studies, and vocal performance), COMPUTER AND PHYSICAL SCIENCE (applied science, chemistry, Computer Engineering Technology, computer information systems, computer science, industrial technology, mathematics, mathematics/computational, physics and mathematics, physics, radiological technology, science, and science technology), EDUCATION (business education, (Education) Childhood Education, computer education, early childhood education, elementary education, English education, mathematics education, middle school education, physical education, reading education, science education, social science education, social studies education, social studies secondary school education, spanish education K-12, special education, and teaching English as a second/

foreign language (TESOL/TEFOL)), ENGINEERING AND ENVIRONMENTAL DESIGN (manufacturing technology and transportation technology), HEALTH PROFESSIONS (dental hygiene, environmental health science, health, health promotion, health science, medical technology, predentistry, premedicine, preoptometry, pre-occupational therapy, prepharmacy, pre-physician assistant, pre-physical therapy, preveterinary science, and respiratory therapy), SOCIAL SCIENCE (criminal justice, early childhood studies, economics, forensic studies, history, justice and society, law enforcement and corrections, political science/government, psychology, social studies, and sociology). Criminal Justice, health professions and related programs, and business/marketing are the strongest academically. Teacher education, criminal justice, and biology-environmental health have the largest enrollments.

ACTIVITIES: There are 77 groups on campus, including art, band, cheerleading, chess, choir, chorale, chorus, communications, computers, dance, debate, drama, ethnic, film, forensics, honors, international, jazz band, literary magazine, marching band, musical theater, newspaper, orchestra, pep band, photography, political, professional, radio and TV, religious, social, social service, student government, and symphony. Popular campus events include Spring Fling, Natural High, and International Semesters. **Sports:** There are 7 intercollegiate sports for men and 7 for women, and 10 intramural sports for men and 10 for women. Facilities include a 10,000-seat Astroturf football stadium, 4000-seat gym, 4000-seat auditorium, a natatorium, student life center, black-box theater, 3240-seat gym with basketball court, 6-lane 200-meter indoor track, training and weight room, cross-country course, and soccer, softball, and baseball fields. **Graduates:** From July 1, 2013 to June 30, 2014, 804 bachelor's degrees were awarded. The most popular majors were criminal justice (20%), health professions and related programs (19%), and business/marketing (19%). 236 companies recruited on campus in 2013-2014. In an average class, 15% graduate in 4 years or less, 31% graduate in 5 years or less, and 36% graduate in 6 years or less.

SERVICES: Counseling and information services are available, as is tutoring in some subjects, and business courses. There is a reader service for the blind, and remedial math, reading, and writing. Assistance is also provided for improving time management and test-taking skills. **Library/Resources:** The library contains 1.3 million volumes, 782,282 microform items, 4,990 audio/video tapes/CDs/DVDs, and subscribes to 265 periodicals including electronic. Computerized library services include interlibrary loans, database searching, Internet access, and Wi-Fi capability. Special learning facilities include an art gallery, radio station, TV station, a biology pond, child development center, crime lab, small business development center, performing arts center, greenhouse, and an international trade and quality center. **Physically Challenged Students:** 99% of the campus is accessible. Facilities include wheelchair ramps, elevators, special parking, specially equipped restrooms, special class scheduling, lowered drinking fountains, lowered telephones, and special housing. **Special:** There are co-op programs in radiological and medical technology, respiratory therapy, paramedical studies, aviation, and engineering. Students may study abroad at Oxford or Cambridge and in 100 countries through ISEP. Missouri Southern also offers internships in many majors, accelerated degree programs in all majors, a 3-2 engineering degree with the University of Missouri-Rolla, a general studies degree, and credit for life experience. Nondegree study is possible. There are 12 national honor societies, a freshman honors program, and 1 departmental honors programs. **Visiting:** There are regularly scheduled orientations for prospective students, including a preenrollment tour during the summer. There are guides for informal visits, visitors may sit in on classes, and stay overnight. To schedule a visit, contact Derek Skaggs at skaggs-d@mssu.edu. **Campus Safety and Security:** Measures include 24-hour foot and vehicle patrol, emergency notification system, and self-defense education. There are emergency telephones, lighted pathways/sidewalks, controlled access to dorms/residences, officers on duty 24/7, even on holidays. We have a redundancy of notification systems, including Rave messaging. The RAD self-defense for girls is taught as a regular class in Fall/Spring. We also teach the ALICE concepts (active shooter response) to students in the University Experience classes.

REQUIREMENTS: The ACT is required. Applicants must be graduates of accredited secondary schools or have earned a GED. The college requires completion of 16 Carnegie units in core courses for high school graduates. A GPA of 2.0 is required. AP and CLEP credits are accepted. General education requirements include a total of 51 credit hours, with 15 in basic studies, 12 each in science and cultural studies, 9 in humanities, and 3 in international studies. Students must also demonstrate proficiency in computer skills and writing. To graduate, students must complete at least 124 credit hours, including a minimum of 40 in the major, and present a minimum GPA of 2.0 (2.75 for the B.S.E.). **Procedure:** Freshmen are admitted to all sessions. Entrance exams should be taken during the junior or senior year of high school. There are deferred admissions and rolling admissions plans. Applications should be filed by September 1 for fall entry, along with a $25 fee. Notification is sent on a rolling basis. Applications are accepted on-line. **Transfer Students:** 582 transfer students enrolled in 2013-2014. Applicants must have a GPA of 2.0 and must be able to return to their previous college. 30 of 124 credits required for the bachelor's degree must be completed at Missouri Southern. **International Students:** There are 193 international students enrolled. The school actively recruits these students. They must take the TOEFL or MELAB. They must also take the ACT, scoring 18.

ADMISSIONS: 96% of the 2014-2015 applicants were accepted. The ACT scores were 18% below 21, and 53% between 21 and 23. 29% of the current freshmen were in the top fifth of their class; 57% were in the top two fifths. **Admissions Contact:** Derek S. Skaggs, Director of Admissions. E-Mail: *admissions@mssu.edu* Web: *www.mssu.edu*

FINANCIAL AID: In 2014-2015, 95% of all full-time freshmen and 90% of continuing full-time students received some form of financial aid. 73% of all full-time freshmen and 75% of continuing full-time students received need-based aid. The average freshman award was $4,352. Need-based scholarships or need-based grants averaged $2,429 ($3,865 maximum); need-based self-help aid (loans and jobs) averaged $1,663 ($3,464 maximum); non-need-based athletic scholarships averaged $2,798 ($5,256 maximum); and other non-need-based awards and non-need-based scholarships averaged $2,026 ($8,666 maximum). The average financial indebtedness of the 2014 graduate was $18,690. The FAFSA is required. The priority date for freshman financial aid applications for fall entry is April 1. The deadline for filing freshman financial aid applications for fall entry is October 1.

MISSOURI STATE UNIVERSITY   **B-3**
www.missouristate.edu

Springfield, MO 65897   **(417) 836-5000**
                                             (800) 492-7900
Fax: (417) 836-6334   Email: info@missouristate.edu
Full-time: 5910 men, 8085 women   **Faculty:** IIA, -$
Part-time: 1025 men, 1157 women   **Ph.D.s:** 71%
Graduate: 1095 men, 1838 women   **Student/Faculty:** 20 to 1
Year: semesters, summer session   **Tuition:** $7008 ($13,668)
Room & Board: $7864   **Freshman Class:** 8044
                                       applied, 6840 accepted,
                                       2801 enrolled
SAT CR/M: 545/535 **ACT:** 24   **CEEB CODE:** 6665
Application Deadline: July 20   **COMPETITIVE+**

Missouri State University, founded in 1905, is a public institution offering undergraduate programs in arts and letters, business administration, humanities and social sciences, education and psychology, health and applied sciences, and science and math. There are 7 undergraduate schools and 1 graduate school. In addition to regional accreditation, MSU has baccalaureate program accreditation with AACSB, ABET, ACCE, ACPE, APTA, CSWE, NASM, NCATE, ACEND, ACPHA, and ARC-PA. The 304-acre campus is in a suburban area 220 miles southwest of St. Louis. Including any residence halls, there are 61 buildings.

STUDENT LIFE: 84% of undergraduates are from Missouri. Others are from 50 states, 83 foreign countries, and Canada. 84% are White. The average age of freshmen is 18; all undergraduates, 22. 25% do not continue beyond their first year; 55% remain to graduate. **Housing:** 4000 students can be accommodated in college housing, which includes coed dorms, on-campus apartments, and married student housing. In addition, there are honors houses, fraternity houses, sorority houses, coed dorms, apartments for single students and housing for disabled students, and theme housing. On-campus housing is guaranteed for all 4 years. 73% of students commute. Alcohol is not permitted. All students may keep cars.

FACULTY/CLASSROOMS: 52% of faculty are male; 48% are female. No introductory courses are taught by graduate students. The average class size in a regular course is 23.

PROGRAMS OF STUDY: MSU confers B.S.A.T., B.A., B.A.S., B.F.A., B.M.U.S., B.M.E., B.S., B.S.Ed., B.S.N. and B.S.W. degrees. Master's and Doctoral degrees are also awarded. Bachelor's degrees are awarded in AGRICULTURE (agriculture, animal science, environmental studies, plant science, and wildlife management), BIOLOGICAL SCIENCE (biology/biological science and cell biology), BUSINESS (accounting, apparel and textiles, business administration and management, entrepreneurial studies, fashion merchandising, finance, logistics, management science, marketing/retailing/merchandising, and recreation and leisure services), COMMUNICATIONS AND THE ARTS (art history, art, communications, communication science, design, English, French, German, information technology, journalism, Latin, music, musical theater, performing arts, Spanish, speech/debate/rhetoric, and theatre arts), COMPUTER AND PHYSICAL SCIENCE (chemistry, computer science, geology, mathematics, and natural sciences), EDUCATION (agricultural education, athletic training, business education, computer education, early childhood education, education administration, elementary education, middle school education, physical education, science education, and special education), ENGINEERING AND ENVIRONMENTAL DESIGN (construction management, interior design, and materials science), HEALTH PROFESSIONS (clinical science, exercise science, health care administration, health promotion, hospital administration, nursing, physical therapy, physician's assistant, radiological science, respiratory therapy, and speech pathology/audiology), SOCIAL SCIENCE (anthropology, child psychology/development, counseling/psychology, criminology, dietetics, economics, family/consumer studies, fashion design and technology, geography, gerontology, (Social Science) Global Studies, history, philosophy, political science/government, religion, social work, and sociology). Business and education have the largest enrollments.

ACTIVITIES: Groups on campus include art, band, campus ministries, cheerleading, chess, choir, chorale, chorus, communications, computers, dance, drama, drill team, environmental, ethnic, film, gay, honors, international, jazz band, literary magazine, marching band, musical theater, newspaper, opera, orchestra, pep band, political, professional, radio and TV, religious, social, social service, student government, and symphony. Popular campus events include Tent Theater, Spring Fling, Community Service Fair and Leadership Conference. **Sports:** There are 6 intercollegiate sports for men and 10 for women, and 23 intramural sports for men and 22 for women. Facilities include a 16,600-seat stadium, 11,000-seat arena, 8,858 seat arena, a swimming pool, softball and practice fields, tennis courts, bowling lanes, and the state-of-the-art Foster recreation center. **Graduates:** From July 1, 2013 to June 30, 2014, 3060 bachelor's degrees were awarded. The most popular majors were business/marketing (27%), education (13%), and social sciences (8%). 610 companies recruited on campus in 2013-2014. In an average class, 32% graduate in 4 years or less, 50% graduate in 5 years or less, and 55% graduate in 6 years or less. Of the 2013 graduating class, 70% were employed within 6 months of graduation.

SERVICES: Counseling and information services are available, as is tutoring in some subjects. There is a reader service for the blind, and remedial math, reading, and writing. A math center and a writing center are available for student use. Proctors are available for tests given to those with disabilities. **Library/Resources:** The library contains 782,257 volumes, 1.1 million microform items, 19,708 audio/video tapes/CDs/DVDs, and subscribes to 37,000 periodicals including electronic. Computerized library services include interlibrary loans, database searching, Internet access, and Wi-Fi capability. Special learning facilities include an art gallery, radio station, and TV station. **Physically Challenged Students:** All of the campus is accessible. Facilities include wheelchair ramps, elevators, special parking, specially equipped restrooms, special class scheduling, lowered drinking fountains, lowered telephones, special housing. **Special:** MSU offers

co-op programs, internships, study abroad in 40 countries, and work-study programs. Also available are B.A.-B.S. degrees in 12 majors, preprofessional programs in law and medicine, accelerated degree programs and student-designed and interdisciplinary majors, including antiquities, agriculture business and agriculture education, chemistry/biochemistry, communication management, and finance/real estate. A 3-2 engineering degree is available through the University of Missouri-Rolla. Credit for military experience and pass/not-pass options are offered. There are 27 national honor societies and a freshman honors program. **Visiting:** There are regularly scheduled orientations for prospective students, guests can request an appointment with an admissions advisor, an academic department, or other areas of interest.. There are guides for informal visits. To schedule a visit, contact the Admissions Office. **Campus Safety and Security:** Measures include 24-hour foot and vehicle patrol, emergency notification system, self-defense education, and security escort services. There are shuttle buses, emergency telephones, lighted pathways/sidewalks, and controlled access to dorms/residences.

REQUIREMENTS: Either SAT or ACT is required for admittance; the ACT is preferred. Admission is based on a sliding scale of rank or GPA and test score. Freshmen must also have a 17-unit high school core curriculum, including 4 in English, 3 each in math, science (with 1 lab), and academic electives, 2 in social studies and 1 each in visual and performing arts, and history. AP and CLEP credits are accepted. Important factors in the admissions decision are advanced placement or honors courses and extracurricular activities record.A total of 125 to 130 semester hours, including 30 to 60 in the major, and a minimum GPA of 2.0 are required. 45 general education semester hours are required, to include 8 in natural sciences, 6 to 9 each in social sciences and humanities, 6 in American studies, 4 in phys ed, 3 to 6 in English composition, 3 each in math and speech, and 1 in freshman orientation. Arts/fine arts and computer literacy classes are also required. **Procedure:** Freshmen are admitted fall, spring, and summer. Entrance exams should be taken as early as possible. There is a rolling admissions plan. Applications should be filed by July 20 for fall entry, along with a $35 fee. Notification is sent on a rolling basis. Applications are accepted on-line. Application fees are waived if application is completed on-line. **Transfer Students:** 1707 transfer students enrolled in 2013-2014. Applicants must present a minimum GPA of 2.0 on transferable courses. College transcripts are required. If they have completed less than 24 semester hours, they are also required to meet freshman admission requirements. 30 of 125 credits required for the bachelor's degree must be completed at MSU. **International Students:** There are 780 international students enrolled. The school actively recruits these students. They must take the TOEFL with a minimum score of 500 on the paper-based TOEFL (PBT) or 61 on the Internet-based version (iBT). They must also take the ACT.

ADMISSIONS: 85% of the 2014-2015 applicants were accepted. The SAT scores for the 2014-2015 freshman class were: Critical Reading--33% below 500, 38% between 500 and 599, 25% between 600 and 699, and 5% between 700 and 800; Math--33% below 500, 40% between 500 and 599, 27% between 600 and 699, and 1% between 700 and 800. The ACT scores were 2% below 21, 45% between 21 and 23, 45% between 27 and 28, and 9% above 28. 37% of the current freshmen were in the top fifth of their class; 62% were in the top two fifths. **Admissions Contact:** Benjamin P. Metzger, Assistant Director Admissons-Office Oper. E-Mail: *info@missouristate.edu* Web: *www.missouristate.edu*

FINANCIAL AID: In 2014-2015, 64% of all full-time freshmen and 59% of continuing full-time students received some form of financial aid. 64% of all full-time freshmen and 59% of continuing full-time students received need-based aid. The average freshman award was $9,457. Need-based scholarships or need-based grants averaged $6,147; need-based self-help aid (loans and jobs) averaged $5,591; non-need-based athletic scholarships averaged $11,221; other non-need-based awards and non-need-based scholarships averaged $3,471; and $3,235 from other forms of aid. The average financial indebtedness of the 2014 graduate was $24,655. MSU is a member of CSS. The FAFSA is required. The priority date for freshman financial aid applications for fall entry is March 30. The deadline for filing freshman financial aid applications for fall entry is rolling.

MISSOURI UNIVERSITY OF SCIENCE AND   C-3 TECHNOLOGY
www.futurestudents.mst.edu

Rolla, MO 65409

(573) 341-4164
(800) 522-0938

Fax: (573) 341-4082

Email: admissions@mst.edu

Full-time: 4227 men, 1245 women

Faculty: 361; I, av$

Part-time: 487 men, 187 women

Ph.D.s: 89%

Graduate: 1577 men, 407 women

Student/Faculty: 15 to 1

Year: semesters, summer session

Tuition: $9510 ($24,675)

Room & Board: $9145

Freshman Class: n/av

SAT CR/M: 590/640 ACT: 28

CEEB CODE: 6876

Application Deadline: July 1

VERY COMPETITIVE+

Missouri University of Science and Technology, founded in 1870, is part of the University of Missouri system. A public research institution, it offers comprehensive undergraduate and graduate programs and confers degrees in arts and sciences, engineering, mines and metallurgy, and management and information systems. In addition to regional accreditation, Missouri S&T has baccalaureate program accreditation with AACSB, ABET, CSAB, EAC, and CAC. The 284-acre campus is in a small town 100 miles southwest of St. Louis, MO and 100 miles northeast of Springfield, MO. Including any residence halls, there are 72 buildings.

STUDENT LIFE: 77% of undergraduates are from Missouri. Others are from 49 states, 60 foreign countries, and Canada. 78% are White. **Male To Female Ratio:** 0.3:1. The average age of freshmen is 18; all undergraduates, 21. 17% do not continue beyond their first year; 63% remain to graduate. **Housing:** 2152 students can be accommodated in college housing, which includes coed dorms, on-campus apartments, and married student housing. In addition, there are honors houses, fraternity houses, sorority houses, Residential college, learning community, and holistic community. On-campus housing is guaranteed for the freshman year only, is available on a first-come, and first-served basis. Alcohol is not permitted. All students may keep cars.

FACULTY/CLASSROOMS: 75% of faculty are male; 25% are female. No introductory courses are taught by graduate students.

PROGRAMS OF STUDY: Missouri S&T confers B.A., and B.S. degrees. Master's and Doctoral degrees are also awarded. Bachelor's degrees are awarded in BIOLOGICAL SCIENCE (biology/biological science, environmental biology, and life science), BUSINESS (business administration and management and management information systems), COMMUNICATIONS AND THE ARTS (English and technical and business writing), COMPUTER AND PHYSICAL SCIENCE (applied mathematics, chemistry, computer science, geology, geophysics and seismology, information sciences and systems, mathematics, physics, and statistics), EDUCATION (secondary education), ENGINEERING AND ENVIRONMENTAL DESIGN (aeronautical engineering, architectural engineering, ceramic engineering, chemical engineering, civil engineering, computer engineering, electrical/electronics engineering, engineering management, engineering mechanics, environmental engineering, geological engineering, manufacturing engineering, materials engineering, mechanical engineering, metallurgical engineering, mining and mineral engineering, nuclear engineering, petroleum/natural gas engineering, and systems engineering), HEALTH PROFESSIONS (premedicine), SOCIAL SCIENCE (economics, history, philosophy, prelaw, and psychology). Engineering, science and technology are the strongest academically. Engineering, arts, sciences, mines and metallurgy have the largest enrollments.

ACTIVITIES: 21% of men belong to 23 national fraternities; 19% of women belong to 5 national sororities. There are 221 groups on campus, including art, band, cheerleading, chess, choir, chorale, chorus, computers, dance, drama, drill team, ethnic, gay, honors, international, jazz band, literary magazine, marching band, musical theater, newspaper, orchestra, pep band, political, professional, radio and TV, religious, social, social service, student government, symphony, and yearbook. Popular campus events include St. Patrick's Day, Homecoming, Campus Block Party and Celebration of Nations. **Sports:** There are 8 intercollegiate sports for men and 7 for women,

and 20 intramural sports for men and 19 for women. Facilities include a gym, weight room, pool, a nine hole golf course, track, racquetball and tennis courts, baseball and soccer fields, and a 5000-seat stadium. **Graduates:** From July 1, 2013 to June 30, 2014, 1118 bachelor's degrees were awarded. The most popular majors were mechanical engineering (15%), civil engineering (12%), and electrical engineering (8%). 872 companies recruited on campus in 2013-2014. In an average class, 63% graduate in 6 years or less. Of the 2013 graduating class, 16% were enrolled in graduate school within 6 months of graduation, and 57% were employed.

SERVICES: Counseling and information services are available, as is tutoring in most subjects. There is a reader service for the blind. **Library/Resources:** The library contains 479,874 volumes, 423,403 microform items, 4,634 audio/video tapes/CDs/DVDs, and subscribes to 3,901 periodicals including electronic. Computerized library services include interlibrary loans, database searching, Internet access, and Wi-Fi capability. Special learning facilities include a radio station, a writing center, student design center, nuclear reactor, observatory, explosives testing labs, and underground mine, hot glass shop. **Physically Challenged Students:** 95% of the campus is accessible. Facilities include wheelchair ramps, elevators, special parking, specially equipped restrooms, special class scheduling, lowered drinking fountains, lowered telephones, special housing. **Special:** MS&T offers internships in business and government, co-op programs in which students work and attend school on alternating schedules, and study abroad in more than 40 countries. Accelerated degrees in science and engineering, dual majors, B.A.-B.S. degrees, a 3-2 engineering degree, work-study programs, credit for life/military/work experience, and pass/fail options in certain courses are also available. There are 28 national honor societies, a freshman honors program, and 16 departmental honors programs. **Visiting:** There are regularly scheduled orientations for prospective students, including a tour with a student, admissions and financial aid counseling, special interest contact, and a departmental visit with a faculty member. There are guides for informal visits, visitors may sit in on classes, and stay overnight. To schedule a visit, contact Admissions Office at admissions@mst.edu. **Campus Safety and Security:** Measures include 24-hour foot and vehicle patrol, emergency notification system, self-defense education, and security escort services. There are shuttle buses, emergency telephones, lighted pathways/sidewalks, crime prevention and rape/sexual assault programs.

REQUIREMENTS: The SAT or ACT is required. In addition, the sum of the high school student's class rank percentile and aptitude exam percentile must be 120 or higher. Candidates must be graduates of an accredited secondary school or have the GED. The applicant must have completed 16 academic credit units, including 4 each in English and math, 3 each in science and social studies, and 2 in a foreign language. AP and CLEP credits are accepted. Important factors in the admissions decision are leadership record, extracurricular activities record, and advanced placement or honors courses. Candidates for graduation must maintain at least a 2.0 GPA. A total of 120 credits is required. A Senior assessment exam is required. **Procedure:** Freshmen are admitted fall, winter, and summer. Entrance exams should be taken late in the junior year or early in the senior year. There are deferred admissions and rolling admissions plans. Early decision applications should be filed by December 1; regular applications, by July 1 for fall entry; December 1 for spring entry; and May 1 for summer entry, along with a $50 fee. Applications are accepted on-line. **Transfer Students:** 427 transfer students enrolled in 2013-2014. Applicants with fewer than 24 semester hours of college-level work must apply as freshmen; those with 24 or more must have attained at least a 2.0 GPA in all college-level courses. 60 of 120 credits required for the bachelor's degree must be completed at Missouri S&T . **International Students:** There are 384 international students enrolled. The school actively recruits these students. They must take the TOEFL with a minimum score of 550 on the paper-based TOEFL (PBT) or 79 on the Internet-based version (iBT). They must also take the SAT or ACT.

ADMISSIONS: The SAT scores for the 2014-2015 freshman class were: Critical Reading--14% below 500, 35% between 500 and 599, 36% between 600 and 699, and 15% between 700 and 800; Math--5% below 500, 21% between 500 and 599, 54% between 600 and 699, and 21% between 700 and 800. The ACT scores were 1% below 21, 8%

between 21 and 23, 26% between 24 and 26, 19% between 27 and 28, and 46% above 28. 60% of the current freshmen were in the top fifth of their class; 88% were in the top two fifths. **Admissions Contact:** Lynn Stichnote, Director. E-Mail: *admissions@mst.edu* Web: *www. futurestudents.mst.edu*

FINANCIAL AID: In 2014-2015, 88% of all full-time freshmen and 90% of continuing full-time students received some form of financial aid. 43% of all full-time freshmen and 52% of continuing full-time students received need-based aid. The average freshman award was $11,773. Need-based scholarships or need-based grants averaged $9,131; need-based self-help aid (loans and jobs) averaged $3,755; non-need-based athletic scholarships averaged $5,569; and other non-need-based awards and non-need-based scholarships averaged $6,300. The average financial indebtedness of the 2014 graduate was $6,166. Missouri S&T is a member of CSS. The FAFSA is required. The priority date for freshman financial aid applications for fall entry is March 1.

MISSOURI VALLEY COLLEGE	B-2
www.moval.edu	
Marshall, MO 65340	(660) 831-4157
	n/av
Fax: (660) 831-4233	Email: langdond@moval.edu
Full-time: 840 men, 550 women	**Faculty:** n/av
Part-time: 20 men, 20 women	**Ph.D.s:** 44%
Graduate: n/av	**Student/Faculty:** n/av
Year: semesters, summer session	**Tuition:** $18,280
Room & Board: $7200	**Freshman Class:** n/av
SAT or ACT: required	**CEEB CODE:** 6413
Application Deadline: open	**COMPETITIVE**

Missouri Valley College, founded in 1889, is a private liberal arts college, affiliated with the Presbyterian Church, offering 27 majors. The figures in the above capsule and in this profile are approximate. In addition to regional accreditation, MVC has baccalaureate program accreditation with CAHEA. The 150-acre campus is in a small town 50 miles northwest of Columbia and 80 miles northeast of Kansas City. Including any residence halls, there are 17 buildings.

STUDENT LIFE: 66% of undergraduates are from Missouri. Others are from 43 states, 26 foreign countries, and Canada. 75% are from public schools. 83% are White; 17% African American. 45% are Protestant; 32% Islamic, Mormon, Orthodox, Agnostic and unknown; 14% Catholic. **Male To Female Ratio:** 0.7:1. The average age of freshmen is 19; all undergraduates, 21. 48% do not continue beyond their first year; 20% remain to graduate. **Housing:** 1100 students can be accommodated in college housing, which includes single-sex and coed dorms and on-campus apartments. In addition, there are honors houses, special-interest houses, fraternity houses, and sorority houses. On-campus housing is guaranteed for all 4 years. 72% of students live on campus; of those, 50% remain on campus on weekends. Alcohol is not permitted. All students may keep cars.

FACULTY/CLASSROOMS: 73% of faculty are male; 27% are female. All teach undergraduates. No introductory courses are taught by graduate students. The average class size in an introductory lecture is 30; in a laboratory is 25; and in a regular course is 18.

PROGRAMS OF STUDY: MVC confers B.A., B.S. and B.F.A. degrees. Associate degrees are also awarded. Bachelor's degrees are awarded in BIOLOGICAL SCIENCE (biology/biological science), BUSINESS (accounting, business administration and management, and recreational facilities management), COMMUNICATIONS AND THE ARTS (art, communications, dramatic arts, English, and speech/debate/rhetoric), COMPUTER AND PHYSICAL SCIENCE (information sciences and systems and mathematics), EDUCATION (elementary education, physical education, and social studies education), HEALTH PROFESSIONS (exercise science), SOCIAL SCIENCE (addiction studies, anthropology, criminal justice, economics, history, human services, liberal arts/general studies, philosophy, political science/government, psychology, public administration, religion, and sociology). Education is the strongest academically. Business administration, phys ed, and psychology have the largest enrollments.

ACTIVITIES: 15% of men belong to 4 national fraternities; 8% of women belong to 2 national sororities. There are 40 groups on campus, including art, cheerleading, choir, chorale, chorus, computers, dance, drama, ethnic, film, honors, international, jazz band, literary magazine, musical theater, newspaper, photography, radio and TV, religious, SADD, social, social service, student government, and yearbook. Popular campus events include Springfest, Maastricht Institute of Entrepreneurship, and Guerilla Film Festival. **Sports:** There are 13 intercollegiate sports for men and 12 for women, and 7 intramural sports for men and 7 for women. Facilities include a 2000-seat gym, tennis and basketball courts, football and soccer fields, a 1000-seat stadium, and horse stables. **Graduates:** From July 1, 2013 to June 30, 2014, 251 bachelor's degrees were awarded. The most popular majors were business administration (18%), criminal justice (16%), and education (6%). In an average class, 3% graduate in 3 years or less, 20% graduate in 4 years or less, 27% graduate in 5 years or less, and 22% graduate in 6 years or less.

SERVICES: Counseling and information services are available, as is tutoring in most subjects. There is remedial math, reading, and writing. **Library/Resources:** The 2 libraries contain 75,000 volumes, 27,000 microform items, 1,600 audio/video tapes/CDs/DVDs, and subscribe to 250 periodicals including electronic. Computerized library services include interlibrary loans, database searching, Internet access, and Wi-Fi capability. Special learning facilities include a radio station and TV station. **Physically Challenged Students:** 65% of the campus is accessible. Facilities include wheelchair ramps, elevators, special parking, specially equipped restrooms, and special class scheduling. **Special:** Accelerated degree programs, internships, study abroad, work-study, co-op programs, nondegree study, and pass/fail options are available. There are 3 national honor societies and 3 departmental honors programs. **Visiting:** There are regularly scheduled orientations for prospective students, including jump-start days in the summer and registration days during the school year. There are guides for informal visits, visitors may sit in on classes, and stay overnight. To schedule a visit, contact the Admission Coordinator. **Campus Safety and Security:** Measures include emergency notification system and security escort services. There are shuttle buses, emergency telephones, and lighted pathways/sidewalks.

REQUIREMENTS: The SAT or ACT is required. Students must have graduated from an accredited secondary school or have the GED. Auditions required for performance-based scholarships MVC requires applicants to be in the upper 50% of their class. A GPA of 2.0 is required. AP and CLEP credits are accepted. Important factors in the admissions decision are advanced placement or honors courses, evidence of special talent, and extracurricular activities record. Students must complete 128 hours, with 30 to 50 hours in the major and 40 hours in a core curriulum. A 2.0 GPA is also required. **Procedure:** Freshmen are admitted to all sessions. Entrance exams should be taken as early as possible. There is a rolling admissions plan. Application deadlines are open. Application fee is $15. Notification is sent on a rolling basis. Applications are accepted on-line. **Transfer Students:** A minimum GPA of 2.0 is recommended; D grades do not transfer. Official transcripts are required for all previous colleges attended. Students with fewer than 27 credits transferring must submit high school transcripts as well. 30 of 128 credits required for the bachelor's degree must be completed at MVC. **International Students:** There are 131 international students enrolled. The school actively recruits these students. They must take the TOEFL. They must also take the SAT or ACT.

ADMISSIONS: Tennille Langdon, Director of Admissions. E-Mail: *langdond@moval.edu* Web: *www.moval.edu*

FINANCIAL AID: MVC is a member of CSS. The FAFSA is required. Check with the school for current application deadlines.

MISSOURI WESTERN STATE UNIVERSITY (*The complete profile is made available exclusively on our website, www.barronspac.com*)

NORTHWEST MISSOURI STATE UNIVERSITY   A-1
www.nwmissouri.edu

Maryville, MO 64468	(660) 562-1146
	(800) 633-1175
Fax: (660) 562-1121	Email: tammi@nwmissouri.edu
Full-time: 2196 men, 2784 women	Faculty: 250; IIA, --$
Part-time: 259 men, 252 women	Ph.D.s: 64%
Graduate: 687 men, 542 women	Student/Faculty: 22 to 1
Year: trimesters, summer session	Tuition: $8155 ($14,407)
Room & Board: $9192	Freshman Class: 5570 applied, 4165 accepted, 1297 enrolled
SAT CR/M: 473/523 ACT: 22	CEEB CODE: 6488
Application Deadline: open	COMPETITIVE

Northwest Missouri State University, founded in 1905, is a public institution offering undergraduate courses in agriculture, science, arts and humanities, business, government, computer science, and education. There are 3 undergraduate schools and 1 graduate school. In addition to regional accreditation, Northwest has baccalaureate program accreditation with AACSB, ADA, AHEA, NASM, NCATE, AACTE, AAFCS, and ACS. The 370-acre campus is in a small town 90 miles north of Kansas City. Including any residence halls, there are 35 buildings.

STUDENT LIFE: 68% of undergraduates are from Missouri. Others are from 44 states, and 24 foreign countries. 97% are from public schools. 80% are White. **Male To Female Ratio:** 1.1:1. The average age of freshmen is 18; all undergraduates, 21. 34% do not continue beyond their first year; 59% remain to graduate. **Housing:** 2987 students can be accommodated in college housing, which includes single-sex and coed dorms, on-campus apartments, and married student housing. In addition, there are fraternity houses and sorority houses. On-campus housing is guaranteed for all 4 years and is guaranteed for the freshman year only. 59% of students commute. Alcohol is not permitted. All students may keep cars.

FACULTY/CLASSROOMS: 52% of faculty are male; 48% are female. All teach undergraduates. No introductory courses are taught by graduate students. The average class size in an introductory lecture is 40; in a laboratory is 20; and in a regular course is 25.

PROGRAMS OF STUDY: Northwest confers B.A., B.S., B.F.A., B.S.Ed., B.S.Med.Tech., B.S.N. and B.Tech. degrees. Master's degrees are also awarded. Bachelor's degrees are awarded in AGRICULTURE (agricultural business management, agricultural economics, agricultural mechanics, agriculture, agronomy, animal science, conservation and regulation, forestry and related sciences, horticulture, and wildlife management), BIOLOGICAL SCIENCE (biology/biological science, botany, ecology, marine biology, and zoology), BUSINESS (accounting, apparel and textiles, banking and finance, business administration and management, business economics, international business, international business management, marketing/retailing/merchandising, and recreation and leisure services), COMMUNICATIONS AND THE ARTS (advertising, American Sign Language, art, broadcasting, communications, dramatic arts, English, fine arts, journalism, music, public relations, Spanish, and speech/debate/rhetoric), COMPUTER AND PHYSICAL SCIENCE (chemistry, computer management, computer science, data processing, earth science, geology, information sciences and systems, mathematics, physics, science, and statistics), EDUCATION (agricultural education, art education, business education, early childhood education, education of the mentally handicapped, elementary education, English education, mathematics education, middle school education, music education, physical education, recreation education, science education, secondary education, special education, and specific learning disabilities), ENGINEERING AND ENVIRONMENTAL DESIGN (emergency/disaster science and preengineering), HEALTH PROFESSIONS (biology, predentistry, premedicine, prepharmacy, and preveterinary science), SOCIAL SCIENCE (child care/child and family studies, economics, family/consumer resource management, food science, geography, history, humanities, industrial and organizational psychology, philosophy, political science/government, prelaw, psychol-

ogy, public administration, social psychology, social science, sociology, and textiles and clothing). Teacher education, business management , psychology, and agriculture are the strongest and have the largest enrollments.

ACTIVITIES: 19% of men belong to 10 national fraternities; 18% of women belong to 7 national sororities. There are 152 groups on campus, including band, cheerleading, choir, chorale, chorus, computers, dance, debate, drama, drill team, drum and bugle corps, ethnic, film, forensics, gay, international, jazz band, literary magazine, marching band, newspaper, orchestra, pep band, photography, political, professional, radio and TV, religious, social, student government, symphony, and yearbook. Popular campus events include SAC Fall and Spring Concerts, Homecoming Events, Football Games, Arrowhead (Fall Classic), Up 'Til Dawn Colden Pond Plunge, SAC Grocery Bingo, SAC Late Night events, Greek Life Bid Day, and Advantage Week Fireworks. **Sports:** There are 7 intercollegiate sports for men and 9 for women, and 12 intramural sports for men and 13 for women. Facilities include a 7000-seat stadium, a 3000-seat basketball arena, 3 gyms, 4 racquetball courts, a weight-lifting area,baseball and softball fields, volleyball and tennis courts,dance areas, frisbee golf course, brand new cricket pitch (first in the region). **Graduates:** From July 1, 2013 to June 30, 2014, 1022 bachelor's degrees were awarded. The most popular majors were business/marketing (23%), education (19%), and agriculture (10%). 180 companies recruited on campus in 2013-2014. In an average class, 29% graduate in 4 years or less, 47% graduate in 5 years or less, and 50% graduate in 6 years or less. Of the 2013 graduating class, 17% were enrolled in graduate school within 6 months of graduation, and 80% were employed.

SERVICES: Counseling and information services are available, as is tutoring in most subjects. There is a reader service for the blind, and remedial math, reading, and writing. **Library/Resources:** The library contains 359,371 volumes, 11,515 microform items, 4,920 audio/video tapes/CDs/DVDs, and subscribes to 34,096 periodicals including electronic. Computerized library services include interlibrary loans, database searching, Internet access, and Wi-Fi capability. Special learning facilities include an art gallery, radio station, TV station, Missouri Arboretum, Mozingo Outdoor Education Recreation Area (observatory, ropes challenge course, trap and archery, canoes and kayaks), Horace Mann Laboratory School, R.T. Wright Farm (dairy operation, swine herd, horticulture complex, experimental farmland), Center for Innovation and Entrepreneurship (business incubator), Studio Theater and Black Box experimental theater, online Northwest History Museum, Science Museum, Agriculture Museum, Jean Jennings Bartik Computing Museum, Warren Stucki Museum of Broadcasting, Student Media Converged Newsroom, Joyce and Harvey White International Plaza. **Physically Challenged Students:** All of the campus is accessible. Facilities include wheelchair ramps, elevators, special parking, specially equipped restrooms, special class scheduling, lowered drinking fountains, and lowered telephones. **Special:** Campus-wide internships, study abroad program (England, Mexico, Spain, Netherlands, etc. Work-study programs, student designed majors, a 3-2 engineering degree with the Missouri University of Science and Technology, credit for military experience, service learning, nondegree study, and pass/fail options are possible. There are 3 national honor societies and a freshman honors program. **Visiting:** There are regularly scheduled orientations for prospective students. There are guides for informal visits, visitors may sit in on classes, and stay overnight. To schedule a visit, contact Mabel Cook Recruitment and Visitors Center at admissions@nwmissouri.edu. **Campus Safety and Security:** Measures include 24-hour foot and vehicle patrol, emergency notification system, self-defense education, and security escort services. There are shuttle buses, lighted pathways/sidewalks, and controlled access to dorms/residences.

REQUIREMENTS: The ACT is required. A minimum composite score of 970 on the SAT or 21 on the ACT; if scores are below those levels, a combined percentile index obtained from the SAT or ACT score and high school rank will be used. A GPA of 2.0 is required. AP and CLEP credits are accepted. Important factors in the admissions decision are evidence of special talent and personality/intangible qualities. All students must maintain a minimum GPA of 2.0 while taking at least 124 credit hours. Distribution requirements include 9 hours each in social science and humanities, 8 in natural science, 6 in composition, 4 each in math and phys ed, 3 each in oral communications and behavioral sciences, and 1 in the freshman seminar. **Procedure:** Freshmen are admitted fall, spring, and summer. Entrance exams should be taken in the fall of the senior year. There is a rolling admissions plan. Application deadlines are open. Application fee is $25. Notifications are sent September 1. Applications are accepted on-line. Application fees are waived if application is completed on-line. **Transfer Students:** 236 transfer students enrolled in 2013-2014. Applicants must present a minimum GPA of 2.0. 30 of 124 credits required for the bachelor's degree must be completed at Northwest. **International Students:** There are 195 international students enrolled. The school actively recruits these students. They must take the TOEFL with a minimum score of 500 on the paper-based TOEFL (PBT) or 61 on the Internet-based version (iBT).

ADMISSIONS: 75% of the 2014-2015 applicants were accepted. The ACT scores were 29% below 21, 33% between 21 and 23, 21% between 24 and 26, 9% between 27 and 28, and 8% above 28. 31% of the current freshmen were in the top fifth of their class; 63% were in the top two fifths. 39 freshmen graduated first in their class. **Admissions Contact:** Tamera Grow, Associate Director of Admissions. E-Mail: *tammi@nwmissouri.edu* Web: *www.nwmissouri.edu/admissions*

FINANCIAL AID: In 2014-2015, 73% of all full-time freshmen and 69% of continuing full-time students received some form of financial aid. 63% of all full-time freshmen and 55% of continuing full-time students received need-based aid. The average freshman award was $11,121. Need-based scholarships or need-based grants averaged $7,028; need-based self-help aid (loans and jobs) averaged $3,409; and non-need-based athletic scholarships averaged $5,363. 53% of undergraduate students work part-time. Average annual earnings from campus work are $2390. The FAFSA is required. The priority date for freshman financial aid applications for fall entry is April 1.

PARK UNIVERSITY — A-2
www.park.edu

Parkville, MO 64152

(816) 584-6215
(800) 745-7275

Fax: (816) 741-4462

Email: admissions@park.edu

Full-time: 547 men, 657 women	Faculty: 94
Part-time: 182 men, 288 women	Ph.D.s: 54%
Graduate: 336 men, 448 women	Student/Faculty: 11 to 1
Year: semesters, summer session	Tuition: $10,480
Room & Board: $7045	Freshman Class: 778 applied, 539 accepted, 212 enrolled
ACT: 21	CEEB CODE: 6574
Application Deadline: n/av	COMPETITIVE

Park University, founded in 1875, is a private institution offering degree programs in the humanities, performing arts, natural and life sciences, and social and administrative sciences. Figures in the above capsule and in this profile are approximate. There are 3 undergraduate schools and 1 graduate school. In addition to regional accreditation, Park has baccalaureate program accreditation with NLN and CAATE. The 700-acre campus is in a suburban area 12 miles north of Kansas City. Including any residence halls, there are 17 buildings.

STUDENT LIFE: 80% of undergraduates are from Missouri. Others are from 50 states, 103 foreign countries, and Canada. 80% are from public schools. 52% are White; 19% Foreign. 88% claim no religious affiliation. **Male To Female Ratio:** 1.3:1. The average age of freshmen is 18; all undergraduates, 24. 39% do not continue beyond their first year; 41% remain to graduate. **Housing:** 410 students can be accommodated in college housing, which includes coed dorms and on-campus apartments. In addition, there are honors houses. On-campus housing is guaranteed for all 4 years. 80% of students commute. Alcohol is not permitted. All students may keep cars.

FACULTY/CLASSROOMS: 62% of faculty are male; 38% are female. All teach undergraduates, and 80% do research. No introductory courses are taught by graduate students. The average class size in an introductory lecture is 20; in a laboratory is 10; and in a regular course is 15.

PROGRAMS OF STUDY: Park confers B.A., B.S., B.P.A., B.S.W., B.S.N. and B.F.A. degrees. Associate and Master's degrees are also awarded. Bachelor's degrees are awarded in BIOLOGICAL SCIENCE (biology/biological science), BUSINESS (accounting, business administration and management, business economics, human resources, management information systems, and marketing management), COMMUNICATIONS AND THE ARTS (communications, dramatic arts, English, fine arts, graphic design, music, public relations, and Spanish), COMPUTER AND PHYSICAL SCIENCE (chemistry, computer science, information sciences and systems, mathematics, and natural sciences), EDUCATION (athletic training, early childhood education, and elementary education), ENGINEERING AND ENVIRONMENTAL DESIGN (aviation administration/management, computational sciences, engineering management, and interior design), HEALTH PROFESSIONS (health care administration), SOCIAL SCIENCE (child care/child and family studies, criminal justice, economics, fire protection, fire services administration, geography, history, human services, law, liberal arts/general studies, political science/government, psychology, public administration, social psychology, social work, and sociology). Management, management/computer information systems, and management/human resources have the largest enrollments.

ACTIVITIES: There are 30 groups on campus, including cheerleading, computers, drama, ethnic, honors, international, literary magazine, newspaper, photography, political, professional, radio and TV, religious, social, social service, and student government. Popular campus events include Fall Harvest Festival, Spring Fling and International Week. **Sports:** There are 6 intercollegiate sports for men and 7 for women, and 3 intramural sports for men and 3 for women. Facilities include 2 indoor gyms with basketball and volleyball courts, an all-weather outdoor track, soccer and softball fields, a sports medicine room, 4 tennis courts, and outdoor sand volleyball and basketball courts. **Graduates:** From July 1, 2013 to June 30, 2014, 398 bachelor's degrees were awarded. The most popular majors were business/management (24%), education (14%), and computer and information systems (13%). 15 companies recruited on campus in 2013-2014. In an average class, 6% graduate in 3 years or less, 53% graduate in 4 years or less, 36% graduate in 5 years or less, and 5% graduate in 6 years or less.

SERVICES: Counseling and information services are available, as is tutoring in most subjects. There is a reader service for the blind, and remedial math, reading, and writing. **Library/Resources:** The library contains 158,422 volumes, 195,530 microform items, 670 audio/video tapes/CDs/DVDs, and subscribes to 775 periodicals including electronic. Computerized library services include interlibrary loans and database searching. Special learning facilities include an art gallery, radio station, and TV station. **Physically Challenged Students:** 95% of the campus is accessible. Facilities include wheelchair ramps, elevators, special parking, specially equipped restrooms, special class scheduling, and lowered drinking fountains. **Special:** Cross-registration is available through a Kansas City consortium, and study abroad is possible through other schools. The university also offers internships in most majors, work-study programs with local companies, a Washington semester, credit for life and military experience, pass/fail options, and nondegree study. An accelerated degree program is offered in some majors. There are 2 national honor societies and a freshman honors program. **Visiting:** There are regularly scheduled orientations for prospective students, including a campus tour, lunch, an information session with a student panel, sessions on admissions, scholarships, and financial aid, and a chance to attend a class and meet with a faculty member. There are guides for informal visits, visitors may sit in on classes, and stay overnight. To schedule a visit, contact the Admissions and Student Financial Services. **Campus Safety and Security:** Measures include 24-hour foot and vehicle patrol and security escort services. There are emergency telephones and lighted pathways/sidewalks.

REQUIREMENTS: The ACT is required. The GED is accepted with a minimum total score of 225 and no area less than 35. Park requires applicants to be in the upper 50% of their class. A GPA of 2.0 is required. AP and CLEP credits are accepted. Important factors in the admissions decision are advanced placement or honors courses, leadership record, and extracurricular activities record. All students must complete core requirements, including 3 semesters of English composition and 1 of algebra, as well as 1 science course. They must also complete 24 to 27 hours of general education courses and 9 hours of liberal learning courses. Of the 120 credit hours needed for the bachelor's degree, 45 must be completed in upper-division work and 30 to 60 in the major, with a minimum GPA of 2.0. **Procedure:** Freshmen are admitted fall, spring, and summer. Entrance exams should be taken during the junior year or early in the senior year. There is a rolling admissions plan. Check with the school for current application deadlines. The application fee is $25. Notification is sent on a rolling basis. Applications are accepted on-line. **Transfer Students:** The college requires a GPA of at least 2.0. A minimum ACT composite score of 20 is recommended but is waived for students age 25 or older. 30 of 120 credits required for the bachelor's degree must be completed at Park. **International Students:** There are 324 international students enrolled. The school actively recruits these students. They must take the TOEFL. They must also take the ACT.

ADMISSIONS: 69% of the 2014-2015 applicants were accepted. The ACT scores were 50% below 21, 29% between 21 and 23, 9% between 24 and 26, 5% between 27 and 28, and 7% above 28. 29% of the current freshmen were in the top fifth of their class; 54% were in the top two fifths. **Admissions Contact:** Eric Blair, Director of Undergraduate Admissions. E-Mail: *admissions@park.edu* Web: *www.park.edu*

FINANCIAL AID: In 2014-2015, 62% of all full-time freshmen and 57% of continuing full-time students received some form of financial aid. 49% of all full-time freshmen and 42% of continuing full-time students received need-based aid. The average freshman award was $10,524. The average financial indebtedness of the 2014 graduate was $22,218. The FAFSA and the college's own financial statement are required. The priority date for freshman financial aid applications for fall entry is March 15. The deadline for filing freshman financial aid applications for fall entry is August 1.

RESEARCH COLLEGE OF NURSING (*The complete profile is made available exclusively on our website, www.barronspac.com*)

ROCKHURST UNIVERSITY	A-2
www.rockhurst.edu	

Kansas City, MO 64110	**(816) 501-4100**
	(800) 842-6776
Fax: (816) 501-4241	**Email:** admission@rockhurst.edu
Full-time: 615 men, 850 women	**Faculty:** IIA, --$
Part-time: 320 men, 540 women	**Ph.D.s:** 84%
Graduate: 335 men, 475 women	**Student/Faculty:** n/av
Year: semesters, summer session	**Tuition:** $13,225
Room & Board: $7400	**Freshman Class:** n/av
ACT: required **SAT:** recommended	**CEEB CODE:** 6611
Application Deadline: n/av	**COMPETITIVE**

Rockhurst University, founded in 1910, is a private Catholic Jesuit institution that offers undergraduate programs in the arts and sciences, education, nursing, and business. The figures in the above capsule and in this profile are approximate. There are 4 undergraduate schools and 2 graduate schools. In addition to regional accreditation, Rockhurst has baccalaureate program accreditation with APTA, CAHEA, NLN, TEAC, and AACTE. The 55-acre campus is in an urban area in Kansas City. Including any residence halls, there are 19 buildings.

STUDENT LIFE: 58% of undergraduates are from Missouri. Others are from 17 states. 49% are from public schools. 82% are White. 46% are Catholic; 34% Buddhist, Hindu, Muslim, and Islamic; 20% Protestant. **Male To Female Ratio:** 1.5:1. The average age of freshmen is 18; all undergraduates, 21. 11% do not continue beyond their first year; 66% remain to graduate. **Housing:** 815 students can be accommodated in college housing, which includes single-sex and coed dorms and on-campus apartments. In addition, there are honors houses and special-interest houses. On-campus housing is available on a first-come and first-served basis. Priority is given to out-of-town students. 61% of students live on campus; of those, 45% remain on campus on weekends. All students may keep cars.

FACULTY/CLASSROOMS: 52% of faculty are male; 48% are female. 87% teach undergraduates. No introductory courses are taught by graduate students. The average class size in an introductory lecture is 20; in a laboratory is 14; and in a regular course is 21.

PROGRAMS OF STUDY: Rockhurst confers B.A., B.S., B.S.B.A. and B.S.N. degrees. Master's and Doctoral degrees are also awarded. Bachelor's degrees are awarded in BIOLOGICAL SCIENCE (biochemistry, bioinformatics, and biology/biological science), BUSINESS (business administration and management, business communications, business economics, and nonprofit/public organization management), COMMUNICATIONS AND THE ARTS (communications, English, French, and Spanish), COMPUTER AND PHYSICAL SCIENCE (chemistry, computer science, mathematics, and physics), EDUCATION (elementary education, foreign languages education, and secondary education), ENGINEERING AND ENVIRONMENTAL DESIGN (computer technology), HEALTH PROFESSIONS (clinical science, nursing, and speech pathology/audiology), SOCIAL SCIENCE (economics, history, international relations, philosophy, political science/government, psychology, and theological studies). Nursing and business administration are the strongest academically.

ACTIVITIES: 7% of men belong to 4 national fraternities; 7% of women belong to 2 national sororities. There are 55 groups on campus, including art, cheerleading, choir, chorale, chorus, computers, drama, ethnic, honors, international, literary magazine, musical theater, newspaper, photography, political, professional, radio and TV, religious, social, social service, and student government. Popular campus events include Fraternity Socials, Coffee House Events, and Rockstock (live bands). **Sports:** There are 5 intercollegiate sports for men and 5 for women, and 12 intramural sports for men and 12 for women. Facilities include athletic and soccer fields, tennis, handball, racquetball, badminton, basketball, and volleyball courts, a weight and exercise room, gymnastics facilities, and a NCAA baseball field. **Graduates:** From July 1, 2013 to June 30, 2014, 366 bachelor's degrees were awarded. The most popular majors were business (35%), nursing/health professions (21%), and psychology/social science/history (13%). In an average class, 51% graduate in 4 years or less, 63% graduate in 5 years or less, and 66% graduate in 6 years or less.

SERVICES: Counseling and information services are available, as is tutoring in most subjects. The Learning Center offers tutoring in many subjects, assistance with any college writing task, and study strategies, SI courses, support for various professional tests. **Library/Resources:** The library contains 314,890 volumes, 596,850 microform items, 8,078 audio/video tapes/CDs/DVDs, and subscribes to 38,934 periodicals including electronic. Computerized library services include interlibrary loans, database searching, Internet access, and Wi-Fi capability. Special learning facilities include an art gallery, radio station, multimedia classrooms. **Physically Challenged Students:** 90% of the campus is accessible. Facilities include wheelchair ramps, elevators, special parking, specially equipped restrooms, lowered drinking fountains, and lowered telephones. **Special:** Students may obtain career-related work experience through the Cooperative Education Program. Internships for credit and salary are available. Students are encouraged to study abroad in 1 of 5 countries for a semester, to take a semester in New York at Fordham University, or to participate in a congressional intern/study program in Washington, D.C., through Marquette University. B.A.-B.S. degrees are available in business administration. Work-study and an accelerated degree in nursing are also available. Students may pursue dual majors, a 3-2 engineering degree, and interdisciplinary majors. There are 7 national honor societies, including Phi Beta Kappa, a freshman honors program, and 12 departmental honors programs. **Visiting:** There are regularly scheduled orientations for prospective students, including a campus tour, an interview with an admissions counselor, and a classroom visit or meeting with a faculty member. There are guides for informal visits, visitors may sit in on classes, and stay overnight. To schedule a visit, contact the Admissions Office. **Campus Safety and Security:** Measures include 24-hour foot and vehicle patrol, self-defense education, and security escort services. There are shuttle buses, emergency telephones, lighted pathways/sidewalks, formal presentations, and a full in-house security program geared toward integration of security into the overall campus operation.

REQUIREMENTS: The ACT is required. The SAT is recommended. In addition, an applicants must be a graduate of an accredited secondary school or have earned a GED. The university requires completion of 15 academic credits, including 4 years of English, 3 to 4 of history/social science, 3 of math, 2 to 4 of a foreign language, and 1 of visual or performing arts. An interview is recommended, and a recommendation is required. Rockhurst requires applicants to be in the upper 50% of their class. A GPA of 2.0 is required. AP and CLEP credits are accepted. Important factors in the admissions decision are advanced placement or honors courses, recommendations by school officials, and leadership record. Students must complete 128 credit hours with a minimum of 18 in the major, with at least a 2.0 GPA. 52 prescribed semester hours in philosophy, theology, history, literature, science, social studies, and the arts are required. Students must also demonstrate proficiency in oral and written communication and math. **Procedure:** Freshmen are admitted to all sessions. Entrance exams should be taken in April or June of the junior year or October, December, or February of the senior year. There are deferred admissions and rolling admissions plans. Check with the school for current application deadlines. The application fee is $25. Applications are accepted on-line. **Transfer Students:** 95 transfer students enrolled in 2013-2014. Transfer applicants must have a GPA of at least 2.25. An interview is recommended. All college transcripts must be submitted; a high school transcript and test scores are required if the applicant has completed fewer than 24 college semester hours. 30 of 128 credits required for the bachelor's degree must be completed at Rockhurst. **International Students:** There are 2 international students enrolled. The school actively recruits these students. They must take the TOEFL with a minimum score of 550 on the paper-based TOEFL (PBT) or 79 on the Internet-based version (iBT). They must also take the SAT or ACT, scoring 20.

ADMISSIONS: 5 freshmen graduated first in their class. **Admissions Contact:** Phil Gebauer, Associate Vice President for Enrollment. E-Mail: *admission@rockhurst.edu* Web: *www.rockhurst.edu*

FINANCIAL AID: In 2014-2015, 91% of all full-time freshmen and 81% of continuing full-time students received some form of financial aid. 69% of all full-time freshmen and 67% of continuing full-time students received need-based aid. The average freshman award was $21,879. Need-based scholarships or need-based grants averaged $4,855 ($25,966 maximum); need-based self-help aid (loans and jobs) averaged $4,097 ($5,975 maximum); and non-need-based athletic scholarships averaged $9,338 ($23,930 maximum). 22% of undergraduate students work part-time. Average annual earnings from campus work are $1500. The average financial indebtedness of the 2014 graduate was $16,579. The FAFSA is required. Check with the school for current application deadlines.

SAINT LOUIS UNIVERSITY　　　　D-2
www.slu.edu

St. Louis, MO 63103	(314) 977-2500
	(800) SLUFORU
Fax: (314) 977-7136	Email: admission@slu.edu
Full-time: 3288 men, 4415 women	Faculty: 671; I, -$
Part-time: 270 men, 591 women	Ph.D.s: 92%
Graduate: 1900 men, 2823 women	Student/Faculty: 12 to 1
Year: semesters, summer session	Tuition: $37,966
Room & Board: $10,380	Freshman Class: 13911 applied, 8383 accepted, 1605 enrolled
SAT: required ACT: 28	CEEB CODE: 6629
Application Deadline: December 1	HIGHLY COMPETITIVE

Saint Louis University is a Catholic, Jesuit institution that values academic excellence, life-changing research, compassionate health care, and a strong commitment to faith and service. Founded in 1818, SLU is the second oldest Jesuit university in the United States. Offering a complete range of undergraduate, graduate and professional programs including law and medicine the University fosters the intellectual and character development of more than 13,300 students on campuses in St. Louis and Madrid, Spain. Building on a legacy of nearly 200 years, Saint Louis University continues to move forward with an unwavering commitment to a higher purpose, a greater good. There are 9 undergraduate schools and 9 graduate schools. In addition to regional accreditation, SLU has baccalaureate program

accreditation with AACSB, ABET, ADA, CSWE, NASAD, NCATE, ACS, AABI, CEPH, CAHIIM, CAAHEP, CCNE, JRCERT, JRCNMT, NAACLS, and DESE. The 271-acre campus is in an urban area midtown section of St. Louis, approximately 4 miles west of the Gateway Arch. Including any residence halls, there are 134 buildings.

STUDENT LIFE: 63% of undergraduates are from out of state, mostly the Midwest. Students are from 48 states, 53 foreign countries, and Canada. 65% are White. 41% claim no religious affiliation; 38% Catholic; 14% Protestant. **Male To Female Ratio:** 1.4:1. The average age of freshmen is 18; all undergraduates, 21. 11% do not continue beyond their first year; 71% remain to graduate. **Housing:** 3866 students can be accommodated in college housing, which includes single-sex and coed dorms and on-campus apartments. In addition, there are honors houses, special-interest houses, fraternity houses, sorority houses, Women's dorms, men's dorms, special housing for disabled students, learning community houses. On-campus housing is guaranteed for the freshman year only, is available on a first-come, first-served basis, and is available on a lottery system for upperclassmen. 52% of students live on campus; of those, 80% remain on campus on weekends. All students may keep cars.

FACULTY/CLASSROOMS: 59% of faculty are male; 41% are female. 40% teach undergraduates, 45% do research, and 23% do both. Graduate students teach 7% of introductory courses. The average class size in an introductory lecture is 23; in a laboratory is 19; and in a regular course is 22.

PROGRAMS OF STUDY: SLU confers B.A., and B.S. degrees. Master's and Doctoral degrees are also awarded. Bachelor's degrees are awarded in BIOLOGICAL SCIENCE (biochemistry, biology/biological science, neurosciences, nutrition, and nutritional sciences), BUSINESS (business administration and management, management information systems, marketing, organizational behavior, and organizational leadership and management), COMMUNICATIONS AND THE ARTS (art history, classical languages, classics, communications, communication science, dramatic arts, English, English literature, fine arts, French, Germanic languages and literature, Italian, music, Russian languages and literature, Spanish, studio art, theatre arts, and theater management), COMPUTER AND PHYSICAL SCIENCE (atmospheric sciences and meteorology, chemistry, clinical laboratory science, computer information systems, earth science, geology, mathematics, and physics), EDUCATION (education, elementary education, general studies, and health information management), ENGINEERING AND ENVIRONMENTAL DESIGN (aeronautical engineering, aeronautical technology, aerospace studies, airline piloting and navigation, aviation administration/management, biomedical engineering, civil engineering, computer engineering, electrical/electronics engineering, emergency/disaster science, engineering, engineering physics, mechanical engineering, and nuclear medicine technology), HEALTH PROFESSIONS (allied health, biology, cytotechnology, exercise science, health care administration, health services technology, kinesiology, medical laboratory science, medical technology, nursing, nutrition and dietetics, occupational therapy, public health, radiation therapy, radiologic imaging modalities, and speech pathology/audiology), SOCIAL SCIENCE (African American studies, American studies, anthropology, criminal justice, French studies, history, humanities, international relations, Latin American studies, liberal arts/general studies, philosophy, political science/government, psychology, social work, sociology, theology, theological studies, urban studies, and women's studies). Psychology, physician's assistant, physical therapy, and dental education are the strongest academically. Nursing, physical therapy, and accounting have the largest enrollments.

ACTIVITIES: 18% of men belong to 8 national fraternities; 26% of women belong to 6 national sororities. There are 140 groups on campus, including basketball games, improvisational comedy, midnight breakfast at finals, Model UN, relay for life, singing groups, art, band, cheerleading, chess, choir, chorale, chorus, computers, dance, debate, drama, drill team, environmental, ethnic, games/hobbies, gay, honors, international, jazz band, literary magazine, musical theater, newspaper, pep band, photography, political, professional, radio and TV, religious, social, social service, and student government. Popular campus events include Make a Difference Day, SLU Involvement Fair, International Banquet, Homecoming, Sunday Night Mass, Major concerts in Fall and Spring, Comedians, Billikens After Dark

Events, Atlas Week, and Dance Marathon. **Sports:** There are 8 intercollegiate sports for men and 10 for women, and 21 intramural sports for men and 21 for women. Facilities include Chaifetz Arena (men's/women's basketball home court) and Chaifetz Pavilion, a two-court practice facility (which accommodates volleyball home matches and volleyball/basketball practices); Robert R. Hermann Stadium (men's and women's soccer playing field) and an adjacent practice soccer field; Billiken Sports Center includes baseball and softball fields; Simon Recreation Center includes various facilities for student use, but specifically includes a pool utilized by SLU's swimming and diving teams; Dwight Davis Tennis Center/Sunset Hills Tennis Center is outdoor/indoor tennis courts utilized by SLU's tennis teams; St. Louis Soccer Park includes an Astroturf field utilized by SLU's field hockey team. **Graduates:** From July 1, 2013 to June 30, 2014, 1828 bachelor's degrees were awarded. The most popular majors were business administration (17%), nursing (8%), and biology (6%). 282 companies recruited on campus in 2013-2014. In an average class, 61% graduate in 4 years or less, 72% graduate in 5 years or less, and 73% graduate in 6 years or less. Of the 2013 graduating class, 40% were enrolled in graduate school within 6 months of graduation, and 53% were employed.

SERVICES: Counseling and information services are available, as is tutoring in most subjects. **Library/Resources:** The 3 libraries contain 1.9 million volumes, 2.7 million microform items, 75,635 audio/video tapes/CDs/DVDs, and subscribe to 9,953 periodicals including electronic. Computerized library services include interlibrary loans, database searching, Internet access, and Wi-Fi capability. Special learning facilities include an art gallery, radio station, TV station, The Vatican Manuscripts microfilm library, athletics baseball/softball hitting facility, biological station, entrepreneurial studies center, earthquake research center, performing arts center, supersonic wind tunnel, water tunnel, shock tube, fabrication labs, airport, flight simulators, sculpture/ceramics studio, physiology/gait research labs, Madrid, Spain Campus, demonstration clinics, 8 lane NCAA regulation track and field, NCAA competion hammer, discus and shot put throwing area,3 student unions, LEED Certified Research Facility, Doisy Research Center, Chaifetz Arena, recreation complex, hotels, religious facilities and chapels, Sculpture dog park, Law School in the heart of the downtown legal community, demonstration clinics (practice with actual patients), counseling and family therapy, child development, speech and hearing, psychology, dental, occupational and physical therapy, organic garden and food service. **Physically Challenged Students:** 95% of the campus is accessible. Facilities include wheelchair ramps, elevators, special parking, specially equipped restrooms, special class scheduling, lowered drinking fountains, lowered telephones, and special housing. **Special:** Students may study abroad in 29 countries. Cross-registration with Washington University, the University of Missouri at St. Louis, Aquinas Institute of Theology and Harris-Stowe State College. There are internships, work-study programs on campus, an accelerated degree program in nursing, a 3-2 engineering degree program with Washington University in St. Louis, dual majors, student-designed majors. Students may also participate in university-sponsored mission trips. There are 3 national honor societies, including Phi Beta Kappa, a freshman honors program, and 1 departmental honors programs. **Visiting:** There are regularly scheduled orientations for prospective students, visits are available year round. Options include campus tours, residence hall tours, academic meetings, class visits, and presentations on admission, student development, studying abroad, student life/campus culture. There are guides for informal visits, visitors may sit in on classes, and stay overnight. To schedule a visit, contact Andrea Hitsman at admission@slu.edu. **Campus Safety and Security:** Measures include 24-hour foot and vehicle patrol, emergency notification system, self-defense education, and security escort services. There are shuttle buses, emergency telephones, lighted pathways/sidewalks, controlled access to dorms/residences, video cameras, identification of valuables, smoke detectors in halls, informal safety and security discussions, bike patrols, prevention/awareness programs, mobile security patrols, motorist assistance, security officers who have police powers on campus including the power to arrest individuals, 24 hour emergency telephone/alarm devices.

REQUIREMENTS: The SAT or ACT is required. A complete application is required for admission consideration, which consists of an application, an essay, a high school transcript, and test scores. Auditions and portfolios are required for the music and art programs. AP and CLEP credits are accepted. Important factors in the admissions decision are advanced placement or honors courses, leadership record, and extracurricular activities record. Students must maintain a 2.0 GPA while completing a minimum of 120 credit hours. The core curriculum includes courses in English, Philosophy, Theology, Math, and Cultural Diversity. **Procedure:** Freshmen are admitted fall, spring, and summer. Entrance exams should be taken Junior or Senior year. Junior is recommended. There are deferred admissions and rolling admissions plans. Applications should be filed by December 1 for fall entry; January 1 for spring entry; and June 1 for summer entry. Notification is sent on a rolling basis. 291 applicants were on the 2014 waiting list; 97 were admitted. Applications are accepted on-line. Application fees are waived if application is completed on-line. **Transfer Students:** 287 transfer students enrolled in 2013-2014. The university requires original transcripts from each institution (high school and college) the student attended, as well as, a minimum GPA of at least 2.5 (on a scale of 4.0). 30 of 120 credits required for the bachelor's degree must be completed at SLU. **International Students:** There are 651 international students enrolled. The school actively recruits these students. They must take the TOEFL with a minimum score of 550 on the paper-based TOEFL (PBT) or 80 on the Internet-based version (iBT) and the college's own test, or take the IELTS.

ADMISSIONS: 60% of the 2014-2015 applicants were accepted. The SAT scores for the 2014-2015 freshman class were: Critical Reading--13% below 500, 35% between 500 and 599, 41% between 600 and 699, and 11% between 700 and 800; Math--9% below 500, 33% between 500 and 599, 40% between 600 and 699, and 18% between 700 and 800. The ACT scores were 2% below 21, 10% between 21 and 23, 27% between 24 and 26, 20% between 27 and 28, and 41% above 28. 65% of the current freshmen were in the top fifth of their class; 87% were in the top two fifths. There were 10 National Merit finalists. **Admissions Contact:** Jean M. Gilman, Dean of Admissions. E-Mail: *admission@slu.edu* Web: *www.slu.edu*

FINANCIAL AID: In 2014-2015, 95% of all full-time freshmen and 90% of continuing full-time students received some form of financial aid. 54% of all full-time freshmen and 55% of continuing full-time students received need-based aid. 20% of undergraduate students work part-time. Average annual earnings from campus work are $3435. The average financial indebtedness of the 2014 graduate was $33,320. SLU is a member of CSS. The FAFSA is required. The priority date for freshman financial aid applications for fall entry is March 1. The deadline for filing freshman financial aid applications for fall entry is May 1.

SOUTHEAST MISSOURI STATE UNIVERSITY (*The complete profile is made available exclusively on our website, www.barronspac.com*)

SOUTHWEST BAPTIST UNIVERSITY	B-3
www.sbuniv.edu	

Bolivar, MO 65613	(417) 328-1817
	(800) 526-5859
Fax: (417) 328-1514	Email: dcrowder@sbuniv.edu
Full-time: 833 men, 1232 women	Faculty: n/av
Part-time: 244 men, 700 women	Ph.Ds: 71%
Graduate: 313 men, 542 women	Student/Faculty: n/av
Year: 4-1-4, summer session	Tuition: $18,360
Room & Board: $6350	Freshman Class: n/av
SAT or ACT: required	CEEB CODE: 6664
Application Deadline: n/av	COMPETITIVE

Southwest Baptist University, founded in 1878, is a private liberal arts institution affiliated with the Southern Baptist Convention. There are 6 undergraduate schools and 3 graduate schools. In addition to regional accreditation, SBU has baccalaureate program accreditation with ACBSP, NASM, NLN, CAATE, CAPTE, and NASM. The 180-acre campus is in a small town 28 miles north of Springfield Missouri. Including any residence halls, there are 26 buildings.

STUDENT LIFE: 71% of undergraduates are from Missouri. Others are from 40 states, 19 foreign countries, and Canada. 73% are White. 87% are Protestant. **Male To Female Ratio:** 1.8:1. The average age of freshmen is 18; all undergraduates, 21. 28% do not continue beyond their first year. **Housing:** 1071 students can be accommodated in college housing, which includes single-sex dorms and on-campus apartments. On-campus housing is guaranteed for all 4 years. 62% of students live on campus; of those, 65% remain on campus on weekends. Alcohol is not permitted. All students may keep cars.

FACULTY/CLASSROOMS: 80% teach undergraduates. No introductory courses are taught by graduate students. The average class size in an introductory lecture is 40; in a laboratory is 20; and in a regular course is 20.

PROGRAMS OF STUDY: SBU confers B.A., B.S., B.A.S., B.M. and B.S.N. degrees. Associate, Master's, and Doctoral degrees are also awarded. Bachelor's degrees are awarded in BIOLOGICAL SCIENCE (biology/biological science), BUSINESS (accounting, business administration and management, international business management, marketing and distribution, recreation and leisure services, and sports management), COMMUNICATIONS AND THE ARTS (art, communications, English, journalism, music, performing arts, and Spanish), COMPUTER AND PHYSICAL SCIENCE (chemistry, computer science, information sciences and systems, and mathematics), EDUCATION (art education, athletic training, early childhood education, elementary education, health education, mathematics education, middle school education, music education, physical education, secondary education, and social studies education), ENGINEERING AND ENVIRONMENTAL DESIGN (commercial art and occupational safety and health), HEALTH PROFESSIONS (medical technology and nursing), SOCIAL SCIENCE (biblical studies, criminal justice, economics, history, human services, interdisciplinary studies, ministries, missions, parks and recreation management, pastoral studies, political science/government, psychology, religious education, religious music, and sociology). Education, psychology, and business administration have the largest enrollments.

ACTIVITIES: There are 36 groups on campus, including art, band, cheerleading, choir, chorale, chorus, computers, debate, drama, forensics, honors, international, jazz band, musical theater, newspaper, opera, orchestra, pep band, photography, political, professional, religious, social service, and student government. Popular campus events include Welcome Week, Concerts and Courtwarming. **Sports:** Facilities include a Jane and Ken Meyer Wellness and Sports Center, which houses intramural basketball courts, racquetball courts, a rock-climbing wall, weight rooms, an aerobics room, an indoor walking/jogging track, health and phys ed classrooms, and an Olympic-size swimming pool. The sports arena has seating for 2800 people. **Graduates:** From July 1, 2013 to June 30, 2014, 419 bachelor's degrees were awarded. In an average class, 41% graduate in 4 years or less, 50% graduate in 5 years or less, and 53% graduate in 6 years or less.

SERVICES: Counseling and information services are available, as is tutoring in every subject. There is remedial math, reading, and writing. **Library/Resources:** The library contains 724,203 volumes, 482,190 microform items, 11,451 audio/video tapes/CDs/DVDs, and subscribes to 22,679 periodicals including electronic. Computerized library services include interlibrary loans, database searching, Internet access, and Wi-Fi capability. Special learning facilities include an art gallery. **Physically Challenged Students:** 95% of the campus is accessible. Facilities include wheelchair ramps, elevators, special parking, specially equipped restrooms, special class scheduling, and lowered drinking fountains. **Special:** SBU offers internships, study abroad in 80 countries, an Oxford honors program, a Washington semester, work-study programs. There are also American studies, contemporary music, family film, and journalism programs. There are a freshman honors program. **Visiting:** There are regularly scheduled orientations for prospective students, including fall and spring visitation days. There are guides for informal visits, visitors may sit in on classes, and stay overnight. To schedule a visit, contact the Director of Admissions. **Campus Safety and Security:** Measures include 24-hour foot and vehicle patrol. There are emergency telephones and lighted pathways/sidewalks.

REQUIREMENTS: The SAT or ACT is required. An SBU applicant must present either proof of graduation from an accredited or approved high school or a homeschool transcript. Additionally, students must meet 2 of the following 3 qualifiers: 2.5 high school GPA

on a 4.0 scale; 21 ACT or satisfactory SAT composite score; or top 50% of high school rank. Applicants are recommended to have 13 academic credits, including a recommended 4 credits in English, 3 in math, 2 each in natural science and history or social science, and 2 elective units. AP and CLEP credits are accepted. To graduate, students must complete 128 credit hours, with 40 in upper-division courses and 52 in general education requirements, and maintain a 2.0 GPA. The number of hours in the major varies. **Procedure:** Freshmen are admitted to all sessions. Entrance exams should be taken at any time prior to admission. There are deferred admissions and rolling admissions plans. Application deadlines are open. Application fee is $30. Applications are accepted on-line. **Transfer Students:** 114 transfer students enrolled in 2013-2014. Applicants must submit official college and high school transcripts and have a minimum GPA of 2.0. An interview is encouraged. Students who have not yet met SBU's English and math requirements must present scores from the ACT, SAT, or other approved placement test. Only 6 hours of D credit can be transferred. 30 of 128 credits required for the bachelor's degree must be completed at SBU. **International Students:** There are 30 international students enrolled. They must take the TOEFL. They must also take the SAT or ACT.

ADMISSIONS: Darren Crowder, Director of Admissions. E-Mail: *dcrowder@sbuniv.edu* Web: *www.sbuniv.edu*

FINANCIAL AID: The FAFSA and the college's own financial statement are required. Check with the school for current application deadlines.

STEPHENS COLLEGE   C-2
www.stephens.edu

Columbia, MO 65215	(573)876-2391
	n/av
Fax: (573)876-7237	Email: tgoalder@stephens.edu
Full-time: 1 men, 556 women	Faculty: n/av
Part-time: 6 men, 116 women	Ph.D.s: 83%
Graduate: 24 men, 172 women	Student/Faculty: n/av
Year: semesters, summer session	Tuition: $28,510
Room & Board: $9532	Freshman Class: 748 applied, 725 accepted, 259 enrolled
SAT or ACT: required	CEEB CODE: 6683
Application Deadline: n/av	VERY COMPETITIVE

Stephens College, founded in 1833, is a private college primarily for women, offering undergraduate programs in the arts and sciences, business, education, and fine arts. There are 5 undergraduate schools and 3 graduate schools. The 59-acre campus is in an urban area 120 miles west of St. Louis. Including any residence halls, there are 35 buildings.

STUDENT LIFE: 64% of undergraduates are from Missouri. Others are from 41 states, and 2 foreign countries. 93% are from public schools. 73% are White; 13% African American. **Male To Female Ratio:** 27.2:1. The average age of freshmen is 18; all undergraduates, 24. 33% do not continue beyond their first year; 45% remain to graduate. **Housing:** 724 students can be accommodated in college housing, which includes single-sex dorms and on-campus apartments. In addition, there are honors houses, special interest houses for intercultural scholars and fine arts majors, and houses with designated academic floors, nonsmoking floors and pet floors. On-campus housing is guaranteed for all 4 years. 72% of students live on campus; of those, 90% remain on campus on weekends. All students may keep cars.

FACULTY/CLASSROOMS: 40% of faculty are male; 60% are female. 92% teach undergraduates, and all teach and do research. No introductory courses are taught by graduate students. The average class size in an introductory lecture is 30; in a laboratory is 12; and in a regular course is 20.

PROGRAMS OF STUDY: Stephens confers B.A., B.S. and B.F.A. degrees. Master's degrees are also awarded. Bachelor's degrees are awarded in AGRICULTURE (equine science), BIOLOGICAL SCIENCE (biology/biological science), BUSINESS (accounting, business administration and management, and fashion merchandising),

COMMUNICATIONS AND THE ARTS (creative writing, dance, dramatic arts, English, film arts, graphic design, public relations, and theater design), EDUCATION (early childhood education and elementary education), ENGINEERING AND ENVIRONMENTAL DESIGN (interior design), SOCIAL SCIENCE (fashion design and technology and liberal arts/general studies). Education, and biology are the strongest academically. Performing arts, fashion, and biology have the largest enrollments.

ACTIVITIES: 8% of women belong to 2 national sororities. There are 38 groups on campus, including art, choir, chorale, chorus, dance, drama, ethnic, gay, honors, international, literary magazine, musical theater, newspaper, photography, political, professional, radio and TV, religious, social, social service, student government, and yearbook. Popular campus events include Opening Convocation, Honors Convocation, and Performing Arts Events. **Sports:** There are 4 intercollegiate sports for women. Facilities include a 300-seat gym and tennis courts. **Graduates:** From July 1, 2013 to June 30, 2014, 164 bachelor's degrees were awarded. The most popular majors were health information administration (11%), fashion - marketing and manegment (10%), and counseling (7%). In an average class, 71% graduate in 3 years or less, 96% graduate in 4 years or less, 99% graduate in 5 years or less, and 100% graduate in 6 years or less. Of the 2013 graduating class, 2% were enrolled in graduate school within 6 months of graduation.

SERVICES: Counseling and information services are available, as is tutoring in most subjects. There is remedial writing. **Library/ Resources:** The library contains 143,229 volumes, 10,792 microform items, 3,356 audio/video tapes/CDs/DVDs, and subscribes to 45,699 periodicals including electronic. Computerized library services include interlibrary loans, database searching, and Internet access. Special learning facilities include an art gallery, radio station, and TV station. **Physically Challenged Students:** 80% of the campus is accessible. Facilities include wheelchair ramps, elevators, special parking, specially equipped restrooms, special class scheduling, lowered drinking fountains, and special housing. **Special:** Students may study abroad in England, Italy, Mexico, France, Ecuador, South Korea, and Spain. Stephens also offers cross-registration with the Mid-Missouri Association of Colleges and Universities, many internships, a Washington semester, dual and student-designed majors, a 3-2 occupational therapy degree program with Washington University, accelerated degree programs in dance and theater arts, and pass/fail options for electives. There are 8 national honor societies and a freshman honors program. **Visiting:** There are regularly scheduled orientations for prospective students, consisting of attendance at classes, a campus tour, an appointment with instructors, and an interview. There are guides for informal visits, visitors may sit in on classes, and stay overnight. To schedule a visit, contact the Campus Visit Coordinator at apply@stephens.edu. **Campus Safety and Security:** Measures include 24-hour foot and vehicle patrol, emergency notification system, self-defense education, and security escort services. There are emergency telephones, lighted pathways/sidewalks, and controlled access to dorms/residences.

REQUIREMENTS: The SAT or ACT is required. Applicants must be graduates of accredited secondary schools or have earned a GED. An essay is also required, and an interview is recommended. A GPA of 2.5 is required. AP and CLEP credits are accepted. Important factors in the admissions decision are advanced placement or honors courses, leadership record, and recommendations by school officials.All students must complete 6 hours of English and a distribution of 9 courses in lower-division work, including 6 hours of social sciences and 3 hours each of math, science, literary studies, history, cultural studies, and ethics. The bachelor's degree requires completion of at least 120 semester hours, including 30 to 72 in a major field, with a minimum GPA of 2.0. **Procedure:** Freshmen are admitted fall and spring. There are deferred admissions and rolling admissions plans. Application deadlines are open. Application fee is $50. Applications are accepted on-line. **Transfer Students:** 68 transfer students enrolled in 2013-2014. Applicants must submit official transcripts from all college work attempted or completed as well as a recommendation from an academic college instructor. Transfers must submit an official high school transcript. 36 of 120 credits required for the bachelor's degree must be completed at Stephens. **International Students:** There are 2 international students enrolled. The school actively recruits these stu-

dents. They must take the TOEFL with a minimum score of 79 on the Internet-based version (iBT).

ADMISSIONS: 97% of the 2014-2015 applicants were accepted. The ACT scores were 29% below 21, 14% between 24 and 26, and 43% between 27 and 28. 27% of the current freshmen were in the top fifth of their class; 60% were in the top two fifths. **Admissions Contact:** Tiffany Goalder E-Mail: *tgoalder@stephens.edu* Web: *www.stephens .edu*

FINANCIAL AID: In 2014-2015, 99% of all full-time freshmen and 54% of continuing full-time students received some form of financial aid. 82% of all full-time freshmen and 49% of continuing full-time students received need-based aid. The average freshman award was $7,025. Need-based scholarships or need-based grants averaged $9,878; need-based self-help aid (loans and jobs) averaged $3,574; non-need-based athletic scholarships averaged $7,656; and other non-need-based awards and non-need-based scholarships averaged $15,398. 10% of undergraduate students work part-time. Average annual earnings from campus work are $1630. The average financial indebtedness of the 2014 graduate was $37,467. The FAFSA is required. The priority date for freshman financial aid applications for fall entry is March 1.

TRUMAN STATE UNIVERSITY   C-1
www.truman.edu

Kirksville, MO 63501

(660) 785-4114
n/av

Fax: (660) 785-7456

Email: admissions@truman.edu

Full-time: 2169 men, 3126 women
Part-time: 242 men, 373 women
Graduate: 84 men, 254 women
Year: semesters, summer session
Room & Board: $8167

Faculty: 318; IIA, --$
Ph.Ds: 87%
Student/Faculty: 17 to 1
Tuition: $7374 ($13,438)
Freshman Class: 4095 applied, 3050 accepted, 1320 enrolled

SAT CR/M: 630/610 ACT: 27
Application Deadline: March 1

CEEB CODE: 6483
HIGHLY COMPETITIVE

Truman State University, founded in 1867, is a highly selective public liberal arts and sciences institution offering 37 undergraduate areas of study and 8 graduate degrees within the liberal arts and sciences and select pre-professional programs. There are 5 undergraduate schools and 5 graduate schools. In addition to regional accreditation, Truman has baccalaureate program accreditation with AACSB, NASM, NCATE, ACS ASHA CCNE, and CAATE. The 140-acre campus is in a small town in the northeast corner of Missouri. 170 miles from Kansas City, 200 miles from St. Louis, and 90 miles north of Columbia, MO. Including any residence halls, there are 32 buildings.

STUDENT LIFE: 81% of undergraduates are from Missouri. Others are from 40 states, 50 foreign countries, and Canada. 87% are from public schools. 80% are White. 43% claim no religious affiliation; 33% Protestant; 21% Catholic. **Male To Female Ratio:** 1.5:1. The average age of freshmen is 18; all undergraduates, 20. 12% do not continue beyond their first year; 71% remain to graduate. **Housing:** 2864 students can be accommodated in college housing, which includes single-sex and coed dorms, on-campus apartments, and married student housing. In addition, there are honors houses, language houses, and special-interest houses. On-campus housing is guaranteed for the freshman year only, is available on a first-come, first-served basis, and is available on a lottery system for upperclassmen. 55% of students commute. Alcohol is not permitted. All students may keep cars.

FACULTY/CLASSROOMS: 57% of faculty are male; 43% are female. All teach undergraduates. Graduate students teach 3% of introductory courses. The average class size in an introductory lecture is 24; in a laboratory is 17; and in a regular course is 19.

PROGRAMS OF STUDY: Truman confers B.A., B.S., B.F.A., B.M. and B.S.N. degrees. Master's degrees are also awarded. Bachelor's degrees are awarded in AGRICULTURE (agricultural business management, agriculture, agronomy, animal science, equine science, and horticulture), BIOLOGICAL SCIENCE (biology/biological science), BUSINESS (accounting, business administration and management, and international business management), COMMUNICATIONS AND THE ARTS (art, art history and appreciation, classics, communications, creative writing, dramatic arts, English, fine arts, French, German, journalism, linguistics, music, music performance, romance languages and literature, Russian, Spanish, studio art, and visual design), COMPUTER AND PHYSICAL SCIENCE (chemistry, computer science, mathematics, and physics), EDUCATION (athletic training and physical education), ENGINEERING AND ENVIRONMENTAL DESIGN (preengineering), HEALTH PROFESSIONS (clinical science, exercise science, health science, nursing, physical therapy, predentistry, premedicine, prepharmacy, preveterinary science, public health, and speech pathology/audiology), SOCIAL SCIENCE (anthropology, criminal justice, economics, history, interdisciplinary studies, philosophy, physical fitness/movement, political science/government, prelaw, psychology, religion, and sociology). Chemistry, biology, and accounting are the strongest academically. Business administration, biology, and English have the largest enrollments.

ACTIVITIES: 24% of men belong to 12 national fraternities; 18% of women belong to 1 local and 5 national sororities. There are 213 groups on campus, including art, band, cheerleading, chess, choir, chorale, chorus, computers, dance, debate, drama, drill team, environmental, ethnic, film, forensics, gay, honors, international, jazz band, literary magazine, marching band, musical theater, newspaper, opera, orchestra, pep band, political, professional, radio and TV, religious, social, social service, student government, and symphony. Popular campus events include Final Blowout, Kohlenberg Lyceum Series, and the Big Event. **Sports:** There are 10 intercollegiate sports for men and 10 for women, and 35 intramural sports for men and 35 for women. Facilities include a 5,000-seat football stadium, a soccer field, tennis courts, softball diamond, baseball diamond, 3,000-seat arena with 3 basketball courts, an Olympic-size pool, weight training rooms, indoor and outdoor track facilities, and a 60,000-square-foot student recreation center. **Graduates:** From July 1, 2013 to June 30, 2014, 1236 bachelor's degrees were awarded. The most popular majors were business administration (14%), health & exercise sciences (12%), and psychology (10%). 161 companies recruited on campus in 2013-2014. In an average class, 2% graduate in 3 years or less, 57% graduate in 4 years or less, 70% graduate in 5 years or less, and 71% graduate in 6 years or less. Of the 2013 graduating class, 45% were enrolled in graduate school within 6 months of graduation, and 54% were employed.

SERVICES: Counseling and information services are available, as is tutoring in most subjects. Services for the hearing impaired, including a braille scanner and printer. Disability services provides reasonable accommodations to qualified students which include, but are not limited to: classroom accommodations such as test or note taking services, housing include placement and bathroom configurations, assistance for hearing and visually impaired students. Client accommodations are based on individualized, qualified guidelines per ADA standards and are determined through a collaborative approach between the student and the Disability Services Coordinator. **Library/Resources:** The library contains 512,441 volumes, 1.6 million microform items, 40,525 audio/video tapes/CDs/DVDs, and subscribes to 3,481 periodicals including electronic. Computerized library services include interlibrary loans, database searching, Internet access, and Wi-Fi capability. Special learning facilities include an art gallery, planetarium, radio station, nursing simulation lab, an observatory, greenhouse chamber, speech and hearing clinic, a broadcasting studio, language learning center, farm, herpetology lab, writing center, convergent media center, midi music studio and various labs for science programs. **Physically Challenged Students:** 99% of the campus is accessible. Facilities include wheelchair ramps, elevators, special parking, specially equipped restrooms, special class scheduling, lowered drinking fountains, special housing. the swimming pool is equipped with a lift to assist physically disabled swimmers. **Special:** Study abroad in over 50 countries is offered through Truman's own programs and those of the College Consortium for International Studies, the Council on International Educational Exchange, and the International Student Exchange Program. The university requires internships in education and health and exercise science. Voluntary

legislative internships are offered to all students at the state capitol, and internships through the Washington Center. There is a dual-degree program with Physics and Engineering where Truman provides the Physics and the student then transfers to another institution for Engineering and upon completion of that work Truman will award a Physics degree along with earned Engineering degree from the other school. Work-study programs, B.A.-B.S. degrees, dual majors, student-designed interdisciplinary majors, credit for military experience, pass/fail options for internships, and non-degree study are available. There are 18 national honor societies, including Phi Beta Kappa, a freshman honors program, and 21 departmental honors programs. **Visiting:** There are regularly scheduled orientations for prospective students. Campus visits include a personalized meeting with an admission counselor, a student-led campus tour, and appointments with a faculty member in the student's major or in any areas of special interest upon request. There are guides for informal visits, visitors may sit in on classes, and stay overnight. To schedule a visit, contact Carrie Riley at (660) 785-4114. **Campus Safety and Security:** Measures include 24-hour foot and vehicle patrol, emergency notification system, self-defense education, and security escort services. There are emergency telephones, lighted pathways/sidewalks, and controlled access to dorms/residences.

REQUIREMENTS: The ACT is required. Truman must have a standardized test score on file for admission consideration, either the ACT or the SAT. Applicants should have completed 4 units of English, 3 each of science and social studies, 2 of foreign language, and 1 of art or music. 4 units of math are strongly recommended. An essay is required and list of activities is strongly recommended. AP and CLEP credits are accepted. Important factors in the admissions decision are advanced placement or honors courses, leadership record, and extracurricular activities record. All students must complete 63 hours of course work in the liberal arts, 16 of which must be in written and oral communication, math and statistics, computer literacy, and personal well-being, and 23 of which must be in history, science, social science, philosophy/religion, math, and aesthetics. Elementary proficiency in a foreign language is required of all majors. The B.A., B.F.A., and B.M. degree require intermediate proficiency in one foreign language, and the B.S. and B.S.N. require additional course work in science, math, statistics, computer science, social sciences, or logic. Skills such as writing, quantitative analysis, problem solving, and critical thinking are reinforced throughout the curriculum, and all seniors end their studies with a capstone, or culminating experience, in their majors. Students must also complete a nationally normed exam in their subject areas as part of Truman's assessment program. **Procedure:** Freshmen are admitted fall, spring, and summer. Entrance exams should be taken Spring of Junior year, Summer, or Fall of Senior year. There are deferred admissions and rolling admissions plans. Applications should be filed by March 1 for fall entry; November 15 for spring entry; and March 1 for summer entry. Notification is sent on a rolling basis. Applications are accepted on-line. **Transfer Students:** 164 transfer students enrolled in 2013-2014. Transfer applicants are considered for admission through a competitive individualized review process that emphasizes preparedness for study based upon a variety of criteria. Cumulative grade point average in transferable college credit, strength of college curriculum, and the admission essay are considered for all transfer admission candidates. Cumulative high school record and ACT/SAT scores will also be reviewed for applicants who have completed fewer than 24 hours of transferable post high school college credit at the time of application. 45 of 120 credits required for the bachelor's degree must be completed at Truman. **International Students:** There are 349 international students enrolled. The school actively recruits these students. They must take the TOEFL with a minimum score of 550 on the paper-based TOEFL (PBT) or 79 on the Internet-based version (iBT) and the Comprehensive English Language Test. They must also take the SAT or ACT.

ADMISSIONS: 74% of the 2014-2015 applicants were accepted. The SAT scores for the 2014-2015 freshman class were: Critical Reading--6% below 500, 24% between 500 and 599, 49% between 600 and 699, and 21% between 700 and 800; Math--9% below 500, 35% between 500 and 599, 35% between 600 and 699, and 21% between 700 and 800. The ACT scores were 3% below 21, 15% between 21 and 23, 29% between 24 and 26, 17% between 27 and 28, and 36% above

28. 72% of the current freshmen were in the top fifth of their class; 94% were in the top two fifths. There were 6 National Merit finalists. 183 freshmen graduated first in their class. **Admissions Contact:** Melody Chambers, Director of Admissions. E-Mail: *admissions@ truman.edu* Web: *www.truman.edu*

FINANCIAL AID: In 2014-2015, 99% of all full-time freshmen and 79% of continuing full-time students received some form of financial aid. 45% of all full-time freshmen and 37% of continuing full-time students received need-based aid. The average freshman award was $12,706. Need-based scholarships or need-based grants averaged $4,609 ($14,326 maximum); need-based self-help aid (loans and jobs) averaged $4,342 ($8,500 maximum); non-need-based athletic scholarships averaged $4,096 ($22,935 maximum); and other non-need-based awards and non-need-based scholarships averaged $9,127 ($26,500 maximum). 31% of undergraduate students work part-time. Average annual earnings from campus work are $1207. The average financial indebtedness of the 2014 graduate was $22,109. The FAFSA is required. The priority date for freshman financial aid applications for fall entry is February 15. The deadline for filing freshman financial aid applications for fall entry is April 1.

UNIVERSITY OF CENTRAL MISSOURI   B-2
www.ucmo.edu

Warrensburg, MO 64093   (660) 543-4290

Fax: (660) 543-8517	Email: admit@ucmo.edu
Full-time: 3764 men, 4428 women	Faculty: 452; IIA, --$
Part-time: 680 men, 867 women	Ph.D.s: 67%
Graduate: 810 men, 1399 women	Student/Faculty: 17 to 1
Year: semesters, summer session	Tuition: $7147 ($13,435)
Room & Board: $7458	Freshman Class: n/av CEEB CODE: 6090
Application Deadline: open	COMPETITIVE

University of Central Missouri, founded in 1871, is a public liberal arts institution offering a comprehensive range of degree programs. There are 4 undergraduate schools and 1 graduate school. In addition to regional accreditation, Central has baccalaureate program accreditation with AACSB, ABET, ACCE, ADA, ASLA, CSWE, NASAD, NASM, NCATE, NLN, ACS, ADDA, ASLHA, CAA, CADE, CCNE, NAIT, NASPE, and and SOA. The 1561-acre campus is in a small town 50 miles southeast of Kansas City. Including any residence halls, there are 107 buildings.

STUDENT LIFE: 89% of undergraduates are from Missouri. Others are from 42 states, 59 foreign countries, and Canada. 92% are from public schools. 85% are White. 54% are Protestant; 20% Catholic; 12% claim no religious affiliation. **Male To Female Ratio:** 1.3:1. The average age of freshmen is 19; all undergraduates, 22. 32% do not continue beyond their first year; 51% remain to graduate. **Housing:** 3540 students can be accommodated in college housing, which includes single-sex and coed dorms, on-campus apartments, off-campus apartments, and married student housing. In addition, there are honors houses, special-interest houses, fraternity houses, sorority houses, and quiet dorms. On-campus housing is guaranteed for the freshman year only, is available on a first-come, first-served basis. 72% of students commute. All students may keep cars.

FACULTY/CLASSROOMS: 54% of faculty are male; 46% are female. No introductory courses are taught by graduate students. The average class size in an introductory lecture is 30 and in a regular course is 23.

PROGRAMS OF STUDY: Central confers B.A., B.S., B.F.A., B.M., B.M.E., B.S.B.A., B.S.Ed. and B.S.W. degrees. Associate and Master's degrees are also awarded. Bachelor's degrees are awarded in AGRI-CULTURE (agricultural business management and conservation and regulation), BIOLOGICAL SCIENCE (biology/biological science), BUSINESS (accounting, business administration and management, hotel/motel and restaurant management, human resources, management science, marketing/retailing/merchandising, organizational behavior, recreation and leisure services, and tourism), COMMUNI-CATIONS AND THE ARTS (broadcasting, communications,

English, French, German, journalism, music, photography, public relations, Spanish, speech/debate/rhetoric, studio art, and theater design), COMPUTER AND PHYSICAL SCIENCE (actuarial science, chemistry, computer science, earth science, geology, information sciences and systems, mathematics, and physics), EDUCATION (agricultural education, art education, business education, early childhood education, elementary education, English education, foreign languages education, industrial arts education, mathematics education, middle school education, music education, physical education, science education, secondary education, social studies education, and special education), ENGINEERING AND ENVIRONMENTAL DESIGN (agricultural engineering technology, automotive technology, aviation computer technology, commercial art, construction management, drafting and design technology, electrical/electronics engineering, electrical/electronics engineering technology, engineering, engineering technology, graphic arts technology, industrial engineering technology, interior design, manufacturing technology, and occupational safety and health), HEALTH PROFESSIONS (medical laboratory technology, nursing, predentistry, premedicine, preveterinary science, and speech pathology/audiology), SOCIAL SCIENCE (criminal justice, dietetics, economics, geography, history, political science/government, prelaw, psychology, safety management, social work, sociology, and textiles and clothing). School of technology, elementary education and early childhood, criminal justice and nursing have the largest enrollments.

ACTIVITIES: 6% of men belong to 12 national fraternities; 6% of women belong to 11 national sororities. There are 250 groups on campus, including art, band, cheerleading, chess, choir, chorale, chorus, computers, dance, debate, drama, drill team, ethnic, film, forensics, gay, honors, international, jazz band, literary magazine, marching band, musical theater, newspaper, opera, orchestra, pep band, photography, political, professional, radio and TV, religious, social, social service, student government, and symphony. Popular campus events include Performing Arts Series, Technology Fair, and Repertory Theater. **Sports:** There are 7 intercollegiate sports for men and 7 for women, and 32 intramural sports for men and 32 for women. Facilities include a stadium seating more than 12,000, 3 gyms, baseball, softball, women's soccer, and practice fields, a bowling alley, tennis courts, and a multipurpose building that contains a swimming pool, weight rooms, and courts for basketball, racquetball, and volleyball. A nearby outdoor recreation area has an 18-hole golf course and facilities for swimming and other activities. The Student Recreation and Wellness Center includes 3 fitness rooms for aerobics, spinning, kickboxing, 3 new sport courts, a free weight room, 4 additional fitness areas that houses nearly a half-million dollars of fitness equipment, a passive recreation room, inside walking track, outside patio area for lounging, climbing wall. **Graduates:** From July 1, 2013 to June 30, 2014, 1805 bachelor's degrees were awarded. The most popular majors were technology (8%), criminal justice (7%), and elementary education and early childhood (6%). 330 companies recruited on campus in 2013-2014. In an average class, 28% graduate in 4 years or less, 45% graduate in 5 years or less, and 49% graduate in 6 years or less. Of the 2013 graduating class, 18% were enrolled in graduate school within 6 months of graduation, and 91% were employed.

SERVICES: Counseling and information services are available, as is tutoring in some subjects, for a fee including math, chemistry, physics, biology, accounting, economics, and business. There is a reader service for the blind, and remedial math. Writing and learning labs are available for all students. Tutoring is available through TRIO Student Support Services. **Library/Resources:** The library contains 2.2 million volumes, 815,787 microform items, 20,544 audio/video tapes/CDs/DVDs, and subscribes to 783 periodicals including electronic. Computerized library services include interlibrary loans, database searching, Internet access, and Wi-Fi capability. Special learning facilities include an art gallery, natural history museum, planetarium, radio station, TV station, an instructional airport, a 200-acre farm, a driving/safety range, a speech and hearing clinic, a child development lab, and an English Language Center. **Physically Challenged Students:** 95% of the campus is accessible. Facilities include wheelchair ramps, elevators, special parking, specially equipped restrooms, special class scheduling, lowered drinking fountains, lowered telephones, and special housing. **Special:** Central offers cross-registration with the Midwest Student Exchange program, credit and non-credit internships, study abroad in more than 15 countries, a B.A. - B.S. degree, dual and student-designed majors, credit for military service, pass/fail options, nondegree study, and a 3-2 engineering degree with the University of Missouri at Columbia and at Rolla and with the University of Indiana. There are 25 national honor societies, a freshman honors program, and 7 departmental honors programs. **Visiting:** There are regularly scheduled orientations for prospective students, including orientation sessions on housing, general education requirements, and enrollment for fall classes. There are guides for informal visits, visitors may sit in on classes, and stay overnight. To schedule a visit, contact the Office of Admissions. **Campus Safety and Security:** Measures include 24-hour foot and vehicle patrol, emergency notification system, self-defense education, and security escort services. There are emergency telephones, lighted pathways/sidewalks, a bike patrol, and a canine patrol.

REQUIREMENTS: The ACT is required. Applicants must have completed 16 academic credits, including 4 in English with a writing emphasis, 3 each in math (algebra and beyond) and social science, 2 in natural sciences, and 1 in fine or performing arts, as well as 3 in academic electives. A foreign language is recommended. The GED is accepted. AP and CLEP credits are accepted. To graduate, students must complete a minimum of 120 hours, including 35 to 64 in the major, and have a minimum GPA of 2.0; several majors require a higher cumulative GPA. General education requirements include a total of 39 to 45 hours in humanities, social sciences, multicultural studies, technology, English and oral communications, math, science, and individual development. A comprehensive exam may be part of the exit assessment in selected majors. **Procedure:** Freshmen are admitted to all sessions. Entrance exams should be taken in the junior year of high school. There is a rolling admissions plan. Application deadlines are open. Application fee is $30. Notification is sent on a rolling basis. Applications are accepted on-line. **Transfer Students:** 1006 transfer students enrolled in 2013-2014. Applicants must have a minimum GPA of 2.0, as indicated by an official college transcript. 30 of 120 credits required for the bachelor's degree must be completed at Central. **International Students:** There are 540 international students enrolled. The school actively recruits these students. They must take the TOEFL with a minimum score of 500 on the paper-based TOEFL (PBT), participate in institutional assessment. They must also take the ACT.

ADMISSIONS: 24% of the current freshmen were in the top fifth of their class; 55% were in the top two fifths. 20 freshmen graduated first in their class. **Admissions Contact:** Dr. Richard Sluder, Assistant Provost of Enrollment Management. E-Mail: *admit@ucmo.edu* Web: *www.ucmo.edu*

FINANCIAL AID: In 2014-2015, 94% of all full-time freshmen and 71% of continuing full-time students received some form of financial aid. 66% of all full-time freshmen and 62% of continuing full-time students received need-based aid. The average freshman award was $9,825. 11% of undergraduate students work part-time. Average annual earnings from campus work are $3300. The average financial indebtedness of the 2014 graduate was $23,766. Central is a member of CSS. The FAFSA is required. The priority date for freshman financial aid applications for fall entry is April 1.

UNIVERSITY OF MISSOURI SYSTEM

The University of Missouri System, established in 1963, is a public system in Missouri. It is governed by a board of curators, whose chief administrator is the president. The primary goal of the system is teaching, research, extension, and public service. The main priorities are access to quality learning, teaching, academic and research achievement, and quality community-university engagement. The total student enrollment of all 4 campuses is usually 75,000, with 8000 faculty members. Altogether there are 236 baccalaureate, 219 master's, and 135 doctoral programs offered in University of Missouri System. 4-year campuses are located in Columbia, Kansas City, Rolla, and St. Louis. Profiles of the 4-year campuses are included in this section.

UNIVERSITY OF MISSOURI/COLUMBIA C-2
www.missouri.edu

Columbia, MO 65211

(573) 882-7786
n/av

Fax: (573) 882-7887
Full-time: 12097 men, 13081 women
Part-time: 924 men, 894 women
Graduate: 3290 men, 4462 women
Year: semesters, summer session
Room & Board: $8944
ACT: required
Application Deadline: May 1

Email: MU4U@missouri.edu
Faculty: 1241; I, -$
Ph.D.s: 93%
Student/Faculty: 20 to 1
Tuition: $9257 ($23,366)
Freshman Class: n/av

CEEB CODE: 6875
MOST COMPETITIVE

The University of Missouri/Columbia, established in 1839, offers a comprehensive array of undergraduate and graduate programs as well as professional training in law, medicine, and veterinary medicine. There are 16 undergraduate schools and 19 graduate schools. In addition to regional accreditation, Mizzou has baccalaureate program accreditation with AACSB, ABET, ACEJMC, ADA, APTA, CAHEA, CSWE, FIDER, NASM, NCATE, NRPA, SAF, ACOTE, CAAHEP, and CADE. The 1262-acre campus is in a suburban area 120 miles west of St. Louis and 120 miles east of Kansas City. Including any residence halls, there are 350 buildings.

STUDENT LIFE: 71% of undergraduates are from Missouri. Others are from 50 states, 115 foreign countries, and Canada. 81% are White. **Male To Female Ratio:** 1.1:1. The average age of freshmen is 18; all undergraduates, 20. 16% do not continue beyond their first year; 71% remain to graduate. **Housing:** 7177 students can be accommodated in college housing, which includes single-sex and coed dorms, off-campus apartments, and married student housing. In addition, there are honors houses, language houses, special-interest houses, fraternity houses, sorority houses, International houses, quiet houses, graduate/professional houses, and learning/living communities by major. 74% of students commute. Alcohol is not permitted. All students may keep cars.

FACULTY/CLASSROOMS: 63% of faculty are male; 37% are female. No introductory courses are taught by graduate students.

PROGRAMS OF STUDY: Mizzou confers B.A., B.S., B.E.S., B.F.A., B.G.S., B.H.S., B.J., B.M., B.S.Acc., B.S.B.A., B.S.B.E., B.S.ChE., B.S.CiE., B.O.S., B.S.E.E., B.S.Ed., B.S.F., B.S.F.W., B.S.H.E.S., B.S.I.E., B.S.M.E., B.S.N. and B.S.W. degrees. Master's and Doctoral degrees are also awarded. Bachelor's degrees are awarded in AGRICULTURE (agricultural business management, agricultural economics, agriculture, animal science, fishing and fisheries, forestry and related sciences, plant science, and soil science), BIOLOGICAL SCIENCE (biochemistry, biology/biological science, microbiology, and nutrition), BUSINESS (accounting, banking and finance, business administration and management, business economics, hotel/motel and restaurant management, marketing/retailing/merchandising, real estate, and tourism), COMMUNICATIONS AND THE ARTS (advertising, art, art history and appreciation, broadcasting, classics, communications, creative writing, design, dramatic arts, English, English literature, French, German, journalism, linguistics, music, Russian, and Spanish), COMPUTER AND PHYSICAL SCIENCE (atmospheric sciences and meteorology, chemistry, computer science, geology, mathematics, physics, and statistics), EDUCATION (art education, early childhood education, education, education administration, elementary education, English education, mathematics education, middle school education, music education, science education, secondary education, and social studies education), ENGINEERING AND ENVIRONMENTAL DESIGN (biomedical engineering, chemical engineering, civil engineering, computer engineering, electrical/electronics engineering, engineering, industrial engineering, and mechanical engineering), HEALTH PROFESSIONS (nursing, occupational therapy, physical therapy, public health, radiological science, respiratory therapy, and veterinary science), SOCIAL SCIENCE (anthropology, archeology, child care/child and family studies, counseling/psychology, early childhood studies, economics, family/consumer resource management, food science, geography, history, human development, international studies, liberal arts/general studies, parks and recreation management, philosophy, political science/government, psychology, public administration, public affairs, religion, rural sociology, social science, social work, sociology, and textiles and clothing). Biological sciences, accounting, and journalism are the strongest academically. Business administration, journalism, and biological sciences have the largest enrollments.

ACTIVITIES: 22% of men belong to 32 national fraternities; 28% of women belong to 18 national sororities. There are 700 groups on campus, including art, band, cheerleading, chess, choir, chorale, chorus, computers, dance, debate, drama, drill team, drum and bugle corps, environmental, ethnic, film, gay, honors, international, jazz band, literary magazine, marching band, musical theater, newspaper, orchestra, pep band, photography, political, professional, radio and TV, religious, social, social service, student government, symphony, and yearbook. Popular campus events include Big Twelve athletics, academic weeks, and meet mizzou day. **Sports:** There are 8 intercollegiate sports for men and 10 for women, and 35 intramural sports for men and 37 for women. Facilities include recreation complex with a 50-meter competition pool and diving well, a club pool, a high-tech fitness club, a heavy-lifting gym, a climbing and bouldering wall, multicourts, racquetball courts, and an indoor track. There is a 62,000-seat stadium, a 1,300-seat indoor gym, and an 18,000-seat auditorium. **Graduates:** From July 1, 2013 to June 30, 2014, 5528 bachelor's degrees were awarded. The most popular majors were business (17%), journalism (12%), and health professions and related sciences (10%). 1786 companies recruited on campus in 2013-2014. In an average class, 46% graduate in 4 years or less, 67% graduate in 5 years or less, and 71% graduate in 6 years or less.

SERVICES: Counseling and information services are available, as is tutoring in some subjects. There is a reader service for the blind. **Library/Resources:** The 11 libraries contain 2.7 million volumes, 8.1 million microform items, 35,711 audio/video tapes/CDs/DVDs, and subscribe to 0 periodicals including electronic. Computerized library services include interlibrary loans, database searching, Internet access, and Wi-Fi capability. Special learning facilities include an art gallery, natural history museum, radio station, TV station, astronomy observatory; freedom of information center; herbarium; State Historical Society of Missouri; Western Historical Manuscripts; and anthropology, fishery, wildlife collections, Life Sciences Center. **Physically Challenged Students:** All of the campus is accessible. Facilities include wheelchair ramps, elevators, special parking, specially equipped restrooms, special class scheduling, lowered drinking fountains, lowered telephones, and special housing. **Special:** Available academic programs include co-op programs and cross-registration with other schools, internships, study abroad, a Washington semester, and work-study programs. Special degrees or studies include an accelerated degree, dual majors, a general studies degree, and student-designed majors. For highly motivated students, there is an honors college and the possibility of early admission to the schools of law and medicine. There are 25 national honor societies, including Phi Beta Kappa, a freshman honors program, and 34 departmental honors programs. **Visiting:** There are regularly scheduled orientations for prospective students, consisting of a campus tour, a visit with an admissions representative, and a visit with an academic representative on request. There are guides for informal visits and visitors may sit in on classes. To schedule a visit, contact the Admissions Office at (573) 882-2456. **Campus Safety and Security:** Measures include 24-hour foot and vehicle patrol, emergency notification system, self-defense education, and security escort services. There are shuttle buses, emergency telephones, lighted pathways/sidewalks, a 24-hour bicycle patrol.

REQUIREMENTS: The ACT is required. Students may gain probationary admission with sufficient GED scores. The usual requirements are completion of 17 Carnegie units, including 4 each in English and math, 3 each in social studies and science, 2 in a foreign language, and 1 in fine arts. Admission is determined by these units and a combination of class rank and ACT score. AP and CLEP credits are accepted. Important factors in the admissions decision are advanced placement or honors courses and evidence of special talent.To graduate, students must maintain a minimum 2.0 GPA and complete at least 120 credits, of which at least 30 must be in their major, although credit requirements can vary by degree program. All students must take English, plus 2 additional writing-intensive

courses, demonstrate competency in college algebra, take 1 additional course in development math and reasoning skills, and complete a course in American history or government. Students must complete 9 hours in social and behavioral sciences, 9 in physical and biological sciences (including 1 lab course), and 9 in humanities and fine arts. A capstone experience is also required. **Procedure:** Freshmen are admitted to all sessions. Entrance exams should be taken late in the junior year or in the senior year. There are deferred admissions and rolling admissions plans. Applications should be filed by May 1 for fall entry, along with a $50 fee. Notification is sent on a rolling basis. Applications are accepted on-line. **Transfer Students:** 1407 transfer students enrolled in 2013-2014. Transfer students must present 24 hours of completed college-level course work with a minimum 2.5 GPA. Students must also complete college algebra or equivalent as well as freshman English or equivalent with a C- or better. 30 of 120 credits required for the bachelor's degree must be completed at Mizzou. **International Students:** There are 798 international students enrolled. The school actively recruits these students. They must take the TOEFL.

ADMISSIONS: The ACT scores were 6% below 21, 23% between 21 and 23, 31% between 24 and 26, 18% between 27 and 28, and 23% above 28. There were 29 National Merit finalists. 235 freshmen graduated first in their class. **Admissions Contact:** Barbara Rupp, Director of Undergraduate Admissions. E-Mail: *MU4U@missouri.edu* Web: *www.missouri.edu*

FINANCIAL AID: In 2014-2015, 52% of all full-time freshmen and 48% of continuing full-time students received some form of financial aid. 46% of all full-time freshmen and 39% of continuing full-time students received need-based aid. The average financial indebtedness of the 2014 graduate was $23,588. The FAFSA is required. The priority date for freshman financial aid applications for fall entry is March 1.

UNIVERSITY OF MISSOURI-KANSAS CITY   A-2
www.umkc.edu

Kansas City, MO 64110	(816) 235-1111
	1-800-775-8652
Fax: (816) 235-5544	Email: admit@umkc.edu
Full-time: 2950 men, 3863 women	Faculty: 1, -$
Part-time: 1386 men, 2048 women	Ph.D.s: 85%
Graduate: 2519 men, 2980 women	Student/Faculty: 13 to 1
Year: semesters, summer session	Tuition: $8103 ($20,850)
Room & Board: $11,500	Freshman Class: 4462 applied, 2919 accepted, 1078 enrolled
SAT M/W: 570/540	CEEB CODE: 6872
Application Deadline: open	COMPETITIVE

The University of Missouri/Kansas City, which opened in 1933, is a public institution offering undergraduate and graduate programs in the arts and sciences, engineering, business, education, health fields, preprofessional, and professional studies. There are 10 undergraduate schools and 12 graduate schools. In addition to regional accreditation, UMKC has baccalaureate program accreditation with AACSB, ABET, ACPE, ADA, NASM, NCATE, NLN, NASM, NAST, and CCNE. The 149-acre campus is in an urban area in Kansas City. Including any residence halls, there are 68 buildings.

STUDENT LIFE: 73% of undergraduates are from Missouri. Others are from 42 states, 42 foreign countries, and Canada. 60% are White; 14% African American. **Male To Female Ratio:** 1.3:1. The average age of freshmen is 18; all undergraduates, 23. 27% do not continue beyond their first year; 73% remain to graduate. **Housing:** 1399 students can be accommodated in college housing, which includes coed dorms, on-campus apartments, and married student housing. In addition, there are fraternity houses and sorority houses. On-campus housing is available on a first-come, first-served basis. 95% of students commute. Alcohol is not permitted. All students may keep cars.

FACULTY/CLASSROOMS: 54% of faculty are male; 46% are female. No introductory courses are taught by graduate students. The average class size in an introductory lecture is 30; in a laboratory is 16; and in a regular course is 24.

PROGRAMS OF STUDY: UMKC confers B.A., B.S., B.B.A., B.F.A., B.I.T., B.L.A., B.M., B.M.E., B.S.C.I.E., B.S.D.H., B.S.E.E., B.S.M.E., B.H.S. and B.S.N. degrees. Master's and Doctoral degrees are also awarded. Bachelor's degrees are awarded in BIOLOGICAL SCIENCE (bioinformatics, biology/biological science, and biotechnology), BUSINESS (accounting and business administration and management), COMMUNICATIONS AND THE ARTS (art history and appreciation, communications, dance, dramatic arts, English, French, German, information technology, music, music performance, music theory and composition, performing arts, Spanish, and studio art), COMPUTER AND PHYSICAL SCIENCE (chemistry, computer science, geology, mathematics, and physics), EDUCATION (early childhood education, elementary education, middle school education, music education, and secondary education), ENGINEERING AND ENVIRONMENTAL DESIGN (civil engineering, electrical/electronics engineering, environmental science, and mechanical engineering), HEALTH PROFESSIONS (dental hygiene, health, health science, music therapy, and nursing), SOCIAL SCIENCE (criminal justice, economics, geography, history, Judaic studies, liberal arts/general studies, philosophy, political science/government, psychology, sociology, and urban studies). Health sciences and performing arts is the strongest academically. Liberal arts has the largest enrollment.

ACTIVITIES: 4% of men belong to 6 national fraternities; 6% of women belong to 2 local and 7 national sororities. There are 255 groups on campus, including art, band, cheerleading, chess, choir, chorale, chorus, computers, dance, debate, drama, ethnic, gay, honors, international, jazz band, literary magazine, newspaper, opera, orchestra, photography, political, professional, radio and TV, religious, social, social service, student government, and yearbook. Popular campus events include International Food and Culture Night, Welcome Back Week and Spring Fling, Homecoming and Court Warming. **Sports:** There are 6 intercollegiate sports for men and 8 for women, and 13 intramural sports for men and 13 for women. Facilities include a recreation center with 5 gyms, an indoor/outdoor pool, indoor and outdoor tracks, a fitness center, and handball, racquetball, and squash courts. There are also recreation facilities at the university center. **Graduates:** From July 1, 2013 to June 30, 2014, 1759 bachelor's degrees were awarded. The most popular majors were liberal arts (14%), business administration (11%), and nursing (10%). In an average class, 2% graduate in 3 years or less, 23% graduate in 4 years or less, 40% graduate in 5 years or less, and 47% graduate in 6 years or less.

SERVICES: Counseling and information services are available, as is tutoring in some subjects, accounting, biology, chemistry, foreign languages, writing, and math and statistics. There is a reader service for the blind. **Library/Resources:** The 4 libraries contain 1.1 million volumes, 1.2 million microform items, 353,243 audio/video tapes/CDs/DVDs, and subscribe to 7,222 periodicals including electronic. Computerized library services include interlibrary loans, database searching, and Internet access. Special learning facilities include a planetarium and radio station. **Physically Challenged Students:** 95% of the campus is accessible. Facilities include wheelchair ramps, elevators, special parking, specially equipped restrooms, special class scheduling, lowered drinking fountains, lowered telephones, and special housing. **Special:** Special academic programs include co-op programs and internships in several majors, study abroad in 8 countries, an accelerated degree program, and dual majors. Special degrees include a B.A.-B.S. degree in the computer science program and a liberal arts degree offered by the adult program. The pass/fail option is available in some courses. Freshmen may enter 6-year medical and dental programs. There are 4 national honor societies, a freshman honors program, and 1 departmental honors programs. **Visiting:** There are regularly scheduled orientations for prospective students, consisting of a 1-day program for new freshmen or a half-day optional program for transfer students. There are guides for informal visits. To schedule a visit, contact the UMKC Welcome Center at (816) 235-8652. **Campus Safety and Security:** Measures include 24-hour foot and vehicle patrol, emergency notification system, self-defense education, and security escort services. There are shuttle buses, emergency telephones, lighted pathways/sidewalks, and controlled access to dorms/residences.

REQUIREMENTS: The ACT is required. A combination of the student's test score and class rank determines admissibility; if the rank is 47 or below, the ACT score must be 23 or higher. Graduation from an accredited secondary school is a requirement for admission; the GED is also accepted. Required high school subjects include 4 units each of English and math, 3 each of social studies and science, 1 of arts, and 2 of a foreign language. A portfolio is required for art majors, an audition for music majors, and an interview for only those students applying for the pharmacy degree or the 6-year medical and dental programs. AP and CLEP credits are accepted. Most candidates for the B.A. and B.S. degrees must complete a core curriculum that consists of courses in English, a foreign language, math, philosophy, fine arts, history, literature, natural sciences, and social sciences. They must complete 120 credit hours, including 30 in their major, with a 2.0 GPA. **Procedure:** Freshmen are admitted to all sessions. Entrance exams should be taken by March of the senior year. There is a rolling admissions plan. Application deadlines are open. Application fee is $45. Applications are accepted on-line. **Transfer Students:** 1371 transfer students enrolled in 2013-2014. Transfer Students need to have an overall 2.0 GPA on a 4.0 scale in all coursework, which includes repeated coursework, attempted at previous institutions. Transfer students must send in all official college transcripts from all colleges and universities where coursework was attempted. Transfer students with fewer than 24 hours of transferable college credit must also send in official high school transcripts. Some academic units and departments have specific admission requirements in addition to general university requirements. 30 of 120 credits required for the bachelor's degree must be completed at UMKC. **International Students:** There are 822 international students enrolled. The school actively recruits these students. They must take the TOEFL with a minimum score of 550 on the paper-based TOEFL (PBT) or 79 on the Internet-based version (iBT).

ADMISSIONS: 65% of the 2014-2015 applicants were accepted. The SAT scores for the 2014-2015 freshman class were: Math--24% below 500, 34% between 500 and 599, 25% between 600 and 699, and 17% between 700 and 800; Writing--19% below 500, 43% between 500 and 599, 19% between 600 and 699, and 17% between 700 and 800. The ACT scores were 22% below 21, 25% between 21 and 23, 24% between 24 and 26, 11% between 27 and 28, and 18% above 28. 44% of the current freshmen were in the top fifth of their class; 77% were in the top two fifths. **Admissions Contact:** Tamara Byland, Director of Admissions. E-Mail: *admit@umkc.edu* Web: *www.umkc.edu/admissions*

FINANCIAL AID: In 2014-2015, 69% of all full-time freshmen and continuing full-time students received some form of financial aid. 66% of all full-time freshmen and continuing full-time students received need-based aid. The average freshman award was $10,463. Need-based scholarships or need-based grants averaged $7,401; and need-based self-help aid (loans and jobs) averaged $6,935. The FAFSA is required. The priority date for freshman financial aid applications for fall entry is March 1.

UNIVERSITY OF MISSOURI-ST. LOUIS   D-2
www.umsl.edu

St. Louis, MO 63121	**(314) 516-UMSL**
	n/av
Fax: (314) 516-5310	**Email: admissions@umsl.edu**
Full-time: 2558 men, 3513 women	**Faculty:** 712; I, --$
Part-time: 3258 men, 4558 women	**Ph.D.s:** 74%
Graduate: 1062 men, 2136 women	**Student/Faculty:** 17 to 1
Year: semesters, summer session	**Tuition:** $9474 ($24,429)
Room & Board: n/ap	**Freshman Class:** 1733 applied, 1312 accepted, 513 enrolled
SAT CR/M/W: 550/612/510 **ACT:** 24	**CEEB CODE:** 6889
Application Deadline: July 1	**VERY COMPETITIVE**

The University of Missouri/St. Louis, founded in 1963, is a public institution offering undergraduate and graduate programs and conferring degrees in arts and sciences, business, nursing, education, engineering, and optometry. UMSL is recognized for its contributions to the social and economic advancement of the St. Louis region.

Awards include ranking 14th nationally in "Best College and University Civic Partnerships" for economic, social, and cultural impact on metro regions. UMSL also achieved the Carnegie Foundation's Community Engagement Classification for exceptional collaboration with the community for the mutually beneficial exchange of knowledge and resources. Nationally recognized programs include criminology and criminal justice, biology and the Harris World Ecology Center, business, and counseling. UMSL students consistently score high on licensing exams in nursing, optometry, clinical psychology, and education. There are 7 undergraduate schools and 5 graduate schools. In addition to regional accreditation, UMSL has baccalaureate program accreditation with AACSB, ABET, CSWE, NASM, NCATE, and CCNE. The 350-acre campus is in an urban area 10 miles north of downtown St. Louis, Missouri. Including any residence halls, there are 44 buildings.

STUDENT LIFE: 84% of undergraduates are from Missouri. Others are from 48 states, 69 foreign countries, and Canada. 80% are from public schools. 70% are White; 15% African American. **Male To Female Ratio:** 1.5:1. The average age of freshmen is 18; all undergraduates, 26. 21% do not continue beyond their first year; 42% remain to graduate. **Housing:** 1202 students can be accommodated in college housing, which includes coed dorms, on-campus apartments, and married student housing. In addition, there are honors houses, language houses, special-interest houses, fraternity houses, sorority houses, Including theme house, wellness house, students over 21 apartments, and graduate/professional school housing. On-campus housing is available on a first-come and first-served basis. 91% of students commute. All students may keep cars.

FACULTY/CLASSROOMS: 43% of faculty are male; 577% are female. 41% teach undergraduates, 11% do research, and 20% do both. Graduate students teach 21% of introductory courses. The average class size in an introductory lecture is 29; in a laboratory is 16; and in a regular course is 19.

PROGRAMS OF STUDY: UMSL confers B.A., B.S., B.F.A., B.L.S., B.M., B.M.E., B.M, B.S.Acc., B.S.B.A., B.S.C.I.E., B.S.Ed., B.S.E.E., B.S.M.E., B.E.S., B.S.N., B.S.P.P.A., B.S.W., B.I.S. and B.S.I.S. degrees. Master's and Doctoral degrees are also awarded. Bachelor's degrees are awarded in BIOLOGICAL SCIENCE (biochemistry, biology/biological science, and biotechnology), BUSINESS (accounting, business administration and management, finance, international business management, logistics, management information systems, marketing management, and operations management), COMMUNICATIONS AND THE ARTS (art history and appreciation, communications, dance, dramatic arts, English, French, German, Germanic languages and literature, Japanese, media arts, music, Spanish, and studio art), COMPUTER AND PHYSICAL SCIENCE (chemistry, computer science, information sciences and systems, mathematics, and physics), EDUCATION (early childhood education, education, elementary education, music education, physical education, secondary education, and special education), ENGINEERING AND ENVIRONMENTAL DESIGN (civil engineering, electrical/electronics engineering, and mechanical engineering), HEALTH PROFESSIONS (nursing), SOCIAL SCIENCE (anthropology, criminal justice, economics, history, interdisciplinary studies, liberal arts/general studies, philosophy, political science/government, psychology, public administration, social work, and sociology). Biology, chemistry, biochem/biotech, nursing, and international business are the strongest academically. Business, education, and nursing have the largest enrollments.

ACTIVITIES: 3% of men belong to 3 national fraternities; 2% of women belong to 3 national sororities. There are 96 groups on campus, including art, band, cheerleading, choir, chorale, chorus, computers, dance, debate, drama, environmental, ethnic, forensics, gay, honors, international, jazz band, literary magazine, newspaper, opera, pep band, photography, political, professional, radio and TV, religious, social, social service, and student government. Popular campus events include Expo, Weeks of Welcome, Family Weekend, MLK Day of Service, and Mirthday. **Sports:** There are 6 intercollegiate sports for men and 7 for women, and 12 intramural sports for men and 12 for women. Facilities include indoor jogging track, fitness center, handball/racquetball, basketball, volleyball, and badminton courts; wrestling, dance, and conditioning rooms, and a swimming pool; outdoors, there are intramural fields and facilities for baseball, soccer, handball, racquetball, and tennis. **Graduates:** From July 1,

2013 to June 30, 2014, 1974 bachelor's degrees were awarded. The most popular majors were business administration (25%), health professions (12%), and education (11%). 325 companies recruited on campus in 2013-2014. In an average class, 20% graduate in 3 years or less, 18% graduate in 4 years or less, 7% graduate in 5 years or less, and 46% graduate in 6 years or less. Of the 2013 graduating class, 12% were enrolled in graduate school within 6 months of graduation, and 76% were employed.

SERVICES: Counseling and information services are available, as is tutoring in most subjects, math and writing labs. There is remedial math. **Library/Resources:** The 2 libraries contain 1.3 million volumes, 1.3 million microform items, 4,058 audio/video tapes/CDs/DVDs, and subscribe to 2,374 periodicals including electronic. Computerized library services include interlibrary loans, database searching, Internet access, and Wi-Fi capability. Special learning facilities include an art gallery, planetarium, radio station, TV station, libraries include the Thomas Jefferson library, and the St. Louis Mercantile library includes a collection of American art and realia, including are art galleries, observatory, on-campus pre-school, honors college, nonprofit management/leadership program, women in public life institute; centers for nanoscience, neurodynamics, emerging technologies, entrepreneurship and economic education, international studies, transportation studies, gerontology, teaching and learning; performing arts, world ecology, technology and learning, math, science education, eye care, ELS language, trauma recovery, student success, and French, German, and Greek cultural centers. **Physically Challenged Students:** All of the campus is accessible. Facilities include wheelchair ramps, elevators, special parking, specially equipped restrooms, special class scheduling, lowered drinking fountains, lowered telephones, and special housing. **Special:** Cross-registration with Washington University, St. Louis University, and St. Louis Community College and cooperative programs in all majors are offered. Study abroad in 32 countries, including England, France, and Germany are available. Most degree programs are available through the Evening Courses. There is an accelerated nursing degree program and student-designed majors for the B.L.S. There are 24 national honor societies and a freshman honors program. **Visiting:** There are regularly scheduled orientations for prospective students, 20-minute info session, special appointments if needed and a campus walking tour. There are guides for informal visits, visitors may sit in on classes, and stay overnight. To schedule a visit, contact Yolanda Weathersby at (314) 516-6877. **Campus Safety and Security:** Measures include 24-hour foot and vehicle patrol, emergency notification system, self-defense education, and security escort services. There are shuttle buses, emergency telephones, lighted pathways/sidewalks, controlled access to dorms/residences, criminal investigations.

REQUIREMENTS: The SAT or ACT is required. Applicants are required to have a total of 17 units, including 4 each in English and math, 3 each in social studies and science, 2 in the same foreign language, and 1 in fine arts. Class rank and test scores are used to determine eligibility for admission. AP and CLEP credits are accepted. To graduate, students must complete 120 credit hours, 42 of which must be in the area of general education. They must maintain a 2.3 GPA. The number of hours required for the major varies. **Procedure:** Freshmen are admitted fall, spring, and summer. Entrance exams should be taken in the junior year. There is a rolling admissions plan. Application deadlines are open. Application fee is $35. Notification is sent on a rolling basis. Applications are accepted on-line. **Transfer Students:** 1572 transfer students enrolled in 2013-2014. Transfer students must have earned a minimum of 24 credit hours and maintained a minimum 2.3 GPA. 30 of 120 credits required for the bachelor's degree must be completed at UMSL. **International Students:** There are 352 international students enrolled. The school actively recruits these students. They must take the TOEFL with a minimum score of 500 on the paper-based TOEFL (PBT) or 61 on the Internet-based version (iBT) and the college's own test.

ADMISSIONS: 76% of the 2014-2015 applicants were accepted. The SAT scores for the 2014-2015 freshman class were: Critical Reading--36% below 500, 37% between 500 and 599, and 27% between 600 and 699; Math--33% below 500, 33% between 600 and 699, and 25% between 700 and 800; Writing--46% below 500, 27% between 500 and 599, and 27% between 600 and 699. The ACT scores were 17% below 21, 28% between 21 and 23, 28% between 24 and 26, 13%

between 27 and 28, and 14% above 28. 51% of the current freshmen were in the top fifth of their class; 76% were in the top two fifths. **Admissions Contact:** Jerry D. Hoffman, Associate Director of Admissions. E-Mail: *admissions@umsl.edu* Web: *www.umsl.edu*

FINANCIAL AID: The average freshman award was $16,179. Need-based scholarships or need-based grants averaged $5,831 ($12,045 maximum); need-based self-help aid (loans and jobs) averaged $3,499 ($8,000 maximum); non-need-based athletic scholarships averaged $9,581 ($25,180 maximum); and other non-need-based awards and non-need-based scholarships averaged $9,572 ($32,572 maximum). Average annual earnings from campus work are $3727. The average financial indebtedness of the 2014 graduate was $23,617. The FAFSA is required. The priority date for freshman financial aid applications for fall entry is March 1.

WASHINGTON UNIVERSITY IN ST. LOUIS D-3
www.wustl.edu

St. Louis, MO 63130	(314) 935-6000
	(800) 638-0700
Fax: (314) 935-4290	Email: admissions@wustl.edu
Full-time: 3308 men, 3378 women	Faculty: I
Part-time: 259 men, 456 women	Ph.D.s: 94%
Graduate: 3494 men, 3453 women	Student/Faculty: 8 to 1
Year: semesters, summer session	Tuition: $55,467
Room & Board: $14,377	Freshman Class: 29211 applied, 5004 accepted, 1734 enrolled
SAT or ACT: required	CEEB CODE: 6929
Application Deadline: January 15	MOST COMPETITIVE

Washington University, founded in 1853, is a private institution offering undergraduate and graduate programs in arts and sciences, business, architecture, engineering, art, and professional programs in law, medicine (including physical therapy and occupational therapy), and social work. There are 5 undergraduate schools and 8 graduate schools. In addition to regional accreditation, Washington U. has baccalaureate program accreditation with AACSB, ABET, and NASAD. The 169-acre campus is in a suburban area 7 miles west of St. Louis, MO. Including any residence halls, there are 113 buildings.

STUDENT LIFE: 93% of undergraduates are from out of state, mostly the Midwest. Students are from 50 states, 50 foreign countries, and Canada. 56% are from public schools. 55% are White; 17% Asian American. **Male To Female Ratio:** 1.0:1. The average age of freshmen is 18; all undergraduates, 21. 3% do not continue beyond their first year; 95% remain to graduate. **Housing:** 5406 students can be accommodated in college housing, which includes single-sex and coed dorms, on-campus apartments, off-campus apartments, and married student housing. In addition, there are special-interest houses, fraternity houses, special-interest suites, upper-class housing, and small group housing for students who share common interests and goals. On-campus housing is guaranteed for the freshman year only and is available on a lottery system for upperclassmen. 65% of students live on campus; of those, 97% remain on campus on weekends. Upperclassmen may keep cars.

FACULTY/CLASSROOMS: 62% of faculty are male; 38% are female. No introductory courses are taught by graduate students. The average class size in an introductory lecture is 33.

PROGRAMS OF STUDY: Washington U. confers B.A., B.S., B.F.A., B.M., B.S.B.A., B.S.B.M.E., B.S.C.E., B.S.Ch.E., B.S.C.S., B.S.Co.E., B.S.E.E., B.S.I.M., B.S.M.E. and B.S.S.S.E. degrees. Associate, Master's, and Doctoral degrees are also awarded. Bachelor's degrees are awarded in AGRICULTURE (environmental studies, natural resource management, and plant science), BIOLOGICAL SCIENCE (biochemistry, bioinformatics, biology/biological science, biomathematics, biophysics, ecology, and neurosciences), BUSINESS (accounting, banking and finance, business administration and management, business economics, entrepreneurial studies, human resources, international business management, international economics, marketing management, marketing/retailing/merchandising, and trade and industrial supervision and management), COMMUNI-

CATIONS AND THE ARTS (advertising, American literature, Arabic, art history and appreciation, ceramic art and design, Chinese, classical languages, classics, communications, comparative literature, creative writing, dance, design, dramatic arts, drawing, East Asian languages and literature, English, English literature, film arts, fine arts, French, German, Germanic languages and literature, graphic design, Greek (classical), Hebrew, illustration, Italian, Japanese, journalism, languages, Latin, linguistics, literature, music, music theory and composition, painting, performing arts, photography, printmaking, romance languages and literature, sculpture, Spanish, studio art, and visual and performing arts), COMPUTER AND PHYSICAL SCIENCE (applied mathematics, chemistry, computer programming, computer science, earth science, geology, geophysics and seismology, information sciences and systems, mathematics, physical sciences, physics, and statistics), EDUCATION (art education, education, elementary education, foreign languages education, mathematics education, middle school education, science education, secondary education, social science education, and social studies education), ENGINEERING AND ENVIRONMENTAL DESIGN (architectural technology, architecture, bioengineering, biomedical engineering, chemical engineering, civil engineering, commercial art, computer engineering, electrical/electronics engineering, engineering, engineering mechanics, environmental science, mechanical engineering, systems engineering, and technology and public affairs), HEALTH PROFESSIONS (allied health, health care administration, health science, pharmacy, predentistry, premedicine, prepharmacy, and preveterinary science), SOCIAL SCIENCE (African studies, African American studies, American studies, anthropology, archeology, area studies, Asian/Oriental studies, biopsychology, East Asian studies, Eastern European studies, economics, ethnic studies, European studies, fashion design and technology, history, humanities, industrial and organizational psychology, interdisciplinary studies, international relations, international studies, Islamic studies, Judaic studies, Latin American studies, Middle Eastern studies, Near Eastern studies, philosophy, political science/government, psychology, religion, social science, South Asian studies, systems science, urban studies, Western European studies, and women's studies). Social sciences, engineering, business, biological/life sciences, and psychology are the strongest academically. Social sciences, engineering, and business have the largest enrollments.

ACTIVITIES: 25% of men belong to 10 national fraternities; 25% of women belong to 8 national sororities. There are 300 groups on campus, including art, band, cheerleading, chess, choir, chorale, chorus, computers, dance, debate, drama, environmental, ethnic, film, forensics, gay, honors, international, jazz band, literary magazine, musical theater, newspaper, opera, orchestra, pep band, photography, political, professional, radio and TV, religious, social, social service, student government, symphony, and yearbook. Popular campus events include Multicultural Celebrations, W.I.L.D. (concert festival), and student-run carnival. **Sports:** There are 9 intercollegiate sports for men and 10 for women, and 33 intramural sports for men and 33 for women. Facilities include a swimming pool, tracks, a weight room, saunas, recreational playing fields, a football stadium, a fitness center, and racquetball, tennis, handball, wallyball, and squash courts. **Graduates:** From July 1, 2013 to June 30, 2014, 1798 bachelor's degrees were awarded. The most popular majors were biology and psychology (18%), engineering (16%), and business (14%). 400 companies recruited on campus in 2013-2014. In an average class, 90% graduate in 4 years or less, 94% graduate in 5 years or less, and 95% graduate in 6 years or less. Of the 2013 graduating class, 33% were enrolled in graduate school within 6 months of graduation, and 62% were employed.

SERVICES: Counseling and information services are available, as is tutoring in every subject. There is a reader service for the blind. **Library/Resources:** The 12 libraries contain 5.2 million volumes, 3.5 million microform items, 96,234 audio/video tapes/CDs/DVDs, and subscribe to 116,120 periodicals including electronic. Computerized library services include interlibrary loans, database searching, Internet access, and Wi-Fi capability. Special learning facilities include an art gallery, planetarium, radio station, TV station, a dance studio, a professional theater, observatory, and studio theater. **Physically Challenged Students:** 95% of the campus is accessible. Facilities include wheelchair ramps, elevators, special parking, specially equipped restrooms, special class scheduling, lowered drinking fountains, lowered telephones. **Special:** Opportunities are provided for cooperative programs with other schools, internships, work-study programs, study abroad, a Washington (D.C.) semester, accelerated degree programs, a B.A.-B.S. engineering degree, credit by examination, nondegree study, pass/fail options, and dual and student-designed majors. There are 19 national honor societies and including Phi Beta Kappa. **Visiting:** There are regularly scheduled orientations for prospective students, student visits consist of group presentations followed by a campus tour, as well as class visits and meetings with current students and faculty. There are guides for informal visits, visitors may sit in on classes, and stay overnight. To schedule a visit, contact the Office of Undergraduate Admissions at (800) 638-0700. **Campus Safety and Security:** Measures include 24-hour foot and vehicle patrol, emergency notification system, self-defense education, and security escort services. There are shuttle buses, emergency telephones, lighted pathways/sidewalks, and controlled access to dorms/residences.

REQUIREMENTS: The SAT or ACT is required. An essay is required from all applicants. Portfolios are required for students applying to the College of Art. Portfolios are encouraged for students applying to the College of Architecture. 4 years of English, math, science, and social studies are recommended. Up to 4 years of a foreign language and history are recommended. Also required are recommendations from a teacher and a counselor. AP credits are accepted. **Procedure:** Freshmen are admitted fall. Entrance exams should be taken By December of the senior year. There are early decision and deferred admissions plans. Early decision applications should be filed by November 15; regular applications, by January 15 for fall entry, along with a $75 fee. Notification of early decision is sent December 15; regular decision, April 1. 637 early decision candidates were accepted for the 2014-2015 class. Applications are accepted on-line. **Transfer Students:** 93 transfer students enrolled in 2013-2014. **International Students:** There are 598 international students enrolled. The school actively recruits these students. They must take the TOEFL with a minimum score of 550 on the paper-based TOEFL (PBT) or 100 on the Internet-based version (iBT). They must also take the SAT or ACT.

ADMISSIONS: 17% of the 2014-2015 applicants were accepted. The SAT scores for the 2014-2015 freshman class were: Critical Reading--1% between 500 and 599, 21% between 600 and 699, and 78% between 700 and 800; Math--11% between 600 and 699, and 89% between 700 and 800; Writing--1% between 500 and 599, 21% between 600 and 699, and 78% between 700 and 800. The ACT scores were 1% between 27 and 28, and 99% above 28. **Admissions Contact:** Office of Undergraduate Admissions E-Mail: *admissions@wustl.edu* Web: *www.wustl.edu*

FINANCIAL AID: In 2014-2015, 55% of all full-time freshmen and 51% of continuing full-time students received some form of financial aid. 41% of all full-time freshmen and 38% of continuing full-time students received need-based aid. Average annual earnings from campus work are $2139. Washington U. is a member of CSS. The CSS/Profile and FAFSA, and Finalized FAFSA using IRS Data Retrieval Tool are required. The deadline for filing freshman financial aid applications for fall entry is February 1.

Webster University is committed to delivering high-quality learning experiences that transform students for global citizenship and individual excellence. With its home campus in St. Louis, Webster University is the only Tier 1, private, non-profit U.S.-based university providing a network of international residential campuses. Founded in 1915, Webster University's campus network includes traditional, metropolitan, military and corporate locations around the world. Webster University is an independent institution with programs in fine and performing arts, liberal arts and sciences, media communications, education, nursing, and business. There are 5 undergraduate schools and 5 graduate schools. In addition to regional accreditation, Webster has baccalaureate program accreditation with ACBSP, NASM, NCATE, NLN, ABA, and COA. The 47-acre campus is in a suburban area 6 miles southwest of St. Louis. Including any residence halls, there are 41 buildings.

STUDENT LIFE: 73% of undergraduates are from Missouri. Others are from 44 states, 71 foreign countries, and Canada. 67% are White; 13% African American. **Male To Female Ratio:** 1.4:1. The average age of freshmen is 18; all undergraduates, 23. 23% do not continue beyond their first year; 64% remain to graduate. **Housing:** 730 students can be accommodated in college housing, which includes single-sex and coed dorms and on-campus apartments. In addition, there are special-interest houses. On-campus housing is available on a first-come, first-served basis, and is available on a lottery system for upperclassmen. Priority is given to out-of-town students. 75% of students commute. All students may keep cars.

FACULTY/CLASSROOMS: 55% of faculty are male; 45% are female. All teach undergraduates. No introductory courses are taught by graduate students. The average class size in an introductory lecture is 14; in a laboratory is 11; and in a regular course is 13.

PROGRAMS OF STUDY: Webster confers B.A., B.S., B.F.A., B.M., B.M.Ed. and B.S.N. degrees. Master's and Doctoral degrees are also awarded. Bachelor's degrees are awarded in AGRICULTURE (environmental studies), BIOLOGICAL SCIENCE (biology/biological science), BUSINESS (accounting, business administration and management, finance, management science, and marketing management), COMMUNICATIONS AND THE ARTS (acting, advertising, animation, art history, art, art history and appreciation, audio technology, ballet, ceramic art and design, choral music, communications, costume design, creative writing, dance, digital communications, dramatic arts, English, film arts, French, German, graphic design, information technology, instrumental performance, instrumental music education, jazz, journalism, media arts, music, music performance, music theory and composition, musical theater, painting, photography, piano performance, playwriting/screenwriting, printmaking, public relations, scenic and lighting design, sculpture, Spanish, studio art, theater design, video, vocal performance, voice, and vocal music education), COMPUTER AND PHYSICAL SCIENCE (computer management, computer science, information sciences and systems, and mathematics), EDUCATION (art education, early childhood education, education, elementary education, foreign languages education, journalism education, mathematics education, middle school education, music education, secondary education, social studies education, social studies secondary school education, and special education), HEALTH PROFESSIONS (nursing), SOCIAL SCIENCE (American studies, area studies, cultural anthropology, economics, European studies, history, interdisciplinary studies, international relations, legal studies, philosophy, political science/government, psychology, religion, religious studies, social science, sociology, and women's studies). Fine arts is the strongest academically. Business has the largest enrollment.

ACTIVITIES: 3% of women belong to 1 local sororities. There are 67 groups on campus, including and international, art, band, cheerleading, chess, choir, chorale, chorus, communications, computers, dance, debate, departmental, drama, environmental, ethnic, film, forensics, gay, international, jazz band, literary magazine, musical theater, newspaper, opera, orchestra, photography, political, professional, radio and TV, religious, social, social service, student government, and symphony. Popular campus events include Homecoming, Webster Works Worldwide and Spring Fest. **Sports:** There are 8 intercollegiate sports for men and 8 for women, and 4 intramural sports for men and 4 for women. Facilities include a gym, an athletic training center, a sauna, a fitness center, a 25-yard 6-lane indoor

---

WEBSTER UNIVERSITY   D-2
www.webster.edu

St. Louis, MO 63119	(314) 246-7080
	1-800-753-6765
Fax: 314-246-7116	Email: jamesmyers79@webster.edu
Full-time: 1126 men, 1318 women	Faculty: 198
Part-time: 230 men, 254 women	Ph.D.s: 82%
Graduate: 596 men, 1168 women	Student/Faculty: 12 to 1
Year: semesters, summer session	Tuition: $24,500
Room & Board: $10,600	Freshman Class: 1863 applied, 1038 accepted, 457 enrolled
ACT: 24	CEEB CODE: 6933
Application Deadline: August 1	COMPETITIVE+

swimming pool. **Graduates:** From July 1, 2013 to June 30, 2014, 746 bachelor's degrees were awarded. The most popular majors were management (16%), education (5%), and psychology (5%). 52 companies recruited on campus in 2013-2014. In an average class, 8% graduate in 3 years or less, 43% graduate in 4 years or less, 61% graduate in 5 years or less, and 64% graduate in 6 years or less.

SERVICES: Counseling and information services are available, as is tutoring in most subjects. There is a reader service for the blind. Peer tutoring and study skills training are available. **Library/Resources:** The library contains 277,838 volumes, 137,800 microform items, 29,328 audio/video tapes/CDs/DVDs, and subscribes to 1,419 periodicals including electronic. Computerized library services include interlibrary loans, database searching, Internet access, and Wi-Fi capability. Special learning facilities include an art gallery, radio station, TV station, a media center, a theater, and a community music school. **Physically Challenged Students:** 75% of the campus is accessible. Facilities include wheelchair ramps, elevators, special parking, specially equipped restrooms, special class scheduling, lowered drinking fountains, lowered telephones, special housing. Telephones for the hearing impaired, automatic door openers, a reading machine, computer for paraplegic students, reading and writing software, deaf interpreters, note takers, and textbooks on tape. All TV monitors in classrooms have closed caption capabilities. **Special:** Webster University offers co-op programs, work-study programs, internships, dual majors, student-designed majors, and a 3-2 engineering degree with the University of Missouri/Columbia and Washington University. Study abroad in at least 12 countries is available. **Visiting:** There are regularly scheduled orientations for prospective students, consisting of an open house, which includes classes, meetings with faculty, a financial aid workshop, a tour of the university, and a student activities overview. There are guides for informal visits, visitors may sit in on classes, and stay overnight. To schedule a visit, contact the Visit Coordinator at (800) 753-6765. **Campus Safety and Security:** Measures include 24-hour foot and vehicle patrol, emergency notification system, self-defense education, and security escort services. There are emergency telephones, lighted pathways/sidewalks, and controlled access to dorms/residences.

REQUIREMENTS: The ACT is required. Applicants must be graduates of an accredited secondary school. The GED is accepted. Webster recommends that students complete 16 high school academic units, including 4 units of English, 3 each of social studies/history and math, and 2 each of foreign language, science, and electives. An essay is required of all students, and a portfolio or audition is required for art, dance, music, musical theater, and film. Webster requires applicants to be in the upper 50% of their class. AP and CLEP credits are accepted. Important factors in the admissions decision are advanced placement or honors courses, leadership record, and recommendations by school officials. To graduate, students must complete at least 128 semester hours, with a minimum GPA of 2.0. They must successfully complete an approved major, which may or may not require more than 128 credit hours, and successfully complete the global citizenship program or general education program requirements. All new degree-seeking freshmen with fewer than 16 college credit hours are required to take a freshman seminar. At least 30 semester credits of a student's final 36 credits must be earned at Webster. **Procedure:** Freshmen are admitted fall, spring, and summer. Entrance exams should be taken in the spring of the junior year. There are deferred admissions and rolling admissions plans. Applications should be filed by August 1 for fall entry; December 1 for spring entry, along with a $35 fee. Notification is sent on a rolling basis. Applications are accepted on-line. **Transfer Students:** 319 transfer students enrolled in 2013-2014. Applicants for transfer must have a minimum GPA of 2.0 for college credit completed. If they have fewer than 30 transferable hours, they must submit high school transcripts. 30 of 128 credits required for the bachelor's degree must be completed at Webster. **International Students:** There are 93 international students enrolled. The school actively recruits these students. They must take the TOEFL with a minimum score of 550 on the paper-based TOEFL (PBT) or 80 on the Internet-based version (iBT) and the Comprehensive English Language Test, written and oral/listening tests, or take the IELTS, SAT or ACT if they are graduates of U.S. high schools or international secondary schools that use English as the language of instruction.

ADMISSIONS: 56% of the 2014-2015 applicants were accepted. The ACT scores were 25% below 21, 27% between 21 and 23, 22% between 24 and 26, 11% between 27 and 28, and 15% above 28. 35% of the current freshmen were in the top fifth of their class; 64% were in the top two fifths. 3 freshmen graduated first in their class. **Admissions Contact:** James Myers, Associate VP Undergraduate Admissions. E-Mail: *jamesmyers79@webster.edu* Web: *www.webster.edu/admissions/undergraduate/*

FINANCIAL AID: In 2014-2015, 97% of all full-time freshmen and 91% of continuing full-time students received some form of financial aid. 75% of all full-time freshmen and 69% of continuing full-time students received need-based aid. The average freshman award was $25,457. Need-based scholarships or need-based grants averaged $10,659; need-based self-help aid (loans and jobs) averaged $9,262; other non-need-based awards and non-need-based scholarships averaged $11,679; and $3,756 from other forms of aid. 20% of undergraduate students work part-time. Average annual earnings from campus work are $3840. The average financial indebtedness of the 2014 graduate was $23,704. Webster is a member of CSS. The FAFSA and the college's own financial statement are required. The priority date for freshman financial aid applications for fall entry is March 1. The deadline for filing freshman financial aid applications for fall entry is August 1.

WESTMINSTER COLLEGE   C-2
www.westminister-mo.edu

Fulton, MO 65251	**(573) 592-5251**
	(800) 475-3361
Fax: (573) 592-5255	**Email:** kelle.silvey@westminster-mo.edu
Full-time: 540 men, 394 women	**Faculty:** 59; IIB, --$
Part-time: 2 men, 8 women	**Ph.D.s:** 91%
Graduate: none	**Student/Faculty:** 14 to 1
Year: semesters, summer session	**Tuition:** $22,560
Room & Board: $9160	**Freshman Class:** 1356 applied, 910 accepted, 219 enrolled
SAT: recommended **ACT:** 24	**CEEB CODE:** 6937
Application Deadline: open	**VERY COMPETITIVE**

Westminster College, founded in 1851, is a private liberal arts and sciences college affiliated with the Presbyterian Church. There is 1 undergraduate school. The 87-acre campus is in a small town 20 miles east of Columbia and 25 miles north of Jefferson City. Including any residence halls, there are 26 buildings.

STUDENT LIFE: 63% of undergraduates are from Missouri. Others are from 28 states, and 70 foreign countries. 75% are from public schools. 65% are White; 16% Foreign. 56% are Protestant; 20% Catholic; 15% claim no religious affiliation. **Male To Female Ratio:** 0.7:1. The average age of freshmen is 18; all undergraduates, 20. 22% do not continue beyond their first year; 68% remain to graduate. **Housing:** 900 students can be accommodated in college housing, which includes single-sex and coed dorms and off-campus apartments. In addition, there are special-interest houses and fraternity houses. On-campus housing is guaranteed for all 4 years. 84% of students live on campus; of those, 95% remain on campus on weekends. All students may keep cars.

FACULTY/CLASSROOMS: 57% of faculty are male; 43% are female. All teach undergraduates, 75% do research, and 75% do both. No introductory courses are taught by graduate students. The average class size in an introductory lecture is 19; in a laboratory is 20; and in a regular course is 15.

PROGRAMS OF STUDY: Westminster confers B.A. degrees. Bachelor's degrees are awarded in BIOLOGICAL SCIENCE (biochemistry and biology/biological science), BUSINESS (accounting, business administration and management, business communications, international business management, management information systems, and sports management), COMMUNICATIONS AND THE ARTS (English, French, and Spanish), COMPUTER AND PHYSICAL SCIENCE (chemistry, computer science, mathematics, and physics), EDUCATION (elementary education, middle school education, physical education, secondary education, and sports and wellness studies), ENGINEERING AND ENVIRONMENTAL DESIGN (environmental science), HEALTH PROFESSIONS (nursing), SOCIAL SCIENCE (anthropology, economics, history, international studies, philosophy, political science/government, psychology, religion, and sociology). English, biology, psychology, leadership studies, and transnational/international studies are the strongest academically. Business administration, biology, and psychology have the largest enrollments.

ACTIVITIES: 45% of men belong to 6 national fraternities; 34% of women belong to 4 national sororities. There are 65 groups on campus, including and Multicultural Club, International Club, art, Blue Blazers investment club, cheerleading, choir, chorale, chorus, computers, dance, drama, environmental, ethnic, gay, honors, international, jazz band, literary magazine, musical theater, newspaper, pep band, photography, political, professional, religious, social, social service, and student government. Popular campus events include Alumni Weekend, Westminster Symposium, Undergraduate Scholars Forum, What if...? Conference and International Week. **Sports:** There are 8 intercollegiate sports for men and 8 for women, and 16 intramural sports for men and 10 for women. Facilities include an 800-seat gym, aerobic training center, weight room, training room, football, baseball, softball, soccer fields, field sports area, tennis, racquetball, sand volleyball courts, a swimming pool, indoor rifle range, and a 1500-seat auditorium/arena. **Graduates:** From July 1, 2013 to June 30, 2014, 253 bachelor's degrees were awarded. The most popular majors were business administration/management (29%), biology and psychology (19%), and education (10%). 71 companies recruited on campus in 2013-2014. In an average class, 48% graduate in 4 years or less, 64% graduate in 5 years or less, and 68% graduate in 6 years or less. Of the 2013 graduating class, 24% were enrolled in graduate school within 6 months of graduation, and 90% were employed.

SERVICES: Counseling and information services are available, as is tutoring in most subjects. There is remedial math, reading, and writing. **Library/Resources:** The 2 libraries contain 100,265 volumes, 6,912 microform items, 9,691 audio/video tapes/CDs/DVDs, and subscribe to 30,201 periodicals including electronic. Computerized library services include interlibrary loans, database searching, Internet access, and Wi-Fi capability. **Physically Challenged Students:** 80% of the campus is accessible. Facilities include wheelchair ramps, elevators, special parking, specially equipped restrooms, special class scheduling, lowered drinking fountains, and lowered telephones. **Special:** Westminster offers co-op programs with colleges of the Mid-Missouri Associated Colleges and Universities, cross-registration with William Woods University, internships in all areas, study abroad in 15 countries, a Washington semester, a United Nations semester, and an urban studies program in Chicago. Student-designed majors are available as well as a dual degree nursing program with Golfarb School of Nursing at Barnes-Jewish College, dual degree program with Logan University of Chiropractic, and a 3-2 engineering degree with Washington University in St. Louis. The pass/fail option and dual majors are available. There are 16 national honor societies, a freshman honors program, and 8 departmental honors programs. **Visiting:** There are regularly scheduled orientations for prospective students, including 1-day summer programs with a general orientation and class registration. There are guides for informal visits, visitors may sit in on classes, and stay overnight. To schedule a visit, contact Kelle Silvey, Director of Admissions. **Campus Safety and Security:** Measures include 24-hour foot and vehicle patrol, emergency notification system, self-defense education, and security escort services. There are emergency telephones and lighted pathways/sidewalks.

REQUIREMENTS: The ACT is required. The SAT is recommended. Applicants must be graduates of an accredited secondary school. The GED is also accepted. Students must have completed 4 years each of social studies and English, 3 years each of math and science, and 2 years each of a foreign language and history. An essay is required and an interview is recommended. Westminster requires applicants to be in the upper 50% of their class. AP and CLEP credits are accepted. Important factors in the admissions decision are advanced placement or honors courses, leadership record, and extracurricular activities record. To graduate, students must complete 122 credit hours, including a maximum of 40 hours in their major, with a minimum GPA

of 2.0. All students are required to take Westminster seminar, academic writing, statistics or calculus, 4 hours of foreign language, and 1 hour of phys ed. Students must also take 6 to 10 hours (37 to 42 total) in scientific inquiry, historical awareness, fundamental questions, artistic expression, human behaviors and institutions, cultural diversity, and global interdependence. In addition, an integrative upper-level course, 2 writing intensive courses, and an upper-level course from a non-major academic division are required. **Procedure:** Freshmen are admitted to all sessions. Entrance exams should be taken in the junior year of high school. There are early decision, deferred admissions, and rolling admissions plans. Application deadlines are open. Applications are accepted on-line. **Transfer Students:** 65 transfer students enrolled in 2013-2014. Applicants must have taken either the ACT or the SAT and must complete at least 4 semesters at Westminster as full-time students. 60 of 122 credits required for the bachelor's degree must be completed at Westminster. **International Students:** There are 159 international students enrolled. The school actively recruits these students. They must take the TOEFL.

ADMISSIONS: 67% of the 2014-2015 applicants were accepted. The ACT scores were 17% below 21, 28% between 21 and 23, 22% between 24 and 26, 17% between 27 and 28, and 18% above 28. 44% of the current freshmen were in the top fifth of their class; 69% were in the top two fifths. 5 freshmen graduated first in their class. **Admissions Contact:** Kille Silvey, Director of Admissions. E-Mail: kelle.silvey@westminster-mo.edu Web: www.westminister-mo.edu

FINANCIAL AID: In 2014-2015, 99% of all full-time freshmen and 99% of continuing full-time students received some form of financial aid. 53% of all full-time freshmen and 57% of continuing full-time students received need-based aid. The average freshman award was $20,155. Need-based scholarships or need-based grants averaged $15,940; and need-based self-help aid (loans and jobs) averaged $4,660. 66% of undergraduate students work part-time. Average annual earnings from campus work are $2000. The average financial indebtedness of the 2014 graduate was $26,723. The FAFSA is required. The priority date for freshman financial aid applications for fall entry is February 15.

WILLIAM JEWELL COLLEGE　　　　　　B-2
www.jewell.edu

Liberty, MO 64068	**(816) 781-7700, ext. 5137**
	(800) 753-7009
Fax: (816) 415-5027	**Email: admission@william.jewell.edu**
Full-time: 414 men, 616 women	**Faculty:** 70
Part-time: none	**Ph.D.s:** 86%
Graduate: n/av	**Student/Faculty:** 15 to 1
Year: semesters, summer session	**Tuition:** $24,300
Room & Board: $6700	**Freshman Class:** 2497 applied, 1374 accepted, 282 enrolled
SAT: required **ACT:** 26	**CEEB CODE:** 6941
Application Deadline: August 15	**VERY COMPETITIVE+**

William Jewell College, founded in 1849, is an academically selective liberal arts college and offers undergraduate programs in the arts and sciences, business, education, and nursing fields. The figures in the above capsule and in this profile are approximate. In addition to regional accreditation, Jewell has baccalaureate program accreditation with NASM and CCNE. The 200-acre campus is in a suburban area 15 miles northeast of Kansas City. Including any residence halls, there are 28 buildings.

STUDENT LIFE: 69% of undergraduates are from Missouri. Others are from 30 states, and 11 foreign countries. 91% are from public schools. 82% are White. 51% are Protestant; 35% claim no religious affiliation; 11% Catholic. **Male To Female Ratio:** 1.5:1. The average age of freshmen is 19; all undergraduates, 20. 22% do not continue beyond their first year; 63% remain to graduate. **Housing:** 1013 students can be accommodated in college housing, which includes single-sex and coed dorms. In addition, there are honors houses, language houses, fraternity houses, and sorority houses. On-campus housing is guaranteed for all 4 years. 75% of students live on campus; of those, 60% remain on campus on weekends. Alcohol is not permitted. All students may keep cars.

FACULTY/CLASSROOMS: 51% of faculty are male; 49% are female. 80% teach undergraduates, and 20% do both. No introductory courses are taught by graduate students. The average class size in an introductory lecture is 20; in a laboratory is 18; and in a regular course is 15.

PROGRAMS OF STUDY: Jewell confers B.A., and B.S. degrees. Bachelor's degrees are awarded in BIOLOGICAL SCIENCE (biochemistry and biology/biological science), BUSINESS (accounting, business administration and management, business economics, and international business management), COMMUNICATIONS AND THE ARTS (art, communications, dramatic arts, English, French, music, and Spanish), COMPUTER AND PHYSICAL SCIENCE (chemistry, mathematics, and physics), EDUCATION (elementary education, music education, and secondary education), HEALTH PROFESSIONS (medical laboratory technology and nursing), SOCIAL SCIENCE (history, international relations, Japanese studies, philosophy, political science/government, psychology, and religion). Business has the largest enrollment.

ACTIVITIES: 31% of men belong to 3 national fraternities; 34% of women belong to 4 national sororities. There are 60 groups on campus, including cheerleading, choir, chorale, chorus, computers, dance, debate, drama, drill team, ethnic, gay, honors, international, jazz band, ministries, musical theater, newspaper, orchestra, pep band, photography, political, professional, radio and TV, religious, social, social service, student government, and symphony. Popular campus events include Hanging of the Green/Lighting of the Quad and Family Weekend. **Sports:** There are 9 intercollegiate sports for men and 9 for women, and 12 intramural sports for men and 12 for women. Facilities include a football and soccer stadium, a complex for baseball and softball, and a phys ed center with an indoor track, a dance room, and facilities for basketball, racquetball, swimming, indoor tennis, volleyball, and weight lifting. The total seating capacity of the stadium is 3200 and that of the indoor gym is 1000. **Graduates:** From July 1, 2013 to June 30, 2014, 267 bachelor's degrees were awarded. The most popular majors were business/marketing (22%), health professions and related sciences (17%), and psychology (11%). 36 companies recruited on campus in 2013-2014. In an average class, 54% graduate in 4 years or less, 62% graduate in 5 years or less, and 63% graduate in 6 years or less. Of the 2013 graduating class, 25% were enrolled in graduate school within 6 months of graduation, and 75% were employed.

SERVICES: Counseling and information services are available, as is tutoring in most subjects. **Library/Resources:** The library contains 231,031 volumes, 1,050 microform items, 11,232 audio/video tapes/CDs/DVDs, and subscribes to 500 periodicals including electronic. Computerized library services include interlibrary loans, database searching, and Internet access. Special learning facilities include an art gallery, planetarium, and radio station. **Physically Challenged Students:** 85% of the campus is accessible. Facilities include wheelchair ramps, elevators, special parking, specially equipped restrooms, special class scheduling, lowered drinking fountains, lowered telephones, and special housing. **Special:** Internships for juniors or seniors, study abroad in Europe, Japan, Mexico, Australia, and Hong Kong, and a Washington semester are offered. B.A.-B.S. degrees, dual majors of any combination, internships, an accelerated degree in nursing, student-designed majors, and 3-2 engineering degrees with Washington University and the Universities of Missouri and Kansas are available. The Oxbridge Honors Program for major study is patterned after the teaching methods of Oxford and Cambridge and includes a year at either Oxford or Cambridge. Leadership and service learning programs are offered. There are 13 national honor societies, a freshman honors program, and 13 departmental honors programs. **Visiting:** There are regularly scheduled orientations for prospective students, and personalized visits can be arranged upon request. There are guides for informal visits and visitors may sit in on classes. To schedule a visit, contact the Admission Office. **Campus Safety and Security:** Measures include 24-hour foot and vehicle patrol, emergency notification system, and self-defense education. There are emergency telephones, lighted pathways/sidewalks, and controlled access to dorms/residences.

REQUIREMENTS: The SAT or ACT is required. Students must be graduates of an accredited secondary school; the GED is also accepted. The college requires that applicants have taken 4 English courses and 4 academic electives, 3 courses each in math, social studies, and science; of these, 1 must be a lab, 2 in foreign language. An interview is recommended. An audition is advised for music applicants. AP and CLEP credits are accepted. Important factors in the admissions decision are advanced placement or honors courses, extracurricular activities record, and leadership record. To graduate, students must complete a minimum of 124 credits with a minimum 2.0 GPA, fulfilling the proper core requirements for their major and degree. All students must take The Responsible Self in their first year, and must also take courses in oral and written communication, phys ed, math, and foreign language, interdisciplinary courses in 4 categories, and a core curriculum capstone course. Comprehensive exams in most majors are required. **Procedure:** Freshmen are admitted fall, spring, and summer. Entrance exams should be taken in the junior year. There are deferred admissions and rolling admissions plans. Applications should be filed by August 15 for fall entry, along with a $25 fee. Notification is sent on a rolling basis. Applications are accepted on-line. **Transfer Students:** 44 transfer students enrolled in 2013-2014. Transfer students must have maintained a 2.5 GPA and be in good academic standing with their former schools and submit all college transcripts. Education majors must take the ACT, achieving a minimum score of 20. An interview is recommended for all students. 30 of 124 credits required for the bachelor's degree must be completed at Jewell. **International Students:** There are 22 international students enrolled. The school actively recruits these students. They must take the TOEFL with a minimum score of 550 on the paper-based TOEFL (PBT) or 80 on the Internet-based version (iBT) or take the MELAB.

ADMISSIONS: 55% of the 2014-2015 applicants were accepted. The SAT scores for the 2014-2015 freshman class were: Critical Reading--24% below 500, 30% between 500 and 599, 39% between 600 and 699, and 7% between 700 and 800; Math--21% below 500, 34% between 500 and 599, 39% between 600 and 699, and 11% between 700 and 800. The ACT scores were 9% below 21, 22% between 21 and 23, 25% between 24 and 26, 18% between 27 and 28, and 26% above 28. 68% of the current freshmen were in the top fifth of their class; 92% were in the top two fifths. 28 freshmen graduated first in their class. **Admissions Contact:** Bridget Gramling, Dean of Admissions. E-Mail: *admission@william.jewell.edu* Web: *www.jewell.edu*

FINANCIAL AID: In 2014-2015, 99% of all full-time freshmen and 96% of continuing full-time students received some form of financial aid. 72% of all full-time freshmen and 69% of continuing full-time students received need-based aid. The average freshman award was $25,316. Need-based self-help aid (loans and jobs) averaged $6,783 ($16,500 maximum). The average financial indebtedness of the 2014 graduate was $24,102. Jewell is a member of CSS. The FAFSA is required. The priority date for freshman financial aid applications for fall entry is March 1.

WILLIAM WOODS UNIVERSITY C-2
www.williamwoods.edu

Fulton, MO 65251	**(573) 592-4221**
	(800) 995-3159
Fax: (573) 592-1146	Email: admissions@williamwoods.edu
Full-time: 207 men, 657 women	**Faculty:** 56
Part-time: 51 men, 154 women	**Ph.D.s:** 60%
Graduate: 512 men, 802 women	**Student/Faculty:** 14 to 1
Year: semesters, summer session	**Tuition:** $17,310
Room & Board: $6950	**Freshman Class:** 877 applied, 672 accepted, 243 enrolled
SAT CR/M: 560/510 **ACT:** 23	**CEEB CODE:** 6944
Application Deadline: open	**COMPETITIVE**

William Woods University, founded in 1870, is an independent professions-oriented, liberal arts institution affiliated with the Christian Church (Disciples of Christ). Unique programs of study include an equestrian studies program and a four-year American Sign Language Interpreting program. Figures in the above capsule and in this profile are approximate. There is one undergraduate school and one graduate school. In addition to regional accreditation, William Woods has baccalaureate program accreditation with CSWE, CAATE, and CAAHEP. The 170-acre campus is in a small town 100 miles west of St. Louis. Including any residence halls, there are 35 buildings.

STUDENT LIFE: 70% of undergraduates are from Missouri. Others are from 44 states, 5 foreign countries, and Canada. 83% are White. 42% are Baptist, Christian, Methodist, Lutheran, Presbyterian, Pentecost; 30% claim no religious affiliation; 21% Catholic. **Male To Female Ratio:** 2.1:1. The average age of freshmen is 19; all undergraduates, 21. 22% do not continue beyond their first year; 55% remain to graduate. **Housing:** 760 students can be accommodated in college housing, which includes single-sex and coed dorms and on-campus apartments. In addition, there are special-interest houses, fraternity houses, sorority houses, Nonsmoking and independent housing. On-campus housing is guaranteed for all 4 years. 80% of students live on campus; of those, 60% remain on campus on weekends. All students may keep cars.

FACULTY/CLASSROOMS: 46% of faculty are male; 54% are female. All teach undergraduates. No introductory courses are taught by graduate students. The average class size in an introductory lecture is 25; in a laboratory is 15; and in a regular course is 20.

PROGRAMS OF STUDY: William Woods confers B.A., B.S., B.F.A. and B.S.W. degrees. Associate and Master's degrees are also awarded. Bachelor's degrees are awarded in AGRICULTURE (equine science), BIOLOGICAL SCIENCE (biology/biological science), BUSINESS (accounting and business administration and management), COMMUNICATIONS AND THE ARTS (art, communications, dramatic arts, English, graphic design, journalism, and studio art), COMPUTER AND PHYSICAL SCIENCE (computer science, information sciences and systems, mathematics, and science), EDUCATION (athletic training, early childhood education, elementary education, middle school education, physical education, and special education), SOCIAL SCIENCE (family/juvenile justice, history, interdisciplinary studies, international studies, interpreter for the deaf, paralegal studies, political science/government, psychology, and social work). Business, equestrian studies, and education are the strongest academically, and have the largest enrollments.

ACTIVITIES: 22% of men belong to 2 national fraternities; 30% of women belong to 4 national sororities. There are 40 groups on campus, including art, cheerleading, choir, drama, honors, international, musical theater, newspaper, professional, radio and TV, religious, social, social service, and student government. Popular campus events include Salute to the Arts, Campus Involvement and Activities Fair, and Autumn at the Woods. **Sports:** There are 5 intercollegiate sports for men and 6 for women, and 7 intramural sports for men and 7 for women. Facilities include a gym, a fitness center, a sand volleyball court, tennis courts, soccer, baseball, and softball fields, a weight room, a lake with a sand beach, table tennis and pool tables, a cross-country trail equipped with FitTrail stations, and a sauna.

Graduates: From July 1, 2013 to June 30, 2014, 215 bachelor's degrees were awarded. The most popular majors were business (29%), education (16%), and equestrian studies/equestrian (16%). 50 companies recruited on campus in 2013-2014. In an average class, 44% graduate in 4 years or less and 48% graduate in 6 years or less.

SERVICES: Counseling and information services are available, as is tutoring in most subjects. There is a reader service for the blind, and remedial math and writing. Interpreting is provided for the deaf upon request and receipt of supporting documentation. **Library/ Resources:** The library contains 134,538 volumes, 11,072 microform items, and 28,711 audio/video tapes/CDs/DVDs, and subscribes to 15,796 periodicals including electronic. Computerized library services include interlibrary loans, database searching, and Internet access. Special learning facilities include an art gallery, radio station, 12 "smart classrooms" equipped with Smartboards and networked computers, labs for photography, foreign languages, art, and American Sign Language interpreting, equestrian studies stables, a model courtroom, and an observatory. **Physically Challenged Students:** 85% of the campus is accessible. Facilities include wheelchair ramps, elevators, special parking, specially equipped restrooms, special class scheduling, lowered telephones. Campus access to TTY phones. **Special:** William Woods University offers cross-registration with schools in the Mid-Missouri Association of Colleges and Universities, internships in various fields, including equestrian studies and computer

information systems, study abroad, a Washington semester, and work-study. An accelerated degree program in most majors, B.A.-B.S. degrees, and student-designed and dual majors are possible. Credit for life, military, and work experience and pass/fail are available. The LEAD (Leading, Educating, Achieving, and Developing) program provides awards ($5000 to residential students) to any incoming student who makes a commitment to attend a minimum number of campus activities and participate within the surrounding community. There are 12 national honor societies and a freshman honors program. **Visiting:** There are regularly scheduled orientations for prospective students, including the opportunity to talk with an academic adviser and an extensive student development-directed orientation to campus life. There are guides for informal visits, visitors may sit in on classes, and stay overnight. To schedule a visit, contact the Office of Enrollment Services. **Campus Safety and Security:** Measures include 24-hour foot and vehicle patrol, self-defense education, and security escort services. There are emergency telephones and lighted pathways/sidewalks.

REQUIREMENTS: The SAT or ACT is required, with a score of 870 on the SAT or 18 on the ACT. Students must graduate within the top 50% of an accredited high school class to be admitted. The GED is also accepted. They must have completed 16 course units, 11 of which must be distributed among English, a foreign language, math, natural sciences, and social sciences. 2 references are required, and an interview is recommended. William Woods requires applicants to be in the upper 50% of their class. AP and CLEP credits are accepted. Important factors in the admissions decision are personality/intangible qualities, leadership record, and recommendations by school officials.Students must complete a minimum of 122 credits to graduate, including at least 30 in the major and 52 in Common Studies, with 7 in the natural sciences, 6 each in English, the humanities, and behavioral and social sciences, 3 each in oral communication, math, and fine or performing arts, and 2 in freshman seminar. They must have maintained a minimum GPA of 2.0. An internship or other culimating project is required for many majors. **Procedure:** Freshmen are admitted to all sessions. Entrance exams should be taken in the spring of the junior year or the fall of the senior year. There are deferred admissions and rolling admissions plans. Application deadlines are open. Application fee is $25. Applications are accepted on-line. **Transfer Students:** 114 transfer students enrolled in 2013-2014. Transfer students must submit high school transcripts or GED and all college transcripts. They must also provide 2 references and be in good standing with their previous institution. 30 of 122 credits required for the bachelor's degree must be completed at William Woods. **International Students:** There are 8 international students enrolled. The school actively recruits these students. They must take the TOEFL with a minimum score of 500 on the paper-based TOEFL (PBT) or 61 on the Internet-based version (iBT), or pass the STEP-EIKEN Grade Pre-1 test. They must also take the SAT or ACT, scoring 19.

ADMISSIONS: 77% of the 2014-2015 applicants were accepted. The SAT scores for the 2014-2015 freshman class were: Critical Reading--30% below 500, 39% between 500 and 599, 29% between 600 and 699, and 2% between 700 and 800; Math--44% below 500, 44% between 500 and 599, and 12% between 600 and 699. The ACT scores were 37% below 21, 22% between 21 and 23, 20% between 24 and 26, 9% between 27 and 28, and 12% above 28. 29% of the current freshmen were in the top fifth of their class; 58% were in the top two fifths. 5 freshmen graduated first in their class. **Admissions Contact:** Sarah Munns, Dean of Enrollment Services. E-Mail: *admissions@ williamwoods.edu* Web: *www.williamwoods.edu*

FINANCIAL AID: In 2014-2015, 100% of all full-time freshmen and 95% of continuing full-time students received some form of financial aid. 70% of all full-time freshmen and continuing full-time students received need-based aid. The average freshman award was $16,124. Need-based scholarships or need-based grants averaged $12,823; need-based self-help aid (loans and jobs) averaged $4,324; and non-need-based athletic scholarships averaged $6,415. 41% of undergraduate students work part-time. Average annual earnings from campus work are $1000. The average financial indebtedness of the 2014 graduate was $18,969. The FAFSA and the college's own financial statement are required. The deadline for filing freshman financial aid applications for fall entry is March 1.

MONTANA

College Location

0 20 40 60 80 100
Miles

CARROLL COLLEGE   C-3
www.carroll.edu

Helena, MT 59625

          (406) 447-4384
          (800) 992-3648

Fax: (406) 447-4533	**Email:** admissions@caroll.edu
Full-time: 575 men, 750 women	**Faculty:** n/av
Part-time: 95 men, 130 women	**Ph.D.s:** n/av
Graduate: n/av	**Student/Faculty:** n/av
Year: semesters, summer session	**Tuition:** $21,000
Room & Board: $7000	**Freshman Class:** n/av
SAT or ACT: required	**CEEB CODE:** 4041
Application Deadline: June 1	**COMPETITIVE**

Carroll College, founded in 1909, is a small liberal arts college affiliated with the Roman Catholic Church. It offers undergraduate programs in arts and sciences, business, engineering, nursing, education, religion, and selected preprofessional training. The figures in the above capsule and in this profile are approximate. In addition to regional accreditation, Carroll has baccalaureate program accreditation with CAHEA, CSWE, NLN, and NRPA. The 64-acre campus is in a small town 110 miles east of Missoula and 100 miles west of Bozeman. Including any residence halls, there are 16 buildings.

STUDENT LIFE: 64% of undergraduates are from Montana. Others are from 30 states, 11 foreign countries, and Canada. 81% are from public schools. 67% are White. 67% are Catholic; 31% Lutheran, Methodist and Baptist. **Male To Female Ratio:** 1.3:1. The average age of freshmen is 18; all undergraduates, 21. 21% do not continue beyond their first year; 60% remain to graduate. **Housing:** 830 students can be accommodated in college housing, which includes single-sex and coed dorms and on-campus apartments. On-campus housing is guaranteed for all 4 years. 54% of students live on campus; of those, 95% remain on campus on weekends. All students may keep cars.

FACULTY/CLASSROOMS: 62% of faculty are male; 38% are female.

All teach undergraduates. No introductory courses are taught by graduate students. The average class size in an introductory lecture is 22; in a laboratory is 13; and in a regular course is 17.

PROGRAMS OF STUDY: Carroll confers B.A. degrees. Associate degrees are also awarded. Bachelor's degrees are awarded in BIOLOGICAL SCIENCE (biology/biological science), BUSINESS (accounting and business administration and management), COMMUNICATIONS AND THE ARTS (classical languages, communications, creative writing, dramatic arts, English, French, performing arts, public relations, and Spanish), COMPUTER AND PHYSICAL SCIENCE (chemistry, computer science, and mathematics), EDUCATION (elementary education, foreign languages education, physical education, secondary education, and teaching English as a second/foreign language (TESOL/TEFOL)), ENGINEERING AND ENVIRONMENTAL DESIGN (civil engineering and environmental science), HEALTH PROFESSIONS (clinical science, health care administration, nursing, predentistry, premedicine, preoptometry, prepharmacy, and preveterinary science), SOCIAL SCIENCE (history, international relations, philosophy, political science/government, prelaw, psychology, public administration, religion, social science, and sociology). Business, nursing, and biology have the largest enrollments.

ACTIVITIES: There are no fraternities or sororities. There are 35 groups on campus, including art, cheerleading, choir, dance, drama, drill team, ethnic, film, forensics, honors, international, jazz band, literary magazine, musical theater, newspaper, pep band, political, professional, radio and TV, religious, social, social service, student government, and yearbook. Popular campus events include Theme Dances, Casino Night and Softball Tournament. **Sports:** There are 3 intercollegiate sports for men and 5 for women, and 10 intramural sports for men and 10 for women. Facilities include basketball, tennis, and racquetball courts, weight-lifting, aerobics, and dance rooms, a swimming pool, football stadium, soccer field, new fitness center, and a 4200-seat gym.

SERVICES: Counseling and information services are available, as is

tutoring in most subjects. There is remedial math, reading, and writing. **Library/Resources:** The library contains 89,003 volumes, 64,500 microform items, 3,890 audio/video tapes/CDs/DVDs, and subscribes to 504 periodicals including electronic. Computerized library services include interlibrary loans, database searching, and Internet access. Special learning facilities include a radio station, civil engineering lab, nursing lab (SimMan), performing arts theater and astronomical observatory. **Physically Challenged Students:** 90% of the campus is accessible. Facilities include wheelchair ramps, elevators, special parking, specially equipped restrooms, special class scheduling, and lowered drinking fountains. **Special:** Carroll College offers a 3-2 engineering program leading to acceptance to any of 6 cooperating universities. In addition, internships, study abroad in Paris, Japan, Spain, Germany, Korea, and many other countries through a consortium for international studies, and work-study programs in certain fields are available. Students may take a dual major in any two fields of study, select an interdisciplinary major such as health information management, earn credit for life, military, and work experience, or pursue nondegree study. The pass/fail option is available. There are 6 national honor societies, including Phi Beta Kappa, a freshman honors program, and 5 departmental honors programs. **Visiting:** There are regularly scheduled orientations for prospective students. There are guides for informal visits, visitors may sit in on classes, and stay overnight. To schedule a visit, contact the Admissions Office. **Campus Safety and Security:** Measures include security escort services. There are lighted pathways/sidewalks.

REQUIREMENTS: The SAT or ACT is required. Students must be graduates of an accredited secondary school or have a GED. An essay is required. A GPA of 2.5 is required. AP and CLEP credits are accepted. Important factors in the admissions decision are advanced placement or honors courses, recommendations by school officials, and leadership record. To graduate, students must complete 122 semester hours and maintain the specific GPA and credit concentration required by their major. The college's general liberal arts requirements include courses in writing, communications, history, math, natural and social sciences, philosophy, theology, and fine arts. **Procedure:** Freshmen are admitted fall and spring. Entrance exams should be taken in the fall of the senior year. There are deferred admissions and rolling admissions plans. Applications should be filed by June 1 for fall entry, along with a $35 fee. Notification is sent on a rolling basis. Applications are accepted on-line. **Transfer Students:** Transfer students need a 2.5 GPA and must submit ACT or SAT scores if fewer than 30 college credits have been completed. Letters of recommendation are required. 30 of 122 credits required for the bachelor's degree must be completed at Carroll. **International Students:** The school actively recruits these students. They must take the TOEFL. English-speaking students must submit SAT or ACT scores.

ADMISSIONS: Director of Admissions. E-Mail: *admissions@caroll .edu* Web: *www.carroll.edu*

FINANCIAL AID: The FAFSA is required. Check with the school for current application deadlines.

MONTANA STATE UNIVERSITY   C-3
www.montana.edu

Bozeman, MT 59717	(406) 994-2452
	888-MSU-CATS
Fax: (406) 994-1923	Email: admissions@montana.edu
Full-time: 5269 men, 4246 women	Faculty: 592
Part-time: 1049 men, 1015 women	Ph.D.s: 79%
Graduate: 911 men, 1069 women	Student/Faculty: 17 to 1
Year: semesters, summer session	Tuition: $6168 ($18,291)
Room & Board: $7900	Freshman Class: 5786 accepted, 2623 enrolled
SAT CR/M/W: 550/560/540 ACT: 24	CEEB CODE: 4488
Application Deadline: n/av	COMPETITIVE

Montana State University's missions is to provide a challenging and richly diverse learning environment in which the entire university community is fully engaged in supporting student success. To provide an environment that promotes the exploration, discovery, and

dissemination of new knowledge. To provide a collegial environment for faculty and students in which discovery and learning are closely integrated and highly valued. To serve the people and communities of Montana by sharing our expertise and collaborating with others to improve the lives and prosperity of Montanans. In accomplishing our mission, we remain committed to the wise stewardship of resources through meaningful assessment and public accountability. Figures in the above capsule and in this profile are approximate. There are 9 undergraduate schools and 1 graduate school. In addition to regional accreditation, MSU has baccalaureate program accreditation with AACSB, ABET, ADA, CSAB, NAAB, NASAD, NASM, NCATE, NLN, AAFCS, CACREP, and CCNE. The 1781-acre campus is in a small town 140 miles west of Billings and 90 miles north of Yellowstone National Park. Including any residence halls, there are 90 buildings.

STUDENT LIFE: 69% of undergraduates are from Montana. Others are from 50 states, 65 foreign countries, and Canada. 84% are White. **Male To Female Ratio:** 0.9:1. The average age of freshmen is 19; all undergraduates, 22. 29% do not continue beyond their first year; 47% remain to graduate. **Housing:** 5400 students can be accommodated in college housing, which includes coed dorms and married student housing. In addition, there are honors houses, floors for older students, nonsmoking floors, and wellness floors. On-campus housing is guaranteed for the freshman year only, and is available on a first-come, first-served basis. 75% of students commute. All students may keep cars.

FACULTY/CLASSROOMS: 62% of faculty are male; 38% are female. All teach and do research. Graduate students teach 21% of introductory courses. The average class size in an introductory lecture is 66; in a laboratory is 18; and in a regular course is 22.

PROGRAMS OF STUDY: MSU confers B.A., B.S., B.F.A. and B.Mus.Ed. degrees. Master's and Doctoral degrees are also awarded. Bachelor's degrees are awarded in AGRICULTURE (agricultural business management, animal science, horticulture, natural resource management, and plant science), BIOLOGICAL SCIENCE (biology/biological science, biotechnology, cell biology, microbiology, and neurosciences), BUSINESS (business administration and management), COMMUNICATIONS AND THE ARTS (art, English, fine arts, media arts, modern language, and music), COMPUTER AND PHYSICAL SCIENCE (chemistry, computer science, earth science, mathematics, and physics), EDUCATION (agricultural education, elementary education, music education, secondary education, and technical education), ENGINEERING AND ENVIRONMENTAL DESIGN (agricultural engineering technology, chemical engineering, civil engineering, computer engineering, construction engineering, electrical/electronics engineering, environmental design, environmental science, industrial engineering, land use management and reclamation, mechanical engineering, and mechanical engineering technology), HEALTH PROFESSIONS (health and nursing), SOCIAL SCIENCE (anthropology, economics, history, human development, liberal arts/general studies, philosophy, political science/government, psychology, and sociology). Engineering, physical science, and architecture are the strongest academically. Business, education, and nursing have the largest enrollments.

ACTIVITIES: 3% of men belong to 7 national fraternities; 3% of women belong to 4 national sororities. There are 150 groups on campus, including art, band, cheerleading, chess, choir, chorale, chorus, computers, dance, drama, drill team, environmental, ethnic, film, gay, honors, international, jazz band, marching band, musical theater, newspaper, orchestra, pep band, photography, political, professional, radio and TV, religious, social, social service, student government, and symphony. Popular campus events include International Food Bazaar and Native American Pow-Wow. **Sports:** There are 6 intercollegiate sports for men and 7 for women, and 38 intramural sports for men and 40 for women. **Graduates:** The most popular majors were engineering (12%), business (12%), and health professions and related sciences (10%). 126 companies recruited on campus in 2013-2014. In an average class, 17% graduate in 4 years or less, 40% graduate in 5 years or less, and 47% graduate in 6 years or less. Of the 2013 graduating class, 15% were enrolled in graduate school within 6 months of graduation, and 95% were employed.

SERVICES: Counseling and information services are available, as is tutoring in most subjects. There is a reader service for the blind, and remedial math, reading, and writing. **Library/Resources:** The 2 libraries contain 744,989 volumes, 2.2 million microform items, 13,446 audio/video tapes/CDs/DVDs, and subscribe to 10,131 periodicals including electronic. Computerized library services include interlibrary loans, database searching, and Internet access. Special learning facilities include an art gallery, natural history museum, planetarium, radio station, TV station, a center for biofilm engineering, Burns Telecommunication Center, and a geographic information and analysis center. **Physically Challenged Students:** 90% of the campus is accessible. Facilities include wheelchair ramps, elevators, special parking, specially equipped restrooms, special class scheduling, lowered drinking fountains, lowered telephones, services through the resource center, and a taping service for the blind. **Special:** Montana State University offers internships in selected majors, study in 40 countries, cross-registration in selected programs, B.A.-B.S. degrees, dual and interdisciplinary majors, nondegree study, and pass/fail options. There are 23 national honor societies and a freshman honors program. **Visiting:** There are regularly scheduled orientations for prospective students. There are guides for informal visits, visitors may sit in on classes, and stay overnight. To schedule a visit, contact the Office of New Student Services at orientation@montana .edu. **Campus Safety and Security:** Measures include 24-hour foot and vehicle patrol, emergency notification system, self-defense education, and security escort services. There are emergency telephones, lighted pathways/sidewalks, and controlled access to dorms/residences.

REQUIREMENTS: The SAT or ACT is required. MSU requires applicants to have a minimum GPA of 2.5, rank in the upper 50% of their graduating class or have minimum composite scores of 22 on the ACT or a satisfactory score on the SAT. They must be graduates of an accredited secondary school. The GED is accepted. Students should have completed 4 years of English, 3 years each of social studies and math, 2 years of lab science, and 2 years of language, computer science, visual and performing arts, or vocational education. AP and CLEP credits are accepted.To graduate, students must complete a core curriculum of 8 credits of natural sciences, 6 credits each of multicultural studies, humanities, social science, and communications, and 3 credits each of fine arts and math. The total number of credits required varies by program, with 120 being the minimum; at least one third must be in upper-division courses. A minimum 2.0 GPA is needed. Students must be officially registered in their chosen curriculum for at least 2 semesters before graduation. **Procedure:** Freshmen are admitted fall, spring, and summer. Entrance exams should be taken in the fall of the senior year. There are deferred admissions and rolling admissions plans. Application deadlines are open. The fall 2014 application fee was $30. Notification is sent on a rolling basis. Applications are accepted on-line. **Transfer Students:** 790 transfer students enrolled in 2013-2014. Applicants must have a minimum GPA of 2.0; grades of D or better transfer for credit. 30 of 120 credits required for the bachelor's degree must be completed at MSU. **International Students:** The school actively recruits these students. They must take the TOEFL with a minimum score of 525 on the paper-based TOEFL (PBT). Students must also submit proof of American Cultural Exchange Language Institute Level 6 (available at MSU).

ADMISSIONS: The SAT scores for the 2014-2015 freshman class were: Critical Reading--27% below 500, 39% between 500 and 599, 27% between 600 and 699, and 6% between 700 and 800; Math--24% below 500, 39% between 500 and 599, 29% between 600 and 699, and 7% between 700 and 800; Writing--31% below 500, 43% between 500 and 599, 21% between 600 and 699, and 4% between 700 and 800. The ACT scores were 21% below 21, 24% between 21 and 23, 23% between 24 and 26, 13% between 27 and 28, and 19% above 28. There were 6 National Merit finalists. 114 freshmen graduated first in their class. **Admissions Contact:** Ronda Russell, Director, Admissions. E-Mail: *admissions@montana.edu* Web: *www.montana.edu*

FINANCIAL AID: In 2014-2015, 54% of all full-time freshmen and 56% of continuing full-time students received some form of financial aid. 50% of undergraduate students work part-time. The average financial indebtedness of the 2014 graduate was $24,421. The FAFSA is required. Check with the school for current application deadlines.

MONTANA STATE UNIVERSITY-BILLINGS (*The complete profile is made available exclusively on our website, www.barronspac.com*)

MONTANA STATE UNIVERSITY-NORTHERN (*The complete profile is made available exclusively on our website, www.barronspac.com*)

MONTANA TECH OF THE UNIVERSITY OF MONTANA   B-3
www.mtech.edu

Butte, MT 59701	(406) 496-4568
	(800) 445-TECH
Fax: (406) 496-4710	Email: enrollment@mtech.edu
Full-time: 1421 men, 769 women	Faculty: IIB, -$
Part-time: 243 men, 324 women	Ph.D.s: 60%
Graduate: 106 men, 60 women	Student/Faculty: n/av
Year: semesters, summer session	Tuition: $6722 ($19,500)
Room & Board: $7928	Freshman Class: 877 applied, 773 accepted, 441 enrolled
SAT CR/M/W: 545/610/530 ACT: 24	CEEB CODE: 4487
Application Deadline: open	VERY COMPETITIVE

Montana Tech possesses an internationally esteemed, century-old tradition of excellence in higher education. The university offers degrees and certificates focused in areas such as nursing, health and safety, responsible development of natural resources, engineering, ecology and restoration, business, information technology, energy, and workforce development. Montana Tech has a long-standing reputation for producing outstanding graduates. Figures in the above capsule and in this profile are approximate. There are 3 undergraduate schools and 1 graduate school. In addition to regional accreditation, Montana Tech has baccalaureate program accreditation with ABET, CSAB, ACS, and IACBE. The 56-acre campus is in a small town in Butte, Montana. Including any residence halls, there are 19 buildings.

STUDENT LIFE: 77% of undergraduates are from Montana. Others are from 42 states, 20 foreign countries, and Canada. 82% are White. **Male To Female Ratio:** 0.7:1. 37% do not continue beyond their first year; 44% remain to graduate. **Housing:** College-sponsored housing includes coed dorms, off-campus apartments, and married student housing. On-campus housing is guaranteed for the freshman year only, and is available on a first-come, first-served basis. Priority is given to out-of-town students. 89% of students commute. All students may keep cars.

FACULTY/CLASSROOMS: 61% of faculty are male; 39% are female. No introductory courses are taught by graduate students.

PROGRAMS OF STUDY: Montana Tech confers B.S. and B.A.S degrees. Associate and Master's degrees are also awarded. Bachelor's degrees are awarded in BIOLOGICAL SCIENCE (biology/biological science), BUSINESS (business systems analysis), COMMUNICATIONS AND THE ARTS (communications and communications technology), COMPUTER AND PHYSICAL SCIENCE (chemistry, computer programming, computer science, mathematics, science, and statistics), EDUCATION (health information management), ENGINEERING AND ENVIRONMENTAL DESIGN (computer engineering, engineering, environmental engineering, geological engineering, geophysical engineering, metallurgical engineering, mining and mineral engineering, occupational safety and health, and petroleum/natural gas engineering), HEALTH PROFESSIONS (nursing), SOCIAL SCIENCE (liberal arts/general studies).

ACTIVITIES: There are 50 groups on campus, including band, cheerleading, chess, choir, chorale, computers, environmental, ethnic, gay, honors, international, newspaper, pep band, political, professional, radio and TV, religious, social, social service, and student government. Popular campus events include M-Day, and Homecoming. **Sports:** There are 3 intercollegiate sports for men and 3 for women. Facilities include Kelvin Sampson Court, cardio room, weight room, racquetball courts, locker rooms, classrooms, and offices. The Alumni Coliseum provides an outstanding football experience for Digger home games. **Graduates:** From July 1, 2013 to June 30, 2014, 278 bachelor's degrees were awarded. The most popular majors were petroleum engineering (21%), general engineering (17%), and business (15%). 127 companies recruited on campus in

2013-2014. In an average class, 18% graduate in 4 years or less, 42% graduate in 5 years or less, and 48% graduate in 6 years or less.

SERVICES: Counseling and information services are available, as is tutoring in most subjects. There is a reader service for the blind, and remedial math and writing. **Library/Resources:** The library contains 140,851 volumes, 60,390 microform items, 5,329 audio/video tapes/CDs/DVDs, and subscribes to 41,874 periodicals including electronic. Computerized library services include interlibrary loans, database searching, Internet access, and Wi-Fi capability. Special learning facilities include a radio station, a mineral museum, and METNET 2-way interactive communication studio. **Physically Challenged Students:** 75% of the campus is accessible. Facilities include wheelchair ramps, elevators, special parking, specially equipped restrooms, special class scheduling, lowered drinking fountains, lowered telephones, and special housing. **Special:** There is a 3-2 liberal arts-engineering program with Carroll College, dual enrollment agreement with Flathead Valley Community College, collaborative programs with UM Helena (BAS Business, BS BIT, BAS General Studies), UM Western (Elementary Education Certification and Secondary Education Certification in Biological Sciences, General Sciences, and Mathematical Sciences), and UM-COT (AAS Surgical Technology). Additionally, Tech offers double majors, honors program, independent study, internships, and work study. There are 3 national honor societies, including Phi Beta Kappa, and a freshman honors program. **Visiting:** There are regularly scheduled orientations for prospective students. There is an official fall orientation, though visits are welcome any time. There are guides for informal visits, visitors may sit in on classes, and stay overnight. To schedule a visit, contact the Enrollment Services at (406) 496-4256. **Campus Safety and Security:** Measures include 24-hour foot and vehicle patrol, emergency notification system, self-defense education, and security escort services. There are emergency telephones and lighted pathways/sidewalks.

REQUIREMENTS: The SAT or ACT is required. The ACT Optional Writing test is also required. Applicants must be graduates of an accredited secondary school. The GED is accepted. 14 academic credits are required, including English, 4 years; math and social studies, 3 years each; science, 2 years; plus 2 years chosen from foreign language, computer science, visual and performing arts, or vocational education. Applicants must have minimum composite scores of 22 on the ACT or satisfactory scores on the SAT or a 2.5 GPA, or be in the top half of their graduating class. Other factors regarding admissions are considered only if the preceding standards are not met. AP and CLEP credits are accepted. For graduation, students must complete at least 120 semester credits (more for engineering degrees) and maintain a minimum 2.0 GPA. Requirements include 6 hours each of communications, humanities/fine arts, mathematical sciences, and social sciences, and 6 to 7 hours of physical and life sciences with a lab required for 1 course. Engineering students must satisfy specific requirements within the individual curriculum. **Procedure:** Freshmen are admitted to all sessions. Entrance exams should be taken in the senior year. There are deferred admissions and rolling admissions plans. Application deadlines are open. Application fee is $30. Notification is sent on a rolling basis. Applications are accepted on-line. **Transfer Students:** 226 transfer students enrolled in 2013-2014. Transfer applicants must have a minimum GPA of 2.0. Grades of C and above transfer for credit. **International Students:** There are 183 international students enrolled. The school actively recruits these students. They must take the TOEFL with a minimum score of 525 on the paper-based TOEFL (PBT) or 71 on the Internet-based version (iBT). They must also take the SAT or ACT, scoring 22.

ADMISSIONS: 88% of the 2014-2015 applicants were accepted. The SAT scores for the 2014-2015 freshman class were: Critical Reading--25% below 500, 44% between 500 and 599, 26% between 600 and 699, and 4% between 700 and 800; Math--11% below 500, 31% between 500 and 599, 46% between 600 and 699, and 13% between 700 and 800; Writing--38% below 500, 36% between 500 and 599, 24% between 600 and 699, and 3% between 700 and 800. The ACT scores were 14% below 21, 31% between 21 and 23, 31% between 24 and 26, 12% between 27 and 28, and 12% above 28. 24 freshmen graduated first in their class. **Admissions Contact:** Stephanie Crowe, Director of Recruiting. E-Mail: *enrollment@mtech.edu* Web: *www.mtech.edu*

FINANCIAL AID: In 2014-2015, 63% of all full-time freshmen and 61% of continuing full-time students received some form of financial aid. 60% of all full-time freshmen and 54% of continuing full-time students received need-based aid. The average freshman award was $9,725. Need-based scholarships or need-based grants averaged $5,496; need-based self-help aid (loans and jobs) averaged $3,239; non-need-based athletic scholarships averaged $7,534; and other non-need-based awards and non-need-based scholarships averaged $3,230. The FAFSA and the college's own financial statement are required. Check with the school for current application deadlines.

MONTANA UNIVERSITY SYSTEM

The Montana University System, established in 1972, is a private system in Montana. It is governed by a Board of Regents, whose chief administrator is the commissioner of higher education. The goal of the system is teaching first, then research and public service. The main priorities are funding, system structure, and transfer articulation. The total student enrollment is usually about 47,000 with 1200 faculty members. Altogether there are 148 baccalaureate, 92 master's, and 26 doctoral programs offered in the Montana University System. Profiles of the 4-year campuses are included in this section.

ROCKY MOUNTAIN COLLEGE D-3
www.rocky.edu

Billings, MT 59102	(406) 657-1000 or 657-1026
	(800) 877-6259
Fax: (406) 657-1189	Email: admissions@rocky.edu
Full-time: 462 men, 417 women	Faculty: 64; IIB, --$
Part-time: 9 men, 15 women	Ph.D.s: 85%
Graduate: 45 men, 46 women	Student/Faculty: 12 to 1
Year: semesters, summer session	Tuition: $24,530
Room & Board: $7712	Freshman Class: 1469 applied, 962 accepted, 221 enrolled
SAT CR/M/W: 511/504/478 ACT: 23	CEEB CODE: 4660
Application Deadline: n/av	COMPETITIVE

Rocky Mountain College is a private college founded on the unique practice of joining the liberal arts tradition along with practical training for professional development. Established in 1878, RMC functions on a mission of educating students through liberal arts and professional programs that cultivate critical thinking, creative expression, ethical decision-making, informed citizenship, and professional excellence. The College supports its mission through core themes of academic excellence, transformational learning, and shared responsibility and stewardship. There is 1 undergraduate school and 1 graduate school. In addition to regional accreditation, Rocky has baccalaureate program accreditation with ARC-PA and AABI. The 60-acre campus is in a suburban area in a residential section of Billings, Montana. Including any residence halls, there are 16 buildings.

STUDENT LIFE: 55% of undergraduates are from Montana. Others are from 42 states, 18 foreign countries, and Canada. 77% are White. **Male To Female Ratio:** 0.9:1. The average age of freshmen is 18; all undergraduates, 21. 29% do not continue beyond their first year; 71% remain to graduate. **Housing:** 570 students can be accommodated in college housing, which includes coed dorms, on-campus apartments, and married student housing. On-campus housing is guaranteed for the freshman year only, and is available on a first-come, first-served basis. 53% of students commute. Alcohol is not permitted. All students may keep cars.

FACULTY/CLASSROOMS: 55% of faculty are male; 45% are female. All teach undergraduates, and 5% do both. No introductory courses are taught by graduate students. The average class size in an introductory lecture is 14; in a laboratory is 12; and in a regular course is 14.

PROGRAMS OF STUDY: Rocky confers B.A., and B.S. degrees. Associate and Master's degrees are also awarded. Bachelor's degrees are awarded in AGRICULTURE (environmental studies, equestrian studies, and equine science), BUSINESS (accounting, business administration and management, and sports management), COMMUNICATIONS AND THE ARTS (art, communications, creative writing, literature, music performance, and theatre arts), COM-

PUTER AND PHYSICAL SCIENCE (chemistry, computer science, geology, mathematics, and petroleum systems / geology), EDUCATION (art education, athletic training, education, elementary education, English education, health and physical education, mathematics education, music education, psychology education, science education, social science education, and social studies education), ENGINEERING AND ENVIRONMENTAL DESIGN (aeronautical science, aviation administration/management, and environmental science), HEALTH PROFESSIONS (biology and exercise science), SOCIAL SCIENCE (history, philosophy and religion, political science/government, psychology, and sociology). Business, biology, and health and human performance have the largest enrollments.

ACTIVITIES: There are no fraternities or sororities. There are 13 groups on campus, including aviation and equestrian, band, cheerleading, choir, chorale, chorus, computers, debate, drama, environmental, forensics, gay, honors, international, jazz band, literary magazine, musical theater, newspaper, pep band, professional, religious, social, social service, student government, and yearbook. Popular campus events include convocations, intercollegiate athletics, Candlelight Dinner, Yule Log Dinner, and International Week. **Sports:** There are 8 intercollegiate sports for men and 8 for women, and 10 intramural sports for men and 10 for women. Facilities include a football stadium, soccer field, gymnasium, auxiliary exercise areas, weight room, swimming pool, and a climbing wall. **Graduates:** From July 1, 2013 to June 30, 2014, 202 bachelor's degrees were awarded. The most popular majors were business (19%), physical education and health (11%), and biology (9%). 18 companies recruited on campus in 2013-2014. In an average class, 20% graduate in 4 years or less, 38% graduate in 5 years or less, and 40% graduate in 6 years or less. Of the 2013 graduating class, 16% were enrolled in graduate school within 6 months of graduation, and 80% were employed.

SERVICES: Counseling and information services are available, as is tutoring in most subjects. There is a reader service for the blind, and remedial math, reading, and writing. Note-taking is available for qualified students. **Library/Resources:** The library contains 81,432 volumes, 1,664 audio/video tapes/CDs/DVDs, and subscribes to 31,742 periodicals including electronic. Computerized library services include interlibrary loans, database searching, Internet access, and Wi-Fi capability. Special learning facilities include an art gallery, a flight school and equestrian facilities. **Physically Challenged Students:** 75% of the campus is accessible. Facilities include wheelchair ramps, elevators, special parking, specially equipped restrooms, special class scheduling, lowered drinking fountains, and special housing. **Special:** Rocky Mountain College offers internships with local, regional, and national employers; various study abroad opportunities with formal exchange contracts in the United Kingdom, Finland, Japan, Sweden, and China; dual majors; individualized programs of study; and credit for life, military, and work experience. Juniors and seniors may elect to take 1 course on a pass/fail basis each semester. There is 1 national honor society and 1 departmental honors program. **Visiting:** There are regularly scheduled orientations for prospective students. Students may visit year-round and will meet with admission representatives, tour campus, with opportunities to sit in on a class and meet with a faculty member. To schedule a visit, contact Megan Cabe at (406) 657-1026. **Campus Safety and Security:** Measures include emergency notification system, self-defense education, and security escort services. There are emergency telephones, lighted pathways/sidewalks, controlled access to dorms/residences, security cameras and electronic access systems.

REQUIREMENTS: The SAT or ACT is required. Applicants must be graduates of an accredited secondary school. The GED is also accepted. Students must have completed 4 units of English, 4 units of math, 3 units in the natural sciences, 3 units in the social sciences, and 2 units of history. The school recommends a portfolio for admission to the art program, an audition for admission to the music or theatre program, and an interview for academically challenged students. A GPA of 2.5 is required. AP and CLEP credits are accepted. Important factors in the admissions decision are ability to finance college education, extracurricular activities record, and personality/intangible qualities. To graduate, students must complete a minimum of 124 credit hours, complete all major requirements with a minimum overall GPA of 2.0 and 2.25 in the major. If a minor area is chosen, a minimum of 18 hours is required. There are core curriculum requirements in fine arts, humanities, communication, and the natural and social sciences, as well as writing, communication, and math. **Procedure:** Freshmen are admitted fall, spring, and summer. Entrance exams should be taken during the first half of the senior year. There are early admissions, deferred admissions, and rolling admissions plans. Application deadlines are open. Application fee is $35. Applications are accepted on-line. Application fees are waived if application is completed on-line. **Transfer Students:** 68 transfer students enrolled in 2013-2014. Transfer students must have a minimum GPA of 2.0 and grades of 2.0 and higher transfer for credit. Transfers are admitted every term. 30 of 124 credits required for the bachelor's degree must be completed at Rocky. **International Students:** There are 37 international students enrolled. The school actively recruits these students. They must take the TOEFL with a minimum score of 570 on the paper-based TOEFL (PBT) or 88 on the Internet-based version (iBT), or take the IELTS. They must also take the SAT or ACT, scoring 860/SAT (critical reading and math) or 18/ACT.

ADMISSIONS: 65% of the 2014-2015 applicants were accepted. The SAT scores for the 2014-2015 freshman class were: Critical Reading--43% below 500, 38% between 500 and 599, 16% between 600 and 699, and 2% between 700 and 800; Math--40% below 500, 48% between 500 and 599, 12% between 600 and 699, and 1% between 700 and 800; Writing--62% below 500, 26% between 500 and 599, 11% between 600 and 699, and 2% between 700 and 800. The ACT scores were 32% below 21, 26% between 21 and 23, 22% between 24 and 26, 8% between 27 and 28, and 11% above 28. **Admissions Contact:** Austin Mapston, Director of Admissions. E-Mail: *admissions@ rocky.edu* Web: *www.rocky.edu*

FINANCIAL AID: In 2014-2015, 99% of all full-time freshmen and continuing full-time students received some form of financial aid. 80% of all full-time freshmen and 69% of continuing full-time students received need-based aid. The average freshman award was $26,860. 31% of undergraduate students work part-time. Average annual earnings from campus work are $1420. The FAFSA and the college's own financial statement are required. The priority date for freshman financial aid applications for fall entry is March 1.

UNIVERSITY OF GREAT FALLS
www.ugf.edu

C-2

Great Falls, MT 59405	(406) 791-5200
	(800) 856-9544
Fax: (406) 791-5209	Email: enroll@ugf.edu
Full-time: 210 men, 310 women	Faculty: n/av
Part-time: 110 men, 210 women	Ph.Ds: n/av
Graduate: 40 men, 110 women	Student/Faculty: n/av
Year: semesters, summer session	Tuition: $17,970
Room & Board: $7000	Freshman Class: n/av
SAT or ACT: recommended	CEEB CODE: 4058
Application Deadline: n/av	COMPETITIVE

The University of Great Falls, established in 1932, is a private, liberal arts institution affiliated with the Roman Catholic Church. The figures in the above capsule and in this profile are approximate. There are 2 undergraduate schools and 1 graduate school. The 40-acre campus is in an urban area. Including any residence halls, there are 13 buildings.

STUDENT LIFE: 93% of undergraduates are from Montana. Others are from 20 states and Canada. 99% are from public schools. 80% are White. 28% are Catholic; 22% claim no religious affiliation; 19% Protestant. **Male To Female Ratio:** 1.8:1. The average age of freshmen is 26; all undergraduates, 33. 46% do not continue beyond their first year; 20% remain to graduate. **Housing:** 189 students can be accommodated in college housing, which includes single-sex and coed dorms, off-campus apartments, and married student housing. On-campus housing is guaranteed for the freshman year only, and is available on a first-come, first-served basis. Priority is given to out-of-town students. 88% of students commute. Alcohol is not permitted. All students may keep cars.

FACULTY/CLASSROOMS: 59% of faculty are male; 42% are female.

All teach undergraduates. No introductory courses are taught by graduate students. The average class size in an introductory lecture is 15; in a laboratory is 10; and in a regular course is 14.

PROGRAMS OF STUDY: UGF confers B.A. and B.S. degrees. Associate and Master's degrees are also awarded. Bachelor's degrees are awarded in BIOLOGICAL SCIENCE (biology/biological science, botany, microbiology, molecular biology, and physiology), BUSINESS (accounting, business administration and management, management science, and marketing/retailing/merchandising), COMMUNICATIONS AND THE ARTS (art, English, and fine arts), COMPUTER AND PHYSICAL SCIENCE (computer management, computer programming, computer science, mathematics, physical sciences, and science), EDUCATION (education of the exceptional child, elementary education, health education, mathematics education, middle school education, physical education, reading education, science education, secondary education, social studies education, and special education), ENGINEERING AND ENVIRONMENTAL DESIGN (computer graphics), HEALTH PROFESSIONS (health care administration, predentistry, and premedicine), SOCIAL SCIENCE (counseling/psychology, criminal justice, history, human services, law enforcement and corrections, paralegal studies, political science/government, prelaw, psychology, religion, social science, sociology, and theological studies). Biology, paralegal studies, and computer science are the strongest academically. Education, criminal justice, and business have the largest enrollments.

ACTIVITIES: There are 15 groups on campus, including art, cheerleading, chess, choir, chorus, computers, drama, ethnic, forensics, honors, literary magazine, musical theater, newspaper, orchestra, photography, professional, religious, social, social service, student government, students in free enterprise (SIFE), and symphony. Popular campus events include Orientation Barbecue, Halloween Dance, and Intramural Festival. **Sports:** There is 1 intercollegiate sports for men and 2 for women, and 7 intramural sports for men and 7 for women. Facilities include a gym, Olympic-size pool, a game room, and workout room.

SERVICES: Counseling and information services are available, as is tutoring in some subjects. There is a reader service for the blind, and remedial math, reading, and writing. Tutoring in basic skills. **Library/Resources:** The library contains 106,135 volumes, 124,608 microform items, 3,894 audio/video tapes/CDs/DVDs, and subscribes to 587 periodicals including electronic. Computerized library services include interlibrary loans and database searching. Special learning facilities include an art gallery. **Physically Challenged Students:** All of the campus is accessible. Facilities include wheelchair ramps, elevators, special parking, specially equipped restrooms, special class scheduling, and lowered drinking fountains. **Special:** Internships are offered in sociology, criminal justice, paralegal studies, health care administration, and chemical-dependency counseling. Opportunities are provided for work-study programs, B.A.-B.S. degrees in most majors, dual majors, a general studies degree, credit by exam or for military service, and nondegree study. A 3-2 engineering degree for applied computer science and applied math majors is offered with Montana State University-Bozeman. Specialized instruction is available through the use of videotape and telephone discussions in 14 locations throughout Montana and Canada. There is 1 national honor society. **Visiting:** There are regularly scheduled orientations for prospective students, including meeting with prospective advisers and staff, financial aid presentation, campus tour, and lunch. There are guides for informal visits, visitors may sit in on classes, and stay overnight. To schedule a visit, contact the Office of Admissions. **Campus Safety and Security:** Measures include 24-hour foot and vehicle patrol, self-defense education, and security escort services. There are emergency telephones and lighted pathways/sidewalks.

REQUIREMENTS: The SAT or ACT is recommended. Graduation from an accredited secondary school is required; the GED is accepted. Applicants should have 4 years of English, 3 of math, and 2 each of social studies, science, and electives, including foreign language, art, music, and vocational education. An interview is recommended. A GPA of 2.0 is required. AP and CLEP credits are accepted. Students must complete 128 credit hours, including 30 to 65 in the major, plus 15 to 21 minor credits, maintaining a minimum GPA of 2.0. The 52-credit-hour core curriculum includes math, computer science, art, behavioral science, history, literature, philosophy, science, writing,

theology, and religion. **Procedure:** Freshmen are admitted fall, spring, and summer. Entrance exams should be taken prior to registration. There is a rolling admissions plan. Check with the school for current application deadlines. The fall 2014 application fee was $25. **Transfer Students:** Transfer applicants must be in good academic standing from another accredited college or university and must submit official transcripts from all colleges or universities attended. Those without a bachelor's degree must also submit an official high school transcript. 30 of 128 credits required for the bachelor's degree must be completed at UGF. **International Students:** The school actively recruits these students. They must take the TOEFL.

ADMISSIONS: Director of Admissions. E-Mail: *enroll@ugf.edu* Web: *www.ugf.edu*

FINANCIAL AID: UGF is a member of CSS. The FAFSA is required. Check with the school for current application deadlines.

UNIVERSITY OF MONTANA B-2
www.umt.edu

Missoula, MT 59812
(406) 243-6266
(800) 462-8636

Fax: (406) 243-5711
Full-time: 4465 men, 4981 women
Part-time: 1211 men, 1597 women
Graduate: 947 men, 1324 women
Year: semesters, summer session
Room & Board: $7625
SAT or ACT: required
Application Deadline: March 1

Email: admiss@umontana.edu
Faculty: I
Ph.D.s: 80%
Student/Faculty: 18 to 1
Tuition: $6045 ($21,719)
Freshman Class: n/av
CEEB CODE: 4489
COMPETITIVE

The University of Montana, founded in 1893, is a public institution with programs in arts and sciences, business administration, fine arts, education, forestry, journalism, and pharmacy and allied health sciences. It is part of the Montana university system. The figures in the above capsule and in this profile are approximate. There are 8 undergraduate schools and 2 graduate schools. In addition to regional accreditation, U of M has baccalaureate program accreditation with AACSB, ACCE, ACPE, APTA, CAHEA, CSAB, CSWE, NASAD, NASDTEC, NASM, NCATE, and SAF. The 220-acre campus is in an urban area 200 miles east of Spokane. Including any residence halls, there are 57 buildings.

STUDENT LIFE: 74% of undergraduates are from Montana. Others are from 50 states, 58 foreign countries, and Canada. 80% are from public schools. 77% are White. **Male To Female Ratio:** 1.2:1. The average age of freshmen is 19; all undergraduates, 25. 26% do not continue beyond their first year; 48% remain to graduate. **Housing:** 3430 students can be accommodated in college housing, which includes single-sex and coed dorms, off-campus apartments, and married student housing. In addition, there are honors houses, special-interest houses, an international house, and nontraditional houses. On-campus housing is guaranteed for the freshman year only. 75% of students commute. All students may keep cars.

FACULTY/CLASSROOMS: 57% of faculty are male; 43% are female. All teach and do research. Graduate students teach 2% of introductory courses. The average class size in an introductory lecture is 35; in a laboratory is 25; and in a regular course is 35.

PROGRAMS OF STUDY: U of M confers B.A., B.S., B.A.E., B.S.H.P.E. and B.S.M. degrees. Associate, Master's, and Doctoral degrees are also awarded. Bachelor's degrees are awarded in AGRICULTURE (environmental studies and forestry and related sciences), BIOLOGICAL SCIENCE (biology/biological science, botany, microbiology, wildlife biology, and zoology), BUSINESS (accounting, banking and finance, business administration and management, marketing/retailing/merchandising, personnel management, and small business management), COMMUNICATIONS AND THE ARTS (classics, communications, dramatic arts, English, fine arts, French, German, Japanese, journalism, music, music performance, radio/television technology, Russian, and Spanish), COMPUTER AND PHYSICAL SCIENCE (chemistry, computer science, geology, mathematics, and physics), EDUCATION (elementary education, music education, physical education, science education, and secondary education), HEALTH PROFESSIONS (medical technology and pharmacy), SOCIAL SCIENCE (anthropology, economics, geography, history, liberal arts/general studies, Native American studies, philosophy, political science/government, psychology, social work, sociology, and women's studies). Journalism, forestry, and liberal arts are the strongest academically. Business, forestry, and education have the largest enrollments.

ACTIVITIES: 10% of men belong to 9 national fraternities; 8% of women belong to 4 national sororities. There are 130 groups on campus, including academic, and forestry, art, band, cheerleading, chess, choir, chorale, chorus, computers, creative writing, dance, drill team, ethnic, gay, honors, international, jazz band, literary magazine, marching band, newspaper, opera, orchestra, pep band, political, professional, radio and TV, religious, social, social service, student government, and symphony. Popular campus events include Foresters Day, Founders Day, and International Week. **Sports:** There are 6 intercollegiate sports for men and 9 for women, and 16 intramural sports for men and 12 for women. Facilities include a field house, a 10,000-seat arena, a 26,000-seat stadium, a fitness center, a golf course, soccer and rugby fields, an Olympic-size pool, a game room, a climbing wall, weight rooms, and mountain trails.

SERVICES: Counseling and information services are available, as is tutoring in every subject. There is a reader service for the blind, and remedial math, reading, and writing. Mentors and note takers are available, as are books on tape for LD students. **Library/Resources:** The 4 libraries contain 1.4 million volumes, 343,000 microform items, 70,000 audio/video tapes/CDs/DVDs, and subscribe to 5,000 periodicals including electronic. Computerized library services include interlibrary loans, database searching, Internet access, and Wi-Fi capability. Special learning facilities include an art gallery, radio station, TV station, experimental forest, biological station, ranch, center for people and forests, geology field camp, international language lab, wilderness institute, observatory, and freshwater research center. **Physically Challenged Students:** 75% of the campus is accessible. Facilities include wheelchair ramps, elevators, special parking, specially equipped restrooms, special class scheduling, lowered drinking fountains, lowered telephones, special housing. **Special:** Students may cross-register with Montana Tech and Western Montana College. Co-op programs exist in business, communications, economics, management, and liberal studies; internships in most majors, work-study programs with nonprofit organizations, and study abroad in 12 countries are available. The school offers a B.A.-B.S. degree in chemistry, pass/fail options in classes other than major requirements, and dual majors in physics and computer science as well as history and political science. There are 7 national honor societies, Phi Beta Kappa, a freshman honors program, and 5 departmental honors programs. **Visiting:** There are regularly scheduled orientations for prospective students, including placement testing, advising, workshops, and social events. There are guides for informal visits and visitors may sit in on classes. To schedule a visit, contact the Office of Admissions. **Campus Safety and Security:** Measures include 24-hour foot and vehicle patrol, self-defense education, and security escort services. There are emergency telephones and lighted pathways/sidewalks.

REQUIREMENTS: The SAT or ACT is required, with a minimum composite ACT score of 22 or a satisfactory SAT verbal-math-writing composite score. Applicants must be graduates of an accredited secondary school. The GED is accepted. Students should have completed 4 years of English, 3 of math, 3 of social studies, 2 of lab science, and 2 of foreign language, computer science, visual arts, or vocational education. U of M requires applicants to be in the upper 50% of their class. A GPA of 2.5 is required. AP and CLEP credits are accepted. Important factors in the admissions decision are advanced placement or honors courses, evidence of special talent, and geographical diversity. A total of 120 credits is required for graduation in most majors. The number of hours in the major varies; some majors require a thesis. There are competency requirements in writing, math, and foreign language or symbolic systems. Juniors must pass writing exams. Distribution requirements include courses in expressive arts, literary and artistic studies, historical and cultural studies, social sciences, ethical and human values, and natural sciences. A minimum GPA of 2.0 must be maintained. **Procedure:** Freshmen are admitted to all sessions. There are deferred admissions and rolling admissions plans. Applications should be filed by March 1 for fall entry; November 15 for spring entry, along with a $30 fee. Notification is sent on a rolling basis. Applications are accepted on-line. **Transfer Students:** Applicants must have a minimum GPA of 2.0. Grades of 2.0 or better transfer for credit. 30 of 120 credits required for the bachelor's degree must be completed at U of M. **International Students:** The school actively recruits these students. They must take the TOEFL.

ADMISSIONS: Jed Liston, Assistant VP for Enrollment. E-Mail: *admiss@umontana.edu* Web: *www.umt.edu*

FINANCIAL AID: U of M is a member of CSS. The FAFSA is required. Check with the school for current application deadlines.

UNIVERSITY OF MONTANA-WESTERN (*The complete profile is made available exclusively on our website, www.barronspac.com*)

NEBRASKA

• College Location

0 20 40 60 80 100
Miles

BELLEVUE UNIVERSITY (*The complete profile is made available exclusively on our website, www.barronspac.com*)

CHADRON STATE COLLEGE (*The complete profile is made available exclusively on our website, www.barronspac.com*)

CLARKSON COLLEGE   F-3
www.clarksoncollege.edu

Omaha, NE 68131	(402) 552-3041
	(800) 647-5500
Fax: (402) 552-6057	Email: workdenise@clarksoncollege.edu
Full-time: n/av	Faculty: n/av
Part-time: n/av	Ph.D.s: n/av
Graduate: n/av	Student/Faculty: n/av
Year: semesters, summer session	Tuition: $14,405
Room & Board: $7200	Freshman Class: n/av
SAT or ACT: required	CEEB CODE: 2250
Application Deadline: open	**VERY COMPETITIVE**

Clarkson College, established in 1888 and affiliated with the Episcopal Church, offers undergraduate and graduate degrees in the health care professions and business. The figures in the above capsule and in this profile are approximate. There are 3 undergraduate schools and 2 graduate schools. In addition to regional accreditation, Clarkson has baccalaureate program accreditation with NLN. The 3-acre campus is in an urban area in Omaha. Including any residence halls, there are 4 buildings.

STUDENT LIFE: 61% of undergraduates are from Nebraska. Others are from 13 states and 2 foreign countries. 90% are from public schools. 90% are White. 50% are Catholic; 45% Protestant. The average age of all undergraduates is 22. 87% remain to graduate. **Housing:** 140 students can be accommodated in college housing, which includes coed on-campus apartments. On-campus housing is available on a first-come, first-served basis. Priority is given to out-of-town students. 90% of students commute. Alcohol is not permitted. All students may keep cars.

FACULTY/CLASSROOMS: 16% of faculty are male; 84% are female.

All teach undergraduates. No introductory courses are taught by graduate students. The average class size in an introductory lecture is 30; in a laboratory is 20; and in a regular course is 20.

PROGRAMS OF STUDY: Clarkson confers B.S. and B.S.N. degrees. Associate and Master's degrees are also awarded. Bachelor's degrees are awarded in BUSINESS (business administration and management), COMPUTER AND PHYSICAL SCIENCE (radiological technology), HEALTH PROFESSIONS (nursing and radiograph medical technology). Radiological technology and nursing are the strongest academically. Nursing has the largest enrollment.

ACTIVITIES: There are no fraternities or sororities. There are 12 groups on campus, including newspaper, professional, religious, social, social service, and student government. Popular campus events include talent show, game nights, and intramural volleyball. **Sports:** There is no sports program at Clarkson. Facilities include there is an exercise room available 24 hours, and a small gym area with basketball hoops and volleyball courts.

SERVICES: Counseling and information services are available, as is tutoring in every subject. **Library/Resources:** The library contains 7,613 volumes, 698 audio/video tapes/CDs/DVDs, and subscribes to 217 periodicals including electronic. Computerized library services include interlibrary loans, database searching, and Internet access. **Physically Challenged Students:** 95% of the campus is accessible. Facilities include wheelchair ramps, elevators, special parking, specially equipped restrooms, special class scheduling, lowered drinking fountains, lowered telephones, and special housing. **Special:** A co-op program in nursing, work-study programs, and dual majors are available. Credit is given for military experience, and nondegree study is possible. The distance education option allows advanced placement students living a distance from the campus to complete their studies at home. There is 1 national honor society. **Visiting:** There are regularly scheduled orientations for prospective students. There are guides for informal visits and visitors may sit in on classes. To schedule a visit, contact the Admissions Office. **Campus Safety and Security:** Measures include 24-hour foot and vehicle patrol, emergency notification system, self-defense education, and security escort services. There are emergency telephones and lighted pathways/sidewalks.

REQUIREMENTS: The SAT or ACT is required, with a minimum composite score of 20 on the ACT or a satisfactory score on the SAT. The ACT is preferred. Tests are not required for applicants more than 2 years out of high school. Applicants must be graduates of an accredited secondary school, with 3 years of English and 2 each of social science, algebra, and science (including lab science). The GED is accepted. Clarkson requires applicants to be in the upper 50% of their class. A GPA of 2.5 is required. AP and CLEP credits are accepted. Important factors in the admissions decision are advanced placement or honors courses, extracurricular activities record, and evidence of special talent.To graduate, students must complete 128 credit hours, including 68 in the major, and maintain a minimum GPA of 2.0. General education requirements include courses in the humanities, English, behavioral and social sciences, science and math, and phys ed. A 9-hour core curriculum is also required. **Procedure:** Freshmen are admitted to all sessions. Entrance exams should be taken during the junior year or first semester of the senior year. There is a deferred admissions plan. Application deadlines are open. Application fee is $35. Notification of early decision is sent April 1; regular decision, June 1. **Transfer Students:** Transfer students must have a minimum GPA of 2.5. Grades of C or better transfer for credit. Transfers are admitted for fall and spring. An interview is sometimes required. 64 of 128 credits required for the bachelor's degree must be completed at Clarkson. **International Students:** They must take the TOEFL, or score 85 on the MELAB, or 5 on the TWE. They must also take the SAT or ACT.

ADMISSIONS: Denise Work, Director of Admissions. E-Mail: *workdenise@clarksoncollege.edu* Web: *www.clarksoncollege.edu*

FINANCIAL AID: In 2014-2015, 90% of all full-time freshmen and 90% of continuing full-time students received some form of financial aid. 75% of continuing full-time students received need-based aid. Clarkson is a member of CSS. The FAFSA and the college's own financial statement are required. Check with the school for current application deadlines.

COLLEGE OF SAINT MARY   F-3
www.csm.edu

Omaha, NE 68106

	402-399-2407
	(800) 926-5534
Fax: (402) 399-2412	Email: enroll@csm.edu
Full-time: 679 women	Faculty: 40
Part-time: 9 men, 82 women	Ph.D.s: 70%
Graduate: 14 men, 234 women	Student/Faculty: 15 to 1
Year: semesters, summer session	Tuition: $27,984
Room & Board: $7200	Freshman Class: 193 applied, 183 accepted, 71 enrolled
ACT: 23	CEEB CODE: 6106
Application Deadline: open	COMPETITIVE

College of Saint Mary, founded in 1923, is a women's college committed to the works, values and aspirations of the Sisters of Mercy and dedicated to the education of women in an environment that calls forth potential and fosters leadership. There is 1 undergraduate school and 1 graduate school. In addition to regional accreditation, CSM has baccalaureate program accreditation with NLN, ACOTE, IACBE, and ABA. The 40-acre campus is in an urban area within metro Omaha. Including any residence halls, there are 9 buildings.

STUDENT LIFE: 80% of undergraduates are from Nebraska. Others are from 21 states, and 9 foreign countries. 90% are from public schools. 78% are White. 58% are Unknown religion; 42% Catholic. **Male To Female Ratio:** 43.3:1. The average age of freshmen is 20; all undergraduates, 25. 21% do not continue beyond their first year; 49% remain to graduate. **Housing:** 289 students can be accommodated in college housing, which includes single-sex dorms. There is a residence hall for single student mothers with children. On-campus housing is guaranteed for all 4 years. 68% of students commute. All students may keep cars.

FACULTY/CLASSROOMS: 16% of faculty are male; 84% are female. 95% teach undergraduates, and 10% do research. No introductory courses are taught by graduate students. The average class size in an introductory lecture is 16; in a laboratory is 14; and in a regular course is 14.

PROGRAMS OF STUDY: CSM confers B.A., B.S., B.B.L.M., B.G.S. and B.R.S. degrees. Associate, Master's, and Doctoral degrees are also awarded. Bachelor's degrees are awarded in BIOLOGICAL SCIENCE (biology/biological science), BUSINESS (business intelligence and analytics), COMMUNICATIONS AND THE ARTS (art, English, language arts, and Spanish), COMPUTER AND PHYSICAL SCIENCE (chemistry, mathematics, and natural sciences), EDUCATION (early childhood education, education, elementary education, and special education), HEALTH PROFESSIONS (medical laboratory technology and nursing), SOCIAL SCIENCE (applied psychology, humanities, liberal arts/general studies, paralegal studies, psychology, social science, and theological studies). Biology, chemistry, occupational therapy and nursing are the strongest academically. Occupational therapy, nursing, and education have the largest enrollments.

ACTIVITIES: There are no fraternities or sororities. There are 20 groups on campus, including and campus activities board, business, green team, art, choir, chorus, dance, drama, environmental, ethnic, forensics, honors, international, multicultural, professional, religious, social, social service, and student government. Popular campus events include Heritage Week, Queen of Hearts Celebration, Casino and Comedian Night. **Sports:** There are 8 intercollegiate sports for women and 5 intramural sports for women. Facilities include a gym, a 6-lane swimming pool, weight room, an elevated running track, exercise room, a training room, 2 soccer fields, and 2 softball fields. **Graduates:** From July 1, 2013 to June 30, 2014, 132 bachelor's degrees were awarded. The most popular majors were rehabilitation studies/ occupational therapy (33%), nursing (17%), and business (9%). 30 companies recruited on campus in 2013-2014. In an average class, 41% graduate in 4 years or less, 43% graduate in 5 years or less, and 49% graduate in 6 years or less. Of the 2013 graduating class, 37% were enrolled in graduate school within 6 months of graduation, and 39% were employed.

SERVICES: Counseling and information services are available, as is tutoring in most subjects. There is a reader service for the blind, and remedial math, reading, and writing. There are also study groups and learning circles. **Library/Resources:** The library contains 89,613 volumes, 2,770 audio/video tapes/CDs/DVDs, and subscribes to 375 periodicals including electronic. Computerized library services include interlibrary loans, database searching, Internet access, and Wi-Fi capability. Special learning facilities include an art gallery, cadaver lab, digital piano lab, native fish acquarium, nursing/ occupational therapy/physician assistant laboratories, lecture capture system, online learning platform. **Physically Challenged Students:** All of the campus is accessible. Facilities include wheelchair ramps, elevators, special parking, specially equipped restrooms, special class scheduling, lowered drinking fountains, special housing. **Special:** Students may pursue internships in any major, including research courses in the sciences. CSM also offers dual majors, study abroad, nondegree study, pass/fail options, an accelerated degree program in business leadership and management, and credit for military and work experience. There are 2 national honor societies, a freshman honors program, and 30 departmental honors programs. **Visiting:** There are regularly scheduled orientations for prospective students, consisting of a tour of the campus, a meeting with a financial aid representative, student-life presentations, and lunch. There are guides for informal visits, visitors may sit in on classes, and stay overnight. To schedule a visit, contact Amy Miller at (402) 399-2355. **Campus Safety and Security:** Measures include 24-hour foot and vehicle patrol, emergency notification system, self-defense education, and security escort services. There are lighted pathways/sidewalks, controlled access to dorms/residences, camera-monitored entrances to residence halls.

REQUIREMENTS: Students are accepted with a minimum composite score of 18 on the ACT or comparable SAT score. Students must also have a GPA of at least 2.0. Applicants must be graduates of an accredited secondary school. The GED is accepted. Students should have completed 16 academic units, including 4 years of English and 2 each of math, social studies, and science, with biology and chemistry required for the various health profession majors. An interview is recommended. A GPA of 2.0 is required. AP and CLEP credits are accepted.To graduate, students must complete 128 semester hours, with a minimum of 30 hours in the major and a 2.0 GPA in the major and overall. Required general education courses total 47 hours, with 10 in quantitative reasoning and science, 6 each in English and theology, 3 each in communications, moral reasoning, fine arts, global cultural diversity, history, philosophy, and social science, and 1 in a first year seminar. Each student prior to graduation completes and presents a research project in her major either individually or with a team. **Procedure:** Freshmen are admitted fall, spring, and summer. Entrance exams should be taken in the junior or senior year. There are deferred admissions and rolling admissions plans. Application deadlines are open. Application fee is $30. Applications are accepted on-line. **Transfer Students:** 149 transfer students enrolled in 2013-2014. Applicants should have a minimum GPA of 2.0 and submit official transcripts from previous colleges attended. Students with fewer than 12 credit hours must also submit ACT or SAT scores. Grades of C or better transfer for credit. Students are admitted every term. 30 of 128 credits required for the bachelor's degree must be completed at CSM. **International Students:** There are 7 international students enrolled. They must take the TOEFL with a minimum score of 550 on the paper-based TOEFL (PBT) or 79 on the Internet-based version (iBT). They must also take the SAT or ACT, scoring 18.

ADMISSIONS: 95% of the 2014-2015 applicants were accepted. The ACT scores were 26% below 21, 35% between 21 and 23, 23% between 24 and 26, 10% between 27 and 28, and 6% above 28. 41% of the current freshmen were in the top fifth of their class; 81% were in the top two fifths. **Admissions Contact:** Greg Fritz, VP Enrollment Services. E-Mail: *enroll@csm.edu* Web: *www.csm.edu*

FINANCIAL AID: In 2014-2015, 100% of all full-time freshmen and 99% of continuing full-time students received some form of financial aid. 77% of all full-time freshmen and 84% of continuing full-time students received need-based aid. The average freshman award was $29,270. Need-based scholarships or need-based grants averaged $9,933; need-based self-help aid (loans and jobs) averaged $5,598; non-need-based athletic scholarships averaged $6,257; and other non-need-based awards and non-need-based scholarships averaged $14,356. 80% of undergraduate students work part-time. Average annual earnings from campus work are $1556. The average financial indebtedness of the 2014 graduate was $29,538. The FAFSA is required. The priority date for freshman financial aid applications for fall entry is March 15.

CONCORDIA UNIVERSITY NEBRASKA   **E-3**
www.cune.edu

Seward, NE 68434	(402) 643-7233
	(800) 535-5494
Fax: (402) 643-4073	Email: admiss@cune.edu
Full-time: n/av	Faculty: IIB, --$
Part-time: n/av	Ph.D.s: n/av
Graduate: n/av	Student/Faculty: n/av
Year: semesters, summer session	Tuition: $20,000
Room & Board: $6000	Freshman Class: n/av
SAT or ACT: required	CEEB CODE: 6116
Application Deadline: n/av	VERY COMPETITIVE

Concordia University Nebraska, founded in 1894, is a private university owned and operated by the Lutheran Church-Missouri Synod, with degree programs in professional education and liberal arts. Among Concordia's major programs are those for professional work in the Lutheran Church, teacher education, director of Christian education, preseminary pastoral training, and church music. The figures in the above capsule and in this profile are approximate. There is 1 graduate school. In addition to regional accreditation, Concordia has baccalaureate program accreditation with NCATE. The 120-acre campus is in a small town 25 miles west of Lincoln. Including any residence halls, there are 26 buildings.

STUDENT LIFE: 59% of undergraduates are from out of state, mostly the Midwest. Students are from 37 states and 9 foreign countries. 95% are White. 95% are Protestant. The average age of freshmen is 18; all undergraduates, 21. 22% do not continue beyond their first year; 48% remain to graduate. **Housing:** 815 students can be accommodated in college housing, which includes single-sex dorms, off-campus apartments, and married student housing. On-campus housing is guaranteed for all 4 years. 85% of students live on campus; of those, 90% remain on campus on weekends. Alcohol is not permitted. All students may keep cars.

FACULTY/CLASSROOMS: 71% of faculty are male; 29% are female. All teach undergraduates. Graduate students teach 1% of introductory courses. The average class size in an introductory lecture is 20; in a laboratory is 15; and in a regular course is 15.

PROGRAMS OF STUDY: Concordia confers B.A., B.S., B.F.A., B.S.Med.Tech., B.Mus. and B.Sacred Music degrees. Master's degrees are also awarded. Bachelor's degrees are awarded in BIOLOGICAL SCIENCE (biology/biological science), BUSINESS (accounting, business administration and management, and sports management), COMMUNICATIONS AND THE ARTS (communications, dramatic arts, English, fine arts, music, speech/debate/rhetoric, and studio art), COMPUTER AND PHYSICAL SCIENCE (chemistry, computer science, mathematics, natural sciences, and physical sciences), EDUCATION (business education, Christian education, early childhood education, elementary education, home economics education, industrial arts education, middle school education, music education, physical education, science education, secondary education, and special education), HEALTH PROFESSIONS (exercise science, health, medical laboratory technology, predentistry, and premedicine), SOCIAL SCIENCE (behavioral science, geography, history, physical fitness/movement, prelaw, psychology, and theological studies). Education, business, and art are the strongest academically. Education has the largest enrollment.

ACTIVITIES: There are no fraternities or sororities. There are 35 groups on campus, including band, cheerleading, choir, chorale, chorus, computers, dance, debate, drama, drill team, ethnic, forensics, honors, international, jazz band, literary magazine, musical theater, newspaper, orchestra, pep band, photography, professional, religious, social, social service, student government, and yearbook. Popular campus events include Spring Weekend and Multicultural Awareness Week. **Sports:** There are 8 intercollegiate sports for men and 8 for women, and 7 intramural sports for men and 7 for women. Facilities include a gym, a weight-training room, an indoor pool, football, baseball, and soccer fields, and a track and field stadium.

SERVICES: Counseling and information services are available, as is tutoring in every subject. There is a reader service for the blind. **Library/Resources:** The 3 libraries contain 177,683 volumes, 10,719 microform items, 13,214 audio/video tapes/CDs/DVDs, and subscribe to 545 periodicals including electronic. Computerized library services include database searching. Special learning facilities include an art gallery, natural history museum, an observatory. **Physically Challenged Students:** 35% of the campus is accessible. Facilities include wheelchair ramps, elevators, special parking, specially equipped restrooms, lowered drinking fountains, and lowered telephones. **Special:** Concordia offers cross-registration with the University of Nebraska in Lincoln. Internships are available in education, business, and Christian education. B.A.-B.S. degrees, student-designed majors, dual majors, study abroad in England and China, nondegree studies, and pass/fail options are available. There is an accelerated degree program in organizational management. There is a freshman honors program. **Visiting:** There are regularly scheduled orientations for prospective students, including a campus tour, visits with professors/coaches, and an admission interview. There are guides for informal visits, visitors may sit in on classes, and stay overnight. To schedule a visit, contact the Office of Admission. **Campus Safety and Security:** Measures include 24-hour foot and vehicle patrol, self-defense education, and security escort services. There are emergency telephones, lighted pathways/sidewalks, vehicle and bicycle registration, and a possession ID engraving program.

REQUIREMENTS: The SAT or ACT is required. A minimum composite score of 18 is recommended for the ACT. Applicants need not be graduates of an accredited secondary school. The GED is accepted. The school strongly encourages high school courses in art, English, foreign language, history, math, music, phys ed, science, and social studies. An interview is recommended. A GPA of 2.8 is required. AP and CLEP credits are accepted. Important factors in the admissions decision are ability to finance college education, leadership record, and recommendations by alumni.To graduate, students must complete a minimum of 128 credits with a GPA of at least 2.0. Required general education courses include 12 hours of theology, 9 hours each of English/speech, social science, and science, 6 of fine arts, 3 each of math and health and phys ed, 2 to 3 of electives, and 1 hour minimum of computer literacy. **Procedure:** Freshmen are admitted to all sessions. Entrance exams should be taken in the junior or senior year. There is a rolling admissions plan. Application deadlines are open. Applications are accepted on-line. **Transfer Students:** 58 transfer students enrolled in 2013-2014. Applicants should have a minimum GPA of 2.5 and a minimum ACT score of 18. An interview is recommended. Passing grades transfer for credit. Transfers are admitted every term. 30 of 128 credits required for the bachelor's degree must be completed at Concordia. **International Students:** There are 9 international students enrolled. They must take the TOEFL. They must also take the SAT or ACT.

ADMISSIONS: Office of Admissions. E-Mail: *admiss@cune.edu* Web: *www.cune.edu*

FINANCIAL AID: In 2014-2015, 98% of all full-time freshmen received some form of financial aid. The FAFSA and the college's own financial statement are required. Check with the school for current application deadlines.

CREIGHTON UNIVERSITY F-3
www.creighton.edu

Omaha, NE 68178

(402) 280-2703
(800) 282-5835

Fax: (402) 280-2685   Email: SarahRichardson@creighton.edu

Full-time: 1545 men, 2270 women	Faculty: 290; IIA, +$
Part-time: 119 men, 142 women	Ph.D.s: 89%
Graduate: 1801 men, 2142 women	Student/Faculty: 13 to 1
Year: semesters, summer session	Tuition: $34,330
Room & Board: $9728	Freshman Class: 5336 applied, 4090 accepted, 966 enrolled
SAT CR/M/W: 580/600/560 ACT: 27	CEEB CODE: 6121
Application Deadline: February 15	VERY COMPETITIVE

Creighton University, founded in 1878, is a private Jesuit Catholic institution offering undergraduate programs in arts and sciences, business administration, and nursing as well as graduate, dental, medical, law, pharmacy, physical therapy, and occupational therapy programs. There are 3 undergraduate schools and 1 graduate school. In addition to regional accreditation, Creighton has baccalaureate program accreditation with AACSB, ACPE, ADA, CSWE, NCATE, ABA, LCME, ACCME, ACGME, ACOTE, CAPTE, CCNE, ACS, CoAEMSP, and ANCC. The 139-acre campus is in an urban area near downtown Omaha Nebraska. Including any residence halls, there are 61 buildings.

STUDENT LIFE: 70% of undergraduates are from out of state, mostly the Midwest. Students are from 50 states, 45 foreign countries, and Canada. 50% are from public schools. 73% are White. 58% are Catholic; 21% Protestant; 18% Jewish, Hinduism, Buddhism, Islam and Unknown. **Male To Female Ratio:** 1.3:1. The average age of freshmen is 18; all undergraduates, 21. 9% do not continue beyond their first year; 75% remain to graduate. **Housing:** 2444 students can be accommodated in college housing, which includes single-sex and coed dorms, on-campus apartments, and married student housing. In addition, there are honors houses, special-interest houses, Cortina Community and Freshman Leadership Program housing. On-campus housing is available on a first-come, first-served basis and is available on a lottery system for upperclassmen. 62% of students live on campus; of those, 90% remain on campus on weekends. All students may keep cars.

FACULTY/CLASSROOMS: 54% of faculty are male; 46% are female. All teach and do research. No introductory courses are taught by graduate students. The average class size in an introductory lecture is 22; in a laboratory is 9; and in a regular course is 21.

PROGRAMS OF STUDY: Creighton confers B.A., B.F.A., B.S., B.S.Atmospheric Science, B.S.B.A., B.S.Chemistry, B.S.Dental Hygiene, B.S.Emergency Medical Services, B.S.Environmental Sci-

ence, B.S.Health Sciences, B.S. Mathematics, B.S.N., B.S.Physics and B.S.W. degrees. Associate, Master's, and Doctoral degrees are also awarded. Bachelor's degrees are awarded in BIOLOGICAL SCIENCE (biochemistry and biology/biological science), BUSINESS (accounting, banking and finance, business administration and management, business intelligence and analytics, entrepreneurial studies, integrated leadership studies, international business management, management information systems, management science, and marketing/retailing/merchandising), COMMUNICATIONS AND THE ARTS (art history, art, classical languages, communication studies, dance, dramatic arts, English, fine arts, french and francophone studies, german studies, graphic design and media, Greek, journalism, Latin, music, musical theater, studio art, theatre arts, and visual and performing arts), COMPUTER AND PHYSICAL SCIENCE (applied physics, chemistry, computer science, energy science, informatics and computer science, mathematics, physical sciences, and physics), EDUCATION (elementary education and secondary education), ENGINEERING AND ENVIRONMENTAL DESIGN (computational sciences, energy management technology, and environmental science), HEALTH PROFESSIONS (dental hygiene, emergency medical services, exercise science, health administration and policy, health science, and nursing), SOCIAL SCIENCE (African studies, American studies, anthropology, classical and near eastern civilization, cultural anthropology, economics, history, international relations, justice and society, medical anthropology, Native American studies, Near Eastern studies, peace studies, philosophy, political science/government, psychology, social work, sociology, Spanish studies, Spanish and Hispanic studies, and theology). Business, science, health science, nursing, biological sciences and psychology are the strongest academically and have the largest enrollments.

ACTIVITIES: 30% of men belong to 5 national fraternities; 33% of women belong to 7 national sororities. There are 212 groups on campus, including art, band, cheerleading, chess, choir, chorale, chorus, computers, dance, debate, drama, drill team, environmental, ethnic, forensics, gay, honors, international, jazz band, literary magazine, musical theater, newspaper, orchestra, pep band, photography, political, professional, radio and TV, religious, social, social service, student government, and symphony. Popular campus events include Diversity Week, Fallapalooza Concert, CUNITY Week, Spring Fling Week, Luau, Pow Wow, Greek Week, FLP Thanksgiving Dinner, and Greek Philanthropies. **Sports:** There are 6 intercollegiate sports for men and 8 for women, and 22 intramural sports for men and 22 for women. Facilities include a sports complex (an outdoor artificial turf area) along with a baseball/softball facility, an intercollegiate soccer facility, and 2 physical fitness centers with space for basketball, volleyball, badminton, soccer and open recreational play, a weight room and a jogging track. Another facility houses an arena for women's basketball and volleyball as well as locker rooms, athletic training rooms and offices for the coaching staff. Creighton is in the process of building a new basketball practice facility to replace its existing practice arena. **Graduates:** From July 1, 2013 to June 30, 2014, 1011 bachelor's degrees were awarded. The most popular majors were health professions and related programs (29%), business/marketing (15%), and biological/life sciences (9%). 250 companies recruited on campus in 2013-2014. In an average class, 1% graduate in 3 years or less, 67% graduate in 4 years or less, 75% graduate in 5 years or less, and 76% graduate in 6 years or less. Of the 2013 graduating class, 32% were enrolled in graduate school within 6 months of graduation, and 56% were employed.

SERVICES: Counseling and information services are available, as is tutoring in most subjects. **Library/Resources:** The 3 libraries contain 681,198 volumes, 1.8 million microform items, 14,928 audio/video tapes/CDs/DVDs, and subscribe to 60,732 periodicals including electronic. Computerized library services include interlibrary loans, database searching, Internet access, and Wi-Fi capability. Special learning facilities include an art gallery, radio station, TV station, solar array used for prototype testing of solar cells. **Physically Challenged Students:** 85% of the campus is accessible. Facilities include wheelchair ramps, elevators, special parking, specially equipped restrooms, special class scheduling, lowered drinking fountains, special housing. **Special:** The University offers study abroad in 56 countries, a Washington semester, and numerous internship opportunities. Students may take an accelerated degree program in organizational communication and creative writing. B.A.-B.S. degrees and dual majors are possible as well as a 3-2 engineering degree with the University of Detroit Mercy. Army ROTC is offered on campus; Air Force ROTC is available through an arrangement with University of Nebraska, Omaha. There are 15 national honor societies, including Phi Beta Kappa, and a freshman honors program. **Visiting:** There are regularly scheduled orientations for prospective students, consisting of open house programs with various presentations and campus tours. A daily visit can be scheduled by either calling the Admissions office or completing online request. There are guides for informal visits, visitors may sit in on classes, and stay overnight. To schedule a visit, contact the Admissions Office. **Campus Safety and Security:** Measures include 24-hour foot and vehicle patrol, emergency notification system, self-defense education, and security escort services. There are shuttle buses, emergency telephones, lighted pathways/sidewalks, controlled access to dorms/residences, a pedestrian escort service, full-time crime prevention officer, violence intervention and prevention center, electronic card access systems, and surveillance cameras.

REQUIREMENTS: The SAT or ACT is required. Applicants must be graduates of an accredited secondary school. The GED is accepted. Students should have completed 16 credits including 4 credits in English, 3 each in math and electives, and 2 each in foreign language, science, and social studies. Home-schooled students are welcome. Creighton requires applicants to be in the upper 50% of their class. A GPA of 2.5 is required. AP and CLEP credits are accepted. Important factors in the admissions decision are advanced placement or honors courses, extracurricular activities record, and recommendations by school officials. For graduation, students must complete a minimum of 128 credit hours and maintain a GPA of 2.0. Each school has general education requirements. Total number of hours required in major and specific disciplines varies by college and major. **Procedure:** Freshmen are admitted fall, spring, and summer. Entrance exams should be taken Fall of the senior year. There are deferred admissions and rolling admissions plans. Applications should be filed by February 15 for fall entry; December 15 for spring entry, along with a $40 fee. Notification is sent on a rolling basis. Applications are accepted on-line. Application fees are waived if application is completed on-line. **Transfer Students:** 46 transfer students enrolled in 2013-2014. Applicants must have a 2.0 minimum GPA in a regionally accredited school. A minimum score of 21 on the ACT or 990 on the SAT is recommended. Grades of C or better transfer for credit. Transfers are admitted every semester. 48 of 128 credits required for the bachelor's degree must be completed at Creighton. **International Students:** There are 79 international students enrolled. The school actively recruits these students. They must take the TOEFL with a minimum score of 550 on the paper-based TOEFL (PBT) or 80 on the Internet-based version (iBT), or take the IELTS.

ADMISSIONS: 77% of the 2014-2015 applicants were accepted. The SAT scores for the 2014-2015 freshman class were: Critical Reading--14% below 500, 45% between 500 and 599, 32% between 600 and 699, and 9% between 700 and 800; Math--8% below 500, 38% between 500 and 599, 40% between 600 and 699, and 14% between 700 and 800; Writing--21% below 500, 42% between 500 and 599, 31% between 600 and 699, and 6% between 700 and 800. The ACT scores were 4% below 21, 16% between 21 and 23, 29% between 24 and 26, 17% between 27 and 28, and 34% above 28. 64% of the current freshmen were in the top fifth of their class; 87% were in the top two fifths. There were 3 National Merit finalists. 55 freshmen graduated first in their class. **Admissions Contact:** Sarah Richardson, Director of Admissions and Scholarships. E-Mail: *SarahRichardson@creighton.edu* Web: *www.creighton.edu/admissions*

FINANCIAL AID: In 2014-2015, 99% of all full-time freshmen and 96% of continuing full-time students received some form of financial aid. 62% of all full-time freshmen and 57% of continuing full-time students received need-based aid. The average freshman award was $27,298. Need-based scholarships or need-based grants averaged $21,989; need-based self-help aid (loans and jobs) averaged $6,220; non-need-based athletic scholarships averaged $24,871; and $15,527 from other forms of aid. 119% of undergraduate students work part-time. Average annual earnings from campus work are $2372. The average financial indebtedness of the 2014 graduate was $35,510. The FAFSA is required. The priority date for freshman financial aid applications for fall entry is April 1.

DOANE COLLEGE
E-3
www.doane.edu

Crete, NE 68333	(402) 826-8222
	(800) 333-6263
Fax: (402) 826-8600	Email: admissions@doane.edu
Full-time: 533 men, 524 women	Faculty: 83; IIB, --$
Part-time: 2 men, 8 women	Ph.D.s: 82%
Graduate: n/av	Student/Faculty: 12 to 1
Year: 4-1-4	Tuition: $27,200
Room & Board: $8030	Freshman Class: 1627 applied, 1291 accepted, 268 enrolled
SAT: recommended ACT: 23	CEEB CODE: 6165
Application Deadline: n/av	COMPETITIVE

Doane College, founded in 1872, is a private liberal arts and science college. There are 3 undergraduate schools and 3 graduate schools. In addition to regional accreditation, Doane has baccalaureate program accreditation with NCATE. The 300-acre campus is in a small town 25 miles southwest of Lincoln. Including any residence halls, there are 28 buildings.

STUDENT LIFE: 77% of undergraduates are from Nebraska. Others are from 29 states, 4 foreign countries, and Canada. 75% are from public schools. 82% are White. 19% are Catholic. **Male To Female Ratio:** 1.0:1. The average age of freshmen is 18; all undergraduates, 20. 23% do not continue beyond their first year; 77% remain to graduate. **Housing:** 832 students can be accommodated in college housing, which includes single-sex and coed dorms and on-campus apartments. In addition, there are honors houses and special-interest houses. On-campus housing is guaranteed for all 4 years. 78% of students live on campus; of those, 79% remain on campus on weekends. All students may keep cars.

FACULTY/CLASSROOMS: 48% of faculty are male; 52% are female. All teach undergraduates. No introductory courses are taught by graduate students. The average class size in an introductory lecture is 24; in a laboratory is 16; and in a regular course is 18.

PROGRAMS OF STUDY: Doane confers B.A. and B.S. degrees. Bachelor's degrees are awarded in BIOLOGICAL SCIENCE (biochemistry and biology/biological science), BUSINESS (accounting and business administration and management), COMMUNICATIONS AND THE ARTS (art, dramatic arts, English, English as a second/foreign language, French, German, journalism, music, and Spanish), COMPUTER AND PHYSICAL SCIENCE (chemistry, computer science, information sciences and systems, mathematics, natural sciences, physical sciences, and physics), EDUCATION (business education, elementary education, physical education, and special education), ENGINEERING AND ENVIRONMENTAL DESIGN (environmental science), SOCIAL SCIENCE (economics, history, international studies, philosophy, political science/government, psychology, public administration, religion, and sociology). Biology and economics are the strongest academically. Education and business administration have the largest enrollments.

ACTIVITIES: 17% of men belong to 5 local fraternities; 22% of women belong to 4 local sororities. There are 50 groups on campus, including alternative spring break, and wildlife/conservation, Hanson Leadership program, investment, art, band, cheerleading, choir, chorale, chorus, computers, dance, drama, ethnic, forensics, gay, honors, international, jazz band, literary magazine, marching band, musical theater, newspaper, pep band, photography, political, professional, radio and TV, religious, social, social service, speech team, and student government. Popular campus events include Parents Day, Stop Day, Christmas Festival and Concert. **Sports:** There are 6 intercollegiate sports for men and 6 for women, and 4 intramural sports for men and 4 for women. Facilities include a phys ed building, field house, sports field, fitness center, a gym, pool, nature and cross-country trails, challenge course, indoor and outdoor tracks. **Graduates:** From July 1, 2013 to June 30, 2014, 228 bachelor's degrees were awarded. The most popular majors were elementary education (23%), biology (13%), and business (10%). 45 companies recruited on campus in 2013-2014. In an average class, 1% graduate in 3 years or less, 60% graduate in 4 years or less, 63% graduate in 5 years or less, and 66% graduate in 6 years or less. Of the 2013 graduating class, 20% were enrolled in graduate school within 6 months of graduation, and 79% were employed.

SERVICES: Counseling and information services are available, as is tutoring in every subject. There is remedial math, reading, and writing. **Library/Resources:** The library contains 346,771 volumes, 7,410 microform items, 11,082 audio/video tapes/CDs/DVDs, and subscribes to 59,834 periodicals including electronic. Computerized library services include interlibrary loans, database searching, Internet access, and Wi-Fi capability. Special learning facilities include an art gallery, radio station, TV station, an observatory. **Physically Challenged Students:** 60% of the campus is accessible. Facilities include wheelchair ramps, elevators, special parking, specially equipped restrooms, and special class scheduling. **Special:** Internships for sophomores through seniors, a Washington semester, and study abroad in numerous countries are possible. A 3-2 engineering program in conjunction with Washington University and Columbia University, work-study, student-designed and interdisciplinary majors, dual majors and accelerated degrees in all areas, credit by exam, nondegree study, and pass/fail options are available. Doane also offers the HELPS program, designed for Doane college graduates who wish to return as full-time students to seek further education in preparation for career advancement. Students may pursue a 3-2 environmental studies/forestry degree in conjunction with Duke University. Doane's Lincoln campus, designed for adults, offers intensive 8-week classes in the evening and on weekends in both undergraduate and graduate programs. Doane offers an honors program, leadership development program, and the opportunity to conduct summer research projects with faculty. There are 7 national honor societies, a freshman honors program, and 3 departmental honors programs. **Visiting:** There are regularly scheduled orientations for prospective students, including 4 scheduled half-day visits that incorporate a parents program. There are guides for informal visits, visitors may sit in on classes, and stay overnight. To schedule a visit, contact the Admissions Office at (800) 333-6263. **Campus Safety and Security:** Measures include security escort services. There are emergency telephones, lighted pathways/sidewalks, evening patrols by trained security personnel.

REQUIREMENTS: The ACT is required. The SAT is recommended. Applicants must be graduates of an accredited secondary school. The GED is accepted. It is recommended that 4 units of English and 3 units each of math, science, and the social sciences be completed. An interview is recommended. Art students must submit a portfolio, and music and drama students must audition. A GPA of 2.0 is required. AP and CLEP credits are accepted. Important factors in the admissions decision are advanced placement or honors courses, leadership record, parents or siblings attended your school, evidence of special talent, personality/intangible qualities, extracurricular activities record, recommendations by alumni, geographical diversity, recommendations by school officials, and ability to finance college education. The Doane Plan requires students to complete 60 to 70 credits in heritage studies, contemporary issues, international/multicultural perspective, natural science, quantitative reasoning, communication, aesthetic perspective, health and well-being, and community and leadership. Students are also required to complete 2 hours of phys ed, demonstrate computer skills in word processing, and in most disciplines, complete a senior seminar. Students must complete 132 credit hours and have a minimum GPA of 2.0 in the major to graduate. **Procedure:** Freshmen are admitted fall, winter, and spring. Entrance exams should be taken by spring of the junior year or early senior year. There are deferred admissions and rolling admissions plans. Application deadlines are open. Notification is sent on a rolling basis. Applications are accepted on-line. **Transfer Students:** 44 transfer students enrolled in 2013-2014. Transfer students must submit a transcript from previously attended colleges and have been in good standing. The SAT or ACT is usually required. Grades of 2.0 or higher generally transfer for credit. 30 of 132 credits required for the bachelor's degree must be completed at Doane. **International Students:** There are 14 international students enrolled. The school actively recruits these students. They must take the TOEFL with a minimum score of 525 on the paper-based TOEFL (PBT) or 70 on the Internet-based version (iBT), or take the IELTS with a minimum score of 5.5. They must also take the SAT or ACT.

ADMISSIONS: 79% of the 2014-2015 applicants were accepted. The ACT scores were 24% below 21, 35% between 21 and 23, 25% between 24 and 26, 10% between 27 and 28, and 6% above 28. 38% of the current freshmen were in the top fifth of their class; 88% were in the top two fifths. There were 2 National Merit finalists. 9 freshmen graduated first in their class. **Admissions Contact:** Joel Weyand, Vice President for Enrollment . E-Mail: *admissions@doane.edu* Web: *www.doane.edu*

FINANCIAL AID: In 2014-2015, 100% of all full-time freshmen and 98% of continuing full-time students received some form of financial aid. 90% of all full-time freshmen and 89% of continuing full-time students received need-based aid. The average freshman award was $21,353. Need-based scholarships or need-based grants averaged $17,884 ($25,560 maximum); need-based self-help aid (loans and jobs) averaged $4,641 ($9,150 maximum); non-need-based athletic scholarships averaged $10,509 ($23,000 maximum); and other non-need-based awards and non-need-based scholarships averaged $8,638 ($25,560 maximum). 43% of undergraduate students work part-time. Average annual earnings from campus work are $920. The average financial indebtedness of the 2014 graduate was $24,578. The FAFSA is required. The deadline for filing freshman financial aid applications for fall entry is March 1.

HASTINGS COLLEGE — D-3
www.hastings.edu

Hastings, NE 68901	**(402) 461-7403**
	(800) 532-7642
Fax: (402) 461-7490	**Email:** mmolliconi@hastings.edu
Full-time: 564 men, 519 women	**Faculty:** 86; IIB, --$
Part-time: 10 men, 11 women	**Ph.D.s:** 72%
Graduate: 22 men, 28 women	**Student/Faculty:** 13 to 1
Year: 4-1-4, summer session	**Tuition:** $23,325
Room & Board: $8228	**Freshman Class:** 11186 applied, 1126 accepted, 289 enrolled
SAT: required **ACT:** 24	**CEEB CODE:** 6270
Application Deadline: August 1	**COMPETITIVE+**

Hastings College, founded in 1882 and affiliated with the Presbyterian Church, offers programs in the liberal arts and sciences, education, business, and pre-health professions. Figures in the above capsule and in this profile are approximate. There is 1 graduate school. In addition to regional accreditation, Hastings College has baccalaureate program accreditation with NASM and NCATE. The 109-acre campus is in a rural area 150 miles west of Omaha. Including any residence halls, there are 42 buildings.

STUDENT LIFE: 69% of undergraduates are from Nebraska. Others are from 31 states, 8 foreign countries, and Canada. 86% are from public schools. 89% are White. 38% are Protestant; 34% claim no religious affiliation; 21% Catholic. **Male To Female Ratio:** 0.9:1. The average age of freshmen is 19; all undergraduates, 21. 27% do not continue beyond their first year; 63% remain to graduate. **Housing:** 842 students can be accommodated in college housing, which includes single-sex and coed dorms and on-campus apartments. In addition, there are honors houses, non-honors houses. On-campus housing is guaranteed for the freshman year only, and is available on a first-come, first-served basis. Priority is given to out-of-town students. 73% of students live on campus; of those, 60% remain on campus on weekends. All students may keep cars.

FACULTY/CLASSROOMS: 56% of faculty are male; 44% are female. All teach undergraduates, and 25% do both. No introductory courses are taught by graduate students. The average class size in an introductory lecture is 25; in a laboratory is 24; and in a regular course is 23.

PROGRAMS OF STUDY: Hastings College confers B.A. and B.M. degrees. Master's degrees are also awarded. Bachelor's degrees are awarded in BIOLOGICAL SCIENCE (biology/biological science), BUSINESS (accounting and business administration and management), COMMUNICATIONS AND THE ARTS (broadcasting, communications, dramatic arts, English, fine arts, German, music, Spanish, and speech/debate/rhetoric), COMPUTER AND PHYSICAL SCIENCE (chemistry, computer science, mathematics, and physics),

EDUCATION (art education, business education, elementary education, foreign languages education, music education, science education, secondary education, and special education), HEALTH PROFESSIONS (health care administration), SOCIAL SCIENCE (economics, history, human services, philosophy, political science/government, psychology, religion, social science, and sociology). Physics, mathematics, and religion are the strongest academically. Business administration, teacher education, and biology have the largest enrollments.

ACTIVITIES: 30% of men belong to 4 local fraternities; 30% of women belong to 4 local sororities. There are 80 groups on campus, including and public relations, health advisory council, nontraditional students, peer educators, art, band, cheerleading, choir, chorus, computers, dance, debate, drama, environmental, ethnic, flag team, forensics, gay, honors, international, jazz band, literary magazine, marching band, musical theater, newspaper, orchestra, pep band, photography, political, professional, radio and TV, religious, social, social service, student government, and symphony. Popular campus events include May Fete, Festival of Lessons and Carols, and Artist Lecture Series. **Sports:** There are 9 intercollegiate sports for men and 10 for women, and 12 intramural sports for men and 12 for women. Facilities include a physical fitness center, a pool, a weight room, indoor and outdoor tennis courts, a 3000-seat stadium, a 2500-seat gym, a wellness center, and an all-weather track. **Graduates:** From July 1, 2013 to June 30, 2014, 238 bachelor's degrees were awarded. The most popular majors were business administration (9%), psychology (9%), and biology (8%). 80 companies recruited on campus in 2013-2014. In an average class, 52% graduate in 4 years or less, 62% graduate in 5 years or less, and 63% graduate in 6 years or less. Of the 2013 graduating class, 27% were enrolled in graduate school within 6 months of graduation, and 71% were employed.

SERVICES: Counseling and information services are available, as is tutoring in most subjects. **Library/Resources:** The library contains 135,450 volumes, 87,723 microform items, and 3,802 audio/video tapes/CDs/DVDs, and subscribes to 1,050 periodicals including electronic. Computerized library services include interlibrary loans, database searching, Internet access, and Wi-Fi capability. Special learning facilities include an art gallery, radio station, TV station, an observatory, a glass blowing studio, greenhouse, and infant study lab. **Physically Challenged Students:** 90% of the campus is accessible. Facilities include wheelchair ramps, elevators, special parking, specially equipped restrooms, special class scheduling, lowered drinking fountains, and lowered telephones. **Special:** There is a co-op nursing program, a 3-2 engineering program with Columbia and Washington Universities and Georgia Institute of Technology, and a 3-2 degree in occupational therapy with Boston and Washington Universities. Internships, study abroad in England, Spain, Russia, Ireland, Holland, and Germany, dual majors in all areas, and student-designed majors are possible. There are 12 national honor societies. **Visiting:** There are regularly scheduled orientations for prospective students, including academic department presentations, a financial aid session, a student panel discussion, a student guided tour, and an activities fair. There are guides for informal visits, visitors may sit in on classes, and stay overnight. To schedule a visit, contact the Admissions Office. **Campus Safety and Security:** Measures include emergency notification system and security escort services. There are emergency telephones, lighted pathways/sidewalks, a night security patrol.

REQUIREMENTS: The SAT or ACT is required. Applicants should graduate from an accredited secondary school with a minimum of 4 academic credits in English and 2 each in math, science, social studies, and a foreign language. Generally, placement in the upper half of the graduating class, a minimum GPA of 2.0, or a composite score of 20 on the enhanced ACT, is a minimal requirement for consideration for admission. AP and CLEP credits are accepted. Important factors in the admissions decision are advanced placement or honors courses, leadership record, and personality/intangible qualities. Students are required to take courses in written and oral communication, physical and life science, foreign language, history, social and political science, literature, philosophy, religion, health/wellness, computer science, the fine arts, and phys ed. A minimum 2.0 GPA and 127 credit hours, with 30 to 36 in the major, are required to graduate. **Procedure:** Freshmen are admitted to all sessions. Entrance exams should be taken before November. There is a rolling admission plan. Applications should be filed by August 1 for fall entry; December 1 for winter entry; January 1 for spring entry; and May 15 for summer entry. The fall 2014 application fee was $20. Applications are accepted on-line. **Transfer Students:** 48 transfer students enrolled in 2013-2014. Transfer students must have completed course work equivalent by description to that of Hastings and have earned grades of C or better. 30 of 127 credits required for the bachelor's degree must be completed at Hastings College. **International Students:** There are 16 international students enrolled. The school actively recruits these students. They must take the TOEFL.

ADMISSIONS: 100% of the 2014-2015 applicants were accepted. The ACT scores were 37% below 21, 23% between 21 and 23, 20% between 24 and 26, 10% between 27 and 28, and 10% above 28. 36% of the current freshmen were in the top fifth of their class; 64% were in the top two fifths. 18 freshmen graduated first in their class. **Admissions Contact:** Mary Molliconi, Director of Admissions. E-Mail: *mmolliconi@hastings.edu* Web: *www.hastings.edu*

FINANCIAL AID: In 2014-2015, 99% of all full-time freshmen and 99% of continuing full-time students received some form of financial aid. 78% of all full-time freshmen and 73% of continuing full-time students received need-based aid. 40% of undergraduate students work part-time. Average annual earnings from campus work are $1200. The average financial indebtedness of the 2014 graduate was $22,882. Hastings College is a member of CSS. The FAFSA is required. The deadline for filing freshman financial aid applications for fall entry is May 1.

MIDLAND UNIVERSITY	E-3
www.MidlandU.edu	

Fremont, NE 68025	**(402) 941-6501**
	(800) 642-8382
Fax: (402)-941-6513	Email: Ferzely@MidlandU.edu
Full-time: n/av	Faculty: n/av
Part-time: n/av	Ph.D.s: n/av
Graduate: n/av	Student/Faculty: n/av
Year: 4-1-4, summer session	Tuition: $27,000
Room & Board: $7000	Freshman Class: n/av
SAT or ACT: required	CEEB CODE: 6406
Application Deadline: n/av	**COMPETITIVE**

Midland University is a private liberal arts institution. Affiliated with the ELCA, Midland offers more than 40 programs of study, 27 varsity sports, a plethora of arts opportunities, and several student organizations. Figures in the above capsule and in this profile are approximate. There are 2 graduate schools. In addition to regional accreditation, Midland has baccalaureate program accreditation with NLN. The 27-acre campus is in an urban area 30 minutes northwest of Omaha. Including any residence halls, there are 18 buildings.

STUDENT LIFE: 75% of undergraduates are from Nebraska. Others are from 23 states, 10 foreign countries, and Canada. 94% are from public schools. 91% are White. 57% are Protestant; 32% Catholic. The average age of freshmen is 18; all undergraduates, 20. 16% do not continue beyond their first year; 56% remain to graduate. **Housing:** 600 students can be accommodated in college housing, which includes single-sex and coed dorms, on-campus apartments, and off-campus apartments. On-campus housing is available on a first-come, first-served basis and is available on a lottery system for upperclassmen. 30% of students commute. Alcohol is not permitted. All students may keep cars.

FACULTY/CLASSROOMS: 60% of faculty are male; 40% are female. All teach undergraduates. No introductory courses are taught by graduate students. The average class size in a laboratory is 20 and in a regular course is 20.

PROGRAMS OF STUDY: Midland confers B.A., B.S., B.S.B.A. and B.S.N. degrees. Master's degrees are also awarded. Bachelor's degrees are awarded in BIOLOGICAL SCIENCE (biology/biological science), BUSINESS (accounting, business administration and management, business economics, management information systems, and marketing/retailing/merchandising), COMMUNICATIONS AND THE ARTS (advertising, communications, English, fine arts, journalism, and music), COMPUTER AND PHYSICAL SCIENCE (chemistry, computer programming, computer science, and mathematics), EDUCATION (art education, business education, early childhood education, elementary education, middle school education, music education, science education, and secondary education), HEALTH PROFESSIONS (nursing, predentistry, and premedicine), SOCIAL SCIENCE (community services, economics, history, parks and recreation management, prelaw, psychology, religion, social science, and sociology). Business, journalism, and education are the strongest academically. Business, education, and nursing have the largest enrollments.

ACTIVITIES: 20% of men belong to 4 local fraternities; 20% of women belong to 4 local sororities. There are 36 groups on campus, including art, band, cheerleading, choir, chorale, chorus, computers, drama, drill team, drum and bugle corps, ethnic, film, forensics, gay, honors, jazz band, literary magazine, musical theater, newspaper, orchestra, pep band, photography, political, professional, radio and TV, religious, social, social service, student government, and yearbook. Popular campus events include Greek Games, Snow Week, Martin Luther King Day, Midland U's Got Talent, and Festival of the Arts. **Sports:** There are 12 intercollegiate sports for men and 15 for women. Facilities include a phys ed center, an athletic practice field, an indoor pool, an indoor track, and a weight room. Students also have access to the second largest YMCA in the world at no cost to them.

SERVICES: Counseling and information services are available, as is tutoring in every subject. There is remedial reading and writing. **Library/Resources:** The library contains 105,000 volumes, 1,000 audio/video tapes/CDs/DVDs, and subscribes to 900 periodicals including electronic. Computerized library services include interlibrary loans, database searching, Internet access, and Wi-Fi capability. Special learning facilities include an art gallery, planetarium, and radio station. **Physically Challenged Students:** 90% of the campus is accessible. Facilities include wheelchair ramps, elevators, special parking, specially equipped restrooms, special class scheduling, lowered drinking fountains, and lowered telephones. **Special:** There is cross-registration with Dana College in Blair, internships in business, public relations, journalism, and art, study abroad in 3 countries, student-designed majors, work-study programs, and a 3-2 engineering degree with Washington University. Other options include dual majors, independent study, directed study, and the pass/no credit grading system. There are 2 national honor societies. **Visiting:** There are regularly scheduled orientations for prospective students. Campus visits are scheduled on an individual basis and as much as possible include visits with faculty, students, and financial aid counselors. There are guides for informal visits, visitors may sit in on classes, and stay overnight. To schedule a visit, contact the Admissions Office at admissions@MidlandU.edu. **Campus Safety and Security:** Measures include 24-hour foot and vehicle patrol, emergency notification system, and security escort services. There are lighted pathways/sidewalks and controlled access to dorms/residences.

REQUIREMENTS: The SAT or ACT is required. Applicants should be graduates of an accredited secondary school. The GED is accepted. Recommended preparation includes 3 units of English, 2 each of math and foreign language, and 10 of electives. An interview is recommended. AP and CLEP credits are accepted. Important factors in the admissions decision are leadership record, extracurricular activities record, and evidence of special talent. To graduate, students need a total of 120 credit hours, with 33 of these in distribution requirements of the student's selection. 1 English, speech, and math course is required, as well as 1 year of foreign language on the high school or college level. The total number of hours in the major varies from 34 to 48, and students must maintain a GPA of at least 2.0 overall and 2.25 in the major, with some departments requiring a higher minimum GPA. **Procedure:** Freshmen are admitted fall and winter. Entrance exams should be taken during the fall of the senior year. There are deferred admissions and rolling admissions plans. Application deadlines are open. Notification is sent on a rolling basis. Applications are accepted on-line. **Transfer Students:** 125 transfer students enrolled in 2013-2014. Applicants must be in good standing at their previous college and generally have a 2.0 minimum GPA. Grades of C or higher transfer for credit. 30 of 120 credits required for the bach-

elor's degree must be completed at Midland. **International Students:** The school actively recruits these students. They must take the TOEFL.

ADMISSIONS: Eliza Ferzely, VP for Admissions & Enrollment Mgmnt. E-Mail: *Ferzely@MidlandU.edu* Web: *www.MidlandU.edu*

FINANCIAL AID: In 2014-2015, 98% of all full-time freshmen and 97% of continuing full-time students received some form of financial aid. Midland is a member of CSS. The FAFSA and FFS are required. Check with the school for current application deadlines.

NEBRASKA METHODIST COLLEGE OF NURSING AND ALLIED HEALTH *(The complete profile is made available exclusively on our website, www.barronspac.com)*

NEBRASKA WESLEYAN UNIVERSITY   E-3
www.nebrwesleyan.edu

Lincoln, NE 68504	(402) 465-2144
	n/av
Fax: (402) 465-2179	Email: admissions@nebrwesleyan.edu
Full-time: 690 men, 980 women	Faculty: 105; IIB, --$
Part-time: 78 men, 155 women	Ph.D.s: 89%
Graduate: 66 men, 179 women	Student/Faculty: 12 to 1
Year: semesters, summer session	Tuition: $23,974
Room & Board: $6800	Freshman Class: n/av
SAT: required ACT: 25	CEEB CODE: 6470
Application Deadline: May 1	COMPETITIVE+

Nebraska Wesleyan University, founded in 1887, is a private liberal arts institution affiliated with the United Methodist Church. Figures in the above capsule and in this profile are approximate. There are 18 undergraduate schools and 3 graduate schools. In addition to regional accreditation, NWU has baccalaureate program accreditation with ACBSP, CSWE, NASM, NCATE, and NLN. The 50-acre campus is in a suburban area 50 miles west of Omaha. Including any residence halls, there are 31 buildings.

STUDENT LIFE: 88% of undergraduates are from Nebraska. Others are from 25 states, 14 foreign countries, and Canada. 93% are White. 36% are Protestant; 24% Catholic; 14% claim no religious affiliation. **Male To Female Ratio:** 1.6:1. The average age of freshmen is 18; all undergraduates, 20. 18% do not continue beyond their first year; 70% remain to graduate. **Housing:** 1055 students can be accommodated in college housing, which includes single-sex and coed dorms, on-campus apartments, and off-campus apartments. In addition, there are fraternity houses and sorority houses. On-campus housing is guaranteed for all 4 years. 65% of students live on campus; of those, 70% remain on campus on weekends. All students may keep cars.

FACULTY/CLASSROOMS: 45% of faculty are male; 55% are female. All teach undergraduates. No introductory courses are taught by graduate students. The average class size in an introductory lecture is 22; in a laboratory is 17; and in a regular course is 19.

PROGRAMS OF STUDY: NWU confers B.A., B.S., B.F.A., B.M. and B.S.N. degrees. Master's degrees are also awarded. Bachelor's degrees are awarded in BIOLOGICAL SCIENCE (biochemistry, biology/biological science, and molecular biology), BUSINESS (accounting, business administration and management, international business management, and sports management), COMMUNICATIONS AND THE ARTS (applied music, art, communications, dramatic arts, English, French, German, language arts, music, Spanish, and studio art), COMPUTER AND PHYSICAL SCIENCE (chemistry, computer science, information sciences and systems, mathematics, and physics), EDUCATION (athletic training, elementary education, English education, middle school education, music education, physical education, science education, social science education, and special education), HEALTH PROFESSIONS (exercise science, health, and nursing), SOCIAL SCIENCE (biopsychology, economics, history, international studies, paralegal studies, philosophy, political science/government, psychology, religion, social work, sociology, and women's studies). Business administration, biology, and psychology have the largest enrollments.

ACTIVITIES: 12% of men belong to 1 local and 3 national fraterni-

ties; 19% of women belong to 2 local and 2 national sororities. There are 80 groups on campus, including art, band, cheerleading, choir, chorus, computers, debate, drama, drill team, ethnic, forensics, gay, honors, international, jazz band, literary magazine, musical theater, newspaper, opera, orchestra, pep band, political, professional, religious, social, social service, student government, and yearbook. Popular campus events include international dinners, Mosaic Week (week emphasizing multicultural activities), and Visions. **Sports:** There are 8 intercollegiate sports for men and 8 for women, and 8 intramural sports for men and 8 for women. Facilities include a recreation and fitness center, a field house and gym, a football/soccer stadium, a swimming pool, an outdoor track, football and baseball fields, tennis courts, racquetball courts, and volleyball courts. **Graduates:** From July 1, 2013 to June 30, 2014, 403 Bachelor's degrees were awarded. The most popular majors were business administration (23%), nursing (13%), and education (9%). 82 companies recruited on campus in 2013-2014. In an average class, 1% graduate in 3 years or less, 52% graduate in 4 years or less, 64% graduate in 5 years or less, and 70% graduate in 6 years or less.

SERVICES: Counseling and information services are available, as is tutoring in some subjects. **Library/Resources:** The library contains 221,084 volumes, 4,897 microform items, 8,826 audio/video tapes/CDs/DVDs, and subscribes to 832 periodicals including electronic. Computerized library services include interlibrary loans, database searching, Internet access, and Wi-Fi capability. Special learning facilities include an art gallery, planetarium, laboratory theater, sleep lab, greenhouse, herbarium, and nuclear magnetic resonance lab. **Physically Challenged Students:** 92% of the campus is accessible. Facilities include wheelchair ramps, elevators, special parking, specially equipped restrooms, special class scheduling, lowered drinking fountains, lowered telephones, special housing. All academic programs can be moved or adapted as needed to accommodate students. **Special:** NWU offers the Capitol Hill Internship Program; study abroad in 38 countries through the International Student Exchange Program and sister schools in Mexico, Japan, and Estonia; a global studies major; and many other interdisciplinary studies majors and minors. Internships are available in most departments and required in many. Natural sciences majors can complete summer research fellowships at labs, universities, and agencies nationwide and internationally. Other options include pass/fail options, dual majors, credit by exam, and a 3-2 engineering degree in conjunction with Washington and Columbia Universities. There are 25 national honor societies. **Visiting:** There are regularly scheduled orientations for prospective students, consisting of a tour, classroom visits, and meetings with faculty, financial aid and admissions personnel, and current students. There are guides for informal visits, visitors may sit in on classes, and stay overnight. To schedule a visit, contact the Admissions Office. **Campus Safety and Security:** Measures include emergency notification system and security escort services. There are emergency telephones, lighted pathways/sidewalks, controlled access to dorms/residences, security service, night time foot patrol, and a uniformed police officer during the day.

REQUIREMENTS: The SAT or ACT is required. Freshmen must be graduates of an accredited secondary school or submit the GED. A campus visit is recommended. NWU requires applicants to be in the upper 50% of their class. AP and CLEP credits are accepted. To graduate, students must complete approximately 42 to 48 hours of general education requirements, including 9 hours in First-year Experience, 8 in Developing Foundations courses, 7 in Scientific Inquiry, 6 in U.S. Culture and Society, 3 to 11 in Global Perspectives, 3 in Western Intellectual and Religious Traditions, and 3 in Fine Arts. At least 126 credit hours, including 30 in the major, must be completed with a minimum GPA of 2.0. A senior comprehensive is also needed, consisting of a comprehensive exam in the major discipline, a thesis or independent study, or an internship, presentation, or performance. **Procedure:** Freshmen are admitted fall and spring. Entrance exams should be taken no later than December of the senior year. There are early decision and deferred admissions plans. Early decision applications should be filed by November 15; regular applications, by May 1 for fall entry; December 15 for spring entry; and April 15 for summer entry, along with a $20 fee. Notification of early decision is sent December 15; regular decision, January 15. 338 early decision candidates were accepted for the 2014-2015 class. Applications are accepted on-line. **Transfer Students:** 61 transfer students enrolled in 2013-2014. Applicants must be in good standing at their previous school and have a 2.0 GPA or higher. Grades of C- or better transfer for credit. 30 of 126 credits required for the bachelor's degree must be completed at NWU. **International Students:** There are 33 international students enrolled. The school actively recruits these students. They must take the TOEFL with a minimum score of 525 on the paper-based TOEFL (PBT) or 71 on the Internet-based version (iBT). The SAT or ACT is recommended.

ADMISSIONS: The ACT scores were 10% below 21, 27% between 21 and 23, 28% between 24 and 26, 18% between 27 and 28, and 17% above 28. 48% of the current freshmen were in the top fifth of their class; 79% were in the top two fifths. 22 freshmen graduated first in their class. **Admissions Contact:** David Duzik, Director of Admissions. E-Mail: *admissions@nebrwesleyan.edu* Web: *www.nebrwesleyan.edu*

FINANCIAL AID: In 2014-2015, 99% of all full-time freshmen and 96% of continuing full-time students received some form of financial aid. 77% of all full-time freshmen and 71% of continuing full-time students received need-based aid. The average freshman award was $16,769. Need-based scholarships or need-based grants averaged $10,040 ($28,500 maximum); need-based self-help aid (loans and jobs) averaged $3,648 ($16,541 maximum); and other non-need-based awards and non-need-based scholarships averaged $2,690 ($19,625 maximum). 102% of undergraduate students work part-time. Average annual earnings from campus work are $1318. The average financial indebtedness of the 2014 graduate was $19,636. The FAFSA is required. The priority date for freshman financial aid applications for fall entry is rolling. The deadline for filing freshman financial aid applications for fall entry is rolling.

PERU STATE COLLEGE (*The complete profile is made available exclusively on our website, www.barronspac.com*)

UNION COLLEGE   E-3
www.ucollege.edu

Lincoln, NE 68506   (402) 486-2504
  (800) 228-4600
Fax: (402) 486-2895   **Email:** ucenrol@ucollege.edu
Full-time: 284 men, 380 women   **Faculty:** 53
Part-time: 53 men, 69 women   **Ph.D.s:** 52%
Graduate: 21 men, 49 women   **Student/Faculty:** 15 to 1
Year: semesters, summer session   **Tuition:** $17,430
Room & Board: $5840   **Freshman Class:** n/av
ACT: 22   **CEEB CODE:** 6865
Application Deadline: open   **COMPETITIVE**

Union College, established in 1891, is a private liberal arts institution affiliated with the Seventh-Day Adventist Church. In addition to regional accreditation, has baccalaureate program accreditation with CSWE and NCATE. The 26-acre campus is in a suburban area in southeast Lincoln Nebraska. Including any residence halls, there are 13 buildings.

STUDENT LIFE: 86% of undergraduates are from out of state, mostly the Mid-West. Students are from 45 states, 21 foreign countries, and Canada. 30% are from public schools. 72% are White. **Male To Female Ratio:** 1.4:1. The average age of freshmen is 18; all undergraduates, 22. 35% do not continue beyond their first year; 54% remain to graduate. **Housing:** 642 students can be accommodated in college housing, which includes single-sex dorms, on-campus apartments, and married student housing. On-campus housing is guaranteed for the freshman year only, and is available on a first-come, first-served basis. 52% of students commute. Alcohol is not permitted. All students may keep cars.

FACULTY/CLASSROOMS: 55% of faculty are male; 45% are female. No introductory courses are taught by graduate students. The average class size in an introductory lecture is 21 and in a regular course is 16.

PROGRAMS OF STUDY: confers B.A., B.S., B.A.T., B.Ed., B.M., B.S.W. and B.T. degrees. Associate and Master's degrees are also awarded. Bachelor's degrees are awarded in BIOLOGICAL SCIENCE (biology/biological science), BUSINESS (accounting, banking and finance, business administration and management, management science, marketing and distribution, and small business management), COMMUNICATIONS AND THE ARTS (communications, English, French, German, graphic design, journalism, literature, music, music performance, public relations, Spanish, and studio art), COMPUTER AND PHYSICAL SCIENCE (chemistry, computer science, mathematics, physics, and science), EDUCATION (art education, business education, computer education, elementary education, English education, mathematics education, music education, physical education, secondary education, and social science education), HEALTH PROFESSIONS (medical laboratory technology, nursing, and physician's assistant), SOCIAL SCIENCE (history, international public service, international studies, pastoral studies, physical fitness/movement, psychology, religion, religious education, social science, social work, and theological studies). Physician's assistant and physical science are the strongest academically. Nursing and international rescue and relief have the largest enrollments.

ACTIVITIES: There are no fraternities or sororities. There are 18 groups on campus, including art, band, choir, chorale, chorus, computers, drama, ethnic, honors, international, literary magazine, newspaper, orchestra, photography, religious, social, student government, and yearbook. **Sports:** There are 2 intercollegiate sports for men and 3 for women, and 8 intramural sports for men and 8 for women. Facilities include an Olympic-size indoor swimming pool, a weight room, tennis courts, and a sandlot volleyball court. **Graduates:** From July 1, 2013 to June 30, 2014, 170 bachelor's degrees were awarded. The most popular majors were nursing (16%), business administration (15%), and elementary education (8%). 32 companies recruited on campus in 2013-2014. In an average class, 29% graduate in 4 years or less and 57% graduate in 6 years or less. Of the 2013 graduating class, 15% were enrolled in graduate school within 6 months of graduation, and 80% were employed.

SERVICES: Counseling and information services are available, as is tutoring in most subjects. There is a reader service for the blind, and remedial math, reading, and writing. **Library/Resources:** The library contains 161,728 volumes, 1,938 microform items, 2,066 audio/video tapes/CDs/DVDs, and subscribes to 604 periodicals including electronic. Computerized library services include interlibrary loans, database searching, Internet access, and Wi-Fi capability. Special learning facilities include an art gallery, a state-run natural arboretum. **Physically Challenged Students:** 75% of the campus is accessible. Facilities include wheelchair ramps, elevators, special parking, specially equipped restrooms, and lowered telephones. **Special:** Special academic programs include study abroad in 7 countries, co-op programs with 9 Adventist institutions abroad, and cross-registration with the University of Nebraska, Nebraska Wesleyan University, and Southeast Community College. Student-designed majors are available through the Personalized Bachelor's Degree Program. There are pass/fail options in electives for upperclassmen with a minimum cumulative GPA of 2.0. Some internships are available. There is a freshman honors program. **Visiting:** There are regularly scheduled orientations for prospective students. There are guides for informal visits, visitors may sit in on classes, and stay overnight. To schedule a visit, contact the Admissions Office Campus Hostess. **Campus Safety and Security:** Measures include 24-hour foot and vehicle patrol and security escort services. There are emergency telephones and lighted pathways/sidewalks.

REQUIREMENTS: The ACT is required. Freshmen with a high school GPA below 2.5 and/or an ACT composite score below the 20th percentile will be enrolled in the freshman development program. Applicants must have graduated from an accredited secondary school with 18 academic credits, including 3 units of English and 1 unit each of math, science, and history. For math and science programs, 2 units of algebra and 1 unit each of geometry and trigonometry are recommended. For majors in nursing, biology, chemistry, physics, or engineering, applicants should complete physics and chemistry courses. The GED is also accepted. An essay and interview are advised, and music students should audition. A GPA of 2.5 is required. AP and CLEP credits are accepted. Students must complete 128 semester hours, with fulfillment of a major, and maintain a minimum GPA of 2.0. There are 56 hours of core classes, including those in art/fine arts,

computer science, English, history, math, science, and philosophy/religion. Courses in phy ed are also required. **Procedure:** Freshmen are admitted fall and spring. Entrance exams should be taken by fall of the senior year. There is a rolling admissions plan. Application deadlines are open. **Transfer Students:** Transfer students must have a minimum GPA of 2.0. The ACT is required, and high school and college transcripts must be submitted. 30 of 128 credits required for the bachelor's degree must be completed at Union. **International Students:** There are 109 international students enrolled. The school actively recruits these students. They must take the TOEFL with a minimum score of 550 on the paper-based TOEFL (PBT) or 80 on the Internet-based version (iBT). They must also take the ACT, scoring 18.

ADMISSIONS: 32% of the current freshmen were in the top fifth of their class; 69% were in the top two fifths. **Admissions Contact:** Huda McClelland, Director of Admissions. E-Mail: *ucenrol@ucollege .edu* Web: *www.ucollege.edu*

FINANCIAL AID: In 2014-2015, 99% of all full-time freshmen and 91% of continuing full-time students received some form of financial aid. 97% of all full-time freshmen and 79% of continuing full-time students received need-based aid. 54% of undergraduate students work part-time. Average annual earnings from campus work are $2400. The FAFSA is required. Check with the school for current application deadlines.

UNIVERSITY OF NEBRASKA SYSTEM

The University of Nebraska System, established in 1869, is a public system in Nebraska. It is governed by a board of regents and a central administration, whose chief administrator is the president. The primary mission and priorities of the system are teaching, research, and service. The total student enrollment of all 5 campuses is usually 50,000, with 4230 faculty members. Altogether there are 449 baccalaureate, 169 master's, and 51 doctoral programs offered in the University of Nebraska System. 4-year campuses are located in Kearney, Lincoln, and Omaha. Profiles of the 4-year campuses are included in this section.

UNIVERSITY OF NEBRASKA - LINCOLN E-3
www.admissions.unl.edu

Lincoln, NE 68588	(402) 472-2023
	(800) 742-8800
Fax: (402) 472-0670	Email: admissions@unl.edu
Full-time: 9887 men, 8773 women	Faculty: 1052; I, av$
Part-time: 767 men, 552 women	Ph.D.s: 94%
Graduate: 2408 men, 2619 women	Student/Faculty: 18 to 1
Year: semesters, summer session	Tuition: $8475 ($26,302)
Room & Board: $10,032	Freshman Class: 11865 applied, 8293 accepted, 4652 enrolled
SAT CR/M: 570/590 ACT: 25	CEEB CODE: 6877
Application Deadline: May 1	VERY COMPETITIVE

The University of Nebraska–Lincoln is a public institution, founded in 1869. UNL is an educational institution of international stature, listed by the Carnegie Foundation within the "Research Universities (very high research activity)" category. UNL is a land-grant university and a member of the Association of Public and Land-grant Universities (APLU). The university is accredited by the Higher Learning Commission of the North Central Association of Colleges and Schools. Programs are offered through the Colleges of Agricultural Sciences and Natural Resources, Architecture, Arts and Sciences, Business Administration, Education and Human Sciences, Engineering, Fine and Performing Arts, Journalism and Mass Communications, Law and the Exploratory and Pre-Professonal Advising Center. There are 8 undergraduate schools and 1 graduate school. In addition to regional accreditation, UNL has baccalaureate program accreditation with AACSB, ABET, ACCE, ACEJMC, ADA, ASLA, NAAB, NASAD, NASM, TEAC, NASD, NAST, and CAEP. The 622-acre campus is in an urban area 55 miles southwest of Omaha. Including any residence halls, there are 266 buildings.

STUDENT LIFE: 79% of undergraduates are from Nebraska. Others are from 49 states, 107 foreign countries, and Canada. 78% are White. **Male To Female Ratio:** 0.9:1. The average age of freshmen is 18; all undergraduates, 20.5. 16% do not continue beyond their first year; 67% remain to graduate. **Housing:** 10122 students can be accommodated in college housing, which includes single-sex and coed dorms, on-campus apartments, off-campus apartments, and married student housing. In addition, there are honors houses, special-interest houses, fraternity houses, sorority houses, special floors/sections for first-year students in 26 interest groups, and 9 scholar communities. On-campus housing is guaranteed for the freshman year only, and is available on a first-come, first-served basis. 57% of students commute. Alcohol is not permitted. All students may keep cars.

FACULTY/CLASSROOMS: 69% of faculty are male; 31% are female. 89% teach undergraduates, 95% do research, and 86% do both. No introductory courses are taught by graduate students. The average class size in an introductory lecture is 42; in a laboratory is 21; and in a regular course is 28.

PROGRAMS OF STUDY: UNL confers B.A., B.S., B.F.A., B.J., B.M., B.M.Ed. and B.L.A. degrees. Master's and Doctoral degrees are also awarded. Bachelor's degrees are awarded in AGRICULTURE (agricultural business management, agricultural communications, agricultural economics, agricultural mechanics, agriculture, agronomy, animal science, environmental studies, fish and game management, food technology for companion animals, great plains studies, horticulture, natural resource/environmental economics, natural resource management, plant science, ranch management, range/farm management, turfgrass and landscape management, and wildlife management), BIOLOGICAL SCIENCE (biochemistry, biology/biological science, entomology, forensic science, life science secondary school education, microbiology, and nutrition), BUSINESS (accounting, apparel and accessories marketing, apparel and textiles, banking and finance, business administration and management, business economics, entrepreneurial studies, fashion merchandising, finance, hospitality management services, human resources, insurance and risk management, international business management, investments and securities, management science, marketing management, marketing/retailing/merchandising, organizational leadership and management, and supply chain management), COMMUNICATIONS AND THE ARTS (advertising, apparel design, art history, art, art history and appreciation, broadcasting, classical languages, classics, communications, communication rhetoric/communication, dance, dramatic arts, English, English as a second/foreign language, film arts, film, television and digital media, fine arts, French, German, information technology, journalism, language arts, Latin, music, public relations, Russian, Spanish, speech/debate/rhetoric, studio art, theatre arts, and theater design), COMPUTER AND PHYSICAL SCIENCE (actuarial science, applied science, astronomy, atmospheric sciences and meteorology, chemistry, chemistry/adolescence education, computer science, earth science / adolescence education, geology, mathematics, physics, physics with astrophysics option, and science), EDUCATION (agricultural education, athletic training, business education, (Education) Childhood Education, computer education, drama education, early childhood education, education, education of the deaf and hearing impaired, elementary education, English education, environmental education, foreign languages education, golf enterprise management, home economics education, journalism education, marketing and distribution education, mathematics education, music education, physical science secondary school education, science education, secondary education, social science education, special education, and teaching English as a second/foreign language (TESOL/TEFOL)), ENGINEERING AND ENVIRONMENTAL DESIGN (agricultural engineering, architectural engineering, architecture, bioengineering, chemical engineering, civil engineering, computer engineering, construction engineering, construction management, electrical/electronics engineering, environmental science, interior design, landscape architecture, landscape architecture/design, and mechanical engineering), HEALTH PROFESSIONS (exercise science, health science, predentistry, premedicine, prepharmacy, speech pathology/audiology, and veterinary science), SOCIAL SCIENCE (anthropology, architectural studies, child care/child and family studies, classical/ancient civilization, culinary arts, dietetics, early childhood studies, economics, ethnic studies, European studies, family/consumer studies, food production/management/services, food science, geography, (Social Science) Global Studies, history, interdisciplinary studies, international studies, Latin American studies, liberal arts/general studies, medieval studies, parks and recreation management, philosophy, political science/government, prelaw, psychology, religious studies, sociology, textiles and clothing, water resources, and women and gender studies). Agriculture, biochemistry, and biological sciences are the strongest academically. Business administration, psychology, and pre-health have the largest enrollments.

ACTIVITIES: 19% of men belong to 28 national fraternities; 23% of women belong to 20 national sororities. There are 658 groups on campus, including art, band, cheerleading, chess, choir, chorale, chorus, communications, computers, dance, debate, drama, drill team, environmental, ethnic, film, forensics, gay, honors, international, jazz band, literary magazine, marching band, musical theater, newspaper, opera, orchestra, pep band, photography, political, professional, radio and TV, religious, social, social service, student government, and symphony. Popular campus events include homecoming, Big Red Welcome, The Big Event, dance marathon and football games. **Sports:** There are 9 intercollegiate sports for men and 13 for women, and 80 intramural sports for men and 78 for women. Facilities include campus recreation center, athleietic conditioning and training center, football stadium, multisport competition center, soccer and tennis complex, indoor and outdoor practice facilities, soccer fields, track, tennis courts, swimming pools, bowling alley, rifle range, arena and baseball/softball stadiums shared with city of Lincoln; public city golf courses. **Graduates:** From July 1, 2013 to June 30, 2014, 3864 bachelor's degrees were awarded. The most popular majors were business marketing (23%), engineering (10%), and agriculture (8%). 221 companies recruited on campus in 2013-2014. In an average class, 33% graduate in 4 years or less, 61% graduate in 5 years or less, and 67% graduate in 6 years or less. Of the 2013 graduating class, 23% were enrolled in graduate school within 6 months of graduation, and 71% were employed.

SERVICES: There is a reader service for the blind. **Library/Resources:** The 8 libraries contain 3.8 million volumes, 251,550 microform items, 320,339 audio/video tapes/CDs/DVDs, and subscribe to 62,500 periodicals including electronic. Computerized library services include interlibrary loans, database searching, Internet access, and Wi-Fi capability. Special learning facilities include an art gallery, natural history museum, planetarium, radio station, TV station, Nebraska State Museum, International Quilt Study Center and Museum, Sheldon Museum of Art, Diocles Laser/Extreme Light Lab, Krueger Collection of Miniatures, Jackie Gaughan Multicultural Center, Larsen Tractor Test and Power Museum, Great Plains Art Museum, Behlen Observatory, Midwest Roadside Safety Facility. **Physically Challenged Students:** All of the campus is accessible. Facilities include wheelchair ramps, elevators, special parking, specially equipped restrooms, special class scheduling, lowered drinking fountains, lowered telephones, special housing, assistance from Services for Students with Disabilities. **Special:** There is cross-registration with many schools, and co-op programs are available in the College of Engineering and Agriculture. Through membership in the International Student Exchange Program, the university can place students in more than 90 universities around the world. Internship opportunities abound, as do work-study programs and undergraduate research opportunities. Accelerated degree programs, a Washington semester, B.A.-B.S. degrees, dual majors, combined pre-professional programs, student-designed majors, credit by exam, nondegree study, and pass/fail options are also available. There are 37 national honor societies, including Phi Beta Kappa, a freshman honors program, and 41 departmental honors programs. **Visiting:** There are regularly scheduled orientations for prospective students, including a campus tour, an information session about academics, scholarships and financial aid, living and dining options, how to get involved, Greek life and career connections for your future sessions. There are guides for informal visits and visitors may sit in on classes. To schedule a visit, contact the Admissions Office. **Campus Safety and Security:** Measures include 24-hour foot and vehicle patrol, emergency notification system, self-defense education, and security escort services. There are shuttle buses, emergency telephones, lighted pathways/sidewalks, and controlled access to dorms/residences.

REQUIREMENTS: The SAT or ACT is recommended. Applicants

must be graduates of an accredited secondary school. The GED is accepted. Students must have completed 4 years each of English and math, 3 years of science and social studies, and 2 years of a foreign language. Applicants must have a minimum composite ACT score of 20, or a combined SAT score of 950, or rank in the top 50% of their high school class. AP and CLEP credits are accepted. Important factors in the admissions decision are advanced placement or honors courses, recommendations by school officials, and evidence of special talent. All students must complete the general education requirements for the Achievement-Centered Education (ACE) program. The program is based on a set of four institutional objectives and 10 student learning outcomes. Students complete the equivalent of 3 credit hours for each of the ten student learning outcomes. A minimum GPA of 2.0 is required. Each college and major has its own requirements; few graduation requirements apply to all students. **Procedure:** Freshmen are admitted to all sessions. Entrance exams should be taken in April of the junior year. There is a rolling admissions plan. Applications should be filed by May 1 for fall entry; December 1 for spring entry; and May 1 for summer entry, along with a $45 fee. Applications are accepted on-line. **Transfer Students:** 980 transfer students enrolled in 2013-2014. Transfer students must have a 2.0 GPA for both the cumulative average of all post-secondary school attended and for the most recent term of attendance. In certain majors, a higher GPA and/or extra course work may be required. **International Students:** There are 1450 international students enrolled. The school actively recruits these students. ACT or SAT may be required for admission into some colleges.

ADMISSIONS: 70% of the 2014-2015 applicants were accepted. The SAT scores for the 2014-2015 freshman class were: Critical Reading--24% below 500, 34% between 500 and 599, 29% between 600 and 699, and 13% between 700 and 800; Math--19% below 500, 31% between 500 and 599, 32% between 600 and 699, and 18% between 700 and 800. The ACT scores were 14% below 21, 21% between 21 and 23, 26% between 24 and 26, 14% between 27 and 28, and 25% above 28. 43% of the current freshmen were in the top fifth of their class; 73% were in the top two fifths. There were 48 National Merit finalists. 284 freshmen graduated first in their class. **Admissions Contact:** Amber Williams, Associate Dean of Enrollment Management. E-Mail: *admissions@unl.edu* Web: *http://admissions.unl.edu*

FINANCIAL AID: In 2014-2015, 93% of all full-time freshmen and 69% of continuing full-time students received some form of financial aid. 60% of all full-time freshmen and 41% of continuing full-time students received need-based aid. The average freshman award was $15,073. Need-based scholarships or need-based grants averaged $8,157; need-based self-help aid (loans and jobs) averaged $4,046; non-need-based athletic scholarships averaged $13,033; and other non-need-based awards and non-need-based scholarships averaged $5,601. 71% of undergraduate students work part-time. Average annual earnings from campus work are $4447. The average financial indebtedness of the 2014 graduate was $20,567. The FAFSA is required. The priority date for freshman financial aid applications for fall entry is April 1.

UNIVERSITY OF NEBRASKA AT KEARNEY (*The complete profile is made available exclusively on our website, www.barronspac.com*)

UNIVERSITY OF NEBRASKA AT OMAHA   F-3
www.unomaha.edu

Omaha, NE 68182	(402) 554-2393
	n/av
Fax: (402) 554-3472	Email: unoadm@unomaha.edu
Full-time: 4000 men, 4725 women	Faculty: n/av
Part-time: 1300 men, 1500 women	Ph.D.s: n/av
Graduate: 1090 men, 1720 women	Student/Faculty: n/av
Year: semesters, summer session	Tuition: $5780 ($16,300)
Room & Board: $8640	Freshman Class: n/av
SAT or ACT: required	CEEB CODE: 6420
Application Deadline: August 1	COMPETITIVE

The University of Nebraska at Omaha, established in 1908, is a public institution and part of the University of Nebraska system. The figures in the above capsule and in this profile are approximate. There are 9 undergraduate schools and 1 graduate school. In addition to regional accreditation, UNOmaha has baccalaureate program accreditation with AACSB, ABET, CSWE, NASAD, NASM, NCATE, CACREP, NASPAA, CAAHEP, CAA, and ACS. The 158-acre campus is in a suburban area within the Omaha city limits. Including any residence halls, there are 46 buildings.

STUDENT LIFE: 93% of undergraduates are from Nebraska. Others are from 34 states, 78 foreign countries, and Canada. 86% are from public schools. 82% are White. **Male To Female Ratio:** 1.2:1. The average age of freshmen is 18; all undergraduates, 23. 29% do not continue beyond their first year; 39% remain to graduate. **Housing:** 1212 students can be accommodated in college housing, which includes single-sex and coed dorms and on-campus apartments. In addition, there are honors houses. On-campus housing is available on a first-come, first-served basis. 91% of students commute. Alcohol is not permitted. All students may keep cars.

FACULTY/CLASSROOMS: 59% of faculty are male; 41% are female. 97% teach undergraduates. Graduate students teach 4% of introductory courses. The average class size in an introductory lecture is 38; in a laboratory is 12; and in a regular course is 21.

PROGRAMS OF STUDY: UNOmaha confers B.A., B.S., B.A.A.H., B.A.S.A., B.A.T.H., B.F.A., B.I.S., B.G.S., B.M., B.S.B.A., B.S.C.N., B.S.C.S., B.S.E.D., B.S.P.A. and B.S.S.W. degrees. Master's and Doctoral degrees are also awarded. Bachelor's degrees are awarded in AGRICULTURE (environmental studies), BIOLOGICAL SCIENCE (bioinformatics, biology/biological science, and biotechnology), BUSINESS (accounting, banking and finance, business communications, management information systems, management science, marketing/retailing/merchandising, real estate, and recreation and leisure services), COMMUNICATIONS AND THE ARTS (art, art history and appreciation, broadcasting, communications, creative writing, dramatic arts, English, fine arts, French, German, journalism, music, Spanish, and speech/debate/rhetoric), COMPUTER AND PHYSICAL SCIENCE (chemistry, computer science, geology, information sciences and systems, mathematics, and physics), EDUCATION (elementary education, library science, physical education, and secondary education), ENGINEERING AND ENVIRONMENTAL DESIGN (aviation administration/management and engineering physics), HEALTH PROFESSIONS (community health work and health care administration), SOCIAL SCIENCE (African American studies, criminal justice, economics, geography, history, interdisciplinary studies, international studies, Latin American studies, liberal arts/general studies, philosophy, political science/government, psychology, public administration, social work, sociology, and women's studies). Elementary education, criminal justice, and marketing management have the largest enrollments.

ACTIVITIES: 2% of men belong to 7 national fraternities; 2% of women belong to 9 national sororities. There are 112 groups on campus, including band, cheerleading, chess, choir, chorale, chorus, dance, drama, drill team, ethnic, film, gay, honors, international, jazz band, literary magazine, marching band, musical theater, newspaper, opera, orchestra, pep band, political, professional, radio and TV, religious, social, social service, student government, and symphony. Popular campus events include Celebrate UNO, International Week, and Black History Month. **Sports:** There are 5 intercollegiate sports for men and 8 for women, and 16 intramural sports for men and 16 for women. Facilities include a football field, a field house, and a recreation building housing basketball and volleyball courts, weight rooms, and a swimming pool.

SERVICES: Counseling and information services are available, as is tutoring in some subjects. There is a reader service for the blind. **Library/Resources:** The library contains 700,000 volumes, 2.0 million microform items, 7,000 audio/video tapes/CDs/DVDs, and subscribes to 3,000 periodicals including electronic. Computerized library services include interlibrary loans, database searching, and Internet access. Special learning facilities include an art gallery, radio station, and TV station. **Physically Challenged Students:** 99% of the campus is accessible. Facilities include wheelchair ramps, elevators, special parking, specially equipped restrooms, special class scheduling, lowered drinking fountains, and lowered telephones. **Special:** UNOmaha offers internships for business students, cooperative programs, and credit by examination. Students may study abroad in various European countries. There are 15 national honor societies, a freshman honors program, and 10 departmental honors programs. **Visiting:** There are regularly scheduled orientations for prospective students. There are guides for informal visits and visitors may sit in on classes. To schedule a visit, contact the Office of Orientation at (402) 554-2677. **Campus Safety and Security:** Measures include 24-hour foot and vehicle patrol, self-defense education, and security escort services. There are shuttle buses, emergency telephones, and lighted pathways/sidewalks.

REQUIREMENTS: The SAT or ACT is required. Students must be graduates of an accredited secondary school. The GED is accepted. Students must have completed 4 units of English and 2 each of math, social sciences, and sciences. UNOmaha requires applicants to be in the upper 50% of their class. A GPA of 2.0 is required. AP and CLEP credits are accepted. Important factors in the admissions decision are recommendations by school officials, evidence of special talent, and personality/intangible qualities.To graduate, students must complete 30 hours of distribution requirements in natural and physical sciences, humanities and fine arts, and social and behavioral sciences; 15 hours in fundamental academic skills in English, writing, math, and public speaking; and 6 hours in cultural diversity. **Procedure:** Freshmen are admitted fall, spring, and summer. Entrance exams should be taken by the senior year. There is a rolling admissions plan. Applications should be filed by August 1 for fall entry; December 1 for spring entry; and June 1 for summer entry, along with a $45 fee. Applications are accepted on-line. **Transfer Students:** Applicants must present evidence of good standing at the last institution they attended. Grades of C or better transfer for credit. A minimum GPA of 2.0 is required. 30 of 125 credits required for the bachelor's degree must be completed at UNOmaha. **International Students:** The school actively recruits these students. They must take the TOEFL.

ADMISSIONS: 27 freshmen graduated first in their class. **Admissions Contact:** Jolene Adams, Director of Admissions. E-Mail: unoadm@unomaha.edu Web: www.unomaha.edu

FINANCIAL AID: The FAFSA is required. Check with the school for current application deadlines.

WAYNE STATE COLLEGE (*The complete profile is made available exclusively on our website, www.barronspac.com*)

YORK COLLEGE   E-3
www.york.edu

York, NE 68467	(402) 363-5608
	(800) 950-9675
Fax: (402) 363-5623	Email: clones@york.edu
Full-time: 180 men, 190 women	Faculty: n/av
Part-time: 25 men, 20 women	Ph.D.s: n/av
Graduate: n/av	Student/Faculty: n/av
Year: semesters, summer session	Tuition: $15,300
Room & Board: $5850	Freshman Class: n/av
ACT: recommended	CEEB CODE: 6984
Application Deadline: n/av	COMPETITIVE

York College, founded in 1890, is an independent undergraduate college affiliated with the Churches of Christ. The figures in the above capsule and in this profile are approximate. In addition to regional accreditation, York has baccalaureate program accreditation with NCATE. The 40-acre campus is in a small town 45 miles west of Lincoln. Including any residence halls, there are 18 buildings. **STUDENT LIFE:** 67% of undergraduates are from out of state, mostly the Midwest. Students are from 30 states, 5 foreign countries, and Canada. 90% are from public schools. 87% are White. 22% are Protestant. **Male To Female Ratio:** 1.0:1. The average age of freshmen is 18; all undergraduates, 21. 15% do not continue beyond their first year; 50% remain to graduate. **Housing:** 472 students can be accommodated in college housing, which includes single-sex dorms and on-campus apartments. On-campus housing is guaranteed for all 4 years. 72% of students live on campus; of those, 85% remain on campus on weekends. Alcohol is not permitted. All students may keep cars. **FACULTY/CLASSROOMS:** 67% of faculty are male; 33% are female.

All teach undergraduates. No introductory courses are taught by graduate students. The average class size in an introductory lecture is 30; in a laboratory is 20; and in a regular course is 25.

PROGRAMS OF STUDY: York confers B.A., B.S., B.B.A. and B.Mus. degrees. Associate and Master's degrees are also awarded. Bachelor's degrees are awarded in BIOLOGICAL SCIENCE (biology/biological science), BUSINESS (accounting, business administration and management, and human resources), COMMUNICATIONS AND THE ARTS (communications, English, music performance, and voice), COMPUTER AND PHYSICAL SCIENCE (natural sciences), EDUCATION (drama education, education, elementary education, English education, middle school education, music education, psychology education, science education, secondary education, social science education, and special education), SOCIAL SCIENCE (biblical studies, biopsychology, history, human services, liberal arts/general studies, psychology, and youth ministry). Education, natural science and psychology are the strongest academically. Education and business have the largest enrollments.

ACTIVITIES: 57% of men belong to 4 local fraternities; 62% of women belong to 4 local sororities. There are 25 groups on campus, including art, choir, chorus, computers, drama, honors, international, literary magazine, musical theater, newspaper, photography, political, professional, religious, social, social service, student government, and yearbook. Popular campus events include High School Days, Fall Musical and an All School Banquet. **Sports:** There are 4 intercollegiate sports for men and 3 for women, and 6 intramural sports for men and 6 for women. Facilities include a gym, basketball and volleyball courts, soccer, baseball, and intramural fields, a weight room and an indoor track. **Graduates:** From July 1, 2013 to June 30, 2014, 57 bachelor's degrees were awarded. The most popular majors were education (29%), business (26%), and psychology (9%). 7 companies recruited on campus in 2013-2014. In an average class, 8% graduate in 3 years or less, 35% graduate in 4 years or less, 49% graduate in 5 years or less, and 50% graduate in 6 years or less. Of the 2013 graduating class, 6% were enrolled in graduate school within 6 months of graduation, and 90% were employed.

SERVICES: Counseling and information services are available, as is tutoring in most subjects. There is remedial math, reading, and writing. **Library/Resources:** The library contains 126,086 volumes, 21,578 microform items, and 7,017 audio/video tapes/CDs/DVDs, and subscribes to 301 periodicals including electronic. Computerized library services include interlibrary loans and database searching. **Physically Challenged Students:** 50% of the campus is accessible. Facilities include wheelchair ramps, elevators, special parking, specially equipped restrooms, lowered drinking fountains, lowered telephones, and special housing. **Special:** Summer internships are required in biblical studies,and psychology, and work-study is available on campus. Honors and independent study are available as adjuncts to a normal course load. There are 2 national honor societies, a freshman honors program, and 2 departmental honors programs. **Visiting:** There are regularly scheduled orientations for prospective students, including a campus tour, visit with financial aid and admissions representatives, visit with the registrar and a possibly, with a faculty member within the student's major area of concentration. There are guides for informal visits, visitors may sit in on classes, and stay overnight. **Campus Safety and Security:** Measures include self-defense education. There are emergency telephones, lighted pathways/sidewalks, and an evening/night foot patrol.

REQUIREMENTS: The ACT is recommended. For regular acceptance, students must meet 2 of the following 3 requirements: a 2.0 cumulative GPA; graduate in the top half of their graduating class; achieve satisfactory scores on the ACT or SAT. AP and CLEP credits are accepted. Important factors in the admissions decision are ability to finance college education, personality/intangible qualities, and evidence of special talent.To graduate, students must complete a minimum of 128 credits with a 2.0 GPA. Course work includes a general education requirement of 18 hours of humanities, 16 of Bible, 12 of social science, 6 of science, and 3 of math or computer science. The major requirements vary according to concentration; typically, 40 hours or more are required. Some majors and minors require a 2.5 GPA. **Procedure:** Freshmen are admitted to all sessions. Entrance exams should be taken during March or April. There is a rolling admissions plan. Application deadlines are open. Application fee is

$20. **Transfer Students:** 48 transfer students enrolled in 2013-2014. Transfer students with less than 24 semester hours must have a high school transcript, ACT scores, college transcripts, and 1 reference. Transfers with 24 to 60 hours must have proof of high school graduation (diploma or final), a college transcript, and 1 reference. Transfers with more than 60 hours must have a college transcript and 1 reference letter. 30 of 128 credits required for the bachelor's degree must be completed at York. **International Students:** There are 6 international students enrolled. They must take the TOEFL. They must also take the SAT or ACT.

ADMISSIONS: 7 freshmen graduated first in their class. **Admissions Contact:** Director of Admissions E-Mail: *clones@york.edu* Web: *www.york.edu*

FINANCIAL AID: In 2014-2015, 99% of all full-time freshmen and 99% of continuing full-time students received some form of financial aid. 98% of all full-time freshmen and 99% of continuing full-time students received need-based aid. The average freshman award was $14,765. Need-based scholarships or need-based grants averaged $7,182; need-based self-help aid (loans and jobs) averaged $2,762; non-need-based athletic scholarships averaged $1,835; and other non-need-based awards and non-need-based scholarships averaged $2,986. 72% of undergraduate students work part-time. Average annual earnings from campus work are $825. The average financial indebtedness of the 2014 graduate was $19,634. The FAFSA is required. Check with the school for current application deadlines.

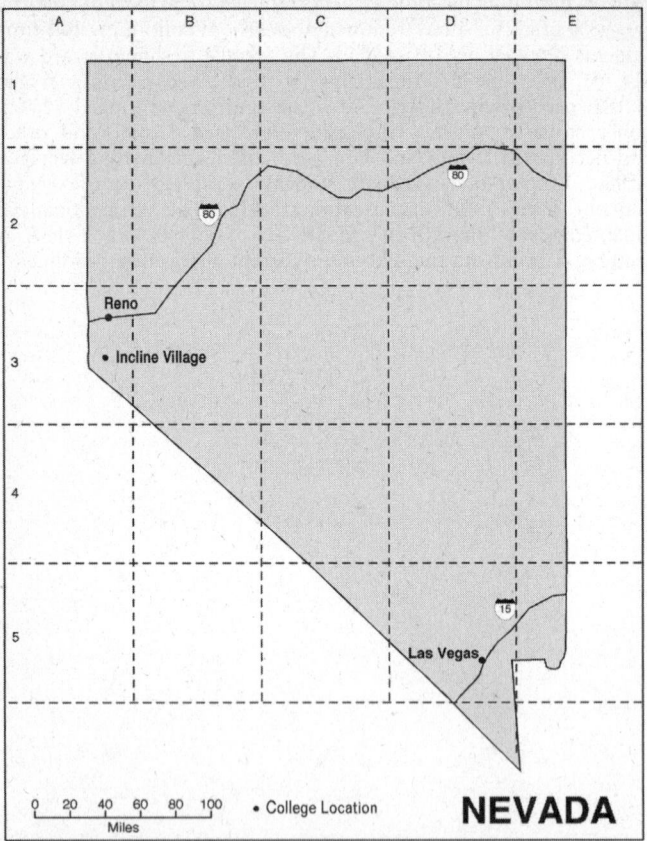

NEVADA

0 20 40 60 80 100
Miles

• College Location

SIERRA NEVADA COLLEGE   A-3
www.sierranevada.edu

Incline Village, NV 89451	(775) 831-1314
	(866) 412-4636
Fax: (775) 831-6223	Email: admissions@sierranevada.edu
Full-time: 70 men, 90 women	Faculty: n/av
Part-time: 25 men, 10 women	Ph.D.s: n/av
Graduate: 95 men, 245 women	Student/Faculty: n/av
Year: semesters, summer session	Tuition: $24,200
Room & Board: $9500	Freshman Class: n/av
ACT: required	CEEB CODE: 4757
Application Deadline: February 15	VERY COMPETITIVE

Sierra Nevada College, founded in 1969, is a private institution offering programs in liberal arts, fine arts, business, hotel resort management, ski business management, environmental science, and teacher education. The figures in the above capsule and in this profile are approximate. There are 7 undergraduate schools. The 17-acre campus is in a rural area 25 miles west of Reno. Including any residence halls, there are 7 buildings.

STUDENT LIFE: 70% of undergraduates are from out of state, mostly the West. Students are from 35 states, 8 foreign countries, and Canada. 60% are from public schools. 93% are White. **Male To Female Ratio:** 1.8:1. The average age of freshmen is 19; all undergraduates, 22. 14% do not continue beyond their first year; 62% remain to graduate. **Housing:** 120 students can be accommodated in college housing, which includes coed dorms and on-campus apartments. On-campus housing is guaranteed for all 4 years. 60% of students commute. Alcohol is not permitted. All students may keep cars.

FACULTY/CLASSROOMS: 60% of faculty are male; 40% are female. All teach undergraduates, 15% do research, and 25% do both. No introductory courses are taught by graduate students. The average class size in an introductory lecture is 12; in a laboratory is 8; and in a regular course is 12.

PROGRAMS OF STUDY: SNC confers B.A., B.S. and B.F.A. degrees.

Bachelor's degrees are awarded in BUSINESS (business administration and management and recreational facilities management), COMMUNICATIONS AND THE ARTS (fine arts and music), COMPUTER AND PHYSICAL SCIENCE (science), ENGINEERING AND ENVIRONMENTAL DESIGN (environmental science), SOCIAL SCIENCE (humanities). Environmental and science/ecology are the strongest academically. Business administration has the largest enrollment.

ACTIVITIES: There are no fraternities or sororities. Groups on campus include art, choir, chorale, chorus, computers, dance, environmental, ethnic, honors, international, musical theater, newspaper, political, professional, social, social service, student government, and yearbook. Popular campus events include Bohemia Night, Nevada Day, and Game Show Take-off. **Sports:** There are 2 intercollegiate sports for men and 2 for women, and 2 intramural sports for men and 2 for women. Facilities include nearby ski areas, hiking and mountain biking trails, volleyball and softball areas, community tennis courts and golf courses, and sites for water sports and beach volleyball at Lake Tahoe.

SERVICES: Counseling and information services are available, as is tutoring in every subject. There is remedial math, reading, and writing. **Library/Resources:** The library contains 20,000 volumes, 10,000 microform items, and subscribes to 100 periodicals including electronic. Computerized library services include interlibrary loans, database searching, Internet access, and Wi-Fi capability. Special learning facilities include an art gallery, an observatory, and a recording studio. **Physically Challenged Students:** All of the campus is accessible. Facilities include wheelchair ramps, elevators, special parking, specially equipped restrooms, special class scheduling, and special housing. **Special:** Business administration concentrations are offered in ski business and resort management and in hotel, restaurant, and resort management. Student-designed majors, work-study programs, internships, credit for life experiences and volunteer community work, and nondegree study are available. **Visiting:** There are regularly scheduled orientations for prospective students, including a student-led campus tour that is available by appointment and 1-night overnight stays. To schedule a visit, contact the Office of Admissions. **Campus Safety and Security:** Measures include 24-hour foot and vehicle patrol, emergency notification system, and security escort services. There are lighted pathways/sidewalks and controlled access to dorms/residences.

REQUIREMENTS: The ACT is required. The ACT Optional Writing test is also required. All applicants are reviewed individually. Official transcripts, an essay, and 2 letters of recommendation are required, and an interview is recommended. AP and CLEP credits are accepted. Important factors in the admissions decision are advanced placement or honors courses, recommendations by school officials, and personality/intangible qualities. All students must complete at least 120 semester hours, including 40 in upper-division courses with a minimum GPA of 2.0. Students also must pass the writing proficiency exam and meet distribution requirements in 4 interdisciplinary themes: symbols, relationships with nature and humans, memberships in groups and institutions, and ethics, values, and beliefs. **Procedure:** Freshmen are admitted to all sessions. Entrance exams should be taken in the spring of junior year or fall of senior year. There are early decision, early admissions, deferred admissions, and rolling admissions plans. Applications should be filed by February 15 for fall entry. Notification is sent on a rolling basis. Applications are accepted on-line. **Transfer Students:** 46 transfer students enrolled in 2013-2014. The college accepts applications from students who have completed course work at an accredited post-secondary institution. If fewer than 15 credits have been earned, the high school transcript and standardized test scores are also required. Transfer applicants are expected to be in good academic standing at their college or university. 96 of 120 credits required for the bachelor's degree must be completed at SNC. **International Students:** The school actively recruits these students. They must take the TOEFL, or take any other English proficiency test.

ADMISSIONS: Admissions Department, Dean of Admission and Financial Aid. E-Mail: *admissions@sierranevada.edu* Web: *www.sierranevada.edu*

FINANCIAL AID: In 2014-2015, 80% of all full-time freshmen and

80% of continuing full-time students received some form of financial aid. 80% of all full-time freshmen and continuing full-time students received need-based aid. Need-based scholarships or need-based grants averaged $7,000 ($16,000 maximum); need-based self-help aid (loans and jobs) averaged $3,800 ($7,500 maximum); and other non-need-based awards and non-need-based scholarships averaged $3,000 ($10,000 maximum). The FAFSA and the college's own financial statement are required. Check with the school for current application deadlines.

UNIVERSITY AND COMMUNITY COLLEGE SYSTEM OF NEVADA

The University and Community College System of Nevada, established in 1865, is a public system in Nevada. It is governed by a board of regents, whose chief administrator is the chancellor. The primary goal of the system is teaching, research, and public service. The main priorities are to provide all public programs of postsecondary instruction in Nevada, to sponsor programs of basic and applied research that contribute to the cultural, economic, and social development of Nevada, and to sponsor programs of public service for citizens of the state. The total student enrollment for all seven campuses is usually about 108,000 with 1750 faculty members. Altogether there are approximate 135 baccalaureate, 97 master's, 34 doctoral programs offered in the University and Community College System of Nevada. Profiles of the 4-year campuses are included in this section.

UNIVERSITY OF NEVADA, LAS VEGAS D-5
www.unlv.edu

Las Vegas, NV 89154	(702) 774-UNLV
Fax: (702) 774-8008	
Full-time: 7372 men, 9019 women	**Faculty:** 676; I, av$
Part-time: 3451 men, 2866 women	**Ph.D.s:** 95%
Graduate: 2201 men, 3355 women	**Student/Faculty:** 24 to 1
Year: semesters, summer session	**Tuition:** $4783 ($17,123)
Room & Board: $12,250	**Freshman Class:** n/av
	CEEB CODE: 4861
Application Deadline: February 1	**COMPETITIVE**

University of Nevada, Las Vegas, established in 1957, is a state-supported institution offering undergraduate and graduate programs in business, education, health science, engineering, science and math, hotel administration, fine arts, liberal arts, urban affairs, and honors. Figures in the above capsule and in this profile are approximate. There are 10 undergraduate schools and 1 graduate school. In addition to regional accreditation, UNLV has baccalaureate program accreditation with AACSB, ABET, ACCE, ADA, APTA, ASLA, CSAB, CSWE, FIDER, NAAB, NASAD, NASM, NCATE, and NLN. The 353-acre campus is in an urban area on the southern tip of Nevada, just east of the Las Vegas strip. Including any residence halls, there are 90 buildings.

STUDENT LIFE: 80% of undergraduates are from Nevada. Others are from 50 states, 57 foreign countries, and Canada. 46% are White; 18% Asian American; 14% Hispanic. **Male To Female Ratio:** 1.2:1. The average age of freshmen is 18; all undergraduates, 25. 26% do not continue beyond their first year; 39% remain to graduate. **Housing:** 2500 students can be accommodated in college housing, which includes single-sex and coed dorms. In addition, there are honors houses, special-interest houses, substance-free houses, study-intensive recess housing, major-specific houses, a global house, and a leadership focus house. On-campus housing is guaranteed for the freshman year only, and is available on a first-come, first-served basis. Priority is given to out-of-town students. 90% of students commute. All students may keep cars.

FACULTY/CLASSROOMS: 65% of faculty are male; 35% are female. 95% teach undergraduates, and 5% do research. No introductory courses are taught by graduate students. The average class size in an introductory lecture is 21 and in a laboratory is 20.

PROGRAMS OF STUDY: UNLV confers B.A., B.S. and B.F.A. degrees. Master's and Doctoral degrees are also awarded. Bachelor's degrees are awarded in BIOLOGICAL SCIENCE (biology/biological science), BUSINESS (accounting, banking and finance, hotel/motel and restaurant management, human resources, international business management, management information systems, management science, marketing/retailing/merchandising, real estate, and recreational facilities management), COMMUNICATIONS AND THE ARTS (art history and appreciation, communications, dance, dramatic arts, English, film arts, fine arts, French, German, music, romance languages and literature, and Spanish), COMPUTER AND PHYSICAL SCIENCE (applied physics, chemistry, computer science, earth science, geology, mathematics, physics, and radiological technology), EDUCATION (elementary education, health education, physical education, recreation education, secondary education, special education, and trade and industrial education), ENGINEERING AND ENVIRONMENTAL DESIGN (architectural engineering, civil engineering, computer engineering, construction management, electrical/electronics engineering, environmental science, interior design, landscape architecture/design, mechanical engineering, and urban planning technology), HEALTH PROFESSIONS (clinical science, exercise science, health care administration, nuclear medical technology, nursing, and sports medicine), SOCIAL SCIENCE (anthropology, criminal justice, economics, food production/management/services, history, interdisciplinary studies, philosophy, physical fitness/movement, political science/government, psychology, public administration, social science, social work, sociology, and women's studies). Hotel administration, fine arts, and engineering are the strongest academically.

ACTIVITIES: 5% of men belong to 18 national fraternities; 3% of women belong to 11 national sororities. There are 160 groups on campus, including art, band, cheerleading, chess, choir, chorus, computers, dance, debate, drama, drill team, ethnic, film, gay, honors, international, jazz band, literary magazine, marching band, musical theater, newspaper, orchestra, pep band, photography, political, professional, radio and TV, religious, social, social service, student government, and symphony. Popular campus events include Weeks of Welcome, Premier UNLV, and Unityfest. **Sports:** There are 8 intercollegiate sports for men and 9 for women, and 47 intramural sports for men and 47 for women. Facilities include a recreation and wellness center that includes a lap pool, cardio machines, weight room, running track, racquetball courts, and 5 multiuse courts. There is a 19,000-seat indoor arena for basketball, a 3,000-seat arena for basketball and volleyball, a 40,000-seat football stadium, football practice fields, tennis courts, a softball stadium, a baseball stadium, soccer fields, track facilities, a boxing gym, and separate athletic/training facilities and weight room facilities for intercollegiate athletes. **Graduates:** The most popular majors were education (9%), psychology (7%), and communications/journalism (6%).

SERVICES: Counseling and information services are available, as is tutoring in every subject. There is a reader service for the blind, and remedial math, reading, and writing. **Library/Resources:** The 6 libraries contain 950,600 volumes, 1.8 million microform items, 13,500 audio/video tapes/CDs/DVDs, and subscribe to 1,759 periodicals including electronic. Computerized library services include interlibrary loans, database searching, Internet access, and Wi-Fi capability. Special learning facilities include an art gallery, natural history museum, and radio station. **Physically Challenged Students:** All of the campus is accessible. Facilities include wheelchair ramps, elevators, special parking, specially equipped restrooms, special class scheduling, lowered drinking fountains, lowered telephones, and special housing. **Special:** Opportunities are provided for internships, an accelerated degree program, B.A.-B.S. degrees, dual majors, credit by examination, credit for military service, nondegree study, pass/fail options, and study abroad in 25 countries. There are 16 national honor societies, including Phi Beta Kappa, a freshman honors program, and 11 departmental honors programs. **Visiting:** There are regularly scheduled orientations for prospective students, consisting of a complete introduction to the campus, student services, and parent orientation. There are guides for informal visits and visitors may sit in on classes. To schedule a visit, contact the Office of Admissions. **Campus Safety and Security:** Measures include 24-hour foot and vehicle patrol, emergency notification system, self-defense education, and security escort services. There are shuttle buses, emergency telephones, and lighted pathways/sidewalks.

REQUIREMENTS: Graduation from an accredited secondary school is required. Applicants must also meet the academic core requirements, which include 4 credits in English and 3 each in history, social studies, math, and science. A GPA of 3.0 is required. AP and CLEP credits are accepted. Important factors in the admissions decision are recommendations by school officials, advanced placement or honors courses, and geographical diversity. Students must complete 124 credits, with 45 in the major, and maintain a minimum GPA of 2.0. All students must meet core requirements that include courses in English, logic and math, the Constitution, social science, fine arts, science, humanities, and international and multicultural diversity. **Procedure:** Freshmen are admitted to all sessions. Entrance exams should be taken by February 1. There is a rolling admissions plan. Applications should be filed by February 1 for fall entry; October 1 for spring entry; and February 1 for summer entry, along with a $60 fee. Applications are accepted on-line. **Transfer Students:** 1934 transfer students enrolled in 2013-2014. Applicants should present a minimum GPA of 2.5 and a minimum of 24 credits for transfer. The SAT or the ACT is recommended. Applicants must be in good academic standing and eligible to return to the educational institution last attended. 30 of 124 credits required for the bachelor's degree must be completed at UNLV. **International Students:** They must take the TOEFL with a minimum score of 500 on the paper-based TOEFL (PBT) or 61 on the Internet-based version (iBT), or take the MELAB, or IELTS.

ADMISSIONS: The SAT scores for the 2014-2015 freshman class were: Critical Reading--50% below 500, 36% between 500 and 599, 13% between 600 and 699, and 1% between 700 and 800; Math--42% below 500, 38% between 500 and 599, 17% between 600 and 699, and 3% between 700 and 800. The ACT scores were 16% below 21, 52% between 21 and 23, 15% between 24 and 26, 14% between 27 and 28, and 3% above 28. 52% of the current freshmen were in the top fifth of their class; 85% were in the top two fifths. There were 3 National Merit finalists. **Admissions Contact:** Wendell Staszkow, Assistant Director of Admissions. Web: *www.unlv.edu*

FINANCIAL AID: The average freshman award was $4,711. Need-based scholarships or need-based grants averaged $3,791; and need-based self-help aid (loans and jobs) averaged $3,336. 75% of undergraduate students work part-time. UNLV is a member of CSS. The CCS/Profile, FAFSA, FFS, or SFS, and the college's own financial statement and a singlefile form are required. The priority date for freshman financial aid applications for fall entry is February 1.

UNIVERSITY OF NEVADA/RENO   A-3
www.unr.edu

Reno, NV 89557	(775) 784-1110
Fax: (775) 784-4283	**Email:** asknevada@unr.edu
Full-time: 6601 men, 7398 women	**Faculty:** I, -$
Part-time: 1408 men, 1432 women	**Ph.D.s:** 93%
Graduate: 1436 men, 1659 women	**Student/Faculty:** n/av
Year: semesters, summer session	**Tuition:** $6639 ($20,549)
Room & Board: $10,868	**Freshman Class:** 8859 applied, 7418 accepted, 3387 enrolled
SAT CR/M/W: 540/540/520 **ACT:** 23	**CEEB CODE:** 4844
Application Deadline: February 1	**COMPETITIVE**

The University of Nevada/Reno, established in 1874, is a land-grant institution and part of the Nevada System of Higher Education. It offers programs in agriculture, arts and science, business administration, education, engineering, human and community sciences, journalism, medicine, and mining, as well as interdisciplinary studies. There are 10 undergraduate schools and 1 graduate school. In addition to regional accreditation, Nevada has baccalaureate program accreditation with AACSB, ABET, ACEJMC, AHEA, CSWE, NASM, NCATE, and NLN. The 268-acre campus is in an urban area 200 miles east of San Francisco, 35 miles from Lake Tahoe. Including any residence halls, there are 128 buildings.

STUDENT LIFE: 82% of undergraduates are from Nevada. Others are from 47 states, 77 foreign countries, and Canada. 62% are White; 16% Hispanic. **Male To Female Ratio:** 1.1:1. The average age of freshmen is 18; all undergraduates, 22. 19% do not continue beyond their

first year; 55% remain to graduate. **Housing:** 2611 students can be accommodated in college housing, which includes single-sex and coed dorms, on-campus apartments, off-campus apartments, and married student housing. In addition, there are honors houses, and a living learning center. On-campus housing is available on a first-come, first-served basis. 84% of students commute. Alcohol is not permitted. All students may keep cars.

FACULTY/CLASSROOMS: 58% of faculty are male; 42% are female. All teach and do research. Graduate students teach 10% of introductory courses. The average class size in an introductory lecture is 43; in a laboratory is 19; and in a regular course is 31.

PROGRAMS OF STUDY: Nevada confers B.A., B.S., B.A.C.J., B.A.Ed., B.F.A., B.G.S., B.M., B.S.Bus.Ad., B.S.C.E., B.S.Chem.E., B.S.Chem., B.S.C.S., B.S.Ed., B.S.E.E., B.S.E.P., B.S.Geog., B.S.Geol., B.S.Geol.E., B.S.Geophys., B.S.M.E., B.S.Met.E., B.S.Min.E., B.S.Nurs. and B.S.Vet.Sc. degrees. Master's and doctoral degrees are also awarded. Bachelor's degrees are awarded in AGRICULTURE (agricultural sciences, natural resource management, and wildlife management), BIOLOGICAL SCIENCE (biochemistry, biology/biological science, biotechnology, nutrition, and nutritional sciences), BUSINESS (accounting, business administration - international, finance, management science, marketing, and marketing/retailing/merchandising), COMMUNICATIONS AND THE ARTS (applied music, art history, art, communications, dramatic arts, English, French, journalism, music, and Spanish), COMPUTER AND PHYSICAL SCIENCE (chemistry, computer science, geology, geophysics and seismology, hydrology, information sciences and systems, mathematics, and physics), EDUCATION (early childhood education, elementary education, general studies, music education, secondary education, and special education), ENGINEERING AND ENVIRONMENTAL DESIGN (chemical engineering, civil engineering, civil and environmental engineering, electrical/electronics engineering, engineering physics, environmental science, geological engineering, mechanical engineering, metallurgical engineering, and mining and mineral engineering), HEALTH PROFESSIONS (kinesiology, nursing, nutrition and dietetics, and speech pathology/audiology), SOCIAL SCIENCE (anthropology, child care/child and family studies, criminal justice, economics, geography, history, international relations, philosophy, political science/government, psychology, social work, sociology, and women's studies). Biology, psychology, and criminal justice have the largest enrollments.

ACTIVITIES: 7% of men belong to 2 local and 17 national fraternities; 7% of women belong to 9 national sororities. There are 100 groups on campus, including art, band, cheerleading, chess, choir, chorale, chorus, computers, dance, debate, drama, drill team, ethnic, film, forensics, gay, honors, international, jazz band, literary magazine, marching band, musical theater, newspaper, orchestra, pep band, photography, political, professional, radio and TV, religious, social, social service, student government, and symphony. Popular campus events include Mackay Week. **Sports:** There are 6 intercollegiate sports for men and 10 for women, and 6 intramural sports for men and 6 for women. Facilities include a recreation center, a 30,000-seat stadium, a 2,200-seat gym, a 3,000-seat baseball field, a 200-seat movie theater, and an 11,600-seat indoor events center. **Graduates:** From July 1, 2013 to June 30, 2014, 2743 bachelor's degrees were awarded. The most popular majors were business (15%), health professions (12%), and biological sciences (11%). In an average class, 22% graduate in 4 years or less, 48% graduate in 5 years or less, and 55% graduate in 6 years or less.

SERVICES: Counseling and information services are available, as is tutoring in most subjects. There is a reader service for the blind, and remedial math, reading, and writing. Students are mainstreamed with special services for the disabled. **Library/Resources:** The 6 libraries contain 1.2 million volumes, 3.3 million microform items, 49,433 audio/video tapes/CDs/DVDs, and subscribe to 19,058 periodicals including electronic. Computerized library services include interlibrary loans, database searching, and Internet access. Special learning facilities include an art gallery, planetarium, radio station, TV station, the Nevada Historical Society Museum, and Keck Mineral Museum. **Physically Challenged Students:** 99% of the campus is accessible. Facilities include wheelchair ramps, elevators, special parking, specially equipped restrooms, special class scheduling, lowered drinking fountains, lowered telephones, special housing, and automatic door openers. **Special:** Students may study abroad in 24 countries, pursue internships, and complete dual majors in many subject areas. There is 1 national honor society and a freshman honors program. **Visiting:** There are regularly scheduled orientations for prospective students and meetings with academic representatives. Campus tours include visiting residence halls. There are guides for informal visits and visitors may sit in on classes. To schedule a visit, contact the Office for Prospective Students. **Campus Safety and Security:** Measures include 24-hour foot and vehicle patrol, emergency notification system, self-defense education, and security escort services. There are shuttle buses, emergency telephones, lighted pathways/sidewalks, and controlled access to dorms/residences.

REQUIREMENTS: The SAT or ACT is required. Applicants should have completed 13 1/2 academic credits, including 4 in English, 3 each in math, science, and social studies/history, and a half credit in computer literacy. The GED is not accepted. A GPA of 3.0 is required. AP and CLEP credits are accepted.To graduate, all students must complete 124 to 138 semester credits and earn a GPA of 2.0. The core curriculum includes 9 credits of Western Traditions, 6 each of capstone courses and natural science, 3 to 6 of writing, 3 each of math, social science, and fine arts, and fulfillment of the diversity requirement. **Procedure:** Freshmen are admitted fall and spring. Entrance exams should be taken in October of the senior year. There are deferred admissions and rolling admissions plans. Applications should be filed by February 1 for fall entry; November 1 for spring entry. The fall 2014 application fee was $60. Notification is sent on a rolling basis. **Transfer Students:** 1431 transfer students enrolled in 2013-2014. Applicants should have a GPA of 2.5 and 24 transferable credits. College transcripts are required. 32 of 124 credits required for the bachelor's degree must be completed at Nevada. **International Students:** There are 238 international students enrolled. The school actively recruits these students. They must take the TOEFL. The SAT or ACT may also be submitted.

ADMISSIONS: 84% of the 2014-2015 applicants were accepted. The SAT scores for the 2014-2015 freshman class were: Critical Reading--32% below 500, 45% between 500 and 599, 20% between 600 and 699, and 3% between 700 and 800; Math--28% below 500, 45% between 500 and 599, 23% between 600 and 699, and 4% between 700 and 800; Writing--42% below 500, 42% between 500 and 599, 14% between 600 and 699, and 2% between 700 and 800. The ACT scores were 22% below 21, 33% between 21 and 23, 25% between 24 and 26, 10% between 27 and 28, and 10% above 28. 45% of the current freshmen were in the top fifth of their class; 76% were in the top two fifths. 52 freshmen graduated first in their class. **Admissions Contact:** Dr. Melisa N. Choroszy, Assistant Vice President, Records/Enrollment Services. E-Mail: *asknevada@unr.edu* Web: *www.unr.edu*

FINANCIAL AID: In 2014-2015, 27% of all full-time freshmen and 32% of continuing full-time students received some form of financial aid. 25% of all full-time freshmen and 29% of continuing full-time students received need-based aid. The average financial indebtedness of the 2014 graduate was $12,285. The FAFSA is required. Check with the school for current application deadlines.

NEW HAMPSHIRE

• College Location

0 10 20 30 40 50
Miles

Plymouth

93

Hanover

89

New London

Henniker • Concord Durham

Manchester
Keene Merrimack 93 95

• Rindge Nashua

COLBY-SAWYER COLLEGE   C-5
www.colby-sawyer.edu

New London, NH 03257   (603) 526-3700
                                  (800) 272-1015
Fax: (603) 526-3452   Email: admissions@colby-sawyer.edu

Full-time: n/av	Faculty: n/av
Part-time: 6 men, 12 women	Ph.D.s: n/av
Graduate: n/av	Student/Faculty: 14 to 1
Year: semesters	Tuition: $38,040
Room & Board: $12,750	Freshman Class: n/av
SAT or ACT: required	CEEB CODE: 3281
Application Deadline: open	**COMPETITIVE**

Colby-Sawyer College, established in 1837, is a private, independent institution offering programs of study that innovatively integrate liberal arts and sciences with professional preparation. Undergraduate majors include environmental studies, graphic design, child development, education, exercise and sport sciences, studio arts, nursing, business, biology, English, psychology, communications, and history, society, and culture, as well as education certification. The figures in the above capsule and in this profile are approximate. In addition to regional accreditation, Colby-Sawyer has baccalaureate program accreditation with CCNE and CAATE. The 200-acre campus is in a small town 90 minutes north of Boston. Including any residence halls, there are 30 buildings.

STUDENT LIFE: 68% of undergraduates are from out of state, mostly the Northeast. Students are from 28 states, 38 foreign countries, and Canada. 83% are from public schools. 89% are White. **Male To Female Ratio:** 2.0:1. The average age of freshmen is 18; all undergraduates, 19. 19% do not continue beyond their first year; 64% remain to graduate. **Housing:** 870 students can be accommodated in college housing, which includes single-sex and coed dorms, on-campus apartments, off-campus apartments, and a substance-free residence hall. On-campus housing is guaranteed for all 4 years. 90% of students live on campus; of those, 70% remain on campus on weekends. All students may keep cars.

FACULTY/CLASSROOMS: 48% of faculty are male; 52% are female. All teach undergraduates. No introductory courses are taught by graduate students. The average class size in a regular course is 17.

PROGRAMS OF STUDY: Colby-Sawyer confers B.A., B.S. and B.F.A. degrees. Associate degrees are also awarded. Bachelor's degrees are awarded in AGRICULTURE (environmental studies), BIOLOGICAL SCIENCE (biology/biological science), BUSINESS (accounting, business administration and management, and sports management), COMMUNICATIONS AND THE ARTS (art, communications, creative writing, English, graphic design, performing arts, and studio art), COMPUTER AND PHYSICAL SCIENCE (natural sciences), EDUCATION (art education, athletic training, early childhood education, English education, social science education, and social studies education), ENGINEERING AND ENVIRONMENTAL DESIGN (environmental science), HEALTH PROFESSIONS (exercise science, nursing, and public health), SOCIAL SCIENCE (child psychology/development, history, humanities, philosophy, psychology, and sociology). Exercise and sport sciences, business administration and nursing have the largest enrollments.

ACTIVITIES: There are no fraternities or sororities. There are 40 groups on campus, including student academic counselors, key association (campus tour guides), art, chorus, dance, drama, environmental, film, gay, honors, international, literary magazine, musical theater, newspaper, outing, photography, political, professional, radio and TV, religious, social, social service, and student government. Popular campus events include fall and spring weekends and Mountain Day. **Sports:** There are 8 intercollegiate sports for men and 9 for women, and 15 intramural sports for men and 15 for women. Facilities include 6 outdoor and 3 indoor tennis courts, a fitness center, an NCAA-approved swimming pool, a suspended indoor track, squash and racquetball courts, 4 outdoor competitive fields, nearby golf courses, ski and biking trails, and an indoor riding arena. **Graduates:** From July 1, 2013 to June 30, 2014, 216 bachelor's degrees were awarded. The most popular majors were business administration (22%), health and physical education (13%), and teacher education (11%). In an average class, 51% graduate in 4 years or less, 59% graduate in 5 years or less, and 60% graduate in 6 years or less. Of the 2013 graduating class, 11% were enrolled in graduate school within 6 months of graduation, and 90% were employed.

SERVICES: Counseling and information services are available, as is tutoring in every subject. There is a reader service for the blind, and remedial math, reading, and writing. **Library/Resources:** The library contains 93,861 volumes, 204,109 microform items, 2,400 audio/video tapes/CDs/DVDs, and subscribes to 32,019 periodicals including electronic. Computerized library services include interlibrary loans, database searching, and Internet access. Special learning facilities include an art gallery, radio station, academic development center, Windy Hill laboratory school (K-3), weather station, and the Curtis L. Ivey science center. **Physically Challenged Students:** 50% of the campus is accessible. Facilities include wheelchair ramps, elevators, special parking, specially equipped restrooms, special class scheduling, and special housing. **Special:** There is cross-registration through the New Hampshire College and University Council. Students may choose internships (required in some majors) and may study abroad in Australia, Canada, and several European countries. A Washington semester with American University is available. Other options include education certification, credit by exam, and interdisciplinary majors such as history, society, and culture. There are 4 national honor societies and a freshman honors program. **Visiting:** There are regularly scheduled orientations for prospective students, including tours and interviews. Open house programs offer tours as well as academic, athletic, campus life, career development, and academic development presentations; several visiting-day programs offer tours, interviews, and class visits. There are guides for informal visits, visitors may sit in on classes, and stay overnight. To schedule a visit, contact the Admissions Office. **Campus Safety and Security:** Measures include 24-hour foot and vehicle patrol, emergency notification system, self-defense education, and security escort services. There are shuttle buses, emergency telephones, lighted pathways/sidewalks, controlled access to dorms/residences, monthly meetings between students and campus safety personnel.

REQUIREMENTS: The SAT or ACT is required. The ACT Optional

Writing test is also required. The GED is accepted. A minimum of 15 college preparatory credits is recommended for admission, including 4 years of English, 3 or more of social studies, 3 of math, 2 of the same foreign language, and 3 or more of lab science. An essay is required, as are 2 letters of recommendation. Interviews are strongly recommended. A GPA of 2.0 is required. AP and CLEP credits are accepted. Required courses include writing, math, and computer literacy. Each pathway is a set of five courses that all relate to a theme. Each student is required to take a total of eight Exploration courses: 1 course each in fine and performing arts, history, humanities, literature, social sciences, and laboratory science course, and 1 course from 2 of the following areas: environmental literacy, media literacy, global perspectives, and wellness. Most majors must also complete an internship or a senior research project. A total of 120 credit hours, with a minimum GPA of 2.0, is required for graduation. **Procedure:** Freshmen are admitted fall and spring. Entrance exams should be taken in the fall of the senior year. There are early decision, deferred admissions, and rolling admissions plans. Early decision applications should be filed by December 1, along with a $45 fee. Notification of early decision is sent December 15; regular decision, on a rolling basis. Applications are accepted on-line. **Transfer Students:** 17 transfer students enrolled in 2013-2014. College-level work will be emphasized. College transcripts, course descriptions, and a dean's form are required in addition to the standard requirements. 60 of 120 credits required for the bachelor's degree must be completed at Colby-Sawyer. **International Students:** There are 13 international students enrolled. The school actively recruits these students. They must take the TOEFL.

ADMISSIONS: Admissions Office. E-Mail: *admissions@colby-sawyer .edu* Web: *www.colby-sawyer.edu*

FINANCIAL AID: In 2014-2015, 97% of all full-time freshmen and 78% of continuing full-time students received some form of financial aid. 81% of all full-time freshmen and 78% of continuing full-time students received need-based aid. The average freshman award was $24,043. The average financial indebtedness of the 2014 graduate was $13,578. Colby-Sawyer is a member of CSS. The FAFSA is required. Check with the school for current application deadlines.

DANIEL WEBSTER COLLEGE — D-6
www.dwc.edu

Nashua, NH 03063	**(603) 577-6600**
	(800) 325-6876
Fax: (603) 577-6001	Email: admissions@dwc.edu
Full-time: 555 men, 135 women	Faculty: n/av
Part-time: 25 men, 10 women	Ph.D.s: n/av
Graduate: 75 men, 70 women	Student/Faculty: 16 to 1
Year: semesters, summer session	Tuition: $15,090
Room & Board: $10,290	Freshman Class: n/av
SAT: required	CEEB CODE: 3648
Application Deadline: open	**COMPETITIVE**

Daniel Webster College, founded in 1965, is a non-denominational private college offering study in the fields of aviation, business, computer sciences, engineering, sports management, and social sciences. The figures in the above capsule and in this profile are approximate. There are 4 undergraduate schools and 1 graduate school. In addition to regional accreditation, DWC has baccalaureate program accreditation with AABI, AT-CTl, CAA, FAA, NASSM, and SMPRC. The 54-acre campus is in a suburban area in southern New Hampshire, 36 miles from Boston and 20 miles from Manchester. Including any residence halls, there are 14 buildings.

STUDENT LIFE: 66% of undergraduates are from out of state, mostly the Northeast. Students are from 22 states, 15 foreign countries, and Canada. 91% are White. **Male To Female Ratio:** 0.3:1. The average age of freshmen is 18; all undergraduates, 21. 24% do not continue beyond their first year. **Housing:** 500 students can be accommodated in college housing, which includes single-sex and coed dorms and on-campus apartments. Suites, quiet floors in residence halls, smoke-free areas, and a substance-free, 10-month housing option. On-campus housing is guaranteed for all 4 years. 68% of students live on campus; of those, 80% remain on campus on weekends. All students may keep cars.

FACULTY/CLASSROOMS: 80% of faculty are male; 20% are female. All teach and do research. No introductory courses are taught by graduate students. The average class size in an introductory lecture is 17; in a laboratory is 12; and in a regular course is 20.

PROGRAMS OF STUDY: DWC confers B.S. and M.B.A. degrees. Associate and Master's degrees are also awarded. Bachelor's degrees are awarded in BUSINESS (business administration and management, management information systems, marketing management, and sports management), COMPUTER AND PHYSICAL SCIENCE (computer science and information sciences and systems), ENGINEERING AND ENVIRONMENTAL DESIGN (aeronautical engineering, air traffic control, airline piloting and navigation, aviation administration/management, computer technology, and mechanical engineering), SOCIAL SCIENCE (psychology and social science). Aviation, computer science, and information systems are the strongest academically. Aviation has the largest enrollment.

ACTIVITIES: There are no fraternities or sororities. There are 26 groups on campus, including golf and culinary club, ski club, computers, drama, film, honors, jazz band, newspaper, off reading club, professional, religious, social, social service, student government, and yearbook. Popular campus events include Ski Day, Family Weekend, and Whitewater Rafting Trip. **Sports:** There are 7 intercollegiate sports for men and 7 for women, and 6 intramural sports for men and 5 for women. Facilities include an indoor basketball/volleyball court, a weight room, soccer, lacrosse, and softball fields, and cross-country trails.

SERVICES: Counseling and information services are available, as is tutoring in every subject. There is remedial math and writing. Study skills and test skills workshops, study groups, a math/science center, a writing center, and accommodations for students with learning disabilities are available. **Library/Resources:** The library contains 32,000 volumes, 55,294 microform items, 1,457 audio/video tapes/CDs/DVDs, and subscribes to 390 periodicals including electronic. Computerized library services include interlibrary loans, database searching, and Internet access. Special learning facilities include a **Physically Challenged Students:** 75% of the campus is accessible. Facilities include wheelchair ramps, elevators, special parking, specially equipped restrooms, special class scheduling, and lowered drinking fountains. **Special:** There is cross-registration with the New Hampshire College and University Council. All programs offer credit by exam. Interdisciplinary majors, including aviation flight operations and aviation management/air traffic management, are available. Study abroad, internships in aviation, business management, computer sciences, and sport management, a general studies degree, and a 2-2 engineering program with the universities of New Hampshire and Massachusetts at Lowell, Kettering University, and Clarkson University are additional options. There is 1 national honor society and 1 departmental honors program. **Visiting:** There are regularly scheduled orientations for prospective students, including a tour and an admissions interview; also available are meetings with faculty and coaches and an aerial tour of the campus as well as sitting in on class. There are guides for informal visits, visitors may sit in on classes, and stay overnight. To schedule a visit, contact the Office of Admissions. **Campus Safety and Security:** Measures include 24-hour foot and vehicle patrol, emergency notification system, self-defense education, and security escort services. There are emergency telephones, lighted pathways/sidewalks, and controlled access to dorms/residences.

REQUIREMENTS: The SAT is required. Applicants must be graduates of an accredited secondary school or submit the GED. Students should have taken 4 years of English, 3 of math, 2 each of social studies and science, and 1 of history. An essay and an interview are recommended. A GPA of 2.0 is required. AP and CLEP credits are accepted. Important factors in the admissions decision are advanced placement or honors courses, recommendations by school officials, and leadership record. Students must complete general education courses in communication, computer literacy, math, natural science, the humanities, and the social sciences. At least 120 credits, with 45 to 58 in the major, are required for graduation. Students must maintain a minimum overall GPA of 2.0. and grades of C or better in their major. **Procedure:** Freshmen are admitted to all sessions. There are early decision, deferred admissions, and rolling admissions plans.

Application deadlines are open. Application fee is $35. Applications are accepted on-line. **Transfer Students:** Transfer students must have a minimum college GPA of 2.0. The SAT is required. Grades of C or better transfer for credit. 30 of 120 credits required for the bachelor's degree must be completed at DWC. **International Students:** They must take the TOEFL. They must also take the SAT or ACT.

ADMISSIONS: Daniel P. Monahan, Dean of Admissions. E-Mail: *admissions@dwc.edu* Web: *www.dwc.edu*

FINANCIAL AID: The FAFSA and the college's own financial statement are required. Check with the school for current application deadlines.

DARTMOUTH COLLEGE   **B-4**
www.dartmouth.edu

Hanover, NH 03755   **(603) 646-2875**
    n/av

Fax: (603) 646-1216   Email: admissions.office@dartmouth.edu

Full-time: 2064 men, 2037 women   **Faculty:** 482; I, ++$

Part-time: 25 men, 21 women   **Ph.D.s:** n/av

Graduate: 988 men, 713 women   **Student/Faculty:** 8 to 1

Year: quarters, summer session   **Tuition:** $45,042

Room & Board: $12,954   **Freshman Class:** 18132 applied, 2279 accepted, 1094 enrolled

SAT or ACT: required   **CEEB CODE:** 3351

Application Deadline: January 1   **MOST COMPETITIVE**

Dartmouth College, chartered in 1769, is a private liberal arts institution offering a wide range of graduate and undergraduate programs. There is a year-round academic calendar of 4 10-week terms. Figures in the above capsule and in this profile are approximate. There are 4 graduate schools. The 269-acre campus is in a rural area 140 miles northwest of Boston. Including any residence halls, there are 160 buildings.

STUDENT LIFE: 96% of undergraduates are from out of state, mostly the Middle Atlantic. Students are from 50 states, 80 foreign countries, and Canada. 62% are from public schools. 53% are White; 14% Asian American. 30% are Protestant; 28% claim no religious affiliation; 23% Catholic; 11% Jewish. **Male To Female Ratio:** 0.9:1. The average age of freshmen is 18; all undergraduates, 20. 2% do not continue beyond their first year; 95% remain to graduate. **Housing:** 3500 students can be accommodated in college housing, which includes coed dorms, on-campus apartments, off-campus apartments, and married student housing. In addition, there are language houses, special-interest houses, fraternity houses, sorority houses, substance- and smoke-free residence halls, and faculty-in-residence and academic affinity programs. On-campus housing is guaranteed for the freshman year only and is available on a lottery system for upperclassmen. 85% of students live on campus. Upperclassmen may keep cars.

FACULTY/CLASSROOMS: 62% of faculty are male; 38% are female. All teach and do research. No introductory courses are taught by graduate students. The average class size in an introductory lecture is 34; in a laboratory is 16; and in a regular course is 23.

PROGRAMS OF STUDY: Dartmouth confers B.A. and B.Eng. degrees. Master's and Doctoral degrees are also awarded. Bachelor's degrees are awarded in AGRICULTURE (environmental studies), BIOLOGICAL SCIENCE (biochemistry, biology/biological science, genetics, and neurosciences), COMMUNICATIONS AND THE ARTS (Arabic, art history and appreciation, Chinese, classical languages, classics, comparative literature, dramatic arts, English, film arts, French, German, Italian, linguistics, music, Portuguese, romance languages and literature, Russian, Spanish, and studio art), COMPUTER AND PHYSICAL SCIENCE (astrophysics, chemistry, computer science, earth science, mathematics, and physics), ENGINEERING AND ENVIRONMENTAL DESIGN (engineering and applied science, engineering physics, and environmental science), SOCIAL SCIENCE (African American studies, anthropology, Asian/Oriental studies, classical/ancient civilization, cognitive science, economics, French studies, geography, German area studies, history,

Latin American studies, Middle Eastern studies, Native American studies, philosophy, psychology, religion, Russian and Slavic studies, sociology, Spanish studies, and women's studies). Economics, government, psychological and brain sciences have the largest enrollments.

ACTIVITIES: 39% of men belong to 9 local and 5 national fraternities; 34% of women belong to 3 local and 6 national sororities. There are 300 groups on campus, including art, band, cheerleading, chess, choir, chorale, chorus, computers, dance, debate, drama, environmental, ethnic, film, forensics, gay, honors, international, jazz band, literary magazine, marching band, musical theater, newspaper, opera, orchestra, pep band, photography, political, professional, radio and TV, religious, social, social service, student government, symphony, and yearbook. Popular campus events include Dartmouth Night/Homecoming Weekend, Winter Carnival and Green Key Service Weekend. **Sports:** There are 17 intercollegiate sports for men and 17 for women, and 25 intramural sports for men and 25 for women. Facilities include a 2100-seat arena, 16,000-square-foot fitness center, squash and racquetball courts, dance studio, 5000-seat ice-hockey arena, a gym, 20,000-seat football stadium, boat house, tennis center with indoor and outdoor courts, golf course, ski slope with 3 chairlifts, and a riding farm. **Graduates:** From July 1, 2013 to June 30, 2014, 1084 bachelor's degrees were awarded. The most popular majors were economics, government, and psychological and brain sciences. In an average class, 95% graduate in 6 years or less.

SERVICES: Counseling and information services are available, as is tutoring in every subject. There is a reader service for the blind. There is an academic skills center for all students. Readers, note takers, tape recorders and support for learning-disabled students are available.

Library/Resources: The 10 libraries contain 2.5 million volumes, 2.6 million microform items, 772,660 audio/video tapes/CDs/DVDs, and subscribe to 42,116 periodicals including electronic. Computerized library services include interlibrary loans, database searching, Internet access, and Wi-Fi capability. Special learning facilities include an art gallery, radio station, a creative and performing arts center, life sciences lab, a physical and social sciences centers and observatory.

Physically Challenged Students: All of the campus is accessible. Facilities include wheelchair ramps, elevators, special parking, specially equipped restrooms, special class scheduling, lowered drinking fountains, lowered telephones, and special housing. **Special:** Students may design programs using the college's unique Dartmouth Plan, which divides the academic calendar into 4 10-week terms, based on the seasons. The plan permits greater flexibility for vacations and for the 45 study-abroad programs in 23 countries in Latin America, Europe, Asia, and Africa. Cross-registration is offered through the Twelve College Exchange Network. Exchange programs also exist with the University of California at San Diego, Stanford, Oxford, and McGill Universities, selected German universities, Keio University in Tokyo, and Beijing Normal University in China. Students may design their own interdisciplinary majors involving multiple departments, take dual majors in all fields, or create a modified major involving 2 departments, with emphasis in 1. Hands-on computer science education, internships, and work-study programs also are available. A 3-2 engineering degree is offered with Dartmouth's Thayer School of Engineering. There are 3 national honor societies, including Phi Beta Kappa. **Visiting:** There are regularly scheduled orientations for prospective students, including a campus tour, a group information session, and a student forum. There are guides for informal visits, visitors may sit in on classes, and stay overnight. To schedule a visit, contact the Office of Admissions. **Campus Safety and Security:** Measures include 24-hour foot and vehicle patrol, emergency notification system, self-defense education, and security escort services. There are shuttle buses, emergency telephones, and lighted pathways/sidewalks.

REQUIREMENTS: The SAT or ACT is required. The ACT Optional Writing test is also required. Evidence of intellectual capacity, motivation, and personal integrity are important factors in the highly competitive admissions process, which also considers talent, accomplishment, and involvement in nonacademic areas. Course requirements are flexible, but students are urged to take English, foreign language, math, lab science, and history. The GED is accepted. AP credits are accepted. All students must pass 35 courses, 10 of which must be distributed in the following fields: arts; social analysis; literature; quantitative or deductive science; philosophical, religious, or historical analysis; natural science; technology or applied science; and international or comparative study. 3 world culture courses are required from the U.S., Europe, and at least 1 non-Western society. A multidisciplinary or interdisciplinary course, a freshman seminar, a senior project, and foreign language proficiency are also required. **Procedure:** Freshmen are admitted fall. Entrance exams should be taken no later than November or January of the senior year. There are early decision and deferred admissions plans. Early decision applications should be filed by November 1; regular applications, by January 1 for fall entry. The fall 2014 application fee was $70. Notification of early decision is sent December 15; regular decision, April 1. 958 applicants were on the 2014 waiting list; 95 were admitted. Applications are accepted on-line. **Transfer Students:** 23 transfer students enrolled in 2013-2014. Applicants must demonstrate high achievement and intellectual motivation through college transcripts as well as standardized test scores and high school transcripts. 18 of 35 credits required for the bachelor's degree must be completed at Dartmouth. **International Students:** There are 286 international students enrolled. The school actively recruits these students. They must take the TOEFL. They must also take the SAT or ACT.

ADMISSIONS: 13% of the 2014-2015 applicants were accepted. 95% of the current freshmen were in the top fifth of their class; 100% were in the top two fifths. 323 freshmen graduated first in their class. **Admissions Contact:** Maria Laskaris, Dean of Admissions. E-Mail: *admissions.office@dartmouth.edu* Web: *www.dartmouth.edu*

FINANCIAL AID: In 2014-2015, 49% of all full-time freshmen and 53% of continuing full-time students received some form of financial aid. 49% of all full-time freshmen and 53% of continuing full-time students received need-based aid. The average freshman award was $37,055. Need-based scholarships or need-based grants averaged $34,927; and need-based self-help aid (loans and jobs) averaged $2,870. The average financial indebtedness of the 2014 graduate was $18,095. Dartmouth is a member of CSS. The CSS/Profile, FAFSA, and parents' and student's federal income tax returns are required. The deadline for filing freshman financial aid applications for fall entry is February 1.

FRANKLIN PIERCE UNIVERSITY   C-6
www.franklinpierce.edu

Rindge, NH 03461	(603) 899-4050
	(800) 437-0048
Fax: (603) 899-4394	Email: admissions@franklinpierce.edu
Full-time: 591 men, 716 women	**Faculty:** 71; IIB, -$
Part-time: 95 men, 285 women	**Ph.D.s:** 70%
Graduate: 205 men, 324 women	**Student/Faculty:** 14 to 1
Year: semesters, summer session	**Tuition:** $31,000
Room & Board: $11,598	**Freshman Class:** 4419 applied, 3681 accepted, 450 enrolled
SAT CR/M/W: 480/480/470 **ACT:** 21	**CEEB CODE:** 3395
Application Deadline: n/av	**COMPETITIVE**

Franklin Pierce University, founded in 1962, is a private liberal arts institution with an extensive continuing education program. Many degrees are offered with emphasis in health care, business, education, mass communications, psychology, humanities, visual and performing arts, and leadership studies. Figures in the above capsule and in this profile are approximate. There are 2 undergraduate schools and 1 graduate school. In addition to regional accreditation, FPU has baccalaureate program accreditation with NEASC. The 1200-acre campus is in a rural area 65 miles northwest of Boston. Including any residence halls, there are 30 buildings.

STUDENT LIFE: 78% of undergraduates are from out of state, mostly the Northeast. Students are from 34 states, 29 foreign countries, and Canada. 83% are from public schools. 78% are White; 13% race unknown. **Male To Female Ratio:** 1.5:1. The average age of freshmen is 18; all undergraduates, 20. 31% do not continue beyond their first year; 52% remain to graduate. **Housing:** 1492 students can be accommodated in college housing, which includes coed dorms, on-campus apartments, and off-campus apartments. In addition, there are special-interest houses, wellness living, and apartments for

single students. On-campus housing is guaranteed for all 4 years. 94% of students live on campus; of those, 70% remain on campus on weekends. All students may keep cars.

FACULTY/CLASSROOMS: 48% of faculty are male; 52% are female. All teach undergraduates, and 50% do both. No introductory courses are taught by graduate students. The average class size in an introductory lecture is 60; in a laboratory is 16; and in a regular course is 16.

PROGRAMS OF STUDY: FPU confers B.A., and B.S. degrees. Associate, Master's, and Doctoral degrees are also awarded. Bachelor's degrees are awarded in BIOLOGICAL SCIENCE (biology/biological science), BUSINESS (accounting, banking and finance, business administration and management, management science, marketing/retailing/merchandising, and sports management), COMMUNICATIONS AND THE ARTS (arts administration/management, communications, dance, dramatic arts, English, fine arts, graphic design, music, and theatre arts), COMPUTER AND PHYSICAL SCIENCE (mathematics), EDUCATION (education, elementary education, and secondary education), ENGINEERING AND ENVIRONMENTAL DESIGN (environmental science), HEALTH PROFESSIONS (health care administration, health science, and nursing), SOCIAL SCIENCE (American studies, anthropology, criminal justice, history, interdisciplinary studies, political science/government, psychology, and social work). Anthropology, health sciences, biology and history are the strongest academically. Biology, health sciences, criminal justice, psychology, education and management have the largest enrollments.

ACTIVITIES: There are no fraternities or sororities. There are 35 groups on campus, including art, cheerleading, choir, chorale, chorus, computers, dance, drama, environmental, ethnic, film, forensics, gay, honors, international, jazz band, literary magazine, musical theater, newspaper, photography, political, professional, radio and TV, religious, social, social service, student government, and yearbook. Popular campus events include Winter Carnival, Spring and Fall Weekend and Up All Night Mardi Gras. **Sports:** There are 9 intercollegiate sports for men and 11 for women, and 32 intramural sports for men and 32 for women. Facilities include a 72,000-square-foot airframe activity center, (with tennis courts, indoor turf soccer field, basketball courts, track, fitness center, and volleyball courts), a field house, a fitness center, an 800-seat gym, an athletic training facility, playing fields including an artificial turf baseball field, and artificial turf soccer/lacrosse and field hockey field, a softball field, and another all-purpose field, a lake with a beach, fleet of sailboats and kayaks, cross-country and hiking trails, courts for tennis, basketball, and volleyball. **Graduates:** From July 1, 2013 to June 30, 2014, 378 bachelor's degrees were awarded. The most popular majors were business/marketing (18%), health professions and related sciences (14%), and biological/life sciences (7%). In an average class, 2% graduate in 3 years or less, 37% graduate in 4 years or less, 48% graduate in 5 years or less, and 50% graduate in 6 years or less. Of the 2013 graduating class, 37% were enrolled in graduate school within 6 months of graduation, and 79% were employed.

SERVICES: Counseling and information services are available, as is tutoring in every subject. There is a reader service for the blind, and remedial math, reading, and writing. Note takers, a professional reading specialist, alternative testing, reduced course loads, study skills workshops, and content-area study skills courses are available. **Library/Resources:** The library contains 144,770 volumes, 26,182 microform items, 10,312 audio/video tapes/CDs/DVDs, and subscribes to 10,275 periodicals including electronic. Computerized library services include interlibrary loans, database searching, Internet access, and Wi-Fi capability. Special learning facilities include an art gallery, radio station, TV station, computer labs, theaters, recording studios, athletic training facility, glassblowing hut. **Physically Challenged Students:** 70% of the campus is accessible. Facilities include wheelchair ramps, elevators, special parking, specially equipped restrooms, special class scheduling, and special housing. **Special:** Cross-registration is offered in nearly every subject through the New Hampshire College and University Council, a 13-member consortium of area institutions. Study abroad in 9 countries, Pierce on the Camino, internships in most majors on or off campus, a Washington semester, and work-study through the college are possible. In addition, accelerated degree programs in all majors, dual majors in most fields, student-designed majors, credit for life experience, and nondegree study are available. Pathway programs from undergraduate to M.D. and D.V.M. programs at St. George's University in Grenada afford students special graduate study opportunities, along with pathways and consideration to Franklin Pierce's Doctor of Physical Therapy and Master of Physician Assistant Studies programs. Pathway and accelerated Franklin Pierce M.B.A., M.Ed., and M.S. in Information Technology Management degree programs provide additional options. There are 7 national honor societies and a freshman honors program. **Visiting:** There are regularly scheduled orientations for prospective students, including open houses held each spring and fall and interviews and tours available weekdays and most Saturdays. There are guides for informal visits, visitors may sit in on classes, and stay overnight. To schedule a visit, contact the Admissions Office. **Campus Safety and Security:** Measures include 24-hour foot and vehicle patrol, emergency notification system, self-defense education, and security escort services. There are shuttle buses, emergency telephones, lighted pathways/sidewalks, on campus student-run fire department and EMS squad.

REQUIREMENTS: The SAT is required. The ACT and ACT Writing Test are recommended. Applicants must have earned 10 academic units or 16 Carnegie units in high school, including 4 years of English, 3 each in math and social studies, and 3 in science. An interview is recommended. The GED is accepted. FPU requires applicants to be in the upper 60% of their class. A GPA of 2.9 is required. AP and CLEP credits are accepted. Important factors in the admissions decision are recommendations by school officials, advanced placement or honors courses, and extracurricular activities record. Students must complete 120 semester hours with a cumulative GPA of at least 2.0 and pass exams for writing and math competency. General and liberal education core curricular requirements include mastery of an established set of learning outcomes in the following areas: Knowledge and Understanding, Intellectual and Practical Skills, Personal and Social Responsibility, and Engaged Learning and Thinking. **Procedure:** Freshmen are admitted to all sessions. Entrance exams should be taken in the spring of junior year or the fall of the senior year. There are deferred admissions and rolling admissions plans. Application deadlines are open. Application fee is $40. Notification is sent on a rolling basis. Applications are accepted on-line. **Transfer Students:** 21 transfer students enrolled in 2013-2014. A minimum 2.0 GPA in college work is required. Students with fewer than 30 credits must submit SAT results (no minimum score) and official high school transcripts. A personal recommendation is necessary, and an interview is recommended. 30 of 120 credits required for the bachelor's degree must be completed at FPU. **International Students:** There are 25 international students enrolled. The school actively recruits these students. They must take the TOEFL with a minimum score of 61 on the Internet-based version (iBT) and also take ELS Level 109. The SAT or ACT may be substituted for the TOEFL.

ADMISSIONS: 83% of the 2014-2015 applicants were accepted. The SAT scores for the 2014-2015 freshman class were: Critical Reading-58% below 500, 36% between 500 and 599, and 6% between 600 and 699; Math--54% below 500, 37% between 500 and 599, and 7% between 600 and 699; Writing--63% below 500, 32% between 500 and 599, and 5% between 600 and 699. The ACT scores were 9% below 21, 72% between 21 and 23, and 19% above 28. 44% of the current freshmen were in the top fifth of their class; 56% were in the top two fifths. **Admissions Contact:** Linda Quimby, Director. E-Mail: *admissions@franklinpierce.edu* Web: *www.franklinpierce.edu/admissions*

FINANCIAL AID: In 2014-2015, 86% of all full-time freshmen and 85% of continuing full-time students received some form of financial aid. 86% of all full-time freshmen and 85% of continuing full-time students received need-based aid. The average freshman award was $23,887. Need-based scholarships or need-based grants averaged $19,445; need-based self-help aid (loans and jobs) averaged $5,484; non-need-based athletic scholarships averaged $12,919; and other non-need-based awards and non-need-based scholarships averaged $13,304. 50% of undergraduate students work part-time. Average annual earnings from campus work are $618. The average financial indebtedness of the 2014 graduate was $36,087. FPU is a member of CSS. The FAFSA is required. The priority date for freshman financial aid applications for fall entry is March 1.

GRANITE STATE COLLEGE (*The complete profile is made available exclusively on our website, www.barronspac.com*)

KEENE STATE COLLEGE (*The complete profile is made available exclusively on our website, www.barronspac.com*)

NEW ENGLAND COLLEGE (*The complete profile is made available exclusively on our website, www.barronspac.com*)

PLYMOUTH STATE UNIVERSITY (*The complete profile is made available exclusively on our website, www.barronspac.com*)

RIVIER UNIVERSITY	**D-6**
www.rivier.edu	
Nashua, NH 03060	**(603) 897-8507**
	(800) 44-RIVIER
Fax: (603) 891-1799	Email: rivadmit@rivier.edu
Full-time: 310 men, 610 women	**Faculty:** n/av
Part-time: 205 men, 505 women	**Ph.Ds:** n/av
Graduate: 255 men, 625 women	**Student/Faculty:** n/av
Year: semesters, summer session	**Tuition:** $26,000
Room & Board: $9000	**Freshman Class:** n/av
SAT: required	**CEEB CODE:** 3728
Application Deadline: open	**VERY COMPETITIVE**

Rivier College, founded in 1933 by the Sisters of the Presentation of Mary, is a private Roman Catholic college offering a liberal arts and professional curriculum. The figures in the above capsule and in this profile are approximate. There is 1 graduate school. In addition to regional accreditation, Rivier has baccalaureate program accreditation with NLN. The 68-acre campus is in a suburban area 45 miles north of Boston. Including any residence halls, there are 44 buildings.

STUDENT LIFE: 68% of undergraduates are from New Hampshire. Others are from 13 states, 13 foreign countries, and Canada. 80% are from public schools. 93% are White. 80% are Catholic. **Male To Female Ratio:** 2.3:1. The average age of freshmen is 18; all undergraduates, 28. 29% do not continue beyond their first year. **Housing:** 425 students can be accommodated in college housing, which includes coed dorms, and a substance-free/wellness residence hall. On-campus housing is guaranteed for all 4 years, and is available on a first-come, first-served basis. 56% of students commute. All students may keep cars.

FACULTY/CLASSROOMS: 38% of faculty are male; 62% are female. 88% teach undergraduates. No introductory courses are taught by graduate students. The average class size in an introductory lecture is 25; in a laboratory is 20; and in a regular course is 17.

PROGRAMS OF STUDY: Rivier confers B.A., B.S. and B.F.A. degrees. Associate and Master's degrees are also awarded. Bachelor's degrees are awarded in BIOLOGICAL SCIENCE (biology/biological science), BUSINESS (business administration and management, management information systems, and management science), COMMUNICATIONS AND THE ARTS (communications, English, graphic design, illustration, and studio art), COMPUTER AND PHYSICAL SCIENCE (computer science and mathematics), EDUCATION (art education, early childhood education, elementary education, English education, mathematics education, secondary education, and social studies education), HEALTH PROFESSIONS (nursing, predentistry, premedicine, and preveterinary science), SOCIAL SCIENCE (history, human development, liberal arts/general studies, political science/government, prelaw, psychology, and sociology). Art, education, and nursing are the strongest academically. Education, psychology, and business have the largest enrollments.

ACTIVITIES: There are no fraternities or sororities. There are 32 groups on campus, including and nursing, behavioral sciences, history, paralegal, art, chorus, computers, debate, drama, ethnic, honors, international, literary magazine, newspaper, political, professional, religious, social, social sciences, social service, student government, and yearbook. Popular campus events include Spirit Week, Black History Month, and Women's History Month. **Sports:** There are 5 intercollegiate sports for men and 5 for women, and 7 intramural sports for men and 7 for women. Facilities include a 300-seat gym, a weight room, and soccer and softball fields.

SERVICES: Counseling and information services are available, as is

tutoring in some subjects, including math, English, business, and languages. Tutoring is available in other subjects. There is remedial math and writing. There is a full-service writing center. **Library/Resources:** The library contains 107,200 volumes, 89,572 microform items, 29,094 audio/video tapes/CDs/DVDs, and subscribes to 480 periodicals including electronic. Computerized library services include interlibrary loans and database searching. Special learning facilities include an art gallery, TV station, education curriculum resources center, legal reference center, early childhood center/laboratory school, and language lab. **Physically Challenged Students:** 75% of the campus is accessible. Facilities include wheelchair ramps, elevators, special parking, specially equipped restrooms, and lowered drinking fountains. **Special:** Rivier offers cross-registration through the New Hampshire College and University Council, internships in most majors, an accelerated master's program in English, dual majors, a liberal studies degree, credit by challenge examination, nondegree study, and pass/fail options. There is 1 national honor society and a freshman honors program. **Visiting:** There are regularly scheduled orientations for prospective students, including an opportunity to interview, a tour, class visits, and opportunities to meet with faculty, coaches, and current students. There are guides for informal visits, visitors may sit in on classes, and stay overnight. To schedule a visit, contact the Office of Undergraduate Admissions. **Campus Safety and Security:** Measures include 24-hour foot and vehicle patrol and security escort services. There are emergency telephones, lighted pathways/sidewalks, 24-hour access by telephone or walkie-talkie, and electronically operated dorm entrances using security cards.

REQUIREMENTS: The SAT is required. Applicants must be high school graduates or hold the GED. The recommended college preparatory curriculum includes 4 years of English, 3 of math, 2 or more each of foreign language and social studies, 1 of lab science, and 4 academic electives. An essay and 1 or 2 letters of recommendation are required, and an interview is highly recommended. Prospective art majors must submit a portfolio. A GPA of 2.5 is required. AP and CLEP credits are accepted. Important factors in the admissions decision are advanced placement or honors courses, recommendations by school officials, and extracurricular activities record. A writing sample is required at entry, and a demonstration of writing proficiency must be shown prior to graduation. Students must complete at least 120 credit hours, ordinarily consisting of 40 3-credit courses, with 35 to 60 credits in the student's major, and they must maintain a minimum GPA of 2.0. Distribution requirements include 17 core courses in basic skills of writing and math, the humanities, and the sciences. These courses include religious studies, philosophy, physical and life sciences, fine arts, modern languages, literature, behavioral and social sciences, and Western civilization. **Procedure:** Freshmen are admitted fall and spring. Entrance exams should be taken in the junior or senior year. There are deferred admissions and rolling admissions plans. Application deadlines are open. The fall 2014 application fee was $25. Notification of early decision is sent December 1; regular decision, on a rolling basis. Applications are accepted on-line. **Transfer Students:** Transfer applicants should have a minimum GPA of 2.5 and submit SAT I or ACT scores if they have earned fewer than 12 credits at the previous institution. Official college transcripts are required and an interview is recommended. 60 of 120 credits required for the bachelor's degree must be completed at Rivier. **International Students:** The school actively recruits these students. They must take the TOEFL and the college's own test.

ADMISSIONS: David A. Boisvert, Director of Undergraduate Admissions. E-Mail: *rivadmit@rivier.edu* Web: *www.rivier.edu*

FINANCIAL AID: Rivier is a member of CSS. The FAFSA is required. Check with the school for current application deadlines.

SAINT ANSELM COLLEGE D-6
www.anselm.edu

Manchester, NH 03102	(603) 641-7500
	(888)-4-ANSELM
Fax: (603) 641-7550	Email: admission@anselm.edu
Full-time: 762 men, 1116 women	Faculty: 146; IIB, +$
Part-time: 17 men, 28 women	Ph.D.s: 98%
Graduate: n/av	Student/Faculty: 11 to 1
Year: semesters, summer session	Tuition: $36,336
Room & Board: $13,040	Freshman Class: 3568 applied, 2716 accepted, 532 enrolled
SAT CR/M/W: 560/570/570 ACT: 25	CEEB CODE: 3748
Application Deadline: February 1	VERY COMPETITIVE

Saint Anselm College, founded in 1889, is a private Roman Catholic institution offering a liberal arts education. There is 1 undergraduate school. In addition to regional accreditation, Saint Anselm has baccalaureate program accreditation with NLN. The 380-acre campus is in a suburban area in Southern New Hampshire, minutes from downtown Manchester, 50 miles north of Boston and under an hour from the White Mountains and seacoast. Including any residence halls, there are 64 buildings.

STUDENT LIFE: 79% of undergraduates are from out of state, mostly the Northeast. Students are from 28 states, 21 foreign countries, and Canada. 67% are from public schools. 78% are White; 13% race unknown. 55% are Catholic. **Male To Female Ratio:** 1.5:1. The average age of freshmen is 18; all undergraduates, 20. 12% do not continue beyond their first year; 75% remain to graduate. **Housing:** 1794 students can be accommodated in college housing, which includes single-sex and coed dorms and on-campus apartments. In addition, there are special-interest houses, and substance-free housing. On-campus housing is guaranteed for all 4 years. 90% of students live on campus; of those, 88% remain on campus on weekends. All students may keep cars.

FACULTY/CLASSROOMS: 60% of faculty are male; 40% are female. All teach undergraduates. No introductory courses are taught by graduate students. The average class size in a laboratory is 18 and in a regular course is 18.

PROGRAMS OF STUDY: Saint Anselm confers B.A., and B.S.N. degrees. Bachelor's degrees are awarded in BIOLOGICAL SCIENCE (biochemistry and biology/biological science), BUSINESS (accounting, banking and finance, and business administration and management), COMMUNICATIONS AND THE ARTS (classics, English, fine arts, French, and Spanish), COMPUTER AND PHYSICAL SCIENCE (chemistry, computer science, mathematics, and natural sciences), EDUCATION (education and secondary education), ENGINEERING AND ENVIRONMENTAL DESIGN (engineering and environmental science), HEALTH PROFESSIONS (nursing, predentistry, and premedicine), SOCIAL SCIENCE (criminal justice, economics, forensic studies, German area studies, history, liberal arts/general studies, philosophy, political science/government, prelaw, psychology, sociology, and theological studies). Nursing is the strongest academically. Nursing, business, and biology have the largest enrollments.

ACTIVITIES: There are no fraternities or sororities. There are 60 groups on campus, including art, band, chess, choir, chorale, chorus, communications, computers, dance, debate, drama, environmental, ethnic, film, forensics, gay, honors, international, jazz band, literary magazine, musical theater, newspaper, orchestra, pep band, photography, political, professional, radio and TV, religious, social, social service, student government, and yearbook. Popular campus events include Family Weekend, Road for Hope, Spring Weekend, Running of the Bells, Gingerbread House Competition, and Shakespeare's Birthday. **Sports:** There are 10 intercollegiate sports for men and 10 for women, and 8 intramural sports for men and 8 for women. Facilities include a 1500-seat gym, an ice hockey arena, activity center that houses basketball, volleyball, tennis, racquetball courts, weight and training rooms, a 2500-seat football stadium, a 500-seat baseball stadium, athletic fields and state-of-the-art fitness center. **Graduates:** From July 1, 2013 to June 30, 2014, 417 bachelor's degrees were awarded. The most popular majors were social sciences (20%), business/marketing (19%), and health professions and related programs (19%). In an average class, 71% graduate in 4 years or less, 74% graduate in 5 years or less, and 75% graduate in 6 years or less. **SERVICES:** Counseling and information services are available, as is tutoring in most subjects. There is a reader service for the blind. **Library/Resources:** The library contains 219,000 volumes, 65,000 microform items, 8,000 audio/video tapes/CDs/DVDs, and subscribes to 3,900 periodicals including electronic. Computerized library services include interlibrary loans, database searching, Internet access, and Wi-Fi capability. Special learning facilities include an art gallery, planetarium, radio station, TV station, New Hampshire Institute of Politics and Political Library. **Physically Challenged Students:** 80% of the campus is accessible. Facilities include wheelchair ramps, elevators, special parking, specially equipped restrooms, special class scheduling, lowered drinking fountains, lowered telephones, and special housing. **Special:** Saint Anselm offers a 5-year liberal arts and a 3-2 engineering program in cooperation with Manhattan College, University of Notre Dame, University of Massachusetts Lowell, and Catholic University of America. Cross-registration is possible. In addition, internships, work-study, a Washington semester, a New York City semester, study abroad, and nondegree study are available. There are 11 national honor societies and a freshman honors program. **Visiting:** There are regularly scheduled orientations for prospective students, consisting of daily individual interviews and/or group information sessions followed by a campus tour. There are guides for informal visits and visitors may sit in on classes. To schedule a visit, contact the Office of Admission. **Campus Safety and Security:** Measures include 24-hour foot and vehicle patrol, emergency notification system, and self-defense education. There are emergency telephones, lighted pathways/sidewalks, and controlled access to dorms/residences.

REQUIREMENTS: Applicants must have 16 academic credits and 16 Carnegie units, including 4 years of English, 3 each of math and science, 2 of foreign language, and 1 each of history and social studies. An essay is required, and an interview is recommended. The GED is accepted. AP and CLEP credits are accepted. Important factors in the admissions decision are advanced placement or honors courses, leadership record, extracurricular activities record, recommendations by school officials, parents or siblings attended your school, evidence of special talent, personality/intangible qualities, recommendations by alumni, and geographical diversity. In the spirit of what is best in a liberal arts education, the academic core at Saint Anselm College has been designed to offer students a breadth of experience that will prepare them for life; an education that not only provides professional and career preparation, but also encourages a lifelong pursuit of truth that will sustain and enrich their lives. This education is facilitated through a core curriculum composed of a set of common courses and learning outcomes considered essential for the education of students in all majors. **Procedure:** Freshmen are admitted fall and spring. Entrance exams should be taken during the spring of the junior year or fall of the senior year. There are early admissions and deferred admissions plans. Early decision applications should be filed by November 15; regular applications, by February 1 for fall entry; and November 15 for spring entry, along with a $50 fee. Notifications are sent March 10. 196 applicants were on the 2014 waiting list; 38 were admitted. Applications are accepted on-line. **Transfer Students:** 21 transfer students enrolled in 2013-2014. 20 of 40 credits required for the Bachelor's degree must be completed at Saint Anselm. **International Students:** There are 12 international students enrolled. They must take the TOEFL with a minimum score of 80 on the Internet-based version (iBT).

ADMISSIONS: 76% of the 2014-2015 applicants were accepted. The SAT scores for the 2014-2015 freshman class were: Critical Reading--10% below 500, 57% between 500 and 599, 29% between 600 and 699, and 4% between 700 and 800; Math--11% below 500, 51% between 500 and 599, 36% between 600 and 699, and 2% between 700 and 800; Writing--11% below 500, 51% between 500 and 599, 34% between 600 and 699, and 4% between 700 and 800. The ACT scores were 6% below 21, 23% between 21 and 23, 37% between 24 and 26, 22% between 27 and 28, and 12% above 28. 56% of the current freshmen were in the top fifth of their class; 87% were in the top two fifths. **Admissions Contact:** Eric Nichols, Dean of Admission. E-Mail: *admission@anselm.edu* Web: *www.anselm.edu*

FINANCIAL AID: In 2014-2015, 96% of all full-time freshmen and 97% of continuing full-time students received some form of financial aid. The average freshman award was $25,200. Need-based scholarships or need-based grants averaged $20,050. Saint Anselm is a member of CSS. The CSS/Profile and FAFSA are required. The deadline for filing freshman financial aid applications for fall entry is March 15.

SOUTHERN NEW HAMPSHIRE UNIVERSITY · D-6
www.snhu.edu

Manchester, NH 03106

(603) 645-9611
(800) 642-4968

Fax: (603) 645-9693	Email: admission@snhu.edu
Full-time: 870 men, 1070 women	Faculty: n/av
Part-time: 25 men, 30 women	Ph.D.s: n/av
Graduate: 965 men, 1415 women	Student/Faculty: n/av
Year: semesters, summer session	Tuition: $28,380
Room & Board: $9720	Freshman Class: n/av
SAT or ACT: required	CEEB CODE: 3649
Application Deadline: n/av	COMPETITIVE

Southern New Hampshire University, founded in 1932, is a private university offering academic programs in business, education, liberal arts, culinary arts, and community economic development. SNHU also has continuing education and online education programs. The figures in the above capsule and in this profile are approximate. There are 5 undergraduate schools and 4 graduate schools. In addition to regional accreditation, SNHU has baccalaureate program accreditation with ACBSP and NASPE. The 280-acre campus is in a suburban area 55 miles north of Boston. Including any residence halls, there are 28 buildings.

STUDENT LIFE: 54% of undergraduates are from out of state, mostly the Northeast. Students are from 28 states, 54 foreign countries, and Canada. 88% are from public schools. 77% are White. 36% are Catholic; 29% claim no religious affiliation; 20% Protestant. **Male To Female Ratio:** 1.4:1. The average age of freshmen is 19; all undergraduates, 20. 25% do not continue beyond their first year; 50% remain to graduate. **Housing:** 1668 students can be accommodated in college housing, which includes single-sex and coed dorms and on-campus apartments. In addition, there are special-interest houses, and a wellness housing area. On-campus housing is guaranteed for all 4 years. 76% of students live on campus; of those, 65% remain on campus on weekends. All students may keep cars.

FACULTY/CLASSROOMS: 60% of faculty are male; 40% are female. 90% teach undergraduates, 78% do research, and 73% do both. No introductory courses are taught by graduate students. The average class size in an introductory lecture is 20; in a laboratory is 15; and in a regular course is 21.

PROGRAMS OF STUDY: SNHU confers B.A., B.S. and B.A.S.H.A. degrees. Associate, Master's, and Doctoral degrees are also awarded. Bachelor's degrees are awarded in AGRICULTURE (environmental studies), BUSINESS (accounting, business administration and management, fashion merchandising, hospitality management services, international business management, marketing management, marketing/retailing/merchandising, retailing, sports management, and tourism), COMMUNICATIONS AND THE ARTS (advertising, communications, creative writing, English, English as a second/foreign language, English literature, and graphic design), COMPUTER AND PHYSICAL SCIENCE (computer science, digital arts/technology, and information sciences and systems), EDUCATION (business education, early childhood education, education, elementary education, English education, secondary education, social studies education, and special education), ENGINEERING AND ENVIRONMENTAL DESIGN (technological management), SOCIAL SCIENCE (child psychology/development, culinary arts, history, liberal arts/general studies, political science/government, psychology, public affairs, and social science). Business administration is the strongest academically. Business administration, sports management, and psychology have the largest enrollments.

ACTIVITIES: 4% of men belong to 2 national fraternities; 5% of

women belong to 3 local and 1 national sororities. There are 52 groups on campus, including and field hockey, crew club, cheerleading, chess, chorus, dance, debate, drama, ethnic, gay, honors, international, musical theater, newspaper, political, professional, radio and TV, religious, social, social service, sports club, student government, and yearbook. Popular campus events include fall, winter, and spring weekends, and International Night. **Sports:** There is no sports program at SNHU. Facilities include 2 gyms, an Olympic-sized swimming pool, 4 lighted tennis courts, a lighted artificial surface game field, a fitness room, natural grass baseball, softball, and practice fields, a racquetball court, and an aerobic/excercise room. **Graduates:** From July 1, 2013 to June 30, 2014, 1141 bachelor's degrees were awarded. The most popular majors were business administration (42%), psychology (6%), and accounting (6%). 75 companies recruited on campus in 2013-2014. In an average class, 40% graduate in 4 years or less, 48% graduate in 5 years or less, and 50% graduate in 6 years or less. Of the 2013 graduating class, 11% were enrolled in graduate school within 6 months of graduation, and 85% were employed.

SERVICES: Counseling and information services are available, as is tutoring in every subject. There is a reader service for the blind, and remedial math and writing. Peer mentoring and structured learning assistance services are also available. There is also a Jump Start program available for the summer of pre-college. **Library/Resources:** The library contains 94,042 volumes, 378,319 microform items, 3,170 audio/video tapes/CDs/DVDs, and subscribes to 755 periodicals including electronic. Computerized library services include interlibrary loans, database searching, Internet access, and Wi-Fi capability. Special learning facilities include an art gallery, radio station, a center for financial studies, an advertising agency (on campus), an audiovisual studio, a psychology observation lab, a career development center, and an iMAC graphics lab. **Physically Challenged Students:** 80% of the campus is accessible. Facilities include wheelchair ramps, elevators, special parking, specially equipped restrooms, special class scheduling, lowered drinking fountains, lowered telephones, special housing. **Special:** There are co-ops available, a choice of over 35 study abroad opportunities through the University Studies Abroad Consortium, work-study positions throughout the campus, dual majors, and a 3-year bachelor's degree that is an accelerated degree program in business administration. There are 6 national honor societies, a freshman honors program, and 1 departmental honors program. **Visiting:** There are regularly scheduled orientations for prospective students, including a greeting from college administrators, campus tours with students, and informal presentation/discussions with faculty and staff. There are guides for informal visits and visitors may sit in on classes. To schedule a visit, contact the Admission Office. **Campus Safety and Security:** Measures include 24-hour foot and vehicle patrol, emergency notification system, and security escort services. There are emergency telephones, lighted pathways/sidewalks, controlled access to dorms/residences, winter driving seminars for international students, and public safety officers.

REQUIREMENTS: The SAT or ACT is required. The ACT Optional Writing test is also required. Students must have completed 4 years of English and 3 of math. An essay, high school transcript, SAT or ACT (with writing), and a letter of recommendation from a guidance counselor or 2 teachers are required. An interview is strongly recommended. The GED is accepted. A GPA of 2.0 is required. AP and CLEP credits are accepted.To graduate, students must complete a minimum of 120 credit hours, including 39 in their majors, with a GPA of 2.0. Distribution requirements total 45 credits from the college core, including 2 to 3 courses in writing, and 2 math, information technology, public speaking, statistics, behavioral, social and natural sciences, and electives in fine arts and literature. **Procedure:** Freshmen are admitted fall and spring. There are deferred admissions and rolling admissions plans. Application deadlines are open. Application fee is $40. Notification is sent on a rolling basis. Applications are accepted on-line. **Transfer Students:** 164 transfer students enrolled in 2013-2014. Transfer applicants must submit a completed application, essay, official high school transcript, official college transcripts, supplemental transfer form, and a letter of recommendation. An interview is also highly recommended. Most successful applicants for transfer admission have a cumulative GPA of 2.5 or higher. 30 of 120 credits required for the bachelor's degree must be completed at

SNHU. **International Students:** There are 89 international students enrolled. The school actively recruits these students. They must take the TOEFL.

ADMISSIONS: Steven Soba, Director of Admission. E-Mail: *admission@snhu.edu* Web: *www.snhu.edu*

FINANCIAL AID: In 2014-2015, 95% of all full-time freshmen and 92% of continuing full-time students received some form of financial aid. 76% of all full-time freshmen and 68% of continuing full-time students received need-based aid. SNHU is a member of CSS. The FAFSA is required. Check with the school for current application deadlines.

THOMAS MORE COLLEGE OF LIBERAL ARTS   D-6
www.thomasmorecollege.edu

Merrimack, NH 03054   (603) 880-8308 / (800) 880-8308

Fax: (603) 880-9280   Email: admissions@thomasmorecollege.edu

Full-time: 52 men, 44 women	**Faculty:** 5
Part-time: n/av	**Ph.D.s:** 100%
Graduate: n/av	**Student/Faculty:** 14 to 1
Year: semesters	**Tuition:** $19,200
Room & Board: $9400	**Freshman Class:** n/av
SAT or ACT: required	**CEEB CODE:** 3892
Application Deadline: open	**COMPETITIVE**

Thomas More College of Liberal Arts, founded in 1978 by Roman Catholic educators, is an undergraduate institution that combines intensive reading of the great books with lectures and seminar discussions placing those works in their historical, cultural, and theological context. Thomas More welcomes students of all faiths. Figures in the above capsule and in this profile are approximate. There is 1 undergraduate school. In addition to regional accreditation, Thomas More College has baccalaureate program accreditation with AALE. The 17-acre campus is in a small town between Nashua and Manchester, 40 miles north of Boston. Including any residence halls, there are 5 buildings.

STUDENT LIFE: 81% of undergraduates are from out of state, mostly the Northeast. Students are from 20 states, 2 foreign countries, and Canada. 84% are White. **Male To Female Ratio:** 0.8:1. The average age of freshmen is 18; all undergraduates, 20. 9% do not continue beyond their first year. **Housing:** All students commute. All students may keep cars.

FACULTY/CLASSROOMS: 80% of faculty are male; 20% are female. All teach undergraduates, 80% do research, and 80% do both. No introductory courses are taught by graduate students.

PROGRAMS OF STUDY: Thomas More College confers B.A. degrees. Bachelor's degrees are awarded in SOCIAL SCIENCE (liberal arts/general studies).

ACTIVITIES: There are no fraternities or sororities. Groups on campus include art, choir, chorale, chorus, dance, debate, drama, literary magazine, musical theater, newspaper, photography, radio and TV, and yearbook. Popular campus events include St. Patrick's Day. **Graduates:** From July 1, 2013 to June 30, 2014, 12 bachelor's degrees were awarded. The most popular majors were liberal arts (100%). In an average class, 100% graduate in 4 years or less. Of the 2013 graduating class, 27% were enrolled in graduate school within 6 months of graduation, and 73% were employed.

SERVICES: Counseling and information services are available, as is tutoring in most subjects. Informal tutoring is available by request. **Library/Resources:** The library contains 50,000 volumes, and subscribes to 20 periodicals including electronic. Computerized library services include Internet access. Special learning facilities include a radio station. **Physically Challenged Students:** 70% of the campus is accessible. Facilities include wheelchair ramps, special parking, and specially equipped restrooms. **Special:** A semester in Rome for sophomores is required. Internships are available at Vatican Radio, Zenit News, and the United Nations. **Visiting:** There are regularly scheduled orientations for prospective students. There are guides for informal visits and visitors may sit in on classes. To schedule a visit, contact the Director of Admissions. **Campus Safety and Security:** Measures include security escort services. There are lighted pathways/sidewalks.

REQUIREMENTS: The SAT or ACT is required. Applicants should be high school graduates with 4 college preparatory units of English, 3 of math, and 2 each of foreign language, social science, and lab science. The GED is accepted. An essay and 2 letters of recommendation are required. An interview is strongly recommended. Important factors in the admissions decision are personality/intangible qualities, evidence of special talent, and leadership record. To graduate, students in the classes of 2013 and beyond must complete 121 credit hours, including 32 in humanities, 12 each in classical languages, tutorials, philosophy, and sacred scripture, 9 in writing/rhetoric/poetics, 7 in fine arts, and 6 each in math, natural science, and theology. In addition, students must complete a junior project of independent study and a senior thesis and seminar. **Procedure:** Freshmen are admitted fall and spring. There is a rolling admissions plan. Application deadlines are open. Applications are accepted on-line. **Transfer Students:** 4 transfer students enrolled in 2013-2014. Applicants must submit a transcript from all higher institutions attended. **International Students:** There are 2 international students enrolled. The school actively recruits these students.

ADMISSIONS: There were 2 National Merit finalists. **Admissions Contact:** Mark Schwerdt, Director of Admissions. E-Mail: *admissions@thomasmorecollege.edu* Web: *www.thomasmorecollege.edu*

FINANCIAL AID: In 2014-2015, 80% of all full-time freshmen and 90% of continuing full-time students received some form of financial aid. 65% of all full-time freshmen and 77% of continuing full-time students received need-based aid. The average freshman award was $8,768. 59% of undergraduate students work part-time. Average annual earnings from campus work are $1960. The average financial indebtedness of the 2014 graduate was $13,056. Thomas More College is a member of CSS. The FAFSA is required. Check with the school for current application deadlines.

UNIVERSITY OF NEW HAMPSHIRE   E-5
www.unh.edu

Durham, NH 03824	(603) 862-1360
	n/av
Fax: (603) 862-0077	Email: admissions@unh.edu
Full-time: 5628 men, 6749 women	Faculty: 620; 1, +$
Part-time: 254 men, 209 women	Ph.D.s: 87%
Graduate: 988 men, 1344 women	Student/Faculty: 20 to 1
Year: semesters, summer session	Tuition: $16,552 ($29,532)
Room & Board: $10,360	Freshman Class: 18420 applied, 14740 accepted, 3227 enrolled
SAT CR/M/W: 536/552/536 ACT: 24	CEEB CODE: 3918
Application Deadline: February 1	COMPETITIVE

The University of New Hampshire, founded in 1866, is part of the public university system of New Hampshire and offers degree programs in liberal arts, engineering, physical sciences, business, economics, life sciences, agriculture, and health and human services. There are 6 undergraduate schools and 1 graduate school. In addition to regional accreditation, UNH has baccalaureate program accreditation with AACSB, ABET, ADA, CSWE, NASM, NRPA, SAF, TEAC, AACN, ACOTE, AEE, ASHA, AUPHA, CCIE, CEPH, COAMFTE, JRC-AT, NAACLS, and NAEYC. The 2600-acre campus is in a small town 50 miles north of Boston. Including any residence halls, there are 149 buildings.

STUDENT LIFE: 50% of undergraduates are from out of state, mostly the Northeast. Students are from 44 states, 34 foreign countries, and Canada. 81% are from public schools. 80% are White. **Male To Female Ratio:** 1.2:1. The average age of freshmen is 18; all undergraduates, 20. 14% do not continue beyond their first year; 77% remain to graduate. **Housing:** 7500 students can be accommodated in college housing, which includes coed dorms, on-campus apartments, and married student housing. In addition, there are honors houses, language houses, special-interest houses, international and substance-free residence halls. On-campus housing is guaranteed for the freshman year only, and is available on a first-come, first-served basis. 56% of students live on campus; of those, 65% remain on campus on weekends. Upperclassmen may keep cars.

FACULTY/CLASSROOMS: 50% of faculty are male; 50% are female. 90% teach undergraduates, all do research, and 90% do both. Graduate students teach 2% of introductory courses. The average class size in an introductory lecture is 52; in a laboratory is 22; and in a regular course is 24.

PROGRAMS OF STUDY: UNH confers B.A., B.F.A., B.Mus., B.S. and B.S.Forestry degrees. Associate, Master's, and Doctoral degrees are also awarded. Bachelor's degrees are awarded in AGRICULTURE (animal science, dairy science, environmental studies, forestry and related sciences, horticulture, and wildlife management), BIOLOGICAL SCIENCE (biochemistry, biology/biological science, genetics, microbiology, molecular biology, neurosciences, nutrition, and zoology), BUSINESS (applied management, business administration and management, hospitality management services, and tourism), COMMUNICATIONS AND THE ARTS (art history, classics, communications, English, fine arts, French, German, Greek, information technology, Latin, linguistics, music, recreation administration, Russian, Spanish, studio art, and theatre acting), COMPUTER AND PHYSICAL SCIENCE (applied mathematics, chemistry, computer information systems, computer science, earth science, geology, hydrology, mathematics, and physics), EDUCATION (athletic training, mathematics education, and physical education), ENGINEERING AND ENVIRONMENTAL DESIGN (bioengineering, chemical engineering, city/community/regional planning, civil engineering, computer engineering, electrical/electronics engineering, environmental engineering, environmental science, and mechanical engineering), HEALTH PROFESSIONS (biomedical science, health administration and policy, medical laboratory science, nursing, occupational therapy, speech pathology/audiology, and veterinary science), SOCIAL SCIENCE (anthropology, culinary arts, economics, European studies, family/consumer studies, French studies, geography, history, humanities, philosophy, physical fitness/movement, political science/government, psychology, social work, sociology, and women's studies). Marine biology, engineering, and English are the strongest academically. Business administration, psychology, and biomedical science have the largest enrollments.

ACTIVITIES: 12% of men belong to 12 national fraternities; 12% of women belong to 7 national sororities. There are 262 groups on campus, including art, band, cheerleading, chess, choir, chorale, chorus, computers, dance, debate, drama, environmental, ethnic, film, gay, honors, international, jazz band, literary magazine, marching band, musical theater, newspaper, orchestra, pep band, political, professional, radio and TV, religious, social, social service, student government, symphony, and yearbook. Popular campus events include Jukebox, Student Activities Fair, Concerts and Comedians, Winter Carnival, Athletic Events, Homecoming, MUB Lecture Series, May Day, and Kwanzaa Celebration. **Sports:** There are 31 intercollegiate sports for men and 36 for women, and 25 intramural sports for men and 26 for women. Facilities include indoor and outdoor swimming pools, tracks, tennis courts, gyms, wrestling and gymnastics rooms, dance studio, playing fields, indoor ice rink, cross-country ski trails, pond for sailing. A 3-story recreation and sports complex, which seats 6,500 for hockey and 7,500 for basketball games and special events, includes a fitness center, jogging track, weight room, racquetball courts, international squash court, aerobics and martial arts studios, multipurpose courts, and basketball courts. **Graduates:** From July 1, 2013 to June 30, 2014, 2671 bachelor's degrees were awarded. The most popular majors were business administration (16%), psychology (7%), speech, communication, and and rhetoric (5%). 200 companies recruited on campus in 2013-2014. In an average class, 66% graduate in 4 years or less, 76% graduate in 5 years or less, and 77% graduate in 6 years or less. Of the 2013 graduating class, 30% were enrolled in graduate school within 6 months of graduation, and 50% were employed.

SERVICES: Counseling and information services are available, as is tutoring in most subjects. Instruction in learning strategies, study skills, time management, and organizational skills is available. The university writing center offers free assistance by trained consultants.

Library/Resources: The 4 libraries contain 2.1 million volumes, 2.9 million microform items, 43,024 audio/video tapes/CDs/DVDs, and subscribe to 57,847 periodicals including electronic. Computerized library services include interlibrary loans, database searching, Internet access, and Wi-Fi capability. Special learning facilities include an art gallery, radio station, optical observatory, marine research labs, interoperability lab, flow physics facility, experiential learning center, electron microscope, child development center, journalism lab, wind tunnel, various agricultural and equine facilities, sawmill, language labs, performing arts center, and survey center. **Physically Challenged Students:** 88% of the campus is accessible. Facilities include wheelchair ramps, elevators, special parking, specially equipped restrooms, special class scheduling, lowered drinking fountains, lowered telephones, special housing. Accommodations made on a case-by-case basis include sign language interpreters, reduced course loads, extended exam time, accessible transportation, academic modifications, note takers, text on tape, and note takers. **Special:** Joint programs with Cornell University in marine science are available. Extensive cross-registration is possible through the New Hampshire College and University Council Consortium. There also is nationwide study through the National Student Exchange and worldwide study through the Center for International Education. Internships, study abroad throughout the world, a Washington semester, work-study, and B.A.-B.S. degrees, dual majors, a general studies degree, student-designed majors, extensive 3-2 B.S./M.B.A. programs and other bachelor's/graduate degree plans, nondegree study, and pass/fail options are also available. A 3-2 engineering degree is offered with the New Hampshire Technical Institute, Vermont Technical College, Keene State College, and other institutions. There are 20 national honor societies, including Phi Beta Kappa, a freshman honors program, and 67 departmental honors programs. **Visiting:** There are regularly scheduled orientations for prospective students, including campus tours, group information session, and open house programs. There are guides for informal visits and visitors may sit in on classes. To schedule a visit, contact the Admissions Office. **Campus Safety and Security:** Measures include 24-hour foot and vehicle patrol, emergency notification system, self-defense education, and security escort services. There are shuttle buses, emergency telephones, lighted pathways/sidewalks, controlled access to dorms/residences, prevention awareness programs.

REQUIREMENTS: The SAT or ACT is required. The ACT Optional Writing test is also required. Required: 15 academic units: 4 English, 3 mathematics, 3 science (at least 2 must include lab), 2 foreign language, 3 social studies. Recommended: 19 academic units: 4 English, 4 mathematics, 4 science (3 that include lab), 3 foreign language, 3 social studies, 1 visual/performing arts. Essay required for all students. Audition is required for music students. AP credits are accepted. Important factors in the admissions decision are advanced placement or honors courses, recommendations by school officials, and evidence of special talent. To graduate, all students must maintain a GPA of 2.0 and complete at least 128 credits, with a minimum of 36 credits and 10 classes in the major. General education requirements include 4 writing-intensive courses, including freshman composition, 3 courses in biological/physical science, 1 course each in quantitative reasoning, historical perspectives, social science, fine arts, foreign culture, and philosophy/literature. All seniors must complete a senior thesis or project. **Procedure:** Freshmen are admitted fall

and spring. Entrance exams should be taken before February 1 of the senior year. There are early decision and deferred admissions plans. Early decision applications should be filed by November 15; regular applications, by February 1 for fall entry; and October 15 for spring entry. The fall 2014 application fee was $50. Notification of early decision is sent January 15; regular decision, April 15. 8590 early decision candidates were accepted for the 2014-2015 class. Applications are accepted on-line. **Transfer Students:** 503 transfer students enrolled in 2013-2014. Applicants must submit an overall minimum GPA of 2.8 in a general education curriculum. The SAT or the ACT is required unless waived. An essay is required. A letter of recommendation is optional. 32 of 128 credits required for the bachelor's degree must be completed at UNH. **International Students:** There are 230 international students enrolled. The school actively recruits these students. They must take the TOEFL with a minimum score of 550 on the paper-based TOEFL (PBT) or 80 on the Internet-based version (iBT). They must also take the SAT or ACT.

ADMISSIONS: 80% of the 2014-2015 applicants were accepted. The SAT scores for the 2014-2015 freshman class were: Critical Reading--30% below 500, 50% between 500 and 599, 18% between 600 and 699, and 2% between 700 and 800; Math--21% below 500, 50% between 500 and 599, 26% between 600 and 699, and 3% between 700 and 800; Writing--29% below 500, 49% between 500 and 599, 20% between 600 and 699, and 2% between 700 and 800. 39% of the current freshmen were in the top fifth of their class; 73% were in the top two fifths. 37 freshmen graduated first in their class. **Admissions Contact:** Robert McGann, Director of Admissions. E-Mail: *admissions@unh.edu* Web: *www.unh.edu*

FINANCIAL AID: In 2014-2015, 85% of all full-time freshmen and 81% of continuing full-time students received some form of financial aid. 71% of all full-time freshmen and 66% of continuing full-time students received need-based aid. The average freshman award was $22,663. Need-based scholarships or need-based grants averaged $10,866 ($28,000 maximum); need-based self-help aid (loans and jobs) averaged $5,837 ($8,000 maximum); non-need-based athletic scholarships averaged $23,879 ($39,272 maximum); and other non-need-based awards and non-need-based scholarships averaged $10,042 ($40,000 maximum). 15% of undergraduate students work part-time. Average annual earnings from campus work are $2507. The average financial indebtedness of the 2014 graduate was $36,965. The FAFSA is required. The deadline for filing freshman financial aid applications for fall entry is March 1.

UNIVERSITY SYSTEM OF NEW HAMPSHIRE

The University System of New Hampshire, established in 1963, is a public system in New Hampshire. It is governed by a board of trustees, whose chief administrator is the chancellor. The primary goal of the system is to serve the higher educational needs of the people of New Hampshire. The main priorities are to provide a well-coordinated system of higher education, student access and diversity, and quality programs with a commitment to excellence. The total student enrollment of all four campuses is usually about 31,000 with 1080 faculty members. Altogether there are 131 baccalaureate, 68 master's, and 21 doctoral programs offered in the University System of New Hampshire. Profiles of the 4-year campuses are included in this section.

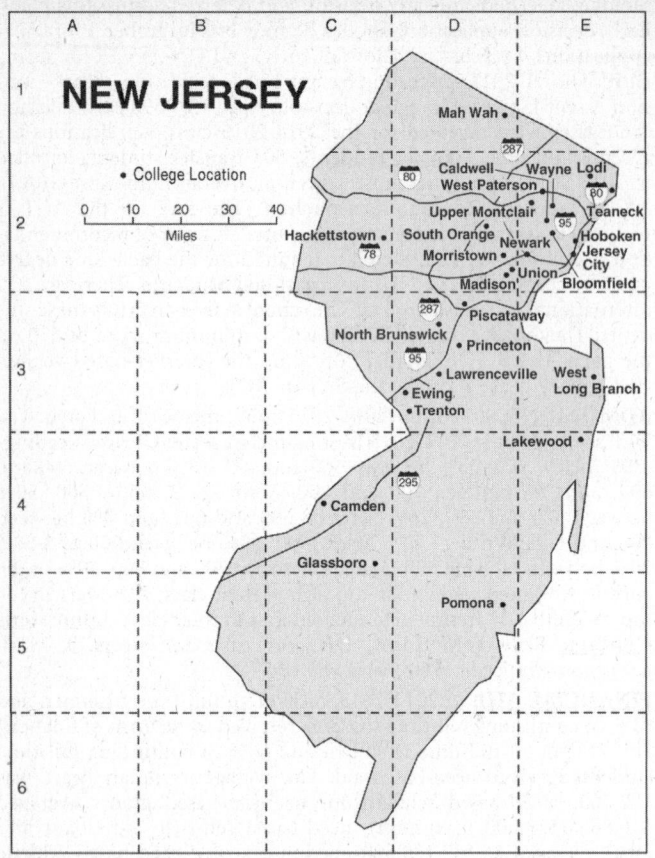

NEW JERSEY

- College Location

Miles 0 10 20 30 40

Mah Wah
Caldwell · Wayne Lodi
West Paterson
Upper Montclair · Teaneck
Hackettstown · South Orange · Hoboken
Morristown · Newark · Jersey City
Madison · Union · Bloomfield
Piscataway
North Brunswick · Princeton
Lawrenceville · West Long Branch
Ewing · Trenton
Lakewood
Camden
Glassboro
Pomona

BERKELEY COLLEGE/NEW JERSEY (*The complete profile is made available exclusively on our website, www.barronspac.com*)

BLOOMFIELD COLLEGE (*The complete profile is made available exclusively on our website, www.barronspac.com*)

CALDWELL COLLEGE (*The complete profile is made available exclusively on our website, www.barronspac.com*)

CENTENARY COLLEGE   C-2
www.centenarycollege.edu

Hackettstown, NJ 07840   (908) 852-1400
                                              (800) 236-8679
Fax: (908) 852-3454   Email: admissions@centenarycollege.edu
Full-time: 680 men, 1160 women   Faculty: 72; IIB, -$
Part-time: 58 men, 95 women   Ph.D.s: 54%
Graduate: 229 men, 472 women   Student/Faculty: 26 to 1
Year: semesters, summer session   Tuition: $28,890
Room & Board: $9720   Freshman Class: 753
                                   applied, 672 accepted, 272
                                   enrolled
SAT CR/M: 465/463 ACT: 21   CEEB CODE: 2080
Application Deadline: open   COMPETITIVE

Centenary College, founded in 1867, is a private institution affiliated with the United Methodist Church. The college offers undergraduate and graduate programs in liberal arts, business, international studies, education, equine studies, fashion, and fine arts. Figures in the above capsule and in this profile are approximate. There is one graduate school. In addition to regional accreditation, Centenary has baccalaureate program accreditation with CSWE, NASDTEC, and TEAC. The 42-acre campus is in a suburban area 55 miles west of New York City. Including any residence halls, there are 22 buildings.

STUDENT LIFE: 88% of undergraduates are from New Jersey.

Others are from 21 states, 8 foreign countries, and Canada. 85% are from public schools. 66% are White. **Male To Female Ratio:** 1.8:1. The average age of freshmen is 18; all undergraduates, 24. 24% do not continue beyond their first year; 51% remain to graduate. **Housing:** 756 students can be accommodated in college housing, which includes single-sex and coed dorms and on-campus apartments. On-campus housing is available on a first-come, first-served basis, and is available on a lottery system for upperclassmen. 54% of students live on campus; of those, 70% remain on campus on weekends. All students may keep cars.

FACULTY/CLASSROOMS: 44% of faculty are male; 56% are female. All teach and do research. No introductory courses are taught by graduate students. The average class size in an introductory lecture is 25; in a laboratory is 20; and in a regular course is 15.

PROGRAMS OF STUDY: Centenary confers B.A., B.F.A. and B.S. degrees. Associate and Master's degrees are also awarded. Bachelor's degrees are awarded in AGRICULTURE (equine science), BIOLOGICAL SCIENCE (biology/biological science), BUSINESS (accounting and business administration and management), COMMUNICATIONS AND THE ARTS (applied art, communications, dramatic arts, and English), COMPUTER AND PHYSICAL SCIENCE (mathematics), EDUCATION (elementary education and secondary education), SOCIAL SCIENCE (criminal justice, fashion design and technology, history, interdisciplinary studies, international studies, political science/government, psychology, and sociology). Equine studies, business, and education are the strongest academically.

ACTIVITIES: 3% of men belong to 1 local fraternity; 5% of women belong to 3 local sororities. There are 30 groups on campus, including art, chorus, dance, debate, drama, environmental, ethnic, gay, honors, international, literary magazine, newspaper, photography, political, professional, radio and TV, religious, social, social service, student government, and yearbook. Popular campus events include President's Ball, Community Plunge, and Tis the Season. **Sports:** There are 7 intercollegiate sports for men and 7 for women. Facilities include a gym, a fitness center and indoor pool, tennis courts, playing fields, and an equine center and stables. **Graduates:** From July 1, 2013 to June 30, 2014, 524 bachelor's degrees were awarded. The most popular majors were business administration (51%), social sciences (9%), and psychology (8%). 35 companies recruited on campus in 2013-2014. In an average class, 51% graduate in 4 years or less, 51% graduate in 5 years or less, and 52% graduate in 6 years or less. Of the 2013 graduating class, 10% were enrolled in graduate school within 6 months of graduation, and 75% were employed.

SERVICES: Counseling and information services are available, as is tutoring in every subject, as requested. There is remedial math, reading, and writing. Learning associates provide personalized subject matter support. **Library/Resources:** The library contains 68,000 volumes, 20,000 microform items, 5,000 audio/video tapes/CDs/DVDs, and subscribes to 375 periodicals including electronic. Computerized library services include interlibrary loans, database searching, Internet access, and Wi-Fi capability. Special learning facilities include a radio station, TV station, an equestrian center, CAD lab, and wireless network. **Physically Challenged Students:** 60% of the campus is accessible. Facilities include wheelchair ramps, special parking, specially equipped restrooms, special class scheduling, and lowered telephones. **Special:** Centenary offers internships in every major. The college offers study abroad in England and other countries, dual majors, as long as they are covered under the same degree, an accelerated degree program in liberal arts and business administration, student-designed majors, work-study on-campus, and a pass/fail option. Students ages 25 or older may earn life experience credits. There is 1 national honor society and a freshman honors program. **Visiting:** There are regularly scheduled orientations for prospective students, including basic skills testing, advising, registration, and social events. Visitors may sit in on classes and stay overnight. To schedule a visit, contact the Admissions Office. **Campus Safety and Security:** Measures include 24-hour foot and vehicle patrol, emergency notification system, and security escort services. There are emergency telephones, lighted pathways/sidewalks, and controlled access to dorms/residences.

REQUIREMENTS: The SAT or ACT is required. Minimum scores include a satisfactory SAT score or an ACT composite of 18. Applicants must be graduates of accredited secondary schools or have earned a GED. Centenary requires 16 academic credits or Carnegie units, based on 4 years of English, math, and science, and 2 years each of foreign language and history. An essay is required for freshmen, and an interview is recommended. Applicants to specific fine arts programs must also submit a portfolio. A GPA of 2.0 is required. AP and CLEP credits are accepted. Important factors in the admissions decision are advanced placement or honors courses, leadership record, and ability to finance college education. Students must complete a distribution of 40 to 46 semester hours in core courses, including college seminars, and 9 credits in liberal arts studies, as well as the required number of credits, usually 48, for their majors. At least 128 semester hours and a minimum GPA of 2.0 are needed to earn the bachelor's degree. **Procedure:** Freshmen are admitted fall and spring. Entrance exams should be taken as early as possible in the senior year. There are deferred admissions and rolling admissions plans. Application deadlines are open. Application fee is $30. Notification is sent on a rolling basis. Applications are accepted on-line. **Transfer Students:** 178 transfer students enrolled in 2013-2014. Applicants must have a minimum college GPA of 2.0 and submit proof of high school graduation or the equivalent. 32 of 128 credits required for the bachelor's degree must be completed at Centenary. **International Students:** There are 54 international students enrolled. The school actively recruits these students. They must take the TOEFL with a minimum score of 520 on the paper-based TOEFL (PBT) or 80 on the Internet-based version (iBT), or IELTS with a score of 5.0. They must also take the SAT or ACT.

ADMISSIONS: 89% of the 2014-2015 applicants were accepted. The SAT scores for the 2014-2015 freshman class were: Critical Reading--67% below 500, 25% between 500 and 599, 7% between 600 and 699, and 1% between 700 and 800; Math--65% below 500, 30% between 500 and 599, and 5% between 600 and 699. The ACT scores were 29% below 21, 43% between 21 and 23, 7% between 24 and 26, 7% between 27 and 28, and 14% above 28. **Admissions Contact:** Glenna Warren, Dean of Admissions and Financial Aid. E-Mail: *admissions@ centenarycollege.edu* Web: *www.centenarycollege.edu*

FINANCIAL AID: In 2014-2015, 85% of all full-time freshmen and 88% of continuing full-time students received some form of financial aid. 84% of all full-time freshmen and 85% of continuing full-time students received need-based aid. The average freshman award was $19,100. Need-based scholarships or need-based grants averaged $14,806; and need-based self-help aid (loans and jobs) averaged $5,279. 75% of undergraduate students work part-time. Average annual earnings from campus work are $1200. The average financial indebtedness of the 2014 graduate was $28,104. The FAFSA, and other forms as requested is required. The priority date for freshman financial aid applications for fall entry is March 15. The deadline for filing freshman financial aid applications for fall entry is September 1.

COLLEGE OF NEW JERSEY

D-3

www.tcnj.edu

Ewing, NJ 08628	(609) 771-2131
	(800) 624-0967
Fax: (609) 637-5174	Email: tcnjinfo@tcnj.edu
Full-time: 2775 men, 3680 women	Faculty: 342; IIA, ++$
Part-time: 76 men, 122 women	Ph.D.s: 88%
Graduate: 107 men, 580 women	Student/Faculty: 13 to 1
Year: semesters, summer session	Tuition: $14,730 ($25,135)
Room & Board: $11,343	Freshman Class: 11145 applied, 4828 accepted, 1404 enrolled
SAT CR/M/W: 610/640/620	CEEB CODE: 2519
Application Deadline: January 15	HIGHLY COMPETITIVE

The College of New Jersey, founded in 1855, is a public institution offering programs in the liberal arts, sciences, business, engineering, nursing, and education. There are 7 undergraduate schools and 1 graduate school. In addition to regional accreditation, TCNJ has baccalaureate program accreditation with AACSB, ABET, NASM,

NCATE, and NLN. The 289-acre campus is in a suburban area between Princeton and Trenton, NJ. Including any residence halls, there are 61 buildings.

STUDENT LIFE: 94% of undergraduates are from New Jersey. Others are from 23 states, 30 foreign countries, and Canada. 70% are from public schools. 66% are White; 11% Hispanic. 48% are Catholic; 17% Protestant; 15% claim no religious affiliation; 15% Eastern Orthodox, Buddhist, Muslim, Islamic and Quaker. **Male To Female Ratio:** 1.5:1. The average age of freshmen is 18; all undergraduates, 20. 6% do not continue beyond their first year; 86% remain to graduate. **Housing:** 4000 students can be accommodated in college housing, which includes single-sex and coed dorms, on-campus apartments, and off-campus apartments. In addition, there are special-interest houses. All freshman participate in the First Seminar Program and are housed in learning communities that connect the academic and social aspects of the college environment. On-campus housing is guaranteed for the freshman year only and is available on a lottery system for upperclassmen. 52% of students commute. Upperclassmen may keep cars.

FACULTY/CLASSROOMS: 49% of faculty are male; 51% are female. All teach undergraduates, and 85% do both. No introductory courses are taught by graduate students. The average class size in an introductory lecture is 25; in a laboratory is 17; and in a regular course is 21.

PROGRAMS OF STUDY: TCNJ confers B.A., B.S., B.A.B.M.E., B.F.A., B.M., B.S.C.E., B.S.Co.E., B.S.E.E., B.S.M.E. and B.S.N. degrees. Master's degrees are also awarded. Bachelor's degrees are awarded in BIOLOGICAL SCIENCE (biology/biological science), BUSINESS (accounting and business administration and management), COMMUNICATIONS AND THE ARTS (art, art history and appreciation, communications, English, fine arts, graphic design, multimedia, music, and Spanish), COMPUTER AND PHYSICAL SCIENCE (chemistry, computer science, digital arts/technology, mathematics, and physics), EDUCATION (art education, early childhood education, education of the deaf and hearing impaired, elementary education, English education, health education, mathematics education, music education, physical education, science education, social science education, social studies education, special education, and technical education), ENGINEERING AND ENVIRONMENTAL DESIGN (biomedical engineering, civil engineering, computer engineering, electrical/electronics engineering, engineering and applied science, and mechanical engineering), HEALTH PROFESSIONS (exercise science and nursing), SOCIAL SCIENCE (criminal justice, economics, history, international studies, philosophy, political science/government, psychology, sociology, and women's studies). Biology, education, and engineering are the strongest academically. Psychology, biology, and elementary education have the largest enrollment.

ACTIVITIES: 9% of men belong to 14 national fraternities; 11% of women belong to 13 national sororities. There are 226 groups on campus, including foreign language, art, band, cheerleading, chess, choir, chorale, chorus, computers, dance, drama, environmental, ethnic, film, forensics, gay, honors, international, jazz band, literary magazine, musical theater, newspaper, opera, orchestra, pep band, photography, political, professional, radio and TV, recreational, religious, social, social service, student government, symphony, and yearbook. Popular campus events include Lallanobozza, Mystique of the EAST, and TCNJ Later Nighter. **Sports:** There are 9 intercollegiate sports for men and 9 for women, and 14 intramural sports for men and 14 for women. Facilities include a 5000-seat stadium with an Astroturf field, an aquatic center, baseball and softball diamonds, a Sportexe-surface soccer/multipurpose field, an all-weather track, a sand volleyball court, 5 grass playing fields, a 1200-seat gym, a physical enhancement center, a student recreation center, tennis, racquetball, and basketball/volleyball courts, and a free weight room. **Graduates:** From July 1, 2013 to June 30, 2014, 1568 bachelor's degrees were awarded. The most popular majors were business/finance (18%), psychology (7%), and education (3%). 400 companies recruited on campus in 2013-2014. In an average class, 1% graduate in 3 years or less, 76% graduate in 4 years or less, 87% graduate in 5 years or less, and 87% graduate in 6 years or less. Of the 2013 graduating class, 33% were enrolled in graduate school within 6 months of graduation, and 95% were employed.

SERVICES: Counseling and information services are available, as is

tutoring in most subjects. There is a reader service for the blind, and remedial math, reading, and writing. **Library/Resources:** The library contains 694,144 volumes, 426,253 microform items, 40,127 audio/video tapes/CDs/DVDs, and subscribes to 73,733 periodicals including electronic. Computerized library services include interlibrary loans, database searching, Internet access, and Wi-Fi capability. Special learning facilities include an art gallery, planetarium, radio station, TV station, electron microscopy lab, nuclear magnetic resonance lab, optical spectroscopy lab, observatory, planetarium, and greenhouse. **Physically Challenged Students:** 90% of the campus is accessible. Facilities include wheelchair ramps, elevators, special parking, specially equipped restrooms, special class scheduling, lowered drinking fountains, lowered telephones, special housing. **Special:** TCNJ offers cross-registration with the New Jersey Marine Science Consortium, a limited number of overseas internship possibilities, numerous internships in the public and private sectors, a Washington semester, and study abroad in more than a dozen countries. Pass/fail options and some dual majors are possible. Specially designed research courses allow students to participate in collaborative scholarly projects with members of the faculty, and the Bonner Center offers opportunities for community-engaged initiatives. Combined advanced and accelerated degree programs are offered in education of the deaf and hard of hearing, special education, medicine, and optometry. There are 16 national honor societies, including Phi Beta Kappa, a freshman honors program, and 40 departmental honors programs. **Visiting:** There are regularly scheduled orientations for prospective students, consisting of an admissions presentation and a tour of campus. Reservations are required. There are guides for informal visits, visitors may sit in on classes, and stay overnight. To schedule a visit, contact the Admissions Office. **Campus Safety and Security:** Measures include 24-hour foot and vehicle patrol, emergency notification system, self-defense education, and security escort services. There are emergency telephones, lighted pathways/sidewalks, and controlled access to dorms/residences.

REQUIREMENTS: The SAT is required. Applicants must have earned 16 academic credits in high school, consisting of 4 in English, 3 each in math and science, 2 each in foreign language and social studies, and 6 others distributed among math, science, social studies, and a foreign language. An essay is required. Art majors must submit a portfolio, and music majors must audition. The GED is accepted. A GPA of 2.0 is required. AP and CLEP credits are accepted. Important factors in the admissions decision are advanced placement or honors courses, leadership record, and evidence of special talent. To graduate, students must complete a liberal learning curriculum of 128 to 136 credit hours that includes at least 1 major, as well as a suite of courses that address 3 interdependent structural elements: intellectual and scholarly growth; civic responsibilities; and the broad sectors of human inquiry within the arts and humanities, social sciences, natural sciences, and quantitative reasoning. **Procedure:** Freshmen are admitted fall and spring. Entrance exams should be taken by the end of the junior year or early in the senior year. There are early decision and rolling admissions plans. Early decision applications should be filed by November 15; regular applications, by January 15 for fall entry; and November 15 for spring entry, along with a $75 fee. Notification of early decision is sent December 15; regular decision, January 15. 344 early decision candidates were accepted for the 2014-2015 class. 529 applicants were on the 2014 waiting list; 37 were admitted. Applications are accepted on-line. **Transfer Students:** 258 transfer students enrolled in 2013-2014. Transfer students must have a minimum GPA of 2.5, and those with fewer than 33 credits must submit SAT scores. An associate degree is recommended. All transfer students must submit high school transcripts. 12 of 34 credits required for the bachelor's degree must be completed at TCNJ. **International Students:** There are 23 international students enrolled. They must take the TOEFL with a minimum score of 550 on the paper-based TOEFL (PBT) or 90 on the Internet-based version (iBT). They must also take the SAT or ACT. The SAT is required for merit scholarship consideration.

ADMISSIONS: 43% of the 2014-2015 applicants were accepted. The SAT scores for the 2014-2015 freshman class were: Critical Reading--7% below 500, 38% between 500 and 599, 43% between 600 and 699, and 12% between 700 and 800; Math--4% below 500, 27% between 500 and 599, 51% between 600 and 699, and 18% between

700 and 800; Writing--8% below 500, 32% between 500 and 599, 44% between 600 and 699, and 16% between 700 and 800. 87% of the current freshmen were in the top fifth of their class; 98% were in the top two fifths. 13 freshmen graduated first in their class. **Admissions Contact:** Grecia Montero, Director of Admissions. E-Mail: *tcnjinfo@tcnj.edu* Web: *www.tcnj.edu*

FINANCIAL AID: In 2014-2015, 70% of all full-time freshmen and 62% of continuing full-time students received some form of financial aid. 55% of all full-time freshmen and 52% of continuing full-time students received need-based aid. The average freshman award was $11,034. Need-based scholarships or need-based grants averaged $14,369; need-based self-help aid (loans and jobs) averaged $3,636; and other non-need-based awards and non-need-based scholarships averaged $5,798. 21% of undergraduate students work part-time. Average annual earnings from campus work are $2400. The average financial indebtedness of the 2014 graduate was $21,032. TCNJ is a member of CSS. The FAFSA, and copies of students' and parents' tax returns as applicable is required. The priority date for freshman financial aid applications for fall entry is March 1. The deadline for filing freshman financial aid applications for fall entry is October 1.

COLLEGE OF SAINT ELIZABETH *(The complete profile is made available exclusively on our website, www.barronspac.com)*

DREW UNIVERSITY/COLLEGE OF LIBERAL ARTS www.drew.edu	D-2
Madison, NJ 07940	(973) 408-DREW
	n/av
Fax: (973) 408-3068	Email: cadm@drew.edu
Full-time: 515 men, 842 women	Faculty: 123; IIA, +$
Part-time: 20 men, 40 women	Ph.D.s: 99%
Graduate: 331 men, 365 women	Student/Faculty: 11 to 1
Year: semesters, summer session	Tuition: $45,214
Room & Board: $12,302	Freshman Class: n/av
SAT CR/M/W: 550/550/560 ACT: 25	CEEB CODE: 2193
Application Deadline: February 15	COMPETITIVE

The College of Liberal Arts was added to Drew University in 1928 and is part of an educational complex that includes a theological school and a graduate school. Drew is a private, independent institution. There is 1 undergraduate school and 2 graduate schools. The 186-acre campus is in a suburban area 30 miles west of New York City. Including any residence halls, there are 57 buildings.

STUDENT LIFE: 65% of undergraduates are from New Jersey. Others are from 39 states, and 25 foreign countries. 54% are White; 12% Hispanic. **Male To Female Ratio:** 1.4:1. The average age of freshmen is 18; all undergraduates, 20. 16% do not continue beyond their first year; 69% remain to graduate. **Housing:** 1263 students can be accommodated in college housing, which includes single-sex and coed dorms and on-campus apartments. In addition, there are special-interest houses. On-campus housing is guaranteed for all 4 years. 74% of students live on campus; of those, 70% remain on campus on weekends. Upperclassmen may keep cars.

FACULTY/CLASSROOMS: 49% of faculty are male; 51% are female. 74% teach undergraduates. No introductory courses are taught by graduate students. The average class size in an introductory lecture is 25; in a laboratory is 20; and in a regular course is 17.

PROGRAMS OF STUDY: Drew confers B.A. degrees. Master's and Doctoral degrees are also awarded. Bachelor's degrees are awarded in AGRICULTURE (environmental studies), BIOLOGICAL SCIENCE (biochemistry, biology/biological science, and neurosciences), COMMUNICATIONS AND THE ARTS (art, art history and appreciation, Chinese, classics, English, French, German, music, Spanish, and theatre arts), COMPUTER AND PHYSICAL SCIENCE (chemistry, computer science, mathematics, and physics), SOCIAL SCIENCE (African studies, anthropology, economics, history, international relations, philosophy, political science/government, psychology, religion, sociology, and women's studies). Theatre arts, business studies, and neuroscience arts are the strongest academically. Psychology, economics, and business studies have the largest enrollments.

ACTIVITIES: There are 80 groups on campus, including On A Different Note and All of the Above a Capela Ensembles, 36 Madison Avenue, art, cheerleading, choir, chorale, chorus, computers, dance, drama, environmental, ethnic, film, gay, honors, international, jazz band, literary magazine, newspaper, orchestra, photography, political, professional, radio and TV, religious, social, social service, student government, and yearbook. Popular campus events include Drew Forum Lecture Series, First Annual Picnic, Holiday Ball, Jam-Fest a Capella Concert, Chamber Music Society of Lincoln Center Concert Series, Drew Theatre productions, MedFest - That Medieval Thing, Bear-B-Que, Boardwalk Night, Hoyt Halloween,. **Sports:** There are 11 intercollegiate sports for men and 12 for women, and 12 intramural sports for men and 12 for women. Facilities include an artificial turf athletic field with a 1000-seat gym, a 1000-seat auditorium, a swimming pool, a lighted tennis complex, a weight training room, a game room, an indoor track, a forest preserve, and an arboretum. **Graduates:** From July 1, 2013 to June 30, 2014, 349 bachelor's degrees were awarded. The most popular majors were economics (9%), psychology (9%), and business studies (8%). In an average class, 65% graduate in 4 years or less, 68% graduate in 5 years or less, and 69% graduate in 6 years or less.

SERVICES: Counseling and information services are available, as is tutoring in most subjects. There is a reader service for the blind. **Library/Resources:** The library contains 642,749 volumes, 517,242 microform items, and 6,459 audio/video tapes/CDs/DVDs. Computerized library services include interlibrary loans, database searching, Internet access, and Wi-Fi capability. Special learning facilities include an art gallery, radio station, Drew has an observatory and an arboretum. It is also home to the Charles A. Dana Center for Research Scientists Emeriti and the Shakespeare Theatre of New Jersey. **Physically Challenged Students:** Facilities include wheelchair ramps, elevators, special parking, specially equipped restrooms, special class scheduling, lowered drinking fountains, lowered telephones, special housing. The main dining facility, the student center and commons, and the ground floor of every dorm and classroom building are accessible to students with physical disabilities. **Special:** Civic Scholars program, seven-year dual degree program (BA/MD) with Rutgers-New Jersey Medical School, dual degree program (BA/BS) in engineering with Columbia University, five-year dual degree (BA/MA) in teaching at Drew University, student-designed majors, internships, cross-registration with the College of Saint Elizabeth and Fairleigh Dickinson University, Wall Street semester, United Nations semester, Semester on Contemporary Art, Semester on Communications and Media, study-abroad opportunities. There are 11 national honor societies, Phi Beta Kappa, a freshman honors program, and 12 departmental honors programs. **Visiting:** There are regularly scheduled orientations for prospective students, traditionally, open houses begin early in the morning and run through early afternoon. The day includes campus tours, information sessions about admissions and financial assistance, and presentations about student life and academics. There are guides for informal visits and visitors may sit in on classes. To schedule a visit, contact the Office of College Admissions. **Campus Safety and Security:** Measures include 24-hour foot and vehicle patrol, emergency notification system, self-defense education, and security escort services. There are shuttle buses, emergency telephones, lighted pathways/sidewalks, and controlled access to dorms/residences.

REQUIREMENTS: The SAT or ACT is required. The university strongly recommends 18 academic credits or Carnegie units, including 4 in English, 3 in math, 3 in the same foreign language, 3 in science including 2 lab courses, 3 in history, with the remaining 2 in other academic courses. An essay is also required, and an interview is recommended. AP and CLEP credits are accepted.To graduate, students must earn at least 128 credits, of which at least 64 must be beyond the lower level and at least 32 must be at the upper level. All students must fulfill the requirements of a major and those of the general education program. For graduation, the cumulative GPA, both overall and in the major, must be at least 2.0. General education requirements include a first-year seminar, demonstration of writing competency, at least 8 credits in foreign language and fulfillment of a language-in-context requirement, and completion of at least 4 cred-

its in each of 2 different departments in the following 4 divisions: natural and mathematical sciences, social sciences, humanities, and arts and literature. Each student may also complete a minor. **Procedure:** Freshmen are admitted fall and spring. Entrance exams should be taken by January of the senior year. There are early decision, early admissions, and deferred admissions plans. Early decision applications should be filed by December 1; regular applications, by February 15 for fall entry, along with a $60 fee. Notification of early decision is sent December 15; regular decision, March 30. 58 early decision candidates were accepted for the 2014-2015 class. Applications are accepted on-line. **Transfer Students:** Applicants must submit official high school and college transcripts, a personal essay, and a statement of good standing from previous schools attended. An interview also may be required. Students with fewer then 12 credits must apply as entering freshman. 48 of 128 credits required for the bachelor's degree must be completed at Drew. **International Students:** There are 64 international students enrolled. The school actively recruits these students. They must take the TOEFL with a minimum score of 550 on the paper-based TOEFL (PBT) or 80 on the Internet-based version (iBT).

ADMISSIONS: The SAT scores for the 2014-2015 freshman class were: Critical Reading--24% below 500, 41% between 500 and 599, 30% between 600 and 699, and 5% between 700 and 800; Math--22% below 500, 50% between 500 and 599, 26% between 600 and 699, and 3% between 700 and 800; Writing--25% below 500, 43% between 500 and 599, 27% between 600 and 699, and 5% between 700 and 800. The ACT scores were 19% below 21, 20% between 21 and 23, 26% between 24 and 26, 12% between 27 and 28, and 23% above 28. **Admissions Contact:** Mark Kopenski, Vice President of Enrollment Management. E-Mail: *cadm@drew.edu* Web: *www.drew.edu*

FINANCIAL AID: The average freshman award was $33,797. Need-based scholarships or need-based grants averaged $32,927; need-based self-help aid (loans and jobs) averaged $4,162; and other non-need-based awards and non-need-based scholarships averaged $18,346. The average financial indebtedness of the 2014 graduate was $24,778. The FAFSA is required. The deadline for filing freshman financial aid applications for fall entry is February 15.

FAIRLEIGH DICKINSON UNIVERSITY SYSTEM

The Fairleigh Dickinson University System, established in 1942, is a private system in New Jersey. It is governed by a board of trustees, whose chief administrator is the president. The primary goal of the system is teaching/research. The main priorities are to provide an academically challenging learning experience to prepare students for employment or enrollment in graduate and professional schools; to promote independent thinking and collaborative learning in students; to cultivate a holistic, integrated living-learning experience as part of the educational process; and to foster the ideals of good citizenship and community service. The total student enrollment is usually about 12,000 with 700 faculty members. Altogether there are 38 baccalaureate, 51 master's, and 1 doctoral program offered in the Fairleigh Dickinson University System. Profiles of the 4-year campuses are included in this section.

FAIRLEIGH DICKINSON UNIVERSITY/ COLLEGE AT FLORHAM www.fdu.edu	**D-2**
Madison, NJ 07940	**(973) 443-8900** **(800) 338-8803**
Fax: (973) 443-8088	**Email:** globaleducation@fdu.edu
Full-time: 1076 men, 1205 women	**Faculty:** IIA, +$
Part-time: 98 men, 101 women	**Ph.Ds:** n/av
Graduate: 512 men, 517 women	**Student/Faculty:** n/av
Year: semesters, summer session	**Tuition:** $31,084
Room & Board: $11,058	**Freshman Class:** 3907 applied, 2601 accepted, 646 enrolled
SAT CR/M/W: 520/530/520 **ACT:** required	
	CEEB CODE: 2262
Application Deadline: open	**COMPETITIVE**

Fairleigh Dickinson University/College at Florham, founded in 1942, is an independent university offering undergraduate, graduate, and professional level programs. Studies are rooted in the liberal arts but also offer hands-on opportunities in business and professional internships, cooperative education, and global studies abroad. Figures in the above capsule and in this profile are approximate. There are 3 undergraduate schools and 2 graduate schools. In addition to regional accreditation, College at Florham has baccalaureate program accreditation with AACSB, NASDTEC, and ACS. The 166-acre campus is in a suburban area 27 miles west of New York City. Including any residence halls, there are 36 buildings.

STUDENT LIFE: 85% of undergraduates are from New Jersey. Others are from 27 states, 12 foreign countries, and Canada. 69% are White. **Male To Female Ratio:** 1.1:1. The average age of freshmen is 18; all undergraduates, 20. 25% do not continue beyond their first year; 52% remain to graduate. **Housing:** 1500 students can be accommodated in college housing, which includes coed dorms. In addition, there are honors houses and special-interest houses. On-campus housing is available on a first-come and first-served basis. Priority is given to out-of-town students. 60% of students live on campus; of those, 75% remain on campus on weekends. Upperclassmen may keep cars.

FACULTY/CLASSROOMS: No introductory courses are taught by graduate students.

PROGRAMS OF STUDY: College at Florham confers B.A., B.S., B.S.A.H.T., B.S.C.L.S. and B.S.N. degrees. Master's degrees are also awarded. Bachelor's degrees are awarded in BIOLOGICAL SCIENCE (biochemistry and biology/biological science), BUSINESS (accounting, banking and finance, business administration and management, entrepreneurial studies, hotel/motel and restaurant management, and marketing/retailing/merchandising), COMMUNICATIONS AND THE ARTS (animation, communications, creative writing, dramatic arts, film arts, fine arts, literature, and video), COMPUTER AND PHYSICAL SCIENCE (chemistry, computer science, mathematics, and radiological technology), HEALTH PROFESSIONS (allied health, clinical science, medical laboratory technology, and nursing), SOCIAL SCIENCE (economics, French studies, history, humanities, liberal arts/general studies, philosophy, political science/government, psychology, sociology, and Spanish studies). Psychology, business management, and communications have the largest enrollments.

ACTIVITIES: There are 44 groups on campus, including cheerleading, chorale, computers, dance, environmental, ethnic, gay, honors, international, literary magazine, newspaper, political, professional, radio and TV, religious, social, social service, and student government. Popular campus events include Florham Fest and Haunted Mansion. **Sports:** There are 9 intercollegiate sports for men and 9 for women, and 7 intramural sports for men and 5 for women. Facilities include a state-of-the-art synthetic turf field for football, field hockey, soccer, and lacrosse. **Graduates:** From July 1, 2013 to June 30, 2014, 522 bachelor's degrees were awarded. The most popular majors were psychology (14%), business/marketing (12%), and communications (8%). 200 companies recruited on campus in 2013-2014. In an average class, 35% graduate in 4 years or less, 48% graduate in 5 years or less, and 52% graduate in 6 years or less.

SERVICES: Counseling and information services are available, as is tutoring in most subjects. There is a reader service for the blind, and remedial math, reading, and writing. Oral interpretation for the hearing impaired. Workshops also offer assistance with study skills and time management, and support services for basic skills students and freshmen are available. There is a Regional Center for College Students with Learning Disabilities that offers comprehensive support to students admitted to the program. **Library/Resources:** The library contains 149,850 volumes, 19,236 microform items, 689 audio/video tapes/CDs/DVDs, and subscribes to 1,182 periodicals including electronic. Computerized library services include interlibrary loans, database searching, Internet access, and Wi-Fi capability. Special learning facilities include an art gallery, radio station, an web-lab, ITV multimedia classrooms, and theaters. **Physically Challenged Students:** 34% of the campus is accessible. Facilities include wheelchair ramps, elevators, special parking, specially equipped restrooms, special class scheduling, lowered drinking fountains, lowered telephones, and special housing. **Special:** The college offers co-op programs in most majors, internships, and study abroad. A Washington semester,

work-study, accelerated degrees, and student-designed majors in the humanities and general studies are possible. Prepharmacy and joint baccalaureate dental programs are available. There are 10 national honor societies, a freshman honors program, and 11 departmental honors programs. **Visiting:** There are regularly scheduled orientations for prospective students, including standardized placement testing, faculty advisement, class registration, and educational and social activities to prepare students for entrance. There are guides for informal visits, visitors may sit in on classes, and stay overnight. To schedule a visit, contact the Admissions Office. **Campus Safety and Security:** Measures include 24-hour foot and vehicle patrol, emergency notification system, self-defense education, and security escort services. There are shuttle buses, emergency telephones, and lighted pathways/sidewalks.

REQUIREMENTS: The SAT or ACT is required. Applicants should be graduates of an accredited high school or have a GED certificate. They should have completed a minimum of 16 academic units, including 4 in English, 3 in math, 2 each in history, foreign language, and lab science (3 are recommended), and 3 in electives. Those students applying to science and health sciences programs must meet additional requirements. An interview may be requested. AP and CLEP credits are accepted. Important factors in the admissions decision are leadership record, recommendations by school officials, and extracurricular activities record. To graduate, students must complete a 120 to 128 credits, including 30 to 44 in the major, with an overall minimum 2.0 GPA (2.5 in the major). Distribution requirements include courses in English, communications, math, phys ed, foreign language, humanities, social and behavioral sciences, lab and computer science, an integrated, interdisciplinary university core sequence, and freshman seminar. **Procedure:** Freshmen are admitted to all sessions. Entrance exams should be taken May of their junior year. There are early admissions, deferred admissions, and rolling admissions plans. Check with the school for current application deadlines. The application fee is $40. Notification is sent on a rolling basis. Applications are accepted on-line. **Transfer Students:** 131 transfer students enrolled in 2013-2014. All transfer applicants must submit official transcripts for all college work taken. Those students with fewer than 24 credits must also submit a high school transcript or a copy of their state department of education's equivalency score and SAT scores. 32 of 120 credits required for the bachelor's degree must be completed at College at Florham. **International Students:** There are 14 international students enrolled. The school actively recruits these students. They must take the TOEFL with a minimum score of 550 on the paper-based TOEFL (PBT) or 79 on the Internet-based version (iBT), or take the IELTS. SAT or ACT is highly recommended.

ADMISSIONS: 67% of the 2014-2015 applicants were accepted. The SAT scores for the 2014-2015 freshman class were: Critical Reading--36% below 500, 51% between 500 and 599, 13% between 600 and 699, and 1% between 700 and 800; Math--31% below 500, 49% between 500 and 599, 18% between 600 and 699, and 1% between 700 and 800; Writing--36% below 500, 50% between 500 and 599, 13% between 600 and 699, and 1% between 700 and 800. 32% of the current freshmen were in the top fifth of their class; 62% were in the top two fifths. 5 freshmen graduated first in their class. **Admissions Contact:** Jonathan Wexler, Associate Vice President of Enrollment Management. E-Mail: *globaleducation@fdu.edu* Web: *www.fdu.edu*

FINANCIAL AID: The FAFSA is required. The priority date for freshman financial aid applications for fall entry is February 15.

FAIRLEIGH DICKINSON UNIVERSITY/ METROPOLITAN CAMPUS   E-2
www.fdu.edu

Teaneck, NJ 07666	(201) 692-2553
	(800) 338-8803
Fax: (201) 692-7319	Email: globaleducation@fdu.edu
Full-time: 983 men, 1488 women	Faculty: n/av
Part-time: 1567 men, 2006 women	Ph.D.s: n/av
Graduate: 1126 men, 1634 women	Student/Faculty: n/av
Year: semesters, summer session	Tuition: $28,886
Room & Board: $11,368	Freshman Class: 5108 applied, 2916 accepted, 711 enrolled
SAT CR/M/W: 510/530/500 ACT: required	
	CEEB CODE: 2263
Application Deadline: March 15	COMPETITIVE

Farleigh Dickinson University/Metropolitan Campus, founded in 1942, is an independent university offering undergraduate and graduate degrees in business, arts and sciences, professional studies, public administration, and hotel, restaurant, and tourism management. There are 3 undergraduate schools and 3 graduate schools. In addition to regional accreditation, FDU has baccalaureate program accreditation with AACSB, ABET, TEAC, JR, and ABA. The 92-acre campus is in a suburban area 13 miles from midtown Manhattan, New York City. Including any residence halls, there are 55 buildings.

STUDENT LIFE: 87% of undergraduates are from New Jersey. Others are from 25 states, 64 foreign countries, and Canada. 33% are White; 20% Hispanic; 18% African American. **Male To Female Ratio:** 1.4:1. The average age of freshmen is 18; all undergraduates, 22. 27% do not continue beyond their first year; 40% remain to graduate.

Housing: 982 students can be accommodated in college housing, which includes single-sex and coed dorms. In addition, there are honors houses, special-interest houses, L.I.F.E. house and Global Scholar houses. On-campus housing is available on a first-come, first-served basis, and is available on a lottery system for upperclassmen. 79% of students commute. Alcohol is not permitted. All students may keep cars.

FACULTY/CLASSROOMS: No introductory courses are taught by graduate students.

PROGRAMS OF STUDY: FDU confers B.A., B.S., B.S.Civ.E.T., B.S.C.L.S., B.S.Con.E.T., B.S.E.E., B.S.E.E.T., B.S.M.E.T. and B.S.N. degrees. Associate, Master's, and Doctoral degrees are also awarded. Bachelor's degrees are awarded in BIOLOGICAL SCIENCE (biochemistry, biology/biological science, and marine biology), BUSINESS (accounting, business administration and management, business economics, entrepreneurial studies, hotel/motel and restaurant management, and marketing/retailing/merchandising), COMMUNICATIONS AND THE ARTS (communications, English literature, and fine arts), COMPUTER AND PHYSICAL SCIENCE (chemistry, computer science, information sciences and systems, mathematics, radiological technology, and science), ENGINEERING AND ENVIRONMENTAL DESIGN (civil engineering technology, construction engineering, electrical/electronics engineering, electrical/electronics engineering technology, and mechanical engineering technology), HEALTH PROFESSIONS (allied health, clinical science, medical laboratory technology, nursing, and physical therapy), SOCIAL SCIENCE (criminal justice, economics, history, humanities, interdisciplinary studies, international studies, liberal arts/general studies, philosophy, political science/government, psychology, and Spanish studies). Nursing, psychology, and business management have the largest enrollments.

ACTIVITIES: 1% of men belong to 5 national fraternities; 1% of women belong to 7 national sororities. There are 72 groups on campus, including cheerleading, chorus, computers, dance, drama, environmental, ethnic, film, gay, honors, international, literary magazine, newspaper, pep band, photography, political, professional, radio and TV, religious, social, social service, student government, and student programming board. Popular campus events include Welcome Back Week, Spring Fest, and Dances. **Sports:** There are 7 intercollegiate sports for men and 10 for women, and 7 intramural sports for men and 7 for women. Facilities include a 5,000-seat facility with a 6-lane, 200-meter track, 4 full basketball courts, 2 volleyball courts, 4 racquetball courts, and a fully equipped weight room; 6 outdoor tennis courts; a baseball field and soccer field with bleachers; 2 training room facilities; a softball field; and a state-of-the-art fitness center with aerobics room, selectorized weight room, and cardio room. **Graduates:** From July 1, 2013 to June 30, 2014, 784 bachelor's degrees were awarded. The most popular majors were psychology (7%), nursing (6%), and criminal justice (6%). 201 companies recruited on campus in 2013-2014. In an average class, 21% graduate in 4 years or less, 37% graduate in 5 years or less, and 40% graduate in 6 years or less.

SERVICES: Counseling and information services are available, as is tutoring in every subject. There is a reader service for the blind, and remedial math, reading, and writing. Workshops offer assistance with academic study skills, time management, and advanced reading and writing. Support services for basic skills students and freshmen are available. There is also a Regional Center for College Students with Learning Disabilities that offers comprehensive support to students

admitted to the program. **Library/Resources:** The 3 libraries contain 196,703 volumes, 103,808 microform items, 1,311 audio/video tapes/CDs/DVDs, and subscribe to 1,601 periodicals including electronic. Computerized library services include interlibrary loans, database searching, and Internet access. Special learning facilities include an art gallery, radio station, computer labs, ITV multimedia classrooms, photonics lab, theater, art galleries, web-lab, cyber crime lab, and the Regional Center for College Students with Learning Disabilities. **Physically Challenged Students:** 41% of the campus is accessible. Facilities include wheelchair ramps, elevators, special parking, specially equipped restrooms, special class scheduling, lowered drinking fountains, lowered telephones, special housing. oral interpretation for the hearing impaired. **Special:** FDU offers co-op programs in most majors, cross-registration, internships, and study abroad in England and Vancouver. A Washington semester, work-study, accelerated degrees, and student-designed majors in the humanities and general studies are possible. A 7-year medical program is available with Karol Marcinkowski School of Medicine in Poland, as is an accelerated chiropractic program with New York Chiropractic College and Logan Chiropractic College (B.S.,B.A./M.A.T.). There are 12 national honor societies, a freshman honors program, and 16 departmental honors programs. **Visiting:** There are regularly scheduled orientations for prospective students, including standardized placement testing, faculty advisement, class registration, and educational and social activities to prepare students for entrance. There are guides for informal visits, visitors may sit in on classes, and stay overnight. To schedule a visit, contact the Admissions Office. **Campus Safety and Security:** Measures include 24-hour foot and vehicle patrol, emergency notification system, self-defense education, and security escort services. There are emergency telephones and lighted pathways/sidewalks.

REQUIREMENTS: The SAT or ACT is required. Applicants should be graduates of an accredited high school or have a GED certificate. They should have completed a minimum of 16 academic units, including 4 in English, 3 in math, 2 each in history, foreign language, and lab science (3 are recommended), and 3 in electives. Those students applying to science, engineering, and health sciences programs must meet additional requirements. An interview may be required. AP and CLEP credits are accepted. Important factors in the admissions decision are leadership record, recommendations by school officials, and extracurricular activities record. To graduate, students must complete 120 to 128 credits, including 30 to 44 in the major, with an overall minimum 2.0. GPA. Students must complete a 4-semester interdisciplinary sequence and 1 course in freshman seminar. The core curriculum includes 6 credits in English, 12 in university core, and 3 each in math and computer science. **Procedure:** Freshmen are admitted to all sessions. Entrance exams should be taken by May of the junior year. There are deferred admissions and rolling admissions plans. Applications should be filed by March 15 for fall entry, along with a $40 fee. Notification is sent on a rolling basis. Applications are accepted on-line. **Transfer Students:** 499 transfer students enrolled in 2013-2014. All applicants must submit official transcripts for all college work taken. Those students with fewer than 24 credits must also submit a high school transcript or a copy of their state department of education's equivalency score and SAT scores. 32 of 128 credits required for the bachelor's degree must be completed at FDU. **International Students:** There are 243 international students enrolled. The school actively recruits these students. They must take the TOEFL with a minimum score of 550 on the paper-based TOEFL (PBT) or 79 on the Internet-based version (iBT), or take the IELTS. The ACT or SAT is highly recommended.

ADMISSIONS: 57% of the 2014-2015 applicants were accepted. The SAT scores for the 2014-2015 freshman class were: Critical Reading--42% below 500, 46% between 500 and 599, and 11% between 600 and 699; Math--30% below 500, 52% between 500 and 599, 16% between 600 and 699, and 2% between 700 and 800; Writing--43% below 500, 49% between 500 and 599, 8% between 600 and 699. 30% of the current freshmen were in the top fifth of their class; 62% were in the top two fifths. 1 freshman graduated first in the class. **Admissions Contact:** Jonathan Wexler, Associate Vice President of Enrollment Management. E-Mail: *globaleducation@fdu.edu* Web: *www.fdu.edu*

FINANCIAL AID: Check with the school for current application deadlines.

FELICIAN COLLEGE (*The complete profile is made available exclusively on our website, www.barronspac.com*)

GEORGIAN COURT UNIVERSITY (*The complete profile is made available exclusively on our website, www.barronspac.com*)

KEAN UNIVERSITY	D-2
www.kean.edu	
Union, NJ 07083	(908) 737-7100 n/av
Fax: (908) 737-7105	Email: admitme@kean.edu
Full-time: 3784 men, 5499 women	Faculty: IIA, ++$
Part-time: 1011 men, 1693 women	Ph.D.s: 85%
Graduate: 530 men, 1842 women	Student/Faculty: 17 to 1
Year: semesters, summer session	Tuition: $11,244 ($17,653)
Room & Board: $12,200	Freshman Class: 5718 applied, 4023 accepted, 1502 enrolled
SAT: required	CEEB CODE: 2517
Application Deadline: May 31	COMPETITIVE

Kean University is a public university serving undergraduate and graduate students in the liberal arts, the sciences, and the professions. There are 6 undergraduate schools and 1 graduate school. In addition to regional accreditation, Kean has baccalaureate program accreditation with NASAD, NASM, NCATE, NLN, NAST, CIDA, CAATE, and CAHIIM. The 185-acre campus is in a suburban area in Union, NJ additional locations in Toms River, NJ and Wenzhou, China. Including any residence halls, there are 47 buildings.

STUDENT LIFE: 98% of undergraduates are from New Jersey. Others are from 20 states, 49 foreign countries, and Canada. 38% are White; 25% Hispanic; 20% African American. **Male To Female Ratio:** 1.7:1. The average age of freshmen is 18; all undergraduates, 24. 25% do not continue beyond their first year; 48% remain to graduate.

Housing: 2039 students can be accommodated in college housing, which includes single-sex and coed dorms and on-campus apartments. In addition, there are special-interest houses, Freshman housing, and women-only floor, living learning communities for SIMS (Success in Math and Science), GREEN (Gearing Residents toward Environment, Exercise and Nutrition) and WELL(Women Empowered toward Leadership and Learning). On-campus housing is available on a first-come and first-served basis. 86% of students commute. Alcohol is not permitted. Upperclassmen may keep cars.

FACULTY/CLASSROOMS: 48% of faculty are male; 52% are female. No introductory courses are taught by graduate students. The average class size in a regular course is 21.

PROGRAMS OF STUDY: Kean confers B.A., B.S., B.F.A., B.I.D. and B.S.N. degrees. Master's and Doctoral degrees are also awarded. Bachelor's degrees are awarded in BIOLOGICAL SCIENCE (biology/biological science), BUSINESS (accounting, finance, international business management, management science, marketing management, recreational facilities management, and sustainable management), COMMUNICATIONS AND THE ARTS (art history and appreciation, communications, English, fine arts, fine/studio arts, general, industrial design, information technology, music, music performance, performing arts, Spanish, studio art, theatre arts, theater design, and visual and performing arts), COMPUTER AND PHYSICAL SCIENCE (chemistry, computer science, earth science, mathematics, and science and technology studies), EDUCATION (athletic training, early childhood education, elementary education, health information management, middle school education, music education, physical education, secondary education, and special education), ENGINEERING AND ENVIRONMENTAL DESIGN (interior design), HEALTH PROFESSIONS (medical technology, nursing, and speech pathology/audiology), SOCIAL SCIENCE (Asian/Oriental studies, criminal justice, economics, history, political science/government, psychology, public administration, and sociology). Science/technology and education is the strongest academically. Business and education have the largest enrollments.

ACTIVITIES: There are 137 groups on campus, including art, band, choir, chorale, chorus, communications, computers, dance, drama, environmental, ethnic, film, forensics, gay, honors, international, jazz band, literary magazine, musical theater, newspaper, orchestra, pep band, photography, political, professional, radio and TV, religious, social, social service, student government, symphony, and yearbook. Popular campus events include Homecoming, Campus Awareness Festival, Comedy Show, Unity Week, Concerts, Class Events and Meet the Greeks, Food Bank Luncheon, Student Group Expo, and Martin Luther King Jr. Day of Service. **Sports:** There are 6 intercollegiate sports for men and 7 for women, and 6 intramural sports for men and 6 for women. Facilities include 5300-seat stadium, an 8-lane track, 800-seat soccer stadium, 350-seat baseball stadium, 250-seat softball stadium, practice fields, 3000-seat arena, 5 indoor basketball courts, 2 outdoor basketball courts, 10 outdoor tennis courts, indoor swimming pool, 3 fitness rooms and pool tables. **Graduates:** From July 1, 2013 to June 30, 2014, 2582 bachelor's degrees were awarded. The most popular majors were psychology (16%), management science (7%), and criminal justice (6%). 120 companies recruited on campus in 2013-2014. In an average class, 18% graduate in 4 years or less, 41% graduate in 5 years or less, and 48% graduate in 6 years or less.

SERVICES: Counseling and information services are available, as is tutoring in most subjects. There is remedial math, reading, and writing. **Library/Resources:** The library contains 221,225 volumes, and subscribes to 48,982 periodicals including electronic. Computerized library services include interlibrary loans, database searching, Internet access, and Wi-Fi capability. Special learning facilities include an art gallery, planetarium, radio station, TV station, New Jersey Center for Science, Technology, and Mathematics; Holocaust Resource Center; Wynona Moore Lipman Ethnic Studies Center; Liberty Hall Museum; Human Rights Institute and New Jersey Highlands. **Physically Challenged Students:** All of the campus is accessible. Facilities include wheelchair ramps, elevators, special parking, specially equipped restrooms, special class scheduling, lowered drinking fountains, lowered telephones, and special housing. **Special:** There are 27 national honor societies, a freshman honors program, and 8 departmental honors programs. **Visiting:** There are regularly scheduled orientations for prospective students. There are guides for informal visits and visitors may sit in on classes. To schedule a visit, contact the Office of Undergraduate Admissions. **Campus Safety and Security:** Measures include 24-hour foot and vehicle patrol, emergency notification system, self-defense education, and security escort services. There are shuttle buses, emergency telephones, lighted pathways/sidewalks, controlled access to dorms/residences, all residence halls have surveillance cameras in floors, lounges, elevators and exit doors; All residence halls have fire sprinkler systems.

REQUIREMENTS: The SAT is required. Applicants must be graduates of accredited secondary schools or have earned a GED. College preparatory study includes 4 courses in English, 3 in math, 2 each in lab science and history, and 5 in academic electives. An essay and 2 letters of recommendation, official transcript and SAT/ACT are also required. AP and CLEP credits are accepted. **Procedure:** Freshmen are admitted fall and spring. Entrance exams should be taken April-June of the junior year Oct./Nov. of the senior year. There are deferred admissions and rolling admissions plans. Applications should be filed by May 31 for fall entry; December 1 for spring entry, along with a $75 fee. Notifications are sent November 1. Applications are accepted on-line. **Transfer Students:** 1438 transfer students enrolled in 2013-2014. NACES evaluation of transcripts for any foreign institution attended. The minimum number of credits to transfer with a 2.0 is 30. Between 15-30 credit (semester) hours students must have a 3.0 GPA. 32 of 124 credits required for the bachelor's degree must be completed at Kean. **International Students:** There are 121 international students enrolled. The school actively recruits these students. They must take the TOEFL with a minimum score of 550 on the paper-based TOEFL (PBT) or 80 on the Internet-based version (iBT), or take the IELTS - International English Language Testing System. SAT or ACT is required of some applicants.

ADMISSIONS: 70% of the 2014-2015 applicants were accepted. 27% of the current freshmen were in the top fifth of their class; 61% were in the top two fifths. **Admissions Contact:** Marsha McCarthy, Director of Admissions. E-Mail: *admitme@kean.edu* Web: *www.kean.edu*

FINANCIAL AID: In 2014-2015, 80% of all full-time freshmen students received some form of financial aid. 73% of all full-time freshmen students received need-based aid. The average freshman award was $10,305. Need-based scholarships or need-based grants averaged

$8,479; need-based self-help aid (loans and jobs) averaged $3,695; and other non-need-based awards and non-need-based scholarships averaged $4,463. 8% of undergraduate students work part-time. Average annual earnings from campus work are $4320. The average financial indebtedness of the 2014 graduate was $32,886. The FAFSA is required. The priority date for freshman financial aid applications for fall entry is April 17.

MONMOUTH UNIVERSITY E-3
www.monmouth.edu

| West Long Branch, NJ 07764 | (732) 571-3456 |
| | (800) 543-9671 |

Fax: (732) 263-5166	Email: admission@monmouth.edu
Full-time: 1775 men, 2595 women	Faculty: 262; IIA, +$
Part-time: 103 men, 161 women	Ph.D.s: 80%
Graduate: 444 men, 1317 women	Student/Faculty: 17 to 1
Year: semesters, summer session	Tuition: $32,310
Room & Board: $11,798	Freshman Class: 7691 applied, 5706 accepted, 1056 enrolled
SAT CR/M/W: 520/537/531 ACT: 23	CEEB CODE: 2416
Application Deadline: March 1	COMPETITIVE

Monmouth University, founded in 1933, is a private comprehensive institution offering both undergraduate and graduate programs in the arts and sciences, business, education, nursing, technology, and professional training. Figures in the above capsule and in this profile are approximate. There are 7 undergraduate schools and 1 graduate school. In addition to regional accreditation, Monmouth has baccalaureate program accreditation with AACSB, ABET, CSWE, NCATE, NLN, ACS, CCNE, and CACREP. The 159-acre campus is in a suburban area 55 miles from New York City, and 75 miles from Philadelphia. Including any residence halls, there are 54 buildings.
STUDENT LIFE: 86% of undergraduates are from New Jersey. Others are from 30 states, 24 foreign countries, and Canada. 85% are from public schools. 76% are White. **Male To Female Ratio:** 1.8:1. The average age of freshmen is 18; all undergraduates, 20. 17% do not continue beyond their first year; 67% remain to graduate. **Housing:** 2063 students can be accommodated in college housing, which includes coed dorms, on-campus apartments, and off-campus apartments. In addition, there are honors houses. On-campus housing is available on a first-come, first-served basis, and is available on a lottery system for upperclassmen. Priority is given to out-of-town students. 59% of students commute. All students may keep cars.
FACULTY/CLASSROOMS: 46% of faculty are male; 54% are female. 91% teach undergraduates, 57% do research, and 50% do both. No introductory courses are taught by graduate students. The average class size in an introductory lecture is 23; in a laboratory is 16; and in a regular course is 22.
PROGRAMS OF STUDY: Monmouth confers B.A., B.S., B.F.A., B.S.N. and B.S.W. degrees. Associate, Master's, and Doctoral degrees are also awarded. Bachelor's degrees are awarded in BIOLOGICAL SCIENCE (biology/biological science and marine biology), BUSINESS (accounting, banking and finance, business administration and management, business administration -international, business administration marketing, business economics, international business management, marketing management, and real estate), COMMUNICATIONS AND THE ARTS (art, art history and appreciation, communications, English, graphic design, modern language, music, music business management, music industry, and Spanish), COMPUTER AND PHYSICAL SCIENCE (chemistry, clinical laboratory science, chemistry education, computer science, mathematics, and software engineering), EDUCATION (art education, early childhood education, education, elementary education, English education, foreign languages education, health education, mathematics education, music education, physical education, science education, secondary education, social studies education, social studies secondary school education, spanish education K-12, and special education), ENGINEERING AND ENVIRONMENTAL DESIGN (computer graphics), HEALTH PROFESSIONS (medical laboratory science, medical laboratory technology, nursing, and premedicine), SOCIAL SCIENCE

(anthropology, criminal justice, history, homeland security, legal studies, political science/government, prelaw, psychology, social work, and sociology). Business, education, and communication have the largest enrollments.
ACTIVITIES: 15% of men belong to 8 national fraternities; 13% of women belong to 8 national sororities. There are 104 groups on campus, including and mock trial, veterans, art, band, cheerleading, choir, chorus, computers, dance, debate, drama, environmental, ethnic, gay, honors, international, jazz band, literary magazine, musical theater, newspaper, pep band, photography, political, professional, radio and TV, religious, social, social service, student activities board, student government, and yearbook. Popular campus events include The Big Event, Springfest, Ebony Night, and Winter Ball. **Sports:** There are 16 intercollegiate sports for men and 16 for women, and 15 intramural sports for men and 12 for women. Facilities include a 4,100 seat state-of-the-art arena, 200 meter, 6-lane indoor track, an indoor practice facility with 2 full basketball courts, a 3,500-seat football field with Field Turf, soccer field with lighting and Field-Turf, six outdoor tennis courts, an 8-lane all-weather track, an indoor pool, exercise and weight facility, a varsity athletics weight room, baseball, softball, and field hockey fields. **Graduates:** From July 1, 2013 to June 30, 2014, 1147 bachelor's degrees were awarded. The most popular majors were business (24%), communication (12%), and education (11%). 205 companies recruited on campus in 2013-2014. In an average class, 55% graduate in 4 years or less, 66% graduate in 5 years or less, and 67% graduate in 6 years or less. Of the 2013 graduating class, 42% were enrolled in graduate school within 6 months of graduation, and 65% were employed.
SERVICES: Counseling and information services are available, as is tutoring in every subject. There is a reader service for the blind, and remedial math, reading, and writing. **Library/Resources:** The library contains 290,000 volumes, 1,024 audio/video tapes/CDs/DVDs, and subscribes to 61,000 periodicals including electronic. Computerized library services include interlibrary loans, database searching, Internet access, and Wi-Fi capability. Special learning facilities include an art gallery, radio station, TV station, including a theater, financial markets lab, greenhouse, and a community garden. **Physically Challenged Students:** 95% of the campus is accessible. Facilities include wheelchair ramps, elevators, special parking, specially equipped restrooms, special class scheduling, lowered drinking fountains, special housing. Academic assistance provided within the classroom. **Special:** Students may study abroad in England, Australia, Italy, and Spain or through The College Consortium for International Studies (CCIS) program. There are cooperative and internship programs and a Washington semester. Five year Baccalaureate/Mater's programs in many academic areas. Monmouth also offers work-study programs, dual majors, flexible studies programs, and credit for life experience. Nondegree study is possible. There are 22 national honor societies and a freshman honors program. **Visiting:** There are regularly scheduled orientations for prospective students, students visits include campus tours. There are guides for informal visits and visitors may sit in on classes. To schedule a visit, contact the Admission Office at visitmu@monmouth.edu. **Campus Safety and Security:** Measures include 24-hour foot and vehicle patrol, emergency notification system, self-defense education, and security escort services. There are emergency telephones, lighted pathways/sidewalks, controlled access to dorms/residences, and university police force.
REQUIREMENTS: The SAT or ACT is required. The ACT Optional Writing test is also required. Applicants must be graduates of accredited secondary schools or have earned a GED. The university requires 16 Carnegie units, based on 4 years of English, 3 of math, and 2 each of social studies/history and science, with the remaining 5 units in academic electives. An essay and a letter of recommendation are required. AP and CLEP credits are accepted. Important factors in the admissions decision are advanced placement or honors courses, leadership record, and extracurricular activities record. To graduate, students must earn at least 128 credits, including 30 to 81 in a major, with a minimum GPA of 2.0 overall and 2.1 in the major. Education majors are required to have a cumulative GPA of 3.0. **Procedure:** Freshmen are admitted fall and spring. Entrance exams should be taken by December of the senior year. There is a deferred admissions plan. Applications should be filed by March 1 for fall entry; January 1 for spring entry, along with a $50 fee. Notifications are sent April

1. Applications are accepted on-line. **Transfer Students:** 477 transfer students enrolled in 2013-2014. Transfer applicants with fewer than 24 transferable college credits must provide a high school transcript and SAT or ACT scores. All transfer applicants must submit official college transcripts for all institutions attended. A 2.25 minimum college GPA is required for general admission consideration, does not guarantee acceptance. For education majors, a minimum cumulative GPA of 3.00 is required. 32 of 128 credits required for the bachelor's degree must be completed at Monmouth. **International Students:** There are 35 international students enrolled. The school actively recruits these students. They must take the TOEFL with a minimum score of 550 on the paper-based TOEFL (PBT) or 79 on the Internet-based version (iBT) or take the MELAB, or take the IELTS, or the Cambridge ESOL (CAE). They must also take the SAT or ACT, scoring varies by student profile. Students from English speaking countries must take the SAT or ACT.

ADMISSIONS: 74% of the 2014-2015 applicants were accepted. The SAT scores for the 2014-2015 freshman class were: Critical Reading--39% below 500, 47% between 500 and 599, 13% between 600 and 699, and 1% between 700 and 800; Math--28% below 500, 52% between 500 and 599, 18% between 600 and 699, and 2% between 700 and 800; Writing--32% below 500, 51% between 500 and 599, 16% between 600 and 699, and 1% between 700 and 800. The ACT scores were 16% below 21, 41% between 21 and 23, 27% between 24 and 26, 13% between 27 and 28, and 3% above 28. 40% of the current freshmen were in the top fifth of their class; 69% were in the top two fifths. 2 freshmen graduated first in their class. **Admissions Contact:** Victoria Bobik, Director of Undergraduate Admission. E-Mail: *admission@monmouth.edu* Web: *www.monmouth.edu*

FINANCIAL AID: In 2014-2015, 99% of all full-time freshmen and 93% of continuing full-time students received some form of financial aid. 67% of all full-time freshmen and 57% of continuing full-time students received need-based aid. The average freshman award was $30,434. Need-based scholarships or need-based grants averaged $14,132 ($43,099 maximum); need-based self-help aid (loans and jobs) averaged $5,133 ($9,500 maximum); non-need-based athletic scholarships averaged $21,966 ($51,138 maximum); other non-need-based awards and non-need-based scholarships averaged $12,230 ($36,882 maximum); and $11,237 from other forms of aid. 25% of undergraduate students work part-time. Average annual earnings from campus work are $1303. The average financial indebtedness of the 2014 graduate was $24,141. The FAFSA and the state aid form are required. Check with the school for current application deadlines.

MONTCLAIR STATE UNIVERSITY　　　　E-2
www.montclair.edu

Montclair, NJ 07042	(973) 655-4444
	(800) 331-9205
Fax: (973) 655-7700	Email: msuadm@mail.montclair.edu
Full-time: 4784 men, 7596 women	Faculty: IIA, ++$
Part-time: 829 men, 1223 women	Ph.D.s: 92%
Graduate: 1066 men, 2884 women	Student/Faculty: 17 to 1
Year: semesters, summer session	Tuition: $11,058 ($20,136)
Room & Board: $11,556	Freshman Class: n/av
SAT CR/M/W: 487/502/497	CEEB CODE: 2520
Application Deadline: March 1	COMPETITIVE

Montclair State University, established in 1908, is a public institution offering programs in liberal arts and sciences, business administration, fine and performing arts, and professional studies. Figures in the above capsule and in this profile are approximate. There are 5 undergraduate schools and 1 graduate school. In addition to regional accreditation, Montclair has baccalaureate program accreditation with AACSB, ABET, ADA, CSAB, NASAD, NASDTEC, NASM, NCATE, NRPA, CAAHEP, NASD, and NAST. The 275-acre campus is in a suburban area 14 miles west of New York City. Including any residence halls, there are 66 buildings.

STUDENT LIFE: 97% of undergraduates are from New Jersey. Others are from 33 states, 110 foreign countries, and Canada. 53% are White; 21% Hispanic. **Male To Female Ratio:** 1.8:1. The average

age of freshmen is 19; all undergraduates, 22. 63% remain to graduate. **Housing:** 5200 students can be accommodated in college housing, which includes single-sex and coed dorms and on-campus apartments. In addition, there are honors houses, special-interest houses, living learning communities. On-campus housing is available on a first-come and first-served basis. Priority is given to out-of-town students. 74% of students commute. Alcohol is not permitted. Upperclassmen may keep cars.

FACULTY/CLASSROOMS: 47% of faculty are male; 53% are female. All teach undergraduates. No introductory courses are taught by graduate students. The average class size in an introductory lecture is 25; in a laboratory is 18; and in a regular course is 24.

PROGRAMS OF STUDY: Montclair confers B.A., B.S., B.F.A., B.S./M.S., B.S./M.A.T. and B.Mus. degrees. Master's and Doctoral degrees are also awarded. Bachelor's degrees are awarded in BIOLOGICAL SCIENCE (biochemistry, biology/biological science, environmental biology, marine science, molecular biology, and nutrition), BUSINESS (accounting, banking and finance, business administration and management, business economics, hospitality management services, international business management, management information systems, marketing management, recreation and leisure services, retailing, and tourism), COMMUNICATIONS AND THE ARTS (art, art history and appreciation, broadcasting, classics, communications, communications technology, creative writing, dance, dramatic arts, English, film arts, fine arts, French, graphic design, Italian, Latin, linguistics, music, music performance, music theory and composition, musical theater, public relations, Spanish, speech/debate/rhetoric, studio art, and theater design), COMPUTER AND PHYSICAL SCIENCE (applied mathematics, astronomy, chemistry, computer science, geoscience, information sciences and systems, mathematics, and physics), EDUCATION (art education, athletic training, business education, early childhood education, health education, home economics education, middle school education, music education, and physical education), HEALTH PROFESSIONS (allied health, community health work, music therapy, predentistry, premedicine, prepharmacy, and public health), SOCIAL SCIENCE (anthropology, criminal justice, dietetics, economics, family and community services, food production/management/services, geography, gerontology, history, home economics, human ecology, humanities, law, paralegal studies, parks and recreation management, philosophy, political science/government, psychology, religion, sociology, and women's studies). Business administration, family and child studies, and psychology have the largest enrollments.

ACTIVITIES: 5% of men belong to 2 local and 13 national fraternities; 4% of women belong to 4 local and 12 national sororities. There are 142 groups on campus, including band, cheerleading, choir, chorus, dance, drama, environmental, ethnic, film, gay, honors, international, jazz band, literary magazine, marching band, musical theater, newspaper, orchestra, pep band, political, professional, radio and TV, religious, social, social service, student government, and yearbook. Popular campus events include Fall Frenzy, Homecoming, Greek Week and World's Fair. **Sports:** There are 8 intercollegiate sports for men and 9 for women, and 12 intramural sports for men and 12 for women. Facilities include Panzer Athletic Center is the home of intercollegiate athletics and physical education classes. The athletic center has a pool, competition gymnasium, auxiliary gymnasium, offices, athletic training facility and locker rooms. There is a turf multi-purpose stadium called Sprague field, which is the home to field hockey, football, and men's and women's lacrosse. Pit taser field is a turf soccer park, home to men's and women's soccer. Intramurals are also played on Sprague field. There is a baseball stadium and a softball stadium and an 8 lane track. **Graduates:** From July 1, 2013 to June 30, 2014, 314 bachelor's degrees were awarded. The most popular majors were business administration (14%), family and child studies (14%), and psychology (9%). In an average class, 1% graduate in 3 years or less, 35% graduate in 4 years or less, 58% graduate in 5 years or less, and 63% graduate in 6 years or less. Of the 2013 graduating class, 16% were enrolled in graduate school within 6 months of graduation.

SERVICES: Counseling and information services are available, as is tutoring in most subjects. There is a reader service for the blind, remedial math, reading, and writing. Audio textbooks are available. **Library/Resources:** The library contains 459,034 volumes, 1.2 million microform items, 21,145 audio/video tapes/CDs/DVDs, and subscribes to 21,145 periodicals including electronic. Computerized library services include interlibrary loans, database searching, and Internet access. Special learning facilities include an art gallery, radio station, and TV station. **Physically Challenged Students:** 90% of the campus is accessible. Facilities include wheelchair ramps, elevators, special parking, specially equipped restrooms, special class scheduling, lowered drinking fountains, lowered telephones, special housing. curb cuts, speaker phones, special building signs, TDDs, and priority registration. There is a disability resource center on campus. **Special:** Internships, co-op programs in all majors, credit by exam, pass/fail options, work-study, credit for life experience, independent study, and study abroad in 51 countries are offered. Joint-degree programs are offered in practical anthropology and applied economics, and a 5-year B.A.-B.Mus. program in music is available, as is an articulated medical, dental, physical therapy, and physician assistant program with the University of Medicine and Dentistry of New Jersey and an articulated program leading to a Pharm.D. with Rutgers University. There are 28 national honor societies, a freshman honors program, and 3 departmental honors programs. **Visiting:** There are regularly scheduled orientations for prospective students, Students engage in activities, registration, learn MSU policies and procedures, learn about connecting in and out of the classroom, and obtain an MSU ID. There are guides for informal visits. To schedule a visit, contact the Admissions Office. **Campus Safety and Security:** Measures include 24-hour foot and vehicle patrol, emergency notification system, self-defense education, and security escort services. There are shuttle buses, emergency telephones, lighted pathways/sidewalks, controlled access to dorms/residences, a full-time campus police force, and crime prevention officer.

REQUIREMENTS: The SAT is required. Applicants must submit 16 Carnegie units, including 4 in English, 3 to 4 in math (including algebra I and II and geometry), 2 each in lab science, social studies, and a foreign language, and the remainder in additional courses in these fields. The GED is accepted. A portfolio, audition, or interview is required for students planning to major in fine arts, music, speech, or theater. Admission to computer science requires 4 years of math, including trigonometry. AP and CLEP credits are accepted. Important factors in the admissions decision are advanced placement or honors courses, recommendations by school officials, and leadership record. Students must successfully complete a minimum of 120 semester hours, with 33 to 82 in the major, while maintaining a minimum GPA of 2.0. General education requirements include courses in communications, contemporary issues, art appreciation, a foreign language, humanities, math, natural/physical science, social sciences, and multicultural awareness, as well as 1 semester hour in phys ed and 3 semester hours in computer science. **Procedure:** Freshmen are admitted fall and spring. Entrance exams should be taken October, November, or December of the senior year. There is a rolling admissions plan. Applications should be filed by March 1 for fall entry; November 1 for spring entry, along with a $65 fee. Notification is sent on a rolling basis. Applications are accepted on-line. **Transfer Students:** 1379 transfer students enrolled in 2013-2014. Applicants must have completed a minimum of 15 credits from an accredited college. A cumulative GPA of 2.5 is required for most majors, with higher required in select programs. Applicants must have completed English composition. High school and college transcripts are required. 32 of 128 credits required for the bachelor's degree must be completed at Montclair. **International Students:** There are 282 international students enrolled. The school actively recruits these students. They must take the TOEFL with a minimum score of 80 on the Internet-based version (iBT). They must also take the SAT.

ADMISSIONS: The SAT scores for the 2014-2015 freshman class were: Critical Reading--58% below 500, 34% between 500 and 599, 7% between 600 and 699, and 1% between 700 and 800; Math--48% below 500, 42% between 500 and 599, 9% between 600 and 699, and 1% between 700 and 800; Writing--52% below 500, 39% between 500 and 599, 8% between 600 and 699, and 1% between 700 and 800. 32% of the current freshmen were in the top fifth of their class; 70% were in the top two fifths. **Admissions Contact:** Lisa Kasper, Director of Admissions. E-Mail: *msuadm@mail.montclair.edu* Web: *www.montclair.edu*

FINANCIAL AID: In 2014-2015, 83% of all full-time freshmen and 53% of continuing full-time students received some form of financial aid. 80% of all full-time freshmen and 67% of continuing full-time students received need-based aid. The average freshman award was $8,461. Need-based scholarships or need-based grants averaged $8,868 ($15,268 maximum); need-based self-help aid (loans and jobs) averaged $3,435 ($8,500 maximum); and other non-need-based awards and non-need-based scholarships averaged $10,454 ($12,000 maximum). 13% of undergraduate students work part-time. Average annual earnings from campus work are $1661. The average financial indebtedness of the 2014 graduate was $20,993. The FAFSA is required. The priority date for freshman financial aid applications for fall entry is March 1.

NEW JERSEY CITY UNIVERSITY *(The complete profile is made available exclusively on our website, www.barronspac.com)*

NEW JERSEY INSTITUTE OF TECHNOLOGY www.njit.edu	E-2
Newark, NJ 07102	**(973) 596-3300** n/av
Fax: (973) 596-3461	Email: admissions@njit.edu
Full-time: 4352 men, 1177 women	Faculty: 418; I, +$
Part-time: 1072 men, 510 women	Ph.D.s: 100%
Graduate: 1948 men, 885 women	Student/Faculty: 13 to 1
Year: semesters, summer session	Tuition: $14,740 ($27,140)
Room & Board: $11,750	Freshman Class: 4216 applied, 2684 accepted, 1626 enrolled
SAT CR/M/W: 549/614/540	CEEB CODE: 2513
Application Deadline: June 1	COMPETITIVE+

New Jersey Institute of Technology is a public research university providing instruction, research, and public service in engineering, computer science, management, architecture, digital design, industrial design, interior design, engineering technology, applied sciences, and related fields. Figures in the above capsule and in this profile are approximate. There are 6 undergraduate schools and 1 graduate school. In addition to regional accreditation, NJIT has baccalaureate program accreditation with AACSB, ABET, NAAB, and CIDA. The 45-acre campus is in an urban area 10 miles west of New York City. Including any residence halls, there are 27 buildings.

STUDENT LIFE: 93% of undergraduates are from New Jersey. Others are from 24 states, 86 foreign countries, and Canada. 80% are from public schools. 35% are White; 21% Asian American; 14% Hispanic. **Male To Female Ratio:** 0.3:1. The average age of freshmen is 18; all undergraduates, 22. 18% do not continue beyond their first year; 54% remain to graduate. **Housing:** 1663 students can be accommodated in college housing, which includes coed dorms. On-campus housing is available on a first-come, first-served basis, and is available on a lottery system for upperclassmen. Priority is given to out-of-town students. 74% of students commute. All students may keep cars.

FACULTY/CLASSROOMS: 82% of faculty are male; 18% are female. All teach undergraduates, all do research, and 74% do both. Graduate students teach 10% of introductory courses. The average class size in an introductory lecture is 30; in a laboratory is 27; and in a regular course is 25.

PROGRAMS OF STUDY: NJIT confers B.A., B.S. and B.Arch. degrees. Master's and Doctoral degrees are also awarded. Bachelor's degrees are awarded in BIOLOGICAL SCIENCE (biology/biological science), BUSINESS (management science), COMMUNICATIONS AND THE ARTS (communications and technical and business writing), COMPUTER AND PHYSICAL SCIENCE (applied mathematics, applied physics, chemistry, computer management, computer science, information sciences and systems, and mathematics), ENGINEERING AND ENVIRONMENTAL DESIGN (architecture, biomedical engineering, chemical engineering, civil engineering, computer engineering, computer technology, electrical/electronics engineering, engineering and applied science, engineering technology, environmental engineering, environmental science, geophysical engineering, industrial engineering, manufacturing engineering, mechanical engineering, technological management, and technology and public affairs), SOCIAL SCIENCE (history). Engineering, computer science and architecture are the strongest academically.

ACTIVITIES: 8% of men belong to 19 local and 10 national fraternities; 5% of women belong to 4 local and 5 national sororities. There are 92 groups on campus, including art, chess, computers, drama, drum and bugle corps, ethnic, gay, honors, international, musical theater, newspaper, photography, professional, radio and TV, religious, social, social service, student government, and yearbook. Popular campus events include Miniversity, International Students Food Festival, and Leadership Training Weekend. **Sports:** There are 9 intercollegiate sports for men and 6 for women, and 13 intramural sports for men and 7 for women. Facilities include a 1000-seat stadium, a fitness center with an indoor track, a 6-lane swimming pool, 4 tennis courts, 4 racquet sport courts, playing fields, bowling lanes, a table tennis and billiards area, and 3 gyms, the largest of which seats 1200. **Graduates:** From July 1, 2013 to June 30, 2014, 1006 bachelor's degrees were awarded. The most popular majors were architecture (10%), mechanical engineering (9%), and civil engineering (7%). 170 companies recruited on campus in 2013-2014. In an average class, 1% graduate in 3 years or less, 23% graduate in 4 years or less, 46% graduate in 5 years or less, and 54% graduate in 6 years or less. Of the 2013 graduating class, 27% were enrolled in graduate school within 6 months of graduation, and 51% were employed.

SERVICES: Counseling and information services are available, as is tutoring in most subjects. There is a reader service for the blind, and remedial math, reading, and writing. **Library/Resources:** The 2 libraries contain 171,180 volumes, 7,650 microform items, and 100,502 audio/video tapes/CDs/DVDs. Computerized library services include interlibrary loans and database searching. Special learning facilities include an art gallery, radio station, 3 TV studios. NJIT is home to many government- and industry-sponsored labs and research centers, including the EPA Northeast Hazardous Substance Research Center, the National Center for Transportation and Industrial Productivity, the Center for Manufacturing Systems, the Emission Reduction Research Center, the Microelectronics Research Center, the Center for Microwave and Lightwave Engineering, and the Multi-Lifecycle Engineering Center. **Physically Challenged Students:** 95% of the campus is accessible. Facilities include wheelchair ramps, elevators, special parking, specially equipped restrooms, special class scheduling, lowered drinking fountains, and lowered telephones. **Special:** Cross-registration is offered in conjunction with Essex County College, Rutgers University's Newark campus, and the University of Medicine and Dentistry of New Jersey. Cooperative programs, available in all majors, include two 6-month internships. There are 3-2 engineering degree programs with Stockton State College and Lincoln and Seton Hall Universities. NJIT also offers work-study programs, study abroad in 18 countries, dual and interdisciplinary majors, accelerated degree programs, distance learning, and nondegree study. There is 1 national honor society, a freshman honors program, and 17 departmental honors programs. **Visiting:** There are regularly scheduled orientations for prospective students, including tours and meetings with admissions personnel, students, and faculty. There are guides for informal visits, visitors may sit in on classes, and stay overnight. To schedule a visit, contact the Director of Admissions. **Campus Safety and Security:** Measures include 24-hour foot and vehicle patrol, self-defense education, and security escort services. There are shuttle buses, emergency telephones, and lighted pathways/sidewalks.

REQUIREMENTS: The SAT is required. SAT: Subject test in math I or II is also required. Applicants should have completed 16 secondary school units, including 4 each in English and math, 2 in a lab science, and 6 in a distribution of social studies, foreign language, math, and science courses. NJIT requires applicants to be in the upper 30% of their class. AP and CLEP credits are accepted. Important factors in the admissions decision are advanced placement or honors courses, recommendations by school officials, and geographical diversity. General university requirements include 9 credits of humanities and social science electives, 7 of natural sciences, 6 each of math, cultural history, basic social sciences, and engineering technology, 3 each of English and management, and 2 of computer science. Students must also complete 2 courses in phys ed. To graduate,

students must earn between 124 and 164 credits, depending on the program, including 50 in the major, with a minimum GPA of 2.0 in upper-level major courses. **Procedure:** Freshmen are admitted fall and spring. Entrance exams should be taken in May of the junior year or November of the senior year. There is a rolling admissions plan. Applications should be filed by June 1 for fall entry; November 15 for spring entry, along with a $70 fee. Notifications are sent January 2. Applications are accepted on-line. **Transfer Students:** 616 transfer students enrolled in 2013-2014. A minimum college GPA of 2.0 is required, but 2.5 or higher is recommended. Students must submit transcripts of all attempted postsecondary academic work. Applicants with fewer than 30 credits may be asked to provide scores on the SAT and the SAT: Subject test in math, as well as high school transcripts. Engineering technology students must present an associate degree. Admission to the School of Architecture is very competitive for transfer students. 33 of 124 credits required for the bachelor's degree must be completed at NJIT. **International Students:** There are 271 international students enrolled. The school actively recruits these students. They must take the TOEFL with a minimum score of 550 on the paper-based TOEFL (PBT) or 79 on the Internet-based version (iBT). They must also take the SAT.

ADMISSIONS: 64% of the 2014-2015 applicants were accepted. The SAT scores for the 2014-2015 freshman class were: Critical Reading--34% below 500, 40% between 500 and 599, 21% between 600 and 699, and 5% between 700 and 800; Math--4% below 500, 43% between 500 and 599, 40% between 600 and 699, and 13% between 700 and 800; Writing--37% below 500, 41% between 500 and 599, 18% between 600 and 699, and 4% between 700 and 800. 40% of the current freshmen were in the top fifth of their class; 73% were in the top two fifths. **Admissions Contact:** Kathy Kelly, Director of Admissions. E-Mail: *admissions@njit.edu* Web: *www.njit.edu*

FINANCIAL AID: In 2014-2015, 94% of all full-time freshmen and 71% of continuing full-time students received some form of financial aid. 88% of all full-time freshmen and 66% of continuing full-time students received need-based aid. The average freshman award was $16,000. Need-based scholarships or need-based grants averaged $11,792 ($31,190 maximum); need-based self-help aid (loans and jobs) averaged $3,392 ($5,500 maximum); non-need-based athletic scholarships averaged $28,016 ($28,285 maximum); and other non-need-based awards and non-need-based scholarships averaged $7,579 ($38,120 maximum). 100% of undergraduate students work part-time. Average annual earnings from campus work are $2293. The average financial indebtedness of the 2014 graduate was $32,000. The priority date for freshman financial aid applications for fall entry is March 15.

PRINCETON UNIVERSITY　　　　　　　　　**D-3**
www.princeton.edu

Princeton, NJ 08544	609-258-3060
	n/av
Fax: (609) 258-6743	Email: uaoffice@princeton.edu
Full-time: 2673 men, 2571 women	Faculty: 904; I, ++$
Part-time: n/av	Ph.D.s: 94%
Graduate: 1675 men, 1016 women	Student/Faculty: 6 to 1
Year: semesters	Tuition: $40,715
Room & Board: $13,080	Freshman Class: 26498 applied, 1963 accepted, 1285 enrolled
SAT CR/M/W: 740/760/750 **ACT:** 33	CEEB CODE: 2672
Application Deadline: January 1	MOST COMPETITIVE

Princeton University, established in 1746, is a private institution offering degrees in the liberal arts and sciences, engineering, applied science, architecture, public and international affairs, interdisciplinary and regional studies, and the creative arts. There are 4 graduate schools. In addition to regional accreditation, Princeton has baccalaureate program accreditation with ABET and NAAB. The 500-acre campus is in a small town 50 miles south of New York City. Including any residence halls, there are 160 buildings.

STUDENT LIFE: 84% of undergraduates are from out of state, mostly the Middle Atlantic. Students are from 50 states, 88 foreign countries, and Canada. 47% are White; 20% Asian American; 11% Foreign. **Male To Female Ratio:** 0.8:1. The average age of freshmen is 18; all undergraduates, 20. 2% do not continue beyond their first year; 96% remain to graduate. **Housing:** 6729 students can be accommodated in college housing, which includes single-sex and coed dorms, on-campus apartments, off-campus apartments, and married student housing. Freshmen and sophomores are assigned to 1 of 6 residential colleges; most juniors and seniors live in upper-class dorms and select from among such dining options as co-ops and private clubs. On-campus housing is guaranteed for all 4 years. 98% of students live on campus. Upperclassmen may keep cars.

FACULTY/CLASSROOMS: 68% of faculty are male; 32% are female. All teach and do research. No introductory courses are taught by graduate students.

PROGRAMS OF STUDY: Princeton confers A.B., and B.S.E. degrees. Master's and Doctoral degrees are also awarded. Bachelor's degrees are awarded in BIOLOGICAL SCIENCE (ecology, evolutionary biology, and molecular biology), BUSINESS (operations research), COMMUNICATIONS AND THE ARTS (classics, comparative literature, English, French, German, Italian, music, Portuguese, Slavic languages, and Spanish), COMPUTER AND PHYSICAL SCIENCE (astrophysics, chemistry, computer science, geoscience, mathematics, and physics), ENGINEERING AND ENVIRONMENTAL DESIGN (aeronautical engineering, architectural engineering, architecture, chemical engineering, civil engineering, electrical/electronics engineering, and mechanical engineering), SOCIAL SCIENCE (anthropology, archeology, East Asian studies, economics, history, international relations, Near Eastern studies, philosophy, political science/government, psychology, religion, and sociology). Economics, politics, and public policy have the largest enrollments.

ACTIVITIES: There are 250 groups on campus, including art, band, cheerleading, chess, choir, chorale, chorus, communications, computers, dance, debate, drama, environmental, ethnic, forensics, gay, honors, international, jazz band, literary magazine, marching band, Model UN, musical theater, newspaper, opera, orchestra, pep band, photography, political, professional, religious, social, social service, student government, symphony, and yearbook. Popular campus events include communiversity. **Sports:** There are 20 intercollegiate sports for men and 18 for women, and 20 intramural sports for men and 20 for women. Facilities include a 250,000-square-foot gymnasium for intercollegiate sports; a gymnasium for recreational sports; a fitness center; an Olympic-size pool with complete diving facilities; separate stadiums for football (28,000 seats), track and field, and lacrosse and field hockey; a hockey rink; and outdoor facilities such as tennis courts, an 18-hole golf course, and more than 50 acres of fields for baseball, lacrosse, rugby, soccer, and softball. **Graduates:** From July 1, 2013 to June 30, 2014, 1271 bachelor's degrees were awarded. The most popular majors were social science (26%), engineering (20%), and life sciences (10%). In an average class, 88% graduate in 4 years or less, 95% graduate in 5 years or less, and 97% graduate in 6 years or less.

SERVICES: Counseling and information services are available, as is tutoring in every subject. There is a reader service for the blind. Princeton's McGraw Center for Teaching and Learning offers workshops and individual consultations in which students can learn to manage large reading loads, problem-solve, take effective notes and create study tools, prepare for long-term projects and oral presentations; prepare for exams, manage time, and overcome test anxiety. Princeton's Writing Program works to ensure freshmen and others can master college-level writing. **Library/Resources:** The 11 libraries contain 8.2 million volumes, 395,285 microform items, 120,600 audio/video tapes/CDs/DVDs, and subscribe to 84,283 periodicals including electronic. Computerized library services include interlibrary loans, database searching, Internet access, and Wi-Fi capability. Special learning facilities include an art gallery, natural history museum, a music center, a visual and performing arts center, several theaters, an observatory, a plasma physics lab, and a center for environmental and energy studies. **Physically Challenged Students:** Facilities include wheelchair ramps, elevators, special parking, specially equipped restrooms, lowered drinking fountains, lowered telephones, special housing. Each student's needs are assessed individually. Accommodations may include additional testing time, sign language translators, and dietary accommodations for food aller-

gies. Princeton has an Office of Disability Services. **Special:** Princeton offers independent study, accelerated degree programs, student-proposed courses and majors, field study, community-based learning courses that enrich course work with related service projects, study abroad, freshman seminars, and independent work in the junior and senior year. They also offer a Program in Teacher Preparation. There are 2 national honor societies and Phi Beta Kappa. **Visiting:** There are regularly scheduled orientations for prospective students, Including information sessions on Monday to Friday within the Admission Office, and some Saturdays in the fall. Also, Princeton has an open campus, with many free and public events, and students are welcome to attend such events. They may visit www.princeton.edu/admission for more information. Visitors may sit in on classes. To schedule a visit, contact the Undergraduate Admission Office. **Campus Safety and Security:** Measures include 24-hour foot and vehicle patrol, emergency notification system, self-defense education, and security escort services. There are shuttle buses, emergency telephones, lighted pathways/sidewalks, and controlled access to dorms/residences.

REQUIREMENTS: The SAT or ACT is required. The ACT is accepted in lieu of SAT Reasoning test when every other school to which the student applies requires only the ACT. Three SAT Subject tests are also required for all applicants. Recommended college preparatory courses include 4 years each of English, math, science, and a foreign language; 2 years each of lab science and history; and some study of art and music. Essays are required as part of the application and an interview is recommended. Students with special talent in visual or performing arts may supplement tapes, CDs or DVDs. AP credits are accepted. Important factors in the admissions decision are personality/intangible qualities, recommendations by school officials, and advanced placement or honors courses. To graduate, students must complete 8 semesters, or academic units. Candidates for the A.B. degree must demonstrate proficiency in English composition and a foreign language and they must complete distribution requirements in 7 academic areas. Candidates for the B.S.E. must satisfy the English composition requirement and complete a minimum of 7 courses in the humanities and social sciences spread over 4 distribution areas. A junior project and senior thesis are required of virtually all students. **Procedure:** Freshmen are admitted fall. Entrance exams should be taken by January of the senior year at the latest. There are early admissions and deferred admissions plans. Applications should be filed by January 1 for fall entry, along with a $65 fee. Notifications are sent April 1. 1395 applicants were on the 2014 waiting list; 33 were admitted. Applications are accepted on-line. **Transfer Students:** Princeton does not have a transfer admissions option. **International Students:** There are 569 international students enrolled. The school actively recruits these students. They must take the TOEFL, The SAT: Writing Test may be substituted for the TOEFL. They must also take the SAT or ACT. Students must take the SAT or ACT, plus three SAT Subject Tests.

ADMISSIONS: 7% of the 2014-2015 applicants were accepted. The SAT scores for the 2014-2015 freshman class were: Critical Reading--3% between 500 and 599, 21% between 600 and 699, and 76% between 700 and 800; Math--1% between 500 and 599, 19% between 600 and 699, and 80% between 700 and 800; Writing--3% between 500 and 599, 18% between 600 and 699, and 79% between 700 and 800. The ACT scores were 1% between 24 and 26, 6% between 27 and 28, and 93% above 28. 98% of the current freshmen were in the top fifth of their class; 99% were in the top two fifths. 137 freshmen graduated first in their class. **Admissions Contact:** Janet Lavin Rapelye, Dean of Admissions. E-Mail: *uaoffice@princeton.edu* Web: *http://www.princeton.edu/admission/*

FINANCIAL AID: Princeton is a member of CSS. Check with the school for current application deadlines.

RAMAPO COLLEGE OF NEW JERSEY   D-1
www.ramapo.edu

Mahwah, NJ 07430   (201) 684-7300
                                             (800) 9-RAMAPO
Fax: (201) 684-7964   **Email:** admissions@ramapo.edu
Full-time: 2239 men, 2753 women   **Faculty:** 218
Part-time: 255 men, 367 women   **Ph.D.s:** 94%
Graduate: 82 men, 156 women   **Student/Faculty:** 18 to 1
Year: semesters, summer session   **Tuition:** $13,388 ($22,038)
Room & Board: $11,550   **Freshman Class:** 6297
                                       applied, 3480 accepted,
                                       889 enrolled
SAT CR/M/W: 540/555/530 **ACT:** 23   **CEEB CODE:** 2884
Application Deadline: March 1   **COMPETITIVE**

Ramapo College, founded in 1969, is a public institution offering undergraduate programs in the arts and sciences, American and international studies, business administration, and human services. Personal interaction is incorporated throughout the curriculum as is an international and multicultural component including telecommunications and computer technology. Figures in the above capsule and in this profile are approximate. There are 5 undergraduate schools and 4 graduate schools. In addition to regional accreditation, Ramapo has baccalaureate program accreditation with AACSB, CSWE, TEAC, MSCHE, NLNAC, and ACS. The 314-acre campus is in a suburban area 25 miles northwest of New York City. Including any residence halls, there are 62 buildings.

STUDENT LIFE: 95% of undergraduates are from New Jersey. Others are from 17 states, and 27 foreign countries. 66% are White; 13% Hispanic. **Male To Female Ratio:** 1.3:1. The average age of freshmen is 18; all undergraduates, 22. 12% do not continue beyond their first year; 72% remain to graduate. **Housing:** 3062 students can be accommodated in college housing, which includes coed dorms and on-campus apartments. In addition, there are honors houses, special-interest houses, blocks of rooms are reserved for scholars and honors students. On-campus housing is guaranteed for all 4 years, is available on a first-come, and first-served basis. 53% of students live on campus. All students may keep cars.

FACULTY/CLASSROOMS: 51% of faculty are male; 49% are female. All teach undergraduates. No introductory courses are taught by graduate students. The average class size in an introductory lecture is 26; in a laboratory is 19; and in a regular course is 23.

PROGRAMS OF STUDY: Ramapo confers B.A., B.S., B.S.N. and B.S.W. degrees. Master's degrees are also awarded. Bachelor's degrees are awarded in AGRICULTURE (environmental studies), BIOLOGICAL SCIENCE (biochemistry, bioinformatics, and biology/biological science), BUSINESS (accounting, business administration and management, and international business management), COMMUNICATIONS AND THE ARTS (art, communications, dramatic arts, literature, music, and visual and performing arts), COMPUTER AND PHYSICAL SCIENCE (chemistry, computer science, information sciences and systems, and mathematics), ENGINEERING AND ENVIRONMENTAL DESIGN (engineering physics and environmental science), HEALTH PROFESSIONS (allied health, clinical science, and nursing), SOCIAL SCIENCE (African studies, American studies, economics, history, international studies, law, liberal arts/general studies, political science/government, psychology, science and society, social science, social work, sociology, and Spanish studies). Physics, bioinformatics, and biology are the strongest academically. Business administration, psychology, and communication arts have the largest enrollments.

ACTIVITIES: 17% of men belong to 15 national fraternities; 17% of women belong to 13 national sororities. There are 100 groups on campus, including and theme housing, and environmental clubs, cheerleading, choir, chorale, chorus, computers, dance, debate, drama, environmental, ethnic, film, gay, honors, international, jazz band, literary magazine, musical theater, newspaper, pep band, photography, political, professional, radio and TV, religious, social, social service, student government, volunteer/community service, and yearbook. Popular campus events include LollaNoBooza, Octoberfest, and Stress Busters. **Sports:** There are 8 intercollegiate sports for men

and 10 for women, and 16 intramural sports for men and 16 for women. Facilities include 10% Varsity and 80% Intramural participation. Facilities include a 1200-seat stadium that includes an 8-lane, 400-meter track and a FieldTurf field, 12 lighted tennis courts, and baseball, softball, field hockey, and soccer fields. A 1457-seat competition arena houses basketball and volleyball courts, and there is an auxiliary gym for intramurals and recreation. A 5000-square-foot fitness center includes cardio machines, machine weight stations, and free weights. Also available is a new athletic training room, a 6-lane swimming pool, and multiple locker rooms. **Graduates:** From July 1, 2013 to June 30, 2014, 1325 bachelor's degrees were awarded. The most popular majors were business/marketing (21%), psychology (15%), and communication arts (11%). 130 companies recruited on campus in 2013-2014. In an average class, 2% graduate in 3 years or less, 60% graduate in 4 years or less, 70% graduate in 5 years or less, and 72% graduate in 6 years or less.

SERVICES: Counseling and information services are available, as is tutoring in every subject. There is a reader service for the blind, and remedial math, reading, and writing. Students have access to resources at the Center for Academic Success **Library/Resources:** The library contains 191,031 volumes, 2,500 microform items, 9,373 audio/video tapes/CDs/DVDs, and subscribes to 488 periodicals including electronic. Computerized library services include interlibrary loans, database searching, Internet access, and Wi-Fi capability. Special learning facilities include a radio station, TV station, astronomical observatory, international telecommunications satellite center, the Marge Roukema Center for International Education and Entrepreneurship, a solar greenhouse center, a spirituality center, and a sustainability education center. **Physically Challenged Students:** All of the campus is accessible. Facilities include wheelchair ramps, elevators, special parking, specially equipped restrooms, special class scheduling, lowered drinking fountains, lowered telephones, and special housing. **Special:** Ramapo's curriculum emphasizes the interdependence of global society and includes an international dimension in all academic programs. Students may study abroad in many countries. Cooperative programs are available with various corporations and in foreign countries. Cross-registration is possible with local state colleges. Ramapo offers accelerated degree programs, dual and student-designed majors, credit for life experience, pass/fail options, internships, work-study programs, and certificate programs in gerontology and substance abuse. A teachers education program is offered. There are 23 national honor societies, a freshman honors program, and 5 departmental honors programs. **Visiting:** There are regularly scheduled orientations for prospective students, Student visits include orientation, advisement, registration, and immediate decision days (that follow the early action plan). There are guides for informal visits and visitors may sit in on classes. To schedule a visit, contact the Admissions Office at admissions@ramapo.edu. **Campus Safety and Security:** Measures include 24-hour foot and vehicle patrol, emergency notification system, and security escort services. There are shuttle buses, emergency telephones, lighted pathways/sidewalks, surveillance cameras.

REQUIREMENTS: The SAT is required. Applicants must be graduates of an accredited secondary schools or have earned a GED. The college requires 18 academic credits, including 4 in English, 3 each in math, science, and social studies, 2 in foreign language, and the remaining 3 in academic electives. Students must also submit an essay. An interview is recommended. AP and CLEP credits are accepted. Important factors in the admissions decision are advanced placement or honors courses, recommendations by school officials, and evidence of special talent.Students must complete general education requirements of approximately 50 credits in science, social science, humanities, and English composition, as well as core requirements in their school of study and their particular major. A senior seminar is also required. To graduate, students must earn at least 128 credits with a minimum GPA of 2.0. **Procedure:** Freshmen are admitted fall and spring. Entrance exams should be taken during the senior year. There are early admissions, deferred admissions, and rolling admissions plans. Applications should be filed by March 1 for fall entry; December 1 for spring entry. The fall 2014 application fee was $60. Notification is sent on a rolling basis. Applications are accepted on-line. **Transfer Students:** 596 transfer students enrolled in 2013-2014. Applicants must supply a completed admission application, official transcripts from all previously attended colleges, and an official high school transcript (if fewer than 60 credits from another college attempted). 48 of 128 credits required for the bachelor's degree must be completed at Ramapo. **International Students:** There are 77 international students enrolled. The school actively recruits these students. They must take the TOEFL with a minimum score of 550 on the paper-based TOEFL (PBT) or 90 on the Internet-based version (iBT) and the Comprehensive English Language Test. They must also take the SAT.

ADMISSIONS: 55% of the 2014-2015 applicants were accepted. The SAT scores for the 2014-2015 freshman class were: Critical Reading--29% below 500, 51% between 500 and 599, 18% between 600 and 699, and 3% between 700 and 800; Math--21% below 500, 49% between 500 and 599, 25% between 600 and 699, and 5% between 700 and 800; Writing--32% below 500, 47% between 500 and 599, 18% between 600 and 699, and 3% between 700 and 800. The ACT scores were 12% below 21, 42% between 21 and 23, 40% between 24 and 26, and 6% above 28. 57% of the current freshmen were in the top fifth of their class; 89% were in the top two fifths. 2 freshmen graduated first in their class. **Admissions Contact:** Peter Rice, Director of Admissions. E-Mail: *admissions@ramapo.edu* Web: *www.ramapo.edu*

FINANCIAL AID: In 2014-2015, 80% of all full-time freshmen and 82% of continuing full-time students received some form of financial aid. 60% of all full-time freshmen and 50% of continuing full-time students received need-based aid. The average freshman award was $11,368. Need-based scholarships or need-based grants averaged $10,305; need-based self-help aid (loans and jobs) averaged $4,525; other non-need-based awards and non-need-based scholarships averaged $4,437; and $10,254 from other forms of aid. 4% of undergraduate students work part-time. Average annual earnings from campus work are $2000. The average financial indebtedness of the 2014 graduate was $22,309. The FAFSA is required. The priority date for freshman financial aid applications for fall entry is March 1. The deadline for filing freshman financial aid applications for fall entry is March 15.

RICHARD STOCKTON COLLEGE OF NEW JERSEY   D-5

www.stockton.edu

Pomona, NJ 08240

(609) 652-4261
n/av

Fax: (609) 748-5541

Email: admissions@stockton.edu

Full-time: 2460 men, 3420 women	**Faculty:** IIA, ++$
Part-time: 350 men, 560 women	**Ph.D.s:** n/av
Graduate: 160 men, 440 women	**Student/Faculty:** n/av
Year: semesters, summer session	**Tuition:** $12,500 ($18,700)
Room & Board: $11,100	**Freshman Class:** n/av
SAT or ACT: required	**CEEB CODE:** 2889
Application Deadline: n/av	**VERY COMPETITIVE**

Richard Stockton College of New Jersey, founded in 1969, is a public liberal arts college with 28 undergraduate programs and 6 graduate specialty areas. The figures in the above capsule and in this profile are approximate. There is one graduate school. In addition to regional accreditation, Stockton has baccalaureate program accreditation with APTA, CSWE, NASDTEC, NLN, ACS, ACOTE, AOTA, and NEHS-PAC. The 1600-acre campus is in a suburban area 12 miles northwest of Atlantic City. Including any residence halls, there are 55 buildings.
STUDENT LIFE: 98% of undergraduates are from New Jersey. Others are from 21 states, 10 foreign countries, and Canada. 74% are from public schools. 78% are White. **Male To Female Ratio:** 1.5:1. The average age of freshmen is 18; all undergraduates, 22. 17% do not continue beyond their first year; 67% remain to graduate. **Housing:** 2081 students can be accommodated in college housing, which includes coed dorms and on-campus apartments. In addition, there are special-interest houses, wellness, substance-free, academic, and smoke-free housing. On-campus housing is guaranteed for the freshman year only, is available on a first-come, first-served basis, and is available on a lottery system for upperclassmen. 68% of students commute. All students may keep cars.

FACULTY/CLASSROOMS: 54% of faculty are male; 46% are female. No introductory courses are taught by graduate students. The average class size in an introductory lecture is 33; in a laboratory is 18; and in a regular course is 19.
PROGRAMS OF STUDY: Stockton confers B.A., B.S. and B.S.N. degrees. Master's and Doctoral degrees are also awarded. Bachelor's degrees are awarded in BIOLOGICAL SCIENCE (biochemistry, biology/biological science, and marine science), BUSINESS (accounting, banking and finance, business administration and management, and management science), COMMUNICATIONS AND THE ARTS (communications, dance, dramatic arts, fine arts, languages, literature, and music), COMPUTER AND PHYSICAL SCIENCE (chemistry, computer science, geology, information sciences and systems, mathematics, and physics), EDUCATION (education), ENGINEERING AND ENVIRONMENTAL DESIGN (computational sciences, environmental science, and preengineering), HEALTH PROFESSIONS (nursing, physical therapy, public health, and speech pathology/audiology), SOCIAL SCIENCE (anthropology, criminal justice, economics, history, liberal arts/general studies, philosophy, political science/government, psychology, and social work). Sciences is the strongest academically. Business, psychology, and criminal justice have the largest enrollments.

ACTIVITIES: 4% of men belong to 11 national fraternities; 5% of women belong to 10 national sororities. There are 94 groups on campus, including art, band, cheerleading, chess, choir, chorale, chorus, computers, dance, drama, ethnic, gay, honors, international, jazz band, literary magazine, newspaper, orchestra, pep band, photography, political, professional, radio and TV, religious, social, social service, and student government. Popular campus events include Spring Concert, Spring Fling, and Black History Month. **Sports:** There are 7 intercollegiate sports for men and 10 for women, and 10 intramural sports for men and 10 for women. Facilities include an indoor 6-lane swimming pool, an outdoor track, a weight-lifting gym, 2 multipurpose gyms, a sauna, steam baths, and dance studios, as well as playing fields, a 60-acre lake for fishing and canoeing, cross-country courses, bike trails, an all-weather track, and tennis, racquetball, and basketball courts. There are 9 club sports in addition to intramurals. **Graduates:** From July 1, 2013 to June 30, 2014, 1632 bachelor's degrees were awarded. The most popular majors were social science (30%), business and management (19%), and natural sciences (15%). 250 companies recruited on campus in 2013-2014. In an average class, 2% graduate in 3 years or less, 43% graduate in 4 years or less, 65% graduate in 5 years or less, and 67% graduate in 6 years or less. Of the 2013 graduating class, 34% were enrolled in graduate school within 6 months of graduation, and 83% were employed.

SERVICES: Counseling and information services are available, as is tutoring in most subjects. There is a reader service for the blind, and remedial math, reading, and writing. There is a skills center and a learning access program for learning-disabled students. **Library/Resources:** The library contains 627,318 volumes, 1.1 million microform items, 15,342 audio/video tapes/CDs/DVDs, and subscribes to 26,375 periodicals including electronic. Computerized library services include interlibrary loans, database searching, and Internet access. Special learning facilities include an art gallery, radio station, TV station, astronomical observatory, marine science field lab, marina with a fleet of small boats, Holocaust resource center, educational technology, training center, and performing arts center. **Physically Challenged Students:** 99% of the campus is accessible. Facilities include wheelchair ramps, elevators, special parking, specially equipped restrooms, special class scheduling, lowered drinking fountains, lowered telephones. **Special:** Stockton offers internships in all fields with a wide variety of companies, work-study with various government agencies and corporations, a Washington semester, independent study, and study abroad in 53 countries. Dual majors in all programs, student-designed majors, an accelerated degree in medicine and criminal justice, 3-2 engineering degrees with the New Jersey Institute of Technology and Rutgers University, and general studies degrees are also offered. Nondegree study, pass/fail options, and credit for life, military, and work experience are possible. There are 5 national honor societies and a freshman honors program. **Visiting:** There are regularly scheduled orientations for prospective students, including academic advising and orientation. There are guides for informal visits and visitors may sit in on classes. To schedule a visit, contact Enrollment Management at (609) 652-4251. **Campus Safety and Security:** Measures include 24-hour foot and vehicle patrol, emergency notification system, self-defense education, and security escort services. There are emergency telephones, lighted pathways/sidewalks, a fully commissioned police department.

REQUIREMENTS: The SAT or ACT is required. Applicants must be high school graduates; the GED is accepted. 16 academic credits are required, including 4 years in English, 3 each in math and social studies, 2 in science, and 4 additional years of any of the above or a foreign language, or both. An essay and an interview are recommended, and a portfolio or audition is necessary where appropriate. AP and CLEP credits are accepted. Important factors in the admissions decision are advanced placement or honors courses, leadership record, and evidence of special talent. To graduate, students must earn 128 credit hours, with 32 in the general studies curriculum and maintain a minimum GPA of 2.0. 3 quantitative reasoning and 4 writing courses as well as freshman seminar are required. **Procedure:** Freshmen are admitted fall and spring. Entrance exams should be taken once in the junior year and again before January in the senior year. There is a rolling admissions plan. Applications should be filed by December 1 for spring entry. The fall 2014 application fee was $50. Notification is sent on a rolling basis. Applications are accepted online. **Transfer Students:** 1088 transfer students enrolled in 2013-2014. Transfer students must have earned at least 16 credits at other colleges and must submit college and high school transcripts as well as SAT scores. 32 of 128 credits required for the bachelor's degree must be completed at Stockton. **International Students:** There are 25 international students enrolled. They must take the TOEFL. They must also take the SAT or ACT.

ADMISSIONS: John Lacovelli, Interim Dean, Enrollment Management. E-Mail: *admissions@stockton.edu* Web: *www.stockton.edu*

FINANCIAL AID: In 2014-2015, 77% of all full-time freshmen and 90% of continuing full-time students received some form of financial aid. 40% of all full-time freshmen and 41% of continuing full-time students received need-based aid. The average freshman award was $11,772. Need-based scholarships or need-based grants averaged $8,170 ($15,396 maximum); need-based self-help aid (loans and jobs) averaged $3,702 ($9,900 maximum); and other non-need-based awards and non-need-based scholarships averaged $3,602 ($23,555 maximum). 16% of undergraduate students work part-time. Average annual earnings from campus work are $1394. The average financial indebtedness of the 2014 graduate was $15,624. The FAFSA is required. Check with the school for current application deadlines.

RIDER UNIVERSITY   D-3
www.rider.edu

Lawrenceville, NJ 08648	(609) 896-5042
	(800) 257-9026
Fax: (609) 895-6645	Email: admissions@rider.edu
Full-time: 1648 men, 2280 women	**Faculty:** 237; IIA, ++$
Part-time: 246 men, 375 women	**Ph.D.s:** 98%
Graduate: 329 men, 607 women	**Student/Faculty:** 17 to 1
Year: semesters, summer session	**Tuition:** $33,420
Room & Board: $12,340	**Freshman Class:** 7903 applied, 5701 accepted, 919 enrolled
SAT CR/M/W: 510/520/520 **ACT:** 22	**CEEB CODE:** 2758
Application Deadline: n/av	**COMPETITIVE**

Rider University, founded in 1865, is a private institution offering undergraduate programs in the areas of business administration, liberal arts, education, sciences, and continuing studies. Westminster Choir College, located in nearby Princeton, is Rider's fourth college. Figures in the above capsule and in this profile are approximate. There are 4 undergraduate schools and 2 graduate schools. In addition to regional accreditation, Rider has baccalaureate program accreditation with AACSB, NASM, NCATE, CACREP, and NASP. The 280-acre campus is in a suburban area 3 miles north of Trenton and 7 miles south of Princeton. Including any residence halls, there are 41 buildings.

STUDENT LIFE: 78% of undergraduates are from New Jersey. Others are from 51 states, 64 foreign countries, and Canada. 66% are White. **Male To Female Ratio:** 1.5:1. The average age of freshmen is 18; all undergraduates, 22. 23% do not continue beyond their first year; 66% remain to graduate. **Housing:** 2515 students can be accommodated in college housing, which includes single-sex and coed dorms and on-campus apartments. In addition, there are honors houses, language houses, special-interest houses, fraternity houses, sorority houses, learning community, wellness, quiet, science area, and first-year experience housing. On-campus housing is available on a lottery system for upperclassmen. 57% of students live on campus; of those, 50% remain on campus on weekends. All students may keep cars.

FACULTY/CLASSROOMS: 56% of faculty are male; 44% are female. All teach and do research. No introductory courses are taught by graduate students. The average class size in an introductory lecture is 26; in a laboratory is 14; and in a regular course is 20.

PROGRAMS OF STUDY: Rider confers B.A., B.M., B.S. and B.S.B.A. degrees. Associate and Master's degrees are also awarded. Bachelor's degrees are awarded in BIOLOGICAL SCIENCE (biochemistry, biology/biological science, and marine science), BUSINESS (accounting, banking and finance, business administration and management, business economics, human resources, international business management, management science, marketing/retailing/merchandising, and office supervision and management), COMMUNICATIONS AND THE ARTS (advertising, communications, dance, dramatic arts, English, English literature, fine arts, French, German, journalism, multimedia, music, piano/organ, public relations, Russian, Spanish, and voice), COMPUTER AND PHYSICAL SCIENCE (actuarial science, chemistry, geoscience, information sciences and systems, mathematics, and physics), EDUCATION (business education, early childhood education, elementary education, English education, foreign languages education, marketing and distribution education, mathematics education, music education, science education, secondary education, and social studies education), ENGINEERING AND ENVIRONMENTAL DESIGN (environmental science), HEALTH PROFESSIONS (premedicine), SOCIAL SCIENCE (American studies, biopsychology, economics, history, liberal arts/general studies, philosophy, political science/government, prelaw, psychology, and sociology). Elementary education, accounting, and business administration have the largest enrollments.

ACTIVITIES: 5% of men belong to 4 national fraternities; 9% of women belong to 8 national sororities. There are 130 groups on campus, including art, band, cheerleading, choir, chorale, chorus, computers, dance, drama, environmental, ethnic, film, gay, honors, international, jazz band, literary magazine, musical theater, newspaper, opera, orchestra, pep band, photography, political, professional, religious, social, social service, student government, symphony, and yearbook. Popular campus events include Cranberry Fest, Family Day and Unity Day. **Sports:** There are 10 intercollegiate sports for men and 10 for women, and 10 intramural sports for men and 6 for women. Facilities include a recreation center with basketball, volleyball, and tennis courts, and an elevated jogging/walking track, and a fitness center with cardio equipment, weight room machines, and free weights. **Graduates:** From July 1, 2013 to June 30, 2014, 865 bachelor's degrees were awarded. The most popular majors were business (35%), education (15%), and English (12%). 150 companies recruited on campus in 2013-2014. In an average class, 57% graduate in 4 years or less, 65% graduate in 5 years or less, and 67% graduate in 6 years or less.

SERVICES: Counseling and information services are available, as is tutoring in most subjects. There is remedial math, reading, and writing. **Library/Resources:** The library contains 448,025 volumes, 657,600 microform items, 5,444 audio/video tapes/CDs/DVDs, and subscribes to 50,594 periodicals including electronic. Computerized library services include interlibrary loans, database searching, Internet access, and Wi-Fi capability. Special learning facilities include an art gallery, TV station, journalism and sociology labs, and a holocaust/genocide center. **Physically Challenged Students:** 75% of the campus is accessible. Facilities include wheelchair ramps, elevators, special parking, specially equipped restrooms, special class scheduling, lowered drinking fountains, and lowered telephones. **Special:** Internships in many programs, a co-op program in retail marketing, work-study, study abroad in 14 countries, a B.A.-B.S. degree in all liberal arts and sciences, dual majors in education, a liberal studies degree, and nondegree study are possible. There are 24 national honor societies, a freshman honors program, and 17 departmental honors programs. **Visiting:** There are regularly scheduled orientations for prospective students, including 3 open houses, Saturday information sessions and other programs that consist of a welcome, a campus tour, and a variety of formal and informal activities to meet faculty, staff, current students, and alumni. There are guides for informal visits and visitors may sit in on classes. To schedule a visit, contact the Office of Admissions at (609) 896-5042. **Campus Safety and Security:** Measures include 24-hour foot and vehicle patrol, emergency notification system, self-defense education, and security escort services. There are shuttle buses, emergency telephones, lighted pathways/sidewalks shuttle car, a staffed kiosk at the entrance, a security system in residence halls, video camera surveillance, bike patrol, and a property ID program.

REQUIREMENTS: The SAT or ACT is required. Applicants need 16 Carnegie units, including 4 years of English and 2 of math. 3 units of math are required for prospective math, science, and business majors. An essay is recommended. An audition is required for theater scholarships. The GED is accepted. AP and CLEP credits are accepted. Important factors in the admissions decision are advanced placement or honors courses, extracurricular activities record, and leadership record. To graduate, all students must maintain a minimum GPA of 2.0 while taking 120 semester hours. Students also must fulfill core curriculum requirements, including 9 hours in humanities, 7 to 8 in science, 6 each in English writing and foreign language (may be waived if proficiency is demonstrated), social sciences/communications, and history, and 3 in math. 30 to 76 credits are required in the major. A thesis is required in the honors program and some science majors. **Procedure:** Freshmen are admitted fall and spring. Entrance exams should be taken by January of the senior year. There are deferred admissions and rolling admissions plans. Application deadlines are open. Application fee is $50. Notification is sent on a rolling basis. 70 applicants were on the 2014 waiting list; 49 were admitted. Applications are accepted on-line. **Transfer Students:** 262 transfer students enrolled in 2013-2014. A GPA of 2.5 or better is required for applicants. If students have fewer than 30 credits, they also must submit high school transcripts and SAT scores. An essay or personal statement is required, and an interview is recommended. 30 of 120 credits required for the bachelor's degree must be completed at Rider. **International Students:** There are 74 international students enrolled. The school actively recruits these students. They must take the TOEFL with a minimum score of 550 on the paper-based TOEFL (PBT) or 80 on the Internet-based version (iBT). They must also take the SAT or ACT.

ADMISSIONS: 72% of the 2014-2015 applicants were accepted. The SAT scores for the 2014-2015 freshman class were: Critical Reading--44% below 500, 42% between 500 and 599, 12% between 600 and 699, and 2% between 700 and 800; Math--35% below 500, 44% between 500 and 599, 18% between 600 and 699, and 2% between 700 and 800; Writing--43% below 500, 40% between 500 and 599, 14% between 600 and 699, and 2% between 700 and 800. **Admissions Contact:** Susan C. Christian, Director of Admissions. E-Mail: *admissions@rider.edu* Web: *www.rider.edu*

FINANCIAL AID: In 2014-2015, 78% of all full-time freshmen and 71% of continuing full-time students received some form of financial aid. 77% of all full-time freshmen and 69% of continuing full-time students received need-based aid. The average freshman award was $25,177. Need-based scholarships or need-based grants averaged $20,455; need-based self-help aid (loans and jobs) averaged $5,627; and $3,226 from other forms of aid. The average financial indebtedness of the 2014 graduate was $32,718. The FAFSA is required. The priority date for freshman financial aid applications for fall entry is March 1.

ROWAN UNIVERSITY   C-4
www.rowan.edu

Glassboro, NJ 08028	**(855) 256-4200**
	1.877.RU.ROWAN
Fax: (856) 256-4430	**Email: admissions@rowan.edu**
Full-time: 5677 men, 4822 women	**Faculty:** 362
Part-time: 635 men, 888 women	**Ph.D.s:** 80%
Graduate: 1036 men, 1720 women	**Student/Faculty:** 17 to 1
Year: semesters, summer session	**Tuition:** $12,616 ($20,570)
Room & Board: $11,406	**Freshman Class:** 10078 applied, 6600 accepted, 1920 enrolled
SAT CR/M/W: 582/622/565	**CEEB CODE:** 2515
Application Deadline: March 1	**VERY COMPETITIVE+**

Rowan University, a leading state-designated comprehensive public research institution, combines liberal education with professional preparation from the baccalaureate through the doctorate. Rowan provides a collaborative, learning-centered environment in which highly qualified and diverse faculty, staff, and students integrate teaching, research, scholarship, creative activity, and community service. There are 9 undergraduate schools and 1 graduate school. In addition to regional accreditation, Rowan has baccalaureate program accreditation with AACSB, ABET, CSAB, NASAD, NASDTEC, NASM, NCATE, LCME, LOCA, COPTI, MUS, CAATE, THEA, NASD, and NAST. The 921-acre campus is in a suburban area 20 miles southeast of Philadelphia. Including any residence halls, there are 85 buildings.

STUDENT LIFE: 95% of undergraduates are from New Jersey. Others are from 33 states, and 19 foreign countries. 90% are from public schools. 69% are White. **Male To Female Ratio:** 1.0:1. The average age of freshmen is 18; all undergraduates, 22. 14% do not continue beyond their first year; 67% remain to graduate. **Housing:** 4385 students can be accommodated in college housing, which includes coed dorms and on-campus apartments. In addition, there are honors houses and special-interest houses. On-campus housing is guaranteed for the freshman year only and is available on a lottery system for upperclassmen. Priority is given to out-of-town students. 64% of students commute. Upperclassmen may keep cars.

FACULTY/CLASSROOMS: 53% of faculty are male; 47% are female. 92% teach undergraduates, and 8% do both. No introductory courses are taught by graduate students. The average class size in an introductory lecture is 22; in a laboratory is 16; and in a regular course is 22.

PROGRAMS OF STUDY: Rowan confers B.A., B.S., B.S.N., B.F.A., B.G.S. and B.M. degrees. Master's and Doctoral degrees are also awarded. Bachelor's degrees are awarded in AGRICULTURE (environmental studies), BIOLOGICAL SCIENCE (biochemistry, bioinformatics, and biology/biological science), BUSINESS (accounting, business administration and management, entrepreneurial studies, human resources, marketing/retailing/merchandising, personnel management, and small business management), COMMUNICATIONS AND THE ARTS (advertising, art, broadcasting, communications, dramatic arts, English, fine arts, jazz, journalism, music, public relations, radio/television technology, Spanish, speech/debate/rhetoric, and theatre arts), COMPUTER AND PHYSICAL SCIENCE (chemistry, computer science, mathematics, physical sciences, and physics), EDUCATION (art education, athletic training, collaborative education, early childhood education, education, elementary education, foreign languages education, general studies, music education, and science education), ENGINEERING AND ENVIRONMENTAL DESIGN (biomedical engineering, chemical engineering, civil engineering, engineering, and mechanical engineering), HEALTH PROFESSIONS (health and nursing), SOCIAL SCIENCE (African studies, American studies, criminal justice, economics, geography, history, liberal arts/general studies, philosophy and religion, political science/government, psychology, and sociology). Engineering, biology, and education are the strongest academically. Biological science, psychology, and elementary education have the largest enrollments.

ACTIVITIES: 5% of men belong to 16 national fraternities; 4% of women belong to 10 national sororities. There are 150 groups on campus, including and concert band, art, band, cheerleading, chess, choir, chorale, chorus, communications, computers, dance, drama, environmental, ethnic, film, gay, honors, international, jazz band, literary magazine, music ensembles, musical theater, newspaper, opera, orchestra, pep band, photography, political, professional, radio and TV, religious, social, social service, student government, symphony, and yearbook. Popular campus events include Prof Stock, Back to the Boro, Senior Send Off, Home Coming, and Leadership Conference. **Sports:** The NCAA sports for men are football, soccer, cross country, basketball, swimming, indoor track, outdoor track and baseball. For women there are volleyball, cross country, field hockey, soccer, basketball, indoor track, swimming, lacrosse, outdoor track and softball. Regarding men's and women's intramural sports breakdown: many of our sports are either open to either gender or we have co-rec or co-ed divisions available. The majority of open divisions are men's teams – such as wiffleball, bowling, billiards, racquetball, ping pong, tennis, badminton, dodgeball, battleship, horse, golf, sand volleyball, punt, pass and kick, free throw and 3 point competition (15 offerings). Men's specific – basketball, outdoor soccer, softball, volleyball, flag football, indoor soccer, 1 on 1 basketball, kickball, regional dodgeball (9 offerings). Women's specific – basketball, outdoor soccer, softball, volleyball, flag football, indoor soccer, 1 on 1 basketball, regional dodgeball (8 offerings). 76,000 square foot student recreation center including: (2) 25 yard competition pools, 3 court recreational multi-purpose wood courts, indoor jogging track, group fitness studio, cycling studio, 4 racquetball courts, free weight room, cardiovascular and selectorized equipment areas, multi-purpose outdoor recreational field, and café area. **Graduates:** From July 1, 2013 to June 30, 2014, 2636 bachelor's degrees were awarded. The most popular majors were psychology (8%), elementary education (7%), and law/justice (7%). 106 companies recruited on campus in 2013-2014. In an average class, 43% graduate in 4 years or less, 64% graduate in 5 years or less, and 67% graduate in 6 years or less.

SERVICES: Counseling and information services are available, as is tutoring in every subject. There is a reader service for the blind, and remedial math, reading, and writing. **Library/Resources:** The 4 libraries contain 641,430 volumes, 519,817 microform items, 18,984 audio/video tapes/CDs/DVDs, and subscribe to 77,727 periodicals including electronic. Computerized library services include interlibrary loans, database searching, Internet access, and Wi-Fi capability. Special learning facilities include an art gallery, planetarium, radio station, TV station, virtual reality cave, exercise science research laboratory, assessment and learning center. **Physically Challenged Students:** 95% of the campus is accessible. Facilities include wheelchair ramps, elevators, special parking, specially equipped restrooms, special class scheduling, lowered drinking fountains, lowered telephones, and special housing. **Special:** Honors program is a special interdisciplinary program that is not housed in any department per se; rather departments provide courses to the stand alone honors program. Students may study abroad in 40 countries. Internships are available in all majors both with and without pay. Rowan also offers accelerated degree programs and 3-2 degrees in optometry, podiatry, and pharmacy as well as a 4-1 degree in business. There are dual majors, pass/fail options, and credit for military experience. BS/MS accelerated degrees. Joint BS/MS accelerated degrees with Stockton College. There are 12 national honor societies and a freshman honors program. **Visiting:** There are regularly scheduled orientations for prospective students, visiting students may participate in a 2-day summer program providing schedule confirmation/adjustment, student activities updates, and workshops for students and parents. There are guides for informal visits and visitors may sit in on classes. To schedule a visit, contact Albert Betts at betts@rowan.edu. **Campus Safety and Security:** Measures include 24-hour foot and vehicle patrol, emergency notification system, self-defense education, and security escort services. There are shuttle buses, emergency telephones, lighted pathways/sidewalks, controlled access to dorms/residences, Rowan Dept. of Public Safety also has an EMS service which include 2 ambulances.

REQUIREMENTS: The SAT is required. Students are required to score an 1080, or no less than 500 on either part. Students submitting ACT scores should have a minimum composite score of 23. Applicants must be graduates of accredited secondary schools or have earned a GED. Rowan requires 16 academic credits or Carnegie units, including 4 in English, 3 each in math and college preparatory elec-

tives, and 2 each in foreign language, history, and lab science. A portfolio or audition is required for specific majors. AP and CLEP credits are accepted. Important factors in the admissions decision are advanced placement or honors courses, evidence of special talent, and leadership record. General education requirements include 6-12 credits of social and behavior sciences; 6-12 credits of history, humanities and language; 7-15 credits of math and science (one science course must be 4 credits with a lab component), 9 credits of communication, and 6 credits in non-program courses. Students also take requirements in the Rowan Experience, which includes the Rowan Seminar and courses with the following designations: Multicultural/Global, Artistic/Creative Experience, Literature, and Writing Intensive. The bachelor's degree requires 120-132 semester hours, including 30-42 in a major field, with a minimum GPA of 2.0. **Procedure:** Freshmen are admitted fall and spring. Entrance exams should be taken by May or June of the junior year, or by December of the sen. There is a deferred admissions plan. Applications should be filed by March 1 for fall entry; November 1 for spring entry, along with a $65 fee. Notifications are sent April 15. 150 applicants were on the 2014 waiting list; 56 were admitted. Applications are accepted on-line. **Transfer Students:** 1429 transfer students enrolled in 2013-2014. Applicants must have a minimum GPA of 2.0, but should present a GPA of 2.5 to be competitive. An associate degree is recommended. Students who have earned fewer than 24 semester hours must also submit a high school transcript and SAT I results. 30 of 120 credits required for the bachelor's degree must be completed at Rowan. **International Students:** There are 110 international students enrolled. The school actively recruits these students. They must take the TOEFL with a minimum score of 550 on the paper-based TOEFL (PBT) or 79 on the Internet-based version (iBT), or take the IELTS. They must also take the SAT or ACT. SAT for students whose first language is English and all engineering majors.

ADMISSIONS: 65% of the 2014-2015 applicants were accepted. The SAT scores for the 2014-2015 freshman class were: Critical Reading--6% below 500, 57% between 500 and 599, 32% between 600 and 699, and 5% between 700 and 800; Math--1% below 500, 34% between 500 and 599, 53% between 600 and 699, and 12% between 700 and 800; Writing--14% below 500, 55% between 500 and 599, 28% between 600 and 699, and 3% between 700 and 800. **Admissions Contact:** Albert Betts, Director of Admissions. E-Mail: *admissions@ rowan.edu* Web: *http://www.rowan.edu/home/admissions-aid/ undergraduate-admissions*

FINANCIAL AID: The average freshman award was $10,558. Need-based scholarships or need-based grants averaged $9,868; need-based self-help aid (loans and jobs) averaged $3,405; and other non-need-based awards and non-need-based scholarships averaged $8,566. 10% of undergraduate students work part-time. Average annual earnings from campus work are $1200. The average financial indebtedness of the 2014 graduate was $26,748. The FAFSA is required. The priority date for freshman financial aid applications for fall entry is January 1. The deadline for filing freshman financial aid applications for fall entry is March 15.

RUTGERS, THE STATE UNIVERSITY OF NEW JERSEY

Rutgers, the State University of New Jersey, established in 1766, is a public system in New Jersey. It is governed by a board of governors, whose chief administrator is the president. The primary goal of the system is instruction, research, and service. The main priorities are to continue development as a distinguished comprehensive public university, to enhance undergraduate education, to strengthen graduate education and research, and to develop and improve programs to serve society New Jersey's needs. The total student enrollment is usually about 65,512 with 1,900 faculty members. Altogether there are approximately 117 baccalaureate, 116 master's, and 83 doctoral programs offered by the school. Profiles of the 4-year campuses are included in this section.

RUTGERS, THE STATE UNIVERSITY OF NEW JERSEY/CAMDEN CAMPUS
C-4

www.camden.rutgers.edu/

Camden, NJ 08102	(856) 225-6104
	n/av
Fax: n/av	**Email: admissions@ugadm.rutgers.edu**
Full-time: 1797 men, 2193 women	**Faculty:** 310; IIA, ++$
Part-time: 335 men, 532 women	**Ph.D.s:** 99%
Graduate: 740 men, 724 women	**Student/Faculty:** 13 to 1
Year: semesters, summer session	**Tuition:** $13,683 ($27,978)
Room & Board: $11,438	**Freshman Class:** 6550 applied, 3955 accepted, 431 enrolled
SAT CR/M/W: 510/530/510 **ACT:** required	
	CEEB CODE: 2742
Application Deadline: open	**COMPETITIVE**

Rutgers, The State University of New Jersey/Camden Campus was founded in 1926. On July 1, 2013, the New Jersey Medical and Health Sciences Education Restructuring Act went into effect, integrating Rutgers, The State University of New Jersey, with all units of the University of Medicine and Dentistry of New Jersey (UMDNJ), except University Hospital in Newark and the School of Osteopathic Medicine in Stratford. The integration of the legacy elements of UMDNJ into Rutgers has created a fourth unit, Rutgers Biomedical and Health Sciences (RBHS), which consists of a number of schools and units located on various sites but closely aligned with the campuses in Newark and New Brunswick. The campus is comprised of 4 undergraduate, degree-granting schools: College of the Arts and Sciences, University College--Camden, the School of Nursing-Camden and the School of Business--Camden. Each school has individual requirements, policies, and fees. There are 4 undergraduate schools and 4 graduate schools. In addition to regional accreditation, RU-Camden has baccalaureate program accreditation with AACSB, APTA, CSWE, TEAC, and CCNE. The 32-acre campus is in an urban area 1 mile east of Philadelphia. Including any residence halls, there are 47 buildings.

STUDENT LIFE: 96% of undergraduates are from New Jersey. Others are from 23 states, 18 foreign countries, and Canada. 55% are White; 16% African American; 12% Hispanic. **Male To Female Ratio:** 1.2:1. The average age of freshmen is 18; all undergraduates, 22. 18% do not continue beyond their first year; 82% remain to graduate.

Housing: 613 students can be accommodated in college housing, which includes coed dorms and on-campus apartments. In addition, there are fraternity houses, sorority houses, Coed dorms,. 94% of students commute. Alcohol is not permitted.

FACULTY/CLASSROOMS: 53% of faculty are male; 47% are female. No introductory courses are taught by graduate students. The average class size in an introductory lecture is 30; in a laboratory is 20; and in a regular course is 30.

PROGRAMS OF STUDY: RU-Camden confers B.A., B.S. and B.H.M. degrees. Master's and Doctoral degrees are also awarded. Bachelor's degrees are awarded in BIOLOGICAL SCIENCE (biochemistry and biology/biological science), BUSINESS (accounting, banking and finance, hospitality management services, management science, and marketing/retailing/merchandising), COMMUNICATIONS AND THE ARTS (art, art history and appreciation, dramatic arts, English, French, German, music, and Spanish), COMPUTER AND PHYSICAL SCIENCE (chemistry, computer science, mathematics, physics, and science), HEALTH PROFESSIONS (medical laboratory technology and nursing), SOCIAL SCIENCE (African American studies, child care/child and family studies, criminal justice, economics, history, interdisciplinary studies, liberal arts/general studies, philosophy, political science/government, psychology, religion, social work, sociology, and urban studies). Nursing, business management, and psychology have the largest enrollments.

ACTIVITIES: There are 75 groups on campus, including computers, drama, ethnic, gay, honors, international, newspaper, political, professional, radio and TV, religious, social, social service, student government, and yearbook. Popular campus events include Raptor Day, Springfest and Basketball Team Sports. **Sports:** There are 9 intercollegiate sports for men and 10 for women. **Graduates:** From July 1, 2013

to June 30, 2014, 1119 bachelor's degrees were awarded. The most popular majors were business/marketing (24%), psychology (14%), and social sciences (10%). In an average class, 48% graduate in 5 years or less and 55% graduate in 6 years or less.

SERVICES: Counseling and information services are available, as is tutoring in some subjects, and introductory classes There is a reader service for the blind, and remedial math, reading, and writing. **Library/Resources:** The 2 libraries contain 729,987 volumes, 974,491 microform items, 591 audio/video tapes/CDs/DVDs, and subscribe to 15,013 periodicals including electronic. Computerized library services include interlibrary loans, database searching, and Internet access. Special learning facilities include an art gallery and radio station. **Physically Challenged Students:** 95% of the campus is accessible. Facilities include wheelchair ramps, elevators, special parking, specially equipped restrooms, special class scheduling, lowered drinking fountains, lowered telephones, special housing. Facilities vary from building to building. However, all classes are scheduled in accessible locations for disabled students. **Special:** The University offers a cooperative baccalaureate program in engineering with School of Engineering (New Brunswick Campus). Interdisciplinary programs in African-American studies, general science. Cooperative baccalaureate in medical technology with approved hospital. B.A./M.A. in Childhood Studies, English, history, liberal studies or psychology; B.A./M.S. in biology, chemistry or mathematics (with the Graduate School-Camden). B.A. in economics or political science/Master of Public Administration (with the Graduate School-Camden); BS/ Master of Business and Science (MBS). In addition, there is an 8-year B.A./M.D. program and many combined bachelor's and master's programs. There are distance learning, English as a Second Language, honors and independent study programs. There is a freshman honors program. **Visiting:** There are regularly scheduled orientations for prospective students, including an information session with an admissions officer and a campus tour. Visitors may sit in on classes. To schedule a visit, contact the Admissions Office (Camden). **Campus Safety and Security:** Measures include 24-hour foot and vehicle patrol, emergency notification system, self-defense education, and security escort services. There are shuttle buses, emergency telephones, lighted pathways/sidewalks, the police department is supplemented by security guards.

REQUIREMENTS: The SAT or ACT is required, but not for students who have been out of high school for 2 years or more. SAT: Subject tests are required of students without a high school diploma from an accredited high school and from some GED holders. A high school diploma is required; the GED is accepted. Students must have completed a general college-preparatory program, including 16 academic credits or Carnegie units, with 4 years of English, 3 years of math (4 recommended), and 2 years each of a foreign language and science, plus 5 in electives. AP and CLEP credits are accepted. Important factors in the admissions decision are advanced placement or honors courses, evidence of special talent, and leadership record. To graduate, students must complete 120 credits, with 30 to 48 in the major, and maintain a minimum GPA of 2.0. A core curriculum of 60 credits is required, including 3 credits each in literary masterpieces, art, music or theater arts, and a foreign language, with an additional 3 credits in English or a foreign language; and 3 credits in math, with an additional 3 credits in math, computer science, or statistics. 1 interdisciplinary course is required, as are 9 credits from social science disciplines, 6 credits in English composition, 6 credits in history, 6 credits in the natural science disciplines, and an additional 9 credits in courses offered outside the major department. **Procedure:** Freshmen are admitted fall. Entrance exams should be taken by December of senior year is recommended, but not required. There are early admissions and rolling admissions plans. Application deadlines are open. Application fee is $65. Notifications are sent March 1. Applications are accepted on-line. **Transfer Students:** 837 transfer students enrolled in 2013-2014. Applicants must have a minimum of 12 credit hours. Grades of C or better in courses that correspond in content and credit to those offered by the college transfer for credit. Transfer students are admitted in the fall and spring semesters. All high school and previous college transcripts are required. 30 of 120 credits required for the bachelor's degree must be completed at RU-Camden. **International Students:** There are 68 international students enrolled. They must take the TOEFL with a minimum score of 550 on the paper-based TOEFL (PBT) or 79 on the Internet-based version (iBT). They must also take the SAT or ACT or the IELTS, scoring 7.

ADMISSIONS: 60% of the 2014-2015 applicants were accepted. The SAT scores for the 2014-2015 freshman class were: Critical Reading--39% below 500, 46% between 500 and 599, 13% between 600 and 699, and 2% between 700 and 800; Math--30% below 500, 50% between 500 and 599, 17% between 600 and 699, and 3% between 700 and 800; Writing--41% below 500, 44% between 500 and 599, 13% between 600 and 699, and 2% between 700 and 800. 37% of the current freshmen were in the top fifth of their class; 70% were in the top two fifths. **Admissions Contact:** Mary Beth Daisey, Assoc Chancellor Enroll Mngmt (Acting). E-Mail: *admissions@ugadm.rutgers.edu* Web: *www.camden.rutgers.edu*

FINANCIAL AID: In 2014-2015, 93% of all full-time freshmen and 93% of continuing full-time students received some form of financial aid. 69% of all full-time freshmen and 73% of continuing full-time students received need-based aid. The average freshman award was $7,998. Need-based scholarships or need-based grants averaged $9,146; need-based self-help aid (loans and jobs) averaged $4,676; and other non-need-based awards and non-need-based scholarships averaged $7,998. Average annual earnings from campus work are $1424. The average financial indebtedness of the 2014 graduate was $25,483. The FAFSA is required. The priority date for freshman financial aid applications for fall entry is March 15. The deadline for filing freshman financial aid applications for fall entry is open.

RUTGERS, THE STATE UNIVERSITY OF NEW JERSEY/NEW BRUNSWICK　　D-3
www.newbrunswick.rutgers.edu

Piscataway, NJ 08854	(732) 932-4636
	n/av
Fax: (732) 445-0237	Email: admissions@ugadm.rutgers.edu
Full-time: 16238 men, 16173 women	Faculty: 3083; I, +$
	Ph.D.s: 99%
Part-time: 906 men, 1227 women	Student/Faculty: 11 to 1
Graduate: 5356 men, 8478 women	Tuition: $13,813 ($28,591)
Year: semesters, summer session	Freshman Class: 31941
Room & Board: $11,749	applied, 19324 accepted, 6348 enrolled
SAT CR/M/W: 600/640/610 ACT: required	
	CEEB CODE: 2753
Application Deadline: n/av	VERY COMPETITIVE

Rutgers, The State University of New Jersey, New Brunswick was founded in 1766. On July 1, 2013, the New Jersey Medical and Health Sciences Education Restructuring Act went into effect, integrating Rutgers, The State University of New Jersey, with all units of the University of Medicine and Dentistry of New Jersey (UMDNJ), except University Hospital in Newark and the School of Osteopathic Medicine in Stratford. The integration of the legacy elements of UMDNJ into Rutgers has created a fourth unit, Rutgers Biomedical and Health Sciences (RBHS), which consists of a number of schools and units located on various sites but closely aligned with the campus in New Brunswick. The campus is comprised of 12 undergraduate units. Undergraduate students in New Brunswick enroll in the School of Arts and Sciences, the liberal arts college, and/or in one of the professional schools: School of Environmental and Biological Sciences (formerly Cook College); Mason Gross School of the Arts; Rutgers Business School: Undergraduate-New Brunswick; School of Communication, and Information; School of Engineering; Edward J. Bloustein School of Planning and Public Policy; the School of Management and Labor Relations; Ernest Mario School of Pharmacy; College of Nursing; School of Nursing; School of Health Related Professions; or the School of Public Health. Some schools located in New Brunswick and/or Newark are also part of the Rutgers Biomedical and Health Sciences unit and are listed for each campus. Each school has individual requirements, policies, and fees. There are 12 undergraduate schools and 17 graduate schools. In addition to regional accreditation, RU-New Brunswick has baccalaureate program accreditation with AACSB, ABET, ACPE, ADA, APTA, ASLA, CSWE, NASM, TEAC, ABOG, ACEND, ACGME, ACME, ACOTE, ANFP, APA, ARC-PA, ARRT, CAAHEP, CACREP, CAHIIM, CCNE, CEPH, COA, COARC, CORE, LCME, NAACLS, and NASD. The 2688-acre campus is in an urban area 33 miles south of New York City. Including any residence halls, there are 670 buildings.

STUDENT LIFE: 88% of undergraduates are from New Jersey. Others are from 45 states, 54 foreign countries, and Canada. 43% are White; 26% Asian American; 12% Hispanic. **Male To Female Ratio:** 1.2:1. The average age of freshmen is 18; all undergraduates, 21. 8% do not continue beyond their first year; 92% remain to graduate.

Housing: 15270 students can be accommodated in college housing, which includes single-sex and coed dorms and married student housing. In addition, there are language houses, special-interest houses, fraternity houses, sorority houses, substance-free house, Math/Science/Engineering House for women, first-year residence, transfer center, and residence for single mothers and children. 58% of students commute. Alcohol is not permitted. Upperclassmen may keep cars.

FACULTY/CLASSROOMS: 52% of faculty are male; 48% are female. No introductory courses are taught by graduate students. The average class size in an introductory lecture is 30; in a laboratory is 20; and in a regular course is 30.

PROGRAMS OF STUDY: RU-New Brunswick confers B.A., B.S., B.F.A. and B.Mus. and B.S.N. degrees. Associate, Master's, and Doctoral degrees are also awarded. Bachelor's degrees are awarded in AGRICULTURE (agriculture, animal science, natural resource/environmental economics, natural resource management, and plant science), BIOLOGICAL SCIENCE (biochemistry, biology/biological science, biomathematics, biotechnology, botany, cell biology, ecology, evolutionary biology, genetics, marine science, microbiology, molecular biology, nutrition, and physiology), BUSINESS (accounting, banking and finance, business administration and management, finance, human resources, labor studies, management information systems, management science, marketing, and marketing/retailing/merchandising), COMMUNICATIONS AND THE ARTS (art, art history and appreciation, Chinese, classics, communications, comparative literature, dance, dramatic arts, East Asian languages and literature, English, French, German, Italian, journalism, Latin, linguistics, music, Portuguese, Russian, Spanish, and visual and performing arts), COMPUTER AND PHYSICAL SCIENCE (astrophysics, atmospheric sciences and meteorology, chemistry, computer science, geology, information sciences and systems, mathematics, physics, and statistics), EDUCATION (health information management), ENGINEERING AND ENVIRONMENTAL DESIGN (biomedical engineering, bioresource engineering, ceramic engineering, chemical engineering, civil engineering, electrical/electronics engineering, engineering and applied science, environmental design, environmental science, industrial engineering, materials science and engineering, and mechanical engineering), HEALTH PROFESSIONS (allied health, biomedical science, exercise science, medical laboratory technology, medical technology, nursing, pharmacy, public health, and rehabilitation therapy), SOCIAL SCIENCE (African American studies, American studies, anthropology, Asian/Oriental studies, criminal justice, economics, food science, geography, Hispanic American studies, history, humanities, Judaic studies, Latin American studies, medieval studies, Middle Eastern studies, philosophy, political science/government, psychology, religion, Russian and Slavic studies, social work, sociology, urban studies, and women's studies). Management, pharmacy, and biology have the largest enrollments.

ACTIVITIES: 9% of men belong to 27 national fraternities. There are 400 groups on campus, including art, band, cheerleading, chess, choir, chorale, chorus, computers, dance, drama, drill team, ethnic, film, gay, honors, international, jazz band, literary magazine, marching band, musical theater, newspaper, opera, orchestra, pep band, photography, political, professional, radio and TV, religious, social, social service, student government, symphony, and yearbook. Popular campus events include Theater Trips, Rutgers Day, Football and Basketball. **Sports:** There are 9 intercollegiate sports for men and 13 for women, and 50 intramural sports for men and 50 for women. **Graduates:** From July 1, 2013 to June 30, 2014, 7244 bachelor's degrees were awarded. The most popular majors were business/marketing (14%), social sciences (11%), and engineering (10%). 1000 companies recruited on campus in 2013-2014. In an average class, 76% graduate in 5 years or less and 79% graduate in 6 years or less.

SERVICES: Counseling and information services are available, as is

tutoring in most subjects, with specific assistance in difficult first- and second-level courses, as well as reading assistance. There is remedial math, reading, and writing. There is computer software with aids, library technology, and assistance. **Library/Resources:** The 15 libraries contain 5.5 million volumes, 3.6 million microform items, 57,166 audio/video tapes/CDs/DVDs, and subscribe to 195,296 periodicals including electronic. Computerized library services include interlibrary loans, database searching, Internet access, and Wi-Fi capability. Special learning facilities include an art gallery, radio station, TV station, a geology museum, and various research centers. **Physically Challenged Students:** Facilities include wheelchair ramps, elevators, special parking, specially equipped restrooms, special class scheduling, lowered drinking fountains, lowered telephones, and special housing. Facilities vary from building to building. However, all classes are scheduled in accessible locations for disabled students. **Special:** 5-year B.A. or B.S./MBA program in Rutgers Business School; BS in Business Discipline/MBA; BA or BS in Science Discipline/MBA; 8-year Bachelor/Medical Dual Degree program with Robert Wood Johnson Medical School; 5-year BS/BS in Bioenvironmental engineering with the School of Engineering; 5-year accelerated baccalaureate-M.B.A with Rutgers Business School, Bureau of Engineering Research, supported by the university, industry, state and federal government, provides research opportunities for students and faculty; Continuing professional education; Exchange program between School of Engineering and the City University of London for qualified students majoring in civil, electrical, or mechanical engineering; 5-year (BA/BS degree) program in liberal arts and engineering; 5-year BA or BS/M.Ed. with the Graduate School of Education; Interdepartmental programs and certificate programs are available; Study Abroad in England, France, Italy, Ireland, Germany, Greece, Mexico, Israel, Australia, India, Japan, Netherlands, Scotland, South Africa, South Korea, Spain and several others; Alumnae externship program; Language and Cultural House Program; B.A. in Religion/M.A. in Religious Studies; B.A./Master of Communication and Information Studies (with SC&I); B.A./MLER (with School of Management and Labor Relations); Baccalaureate/M.C.R.P., or M.P.P with EJB School of Planning and Public Policy;Baccalaureate in Business major/Master of Human Resource Management (with School of Management and Labor Relations-SMLR); BS/Master of Business and Science (MBS). Pharm.D./MBA program with Rutgers Business School; Pharm.D./M.P.H.;Pharm.D./Ph.D.in Pharmaceutical Science; Pharm.D./Ph.D. in Toxicology; Pharm.D./M.D. There are 2 national honor societies, Phi Beta Kappa, and a freshman honors program. **Visiting:** There are regularly scheduled orientations for prospective students, including a preadmission orientation for prospective students. To schedule a visit, contact the University Undergraduate Admissions at (732) 445-4636. **Campus Safety and Security:** Measures include 24-hour foot and vehicle patrol, self-defense education, and security escort services. There are shuttle buses, emergency telephones, lighted pathways/sidewalks, the police department is supplemented by security guards and student safety officers.

REQUIREMENTS: The SAT or ACT is required. A high school diploma is required. The GED is accepted. Students must have completed a general college-preparatory program, including 16 academic credits or Carnegie units, with 4 years of English, 3 years of math 4 recommended, including (algebra I and II, and geometry), 2 years each of a foreign language and science, and 5 in electives. Engineering students need 4 years of math and must take chemistry and physics for sciences; nursing and pharmacy students must take biology and chemistry. SAT: Subject tests are required for students without a high school diploma from an accredited high school and from some GED holders. AP and CLEP credits are accepted. Important factors in the admissions decision are evidence of special talent, extracurricular activities record, and ability to finance college education. To graduate, students must complete 120 credits, with a minimum GPA of 2.0. A liberal arts core requirement includes Writing (6 credits); Quantitative Reasoning (6 credits); Natural Sciences (6 credits); Social Sciences and Humanities (12 credits); Diversity (3 credits); and Global Awareness (3 credits). Check with the individual college for specific program requirements. **Procedure:** Freshmen are admitted fall. Entrance exams should be taken December of senior year is recommended but not required. There are early admissions and rolling

admissions plans. Application deadlines are open. Application fee is $65. Notifications are sent March 1. Applications are accepted online. **Transfer Students:** 2521 transfer students enrolled in 2013-2014. Applicant must have a minimum of 12 credit hours earned. High school and college transcripts are required. Transfers are admitted in the fall or spring. 30 of 120 credits required for the bachelor's degree must be completed at RU-New Brunswick. **International Students:** There are 1963 international students enrolled. They must take the TOEFL with a minimum score of 550 on the paper-based TOEFL (PBT) or 79 on the Internet-based version (iBT). Student's are required to take the IELTS, scoring 7.

ADMISSIONS: 60% of the 2014-2015 applicants were accepted. The SAT scores for the 2014-2015 freshman class were: Critical Reading--7% below 500, 42% between 500 and 599, 38% between 600 and 699, and 13% between 700 and 800; Math--2% below 500, 27% between 500 and 599, 44% between 600 and 699, and 27% between 700 and 800; Writing--5% below 500, 38% between 500 and 599, 39% between 600 and 699, and 18% between 700 and 800. 64% of the current freshmen were in the top fifth of their class; 91% were in the top two fifths. **Admissions Contact:** Office of University Undergraduate Admissions E-Mail: *admissions@ugadm.rutgers.edu* Web: *http:/newbrunswick.rutgers.edu*

FINANCIAL AID: In 2014-2015, 58% of all full-time freshmen and continuing full-time students received some form of financial aid. 52% of all full-time freshmen and 60% of continuing full-time students received need-based aid. The average freshman award was $22,212. Need-based scholarships or need-based grants averaged $10,236; need-based self-help aid (loans and jobs) averaged $4,851; non-need-based athletic scholarships averaged $20,641; and other non-need-based awards and non-need-based scholarships averaged $8,664. The average financial indebtedness of the 2014 graduate was $26,656. The FAFSA is required. The priority date for freshman financial aid applications for fall entry is March 15.

RUTGERS, THE STATE UNIVERSITY OF NEW JERSEY/NEWARK CAMPUS   E-2
www.newark.rutgers.edu

Newark, NJ 07102	(973) 353-5205 n/av
Fax: (973) 353-1440	Email: newarkadmissions@ugadm.rutgers.edu

Full-time: 2884 men, 3059 women	**Faculty:** 477; I, ++$
Part-time: 709 men, 756 women	**Ph.D.s:** 99%
Graduate: 2180 men, 1726 women	**Student/Faculty:** 12 to 1
Year: semesters, summer session	**Tuition:** $13,297 ($28,075)
Room & Board: $12,509	**Freshman Class:** 10332 applied, 6483 accepted, 1081 enrolled

SAT CR/M/W: 510/550/520 **ACT:** required	
	CEEB CODE: 2753
Application Deadline: open	**COMPETITIVE**

Rutgers, The State University of New Jersey/Newark Campus was founded in 1908. On July 1, 2013, the New Jersey Medical and Health Sciences Education Restructuring Act went into effect, integrating Rutgers, The State University of New Jersey, with all units of the University of Medicine and Dentistry of New Jersey (UMDNJ), except University Hospital in Newark and the School of Osteopathic Medicine in Stratford. The integration of the legacy elements of UMDNJ into Rutgers has created a fourth unit, Rutgers Biomedical and Health Sciences (RBHS), which consists of a number of schools and units located on various sites but closely aligned with the campus in New Brunswick. The campus is comprised of 5 undergraduate, degree-granting schools: Newark College of Arts and Sciences, University College-Newark, Rutgers Business School, Undergraduate-Newark, College of Nursing, School of Nursing, School of Criminal Justice and the School of Public Affairs and Administration. Some schools located in Newark and/or New Brunswick are also part of the Rutgers Biomedical and Health Sciences unit and are listed for each campus. Each school has individual requirements, policies, and fees. There are 5 undergraduate schools and 5 graduate schools. In addition to regional accreditation, RU-Newark has baccalaureate program accreditation with AACSB, CSWE, TEAC, and CCNE. The 106-acre campus is in an urban area 7 miles west of New York City. Including any residence halls, there are 51 buildings.

STUDENT LIFE: 95% of undergraduates are from New Jersey. Others are from 27 states, 41 foreign countries, and Canada. 25% are White; 24% Hispanic; 21% Asian American; 18% African American. **Male To Female Ratio:** 1.0:1. The average age of freshmen is 18; all undergraduates, 23. 14% do not continue beyond their first year; 86% remain to graduate. **Housing:** 1722 students can be accommodated in college housing, which includes coed dorms and on-campus apartments. In addition, there are fraternity houses. 90% of students commute. Alcohol is not permitted.

FACULTY/CLASSROOMS: 64% of faculty are male; 36% are female. All teach and do research. No introductory courses are taught by graduate students. The average class size in an introductory lecture is 30; in a laboratory is 20; and in a regular course is 30.

PROGRAMS OF STUDY: RU-Newark confers B.A., B.S. and B.F.A. degrees. Associate, Master's, and Doctoral degrees are also awarded. Bachelor's degrees are awarded in BIOLOGICAL SCIENCE (biology/ biological science, botany, and zoology), BUSINESS (accounting, banking and finance, business administration and management, finance, management science, marketing, marketing/retailing/ merchandising, and supply chain management), COMMUNICA-TIONS AND THE ARTS (art, creative writing, dramatic arts, English, French, German, Italian, journalism, music, Portuguese, Spanish, and visual and performing arts), COMPUTER AND PHYSICAL SCI-ENCE (applied mathematics, applied physics, chemistry, computer science, geology, geoscience, information sciences and systems, mathematics, and physics), ENGINEERING AND ENVIRONMENTAL DESIGN (environmental science and geological engineering), HEALTH PROFESSIONS (allied health, clinical science, medical laboratory technology, and nursing), SOCIAL SCIENCE (African American studies, American studies, anthropology, area studies, classical/ ancient civilization, criminal justice, Eastern European studies, economics, history, interdisciplinary studies, medieval studies, philosophy, political science/government, psychology, public administration, Puerto Rican studies, science and society, social work, sociology, and women's studies). Accounting, criminal justice, psychology and finance have the largest enrollments.

ACTIVITIES: There are 85 groups on campus, including chess, chorale, chorus, drama, newspaper, outreach, radio and TV, and student government. Popular campus events include Alpha Sigma Lambda, Black History Month and Honors Convocation. **Sports:** There are 7 intercollegiate sports for men and 7 for women. Facilities include The mission of the Rutgers-Newark Department of Athletics and Recreation is to provide University constituencies, including students, faculty, staff, alumni, and the community at-large with a diverse range of programs and activities to enhance the overall quality of life and participation in the "Rutgers Experience." The department mission supports the Rutgers-Newark tradition of providing a "first-rate education to students of modest means, to first-generation college attendees, and to students of diverse racial, ethnic and religious backgrounds." The program addresses the varied interests of constituents participating in intercollegiate competition, practices, and instruction as well as social and tournament play. The Rutgers-Newark intercollegiate athletics program gives undergraduate students an opportunity to participate and represent their institution in competition while providing all constituencies the chance to witness and support on-campus events. The athletics program provides the campus community with a high degree of visibility, enhancing the stature of the institution and its programs while conducting affairs within the moral and ethical principles of the University and the spirit of fair play. Rutgers-Newark is committed to providing its student-athletes with qualified professionals and facilities to support their athletic endeavors, and experienced educational support to enhance their academic progress, regardless of sport or gender. The department places the welfare of the student above any consideration, with the primary concern being the overall development of the participant, leading to the completion of a degree. The Rutgers-Newark recreation program offers a multitude of programs designed to encourage participation and enhance individual health, wellness and overall quality of life. The programs and activities offered are designed to enhance institutional and community relationships, emphasizing the educational, health, social and recreational values of individual and competitive sports. Athletics facilities, utilized by varsity sports and recreation, are available to all members of the Rutgers community. The facilities complement the diversified program offerings. Rutgers-Newark pledges to provide its constituencies modern facilities and equipment in sufficient numbers that conform to optimum standards for health and safety. **Graduates:** From July 1, 2013 to June 30, 2014, 1471 bachelor's degrees were awarded. The most popular majors were business/marketing (41%), criminal justice (13%), and psychology (12%). In an average class, 60% graduate in 5 years or less and 67% graduate in 6 years or less.

SERVICES: Counseling and information services are available, as is tutoring in most subjects. There is a reader service for the blind, and remedial math, reading, and writing. **Library/Resources:** The 4 libraries contain 729,987 volumes, 974,491 microform items, 591 audio/video tapes/CDs/DVDs, and subscribe to 15,013 periodicals including electronic. Computerized library services include interlibrary loans, database searching, and Internet access. Special learning facilities include an art gallery, radio station, a molecular and behavioral neuroscience center, and institutes of jazz and animal behavior. **Physically Challenged Students:** 80% of the campus is accessible. Facilities include wheelchair ramps, elevators, special parking, specially equipped restrooms, special class scheduling, lowered drinking fountains, lowered telephones, special housing. Facilities vary from building to building. However, all classes are scheduled in accessible locations for disabled students. **Special:** Students may cross-register with the New Jersey Institute of Technology. Internships are available. The school offers study abroad in over 30 countries, accelerated degree programs in business administration and criminal justice, co-op programs, independent study, distance learning, English as a Second Language, dual majors, student-designed majors, nondegree study, and pass/fail options. Contact the school for information on the Honors College. 5-year baccalaureate-MBA with Rutgers Business School; BS in Business Discipline/MBA; BA or BS in Science Discipline/MBA; Baccalaureate/M.A. in Criminal Justice with the School of Criminal Justice; Baccalaureate/MPA with the School of Public Affairs and Administration; Cooperative baccalaureate program with School of Engineering (New Brunswick campus); Cooperative baccalaureate in medical technology with affiliated hospitals; Interdisciplinary programs in archaeology, international affairs, legal studies, women's studies; continuing professional education; Baccalaureate in Business Major/Master of Human Resource Management (with School of Management and Labor Relations in New Brunswick); Baccalaureate-master's dual degree programs with the School of Criminal Justice and Rutgers Business School; BA or BS in Biology/ MS in Biology; BA in Chemistry/MS in Chemistry; BA in Economics/ MA in Economics; BS in Environmental Sciences/MS In Environmental Geology; BS in Environmental Sciences/MS in Environmental Sciences; BA in Political Science, Sociology or Anthropology/MS in Global Affairs; BA in History/MA in History; BA in History, Sociology or Anthropology/MA in Jazz History and Research; BA in Political Science/MA in Political Science; BA/MA in Peace and Conflict Studies; BS in Computer Science or Information Science/Master of Information Technology; BS in Accounting/Master of Accountancy (Governmental Accounting or Financial Accounting); BS in Accounting/MBA in Professional Accounting; BS in Finance/Master of Quantitative Finance; BS/Master of Business and Science (MBS); BS in Nursing/MS in Nursing; BA in Psychology/MA in Psychology; Master of Public Administration/Master of Accountancy in Governmental Accounting; MS in Global Affairs/Master of Public Policy (with Bloustein School in New Brunswick); Pharm.D./M.B.A. program with Rutgers Business School. There are 12 national honor societies, including Phi Beta Kappa, and a freshman honors program. **Visiting:** There are regularly scheduled orientations for prospective students, including an information session with an admissions counselor and a tour of the campus. There are guides for informal visits and visitors may sit in on classes. To schedule a visit, contact the Admissions Office (Newark). **Campus Safety and Security:** Measures include 24-hour foot and vehicle patrol, self-defense education, and security escort services. There are shuttle buses, emergency telephones, lighted pathways/sidewalks, Security guards assist Rutgers police in providing public safety services. There is also a student marshal program.

REQUIREMENTS: The SAT or ACT is required. A high school diploma is required; the GED is accepted. SAT: Subject tests are required of students without a high school diploma from an accredited high school and from some GED holders. Students should have completed 16 high school academic credits or Carnegie units, with 4 years of English, 3 years of math, (4 recommended) 2 years each of science, a general college-preparatory program, including and a foreign language, and 5 electives. Biology and chemistry are required for nursing students. AP and CLEP credits are accepted. Important factors in the admissions decision are advanced placement or honors courses, evidence of special talent, and leadership record. To graduate, students must complete 124 credits with a minimum GPA of 2.0. Distribution requirements include 8 credits in natural science/math or 3 courses in non-lab science, math, or computer science; 6 credits each in history, literature, social sciences, humanities, and fine arts; 1 course in critical thinking; and 15 credits of electives. All students must take English composition and demonstrate math proficiency either by exam or by successfully completing a college algebra course or any other advanced course in math, a college calculus course, (with a grade of C or better) or a precalculus course (with a grade of B or better). **Procedure:** Freshmen are admitted fall. Entrance exams should be taken by December of senior year is recommended, but not required. There are early admissions and rolling admissions plans. Application deadlines are open. Application fee is $65. Notifications are sent March 1. Applications are accepted on-line. **Transfer Students:** 779 transfer students enrolled in 2013-2014. Students who have completed at least 12 credit hours at another college with a cumulative GPA of 2.0 are considered for admission as transfer students. Transfers are admitted in the fall and spring. High school and college transcripts are required. 30 of 124 credits required for the bachelor's degree must be completed at RU-Newark. **International Students:** There are 184 international students enrolled. They must take the TOEFL with a minimum score of 550 on the paper-based TOEFL (PBT) or 79 on the Internet-based version (iBT) and the college's own test or the IELTS, scoring 6.

ADMISSIONS: 63% of the 2014-2015 applicants were accepted. The SAT scores for the 2014-2015 freshman class were: Critical Reading--42% below 500, 43% between 500 and 599, 13% between 600 and 699, and 2% between 700 and 800; Math--21% below 500, 50% between 500 and 599, 25% between 600 and 699, and 4% between 700 and 800; Writing--36% below 500, 46% between 500 and 599, 14% between 600 and 699, and 4% between 700 and 800. 39% of the current freshmen were in the top fifth of their class; 75% were in the top two fifths. **Admissions Contact:** Ben Rohdin, Assistant Provost for Enrollment Managmt. E-Mail: *newarkadmissions@ugadm.rutgers .edu* Web: *http://www.newark.rutgers.edu/*

FINANCIAL AID: In 2014-2015, 85% of all full-time freshmen and 89% of continuing full-time students received some form of financial aid. 71% of all full-time freshmen and 83% of continuing full-time students received need-based aid. Average annual earnings from campus work are $1272. The average financial indebtedness of the 2014 graduate was $24,837. The FAFSA is required. The priority date for freshman financial aid applications for fall entry is March 15. The deadline for filing freshman financial aid applications for fall entry is open.

Saint Peter's University, formerly Saint Peter's College, founded in 1872, is a private liberal arts and business college affiliated with the Roman Catholic Church and known as New Jersey's Jesuit College. The figures in the above capsule and in this profile are approximate. There are 2 undergraduate schools and 3 graduate schools. In addition to regional accreditation, SPC has baccalaureate program accreditation with NLN. The 15-acre campus is in an urban area 2 miles west of New York City. Including any residence halls, there are 29 buildings.

STUDENT LIFE: 87% of undergraduates are from New Jersey. Others are from 26 states, and 10 foreign countries. 56% are from public schools. 44% are White; 27% Hispanic; 21% African American. 68% are Catholic. **Male To Female Ratio:** 1.5:1. The average age of freshmen is 18; all undergraduates, 24. 23% do not continue beyond their first year; 51% remain to graduate. **Housing:** 863 students can be accommodated in college housing, which includes single-sex and coed dorms and on-campus apartments. In addition, there are special-interest houses, community service houses. On-campus housing is guaranteed for all 4 years. 50% of students commute. Upperclassmen may keep cars.

FACULTY/CLASSROOMS: 50% of faculty are male; 50% are female. All teach undergraduates. No introductory courses are taught by graduate students. The average class size in an introductory lecture is 23; in a laboratory is 14; and in a regular course is 16.

PROGRAMS OF STUDY: SPC confers B.A., B.S. and B.S.N. degrees. Associate, Master's, and Doctoral degrees are also awarded. Bachelor's degrees are awarded in BIOLOGICAL SCIENCE (biochemistry and biology/biological science), BUSINESS (accounting, business administration and management, international business management, and marketing/retailing/merchandising), COMMUNICATIONS AND THE ARTS (art history and appreciation, classical languages, communications, English, fine arts, graphic design, modern language, Spanish, and visual and performing arts), COMPUTER AND PHYSICAL SCIENCE (chemistry, computer science, mathematics, natural sciences, and physics), EDUCATION (elementary education and secondary education), HEALTH PROFESSIONS (biomedical science, health care administration, medical laboratory technology, nursing, predentistry, and premedicine), SOCIAL SCIENCE (African American studies, American studies, classical/ancient civilization, criminal justice, economics, history, humanities, interdisciplinary studies, international studies, Latin American studies, philosophy, political science/government, prelaw, psychology, social science, sociology, theological studies, and urban studies). Natural sciences and accounting is the strongest academically. Business management, accounting, and computer sciences have the largest enrollments.

ACTIVITIES: There are 50 groups on campus, including cheerleading, chess, chorus, computers, debate, drama, ethnic, forensics, honors, international, literary magazine, newspaper, pep band, political, professional, radio and TV, religious, social, social service, and student government. Popular campus events include International Day, Career Fairs and SpringFest. **Sports:** There are 10 intercollegiate sports for men and 8 for women, and 20 intramural sports for men and 18 for women. Facilities include a recreational center, a 2000-seat gym, and an athletic field. **Graduates:** From July 1, 2013 to June 30, 2014, 489 bachelor's degrees were awarded. The most popular majors were business/marketing (29%), biological/life sciences (10%), and health professions and related programs (9%). In an average class, 53% graduate in 6 years or less.

SERVICES: Counseling and information services are available, as is tutoring in every subject. There is a reader service for the blind, and remedial math, reading, and writing. **Library/Resources:** The 2 libraries contain 285,000 volumes, 70,000 microform items, 3,800 audio/video tapes/CDs/DVDs, and subscribe to 1,800 periodicals including electronic. Computerized library services include interlibrary loans and database searching. Special learning facilities include an art gallery, radio station, and TV station. **Physically Challenged Students:** 80% of the campus is accessible. Facilities include wheelchair ramps, elevators, special parking, specially equipped restrooms, special class scheduling, lowered drinking fountains, lowered telephones. **Special:** There are co-op programs with local companies, as well as departmental programs, and many internships available in Jersey City and nearby New York City. A Washington semester and

SAINT PETER'S UNIVERSITY   E-2
www.spc.edu

Jersey City, NJ 07306	(201) 915-9213
	(888) SPC-9933
Fax: (201) 432-5860	**Email:** admissions@spc.edu
Full-time: 825 men, 1077 women	**Faculty:** IIA, av$
Part-time: 101 men, 314 women	**Ph.D.s:** n/av
Graduate: 282 men, 446 women	**Student/Faculty:** 12 to 1
Year: semesters, summer session	**Tuition:** $31,222
Room & Board: $13,020	**Freshman Class:** 3256 applied, 1973 accepted, 393 enrolled
SAT or ACT: required	**CEEB CODE:** 2806
Application Deadline: open	**COMPETITIVE**

study abroad in any of 60 countries are offered. There are preprofessional programs in dentistry, pharmacy, physician assistant, and physical therapy. The college also offers dual majors and student-designed majors, credit for life, military, and work experience, non-degree study, and pass/fail options. There are 9 national honor societies, a freshman honors program, and 1 departmental honors program. **Visiting:** There are regularly scheduled orientations for prospective students, including open houses, weekend and weekday visit days with a tour and class and information sessions, as well as tours and interviews by appointment. There are guides for informal visits, visitors may sit in on classes, and stay overnight. To schedule a visit, contact the Admissions Office. **Campus Safety and Security:** Measures include 24-hour foot and vehicle patrol, self-defense education, and security escort services. There are shuttle buses, emergency telephones, security desk monitoring of access to residence halls.

REQUIREMENTS: The SAT or ACT is required. Applicants must be high school graduates or submit the GED certificate. Students should have completed 16 Carnegie units of high school study, including 4 years of English, 3 of math, 2 each of science, history, and a foreign language, and another 3 of additional work in any of these subjects. An essay and 2 letters of recommendation are required, and an interview is recommended. SPC requires applicants to be in the upper 97% of their class. A GPA of 3.1 is required. AP and CLEP credits are accepted. Important factors in the admissions decision are advanced placement or honors courses, extracurricular activities record, and recommendations by school officials. To graduate, students must complete 129 credit hours, including 57 in the core curriculum, 12 in core electives, between 30 and 45 in the major, and the rest in subjects related to the major. The core curriculum requires 9 credits of natural sciences, 6 to 8 of math, and 3 each of social science, philosophy, history, literature, a modern language, fine arts, and composition. Students must earn a GPA of 2.0. **Procedure:** Freshmen are admitted fall and spring. Entrance exams should be taken by the fall of the senior year. There are early admissions, deferred admissions, and rolling admissions plans. Application deadlines are open. Notification is sent on a rolling basis. 299 applicants were on the 2014 waiting list; 290 were admitted. Applications are accepted on-line. **Transfer Students:** 164 transfer students enrolled in 2013-2014. The school requires a 2.0 college GPA of transfer students, as well as a high school transcript and a satisfactory composite SAT score for students less than 2 years out of high school. An interview is recommended. 30 of 129 credits required for the bachelor's degree must be completed at SPC. **International Students:** The school actively recruits these students. They must take the TOEFL.

ADMISSIONS: 61% of the 2014-2015 applicants were accepted. **Admissions Contact:** Joseph Giglio, Director of Admissions. E-Mail: *admissions@spc.edu* Web: *www.spc.edu*

FINANCIAL AID: SPC is a member of CSS. The FAFSA is required. Check with the school for current application deadlines.

SETON HALL UNIVERSITY　　　　　　　　D-2
www.shu.edu

South Orange, NJ 07079	(973) 313-6146
	(800) THE-HALL
Fax: (973) 275-2040	Email: thehall@shu.edu
Full-time: 1939 men, 2698 women	Faculty: 339; I, -$
Part-time: 189 men, 322 women	Ph.D.s: 88%
Graduate: 1992 men, 2516 women	Student/Faculty: 14 to 1
Year: semesters, summer session	Tuition: $33,490
Room & Board: $12,412	Freshman Class: 6436 applied, 5474 accepted, 993 enrolled
SAT CR/M/W: 530/540/550 ACT: 23	CEEB CODE: 2811
Application Deadline: March 1	COMPETITIVE

Seton Hall University, founded in 1856, is a major Catholic University. The University is home to 10,000 students and eight schools that offer degrees at the baccalaureate, master, and doctoral and professional levels. Figures in the above capsule and in this profile are approximate. There are 6 undergraduate schools and 8 graduate schools. In addition to regional accreditation, Seton Hall has bacca-

laureate program accreditation with AACSB, CSWE, NCATE, and CCNE. The 58-acre campus is in a suburban area 14 miles west of New York City. Including any residence halls, there are 35 buildings.

STUDENT LIFE: 76% of undergraduates are from New Jersey. Others are from 43 states, 46 foreign countries, and Canada. 69% are from public schools. 51% are White; 14% Hispanic; 13% African American. 69% are Catholic; 14% Protestant. **Male To Female Ratio:** 1.3:1. The average age of freshmen is 18; all undergraduates, 21. 19% do not continue beyond their first year; 65% remain to graduate. **Housing:** 2236 students can be accommodated in college housing, which includes coed dorms and off-campus apartments. In addition, there are honors houses and special-interest houses. On-campus housing is available on a lottery system for upperclassmen. Priority is given to out-of-town students. 58% of students commute. Upperclassmen may keep cars.

FACULTY/CLASSROOMS: 53% of faculty are male; 47% are female. No introductory courses are taught by graduate students. The average class size in an introductory lecture is 26; in a laboratory is 17; and in a regular course is 21.

PROGRAMS OF STUDY: Seton Hall confers B.A., B.S., B.A.B.A., B.S.B., B.S.E., B.S.I.R. and B.S.N. degrees. Master's and Doctoral degrees are also awarded. Bachelor's degrees are awarded in AGRICULTURE (environmental studies), BIOLOGICAL SCIENCE (biochemistry and biology/biological science), BUSINESS (accounting, business administration and management, business economics, finance, management information systems, marketing management, and sports management), COMMUNICATIONS AND THE ARTS (applied music, art history, broadcasting, classics, communications, creative writing, English, fine arts, French, graphic design, Italian, journalism, modern language, music, Spanish, and theatre arts), COMPUTER AND PHYSICAL SCIENCE (chemistry, computer science, mathematics, and physics), EDUCATION (elementary education, secondary education, and special education), HEALTH PROFESSIONS (nursing), SOCIAL SCIENCE (African American studies, anthropology, Asian/Oriental studies, criminal justice, economics, history, international relations, Latin American studies, liberal arts/general studies, philosophy, political science/government, psychology, religion, social science, social work, sociology, and theological studies). Business, biology, and diplomacy are the strongest academically. Nursing has the largest enrollment.

ACTIVITIES: 7% of men belong to 11 national fraternities; 11% of women belong to 14 national sororities. There are 124 groups on campus, including recreation, student Ambassador Society, art, cheerleading, chess, choir, chorus, commuter council, computers, dance, drama, drill team, environmental, ethnic, film, forensics, honors, international, literary magazine, musical theater, newspaper, pep band, photography, political, professional, radio and TV, religious, social, social service, and student government. Popular campus events include University Day, Theatre-in-the-Round, and Career Day. **Sports:** There are 6 intercollegiate sports for men and 8 for women, and 13 intramural sports for men and 13 for women. Facilities include A 2000-seat on-campus arena, recreational field house, indoor track, indoor pool, fitness and aerobics rooms, a soccer and baseball field, a softball field, and tennis and racquetball courts; men's basketball also uses the Prudential Center, which seats 10,000. **Graduates:** From July 1, 2013 to June 30, 2014, 993 bachelor's degrees were awarded. The most popular majors were nursing (10%), finance (7%), and biology (7%). 400 companies recruited on campus in 2013-2014. In an average class, 51% graduate in 4 years or less, 62% graduate in 5 years or less, and 65% graduate in 6 years or less. Of the 2013 graduating class, 29% were enrolled in graduate school within 6 months of graduation, and 77% were employed.

SERVICES: Counseling and information services are available, as is tutoring in most subjects. There is a reader service for the blind, and remedial math, reading, and writing. The Academic Resource Center also offers support for students interested in national scholarship opportunities and aids students who are pursuing interdisciplinary and pre-professional majors. **Library/Resources:** The 2 libraries contain 629,978 volumes, 500,000 microform items, 5,340 audio/video tapes/CDs/DVDs, and subscribe to 29,000 periodicals including electronic. Computerized library services include interlibrary loans, database searching, Internet access, and Wi-Fi capability. Special learning facilities include an art gallery, radio station, TV station, various institutes, and centers for learning and research. **Physically Challenged Students:** 95% of the campus is accessible. Facilities include wheelchair ramps, elevators, special parking, specially equipped restrooms, special class scheduling, lowered drinking fountains, and the School of Business; internships are available through the College of Arts and Sciences and School of Diplomacy. Education majors go into the field during their sophomore year. Engineering 3+2 degrees are available with the New Jersey Institute of Technology. Study abroad is available in 15 countries. An accelerated B.S.N. degree is offered. There are a total of 17 bachelor/graduate dual degree programs. Non-degree study is permitted. There are 27 national honor societies, a freshman honors program, and 5 departmental honors programs. **Visiting:** There are regularly scheduled orientations for prospective students, including campus tours weekdays and Saturdays during the academic year and on weekdays during the summer. Open houses for prospective applicants are available each fall. Visitors may sit in on classes. To schedule a visit, contact the Enrollment Services Office. **Campus Safety and Security:** Measures include 24-hour foot and vehicle patrol, emergency notification system, self-defense education, and security escort services. There are shuttle buses, emergency telephones, lighted pathways/sidewalks, controlled access to dorms/residences, security attendants are posted at residence hall entrances.

REQUIREMENTS: The SAT or ACT is required. Seton Hall recommends a satisfactory score on the SAT or a minimum composite score on the ACT. Applicants must supply high school transcripts or a GED certificate. Students should have completed 16 Carnegie units of high school study, including 4 years of English, 3 of Math, 2 each of a Foreign Language and either History or Social Studies, 1 of Science, and 4 Academic Electives. An essay is required and an interview is recommended. AP and CLEP credits are accepted. Important factors in the admissions decision are advanced placement or honors courses, leadership record, and parents or siblings attended your school. To graduate, students must complete the University Core Curriculum and complete at least 120 credit hours earning a minimum GPA of 2.0. **Procedure:** Freshmen are admitted fall and spring. Entrance exams should be taken by January of the senior year. There are early admissions, deferred admissions, and rolling admissions plans. Application deadlines are open. Application fee is $55. Notification is sent on a rolling basis. Applications are accepted on-line. **Transfer Students:** 315 transfer students enrolled in 2013-2014. Applicants should have earned 30 hours of college credit, with a minimum GPA of 2.5, or 2.8 for the business and science schools. The SAT is required for students with fewer than 30 credits of college-level work at the time of application, and an interview is recommended. 30 of 120 credits required for the bachelor's degree must be completed at Seton Hall. **International Students:** There are 90 international students enrolled. The school actively recruits these students. They must take the TOEFL with a minimum score of 550 on the paper-based TOEFL (PBT) or 79 on the Internet-based version (iBT). They must also take the SAT.

ADMISSIONS: 85% of the 2014-2015 applicants were accepted. The SAT scores for the 2014-2015 freshman class were: Critical Reading--29% below 500, 49% between 500 and 599, 21% between 600 and 699, and 1% between 700 and 800; Math--26% below 500, 49% between 500 and 599, 24% between 600 and 699, and 2% between 700 and 800; Writing--24% below 500, 48% between 500 and 599, 26% between 600 and 699, and 2% between 700 and 800. The ACT scores were 20% below 21, 33% between 21 and 23, 27% between 24 and 26, 8% between 27 and 28, and 13% above 28. 48% of the current freshmen were in the top fifth of their class; 72% were in the top two fifths. 1 freshman graduated first in the class. **Admissions Contact:** Wendy Lin-Cook, Assistant Vice President for Admissions. E-Mail: *thehall@shu.edu* Web: *www.shu.edu*

FINANCIAL AID: The FAFSA is required. The priority date for freshman financial aid applications for fall entry is March 1. The deadline for filing freshman financial aid applications for fall entry is open.

STEVENS INSTITUTE OF TECHNOLOGY   E-2
www.stevens.edu

Hoboken, NJ 07030

(201) 216-5194
(800) 458-5323

Fax: (201) 216-8348
Email: admissions@stevens.edu

Full-time: 1654 men, 579 women
Part-time: 1 men
Graduate: 2761 men, 867 women
Year: semesters, summer session
Room & Board: $12,150

Faculty: 226
Ph.D.s: 90%
Student/Faculty: 10 to 1
Tuition: $37,980
Freshman Class: 3232 applied, 1609 accepted, 614 enrolled

SAT CR/M/W: 600/670/600 **ACT:** 27
Application Deadline: February 1

CEEB CODE: 2819
HIGHLY COMPETITIVE

Stevens Institute of Technology, founded in 1870, is a private institution offering programs of study in science, computer science, engineering, business, and humanities. Figures in the above capsule and in this profile are approximate. There are 4 undergraduate schools and 3 graduate schools. In addition to regional accreditation, Stevens has baccalaureate program accreditation with ABET and CSAB. The 55-acre campus is in an urban area on the banks of the Hudson River, overlooking the Manhattan skyline. Including any residence halls, there are 25 buildings.

STUDENT LIFE: 60% of undergraduates are from New Jersey. Others are from 42 states, 30 foreign countries, and Canada. 80% are from public schools. 54% are White; 11% Asian American. **Male To Female Ratio:** 0.3:1. The average age of freshmen is 18; all undergraduates, 20. 10% do not continue beyond their first year; 76% remain to graduate. **Housing:** 1358 students can be accommodated in college housing, which includes coed dorms, on-campus apartments, off-campus apartments, and married student housing. In addition, there are special-interest houses, fraternity houses, and sorority houses. On-campus housing is guaranteed for all 4 years. 85% of students live on campus; of those, 70% remain on campus on weekends. Alcohol is not permitted. Upperclassmen may keep cars.

FACULTY/CLASSROOMS: 80% of faculty are male; 20% are female. 75% do both. No introductory courses are taught by graduate students. The average class size in an introductory lecture is 75; in a laboratory is 20; and in a regular course is 25.

PROGRAMS OF STUDY: Stevens confers B.A., B.S. and B.E. degrees. Master's and Doctoral degrees are also awarded. Bachelor's degrees are awarded in BIOLOGICAL SCIENCE (biochemistry and bioinformatics), BUSINESS (business administration and management), COMMUNICATIONS AND THE ARTS (literature and music technology), COMPUTER AND PHYSICAL SCIENCE (chemistry, computer science, computer security and information assurance, digital arts/technology, information sciences and systems, mathematics, physics, and science technology), ENGINEERING AND ENVIRONMENTAL DESIGN (biomedical engineering, chemical engineering, civil engineering, computational sciences, computer engineering, electrical/electronics engineering, engineering management, engineering physics, environmental engineering, mechanical engineering, naval architecture and marine engineering, and systems engineering), SOCIAL SCIENCE (history and philosophy). Engineering is the strongest academically. Mechanical engineering, civil engineering, and business have the largest enrollments.

ACTIVITIES: 19% of men belong to 11 national fraternities; 20% of women belong to 1 local and 3 national sororities. There are 105 groups on campus, including anime, gamers, paintball, SAE, art, band, chess, choir, chorus, computers, dance, debate, drama, engineers without borders, environmental, ethnic, film, honors, international, jazz band, literary magazine, musical theater, newspaper, pep band, photography, political, professional, radio and TV, religious, social, social service, and student government. Popular campus events include Fall Tech Fest, Spring Boken Festival and Midnight Breakfast. **Sports:** There are 13 intercollegiate sports for men and 13 for women, and 12 intramural sports for men and 12 for women. Facilities include a 60,000-square-foot complex with an NCAA regulation swimming pool, a 1,400-seat basketball arena, fitness rooms, racquetball/squash courts, a playing field, a student union, and several outdoor courts. **Graduates:** From July 1, 2013 to June 30, 2014, 419 bachelor's degrees were awarded. The most popular majors were mechanical engineering (18%), electrical engineering (12%), and business (11%). 380 companies recruited on campus in 2013-2014. In an average class, 25% graduate in 4 years or less, 72% graduate in 5 years or less, and 76% graduate in 6 years or less. Of the 2013 graduating class, 20% were enrolled in graduate school within 6 months of graduation, and 75% were employed.

SERVICES: Counseling and information services are available, as is tutoring in every subject. **Library/Resources:** The library contains 123,063 volumes, and subscribes to 39,500 periodicals including electronic. Computerized library services include interlibrary loans, database searching, Internet access, and Wi-Fi capability. Special learning facilities include a radio station, TV station, a lab for ocean and coastal engineering, an environmental lab, a design and manufacturing institute, a technology center, a telecommunications institute, a computer vision lab, an ultrafast laser spectroscopy and high-speed communications lab, and a wireless network security center. **Physically Challenged Students:** All of the campus is accessible. Facilities include wheelchair ramps, elevators, special parking, specially equipped restrooms, lowered drinking fountains, and special housing. **Special:** Stevens offers cross-registration and a 3-2 engineering degree with New York University, a work-study program within the school, co-op programs, corporate and research internships through the Undergraduate Projects in Technology and Medicine, study abroad in 7 countries, and pass/fail options for extra courses. Students may undertake dual majors as well as accelerated degree programs in medicine, dentistry, and law and can receive a B.A.-B.E. degree or a B.A.-B.S. degree in all majors. Undergraduates may take graduate courses. There are 9 national honor societies and a freshman honors program. **Visiting:** There are regularly scheduled orientations for prospective students, including interviews and campus tours. There are guides for informal visits, visitors may sit in on classes, and stay overnight. To schedule a visit, contact the Admissions Office. **Campus Safety and Security:** Measures include 24-hour foot and vehicle patrol, emergency notification system, self-defense education, and security escort services. There are emergency telephones, lighted pathways/sidewalks, and controlled access to dorms/residences.

REQUIREMENTS: The SAT or ACT is required. Applicants must provide official high school transcripts. Students should have taken 4 years of English, math, and science. An interview, essay, and 2 letters of recommendation are required. AP credits are accepted. Important factors in the admissions decision are advanced placement or honors courses, extracurricular activities record, and personality/intangible qualities. To graduate, the student must have earned 122 to 150 credit hours (dependent on program) with a minimum 2.0 GPA; the total hours in the major vary by program. The core curriculum includes courses in engineering, science, computer science, math, liberal arts, and phys ed. **Procedure:** Freshmen are admitted fall. Entrance exams should be taken by February of the senior year. There are early decision and deferred admissions plans. Early decision applications should be filed by November 15; regular applications, by February 1 for fall entry; and December 1 for spring entry, along with a $55 fee. Notification of early decision is sent December 15; regular decision, March 21. 338 early decision candidates were accepted for the 2014-2015 class. 481 applicants were on the 2014 waiting list; 30 were admitted. Applications are accepted on-line. **Transfer Students:** 45 transfer students enrolled in 2013-2014. Applicants should have a minimum GPA of 3.0. They must submit all college transcripts, including course descriptions; SAT or ACT scores are required of those students with fewer than 30 hours of college credit. 50 of 122 credits required for the bachelor's degree must be completed at Stevens. **International Students:** There are 92 international students enrolled. The school actively recruits these students. They must take the TOEFL with a minimum score of 550 on the paper-based TOEFL (PBT) or 83 on the Internet-based version (iBT). They must also take the SAT or ACT.

ADMISSIONS: 50% of the 2014-2015 applicants were accepted. The SAT scores for the 2014-2015 freshman class were: Critical Reading--9% below 500, 41% between 500 and 599, 41% between 600 and 699, and 9% between 700 and 800; Math--14% between 500 and 599, 58% between 600 and 699, and 28% between 700 and 800; Writing--11% below 500, 39% between 500 and 599, 41% between 600 and

699, and 9% between 700 and 800. The ACT scores were 18% between 21 and 23, % between 24 and 26, 58% between 27 and 28, and 24% above 28. 78% of the current freshmen were in the top fifth of their class; 95% were in the top two fifths. 9 freshmen graduated first in their class. **Admissions Contact:** Daniel Gallagher, Dean of University Admissions. E-Mail: *admissions@stevens.edu* Web: *www.stevens.edu*

FINANCIAL AID: In 2014-2015, 93% of all full-time freshmen and 90% of continuing full-time students received some form of financial aid. 84% of all full-time freshmen and 80% of continuing full-time students received need-based aid. 24% of undergraduate students work part-time. Average annual earnings from campus work are $1202. The average financial indebtedness of the 2014 graduate was $1,587. Stevens is a member of CSS. The CSS/Profile and FAFSA are required. The priority date for freshman financial aid applications for fall entry is February 15.

THOMAS EDISON STATE COLLEGE (*The complete profile is made available exclusively on our website, www.barronspac.com*)

WESTMINSTER CHOIR COLLEGE (*The complete profile is made available exclusively on our website, www.barronspac.com*)

WILLIAM PATERSON UNIVERSITY OF NEW JERSEY
E-2
www.wpunj.edu

Wayne, NJ 07470	(973) 720-2125
	n/av
Fax: (973) 720-2910	Email: admissions@wpunj.edu
Full-time: 3814 men, 4522 women	Faculty: 400; IIA, ++$
Part-time: 755 men, 935 women	Ph.D.s: 92%
Graduate: 322 men, 1004 women	Student/Faculty: 21 to 1
Year: semesters, summer session	Tuition: $12,194 ($19,574)
Room & Board: $10,500	Freshman Class: 6968 applied, 4234 accepted, 1240 enrolled
SAT CR/M: 517/526 ACT: required	CEEB CODE: 2518
Application Deadline: June 1	COMPETITIVE

William Paterson University of New Jersey, founded in 1855 as a college, is a public institution comprised of the colleges of Arts and Communication; Education; Humanities, and Social Sciences; Science and Health; and Business. Figures in the above capsule and in this profile are approximate. There are 5 undergraduate schools and 5 graduate schools. In addition to regional accreditation, WPUNJ has baccalaureate program accreditation with ASLA, NASM, NCATE, and NLN. The 370-acre campus is in a suburban area 25 miles west of New York City. Including any residence halls, there are 35 buildings.

STUDENT LIFE: 98% of undergraduates are from New Jersey. Others are from 22 states, 58 foreign countries, and Canada. 75% are from public schools. 63% are White; 15% Hispanic; 12% African American. **Male To Female Ratio:** 1.3:1. The average age of freshmen is 18; all undergraduates, 24. **Housing:** College-sponsored housing includes coed dorms and on-campus apartments. In addition, there are honors houses. On-campus housing is guaranteed for all 4 years. 77% of students commute. Upperclassmen may keep cars.

FACULTY/CLASSROOMS: 51% of faculty are male; 49% are female. All teach undergraduates, all do research, and all teach and do research. No introductory courses are taught by graduate students. The average class size in an introductory lecture is 32; in a laboratory is 24; and in a regular course is 19.

PROGRAMS OF STUDY: WPUNJ confers B.A., B.S., B.F.A. and B.M. degrees. Master's and Doctoral degrees are also awarded. Bachelor's degrees are awarded in BIOLOGICAL SCIENCE (biology/biological science and biotechnology), BUSINESS (accounting, banking and finance, and business administration and management), COMMUNICATIONS AND THE ARTS (art history and appreciation, communications, dramatic arts, English, fine arts, music, Spanish, and studio art), COMPUTER AND PHYSICAL SCIENCE (chemistry, computer science, and mathematics), EDUCATION (health education, music education, physical education, and special education), ENGINEERING AND ENVIRONMENTAL DESIGN (environmental science), HEALTH PROFESSIONS (community health work, health science, and nursing), SOCIAL SCIENCE (African American studies, anthropology, economics, geography, history, philosophy, political science/government, psychology, and sociology). Biology/biotechnology, computer science, and English are the strongest academically. Management, communications, and education have the largest enrollments.

ACTIVITIES: 2% of men belong to 13 national fraternities; 3% of women belong to 12 national sororities. There are 100 groups on campus, including art, cheerleading, chorus, computers, dance, drama, ethnic, film, gay, honors, international, jazz band, literary magazine, musical theater, newspaper, opera, orchestra, photography, political, professional, radio and TV, religious, social, social service, student government, and yearbook. Popular campus events include Pioneer Pride Week, Latin Heritage Celebration, Welcome Week, African Heritage Celebration, WinterFest, Springfest and Meet the Greeks. **Sports:** There are 7 intercollegiate sports for men and 7 for women, and 24 intramural sports for men and 24 for women. Facilities include a recreation center with courts for basketball, tennis, racquetball, volleyball, and badminton, weight and exercise rooms, saunas and whirlpools, and a 4000-seat auditorium. The university also offers an Olympic-size pool, 8 additional tennis courts, and an athletic complex with fields for baseball, field hockey, football, soccer, softball, and track. **Graduates:** From July 1, 2013 to June 30, 2014, 1984 bachelor's degrees were awarded. The most popular majors were business/marketing (19%), education (13%), and psychology (11%). In an average class, 14% graduate in 4 years or less, 40% graduate in 5 years or less, and 47% graduate in 6 years or less.

SERVICES: Counseling and information services are available, as is tutoring in most subjects. There is remedial math, reading, and writing. There is a science enrichment center, a writing center, and a business tutorial lab. **Library/Resources:** The library contains 300,000 volumes, 1,000,000 microform items, 20,000 audio/video tapes/CDs/DVDs, and subscribes to 5,000 periodicals including electronic. Computerized library services include interlibrary loans and database searching. Special learning facilities include an art gallery, radio station, TV station, a speech and hearing clinic, an academic support center, a computerized writing center, and a teleconference center. **Physically Challenged Students:** Facilities include wheelchair ramps, elevators, special parking, specially equipped restrooms, special class scheduling, lowered drinking fountains, lowered telephones, and special housing. **Special:** Study abroad in 33 countries, cross-registration, internships, work-study programs on campus, accelerated degree programs, dual majors, individual curriculum design, and credit for military experience are available. Nondegree study and some pass/fail options are also possible. In the Learning Clusters Project, students experience how 3 general education courses, taken together, reinforce and better integrate each other. There is a professional program in teacher education leading to certification in early childhood, elementary, middle, and secondary education. There are 19 national honor societies, a freshman honors program, and 11 departmental honors programs. **Visiting:** There are regularly scheduled orientations for prospective students, including a campus tour, guest speakers, and dissemination of printed information. There are guides for informal visits and visitors may sit in on classes. To schedule a visit, contact the Admissions Office. **Campus Safety and Security:** Measures include 24-hour foot and vehicle patrol, emergency notification system, and security escort services. There are shuttle buses, emergency telephones, lighted pathways/sidewalks, and controlled access to dorms/residences.

REQUIREMENTS: The SAT or ACT is required. Applicants must

have 16 academic credits or Carnegie units, including 4 in English, 3 in math, 2 each in science lab and social studies, and 5 electives such as foreign language and history. An essay and interview are recommended for some applicants, as are a portfolio and audition. The GED is accepted. AP and CLEP credits are accepted. Important factors in the admissions decision are advanced placement or honors courses, recommendations by school officials, and evidence of special talent. All students must maintain a cumulative GPA of at least 2.0 and take 120 credit hours, typically including 30 to 40 in their major. The University Core Curriculum (the Core) will be the general education program of William Paterson it is a 40 credit program, which constitutes a third of the entire undergraduate curriculum. Students create their Core experience by choosing a sequence of 13 courses from each of the following six areas of study. Each area and sub-area will have a variety of courses to choose from. Also required are 1 course in health or movement science, 1 course dealing with racism or sexism. Courses in areas Four, Five and Six (Diversity and Justice, Community and Civic Engagement, and Global Awareness) may be within student majors. Such courses can thus be used to satisfy both, Core and major requirements. Students at WPU are required to complete four Writing Intensive courses and two Technology Intensive courses. These courses are not additional "stand-alone" courses but any course   within the Core, or any major or any minor or any free elective   that has been designated as a WI or TI course. **Procedure:** Freshmen are admitted fall and spring. Entrance exams should be taken by January 31. There are early admissions, deferred admissions, and rolling admissions plans. Applications should be filed by June 1 for fall entry; December 1 for spring entry, along with a $50 fee. Notification is sent on a rolling basis. Applications are accepted on-line. **Transfer Students:** Transfer students must present at least 12 college level credits with a minimum 2.0 GPA. Nursing Majors are encouraged to have a minimum of a 3.0 GPA or higher. Communication Disorders must have a minimum GPA of 3.5. Allied Health, Public Health, and Business Majors have specific requirements for admission please check our website, www.wpunj.edu for those requirements. 30 of 120 credits required for the bachelor's degree must be completed at WPUNJ. **International Students:** There are 99 international students enrolled. They must take the TOEFL with a minimum score of 550 on the paper-based TOEFL (PBT) or 80 on the Internet-based version (iBT), or take the IELTS - overall band score of 6.0 or higher. TOEFL could be waived based on submission of sufficient SAT/ACT scores.

ADMISSIONS: 61% of the 2014-2015 applicants were accepted. The SAT scores for the 2014-2015 freshman class were: Critical Reading--49% below 500, 39% between 500 and 599, 9% between 600 and 699, and 2% between 700 and 800; Math--42% below 500, 46% between 500 and 599, and 12% between 600 and 699. **Admissions Contact:** Rohan Howell, Director of Undergraduate Admissions. E-Mail: *admissions@wpunj.edu* Web: *www.wpunj.edu*

FINANCIAL AID: In 2014-2015, 86% of all full-time freshmen and 84% of continuing full-time students received some form of financial aid. 64% of all full-time freshmen and 66% of continuing full-time students received need-based aid. The average freshman award was $13,247. Need-based scholarships or need-based grants averaged $8,359 ($13,800 maximum); need-based self-help aid (loans and jobs) averaged $3,285 ($5,000 maximum); and other non-need-based awards and non-need-based scholarships averaged $5,622 ($18,000 maximum). 72% of undergraduate students work part-time. Average annual earnings from campus work are $1500. The average financial indebtedness of the 2014 graduate was $29,906. WPUNJ is a member of CSS. The FAFSA is required. The priority date for freshman financial aid applications for fall entry is April 1.

College Location

NEW MEXICO

0 20 40 60 80 100
Miles

EASTERN NEW MEXICO UNIVERSITY   E-3
www.enmu.edu

Portales, NM 88130	**(575) 562-2178**
	(800) 367-3668
Fax: (575) 562-2118	**Email: enrollment.services@enmu.edu**
Full-time: 1204 men, 1555 women	**Faculty:** 151
Part-time: 796 men, 1017 women	**Ph.D.s:** 80%
Graduate: 324 men, 959 women	**Student/Faculty:** 17 to 1
Year: semesters, summer session	**Tuition:** $4592 ($9862)
Room & Board: $6090	**Freshman Class:** 2291 applied, 1515 accepted, 709 enrolled
SAT CR/M: 470/490 **ACT:** 21	**CEEB CODE:** 4116
Application Deadline: open	**COMPETITIVE**

Eastern New Mexico University, founded in 1934, is a public institution offering programs in the liberal arts and sciences, as well as education, business, fine arts, and vocational and technical fields. Figures in the above capsule and in this profile are approximate. There are 4 undergraduate schools and 1 graduate school. In addition to regional accreditation, Eastern has baccalaureate program accreditation with ACBSP, ASLA, CSWE, NASM, NCATE, NLN, and TEAC. The 400-acre campus is in a small town in Portales, NM. Including any residence halls, there are 40 buildings.

STUDENT LIFE: 80% of undergraduates are from New Mexico. Others are from 47 states, 16 foreign countries, and Canada. 47% are White; 33% Hispanic. **Male To Female Ratio:** 1.5:1. The average age of freshmen is 19; all undergraduates, 25. 39% do not continue beyond their first year. **Housing:** 1098 students can be accommodated in college housing, which includes single-sex and coed dorms, on-campus apartments, and married student housing. In addition, there are sorority houses, female freshmen-only living areas. On-campus housing is guaranteed for all 4 years. 67% of students commute. Alcohol is not permitted. All students may keep cars.

FACULTY/CLASSROOMS: 49% of faculty are male; 51% are female.

93% teach undergraduates, all do research, and 93% do both. Graduate students teach 10% of introductory courses. The average class size in an introductory lecture is 30; in a laboratory is 15; and in a regular course is 19.

PROGRAMS OF STUDY: Eastern confers B.A., B.S., B.A.E., B.B.A., B.F.A., B.M., B.M.E., B.S.E., B.U.S., B.A.A.S., B.S.N., B.S.W. and B.O.E. degrees. Associate and Master's degrees are also awarded. Bachelor's degrees are awarded in AGRICULTURE (agricultural business management, agriculture, animal science, and wildlife management), BIOLOGICAL SCIENCE (avian sciences, biochemistry, and biology/biological science), BUSINESS (accounting, business administration and management, and marketing/retailing/merchandising), COMMUNICATIONS AND THE ARTS (art, communications, dramatic arts, English, music, Spanish, and visual design), COMPUTER AND PHYSICAL SCIENCE (chemistry, computer science, geology, information sciences and systems, and mathematics), EDUCATION (agricultural education, business education, early childhood education, elementary education, home economics education, music education, physical education, special education, and technical education), ENGINEERING AND ENVIRONMENTAL DESIGN (electrical/electronics engineering technology and environmental science), HEALTH PROFESSIONS (medical laboratory technology, nursing, and speech pathology/audiology), SOCIAL SCIENCE (anthropology, counseling/psychology, criminal justice, forensic studies, history, human services, political science/government, psychology, religion, social studies, social work, and sociology). Elementary education, business administration, nursing (BSN only) and biology are the strongest academically. Business, education, criminal justice and biology have the largest enrollments.

ACTIVITIES: There are 55 groups on campus, including art, band, cheerleading, choir, chorus, communications, computers, dance, debate, drama, drill team, environmental, ethnic, film, forensics, gay, honors, international, jazz band, marching band, musical theater, newspaper, pep band, photography, political, professional, radio and TV, religious, social, social service, student government, symphony, and yearbook. Popular campus events include Green and Silver Preview and Dawg Days (freshman orientation). **Sports:** There are 7 intercollegiate sports for men and 7 for women, and 15 intramural sports for men and 15 for women. Facilities include an indoor 4,800-seat arena, 5,000-seat outdoor stadium, indoor/outdoor tennis courts, handball and racquetball courts, and an indoor pool. **Graduates:** From July 1, 2013 to June 30, 2014, 615 bachelor's degrees were awarded. The most popular majors were university studies (9%), elementary education (9%), and applied arts and science (9%). 91 companies recruited on campus in 2013-2014. In an average class, 11% graduate in 4 years or less, 24% graduate in 5 years or less, and 29% graduate in 6 years or less.

SERVICES: Counseling and information services are available, as is tutoring in every subject. There is a reader service for the blind, and remedial math, reading, and writing. **Library/Resources:** The 3 libraries contain 329,003 volumes, 467,017 microform items, 28,321 audio/video tapes/CDs/DVDs, and subscribe to 62,670 periodicals including electronic. Computerized library services include interlibrary loans, database searching, and Internet access. Special learning facilities include an art gallery, natural history museum, radio station, TV station. Eastern New Mexico University is home to a broadcasting center, with one of the largest viewing areas in the nation, and serves as a PBS and NPR affiliate. ENMU also has a science fiction library, a teacher education library, a mineral museum, an anthropology museum, an archeological dig site, and a corresponding museum to the dig site at Blackwater Draw. **Physically Challenged Students:** All of the campus is accessible. Facilities include wheelchair ramps, elevators, special parking, specially equipped restrooms, special class scheduling, lowered drinking fountains, special housing, ADA compliant campus, reserved parking, automatic doors, curb cuts, and elevators. **Special:** The school offers co-op programs in wildlife and fisheries and communication, internships, work-study programs, student-designed majors, a general studies degree, credit for military experience, and non-degree study. There are 2 national honor societies. **Visiting:** There are regularly scheduled orientations for prospective students, including meetings with admissions, financial aid, and faculty advisor, a tour of campus, and a meal in the dining hall. There are guides for informal visits, visitors may sit in on classes, and stay overnight. To schedule a visit, contact the Admissions Office. **Campus Safety and Security:** Measures include 24-hour foot and vehicle patrol, emergency notification system, self-defense education, and security escort services. There are emergency telephones, lighted pathways/sidewalks, controlled access to dorms/residences, new security cameras to deter crime/theft.

REQUIREMENTS: The SAT or ACT is required. A minimum composite score of 17 on the ACT or 810 on the SAT, or a GPA of 2.5, is required. Applicants must be high school graduate or possess a GED certificate and be in good standing with all previously attended institutions. AP and CLEP credits are accepted. To graduate, students must earn 128 credit hours, 36 in the major, 40 total upper division, with a minimum GPA of 2.0. Minimum 32 hours must be from ENMU-main campus; 15 of final 33 hours must be upper division. **Procedure:** Freshmen are admitted fall, spring, and summer. Entrance exams should be taken in the junior or senior year of high school. There is a rolling admissions plan. Application deadlines are open. Applications are accepted on-line. **Transfer Students:** 615 transfer students enrolled in 2013-2014. Transfer students must have a minimum cumulative college GPA of 2.0 and be in good standing with all previously attended institutions. 32 of 128 credits required for the bachelor's degree must be completed at Eastern. **International Students:** There are 151 international students enrolled. They must take the TOEFL with a minimum score of 550 on the paper-based TOEFL (PBT) or 61 on the Internet-based version (iBT).

ADMISSIONS: 66% of the 2014-2015 applicants were accepted. The SAT scores for the 2014-2015 freshman class were: Critical Reading--60% below 500, 23% between 500 and 599, and 9% between 600 and 699; Math--54% below 500, 33% between 500 and 599, 9% between 600 and 699, and 1% between 700 and 800. The ACT scores were 56% below 21, 25% between 21 and 23, 15% between 24 and 26, 2% between 27 and 28, and 2% above 28. 36% of the current freshmen were in the top fifth of their class; 68% were in the top two fifths. 14 freshmen graduated first in their class. **Admissions Contact:** Cody Spitz, Director of Enrollment Services. E-Mail: *enrollment.services@enmu.edu* Web: *www.enmu.edu*

FINANCIAL AID: In 2014-2015, 98% of all full-time freshmen and 89% of continuing full-time students received some form of financial aid. 42% of all full-time freshmen and 44% of continuing full-time students received need-based aid. The average freshman award was $10,356. Need-based scholarships or need-based grants averaged $4,736; need-based self-help aid (loans and jobs) averaged $3,892; non-need-based athletic scholarships averaged $3,382; other non-need-based awards and non-need-based scholarships averaged $4,213; and $2,905 from other forms of aid. The average financial indebtedness of the 2014 graduate was $14,821. The FAFSA, the college's own financial statement, and the institutional scholarship application are required. The priority date for freshman financial aid applications for fall entry is March 1. The deadline for filing freshman financial aid applications for fall entry is August 15.

NEW MEXICO HIGHLANDS UNIVERSITY *(The complete profile is made available exclusively on our website, www.barronspac.com)*

NEW MEXICO INSTITUTE OF MINING AND TECHNOLOGY   **C-3**
www.nmt.edu

Socorro, NM 87801

	(575) 835-5424
	(800) 428-TECH
Fax: (575) 835-5989	Email: tortiz@admin.nmt.edu
Full-time: 1057 men, 385 women	Faculty: 121
Part-time: 58 men, 24 women	Ph.D.s: 97%
Graduate: 248 men, 134 women	Student/Faculty: 13 to 1
Year: semesters, summer session	Tuition: $6256 ($18,184)
Room & Board: $7336	Freshman Class: 1003 applied, 365 accepted, 285 enrolled
SAT CR/M: 600/620 ACT: 26	CEEB CODE: 4533
Application Deadline: August 1	VERY COMPETITIVE

New Mexico Institute of Mining and Technology, founded in 1889 as the New Mexico School of Mines, is a science and engineering university. It has 4 research-associated divisions: the New Mexico Bureau of Geology and Mineral Resources, the Energetic Materials Research and Testing Center, the Petroleum Recovery Research Center, and the Langmuir Laboratory for Atmospheric Research. Figures in the above capsule and in this profile are approximate. There is 1 undergraduate school and 1 graduate school. In addition to regional accreditation, New Mexico Tech has baccalaureate program accreditation with ABET. The 320-acre campus is in a small town 75 miles south of Albuquerque. Including any residence halls, there are 28 buildings.

STUDENT LIFE: 81% of undergraduates are from New Mexico. Others are from 43 states, 27 foreign countries, and Canada. 56% are White; 24% Hispanic. **Male To Female Ratio:** 0.4:1. The average age of freshmen is 18; all undergraduates, 22. 22% do not continue beyond their first year; 45% remain to graduate. **Housing:** 807 students can be accommodated in college housing, which includes single-sex and coed dorms, on-campus apartments, off-campus apartments, and married student housing. On-campus housing is available on a first-come, first-served basis. 50% of students commute. Alcohol is not permitted. All students may keep cars.

FACULTY/CLASSROOMS: 80% of faculty are male; 20% are female. 95% do both. No introductory courses are taught by graduate students. The average class size in an introductory lecture is 18; in a laboratory is 12; and in a regular course is 18.

PROGRAMS OF STUDY: New Mexico Tech confers B.S. and B.G.S. degrees. Associate, Master's, and Doctoral degrees are also awarded. Bachelor's degrees are awarded in BIOLOGICAL SCIENCE (biology/biological science), BUSINESS (business administration and management), COMMUNICATIONS AND THE ARTS (technical and business writing), COMPUTER AND PHYSICAL SCIENCE (chemistry, computer science, earth science, information sciences and systems, mathematics, and physics), ENGINEERING AND ENVIRONMENTAL DESIGN (chemical engineering, civil engineering, electrical/electronics engineering, environmental engineering, environmental science, materials engineering, mechanical engineering, mining and mineral engineering, and petroleum/natural gas engineering), SOCIAL SCIENCE (liberal arts/general studies and psychology). Physics and electrical engineering are the strongest academically. Mechanical engineering, computer science, and electrical engineering have the largest enrollments.

ACTIVITIES: There are no fraternities or sororities. There are 55 groups on campus, including art, band, chess, chorus, computers, drama, ethnic, gay, honors, international, jazz band, musical theater, orchestra, political, professional, radio and TV, religious, social, social service, student government, and yearbook. Popular campus events include 49ers, Spring Fling, and International Student Exhibit. **Sports:** There are 9 intramural sports for men and 9 for women. Facilities include a swimming pool, two gyms, an 18-hole golf course, an athletic field, a climbing wall, a weight/fitness room, racquetball/squash and tennis courts, sand volleyball court, a Ping-Pong area, and a martial arts/combatives room. **Graduates:** From July 1, 2013 to June 30, 2014, 223 bachelor's degrees were awarded. The most popular majors were mechanical engineering (20%), petroleum engineering (12%), and chemical engineering (10%). In an average class, 22% graduate in 4 years or less, 40% graduate in 5 years or less, and 45% graduate in 6 years or less.

SERVICES: Counseling and information services are available, as is tutoring in most subjects. There is a reader service for the blind. **Library/Resources:** The library contains 385,987 volumes, 79,926 microform items, and 2,899 audio/video tapes/CDs/DVDs, and subscribes to 50,000 periodicals including electronic. Computerized library services include interlibrary loans, database searching, Internet access, and Wi-Fi capability. Special learning facilities include a radio station, a mineral museum, a seismic research mine, and a campus astronomical observatory. **Physically Challenged Students:** Facilities include wheelchair ramps, elevators, special parking, specially equipped restrooms, lowered drinking fountains, lowered telephones. The majority of the campus is wheelchair accessible. **Special:** New Mexico Tech offers co-op programs in computer science and all engineering majors, internships in technical communications, and cross-registration with New Mexico State, University of New Mexico, and Los Alamos National Laboratories in the WERC consortium.

Dual majors are offered in engineering, computer science, physics, and math. Work-study, student-designed majors in environmental science, general studies, and basic science, nondegree study, and pass/fail options are also available. There are 4 national honor societies. **Visiting:** There are regularly scheduled orientations for prospective students, including 2 days of get-acquainted social activities, information sessions for parents and students, and transition sessions for parents. There are guides for informal visits, visitors may sit in on classes, and stay overnight. To schedule a visit, contact the Admission Office at admissions@admin.nmt.edu. **Campus Safety and Security:** Measures include 24-hour foot and vehicle patrol, self-defense education, and security escort services. There are emergency telephones and lighted pathways/sidewalks.

REQUIREMENTS: The SAT or ACT is required. Applicants must be high school graduates or present a GED certificate. Students should have earned 15 academic credits, consisting of 4 units of English, 3 each of social science and math (2 beyond general math), 2 of lab science, and electives. A GPA of 2.5 is required. AP credits are accepted. Important factors in the admissions decision are advanced placement or honors courses, evidence of special talent, and extracurricular activities record. Students must earn at least 130 credit hours to graduate, including 42 hours of basic science, consisting in part of 10 hours of physics and 8 each of chemistry, calculus, biology, geology, and engineering. Further distribution requirements include 9 hours each of written and spoken English, 18 hours of literature, philosophy, the arts, and social science, and a senior seminar or senior design project. The credit hours required in the major vary by program. The student must also maintain a cumulative GPA of 2.0. **Procedure:** Freshmen are admitted to all sessions. Entrance exams should be taken by December of the senior year. There are early decision, early admissions, deferred admissions, and rolling admissions plans. Applications should be filed by August 1 for fall entry; December 1 for spring entry, along with a $15 fee. Notifications are sent March 1. **Transfer Students:** 109 transfer students enrolled in 2013-2014. Transfer students must have a GPA of 2.0 and have completed 30 semester hours of transferable credit. Those who have fewer than 30 credit hours, or who have not completed freshman English, must present a minimum ACT score of 21, as well as high school transcripts. 30 of 130 credits required for the bachelor's degree must be completed at New Mexico Tech. **International Students:** There are 54 international students enrolled. They must take the TOEFL with a minimum score of 540 on the paper-based TOEFL (PBT) or 76 on the Internet-based version (iBT).

ADMISSIONS: 36% of the 2014-2015 applicants were accepted. The SAT scores for the 2014-2015 freshman class were: Critical Reading--6% below 500, 40% between 500 and 599, 39% between 600 and 699, and 15% between 700 and 800; Math--4% below 500, 28% between 500 and 599, 45% between 600 and 699, and 23% between 700 and 800. The ACT scores were 3% below 21, 22% between 21 and 23, 28% between 24 and 26, 18% between 27 and 28, and 29% above 28. 55% of the current freshmen were in the top fifth of their class; 80% were in the top two fifths. 6 freshmen graduated first in their class. **Admissions Contact:** Tony Ortiz, Director of Admission. E-Mail: *tortiz@admin.nmt.edu* Web: *www.nmt.edu*

FINANCIAL AID: The average financial indebtedness of the 2014 graduate was $20,944. The FAFSA is required. The priority date for freshman financial aid applications for fall entry is March 1. The deadline for filing freshman financial aid applications for fall entry is May 1.

NEW MEXICO STATE UNIVERSITY   C-4
www.nmsu.edu

Las Cruces, NM 88003	(505) 646-3121
	(800) 662-6678
Fax: (505) 646-6330	Email: admissions@nmsu.edu
Full-time: 5036 men, 5632 women	Faculty: 555; I, --$
Part-time: 966 men, 1150 women	Ph.D.s: 79%
Graduate: 1329 men, 1716 women	Student/Faculty: 19 to 1
Year: semesters, summer session	Tuition: $5950 ($19,112)
Room & Board: $8100	Freshman Class: 7116 applied, 4952 accepted, 1862 enrolled
SAT CR/M/W: 460/480/450 ACT: 21	CEEB CODE: 4531
Application Deadline: open	COMPETITIVE

New Mexico State University, founded in 1888, is a public institution offering undergraduate and graduate programs that include study in liberal arts, agriculture, business, engineering, health science, education, and visual and performing arts. Figures in the above capsule and in this profile are approximate. There are 6 undergraduate schools and 1 graduate school. In addition to regional accreditation, NMSU has baccalaureate program accreditation with AACSB, ABET, ADA, CSWE, NASM, NCATE, AAHE, ACS, NASPAA, ASHA, ASEE, AAAHC, AER, APA, CADE, CACREP, CAATE, CAA, CEPH, IACS, NASP, CCNE, NMPED, and SRM. The 900-acre campus is in a small town 40 miles north of El Paso . Including any residence halls, there are 294 buildings.

STUDENT LIFE: 71% of undergraduates are from New Mexico. Others are from 48 states, 44 foreign countries, and Canada. 49% are Hispanic; 32% White. **Male To Female Ratio:** 1.2:1. The average age of freshmen is 19; all undergraduates, 23. 26% do not continue beyond their first year; 74% remain to graduate. **Housing:** 3385 students can be accommodated in college housing, which includes single-sex and coed dorms, on-campus apartments, and married student housing. In addition, there are honors houses, fraternity houses, and sorority houses. On-campus housing is available on a first-come, first-served basis. 81% of students commute. All students may keep cars.

FACULTY/CLASSROOMS: 51% of faculty are male; 49% are female. Graduate students teach 23% of introductory courses. The average class size in an introductory lecture is 40 and in a laboratory is 20.

PROGRAMS OF STUDY: NMSU confers B.A., and B.S. degrees. Associate, Master's, and Doctoral degrees are also awarded. Bachelor's degrees are awarded in AGRICULTURE (agricultural business management, agricultural economics, agriculture, agronomy, animal science, horticulture, natural resource management, range/farm management, soil science, turfgrass and landscape management, and wildlife science), BIOLOGICAL SCIENCE (biochemistry, biology/biological science, ecology, genetics, microbiology, molecular biology, nutrition, and plant pathology), BUSINESS (accounting, business administration and management, business economics, fashion merchandising, finance, hotel/motel and restaurant management, international business management, management information systems, marketing, marketing/retailing/merchandising, and tourism), COMMUNICATIONS AND THE ARTS (animation, art, communications, dance, dramatic arts, English, film arts, fine arts, foreign language, journalism, music, music performance, theatre arts, video, and visual and performing arts), COMPUTER AND PHYSICAL SCIENCE (astronomy, chemistry, computer science, geology, information sciences and systems, mathematics, and physics), EDUCATION (agricultural education, athletic training, bilingual/bicultural education, early childhood education, elementary education, home economics education, music education, physical education, secondary education, and special education), ENGINEERING AND ENVIRONMENTAL DESIGN (aerospace engineering, aerospace studies, chemical engineering, city/community/regional planning, civil engineering, computer technology, electrical/electronics engineering, engineering physics, engineering technology, environmental engineering, environmental science, industrial engineering, mechanical engineering, and surveying engineering), HEALTH PROFESSIONS (clinical science, community health work, environmental health science, kinesiology, nursing, and speech pathology/audiology), SOCIAL SCIENCE (anthropology, community services, criminal justice, economics, family/consumer studies, geography, history, philosophy, physical fitness/movement, political science/government, psychology, social work, sociology, textiles and clothing, and women's studies). Criminal justice, nursing, and biology have the largest enrollments.

ACTIVITIES: 2% of men belong to 10 national fraternities; 2% of women belong to 6 national sororities. There are 226 groups on campus, including art, band, cheerleading, choir, chorale, chorus, computers, dance, drama, drill team, drum and bugle corps, environmental, ethnic, film, gay, honors, international, jazz band, literary magazine, marching band, musical theater, newspaper, opera, orchestra, pep band, photography, political, professional, radio and TV, religious, social, social service, student government, and symphony. Popular campus events include Fiestas Latinas, American Indian Week, Noche De Luminarias, Greek Week, Halloween Howl and NMSU Homecoming. **Sports:** There are 6 intercollegiate sports for men and 9 for women, and 21 intramural sports for men and 21 for women. Facilities include a game room, natatorium, tennis courts, playing fields, a gym, and rodeo grounds. One campus stadium seats 30,342 while the other seats more than 13,000. **Graduates:** From July 1, 2013 to June 30, 2014, 2714 bachelor's degrees were awarded. The most popular majors were criminal justice (7%), individualized studies (5%), and psychology (4%). 341 companies recruited on campus in 2013-2014. In an average class, 16% graduate in 4 years or less, 37% graduate in 5 years or less, and 46% graduate in 6 years or less.

SERVICES: Counseling and information services are available, as is tutoring in most subjects. There is a reader service for the blind. Remedial classes are offered at the Dona Ana Branch Community College. There is also an interpreter for the hearing impaired. **Library/Resources:** The 2 libraries contain 1.8 million volumes, 1.5 million microform items, 17,232 audio/video tapes/CDs/DVDs, and subscribe to 79,830 periodicals including electronic. Computerized library services include interlibrary loans, database searching, Internet access, and Wi-Fi capability. Special learning facilities include an art gallery, natural history museum, radio station, TV station, a 289-acre experimental farm and orchard, a 61,760-acre cattle and experimental ranch, and a 2160-acre recreational area in the Organ Mountains. **Physically Challenged Students:** 95% of the campus is accessible. Facilities include wheelchair ramps, elevators, special parking, specially equipped restrooms, lowered drinking fountains, lowered telephones. **Special:** Internships, cooperative programs in engineering, math, science, teacher education, business, agriculture, social services, health, government, and other majors, dual majors, study abroad in 56 countries, work-study, and B.A.-B.S. degrees are available. WICHE and National Student Exchange are also available. There are 25 national honor societies, a freshman honors program, and 18 departmental honors programs. **Visiting:** There are regularly scheduled orientations for prospective students, including a tour of the campus and meetings with admissions counselors, faculty members, and financial aid advisers. There are guides for informal visits, visitors may sit in on classes, and stay overnight. To schedule a visit, contact the Office of Admissions. **Campus Safety and Security:** Measures include 24-hour foot and vehicle patrol, emergency notification system, self-defense education, and security escort services. There are shuttle buses, lighted pathways/sidewalks, controlled access to dorms/residences, recycled phones with 911 programmed in for emergencies.

REQUIREMENTS: The ACT is required. Applicants must score 20 on the ACT or may take the SAT (accepted, but not recommended) and submit a composite score of 780. The GED is accepted. Minimum high school preparation includes 4 units of English, 3 of math, 2 beyond general science, and 1 foreign language/fine arts. A GPA of 2.0 is required. AP and CLEP credits are accepted. All students must complete a minimum of 128 credits, including at least 50 upper-division credits. A minimum GPA of 2.0 is needed. Distribution requirements include communications, humanities, math, natural sciences, and social sciences. **Procedure:** Freshmen are admitted to all sessions. Entrance exams should be taken during the high school junior or senior year. There is a rolling admissions plan. Application deadlines are open. Application fee is $20. Notification is sent on a rolling basis. Applications are accepted on-line. **Transfer Students:** 1019 transfer students enrolled in 2013-2014. Applicants must have a minimum GPA of 2.0. 30 credits are required to avoid freshman admission requirements. If the applicant has earned 30 academic credit hours or more, the ACT score will be waived. If the applicant has earned 48 academic credit hours or more, the high school transcript will be waived. 30 of 128 credits required for the bachelor's degree must be completed at NMSU. **International Students:** There are 570 international students enrolled. The school actively recruits these students. They must take the TOEFL with a minimum score of 550 on the paper-based TOEFL (PBT) or 79 on the Internet-based version (iBT), or take the MELAB.

ADMISSIONS: 70% of the 2014-2015 applicants were accepted. The SAT scores for the 2014-2015 freshman class were: Critical Reading--60% below 500, 30% between 500 and 599, 9% between 600 and 699, and 1% between 700 and 800; Math--55% below 500, 34% between 500 and 599, and 11% between 600 and 699; Writing--65% below 500, 28% between 500 and 599, 7% between 600 and 699. The ACT scores were 49% below 21, 24% between 21 and 23, 17% between 24 and 26, 6% between 27 and 28, and 4% above 28. 33% of the current freshmen were in the top fifth of their class; 57% were in the top two fifths. 28 freshmen graduated first in their class. **Admissions Contact:** Delia De Leon, Interim Director of Admissions. E-Mail: *admissions@nmsu.edu* Web: *www.nmsu.edu*

FINANCIAL AID: In 2014-2015, 97% of all full-time freshmen and 88% of continuing full-time students received some form of financial aid. 70% of all full-time freshmen and 66% of continuing full-time students received need-based aid. The average freshman award was $11,033. Need-based scholarships or need-based grants averaged $6,651 ($24,840 maximum); need-based self-help aid (loans and jobs) averaged $4,140 ($13,392 maximum); non-need-based athletic scholarships averaged $10,006 ($20,358 maximum); other non-need-based awards and non-need-based scholarships averaged $4,200 ($16,971 maximum); and $11,577 from other forms of aid. 7% of undergraduate students work part-time. Average annual earnings from campus work are $7566. The average financial indebtedness of the 2014 graduate was $21,589. The FAFSA is required. The deadline for filing freshman financial aid applications for fall entry is March 1.

SANTA FE UNIVERSITY OF ART AND DESIGN (*The complete profile is made available exclusively on our website, www.barronspac.com*)

ST. JOHN'S COLLEGE, SANTA FE   C-2
www.sjcsf.edu

Santa Fe, NM 87505	(505) 984-6060
	(800) 331-5232
Fax: (505) 984-6162	Email: admissions@sjcsf.edu
Full-time: 198 men, 147 women	Faculty: 66
Part-time: 1 men, 3 women	Ph.D.s: 53%
Graduate: 56 men, 25 women	Student/Faculty: 8 to 1
Year: semesters, summer session	Tuition: $45,004
Room & Board: $9994	Freshman Class: 251 applied, 211 accepted, 100 enrolled
SAT CR/M: 680/630 ACT: 28	CEEB CODE: 4737
Application Deadline: March 1	HIGHLY COMPETITIVE+

St. John's College, founded in 1696, offers a curriculum based on the great books of western civilization in which students and faculty learn together in small discussion-based classes. Figures in the above capsule and in this profile are approximate. There is 1 graduate school. The 250-acre campus is in a suburban area in Santa Fe, New Mexico. Including any residence halls, there are 31 buildings.

STUDENT LIFE: 94% of undergraduates are from out of state, mostly the Southwest. Students are from 46 states, 17 foreign countries, and Canada. 68% are from public schools. 74% are White. **Male To Female Ratio:** 0.7:1. The average age of freshmen is 20; all undergraduates, 21. 10% do not continue beyond their first year; 60% remain to graduate. **Housing:** 327 students can be accommodated in college housing, which includes single-sex and coed dorms, on-campus apartments, and married student housing. In addition, there are special-interest houses, substance free residences, and green/sustainable housing. On-campus housing is guaranteed for the freshman year only and is available on a lottery system for upperclassmen. 75% of students live on campus; of those, 75% remain on campus on weekends. All students may keep cars.

FACULTY/CLASSROOMS: 75% of faculty are male; 25% are female. All teach undergraduates. No introductory courses are taught by graduate students. The average class size in a laboratory is 15 and in a regular course is 15.

PROGRAMS OF STUDY: St. John's confers B.A. degrees. Master's degrees are also awarded. Bachelor's degrees are awarded in COMPUTER AND PHYSICAL SCIENCE (mathematics and science), SOCIAL SCIENCE (liberal arts/general studies and philosophy).

ACTIVITIES: There are no fraternities or sororities. There are 27 groups on campus, including and fencing, art, chess, chorus, dance, drama, environmental, film, gay, international, literary magazine, musical theater, newspaper, orchestra, photography, religious, search and rescue, social service, and student government. Popular campus events include Oktoberfest, Halloween and Christmas parties. **Sports:** 5 intramural sports for men and 5 for women. Facilities include soccer field, track, outdoor tennis courts, gym with weight room and cardio equipment, racquetball, squash, and basketball courts, and nearby mountains. **Graduates:** From July 1, 2013 to June 30, 2014, 104 bachelor's degrees were awarded. The most popular majors were liberal arts/general studies (100%). 29 companies recruited on campus in 2013-2014. In an average class, 65% graduate in 4 years or less and 15% graduate in 5 years or less. Of the 2013 graduating class, 13% were enrolled in graduate school within 6 months of graduation, and 62% were employed.

SERVICES: Counseling and information services are available, as is tutoring in every subject. **Library/Resources:** The library contains 67,800 volumes, 4,192 audio/video tapes/CDs/DVDs, and subscribes to 95 periodicals including electronic. Computerized library services include interlibrary loans, database searching, and Internet access. Special learning facilities include an art gallery, music practice rooms, Ptolemy stone, and laboratories. **Physically Challenged Students:** 75% of the campus is accessible. Facilities include wheelchair ramps, elevators, special parking, specially equipped restrooms, special class scheduling, and special housing. **Special:** Internships with alumni in a wide range of fields are available and students may transfer between the Santa Fe and Annapolis campuses. Ariel Internship Program provides stipends to undergraduates for a limited number of summer intership opportunities. Work-study programs are available with the state government, museums, galleries, the Santa Fe Institute, businesses, and schools. There are guides for informal visits, visitors may sit in on classes, and stay overnight. To schedule a visit, contact the Admissions Office. **Campus Safety and Security:** Measures include 24-hour foot and vehicle patrol, emergency notification system, self-defense education, and security escort services. There are shuttle buses, emergency telephones, lighted pathways/sidewalks, controlled access to dorms/residences, informal discussions and pamphlets/posters/films.

REQUIREMENTS: Applicants must write 3 personal essays and submit 2 teacher references, a secondary school report including a reference from a school official, and transcripts of all academic work in high school and college. A campus visit and interview are recommended. 3 years of math and 2 years of foreign language are required; 4 years each of math, foreign language, and English, and 3 years of science are recommended. The GED is accepted. The college has 1 curriculum, based on the great books of Western civilization for a total of 136 credits. Students attend seminars, preceptorials on specific works or topics, language, music, and math tutorials, and a 3-year science lab. Students take oral exams each semester and write annual essays. Sophomores take a math exam and seniors write a final essay and take an oral exam. **Procedure:** Freshmen are admitted fall and spring. There are deferred admissions and rolling admissions plans. Application deadlines are open. Applications are accepted online. **Transfer Students:** 21 transfer students enrolled in 2013-2014. St. John's accepts transfer students only for its freshman class; no previous college credit is recognized. Admission requirements are the same as for freshmen. 136 of 136 credits required for the bachelor's degree must be completed at St. John's. **International Students:** There are 36 international students enrolled. The school actively recruits these students. They must take the TOEFL with a minimum score of 550 on the paper-based TOEFL (PBT).

ADMISSIONS: 84% of the 2014-2015 applicants were accepted. The SAT scores for the 2014-2015 freshman class were: Critical Reading--4% below 500, 19% between 500 and 599, 29% between 600 and 699, and 48% between 700 and 800; Math--20% below 500, 21% between 500 and 599, 40% between 600 and 699, and 19% between 700 and 800. There were 2 National Merit finalists. **Admissions Contact:** Larry Clendenin, Director of Admissions. E-Mail: *admissions@sjcsf.edu* Web: *www.sjcsf.edu*

FINANCIAL AID: In 2014-2015, 81% of all full-time freshmen and 75% of continuing full-time students received some form of financial aid. 80% of all full-time freshmen and 70% of continuing full-time students received need-based aid. The average freshman award was $36,445. Need-based scholarships or need-based grants averaged $31,970 need-based self-help aid (loans and jobs) averaged $7,200;

other non-need-based awards and non-need-based scholarships averaged $5,250; and $25,328 from other forms of aid. 115% of undergraduate students work part-time. Average annual earnings from campus work are $2880. The average financial indebtedness of the 2014 graduate was $26,750. The CSS/Profile, FAFSA, Business/FARM supplement, and non-custodial parent statement are required. The priority date for freshman financial aid applications for fall entry is February 15.

UNIVERSITY OF NEW MEXICO   C-2
www.unm.edu

Albuquerque, NM 87131   (505) 277-8900
1-800-CALL UNM ext. 1
Fax: (505) 277-6809   **Email:** apply@unm.edu
Full-time: 7401 men, 8939 women   **Faculty:** I, -$
Part-time: 1875 men, 2637 women   **Ph.D.s:** 85%
Graduate: 2744 men, 3425 women   **Student/Faculty:** 20 to 1
Year: semesters, summer session   **Tuition:** $6846 ($20,688)
Room & Board: $8454   **Freshman Class:** 11652 applied, 7350 accepted, 3518 enrolled
SAT or ACT: required   **CEEB CODE:** 4845
Application Deadline: June 15   **COMPETITIVE**

The University of New Mexico, founded in 1889, is a public university offering instruction in liberal and fine arts, business, engineering, health science, teacher preparation, law, and technology. In addition, to the main campus there are four branch campuses. The figures provided in this profile are approximate. There are 10 undergraduate schools and 5 graduate schools. In addition to regional accreditation, UNM has baccalaureate program accreditation with AACSB, ABET, ACCE, ACEJMC, ACPE, ADA, CAHEA, NAAB, NASM, NCATE, CDA, CAATE, and NAST/NASD. The 783-acre campus is in an urban area within the city of Albuquerque. Including any residence halls, there are 339 buildings.

STUDENT LIFE: 90% of undergraduates are from New Mexico. Others are from 50 states, 56 foreign countries, and Canada. 45% are Hispanic; 37% White. **Male To Female Ratio:** 1.2:1. The average age of freshmen is 19; all undergraduates, 23. 22% do not continue beyond their first year; 48% remain to graduate. **Housing:** 3700 students can be accommodated in college housing, which includes single-sex and coed dorms, on-campus apartments, and married student housing. In addition, there are honors houses, special-interest houses, fraternity houses, sorority houses, freshman living learning communities, scholar's wings, graduates and senior undergraduate units, global learning community, and combined BA/MD degree program quarters. 89% of students commute. Alcohol is not permitted. All students may keep cars.

FACULTY/CLASSROOMS: 52% of faculty are male; 48% are female. No introductory courses are taught by graduate students.

PROGRAMS OF STUDY: UNM confers B.A., B.S., B.A.A., B.A.E.P.D., B.A.Ed., B.A.F.A., B.B.A., B.F.A., B.I.S., B.L.A., B.M., B.M.E., B.S.C.E., B.S.Ch.E., B.S.Cp.E., B.S.Cn.E., B.S.C.S., B.S.D.H., B.S.E.E., B.S.Ed., B.S.M.E., B.S.M.L., B.S.N., B.S.D.H. and B.S.N.E degrees. Associate, master's, and doctoral degrees are also awarded. Bachelor's degrees are awarded in BIOLOGICAL SCIENCE (biochemistry, biology/biological science, and nutrition), BUSINESS (business administration and management), COMMUNICATIONS AND THE ARTS (American Sign Language, art history, art, classics, communications, comparative literature, dance, English, film, television and digital media, French, German, journalism, languages, linguistics, media arts, music, Portuguese, Russian, Spanish, studio art, theater design, and theatre studies), COMPUTER AND PHYSICAL SCIENCE (astrophysics, chemistry, computer science, earth science, mathematics, physics, and statistics), EDUCATION (art education, athletic training, drama education, early childhood education, elementary education, health education, music education, physical education, secondary education, special education, and technical education), ENGINEERING AND ENVIRONMENTAL DESIGN (architecture, chemical engineering, civil engineering, computer engineering, construction engineering, construction management, electrical/electronics engineering, environmental design, environmental science, mechanical engineering, and nuclear engineering), HEALTH PROFESSIONS (dental hygiene, emergency medical technologies, exercise science, health, medical laboratory technology, nursing, radiological science, and speech pathology/audiology), SOCIAL SCIENCE (africana studies, American studies, anthropology, Asian/Oriental studies, child care/child and family studies, criminology, economics, European studies, family/consumer studies, geography, history, human development, human services, interdisciplinary studies, international studies, Latin American studies, liberal arts/general studies, Mexican-American/Chicano studies, Native American studies, philosophy, political science/government, psychology, religion, sociology, and women's studies). Business administration, psychology, and biology have the largest enrollments.

ACTIVITIES: 2% of men belong to 15 national fraternities; 3% of women belong to 10 national sororities. There are 400 groups on campus, including art, band, cheerleading, chess, choir, chorale, chorus, communications, dance, drama, drill team, environmental, ethnic, gay, honors, international, jazz band, literary magazine, marching band, musical theater, opera, orchestra, pep band, political, professional, religious, social, social service, student government, and symphony. Popular campus events include Spring Fiesta, Welcome Back Days, and Hanging of the Greens. **Sports:** There are 8 intercollegiate sports for men and 11 for women, and 5 intramural sports for men and 5 for women. Facilities include a football field, 2 gyms, 2 pools, weights, racquetball, basketball, and tennis courts. The stadium seats 38,370, the gym 7,000, and the largest arena 18,018. **Graduates:** From July 1, 2013 to June 30, 2014, 3493 bachelor's degrees were awarded. The most popular majors were business administration (20%), psychology (8%), and elementary education (6%). 414 companies recruited on campus in 2013-2014. In an average class, 48% graduate in 6 years or less.

SERVICES: Counseling and information services are available, as is tutoring in most subjects. There is remedial math, reading, and writing. **Library/Resources:** The 8 libraries contain 3.6 million volumes, 713,958 microform items, 54,238 audio/video tapes/CDs/DVDs, and subscribe to 71,932 periodicals including electronic. Computerized library services include interlibrary loans, database searching, Internet access, and Wi-Fi capability. Special learning facilities include an art gallery, planetarium, TV station, a robotics lab, lithography and meteoritic institutes, observatory, arts lab, and museums of geology, anthropology, biology, and art. **Physically Challenged Students:** All of the campus is accessible. Facilities include wheelchair ramps, elevators, special parking, specially equipped restrooms, lowered drinking fountains, and special housing. **Special:** There is a 3-2 engineering program with the Anderson School of Management. Study abroad is available in 28 countries. The university offers cooperative programs in arts and sciences management, engineering, and fine arts, a Washington semester, work-study, dual and student-designed majors, a general studies degree, credit for military experience, nondegree study, and pass/fail options. There are 20 national honor societies, including Phi Beta Kappa, a freshman honors program, and 46 departmental honors programs. **Visiting:** There are regularly scheduled orientations for prospective students, includeing academic advisement and registration. There are guides for informal visits, visitors may sit in on classes, and stay overnight. To schedule a visit, contact Admissions and Recrutment Services at (505) 277-2260. **Campus Safety and Security:** Measures include 24-hour foot and vehicle patrol, emergency notification system, self-defense education, and security escort services. There are shuttle buses, emergency telephones, lighted pathways/sidewalks, crime stoppers, jump starts, operation ID, bicycle registration, and a 911 emergency system.

REQUIREMENTS: The SAT or ACT is required. A total of 13 academic credits is required, including 4 years of English, 3 years of math, and 2 years each of foreign language, natural science (1 lab), and social science (1 U.S. history). A GED is accepted. Freshman applicants must be graduates of a high school accredited by a regional accrediting association or by the state department of education or state university of the state in which the high school is located. The minimum GPA requirement for admission to bachelor degree programs is 2.25 (on a 4.0 scale) in all previous academic work from an accredited high school. Grades in all courses allowed toward high school graduation are computed in the average. AP and CLEP credits

are accepted. All students must take 2 English courses or pass an English composition competence examination and complete the University Core Curriculum. A minimum of 128 credit hours is required. **Procedure:** Freshmen are admitted fall, spring, and summer. Entrance exams should be taken during the summer following the junior year. There are early admissions, deferred admissions, and rolling admissions plans. June 15 for fall entry; November 15 for spring entry; and May 1 for summer entry. The fall 2014 application fee was $20. Notification is sent on a rolling basis. Applications are accepted on-line. **Transfer Students:** 927 transfer students enrolled in 2013-2014. Applicants must have at least a 2.0 GPA in all transferable courses. 30 of 128 credits required for the bachelor's degree must be completed at UNM. **International Students:** There are 208 international students enrolled. The school actively recruits these students. They must take the TOEFL, University of Cambridge English Examination (CPE or CAE) and IELTS. They must also take the SAT or ACT.

ADMISSIONS: 63% of the 2014-2015 applicants were accepted. **Admissions Contact:** Matthew Hulett, Director of Admissions. E-Mail: *apply@unm.edu* Web: *www.unm.edu*

FINANCIAL AID: In 2014-2015, 85% of continuing full-time students received some form of financial aid. The FAFSA is required. Check with the school for current application deadlines.

UNIVERSITY OF THE SOUTHWEST   E-4
www.csw.edu

Hobbs, NM 88240	(505) 392-6563
	(800) 530-4400
Fax: (505) 392-6006	Email: ataylor@csw.edu
Full-time: 150 men, 200 women	Faculty: IIB, --$
Part-time: 20 men, 55 women	Ph.D.s: n/av
Graduate: 40 men, 125 women	Student/Faculty: n/av
Year: semesters, summer session	Tuition: $11,000
Room & Board: $4000	Freshman Class: n/av
SAT or ACT: required	CEEB CODE: 4116
Application Deadline: open	COMPETITIVE

University of the Southwest, founded in 1962, is an independent college offering undergraduate programs in arts and sciences, business, education, psychology, and criminal justice. Graduate programs are offered in education. The figures in the above capsule and in this profile are approximate. There is 1 graduate school. The 162-acre campus is in a small town 110 miles southwest of Lubbock, TX. Including any residence halls, there are 11 buildings.

STUDENT LIFE: 70% of undergraduates are from New Mexico. Others are from 11 states, 5 foreign countries, and Canada. 43% are White; 38% Hispanic. **Male To Female Ratio:** 1.8:1. The average age of freshmen is 20; all undergraduates, 26. 35% do not continue beyond their first year; 35% remain to graduate. **Housing:** 172 students can be accommodated in college housing, which includes single-sex and coed dorms and on-campus apartments. On-campus housing is available on a first-come, first-served basis. Priority is given to out-of-town students. 77% of students commute. Alcohol is not permitted. All students may keep cars.

FACULTY/CLASSROOMS: 51% of faculty are male; 49% are female. 99% teach undergraduates. No introductory courses are taught by graduate students. The average class size in an introductory lecture is 11; in a laboratory is 7; and in a regular course is 12.

PROGRAMS OF STUDY: confers B.S., B.A.S. and B.B.A. degrees. Master's degrees are also awarded. Bachelor's degrees are awarded in BIOLOGICAL SCIENCE (biology/biological science), BUSINESS (accounting and business administration and management), COMMUNICATIONS AND THE ARTS (English and fine arts), COMPUTER AND PHYSICAL SCIENCE (mathematics), EDUCATION (elementary education, secondary education, and special education), SOCIAL SCIENCE (criminal justice, history, humanities, psychology, and sociology). Education and business are the strongest academically. Education, business, and criminal justice have the largest enrollments.

ACTIVITIES: There are no fraternities or sororities. There are 7

groups on campus, including debate, drama, honors, international, newspaper, professional, religious, and student government. Popular campus events include Annual Students in Free Enterprise Dinner and Award Presentation, Family Week, and Speakers' Presentations. **Sports:** There are 4 intercollegiate sports for men and 6 for women, and 5 intramural sports for men and 5 for women. Facilities include soccer and baseball fields, a game room, and a physical fitness center with a multipurpose gym, racquetball courts, and physiology lab. **Graduates:** From July 1, 2013 to June 30, 2014, 98 bachelor's degrees were awarded. The most popular majors were education (29%), psychology (11%), and accounting (10%). 10 companies recruited on campus in 2013-2014. In an average class, 19% graduate in 5 years or less. Of the 2013 graduating class, 5% were enrolled in graduate school within 6 months of graduation.

SERVICES: Counseling and information services are available, as is tutoring in most subjects. There is remedial math and writing. **Library/Resources:** The library contains 76,450 volumes, 25,750 microform items, 1,553 audio/video tapes/CDs/DVDs, and subscribes to 333 periodicals including electronic. Computerized library services include interlibrary loans, database searching, and Internet access. **Physically Challenged Students:** All of the campus is accessible. Facilities include wheelchair ramps, special parking, and specially equipped restrooms. **Special:** The school offers co-op programs in early childhood education. Internships are available for students majoring in business, psychology, and education. CSW also offers nondegree study and credit for military experience. There are 2 national honor societies and 1 departmental honors program. **Visiting:** There are guides for informal visits, visitors may sit in on classes, and stay overnight. To schedule a visit, contact Coordinator of Admissions. **Campus Safety and Security:** Measures include 24-hour foot and vehicle patrol.

REQUIREMENTS: The SAT or ACT is required. The ACT Optional Writing test is also required. Students must have a minimum composite score of 18 on the ACT or a satisfactory score on the SAT. Applicants must be graduates of an accredited secondary school or have a GED certificate. A GPA of 2.0 is required. AP and CLEP credits are accepted. Important factors in the admissions decision are advanced placement or honors courses, extracurricular activities record, and ability to finance college education.To graduate, students must complete 128 semester hours with a minimum GPA of 2.0 (2.5 for education majors). General education requirements include 12 semester hours each of social science and math/science, 9 each of humanities/fine arts and communications, 6 of religion, and 3 of economics, as well as a course in free enterprise and a senior seminar in leadership and ethics. **Procedure:** Freshmen are admitted to all sessions. There is a rolling admissions plan. Application deadlines are open. Application fee is $25. Notification is sent on a rolling basis. Applications are accepted on-line. **Transfer Students:** 135 transfer students enrolled in 2013-2014. Applicants must present a minimum GPA of 2.0 and official transcripts from all colleges attended. 30 of 128 credits required for the bachelor's degree must be completed at University of Southwest. **International Students:** There are 27 international students enrolled. They must take the TOEFL. They must also take the SAT or ACT.

ADMISSIONS: Ashley Taylor, Coordinator of Admissions. E-Mail: *ataylor@csw.edu* Web: *www.csw.edu*

FINANCIAL AID: In 2014-2015, 97% of all full-time freshmen and 88% of continuing full-time students received some form of financial aid. 64% of all full-time freshmen and 70% of continuing full-time students received need-based aid. The FAFSA and the college's own financial statement are required. Check with the school for current application deadlines.

WESTERN NEW MEXICO UNIVERSITY (*The complete profile is made available exclusively on our website, www.barronspac.com*)

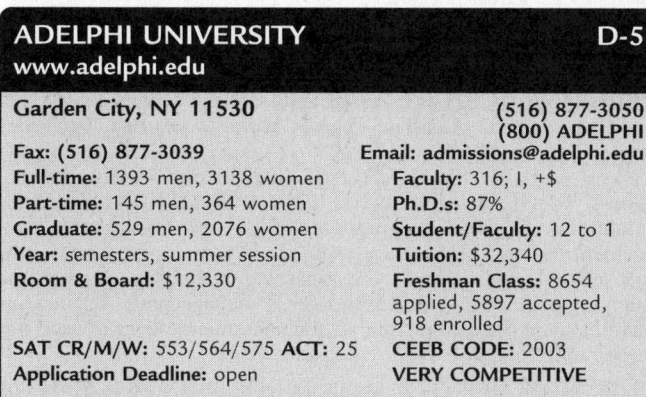

NEW YORK

· College Location

0 20 40 60 80 100

Miles

ADELPHI UNIVERSITY D-5
www.adelphi.edu

Garden City, NY 11530	**(516) 877-3050**
	(800) ADELPHI
Fax: (516) 877-3039	**Email: admissions@adelphi.edu**
Full-time: 1393 men, 3138 women	**Faculty:** 316; I, +$
Part-time: 145 men, 364 women	**Ph.D.s:** 87%
Graduate: 529 men, 2076 women	**Student/Faculty:** 12 to 1
Year: semesters, summer session	**Tuition:** $32,340
Room & Board: $12,330	**Freshman Class:** 8654 applied, 5897 accepted, 918 enrolled
SAT CR/M/W: 553/564/575 **ACT:** 25	**CEEB CODE:** 2003
Application Deadline: open	**VERY COMPETITIVE**

Adelphi University, founded in 1896, is a private institution. The figure for tuition and fees in the above capsule is for first-year students. There are 8 undergraduate schools and 7 graduate schools. In addition to regional accreditation, Adelphi has baccalaureate program accreditation with AACSB, CSWE, NCATE, NLN, APA, ASHA, and CCNE. The 75-acre campus is in a suburban area 20 miles east of New York City. Including any residence halls, there are 26 buildings.

STUDENT LIFE: 92% of undergraduates are from New York. Others are from 38 states, 40 foreign countries, and Canada. 74% are from public schools. 61% are White; 15% Hispanic; 12% African American. 47% are Catholic; 17% Hindu, Buddhist, Muslim, Christian, 16% claim no religious affiliation; 12% Jewish. **Male To Female Ratio:** 2.7:1. The average age of freshmen is 18; all undergraduates, 20. 19% do not continue beyond their first year; 67% remain to graduate. **Housing:** 1282 students can be accommodated in college housing, which includes coed dorms. In addition, there are honors houses and special-interest houses. On-campus housing is available on a first-come, first-served basis, and is available on a lottery system for upperclassmen. Priority is given to out-of-town students. 77% of students commute. Alcohol is not permitted. All students may keep cars.

FACULTY/CLASSROOMS: 46% of faculty are male; 54% are female.

All teach undergraduates. No introductory courses are taught by graduate students. The average class size in a regular course is 20.

PROGRAMS OF STUDY: Adelphi confers B.A., B.S., B.B.A., B.F.A., B.S.Ed. and B.S.S.W. degrees. Associate, Master's, and Doctoral degrees are also awarded. Bachelor's degrees are awarded in AGRICULTURE (environmental studies), BIOLOGICAL SCIENCE (biochemistry and biology/biological science), BUSINESS (accounting, banking and finance, business administration and management, human resources, and management information systems), COMMUNICATIONS AND THE ARTS (art history and appreciation, communications, dance, design, dramatic arts, English, fine arts, French, languages, music, performing arts, Spanish, and theater design), COMPUTER AND PHYSICAL SCIENCE (chemistry, computer science, mathematics, and physics), EDUCATION (art education and physical education), HEALTH PROFESSIONS (nursing and speech pathology/audiology), SOCIAL SCIENCE (anthropology, criminal justice, economics, history, Latin American studies, philosophy, political science/government, psychology, social science, social work, and sociology). Nursing, business, and social work are the strongest academically. Nursing, biology, and psychology have the largest enrollments.

ACTIVITIES: 11% of men belong to 7 national fraternities; 9% of women belong to 10 national sororities. There are 80 groups on campus, including art, band, cheerleading, chorale, chorus, computers, dance, debate, drama, environmental, ethnic, film, gay, honors, international, jazz band, literary magazine, musical theater, newspaper, opera, orchestra, political, professional, radio and TV, religious, social, social service, student government, and yearbook. Popular campus events include Family Week, Student Holiday Party, Spring-In Festival, Spring Concert and Commuter Appreciation Week. **Sports:** There are 9 intercollegiate sports for men and 11 for women, and 14 intramural sports for men and 14 for women. Facilities include a 3000-seat stadium, a 600-seat gym, a 4-lane swimming pool, fitness center, racquetball, squash, and tennis courts, a dance studio, an indoor track, baseball field, and a softball field. **Graduates:** From July 1, 2013 to June 30, 2014, 1250 bachelor's degrees were awarded. The most popular majors were health professions (23%), business (13%), and social science (12%). 200 companies recruited on campus in 2013-2014. In an average class, 5% graduate in 3 years or less, 54% graduate in 4 years or less, 61% graduate in 5 years or less, and 66% graduate in 6 years or less. Of the 2013 graduating class, 41% were enrolled in graduate school within 6 months of graduation, and 88% were employed.

SERVICES: Counseling and information services are available, as is tutoring in most subjects, a learning center offers tutoring in writing, quantitative skills and help with class assignments. There is a reader service for the blind. A writing center is also available. **Library/Resources:** The library contains 632,180 volumes, 789,749 microform items, 26,746 audio/video tapes/CDs/DVDs, and subscribes to 929 periodicals including electronic. Computerized library services include interlibrary loans, database searching, Internet access, and Wi-Fi capability. Special learning facilities include an art gallery, radio station, an observatory, a theater, sculpture and ceramics studios, a bronze casting foundry, and language labs. **Physically Challenged Students:** 95% of the campus is accessible. Facilities include wheelchair ramps, elevators, special parking, specially equipped restrooms, special class scheduling, lowered drinking fountains, lowered telephones, and special housing. **Special:** Cross-registration is possible with New York University College of Dentistry, Tufts University School of Dental Medicine, Columbia University, New York Law School, SUNY State College of Optometry, and New York Medical College. Internships are available in accounting, banking and money management, and communications. Study abroad is available in 65 countries, including Spain, France, Denmark, and England. A 5-year bachelor's/master's degree in a number of fields, including biology, social work, and education is offered. In addition, work-study programs, double majors, the B.A.-B.S. degree, an accelerated degree program, student-designed majors, and a Washington semester are available. A 3-2 engineering degree is offered with Rensselaer Polytechnic, Columbia, Polytechnic, and Stevens Institute of Technology, and joint degree programs are offered in computer science, dentistry, engineering, environmental studies, law, optometry, and physical therapy with other universities and technical institutions. Credit for life experience for adult students, nondegree study in special cases, and pass/fail options are possible. There are 27 national honor societies and a freshman honors program. **Visiting:** There are regularly scheduled orientations for prospective students, including a campus tour, an interview, and information sessions. There are guides for informal visits and visitors may sit in on classes. To schedule a visit, contact the Undergraduate Admissions at undergraduate@adelphi.edu. **Campus Safety and Security:** Measures include 24-hour foot and vehicle patrol, emergency notification system, self-defense education, and security escort services. There are shuttle buses, emergency telephones, lighted pathways/sidewalks, dorm main entrances are videotaped and dorm doors are locked 24 hours a day.

REQUIREMENTS: Applicants should have 16 academic credits, including a recommended 4 units of English, history, and social studies, 3 each of math and science, and 2 or 3 of foreign language. An essay is required and An interview recommended for all applicants. A portfolio for art and technical theater candidates, an audition for music, dance, and theater candidates, and an interview for nursing, social work, and honors candidates are required. The SAT is recommended for the general studies and learning disabilities programs. A GPA of 2.5 is required. AP credits are accepted. Important factors in the admissions decision are advanced placement or honors courses, leadership record, and personality/intangible qualities.To graduate, students need at least a 2.0 cumulative GPA (higher in some programs) and 120 credit hours with a minimum of 27 in the major. 6 credits each are required in the arts, humanities, and languages, natural sciences and math, and social sciences. Other course requirements include English composition, freshman seminar (3 credits each), and a 1-credit freshman orientation experience, and a capstone experience for seniors. **Procedure:** Freshmen are admitted fall and spring. Entrance exams should be taken in October of the senior year or May of the junior year. There are early admissions, deferred admissions, and rolling admissions plans. Application deadlines are open. The fall 2014 application fee was $40. Applications are accepted online. **Transfer Students:** 541 transfer students enrolled in 2013-2014. A GPA of 2.5 is recommended in addition to an essay, an official high school transcript, and official records of all work completed or in progress from previous colleges and universities. An interview is required for students in social work and nursing, while an audition is needed for music, dance, and theater students and a portfolio for art and technical theater students. 30 of 120 credits required for the bachelor's degree must be completed at Adelphi. **International Students:** There are 203 international students enrolled. The school actively recruits these students. They must take the TOEFL with a minimum score of 550 on the paper-based TOEFL (PBT) or 80 on the Internet-based version (iBT). They must also take the SAT or ACT.

ADMISSIONS: 68% of the 2014-2015 applicants were accepted. The SAT scores for the 2014-2015 freshman class were: Critical Reading--25% below 500, 50% between 500 and 599, 20% between 600 and 699, and 5% between 700 and 800; Math--18% below 500, 48% between 500 and 599, 29% between 600 and 699, and 5% between 700 and 800; Writing--19% below 500, 47% between 500 and 599, 29% between 600 and 699, and 5% between 700 and 800. 46% of the current freshmen were in the top fifth of their class; 81% were in the top two fifths. **Admissions Contact:** Christine Murphy, Director of Admissions. E-Mail: *admissions@adelphi.edu* Web: *www.adelphi.edu*

FINANCIAL AID: In 2014-2015, 99% of all full-time freshmen and 88% of continuing full-time students received some form of financial aid. 75% of all full-time freshmen and 72% of continuing full-time students received need-based aid. The average freshman award was $19,000. Need-based scholarships or need-based grants averaged $6,837 need-based self-help aid (loans and jobs) averaged $5,139; and non-need-based athletic scholarships averaged $13,490. Adelphi is a member of CSS. The FAFSA and the state aid form are required. The priority date for freshman financial aid applications for fall entry is March 1. The deadline for filing freshman financial aid applications for fall entry is February 15.

ALBANY COLLEGE OF PHARMACY AND HEALTH SCIENCES
(The complete profile is made available exclusively on our website, www. barronspac.com)

ALFRED STATE/SUNY COLLEGE OF TECHNOLOGY   B-4
www.alfredstate.edu

Alfred, NY 14802	(607) 587-4215
	(800) 4-ALFRED
Fax: (607) 587-4299	Email: admissions@alfredstate.edu
Full-time: n/av	Faculty: n/av
Part-time: n/av	Ph.D.s: n/av
Graduate: n/av	Student/Faculty: n/av
Year: semesters, summer session	Tuition: $6874 ($16,124)
Room & Board: $11,160	Freshman Class: n/av
SAT CR/M/W: 520/540/490 ACT: 23	CEEB CODE: 2522
Application Deadline: n/av	COMPETITIVE

The State University of New York College of Technology at Alfred, founded in 1908, is a public institution conferring associate and bachelor's degrees. Figures in the above capsule and in this profile are approximate. There are 3 undergraduate schools. In addition to regional accreditation, Alfred State College has baccalaureate program accreditation with ABET. The 150-acre campus is in a rural area 15 miles north of Pennsylvania, 75 miles south of Rochester, and 90 miles southeast of Buffalo. Including any residence halls, there are 50 buildings.

STUDENT LIFE: 97% of undergraduates are from New York. Others are from 7 states, 12 foreign countries, and Canada. 73% are White; 11% African American. The average age of freshmen is 18; all undergraduates, 19. 67% remain to graduate. **Housing:** College-sponsored housing includes coed dorms and on-campus apartments. In addition, there are honors houses, language houses, special-interest houses, wellness, computerized, and adult housing. On-campus housing is guaranteed for all 4 years. 70% of students live on campus; of those, 50% remain on campus on weekends. Alcohol is not permitted. All students may keep cars.

FACULTY/CLASSROOMS: 66% of faculty are male; 34% are female. All teach undergraduates. No introductory courses are taught by graduate students. The average class size in an introductory lecture is 40; in a laboratory is 20; and in a regular course is 20.

PROGRAMS OF STUDY: Alfred State College confers B.S., B.B.A. and B.T. degrees. Associate degrees are also awarded. Bachelor's degrees are awarded in BUSINESS (banking and finance), COMPUTER AND PHYSICAL SCIENCE (information sciences and systems), ENGINEERING AND ENVIRONMENTAL DESIGN (architectural technology, computer technology, construction management, electrical/electronics engineering technology, manufacturing technology, mechanical engineering technology, survey and mapping technology, and technological management). Engineering technology programs are the strongest academically and have the largest enrollments.

ACTIVITIES: There are 90 groups on campus, including rescue and response team, band, cheerleading, chess, choir, chorale, chorus, computers, dance, drama, environmental, ethnic, forensics, gay, honors, international, jazz band, literary magazine, musical theater, newspaper, orchestra, peer education network, pep band, professional, radio and TV, social, social service, student government, and yearbook. Popular campus events include Family Weekend and Hot Dog Day. **Sports:** There are 9 intercollegiate sports for men and 7 for women, and 26 intramural sports for men and 23 for women. Facilities include a fitness center/weight room, an indoor swimming pool, wrestling room, a full gym, tennis courts, an outdoor track, baseball and softball fields, and practice fields. **Graduates:** Of the 2013 graduating class, 99% were enrolled in graduate school within 6 months of graduation, and 99% were employed.

SERVICES: Counseling and information services are available, as is tutoring in most subjects. There is a reader service for the blind, and remedial math, reading, and writing. **Library/Resources:** The 2 libraries contain 61,500 volumes, 8,148 audio/video tapes/CDs/DVDs, and subscribe to 5,500 periodicals including electronic. Computerized library services include interlibrary loans, database searching, Internet access, and Wi-Fi capability. Special learning facilities include an art gallery and radio station. **Physically Challenged Students:** All of the campus is accessible. Facilities include wheelchair ramps, elevators, special parking, specially equipped restrooms, special class scheduling, lowered drinking fountains, lowered telephones, and special housing. **Special:** Cross-registration is offered with Alfred University, Houghton College, Rochester area colleges, and the Western New York Consortium. On-campus work-study programs are available, as are summer internships. There are 2 national honor societies, a freshman honors program, and 52 departmental honors programs. **Visiting:** There are regularly scheduled orientations for prospective students, including open houses during the fall and spring semesters. All aspects of the campus are open for visitation, and accepted students are invited to participate in an overnight visit. There are guides for informal visits, visitors may sit in on classes, and stay overnight. To schedule a visit, contact the Admissions Office. **Campus Safety and Security:** Measures include 24-hour foot and vehicle patrol, emergency notification system, self-defense education, and security escort services. There are shuttle buses, emergency telephones, lighted pathways/sidewalks, and controlled access to dorms/residences.

REQUIREMENTS: The SAT or ACT is required. Applicants must have graduated from an accredited secondary school or earned a GED. Specific course requirements vary by curriculum. A portfolio is required for applicants interested in computer art and design and Digital Media and Animation. AP and CLEP credits are accepted. Important factors in the admissions decision are advanced placement or honors courses, extracurricular activities record, and recommendations by school officials.To graduate, candidates for a bachelor's degree must complete a total of 120 credits. A core sequence, including courses in math, physical sciences, and liberal studies, and a year-long senior technical project, are required. A phys ed course is also required. **Procedure:** Freshmen are admitted to all sessions. Entrance exams should be taken November 1. There is a rolling admissions plan. Application deadlines are open. Application fee is $50. Notifications are sent November 1. Applications are accepted on-line. **Transfer Students:** 263 transfer students enrolled in 2013-2014. Transfer applicants must have a minimum 2.4 GPA. 30 of 120 credits required for the bachelor's degree must be completed at Alfred State College. **International Students:** There are 50 international students enrolled. The school actively recruits these students. They must take the TOEFL.

ADMISSIONS: Deborah Goodrich, Associate Vice President for Enrollment Management. E-Mail: *admissions@alfredstate.edu* Web: *www.alfredstate.edu*

FINANCIAL AID: In 2014-2015, 80% of all full-time freshmen students received some form of financial aid. 80% of all full-time freshmen and 80% of continuing full-time students received need-based aid. Average annual earnings from campus work are $1000. The FAFSA is required. Check with the school for current application deadlines.

ALFRED UNIVERSITY	B-4
www.alfred.edu	

Alfred, NY 14802	(607) 871-2115
	(800) 541-9229
Fax: (607) 871-2198	Email: admissions@alfred.edu
Full-time: 939 men, 970 women	Faculty: 150; III, av$
Part-time: 24 men, 27 women	Ph.D.s: 93%
Graduate: 157 men, 314 women	Student/Faculty: 13 to 1
Year: semesters, summer session	Tuition: $29,610
Room & Board: $12,160	Freshman Class: 3417 applied, 2385 accepted, 535 enrolled
SAT CR/M/W: 530/550/510 **ACT:** 24	CEEB CODE: 2005
Application Deadline: February 1	COMPETITIVE

Alfred University, founded in 1836, is composed of the privately endowed college of Liberal Arts and Sciences, college of ceramics (Inamori School of Engineering and School of Art and Design). Bachelors, masters, certificates of advanced study, and doctoral degrees are awarded as the culmination of Alfred University's academic and professional programs. There are 5 undergraduate schools and 1 graduate school. In addition to regional accreditation, AU has baccalaureate program accreditation with AACSB, ABET, NASAD, TEAC, CAATE, and ACS. The 232-acre campus is in a rural area between the foothills of the Allegheny Mountains and the Finger Lakes region in western NY. Including any residence halls, there are 52 buildings.

STUDENT LIFE: 76% of undergraduates are from New York. Others are from 42 states, 19 foreign countries, and Canada. 66% are White; 12% race unknown. **Male To Female Ratio:** 1.2:1. The average age of freshmen is 18; all undergraduates, 20. 26% do not continue beyond their first year; 62% remain to graduate. **Housing:** 1469 students can be accommodated in college housing, which includes single-sex and coed dorms and on-campus apartments. In addition, there are honors houses, language houses, special-interest houses, and theme housing. On-campus housing is guaranteed for the freshman year only, is available on a first-come, first-served basis, and is available on a lottery system for upperclassmen. 76% of students live on campus; of those, 90% remain on campus on weekends. All students may keep cars.

FACULTY/CLASSROOMS: 54% of faculty are male; 46% are female. 90% do both. No introductory courses are taught by graduate students. The average class size in an introductory lecture is 30; in a laboratory is 20; and in a regular course is 18.

PROGRAMS OF STUDY: AU confers B.A., B.F.A. and B.S. degrees. Master's and Doctoral degrees are also awarded. Bachelor's degrees are awarded in AGRICULTURE (environmental studies), BIOLOGICAL SCIENCE (biology/biological science), BUSINESS (accounting, business administration and management, and marketing/retailing/merchandising), COMMUNICATIONS AND THE ARTS (art history and appreciation, ceramic art and design, communications, dramatic arts, English, fine arts, glass, Spanish, and theatre arts), COMPUTER AND PHYSICAL SCIENCE (chemistry, geology, mathematics, physics, and science), EDUCATION (art education, athletic training, business education, early childhood education, mathematics education, science education, secondary education, and social studies education), ENGINEERING AND ENVIRONMENTAL DESIGN (ceramic engineering, materials engineering, and mechanical engineering), SOCIAL SCIENCE (criminal justice, crosscultural studies, gerontology, history, interdisciplinary studies, philosophy, political science/government, psychology, and sociology). Engineering is the strongest academically. Art and design, business administration, and mechanical engineering have the largest enrollments.

ACTIVITIES: There are no fraternities or sororities. There are 90 groups on campus, including honors, business, communications, cultural, diversity and multicultural, engineering, entertainment, math and science, service and leadership, spiritual life, art, athletics, band, cheerleading, chorale, chorus, computers, dance, drama, environmental, ethnic, film, gay, honors, international, jazz band, literary magazine, musical theater, newspaper, orchestra, pep band, photography, political, professional, radio and TV, religious, social, social service, student government, and yearbook. Popular campus events include Homecoming Weekend, Family Weekend and Hot Dog Day. **Sports:** There are 10 intercollegiate sports for men and 11 for women, and 14 intramural sports for men and 13 for women. Facilities include a multi-purpose field for football, soccer, and lacrosse, an Olympic-size pool, softball field, tennis courts, racquetball and squash courts, a weight room, dance and exercise studios. Merrill Field seats approximately 5,000; the indoor gym seats approximately 3,500. There is also a fitness center, an equestrian center, many hiking trails, and easy access to cross-country skiing, a four-lane indoor track, basketball courts, and storage and locker facilities. **Graduates:** From July 1, 2013 to June 30, 2014, 356 bachelor's degrees were awarded. The most popular majors were fine arts (31%), engineering (17%), and biology (8%). 80 companies recruited on campus in 2013-2014. In an average class, 44% graduate in 4 years or less, 61% graduate in 5 years or less, and 62% graduate in 6 years or less.

SERVICES: Counseling and information services are available, as is tutoring in most subjects, depends on tutor availability. Time management, study skills workshops, and a writing center are available. There are also services for students with learning and physical disabilities. **Library/Resources:** The 2 libraries contain 286,995 volumes, 79,704 microform items, 179,255 audio/video tapes/CDs/DVDs, and subscribe to 93,502 periodicals including electronic. Computerized library services include interlibrary loans, database searching, Internet access, and Wi-Fi capability. Special learning facilities include an art gallery, radio station, TV station, observatory, and a museum of ceramic art. **Physically Challenged Students:** 45% of the campus is accessible. Facilities include wheelchair ramps, elevators, special parking, specially equipped restrooms, special class scheduling, lowered drinking fountains. **Special:** There are cooperative programs in engineering with Duke and Columbia Universities. AU participates in a cross-registration program with more than 15 area colleges and universities through the Rochester Area Colleges consortium. AU also offers study abroad, Washington and Albany semesters, student-designed majors, and a 4+1 MBA program for students majoring in Liberal Arts and Sciences or Engineering. There are 16 national honor societies including Phi Beta Kappa. **Visiting:** There are regularly scheduled orientations for prospective students, agenda is customized per student's needs. There are guides for informal visits, visitors may sit in on classes, and stay overnight. To schedule a visit, contact the Admissions Office at (800) 541-9229. **Campus Safety and Security:** Measures include emergency notification system and security escort services. There are emergency telephones, lighted pathways/ sidewalks, controlled access to dorms/residences, vehicle and foot patrol.

REQUIREMENTS: The SAT or ACT is required. A GED is accepted. A minimum of 16 Carnegie units is required, including 4 years of English, 2 to 3 years each of math, history/social studies, and science. Depending on the school/college applied to, the remaining units may be either in a foreign language, the categories listed above, or business, art, or computer science. Official high school transcripts, one letter of recommendation, an essay, and a $50 fee (may be waived by visiting campus or with a NACAC or College Board waiver) is required of all applicants. Applicants to the School of Art and Design must submit a portfolio. Interviews are encouraged. AP credits are accepted. Important factors in the admissions decision are recommendations by school officials, extracurricular activities record, and leadership record. To satisfy the requirements for a Bachelors Degree a student must: Complete all course requirements, including those required for the major, general education, and the minimum number of credits for the degree sought depending on the school or college of enrollment; Earn a cumulative GPA of at least 2.0; Satisfy the Global Perspective Requirement; Satisfy the Physical Education requirement; Request legal conferral of degree and satisfy financial obligations to the University; Earn at least 45 semester credit hours at AU; and be in residence at AU at least during the final 30 credit hours earned toward the degree. **Procedure:** Freshmen are admitted fall and spring. Entrance exams should be taken spring of junior year. There are early decision, deferred admissions, and rolling admissions plans. Early decision applications should be filed by December 1; regular applications, by February 1 for fall entry; and December 1 for spring entry, along with a $50 fee. Notification of early decision is sent December 15; regular decision, on a rolling basis. 45 early decision candidates were accepted for the 2014-2015 class. 91 applicants were on the 2014 waiting list; 11 were admitted. Applications are accepted on-line. **Transfer Students:** 49 transfer students enrolled in 2013-2014. Transfer applicants must have a GPA of at least 2.5 on a 4.0 scale. They must submit at least 1 letter of recommendation and official high school and college transcripts. Applicants to the School of Art and Design must also submit a portfolio. 45 of 120 credits required for the bachelor's degree must be completed at AU. **International Students:** There are 51 international students enrolled. The school actively recruits these students. They must take the TOEFL with a minimum score of 550 on the paper-based TOEFL (PBT) or 80 on the Internet-based version (iBT), they must take the TOEFL or IELTS if they do not submit the SAT or ACT.

ADMISSIONS: 70% of the 2014-2015 applicants were accepted. The SAT scores for the 2014-2015 freshman class were: Critical Reading--27% below 500, 51% between 500 and 599, 19% between 600 and 699, and 3% between 700 and 800; Math--20% below 500, 49% between 500 and 599, 27% between 600 and 699, and 4% between 700 and 800; Writing--43% below 500, 40% between 500 and 599, 15% between 600 and 699, and 2% between 700 and 800. The ACT scores were 16% below 21, 28% between 21 and 23, 30% between 24 and 26, 15% between 27 and 28, and 11% above 28. 36% of the current freshmen were in the top fifth of their class; 70% were in the top two fifths. 3 freshmen graduated first in their class. **Admissions Contact:** Earl E. Pierce, VP for Enrollment Management. E-Mail: *admissions@alfred.edu* Web: *www.alfred.edu*

FINANCIAL AID: In 2014-2015, 97% of all full-time freshmen and continuing full-time students received some form of financial aid. 97% of all full-time freshmen and continuing full-time students received need-based aid. The average freshman award was $26,623. Need-based scholarships or need-based grants averaged $20,371; need-based self-help aid (loans and jobs) averaged $6,640; and $4,986 from other forms of aid. 40% of undergraduate students work part-time. Average annual earnings from campus work are $1800. The average financial indebtedness of the 2014 graduate was $33,467. AU is a member of CSS. The FAFSA, the state aid form, and the college's own financial statement, and the business/farm supplement, and the noncustodial parent statement are required. The priority date for freshman financial aid applications for fall entry is March 15. The deadline for filing freshman financial aid applications for fall entry is May 1.

BARD COLLEGE D-4
www.bard.edu

Annandale-on-Hudson, NY 12504	(845) 758-7472
	n/av
Fax: (845) 758-5208	**Email:** admission@bard.edu
Full-time: 848 men, 1077 women	**Faculty:** 149; IIB, ++$
Part-time: 47 men, 50 women	**Ph.D.s:** 96%
Graduate: 91 men, 165 women	**Student/Faculty:** 10 to 1
Year: 4-1-4	**Tuition:** $48,465
Room & Board: $13,772	**Freshman Class:** 5466 applied, 2056 accepted, 489 enrolled
SAT CR/M: 650/620	**CEEB CODE:** 2037
Application Deadline: January 1	**HIGHLY COMPETITIVE**

Bard College, founded in 1860, is an independent liberal arts and sciences institution affiliated historically with the Association of Episcopal Colleges. Discussion-oriented seminars and independent study are encouraged, tutorials are on a one-to-one basis, and most classes are kept small. Figures in the above capsule and in this profile are approximate. There is 1 undergraduate school and 13 graduate schools. The 600-acre campus is in a rural area 100 miles north of New York City. Including any residence halls, there are 70 buildings.

STUDENT LIFE: 65% of undergraduates are from out of state, mostly the Middle Atlantic. Students are from 34 states, 22 foreign countries, and Canada. 60% are from public schools. 38% are White; 13% Asian American. 22% are unknown denominations. **Male To Female Ratio:** 1.3:1. The average age of freshmen is 18; all undergraduates, 20. 13% do not continue beyond their first year; 74% remain to graduate. **Housing:** 1450 students can be accommodated in college housing, which includes single-sex and coed dorms. In addition, there are special-interest houses, single-sex dorm, suites, and quiet dorms. On-campus housing is guaranteed for the freshman year only and is available on a lottery system for upperclassmen. 73% of students live on campus; of those, 75% remain on campus on weekends. All students may keep cars.

FACULTY/CLASSROOMS: 58% of faculty are male; 42% are female. All teach and do research. No introductory courses are taught by graduate students. The average class size in a regular course is 17.

PROGRAMS OF STUDY: Bard confers B.A., B.S., B.Music, and B.P.S. degrees. Associate, Master's, and Doctoral degrees are also awarded. Bachelor's degrees are awarded in AGRICULTURE (environmental studies), BIOLOGICAL SCIENCE (biology/biological science), COMMUNICATIONS AND THE ARTS (Arabic, art history and appreciation, Chinese, classical languages, creative writing, dance, dramatic arts, English literature, film arts, French, Germanic languages and literature, Hebrew, Italian, literature, music, photography, Russian, Spanish, studio art, and theatre arts), COMPUTER AND PHYSICAL SCIENCE (chemistry, computer science, mathematics, and physics), SOCIAL SCIENCE (African studies, American studies, anthropology, area studies, Asian/Oriental studies, Celtic studies, classical/ancient civilization, cognitive science, economics,

French studies, gender studies, German area studies, history, interdisciplinary studies, international studies, Italian studies, Judaic studies, Latin American studies, medieval studies, Middle Eastern studies, philosophy, political science/government, psychology, religion, Russian and Slavic studies, Sanskrit and Indian studies, science and society, sociology, Spanish studies, theological studies, and Victorian studies). Social studies, visual and performing arts, languages and literatures have the largest enrollments.

ACTIVITIES: There are no fraternities or sororities. There are 150 groups on campus, including and Model UN, art, band, chamber groups, chess, choir, chorus, computers, dance, debate, drama, environmental, ethnic, film, forensics, gay, international, jazz band, literary magazine, musical theater, newspaper, opera, orchestra, photography, political, radio and TV, religious, social, social service, student government, and symphony. Popular campus events include Winter Carnival, Spring Festival and International Students Cultural Show. **Sports:** There are 10 intercollegiate sports for men and 8 for women, and 9 intramural sports for men and 9 for women. Facilities include a gym and pool, baseball field, fitness and weight facilities, rugby, soccer and lacrosse fields, squash and tennis courts, cross-country trails, bike paths, and multi-purpose fields for activities such as ultimate frisbee and open recreation. **Graduates:** From July 1, 2013 to June 30, 2014, 489 bachelor's degrees were awarded. The most popular majors were social studies (32%), visual and performing arts (31%), and language and literature (20%). In an average class, 60% graduate in 4 years or less, 72% graduate in 5 years or less, and 74% graduate in 6 years or less.

SERVICES: Counseling and information services are available, as is tutoring in every subject. There is a reader service for the blind. **Library/Resources:** The library contains 400,000 volumes, 8,002 microform items, 5,337 audio/video tapes/CDs/DVDs, and subscribes to 37,293 periodicals including electronic. Computerized library services include interlibrary loans, database searching, Internet access, and Wi-Fi capability. Special learning facilities include an art gallery, radio station, an ecology field station, the Levy economics institute, the institute for writing and thinking, the institute for advanced theology, the center for curatorial studies and art in contemporary culture, and an archeological station. **Physically Challenged Students:** 70% of the campus is accessible. Facilities include wheelchair ramps, elevators, special parking, specially equipped restrooms, lowered drinking fountains, and lowered telephones. **Special:** Bard offers opportunities for study abroad, internships, Washington and New York semesters, dual majors, student-designed majors, accelerated degree programs, and pass/fail options. A 3-2 engineering degree is available with the Columbia University, Washington University (St. Louis), and Dartmouth College Schools of Engineering. Other 3-2 degrees are available in forestry and environmental studies, social work, architecture, city and regional planning, public health, and business administration. There are also opportunities for independent study, multicultural and ethnic studies, area studies, human rights, and globalization and international affairs. **Visiting:** There are regularly scheduled orientations for prospective students, consisting of regularly scheduled daily tours and information sessions. Visitors may sit in on classes. To schedule a visit, contact the Admissions Office. **Campus Safety and Security:** Measures include 24-hour foot and vehicle patrol, emergency notification system, self-defense education, and security escort services. There are shuttle buses, emergency telephones, lighted pathways/sidewalks, volunteer emergency medical technicians on call 24 hours a day, and Bard response to Rape and Associated Violence Education (BRAVE).

REQUIREMENTS: Bard places strong emphasis on the academic background and intellectual curiosity of applicants, as well as indications of the student's commitment to social and environmental concerns, independent research, volunteer work, and other important extracurricular activities. Students applying for admission are expected to have graduated from an accredited secondary school (the GED is accepted) and must submit written essays with the application. The High School record should include a full complement of college-preparatory courses. Honors and advanced placement courses are also considered. A GPA of 3.0 is required. AP credits are accepted. Important factors in the admissions decision are advanced placement or honors courses, recommendations by school officials, and extracurricular activities record. All students must complete a

3-week workshop in Language and Thinking (August of first year), a two and a half week Citizen Science program (January of first year); a first-year seminar; and a senior project. A conference in the junior year is required, and through a moderation process in the sophomore year, the student chooses a concentration in an academic department. A distribution of at least 1 course in each of the 9 academic areas is required, with 40 credits outside the division of the student's major and a total of 128 credit hours needed to graduate. "Rethinking Differences," a course fulfilling the diversity requirement, is also required. **Procedure:** Freshmen are admitted in the fall. There are early admissions and deferred admissions plans. Applications should be filed by January 1 for fall entry; November 1 for spring entry, along with a $50 fee. Notifications are sent April 1. 404 applicants were on the 2014 waiting list; 88 were admitted. Applications are accepted online. **Transfer Students:** 61 transfer students enrolled in 2013-2014. Admission requirements are the same as for regular applicants. A minimum GPA of 3.0 and an interview are recommended. High School transcript (when less than 2 years of college-level study completed), transfer questionnaire, and dean's report are required. 64 of 128 credits required for the bachelor's degree must be completed at Bard. **International Students:** There are 237 international students enrolled. The school actively recruits these students. They must take the TOEFL with a minimum score of 600 on the paper-based TOEFL (PBT).

ADMISSIONS: 38% of the 2014-2015 applicants were accepted. **Admissions Contact:** Mary Backlund, Director of Admissions. E-Mail: *admission@bard.edu* Web: *www.bard.edu*

FINANCIAL AID: In 2014-2015, 70% of all full-time freshmen and 70% of continuing full-time students received some form of financial aid. 68% of all full-time freshmen and 68% of continuing full-time students received need-based aid. The average freshman award was $42,888. Need-based scholarships or need-based grants averaged $33,525; need-based self-help aid (loans and jobs) averaged $6,512; and other non-need-based awards and non-need-based scholarships averaged $21,973. 30% of undergraduate students work part-time. Average annual earnings from campus work are $2000. The average financial indebtedness of the 2014 graduate was $25,644. Bard is a member of CSS. The CSS/Profile, FAFSA, and the state aid form, and Non-custodial profile and/or Business/Farm supplement if applicable are required. The priority date for freshman financial aid applications for fall entry is February 1. The deadline for filing freshman financial aid applications for fall entry is February 15.

BARNARD COLLEGE/COLUMBIA UNIVERSITY D-5
www.barnard.edu

New York, NY 10027 (212) 854-5262

Fax: (212) 854-6220	Email: admissions@barnard.edu
Full-time: 2300 women	Faculty: n/av
Part-time: 55 women	Ph.D.s: n/av
Graduate: n/av	Student/Faculty: n/av
Year: semesters	Tuition: $29,000
Room & Board: $12,000	Freshman Class: n/av
SAT or ACT: required	CEEB CODE: 2038
Application Deadline: January 1	MOST COMPETITIVE

Barnard College, founded in 1889, is an independent affiliate of Columbia University. It is an undergraduate womens' liberal arts college. The figures in the above capsule and in this profile are approximate. The 4-acre campus is in an urban area Manhattan's Upper West Side. Including any residence halls, there are 15 buildings.

STUDENT LIFE: 68% of undergraduates are from out of state, mostly the Middle Atlantic. Students are from 48 states, 35 foreign countries, and Canada. 53% are from public schools. 66% are White; 16% Asian American. The student base is all female. The average age of freshmen is 18; all undergraduates, 20. 5% do not continue beyond their first year; 84% remain to graduate. **Housing:** 2057 students can be accommodated in college housing, which includes single-sex and coed dorms, on-campus apartments, and off-campus apartments. In addition, there are special-interest houses. On-campus housing is guaranteed for all 4 years. 90% of students live on campus; of those, 75% remain on campus on weekends. Alcohol is not permitted. All students may keep cars.

FACULTY/CLASSROOMS: 35% of faculty are male; 65% are female. All teach and do research. No introductory courses are taught by graduate students. The average class size in an introductory lecture is 30; in a laboratory is 11; and in a regular course is 13.

PROGRAMS OF STUDY: Barnard College confers B.A. degrees. Bachelor's degrees are awarded in BIOLOGICAL SCIENCE (biochemistry and biology/biological science), COMMUNICATIONS AND THE ARTS (art history and appreciation, classics, comparative literature, dance, dramatic arts, English, film arts, French, German, Greek, Italian, Latin, linguistics, music, Russian, and Spanish), COMPUTER AND PHYSICAL SCIENCE (astronomy, chemistry, computer science, mathematics, physics, and statistics), ENGINEERING AND ENVIRONMENTAL DESIGN (architecture and environmental science), SOCIAL SCIENCE (American studies, anthropology, biopsychology, classical/ancient civilization, East Asian studies, economics, European studies, history, international studies, medieval studies, Middle Eastern studies, philosophy, political science/government, psychology, religion, sociology, urban studies, and women's studies). English, psychology, and economics are the strongest academically, and have the largest enrollments.

ACTIVITIES: There are no fraternities or sororities. There are 100 groups on campus, including art, band, cheerleading, choir, chorale, chorus, dance, debate, drama, ethnic, film, gay, international, jazz band, literary magazine, marching band, Model UN, musical theater, newspaper, opera, orchestra, pep band, photography, political, professional, radio and TV, religious, social, social service, student government, symphony, and yearbook. Popular campus events include Spring and Winter Festivals, Founders Day and Take Back the Night. **Sports:** There are 15 intercollegiate sports for women, and 16 intramural sports for women. Facilities include pools, weight rooms, gyms, tennis courts, an indoor track, and a boat slip. **Graduates:** From July 1, 2013 to June 30, 2014, 597 bachelor's degrees were awarded. The most popular majors were social sciences (25%), psychology (14%), and English (11%). In an average class, 2% graduate in 3 years or less, 82% graduate in 4 years or less, 88% graduate in 5 years or less, and 89% graduate in 6 years or less.

SERVICES: Counseling and information services are available, as is tutoring in every subject. There is a reader service for the blind. A student-staffed writing room is available for students of all levels of writing ability, and a math help room is also available to students in all math courses. **Library/Resources:** The library contains 204,906 volumes, 17,705 microform items, 17,448 audio/video tapes/CDs/DVDs, and subscribes to 543 periodicals including electronic. Computerized library services include interlibrary loans, database searching, and Internet access. Special learning facilities include an art gallery, radio station, TV station, a greenhouse, history of physics lab, child development research and study center, dance studio, modern theater, womens' research archives within a womens' center, and multimedia labs and classrooms. **Physically Challenged Students:** 90% of the campus is accessible. Facilities include wheelchair ramps, elevators, special parking, specially equipped restrooms, special class scheduling, lowered drinking fountains, lowered telephones, special housing. The Office of Disability Services provides a variety of support services to students with permanent and temporary disabilities. **Special:** Barnard offers cross-registration with Columbia University, more than 2500 internships with New York City firms and institutions, and study abroad worldwide. A 3-2 engineering program with the Columbia School of Engineering and double-degree programs with the Columbia University Schools of International and Public Affairs, Law, and Dentistry, the Juilliard School, and the Jewish Theological Seminary are possible. The college offers dual and student-designed majors and multidisciplinary majors, including economic history. There is 1 national honor society including Phi Beta Kappa. **Visiting:** There are regularly scheduled orientations for prospective students, consisting of open house programs for prospective students regularly scheduled throughout the fall. There are guides for informal visits, visitors may sit in on classes, and stay overnight. To schedule a visit, contact the Office of Admissions. **Campus Safety and Security:** Measures include 24-hour foot and vehicle patrol and security escort services. There are shuttle buses, emergency telephones, lighted pathways/sidewalks, safety and security education programs.

REQUIREMENTS: The SAT or ACT is required. If taking the SAT, an applicant must also take 3 SAT Subject tests, one of which must be in writing or literature. A GED is accepted. Applicants should prepare with 4 years of English, 3 of math and science, 3 or 4 of a foreign language, 2 of a lab science, and 1 of history. An interview is recommended. AP credits are accepted. Important factors in the admissions decision are advanced placement or honors courses, evidence of special talent, and extracurricular activities record. A total of 120 credits is required, with a minimum GPA of 2.0. All students must take 4 semesters each of a foreign language, humanities, or social sciences outside the major, and geographic and cultural diversity courses that may satisfy the major or other requirements, 2 semesters each of lab science and phys ed, and 1 semester each in first-year seminar, first-year English, and quantitative reasoning. **Procedure:** Freshmen are admitted fall. Entrance exams should be taken by January of the senior year. There are early decision, early admissions, and deferred admissions plans. Early decision applications should be filed by November 15; regular applications, by January 1 for fall entry, along with a $55 fee. Notification of early decision is sent December 15; regular decision, April 1. Applications are accepted on-line. **Transfer Students:** 80 transfer students enrolled in 2013-2014. Applicants must complete at least 1 college course. The SAT or ACT is required. Deadline for transfer applicants is April 1 (fall term) and November 1 (spring term). They must submit high school and college transcripts. They must be in good standing from prior institutions attended and submit an essay or personal statement. 60 of 120 credits required for the bachelor's degree must be completed at Barnard College. **International Students:** The school actively recruits these students. They must take the TOEFL. They must also take the SAT or ACT. Applicants who take the SAT must also take SAT Subject tests in writing or literature and 2 others.

ADMISSIONS: Jennifer Fondiller, Dean of Admissions. E-Mail: *admissions@barnard.edu* Web: *www.barnard.edu*

FINANCIAL AID: In 2014-2015, 44% of all full-time freshmen and 44% of continuing full-time students received some form of financial aid. 41% of all full-time freshmen and 42% of continuing full-time students received need-based aid. The average freshman award was $30,644. Need-based scholarships or need-based grants averaged $29,509; and need-based self-help aid (loans and jobs) averaged $3,529. 46% of undergraduate students work part-time. The average financial indebtedness of the 2014 graduate was $17,630. Barnard College is a member of CSS. The CSS/Profile, FAFSA, the state aid form, and the college's own financial statement, and the parents' and student's federal tax returns, and the business and/or farm supplement. Check with the school for current application deadlines.

BERKELEY COLLEGE OF NEW YORK CITY *(The complete profile is made available exclusively on our website, www.barronspac.com)*

BERKELEY COLLEGE/WESTCHESTER CAMPUS *(The complete profile is made available exclusively on our website, www.barronspac.com)*

BINGHAMTON UNIVERSITY/THE STATE UNIVERSITY OF NEW YORK   C-4
www.binghamton.edu

Binghamton, NY 13902	(607) 777-2171
	n/av
Fax: (607) 777-4445	Email: admit@binghamton.edu
Full-time: 6746 men, 6162 women	Faculty: 661; I, -$
Part-time: 284 men, 220 women	Ph.D.s: 94%
Graduate: 1713 men, 1570 women	Student/Faculty: 20 to 1
Year: semesters, summer session	Tuition: $8620 ($20,260)
Room & Board: $13,028	Freshman Class: 28518 applied, 12564 accepted, 2602 enrolled
SAT CR/M/W: 630/660/620 ACT: 29	CEEB CODE: 2335
Application Deadline: January 15	HIGHLY COMPETITIVE+

Part of the State University of New York (SUNY) system, Binghamton University was founded in 1946. The university offers programs in arts and sciences, education, nursing, business administration, engineering and applied science, and community and public affairs. There are 5 undergraduate schools and 2 graduate schools. In addition to regional accreditation, Binghamton University has baccalaureate program accreditation with AACSB, ABET, CSWE, NASM, TEAC, APA, NASPAA, and CCNE. The 930-acre campus is in a suburban area 1 mile west of Binghamton. Including any residence halls, there are 102 buildings.

STUDENT LIFE: 90% of undergraduates are from New York. Others are from 48 states, 97 foreign countries, and Canada. 88% are from public schools. 55% are White; 14% Asian American; 11% Foreign.
Male To Female Ratio: 0.9:1. The average age of freshmen is 18; all undergraduates, 20. 11% do not continue beyond their first year; 81% remain to graduate. **Housing:** 7457 students can be accommodated in college housing, which includes coed dorms, on-campus apartments, and off-campus apartments. In addition, there are special-interest houses, chemical and smoke-free housing, living learning communities, quiet living, gender inclusive housing and family housing. On-campus housing is guaranteed for the freshman year only, is available on a first-come, and first-served basis. 52% of students live on campus; of those, 95% remain on campus on weekends. Upperclassmen may keep cars.

FACULTY/CLASSROOMS: 59% of faculty are male; 41% are female. All teach and do research. Graduate students teach 5% of introductory courses. The average class size in an introductory lecture is 54; in a laboratory is 21; and in a regular course is 33.

PROGRAMS OF STUDY: Binghamton University confers B.A., B.S. and Mus.B. degrees. Master's and Doctoral degrees are also awarded. Bachelor's degrees are awarded in AGRICULTURE (environmental studies), BIOLOGICAL SCIENCE (biochemistry, biology/biological science, cell biology, environmental earth resources, evolutionary biology, molecular biology, and neurosciences), BUSINESS (accounting, business administration and management, entrepreneurial studies, finance, management information systems, management science, marketing management, and supply chain management), COMMUNICATIONS AND THE ARTS (Arabic, art history, art, classics, comparative literature, creative writing, dance, dramatic arts, drawing, English, English literature, film arts, French, German, Germanic languages and literature, Hebrew, Italian, Korean, Latin, linguistics, literature, music, music performance, painting, printmaking, sculpture, Spanish, speech/debate/rhetoric, studio art, theatre arts, theater design, and visual and performing arts), COMPUTER AND PHYSICAL SCIENCE (actuarial mathematics, chemistry, computer science, environmental chemistry, environmental geology, geology, information sciences and systems, mathematics, and physics), ENGINEERING AND ENVIRONMENTAL DESIGN (bioengineering, biomedical engineering, computer engineering, electrical/electronics engineering, engineering, environmental design, environmental science, industrial engineering, mechanical engineering, and systems engineering), HEALTH PROFESSIONS (nursing and Pre-Health Studies), SOCIAL SCIENCE (Africana studies, anthropology, Asian/American studies, Caribbean studies, Chinese Studies, classical/ancient civilization, East Asian studies, economics, geography, history, human development, interdisciplinary studies, international studies, Japanese studies, Judaic studies, Latin American studies, medieval studies, philosophy, political science/government, psychobiology, psychology, sociology, and South Asian studies). Business administration, political science, biology and engineering are the strongest academically. Engineering, business administration, and psychology have the largest enrollments.

ACTIVITIES: 12% of men belong to 33 national fraternities; 10% of women belong to 17 national sororities. There are 373 groups on campus, including club sports/intramurals, special interest groups, art, band, cheerleading, chess, choir, chorale, chorus, communications, computers, cultural, dance, debate, drama, environmental, ethnic, film, gay, honors, international, jazz band, literary magazine, musical theater, newspaper, opera, orchestra, pep band, photography, political, professional, radio and TV, religious, social, social service, student government, symphony, and yearbook. Popular campus events include Spring Fling, University Fest, China Night, Frost Fest, Welcome Weekend, Shabbat 1500 Dinner, Homecoming, Family Weekend, Relay for Life, Basketball/Soccer/Lacrosse Games, Concerts and Stand-up Comedian Performances. **Sports:** There are 11 intercollegiate sports for men and 10 for women, and 13 intramural sports for men and 13 for women. Facilities include a 5,000-seat events center with basketball and tennis courts and a 200-meter track; 2 additional gyms also equipped with swimming pools; fitness center, all-purpose courts for basketball, volleyball, and other activities; racquetball and squash courts; dance and karate studios. The campus has a 2,500-seat soccer and lacrosse complex and separate facilities for baseball, softball, track and field, tennis, and cross-country. The campus also features a 190-acre nature preserve. **Graduates:** From July 1, 2013 to June 30, 2014, 3064 bachelor's degrees were awarded. The most popular majors were management (13%), psychology (12%), and engineering (10%). 250 companies recruited on campus in 2013-2014. In an average class, 5% graduate in 3 years or less, 69% graduate in 4 years or less, 79% graduate in 5 years or less, and 81% graduate in 6 years or less. Of the 2013 graduating class, 30% were enrolled in graduate school within 6 months of graduation.

SERVICES: Counseling and information services are available, as is tutoring in most subjects, alternate format reading materials for those with visual/reading disabilities, and academic success consultation/instruction sessions provided for SSD-registered students There is a reader service for the blind. Walk-in and by appointment tutoring available 7 days per week **Library/Resources:** The 3 libraries contain 2.6 million volumes, 1.9 million microform items, 126,483 audio/video tapes/CDs/DVDs, and subscribe to 87,696 periodicals including electronic. Computerized library services include interlibrary loans, database searching, Internet access, and Wi-Fi capability. Special learning facilities include an art gallery, radio station, TV station, theaters, art/dance studios, sculpture foundry, art museum, nature preserve, teaching greenhouse, information commons/workstations, public archaeology facility, child development institute, GIS core facility, biotechnology start-up suites, innovative technologies complex, analytical diagnostics laboratory, electron microscopy laboratory, innovative practice center simulation lab, collaboratory, learning studio, and centers for performing arts, learning and teaching, organized research, integrated electronics engineering, advanced microelectronics manufacturing and autonomous solar power. **Physically Challenged Students:** 95% of the campus is accessible. Facilities include wheelchair ramps, elevators, special parking, specially equipped restrooms, lowered drinking fountains, lowered telephones, special housing. Comprehensive array of services for students with physical, learning, or other disabilities. **Special:** The university offers a number of accelerated programs (3-2 and 4-1) to earn combined bachelor's and master's degrees; 600 study-abroad opportunities in over 100 countries; internship opportunities in New York City and other major cities; dual and interdisciplinary majors such as philosophy, politics, and law; individualized major program in Harpur College of Arts and Sciences; pre-health programs in medicine - dentistry, optometry, veterinary medicine, podiatry, nutrition, physical and occupational therapy, and chiropractic. Early assurance programs guarantee graduate admission at partner SUNY schools (Buffalo, Upstate Medical-Syracuse, and College of Optometry). There are 28 national honor societies, including Phi Beta Kappa, a freshman honors program, and 34 departmental honors programs. **Visiting:** There are regularly scheduled orientations for prospective students, including an information session and a student-led tour of campus. To schedule a visit, contact the Office of Undergraduate Admissions. **Campus Safety and Security:** Measures include 24-hour foot and vehicle patrol, emergency notification system, self-defense education, and security escort services. There are shuttle buses, emergency telephones, lighted pathways/sidewalks, controlled access to dorms/residences, police officers on foot, bike and car patrols, monitored entrance to campus with proper identification between midnight and 5 a.m.; LED vehicle speed monitoring signs; emergency text messaging/communications; and formal personal safety programs.

REQUIREMENTS: The SAT or ACT is required. The ACT Optional Writing test is also required. Applicants must be graduates of an accredited secondary school or have a GED certificate and complete 16 academic credits. These include 4 units of English, 3 units of 1 foreign language or 2 units each of 2 foreign languages, 3 of math, and 2 each of science and social studies. Students may submit slides of artwork, request an audition for music, prepare a videotape for dance or theater, or share athletic achievements. An essay is required. Binghamton University requires that each enrolling student fulfills the graduation requirements at their high school. AP and CLEP credits are accepted.To graduate, all students must complete 124 to 130 credit hours, with 36 to 72 in the major and a minimum GPA of 2.0. General education requirements include courses in language and communication, global vision, science, aesthetic perspective, foreign language, humanities, math, social science, physical activity/wellness, and pluralism. Other requirements vary by school. **Procedure:** Freshmen are admitted fall and spring. Entrance exams should be taken in the spring of the junior year or the fall of the senior year. There are early admissions, deferred admissions, and rolling admissions plans. Application deadlines are open. Application fee is $50. Notification is sent on a rolling basis. 3407 applicants were on the 2014 waiting list; 281 were admitted. Applications are accepted on-line. **Transfer Students:** 1538 transfer students enrolled in 2013-2014. Applicants must submit college transcripts; students who wish to transfer after their first year of college must also submit their high school transcripts. 44 of 126 credits required for the bachelor's degree must be completed at Binghamton University. **International Students:** There are 1414 international students enrolled. The school actively recruits these students. They must take the TOEFL with a minimum score of 560 on the paper-based TOEFL (PBT) or 83 on the Internet-based version (iBT). If the student attends a h/s in the US or a h/s where the primary language of instruction is English, SAT/ACT required. They must also take the SAT or ACT. If the student attends a High School in the US or a High School where the primary language of instruction is English, SAT/ACT required.

ADMISSIONS: 44% of the 2014-2015 applicants were accepted. The SAT scores for the 2014-2015 freshman class were: Critical Reading--4% below 500, 24% between 500 and 599, 57% between 600 and 699, and 15% between 700 and 800; Math--1% below 500, 14% between 500 and 599, 57% between 600 and 699, and 28% between 700 and 800; Writing--2% below 500, 20% between 500 and 599, 57% between 600 and 699, and 21% between 700 and 800. The ACT scores were 1% below 21, 4% between 21 and 23, 16% between 24 and 26, 25% between 27 and 28, and 54% above 28. 77% of the current freshmen were in the top fifth of their class; 94% were in the top two fifths. **Admissions Contact:** Randall Edouard, Asst Provost for Undergraduate Admission. E-Mail: *admit@binghamton.edu* Web: *www.binghamton.edu/admissions*

FINANCIAL AID: In 2014-2015, 83% of all full-time freshmen and 67% of continuing full-time students received some form of financial aid. 63% of all full-time freshmen and 57% of continuing full-time students received need-based aid. The average freshman award was $14,097. Need-based scholarships or need-based grants averaged $4,864; need-based self-help aid (loans and jobs) averaged $2,633; non-need-based athletic scholarships averaged $593; and other non-need-based awards and non-need-based scholarships averaged $7,513. 17% of undergraduate students work part-time. Average annual earnings from campus work are $1316. The average financial indebtedness of the 2014 graduate was $25,727. The FAFSA and the state aid form are required. The priority date for freshman financial aid applications for fall entry is February 1.

tion. Figures in the above capsule and in this profile are approximate. There are 4 undergraduate schools and 2 graduate schools. The campus locations are in urban areas in the Bronx, Manhattan and Brooklyn. Including any residence halls, there are 4 buildings.

STUDENT LIFE: 100% of undergraduates are from New York. 70% are from public schools. 85% are Hispanic. 85% are Catholic. **Male To Female Ratio:** 3.5:1. The average age of freshmen is 29; all undergraduates, 32. 12% do not continue beyond their first year; 80% remain to graduate. **Housing:** College-sponsored housing includes Alcohol is not permitted. No one may keep cars.

FACULTY/CLASSROOMS: No introductory courses are taught by graduate students.

PROGRAMS OF STUDY: Boricua confers B.A. degrees. Associate degrees are also awarded. Bachelor's degrees are awarded in BUSINESS (business administration and management), EDUCATION (elementary education), SOCIAL SCIENCE (human services and liberal arts/general studies). Applied science paralegal studies is the strongest academically. Human services has the largest enrollment.

ACTIVITIES: There are no fraternities or sororities. There are 5 groups on campus, including art, chorus, drama, newspaper, and student government. Popular campus events include Cultural Programs, Puerto Rican Discovery Day, Christmas and Spring concerts with Chorus and Orchestra. **Sports:** Facilities include a gym. **Graduates:** From July 1, 2013 to June 30, 2014, 90 bachelor's degrees were awarded. The most popular majors were human services, early childhood education, and business administration. In an average class, 65% graduate in 4 years or less and 35% graduate in 5 years or less.

SERVICES: Counseling and information services are available, as is tutoring in most subjects. **Library/Resources:** The 4 libraries contain 128,727 volumes, 3,000 audio/video tapes/CDs/DVDs, and subscribe to 227 periodicals including electronic. Computerized library services include database searching, Internet access, and Wi-Fi capability. Special learning facilities include an art gallery. **Physically Challenged Students:** Facilities include elevators and specially equipped restrooms. **Visiting:** There are regularly scheduled orientations for prospective students, letters are sent to prospective students advising them of scheduled orientations. To schedule a visit, contact Abraham Cruzat or Miriam Prefferat at (212) 694-1000. **Campus Safety and Security:** There are shuttle buses, emergency telephones, and lighted pathways/sidewalks.

REQUIREMENTS: Boricua administers its own tests to prospective students, although either the SAT or ACT is accepted. Applicants must be graduates of an accredited secondary school or have a GED. 2 letters of recommendation and an admissions interview are required. Applicants must demonstrate a working knowledge of English and Spanish to a faculty panel. CLEP credits are accepted. Important factors in the admissions decision are leadership record, personality/intangible qualities, and recommendations by school officials.132 Credits **Procedure:** Freshmen are admitted fall, spring, and summer. Entrance exams should be taken students will receive a call by the admissions staff. There are early decision and rolling admissions plans. Application deadlines are open. Application fee is $30. **Transfer Students:** Applicants with associate degrees may transfer up to 60 credits. All college credits passed with grade C and above are accepted. 80 of 124 credits required for the bachelor's degree must be completed at Boricua.

ADMISSIONS: Abraham Cruz, Director of Student Services. E-Mail: *mpfeffer@boricuacolleg* Web: *www.boricuacollege.edu*

FINANCIAL AID: In 2014-2015, 100% of all full-time freshmen and 100% of continuing full-time students received some form of financial aid. 100% of all full-time freshmen and 100% of continuing full-time students received need-based aid. The average freshman award was $100. Boricua is a member of CSS. The FAFSA, and income tax forms is required. Check with the school for current application deadlines.

BORICUA COLLEGE	**D-5**
www.boricuacollege.edu	

New York, NY 10032	**(212) 694-1000 or (718) 782-2200**
	n/av
Fax: (212) 694-1015 or (718) 782-2050	Email: mpfeffer@
	boricuacolleg
Full-time: 260 men, 910 women	**Faculty:** n/av
Part-time: n/av	**Ph.D.s:** n/av
Graduate: n/av	**Student/Faculty:** n/av
Year: 4-1-4, summer session	**Tuition:** $8600
Room & Board: n/app	**Freshman Class:** n/av
	CEEB CODE: 2901
Application Deadline: n/av	**COMPETITIVE**

Boricua College, founded in 1974, is a private college for bilingual students, designed to meet the needs of a Spanish-speaking popula-

BUFFALO STATE COLLEGE / STATE UNIVERSITY OF NEW YORK   A-3
www.buffalostate.edu

Buffalo, NY 14222	**(716) 878-4017**
Fax: (716) 878-6100	**Email: admissions@buffalostate.edu**
Full-time: 3570 men, 5220 women	**Faculty:** n/av; IIA, -$
Part-time: 495 men, 555 women	**Ph.D.s:** 84%
Graduate: 570 men, 1330 women	**Student/Faculty:** n/av
Year: semesters, summer session	**Tuition:** $71600 ($16,150)
Room & Board: $11,320	**Freshman Class:** n/av
SAT: required	**CEEB CODE:** 2925
Application Deadline: open	**COMPETITIVE+**

The State University of New York/College at Buffalo, established in 1867, is a public institution conferring undergraduate liberal arts degrees. The figures in the above capsule and in this profile are approximate. There are 4 undergraduate schools and 1 graduate school. In addition to regional accreditation, Buffalo State College has baccalaureate program accreditation with ABET, ACS, ADA, ASLA, CSWE, FIDER, IACBE, NASAD, NAST, and NCATE. The library contains 618,429 volumes, 1.0 million microform items, and 18,500 audio/video tapes/CDs/DVDs, and subscribes to 2948 periodicals including electronic. Computerized library services include interlibrary loans, database searching, and Internet access. Special learning facilities include a learning resource center, art gallery, planetarium, radio station, TV station, speech, language, and hearing clinic, and a center for performing arts. The 115-acre campus is in an urban area in Buffalo. Including any residence halls, there are 38 buildings.

STUDENT LIFE: 99% of undergraduates are from New York. Others are from 26 states, 20 foreign countries, and Canada. 85% are from public schools. 65% are white; 13% African American. The average age of freshmen is 19; all undergraduates, 25. 22% do not continue beyond their first year; 48% remain to graduate.

FACULTY/CLASSROOMS: 51% of faculty are male; 49% are female. All teach undergraduates. No introductory courses are taught by graduate students. The average class size in an introductory lecture is 34; in a laboratory, 12; and in a regular course, 18.

PROGRAMS OF STUDY: Buffalo State College confers B.A., B.S., B.F.A., B.Mus., B.S.Ed., and B.Tech degrees. Master's degrees are also awarded. Bachelor's degrees are awarded in BIOLOGICAL SCIENCE (biology/biological science), BUSINESS (business administration and management and hospitality management services), COMMUNICATIONS AND THE ARTS (art, art history and appreciation, broadcasting, communications, design, dramatic arts, English, fine arts, French, journalism, music, painting, photography, printmaking, sculpture, and Spanish), COMPUTER AND PHYSICAL SCIENCE (chemistry, earth science, geology, information sciences and systems, mathematics, and physics), EDUCATION (art education, business education, elementary education, foreign languages education, industrial arts education, science education, secondary education, and special education), ENGINEERING AND ENVIRONMENTAL DESIGN (electrical/electronics engineering technology, industrial engineering technology, and mechanical engineering technology), HEALTH PROFESSIONS (health and speech pathology/audiology), SOCIAL SCIENCE (anthropology, criminal justice, dietetics, economics, geography, history, humanities, philosophy, political science/government, psychology, social work, sociology, and urban studies). Elementary education and exceptional education are the strongest academically. Elementary education, communication, and business have the largest enrollments.

ACTIVITIES: 1% of men belong to 1 local fraternity and 9 national fraternities; 1% of women belong to 3 local and 7 national sororities. There are 75 groups on campus, including art, cheerleading, chess, choir, chorus, computers, dance, drama, ethnic, gay, honors, international, jazz band, literary magazine, musical theater, newspaper, orchestra, political, professional, radio and TV, religious, social, social service, and student government. Popular campus events include Commuter Daze, the Gathering, and Welcome Back Week.

SERVICES: Counseling and information services are available, as is tutoring in every subject. There is a reader service for the blind, and remedial math, reading, and writing. Tutors for visually impaired and hearing impaired students are also available.

REQUIREMENTS: The SAT is required. Students must graduate from an accredited secondary school or have a GED. They must complete 4 years of English, 3 years each of math, science, and social studies, and 2 years of a foreign language. A portfolio is required for fine arts applicants. AP and CLEP credits are accepted. Important factors in the admissions decision are advanced placement or honors courses, evidence of special talent, and recommendations by school officials.

FINANCIAL AID: Buffalo State College is a member of CSS. The FAFSA and TAP are required. Check with the school for current application deadlines.

CANISIUS COLLEGE   A-3
www.canisius.edu

Buffalo, NY 14208	**(716) 888-2200**
	(800) 843-1517
Fax: (716) 888-3230	**Email: admissions@canisius.edu**
Full-time: 1328 men, 1497 women	**Faculty:** 210; IIA, +$
Part-time: 205 men, 54 women	**Ph.D.s:** 97%
Graduate: 545 men, 908 women	**Student/Faculty:** 12 to 1
Year: semesters, summer session	**Tuition:** $33,972
Room & Board: $12,270	**Freshman Class:** 4322 applied, 3134 accepted, 682 enrolled
SAT CR/M: 520/500 **ACT:** 24	**CEEB CODE:** 2073
Application Deadline: March 1	**COMPETITIVE**

Canisius College, founded in 1870, is a private Roman Catholic college in the Jesuit tradition. It offers undergraduate programs in the liberal arts and sciences, business, education, and human services. There are 3 undergraduate schools and 3 graduate schools. In addition to regional accreditation, Canisius has baccalaureate program accreditation with AACSB, CAHEA, NCATE, CACREP, CAATE, and CED. The 72-acre campus is in an urban area in Buffalo NY. Including any residence halls, there are 51 buildings.

STUDENT LIFE: 92% of undergraduates are from New York. Others are from 29 states, 18 foreign countries, and Canada. 70% are from public schools. 73% are White. **Male To Female Ratio:** 1.2:1. The average age of freshmen is 18; all undergraduates, 20. 20% do not continue beyond their first year; 68% remain to graduate. **Housing:** 1422 students can be accommodated in college housing, which includes single-sex and coed dorms, on-campus apartments, and off-campus apartments. In addition, there are honors houses, special-interest houses, An intercultural hall, and townhouses plus an honor's dorm, and Bosch or Frisch halls (suite-style rooms) for first-year students. On-campus housing is guaranteed for all 4 years, is available on a first-come, first-served basis, and is available on a lottery system for upperclassmen. 52% of students commute. All students may keep cars.

FACULTY/CLASSROOMS: 55% of faculty are male; 45% are female. All teach and do research. No introductory courses are taught by graduate students. The average class size in an introductory lecture is 23; in a laboratory is 18; and in a regular course is 20.

PROGRAMS OF STUDY: Canisius confers B.A., B.S., B.A.Ed. and B.S.Ed. degrees. Master's degrees are also awarded. Bachelor's degrees are awarded in AGRICULTURE (environmental studies), BIOLOGICAL SCIENCE (biochemistry, bioinformatics, biology/biological science, cell biology, neurosciences, and zoology), BUSINESS (accounting, banking and finance, business administration and management, business communications, business economics, entrepreneurial studies, fashion merchandising, finance, international business management, management information systems, management science, marketing management, marketing/retailing/merchandising, operations research, and sports management), COMMUNICATIONS AND THE ARTS (art history, classical languages, communications, creative writing, digital communications, English, fine arts, French, German, journalism, media arts, modern language, music, music performance, Spanish, speech/debate/rhetoric, and theatre arts), COMPUTER AND PHYSICAL SCIENCE (chemistry, computer science, information sciences and systems, mathematics, and physics), EDUCATION (athletic training, business education, (Education) Childhood Education, early childhood education, education, education administration, education of the deaf and hearing impaired, education of the exceptional child, elementary education, English education, foreign languages education, mathematics education, middle school education, physical education, science education, social studies education, special education, and teaching English as a second/foreign language (TESOL/TEFOL)), ENGINEERING AND ENVIRONMENTAL DESIGN (computational sciences, environmental science, and preengineering), HEALTH PROFESSIONS (clinical science, exercise science, medical laboratory technology, predentistry, premedicine, prepharmacy, preveterinary science, and sports medicine), SOCIAL SCIENCE (anthropology, biblical studies, cognitive science, criminal justice, European studies, gerontology, history, humanities and social science, international relations, Latin American studies, liberal arts/general studies, philosophy, prelaw, psychology, social science, sociology, urban studies, and women's studies). Accounting, biology, and finance are the strongest academically. Psychology, business administration/management, and communication studies have the largest enrollments.

ACTIVITIES: 1% of men belong to 1 national fraternity; 1% of women belong to 1 national sorority. There are 140 groups on campus, including art, band, cheerleading, chess, choir, chorale, computers, dance, drama, drill team, environmental, ethnic, gay, honors, international, jazz band, literary magazine, musical theater, newspaper, orchestra, pep band, political, professional, radio and TV, religious, social, social service, student government, and yearbook. Popular campus events include Fall Semiformal, International Fest, and Canisius Concert Series. **Sports:** There are 8 intercollegiate sports for men and 9 for women, and 12 intramural sports for men and 12 for women. Facilities include an 1800-seat athletic center with a 25-yard pool, training rooms, a 1000-seat sports complex with Astroturf playing fields, a rifle range, and a mirrored dance studio. **Graduates:** From July 1, 2013 to June 30, 2014, 682 bachelor's degrees were awarded. The most popular majors were business/marketing (27%), education (14%), and biological/life sciences (12%). 30 companies recruited on campus in 2013-2014. In an average class, 58% graduate in 4 years or less, 67% graduate in 5 years or less, and 68% graduate in 6 years or less.

SERVICES: Counseling and information services are available, as is tutoring in every subject. There is a reader service for the blind, and remedial math, reading, and writing. **Library/Resources:** The library contains 464,755 volumes, 599,947 microform items, 14,762 audio/video tapes/CDs/DVDs, and subscribes to 52,472 periodicals including electronic. Computerized library services include interlibrary loans, database searching, Internet access, and Wi-Fi capability. Special learning facilities include an art gallery, radio station, TV station, a television studio, foreign language lab, 85+ media-assisted classrooms, digital media lab, and musical instrument digital interface classroom. **Physically Challenged Students:** 90% of the campus is accessible. Facilities include wheelchair ramps, elevators, special parking, specially equipped restrooms, special class scheduling, lowered drinking fountains, lowered telephones. Automatic doors, TDD, a shuttle service for students with disabilities, distraction-free testing spaces, and adjustable classroom desks. **Special:** Canisius offers internships, credit by exam, pass/fail options, dual majors, a Washington semester, work-study programs, and study abroad in over a dozen countries. Cooperative programs are available with the Fashion Institute of Technology in New York City. Cross-registration is permitted with the schools in the Western New York Consortium of Higher Education. Canisius also offers early assurance and joint degree programs, with SUNY health professions schools in Buffalo and Syracuse, and a 3-2 MBA. There are 16 national honor societies, a freshman honors program, and 5 departmental honors programs. **Visiting:** There are regularly scheduled orientations for prospective students, including an admissions interview or group session, campus tour, and financial aid appointment by request. Also available are summer visitations for families, selected Saturday visits, multiple Fall Open Houses and an Open House in the Spring, a Financial Aid Workshop Workshop in January, and overnights for admitted students. There are guides for informal visits and visitors may sit in on classes. To schedule a visit, contact the Admissions Office. **Campus Safety and Security:** Measures include 24-hour foot and vehicle patrol, emergency notification system, self-defense education, and security escort services. There are shuttle buses, emergency telephones, lighted pathways/sidewalks, controlled access to dorms/residences, Crime prevention officer, bicycle patrols, and crime prevention programs. Also blue light emergency stations around campus.

REQUIREMENTS: The SAT or ACT is required. All students must submit official high school transcript (or GED) and SAT or ACT results. College preparatory course work should include 4 units each of English and social science, 3 units each of math, science, and foreign language. Students with a B+ average and a satisfactory SAT score are most competitive. An essay and an interview are recommended. A GPA of 2.0 is required. AP and CLEP credits are accepted. Important factors in the admissions decision are leadership record, recommendations by school officials, and advanced placement or honors courses. Students take 12 required courses and complete 6 knowledge and skills requirement areas to satisfy their requirements. In addition, students must take 10 3-credit courses in the major. A minimum of 120 credit hours and a GPA of 2.0 are required for graduation. **Procedure:** Freshmen are admitted fall, spring, and summer. Entrance exams should be taken during the junior or senior year. There are deferred admissions and rolling admissions plans. Applications should be filed by March 1 for fall entry, along with a $40 fee. Notification is sent on a rolling basis. Applications are accepted online. **Transfer Students:** 119 transfer students enrolled in 2013-2014. Applicants must present a minimum GPA of 2.0 and a Transfer Recommendation Form. 30 of 120 credits required for the bachelor's degree must be completed at Canisius. **International Students:** There are 131 international students enrolled. The school actively recruits these students. They must take the TOEFL with a minimum score of 500 on the paper-based TOEFL (PBT) or 61 on the Internet-based version (iBT), or take the IELTS or STEPs are also acceptable. They must also take the SAT or ACT.

ADMISSIONS: 73% of the 2014-2015 applicants were accepted. The SAT scores for the 2014-2015 freshman class were: Critical Reading--40% below 500, 40% between 500 and 599, 17% between 600 and 699, and 3% between 700 and 800; Math--35% below 500, 38% between 500 and 599, 23% between 600 and 699, and 4% between 700 and 800. The ACT scores were 21% below 21, 28% between 21 and 23, 23% between 24 and 26, 14% between 27 and 28, and 14% above 28. 39% of the current freshmen were in the top fifth of their class; 68% were in the top two fifths. 7 freshmen graduated first in their class. **Admissions Contact:** Mollie Ballaro, Dean of Admissions. E-Mail: *admissions@canisius.edu* Web: *www.canisius.edu*

FINANCIAL AID: In 2014-2015, 98% of all full-time freshmen and 97% of continuing full-time students received some form of financial aid. 86% of all full-time freshmen and 79% of continuing full-time students received need-based aid. The average freshman award was $31,604. Need-based scholarships or need-based grants averaged $10,219 ($42,332 maximum); need-based self-help aid (loans and jobs) averaged $4,888 ($7,800 maximum); non-need-based athletic scholarships averaged $17,946 ($47,900 maximum); and other non-need-based awards and non-need-based scholarships averaged $15,391 ($45,907 maximum). 19% of undergraduate students work part-time. Average annual earnings from campus work are $1662. The average financial indebtedness of the 2014 graduate was $37,903. Canisius is a member of CSS. The FAFSA is required. The priority date for freshman financial aid applications for fall entry is February 15.

CAZENOVIA COLLEGE	C-3
www.cazenovia.edu	

Cazenovia, NY 13035	(315) 655-7208
	(800) 654-3210
Fax: (315) 655-2190	Email: admission@cazcollege.edu
Full-time: 250 men, 700 women	**Faculty:** IIB, -$
Part-time: 35 men, 120 women	**Ph.D.s:** n/av
Graduate: n/av	**Student/Faculty:** n/av
Year: semesters, summer session	**Tuition:** $30,560
Room & Board: $12,904	**Freshman Class:** n/av
SAT or ACT: recommended	**CEEB CODE:** 2078
Application Deadline: open	**COMPETITIVE**

Cazenovia College, founded in 1824, is a private institution offering degree programs in liberal arts and pre-professional studies. The figures in the above capsule and in this profile are approximate. The 40-acre campus is in a small town 18 miles southeast of Syracuse, NY. Including any residence halls, there are 26 buildings.

STUDENT LIFE: 80% of undergraduates are from New York. Others are from 24 states, 4 foreign countries, and Canada. 90% are from public schools. 86% are White. **Male To Female Ratio:** 2.9:1. The average age of freshmen is 18. **Housing:** 817 students can be accommodated in college housing, which includes single-sex and coed dorms, on-campus apartments, and off-campus apartments. All-female residence hall, and upperclass-only housing. 90% of students live on campus. Upperclassmen may keep cars.

FACULTY/CLASSROOMS: 40% of faculty are male; 60% are female. All teach undergraduates, and 1% do research. No introductory courses are taught by graduate students. The average class size in an introductory lecture is 20; in a laboratory is 15; and in a regular course is 16.

PROGRAMS OF STUDY: Cazenovia confers B.A., B.S., B.F.A. and B.P.S. degrees. Associate degrees are also awarded. Bachelor's degrees are awarded in AGRICULTURE (environmental studies), BUSINESS (business administration and management and management science), COMMUNICATIONS AND THE ARTS (communications, English, studio art, and visual design), EDUCATION (early childhood education and elementary education), ENGINEERING AND ENVIRONMENTAL DESIGN (commercial art and interior design), SOCIAL SCIENCE (criminology, fashion design and technology, human services, liberal arts/general studies, psychology, and social science). Interior design and equine management is the strongest academically. Management has the largest enrollment.

ACTIVITIES: There are no fraternities or sororities. There are 52 groups on campus, including art, band, cheerleading, choir, chorale, computers, debate, drama, environmental, ethnic, gay, honors, literary magazine, musical theater, newspaper, political, professional, religious, social, social service, student government, and yearbook. **Sports:** There are 10 intercollegiate sports for men and 10 for women, and 9 intramural sports for men and 9 for women. Facilities include an athletic center with a pool, 2 gyms, a fitness center, outdoor tennis courts, and athletic fields. **Graduates:** From July 1, 2013 to June 30, 2014, 163 bachelor's degrees were awarded. The most popular majors were management (39%), human services (25%), and visual communications (19%).

SERVICES: Counseling and information services are available, as is tutoring in most subjects. There is a reader service for the blind, and remedial math, reading, and writing. **Library/Resources:** The library contains 83,340 volumes, 14,727 microform items, 4,160 audio/video tapes/CDs/DVDs, and subscribes to 61,000 periodicals including electronic. Computerized library services include interlibrary loans, database searching, Internet access, and Wi-Fi capability. Special learning facilities include an art gallery, a nearby campus farm with equine center. **Physically Challenged Students:** 86% of the campus is accessible. Facilities include wheelchair ramps, elevators, special parking, specially equipped restrooms, special class scheduling, lowered telephones, and special housing. **Special:** Cazenovia offers internships, a Washington semester, work-study, B.A.-B.S. degrees in liberal studies and liberal and professional studies. There is a study-abroad program at Canterbury Christ Church University in the United Kingdom. There are 3 national honor societies, a freshman honors program, and 2 departmental honors programs. **Visiting:** There are regularly scheduled orientations for prospective students, student orientations consist of a welcome by the president and deans, financial aid sessions, placement testing, academic advising, and registration. There are guides for informal visits, visitors may sit in on classes, and stay overnight. To schedule a visit, contact The Admissions Office. **Campus Safety and Security:** Measures include 24-hour foot and vehicle patrol, emergency notification system, and security escort services. There are emergency telephones, lighted pathways/sidewalks, and controlled access to dorms/residences.

REQUIREMENTS: The SAT or ACT is recommended. Applicants should be graduates of an accredited secondary school or the equivalent. A recommendation from a guidance counselor or teacher is required. AP and CLEP credits are accepted. Important factors in the admissions decision are advanced placement or honors courses and leadership record. A total of 120 semester credits and a GPA of 2.0 are required for the bachelor's degree. Students must take courses in speech, academic writing, diversity and social consciousness, science or math, visual literacy, communications, ethics, cultural literacy, and research methods. They must also demonstrate math proficiency and complete a senior capstone course. **Procedure:** Freshmen are admitted fall and spring. Entrance exams should be taken by the fall of the senior year. There are deferred admissions and rolling admissions plans. Application deadlines are open. Application fee is $30. Applications are accepted on-line. **Transfer Students:** 66 transfer students enrolled in 2013-2014. Applicants must present at least 12 college credits, with a minimum GPA of 2.0, and official transcripts from previous colleges attended. Students with fewer than 24 credits must also submit a high school transcript. 30 of 120 credits required for the bachelor's degree must be completed at Cazenovia. **International Students:** There are 4 international students enrolled. The school actively recruits these students. They must take the TOEFL.

ADMISSIONS: Robert A. Croot, Dean for Admissions and Financial Aid. E-Mail: *admission@cazcollege.edu* Web: *www.cazenovia.edu*

FINANCIAL AID: Cazenovia is a member of CSS. The FAFSA, and and Express TAP is required. Check with the school for current application deadlines.

CITY UNIVERSITY OF NEW YORK

The City University of New York, established in 1847, is a public system in New York. It is governed by a board of trustees, whose chief administrator is the chancellor. The primary goal of the system is to maintain and expand its commitment to academic excellence and to provide equal access and opportunity. The main priorities are providing access for all students who seek to enroll, insuring student success, and enhancing instructional and research excellence. The total student enrollment for all 4 campuses is usually 269,144 with 7313 faculty members. Altogether there are 573 baccalaureate, 451 master's and 65 doctoral programs offered in the City University of New York System. Profiles of the 4-year campuses are included in this section.

CITY UNIVERSITY OF NEW YORK/ BARUCH COLLEGE	D-5
www.cuny.edu	

New York, NY 10010	(646) 312-1400 n/av
Fax: (646) 312-1361	Email: marisa.delacruz@baruch.cuny.edu
Full-time: 5530 men, 4866 women	Faculty: n/av
Part-time: 1752 men, 1934 women	Ph.D.s: 59%
Graduate: 1632 men, 1791 women	Student/Faculty: 16 to 1
Year: semesters, summer session	Tuition: $6261 ($15,831)
Room & Board: n/app	Freshman Class: 19423 applied, 5153 accepted, 1254 enrolled
SAT or ACT: required	CEEB CODE: 2034
Application Deadline: February 1	HIGHLY COMPETITIVE

Baruch College was founded in 1919 and became a separate unit of the City University of New York in 1968. It offers undergraduate programs in business and public administration and liberal arts and sciences. There are 3 undergraduate schools and 3 graduate schools. In addition to regional accreditation, Baruch has baccalaureate program accreditation with AACSB. The 4-acre campus is in an urban area in New York City. Including any residence halls, there are 6 buildings.

STUDENT LIFE: 85% of undergraduates are from New York. Others are from 2 states, and 164 foreign countries. 62% are from public schools. 34% are Asian American; 30% White; 13% Hispanic; 12% Foreign. **Male To Female Ratio:** 1.0:1. The average age of freshmen is 18; all undergraduates, 24. 12% do not continue beyond their first year; 66% remain to graduate. **Housing:** 242 students can be accommodated in college housing, which includes dorms. On-campus housing is available on a lottery system for upperclassmen. Alcohol is not permitted. All students commute. No one may keep cars.

FACULTY/CLASSROOMS: 60% of faculty are male; 40% are female.

93% teach undergraduates, and 89% do research. Graduate students teach 8% of introductory courses. The average class size in an introductory lecture is 275; in a laboratory is 20; and in a regular course is 35.

PROGRAMS OF STUDY: Baruch confers B.A., B.S. and B.B.A. degrees. Master's degrees are also awarded. Bachelor's degrees are awarded in BUSINESS (accounting, investments and securities, management science, marketing management, marketing/retailing/merchandising, operations research, personnel management, and real estate), COMMUNICATIONS AND THE ARTS (advertising, communications, English, journalism, music, and Spanish), COMPUTER AND PHYSICAL SCIENCE (actuarial science, information sciences and systems, mathematics, and statistics), SOCIAL SCIENCE (economics, history, industrial and organizational psychology, philosophy, political science/government, psychology, public affairs, and sociology). Economics, English, and math are the strongest academically. Accounting, finance, and marketing have the largest enrollments.

ACTIVITIES: 1% of men belong to 2 national fraternities; 1% of women belong to 2 national sororities. There are 172 groups on campus, including cheerleading, chess, chorus, computers, dance, debate, drama, ethnic, gay, honors, international, literary magazine, newspaper, photography, political, professional, radio and TV, religious, social, social service, student government, and yearbook. Popular campus events include Club Fairs, Relay for Life and Caribbean Week. **Sports:** There are 7 intercollegiate sports for men and 7 for women, and 5 intramural sports for men and 5 for women. Facilities include a swimming pool, two gyms, a weight room, an exercise room, and racquetball courts. **Graduates:** From July 1, 2013 to June 30, 2014, 3042 bachelor's degrees were awarded. The most popular majors were finance and investments (23%), accounting (20%), and marketing (10%). 200 companies recruited on campus in 2013-2014. In an average class, 5% graduate in 4 years or less, 63% graduate in 5 years or less, and 67% graduate in 6 years or less.

SERVICES: Counseling and information services are available, as is tutoring in most subjects. There is a reader service for the blind, and remedial math and writing. Note takers and large-print computer screens are available. There are also interpreters for the deaf. **Library/Resources:** The library contains 626,753 volumes, 2.1 million microform items, 52,020 audio/video tapes/CDs/DVDs, and subscribes to 89,951 periodicals including electronic. Computerized library services include interlibrary loans, database searching, Internet access, and Wi-Fi capability. Special learning facilities include an art gallery, radio station, an journalism lab, and a newspaper lab. **Physically Challenged Students:** All of the campus is accessible. Facilities include wheelchair ramps, elevators, specially equipped restrooms, special class scheduling, lowered drinking fountains, and lowered telephones. **Special:** Students may take courses at all CUNY schools. The college offers internships and study abroad in Great Britain, France, Germany, Mexico, and Israel. Students may design their own liberal arts major. A federal work-study program is available, and pass/fail options are permitted for liberal arts majors. Students may combine any undergraduate major with a master's in accountancy. There are 4 national honor societies, a freshman honors program, and 17 departmental honors programs. **Visiting:** There are regularly scheduled orientations for prospective students, including a meeting with an admissions counselor. There are guides for informal visits. To schedule a visit, contact the Admissions Office. **Campus Safety and Security:** Measures include 24-hour foot and vehicle patrol, self-defense education, and security escort services. There are lighted pathways/sidewalks, controlled access to dorms/residences, There are fire safety directors and an ID system that uses card swipe in turnstiles for entry.

REQUIREMENTS: The SAT or ACT is required. Applicants must present an official high school transcript (a GED will be accepted) indicating a minimum average grade of 81% in academic subjects (minimum of 14 credits). AP and CLEP credits are accepted. Important factors in the admissions decision are personality/intangible qualities, advanced placement or honors courses, and leadership record.Students must complete a minimum of 120 credits for the B.A. or B.S. and 124 for the B.B.A., with at least 24 hours in the major, and maintain a GPA of 2.0 overall in the major. Students' core curriculum should include courses in English, literature, communications,

history, philosophy, psychology, microeconomics, and fine and performing arts. **Procedure:** Freshmen are admitted fall and spring. Entrance exams should be taken March 1. There are early decision and rolling admissions plans. Early decision applications should be filed by December 1; regular applications, by February 1 for fall entry; and October 1 for spring entry, along with a $65 fee. Notifications are sent February 1. Applications are accepted on-line. **Transfer Students:** 1571 transfer students enrolled in 2013-2014. Applicants must have a minimum GPA of 2.5 for 12 to 34.9 credits submitted, a minimum GPA of 2.25 for 35 to 59.9 credits, and a minimum GPA of 2.0 for 60 or more credits. Business applicants must have a 2.75 GPA. Students applying for transfer with fewer than 12 credits earned must have a minimum GPA of 2.5 and a minimum high school average of 80%. 32 of 128 credits required for the bachelor's degree must be completed at Baruch. **International Students:** There are 1669 international students enrolled. They must take the TOEFL with a minimum score of 550 on the paper-based TOEFL (PBT) or 80 on the Internet-based version (iBT). They must also take the SAT or ACT.

ADMISSIONS: 27% of the 2014-2015 applicants were accepted. The SAT scores for the 2014-2015 freshman class were: Critical Reading--12% below 500, 48% between 500 and 599, 31% between 600 and 699, and 8% between 700 and 800; Math--1% below 500, 21% between 500 and 599, 50% between 600 and 699, and 27% between 700 and 800. **Admissions Contact:** Marisa Delacruz, Director of Undergraduate Admissions. E-Mail: *marisa.delacruz@baruch.cuny .edu* Web: *www.cuny.edu*

FINANCIAL AID: The FAFSA is required. Check with the school for current application deadlines.

CITY UNIVERSITY OF NEW YORK/ BROOKLYN COLLEGE	D-5
www.brooklyn.cuny.edu	

Brooklyn, NY 11210	(718) 951-5001
	n/av
Fax: (718) 951-4506	Email: adminqry@brooklyn.cuny.edu

Full-time: 3852 men, 5386 women	Faculty: 543
Part-time: 1472 men, 2389 women	Ph.Ds: 96%
Graduate: 1169 men, 2256 women	Student/Faculty: 15 to 1
Year: semesters, summer session	Tuition: $5884 ($15,004)
Room & Board: n/app	Freshman Class: n/av
SAT or ACT: required	CEEB CODE: 2046
Application Deadline: October 1	COMPETITIVE+

Brooklyn College, established in 1930, is a publicly supported college of liberal arts, sciences, pre-professional, and professional studies. It is part of the City University of New York and serves the commuter student. Figures in the above capsule and in this profile are approximate. There are 5 undergraduate schools and 5 graduate schools. In addition to regional accreditation, Brooklyn College has baccalaureate program accreditation with ADA, NCATE, and ASLHA. The 36-acre campus is in an urban area in Brooklyn, NY. Including any residence halls, there are 15 buildings.

STUDENT LIFE: 99% of undergraduates are from New York. Others are from 10 states, 140 foreign countries, and Canada. 78% are from public schools. 40% are White; 25% African American; 16% Asian American; 14% Hispanic. **Male To Female Ratio:** 1.5:1. The average age of freshmen is 18; all undergraduates, 23. 16% do not continue beyond their first year; 84% remain to graduate. Alcohol is not permitted. All students commute. No one may keep cars.

FACULTY/CLASSROOMS: 51% of faculty are male; 49% are female. No introductory courses are taught by graduate students. The average class size in a laboratory is 16 and in a regular course is 32.

PROGRAMS OF STUDY: Brooklyn College confers B.A., B.S., B.F.A., B.B.A., and B.Mus. degrees. Master's degrees are also awarded. Bachelor's degrees are awarded in AGRICULTURE (environmental studies), BIOLOGICAL SCIENCE (biology/biological science), BUSINESS (accounting, banking and finance, business administration and management, business (dual major program), business information systems, and business systems analysis), COMMUNICATIONS AND THE ARTS (art, art history and appreciation, broadcasting, classics, communications, comparative literature, creative writing, English, film arts, French, Italian, journalism, linguistics, multimedia, music, music performance, music theory and composition, radio/television technology, Russian, Spanish, speech/debate/rhetoric, theater management, and visual and performing arts), COMPUTER AND PHYSICAL SCIENCE (chemistry, computer science, earth science, geology, information sciences and systems, mathematics, and physics), EDUCATION (art education, bilingual/bicultural education, (Education) Childhood Education, childhood education: 1-6, early childhood education, elementary education, English education, foreign languages education, mathematics education, music education, physical education, science education, secondary education, and social studies education), HEALTH PROFESSIONS (health science and speech pathology/audiology), SOCIAL SCIENCE (African studies, American studies, anthropology, Caribbean studies, child care/child and family studies, economics, Hispanic American studies, history, interdisciplinary studies, Judaic studies, Latin American studies, philosophy, political science/government, psychology, Puerto Rican studies, religion, sociology, and women's studies). Business, accounting, and education have the largest enrollments.

ACTIVITIES: 3% of men belong to 2 local and 6 national fraternities; 3% of women belong to 4 local and 4 national sororities. There are 161 groups on campus, including academic club, art, chess, computers, dance, drama, ethnic, film, forensics, gay, honors, international, literary magazine, musical theater, newspaper, political, professional, radio and TV, religious, social, social service, student government, symphony, and yearbook. Popular campus events include Welcome Back Bash, Fall Festival and Make a Difference Day. **Sports:** There are 6 intercollegiate sports for men and 7 for women, and 3 intramural sports for men and 3 for women. Facilities include a swimming pool, soccer field, softball field, volleyball, tennis, and basketball courts, a fitness center, and a jogging track. **Graduates:** From July 1, 2013 to June 30, 2014, 2474 bachelor's degrees were awarded. The most popular majors were business (21%), psychology (13%), and accounting (11%). 330 companies recruited on campus in 2013-2014. In an average class, 46% graduate in 5 years or less and 54% graduate in 6 years or less.

SERVICES: Counseling and information services are available, as is tutoring in every subject. There is a reader service for the blind. **Library/Resources:** The library contains 1.7 million volumes, 1.3 million microform items, 130,093 audio/video tapes/CDs/DVDs, and subscribes to 185,516 periodicals including electronic. Computerized library services include interlibrary loans, database searching, and Internet access. Special learning facilities include an art gallery, radio station, TV station, three color studios, and a speech and hearing clinic. **Physically Challenged Students:** All of the campus is accessible. Facilities include wheelchair ramps, elevators, special parking, specially equipped restrooms, special class scheduling, and lowered drinking fountains. **Special:** There are numerous cross-registration programs with colleges and universities in the area. Many internships and work-study programs are available. Study abroad is possible in more than 29 countries. A B.A.-M.D., B.S.-M.P.S., and accelerated B.A.-M.A. programs are available. A number of B.A.-B.S. degrees, dual majors, a 3-2 engineering degree, and student-designed majors are possible. Credit by exam, credit for life experience, non-degree study, and pass/fail options are offered. There is a Latin and Greek Institute offered during the summer through the Graduate Center. There are 9 national honor societies, including Phi Beta Kappa, a freshman honors program, and 6 departmental honors programs. **Visiting:** There are regularly scheduled orientations for prospective students, including campus tours, presentations, and meetings with faculty. There are guides for informal visits. To schedule a visit, contact Christopher Milton, Director for Recruitment at (718) 951-5001. **Campus Safety and Security:** Measures include 24-hour foot and vehicle patrol, emergency notification system, and security escort services. There are shuttle buses, emergency telephones, lighted pathways/sidewalks, CCTV cameras, and informational assistants.

REQUIREMENTS: The SAT or ACT is required. Applicants applying directly from high school must have completed 81% GPA with 5 units of math and English with no less than 2 years of either combined (critical reading and math) SAT score or ACT equivalent of 1000 for regular freshmen admissions. Students will be admitted with GED score of 3000 and have the equivalent of 2 years of high school

math. A GPA of 3.0 is required. AP and CLEP credits are accepted. There are 11 required, interrelated courses that cover the following core curriculum areas: classics, art, music, political science, sociology, history, literature, math, computer science, chemistry, physics, biology, geology, philosophy, and comparative cultures. There are basic skills requirements in reading, composition, speech, and math, as well as a foreign language requirement. A 2.0 GPA and a minimum of 120 credit hours, with 31 to 36 in the major (67 to 70 for chemistry), are required to graduate. **Procedure:** Freshmen are admitted fall and spring. There are early admissions and rolling admissions plans. Applications should be filed by October 1 for fall entry; February 1 for spring entry, along with a $65 fee. Notification of early decision is sent December 15; regular decision, on a rolling basis. Applications are accepted on-line. **Transfer Students:** 2879 transfer students enrolled in 2013-2014. Transfer students must have up to 24 credits; 2.5 GPA and freshman requirements: 25 and over credits, a 2.3 GPA. 30 of 120 credits required for the bachelor's degree must be completed at Brooklyn College. **International Students:** There are 352 international students enrolled. The school actively recruits these students. They must take the TOEFL with a minimum score of 500 on the paper-based TOEFL (PBT) or 61 on the Internet-based version (iBT) and the college's own test.

ADMISSIONS: Admissions Office. E-Mail: *adminqry@brooklyn.cuny .edu* Web: *www.brooklyn.cuny.edu*

FINANCIAL AID: In 2014-2015, 69% of all full-time freshmen and 76% of continuing full-time students received some form of financial aid. 61% of all full-time freshmen and 74% of continuing full-time students received need-based aid. The average freshman award was $7,500. Need-based scholarships or need-based grants averaged $3,300 ($10,500 maximum); need-based self-help aid (loans and jobs) averaged $3,200 ($3,500 maximum); and other non-need-based awards and non-need-based scholarships averaged $1,500 ($10,500 maximum). 71% of undergraduate students work part-time. Average annual earnings from campus work are $1200. The average financial indebtedness of the 2014 graduate was $12,300. The FAFSA is required. The priority date for freshman financial aid applications for fall entry is April 1.

CITY UNIVERSITY OF NEW YORK/CITY COLLEGE   D-5
www.ccny.cuny.edu

New York, NY 10031	**(212) 650-6977**
Fax: (212) 650-6417	**Email:** admissions@ccny.cuny.edu
Full-time: 4727 men, 5122 women	**Faculty:** 510
Part-time: 1512 men, 1548 women	**Ph.D.s:** 87%
Graduate: 1094 men, 1394 women	**Student/Faculty:** 14 to 1
Year: semesters, summer session	**Tuition:** $6471 ($13,281)
Room & Board: $13,848	**Freshman Class:** 24497 applied, 1530 accepted, 1441 enrolled
SAT CR/M/W: 520/580/515	**CEEB CODE:** 2083
Application Deadline: December 1	**HIGHLY COMPETITIVE+**

City College, founded in 1847, is a public liberal arts college that is part of the City University of New York. The college offers programs through 4 undergraduate and 4 graduate schools and 2 professional centers. There are 6 undergraduate schools and 6 graduate schools. In addition to regional accreditation, CCNY has baccalaureate program accreditation with ABET, ABFSE, NAAB, and NCATE. The 35-acre campus is in an urban area in New York City. Including any residence halls, there are 14 buildings.

STUDENT LIFE: 96% of undergraduates are from New York. Others are from 40 states, 158 foreign countries, and Canada. 84% are from public schools. 25% are Hispanic; 23% African American; 21% Asian American; 20% White. **Male To Female Ratio:** 1.1:1. The average age of freshmen is 19; all undergraduates, 24. 22% do not continue beyond their first year; 42% remain to graduate. **Housing:** 580 students can be accommodated in college housing, which includes single-sex and coed on-campus apartments and married student housing. Apartments for single students. On-campus housing is available on a first-come and first-served basis. Priority is given to out-of-town students. 97% of students commute. Alcohol is not permitted. All students may keep cars.

FACULTY/CLASSROOMS: 56% of faculty are male; 44% are female. 77% teach undergraduates, 65% do research, and 53% do both. No introductory courses are taught by graduate students. The average class size in an introductory lecture is 29; in a laboratory is 15; and in a regular course is 19.

PROGRAMS OF STUDY: CCNY confers B.A., B.S., B.Arch., B.E., B.F.A., B.M.E. and B.S.Ed. degrees. Master's and Doctoral degrees are also awarded. Bachelor's degrees are awarded in BIOLOGICAL SCIENCE (biology/biological science), BUSINESS (business administration and management), COMMUNICATIONS AND THE ARTS (art, communications, comparative literature, dramatic arts, English, film arts, fine arts, French, multimedia, music, performing arts, romance languages and literature, Spanish, and video), COMPUTER AND PHYSICAL SCIENCE (atmospheric sciences and meteorology, chemistry, computer science, earth science, geology, mathematics, physics, and quantitative methods), EDUCATION (art education, bilingual/bicultural education, early childhood education, education of the emotionally handicapped, education of the mentally handicapped, elementary education, English education, foreign languages education, mathematics education, secondary education, social studies education, and special education), ENGINEERING AND ENVIRONMENTAL DESIGN (architecture, biomedical engineering, chemical engineering, civil engineering, computer engineering, electrical/electronics engineering, environmental engineering, environmental science, landscape architecture/design, and mechanical engineering), HEALTH PROFESSIONS (biomedical science, physician's assistant, predentistry, and premedicine), SOCIAL SCIENCE (American studies, anthropology, area studies, Asian/Oriental studies, economics, ethnic studies, history, international studies, Latin American studies, philosophy, political science/government, prelaw, psychology, sociology, and urban studies). Engineering, architecture, and sciences are the strongest academically. Engineering, architecture, and psychology have the largest enrollments.

ACTIVITIES: There are 170 groups on campus, including and choral groups, art, band, cheerleading, chess, chorus, computers, dance, debate, drama, ethnic, film, gay, honors, international, jazz band, literary magazine, Model UN, newspaper, orchestra, photography, political, professional, radio and TV, religious, social, social service, student government, and yearbook. Popular campus events include Langston Hughes Poetry Contest, Dance Theater of Harlem Performances at Davis Center and Architecture Lecture Series. **Sports:** There are 9 intercollegiate sports for men and 9 for women, and 9 intramural sports for men and 9 for women. Facilities include a weight room, swimming pools, and two gyms. **Graduates:** From July 1, 2013 to June 30, 2014, 2126 bachelor's degrees were awarded. The most popular majors were psychology (15%), engineering (13%), and social sciences (11%). 850 companies recruited on campus in 2013-2014. In an average class, 8% graduate in 4 years or less, 30% graduate in 5 years or less, and 42% graduate in 6 years or less. Of the 2013 graduating class, 18% were enrolled in graduate school within 6 months of graduation.

SERVICES: There are 170 groups on campus, including and choral groups, art, band, cheerleading, chess, chorus, computers, dance, debate, drama, ethnic, film, gay, honors, international, jazz band, literary magazine, Model UN, newspaper, orchestra, photography, political, professional, radio and TV, religious, social, social service, student government, and yearbook. Popular campus events include Langston Hughes Poetry Contest, Dance Theater of Harlem Performances at Davis Center and Architecture Lecture Series. **Sports:** There are 9 intercollegiate sports for men and 9 for women, and 9 intramural sports for men and 9 for women. Facilities include a weight room, swimming pools, and two gyms. **Graduates:** From July 1, 2013 to June 30, 2014, 2126 bachelor's degrees were awarded. The most popular majors were psychology (15%), engineering (13%), and social sciences (11%). 850 companies recruited on campus in 2013-2014. In an average class, 8% graduate in 4 years or less, 30% graduate in 5 years or less, and 42% graduate in 6 years or less. Of the 2013 graduating class, 18% were enrolled in graduate school within 6 months of graduation.

REQUIREMENTS: The SAT is required. Students who apply should have a recommended satisfactory minimum SAT score or an ACT score of 22. Graduation from an accredited secondary school is generally required, but a GED will be accepted. 14 academic credits should be presented with a minimum grade average of 80%. AP credits are accepted. Students must successfully complete 120 credits, with 32 to 48 in the major, and maintain a minimum GPA of 2.0. A core curriculum must be met, including courses in anthropology, art, English, psychology, and sociology. Students must complete a college proficiency exam. **Procedure:** Freshmen are admitted to all sessions. Entrance exams should be taken prior to registration. There is a rolling admissions plan. Applications should be filed by December 1 for fall entry; October 15 for spring entry, along with a $65 fee. Notifications are sent January 15. Applications are accepted on-line. **Transfer Students:** 1498 transfer students enrolled in 2013-2014. Transfer applicants must have earned a minimum of 24 credit hours and maintained a GPA of 2.0. Selected programs have more competitive requirements. 32 of 120 credits required for the bachelor's degree must be completed at CCNY. **International Students:** There are 1758 international students enrolled. They must take the TOEFL with a minimum score of 500 on the paper-based TOEFL (PBT) or 61 on the Internet-based version (iBT). They must also take the ACT, and the CUNY Placement Exam.

ADMISSIONS: 6% of the 2014-2015 applicants were accepted. The SAT scores for the 2014-2015 freshman class were: Critical Reading--43% below 500, 34% between 500 and 599, 16% between 600 and 699, and 6% between 700 and 800; Math--14% below 500, 45% between 500 and 599, 29% between 600 and 699, and 12% between 700 and 800. 60% of the current freshmen were in the top fifth of their class; 87% were in the top two fifths. **Admissions Contact:** Joe Fantozzi, Director of Admissions. E-Mail: *admissions@ccny.cuny.edu* Web: *www.ccny.cuny.edu*

FINANCIAL AID: In 2014-2015, 84% of all full-time freshmen and 82% of continuing full-time students received some form of financial aid. 84% of all full-time freshmen and 82% of continuing full-time students received need-based aid. The average freshman award was $8,757. Need-based scholarships or need-based grants averaged $7,989; need-based self-help aid (loans and jobs) averaged $7,210; other non-need-based awards and non-need-based scholarships averaged $3,106; and $5,530 from other forms of aid. The average financial indebtedness of the 2014 graduate was $16,944. The FAFSA and the state aid form are required. The priority date for freshman financial aid applications for fall entry is April 1. The deadline for filing freshman financial aid applications for fall entry is rolling.

CLARKSON UNIVERSITY   D-2
www.clarkson.edu

Potsdam, NY 13699   (315) 268-6480
n/av

Fax: (315) 268-7647	Email: bgrant@clarkson.edu
Full-time: n/av	Faculty: 178
Part-time: n/av	Ph.D.s: 89%
Graduate: n/av	Student/Faculty: 13 to 1
Year: semesters, summer session	Tuition: $42,530
Room & Board: $14,800	Freshman Class: 6747 applied, 4320 accepted, 757 enrolled
SAT CR/M/W: 560/620/550 ACT: 26	CEEB CODE: 2084
Application Deadline: January 15	HIGHLY COMPETITIVE

Clarkson University, is a private, nationally ranked research university with 50+ academic programs in engineering, business, arts, sciences and health professions. We are the institution of choice for enterprising, high-ability scholars from diverse backgrounds who embrace challenge and thrive in a rigorous, highly collaborative learning environment. In partnership with leading businesses and industries, we are reshaping education to meet the needs of a modern world by connecting knowledge, discipline, nations and cultures. We encourage our students to push the limits of what is known, and to apply their ingenuity to develop fresh solutions to real-world challenges. For more than 100 years, our graduates have achieved extraordinary professional success and advanced the global economy ethically and responsibly. One in five alumni already leads as a CEO, VP or equivalent senior executive of a company. There are 4 undergraduate schools and 4 graduate schools. In addition to regional accreditation, Clarkson has baccalaureate program accreditation with AACSB, ABET, APTA, and ARC-PA. The 640-acre campus is in a rural area in Potsdam, 135 miles northeast of Syracuse, 85 miles south of Ottawa, Canada and 69 miles northwest of the Olympic Village in Lake Placid. Including any residence halls, there are 71 buildings.

STUDENT LIFE: 74% of undergraduates are from New York. Others are from 46 states, 52 foreign countries, and Canada. 85% are from public schools. 83% are White. The average age of freshmen is 18; all undergraduates, 20. 12% do not continue beyond their first year; 75% remain to graduate. **Housing:** 2510 students can be accommodated in college housing, which includes single-sex and coed dorms, on-campus apartments, and off-campus apartments. In addition, there are honors houses, special-interest houses, fraternity houses, and sorority houses. On-campus housing is guaranteed for all 4 years and is available on a lottery system for upperclassmen. 84% of students live on campus; of those, 90% remain on campus on weekends. All students may keep cars.

FACULTY/CLASSROOMS: 71% of faculty are male; 29% are female. 80% teach undergraduates, all do research, and 80% do both. No introductory courses are taught by graduate students. The average class size in an introductory lecture is 35; in a laboratory is 21; and in a regular course is 29.

PROGRAMS OF STUDY: Clarkson confers B.S., and B.P.S. degrees. Master's and Doctoral degrees are also awarded. Bachelor's degrees are awarded in BIOLOGICAL SCIENCE (biology/biological science and molecular biology), BUSINESS (accounting, business administration and management, business systems analysis, entrepreneurial studies, finance, management information systems, and supply chain management), COMMUNICATIONS AND THE ARTS (communications and technical and business writing), COMPUTER AND PHYSICAL SCIENCE (applied mathematics, chemistry, computer science, digital arts/technology, information sciences and systems, mathematics, physics, science, and software engineering), ENGINEERING AND ENVIRONMENTAL DESIGN (aeronautical engineering, chemical engineering, civil engineering, computer engineering, electrical/electronics engineering, engineering management, environmental engineering, environmental science, and mechanical engineering), HEALTH PROFESSIONS (environmental health science), SOCIAL SCIENCE (American studies, history, humanities, interdisciplinary studies, political science/government, psychology, and social science). Engineering, business, and physical/life sciences are the strongest academically. Engineering, and physical/life sciences have the largest enrollments.

ACTIVITIES: 12% of men belong to 3 local and 8 national fraternities; 15% of women belong to 4 national sororities. There are 147 groups on campus, including cheerleading, chorus, computers, drama, drill team, environmental, ethnic, gay, honors, international, jazz band, musical theater, newspaper, orchestra, pep band, photography, political, professional, radio and TV, religious, social, social service, SPEED Teams (Student Projects for Engineering Experience & Design), student government, and yearbook. Popular campus events include Spring and WinterFest, World in Potsdam Diversity Festival, and NCAA Division I Championship Hockey Games. **Sports:** There are 10 intercollegiate sports for men and 10 for women, and 6 intramural sports for men and 6 for women. Facilities include 3000-seat multipurpose ice arena, fitness center, gym, swimming pool, weight room, field house, tennis courts, and all-purpose indoor and outdoor turf fields. **Graduates:** From July 1, 2013 to June 30, 2014, 639 bachelor's degrees were awarded. The most popular majors were mechanical engineering (16%), civil engineering (11%), and engineering management (9%). 251 companies recruited on campus in 2013-2014. In an average class, 1% graduate in 3 years or less, 63% graduate in 4 years or less, 75% graduate in 5 years or less, and 75% graduate in 6 years or less. Of the 2013 graduating class, 15% were enrolled in graduate school within 6 months of graduation, and 70% were employed.

SERVICES: Counseling and information services are available, as is tutoring in most subjects. There is a reader service for the blind, and remedial math and writing. **Library/Resources:** The 2 libraries contain 371,937 volumes, 256,398 microform items, 458 audio/video tapes/CDs/DVDs, and subscribe to 23,962 periodicals including electronic. Computerized library services include interlibrary loans, database searching, Internet access, and Wi-Fi capability. Special learning facilities include a radio station, TV station, Design, prototyping and testing facilities for SPEED Team competitions (Student Projects for Engineering Experience and Design), Institute for a Sustainable Environment, wind turbine test site, wind tunnel facility, greenhouse, observatory, nature preserve with hiking/cross-country ski trails, machine and electrical fabrication shops, welding shop, sustainable energy systems, air resources engineering and science, advanced materials processing, Great Rivers, innovation, and rehabilitation engineering, science, and technology centers. **Physically Challenged Students:** 85% of the campus is accessible. Facilities include wheelchair ramps, elevators, special parking, specially equipped restrooms, special class scheduling, lowered drinking fountains, lowered telephones, and special housing. **Special:** Students can take advantage of many unique educational experiences at Clarkson. Students can sign up for the Washington Semester, Adirondack Semester or Semester at Sea. Students can cross-register at St. Lawrence University, SUNY Potsdam or SUNY Canton, or transfer to Clarkson through one of our many 3-2 engineering degree agreements. Our 3-2 agreements allow students to take their first 3 years of college at a 4-year liberal arts institution and then transfer with junior standing into one of Clarkson's 4-year engineering programs. Students can choose one of Clarkson's may pre-designed interdisciplinary majors, or design their own with a dual major or BPS degree. All Clarkson students are required to complete a professional experience, which usually takes place through a co-op or internship, with one of Clarkson's many industry partners including General Dynamics, General Electric, IBM, Lockheed Martin, and Proctor and Gamble. Many programs of study also require a study abroad experience, which can take place through instructor-led summer trips or a semester/year abroad in Australia, Austria, China, Denmark, France, Germany, Hong Kong, Hungary, India, Ireland, Japan, South Korea, Mexico, New Zealand, Singapore, Spain, Sweden, or the United Kingdom. Work-study programs are also available. There are 15 national honor societies, a freshman honors program, and 9 departmental honors programs. **Visiting:** There are regularly scheduled orientations for prospective students, visits are individually customized to your interests, and include a personalized tour with a Clarkson student and one-on-one meetings with admissions officers, faculty members, and coaches. There are guides for informal visits, visitors may sit in on classes, and stay overnight. To schedule a visit, contact the Undergraduate Admissions. **Campus Safety and Security:** Measures include 24-hour foot and vehicle patrol, emergency notification system, and security escort services. There are emergency telephones, lighted pathways/sidewalks, and controlled access to dorms/residences.

REQUIREMENTS: SAT or ACT scores are required. SAT subject tests are recommended. Applicants must have graduated from an accredited secondary school or have a GED. A campus visit and interview are also recommended. AP and CLEP credits are accepted. Important factors in the admissions decision are advanced placement or honors courses, recommendations by school officials, and extracurricular activities record. Students must complete a least 120 credit hours, 30 in a major field of study, with a minimum 2.0 cumulative GPA. Students must meet the requirements of the Clarkson Common Experience, which includes a professional experience such as a co-op or internship, and any additional requirements determined by their major department. A student entering as a first-year freshman must have been in residence for at least four semesters including the final undergraduate semester or, if entering with advanced standing, have completed at least half the remaining upper-level undergraduate work in residence at Clarkson. **Procedure:** Freshmen are admitted fall and spring. Entrance exams should be taken by November. There are early decision, early admissions, and deferred admissions plans. Early decision applications should be filed by December 1; regular applications, by January 15 for fall entry; and October 15 for spring entry, along with a $50 fee. Notification of early decision is sent January 1; regular decision, February 1. 120 early decision candidates were accepted for the 2014-2015 class. 159 applicants were on the 2014 waiting list; 17 were admitted. Applications are accepted on-line. Application fees are waived if application is completed on-line. **Transfer Students:** 121 transfer students enrolled in 2013-2014.

Transfer applicants must submit two letters of recommendation, including one from an academic professor or instructor. Applicants must also submit official secondary school transcripts if not earning an Associate's Degree, and SAT or ACT scores if less than 24 credits at time of application. Transfer applicants into engineering or other majors requiring calculus should have completed at least one college-level calculus course. International students whose first language is not English must submit TOEFL or IELTS scores. 30 of 120 credits required for the bachelor's degree must be completed at Clarkson. **International Students:** There are 110 international students enrolled. The school actively recruits these students. They must take the TOEFL with a minimum score of 550 on the paper-based TOEFL (PBT) or 80 on the Internet-based version (iBT). They must also take the SAT or ACT.

ADMISSIONS: 64% of the 2014-2015 applicants were accepted. The SAT scores for the 2014-2015 freshman class were: Critical Reading--15% below 500, 50% between 500 and 599, 28% between 600 and 699, and 7% between 700 and 800; Math--5% below 500, 31% between 500 and 599, 51% between 600 and 699, and 13% between 700 and 800; Writing--23% below 500, 50% between 500 and 599, 22% between 600 and 699, and 4% between 700 and 800. The ACT scores were 4% below 21, 20% between 21 and 23, 32% between 24 and 26, 20% between 27 and 28, and 24% above 28. 67% of the current freshmen were in the top fifth of their class; 92% were in the top two fifths. 24 freshmen graduated first in their class. **Admissions Contact:** Brian T. Grant, Dean of Admissions. E-Mail: *bgrant@ clarkson.edu* Web: *www.clarkson.edu*

FINANCIAL AID: In 2014-2015, 98% of all full-time freshmen and 99% of continuing full-time students received some form of financial aid. 81% of all full-time freshmen and 84% of continuing full-time students received need-based aid. The average freshman award was $37,165. Need-based scholarships or need-based grants averaged $30,384 ($57,848 maximum); need-based self-help aid (loans and jobs) averaged $5,015 ($10,700 maximum); non-need-based athletic scholarships averaged $40,705 ($53,728 maximum); and other non-need-based awards and non-need-based scholarships averaged $24,683 ($45,997 maximum). 38% of undergraduate students work part-time. Average annual earnings from campus work are $1476. The average financial indebtedness of the 2014 graduate was $26,832. The FAFSA, and For need -based aid file the FAFSA by February 1 is required. The priority date for freshman financial aid applications for fall entry is February 15. The deadline for filing freshman financial aid applications for fall entry is March 1.

COLGATE UNIVERSITY   **D-5**
www.colgate.edu

Hamilton, NY 13346	(315) 228-7401
	n/av
Fax: (315) 228-7544	Email: admission@mail.colgate.edu
Full-time: 1313 men, 1487 women	Faculty: 266; IIB, ++$
Part-time: 10 men, 15 women	Ph.D.s: 96%
Graduate: 4 men, 8 women	Student/Faculty: 11 to 1
Year: semesters	Tuition: $48,255
Room & Board: $9910	Freshman Class: 7816 applied, 2464 accepted, 750 enrolled
SAT CR/M: 661/680 ACT: 30	CEEB CODE: 2086
Application Deadline: January 15	MOST COMPETITIVE

Colgate University, founded in 1819, is a private liberal arts institution. The figures in the above capsule and in this profile are approximate. There is one graduate school. The 515-acre campus is in a rural area 45 miles southeast of Syracuse, NY and 35 miles southwest of Utica, NY. Including any residence halls, there are 87 buildings. **STUDENT LIFE:** 72% of undergraduates are from out of state, mostly the Northeast. Students are from 49 states, 35 foreign countries, and Canada. 62% are from public schools. 74% are White. **Male To Female Ratio:** 1.1:1. The average age of freshmen is 18; all undergraduates, 20. 5% do not continue beyond their first year; 91% remain to graduate. **Housing:** 2400 students can be accommodated in college housing, which includes coed dorms and on-campus apart-

ments. In addition, there are language houses, special-interest houses, and fraternity houses. On-campus housing is guaranteed for all 4 years. 93% of students live on campus; of those, 96% remain on campus on weekends. All students may keep cars.

FACULTY/CLASSROOMS: 57% of faculty are male; 43% are female. All teach and do research. No introductory courses are taught by graduate students. The average class size in an introductory lecture is 21; in a laboratory is 17; and in a regular course is 19.

PROGRAMS OF STUDY: Colgate confers B.A. degrees. Master's degrees are also awarded. Bachelor's degrees are awarded in BIOLOGICAL SCIENCE (biochemistry, biology/biological science, molecular biology, and neurosciences), COMMUNICATIONS AND THE ARTS (art history and appreciation, Chinese, classics, dramatic arts, English, French, German, Greek, Japanese, Latin, music, Russian, Spanish, and studio art), COMPUTER AND PHYSICAL SCIENCE (astronomy, astrophysics, chemistry, computer science, geology, geophysics and seismology, mathematics, natural sciences, physical sciences, and physics), EDUCATION (education), ENGINEERING AND ENVIRONMENTAL DESIGN (environmental science), SOCIAL SCIENCE (African studies, Asian/Oriental studies, economics, geography, history, humanities, international relations, Latin American studies, Native American studies, peace studies, philosophy, political science/government, psychology, religion, Russian and Slavic studies, social science, sociology, and women's studies). English, economics, and history have the largest enrollments.

ACTIVITIES: 40% of men belong to 6 national fraternities; 38% of women belong to 3 national sororities. There are 180 groups on campus, including art, band, cheerleading, chess, choir, chorale, chorus, computers, dance, debate, drama, environmental, ethnic, film, forensics, gay, honors, international, jazz band, literary magazine, musical theater, newspaper, orchestra, pep band, photography, political, professional, radio and TV, religious, social, social service, student government, symphony, and yearbook. Popular campus events include Winter Olympics, DanceFest and Spring Party Weekend. **Sports:** There are 11 intercollegiate sports for men and 12 for women, and 19 intramural sports for men and 19 for women. Facilities include a softball diamond, numerous athletic fields, an outdoor artificial surface field, a football stadium, an athletic center, a 3000-seat gym, a golf course, a field house, a 50-meter pool, a bowling center, a hockey rink, a 9000-square-foot fitness center, running trails, a trap range, and courts for basketball, tennis, squash, handball, and racquetball. **Graduates:** From July 1, 2013 to June 30, 2014, 704 bachelor's degrees were awarded. 200 companies recruited on campus in 2013-2014. In an average class, 1% graduate in 3 years or less, 88% graduate in 4 years or less, 90% graduate in 5 years or less, and 91% graduate in 6 years or less. Of the 2013 graduating class, 20% were enrolled in graduate school within 6 months of graduation, and 80% were employed.

SERVICES: Counseling and information services are available, as is tutoring in every subject. There is a reader service for the blind, and remedial writing. There is a note-taking service for students with learning and sensory disabilities, and a writing center. **Library/ Resources:** The 2 libraries contain 734,812 volumes, 593,646 microform items, and subscribe to 36,752 periodicals including electronic. Computerized library services include interlibrary loans, database searching, Internet access, and Wi-Fi capability. Special learning facilities include an art gallery, radio station, TV station, an anthropology museum, and an observatory. **Physically Challenged Students:** 20% of the campus is accessible. Facilities include wheelchair ramps, elevators, special parking, specially equipped restrooms, special class scheduling, and lowered drinking fountains. **Special:** Colgate offers various internships, semester and summer research opportunities with faculty, work-study, study abroad in 22 countries, accelerated degree programs, dual majors, and student-designed majors. A 3-2 engineering degree with Columbia and Washington Universities and Rensselaer Polytechnic Institute, an early assurance medical program with George Washington University, credit by exam, and pass/fail options are available. There are 12 national honor societies, including Phi Beta Kappa, and 10 departmental honors programs. **Visiting:** There are regularly scheduled orientations for prospective students, including nonevaluative interviews, group information sessions, and student-led tours. There are guides for informal visits, visitors may sit in on classes, and stay overnight. To schedule a visit, contact the

Office of Admission. **Campus Safety and Security:** Measures include 24-hour foot and vehicle patrol, emergency notification system, self-defense education, and security escort services. There are shuttle buses, emergency telephones, and lighted pathways/sidewalks.

REQUIREMENTS: The SAT or ACT is required. Students must submit 2 teacher recommendations and a counselor's report. An interview, though not evaluated, is recommended. Students should present 16 or more Carnegie credits, based on 4 years each of English and math and at least 3 of lab science, social science, and a foreign language, with electives in the arts. AP credits are accepted. Important factors in the admissions decision are advanced placement or honors courses, recommendations by school officials, and leadership record.To graduate, students must complete a first-year seminar course and the core curriculum, including 4 general education courses and 2 courses each in the natural sciences, social sciences, and humanities. A total of 32 courses is required, with 8 to 12 courses in the major. Study in a foreign language, phys ed, and a swimming test are also required. Students need a minimum 2.0 GPA. **Procedure:** Freshmen are admitted fall. Entrance exams should be taken in time for score reports to reach the University by January 15. There are early decision and deferred admissions plans. Early decision applications should be filed by November 15; regular applications, by January 15 for fall entry, along with a $55 fee. Notification of early decision is sent December 15; regular decision, April 1. 363 early decision candidates were accepted for the 2014-2015 class. 709 applicants were on the 2014 waiting list; 22 were admitted. Applications are accepted on-line. **Transfer Students:** 22 transfer students enrolled in 2013-2014. Either the SAT or the ACT is required, as well as college and high school transcripts, a dean's report, and faculty recommendations. 16 of 32 credits required for the bachelor's degree must be completed at Colgate. **International Students:** There are 133 international students enrolled. The school actively recruits these students. They must take the TOEFL. They must also take the SAT or ACT.

ADMISSIONS: 32% of the 2014-2015 applicants were accepted. The SAT scores for the 2014-2015 freshman class were: Critical Reading--4% below 500, 12% between 500 and 599, 47% between 600 and 699, and 37% between 700 and 800; Math--2% below 500, 11% between 500 and 599, 45% between 600 and 699, and 42% between 700 and 800. The ACT scores were 1% below 21, 3% between 21 and 23, 9% between 24 and 26, 13% between 27 and 28, and 76% above 28. 86% of the current freshmen were in the top fifth of their class; 98% were in the top two fifths. 23 freshmen graduated first in their class. **Admissions Contact:** Gary L. Ross, Dean of Admission. E-Mail: *admission@mail.colgate.edu* Web: *www.colgate.edu*

FINANCIAL AID: In 2014-2015, 34% of all full-time freshmen and 35% of continuing full-time students received some form of financial aid. 34% of all full-time freshmen and 35% of continuing full-time students received need-based aid. The average freshman award was $39,758. Need-based scholarships or need-based grants averaged $35,526; need-based self-help aid (loans and jobs) averaged $4,185; and non-need-based athletic scholarships averaged $33,771. The average financial indebtedness of the 2014 graduate was $14,170. Colgate is a member of CSS. The CSS/Profile and FAFSA, and International students need the International Student's Financial Aid Application are required. The deadline for filing freshman financial aid applications for fall entry is January 15.

COLLEGE OF MOUNT SAINT VINCENT　　　　D-5
www.cmsv.edu

Riverdale, NY 10471	(718) 405-3304
	(800) 665-CMSV
Fax: (718) 549-7945	Email: admissns@mountsaintvincent.edu
Full-time: 305 men, 1105 women	Faculty: IIB, +$
Part-time: 30 men, 155 women	Ph.D.s: n/av
Graduate: 105 men, 310 women	Student/Faculty: n/av
Year: semesters, summer session	Tuition: $24,120
Room & Board: $12,060	Freshman Class: n/av
SAT or ACT: required	CEEB CODE: 2088
Application Deadline: April 2	MOST COMPETITIVE

The College of Mount Saint Vincent, founded as an academy in 1847 and chartered as a college in 1911, is a private liberal arts institution in the Catholic tradition. The figures in the above capsule and in this profile are approximate. There is one graduate school. In addition to regional accreditation, The Mount has baccalaureate program accreditation with ACBSP and NLN. The 70-acre campus is in an urban area 11 miles north of New York City. Including any residence halls, there are 11 buildings.

STUDENT LIFE: 89% of undergraduates are from New York. Others are from 19 states, and 4 foreign countries. 46% are from public schools. 38% are White; 32% Hispanic; 14% African American. 81% are Catholic. **Male To Female Ratio:** 3.6:1. The average age of freshmen is 18; all undergraduates, 22. 25% do not continue beyond their first year; 62% remain to graduate. **Housing:** 778 students can be accommodated in college housing, which includes coed dorms. On-campus housing is guaranteed for all 4 years, is available on a first-come, first-served basis, and is available on a lottery system for upperclassmen. 54% of students live on campus; of those, 65% remain on campus on weekends. All students may keep cars.

FACULTY/CLASSROOMS: 39% of faculty are male; 61% are female. All teach undergraduates, and 80% do both. No introductory courses are taught by graduate students. The average class size in an introductory lecture is 25; in a laboratory is 15; and in a regular course is 15.

PROGRAMS OF STUDY: The Mount confers B.A. and B.S. degrees. Associate and Master's degrees are also awarded. Bachelor's degrees are awarded in BIOLOGICAL SCIENCE (biochemistry and biology/biological science), BUSINESS (business administration and management), COMMUNICATIONS AND THE ARTS (communications, English, French, modern language, and Spanish), COMPUTER AND PHYSICAL SCIENCE (chemistry, computer science, mathematics, and physics), EDUCATION (health education, physical education, and special education), HEALTH PROFESSIONS (allied health and nursing), SOCIAL SCIENCE (economics, history, liberal arts/general studies, philosophy, psychology, religion, sociology, and urban studies). Nursing and biology is the strongest academically. Nursing, psychology, and business have the largest enrollments.

ACTIVITIES: There are no fraternities or sororities. There are 30 groups on campus, including art, cheerleading, chess, choir, chorus, computers, dance, debate, drama, ethnic, film, gay, honors, international, literary magazine, musical theater, newspaper, photography, professional, radio and TV, religious, social, social service, student government, and yearbook. Popular campus events include Phin Fest, Mount Madness, Brown Bag Bingo, Spring Concert and Theater Thursdays. **Sports:** There are 8 intercollegiate sports for men and 7 for women, and 5 intramural sports for men and 5 for women. Facilities include two gyms (main Peter Jay Sharp Athletic and Recreation Center and a smaller upstairs gym in the same building), a weight room, a dance studio, a recreation room, a fitness center with aerobic and Nautilus facilities, basketball court, and squash.

SERVICES: Counseling and information services are available, as is tutoring in most subjects, computer science, math, chemistry, biology, languages, psychology, sociology, writing, and economics. There is a reader service for the blind, and remedial math, reading, and writing. **Library/Resources:** The library contains 129,000 volumes, 7,000 microform items, 6,500 audio/video tapes/CDs/DVDs, and subscribes to 234 periodicals including electronic. Computerized library services include interlibrary loans, database searching, and Internet access. Special learning facilities include a radio station and TV station. **Physically Challenged Students:** 90% of the campus is accessible. Facilities include wheelchair ramps, elevators, special parking, specially equipped restrooms, lowered drinking fountains, and lowered telephones. **Special:** Cross-registration with Manhattan College offers cooperative B.A. programs in international studies, philosophy, phys ed, physics, religious studies, and urban affairs. Internships, work-study, study abroad in 6 countries, a 3-2 engineering degree with Manhattan College, dual majors, and student-designed majors in liberal arts are available. B.A.-B.S. degrees in computer science, health education, math, and psychology, and teacher dual certification programs with special education and elementary, middle school, and secondary education are possible. There are 15 national honor societies, a freshman honors program, and 5 departmental honors programs. **Visiting:** There are regularly scheduled orientations for prospective students, Upon request, students may have an interview with an admissions counselor, sit in on classes, and tour the campus. All students are invited to an open house. Accepted students may have a one-on-one meeting with a student on campus. There are guides for informal visits, visitors may sit in on classes, and stay overnight. To schedule a visit, contact the Admissions Office. **Campus Safety and Security:** Measures include 24-hour foot and vehicle patrol and security escort services. There are shuttle buses, emergency telephones, lighted pathways/sidewalks, a college committee on safety and security on campus.

REQUIREMENTS: The SAT or ACT is required. Applicants should have completed 4 high school academic units of English, 3 of science, and 2 each of math, foreign language, and social sciences, as well as electives. An essay is required, and an interview is recommended. One letter of recommendation is required, and additional letters are encouraged. AP and CLEP credits are accepted. Important factors in the admissions decision are advanced placement or honors courses, recommendations by school officials, and extracurricular activities record.All students must complete a 49-credit core curriculum with courses in humanities, social sciences, math and computers, and natural sciences. A total of 120 credits for a B.A. or 126 credits for a B.S., with a minimum of 30 credits in the major, and a minimum GPA of 2.0 are required. **Procedure:** Freshmen are admitted fall and spring. Entrance exams should be taken during the junior year and/or fall of the senior year. There are early admissions and rolling admissions plans. Early decision applications should be filed by November 15; regular applications, by April 2 for fall entry. The fall 2014 application fee was $35. Notification is sent on a rolling basis. Applications are accepted on-line. **Transfer Students:** Transfer applicants should have a minimum GPA of 2.0. Those majoring in nursing, the sciences, math, or computer science need at least a 2.5 GPA. An interview is recommended. 45 of 120 credits required for the bachelor's degree must be completed at The Mount. **International Students:** The school actively recruits these students. They must take the TOEFL, or complete ELS Level 109, available on campus. They must also take the SAT or ACT, scoring 900.

ADMISSIONS: Timothy P. Nash, Dean of Admission and Financial Aid. E-Mail: *admissns@mountsaintvincent.edu* Web: *www.cmsv.edu*

FINANCIAL AID: The Mount is a member of CSS. The FAFSA, and the TAP application for New York state residents is required. Check with the school for current application deadlines.

COLLEGE OF NEW ROCHELLE   **D-5**
www.cnr.edu

New Rochelle, NY 10805	(914) 654-5452
	(800) 933-5923
Fax: (914) 654-5464	Email: sdecker@cnr.edu
Full-time: 25 men, 605 women	Faculty: n/av
Part-time: 60 men, 335 women	Ph.D.s: n/av
Graduate: 105 men, 930 women	Student/Faculty: n/av
Year: semesters, summer session	Tuition: $24,600
Room & Board: $9000	Freshman Class: n/av
SAT: required	CEEB CODE: 2089
Application Deadline: August 15	VERY COMPETITIVE

The College of New Rochelle was founded in 1904 by the Ursuline order as the first Catholic college for women in New York State. Now independent, there are 3 undergraduate schools. The School of Arts and Sciences offers liberal arts baccalaureate education for women only and the School of Nursing is coeducational. The figures in the above profile and in this capsule are approximate. There are 3 undergraduate schools and 1 graduate school. In addition to regional accreditation, CNR has baccalaureate program accreditation with CSWE, NLN, and CCNE. The 20-acre campus is in a suburban area 12 miles north of New York City. Including any residence halls, there are 20 buildings.

STUDENT LIFE: 87% of undergraduates are from New York. Others are from 17 states, and 10 foreign countries. 73% are from public schools. 52% are African American; 22% Hispanic; 18% White. 77% are Catholic; 18% Protestant. The average age of freshmen is 20; all undergraduates, 27. 29% do not continue beyond their first year; 71%

remain to graduate. **Housing:** 410 students can be accommodated in college housing, which includes single-sex dorms. On-campus housing is guaranteed for all 4 years. 56% of students live on campus; of those, 50% remain on campus on weekends. All students may keep cars.

FACULTY/CLASSROOMS: 25% of faculty are male; 75% are female. All teach and do research. No introductory courses are taught by graduate students. The average class size in an introductory lecture is 25; in a laboratory is 10; and in a regular course is 15.

PROGRAMS OF STUDY: CNR confers B.A., B.S., B.F.A. and B.S.N. degrees. Master's degrees are also awarded. Bachelor's degrees are awarded in AGRICULTURE (environmental studies), BIOLOGICAL SCIENCE (biology/biological science), BUSINESS (business administration and management), COMMUNICATIONS AND THE ARTS (art history and appreciation, classics, communications, English, French, and Spanish), COMPUTER AND PHYSICAL SCIENCE (chemistry and mathematics), EDUCATION (art education), HEALTH PROFESSIONS (art therapy and nursing), SOCIAL SCIENCE (economics, history, international studies, philosophy, political science/government, psychology, religion, social work, sociology, and women's studies). Nursing, art, and psychology have the largest enrollments.

ACTIVITIES: There are no fraternities or sororities. There are 18 groups on campus, including art, cheerleading, choir, chorus, drama, environmental, ethnic, film, honors, international, literary magazine, musical theater, newspaper, photography, political, professional, religious, social, social service, and student government. Popular campus events include Junior Celebration, Family Weekend, and Strawberry Festival. **Sports:** There are 6 intercollegiate sports for women. Facilities include a fitness center and tennis courts. **Graduates:** From July 1, 2013 to June 30, 2014, 241 bachelor's degrees were awarded. The most popular majors were nursing (67%), psychology (9%), and commercial arts (4%). 27 companies recruited on campus in 2013-2014. In an average class, 50% graduate in 4 years or less, 51% graduate in 5 years or less, and 52% graduate in 6 years or less. Of the 2013 graduating class, 20% were enrolled in graduate school within 6 months of graduation, and 60% were employed.

SERVICES: Counseling and information services are available, as is tutoring in some subjects, science, languages There is remedial math, reading, and writing. Individual counseling and educational workshops about self-development and personal concerns are available, as are self-help materials. **Library/Resources:** The library contains 224,000 volumes, 277 microform items, 5,700 audio/video tapes/CDs/DVDs, and subscribes to 1,432 periodicals including electronic. Computerized library services include interlibrary loans, database searching, and Internet access. Special learning facilities include an art gallery, a Learning Center for Nursing. **Physically Challenged Students:** 50% of the campus is accessible. Facilities include wheelchair ramps, elevators, special parking, specially equipped restrooms, and special class scheduling. **Special:** CNR provides cooperative programs in all disciplines, work-study programs, dual majors in all majors, interdisciplinary studies, an accelerated degree program in nursing, a Washington semester, internships, study abroad in 9 countries, non-degree study, pass/fail options, student-designed majors, and a general studies degree. There are 1 national honor society and a freshman honors program. **Visiting:** There are regularly scheduled orientations for prospective students, including several open houses providing information on admission. There are guides for informal visits, visitors may sit in on classes, and stay overnight. To schedule a visit, contact the Office of Admissions. **Campus Safety and Security:** Measures include 24-hour foot and vehicle patrol, self-defense education, and security escort services. There are shuttle buses, emergency telephones, lighted pathways/sidewalks, card access to dorms, and surveillance cameras.

REQUIREMENTS: The SAT is required. Graduation from an accredited secondary school is required. The GED is accepted. Applicants must have completed 15 academic credits, with 4 in English, 3 each in math, science, and social studies, and 2 in a foreign language. A portfolio is required for art majors. An essay and interview are recommended. AP and CLEP credits are accepted. Important factors in the admissions decision are advanced placement or honors courses, recommendations by school officials, and leadership record.Students must complete 120 credit hours, 60 to 90 in liberal arts courses, depending on the major, meet specific course distribution requirements, and maintain a minimum GPA of 2.0 to graduate. 4 phys ed courses are also required. **Procedure:** Freshmen are admitted to all sessions. Entrance exams should be taken in the junior year or fall of the senior year. There are early decision, early admissions, deferred admissions, and rolling admissions plans. Early decision applications should be filed by November 1; regular applications, by August 15 for fall entry; and January 10 for spring entry. The fall 2014 application fee was $20. Notification of early decision is sent December 15; regular decision, on a rolling basis. **Transfer Students:** 68 transfer students enrolled in 2013-2014. Transfer students must submit a transcript from their previous college showing courses completed and a minimum GPA of 2.0. High school records and SAT scores are required. An interview is recommended. 30 of 120 credits required for the bachelor's degree must be completed at CNR. **International Students:** They must take the TOEFL, or the ESL Language Test. They must also take the SAT or ACT, the SAT is preferred.

ADMISSIONS: Stephanie Decker, Director of Admission. E-Mail: *sdecker@cnr.edu* Web: *www.cnr.edu*

FINANCIAL AID: The FAFSA, CCS/Profile, or FAFSA, or FFS, or SFS, and the college's own financial statement, and income documentation are required. Check with the school for current application deadlines.

COLLEGE OF SAINT ROSE — D-3
www.strose.edu

Albany, NY 12203

(518) 454-5150
(800) 637-8556

Fax: (518) 454-2013

Email: admit@strose.edu

Full-time: 887 men, 1777 women
Faculty: 209

Part-time: 82 men, 145 women
Ph.D.s: 96%

Graduate: 377 men, 1036 women
Student/Faculty: 13 to 1

Year: semesters, summer session
Tuition: $27,684

Room & Board: $11,250
Freshman Class: 4651 applied, 3605 accepted, 621 enrolled

SAT CR/M: 520/520 ACT: 23
CEEB CODE: 2091

Application Deadline: February 1
COMPETITIVE

The College of Saint Rose offers students the benefits of an urban environment as well as a close-knit campus community. The College offers 70 undergraduate majors and 52 graduate programs through its four schools: School of Arts and Humanities, School of Business, School of Education, and School of Mathematics and Sciences. Saint Rose is distinguished by its rigorous academics taught in a highly personal learning environment in state-of-the-art facilities. There are 4 undergraduate schools and 4 graduate schools. In addition to regional accreditation, College of Saint Rose has baccalaureate program accreditation with ACBSP, ASLA, CSWE, NASAD, NASM, NCATE, and NASP. The 49-acre campus is in an urban area in the Capital Region of New York State. Including any residence halls, there are 88 buildings.

STUDENT LIFE: 88% of undergraduates are from New York. Others are from 29 states, 22 foreign countries, and Canada. 72% are White. The average age of freshmen is 18; all undergraduates, 21. 25% do not continue beyond their first year; 66% remain to graduate. **Housing:** 1408 students can be accommodated in college housing, which includes single-sex and coed dorms and on-campus apartments. Apartments for single students and special housing for disabled students are also available. On-campus housing is guaranteed for all 4 years, is available on a first-come, first-served basis, and is available on a lottery system for upperclassmen. 56% of students commute. Upperclassmen may keep cars.

FACULTY/CLASSROOMS: 44% of faculty are male; 56% are female. All teach and do research. No introductory courses are taught by graduate students. The average class size in an introductory lecture is 19; in a laboratory is 18; and in a regular course is 13.

PROGRAMS OF STUDY: College of Saint Rose confers B.A., B.S. and B.F.A. degrees. Master's degrees are also awarded. Bachelor's degrees are awarded in BIOLOGICAL SCIENCE (biochemistry, bioinformatics, biology/adolescence education, biology/biological science, forensic psychology, and forensic science), BUSINESS (accounting and business administration and management), COMMUNICATIONS AND THE ARTS (communications, English, graphic design, information technology, music, music industry, Spanish, spanish / adolescence education, and studio art), COMPUTER AND PHYSICAL SCIENCE (chemistry, chemistry/adolescence education, computer science, earth science / adolescence education, geology, and mathematics), EDUCATION (art education, childhood education: 1-6, early childhood education, English education, mathematics education, music education, science education, social studies secondary school education, and special education), HEALTH PROFESSIONS (cytotechnology and medical technology), SOCIAL SCIENCE (American studies, communication sciences and disorders, criminal justice, economics, history, interdisciplinary studies, law, philosophy, political science/government, psychology, religion, social work, sociology, and women & gender studies). Communication sciences and disorders, art, music, education, and business administration are the strongest academically. Business administration, communications, special education/ childhood education, communication sciences and disorders have the largest enrollments.

ACTIVITIES: There are no fraternities or sororities. There are 33 groups on campus, including Habitat for Humanity, Geology Club, Girls for God (G4G), Student Events Board, Adventure Club, band, cheerleading, chorale, dance, drama, environmental, ethnic, international, jazz band, literary magazine, musical theater, newspaper, pep band, political, professional, radio and TV, religious, social, social service, student government, symphony, and yearbook. Popular campus events include Harvest Fest, Rose Rock Music Festival, Midnight Madnes and Dodgeball Madness. **Sports:** There are 9 intercollegiate sports for men and 9 for women, and 9 intramural sports for men and 9 for women. Facilities include Nolan Gym has 1 full sized basketball court, 2 smaller basketball courts, 1 full sized volleyball court, 2 smaller sized volleyball courts, 4 lane indoor pool, and fitness center. Plumeri Sports Complex has synthetic turf field lined for men's lacrosse and soccer, NCAA baseball field, NCAA softball field, and a practice field. **Graduates:** From July 1, 2013 to June 30, 2014, 613 bachelor's degrees were awarded. The most popular majors were childhood education (10%), business administration (10%), and special education (9%). 59 companies recruited on campus in 2013-2014. In an average class, 47% graduate in 4 years or less, 64% graduate in 5 years or less, and 66% graduate in 6 years or less. Of the 2013 graduating class, 50% were enrolled in graduate school within 6 months of graduation, and 70% were employed.

SERVICES: Counseling and information services are available, as is tutoring in every subject. There is a reader service for the blind, and remedial math, reading, and writing. There is also a full-time director of disabled student services. **Library/Resources:** The 3 libraries contain 224,616 volumes, 313,339 microform items, 5,010 audio/video tapes/CDs/DVDs, and subscribe to 562 periodicals including electronic. Computerized library services include interlibrary loans, database searching, Internet access, and Wi-Fi capability. Special learning facilities include an art gallery, internship office, entrepreneurship center, TV and radio studios, music recording studio, performance venue, music/video editing computer labs, recital hall, rehearsal rooms, and labs for geology, biology, chemistry, computer science and neuro-psychology. **Physically Challenged Students:** 71% of the campus is accessible. Facilities include wheelchair ramps, elevators, special parking, specially equipped restrooms, lowered drinking fountains, lowered telephones, special housing. **Special:** CSR offers cross-registration with several local colleges, internships, work-study programs, study abroad in several countries, dual and student-designed majors, non-degree study, and pass/fail options. There are 3-2 engineering degree programs with Alfred and Clarkson Universities, Union College, and Rensselaer Polytechnic University, as well as a 6-year law program with Albany Law School. There are 14 national honor societies and 11 departmental honors programs. **Visiting:** There are regularly scheduled orientations for prospective students, tours begin at 8:30 a.m. followed by a formal presentation at 10:00 a.m. Tours of specific facilities and faculty presentations follow morning events. There are guides for informal visits, visitors may sit in on classes, and stay overnight. To schedule a visit, contact the

Undergraduate Admissions. <u>Campus Safety and Security:</u> Measures include 24-hour foot and vehicle patrol, emergency notification system, and security escort services. There are shuttle buses, emergency telephones, lighted pathways/sidewalks, and controlled access to dorms/residences.

<u>REQUIREMENTS:</u> The SAT or ACT is recommended. Applicants must be graduates of an accredited secondary school or have a GED certificate. They should have completed college preparatory programs including 4 years of English and history, and 3 years of math, science, and foreign language. All students must submit a letter of recommendation and an essay. Art students must submit portfolios, and music students must audition. AP and CLEP credits are accepted. Important factors in the admissions decision are advanced placement or honors courses, extracurricular activities record, and leadership record. To graduate, students must complete 122 credits with a minimum GPA of 2.0 overall and in the major; these requirements are higher for certain majors. Liberal education requirements consist of 4 credits in college writing and speech and 30 credits in the humanities, science and math, social science and business, English, computer literacy, foreign languages, history, philosophy, and the arts. Students must also complete 2 credits in physical education. <u>Procedure:</u> Freshmen are admitted fall and spring. Entrance exams should be taken during the spring of junior year or the fall of senior year. There are early admissions, deferred admissions, and rolling admissions plans. Early decision applications should be filed by December 1; regular applications, by February 1 for fall entry; and December 1 for spring entry, along with a $40 fee. Notification is sent on a Rolling basis. Applications are accepted on-line. <u>Transfer Students:</u> 248 transfer students enrolled in 2013-2014. Applicants must submit official transcripts from all colleges attended, a letter of recommendation, and an essay of the reasons for seeking transfer. An interview is recommended. Art majors must submit a portfolio, and music majors must audition. The minimum overall college GPA is a 2.5. 60 of 122 credits required for the bachelor's degree must be completed at College of Saint Rose. <u>International Students:</u> There are 35 international students enrolled. The school actively recruits these students. They must take the TOEFL with a minimum score of 80 on the paper-based TOEFL (PBT) or 82 on the Internet-based version (iBT), or take the IELTS . They must also take the SAT or ACT. Test-optional if students have alternate English proficiency (IB, A-levels, for example).

<u>ADMISSIONS:</u> 78% of the 2014-2015 applicants were accepted. The SAT scores for the 2014-2015 freshman class were: Critical Reading--37% below 500, 44% between 500 and 599, 17% between 600 and 699, and 2% between 700 and 800; Math--35% below 500, 47% between 500 and 599, 16% between 600 and 699, and 3% between 700 and 800. The ACT scores were 28% below 21, 23% between 21 and 23, 28% between 24 and 26, 11% between 27 and 28, and 11% above 28. 36% of the current freshmen were in the top fifth of their class; 68% were in the top two fifths. 1 freshman graduated first in the class. <u>Admissions Contact:</u> Jeremy Bogan, Assistant VP of Undergraduate Admissions. E-Mail: *admit@strose.edu* Web: *www.strose.edu*

<u>FINANCIAL AID:</u> In 2014-2015, 98% of all full-time freshmen and continuing full-time students received some form of financial aid. 95% of all full-time freshmen and 91% of continuing full-time students received need-based aid. The average freshman award was $23,415. Need-based scholarships or need-based grants averaged $11,730; need-based self-help aid (loans and jobs) averaged $3,963; non-need-based athletic scholarships averaged $15,545; and other non-need-based awards and non-need-based scholarships averaged $10,584. 70% of undergraduate students work part-time. Average annual earnings from campus work are $1700. The average financial indebtedness of the 2014 graduate was $25,780. College of Saint Rose is a member of CSS. The FAFSA is required. The priority date for freshman financial aid applications for fall entry is February 1. The deadline for filing freshman financial aid applications for fall entry is April 1.

COLLEGE OF STATEN ISLAND/THE CITY OF NEW YOK (*The complete profile is made available exclusively on our website, www. barronspac.com*)

COLUMBIA UNIVERSITY SYSTEM

The Columbia University System, established in 1754, is a public system in New York. It is governed by a board of trustees, whose chief administrator is the president. The primary goal of the system is teaching and research. The main priorities are providing outstanding undergraduate instruction; conducting research to develop new knowledge and methods; and training of professionals in law, business, social work, and medicine. The total student enrollment is usually about 29,200 with 2500 faculty members. Altogether there are 110 baccalaureate, 159 master's, and 79 doctoral programs offered in the Columbia University System. Profiles of the 4-year campuses are included in this section.

COLUMBIA UNIVERSITY/CITY OF NEW YORK	D-5
www.columbia.edu	

New York, NY 10027	(212) 854-2522
	n/av
Fax: (212) 854-1209	Email: ugrad-ask@columbia.edu
Full-time: 3174 men, 2910 women	Faculty: I, ++$
Part-time: n/av	Ph.D.s: n/av
Graduate: n/av	Student/Faculty: 6 to 1
Year: semesters, summer session	Tuition: $49,138
Room & Board: $11,978	Freshman Class: 33531 applied, 2131 accepted, 1416 enrolled
SAT CR/M/W: 740/750/750 ACT: 33	CEEB CODE: 2116
Application Deadline: January 1	MOST COMPETITIVE

Columbia University in the City of New York was founded in 1754. 4,500 undergraduates study liberal arts and science programs in Columbia College and 1,500 major in The Fu Foundation School of Engineering and Applied Science. Students also have access to our more than a dozen graduate and professional schools, a traditional college campus in the neighborhood of Morningside Heights, and all that New York City has to offer professionally, socially, and culturally. The figures in the above capsule and in this profile are approximate. The 36-acre campus is in an urban area in New York City. Including any residence halls, there are 50 buildings.

<u>STUDENT LIFE:</u> 77% of undergraduates are from out of state, mostly the Middle Atlantic. Students are from 50 states, 90 foreign countries, and Canada. 36% are White; 22% Asian American; 13% Hispanic; 13% Foreign; 11% African American. <u>Male To Female Ratio:</u> 0.9:1. The average age of freshmen is 18; all undergraduates, 20. 1% do not continue beyond their first year; 99% remain to graduate. <u>Housing:</u> 5606 students can be accommodated in college housing, which includes single-sex and coed dorms and on-campus apartments. In addition, there are language houses, special-interest houses, and fraternity houses. On-campus housing is guaranteed for all 4 years and is available on a lottery system for upperclassmen. 94% of students live on campus. All students may keep cars.

<u>FACULTY/CLASSROOMS:</u> All teach and do research. No introductory courses are taught by graduate students.

<u>PROGRAMS OF STUDY:</u> Columbia confers B.A., and B.S. degrees. Master's and Doctoral degrees are also awarded. Bachelor's degrees are awarded in BIOLOGICAL SCIENCE (biochemistry, biology/biological science, biophysics, environmental biology, and neurosciences), BUSINESS (operations research), COMMUNICATIONS AND THE ARTS (art history and appreciation, classics, comparative literature, dance, dramatic arts, English, film arts, French, German, Germanic languages and literature, Greek, Latin, linguistics, music, Russian, Spanish, and visual and performing arts), COMPUTER AND PHYSICAL SCIENCE (applied mathematics, applied physics, astronomy, astrophysics, chemistry, computer science, earth science, geochemistry, geology, geophysics and seismology, mathematics, physics, and statistics), EDUCATION (education), ENGINEERING AND ENVIRONMENTAL DESIGN (architecture, biomedical engineering, chemical engineering, civil engineering, computer engineering, electrical/electronics engineering, engineering management, engineering mechanics, environmental science, industrial engineering technology, materials science, mechanical engineering, metallurgical engineering, and mining and mineral engineering), SOCIAL

SCIENCE (African American studies, American studies, anthropology, archeology, area studies, Asian/American studies, classical/ancient civilization, East Asian studies, economics, Hispanic American studies, history, Italian studies, Latin American studies, medieval studies, Middle Eastern studies, philosophy, political science/government, psychology, religion, Russian and Slavic studies, sociology, urban studies, and women's studies). Political science, economics, engineering, history, English, psychology have the largest enrollments.

ACTIVITIES: 19% of men belong to 22 national fraternities; 9% of women belong to 11 national sororities. There are 500 groups on campus, including art, band, cheerleading, chess, choir, chorale, chorus, communications, computers, dance, debate, drama, environmental, ethnic, film, forensics, gay, honors, international, jazz band, literary magazine, marching band, musical theater, newspaper, opera, orchestra, pep band, photography, political, professional, radio and TV, religious, social, social service, student government, symphony, and yearbook. Popular campus events include New Student Orientation Program, Orgo Night, Bacchanal Spring Concert and Tree Lighting Ceremony/Yule Log. **Sports:** There are 14 intercollegiate sports for men and 15 for women, and 20 intramural sports for men and 20 for women. Facilities include a football stadium, indoor and outdoor track and field facilities, a baseball field, a soccer stadium, a recreational gym with a swimming pool, basketball/volleyball courts, aerobic, fencing, wrestling, martial arts, and weight rooms, a boat house, and tennis, squash, handball, and racquetball courts. **Graduates:** From July 1, 2013 to June 30, 2014, 1580 bachelor's degrees were awarded. The most popular majors were social sciences (22%), engineering (21%), and biological/life sciences (10%). 370 companies recruited on campus in 2013-2014. In an average class, 89% graduate in 4 years or less, 94% graduate in 5 years or less, and 96% graduate in 6 years or less.

SERVICES: Counseling and information services are available, as is tutoring in every subject. There is a reader service for the blind. **Library/Resources:** The 22 libraries contain 12.0 million volumes. Computerized library services include interlibrary loans, database searching, Internet access, and Wi-Fi capability. Special learning facilities include an art gallery, planetarium, radio station, TV station, an observatory. **Physically Challenged Students:** All of the campus is accessible. Facilities include wheelchair ramps, elevators, special parking, specially equipped restrooms, special class scheduling, lowered drinking fountains, lowered telephones, special housing. **Special:** There are study abroad programs at more than 200 locations, including France, Oxford, Cambridge,Universities in England, and the Kyoto Center for Japanese Studies in Japan, and Biosphere 2 (Arizona). Cross-registration is possible with the Juilliard School and Barnard College. Combined B.A.-B.S. degrees are offered via 3-2 or 4-1 engineering programs. A 3-2 engineering degree is offered with Columbia's Fu Foundation School of Engineering and Applied Science. There is also a 5-year B.A./M.I.A. with Columbia's School of International and Public Affairs. The college offers work-study, internships, credit by exam, pass/fail options, and dual, student-designed, and interdisciplinary majors, including regional studies and ancient studies. There is a Phi Beta Kappa chapter. **Visiting:** There are regularly scheduled orientations for prospective students, consisting of group information sessions and student-led tours as well as special science tours and engineering tours. There are guides for informal visits, visitors may sit in on classes, and stay overnight. To schedule a visit, contact the Visitors Center at (212) 854-4900. **Campus Safety and Security:** Measures include 24-hour foot and vehicle patrol, emergency notification system, self-defense education, and security escort services. There are shuttle buses, emergency telephones, lighted pathways/sidewalks, and controlled access to dorms/residences.

REQUIREMENTS: The SAT or ACT is required. The ACT Optional Writing test is also required. The admissions application consists of the Common Application and Columbia Supplement; HS transcript; SAT and 2 SAT Subject Tests or ACT with Writing; 3 letters of reference; and an essay. AP credits are accepted. All students complete a core curriculum consisting of classes in Western and non-Western cultures, literature and philosophy, history, social science, art, sculpture and architecture, and music of the Western tradition and science; 2 courses in non-Western areas are also required. Distribution

requirements include 2 years of foreign language (unless competency can be demonstrated), 2 semesters of science, 1 year of phys ed, and 1 semester of writing. A thesis may be required for departmental honors in certain departments. A total of 124 credit hours is required; usually 30 to 40 of these are in the major. The engineering students are required to take calculus, physics, chemistry and economics and specific introductory engineering design courses in addition to half of the Columbia College core. The minimum required GPA is 2.0. **Procedure:** Freshmen are admitted fall. Entrance exams should be taken by Jan. of the senior year (RD) or Nov. (if ED). There are early decision and deferred admissions plans. Early decision applications should be filed by November 1; regular applications, by January 1 for fall entry, along with a $85 fee. Notification of early decision is sent December 15; regular decision, April 1. Applications are accepted online. **Transfer Students:** 123 transfer students enrolled in 2013-2014. Applicants must have completed 1 full year of college (24 credits). They must submit high school and college transcripts. 60 of 128 credits required for the bachelor's degree must be completed at Columbia. **International Students:** The school actively recruits these students. They must take the TOEFL with a minimum score of 100 on the Internet-based version (iBT), or take the IELTS. They must also take the SAT or ACT.

ADMISSIONS: 6% of the 2014-2015 applicants were accepted. The SAT scores for the 2014-2015 freshman class were: Critical Reading--3% between 500 and 599, 21% between 600 and 699, and 76% between 700 and 800; Math--2% between 500 and 599, 20% between 600 and 699, and 78% between 700 and 800; Writing--2% between 500 and 599, 24% between 600 and 699, and 74% between 700 and 800. The ACT scores were 10% between 27 and 28, and 90% above 28. **Admissions Contact:** Admissions Officer, Office of Undergraduate Admissions. E-Mail: *ugrad-ask@columbia.edu* Web: *undergrad.admissions.columbia.edu*

FINANCIAL AID: In 2014-2015, 51% of all full-time freshmen and 52% of continuing full-time students received some form of financial aid. 49% of all full-time freshmen and 50% of continuing full-time students received need-based aid. The average freshman award was $43,087. Need-based scholarships or need-based grants averaged $42,785 and need-based self-help aid (loans and jobs) averaged $2,263. Columbia is a member of CSS. The CSS/Profile, FAFSA, and the college's own financial statement, and federal tax returns, the business/farm supplement, and/or the divorced/separated parents statement, if applicable, are required. are required. The deadline for filing freshman financial aid applications for fall entry is March 1.

COLUMBIA UNIVERSITY/SCHOOL OF GENERAL STUDIES　　　D-5
www.gs.columbia.edu

New York, NY 10027	**(212) 854-2772**
	(800) 895-1169
Fax: (212) 854-6316	**Email:** gsdegree@columbia.edu
Full-time: 813 men, 532 women	**Faculty:** 1823
Part-time: 206 men, 212 women	**Ph.D.s:** 100%
Graduate: n/av	**Student/Faculty:** 6 to 1
Year: semesters, summer session	**Tuition:** $47,781
Room & Board: $10,450	**Freshman Class:** n/av
SAT or ACT: recommended	**CEEB CODE:** 2095
Application Deadline: June 1	**MOST COMPETITIVE**

The School of General Studies of Columbia University is a liberal arts college created specifically for returning and nontraditional students seeking a rigorous, traditional, Ivy League undergraduate degree full- or part-time. GS is also home to the oldest and largest Postbaccalaureate Premedical program in the United States, the Joint program with Jewish Theological Seminary, and the Dual BA program between Columbia University and the Sciences. The figures in the above capsule and in this profile are approximate. There are 3 undergraduate schools and 14 graduate schools. The 36-acre campus is in an urban area on the upper west side of Manhattan in New York City.

STUDENT LIFE: 68% of undergraduates are from New York. Others are from states, 62 foreign countries, and Canada. 50% are White;

17% Foreign; 11% Hispanic. **Male To Female Ratio:** 0.7:1. The average age of freshmen is 20; all undergraduates, 28. **Housing:** 645 students can be accommodated in college housing, which includes single-sex and coed off-campus apartments and married student housing. In addition, there are special-interest houses, fraternity houses, an international house. On-campus housing is available on a first-come and first-served basis. Priority is given to out-of-town students. 74% of students commute. Alcohol is not permitted. No one may keep cars.

FACULTY/CLASSROOMS: 66% of faculty are male; 34% are female. No introductory courses are taught by graduate students.

PROGRAMS OF STUDY: GS confers B.A. degrees. Bachelor's degrees are awarded in BIOLOGICAL SCIENCE (biology/biological science), COMMUNICATIONS AND THE ARTS (art history and appreciation, classics, comparative literature, dance, dramatic arts, English literature, film arts, French, German, Italian, literature, music, Slavic languages, Spanish, and visual and performing arts), COMPUTER AND PHYSICAL SCIENCE (applied mathematics, astronomy, chemistry, computer science, geoscience, mathematics, physics, and statistics), ENGINEERING AND ENVIRONMENTAL DESIGN (architecture and environmental science), SOCIAL SCIENCE (African American studies, anthropology, archeology, classical/ancient civilization, East Asian studies, economics, French studies, German area studies, Hispanic American studies, history, Italian studies, Latin American studies, Middle Eastern studies, philosophy, political science/government, psychology, religion, sociology, urban studies, and women's studies). Political science, economics, and English have the largest enrollments.

ACTIVITIES: 1% of men belong to 17 national fraternities; 1% of women belong to 10 national sororities. There are 541 groups on campus, including and women's, art, band, cheerleading, chess, choir, chorale, chorus, computers, dance, debate, drama, environmental, ethnic, film, gay, honors, international, jazz band, literary magazine, marching band, musical theater, newspaper, opera, orchestra, photography, political, professional, radio and TV, religious, social, social service, student government, symphony, writers, and yearbook. **Sports:** There are 14 intercollegiate sports for men and 15 for women, and 9 intramural sports for men and 9 for women. Facilities include 2 gyms, a swimming pool, tennis, squash, and racquetball courts, a training center, 2 dance/martial arts studios, a fencing room, a wrestling room, and an indoor track. **Graduates:** From July 1, 2013 to June 30, 2014, 374 bachelor's degrees were awarded. The most popular majors were economics, political science, and history. 300 companies recruited on campus in 2013-2014.

SERVICES: Counseling and information services are available, as is tutoring in some subjects, English composition, math, languages, and sciences. **Library/Resources:** The 22 libraries contain 1.0 million volumes, 6.4 million microform items, 156,717 audio/video tapes/CDs/DVDs, and subscribe to 144,787 periodicals including electronic. Computerized library services include interlibrary loans, database searching, Internet access, and Wi-Fi capability. Special learning facilities include an art gallery, planetarium, radio station, and TV station. **Physically Challenged Students:** All of the campus is accessible. Facilities include wheelchair ramps, elevators, specially equipped restrooms, lowered drinking fountains, and lowered telephones. **Special:** Pre-professional studies in allied health and medical fields and interdisciplinary majors, minors, and concentrations are offered. Internships in New York City, work-study programs on campus, study abroad, a 3-2 engineering degree at Columbia University School of Engineering and Applied Science, and dual majors are available. There is a Phi Beta Kappa chapter. **Visiting:** There are regularly scheduled orientations for prospective students, consisting of an admissions information session every other Wednesday, preceded by a campus tour. There are guides for informal visits and visitors may sit in on classes. To schedule a visit, contact the Office of Admissions and Financial Aid. **Campus Safety and Security:** Measures include 24-hour foot and vehicle patrol, emergency notification system, self-defense education, and security escort services. There are shuttle buses, emergency telephones, and lighted pathways/sidewalks.

REQUIREMENTS: SAT, ACT, or Columbia's General Studies Admissions Exam scores should be submitted along with high school and all college transcripts. An autobiographical statement is required. An interview is encouraged. AP credits are accepted. Important fac-

tors in the admissions decision are personality/intangible qualities, extracurricular activities record, and evidence of special talent. All students must complete 124 credit hours, including 56 distribution requirement credits in literature, humanities, foreign language or literature, social science, science, and global studies. At least 64 of the 124 credit hours required to graduate must be completed at Columbia University. Proficiency in English composition and math is required. A GPA of 2.0 is necessary to graduate. **Procedure:** Freshmen are admitted fall, spring, and summer. Entrance exams should be taken as early as possible. There are deferred admissions and rolling admissions plans. Early decision applications should be filed by March 1; regular applications, by June 1 for fall entry; November 1 for spring entry; and April 1 for summer entry, along with a $80 fee. Notification of early decision is sent May 1; regular decision, July 30. applicants were on the 2014 waiting list; were admitted. Applications are accepted on-line. **Transfer Students:** 451 transfer students enrolled in 2013-2014. Most students come to GS with some college credit. 64 of 124 credits required for the bachelor's degree must be completed at GS. **International Students:** There are 225 international students enrolled. The school actively recruits these students. They must take the TOEFL with a minimum score of 600 on the paper-based TOEFL (PBT) or 100 on the Internet-based version (iBT) and the college's own test, International students must take either the TOEFL or an English placement test administered by Columbia's American Language Program. They must also take the SAT or ACT, and the college's own entrance exam. Submission of recent SAT scores is encouraged. Students with no scores must take the General Studies Admissions Exam.

ADMISSIONS: Curtis Rodgers, Dean of Admissions. E-Mail: *gsdegree@columbia.edu* Web: *www.gs.columbia.edu*

FINANCIAL AID: The average freshman award was $8,000. 75% of undergraduate students work part-time. Average annual earnings from campus work are $2500. GS is a member of CSS. The FAFSA and the college's own financial statement are required. The priority date for freshman financial aid applications for fall entry is March 1. The deadline for filing freshman financial aid applications for fall entry is June 1.

CONCORDIA COLLEGE - NEW YORK (*The complete profile is made available exclusively on our website, www.barronspac.com*)

COOPER UNION FOR THE ADVANCEMENT OF SCIENCE AND ART www.cooper.edu	**D-5**
New York, NY 10003	**(212) 353-4120** n/av
Fax: (212) 353-4342	**Email:** admissions@cooper.edu
Full-time: 556 men, 307 women	**Faculty:** 50; IIB, ++$
Part-time: 1 men, 4 women	**Ph.D.s:** 90%
Graduate: 36 men, 16 women	**Student/Faculty:** 17 to 1
Year: semesters, summer session	**Tuition:** $39,600
Room & Board: $15,000	**Freshman Class:** 3193 applied, 247 accepted, 186 enrolled
SAT CR/M: 650/730 **ACT:** 31	**CEEB CODE:** 2097
Application Deadline: January 1	**MOST COMPETITIVE**

The Cooper Union for the Advancement of Science and Art. It offers degrees in architecture, art, and engineering. Starting in the Fall of 2014, new students will receive a half-tuition scholarship plus additional financial aid to help offset the costs of attendance. There are 3 undergraduate schools and 1 graduate school. In addition to regional accreditation, Cooper Union has baccalaureate program accreditation with ABET, NAAB, and NASAD. The campus is in an urban area in New York City. Including any residence halls, there are 4 buildings.

STUDENT LIFE: 55% of undergraduates are from New York. Others are from 39 states, 14 foreign countries, and Canada. 70% are from public schools. 37% are White; 19% Asian American; 14% race unknown. **Male To Female Ratio:** 0.6:1. The average age of freshmen is 18; all undergraduates, 20. 5% do not continue beyond their first year; 81% remain to graduate. **Housing:** 178 students can be accommodated in college housing, which includes coed dorms. On-campus housing is available on a first-come, first-served basis, and is available on a lottery system for upperclassmen. 80% of students commute. Some may keep cars.

FACULTY/CLASSROOMS: 73% of faculty are male; 27% are female. All teach and do research. No introductory courses are taught by graduate students. The average class size in an introductory lecture is 25; in a laboratory is 16; and in a regular course is 20.

PROGRAMS OF STUDY: Cooper Union confers B.S., B.Arch., B.E. and B.F.A. degrees. Master's degrees are also awarded. Bachelor's degrees are awarded in COMMUNICATIONS AND THE ARTS (fine arts and graphic design), ENGINEERING AND ENVIRONMENTAL DESIGN (architecture, chemical engineering, civil engineering, electrical/electronics engineering, engineering, and mechanical engineering). Architecture, fine art and engineering are the strongest academically. Engineering has the largest enrollment.

ACTIVITIES: 10% of men belong to 2 national fraternities. There are no sororities. There are 90 groups on campus, including art, band, chess, chorale, computers, dance, drama, environmental, ethnic, ethnic and musical, film, gay, honors, international, jazz band, literary magazine, musical theater, newspaper, orchestra, photography, political, professional, religious, social, social service, student government, and yearbook. Popular campus events include Annual Culture Show, Annual Talent Show, End-of-the-Year Student Art, Architecture and Engineering Exhibit and ongoing events in the Great Hall. **Sports:** There are 5 intercollegiate sports for men and 3 for women, and 12 intramural sports for men and 12 for women. Facilities include access to local gyms on weekends, a nearby swimming pool, and basketball courts. **Graduates:** From July 1, 2013 to June 30, 2014, 184 bachelor's degrees were awarded. The most popular majors were fine arts (30%), electrical engineering (16%), and mechanical engineering (15%). 110 companies recruited on campus in 2013-2014. In an average class, 1% graduate in 3 years or less, 70% graduate in 4 years or less, 81% graduate in 5 years or less, and 82% graduate in 6 years or less. Of the 2013 graduating class, 42% were enrolled in graduate school within 6 months of graduation, and 42% were employed.

SERVICES: Counseling and information services are available, as is tutoring in some subjects, math, physics, speech, writing, and other forms of communication. **Library/Resources:** The library contains 147,552 volumes, 24,217 microform items, 2,228 audio/video tapes/CDs/DVDs, and subscribes to 9,730 periodicals including electronic. Computerized library services include interlibrary loans, database searching, and Internet access. Special learning facilities include an art gallery, a center for speaking and writing, an electronic resources center, and a visual resources center. **Physically Challenged Students:** 80% of the campus is accessible. Facilities include wheelchair ramps, elevators, specially equipped restrooms, special class scheduling, and special housing. **Special:** Cross-registration with New School University, internships, formal study abroad for art and engineering students. Non-degree study is possible. An accelerated degree in engineering is also available (combined bachelors and masters degree program). Cooper Union also participates in a joint MEng/MD degree program with SUNY Downstate Medical Center. Students are permitted with approval, to take an elective leave to further pursue their interests and long term goals. There are 4 national honor societies and 1 departmental honors programs. **Visiting:** There are regularly scheduled orientations for prospective students, consisting of open house and portfolio review days for art and open house for engineering; architecture tours are by appointment. There are guides for informal visits and visitors may sit in on classes. To schedule a visit, contact the Office of Admissions and Records. **Campus Safety and Security:** Measures include emergency notification system. There are emergency telephones, lighted pathways/sidewalks, controlled access to dorms/residences, There are security guards in all building lobbies and hand-scan technology in the residence hall.

REQUIREMENTS: The SAT or ACT is required. Engineering applicants must take SAT Subject Tests in mathematics I or II and physics or chemistry. Graduation from an approved secondary school is required. Applicants should have completed 16 to 18 high school academic credits, depending on their major. An essay is part of the application process. Art students must submit a portfolio. Art and architecture applicants must complete a project called the home test. AP credits are accepted. Important factors in the admissions decision are personality/intangible qualities, evidence of special talent, and advanced placement or honors courses. The 5-year architecture program requires 160 credits, including 30 in liberal arts and electives, for graduation. Art students must complete 128 credits, including 38 in liberal arts and electives. Engineering students are required to complete a minimum of 135 credits, including a computer programming course and approximately 12-28 credits in humanities and social sciences, with a minimum GPA of 2.0. All students must complete a four semester sequence of humanities and social science courses. **Procedure:** Freshmen are admitted fall. Entrance exams should be taken before February 1. There are early decision, early admissions, and deferred admissions plans. Early decision applications should be filed by December 1; regular applications, by January 1 for fall entry, along with a $70 fee. Notification of early decision is sent February 1; regular decision, April 1. 75 early decision candidates were accepted for the 2014-2015 class. 75 applicants were on the 2014 waiting list; 15 were admitted. Applications are accepted on-line. **Transfer Students:** Art and architecture transfer applicants must present a portfolio and a minimum of 24 credits in studio classes. Engineering transfer applicants must submit a transcript with grades of B or better in at least 24 credits of appropriate courses. 68 of 128 credits required for the bachelor's degree must be completed at Cooper Union. **International Students:** There are 86 international students enrolled. They must take the TOEFL with a minimum score of 600 on the paper-based TOEFL (PBT) or 100 on the Internet-based version (iBT). They must also take the SAT or ACT, and the college's own entrance exam. All freshman applicants must take the SAT; art and architecture students must also take the home test.

ADMISSIONS: 8% of the 2014-2015 applicants were accepted. The SAT scores for the 2014-2015 freshman class were: Critical Reading--3% below 500, 19% between 500 and 599, 47% between 600 and 699, and 31% between 700 and 800; Math--9% below 500, 17% between 500 and 599, 18% between 600 and 699, and 57% between 700 and 800. The ACT scores were 25% between 27 and 28, and 75% above 28. 90% of the current freshmen were in the top fifth of their class; 95% were in the top two fifths. 10 freshmen graduated first in their class. **Admissions Contact:** Mitchell Lipton, Dean of Admissions and Records. E-Mail: *admissions@cooper.edu* Web: *http:/cooper.edu*

FINANCIAL AID: In 2014-2015, 100% of all full-time freshmen and 100% of continuing full-time students received some form of financial aid. 36% of all full-time freshmen and 35% of continuing full-time students received need-based aid. The average freshman award was $37,500. Need-based scholarships or need-based grants averaged $5,254 ($5,500 maximum); need-based self-help aid (loans and jobs) averaged $3,217 ($3,768 maximum); and other non-need-based awards and non-need-based scholarships averaged $37,500 ($37,500 maximum). 47% of undergraduate students work part-time. Cooper Union is a member of CSS. The CSS/Profile and FAFSA are required. The priority date for freshman financial aid applications for fall entry is April 15. The deadline for filing freshman financial aid applications for fall entry is May 1.

CORNELL UNIVERSITY   C-4
www.cornell.edu

Ithaca, NY 14850	(607) 255-5241
Fax: (607) 255-0659	**Email:** admissions@cornell.edu
Full-time: 7082 men, 7371 women	**Faculty:** n/av
Part-time: n/av	**Ph.D.s:** n/av
Graduate: 4148 men, 3249 women	**Student/Faculty:** n/av
Year: semesters, summer session	**Tuition:** $47,286
Room & Board: $13,678	**Freshman Class:** 43037 applied, 6105 accepted, 3225 enrolled
SAT or ACT: required	**CEEB CODE:** 2098
Application Deadline: January 2	**MOST COMPETITIVE**

Cornell University was founded in 1865 as the federal land-grant institution of New York State. It is a private endowed university, a member of the Ivy League/Ancient Eight, and a partner of the State University, 2 medical graduate and professional units in New York City, and 1 in Doha, Qatar. The Cornell NYC Tech Campus in New York City is the latest addition. There are 7 undergraduate schools and 4 graduate schools. In addition to regional accreditation, Cornell has baccalaureate program accreditation with AACSB, ABET, ASLA, NAAB, and CIDA. The 745-acre campus is in a rural area 60 miles south of Syracuse, NY. Including any residence halls, there are 613 buildings.

STUDENT LIFE: 68% of undergraduates are from out of state, mostly the Middle Atlantic. Students are from 50 states, 85 foreign countries, and Canada. 42% are White; 17% Asian American; 12% Hispanic. **Male To Female Ratio:** 0.9:1. The average age of freshmen is 18; all undergraduates, 20. 4% do not continue beyond their first year; 93% remain to graduate. **Housing:** 9187 students can be accommodated in college housing, which includes single-sex and coed dorms, on-campus apartments, and married student housing. In addition, there are language houses, special-interest houses, fraternity houses, and sorority houses. On-campus housing is available on a lottery system for upperclassmen. 55% of students live on campus; of those, 90% remain on campus on weekends. All students may keep cars.

FACULTY/CLASSROOMS: No introductory courses are taught by graduate students.

PROGRAMS OF STUDY: Cornell confers B.A., B.S., B.Arch. and B.F.A. degrees. Master's and Doctoral degrees are also awarded. Bachelor's degrees are awarded in AGRICULTURE (agricultural sciences, animal science, international agriculture/rural development, plant science, and viticulture and enology), BIOLOGICAL SCIENCE (biology/biological science, biology and society, biometrics and biostatistics, entomology, human biology, health, and society, and nutritional sciences), BUSINESS (applied economics / management, hotel and restaurant administration, industrial and labor relations, and policy analysis and management), COMMUNICATIONS AND THE ARTS (art history, classics, communication, comparative literature, design and environmental analysis, English, fiber science and apparel design, fine arts, French, German, Italian, linguistics, music, performing and media arts, and Spanish), COMPUTER AND PHYSICAL SCIENCE (astronomy, atmospheric science, chemistry / chemical biology, computer science, inform, science, systms and tech, information science, mathematics, physics, science of earth systems, science of natural and environmental systems, science and technology studies, and statistics), ENGINEERING AND ENVIRONMENTAL DESIGN (architecture, bioengineering, chemical engineering, civil engineering, electrical and computer engineering, engineering physics, environmental engineering, landscape architecture, materials science and engineering, mechanical engineering, and operations research and engineering), HEALTH PROFESSIONS (global and public health science, China/Asia-pacific studies, developmental sociology, economics, government, feminist, gender, sexuality studies, food science, German area studies, history, human development, Near Eastern studies, philosophy, psychology, religious studies, sociology, and urban and regional studies). Engineering, business, agriculture and life sciences have the largest enrollments.

ACTIVITIES: 27% of men belong to 2 local and 39 national fraternities; 23% of women belong to 20 national sororities. There are 1017 groups on campus, including art, band, cheerleading, chess, choir, chorale, chorus, communications, computers, dance, debate, drama, drill team, environmental, ethnic, film, forensics, gay, honors, international, jazz band, literary magazine, marching band, musical theater, newspaper, orchestra, pep band, photography, political, professional, radio and TV, religious, social, social service, student government, symphony, and yearbook. Popular campus events include Dragon Day, New Student Reading Project, and Third World Festival of the Arts. **Sports:** There are 18 intercollegiate sports for men and 19 for women, and 20 intramural sports for men and 20 for women. Facilities include Barton indoor and Robert J. Kane outdoor track, a 5000-seat indoor Newman Arena, 3 swimming pools, 25000-seat Schoellkopf football/lacrosse stadium, 16 intercollegiate fields, Helen Newman bowling alley, Jessup intramural fields, Collyer Boat House, Reis indoor and outdoor tennis courts, Merrill Sailing Center,

and the Lindseth climbing wall. **Graduates:** From July 1, 2013 to June 30, 2014, 3570 bachelor's degrees were awarded. The most popular majors were engineering (18%), business (14%), and biological/life sciences (14%). In an average class, 9% graduate in 3 years or less, 87% graduate in 4 years or less, 92% graduate in 5 years or less, and 93% graduate in 6 years or less.

SERVICES: Counseling and information services are available, as is tutoring in some subjects, many introductory courses in math, the sciences, and economics. There is a reader service for the blind. Biology and math student support centers, and writing workshops are also available. In addition, supplemental instruction in introductory math, chemistry, biology, economics, and physics courses are provided. **Library/Resources:** The 17 libraries contain 8.9 million volumes, 170,344 audio/video tapes/CDs/DVDs, and subscribe to 118,894 periodicals including electronic. Computerized library services include interlibrary loans, database searching, Internet access, and Wi-Fi capability. Special learning facilities include an art gallery, radio station, TV station, biotechnology institute, woods sanctuary, 4 designated national resource centers, 2 local optical observatories, Africana Studies and research center, arboretum, particle accelerator, supercomputers, national research centers, performing arts center, lab of ornithology, vertebrates museum, living and learning communities, campus orchard, dairy pilot plant, mineralogical museum, animal teaching hospital, 2 agricultural experiment stations, and a marine laboratory. **Physically Challenged Students:** Facilities include wheelchair ramps, elevators, special parking, specially equipped restrooms, special class scheduling, lowered drinking fountains, lowered telephones, special housing. Testing accommodations, course materials in alternate formats, transportation assistance around campus, assistive listening devices, assistive technology, dining options to address dietary restrictions. **Special:** Cornell's colleges and schools offer nearly unlimited opportunities for international study internships and exchanges. There are opportunities for dual-majors and minors throughout the university. Refer to information provided by the individual schools, colleges, and programs for details. There are 7 national honor societies including Phi Beta Kappa. **Visiting:** There are regularly scheduled orientations for prospective students, consist of campus tours and information sessions. There are guides for informal visits, visitors may sit in on classes, and stay overnight. To schedule a visit, contact the Red Carpet Society at (607) 255-3447. **Campus Safety and Security:** Measures include 24-hour foot and vehicle patrol, emergency notification system, self-defense education, and security escort services. There are shuttle buses, emergency telephones, lighted pathways/sidewalks, controlled access to dorms/residences, Specially assigned Crime Prevention officers who create and maintain educational outreach programs and conduct security reviews of on campus locations. Building Security Committee which is comprised of Crime Prevention, the Chief's office, University Architect, Planning and Construction and Project Management personnel to ensure new facilities and major renovations take full advantage of reasonable security devices and measures. Public Safety Advisory Committee which is comprised of students, staff and faculty representatives who meet regularly tor review on campus crime prevention and education efforts. Larger Councils on Hazing, Alcohol, Sexual and Domestic Violence and Mental Health and Wellness which are comprise of students, faculty and staff, chaired by executive level administrators. These committees include more members and meet more often. Alert Team- staff from police, fraternity and sorority offices, mental health, campus life academic and others as needed to address students who of concern to the community for behavioral reasons who may have "fallen through the cracks" systemically.

REQUIREMENTS: The SAT or ACT is required. The ACT Optional Writing test is also required. An essay is required as part of the application process. Other requirements vary by division or program, including specific SAT Subject tests and selection of courses within the minimum 16 secondary-school academic units needed. An interview and/or portfolio is required for specific majors. AP credits are accepted. A student's college determines degree requirements such as residency, number of credits, distribution of credits, and grade averages. See the individual requirements listed by each college or school or contact the college registrar's office. **Procedure:** Freshmen are admitted fall. There are early decision and deferred admissions plans.

Early decision applications should be filed by November 1; regular applications, by January 2 for fall entry, along with a $75 fee. Notifications are sent in April. 1338 early decision candidates were accepted for the 2014-2015 class. 2026 applicants were on the 2014 waiting list; 96 were admitted. Applications are accepted on-line. **Transfer Students:** 542 transfer students enrolled in 2013-2014. All applicants must submit high school and college transcripts, as well as scores from the SAT or ACT if taken previously. Other admission requirements vary by program, including the number of credits that must be completed at Cornell. 60 of 120 credits required for the bachelor's degree must be completed at Cornell. **International Students:** There are 1464 international students enrolled. The school actively recruits these students. They must take the TOEFL with a minimum score of 600 on the paper-based TOEFL (PBT) or 100 on the Internet-based version (iBT), or take the IELTS (International English Language Testing System) is also accepted. They must also take the SAT or ACT. Take the TOEFL or IELTS.

ADMISSIONS: 14% of the 2014-2015 applicants were accepted. The SAT scores for the 2014-2015 freshman class were: Critical Reading--8% between 500 and 599, 40% between 600 and 699, and 51% between 700 and 800; Math--4% between 500 and 599, 26% between 600 and 699, and 69% between 700 and 800. **Admissions Contact:** Shawn Felton, Director of Undergraduate Admissions. E-Mail: *admissions@cornell.edu* Web: *admissions.cornell.edu*

FINANCIAL AID: 47% of all full-time freshmen and 48% of continuing full-time students received need-based aid. The average freshman award was $44,400. Need-based scholarships or need-based grants averaged $38,758 ; and need-based self-help aid (loans and jobs) averaged $5,126. The average financial indebtedness of the 2014 graduate was $21,411. The CSS/Profile, FAFSA, and the college's own financial statement, and The IRS form is required after enrollment. are required. The deadline for filing freshman financial aid applications for fall entry is February 15.

DAEMEN COLLEGE — A-3
www.daemen.edu

Amherst, NY 14226	**(716) 839-8225**
	(800) 462-7652
Fax: (716) 839-8370	Email: admissions@daemen.edu
Full-time: 390 men, 975 women	Faculty: IIB, -$
Part-time: 60 men, 260 women	Ph.D.s: n/av
Graduate: 125 men, 725 women	Student/Faculty: n/av
Year: semesters, summer session	Tuition: $24,480
Room & Board: $10,290	Freshman Class: n/av
SAT or ACT: required	CEEB CODE: 2762
Application Deadline: open	**COMPETITIVE**

Daemen College, founded in 1947, is a private institution offering undergraduate and graduate programs in the liberal and fine arts, business, education, allied health professions, and natural sciences. There is 1 undergraduate school and 1 graduate school. In addition to regional accreditation, Daemen has baccalaureate program accreditation with APTA, CSWE, NLN, ARC-PA, and IACBE. The 35-acre campus is in a suburban area 9 miles northeast of downtown Buffalo. Including any residence halls, there are 18 buildings.

STUDENT LIFE: 96% of undergraduates are from New York. Others are from 16 states, 4 foreign countries, and Canada. 85% are White. 42% are Catholic; 15% Protestant. **Male To Female Ratio:** 3.4:1. The average age of freshmen is 18; all undergraduates, 23. 26% do not continue beyond their first year; 54% remain to graduate. **Housing:** 524 students can be accommodated in college housing, which includes coed dorms and on-campus apartments. Quiet dorms. On-campus housing is guaranteed for all 4 years. 65% of students commute. All students may keep cars.

FACULTY/CLASSROOMS: 40% of faculty are male; 60% are female. 64% teach undergraduates, and 1% do both. No introductory courses are taught by graduate students. The average class size in an introductory lecture is 17; in a laboratory is 10; and in a regular course is 14.

PROGRAMS OF STUDY: Daemen confers B.A., B.S., B.S./M.S., and B.F.A. degrees. Master's and Doctoral degrees are also awarded. Bach-

elor's degrees are awarded in AGRICULTURE (environmental studies), BIOLOGICAL SCIENCE (biochemistry and biology/biological science), BUSINESS (accounting and business administration and management), COMMUNICATIONS AND THE ARTS (animation, applied art, art, arts administration/management, English, fine arts, French, graphic design, and Spanish), COMPUTER AND PHYSICAL SCIENCE (mathematics and natural sciences), EDUCATION (art education, early childhood education, elementary education, English education, foreign languages education, mathematics education, science education, and social studies education), HEALTH PROFESSIONS (health science, nursing, physician's assistant, and preventive/wellness health care), SOCIAL SCIENCE (history, paralegal studies, political science/government, psychology, religion, and social work). Physical therapy, physician assistant, and natural science. are the strongest academically. Nursing, childhood education, physical therapy, and natural science have the largest enrollments.

ACTIVITIES: 6% of men belong to 1 local fraternity; 4% of women belong to 4 local sororities. There are 47 groups on campus, including amnesty international, academic clubs, athletic clubs, pre-law association, student without borders, art, cheerleading, choir, dance, drama, environmental, ethnic, gay, honors, literary magazine, newspaper, professional, social, social service, student government, wellness club, and yearbook. Popular campus events include Homecoming, Battle of the Bands, and Spring Fest. **Sports:** There are 4 intercollegiate sports for men and 4 for women, and 4 intramural sports for men and 2 for women. Facilities include a gym, weight and exercise rooms, saunas, and a volleyball sand court. **Graduates:** From July 1, 2013 to June 30, 2014, 279 bachelor's degrees were awarded. The most popular majors were nursing (18%), natural science (16%), and early childhood/childhood education (15%). 80 companies recruited on campus in 2013-2014. In an average class, 35% graduate in 4 years or less, 50% graduate in 5 years or less, and 54% graduate in 6 years or less. Of the 2013 graduating class, 25% were enrolled in graduate school within 6 months of graduation, and 90% were employed.

SERVICES: Counseling and information services are available, as is tutoring in every subject. There is remedial math, reading, and writing. **Library/Resources:** The library contains 140,576 volumes, 28,055 microform items, 2,354 audio/video tapes/CDs/DVDs, and subscribes to 31,925 periodicals including electronic. Computerized library services include interlibrary loans, database searching, Internet access, and Wi-Fi capability. Special learning facilities include an art gallery, video conference center. **Physically Challenged Students:** 83% of the campus is accessible. Facilities include wheelchair ramps, elevators, special parking, specially equipped restrooms, lowered drinking fountains, and lowered telephones. **Special:** Daemen offers cooperative programs in all majors, internships, cross-registration within the Western New York Consortium of Colleges and Universities, student-designed majors, work-study programs, an accelerated degree program in nursing, dual majors, a Washington semester, and study abroad in 6 countries. There is an International Studies Program that leads to a minor in international studies. There are 8 national honor societies, a freshman honors program, and 20 departmental honors programs. **Visiting:** There are regularly scheduled orientations for prospective students, Two 5-day orientations that includes a campus tour, an interview, and placement testing in math and English during July and August. Fall Open House in October, College Night in September, and Day @ Daemen in September and November are other regularly. There are guides for informal visits, visitors may sit in on classes, and stay overnight. To schedule a visit, contact the Admissions Office. **Campus Safety and Security:** Measures include 24-hour foot and vehicle patrol and security escort services. There are emergency telephones, lighted pathways/sidewalks, and video monitors.

REQUIREMENTS: The SAT or ACT is required. Applicants must be graduates of an accredited secondary school or have the GED equivalent. Some departments have further admissions requirements, including a portfolio review for art majors, 3-year sequences of math and science for all natural science programs, and 2 essays, 3 letters of recommendation, and a supplemental application for the physician assistant program. A GPA of 2.0 is required. AP and CLEP credits are accepted. Important factors in the admissions decision are advanced placement or honors courses, leadership record, and evidence of special talent.To graduate, students must complete 120 to 199 hours (depending on the degree program) with a minimum GPA of 2.0. Students are required to complete a minimum of 30 credit hours of course work in residence. The final semester's course work must be taken in residence. **Procedure:** Freshmen are admitted fall, spring, and summer. Entrance exams should be taken by the summer following the senior year. There are early admissions, deferred admissions, and rolling admissions plans. Application deadlines are open. The fall 2014 application fee was $25. Notification is sent on a rolling basis. Applications are accepted on-line. **Transfer Students:** 243 transfer students enrolled in 2013-2014. Applicants must present college transcripts and an indication of good standing from the last institution attended and a minimum GPA of 2.0. to 2.8. Physician assistant applicants should submit essays, 3 letters of recommendation, and supplemental applications. 30 of 120 credits required for the bachelor's degree must be completed at Daemen. **International Students:** There are 10 international students enrolled. They must take the TOEFL.

ADMISSIONS: Donna Shaffner, Dean of Admissions. E-Mail: *admissions@daemen.edu* Web: *www.daemen.edu*

FINANCIAL AID: In 2014-2015, 88% of all full-time freshmen and 90% of continuing full-time students received some form of financial aid. 83% of all full-time freshmen and 82% of continuing full-time students received need-based aid. The average freshman award was $12,769. Need-based scholarships or need-based grants averaged $8,931; need-based self-help aid (loans and jobs) averaged $4,356; non-need-based athletic scholarships averaged $6,833; and other non-need-based awards and non-need-based scholarships averaged $3,149. 20% of undergraduate students work part-time. The FAFSA and the state aid form, and foreign student certification of finances are required. Check with the school for current application deadlines.

DOMINICAN COLLEGE *(The complete profile is made available exclusively on our website, www.barronspac.com)*

DOWLING COLLEGE *(The complete profile is made available exclusively on our website, www.barronspac.com)*

D'YOUVILLE COLLEGE   A-3
www.dyc.edu

Buffalo, NY 14201	(716) 829-7600
	(800) 777-3921
Fax: (716) 829-7900	Email: admiss@dyc.edu
Full-time: 404 men, 1063 women	Faculty: 146
Part-time: 77 men, 322 women	Ph.Ds: n/av
Graduate: 329 men, 776 women	Student/Faculty: 12 to 1
Year: semesters, summer session	Tuition: $20,050
Room & Board: $9800	Freshman Class: 822 applied, 791 accepted, 155 enrolled
SAT CR/M/W: 520/530/510 ACT: 23	CEEB CODE: 2197
Application Deadline: n/av	COMPETITIVE

D'Youville College, founded in 1908, is a private, nonsectarian liberal arts institution granting degrees at the Bachelors, Masters, First Professional and Doctoral levels. Figures in the above capsule and in this profile are approximate. There is one graduate school. In addition to regional accreditation, D'Youville has baccalaureate program accreditation with ADA, APTA, and CCNE. The 10-acre campus is in an urban area 1 mile north of Downtown Buffalo, and 1 mile from the Peace Bridge border crossing to Canada. Including any residence halls, there are 12 buildings.

STUDENT LIFE: 95% of undergraduates are from New York. Others are from 20 states, 48 foreign countries, and Canada. 80% are from public schools. 65% are White; 12% African American. 46% are Anglican, Buddhist, Christian, and Hindu, 25% Catholic. **Male To Female Ratio:** 2.7:1. The average age of freshmen is 18; all undergraduates, 24. 27% do not continue beyond their first year; 63% remain

to graduate. **Housing:** 478 students can be accommodated in college housing, which includes single-sex and coed dorms and on-campus apartments. Quiet floors, and 21 and older floors. On-campus housing is guaranteed for all 4 years. 87% of students commute. All students may keep cars.

FACULTY/CLASSROOMS: 43% of faculty are male; 67% are female. All teach and do research. No introductory courses are taught by graduate students.

PROGRAMS OF STUDY: D'Youville confers B.A., B.S., B.S./M.S. and B.S.N. degrees. Master's and Doctoral degrees are also awarded. Bachelor's degrees are awarded in BIOLOGICAL SCIENCE (biology/ biological science), BUSINESS (accounting and business administration and management), COMMUNICATIONS AND THE ARTS (English), COMPUTER AND PHYSICAL SCIENCE (information sciences and systems and mathematics), HEALTH PROFESSIONS (exercise science, health care administration, nursing, and physician's assistant), SOCIAL SCIENCE (dietetics, history, interdisciplinary studies, international studies, philosophy, psychology, and sociology). Education, and health professions are the strongest academically. Health professions, business, and nursing have the largest enrollments.

ACTIVITIES: There are no fraternities or sororities. There are 35 groups on campus, including cheerleading, chorus, computers, dance, drama, drill team, ethnic, gay, honors, international, literary magazine, newspaper, professional, religious, social, social service, and student government. Popular campus events include Moving Up Days, International Fiesta and Honors Convocation. **Sports:** There are 7 intercollegiate sports for men and 7 for women. Facilities include a 500-seat gym that houses basketball and volleyball courts, an indoor batting cage, a fitness facility with aerobic and free weights, swimming pool, and dance studio. **Graduates:** From July 1, 2013 to June 30, 2014, 318 bachelor's degrees were awarded. The most popular majors were health professions and related sciences (49%), business/marketing (20%), and interdisciplinary studies (10%). 92 companies recruited on campus in 2013-2014. In an average class, 40% graduate in 4 years or less, 63% graduate in 5 years or less, and 63% graduate in 6 years or less.

SERVICES: Counseling and information services are available, as is tutoring in some subjects, based on tutor accessibility. There is a reader service for the blind, and remedial math, reading, and writing. **Library/Resources:** The library contains 96,876 volumes, 205,411 microform items, 4,246 audio/video tapes/CDs/DVDs, and subscribes to 683 periodicals including electronic. Computerized library services include interlibrary loans, database searching, Internet access, and Wi-Fi capability. **Physically Challenged Students:** 95% of the campus is accessible. Facilities include wheelchair ramps, elevators, special parking, specially equipped restrooms, lowered drinking fountains, and special housing. **Special:** D'Youville has cross-registration with member colleges of the Western New York Consortium. Internships, work-study programs, dual majors, study abroad in 5 countries, and pass/fail options are available. Accelerated 5-year B.S.-M.S. programs in occupational therapy, intenational business, elementary education, physician's assistant, nursing, and dietetics are offered. For freshmen with undecided majors, the Career Discovery Program offers special courses, internships, and faculty advisers. There are 3 national honor societies and 2 departmental honors programs. **Visiting:** There are regularly scheduled orientations for prospective students. There are guides for informal visits, visitors may sit in on classes, and stay overnight. To schedule a visit, contact the Admissions Office. **Campus Safety and Security:** Measures include 24-hour foot and vehicle patrol, emergency notification system, self-defense education, and security escort services. There are emergency telephones, lighted pathways/sidewalks, a special focus program, and a security committee.

REQUIREMENTS: The SAT or ACT is required. Applicants should have completed 16 Carnegie units, including 4 years of high school English, 3 of social studies, and 1 each of math and science; some majors require additional years of math and science. The GED is accepted. A GPA of 2.0 is required. AP and CLEP credits are accepted. All students must complete general program and core curriculum requirements, including 5 courses in humanities, 2 each in English and natural sciences, and 1 each in ethics, philosophy or religion, history, sociology, psychology, economics or political science, math, and computer science. A minimum of 120 to 144 credit hours, varying by major, with a minimum GPA of 2.0, (higher for some programs), is required to graduate. **Procedure:** Freshmen are admitted fall and spring. Entrance exams should be taken by the end of the junior year. There are deferred admissions and rolling admissions plans. Application deadlines are open. Application fee is $25. Applications are accepted on-line. **Transfer Students:** 235 transfer students enrolled in 2013-2014. Applicants need a minimum GPA of 2.0, or 2.5 for some programs. 30 of 120 credits required for the bachelor's degree must be completed at D'Youville. **International Students:** There are 156 international students enrolled. The school actively recruits these students. They must take the TOEFL with a minimum score of 500 on the paper-based TOEFL (PBT) or 61 on the Internet-based version (iBT). They must also take the SAT or ACT, scoring 900.

ADMISSIONS: 96% of the 2014-2015 applicants were accepted. The SAT scores for the 2014-2015 freshman class were: Critical Reading--44% below 500, 48% between 500 and 599, and 8% between 600 and 699; Math--33% below 500, 53% between 500 and 599, 14% between 600 and 699, and 1% between 700 and 800; Writing--49% below 500, 46% between 500 and 599, and 6% between 600 and 699. The ACT scores were 20% below 21, 37% between 21 and 23, 27% between 24 and 26, 10% between 27 and 28, and 7% above 28. 40% of the current freshmen were in the top fifth of their class; 80% were in the top two fifths. **Admissions Contact:** Steven Smith, Director of Undergraduate Admissions. E-Mail: *admiss@dyc.edu* Web: *www.dyc.edu*

FINANCIAL AID: In 2014-2015, 86% of all full-time freshmen and 87% of continuing full-time students received some form of financial aid. 84% of all full-time freshmen and 84% of continuing full-time students received need-based aid. The average freshman award was $20,127. Need-based scholarships or need-based grants averaged $14,155 ($20,127 maximum); need-based self-help aid (loans and jobs) averaged $8,108 ($9,900 maximum); and other non-need-based awards and non-need-based scholarships averaged $11,709 ($9,900 maximum). The average financial indebtedness of the 2014 graduate was $31,401. The FAFSA and the state aid form are required. The priority date for freshman financial aid applications for fall entry is March 1. The deadline for filing freshman financial aid applications for fall entry is April 15.

EASTMAN SCHOOL OF MUSIC *(The complete profile is made available exclusively on our website, www.barronspac.com)*

ELMIRA COLLEGE   B-4
www.elmira.edu

Elmira, NY 14901	(607) 735-1724
	(800) 935-6472
Fax: (607) 735-1718	Email: admissions@elmira.edu
Full-time: 347 men, 841 women	**Faculty:** 82
Part-time: 52 men, 168 women	**Ph.D.s:** 100%
Graduate: 12 men, 122 women	**Student/Faculty:** 14 to 1
Year: other, summer session	**Tuition:** $38,150
Room & Board: $11,800	**Freshman Class:** 2083 applied, 1648 accepted, 396 enrolled
SAT CR/M: 540/530 **ACT:** 24	**CEEB CODE:** 2226
Application Deadline: rolling	**COMPETITIVE+**

Elmira College, founded in 1855, is a private liberal arts institution offering general and preprofessional programs. The figures in the above capsule and in this profile are approximate. In addition to regional accreditation, Elmira has baccalaureate program accreditation with NLN. The 42-acre campus is in a suburban area 90 miles southwest of Syracuse and 50 miles west of Binghamton. Including any residence halls, there are 26 buildings.

STUDENT LIFE: 52% of undergraduates are from out of state, mostly the Northeast. Students are from 35 states, 21 foreign countries, and Canada. 59% are from public schools. 71% are White. **Male To Female Ratio:** 2.8:1. The average age of freshmen is 18; all undergraduates, 20. 25% do not continue beyond their first year; 66% remain to graduate. **Housing:** 1097 students can be accommodated in college housing, which includes single-sex and coed dorms and on-campus apartments. quiet floors and alcohol- and tobacco-free floors. On-campus housing is guaranteed for all 4 years. 93% of students live on campus; of those, 90% remain on campus on weekends. All students may keep cars.

FACULTY/CLASSROOMS: 63% of faculty are male; 37% are female. All teach and do research. No introductory courses are taught by graduate students. The average class size in an introductory lecture is 24; in a laboratory is 10; and in a regular course is 16.

PROGRAMS OF STUDY: Elmira confers B.A., and B.S. degrees. Associate and Master's degrees are also awarded. Bachelor's degrees are awarded in BIOLOGICAL SCIENCE (biochemistry and biology/biological science), BUSINESS (accounting, business administration and management, business economics, international business management, and marketing/retailing/merchandising), COMMUNICATIONS AND THE ARTS (art, classics, dramatic arts, English literature, fine arts, French, languages, music, and Spanish), COMPUTER AND PHYSICAL SCIENCE (chemistry and mathematics), EDUCATION (art education, elementary education, foreign languages education, science education, and secondary education), ENGINEERING AND ENVIRONMENTAL DESIGN (environmental science), HEALTH PROFESSIONS (medical laboratory technology, nursing, predentistry, premedicine, and speech pathology/audiology), SOCIAL SCIENCE (American studies, anthropology, criminal justice, history, human services, international studies, philosophy, political science/government, prelaw, psychology, and sociology). History, theater, and premedicine are the strongest academically. Psychology, business administration, and education have the largest enrollments.

ACTIVITIES: There are no fraternities or sororities. There are 119 groups on campus, including active minds, and hall council, classics society, model UN, orientation leaders, silent voices, student alumni council, art, chorale, chorus, dance, drama, environmental, ethnic, gay, honors, international, literary magazine, musical theater, newspaper, photography, political, professional, religious, social, social service, student activities board, student government, and yearbook. Popular campus events include Mountain Day, Finals breakfast, and May Days. **Sports:** There are 8 intercollegiate sports for men and 11 for women, and 17 intramural sports for men and 17 for women. Facilities include 2500-seat and 950-seat gyms, indoor tennis facilities, a 3500-seat hockey arena, racquetball courts, fitness center, dance studio, and a swimming pool. **Graduates:** From July 1, 2013 to June 30, 2014, 274 bachelor's degrees were awarded. The most popular majors were education (19%), business administration (17%), and nursing (13%). 60 companies recruited on campus in 2013-2014. In an average class, 60% graduate in 4 years or less, 2% graduate in 5 years or less, and 1% graduate in 6 years or less.

SERVICES: Counseling and information services are available, as is tutoring in most subjects. There is a reader service for the blind. Tutoring in math and freshman English is available in each freshman dorm. **Library/Resources:** The library contains 203,343 volumes, 591,429 microform items, 5,897 audio/video tapes/CDs/DVDs, and subscribes to 337 periodicals including electronic. Computerized library services include interlibrary loans, database searching, Internet access, and Wi-Fi capability. Special learning facilities include an art gallery, speech/hearing clinic and Mark Twain's study and exhibit. **Physically Challenged Students:** 25% of the campus is accessible. Facilities include wheelchair ramps, elevators, special parking, specially equipped restrooms, special class scheduling, lowered drinking fountains, and special housing. **Special:** The required field experience program provides a career-related internship as well as community service. A junior year abroad program, an accelerated degree program, a general studies degree, student-designed majors, and pass/fail options are available. A 3-2 chemical engineering degree is offered with Clarkson University. B.A.-B.S. degrees are offered in biochemistry, biology, chemistry, economics, education, environmental studies, history, math, political science, and psychology. There are 20 national honor societies including Phi Beta Kappa. **Visiting:** There are regularly scheduled orientations for prospective students, consisting of an open house format and overview, a tour, lunch, a student panel, a faculty panel, general admissions and scholarship information, and an optional interview. Individual visits for interviews and tours are available year-round, including Saturday mornings. There are guides for informal visits, visitors may sit in on classes, and stay overnight. To schedule a visit, contact the Office of Admissions. **Campus Safety and Security:** Measures include 24-hour foot and vehicle patrol, emergency notification system, and security escort services. There are emergency telephones, lighted pathways/sidewalks, and controlled access to dorms/residences.

REQUIREMENTS: The SAT or ACT is required. Applicants should have completed 4 years of high school English, 3 of math, and 2 of science. An essay is part of the application process. An interview is strongly recommended. A GPA of 2.0 is required. AP and CLEP credits are accepted. Important factors in the admissions decision are advanced placement or honors courses, extracurricular activities record, and recommendations by school officials. All students must complete general degree requirements, including communication skills, writing courses, math competency, and a core curriculum; distribution requirements in culture and civilization, contemporary social institutions, the scientific method, the creative process, and phys ed; and a field experience program. A total of 120 credit hours with a minimum GPA of 2.0 overall and in the major is required to graduate. **Procedure:** Freshmen are admitted fall and winter. Entrance exams should be taken by January of the entry year. There are early decision, deferred admissions, and rolling admissions plans. Early decision applications should be filed by November 15, along with a $50 fee. Notification of early decision is sent December 15; regular decision, on a rolling basis. 71 early decision candidates were accepted for the 2014-2015 class. 26 applicants were on the 2014 waiting list; 2 were admitted. Applications are accepted on-line. **Transfer Students:** 49 transfer students enrolled in 2013-2014. Applicants should have a minimum GPA of 2.0. An interview is strongly recommended. 30 of 120 credits required for the bachelor's degree must be completed at Elmira. **International Students:** There are 74 international students enrolled. The school actively recruits these students. They must take the TOEFL with a minimum score of 500 on the paper-based TOEFL (PBT) or 61 on the Internet-based version (iBT) and the Comprehensive English Language Test.

ADMISSIONS: 79% of the 2014-2015 applicants were accepted. The SAT scores for the 2014-2015 freshman class were: Critical Reading--37% below 500, 42% between 500 and 599, 16% between 600 and 699, and 5% between 700 and 800; Math--35% below 500, 46% between 500 and 599, 16% between 600 and 699, and 3% between 700 and 800. The ACT scores were 2% below 21, 5% between 21 and 23, 16% between 24 and 26, 20% between 27 and 28, and 7% above 28. 56% of the current freshmen were in the top fifth of their class; 91% were in the top two fifths. There were 2 National Merit finalists. 24 freshmen graduated first in their class. **Admissions Contact:** Brett Moore, Director of Admissions. E-Mail: *admissions@elmira.edu* Web: *www.elmira.edu*

FINANCIAL AID: In 2014-2015, 98% of all full-time freshmen and 98% of continuing full-time students received some form of financial aid. 87% of all full-time freshmen and 84% of continuing full-time students received need-based aid. The average freshman award was $30,064. Need-based scholarships or need-based grants averaged $26,776; and need-based self-help aid (loans and jobs) averaged $4,151. 50% of undergraduate students work part-time. Average annual earnings from campus work are $1500. The average financial indebtedness of the 2014 graduate was $27,426. The FAFSA and the state aid form are required. The priority date for freshman financial aid applications for fall entry is February 1. The deadline for filing freshman financial aid applications for fall entry is March 15.

EUGENE LANG COLLEGE/THE NEW SCHOOL FOR LIBERAL ARTS D-5

www.newschool.edu/lang

New York, NY 10011	**212.229.5150**
	800.292.3040
Fax: 212.229.5355	Email: lang@newschool.edu
Full-time: 425 men, 930 women	**Faculty:** 65
Part-time: 42 men, 60 women	**Ph.D.s:** 80%
Graduate: n/av	**Student/Faculty:** 22 to 1
Year: semesters	**Tuition:** $39,976
Room & Board: $15,674	**Freshman Class:** n/av
	CEEB CODE: 2521
Application Deadline: January 6	**COMPETITIVE**

Eugene Lang College, established in 1978, is the liberal arts undergraduate division of the New School. Figures in the above capsule and in this profile are approximate. There is one undergraduate school. In addition to regional accreditation, Eugene Lang College has baccalaureate program accreditation with MSCHE. The 37-acre campus is in an urban area in Greenwich Village, Manhatten, New York City. Including any residence halls, there are 23 buildings.

STUDENT LIFE: 72% of undergraduates are from out of state, mostly the Middle Atlantic. Students are from 43 states, 46 foreign countries, and Canada. 61% are from public schools. 57% are White; 13% Hispanic. **Male To Female Ratio:** 2.1:1. The average age of freshmen is 19; all undergraduates, 20. 20% do not continue beyond their first year; 52% remain to graduate. **Housing:** 1945 students can be accommodated in college housing, which includes coed dorms. In addition, there are special-interest houses, Honors community housing is focused more on Academics than an actual GPA. On-campus housing is available on a first-come, first-served basis, and is available on a lottery system for upperclassmen. 70% of students commute. Alcohol is not permitted. All students may keep cars.

FACULTY/CLASSROOMS: 43% of faculty are male; 57% are female. All teach undergraduates. No introductory courses are taught by graduate students.

PROGRAMS OF STUDY: Eugene Lang College confers B.A. degrees. Bachelor's degrees are awarded in AGRICULTURE (environmental studies), COMMUNICATIONS AND THE ARTS (dance, dramatic arts, literature, music, theatre acting, theater design, and theatre studies), EDUCATION (education and foreign languages education), SOCIAL SCIENCE (anthropology, Chinese Studies, economics, gender studies, history, interdisciplinary studies, philosophy, political science/government, psychology, religion, sociology, and urban studies). Creative writing, history, urban studies, and education are the strongest academically. Writing and cultural studies have the largest enrollments.

ACTIVITIES: There are no fraternities or sororities. There are 46 groups on campus, including dress practice collective, games clubs, international interest clubs, textile association, art, band, choir, chorus, communications, computers, dance, debate, drama, environmental, ethnic, film, gay, honors, international, jazz band, literary magazine, museum club, musical theater, newspaper, opera, orchestra, photography, political, professional, radio and TV, religious, social, social service, student government, and symphony. Popular campus events include Welcome Back Block party, Seek relief Week, Midnight Breakfast, 100 Nights Dinner, Leadership Retreat, Service Trips, and Leadership Banquet Awards. **Sports:** There are 4 intramural sports for men and 4 for women. We do not have a fitness facility, but we do have a fitness room where we host group fitness classes and personal training. **Graduates:** From July 1, 2013 to June 30, 2014, 420 bachelor's degrees were awarded. The most popular majors were liberal arts (32%), literary studies (16%), and arts (15%). In an average class, 39% graduate in 4 years or less, 48% graduate in 5 years or less, and 52% graduate in 6 years or less. Of the 2013 graduating class, 10% were enrolled in graduate school within 6 months of graduation, and 6% were employed.

SERVICES: **Library/Resources:** The 3 libraries contain 15.7 million volumes, 1,184 microform items, 17,426 audio/video tapes/CDs/DVDs, and subscribe to 76,012 periodicals including electronic. Computerized library services include interlibrary loans, database searching, Internet access, and Wi-Fi capability. Special learning facilities include an art gallery, radio station, and a writing center. **Physically Challenged Students:** 95% of the campus is accessible. Facilities include wheelchair ramps, elevators, specially equipped restrooms, special class scheduling, lowered drinking fountains, and special housing. **Special:** Lang College offers a concentration rather than a traditional major; there is no core curriculum and students are instructed in small seminars. Students may cross-register with other New School divisions. A large variety of internships for credit, study abroad, B.A./M.A. and B.A./M.S.T. options, a B.A./B.F.A. degree with Parsons The New School for Design and The New School for Jazz and Contemporary Music Program, student-designed majors, and nondegree study are available. **Visiting:** There are regularly scheduled orientations for prospective students, consisting of information sessions every weekday at 2:00; tours every weekday at 3:00. Walk in meetings with counselors available every weekday between 9 am and 5 pm.

There are guides for informal visits and visitors may sit in on classes. To schedule a visit, contact Denise Rodriguez at rodrigud@newschool.edu. **Campus Safety and Security:** Measures include self-defense education. Honors community housing is focused more on Academics than an actual GPA.

REQUIREMENTS: Freshmen: Common App (online); 2 essays; secondary school transcript; counselor recommendation; teacher evaluation; SAT or ACT scores (or a graded academic paper); TOEFL score (for ESL students). Transfers: college transcripts. AP and CLEP credits are accepted. Important factors in the admissions decision are recommendations by school officials, advanced placement or honors courses, and extracurricular activities record.To graduate, students must complete 120 credit hours, with a GPA of 2.0 and a minimum of 36 hours in 1 of 11 paths of study: writing, literature, the arts (includes dance and theater, urban studies, social and historical inquiry, cultural studies, media, philosophy, religious studies, psychology, education studies, and science, technology, and society. Also required are 88 credit hours in Lang College courses and 4 credits of senior work. Required courses include a first-year writing seminar and a freshman workshop program. **Procedure:** Freshmen are admitted fall and spring. Entrance exams should be taken in May of the junior year or October of the senior year. There are early decision and deferred admissions plans. Early decision applications should be filed by November 1; regular applications, by January 6 for fall entry; and November 1 for spring entry, along with a $50 fee. Notification of early decision is sent December 15; regular decision, April 1. Applications are accepted on-line. Application fees are waived if application is completed on-line. **Transfer Students:** Applicants must have a minimum college GPA of 2.5 and must submit high school transcripts, ACT or SAT scores (if taken in the last 5 years), and 2 recommendations. An interview is recommended. Grades of C or better transfer for credit. 60 of 120 credits required for the bachelor's degree must be completed at Eugene Lang College. **International Students:** There are 96 international students enrolled. The school actively recruits these students. They must take the TOEFL with a minimum score of 100 on the paper-based TOEFL (PBT) or 100 on the Internet-based version (iBT), or take the IELTS, or the PTE.

ADMISSIONS: Karen Williams, Director of Admissions. E-Mail: *lang@newschool.edu* Web: *www.newschool.edu/lang*

FINANCIAL AID: In 2014-2015, 47% of all full-time freshmen students received some form of financial aid. 41% of all full-time freshmen students received need-based aid. The average financial indebtedness of the 2014 graduate was $23,170. Eugene Lang College is a member of CSS. The FAFSA and the state aid form are required. The priority date for freshman financial aid applications for fall entry is March 1. The deadline for filing freshman financial aid applications for fall entry is June 30.

EXCELSIOR COLLEGE *(The complete profile is made available exclusively on our website, www.barronspac.com)*

FARMINGDALE STATE COLLEGE   E-5
www.farmingdale.edu

Farmingdale, NY 11735	(631) 420-2200 n/av
Fax: (631) 420-2633	Email: admissions@farmingdale.edu
Full-time: 3791 men, 2496 women	Faculty: 209; IIB, +$
Part-time: 1003 men, 1104 women	Ph.D.s: 75%
Graduate: n/av	Student/Faculty: 30 to 1
Year: semesters, summer session	Tuition: $7483 ($17,133)
Room & Board: $12,190	Freshman Class: 5183 applied, 2418 accepted, 1101 enrolled
SAT CR/M/W: 480/500/470 ACT: 21	CEEB CODE: 2526
Application Deadline: June 1	COMPETITIVE

Farmingdale State College, formerly State University of New York/College of Technology at Farmingdale founded in 1912, is a public institution offering associate and bachelor's degrees in the applied sciences and technology. There are 4 undergraduate schools. In addition to regional accreditation, SUNY Farmingdale has baccalaureate program accreditation with ABET, ADA, ATMAE, NAACLS, and ACEN. The 380-acre campus is in a suburban area on Long Island, about 35 miles east of New York City. Including any residence halls, there are 40 buildings.

STUDENT LIFE: 97% of undergraduates are from New York. Others are from 11 states, 80 foreign countries, and Canada. 92% are from public schools. 61% are White; 16% Hispanic. **Male To Female Ratio:** 0.8:1. The average age of freshmen is 18; all undergraduates, 24. 20% do not continue beyond their first year; 43% remain to graduate. **Housing:** 600 students can be accommodated in college housing, which includes coed dorms. On-campus housing is available on a first-come and first-served basis. 92% of students commute. Alcohol is not permitted. All students may keep cars.

FACULTY/CLASSROOMS: 56% of faculty are male; 44% are female. No introductory courses are taught by graduate students. The average class size in an introductory lecture is 28; in a laboratory is 22; and in a regular course is 28.

PROGRAMS OF STUDY: SUNY Farmingdale confers B.S., and B.Tech. degrees. Associate degrees are also awarded. Bachelor's degrees are awarded in AGRICULTURE (horticulture), BIOLOGICAL SCIENCE (biology/biological science), BUSINESS (applied economics / management, business administration and management, facilities management, global management, and sports management), COMMUNICATIONS AND THE ARTS (English and professional communication, telecommunications engineering technology, and visual design), COMPUTER AND PHYSICAL SCIENCE (applied mathematics, computer engineering technology, computer programming, and information sciences and systems), ENGINEERING AND ENVIRONMENTAL DESIGN (aeronautical science, architectural technology, automotive technology, aviation administration/management, construction technology, electrical/electronics engineering technology, industrial engineering technology, manufacturing technology, and mechanical engineering technology), HEALTH PROFESSIONS (dental hygiene, medical technology, and nursing), SOCIAL SCIENCE (applied psychology, criminal justice, and safety and security technology). Nursing, Dental Hygiene, Bioscience, Engineering Technology, and Computer Science are the strongest academically. Business Management, Criminal Justice: Law Enforcement Technology, and Computer Programming and Information Systems have the largest enrollments.

ACTIVITIES: There are 70 groups on campus, including art, computers, dance, ethnic, honors, musical theater, newspaper, photography, professional, radio and TV, religious, social, social service, student government, and yearbook. Popular campus events include Homecoming Week, Bingo for Books, Casino Night, and Farewell to Farmingdale. **Sports:** There are 9 intercollegiate sports for men and 9 for women, and 11 intramural sports for men and 11 for women. Facilities include basketball, badminton, volleyball, racquetball, handball, squash, and tennis courts, a wrestling room, weight training rooms, indoor and outdoor tracks, a golf driving range and 3-hole golf layout, and baseball, softball, soccer/lacrosse, and multipurpose fields. **Graduates:** From July 1, 2013 to June 30, 2014, 1230 bachelor's degrees were awarded. The most popular majors were Business Management (27%), Criminal Justice (7%), and Nursing (7%). 50 companies recruited on campus in 2013-2014. In an average class, 43% graduate in 6 years or less. Of the 2013 graduating class, 45% were employed within 6 months of graduation.

SERVICES: Counseling and information services are available, as is tutoring in most subjects. There is a reader service for the blind, and remedial math, reading, and writing. There is a learning disabilities specialist counselor available. **Library/Resources:** The library contains 180,000 volumes, 27,000 microform items, 1,446 audio/video tapes/CDs/DVDs, and subscribes to 706 periodicals including electronic. Computerized library services include interlibrary loans, database searching, Internet access, and Wi-Fi capability. Special learning facilities include an art gallery, radio station, a dental hygiene clinic, CAD/CAM and CIM labs, fleet of multi- and single-engine airplanes, and a greenhouse complex. **Physically Challenged Students:** 90% of the campus is accessible. Facilities include wheelchair ramps, elevators, special parking, specially equipped restrooms, special class scheduling, lowered drinking fountains, and lowered telephones. **Special:** Internships are available, as well as study abroad in Italy. There are 6 national honor societies. **Visiting:** There are regularly scheduled orientations for prospective students, including a tour of the campus and general information about the college, admissions, financial aid, and residence life. There are guides for informal visits. To schedule a visit, contact the Admissions Office at (631) 420-2200. **Campus Safety and Security:** Measures include 24-hour foot and vehicle patrol, emergency notification system, and security escort services. There are emergency telephones, lighted pathways/sidewalks, and controlled access to dorms/residences.

REQUIREMENTS: The SAT is required. Applicants must be graduates of an accredited secondary school or have earned a GED. Specific entrance requirements vary by program, but recommended preparation includes 4 units of English and 3 each of math, science, and social science. Either the SAT or the ACT is required. A GPA of 3.0 is required. AP and CLEP credits are accepted. Important factors in the admissions decision are advanced placement or honors courses, recommendations by school officials, and extracurricular activities record. To graduate, students must complete 120 to 130 credits with a minimum GPA of 2.0. The core curriculum includes at least 60 credits of liberal arts and sciences courses in the Bachelor of Science programs and 45 credits in the Bachelor of Technology programs, as well as credits in major coursework. One writing-intensive course and all general education requirements must be satisfactorily completed. **Procedure:** Freshmen are admitted fall and spring. There are deferred admissions and rolling admissions plans. Application deadlines are open. Application fee is $50. Notification is sent on a rolling basis. Applications are accepted on-line. **Transfer Students:** 1333 transfer students enrolled in 2013-2014. Applicants must have a minimum GPA of 2.5. 30 of 120 credits required for the bachelor's degree must be completed at SUNY Farmingdale. **International Students:** There are 220 international students enrolled. They must take the TOEFL with a minimum score of 520 on the paper-based TOEFL (PBT) or 68 on the Internet-based version (iBT). They must also take the SAT or ACT, scoring 1000.

ADMISSIONS: 47% of the 2014-2015 applicants were accepted. The SAT scores for the 2014-2015 freshman class were: Critical Reading--60% below 500, 35% between 500 and 599, and 5% between 600 and 699; Math--45% below 500, 46% between 500 and 599, and 9% between 600 and 699. The ACT scores were 46% below 21, 37% between 21 and 23, 12% between 24 and 26, 4% between 27 and 28, and 1% above 28. **Admissions Contact:** Jim Hall, Director of Admissions. E-Mail: *admissions@farmingdale.edu* Web: *www.farmingdale.edu*

FINANCIAL AID: In 2014-2015, 79% of all full-time freshmen and 66% of continuing full-time students received some form of financial aid. 54% of all full-time freshmen and 48% of continuing full-time students received need-based aid. The average freshman award was $7,939. Need-based scholarships or need-based grants averaged $5,770 ($16,857 maximum); need-based self-help aid (loans and jobs) averaged $3,332 ($6,500 maximum); and other non-need-based awards and non-need-based scholarships averaged $1,825 ($12,627 maximum). The FAFSA, the state aid form, and the college's own financial statement are required. Check with the school for current application deadlines.

FASHION INSTITUTE OF TECHNOLOGY/STATE UNIVERSITY OF NEW YORK (*The complete profile is made available exclusively on our website, www.barronspac.com*)

Five Towns College, founded in 1972, is a private institution offering undergraduate programs in music, music business, business, liberal arts, theater, elementary education, mass communication (broadcasting, journalism), audio recording technology, and film/video. Graduate programs in music, music education, and childhood education are also offered. Figures in the above capsule and in this profile are approximate. There is 1 undergraduate school and 1 graduate school. In addition to regional accreditation, FTC has baccalaureate program accreditation with NCATE. The 40-acre campus is in a suburban area 48 miles east of New York City. Including any residence halls, there are 5 buildings.

STUDENT LIFE: 94% of undergraduates are from New York. Others are from 9 states, and 1 foreign countries. 91% are from public schools. 51% are White; 20% African American; 13% Hispanic. **Male To Female Ratio:** 0.4:1. The average age of freshmen is 19; all undergraduates, 21. 23% do not continue beyond their first year; 55% remain to graduate. **Housing:** 200 students can be accommodated in college housing, which includes coed dorms. Priority is given to out-of-town students. 80% of students commute. Alcohol is not permitted. Upperclassmen may keep cars.

FACULTY/CLASSROOMS: 56% of faculty are male; 42% are female. 98% teach undergraduates, 20% do research, and 20% do both. No introductory courses are taught by graduate students. The average class size in an introductory lecture is 30 and in a regular course is 15.

PROGRAMS OF STUDY: FTC confers B.S., B.F.A., B.P.S. and Mus.B. degrees. Associate, Master's, and Doctoral degrees are also awarded. Bachelor's degrees are awarded in COMMUNICATIONS AND THE ARTS (audio technology, communications, dramatic arts, jazz, music business management, music performance, music theory and composition, and video), EDUCATION (elementary education and music education). Music, business, and childhood education are the strongest academically. Business management with a concentration in audio recording technology, film and video have the largest enrollments.

ACTIVITIES: There are no fraternities or sororities. There are 16 groups on campus, including and broadcasting, barbershop quartets, hip-hop, music business, readers theater, theatrical concert, art, band, choir, chorale, chorus, dance, drama, film, international, jazz band, live audio, musical theater, newspaper, orchestra, professional, radio and TV, social, student government, symphony, and yearbook. Popular campus events include Lunch and Lecture Series, Annual Picnic and Spring and Fall Festivals. **Sports:** There is no sports program at FTC. Facilities include a gym with basketball and volleyball courts, an outdoor baseball/soccer field, and a fitness center. **Graduates:** From July 1, 2013 to June 30, 2014, 178 bachelor's degrees were awarded. The most popular majors were business management (48%), film and video (16%), and music (11%). 64 companies recruited on campus in 2013-2014. In an average class, 54% graduate in 4 years or less, 64% graduate in 5 years or less, and 75% graduate in 6 years or less. Of the 2013 graduating class, 15% were enrolled in graduate school within 6 months of graduation, and 81% were employed.

SERVICES: Counseling and information services are available, as is tutoring in most subjects. There is a reader service for the blind. **Library/Resources:** The 2 libraries contain 44,771 volumes, 50 microform items, 16,416 audio/video tapes/CDs/DVDs, and subscribe to 500 periodicals including electronic. Computerized library services include interlibrary loans, database searching, Internet access, and Wi-Fi capability. Special learning facilities include a radio station, 72-, 48-, and 24-track recording studios, a MIDI studio, and a film video/TV studio. **Physically Challenged Students:** All of the campus is accessible. Facilities include wheelchair ramps, special parking, specially equipped restrooms, and special housing. **Special:** Internships are required in business management (concentrations in audio recording technology and music business), mass communication (concentrations in broadcasting and journalism), and are available for all other degree programs. There is 1 national honor society. **Visiting:** There are regularly scheduled orientations for prospective students, including a campus tour, academic counseling, financial aid counseling, and educational workshops. Students also learn about student support services and how to become involved in student activities. There are guides for informal visits and visitors may sit in

FIVE TOWNS COLLEGE	E-5
www.ftc.edu	
Dix Hills, NY 11746	**(631) 656-2110**
Fax: (631) 656-2172	Email: admissions@ftc.edu
Full-time: 479 men, 213 women	Faculty: 24
Part-time: 41 men, 16 women	Ph.D.s: 33%
Graduate: 29 men, 10 women	Student/Faculty: 14 to 1
Year: semesters, summer session	Tuition: $20,880
Room & Board: $13,610	Freshman Class: 598 applied, 331 accepted, 239 enrolled
SAT CR/M/W: 450/430/430 ACT: 21	CEEB CODE: 3142
Application Deadline: rolling	COMPETITIVE

on classes. To schedule a visit, contact the Admissions Office. **Campus Safety and Security:** Measures include 24-hour foot and vehicle patrol, emergency notification system, and security escort services. There are shuttle buses, lighted pathways/sidewalks, and controlled access to dorms/residences.

REQUIREMENTS: The SAT or ACT is required. A minimum high school average of 80 is required. A GED with a minimum score of 2500 is accepted. An audition is required for students in music and theater. We recommend a 1350 on all three parts of the SAT and a 19 on the ACT. We offer an entrance exam for students that do not meet our academic standards. AP and CLEP credits are accepted. Important factors in the admissions decision are evidence of special talent, recommendations by school officials, and extracurricular activities record.To graduate, all students must complete a total of 134 credits for a Mus.B. or B.F.A. degree, 127 for a B.S. degree, or 121 for a B.P.S. degree. Students must maintain at least a C average in their major concentration and have a minimum GPA of 2.0 to graduate. Distribution requirements include 45 credits in core courses in liberal arts. The core curriculum consists of English Composition 101 and 102, Speech 101, 3 credits each of either psychology or sociology, and various upper-division liberal arts and social science courses. All music students must pass a jury exam. Music majors and elementary education majors must take a comprehensive exam. **Procedure:** Freshmen are admitted fall, spring, and summer. Entrance exams should be taken prior to admission. There are early decision, deferred admissions, and rolling admissions plans. Early decision applications should be filed by December 1, along with a $35 fee. Notification is sent on a rolling basis. 5 early decision candidates were accepted for the 2014-2015 class. Applications are accepted on-line. **Transfer Students:** 70 transfer students enrolled in 2013-2014. Students must be in good academic standing at their former school and have a minimum GPA of 2.5. 60 of 121 credits required for the bachelor's degree must be completed at FTC. **International Students:** There are 7 international students enrolled. The school actively recruits these students. They must take the TOEFL with a minimum score of 520 on the paper-based TOEFL (PBT) or 79 on the Internet-based version (iBT).

ADMISSIONS: 55% of the 2014-2015 applicants were accepted. The SAT scores for the 2014-2015 freshman class were: Critical Reading--67% below 500, 26% between 500 and 599, 5% between 600 and 699, and 2% between 700 and 800; Math--68% below 500, 24% between 500 and 599, 7% between 600 and 699, and 1% between 700 and 800; Writing--75% below 500, 21% between 500 and 599, 3% between 600 and 699, and 1% between 700 and 800. The ACT scores were 40% below 21, 45% between 21 and 23, and 15% between 24 and 26. 15% of the current freshmen were in the top fifth of their class; 40% were in the top two fifths. **Admissions Contact:** Jerry Cohen, Dean of Enrollment Services. E-Mail: *admissions@ftc.edu* Web: *www.ftc.edu*

FINANCIAL AID: In 2014-2015, 92% of all full-time freshmen and 90% of continuing full-time students received some form of financial aid. 73% of all full-time freshmen and 75% of continuing full-time students received need-based aid. The average freshman award was $14,000. Need-based scholarships or need-based grants averaged $3,900; need-based self-help aid (loans and jobs) averaged $4,000; and other non-need-based awards and non-need-based scholarships averaged $7,000. 90% of undergraduate students work part-time. Average annual earnings from campus work are $3000. The average financial indebtedness of the 2014 graduate was $22,000. The FAFSA and the college's own financial statement are required. The priority date for freshman financial aid applications for fall entry is March 31. The deadline for filing freshman financial aid applications for fall entry is August 25.

FORDHAM UNIVERSITY SYSTEM

The Fordham University System, established in 1841, is a private system in New York affiliated with the Catholic Church in the Jesuit tradition. It is governed by a board of trustees, whose chief administrator is the president. The primary goal of the system is to foster the intellectual, moral, and religious development of its students and prepare them for leadership in a global society. The main priorities are excellence in undergraduate and graduate/professional programs, and commitment to teaching, research, and service. The total student enrollment in a recent year was 14,448 with 1403 faculty members. Altogether there are approximately 69 baccalaureate, 71 master's, and 25 doctoral programs offered in the Fordham University System. Profiles of the 4-year campuses are included in this section.

FORDHAM UNIVERSITY   D-5
www.fordham.edu

Bronx, NY 10458	**(718) 817-4000**
	(800) FORDHAM
Fax: (718) 367-9404	**Email:** enroll@fordham.edu
Full-time: 3676 men, 4382 women	**Faculty:** I, av$
Part-time: 237 men, 338 women	**Ph.D.s:** 93%
Graduate: 2415 men, 4183 women	**Student/Faculty:** 13 to 1
Year: semesters, summer session	**Tuition:** $45,623
Room & Board: $15,965	**Freshman Class:** 40912 applied, 19685 accepted, 2258 enrolled
SAT CR/M/W: 620/620/630 **ACT:** 28	**CEEB CODE:** 2259
Application Deadline: January 1	**HIGHLY COMPETITIVE+**

Fordham University, an independent institution offering an education based in the Jesuit tradition, has two major campuses in New York City. Fordham has four full-time undergraduate colleges, and six graduate/professional schools, offering a broad range of studies in liberal arts and sciences, business administration, social service, education and law. Pre-professional studies in law and medicine are popular programs, as well as the opportunity to study abroad. Fordham also works with more than 2,000 organizations in the New York metropolitan area to arrange internships for students in fields such as business, communications, medicine, law and education. There are 4 undergraduate schools and 6 graduate schools. In addition to regional accreditation, has baccalaureate program accreditation with AACSB and NCATE. The 93-acre campus is in an urban area Rose Hill campus is located in the Bronx adjacent to the Bronx Zoo and New York Botanical Gardens. The Lincoln Center campus is located in Manhattan at 60th Street and Columbus Avenue. Including any residence halls, there are 42 buildings.

STUDENT LIFE: 53% of undergraduates are from out of state, mostly the Northeast. Students are from 48 states, 65 foreign countries, and Canada. 60% are White; 14% Hispanic. 51% are Catholic; 13% Buddhist, Greek Orthodox, Hindu, and Muslim. **Male To Female Ratio:** 1.4:1. The average age of freshmen is 18; all undergraduates, 21. **Housing:** 4490 students can be accommodated in college housing, which includes coed dorms, on-campus apartments, and off-campus apartments. Integrated learning communities. On-campus housing is guaranteed for all 4 years, is available on a first-come, first-served basis, and is available on a lottery system for upperclassmen. 57% of students live on campus. All students may keep cars.

FACULTY/CLASSROOMS: 53% of faculty are male; 47% are female. No introductory courses are taught by graduate students. The average class size in an introductory lecture is 22.

PROGRAMS OF STUDY: Fordham confers B.A., B.S. and B.F.A. degrees. Master's and Doctoral degrees are also awarded. Bachelor's degrees are awarded in BIOLOGICAL SCIENCE (biology/biological science and neurosciences), BUSINESS (accounting, business administration and management, business economics, finance, international business management, and marketing management), COMMUNICATIONS AND THE ARTS (art history, classical languages, classics, communication, communications, comparative literature, dance, dramatic arts, English, English literature, English Writing, fine arts, French, German, graphic design, Italian, journalism, Latin, music, music theory and composition, performing arts, Spanish, studio art, theatre acting, theater design, theatre production, and visual and performing arts), COMPUTER AND PHYSICAL SCIENCE (chemistry, computer science, information sciences and systems, mathematics, mathematics – economics, natural sciences, physics, science, and statistics), ENGINEERING AND ENVIRONMENTAL DESIGN (engineering physics and environmental science), SOCIAL SCIENCE (African studies, African American studies, American studies, anthropology, classical/ancient civilization, economics,

French studies, German area studies, history, international studies, Italian studies, Latin American studies, medieval studies, Middle Eastern studies, philosophy, political science/government, psychology, religion, social science, social work, sociology, Spanish studies, theological studies, urban studies, and women's studies). Biology, political science, English, and business administration are the strongest academically. Business, communication and media studies, and psychology have the largest enrollments.

ACTIVITIES: There are no fraternities or sororities. There are 165 groups on campus, including campus activities board, art, band, cheerleading, choir, chorale, chorus, computers, dance, debate, drama, environmental, ethnic, film, gay, honors, international, jazz band, literary magazine, marching band, musical theater, newspaper, orchestra, pep band, photography, political, professional, radio and TV, religious, social, social service, student admission ambassadors, student government, symphony, and yearbook. Popular campus events include Fall in Love with Fordham Festival, Spring Weekend, Spring Semiformal and Senior Week. **Sports:** There are 12 intercollegiate sports for men and 10 for women, and 5 intramural sports for men and 5 for women. Facilities include A 6000-seat football stadium, an Olympic-size pool with a separate diving area, an indoor track, a 3200-seat gym, and tennis, squash, and racquetball courts, a newly renovated student workout room. **Graduates:** The most popular majors were business administration (29%), social sciences (18%), and communication and media studies (13%). Of the 2013 graduating class, 29% were enrolled in graduate school within 6 months of graduation, and 76% were employed.

SERVICES: Counseling and information services are available, as is tutoring in most subjects. **Library/Resources:** The 4 libraries contain 228.0 million volumes, 3.2 million microform items, 64,833 audio/video tapes/CDs/DVDs, and subscribe to 68,957 periodicals including electronic. Computerized library services include interlibrary loans, database searching, internet access, and Wi-Fi capability. Special learning facilities include an art gallery, radio station, a seismic station, an archeological site, and a biological field station. **Physically Challenged Students:** 80% of the campus is accessible. Facilities include wheelchair ramps, elevators, special parking, specially equipped restrooms, special class scheduling, and lowered drinking fountains. **Special:** Fordham University offers career-oriented internships during the junior or senior year with New York City companies and institutions. A combined 3-2 engineering program is available with Columbia and Case Western Reserve Universities. Accelerated degrees, dual and student-designed majors, and pass/fail options are available. Study abroad programs are available around the globe and include Fordham specific programs in London, England; Grenada, Spain; and Pretoria, South Africa. Fordham additionally offers a B.F.A program in conjunction with the Alvin Ailey School of Dance and a B.A. program in Theatre. There are 6 national honor societies, Phi Beta Kappa, and a freshman honors program. **Visiting:** There are regularly scheduled orientations for prospective students. There are guides for informal visits and visitors may sit in on classes. To schedule a visit, contact the Office of Undergraduate Admission. **Campus Safety and Security:** Measures include 24-hour foot and vehicle patrol, emergency notification system, and security escort services. There are shuttle buses, emergency telephones, lighted pathways/sidewalks, and controlled access to dorms/residences.

REQUIREMENTS: The SAT or ACT is required. The ACT Optional Writing test is also required. Applicants should complete 4 years of high school English, 3 years of math, science, social studies, and history, and 2 years of a foreign language. Applicants should submit the Common Application which includes an essay and questions on the Fordham member screen. A secondary school report or guidance counselor letter of recommendation is required. Fordham requires either the SAT or ACT. SAT II subject tests are not required. Auditions are required for theatre and dance majors. Additionally, Fordham has a no interview policy. AP credits are accepted. Important factors in the admissions decision are advanced placement or honors courses, leadership record, extracurricular activities record, parents or siblings attended your school, evidence of special talent, personality/intangible qualities, geographical diversity, and recommendations by school officials.All students must complete a core curriculum, including courses each in literature, history, philosophy, theology, natural sciences, social sciences, math, English composi-

tion, fine arts and foreign language competency. A total of 124 credits and a 2.0 minimum GPA are required for graduation. **Procedure:** Freshmen are admitted fall and spring. Entrance exams should be taken by January of the senior year. There are early admissions and deferred admissions plans. Early decision applications should be filed by November 1; regular applications, by January 1 for fall entry; and December 1 for spring entry, along with a $70 fee. Notification of early decision is sent December 15; regular decision, April 1. 2366 applicants were on the 2014 waiting list; 297 were admitted. Applications are accepted on-line. **Transfer Students:** 339 transfer students enrolled in 2013-2014. A 3.0 minimum GPA is recommended. All applicants are required to submit the Common Application and essay, official high school and college transcripts, and a letter of good standing from the Dean or University Registrar from the institution the student currently attends. Applicants with less than one full year of full-time course work at a post-secondary institution must submit SAT or ACT scores. 64 of 124 credits required for the bachelor's degree must be completed a Fordham. **International Students:** There are 554 international students enrolled. The school actively recruits these students. They must take the TOEFL with a minimum score of 90 on the Internet-based version (iBT) and the college's own test. They must also take the SAT or ACT.

ADMISSIONS: 48% of the 2014-2015 applicants were accepted. The SAT scores for the 2014-2015 freshman class were: Critical Reading--4% below 500, 32% between 500 and 599, 47% between 600 and 699, and 17% between 700 and 800; Math--3% below 500, 30% between 500 and 599, 52% between 600 and 699, and 15% between 700 and 800; Writing--5% below 500, 26% between 500 and 599, 51% between 600 and 699, and 19% between 700 and 800. The ACT scores were 2% below 21, 6% between 21 and 23, 23% between 24 and 26, 23% between 27 and 28, and 47% above 28. 71% of the current freshmen were in the top fifth of their class; 92% were in the top two fifths. **Admissions Contact:** Patricia Peek, Ph.D., Director of Admission. E-Mail: *enroll@fordham.edu* Web: *www.fordham.edu*

FINANCIAL AID: In 2014-2015, 91% of all full-time freshmen and continuing full-time students received some form of financial aid. Fordham is a member of CSS. The CSS/Profile and FAFSA, and noncustodial profile, business and farm supplement are required. The deadline for filing freshman financial aid applications for fall entry is February 10.

HAMILTON COLLEGE   C-3
www.hamilton.edu

Clinton, NY 13323   (315) 859-4421
                                          (800) 843-2655
Fax: (315) 859-4457   Email: admission@hamilton.edu
Full-time: 910 men, 958 women   Faculty: 188; IIB, ++$
Part-time: 7 men, 9 women   Ph.Ds: 94%
Graduate: n/av   Student/Faculty: 10 to 1
Year: semesters   Tuition: $44,350
Room & Board: $11,270   Freshman Class: 5107
                                   applied, 1389 accepted,
                                   469 enrolled
SAT CR/M/W: 700/700/700 ACT: 31   CEEB CODE: 2286
Application Deadline: January 1   MOST COMPETITIVE

Hamilton College, chartered in 1812, is a private, nonsectarian, liberal arts school offering undergraduate programs in the arts and sciences. Figures in the above capsule and in this profile are approximate. The 1300-acre campus is in a rural area 9 miles southwest of Utica. Including any residence halls, there are 106 buildings.

STUDENT LIFE: 67% of undergraduates are from out of state, mostly the Middle Atlantic. Students are from 46 states, 39 foreign countries, and Canada. 61% are from public schools. 63% are White; 11% race unknown. 40% claim no religious affiliation; 24% Protestant; 21% Catholic. **Male To Female Ratio:** 1.1:1. The average age of freshmen is 18; all undergraduates, 20. 4% do not continue beyond their first year; 91% remain to graduate. **Housing:** 1835 students can be accommodated in college housing, which includes coed dorms, on-campus apartments, and married student housing. In addition, there are special-interest houses, quiet floors, and substance-free areas. On-campus housing is guaranteed for all 4 years. 98% of students live on campus; of those, 90% remain on campus on weekends. Upperclassmen may keep cars.

FACULTY/CLASSROOMS: 57% of faculty are male; 43% are female. All teach undergraduates. No introductory courses are taught by graduate students. The average class size in a regular course is 16.

PROGRAMS OF STUDY: Hamilton confers A.B. degrees. Bachelor's degrees are awarded in AGRICULTURE (environmental studies), BIOLOGICAL SCIENCE (biochemistry, biology/biological science, and neurosciences), COMMUNICATIONS AND THE ARTS (art, art history and appreciation, Chinese, classics, communications, comparative literature, creative writing, dance, dramatic arts, English, English literature, French, languages, music, and studio art), COMPUTER AND PHYSICAL SCIENCE (chemical physics, chemistry, computer science, geoscience, mathematics, and physics), SOCIAL SCIENCE (African studies, American studies, anthropology, archeology, Asian/Oriental studies, economics, German area studies, Hispanic American studies, history, interdisciplinary studies, international relations, philosophy, political science/government, psychobiology, psychology, public affairs, religion, Russian and Slavic studies, sociology, and women's studies). Economics, mathematics, and psychology have the largest enrollments.

ACTIVITIES: 26% of men belong to 11 national fraternities; 17% of women belong to 6 local and 1 national sororities. There are 189 groups on campus, including art, band, chess, choir, chorale, chorus, communications, computers, dance, debate, drama, environmental, ethnic, film, gay, honors, international, jazz band, literary magazine, musical theater, newspaper, orchestra, photography, political, professional, radio and TV, religious, social, social service, student government, and yearbook. Popular campus events include Class and Charter Day, and Feb Fest (Winter Carnival). **Sports:** There are 14 intercollegiate sports for men and 15 for women, and 16 intramural sports for men and 16 for women. Facilities include a gym, a field house, a fitness and dance center, squash and racquetball courts, indoor and outdoor tennis courts, an artificial grass football stadium, a 9-hole golf course, a swimming pool, indoor and outdoor tracks, baseball and softball fields, numerous grass fields, an artificial turf field, paddle tennis courts, and an ice rink. **Graduates:** From July 1, 2013 to June 30, 2014, 462 bachelor's degrees were awarded. The most popular majors were economics (16%), mathematics (10%), and government (8%). In an average class, 85% graduate in 4 years or less, 90% graduate in 5 years or less, and 91% graduate in 6 years or less.

SERVICES: Counseling and information services are available, as is tutoring in some subjects, through the New York State Higher Education Opportunity Program (HEOP). **Library/Resources:** The 2 libraries contain 625,376 volumes, 293,834 microform items, 35,217 audio/video tapes/CDs/DVDs, and subscribe to 4,546 periodicals including electronic. Computerized library services include interlibrary loans, database searching, Internet access, and Wi-Fi capability. Special learning facilities include an art gallery, radio station, TV station, an observatory; electron microscope; Wellin Museum of Art. **Physically Challenged Students:** Facilities include wheelchair ramps, elevators, special parking, specially equipped restrooms, special class scheduling, and special housing. **Special:** Cross-registration is permitted with Colgate University and Utica College. Opportunities are provided for a Washington semester and a New York City semester. Student-designed majors and study abroad in many countries are available, and 3-2 engineering degrees are offered with Washington University in St. Louis, Rensselaer Polytechnic Institute, and Columbia University. There are 8 national honor societies including Phi Beta Kappa. **Visiting:** There are regularly scheduled orientations for prospective students, consisting of an interview, tour, class visit, and open house program. There are guides for informal visits, visitors may sit in on classes, and stay overnight. To schedule a visit, contact the Office of Admission. **Campus Safety and Security:** Measures include 24-hour foot and vehicle patrol, emergency notification system, self-defense education, and security escort services. There are shuttle buses, emergency telephones, lighted pathways/sidewalks, and controlled access to dorms/residences.

REQUIREMENTS: The SAT or ACT is required. Although graduation from an accredited secondary school or a GED is desirable, and a full complement of college-preparatory courses is recommended,

Hamilton will consider all highly recommended candidates who demonstrate an ability and desire to perform at intellectually demanding levels. Students can fulfill test requirements with the SAT, ACT, 3 SAT Subject tests, 3 AP exams, or any combination of these. An essay is required, and an interview is recommended. AP credits are accepted. Important factors in the admissions decision are advanced placement or honors courses, recommendations by school officials, and parents or siblings attended your school. Students must successfully complete 128 credits, with 32 to 40 of these in the student's major, and must maintain at least a 72 average in half the courses taken. **Procedure:** Freshmen are admitted fall. Entrance exams should be taken prior to February of the senior year. There are early decision and deferred admissions plans. Early decision applications should be filed by November 15; regular applications, by January 1 for fall entry. The fall 2014 application fee was $60. Notification of early decision is sent December 15; regular decision, April 1. 251 early decision candidates were accepted for the 2014-2015 class. 1016 applicants were on the 2014 waiting list; 3 were admitted. Applications are accepted on-line. **Transfer Students:** 14 transfer students enrolled in 2013-2014. Transfer applicants must submit high school and college transcripts, an essay or personal statement, and standardized test scores and must present a minimum GPA of 3.0 in all college-level work. 64 of 128 credits required for the bachelor's degree must be completed at Hamilton. **International Students:** There are 90 international students enrolled. The school actively recruits these students. They must take the TOEFL. They must also take the SAT or ACT.

ADMISSIONS: 27% of the 2014-2015 applicants were accepted. The SAT scores for the 2014-2015 freshman class were: Critical Reading--1% below 500, 10% between 500 and 599, 38% between 600 and 699, and 51% between 700 and 800; Math--1% below 500, 7% between 500 and 599, 42% between 600 and 699, and 51% between 700 and 800; Writing--1% below 500, 11% between 500 and 599, 36% between 600 and 699, and 52% between 700 and 800. The ACT scores were 1% below 21, 1% between 21 and 23, 9% between 24 and 26, 8% between 27 and 28, and 82% above 28. 95% of the current freshmen were in the top fifth of their class; 100% were in the top two fifths. 20 freshmen graduated first in their class. **Admissions Contact:** Monica Inzer, Vice President and Dean of Admission and Financial Aid. E-Mail: *admission@hamilton.edu* Web: *www.hamilton.edu*

FINANCIAL AID: In 2014-2015, 54% of all full-time freshmen and 44% of continuing full-time students received some form of financial aid. 54% of all full-time freshmen and 44% of continuing full-time students received need-based aid. The average freshman award was $40,594. Need-based scholarships or need-based grants averaged $37,569; and need-based self-help aid (loans and jobs) averaged $3,814. 53% of undergraduate students work part-time. Average annual earnings from campus work are $887. The average financial indebtedness of the 2014 graduate was $18,568. Hamilton is a member of CSS. The CSS/Profile, FAFSA, and the college's own financial statement are required. The deadline for filing freshman financial aid applications for fall entry is February 15.

HARTWICK COLLEGE D-3
www.hartwick.edu

Oneonta, NY 13820 (607) 431-4150
(888) HARTWICK

Fax: (607) 431-4102	Email: admissions@hartwick.edu
Full-time: 591 men, 916 women	Faculty: 111; IIB, +$
Part-time: 13 men, 20 women	Ph.D.s: 87%
Graduate: n/av	Student/Faculty: 14 to 1
Year: 4-1-4, summer session	Tuition: $40,470
Room & Board: $10,800	Freshman Class: n/av
	CEEB CODE: 2288
Application Deadline: rolling	COMPETITIVE

Hartwick College, founded in 1797, is a private undergraduate liberal arts and sciences college. There is one undergraduate school. In addition to regional accreditation, Hartwick has baccalaureate program accreditation with NASAD, NASM, TEAC, CCNE, and ACS. The 425-acre campus is in a small town 75 miles southwest of Albany, NY. Including any residence halls, there are 22 buildings.

STUDENT LIFE: 75% of undergraduates are from New York. Others are from 26 states, 26 foreign countries, and Canada. 85% are from public schools. 70% are White; 12% race unknown. 32% claim no religious affiliation; 30% Protestant; 25% Catholic. **Male To Female Ratio:** 1.5:1. The average age of freshmen is 19; all undergraduates, 20. 22% do not continue beyond their first year; 61% remain to graduate. **Housing:** 1201 students can be accommodated in college housing, which includes coed dorms and on-campus apartments. In addition, there are honors houses, fraternity houses, sorority houses, substance-free housing, community engagement floor, and an environmental campus. On-campus housing is guaranteed for all 4 years and is available on a lottery system for upperclassmen. 81% of students live on campus; of those, 80% remain on campus on weekends. All students may keep cars.

FACULTY/CLASSROOMS: 60% of faculty are male; 40% are female. All teach undergraduates. No introductory courses are taught by graduate students. The average class size in an introductory lecture is 20; in a laboratory is 20; and in a regular course is 17.

PROGRAMS OF STUDY: Hartwick confers B.A., and B.S. degrees. Bachelor's degrees are awarded in BIOLOGICAL SCIENCE (biochemistry and biology/biological science), BUSINESS (accounting and business administration and management), COMMUNICATIONS AND THE ARTS (art, art history and appreciation, dramatic arts, English, French, German, languages, music, and Spanish), COMPUTER AND PHYSICAL SCIENCE (chemistry, computer science, geology, information sciences and systems, mathematics, and physics), EDUCATION (music education), ENGINEERING AND ENVIRONMENTAL DESIGN (environmental science), HEALTH PROFESSIONS (medical technology and nursing), SOCIAL SCIENCE (anthropology, economics, history, philosophy, political science/government, psychology, religion, and sociology). Psychology, business administration/accounting, and nursing have the largest enrollments.

ACTIVITIES: 10% of men belong to 2 national fraternities; 8% of women belong to 2 local and 1 national sororities. There are 70 groups on campus, including art, band, cheerleading, choir, chorale, chorus, dance, drama, environmental, ethnic, gay, honors, international, jazz band, literary magazine, musical theater, newspaper, pep band, political, professional, radio and TV, religious, social, social service, student government, and yearbook. Popular campus events include Wick Wars (traditional fair-day contests), Oneonta State and Hartwick Fest (street fair and concert), and Scholar Showcase. **Sports:** There are 7 intercollegiate sports for men and 10 for women, and 5 intramural sports for men and 5 for women. Facilities include 2 gyms, an indoor pool, dance room, athletic and training facilities, track, 2 fitness centers, lighted all-weather playing field, lighted soccer field, an equestrian complex (off-campus), courts for handball, racquetball, squash, and tennis. **Graduates:** From July 1, 2013 to June 30, 2014, 354 bachelor's degrees were awarded. The most popular majors were business administration (19%), nursing (14%), and sociology. In an average class, 53% graduate in 4 years or less, 60% graduate in 5 years or less, and 61% graduate in 6 years or less. Of the 2013 graduating class, 16% were enrolled in graduate school within 6 months of graduation, and 26% were employed.

SERVICES: Counseling and information services are available, as is tutoring in most subjects. There is a reader service for the blind. Writing center and an academic support center. **Library/Resources:** The library contains 300,606 volumes, 29,700 microform items, 3,644 audio/video tapes/CDs/DVDs, and subscribes to 13,112 periodicals including electronic. Computerized library services include interlibrary loans, database searching, Internet access, and Wi-Fi capability. Special learning facilities include an art gallery, radio station, an 200-acre environmental campus, the Yager museum of art, culture and an observatory. **Physically Challenged Students:** 50% of the campus is accessible. Facilities include wheelchair ramps, elevators, special parking, and specially equipped restrooms. **Special:** Hartwick's innovative approach emphasizes personalized instruction and practical experiences both inside and outside the classroom: study abroad, internships, collaborative research, and more. Hartwick offers more thane than 30 courses of study leading to a bachelor of arts (B.A.) or bachelor of science (B.S.) degree, four pre-professional programs, five cooperative programs, and a series of interesting minors and other options, including certification in education. Plus, you can design

you own major. Within Hartwick's Three-Year Bachelor's Degree Program, there are 24 major areas of study leading to a bachelor of arts (B.A.) or bachelor of science (B.S.) degree. There is a 3-2 engineering program with Clarkson University or Columbia University, and a 3-3 program with Albany Law School. There are 9 national honor societies and a freshman honors program. **Visiting:** There are regularly scheduled orientations for prospective students, consisting of an interview and tour, lunch, departmental open houses, presentations on student life, off-campus programs, and a career planning process. There are guides for informal visits, visitors may sit in on classes, and stay overnight. To schedule a visit, contact the Admissions Office at admissions@hartwick.edu. **Campus Safety and Security:** Measures include 24-hour foot and vehicle patrol, emergency notification system, self-defense education, and security escort services. There are emergency telephones, lighted pathways/sidewalks, and controlled access to dorms/residences.

REQUIREMENTS: Reporting of SAT and ACT scores is optional. The recommended secondary course of study includes 4 years of English and 3 years each of math, a foreign language, history, and lab science. Hartwick strongly recommends that applicants plan a campus visit and interview. Prospective art majors should submit a portfolio, and music majors must audition. A GPA of 2.5 is required. AP and CLEP credits are accepted. Important factors in the admissions decision are advanced placement or honors courses, recommendations by school officials, and ability to finance college education.Students must complete 120 credit hours with at least a 2.0 GPA. The core curriculum consists of Hartwick's Liberal Arts in Practice. Distribution requirements include a first-year seminar; 9 credits spread through humanities, physical and life sciences, and social and behavioral sciences; 3 credits in quantitative and formal reasoning; foreign language (intermediate-level proficiency); attainment of writing level 4; and a senior capstone. **Procedure:** Freshmen are admitted fall and spring. Entrance exams should be taken in the spring of the junior year and/or the fall of the senior year. There are early decision, deferred admissions, and rolling admissions plans. Application deadlines are open. Notification is sent on a rolling basis. 33 early decision candidates were accepted for the 2014-2015 class. 51 applicants were on the 2014 waiting list; 45 were admitted. Applications are accepted on-line. **Transfer Students:** 36 transfer students enrolled in 2013-2014. Applicants should present a minimum GPA of 2.0. 60 of 120 credits required for the bachelor's degree must be completed at Hartwick. **International Students:** There are 52 international students enrolled. They must take the TOEFL with a minimum score of 550 on the paper-based TOEFL (PBT) or 79 on the Internet-based version (iBT). They must also take the SAT, scoring 420.

ADMISSIONS: 15% of the current freshmen were in the top fifth of their class; 45% were in the top two fifths. **Admissions Contact:** Lisa Starkey-Wood, Director of Admissions. E-Mail: admissions@hartwick .edu Web: www.hartwick.edu

FINANCIAL AID: In 2014-2015, 100% of all full-time freshmen and 99% of continuing full-time students received some form of financial aid. The average freshman award was $21,632. 66% of undergraduate students work part-time. Average annual earnings from campus work are $1640. Hartwick is a member of CSS. The FAFSA and the college's own financial statement are required. The deadline for filing freshman financial aid applications for fall entry is February 15.

HILBERT COLLEGE	A-4
www.hilbert.edu	

Hamburg, NY 14075	(716) 649-7900
	(800) 649-8003
Fax: (716) 649-0702	Email: admissions@hilbert.edu
Full-time: 404 men, 480 women	Faculty: 47; IIB, -$
Part-time: 52 men, 83 women	Ph.Ds: 53%
Graduate: 21 men, 29 women	Student/Faculty: 18 to 1
Year: semesters, summer session	Tuition: $19,900
Room & Board: $8650	Freshman Class: n/av
	CEEB CODE: 2334
Application Deadline: n/av	COMPETITIVE

Hilbert College, located in suburban Hamburg, N.Y., is a private four-year college founded in 1957 in the Catholic Franciscan tradition. Hilbert is a dynamic Western New York college that offers career-focused majors, including one of the top criminal justice programs in the region, and more than 50 minors and concentrations. The college's engaging, student-centered campus community offers numerous leadership, internship, and service learning opportunities from which students launch successful careers while making positive changes in their communities. The Hilbert Blueprint promotes a well-rounded student experience over four years – starting with the Foundations Seminar in the freshman year, followed by Sophomore Service, Junior Symposium, and culminating with the Senior Capstone. Hilbert has expanded its academic offerings with the college's first graduate programs and new Accelerated Degree Programs geared to adult learners. There is 1 undergraduate school and 1 graduate school. The 44-acre campus is in a suburban area about 10 miles south of Buffalo. Including any residence halls, there are 11 buildings.

STUDENT LIFE: 95% of undergraduates are from New York. Others are from 12 states, 2 foreign countries, and Canada. 80% are from public schools. 73% are White. **Male To Female Ratio:** 1.2:1. The average age of freshmen is 18; all undergraduates, 22. 25% do not continue beyond their first year; 39% remain to graduate. **Housing:** 304 students can be accommodated in college housing, which includes coed dorms and on-campus apartments. On-campus housing is guaranteed for the freshman year only, is available on a first-come, first-served basis, and is available on a lottery system for upperclassmen. 71% of students commute. All students may keep cars.

FACULTY/CLASSROOMS: 51% of faculty are male; 49% are female. All teach undergraduates, and 10% do both. No introductory courses are taught by graduate students. The average class size in an introductory lecture is 20 and in a regular course is 15.

PROGRAMS OF STUDY: Hilbert confers B.A., and B.S. degrees. Associate and Master's degrees are also awarded. Bachelor's degrees are awarded in BIOLOGICAL SCIENCE (forensic science), BUSINESS (accounting, business administration and management, international business management, organizational leadership and management, and sports management), COMMUNICATIONS AND THE ARTS (digital communications and English), COMPUTER AND PHYSICAL SCIENCE (computer security and information assurance), HEALTH PROFESSIONS (rehabilitation therapy), SOCIAL SCIENCE (criminal justice, criminology, forensic studies, human services, liberal arts/general studies, paralegal studies, political science/government, and psychology). Paralegal studies, psychology, and accounting are the strongest academically. Criminal justice, forensic science, and business administration have the largest enrollments.

ACTIVITIES: There are no fraternities or sororities. There are 20 groups on campus, including and human services), criminal justice, psychology, academic (e.g., cheerleading, ethnic, film, honors, literary magazine, newspaper, professional, religious, social, social service, and student government. Popular campus events include Quad Party, Fall Fest, and Fall Family Weekend. **Sports:** There are 5 intercollegiate sports for men and 6 for women, and 4 intramural sports for men and 4 for women. Facilities include a soccer/lacrosse field, baseball and softball diamonds, a practice field, fitness center, and a 900-seat NCAA regulation indoor athletic facility. **Graduates:** From July 1, 2013 to June 30, 2014, 227 bachelor's degrees were awarded. The most popular majors were criminal justice (37%), forensic science/crime scene invetigation (22%), and business administration (8%). 50 companies recruited on campus in 2013-2014. In an average class, 36% graduate in 4 years or less, 38% graduate in 5 years or less, and 39% graduate in 6 years or less. Of the 2013 graduating class, 15% were enrolled in graduate school within 6 months of graduation, and 75% were employed.

SERVICES: Counseling and information services are available, as is tutoring in some subjects, writing, accounting, and math. There is remedial math and writing. **Library/Resources:** The library contains 36,076 volumes, 3,616 microform items, 1,500 audio/video tapes/CDs/DVDs, and subscribes to 23,190 periodicals including electronic. Computerized library services include interlibrary loans, database searching, Internet access, and Wi-Fi capability. Special learning facilities include a **Physically Challenged Students:** 95% of the campus is accessible. Facilities include wheelchair ramps, elevators, special parking, specially equipped restrooms, special class scheduling, low-

ered drinking fountains, and lowered telephones. **Special:** Hilbert offers study abroad, cross-registration with the 17-member Western New York College Consortium, internships in most majors, and work-study programs. The college maintains articulation agreements with 22 New York State community colleges. There are 4 national honor societies, a freshman honors program, and 3 departmental honors programs. **Visiting:** There are regularly scheduled orientations for prospective students. There are guides for informal visits and visitors may sit in on classes. To schedule a visit, contact Office of Admissions at admissions@hilbert.edu. **Campus Safety and Security:** Measures include 24-hour foot and vehicle patrol, emergency notification system, self-defense education, and security escort services. There are emergency telephones, lighted pathways/sidewalks, and controlled access to dorms/residences.

REQUIREMENTS: The SAT or ACT is recommended. Admission is based upon past academic performance, demonstrated ability, and personal characteristics. Applicants must submit an official high school transcript or GED certificate. AP and CLEP credits are accepted. Important factors in the admissions decision are leadership record, advanced placement or honors courses, and recommendations by school officials. To graduate, students must complete 120 credit hours, including at least 36 in the major and 60 in liberal arts, with a minimum 2.0 GPA. Students must fulfill General Education requirements in interdisciplinary studies,intercultural awareness, arts and literature, math, religious studies, moral reasoning, political science/geography/history, sociology/psychology/economics, and physical sciences. **Procedure:** Freshmen are admitted to all sessions. There are deferred admissions and rolling admissions plans. Application deadlines are open. Application fee is $25. Applications are accepted on-line. Application fees are waived if application is completed on-line. **Transfer Students:** 301 transfer students enrolled in 2013-2014. Applicants must submit official transcripts from all colleges attended and, in some cases, the high school transcript. 30 of 120 credits required for the bachelor's degree must be completed at Hilbert. **International Students:** There are 6 international students enrolled. They must take the TOEFL.

ADMISSIONS: Justin Rogers, Director of Admissions. E-Mail: *admissions@hilbert.edu* Web: *www.hilbert.edu*

FINANCIAL AID: In 2014-2015, 88% of all full-time freshmen and 83% of continuing full-time students received some form of financial aid. 100% of all full-time freshmen and 98% of continuing full-time students received need-based aid. The average freshman award was $15,206. Need-based scholarships or need-based grants averaged $11,620; need-based self-help aid (loans and jobs) averaged $3,971; and other non-need-based awards and non-need-based scholarships averaged $5,087. 7% of undergraduate students work part-time. Average annual earnings from campus work are $1735. Hilbert is a member of CSS. The FAFSA is required. The priority date for freshman financial aid applications for fall entry is March 1. The deadline for filing freshman financial aid applications for fall entry is December 1.

HOBART AND WILLIAM SMITH COLLEGES B-3
www.hws.edu

Geneva, NY 14456	H: (315) 781-3622
	n/av
Fax: (315) 781-3471	Email: jyoung@hws.edu
Full-time: 1101 men, 1261 women	Faculty: IIB, +$
Part-time: 57 men, 2 women	Ph.D.s: n/av
Graduate: 4 women	Student/Faculty: 11 to 1
Year: semesters	Tuition: $47,908
Room & Board: $12,126	Freshman Class: 5093 applied, 2528 accepted, 643 enrolled
SAT CR/M/W: 620/620/610 **ACT:** 29	CEEB CODE: 2294
Application Deadline: February 1	HIGHLY COMPETITIVE+

Hobart and William Smith are independent liberal arts colleges distinctive for providing highly individualized educations. Guided by an interdisciplinary curriculum grounded in exploration and rigor, the colleges prepare students to think critically. In partnership with the Geneva and global communities and through robust programs in career development, study-abroad, service, leadership and athletics, the colleges foster an environment that values global citizenship, teamwork, ethics, inclusive excellence, and cultural competence. There are 1 undergraduate school and 1 graduate school. The 195-acre campus is in a small town in the heart of New York State's Finger Lake region, 50 miles west of Syracuse and 50 miles east of Rochester, on the north shore of Seneca Lake. Including any residence halls, there are 95 buildings.

STUDENT LIFE: 55% of undergraduates are from out of state, mostly the Northeast. Students are from 43 states, 24 foreign countries, and Canada. 59% are from public schools. 69% are White. 30% are Catholic; 30% Protestant; 20% claim no religious affiliation; 15% Jewish. **Male To Female Ratio:** 1.1:1. The average age of freshmen is 18; all undergraduates, 20. 12% do not continue beyond their first year; 75% remain to graduate. **Housing:** 1930 students can be accommodated in college housing, which includes single-sex and coed dorms and on-campus apartments. In addition, there are honors houses, language houses, special-interest houses, fraternity houses, cooperative, themed houses in which students plan and prepare their own meals, and townhouses for upperclassmen. On-campus housing is guaranteed for all 4 years. 90% of students live on campus; of those, 93% remain on campus on weekends. All students may keep cars.

FACULTY/CLASSROOMS: 60% of faculty are male; 40% are female. All teach and do research. No introductory courses are taught by graduate students. The average class size in an introductory lecture is 40; in a laboratory is 18; and in a regular course is 18.

PROGRAMS OF STUDY: HWS confers B.A., and B.S. degrees. Master's degrees are also awarded. Bachelor's degrees are awarded in BIOLOGICAL SCIENCE (biochemistry and biology/biological science), COMMUNICATIONS AND THE ARTS (art history, classics, communication rhetoric/communication, comparative literature, dance, English, film, television and digital media, fine arts, French, Greek, Latin, modern language, music, Russian languages and literature, and studio art), COMPUTER AND PHYSICAL SCIENCE (chemistry, computer science, geoscience, mathematics, and physics), ENGINEERING AND ENVIRONMENTAL DESIGN (architecture and environmental science), SOCIAL SCIENCE (African studies, Africana studies, American studies, anthropology, architectural studies, Asian/Oriental studies, economics, European studies, history, international relations, Latin American studies, philosophy, political science/government, psychology, religion, Russian and Slavic studies, sociology, Spanish studies, Hispanic studies, urban studies, and women's studies). Natural sciences, environmental studies, women's studies and architecture are the strongest academically. English, economics, political science, media and society have the largest enrollments.

ACTIVITIES: 20% of men belong to 7 national fraternities. There are no sororities. There are 70 groups on campus, including and women's collective, club sports, crossfit, first generation, art, chess, choir, chorale, chorus, computers, dance, debate, debate team, drama, environmental, ethnic, film, gay, honors, international, jazz band, literary magazine, musical theater, newspaper, orchestra, photography, political, professional, radio and TV, religious, social, social service, student government, symphony, and yearbook. Popular campus events include The Pitch Entrepreneurial Competition, Charter Day and Moving Up Day, as well as Convocation and Homecoming. **Sports:** There are 11 intercollegiate sports for men and 12 for women, and 22 intramural sports for men and 22 for women. Facilities include a sport and recreation center, 2 gyms, numerous athletic fields, a swimming pool, 5 indoor tennis courts, 8 outdoor tennis courts, 3 weight rooms, basketball and racquetball courts, an indoor track, international squash courts, a boathouse, and a crew facility. **Graduates:** From July 1, 2013 to June 30, 2014, 484 bachelor's degrees were awarded. The most popular majors were economics (12%), English (10%), and media and society (9%). In an average class, 74% graduate in 4 years or less, 79% graduate in 5 years or less, and 79% graduate in 6 years or less. Of the 2013 graduating class, 12% were enrolled in graduate school within 6 months of graduation, and 75% were employed.

SERVICES: Counseling and information services are available, as is

tutoring in every subject. There is a reader service for the blind, and remedial math, reading, and writing. There is a counseling center staffed by 5 therapists/counselors as well as various support groups and educational workshops. **Library/Resources:** The library contains 504,379 volumes, 47,714 microform items, 15,176 audio/video tapes/CDs/DVDs, and subscribes to 5,011 periodicals including electronic. Computerized library services include interlibrary loans, database searching, Internet access, and Wi-Fi capability. Special learning facilities include an art gallery, radio station, a 100-acre natural preserve, 35 acres of farmland, the Finger Lakes Institute at HWS, Finger Lakes Community Design Center and a 70-foot research vessel. **Physically Challenged Students:** 65% of the campus is accessible. Facilities include wheelchair ramps, elevators, special parking, specially equipped restrooms, special class scheduling, and lowered drinking fountains. **Special:** Students are encouraged to spend at least 1 term in a study-abroad program, offered in more than 33 countries and locales within the United States. Additionally, the Colleges offer a semester in Washington, D.C. HWS accepts a maximum of 7 AP credits, participate in the College Level Examination Program (CLEP) and Regents College Examination Program (RCE),and recognize academic work taken toward the International Baccalaureate. There are also advanced business degree programs with Clarkson University and Rochester Institute of Technology and 3-2 engineering degrees with Columbia University, Rensselaer Polytechnic Institute, and Dartmouth College. Through the Salisbury Center for Career, Professional and Experiential Learning, students have numerous opportunities to find credit-bearing internships nationally and internationally. There are 8 national honor societies, including Phi Beta Kappa, and 100 departmental honors programs. **Visiting:** There are regularly scheduled orientations for prospective students, including 7 open houses in the spring, summer, and fall, daily tours and personal interviews year round. Information sessions are offered February through April and on Saturdays in the summer. There are guides for informal visits, visitors may sit in on classes, and stay overnight. To schedule a visit, contact the Office of Admissions. **Campus Safety and Security:** Measures include 24-hour foot and vehicle patrol, emergency notification system, self-defense education, and security escort services. There are shuttle buses, emergency telephones, lighted pathways/sidewalks, and controlled access to dorms/residences.

REQUIREMENTS: SAT: Subject tests are not required but will be considered if taken. A GED may be is accepted. A total of 19 academic credits is required, including 4 years of English, 3 of math, and at least 3 each of lab science, foreign language, and history. An essay is required; an interview is recommended. AP credits are accepted. Important factors in the admissions decision are advanced placement or honors courses, evidence of special talent, and leadership record. All first-year students must take a seminar. Students should complete a major of 14 to 18 courses and a minor of 6 to 8 courses, or a second major. Of the major or the minor (or second major), one must be disciplinary and the other interdisciplinary. Minimum grade and GPA standards apply. In addition, all students must meet the 8 goals established by the faculty to ensure breadth across the disciplines as well as depth in the major. **Procedure:** Freshmen are admitted fall. Entrance exams should be taken no later than December of the senior year. There are early decision, early admissions, and deferred admissions plans. Early decision applications should be filed by November 15; regular applications, by February 1 for fall entry, along with a $45 fee. Notification of early decision is sent December 15; regular decision, in March. 345 early decision candidates were accepted for the 2014-2015 class. 759 applicants were on the 2014 waiting list; 31 were admitted. Applications are accepted on-line. Application fees are waived if application is completed on-line. **Transfer Students:** 9 transfer students enrolled in 2013-2014. Applicants must have a 2.5 GPA and have completed 1 year of college study. They are required to take the SAT or ACT. An interview is recommended. 16 of 32 credits required for the bachelor's degree must be completed at HWS. **International Students:** There are 119 international students enrolled. The school actively recruits these students. They must take the TOEFL. They must also take the SAT or ACT.

ADMISSIONS: 50% of the 2014-2015 applicants were accepted. The SAT scores for the 2014-2015 freshman class were: Critical Reading--3% below 500, 35% between 500 and 599, 50% between 600 and

699, and 12% between 700 and 800; Math--2% below 500, 29% between 500 and 599, 57% between 600 and 699, and 12% between 700 and 800; Writing--3% below 500, 33% between 500 and 599, 54% between 600 and 699, and 10% between 700 and 800. The ACT scores were 1% below 21, 1% between 21 and 23, 16% between 24 and 26, 25% between 27 and 28, and 59% above 28. **Admissions Contact:** John W. Young, Director of Admissions. E-Mail: *jyoung@hws.edu* Web: *www.hws.edu*

FINANCIAL AID: In 2014-2015, 86% of all full-time freshmen and 85% of continuing full-time students received some form of financial aid. 54% of all full-time freshmen and 50% of continuing full-time students received need-based aid. The average freshman award was $34,571. Need-based scholarships or need-based grants averaged $29,733 ($47,908 maximum); need-based self-help aid (loans and jobs) averaged $4,012 ($9,500 maximum); and other non-need-based awards and non-need-based scholarships averaged $13,782 ($47,908 maximum). 28% of undergraduate students work part-time. Average annual earnings from campus work are $861. The average financial indebtedness of the 2014 graduate was $34,209. HWS is a member of CSS. The CSS/Profile and FAFSA are required. The priority date for freshman financial aid applications for fall entry is February 1. The deadline for filing freshman financial aid applications for fall entry is February 1.

HOFSTRA UNIVERSITY	**D-5**
www.hofstra.edu	

Hempstead, NY 11549	**(516) 463-6700**
	(800) HOFSTRA
Fax: (516) 463-7660	**Email:** admission@hofstra.edu
Full-time: 2989 men, 3485 women	**Faculty:** 371; I, +$
Part-time: 219 men, 211 women	**Ph.D.s:** 92%
Graduate: 1606 men, 2443 women	**Student/Faculty:** 17 to 1
Year: semesters, summer session	**Tuition:** $38,900
Room & Board: $12,910	**Freshman Class:** 26388 applied, 16258 accepted, 1714 enrolled
SAT CR/M: 560/570 **ACT:** 25	**CEEB CODE:** 2295
Application Deadline: open	**VERY COMPETITIVE+**

Hofstra University, founded in 1935, is an independent institution offering programs in liberal arts and sciences, business, communications, education, engineering and applied sciences, health and human services, honors studies, law, and medicine. There are 7 undergraduate schools and 8 graduate schools. In addition to regional accreditation, Hofstra has baccalaureate program accreditation with AACSB, ABET, ACEJMC, TEAC, ABA, ACS, APA, MSCHE, ARC-PA, CAATE, CAA, AATA, CORE, LCME, NASP, and TEAC. The 240-acre campus is in a suburban area 25 miles east of New York City. Including any residence halls, there are 115 buildings.

STUDENT LIFE: 63% of undergraduates are from New York. Others are from 46 states, 51 foreign countries, and Canada. 56% are White; 14% Hispanic. **Male To Female Ratio:** 1.3:1. The average age of freshmen is 18; all undergraduates, 20. 20% do not continue beyond their first year; 60% remain to graduate. **Housing:** 3600 students can be accommodated in college housing, which includes single-sex and coed dorms and on-campus apartments. In addition, there are honors houses, special-interest houses, There also is a living-learning center, quiet floors, women's floors, themed living communities and freshman housing. On-campus housing is guaranteed for all 4 years, is available on a first-come, first-served basis, and is available on a lottery system for upperclassmen. Priority is given to out-of-town students. 50% of students commute. All students may keep cars.

FACULTY/CLASSROOMS: 55% of faculty are male; 45% are female. 81% teach undergraduates, all do research, and 90% do both. No introductory courses are taught by graduate students. The average class size in an introductory lecture is 28; in a laboratory is 16; and in a regular course is 21.

PROGRAMS OF STUDY: Hofstra confers B.A., B.S., B.B.A., B.E., B.F.A. and B.S.Ed. degrees. Master's and Doctoral degrees are also awarded. Bachelor's degrees are awarded in AGRICULTURE (environmental studies), BIOLOGICAL SCIENCE (biochemistry and biology/biological science), BUSINESS (accounting, banking and finance, business administration and management, business economics, business law, entrepreneurial studies, international business management, labor studies, management information systems, marketing management, and supply chain management), COMMUNICATIONS AND THE ARTS (American literature, art history and appreciation, audio technology, ceramic art and design, Chinese, classics, comparative literature, creative writing, dance, design, dramatic arts, film arts, fine arts, French, German, Hebrew, Italian, Japanese, jazz, journalism, Latin, linguistics, media arts, metal/jewelry, music, music business management, music history and appreciation, music performance, music theory and composition, painting, photography, public relations, publishing, radio/television technology, Russian, Spanish, speech/debate/rhetoric, theater design, theater management, video, and visual and performing arts), COMPUTER AND PHYSICAL SCIENCE (applied mathematics, applied physics, chemistry, computer science, geology, information sciences and systems, mathematics, physics, and Urban Ecology), EDUCATION (art education, athletic training, business education, (Education) Childhood Education, dance education, elementary education, English education, foreign languages education, health education, mathematics education, music education, physical education, science education, secondary education, and social studies education), ENGINEERING AND ENVIRONMENTAL DESIGN (biomedical engineering, civil engineering, computer engineering, electrical/electronics engineering, engineering and applied science, industrial engineering, manufacturing engineering, and mechanical engineering), HEALTH PROFESSIONS (allied health, community health work, exercise science, health science, Pre-Health Studies, predentistry, premedicine, preoptometry, preosteopathy, prepodiatry, preveterinary science, and speech pathology/audiology), SOCIAL SCIENCE (African studies, American studies, anthropology, Caribbean studies, Chinese Studies, china asia-pacific studies, criminology, economics, forensic studies, geography, (Social Science) Global Studies, Hispanic American studies, history, Japanese studies, Judaic studies, Latin American studies, liberal arts/general studies, philosophy, political science/government, psychology, religion, sociology, and women's studies). Accounting, biology, and communication are the strongest academically. Biology, psychology, and accounting have the largest enrollments.

ACTIVITIES: 5% of men and 1% of women belong to 17 national fraternities; 7% of women belong to 1 local and 11 national sororities. There are 249 groups on campus, including and a resident student association, art, band, cheerleading, chess, choir, chorale, chorus, communications, computers, dance, debate, drama, environmental, ethnic, film, forensics, gay, honors, international, jazz band, literary magazine, musical theater, newspaper, opera, orchestra, pep band, photography, political, professional, radio and TV, religious, social, social service, student government, symphony, and yearbook. Popular campus events include New Student Convocation, Welcome Week, Hofstra Celebrates the Holidays, Student Leadership Awards, Hofstra Music Fest, Hofstra Fall Festival, Jail and Bail, Alt Spring Break, Greek Week, Relay for Life, Leadership Programs, Senior Week, Heritage Month. **Sports:** There are 8 intercollegiate sports for men and 9 for women, and 6 intramural sports for men and 6 for women. Facilities include a 15,000-seat stadium, 5,000-seat arena, 1,600-seat soccer stadium, physical education building, swim center with an Olympic-size swimming pool and high-dive area, softball stadium, intramural fields, and a fitness center with a multipurpose gym, an indoor track, and weight room. **Graduates:** From July 1, 2013 to June 30, 2014, 1403 bachelor's degrees were awarded. The most popular majors were psychology (8%), marketing (6%), and management (6%). 239 companies recruited on campus in 2013-2014. In an average class, 50% graduate in 4 years or less, 59% graduate in 5 years or less, and 60% graduate in 6 years or less. Of the 2013 graduating class, 27% were enrolled in graduate school within 6 months of graduation, and 76% were employed.

SERVICES: Counseling and information services are available, as is tutoring in most subjects. There is a reader service for the blind. **Library/Resources:** The 3 libraries contain 1.2 million volumes, 3.4 million microform items, 17,433 audio/video tapes/CDs/DVDs, and subscribe to 14,628 periodicals including electronic. Computerized library services include interlibrary loans, database searching, Internet access, and Wi-Fi capability. Special learning facilities include an art gallery, radio station, TV station, science labs and state-of-the-art bio-engineering labs; robotics and big data labs; rooftop observatory; 6 theaters including a black box teaching theater; financial trading room; multi-media converged news room; comprehensive media production facility including a 24-hr radio station; multiple 3-D printers; digital language lab; state-of-the-art medical school; 100% wireless campus; child care institute; cultural center; museum, arboretum, and bird sanctuary. **Physically Challenged Students:** All of the campus is accessible. Facilities include wheelchair ramps, elevators, special parking, specially equipped restrooms, special class scheduling, lowered drinking fountains, lowered telephones, and special housing. **Special:** Internships in numerous career fields, Engineering Co-Op Program, SUNY Brockport/Washington Semester, utilization of the Washington Center for internship conferences and programming, an Albany internship with the NY State Assembly, NY State Senate Internship, Study Abroad, and dual and individually designed majors are offered. Credits for prior learning and credit by exam are given with proper credentials. Hofstra offers over 100 dual degree programs. There are 36 national honor societies, Phi Beta Kappa, a freshman honors program, and 35 departmental honors programs. **Visiting:** There are regularly scheduled orientations for prospective students, a group information session, a campus tour and an optional interview with a admission counselor. There are guides for informal visits, visitors may sit in on classes, and stay overnight. To schedule a visit, contact Andrea Nadler at (516) 463-6798. **Campus Safety and Security:** Measures include 24-hour foot and vehicle patrol, emergency notification system, self-defense education, and security escort services. There are shuttle buses, emergency telephones, lighted pathways/sidewalks, controlled access to dorms/residences. Residence halls have security cameras, require card access to enter, and entrance is monitored by resident student safety representative 24/7 and CCTV; bike patrol; and a motorist assistance program.

REQUIREMENTS: Applicants should graduate from an accredited secondary school or have a GED. Preparatory work should include 4 years of English, 3 each of history and social studies, math, and science, and 2 of foreign language. Engineering students are required to have 4 years of math and 1 each of chemistry and physics. An essay is required. Interviews are recommended. One counselor or teacher recommendation is recommended. Hofstra is test optional, standardized test scores are not required for most programs with the exception of home schooled and international applicants. AP and CLEP credits are accepted. Important factors in the admissions decision are advanced placement or honors courses, recommendations by school officials, and leadership record. A total of 124 to 134 credit hours is required for graduation, (152 for 5 year Accounting) with approximately 30 to 60 in the major depending on degree program and a minimum GPA of 2.0. (Some majors have a higher GPA requirement). Students must pass Writing Studies and Composition (WSC) 1 and 2 and pass a writing proficiency exam. For the B.A. degree, 33 credits in distribution/general education are required: (Humanities (9), Social Science (9), Natural Science/Math/Computer Science (9), Cross Culture (3), Interdisciplinary (3). Foreign language study is required for the B.A., the B.B.A. in International Business, and some B.S. programs. **Procedure:** Freshmen are admitted fall and spring. Entrance exams should be taken in the junior or senior year. There are early admissions, deferred admissions, and rolling admissions plans. Early decision applications should be filed by December 15, along with a $70 fee. Notification of early decision is sent January 15; regular decision, February 1. 47 applicants were on the 2014 waiting list; 10 were admitted. Applications are accepted on-line. **Transfer Students:** 599 transfer students enrolled in 2013-2014. Admission is based primarily on prior college work. A maximum of 64 credits from a 2-year school or 94 credits from a 4-year school is accepted. There is a 30-credit maximum on AP/CLEP credits. 30 of 124 credits required for the bachelor's degree must be completed at Hofstra. **International Students:** There are 294 international students enrolled. The school actively recruits these students. They must take the TOEFL with a minimum score of 550 on the paper-based TOEFL (PBT) or 80 on the Internet-based version (iBT). **ADMISSIONS:** 62% of the 2014-2015 applicants were accepted. The

SAT scores for the 2014-2015 freshman class were: Critical Reading--12% below 500, 56% between 500 and 599, 27% between 600 and 699, and 5% between 700 and 800; Math--9% below 500, 52% between 500 and 599, 33% between 600 and 699, and 6% between 700 and 800. The ACT scores were 3% below 21, 28% between 21 and 23, 32% between 24 and 26, 17% between 27 and 28, and 21% above 28. 50% of the current freshmen were in the top fifth of their class; 78% were in the top two fifths. 8 freshmen graduated first in their class. **Admissions Contact:** Jessica Eads, Vice President of Enrollment Management . E-Mail: *admission@hofstra.edu* Web: *www.hofstra.edu*

FINANCIAL AID: In 2014-2015, 93% of all full-time freshmen and 88% of continuing full-time students received some form of financial aid. 71% of all full-time freshmen and 64% of continuing full-time students received need-based aid. The average freshman award was $27,000. Need-based scholarships or need-based grants averaged $22,000 ($53,000 maximum); need-based self-help aid (loans and jobs) averaged $7,000 ($14,000 maximum); non-need-based athletic scholarships averaged $22,000 ($48,000 maximum); and other non-need-based awards and non-need-based scholarships averaged $18,000 ($40,000 maximum). 41% of undergraduate students work part-time. Average annual earnings from campus work are $3000. The FAFSA and the state aid form are required. The priority date for freshman financial aid applications for fall entry is February 15.

HOUGHTON COLLEGE   B-3
www.houghton.edu

Houghton, NY 14744

(585) 567-9353
(800) 777-2556

Fax: (585) 567-9522
Full-time: 363 men, 660 women
Part-time: 22 men, 36 women
Graduate: 12 men, 7 women
Year: semesters, summer session
Room & Board: $8252

Email: admission@houghton.edu
Faculty: 73
Ph.D.s: 88%
Student/Faculty: 14 to 1
Tuition: $28,556
Freshman Class: 807 applied, 735 accepted, 223 enrolled

SAT CR/M/W: 569/548/547 **ACT:** 25
Application Deadline: n/av

CEEB CODE: 2299
COMPETITIVE+

Houghton College, founded in 1883, provides a residential educational experience integrating academic instruction with Christian faith. Figures in the above capsule and in this profile are approximate. In addition to regional accreditation, Houghton has baccalaureate program accreditation with NASM and TEAC. The 1300-acre campus is in a rural area 65 miles southeast of Buffalo and 70 miles southwest of Rochester. Including any residence halls, there are 20 buildings. **STUDENT LIFE:** 58% of undergraduates are from New York. Others are from 36 states, 31 foreign countries, and Canada. 66% are from public schools. 84% are White. 95% are Protestant. **Male To Female Ratio:** 1.8:1. The average age of freshmen is 18; all undergraduates, 22. 12% do not continue beyond their first year; 74% remain to graduate. **Housing:** 1066 students can be accommodated in college housing, which includes single-sex dorms, on-campus apartments, and married student housing. In addition, there are special-interest houses, Equestrian students have the opportunity to live in housing on site. On-campus housing is guaranteed for all 4 years. Priority is given to out-of-town students. 87% of students live on campus; of those, 67% remain on campus on weekends. Alcohol is not permitted. All students may keep cars.

FACULTY/CLASSROOMS: 64% of faculty are male; 36% are female. All teach undergraduates, 20% do research, and 20% do both. No introductory courses are taught by graduate students. The average class size in an introductory lecture is 26; in a laboratory is 13; and in a regular course is 17.

PROGRAMS OF STUDY: Houghton confers B.A., B.S., B.F.A. and B.Mus. degrees. Associate and Master's degrees are also awarded. Bachelor's degrees are awarded in AGRICULTURE (equine science), BIOLOGICAL SCIENCE (biochemistry, biology/adolescence education, biology/biological science, and environmental biology), BUSI-

NESS (accounting, business administration and management, recreation and leisure services, and recreational facilities management), COMMUNICATIONS AND THE ARTS (art, communication, English, English as a second/foreign language, English literature, English Writing, instrumental performance, media arts, music, music performance, music theory and composition, organ performance, printmaking, Spanish, studio art, vocal performance, voice, vocal music education, and writing), COMPUTER AND PHYSICAL SCIENCE (applied physics, chemistry, chemistry/adolescence education, computer science, mathematics, physics, and science), EDUCATION (art education, (Education) Childhood Education, childhood education: 1-6, Christian education, education of the exceptional child, elementary education, English education, foreign languages education, general studies, health education, mathematics education, music education, physical education, science education, secondary education, special education, and teaching English as a second/foreign language (TESOL/TEFOL)), ENGINEERING AND ENVIRONMENTAL DESIGN (environmental science and preengineering), HEALTH PROFESSIONS (medical technology, predentistry, premedicine, preoptometry, prepharmacy, prephysical therapy, preveterinary science, and recreation therapy), SOCIAL SCIENCE (biblical studies, Christian studies, counseling/psychology, crosscultural studies, history, humanities, interdisciplinary studies, international studies, liberal arts/general studies, ministries, parks and recreation management, pastoral studies, philosophy, political science/government, prelaw, psychobiology, psychology, religion, religious education, religious studies, religious music, and sociology). Biology, religion, art, music, psychology, communications, and businesss administration are the strongest academically. Management/business administration, biology, and inclusive childhood education have the largest enrollments.

ACTIVITIES: There are no fraternities or sororities. There are 50 groups on campus, including mission organizations, ministry, art, bagpipe, band, choir, chorale, chorus, communications, drama, environmental, ethnic, film, honors, international, jazz band, literary magazine, musical theater, newspaper, opera, orchestra, pep band, photography, political, professional, religious, social, social service, student government, symphony, volunteer service, and yearbook. Popular campus events include Christian Life Emphasis Week, Film Festival, SPOT Variety Show, Purple and Gold Week, Faith and Justice Symposium and Martin Luther King Jr. Service Day. **Sports:** There are 7 intercollegiate sports for men and 9 for women, and 7 intramural sports for men and 7 for women. Facilities include 3 basketball and 4 racquetball courts, a swimming pool, an indoor track, a downhill ski slope, cross-country ski trails, 6 tennis courts, a climbing wall, an 8-lane all-weather track, a ropes course, and a 386-acre equestrian center with an indoor riding ring. The gym seats 1800; the auditorium, 1300, baseball and softball fields under construction along with new athletic complex/field house. **Graduates:** From July 1, 2013 to June 30, 2014, 348 bachelor's degrees were awarded. The most popular majors were business administration (21%), education (13%), and biology (11%). 54 companies recruited on campus in 2013-2014. In an average class, 2% graduate in 3 years or less, 64% graduate in 4 years or less, 72% graduate in 5 years or less, and 74% graduate in 6 years or less. Of the 2013 graduating class, 18% were enrolled in graduate school within 6 months of graduation, and 86% were employed.

SERVICES: Counseling and information services are available, as is tutoring in some subjects, general education courses. There is a reader service for the blind. There is support for students with learning-related disabilities. **Library/Resources:** The 2 libraries contain 314,183 volumes, 47,163 microform items, 21,092 audio/video tapes/CDs/DVDs, and subscribe to 57,591 periodicals including electronic. Computerized library services include interlibrary loans, database searching, Internet access, and Wi-Fi capability. Special learning facilities include an art gallery, an equestrian center, a ropes course, digital media lab, greenhouse, outdoor classroom. **Physically Challenged Students:** 85% of the campus is accessible. Facilities include wheelchair ramps, elevators, special parking, specially equipped restrooms, special class scheduling, lowered drinking fountains, lowered telephones, and special housing. **Special:** Students may cross-register with members of the Western New York Consortium, the Christian College Consortium, and the Five College Committee. Internships are available in psychology, social work, business, educational minis-

tries, physical fitness, political science, graphic design, communication, athletic training, recreation, English, and Christian education. Study abroad in 25 countries, a Washington semester, and dual majors. A 3-2 engineering degree with Clarkson and Washington Universities are available as well as a 4-1 BS/MBA degree with Alfred U, Clarkson U, Niagara U and Rochester Institute of Technology. A PharmD 3-4 degree program with University of Buffalo is also available. Students may design their own major as an Interdisciplinary Studies major. Credit for military experience and nondegree study are possible. There are 3 national honor societies, Phi Beta Kappa, a freshman honors program, and 3 departmental honors programs. **Visiting:** There are regularly scheduled orientations for prospective students, including a campus tour, an admissions interview, a financial aid session, a class visit, and an academic information session. There are guides for informal visits, visitors may sit in on classes, and stay overnight. To schedule a visit, contact the Visit Office. **Campus Safety and Security:** Measures include 24-hour foot and vehicle patrol, emergency notification system, and security escort services. There are emergency telephones, lighted pathways/sidewalks, controlled access to dorms/residences, campus emergency preparedness plan includes agreements with local police departments, American Red Cross, and local schools/businesses for cooperative assistance as needed.

REQUIREMENTS: The SAT or ACT is required. Applicants must graduate from an accredited secondary school, be home-schooled, or have a GED. A total of 16 academic credits is recommended, including 4 of English, 3 of social studies, and 2 each of foreign language, math, and science. An essay is required. Music students must audition. An interview is recommended. AP and CLEP credits are accepted. Important factors in the admissions decision are personality/intangible qualities, advanced placement or honors courses, and recommendations by school officials. Integrative studies courses are required in the following disciplines: writing, literature, Bible, foreign language, history, math, science, physical education, theology, philosophy, fine arts, social science, and humanities. A minimum GPA of 2.0 is required to graduate. **Procedure:** Freshmen are admitted fall and spring. Entrance exams should be taken in the spring of the junior year or fall of the senior year. There are deferred admissions and rolling admissions plans. Application deadlines are open. Application fee is $40. Notifications are sent January 1. Applications are accepted on-line. **Transfer Students:** 60 transfer students enrolled in 2013-2014. Applicants should have a 2.75 or better GPA. A character recommendation and high school transcripts must be submitted. The essay, an SAT or ACT and an interview are optional but encouraged. 30 of 125 credits required for the bachelor's degree must be completed at Houghton. **International Students:** There are 64 international students enrolled. The school actively recruits these students. They must take the TOEFL with a minimum score of 550 on the paper-based TOEFL (PBT) or 80 on the Internet-based version (iBT). They must also take the SAT or ACT or take the TOEFL.

ADMISSIONS: 91% of the 2014-2015 applicants were accepted. The SAT scores for the 2014-2015 freshman class were: Critical Reading--22% below 500, 41% between 500 and 599, 29% between 600 and 699, and 8% between 700 and 800; Math--27% below 500, 44% between 500 and 599, 25% between 600 and 699, and 4% between 700 and 800; Writing--32% below 500, 36% between 500 and 599, 28% between 600 and 699, and 4% between 700 and 800. The ACT scores were 17% below 21, 20% between 21 and 23, 26% between 24 and 26, 19% between 27 and 28, and 19% above 28. 51% of the current freshmen were in the top fifth of their class; 80% were in the top two fifths. There were 1 National Merit finalists. 8 freshmen graduated first in their class. **Admissions Contact:** Eric Currie, Vice President for Enrollment Management. E-Mail: *admission@houghton.edu* Web: *www.houghton.edu*

FINANCIAL AID: In 2014-2015, 100% of all full-time freshmen and 97% of continuing full-time students received some form of financial aid. 85% of all full-time freshmen and 86% of continuing full-time students received need-based aid. The average freshman award was $22,221. Need-based scholarships or need-based grants averaged $7,116 ($14,000 maximum); need-based self-help aid (loans and jobs) averaged $4,232 ($5,500 maximum); other non-need-based awards and non-need-based scholarships averaged $8,468 ($26,924 maximum); and $2,405 from other forms of aid. 43% of undergraduate students work part-time. Average annual earnings from campus work are $1561. The average financial indebtedness of the 2014 graduate was $22,197. Houghton is a member of CSS. The FAFSA is required. The priority date for freshman financial aid applications for fall entry is March 1.

HUNTER COLLEGE   D-5
www.hunter.cuny.edu

New York, NY 10065

	(212) 772-4490
	(800) 772-4000
Fax: n/av	**Email:** admissions@hunter.cuny.edu
Full-time: 4185 men, 7611 women	**Faculty:** 750
Part-time: 1664 men, 3178 women	**Ph.D.s:** 86%
Graduate: 1434 men, 4752 women	**Student/Faculty:** 15 to 1
Year: semesters, summer session	**Tuition:** $6129 ($15,699)
Room & Board: $5300	**Freshman Class:** n/av
SAT CR/M: 574/598	**CEEB CODE:** 2301
Application Deadline: open	**VERY COMPETITIVE**

Hunter College, a comprehensive, institution established in 1870, is part of the City University of New York and is both city and state-supported. Primarily a commuter college, it emphasizes liberal arts in its undergraduate and graduate programs. Figures in the above capsule and in this profile are approximate. There are 3 undergraduate schools and 4 graduate schools. In addition to regional accreditation, Hunter has baccalaureate program accreditation with ADA, APTA, ASLA, CSWE, NCATE, and NLN. The 3-acre campus is in an urban area in New York City. Including any residence halls, there are 6 buildings.

STUDENT LIFE: 98% of undergraduates are from New York. Others are from 42 states, 151 foreign countries, and Canada. 71% are from public schools. 44% are White; 21% Asian American; 17% Hispanic; 12% African American. **Male To Female Ratio:** 2.1:1. The average age of freshmen is 18; all undergraduates, 24. 17% do not continue beyond their first year. **Housing:** 662 students can be accommodated in college housing, which includes coed dorms. On-campus housing is available on a first-come, first-served basis, and is available on a lottery system for upperclassmen. 99% of students commute. No one may keep cars.

FACULTY/CLASSROOMS: No introductory courses are taught by graduate students. The average class size in a laboratory is 20 and in a regular course is 30.

PROGRAMS OF STUDY: Hunter confers B.A., B.S., B.F.A., B.Mus. and B.S.Ed degrees. Master's degrees are also awarded. Bachelor's degrees are awarded in BIOLOGICAL SCIENCE (biology/biological science and nutrition), BUSINESS (accounting), COMMUNICATIONS AND THE ARTS (Chinese, classics, comparative literature, creative writing, dance, dramatic arts, English, English literature, film arts, fine arts, French, German, Greek, Hebrew, Italian, languages, Latin, media arts, music, Russian, and Spanish), COMPUTER AND PHYSICAL SCIENCE (chemistry, computer science, mathematics, physics, and statistics), EDUCATION (art education, early childhood education, elementary education, foreign languages education, health education, middle school education, music education, science education, and secondary education), ENGINEERING AND ENVIRONMENTAL DESIGN (energy management technology, environmental science, and preengineering), HEALTH PROFESSIONS (medical laboratory technology, nursing, physical therapy, predentistry, premedicine, and public health), SOCIAL SCIENCE (African American studies, anthropology, archeology, economics, geography, Hispanic American studies, history, international relations, Judaic studies, Latin American studies, philosophy, political science/government, prelaw, psychology, religion, social science, sociology, urban studies, and women's studies). Nursing is the strongest academically. Psychology has the largest enrollment.

ACTIVITIES: 2% of men belong to 1 local and 1 national fraternities. There are 150 groups on campus, including art, band, cheerleading, choir, chorale, chorus, drama, ethnic, film, gay, honors, international, jazz band, literary magazine, musical theater, newspaper, orchestra, political, professional, radio and TV, religious, social, social service,

student government, and symphony. Popular campus events include Major Day Fair. **Sports:** There are 9 intercollegiate sports for men and 11 for women. Facilities include fencing, dance, and weight rooms, racquetball courts, a pool, outdoor tennis courts, and a gym. **Graduates:** From July 1, 2013 to June 30, 2014, 2707 bachelor's degrees were awarded. The most popular majors were psychology (21%), social sciences (18%), and English (14%). In an average class, 46% graduate in 6 years or less.

SERVICES: Counseling and information services are available, as is tutoring in every subject. There is a reader service for the blind, and remedial math, reading, and writing. Review of graduate-level papers through the writing center and a math tutoring center are available. **Library/Resources:** The library contains 865,240 volumes, 651,000 microform items, 75,000 audio/video tapes/CDs/DVDs, and subscribes to 36,000 periodicals including electronic. Computerized library services include database searching. Special learning facilities include an art gallery, radio station, a geography/geology lab, on-campus elementary and secondary schools, and a theater. **Physically Challenged Students:** All of the campus is accessible. Facilities include wheelchair ramps, elevators, special parking, specially equipped restrooms, special class scheduling, lowered drinking fountains, lowered telephones. **Special:** Special academic programs include internships, student-designed majors, work-study, study abroad in 24 countries, and dual majors. There is cross-registration with the Brooklyn School of Law, Marymount Manhattan College, and the YIVO Institute. Through the National Student Exchange Program, Hunter students can study for 1 or 2 semesters at any of 150 U.S. campuses. Accelerated degree programs are offered in anthropology, biopharmacology, economics, English, history, math, physics, sociology, and social research. Exchange programs in Paris or Puerto Rico are possible. There are 2 national honor societies, Phi Beta Kappa, a freshman honors program, and 19 departmental honors programs. **Visiting:** There are regularly scheduled orientations for prospective students, consisting of presentations and tours every Friday. There are guides for informal visits and visitors may sit in on classes. To schedule a visit, contact the Admissions Office. **Campus Safety and Security:** Measures include self-defense education. There are shuttle buses, emergency telephones, 24-hour foot patrol.

REQUIREMENTS: The SAT is required. Student admission is based on a combination of high school grade average, high school academic credits, including English and math, and SAT scores. AP and CLEP credits are accepted. To graduate, students must complete 120 credits. The total number of hours in a major varies from 24 credits for a liberal arts major to 63 credits for a professional concentration; a minimum GPA of 2.0 is needed overall and in the major. Distribution requirements include 12 credits of social sciences, up to 12 credits of a foreign language, 10 or more of math and science, 9 of humanities and the arts, 6 of literature, and 3 of English composition. **Procedure:** Freshmen are admitted fall and spring. Entrance exams should be taken by October of the junior year. There are early admissions, deferred admissions, and rolling admissions plans. Application deadlines are open. Application fee is $65. Notification of early decision is sent December 15; regular decision, January 1. 4 early decision candidates were accepted for the 2014-2015 class. Applications are accepted on-line. **Transfer Students:** 1877 transfer students enrolled in 2013-2014. Applicants must have at least a 2.0 GPA. All students must complete 30 of the 120 to 131 credits required for a bachelor's degree at the college, including half of those needed for both the major and the minor. **International Students:** There are 1352 international students enrolled. They must take the TOEFL with a minimum score of 500 on the paper-based TOEFL (PBT) and the college's own test.

ADMISSIONS: The SAT scores for the 2014-2015 freshman class were: Critical Reading--12% below 500, 54% between 500 and 599, 26% between 600 and 699, and 8% between 700 and 800; Math--3% below 500, 50% between 500 and 599, 37% between 600 and 699, and 10% between 700 and 800. **Admissions Contact:** Bill Zlata, Director of Admissions. E-Mail: *admissions@hunter.cuny.edu* Web: *www.hunter.cuny.edu*

FINANCIAL AID: The FAFSA and the college's own financial statement are required. The deadline for filing freshman financial aid applications for fall entry is May 1.

IONA COLLEGE   D-5
www.iona.edu

New Rochelle, NY 10801

(914) 633-2502
(800) 231-IONA

Fax: (914) 633-2182
Full-time: 1267 men, 1660 women
Part-time: 248 men, 287 women
Graduate: 320 men, 459 women
Year: semesters, summer session
Room & Board: $12,488

Email: admissions@iona.edu
Faculty: 169; IIA, +$
Ph.D.s: 90%
Student/Faculty: 17 to 1
Tuition: $31,540
Freshman Class: 8741 applied, 7556 accepted, 722 enrolled

SAT CR/M: 500/500 ACT: 22
Application Deadline: February 15

CEEB CODE: 2324
COMPETITIVE

Iona College, founded in 1940, is a private college offering programs through schools of general studies, arts and science, and business. It has a graduate campus in Rockland County in addition to the main campus in New Rochelle. Figures in the above capsule and in this profile are approximate. There are 2 undergraduate schools and 2 graduate schools. In addition to regional accreditation, Iona has baccalaureate program accreditation with AACSB, ABET, ACEJMC, CSWE, and NCATE. The 43-acre campus is in a suburban area 17 miles northeast of New York City. Including any residence halls, there are 49 buildings.

STUDENT LIFE: 76% of undergraduates are from New York. Others are from 34 states, 32 foreign countries, and Canada. 57% are White; 17% race unknown; 16% Hispanic. **Male To Female Ratio:** 1.3:1. The average age of freshmen is 18; all undergraduates, 19. 19% do not continue beyond their first year; 65% remain to graduate. **Housing:** 1358 students can be accommodated in college housing, which includes single-sex dorms, on-campus apartments, and off-campus apartments. Honors floor, in suite style residence hall; science floor, in suite style residence hall; an Education floor, in suite style residence hall. On-campus housing is available on a first-come, first-served basis, and is available on a lottery system for upperclassmen. 57% of students commute. Upperclassmen may keep cars.

FACULTY/CLASSROOMS: 58% of faculty are male; 42% are female. 88% teach undergraduates. No introductory courses are taught by graduate students. The average class size in an introductory lecture is 25; in a laboratory is 17; and in a regular course is 14.

PROGRAMS OF STUDY: Iona confers B.A., B.S., B.B.A. and B.P.S. degrees. Master's degrees are also awarded. Bachelor's degrees are awarded in BIOLOGICAL SCIENCE (biochemistry and biology/biological science), BUSINESS (accounting, business administration and management, finance, international business management, management science, and marketing management), COMMUNICATIONS AND THE ARTS (communications, English, French, Italian, Spanish, and speech/debate/rhetoric), COMPUTER AND PHYSICAL SCIENCE (applied mathematics, chemistry, computer science, information sciences and systems, mathematics, and physics), EDUCATION ((Education) Childhood Education and early childhood education), ENGINEERING AND ENVIRONMENTAL DESIGN (environmental science), HEALTH PROFESSIONS (speech pathology/audiology), SOCIAL SCIENCE (criminal justice, economics, history, international studies, liberal arts/general studies, philosophy, political science/government, psychology, religion, social work, and sociology). Psychology, marketing, and mass communication are the strongest academically. Mass communication, psychology, and criminal justice are the largest.

ACTIVITIES: 6% of men belong to 1 local and 2 national fraternities; 9% of women belong to 4 local and 1 national sororities. There are 70 groups on campus, including black student union, democracy matters, Gaelic society club sports- Rugby, Hispanic organization of Latin awareness, Italian society, karate club, national student speech and hearing/language association general interest - inter-residence hall council, students against destructive, students association, community sevice and Religious groups, students for veterans students for peace, bagpipe, cheerleading, cheerleading and dance academic professional groups - public relations student society of America, chorale, computers, dance, debate, drama, environmental, film, gay,

honors, literary magazine, multi cultural groups, students Caribbean ancestry, musical theater, newspaper, political, professional, radio and TV, religious, social, social service, student government, and yearbook. Popular campus events include Spring Weekend/Concert Event, Travel Series, Heritage Week, Fashion Show, Campus Coffee House, Homecoming Carnivel, Week of the Peacemaker and Make a Difference Week, Black History Month, Hispanic Heritage Month and Alcohol Awareness Week. **Sports:** There are 10 intercollegiate sports for men and 11 for women, and 10 intramural sports for men and 10 for women. Facilities include an indoor facilities: 2 gymnasiums, 2 weight rooms, cardio room, core studio, aerobics studio, rowing tank and a swimming pool. Outdoor facilities: soccer/lacrosse field and softball field. **Graduates:** From July 1, 2013 to June 30, 2014, 727 bachelor's degrees were awarded. The most popular majors were business (38%), mass communication (17%), and Education (10%). 65 companies recruited on campus in 2013-2014. In an average class, 1% graduate in 3 years or less, 56% graduate in 4 years or less, 63% graduate in 5 years or less, and 65% graduate in 6 years or less. Of the 2013 graduating class, 40% were enrolled in graduate school within 6 months of graduation, and 68% were employed.

SERVICES: Counseling and information services are available, as is tutoring in most subjects. There is a reader service for the blind. Assist students with acquiring electronic versions of texts **Library/Resources:** The 3 libraries contain 268,476 volumes, 510,213 microform items, 4,176 audio/video tapes/CDs/DVDs, and subscribe to 742 periodicals including electronic. Computerized library services include interlibrary loans, database searching, Internet access, and Wi-Fi capability. Special learning facilities include an art gallery, radio station, TV station, an electron microscope, and a speech and hearing clinic. **Physically Challenged Students:** 70% of the campus is accessible. Facilities include wheelchair ramps, elevators, special parking, specially equipped restrooms, special class scheduling, lowered drinking fountains, special housing. All classes are on the first floor. **Special:** There are internships available for students. Study abroad is available in 9 countries. Work-study positions are available in several locations throughout the College. Students may earn either a BA or BS degree in Adolescent Education, Computer Science, Economics, or Mathematics. There is an articulation agreement with New York Medical College for Physical Therapy. Five-year programs are offered in the following areas: Chemistry and Adolescent Education; Chemistry and Computer Science; Computer Science; Criminal Justice; English; History, Mathematics and Computer Science; and Psychology. There are 2 national honor societies, a freshman honors program, and 24 departmental honors programs. **Visiting:** There are regularly scheduled orientations for prospective students, including a meeting with an admissions counselor, a campus tour, and a variety of on-campus programs during the summer and fall. There are guides for informal visits and visitors may sit in on classes. To schedule a visit, contact Elizabeth English at (914) 633-2622. **Campus Safety and Security:** Measures include 24-hour foot and vehicle patrol, emergency notification system, and security escort services. There are shuttle buses, emergency telephones, lighted pathways/sidewalks, and controlled access to dorms/residences.

REQUIREMENTS: The SAT or ACT is required. Applicants must complete 16 academic credits, including 4 units of English, 3 of math,3 science, 2 each of foreign language and social studies, and 1 each of history, and academic electives. A GED is accepted. An essay is required, and an interview is recommended. AP and CLEP credits are accepted. Important factors in the admissions decision are recommendations by school officials, extracurricular activities record, and leadership record.All students are required to take courses in the humanities courses, social sciences, science and technology, natural and/or symbolic languages, and communication skills as a part of the College Core. Students enrolled in BBA programs, BS programs, and the Honors Program take specific core courses that are unique to each program. Students who earn BA degrees must take a total of 90 liberal arts credits; students who earn BS degrees must take a total of 60 liberal arts credits; and students who earn BBA degrees must take a total of 63 liberal arts credits in order to complete the bachelor's degree. Computer literacy is required. The total number of credits required to graduate is at least 120, depending on the major, with at least 30 in the major. The minimum GPA requirement is 2.0. **Procedure:** Freshmen are admitted fall and spring. Entrance exams should be taken in the spring of the junior year. There are early admissions and deferred admissions plans. Applications should be filed by February 15 for fall entry; January 1 for spring entry, along with a $50 fee. 1184 applicants were on the 2014 waiting list; 1120 were admitted. Applications are accepted on-line. **Transfer Students:** 161 transfer students enrolled in 2013-2014. Transfer applicants must have a GPA of at least 2.0 and must submit high school transcripts if they have earned fewer than 30 college credits. An interview is recommended. 30 of 120 credits required for the bachelor's degree must be completed at Iona. **International Students:** There are 48 international students enrolled. The school actively recruits these students. They must take the TOEFL with a minimum score of 550 on the paper-based TOEFL (PBT). They must also take the SAT or ACT.

ADMISSIONS: 86% of the 2014-2015 applicants were accepted. The SAT scores for the 2014-2015 freshman class were: Critical Reading--49% below 500, 41% between 500 and 599, 9% between 600 and 699, and 1% between 700 and 800; Math--44% below 500, 42% between 500 and 599, 13% between 600 and 699, and 2% between 700 and 800. The ACT scores were 28% below 21, 37% between 21 and 23, 20% between 24 and 26, 6% between 27 and 28, and 10% above 28. 34% of the current freshmen were in the top fifth of their class; 66% were in the top two fifths. **Admissions Contact:** Katherine Reilly, Director for Undergraduate Admissions. E-Mail: *admissions@iona .edu* Web: *www.iona.edu*

FINANCIAL AID: In 2014-2015, 98% of all full-time freshmen and 96% of continuing full-time students received some form of financial aid. 72% of all full-time freshmen and 65% of continuing full-time students received need-based aid. The average freshman award was $27,908. Need-based scholarships or need-based grants averaged $6,704 ($20,400 maximum); need-based self-help aid (loans and jobs) averaged $3,871 ($9,800 maximum); non-need-based athletic scholarships averaged $17,643 ($49,102 maximum); and other non-need-based awards and non-need-based scholarships averaged $20,153 ($48,611 maximum). 15% of undergraduate students work part-time. Average annual earnings from campus work are $1261. The average financial indebtedness of the 2014 graduate was $31,960. Iona is a member of CSS. The FAFSA and the state aid form are required. The priority date for freshman financial aid applications for fall entry is April 15. The deadline for filing freshman financial aid applications for fall entry is April 15.

ITHACA COLLEGE   C-4
www.ithaca.edu

Ithaca, NY 14850	(607) 274-3124
	(800) 429-4274
Fax: (607) 274-1900	**Email:** admission@ithaca.edu
Full-time: 2670 men, 3461 women	**Faculty:** 489; IIA, av$
Part-time: 55 men, 48 women	**Ph.D.s:** 94%
Graduate: 140 men, 349 women	**Student/Faculty:** 11 to 1
Year: semesters, summer session	**Tuition:** $38,400
Room & Board: $13,900	**Freshman Class:** 15658 applied, 10429 accepted, 1789 enrolled
SAT CR/M/W: 590/590/590	**CEEB CODE:** 2325
Application Deadline: February 1	**HIGHLY COMPETITIVE**

Located in New York's Finger Lakes region, Ithaca College (IC) is home to 6,100 undergraduates and 400 graduate students and offers more than 100 degree programs in its schools. There are 5 undergraduate schools and one graduate school. In addition to regional accreditation, Ithaca has baccalaureate program accreditation with AACSB, APTA, NASM, and NRPA. The library contains 318,480 volumes, 21,143 microform items, and 34,988 audio/video tapes/CDs/DVDs, and subscribes to 60,197 periodicals including electronic. Computerized library services include interlibrary loans, database searching, Internet access, and Wi-Fi capability. Special learning facilities include an art gallery, radio station, and a TV station. The 669-acre campus is in a small town 250 miles northwest of New York City. Including any residence halls, there are 86 buildings.

STUDENT LIFE: 56% of undergraduates are from out of state, mostly the Middle Atlantic. Students are from 47 states, 68 foreign countries, and Canada. 84% are from public schools. 69% are White; 11% race unknown. The average age of freshmen is 18; all undergraduates, 20. 13% do not continue beyond their first year; 76% remain to graduate.

FACULTY/CLASSROOMS: 51% of faculty are male; 49% are female. All teach undergraduates. Graduate students teach 6% of introductory courses. The average class size in an introductory lecture is 24.

PROGRAMS OF STUDY: Ithaca confers B.A., B.S., B.F.A. and Mus.B. degrees. Master's and doctoral degrees are also awarded. Bachelor's degrees are awarded in AGRICULTURE (environmental studies), BIOLOGICAL SCIENCE (biochemistry and biology/ biological science), BUSINESS (accounting, applied economics / management, business administration and management, business communications, organizational behavior, recreation and leisure services, and sports management), COMMUNICATIONS AND THE ARTS (art history, art, art history and appreciation, audio technology, broadcasting, communication, communications, creative writing, dramatic arts, English, English literature, English Writing, film arts, fine arts, French, German, jazz, journalism, languages, media arts, modern language, music, music performance, music theory and composition, musical theater, performing arts, photography, piano pedagogy, public relations, Spanish, sports media, studio art, telecommunications, theater design, theater management, video, and visual and performing arts), COMPUTER AND PHYSICAL SCIENCE (chemistry, computer mathematics, computer science, information sciences and systems, mathematics, mathematics — economics, and physics), EDUCATION (art education, athletic training, education, education of the deaf and hearing impaired, English education, foreign languages education, health education, mathematics education, middle school education, music education, physical education, secondary education, social studies education, speech correction, sports and wellness studies, and sports studies), ENGINEERING AND ENVIRONMENTAL DESIGN (engineering chemistry, engineering physics, and environmental science), HEALTH PROFESSIONS (allied health, clinical science, community health work, exercise science, health, health science, occupational therapy, physical therapy, preallied health, Pre-Health Studies, predentistry, premedicine, preoptometry, public health, recreation therapy, rehabilitation therapy, speech pathology/audiology, speech therapy, and sports medicine), SOCIAL SCIENCE (anthropology, applied psychology, architectural studies, area studies, economics, German area studies, gerontology, history, industrial and organizational psychology, interdisciplinary studies, Italian studies, legal studies, liberal arts/general studies, philosophy, philosophy and religion, physical fitness/ movement, political science/government, prelaw, psychology, social studies, and sociology). Physical therapy, theater, and music are the strongest academically. Music, business administration, and television/radio have the largest enrollments.

ACTIVITIES: 1% of men belong to 4 national fraternities; 1% of women belong to 1 local sorority. There are 200 groups on campus, including cultural and academic clubs, art, band, cheerleading, chess, choir, chorale, chorus, computers, dance, drama, drum and bugle corps, environmental, ethnic, film, forensics, gay, honors, international, jazz band, literary magazine, musical theater, newspaper, opera, orchestra, pep band, photography, political, professional, radio and TV, religious, social, social service, sports clubs, student government, and symphony. Popular campus events include Pep Rallies, Student Involvement Fair, and Various Multicultural Awareness Events.

SERVICES: Nonremedial tutoring is available.

REQUIREMENTS: Applicants should be graduates of an accredited secondary school with a minimum of 16 Carnegie units, including 4 years of English, 3 each of math, science, and social studies, 2 of foreign language, and other college-preparatory electives. The GED is accepted. An essay is required, as is an audition for music and theater students. In some majors, a portfolio and an interview are recommended. AP and CLEP credits are accepted.

ADMISSIONS: 67% of the 2013-2014 applicants were accepted. The SAT scores for the 2013-2014 freshman class were: Critical Reading--9% below 500, 46% between 500 and 599, 38% between 600 and 699, and 7% between 700 and 800; Math--9% below 500, 44% between 500 and 599, 41% between 600 and 699, and 6% between

700 and 800; Writing--11% below 500, 41% between 500 and 599, 41% between 600 and 699, and 7% between 700 and 800. 53% of the current freshmen were in the top fifth of their class; 82% were in the top two fifths. There were 6 National Merit finalists. 12 freshmen graduated first in their class.

FINANCIAL AID: In 2013-2014, 95% of all full-time freshmen and 90% of continuing full-time students received some form of financial aid. 71% of all full-time freshmen and 67% of continuing full-time students received need-based aid. The average freshman award was $34,366. Need-based scholarships or need-based grants averaged $23,407 ($53,695 maximum); need-based self-help aid (loans and jobs) averaged $7,371 ($14,100 maximum); and other non-need-based awards and non-need-based scholarships averaged $9,617 ($55,587 maximum). 39% of undergraduate students work part-time. Average annual earnings from campus work are $2361. Ithaca is a member of CSS. The CSS/Profile and FAFSA are required. The deadline for filing freshman financial aid applications for fall entry is February 1.

JOHN JAY COLLEGE OF CRIMINAL JUSTICE/THE CITY UNIVERSITY OF NEW YORK (*The complete profile is made available exclusively on our website, www.barronspac.com*)

JUILLIARD SCHOOL (*The complete profile is made available exclusively on our website, www.barronspac.com*)

KEUKA COLLEGE	**B-3**
www.keuka.edu	

Keuka Park, NY 14478	(315) 536-5254, ext. 254
	(800) 33-KEUKA
Fax: (315) 536-5386	Email: admissions@mail.keuka.edu
Full-time: 383 men, 1131 women	Faculty: 80; IIA, -$
Part-time: 34 men, 281 women	Ph.D.s: 75%
Graduate: 48 men, 156 women	Student/Faculty: 15 to 1
Year: 4-1-4, summer session	Tuition: $27,240
Room & Board: $10,590	Freshman Class: 1375 applied, 1207 accepted, 224 enrolled
SAT or ACT: required	CEEB CODE: 2350
Application Deadline: open	**COMPETITIVE**

Keuka College, founded in 1890, is an independent college affiliated with American Baptist Churches and offers instruction in the liberal arts. Figures in the above capsule and in this profile are approximate. In addition to regional accreditation, Keuka has baccalaureate program accreditation with AHEA, CSWE, and NLN. The 203-acre campus is in a rural area 60 miles south of Rochester. Including any residence halls, there are 19 buildings.

STUDENT LIFE: 94% of undergraduates are from New York. Others are from 26 states, 9 foreign countries, and Canada. 80% are from public schools. 90% are White. **Male To Female Ratio:** 3.4:1. The average age of freshmen is 18; all undergraduates, 23. 27% do not continue beyond their first year; 52% remain to graduate. **Housing:** 719 students can be accommodated in college housing, which includes single-sex and coed dorms. In addition, there are honors houses, special-interest houses, cooperative living, and leadership and wellness housing. On-campus housing is guaranteed for all 4 years. 55% of students live on campus; of those, 60% remain on campus on weekends. Alcohol is not permitted. Upperclassmen may keep cars.

FACULTY/CLASSROOMS: 32% of faculty are male; 68% are female. All teach undergraduates. No introductory courses are taught by graduate students. The average class size in an introductory lecture is 20; in a laboratory is 15; and in a regular course is 20.

PROGRAMS OF STUDY: Keuka confers B.A., and B.S. degrees. Master's degrees are also awarded. Bachelor's degrees are awarded in BIOLOGICAL SCIENCE (biochemistry and biology/biological science), BUSINESS (accounting, business administration and management, hotel/motel and restaurant management, and marketing/retailing/merchandising), COMMUNICATIONS AND THE ARTS (American Sign Language, communications, and English), EDUCATION (elementary education and secondary education), ENGINEERING AND ENVIRONMENTAL DESIGN (environmental science), HEALTH PROFESSIONS (medical laboratory technology, nursing, occupational therapy, predentistry, premedicine, and preveterinary science), SOCIAL SCIENCE (criminal justice, political science/government, prelaw, psychology, social work, and sociology). Occupational therapy, biology, and education are the strongest academically. Occupational therapy, education, and management have the largest enrollments.

ACTIVITIES: There are no fraternities or sororities. There are 45 groups on campus, including and leadership, art, cheerleading, choir, chorale, community service, dance, drama, ethnic, gay, honors, international, literary magazine, newspaper, political, professional, religious, social, social service, student government, and yearbook. Popular campus events include Spring Weekend, May Day and Family Weekend. **Sports:** There are 7 intercollegiate sports for men and 8 for women, and 8 intramural sports for men and 8 for women. Facilities include a gym, a fitness center, a weight room, and an outdoor athletic facility. **Graduates:** From July 1, 2013 to June 30, 2014, 462 bachelor's degrees were awarded. The most popular majors were business (29%), nursing (16%), and criminal justice (14%). In an average class, 45% graduate in 4 years or less, 5% graduate in 5 years or less, and 1% graduate in 6 years or less. Of the 2013 graduating class, 39% were enrolled in graduate school within 6 months of graduation, and 90% were employed.

SERVICES: Counseling and information services are available, as is tutoring in every subject. There is a reader service for the blind, and remedial math, reading, and writing. Individual and group tutoring is available free through the college's academic support services. **Library/Resources:** The library contains 112,297 volumes, 4,190 microform items, 4,190 audio/video tapes/CDs/DVDs, and subscribes to 18,151 periodicals including electronic. Computerized library services include interlibrary loans and database searching. Special learning facilities include an art gallery. **Physically Challenged Students:** 60% of the campus is accessible. Facilities include wheelchair ramps, elevators, special parking, specially equipped restrooms, special class scheduling, lowered drinking fountains, and special housing. **Special:** There are co-op programs with other members of the Rochester Area Colleges Consortium. The college offers internships, study abroad, a Washington semester, dual majors, and student-designed majors. Credit is also given by exam and for work experience. There are 16 national honor societies. **Visiting:** There are regularly scheduled orientations for prospective students, including open houses held in October and April, when students can speak with faculty, student affairs and financial aid representatives, and current students. There are guides for informal visits, visitors may sit in on classes, and stay overnight. To schedule a visit, contact the Admissions Office. **Campus Safety and Security:** Measures include 24-hour foot and vehicle patrol and self-defense education. There are shuttle buses, emergency telephones, and lighted pathways/sidewalks.

REQUIREMENTS: The SAT or ACT is required. Students should graduate from an accredited secondary school with a minimum GPA of 2.8. The GED is accepted. A minimum of 15 Carnegie units is required, including 4 years of English, 3 of history, 2 to 3 of math and science, 2 of foreign language, and 1 of social studies. An essay is required, and an interview is recommended. AP and CLEP credits are accepted. Important factors in the admissions decision are recommendations by school officials, extracurricular activities record, and leadership record.Students must complete 1 field period combining academic study and professional experience for each year of enrollment. The core curriculum consists of 43 to 46 credits, including but not limited to required courses in phys ed, computer science, and integrative studies. A total of 120 credit hours is required for graduation with a minimum of 30 credits in the major and a major and cumulative GPA of 2.0. **Procedure:** Freshmen are admitted fall and spring. Entrance exams should be taken in the spring of the junior year or the fall of the senior year. There are early decision, deferred admissions, and rolling admissions plans. Check with the school for current application deadlines. The application fee is $50. Notification is sent on a rolling basis. Applications are accepted on-line. **Transfer Students:** Applicants must take the SAT or ACT and submit transcripts. An interview is recommended. A minimum GPA of 2.5 is required in college work. 30 of 120 credits required for the bachelor's degree must be completed at Keuka. **International Students:** There are 76 international students enrolled. The school actively recruits these students. They must take the TOEFL.

ADMISSIONS: 88% of the 2014-2015 applicants were accepted. The SAT scores for the 2014-2015 freshman class were: Critical Reading--59% below 500, 36% between 500 and 599, and 5% between 600 and 699; Math--61% below 500, 31% between 500 and 599, and 8% between 600 and 699; Writing--73% below 500, 26% between 500 and 599, and 1% between 600 and 699. The ACT scores were 79% below 21, and 2% above 28. 26% of the current freshmen were in the top fifth of their class; 63% were in the top two fifths. **Admissions Contact:** Gary Boyer, Director of Admissions. E-Mail: *admissions@ mail.keuka.edu* Web: *www.keuka.edu*

FINANCIAL AID: In 2014-2015, 95% of all full-time freshmen and 93% of continuing full-time students received some form of financial aid. 93% of all full-time freshmen and 90% of continuing full-time students received need-based aid. The average freshman award was $22,711. Need-based scholarships or need-based grants averaged $14,206 ($7,852 maximum). 65% of undergraduate students work part-time. Average annual earnings from campus work are $1250. The average financial indebtedness of the 2014 graduate was $19,507. The FAFSA and the college's own financial statement are required. Check with the school for current application deadlines.

LE MOYNE COLLEGE — C-3
www.lemoyne.edu

Syracuse, NY 13214

Fax: (315) 445-4711
Full-time: 1107 men, 1393 women
Part-time: 90 men, 259 women
Graduate: 174 men, 358 women
Year: semesters, summer session
Room & Board: $12,130

SAT CR/M: 520/530 ACT: 23
Application Deadline: February 1

(315) 445-4300
(800) 333-4733
Email: admission@lemoyne.edu
Faculty: 143; IIA, +$
Ph.D.s: 94%
Student/Faculty: 15 to 1
Tuition: $31,340
Freshman Class: 6353 applied, 4124 accepted, 678 enrolled
CEEB CODE: 2366
COMPETITIVE

Le Moyne College, founded in 1946, is a private liberal arts and sciences institution affiliated with the Roman Catholic Society of Jesus (Jesuit) and offers undergraduate and graduate degrees in a variety of disciplines. In addition to regional accreditation, Le Moyne has baccalaureate program accreditation with AACSB, TEAC, CCNE, and ACS. The 161-acre campus is in a suburban area on the eastern edge of Syracuse. Including any residence halls, there are 46 buildings.

STUDENT LIFE: 94% of undergraduates are from New York. Others are from 26 states, 37 foreign countries, and Canada. 83% are from public schools. 78% are White. 51% claim no religious affiliation; 35% Catholic. **Male To Female Ratio:** 1.5:1. The average age of freshmen is 18; all undergraduates, 22. 14% do not continue beyond their first year; 72% remain to graduate. **Housing:** 1609 students can be accommodated in college housing, which includes coed dorms, on-campus apartments, and off-campus apartments. In addition, there are special-interest houses, living learning communities. On-campus housing is guaranteed for all 4 years, is available on a first-come, first-served basis, and is available on a lottery system for upperclassmen. Priority is given to out-of-town students. 59% of students live on campus; of those, 85% remain on campus on weekends. All students may keep cars.

FACULTY/CLASSROOMS: 58% of faculty are male; 42% are female. 97% do both. No introductory courses are taught by graduate students. The average class size in an introductory lecture is 21; in a laboratory is 16; and in a regular course is 20.

PROGRAMS OF STUDY: Le Moyne confers B.A., and B.S. degrees. Master's degrees are also awarded. Bachelor's degrees are awarded in BIOLOGICAL SCIENCE (biochemistry, biology/biological science, and ecology), BUSINESS (accounting, banking and finance, business administration and management, human resources, management

information systems, marketing management, operations management, and organizational leadership and management), COMMUNICATIONS AND THE ARTS (advertising, communications, creative writing, dramatic arts, English, film arts, French, journalism, literature, media arts, music, public relations, radio/television technology, and Spanish), COMPUTER AND PHYSICAL SCIENCE (actuarial science, applied mathematics, chemistry, computer programming, computer science, information sciences and systems, mathematics, physical sciences, physics, science, and statistics), EDUCATION (elementary education, English education, foreign languages education, mathematics education, science education, secondary education, social studies education, special education, and teaching English as a second/foreign language (TESOL/TEFOL)), ENGINEERING AND ENVIRONMENTAL DESIGN (environmental science and preengineering), HEALTH PROFESSIONS (nursing, predentistry, premedicine, preoptometry, prepharmacy, prepodiatry, and preveterinary science), SOCIAL SCIENCE (anthropology, criminology, economics, history, human services, international relations, international studies, law enforcement and corrections, peace studies, philosophy, political science/government, prelaw, psychology, religion, and sociology). Biology, psychology, and accounting, are the strongest academically, and have the largest enrollments.

ACTIVITIES: There are no fraternities or sororities. There are 90 groups on campus, including art, band, cheerleading, choir, chorale, chorus, communications, computers, dance, drama, environmental, ethnic, film, gay, honors, international, jazz band, literary magazine, musical theater, newspaper, orchestra, photography, political, professional, radio and TV, religious, social, social service, student government, and yearbook. Popular campus events include Spring Olympics, Halloween Dance, Snow Ball Holiday Party, Senior Week Activities and Fall Fest. **Sports:** There are 10 intercollegiate sports for men and 11 for women, and 12 intramural sports for men and 12 for women. Facilities include a 2500-seat gym, an athletic weightroom, team rooms, a 25-yard lap pool with diving board, a fitness center, an athletic training room, a jogging track, racquetball courts, a recreational gym, and locker rooms. Outdoor facilities include fields for intercollegiate baseball, softball, soccer, and lacrosse, a cross-country trail, and several intramural and club sports fields. **Graduates:** From July 1, 2013 to June 30, 2014, 592 bachelor's degrees were awarded. The most popular majors were psychology (18%), biology (13%), and English (7%). 275 companies recruited on campus in 2013-2014. In an average class, 56% graduate in 4 years or less, 66% graduate in 5 years or less, and 72% graduate in 6 years or less. Of the 2013 graduating class, 24% were enrolled in graduate school within 6 months of graduation, and 28% were employed.

SERVICES: Counseling and information services are available, as is tutoring in some subjects, math, biology, chemistry, physics, economics, philosophy, Spanish, French, German, Latin, Arabic, history, Japanese, Italian, Chinese, psychology, finance and statistics. There is a reader service for the blind, and remedial math and writing. Study groups are available for selected courses. Writing tutor support for all subjects. **Library/Resources:** The library contains 225,172 volumes, 277,313 microform items, 9,375 audio/video tapes/CDs/DVDs, and subscribes to 146,883 periodicals including electronic. Computerized library services include interlibrary loans, database searching, Internet access, and Wi-Fi capability. Special learning facilities include an art gallery, radio station, TV station, W.Carroll Coyne Performing Arts Center, a media center, and a tutor/writing center. **Physically Challenged Students:** 98% of the campus is accessible. Facilities include wheelchair ramps, elevators, special parking, specially equipped restrooms, lowered drinking fountains, lowered telephones, special housing. Automatic door openers, strobe fire alarm system, wheelchair tables in classrooms and braille signage. **Special:** Internships are available to students in all majors. A campus work-study program, study abroad in 11 countries, dual majors, and a Washington semester are offered. A bachelor plus Master's articulation arrangement with L.C. Smith School of Engineering at Syracuse University as well as early assurance collaborative partnerships in medical, dental, podiatry and optometry fields of graduate study, e.g., a DPT with Upstate Medical University, dental with University of Buffalo and accelerated entry into Physician Assistant Studies. There are 14 national honor societies, a freshman honors program, and 15 departmental honors programs. **Visiting:** There are regularly scheduled orientations for prospective students, including a campus tour and an interview with admissions counselors. Accepted students are invited to attend class, meet with faculty and stay overnight in a residence hall. There are guides for informal visits, visitors may sit in on classes, and stay overnight. To schedule a visit, contact the Admission Office. **Campus Safety and Security:** Measures include 24-hour foot and vehicle patrol, emergency notification system, self-defense education, and security escort services. There are shuttle buses, emergency telephones, lighted pathways/sidewalks, controlled access to dorms/residences, 8 blue light security phones, 190 stationary closed-circuit security cameras, AT&T campuswide card access, and 10 pan tilt zoom closed-circuit security cameras.

REQUIREMENTS: The SAT or ACT is required. Students should graduate from an accredited high school having completed 17 academic units that include 4 in English and social studies, 3 to 4 each in math and science, and 3 in foreign language. A personal statement and letters of recommendation from a teacher and a counselor are required. AP and CLEP credits are accepted. Important factors in the admissions decision are recommendations by school officials, advanced placement or honors courses, and extracurricular activities record.A core curriculum of courses in the humanities, natural sciences, and social sciences is required. Students must earn a GPA of 2.0 overall and in their major, complete one half of their major in residence and 120 total credit hours to graduate. **Procedure:** Freshmen are admitted fall and spring. Entrance exams should be taken in the spring of the junior year or fall of the senior year. There are early admissions, deferred admissions, and rolling admissions plans. Applications should be filed by February 1 for fall entry; December 1 for spring entry, along with a $35 fee. Notification is sent on a rolling basis. 67 applicants were on the 2014 waiting list; 42 were admitted. Applications are accepted on-line. Application fees are waived if application is completed on-line. **Transfer Students:** 263 transfer students enrolled in 2013-2014. A 2.6 GPA is required for admission to most programs. A completed application for transfer admission, official college transcripts, and a personal statement must be submitted. Official high school transcripts and SAT or ACT scores are needed for students with fewer than 24 completed college credits at the time of application. 30 of 120 credits required for the bachelor's degree must be completed at Le Moyne. **International Students:** There are 26 international students enrolled. The school actively recruits these students. They must take the TOEFL with a minimum score of 550 on the paper-based TOEFL (PBT) or 79 on the Internet-based version (iBT). They must also take the SAT or ACT.

ADMISSIONS: 65% of the 2014-2015 applicants were accepted. The SAT scores for the 2014-2015 freshman class were: Critical Reading--34% below 500, 47% between 500 and 599, 17% between 600 and 699, and 2% between 700 and 800; Math--30% below 500, 45% between 500 and 599, 22% between 600 and 699, and 3% between 700 and 800. The ACT scores were 19% below 21, 31% between 21 and 23, 24% between 24 and 26, 12% between 27 and 28, and 14% above 28. 45% of the current freshmen were in the top fifth of their class; 76% were in the top two fifths. 6 freshmen graduated first in their class. **Admissions Contact:** Mary M. Chandler, Sr. Director of Admission. E-Mail: *admission@lemoyne.edu* Web: *www.lemoyne.edu/admissions*

FINANCIAL AID: In 2014-2015, 96% of all full-time freshmen and 90% of continuing full-time students received some form of financial aid. 86% of all full-time freshmen and 83% of continuing full-time students received need-based aid. The average freshman award was $24,792. Need-based scholarships or need-based grants averaged $20,669 ($41,474 maximum); need-based self-help aid (loans and jobs) averaged $4,293 ($7,500 maximum); non-need-based athletic scholarships averaged $8,650 ($42,890 maximum); and other non-need-based awards and non-need-based scholarships averaged $7,356 ($23,750 maximum). 33% of undergraduate students work part-time. Average annual earnings from campus work are $975. The average financial indebtedness of the 2014 graduate was $29,984. Le Moyne is a member of CSS. The FAFSA and the state aid form are required. The deadline for filing freshman financial aid applications for fall entry is February 15.

LEHMAN COLLEGE/THE CITY UNIVERSITY OF NEW YORK *(The complete profile is made available exclusively on our website, www. barronspac.com)*

LIM COLLEGE *(The complete profile is made available exclusively on our website, www.barronspac.com)*

LIST COLLEGE *(The complete profile is made available exclusively on our website, www.barronspac.com)*

LIU BROOKLYN *(The complete profile is made available exclusively on our website, www.barronspac.com)*

LIU POST   D-5
www.liu.edu/post

Brookville, NY 11548	(516) 299-2900
	1-800-LIU-PLAN
Fax: (516) 299-2137	Email: post-enroll@liu.edu
Full-time: 1333 men, 2054 women	Faculty: 198; IIA, ++$
Part-time: 1666 men, 2064 women	Ph.D.s: 89%
Graduate: 917 men, 1452 women	Student/Faculty: 17 to 1
Year: semesters, summer session	Tuition: $34,852
Room & Board: $12,808	Freshman Class: 6550 applied, 5437 accepted, 563 enrolled
SAT CR/M/W: 490/500/490 ACT: 21	CEEB CODE: 2070
Application Deadline: rolling	COMPETITIVE

LIU Post a comprehensive, private university in Brookville, N.Y., situated on Long Island's Gold Coast offers more than 200 academic programs through its School of Computer Science, Innovation and Management Engineering; School of Business; School of Professional Accountancy; School of Visual and Performing Arts; College of Education, Information and Technology; College of Liberal Arts and Sciences; and the School of Health Professions and Nursing. Our students receive all of the resources of a major university, with world-class faculty that includes Fulbright fellows, a vibrant campus life, and 22 championship award-winning NCAA Division II athletic teams. There are 5 undergraduate schools and 5 graduate schools. In addition to regional accreditation, has baccalaureate program accreditation with AACSB, CSWE, TEAC, AACN, JRCERT, and NAACLS. The 308-acre campus is in a suburban area 25 miles east of New York City. Including any residence halls, there are 46 buildings.

STUDENT LIFE: 93% of undergraduates are from New York. Others are from 35 states, 39 foreign countries, and Canada. 40% are White; 34% race unknown. **Male To Female Ratio:** 1.4:1. The average age of freshmen is 19; all undergraduates, 21. 25% do not continue beyond their first year; 75% remain to graduate. **Housing:** 1356 students can be accommodated in college housing, which includes coed dorms. Intensified study, 10-month housing, special housing for disabled students. On-campus housing is guaranteed for all 4 years, is available on a first-come, and first-served basis. 69% of students commute. All students may keep cars.

FACULTY/CLASSROOMS: 49% of faculty are male; 51% are female. No introductory courses are taught by graduate students.

PROGRAMS OF STUDY: LIU Post confers B.A., B.F.A., B.S. and B.M. degrees. Associate, Master's, and Doctoral degrees are also awarded. Bachelor's degrees are awarded in BIOLOGICAL SCIENCE (biology/adolescence education, biology/biological science, cell biology, and nutrition), BUSINESS (accounting, business administration and management, and marketing/retailing/merchandising), COMMUNICATIONS AND THE ARTS (art, art history and appreciation, arts administration/management, broadcasting, dance, dramatic arts, English, film arts, fine arts, French, information technology, instrumental performance, Italian, journalism, music, music performance, opera, photography, public relations, radio/TV, Spanish, Spanish/adolescence education, theatre arts, and vocal performance), COMPUTER AND PHYSICAL SCIENCE (applied mathematics, chemistry, chemistry/adolescence education, computer science, digital arts/technology, earth science/adolescence education, geology, information sciences and systems, mathematics, physics, and radiological technology), EDUCATION (art education, early childhood education, elementary education, English education, foreign languages education, health education, mathematics education, music education, physical education, secondary education, and social studies education), ENGINEERING AND ENVIRONMENTAL DESIGN (commercial art), HEALTH PROFESSIONS (art therapy, biomedical science, clinical science, health care administration, health science, medical laboratory technology, medical records administration/services, nursing, and speech pathology/audiology), SOCIAL SCIENCE (American studies, criminal justice, economics, forensic studies, geography, history, interdisciplinary studies, international studies, liberal arts, sciences, general studies, humanities, philosophy, political science/government, psychology, public administration, social work, and sociology). Business administration, criminal justice, and health sciences have the largest enrollments.

ACTIVITIES: There are 72 groups on campus, including art, band, cheerleading, choir, chorale, chorus, computers, dance, drama, environmental, ethnic, forensics, gay, honors, international, jazz band, literary magazine, musical theater, newspaper, orchestra, pep band, political, professional, radio and TV, religious, social, social service, student government, and yearbook. Popular campus events include Homecoming, Pratt After Dark, Midnight Breakfast, Pep Rally, and Midnight Madness. **Sports:** There are 8 intercollegiate sports for men and 12 for women, and 9 intramural sports for men and 9 for women. Facilities include LIU Post's, Pratt Recreation Center is a state-of-the-art health and fitness facility featuring an eight-lane swimming pool, three full-size basketball courts, racquetball courts, and an elevated jogging track. Home to the LIU Post Pioneers' 22 Division II NCAA men's and women's sports teams, the campus has 70-acres of playing fields, including the Bethpage Federal Credit Union Stadium. **Graduates:** From July 1, 2013 to June 30, 2014, 871 bachelor's degrees were awarded. The most popular majors were business/marketing (19%), education (17%), and health professions (16%). 139 companies recruited on campus in 2013-2014. In an average class, 1% graduate in 3 years or less, 22% graduate in 4 years or less, 37% graduate in 5 years or less, and 40% graduate in 6 years or less.

SERVICES: Counseling and information services are available, as is tutoring in every subject. There is a reader service for the blind, and remedial math, reading, and writing. **Library/Resources:** The library contains 2.1 million volumes, 406,806 microform items, 4,483 audio/video tapes/CDs/DVDs, and subscribes to 223,335 periodicals including electronic. Computerized library services include interlibrary loans, database searching, Internet access, and Wi-Fi capability. Special learning facilities include an art gallery, radio station, TV station, Honors College: A school for highly motivated students seeking challenging, rigorous academics. Tilles Center for the Performing Arts: A 2,242-seat concert hall that features a wide range of dance, music, and theater events, where students in the School of Visual and Performing Arts are able to perform alongside world-renowned performers and engage in live stage productions. Student-Run Businesses: These fully functional business operations afford students unique experiential learning opportunities as they make executive-level decisions. They include: Browse: A high-tech, Apple-licensed technology store, with "Genius Bar" customer service that employs students; PR and Marketing Agency: A full-service agency managed by students; Student Innovation Incubator: A physical and virtual workspace for students to launch startup businesses and collaborate with successful entrepreneurs; The Student Body Boutique: A trendy clothing boutique that sells the latest fashions at an affordable price; Art Gallery Shop: A sophisticated gallery where students can showcase and sell original artwork; Eateries that include: The Post Treat Shoppe, which offers traditional snacks like lollipops and soda in addition to healthy options; The End Zone, a lounge that offers a full menu and HD televisions for watching sports and other entertainment; and The Pratt Smoothie Bar, a juice bar that sells nutritious offerings for students on the go; Wall Street Trading Floor: Featuring Bloomberg terminals and other business technology, this simulated trading floor empowers students to utilize the latest financial tools and learn in a real-time trading environment; Equestrian Stables: Northshore Equestrian Center houses the LIU Post Equine Studies program, offering a large indoor arena, two spacious outdoor rings, a viewing area, and a café. **Physically Challenged Students:** Facilities include wheelchair ramps, elevators, special parking, specially equipped restrooms, special class scheduling, lowered drinking fountains, lowered telephones, and special housing. **Special:** Paid internships help students build a resume while still taking classes. Study abroad options include Europe, Asia,

China, Australia and many other locations. LIU Global offers study options in several locations around the world. Dual majors, accelerated degrees, and a nationally recognized Honors Program help motivated students shape a challenging academic schedule. The Higher Education Opportunity Program is specially designed for New York State residents who are economically disadvantaged and educationally underprepared. LIU Post also offers a wide range of support services including tutoring, academic advisement, financial aid, and career and personal counseling. There are a freshman honors program. **Visiting:** There are regularly scheduled orientations for prospective students, events include a guided campus tour, admissions overview, a meet-and-greet with faculty and deans, interacting with student leaders, attending mini classes, becoming a student for a day, and touring our student-run businesses and high tech incubato. There are guides for informal visits and visitors may sit in on classes. To schedule a visit, contact Celeste LaCasse at celeste.lacasse@liu.edu. **Campus Safety and Security:** Measures include 24-hour foot and vehicle patrol, emergency notification system, and security escort services. There are shuttle buses, emergency telephones, lighted pathways/sidewalks, and controlled access to dorms/residences.

REQUIREMENTS: SAT or ACT is required. Average GPA: Solid "B" (82–85) 3.0, Average SAT: Math and Critical Reading combined: 1000 or ACT Composite: 20. High school students seeking admission to LIU Post are expected to have completed a college preparatory program (includes 4 years of English, 3 years each of math, social studies, and science, and 2 years of foreign language). Students applying for admission to programs in the visual and performing arts must schedule an audition or portfolio review through the department. Students must also submit the following: completed application for admission, official high school transcript or evidence of completion of high school graduation requirements (GED), Non-refundable application fee, tests results from the SAT or ACT (school codes: ACT-2687; SAT-2070), personal statement/essay, and letters of recommendation from high school teacher or guidance counselor AP and CLEP credits are accepted. General Requirements for Graduation: 2.00 cumulative average (higher in some areas), 2.25 minor subject average (higher in some areas) if attempted, core and major requirements fulfilled, and minor requirements if attempted, 128 credits (more in some departments), 129 credits including freshman seminar, writing across the curriculum courses 3-5 depending on admissions status, and minimum liberal arts requirements (varies depending on degree being earned). Core: Competency Requirements (library use, computer literacy, oral communication competency), English Comp (6 credits), laboratory sciences (8 credits), history and philosophy (9 credits), literature or foreign language (6 credits), arts (6 credits), economics or political science (6 credits), anthropology, geography, psychology or sociology (6 credits), and mathematics (3 credits). **Procedure:** Freshmen are admitted fall and spring. Entrance exams should be taken by Spring 2015. There are early admissions, deferred admissions, and rolling admissions plans. Application deadlines are open. Application fee is $50. Notification is sent on a rolling basis. Applications are accepted on-line. **Transfer Students:** 437 transfer students enrolled in 2013-2014. A high school GPA of 2.5 or college GPA of 2.0 is required. 32 of 128 credits required for the bachelor's degree must be completed at LIU Post. **International Students:** There are 398 international students enrolled. The school actively recruits these students. They must take the TOEFL with a minimum score of 527 on the paper-based TOEFL (PBT) or 75 on the Internet-based version (iBT).

ADMISSIONS: 83% of the 2014-2015 applicants were accepted. The SAT scores for the 2014-2015 freshman class were: Critical Reading--53% below 500, 40% between 500 and 599, 6% between 600 and 699, and 1% between 700 and 800; Math--49% below 500, 41% between 500 and 599, 9% between 600 and 699, and 1% between 700 and 800; Writing--57% below 500, 36% between 500 and 599, 6% between 600 and 699, and 1% between 700 and 800. The ACT scores were 40% below 21, 33% between 21 and 23, 17% between 24 and 26, 6% between 27 and 28, and 4% above 28. **Admissions Contact:** Dr. Jackie Nealon, VP & Acting Dean of Admissions. E-Mail: *post-enroll@liu.edu* Web: *www.liu.edu/post*

FINANCIAL AID: In 2014-2015, 90% of all full-time freshmen and 85% of continuing full-time students received some form of financial aid. 66% of all full-time freshmen and 62% of continuing full-time students received need-based aid. The average freshman award was

$22,300. Need-based scholarships or need-based grants averaged $10,500; need-based self-help aid (loans and jobs) averaged $8,100; non-need-based athletic scholarships averaged $14,600; and other non-need-based awards and non-need-based scholarships averaged $13,200. The average financial indebtedness of the 2014 graduate was $21,700. LIU Post is a member of CSS. The FAFSA and the state aid form are required. The priority date for freshman financial aid applications for fall entry is February 15. The deadline for filing freshman financial aid applications for fall entry is February 15.

MANHATTAN COLLEGE　　　　　　　　D-5
www.manhattan.edu

Riverdale, NY 10471	(718) 862-7200
	(800) 622-9235
Fax: (718) 862-8019	Email: admit@manhattan.edu
Full-time: 1713 men, 1428 women	Faculty: IIA, ++$
Part-time: 151 men, 59 women	Ph.D.s: 95%
Graduate: 196 men, 253 women	Student/Faculty: 12 to 1
Year: semesters, summer session	Tuition: $35,968
Room & Board: $13,620	Freshman Class: 6546 applied, 4555 accepted, 842 enrolled
SAT CR/M/W: 526/535/528 ACT: 24	CEEB CODE: 2395
Application Deadline: March 1	COMPETITIVE+

Founded in 1853, Manhattan College offers an exceptional college education enriched by Lasallian Catholic values and access to New York City. Our celebrated faculty and students are committed to the lifelong pursuit of academic excellence, career achievement, and reflection on values, ethics and principles. It offers degree programs in the arts and sciences, education and health, business, and engineering. Figures in the above capsule and in this profile are approximate. There are 5 undergraduate schools and 3 graduate schools. In addition to regional accreditation, Manhattan has baccalaureate program accreditation with AACSB, ABET, AHEA, CAHEA, and TEAC. The 22-acre campus is in an urban area in Riverdale NY, 10 miles north of midtown Manhattan. Including any residence halls, there are 21 buildings.

STUDENT LIFE: 75% of undergraduates are from New York. Others are from 36 states, 46 foreign countries, and Canada. 60% are from public schools. 60% are White; 17% Hispanic. 55% are Catholic. **Male To Female Ratio:** 0.8:1. The average age of freshmen is 18; all undergraduates, 21. 12% do not continue beyond their first year; 75% remain to graduate. **Housing:** 2095 students can be accommodated in college housing, which includes coed dorms, on-campus apartments, off-campus apartments, and married student housing. Arches a living/learning environment. On-campus housing is guaranteed for all 4 years. 65% of students live on campus; of those, 80% remain on campus on weekends. All students may keep cars.

FACULTY/CLASSROOMS: 60% of faculty are male; 40% are female. All teach undergraduates, and 80% do both. No introductory courses are taught by graduate students. The average class size in an introductory lecture is 15 and in a regular course is 22.

PROGRAMS OF STUDY: Manhattan confers B.A., B.S. and B.S.E. degrees. Master's degrees are also awarded. Bachelor's degrees are awarded in BIOLOGICAL SCIENCE (biochemistry and biology/biological science), BUSINESS (accounting, banking and finance, business economics, international business management, labor studies, and marketing/retailing/merchandising), COMMUNICATIONS AND THE ARTS (broadcasting, communications, English, French, journalism, and Spanish), COMPUTER AND PHYSICAL SCIENCE (chemistry, computer science, information sciences and systems, mathematics, and physics), EDUCATION (early childhood education, education, education of the emotionally handicapped, elementary education, foreign languages education, health education, middle school education, physical education, science education, secondary education, and special education), ENGINEERING AND ENVIRONMENTAL DESIGN (chemical engineering, civil engineering, electrical/electronics engineering, environmental engineering, and mechanical engineering), HEALTH PROFESSIONS (predentistry, premedicine, and radiological science), SOCIAL SCIENCE

(economics, history, peace studies, philosophy, political science/government, prelaw, psychology, religion, sociology, and urban studies). Engineering and business is the strongest academically. Engineering, business, and arts have the largest enrollments.

ACTIVITIES: 3% of men belong to 2 local and 1 national fraternities; 1% of women belong to 2 local sororities. There are 70 groups on campus, including bagpipe, cheerleading, choir, chorus, computers, dance, debate, drama, ethnic, honors, international, jazz band, literary magazine, musical theater, newspaper, orchestra, pep band, political, professional, radio and TV, religious, social, social service, student government, and yearbook. Popular campus events include Annual Springfest, Special Olympics and Jasper Jingle. **Sports:** There are 8 intercollegiate sports for men and 8 for women, and 7 intramural sports for men and 7 for women. Facilities include Draddy Gym has 3 hardwood basketball courts used for basketball, volleyball, dodge ball, indoor soccer, dorm wars; has an indoor track and a weight room with free weights and weightlifting machines. Alumni Hall - has a fitness center with many different cardio machines and a dance studio use for dancing and fitness classes. Gaelic Park - a large turf field used for football, soccer, lacrosse, softball and Ultimate Frisbee. **Graduates:** From July 1, 2013 to June 30, 2014, 784 bachelor's degrees were awarded. The most popular majors were engineering (25%), business (22%), and education (13%). In an average class, 63% graduate in 4 years or less and 70% graduate in 6 years or less. Of the 2013 graduating class, 18% were enrolled in graduate school within 6 months of graduation, and 65% were employed.

SERVICES: Counseling and information services are available, as is tutoring in every subject. Center for Academic Success is comprised of 3 offices with open door policy and extended hours. **Library/Resources:** The library contains 292,438 volumes, 675,489 microform items, 2,676 audio/video tapes/CDs/DVDs, and subscribes to 343 periodicals including electronic. Computerized library services include interlibrary loans, database searching, Internet access, and Wi-Fi capability. Special learning facilities include a radio station, TV station, an research and learning center, 24-hour Internet cafe, Holocaust, Genocide and Interfaith Education Center, and Center for Academic Success. **Physically Challenged Students:** All of the campus is accessible. Facilities include wheelchair ramps, elevators, special parking, specially equipped restrooms, and special housing. **Special:** Manhattan offers credit and non-credit based internships and experiential learning opportunities in for-profit, not-for-profit, social, cultural, educational, religious, government and non-government organizations. Students may enroll in numerous study abroad programs that are offered throughout the world. Five year Bachelors/Masters degrees in Business, Education and Engineering are offered and a dual major in international business, credit by exam, and non-degree study are also available. There are 22 national honor societies, including Phi Beta Kappa, a freshman honors program, and 28 departmental honors programs. **Visiting:** There are regularly scheduled orientations for prospective students, during 2 days in the summer, which include scheduling, parent workshops, loan seminars, and English and math testing. There are guides for informal visits, visitors may sit in on classes, and stay overnight. To schedule a visit, contact the Admission Center. **Campus Safety and Security:** Measures include 24-hour foot and vehicle patrol and emergency notification system. There are emergency telephones, lighted pathways/sidewalks, and controlled access to dorms/residences.

REQUIREMENTS: The SAT or ACT is required. Applicants must graduate from an accredited secondary school or have earned a GED. 16 academic units are required, including 4 of English, 3 each of math and social studies, and 2 of foreign language, lab sciences, and electives. An essay is required and an interview is recommended. AP and CLEP credits are accepted. Important factors in the admissions decision are advanced placement or honors courses, leadership record, and recommendations by school officials. All students must take courses in English composition and literature, religious studies, philosophy, humanities, social science, science, math, and a modern foreign language. About 130 credit hours are required for graduation, with about 36 in the major. The minimum GPA is 2.0. **Procedure:** Freshmen are admitted fall and spring. Entrance exams should be taken in the spring of the junior year or the fall of the senior year. There are early decision, deferred admissions, and rolling admissions plans. Early decision applications should be filed by November 15;

regular applications, by March 1 for fall entry; and December 1 for spring entry, along with a $60 fee. Notification of early decision is sent December 15; regular decision, December 15. 38 early decision candidates were accepted for the 2014-2015 class. 272 applicants were on the 2014 waiting list; 52 were admitted. Applications are accepted on-line. **Transfer Students:** 143 transfer students enrolled in 2013-2014. Applicants must have a GPA of 2.5 and meet subject course requirements according to their course of study. They must submit transcripts from colleges and high schools attended. An interview is recommended. 66 of 130 credits required for the bachelor's degree must be completed at Manhattan. **International Students:** There are 85 international students enrolled. The school actively recruits these students. They must take the TOEFL with a minimum score of 550 on the paper-based TOEFL (PBT) or 80 on the Internet-based version (iBT). They must also take the SAT or ACT.

ADMISSIONS: 70% of the 2014-2015 applicants were accepted. The SAT scores for the 2014-2015 freshman class were: Critical Reading--38% below 500, 44% between 500 and 599, 16% between 600 and 699, and 2% between 700 and 800; Math--29% below 500, 40% between 500 and 599, 27% between 600 and 699, and 4% between 700 and 800; Writing--35% below 500, 45% between 500 and 599, 19% between 600 and 699, and 2% between 700 and 800. The ACT scores were 16% below 21, 27% between 21 and 23, 30% between 24 and 26, 12% between 27 and 28, and 15% above 28. **Admissions Contact:** William J. Bisset, Jr., Vice President for Enrollment Management. E-Mail: *admit@manhattan.edu* Web: *www.manhattan.edu*

FINANCIAL AID: In 2014-2015, 75% of all full-time freshmen and 72% of continuing full-time students received some form of financial aid. 74% of all full-time freshmen and 72% of continuing full-time students received need-based aid. The average freshman award was $22,566. Need-based scholarships or need-based grants averaged $14,551; need-based self-help aid (loans and jobs) averaged $4,900; and non-need-based athletic scholarships averaged $31,336. 26% of undergraduate students work part-time. Average annual earnings from campus work are $1500. The average financial indebtedness of the 2014 graduate was $34,375. The FAFSA and the college's own financial statement are required. The priority date for freshman financial aid applications for fall entry is February 15.

MANHATTAN SCHOOL OF MUSIC (*The complete profile is made available exclusively on our website, www.barronspac.com*)

MANHATTANVILLE COLLEGE   **D-5**
www.manhattanville.edu

Purchase, NY 10577   **(914) 323-5129**
    (800) 32 VILLE

Fax: **(914) 694-1732**	Email: **admissions@mville.edu**
Full-time: 608 men, 1100 women	Faculty: 110
Part-time: 39 men, 51 women	Ph.D.s: 74%
Graduate: 339 men, 728 women	Student/Faculty: 15 to 1
Year: semesters, summer session	Tuition: $36,220
Room & Board: $14,520	Freshman Class: 3929 applied, 2902 accepted, 459 enrolled
SAT or ACT: recommended	CEEB CODE: 2397
Application Deadline: August 1	**VERY COMPETITIVE**

Manhattanville College, founded in 1841 is an independent, co-educational liberal arts institution dedicated to academic excellence. Manhattanville prepares students to be ethical and socially responsible leaders in a global community. The college has a rich history of preparing highly motivated students who value ethical integrity and social responsibility with the highest-quality education amongst a globally diverse campus community. The undergraduate programs combine the intellectual strength and passion of a liberal arts education with the hands-on, real-world experiences to turn a student's passion into an exciting career. The college offers more than 50 undergraduate areas of study including newly developed majors in sport studies, digital media production, accounting and marketing. Students can combine in-class learning with on-the-job experiences through access to over 700 internships ranging from Fortune 500 companies to non-profits, arts and entertainment venues to research opportunities and more. At Manhattanville, students get an insider's view of how the world works through powerful internships, international study and services learning, and four years of life on a campus just minutes from the world's most cosmopolitan city. The Manhattanville School of Business offers six master's degrees, including, Business Leadership, Finance, Human Resource Management and Organizational Effectiveness, International Management, Marketing Communication Management and Sport Business Management. Manhattanville welcomes writers and aspiring writers to join its dynamic literary community. There is 1 undergraduate school and 2 graduate schools. In addition to regional accreditation, M'ville has baccalaureate program accreditation with NCATE and IACBE. The 100-acre campus is in a suburban area 30 miles north of New York City. Including any residence halls, there are 20 buildings.

STUDENT LIFE: 64% of undergraduates are from New York. Others are from 43 states, 47 foreign countries, and Canada. 40% are race unknown; 28% White; 13% Hispanic. **Male To Female Ratio:** 1.9:1. The average age of freshmen is 18; all undergraduates, 20. 21% do not continue beyond their first year; 54% remain to graduate. **Housing:** 1260 students can be accommodated in college housing, which includes coed dorms. In addition, there are honors houses, Wellness community housing available which promotes a substance-free, holistic environment. On-campus housing is guaranteed for all 4 years, is available on a first-come, and first-served basis. 64% of students live on campus; of those, 70% remain on campus on weekends. All students may keep cars.

FACULTY/CLASSROOMS: 50% of faculty are male; 50% are female. All teach undergraduates. No introductory courses are taught by graduate students. The average class size in a regular course is 19.

PROGRAMS OF STUDY: M'ville confers B.A., B.S., B.F.A. and B.Mus. degrees. Master's and Doctoral degrees are also awarded. Bachelor's degrees are awarded in AGRICULTURE (environmental studies), BIOLOGICAL SCIENCE (biochemistry and biology/biological science), BUSINESS (accounting, banking and finance, business administration and management, and marketing), COMMUNICATIONS AND THE ARTS (art history and appreciation, communications, dance, digital media, dramatic arts, English, French, music, Spanish, and studio art), COMPUTER AND PHYSICAL SCIENCE (chemistry, computer science, and mathematics), EDUCATION (education and sports studies), SOCIAL SCIENCE (American studies, Asian/Oriental studies, economics, history, international studies, legal studies, philosophy, political science/government, psychology, religion, and sociology). Psychology, business management, and communication studies have the largest enrollments.

ACTIVITIES: There are no fraternities or sororities. There are 40 groups on campus, including art, band, cheerleading, chess, chorale, chorus, computers, dance, debate, drama, environmental, ethnic, film, gay, honors, international, jazz band, literary magazine, musical theater, newspaper, opera, orchestra, photography, political, professional, radio and TV, religious, social, social service, student government, and yearbook. Popular campus events include Fall Fest'ville, Quad Jam, End of semester Brunches and Nights parties which countdown to graduation. **Sports:** There are 8 intercollegiate sports for men and 11 for women. Facilities include Manhattanville's athletic and recreation facilities include a 1000-seat gym, state-of-the-art scoreboard, indoor batting cages, 6 lane indoor pool, 6 Har-Tru tennis courts, strength and conditioning center, turf field that houses lacrosse, field hockey and soccer, as well as a grass soccer field, baseball field and softball field. **Graduates:** From July 1, 2013 to June 30, 2014, 292 bachelor's degrees were awarded. The most popular majors were management (13%), psychology (12%), and communications (8%). 80 companies recruited on campus in 2013-2014. In an average class, 54% graduate in 4 years or less, 58% graduate in 5 years or less, and 58% graduate in 6 years or less. Of the 2013 graduating class, 21% were enrolled in graduate school within 6 months of graduation, and 52% were employed.

SERVICES: Counseling and information services are available, as is tutoring in every subject. **Library/Resources:** The library contains 429,051 volumes, 259,230 microform items, 12,786 audio/video tapes/CDs/DVDs, and subscribes to 56,314 periodicals including electronic. Computerized library services include interlibrary loans, database searching, Internet access, and Wi-Fi capability. Special learning facilities include an art gallery, radio station, Multimedia Production Labs, Environmental Sciences Lab, Performance Theatre and Dance Studio. **Physically Challenged Students:** 70% of the campus is accessible. Facilities include wheelchair ramps, elevators, special parking, specially equipped restrooms, special class scheduling, and special housing. **Special:** Manhattanville college offers two Study Abroad programs (cooperative and non-cooperative) to successful candidates to further their education through international institutions. Manhattanville is pleased to announce a new partnership with EF International Language Centers (EF). Manhattanville offers cross-registration with SUNY Purchase. Dual, student-designed and interdisciplinary majors are also available at the college. There are 3 national honor societies, a freshman honors program, and 18 departmental honors programs. **Visiting:** There are regularly scheduled orientations for prospective students, consisting of weekday information sessions and tours at 10 am, 12 pm, and 2 pm (except for holiday closures). There are also spring and fall Saturday and Sunday sessions. There are guides for informal visits, visitors may sit in on classes, and stay overnight. To schedule a visit, contact the Office of Admissions at joseph.garzione@mville.edu. **Campus Safety and Security:** Measures include 24-hour foot and vehicle patrol, emergency notification system, and security escort services. There are shuttle buses, emergency telephones, lighted pathways/sidewalks, and controlled access to dorms/residences.

REQUIREMENTS: The SAT or ACT is recommended. Applicants should graduate in the upper 50% of their class with 4 years of English, 3 each of history, math, and science, including 2 of lab science, and 1 half-year each of art and music. The GED is accepted. Interviews are strongly encouraged. Art applicants must submit a portfolio, music applicants must audition. A GPA of 2.5 is required. AP and CLEP credits are accepted. Important factors in the admissions decision are advanced placement or honors courses, evidence of special talent, and extracurricular activities record. To qualify for a Bachelor's degree and be eligible for participation in the College's commencement ceremony, undergraduate students must complete all of the following degree requirements: General Education requirements(for ALL students regardless of major or program). A minimum of 120 total credits (though some major programs may exceed 120). A minimum cumulative G.P.A. of 2.0. Completion of a Major (normally with final grades of C or better, though some majors accept C- or higher). Minimum number of liberal arts credits for B.A. degree: 90 liberal arts credits, B.S. degree: 60 liberal arts credits, B.F.A. degree: 30 liberal arts credits, B.Mus degree: 30 liberal arts credits. All undergraduate students must complete all of the the following general education credit requirements (Competency and Distribution) to fulfill the College's General Education requirements for degree completion. A minimum letter grade of "C-" must be earned to fulfill a requirement. I: Competency Requirements • Quantitative Reasoning (6 credits) • Critical Analysis and Reasoning (6 credits) • Scientific Reasoning (6 credits) • Oral Communication (3 credits) • Written Communication (6 credits) • Second Language (minimum of 6 introductory-level credits in one language or demonstration of equivalent competency) • Technological Competency (3 credits) II: Distribution Area Requirements All Manhattanville undergraduates must complete the indicated credit requirement in all four of the following curricular distribution areas in addition to Competency requirements: • Humanities (6 credits) • Social Science (6 credits) • Mathematical (3 credits) AND Scientific (3 credits) • Fine Arts (6 credits) A minimum C- letter grade must be earned in any general education competency or distribution course to fulfill a requirement. **Procedure:** Freshmen are admitted fall and spring. Entrance exams should be taken we adhere to Early Action Policy, December 1 Deadline Application. There are early admissions, deferred admissions, and rolling admissions plans. Application deadlines are open. Application fee is $50. Notification of early decision is sent December 31; regular decision, Applications are accepted on-line. **Transfer Students:** 77 transfer students enrolled in 2013-2014. 30 or more credits - Application, recommendations, college transcripts, applicants can adhere to college-wide test-optional policy, interview recommended for some. If less than 30 credits - Application, recommendations, college/high school transcripts, applicants can adhere to college-wide test-optional policy, interview recommended for some. 30 of 120 credits required

for the bachelor's degree must be completed at M'ville. **International Students:** There are 236 international students enrolled. The school actively recruits these students. They must take the TOEFL with a minimum score of 550 on the paper-based TOEFL (PBT) or 80 on the Internet-based version (iBT), or take the IELTS, Cambridge English, CEFR B2 or higher, IB. They must also take the SAT or ACT. **ADMISSIONS:** 74% of the 2014-2015 applicants were accepted. The SAT scores for the 2014-2015 freshman class were: Critical Reading--26% below 500, 57% between 500 and 599, 15% between 600 and 699, and 2% between 700 and 800; Math--32% below 500, 48% between 500 and 599, 17% between 600 and 699, and 3% between 700 and 800; Writing--29% below 500, 48% between 500 and 599, 21% between 600 and 699, and 2% between 700 and 800. **Admissions Contact:** Nik Kumar, Vice President, Enrollment Management. E-Mail: *admissions@mville.edu* Web: *www.manhattanville.edu*

FINANCIAL AID: In 2014-2015, 97% of all full-time freshmen and 95% of continuing full-time students received some form of financial aid. 61% of all full-time freshmen and 66% of continuing full-time students received need-based aid. The average freshman award was $26,805. Need-based scholarships or need-based grants averaged $4,883 ($45,410 maximum); need-based self-help aid (loans and jobs) averaged $2,227 ($8,500 maximum); and other non-need-based awards and non-need-based scholarships averaged $17,718 ($34,870 maximum). The average financial indebtedness of the 2014 graduate was $25,171. The FAFSA and the state aid form, and International students can apply for need based aid using the International Student Financial Aid Application (ISFAA) are required. The priority date for freshman financial aid applications for fall entry is March 1. The deadline for filing freshman financial aid applications for fall entry is March 1.

MANNES COLLEGE NEW SCHOOL FOR MUSIC (*The complete profile is made available exclusively on our website, www.barronspac.com*)

MARIST COLLEGE	D-4
www.marist.edu	
Poughkeepsie, NY 12601	(845) 575-3226
	(800) 436-5483
Fax: (845) 575-3215	Email: admissions@marist.edu
Full-time: 1900 men, 2600 women	Faculty: IIA, +$
Part-time: 185 men, 190 women	Ph.D.s: n/av
Graduate: 405 men, 485 women	Student/Faculty: n/av
Year: semesters, summer session	Tuition: $28,800
Room & Board: $12.600	Freshman Class: n/av
SAT or ACT: required	CEEB CODE: 2400
Application Deadline: February 15	COMPETITIVE

Marist College, founded in 1929, is private liberal arts college with a Catholic tradition. The figures in the above capsule and in this profile are approximate. There are 7 undergraduate schools and 4 graduate schools. In addition to regional accreditation, Marist has baccalaureate program accreditation with AACSB, CSWE, and NAACLS. The 180-acre campus is in a suburban area 75 miles north of New York City on the Hudson River. Including any residence halls, there are 49 buildings.

STUDENT LIFE: 59% of undergraduates are from New York. Others are from 39 states, 9 foreign countries, and Canada. 70% are from public schools. 77% are White. **Male To Female Ratio:** 1.3:1. The average age of freshmen is 18; all undergraduates, 22. 9% do not continue beyond their first year; 78% remain to graduate. **Housing:** 2858 students can be accommodated in college housing, which includes coed dorms, on-campus apartments, and off-campus apartments. In addition, there are special-interest houses, Freshman dorms with mentors, and housing for upperclassmen. 72% of students live on campus; of those, 90% remain on campus on weekends. Alcohol is not permitted. Upperclassmen may keep cars.

FACULTY/CLASSROOMS: 56% of faculty are male; 44% are female. 95% teach undergraduates, 68% do research, and 66% do both. No introductory courses are taught by graduate students. The average

class size in an introductory lecture is 20; in a laboratory is 20; and in a regular course is 18.

PROGRAMS OF STUDY: Marist confers B.A., B.S. and B.P.S. degrees. Master's degrees are also awarded. Bachelor's degrees are awarded in BIOLOGICAL SCIENCE (biology/biological science), BUSINESS (accounting, business administration and management, and fashion merchandising), COMMUNICATIONS AND THE ARTS (communications, English, fine arts, French, and Spanish), COMPUTER AND PHYSICAL SCIENCE (chemistry, computer mathematics, computer science, digital arts/technology, information sciences and systems, and mathematics), EDUCATION (athletic training and special education), ENGINEERING AND ENVIRONMENTAL DESIGN (environmental science), HEALTH PROFESSIONS (medical technology), SOCIAL SCIENCE (American studies, criminal justice, economics, fashion design and technology, history, interdisciplinary studies, philosophy, political science/government, psychology, and social work). Business administration, communications, and childhood/special education have the largest enrollments.

ACTIVITIES: 1% of men belong to 3 national fraternities; 3% of women belong to 1 local and 3 national sororities. There are 81 groups on campus, including art, band, cheerleading, chess, choir, chorale, chorus, computers, dance, debate, drama, ethnic, film, gay, honors, international, jazz band, literary magazine, marching band, musical theater, newspaper, orchestra, pep band, photography, political, professional, radio and TV, religious, social, social service, student government, and symphony. Popular campus events include Activities Fair, Foxfest, and Giving Tree Program. **Sports:** There are 11 intercollegiate sports for men and 12 for women, and 4 intramural sports for men and 4 for women. Facilities include a boathouse, a 3600-seat basketball arena, a 5000-seat stadium, 30 acres of playing fields, a field house, a swimming pool, a diving well, racquetball courts, a tennis pavilion, a dance and aerobics studio, a weight room, intramural basketball courts, an all-purpose playing space, and a fitness center. **Graduates:** From July 1, 2013 to June 30, 2014, 1152 bachelor's degrees were awarded. The most popular majors were business (24%), communications (20%), and childhood/special education (9%). 200 companies recruited on campus in 2013-2014. In an average class, 69% graduate in 4 years or less, 78% graduate in 5 years or less, and 78% graduate in 6 years or less. Of the 2013 graduating class, 22% were enrolled in graduate school within 6 months of graduation, and 85% were employed.

SERVICES: Counseling and information services are available, as is tutoring in every subject. There is a reader service for the blind, and remedial math, reading, and writing. **Library/Resources:** The library contains 207,750 volumes, 12,206 microform items, 5,657 audio/video tapes/CDs/DVDs, and subscribes to 30,127 periodicals including electronic. Computerized library services include interlibrary loans, database searching, Internet access, and Wi-Fi capability. Special learning facilities include an art gallery, radio station, TV station, a gallery of Lowell Thomas memorabilia, estuarine and environmental studies lab, public opinion institute, and economic research center. **Physically Challenged Students:** All of the campus is accessible. Facilities include wheelchair ramps, elevators, special parking, specially equipped restrooms, special class scheduling, lowered drinking fountains, and lowered telephones. **Special:** Marist offers cross-registration with schools in the Mid-Hudson Career Consortium and study abroad in 38 countries. The school also offers a 3-year degree in social work, co-op programs in computer science and computer information systems, information technology, accounting, and business, work-study programs, and dual and student-designed majors. There are internships available with more than 1100 organizations in the United States and abroad, including New York State Legislature and White House programs. There are 14 national honor societies and a freshman honors program. **Visiting:** There are regularly scheduled orientations for prospective students, including 1-day June visits for freshmen and a 1-week welcome program. There are guides for informal visits, visitors may sit in on classes, and stay overnight. To schedule a visit, contact the Admissions Office. **Campus Safety and Security:** Measures include 24-hour foot and vehicle patrol and security escort services. There are emergency telephones and lighted pathways/sidewalks.

REQUIREMENTS: The SAT or ACT is required. The ACT Optional Writing test is also required. Applicants should have 17 high school units, including at least 4 years in English, 3 each in math and science, 2 each in social studies, foreign language, and an elective, and 1 in American history. An essay and 2 letters of recommendation are also required. Marist requires applicants to be in the upper 50% of their class. AP and CLEP credits are accepted. Important factors in the admissions decision are advanced placement or honors courses, leadership record, and recommendations by school officials. To graduate, students must maintain a GPA of 2.0 in the major while taking 120 credits. A 30-credit core curriculum and 30 to 36 credits in a major are required. Distribution requirements include 6 credits each in natural sciences, social sciences, history, literature, and math and 3 credits each in fine arts and philosophy/religious studies. Specific course requirements include English writing skills and foundation courses in those areas defined by major programs. **Procedure:** Freshmen are admitted fall and spring. Entrance exams should be taken during the fall of the senior year. There are early decision and deferred admissions plans. Early decision applications should be filed by November 15; regular applications, by February 15 for fall entry; and November 1 for spring entry, along with a $50 fee. Notification of early decision is sent December 15; regular decision, March 15. Applications are accepted on-line. **Transfer Students:** 158 transfer students enrolled in 2013-2014. Applicants must have at least a 2.8 GPA (depending on the college and major program) in at least 30 college credits. Students with fewer than 25 credits will be treated as freshmen. Grades of C or better transfer. 30 of 120 credits required for the bachelor's degree must be completed at Marist. **International Students:** There are 12 international students enrolled. The school actively recruits these students. They must take the TOEFL and the college's own test. The IELTS is accepted.

ADMISSIONS: Kent Rinehart, Dean of Admission. E-Mail: *admissions@marist.edu* Web: *www.marist.edu*

FINANCIAL AID: In 2014-2015, 91% of all full-time freshmen and 80% of continuing full-time students received some form of financial aid. 59% of all full-time freshmen and 56% of continuing full-time students received need-based aid. The average freshman award was $15,909. Need-based scholarships or need-based grants averaged $11,723 ($35,515 maximum); need-based self-help aid (loans and jobs) averaged $5,390 ($8,200 maximum); and non-need-based athletic scholarships averaged $9,804 ($36,885 maximum). 33% of undergraduate students work part-time. Average annual earnings from campus work are $2088. The average financial indebtedness of the 2014 graduate was $28,374. The FAFSA is required. Check with the school for current application deadlines.

**MARITIME COLLEGE/STATE UNIVERSITY   D-5
OF NEW YORK**
www.sunymaritime.edu

Throgs Neck, NY 10465	**(718) 409-7221**
	(800) 642-1874
Fax: (718) 409-7465	Email: sunymaritime.edu
Full-time: 1326 men, 137 women	Faculty: 69; IIA
Part-time: 97 men, 15 women	Ph.D.s: 49%
Graduate: 151 men, 31 women	Student/Faculty: 21 to 1
Year: semesters, summer session	Tuition: $6956 ($15,996)
Room & Board: $10,900	Freshman Class: 1397 applied, 888 accepted, 356 enrolled
SAT CR/M: 510/550 ACT: 22	CEEB CODE: 2536
Application Deadline: open	COMPETITIVE

The Maritime College of the State University of New York, founded in 1874, is a public institution that prepares students for the U.S. Merchant Marine officers' license and for bachelor's degrees in engineering, naval architecture, marine environmental science, and marine transportation/business administration. Figures in the above capsule and in this profile are approximate. There is one graduate school. In addition to regional accreditation, New York Maritime has baccalaureate program accreditation with ABET. The 52-acre campus is in a suburban area on the Throgs Neck peninsula where Long Island Sound meets the East River. Including any residence halls, there are 31 buildings.

STUDENT LIFE: 65% of undergraduates are from New York. Others

are from 28 states, and 20 foreign countries. 70% are from public schools. 71% are White. **Male To Female Ratio:** 0.1:1. The average age of freshmen is 19; all undergraduates, 21. 23% do not continue beyond their first year; 77% remain to graduate. **Housing:** 1281 students can be accommodated in college housing, which includes single-sex and coed dorms. On-campus housing is guaranteed for all 4 years, is available on a first-come, and first-served basis. 82% of students live on campus; of those, 25% remain on campus on weekends. Alcohol is not permitted. Upperclassmen may keep cars.

FACULTY/CLASSROOMS: 89% of faculty are male; 11% are female. 96% teach undergraduates, and 20% do both. No introductory courses are taught by graduate students. The average class size in an introductory lecture is 28; in a laboratory is 16; and in a regular course is 30.

PROGRAMS OF STUDY: New York Maritime confers B.E., and B.S. degrees. Associate and Master's degrees are also awarded. Bachelor's degrees are awarded in BIOLOGICAL SCIENCE (marine science), BUSINESS (business administration and management and transportation management), COMPUTER AND PHYSICAL SCIENCE (atmospheric sciences and meteorology), ENGINEERING AND ENVIRONMENTAL DESIGN (electrical/electronics engineering, engineering, environmental science, marine engineering, maritime science, and naval architecture and marine engineering), SOCIAL SCIENCE (humanities). Marine operations, marine environmental science, and electrical engineering are the strongest academically. Marine transportation, marine engineering, and international transportation and trade have the largest enrollments.

ACTIVITIES: There are no fraternities or sororities. There are 30 groups on campus, including art, bagpipe, band, chorus, computers, drill team, ethnic, honors, international, jazz band, marching band, newspaper, pep band, photography, political, professional, religious, social, social service, and student government. Popular campus events include Thursdays in the TIV, Ring Dance and Super Bowl Party. **Sports:** There are 9 intercollegiate sports for men and 9 for women, and 6 intramural sports for men and 6 for women. Facilities include an athletic center containing a 2,000-seat gym, a swimming pool, exercise and weight rooms, a rifle and pistol range, and 3 handball/racquetball and squash courts; a sailing center; and football, baseball, lacrosse, and soccer fields. **Graduates:** From July 1, 2013 to June 30, 2014, 306 bachelor's degrees were awarded. The most popular majors were marine transportation (30%), international transportation and trade (18%), and naval architecture (9%). 22 companies recruited on campus in 2013-2014. In an average class, 31% graduate in 4 years or less, 47% graduate in 5 years or less, and 49% graduate in 6 years or less. Of the 2013 graduating class, 4% were enrolled in graduate school within 6 months of graduation, and 100% were employed.

SERVICES: Counseling and information services are available, as is tutoring in every subject. **Library/Resources:** The library contains 85,984 volumes, 28,400 microform items, 774 audio/video tapes/CDs/DVDs, and subscribes to 38,735 periodicals including electronic. Computerized library services include interlibrary loans, database searching, and Internet access. Special learning facilities include a **Physically Challenged Students:** 81% of the campus is accessible. Facilities include wheelchair ramps, elevators, special parking, and specially equipped restrooms. **Special:** The college offers co-op programs in engineering, an accelerated degree program in marine transportation/transportation management, and internships as cadet observers aboard commercial ships. There are 2 national honor societies, a freshman honors program, and 2 departmental honors programs. **Visiting:** There are regularly scheduled orientations for prospective students, including a tour of the campus and facilities and meetings with faculty and students. There are guides for informal visits, visitors may sit in on classes, and stay overnight. To schedule a visit, contact the Admissions Office. **Campus Safety and Security:** Measures include 24-hour foot and vehicle patrol, emergency notification system, self-defense education, and security escort services. There are emergency telephones, lighted pathways/sidewalks, and controlled access to dorms/residences.

REQUIREMENTS: The SAT is required. Applicants must be high school graduates or hold a GED. 16 Carnegie units are required, including 4 years of English, 3 of math (4 are preferred), and 1 of physics or chemistry. An essay is required and an interview is recommended. AP and CLEP credits are accepted. Important factors in the admissions decision are advanced placement or honors courses, extracurricular activities record, and leadership record.Bachelor's degree candidates must earn 126 to 181 credit hours, with a GPA of 2.0 and distribution requirements vary by the major. If pursuing the U.S. Merchant Marine officers' license, all students must spend 3 summer semesters at sea acquiring hands-on experience aboard the college's training vessel. **Procedure:** Freshmen are admitted fall and spring. Entrance exams should be taken during the junior or senior year. There are early decision, early admissions, deferred admissions, and rolling admissions plans. Early decision applications should be filed by November 15, along with a $40 fee. Notification of early decision is sent December 15; regular decision, Applications are accepted on-line. **Transfer Students:** 77 transfer students enrolled in 2013-2014. Transfer students must have a 2.5 GPA. **International Students:** There are 94 international students enrolled. The school actively recruits these students. They must take the TOEFL. They must also take the SAT or ACT.

ADMISSIONS: 64% of the 2014-2015 applicants were accepted. The SAT scores for the 2014-2015 freshman class were: Critical Reading--42% below 500, 45% between 500 and 599, 11% between 600 and 699, and 2% between 700 and 800; Math--20% below 500, 52% between 500 and 599, 26% between 600 and 699, and 2% between 700 and 800. The ACT scores were 35% below 21, 40% between 21 and 23, 16% between 24 and 26, 4% between 27 and 28, and 5% above 28. 19% of the current freshmen were in the top fifth of their class; 52% were in the top two fifths. **Admissions Contact:** Jonathan White, Dean of Admissions. E-Mail: *sunymaritime.edu* Web: *www.sunymaritime.edu*

FINANCIAL AID: In 2014-2015, 77% of all full-time freshmen and 80% of continuing full-time students received some form of financial aid. 44% of all full-time freshmen and 47% of continuing full-time students received need-based aid. The average financial indebtedness of the 2014 graduate was $17,345. The FAFSA and the college's own financial statement, and student and parent federal income tax returns are required. The priority date for freshman financial aid applications for fall entry is March 1. The deadline for filing freshman financial aid applications for fall entry is July 15.

MARYMOUNT MANHATTAN COLLEGE D-5
www.mmm.edu

New York, NY 10021

(212) 517-0555
(800) 627-9668

Fax: (212) 517-0448
Email: admissions@mmm.edu

Full-time: 396 men, 1296 women
Faculty: 96; IIB, +$

Part-time: 42 men, 211 women
Ph.D.s: 91%

Graduate: n/av
Student/Faculty: 17 to 1

Year: semesters, summer session
Tuition: $25,688

Room & Board: $14,430
Freshman Class: 4174 applied, 2995 accepted, 504 enrolled

SAT or ACT: required
CEEB CODE: 2405

Application Deadline: open
VERY COMPETITIVE

Marymount Manhattan College is an urban, independent liberal arts college, offering programs in the arts and sciences for all ages, as well as substantial preprofessional preparation. Figures in the above capsule and in this profile are approximate. There is one undergraduate school. The 1-acre campus is in an urban area in Manhattan. Including any residence halls, there are 3 buildings.

STUDENT LIFE: 55% of undergraduates are from out of state, mostly the Middle Atlantic. Students are from 44 states, 26 foreign countries, and Canada. 57% are from public schools. 68% are White; 14% Hispanic; 12% African American. **Male To Female Ratio:** 3.4:1. The average age of freshmen is 19; all undergraduates, 21. 38% do not continue beyond their first year; 49% remain to graduate. **Housing:** 780 students can be accommodated in college housing, which includes single-sex and coed dorms and off-campus apartments. On-campus housing is available on a first-come, first-served basis, and is available on a lottery system for upperclassmen. Priority is given to out-of-town students. 64% of students commute. Alcohol is not permitted. All students may keep cars.

FACULTY/CLASSROOMS: 49% of faculty are male; 51% are female. 65% teach undergraduates, and 35% do both. No introductory courses are taught by graduate students. The average class size in an introductory lecture is 25; in a laboratory is 15; and in a regular course is 20.

PROGRAMS OF STUDY: MMC confers B.A., B.S. and B.F.A. degrees. Associate degrees are also awarded. Bachelor's degrees are awarded in BIOLOGICAL SCIENCE (biology/biological science), BUSINESS (accounting and business administration and management), COMMUNICATIONS AND THE ARTS (communications, dance, dramatic arts, English, and fine arts), COMPUTER AND PHYSICAL SCIENCE (information sciences and systems), EDUCATION (elementary education), HEALTH PROFESSIONS (premedicine and speech pathology/audiology), SOCIAL SCIENCE (history, international studies, liberal arts/general studies, philosophy and religion, political science/government, psychology, and sociology). Theater, communications, business, dance, psychology, and English are the strongest academically.

ACTIVITIES: There are no fraternities; 1% of women belong to 2 national sororities. There are 29 groups on campus, including art, choir, computers, dance, drama, ethnic, gay, honors, international, literary magazine, musical theater, newspaper, photography, political, professional, radio and TV, religious, social, social service, student government, and yearbook. Popular campus events include Strawberry Festival, Honors Day and Holiday Soiree. **Sports:** There are 3 intramural sports for men and 3 for women. Facilities include a 300-seat auditorium. **Graduates:** From July 1, 2013 to June 30, 2014, 389 bachelor's degrees were awarded. The most popular majors were visual/performing arts (38%), journalism (27%), and business/marketing (9%). 37 companies recruited on campus in 2013-2014. In an average class, 39% graduate in 4 years or less, 48% graduate in 5 years or less, and 49% graduate in 6 years or less. Of the 2013 graduating class, 23% were enrolled in graduate school within 6 months of graduation, and 63% were employed.

SERVICES: Counseling and information services are available, as is tutoring in every subject. There is remedial math, reading, and writing. **Library/Resources:** The library contains 75,000 volumes, 70 microform items, 4,000 audio/video tapes/CDs/DVDs, and subscribes to 2,740 periodicals including electronic. Computerized library services include interlibrary loans, database searching, Internet access, and Wi-Fi capability. Special learning facilities include an art gallery, radio station, TV station, a communications arts multimedia suite featuring digital editing technology. **Physically Challenged Students:** All of the campus is accessible. Facilities include wheelchair ramps, elevators, specially equipped restrooms, special class scheduling, and lowered drinking fountains. **Special:** MMC offers study abroad, interdisciplinary courses, pass/fail options, nondegree study, credit for life experience, and some 250 internships in all majors. Cooperative programs in business and finance, dance, music, languages, nursing, and urban education are offered in conjunction with local colleges and institutes. There is a January mini-session, cross-registration with Hunter College, and the China Institute, and a 5-year masters in publishing with Pace University. There are 7 national honor societies and 5 departmental honors programs. **Visiting:** There are regularly scheduled orientations for prospective students, including an interview with an admissions counselor, a tour of the school and dorms, and a meeting with a financial aid adviser. There are guides for informal visits and visitors may sit in on classes. To schedule a visit, contact the Admissions Office. **Campus Safety and Security:** Measures include 24-hour foot and vehicle patrol and self-defense education. There are shuttle buses, lighted pathways/sidewalks, security cameras, and photo ID check-in.

REQUIREMENTS: The SAT or ACT is required. Applicants should be graduates of an accredited secondary school or have a GED certificate. MMC recommends completion of 16 academic units, including 4 each in English and electives, and 3 each in language, math, social science, and science. Recommendations are required, and an interview is strongly advised. Applicants to the dance and acting programs must audition. A GPA of 2.5 is required. AP and CLEP credits are accepted. Important factors in the admissions decision are personality/intangible qualities, evidence of special talent, and leadership record.To graduate, students must complete 120 credit hours, including 31 to 71 in the major, with a minimum GPA of 2.0. The

core plus shared curriculum totals 48 credits in the areas of critical thinking, psychology and philosophy, quantitative reasoning and science, the modern world, communications/language, and the arts. **Procedure:** Freshmen are admitted to all sessions. Entrance exams should be taken as early as possible. There are deferred admissions and rolling admissions plans. Application deadlines are open. Application fee is $60. Notification of early decision is sent December 15; regular decision, on a rolling basis. Applications are accepted on-line. **Transfer Students:** 141 transfer students enrolled in 2013-2014. Applicants who have graduated from high school less then 5 years ago must meet standard freshman requirements and must submit official transcripts from all colleges attended. 30 of 120 credits required for the bachelor's degree must be completed at MMC. **International Students:** There are 58 international students enrolled. The school actively recruits these students. They must take the TOEFL. They must also take the SAT or ACT, scoring 900.

ADMISSIONS: 72% of the 2014-2015 applicants were accepted. **Admissions Contact:** James Rogers, Dean of Admissions. E-Mail: *admissions@mmm.edu* Web: *www.mmm.edu*

FINANCIAL AID: In 2014-2015, 77% of all full-time freshmen and 75% of continuing full-time students received some form of financial aid. 77% of all full-time freshmen and 59% of continuing full-time students received need-based aid. The average freshman award was $13,068. Need-based scholarships or need-based grants averaged $10,521; need-based self-help aid (loans and jobs) averaged $3,477; and $3,477 from other forms of aid. 75% of undergraduate students work part-time. Average annual earnings from campus work are $2500. The average financial indebtedness of the 2014 graduate was $15,206. The FAFSA, and TAP for (New York state residents) is required. The deadline for filing freshman financial aid applications for fall entry is March 15.

MEDAILLE COLLEGE	A-1
www.medaille.edu	

Buffalo, NY 14214	**(716) 880-2200**
	n/av
Fax: (716) 880-2007	Email: admissionsug@medaille.edu
Full-time: 580 men, 1069 women	**Faculty:** IIA
Part-time: 42 men, 152 women	**Ph.D.s:** 62%
Graduate: 179 men, 611 women	**Student/Faculty:** 16 to 1
Year: semesters, summer session	**Tuition:** $23,812
Room & Board: $11,300	**Freshman Class:** 1497 applied, 895 accepted, 400 enrolled
SAT CR/M: 460/460 **ACT:** 21	**CEEB CODE:** 2422
Application Deadline: n/av	**COMPETITIVE**

Medaille College, founded in 1875, is a private, nonsectarian institution offering undergraduate programs in liberal arts, education, business, and sciences, and graduate programs in business and education, to a primarily commuter student body. There is one graduate school. In addition to regional accreditation, Medaille has baccalaureate program accreditation with AVMA. The 13-acre campus is in an urban area 3 miles from downtown Buffalo. Including any residence halls, there are 17 buildings.

STUDENT LIFE: 92% of undergraduates are from New York. Others are from 17 states, 4 foreign countries, and Canada. 61% are White; 16% African American. **Male To Female Ratio:** 2.3:1. The average age of freshmen is 18; all undergraduates, 24. 32% do not continue beyond their first year; 68% remain to graduate. **Housing:** 420 students can be accommodated in college housing, which includes single-sex and coed dorms and on-campus apartments. On-campus housing is available on a first-come and first-served basis. 80% of students commute. All students may keep cars.

FACULTY/CLASSROOMS: 50% of faculty are male; 50% are female. No introductory courses are taught by graduate students. The average class size in an introductory lecture is 20; in a laboratory is 10; and in a regular course is 14.

PROGRAMS OF STUDY: Medaille confers B.A., B.S., B.B.A. and B.S.Ed. degrees. Associate and Master's degrees are also awarded.

Bachelor's degrees are awarded in BIOLOGICAL SCIENCE (biology/biological science), BUSINESS (business administration and management and sports management), COMMUNICATIONS AND THE ARTS (communications and English), EDUCATION (early childhood education, elementary education, and middle school education), HEALTH PROFESSIONS (veterinary science), SOCIAL SCIENCE (criminal justice, liberal arts/general studies, psychology, and social science). Education, business, communication, and veterinary technology are the strongest academically. Education, business administration, and veterinary technology have the largest enrollments.

ACTIVITIES: There are no fraternities or sororities. There are 26 groups on campus, including academic clubs, art, cheerleading, dance, drama, environmental, ethnic, gay, honors, literary magazine, musical theater, newspaper, photography, professional, radio and TV, social, and student government. Popular campus events include Founders Day, Silent Auction, Campus Carnival and Honors Convocation. **Sports:** There are 7 intercollegiate sports for men and 8 for women, and 3 intramural sports for men and 3 for women. Facilities include an NCAA regulation gym located in the student center, and a softball and soccer field. **Graduates:** From July 1, 2013 to June 30, 2014, 316 bachelor's degrees were awarded. The most popular majors were business administration (34%), veterinary technology (18%), and Education (9%). 75 companies recruited on campus in 2013-2014. In an average class, 35% graduate in 4 years or less, 41% graduate in 5 years or less, and 45% graduate in 6 years or less. Of the 2013 graduating class, 28% were enrolled in graduate school within 6 months of graduation, and 95% were employed.

SERVICES: Counseling and information services are available, as is tutoring in most subjects. There is a reader service for the blind, and remedial math, reading, and writing. **Library/Resources:** The library contains 55,690 volumes, 1,411 audio/video tapes/CDs/DVDs, and subscribes to 236 periodicals including electronic. Computerized library services include interlibrary loans, database searching, Internet access, and Wi-Fi capability. Special learning facilities include a radio station, TV station, new media institute. **Physically Challenged Students:** All of the campus is accessible. Facilities include wheelchair ramps, elevators, special parking, specially equipped restrooms, lowered drinking fountains, and lowered telephones. **Special:** Cross-registration is available with colleges in the Western New York Consortium. Most degree programs require internships. Opportunities are provided for student-designed majors, credit by examination, pass/fail options, accelerated degrees, dual majors, and credit for work experience. There are 2 national honor societies and a freshman honors program. **Visiting:** There are regularly scheduled orientations for prospective students, including campus tours, academic program meetings, ice-breakers, and a review of policies and procedures. There are guides for informal visits, visitors may sit in on classes, and stay overnight. To schedule a visit, contact Karen McGrath at (716) 880-2200. **Campus Safety and Security:** Measures include 24-hour foot and vehicle patrol, emergency notification system, self-defense education, and security escort services. There are shuttle buses, emergency telephones, lighted pathways/sidewalks, and controlled access to dorms/residences.

REQUIREMENTS: The SAT is required. Applicants must be graduates of an accredited secondary school or hold the GED. An essay and an interview are required. AP and CLEP credits are accepted. Important factors in the admissions decision are advanced placement or honors courses, personality/intangible qualities, and leadership record. The bachelor's degree requires successful completion of 120 credit hours or 128 for elementary education and biology majors. In addition to specific course requirements for each major, students must maintain a minimum GPA of 2.0. Students must also complete a general education core curriculum of 30 required credits in Self and Others (3 credits); U.S. Colonial History (3 credits); Creative Expression (3 credits); Scientific Discovery, (3 credits); Mathematics (3 credits); Communication (9 credits) and 6 credits in baccalaureate capstone courses. **Procedure:** Freshmen are admitted to all sessions. Entrance exams should be taken in May. There are deferred admissions and rolling admissions plans. Applications should be filed by January 15 for spring entry; May 15 for summer entry, along with a $25 fee. Notification is sent on a rolling basis. Applications are accepted on-line. **Transfer Students:** 205 transfer students enrolled

in 2013-2014. Transfer applicants must have a minimum GPA of 2.0 in their previous college work. An interview and recommendations are required. 30 of 120 credits required for the bachelor's degree must be completed at Medaille. **International Students:** There are 4 international students enrolled. The school actively recruits these students. They must take the TOEFL with a minimum score of 550 on the paper-based TOEFL (PBT) or 61 on the Internet-based version (iBT). They must also take the SAT.

ADMISSIONS: 60% of the 2014-2015 applicants were accepted. The SAT scores for the 2014-2015 freshman class were: Critical Reading--80% below 500, 17% between 500 and 599, 2% between 600 and 699, and 1% between 700 and 800; Math--72% below 500, 22% between 500 and 599, and 6% between 600 and 699. **Admissions Contact:** Karen McGrath, Vice President for Enrollment Management. E-Mail: *admissionsug@medaille.edu* Web: *www.medaille.edu*

FINANCIAL AID: In 2014-2015, 100% of all full-time freshmen and 98% of continuing full-time students received some form of financial aid. 100% of all full-time freshmen and 97% of continuing full-time students received need-based aid. The average freshman award was $13,473. 15% of undergraduate students work part-time. Average annual earnings from campus work are $1500. Medaille is a member of CSS. The FAFSA, the state aid form, and the college's own financial statement are required. The deadline for filing freshman financial aid applications for fall entry is March 1.

MEGAR EVERS COLLEGE/THE CITY UNIVERSITY OF NEW YORK (*The complete profile is made available exclusively on our website, www.barronspac.com*)

MERCY COLLEGE	**D-5**
www.mercy.edu	

Dobbs Ferry, NY 10522	(877) 637-2946
	(877) MERCY-GO
Fax: 914-674-7382	Email: admissions@mercy.edu
Full-time: 1699 men, 3590 women	**Faculty:** 197
Part-time: 752 men, 1898 women	**Ph.D.s:** 84%
Graduate: 622 men, 2711 women	**Student/Faculty:** 18 to 1
Year: semesters, summer session	**Tuition:** $17,766
Room & Board: $12,690	**Freshman Class:** 6394 applied, 4013 accepted, 753 enrolled
	CEEB CODE: 2409
Application Deadline: open	**COMPETITIVE**

Mercy College, founded in 1950, is a private institution dedicated to offering a curriculum of liberal arts and sciences as well as preprofessional and professional programs. Graduate programs provide advanced preparation in selected disciplines. Figures in the above capsule and in this profile are approximate. There are 5 undergraduate schools and 5 graduate schools. In addition to regional accreditation, Mercy has baccalaureate program accreditation with CSWE, NASAD, NCATE, ACOTE, CCNE, CAPTE, AVMA, and CAEP. The 66-acre campus is in a suburban area 25 miles north of New York City. Including any residence halls, there are 6 buildings.

STUDENT LIFE: 93% of undergraduates are from New York. Others are from 36 states, 37 foreign countries, and Canada. 32% are White; 32% Hispanic; 24% African American. **Male To Female Ratio:** 2.7:1. The average age of freshmen is 19; all undergraduates, 24. 34% do not continue beyond their first year; 30% remain to graduate. **Housing:** 600 students can be accommodated in college housing, which includes coed dorms. On-campus housing is available on a first-come and first-served basis. Priority is given to out-of-town students. 92% of students commute. Alcohol is not permitted. All students may keep cars.

FACULTY/CLASSROOMS: 38% of faculty are male; 62% are female. All teach undergraduates. No introductory courses are taught by graduate students. The average class size in an introductory lecture is 18 and in a regular course is 18.

PROGRAMS OF STUDY: Mercy confers B.A., B.F.A and B.S. degrees. Associate, Master's, and Doctoral degrees are also awarded.

Bachelor's degrees are awarded in BIOLOGICAL SCIENCE (biology/ biological science), BUSINESS (accounting, banking and finance, business administration and management, business (dual major program), entrepreneurial studies, and human resources/organizational mgmt), COMMUNICATIONS AND THE ARTS (broadcasting, communications, English, film, television and digital media, fine arts, journalism, media arts, music, music industry, music technology, and Spanish), COMPUTER AND PHYSICAL SCIENCE (computer science, digital arts/technology, information sciences and systems, and mathematics), EDUCATION (elementary education, special education, sports and wellness studies, and teaching English as a second/ foreign language (TESOL/TEFOL)), HEALTH PROFESSIONS (exercise science, health science, medical laboratory technology, nursing, speech pathology/audiology, and veterinary science), SOCIAL SCIENCE (behavioral science, communication sciences and disorders, criminal justice, history, interdisciplinary studies, legal studies, liberal arts/general studies, paralegal studies, political science/government, psychology, social work, and sociology). Health professions programs is the strongest academically. Business, education and psychology have the largest enrollments.

ACTIVITIES: There are no fraternities or sororities. There are 36 groups on campus, including veterinary club and STEM club, communications, computers, dance, drama, environmental, ethnic, film, honors, international, newspaper, political, professional, religious, social, social service, student government, and student military veteran club. Popular campus events include Veterans Day Activities, Founders Day/Alumni Weekend, Open Houses, Major League Baseball Events, Broadway Shows, Spring Fling Festival, Poetry Readings and Club Fairs. **Sports:** There are 4 intercollegiate sports for men and 6 for women, and 1 intramural sports for men and 2 for women. Facilities include a gym, a soccer/baseball/softball field, 3 swimming pools, 2 tennis courts, a track, basketball/volleyball court and a fitness center. **Graduates:** From July 1, 2013 to June 30, 2014, 1340 bachelor's degrees were awarded. The most popular majors were behavioral science (25%), psychology (12%), and health professions (12%). 242 companies recruited on campus in 2013-2014. In an average class, 23% graduate in 4 years or less, 32% graduate in 5 years or less, and 35% graduate in 6 years or less.

SERVICES: Counseling and information services are available, as is tutoring in every subject. There is a reader service for the blind. **Library/Resources:** The 4 libraries contain 150,000 volumes, 3,000 audio/video tapes/CDs/DVDs, and subscribe to 20,040 periodicals including electronic. Computerized library services include interlibrary loans, database searching, Internet access, and Wi-Fi capability. Special learning facilities include a TV station, an computer lab, reference library and a digital arts center. **Physically Challenged Students:** 75% of the campus is accessible. Facilities include wheelchair ramps, elevators, special parking, specially equipped restrooms, special class scheduling, and lowered drinking fountains. **Special:** Mercy offers internships and cooperative education in each major, an on-campus employment program with a community service component, study abroad, dual majors and degrees, credit for life experience, non-degree study, and pass/fail options. There are 7 national honor societies, including Phi Beta Kappa, a freshman honors program, and 14 departmental honors programs. **Visiting:** There are regularly scheduled orientations for prospective students, including spring and fall open houses and information sessions. There are guides for informal visits and visitors may sit in on classes. To schedule a visit, contact the Admissions Office. **Campus Safety and Security:** Measures include 24-hour foot and vehicle patrol, emergency notification system, self-defense education, and security escort services. There are emergency telephones, lighted pathways/sidewalks, and controlled access to dorms/residences.

REQUIREMENTS: Applicants must be graduates of an accredited secondary school or have a GED certificate. They should have completed at least 16 academic units. A GPA of 2.5 is required. AP and CLEP credits are accepted. Important factors in the admissions decision are recommendations by school officials, personality/intangible qualities, and leadership record. To graduate, students must complete 120 semester hours with a minimum GPA of 2.0 overall. In total, 30 semester hours must be completed at Mercy. The Mercy College General Education Curriculum includes: 6 English credits, 3 speech credits, 6 history credits, 9 social science credits, 3 philosophy/religion credits, 3 art/music credits, 3 foreign language credits, 3 math credits, 3 computer science credits, and 3 natural science credits. **Procedure:** Freshmen are admitted fall, spring, and summer. Entrance exams should be taken between January and August of their senior year. There are early decision, deferred admissions, and rolling admissions plans. Application deadlines are open. Application fee is $40. Notification is sent on a rolling basis. Applications are accepted on-line. **Transfer Students:** 1798 transfer students enrolled in 2013-2014. Applicants must submit official transcripts from all colleges attended and must also submit their high school transcript. 30 of 120 credits required for the bachelor's degree must be completed at Mercy. **International Students:** There are 77 international students enrolled. The school actively recruits these students. They must take the TOEFL with a minimum score of 550 on the paper-based TOEFL (PBT) or 79 on the Internet-based version (iBT) and the college's own test.

ADMISSIONS: 63% of the 2014-2015 applicants were accepted. **Admissions Contact:** Deirdre Whitman, Vice President for Enrollment Management. E-Mail: *admissions@mercy.edu* Web: *www.mercy .edu*

FINANCIAL AID: In 2014-2015, 91% of all full-time freshmen and 85% of continuing full-time students received some form of financial aid. 83% of all full-time freshmen and 78% of continuing full-time students received need-based aid. The average freshman award was $15,144. Need-based scholarships or need-based grants averaged $10,789; need-based self-help aid (loans and jobs) averaged $2,979; non-need-based athletic scholarships averaged $5,178; and other non-need-based awards and non-need-based scholarships averaged $4,964. 1% of undergraduate students work part-time. The average financial indebtedness of the 2014 graduate was $17,399. The FAFSA and the state aid form are required. The priority date for freshman financial aid applications for fall entry is February 15.

METROPOLITAN COLLEGE OF NEW YORK   D-5
www.metropolitan.edu

New York, NY 10013	**(212) 343-1234, ext. 5001**
Fax: (212) 343-8470	**Email:** slenhart@metropolitan.edu
Full-time: n/av	**Faculty:** n/av
Part-time: n/av	**Ph.D.s:** 84%
Graduate: n/av	**Student/Faculty:** 14 to 1
Year: semesters, summer session	**Tuition:** $17,00
Room & Board: n/app	**Freshman Class:** 650 applied, 330 accepted, 126 enrolled
	CEEB CODE: 4802
Application Deadline: n/av	**VERY COMPETITIVE**

Metropolitan College of New York, founded in 1964, is a private institution offering programs in human services and business management. The college operates on a 3-semester calendar, including a complete summer semester. All bachelor degree programs involve a combination of class work and field work and may be completed in 2 years and 8 months. Most Masters degree programs can be completed in 1 year. The figures in the above capsule and in this profile are approximate. There are 2 undergraduate schools and 2 graduate schools. The campus is in an urban area in New York City, NY. Including any residence halls, there is 1 building.

STUDENT LIFE: 99% of undergraduates are from New York. Others are from 4 states, 9 foreign countries, and Canada. 68% are from public schools. 63% are African American; 19% Hispanic. The average age of freshmen is 32; all undergraduates, 32. 40% do not continue beyond their first year; 43% remain to graduate. Alcohol is not permitted. All students commute.

FACULTY/CLASSROOMS: 51% of faculty are male; 49% are female. 95% teach undergraduates, 10% do research, and 99% do both. No introductory courses are taught by graduate students. The average class size in a laboratory is 15 and in a regular course is 15.

PROGRAMS OF STUDY: The college confers B.B.A., and B.P.S. degrees. Associate and Master's degrees are also awarded. Bachelor's degrees are awarded in BUSINESS (business administration and management), EDUCATION (early childhood education), HEALTH PROFESSIONS (mental health/human services), SOCIAL SCIENCE (child care/child and family studies, community services, gerontology, human services, prelaw, psychology, and social work). Business management is the strongest academically. Human services has the largest enrollment.

ACTIVITIES: There are no fraternities or sororities. There are 10 groups on campus, including computers, ethnic, gay, honors, newspaper, professional, social, social service, and student government. Popular campus events include Career fairs, Admissions Open House and Dean's List Ceremonies. **Sports:** There is no sports program at The college. **Graduates:** From July 1, 2013 to June 30, 2014, 166 bachelor's degrees were awarded. 70 companies recruited on campus in 2013-2014. In an average class, 42% graduate in 4 years or less. Of the 2013 graduating class, 50% were enrolled in graduate school within 6 months of graduation, and 80% were employed.

SERVICES: Counseling and information services are available, as is tutoring in every subject. There is remedial math, reading, and writing. **Library/Resources:** The library contains 32,000 volumes, 1,800 microform items, and subscribes to 3,300 periodicals including electronic. Computerized library services include interlibrary loans, database searching, and Internet access. **Physically Challenged Students:** All of the campus is accessible. Facilities include wheelchair ramps, elevators, specially equipped restrooms, special class scheduling, lowered drinking fountains, and lowered telephones. **Special:** Internships, which include required weekly 14-hour field sites, study abroad in 3 countries, work-study programs, B.A.-B.S. degrees, and accelerated degree programs in human services, business management, and American urban studies are offered, as well as credit by exam, and credit for life experience. **Visiting:** There are regularly scheduled orientations for prospective students. There are guides for informal visits and visitors may sit in on classes. To schedule a visit, contact The Admissions Office. **Campus Safety and Security:** Measures include 24-hour foot and vehicle patrol and emergency notification system. There are lighted pathways/sidewalks, fire drills, and a fire escape stairwell.

REQUIREMENTS: Students must take the ETS's Accuplacer Test in reading and math. Recent high school graduates who have a satisfactory SAT score may present the SAT instead. Applicants must have graduated from an accredited secondary school. The GED is accepted. An essay and an interview are required. CLEP credits are accepted. Important factors in the admissions decision are evidence of special talent, leadership record, and personality/intangible qualities. To graduate, students must complete 128 credit hours with a minimum GPA of 2.0. The curriculum is prescribed; no electives are featured. A constructive action document based on performance in the field and mastery of course work is required each semester. **Procedure:** Freshmen are admitted to all sessions. Entrance exams should be taken in the senior year. There are deferred admissions and rolling admissions plans. Applications should be filed by December 1 for spring entry; April 1 for summer entry, along with a $30 fee. Applications are accepted on-line. **Transfer Students:** 45 transfer students enrolled in 2013-2014. Admission is based on current skills and abilities as measured on the entrance exam and essay. 64 of 128 credits required for the bachelor's degree must be completed at The college. **International Students:** The school actively recruits these students. They must take the TOEFL.

ADMISSIONS: 51% of the 2014-2015 applicants were accepted. **Admissions Contact:** Steven Lenhart, Dean of Admissions. E-Mail: *slenhart@metropolitan.edu* Web: *www.metropolitan.edu*

FINANCIAL AID: In 2014-2015, 96% of all full-time freshmen and 90% of continuing full-time students received some form of financial aid. The average freshman award was $13,611. Need-based scholarships or need-based grants averaged $10,154; and need-based self-help aid (loans and jobs) averaged $3,517. The CSS/Profile and FAFSA, and the New York State Higher Education Financial Statement. are required. The deadline for filing freshman financial aid applications for fall entry is August 15.

MOLLOY COLLEGE — D-5
www.molloy.edu

Rockville Centre, NY 11570	**(516) 323-4000**
	n/av
Fax: (516) 256-2247	Email: mlane@molloy.edu
Full-time: 713 men, 1966 women	Faculty: IIA, ++$
Part-time: 135 men, 522 women	Ph.D.s: 75%
Graduate: 211 men, 950 women	Student/Faculty: 10 to 1
Year: 4-1-4, summer session	Tuition: $26,850
Room & Board: $13,590	Freshman Class: 3277 applied, 2471 accepted, 492 enrolled
SAT CR/M/W: 520/530/510 ACT: 24	CEEB CODE: 2415
Application Deadline: open	COMPETITIVE

Molloy offers students a rich and multidimensional educational experience where students are encouraged to think critically and explore creatively. Combining the strengths of academic excellence and leadership with personal, compassionate mentoring, we bring out the best in every student - here and around the globe. Molloy College students develop that all-important confidence, that strong, "I will" attitude that enables them to succeed in their careers, and more importantly, to make a difference in our world. There are no undergraduate schools and 6 graduate schools. In addition to regional accreditation, Molloy has baccalaureate program accreditation with CSWE, NCATE, NLN, CAAHEP, and CCNE. The 30-acre campus is in a suburban area 20 miles east of New York City. Including any residence halls, there are 6 buildings.

STUDENT LIFE: 98% of undergraduates are from New York. Others are from 20 states, and 9 foreign countries. 63% are White; 14% Hispanic; 12% African American. 61% are Catholic; 13% claim no religious affiliation. **Male To Female Ratio:** 3.2:1. The average age of freshmen is 18; all undergraduates, 24. 10% do not continue beyond their first year; 70% remain to graduate. **Housing:** 258 students can be accommodated in college housing, which includes coed dorms. Priority is given to out-of-town students. 92% of students commute. Alcohol is not permitted. All students may keep cars.

FACULTY/CLASSROOMS: 31% of faculty are male; 69% are female. No introductory courses are taught by graduate students. The average class size in an introductory lecture is 17; in a laboratory is 12; and in a regular course is 17.

PROGRAMS OF STUDY: Molloy confers B.A., B.S., B.F.A. and B.S.W degrees. Associate, Master's, and Doctoral degrees are also awarded. Bachelor's degrees are awarded in AGRICULTURE (environmental studies), BIOLOGICAL SCIENCE (biology/biological science), BUSINESS (accounting, business administration and management, finance, and marketing), COMMUNICATIONS AND THE ARTS (art, communication, English, music, and theatre arts), COMPUTER AND PHYSICAL SCIENCE (computer information systems, computer science, and mathematics), EDUCATION (childhood education: 1-6, early childhood education, and music education), ENGINEERING AND ENVIRONMENTAL DESIGN (nuclear medicine technology), HEALTH PROFESSIONS (health, music therapy, nursing, and speech pathology/audiology), SOCIAL SCIENCE (criminal justice, history, interdisciplinary studies, philosophy, political science/government, psychology, social work, sociology, Spanish and Hispanic studies, and theology). Nursing, education, and business are the strongest academically and have the largest enrollments.

ACTIVITIES: There are no fraternities or sororities. There are 60 groups on campus, including art, band, cheerleading, chess, chorus, dance, drama, ethnic, honors, international, jazz band, literary magazine, newspaper, professional, religious, social, social service, student government, and yearbook. Popular campus events include Scavenger Hunt, Halloween Party, Relay for Life, Safe Halloween, Hats and Stockings, Stuff a Bear, Maroon Madness, Santa's Workshop, Bunny Brunch. **Sports:** There are 7 intercollegiate sports for men and 9 for women, and 3 intramural sports for men and 3 for women. Facilities include a gym, dance studio, weight room, sports fields, basketball and tennis courts. **Graduates:** From July 1, 2013 to June 30, 2014, 775 bachelor's degrees were awarded. The most popular majors were nursing (53%), education (10%), and business (7%). In an average class, 40% graduate in 4 years or less, 65% graduate in 5 years or less, and 70% graduate in 6 years or less.

SERVICES: Counseling and information services are available, as is tutoring in every subject. There is a reader service for the blind, and remedial math, reading, and writing. **Library/Resources:** The library contains 72,697 volumes, 427 microform items, 4,947 audio/video tapes/CDs/DVDs, and subscribes to 52,928 periodicals including electronic. Computerized library services include interlibrary loans, database searching, and Internet access. Special learning facilities include an art gallery. **Physically Challenged Students:** All of the campus is accessible. Facilities include wheelchair ramps, elevators, special parking, specially equipped restrooms, special class scheduling, lowered drinking fountains, and lowered telephones. **Special:** The college offers study abroad programs, dual degree programs, and other unique internship opportunities. There are 18 national honor societies and a freshman honors program. **Visiting:** There are regularly scheduled orientations for prospective students, including an address by the president of the college, department presentations, campus tours, admissions, financial aid, and scholarship information. There are guides for informal visits and visitors may sit in on classes. To schedule a visit, contact the Admissions Office. **Campus Safety and Security:** Measures include 24-hour foot and vehicle patrol, emergency notification system, and security escort services. There are shuttle buses, emergency telephones, lighted pathways/sidewalks, campus concerns committee.

REQUIREMENTS: The SAT or ACT is required. The ACT Optional Writing test is also required. Applicants should be graduates of a secondary school or have a GED. Preparation should include 4 units of English and social studies, 3 units of math, science, foreign language and history. An essay is required and an interview is recommended. Music students must audition and take a theory exam. A GPA of 3.0 is required. AP and CLEP credits are accepted. Important factors in the admissions decision are advanced placement or honors courses, recommendations by school officials, and extracurricular activities record. General Education requirements consist of 45 to 54 credits. A total of 128 to 137 credit hours is required for graduation. **Procedure:** Freshmen are admitted fall and spring. Entrance exams should be taken in the fall of the senior year. There are early admissions, deferred admissions, and rolling admissions plans. Application deadlines are open. Application fee is $40. Notifications are sent 10 15. Applications are accepted on-line. **Transfer Students:** 384 transfer students enrolled in 2013-2014. A minimum college GPA of 2.0 is required, with some majors requiring a higher GPA. An interview is recommended. 30 of 128 credits required for the bachelor's degree must be completed at Molloy. **International Students:** There are 8 international students enrolled. They must take the TOEFL with a minimum score of 500 on the paper-based TOEFL (PBT).

ADMISSIONS: 75% of the 2014-2015 applicants were accepted. The SAT scores for the 2014-2015 freshman class were: Critical Reading--29% below 500, 58% between 500 and 599, 11% between 600 and 699, and 2% between 700 and 800; Math--26% below 500, 53% between 500 and 599, 19% between 600 and 699, and 2% between 700 and 800; Writing--39% below 500, 45% between 500 and 599, 15% between 600 and 699, and 1% between 700 and 800. The ACT scores were 14% below 21, 34% between 21 and 23, 36% between 24 and 26, 10% between 27 and 28, and 6% above 28. **Admissions Contact:** Marguerite Lane, Dean of Admissions. E-Mail: *mlane@molloy.edu* Web: *www.molloy.edu*

FINANCIAL AID: Molloy is a member of CSS. The FAFSA is required. The priority date for freshman financial aid applications for fall entry is April 15. The deadline for filing freshman financial aid applications for fall entry is May 1.

MONROE COLLEGE   **D-5**
www.monroecollege.edu

Bronx, NY 10468	(718) 933-6700
	(800) 55 MONROE
Fax: (718) 364-3552	Email: admissions@monroecollege.edu
Full-time: 1410 men, 3510 women	Faculty: III, av$
Part-time: 155 men, 405 women	Ph.D.s: n/av
Graduate: n/av	Student/Faculty: n/av
Year: varies, summer session	Tuition: $13,740
Room & Board: $6500	Freshman Class: n/av
SAT: recommended	CEEB CODE: 2462
Application Deadline: August 15	**COMPETITIVE**

Monroe College, founded in 1933, offers bachelor's degrees in accounting, business management, computer information systems, criminal justice, hospitality management, and health services administration. The figures in the above capsule and in this profile are approximate. The campus in the Fordham Road section of the Bronx. Including any residence halls, there are 5 buildings.

STUDENT LIFE: 96% of undergraduates are from New York. Others are from states. 46% are African American; 42% Hispanic. **Male To Female Ratio:** 2.5:1. The average age of freshmen is 23; all undergraduates, 26. **Housing:** 620 students can be accommodated in college housing, which includes single-sex and coed dorms and off-campus apartments. In addition, there are honors houses. On-campus housing is guaranteed for all 4 years. 90% of students commute. All students may keep cars.

FACULTY/CLASSROOMS: All teach undergraduates. No introductory courses are taught by graduate students. The average class size in an introductory lecture is 30.

PROGRAMS OF STUDY: Monroe confers B.S., and B.B.A. degrees. Associate and Master's degrees are also awarded. Bachelor's degrees are awarded in BUSINESS (accounting, business administration and management, and hospitality management services), COMPUTER AND PHYSICAL SCIENCE (information sciences and systems), HEALTH PROFESSIONS (health care administration), SOCIAL SCIENCE (criminal justice). Business management, criminal justice, and health services administration have the largest enrollments.

ACTIVITIES: There are no fraternities or sororities. Groups on campus include cheerleading, computers, dance, drama, honors, literary magazine, newspaper, professional, and social service. Popular campus events include Talent Shows, President's and Deans' List Galas and Cultural Trips to New York City. **Sports:** There is no sports program at Monroe.

SERVICES: Counseling and information services are available, as is tutoring in every subject. There is a reader service for the blind, and remedial math, reading, and writing. **Library/Resources:** Computerized library services include interlibrary loans, database searching, Internet access, and Wi-Fi capability. **Physically Challenged Students:** All of the campus is accessible. Facilities include wheelchair ramps, elevators, special parking, specially equipped restrooms, special class scheduling, lowered drinking fountains, lowered telephones, and special housing. **Special:** Co-op programs are available in all degree programs. Study abroad is available for culinary students interested in studying in Italy. There are 1 national honor society, a freshman honors program, and 1 departmental honors program. **Visiting:** There are regularly scheduled orientations for prospective students, including a variety of open houses during the semester in which applicants can tour the campus and talk with faculty and/pr chairs of individual departments. There are guides for informal visits, visitors may sit in on classes, and stay overnight. **Campus Safety and Security:** Measures include 24-hour foot and vehicle patrol, self-defense education, and security escort services. There are shuttle buses, emergency telephones, and lighted pathways/sidewalks.

REQUIREMENTS: The SAT is recommended. An application, an essay, and an interview are required. Monroe requires applicants to be in the upper 50% of their class. AP and CLEP credits are accepted. To graduate, students must have 120 credit hours and at least a 2.0 GPA. The core curriculum includes courses in writing/literature, math, liberal arts, and business or technology. **Procedure:** Freshmen are admitted fall, winter, and spring. There are early decision and rolling admissions plans. Early decision applications should be filed by February 1; regular applications, by August 15 for fall entry; January 5 for winter entry; and April 15 for spring entry. The fall 2014 application fee was $35. **Transfer Students:** Transfer students must provide an official transcript from any prior institution they have attended in addition to the application and an essay. 30 of 120 credits required for the bachelor's degree must be completed at Monroe. **International Students:** The school actively recruits these students.

ADMISSIONS: Evan Jerome, Director of Admissions. E-Mail: *admissions@monroecollege.edu* Web: *www.monroecollege.edu*

FINANCIAL AID: The FAFSA, the state aid form, and the college's own financial statement are required. Check with the school for current application deadlines.

MOUNT SAINT MARY COLLEGE   D-4

www.msmc.edu

Newburgh, NY 12550

Fax: (845) 562-6762

Full-time: 538 men, 1024 women
Part-time: 121 men, 340 women
Graduate: 95 men, 258 women
Year: semesters, summer session
Room & Board: $13,556

Application Deadline: open

(845) 569-3255
(888) YES-MSMC
Email: nancy.scaffidi@msmc.edu

Faculty: 92; IIB, +$
Ph.D.s: 91%
Student/Faculty: 20 to 1
Tuition: $27,582
Freshman Class: 3551 applied, 3054 accepted, 449 enrolled
CEEB CODE: 2423
COMPETITIVE

MSMC founded in 1959, is a private liberal arts college offering undergraduate programs leading to Bachelor of Arts and Bachelor of Science degrees, and graduate programs leading to the masters in education, nursing, and business administration. An accelerated evening program is offered for nontraditional and adult students. Figures in the above capsule and in this profile are approximate. There are 3 graduate schools. In addition to regional accreditation, the Mount has baccalaureate program accreditation with NCATE and CCNE. The 86-acre campus is in a suburban area 58 miles north of New York City. Including any residence halls, there are 41 buildings.

STUDENT LIFE: 89% of undergraduates are from New York. Others are from 13 states. 76% are from public schools. 64% are White; 13% race unknown; 12% Hispanic. 49% are Baptist, Christian, Episcopalian, Lutheran and Methodist.; 45% Catholic. **Male To Female Ratio:** 2.2:1. The average age of freshmen is 18; all undergraduates, 23. 31% do not continue beyond their first year; 52% remain to graduate. **Housing:** 1064 students can be accommodated in college housing, which includes single-sex and coed dorms. On-campus townhouses. On-campus housing is guaranteed for all 4 years. 54% of students commute. Upperclassmen may keep cars.

FACULTY/CLASSROOMS: 42% of faculty are male; 58% are female. 94% teach undergraduates. No introductory courses are taught by graduate students. The average class size in an introductory lecture is 20; in a laboratory is 11; and in a regular course is 19.

PROGRAMS OF STUDY: Mount confers B.A., B.S. and B.S.Ed. degrees. Master's degrees are also awarded. Bachelor's degrees are awarded in BIOLOGICAL SCIENCE (biology/biological science), BUSINESS (accounting and business administration and management), COMMUNICATIONS AND THE ARTS (English, information technology, media arts, and public relations), COMPUTER AND PHYSICAL SCIENCE (chemistry, mathematics, and science), EDUCATION (education), HEALTH PROFESSIONS (nursing), SOCIAL SCIENCE (Hispanic American studies, history, human services, interdisciplinary studies, political science/government, psychology, social science, social work, and sociology). Education, nursing, and business are the strongest academically and have the largest enrollments.

ACTIVITIES: There are 37 groups on campus, including art, cheerleading, choir, computers, dance, drama, environmental, ethnic, gay, honors, literary magazine, musical theater, newspaper, photography, political, professional, radio and TV, religious, social, student government, and yearbook. Popular campus events include Spring Weekend, Siblings Weekend and Holiday Formal. **Sports:** There are 9 intercollegiate sports for men and 9 for women, and 10 intramural sports for men and 10 for women. Facilities include an Elaine and William Kaplan Physical Recreation Center houses 3 regulation basketball courts, an elevated running track, cardiovascular room, fully equipped weight room, aerobics studio, indoor full-length swimming pool and a multipurpose room. The outdoor athletic complex features an all-weather, synthetic turf field, a natural grass field, and six hard court tennis courts. **Graduates:** From July 1, 2013 to June 30, 2014, 554 bachelor's degrees were awarded. The most popular majors were nursing (19%), business (18%), and psychology (11%). 91 companies recruited on campus in 2013-2014. In an average class, 1% graduate in 3 years or less, 41% graduate in 4 years or less, 50% graduate in 5 years or less, and 52% graduate in 6 years or less. Of the 2013 graduating class, 26% were enrolled in graduate school within 6 months of graduation, and 84% were employed.

SERVICES: Counseling and information services are available, as is tutoring in every subject. There is remedial math, reading, and writing. **Library/Resources:** The 2 libraries contain 76,888 volumes, 8,231 audio/video tapes/CDs/DVDs, and subscribe to 51,095 periodicals including electronic. Computerized library services include interlibrary loans, database searching, Internet access, and Wi-Fi capability. Special learning facilities include a radio station, elementary school, herbarium field station, and an arboretum. **Physically Challenged Students:** 95% of the campus is accessible. Facilities include wheelchair ramps, elevators, special parking, specially equipped restrooms, lowered telephones. Special equipment in the library and computer centers to accommodate students with low vision. **Special:** Co-op programs and internships are available in all majors. There is cross-registration with other mid-Hudson area colleges, as well as accelerated degree programs in business, accounting, and nursing, among others. There are several collaborative programs. The college also offers study abroad in more than 22 countries, a Washington semester, work-study, and dual and student-designed majors. Credit by exam and for life, military, and work experience is available for a maximum of 30 credits. There are 12 national honor societies and a freshman honors program. **Visiting:** There are regularly scheduled orientations for prospective students, student visits include 4 open houses per year, a summer orientation program, and Spend a Day with a Current Student program in the spring. There are guides for informal visits, visitors may sit in on classes, and stay overnight. To schedule a visit, contact the Admissions Office at admissions@msmc .edu. **Campus Safety and Security:** Measures include 24-hour foot and vehicle patrol, emergency notification system, self-defense education, and security escort services. There are shuttle buses, emergency telephones, lighted pathways/sidewalks, and controlled access to dorms/residences.

REQUIREMENTS: The SAT or ACT is required. Students should be graduates of an accredited secondary school. The GED is accepted. Applicants should prepare with 4 years each of English and history, and at least 3 each of math and science and 2 of foreign language. An essay and an interview are recommended. AP and CLEP credits are accepted. Important factors in the admissions decision are advanced placement or honors courses, evidence of special talent, and personality/intangible qualities. A total of 120 credit hours is required for the B.A. or B.S., with 24 to 40 in the major and a minimum GPA of 2.0. Overall requirements are higher for nursing, medical technology, and education students. All students must achieve computer literacy before graduation. **Procedure:** Freshmen are admitted to all sessions. Entrance exams should be taken by the junior year. There are deferred admissions and rolling admissions plans. Application deadlines are open. Application fee is $45. Notification is sent on a rolling basis. Applications are accepted on-line. Application fees are waived if application is completed on-line. **Transfer Students:** 199 transfer students enrolled in 2013-2014. Applicants must have a GPA of at least 2.5 in all college work. The SAT or ACT, and an interview are recommended. 30 of 120 credits required for the bachelor's degree must be completed at the Mount. **International Students:** They must take the TOEFL with a minimum score of 550 on the paper-based TOEFL (PBT) or 80 on the Internet-based version (iBT). They must also take the SAT or ACT, and the college's own entrance exam. freshman are required to take standard placement test.

ADMISSIONS: 86% of the 2014-2015 applicants were accepted. 27% of the current freshmen were in the top fifth of their class; 61% were in the top two fifths. **Admissions Contact:** Nancy Scaffidi, Director of Admissions. E-Mail: *nancy.scaffidi@msmc.edu* Web: *www.msmc .edu*

FINANCIAL AID: In 2014-2015, 97% of all full-time freshmen and 95% of continuing full-time students received some form of financial aid. 91% of all full-time freshmen and 87% of continuing full-time students received need-based aid. The average freshman award was $23,266. Need-based scholarships or need-based grants averaged $8,096 ($46,186 maximum); need-based self-help aid (loans and jobs) averaged $7,375 ($36,665 maximum); and other non-need-based awards and non-need-based scholarships averaged $10,897 ($38,110 maximum). 11% of undergraduate students work part-time. Average annual earnings from campus work are $1200. The average financial indebtedness of the 2014 graduate was $28,645. The FAFSA is required. The priority date for freshman financial aid applications for fall entry is February 15. The deadline for filing freshman financial aid applications for fall entry is March 15.

NAZARETH COLLEGE OF ROCHESTER   B-3
ww.naz.edu

Rochester, NY 14618	**(585) 389-2860**
	(800) 462-3944
Fax: (585) 389-2826	**Email:** admissions@naz.edu
Full-time: 511 men, 1390 women	**Faculty:** 163
Part-time: 37 men, 96 women	**Ph.Ds:** 73%
Graduate: 168 men, 621 women	**Student/Faculty:** 12 to 1
Year: semesters, summer session	**Tuition:** $30,562
Room & Board: $12,466	**Freshman Class:** 3838 applied, 2625 accepted, 423 enrolled
SAT CR/M/W: 540/540/520 **ACT:** 25	**CEEB CODE:** 2511
Application Deadline: February 1	**COMPETITIVE+**

Nazareth College of Rochester, founded in 1924, is an independent institution offering programs in the liberal arts and sciences and pre-professional areas. Figures in the above capsule and in this profile are approximate. There are 4 undergraduate schools and 4 graduate schools. In addition to regional accreditation, Nazareth has baccalaureate program accreditation with CSWE, NASM, TEAC, ACS, CCNE, and IACBE. The 150-acre campus is in a suburban area 7 miles east of Rochester. Including any residence halls, there are 29 buildings.

STUDENT LIFE: 93% of undergraduates are from New York. Others are from 27 states, 22 foreign countries, and Canada. 88% are from public schools. 72% are White; 13% race unknown. **Male To Female Ratio:** 2.9:1. The average age of freshmen is 18; all undergraduates, 21. 21% do not continue beyond their first year; 68% remain to graduate. **Housing:** 1232 students can be accommodated in college housing, which includes single-sex and coed dorms and on-campus apartments. In addition, there are language houses, special-interest houses, Substance-free floors, freshman experience floors, and honors floors. On-campus housing is guaranteed for all 4 years. 53% of students live on campus; of those, 88% remain on campus on weekends. All students may keep cars.

FACULTY/CLASSROOMS: 37% of faculty are male; 63% are female. 93% teach undergraduates. No introductory courses are taught by graduate students. The average class size in an introductory lecture is 21; in a laboratory is 11; and in a regular course is 19.

PROGRAMS OF STUDY: Nazareth confers B.A., B.S., B.F.A., and B.Mus. degrees. Master's and Doctoral degrees are also awarded. Bachelor's degrees are awarded in BIOLOGICAL SCIENCE (biochemistry, biology/adolescence education, biology/biological science, and toxicology), BUSINESS (accounting, business administration and management, finance, international business management, and marketing and distribution), COMMUNICATIONS AND THE ARTS (art history, art, Chinese, communication rhetoric/communication, English, fine arts, French, German, information technology, Italian, literature, music, music business management, music history and appreciation, music performance, music theory and composition, musical theater, Spanish, spanish / adolescence education, studio art, theatre arts, and visual design), COMPUTER AND PHYSICAL SCIENCE (chemistry, chemistry/adolescence education, and mathematics), EDUCATION (art education, business education, elementary education, English education, foreign languages education, mathematics education, middle school education, music education, psychology education, and social science education), ENGINEERING AND ENVIRONMENTAL DESIGN (environmental science), HEALTH PROFESSIONS (health science, music therapy, nursing, and speech pathology/audiology), SOCIAL SCIENCE (American studies, anthropology, Asian studies, communication sciences and disorders, economics, history, international studies, legal studies, peace studies, philosophy, political science/government, psychology, religion, social science, social work, sociology, and women's studies). Physical therapy, and history are the strongest academically. Physical therapy, nursing, and business have the largest enrollments.

ACTIVITIES: There are no fraternities or sororities. There are 48 groups on campus, including art, band, choir, chorale, chorus, communications, computers, dance, drama, ethnic, gay, honors, international, jazz band, literary magazine, musical theater, newspaper, opera, orchestra, political, professional, radio station, religious, social, student government, and yearbook. Popular campus events include Springfest and Siblings Weekend, Welcome Week, Battle of the Beaks and Family Weekend; Formal. **Sports:** There is no sports program at Nazareth. Facilities include a gym, a 25-meter swimming pool, soccer and lacrosse fields, including an outdoor turf field, tennis and racquetball courts, a fitness center, sauna, 2,200-seat stadium, and a 400-meter all-weather track. **Graduates:** From July 1, 2013 to June 30, 2014, 520 bachelor's degrees were awarded. The most popular majors were education (17%), health (17%), and business (10%). 36 companies recruited on campus in 2013-2014. In an average class, 59% graduate in 4 years or less, 67% graduate in 5 years or less, and 68% graduate in 6 years or less. Of the 2013 graduating class, 49% were enrolled in graduate school within 6 months of graduation, and 72% were employed.

SERVICES: Counseling and information services are available, as is tutoring in every subject. **Library/Resources:** The library contains 237,203 volumes, 470,000 microform items, 181,114 audio/video tapes/CDs/DVDs, and subscribes to 86,321 periodicals including electronic. Computerized library services include interlibrary loans, database searching, Internet access, and Wi-Fi capability. Special learning facilities include an art gallery. **Physically Challenged Students:** 80% of the campus is accessible. Facilities include wheelchair ramps, elevators, special parking, specially equipped restrooms, special class scheduling, lowered drinking fountains, and special housing. **Special:** Nazareth offers cross-registration with members of the Rochester Area College Consortium (about 15 colleges participate in this program). Full-time students can register for courses at any of these institutions. Internships are available in any of our academic programs and are arranged through the student's academic adviser and Director of Internships. Nazareth participates in the Washington and Albany internship programs. There is study abroad in France, Spain, Italy, and Germany, and there are exchange programs in Australia, Japan, Italy, France, Peru, United Kingdom, Hungary, Wales. There are 25 national honor societies, a freshman honors program, and 13 departmental honors programs. **Visiting:** There are regularly scheduled orientations for prospective students, including individual appointments, group sessions, campus tours, open houses, and summer academic orientation. There are guides for informal visits, visitors may sit in on classes, and stay overnight. To schedule a visit, contact the Admissions Office at visit@naz.edu. **Campus Safety and Security:** Measures include 24-hour foot and vehicle patrol, emergency notification system, and security escort services. There are shuttle buses, emergency telephones, lighted pathways/sidewalks, controlled access to dorms/residences, alarm system, and security beepers free to all students.

REQUIREMENTS: Applicants should graduate from an accredited secondary school or have a GED. A minimum of 16 academic credits is required, including 4 years of English and 3 each of social studies, foreign language, math, and science. An essay is required, as is an audition for music and theater students and a portfolio for art students. An interview is recommended. Nazareth requires applicants to be in the upper 50% of their class. A GPA of 2.8 is required. AP and CLEP credits are accepted. Important factors in the admissions decision are geographical diversity, advanced placement or honors courses, and evidence of special talent.Nazareth's new Core Curriculum is all about integration integrating the various ways that different disciplines explore Enduring Questions, engaging in three Integrative Studies courses that help you explore a question of your own, and participating in an Experiential Learning Pathway that helps you integrate what you have learned in the classroom with what is happening in the world. Additional requirements vary by major program. A total of 120 credit hours are required to graduate, with a minimum GPA of 2.0. **Procedure:** Freshmen are admitted fall and spring. Entrance exams should be taken by December of the senior year. There are early decision, early admissions, and deferred admissions plans. Early decision applications should be filed by November 1; regular applications, by February 1 for fall entry; and November 1 for spring entry, along with a $45 fee. Notification of early decision is sent December 1; regular decision, March 1. 59 early decision candidates were accepted for the 2014-2015 class. 58 applicants were on the 2014 waiting list; 6 were admitted. Applications are accepted online. **Transfer Students:** 168 transfer students enrolled in 2013-2014. Applicants must have a college GPA of 2.5 (2.75 for education and physical therapy students). Those with fewer than 30 credits must submit high school transcripts. 30 of 120 credits required for the bachelor's degree must be completed at Nazareth. **International Students:** There are 62 international students enrolled. The school actively recruits these students. They must take the TOEFL with a minimum score of 550 on the paper-based TOEFL (PBT) or 79 on the Internet-based version (iBT).

ADMISSIONS: 68% of the 2014-2015 applicants were accepted. The SAT scores for the 2014-2015 freshman class were: Critical Reading- -29% below 500, 49% between 500 and 599, 20% between 600 and 699, and 2% between 700 and 800; Math--24% below 500, 49% between 500 and 599, 23% between 600 and 699, and 4% between 700 and 800; Writing--33% below 500, 45% between 500 and 599, 19% between 600 and 699, and 3% between 700 and 800. The ACT scores were 15% below 21, 26% between 21 and 23, 31% between 24 and 26, 14% between 27 and 28, and 14% above 28. 55% of the current freshmen were in the top fifth of their class; 81% were in the top two fifths. 6 freshmen graduated first in their class. **Admissions Contact:** Ian Mortimer, Vice President of Enrollment Management. E-Mail: *admissions@naz.edu* Web: *ww.naz.edu*

FINANCIAL AID: In 2014-2015, 100% of all full-time freshmen and 99% of continuing full-time students received some form of financial aid. 81% of all full-time freshmen and 81% of continuing full-time students received need-based aid. The average freshman award was $25,702. Need-based scholarships or need-based grants averaged $17,253; need-based self-help aid (loans and jobs) averaged $4,991; and other non-need-based awards and non-need-based scholarships averaged $18,469. 25% of undergraduate students work part-time. Average annual earnings from campus work are $1009. The average financial indebtedness of the 2014 graduate was $28,938. Nazareth is a member of CSS. The FAFSA, and The CSS Profile is required for early decision applicants only. is required. The priority date for freshman financial aid applications for fall entry is February 1.

NEW YORK COLLEGE OF TECHNOLOGY/THE CITY UNIVERSITY OF NEW YORK (*The complete profile is made available exclusively on our website, www.barronspac.com*)

NEW YORK INSTITUTE OF TECHNOLOGY   D-5
www.nyit.edu

Old Westbury, NY 11568   (800) 345-NYIT
                                             (800) 345-NYIT

Fax: (516) 686-7613	Email: admissions@nyit.edu
Full-time: 2308 men, 1396 women	Faculty: IIA, ++$
Part-time: 485 men, 267 women	Ph.D.s: 90%
Graduate: 1527 men, 1562 women	Student/Faculty: 11 to 1
Year: semesters, summer session	Tuition: $32,180
Room & Board: $12,830	Freshman Class: n/av
SAT or ACT: required	CEEB CODE: 2561
Application Deadline: n/av	**VERY COMPETITIVE**

New York Institute of Technology (NYIT) offers 90 degree programs, including undergraduate, graduate, and professional degrees, in more than 50 fields of study, including architecture and design; arts and sciences; education; engineering and computing sciences; health professions; management; and osteopathic medicine. A non-profit independent, private institution of higher education, NYIT has 12,000 students attending campuses on Long Island and in Manhattan, online, and at its global campuses. NYIT sponsors 11 NCAA Division II programs and one Division I team at its Old Westbury Campus. Led by President Edward Guiliano, NYIT is guided by its mission to provide career-oriented professional education, offer access to opportunity to all qualified students, and support applications-oriented research that benefits the larger world. There are 5 undergraduate schools and 7 graduate schools. In addition to regional accreditation, NYIT has baccalaureate program accreditation with

ABET, NAAB, CCNE, and CIDA. The 215-acre campus is in a suburban area 25 miles east of New York City. Including any residence halls, there are 57 buildings.

STUDENT LIFE: 91% of undergraduates are from New York. Others are from 48 states, 100 foreign countries, and Canada. 26% are White; 24% race unknown; 17% Foreign; 15% Asian American. **Male To Female Ratio:** 0.7:1. The average age of freshmen is 19; all undergraduates, 22. **Housing:** 884 students can be accommodated in college housing, which includes coed dorms. On-campus housing is available on a first-come and first-served basis. 88% of students commute. Alcohol is not permitted. All students may keep cars.

FACULTY/CLASSROOMS: 62% of faculty are male; 38% are female. No introductory courses are taught by graduate students.

PROGRAMS OF STUDY: NYIT confers B.A., B.S., B.Arch., B.F.A. and B.P.S. degrees. Associate, Master's, and Doctoral degrees are also awarded. Bachelor's degrees are awarded in BIOLOGICAL SCIENCE (biotechnology and life science), BUSINESS (accounting/CPA, business administration and management, entrepreneurial studies, finance, hospitality management services, human resources/ organizational mgmt, international business management, marketing management, and urban administration), COMMUNICATIONS AND THE ARTS (advertising, communications, English, graphic design, radio/TV, and telecommunications), COMPUTER AND PHYSICAL SCIENCE (chemistry, computer information technology, and computer science), ENGINEERING AND ENVIRONMENTAL DESIGN (architectural technology, architecture, computer graphics, construction management, electrical and computer engineering, engineering management, interior design, and mechanical engineering), HEALTH PROFESSIONS (biology, health science, nursing, and premedicine), SOCIAL SCIENCE (behavioral science, criminal justice, interdisciplinary studies, political science/government, psychology, social work, and sociology). Computer science, life sciences, and architectural technology have the largest enrollments.

ACTIVITIES: 3% of men belong to 1 local and 7 national fraternities; 2% of women belong to 1 local and 5 national sororities. There are 50 groups on campus, including art, cheerleading, chorale, computers, dance, drama, environmental, ethnic, film, honors, international, literary magazine, musical theater, newspaper, political, professional, radio and TV, religious, social, social service, and student government. Popular campus events include May Fest, Relay for Life, Greek Week, and Welcome Week. **Sports:** There are 6 intercollegiate sports for men and 6 for women, and 2 intramural sports for men and 5 for women. Facilities include the campus recreation center, located in the student activities center (SAC), houses a weight room, basketball gymnasium, and recreation room with table tennis, billiards, and TV. There are outdoor tennis and basketball courts adjacent to the SAC and fields for softball, lacrosse, baseball, and soccer. **Graduates:** From July 1, 2013 to June 30, 2014, 921 bachelor's degrees were awarded. The most popular majors were architectural technology (9%), business administration (9%), and electrical and computer engineering (9%). In an average class, 25% graduate in 4 years or less, 43% graduate in 5 years or less, and 47% graduate in 6 years or less.

SERVICES: Counseling and information services are available, as is tutoring in every subject. There is remedial math, reading, and writing. **Library/Resources:** The 4 libraries contain 148,963 volumes, 687,410 microform items. Computerized library services include interlibrary loans, database searching, Internet access, and Wi-Fi capability. Special learning facilities include an art gallery, radio station, Motion Capture Lab; Math Resource Center; Writing Center; Specialized Teaching Labs; online and in-person tutoring services (Learning Center); School of Management Simulated Trading Floor (Manhattan Campus). **Physically Challenged Students:** All of the campus is accessible. Facilities include wheelchair ramps, elevators, special parking, specially equipped restrooms, and lowered drinking fountains. **Special:** NYIT offers a semester-long study abroad program at its Nanjing, China campus. Although this program is primarily open to undergraduates majoring in business, computer sciences, electrical engineering, and communication arts, students from all disciplines are welcome to apply. A semester- or year-long study abroad program is offered at NYIT's campus in Abu Dhabi, United Arab Emirates. Additionally, NYIT offers study abroad programs at institutions in the Netherlands, Turkey, and the Dominican Republic, and short-term summer and intersession programs in France (Summer

Engineering School), Germany (Summer Business Program), and India (Intersession Business School), as well as other locations that vary each year (Summer Architecture Studio Abroad). NYIT offers the following combined programs: •B.S. Life Sciences/M.S. Occupational Therapy •B.S. Life Sciences/M.S. Physician Assistant Studies •B.S. Life Sciences/Doctor of Physical Therapy •B.S. Life Sciences/ Doctor of Osteopathic Medicine •B.F.A./M.A. Communication Arts •B.S. Mechanical Engineering/M.S. Energy Management •B.S. Architectural Technology/M.S. Energy Management •B.S./M.B.A. Accounting – CPA Track There are 9 national honor societies, a freshman honors program, and 1 departmental honors program. **Visiting:** There are regularly scheduled orientations for prospective students, a number of of admissions events are held throughout the year, including Fall Open House, Spring Preview Days, Student for a Day events, and transfer and graduate information sessions. There are guides for informal visits and visitors may sit in on classes. To schedule a visit, contact the Office of Admissions. **Campus Safety and Security:** Measures include 24-hour foot and vehicle patrol, emergency notification system, and security escort services. There are shuttle buses, emergency telephones, lighted pathways/sidewalks, controlled access to dorms/residences, NYIT Alerts, a mass text and voice messaging notification system for emergency communications and student outreach.

REQUIREMENTS: The SAT or ACT is required. Completed application for admission and $50 application fee; essay; transcripts of all high school and previous college work; SAT or ACT scores; and two letters of recommendation. There are additional requirements for admission to the School of Architecture and Design, School of Engineering and Computing Sciences, School of Health Professions, and the B.F.A. program. AP and CLEP credits are accepted. All students take courses in NYIT's Discovery Core Curriculum, which is designed to build core competencies in the following areas: Interdisciplinary Mindset; Global Perspective; Literacy; Ethical and Civic Engagement; Process and Nature of Science and the Arts; Critical Thinking; and Communication. **Procedure:** Freshmen are admitted fall, spring, and summer. There are early admissions, deferred admissions, and rolling admissions plans. Application deadlines are open. The fall 2014 application fee was $50. Notification is sent on a rolling basis. Applications are accepted on-line. **Transfer Students:** 396 transfer students enrolled in 2013-2014. Completed application for admission and $50 application fee; official transcript(s) from all colleges attended (if less than 24 credits of college coursework have been completed, official high school transcript(s) and SAT or ACT exam scores are required); GPA, essay, and letters of recommendation are recommended and may be required for admission to specific programs. 30 of 120 credits required for the bachelor's degree must be completed at NYIT. **International Students:** There are 460 international students enrolled. The school actively recruits these students. They must take the TOEFL with a minimum score of 550 on the paper-based TOEFL (PBT) or 79 on the Internet-based version (iBT), or take the IELTS. They must also take the SAT or ACT.

ADMISSIONS: The SAT scores for the 2014-2015 freshman class were: Critical Reading--33% below 500, 49% between 500 and 599, 16% between 600 and 699, and 2% between 700 and 800; Math--10% below 500, 45% between 500 and 599, 34% between 600 and 699, and 11% between 700 and 800. **Admissions Contact:** Karen Vahey, Dean of Admissions and Financial Aid. E-Mail: *admissions@nyit.edu* Web: *www.nyit.edu*

FINANCIAL AID: In 2014-2015, 80% of all full-time freshmen and 75% of continuing full-time students received some form of financial aid. The average freshman award was $20,191. Need-based scholarships or need-based grants averaged $7,331; and need-based self-help aid (loans and jobs) averaged $3,722. The FAFSA and the state aid form, and New York State residents submit Tuition Assistance Program (TAP) form are required. The priority date for freshman financial aid applications for fall entry is March 1.

NEW YORK UNIVERSITY — D-5

www.nyu.edu

New York, NY 10011   (212) 998-4500
n/av

Fax: (212) 995-4902

Full-time: 8567 men, 12798 women	**Faculty:** I, ++$
Part-time: 499 men, 751 women	**Ph.D.s:** n/av
Graduate: 9553 men, 12431 women	**Student/Faculty:** n/av
Year: semesters, summer session	**Tuition:** $44,848
Room & Board: $16,622	**Freshman Class:** 45329 applied, 14423 accepted, 4984 enrolled
SAT CR/M/W: 670/680/680 **ACT:** 30	**CEEB CODE:** 2562
Application Deadline: January 1	**MOST COMPETITIVE**

New York University, founded in 1831, is the largest private university in the United States. NYU, which is composed of 18 schools, colleges, and divisions, occupies 5 major centers in Manhattan and operates branch campus and research programs in other parts of the United States and abroad. In addition to its Manhattan locations, the University is also formally affiliated the Polytechnic Institute of NYU in Brooklyn, the second oldest school of engineering and technology in the country, and has research facilities, notably the Nelson Institute of Environmental Medicine, in Sterling Forest, near Tuxedo, New York. NYU has established itself as the first global network university, with a comprehensive liberal arts campus in Abu Dhabi – the first to be operated abroad by a major U.S. research university – and other sites for study and research in Accra, Ghana; Berlin, Germany; Buenos Aires, Argentina; Florence, Italy; London, England; Madrid, Spain; Paris, France; Prague, the Czech Republic; Shanghai, China; and Tel Aviv, Israel, among other locations. There are 9 undergraduate schools and 11 graduate schools. In addition to regional accreditation, NYU has baccalaureate program accreditation with AACSB, ACEJMC, ADA, CSWE, NLN, ACS, and APA. The -acre campus is in an urban area in New York City's Greenwich Village. Including any residence halls, there are 82 buildings.

STUDENT LIFE: 70% of undergraduates are from out of state, mostly the Northeast. Students are from 50 states, 144 foreign countries, and Canada. 39% are White; 18% Asian American; 14% Foreign; 11% race unknown. **Male To Female Ratio:** 1.4:1. The average age of freshmen is 18; all undergraduates, 21. 8% do not continue beyond their first year; 84% remain to graduate. **Housing:** 10774 students can be accommodated in college housing, which includes coed dorms and on-campus apartments. In addition, there are special-interest houses, fraternity houses, SAFE (Substance and Alcohol-Free Environment), First Year Residential Experience, Sophomore Residential Experience, and Explorations Learning Communities. On-campus housing is guaranteed for all 4 years. 52% of students commute. All students may keep cars.

FACULTY/CLASSROOMS: No introductory courses are taught by graduate students.

PROGRAMS OF STUDY: NYU confers B.A., B.S., B.F.A., B.S./B.E. and Mus.B. degrees. Associate, Master's, and Doctoral degrees are also awarded. Bachelor's degrees are awarded in AGRICULTURE (environmental studies), BIOLOGICAL SCIENCE (biochemistry, biology/biological science, cell biology, microbiology, neurosciences, and nutrition), BUSINESS (accounting, banking and finance, business administration and management, business economics, business law, finance, hotel/motel and restaurant management, human resources, industrial and labor relations, international business management, management information systems, management science, marketing management, marketing/retailing/merchandising, operations management, operations research, organizational behavior, property management, real estate, recreation and leisure services, and sports management), COMMUNICATIONS AND THE ARTS (American literature, animation, Arabic, art history, art history and appreciation, arts administration/management, classical languages, classics, communications, communications technology, comparative literature, creative writing, dance, design, digital communications, dramatic arts, English, English literature, film arts, fine arts, French, German, Germanic languages and literature, graphic design, Greek, Greek (classical), Greek (modern), Hebrew, information technology, instrumental performance, Italian, journalism, languages, Latin, linguistics, literature, media arts, music, music business management, music composition, music performance, music technology, music theory and composition, performing arts, photography, piano performance, Portuguese, public relations, publishing, radio/television technology, romance languages and literature, Russian, Slavic languages, Spanish, speech/debate/rhetoric, studio art, technical and business writing, theater management, vocal performance, voice, and writing), COMPUTER AND PHYSICAL SCIENCE (actuarial science, chemistry, Computer Engineering Technology, computer mathematics, computer science, digital arts/technology, earth science, information sciences and systems, mathematics, mathematics – economics, physics, and statistics), EDUCATION (art education, bilingual/bicultural education, (Education) Childhood Education, childhood education: 1-6, dance education, early childhood education, education, elementary education, English education, foreign languages education, general studies, mathematics education, music education, nursing education, school psychology, science education, secondary education, social science education, social studies education, social studies secondary school education, special education, and speech correction), ENGINEERING AND ENVIRONMENTAL DESIGN (biomedical engineering, chemical engineering, civil engineering, computational sciences, computer engineering, construction management, electrical and computer engineering, electrical/electronics engineering, engineering, engineering chemistry, engineering mechanics, engineering physics, graphic arts technology, mechanical engineering, and urban design), HEALTH PROFESSIONS (art therapy, dental hygiene, environmental health science, health care administration, music therapy, nursing, nursing home administration, occupational therapy, pharmacology, physical therapy, Pre-Health Studies, predentistry, premedicine, public health, and speech pathology/audiology), SOCIAL SCIENCE (African studies, African American studies, American studies, anthropology, applied psychology, architectural studies, area studies, Asian/American studies, Asian/Oriental studies, child care/child and family studies, classical/ancient civilization, counseling/psychology, developmental psychology, early childhood studies, East Asian studies, economics, ethnic studies, European studies, French studies, gender studies, (Social Science) Global Studies, history, humanities, humanities and social science, Iberian studies, international relations, Islamic studies, Italian studies, Japanese studies, Judaic studies, Latin American studies, law, Luso-Brazilian studies, medieval studies, Middle Eastern studies, Pacific area studies, philosophy, philosophy and religion, political science/government, psychology, public administration, religion, religious studies, Russian and Slavic studies, social science, social studies, social work, sociology, and urban studies). Business, individualized major, and theatre have the largest enrollments.

ACTIVITIES: 7% of men belong to 19 national fraternities; 5% of women belong to 12 national sororities. Groups on campus include art, bagpipe, band, cheerleading, chess, choir, chorale, chorus, computers, dance, debate, drama, environmental, ethnic, film, forensics, gay, honors, international, jazz band, literary magazine, marching band, musical theater, newspaper, opera, orchestra, pep band, photography, political, professional, radio and TV, religious, social, social service, student government, and symphony. Popular campus events include Spring Strawberry Festival, Grad Alley and Career Services Fair. **Sports:** There are 10 intercollegiate sports for men and 9 for women, and 9 intramural sports for men and 9 for women. Facilities include 2 state-of-the-art sports and recreation facilities. The sports center houses multipurpose courts for basketball, volleyball, tennis, and badminton, squash courts, handball and racquetball courts, rooftop tennis courts and running track, a 25-meter swimming pool, a diving tank, saunas, weight-training facilities, an aerobic fitness room, rooms for wrestling, judo, fencing, physical fitness, exercise prescription, and dance, and a rock-climbing wall. The athletic center is equipped with a 25-yard swimming pool, basketball/activities courts, a foot aerobic fitness room with cardio equipment, and a 30-foot indoor climbing center. **Graduates:** From July 1, 2013 to June 30, 2014, 6310 bachelor's degrees were awarded. The most popular majors were social science (38%), visual and performing arts (16%), culture, education, and and human development (12%). 800 companies recruited on campus in 2013-2014. In an average class, 77% graduate in 4 years or less, 82% graduate in 5 years or less, and 84% graduate in 6 years or less.

SERVICES: Counseling and information services are available, as is tutoring in every subject. There is a reader service for the blind. Services include sign language interpreters, scribes, research aides, and note takers for special needs. **Library/Resources:** Computerized library services include interlibrary loans, database searching, Internet access, and Wi-Fi capability. Special learning facilities include an art gallery, radio station, TV station, a speech-language-hearing clinic, a center for students with disabilities, and Speaking Freely (free noncredit foreign language classes). **Physically Challenged Students:** 95% of the campus is accessible. Facilities include wheelchair ramps, elevators, specially equipped restrooms, special class scheduling, lowered drinking fountains, lowered telephones, special housing. buses with hydraulic lifts, adaptive computer equipment, CART or C-print services, a CTV enlargement system, a JAWS speech synthesizer, Dragon Dictate Voice Recognition, and Kurzweil Personal Readers. **Special:** A vast array of internships is available, as well as study worldwide at NYU's 10 sites: Berlin, Buenos Aires, Florence, Ghana, London, Madrid, Paris, Prague, Shanghai, and Tel Aviv. B.A.-B.S. degree options, accelerated degrees in more than 230 majors, dual and student-designed majors, credit by exam, and pass/fail options are also available. A Washington semester is available to political science majors. There are exchange programs with several historically black colleges. There are Phi Beta Kappa and a freshman honors program. **Visiting:** There are regularly scheduled orientations for prospective students, including campus tours and weekday information sessions by appointment. There are also 2 fall open houses. To schedule a visit, contact the Office of Undergraduate Admissions. **Campus Safety and Security:** Measures include 24-hour foot and vehicle patrol, emergency notification system, self-defense education, and security escort services. There are shuttle buses, emergency telephones, lighted pathways/sidewalks, 24-hour security in residence halls, and a neighborhood-merchant emergency help service.

REQUIREMENTS: The SAT or ACT is required. The ACT Optional Writing test is also required. Applicants must graduate from an accredited secondary school. The GED is accepted. Students must present at least 16 Carnegie units, including 4 in English. Some majors require an audition or submission of a creative portfolio. All applicants must submit an essay and 2 letters of recommendation. Applicants can submit the SAT and 2 SAT: Subject tests; the ACT with Writing; the SAT and 2 Advanced Placement (AP) exam scores; 3 SAT: Subject tests (1 in literature or the humanities, 1 in math/science, and 1 in any non-language area); or 3 AP exam scores (1 in literature/humanities, 1 in math/science, and 1 in any nonlanguge area). AP credits are accepted.All students must complete a minimum of 128 credit hours and maintain a minimum GPA of 2.0. A course in expository writing is required. Students must complete a core liberal arts curriculum in addition to major and elective credit. **Procedure:** Freshmen are admitted fall and spring. Entrance exams should be taken by November of the senior year. There is a early decision plan. Early decision applications should be filed by November 1; regular applications, by January 1 for fall entry, along with a $70 fee. Notification of early decision is sent December 15; regular decision, April 1. 1967 early decision candidates were accepted for the 2014-2015 class. Applications are accepted on-line. **Transfer Students:** 607 transfer students enrolled in 2013-2014. Students must submit official college transcripts from all postsecondary institutions attended, a final high school transcript, and SAT scores. 64 of 128 credits required for the bachelor's degree must be completed at NYU. **International Students:** There are 3024 international students enrolled. The school actively recruits these students. They must take the TOEFL and the college's own test, or take the IELTS or have ESL testing. They must also take the SAT or ACT.

ADMISSIONS: 32% of the 2014-2015 applicants were accepted. The SAT scores for the 2014-2015 freshman class were: Critical Reading--1% below 500, 14% between 500 and 599, 50% between 600 and 699, and 35% between 700 and 800; Math--1% below 500, 13% between 500 and 599, 43% between 600 and 699, and 43% between 700 and 800; Writing--1% below 500, 10% between 500 and 599, 47% between 600 and 699, and 42% between 700 and 800. The ACT scores were 1% between 21 and 23, 10% between 24 and 26, 18% between 27 and 28, and 71% above 28. **Admissions Contact:** Office of Undergraduate Admissions Web: *http://www.nyu.edu/admissions/undergraduate-admissions.html*

FINANCIAL AID: The CSS/Profile, FAFSA, and the state aid form are required. The deadline for filing freshman financial aid applications for fall entry is February 15.

NIAGARA UNIVERSITY
A-3
www.niagara.edu

Niagara University, NY 14109	(716) 286-8700
	(800) 462-2111
Fax: (716) 286-8710	Email: admissions@niagara.edu
Full-time: 1153 men, 1680 women	Faculty: 140; IIA, av$
Part-time: 88 men, 255 women	Ph.D.s: n/av
Graduate: 293 men, 604 women	Student/Faculty: 18 to 1
Year: semesters, summer session	Tuition: $29,060
Room & Board: $11,950	Freshman Class: 3565 applied, 2348 accepted, 616 enrolled
SAT CR/M/W: 510/530/500 ACT: 23	CEEB CODE: 2558
Application Deadline: n/av	COMPETITIVE

Niagara University, founded in 1856 by the Vincentian fathers and brothers, is a private institution rooted in a Roman Catholic tradition. Programs offered include those in liberal arts, business, education, nursing, and travel, hotel, and restaurant administration. There are 4 undergraduate schools and 4 graduate schools. In addition to regional accreditation, Niagara has baccalaureate program accreditation with AACSB, CSWE, NCATE, ACPHA, ACS, and CCNE. The 160-acre campus is in a suburban area 4 miles north of Niagara Falls, 20 miles north of Buffalo, 90 miles from Toronto, Canada. Including any residence halls, there are 32 buildings.

STUDENT LIFE: 78% of undergraduates are from New York. Others are from 32 states, 26 foreign countries, and Canada. 71% are White. 31% are Catholic. **Male To Female Ratio:** 1.7:1. The average age of freshmen is 18; all undergraduates, 21. 16% do not continue beyond their first year; 64% remain to graduate. **Housing:** 1455 students can be accommodated in college housing, which includes single-sex and coed dorms and on-campus apartments. In addition, there are special-interest houses. On-campus housing is guaranteed for all 4 years and is available on a lottery system for upperclassmen. 52% of students live on campus. All students may keep cars.

FACULTY/CLASSROOMS: 60% of faculty are male; 40% are female. 89% teach undergraduates. No introductory courses are taught by graduate students. The average class size in an introductory lecture is 23; in a laboratory is 16; and in a regular course is 23.

PROGRAMS OF STUDY: Niagara confers B.A., B.S., B.B.A. and B.F.A. degrees. Associate, Master's, and Doctoral degrees are also awarded. Bachelor's degrees are awarded in AGRICULTURE (environmental studies), BIOLOGICAL SCIENCE (biochemistry, bioinformatics, biology/adolescence education, biology/biological science, and life science), BUSINESS (accounting, accounting/CPA, business administration and management, business administration marketing, business economics, finance, hotel/motel and restaurant management, human resources, international business, marketing/retailing/merchandising, sports management, tourism, and transportation management), COMMUNICATIONS AND THE ARTS (art history, communication studies, communications, dramatic arts, English, foreign language, French, Spanish, Spanish/adolescence education, theatre arts, and theater design), COMPUTER AND PHYSICAL SCIENCE (chemistry, chemistry/adolescence education, chemistry education, computer information technology, computer information systems, computer science, information science and systems, information science, and mathematics), EDUCATION (business education, (Education) Childhood Education, childhood education: 1-6, early childhood education, education, education of the exceptional child, elementary education, English education, foreign languages education, mathematics education, middle school education, museum studies, science education, secondary education, social studies education, social studies secondary school education, Spanish studies, education K-12, special education, and teaching English as a second/foreign language (TESOL/TEFOL)), HEALTH PROFESSIONS (biology and nursing), SOCIAL SCIENCE (child psychology/development, criminal justice, criminology, early childhood studies, economics, history, international studies, liberal arts/general studies,

philosophy, political science/government, psychology, religion, religious studies, social science, social work, and sociology). Business, social sciences, and biology are the strongest academically. Business, hospitality and Tourism management have the largest enrollments.

ACTIVITIES: 4% of men belong to 1 local and 1 national fraternities; 4% of women belong to 2 national sororities. There are 81 groups on campus, including art, cheerleading, choir, dance, drama, drill team, environmental, ethnic, honors, international, literary magazine, musical theater, newspaper, pep band, political, professional, radio and TV, religious, social, social service, student government, and yearbook. Popular campus events include Orientation, CARE, and RidgeFest. **Sports:** There are 8 intercollegiate sports for men and 10 for women, and 25 intramural sports for men and 25 for women. Facilities include a 2400-seat gym, a 6-lane swimming and diving pool, exercise and weight rooms, saunas and dance areas, outdoor tennis and basketball courts, baseball and soccer fields, rugby pitch, basketball and racquetball courts, a 2100-seat hockey arena, and multipurpose courts with an indoor track. Hiking and biking trails are nearby. **Graduates:** From July 1, 2013 to June 30, 2014, 880 bachelor's degrees were awarded. The most popular majors were education (33%), business (17%), and hospitality and tourism management (14%). 299 companies recruited on campus in 2013-2014. In an average class, 3% graduate in 3 years or less, 59% graduate in 4 years or less, 64% graduate in 5 years or less, and 64% graduate in 6 years or less. Of the 2013 graduating class, 26% were enrolled in graduate school within 6 months of graduation, and 80% were employed.

SERVICES: Counseling and information services are available, as is tutoring in most subjects. There is a reader service for the blind, and remedial math and writing. Study skills development, note taking, and escort-assistance services are available, as are educational assistant services for the vision-impaired, educational/classroom assistance and machines for the hearing-impaired, and services for the learning disabled **Library/Resources:** The library contains 165,444 volumes, 6,450 microform items, 6,603 audio/video tapes/CDs/DVDs, and subscribes to 23,500 periodicals including electronic. Computerized library services include interlibrary loans, database searching, Internet access, and Wi-Fi capability. Special learning facilities include an art gallery, radio station, an theatre, greenhouse, nursing simulation lab, and family literacy center. **Physically Challenged Students:** 75% of the campus is accessible. Facilities include wheelchair ramps, elevators, special parking, specially equipped restrooms, special class scheduling, lowered drinking fountains, special housing. **Special:** Niagara offers a Washington semester, a semester at the state capitol in Albany, on-campus work-study, internships in most majors with such companies as the Big 6 accounting firms and Walt Disney World, and co-op programs in all areas except nursing, education, and social work. Students may study abroad in 8 countries and cross-register through the Western New York Consortium. An accelerated degree program in business, B.A.-B.S. degrees, dual majors, non-degree study, credit for life, military, and work experience, pass/fail options, and research are also available. There is also an academic exploration program for undeclared majors. There are 19 national honor societies and a freshman honors program. **Visiting:** There are regularly scheduled orientations for prospective students, includes individual interviews and campus tours. Other arrangements can be made individually, such as to attend a class, eat in the student cafeteria, and/or speak with a faculty member. There are guides for informal visits, visitors may sit in on classes, and stay overnight. To schedule a visit, contact the Admissions Office at admissions@niagara.edu. **Campus Safety and Security:** Measures include 24-hour foot and vehicle patrol, emergency notification system, self-defense education, and security escort services. There are emergency telephones, lighted pathways/sidewalks, controlled access to dorms/residences, and a campus security advisory board.

REQUIREMENTS: The SAT or ACT is required. Applicants should be graduates of an accredited high school. The GED is accepted. The high school program should include 16 academic credits, with 4 in English and 2 each in foreign language, history, math, science, and social studies, as well as academic electives. Science, math, and computer majors should have 3 credits each in math and science. AP and CLEP credits are accepted. Important factors in the admissions decision are advanced placement or honors courses, parents or siblings attended your school, and recommendations by school officials. To graduate, students must earn 120 to 126 credit hours and a GPA of at least 2.0; 60 to 66 such hours are required in the major, 20 in specific disciplines, and 20 in liberal arts classes. A comprehensive exam is required in some majors; a thesis is required of honor students and some majors. **Procedure:** Freshmen are admitted to all sessions. Entrance exams should be taken In the junior year or fall of the senior year. There are early decision, early admissions, deferred admissions, and rolling admissions plans. Check with the school for current application deadlines. Notification is sent on a rolling basis. Applications are accepted on-line. **Transfer Students:** 174 transfer students enrolled in 2013-2014. Applicants must have a minimum GPA of 2.0 in travel, hotel, and restaurant administration, arts and sciences, and academic exploration (except for 2.25 in business and 2.5 for nursing and education majors) and submit all high school and college transcripts. The SAT or ACT is recommended. 30 of 120 credits required for the bachelor's degree must be completed at Niagara. **International Students:** There are 302 international students enrolled. The school actively recruits these students. They must take the TOEFL with a minimum score of 550 on the paper-based TOEFL (PBT) or 79 on the Internet-based version (iBT).

ADMISSIONS: 66% of the 2014-2015 applicants were accepted. The SAT scores for the 2014-2015 freshman class were: Critical Reading-10% below 500, 48% between 500 and 599, 11% between 600 and 699, and 1% between 700 and 800; Math--32% below 500, 51% between 500 and 599, 17% between 600 and 699, and 1% between 700 and 800; Writing--49% below 500, 40% between 500 and 599, 10% between 600 and 699, and 1% between 700 and 800. The ACT scores were 27% below 21, 29% between 21 and 23, 26% between 24 and 26, 13% between 27 and 28, and 5% above 28. **Admissions Contact:** Harry Gong, Director of Admissions. E-Mail: *admissions@ niagara.edu* Web: *www.niagara.edu*

FINANCIAL AID: Niagara is a member of CSS. The FAFSA is required. The priority date for freshman financial aid applications for fall entry is February 15.

NYACK COLLEGE   D-4
www.nyack.edu

Nyack, NY 10960	**(845) 675-4401**
	(800) 336-9225
Fax: (845) 358-3047	Email: admissions@nyack.edu
Full-time: 544 men, 872 women	Faculty: 83
Part-time: 103 men, 186 women	Ph.D.s: 77%
Graduate: 519 men, 672 women	Student/Faculty: 12 to 1
Year: semesters, summer session	Tuition: $24,300
Room & Board: $8950	Freshman Class: 625 applied, 621 accepted, 250 enrolled
SAT or ACT: required	CEEB CODE: 2560
Application Deadline: n/av	COMPETITIVE

Nyack College, founded in 1882, is a private, coeducational Christian college, liberal arts institution affiliated with the Christian and Missionary Alliance. In addition to regional accreditation, Nyack has baccalaureate program accreditation with CSWE, NASM, NCATE, TATS, ACSI, and CCNE. The 125-acre campus is in a suburban area in Nyack, NY (20 miles north of New York City) and lower Manhattan. Including any residence halls, there are 40 buildings.

STUDENT LIFE: 66% of undergraduates are from New York. Others are from 41 states, 53 foreign countries, and Canada. 31% are African American; 27% Hispanic; 19% White; 12% Asian American. 95% are Protestant. **Male To Female Ratio:** 1.5:1. The average age of freshmen is 20; all undergraduates, 26. 33% do not continue beyond their first year. **Housing:** College-sponsored housing includes single-sex dorms, on-campus apartments, and married student housing. On-campus housing is guaranteed for all 4 years. Priority is given to out-of-town students. Alcohol is not permitted. Upperclassmen may keep cars.

FACULTY/CLASSROOMS: 56% of faculty are male; 44% are female. No introductory courses are taught by graduate students.

PROGRAMS OF STUDY: Nyack confers B.A., B.S., B.Mus., S.M.B. and B.P.S degrees. Associate, Master's, and Doctoral degrees are also awarded. Bachelor's degrees are awarded in BUSINESS (accounting, business administration and management, and organizational leadership and management), COMMUNICATIONS AND THE ARTS (church music, communications, communication rhetoric/ communication, English, music, music performance, music theory and composition, piano/organ, and voice), COMPUTER AND PHYSICAL SCIENCE (computer science and mathematics), EDUCATION ((Education) Childhood Education, early childhood education, elementary education, English education, history education, mathematics education, music education, secondary education, and teaching English as a second/foreign language (TESOL/TEFOL)), HEALTH PROFESSIONS (biology and nursing), SOCIAL SCIENCE (biblical studies, criminal justice, crosscultural studies, history, interdisciplinary studies, pastoral studies, philosophy, philosophy and religion, psychology, religion, religious music, social work, sociology, theological studies, and youth ministry). Biblical/ministry-related programs, psychology, and business administration have the largest enrollments.

ACTIVITIES: There are no fraternities or sororities. There are 40 groups on campus, including musical ensembles, band, campus ministry teams, chorale, dance, drama, ethnic, honors, international, literary magazine, musical theater, newspaper, opera, orchestra, professional, radio and TV, religious, social, social service, and student government. Popular campus events include Homecoming, Spiritual Emphasis Week, Christmas Concert, and Midnight Breakfast. **Sports:** There are 5 intercollegiate sports for men and 6 for women, and 7 intramural sports for men and 7 for women. Facilities include a gym, soccer field, a fitness center, field house, baseball and softball fields, and tennis courts. **Graduates:** From July 1, 2013 to June 30, 2014, 408 bachelor's degrees were awarded. The most popular majors were business and marketing (41%), interdisciplinary studies (14%), and theology and religious vocations (9%).

SERVICES: Counseling and information services are available, as is tutoring in some subjects. There is remedial math, reading, and writing. **Library/Resources:** The 3 libraries contain 170,625 volumes, 34,744 microform items, 7,770 audio/video tapes/CDs/DVDs, and subscribe to 188 periodicals including electronic. Computerized library services include interlibrary loans, database searching, Internet access, and Wi-Fi capability. Special learning facilities include a radio station. **Physically Challenged Students: Special:** There are a freshman honors program. **Visiting:** There are regularly scheduled orientations for prospective students. There are guides for informal visits, visitors may sit in on classes, and stay overnight.. **Campus Safety and Security:** Measures include 24-hour foot and vehicle patrol. There are emergency telephones and lighted pathways/ sidewalks.

REQUIREMENTS: The SAT or ACT is required. High School graduation or its equivalent is essential. Completion of 15 academic credits is highly recommended: 4 units of English, 3 of mathematics, 3 of science, 3 of social science, and 2 of a foreign language. Students must demonstrate sound Christian character through personal testimony and recommendations. An interview may be required. A GPA of 2.0 is required. AP and CLEP credits are accepted. Important factors in the admissions decision are advanced placement or honors courses, personality/intangible qualities, recommendations by alumni, recommendations by school officials, parents or siblings attended your school, evidence of special talent, extracurricular activities record, and geographical diversity.120 credits (bachelor), 2.0 minimum GPA, core curriculum, Bible and Ministry minor curriculum **Procedure:** Freshmen are admitted fall, spring, and summer. There are deferred admissions and rolling admissions plans. Application deadlines are open. Application fee is $25. Notification is sent on a rolling basis. Applications are accepted on-line. **Transfer Students:** 227 transfer students enrolled in 2013-2014. Applicants must provide all transcripts from previous schools attended. 30 of 120 credits required for the bachelor's degree must be completed at Nyack. **International Students:** There are 85 international students enrolled. The school actively recruits these students. They must take the TOEFL with a minimum score of 550 on the paper-based TOEFL (PBT) or 83 on the Internet-based version (iBT). They must also take the SAT or ACT.

ADMISSIONS: 99% of the 2014-2015 applicants were accepted. The SAT scores for the 2014-2015 freshman class were: Critical Reading-

-70% below 500, 27% between 500 and 599, 2% between 600 and 699, and 1% between 700 and 800; Math--74% below 500, 21% between 500 and 599, 4% between 600 and 699, and 1% between 700 and 800. **Admissions Contact:** Dan Bailey, Director of Admissions. E-Mail: *admissions@nyack.edu* Web: *www.nyack.edu/admissions*

FINANCIAL AID: In 2014-2015, 89% of all full-time freshmen and continuing full-time students received some form of financial aid. 89% of all full-time freshmen and continuing full-time students received need-based aid. The average freshman award was $20,158. Need-based scholarships or need-based grants averaged $10,89; need-based self-help aid (loans and jobs) averaged $4,352; non-need-based athletic scholarships averaged $15,529; other non-need-based awards and non-need-based scholarships averaged $3,307; and $4,930 from other forms of aid. The average financial indebtedness of the 2014 graduate was $37,877. The FAFSA and the college's own financial statement are required. Check with the school for current application deadlines.

OSWEGO / STATE UNIVERSITY OF NEW YORK   C-3
www.oswego.edu

Oswego, NY 13126	**(315) 312-2250**
	n/av
Fax: (315) 312-3260	**Email: admiss@oswego.edu**
Full-time: 3361 men, 3593 women	**Faculty:** IIA, -$
Part-time: 192 men, 182 women	**Ph.Ds:** 88%
Graduate: 320 men, 469 women	**Student/Faculty:** 18 to 1
Year: semesters, summer session	**Tuition:** $7181 ($16,631)
Room & Board: $12,610	**Freshman Class:** 9746 applied, 4719 accepted, 1270 enrolled
SAT CR/M: 540/560 **ACT:** 24	**CEEB CODE:** 2543
Application Deadline: January 15	**VERY COMPETITIVE**

State University of New York at Oswego, founded in 1861, is a comprehensive institution offering more than 110 cooperative, preprofessional, and graduate programs through the College of Liberal Arts and Sciences, School of Business, School of Communication, Media and the Arts and School of Education. There are 4 undergraduate schools and 1 graduate school. In addition to regional accreditation, Oswego has baccalaureate program accreditation with AACSB, NASAD, NASM, NCATE, ACS, and NASP. The 696-acre campus is in a small town on the southeast shore of Lake Ontario, 35 miles northwest of Syracuse. Including any residence halls, there are 40 buildings.

STUDENT LIFE: 96% of undergraduates are from New York. Others are from 26 states, 15 foreign countries, and Canada. 90% are from public schools. 79% are White. **Male To Female Ratio:** 1.1:1. The average age of freshmen is 18; all undergraduates, 21. 18% do not continue beyond their first year; 62% remain to graduate. **Housing:** 4600 students can be accommodated in college housing, which includes coed dorms and on-campus apartments. In addition, there are special-interest houses, resident hall living and learning communities, a freshmen-only building, upperclassmen suites and upperclassmen townhouses. On-campus housing is guaranteed for all 4 years. 65% of students live on campus; of those, 90% remain on campus on weekends. All students may keep cars.

FACULTY/CLASSROOMS: 53% of faculty are male; 47% are female. 96% teach undergraduates. No introductory courses are taught by graduate students. The average class size in an introductory lecture is 40; in a laboratory is 15; and in a regular course is 24.

PROGRAMS OF STUDY: Oswego confers B.A., B.S. and B.F.A. degrees. Master's degrees are also awarded. Bachelor's degrees are awarded in BIOLOGICAL SCIENCE (biochemistry, biology/adolescence education, biology/biological science, (Biological) Pre-Health Studies, and zoology), BUSINESS (accounting, business administration and management, finance, human resources, insurance and risk management, management science, marketing/retailing/merchandising, operations management, and recreational facilities management), COMMUNICATIONS AND THE ARTS (art,

broadcasting, communications, creative writing, dramatic arts, English, English as a second/foreign language, English Writing, film arts, French, German, graphic design, journalism, linguistics, music, musical theater, public relations, Spanish, spanish / adolescence education, theatre acting, theatre arts, and theatre production), COMPUTER AND PHYSICAL SCIENCE (applied mathematics, atmospheric sciences and meteorology, chemistry, computer science, earth science, earth science / adolescence education, environmental geology, geochemistry, geology, information sciences and systems, mathematics, physics, and software engineering), EDUCATION (agricultural education, business education, (Education) Childhood Education, elementary education, English education, foreign languages education, mathematics education, secondary education, social studies education, teaching English as a second/foreign language (TESOL/TEFOL), technical education, trade and industrial education, and vocational education), ENGINEERING AND ENVIRONMENTAL DESIGN (electrical and computer engineering, pre-engineering, and technological management), HEALTH PROFESSIONS (Pre-Health Studies, predentistry, premedicine, pre-optometry, prephysical therapy, and preveterinary science), SOCIAL SCIENCE (American studies, anthropology, cognitive science, criminal justice, economics, family/consumer studies, French studies, history, human development, international studies, philosophy, political science/government, prelaw, psychology, sociology, women & gender studies, and women's studies). Biological sciences, chemistry, computer science, meteorology, education and accounting are the strongest academically. Childhood/adolescence education, business administration, and biological sciences have the largest enrollments.

ACTIVITIES: 7% of men belong to 7 local and 10 national fraternities; 6% of women belong to 5 local and 7 national sororities. There are 186 groups on campus, including cheerleading and Equestrian Teams, ice hockey, rugby, art, athletics: crew, band, cheerleading, choir, chorale, chorus, communications, computers, dance, drama, environmental, ethnic, film, gay, honors, international, jazz band, literary magazine, musical theater, newspaper, opera, orchestra, pep band, photography, political, professional, radio and TV, religious, social, social service, student government, symphony, and yearbook. Popular campus events include Honors Convocations, Quest, May Day, Fall and Spring Concerts, Family and Friends Weekend and Hockey Nights in Oswego. **Sports:** There are 12 intercollegiate sports for men and 12 for women, and 21 intramural sports for men and 21 for women. Facilities include an ice hockey rink, a field house with an artificial-grass practice area, 18 tennis courts, an outdoor track, 3 soccer and 3 lacrosse fields, baseball and softball fields, numerous basketball courts, racquetball and squash courts, 2 indoor pools, and a diving well. The gym seats 3500. There are also 2 membership fitness centers and weight rooms, a cross-country ski lodge, and a martial arts/dance studio. **Graduates:** From July 1, 2013 to June 30, 2014, 1668 bachelor's degrees were awarded. The most popular majors were education (23%), business (23%), and communications (11%). 150 companies recruited on campus in 2013-2014. In an average class, 38% graduate in 4 years or less, 54% graduate in 5 years or less, and 58% graduate in 6 years or less. Of the 2013 graduating class, 26% were enrolled in graduate school within 6 months of graduation, and 95% were employed.

SERVICES: Counseling and information services are available, as is tutoring in every subject. There is a reader service for the blind, and remedial math, reading, and writing. In addition, the Office of Disability Services provides general foundation support. **Library/Resources:** The library contains 554,986 volumes, 1.6 million microform items, 31,384 audio/video tapes/CDs/DVDs, and subscribes to 52,600 periodicals including electronic. Computerized library services include interlibrary loans, database searching, Internet access, and Wi-Fi capability. Special learning facilities include an art gallery, planetarium, radio station, TV station, 330-acre biological Rice Creek Field Station. **Physically Challenged Students:** 85% of the campus is accessible. Facilities include wheelchair ramps, elevators, special parking, specially equipped restrooms, special class scheduling, lowered drinking fountains, lowered telephones, special housing. Student support group. **Special:** Oswego offers cross-registration with ACUSNY-Visiting Student Program. More than 1000 internships are available with business, social, cultural, and government agencies. In addition 12 departments offer co-op opportunities as well. The university also offers a Washington semester, study abroad in more than 80 programs, a 5-year accounting B.S./M.B.A. program, dual majors, B.A.-B.S. degrees in several sciences and a B.A.-B.F.A. in art, credit for military experience, nondegree study, and pass/fail options. A pre-engineering option is available. A 3-4 degree in optometry with SUNY College of Optometry, and 2+2 medical imaging/ 3+3 physical therapy with SUNY Upstate Medical Center are also possible. There are 21 national honor societies, a freshman honors program, and 9 departmental honors programs. **Visiting:** There are regularly scheduled orientations for prospective students, usually including a campus tour and a meeting/presentation with a counselor. There are guides for informal visits, visitors may sit in on classes, and stay overnight. To schedule a visit, contact the Office of Admissions at admiss@oswego.edu. **Campus Safety and Security:** Measures include 24-hour foot and vehicle patrol, emergency notification system, self-defense education, and security escort services. There are shuttle buses, emergency telephones, lighted pathways/sidewalks, controlled access to dorms/residences, an electronic device that locates students and alerts the police when pressed.

REQUIREMENTS: The SAT or ACT is required. Applicants must be graduates of an accredited secondary school or have a GED certificate. 18 academic units are required, preferring 4 years each of English and social studies, 7 years combined of math and science, and 2 of a foreign language. An essay and interview are strongly recommended. A GPA of 82.0 is required. AP and CLEP credits are accepted. Important factors in the admissions decision are advanced placement or honors courses, extracurricular activities record, and personality/intangible qualities. To graduate, all students must complete 30 to 33 general education credits, including 9-12 in writing, mathematics, foreign language, natural science and 15 credits from areas of natural sciences, social and behavior sciences, american history, western civilization, humanities, fine and performing arts and world awareness. Students must have a minimum 2.0 GPA and complete 122 total credit hours (127 hours for technology and vocational education students). The total number of hours in the major varies from 33 to 95. **Procedure:** Freshmen are admitted fall and spring. Entrance exams should be taken during the spring of the junior year and fall of the senior year. There are early decision, early admissions, deferred admissions, and rolling admissions plans. Early decision applications should be filed by November 29; regular applications, by January 15 for fall entry, along with a $50 fee. Notification of early decision is sent December 15; regular decision, in January. 140 early decision candidates were accepted for the 2014-2015 class. Applications are accepted on-line. **Transfer Students:** 762 transfer students enrolled in 2013-2014. Applicants must submit official transcripts from previously attended colleges. Students with a minimum GPA of 2.3 are encouraged to apply. SUNY associate degree holders are given preference. Secondary school records may be required for 1-year transfers. 30 of 122 credits required for the bachelor's degree must be completed at Oswego. **International Students:** There are 147 international students enrolled. The school actively recruits these students. They must take the TOEFL with a minimum score of 550 on the paper-based TOEFL (PBT) or 80 on the Internet-based version (iBT).

ADMISSIONS: 48% of the 2014-2015 applicants were accepted. The SAT scores for the 2014-2015 freshman class were: Critical Reading--22% below 500, 58% between 500 and 599, 18% between 600 and 699, and 2% between 700 and 800; Math--16% below 500, 59% between 500 and 599, 23% between 600 and 699, and 2% between 700 and 800. The ACT scores were 11% below 21, 40% between 21 and 23, 29% between 24 and 26, 15% between 27 and 28, and 5% above 28. 51% of the current freshmen were in the top fifth of their class; 80% were in the top two fifths. **Admissions Contact:** Daniel Griffin, Interim Director of Admissions. E-Mail: *admiss@oswego.edu* Web: *www.oswego.edu*

FINANCIAL AID: In 2014-2015, 70% of all full-time freshmen and 70% of continuing full-time students received some form of financial aid. 65% of all full-time freshmen and 66% of continuing full-time students received need-based aid. The average freshman award was $7,044. Need-based scholarships or need-based grants averaged $6,391; need-based self-help aid (loans and jobs) averaged $3,843; other non-need-based awards and non-need-based scholarships averaged $3,728; and $3,204 from other forms of aid. 65% of undergradu-

ate students work part-time. Average annual earnings from campus work are $1500. The average financial indebtedness of the 2014 graduate was $26,611. Oswego is a member of CSS. The FAFSA and the state aid form are required. The priority date for freshman financial aid applications for fall entry is March 1.

PACE UNIVERSITY — D-5
www.pace.edu

New York, NY 10038	(212) 346-1323 or (914) 773-3746 (800) 874-PACE
Fax: (212) 346-1831 or (914) 773-3851	**Email:** infoctr@pace.edu
Full-time: 2881 men, 4381 women	**Faculty:** 422; I, +$
Part-time: 660 men, 772 women	**Ph.D.s:** 89%
Graduate: 1533 men, 2630 women	**Student/Faculty:** 16 to 1
Year: semesters, summer session	**Tuition:** $39,747
Room & Board: $13,620	**Freshman Class:** 15226 applied, 13366 accepted, 1938 enrolled
SAT CR/M: 550/554 **ACT:** required	**CEEB CODE:** 2635
Application Deadline: February 15	**COMPETITIVE**

Pace University, founded 1906, has produced thinking professionals by providing high-quality education for the professions with a firm base in liberal learning amid the advantages of the New York Metropolitan area. A private univeriity, Pace has campuses in New York City and Westchester County, enrolling students in bachelor's, master's, and doctoral programs in its College of Health Professions, Dyson College of Arts and Sciences, Lubin School of Business, School of Education, School of Law, and Seidenberg School of Computer Science and Information Systems. There are 5 undergraduate schools and 6 graduate schools. In addition to regional accreditation, Pace has baccalaureate program accreditation with AACSB, ABET, NCATE, CCNE, ARC-PA, and ACE. The 265-acre campus is in an urban area Pace University's lower Manhattan campus, is in the heart of the Financial District. The Pleasantville campus, is in Westchester County. Including any residence halls, there are 65 buildings.

STUDENT LIFE: 53% of undergraduates are from New York. Others are from 46 states, 105 foreign countries, and Canada. 75% are from public schools. 48% are White; 14% Hispanic; 11% Foreign. **Male To Female Ratio:** 1.5:1. The average age of freshmen is 18; all undergraduates, 22. 24% do not continue beyond their first year; 51% remain to graduate. **Housing:** 3524 students can be accommodated in college housing, which includes coed dorms and on-campus apartments. In addition, there are honors houses, special-interest houses, and a wellness floor. 54% of students commute. Some may keep cars.

FACULTY/CLASSROOMS: 53% of faculty are male; 47% are female. 84% teach undergraduates, and 24% do research. No introductory courses are taught by graduate students. The average class size in an introductory lecture is 35; in a laboratory is 11; and in a regular course is 23.

PROGRAMS OF STUDY: Pace confers B.A., B.S., B.B.A., B.F.A. and B.S.N. degrees. Associate, Master's, and Doctoral degrees are also awarded. Bachelor's degrees are awarded in AGRICULTURE (environmental studies), BIOLOGICAL SCIENCE (biology/adolescence education, biology/biological science, and forensic science), BUSINESS (accounting, banking and finance, business administration and management, business economics, entrepreneurial studies, finance, hospitality management services, international business management, international marketing, and marketing/retailing/merchandising), COMMUNICATIONS AND THE ARTS (acting, advertising, art history, art, art history and appreciation, communications, dance, English, film arts, fine arts, modern language, musical theater, Spanish, theatre acting, theatre arts, theater design, theatre production, and theater management), COMPUTER AND PHYSICAL SCIENCE (chemistry, computer science, computer security and information assurance, earth science/adolescence education, information sciences and systems, mathematics, and physics), EDUCATION (education of the deaf and hearing impaired and elementary education), ENGINEERING AND ENVIRONMENTAL DESIGN (environmental science), HEALTH PROFESSIONS (nursing and speech pathology/audiology), SOCIAL SCIENCE (American studies, applied psychology, Asian studies, biopsychology, criminal justice, economics, forensic studies, history, Latin American studies, philosophy and religion, political science/government, psychology, social science, sociology, and women and gender studies). Accounting is the strongest academically. Business and finance has the largest enrollment.

ACTIVITIES: 2% of men belong to 1 local and 11 national fraternities; 3% of women belong to 3 local and 11 national sororities. There are 83 groups on campus, including art, cheerleading, chorus, computers, dance, debate, drama, environmental, ethnic, film, gay, honors, international, literary magazine, musical theater, newspaper, photography, political, professional, radio and TV, religious, social, social service, student government, and yearbook. Popular campus events include Homecoming, CariCulture and Live Love Laugh. **Sports:** There are 6 intercollegiate sports for men and 8 for women, and 9 intramural sports for men and 9 for women. Facilities include The Civic Center gym in New York City. There are football, lacrosse, soccer,softball, baseball fields and tennis courts,and a health, fitness, and recreation center at the Pleasantville/Briarcliff Manor campus. **Graduates:** From July 1, 2013 to June 30, 2014, 1652 bachelor's degrees were awarded. The most popular majors were finance (8%), accounting (8%), and communication studies (5%). 359 companies recruited on campus in 2013-2014. In an average class, 1% graduate in 3 years or less, 39% graduate in 4 years or less, 53% graduate in 5 years or less, and 56% graduate in 6 years or less. Of the 2013 graduating class, 5% were enrolled in graduate school within 6 months of graduation, and 53% were employed.

SERVICES: Counseling and information services are available, as is tutoring in every subject. There is remedial math, reading, and writing. All services are provided in the University's Center for Academic Excellence. **Library/Resources:** The 3 libraries contain 790,086 volumes, 53,517 microform items, 5,668 audio/video tapes/CDs/DVDs, and subscribe to 209,896 periodicals including electronic. Computerized library services include interlibrary loans, database searching, Internet access, and Wi-Fi capability. Special learning facilities include an art gallery, radio station, TV station, 2 art galleries, a performing arts center, biological research labs, an environmental center, a language lab, and computer labs. **Physically Challenged Students:** 70% of the campus is accessible. Facilities include wheelchair ramps, elevators, special parking, special class scheduling, lowered drinking fountains, lowered telephones, other facilities that vary by campus; there is no student parking in NYC. **Special:** Internships, study abroad, and a cooperative education program in all majors are available. Pace also offers accelerated degree programs, B.A.-B.S. degrees, dual majors, general studies degrees, and 3-2 engineering degrees with Manhattan College and Rensselaer Polytechnic Institute. Credit for life, military, and work experience, nondegree study, and pass/fail options are available. There are 25 national honor societies, a freshman honors program, and 19 departmental honors programs. **Visiting:** There are regularly scheduled orientations for prospective students, including student-for-a-day programs and overnight visits by appointment. There are guides for informal visits, visitors may sit in on classes, and stay overnight. To schedule a visit, contact the Office of Undergraduate Admission at ugnyc@pace.edu. **Campus Safety and Security:** Measures include 24-hour foot and vehicle patrol, emergency notification system, and security escort services. There are shuttle buses, emergency telephones, lighted pathways/sidewalks, controlled access to dorms/residences, including closed circuit TV.

REQUIREMENTS: The SAT or ACT is required. Applicants should be graduates of an accredited secondary school with at least 16 academic credits, including 4 in English, 3 to 4 each in math, science, and history, and 2 to 3 in a foreign language. The GED is accepted, official SAT or ACT scores. An essay is required. Two letters of recommendations from a teacher or counselor who can attest to your academic potential and personal characteristics. A GPA of 3.0 is required. AP and CLEP credits are accepted. Important factors in the admissions decision are advanced placement or honors courses, recommendations by school officials, and leadership record.To graduate, students must complete 128 to 133 credit hours depending on the major, including 32 to 50 in the major, with a minimum GPA of 2.0. A core curriculum with a minimum of 44 credits that includes an introductory computer science course as well as a community-based

learning experience and 2 enhanced writing courses is also required. **Procedure:** Freshmen are admitted fall and spring. Entrance exams should be taken by December of the senior year. There are early admissions, deferred admissions, and rolling admissions plans. February 15 for fall entry, along with a $50 fee. Notifications are sent December 15. Applications are accepted on-line. **Transfer Students:** 927 transfer students enrolled in 2013-2014. Applicants are admitted in the fall or spring. A college GPA of 2.5 is required. Grades of C or better transfer for credit. A maximum of 68 credits will be accepted from a 2-year school. Students who transfer with less than 32 credits also need to submit SAT or ACT scores 32 of 128 credits required for the bachelor's degree must be completed at Pace. **International Students:** There are 610 international students enrolled. The school actively recruits these students. They must take the TOEFL with a minimum score of 570 on the paper-based TOEFL (PBT) or 89 on the Internet-based version (iBT) and the college's own test.

ADMISSIONS: 88% of the 2014-2015 applicants were accepted. The SAT scores for the 2014-2015 freshman class were: Critical Reading--20% below 500, 56% between 500 and 599, 22% between 600 and 699, and 3% between 700 and 800; Math--19% below 500, 55% between 500 and 599, 23% between 600 and 699, and 3% between 700 and 800. The ACT scores were 24% below 21, 30% between 21 and 23, 25% between 24 and 26, 13% between 27 and 28, and 8% above 28. 32% of the current freshmen were in the top fifth of their class; 64% were in the top two fifths. **Admissions Contact:** Donna J. Grand Pre, Dean of Admissions. E-Mail: *infoctr@pace.edu* Web: *www.pace.edu*

FINANCIAL AID: In 2014-2015, 98% of all full-time freshmen and 95% of continuing full-time students received some form of financial aid. 76% of all full-time freshmen and 71% of continuing full-time students received need-based aid. The average freshman award was $39,492. Need-based scholarships or need-based grants averaged $26,448; need-based self-help aid (loans and jobs) averaged $13,697; non-need-based athletic scholarships averaged $13,604; and other non-need-based awards and non-need-based scholarships averaged $17,474. Average annual earnings from campus work are $2156. The average financial indebtedness of the 2014 graduate was $35,580. The FAFSA is required. The deadline for filing freshman financial aid applications for fall entry is February 15.

PARSONS THE NEW SCHOOL FOR DESIGN *(The complete profile is made available exclusively on our website, www.barronspac.com)*

POLYTECHNIC INSTITUTE OF NEW YORK   D-5 UNIVERSITY
www.poly.edu

Brooklyn, NY 11201	**(718) 260-3100**
	(800) 765-8324
Fax: (718) 260-3446	**Email: uadmit@poly.edu**
Full-time: 1517 men, 435 women	**Faculty:** 157; I, av$
Part-time: 88 men, 31 women	**Ph.D.s:** n/av
Graduate: 1946 men, 635 women	**Student/Faculty:** 14 to 1
Year: semesters, summer session	**Tuition:** $39,564
Room & Board: $13,500	**Freshman Class:** 3284 applied, 2453 accepted, 495 enrolled
SAT CR/M/W: 600/680/600 **ACT:** 28	**CEEB CODE:** 2668
Application Deadline: n/av	**HIGHLY COMPETITIVE+**

Polytechnic Institute of New York University is the nation's second oldest private engineering institution. Today, it is the New York metropolitan area's preeminent resource in science, engineering and technology education and research. A private coeducational institution, Polytechnic has a distinguished history in electrical engineering, polymer chemistry and aerospace and microwave engineering. The Institute is a leader in telecommunications, information science and technology management and is focused on demanding societal issues in the areas of urban systems, health and wellness and global information technology. The Institute prepares graduates to play leading roles in these overarching areas through invention, innovation and entrepreneurship (i2e). Figures in the above capsule and in this profile are approximate. There is 1 undergraduate school and 1 graduate school. In addition to regional accreditation, NYU-Poly has baccalaureate program accreditation with ABET and CSAB. The 3-acre campus is in an urban area 2 Miles from New York City. Including any residence halls, there are 6 buildings.

STUDENT LIFE: 68% of undergraduates are from New York. Others are from 26 states, 31 foreign countries, and Canada. 88% are from public schools. 38% are Foreign; 21% White; 20% Asian American. **Male To Female Ratio:** 0.3:1. The average age of freshmen is 18; all undergraduates, 20. 14% do not continue beyond their first year; 55% remain to graduate. **Housing:** 400 students can be accommodated in college housing, which includes coed dorms. On-campus housing is available on a first-come and first-served basis. Priority is given to out-of-town students. 75% of students commute. Alcohol is not permitted. No one may keep cars.

FACULTY/CLASSROOMS: 80% of faculty are male; 20% are female. 68% teach undergraduates. No introductory courses are taught by graduate students. The average class size in an introductory lecture is 29; in a laboratory is 16; and in a regular course is 22.

PROGRAMS OF STUDY: NYU-Poly confers B.S. degrees. Master's and Doctoral degrees are also awarded. Bachelor's degrees are awarded in BIOLOGICAL SCIENCE (molecular biology), BUSINESS (business administration and management), COMPUTER AND PHYSICAL SCIENCE (chemistry, computer science, information sciences and systems, mathematics, and physics), ENGINEERING AND ENVIRONMENTAL DESIGN (chemical engineering, civil engineering, computer engineering, construction management, electrical/electronics engineering, and mechanical engineering), SOCIAL SCIENCE (humanities, liberal arts/general studies, and social science). Engineering, management, and physical science are the strongest academically. Electrical engineering, mechanical engineering, and civil engineering have the largest enrollments.

ACTIVITIES: 2% of men and 1% of women belong to 2 local and 3 national fraternities; 1% of women belong to 1 national sorority. There are 46 groups on campus, including chess, computers, dance, ethnic, film, honors, international, literary magazine, newspaper, photography, professional, radio and TV, religious, social, social service, student government, and yearbook. Popular campus events include Chinese New Year, Film Festivals and International Food Fair. **Sports:** There are 7 intercollegiate sports for men and 7 for women, and 13 intramural sports for men and 12 for women. Facilities include soccer, lacrosse, and baseball fields, basketball courts, ping-pong tables, and 2 student centers. **Graduates:** From July 1, 2013 to June 30, 2014, 276 bachelor's degrees were awarded. The most popular majors were electrical engineering (17%), civil engineering (15%), and mechanical engineering (12%). 285 companies recruited on campus in 2013-2014. In an average class, 41% graduate in 4 years or less, 58% graduate in 5 years or less, and 62% graduate in 6 years or less. Of the 2013 graduating class, 20% were enrolled in graduate school within 6 months of graduation, and 64% were employed.

SERVICES: Counseling and information services are available, as is tutoring in every subject. There is remedial math and writing. **Library/Resources:** The library contains 120,863 volumes, 20,000 microform items, 460 audio/video tapes/CDs/DVDs, and subscribes to 43,500 periodicals including electronic. Computerized library services include interlibrary loans, database searching, Internet access, and Wi-Fi capability. Special learning facilities include a radio station. **Physically Challenged Students:** All of the campus is accessible. Facilities include wheelchair ramps, elevators, special parking, specially equipped restrooms, lowered drinking fountains, and lowered telephones. **Special:** Cooperative programs are available in all majors. Opportunities are provided for internships, work-study programs, study abroad, accelerated degree programs in engineering and computer science, dual majors, student-designed majors, and nondegree study. There are 9 national honor societies, a freshman honors program, and 3 departmental honors programs. **Visiting:** There are regularly scheduled orientations for prospective students, including a keynote speaker, major presentations, financial aid and scholarship sessions, and student life and career services sessions. There are guides for informal visits and visitors may stay overnight. To schedule a visit, contact the Dean of Admission. **Campus Safety and Security:** Measures include 24-hour foot and vehicle patrol. There are emergency telephones and lighted pathways/sidewalks.

REQUIREMENTS: The SAT is required. Graduation from an accredited secondary school is required; a GED will be accepted. The preferred secondary school course of study is: 4 course years of English, 4 of Science (Chemistry is required and physics is strongly recommended), and 4 of Mathematics (Sequential I, II, III, precalculus, calculus). An essay and an interview are recommended. AP credits are accepted. Important factors in the admissions decision are advanced placement or honors courses, leadership record, and evidence of special talent. Students must complete all university and departmental course requirements, including 24 credits in Humanities/Social Science, 16 in Math, 12 in Chemistry/Physics, 4 in Engineering Design, and 3 in Programming Methodology. A total of 120 to 128 credits must be earned, with 32 in the major, and a minimum GPA of 2.0 is required to graduate. A senior design project is also required of engineering students. **Procedure:** Freshmen are admitted fall, spring, and summer. Entrance exams should be taken by November of the senior year. There are early admissions, deferred admissions, and rolling admissions plans. Application deadlines are open. Application fee is $65. Notification is sent on a rolling basis. Applications are accepted on-line. **Transfer Students:** 81 transfer students enrolled in 2013-2014. Transfer applicants must have a 2.5 cumulative GPA. Students with fewer than 30 credits must submit SAT scores and secondary school transcripts in addition to official college-level transcripts. 64 of 124 credits required for the bachelor's degree must be completed at NYU-Poly. **International Students:** There are 207 international students enrolled. The school actively recruits these students. They must take the TOEFL with a minimum score of 550 on the paper-based TOEFL (PBT) or 80 on the Internet-based version (iBT). They must also take the SAT or ACT.

ADMISSIONS: 75% of the 2014-2015 applicants were accepted. The SAT scores for the 2014-2015 freshman class were: Critical Reading--11% below 500, 38% between 500 and 599, 40% between 600 and 699, and 11% between 700 and 800; Math--1% below 500, 10% between 500 and 599, 45% between 600 and 699, and 44% between 700 and 800; Writing--9% below 500, 40% between 500 and 599, 41% between 600 and 699, and 10% between 700 and 800. The ACT scores were 25% between 24 and 26, 26% between 27 and 28, and 48% above 28. **Admissions Contact:** Joy Colelli, Dean of Undergraduate Admissions. E-Mail: uadmit@poly.edu Web: www.poly.edu

FINANCIAL AID: In 2014-2015, 73% of all full-time freshmen and 75% of continuing full-time students received some form of financial aid. 67% of all full-time freshmen and 71% of continuing full-time students received need-based aid. The average freshman award was $28,428. Need-based scholarships or need-based grants averaged $14,348; need-based self-help aid (loans and jobs) averaged $3,817; and other non-need-based awards and non-need-based scholarships averaged $13,261. 30% of undergraduate students work part-time. Average annual earnings from campus work are $6360. The average financial indebtedness of the 2014 graduate was $36,574. NYU-Poly is a member of CSS. The FAFSA and the college's own financial statement are required. The priority date for freshman financial aid applications for fall entry is March 1.

PRATT INSTITUTE (*The complete profile is made available exclusively on our website, www.barronspac.com*)

QUEENS COLLEGE/THE CITY UNIVERSITY OF NEW YORK   D-5
www.qc.cuny.edu

Flushing, NY 11367	(718) 997-5608
	n/av
Fax: (718) 997-5617	Email: vincent.angrisani@qc.cuny.edu
Full-time: 4783 men, 5986 women	Faculty: n/av
Part-time: 1913 men, 2669 women	Ph.D.s: 85%
Graduate: 1034 men, 2589 women	Student/Faculty: 16 to 1
Year: semesters, summer session	Tuition: $6207 ($15,027)
Room & Board: $10,900	Freshman Class: 19032 applied, 7045 accepted, 890 enrolled
SAT CR/M: 540/574	CEEB CODE: 2750
Application Deadline: February 1	VERY COMPETITIVE

Queens College, founded in 1937, was hailed by the people of the borough as "the college of the future." Now part of the City University of New York (CUNY), Queens College offers a rigorous education in the liberal arts and sciences under the guidance of a faculty dedicated to both teaching and research. Students graduate with the ability to think critically, address complex problems, explore various cultures, and use modern technologies and information resources. The college has students from more than 150 nations. Queens College was cited as being one of only five colleges in the U.S. that serves low-income students. This was based on the college's graduation rate, low tuition, and the amount of need-based financial aid it awards to students. The beautiful campus consists of 92 acres lined with trees surrounding grassy open spaces and a traditional quad. The college boasts state-of-the-art computer and science laboratories, a spectacular music building, and the six-story Rosenthal Library. The major classroom building, Powdermaker Hall, has the latest technology throughout. The administration is committed to making the college a home away from home for its students with over 100 clubs and teams. The only CUNY college that participates in NCAA Division II sports, Queens sponsors men's and women's teams and has some of the finest athletics facilities in the metropolitan area. The college continues to improve the Student Union; and embark on a variety of beautification projects. Academic programs are organized into four divisions, which offer both day and evening courses: Arts and Humanities; Mathematics and the Natural Sciences; the Social Sciences; and Education (Queens College educates more teachers than any other college in the New York City region). Queens College participates in CUNY's Macaulay Honors College, a challenging program open to the most academically gifted students, and offers qualified students its own honors programs in the arts and humanities, sciences, and social sciences. An Honors Center with lounges and labs is available for students participating in the college's various honors programs. The college's centers and institutes serve students and the larger community by addressing society's most important challenges, including cancer, pollution, and racism, as well as celebrating the borough's many ethnic communities. The college's arts scene is vibrant thanks to the Kupferberg Center for the Visual and Performing Arts, which brings together the college's academic departments in the arts (Music, Drama, Art, and Media Studies) and its museums (the Godwin-Ternbach, the Queens College Art Center, and the Louis Armstrong House Museum). The celebrated Evening Readings Series has brought some of the world's finest writers to campus. There is 1 undergraduate school and 1 graduate school. In addition to regional accreditation, Queens has baccalaureate program accreditation with ADA, NASM, NCATE, TEAC, APA, ACTFL, CEC, ELCC, AAHPERD, ADE, ASHA, CADE, ACS, AASLP, CAA, CAEP, ACEI, ACEND, IRA, NAEYC, NASP, NCSS, NCTE, NCTM, NSTA, and TESOL. The 92-acre campus is in an urban area 12 miles from Manhattan. Including any residence halls, there are 17 buildings.

STUDENT LIFE: 99% of undergraduates are from New York. Others are from 15 states, 90 foreign countries, and Canada. 70% are from public schools. 45% are White; 26% Asian American; 16% Hispanic. **Male To Female Ratio:** 1.5:1. The average age of freshmen is 19; all undergraduates, 24. 13% do not continue beyond their first year; 55% remain to graduate. **Housing:** 494 students can be accommodated in college housing, which includes coed dorms. On-campus housing is available on a first-come and first-served basis. 97% of students commute. Alcohol is not permitted. All students may keep cars.

FACULTY/CLASSROOMS: 52% of faculty are male; 48% are female. 85% do both. Graduate students teach 1% of introductory courses.

PROGRAMS OF STUDY: Queens confers B.A.,B.S., B.B.A., B.F.A. and B.Mus. degrees. Master's degrees are also awarded. Bachelor's degrees are awarded in AGRICULTURE (environmental studies), BIOLOGICAL SCIENCE (biology/biological science, environmental biology, neurosciences, and nutrition), BUSINESS (accounting, banking and finance, business administration and management, international business management, and labor studies), COMMUNICATIONS AND THE ARTS (art, art history and appreciation, Chinese, comparative literature, dance, dramatic arts, English, film arts, French, German, graphic design, Greek (modern), Hebrew, Italian, linguistics, media arts, music, music performance, Russian, Spanish, and studio art), COMPUTER AND PHYSICAL SCIENCE (actuarial science, chemistry, computer science, environmental geology, geol-

ogy, mathematics, and physics), EDUCATION (art education, early childhood education, home economics education, music education, physical education, and science education), ENGINEERING AND ENVIRONMENTAL DESIGN (environmental science), HEALTH PROFESSIONS (exercise science and speech pathology/audiology), SOCIAL SCIENCE (African studies, American studies, anthropology, classical/ancient civilization, East Asian studies, economics, family/consumer studies, history, home economics, interdisciplinary studies, Judaic studies, Latin American studies, philosophy, political science/government, psychology, religion, sociology, urban studies, and women's studies). Accounting, psychology, and economics have the largest enrollments.

ACTIVITIES: 1% of men and 1% of women belong to 3 national fraternities. There are 81 groups on campus, including art, band, choir, chorus, communications, computers, dance, debate, drama, environmental, ethnic, film, gay, honors, international, jazz band, literary magazine, musical theater, newspaper, orchestra, political, professional, radio and TV, religious, social, social service, student government, symphony, and yearbook. Popular campus events include Fall and Spring Campus Fests, Spring Job Fair and Transfer Student Day. **Sports:** There are 9 intercollegiate sports for men and 12 for women, and 9 intramural sports for men and 9 for women. Facilities include a gym complex, swimming pool, dance studios, weight rooms, outdoor quarter-mile track, soccer, lacrosse, and baseball fields, and 18 tennis courts. **Graduates:** From July 1, 2013 to June 30, 2014, 3207 bachelor's degrees were awarded. The most popular majors were psychology (18%), accounting (14%), and economics/ sociology (10%). 55 companies recruited on campus in 2013-2014. In an average class, 4% graduate in 3 years or less, 25% graduate in 4 years or less, 45% graduate in 5 years or less, and 55% graduate in 6 years or less. Of the 2013 graduating class, 25% were enrolled in graduate school within 6 months of graduation, and 67% were employed.

SERVICES: Counseling and information services are available, as is tutoring in most subjects. There is a reader service for the blind. **Library/Resources:** The library contains 1.1 million volumes, 978,608 microform items, 41,563 audio/video tapes/CDs/DVDs, and subscribes to 42,000 periodicals including electronic. Computerized library services include interlibrary loans, database searching, Internet access, and Wi-Fi capability. Special learning facilities include an art gallery, radio station, TV station, a small museums, and a theater. **Physically Challenged Students:** All of the campus is accessible. Facilities include wheelchair ramps, elevators, special parking, specially equipped restrooms, special class scheduling, lowered drinking fountains, lowered telephones, and special housing. **Special:** Queens offers co-op programs, cross-registration with other CUNY campuses, internships in business, liberal arts, journalism, and social sciences, study abroad, work-study, accelerated degrees, dual majors, pass/fail options, and nondegree study. There are preprofessional programs in engineering, law, and prehealth. The SEEK program provides financial and educational resources for underprepared freshmen. There are 15 national honor societies, including Phi Beta Kappa, and a freshman honors program. **Visiting:** There are regularly scheduled orientations for prospective students, including information sessions and a campus tour. Visitors may sit in on classes. To schedule a visit, contact the Admissions Office. **Campus Safety and Security:** Measures include 24-hour foot and vehicle patrol and emergency notification system. There are emergency telephones, lighted pathways/sidewalks, and controlled access to dorms/residences.

REQUIREMENTS: The SAT is required. High school preparation should include 4 years each of English and social studies, 3 each of math and foreign language, and 2 of lab science. A GPA of 3.0 is required. AP and CLEP credits are accepted.To graduate, students must complete 120 credits with a minimum GPA of 2.0. They must fulfill requirements in the major and liberal arts core curriculum. Effective Fall 2013, entering freshmen and transfer students will follow a revised liberal arts curriculum to meet the requirements of the CUNY Pathways Initiative. The Pathways General Education framework is common to all CUNY colleges. This guarantees that the core curriculum requirements fulfilled at one CUNY college will carry over seamesly if a student transfers to another CUNY college. **Procedure:** Freshmen are admitted fall and spring. Entrance exams should be taken in the spring of the junior year or the fall of the senior year. There are early admissions and rolling admissions plans. Application deadlines are open. Application fee is $65. Notifications are sent February 1. **Transfer Students:** 3431 transfer students enrolled in 2013-2014. Admissions requirements vary depending on the number of credits to be transferred; students should consult with the Admissions Office. 45 of 120 credits required for the bachelor's degree must be completed at Queens. **International Students:** There are 736 international students enrolled. They must take the TOEFL with a minimum score of 600 on the paper-based TOEFL (PBT) or 62 on the Internet-based version (iBT). They must also take the SAT or the CUNY Skills Assessment Test.

ADMISSIONS: 37% of the 2014-2015 applicants were accepted. The SAT scores for the 2014-2015 freshman class were: Critical Reading--35% below 500, 47% between 500 and 599, 13% between 600 and 699, and 5% between 700 and 800; Math--6% below 500, 60% between 500 and 599, 28% between 600 and 699, and 6% between 700 and 800; Writing--39% below 500, 45% between 500 and 599, 13% between 600 and 699, and 4% between 700 and 800. **Admissions Contact:** Dr. Vincent J. Angrisani, Executive Director of Admissions, Marketing, and Sholarship. E-Mail: *vincent.angrisani@qc.cuny.edu* Web: *http:/www.qc.cuny.edu/admissions*

FINANCIAL AID: In 2014-2015, 65% of all full-time freshmen and 46% of continuing full-time students received some form of financial aid. 68% of all full-time freshmen and 46% of continuing full-time students received need-based aid. The average freshman award was $4,500. Need-based scholarships or need-based grants averaged $6,000; need-based self-help aid (loans and jobs) averaged $4,857; and non-need-based athletic scholarships averaged $5,000. 2% of undergraduate students work part-time. Average annual earnings from campus work are $3474. The average financial indebtedness of the 2014 graduate was $20,000. The FAFSA and the state aid form are required. The priority date for freshman financial aid applications for fall entry is February 15.

RENSSELAER POLYTECHNIC INSTITUTE D-3
www.rpi.edu

Troy, NY 12180	(518) 276-6216
	(800) 448-6562
Fax: (518) 276-4072	Email: admissions@rpi.edu
Full-time: 3819 men, 1604 women	Faculty: 404; I, +$
Part-time: 21 men, 8 women	Ph.D.s: 99%
Graduate: 1112 men, 431 women	Student/Faculty: 15 to 1
Year: semesters, summer session	Tuition: $47,909
Room & Board: $13,620	Freshman Class: 16150 applied, 6654 accepted, 1411 enrolled
SAT CR/M: 660/720 ACT: 29	CEEB CODE: 2757
Application Deadline: January 15	MOST COMPETITIVE

Rensselaer Polytechnic Institute, founded in 1824, is a private institution that offers bachelor's, master's and doctoral degrees in engineering, the sciences, information technology, architecture, management, and the humanities and social sciences. Institute programs serve undergraduates, graduate students, and working professionals around the world. Figures in the above capsule and in this profile are approximate. There are 5 undergraduate schools and 5 graduate schools. In addition to regional accreditation, Rensselaer has baccalaureate program accreditation with AACSB, ABET, NAAB, AAAHC, and ACS. The 295-acre campus is in a suburban area 10 miles north of Albany. Including any residence halls, there are 200 buildings.

STUDENT LIFE: 66% of undergraduates are from out of state, mostly the Northeast. Students are from 49 states, 63 foreign countries, and Canada. 71% are from public schools. 65% are White. **Male To Female Ratio:** 0.4:1. The average age of freshmen is 18; all undergraduates, 20. 7% do not continue beyond their first year; 85% remain to graduate. **Housing:** 3400 students can be accommodated in college housing, which includes single-sex and coed dorms, on-campus apartments, and married student housing. In addition, there are fraternity houses. On-campus housing is available on a first-come, first-served basis, and is available on a lottery system for upperclassmen. 57% of students live on campus. Upperclassmen may keep cars.

FACULTY/CLASSROOMS: 77% of faculty are male; 23% are female.

No introductory courses are taught by graduate students. The average class size in an introductory lecture is 35; in a laboratory is 18; and in a regular course is 28.

PROGRAMS OF STUDY: Rensselaer confers B.S., and B.Arch. degrees. Master's and Doctoral degrees are also awarded. Bachelor's degrees are awarded in BIOLOGICAL SCIENCE (biochemistry, biology/biological science, and biophysics), BUSINESS (management information systems, management science, and recreation and leisure services), COMMUNICATIONS AND THE ARTS (communications and media arts), COMPUTER AND PHYSICAL SCIENCE (applied physics, chemistry, computer science, geology, hydrogeology, mathematics, physics, and science technology), ENGINEERING AND ENVIRONMENTAL DESIGN (aeronautical engineering, architecture, biomedical engineering, chemical engineering, civil engineering, computer engineering, construction engineering, electrical/electronics engineering, engineering, engineering physics, environmental engineering, industrial engineering, materials engineering, mechanical engineering, and nuclear engineering), HEALTH PROFESSIONS (premedicine), SOCIAL SCIENCE (economics, interdisciplinary studies, philosophy, prelaw, and psychology). Engineering, sciences, and architecture are the strongest academically. General engineering, computer science, and management have the largest enrollments.

ACTIVITIES: 30% of men and 1% of women belong to 1 local and 31 national fraternities; 16% of women belong to 1 local and 4 national sororities. There are 161 groups on campus, including Biomedical Engineering Society, Entrepreneurship, Finance, Rensselaer Biotechnology Students Association, art, Astrophysical Society, band, cheerleading, chess, choir, chorale, chorus, computers, dance, drama, drill team, environmental, ethnic, film, gay, honors, international, jazz band, literary magazine, musical theater, orchestra, pep band, photography, political, professional, radio and TV, religious, social, social service, student government, and symphony. Popular campus events include Union Program and Activities Committees-Concerts, Comedy, Cinema , Winter Carnival, Big Red Freak-out. **Sports:** There are 12 intercollegiate sports for men and 11 for women, and 22 intramural sports for men and 21 for women. Facilities include a field house, pool, stadium, 5 gyms, a sports and recreation center, several playing fields, 2 weight rooms, a fitness center, 6 tennis courts, 7 handball/squash courts, 3 artificial turf fields, an indoor track, an ice hockey rink, a stadium and a arena. **Graduates:** From July 1, 2013 to June 30, 2014, 1244 bachelor's degrees were awarded. The most popular majors were engineering (53%), computer science (9%), and management (7%). 370 companies recruited on campus in 2013-2014. In an average class, 60% graduate in 4 years or less, 83% graduate in 5 years or less, and 84% graduate in 6 years or less. Of the 2013 graduating class, 22% were enrolled in graduate school within 6 months of graduation, and 49% were employed.

SERVICES: Counseling and information services are available, as is tutoring in every subject. There is a reader service for the blind, and remedial math, reading, and writing. There is a writing center and an advising and learning assistance center. **Library/Resources:** The 2 libraries contain 476,510 volumes, 125,616 microform items, 137,094 audio/video tapes/CDs/DVDs, and subscribe to 21,036 periodicals including electronic. Computerized library services include interlibrary loans, database searching, Internet access, and Wi-Fi capability. Special learning facilities include an art gallery, radio station, TV station, an observatory. **Physically Challenged Students:** Facilities include wheelchair ramps, elevators, special parking, specially equipped restrooms, special class scheduling, lowered drinking fountains, and lowered telephones. **Special:** Rensselaer offers co-op programs, internships, study abroad/exchange program, and pass/fail options are available. Students may pursue dual and student-designed majors, a 3-2 engineering degree with more than 40 universities, 2-2 agreements, an accelerated degree program in physician-scientist, law and MBA. There are 14 national honor societies and 8 departmental honors programs. **Visiting:** There are regularly scheduled orientations for prospective students, Monday-Friday. Info session at 9 am, tour 10 am M-F 8:30-5:00 pm, and Saturday 10 am March-Nov only. There are guides for informal visits and visitors may sit in on classes. To schedule a visit, contact the Admissions Office. **Campus Safety and Security:** Measures include 24-hour foot and vehicle patrol, self-defense education, and security escort services. There are shuttle buses, emergency telephones, lighted pathways/sidewalks, card-access residence halls, on-campus bicycle patrol, and a student volunteer program.

REQUIREMENTS: The SAT or ACT is required. SAT subject tests in critical reading, math and science are required for accelerated-program applicants or ACT, which must include the optional writing component in lieu of SAT and SAT. AP credits are accepted. Important factors in the admissions decision are advanced placement or honors courses, recommendations by school officials, and leadership record. For graduation, students must earn at least 124 credits in all majors except engineering (128 needed) and the B.Arch. Program (168 needed). The core curriculum includes 48 credits in math, science, humanities, and social sciences. Students must maintain a minimum GPA of 1.8 and must fulfill a writing requirement. **Procedure:** Freshmen are admitted fall, spring, and summer. Entrance exams should be taken in the junior or senior year. There are early decision and deferred admissions plans. Early decision applications should be filed by November 1; regular applications, by January 15 for fall entry; and November 1 for spring entry, along with a $70 fee. Notification of early decision is sent December 14; regular decision, March 8. 340 early decision candidates were accepted for the 2014-2015 class. 3787 applicants were on the 2014 waiting list; 2475 were admitted. Applications are accepted on-line. **Transfer Students:** 126 transfer students enrolled in 2013-2014. Applicants should have completed 12 or more transferable college credits, and must be in good academic standing at the institutions they are attending or attended. 60 of 120 credits required for the bachelor's degree must be completed at Rensselaer. **International Students:** There are 396 international students enrolled. The school actively recruits these students. They must take the TOEFL with a minimum score of 570 on the paper-based TOEFL (PBT) or 88 on the Internet-based version (iBT). They must also take the SAT or ACT.

ADMISSIONS: 41% of the 2014-2015 applicants were accepted. The SAT scores for the 2014-2015 freshman class were: Critical Reading--1% below 500, 17% between 500 and 599, 48% between 600 and 699, and 34% between 700 and 800; Math--3% between 500 and 599, 33% between 600 and 699, and 64% between 700 and 800. The ACT scores were 5% between 21 and 23, 18% between 24 and 26, 21% between 27 and 28, and 56% above 28. 88% of the current freshmen were in the top fifth of their class; 98% were in the top two fifths. 43 freshmen graduated first in their class. **Admissions Contact:** Paul P Marthers, VP Enrollment. E-Mail: *admissions@rpi.edu* Web: *www.rpi.edu*

FINANCIAL AID: In 2014-2015, 93% of all full-time freshmen and 95% of continuing full-time students received some form of financial aid. 70% of all full-time freshmen and 65% of continuing full-time students received need-based aid. The average freshman award was $35,747. Need-based scholarships or need-based grants averaged $30,108; need-based self-help aid (loans and jobs) averaged $5,656; non-need-based athletic scholarships averaged $50,841; and other non-need-based awards and non-need-based scholarships averaged $14,902. Average annual earnings from campus work are $2500. The average financial indebtedness of the 2014 graduate was $32,000. Rensselaer is a member of CSS. The CSS/Profile and FAFSA are required. The priority date for freshman financial aid applications for fall entry is February 1.

Roberts Wesleyan College, founded in 1866, by leaders of the Free Methodist Church, is an innovative and distinctive Christian college offering excellence in liberal arts and professional programs. There are 2 undergraduate schools and 2 graduate schools. In addition to regional accreditation, Roberts has baccalaureate program accreditation with CSWE, NASAD, NASM, IACBE, CCNE, NASP, and RATE. The 75-acre campus is in a suburban area 8 miles southwest of Rochester. Including any residence halls, there are 32 buildings.

STUDENT LIFE: 89% of undergraduates are from New York. Others are from 24 states, 20 foreign countries, and Canada. 72% are White; 11% African American. 62% are Protestant; 17% claim no religious affiliation; 16% Catholic. **Male To Female Ratio:** 2.5:1. The average age of freshmen is 19; all undergraduates, 28. 20% do not continue beyond their first year; 60% remain to graduate. **Housing:** 792 students can be accommodated in college housing, which includes single-sex dorms, on-campus apartments, and off-campus apartments. On-campus housing is guaranteed for all 4 years. 65% of students live on campus; of those, 70% remain on campus on weekends. Alcohol is not permitted. All students may keep cars.

FACULTY/CLASSROOMS: 43% of faculty are male; 57% are female. 85% teach undergraduates. No introductory courses are taught by graduate students. The average class size in an introductory lecture is 30; in a laboratory is 15; and in a regular course is 23.

PROGRAMS OF STUDY: Roberts confers B.A., and B.S. degrees. Associate and Master's degrees are also awarded. Bachelor's degrees are awarded in BIOLOGICAL SCIENCE (biochemistry, biology/adolescence education, biology/biological science, biotechnology, and forensic science), BUSINESS (accounting, business administration and management, international business management, and marketing), COMMUNICATIONS AND THE ARTS (applied art, applied music, art, communication, English, graphic design, music, music performance, piano performance, Spanish, studio art, and vocal performance), COMPUTER AND PHYSICAL SCIENCE (chemistry, chemistry/adolescence education, digital arts/technology, mathematics, and physics), EDUCATION (early childhood education, elementary education, English education, mathematics education, music education, physical education, secondary education, and special education), ENGINEERING AND ENVIRONMENTAL DESIGN (biomedical equipment technology and preengineering), HEALTH PROFESSIONS (biology, nursing, pharmacy, predentistry, premedicine, prepharmacy, prephysical therapy, and preveterinary science), SOCIAL SCIENCE (biblical studies, Christian studies, criminal justice, history, humanities, interdisciplinary studies, liberal arts/general studies, philosophy, prelaw, psychology, religion, and social work). Music, education, nursing, and social work are the strongest academically. Elementary education, nursing, and music have the largest enrollments.

ACTIVITIES: There are no fraternities or sororities. Groups on campus include band, choir, chorale, chorus, dance, drama, environmental, ethnic, honors, international, jazz band, musical theater, newspaper, opera, orchestra, pep band, photography, religious, social, social service, student government, symphony, and yearbook. Popular campus events include Winter Weekend, Spring Formal, Talent and Variety Shows. **Sports:** There are 7 intercollegiate sports for men and 7 for women, and 6 intramural sports for men and 6 for women. Facilities include an athletic center with facilities for basketball, volleyball, tennis, badminton, track, soccer, weight lifting, walleyball, racquetball, exercise machines room, flag football, ultimate Frisbee, and swimming. **Graduates:** From July 1, 2013 to June 30, 2014, 408 bachelor's degrees were awarded. The most popular majors were nursing (20%), education (16%), and psychology (9%). In an average class, 49% graduate in 4 years or less, 61% graduate in 5 years or less, and 63% graduate in 6 years or less. Of the 2013 graduating class, 24% were enrolled in graduate school within 6 months of graduation, and 93% were employed.

SERVICES: Counseling and information services are available, as is tutoring in every subject, note takers for the hearing impaired are available. There is a reader service for the blind, and remedial math, reading, and writing. **Library/Resources:** The library contains 144,199 volumes, 169,823 microform items, 4,462 audio/video tapes/CDs/DVDs, and subscribes to 35,000 periodicals including electronic. Computerized library services include interlibrary loans, database searching, Internet access, and Wi-Fi capability. Special learning facil-

---

ROBERTS WESLEYAN COLLEGE   B-3
www.roberts.edu

Rochester, NY 14624	
	(585) 594-6400
	(800) 777-4792
Fax: (585) 594-6371	Email: anderson_JP@roberts.edu
Full-time: 385 men, 835 women	Faculty: 89
Part-time: 36 men, 80 women	Ph.D.s: 67%
Graduate: 84 men, 342 women	Student/Faculty: 14 to 1
Year: semesters, summer session	Tuition: $28,466
Room & Board: $9840	Freshman Class: 697 applied, 633 accepted, 256 enrolled
SAT CR/M: 553/548 ACT: 24	CEEB CODE: 2759
Application Deadline: February 1	COMPETITIVE+

ities include an art gallery. **Physically Challenged Students:** 85% of the campus is accessible. Facilities include wheelchair ramps, elevators, special parking, specially equipped restrooms, special class scheduling, lowered drinking fountains, and lowered telephones. **Special:** Students may cross-register with members of the Rochester Area Colleges consortium. Internships, study abroad in 8 countries, a Washington semester, co-op programs, B.A.-B.S. degrees, dual majors, and 3-2 engineering degrees with Clarkson University, Rensselaer Polytechnic Institute, and Rochester Institute of Technology are available. 3-4 Pharmacy with University at Buffalo. Nondegree study and credit for life, military, and work experience are also offered. The organizational management program, geared to adults, consists of 4-hour weekly sessions, with reliance on out-of-class work. There are a freshman honors program and 100 departmental honors programs. **Visiting:** There are regularly scheduled orientations for prospective students, including a campus tour, class visits, admissions overview, meetings with faculty, and a financial aid presentation. There are guides for informal visits, visitors may sit in on classes, and stay overnight. To schedule a visit, contact the Admissions Office. **Campus Safety and Security:** Measures include 24-hour foot and vehicle patrol, emergency notification system, self-defense education, and security escort services. There are emergency telephones, lighted pathways/sidewalks, controlled access to dorms/residences, personal-safety education programs.

REQUIREMENTS: The SAT or ACT is required. Applicants must be graduates of an accredited secondary school. The GED is accepted. At least 12 academic credits are required, including 4 years of English and 2 years each of math and science. A foreign language and 3 years of social studies are recommended. The chosen major may modify requirements. An essay is required, and an interview is recommended. Roberts requires applicants to be in the upper 50% of their class. A GPA of 2.5 is required. AP and CLEP credits are accepted. Important factors in the admissions decision are advanced placement or honors courses, personality/intangible qualities, and extracurricular activities record.To graduate, students must complete a minimum of 124 credit hours, with a minimum of 30 hours in the major. Required courses include first-year experience, phys ed, modern technology, world issues, speech, writing, history, Bible, and philosophy. **Procedure:** Freshmen are admitted fall, spring, and summer. There are deferred admissions and rolling admissions plans. Applications should be filed by February 1 for fall entry; December 1 for spring entry. Notification is sent on a rolling basis. Applications are accepted on-line. Application fees are waived if application is completed online. **Transfer Students:** 101 transfer students enrolled in 2013-2014. Applicants must submit transcripts from all previous institutions attended as well as the application and a recommendation. Credit is usually accepted for courses with grade C or better. 30 of 124 credits required for the bachelor's degree must be completed at Roberts. **International Students:** There are 52 international students enrolled. The school actively recruits these students. They must take the TOEFL with a minimum score of 540 on the paper-based TOEFL (PBT) or 75 on the Internet-based version (iBT), or take the IELTS with a minimum score of 6. International students who take the SAT or ACT and score high enough do not need to take the TOEFL or IELTS.

ADMISSIONS: 91% of the 2014-2015 applicants were accepted. The SAT scores for the 2014-2015 freshman class were: Critical Reading-38% below 500, 46% between 500 and 599, 12% between 600 and 699, and 4% between 700 and 800; Math--40% below 500, 37% between 500 and 599, 21% between 600 and 699, and 2% between 700 and 800; Writing--55% below 500, 35% between 500 and 599, 8% between 600 and 699, and 2% between 700 and 800. The ACT scores were 23% below 21, 22% between 21 and 23, 18% between 24 and 26, 22% between 27 and 28, and 15% above 28. 42% of the current freshmen were in the top fifth of their class; 80% were in the top two fifths. 4 freshmen graduated first in their class. **Admissions Contact:** JP Anderson, Associate Vice President of UG Admiss.. E-Mail: *anderson_JP@roberts.edu* Web: *www.roberts.edu*

FINANCIAL AID: In 2014-2015, 98% of all full-time freshmen and 98% of continuing full-time students received some form of financial aid. 90% of all full-time freshmen and 90% of continuing full-time students received need-based aid. The average freshman award was $26,534. Need-based scholarships or need-based grants averaged

$21,096; need-based self-help aid (loans and jobs) averaged $6,466; non-need-based athletic scholarships averaged $9,143; and other non-need-based awards and non-need-based scholarships averaged $13,502. 35% of undergraduate students work part-time. Average annual earnings from campus work are $1080. Roberts is a member of CSS. The FAFSA, and TAP (New York residents only) is required. The priority date for freshman financial aid applications for fall entry is March 15. The deadline for filing freshman financial aid applications for fall entry is rolling.

ROCHESTER INSTITUTE OF TECHNOLOGY   B-3
www.rit.edu

Rochester, NY 14623   **(585) 475-6631**
                                                  n/av
Fax: (585) 475-7424   **Email: admissions@rit.edu**
Full-time: 8531 men, 4212 women   **Faculty:** IIA, ++$
Part-time: 950 men, 531 women   **Ph.D.s:** 70%
Graduate: 1959 men, 1023 women   **Student/Faculty:** 13 to 1
Year: quarters, summer session   **Tuition:** $32,037
Room & Board: $10,413   **Freshman Class:** 14097
                                        applied, 8465 accepted,
                                        2612 enrolled
SAT or ACT: required   **CEEB CODE:** 2760
Application Deadline: March 1   **VERY COMPETITIVE**

Rochester Institute of Technology (RIT) is one of the world's leading career-oriented, technological universities. RIT offers more than ninety undergraduate programs in areas such as engineering, computing, information technology, engineering technology, business, hospitality, science, art, design, photography, biomedical sciences, game design and development, and the liberal arts including psychology, advertising and public relations, and public policy. Students may choose from more than ninety different minors to develop personal and professional interests that complement their academic program. Experiential education is integrated into many programs through cooperative education, internships, study abroad, and undergraduate research. As home to the National Technical Institute for the Deaf (NTID), RIT is a leader in providing access services for deaf and hard-of-hearing students. RIT enrolls students from every state and more than one-hundred countries. Figures in the above capsule and in this profile are approximate. There are 9 undergraduate schools and 9 graduate schools. In addition to regional accreditation, RIT has baccalaureate program accreditation with AACSB, ABET, ADA, CAHEA, CSAB, CSWE, FIDER, NASAD, and CAAHEP. The 1300-acre campus is in a suburban area 5 miles south of Rochester. Including any residence halls, there are 195 buildings.

STUDENT LIFE: 51% of undergraduates are from New York. Others are from 50 states, 107 foreign countries, and Canada. 85% are from public schools. 70% are White. **Male To Female Ratio:** 0.5:1. The average age of freshmen is 18; all undergraduates, 21. 8% do not continue beyond their first year; 69% remain to graduate. **Housing:** 7144 students can be accommodated in college housing, which includes single-sex and coed dorms, on-campus apartments, and married student housing. In addition, there are honors houses, special-interest houses, fraternity houses, and sorority houses. On-campus housing is guaranteed for the freshman year only, is available on a first-come, and first-served basis. 68% of students live on campus; of those, 90% remain on campus on weekends. All students may keep cars.

FACULTY/CLASSROOMS: 65% of faculty are male; 35% are female. 97% teach undergraduates, 3% do research, and 90% do both. No introductory courses are taught by graduate students. The average class size in an introductory lecture is 30; in a laboratory is 16; and in a regular course is 20.

PROGRAMS OF STUDY: RIT confers B.S. and B.F.A. degrees. Associate, Master's, and Doctoral degrees are also awarded. Bachelor's degrees are awarded in BIOLOGICAL SCIENCE (biochemistry, bioinformatics, biology/biological science, biotechnology, and nutrition), BUSINESS (accounting, banking and finance, business administration and management, business systems analysis, hotel/motel and restaurant management, international business management, management information systems, management science, marketing management, and tourism), COMMUNICATIONS AND THE ARTS (animation, applied art, ceramic art and design, communications, communications technology, crafts, design, film arts, fine arts, glass, graphic design, illustration, industrial design, metal/jewelry, photography, publishing, sculpture, studio art, telecommunications, and video), COMPUTER AND PHYSICAL SCIENCE (applied mathematics, chemistry, computer mathematics, computer science, information sciences and systems, mathematics, physics, polymer science, software engineering, statistics, and systems analysis), EDUCATION (education of the deaf and hearing impaired), ENGINEERING AND ENVIRONMENTAL DESIGN (aerospace studies, biomedical engineering, chemical engineering, civil engineering technology, computer engineering, computer graphics, computer technology, electrical/electronics engineering, electrical/electronics engineering technology, engineering, engineering technology, environmental engineering technology, environmental science, furniture design, graphic arts technology, graphic and printing production, industrial engineering, interior design, manufacturing engineering, manufacturing technology, materials science, mechanical engineering, mechanical engineering technology, military science, printing technology, and woodworking), HEALTH PROFESSIONS (allied health, physician's assistant, predentistry, premedicine, preveterinary science, and ultrasound technology), SOCIAL SCIENCE (criminal justice, dietetics, economics, food production/management/services, interpreter for the deaf, philosophy, prelaw, psychology, and public affairs). Mechanical engineering, computer science, film and animation are the strongest academically. Engineering, information technology, and photography have the largest enrollments.

ACTIVITIES: 5% of men belong to 17 national fraternities; 5% of women belong to 12 national sororities. There are 207 groups on campus, including art, band, cheerleading, chess, choir, chorale, chorus, computers, dance, drama, environmental, ethnic, film, gay, gospel choir, honors, international, jazz band, literary magazine, newspaper, orchestra, pep band, photography, political, professional, radio and TV, religious, social, social service, and student government. Popular campus events include Fall, Spring, and Winter Weekends and Martin Luther King Celebration. **Sports:** There are 11 intercollegiate sports for men and 12 for women, and 13 intramural sports for men and 13 for women. Facilities include 3 gyms, an ice rink, 2 swimming pools, 9 tennis courts, a field house, athletic fields, and a student life center with 8 racquetball courts, dance facilities, weight training facilities, and an indoor track. **Graduates:** From July 1, 2013 to June 30, 2014, 2432 bachelor's degrees were awarded. The most popular majors were business administration (7%), mechanical engineering (5%), and information technology (5%). 900 companies recruited on campus in 2013-2014. In an average class, 69% graduate in 6 years or less. Of the 2013 graduating class, 15% were enrolled in graduate school within 6 months of graduation, and 80% were employed.

SERVICES: Counseling and information services are available, as is tutoring in most subjects. There is a reader service for the blind. There are comprehensive support services for students with physical or learning disabilities and for first-generation college students. **Library/Resources:** The library contains 422,281 volumes, 498,703 microform items, 54,935 audio/video tapes/CDs/DVDs, and subscribes to 21,208 periodicals including electronic. Computerized library services include interlibrary loans, database searching, Internet access, and Wi-Fi capability. Special learning facilities include an art gallery, radio station, TV station, a computer chip manufacturing facility, a student-operated restaurant, an electronic prepress lab, an imaging science facility, and an observatory. **Physically Challenged Students:** 95% of the campus is accessible. Facilities include wheelchair ramps, elevators, special parking, specially equipped restrooms, special class scheduling, lowered drinking fountains, lowered telephones, special housing. **Special:** RIT offers internships in social science and allied health majors, and cooperative education programs with 1900 co-op employers. Cooperative education is required or recommended in most programs and provides full-time paid work experience. Cross-registration with Rochester-area colleges is available. There are accelerated dual degree (BS/MS, BS/ME, BS/MBA) programs in science, engineering, public policy, math, computer science,

materials science, imaging science, and business. Students may study abroad in 15 countries, and student-designed majors are permitted in applied arts and sciences. There is an Honors Program in general education and home colleges. There are 6 national honor societies, a freshman honors program, and 7 departmental honors programs. **Visiting:** There are regularly scheduled orientations for prospective students, including academic advising and information on housing and student services. There are guides for informal visits, visitors may sit in on classes, and stay overnight. To schedule a visit, contact the Admissions Receptionist. **Campus Safety and Security:** Measures include 24-hour foot and vehicle patrol, emergency notification system, self-defense education, and security escort services. There are shuttle buses, emergency telephones, lighted pathways/sidewalks, and controlled access to dorms/residences.

REQUIREMENTS: The SAT or ACT is required. Applicants must be high school graduates or have a GED certificate. Applicants are required to submit an essay, and an interview is recommended. The School of Art, the School of Design, and the School for American Crafts emphasize a required portfolio of artwork. Required high school math and science credits vary by program, with 3 years in each area generally acceptable. RIT requires applicants to be in the upper 50% of their class. AP and CLEP credits are accepted. Important factors in the admissions decision are advanced placement or honors courses, recommendations by school officials, and extracurricular activities record. Students must have a GPA of 2.0 and have completed 180 quarter credit hours to graduate. Distribution requirements include 36 credits in the liberal arts (writing, humanities, and social sciences). B.S. programs also require a minimum of 20 quarter credit hours in science and math. There are no general science or math requirements for the B.F.A. programs in art, design, photography, or film/video. **Procedure:** Freshmen are admitted to all sessions. Entrance exams should be taken during the junior or senior year. There are early decision and deferred admissions plans. Early decision applications should be filed by December 1; regular applications, by March 1 for fall entry, along with a $50 fee. Notification of early decision is sent January 15; regular decision, March 15. applicants were on the 2014 waiting list; were admitted. Applications are accepted online. **Transfer Students:** 1079 transfer students enrolled in 2013-2014. Transfer students must have a GPA of 2.5 for admission to most programs; those with fewer than 30 college credits must supply a high school transcript. Other requirements vary by program. 45 of 180 credits required for the bachelor's degree must be completed at RIT. **International Students:** There are 545 international students enrolled. The school actively recruits these students. They must take the TOEFL with a minimum score of 550 on the paper-based TOEFL (PBT) or 79 on the Internet-based version (iBT). They must also take the SAT or ACT.

ADMISSIONS: 60% of the 2014-2015 applicants were accepted. 60% of the current freshmen were in the top fifth of their class; 85% were in the top two fifths. **Admissions Contact:** Daniel Shelley, Director of Admissions. E-Mail: *admissions@rit.edu* Web: *www.rit.edu*

FINANCIAL AID: In 2014-2015, 85% of all full-time freshmen and 89% of continuing full-time students received some form of financial aid. 81% of all full-time freshmen and 83% of continuing full-time students received need-based aid. The average freshman award was $18,900. Need-based scholarships or need-based grants averaged $16,500; and need-based self-help aid (loans and jobs) averaged $5,000. 70% of undergraduate students work part-time. Average annual earnings from campus work are $2500. The average financial indebtedness of the 2014 graduate was $23,800. The FAFSA is required. The priority date for freshman financial aid applications for fall entry is March 1.

RUSSELL SAGE COLLEGE   D-3
www.sage.edu

Troy, NY 12180	(518) 244-2217
	(888) Very-Sage
Fax: (518) 244-6880	Email: rscadm@sage.edu
Full-time: 10 men, 772 women	Faculty: 61; IIA
Part-time: 9 men, 32 women	Ph.D.s: 90%
Graduate: n/av	Student/Faculty: 10 to 1
Year: semesters, summer session	Tuition: $28,000
Room & Board: $11,370	Freshman Class: n/av
	CEEB CODE: 2764
Application Deadline: n/av	COMPETITIVE

Russell Sage College is a comprehensive college for women nestled within the historic district of Troy, NY. RSC offers liberal arts and professional degree programs in an environment aimed at empowering students to become women of influence in their careers and their communities. Figures in the above capsule and in this profile are approximate. There are 2 undergraduate schools and 1 graduate school. In addition to regional accreditation, Russell Sage has baccalaureate program accreditation with ADA, APTA, NASAD, NCATE, NLN, and AOTA. The 14-acre campus is in an urban area 10 miles from Albany and Schenectady. Including any residence halls, there are 38 buildings.

STUDENT LIFE: 93% of undergraduates are from New York. Others are from 16 states, and 1 foreign countries. 67% are White; 12% race unknown. **Male To Female Ratio:** 42.3:1. The average age of freshmen is 18; all undergraduates, 21. 10% do not continue beyond their first year; 73% remain to graduate. **Housing:** 738 students can be accommodated in college housing, which includes single-sex dorms and on-campus apartments. In addition, there are language houses and special-interest houses. On-campus housing is guaranteed for all 4 years and is available on a lottery system for upperclassmen. 52% of students commute. Alcohol is not permitted. All students may keep cars.

FACULTY/CLASSROOMS: 28% of faculty are male; 72% are female. All teach and do research. No introductory courses are taught by graduate students. The average class size in an introductory lecture is 19; in a laboratory is 9; and in a regular course is 16.

PROGRAMS OF STUDY: Russell Sage confers B.A., and B.S. degrees. Master's degrees are also awarded. Bachelor's degrees are awarded in BIOLOGICAL SCIENCE (biochemistry, biology/biological science, and nutrition), COMMUNICATIONS AND THE ARTS (English, musical theater, and Spanish), COMPUTER AND PHYSICAL SCIENCE (chemistry and mathematics), EDUCATION (elementary education), ENGINEERING AND ENVIRONMENTAL DESIGN (environmental science), HEALTH PROFESSIONS (art therapy, nursing, occupational therapy, and physical therapy), SOCIAL SCIENCE (applied psychology, criminal justice, forensic studies, history, interdisciplinary studies, international studies, political science/government, psychology, and sociology). Nursing, nutrition, health sciences, education and psychology are the strongest academically. Health and rehabilitative sciences, education and psychology have the largest enrollments.

ACTIVITIES: There are no fraternities or sororities. There are 26 groups on campus, including choir, chorus, dance, drama, ethnic, gay, honors, literary magazine, musical theater, newspaper, political, religious, social, student government, and yearbook. Popular campus events include Spirit of Sage River Cruise, Rally Day, Sage Fest, and Family Weekend. **Sports:** There are 7 intercollegiate sports for men and 8 for women, and 7 intramural sports for men and 8 for women. Facilities include Neff Athletic Center, Robison Athletic Center, a weight and fitness center, swimming pool, tennis courts, a practice field, 2 gyms, and a large multipurpose room for indoor recreation. **Graduates:** From July 1, 2013 to June 30, 2014, 212 bachelor's degrees were awarded. The most popular majors were nursing (23%), health sciences (9%), and education (9%). 20 companies recruited on campus in 2013-2014. In an average class, 65% graduate in 4 years or less, 71% graduate in 5 years or less, and 73% graduate in 6 years or less. Of the 2013 graduating class, 32% were enrolled in graduate school within 6 months of graduation, and 65% were employed.

SERVICES: Counseling and information services are available, as is tutoring in most subjects. There is remedial math, reading, and writing. **Library/Resources:** The library contains 164,946 volumes, 18,514 microform items, 6,419 audio/video tapes/CDs/DVDs, and subscribes to 65,391 periodicals including electronic. Computerized library services include interlibrary loans and database searching. Special learning facilities include a **Physically Challenged Students:** 75% of the campus is accessible. Facilities include wheelchair ramps, elevators, and special parking. **Special:** Students may cross-register with the 14 area schools of the Hudson-Mohawk Association of Colleges. A theater major is offered in conjunction with Sage Theater Institute. Study abroad, internships, and work-study programs are available. RSC has several accelerated 5-year programs; 3 + 2 M.S., in Occupational Therapy, a 3-2 engineering degree with nearby Rensselaer Polytechnic Institute and our accelerated 4+3 D.P.T. program.

The college confers credit for life, military, or work experience. Non-degree study, student-designed majors, dual majors, and pass/fail options are also available. There are 14 national honor societies and a freshman honors program. **Visiting:** There are regularly scheduled orientations for prospective students, including meetings with faculty, a campus tour, a financial aid session, and an admissions interview. There are guides for informal visits, visitors may sit in on classes, and stay overnight. To schedule a visit, contact Thomas Barresi at rscadm@sage.edu. **Campus Safety and Security:** Measures include 24-hour foot and vehicle patrol, self-defense education, and security escort services. There are emergency telephones, lighted pathways/sidewalks, an evening escort service, and monitored video cameras.

REQUIREMENTS: Applicants must be graduates of an accredited secondary school or have a GED. A minimum of 16 academic units are required. An essay, for applicants still in high school, is required, and an interview is recommended. A GPA of 2.0 is required. AP and CLEP credits are accepted. Important factors in the admissions decision are advanced placement or honors courses, recommendations by school officials, leadership record, recommendations by alumni, parents or siblings attended your school, evidence of special talent, extracurricular activities record, and geographical diversity.A minimum of 120 credit hours is required for the baccalaureate degree. Students must complete at least half the major at Sage. Furthermore, 30 of the last 45 credits must be completed in residence (i.e. at Sage or through the Hudson Mohawk Association). Students must satisfy general education as well as major requirements and must maintain satisfactory standards of scholarship to be eligible for graduation. A Bachelor of Arts degree must include a minimum of 90 credit hours in the liberal arts. A Bachelor of Science degree must include a minimum of 60 credit hours in the liberal arts. Students must achieve a 2.2 grade point average in the major and a 2.0 overall cumulative grade point average. Some majors require a higher grade point average for graduation. The ultimate responsibility for fulfilling graduation requirements rests with the individual student. **Procedure:** Freshmen are admitted fall and spring. Entrance exams should be taken during spring of the junior year or fall of the senior year. There are early admissions, deferred admissions, and rolling admissions plans. Early decision applications should be filed by December 1, along with a $30 fee. Notification of early decision is sent December 15; regular decision, on a rolling basis. Applications are accepted on-line. **Transfer Students:** 84 transfer students enrolled in 2013-2014. Applicants must have a minimum GPA of 2.5. Interviews are strongly encouraged and may be required in some instances. 45 of 120 credits required for the bachelor's degree must be completed at Russell Sage. **International Students:** There are 4 international students enrolled. The school actively recruits these students. They must take the TOEFL. They must also take the SAT or ACT. for international applicants with English as their native language.

ADMISSIONS: Elizabeth Robertson, Associate Vice President for Admissions. E-Mail: *rscadm@sage.edu* Web: *www.sage.edu*

FINANCIAL AID: In 2014-2015, 94% of all full-time freshmen and 91% of continuing full-time students received some form of financial aid. 79% of all full-time freshmen and 74% of continuing full-time students received need-based aid. The FAFSA is required. Check with the school for current application deadlines.

SARAH LAWRENCE COLLEGE   D-5
www.sarahlawrence.edu

Bronxville, NY 10708	(914) 395-2510
	(800) 888-2858
Fax: (914) 395-2515	Email: slcadmit@alc.edu
Full-time: 325 men, 925 women	Faculty: IIB, +$
Part-time: 15 men, 65 women	Ph.D.s: n/av
Graduate: 55 men, 310 women	Student/Faculty: n/av
Year: semesters	Tuition: $37,000
Room & Board: $13,000	Freshman Class: n/av
	CEEB CODE: 2810
Application Deadline: n/av	HIGHLY COMPETITIVE

Sarah Lawrence College, established in 1926, is an independent institution conferring liberal arts degrees. The academic structure is based on the British don system. Students meet biweekly with professors in tutorials and are enrolled in small seminars. While there are no formal majors, students develop individual concentrations that are usually interdisciplinary. Figures in the above capsule and in this profile are approximate. There is one graduate school. The 41-acre campus is in a suburban area 15 miles north of midtown Manhattan. Including any residence halls, there are 50 buildings.

STUDENT LIFE: 81% of undergraduates are from out of state, mostly the Middle Atlantic. Students are from 46 states, 25 foreign countries, and Canada. 65% are from public schools. 70% are White. **Male To Female Ratio:** 3.3:1. The average age of freshmen is 18; all undergraduates, 20. 7% do not continue beyond their first year; 72% remain to graduate. **Housing:** 965 students can be accommodated in college housing, which includes single-sex and coed dorms and on-campus apartments. French Interest House, the Perkins Art Co-op, and the Good Life House. On-campus housing is guaranteed for all 4 years. 87% of students live on campus; of those, 90% remain on campus on weekends. Upperclassmen may keep cars.

FACULTY/CLASSROOMS: 49% of faculty are male; 51% are female. All teach and do research. No introductory courses are taught by graduate students. The average class size in a regular course is 11.

PROGRAMS OF STUDY: Sarah Lawrence confers B.A. degrees. Master's degrees are also awarded. Bachelor's degrees are awarded in BIOLOGICAL SCIENCE (biology/biological science), COMMUNICATIONS AND THE ARTS (art history and appreciation, classics, creative writing, dance, dramatic arts, English, film arts, fine arts, French, German, Greek, Italian, Latin, literature, music, Russian, Spanish, and visual and performing arts), COMPUTER AND PHYSICAL SCIENCE (chemistry and mathematics), HEALTH PROFESSIONS (premedicine), SOCIAL SCIENCE (anthropology, Asian/Oriental studies, economics, history, liberal arts/general studies, philosophy, political science/government, psychology, religion, Russian and Slavic studies, sociology, and women's studies).

ACTIVITIES: There are no fraternities or sororities. There are 30 groups on campus, including philosophy, human rights, art, choir, chorale, chorus, computers, dance, drama, ethnic, film, gay, international, jazz band, literary magazine, musical theater, newspaper, orchestra, photography, poetry, political, radio and TV, religious, social, social service, student government, and yearbook. Popular campus events include Mayfair. **Sports:** There are 5 intercollegiate sports for men and 6 for women, and 9 intramural sports for men and 9 for women. Facilities include a sports center with a gym, a jogging track, a 6-lane swimming pool, a rowing tank, a multipurpose studio, and 3 squash courts; a fitness center and weight room; tennis courts; and a number of open fields and lawns. Off-campus, the college has the use of a boat house, and stables.

SERVICES: Counseling and information services are available, as is tutoring in some subjects, writing There is a reader service for the blind. **Library/Resources:** The 3 libraries contain 282,676 volumes, 24,218 microform items, 9,319 audio/video tapes/CDs/DVDs, and subscribe to 916 periodicals including electronic. Computerized library services include interlibrary loans, database searching, and Internet access. Special learning facilities include an art gallery, radio station, a slide library with 75,000 slides of art and architecture, early childhood center, electronic music studio; music library, student-run theater and student-run art gallery. **Physically Challenged Students:** 50% of the campus is accessible. Facilities include wheelchair ramps, elevators, special parking, specially equipped restrooms, special class scheduling, lowered drinking fountains, and lowered telephones. **Special:** Internships are available in a variety of fields, with the school offering proximity to New York City art galleries and agencies. Study abroad in many countries, work-study programs, dual concentrations, a 3-2 engineering degree with Columbia, and a general degree may be pursued. All concentrations are self-designed and can be combined. **Visiting:** There are regularly scheduled orientations for prospective students, consisting of a full day of faculty and student panels, lectures, tours, and discussion with admissions officers, offered twice per year during the fall. There are guides for informal visits, visitors may sit in on classes, and stay overnight. To schedule a visit, contact the Admissions Office. **Campus Safety and Security:** Measures include 24-hour foot and vehicle patrol, self-defense education, and security escort services. There are shuttle buses, emergency telephones, and lighted pathways/sidewalks.

REQUIREMENTS: Important academic requirements are: secondary school record, teacher recommendation(s) and essay; class rank is considered. Nonacademic requirements include character and personality qualities; extracurricular activities, talent/ability, volunteer work, and work experience. Campus interview, alumnae relations, geographical residence, and minority status are considered. AP credits are accepted. Important factors in the admissions decision are recommendations by school officials, personality/intangible qualities, and extracurricular activities record. To graduate, students must complete 120 credit hours and meet distribution requirements in 3 of 4 academic areas, including history and social sciences, creative and performing arts, natural science and math, and humanities. Students must fulfill a first-year studies requirement in one of 18 areas and meet a phys ed requirement. Students must also take 2 lecture courses, where the average class size is 40. **Procedure:** Freshmen are admitted fall. There are early decision, early admissions, and deferred admissions plans. Early decision applications should be filed by November 15. The fall 2014 application fee was $50. Notification of early decision is sent December 15; regular decision, April 1. applicants were on the 2014 waiting list; were admitted. Applications are accepted on-line. **Transfer Students:** Applicants must submit high school and college transcripts, and a statement of good standing from prior institution(s). A GPA of 3.0 is required and transfer applicants must have a minimum of 30 credits completed, or the equivalent of 2 semesters of full-time college work. Also required are a $50 application fee, Admission Information Form (in-house Form 1), essays, a graded academic paper, and 2 teacher/faculty evaluations. An interview is recommended, but not required. November 15 is the application deadline for spring entry. 60 of 120 credits required for the bachelor's degree must be completed at Sarah Lawrence. **International Students:** The school actively recruits these students. They must take the TOEFL, or SAT II: English as a second language test.

ADMISSIONS: Dean of Admission. E-Mail: *slcadmit@alc.edu* Web: *www.sarahlawrence.edu*

FINANCIAL AID: Sarah Lawrence is a member of CSS. The CSS/Profile and FAFSA, and and non-custodial parent statement are required. Check with the school for current application deadlines.

SCHOOL OF VISUAL ARTS D-5
www.schoolofvisualarts.edu

New York, NY 10010	**(212) 592-2100**
	(800) 436-4204
Fax: (212) 592-2116	**Email:** admissions@sva.edu
Full-time: 1480 men, 1735 women	**Faculty:** n/av
Part-time: 50 men, 70 women	**Ph.Ds:** n/av
Graduate: 175 men, 160 women	**Student/Faculty:** n/av
Year: semesters, summer session	**Tuition:** $24,608
Room & Board: $12,500	**Freshman Class:** n/av
SAT or ACT: required	**CEEB CODE:** 2835
Application Deadline: February 1	**VERY COMPETITIVE**

The School of Visual Arts, established in 1947, is a private college of art and design conferring undergraduate and graduate degrees in fine and commercial arts. The figures in the above capsule and in this profile are approximate. There is one graduate school. In addition to regional accreditation, SVA has baccalaureate program accreditation with FIDER and NASAD. The campus is in an urban area in mid Manhattan. Including any residence halls, there are 14 buildings.

STUDENT LIFE: 55% of undergraduates are from out of state, mostly the Middle Atlantic. Students are from 47 states, 45 foreign countries, and Canada. 53% are White; 13% Asian American; 13% Foreign. **Male To Female Ratio:** 1.2:1. The average age of freshmen is 18; all undergraduates, 21. 16% do not continue beyond their first year; 66% remain to graduate. **Housing:** 1150 students can be accommodated in college housing, which includes single-sex and coed dorms. On-campus housing is available on a first-come and first-served basis. 70% of students commute. Alcohol is not permitted. All students may keep cars.

FACULTY/CLASSROOMS: 64% of faculty are male; 36% are female. 86% teach undergraduates, and 12% do both. No introductory courses are taught by graduate students. The average class size in a regular course is 20.

PROGRAMS OF STUDY: SVA confers B.F.A. degrees. Master's degrees are also awarded. Bachelor's degrees are awarded in COMMUNICATIONS AND THE ARTS (advertising, animation, film arts, fine arts, graphic design, illustration, photography, video, and visual effects), ENGINEERING AND ENVIRONMENTAL DESIGN (computer graphics and interior design). Visual, critical studies, computer art, computer animation and special effects are the strongest academically. Graphic design, film/video and photograph have the largest enrollments.

ACTIVITIES: There are no fraternities or sororities. There are 20 groups on campus, including art, drama, ethnic, film, gay, honors, international, literary magazine, photography, political, professional, radio and TV, religious, social, social service, student government, and yearbook. Popular campus events include Annual Ski Trip, and a Halloween Party. **Sports:** There is no sports program at SVA. **Graduates:** From July 1, 2013 to June 30, 2014, 631 bachelor's degrees were awarded. The most popular majors were graphic design (24%), photography (17%), and film and video (11%). 50 companies recruited on campus in 2013-2014. In an average class, 58% graduate in 4 years or less, 65% graduate in 5 years or less, and 66% graduate in 6 years or less. Of the 2013 graduating class, 6% were enrolled in graduate school within 6 months of graduation, and 76% were employed.

SERVICES: There is remedial reading and writing. **Library/Resources:** The library contains 70,000 volumes, 1,070 microform items, 3,168 audio/video tapes/CDs/DVDs, and subscribes to 307 periodicals including electronic. Computerized library services include database searching, Internet access, and Wi-Fi capability. Special learning facilities include an art gallery, radio station, a design study center and archive, 5 student galleries, 3 media arts workshops, 3 film and 2 video studios, numerous editing facilities, animation studio with 3 pencil test facilities, digital audio room, tape transfer room, and multimedia facility with digital printing and editing systems. **Physically Challenged Students:** All of the campus is accessible. Facilities include wheelchair ramps, elevators, specially equipped restrooms, special class scheduling, and lowered telephones. **Special:** SVA offers for-credit internships with more than 200 media-related, design, and advertising firms, including DC Comics, MTV, and Pentagram Design. A summer internship with Walt Disney Studios is possible for illustration/cartooning majors. There are a freshman honors program. **Visiting:** There are regularly scheduled orientations for prospective students, including Saturday open house receptions and weekly tours. There are guides for informal visits. To schedule a visit, contact the Office of Admissions. **Campus Safety and Security:** Measures include 24-hour foot and vehicle patrol. There are shuttle buses, emergency telephones, lighted pathways/sidewalks, and controlled access to dorms/residences.

REQUIREMENTS: The SAT or ACT is required. Applicants must graduate from an accredited secondary school or have a GED. A statement of intent is required of all students. A portfolio is also required. A personal interview and letters of recommendation are considered helpful. A GPA of 2.7 is required. AP and CLEP credits are accepted. Important factors in the admissions decision are personality/intangible qualities, extracurricular activities record, and evidence of special talent.To graduate, students must complete 120 credits, including at least 72 in the major, with a minimum GPA of 2.0. These credits must include 30 in humanities and sciences, 12 in art history, and 6 in electives. Students must complete 2 introductory courses in literature and writing and must pass a proficiency exam in the first semester. A thesis is required in most programs. **Procedure:** Freshmen are admitted fall. There are early decision, deferred admissions, and rolling admissions plans. Early decision applications should be filed by December 1; regular applications, by February 1 for fall entry. The fall 2014 application fee was $50. Notification of early decision is sent January 15; regular decision, 10 applicants were on the 2014 waiting list; were admitted. Applications are accepted on-line. **Transfer Students:** 265 transfer students enrolled in 2013-2014. College transcripts from all previously attended accredited colleges or universities, portfolio, admissions essay, high school transcripts are required for some, letters of recommendation are encouraged. 60 of 120 credits required for the bachelor's degree must be completed at SVA. **International Students:** There are 434 international students

enrolled. The school actively recruits these students. They must take the TOEFL and the college's own test, or earn a minimum score of 6 in all categories of the NYU English proficiency exam.

ADMISSIONS: Adam Rogers, Director of Admissions. E-Mail: *admissions@sva.edu* Web: *www.schoolofvisualarts.edu*

FINANCIAL AID: 43% of all full-time freshmen and 40% of continuing full-time students received need-based aid. 7% of undergraduate students work part-time. The average financial indebtedness of the 2014 graduate was $30,259. The FAFSA is required. Check with the school for current application deadlines.

SIENA COLLEGE   D-3
www.siena.edu

Loudonville, NY 12211

	(518) 783-2423
	(888) AT SIENA
Fax: (518) 783-2436	Email: admissions@siena.edu
Full-time: 1400 men, 1608 women	Faculty: 210; IIB, +$
Part-time: 86 men, 67 women	Ph.D.s: 89%
Graduate: 35 men, 20 women	Student/Faculty: 12 to 1
Year: semesters, summer session	Tuition: $31,368
Room & Board: $12,495	Freshman Class: 9438 applied, 5428 accepted, 765 enrolled
SAT CR/M/W: 540/550/530 ACT: 25	CEEB CODE: 2814
Application Deadline: February 15	VERY COMPETITIVE

Siena College, founded in 1937, is a learning community advancing the ideals of a liberal arts education, rooted in its identity as a Franciscan and Catholic Institution. There are 3 undergraduate schools and 1 graduate school. In addition to regional accreditation, Siena has baccalaureate program accreditation with AACSB, CSWE, NCATE, and ACS. The 175-acre campus is in a suburban area 2 miles north of Albany. Including any residence halls, there are 33 buildings.

STUDENT LIFE: 78% of undergraduates are from New York. Others are from 33 states, 14 foreign countries, and Canada. 78% are White. **Male To Female Ratio:** 1.1:1. The average age of freshmen is 18; all undergraduates, 20. 14% do not continue beyond their first year; 77% remain to graduate. **Housing:** 2502 students can be accommodated in college housing, which includes coed dorms and on-campus apartments. In addition, there are special-interest houses. On-campus housing is available on a lottery system for upperclassmen. 81% of students live on campus. Upperclassmen may keep cars.

FACULTY/CLASSROOMS: 58% of faculty are male; 42% are female. All teach undergraduates. No introductory courses are taught by graduate students.

PROGRAMS OF STUDY: Siena confers B.A., and B.S degrees. Master's degrees are also awarded. Bachelor's degrees are awarded in BIOLOGICAL SCIENCE (biochemistry and biology/biological science), BUSINESS (accounting, banking and finance, business administration and management, and marketing management), COMMUNICATIONS AND THE ARTS (classics, English, French, Spanish, and visual and performing arts), COMPUTER AND PHYSICAL SCIENCE (actuarial science, chemistry, computer science, mathematics, and physics), ENGINEERING AND ENVIRONMENTAL DESIGN (environmental science), SOCIAL SCIENCE (American studies, economics, history, philosophy, political science/government, psychology, religion, social work, and sociology). Accounting, pyschology, and biology have the largest enrollments.

ACTIVITIES: There are no fraternities or sororities. There are 70 groups on campus, including and community service, cheerleading, chorus, computers, dance, debate, drama, ethnic, film, gay, honors, international, literary magazine, musical theater, newspaper, opera, orchestra, pep band, political, professional, radio and TV, religious, social, social service, student government, and yearbook. Popular campus events include Charity Week, Sienafest and Family Weekend. **Sports:** There are 7 intercollegiate sports for men and 11 for women, and 7 intramural sports for men and 7 for women. Facilities include an athletic complex with free weights, a training facility, an indoor track, an 8-lane, 25-meter pool, fitness equipment, life cycles, 4 multipurpose courts, 6 outdoor tennis courts, 5 outdoor fields, 2 squash courts, and racquetball courts. **Graduates:** From July 1, 2013 to June 30, 2014, 769 bachelor's degrees were awarded. The most popular majors were accounting (14%), psychology (10%), and marketing (9%). 678 companies recruited on campus in 2013-2014. In an average class, 1% graduate in 3 years or less, 72% graduate in 4 years or less, 79% graduate in 5 years or less, and 80% graduate in 6 years or less.

SERVICES: Counseling and information services are available, as is tutoring in most subjects. There is a reader service for the blind, and remedial math and writing. A writing center that offers free one-to-one assistance. **Library/Resources:** The library contains 369,191 volumes, 27,739 microform items, 5,922 audio/video tapes/CDs/DVDs, and subscribes to 280 periodicals including electronic. Computerized library services include interlibrary loans, database searching, Internet access, and Wi-Fi capability. Special learning facilities include an art gallery, radio station, TV station, and the Hickey Financial Technology Center, which features real-time capital market trading room with stock ticker, data screens, workstations, and access to financial information sources and accounting labs. **Physically Challenged Students:** 90% of the campus is accessible. Facilities include wheelchair ramps, elevators, special parking, specially equipped restrooms, special class scheduling, special housing, and an office for students with disabilities that provides various resources. **Special:** The College has opportunities for cross-registration through the Hudson-Mohawk Association. Domestic and international internships, study abroad in 23 countries, a Washington semester, and work-study programs are available. The College offers dual majors in different divisions and a B.A.-B.S. degree in math, economics, and biology as well as a 3-2 engineering degree with Rensselaer Polytechnic Institute, Catholic University, Clarkson University, Manhattan College, SUNY Binghamton, and Western New England College. A 4-4 medical program with Albany Medical College is also offered. There are 15 national honor societies, a freshman honors program, and 4 departmental honors programs. **Visiting:** There are regularly scheduled orientations for prospective students, students may interview with an admissions counselor, tour campus, or attend a group information session. There are guides for informal visits and visitors may sit in on classes. To schedule a visit, contact Admissions Office at admissions@siena .edu. **Campus Safety and Security:** Measures include 24-hour foot and vehicle patrol, emergency notification system, and security escort services. There are emergency telephones, lighted pathways/sidewalks, a card access system for residence halls, radio dispatch, and a 911 on-campus telephone system.

REQUIREMENTS: The SAT or ACT is required. The ACT Optional Writing test is also required. AP and CLEP credits are accepted. Important factors in the admissions decision are advanced placement or honors courses, personality/intangible qualities, and extracurricular activities record.To graduate, students must earn 120 credits, including 30 to 39 depending on major, with at least a 2.0 GPA. At least a C-grade in every major field course used to satisfy the credit hour requirement of the major. The required core curriculum is 42 credits. **Procedure:** Freshmen are admitted fall and spring. Entrance exams should be taken during spring of the junior year or fall of the senior year. There are early decision, early admissions, and deferred admissions plans. Early decision applications should be filed by December 1; regular applications, by February 15 for fall entry; January 15 for spring entry; and May 1 for summer entry. The fall 2014 application fee was $50. 76 early decision candidates were accepted for the 2014-2015 class. 835 applicants were on the 2014 waiting list; 29 were admitted. Applications are accepted on-line. **Transfer Students:** 132 transfer students enrolled in 2013-2014. Applicants must have a minimum 2.5 GPA. An interview is recommended. At least half of the major field requirements must be completed at Siena. 30 of 120 credits required for the bachelor's degree must be completed at Siena. **International Students:** There are 37 international students enrolled. The school actively recruits these students. They must take the TOEFL with a minimum score of 550 on the paper-based TOEFL (PBT) or 79 on the Internet-based version (iBT). They must also take the SAT or ACT.

ADMISSIONS: 58% of the 2014-2015 applicants were accepted. The SAT scores for the 2014-2015 freshman class were: Critical Reading--31% below 500, 44% between 500 and 599, 20% between 600 and 699, and 5% between 700 and 800; Math--29% below 500, 38%

between 500 and 599, 27% between 600 and 699, and 6% between 700 and 800; Writing--30% below 500, 45% between 500 and 599, 22% between 600 and 699, and 3% between 700 and 800. The ACT scores were 16% below 21, 24% between 21 and 23, 27% between 24 and 26, 13% between 27 and 28, and 20% above 28. 48% of the current freshmen were in the top fifth of their class; 81% were in the top two fifths. **Admissions Contact:** Heather Renault, Associate Vice President for Admissions. E-Mail: *admissions@siena.edu* Web: *www. siena.edu*

FINANCIAL AID: In 2014-2015, 97% of all full-time freshmen and 96% of continuing full-time students received some form of financial aid. 72% of all full-time freshmen and 64% of continuing full-time students received need-based aid. The average freshman award was $18,731. Need-based scholarships or need-based grants averaged $9,995 ($33,356 maximum); need-based self-help aid (loans and jobs) averaged $6,000 ($11,500 maximum); non-need-based athletic scholarships averaged $19,522 ($47,121 maximum); and other non-need-based awards and non-need-based scholarships averaged $10,723 ($28,000 maximum). The FAFSA and the state aid form are required. The priority date for freshman financial aid applications for fall entry is February 15. The deadline for filing freshman financial aid applications for fall entry is May 1.

SKIDMORE COLLEGE   D-3
www.skidmore.edu

Saratoga Springs, NY 12866

(518) 580-5570
(800) 867-6007

Fax: (518) 580-5584   **Email:** admissions@skidmore.edu

Full-time: 1035 men, 1661 women	**Faculty:** 260; IIB, +$
Part-time: 17 men, 21 women	**Ph.D.s:** 84%
Graduate: 5 men, 13 women	**Student/Faculty:** 9 to 1
Year: semesters, summer session	**Tuition:** $47,314
Room & Board: $12,628	**Freshman Class:** 8285 applied, 2904 accepted, 660 enrolled

SAT CR/M/W: 620/620/630 **ACT:** 28   **CEEB CODE:** 2815

Application Deadline: January 15   **HIGHLY COMPETITIVE**

Skidmore College, established in 1903, is an independent institution offering undergraduate programs in liberal arts and sciences, as well as preprofessional programs (business, social work, education, studio art, dance, and theater). Figures in the above capsule and in this profile are approximate. There is one undergraduate school and one graduate school. In addition to regional accreditation, Skidmore has baccalaureate program accreditation with CSWE and NASAD. The 1000-acre campus is in a small town in Saratoga Springs, 30 miles north of Albany. Including any residence halls, there are 50 buildings.

STUDENT LIFE: 69% of undergraduates are from out of state, mostly the Northeast. Students are from 44 states, 63 foreign countries, and Canada. 58% are from public schools. 63% are White; 54% two or more races. The average age of freshmen is 18; all undergraduates, 21. 7% do not continue beyond their first year; 86% remain to graduate. **Housing:** College-sponsored housing includes single-sex and coed dorms and on-campus apartments. Theme housing, wellness housing, and housing for disabled students. On-campus housing is guaranteed for all 4 years and is available on a lottery system for upperclassmen. 87% of students live on campus. All students may keep cars.

FACULTY/CLASSROOMS: 44% of faculty are male; 56% are female. All teach undergraduates, all do research, and all teach and do research. No introductory courses are taught by graduate students. The average class size in a regular course is 16.

PROGRAMS OF STUDY: Skidmore confers B.A., and B.S. degrees. Master's degrees are also awarded. Bachelor's degrees are awarded in AGRICULTURE (environmental studies), BIOLOGICAL SCIENCE (biochemistry, biology/biological science, and neurosciences), BUSINESS (business administration and management and business economics), COMMUNICATIONS AND THE ARTS (art, art history and appreciation, classics, dance, dramatic arts, English, French, German, music, and Spanish), COMPUTER AND PHYSICAL SCI-

ENCE (chemistry, computer science, geology, mathematics, and physics), EDUCATION (elementary education), HEALTH PROFESSIONS (exercise science), SOCIAL SCIENCE (American studies, anthropology, Asian/Oriental studies, economics, French studies, gender studies, history, international relations, liberal arts/general studies, philosophy, political science/government, psychology, religion, social science, social work, and sociology). Social sciences, visual and performing arts, business/marketing, English, and psychology have the largest enrollments.

ACTIVITIES: There are no fraternities or sororities. There are 86 groups on campus, including art, band, chorale, chorus, computers, dance, debate, drama, environmental, ethnic, film, gay, honors, international, jazz band, literary magazine, musical theater, newspaper, opera, orchestra, photography, political, professional, radio and TV, religious, social, social service, student government, symphony, and yearbook. Popular campus events include Martin Luther King Week, Oktoberfest, and Spring Fling. **Sports:** There are 9 intercollegiate sports for men and 10 for women. Facilities include an sports and recreation center (main gymnasium with three basketball/volleyball courts, intramural and recreation gyms, swimming pool and diving well, racquetball courts, athletic training room, human-performance laboratory, aerobics and fitness area, and weight room), nine tennis courts (four lighted), artificial-surface field for field hockey, softball diamond with field turf outfield, lighted stadium with 1,400 seats, all-weather track, and field turf playing field for soccer, lacrosse, and intramurals, baseball diamond, golf driving range, heated barn, indoor and outdoor riding rings, hunter course, and riding trails, rowing boathouse, and ice hockey rink (owned by City of Saratoga Springs). **Graduates:** From July 1, 2013 to June 30, 2014, 616 bachelor's degrees were awarded. The most popular majors were social sciences (17%), visual and performing arts (15%), and business/marketing (12%). 51 companies recruited on campus in 2013-2014. In an average class, 83% graduate in 4 years or less, 85% graduate in 5 years or less, and 86% graduate in 6 years or less. Of the 2013 graduating class, 16% were enrolled in graduate school within 6 months of graduation, and 80% were employed.

SERVICES: Counseling and information services are available, as is tutoring in most subjects. There is a reader service for the blind. Diagnostic services, note takers, and books on tape are also offered. **Library/Resources:** Computerized library services include interlibrary loans, database searching, and Internet access. Special learning facilities include an art gallery, radio station, TV station, an electronic music studio, music and art studios, theater teaching facility, anthropology lab, and special biological habitats on campus. **Physically Challenged Students:** 98% of the campus is accessible. Facilities include wheelchair ramps, elevators, special parking, specially equipped restrooms, lowered drinking fountains, and special housing. **Special:** Skidmore offers cross-registration with the Hudson-Mohawk Consortium, individually designed internships, various study-abroad programs, a Washington semester in conjunction with American University, dual and student-designed majors, credit for life and experience, and pass/fail options, as well as a nondegree study program for senior citizens. There are cooperative programs with other schools in engineering, business administration, and health. There are 9 national honor societies, including Phi Beta Kappa, and a freshman honors program. **Visiting:** There are regularly scheduled orientations for prospective students, including full-day open-house programs. There are guides for informal visits, visitors may sit in on classes, and stay overnight. To schedule a visit, contact the Admissions Office. **Campus Safety and Security:** Measures include 24-hour foot and vehicle patrol, emergency notification system, and security escort services. There are shuttle buses, emergency telephones, lighted pathways/sidewalks, controlled access to dorms/residences, Special security alert system, rigorous fire response procedures, and a lock system on dorm entrances.

REQUIREMENTS: The SAT or ACT is required. SAT subject tests recommended. AP and CLEP credits are accepted. Important factors in the admissions decision are advanced placement or honors courses, recommendations by school officials, and evidence of special talent.To graduate, students must complete 120 credits, including at least 24 at the 300 level, with a minimum GPA of 2.0 overall and in the major. B.A. candidates require 90 credits in the liberal arts to graduate; B.S. candidates require 60 credits. Students must fulfill all

core curriculum, distribution, and major requirements. **Procedure:** Freshmen are admitted fall. Entrance exams should be taken by December of the senior year. There are early decision, early admissions, and deferred admissions plans. Early decision applications should be filed by November 15; regular applications, by January 15 for fall entry, along with a $65 fee. Notification of early decision is sent December 15; regular decision, April 1. 283 early decision candidates were accepted for the 2014-2015 class. 430 applicants were on the 2014 waiting list; 21 were admitted. Applications are accepted online. **Transfer Students:** 33 transfer students enrolled in 2013-2014. Transfer students must have a GPA of 2.7 and must submit a high school transcript, all college transcripts, an essay or personal statement, test scores, and a statement of good standing from prior institutions. At least one professor recommendation from the current institution and a mid-term report are also required. 60 of 120 credits required for the bachelor's degree must be completed at Skidmore. **International Students:** There are 182 international students enrolled. The school actively recruits these students. They must take the TOEFL with a minimum score of 590 on the paper-based TOEFL (PBT) or 96 on the Internet-based version (iBT). They must also take the SAT or ACT.

ADMISSIONS: 35% of the 2014-2015 applicants were accepted. The SAT scores for the 2014-2015 freshman class were: Critical Reading--7% below 500, 31% between 500 and 599, 43% between 600 and 699, and 19% between 700 and 800; Math--4% below 500, 34% between 500 and 599, 45% between 600 and 699, and 17% between 700 and 800; Writing--5% below 500, 29% between 500 and 599, 46% between 600 and 699, and 20% between 700 and 800. The ACT scores were 2% below 21, 8% between 21 and 23, 19% between 24 and 26, 28% between 27 and 28, and 43% above 28. 69% of the current freshmen were in the top fifth of their class; 92% were in the top two fifths. **Admissions Contact:** Mary Lou Bates, Director of Admissions. E-Mail: *admissions@skidmore.edu* Web: *www.skidmore.edu*

FINANCIAL AID: In 2014-2015, 51% of all full-time freshmen and 51% of continuing full-time students received some form of financial aid. 46% of all full-time freshmen and 48% of continuing full-time students received need-based aid. The average freshman award was $38,700. Need-based scholarships or need-based grants averaged $35,600 ($58,750 maximum); need-based self-help aid (loans and jobs) averaged $3,900 ($5,500 maximum); and other non-need-based awards and non-need-based scholarships averaged $12,500 ($15,000 maximum). 48% of undergraduate students work part-time. Average annual earnings from campus work are $2220. The average financial indebtedness of the 2014 graduate was $24,371. Skidmore is a member of CSS. The CSS/Profile and FAFSA are required. The deadline for filing freshman financial aid applications for fall entry is February 1.

ST. BONAVENTURE UNIVERSITY   B-4
www.sbu.edu

St. Bonaventure, NY 14778	**(716) 375-2400**
	(800) 462-5050
Fax: (716) 375-4005	**Email:** admissions@sbu.edu
Full-time: 856 men, 869 women	**Faculty:** 139
Part-time: 28 men, 18 women	**Ph.Ds:** 83%
Graduate: 114 men, 262 women	**Student/Faculty:** 11 to 1
Year: semesters, summer session	**Tuition:** $30,475
Room & Board: $11,100	**Freshman Class:** 2682 applied, 1892 accepted, 435 enrolled
SAT CR/M/W: 530/530/510 **ACT:** 24	**CEEB CODE:** 2793
Application Deadline: July 1	**COMPETITIVE**

Saint Bonaventure University, founded in 1858, is a private Roman Catholic institution in the Franciscan tradition, offering programs in the arts and sciences, education, business, and journalism and mass communication. There are 4 undergraduate schools and 1 graduate school. In addition to regional accreditation, SBU has baccalaureate program accreditation with AACSB, NCATE, and CACREP. The 500-acre campus is in a small town 75 miles southeast of Buffalo. Including any residence halls, there are 30 buildings.

STUDENT LIFE: 75% of undergraduates are from New York. Others

are from 34 states, 10 foreign countries, and Canada. 68% are White; 12% race unknown. 58% claim no religious affiliation; 29% Catholic. The average age of freshmen is 18; all undergraduates, 19. 16% do not continue beyond their first year; 68% remain to graduate. **Housing:** 1630 students can be accommodated in college housing, which includes single-sex and coed dorms and on-campus apartments. In addition, there are special-interest houses, living/learning communities. On-campus housing is guaranteed for all 4 years. 76% of students live on campus; of those, 100% remain on campus on weekends. All students may keep cars.

FACULTY/CLASSROOMS: 58% of faculty are male; 42% are female. 90% teach undergraduates. No introductory courses are taught by graduate students. The average class size in an introductory lecture is 18; in a laboratory is 12; and in a regular course is 18.

PROGRAMS OF STUDY: SBU confers B.A., B.S., B.B.A. and B.S.Ed. degrees. Master's degrees are also awarded. Bachelor's degrees are awarded in BIOLOGICAL SCIENCE (biochemistry, bioinformatics, biology/biological science, and biophysics), BUSINESS (accounting, banking and finance, management information systems, management science, and marketing/retailing/merchandising), COMMUNICATIONS AND THE ARTS (art history, classical languages, communications, digital communications, dramatic arts, English, French, journalism, music, Spanish, and visual and performing arts), COMPUTER AND PHYSICAL SCIENCE (chemistry, computer science, mathematics, and physics), EDUCATION (education, elementary education, physical education, special education, and sports studies), ENGINEERING AND ENVIRONMENTAL DESIGN (engineering physics and environmental science), SOCIAL SCIENCE (child care/child and family studies, gerontology, history, international studies, philosophy, political science/government, psychology, sociology, theological studies, and women's studies). Journalism/mass communication, biology, and accounting have the largest enrollments.

ACTIVITIES: There are no fraternities or sororities. There are 65 groups on campus, including art, band, cheerleading, choir, chorale, chorus, computers, dance, drama, ENACTUS, environmental, ethnic, gay, honors, international, jazz band, literary magazine, newspaper, photography, political, professional, radio and TV, religious, social, social service, student government, and yearbook. Popular campus events include Family Weekend, and Spring and Winter Weekends. **Sports:** There are 7 intercollegiate sports for men and 7 for women, and 10 intramural sports for men and 9 for women. Facilities include a 5500-seat basketball arena, an indoor swimming pool, a 9-hole golf course, weight facilities and free weights, and a fitness center with state-of-the-art strength, aerobics and conditioning areas, an indoor track, 3 multi-use courts, and a rock climbing wall. There is also a 77-acre area on campus with soccer, baseball, softball, rugby, and intramural fields, and a recreation trail that winds through campus. **Graduates:** From July 1, 2013 to June 30, 2014, 408 bachelor's degrees were awarded. The most popular majors were communications/journalism (15%), business (13%), and sports studies (8%). In an average class, 1% graduate in 3 years or less, 48% graduate in 4 years or less, 62% graduate in 5 years or less, and 63% graduate in 6 years or less.

SERVICES: Counseling and information services are available, as is tutoring in most subjects. There is remedial math. **Library/Resources:** The library contains 385,874 volumes, 16,950 microform items, 16,539 audio/video tapes/CDs/DVDs, and subscribes to 36,059 periodicals including electronic. Computerized library services include interlibrary loans, database searching, Internet access, and Wi-Fi capability. Special learning facilities include an art gallery, radio station, TV station, an observatory. **Physically Challenged Students:** 90% of the campus is accessible. Facilities include wheelchair ramps, elevators, special parking, and specially equipped restrooms. **Special:** Internships are available in business, mass communication, political science, psychology, sociology. Study abroad in 18 countries, B.A.-B.S. degrees, accelerated degree programs, dual and student-designed majors, a Washington semester with American University, and pass/fail options are offered. Dual admissions with George Washington University School of Medicine, Lake Erie College of Osteopathic Medicine, University at Buffalo School of Dental Medicine, Lake Erie College of Osteopathic Medicine School of Pharmacy, and SUNY-Upstate Medical are also possible. There are 10 national honor

societies and a freshman honors program. **Visiting:** There are regularly scheduled orientations for prospective students, including interviews, tours, class visits, and meetings with professors. There are guides for informal visits, visitors may sit in on classes, and stay overnight. To schedule a visit, contact Christina Sutphen at admissions@sbu.edu. **Campus Safety and Security:** Measures include 24-hour foot and vehicle patrol, emergency notification system, and security escort services. There are shuttle buses, emergency telephones, lighted pathways/sidewalks, and controlled access to dorms/residences.

REQUIREMENTS: The SAT is required. The ACT is recommended, with a satisfactory score on the SAT or 24 on the ACT. Applicants must be graduates of an accredited secondary school or have a GED. 16 academic credits are required, including 4 years each of English and social studies, 3 each of math and science, and 2 of a foreign language. An essay and an interview are recommended. AP and CLEP credits are accepted. To graduate, students must complete 120 credit hours, 30 of them in the major, with a minimum GPA of 2.0. Students must complete general education requirements in addition to major requirements. **Procedure:** Freshmen are admitted to all sessions. Entrance exams should be taken during the spring of the junior year or the fall of the senior year. There are early admissions, deferred admissions, and rolling admissions plans. Applications should be filed by July 1 for fall entry; October 15 for spring entry, along with a $30 fee. Notification is sent on a rolling basis. Applications are accepted on-line. **Transfer Students:** 59 transfer students enrolled in 2013-2014. Applicants must have a minimum 2.0 GPA. High school and college transcripts, essay, and a letter of recommendation are required. 45 of 120 credits required for the bachelor's degree must be completed at SBU. **International Students:** There are 56 international students enrolled. The school actively recruits these students. They must take the TOEFL with a minimum score of 550 on the paper-based TOEFL (PBT) or 79 on the Internet-based version (iBT).

ADMISSIONS: 71% of the 2014-2015 applicants were accepted. The SAT scores for the 2014-2015 freshman class were: Critical Reading--35% below 500, 44% between 500 and 599, 17% between 600 and 699, and 3% between 700 and 800; Math--36% below 500, 43% between 500 and 599, 17% between 600 and 699, and 4% between 700 and 800; Writing--37% below 500, 42% between 500 and 599, 18% between 600 and 699, and 3% between 700 and 800. The ACT scores were 22% below 21, 27% between 21 and 23, 24% between 24 and 26, 10% between 27 and 28, and 17% above 28. 35% of the current freshmen were in the top fifth of their class; 64% were in the top two fifths. 6 freshmen graduated first in their class. **Admissions Contact:** Monica Emery, Director of Recruitment. E-Mail: *admissions@sbu.edu* Web: *www.sbu.edu*

FINANCIAL AID: In 2014-2015, 99% of all full-time freshmen and 97% of continuing full-time students received some form of financial aid. 77% of all full-time freshmen and 76% of continuing full-time students received need-based aid. The average freshman award was $24,722. Need-based scholarships or need-based grants averaged $6,430; need-based self-help aid (loans and jobs) averaged $6,334; non-need-based athletic scholarships averaged $14,331; and other non-need-based awards and non-need-based scholarships averaged $14,273. 36% of undergraduate students work part-time. Average annual earnings from campus work are $882. The average financial indebtedness of the 2014 graduate was $28,425. The FAFSA and the state aid form are required. The priority date for freshman financial aid applications for fall entry is February 15.

ST. FRANCIS COLLEGE   D-5
www.sfc.edu

Brooklyn, NY 11201

(718) 489-5200
n/av

Fax: (718) 802-0453	Email: admissions@sfc.edu
Full-time: 1088 men, 1368 women	Faculty: 80; IIB, +$
Part-time: 129 men, 179 women	Ph.Ds: 86%
Graduate: 31 men, 24 women	Student/Faculty: 18 to 1
Year: semesters, summer session	Tuition: $20,700
Room & Board: $13,500	Freshman Class: n/av
	CEEB CODE: 2796
Application Deadline: April 1	COMPETITIVE

St. Francis College, founded in 1859 by the Franciscan Brothers of Brooklyn. Since its founding, the College has pursued its Franciscan mission to provide an affordable, high-quality education to students from New York City's five boroughs and beyond. The figures in the above capsule and in the profile are approximate. In addition to regional accreditation, St. Francis has baccalaureate program accreditation with TEAC and AACN. The 1-acre campus is in an urban area Brooklyn Heights, NY. Including any residence halls, there are 6 buildings.

STUDENT LIFE: 98% of undergraduates are from New York. Others are from 8 states, 50 foreign countries, and Canada. 49% are from public schools. 37% are White; 22% Hispanic; 19% African American. 51% are Catholic; 29% Protestant; 14% claim no religious affiliation. The average age of freshmen is 19; all undergraduates, 21. 22% do not continue beyond their first year; 52% remain to graduate.

Housing: 173 students can be accommodated in college housing, which includes coed dorms. Students may apply for housing with EHS. On-campus housing is available on a first-come, first-served basis. 100% of students commute. Alcohol is not permitted. All students commute. Some may keep cars.

FACULTY/CLASSROOMS: 59% of faculty are male; 41% are female. All teach and do research. No introductory courses are taught by graduate students. The average class size in an introductory lecture is 22; in a laboratory is 22; and in a regular course is 22.

PROGRAMS OF STUDY: St. Francis confers B.A., and B.S. degrees. Associate and Master's degrees are also awarded. Bachelor's degrees are awarded in BIOLOGICAL SCIENCE (biology/biological science), BUSINESS (accounting, business administration and management, and management science), COMMUNICATIONS AND THE ARTS (communications, English, and Spanish), COMPUTER AND PHYSICAL SCIENCE (chemistry, information sciences and systems, and mathematics), EDUCATION (education, elementary education, middle school education, physical education, and secondary education), HEALTH PROFESSIONS (health care administration, health science, medical laboratory technology, nursing, physician's assistant, and radiological science), SOCIAL SCIENCE (criminal justice, economics, history, international studies, liberal arts/general studies, philosophy, political science/government, psychology, religion, social studies, and sociology). Accounting, management, psychology, and teacher education are the strongest academically. Management, psychology and communications have the largest enrollments.

ACTIVITIES: 10% of men belong to 3 national fraternities; 6% of women belong to 3 local and 1 national sororities. There are 40 groups on campus, including art, cheerleading, choir, chorus, communications, computers, dance, debate, drama, ethnic, honors, international, literary magazine, musical theater, newspaper, photography, political, professional, radio and TV, religious, social, social service, student government, and yearbook. Popular campus events include Terrier Tuesday, Sports Events, Community Day, Valentines Day Auction, Family Day, Battle of Brooklyn, Welcome Back BBQ. **Sports:** There are 9 intercollegiate sports for men and 10 for women, and 5 intramural sports for men and 5 for women. Facilities include a full sized basketball court, a competition-size swimming pool, a weight-training room, and the Genovesi Center, which is a multipurpose facility used for athletic, college, and community events. Home soccer games are played on a brand new field on a pier at Brooklyn Bridge Park. **Graduates:** From July 1, 2013 to June 30, 2014, 578 bachelor's degrees were awarded. The most popular majors were communications (18%), management (13%), and nursing (12%). 20 companies recruited on campus in 2013-2014. In an average class, 1% graduate in 3 years or less, 31% graduate in 4 years or less, 51% graduate in 5 years or less, and 52% graduate in 6 years or less. Of the 2013 graduating class, 37% were enrolled in graduate school within 6 months of graduation, and 51% were employed.

SERVICES: Counseling and information services are available, as is tutoring in most subjects. There is a reader service for the blind, and remedial math, reading, and writing. There are workshops in academic skills such as note taking, test taking, and study skills. **Library/Resources:** The library contains 140,000 volumes, 10,440 microform items, 2,050 audio/video tapes/CDs/DVDs, and subscribes to 14,300 periodicals including electronic. Computerized library services include interlibrary loans, database searching, Internet access, and Wi-Fi capability. Special learning facilities include an art gallery,

radio station, HDTV television studio, a nursing lab with multiple simulators (SYMBaby, SYM Man), and greenhouse. **Physically Challenged Students:** All of the campus is accessible. Facilities include wheelchair ramps, elevators, specially equipped restrooms, lowered drinking fountains, and lowered telephones. **Special:** There are co-op programs in physical therapy, nursing, and computer science. Work-study with Methodist Hospital or the borough president's office, and there are preprofessional health programs with the State University of New York Health Science Center, Methodist Hospital, and St. Vincent's Catholic Medical Center. Study abroad in several countries, dual majors, pass/fail options, and credit for life experience are possible. There are 16 national honor societies, a freshman honors program, and 21 departmental honors programs. **Visiting:** There are regularly scheduled orientations for prospective students, visiting students can participate in a student guided tour of the college, and meetings with faculty if desired. There are guides for informal visits and visitors may sit in on classes. To schedule a visit, contact The Office of Admissions at admissions@sfc.edu. **Campus Safety and Security:** Measures include 24-hour foot and vehicle patrol and emergency notification system.

REQUIREMENTS: The SAT is required. Applicants should graduate from an accredited secondary school or have a GED. An entrance essay is required, as well as the submission of SAT scores and recommendation letters, official high transcript or GED. AP and CLEP credits are accepted. Important factors in the admissions decision are advanced placement or honors courses, extracurricular activities record, and recommendations by school officials. The core curriculum varies according to the major, but all baccalaureate degree programs require courses in communications, English, fine arts, phys ed, history, philosophy, sociology, and science or math. A minimum 2.0 GPA and 128 credit hours are required to graduate. **Procedure:** Freshmen are admitted to all sessions. Entrance exams should be taken In spring of the junior year and fall of the senior year. There are deferred admissions and rolling admissions plans. Applications should be filed by April 1 for fall entry; November 1 for winter entry, along with a $35 fee. Notification is sent on a rolling basis. Applications are accepted on-line. Application fees are waived if application is completed on-line. **Transfer Students:** 183 transfer students enrolled in 2013-2014. A minimum 2.0 GPA is required for transfer students. Official transcripts from previous colleges and high school transcripts, or a graduation certificate, is also required. 30 of 128 credits required for the bachelor's degree must be completed at St. Francis. **International Students:** There are 154 international students enrolled. The school actively recruits these students. They must take the TOEFL with a minimum score of 500 on the paper-based TOEFL (PBT) or 61 on the Internet-based version (iBT). They must also take the SAT or ACT.

ADMISSIONS: Joseph Cummings, AVP Enrollment Services. E-Mail: *admissions@sfc.edu* Web: *www.sfc.edu*

FINANCIAL AID: In 2014-2015, 98% of all full-time freshmen and 83% of continuing full-time students received some form of financial aid. 66% of all full-time freshmen and 58% of continuing full-time students received need-based aid. The average freshman award was $14,300. Need-based scholarships or need-based grants averaged $6,000 ($12,100 maximum); need-based self-help aid (loans and jobs) averaged $7,800 ($29,400 maximum); non-need-based athletic scholarships averaged $9,800 ($32,600 maximum); and other non-need-based awards and non-need-based scholarships averaged $8,300 ($20,700 maximum). 10% of undergraduate students work part-time. Average annual earnings from campus work are $2600. The FAFSA, the state aid form, and the college's own financial statement are required. The priority date for freshman financial aid applications for fall entry is February 15.

ST. JOHN FISHER COLLEGE   B-3
www.sjfc.edu

Rochester, NY 14618	(585) 385-8064
	(800) 444-4640
Fax: (585) 385-8386	Email: admissions@sjfc.edu
Full-time: 1079 men, 1582 women	Faculty: 177; II, +$
Part-time: 77 men, 119 women	Ph.D.s: 89%
Graduate: 332 men, 667 women	Student/Faculty: 12 to 1
Year: semesters, summer session	Tuition: $29,550
Room & Board: $11,158	Freshman Class: 3868 applied, 2605 accepted, 597 enrolled
SAT CR/M/W: 520/560/510 ACT: 25	CEEB CODE: 2798
Application Deadline: rolling	COMPETITIVE+

St. John Fisher College is an independent, liberal arts institution in the Catholic tradition of American higher education. Guided since its inception in 1948 by the educational philosophy of the Congregation of St. Basil, the college emphasizes liberal learning for students in traditional academic disciplines, as well as for those in more directly career-oriented fields. The college welcomes qualified students, faculty, and staff regardless of religious or cultural background. There are 4 undergraduate schools and 5 graduate schools. In addition to regional accreditation, Fisher has baccalaureate program accreditation with AACSB, ACPE, NCATE, ACS, and CCNE. The 154-acre campus is in a suburban area 6 miles southeast of Rochester. Including any residence halls, there are 25 buildings.

STUDENT LIFE: 97% of undergraduates are from New York. Others are from 37 states, 14 foreign countries, and Canada. 84% are from public schools. 84% are White. The average age of freshmen is 18; all undergraduates, 21. 12% do not continue beyond their first year; 72% remain to graduate. **Housing:** 1415 students can be accommodated in college housing, which includes single-sex and coed dorms. On-campus housing is guaranteed for the freshman year only and is available on a lottery system for upperclassmen. Priority is given to out-of-town students. 50% of students commute. Upperclassmen may keep cars.

FACULTY/CLASSROOMS: 41% of faculty are male; 59% are female. 86% teach undergraduates. No introductory courses are taught by graduate students. The average class size in an introductory lecture is 22 and in a laboratory is 14.

PROGRAMS OF STUDY: Fisher confers B.A., and B.S. degrees. Master's and Doctoral degrees are also awarded. Bachelor's degrees are awarded in BIOLOGICAL SCIENCE (biology/biological science), BUSINESS (accounting, business administration and management, marketing management, and sports management), COMMUNICATIONS AND THE ARTS (communications, digital communications, English, French, and Spanish), COMPUTER AND PHYSICAL SCIENCE (chemistry, computer science, mathematics, physics, and statistics), EDUCATION (elementary education, English education, foreign languages education, mathematics education, middle school education, science education, secondary education, social studies education, and special education), HEALTH PROFESSIONS (nursing), SOCIAL SCIENCE (American studies, anthropology, criminology, economics, history, interdisciplinary studies, international studies, legal studies, philosophy, political science/government, psychology, religion, and sociology). Sciences is the strongest academically. Management, nursing, and biological sciences have the largest enrollments.

ACTIVITIES: There are no fraternities or sororities. There are 70 groups on campus, including Commuter Council, Resident Student Association, Student Senate SGA, art, cheerleading, choir, chorus, computers, dance, drama, environmental, ethnic, gay, honors, international, literary magazine, musical theater, newspaper, pep band, photography, political, professional, radio and TV, religious, social, social service, Student Activities Board, student government, and yearbook. Popular campus events include Spring Event, Senior Week, and TEDDI 24-hour Dance Marathon for Charity. **Sports:** There are 11 intercollegiate sports for men and 12 for women, and 4 intramural sports for men and 4 for women. Facilities include Fisher's Student Life Center includes a field house, the Manning and Napier Varsity

Gymnasium for men's and women's basketball teams, a fitness center/weight room, training facilities, and team locker rooms. Growney Stadium, a 2100-seat stadium is home to the football, soccer, and lacrosse teams and is used by many of the college's intramural teams. The Polisseni Track & Field complex features an eight-lane, 400-meter competition track with a grass infield; Dugan Yard baseball complex is home to the men's baseball team. Additional athletic facilites include a softball complex, outdoor tennis courts, regulation-size grass practice field. **Graduates:** From July 1, 2013 to June 30, 2014, 836 bachelor's degrees were awarded. The most popular majors were business (27%), nursing (21%), and education (8%). In an average class, 2% graduate in 3 years or less, 61% graduate in 4 years or less, 70% graduate in 5 years or less, and 72% graduate in 6 years or less.

SERVICES: Counseling and information services are available, as is tutoring in every subject. There is a reader service for the blind. Math and writing centers provide help to students at all levels. 24 Hour Online Tutoring and Peer tutoring is available to all students in most undergraduate subject areas. **Library/Resources:** The library contains 171,467 volumes, 52,323 microform items, 7,968 audio/video tapes/CDs/DVDs, and subscribes to 75,357 periodicals including electronic. Computerized library services include interlibrary loans, database searching, and Internet access. Special learning facilities include an art gallery, radio station, TV station, a multimedia center, "wet" and "dry" multidisciplinary science labs, animal labs, growth chambers, Campus Center, athletics fitness facility. **Physically Challenged Students:** All of the campus is accessible. Facilities include wheelchair ramps, elevators, special parking, specially equipped restrooms, special class scheduling, lowered drinking fountains, lowered telephones. Accessible dorm rooms are available. **Special:** The college has cooperative programs and cross-registration with Rochester area colleges. The college offers internships in most majors, independent research in various majors, study abroad, accelerated degree programs in specific majors, Washington semesters, dual and student-designed majors, and degrees in interdisciplinary studies. A 3-2 engineering degree is offered. Navy and Marine ROTC are available at the University of Rochester and Air Force and Army ROTC is available at Rochester Institute of Technology. There are 10 national honor societies, a freshman honors program, and 8 departmental honors programs. **Visiting:** There are regularly scheduled orientations for prospective students, prospective students can schedule a campus tour; an interview with a member of the admissions staff; a meeting with faculty and coaches; and lunch on campus. There are guides for informal visits, visitors may sit in on classes, and stay overnight. To schedule a visit, contact the Office of Freshman Admissions. **Campus Safety and Security:** Measures include 24-hour foot and vehicle patrol, emergency notification system, self-defense education, and security escort services. There are shuttle buses, emergency telephones, lighted pathways/sidewalks, controlled access to dorms/residences, access to the residence halls is controlled by the ID card access system. Residence halls are patrolled and monitored 24 hours a day by security officers or resident advisers. All other campus facilities are locked and unlocked according to established schedules.

REQUIREMENTS: Applicants are required to submit either SAT or ACT standardized test scores for admission to the College. Applicants must be graduates of an accredited secondary school and have completed 16 academic credits including 4 years each in English and history/social studies, 3 years each in math and science, and 2 years in a foreign language. Interviews are recommended. AP and CLEP credits are accepted. Important factors in the admissions decision are advanced placement or honors courses, extracurricular activities record, and leadership record.To graduate, students must complete at least 120 credit hours, including at least 30 in the major, and maintain a 2.0 minimum GPA. The core curriculum consists of 15 courses that students must successfully complete to graduate; the core is composed of 2 tiers of study: Foundations courses and Perspectives courses. Freshmen must participate in one of the integrative learning communities. **Procedure:** Freshmen are admitted fall. There are early decision, deferred admissions, and rolling admissions plans. Application deadlines are open. Application fee is $30. Notification of early decision is sent January 15; regular decision, on a rolling basis. 108 early decision candidates were accepted for the 2014-2015 class. Applications are accepted on-line. **Transfer Students:** 244 transfer students enrolled in 2013-2014. Applicants must have a minimum GPA of 2.0 to be considered (mean GPA is 2.8). A high school transcript is required for students with fewer than 24 college credits. Interviews are recommended. 30 of 120 credits required for the bachelor's degree must be completed at Fisher. **International Students:** There are 10 international students enrolled. They must take the TOEFL with a minimum score of 550 on the paper-based TOEFL (PBT) or 80 on the Internet-based version (iBT). They must also take the SAT or ACT. International Applicants may submit TOEFL scores or standardized entrance exams such as SAT or ACT.

ADMISSIONS: 67% of the 2014-2015 applicants were accepted. The SAT scores for the 2014-2015 freshman class were: Critical Reading--30% below 500, 54% between 500 and 599, 15% between 600 and 699, and 1% between 700 and 800; Math--17% below 500, 55% between 500 and 599, 25% between 600 and 699, and 3% between 700 and 800; Writing--42% below 500, 44% between 500 and 599, 13% between 600 and 699, and 1% between 700 and 800. The ACT scores were 7% below 21, 34% between 21 and 23, 34% between 24 and 26, 21% between 27 and 28, and 6% above 28. 43% of the current freshmen were in the top fifth of their class; 83% were in the top two fifths. 6 freshmen graduated first in their class. **Admissions Contact:** Stacy Ledermann, Director of Freshman Admissions. E-Mail: *admissions@sjfc.edu* Web: *www.sjfc.edu*

FINANCIAL AID: In 2014-2015, 100% of all full-time freshmen and 99% of continuing full-time students received some form of financial aid. 85% of all full-time freshmen and 83% of continuing full-time students received need-based aid. The average freshman award was $21,225. Need-based scholarships or need-based grants averaged $17,518 ($34,000 maximum); and need-based self-help aid (loans and jobs) averaged $4,733 ($8,000 maximum). 25% of undergraduate students work part-time. Average annual earnings from campus work are $1467. The average financial indebtedness of the 2014 graduate was $32,982. The FAFSA and the state aid form are required. The priority date for freshman financial aid applications for fall entry is February 15.

ST. JOHN'S UNIVERSITY   D-5
www.stjohns.edu

Queens, NY 11439	**(718) 990-2000**
	(888) 9ST-JOHNS
Fax: (718) 990-2096	**Email:** admission@stjohns.edu
Full-time: 4946 men, 5774 women	**Faculty:** 568; I, +$
Part-time: 2114 men, 2931 women	**Ph.D.s:** 92%
Graduate: 1775 men, 2908 women	**Student/Faculty:** 19 to 1
Year: semesters, summer session	**Tuition:** $38,680
Room & Board: $16,390	**Freshman Class:** 44597 applied, 27883 accepted, 2795 enrolled
SAT CR/M: 540/560 **ACT:** 25	**CEEB CODE:** 2799
Application Deadline: open	**COMPETITIVE+**

St. John's University, founded in 1870 by the Vincentian Fathers, is a private Roman Catholic institution offering programs in the arts and sciences, education, business, pharmacy and health sciences, theology, and professional studies. Figures in the above capsule and in this profile are approximate. There are 5 undergraduate schools and 7 graduate schools. In addition to regional accreditation, St. John's has baccalaureate program accreditation with AACSB, ACPE, NASAD, TEAC, ABA, JRCERT, and NAACLS. The 105-acre campus is in a suburban area in a residential section of Queens. There is also campus in Staten Island, a campus in downtown Manhattan, a campus in Rome, Italy and a campus in Oakdale, Long Island. Including any residence halls, there are 52 buildings.

STUDENT LIFE: 70% of undergraduates are from New York. Others are from 48 states, 99 foreign countries, and Canada. 61% are from public schools. 41% are White; 15% Asian American; 14% African American; 14% Hispanic. 48% are Catholic; 20% claim no religious affiliation; 17% Muslim, Hindu, Buddhist, Mormon, Greek and Russian Orthodox; 13% Protestant. The average age of freshmen is 17; all undergraduates, 19. 21% do not continue beyond their first year; 59% remain to graduate. **Housing:** 3649 students can be accommo-

dated in college housing, which includes coed dorms, on-campus apartments, and off-campus apartments. In addition, there are honors houses, special-interest houses, Honors housing (certain beds allocated), and special interest housing (learning communities). On-campus housing is available on a first-come, first-served basis, and is available on a lottery system for upperclassmen. Priority is given to out-of-town students. 79% of students commute. Alcohol is not permitted. Upperclassmen may keep cars.

FACULTY/CLASSROOMS: 56% of faculty are male; 44% are female. 91% teach undergraduates. No introductory courses are taught by graduate students.

PROGRAMS OF STUDY: St. John's confers B.A., B.S., B.F.A. and B.S.Ed. degrees. Associate, Master's, and Doctoral degrees are also awarded. Bachelor's degrees are awarded in AGRICULTURE (environmental studies), BIOLOGICAL SCIENCE (biology/adolescence education, biology/biological science, and toxicology), BUSINESS (accounting, business administration and management, business economics, finance, funeral home services, hospitality management services, information and communication technology, insurance and risk management, management information systems, management science, marketing management, and sports management), COMMUNICATIONS AND THE ARTS (advertising, communications, dramatic arts, English, film, television and digital media, fine arts, French, graphic design, illustration, Italian, journalism, languages, photography, public relations, radio/television technology, Spanish, speech/debate/rhetoric, and telecommunications), COMPUTER AND PHYSICAL SCIENCE (actuarial science, chemistry, computer science, computer security and information assurance, mathematics, physical sciences, and physics), EDUCATION (childhood education: 1-6, early childhood education, education, elementary education, English education, foreign languages education, mathematics education, middle school education, science education, secondary education, social studies education, and special education), HEALTH PROFESSIONS (clinical science, health care administration, pharmacy, physician's assistant, premedicine, radiological science, and speech pathology/audiology), SOCIAL SCIENCE (anthropology, Asian/Oriental studies, criminal justice, economics, history, homeland security, human services, legal studies, liberal arts/general studies, philosophy, political science/government, prelaw, psychology, public administration, social studies, sociology, and theological studies). Pharmacy, biology, and psychology are the strongest academically. Pharmacy has the largest enrollment.

ACTIVITIES: 10% of men belong to 1 local and 16 national fraternities; 8% of women belong to 2 local and 16 national sororities. There are 180 groups on campus, including cheerleading, choir, chorus, computers, dance, debate, drama, environmental, ethnic, film, honors, international, jazz band, literary magazine, musical theater, newspaper, pep band, photography, political, professional, radio and TV, religious, social, social service, student government, and yearbook. Popular campus events include Fall Activities Fair, Spring Fling, Winter Carnival, Pep Rallys and Tailgates and DAC after Dark. **Sports:** There are 7 intercollegiate sports for men and 10 for women, and 14 intramural sports for men and 12 for women. Facilities include gyms, tennis courts, weight and exercise rooms, baseball and softball diamonds, fields for football/lacrosse and soccer, basketball courts, outdoor track. **Graduates:** From July 1, 2013 to June 30, 2014, 2056 bachelor's degrees were awarded. The most popular majors were business/marketing (19%), communications/journalism (11%), and health professions (9%). 251 companies recruited on campus in 2013-2014. In an average class, 1% graduate in 3 years or less, 40% graduate in 4 years or less, 51% graduate in 5 years or less, and 59% graduate in 6 years or less. Of the 2013 graduating class, 46% were enrolled in graduate school within 6 months of graduation, and 66% were employed.

SERVICES: Counseling and information services are available, as is tutoring in most subjects. There is a reader service for the blind. Note-taking services, tape recorders, assistance in study skills, and a program for at-risk freshmen are available. **Library/Resources:** The 4 libraries contain 1.3 million volumes, 376,655 microform items, 5,352 audio/video tapes/CDs/DVDs, and subscribe to 77,908 periodicals including electronic. Computerized library services include interlibrary loans, database searching, Internet access, and Wi-Fi capability. Special learning facilities include an art gallery, radio station, TV station, Health Education Resource Center, Model Pharmacy, Speech and Hearing Clinic, Instructional Materials Center, Instructional Media Center, Institute of Asian Studies, Global Language and Culture Center, Financial Information Lab, Chappell Players Little Theatre, a Math Learning Center and a Writing Center. **Physically Challenged Students:** 95% of the campus is accessible. Facilities include wheelchair ramps, elevators, special parking, specially equipped restrooms, special class scheduling, lowered drinking fountains, and lowered telephones. **Special:** St. John's offers internships, cross-registration, study abroad in Europe, Central and South America, Australia, the Caribbean, Africa, and Asia, accelerated degree programs in many majors, B.A.-B.S. degrees, dual majors and combined degree programs, pass/fail options, and some credit for life, military, and work experience. There are cooperative programs in engineering with Manhattan College, funeral service administration with the McAllister Institute, Dramatic Arts, Film and Television with the American Academy of Dramatic Arts, Biomedical Engineering with Polytechnic University, and Optometry with SUNY College of Optometry. St. John's Staten Island campus offers 14 different 3-year bachelor degree program opportunities. There is a 6-year doctor of pharmacy program for incoming freshmen. Many combined degree programs are available. Eligible students may participate in the University Honors Program. There are 16 national honor societies and a freshman honors program. **Visiting:** There are regularly scheduled orientations for prospective students, including small group presentations and a tour of the campus. Accepted students may also participate in overnight visits scheduled during the Spring semester. There are guides for informal visits and visitors may sit in on classes. To schedule a visit, contact the Office of Admissions. **Campus Safety and Security:** Measures include 24-hour foot and vehicle patrol, emergency notification system, self-defense education, and security escort services. There are shuttle buses, emergency telephones, lighted pathways/sidewalks, controlled access to dorms/residences, a crime prevention awareness program.

REQUIREMENTS: The SAT or ACT is required. Admissions decisions are made by committee and are based on several criteria, including standardized test scores, academic curriculum, and high school average. AP and CLEP credits are accepted. Important factors in the admissions decision are advanced placement or honors courses, recommendations by school officials, and extracurricular activities record. To graduate, students must complete at least 126 credit hours, including core courses and distribution requirements, with a minimum GPA of 2.0 overall and in the major. Other requirements vary by program. Core courses include English, theology, philosophy, Discover NY, history, scientific inquiry, and speech. Distribution requirements include a second language, fine arts, language and culture, math, philosophy, theology, and social sciences. **Procedure:** Freshmen are admitted fall, spring, and summer. Entrance exams should be taken late in the junior year or early in the senior year. There are early admissions, deferred admissions, and rolling admissions plans. Application deadlines are open. Application fee is $50. Notification is sent on a rolling basis. Applications are accepted on-line. Application fees are waived if application is completed on-line. **Transfer Students:** 790 transfer students enrolled in 2013-2014. Applicants must present official transcripts of high school and college work, as well as a list of courses in progress. If the student has been out of school a semester or more, a letter of explanation is also required. Admissions requirements for transfer students to the 6-year pharmacy program are stricter, and placement is limited. 30 of 126 credits required for the bachelor's degree must be completed at St. John's. **International Students:** There are 700 international students enrolled. The school actively recruits these students. They must take the TOEFL with a minimum score of 600 on the paper-based TOEFL (PBT) or 100 on the Internet-based version (iBT). They must also take the SAT or ACT, scoring 1000. This requirement may be waived for international students educated outside of the United States.

ADMISSIONS: 63% of the 2014-2015 applicants were accepted. The SAT scores for the 2014-2015 freshman class were: Critical Reading--27% below 500, 49% between 500 and 599, 20% between 600 and 699, and 4% between 700 and 800; Math--23% below 500, 43% between 500 and 599, 25% between 600 and 699, and 9% between 700 and 800. The ACT scores were 10% below 21, 23% between 21

and 23, 29% between 24 and 26, 16% between 27 and 28, and 22% above 28. 35% of the current freshmen were in the top fifth of their class; 66% were in the top two fifths. **Admissions Contact:** Beth M. Evans, Vise President for Enrollment Management. E-Mail: *admission@stjohns.edu* Web: *www.stjohns.edu/admission*

FINANCIAL AID: In 2014-2015, 98% of all full-time freshmen and 96% of continuing full-time students received some form of financial aid. 90% of all full-time freshmen and 83% of continuing full-time students received need-based aid. The average freshman award was $47,108. Need-based scholarships or need-based grants averaged $9,304 ($28,514 maximum); need-based self-help aid (loans and jobs) averaged $6,473 ($15,500 maximum); non-need-based athletic scholarships averaged $31,260 ($57,429 maximum); other non-need-based awards and non-need-based scholarships averaged $18,362 ($50,942 maximum); and $20,491 from other forms of aid. 9% of undergraduate students work part-time. Average annual earnings from campus work are $2415. The average financial indebtedness of the 2014 graduate was $26,004. The FAFSA is required. The priority date for freshman financial aid applications for fall entry is February 1. The deadline for filing freshman financial aid applications for fall entry is March 1.

ST. JOSEPH'S COLLEGE, NEW YORK/ BROOKLYN CAMPUS   D-5
www.sjcny.edu

Brooklyn, NY 11205	718-940-5800 n/av
Fax: 718-636-8303	Email: brooklynas@sjcny.edu
Full-time: 291 men, 552 women	Faculty: 59; IIB, +$
Part-time: 83 men, 189 women	Ph.D.s: 88%
Graduate: 52 men, 189 women	Student/Faculty: 14 to 1
Year: semesters, summer session	Tuition: $22,630
Room & Board: n/app	Freshman Class: 1573 applied, 1025 accepted, 190 enrolled
SAT CR/M/W: 480/490/470 **ACT:** 21	CEEB CODE: 2802
Application Deadline: August 31	COMPETITIVE

St. Joseph's College, founded in 1916, has provided an affordable liberal arts education to a diverse group of students. Independent and coeducational, St. Joseph's prepares students for lives of integrity, intellectual and spiritual values, social responsibility and service; lives that are worthy of the College's motto: Esse non videri   "To be, not to seem." St. Joseph's Brooklyn Campus challenges its students to develop their full potential and a joy of learning. The College's at the center of one of the nation's most diverse academic and cultural cities. The Brooklyn Academy of Music, the Brooklyn Public Library and the Brooklyn Museum of Art are all minutes away from the College's doors. Students have quick and easy access to such world-renowned institutions as the Metropolitan Museum of Art, the New York Public Library, Madison Square Garden, Carnegie Hall and Lincoln Center. St. Joseph's remains dedicated to maintaining low costs while upholding a strict standard of excellence. While retention rates at most colleges are slipping, St. Joseph's remains above the national average. There are 2 undergraduate schools and one graduate school. In addition to regional accreditation, St. Joseph's College has baccalaureate program accreditation with ACEN, COAPRT, and CAEP. The 5-acre campus is in an urban area 5 miles from midtown Manhattan. Including any residence halls, there are 9 buildings.

STUDENT LIFE: 96% of undergraduates are from New York. Others are from 20 states. 55% are from public schools. 39% are White; 27% African American; 18% Hispanic. The average age of freshmen is 19; all undergraduates, 25. 22% do not continue beyond their first year; 78% remain to graduate. **Housing:** College-sponsored housing includes coed On-campus housing is available on a first-come and first-served basis. Alcohol is not permitted. All students may keep cars.

FACULTY/CLASSROOMS: 43% of faculty are male; 57% are female. All teach undergraduates. No introductory courses are taught by graduate students. The average class size in an introductory lecture is 15; in a laboratory is 13; and in a regular course is 12.

PROGRAMS OF STUDY: St. Joseph's College confers B.A., B.S., B.A./B.S., B.S./M.S. and B.S./M.B.A. degrees. Master's degrees are also awarded. Bachelor's degrees are awarded in BIOLOGICAL SCIENCE (biology/biological science), BUSINESS (accounting, business administration and management, hospitality management services, marketing management, organizational leadership and management, recreation and leisure services, and tourism), COMMUNICATIONS AND THE ARTS (English, journalism, Spanish, and speech/debate/rhetoric), COMPUTER AND PHYSICAL SCIENCE (chemistry, computer information technology, and mathematics), EDUCATION (childhood education: 1-6, elementary education, secondary education, and special education), HEALTH PROFESSIONS (health care administration, medical technology, and nursing), SOCIAL SCIENCE (criminal justice, history, human services, liberal arts/general studies, philosophy and religion, political science/government, psychology, social science, and sociology). Child study and secondary education is the strongest academically. Child study, organizational management and nursing have the largest enrollment.

ACTIVITIES: 2% of men belong to 1 local fraternity; 4% of women belong to 2 local sororities. There are 39 groups on campus, including and psychological counseling, art, computers, dance, drama, environmental, ethnic, film, honors, literary magazine, musical theater, newspaper, personal, political, professional, religious, social, social service, student government, and yearbook. Popular campus events include International Festival, Back-to-School BBQ, Club Fair, Holiday Festival, SJC New Year Party, Spirit Day, Annual Community Service Fair, Junior Class Night, Senior Class Night, Talent Show, Chapel Player Performances. **Sports:** There are 6 intercollegiate sports for men and 7 for women, and 2 intramural sports for men and 1 for women. Facilities include basketball and volleyball courts (on-campus), baseball and softball fields (off-campus), swimming pool (off-campus), tennis courts (off-campus), soccer fields (off-campus).**Graduates:** From July 1, 2013 to June 30, 2014, 282 bachelor's degrees were awarded. The most popular majors were child study (11%), organizational management (9%), and nursing (8%). 131 companies recruited on campus in 2013-2014. In an average class, 56% graduate in 4 years or less, 65% graduate in 5 years or less, and 65% graduate in 6 years or less.

SERVICES: Counseling and information services are available, as is tutoring in most subjects, math, chemistry, biology, speech, psychology, French, Italian, Spanish, computers, economics, business, philosophy, accounting, physics There is remedial math, reading, and writing. **Library/Resources:** The library contains 166,500 volumes, 357 microform items, 3,027 audio/video tapes/CDs/DVDs, and subscribes to 50,875 periodicals including electronic. Computerized library services include interlibrary loans, database searching, Internet access, and Wi-Fi capability. Special learning facilities include an art gallery, an Dillon Child Study Center, Campus Ministry, and Musical Theater. **Physically Challenged Students:** Facilities include wheelchair ramps, elevators, special parking, specially equipped restrooms, lowered drinking fountains. Use of a computer or word processor; use of calculator; tape recorder; class notes enlarged; separate, quiet location for testing; preferential classroom seating; textbooks in alternate format; scribe; sign language interpreters. **Special:** Study abroad in Australia, Spain, Italy and England. The Save Time/Save Money program allows undergraduate students who are accepted into the Graduate Management Studies program to get a head start on an SJC graduate management degree- MBA, MBA in Accounting, MBA in Health Care Management or MS in Management (with concentrations in Organizational Management or Health Care Management or Human Resources Management) by taking graduate courses that would satisfy their undergraduate and graduate degree requirements at the same time at the undergraduate tuition rate. This opportunity is restricted to seniors who have met certain requirements. There are a freshman honors program and 12 departmental honors programs. **Visiting:** There are regularly scheduled orientations for prospective students. There are guides for informal visits and visitors may sit in on classes.. **Campus Safety and Security:** Measures include 24-hour foot and vehicle patrol, emergency notification system, and security escort services. There are shuttle buses, emergency telephones, and lighted pathways/sidewalks.

REQUIREMENTS: The SAT or ACT is required. High School Diploma is required and GED is accepted. Off-campus interview

arranged with admissions representative. A GPA of 2.5 is required. AP and CLEP credits are accepted. Important factors in the admissions decision are advanced placement or honors courses, recommendations by school officials, and extracurricular activities record. **Procedure:** Freshmen are admitted fall, spring, and summer. There are early admissions and deferred admissions plans. Applications should be filed by August 31 for fall entry, along with a $25 fee. Notifications are sent October 1. Applications are accepted on-line. **Transfer Students:** 80 transfer students enrolled in 2013-2014. Chem/Bio Major 2.5 and up and Education Major 2.8 and up. 48 of 128 credits required for the bachelor's degree must be completed at St. Joseph's College. **International Students:** The school actively recruits these students. SAT or ACT are recommended.

ADMISSIONS: 65% of the 2014-2015 applicants were accepted. The SAT scores for the 2014-2015 freshman class were: Critical Reading--56% below 500, 32% between 500 and 599, and 12% between 600 and 699; Math--52% below 500, 34% between 500 and 599, and 14% between 600 and 699; Writing--60% below 500, 28% between 500 and 599, 11% between 600 and 699, and 1% between 700 and 800. The ACT scores were 50% below 21, 25% between 21 and 23, 17% between 24 and 26, % between 27 and 28, and 8% above 28. **Admissions Contact:** Michael Learmond, Director of Admissions Operations. E-Mail: *brooklynas@sjcny.edu* Web: *www.sjcny.edu*

FINANCIAL AID: In 2014-2015, 91% of all full-time freshmen and 92% of continuing full-time students received some form of financial aid. 67% of all full-time freshmen and 67% of continuing full-time students received need-based aid. The average freshman award was $18,716. Need-based scholarships or need-based grants averaged $8,149 ($14,768 maximum); need-based self-help aid (loans and jobs) averaged $3,243 ($5,500 maximum); and other non-need-based awards and non-need-based scholarships averaged $11,847 ($41,700 maximum). 8% of undergraduate students work part-time. Average annual earnings from campus work are $1712. The average financial indebtedness of the 2014 graduate was $23,935. The FAFSA and the state aid form are required. The priority date for freshman financial aid applications for fall entry is February 25.

ST. JOSEPH'S COLLEGE, NEW YORK/ SUFFOLK CAMPUS   E-5
www.sjcny.edu

Patchogue, NY 11772	(631) 687-4500
	n/av
Fax: (631)447-3601	**Email:** longislandas@sjcny.edu
Full-time: 831 men, 1586 women	**Faculty:** 119; IIB, +$
Part-time: 210 men, 396 women	**Ph.D.s:** 76%
Graduate: 137 men, 463 women	**Student/Faculty:** 20 to 1
Year: semesters, summer session	**Tuition:** $22,630
Room & Board: n/app	**Freshman Class:** 1439 applied, 1105 accepted, 321 enrolled
SAT CR/M/W: 530/535/500 **ACT:** 23	**CEEB CODE:** 2841
Application Deadline: n/av	**COMPETITIVE**

St. Joseph's College, founded in 1916, has provided an affordable liberal arts education to a diverse group of students. Independent and coeducational, St. Joseph's prepares students for lives of integrity, intellectual and spiritual values, social responsibility and service; lives that are worthy of the College's motto, Esse non videri   "To be, not to seem." St. Joseph's Long Island Campus challenges its students to develop their full potential and a joy of learning. The College enjoys a student-to-faculty ratio that provides individual attention in an open, supportive atmosphere. St. Joseph's remains dedicated to maintaining low costs while upholding a strict standard of excellence. While retention rates at most colleges are slipping, St. Joseph's remains above the national average. There are 2 undergraduate schools and 1 graduate school. In addition to regional accreditation, St. Joseph's College has baccalaureate program accreditation with ACEN, COAPRT, and CAEP. The 56-acre campus is in a suburban area 55 miles from midtown Manhattan. Including any residence halls, there are 11 buildings.

STUDENT LIFE: 99% of undergraduates are from New York. Others

are from 13 states. 90% are from public schools. 72% are White. **Male To Female Ratio:** 2.1:1. The average age of freshmen is 18; all undergraduates, 24. 15% do not continue beyond their first year; 85% remain to graduate. **Housing:** College-sponsored housing includes Alcohol is not permitted. All students commute. All students may keep cars.

FACULTY/CLASSROOMS: 46% of faculty are male; 54% are female. All teach undergraduates. No introductory courses are taught by graduate students. The average class size in an introductory lecture is 16; in a laboratory is 14; and in a regular course is 15.

PROGRAMS OF STUDY: St. Joseph's College confers B.A., B.S., B.A./M.A., B.S./M.A., B.S./M.S., B.S./M.B.A. degrees. Master's degrees are also awarded. Bachelor's degrees are awarded in BIOLOGICAL SCIENCE (biology/biological science), BUSINESS (accounting, business administration and management, hospitality management services, marketing management, organizational leadership and management, recreation and leisure services, and tourism), COMMUNICATIONS AND THE ARTS (English, journalism, Spanish, and speech/debate/rhetoric), COMPUTER AND PHYSICAL SCIENCE (chemistry, computer information technology, computer science, and mathematics), EDUCATION (education, secondary education, and special education), HEALTH PROFESSIONS (health care administration, medical technology, nursing, and public health), SOCIAL SCIENCE (child psychology/development, criminal justice, history, human services, liberal arts/general studies, philosophy and religion, political science/government, psychology, social science, and sociology). Child study and secondary education is the strongest academically. Child Study, business administration and psychology have the largest enrollments.

ACTIVITIES: 1% of men belong to 2 local fraternities; 1% of women belong to 4 local sororities. There are 52 groups on campus, including art, chess, chorus, computers, dance, drama, environmental, ethnic, film, gay, honors, international, literary magazine, musical theater, newspaper, political, professional, radio and TV, religious, social, social service, student government, and yearbook. Popular campus events include Welcome Back BBQ, Welcome Back Evening Social, Club Fair, Fall Festival, Bowl-a-thon, Charity BINGO, Spring Fling, Spring Gala, Tom DeLuca (Hypnotist), Talent Show. **Sports:** There are 7 intercollegiate sports for men and 9 for women. Facilities include Multi-purpose Turf field for soccer and lacrosse, softball field, baseball field, 6 full tennis courts, natatorium, gymnasium with 2 full courts. **Graduates:** From July 1, 2013 to June 30, 2014, 935 bachelor's degrees were awarded. The most popular majors were child study (20%), psychology (9%), and speech (8%). 131 companies recruited on campus in 2013-2014. In an average class, 52% graduate in 4 years or less, 66% graduate in 5 years or less, and 68% graduate in 6 years or less.

SERVICES: Counseling and information services are available, as is tutoring in most subjects, English, history, psychology, religious studies, speech pathology, speech communications, biology, chemistry, physics, earth science, business administration, accounting, mathematics, computer science, child study, adolescent education, criminal justice, There is a reader service for the blind, and remedial math, reading, and writing. Testing accommodations (for students with documented accommodations), Time management, study skills, test-taking strategies, stress management, organization, note-taking, critical thinking abilities, academic research, academic writing, lab report review, thesis help, public speaking, citation styles and formatting, lesson plan development, and basic computer help (includes helping students learn how to use a flash drive, attach a document to an email, utilize BlackBoard, learn Microsoft Office Word, PowerPoint, and Excel, navigate the databases, and find scholarly sources online). **Library/Resources:** The library contains 196,931 volumes, 1,375 microform items, 2,747 audio/video tapes/CDs/DVDs, and subscribes to 51,068 periodicals including electronic. Computerized library services include interlibrary loans, database searching, Internet access, and Wi-Fi capability. Special learning facilities include an art gallery, radio station, technology building, and computer labs. **Physically Challenged Students:** Facilities include wheelchair ramps, elevators, special parking, specially equipped restrooms, and lowered drinking fountains. **Special:** Study abroad in Australia, Spain, Italy, England. OCICU - Online Consortium of Independent College and Universities. The Save Time/Save Money program allows undergrad-

uate students who are accepted into the Graduate Management Studies program to get a head start on an SJC graduate management degree- MBA, MBA in Accounting, MBA in Health Care Management or MS in Management (with concentrations in Organizational Management or Health Care Management or Human Resources Management) by taking graduate courses that would satisfy their undergraduate and graduate degree requirements at the same time at the undergraduate tuition rate. This opportunity is restricted to seniors who have met certain requirements. There are a freshman honors program and 10 departmental honors programs. **Visiting:** There are regularly scheduled orientations for prospective students, 1-day orientation in August just prior to start of classes. There are guides for informal visits and visitors may sit in on classes.. **Campus Safety and Security:** Measures include 24-hour foot and vehicle patrol, emergency notification system, and security escort services. There are emergency telephones and lighted pathways/sidewalks.

REQUIREMENTS: The SAT or ACT is required. High School diploma is required and GED is accepted. Off-campus interview arranged with admissions representative. A GPA of 3.0 is required. AP and CLEP credits are accepted. Important factors in the admissions decision are advanced placement or honors courses, leadership record, and recommendations by school officials. **Procedure:** Freshmen are admitted fall, spring, and summer. There are early admissions, deferred admissions, and rolling admissions plans. Application deadlines are open. Application fee is $25. Notification of early decision is sent November 1; regular decision, Applications are accepted on-line. **Transfer Students:** 394 transfer students enrolled in 2013-2014. If transferring with less than 24 credits of college level coursework, a high school transcript is required. 48 of 128 credits required for the bachelor's degree must be completed at St. Joseph's College. **International Students:** The school actively recruits these students. SAT or ACT are recommended.

ADMISSIONS: 77% of the 2014-2015 applicants were accepted. The SAT scores for the 2014-2015 freshman class were: Critical Reading--30% below 500, 56% between 500 and 599, 13% between 600 and 699, and 1% between 700 and 800; Math--29% below 500, 52% between 500 and 599, 18% between 600 and 699, and 1% between 700 and 800; Writing--45% below 500, 43% between 500 and 599, 11% between 600 and 699, and 1% between 700 and 800. The ACT scores were 28% below 21, 30% between 21 and 23, 25% between 24 and 26, 11% between 27 and 28, and 6% above 28. **Admissions Contact:** Gigi Lamens, Assoc Vice President for Enrollment Mgmt. E-Mail: *longislandas@sjcny.edu* Web: *www.sjcny.edu*

FINANCIAL AID: In 2014-2015, 98% of all full-time freshmen and 93% of continuing full-time students received some form of financial aid. 67% of all full-time freshmen and 65% of continuing full-time students received need-based aid. The average freshman award was $16,455. Need-based scholarships or need-based grants averaged $5,897 ($22,200 maximum); need-based self-help aid (loans and jobs) averaged $3,499 ($7,500 maximum); and other non-need-based awards and non-need-based scholarships averaged $12,034 ($30,922 maximum). 4% of undergraduate students work part-time. Average annual earnings from campus work are $2623. The average financial indebtedness of the 2014 graduate was $25,707. The FAFSA and the state aid form are required. The priority date for freshman financial aid applications for fall entry is February 25.

ST. LAWRENCE UNIVERSITY   C-2
www.stlwu.edu

Canton, NY 13617	**(315) 229-5261** **(800) 285-1856**
Fax: (315) 229-5818	Email: admissions@stlwu.edu
Full-time: 1978 men, 1257 women	Faculty: 166; IIB, +$
Part-time: 12 men, 14 women	Ph.D.s: 98%
Graduate: 38 men, 58 women	Student/Faculty: 14 to 1
Year: semesters, summer session	Tuition: $47,686
Room & Board: $12,286	Freshman Class: 4273 applied, 1855 accepted, 647 enrolled
SAT CR/M/W: 618/602/620	CEEB CODE: 2805
Application Deadline: February 1	**VERY COMPETITIVE**

St. Lawrence University, established in 1856, is a private liberal arts institution. The figures in the above capsule and in this profile are approximate. There is one graduate school. In addition to regional accreditation, St. Lawrence has baccalaureate program accreditation with ACS. The 1000-acre campus is in a small town 80 miles south of Ottawa, Canada. Including any residence halls, there are 30 buildings.

STUDENT LIFE: 52% of undergraduates are from out of state, mostly the Northeast. Students are from 40 states, 45 foreign countries, and Canada. 69% are from public schools. 83% are White. The average age of freshmen is 18; all undergraduates, 20. 10% do not continue beyond their first year; 79% remain to graduate. **Housing:** 2162 students can be accommodated in college housing, which includes coed dorms and on-campus apartments. In addition, there are special-interest houses, fraternity houses, sorority houses, Theme cottages, such as Habitat for Humanity. On-campus housing is guaranteed for all 4 years. 98% of students live on campus; of those, 90% remain on campus on weekends. All students may keep cars.

FACULTY/CLASSROOMS: 55% of faculty are male; 45% are female. 99% teach undergraduates, and all do research. No introductory courses are taught by graduate students. The average class size in a regular course is 16.

PROGRAMS OF STUDY: St. Lawrence confers B.A., and B.S. degrees. Master's degrees are also awarded. Bachelor's degrees are awarded in AGRICULTURE (conservation and regulation and environmental studies), BIOLOGICAL SCIENCE (biochemistry, biology/biological science, biophysics, and neurosciences), BUSINESS (international economics), COMMUNICATIONS AND THE ARTS (art, art history and appreciation, communications, creative writing, dramatic arts, English, fine arts, French, German, languages, modern language, music, Spanish, studio art, and visual and performing arts), COMPUTER AND PHYSICAL SCIENCE (chemistry, computer science, geology, mathematics, and physics), ENGINEERING AND ENVIRONMENTAL DESIGN (environmental science), SOCIAL SCIENCE (African studies, anthropology, Asian/Oriental studies, Canadian studies, economics, history, interdisciplinary studies, international studies, philosophy, political science/government, psychology, religion, and sociology). Psychology, economics, and government have the largest enrollments.

ACTIVITIES: 4% of men belong to 2 national fraternities; 19% of women belong to 1 local and 3 national sororities. There are 100 groups on campus, including art, choir, chorus, computers, dance, drama, environmental, ethnic, forensics, gay, honors, international, jazz band, literary magazine, newspaper, orchestra, photography, political, professional, radio and TV, religious, social, social service, student government, and yearbook. Popular campus events include Moving-Up Day, 100th Night, and Candlelight Service. **Sports:** There are 16 intercollegiate sports for men and 16 for women, and 11 intramural sports for men and 11 for women. Facilities include basketball, squash, and tennis courts, a swimming pool, and a 133-station fitness center. There are also 2 field houses, an arena, artificial ice rink, 18-hole golf course, riding stables, jogging and cross-country ski trails, indoor and outdoor competition tracks, soccer, baseball, and softball fields. **Graduates:** From July 1, 2013 to June 30, 2014, 444 bachelor's degrees were awarded. The most popular majors were psychology (17%), economics (14%), and environmental studies (10%). 18 companies recruited on campus in 2013-2014. In an average class, 1% graduate in 3 years or less, 78% graduate in 4 years or less, 80% graduate in 5 years or less, and 81% graduate in 6 years or less. Of the 2013 graduating class, 24% were enrolled in graduate school within 6 months of graduation, and 72% were employed.

SERVICES: Counseling and information services are available, as is tutoring in every subject. There is a reader service for the blind. A writing center, science and technology counseling **Library/Resources:** The 2 libraries contain 612,057 volumes, 599,822 microform items, 7,513 audio/video tapes/CDs/DVDs, and subscribe to 41,900 periodicals including electronic. Computerized library services include interlibrary loans, database searching, and Internet access. Special learning facilities include an art gallery, radio station, a science field station. **Physically Challenged Students:** 75% of the campus is accessible. Facilities include wheelchair ramps, elevators, special parking, specially equipped restrooms, special class scheduling, lowered drinking fountains. **Special:** Students may cross-register with the Associated

Colleges of the St. Lawrence Valley. Internships are available through the sociology, psychology, and English departments and through a service learning program. Study-abroad in 15 countries and a Washington semester are offered. Dual majors and student-designed majors can be arranged. Students may earn 3-2 engineering degrees in conjunction with 7 engineering schools. Nondegree study and pass/fail options are available. An Adirondack semester is also offered. There are 20 national honor societies, including Phi Beta Kappa, and 17 departmental honors programs. **Visiting:** There are regularly scheduled orientations for prospective students, including interviews and tours. There are guides for informal visits, visitors may sit in on classes, and stay overnight. To schedule a visit, contact the Admissions Office. **Campus Safety and Security:** Measures include 24-hour foot and vehicle patrol, emergency notification system, self-defense education, and security escort services. There are emergency telephones, lighted pathways/sidewalks, and student patrols.

REQUIREMENTS: Applicants must be graduates of an accredited high school. 16 or more academic credits are required, including 4 years of English and 3 years each of foreign languages, math, science, and social studies. Essays are required and interviews are recommended for all applicants. Submissions of standardized test scores is optional. AP credits are accepted. Important factors in the admissions decision are advanced placement or honors courses, extracurricular activities record, and recommendations by school officials. To graduate, students must maintain a minimum GPA of 2.0 and complete 120 course hours, with 29 to 43 in the major. Freshmen must take a first-year program, a 2-semester team-taught course. Requirements also include 1 course in arts/expression, 1 in humanities, 1 in social science, 1 in math or foreign language, 2 in natural science/science studies, and 2 in diversity. **Procedure:** Freshmen are admitted fall and spring. Entrance exams should be taken during the spring of the junior year or the fall of the senior year. There are early decision and deferred admissions plans. Early decision applications should be filed by November 1; regular applications, by February 1 for fall entry; and December 1 for spring entry, along with a $60 fee. Notification of early decision is sent December 15; regular decision, March 30. 212 early decision candidates were accepted for the 2014-2015 class. 351 applicants were on the 2014 waiting list; 18 were admitted. Applications are accepted on-line. **Transfer Students:** 24 transfer students enrolled in 2013-2014. The high school transcript and SAT scores will be evaluated, but college work is more important. High school and college recommendations are required. 17 of 120 credits required for the bachelor's degree must be completed at St. Lawrence. **International Students:** There are 126 international students enrolled. The school actively recruits these students.

ADMISSIONS: 43% of the 2014-2015 applicants were accepted. The SAT scores for the 2014-2015 freshman class were: Critical Reading--3% below 500, 35% between 500 and 599, 50% between 600 and 699, and 12% between 700 and 800; Math--3% between 500 and 599, 60% between 600 and 699, and 9% between 700 and 800; Writing--6% below 500, 32% between 500 and 599, 49% between 600 and 699, and 12% between 700 and 800. 71% of the current freshmen were in the top fifth of their class; 91% were in the top two fifths. 14 freshmen graduated first in their class. **Admissions Contact:** Teresa Cowdrey, Vice President and Dean of Admissions and Financial Aid. E-Mail: *admissions@stlawu.edu* Web: *www.stlwu.edu*

FINANCIAL AID: In 2014-2015, 92% of all full-time freshmen and 88% of continuing full-time students received some form of financial aid. 63% of all full-time freshmen and 66% of continuing full-time students received need-based aid. The average freshman award was $32,003. Need-based scholarships or need-based grants averaged $37,659; need-based self-help aid (loans and jobs) averaged $6,654; non-need-based athletic scholarships averaged $49,898; and other non-need-based awards and non-need-based scholarships averaged $17,838. 33% of undergraduate students work part-time. Average annual earnings from campus work are $1100. The average financial indebtedness of the 2014 graduate was $26,270. St. Lawrence is a member of CSS. The CSS/Profile and FAFSA, and nocustodial profile are required. The deadline for filing freshman financial aid applications for fall entry is February 1.

ST. THOMAS AQUINAS COLLEGE   D-5
www.stac.edu

Sparkill, NY 10976	(914) 398-4100
	(800) 999-STAC
Fax: (914) 398-4224	Email: thoward@stac.edu
Full-time: n/av	Faculty: IIB, +$
Part-time: n/av	Ph.D.s: n/av
Graduate: 75 men, 125 women	Student/Faculty: n/av
Year: 4-1-4, summer session	Tuition: $27,630
Room & Board: $12,600	Freshman Class: n/av
SAT or ACT: required	CEEB CODE: 0807
Application Deadline: n/av	COMPETITIVE

St. Thomas Aquinas College, founded in 1952, is an independent liberal arts institution. Figures in above capsule and in this profile are approximate. There are 2 graduate schools. The 43-acre campus is in a suburban area 15 miles north of New York City. Including any residence halls, there are 12 buildings.

STUDENT LIFE: 75% of undergraduates are from New York. Others are from 6 states, 8 foreign countries, and Canada. 80% are from public schools. 84% are White. 62% are Catholic; 23% Protestant. The average age of freshmen is 18; all undergraduates, 23. 16% do not continue beyond their first year; 62% remain to graduate. **Housing:** 450 students can be accommodated in college housing, which includes single-sex dorms and on-campus apartments. On-campus housing is guaranteed for all 4 years. 65% of students commute. Alcohol is not permitted. All students may keep cars.

FACULTY/CLASSROOMS: 55% of faculty are male; 45% are female. 99% teach undergraduates, 50% do research, and 50% do both. No introductory courses are taught by graduate students. The average class size in an introductory lecture is 35; in a laboratory is 15; and in a regular course is 20.

PROGRAMS OF STUDY: STAC confers B.A., B.S. and B.S.E. degrees. Associate and Master's degrees are also awarded. Bachelor's degrees are awarded in BUSINESS (accounting, banking and finance, business administration and management, marketing/retailing/merchandising, and recreation and leisure services), COMMUNICATIONS AND THE ARTS (communications, English, fine arts, romance languages and literature, and Spanish), EDUCATION (art education, bilingual/bicultural education, elementary education, foreign languages education, science education, secondary education, and special education), ENGINEERING AND ENVIRONMENTAL DESIGN (commercial art), HEALTH PROFESSIONS (medical laboratory technology and premedicine), SOCIAL SCIENCE (criminal justice, history, philosophy, prelaw, psychology, religion, and social science). Education, business administration, and natural sciences are the strongest academically. Business administration has the largest enrollment.

ACTIVITIES: There are no fraternities or sororities. There are 15 groups on campus, including cheerleading, chorus, computers, drama, honors, international, literary magazine, musical theater, newspaper, professional, radio and TV, religious, social service, student government, and yearbook. Popular campus events include Trips to Broadway shows and Halloween and Christmas mixers. **Sports:** There are 5 intercollegiate sports for men and 4 for women, and 6 intramural sports for men and 5 for women. Facilities include an auditorium, a gym, weight room, basketball and tennis courts.

SERVICES: Counseling and information services are available, as is tutoring in most subjects. There is remedial math and writing. **Library/Resources:** The library contains 102,943 volumes, 45,900 microform items, and subscribes to 108 periodicals including electronic. Computerized library services include interlibrary loans and database searching. Special learning facilities include a radio station and TV station. **Physically Challenged Students:** 90% of the campus is accessible. Facilities include wheelchair ramps, elevators, special parking, specially equipped restrooms, special class scheduling, and lowered telephones. **Special:** The college offers cross-registration with Barry University and Aquinas College and internships in business, criminal justice, commercial design, recreation and leisure, and communications. Study abroad in Europe and Asia, a 3-2 engineering degree with George Washington University and Manhattan College,

and in physical therapy with New York Medical College, and work-study programs are available. Nondegree study and pass/fail options are possible. There are 7 national honor societies, Phi Beta Kappa, and a freshman honors program. **Visiting:** There are guides for informal visits, visitors may sit in on classes, and stay overnight. To schedule a visit, contact the Admissions Office. **Campus Safety and Security:** Measures include 24-hour foot and vehicle patrol and security escort services. There are emergency telephones and lighted pathways/sidewalks.

REQUIREMENTS: The SAT or ACT is required. Applicants must be graduates of an accredited secondary school or have a GED certificate. 16 Carnegie units are recommended, including 4 years of English, and social science, 2 years of math, foreign language, and science, including 2 years of lab science. A GPA of 2.2 is required. AP and CLEP credits are accepted. Important factors in the admissions decision are leadership record, extracurricular activities record, and advanced placement or honors courses.To graduate, all students must complete a total of 120 credit hours, with 36 to 54 in the major and a minimum GPA of 2.0. A core curriculum of 51 credits in liberal arts courses is required. **Procedure:** Freshmen are admitted fall and spring. Entrance exams should be taken by the spring of the junior year. There are early decision, early admissions, deferred admissions, and rolling admissions plans. Check with the school for current application deadlines. The fall 2014 application fee was $30. Notification is sent on a rolling basis. Applications are accepted on-line. **Transfer Students:** Applicants must have a 2.0 GPA from the previous school. 30 of 120 credits required for the bachelor's degree must be completed at STAC. **International Students:** The school actively recruits these students. They must take the TOEFL.

ADMISSIONS: Tracey A. Howard-Ubelhoer, Director of Admissions. E-Mail: *thoward@stac.edu* Web: *www.stac.edu*

FINANCIAL AID: STAC is a member of CSS. The FAFSA is required. Check with the school for current application deadlines.

STATE UNIVERSITY OF NEW YORK

The State University of New York, established in 1948, is a public system in New York. It is governed by a board of trustees, whose chief administrator is the chancellor. The primary goal of the system is teaching, research, and public service. The main priorities are to educate the largest number of people possible at the highest level, including educationally disadvantaged groups; to provide students with enhanced educational skills and techniques; and to enhance the quality of life for all New Yorkers. The total student enrollment is usually about 412,355 with 27000 faculty members. Altogether there are 1423 baccalaureate, 860 master's, and 278 doctoral programs offered in the State University of New York System. Profiles of the 4-year campuses are included in this section.

STATE UNIVERSITY OF NEW YORK /   C-3
COLLEGE OF ENVIRONMENTAL SCIENCE AND FORESTRY
www.esf.edu

Syracuse, NY 13210	(315) 470-6600
Fax: (315) 470-6933	Email: esfinfo@esf.edu
Full-time: 909 men, 618 women	Faculty: 140
Part-time: 303 men, 347 women	Ph.D.s: 96%
Graduate: 315 men, 314 women	Student/Faculty: 13 to 1
Year: semesters	Tuition: $5891 ($13,791)
Room & Board: $12,460	Freshman Class: 1678 applied, 723 accepted, 284 enrolled
SAT CR/M: 584/600 ACT: 25	CEEB CODE: 2530
Application Deadline:	VERY COMPETITIVE

The SUNY College of Environmental Science and Forestry, founded in 1911, is the nation's oldest and largest college focused exclusively on the science, design, engineering, and management of our environment and natural resources. The college offers 21 undergraduate and

28 graduate degree programs, including 8 Ph.D. programs. Students also benefit from a special partnership with Syracuse University (SU) that provides access to courses, housing, and student organizations. There are no undergraduate schools and one graduate school. In addition to regional accreditation, SUNY-ESF has baccalaureate program accreditation with ABET, ASLA, and SAF. The 12-acre campus is in an urban area in Syracuse, NY. Including any residence halls, there are 7 buildings.

STUDENT LIFE: 86% of undergraduates are from New York. Others are from 28 states, and 6 foreign countries. 85% are from public schools. 85% are White. The average age of freshmen is 18; all undergraduates, 21. 22% do not continue beyond their first year; 65% remain to graduate. **Housing:** 475 students can be accommodated in college housing, which includes single-sex and coed dorms, on-campus apartments, and off-campus apartments. In addition, there are special-interest houses, fraternity houses, sorority houses, Substance-free floors, quiet floors, and learning communities. On-campus housing is guaranteed for all 4 years and is available on a lottery system for upperclassmen. 3% of students commute. Alcohol is not permitted. Upperclassmen may keep cars.

FACULTY/CLASSROOMS: 72% of faculty are male; 28% are female. All teach and do research. No introductory courses are taught by graduate students. The average class size in a regular course is 25.

PROGRAMS OF STUDY: SUNY-ESF confers B.S., and B.L.A. degrees. Associate, Master's, and Doctoral degrees are also awarded. Bachelor's degrees are awarded in AGRICULTURE (animal science, environmental studies, fishing and fisheries, forest engineering, forestry and related sciences, natural resource management, plant science, soil science, and wood science), BIOLOGICAL SCIENCE (biology/biological science, biotechnology, botany, ecology, entomology, environmental biology, microbiology, molecular biology, plant genetics, plant pathology, plant physiology, and wildlife biology), COMPUTER AND PHYSICAL SCIENCE (chemistry and polymer science), EDUCATION (environmental education and science education), ENGINEERING AND ENVIRONMENTAL DESIGN (chemical engineering, construction management, environmental design, environmental engineering, environmental science, landscape architecture/design, paper and pulp science, paper engineering, and survey and mapping technology), HEALTH PROFESSIONS (predentistry, premedicine, and prepharmacy), SOCIAL SCIENCE (prelaw). Engineering, chemistry, and biology are the strongest academically. Environmental and forest biology, landscape architecture, and environmental science have the largest enrollments.

ACTIVITIES: 3% of men belong to 20 national fraternities; 3% of women belong to 20 national sororities. There are 300 groups on campus, including art, bagpipe, band, cheerleading, choir, chorale, chorus, computers, dance, debate, drama, environmental, ethnic, film, gay, honors, international, jazz band, literary magazine, marching band, musical theater, newspaper, orchestra, pep band, photography, political, professional, radio and TV, religious, social, social service, student government, symphony, and yearbook. Popular campus events include Earth Week, Awards Banquet and December Soiree. **Sports:** There are 4 intercollegiate sports for men and 3 for women, and 15 intramural sports for men and 15 for women. Facilities include ESF has soccer, golf, cross-country, and woodsman's teams. Students can participate in all Syracuse University club teams, intramural sports, and recreational activities. **Graduates:** From July 1, 2013 to June 30, 2014, 286 bachelor's degrees were awarded. The most popular majors were environmental and forest biology (47%), environmental studies (20%), and landscape architecture (9%). 40 companies recruited on campus in 2013-2014. In an average class, 3% graduate in 3 years or less, 60% graduate in 4 years or less, 71% graduate in 5 years or less, and 72% graduate in 6 years or less. Of the 2013 graduating class, 16% were enrolled in graduate school within 6 months of graduation, and 61% were employed.

SERVICES: Counseling and information services are available, as is tutoring in most subjects. There is a reader service for the blind. **Library/Resources:** The library contains 135,305 volumes, 200,090 microform items, 1,118 audio/video tapes/CDs/DVDs, and subscribes to 2,001 periodicals including electronic. Computerized library services include interlibrary loans, database searching, Internet access, and Wi-Fi capability. Special learning facilities include an art gallery, natural history museum, radio station, and TV station.

Physically Challenged Students: 95% of the campus is accessible. Facilities include wheelchair ramps, elevators, special parking, specially equipped restrooms, lowered drinking fountains, lowered telephones, and special housing. **Special:** Cross-registration is offered with Syracuse University. Co-op programs, internships, and dual options in forest ecosystem science are available. Study abroad is available in landscape architecture and through Syracuse University. There is an Honors Program for outstanding students There are 1 national honor society, a freshman honors program, and 8 departmental honors programs. **Visiting:** There are regularly scheduled orientations for prospective students, including a fall open house, which provides campus tours, faculty sessions, an activities fair, and student affairs presentations. There are guides for informal visits and visitors may sit in on classes. To schedule a visit, contact the Admissions Office. **Campus Safety and Security:** Measures include 24-hour foot and vehicle patrol, emergency notification system, self-defense education, and security escort services. There are shuttle buses, emergency telephones, lighted pathways/sidewalks, and controlled access to dorms/residences.

REQUIREMENTS: The SAT or ACT is required. Applicants are required to have a minimum of 3 years of math and science, including chemistry, in a college preparatory curriculum. A supplemental application form, essay and results of SAT or ACT exams are required. A campus visit, letters of recommendation, and a personal portfolio or resume are recommended. SUNY-ESF requires applicants to be in the upper 50% of their class. AP and CLEP credits are accepted. Important factors in the admissions decision are advanced placement or honors courses, leadership record, and extracurricular activities record.Students must complete 125 to 130 credit hours for the B.S. (160 for the B.L.A.), including 60 in the major, with a minimum 2.0 GPA. Courses in chemistry, English, math, and biology or physics are required. **Procedure:** Freshmen are admitted fall and spring. Entrance exams should be taken by October of the senior year. There are early admissions, deferred admissions, and rolling admissions plans. Early decision applications should be filed by November 15, along with a $40 fee. Notification of early decision is sent December 15; regular decision, March 1. 70 applicants were on the 2014 waiting list; 20 were admitted. Applications are accepted on-line. **Transfer Students:** 226 transfer students enrolled in 2013-2014. Transfer requirements vary by major. Students must successfully complete prerequisite course work and must have a 2.5 or higher GPA to be considered. 24 of 125 credits required for the bachelor's degree must be completed at SUNY-ESF. **International Students:** There are 11 international students enrolled. They must take the TOEFL with a minimum score of 550 on the paper-based TOEFL (PBT) or 79 on the Internet-based version (iBT). They must also take the SAT or ACT.

ADMISSIONS: 43% of the 2014-2015 applicants were accepted. The SAT scores for the 2014-2015 freshman class were: Critical Reading--7% below 500, 50% between 500 and 599, 37% between 600 and 699, and 6% between 700 and 800; Math--5% below 500, 44% between 500 and 599, 46% between 600 and 699, and 5% between 700 and 800. The ACT scores were 6% below 21, 29% between 21 and 23, 35% between 24 and 26, 21% between 27 and 28, and 9% above 28. 77% of the current freshmen were in the top fifth of their class; 96% were in the top two fifths. There were 1 National Merit finalists. **Admissions Contact:** Susan H. Sanford, Director of Admissions, Inter-Instutiona. E-Mail: *esfinfo@esf.edu* Web: *www.esf.edu*

FINANCIAL AID: In 2014-2015, 85% of all full-time freshmen and 85% of continuing full-time students received some form of financial aid. 80% of all full-time freshmen and 80% of continuing full-time students received need-based aid. The average freshman award was $7,200. Need-based scholarships or need-based grants averaged $1,500 ($3,000 maximum); need-based self-help aid (loans and jobs) averaged $4,250 ($5,500 maximum); and other non-need-based awards and non-need-based scholarships averaged $4,500 ($6,000 maximum). 75% of undergraduate students work part-time. Average annual earnings from campus work are $1400. The average financial indebtedness of the 2014 graduate was $21,125. SUNY-ESF is a member of CSS. The FAFSA is required. The priority date for freshman financial aid applications for fall entry is March 1.

STATE UNIVERSITY OF NEW YORK AT POTSDAM — D-2
www.potsdam.edu

Potsdam, NY 13676   (315) 267-2180
                                                            n/av
Fax: (315) 267-2163   Email: admissions@potsdam.edu
Full-time: 1562 men, 2011 women   Faculty: 249; IIA, --$
Part-time: 55 men, 53 women   Ph.D.s: 66%
Graduate: 69 men, 229 women   Student/Faculty: 13 to 1
Year: semesters, summer session   Tuition: $7553 ($17,203)
Room & Board: $10,920   Freshman Class: 5155
                                     applied, 3484 accepted,
                                     830 enrolled
SAT CR/M: 510/510 ACT: 23   CEEB CODE: 2545
Application Deadline: rolling   COMPETITIVE

The State University of New York at Potsdam, founded in 1816, joined the state university system in 1948. SUNY Potsdam offers over 50 programs in Arts and Sciences, 6 in The Crane School of Music and over 20 in The School of Education and Professional Studies as well as programs in Interdisciplinary Studies. Bachelor Degrees are offered in Arts, Science, Fine Arts and Music and Master's degrees in Arts, Education, Science and Music. SUNY Potsdam offers dual degrees with a number of other Universities. There are 3 undergraduate schools and one graduate school. In addition to regional accreditation, SUNY Potsdam has baccalaureate program accreditation with NASM, NCATE, NAST, ICABE, and AAAHC. The 240-acre campus is in a rural area 30 miles from Massena and Ogdensburg, and 140 miles northeast of Syracuse and 80 miles from Montreal, Canada. Including any residence halls, there are 56 buildings.

STUDENT LIFE: 96% of undergraduates are from New York. Others are from 28 states, 14 foreign countries, and Canada. 85% are from public schools. 69% are White. The average age of freshmen is 18; all undergraduates, 21. 20% do not continue beyond their first year; 54% remain to graduate. **Housing:** 2715 students can be accommodated in college housing, which includes single-sex and coed dorms, on-campus apartments, and off-campus apartments. In addition, there are honors houses, special-interest houses, First year experience, quiet study, international house, transfer student housing, sustainability housing,gender neutral,. On-campus housing is guaranteed for all 4 years. 61% of students live on campus; of those, 70% remain on campus on weekends. All students may keep cars.

FACULTY/CLASSROOMS: 51% of faculty are male; 49% are female. All teach undergraduates. No introductory courses are taught by graduate students.

PROGRAMS OF STUDY: SUNY Potsdam confers B.A., B.F.A., B.M. and B.S. degrees. Master's degrees are also awarded. Bachelor's degrees are awarded in AGRICULTURE (environmental studies), BIOLOGICAL SCIENCE (biochemistry and biology/biological science), BUSINESS (business administration and management and business economics), COMMUNICATIONS AND THE ARTS (art history, art, creative writing, dance, English, English literature, English Writing, fine arts, French, literature, music, music business management, music performance, Spanish, communication arts - speech, studio art, theatre arts, and visual and performing arts), COMPUTER AND PHYSICAL SCIENCE (chemistry, computer science, geology, mathematics, and physics), EDUCATION (early childhood education, elementary education, English education, mathematics education, music education, and social studies education), HEALTH PROFESSIONS (community health work), SOCIAL SCIENCE (anthropology, archeology, criminal justice, economics, French studies, history, interdisciplinary studies, philosophy, political science/government, psychology, sociology, Spanish studies, and women's studies). Music education, childhood education and business administration have the largest enrollments.

ACTIVITIES: 1% of men belong to 3 local and 2 national fraternities; 1% of women belong to 7 local and 3 national sororities. There are 81 groups on campus, including art, band, cheerleading, choir, chorale, chorus, computers, dance, drama, environmental, environmental awareness, ethnic, gay, honors, international, jazz band, literary magazine, musical theater, newspaper, opera, orchestra, photography, political, professional, radio and TV, religious, social, social service, student government, and symphony. Popular campus events include Welcome Weekend Carnival, Spring Fest and Crane Candlelight Concert. **Sports:** There are 7 intercollegiate sports for men and 10 for women, and 10 intramural sports for men and 2 for women. Facilities include Maxcy Hall is the center of the sports world here on campus. It's a modern facility that's got it all. 50-foot rock climbing wall, full high ropes course and bouldering cave 8,000 square-foot fitness center with treadmills, spin cycles, ellipticals, strength equipment, free weights, 4,000-seat gymnasium, 2,200-seat hockey rink, Olympic-size swimming pool with a diving well, 33,000 square-foot field house, indoor track, basketball, volleyball and indoor lacrosse courts, 6 racquetball courts, 3 squash courts, dance studio, physical therapy/training room, 50 acres of athletic fields and courts for tennis and basketball, a quarter-mile track, softball soccer, lacrosse and intramural competition. **Graduates:** From July 1, 2013 to June 30, 2014, 742 bachelor's degrees were awarded. The most popular majors were childhood education (11%), music education (10%), and business administration (9%). 46 companies recruited on campus in 2013-2014. In an average class, 36% graduate in 4 years or less, 52% graduate in 5 years or less, and 54% graduate in 6 years or less. Of the 2013 graduating class, 40% were enrolled in graduate school within 6 months of graduation, and 57% were employed.

SERVICES: Counseling and information services are available, as is tutoring in every subject. There is a reader service for the blind. Math labs, and a writing center **Library/Resources:** The 2 libraries contain 437,228 volumes, 772,929 microform items, 13,901 audio/video tapes/CDs/DVDs, and subscribe to 59,000 periodicals including electronic. Computerized library services include interlibrary loans, database searching, Internet access, and Wi-Fi capability. Special learning facilities include an art gallery, natural history museum, planetarium, radio station, Electronic music and recording studios,performance halls, Crane Music Center, seismographic laboratory, anthropology museum, biology museum, Learning and Teaching Excellence Center located in Crumb Library, six fine arts studios. An Art Museum that includes the Gibson Gallery. The Hosmer Hall Gallery, located within the Crane Music Complex, offers concert goers a chance to view art during musical performances. **Physically Challenged Students:** 95% of the campus is accessible. Facilities include wheelchair ramps, elevators, special parking, specially equipped restrooms, special class scheduling, lowered drinking fountains, lowered telephones, special housing, and electric doors. **Special:** Cross-registration is offered with Clarkson University, St. Lawrence University, and SUNY Canton. Over 530 internships available.SUNY Potsdam also offers work-study opportunities, 3-2 engineering degree with Clarkson University, study abroad, 3-2 management and accounting degrees, student-designed majors, dual majors in interdisciplinary natural science, non-degree study, and pass/fail options. Handcrafted education for students who enroll in the Honors Program or engage in Research through the UG Research and Presidential Scholars programs. There are 20 national honor societies, a freshman honors program, and 18 departmental honors programs. **Visiting:** There are regularly scheduled orientations for prospective students, consisting of individual campus visit Monday through Friday. High school juniors, seniors and transfer students will all benefit from our Open House Programs. There are guides for informal visits and visitors may sit in on classes. To schedule a visit, contact the Admissions Office - Lisa Martin at visit@potsdam.edu. **Campus Safety and Security:** Measures include 24-hour foot and vehicle patrol, emergency notification system, self-defense education, and security escort services. There are emergency telephones, lighted pathways/sidewalks, controlled access to dorms/residences, bike patrol, educational programs, campus rescue squad, portable jump-start packs, vehicle lockouts, parking management, and officers are now trained in Narcan administration.

REQUIREMENTS: Applicants must be high school graduates in a college preparatory program or hold a GED. 4 years each of English and social studies, 3 years each of math, foreign language, and science, and 1 year of art or music recommended. An interview is important; an audition when appropriate is required. The majority of our applicants will NOT have to submit an SAT or ACT score. If you would like to have your scores submitted as part of your application, you must request your scores be sent directly from the testing agency. Also, you must submit an SAT or ACT score to be considered for our Mount Emmons Scholarship. Minimum scores for scholarship consideration are a 1300 on the SAT or a 29 on the ACT. AP and CLEP credits are accepted. Important factors in the admissions decision are geographical diversity, parents or siblings attended your school, and recommendations by school officials.To graduate, You must complete a major and earn at least a 2.0 in 30 hours of your major coursework (some majors have higher standards). 15 of those 30 hours must be upper division (U.D.)--level 300 or higher--and if you transfer here, at least 15 U.D. hours must be taken at SUNY Potsdam. 120 credits + 4 P.E. credits (for the B.A., B. F. A and B. S.), 120-130 credits + 4 P.E. credits (for B.M.), Thus, in order to graduate in 4 years (8 semesters) you need to take at least 16 credit hours per semester. NOTE: The college allows students to take 12 credit hours and still maintain full-time student status. This may work well for some students, HOWEVER, unless classes are taken during summer or winterim sessions, a student taking less than 15 credits per semester cannot graduate in 4 years. A certain number of your 120 credits must be designated as liberal arts credits. You must complete the general education requirements You must graduate with an overall G.P.A. of 2.0. Out of your total 120 credits, 45 of those must be designated as upper division courses (level 300 or higher). **Procedure:** Freshmen are admitted fall and spring. Entrance exams should be taken in the junior year or early senior year. There are early admissions, deferred admissions, and rolling admissions plans. Application deadlines are open. Application fee is $50. Notifications are sent October 1. Applications are accepted on-line. **Transfer Students:** 258 transfer students enrolled in 2013-2014. Applicants must have earned 12 hours of college credit. Transfers with fewer than 24 credit hours must submit a high school transcript. College transcript required and essay or personal statement required. 30 of 124 credits required for the bachelor's degree must be completed at SUNY Potsdam. **International Students:** There are 33 international students enrolled. They must take the TOEFL with a minimum score of 550 on the paper-based TOEFL (PBT) or 79 on the Internet-based version (iBT), or take the IELTS.

ADMISSIONS: 68% of the 2014-2015 applicants were accepted. The SAT scores for the 2014-2015 freshman class were: Critical Reading--42% below 500, 40% between 500 and 599, 16% between 600 and 699, and 1% between 700 and 800; Math--42% below 500, 40% between 500 and 599, 14% between 600 and 699, and 3% between 700 and 800. The ACT scores were 7% below 21, 45% between 21 and 23, 37% between 24 and 26, % between 27 and 28, and 10% above 28. **Admissions Contact:** Thomas Nesbitt, Director of Admissions. E-Mail: *admissions@potsdam.edu* Web: *www.potsdam.edu*

FINANCIAL AID: In 2014-2015, 91% of all full-time freshmen and 86% of continuing full-time students received some form of financial aid. 75% of all full-time freshmen and 70% of continuing full-time students received need-based aid. The average freshman award was $16,328. Need-based scholarships or need-based grants averaged $7,826 ($19,269 maximum); need-based self-help aid (loans and jobs) averaged $4,005 ($9,000 maximum); and other non-need-based awards and non-need-based scholarships averaged $3,006 ($20,923 maximum). The average financial indebtedness of the 2014 graduate was $21,531. The FAFSA and the state aid form are required. The priority date for freshman financial aid applications for fall entry is March 1. The deadline for filing freshman financial aid applications for fall entry is May 1.

STATE UNIVERSITY OF NEW YORK AT PURCHASE   D-5
www.purchase.edu

Purchase, NY 10577	(914) 251-6306
Fax: (914) 251-6314	Email: dennis.craig@purchase.edu
Full-time: 1603 men, 2006 women	Faculty: 144; IIB, +$
Part-time: 97 men, 124 women	Ph.D.s: 100%
Graduate: 53 men, 74 women	Student/Faculty: 25 to 1
Year: semesters, summer session	Tuition: $6681 ($14,581)
Room & Board: $10,270	Freshman Class: n/av
SAT: required	CEEB CODE: 2878
Application Deadline: August 15	COMPETITIVE

State University of New York at Purchase, founded in 1967, is a public institution that offers programs in visual arts, music, acting, dance, film, theater/stage design technology, natural science, social science, and humanities. The figures in the above capsule and in this capsule are approximate. There are no undergraduate schools and one graduate school. In addition to regional accreditation, Purchase College SUNY has baccalaureate program accreditation with NASAD and NASM. The 500-acre campus is in a suburban area 35 miles north of midtown Manhattan. Including any residence halls, there are 40 buildings.

STUDENT LIFE: 80% of undergraduates are from New York. Others are from 43 states, 27 foreign countries, and Canada. 55% are White. The average age of freshmen is 18; all undergraduates, 22. 18% do not continue beyond their first year; 51% remain to graduate. **Housing:** 2600 students can be accommodated in college housing, which includes single-sex and coed dorms and on-campus apartments. In addition, there are special-interest houses, transfer student units, nontraditional-aged student units, wellness halls, presidential scholars halls, sophmore communities, conservatory halls, and learning community halls. On-campus housing is guaranteed for the freshman year only, is available on a first-come, and first-served basis. 67% of students live on campus; of those, 75% remain on campus on weekends. All students may keep cars.

FACULTY/CLASSROOMS: 54% of faculty are male; 46% are female. All teach undergraduates. No introductory courses are taught by graduate students. The average class size in an introductory lecture is 27; in a laboratory is 12; and in a regular course is 14.

PROGRAMS OF STUDY: Purchase College SUNY confers B.A., B.S., B.A.L.A., B.F.A. and Mus.B. degrees. Master's degrees are also awarded. Bachelor's degrees are awarded in BIOLOGICAL SCIENCE (biology/biological science), COMMUNICATIONS AND THE ARTS (art history and appreciation, creative writing, dance, dramatic arts, film arts, journalism, literature, music, theater design, and visual and performing arts), COMPUTER AND PHYSICAL SCIENCE (chemistry and mathematics), ENGINEERING AND ENVIRONMENTAL DESIGN (environmental science), SOCIAL SCIENCE (anthropology, economics, ethnic studies, history, liberal arts/general studies, philosophy, political science/government, psychology, sociology, and women's studies). Biology and journalism is the strongest academically. Visual arts, music, and liberal studies have the largest enrollments.

ACTIVITIES: There are no fraternities or sororities. There are 40 groups on campus, including art, band, cheerleading, choir, chorale, computers, dance, drama, environmental, ethnic, jazz band, literary magazine, opera, orchestra, photography, political, professional, religious, social, social service, student government, symphony, and visual arts. Popular campus events include Spring Concert, Alcohol Awareness Week, and Film Programs. **Sports:** There are 7 intercollegiate sports for men and 6 for women, and 20 intramural sports for men and 20 for women. Facilities include a fitness center, 6-lane pool, aerobics studio, 3 basketball courts, 4 raquetball courts, 2 squash courts, 10 tennis courts, outdoor climbing wall, 5 soccer fields, baseball field, softball field, and 4-lane bowling alley. **Graduates:** From July 1, 2013 to June 30, 2014, 499 bachelor's degrees were awarded. The most popular majors were liberal studies (28%), visual arts (23%), and music (17%). 20 companies recruited on campus in 2013-2014. In an average class, 32% graduate in 4 years or less, 44% graduate in 5 years or less, and 47% graduate in 6 years or less.

SERVICES: Counseling and information services are available, as is tutoring in every subject. There is a reader service for the blind, and remedial math, reading, and writing. There are drop-in sessions for math and writing. **Library/Resources:** The library contains 241,984 volumes, 257,609 microform items, 18,273 audio/video tapes/CDs/ DVDs, and subscribes to 37,153 periodicals including electronic. Computerized library services include interlibrary loans, database searching, Internet access, and Wi-Fi capability. Special learning facilities include a TV station, a listening and viewing center, science and photography labs, music practice rooms and instruments, multitrack synthesizers, music composition labs, digital video editing labs, typesetting and computer graphics labs, experimental stage, a performing arts complex, an electron microscope, and the Children's Center. **Physically Challenged Students:** All of the campus is accessible. Facilities include wheelchair ramps, elevators, special parking, specially equipped restrooms. note takers, extended test times, quiet rooms for tests, interpreters for the hearing impaired, readers for the visually impaired, a reading machine in the library, and special note-taking paper. **Special:** Purchase College offers cross-registration with Empire State colleges, internships with corporations, newspapers, and local agencies, and student-designed majors, dual majors, study abroad, work-study, nondegree study, and pass/fail options. There is also an arts conservatory program. **Visiting:** There are regularly scheduled orientations for prospective students, including group question and answer sessions followed by a tour of the campus. To schedule a visit, contact the Admissions Office. **Campus Safety and Security:** Measures include 24-hour foot and vehicle patrol and security escort services. There are emergency telephones and lighted pathways/sidewalks.

REQUIREMENTS: The SAT is required. The ACT is recommended, with minimum required composite scores of 1100 on the SAT or 23 on the ACT. Applicants must be graduates of an accredited secondary school and have completed 16 academic credits and 16 Carnegie units. The GED is accepted. Visual arts students must submit an essay and portfolio and have an interview. Film students need an essay and an interview. Design technology students need a portfolio and an interview. Performing arts students must audition. A GPA of 2.0 is required. AP and CLEP credits are accepted. Important factors in the admissions decision are evidence of special talent, recommendations by school officials, and personality/intangible qualities.A minimum 2.0 GPA is required with a minimum of 120 credits. Students majoring in the arts complete a minimum of 90 professional credits and the SUNY general education curriculum. Students majoring in the liberal arts and sciences complete the general education curriculum and major requirements and must complete a senior thesis. **Procedure:** Freshmen are admitted fall and spring. Entrance exams should be taken by the fall of the senior year. There are early decision, early admissions, deferred admissions, and rolling admissions plans. Early decision applications should be filed by November 15; regular applications, by August 15 for fall entry; and December 1 for spring entry, along with a $30 fee. Notification of early decision is sent December 15; regular decision, on a rolling basis. 18 early decision candidates were accepted for the 2014-2015 class. Applications are accepted on-line. **Transfer Students:** 373 transfer students enrolled in 2013-2014. Students transferring to the School of Arts (visual or performing arts) must pass an audition or portfolio review. Transfer credit is limited; students can contact the Office of Admission to get a preliminary credit evaluation. Students transferring to programs in liberal arts and sciences must have a minimum 2.0 G.P.A. if they have completed 30 or more semester hours; if they have fewer than 30 semester hours, the high school transcript is also reviewed. Liberal arts and science transfers can transfer a maximum of 90 semester hours from 4-year colleges and 75 semester hours from 2-year colleges. 30 of 120 credits required for the bachelor's degree must be completed at Purchase College SUNY. **International Students:** There are 80 international students enrolled. The school actively recruits these students. They must take the TOEFL with a minimum score of 550 on the paper-based TOEFL (PBT) or 80 on the Internet-based version (iBT), or the IELTS or score 430 on the SAT: Verbal test. SAT if the TOEFL has not been taken.

ADMISSIONS: Dennis Craig, Vice President of Admissions. E-Mail: *dennis.craig@purchase.edu* Web: *www.purchase.edu*

FINANCIAL AID: In 2014-2015, 85% of all full-time freshmen and 69% of continuing full-time students received some form of financial aid. 54% of all full-time freshmen and 47% of continuing full-time students received need-based aid. The average freshman award was $7,067. Need-based scholarships or need-based grants averaged $5,343 ($13,450 maximum); need-based self-help aid (loans and jobs) averaged $3,252 ($7,625 maximum); and other non-need-based awards and non-need-based scholarships averaged $3,086 ($17,625 maximum). 12% of undergraduate students work part-time. Average annual earnings from campus work are $1073. The average financial indebtedness of the 2014 graduate was $16,058. Purchase College SUNY is a member of CSS. The FAFSA is required. The deadline for filing freshman financial aid applications for fall entry is February 15.

STATE UNIVERSITY OF NEW YORK/ COLLEGE AT BROCKPORT   B-3
www.brockport.edu

Brockport, NY 14420	(585) 395-2751
	n/av
Fax: (585) 395-5452	Email: admit@brockport.edu
Full-time: 2904 men, 3400 women	Faculty: IIA, av$
Part-time: 295 men, 441 women	Ph.D.s: n/av
Graduate: 362 men, 704 women	Student/Faculty: n/av
Year: semesters, summer session	Tuition: $7562 ($17,212)
Room & Board: $11,440	Freshman Class: 9768 applied, 4781 accepted, 1090 enrolled
SAT CR/M/W: 530/540/510 ACT: 23	CEEB CODE: 2537
Application Deadline: n/av	COMPETITIVE

The State University of New York/College at Brockport, established in 1835, is a comprehensive public liberal arts college with offerings including 49 undergraduate majors, 41 graduate majors, 13 post-master's and 7 advanced certificate programs, teacher certification in 23 areas and combined bachelor's/master's programs. There are 5 undergraduate schools and 1 graduate school. In addition to regional accreditation, SUNY Brockport has baccalaureate program accreditation with AACSB, ABET, CSWE, NCATE, NASD, CCNE, ACS, NAST, CAAHEP, CACREP, NASPAA, COAPRT, NAADAC, and CAATE. The 464-acre campus is in a small town 16 miles west of Rochester. Including any residence halls, there are 68 buildings.

STUDENT LIFE: 99% of undergraduates are from New York. Others are from 22 states, 41 foreign countries, and Canada. 72% are White. The average age of freshmen is 18; all undergraduates, 23. 19% do not continue beyond their first year; 50% remain to graduate. **Housing:** 2771 students can be accommodated in college housing, which includes coed dorms and on-campus apartments. In addition, there are special-interest houses, special residence hall communities for first-year students, and academic excellence floors. On-campus housing is guaranteed for the freshman year only. 62% of students commute. All students may keep cars.

FACULTY/CLASSROOMS: 46% of faculty are male; 54% are female. No introductory courses are taught by graduate students.

PROGRAMS OF STUDY: SUNY Brockport confers B.A., B.S., B.F.A. and B.S.N. degrees. Master's degrees are also awarded. Bachelor's degrees are awarded in BIOLOGICAL SCIENCE (biochemistry and biology/biological science), BUSINESS (accounting, business administration and management, finance, international business management, marketing management, recreation and leisure services, and sports management), COMMUNICATIONS AND THE ARTS (communications, dance, English, French, journalism, Spanish, studio art, and theatre acting), COMPUTER AND PHYSICAL SCIENCE (atmospheric sciences and meteorology, chemistry, computer science, earth science, geology, mathematics, and physics), EDUCATION (physical education), ENGINEERING AND ENVIRONMENTAL DESIGN (computational sciences and environmental science), HEALTH PROFESSIONS (exercise science, health science, kinesiology, medical technology, and nursing), SOCIAL SCIENCE (African studies, African American studies, anthropology, criminal justice, history, international studies, philosophy, political science/government, psychology, social work, sociology, water resources, and women's studies). Nursing, business administration, and criminal justice have the largest enrollments.

ACTIVITIES: 1% of men belong to 2 national fraternities; 2% of women belong to 2 national sororities. There are 257 groups on campus, including and outdoors, criminal justice, art, business, cheerleading, chess, choir, chorus, computers, dance, drama, ethnic, film, gay, honors, international, jazz band, literary magazine, musical theater, newspaper, photography, political, professional, radio and TV, religious, social, social service, and student government. Popular campus events include Scholar's Day, Honors Convocation and Health Week. **Sports:** There are 11 intercollegiate sports for men and 12 for women, and 28 intramural sports for men and 25 for women. Facilities include field hockey, baseball, and softball fields, a soccer pitch, a swimming pool, 6 gyms, a gymnastics area, wrestling and weight rooms, handball, squash, tennis, and racquetball courts, an ice arena, special Olympics stadium with a football field and track, and a recreation center (with weight room, indoor track and field house). **Graduates:** From July 1, 2013 to June 30, 2014, 1885 bachelor's degrees were awarded. The most popular majors were health professions and related sciences (18%), business administration (15%), and recreation and leisure studies (9%). 140 companies recruited on campus in 2013-2014. In an average class, 3% graduate in 3 years or less, 50% graduate in 4 years or less, 66% graduate in 5 years or less, and 68% graduate in 6 years or less.

SERVICES: Counseling and information services are available, as is tutoring in some subjects, wide variety of classes; tutoring for specific classes may vary by semester, depending upon the demand for tutoring and the availability of qualified tutors. Study skills support is available to all students. **Library/Resources:** The library contains 632,976 volumes, 20,269 microform items, 17,076 audio/video tapes/CDs/DVDs, and subscribes to 136,772 periodicals including electronic. Computerized library services include interlibrary loans, database searching, Internet access, and Wi-Fi capability. Special learning facilities include an art gallery, planetarium, radio station, TV station, Special Events Recreation Center with state-of-the-art fitness center, indoor track and event space; Proscenium Theatre and Black Box performance space; modern dance facilities; art galleries; ceramic, painting, photography and sculpture studios; greenhouse; planetarium; electron microscope; nuclear magnetic resonance spectrometer; Faraday Cage; Geographic Information Systems (GIS) lab with Dopplar radar station; aquaculture ponds; environmental science deciduous woodlot; 25-foot research boat; 20 computer labs; "smart" classrooms; student learning center. **Physically Challenged Students:** 95% of the campus is accessible. Facilities include wheelchair ramps, elevators, special parking, specially equipped restrooms, special class scheduling, lowered drinking fountains, lowered telephones, special housing. **Special:** Co-op programs, internships in most majors, and work-study programs in education are available. Brockport offers cross-registration with Rochester area colleges, a Washington semester, study abroad in 16 countries, accelerated degree programs, and an interdisciplinary major in arts for children, emphasizing art, dance, music, and theater. Credit for military and work experience, nondegree study, and pass/fail grading options are available. An alternative general education program, Delta College, is an interdisciplinary program that emphasizes global issues and provides opportunities for work or study in other countries, as well as locally, regionally, and nationally. There are 32 national honor societies, a freshman honors program, and 1 departmental honors programs. **Visiting:** There are regularly scheduled orientations for prospective students, admissions information presentations, campus tours, and class observations. There are guides for informal visits, visitors may sit in on classes, and stay overnight. To schedule a visit, contact Undergraduate Admissions. **Campus Safety and Security:** Measures include 24-hour foot and vehicle patrol, emergency notification system, and security escort services. There are shuttle buses, emergency telephones, lighted pathways/sidewalks, controlled access to dorms/residences, a community policing program, bicycle patrols, and 24-hour locked residence halls.

REQUIREMENTS: The SAT or ACT is required. The College at Brockport will consider many factors when reviewing admissions applications: strength of your academic program, course grades and high school average, standardized test scores (SAT and/or ACT), class rank, supplemental application information, anything additional that you supply (letters of recommendation, resume, portfolio, etc.) Most students who enter Brockport today have: the equivalent of an Advanced Regents Diploma, 4 years of English, 3 years or more of Math, Sciences and Social Studies, 3 years or more of a foreign language, additional electives as appropriate, some college-level course work, including Advanced Placement (AP), International Baccalaureate (IB), and college-affiliated programs such as Syracuse University Project Advance (SUPA). A GPA of 85.0 is required. AP and CLEP credits are accepted. Important factors in the admissions decision are advanced placement or honors courses, leadership record, and extracurricular activities record.To graduate, students must complete a minimum of 120 credits, including 30 or more credits in the major, with a 2.0 GPA. The core curriculum includes the SUNY-wide general education requirements (1 course each in math, natural sciences,

social sciences, American history, Western civilization, world (non-Western) civilization, humanities, the arts, foreign language, and basic communication). All students must take courses in contemporary issues, diversity, and perspectives on women and pass the appropriate competency exams. An academic planning seminar is required of entering freshmen. **Procedure:** Freshmen are admitted fall and spring. Entrance exams should be taken Spring of the junior year and fall of senior year. There are deferred admissions and rolling admissions plans. Application deadlines are open. Application fee is $50. Notification is sent on a rolling basis. Applications are accepted online. **Transfer Students:** 1012 transfer students enrolled in 2013-2014. Applicants must have a minimum GPA of 2.25. Many departments specify pre-requisite courses and a higher GPA (Nursing, Social Work, Education). 30 of 120 credits required for the bachelor's degree must be completed at SUNY Brockport. **International Students:** There are 112 international students enrolled. The school actively recruits these students. They must take the TOEFL with a minimum score of 530 on the paper-based TOEFL (PBT) or 76 on the Internet-based version (iBT), or take the TOEFL, or IETLS, completion of ELS level 112 or 3.7 iTEP is required.

ADMISSIONS: 49% of the 2014-2015 applicants were accepted. The SAT scores for the 2014-2015 freshman class were: Critical Reading--29% below 500, 52% between 500 and 599, 17% between 600 and 699, and 1% between 700 and 800; Math--21% below 500, 57% between 500 and 599, 20% between 600 and 699, and 2% between 700 and 800; Writing--41% below 500, 45% between 500 and 599, 13% between 600 and 699, and 1% between 700 and 800. The ACT scores were 16% below 21, 35% between 21 and 23, 29% between 24 and 26, 13% between 27 and 28, and 6% above 28. 38% of the current freshmen were in the top fifth of their class; 72% were in the top two fifths. 6 freshmen graduated first in their class. **Admissions Contact:** Megan Sarkis , Assistant Director of Admissions. E-Mail: *admit@ brockport.edu* Web: *www.brockport.edu*

FINANCIAL AID: In 2014-2015, 91% of all full-time freshmen and 85% of continuing full-time students received some form of financial aid. 70% of all full-time freshmen and 70% of continuing full-time students received need-based aid. The average freshman award was $14,032. Need-based scholarships or need-based grants averaged $6,225 ($14,868 maximum); need-based self-help aid (loans and jobs) averaged $4,892 ($9,250 maximum); and other non-need-based awards and non-need-based scholarships averaged $6,932 ($26,746 maximum). 34% of undergraduate students work part-time. Average annual earnings from campus work are $1428. The average financial indebtedness of the 2014 graduate was $27,677. The FAFSA and the state aid form are required. The priority date for freshman financial aid applications for fall entry is March 15.

STATE UNIVERSITY OF NEW YORK COLLEGE OF AGRICULTURE AND TECH AT COBLESKILL (*The complete profile is made available exclusively on our website, www.barronspac.com*)

STATE UNIVERSITY OF NEW YORK POLYTECHNIC INSTITUTE   C-3
www.sunypoly.edu

Utica, NY 13502	(315) 792-7500
	1-866-2SUNYIT
Fax: (315) 792-7837	Email: admissions@sunyit.edu
Full-time: 1110 men, 536 women	Faculty: IIA, +$
Part-time: 115 men, 273 women	Ph.D.s: 87%
Graduate: 323 men, 380 women	Student/Faculty: 18 to 1
Year: semesters, summer session	Tuition: $7440 ($17,090)
Room & Board: $12,250	Freshman Class: 2233 applied, 1263 accepted, 347 enrolled
SAT CR/M: 510/550 ACT: 22	CEEB CODE: 0755
Application Deadline: July 15	COMPETITIVE

The State University of New York Polytechnic Institute, founded in 1966, is a public institution offering programs in technology and professional studies. There are 5 undergraduate schools and 5 graduate schools. In addition to regional accreditation, SUNY Poly has baccalaureate program accreditation with AACSB, ABET, AUPHA, CAHIIM, and CCNE. The 800-acre campus is in a suburban area the Utica Campus is at the western end of the Mohawk Valley. The Albany Campus is located at the western end of the City of Albany. Including any residence halls, there are 20 buildings.

STUDENT LIFE: 96% of undergraduates are from New York. Others are from 8 states, and 10 foreign countries. 79% are White. The average age of freshmen is 18; all undergraduates, 26. 25% do not continue beyond their first year; 43% remain to graduate. **Housing:** 823 students can be accommodated in college housing, which includes coed dorms. Special housing for disabled, special housing for international. On-campus housing is available on a first-come, first-served basis, and is available on a lottery system for upperclassmen. 72% of students commute. All students may keep cars.

FACULTY/CLASSROOMS: 60% of faculty are male; 40% are female. No introductory courses are taught by graduate students. The average class size in an introductory lecture is 16; in a laboratory is 10; and in a regular course is 18.

PROGRAMS OF STUDY: SUNY Poly confers B.A., B.S., B.B.A. and B.P.S. degrees. Master's degrees are also awarded. Bachelor's degrees are awarded in BUSINESS (accounting, banking and finance, and business administration and management), COMMUNICATIONS AND THE ARTS (communications technology and telecommunications), COMPUTER AND PHYSICAL SCIENCE (applied mathematics and computer science), ENGINEERING AND ENVIRONMENTAL DESIGN (civil engineering technology, computer technology, electrical/electronics engineering, electrical/electronics engineering technology, and mechanical engineering technology), HEALTH PROFESSIONS (health, health care administration, and nursing), SOCIAL SCIENCE (liberal arts/general studies, psychology, and sociology). Engineering technology, computer science, and business and nursing have the largest enrollments.

ACTIVITIES: There are no fraternities or sororities. There are 36 groups on campus, including Black Latino African Student Union, West Indian African Club, chess, computers, dance, drama, environmental, ethnic, gay, international, literary magazine, newspaper, professional, radio and TV, religious, social, student government, Veteran's, and yearbook. Popular campus events include Wildcat Weekend, Diwali and Holi Festivals, and Apocalypse Week. **Sports:** There are 6 intercollegiate sports for men and 6 for women, and 10 intramural sports for men and 10 for women. Facilities include an indoor and outdoor facilities, a fitness center, fitness trail, and a gym with indoor track, field house, lighted turf field, grass baseball, softball and soccer fields. **Graduates:** From July 1, 2013 to June 30, 2014, 439 bachelor's degrees were awarded. The most popular majors were business administration (17%), nursing (14%), and psychology (9%). 68 companies recruited on campus in 2013-2014.

SERVICES: Counseling and information services are available, as is tutoring in most subjects. There is a reader service for the blind, and remedial math, reading, and writing. **Library/Resources:** The library contains 148,739 volumes, 1,502 audio/video tapes/CDs/DVDs, and subscribes to 1,401 periodicals including electronic. Computerized library services include interlibrary loans, database searching, Internet access, and Wi-Fi capability. Special learning facilities include an art gallery, radio station, and TV station. **Physically Challenged Students:** 99% of the campus is accessible. Facilities include wheelchair ramps, elevators, special parking, specially equipped restrooms, lowered drinking fountains, and special housing. **Special:** SUNY Poly offers cross-registration with the Mohawk Valley Consortium, internships, and work study. An accelerated degree program in nursing, communications and information design, computer information science and Network and Computer Security is possible. There is a joint partnership (1+2+1) with St. Elizabeth College of Nursing. There are 2 national honor societies. **Visiting:** There are regularly scheduled orientations for prospective students, during registration and orientation to campus. There are guides for informal visits, visitors may sit in on classes, and stay overnight. To schedule a visit, contact the Admissions Office. **Campus Safety and Security:** Measures include 24-hour foot and vehicle patrol, emergency notification system, self-defense education, and security escort services. There are emergency telephones, lighted pathways/sidewalks, controlled access to dorms/residences, Emergency call boxes.

REQUIREMENTS: The SAT or ACT is required. Official transcripts,

test scores, essay, and supplemental application are required. A GPA of 3.0 is required. AP and CLEP credits are accepted. Important factors in the admissions decision are advanced placement or honors courses, evidence of special talent, and recommendations by school officials. Students must meet general education requirements and complete 124 to 128 credit hours to graduate. **Procedure:** Freshmen are admitted fall and spring. Entrance exams should be taken by April of year applicant intends to enroll. There are early admissions, deferred admissions, and rolling admissions plans. Applications should be filed by July 15 for fall entry; December 1 for spring entry, along with a $50 fee. Notifications are sent January 15. Applications are accepted on-line. **Transfer Students:** 391 transfer students enrolled in 2013-2014. Transfer students generally must present a minimum cumulative GPA of 2.7 or better. Applicants presenting a GPA below 2.5 will be considered on an individual basis. 30 of 124 credits required for the bachelor's degree must be completed at SUNY Poly. **International Students:** There are 24 international students enrolled. The school actively recruits these students. They must take the TOEFL with a minimum score of 550 on the paper-based TOEFL (PBT) or 79 on the Internet-based version (iBT), or take the IELTS (International English Language Testing Service). They must also take the SAT or ACT. for first-time, full-time students only.

ADMISSIONS: 57% of the 2014-2015 applicants were accepted. The SAT scores for the 2014-2015 freshman class were: Critical Reading--43% below 500, 43% between 500 and 599, 12% between 600 and 699, and 2% between 700 and 800; Math--23% below 500, 49% between 500 and 599, 25% between 600 and 699, and 3% between 700 and 800. The ACT scores were 5% below 21, 52% between 21 and 23, 25% between 24 and 26, 10% between 27 and 28, and 8% above 28. 43% of the current freshmen were in the top fifth of their class; 83% were in the top two fifths. 2 freshmen graduated first in their class. **Admissions Contact:** Gina Liscio, Interim Director of Admissions. E-Mail: admissions@sunyit.edu Web: www.sunyit.edu

FINANCIAL AID: In 2014-2015, 68% of all full-time freshmen and 71% of continuing full-time students received some form of financial aid. 61% of all full-time freshmen and 62% of continuing full-time students received need-based aid. The average freshman award was $9,845. Need-based scholarships or need-based grants averaged $7,472 ; and need-based self-help aid (loans and jobs) averaged $3,277. 9% of undergraduate students work part-time. Average annual earnings from campus work are $1226. The FAFSA and the state aid form are required. The priority date for freshman financial aid applications for fall entry is March 1.

STATE UNIVERSITY OF NEW YORK/EMPIRE STATE COLLEGE
(The complete profile is made available exclusively on our website, www. barronspac.com)

STATE UNIVERSITY OF NEW YORK/UNIVERSITY AT BUFFALO
(See University at Buffalo / The State University of New York)

STONY BROOK UNIVERSITY / STATE UNIVERSITY OF NEW YORK   E-5
www.stonybrook.edu

Stony Brook, NY 11794	(631) 632-6868
Fax: 631) 632-9898	Email: enroll@stonybrook.edu
Full-time: 8361 men, 7024 women	Faculty: 1126; I, +$
Part-time: 595 men, 500 women	Ph.D.s: 97%
Graduate: 3629 men, 4498 women	Student/Faculty: 17 to 1
Year: semesters, summer session	Tuition: $8430 ($21,850)
Room & Board: $11,648	Freshman Class: 33714 applied, 13938 accepted, 2855 enrolled
SAT CR/M/W: 610/660/610 ACT: 28	CEEB CODE: 2548
Application Deadline: January 15	HIGHLY COMPETITIVE+

Stony Brook University, founded in 1957, and part of the State University of New York, is a public institution offering degree programs in arts and sciences, engineering and applied sciences, business, journalism, atmospheric and marine sciences, sustainability studies, public health, nursing, health technology and management, and social work. There are 9 undergraduate schools and 11 graduate schools. In addition to regional accreditation, Stony Brook University has baccalaureate program accreditation with ABET, ADA, APTA, CSWE, NCATE, NLN, AOTA, ACGME, APA, CADE, CCNE, ACEND, ACOTE, ACNM, ARC-PAC, CAAHEP, CAPTE, CAATE , CEPH, CSWE, ASPT, NAACLS, ASPT, CoARC, LCME, AAMC, NAACLS, and NCATE. The 1454-acre campus is in a suburban area on Long Island, 55 miles from New York City. Including any residence halls, there are 202 buildings.

STUDENT LIFE: 80% of undergraduates are from New York. Others are from 47 states, 92 foreign countries, and Canada. 89% are from public schools. 37% are White; 24% Asian American; 13% Foreign. **Male To Female Ratio:** 1.0:1. The average age of freshmen is 18; all undergraduates, 21. 11% do not continue beyond their first year; 72% remain to graduate. **Housing:** 9553 students can be accommodated in college housing, which includes coed dorms, on-campus apartments, and married student housing. In addition, there are honors houses, special-interest houses. On-campus housing is guaranteed for all 4 years. 52% of students live on campus; of those, 65% remain on campus on weekends. Alcohol is not permitted. Upperclassmen may keep cars.

FACULTY/CLASSROOMS: 65% of faculty are male; 35% are female. No introductory courses are taught by graduate students. The average class size in an introductory lecture is 41; in a laboratory is 21; and in a regular course is 34.

PROGRAMS OF STUDY: Stony Brook University confers B.A., B.S. and B.E. degrees. Master's and doctoral degrees are also awarded. Bachelor's degrees are awarded in AGRICULTURE (environmental studies), BIOLOGICAL SCIENCE (biochemistry, biology/biological science, ecology, and marine biology), BUSINESS (business administration and management), COMMUNICATIONS AND THE ARTS (art history and appreciation, comparative literature, dramatic arts, English, film arts, Germanic languages and literature, linguistics, music, Russian languages and literature, and studio art), COMPUTER AND PHYSICAL SCIENCE (applied mathematics, astronomy, atmospheric sciences and meteorology, chemistry, computer science, earth science, geology, information sciences and systems, mathematics, and physics), EDUCATION (athletic training), ENGINEERING AND ENVIRONMENTAL DESIGN (biomedical engineering, chemical engineering, computer engineering, electrical/electronics engineering, engineering and applied science, engineering chemistry, environmental design, environmental science, mechanical engineering, and technological management), HEALTH PROFESSIONS (clinical science, cytotechnology, health science, nursing, occupational therapy, pharmacology, physical therapy, and respiratory therapy), SOCIAL SCIENCE (African studies, American studies, anthropology, Asian/American studies, economics, ethnic studies, European studies, French studies, history, humanities, interdisciplinary studies, Italian studies, liberal arts/general studies, philosophy, political science/government, psychology, religion, social science, social work, sociology, Spanish studies, and women's studies). Biology, business management, and economics are the strongest academically. Biology, psychology, and health science have the largest enrollments.

ACTIVITIES: 3% of men belong to 1 local and 18 national fraternities; 3% of women belong to 2 local and 18 national sororities. There are 341 groups on campus, including band, cheerleading, chess, choir, chorale, computers, dance, debate, drama, environmental, ethnic, film, forensics, gay, honors, international, jazz band, literary magazine, marching band, musical theater, newspaper, opera, orchestra, pep band, photography, political, professional, radio and TV, religious, social, social service, student government, and symphony. Popular campus events include Fall Fest, Opening Week Activities, and Caribbean Weekend. **Sports:** There are 9 intercollegiate sports for men and 9 for women, and 28 intramural sports for men and 28 for women. Facilities include an indoor sports complex houses a 4,000-seat arena, a 1,600-seat gym, a swimming pool, 2 squash and 5 racquetball courts, a dance studio, and exercise and universal gym rooms. Outdoor facilities include an 8,200-seat stadium, a 500-seat softball facility, a 1,000-seat baseball facility, 12 tennis courts, 2 multi-

sport practice facilities, 2 recreational basketball and 4 handball courts, 2 recreational softball fields, and a multi-sport recreational area. A campus recreation center offers 3 floors of state-of-the-art equipment and facilities, including a 3-court gym, fitness studios and workout space. **Graduates:** From July 1, 2013 to June 30, 2014, 3890 bachelor's degrees were awarded. The most popular majors were health sciences (10%), biology (9%), and psychology (8%). 411 companies recruited on campus in 2013-2014. In an average class, 2% graduate in 3 years or less, 45% graduate in 4 years or less, 63% graduate in 5 years or less, and 66% graduate in 6 years or less. Of the 2013 graduating class, 30% were enrolled in graduate school within 6 months of graduation, and 79% were employed.

SERVICES: There is a reader service for the blind, and remedial math and writing. **Library/Resources:** The 7 libraries contain 2.2 million volumes, 3.8 million microform items, 29,149 audio/video tapes/CDs/DVDs, and subscribe to 108,462 periodicals including electronic. Computerized library services include interlibrary loans, database searching, and Internet access. Special learning facilities include an art gallery, radio station, TV station. The Centers for Molecular Medicine and Biology Learning Laboratories, the Institute for Advanced Computational Science, the Louis and Beatrice Laufer Center for Physical and Quantitative Biology, the Marine Sciences Center at Southampton, the Staller Center for the Arts, and the School of Journalism's state-of-the-art newsroom, affording students the opportunity to work across multiple multimedia platforms. **Physically Challenged Students:** 85% of the campus is accessible. Facilities include wheelchair ramps, elevators, special parking, specially equipped restrooms, special class scheduling, lowered drinking fountains, lowered telephones, special housing. **Special:** The university offers a variety of internships in government, including a Washington semester, as well as internships in business and industry, with hospitals and clinics, and in legal and social agencies. The URECA Program promotes undergraduate research and creative projects, both on and off campus including nearby Brookhaven National Labarary, which is co-managed by Stony Brook University. A fast-track MBA program and more than thirty additional combined degree programs are available to undergraduates. Scholars for Medicine, Engineering Scholars for Medicine, and Scholars for Dental Medicine are highly selective programs in which a small number of freshmen are admitted to eight-year combined degree programs in medicine and dental medicine. Women in Science and Engineering, the Honors College, and University Scholars programs provide additional experiences to challenge, inspire, and sustain our most academically talent students. Students may declare double majors or pursue dual degrees. The multidisciplinary studies major is student-designed. Students have the opportunity to study at another college or university through the national student exchange program or our study abroad programs in more than 20 countries, including China, New Zealand, France, Sweden, Taiwan, Denmark, England, Korea, Madagascar, Australia, Costa Rica, Jamaica, Tanzania, Kenya, Spain, Norway, Russia, Japan, Italy, Greece, and Germany. Cross-registration may be arranged through the Long Island Regional Advisory Council for Higher Education. There are 6 national honor societies, including Phi Beta Kappa, a freshman honors program, and 30 departmental honors programs. **Visiting:** There are regularly scheduled orientations for prospective students, Informative sessions about campus life. There are guides for informal visits and visitors may sit in on classes. To schedule a visit, contact the Admissions Office at enroll@stonybrook.edu. **Campus Safety and Security:** Measures include 24-hour foot and vehicle patrol, emergency notification system, self-defense education, and security escort services. There are shuttle buses, emergency telephones, lighted pathways/sidewalks, controlled access to dorms/residences, and a campus crime stoppers program.

REQUIREMENTS: The SAT is required. Applicants must be graduates of an accredited secondary school or have a GED certificate. 16 or 17 academic credits are required, including 4 years each of English and social studies, 3 or 4 of math, 3 of science (4 for engineering majors), and 2 or 3 of a foreign language. 1 letter of recommendation and a supplemental application, including and essay are required. 3 SAT Subject tests, an essay, and an interview are recommended. AP and CLEP credits are accepted. Important factors in the admissions decision are advanced placement or honors courses, extracurricular activities record, and evidence of special talent. To graduate, students must have a minimum 2.0 GPA in 120 credit hours (B.A. and B.S.) or 128 (B.E.). At least 39 credits must be earned in upper-division courses. Students must complete at least 30 credits of general education, through which they are expected to demonstrate versatility, explore interconnectedness, pursue deeper understanding, and prepare for life-long learning. Arts and sciences majors must fulfill a foreign language requirement, unless completed through advanced high-school study. **Procedure:** Freshmen are admitted fall and spring. Entrance exams should be taken during the junior year or in the fall of the senior year. There is a deferred admissions plan. Applications should be filed by January 15 for fall entry; November 1 for spring entry. The fall 2014 application fee was $50. Notifications are sent April 1. 3271 applicants were on the 2014 waiting list; 623 were admitted. Applications are accepted on-line. **Transfer Students:** 2260 transfer students enrolled in 2013-2014. Applicants must have a minimum 2.5 GPA. An associate degree and an interview are recommended. Other requirements vary by program. Applicants who have earned fewer than 24 college credits must submit a high school transcript. 36 of 120 credits required for the bachelor's degree must be completed at Stony Brook University. **International Students:** There are 2082 international students enrolled. They must take the TOEFL with a minimum score of 550 on the paper-based TOEFL (PBT) or 80 on the Internet-based version (iBT).

ADMISSIONS: 41% of the 2014-2015 applicants were accepted. The SAT scores for the 2014-2015 freshman class were: Critical Reading--1% below 500, 38% between 500 and 599, 50% between 600 and 699, and 11% between 700 and 800. Math-- 14% between 500 and 599, 54% between 600 and 699, and 32% between 700 and 800. Writing--3% below 500, 38% between 500 and 599, 45% between 600 and 699, and 14% between 700 and 800. The ACT scores were 2% between 21 and 23, 27% between 24 and 26, 25% between 27 and 28, and 46% above 28. 74% of the current freshmen were in the top fifth of their class; 95% were in the top two fifths. There were 7 National Merit finalists. 27 freshmen graduated first in their class. **Admissions Contact:** Judith Burke-Berhanan, Dean of Admissions. E-Mail: *enroll@stonybrook.edu* Web: *www.stonybrook.edu*

FINANCIAL AID: In 2014-2015, 70% of all full-time freshmen and 65% of continuing full-time students received some form of financial aid. 51% of all full-time freshmen and 54% of continuing full-time students received need-based aid. The average freshman award was $11,172. Need-based scholarships or need-based grants averaged $7,780 ($15,125 maximum); need-based self-help aid (loans and jobs) averaged $5,304 ($15,000 maximum); non-need-based athletic scholarships averaged $20,834 ($37,191 maximum); and other non-need-based awards and non-need-based scholarships averaged $4,492 ($25,840 maximum). 14% of undergraduate students work part-time. Average annual earnings from campus work are $2473. The average financial indebtedness of the 2014 graduate was $24,598. Stony Brook University is a member of CSS. The FAFSA and the state aid form are required. The priority date for freshman financial aid applications for fall entry is March 1.

SUNY COLLEGE AT GENESEO   B-3
www.geneseo.edu

Geneseo, NY 14454   585-245-5571

Fax: (585) 245-5550   Email: admissions@geneseo.edu
Full-time: 2278 men, 3136 women   Faculty: 255; IIA, av$
Part-time: 36 men, 47 women   Ph.D.s: 84%
Graduate: 13 men, 92 women   Student/Faculty: 19 to 1
Year: semesters, summer session   Tuition: $7430 ($16,880)
Room & Board: $11,240   Freshman Class: 9305
                                      applied, 5502 accepted,
                                      1215 enrolled
SAT CR/M: 605/615 ACT: 27   CEEB CODE: 2540
Application Deadline: January 1   HIGHLY COMPETITIVE

The State University of New York/at Geneseo, founded in 1871, is a public institution offering liberal arts, business, and accounting programs, and teaching certification. There are 2 undergraduate schools and 1 graduate school. In addition to regional accreditation, Geneseo

has baccalaureate program accreditation with AACSB, NCATE, and ACS. The 220-acre campus is in a small town 30 miles south of Rochester, NY. Including any residence halls, there are 46 buildings.

STUDENT LIFE: 98% of undergraduates are from New York. Others are from 26 states, 42 foreign countries, and Canada. 75% are White. 17% are Catholic. **Female To Male Ratio:** 1.4:1. The average age of freshmen is 18; all undergraduates, 20. 10% do not continue beyond their first year; 78% remain to graduate. **Housing:** 3255 students can be accommodated in college housing, which includes coed dorms and on-campus apartments. In addition, there are honors houses, special-interest houses, town houses, special housing for disabled, and international housing. On-campus housing is guaranteed for all 4 years, also is available on a first-come, first-served basis. 55% of students live on campus; of those, 98% remain on campus on weekends. All students may keep cars.

FACULTY/CLASSROOMS: 55% of faculty are male; 45% are female. All teach undergraduates. No introductory courses are taught by graduate students. The average class size in an introductory lecture is 48; in a laboratory is 20; and in a regular course is 28.

PROGRAMS OF STUDY: Geneseo confers B.A., B.S. and B.S.Ed. degrees. Master's degrees are also awarded. Bachelor's degrees are awarded in BIOLOGICAL SCIENCE (biochemistry, biology/biological science, and biophysics), BUSINESS (accounting and business administration and management), COMMUNICATIONS AND THE ARTS (art history and appreciation, communications, comparative literature, English, French, music, musical theater, performing arts, Spanish, and theater design), COMPUTER AND PHYSICAL SCIENCE (applied physics, chemistry, geochemistry, geology, geophysics and seismology, mathematics, natural sciences, and physics), EDUCATION (early childhood education, elementary education, and special education), SOCIAL SCIENCE (African American studies, American studies, anthropology, economics, geography, history, international relations, philosophy, political science/government, psychology, and sociology). Education, biology, psychology, English, business, geological science and physics are the strongest academically. Biology, psychology, and business administration have the largest enrollments.

ACTIVITIES: 15% of men belong to 8 local and 3 national fraternities; 24% of women belong to 8 local and 7 national sororities. There are 198 groups on campus, including art, band, cheerleading, chess, choir, chorale, chorus, computers, dance, debate, drama, environmental, ethnic, gay, honors, international, jazz band, literary magazine, musical theater, newspaper, orchestra, pep band, political, professional, radio and TV, religious, social, social service, student government, and symphony. Popular campus events include Siblings Weekend, Blue and White Day, Student Organization Expo, Geneseo Recognizing Excellence, Achievement and Talent Day, Great Day, Relay for Life and Weeks of Welcome. **Sports:** There are 8 intercollegiate sports for men and 12 for women, and 18 intramural sports for men and 18 for women. Facilities include an ice arena, swimming pool, 2 gyms, 3 squash and 8 tennis courts, 4 racquetball courts, an indoor jogging area, nautilus and weight rooms, an outdoor track, and several playing fields. **Graduates:** From July 1, 2013 to June 30, 2014, 1414 bachelor's degrees were awarded. The most popular majors were social sciences (16%), biological/life sciences (15%), and business/marketing (12%). 38 companies recruited on campus in 2013-2014. In an average class, 67% graduate in 4 years or less, 78% graduate in 5 years or less, and 78% graduate in 6 years or less. Of the 2013 graduating class, 33% were enrolled in graduate school within 6 months of graduation, and 45% were employed.

SERVICES: Counseling and information services are available, as is tutoring in some subjects. There is a reader service for the blind. Also a Writing Center and a Math Center for all students. **Library/Resources:** The library contains 484,071 volumes, 172,545 microform items, 23,100 audio/video tapes/CDs/DVDs, and subscribes to 4,126 periodicals including electronic. Computerized library services include interlibrary loans, database searching, Internet access, and Wi-Fi capability. Special learning facilities include an art gallery, planetarium, radio station, TV station, 4 theaters, electron microscopes, integrated science center, particle accelerator, and a wave tank. **Physically Challenged Students:** 95% of the campus is accessible. Facilities include wheelchair ramps, elevators, special parking, specially equipped restrooms, special class scheduling, lowered drinking fountains, lowered telephones, special housing. **Special:** The college offers a cooperative 3-2 engineering degree with Alfred, Case Western Reserve, Clarkson, Columbia, Penn State, and Syracuse Universities, SUNY at Binghamton and Buffalo, and the University of Rochester, as well as a 3-3 degree with Rochester Institute of Technology and Upstate Medical University. Cross-registration is available with the Rochester Area Colleges Consortium. Geneseo offers internships, study abroad, a Washington semester, dual majors, and work-study programs. There are including Phi Beta Kappa and a freshman honors program. **Visiting:** There are regularly scheduled orientations for prospective students, generally including a 90-minute campus tour and a 45-minute information session. Students may also elect to sit in on classes, visit faculty and coaches, or stay overnight. There are guides for informal visits, visitors may sit in on classes, and stay overnight. To schedule a visit, contact the Office of Admissions at admissions@geneseo.edu. **Campus Safety and Security:** Measures include 24-hour foot and vehicle patrol, emergency notification system, self-defense education, and security escort services. There are shuttle buses, emergency telephones, lighted pathways/sidewalks, and controlled access to dorms/residences.

REQUIREMENTS: The SAT or ACT is required. Applicants must be graduates of an accredited secondary school or have a GED certificate. Total 20 academic units recommended. The academic program must have 4 years each of English, math, science, social studies and 4 foreign language. An essay is required. A portfolio or audition for certain programs and an interview are recommended. Rigor of secondary school reviewed. AP and CLEP credits are accepted. Important factors in the admissions decision are advanced placement or honors courses, leadership record, evidence of special talent, extracurricular activities record, recommendations by school officials, ability to finance college education, parents or siblings attended your school, personality/intangible qualities, and geographical diversity. To graduate, students must complete 120 credit hours with a minimum 2.0 GPA. The required core curriculum includes 2 courses each in humanities, fine arts, social sciences, and natural sciences and 1 course each in non-Western tradition, critical writing/reading, numeric and symbolic reasoning, U.S. history, and foreign language proficiency. **Procedure:** Freshmen are admitted fall and spring. Entrance exams should be taken during the spring of the junior year. There are early decision and deferred admissions plans. Early decision applications should be filed by December 1; regular applications, by January 1 for fall entry; and December 1 for spring entry, along with a $50 fee. Notification of early decision is sent December 15; regular decision, March 1. 140 early decision candidates were accepted for the 2014-2015 class. 560 applicants were on the 2014 waiting list; 10 were admitted. Applications are accepted on-line. **Transfer Students:** 314 transfer students enrolled in 2013-2014. Applicants must provide transcripts from all previously attended colleges. A minimum 3.0 GPA is required. Students with fewer than 24 credit hours must submit SAT or ACT scores. 30 of 120 credits required for the bachelor's degree must be completed at Geneseo. **International Students:** There are 144 international students enrolled. The school actively recruits these students. They must take the TOEFL with a minimum score of 525 on the paper-based TOEFL (PBT) or 71 on the Internet-based version (iBT). They must also take the SAT or ACT.

ADMISSIONS: 59% of the 2014-2015 applicants were accepted. The SAT scores for the 2014-2015 freshman class were: Critical Reading--10% below 500, 35% between 500 and 599, 43% between 600 and 699, and 13% between 700 and 800. Math--7% below 500, 30% between 500 and 599, 50% between 600 and 699, and 13% between 700 and 800. The ACT scores were 8% below 21, 75% between 24 and 26, and 17% above 28. **Admissions Contact:** Kevin J Reed, Interim Director Of Admissions. E-Mail: *admissions@geneseo.edu* Web: *www. geneseo.edu/admissions*

FINANCIAL AID: In 2014-2015, 50% of all full-time freshmen received some form of financial aid. 61% of all full-time freshmen received need-based aid. The average freshman award was $10,911. Need-based scholarships or need-based grants averaged $6,494; need-based self-help aid (loans and jobs) averaged $4,556; other non-need-based awards and non-need-based scholarships averaged $3,952; and $4,170 from other forms of aid. The average financial indebtedness of the 2014 graduate was $22,900. Geneseo is a member of CSS. The FAFSA is required. The priority date for freshman financial aid applications for fall entry is February 15.

SUNY COLLEGE AT OLD WESTBURY   D-5
www.oldwestbury.edu

Old Westbury, NY 11568	(516) 876-3073
	n/av
Fax: (516) 876-3307	Email: enroll@oldwestbury.edu
Full-time: 1486 men, 2070 women	Faculty: 145; IIB, +$
Part-time: 277 men, 325 women	Ph.D.s: 85%
Graduate: 86 men, 570 women	Student/Faculty: 25 to 1
Year: semesters, summer session	Tuition: $6624 ($15,874)
Room & Board: $9700	Freshman Class: n/av
	CEEB CODE: 2866
Application Deadline: n/av	COMPETITIVE

The State University of New York/College at Old Westbury, founded in 1965, is a public institution offering degree programs in the arts and sciences, business, education, fine arts, and health science. Figures in the above capsule and in this profile are approximate. There are 3 undergraduate schools and 3 graduate schools. In addition to regional accreditation, SUNY Old Westbury has baccalaureate program accreditation with NCATE and ACS. The 604-acre campus is in a suburban area 20 miles east of New York City. Including any residence halls, there are 23 buildings.

STUDENT LIFE: 97% of undergraduates are from New York. Others are from 13 states, and 9 foreign countries. 85% are from public schools. 33% are White; 30% African American; 21% Hispanic. The average age of freshmen is 19; all undergraduates, 24. 20% do not continue beyond their first year; 35% remain to graduate. **Housing:** 1500 students can be accommodated in college housing, which includes coed dorms. In addition, there are honors houses. On-campus housing is available on a first-come, first-served basis, and is available on a lottery system for upperclassmen. Priority is given to out-of-town students. 77% of students commute. Alcohol is not permitted. All students may keep cars.

FACULTY/CLASSROOMS: 47% of faculty are male; 53% are female. 98% teach undergraduates, 12% do research, and 11% do both. No introductory courses are taught by graduate students. The average class size in an introductory lecture is 25; in a laboratory is 20; and in a regular course is 25.

PROGRAMS OF STUDY: SUNY Old Westbury confers B.A., B.S., B.F.A. and B.P.S. degrees. Master's degrees are also awarded. Bachelor's degrees are awarded in BIOLOGICAL SCIENCE (biochemistry and biology/biological science), BUSINESS (accounting, banking and finance, business administration and management, labor studies, management information systems, and marketing/retailing/merchandising), COMMUNICATIONS AND THE ARTS (communications, media arts, Spanish, and visual and performing arts), COMPUTER AND PHYSICAL SCIENCE (chemistry, computer science, information sciences and systems, and mathematics), EDUCATION (bilingual/bicultural education, early childhood education, elementary education, foreign languages education, mathematics education, middle school education, science education, secondary education, social studies education, and special education), HEALTH PROFESSIONS (community health work and health), SOCIAL SCIENCE (American studies, criminology, history, humanities, philosophy, political science/government, psychology, religion, and sociology). Education, business, and biological sciences are the strongest academically. Psychology, accounting and biological sciences have the largest enrollments.

ACTIVITIES: 1% of men belong to 6 national fraternities; 2% of women belong to 8 national sororities. There are 60 groups on campus, including art, cheerleading, choir, chorale, computers, dance, drama, ethnic, film, gay, honors, international, newspaper, photography, political, professional, radio and TV, religious, social, social service, student government, and yearbook. Popular campus events include Welcome Back Festival, Wellness at Old Westbury and Panther Pride Week. **Sports:** There are 7 intercollegiate sports for men and 7 for women, and 7 intramural sports for men and 7 for women. Facilities include a gym, and a auxiliary gym, a cross-country course, playing fields, a swimming pool, a fitness center, a weight room, jogging trails, a student union building, and courts for tennis, paddleball, handball, racquetball, and squash. **Graduates:** From July

1, 2013 to June 30, 2014, 864 bachelor's degrees were awarded. The most popular majors were psychology (16%), accounting (12%), and media and communications (9%). 75 companies recruited on campus in 2013-2014. In an average class, 1% graduate in 3 years or less, 21% graduate in 4 years or less, 31% graduate in 5 years or less, and 35% graduate in 6 years or less.

SERVICES: Counseling and information services are available, as is tutoring in most subjects, mathematics, and writing There is a reader service for the blind, and remedial math, reading, and writing. **Library/Resources:** The library contains 251,930 volumes, 18,864 microform items, 1,634 audio/video tapes/CDs/DVDs, and subscribes to 2,532 periodicals including electronic. Computerized library services include interlibrary loans, database searching, Internet access, and Wi-Fi capability. Special learning facilities include an art gallery, radio station, TV studio. **Physically Challenged Students:** 90% of the campus is accessible. Facilities include wheelchair ramps, elevators, special parking, specially equipped restrooms, special class scheduling, lowered drinking fountains, lowered telephones. limited volunteer transportation. **Special:** SUNY Old Westbury offers cross-registration with SUNY Empire State, Lirache, and colleges in Nassau and Suffolk counties, internships in teacher education, extensive study-abroad programs, a B.A.-B.S. in psychology, chemistry, industrial labor and relations, and sociology, dual majors, and a 3-2 engineering degree with SUNY at Stony Brook and SUNY Maritime College. An Accelerated B.S. in Biological Sciences/D.O. in Osteopathic Medicine (offered in collaboration with the New York College of Osteopathic Medicine). Credit for military and life experience, nondegree study, and pass/fail options are available. There are 5 national honor societies, a freshman honors program, and 6 departmental honors programs. **Visiting:** There are regularly scheduled orientations for prospective students. There are guides for informal visits. To schedule a visit, contact Enrollment Services at (516) 876-3073. **Campus Safety and Security:** Measures include 24-hour foot and vehicle patrol, emergency notification system, and security escort services. There are shuttle buses, emergency telephones, lighted pathways/sidewalks, an officer patrols dormitories from 6 pm to 2 am

REQUIREMENTS: The SAT is required. Applicants must be graduates of an accredited secondary school or have a GED. An essay, portfolio, and interview are also recommended. Students are evaluated according to qualifying categories of academic achievement, special knowledge and creative ability, paid work experience, and social or personal experience. AP and CLEP credits are accepted. Important factors in the admissions decision are leadership record, recommendations by school officials, and evidence of special talent.General education requirements include courses in writing and reasoning skills, creative arts, ideas and ideology, cross-cultural perspectives, U.S. society and history, physical or life science, and foreign language. A senior project or capstone course is required, based on major. To be eligible for graduation, all candidates must satisfy all College and departmental requirements for the specific degree. Students must complete a minimum of 120 credits of satisfactory work. Some departmental requirements exceed this number. Forty-five of these credits must be earned in course work above the survey and the introductory levels (at or above the 3000 level). To fulfill graduation requirements, School of Education majors must have a 3.00 cumulative grade point average, School of Business majors must have a 2.5 cumulative grade point average as well as for all School of Business courses, all other students must have at least a 2.0 cumulative grade point average (GPA) for all work completed at the College. **Procedure:** Freshmen are admitted fall and spring. There are early decision, deferred admissions, and rolling admissions plans. Application deadlines are open. Application fee is $50. Notification is sent on a rolling basis. Applications are accepted on-line. **Transfer Students:** 1280 transfer students enrolled in 2013-2014. Applicants must submit official transcripts from all colleges attended. Those students with fewer than 24 college credits must also submit a high school transcript. The college requires a minimum overall GPA of 2.0. Specific academic majors may require a higher GPA. 48 of 120 credits required for the bachelor's degree must be completed at SUNY Old Westbury. **International Students:** There are 34 international students enrolled. The school actively recruits these students. They must take the TOEFL with a minimum score of 513 on the paper-based TOEFL (PBT) or 80 on the Internet-based version (iBT) and the college's own test.

ADMISSIONS: Mary Marquez Bell, Vice President for Enrollment Services. E-Mail: *enroll@oldwestbury.edu* Web: *www.oldwestbury.edu*

FINANCIAL AID: In 2014-2015, 69% of all full-time freshmen and 62% of continuing full-time students received some form of financial aid. 65% of all full-time freshmen and 57% of continuing full-time students received need-based aid. The average freshman award was $7,207. Need-based scholarships or need-based grants averaged $7,016; need-based self-help aid (loans and jobs) averaged $7,351; and other non-need-based awards and non-need-based scholarships averaged $1,971. Average annual earnings from campus work are $902. The average financial indebtedness of the 2014 graduate was $17,340. The FAFSA and the college's own financial statement, and the IFAA (Institutional application), and previous year's household income are required. The deadline for filing freshman financial aid applications for fall entry is April 19.

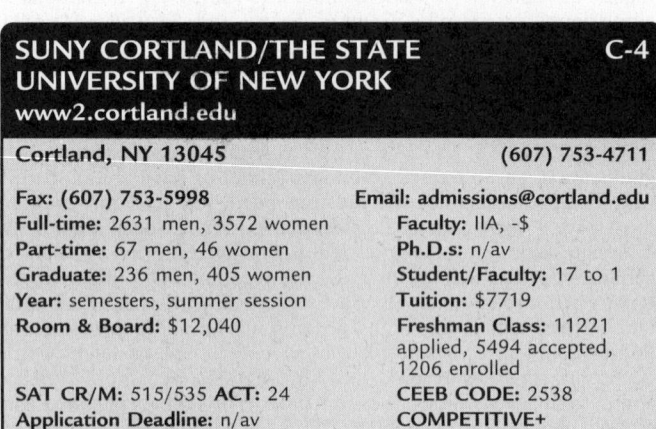

SUNY CORTLAND/THE STATE UNIVERSITY OF NEW YORK   C-4
www2.cortland.edu

Cortland, NY 13045	(607) 753-4711
Fax: (607) 753-5998	Email: admissions@cortland.edu
Full-time: 2631 men, 3572 women	Faculty: IIA, -$
Part-time: 67 men, 46 women	Ph.D.s: n/av
Graduate: 236 men, 405 women	Student/Faculty: 17 to 1
Year: semesters, summer session	Tuition: $7719
Room & Board: $12,040	Freshman Class: 11221 applied, 5494 accepted, 1206 enrolled
SAT CR/M: 515/535 ACT: 24	CEEB CODE: 2538
Application Deadline: n/av	COMPETITIVE+

The State University of New York College at Cortland, founded in 1868, is a public institution offering academic programs leading to baccalaureate and master's degrees in liberal arts and professional studies. There are 3 undergraduate schools and 3 graduate schools. In addition to regional accreditation, SUNY Cortland has baccalaureate program accreditation with CAHEA, NCATE, and NRPA. The 191-acre campus is in a small town 18 miles north of Ithaca and 29 miles south of Syracuse.

STUDENT LIFE: **Female To Male Ratio:** 1.4:1. **Housing:** 3224 students can be accommodated in college housing, which includes coed dorms and off-campus apartments. In addition, there are special-interest houses, fraternity houses, sorority houses, coed dorms, apartments for single students, special housing for disabled students, cooperative housing, wellness housing, leadership house, transfer floor housing, and quiet atmosphere housing. All students may keep cars.

FACULTY/CLASSROOMS: All teach undergraduates, 15% do research, and 15% do both. No introductory courses are taught by graduate students.

PROGRAMS OF STUDY: SUNY Cortland confers B.A., B.S., B.S.Ed. and B.F.A. degrees. Master's degrees are also awarded. Bachelor's degrees are awarded in BIOLOGICAL SCIENCE (biology/biological science), BUSINESS (management science and sports management), COMMUNICATIONS AND THE ARTS (art, communications, English, film arts, and musical theater), COMPUTER AND PHYSICAL SCIENCE (chemistry, geochemistry, geology, geophysics and seismology, mathematics, and physics), EDUCATION (athletic training, education services, foreign languages education, health education, middle school education, physical education, recreation education, and secondary education), ENGINEERING AND ENVIRONMENTAL DESIGN (environmental science), HEALTH PROFESSIONS (health science and speech pathology/audiology), SOCIAL SCIENCE (African American studies, anthropology, economics, geography, history, human services, international studies, philosophy, political science/government, psychology, and sociology).

ACTIVITIES: There are 100 groups on campus, including art, band, cheerleading, chess, choir, chorale, chorus, computers, dance, drama, ethnic, film, gay, honors, international, literary magazine, Model UN, musical theater, newspaper, orchestra, political, professional, radio and TV, religious, social, social service, student government, symphony, and yearbook. Popular campus events include Cortland-

Ithaca College Football Game, Winterfest, and Multicultural Festival. **Sports:** There are 11 intercollegiate sports for men and 14 for women, and 55 intramural sports for men and 55 for women. Facilities include an outdoor multipurpose stadium complex, Olympic-size pool, gym, ice arena, gymnastics arena, wrestling and weight rooms, dance studio, handball/racquetball courts, squash courts, athletic training facility, fitness centers, free-swimming pool, track, baseball field, football/lacrosse/track field, lighted soccer field, field house and 50 acres of athletic fields. **Graduates:** From July 1, 2013 to June 30, 2014, 1625 bachelor's degrees were awarded. The most popular majors were education (29%), parks and recreation (16%), and social sciences (10%).

SERVICES: Counseling and information services are available, as is tutoring in some subjects. There is a fully staffed Academic Support and Achievement Program for writing, math, study skills, and learning strategies. Specific course tutoring is available with peer tutors. **Library/Resources:** The library contains 423,158 volumes, 844,222 microform items, and 2,947 audio/video tapes/CDs/DVDs, and subscribes to 428 periodicals including electronic. Computerized library services include interlibrary loans, database searching, Internet access, and Wi-Fi capability. Special learning facilities include an art gallery, planetarium, radio station, TV station, a greenhouse, a center for speech and hearing disorders, classrooms equipped with integrated technologies (multimedia enhanced instruction), and many specialized labs to support various program offerings. **Physically Challenged Students:** 75% of the campus is accessible. Facilities include wheelchair ramps, elevators, special parking, specially equipped restrooms, special class scheduling, lowered drinking fountains, and lowered telephones. **Special:** Cortland offers cross-registration with Tompkins Cortland Communinty College and has cooperative programs with the State University of New York College of Environmental Science and Forestry, and Centers at Binghamton and Buffalo, and Cornell and Case Western Reserve Universities. Students may study abroad in over 30 countries, and they may enroll in a Washington semester. Work-study programs are available. The college confers an individualized studies degree and allows dual majors. Students may pursue a 3-2 engineering degree in conjunction with Alfred, Case Western Reserve, and Clarkson Universities, and the State University of New York Centers at Binghamton, Buffalo, and Stony Brook. Cortland offers non-degree study opportunities. There are 19 national honor societies, including Phi Beta Kappa, a freshman honors program, and 5 departmental honors programs. **Visiting:** There are regularly scheduled orientations for prospective students, consisting of Autumn Preview Days for prospective students as well as Spring Open House for accepted students. There are guides for informal visits and visitors may sit in on classes. To schedule a visit, contact The Admissions Office at admissions@cortland.edu. **Campus Safety and Security:** Measures include 24-hour foot and vehicle patrol, emergency notification system, self-defense education, and security escort services. There are shuttle buses, emergency telephones, lighted pathways/sidewalks, university police maintain a web site with safety information and links and a silent witness program for reporting crimes anonymously.

REQUIREMENTS: The SAT is required. Applicants must graduate from an accredited secondary school or have a GED. They must have earned 16 Carnegie units and 16 to 20 academic credits, including 4 units each in English and history or social studies and 3 each (4 recommended) in math and science (one of these units must be lab), 3 units in foreign language. Essays and recommendations are required, and in some cases auditions as well. Interviews are strongly recommended. AP and CLEP credits are accepted. Important factors in the admissions decision are advanced placement or honors courses, evidence of special talent, extracurricular activities record, recommendations by alumni, recommendations by school officials, leadership record, parents or siblings attended your school, and geographical diversity. To graduate, undergraduates must complete 6 hours in English Composition, and at least 6 hours of writing-intensive courses, with 3 of those in the major. One course meeting the Quantitative Skills criteria must also be passed; 28 to 29 hours of courses in the General Education program must also be completed, with no more than 2 courses taken in any one of the 8 disciplines in the program. A major of 30 to 36 hours, with no more than 45 credits in discipline-specific courses must be completed. Completion of 90 credits

of Liberal Arts and Science courses toward a B.A., 60 credits toward a B.S.Ed, or 75 credits toward a B.S. is required. A 2.0 GPA, both overall and in all minors and concentrations, must be maintained. Special requirements may be designated by each school of the college. **Procedure:** Freshmen are admitted fall and spring. Entrance exams should be taken during the spring of the junior year or fall of the senior year. There are early decision, early admissions, deferred admissions, and rolling admissions plans. Check with the school for current application deadlines. The application fee is $50. Notification is sent on a rolling basis. Applications are accepted on-line. **Transfer Students:** 645 transfer students enrolled in 2013-2014. Applicants must have a minimum GPA of 2.5. Some programs are more competitive. Interviews are encouraged. 45 of 124 credits required for the bachelor's degree must be completed at SUNY Cortland. **International Students:** The school actively recruits these students. They must take the TOEFL, the SAT I or a General Certificate of Education is acceptable in lieu of the TOEFL. They must also take the SAT or ACT.

ADMISSIONS: 49% of the 2014-2015 applicants were accepted. The SAT scores for the 2014-2015 freshman class were: Critical Reading-- 37% below 500, 53% between 500 and 599, and 9% between 600 and 699. Math-- 23% below 500, 60% between 500 and 599, and 17% between 600 and 699. The ACT scores were 52% between 21 and 23, 44% between 27 and 28, and 4% above 28. **Admissions Contact:** Mark Yacavone, Assistant VP, Enrollment Management. E-Mail: *admissions@cortland.edu* Web: *http://www2.cortland.edu/admissions/*

FINANCIAL AID: In 2014-2015, 76% of all full-time freshmen received some form of financial aid. 76% of all full-time freshmen received need-based aid. The average freshman award was $13,607. Need-based scholarships or need-based grants averaged $5,399; need-based self-help aid (loans and jobs) averaged $3,670; other non-need-based awards and non-need-based scholarships averaged $3,896; and $3,526 from other forms of aid. The average financial indebtedness of the 2014 graduate was $27,472. The FAFSA, and NYS TAP application is required. The deadline for filing freshman financial aid applications for fall entry is April 1.

SUNY FREDONIA/THE STATE UNIVERSITY OF NEW YORK AT FREDONIA A-4
www.fredonia.edu

Fredonia, NY 14063	**(716) 673-3251**
	(800) 252-1212
Fax: (716) 673-3249	**Email: admissions@fredonia.edu**
Full-time: 2192 men, 2633 women	**Faculty:** 251; IIA, -$
Part-time: 64 men, 54 women	**Ph.D.s:** 88%
Graduate: 66 men, 207 women	**Student/Faculty:** 16 to 1
Year: semesters, summer session	**Tuition:** $7740 ($17,390)
Room & Board: $12,100	**Freshman Class:** 6087 applied, 3241 accepted, 1085 enrolled
SAT CR/M: 540/540 **ACT:** 24	**CEEB CODE:** 2539
Application Deadline: open	**VERY COMPETITIVE**

The State University of New York at Fredonia, established in 1826, is a public institution offering undergraduate programs in the arts and sciences, business and professional curricula, teacher preparation, and the fine and performing arts. There are 5 undergraduate schools and 1 graduate school. In addition to regional accreditation, Fredonia has baccalaureate program accreditation with CSWE, NASAD, NASM, NCATE, NAST, and ASHA. The 266-acre campus is in a small town 50 miles south of Buffalo and 45 miles north of Erie, Pennsylvania. Including any residence halls, there are 62 buildings. **STUDENT LIFE:** 94% of undergraduates are from New York. Others are from 24 states, 13 foreign countries, and Canada. 92% are from public schools. 79% are White. The average age of freshmen is 18; all undergraduates, 20. 14% do not continue beyond their first year; 64% remain to graduate. **Housing:** 2900 students can be accommodated in college housing, which includes single-sex and coed dorms and on-campus apartments. In addition, there are honors houses, special-interest houses, living space for fraternities and sororities is available in residence halls. In addition, there are special interest houses for computer and athletics students and quiet-hour centers. On-campus housing is guaranteed for the freshman year only, is available on a first-come, first-served basis, and is available on a lottery system for upperclassmen. Priority is given to out-of-town students. 56% of students live on campus; of those, 96% remain on campus on weekends. All students may keep cars.

FACULTY/CLASSROOMS: 53% of faculty are male; 47% are female. All teach and do research. No introductory courses are taught by graduate students. The average class size in an introductory lecture is 35; in a laboratory is 16; and in a regular course is 23.

PROGRAMS OF STUDY: Fredonia confers B.A., B.F.A., B.S., B.S.Ed. and Mus.B. degrees. Master's degrees are also awarded. Bachelor's degrees are awarded in AGRICULTURE (environmental studies), BIOLOGICAL SCIENCE (biochemistry, biology/adolescence education, biology/biological science, and genetics), BUSINESS (accounting, accounting/CPA, business administration and management, business economics, finance, institutional management, and sports management), COMMUNICATIONS AND THE ARTS (acting, animation, arts administration/management, audio technology, communication, communication studies, communications, dance, dramatic arts, drawing, English, film, television and digital media, fine arts, French, graphic design, illustration, journalism, media arts, music, music performance, music theory and composition, musical theater, painting, photography, public relations, Spanish, theatre arts, theater design, theatre production, theatre studies, and video), COMPUTER AND PHYSICAL SCIENCE (applied mathematics, chemistry, chemistry/adolescence education, computer information systems, computer science, earth science, geochemistry, geology, geoscience, mathematics, and physics), EDUCATION (childhood education: 1-6, early childhood education, education, elementary education, English education, foreign languages education, mathematics education, middle school education, music education, science education, secondary education, social studies education, and social studies secondary school education), ENGINEERING AND ENVIRONMENTAL DESIGN (environmental science), HEALTH PROFESSIONS (health care administration, medical laboratory technology, music therapy, predentistry, premedicine, preoptometry, and speech pathology/audiology), SOCIAL SCIENCE (American studies, early childhood studies, economics, history, interdisciplinary studies, liberal arts/general studies, philosophy, political science/government, prelaw, psychology, social work, sociology, and women's studies). Music, theatre, visual arts, and natural sciences are the strongest academically. STEM, arts, and business have the largest enrollments.

ACTIVITIES: 2% of men belong to 2 national fraternities; 4% of women belong to 3 national sororities. There are 160 groups on campus, including and Spectrum Entertainment Board, art, band, cheerleading, choir, chorale, chorus, communications, computers, dance, debate, drama, drill team, environmental, ethnic, film, gay, honors, international, jazz band, literary magazine, musical theater, newspaper, opera, orchestra, pep band, photography, political, professional, radio and TV, religious, ski club, social, social service, student government, and symphony. Popular campus events include Various Art Center presentations, Fred-Fest, and Little Siblings Weekend. **Sports:** There are 8 intercollegiate sports for men and 9 for women, and 15 intramural sports for men and 15 for women. Facilities include a basketball arena, an ice rink, swimming pool, two gyms, weight rooms, dance studios, soccer fields, indoor and outdoor tracks, racquetball, tennis, and volleyball courts, and a soccer/lacrosse stadium. **Graduates:** From July 1, 2013 to June 30, 2014, 1523 bachelor's degrees were awarded. The most popular majors were education (25%), business administration (13%), and music (10%). 75 companies recruited on campus in 2013-2014. In an average class, 47% graduate in 4 years or less, 62% graduate in 5 years or less, and 64% graduate in 6 years or less.

SERVICES: Counseling and information services are available, as is tutoring in most subjects. There is a reader service for the blind. **Library/Resources:** The library contains 391,121 volumes, 1.1 million microform items, 26,574 audio/video tapes/CDs/DVDs, and subscribes to 1,983 periodicals including electronic. Computerized library services include interlibrary loans, database searching, Internet access, and Wi-Fi capability. Special learning facilities include an art gallery, natural history museum, planetarium, radio station, TV station, a greenhouse, day-care center, speech clinic, and the Rockefeller arts center. **Physically Challenged Students:** 85% of the campus is accessible. Facilities include wheelchair ramps, elevators, special parking, specially equipped restrooms, special class scheduling, lowered drinking fountains, lowered telephones, and special housing. **Special:** Cooperative programs are available with many other institutions. Students may cross-register with colleges in the Western New York Consortium. Fredonia offers a variety of internships, study-abroad programs in more than 60 countries, and a Washington semester. Accelerated degrees, a general studies degree, dual and student-designed majors, a 3-2 engineering degree program with 14 universities, nondegree study, and pass/fail grading options are available. There are 19 national honor societies, a freshman honors program, and 19 departmental honors programs. **Visiting:** There are regularly scheduled orientations for prospective students, including various open house programs and information sessions and tours Monday through Friday, morning and afternoon, and varied Saturday tours. Visitors may sit in on classes and stay overnight. To schedule a visit, contact the Office of Admissions. **Campus Safety and Security:** Measures include 24-hour foot and vehicle patrol, emergency notification system, self-defense education, and security escort services. There are shuttle buses, emergency telephones, lighted pathways/sidewalks, controlled access to dorms/residences, card swipe access to residence halls.

REQUIREMENTS: The SAT or ACT is required, with a satisfactory score on the SAT or 20 on the ACT. Applicants must possess a high school diploma or have a GED. 16 academic credits are recommended, including 4 credits each in English and social studies and 3 each in math, science, and a foreign language. 4 years of math and science are encouraged. Essays are required. Where applicable, an audition or portfolio is required. AP and CLEP credits are accepted. Important factors in the admissions decision are advanced placement or honors courses, leadership record, parents or siblings attended your school, evidence of special talent, personality/intangible qualities, extracurricular activities record, recommendations by alumni, geographical diversity, recommendations by school officials, and ability to finance college education.To graduate, students must complete 120 hours, including 36 to 90 or more in the major, with a 2.0 GPA. Students must take specific courses in English and math and complete 50 hours of general education courses, including writing, statistical/quantitative abilities, oral communication, natural and social sciences, humanities, and arts. **Procedure:** Freshmen are admitted fall and spring. Entrance exams should be taken Spring of the junior year or fall of the senior year. There are early decision, early admissions, deferred admissions, and rolling admissions plans. Early decision applications should be filed by November 1, along with a $50 fee. Notification of early decision is sent December 1; regular decision, December 5. 75 early decision candidates were accepted for the 2014-2015 class. Applications are accepted on-line. **Transfer Students:** 442 transfer students enrolled in 2013-2014. Applicants should have a minimum GPA of 2.0 and appropriate academic course work to be considered. 45 of 120 credits required for the bachelor's degree must be completed at Fredonia. **International Students:** There are 184 international students enrolled. The school actively recruits these students. They must take the TOEFL with a minimum score of 78 on the Internet-based version (iBT), or take the IELTS.

ADMISSIONS: 53% of the 2014-2015 applicants were accepted. The SAT scores for the 2014-2015 freshman class were: Critical Reading--28% below 500, 54% between 500 and 599, 16% between 600 and 699, and 2% between 700 and 800; Math--23% below 500, 58% between 500 and 599, 17% between 600 and 699, and 3% between 700 and 800. The ACT scores were 8% below 21, 39% between 21 and 23, 31% between 24 and 26, 12% between 27 and 28, and 10% above 28. 34% of the current freshmen were in the top fifth of their class; 71% were in the top two fifths. 4 freshmen graduated first in their class. **Admissions Contact:** Cory Bezek, Director of Admissions. E-Mail: *admissions@fredonia.edu* Web: *www.fredonia.edu*

FINANCIAL AID: In 2014-2015, 83% of all full-time freshmen and 77% of continuing full-time students received some form of financial aid. 68% of all full-time freshmen and 68% of continuing full-time students received need-based aid. The average freshman award was $9,280. Need-based scholarships or need-based grants averaged $4,534; need-based self-help aid (loans and jobs) averaged $5,090;

and other non-need-based awards and non-need-based scholarships averaged $527. Average annual earnings from campus work are $1287. The average financial indebtedness of the 2014 graduate was $20,574. The FAFSA and the state aid form, and Express TAP Application (ETA) are required. The priority date for freshman financial aid applications for fall entry is February 1.

SUNY NEW PALTZ
www.newpaltz.edu

D-4

New Paltz, NY 12561	(845) 257-3200 n/av
Fax: (845) 257-3209	Email: admissions@newpaltz.edu
Full-time: 1690 men, 3585 women	Faculty: IIA, -$
Part-time: 295 men, 560 women	Ph.D.s: n/av
Graduate: 490 men, 940 women	Student/Faculty: n/av
Year: semesters, summer session	Tuition: $7128 ($13,828)
Room & Board: $7220	Freshman Class: n/av
SAT or ACT: required	CEEB CODE: 2541
Application Deadline: April 1	COMPETITIVE

State University of New York/University at New Paltz, founded in 1828, is a public institution offering undergraduate and graduate programs in the liberal arts and sciences, business, education, engineering, fine and performing arts, and the health professions. The figures in the above capsule and in this profile are approximate. There are 5 undergraduate schools and 1 graduate school. In addition to regional accreditation, SUNY New Paltz has baccalaureate program accreditation with ABET, CSAB, NASAD, NASM, and NCATE. The 216-acre campus is in a small town 100 miles north of New York City and 65 miles south of Albany. Including any residence halls, there are 53 buildings.

STUDENT LIFE: 92% of undergraduates are from New York. Others are from 28 states, 48 foreign countries, and Canada. 90% are from public schools. 58% are White. The average age of freshmen is 18; all undergraduates, 20. 16% do not continue beyond their first year; 59% remain to graduate. **Housing:** 2800 students can be accommodated in college housing, which includes coed dorms. In addition, there are special-interest houses. On-campus housing is guaranteed for the freshman year only, is available on a first-come, and first-served basis. Priority is given to out-of-town students. 51% of students live on campus; of those, 90% remain on campus on weekends. Upperclassmen may keep cars.

FACULTY/CLASSROOMS: 45% of faculty are male; 55% are female. 97% do both. Graduate students teach 1% of introductory courses. The average class size in an introductory lecture is 19; in a laboratory is 10; and in a regular course is 19.

PROGRAMS OF STUDY: SUNY New Paltz confers B.A., B.S. and B.F.A. degrees. Master's degrees are also awarded. Bachelor's degrees are awarded in BIOLOGICAL SCIENCE (biology/biological science), BUSINESS (accounting, banking and finance, business administration and management, international business management, and marketing/retailing/merchandising), COMMUNICATIONS AND THE ARTS (art history and appreciation, communications, dramatic arts, English, French, German, graphic design, journalism, metal/jewelry, music, painting, photography, sculpture, Spanish, speech/debate/rhetoric, studio art, theater design, and visual and performing arts), COMPUTER AND PHYSICAL SCIENCE (chemistry, computer science, environmental geology, geology, mathematics, and physics), EDUCATION (art education, early childhood education, elementary education, English education, foreign languages education, mathematics education, middle school education, science education, secondary education, and social studies education), ENGINEERING AND ENVIRONMENTAL DESIGN (computer engineering, electrical/electronics engineering, and woodworking), HEALTH PROFESSIONS (music therapy, nursing, and speech pathology/audiology), SOCIAL SCIENCE (African American studies, anthropology, Asian/Oriental studies, economics, geography, history, international relations, Latin American studies, liberal arts/general studies, philosophy, political science/government, psychology, social science, sociology, and women's studies). Business, computer science,

and math are the strongest academically. Business, visual arts, and elementary education have the largest enrollments.

ACTIVITIES: 3% of men belong to 5 local and 5 national fraternities; 2% of women belong to 5 local and 8 national sororities. There are 136 groups on campus, including art, band, cheerleading, chess, choir, chorale, chorus, computers, dance, drama, ethnic, gay, honors, international, jazz band, literary magazine, musical theater, newspaper, orchestra, photography, political, professional, radio and TV, religious, social, social service, student government, and yearbook. Popular campus events include Spirit Weekend, New Paltz Summer Repertory Theater and Rainbow Month. **Sports:** There are 9 intercollegiate sports for men and 11 for women, and 12 intramural sports for men and 9 for women. Facilities include a gym, swimming and diving teams, numerous playing fields, a 35,000-square-foot air-supported structure for tennis, jogging, volleyball, basketball, and softball, crew teams for men and women, riding teams for women, 24 outdoor tennis courts, men's golf, lacrosse, and ice hockey. **Graduates:** From July 1, 2013 to June 30, 2014, 1592 bachelor's degrees were awarded. The most popular majors were education (21%), business and marketing (14%), and social science (11%). 135 companies recruited on campus in 2013-2014. In an average class, 36% graduate in 4 years or less, 59% graduate in 5 years or less, and 61% graduate in 6 years or less.

SERVICES: Counseling and information services are available, as is tutoring in most subjects. There is a reader service for the blind, and remedial math, reading, and writing. **Library/Resources:** The library contains 499,048 volumes, 1.2 million microform items, 4,030 audio/video tapes/CDs/DVDs, and subscribes to 32,361 periodicals including electronic. Computerized library services include interlibrary loans, database searching, Internet access, and Wi-Fi capability. Special learning facilities include a planetarium, radio station, TV station, greenhouse, robotics lab, electron microscope facility, speech and hearing clinic, art museum, music therapy training facility, observatory, Fournier transform mass spectrometer, honors center, electronic media center, electronic classroom, and an IBM e-business virtual lab. **Physically Challenged Students:** 90% of the campus is accessible. Facilities include wheelchair ramps, elevators, special parking, specially equipped restrooms, special class scheduling, lowered drinking fountains, lowered telephones, and special housing. **Special:** There is cross-registration with the Mid-Hudson Consortium of Colleges. The university offers co-op programs and internships in most majors, work-study programs on campus and at the Children's Center of New Paltz, and opportunities for student-designed or dual majors. Students may study abroad in 18 countries. A 3-2 advanced degree in environmental biology is offered with SUNY Environmental Science and Forestry. There are 7-year medical and optometry accelerated degree programs. B.A.-B.S. degrees are offered in liberal arts and science, education, business, science and, engineering, and fine and performing arts. There are 4 national honor societies, a freshman honors program, and 6 departmental honors programs. **Visiting:** There are regularly scheduled orientations for prospective students, including daily information sessions and campus tours. Visitors may sit in on classes. To schedule a visit, contact the Admissions Office. **Campus Safety and Security:** Measures include 24-hour foot and vehicle patrol, self-defense education, and security escort services. There are emergency telephones, lighted pathways/sidewalks, Bicycle patrol, locked residence halls, and a campus 911 system.

REQUIREMENTS: The SAT or ACT is required. 4 units each of English, and social studies, 3 to 4 units each of mathematics and science, including 2 units of lab science, and 2 to 4 units of foreign language are required. The GED is accepted but must be accompanied by a high school transcript and SAT or ACT scores. SUNY New Paltz requires applicants to be in the upper 50% of their class. A GPA of 3.0 is required. AP and CLEP credits are accepted. Important factors in the admissions decision are advanced placement or honors courses, recommendations by school officials, and evidence of special talent. To graduate, students must complete a minimum of 120 credits with a 2.0 GPA. The core curriculum of 16 to 17 credits includes courses in English composition, math and analytical skills, and modern world studies. The number of credits required in the major varies. Distribution requirements include courses in cultures and civilizations, American experience, social sciences, physical and biological sciences, foreign languages, and aesthetic expression, 1 writing-intensive course in the major, and 60 credits in upper-division courses. New York State Teacher Competency Exams are required of education majors. Engineering students must complete a senior project, and art majors must show their work in a senior exhibition. **Procedure:** Freshmen are admitted fall. Entrance exams should be taken before December 31. There are early admissions, deferred admissions, and rolling admissions plans. Applications should be filed by April 1 for fall entry. The fall 2014 application fee was $40. Notification is sent on a rolling basis. Applications are accepted on-line. **Transfer Students:** 1011 transfer students enrolled in 2013-2014. To be considered, applicants must have maintained a minimum GPA of 2.75 in all previous college work at accredited institutions. Some programs require a higher GPA for consideration. 30 of 120 credits required for the bachelor's degree must be completed at SUNY New Paltz. **International Students:** There are 219 international students enrolled. The school actively recruits these students. They must take the TOEFL with a minimum score of 550 on the paper-based TOEFL (PBT) or 80 on the Internet-based version (iBT), or take the SAT or demonstrate English Proficiency. Conditional acceptance is available to both graduate and undergraduate programs. Accepted students must take a placement test upon arrival at SUNY New Paltz. If the student is not yet proficient, he or she must take ESL courses until required proficiency is achieved.

ADMISSIONS: Kimberly Lavoie, Director of Freshman/International Admissions. E-Mail: *admissions@newpaltz.edu* Web: *www.newpaltz.edu*

FINANCIAL AID: In 2014-2015, 70% of all full-time freshmen and 75% of continuing full-time students received some form of financial aid. 55% of all full-time freshmen and 75% of continuing full-time students received need-based aid. The average freshman award was $5,500. Need-based scholarships or need-based grants averaged $2,400; need-based self-help aid (loans and jobs) averaged $2,600; and other non-need-based awards and non-need-based scholarships averaged $500. 45% of undergraduate students work part-time. Average annual earnings from campus work are $900. The average financial indebtedness of the 2014 graduate was $19,000. The FAFSA is required. Check with the school for current application deadlines.

SUNY ONEONTA / STATE UNIVERSITY OF NEW YORK D-3
www.oneonta.edu

Oneonta, NY 13820	(607) 436-2524
	(800) 786-9123
Fax: (607) 436-3074	Email: admissions@oneonta.edu
Full-time: 2294 men, 3430 women	Faculty: 251; IIA, -$
Part-time: 65 men, 74 women	Ph.D.s: 86%
Graduate: 43 men, 163 women	Student/Faculty: 18 to 1
Year: semesters, summer session	Tuition: $6887 ($13,137)
Room & Board: $10,032	Freshman Class: 12031 applied, 5190 accepted, 1146 enrolled
SAT CR/M: 538/563 ACT: 24	CEEB CODE: 2542
Application Deadline: open	COMPETITIVE+

The State University of New York/College at Oneonta, founded in 1889, offers undergraduate and graduate programs in the arts and sciences with a campus-wide emphasis on student engagement, diversity and community service. There is 1 undergraduate school and 1 graduate school. In addition to regional accreditation, SUNY Oneonta has baccalaureate program accreditation with AACSB, ADA, NASM, NCATE, ACS, and AAFCS. The 250-acre campus is in a rural area 75 miles southwest of Albany and 55 miles northeast of Binghamton. Including any residence halls, there are 36 buildings.

STUDENT LIFE: 98% of undergraduates are from New York. Others are from 25 states, and 18 foreign countries. 81% are White. The average age of freshmen is 18; all undergraduates, 20. 16% do not continue beyond their first year; 67% remain to graduate. **Housing:** 3557 students can be accommodated in college housing, which includes coed dorms and on-campus apartments. Freshman housing and special-interest groupings within residence halls. On-campus housing is guaranteed for the freshman year only, is available on a first-come, first-served basis, and is available on a lottery system for upperclassmen. 59% of students live on campus; of those, 60% remain on campus on weekends. Alcohol is not permitted. Upperclassmen may keep cars.

FACULTY/CLASSROOMS: 50% of faculty are male; 50% are female. 96% teach undergraduates. No introductory courses are taught by graduate students. The average class size in an introductory lecture is 28; in a laboratory is 18; and in a regular course is 23.

PROGRAMS OF STUDY: SUNY Oneonta confers B.A., and B.S. degrees. Master's degrees are also awarded. Bachelor's degrees are awarded in BIOLOGICAL SCIENCE (biology/biological science), BUSINESS (accounting, business economics, and fashion merchandising), COMMUNICATIONS AND THE ARTS (art, communications, dramatic arts, English, fine arts, French, music, music business management, and Spanish), COMPUTER AND PHYSICAL SCIENCE (atmospheric sciences and meteorology, chemistry, computer science, earth science, geology, mathematics, physics, and statistics), EDUCATION (business education, elementary education, English education, foreign languages education, home economics education, mathematics education, science education, secondary education, and social science education), ENGINEERING AND ENVIRONMENTAL DESIGN (environmental science), HEALTH PROFESSIONS (predentistry and premedicine), SOCIAL SCIENCE (African studies, anthropology, child care/child and family studies, criminal justice, dietetics, economics, geography, gerontology, Hispanic American studies, history, home economics, international studies, philosophy, political science/government, prelaw, psychology, sociology, and water resources). Physical and natural sciences, business economics, and education are the strongest academically. Elementary education, adolescent education, business, music industry, and fashion are the largest.

ACTIVITIES: 1% of men belong to 5 national fraternities; 1% of women belong to 8 national sororities. There are 112 groups on campus, including academic, cultural and special-interest organizations, art, band, cheerleading, choir, chorale, chorus, computers, dance, debate, drama, environmental, ethnic, film, gay, honors, international, jazz band, literary magazine, musical theater, newspaper, opera, orchestra, photography, political, professional, radio and TV, religious, social, social service, student government, variety of volunteer, and yearbook. Popular campus events include Into the Streets Day of Service, OH-Fest, Battle of the Red Dragons, Red Day and Passing through the Pillars. **Sports:** There are 10 intercollegiate sports for men and 11 for women, and 13 intramural sports for men and 13 for women. Facilities include a gym, field house, dance studios, weight rooms, pool, indoor racquetball courts, tennis courts, indoor and outdoor tracks, athletic fields, and a lighted all-weather field. **Graduates:** From July 1, 2013 to June 30, 2014, 1206 bachelor's degrees were awarded. The most popular majors were education (18%), human ecology (10%), and English (9%). In an average class, 50% graduate in 4 years or less, 63% graduate in 5 years or less, and 64% graduate in 6 years or less.

SERVICES: Counseling and information services are available, as is tutoring in most subjects. There is a reader service for the blind, and remedial math, reading, and writing. Tutoring is also available in all introductory-level courses and most upper-level courses **Library/Resources:** The library contains 482,408 volumes, 1.2 million microform items, 19,174 audio/video tapes/CDs/DVDs, and subscribes to 50,000 periodicals including electronic. Computerized library services include interlibrary loans, database searching, Internet access, and Wi-Fi capability. Special learning facilities include an art gallery, planetarium, radio station, TV station, digital planetarium, science discovery center, community service center, college camp, children's center, and off-campus biological field station. **Physically Challenged Students:** 90% of the campus is accessible. Facilities include wheelchair ramps, elevators, special parking, specially equipped restrooms, special class scheduling, lowered drinking fountains. All academic buildings and most residence halls are accessible. **Special:** Oneonta offers limited cross-registration with Hartwick College, internships in most fields, and dual majors. Students can study abroad through eight exchange programs in Ghana, Finland, Germany, Sweden, Japan and South Korea, as well as more than 500 study abroad programs around the world through the SUNY network. A 3-1 fashion program with the Fashion Institute of Technology, 3-2 engineering degree,and other cooperative programs are offered. There are 20 national honor societies. <u>Visiting:</u> There are regularly scheduled orientations for prospective students, open houses, Friday and Saturday information sessions and individual appointments for prospective students; Academic Exploration Day and summer orientation sessions for admitted students. There are guides for informal visits and visitors may sit in on classes. To schedule a visit, contact the Admissions Office at (800) SUNY-123. <u>Campus Safety and Security:</u> Measures include 24-hour foot and vehicle patrol, emergency notification system, self-defense education, and security escort services. There are shuttle buses, emergency telephones, lighted pathways/sidewalks, and controlled access to dorms/residences.

<u>REQUIREMENTS:</u> The SAT or ACT is required. Applicants should be graduates of an accredited secondary school and have 19 academic credits, including 4 years each of English, social studies, mathematics and science, including lab, 3 units of foreign language is required, (4 units is recommended). The GED is accepted. AP and CLEP credits are accepted. Important factors in the admissions decision are advanced placement or honors courses, evidence of special talent, and leadership record.Students must complete 122 semester hours, with 30 to 36 hours in the major. A minimum GPA of 2.0 (2.5 for education majors) must be maintained. In addition, students must complete a 36-hour general education requirement including courses in math, natural sciences, social sciences, American history, Western civilization, humanities, the arts, foreign language and basic communications. Students must also pass a writing exam. <u>Procedure:</u> Freshmen are admitted fall and spring. Entrance exams should be taken in the spring of the junior year or the fall of the senior year. There are deferred admissions and rolling admissions plans. Application deadlines are open. Application fee is $50. Notifications are sent December 1. Applications are accepted on-line. <u>Transfer Students:</u> 465 transfer students enrolled in 2013-2014. Official transcripts of all previous college work must be submitted. A minimum of 15 semester hours of transferable credit and a GPA of 2.0 (2.5 for education majors) are required. 45 of 122 credits required for the bachelor's degree must be completed at SUNY Oneonta. <u>International Students:</u> There are 111 international students enrolled. The school actively recruits these students. They must take the TOEFL with a minimum score of 500 on the paper-based TOEFL (PBT) or 61 on the Internet-based version (iBT).

<u>ADMISSIONS:</u> 43% of the 2014-2015 applicants were accepted. The SAT scores for the 2014-2015 freshman class were: Critical Reading--23% below 500, 62% between 500 and 599, 14% between 600 and 699, and 1% between 700 and 800; Math--14% below 500, 59% between 500 and 599, 25% between 600 and 699, and 2% between 700 and 800. <u>Admissions Contact:</u> Karen Brown, Director of Admissions. E-Mail: *admissions@oneonta.edu* Web: *www.oneonta.edu*

<u>FINANCIAL AID:</u> In 2014-2015, 83% of all full-time freshmen and 66% of continuing full-time students received some form of financial aid. 42% of all full-time freshmen and 59% of continuing full-time students received need-based aid. The average freshman award was $8,818. Need-based scholarships or need-based grants averaged $6,510; need-based self-help aid (loans and jobs) averaged $3,999; and other non-need-based awards and non-need-based scholarships averaged $2,841. The average financial indebtedness of the 2014 graduate was $15,373. The FAFSA and the state aid form are required. Check with the school for current application deadlines.

SUNY PLATTSBURGH / STATE UNIVERSITY OF NEW YORK   D-2

www.plattsburgh.edu

Plattsburgh, NY 12901	(518) 564-2040
	(888) 673-0012
Fax: (518) 564-2045	Email: higginrj@.plattsburgh.edu
Full-time: 2311 men, 2875 women	Faculty: IIA, -$
Part-time: 159 men, 294 women	Ph.D.s: 81%
Graduate: 107 men, 305 women	Student/Faculty: 16 to 1
Year: semesters, summer session	Tuition: $7159 ($16,609)
Room & Board: $10,924	Freshman Class: n/av
	CEEB CODE: 2844
Application Deadline: August 1	COMPETITIVE

The State University of New York/College at Plattsburgh, founded in 1889, is a public institution offering degree programs in the liberal arts and professional programs. There are 3 undergraduate schools and 2 graduate schools. In addition to regional accreditation, SUNY Plattsburgh has baccalaureate program accreditation with AACSB, ADA, CSWE, NLN, and TEAC. The 300-acre campus is in a suburban area 150 miles north of Albany, 25 miles west of Burlington, Vermont, and 65 miles south of Montreal, Canada. Including any residence halls, there are 36 buildings.

<u>STUDENT LIFE:</u> 90% of undergraduates are from New York. Others are from 27 states, 67 foreign countries, and Canada. 95% are from public schools. 71% are White. The average age of freshmen is 18; all undergraduates, 21. 22% do not continue beyond their first year; 61% remain to graduate. <u>Housing:</u> 2682 students can be accommodated in college housing, which includes single-sex and coed dorms and on-campus apartments. In addition, there are special-interest houses, adult student halls/floors, wellness floors, a substance-free building, and vacation housing. On-campus housing is available on a first-come, first-served basis, and is available on a lottery system for upperclassmen. 56% of students commute. All students may keep cars.

<u>FACULTY/CLASSROOMS:</u> 48% of faculty are male; 52% are female. All teach and do research. No introductory courses are taught by graduate students. The average class size in an introductory lecture is 27; in a laboratory is 17; and in a regular course is 24.

<u>PROGRAMS OF STUDY:</u> SUNY Plattsburgh confers B.A., B.S., B.F.A. and B.S.Ed. degrees. Master's degrees are also awarded. Bachelor's degrees are awarded in BIOLOGICAL SCIENCE (biochemistry, biology/adolescence education, biology/biological science, ecology, and nutrition), BUSINESS (accounting, business administration and management, entrepreneurial studies, finance, hotel/motel and restaurant management, international business management, management information systems, marketing/retailing/merchandising, and supply chain management), COMMUNICATIONS AND THE ARTS (art, communications, English, English literature, English Writing, French, journalism, music, public relations, Spanish, and Spanish / adolescence education), COMPUTER AND PHYSICAL SCIENCE (chemistry, chemistry/adolescence education, computer science, geology, mathematics, and physics), EDUCATION (childhood education: 1-6, English education, mathematics education, special education, and sports and wellness studies), ENGINEERING AND ENVIRONMENTAL DESIGN (environmental science), HEALTH PROFESSIONS (cytotechnology, medical laboratory technology, medical technology, and nursing), SOCIAL SCIENCE (anthropology, Canadian studies, child care/child and family studies, communication sciences and disorders, criminal justice, economics, French studies, gender studies, geography, history, home economics, human development, interdisciplinary studies, Latin American studies, philosophy, political science/government, psychology, social work, sociology, and women's studies). Adolescence education (physics), multimedia journalism, global supply and chain management are the strongest academically. Psychology, education, business, criminal justice, and nursing have the largest enrollments.

<u>ACTIVITIES:</u> 6% of men belong to 1 local and 11 national fraternities; 5% of women belong to 1 local and 8 national sororities. There are 120 groups on campus, including art, band, cheerleading, choir, chorale, chorus, computers, dance, debate, drama, ethnic, film, gay, honors, international, jazz band, literary magazine, musical theater, newspaper, orchestra, pep band, photography, political, professional, radio and TV, religious, social, social service, student government, and yearbook. Popular campus events include Volunteer Opportunities (Relay for Life, Up 'til Dawn), Family Weekend, Night of Nations, President's Gala, Plattsburgh's Best Dance Crew and Plattsburgh's Got Talent Competitions. <u>Sports:</u> There are 7 intercollegiate sports for men and 8 for women, and 9 intramural sports for men and 9 for women. Facilities include a 3500-seat ice arena, a 1500-seat gym, an indoor track, soccer and volleyball areas, an indoor swimming pool, exercise and weight rooms, an aerobics studio, racquetball courts, lighted tennis courts, softball, lacrosse, and rugby fields, and a fitness center. <u>Graduates:</u> From July 1, 2013 to June 30, 2014, 1417 bachelor's degrees were awarded. The most popular majors were business/marketing (22%), communication/journalism (10%), and education (10%). 120 companies recruited on campus in 2013-2014. In an average class, 1% graduate in 3 years or less, 40% graduate in 4 years or

less, 17% graduate in 5 years or less, and 1% graduate in 6 years or less. Of the 2013 graduating class, 12% were enrolled in graduate school within 6 months of graduation, and 79% were employed.

SERVICES: Counseling and information services are available, as is tutoring in every subject. There is a reader service for the blind, and remedial math, reading, and writing. **Library/Resources:** The library contains 541,609 volumes, 723,474 microform items, 25,698 audio/video tapes/CDs/DVDs, and subscribes to 114,144 periodicals including electronic. Computerized library services include interlibrary loans, database searching, Internet access, and Wi-Fi capability. Special learning facilities include an art gallery, planetarium, radio station, TV station, an environmental science institute, a child care center, a research institute, a teacher resource center, a speech and hearing clinic, the Alzheimer's Disease Assistance Center, auditory research labs, a virtual reality simulator, and distance learning facilities. **Physically Challenged Students:** 95% of the campus is accessible. Facilities include wheelchair ramps, elevators, special parking, specially equipped restrooms, special class scheduling, lowered drinking fountains, lowered telephones, special housing. curb cuts, and electronic doors. **Special:** The college offers cross-registration with Clinton Community College and Empire State College, internships, study abroad in 10 countries, cooperative programs in all majors, B.A.-B.S. degrees, dual and student-designed majors, an accelerated degree program in any major except nursing, and B.A./M.S.T. and B.S./MSED combined undergraduate and graduate programs. A 3-2 engineering degree is offered with SUNY Stony Brook and Binghamton, Clarkson, Syracuse, and McGill Universities, and the University of Vermont. There are 31 national honor societies and a freshman honors program. **Visiting:** There are regularly scheduled orientations for prospective students, including a group, student-led tour, and either a group or individual interview. Special overnight events for accepted freshmen include meals with students and faculty, classroom visits, discussions with faculty, and special workshops. There are guides for informal visits, visitors may sit in on classes, and stay overnight. To schedule a visit, contact the Admissions Office. **Campus Safety and Security:** Measures include 24-hour foot and vehicle patrol, emergency notification system, self-defense education, and security escort services. There are shuttle buses, emergency telephones, lighted pathways/sidewalks, controlled access to dorms/residences, bicycle patrols, combination locks on student rooms, a computerized keyless entry system for residence hall access, door viewers, and basement and ground-level security windows in residence halls.

REQUIREMENTS: The SAT or ACT is required. Applicants must have at least 12 academic credits, including 4 years of English, 5 combined years of math and science, and 3 years of social studies. An essay, portfolio, audition, and interview may be recommended in some programs. The GED is accepted. SUNY Plattsburgh requires applicants to be in the upper 50% of their class. AP and CLEP credits are accepted. Important factors in the admissions decision are advanced placement or honors courses, recommendations by school officials, and leadership record.To graduate students must have a 2.0 GPA and complete at least 120 semester hours. Core curriculum courses total 41 to 46 credits. In addition, all students must demonstrate proficiency in writing by completion of English composition and an advanced writing requirement. Specific courses such as library research skills and computer science are offered. A comprehensive exam in some majors and a thesis in the upper-division honors program. Many majors require practicum and/or internship experience to complete a degree. **Procedure:** Freshmen are admitted fall and spring. Entrance exams should be taken during the second half of the junior year or the beginning of the senior year. There is a rolling admissions plan. Early decision applications should be filed by November 15; regular applications, by August 1 for fall entry; and November 1 for spring entry, along with a $50 fee. Notification of early decision is sent December 15; regular decision, January 15. 310 applicants were on the 2014 waiting list; 26 were admitted. Applications are accepted on-line. **Transfer Students:** 612 transfer students enrolled in 2013-2014. Applicants must have a minimum 2.0 GPA. Most academic programs require a 2.5 GPA or better. 36 of 120 credits required for the bachelor's degree must be completed at SUNY Plattsburgh. **International Students:** There are 308 international students enrolled. The school actively recruits these students. They must take the TOEFL with a minimum score of 450 on the paper-based TOEFL (PBT) or 45 on the Internet-based version (iBT).

ADMISSIONS: 34% of the current freshmen were in the top fifth of their class; 75% were in the top two fifths. **Admissions Contact:** Richard Higgins, Director of Admissions. E-Mail: *higginrj@.plattsburgh.edu* Web: *www.plattsburgh.edu*

FINANCIAL AID: In 2014-2015, 65% of all full-time freshmen and continuing full-time students received some form of financial aid. 58% of all full-time freshmen and 59% of continuing full-time students received need-based aid. The average freshman award was $11,845. Need-based scholarships or need-based grants averaged $7,093; need-based self-help aid (loans and jobs) averaged $6,510; and other non-need-based awards and non-need-based scholarships averaged $6,227. 34% of undergraduate students work part-time. Average annual earnings from campus work are $1520. The average financial indebtedness of the 2014 graduate was $26,894. The FAFSA, and In-state students must also file the TAP application. is required. The priority date for freshman financial aid applications for fall entry is February 15.

SYRACUSE UNIVERSITY   C-3
www.syr.edu

Syracuse, NY 13244	**(315) 443-3611**
	n/av
Fax: n/av	Email: orange@syr.edu
Full-time: 6487 men, 8045 women	**Faculty:** n/av
Part-time: 333 men, 359 women	**Ph.D.s:** 89%
Graduate: 3080 men, 3188 women	**Student/Faculty:** n/av
Year: semesters, summer session	**Tuition:** $41,886
Room & Board: $14,460	**Freshman Class:** 27908 applied, 14260 accepted, 3470 enrolled
SAT or ACT: required	**CEEB CODE:** 2823
Application Deadline: January 1	**VERY COMPETITIVE**

Founded in 1870, Syracuse University is a private, coeducational, urban institution Syracuse is recognized as a student-focused global research university renowned for academic rigor, richly diverse learning experiences, and a spirit of discovery. There are 9 undergraduate schools and 11 graduate schools. In addition to regional accreditation, Syracuse has baccalaureate program accreditation with ABET, ACEJMC, CSWE, FIDER, NAAB, NASAD, NASM, NCATE, ACS, and CADE. The 708-acre campus is in an urban area in the city of Syracuse, the heart of Central New York. Including any residence halls, there are 273 buildings.

STUDENT LIFE: 56% of undergraduates are from out of state, mostly the Northeast. Students are from 49 states, 84 foreign countries, and Canada. 67% are from public schools. 56% are White; 11% Hispanic; 11% Foreign. 42% claim no religious affiliation; 24% Catholic; 14% Protestant; 11% Jewish. The average age of freshmen is 18; all undergraduates, 20. 8% do not continue beyond their first year; 82% remain to graduate. **Housing:** 8340 students can be accommodated in college housing, which includes coed dorms and on-campus apartments. In addition, there are special-interest houses, fraternity houses, sorority houses, Theme/wellness housing and special housing for students with disabilities. On-campus housing is available on a lottery system for upperclassmen. 75% of students live on campus; of those, 85% remain on campus on weekends. Upperclassmen may keep cars.

FACULTY/CLASSROOMS: 59% of faculty are male; 41% are female. No introductory courses are taught by graduate students. The average class size in an introductory lecture is 200; in a laboratory is 19; and in a regular course is 24.

PROGRAMS OF STUDY: Syracuse confers B.A., B.S., B.Arch., B.F.A., B.I.D., B.Mus. and B.P.S. degrees. Associate, Master's, and Doctoral degrees are also awarded. Bachelor's degrees are awarded in BIOLOGICAL SCIENCE (biochemistry, biology/adolescence education, biology/biological science, biophysics, biotechnology, neurosciences, and nutrition), BUSINESS (accounting, entrepreneurial studies, finance, management science, marketing management, real estate, retailing, sports management, and supply chain management), COMMUNICATIONS AND THE ARTS (acting, advertising, art history, art, art history and appreciation, broadcasting, ceramic art and design, classics, communication design , communication studies, communication rhetoric/communication, digital communications, dramatic arts, English, English literature, film arts, fine arts, French, Germanic languages and literature, graphic design, illustration, industrial design, journalism, journalism - news and information, linguistics, media arts, metal/jewelry, modern language, music, music history and appreciation, music industry, music production/recording technology, music theory and composition, musical theater, painting, percussion, photography, piano/organ, printmaking, public relations, Russian languages and literature, sculpture, speech/debate/rhetoric, strings, telecommunications, theater design, theater management, video, voice, winds, writing and rhetoric), COMPUTER AND PHYSICAL SCIENCE (applied mathematics, chemistry, chemistry education, Computer Engineering Technology, computer science, earth science, earth science / adolescence education, energy science, geology, information sciences and systems, mathematics, and physics), EDUCATION (art education, early childhood education, education, elementary education, English education, health and physical education, mathematics education, middle school education, music education, physical education, science education, social studies education, and special education), ENGINEERING AND ENVIRONMENTAL DESIGN (aerospace engineering, architectural history, architecture, bioengineering, chemical engineering, civil engineering, computer engineering, computer graphics, electrical/electronics engineering, environmental design, environmental engineering, and mechanical engineering), HEALTH PROFESSIONS (health science, public health, and speech pathology/audiology), SOCIAL SCIENCE (African American studies, anthropology, child care/child and family studies, classical/ancient civilization, communication sciences and disorders, economics, ethics, politics, and social policy, European studies, fashion design and technology, food science, forensic studies, geography, history, international relations, Italian studies, Judaic studies, Latin American studies, liberal arts/general studies, Middle Eastern studies, philosophy, political science/government, psychology, religion, Russian and Slavic studies, social work, sociology, Spanish studies, and women and gender studies). Architecture, public communications, management, life sciences (biology, biochemistry, biophysical science, physics), sport management, drama, and recording and allied entertainment industries (The Bandier Program for Music and the Entertainment Industries Information. Science/studies, psychology (general), architecture have the largest enrollments.

ACTIVITIES: 24% of men belong to 53 national fraternities; 28% of women belong to 22 national sororities. There are 350 groups on campus, including art, band, cheerleading, chess, choir, chorale, chorus, communications, computers, dance, debate, drama, environmental, ethnic, film, forensics, gay, honors, international, jazz band, literary magazine, marching band, musical theater, newspaper, opera, orchestra, pep band, photography, political, professional, radio and TV, religious, social, social service, special interest, student government, and yearbook. Popular campus events include Syracuse Welcome, Winter Carnival, Senior Celebration, Homecoming, University Lectures, PULSE Performing Arts, Veterans Day, Martin Luther King Jr. Dinner, Latino/Hispanic Heritage Month, Asian/Pacific Heritage Month, University Lecture Series. **Sports:** There are 8 intercollegiate sports for men and 12 for women, and 15 intramural sports for men and 15 for women. Facilities include 5 fitness centers, 2 swimming pools, ice skating pavilion, fencing room, racquetball and squash courts, basketball courts, dance studios, volleyball facilities, table-tennis,weight rooms, tennis courts, exercise rooms, indoor track, grass playing fields, multiple outdoor artificial turf fields, an outdoor track, ropes challenge course and zip line, indoor challenge course, soccer stadium, softball stadium, football complex, athlete weight room, fitness classes, country club, golf course, boathouse/rowing facilities, multipurpose domed stadium seats 50,000 for football and 30,000 for basketball. **Graduates:** From July 1, 2013 to June 30, 2014, 3146 bachelor's degrees were awarded. The most popular majors were business and marketing (16%), communications/journalism (14%), and social sciences (11%). 181 companies recruited on campus in 2013-2014. In an average class, 69% graduate in 4 years or less, 79%

graduate in 5 years or less, and 80% graduate in 6 years or less. Of the 2013 graduating class, 23% were enrolled in graduate school within 6 months of graduation, and 91% were employed.

SERVICES: Counseling and information services are available, as is tutoring in most subjects. There is a reader service for the blind. A variety of services are offered by the Syracuse University Tutoring and Study Center including subject specific help, tutoring by academic program, and study resources. Additional services are offered by individual departments and honor societies. The Office of Disability Services provides additional services for those with documented disabilities. **Library/Resources:** The 4 libraries contain 4.1 million volumes, 16,053 microform items, 81,928 audio/video tapes/CDs/DVDs, and subscribe to 33,860 periodicals including electronic. Computerized library services include interlibrary loans, database searching, Internet access, and Wi-Fi capability. Special learning facilities include an art gallery, radio station, TV station, The Syracuse University Library Special Collections Research Center; the Global Collaboratory; the Syracuse Center of Excellence in Environmental and Energy Systems; Center for Science and Technology; Life Sciences Complex; Fidelity MODUS 622i flight simulator; the Dick Clark Studios; the Alan Gerry Center for Media Innovation; the Diane and Bob Miron Digital News Center; Falcone Center for Entreprenuership; Ballentine Investment Institute; Architecture studios; the Dorothea Ilgen Shaffer Art Building; the JP Morgan Chase Technology Center; Syracuse Stage; the Bernice M. Wright Child Development Laboratory; the Belfer Audio Laboratory and Archive; the Gebbie Speech, Language, and Hearing Clinic; Syracuse University Humanities Center. **Physically Challenged Students:** 76% of the campus is accessible. Facilities include wheelchair ramps, elevators, special parking, specially equipped restrooms, lowered drinking fountains, and lowered telephones. **Special:** Co-op programs exist for aerospace engineering, bioengineering, chemical engineering, civil engineering, computer engineering, computer science, electric engineering, environmental engineering, mechanical engineering, and systems and information science. Students are encouraged to undertake internships during both the academic year and summers in the Syracuse community, across the nation and at times internationally. Internships can be for credit or paid, depending upon the field and degree requirements of the student's college of enrollment at SU. The SU Career Services Office aids students in finding internships, as do individual school/college career services units. Syracuse has overseas centers, in Beijing, Florence, Hong Kong, Istanbul, London, Madrid, Santiago (Chile), and Strasbourg (France). Through other programs, SU students have study abroad options in over 30 additional countries. SU also enrolls small cohorts of entering freshmen in the First-Semester Liberal Arts Study Abroad Programs. These students begin their collegiate career at the SU Centers in Florence or Strasbourg in the fall semester. The Maxwell School of Citizenship and Public Affairs offers the Maxwell-Washington semester. There are 10 dual and combined enrollment options through which a variety of major combinations may be undertaken. Student-designed majors may be possible with the assistance of faculty advisors and the approval of the college of enrollment. There are 30 national honor societies, including Phi Beta Kappa, and a freshman honors program. **Visiting:** There are regularly scheduled orientations for prospective students, Prospective students can visit Syracuse University nearly year-round. Options include daily visits which offer an information session and campus tour. Fall and Spring Receptions and Admitted Student Programs are available for admitted students. There are guides for informal visits, visitors may sit in on classes, and stay overnight. To schedule a visit, contact the Office of Admissions. **Campus Safety and Security:** Measures include 24-hour foot and vehicle patrol, emergency notification system, self-defense education, and security escort services. There are shuttle buses, emergency telephones, lighted pathways/sidewalks, controlled access to dorms/residences, Campus wide video security system with central monitoring; crisis alert notification system by email, text message, phone and emergency sirens.

REQUIREMENTS: The SAT or ACT is required. The ACT Optional Writing test is also required. Applicants to Syracuse University must submit the Common Application and Syracuse University Supplement; scores for either the SAT or ACT (for those applicants only taking the ACT, the optional writing test is required); secondary school transcript; counselor evaluation; two academic recommendations; an essay and short written answers to questions. Applicants should have a strong college preparatory record from an accredited secondary school or have a GED equivalent. A portfolio is required for art and architecture majors, and an audition is required for music and drama majors. The SAT and ACT are optional for international applicants studying outside the U.S. who are not prospective student-athletes and not attending an American-system school. AP and CLEP credits are accepted.Portions of the liberal arts core are required by all colleges. New students are required to take a writing course. Liberal arts core courses are required in most majors: writing skills; foreign language or quantitative skills; humanities, natural sciences and mathematics, social sciences; and critical reflections on ethical and social issues. A minimum of 120 credit hours to graduate, but varies by college or major(s). Courses in recreation and physical education and computer science/information management technology are available, but in most majors, are not required. Thesis required of Renee Crown Honors students, to graduate with distinction; some majors require a capstone experience. **Procedure:** Freshmen are admitted fall and spring. Entrance exams should be taken prior to January of the senior year for regular decision. There are early decision and deferred admissions plans. Early decision applications should be filed by November 15; regular applications, by January 1 for fall entry; and November 15 for spring entry. The fall 2014 application fee was $75. Notification of early decision is sent January 1; regular decision, March 15. 1208 early decision candidates were accepted for the 2014-2015 class. 1882 applicants were on the 2014 waiting list; 181 were admitted. Applications are accepted on-line. **Transfer Students:** 408 transfer students enrolled in 2013-2014. Online Common Application Form, $75 Application Fee, an Official Academic Transcripts, Two Academic Recommendations. For applicants with fewer than 30 college credit hours completed, submit SAT or ACT scores and secondary school transcript. A portfolio is required for art and architecture applicants, and an audition for music and drama applicants. TOEFL or IELTS scores are required for students whose native language is not English. Additional requirements may apply to international students. For more information, visit the Apply To Syracuse link at admissions.syr.edu. **International Students:** There are 1627 international students enrolled. The school actively recruits these students. They must take the TOEFL with a minimum score of 550 on the paper-based TOEFL (PBT) or 85 on the Internet-based version (iBT), or take the IELTS. The SAT or ACT are not required for International students who have not studied in an American-based system.

ADMISSIONS: 51% of the 2014-2015 applicants were accepted. The SAT scores for the 2014-2015 freshman class were: Critical Reading--16% below 500, 46% between 500 and 599, 32% between 600 and 699, and 6% between 700 and 800; Math--8% below 500, 36% between 500 and 599, 43% between 600 and 699, and 13% between 700 and 800; Writing--13% below 500, 43% between 500 and 599, 36% between 600 and 699, and 6% between 700 and 800. 62% of the current freshmen were in the top fifth of their class; 87% were in the top two fifths. **Admissions Contact:** Office of Admissions E-Mail: *orange@syr.edu* Web: *http://admissions.syr.edu*

FINANCIAL AID: In 2014-2015, 73% of all full-time freshmen and 73% of continuing full-time students received some form of financial aid. 54% of all full-time freshmen and 57% of continuing full-time students received need-based aid. The average freshman award was $35,510. Need-based scholarships or need-based grants averaged $27,980; and need-based self-help aid (loans and jobs) averaged $7,200. 50% of undergraduate students work part-time. Average annual earnings from campus work are $3000. The average financial indebtedness of the 2014 graduate was $34,584. Syracuse is a member of CSS. The CSS/Profile and FAFSA, and Noncustodial Profile are required. The deadline for filing freshman financial aid applications for fall entry is February 1.

TOURO COLLEGE		D-5
www.touro.edu		

New York, NY 10010		(212) 463-0400
		n/av
Fax: (718) 253-9455	Email: michael.lipkin2@touro.edu	
Full-time: 1635 men, 3452 women	Faculty: n/av	
Part-time: 349 men, 736 women	Ph.D.s: n/av	
Graduate: 301 men, 781 women	Student/Faculty: 16 to 1	
Year: semesters, summer session	Tuition: $15,600	
Room & Board: $12,359	Freshman Class: 1220 applied, 793 accepted, 743 enrolled	
SAT CR/M/W: 590/560/565 ACT: 24	CEEB CODE: 2902	
Application Deadline: April 15	VERY COMPETITIVE	

Touro College, founded in 1971, is a private institution offering undergraduate programs primarily through the Lander College of Liberal Arts and Sciences, the School of General Studies, and the School of Health Sciences. Campuses are in midtown Manhattan, Brooklyn, and Queens. There are 6 undergraduate schools and 8 graduate schools. In addition to regional accreditation, Touro College and University System has baccalaureate program accreditation with APTA, CAHEA, TEAC, AOTA, and ASHA. The campus is in an urban area. Including any residence halls, there are 12 buildings.

STUDENT LIFE: 95% of undergraduates are from New York. Others are from 25 states, 30 foreign countries, and Canada. 27% do not continue beyond their first year; 47% remain to graduate. **Housing:** 200 students can be accommodated in college housing, which includes single-sex dorms, on-campus apartments, and off-campus apartments. On-campus housing is available on a first-come and first-served basis. Priority is given to out-of-town students. Alcohol is not permitted. All students may keep cars.

FACULTY/CLASSROOMS: 49% of faculty are male; 51% are female. No introductory courses are taught by graduate students. The average class size in an introductory lecture is 16; in a laboratory is 12; and in a regular course is 15.

PROGRAMS OF STUDY: Touro College and University System confers B.A., B.S., B.S.N., and B.P.S. degrees. Associate, Master's, and Doctoral degrees are also awarded. Bachelor's degrees are awarded in BIOLOGICAL SCIENCE (biology/biological science), BUSINESS (accounting, banking and finance, business administration and management, management science, and marketing/retailing/merchandising), COMMUNICATIONS AND THE ARTS (English, Hebrew, literature, and speech/debate/rhetoric), COMPUTER AND PHYSICAL SCIENCE (chemistry, computer science, mathematics, and physics), EDUCATION (elementary education and special education), HEALTH PROFESSIONS (nursing, occupational therapy, physical therapy, predentistry, and premedicine), SOCIAL SCIENCE (economics, history, human services, interdisciplinary studies, Judaic studies, liberal arts/general studies, philosophy, political science/government, prelaw, psychology, social science, and sociology). Business/accounting, education, and health sciences are the strongest academically. Psychology, education, and business have the largest enrollments.

ACTIVITIES: There are no fraternities or sororities. There are 8 groups on campus, including computers, debate, ethnic, honors, literary magazine, newspaper, political, professional, religious, social, student government, and yearbook. Popular campus events include Student-sponsored Lecture Series and Student-faculty Social Events. **Sports:** There is no sports program at Touro College and University System. Facilities include 1 baseball field, 2 tennis courts, and 2 basketball courts. **Graduates:** From July 1, 2013 to June 30, 2014, 1459 bachelor's degrees were awarded. The most popular majors were liberal arts (23%), psychology (23%), and business/marketing (16%). 32 companies recruited on campus in 2013-2014.

SERVICES: Counseling and information services are available, as is tutoring in some subjects, accounting, math, English, and natural sciences. There is remedial math, reading, and writing. **Library/Resources:** The 11 libraries contain 271,509 volumes, 14,100 microform items, 4,054 audio/video tapes/CDs/DVDs, and subscribe to 3,163 periodicals including electronic. Computerized library services include interlibrary loans, database searching, Internet access, and Wi-Fi capability. **Physically Challenged Students:** All of the campus is accessible. Facilities include wheelchair ramps, elevators, specially equipped restrooms, lowered drinking fountains, and lowered telephones. **Special:** The college offers cross-registration with the Fashion Institute of Technology, internships for juniors and seniors, study abroad in Israel, work-study programs, interdisciplinary majors, an accelerated degree program, credit for life, military, and work experience, pass/fail options, and dual majors. Early and/or preferential admission to professional programs is also possible. There are 2 national honor societies, a freshman honors program, and 5 departmental honors programs. **Visiting:** There are guides for informal visits, visitors may sit in on classes, and stay overnight. To schedule a visit, contact Steven Toplan at steven.toplan@touro.edu. **Campus Safety and Security:** Measures include 24-hour foot and vehicle patrol and emergency notification system. There are shuttle buses, lighted pathways/sidewalks, and controlled access to dorms/residences.

REQUIREMENTS: The SAT or ACT is recommended. Applicants must be graduates of an accredited secondary school with a satisfactory high school average. High school diploma is required or a GED is accepted. A satisfactory SAT score is recommended. A GPA of 3.0 is required. AP and CLEP credits are accepted. Important factors in the admissions decision are advanced placement or honors courses, recommendations by school officials, leadership record, parents or siblings attended your school, evidence of special talent, personality/intangible qualities, extracurricular activities record, and recommendations by alumni.To graduate, all students must complete at least 120 credit hours (varies by major), with 30 to 70 in the major; 45 of the 120 credits must be from Touro and 1/2 of the student's major has to be completed with Touro. A minimum 2.0 GPA is required, with 2.3 in the major. Specific disciplines include Judaic studies or ethnic studies. Required courses include English composition, history, literature, math, and social and natural sciences. **Procedure:** Freshmen are admitted fall, spring, and summer. Entrance exams should be taken in May of the junior year or fall of the senior year. There are early admissions, deferred admissions, and rolling admissions plans. Early decision applications should be filed by April 15; regular applications, by April 15 for fall entry; December 15 for spring entry; and June 1 for summer entry, along with a $50 fee. Notification of early decision is sent December 1; regular decision, in ongoing. Applications are accepted on-line. **Transfer Students:** 332 transfer students enrolled in 2013-2014. A 2.5 GPA is required. If the student has less than 60 credits, high school documentation is also required. 45 of 120 credits required for the bachelor's degree must be completed at Touro College and University System. **International Students:** There are 159 international students enrolled. They must take the TOEFL with a minimum score of 550 on the paper-based TOEFL (PBT) or 83 on the Internet-based version (iBT) and the college's own test, or take the IELTS. They must also take the SAT or ACT, and the college's own entrance exam. In-house math and English proficiency examinations.

ADMISSIONS: 65% of the 2014-2015 applicants were accepted. The SAT scores for the 2014-2015 freshman class were: Critical Reading--10% below 500, 45% between 500 and 599, 32% between 600 and 699, and 13% between 700 and 800; Math--18% below 500, 49% between 500 and 599, 28% between 600 and 699, and 5% between 700 and 800; Writing--20% below 500, 44% between 500 and 599, 28% between 600 and 699, and 7% between 700 and 800. The ACT scores were 2% below 21, 37% between 21 and 23, % between 24 and 26, 59% between 27 and 28, and 2% above 28. **Admissions Contact:** Michael Lipkin, Office of Institutional Research. E-Mail: *michael.lipkin2@touro.edu* Web: *www.touro.edu*

FINANCIAL AID: The average freshman award was $7,087. Need-based scholarships or need-based grants averaged $4,913; need-based self-help aid (loans and jobs) averaged $341; other non-need-based awards and non-need-based scholarships averaged $2,541; and $849 from other forms of aid. The average financial indebtedness of the 2014 graduate was $16,287. The CSS/Profile is required. The priority date for freshman financial aid applications for fall entry is May 15. The deadline for filing freshman financial aid applications for fall entry is August 15.

UNION COLLEGE   C-3
www.union.edu

Schenectady, NY 12308

(518) 388-6112
(888) 843-6688

Fax: (518) 388-6986
Full-time: 1199 men, 1026 women
Part-time: 11 men, 10 women
Graduate: n/av
Year: trimesters
Room & Board: $11,463

Email: admissions@union.edu
Faculty: 206; IIB, ++$
Ph.D.s: 98%
Student/Faculty: 10 to 1
Tuition: $46,785
Freshman Class: 5725 applied, 2134 accepted, 559 enrolled
CEEB CODE: 2920

Application Deadline: January 15

MOST COMPETITIVE

Union College, founded in 1795, is an independent liberal arts and engineering college. In addition to regional accreditation, Union has baccalaureate program accreditation with ABET. The 100-acre campus is in a small town 15 miles west of Albany. Including any residence halls, there are 100 buildings.

STUDENT LIFE: 62% of undergraduates are from out of state, mostly the Northeast. Students are from 40 states, 29 foreign countries, and Canada. 66% are from public schools. 75% are White. Average age of freshmen is 19; all undergraduates, 20. 8% do not continue beyond their first year; 88% remain to graduate. **Housing:** 1978 students can be accommodated in college housing, which includes single-sex and coed dorms and on-campus apartments. In addition, there are language houses, special-interest houses, fraternity houses, sorority houses, Minerva Houses: up to 45 students live in each of seven distinct houses. All students and faculty members have house affiliations. Each house contributes intellectual, cultural, and social events to the campus. On-campus housing is available on a lottery system for upperclassmen. 86% of students live on campus. Upperclassmen may keep cars.

FACULTY/CLASSROOMS: 56% of faculty are male; 44% are female. No introductory courses are taught by graduate students.

PROGRAMS OF STUDY: Union confers B.A., and B.S degrees. Bachelor's degrees are awarded in AGRICULTURE (environmental studies), BIOLOGICAL SCIENCE (biochemistry, biology/biological science, and neurosciences), COMMUNICATIONS AND THE ARTS (classics, English, fine arts, modern language, and studio art), COMPUTER AND PHYSICAL SCIENCE (astronomy, chemistry, computer science, geology, mathematics, physics, and science), ENGINEERING AND ENVIRONMENTAL DESIGN (bioengineering, computer engineering, electrical/electronics engineering, environmental science, and mechanical engineering), SOCIAL SCIENCE (American studies, anthropology, Asian/Oriental studies, Caribbean studies, economics, French studies, German area studies, history, humanities, interdisciplinary studies, liberal arts/general studies, philosophy, political science/government, psychology, religion, social science, sociology, Spanish studies, and women's studies). Chemistry, geology, classics, and philosophy are the strongest academically. Economics, psychology, and mechanical engineering have the largest enrollments.

ACTIVITIES: 39% of men belong to 13 national fraternities; 39% of women belong to 5 national sororities. There are 101 groups on campus, including art, band, cheerleading, chess, choir, computers, dance, debate, drama, environmental, ethnic, gay, honors, international, jazz band, literary magazine, newspaper, orchestra, pep band, photography, political, professional, radio and TV, religious, social, social service, and student government. Popular campus events include Spring Fest, Lectures and Concerts. **Sports:** Facilities include a field house for volleyball, recreational basketball, indoor track, and intramural activities, 2 synthetic grass fields for soccer, football, field hockey, lacrosse, intramurals, and recreation, basketball/volleyball facility, an ice rink, a gym, that includes a weight room, a fitness center, racquetball/squash courts, aerobics room, and swimming pool, 8 outdoor tennis courts, an outdoor basketball/street hockey court, and boathouse and docks. **Graduates:** From July 1, 2013 to June 30, 2014, 539 bachelor's degrees were awarded. The most popular majors were psychology (13%), economics (11%), and biology (7%). 126 companies recruited on campus in 2013-2014. In an average class, 82% graduate in 4 years or less, 87% graduate in 5 years or less, and 88% graduate in 6 years or less. Of the 2013 graduating class, 30% were enrolled in graduate school within 6 months of graduation, and 67% were employed.

SERVICES: Counseling and information services are available, as is tutoring in most subjects. A writing center and a language center are available. **Library/Resources:** The library contains 624,031 volumes, 829,928 microform items, 14,506 audio/video tapes/CDs/DVDs, and subscribes to 11,181 periodicals including electronic. Computerized library services include interlibrary loans, database searching, Internet access, and Wi-Fi capability. Special learning facilities include a radio station, a theater, high-tech classroom, lab center, multimedia auditorium, music center, and an art, science, history gallery. **Physically Challenged Students:** 80% of the campus is accessible. Facilities include wheelchair ramps, elevators, special parking, specially equipped restrooms, special class scheduling, lowered drinking fountains, lowered telephones, and special housing. **Special:** Cross-registration is permitted with the Hudson Mohawk Consortium. Opportunities are provided for legislative internships in Albany and Washington, D.C., pass/fail options, B.A.-B.S. degrees, dual and student-designed majors, accelerated degree programs in law and medicine, and study abroad in 38 countries. There are 15 national honor societies, including Phi Beta Kappa, a freshman honors program, and 19 departmental honors programs. **Visiting:** There are regularly scheduled orientations for prospective students, including interviews and a tour of the campus. There are guides for informal visits and visitors may sit in on classes. To schedule a visit, contact the Admissions Office, Grant Hall at (518) 388-6112. **Campus Safety and Security:** Measures include 24-hour foot and vehicle patrol, emergency notification system, self-defense education, and security escort services. There are shuttle buses, emergency telephones, lighted pathways/sidewalks, controlled access to dorms/residences, 24-hour locked residence halls, emergency medical assistance, awareness programs, a bicycle patrol, a trolley escort service, a shuttle van, and a security measures sheet.

REQUIREMENTS: Testing is optional except for combined programs. Leadership in Medicine program applicants must submit the SAT I and SAT II or the ACT; Law and Public Policy program applicants must submit the SAT I or the ACT. Applicants to these programs must complete the necessary tests no later than December of the senior year. International students are required to submit the SAT or the ACT, and the TOEFL or IELTS if English is not the first language. Applicants must submit a minimum of 16 full-year credits, distributed as follows: 4 years of English, 2 of a foreign language, 2 1/2 to 3 1/2 years of math, 2 years each of science and social studies, and the remainder in college-preparatory courses. Engineering and math majors are expected to have completed additional math and science courses beyond the minimum requirements. An essay is also required and an interview is recommended. AP credits are accepted. Important factors in the admissions decision are advanced placement or honors courses, extracurricular activities record, and recommendations by school officials. Students must complete a minimum of 36 term courses (engineering may require up to 40), requirements in the major field, degree program, or interdepartmental major, including the major field examination and/or thesis, as applicable, and attain a minimum GPA of 1.8 and 2.0 in the major (2.0 in the minor if a minor has been declared). **Procedure:** Freshmen are admitted fall, winter, and spring. Entrance exams should be taken by January of the senior year. There are early decision, early admissions, and deferred admissions plans. Early decision applications should be filed by November 15; regular applications, by January 15 for fall entry. Notification of early decision is sent December 15; regular decision, April 1. 252 early decision candidates were accepted for the 2014-2015 class. 1059 applicants were on the 2014 waiting list; 62 were admitted. Applications are accepted on-line. **Transfer Students:** 23 transfer students enrolled in 2013-2014. A 3.0 GPA and 1 full year of college academic work are required. Transfer students must study at Union for at least 2 years. 18 of 36 credits required for the bachelor's degree must be completed at Union. **International Students:** There are 134 international students enrolled. The school actively recruits these students. They must take the TOEFL. Testing is optional except for combined programs. International students are required to submit the SAT or ACT.

ADMISSIONS: 37% of the 2014-2015 applicants were accepted. The SAT scores for the 2014-2015 freshman class were: Critical Reading--3% below 500, 25% between 500 and 599, 54% between 600 and 699, and 18% between 700 and 800; Math--12% between 500 and 599, 49% between 600 and 699, and 38% between 700 and 800; Writing--25% between 500 and 599, 54% between 600 and 699, and 21% between 700 and 800. **Admissions Contact:** Ann Fleming Brown, Director of Admission. E-Mail: *admissions@union.edu* Web: *www.union.edu*

FINANCIAL AID: In 2014-2015, 76% of all full-time freshmen and 77% of continuing full-time students received some form of financial aid. 54% of all full-time freshmen and 55% of continuing full-time students received need-based aid. The average freshman award was $32,500. Need-based scholarships or need-based grants averaged $33,500; need-based self-help aid (loans and jobs) averaged $6,200; and other non-need-based awards and non-need-based scholarships averaged $7,400. The average financial indebtedness of the 2014 graduate was $27,911. Union is a member of CSS. The CSS/Profile, FAFSA, and the state aid form, and Noncustodial profile are required. The deadline for filing freshman financial aid applications for fall entry is February 1.

UNITED STATES MERCHANT MARINE ACADEMY D-5
www.usmma.edu

Kings Point, NY 11024	**(516) 726-5641**
	(866) 546-4778
Fax: (516) 773-5390	**Email:** admissions@usmma.edu
Full-time: 851 men, 136 women	**Faculty:** 120
Part-time: n/av	**Ph.D.s:** 34%
Graduate: 23 men, 2 women	**Student/Faculty:** 11 to 1
Year: trimesters	**Tuition:** see profile
Room & Board: see profile	**Freshman Class:** 2252 applied, 354 accepted, 237 enrolled
SAT CR/M: 614/643 **ACT:** required	**CEEB CODE:** 2923
Application Deadline: March 1	**HIGHLY COMPETITIVE+**

The United States Merchant Marine Academy, founded in 1943, is a publicly supported institution offering maritime, military, and engineering programs for the purpose of training officers for the U.S. merchant marine, the maritime industry, and the armed forces. Students make no conventional tuition and room/board payments. Required fees for freshmen are approximately $7,020; costs in subsequent years are less. There are no undergraduate schools. In addition to regional accreditation, Kings Point has baccalaureate program accreditation with ABET. The 82-acre campus is in a suburban area 19 miles east of midtown New York City. Including any residence halls, there are 28 buildings.

STUDENT LIFE: 88% of undergraduates are from out of state, mostly the Middle Atlantic. Students are from 50 states, and 2 foreign countries. 77% are from public schools. 84% are White. 48% are Catholic; 42% Protestant. **Male To Female Ratio:** 0.2:1. The average age of freshmen is 19; all undergraduates, 21. 8% do not continue beyond their first year; 92% remain to graduate. **Housing:** 930 students can be accommodated in college housing, which includes coed dorms. On-campus housing is guaranteed for all 4 years. Alcohol is not permitted. Upperclassmen may keep cars.

FACULTY/CLASSROOMS: 87% of faculty are male; 13% are female. All teach undergraduates, and 25% do both. No introductory courses are taught by graduate students. The average class size in an introductory lecture is 28; in a laboratory is 16; and in a regular course is 28.

PROGRAMS OF STUDY: Kings Point confers B.S. degrees. Master's degrees are also awarded. Bachelor's degrees are awarded in ENGINEERING AND ENVIRONMENTAL DESIGN (marine engineering, marine engineering/shipyard management, marine engineering systems, marine transportation, and maritime logistics and security). Marine engineering systems is the strongest academically. Logistics and intermodal transportation, marine engineering systems, and marine engineering have the largest enrollments.

ACTIVITIES: There are no fraternities or sororities. There are 51

groups on campus, including band, choir, chorus, communications, computers, dance, debate, drill team, drum and bugle corps, ethnic, marching band, newspaper, pep band, photography, professional, religious, and student government. Popular campus events include Regimental Thanksgiving and Holiday Dinners, Battle Standard Dinner, Lanier Lecture Dinners, Ring Dance, Festival of Lights, Holiday Dance, Valentines Dance and Midshipman Appreciation Day. **Sports:** There are 14 intercollegiate sports for men and 9 for women, and 10 intramural sports for men and 10 for women. Facilities include a gymnasium with a swimming pool, basketball and racquetball courts. Outdoor track and football field. **Graduates:** From July 1, 2013 to June 30, 2014, 201 bachelor's degrees were awarded. The most popular majors were marine engineering (23%), marine transportation (22%), and logistics and intermodal transportation (21%). 78 companies recruited on campus in 2013-2014. In an average class, 77% graduate in 4 years or less and 83% graduate in 5 years or less. Of the 2013 graduating class, 100% were employed within 6 months of graduation.

SERVICES: Counseling and information services are available, as is tutoring in most subjects. **Library/Resources:** The library contains 209,217 volumes, 21,306 microform items, 4,750 audio/video tapes/CDs/DVDs, and subscribes to 573 periodicals including electronic. Computerized library services include interlibrary loans, database searching, Internet access, and Wi-Fi capability. Special learning facilities include a planetarium, a maritime museum. **Physically Challenged Students:** 5% of the campus is accessible. Facilities include wheelchair ramps, elevators, special parking, and specially equipped restrooms. **Special:** The college offers internships in the maritime industry and work-study programs with U.S. shipping companies. **Visiting:** There are guides for informal visits, visitors may sit in on classes, and stay overnight. To schedule a visit, contact the Admissions Office. **Campus Safety and Security:** Measures include 24-hour foot and vehicle patrol. There are lighted pathways/sidewalks.

REQUIREMENTS: The SAT or ACT is required. Candidates for admission to the academy must be nominated by a member of the U.S. Congress. They must be between the ages of 17 and 25, U.S. citizens (except by special arrangement), and in excellent physical condition. Applicants should be graduates of an accredited secondary school or have a GED equivalent. 18 academic credits are required, including 4 in English, 3 in math, 1 credit in physics or chemistry with a lab, and 10 in electives. An essay is required. AP credits are accepted. Important factors in the admissions decision are advanced placement or honors courses, leadership record, and extracurricular activities record. To graduate, students must complete a minimum of 163 credit hours according to the new curriculum with a minimum cumulative and major GPA of 2.0. The required curriculum includes courses in math, science, computer science, English, humanities, history, naval science, phys ed, and ship's medicine. Students must complete one year of sea service on U.S flag merchant ships. All students must pass resident and sea project courses, U.S. Coast Guard licensing exam and all required certificates, and the academy physical fitness test. Students must apply for and accept, if offered, a commission in the U.S. uniformed services. **Procedure:** Freshmen are admitted fall. Entrance exams should be taken through January for the SAT and February for ACT. There is a rolling admissions plan. Applications should be filed by March 1 for fall entry. Notifications are sent April 1. 263 applicants were on the 2014 waiting list; were admitted. Applications are accepted on-line. **Transfer Students:** Same as for high school students, except college-level applicants must submit college transcripts (and must have at least a 2.5 cumulative GPA in college level work), and must submit two (2) letters of recommendation from college instructors/professors. 172 credits required for the bachelor's degree must be completed at Kings Point. **International Students:** There are 15 international students enrolled. They must take the TOEFL with a minimum score of 540 on the paper-based TOEFL (PBT) or 76 on the Internet-based version (iBT). They must also take the SAT or ACT.

ADMISSIONS: 16% of the 2014-2015 applicants were accepted. The SAT scores for the 2014-2015 freshman class were: Critical Reading--4% below 500, 40% between 500 and 599, 45% between 600 and 699, and 11% between 700 and 800; Math--15% between 500 and 599, 66% between 600 and 699, and 19% between 700 and 800. The ACT scores were 2% between 21 and 23, 35% between 24 and 26,

35% between 27 and 28, and 28% above 28. 57% of the current freshmen were in the top fifth of their class; 38% were in the top two fifths. There were 13 National Merit finalists. 4 freshmen graduated first in their class. **Admissions Contact:** CPT. Robert E. Johnson, Director of Admissions and Financial Aid. E-Mail: *admissions@usmma.edu* Web: *www.usmma.edu*

FINANCIAL AID: In 2014-2015, 14% of all full-time freshmen and 11% of continuing full-time students received some form of financial aid. 9% of all full-time freshmen and 7% of continuing full-time students received need-based aid. The average freshman award was $4,187. Need-based scholarships or need-based grants averaged $4,071 ($5,550 maximum); need-based self-help aid (loans and jobs) averaged $1,916 ($2,673 maximum); and other non-need-based awards and non-need-based scholarships averaged $3,420 ($5,446 maximum). The FAFSA is required. The deadline for filing freshman financial aid applications for fall entry is May 1.

UNITED STATES MILITARY ACADEMY D-4
www.usma.edu

West Point, NY 10996	(845) 938-4041
	n/av
Fax: (845) 938-8121	Email: admissions@usma.edu
Full-time: 3535 men, 640 women	Faculty: n/av
Part-time: n/av	Ph.D.s: 39%
Graduate: n/av	Student/Faculty: n/av
Year: semesters, summer session	Tuition: see profile
Room & Board: see profile	Freshman Class: n/av
SAT or ACT: required	CEEB CODE: 2924
Application Deadline: n/av	MOST COMPETITIVE

The United States Military Academy, founded in 1802, offers military, engineering, and comprehensive arts and sciences programs leading to a bachelor's degree and a commission as a second lieutenant in the U.S. Army, with a 5-year active duty service obligation. All students receive free tuition and room and board as well as an annual salary of $10,148. An initial deposit of $2900 is required. The figures in the above capsule and in this profile are approximate. In addition to regional accreditation, West Point has baccalaureate program accreditation with ABET. The 16080-acre campus is in a small town 56 miles north of New York City. Including any residence halls, there are 902 buildings.

STUDENT LIFE: 92% of undergraduates are from out of state, mostly the Northeast. Students are from 50 states, and 19 foreign countries. 81% are from public schools. 81% are White. 49% are Protestant; 33% Catholic; 15% claim no religious affiliation. The average age of freshmen is 18; all undergraduates, 20. 8% do not continue beyond their first year; 82% remain to graduate. **Housing:** 4500 students can be accommodated in college housing, which includes coed All cadets live in cadet barracks. On-campus housing is guaranteed for all 4 years. Upperclassmen may keep cars.

FACULTY/CLASSROOMS: 88% of faculty are male; 12% are female. 40% do research, and 40% do both. No introductory courses are taught by graduate students. The average class size in an introductory lecture is 15; in a laboratory is 15; and in a regular course is 15.

PROGRAMS OF STUDY: West Point confers B.S. degrees. Bachelor's degrees are awarded in BIOLOGICAL SCIENCE (life science), BUSINESS (management science and operations research), COMMUNICATIONS AND THE ARTS (languages and literature), COMPUTER AND PHYSICAL SCIENCE (chemistry, computer science, mathematics, and physics), ENGINEERING AND ENVIRONMENTAL DESIGN (civil engineering, electrical/electronics engineering, engineering management, engineering physics, environmental engineering, mechanical engineering, military science, nuclear engineering, and systems engineering), SOCIAL SCIENCE (behavioral science, economics, geography, history, international studies, law, philosophy, and political science/government). Engineering, behavioral sciences, and history have the largest enrollments.

ACTIVITIES: There are no fraternities or sororities. There are 105 groups on campus, including and flying, astronomy, language, art, bagpipe, band, cheerleading, chess, choir, chorale, chorus, computers, dance, debate, debate, drama, drill team, drum and bugle corps, ethnic, film, forensics, honors, international, literary magazine, marching band, musical theater, newspaper, pep band, photography, professional, radio and TV, religious, social, social service, student government, and yearbook. Popular campus events include Ring Weekend and 100th Night for Seniors, 500th Night for Juniors and Yearling Winter Weekend for Sophomores. **Sports:** There are 15 intercollegiate sports for men and 9 for women, and 18 intramural sports for men and 14 for women. Facilities include a 40,000-seat football stadium, baseball fields, a 2500-seat hockey rink, a 5000-seat basketball arena, a gym with 5 gyms for squash, handball, tennis, and racquetball, 3 swimming pools, and workout areas, a field house, indoor/outdoor tracks, a golf course, a ski slope, and hunting, fishing, and boating facilities.

SERVICES: Counseling and information services are available, as is tutoring in every subject. The Center for Enhanced Performance offers 2 courses that provide cadets an opportunity to learn and enhance reading, study, and mental skills. **Library/Resources:** The library contains 442,169 volumes, 748,443 microform items, 12,378 audio/video tapes/CDs/DVDs, and subscribes to 1,963 periodicals including electronic. Computerized library services include interlibrary loans and database searching. Special learning facilities include an art gallery, radio station, TV station, and a military museum. Cadets may conduct research in conjunction with the academic departments through the Operations Research Center, the Photonics Research Center, the Mechanical Engineering Research Center, and the Office of Artificial Intelligence, Analysis, and Evaluation. There is also a visiting artist program featuring painting, sculpture, and photography. **Physically Challenged Students:** Facilities include wheelchair ramps, elevators, special parking, specially equipped restrooms, lowered drinking fountains, and lowered telephones. **Special:** Junior and senior cadets may participate in 3-week summer educational experiences, including Operations Crossroads Africa, research work in technical areas throughout the country, medical internships at Walter Reed Medical Center, workfellow positions with federal and Department of Defense agencies, language training in foreign countries, and study at other military and civilian institutions. There are 7 national honor societies, including Phi Beta Kappa, a freshman honors program, and 5 departmental honors programs. **Visiting:** There are regularly scheduled orientations for prospective students, Candidates are escorted by a cadet, attend class, have lunch with the Corps of Cadets, and talk with cadets about all phases of West Point life. There are guides for informal visits, visitors may sit in on classes, and stay overnight. To schedule a visit, contact the Admissions Office. **Campus Safety and Security:** Measures include 24-hour foot and vehicle patrol and self-defense education. There are shuttle buses and lighted pathways/sidewalks.

REQUIREMENTS: The SAT or ACT is required. Applicants must be qualified academically, physically, and medically. Candidates must be nominated for admission by members of the U.S. Congress or executive sources. West Point recommends that applicants have 4 years each of English and math, 2 years each of foreign language and lab science, such as chemistry and physics, and 1 year of U.S. history. Courses in geography, government, and economics are also suggested. An essay is required, and an interview is recommended. The GED is accepted. Applicants must be 17 to 22 years old, a U.S. citizen at the time of enrollment (except by agreement with another country), unmarried, and not pregnant or legally obligated to support children. AP credits are accepted. Important factors in the admissions decision are leadership record, extracurricular activities record, and recommendations by school officials.All cadets must complete a core of 31 courses and 9 academic electives pertinent to their field of study. The major requires an additional 1 to 3 electives to the field. In addition, all cadets must complete 4 courses each in phys ed and military science and a senior thesis or design project in the major. A total of 140 credits, including 127 academic, 6 military, and 7 physical, with at least a C average, is required to graduate. **Procedure:** Freshmen are admitted summer. Entrance exams should be taken in the spring of the junior year and not later than the fall of the senior year. There are early decision, early admissions, and rolling admissions plans. Check with the school for current application deadlines. **Transfer Students:** All applicants must enter as freshmen. 140 of 140 credits required for the bachelor's degree must be completed at West Point.

International Students: They must take the TOEFL. They must also take the SAT or ACT.

ADMISSIONS: Colonel Michael L. Jones, Director of Admissions. E-Mail: *admissions@usma.edu* Web: *www.usma.edu*

FINANCIAL AID: Check with the school for current application deadlines.

UNIVERSITY AT ALBANY / SUNY   **D-3**
www.albany.edu

Albany, NY 12222	**(518) 956-8220**
	n/av
Fax: **(518) 442-5383**	Email: **ugadmissions@albany.edu**
Full-time: 6177 men, 5791 women	**Faculty:** 701; I, av$
Part-time: 322 men, 252 women	**Ph.D.s:** 95%
Graduate: 1755 men, 2761 women	**Student/Faculty:** 17 to 1
Year: semesters, summer session	**Tuition:** $8040 ($18,360)
Room & Board: $10,634	**Freshman Class:** 21591 applied, 12028 accepted, 2560 enrolled
SAT CR/M: 540/560 **ACT:** 24	**CEEB CODE:** 2532
Application Deadline: August 1	**VERY COMPETITIVE**

The State University of New York/University at Albany, established in 1844, is a public institution conferring undergraduate and graduate degrees in humanities and fine arts, science and math, social and behavioral sciences, business, public policy, education, and social welfare. The figures in the above capsule and in this profile are approximate. There are 8 undergraduate schools and 9 graduate schools. In addition to regional accreditation, University at Albany has baccalaureate program accreditation with AACSB, CSWE, TEAC, ACS, ALA, APA, CEPH, NASPAA, and PAB. The 560-acre campus is in a suburban area about 5 miles west of downtown Albany. Including any residence halls, there are 185 buildings.

STUDENT LIFE: 95% of undergraduates are from New York. Others are from 37 states, 54 foreign countries, and Canada. 58% are White; 11% African American; 11% Hispanic. The average age of freshmen is 18; all undergraduates, 21. 16% do not continue beyond their first year; 65% remain to graduate. **Housing:** 7900 students can be accommodated in college housing, which includes coed dorms, on-campus apartments, and married student housing. In addition, there are honors houses, language houses, and special-interest houses. On-campus housing is available on a first-come, first-served basis, and is available on a lottery system for upperclassmen. Priority is given to out-of-town students. 61% of students live on campus. Alcohol is not permitted. Upperclassmen may keep cars.

FACULTY/CLASSROOMS: 59% of faculty are male; 41% are female. 96% teach undergraduates, and 76% do research. Graduate students teach 13% of introductory courses. The average class size in an introductory lecture is 31; in a laboratory is 15; and in a regular course is 22.

PROGRAMS OF STUDY: University at Albany confers B.A., and B.S. degrees. Master's and Doctoral degrees are also awarded. Bachelor's degrees are awarded in AGRICULTURE (environmental studies), BIOLOGICAL SCIENCE (biochemistry, biology/biological science, and molecular biology), BUSINESS (accounting and business administration and management), COMMUNICATIONS AND THE ARTS (art history and appreciation, Chinese, communications, English, fine arts, linguistics, music, Spanish, and studio art), COMPUTER AND PHYSICAL SCIENCE (actuarial science, applied mathematics, atmospheric sciences and meteorology, chemistry, computer science, earth science, information sciences and systems, mathematics, and physics), ENGINEERING AND ENVIRONMENTAL DESIGN (materials engineering, materials science, and urban design), HEALTH PROFESSIONS (predentistry and premedicine), SOCIAL SCIENCE (African American studies, anthropology, Asian/Oriental studies, Caribbean studies, criminal justice, East Asian studies, economics, geography, Hispanic American studies, history, interdisciplinary studies, Latin American studies, medieval studies, philosophy, political science/government, prelaw, psychology, religion, social work, sociology, and women's studies). Criminal justice, accounting, public administration and policy are the strongest academically. Business, psychology, communication and rhetoric have the largest enrollments.

ACTIVITIES: 4% of men belong to 18 national fraternities; 4% of women belong to 1 local and 18 national sororities. There are 209 groups on campus, including chamber singers, percussion ensemble, art, band, cheerleading, chess, chorale, chorus, computers, dance, debate, drama, electronic music ensemble, environmental, ethnic, film, gay, honors, international, jazz band, literary magazine, marching band, musical theater, newspaper, orchestra, pep band, photography, political, professional, radio and TV, religious, social, social service, student government, symphony, and yearbook. Popular campus events include Relay for Life, and New York State Writer's Series. **Sports:** There are 8 intercollegiate sports for men and 11 for women, and 8 intramural sports for men and 8 for women. Facilities include gym with an Olympic-size pool, ancillary gym with a quarter-mile track, football stadium, softball, soccer, practice fields, an all-weather lacrosse field, and a 5000-seat recreation and convocation center. **Graduates:** From July 1, 2013 to June 30, 2014, 2944 bachelor's degrees were awarded. The most popular majors were English (13%), business (11%), and psychology (11%). 140 companies recruited on campus in 2013-2014. In an average class, 53% graduate in 4 years or less, 64% graduate in 5 years or less, and 65% graduate in 6 years or less.

SERVICES: Counseling and information services are available, as is tutoring in most subjects. There is a reader service for the blind. The Excel program provides low-income and first-generation college students with a variety of mentoring, tutorial, and counseling services. **Library/Resources:** The 3 libraries contain 2.2 million volumes, 2.9 million microform items, 13,718 audio/video tapes/CDs/DVDs, and subscribe to 75,570 periodicals including electronic. Computerized library services include interlibrary loans, database searching, Internet access, and Wi-Fi capability. Special learning facilities include an art gallery, radio station, linear accelerator, sophisticated weather data system, national lightning detection system, interactive media center, extensive art studios, state-of-the-art electronic library, and the Northeast Regional Forensic Institute (NERFI). **Physically Challenged Students:** 99% of the campus is accessible. Facilities include wheelchair ramps, elevators, special parking, specially equipped restrooms, lowered drinking fountains, lowered telephones. disabled student services provides a broad range of personalized services to people with disabilities, including preadmission information and accessible housing information. **Special:** Cross-registration is available with Rensselaer Polytechnic Institute, Albany Law School, and Union, Siena, and Russell Sage Colleges. Internships may be arranged with state government agencies and private organizations. Study abroad in many countries, a Washington semester, B.A.-B.S. degrees, and work-study programs are offered. Dual and student-designed majors, nondegree study, and pass/fail grading options are available. There are accelerated 5-year bachelor's/master's programs in 40 fields; most arts and sciences fields may be combined with an accelerated M.B.A. A 3-2 engineering degree with 1 of 4 institutions is also possible. There are 15 national honor societies, including Phi Beta Kappa, a freshman honors program, and 30 departmental honors programs. **Visiting:** There are regularly scheduled orientations for prospective students, including a 2-day summer orientation session. There are guides for informal visits and visitors may sit in on classes. To schedule a visit, contact the Undergraduate Admissions Office. **Campus Safety and Security:** Measures include 24-hour foot and vehicle patrol, emergency notification system, self-defense education, and security escort services. There are shuttle buses, emergency telephones, lighted pathways/sidewalks, controlled access to dorms/residences, and 5-Quad ambulance service.

REQUIREMENTS: The SAT or ACT is required. Applicants must be graduates of an accredited secondary school or have a GED. 18 academic credits are required, including 2 to 3 units of math, 2 units of lab sciences, and 1 unit of foreign language study. AP and CLEP credits are accepted. Important factors in the admissions decision are advanced placement or honors courses, personality/intangible qualities, and leadership record.To graduate, students must complete a total of 120 credits with a 2.0 GPA in their major and minor, including 30 to 36 credits required in the major for a B.A. degree and 30 to 42 credits for a B.S. degree. B.A. degree candidates must complete

90 credits in liberal arts courses and B.S. candidates must complete 60. The general education program at the University at Albany consists of a minimum of 30 credits of course work in the following areas: disciplinary perspectives, cultural and historical perspectives, and communication and reasoning competencies. **Procedure:** Freshmen are admitted fall, spring, and summer. Entrance exams should be taken by November of the senior year. There are early decision, deferred admissions, and rolling admissions plans. Early decision applications should be filed by November 15; regular applications, by August 1 for fall entry; December 1 for spring entry; and April 1 for summer entry, along with a $50 fee. Notification of early decision is sent January 1; regular decision. Applications are accepted on-line. **Transfer Students:** 1387 transfer students enrolled in 2013-2014. Admission to certain programs is competitive and based not only on a required GPA but also on completion of a certain set of prerequisite core courses. A grade average of B or better is required for applicants to the accounting, business administration, criminal justice, and social welfare programs. 30 of 120 credits required for the bachelor's degree must be completed at University at Albany. **International Students:** There are 615 international students enrolled. The school actively recruits these students. They must take the TOEFL with a minimum score of 550 on the paper-based TOEFL (PBT) or 79 on the Internet-based version (iBT), International students may submit either SAT, ACT, or TOEFL results.

ADMISSIONS: 56% of the 2014-2015 applicants were accepted. The SAT scores for the 2014-2015 freshman class were: Critical Reading--25% below 500, 59% between 500 and 599, 15% between 600 and 699, and 2% between 700 and 800; Math--16% below 500, 54% between 500 and 599, 26% between 600 and 699, and 4% between 700 and 800. The ACT scores were 8% below 21, 33% between 21 and 23, 35% between 24 and 26, 14% between 27 and 28, and 10% above 28. **Admissions Contact:** Timothy Lee, Director of Undergraduate Admissions. E-Mail: ugadmissions@albany.edu Web: www.albany.edu

FINANCIAL AID: In 2014-2015, 62% of all full-time freshmen and 63% of continuing full-time students received some form of financial aid. 62% of all full-time freshmen and 63% of continuing full-time students received need-based aid. The average freshman award was $9,925. Need-based scholarships or need-based grants averaged $6,988; need-based self-help aid (loans and jobs) averaged $4,069; non-need-based athletic scholarships averaged $11,201; and other non-need-based awards and non-need-based scholarships averaged $3,097. 9% of undergraduate students work part-time. The FAFSA, and NY state residents should apply for TAP on-line is required. The priority date for freshman financial aid applications for fall entry is March 15.

UNIVERSITY AT BUFFALO / THE STATE UNIVERSITY OF NEW YORK   A-3
www.buffalo.edu

Buffalo, NY 14214	(716) 645-6900
	(888) UB-ADMIT
Fax: (716) 645-6411	Email: ubadmissions@buffalo.edu
Full-time: 9785 men, 8118 women	Faculty: IIA, av$
Part-time: 780 men, 822 women	Ph.D.s: 96%
Graduate: 4622 men, 4825 women	Student/Faculty: n/av
Year: semesters, summer session	Tuition: $8426 ($20,366)
Room & Board: $11,857	Freshman Class: 23207 applied, 13134 accepted
SAT CR/M: 550/601 **ACT:** 26	CEEB CODE: 2533
Application Deadline: n/av	**VERY COMPETITIVE**

The University at Buffalo, State University of New York, established in 1846, is a public institution offering more than 300 bachelor's, master's, and doctoral degree programs. UB is a comprehensive research-extensive university and the largest campus in the State University of New York system. There are 8 undergraduate schools and 12 graduate schools. In addition to regional accreditation, UB has baccalaureate program accreditation with AACSB, ABET, ACPE, ADA, APTA, CSWE, NAAB, NASAD, ABA, ACCNE, ACOTE, CCNE, COA, LCME, TEAC, APA, ASHA, JRCNM, ACS, ACEND, CORE,

ASHP, NAACLS, CEPH, PAB, ACGME, and ALA. The 1350-acre campus is in a suburban area 3 miles north of Buffalo. Including any residence halls, there are 181 buildings.

STUDENT LIFE: 86% of undergraduates are from New York. Others are from 46 states, 80 foreign countries, and Canada. 52% are White; 16% Foreign; 12% Asian American. The average age of freshmen is 18; all undergraduates, 21. 13% do not continue beyond their first year; 70% remain to graduate. **Housing:** 7019 students can be accommodated in college housing, which includes coed dorms, on-campus apartments, and married student housing. In addition, there are honors houses, special-interest houses, freshmen-only housing and cultural interest housing. On-campus housing is guaranteed for all 4 years, is guaranteed for the freshman year only, is available on a first-come, first-served basis, and is available on a lottery system for upperclassmen. 65% of students commute. All students may keep cars.

FACULTY/CLASSROOMS: 61% of faculty are male; 39% are female. No introductory courses are taught by graduate students.

PROGRAMS OF STUDY: UB confers B.A., B.S., B.F.A. and Mus.B. degrees. Master's and Doctoral degrees are also awarded. Bachelor's degrees are awarded in AGRICULTURE (environmental studies), BIOLOGICAL SCIENCE (biochemistry, bioinformatics, biology/biological science, and biotechnology), BUSINESS (business administration and management), COMMUNICATIONS AND THE ARTS (art, art history and appreciation, classics, communications, dance, English, film arts, French, German, Italian, linguistics, media arts, music, musical theater, Spanish, studio art, and theatre arts), COMPUTER AND PHYSICAL SCIENCE (chemistry, computer science, geology, mathematics, and physics), ENGINEERING AND ENVIRONMENTAL DESIGN (aerospace studies, architecture, biomedical engineering, chemical engineering, civil engineering, computational sciences, computer engineering, electrical/electronics engineering, engineering physics, environmental design, environmental engineering, industrial engineering, and mechanical engineering), HEALTH PROFESSIONS (biomedical science, exercise science, medical technology, nuclear medical technology, nursing, occupational therapy, pharmaceutical science, pharmacology, pharmacy, physical therapy, and speech pathology/audiology), SOCIAL SCIENCE (African American studies, American studies, anthropology, Asian/Oriental studies, cognitive science, economics, geography, history, legal studies, philosophy, political science/government, psychology, social science, sociology, and women's studies). Engineering, business administration, and psychology have the largest enrollments.

ACTIVITIES: 2% of men belong to 2 local and 22 national fraternities; 2% of women belong to 16 national sororities. There are 250 groups on campus, including art, band, cheerleading, chess, choir, chorale, chorus, computers, dance, debate, drama, drill team, environmental, ethnic, film, gay, honors, international, jazz band, literary magazine, marching band, musical theater, newspaper, orchestra, pep band, photography, political, professional, radio and TV, religious, social, social service, student government, and symphony. Popular campus events include Homecoming, Family Weekend and Fallfest. **Sports:** There are 9 intercollegiate sports for men and 9 for women, and 8 intramural sports for men and 8 for women. Facilities include racquetball, squash, tennis, basketball, volleyball, badminton, and handball courts, baseball, soccer, hockey, and multipurpose fields, a football and track and field stadium, an indoor jogging track; an Olympic-size pool and diving well; a triple gym; weight training and wrestling rooms; dance studios; and a spinning room. **Graduates:** From July 1, 2013 to June 30, 2014, 4496 bachelor's degrees were awarded. The most popular majors were business administration (22%), social sciences (14%), and psychology (12%). 274 companies recruited on campus in 2013-2014. In an average class, 3% graduate in 3 years or less, 44% graduate in 4 years or less, 65% graduate in 5 years or less, and 70% graduate in 6 years or less.

SERVICES: Counseling and information services are available, as is tutoring in most subjects. There is a reader service for the blind, and remedial math, reading, and writing. Peer tutoring and some computer-assisted instruction are also available. **Library/Resources:** The 11 libraries contain 4.2 million volumes, 6.2 million microform items, and 283,577 audio/video tapes/CDs/DVDs. Computerized library services include interlibrary loans, database searching, Internet access, and Wi-Fi capability. Special learning facilities include an art gallery, radio station, TV station, an earthquake engineering research center, an arts center, a bio-informatics and life sciences center, a document analysis and Recognition center, a concert hall, an anthropology research center, a computational research center, a poetry and rare books collection, a virtual site museum, center for engineering design and industrial innovation, an electronic poetry center, an archeological center, a pharmacy museum, and clinical and translational research center. **Physically Challenged Students:** 90% of the campus is accessible. Facilities include wheelchair ramps, elevators, special parking, specially equipped restrooms, special class scheduling, lowered drinking fountains, lowered telephones, special housing. **Special:** Students may cross-register with the Western New York Consortium. Internships are available, and students may study abroad in 29 countries. UB offers a Washington semester, work-study programs, accelerated degree programs, B.A.-B.S. degrees, dual, student-designed, and interdisciplinary majors, and credit for military experience. A 3-2 engineering degree can be pursued. Students may choose a successful/unsuccessful (S/U) grading option for selected courses. There is an early assurance of admission program to medical school for undergraduate sophomore students who possess a minimum approximate overall and science GPA of 3.75 and complete particular science courses. There are 34 national honor societies, including Phi Beta Kappa, and a freshman honors program. **Visiting:** There are regularly scheduled orientations for prospective students, including the Visit UB program, in which visitors tour the campus and attend an information session to learn about application procedures, admissions criteria, housing, financial aid, and scholarship programs. The program is offered, with some exceptions, Monday through Friday year-round and on selected Saturdays during the academic year. Reservations are required. Visitors may sit in on classes. To schedule a visit, contact the Office of Admissions at ub-admissions@buffalo.edu. **Campus Safety and Security:** Measures include 24-hour foot and vehicle patrol, emergency notification system, self-defense education, and security escort services. There are shuttle buses, emergency telephones, lighted pathways/sidewalks, controlled access to dorms/residences, an alarm system, routine patrols, student aides in residence halls, some security cameras, bluelight phones, and a university-wide safety committee.

REQUIREMENTS: The SAT is required. Freshmen are evaluated based on secondary school performance, strength of curriculum, standardized test scores, and, in some cases, a supplemental application. A high school diploma is required and the GED is accepted. Dance, music theatre, theatre and music applicants must audition. Architecture requires a portfolio. AP and CLEP credits are accepted. Important factors in the admissions decision are advanced placement or honors courses, recommendations by school officials, and evidence of special talent.To graduate, students must complete 120 semester hours with a minimum GPA of 2.0. General education requirements include writing skills, mathematical sciences, library skills, world civilizations, American pluralism, natural sciences, language, humanities, arts, social and behavioral sciences, and depth requirement. The total number of hours in the major varies. **Procedure:** Freshmen are admitted fall and spring. Entrance exams should be taken during the spring of the junior year or the fall of the senior year. There are early decision and rolling admissions plans. Early decision applications should be filed by November 1. The fall 2014 application fee was $50. Notification of early decision is sent December 15; regular decision, in February. 319 early decision candidates were accepted for the 2014-2015 class. 55 applicants were on the 2014 waiting list; 25 were admitted. Applications are accepted on-line. **Transfer Students:** 1897 transfer students enrolled in 2013-2014. Transfer applicants with fewer than 24 credit hours must supply high school transcripts, SAT and/or ACT test scores, and the previous college academic record. It is recommended that students present a strong record of college study, with a 2.5 GPA. Entry at junior level requires a higher GPA for some programs. Credit may be awarded for military experience and other nontraditional sources. 30 of 120 credits required for the bachelor's degree must be completed at UB. **International Students:** There are 2574 international students enrolled. The school actively recruits these students. They must take the TOEFL with a minimum score of 550 on the paper-based TOEFL (PBT) or 79 on the Internet-based version (iBT). The SAT or ACT is strongly recommended.

ADMISSIONS: 57% of the 2014-2015 applicants were accepted. The

SAT scores for the 2014-2015 freshman class were: Critical Reading--23% below 500, 50% between 500 and 599, 23% between 600 and 699, and 4% between 700 and 800; Math--8% below 500, 40% between 500 and 599, 40% between 600 and 699, and 12% between 700 and 800. **Admissions Contact:** Barry Taylor, Director of Admissions. E-Mail: *ubadmissions@buffalo.edu* Web: *www.buffalo.edu*

FINANCIAL AID: The average freshman award was $9,505. Need-based scholarships or need-based grants averaged $5,770; need-based self-help aid (loans and jobs) averaged $3,675; non-need-based athletic scholarships averaged $17,420; and other non-need-based awards and non-need-based scholarships averaged $6,025. The FAFSA is required. The priority date for freshman financial aid applications for fall entry is March 1.

UNIVERSITY OF ROCHESTER   B-3
www.rochester.edu

Rochester, NY 14627	(585) 275-3221
	(888) 822-2256
Fax: (585) 461-4595	Email: admit@admissions.rochester.edu
Full-time: n/av	Faculty: I, +$
Part-time: n/av	Ph.D.s: 94%
Graduate: n/av	Student/Faculty: 10 to 1
Year: semesters, summer session	Tuition: $46,960
Room & Board: $13,708	Freshman Class: 16393 applied, 6025 accepted, 1337 enrolled
SAT or ACT: recommended	CEEB CODE: 2928
Application Deadline: January 5	MOST COMPETITIVE

The University of Rochester, founded in 1850, is a private research institution offering programs in the arts and sciences, engineering and applied science, nursing, medicine and dentistry, business administration, music, and education. There are 4 undergraduate schools and 7 graduate schools. In addition to regional accreditation, UR has baccalaureate program accreditation with AACSB, ABET, ACPE, ADA, NASM, NCATE, and NLNAC. The 707-acre campus is in a suburban area 2 miles south of downtown Rochester, NY. Including any residence halls, there are 159 buildings.

STUDENT LIFE: 58% of undergraduates are from out of state, mostly the Middle Atlantic. Students are from 50 states, 100 foreign countries, and Canada. 75% are from public schools. 52% are White; 16% Foreign; 11% Asian American. 37% claim no religious affiliation; 19% Catholic; 13% Jewish. The average age of freshmen is 18; all undergraduates, 20. 4% do not continue beyond their first year; 85% remain to graduate. **Housing:** 4112 students can be accommodated in college housing, which includes coed dorms, on-campus apartments, and married student housing. In addition, there are language houses, special-interest houses, and fraternity houses. On-campus housing is guaranteed for the freshman year only and is available on a lottery system for upperclassmen. 93% of students live on campus; of those, 90% remain on campus on weekends. Upperclassmen may keep cars.

FACULTY/CLASSROOMS: No introductory courses are taught by graduate students. The average class size in an introductory lecture is 75; in a laboratory is 20; and in a regular course is 20.

PROGRAMS OF STUDY: UR confers B.A., B.S. and B.M. degrees. Master's and Doctoral degrees are also awarded. Bachelor's degrees are awarded in AGRICULTURE (environmental studies), BIOLOGICAL SCIENCE (biochemistry, biology/biological science, cell biology, ecology, microbiology, molecular biology, and neurosciences), BUSINESS (business administration and management and marketing), COMMUNICATIONS AND THE ARTS (American Sign Language, art history and appreciation, audio technology, classics, comparative literature, digital communications, English, English literature, film arts, French, German, Japanese, jazz, linguistics, media arts, music, music performance, music theory and composition, Russian, Spanish, studio art, and theatre arts), COMPUTER AND PHYSICAL SCIENCE (applied mathematics, astronomy, chemistry, computer science, geology, mathematics, optics, physics, and statistics), EDUCATION (music education), ENGINEERING AND ENVIRON-

MENTAL DESIGN (biomedical engineering, chemical engineering, electrical/electronics engineering, engineering and applied science, environmental science, geological engineering, mechanical engineering, and optical engineering), HEALTH PROFESSIONS (health, nursing, and public health), SOCIAL SCIENCE (African American studies, American studies, anthropology, archeology, cognitive science, East Asian studies, economics, history, interdisciplinary studies, international relations, Latin American studies, philosophy, political science/government, psychology, religion, Russian and Slavic studies, and women's studies). Biomedical engineering, optics, and political science are the strongest academically. Biology, economics, and engineering have the largest enrollments.

ACTIVITIES: 20% of men belong to 19 national fraternities; 20% of women belong to 15 national sororities. There are 250 groups on campus, including art, band, campus activities board, cheerleading, chess, choir, chorale, chorus, computers, dance, debate, drama, drill team, environmental, ethnic, film, gay, honors, international, jazz band, literary magazine, marching band, musical theater, newspaper, opera, orchestra, pep band, photography, political, professional, radio and TV, religious, social, social service, student government, symphony, and yearbook. Popular campus events include Meliora Weekend, Yellowjacket Day and Boar's Head Dinner. **Sports:** There are 11 intercollegiate sports for men and 12 for women, and 7 intramural sports for men and 7 for women. Facilities include an 11,000-square-foot athletic center, a 5,000-seat stadium, a field house, an ice rink, courts for handball, racquetball, squash, and tennis, an indoor track, a fitness center and weight room, a jogging path, and an aquatic center. **Graduates:** The most popular majors were psychology, biology/biological sciences , and engineering. 1000 companies recruited on campus in 2013-2014. In an average class, 77% graduate in 4 years or less, 84% graduate in 5 years or less, and 85% graduate in 6 years or less.

SERVICES: Counseling and information services are available, as is tutoring in most subjects. There is access to screen reading and adaptive software. **Library/Resources:** The 7 libraries contain 4.1 million volumes, 4.7 million microform items, 135,013 audio/video tapes/CDs/DVDs, and subscribe to 42,082 periodicals including electronic. Computerized library services include interlibrary loans, database searching, and Internet access. Special learning facilities include an art gallery, radio station, labs for nuclear structure research and laser energetics; a center for visual science; the Strong Memorial Hospital, an art center, an observatory, an institute of optics, a center for electronic imaging systems, and the National Science Foundation Center for Photoinduced Charge Transfer. **Physically Challenged Students:** 90% of the campus is accessible. Facilities include wheelchair ramps, elevators, special parking, specially equipped restrooms, special class scheduling, lowered drinking fountains, lowered telephones, and special housing. **Special:** Cross-registration is offered with Rochester Area Colleges. Selective programs for exceptional undergraduates in medicine (REMS), engineering (GEAR), and education (GRADE) guarantee admission to professional or graduate school upon completion of the bachelor's degree. The Take Five Scholars Program allows students to stay tuition-free for a fifth year of study. Rochester offers 3-2 programs in business, human development, neuroscience, physics and astronomy, and public health. Study abroad is possible in more than 40 countries. Internships, a Washington semester, B.A.-B.S. degrees, accelerated degree programs, dual and student-designed majors, nondegree study, and pass/fail options are available. There are 8 national honor societies, including Phi Beta Kappa, a freshman honors program, and 13 departmental honors programs. **Visiting:** There are regularly scheduled orientations for prospective students, group information session, campus tour, and interview (optional for seniors). There are guides for informal visits, visitors may sit in on classes, and stay overnight. To schedule a visit, contact Office of Admissions. **Campus Safety and Security:** Measures include 24-hour foot and vehicle patrol, emergency notification system, self-defense education, and security escort services. There are shuttle buses, emergency telephones, lighted pathways/sidewalks, and controlled access to dorms/residences.

REQUIREMENTS: The SAT or ACT is recommended. Applicants should be graduates of an accredited secondary school or have a GED equivalent. An essay or personal statement and recommendations are required. An interview is recommended. An audition is required for music majors. Applicants should complete the Common Application. Admission to the College of Arts, Sciences, and Engineering is based on a holistic review process that includes a "test-flexible" philosophy. As we seek to enroll a diverse and talented class each year, our review procedures incorporate a variety of factors, including many kinds of academic records. In addition to submitting a record of courses and grades during secondary school, applicants must show evidence of preparation through examination results. A wide variety of test results can fulfill this requirement, including SAT Reasoning exams, the ACT, two or more results from SAT Subject exams, Advanced Placement, International Baccalaureate, AS- and A-level exams (in UK and Commonwealth countries), Gao Kao (China), and results from many other national secondary exams. AP credits are accepted. Important factors in the admissions decision are advanced placement or honors courses, personality/intangible qualities, and recommendations by school officials. Students focus on the humanities, social sciences, and natural sciences; one of the three areas will be their major, and they select a 3-course cluster in each of the other two. A total of 128 credit hours with a minimum GPA of 2.0 is required to graduate. Additionally, all students satisfy a freshman writing requirement and take two upper-level courses in their major that are writing intensive. **Procedure:** Freshmen are admitted fall. Entrance exams should be taken by December of the senior year. There are early decision and deferred admissions plans. Early decision applications should be filed by November 1; regular applications, by January 5 for fall entry, along with a $50 fee. Notification of early decision is sent December 15; regular decision, April 1. applicants were on the 2014 waiting list; were admitted. Applications are accepted on-line. **Transfer Students:** 140 transfer students enrolled in 2013-2014. The most important criterion is an applicant's college record. 64 of 128 credits required for the bachelor's degree must be completed at UR. **International Students:** There are 910 international students enrolled. The school actively recruits these students. They must take the TOEFL with a minimum score of 600 on the paper-based TOEFL (PBT) or 100 on the Internet-based version (iBT). They must also take the SAT or ACT.

ADMISSIONS: 37% of the 2014-2015 applicants were accepted. **Admissions Contact:** Jonathan Burdick, Dean of College Admissions. E-Mail: *admit@admissions.rochester.edu* Web: *www.rochester.edu*

FINANCIAL AID: UR is a member of CSS. The CSS/Profile, FAFSA, and the state aid form are required. The deadline for filing freshman financial aid applications for fall entry is February 15.

UTICA COLLEGE   C-3
www.utica.edu

Utica, NY 13502	(315) 792-3006
	(800) 782-8884
Fax: (315) 792-3003	Email: admiss@utica.edu
Full-time: 980 men, 1242 women	Faculty: 143; IIB, av$
Part-time: 175 men, 534 women	Ph.D.s: 85%
Graduate: 542 men, 784 women	Student/Faculty: 11 to 1
Year: semesters, summer session	Tuition: $33,736
Room & Board: $11,934	Freshman Class: n/av
SAT or ACT: recommended	CEEB CODE: 2931
Application Deadline: open	COMPETITIVE

Utica College is a private, comprehensive institution founded by Syracuse University in 1946. There are 4 undergraduate schools and 1 graduate school. In addition to regional accreditation, UC has baccalaureate program accreditation with APTA, NLN, TEAC, AOTA, and AACN. The 128-acre campus is in a suburban area 50 miles east of Syracuse. Including any residence halls, there are 18 buildings.

STUDENT LIFE: 90% of undergraduates are from New York. Others are from 47 states, 32 foreign countries, and Canada. 80% are from public schools. 65% are White; 11% African American. The average age of freshmen is 18; all undergraduates, 21. 28% do not continue beyond their first year; 47% remain to graduate. **Housing:** 1046 students can be accommodated in college housing, which includes single-sex and coed dorms. In addition, there are special-interest houses. On-campus housing is guaranteed for all 4 years and is avail-

able on a lottery system for upperclassmen. 56% of students commute. All students may keep cars.

FACULTY/CLASSROOMS: 49% of faculty are male; 51% are female. All teach and do research. No introductory courses are taught by graduate students. The average class size in an introductory lecture is 23; in a laboratory is 11; and in a regular course is 17.

PROGRAMS OF STUDY: UC confers B.A., and B.S. degrees. Master's and Doctoral degrees are also awarded. Bachelor's degrees are awarded in BIOLOGICAL SCIENCE (biochemistry and biology/biological science), BUSINESS (accounting, business administration and management, business economics, and insurance and risk management), COMMUNICATIONS AND THE ARTS (communications, English, journalism, and public relations), COMPUTER AND PHYSICAL SCIENCE (chemistry, computer science, computer security and information assurance, geoscience, mathematics, and physics), EDUCATION (education and foreign languages education), ENGINEERING AND ENVIRONMENTAL DESIGN (construction management), HEALTH PROFESSIONS (nursing, occupational therapy, physical therapy, and recreation therapy), SOCIAL SCIENCE (child psychology/development, criminal justice, economics, gerontology, history, liberal arts/general studies, philosophy, political science/government, psychology, social studies, and sociology). Occupational therapy, psychology, and biology are the strongest academically. Health studies, nursing, and criminal justice have the largest enrollments.

ACTIVITIES: 2% of men belong to 2 local and 3 national fraternities; 2% of women belong to 2 local and 3 national sororities. There are 86 groups on campus, including art, band, cheerleading, chess, choir, chorus, communications, computers, dance, drama, environmental, ethnic, film, gay, honors, international, jazz band, literary magazine, musical theater, newspaper, orchestra, pep band, photography, political, professional, radio and TV, religious, social, social service, student government, symphony, and yearbook. Popular campus events include Outdoor Concerts, Mock Elections, and Winter Weekend. **Sports:** There are 10 intercollegiate sports for men and 11 for women, and 28 intramural sports for men and 28 for women. Facilities include a 2200-seat gym, a competition-size swimming pool, tennis, racquetball, handball, and squash courts, a sauna, Nautilus and weight rooms, dance and aerobic rooms, playing fields, a stadium, and hockey facilities. **Graduates:** From July 1, 2013 to June 30, 2014, 650 bachelor's degrees were awarded. The most popular majors were health studies (45%), criminal justice (18%), and business and marketing (8%). In an average class, 30% graduate in 4 years or less, 42% graduate in 5 years or less, and 44% graduate in 6 years or less.

SERVICES: Counseling and information services are available, as is tutoring in most subjects. There is a reader service for the blind, and remedial math, reading, and writing. **Library/Resources:** The library contains 145,412 volumes, 34,282 microform items, 10,260 audio/video tapes/CDs/DVDs, and subscribes to 657 periodicals including electronic. Computerized library services include interlibrary loans, database searching, Internet access, and Wi-Fi capability. Special learning facilities include an art gallery, radio station, TV station, an early childhood education lab, a math and writing center, stock trading room, OT, PT, nursing, and physical science labs. **Physically Challenged Students:** 85% of the campus is accessible. Facilities include wheelchair ramps, elevators, special parking, specially equipped restrooms, lowered drinking fountains. **Special:** UC offers co-op programs, internships, work-study programs in all majors, accelerated degrees, dual majors, and cross-registration with Hamilton College and the Mohawk Valley Consortium. Study abroad may be arranged in 9 countries. There is a 3-2 engineering degree with Syracuse University. There are 5 national honor societies and a freshman honors program. **Visiting:** There are regularly scheduled orientations for prospective students, including an interview, financial aid information, and a tour of the campus. There are guides for informal visits, visitors may sit in on classes, and stay overnight. To schedule a visit, contact the Admissions Office at admiss@utica.edu. **Campus Safety and Security:** Measures include 24-hour foot and vehicle patrol, emergency notification system, and security escort services. There are shuttle buses, emergency telephones, lighted pathways/sidewalks, and controlled access to dorms/residences.

REQUIREMENTS: The SAT or ACT and ACT Writing Test are recommended. Graduation from an accredited secondary school or satisfactory scores on the GED are required. Recommended high school courses include 4 years of English, 3 years each of math and social studies, and 2 years each of foreign language and science. An essay and an interview are also recommended. AP and CLEP credits are accepted. Important factors in the admissions decision are advanced placement or honors courses, extracurricular activities record, and leadership record.To graduate, students must complete a total of 120 to 128 hours with a minimum 2.0 GPA. They must complete a general education requirement including basic skills and distribution requirements. **Procedure:** Freshmen are admitted fall and spring. Entrance exams should be taken during the junior year. There are deferred admissions and rolling admissions plans. Application deadlines are open. Application fee is $40. Notification of early decision is sent December 15; regular decision, on a rolling basis. Applications are accepted on-line. **Transfer Students:** 174 transfer students enrolled in 2013-2014. Applicants must have a minimum GPA of 2.0. 30 of 128 credits required for the bachelor's degree must be completed at UC. **International Students:** There are 109 international students enrolled. The school actively recruits these students. They must take the TOEFL with a minimum score of 525 on the paper-based TOEFL (PBT) or 69 on the Internet-based version (iBT) and the Comprehensive English Language Test, or take the IELTS, APIEL, or MELAB. The SAT is recommended if the student's primary language is English.

ADMISSIONS: Jeffery Gates, Vice President for Enrollment Management. E-Mail: *admiss@utica.edu* Web: *www.utica.edu*

FINANCIAL AID: In 2014-2015, 90% of all full-time freshmen and 91% of continuing full-time students received some form of financial aid. 90% of all full-time freshmen and 90% of continuing full-time students received need-based aid. The average freshman award was $30,140. Need-based scholarships or need-based grants averaged $8,708; and need-based self-help aid (loans and jobs) averaged $4,140. Average annual earnings from campus work are $1500. The average financial indebtedness of the 2014 graduate was $42,083. UC is a member of CSS. The FAFSA is required. The priority date for freshman financial aid applications for fall entry is February 15. The deadline for filing freshman financial aid applications for fall entry is April 1.

VASSAR COLLEGE D-4
www.vassar.edu

Poughkeepsie, NY 12604	(845) 437-7300
	(800) 827-7270
Fax: (845) 437-7063	Email: admissions@vassar.edu
Full-time: 1051 men, 1343 women	Faculty: 282; IIB, ++$
Part-time: 14 men, 10 women	Ph.D.s: 95%
Graduate: n/av	Student/Faculty: 8 to 1
Year: semesters	Tuition: $49,570
Room & Board: $11,570	Freshman Class: 7784 applied, 1832 accepted, 665 enrolled
SAT CR/M/W: 704/690/700 ACT: 31	CEEB CODE: 2956
Application Deadline: January 1	MOST COMPETITIVE

Vassar College, founded in 1861, is a highly selective, private college of liberal arts and sciences. There is 1 undergraduate school and 1 graduate school. The 1000-acre campus is in a suburban area 75 miles north of New York City. Including any residence halls, there are 100 buildings.

STUDENT LIFE: 76% of undergraduates are from out of state, mostly the Middle Atlantic. Students are from 49 states, 55 foreign countries, and Canada. 64% are from public schools. 61% are White; 11% Hispanic. The average age of freshmen is 18; all undergraduates, 20. 4% do not continue beyond their first year; 93% remain to graduate. **Housing:** 2383 students can be accommodated in college housing, which includes single-sex and coed dorms, on-campus apartments, off-campus apartments, and married student housing. there is 1 all-women residence hall and 1 cooperative living unit. On-campus housing is guaranteed for all 4 years. 98% of students live on campus; of those, 90% remain on campus on weekends. All students may keep cars.

FACULTY/CLASSROOMS: 54% of faculty are male; 46% are female.

All teach undergraduates, all do research, and all teach and do research. No introductory courses are taught by graduate students. The average class size in an introductory lecture is 21; in a laboratory is 10; and in a regular course is 17.

PROGRAMS OF STUDY: Vassar confers B.A. degrees. Master's degrees are also awarded. Bachelor's degrees are awarded in AGRICULTURE (environmental studies), BIOLOGICAL SCIENCE (biochemistry, biology/biological science, and neurosciences), COMMUNICATIONS AND THE ARTS (art history, art, Chinese, dramatic arts, English, film arts, French, German, Germanic languages and literature, Italian, Japanese, media arts, music, and Russian languages and literature), COMPUTER AND PHYSICAL SCIENCE (astronomy, chemistry, computer science, earth science, geology, mathematics, and physics), EDUCATION (education), HEALTH PROFESSIONS (premedicine), SOCIAL SCIENCE (African studies, American studies, anthropology, Asian/Oriental studies, classical/ancient civilization, cognitive science, economics, geography, Hispanic American studies, history, international studies, Judaic studies, Latin American studies, medieval studies, philosophy, political science/government, prelaw, psychology, religion, science and society, sociology, Spanish studies, urban studies, Victorian studies, and women's studies). English, psychology, biology, economics, and political science have the largest enrollments.

ACTIVITIES: There are no fraternities or sororities. There are 125 groups on campus, including art, band, chess, choir, chorale, chorus, communications, computers, dance, debate, drama, environmental, ethnic, film, gay, honors, international, jazz band, literary magazine, musical theater, newspaper, opera, orchestra, outdoors club, photography, political, professional, radio and TV, religious, social, social service, student government, symphony, and yearbook. Popular campus events include Founders Day, Spring and Fall Formals, and All Parents Weekend. **Sports:** There are 12 intercollegiate sports for men and 13 for women, and 18 intramural sports for men and 18 for women. Facilities include a field house with a swimming pool, 5 indoor tennis courts, weight and conditioning room, 2 gyms with squash and basketball facilities, 9-hole golf course, 13 outdoor tennis courts, an all-weather track, 2 soccer fields, turf field for field hockey and lacrosse, baseball diamond, rugby field, club and intramural fields, competition basketball gym, banked running track, and a 5000-square-foot exercise and fitness center. **Graduates:** From July 1, 2013 to June 30, 2014, 625 bachelor's degrees were awarded. The most popular majors were economics (11%), psychology (10%), and political science and English (9%). 23 companies recruited on campus in 2013-2014. In an average class, 1% graduate in 3 years or less, 88% graduate in 4 years or less, 92% graduate in 5 years or less, and 93% graduate in 6 years or less. Of the 2013 graduating class, 18% were enrolled in graduate school within 6 months of graduation, and 49% were employed.

SERVICES: Counseling and information services are available, as is tutoring in most subjects. There is a reader service for the blind, and remedial math and writing. **Library/Resources:** The 3 libraries contain 1.0 million volumes, 611,076 microform items, 23,590 audio/video tapes/CDs/DVDs, and subscribe to 4,001 periodicals including electronic. Computerized library services include interlibrary loans, database searching, Internet access, and Wi-Fi capability. Special learning facilities include an art gallery, natural history museum, radio station, studio art building with studios, large astronomical observatory, 3 theaters, dance theater and studios, concert halls, environmental field station, intercultural center, and many teaching and research-oriented lab facilities for the sciences. **Physically Challenged Students:** 70% of the campus is accessible. Facilities include wheelchair ramps, elevators, special parking, specially equipped restrooms, special class scheduling, lowered drinking fountains. There is an Office of Disability and Support Services, signage in braille, and assisted listening devices. **Special:** The school offers fieldwork/internships in all academic areas, dual majors, independent/self-designed majors, and non-recorded grade options. Vassar runs study-abroad programs in 7 countries and students have access to study in 250+ other approved programs around the world. A 3-2 engineering degree with Dartmouth College is offered. There are including Phi Beta Kappa. **Visiting:** There are regularly scheduled orientations for prospective students, including a campus tour, an information session, and a class visit when possible. There are guides for informal visits, visitors may sit in on classes, and stay overnight. To schedule a visit, contact the Admissions Office. **Campus Safety and Security:** Measures include 24-hour foot and vehicle patrol, emergency notification system, self-defense education, and security escort services. There are shuttle buses, emergency telephones, lighted pathways/sidewalks, and controlled access to dorms/residences.

REQUIREMENTS: The SAT or ACT is required. The ACT Optional Writing test is also required. SAT and 2 SAT Subject tests, or the ACT with writing, are required. In addition, high school diploma or an approved alternative are required for admission. The high school program should typically include advanced level work with 4 years each of English, social studies, math, foreign language, and science. An essay and 2 letters of recommendation are also required. AP credits are accepted. Important factors in the admissions decision are advanced placement or honors courses, recommendations by school officials, and extracurricular activities record.To graduate, students must have a total of 34 units equivalent to 120 credit hours, with a minimum GPA of 2.0. Of this total, no more than 17 units may be in a single field of concentration and 8 1/2 units must be outside the major field. Entering freshmen must take the freshman writing course. All students must meet the foreign language proficiency requirement and must take a quantitative skills course before their third year. A thesis is required in most departments. **Procedure:** Freshmen are admitted fall. Entrance exams should be taken as early as possible but no later than December of the senior year. There are early decision and deferred admissions plans. Early decision applications should be filed by November 15; regular applications, by January 1 for fall entry, along with a $70 fee. Notification of early decision is sent December 15; regular decision, February 1. 270 early decision candidates were accepted for the 2014-2015 class. 1417 applicants were on the 2014 waiting list; 61 were admitted. Applications are accepted on-line. **Transfer Students:** 16 transfer students enrolled in 2013-2014. Applicants must have a high level of achievement in both high school and college work. 17 of 34 credits required for the bachelor's degree must be completed at Vassar. **International Students:** There are 168 international students enrolled. The school actively recruits these students. They must take the TOEFL with a minimum score of 600 on the paper-based TOEFL (PBT) or 100 on the Internet-based version (iBT), or take the IELTS. They must also take the SAT or ACT.

ADMISSIONS: 24% of the 2014-2015 applicants were accepted. The SAT scores for the 2014-2015 freshman class were: Critical Reading--7% between 500 and 599, 35% between 600 and 699, and 58% between 700 and 800; Math--5% between 500 and 599, 48% between 600 and 699, and 47% between 700 and 800; Writing--7% between 500 and 599, 38% between 600 and 699, and 54% between 700 and 800. The ACT scores were 2% between 24 and 26, 11% between 27 and 28, and 89% above 28. 90% of the current freshmen were in the top fifth of their class; 99% were in the top two fifths. **Admissions Contact:** J.C. Tesone, Director of Admission. E-Mail: *admissions@vassar.edu* Web: *www.vassar.edu*

FINANCIAL AID: In 2014-2015, 65% of all full-time freshmen and 63% of continuing full-time students received some form of financial aid. 60% of all full-time freshmen and 59% of continuing full-time students received need-based aid. The average freshman award was $48,398. Need-based scholarships or need-based grants averaged $45,154 ($60,902 maximum); need-based self-help aid (loans and jobs) averaged $3,577 ($5,660 maximum); and $1,033 from other forms of aid. 65% of undergraduate students work part-time. Average annual earnings from campus work are $1367. The average financial indebtedness of the 2014 graduate was $15,091. Vassar is a member of CSS. The CSS/Profile, FAFSA, FFS, and the college's own financial statement are required. Check with the school for current application deadlines.

VAUGHN COLLEGE OF AERONAUTICS AND TECHNOLOGY D-5
www.vaughn.edu

Flushing, NY 11369	**(718) 429-6600 ext 117** n/av
Fax: **(718) 779-2231**	Email: admitme@vaughn.edu
Full-time: 1190 men, 172 women	Faculty: 41
Part-time: 376 men, 61 women	Ph.D.s: 54%
Graduate: 9 men, 4 women	Student/Faculty: 33 to 1
Year: semesters, summer session	Tuition: $19,460
Room & Board: $11,900	Freshman Class: 723 applied, 618 accepted, 321 enrolled
SAT CR/M: 498/547 ACT: 22	CEEB CODE: 2001
Application Deadline: open	COMPETITIVE

Vaughn College of Aeronautics and Technology, founded in 1932, is a private non-profit institution located in New York City, offering undergraduate and masters degrees in Engineering, Engineering Technology, Management, and Aviation. In addition to regional accreditation, Vaughn has baccalaureate program accreditation with ABET. The 6-acre campus is in an urban area Queens, New York, across the street from LaGuardia Airport, 4 miles east of New York City. Including any residence halls, there are 2 buildings.

STUDENT LIFE: 89% of undergraduates are from New York. Others are from 27 states, and 20 foreign countries. 96% are from public schools. 38% are Hispanic; 19% African American; 17% White. The average age of freshmen is 19; all undergraduates, 23. 20% do not continue beyond their first year; 57% remain to graduate. **Housing:** 200 students can be accommodated in college housing, which includes coed dorms. In addition, there are special-interest houses. On-campus housing is available on a first-come and first-served basis. Priority is given to out-of-town students. 90% of students commute. Alcohol is not permitted. All students may keep cars.

FACULTY/CLASSROOMS: 88% of faculty are male; 12% are female. All teach undergraduates. No introductory courses are taught by graduate students. The average class size in an introductory lecture is 25; in a laboratory is 20; and in a regular course is 20.

PROGRAMS OF STUDY: Vaughn confers B.S. degrees. Associate and Master's degrees are also awarded. Bachelor's degrees are awarded in BUSINESS (business administration and management), ENGINEERING AND ENVIRONMENTAL DESIGN (air traffic control, aircraft mechanics, airline piloting and navigation, aviation administration/management, electrical/electronics engineering technology, mechanical engineering technology, and Mechatronics Engineering). Mechatronic engineering, mechanical engineering technology, and electronic engineering technology are the strongest academically. Aircraft operation (flight), airport management, and mechanical engineering technology have the largest enrollments.

ACTIVITIES: There are no fraternities or sororities. There are 16 groups on campus, including computers, dance, ethnic, gay, honors, international, professional, religious, social, social service, and student government. Popular campus events include Career and Internship Fairs, and Springfest. **Sports:** There are 4 intercollegiate sports for men and 3 for women. Facilities include an state-of-the-art fitness center. **Graduates:** From July 1, 2013 to June 30, 2014, 138 bachelor's degrees were awarded. The most popular majors were airport management (65%), electronic engineering technology (14%), and mechanical engineering technology (11%). 45 companies recruited on campus in 2013-2014. In an average class, 35% graduate in 4 years or less, 52% graduate in 5 years or less, and 57% graduate in 6 years or less.

SERVICES: Counseling and information services are available, as is tutoring in most subjects. There is remedial math, reading, and writing. **Library/Resources:** The library contains 37,455 volumes, 4,252 audio/video tapes/CDs/DVDs, and subscribes to 80,000 periodicals including electronic. Computerized library services include interlibrary loans, database searching, and Internet access. **Physically Challenged Students:** All of the campus is accessible. Facilities include wheelchair ramps, elevators, special parking, specially equipped restrooms, special class scheduling, lowered drinking fountains, and lowered telephones. **Special:** Work-study programs are available with Vaughn College, and internships may be arranged through the career development office. B.S. degrees are offered. **Visiting:** There are regularly scheduled orientations for prospective students, scheduled prior to registration, which include a tour and academic advisement. There are guides for informal visits and visitors may sit in on classes. To schedule a visit, contact the Admissions Office at admitme@vaughn .edu. **Campus Safety and Security:** Measures include 24-hour foot and vehicle patrol, emergency notification system, and security escort services. There are shuttle buses, lighted pathways/sidewalks, and controlled access to dorms/residences.

REQUIREMENTS: The SAT is recommended. SAT or ACT scores are required for all applicants to bachelor of science degree programs. The average SAT score for the engineering program is 1160. The average SAT score for Engineering Technology, Management, and Aricraft Operations programs is 1040. A GPA of 2.0 is required. AP credits are accepted. Important factors in the admissions decision are evidence of special talent, advanced placement or honors courses, and personality/intangible qualities.All students must satisfy English, math, and science requirements and fulfill appropriate licensing requirements while maintaining a GPA of at least 2.0. Students with advanced credit must complete 30 credits in residency. **Procedure:** Freshmen are admitted fall and spring. Entrance exams should be taken March 1. There is a rolling admissions plan. Application deadlines are open. The fall 2014 application fee was $40. Notification is sent on a rolling basis. **Transfer Students:** 245 transfer students enrolled in 2013-2014. A minimum 2.0 GPA is required. 30 of 134 credits required for the bachelor's degree must be completed at Vaughn. **International Students:** There are 40 international students enrolled. The school actively recruits these students. They must take the TOEFL with a minimum score of 80 on the paper-based TOEFL (PBT) or 112 on the Internet-based version (iBT), English Proficiency Certificate. They must also take the SAT. TOEFL accepted in place of SAT for applicants from non-English speaking countries.

ADMISSIONS: 85% of the 2014-2015 applicants were accepted. The SAT scores for the 2014-2015 freshman class were: Critical Reading--54% below 500, 37% between 500 and 599, 8% between 600 and 699, and 1% between 700 and 800; Math--25% below 500, 48% between 500 and 599, 24% between 600 and 699, and 3% between 700 and 800. The ACT scores were 16% below 21, 67% between 21 and 23, and 17% above 28. **Admissions Contact:** David Griffey, Director of Admissions. E-Mail: *admitme@vaughn.edu* Web: *www.vaughn.edu*

FINANCIAL AID: In 2014-2015, 95% of all full-time freshmen and continuing full-time students received some form of financial aid. 80% of all full-time freshmen and continuing full-time students received need-based aid. 60% of undergraduate students work part-time. The average financial indebtedness of the 2014 graduate was $32,500. The CSS/Profile, FAFSA, and the college's own financial statement are required. Check with the school for current application deadlines.

WAGNER COLLEGE   **D-5**
www.wagner.edu

Staten Island, NY 10301	(718) 390-3411
	(800) 221-1010
Fax: (718) 390-3105	Email: admissions@wagner.edu
Full-time: 610 men, 1131 women	Faculty: 102; IIA, av$
Part-time: 23 men, 54 women	Ph.D.s: 85%
Graduate: 128 men, 259 women	Student/Faculty: 13 to 1
Year: semesters, summer session	Tuition: $37,440
Room & Board: $11,160	Freshman Class: 2652 applied, 1907 accepted, 426 enrolled
SAT CR/M/W: 560/540/530 ACT: 25	CEEB CODE: 2966
Application Deadline: February 15	COMPETITIVE+

Wagner College, founded in 1883, is a private liberal arts institution. Figures in the above capsule and in this profile are approximate. There is one graduate school. In addition to regional accreditation, Wagner has baccalaureate program accreditation with AACSB, ACBSP, NCATE, NLN, ARC-PA, and ACS. The 105-acre campus is in a suburban area 10 miles from Manhattan. Including any residence halls, there are 19 buildings.

STUDENT LIFE: 52% of undergraduates are from New York. Others are from 40 states, 20 foreign countries, and Canada. 62% are from public schools. 77% are White; 11% race unknown. The average age of freshmen is 18; all undergraduates, 20. 17% do not continue beyond their first year; 70% remain to graduate. **Housing:** 1600 students can be accommodated in college housing, which includes coed dorms and off-campus apartments. In addition, there are honors houses, special-interest houses, Greek floors, Honors building, quiet floors, medical floors, and themed communities in dorms, and senior year housing. On-campus housing is guaranteed for all 4 years and is available on a lottery system for upperclassmen. 67% of students live on campus; of those, 70% remain on campus on weekends. All students may keep cars.

FACULTY/CLASSROOMS: 45% of faculty are male; 55% are female. All teach undergraduates. No introductory courses are taught by graduate students. The average class size in an introductory lecture is 21; in a laboratory is 13; and in a regular course is 19.

PROGRAMS OF STUDY: Wagner confers B.A., and B.S. degrees. Master's degrees are also awarded. Bachelor's degrees are awarded in BIOLOGICAL SCIENCE (biology/biological science and microbiology), BUSINESS (accounting and business administration and management), COMMUNICATIONS AND THE ARTS (arts administration/management, dramatic arts, English, fine arts, music, theater design, and visual and performing arts), COMPUTER AND PHYSICAL SCIENCE (chemistry, computer science, mathematics, and physics), EDUCATION (elementary education, middle school education, and secondary education), HEALTH PROFESSIONS (nursing and physician's assistant), SOCIAL SCIENCE (anthropology, history, philosophy, political science/government, psychology, public administration, and sociology). Natural sciences and health professions is the strongest academically. Business, nursing, psychology, visual and performing arts have the largest enrollments.

ACTIVITIES: 15% of men and 13% of women belong to 2 local and 2 national fraternities; 13% of women belong to 1 local and 3 national sororities. There are 65 groups on campus, including and women's, academic, art, band, cheerleading, chess, choir, chorale, chorus, communications, computers, dance, debate, drama, environmental, ethnic, gay, honors, international, jazz band, literary magazine, marching band, musical theater, newspaper, opera, pep band, political, professional, religious, social, social service, student government, symphony, and yearbook. Popular campus events include Songfest, WagnerStock, Homecoming, Spring Fling Week, Fall Fest and Family Weekend. **Sports:** There are 8 intercollegiate sports for men and 10 for women, and 5 intramural sports for men and 4 for women. Facilities include a football stadium, a gym, a regulation-sized pool, a fitness center, a track, and a basketball arena, soccer/softball/baseball field. **Graduates:** From July 1, 2013 to June 30, 2014, 417 bachelor's degrees were awarded. The most popular majors were nursing and physician assistants (18%), visual/performing arts (18%), and business administration (17%). 60 companies recruited on campus in 2013-2014. In an average class, 60% graduate in 4 years or less, 64% graduate in 5 years or less, and 66% graduate in 6 years or less. Of the 2013 graduating class, 20% were enrolled in graduate school within 6 months of graduation, and 79% were employed.

SERVICES: Counseling and information services are available, as is tutoring in every subject. There is a reader service for the blind, and remedial math, reading, and writing. **Library/Resources:** The library contains 158,160 volumes, 218 microform items, 2,453 audio/video tapes/CDs/DVDs, and subscribes to 56,399 periodicals including electronic. Computerized library services include interlibrary loans, database searching, Internet access, and Wi-Fi capability. Special learning facilities include an art gallery, planetarium, a nursing resource center. **Physically Challenged Students:** 25% of the campus is accessible. Facilities include wheelchair ramps, elevators, special parking, specially equipped restrooms, special class scheduling, and lowered drinking fountains. **Special:** Internships or field-based research is required of all majors. Students may earn B.A.-B.S. degrees in psychology. Student-designed and dual majors, credit for life experience, a Washington semester, nondegree study, and pass/fail options are available. Study abroad in most countries is possible. Learning Communities for freshmen, sophomores/juniors, and seniors. There are

11 national honor societies and a freshman honors program. **Visiting:** There are regularly scheduled orientations for prospective students, including a presentation by the Admissions Office, a tour of the campus, and meetings with faculty and staff. There are guides for informal visits, visitors may sit in on classes, and stay overnight. To schedule a visit, contact the Admissions Office. **Campus Safety and Security:** Measures include 24-hour foot and vehicle patrol, emergency notification system, and security escort services. There are shuttle buses, emergency telephones, lighted pathways/sidewalks, controlled access to dorms/residences, ID card access into residence halls.

REQUIREMENTS: Graduation from an accredited secondary school is required, with 18 academic credits or Carnegie units, including 4 years of English, 3 years each of history and math, 2 years each of foreign language, science, and social studies, and 1 year each of art and music. An essay is required, and an interview is strongly recommended. Auditions are required for music and theater applicants. An interview is required for the Physician Assistant Program. A GPA of 3.0 is required. AP and CLEP credits are accepted. Important factors in the admissions decision are advanced placement or honors courses, recommendations by school officials, and extracurricular activities record.To graduate, students must complete 36 units with 12 to 18 in the major and a minimum GPA of 2.0. All students must take courses in English, math, and multidisciplinary studies. In addition, students must fulfill distribution requirements in physical science, life science, math and computers, history, literature, philosophy and religion, foreign culture, aesthetics, and human behavior. All students are required to enroll in Learning Communities. **Procedure:** Freshmen are admitted fall and spring. Entrance exams should be taken by December of the senior year. There are early decision and deferred admissions plans. Early decision applications should be filed by December 1; regular applications, by February 15 for fall entry; and November 1 for spring entry, along with a $50 fee. Notification of early decision is sent December 15; regular decision, March 1. 76 early decision candidates were accepted for the 2014-2015 class. 48 applicants were on the 2014 waiting list; 10 were admitted. Applications are accepted on-line. **Transfer Students:** 96 transfer students enrolled in 2013-2014. Transfer students should have a minimum of 30 credit hours earned with a GPA of 2.5. Applicants must submit all college and high school transcripts, a letter of recommendation, and a personal statement. An interview is recommended. SAT or ACT scores taken within the past 5 years may be submitted. 9 of 36 credits required for the bachelor's degree must be completed at Wagner. **International Students:** There are 36 international students enrolled. The school actively recruits these students. They must take the TOEFL with a minimum score of 550 on the paper-based TOEFL (PBT) or 79 on the Internet-based version (iBT).

ADMISSIONS: 72% of the 2014-2015 applicants were accepted. The SAT scores for the 2014-2015 freshman class were: Critical Reading--9% below 500, 42% between 500 and 599, 42% between 600 and 699, and 7% between 700 and 800; Math--10% below 500, 40% between 500 and 599, 42% between 600 and 699, and 7% between 700 and 800; Writing--11% below 500, 39% between 500 and 599, 42% between 600 and 699, and 7% between 700 and 800. The ACT scores were 5% below 21, 28% between 21 and 23, 42% between 24 and 26, 17% between 27 and 28, and 8% above 28. 38% of the current freshmen were in the top fifth of their class; 86% were in the top two fifths. **Admissions Contact:** Robert Herr, Dean of Admissions. E-Mail: *admissions@wagner.edu* Web: *www.wagner.edu*

FINANCIAL AID: In 2014-2015, 91% of all full-time freshmen and 90% of continuing full-time students received some form of financial aid. 72% of all full-time freshmen and 66% of continuing full-time students received need-based aid. The average freshman award was $26,233. Need-based scholarships or need-based grants averaged $16,613 ($48,600 maximum); need-based self-help aid (loans and jobs) averaged $4,468 ($10,000 maximum); non-need-based athletic scholarships averaged $33,347 ($52,076 maximum); and other non-need-based awards and non-need-based scholarships averaged $15,507 ($48,600 maximum). 19% of undergraduate students work part-time. Average annual earnings from campus work are $1004. Wagner is a member of CSS. The FAFSA and the state aid form are required. The priority date for freshman financial aid applications for fall entry is February 15.

WEBB INSTITUTE
www.webb-institute.edu

D-5

Glen Cove, NY 11542

(516) 671-2213
n/av

Fax: (516) 674-9838 — Email: admissions@webb-institute.edu

Full-time: 65 men, 20 women	**Faculty:** n/av
Part-time: n/av	**Ph.D.s:** 50%
Graduate: n/av	**Student/Faculty:** n/av
Year: semesters	**Tuition:** see profile
Room & Board: $14,050	**Freshman Class:** n/av
SAT: required	**CEEB CODE:** 2970
Application Deadline: n/av	**MOST COMPETITIVE**

Webb Institute, founded in 1889, is a private engineering school devoted to professional knowledge of ship construction, design, and motive power. All students receive 4-year, full-tuition scholarships, accepted to students who are U.S. citizens or Green Card holders. The $200 registration fee at the time of acceptance is applied to room and board. The figures for tuition cost ($44,200) is for foreign students for the 2014-15 academic year. In addition to regional accreditation, Webb has baccalaureate program accreditation with ABET. The 26-acre campus is in a suburban area 24 miles east of New York City. Including any residence halls, there are 11 buildings.

STUDENT LIFE: 76% of undergraduates are from out of state, mostly the Northeast. Students are from 22 states, and 1 foreign countries. 70% are from public schools. 96% are White. The average age of freshmen is 18; all undergraduates, 20. 4% do not continue beyond their first year; 73% remain to graduate. **Housing:** 110 students can be accommodated in college housing, which includes single-sex dorms. On-campus housing is guaranteed for all 4 years. All students may keep cars.

FACULTY/CLASSROOMS: 100% of faculty are male. All teach undergraduates, and 40% do both. No introductory courses are taught by graduate students. The average class size in an introductory lecture is 25; in a laboratory is 9; and in a regular course is 25.

PROGRAMS OF STUDY: Webb confers B.S. degrees. Bachelor's degrees are awarded in ENGINEERING AND ENVIRONMENTAL DESIGN (naval architecture and marine engineering).

ACTIVITIES: There are no fraternities or sororities. Groups on campus include chorale, drama, orchestra, professional, social, student government, yachting club, and yearbook. Popular campus events include Parents Day and Webbstock. **Sports:** There are 6 intercollegiate sports for men and 6 for women, and 2 intramural sports for men and 2 for women. Facilities include a 60-seat gym, tennis courts, an athletic field, boat house, and a beach-front dock.

SERVICES: Counseling and information services are available, as is tutoring in most subjects. **Library/Resources:** The library contains 50,598 volumes, 1,633 microform items, 1,851 audio/video tapes/CDs/DVDs, and subscribes to 267 periodicals including electronic. Computerized library services include interlibrary loans, database searching, and Internet access. **Physically Challenged Students:** 90% of the campus is accessible. Facilities include elevators and special parking. **Special:** All students are employed 2 months each year through co-op programs. **Visiting:** There are regularly scheduled orientations for prospective students, including a weekend open house every October. There are guides for informal visits, visitors may sit in on classes, and stay overnight. To schedule a visit, contact the Associate Director of Admissions. **Campus Safety and Security:** Measures include 24-hour foot and vehicle patrol. There are emergency telephones, lighted pathways/sidewalks, and student and professional security services.

REQUIREMENTS: The SAT is required, with a minimum satisfactory score. Applicants should be graduates of an accredited secondary school with 16 academic credits completed, including 4 each in English and math, 2 each in history and science, 1 in foreign language, and 3 in electives. 3 SAT Subject tests in writing, math level I or II, and physics or chemistry are required, as is an interview. A GPA of 3.2 is required. Important factors in the admissions decision are advanced placement or honors courses, evidence of special talent, and personality/intangible qualities. The curriculum is prescribed, with all students taking the same courses in each of the 4 years. The Webb program has 4 practical 8-week paid work periods: freshman year, a helper mechanic in a shipyard; sophomore year, a cadet in the engine room of a ship; and junior and senior years, a draftsman or junior engineer in a design office. All students must complete a senior seminar, thesis, and technical reports, as well as make engineering inspection visits. A total of 146 credits with a minimum passing grade of 70% is required to graduate. **Procedure:** Freshmen are admitted fall. Entrance exams should be taken by January of the senior year. There is a early decision plan. Check with the school for current application deadlines. The application fee is $25. **Transfer Students:** Transfers must enter as freshmen. A 3.2 GPA is required. SAT scores and an interview are required. 146 of 146 credits required for the bachelor's degree must be completed at Webb.

ADMISSIONS: Steven P Ostendorff, Director of Admissions. E-Mail: *admissions@webb-institute.edu* Web: *www.webb-institute.edu*

FINANCIAL AID: The CSS/Profile and the college's own financial statement are required. Check with the school for current application deadlines.

WELLS COLLEGE   C-3
www.wells.edu

Aurora, NY 13026	
	(315) 364-3264
	(800) 952-9355
Fax: (315) 364-3227	Email: admissions@wells.edu
Full-time: 125 men, 415 women	Faculty: IIB, -$
Part-time: 5 men, 15 women	Ph.D.s: 100%
Graduate: n/av	Student/Faculty: n/av
Year: semesters	Tuition: $36,700
Room & Board: $12,700	Freshman Class: n/av
SAT or ACT: required	CEEB CODE: 2971
Application Deadline: n/av	**VERY COMPETITIVE**

Wells College, founded in 1868, is a private liberal arts institution. Historically a women's college, it became coeducational in 2005. The figures in the above capsule and in this profile are approximate. The 365-acre campus is in a small town on Cayuga Lake, in the heart of New York's Finger Lakes, in the villarge of Aurora, and 30 miles north of Ithaca. Including any residence halls, there are 22 buildings.

STUDENT LIFE: 67% of undergraduates are from New York. Others are from 32 states, and 14 foreign countries. 93% are from public schools. 68% are White. **Male To Female Ratio:** 3.3:1. The average age of freshmen is 18; all undergraduates, 20. 20% do not continue beyond their first year; 60% remain to graduate. **Housing:** 450 students can be accommodated in college housing, which includes single-sex and coed dorms and off-campus apartments. In addition, there are special-interest houses, Housing for nontraditional-age students. On-campus housing is guaranteed for all 4 years. 85% of students live on campus. All students may keep cars.

FACULTY/CLASSROOMS: 44% of faculty are male; 56% are female. All teach undergraduates. No introductory courses are taught by graduate students. The average class size in an introductory lecture is 25; in a laboratory is 16; and in a regular course is 13.

PROGRAMS OF STUDY: Wells confers B.A. degrees. Bachelor's degrees are awarded in AGRICULTURE (environmental studies), BIOLOGICAL SCIENCE (biochemistry, biology/biological science, and molecular biology), BUSINESS (business administration and management), COMMUNICATIONS AND THE ARTS (dance, dramatic arts, English, fine arts, French, German, language arts, music, Spanish, and visual and performing arts), COMPUTER AND PHYSICAL SCIENCE (chemistry, computer science, mathematics, and physics), EDUCATION (elementary education), SOCIAL SCIENCE (American studies, anthropology, economics, ethics, politics, and social policy, history, international studies, philosophy, political science/government, psychology, public affairs, religion, sociology, and women's studies). Psychology, English, and biological and chemical sciences have the largest enrollments.

ACTIVITIES: There are 42 groups on campus, including and SAGA, and women's resource center, campus greens, Japanese cultural club, Model UN, Spanish club, WILL (Women in Lifelong Learning), WISA, bell ringers, choir, chorale, dance, drama, environmental,

ethnic, forensics, gay, international, jazz band, literary magazine, newspaper, photography, political, professional, religious, social, social service, and student government. Popular campus events include Odd-Even Basketball Game, Spring Weekend and 100 Days for Seniors. **Sports:** There are 5 intercollegiate sports for men and 7 for women, and 10 intramural sports for men and 10 for women. Facilities include a competition-size swimming pool, a gym, a fitness center with weight and cardio equipment, an athletic training room, 2 indoor tennis courts/practice space, a dance studio, a 9-hole golf course, 4 all-weather tennis courts, a skinned infield softball field, 2 game fields for soccer and lacrosse, a field hockey field, and a boat house and dock with canoes, kayaks, and sailboats. **Graduates:** From July 1, 2013 to June 30, 2014, 82 bachelor's degrees were awarded. The most popular majors were psychology (17%), English (10%), and sociology/anthropology (6%). In an average class, 2% graduate in 3 years or less, 60% graduate in 4 years or less, 61% graduate in 5 years or less, and 62% graduate in 6 years or less. Of the 2013 graduating class, 15% were enrolled in graduate school within 6 months of graduation, and 37% were employed.

SERVICES: Counseling and information services are available, as is tutoring in every subject. Assistance is provided on an individual, as-needed basis. Untimed and extended-time testing options are available. **Library/Resources:** The library contains 218,002 volumes, 14,882 microform items, 1,154 audio/video tapes/CDs/DVDs, and subscribes to 371 periodicals including electronic. Computerized library services include interlibrary loans, database searching, Internet access, and Wi-Fi capability. Special learning facilities include an art gallery, the book arts center. **Physically Challenged Students:** 51% of the campus is accessible. Facilities include wheelchair ramps, elevators, special parking, specially equipped restrooms, special class scheduling, lowered telephones, and special housing. **Special:** Wells offers cross-registration with Cornell University, Cayuga Community College, and Ithaca College, a Washington semester with American University, internships, and accelerated degree programs in all majors. Study abroad in 13 countries is permitted. A 3-2 engineering degree is available with Columbia, Clarkson, and Cornell Universities. Students may also earn 3-2 degrees in business and community health with the University of Rochester and a 3-4 degree in veterinary medicine with Cornell University. Student-designed majors and pass/fail options are available. Work-study, B.A.-B.S. degrees, and dual majors are also available. There are 2 national honor societies including Phi Beta Kappa. **Visiting:** There are regularly scheduled orientations for prospective students, including tours, interviews, class attendance, presentations, open houses, an overnight host program, and meetings with faculty and coaches. There are guides for informal visits, visitors may sit in on classes, and stay overnight. To schedule a visit, contact the Admissions Office. **Campus Safety and Security:** Measures include 24-hour foot and vehicle patrol, self-defense education, and security escort services. There are shuttle buses, emergency telephones, lighted pathways/sidewalks, All students must escort their guests on campus at all times; blue light phones are provided.

REQUIREMENTS: The SAT or ACT is required. In addition, graduation from an accredited secondary school should include 20 academic credits or Carnegie units. High school courses must include 4 years of English, 3 each of a foreign language and math, and 2 each of history and lab science. 2 teacher recommendations and an essay/personal statement are required, and an interview is strongly recommended. AP and CLEP credits are accepted. Important factors in the admissions decision are recommendations by school officials, extracurricular activities record, and advanced placement or honors courses. To graduate, students must complete a total of 120 credit hours, including 33 to 63 in the major, with a minimum GPA of 2.0 overall and in the major. All students must complete 2 first-year experience courses, a comprehensive exam, 3 January intersession internships/courses, and a senior project/thesis. Distribution requirements include 4 courses in phys ed and wellness, 3 each in natural and social sciences and arts and humanities, 2 in a foreign language, and 1 in formal reasoning. **Procedure:** Freshmen are admitted fall. Entrance exams should be taken prior to application. There are early decision and deferred admissions plans. Check with the school for current application deadlines. The application fee is $40. Applications are accepted on-line. **Transfer Students:** 56 transfer students enrolled in 2013-2014. Applicants must be in good standing at the institution last attended. A minimum GPA of 2.0 is required. Wells requires official college and high school transcripts, a personal statement, standardized test scores, and a recommendation from a professor. An interview is strongly recommended. 60 of 120 credits required for the bachelor's degree must be completed at Wells. **International Students:** There are 14 international students enrolled. The school actively recruits these students. They must take the TOEFL with a minimum score of 550 on the paper-based TOEFL (PBT) or 80 on the Internet-based version (iBT). They must also take the SAT or ACT.

ADMISSIONS: 3 freshmen graduated first in their class. **Admissions Contact:** Susan Sloan, Director of Admissions. E-Mail: *admissions@wells.edu* Web: *www.wells.edu*

FINANCIAL AID: In 2014-2015, 91% of all full-time freshmen and 88% of continuing full-time students received some form of financial aid. 71% of all full-time freshmen and 76% of continuing full-time students received need-based aid. The average freshman award was $18,505. Need-based scholarships or need-based grants averaged $13,645 ($21,320 maximum); need-based self-help aid (loans and jobs) averaged $4,900 ($6,600 maximum); and other non-need-based awards and non-need-based scholarships averaged $6,850 ($10,500 maximum). 82% of undergraduate students work part-time. Average annual earnings from campus work are $1600. The average financial indebtedness of the 2014 graduate was $20,355. Wells is a member of CSS. The FAFSA, and early decision applicants must submit the CSS Profile. is required. Check with the school for current application deadlines.

YESHIVA UNIVERSITY   **D-5**
www.yu.edu

New York, NY 10033   (212) 960-5277
                                                       n/av
Fax: (212) 960-0086   Email: yuadmit@ymail.yu.edu
Full-time: 1438 men, 1379 women   Faculty: I, ++$
Part-time: 36 men, 16 women   Ph.D.s: 79%
Graduate: 1701 men, 2183 women   Student/Faculty: n/av
Year: semesters, summer session   Tuition: $36,500
Room & Board: $10,750   Freshman Class: 1898
                                     applied, 1319 accepted,
                                     911 enrolled
                                     CEEB CODE: 2990
Application Deadline: n/av   VERY COMPETITIVE+

Yeshiva University, founded in 1886, is an independent liberal arts institution offering undergraduate programs through Yeshiva College, its undergraduate college for men, Stern College for women, and the Sy Syms School of Business. The figures in the above capsule and in this profile are approximate. There are 7 graduate schools. In addition to regional accreditation, YU has baccalaureate program accreditation with CSWE. The 26-acre campus is in an urban area.

STUDENT LIFE: 44% of undergraduates are from out of state. Students are from 31 states, 16 foreign countries, and Canada. 14% are from public schools. The average age of freshmen is 17; all undergraduates, 19. 8% do not continue beyond their first year; 92% remain to graduate. **Housing:** 1600 students can be accommodated in college housing, which includes single-sex dorms and off-campus apartments. On-campus housing is guaranteed for all 4 years. 85% of students live on campus. Alcohol is not permitted. All students may keep cars.

FACULTY/CLASSROOMS: 73% of faculty are male; 27% are female. 58% teach undergraduates, 60% do research, and 28% do both. No introductory courses are taught by graduate students. The average class size in an introductory lecture is 38; in a laboratory is 15; and in a regular course is 18.

PROGRAMS OF STUDY: YU confers B.A., and B.S. degrees. Associate degrees are also awarded. Bachelor's degrees are awarded in BIOLOGICAL SCIENCE (biology/biological science), BUSINESS (accounting, business administration and management, and marketing/retailing/merchandising), COMMUNICATIONS AND THE ARTS (classical languages, communications, English, French,

Hebrew, music, and speech/debate/rhetoric), COMPUTER AND PHYSICAL SCIENCE (chemistry, computer science, and mathematics), ENGINEERING AND ENVIRONMENTAL DESIGN (preengineering), HEALTH PROFESSIONS (health science), SOCIAL SCIENCE (economics, history, philosophy, political science/government, psychology, religion, and sociology). The dual program of liberal arts and Jewish studies is the strongest academically. Accounting, psychology, and economics have the largest enrollments.

ACTIVITIES: There are 70 groups on campus, including radio, art, choir, computers, drama, honors, international, jazz band, literary magazine, musical theater, newspaper, political, professional, religious, social service, special interest, student government, and yearbook. Popular campus events include Holiday and Dramatic Presentations and Parents Day. **Sports:** There are 8 intercollegiate sports for men and 2 for women, and 5 intramural sports for men and 4 for women. Facilities include The athletic center at Yeshiva College houses a variety of facilities, including a 1000-seat gym. **Graduates:** From July 1, 2013 to June 30, 2014, 631 bachelor's degrees were awarded. The most popular majors were busilness (27%), psychology (17%), and biology (14%).

SERVICES: There is remedial reading and writing. There is also a writing center, which helps students with composition and verbal skills. **Library/Resources:** The 7 libraries contain 900,000 volumes, 759,000 microform items, and 980 audio/video tapes/CDs/DVDs, and subscribe to 7,790 periodicals including electronic. Computerized library services include interlibrary loans and database searching. Special learning facilities include an art gallery, and a museum. **Physically Challenged Students:** 95% of the campus is accessible. Facilities include wheelchair ramps and elevators. **Special:** YU offers a 3-2 degree in occupational therapy with Columbia and New York Universities; a 3-4 degree in podiatry with the New York College of Podiatric Medicine; and a 3-2 or 4-2 degree in engineering with Columbia University. Stern College students may take courses in advertising, photography, and design at the Fashion Institute of Technology. Study-abroad programs may be arranged in Israel. The school offers independent study options and an optional pass/no credit system. There are 9 national honor societies and 20 departmental honors programs. **Visiting:** There are regularly scheduled orientations for prospective students, YU holds open houses for high school students. There are guides for informal visits, visitors may sit in on classes, and stay overnight. To schedule a visit, contact the Office of Admissions. **Campus Safety and Security:** Measures include 24-hour foot and vehicle patrol and security escort services. There are shuttle buses, lighted pathways/sidewalks, ID cards, vulnerability surveys, fire drills, alarm systems, emergency telephone numbers, and transportation for routine and special events.

REQUIREMENTS: The SAT or ACT is required. Graduation from an accredited secondary school with 16 academic credits is required for admission. The GED is accepted under limited and specific circumstances. The SAT Subject test in Hebrew is recommended for placement purposes. An interview and an essay are required. A GPA of 3.3 is required. AP and CLEP credits are accepted. Important factors in the admissions decision are extracurricular activities record, personality/intangible qualities, and evidence of special talent.To graduate, students must complete a total of 128 credit hours. Under the dual program, students pursue a liberal arts or business curriculum together with courses in Hebrew language, literature, and culture. Courses in Jewish learning are geared to the student's level of preparation. **Procedure:** Freshmen are admitted to all sessions. There are early admissions, deferred admissions, and rolling admissions plans. Check with the school for current application deadlines. The application fee is $70. **Transfer Students:** 95 of 128 credits required for the bachelor's degree must be completed at YU. **International Students:** The school actively recruits these students. They must take the TOEFL. They must also take the SAT or ACT.

ADMISSIONS: 69% of the 2014-2015 applicants were accepted. **Admissions Contact:** Michael Kranzler, Director of Undergraduate Admissions. E-Mail: *yuadmit@ymail.yu.edu* Web: *www.yu.edu*

FINANCIAL AID: YU is a member of CSS. The CSS/Profile and the college's own financial statement are required. Check with the school for current application deadlines.

YORK COLLEGE / THE CITY UNIVERSITY OF NEW YORK   D-5
www.york.cuny.edu

Jamaica, NY 11451	(718) 262-2165
	n/av
Fax: (718) 262-2601	Email: admissions@york.cuny.edu
Full-time: 1817 men, 3510 women	Faculty: 201
Part-time: 990 men, 2033 women	Ph.D.s: n/av
Graduate: 4 men, 35 women	Student/Faculty: 19 to 1
Year: semesters, summer session	Tuition: $5496 ($11,406)
Room & Board: n/app	Freshman Class: 13319 applied, 8038 accepted, 1111 enrolled
	CEEB CODE: 2992
Application Deadline: open	VERY COMPETITIVE

York College, established in 1966, is a public liberal arts commuter college and part of the City University of New York. The figures in the above capsule and in this profile are approximate. There are 3 undergraduate schools. In addition to regional accreditation, York has baccalaureate program accreditation with CAHEA, CSWE, NCATE, NLN, ACOTE, ACEN, and ARC-PA. The 50-acre campus is in an urban area in New York City. Including any residence halls, there are 5 buildings.

STUDENT LIFE: 90% of undergraduates are from New York. Others are from 6 states, 77 foreign countries, and Canada. 34% are African American; 27% race unknown; 18% Hispanic; 16% Asian American. The average age of freshmen is 19; all undergraduates, 24. 23% do not continue beyond their first year; 77% remain to graduate. **Housing:** College-sponsored housing includes Alcohol is not permitted. All students commute. All students may keep cars.

FACULTY/CLASSROOMS: 51% of faculty are male; 49% are female. All teach undergraduates, and 7% do both. No introductory courses are taught by graduate students.

PROGRAMS OF STUDY: York confers B.A., and B.S. degrees. Master's degrees are also awarded. Bachelor's degrees are awarded in BIOLOGICAL SCIENCE (biology/biological science and biotechnology), BUSINESS (accounting, business administration and management, and marketing/retailing/merchandising), COMMUNICATIONS AND THE ARTS (art history and appreciation, dramatic arts, English, French, music, Spanish, speech/debate/rhetoric, and studio art), COMPUTER AND PHYSICAL SCIENCE (chemistry, geology, information sciences and systems, mathematics, and physics), EDUCATION (physical education), HEALTH PROFESSIONS (community health work, environmental health science, exercise science, medical laboratory technology, nursing, occupational therapy, and pharmaceutical science), SOCIAL SCIENCE (African American studies, anthropology, economics, gerontology, history, liberal arts/general studies, philosophy, political science/government, psychology, social work, and sociology). Liberal studies, business administration, and accounting have the largest enrollments.

ACTIVITIES: There are 50 groups on campus, including art, cheerleading, choir, chorus, communications, computers, drama, ethnic, honors, international, jazz band, literary magazine, musical theater, newspaper, political, professional, radio and TV, religious, social, social service, and student government. Popular campus events include Club Fairs, Talent Shows, and Ethnic Fairs. **Sports:** There are 9 intercollegiate sports for men and 8 for women, and 9 intramural sports for men and 8 for women. Facilities include a 1200-seat gym, 25-meter, 6-lane swimming pool with diving boards, a health risk appraisal center, an exercise therapy room, outdoor track, tennis courts, soccer field, indoor walking/jogging track, weight room, aerobics room, handball courts, and multipurpose room. **Graduates:** From July 1, 2013 to June 30, 2014, 1000 bachelor's degrees were

awarded. The most popular majors were business administration (20%), psychology (18%), and health professions (18%). 100 companies recruited on campus in 2013-2014. In an average class, 24% graduate in 4 years or less, 84% graduate in 5 years or less, and 56% graduate in 6 years or less.

SERVICES: Counseling and information services are available, as is tutoring in every subject. There is a reader service for the blind, and remedial math, reading, and writing. **Library/Resources:** The library contains 184,799 volumes, 140,461 microform items, 4,613 audio/video tapes/CDs/DVDs, and subscribes to 7,613 periodicals including electronic. Computerized library services include interlibrary loans and database searching. Special learning facilities include an art gallery, radio station, TV station, a cardio-pneumo simulator, flight simulator, and a theater. **Physically Challenged Students:** All of the campus is accessible. Facilities include wheelchair ramps, elevators, special parking, specially equipped restrooms, special class scheduling, lowered drinking fountains, and lowered telephones. **Special:** Cross-registration with all schools in the City University of New York is permitted. Also provided are work-study programs, credit by exam, dual majors in physics and math, nondegree study, pass/fail options, credit for life experience, internships, cooperative programs with other schools, and student-designed majors. There are 6 national honor societies and 4 departmental honors programs. **Visiting:** There are regularly scheduled orientations for prospective students, including workshops and group meetings with faculty and staff on matriculation; registration; financial aid, degree requirements; and advisement for classes. Visitors may sit in on classes. To schedule a visit, contact Michel Hodge at mhodge@york.cuny.edu. **Campus Safety and Security:** Measures include 24-hour foot and vehicle patrol and security escort services. There are emergency telephones and lighted pathways/sidewalks.

REQUIREMENTS: Students should achieve a satisfactory score on the SAT. Applicants must have graduated from an accredited secondary school or present a GED certificate. An audition is recommended for music majors. AP and CLEP credits are accepted.All students are required to complete 120 credits and maintain a minimum GPA of 2.0. The core curriculum of 36-42 credits includes courses in humanities, behavioral science, cultural diversity, math, natural science. Students must also take a 2-credit physical education course, complete 2 semesters of English, two Writing Intensive courses in the lower division of the curriculum (at the 100 or 200 level), and one Writing Intensive course in the upper division of the curriculum (at the 300 level or above) within the major discipline. **Procedure:** Freshmen are admitted fall and spring. There are early admissions, deferred admissions, and rolling admissions plans. Application deadlines are open. The fall 2014 application fee was $65. Notifications are sent in monthly. Applications are accepted on-line. **Transfer Students:** 894 transfer students enrolled in 2013-2014. Students must present a minimum GPA of 2.0. 40 of 120 credits required for the bachelor's degree must be completed at York. **International Students:** There are 120 international students enrolled. They must take the TOEFL. They must also take the SAT or ACT, scoring 1100. Math placement test if student comes from non-English-speaking country.

ADMISSIONS: 60% of the 2014-2015 applicants were accepted. The SAT scores for the 2014-2015 freshman class were: Math--71% below 500, 25% between 500 and 599, and 3% between 600 and 699. **Admissions Contact:** Michel Hodge, Director of Admissions and Enrollment. E-Mail: *admissions@york.cuny.edu* Web: *www.york.cuny.edu*

FINANCIAL AID: In 2014-2015, 69% of all full-time freshmen and 53% of continuing full-time students received some form of financial aid. 24% of all full-time freshmen and 14% of continuing full-time students received need-based aid. The average freshman award was $6,275. The FAFSA and the college's own financial statement are required. The priority date for freshman financial aid applications for fall entry is April 1. The deadline for filing freshman financial aid applications for fall entry is June 1.

NORTH CAROLINA

College Location

0 20 40 60 80 100
Miles

APPALACHIAN STATE UNIVERSITY   B-2
www.appstate.edu

Boone, NC 28608	**(828) 262-2000**
	(828) 262-2120
Fax: (828) 262-3296	Email: admissions@appstate.edu
Full-time: 7097 men, 7740 women	Faculty: 814; IIA, -$
Part-time: 354 men, 521 women	Ph.D.s: 99%
Graduate: 554 men, 1323 women	Student/Faculty: 16 to 1
Year: semesters, summer session	Tuition: $5859 ($17,907)
Room & Board: $7060	Freshman Class: 12248
	applied, 7744 accepted,
	3028 enrolled
SAT CR/M/W: 572/581/548 ACT: 26	CEEB CODE: 5010
Application Deadline: March 15	VERY COMPETITIVE

Appalachian State University, founded in 1899, and a member of the University of North Carolina system, is a comprehensive university offering undergraduate and graduate programs in the arts and sciences, business, teacher education, fine and applied arts, music, and health sciences. Figures in the above capsule and in this profile are approximate. There are 8 undergraduate schools and one graduate school. In addition to regional accreditation, App State has baccalaureate program accreditation with AACSB, CSAB, CSWE, NASAD, NASM, NCATE, and NRPA. The 1300-acre campus is in a small town in northwestern North Carolina. Including any residence halls, there are 90 buildings.

STUDENT LIFE: 92% of undergraduates are from North Carolina. Others are from 46 states, 61 foreign countries, and Canada. 88% are from public schools. 87% are White; 12% race unknown. The average age of freshmen is 18; all undergraduates, 21. 12% do not continue beyond their first year; 66% remain to graduate. **Housing:** 5775 students can be accommodated in college housing, which includes single-sex and coed dorms. In addition, there are sorority houses, Learning communities. On-campus housing is guaranteed for the freshman year only and is available on a lottery system for upperclassmen. 67% of students commute. All students may keep cars.

FACULTY/CLASSROOMS: 53% of faculty are male; 47% are female. 88% teach undergraduates. Graduate students teach 6% of introductory courses. The average class size in a laboratory is 22 and in a regular course is 33.

PROGRAMS OF STUDY: App State confers B.A., B.S., B.F.A., B.M., B.S.B.A., B.S.C.J., B.S.N. and B.S.W. degrees. Master's and Doctoral degrees are also awarded. Bachelor's degrees are awarded in AGRICULTURE (agricultural business management and environmental studies), BIOLOGICAL SCIENCE (biology/biological science, ecology, molecular biology, and nutrition), BUSINESS (accounting,

banking and finance, hospitality management services, insurance and risk management, international business management, management engineering, marketing/retailing/merchandising, and recreational facilities management), COMMUNICATIONS AND THE ARTS (advertising, apparel design, art, arts administration/management, communications, dance, dramatic arts, English, French, graphic design, industrial design, journalism, music business management, music performance, performing arts, photography, public relations, Spanish, and studio art), COMPUTER AND PHYSICAL SCIENCE (actuarial science, chemistry, computer science, geology, mathematics, physics, and statistics), EDUCATION (art education, athletic training, business education, computer education, drama education, education, elementary education, English education, foreign languages education, health education, mathematics education, middle school education, music education, physical education, science education, secondary education, social science education, social studies education, and special education), ENGINEERING AND ENVIRONMENTAL DESIGN (architecture, computer technology, construction management, construction technology, electrical/electronics engineering technology, engineering technology, environmental science, graphic arts technology, industrial engineering technology, and interior design), HEALTH PROFESSIONS (exercise science, health care administration, health science, music therapy, nursing, preventive/wellness health care, and speech pathology/audiology), SOCIAL SCIENCE (anthropology, area studies, child psychology/development, criminal justice, East Asian studies, economics, family/consumer studies, French studies, geography, German area studies, history, interdisciplinary studies, Latin American studies, Middle Eastern studies, philosophy, political science/government, psychology, religion, social work, sociology, South Asian studies, Third World studies, and women's studies). Business/marketing, elementary education, and social sciences have the largest enrollments.

ACTIVITIES: 7% of men belong to 13 national fraternities; 11% of women belong to 9 national sororities. There are 289 groups on campus, including art, band, cheerleading, chess, choir, chorale, chorus, communications, computers, dance, debate, drama, drill team, environmental, ethnic, film, forensics, gay, honors, international, jazz band, literary magazine, marching band, musical theater, newspaper, opera, orchestra, pep band, photography, political, professional, radio and TV, religious, social, social service, student government, and symphony. Popular campus events include Football and Basketball Games, Annual Diversity Celebration, Legends Concerts, and Greek Week. **Sports:** There are 10 intercollegiate sports for men and 10 for women, and 20 intramural sports for men and 20 for women. Facilities include a 9,000-seat convocation center, 7,000-seat varsity gym, 18,000-seat stadium, 3 fitness and recreation centers, facilities for football, soccer, field hockey, basketball, volleyball, wrestling, indoor and outdoor track, golf course, baseball field, tennis courts, 50-meter pool, 50-ft climbing wall, racquetball courts, aerobics studio, weight room, and cardio equipment. **Graduates:** From July 1, 2013 to June 30, 2014, 3435 bachelor's degrees were awarded. The most popular majors were business/ marketing (20%), education (17%), and social sciences (8%). 499 companies recruited on campus in 2013-2014. In an average class, 2% graduate in 3 years or less, 44% graduate in 4 years or less, 65% graduate in 5 years or less, and 66% graduate in 6 years or less.

SERVICES: Counseling and information services are available, as is tutoring in most subjects. There is a reader service for the blind, and remedial math, reading, and writing. **Library/Resources:** The 2 libraries contain 937,956 volumes, 1.5 million microform items, 72,813 audio/video tapes/CDs/DVDs, and subscribe to 23,861 periodicals including electronic. Computerized library services include interlibrary loans, database searching, and Internet access. Special learning facilities include an art gallery, radio station, a dark sky observatory. **Physically Challenged Students:** All of the campus is accessible. Facilities include wheelchair ramps, elevators, special parking, specially equipped restrooms, special class scheduling, lowered drinking fountains, lowered telephones, and special housing. **Special:** App State offers dual degree in Communications with Universidad de las Americas Puebla, a private university in Mexico, a 3-2 engineering degree with Clemson and Auburn Universities, internships, work-study programs, B.A.-B.S. degrees, dual majors, and study abroad. There are 16 national honor societies, a freshman honors program, and 25 departmental honors programs. **Visiting:** There are regularly scheduled orientations for prospective students, starting at the end of May for all new students. There are guides for informal visits and visitors may sit in on classes. **Campus Safety and Security:** Measures include 24-hour foot and vehicle patrol, emergency notification system, self-defense education, and security escort services. There are shuttle buses, emergency telephones, lighted pathways/sidewalks, and controlled access to dorms/residences.

REQUIREMENTS: The SAT or ACT is required. The ACT Optional Writing test is also required. Applicants must be graduates of an accredited secondary school. Applicants must have completed 4 course units in high school English and math, 3 in science, and 2 in foreign languages and social studies. AP and CLEP credits are accepted. Important factors in the admissions decision are advanced placement or honors courses, extracurricular activities record, and evidence of special talent. To graduate, students must complete 122 credit hours for most programs, including 60 in the major, with a minimum 2.0 GPA. General education requirements include courses in math, science, history, phys ed, English, social sciences, and humanities. **Procedure:** Freshmen are admitted fall, spring, and summer. Entrance exams should be taken by November 15, if possible. There are deferred admissions and rolling admissions plans. Applications should be filed by March 15 for fall entry, along with a $55 fee. 630 applicants were on the 2014 waiting list; 200 were admitted. Applications are accepted on-line. **Transfer Students:** 1153 transfer students enrolled in 2013-2014. Transfer students must have earned a minimum 2.0 GPA on collegiate work. They must have a minimum of 30 semester credits or else apply as a freshman. 30 of 128 credits required for the bachelor's degree must be completed at App State. **International Students:** There are 145 international students enrolled. The school actively recruits these students. The SAT or ACT may be accepted in lieu of the TOEFL.

ADMISSIONS: 63% of the 2014-2015 applicants were accepted. The SAT scores for the 2014-2015 freshman class were: Critical Reading--11% below 500, 55% between 500 and 599, 30% between 600 and 699, and 4% between 700 and 800; Math--6% below 500, 52% between 500 and 599, 38% between 600 and 699, and 4% between 700 and 800; Writing--22% below 500, 55% between 500 and 599, 21% between 600 and 699, and 2% between 700 and 800. The ACT scores were 3% below 21, 14% between 21 and 23, 47% between 24 and 26, 19% between 27 and 28, and 17% above 28. 45% of the current freshmen were in the top fifth of their class; 80% were in the top two fifths. **Admissions Contact:** Lloyd Scott, Director of Admissions. E-Mail: *admissions@appstate.edu* Web: *www.appstate.edu*

FINANCIAL AID: In 2014-2015, 67% of all full-time freshmen and 64% of continuing full-time students received some form of financial aid. 47% of all full-time freshmen and 46% of continuing full-time

students received need-based aid. The average freshman award was $10,345. Need-based scholarships or need-based grants averaged $7,710 ($30,679 maximum); need-based self-help aid (loans and jobs) averaged $3,292 ($6,577 maximum); non-need-based athletic scholarships averaged $10,948 ($25,727 maximum); and other non-need-based awards and non-need-based scholarships averaged $2,235 ($12,929 maximum). The average financial indebtedness of the 2014 graduate was $20,016. The FAFSA is required. Check with the school for current application deadlines.

BARTON COLLEGE (*The complete profile is made available exclusively on our website, www.barronspac.com*)

BELMONT ABBEY COLLEGE   C-3
www.belmontabbeycollege.edu

Belmont, NC 28012	(704) 461-6700
	(888) 222-0110
Fax: (704) 461-6220	Email: info@BAC.edu
Full-time: 663 men, 927 women	Faculty: 76; IIB
Part-time: 33 men, 83 women	Ph.D.s: 70%
Graduate: n/av	Student/Faculty: 16 to 1
Year: semesters, summer session	Tuition: $27,622
Room & Board: $10,094	Freshman Class: 1843 applied, 1185 accepted, 303 enrolled
SAT CR/M: 510/510 ACT: 23	CEEB CODE: 5055
Application Deadline: n/av	COMPETITIVE

Belmont Abbey College, founded in 1876, is a private, liberal arts college affiliated with the Roman Catholic Church. Figures in the above capsule and in this profile are approximate. In addition to regional accreditation, Belmont Abbey has baccalaureate program accreditation with NCATE. The 650-acre campus is in a suburban area 12 miles southwest of Charlotte. Including any residence halls, there are 20 buildings.

STUDENT LIFE: 70% of undergraduates are from North Carolina. Others are from 43 states, 24 foreign countries, and Canada. 35% are White; 31% race unknown; 27% African American. 57% are Catholic; 47% claim no religious affiliation. The average age of freshmen is 20; all undergraduates, 28. 37% do not continue beyond their first year; 63% remain to graduate. **Housing:** 747 students can be accommodated in college housing, which includes single-sex and coed dorms, on-campus apartments, and off-campus apartments. In addition, there are special-interest houses, and a quiet residence hall. Single-occupancy housing is available for all students. On-campus housing is guaranteed for all 4 years. 57% of students commute. All students may keep cars.

FACULTY/CLASSROOMS: 55% of faculty are male; 45% are female. All teach undergraduates. No introductory courses are taught by graduate students. The average class size in an introductory lecture is 16; in a laboratory is 15; and in a regular course is 4.

PROGRAMS OF STUDY: Belmont Abbey confers B.A., and B.S. degrees. Bachelor's degrees are awarded in BIOLOGICAL SCIENCE (biology/biological science), BUSINESS (accounting, business administration and management, and sports management), COMMUNICATIONS AND THE ARTS (English), COMPUTER AND PHYSICAL SCIENCE (mathematics), EDUCATION (education and elementary education), SOCIAL SCIENCE (applied psychology, criminal justice, history, liberal arts/general studies, parks and recreation management, philosophy, political science/government, psychology, and theological studies). Psychology, elementary education, and English are the strongest academically. Business administration, education, and elementary education have the largest enrollments.

ACTIVITIES: 6% of men belong to 1 local and 2 national fraternities; 5% of women belong to 4 local sororities. There are 21 groups on campus, including cheerleading, chess, choir, chorus, computers, drama, honors, international, literary magazine, newspaper, political, professional, religious, social, social service, and student government. Popular campus events include Spring Weekend, Special Olympics and Greek Week. **Sports:** There are 8 intercollegiate sports for men and 8 for women. Facilities include a phys ed center with a 1200-seat gym and a college union with a 225-seat auditorium. **Graduates:** From July 1, 2013 to June 30, 2014, 379 bachelor's degrees were awarded. The most popular majors were business management (39%), education (15%), and elementary education (13%). 90 companies recruited on campus in 2013-2014. In an average class, 40% graduate in 4 years or less, 45% graduate in 5 years or less, and 46% graduate in 6 years or less. Of the 2013 graduating class, 16% were enrolled in graduate school within 6 months of graduation, and 88% were employed.

SERVICES: Counseling and information services are available, as is tutoring in some subjects, Math, English, and accounting. There is a reader service for the blind. **Library/Resources:** The library contains 118,827 volumes, 116,173 microform items, 7,418 audio/video tapes/CDs/DVDs, and subscribes to 275 periodicals including electronic. Computerized library services include interlibrary loans, database searching, Internet access, and Wi-Fi capability. **Physically Challenged Students:** 60% of the campus is accessible. Facilities include wheelchair ramps, elevators, special parking, specially equipped restrooms, special class scheduling, and lowered drinking fountains. **Special:** Cross-registration is offered through the Charlotte Area Educational Consortium. There are internships in many majors, including required internships in educational studies, as well as on-campus work-study, accelerated degree programs, nondegree study, dual majors, and study abroad in Guatemala, Germany, and France. There are 5 national honor societies and a freshman honors program. **Visiting:** There are regularly scheduled orientations for prospective students, consisting of a campus tour and meetings with a financial aid adviser, faculty, and students. There are guides for informal visits, visitors may sit in on classes, and stay overnight. To schedule a visit, contact the Admissions Office. **Campus Safety and Security:** Measures include 24-hour foot and vehicle patrol, self-defense education, and security escort services. There are emergency telephones and lighted pathways/sidewalks.

REQUIREMENTS: The SAT is required. Candidates must be graduates of an accredited secondary school and a 2.0 high school GPA. A minimum of 16 academic credits must be completed, including 4 in English, 3 each in math and electives, and 2 each in foreign language, history, and science. AP and CLEP credits are accepted. Important factors in the admissions decision are advanced placement or honors courses, extracurricular activities record, and leadership record. To graduate, all students must complete a minimum of 120 credits, including 60 credits of core curriculum and 30 upper-level credits in the major. Among the core requirements are history, math, natural sciences, theology, philosophy, English, fine arts, and rhetoric. A minimum 2.0 GPA must be maintained. Honors students must submit a thesis. **Procedure:** Freshmen are admitted fall and spring. Entrance exams should be taken by October of the senior year. There are deferred admissions and rolling admissions plans. Check with the school for current application deadlines. The application fee is $35. Applications are accepted on-line. **Transfer Students:** 185 transfer students enrolled in 2013-2014. Students with 24 or more credit hours must submit all college transcripts, and those with fewer than 24 credit hours must also submit a high school transcript and SAT scores. All candidates must have a minimum 2.0 GPA and be eligible to return to the last college attended. An interview is recommended. 30 of 120 credits required for the bachelor's degree must be completed at Belmont Abbey. **International Students:** There are 46 international students enrolled. The school actively recruits these students. They must take the TOEFL with a minimum score of 550 on the paper-based TOEFL (PBT) or 79 on the Internet-based version (iBT). They must also take the SAT or ACT, scoring 900.

ADMISSIONS: 64% of the 2014-2015 applicants were accepted. The SAT scores for the 2014-2015 freshman class were: Critical Reading--54% below 500, 29% between 500 and 599, 13% between 600 and 699, and 3% between 700 and 800; Math--42% below 500, 39% between 500 and 599, 17% between 600 and 699, and 2% between 700 and 800. The ACT scores were 27% below 21, 33% between 21 and 23, 28% between 24 and 26, 4% between 27 and 28, and 7% above 28. 20% of the current freshmen were in the top fifth of their class; 46% were in the top two fifths. 3 freshmen graduated first in their class. **Admissions Contact:** Roger Jones, Director of Admissions. E-Mail: *RogerJones@BAC.edu* Web: *www.belmontabbeycollege.edu*

FINANCIAL AID: In 2014-2015, 98% of all full-time freshmen and 94% of continuing full-time students received some form of financial aid. 72% of all full-time freshmen and 79% of continuing full-time students received need-based aid. The average freshman award was $20,296. Need-based scholarships or need-based grants averaged $17,293 ($20,000 maximum); need-based self-help aid (loans and jobs) averaged $4,023 ($125,800 maximum); non-need-based athletic scholarships averaged $5,053 ($21,000 maximum); and other non-need-based awards and non-need-based scholarships averaged $2,156 ($10,500 maximum). 12% of undergraduate students work part-time. Average annual earnings from campus work are $1800. The average financial indebtedness of the 2014 graduate was $19,516. Belmont Abbey is a member of CSS. The FAFSA and the state aid form are required. The priority date for freshman financial aid applications for fall entry is April 1. The deadline for filing freshman financial aid applications for fall entry is July 1.

BENNETT COLLEGE FOR WOMEN (*The complete profile is made available exclusively on our website, www.barronspac.com*)

CABARRUS COLLEGE OF HEALTH SCIENCES (*The complete profile is made available exclusively on our website, www.barronspac.com*)

CAMPBELL UNIVERSITY E-3
www.campbell.edu

Buies Creek, NC 27506	(910) 893-1200
	(800) 334-4111
Fax: (910) 893-1288	Email: admissions@campbell.edu
Full-time: n/av	Faculty: n/av
Part-time: n/av	Ph.D.s: 92%
Graduate: n/av	Student/Faculty: n/av
Year: semesters, summer session	Tuition: $27,670
Room & Board: $9860	Freshman Class: n/av
SAT or ACT: required	CEEB CODE: 5100
Application Deadline: n/av	**VERY COMPETITIVE**

Campbell University, founded in 1887, is a private, nonsectarian institution offering degree programs in liberal arts and sciences, business, and education. There are 7 undergraduate schools and 6 graduate schools. In addition to regional accreditation, Campbell has baccalaureate program accreditation with ACPE, CSWE, and NCATE. The 1300-acre campus is in a rural area 28 miles south of Raleigh and 30 miles north of Fayetteville. Including any residence halls, there are 84 buildings.

STUDENT LIFE: Students are from 50 states, 42 foreign countries, and Canada. 90% are from public schools. The average age of freshmen is 18; all undergraduates, 20. **Housing:** 2000 students can be accommodated in college housing, which includes single-sex dorms and on-campus apartments. In addition, there are fraternity houses. On-campus housing is guaranteed for all 4 years. Alcohol is not permitted. All students may keep cars.

FACULTY/CLASSROOMS: No introductory courses are taught by graduate students.

PROGRAMS OF STUDY: Campbell confers B.A., B.S., B.Applied Science., B.B.A., B.H.S. and B.S.W. degrees. Associate, Master's, and Doctoral degrees are also awarded. Bachelor's degrees are awarded in BIOLOGICAL SCIENCE (biochemistry and biology/biological science), BUSINESS (accounting, accounting/CPA, banking and finance, business administration and management, business administration - international, business administration, operations, business administration marketing, business economics, international business, international business management, investments and securities, and sports management), COMMUNICATIONS AND THE ARTS (advertising, art, choral music, church music, communications, English, fine arts, French, graphic design, information technology, journalism, music, Spanish, studio art, studio art graphic design, and theatre arts), COMPUTER AND PHYSICAL SCIENCE (chemistry, computer information technology, computer information systems, computer science, information sciences and systems, and mathematics), EDUCATION (athletic training, (Education) Childhood Education, childhood education: 1-6, early childhood education, education, elementary education, English education, and middle school education), ENGINEERING AND ENVIRONMENTAL DESIGN (military science), HEALTH PROFESSIONS (biology, clinical science, exercise science, health communication, health care administration, nursing, predentistry, premedicine, preoptometry, and prepharmacy), SOCIAL SCIENCE (administration of justice, counseling/psychology, criminal justice, economics, history, homeland security, physical fitness/movement, political science/government, prelaw, psychology, religion, and social work). Health science, trust management (business), education, are the strongest academically. Education, pharmacy, biology and business have the largest enrollments.

ACTIVITIES: There are 50 groups on campus, including art, band, cheerleading, choir, chorale, chorus, computers, debate, drama, ethnic, honors, international, jazz band, literary magazine, musical theater, newspaper, orchestra, pep band, photography, political, professional, religious, social, social service, student government, and yearbook. Popular campus events include Staley Lecture Series, Spring Fling,Christmas Formals, Concerts, Plays, Homecoming, and Parents Weekend. **Sports:** Facilities include a 1000-seat gym for intramural sports, 3100 seat gymnasium for Division Sports, football field, athletic complex, 27 hole golf course, a nature trail, NCAA track, 3 workout facilities, tennis courts, baseball, softball, and soccer fields, and an indoor pool. **Graduates:** From July 1, 2013 to June 30, 2014, 932 bachelor's degrees were awarded. The most popular majors were history (4%) and business administration (17%). 14 companies recruited on campus in 2013-2014. In an average class, 31% graduate in 4 years or less, 49% graduate in 5 years or less, and 51% graduate in 6 years or less. Of the 2013 graduating class, 16% were enrolled in graduate school within 6 months of graduation, and 67% were employed.

SERVICES: Counseling and information services are available, as is tutoring in most subjects. There is remedial math and writing. **Library/Resources:** The 2 libraries contain 332,000 volumes, 1,253 microform items, 5,033 audio/video tapes/CDs/DVDs, and subscribe to 15,665 periodicals including electronic. Computerized library services include interlibrary loans, database searching, Internet access, and Wi-Fi capability. Special learning facilities include an art gallery, computer labs, computerized music lab, athletic learning resources center, drug information center for the school of pharmacy, pharmacy research facility, and the Lundy-Fetterman animal museum. **Physically Challenged Students:** 95% of the campus is accessible. Facilities include wheelchair ramps, elevators, special parking, specially equipped restrooms, special class scheduling, lowered drinking fountains, lowered telephones, and special housing. **Special:** Campbell offers co-op programs, internships, study abroad in 7 countries, a Washington semester, numerous apprenticeships, accelerated degrees, dual majors, and a general studies degree. There is credit for military and work experience. Cross-registration with the North Carolina Model Teacher Education Consortium is possible. There are 14 national honor societies, including Phi Beta Kappa, and a freshman honors program. **Visiting:** There are regularly scheduled orientations for prospective students, including a campus tour, student panel and department visits. There are guides for informal visits, visitors may sit in on classes, and stay overnight. To schedule a visit, contact the Admissions Office. **Campus Safety and Security:** Measures include 24-hour foot and vehicle patrol, emergency notification system, self-defense education, and security escort services. There are emergency telephones, lighted pathways/sidewalks, and controlled access to dorms/residences.

REQUIREMENTS: The SAT or ACT is required. Applicants should have completed 12 high school academic credits, including 4 credits of English, 3 of math, and 2 each of history or social studies, science, and foreign language. An essay, an interview, and a portfolio are recommended. An audition is required for some majors. A GPA of 2.7 is required. AP and CLEP credits are accepted. Important factors in the admissions decision are advanced placement or honors courses, leadership record, and personality/intangible qualities.To graduate, students must complete 124 credit hours with a minimum GPA of 2.0 overall and in the major. All students must take a core curriculum of 45 to 65 hours including English, math, science, social science, religion, fine arts, phys ed, and the cultural enrichment program. **Procedure:** Freshmen are admitted to all sessions. Entrance exams should

be taken during the junior year or the fall of the senior year. There are deferred admissions and rolling admissions plans. Application deadlines are open. Applications are accepted on-line. **Transfer Students:** Applicants should have a minimum GPA of 2.5 and supply transcripts from previously attended colleges. 36 of 124 credits required for the bachelor's degree must be completed at Campbell. **International Students:** There are 153 international students enrolled. The school actively recruits these students. They must take the TOEFL with a minimum score of 500 on the paper-based TOEFL (PBT) or 63 on the Internet-based version (iBT). They must also take the SAT or ACT.

ADMISSIONS: 30 freshmen graduated first in their class. **Admissions Contact:** Jason Hall, Assistant Vice President for Admissions. Web: www.campbell.edu

FINANCIAL AID: The FAFSA is required. Check with the school for current application deadlines.

CATAWBA COLLEGE (*The complete profile is made available exclusively on our website, www.barronspac.com*)

DAVIDSON COLLEGE   C-3
www.davidson.edu

Davidson, NC 28035	(704) 894-2000
	(800) 768-0380
Fax: (704) 894-2016	Email: admission@davidson.edu
Full-time: 875 men, 895 women	Faculty: 178; IIB, +$
Part-time: n/av	Ph.D.s: 97%
Graduate: n/av	Student/Faculty: 10 to 1
Year: semesters	Tuition: $45,377
Room & Board: $12,769	Freshman Class: 5560 applied, 1205 accepted, 502 enrolled
SAT CR/M/W: 660/670/670 ACT: 31	CEEB CODE: 5150
Application Deadline: January 2	MOST COMPETITIVE

Davidson College, founded in 1837, is a private liberal arts institution affiliated with the Presbyterian Church. Figures in the above capsule and in this profile are approximate. There is one undergraduate school. In addition to regional accreditation, Davidson has baccalaureate program accreditation with NCATE and ACS. The 665-acre campus is in a small town 19 miles north of Charlotte. Including any residence halls, there are 124 buildings.

STUDENT LIFE: 78% of undergraduates are from out of state, mostly the South. Students are from 48 states, 39 foreign countries, and Canada. 50% are from public schools. 69% are White. The average age of freshmen is 18; all undergraduates, 20. 4% do not continue beyond their first year; 95% remain to graduate. **Housing:** 1758 students can be accommodated in college housing, which includes single-sex and coed dorms, on-campus apartments, and off-campus apartments. In addition, there are special-interest houses, substance-free housing. On-campus housing is guaranteed for the freshman year only and is available on a lottery system for upperclassmen. 93% of students live on campus. All students may keep cars.

FACULTY/CLASSROOMS: 58% of faculty are male; 42% are female. All teach and do research. No introductory courses are taught by graduate students. The average class size in an introductory lecture is 15; in a laboratory is 11; and in a regular course is 15.

PROGRAMS OF STUDY: Davidson confers A.B., and B.S. degrees. Bachelor's degrees are awarded in AGRICULTURE (environmental studies), BIOLOGICAL SCIENCE (biology/biological science), COMMUNICATIONS AND THE ARTS (art, Chinese, classics, dramatic arts, English, French, German, music, and Spanish), COMPUTER AND PHYSICAL SCIENCE (chemistry, mathematics, and physics), SOCIAL SCIENCE (africana studies, anthropology, East Asian studies, economics, gender studies, history, interdisciplinary studies, Latin American studies, philosophy, political science/ government, psychology, religion, and sociology). Biology, economics, and political science have the largest enrollments.

ACTIVITIES: 32% of men belong to 6 national fraternities; 2% of women belong to 4 local and 2 national sororities. There are 200

groups on campus, including art, cheerleading, choir, chorale, chorus, computers, dance, drama, ethnic, gay, honors, international, jazz band, literary magazine, musical theater, newspaper, opera, orchestra, outing, pep band, political, professional, radio and TV, religious, social, social service, student government, symphony, and yearbook. Popular campus events include Fall Concert, Spring Concert, and Convocations. **Sports:** There are 11 intercollegiate sports for men and 10 for women. Facilities include John M. Belk basketball arena, Wilson baseball field, indoor and outdoor tennis courts, 3 racquetball courts, a squash court, a natatorium with a diving well, 2 Nautilus rooms, a gym, wrestling room, dance studio, golf course, cross-country course and trail, a football and soccer stadium, various other playing fields, and facilities for sailing, swimming, water skiing, and canoeing at the Lake campus. **Graduates:** From July 1, 2013 to June 30, 2014, 465 bachelor's degrees were awarded. The most popular majors were political science (13%), economics (11%), and biology (10%). 688 companies recruited on campus in 2013-2014. In an average class, 90% graduate in 4 years or less, 92% graduate in 5 years or less, and 93% graduate in 6 years or less. Of the 2013 graduating class, 21% were enrolled in graduate school within 6 months of graduation, and 69% were employed.

SERVICES: Counseling and information services are available, as is tutoring in some subjects, tutoring is available as needed through the Student Affairs Office. There is a reader service for the blind. Center for Teaching and Learning also provides student support. **Library/Resources:** The 3 libraries contain 561,427 volumes, 601,821 microform items, 17,878 audio/video tapes/CDs/DVDs, and subscribe to 108,090 periodicals including electronic. Computerized library services include interlibrary loans, database searching, Internet access, and Wi-Fi capability. Special learning facilities include an art gallery, radio station, arboretum. **Physically Challenged Students:** 90% of the campus is accessible. Facilities include wheelchair ramps, elevators, special parking, specially equipped restrooms, special class scheduling, lowered drinking fountains, and lowered telephones. **Special:** Davidson offers interdisciplinary international and South Asian studies programs and study abroad in 12 countries as well as through other schools' study-abroad programs. A 3-2 engineering program may be arranged with Georgia Institute of Technology and Columbia, Duke, North Carolina State, and Washington (St. Louis) Universities. Students may design their own majors and cross-register with any college in the Charlotte Area Educational Consortium. There are 15 national honor societies, including Phi Beta Kappa, and 20 departmental honors programs. **Visiting:** There are guides for informal visits, visitors may sit in on classes, and stay overnight. To schedule a visit, contact the Office of Admission. **Campus Safety and Security:** Measures include 24-hour foot and vehicle patrol, emergency notification system, self-defense education, and security escort services. There are shuttle buses, emergency telephones, lighted pathways/sidewalks, and controlled access to dorms/residences.

REQUIREMENTS: The SAT or ACT is required. SAT Subject Tests are strongly recommended. At least 16 high school units are required, although 20 units are recommended. These should include 4 units of English, 3 units of math, 2 units of the same foreign language, 2 units of science, and 2 units of history/social studies. It is strongly recommended that high school students continue for the third and fourth years in science and in the same foreign language, continue math through calculus, and take additional courses in history. AP credits are accepted. Important factors in the admissions decision are advanced placement or honors courses, recommendations by school officials, and leadership record. Students must complete 32 courses, including 10 to 12 in the major, with a 2.0 GPA in order to graduate. Core curriculum requirements include courses in literature, fine arts, history, religion and philosophy, natural science, math, and social sciences. In addition, students must meet foreign language, composition, cultural diversity, and phys ed requirements. Comprehensive exams and a thesis are required in some majors. **Procedure:** Freshmen are admitted fall. Entrance exams should be taken by the end of the junior year. There are early decision and deferred admissions plans. Early decision applications should be filed by November 15; regular applications, by January 2 for fall entry. The fall 2014 application fee was $50. Notification of early decision is sent December 15; regular decision, April 1. 276 early decision candidates were accepted for the 2014-2015 class. Applications are accepted on-line. **Transfer**

Students: 11 transfer students enrolled in 2013-2014. Applicants must have at least 1 full year of college work, generally with a 3.0 GPA. They must submit official college and high school transcripts, as well as required letters of recommendation, and be in good standing at their previous college. 16 of 32 credits required for the bachelor's degree must be completed at Davidson. **International Students:** There are 104 international students enrolled. The school actively recruits these students. They must take the TOEFL with a minimum score of 600 on the paper-based TOEFL (PBT) or 100 on the Internet-based version (iBT). They must also take the SAT or ACT.

ADMISSIONS: 22% of the 2014-2015 applicants were accepted. The SAT scores for the 2014-2015 freshman class were: Critical Reading--2% below 500, 16% between 500 and 599, 49% between 600 and 699, and 33% between 700 and 800; Math--1% below 500, 14% between 500 and 599, 50% between 600 and 699, and 36% between 700 and 800; Writing--3% below 500, 13% between 500 and 599, 49% between 600 and 699, and 35% between 700 and 800. The ACT scores were 1% between 21 and 23, 13% between 24 and 26, 15% between 27 and 28, and 71% above 28. 81% of the current freshmen were in the top fifth of their class; 96% were in the top two fifths. **Admissions Contact:** Christopher J. Gruber, Dean of Admission and Financial Aid. E-Mail: *admission@davidson.edu* Web: *www.davidson.edu*

FINANCIAL AID: In 2014-2015, 45% of all full-time freshmen and continuing full-time students received some form of financial aid. 44% of all full-time freshmen and continuing full-time students received need-based aid. The average freshman award was $36,168. Need-based scholarships or need-based grants averaged $33,367; need-based self-help aid (loans and jobs) averaged $2,801; non-need-based athletic scholarships averaged $17,219; and other non-need-based awards and non-need-based scholarships averaged $18,347. 45% of undergraduate students work part-time. The CSS/Profile, FAFSA, and the college's own financial statement, and Noncustodial (Divorced/Separated) Parent's Statement; corporate tax return and/or noncustodial parent tax return (if app are required. The deadline for filing freshman financial aid applications for fall entry is February 15.

DUKE UNIVERSITY   D-2
www.duke.edu

Durham, NC 27706

(919) 684-8111
(919) 668-1661

Fax: (919) 681-8941   Email: undergrad-admissions@duke.edu

Full-time: 3270 men, 2980 women	Faculty: I, ++$
Part-time: 10 men, 10 women	Ph.D.s: 97%
Graduate: 3845 men, 3375 women	Student/Faculty: n/av
Year: semesters, summer session	Tuition: $39,080
Room & Board: $11,170	Freshman Class: n/av
SAT or ACT: required	CEEB CODE: 5156
Application Deadline: n/av	**MOST COMPETITIVE**

Duke University, founded in 1838, is a private institution affiliated with the United Methodist Church and offering undergraduate programs in arts and sciences and engineering. The figures in the above capsule and in this profile are approximate. There are 2 undergraduate schools and 8 graduate schools. In addition to regional accreditation, Duke has baccalaureate program accreditation with AACSB, ABET, ACPE, AHEA, APTA, NCATE, NLN, and SAF. The 9727-acre campus is in a suburban area 285 miles southwest of Washington, D.C. Including any residence halls, there are 208 buildings.

STUDENT LIFE: 86% of undergraduates are from out of state, mostly the South. Students are from 50 states, 55 foreign countries, and Canada. 60% are from public schools. 56% are White; 14% Asian American. 37% are Protestant; 23% Catholic; 16% claim no religious affiliation. The average age of freshmen is 18; all undergraduates, 20. 4% do not continue beyond their first year; 94% remain to graduate. **Housing:** 5481 students can be accommodated in college housing, which includes single-sex and coed dorms, on-campus apartments, and married student housing. In addition, there are language houses, special-interest houses, Theme houses in women's studies, the arts, and community service (APO). On-campus housing is guaranteed for all 4 years. 82% of students live on campus. All students may keep cars.

FACULTY/CLASSROOMS: 76% of faculty are male; 24% are female. All teach and do research. Graduate students teach 2% of introductory courses. The average class size in an introductory lecture is 39; in a laboratory is 246; and in a regular course is 21.

PROGRAMS OF STUDY: Duke confers B.S., A.B. and B.S.E. degrees. Master's and doctoral degrees are also awarded. Bachelor's degrees are awarded in BIOLOGICAL SCIENCE (anatomy and biology/biological science), COMMUNICATIONS AND THE ARTS (African languages, art history and appreciation, classical languages, dramatic arts, English, Germanic languages and literature, linguistics, literature, music, Slavic languages, Spanish, and visual and performing arts), COMPUTER AND PHYSICAL SCIENCE (chemistry, computer science, geology, mathematics, and physics), ENGINEERING AND ENVIRONMENTAL DESIGN (biomedical engineering, civil engineering, electrical/electronics engineering, environmental science, materials science, and mechanical engineering), SOCIAL SCIENCE (African studies, African American studies, anthropology, area studies, Asian/Oriental studies, Canadian studies, classical/ancient civilization, economics, French studies, history, Italian studies, medieval studies, philosophy, political science/government, psychology, public affairs, religion, sociology, and women's studies). Public policy studies, political science, and economics are the strongest academically. Biology, psychology, and history have the largest enrollments.

ACTIVITIES: 29% of men belong to 17 national fraternities; 42% of women belong to 10 national sororities. There are 400 groups on campus, including art, band, cheerleading, chess, choir, chorale, chorus, computers, dance, debate, drama, drill team, ethnic, film, gay, honors, international, jazz band, literary magazine, marching band, musical theater, newspaper, opera, orchestra, pep band, photography, political, professional, radio and TV, religious, social, social service, student government, and symphony. Popular campus events include College Bowl, Oktoberfest, and Springfest. **Sports:** There are 12 intercollegiate sports for men and 11 for women, and 21 intramural sports for men and 19 for women. Facilities include stadiums for baseball, basketball/volleyball, football, and soccer/lacrosse; squash, racquetball, and tennis courts; an aquatic center; training and weight rooms; a golf course; cross-country and jogging trails; and practice and intramural sport club fields. The largest stadium seats 33,941; the largest arena, seats 8564.

SERVICES: Counseling and information services are available, as is tutoring in every subject. There is a reader service for the blind. **Library/Resources:** The 9 libraries contain 5.5 million volumes, 4.2 million microform items, 61,281 audio/video tapes/CDs/DVDs, and subscribe to 33,934 periodicals including electronic. Computerized library services include interlibrary loans, database searching, and Internet access. Special learning facilities include an art gallery, radio station, TV station, marine lab at Beaufort; primate center; center for international studies; nuclear lab; free electron laser; science research center; institutes of the arts, statistics and decision sciences, policy sciences and public affairs; and centers for teaching and learning, community service, geometric computing, culture, and women. **Physically Challenged Students:** Facilities include wheelchair ramps, elevators, special parking, specially equipped restrooms, special class scheduling, lowered drinking fountains, lowered telephones, special housing. In addition, activities such as concerts can be moved to accessible facilities upon request. **Special:** Duke offers cross-registration with the University of North Carolina/Chapel Hill and North Carolina State and North Carolina Central Universities. Also available are internships through the Career Development Center, study abroad in 36 countries, and a Washington semester. An accelerated degree program is possible, achieving graduation in 3 years or combining the senior year with the first graduate year of the law, business, or environment schools. Several 3-2 and 4-1 medical technology programs (degree completed at Duke) are available. Project Calc, an innovative program in calculus, is also offered. Dual majors of any combination, student-designed majors, nondegree study, and pass/fail options are possible. There are 4 national honor societies, including Phi Beta Kappa, and 38 departmental honors programs. **Visiting:** There are regularly scheduled orientations for prospective students, including student-led tours, counselor-led group information sessions, class visits, and lunch with students. There are guides for informal visits, visitors may sit in on classes, and stay overnight. To schedule a visit, contact the Undergraduate Admissions. **Campus Safety and Security:** Measures include 24-hour foot and vehicle patrol, self-defense education, and security escort services. There are shuttle buses, emergency telephones, lighted pathways/sidewalks, and a crime prevention program.

REQUIREMENTS: The SAT or ACT is required. The ACT Optional Writing test is also required. 3 SAT: Subject tests, including writing, are required. Applicants must be graduates of an accredited secondary school and have completed 15 academic credits, with 4 in English and 3 each in math, science, and foreign language; an additional 2 in social studies or history are recommended. Engineering students must have 4 credit units in math and 1 in physics or chemistry. An essay is required and an interview is recommended. A portfolio or audition is advised in appropriate instances. AP credits are accepted. Important factors in the admissions decision are advanced placement or honors courses, recommendations by school officials, and extracurricular activities record. A minimum of 34 course credits is required for graduation including natural sciences, quantitative reasoning, and social sciences. No more than 17 course credits are allowed in a major for the B.A. and no more than 19 for the B.S. At least 12 courses must be at or above the 100 level. At least 3 courses designated as seminars, tutorials, independent study, or thesis completion are required. Computer proficiency must be demonstrated by engineering students. **Procedure:** Freshmen are admitted fall and spring. Entrance exams should be taken in October of the junior year for early decision applicants and by January of the senior year for regular decision. There are early decision, early admissions, and deferred admissions plans. Check with the school for current application deadlines. The application fee is $75. **Transfer Students:** A minimum 3.6 GPA is recommended. The SAT and 3 SAT: Subject tests or the ACT are required. 17 of 34 credits required for the bachelor's degree must be completed at Duke. **International Students:** The school actively recruits these students. They must also take the SAT or ACT.

ADMISSIONS: Christoph Guttentag, Director of Undergraduate Admissions. E-Mail: *askduke@admiss.duke.edu* Web: *www.duke.edu*

FINANCIAL AID: The CSS/Profile and FAFSA are required. Check with the school for current application deadlines.

EAST CAROLINA UNIVERSITY E-2
www.ecu.edu

Greenville, NC 27858

(252) 328-6131
(252) 328-6640

Fax: (252) 737-1192

Email: admis@ecu.edu

Full-time: 7637 men, 10680 women
Part-time: 1114 men, 1867 women
Graduate: 1981 men, 3668 women
Year: semesters, summer session
Room & Board: $8300

Faculty: I, --$
Ph.D.s: 81%
Student/Faculty: 18 to 1
Tuition: $5869 ($19,683)
Freshman Class: 15535 applied, 9658 accepted, 4015 enrolled

SAT CR/M/W: 510/540/490 **ACT:** 22
Application Deadline: March 15

CEEB CODE: 5180
COMPETITIVE

East Carolina University, founded in 1907, is a state-supported institution offering degree programs in the arts and sciences, business, education, fine arts and communication, health and human performance, human ecology, technology and computer science, medicine, allied health sciences, and nursing. The figures in the above capsule and in this profile are approximate. There are 11 undergraduate schools and 1 graduate school. In addition to regional accreditation, ECU has baccalaureate program accreditation with AACSB, ACCE, ADA, APTA, CSWE, FIDER, NASAD, NASM, NCATE, NLN, and NRPA. The 1401-acre campus is in an urban area 90 miles east of Raleigh. Including any residence halls, there are 239 buildings.

STUDENT LIFE: 88% of undergraduates are from North Carolina. Others are from 42 states, 54 foreign countries, and Canada. 80% are White; 16% African American. The average age of freshmen is 18; all undergraduates, 23. 22% do not continue beyond their first year; 58% remain to graduate. **Housing:** 5497 students can be accommodated in college housing, which includes single-sex and coed dorms. In addition, there are honors houses, fraternity houses, sorority houses, first-year students' floor, a leadership hall, an extended-quiet-hours floor, substance-free hall, nonsmoking floor, and an academic-year hall. On-campus housing is guaranteed for the freshman year only, is available on a first-come, and first-served basis. 76% of students commute. Alcohol is not permitted. All students may keep cars.

FACULTY/CLASSROOMS: 48% of faculty are male; 52% are female. No introductory courses are taught by graduate students. The average class size in an introductory lecture is 42; in a laboratory is 26; and in a regular course is 35.

PROGRAMS OF STUDY: ECU confers B.A., B.S., B.F.A., B.M., B.S.A., B.S.A.P., B.S.B.A., B.S.B.E., B.S.N. and B.S.W. degrees. Master's and Doctoral degrees are also awarded. Bachelor's degrees are awarded in BIOLOGICAL SCIENCE (biochemistry, biology/biological science, and nutrition), BUSINESS (accounting, banking and finance, business administration and management, hospitality management services, management information systems, marketing management, marketing/retailing/merchandising, and recreational facilities management), COMMUNICATIONS AND THE ARTS (art, art history and appreciation, communications, dance, design, dramatic arts, English, French, German, music performance, music theory and composition, speech/debate/rhetoric, and studio art), COMPUTER AND PHYSICAL SCIENCE (applied physics, atmospheric sciences and meteorology, chemistry, computer science, geology, information sciences and systems, mathematics, and physics), EDUCATION (art education, athletic training, business education, dance education, drama education, early childhood education, education of the emotionally handicapped, education of the mentally handicapped, elementary education, English education, foreign languages education, health education, home economics education, marketing and distribution education, mathematics education, middle school education, music education, physical education, science education, social studies education, and special education), ENGINEERING AND ENVIRONMENTAL DESIGN (city/community/regional planning, construction management, electrical/electronics engineering technology, engineering, environmental engineering technology, industrial engineering technology, and interior design), HEALTH PROFESSIONS (environmental health science, exercise science, health care administration, medical records administration/services, medical technology, music therapy, nursing, occupational therapy, public health, recreation therapy, rehabilitation therapy, and speech pathology/audiology), SOCIAL SCIENCE (African American studies, anthropology, applied social science, child care/child and family studies, clothing and textiles management/production/services, criminal justice, dietetics, economics, family and community services, geography, Hispanic American studies, history, liberal arts/general studies, parks and recreation management, philosophy, physical fitness/movement, political science/government, psychology, public history/archives, social work, sociology, and women's studies). Allied health, art, and music are the strongest academically. Elementary education, management, and communication have the largest enrollments.

ACTIVITIES: 9% of men belong to 24 national fraternities; 8% of women belong to 14 national sororities. There are 399 groups on campus, including recreation, military, academic, art, band, cheerleading, choir, chorale, chorus, communications, computers, dance, drama, drill team, environmental, ethnic, gay, honors, international, jazz band, literary magazine, marching band, musical theater, newspaper, opera, orchestra, pep band, photography, political, professional, radio and TV, religious, social, social service, student government, symphony, and yearbook. Popular campus events include Barefoot on the Mall, Midnight Madness and Pirate Palooza. **Sports:** There are 9 intercollegiate sports for men and 9 for women, and 14 intramural sports for men and 14 for women. Facilities include a 43,000-seat stadium, an 8,000-seat basketball coliseum, a baseball and softball field, a track, and a natatorium. The Student Recreation Center is 150,000 square feet, and includes a 6-court multipurpose sports area (basketball courts), a 2 cardiovascular rooms and a weight lifting/training area, 3 exercise studios, indoor and outdoor pools, an indoor track, 30-ft. climbing wall, 7 racquetball courts, wellness center, and a fitness assessment center. The Blount Recreational Sports Complex includes 10 football/soccer fields, 5 softball

fields, ropes challenge course, and a 50-foot Alpine climbing tower. The 129-acre North Recreational Complex has completed Phases I & II (of III), which include: 8 multi-use soccer/rugby/football etc. fields, an 18-hole disc golf course, field house, boathouse, lake and beach area, shade structures, Odyssey team training course, fitness area, sand volleyball courts, grills, walk/jog paths and a maintenance office/storage area. Underway are plans with Construction Management to develop a 6-10 acre experiential large equipment lab. **Graduates:** From July 1, 2013 to June 30, 2014, 4315 bachelor's degrees were awarded. The most popular majors were nursing (7%), communication (7%), and elementary education (6%). In an average class, 33% graduate in 4 years or less, 53% graduate in 5 years or less, and 58% graduate in 6 years or less.

SERVICES: Counseling and information services are available, as is tutoring in most subjects. There is a reader service for the blind, and remedial math and reading. Tutoring is established on a department by department basis. Several learning centers and labs have a established hours of operation, of arrangements can be made by appointment. **Library/Resources:** The 2 libraries contain 2.4 million volumes, 1.2 million microform items, 69,251 audio/video tapes/CDs/DVDs, and subscribe to 73,498 periodicals including electronic. Computerized library services include interlibrary loans, database searching, and Wi-Fi capability. Special learning facilities include an art gallery and radio station. **Physically Challenged Students:** 95% of the campus is accessible. Facilities include wheelchair ramps, elevators, special parking, specially equipped restrooms, special class scheduling, lowered drinking fountains, lowered telephones. Automatic doors and state-of-the art adaptive equipment. **Special:** ECU offers cooperative programs in most majors, internships, study abroad in 42 countries, a Washington semester, accelerated degrees, a B.A.-B.S. in accounting, dual majors, work-study, and a student-designed major in multidisciplinary studies. There are 18 national honor societies, including Phi Beta Kappa, a freshman honors program, and 39 departmental honors programs. **Visiting:** There are regularly scheduled orientations for prospective students, including information sessions and campus tours. There are guides for informal visits. To schedule a visit, contact the Admissions Office. **Campus Safety and Security:** Measures include 24-hour foot and vehicle patrol, emergency notification system, self-defense education, and security escort services. There are shuttle buses, emergency telephones, lighted pathways/sidewalks, controlled access to dorms/residences, residence hall doors locked, bicycle patrols, bicycle registration, motorist assistance lost and found, operation ID, the residence hall liason officer program, on-and off campus crime prevention safety tips, staff and faculty eyes, campus community watch program, and alcohol awareness.

REQUIREMENTS: The SAT or ACT is required. The ACT Optional Writing test is also required. Applicants must be graduates of an accredited secondary school. All degree-seeking students are required to complete 20 academic units, including 4 in English, 4 in math, 3 in science with 1 lab course, 2 in social studies with 1 in U.S. history, 2 units in a foreign language, and 1 unit in fine arts is recommended. Special circumstances exist for applicants with a GED. AP and CLEP credits are accepted. To graduate, students must complete 120 to 128 semester hours with a minimum GPA of 2.0 overall and in the major. General education requirements include 12 hours of social science, 10 of humanities and fine arts, 8 of science, 6 of English, 3 of math, and 3 of health and exercise and sport science. The total must include 12 hours of writing-intensive courses and a course in cultural diversity. **Procedure:** Freshmen are admitted to all sessions. Entrance exams should be taken in the spring of the junior year or the fall of the senior year. There are deferred admissions and rolling admissions plans. Applications should be filed by March 15 for fall entry; November 1 for spring entry; and March 15 for summer entry, along with a $70 fee. Notifications are sent April 15. Applications are accepted on-line. **Transfer Students:** 1427 transfer students enrolled in 2013-2014. Applicants must submit official transcripts from high school and all colleges attended and have a satisfactory GPA in courses attempted. Applicants who will have completed less than 30 semester hours will also be required to meet the freshmen requirements. **International Students:** There are 200 international students enrolled. The school actively recruits these students. They must take the TOEFL with a minimum score of 80 on the Internet-based version (iBT), or take the IELTS. SAT or ACT scores are required if the student will receive an athletic scholarship or if the student will graduate from a U.S. high school.

ADMISSIONS: 62% of the 2014-2015 applicants were accepted. The SAT scores for the 2014-2015 freshman class were: Critical Reading--49% below 500, 43% between 500 and 599, 7% between 600 and 699, and 1% between 700 and 800; Math--32% below 500, 55% between 500 and 599, 12% between 600 and 699, and 1% between 700 and 800; Writing--57% below 500, 37% between 500 and 599, 6% between 600 and 699, and % between 700 and 800. The ACT scores were 18% below 21, 55% between 21 and 23, 19% between 24 and 26, 6% between 27 and 28, and 3% above 28. 35% of the current freshmen were in the top fifth of their class; 68% were in the top two fifths. **Admissions Contact:** James Coker, AssociateDirector of Undergraduate Admissions. E-Mail: *admis@ecu.edu* Web: *www.ecu.edu/admissions*

FINANCIAL AID: In 2014-2015, 60% of all full-time freshmen and 58% of continuing full-time students received some form of financial aid. 55% of all full-time freshmen and 31% of continuing full-time students received need-based aid. The average freshman award was $9,614. Need-based scholarships or need-based grants averaged $8,031; need-based self-help aid (loans and jobs) averaged $3,834; non-need-based athletic scholarships averaged $11,120; and other non-need-based awards and non-need-based scholarships averaged $4,532. The average financial indebtedness of the 2014 graduate was $25,983. ECU is a member of CSS. The FAFSA is required. The priority date for freshman financial aid applications for fall entry is March 1.

ELIZABETH CITY STATE UNIVERSITY   F-2
www.ecsu.edu

Elizabeth City, NC 27909	
	(252) 335-3305
	(800) 347-3278
Fax: (252) 335-3537	Email: admissions@ecsu.edu
Full-time: 1035 men, 1474 women	Faculty: 113; IIB, av$
Part-time: 68 men, 183 women	Ph.D.s: 68%
Graduate: 29 men, 89 women	Student/Faculty: 16 to 1
Year: semesters, summer session	Tuition: $4426 ($15,283)
Room & Board: $7212	Freshman Class: 3925 applied, 2243 accepted, 527 enrolled
SAT or ACT: required	CEEB CODE: 5629
Application Deadline: n/av	COMPETITIVE

Elizabeth City State University, founded in 1891 as part of the University of North Carolina System, is a public institution offering undergraduate programs in liberal arts and sciences, education, and business. Figures in the above capsule and in this profile are approximate. The 829-acre campus is in a small town 55 miles from Norfolk, Virginia.

STUDENT LIFE: 90% of undergraduates are from North Carolina. Others are from 25 states. 73% are African American; 12% White. 12% are Race and ethnicity unknown. 25% do not continue beyond their first year; 50% remain to graduate. **Housing:** 1019 students can be accommodated in college housing, which includes single-sex dorms and on-campus apartments. In addition, there are honors houses, and wellness housing. On-campus housing is guaranteed for all 4 years. 52% of students commute. Alcohol is not permitted. All students may keep cars.

FACULTY/CLASSROOMS: 50% of faculty are male; 50% are female. All teach undergraduates. No introductory courses are taught by graduate students.

PROGRAMS OF STUDY: ECSU confers B.A., B.S. and B.S.Ed. degrees. Master's degrees are also awarded. Bachelor's degrees are awarded in BIOLOGICAL SCIENCE (biology/biological science), BUSINESS (accounting and business administration and management), COMMUNICATIONS AND THE ARTS (art, English, and music), COMPUTER AND PHYSICAL SCIENCE (chemistry, computer science, geology, mathematics, and physics), EDUCATION (business education, elementary education, industrial arts education,

middle school education, physical education, special education, and technical education), ENGINEERING AND ENVIRONMENTAL DESIGN (industrial engineering technology), SOCIAL SCIENCE (criminal justice, history, political science/government, psychology, social science, social work, and sociology).

ACTIVITIES: Groups on campus include band, cheerleading, choir, chorus, dance, drama, honors, international, jazz band, literary magazine, marching band, musical theater, newspaper, pep band, radio and TV, religious, social, student government, symphony, and yearbook. **Sports:** Facilities include a 4500-seat gym, 3500-seat stadium, an all-weather track, golf range, an Olympic pool, weight room, 8 tennis courts, dance and exercise studios, handball and racquetball courts, and playing fields. **Graduates:** From July 1, 2013 to June 30, 2014, 379 bachelor's degrees were awarded. The most popular majors were business/marketing (21%), education (15%), and homeland security (13%). In an average class, 33% graduate in 4 years or less, 46% graduate in 5 years or less, and 49% graduate in 6 years or less. Of the 2013 graduating class, 79% were enrolled in graduate school within 6 months of graduation.

SERVICES: In addition to vocational counseling services, tutoring is available. **Library/Resources:** The library contains 174,566 volumes, 486,884 microform items, 1,220 audio/video tapes/CDs/DVDs, and subscribes to 1,698 periodicals including electronic. Computerized library services include interlibrary loans. Special learning facilities include an art gallery, planetarium, radio station, TV station, a farm, and 639-acre educational research tract. **Physically Challenged Students:** Facilities include wheelchair ramps, elevators, special parking, specially equipped restrooms, and lowered drinking fountains. **Special:** Opportunities are provided for internships, dual majors, weekend/evening degree completion programs, work-study, and credit by exam and for military service. There are 5 national honor societies and a freshman honors program. **Visiting:** There are regularly scheduled orientations for prospective students. There are guides for informal visits. To schedule a visit, contact the Admissions Office. **Campus Safety and Security:** There are emergency telephones, ECSU has its own police department on campus.

REQUIREMENTS: The SAT or ACT is required. Graduation from an accredited secondary school is required; the GED is accepted. Applicants should submit an academic record with 4 courses in English, 3 each in math and 2 in science, and 2 in social studies; it is recommended that applicants have at least 2 course units in foreign languages. Students must also pass the NC Competency Examination or its equivalent. AP and CLEP credits are accepted.Students must have maintained a minimum GPA of 2.0, fulfilled a major, and completed the requirements of general education courses in the fields of grammar, composition, and literature. **Procedure:** Freshmen are admitted fall, spring, and summer. Entrance exams should be taken as early as possible. There are early admissions and deferred admissions plans. Application deadlines are open. Application fee is $30. **Transfer Students:** 201 transfer students enrolled in 2013-2014. Applicants must have a minimum college GPA of 2.0 and submit high school and college transcripts. Those with fewer than 30 credit hours must meet both freshman and transfer admission requirements. 30 credits required for the bachelor's degree must be completed at ECSU. **International Students:** There are 6 international students enrolled. They must take the TOEFL or MELAB. They must also take the SAT or ACT.

ADMISSIONS: 57% of the 2014-2015 applicants were accepted. The SAT scores for the 2014-2015 freshman class were: Critical Reading--89% below 500, 10% between 500 and 599, and 1% between 600 and 699; Math--83% below 500, 16% between 500 and 599, and 1% between 600 and 699; Writing--92% below 500, and 8% between 500 and 599. **Admissions Contact:** Bridgett Golham, Director of Admissions and Recruitment. E-Mail: *admissions@alpha.ecsu.edu* Web: *www.ecsu.edu*

FINANCIAL AID: The FAFSA and the college's own financial statement, and and income tax forms are required. Check with the school for current application deadlines.

ELON UNIVERSITY   D-2
www.elon.edu

Elon, NC 27244	**(336) 278-2000**
	(800) 334-8448
Fax: (336) 278-7699	Email: admissions@elon.edu
Full-time: 2277 men, 3361 women	Faculty: 364; IIA, +$
Part-time: 65 men, 79 women	Ph.D.s: 89%
Graduate: 285 men, 416 women	Student/Faculty: 12 to 1
Year: 4-1-4, summer session	Tuition: $31,247
Room & Board: $10,667	Freshman Class: 10443 applied, 5632 accepted, 1497 enrolled
SAT CR/M/W: 613/612/614 ACT: 27	CEEB CODE: 5183
Application Deadline: January 10	**VERY COMPETITIVE+**

Elon University is a selective, private university renowned as a national model for engaged learning, along with excellence in the liberal arts and sciences and professional programs. There are 4 undergraduate schools and 5 graduate schools. In addition to regional accreditation, Elon has baccalaureate program accreditation with AACSB, ACEJMC, NCATE, CAPTE, and ARC-PA. The 620-acre campus is in a suburban area adjacent to Burlington and 17 miles east of Greensboro. Including any residence halls, there are 186 buildings.
STUDENT LIFE: 79% of undergraduates are from out of state, mostly the Middle Atlantic. Students are from 49 states, 47 foreign countries, and Canada. 60% are from public schools. 82% are White. 36% are Protestant; 26% Catholic. The average age of freshmen is 18; all undergraduates, 20. 9% do not continue beyond their first year; 81% remain to graduate. **Housing:** 3607 students can be accommodated in college housing, which includes single-sex and coed dorms, on-campus apartments, and off-campus apartments. In addition, there are honors houses, language houses, special-interest houses, fraternity houses, sorority houses, Elon's high-tech campus encompasses seven distinct residential neighborhoods for students at various stages of their college careers. On-campus housing is guaranteed for the freshman year only and is available on a lottery system for upperclassmen. 62% of students live on campus; of those, 75% remain on campus on weekends. All students may keep cars.
FACULTY/CLASSROOMS: 52% of faculty are male; 48% are female. 90% teach undergraduates, 65% do research, and 65% do both. No introductory courses are taught by graduate students. The average class size in an introductory lecture is 23; in a laboratory is 19; and in a regular course is 20.
PROGRAMS OF STUDY: Elon confers B.A., B.S., B.F.A. and B.S.B.A degrees. Master's and Doctoral degrees are also awarded. Bachelor's degrees are awarded in AGRICULTURE (environmental studies), BIOLOGICAL SCIENCE (biochemistry and biophysics), BUSINESS (accounting, business administration and management, entrepreneurial studies, finance, international business management, international economics, management information systems, marketing, marketing management, and sports management), COMMUNICATIONS AND THE ARTS (acting, art history, art, arts administration/management, broadcasting, communications, creative writing, dance, dramatic arts, English, film arts, French, journalism, literature, media arts, music, music performance, music technology, musical theater, Spanish, strategic communication, theatre acting, theatre arts, theater design, theatre production, and theatre studies), COMPUTER AND PHYSICAL SCIENCE (applied mathematics, chemistry, computer science, digital arts/technology, information sciences and systems, mathematics, physics, and statistics), EDUCATION (early childhood education, education, elementary education, foreign languages education, health education, mathematics education, middle school education, music education, physical education, science education, secondary education, and special education), ENGINEERING AND ENVIRONMENTAL DESIGN (biomedical engineering, chemical engineering, computer engineering, engineering, engineering physics, environmental engineering, and environmental science), HEALTH PROFESSIONS (biology, exercise science, public health, and sports medicine), SOCIAL SCIENCE (anthropology, economics, history, human services, international studies, philosophy, political science/government, psychology, public administration, religious studies, and sociology). Business, music theater, biology, psychology, interna-

tional studies and communications are the strongest academically. Business, strategic communications, and psychology have the largest enrollments.
ACTIVITIES: 22% of men belong to 11 national fraternities; 39% of women belong to 12 national sororities. There are 228 groups on campus, including art, band, cheerleading, chess, choir, chorale, chorus, communications, computers, dance, debate, drama, drill team, environmental, ethnic, film, gay, honors, international, jazz band, literary magazine, marching band, musical theater, newspaper, orchestra, pep band, photography, political, professional, radio and TV, religious, social, social service, student government, symphony, and yearbook. Popular campus events include Family Weekend, Homecoming, Greek Week, Spring Undergraduate Research Forum (SURF Day), College Coffee and CELEBRATE!, a week-long celebration of Student Achievements in Academics and the Arts, Festival of Holiday Lights. **Sports:** There are 7 intercollegiate sports for men and 9 for women, and 21 intramural sports for men and 21 for women. Facilities include an 8250-seat stadium, lighted tennis courts, softball field, baseball stadium, field house, and 15 athletic fields. The athletic center has racquetball courts, aerobic rooms, a human performance lab, weight room, two-story fitness center, 2 gyms, driving range, and an indoor swimming pool. **Graduates:** From July 1, 2013 to June 30, 2014, 1332 bachelor's degrees were awarded. The most popular majors were marketing (24%), communications (19%), and social sciences (11%). 226 companies recruited on campus in 2013-2014. In an average class, 76% graduate in 4 years or less, 80% graduate in 5 years or less, and 81% graduate in 6 years or less. Of the 2013 graduating class, 19% were enrolled in graduate school within 6 months of graduation, and 66% were employed.
SERVICES: Counseling and information services are available, as is tutoring in most subjects, lower-level courses. Preparatory courses are offered, which count as elective credit toward graduation. We offer texts in alternative formats for students with print disabilities (both learning and visual disabilities). **Library/Resources:** The library contains 420,966 volumes, 284,608 microform items, 24,119 audio/video tapes/CDs/DVDs, and subscribes to 55,046 periodicals including electronic. Computerized library services include interlibrary loans, database searching, Internet access, and Wi-Fi capability. Special learning facilities include a radio station, TV station, a writing center, botanical preserve, a protected Elon Forest, art collection walk, and observatory. **Physically Challenged Students:** 85% of the campus is accessible. Facilities include wheelchair ramps, elevators, special parking, specially equipped restrooms, special class scheduling, lowered drinking fountains, lowered telephones, special housing.
Special: Elon offers co-op programs in most majors, dual majors, student-designed majors, cross-registration with 6 other colleges and universities in North Carolina, paid and unpaid internships, more than 100 study abroad programs, study USA programs, a Washington semester, a Los Angeles semester, a New York semester, work-study programs, pass/fail options, and 3-2 dual engineering degree programs. The month-long January term includes extensive international study opportunities as well as courses focused on domestic travel. There are 31 national honor societies, including Phi Beta Kappa, a freshman honors program, and 25 departmental honors programs. **Visiting:** There are regularly scheduled orientations for prospective students, consisting of 2 weekends in spring for deposited freshmen or a spring open house for nondeposited students. There are guides for informal visits and visitors may sit in on classes. To schedule a visit, contact the Admissions Office. **Campus Safety and Security:** Measures include 24-hour foot and vehicle patrol, emergency notification system, and security escort services. There are shuttle buses, emergency telephones, lighted pathways/sidewalks, controlled access to dorms/residences, Over 200 cameras on campus, annual fire inspections through the County Fire Marshall's Office, Campus Safety and Police operates 24 hours/day 7 days/week, and Operation ID.
REQUIREMENTS: The SAT or ACT is required. The ACT Optional Writing test is also required. Students must be graduates of an accredited secondary school or have a GED certificate. They should have completed 4 credits of English, 3 or more in math (must include algebra 1 and 2, and geometry), 2 or more in a foreign language, 2 or more in science, including at least 1 lab science, and 2 or more in social studies, including U.S. history AP and CLEP credits are

accepted. To graduate, students must complete 132 semester hours, including 32 to 68 in the major, with a minimum GPA of 2.0. All students must fulfill the requirements of the General Studies program, which includes a first-year core, experiential learning, liberal studies, and advanced studies, for a total of 59 semester hours, and must satisfactorily complete a comprehensive exam in the major. **Procedure:** Freshmen are admitted fall and spring. Entrance exams should be taken in the spring of the junior year and the fall of the senior year. There are early decision, early admissions, and deferred admissions plans. Early decision applications should be filed by November 1; regular applications, by January 10 for fall entry; and December 1 for spring entry, along with a $50 fee. Notification of early decision is sent December 1; regular decision, March 15. 494 early decision candidates were accepted for the 2014-2015 class. 3193 applicants were on the 2014 waiting list; 208 were admitted. Applications are accepted on-line. **Transfer Students:** 97 transfer students enrolled in 2013-2014. Applicants must present a high school transcript, 12 credit hours of college transferable classes in the liberal arts and sciences, and a minimum GPA of 2.7 from a two-year or four-year accredited institution. An interview is recommended. A dean's evaluation form is required from all colleges or universities attended, and the applicant must be eligible to return to that institution. 60 of 132 credits required for the bachelor's degree must be completed at Elon. **International Students:** There are 107 international students enrolled. The school actively recruits these students. They must take the TOEFL with a minimum score of 550 on the paper-based TOEFL (PBT) or 79 on the Internet-based version (iBT). They must also take the SAT or ACT, scoring 1330.

ADMISSIONS: 54% of the 2014-2015 applicants were accepted. The SAT scores for the 2014-2015 freshman class were: Critical Reading--5% below 500, 35% between 500 and 599, 49% between 600 and 699, and 11% between 700 and 800; Math--5% below 500, 33% between 500 and 599, 52% between 600 and 699, and 10% between 700 and 800; Writing--4% below 500, 34% between 500 and 599, 50% between 600 and 699, and 12% between 700 and 800. The ACT scores were 3% below 21, 13% between 21 and 23, 27% between 24 and 26, 30% between 27 and 28, and 27% above 28. 52% of the current freshmen were in the top fifth of their class; 82% were in the top two fifths. There were 2 National Merit finalists. 5 freshmen graduated first in their class. **Admissions Contact:** Lisa Keegan, Dean of Admissions. E-Mail: *admissions@elon.edu* Web: *www.elon.edu*

FINANCIAL AID: In 2014-2015, 62% of all full-time freshmen and 62% of continuing full-time students received some form of financial aid. 30% of all full-time freshmen and 31% of continuing full-time students received need-based aid. The average freshman award was $17,421. Need-based scholarships or need-based grants averaged $10,855 ($42,914 maximum); need-based self-help aid (loans and jobs) averaged $4,692 ($9,000 maximum); non-need-based athletic scholarships averaged $28,226 ($43,768 maximum); and other non-need-based awards and non-need-based scholarships averaged $6,517 ($43,348 maximum). 33% of undergraduate students work part-time. Average annual earnings from campus work are $4500. The average financial indebtedness of the 2014 graduate was $27,176. Elon is a member of CSS. The CSS/Profile, FAFSA, and the college's own financial statement are required. The priority date for freshman financial aid applications for fall entry is February 15.

FAYETTEVILLE STATE UNIVERSITY   D-3
www.uncfsu.edu

Fayetteville, NC 28301	
	(910) 672-1111
	(800) 222-2594
Fax: (910) 672-2600	Email: admissions@uncfsu.edu
Full-time: 1297 men, 2619 women	Faculty: 276; IIA, av$
Part-time: 323 men, 1048 women	Ph.D.s: n/av
Graduate: 186 men, 587 women	Student/Faculty: 16 to 1
Year: semesters, summer session	Tuition: $4674 ($15,378)
Room & Board: $6142	Freshman Class: n/av
SAT or ACT: required	CEEB CODE: 5212
Application Deadline: n/av	**COMPETITIVE**

Fayetteville State University, founded in 1867 and today part of the University of North Carolina system, is a public institution offering degree programs in the arts and sciences, business, and teacher preparation. Figures in the above capsule and in this profile are approximate. There are 3 undergraduate schools and 1 graduate school. In addition to regional accreditation, FSU has baccalaureate program accreditation with NCATE. The 156-acre campus is in an urban area 60 miles south of Raleigh. Including any residence halls, there are 43 buildings.

STUDENT LIFE: 95% of undergraduates are from North Carolina. 76% are African American; 20% White. The average age of freshmen is 19; all undergraduates, 27. 24% do not continue beyond their first year; 31% remain to graduate. **Housing:** 1298 students can be accommodated in college housing, which includes single-sex and coed dorms and on-campus apartments. Honors dorm. On-campus housing is available on a first-come and first-served basis. 71% of students commute. Alcohol is not permitted. All students may keep cars.

FACULTY/CLASSROOMS: 54% of faculty are male; 46% are female. All teach and do research. No introductory courses are taught by graduate students. The average class size in an introductory lecture is 30; in a laboratory is 20; and in a regular course is 30.

PROGRAMS OF STUDY: FSU confers B.A., and B.S. degrees. Master's and Doctoral degrees are also awarded. Bachelor's degrees are awarded in BIOLOGICAL SCIENCE (biology/biological science), BUSINESS (accounting, banking and finance, business administration and management, business economics, management information systems, and office supervision and management), COMMUNICATIONS AND THE ARTS (dramatic arts, English, Spanish, speech/debate/rhetoric, and visual and performing arts), COMPUTER AND PHYSICAL SCIENCE (chemistry, computer science, and mathematics), EDUCATION (business education, early childhood education, elementary education, health education, marketing and distribution education, middle school education, music education, secondary education, and social science education), HEALTH PROFESSIONS (medical laboratory technology and nursing), SOCIAL SCIENCE (criminal justice, economics, geography, history, political science/government, psychology, public administration, social science, social work, and sociology).

ACTIVITIES: 1% of men belong to 4 local and 4 national fraternities; 1% of women belong to 3 national sororities. There are 30 groups on campus, including band, cheerleading, choir, chorus, dance, drama, film, honors, international, jazz band, literary magazine, marching band, newspaper, pep band, political, radio and TV, religious, social service, student government, and yearbook. Popular campus events include The Lyceum, Martin Luther King Day and Black History Month. **Sports:** There are 8 intercollegiate sports for men and 8 for women, and 7 intramural sports for men and 5 for women. Facilities include 2 gyms, a stadium, tennis courts, a bowling alley, a dance studio, a swimming pool, and playing fields. **Graduates:** From July 1, 2013 to June 30, 2014, 991 bachelor's degrees were awarded. The most popular majors were criminal justice (16%), psychology (16%), and business administration (14%).

SERVICES: Counseling and information services are available, as is tutoring in some subjects. There is remedial math, reading, and writing. **Library/Resources:** The library contains 335,922 volumes, 1.0 million microform items, 20,676 audio/video tapes/CDs/DVDs. Computerized library services include interlibrary loans and database searching. Special learning facilities include a planetarium and radio station. **Physically Challenged Students:** 75% of the campus is accessible. Facilities include wheelchair ramps, elevators, special parking, specially equipped restrooms, and lowered drinking fountains. **Special:** FSU offers cooperative programs in business, math, and biological and physical sciences with North Carolina State University, internships, B.A.-B.S. degrees, dual majors, 3-2 engineering degree programs, credit for military experience, and nondegree study. There are 17 national honor societies, a freshman honors program, and 7 departmental honors programs. **Visiting:** There are regularly scheduled orientations for prospective students, including a campus tour, recreational activity, placement tests, preregistration, and orientation to FSU services. There are guides for informal visits, visitors may sit in on classes, and stay overnight. To schedule a visit, contact the Director of Enrollment Management at (910) 672-1784. **Campus Safety and Security:** Measures include 24-hour foot and vehicle patrol and security escort services. There are lighted pathways/sidewalks.

REQUIREMENTS: The SAT or ACT is required. Successful scores are also required on the North Carolina Competency Exam. Applicants must be graduates of an accredited secondary school or have the GED. They should have completed 4 academic units of English, 3 each of math and science with 1 lab course, and 2 of social studies; also recommended are 2 units of a foreign language and completion of 1 unit each of foreign language and math in the senior year. AP and CLEP credits are accepted. Important factors in the admissions decision are advanced placement or honors courses, recommendations by school officials, and leadership record.To graduate, students must complete 120 credit hours with a minimum GPA of 2.0 overall and in the major. The core curriculum includes 8 to 11 credits in natural science, 6 to 15 in humanities, 6 to 7 in math, 3 to 9 in social science, 3 each in critical thinking and speech, and 2 each in phys ed/health and university seminar. **Procedure:** Freshmen are admitted to all sessions. Entrance exams should be taken in November. There are early decision, early admissions, deferred admissions, and rolling admissions plans. Check with the school for current application deadlines. The application fee is $35. Notification is sent on a rolling basis. **Transfer Students:** 670 transfer students enrolled in 2013-2014. Applicants must submit official transcripts from all colleges attended, have a minimum GPA of 2.0, and be eligible to return to their previous institution. 33 of 120 credits required for the bachelor's degree must be completed at FSU. **International Students:** They must take the TOEFL, or other English proficiency exam administered in their country. They must also take the SAT or ACT, scoring 800.

ADMISSIONS: Ulisa E. Bowles, Director of Admissions. E-Mail: *admissions@uncfsu.edu* Web: *www.uncfsu.edu*

FINANCIAL AID: FSU is a member of CSS. The FAFSA is required. Check with the school for current application deadlines.

GARDNER-WEBB UNIVERSITY   C-3
www.gardner-webb.edu

Boiling Springs, NC 28017

(704) 406-4000
(800) 253-6472

Fax: (704) 406-4488   Email: admissions@gardner-webb.edu

Full-time: 779 men, 1309 women	**Faculty:** 122; IIA
Part-time: 118 men, 366 women	**Ph.D.s:** 79%
Graduate: 594 men, 1470 women	**Student/Faculty:** 17 to 1
Year: semesters, summer session	**Tuition:** $25,930
Room & Board: $8445	**Freshman Class:** 5456 applied, 2640 accepted, 434 enrolled
SAT or ACT: required	**CEEB CODE:** 5242
Application Deadline: open	**COMPETITIVE+**

Gardner-Webb University, founded in 1905, is an independent institution affiliated with the Baptist Convention of North Carolina and offering undergraduate programs in the arts and sciences, business, education, nursing, and professional studies. The figures in tha above capsule and in this profile are approximate. There are 4 undergraduate schools and 3 graduate schools. In addition to regional accreditation, Webb has baccalaureate program accreditation with ACBSP, NASM, NCATE, NLN, ATS, CAATEP, and NLNAC. The 250-acre campus is in a small town 50 miles west of Charlotte, NC. Including any residence halls, there are 46 buildings.

STUDENT LIFE: 78% of undergraduates are from North Carolina. Others are from 35 states, 21 foreign countries, and Canada. 70% are from public schools. 69% are White; 20% African American. 64% are Protestant. The average age of freshmen is 18; all undergraduates, 21. 26% do not continue beyond their first year; 48% remain to graduate.

Housing: 1368 students can be accommodated in college housing, which includes single-sex dorms and on-campus apartments. In addition, there are honors houses. On-campus housing is guaranteed for all 4 years. 77% of students live on campus; of those, 50% remain on campus on weekends. Alcohol is not permitted. All students may keep cars.

FACULTY/CLASSROOMS: 51% of faculty are male; 49% are female. All teach undergraduates. No introductory courses are taught by graduate students. The average class size in an introductory lecture is 25; in a laboratory is 9; and in a regular course is 18.

PROGRAMS OF STUDY: Webb confers B.A., B.S., B.F.A., B.M. and B.S.N. degrees. Associate, Master's, and Doctoral degrees are also awarded. Bachelor's degrees are awarded in BIOLOGICAL SCIENCE (biology/biological science), BUSINESS (accounting, business administration and management, international business management, and sports management), COMMUNICATIONS AND THE ARTS (American Sign Language, art, communications, English, French, music, and Spanish), COMPUTER AND PHYSICAL SCIENCE (chemistry, computer science, information sciences and systems, and mathematics), EDUCATION (athletic training, elementary education, foreign languages education, health education, middle school education, music education, physical education, and secondary education), ENGINEERING AND ENVIRONMENTAL DESIGN (industrial administration/management), HEALTH PROFESSIONS (health care administration, medical technology, nursing, and physician's assistant), SOCIAL SCIENCE (history, interpreter for the deaf, psychology, religion, religious music, social science, and sociology). Nursing, music, biology, and education are the strongest academically. Business, social science, education, and nursing have the largest enrollments.

ACTIVITIES: There are 65 groups on campus, including art, band, cheerleading, choir, chorale, chorus, debate, drama, drill team, film, honors, international, jazz band, literary magazine, marching band, musical theater, newspaper, opera, orchestra, pep band, photography, political, professional, radio and TV, religious, social, social service, student government, symphony, and yearbook. Popular campus events include Festival of Lights, Bulldog Madness and Spring's Alive. **Sports:** There are 11 intercollegiate sports for men and 10 for women, and 28 intramural sports for men and 28 for women. Facilities include an athletic and recreation facilities include an 8,500-seat stadium, 2 gyms, tennis and racquetball courts, a weight room, a swimming pool, playing fields for softball, soccer, football, and baseball, a 5500-seat arena, an aerobics room, and a ropes course. **Graduates:** From July 1, 2013 to June 30, 2014, 645 bachelor's degrees were awarded. The most popular majors were business administration (27%), social sciences (21%), and nursing and other health related majors (12%). In an average class, 9% graduate in 3 years or less, 37% graduate in 4 years or less, 47% graduate in 5 years or less, and 48% graduate in 6 years or less.

SERVICES: Counseling and information services are available, as is tutoring in every subject. There is a reader service for the blind, and remedial math, reading, and writing. **Library/Resources:** The library contains 244,133 volumes, 653,778 microform items, 12,494 audio/video tapes/CDs/DVDs, and subscribes to 108,251 periodicals including electronic. Computerized library services include interlibrary loans, database searching, Internet access, and Wi-Fi capability. Special learning facilities include an art gallery, radio station, observatory. **Physically Challenged Students:** All of the campus is accessible. Facilities include wheelchair ramps, elevators, special parking, specially equipped restrooms, special class scheduling, lowered drinking fountains, and special housing. **Special:** The university offers work-study programs, internships, and study abroad in 11 countries. There are 11 national honor societies, a freshman honors program, and 3 departmental honors programs. **Visiting:** There are regularly scheduled orientations for prospective students, including a campus tour, and meet with an admissions counselor. There are guides for informal visits, visitors may sit in on classes, and stay overnight. To schedule a visit, contact the Visit Coordinator. **Campus Safety and Security:** Measures include 24-hour foot and vehicle patrol, emergency notification system, self-defense education, and security escort services. There are emergency telephones, lighted pathways/sidewalks, controlled access to dorms/residences, police foot patrol inside of dorms is also provided.

REQUIREMENTS: The SAT or ACT is required. Candidates should be graduates of an accredited secondary school or have a GED certificate. The recommended preparatory curriculum includes 4 units of English, 3 of math, and 2 each of social science, natural science, a foreign language, and electives. One standardized test, either the SAT or the ACT, is required. Webb requires applicants to be in the upper 50% of their class. AP and CLEP credits are accepted. Important factors in the admissions decision are leadership record, extracurricular activities record, and recommendations by school officials.To graduate, students must complete 128 credit hours, including 24 to 36 in the major, with a minimum GPA of 2.0. The required core curriculum consists of 44 hours of general education, liberal arts courses. Students also receive 1 credit hour per year of Dimensions. **Procedure:** Freshmen are admitted to all sessions. Entrance exams should be taken During the junior or senior year of high school. There are deferred admissions and rolling admissions plans. Application deadlines are open. Application fee is $40. Applications are accepted online. **Transfer Students:** 114 transfer students enrolled in 2013-2014. Applicants must submit the standard application and fee, official high school and college transcripts, and SAT or ACT scores. High school transcripts and test scores are waived for applicants with 15 or more semester credits and a GPA of 2.25 and submission of a college transcript. 32 of 128 credits required for the bachelor's degree must be completed at Webb. **International Students:** There are 67 international students enrolled. The school actively recruits these students. They must take the TOEFL with a minimum score of 500 on the paper-based TOEFL (PBT) or 61 on the Internet-based version (iBT). They must also take the SAT or ACT, scoring 870.

ADMISSIONS: 48% of the 2014-2015 applicants were accepted. 42% of the current freshmen were in the top fifth of their class; 66% were in the top two fifths. 3 freshmen graduated first in their class. **Admissions Contact:** Angela Sundell, Assistant Vice President of Admissions. E-Mail: *admissions@gardner-webb.edu* Web: *www.gardner-webb.edu*

FINANCIAL AID: In 2014-2015, 100% of all full-time freshmen and 98% of continuing full-time students received some form of financial aid. The average freshman award was $18,540. Need-based scholarships or need-based grants averaged $7,336; need-based self-help aid (loans and jobs) averaged $4,283; non-need-based athletic scholarships averaged $15,287; and other non-need-based awards and non-need-based scholarships averaged $11,745. Average annual earnings from campus work are $1303. The average financial indebtedness of the 2014 graduate was $19,725. Webb is a member of CSS. The FAFSA and the state aid form, and federal tax returns are required. The priority date for freshman financial aid applications for fall entry is March 1.

GREENSBORO COLLEGE (*The complete profile is made available exclusively on our website, www.barronspac.com*)

GUILFORD COLLEGE — D-2
www.guilford.edu

Greensboro, NC 27410	(336) 316-2220
	(800) 992-7759
Fax: (336) 316-2954	Email: admission@guilford.edu
Full-time: 868 men, 910 women	Faculty: 124; IIB, -$
Part-time: 131 men, 228 women	Ph.D.s: 92%
Graduate: n/av	Student/Faculty: 14 to 1
Year: 4-1-4, summer session	Tuition: $30,430
Room & Board: $8270	Freshman Class: 3001 applied, 1866 accepted, 351 enrolled
SAT CR/M/W: 550/540/520 ACT: 23	CEEB CODE: 5261
Application Deadline: February 15	COMPETITIVE

Guilford's purpose is to provide a transformative, practical, and excellent liberal arts education that produces critical thinkers in an inclusive, diverse environment, guided by Quaker testimonies of community, equality, integrity, peace, and simplicity and emphasizing the creative problem-solving skills, experiences, enthusiasm, and international perspectives necessary to promote positive change in the world. Figures in the above capsule and in this profile are approximate. In addition to regional accreditation, has baccalaureate program accreditation with NCATE. The 340-acre campus is in a suburban area in the western residential area of Greensboro, NC. Including any residence halls, there are 31 buildings.

STUDENT LIFE: 72% of undergraduates are from North Carolina. Others are from 40 states, 15 foreign countries, and Canada. 72% are from public schools. 63% are White; 22% African American. 50%

claim no religious affiliation. The average age of freshmen is 18; all undergraduates, 22. 29% do not continue beyond their first year; 59% remain to graduate. **Housing:** 1043 students can be accommodated in college housing, which includes single-sex and coed dorms and on-campus apartments. In addition, there are special-interest houses. In addition to dormitory and on–campus apartment housing, Guilford offers the opportunity for groups of students to live together in special interest housing or theme houses. These are four houses that accommodate six to ten students and are organized around common social or academic interests, such as the study of languages, science, environmental sustainability, cultural themes, or a community service focus. Students may apply as a group each spring for special interest housing for the following academic year. The houses are not available for first–year students. 74% of students live on campus; of those, 80% remain on campus on weekends. All students may keep cars.

FACULTY/CLASSROOMS: 50% of faculty are male; 50% are female. All teach undergraduates. No introductory courses are taught by graduate students. The average class size in an introductory lecture is 19; in a laboratory is 17; and in a regular course is 19.

PROGRAMS OF STUDY: Guilford confers A.B., B.S., and B.F.A. degrees. Bachelor's degrees are awarded in AGRICULTURE (environmental studies), BIOLOGICAL SCIENCE (biology/biological science), BUSINESS (accounting, business administration and management, information and communication technology, international business management, and sports management), COMMUNICATIONS AND THE ARTS (art, dramatic arts, English, French, German, music, Spanish, theatre arts, and visual and performing arts), COMPUTER AND PHYSICAL SCIENCE (chemistry, geology, information sciences and systems, mathematics, and physics), EDUCATION (education and sports studies), ENGINEERING AND ENVIRONMENTAL DESIGN (computer technology), HEALTH PROFESSIONS (exercise science and health science), SOCIAL SCIENCE (African American studies, anthropology, community services, criminal justice, economics, forensic studies, gender studies, history, interdisciplinary studies, international studies, peace studies, philosophy, political science/government, psychology, religion, sociology, and women's studies). Natural sciences, accounting, psychology, English, art, theater, forensic biology, and community justice are the strongest academically. Business management, psychology, and criminal justice have the largest enrollments.

ACTIVITIES: There are 43 groups on campus, including Yachting, Bayard Rustin Center for LGBTQA Activism, Community Aids Awareness Project, Guilford Peace Society, Inter–Club Council, Men and Women Rugby, Poetry Club, Archery Club. Including art, cheerleading, chess, choir, chorale, chorus, computers, dance, debate, drama, environmental, ethnic, film, gay, honors, international, jazz band, literary magazine, musical theater, newspaper, pep band, photography, political, professional, radio and TV, religious, social, social service, and student government. Popular campus events include Serendipity Spring Festival, Bryan Lecture Series in the Arts, Hip Hop Conference, Eastern Music Festival, International Dinner and Dance Holiday Choir Concerts. **Sports:** There are 8 intercollegiate sports for men and 8 for women, and 3 intramural sports for men and 3 for women. Facilities include Athletic facilities include: 3500-seat football/track stadium with lights (also lacrosse, soccer); 1560-seat field house gymnasium with multiple courts for basketball and volleyball; baseball field; cross–country courses; swimming pool; lighted intramural field; additional playing fields for varsity and club sports; tennis courts; weight room; and a cardio room. **Graduates:** From July 1, 2013 to June 30, 2014, 539 bachelor's degrees were awarded. The most popular majors were business management (18%), psychology (11%), and criminal justice (10%). 183 companies recruited on campus in 2013-2014. In an average class, 50% graduate in 4 years or less, 56% graduate in 5 years or less, and 57% graduate in 6 years or less. Of the 2013 graduating class, 36% were enrolled in graduate school within 6 months of graduation, and 65% were employed.

SERVICES: Counseling and information services are available, as is tutoring in every subject. There is a reader service for the blind, remedial math, reading, and writing. Faculty tutoring for skills development; student tutoring for course-specific help; non–remedial writing; The Learning Commons center devoted to student support. **Library/Resources:** The library contains 256,465 volumes, 21,543 microform items, 5,119 audio/video tapes/CDs/DVDs, and subscribes to 30,561 periodicals including electronic. Computerized library services include interlibrary loans, database searching, Internet access, and Wi-Fi capability. Special learning facilities include an art gallery, planetarium, radio station, Cline observatory (physics and astronomy); photography studio; outdoor sculpture studio; Guilford college farm, community garden, and friends historical collection. **Physically Challenged Students:** 95% of the campus is accessible. Facilities include wheelchair ramps, elevators, special parking, specially equipped restrooms, special class scheduling, lowered drinking fountains, lowered telephones. ATM machine. **Special:** Guilford offers 3-2 degree programs in forestry and environmental studies with Duke University, and in physician assistant training with Bowman Gray School of Medicine at Wake Forest University. Guilford also offers many internships, a Washington semester, work-study programs, accelerated degree programs, dual majors, student-designed majors, study abroad in 13 countries, B.A.-B.S. degrees, and cross-registration with members of the Greater Greensboro Consortium. Pre–professional programs that are designed specifically as preparation for graduate study, dentistry, law, medicine, orthopedic, ministry, veterinary science; past examples include space physics, robotics, crime lab investigation, wildlife rehabilitation, Integrated Lab chemistry research, sports management internships with national or major football, baseball , or soccer leagues, internships with senators, mayors, ACLU, Greenpeace, geology fieldwork in the Andes, Alps, Turkey, archaeology labs, economics experience with cooperatives in Costa Rica, Federal Reserve Bank internships. Domestic Off–campus Semester–away Washington Semester, Washington, D.C., which helps students develop professional skills and career potential through internships with the federal government, lobbying organizations, or public agencies. Formal internship agreements or partnerships: Cooperative program with Duke University leading to graduate studies in natural resources and the environment. Also: Center for Principled Problem Solving, provides opportunities for students to learn about innovation and social change in classes, and participate in programs such as the Clinton Global Initiative University, Unity Hoops Basketball, and the Maryland House of Delegates. Additional Special or Unique Programs Semester abroad (e.g. Africa, China, England, France, Germany, Italy, Japan, the Netherlands, Mexico); Quaker Leadership Program; Bonner Center for Community Service and Learning, provides opportunities to work with non–profit organizations & community groups; Bryan Series, bringing world–class experts in their fields to address the community and meet with students; Student internships with solar conversion; unique majors include forensic biology, forensic accounting, sport management, and peace and conflict studies. Consortia that allow open registration in seven area colleges and universities without additional fees; inter–university Reclaiming Democracy seminar connecting ground–breaking Greensboro civil rights movements with larger social justice issues. There are 2 national honor societies and a freshman honors program. **Visiting:** There are regularly scheduled orientations for prospective students, visits can be scheduled throughout the year. A typical visit includes an information session led by an Admission Counselor followed by a student–led tour. Class visits, professor meetings, and lunch buddies are available when classes are in session. There are guides for informal visits, visitors may sit in on classes, and stay overnight. To schedule a visit, contact the Admission Office. **Campus Safety and Security:** Measures include 24-hour foot and vehicle patrol, emergency notification system, self-defense education, and security escort services. There are emergency telephones, lighted pathways/sidewalks, controlled access to dorms/residences, and a whistle program.

REQUIREMENTS: The SAT is recommended. A minimum SAT composite score of 1000 or ACT score of 22 is recommended. Applicants should have completed 20 Carnegie Units, including 4 in English, 2 each in foreign language and science, and 1 each in history and social studies. The GED is accepted. An essay is required and an interview is recommended. A GPA of 2.0 is required. AP and CLEP credits are accepted. Important factors in the admissions decision are advanced placement or honors courses, leadership record, and evidence of special talent.Students must fulfill requirements in Fine Arts, English, Humanities, Sciences, Social Sciences, and Foreign Language. They must take a first-year experience and an interdisciplinary

capstone course, and courses in historical perspectives, intercultural studies, social justice and environmental responsibility, diversity, business and policy studies, and quantitative literacy. A minimum GPA of 2.0 is required. 128 credit hours must be completed with at least 32 in the major. **Procedure:** Freshmen are admitted fall and spring. Entrance exams should be taken spring of the junior year or fall of the senior year. There are early decision, early admissions, and deferred admissions plans. Early decision applications should be filed by November 15; regular applications, by February 15 for fall entry; and February 15 for spring entry. Notification of early decision is sent February 15; regular decision, April 1. Applications are accepted online. **Transfer Students:** 43 transfer students enrolled in 2013-2014. Applicants for transfer must have a minimum GPA of 2.5 in at least 12 credit hours, submit either SAT or ACT scores, and provide a letter from the academic adviser or dean of the previous school. An interview is recommended. Transfer applicants are evaluated according to the same criteria used for freshman applicants. Consideration is given to the academic reputation of the former college. 32 of 128 credits required for the bachelor's degree must be completed at Guilford. **International Students:** There are 23 international students enrolled. The school actively recruits these students. They must take the TOEFL with a minimum score of 550 on the paper-based TOEFL (PBT) or 80 on the Internet-based version (iBT).

ADMISSIONS: 62% of the 2014-2015 applicants were accepted. The SAT scores for the 2014-2015 freshman class were: Critical Reading--41% below 500, 33% between 500 and 599, 22% between 600 and 699, and 3% between 700 and 800; Math--37% below 500, 41% between 500 and 599, 18% between 600 and 699, and 4% between 700 and 800; Writing--41% below 500, 31% between 500 and 599, 16% between 600 and 699, and 2% between 700 and 800. The ACT scores were 24% below 21, 28% between 21 and 23, 24% between 24 and 26, 10% between 27 and 28, and 14% above 28. 38% of the current freshmen were in the top fifth of their class; 70% were in the top two fifths. 1 freshman graduated first in the class. **Admissions Contact:** Andy Strickler, Director of Admissions. E-Mail: *admission@ guilford.edu* Web: *www.guilford.edu*

FINANCIAL AID: In 2014-2015, 99% of all full-time freshmen and 87% of continuing full-time students received some form of financial aid. 82% of all full-time freshmen and continuing full-time students received need-based aid. The average freshman award was $22,998. Need-based scholarships or need-based grants averaged $20,643 ($30,000 maximum); need-based self-help aid (loans and jobs) averaged $14,646; and other non-need-based awards and non-need-based scholarships averaged $9,351. 18% of undergraduate students work part-time. Average annual earnings from campus work are $1500. The average financial indebtedness of the 2014 graduate was $25,025. The FAFSA is required. The deadline for filing freshman financial aid applications for fall entry is March 1.

HIGH POINT UNIVERSITY	D-2
www.highpoint.edu	

High Point, NC 27262	(336) 841-9000
	(800) 345-6993
Fax: (336) 888-6382	Email: admiss@highpoint.edu
Full-time: 1506 men, 2308 women	Faculty: 212; IIB, -$
Part-time: 60 men, 90 women	Ph.D.s: 77%
Graduate: 64 men, 177 women	Student/Faculty: 15 to 1
Year: semesters, summer session	Tuition: $39,800
Room & Board: n/app	Freshman Class: 4529 applied, 3228 accepted, 1030 enrolled
SAT CR/M/W: 530/545/530 ACT: 22	CEEB CODE: 5293
Application Deadline: March 15	COMPETITIVE

High Point University combines the warmth and intimacy of a small liberal arts college with the academic offerings and amenities of a large state university. High Point University student body is both diverse and dynamic, allowing students to interact with instructors who are well-trained career teachers, not graduate assistants. Students may earn academic credit by participating in internships or by traveling abroad and studying in such locations as England, Mexico, Scotland, and China. High Point University also offers 14 NCAA Division I athletic programs and numerous extra-curricular opportunities. Figures in the above capsule and in this profile are approximate. There are 6 undergraduate schools and 1 graduate school. In addition to regional accreditation, High Point has baccalaureate program accreditation with NCATE, CAATE, and CIDA. The 300-acre campus is in a suburban area 15 miles southeast of Winston-Salem and 12 miles southwest of Greensboro. Including any residence halls, there are 59 buildings.

STUDENT LIFE: 69% of undergraduates are from out of state, mostly the Middle Atlantic. Students are from 46 states, 29 foreign countries, and Canada. 63% are from public schools. 81% are White. 59% are Protestant; 26% Catholic; 11% claim no religious affiliation. The average age of freshmen is 18; all undergraduates, 20. 20% do not continue beyond their first year; 60% remain to graduate. **Housing:** 3004 students can be accommodated in college housing, which includes single-sex and coed dorms, on-campus apartments, and off-campus apartments. In addition, there are honors houses, special-interest houses, fraternity houses, sorority houses, wellness halls, honors housing, and discipline-specific housing. On-campus housing is guaranteed for all 4 years. 93% of students live on campus; of those, 90% remain on campus on weekends. All students may keep cars.

FACULTY/CLASSROOMS: 52% of faculty are male; 48% are female. All teach undergraduates. No introductory courses are taught by graduate students. The average class size in an introductory lecture is 20; in a laboratory is 18; and in a regular course is 18.

PROGRAMS OF STUDY: High Point confers B.A., B.S. and B.S.B.A. degrees. Master's and Doctoral degrees are also awarded. Bachelor's degrees are awarded in BIOLOGICAL SCIENCE (biochemistry and biology/biological science), BUSINESS (accounting, business administration and management, international business management, and nonprofit/public organization management), COMMUNICATIONS AND THE ARTS (art, communications, English literature, English Writing, fine arts, French, graphic design, music, Spanish, and theatre arts), COMPUTER AND PHYSICAL SCIENCE (actuarial science, chemistry, computer science, mathematics, and mathematics – economics), EDUCATION (athletic training, elementary education, middle school education, physical education, and special education), ENGINEERING AND ENVIRONMENTAL DESIGN (interior design), HEALTH PROFESSIONS (exercise science), SOCIAL SCIENCE (criminal justice, history, home furnishings and equipment management/production/services, human services, industrial and organizational psychology, international relations, philosophy, political science/government, psychology, religion, and sociology). Business administration, exercise and sport science, education, psychology, biology, interior design, communications have the largest enrollments.

ACTIVITIES: 15% of men belong to 4 national fraternities; 25% of women belong to 1 local and 4 national sororities. There are 109 groups on campus, including art, band, cheerleading, choir, chorale, chorus, computers, dance, debate, drama, environmental, ethnic, film, honors, international, literary magazine, musical theater, newspaper, orchestra, pep band, political, professional, radio and TV, religious, social, social service, and student government. **Sports:** There are 7 intercollegiate sports for men and 7 for women, and 6 intramural sports for men and 6 for women. Facilities include intramural fields, tennis courts, an intramural gym, a recreation center featuring a swimming pool, racquetball courts, an aerobics center, a weight room, and a 2500-seat arena, 45,000-square-foot student activities center, a soccer stadium and track, a sports center, and a new university park with amphitheater. **Graduates:** From July 1, 2013 to June 30, 2014, 513 bachelor's degrees were awarded. The most popular majors were business (42%), education (9%), and human relations (8%). 15 companies recruited on campus in 2013-2014. In an average class, 50% graduate in 4 years or less, 55% graduate in 5 years or less, and 56% graduate in 6 years or less. Of the 2013 graduating class, 22% were enrolled in graduate school within 6 months of graduation, and 95% were employed.

SERVICES: Counseling and information services are available, as is tutoring in every subject. There is remedial math, reading, and writing. **Library/Resources:** The library contains 288,473 volumes, 84,000 microform items, 12,500 audio/video tapes/CDs/DVDs, and subscribes to 34,000 periodicals including electronic. Computerized

library services include interlibrary loans, database searching, and Internet access. Special learning facilities include an art gallery, radio station, and TV station. **Physically Challenged Students:** 98% of the campus is accessible. Facilities include wheelchair ramps, elevators, special parking, specially equipped restrooms, special class scheduling, and lowered drinking fountains. **Special:** There is cross-registration with the University of North Carolina at Greensboro, North Carolina Agricultural and Technical State University, and Greensboro, Elon, Guilford, and Bennett Colleges. High Point also offers study abroad in many countries, the Student Career Internship Program, accelerated degree programs, unique programs in home furnishings marketing/management studies, work-study programs, student-designed majors, and a 3-2 engineering program with Vanderbilt and Virginia Tech. There are 5 national honor societies, a freshman honors program, and 5 departmental honors programs. **Visiting:** There are regularly scheduled orientations for prospective students, students may visit during approved hours during the weekend and weekday. There are guides for informal visits and visitors may sit in on classes. To schedule a visit, contact the Admissions Office. **Campus Safety and Security:** Measures include 24-hour foot and vehicle patrol, emergency notification system, self-defense education, and security escort services. There are shuttle buses, emergency telephones, lighted pathways/sidewalks, controlled access to dorms/residences, 24-hour secured residence halls and student bike patrols, and valet parking service.

REQUIREMENTS: The SAT or ACT is required. The SAT is preferred. Applicants should be graduates of an accredited secondary school or have a GED certificate. They should have completed 14 academic units, including 4 in English, 3 in math, 2 each in science, social studies, and history, and 1 elective. AP and CLEP credits are accepted. To graduate, students must complete a minimum of 128 credit hours with a minimum GPA of 2.0. The core curriculum consists of 1 course in each of the following subject areas: English, foreign language, mathematics, and ethical reasoning, as well as a First Year Seminar course, President's Seminar, and a PE activity course. Distribution requirements include 2 courses in the social sciences and 1 course in each of the following areas: performing or visual arts, literature, history, religion, and natural science with laboratory. **Procedure:** Freshmen are admitted fall, spring, and summer. Entrance exams should be taken prior to high school graduation. There are early decision, early admissions, deferred admissions, and rolling admissions plans. Early decision applications should be filed by November 6; regular applications, by March 15 for fall entry, along with a $40 fee. Notification of early decision is sent November 27; regular decision, on a rolling basis. 283 early decision candidates were accepted for the 2014-2015 class. Applications are accepted on-line. **Transfer Students:** 50 transfer students enrolled in 2013-2014. Applicants must submit official transcripts from colleges and high schools previously attended, as well as SAT or ACT scores, if available. Generally, a minimum GPA of 2.0 is required. 31 of 124 credits required for the bachelor's degree must be completed at High Point. **International Students:** There are 65 international students enrolled. The school actively recruits these students. The SAT or ACT is required of students who wish to play on varsity athletic teams.

ADMISSIONS: 71% of the 2014-2015 applicants were accepted. The SAT scores for the 2014-2015 freshman class were: Critical Reading--30% below 500, 52% between 500 and 599, 16% between 600 and 699, and 2% between 700 and 800; Math--32% below 500, 49% between 500 and 599, 18% between 600 and 699, and 1% between 700 and 800; Writing--31% below 500, 52% between 500 and 599, 16% between 600 and 699, and 1% between 700 and 800. The ACT scores were 28% below 21, 37% between 21 and 23, 24% between 24 and 26, 7% between 27 and 28, and 5% above 28. 32% of the current freshmen were in the top fifth of their class; 62% were in the top two fifths. 7 freshmen graduated first in their class. **Admissions Contact:** Beth McCarthy, Director of Admissions. E-Mail: *admiss@highpoint.edu* Web: *www.highpoint.edu*

FINANCIAL AID: In 2014-2015, 91% of all full-time freshmen and 78% of continuing full-time students received some form of financial aid. 56% of all full-time freshmen and 56% of continuing full-time students received need-based aid. The average freshman award was $10,875. Need-based scholarships or need-based grants averaged $2,555 ($6,000 maximum); need-based self-help aid (loans and jobs) averaged $4,000 ($4,125 maximum); non-need-based athletic scholarships averaged $17,160 ($19,026 maximum); and other non-need-based awards and non-need-based scholarships averaged $8,576 ($12,000 maximum). 67% of undergraduate students work part-time. Average annual earnings from campus work are $1500. The average financial indebtedness of the 2014 graduate was $11,280. High Point is a member of CSS. The FAFSA and the state aid form are required. The priority date for freshman financial aid applications for fall entry is March 1.

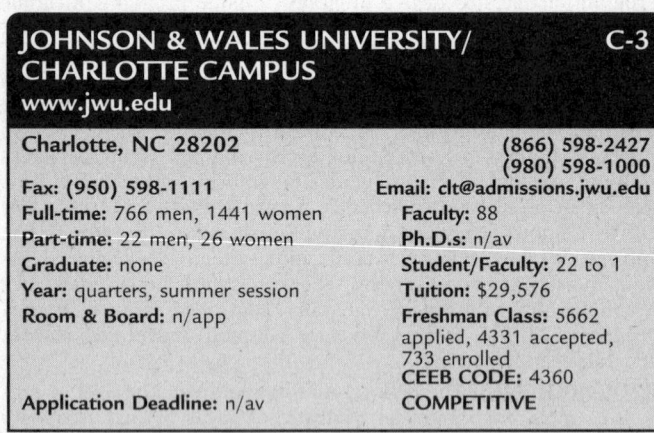

JOHNSON & WALES UNIVERSITY/ CHARLOTTE CAMPUS

C-3

www.jwu.edu

Charlotte, NC 28202	(866) 598-2427
	(980) 598-1000
Fax: (950) 598-1111	Email: clt@admissions.jwu.edu
Full-time: 766 men, 1441 women	Faculty: 88
Part-time: 22 men, 26 women	Ph.D.s: n/av
Graduate: none	Student/Faculty: 22 to 1
Year: quarters, summer session	Tuition: $29,576
Room & Board: n/app	Freshman Class: 5662 applied, 4331 accepted, 733 enrolled
	CEEB CODE: 4360
Application Deadline: n/av	COMPETITIVE

Johnson & Wales University/Charlotte Campus, founded in 2004, offers degree programs in its College of Business, College of Culinary Arts, and Hospitality College. There are 3 undergraduate schools. The campus is in an urban area in the center of the New South, Charlotte. Including any residence halls, there are 6 buildings.

STUDENT LIFE: 61% of undergraduates are from out of state, mostly the South. Students are from 47 states, 22 foreign countries, and Canada. 39% are White; 28% African American. **Female To Male Ratio:** 1.9:1. The average age of freshmen is 18; all undergraduates, 19. 75% remain to graduate. **Housing:** College-sponsored housing includes coed dorms and on-campus apartments, special housing for disabled students, and wellness housing. On-campus housing is available on a lottery system for upperclassmen. 51% of students live on campus. Alcohol is not permitted. All students may keep cars.

FACULTY/CLASSROOMS: All teach undergraduates. No introductory courses are taught by graduate students.

PROGRAMS OF STUDY: JWU confers B.S. degrees. Associate degrees are also awarded. Bachelor's degrees are awarded in BUSINESS (accounting, business administration and management, entrepreneurial studies, hospitality management services, hotel/motel and restaurant management, marketing and distribution, marketing management, marketing/retailing/merchandising, sports management, and tourism), ENGINEERING AND ENVIRONMENTAL DESIGN (food services technology), SOCIAL SCIENCE (clothing and textiles management/production/services, food production/management/services, and parks and recreation management).

ACTIVITIES: There are 36 groups on campus, including cheerleading, gay, honors, international, newspaper, photography, religious, social, student government, and yearbook. Popular campus events include Welcome Week, Western Day, and Spring Week. **Sports: Graduates:** From July 1, 2013 to June 30, 2014, 389 bachelor's degrees were awarded. The most popular majors were family and consumer sciences (56%), business/marketing (30%), and parks and recreation (13%).

SERVICES: Counseling and information services are available, as is tutoring in every subject. **Library/Resources:** The library contains 28,690 volumes, 8,474 audio/video tapes/CDs/DVDs, and subscribes to 196 periodicals including electronic. Computerized library services include interlibrary loans, database searching, Internet access, and Wi-Fi capability. **Physically Challenged Students:** All of the campus is accessible. Facilities include wheelchair ramps, elevators, special parking, specially equipped restrooms, special class scheduling, lowered drinking fountains, lowered telephones, and special housing. **Special:** The university offers co-op programs, accelerated degree

programs, dual majors, study abroad, and worldwide work-study opportunities in business, hospitality, technology, and culinary arts. Most majors require 11-week internships. There is a freshman honors program. **Visiting:** There are regularly scheduled orientations for prospective students, including an introduction to the academic and social aspects of the campus experience through interactive sessions. There are guides for informal visits, visitors may sit in on classes, and stay overnight. To schedule a visit, contact the Admissions Office. **Campus Safety and Security:** Measures include 24-hour foot and vehicle patrol, self-defense education, and security escort services. There are shuttle buses, emergency telephones, and lighted pathways/sidewalks.

REQUIREMENTS: Although SAT and ACT scores are required only for students applying for honors admissions, students who have taken these tests are encouraged to submit their scores. Requirements are 4 years of English, 3 years each of mathematics and science, and 2 years of social studies. High school diploma is required and the GED is accepted. AP and CLEP credits are accepted. Important factors in the admissions decision are advanced placement or honors courses, extracurricular activities record, parents or siblings attended your school, and recommendations by school officials. To graduate, students must complete 180 quarter credit hours, including at least 36 in the major, with a minimum GPA of 2.0. Required courses include English, math, history, economics, science, psychology, sociology, and professional development. **Procedure:** Freshmen are admitted to all sessions. There are deferred admissions and rolling admissions plans. Application deadlines are open. Applications are accepted online. **Transfer Students:** 170 transfer students enrolled in 2013-2014. Applicants are required to submit official high school and college transcripts and must have earned a minimum college GPA of 2.0, 45 of 180 credits required for the bachelor's degree must be completed at JWU. **International Students:** There are 46 international students enrolled. The school actively recruits these students. They must take the TOEFL with a minimum score of 550 on the paper-based TOEFL (PBT) or 80 on the Internet-based version (iBT).

ADMISSIONS: 76% of the 2014-2015 applicants were accepted. **Admissions Contact:** Joseph Campos, Director of Admissions. E-Mail: *clt@admissions.jwu.edu* Web: *www.jwu.edu*

FINANCIAL AID: JWU is a member of CSS. The FAFSA is required. The priority date for freshman financial aid applications for fall entry is March 1.

JOHNSON C. SMITH UNIVERSITY (*The complete profile is made available exclusively on our website, www.barronspac.com*)

LEES-MCRAE COLLEGE

C-2

www.lmc.edu

Banner Elk, NC 28604	(828) 898-5241
	(800) 280-4562
Fax: n/av	Email: admissions@lmc.edu
Full-time: 317 men, 613 women	Faculty: 45; IIB
Part-time: 1 men, 9 women	Ph.D.s: 64%
Graduate: n/av	Student/Faculty: 15 to 1
Year: semesters, summer session	Tuition: $24,150
Room & Board: $9794	Freshman Class: n/av
	CEEB CODE: 5364
Application Deadline: n/av	COMPETITIVE

Lees-McRae is a four-year, coeducational residential college offering diverse baccalaureate degrees, strong athletic programs and outstanding faculty. The College offers online programs and degree-completion opportunities in surrounding communities to nontraditional learners. All academic programs incorporate a broad core curriculum and field-specific career preparation and experiential learning with an emphasis in leadership and service. In addition to regional accreditation, Lees-McRae has baccalaureate program accreditation with TEAC, CAATE, and CCNE. The 460-acre campus is in a rural area 17 miles west of Boone, NC and 115 miles northwest of Charlotte, NC. Including any residence halls, there are 59 buildings.

STUDENT LIFE: 73% of undergraduates are from North Carolina.

Others are from 31 states, 7 foreign countries, and Canada. The average age of freshmen is 18; all undergraduates, 36. **Housing:** 704 students can be accommodated in college housing, which includes single-sex and coed dorms and on-campus apartments. In addition, there are honors houses, special-interest houses, substance-free, and pet-friendly. On-campus housing is guaranteed for all 4 years and is available on a lottery system for upperclassmen. 64% of students live on campus. All students may keep cars.

FACULTY/CLASSROOMS: 45% of faculty are male; 55% are female. All teach undergraduates. No introductory courses are taught by graduate students.

PROGRAMS OF STUDY: Lees-McRae confers B.A., B.S., B.A.A.S and B.F.A. degrees. Bachelor's degrees are awarded in BIOLOGICAL SCIENCE (biology/biological science and wildlife biology), BUSINESS (business administration and management and sports management), COMMUNICATIONS AND THE ARTS (art, communications, design, dramatic arts, English, musical theater, performing arts, and visual and performing arts), COMPUTER AND PHYSICAL SCIENCE (mathematics), EDUCATION (athletic training, drama education, education, and elementary education), HEALTH PROFESSIONS (premedicine and preveterinary science), SOCIAL SCIENCE (criminal justice, history, humanities, psychology, and religion). Wildlife biology, nursing, and education have the largest enrollments.

ACTIVITIES: Groups on campus include art, cheerleading, chorus, communications, dance, drama, environmental, honors, international, musical theater, photography, professional, religious, social, social service, and student government. Popular campus events include Mountain Day, and Stephenson Lecture Series. **Sports:** There are 7 intercollegiate sports for men and 8 for women. Facilities include a main gym that seats 2,000 with basketball/volleyball courts, a match field for soccer/lacrosse, 4 practice fields, a softball field with batting cages, 2 indoor tennis courts, 6 outdoor tennis courts, a secondary gym for intramurals, an indoor Olympic-size pool, fitness center, weight room facility, and outdoor basketball court. **Graduates:** From July 1, 2013 to June 30, 2014, 221 bachelor's degrees were awarded. The most popular majors were health professions (22%), social sciences (22%), and education (19%). In an average class, 30% graduate in 4 years or less, 38% graduate in 5 years or less, and 38% graduate in 6 years or less.

SERVICES: Counseling and information services are available, as is tutoring in most subjects. There is remedial math, reading, and writing. **Library/Resources:** The library contains 216,747 volumes, 7,194 microform items, and 1,488 audio/video tapes/CDs/DVDs. Computerized library services include interlibrary loans, database searching, Internet access, and Wi-Fi capability. Special learning facilities include an art gallery, an wildlife rehabilitation center, academic success center, writing center, technical theatre and design studio. **Physically Challenged Students:** Facilities include wheelchair ramps, special parking, specially equipped restrooms, special class scheduling, and special housing. **Special:** There is a freshman honors program. **Visiting:** There are regularly scheduled orientations for prospective students. There are guides for informal visits, visitors may sit in on classes, and stay overnight. To schedule a visit, contact Candace Silver at (828) 898-8723. **Campus Safety and Security:** Measures include 24-hour foot and vehicle patrol, emergency notification system, and security escort services. There are emergency telephones, lighted pathways/sidewalks, and controlled access to dorms/residences.

REQUIREMENTS: Applicants must have completed 18 units of secondary school academic courses, including 6 of academic electives, 4 of English, 3 of math, 2 of science (1 with lab work), and 1 each of social studies and history. AP and CLEP credits are accepted. **Procedure:** Freshmen are admitted to all sessions. There is a rolling admissions plan. Application deadlines are open. Applications are accepted on-line. **Transfer Students:** 167 transfer students enrolled in 2013-2014. Applicants must submit a college GPA of 2.0 and be in good standing at the previous or current institution. Students who have completed 24 semester hours or more must submit a dean's evaluation form; those with fewer than 24 must also submit high school transcripts 32 of 124 credits required for the bachelor's degree must be completed at Lees-McRae. **International Students:** There are 23 international students enrolled. The school actively recruits these students. They must take the TOEFL.

ADMISSIONS: The SAT scores for the 2014-2015 freshman class were: Critical Reading--59% below 500, 34% between 500 and 599, 6% between 600 and 699, and 1% between 700 and 800; Math--53% below 500, 35% between 500 and 599, and 12% between 600 and 699. **Admissions Contact:** Ginger Hansen, Vice President of Enrollment Management. E-Mail: *admissions@lmc.edu* Web: *www.lmc.edu*

FINANCIAL AID: In 2014-2015, 88% of all full-time freshmen and 80% of continuing full-time students received some form of financial aid. Lees-McRae is a member of CSS. The FAFSA is required. The priority date for freshman financial aid applications for fall entry is April 15.

LENOIR-RHYNE COLLEGE   C-2
www.lr.edu

Hickory, NC 28603	(828) 328-1741
	(828) 328-7330
Fax: (828) 328-7378	Email: admission@lr.edu
Full-time: 569 men, 891 women	Faculty: 107
Part-time: 31 men, 73 women	Ph.Ds: 73%
Graduate: 72 men, 201 women	Student/Faculty: 13 to 1
Year: semesters, summer session	Tuition: $26,524
Room & Board: $9370	Freshman Class: 3316 applied, 2882 accepted, 406 enrolled
SAT CR/M: 480/500 ACT: 21	CEEB CODE: 5363
Application Deadline: open	COMPETITIVE

Lenoir-Rhyne College, founded in 1891, is a private institution affiliated with the Lutheran Church, offering liberal arts programs that focus on business, education, and allied health sciences. Figures in the above capsule and in this profile are approximate. There is one graduate school. In addition to regional accreditation, Lenoir-Rhyne has baccalaureate program accreditation with NCATE and NLN. The 100-acre campus is in a suburban area 45 miles northwest of Charlotte. Including any residence halls, there are 30 buildings.

STUDENT LIFE: 70% of undergraduates are from North Carolina. Others are from 30 states, 9 foreign countries, and Canada. 89% are from public schools. 87% are White. 68% are Protestant; 23% claim no religious affiliation. The average age of freshmen is 18; all undergraduates, 22. 20% do not continue beyond their first year; 63% remain to graduate. **Housing:** 900 students can be accommodated in college housing, which includes single-sex and coed dorms and on-campus apartments. In addition, there are honors houses, special-interest houses, fraternity houses, sorority houses, Hearing-impaired housing, special interest varies by year. On-campus housing is guaranteed for all 4 years and is available on a lottery system for upperclassmen. 65% of students live on campus; of those, 70% remain on campus on weekends. All students may keep cars.

FACULTY/CLASSROOMS: 55% of faculty are male; 45% are female. All teach undergraduates. No introductory courses are taught by graduate students. The average class size in an introductory lecture is 26; in a laboratory is 20; and in a regular course is 20.

PROGRAMS OF STUDY: Lenoir-Rhyne confers B.A., B.S. and B.Mus.Ed. degrees. Master's degrees are also awarded. Bachelor's degrees are awarded in AGRICULTURE (environmental studies), BIOLOGICAL SCIENCE (biology/biological science), BUSINESS (accounting, business administration and management, international business management, management information systems, and sports management), COMMUNICATIONS AND THE ARTS (applied music, communications, dramatic arts, English as a second/foreign language, French, German, graphic design, journalism, music, music performance, piano/organ, and Spanish), COMPUTER AND PHYSICAL SCIENCE (chemistry, computer science, mathematics, and physics), EDUCATION (athletic training, Christian education, early childhood education, elementary education, English education, foreign languages education, health education, middle school education, music education, science education, and secondary education), ENGINEERING AND ENVIRONMENTAL DESIGN (preengineering), HEALTH PROFESSIONS (exercise science, medical laboratory technology, nursing, occupational therapy, predentistry, premedicine, preoptometry, and preveterinary science), SOCIAL SCIENCE (American studies, economics, history, human services, philosophy, political science/government, prelaw, psychology, religion, religious education, religious music, sociology, theological studies, and youth ministry). Business and nursing have the largest enrollments.

ACTIVITIES: 23% of men belong to 3 national fraternities; 27% of women belong to 4 national sororities. There are 50 groups on campus, including art, band, cheerleading, choir, chorus, computers, dance, debate, drama, environmental, ethnic, gay, honors, international, jazz band, literary magazine, musical theater, newspaper, outdoor adventure club, pep band, photography, political, professional, radio and TV, religious, social, social service, student government, symphony, and yearbook. Popular campus events include Spring Fling, Advent Candlelight Service, and Opening of School. **Sports:** There are 10 intercollegiate sports for men and 10 for women, and 14 intramural sports for men and 14 for women. Facilities include an 8500-seat football stadium, a 3600-seat gym, practice fields, racquetball courts, weight rooms, a sauna, a 25-meter swimming pool, 2 intramural fields, and baseball, softball, and soccer fields, and world class Mondotrack track.

SERVICES: Counseling and information services are available, as is tutoring in every subject. There is remedial math and writing. Interpreters and note takers for hearing-impaired students **Library/ Resources:** The library contains 145,960 volumes, 462,878 microform items, 40,379 audio/video tapes/CDs/DVDs, and subscribes to 5,376 periodicals including electronic. Computerized library services include interlibrary loans and database searching. Special learning facilities include a radio station, TV station, and observatory. **Physically Challenged Students:** All of the campus is accessible. Facilities include wheelchair ramps, elevators, special parking, specially equipped restrooms, lowered drinking fountains. **Special:** Lenoir-Rhyne offers study abroad in more than 25 countries and with the nationally known ISEP program, a Washington semester at American University and through the Lutheran College Washington Consortium, internships in most majors, a general studies degree, work-study programs, 3-2 enginering degrees with North Carolina State, North Carolina Agricultural and Technical, and Clemson Universities and the University of North Carolina at Charlotte, pass/fail options, and auditing for most courses. In addition, the Broyhill institute for Business Leadership offers programs to promote understanding of the business community. The university offers an honors program for outstanding students. There are 12 national honor societies, a freshman honors program, and 18 departmental honors programs. **Visiting:** There are regularly scheduled orientations for prospective students, including a meeting with an admissions counselor and a student-guided tour of the campus. There are guides for informal visits, visitors may sit in on classes, and stay overnight. To schedule a visit, contact the Enrollment Management Office. **Campus Safety and Security:** Measures include 24-hour foot and vehicle patrol, emergency notification system, self-defense education, and security escort services. There are emergency telephones, lighted pathways/ sidewalks, and controlled access to dorms/residences.

REQUIREMENTS: The SAT or ACT is required. Applicants need 16 academic credits and should have 4 units in English, 3 in math (algebra 1, geometry, and algebra 2), 2 in the same foreign language, and 1 each in American history and a lab science. An interview is recommended for all students. Music majors must also audition. AP and CLEP credits are accepted. Important factors in the admissions decision are advanced placement or honors courses, personality/ intangible qualities, and leadership record. To graduate, students must complete 128 credit hours, including 56 to 57 in liberal arts courses, with a minimum GPA of 2.0. The total number of hours in a major varies by program. **Procedure:** Freshmen are admitted to all sessions. Entrance exams should be taken in the spring of the junior year and thereafter. There are early admissions, deferred admissions, and rolling admissions plans. Application deadlines are open. Application fee is $35. Notification is sent on a Rolling basis. Applications are accepted on-line. **Transfer Students:** 143 transfer students enrolled in 2013-2014. Applicants with more than 30 semester hours need a 2.0 minimum GPA in general studies programs or a 2.5 minimum GPA in nursing or education programs. Those with fewer than 30 semester hours must meet freshman entrance criteria. 32 of 128 credits required for the bachelor's degree must be completed at

Lenoir-Rhyne. **International Students:** There are 19 international students enrolled. The school actively recruits these students. They must take the TOEFL with a minimum score of 550 on the paper-based TOEFL (PBT) or 79 on the Internet-based version (iBT).

ADMISSIONS: 87% of the 2014-2015 applicants were accepted. The SAT scores for the 2014-2015 freshman class were: Critical Reading-57% below 500, 33% between 500 and 599, and 10% between 600 and 699; Math--46% below 500, 39% between 500 and 599, 14% between 600 and 699, and 1% between 700 and 800. The ACT scores were 74% below 21, 6% between 21 and 23, 17% between 24 and 26, 2% between 27 and 28, and 1% above 28. 42% of the current freshmen were in the top fifth of their class; 75% were in the top two fifths. **Admissions Contact:** Karen Feezor, Director of Admissions. E-Mail: *admission@lr.edu* Web: *www.lr.edu*

FINANCIAL AID: In 2014-2015, 99% of all full-time freshmen and 92% of continuing full-time students received some form of financial aid. 40% of all full-time freshmen and 55% of continuing full-time students received need-based aid. 35% of undergraduate students work part-time. Average annual earnings from campus work are $1000. The average financial indebtedness of the 2014 graduate was $30,000. The FAFSA is required. The deadline for filing freshman financial aid applications for fall entry is March 15.

LIVINGSTONE COLLEGE (*The complete profile is made available exclusively on our website, www.barronspac.com*)

MARS HILL UNIVERSITY (*The complete profile is made available exclusively on our website, www.barronspac.com*)

MEREDITH COLLEGE	D-2
www.meredith.edu	

Raleigh, NC 27607	(919) 760-8600
	(800) MEREDITH
Fax: (919) 760-2348	Email: admissions@meredith.edu
Full-time: 1766 women	Faculty: 138; IIA, --$
Part-time: 9 men, 192 women	Ph.D.s: 91%
Graduate: 32 men, 263 women	Student/Faculty: 13 to 1
Year: semesters, summer session	Tuition: $24,400
Room & Board: $7020	Freshman Class: 1614 applied, 1047 accepted, 1481 enrolled
SAT CR/M: 519/520 ACT: 21	CEEB CODE: 5410
Application Deadline: February 15	COMPETITIVE

Meredith College, founded in 1891, is a private college for women offering a comprehensive undergraduate program with a strong emphasis on the liberal arts. Graduate programs in business, music, education, and nutrition are offered to both women and men. The figures in the above capsule and in this profile are approximate. There are 6 undergraduate schools and one graduate school. In addition to regional accreditation, Meredith has baccalaureate program accreditation with ADA, CSWE, FIDER, NASM, and NCATE. The 225-acre campus is in an urban area in Raleigh, NC. Including any residence halls, there are 30 buildings.

STUDENT LIFE: 90% of undergraduates are from North Carolina. Others are from 36 states, and 17 foreign countries. 77% are White; 11% African American. The average age of freshmen is 18; all undergraduates, 22. 24% do not continue beyond their first year; 76% remain to graduate. **Housing:** 1150 students can be accommodated in college housing, which includes single-sex dorms and on-campus apartments. All nonsmoking halls. On-campus housing is guaranteed for all 4 years. 56% of students commute. Alcohol is not permitted. All students may keep cars.

FACULTY/CLASSROOMS: 31% of faculty are male; 69% are female. All teach undergraduates. No introductory courses are taught by graduate students. The average class size in an introductory lecture is 20; in a laboratory is 11; and in a regular course is 17.

PROGRAMS OF STUDY: Meredith confers B.A., B.S., B.M. and B.S.W. degrees. Master's degrees are also awarded. Bachelor's degrees are awarded in AGRICULTURE (environmental studies), BIOLOGI-

CAL SCIENCE (biology/biological science and nutrition), BUSINESS (accounting, business administration and management, fashion merchandising, and international business management), COMMUNICATIONS AND THE ARTS (applied music, art, communications, dance, dramatic arts, English, fine arts, French, music, music performance, musical theater, and Spanish), COMPUTER AND PHYSICAL SCIENCE (chemistry, computer science, information sciences and systems, and mathematics), EDUCATION (music education), ENGINEERING AND ENVIRONMENTAL DESIGN (interior design), HEALTH PROFESSIONS (exercise science), SOCIAL SCIENCE (American studies, child psychology/development, economics, family/consumer studies, history, international studies, political science/government, psychology, public affairs, religion, social work, and sociology). Interior design, psychology, and biology have the largest enrollments.

ACTIVITIES: There are 91 groups on campus, including and nutrition and wellness, environmental, foreign language, art, chorale, chorus, commuter, computers, dance, drama, ethnic, gay, honors, international, literary magazine, musical theater, newspaper, orchestra, photography, political, professional, religious, social, social service, student government, and symphony. Popular campus events include Academics and Leadership Awards Day, White Iris Ball, and Undergraduate Research Conference. **Sports:** There are 6 intercollegiate sports for women. Facilities include an indoor swimming pool, a dance studio, a fitness center, a horseshoe pit, a putting green and driving range, a softball diamond, tennis courts, a soccer field, and a gym with basketball, volleyball, and badminton courts. **Graduates:** From July 1, 2013 to June 30, 2014, 430 bachelor's degrees were awarded. The most popular majors were psychology (10%), interior design (9%), and child development (7%). In an average class, 14% graduate in 3 years or less, 44% graduate in 4 years or less, 55% graduate in 5 years or less, and 57% graduate in 6 years or less.

SERVICES: Counseling and information services are available, as is tutoring in some subjects, math, writing, computer lab, French, Spanish, biology, chemistry, study skills, German, GRE prep, Praxis prep, and grammar. There is a reader service for the blind. **Library/Resources:** The 2 libraries contain 155,165 volumes, 16,116 microform items, 14,671 audio/video tapes/CDs/DVDs, and subscribe to 2,867 periodicals including electronic. Computerized library services include interlibrary loans, database searching, and Internet access. Special learning facilities include an art gallery, child-care lab, greenhouse, experimental and clinical psychology labs including one on autism, an electron microscope suite, astronomy observation deck, student/faculty research labs, and language lab. **Physically Challenged Students:** 81% of the campus is accessible. Facilities include wheelchair ramps, elevators, special parking, specially equipped restrooms, special class scheduling, lowered drinking fountains, special housing. Handicap lift in the swimming pool, and lowered fire alarms. **Special:** Meredith offers cooperative programs, cross-registration with Cooperating Raleigh Colleges, internships, study abroad in Europe and Asia, a Washington semester at American University, a U.N. semester at Drew University, and work-study programs on campus. Dual majors, interdisciplinary and student-designed majors, preprofessional programs, and pass/fail options are available. Certification in social work and licensure for teaching are possible. Business administration, management, and social work majors can be completed through evening classes. There are 19 national honor societies and a freshman honors program. **Visiting:** There are regularly scheduled orientations for prospective students, students may participate in information sessions for senior students and parents, class visitation, informal conversations with students and faculty/staff, and campus tours. There are guides for informal visits, visitors may sit in on classes, and stay overnight. To schedule a visit, contact the Admissions Office. **Campus Safety and Security:** Measures include 24-hour foot and vehicle patrol, self-defense education, and security escort services. There are emergency telephones, lighted pathways/sidewalks, controlled campus access at night, and 24-hour locked residence halls.

REQUIREMENTS: The SAT or ACT is required. The ACT Optional Writing test is also required. Applicants who submit SAT scores preferred. Applicants must also have a minimum of 16 units of credit, including 4 in English, 3 each in math, history/social studies, and science, 2 in foreign language, and 1 elective. The student is expected to rank in the top half of her class, and grades in academic subjects are very important. An interview may be requested as part of the evaluation process. Meredith requires applicants to be in the upper 50% of their class. AP and CLEP credits are accepted. Important factors in the admissions decision are recommendations by school officials, advanced placement or honors courses, and evidence of special talent. To graduate, students must complete a total of 124 credit hours, including general education requirements, a major field, and electives, with a minimum GPA of 2.0. General Education is comprised of a core curriculum focusing on understanding diverse cultures, fields of knowledge that ensure breadth in the liberal arts, and across-the-curriculum threads and independent learning experiences that build competencies. Some major fields offer or require a concentration, and contract majors are possible. Electives may be used to complete a second major, a minor, teacher licensure, or to explore areas of personal, career or pre-professional interest. **Procedure:** Freshmen are admitted fall and spring. Entrance exams should be taken by January of the senior year. There are early decision, deferred admissions, and rolling admissions plans. Early decision applications should be filed by October 15; regular applications, by February 15 for fall entry, along with a $40 fee. Notification of early decision is sent November 1; regular decision, on a rolling basis. 121 early decision candidates were accepted for the 2014-2015 class. Applications are accepted on-line. **Transfer Students:** 74 transfer students enrolled in 2013-2014. Applicants must have a minimum GPA of 2.0, be eligible to return to the last college attended, and be recommended by college officials. Those students with fewer than 30 hours of credit must also meet freshman admission requirements. 31 of 124 credits required for the bachelor's degree must be completed at Meredith. **International Students:** There are 26 international students enrolled. The school actively recruits these students. They must take the TOEFL. If English is the student's native language or primary language of instruction.

ADMISSIONS: 65% of the 2014-2015 applicants were accepted. The SAT scores for the 2014-2015 freshman class were: Critical Reading--41% below 500, 42% between 500 and 599, 16% between 600 and 699, and 1% between 700 and 800; Math--39% below 500, 43% between 500 and 599, 17% between 600 and 699, and 1% between 700 and 800. The ACT scores were 47% below 21, 24% between 21 and 23, 21% between 24 and 26, 5% between 27 and 28, and 6% above 28. 43% of the current freshmen were in the top fifth of their class; 72% were in the top two fifths. 5 freshmen graduated first in their class. **Admissions Contact:** Cristan Trahey Harris, Director of Admissions. E-Mail: *admissions@meredith.edu* Web: *www.meredith.edu*

FINANCIAL AID: Meredith is a member of CSS. The FAFSA is required. The priority date for freshman financial aid applications for fall entry is February 15.

METHODIST UNIVERSITY   D-3
www.methodist.edu

Fayetteville, NC 28311	**(910) 630-7000**
	(800) 488-7110
Fax: (910) 630-7285	Email: admissions@methodist.edu
Full-time: 1059 men, 960 women	**Faculty:** 142
Part-time: 109 men, 152 women	**Ph.D.s:** 79%
Graduate: 83 men, 113 women	**Student/Faculty:** 13 to 1
Year: semesters, summer session	**Tuition:** $27,082
Room & Board: $10,063	**Freshman Class:** 3823 applied, 2315 accepted, 488 enrolled
SAT CR/M/W: 484/510/466 **ACT:** 21	**CEEB CODE:** 5426
Application Deadline: n/av	**COMPETITIVE**

Methodist University, founded in 1956, is a private institution affiliated with the United Methodist Church. The University offers programs in the arts and sciences, education, business, and professional training. The figures in the above capsule and in this profile are approximate. There are 4 undergraduate schools and 3 graduate schools. In addition to regional accreditation, Methodist has baccalaureate program accreditation with ACBSP, CSWE, NCATE, and

CAAHEP. The 620-acre campus is in a suburban area 5 miles north of Fayetteville. Including any residence halls, there are 38 buildings. **STUDENT LIFE:** 56% of undergraduates are from North Carolina. Others are from 44 states, 31 foreign countries, and Canada. 86% are from public schools. 65% are White; 20% African American. 41% are Protestant; 16% Catholic. The average age of freshmen is 19; all undergraduates, 24. 33% do not continue beyond their first year; 44% remain to graduate. **Housing:** 1095 students can be accommodated in college housing, which includes single-sex dorms and on-campus apartments. In addition, there are honors houses, fraternity houses, sorority houses, first year experience, and a health and wellness hall. On-campus housing is guaranteed for all 4 years. 57% of students live on campus; of those, 70% remain on campus on weekends. Alcohol is not permitted. All students may keep cars.

FACULTY/CLASSROOMS: 52% of faculty are male; 48% are female. All teach undergraduates. No introductory courses are taught by graduate students. The average class size in an introductory lecture is 23; in a laboratory is 20; and in a regular course is 20.

PROGRAMS OF STUDY: Methodist confers B.A., B.S., B.F.A, B.M. and B.S.W. degrees. Associate and Master's degrees are also awarded. Bachelor's degrees are awarded in BIOLOGICAL SCIENCE (biology/biological science), BUSINESS (accounting, business administration and management, marketing/retailing/merchandising, organizational behavior, and sports management), COMMUNICATIONS AND THE ARTS (art, communications, creative writing, dramatic arts, English, French, music, music performance, and Spanish), COMPUTER AND PHYSICAL SCIENCE (chemistry, computer science, and mathematics), EDUCATION (art education, athletic training, elementary education, middle school education, music education, physical education, secondary education, and special education), ENGINEERING AND ENVIRONMENTAL DESIGN (computer technology), HEALTH PROFESSIONS (nursing, physician's assistant, and predentistry), SOCIAL SCIENCE (criminal justice, economics, history, international studies, political science/government, prelaw, psychology, religion, social studies, social work, and sociology). Business administration, biology, and education are the strongest academically, and have the largest enrollments.

ACTIVITIES: 6% of men belong to 1 local and 1 national fraternities; 6% of women belong to 2 local and 1 national sororities. There are 104 groups on campus, including art, band, cheerleading, choir, chorale, chorus, computers, dance, debate, drama, environmental, ethnic, forensics, honors, international, jazz band, literary magazine, marching band, musical theater, newspaper, orchestra, pep band, photography, political, professional, radio and TV, religious, social, social service, student government, and symphony. Popular campus events include Show You Care Day, Annual Woodcutting, and Spring Fest. **Sports:** There are 9 intercollegiate sports for men and 10 for women, and 7 intramural sports for men and 4 for women. Facilities include the Nimocks Fitness center, a 1200-seat stadium, a 1500-seat gym, a golf course, a track and field area, tennis courts, and fields for baseball, softball, and soccer. **Graduates:** From July 1, 2013 to June 30, 2014, 290 bachelor's degrees were awarded. The most popular majors were business (46%), social sciences (11%), and education (7%). 180 companies recruited on campus in 2013-2014. In an average class, 1% graduate in 3 years or less, 33% graduate in 4 years or less, 38% graduate in 5 years or less, and 40% graduate in 6 years or less. Of the 2013 graduating class, 24% were enrolled in graduate school within 6 months of graduation, and 70% were employed.

SERVICES: Counseling and information services are available, as is tutoring in most subjects. There is a reader service for the blind, and remedial math and writing. **Library/Resources:** The library contains 181,833 volumes, 57,759 microform items, 13,412 audio/video tapes/CDs/DVDs, and subscribes to 587 periodicals including electronic. Computerized library services include interlibrary loans, database searching, Internet access, and Wi-Fi capability. Special learning facilities include an art gallery, radio station, 18 hole golf course and pro shop for professional golf and tennis management programs. **Physically Challenged Students:** 90% of the campus is accessible. Facilities include wheelchair ramps, elevators, special parking, specially equipped restrooms, and lowered drinking fountains. **Special:** Methodist offers internships in political science and social work, study abroad in 4 countries, a Washington semester, a general studies degree, a 3-2 engineering degree with North Carolina State Univer-

sity, pass/fail options, dual majors, and nondegree study. The business administration major offers concentrations in professional golf, tennis, and resort management with specialized facilities and co-op programs. There are 7 national honor societies, a freshman honors program, and 5 departmental honors programs. **Visiting:** There are regularly scheduled orientations for prospective students, 3 days prior to the first day of fall semester. There are guides for informal visits, visitors may sit in on classes, and stay overnight. To schedule a visit, contact the Admissions Office. **Campus Safety and Security:** Measures include 24-hour foot and vehicle patrol, emergency notification system, self-defense education, and security escort services. There are shuttle buses, emergency telephones, lighted pathways/sidewalks, and controlled access to dorms/residences.

REQUIREMENTS: The SAT or ACT is required. Applicants should be graduates of an accredited secondary school or have a GED certificate. They must have 16 academic credits, including 4 in English and 3 each in history, math, and science. 2 years of foreign language are recommended. An essay and interview are also recommended. AP and CLEP credits are accepted. Important factors in the admissions decision are recommendations by school officials, evidence of special talent, and advanced placement or honors courses. To graduate, students must complete at least 124 semester hours, including core requirements, with a minimum GPA of 2.0. A liberal arts core, ranging from 36 to 62 hours, is required in all majors. **Procedure:** Freshmen are admitted fall, spring, and summer. There are deferred admissions and rolling admissions plans. Application deadlines are open. Application fee is $25. Applications are accepted on-line. **Transfer Students:** 292 transfer students enrolled in 2013-2014. Applicants must have a minimum GPA of 2.0. They must also submit a high school transcript, college transcripts, and the SAT or ACT scores. 30 of 124 credits required for the bachelor's degree must be completed at Methodist. **International Students:** There are 70 international students enrolled. The school actively recruits these students. They must take the TOEFL with a minimum score of 500 on the paper-based TOEFL (PBT) or 60 on the Internet-based version (iBT). They must also take the SAT or ACT. The student may take the SAT or ACT in place of the TOEFL if English proficiency is demonstrated.

ADMISSIONS: 61% of the 2014-2015 applicants were accepted. The SAT scores for the 2014-2015 freshman class were: Critical Reading--59% below 500, 34% between 500 and 599, 6% between 600 and 699, and 1% between 700 and 800; Math--45% below 500, 40% between 500 and 599, 14% between 600 and 699, and 1% between 700 and 800; Writing--60% below 500, 33% between 500 and 599, 6% between 600 and 699, and 1% between 700 and 800. The ACT scores were 50% below 21, 30% between 21 and 23, 10% between 24 and 26, 6% between 27 and 28, and 4% above 28. 27% of the current freshmen were in the top fifth of their class; 54% were in the top two fifths. 4 freshmen graduated first in their class. **Admissions Contact:** Jamie Legg, Director of Admissions. E-Mail: *jlegg@methodist.edu* Web: *www.methodist.edu*

FINANCIAL AID: In 2014-2015, 92% of all full-time freshmen and continuing full-time students received some form of financial aid. 92% of all full-time freshmen and 85% of continuing full-time students received need-based aid. The average freshman award was $9,780. 60% of undergraduate students work part-time. Average annual earnings from campus work are $1000. The average financial indebtedness of the 2014 graduate was $20,026. The FAFSA is required. The priority date for freshman financial aid applications for fall entry is March 15.

MONTREAT COLLEGE   **B-2**
www.montreat.edu

Montreat, NC 28757	(828) 669-8012
	(800) 622-6968
Fax: (828) 669-2141	Email: admissions@montreat.edu
Full-time: 230 men, 214 women	**Faculty:** 33
Part-time: 110 men, 181 women	**Ph.D.s:** 86%
Graduate: 48 men, 150 women	**Student/Faculty:** 15 to 1
Year: semesters, summer session	**Tuition:** $23,520
Room & Board: $7778	**Freshman Class:** 507 applied, 461 accepted, 148 enrolled
SAT CR/M/W: 475/466/445 **ACT:** required	
	CEEB CODE: 5423
Application Deadline: open	**COMPETITIVE**

Montreat College, founded in 1916, is a private liberal arts institution affiliated with the Association of Presbyterian Colleges and Universities, and committed to the integration of faith and learning. In addition to regional accreditation, Montreat has baccalaureate program accreditation with NCATE, IACBE, and WEAAC. The 139-acre campus is in a small town 15 miles east of Asheville. Including any residence halls, there are 18 buildings.

STUDENT LIFE: 66% of undergraduates are from North Carolina. Others are from 22 states, 11 foreign countries, and Canada. 55% are from public schools. 61% are White; 18% African American. 73% are Protestant. The average age of freshmen is 18; all undergraduates, 28. 39% do not continue beyond their first year; 42% remain to graduate. **Housing:** 392 students can be accommodated in college housing, which includes single-sex dorms and on-campus apartments. On-campus housing is guaranteed for all 4 years. 91% of students live on campus; of those, 50% remain on campus on weekends. Alcohol is not permitted. All students may keep cars.

FACULTY/CLASSROOMS: 58% of faculty are male; 42% are female. All teach undergraduates. No introductory courses are taught by graduate students. The average class size in an introductory lecture is 30; in a laboratory is 15; and in a regular course is 10.

PROGRAMS OF STUDY: Montreat confers B.A., B.S. and B.B.A. degrees. Associate and Masters degrees are also awarded. Bachelor's degrees are awarded in BUSINESS (business administration and management), COMMUNICATIONS AND THE ARTS (church music, communication, English, music business management, and theatre arts), COMPUTER AND PHYSICAL SCIENCE (cyber intelligence/security studies), EDUCATION (elementary education and outdoor leadership/education), ENGINEERING AND ENVIRONMENTAL DESIGN (environmental science), HEALTH PROFESSIONS (biology and exercise science), SOCIAL SCIENCE (American studies, biblical studies, history, human services, liberal arts/general studies, psychology, and religion). English, biology, and environmental studies are the strongest academically. Business, outdoor education, and psychology/human services have the largest enrollments.

ACTIVITIES: There are 25 groups on campus, including art, band, choir, computers, dance, debate, drama, environmental, film, honors, literary magazine, musical theater, newspaper, orchestra, professional, religious, social, social service, and student government. Popular campus events include King of Hearts Male Beauty Pageant, Spring Formal, Homecoming Barn Dance, and Film Contest. **Sports:** There are 8 intercollegiate sports for men and 9 for women, and 4 intramural sports for men and 4 for women. Facilities include standard athletic facilities complemented by opportunities for outdoor recreation activities such as hiking, skiing, whitewater sports, mountain climbing, and camping. **Graduates:** From July 1, 2013 to June 30, 2014, 169 bachelor's degrees were awarded. The most popular majors were business/marketing (44%), psychology and social services (14%), and biology and environmental studies (9%). In an average class, 36% graduate in 4 years or less and 43% graduate in 6 years or less. Of the 2013 graduating class, 70% were employed within 6 months of graduation.

SERVICES: Counseling and information services are available, as is tutoring in most subjects. **Library/Resources:** The library contains 79,165 volumes, 117,155 microform items, 3,119 audio/video tapes/CDs/DVDs, and subscribes to 485 periodicals including electronic. Computerized library services include interlibrary loans, database searching, Internet access, and Wi-Fi capability. Special learning facilities include an art gallery. **Physically Challenged Students:** 75% of the campus is accessible. Facilities include wheelchair ramps, elevators, special parking, specially equipped restrooms, special class scheduling, and lowered telephones. **Special:** Montreat offers internships in all majors, study abroad in numerous countries, a Washington semester, a work-study program, student-designed majors, and dual majors. There are 2 national honor societies, a freshman honors program, and 3 departmental honors programs. **Visiting:** There are regularly scheduled orientations for prospective students, including a campus tour, faculty introduction, and student program. There are guides for informal visits, visitors may sit in on classes, and stay overnight. To schedule a visit, contact the Admissions Office. **Campus Safety and Security:** Measures include 24-hour foot and vehicle patrol and emergency notification system. There are lighted pathways/sidewalks and controlled access to dorms/residences.

REQUIREMENTS: The SAT or ACT is required, with a minimum 860 SAT I score or 18 ACT score needed. Applicants must be graduates of an accredited secondary school and have completed 4 years of English, 3 each of math, science, and social studies, and 1 of foreign language. The GED is accepted. A counselor or teacher recommendation is required, and short autobiographical essay is required unless the student has been interviewed. CLEP credits are accepted. Important factors in the admissions decision are advanced placement or honors courses, extracurricular activities record, and evidence of special talent. To graduate, students must complete 126 credit hours with a minimum GPA of 2.0. 50-53 credits in general education courses are required, including competencies in reading, writing, math, computer skills, and oral communication skills. A thesis is required for some majors. **Procedure:** Freshmen are admitted to all sessions. There is a rolling admissions plan. Application deadlines are open. Application fee is $30. Notification is sent on a rolling basis. **Transfer Students:** 155 transfer students enrolled in 2013-2014. Applicants must submit official college transcripts, be in good standing at their previous institution, and have completed at least 24 semester hours of college credit with a minimum GPA of 2.0. Students with fewer credits must also submit high school transcripts and SAT I or ACT scores. 18 of 126 credits required for the bachelor's degree must be completed at Montreat. **International Students:** There are 29 international students enrolled. The school actively recruits these students. They must take the TOEFL.

ADMISSIONS: 91% of the 2014-2015 applicants were accepted. The SAT scores for the 2014-2015 freshman class were: Critical Reading--20% below 500, 73% between 500 and 599, 7% between 600 and 699, and 1% between 700 and 800; Math--16% below 500, 76% between 500 and 599, 7% between 600 and 699, and 1% between 700 and 800. **Admissions Contact:** Mandi Pike, Senior Admissions Specialist. E-Mail: *admissions@montreat.edu* Web: *www.montreat.edu*

FINANCIAL AID: In 2014-2015, 98% of all full-time freshmen and continuing full-time students received some form of financial aid. 71% of all full-time freshmen and 75% of continuing full-time students received need-based aid. The average freshman award was $21,854. Need-based scholarships or need-based grants averaged $21,414; need-based self-help aid (loans and jobs) averaged $5,345; non-need-based athletic scholarships averaged $8,508; other non-need-based awards and non-need-based scholarships averaged $10,261; and $4,643 from other forms of aid. 30% of undergraduate students work part-time. Average annual earnings from campus work are $1700. The average financial indebtedness of the 2014 graduate was $27,843. Montreat is a member of CSS. The FAFSA and the college's own financial statement are required. The priority date for freshman financial aid applications for fall entry is April 15.

NORTH CAROLINA AGRICULTURAL AND TECHNICAL STATE UNIVERSITY *(The complete profile is made available exclusively on our website, www.barronspac.com)*

NORTH CAROLINA CENTRAL UNIVERSITY   D-2
www.nccu.edu

Durham, NC 27707

(919) 530-6100
(919) 530-6298
Fax: (919) 530-6088   Email: admissions@nccu.edu
Full-time: 1500 men, 2700 women   Faculty: 257; IIA, av$
Part-time: 300 men, 800 women   Ph.D.s: 75%
Graduate: 500 men, 1300 women   Student/Faculty: 16 to 1
Year: semesters, summer session   Tuition: $5000 ($14,000)
Room & Board: $5000   Freshman Class: n/av
SAT or ACT: required   CEEB CODE: 5495
Application Deadline: n/av   COMPETITIVE

North Carolina Central University, founded in 1909, is a publicly funded liberal arts institution in the University of North Carolina system. The figures in the above capsule and in this profile are approximate. There are 3 undergraduate schools and 2 graduate schools. In addition to regional accreditation, NCCU has baccalaureate program accreditation with NCATE and NLN. The 103-acre campus is in an urban area 2 miles from the center of Durham. Including any residence halls, there are 57 buildings.

STUDENT LIFE: 89% of undergraduates are from North Carolina. Others are from 39 states, and 17 foreign countries. 80% are African American; 14% White. The average age of freshmen is 19; all undergraduates, 24. **Housing:** 2377 students can be accommodated in college housing, which includes single-sex and coed dorms and on-campus apartments. In addition, there are honors houses. On-campus housing is available on a first-come, first-served basis, and is available on a lottery system for upperclassmen. 63% of students commute. Alcohol is not permitted. All students may keep cars.

FACULTY/CLASSROOMS: 53% of faculty are male; 47% are female. All teach undergraduates. No introductory courses are taught by graduate students.

PROGRAMS OF STUDY: NCCU confers B.A., B.S., B.B.A., B.M., B.S.N. and B.S.W. degrees. Master's degrees are also awarded. Bachelor's degrees are awarded in BIOLOGICAL SCIENCE (biology/biological science and nutrition), BUSINESS (accounting and business administration and management), COMMUNICATIONS AND THE ARTS (art, dramatic arts, English, French, jazz, music, and Spanish), COMPUTER AND PHYSICAL SCIENCE (chemistry, computer science, mathematics, and physics), EDUCATION (elementary education, health education, middle school education, and physical education), ENGINEERING AND ENVIRONMENTAL DESIGN (environmental science), HEALTH PROFESSIONS (nursing), SOCIAL SCIENCE (child care/child and family studies, child psychology/development, criminal justice, geography, history, human services, political science/government, psychology, social work, and sociology). Criminal justice and business is the strongest academically. Business, biology, and political science have the largest enrollments.

ACTIVITIES: There are 45 groups on campus, including art, band, cheerleading, chess, choir, computers, dance, drama, drill team, ethnic, honors, international, jazz band, literary magazine, marching band, newspaper, political, professional, radio and TV, religious, social, social service, student government, symphony, and yearbook. **Sports:** There are 6 intercollegiate sports for men and 5 for women. Facilities include a 12,000-seat stadium, 4500-seat gym, a swimming pool, handball and tennis courts, a track, bowling alley, dance studios, and a weight room. **Graduates:** From July 1, 2013 to June 30, 2014, 604 bachelor's degrees were awarded. The most popular majors were business administration (21%), education (11%), and criminal justice (9%). 297 companies recruited on campus in 2013-2014.

SERVICES: There is a reader service for the blind, and remedial math, reading, and writing. Assistance for students in obtaining needed documentations, assistance with registration, and appropriate individual accommodations and assistance as needed. **Library/Resources:** The 6 libraries contain 663,913 volumes, 1.2 million microform items, 10,991 audio/video tapes/CDs/DVDs, and subscribe to 6,688 periodicals including electronic. Computerized library services include database searching. Special learning facilities include an art gallery and radio station. **Physically Challenged Students:** 90% of the campus is accessible. Facilities include wheelchair ramps, elevators, special parking, specially equipped restrooms, special class scheduling, lowered drinking fountains, lowered telephones. **Special:** NCCU offers internships, study abroad, a Washington semester, work-study programs, dual majors, and nondegree study. There are 10 national honor societies, a freshman honors program, and 10 departmental honors programs. **Visiting:** There are regularly scheduled orientations for prospective students. There are guides for informal visits, visitors may sit in on classes, and stay overnight.. **Campus Safety and Security:** Measures include 24-hour foot and vehicle patrol and security escort services. There are emergency telephones and lighted pathways/sidewalks.

REQUIREMENTS: The SAT or ACT is required. Applicants must be graduates of an accredited secondary school or have a GED certificate. They must have completed 11 academic credits based on 4 years of English, 3 each of math and science, and 2 each of a foreign language and social studies. Music applicants must audition. AP and CLEP credits are accepted. Important factors in the admissions decision are advanced placement or honors courses, leadership record,

and evidence of special talent.To graduate, students must complete 124 semester hours, including 30 in the major, with a minimum GPA of 2.0. Core requirements include courses in communications, math and natural science, social science, humanities, and health and phys ed. **Procedure:** Entrance exams should be taken in the spring of the junior year. There is a rolling admissions plan. Applications should be filed by November 1 for spring entry. The fall 2014 application fee was $30. Applications are accepted on-line. **Transfer Students:** 373 transfer students enrolled in 2013-2014. Applicants must have a minimum GPA of 2.0 in all college-level courses. 30 of 124 credits required for the bachelor's degree must be completed at NCCU. **International Students:** They must take the TOEFL. They must also take the SAT or ACT. unless these tests are not administered in their country.

ADMISSIONS: Jocelyn L. Foy, Director of Admissions. Web: *www.nccu.edu*

FINANCIAL AID: In 2014-2015, 85% of all full-time freshmen and continuing full-time students received some form of financial aid. 70% of all full-time freshmen and 70% of continuing full-time students received need-based aid. The FAFSA is required. The deadline for filing freshman financial aid applications for fall entry is August 1.

NORTH CAROLINA STATE UNIVERSITY   D-2
www.ncsu.edu

Raleigh, NC 27695   (919) 515-2011
                                                        (919) 515-2434

Fax: (919) 515-5039   Email: undergrad-admissions@ncsu.edu

Full-time: 12264 men, 9557 women	**Faculty:** 1723; I, -$
Part-time: 1744 men, 1268 women	**Ph.D.s:** 91%
Graduate: 5168 men, 4339 women	**Student/Faculty:** 12 to 1
Year: semesters, summer session	**Tuition:** $7788 ($20,953)
Room & Board: $8414	**Freshman Class:** 20298 applied, 10124 accepted, 4225 enrolled
SAT CR/M/W: 590/630/570 **ACT:** 26	**CEEB CODE:** 5496
Application Deadline: November 1	**HIGHLY COMPETITIVE**

North Carolina State University, founded in 1887, is a member of the University of North Carolina System. It's degree programs emphasize the arts and sciences, agriculture, business, education, engineering, and preprofessional training. The figures in the above capsule and in this profile are approximate. There are 10 undergraduate schools and 9 graduate schools. In addition to regional accreditation, NC State has baccalaureate program accreditation with ABET, CSAB, CSWE, NAAB, NCATE, NRPA, and SAF. The 2110-acre campus is in an urban area in Raleigh, NC. Including any residence halls, there are 218 buildings.

STUDENT LIFE: 88% of undergraduates are from North Carolina. Others are from 50 states, 119 foreign countries, and Canada. 91% are from public schools. 70% are White. **Male To Female Ratio:** 0.8:1. The average age of freshmen is 18; all undergraduates, 21. 8% do not continue beyond their first year; 72% remain to graduate. **Housing:** 7300 students can be accommodated in college housing, which includes single-sex and coed dorms, on-campus apartments, off-campus apartments, and married student housing. In addition, there are honors houses, special-interest houses, fraternity houses, sorority houses, international, arts and creative living, computer theme, and first-year-experience halls. On-campus housing is guaranteed for all 4 years. 66% of students commute. Alcohol is not permitted. Upperclassmen may keep cars.

FACULTY/CLASSROOMS: 71% of faculty are male; 29% are female. All teach and do research. Graduate students teach 8% of introductory courses. The average class size in an introductory lecture is 35; in a laboratory is 20; and in a regular course is 30.

PROGRAMS OF STUDY: NC State confers B.A., B.S., B.Arch., B.E.D.A., B.L.A. and B.S.W. degrees. Associate, master's, and doctoral degrees are also awarded. Bachelor's degrees are awarded in AGRICULTURE (agricultural business management, agricultural economics, agriculture, agronomy, animal science, conservation and regulation, fishing and fisheries, forestry and related sciences, horticulture, natural resource management, poultry science, soil science, and wood science), BIOLOGICAL SCIENCE (biochemistry, biology/biological science, botany, microbiology, and zoology), BUSINESS (accounting, business administration and management, business economics, and recreation and leisure services), COMMUNICATIONS AND THE ARTS (communications, design, English, French, graphic design, industrial design, and Spanish), COMPUTER AND PHYSICAL SCIENCE (atmospheric sciences and meteorology, chemistry, computer science, earth science, geology, mathematics, physics, and statistics), EDUCATION (agricultural education, education, foreign languages education, industrial arts education, marketing and distribution education, mathematics education, middle school education, science education, secondary education, social studies education, technical education, and vocational education), ENGINEERING AND ENVIRONMENTAL DESIGN (aeronautical engineering, agricultural engineering, architecture, chemical engineering, civil engineering, computer engineering, construction management, electrical/electronics engineering, engineering, environmental design, environmental engineering, environmental science, furniture design, industrial engineering, landscape architecture/design, materials science, mechanical engineering, nuclear engineering, paper and pulp science, and textile engineering), HEALTH PROFESSIONS (medical laboratory technology, predentistry, premedicine, preveterinary science, and speech pathology/audiology), SOCIAL SCIENCE (clothing and textiles management/production/services, criminal justice, economics, food science, history, interdisciplinary studies, parks and recreation management, philosophy, political science/government, prelaw, psychology, religion, social science, social work, sociology, and textiles and clothing). Electrical engineering, chemical engineering, and architecture are the strongest academically. Business management, mechanical engineering, and electrical engineering have the largest enrollments.

ACTIVITIES: 8% of men belong to 32 national fraternities; 14% of women belong to 19 national sororities. There are 560 groups on campus, including art, bagpipe, band, cheerleading, chess, choir, chorale, chorus, computers, dance, drama, drill team, drum and bugle corps, environmental, ethnic, gay, honors, international, jazz band, literary magazine, marching band, musical theater, orchestra, pep band, photography, political, professional, religious, social, social service, student government, symphony, and yearbook. Popular campus events include Pan African Festival, Wolfstock, and Greek Week. **Sports:** There are 20 intercollegiate sports for men and 16 for women, and 28 intramural sports for men and 26 for women. Facilities include 55,000-seat football stadium, 20,000-seat sports arena, 5000-seat soccer stadium, baseball stadium, 12,500-seat gym, tennis complex, areas for track, 2 indoor pools, and an indoor rock-climbing wall. **Graduates:** The most popular majors were engineering (24%), business/marketing (15%), and biological/life sciences (10%). In an average class, 37% graduate in 4 years or less, 67% graduate in 5 years or less, and 72% graduate in 6 years or less. Of the 2013 graduating class, 20% were enrolled in graduate school within 6 months of graduation, and 59% were employed.

SERVICES: Counseling and information services are available, as is tutoring in most subjects. There is a reader service for the blind, and remedial math and writing. **Library/Resources:** The 5 libraries contain 4.6 million volumes, 66,571 microform items, 177,538 audio/video tapes/CDs/DVDs, and subscribe to 66,000 periodicals including electronic. Computerized library services include interlibrary loans, database searching, Internet access, and Wi-Fi capability. Special learning facilities include an art gallery, TV station, nuclear reactor, phytotron, electron microscope facilities, Materials Research Center, Integrated Manufacturing Systems Engineering Institute, Japan Center, and Precision Engineering Center. **Physically Challenged Students:** 78% of the campus is accessible. Facilities include wheelchair ramps, elevators, special parking, specially equipped restrooms, special class scheduling, lowered drinking fountains, lowered telephones. **Special:** NC State offers cross-registration within the Cooperating Raleigh Colleges network, study abroad in more than 90 countries, internships, work-study programs, an accelerated degree plan, dual majors within any program, a general studies degree in education, a 3-2 engineering degree with the University of North Carolina at Asheville, student-designed multidisciplinary studies majors,

credit by examination, nondegree study, and pass/fail options. There are 15 national honor societies, including Phi Beta Kappa, a freshman honors program, and 44 departmental honors programs. **Visiting:** There are regularly scheduled orientations for prospective students, consisting of admissions information sessions. There are guides for informal visits and visitors may sit in on classes. To schedule a visit, contact the Admissions Office. **Campus Safety and Security:** Measures include 24-hour foot and vehicle patrol, emergency notification system, self-defense education, and security escort services. There are shuttle buses, emergency telephones, lighted pathways/sidewalks, bicycle patrol.

REQUIREMENTS: The SAT or ACT is required. The ACT Optional Writing test is also required. In addition, the SAT: Math test is recommended. Applicants must be graduates of an accredited secondary school or have a GED certificate. They must have completed 20 academic credits, including 4 units of English, 3 each of science and math (4 of math is advised), 2 each of social studies and foreign language, and 1 of history. An essay is recommended for all applicants. A portfolio and interview are required for the School of Design. AP and CLEP credits are accepted. Important factors in the admissions decision are advanced placement or honors courses, leadership record, and evidence of special talent. To graduate, students must complete 120 to 142 semester hours, including 60 to 70 in the major, with a minimum GPA of 2.0. Distribution requirements include 12 to 18 hours in humanities and social sciences, 6 to 8 each in math and science, 6 in English composition, and 4 in phys ed. **Procedure:** Freshmen are admitted to all sessions. Entrance exams should be taken in the spring of the junior year and the fall of the senior year. There is a deferred admissions plan. Early decision applications should be filed by October 15; regular applications, by November 1 for fall entry; November 1 for spring entry; and February 1 for summer entry, along with a $70 fee. Notification of early decision is sent January 30; regular decision, March 15. Applications are accepted on-line. **Transfer Students:** 1027 transfer students enrolled in 2013-2014. Applicants must have completed 30 semester hours of college-level work with a minimum GPA of 2.0. Priority is given to students who have completed 60 hours of relevant course work. An associate degree and an interview are recommended. Applicants must have math, English, and foreign language proficiency. 30 of 120 credits required for the bachelor's degree must be completed at NC State. **International Students:** There are 313 international students enrolled. The school actively recruits these students. They must take the TOEFL. They must also take the SAT or ACT if it is available to students in their country.

ADMISSIONS: 50% of the 2014-2015 applicants were accepted. The SAT scores for the 2014-2015 freshman class were: Critical Reading--7% below 500, 47% between 500 and 599, 28% between 600 and 699, and 8% between 700 and 800; Math--3% below 500, 27% between 500 and 599, 54% between 600 and 699, and 16% between 700 and 800; Writing--13% below 500, 52% between 500 and 599, 30% between 600 and 699, and 5% between 700 and 800. 78% of the current freshmen were in the top fifth of their class; 98% were in the top two fifths. 110 freshmen graduated first in their class. **Admissions Contact:** Thomas Griffin, Director of Admissions. E-Mail: *undergrad_admissions@ncsu.edu* Web: *www.ncsu.edu*

FINANCIAL AID: In 2014-2015, 98% of all full-time freshmen and 97% of continuing full-time students received some form of financial aid. 96% of all full-time freshmen and 94% of continuing full-time students received need-based aid. The average financial indebtedness of the 2014 graduate was $15,823. The FAFSA and the college's own financial statement are required. The deadline for filing freshman financial aid applications for fall entry is March 1.

NORTH CAROLINA WESLEYAN COLLEGE   E-2
www.ncwc.edu

Rocky Mount, NC 27804	(252) 985-5100
	(800) 488-6292
Fax: (252) 985-5295	Email: adm@ncwc.edu
Full-time: 615 men, 515 women	Faculty: IIB
Part-time: 289 men, 337 women	Ph.D.s: 45%
Graduate: n/av	Student/Faculty: n/av
Year: semesters, summer session	Tuition: $23,050
Room & Board: $7890	Freshman Class: 1169 applied, 951 accepted, 288 enrolled
SAT or ACT: required	CEEB CODE: 5501
Application Deadline: n/av	COMPETITIVE

North Carolina Wesleyan College, founded in 1956, is a private liberal arts institution affiliated with the United Methodist Church. The figures in the above capsule and in this prpofile are approximate. In addition to regional accreditation, NCWC has baccalaureate program accreditation with NCATE. The 200-acre campus is in a suburban area 57 miles east of Raleigh. Including any residence halls, there are 18 buildings.

STUDENT LIFE: 85% of undergraduates are from North Carolina. Others are from 24 states, and 9 foreign countries. 70% are from public schools. 45% are African American; 43% White. 70% are Protestant; 16% Catholic; 14% claim no religious affiliation. The average age of freshmen is 19; all undergraduates, 26. 36% do not continue beyond their first year; 26% remain to graduate. **Housing:** 504 students can be accommodated in college housing, which includes single-sex and coed dorms and off-campus apartments. Single-occupancy residence halls with kitchens on each floor and smoke/substance free housing. On-campus housing is guaranteed for all 4 years. 68% of students commute. All students may keep cars.

FACULTY/CLASSROOMS: 62% of faculty are male; 38% are female. All teach undergraduates. No introductory courses are taught by graduate students. The average class size in an introductory lecture is 23; in a laboratory is 15; and in a regular course is 18.

PROGRAMS OF STUDY: NCWC confers B.A., and B.S. degrees. Bachelor's degrees are awarded in BIOLOGICAL SCIENCE (biology/biological science), BUSINESS (accounting, business administration and management, and hotel/motel and restaurant management), COMMUNICATIONS AND THE ARTS (dramatic arts and English), COMPUTER AND PHYSICAL SCIENCE (chemistry, information sciences and systems, and mathematics), EDUCATION (elementary education and middle school education), ENGINEERING AND ENVIRONMENTAL DESIGN (environmental science), HEALTH PROFESSIONS (exercise science and premedicine), SOCIAL SCIENCE (criminal justice, history, political science/government, psychology, religion, and sociology). Business administration, justice studies, and computer information systems are the largest.

ACTIVITIES: 1% of men belong to 3 national fraternities; 1% of women belong to 3 national sororities. There are 23 groups on campus, including cheerleading, chess, choir, chorus, computers, drama, ethnic, gay, honors, international, literary magazine, musical theater, newspaper, political, professional, religious, social, social service, and student government. Popular campus events include Spring Fling, Parents Weekend, and Alumni Homecoming. **Sports:** There are 5 intercollegiate sports for men and 5 for women, and 13 intramural sports for men and 13 for women. Facilities include a 1200-seat gym with areas for basketball, volleyball, and indoor soccer matches; tennis courts; a skeet range; and fields for intramurals and for varsity baseball, softball, and soccer. **Graduates:** From July 1, 2013 to June 30, 2014, 391 bachelor's degrees were awarded. The most popular majors were business/marketing (48%), computer and information sciences (24%), and law/legal studies (10%). In an average class, 15% graduate in 4 years or less, 23% graduate in 5 years or less, and 10% graduate in 6 years or less.

SERVICES: Counseling and information services are available, as is tutoring in most subjects. There is remedial math, reading, and writing. **Library/Resources:** The library contains 65,721 volumes, 2,830 microform items, 4,200 audio/video tapes/CDs/DVDs, and sub-

scribes to 4,645 periodicals including electronic. Computerized library services include interlibrary loans and database searching. Special learning facilities include an art gallery, a performing arts center. **Physically Challenged Students:** 90% of the campus is accessible. Facilities include wheelchair ramps, elevators, special parking, specially equipped restrooms, special class scheduling, lowered drinking fountains, lowered telephones, and special housing. **Special:** NCWC offers cooperative programs in all majors, internships, work-study programs through the college offices, credit for military experience, nondegree study, and pass/fail options. The B.A.-B.S. degree may be earned in all majors. There are 2 national honor societies and a freshman honors program. **Visiting:** There are regularly scheduled orientations for prospective students, including an individual campus tour, an interview, a financial aid session, and meetings with faculty and coaches. There are guides for informal visits, visitors may sit in on classes, and stay overnight. To schedule a visit, contact the Admissions Office. **Campus Safety and Security:** Measures include 24-hour foot and vehicle patrol and security escort services. There are emergency telephones and lighted pathways/sidewalks.

REQUIREMENTS: The SAT or ACT is required, with a satisfactory SAT composite score or ACT score of 19 recommended. Applicants should be graduates of an accredited secondary school or have a GED. They should have completed at least 13 academic courses, including 4 in English, 3 in math, and 2 each in foreign language, social studies, and lab sciences. An essay and an interview are advised. AP and CLEP credits are accepted. Important factors in the admissions decision are advanced placement or honors courses, extracurricular activities record, and leadership record. To graduate, students must complete 124 semester hours, including 30 to 54 in the major, with a minimum GPA of 2.0. Distribution requirements consist of 6 semester hours of English composition or demonstrated proficiency; 4 each of biological and physical science; 3 each of ethics, non-Western culture, math, history, social science, psychology or sociology, religion, literature, and fine arts; 2 of phys ed; and 2 of introduction to college life. Some majors require a thesis. **Procedure:** Freshmen are admitted fall and spring. Entrance exams should be taken in spring of the junior year or fall or winter of the senior year. There are deferred admissions and rolling admissions plans. Application deadlines are open. Application fee is $25. Applications are accepted on-line. **Transfer Students:** Applicants must have a minimum GPA of 2.0 in their college courses. They must submit transcripts of all high school and college work, along with proof of high school graduation. 31 of 124 credits required for the bachelor's degree must be completed at NCWC. **International Students:** They must take the TOEFL. They must also take the SAT. **ADMISSIONS:** 81% of the 2014-2015 applicants were accepted. **Admissions Contact:** Cecelia Summers, Director of Admissions. E-Mail: *adm@ncwc.edu* Web: *www.ncwc.edu*

FINANCIAL AID: 93% of all full-time freshmen and continuing full-time students received need-based aid. The average freshman award was $8,480. Need-based scholarships or need-based grants averaged $2,917; and need-based self-help aid (loans and jobs) averaged $9,193. NCWC is a member of CSS. The FAFSA is required. The priority date for freshman financial aid applications for fall entry is March 15.

PFEIFFER UNIVERSITY (*The complete profile is made available exclusively on our website, www.barronspac.com*)

QUEENS UNIVERSITY OF CHARLOTTE   C-3
www.queens.edu

Charlotte, NC 28274	(704) 337-2200
	(800) 849-0202
Fax: (704) 337-2403	Email: admissions@queens.edu
Full-time: 408 men, 997 women	Faculty: n/av
Part-time: 66 men, 232 women	Ph.D.s: 79%
Graduate: 183 men, 368 women	Student/Faculty: 12 to 1
Year: semesters, summer session	Tuition: $29,045
Room & Board: $10,498	Freshman Class: 1949 applied, 1498 accepted, 316 enrolled
SAT CR/M/W: 520/520/510 ACT: 24	CEEB CODE: 5560
Application Deadline: rolling	COMPETITIVE+

Queens University of Charlotte is a private, co-ed, comprehensive university with a commitment to both liberal arts and professional studies. Located in the heart of historic Charlotte, we serve approximately 2,400 undergraduate and graduate students through the College of Arts and Sciences, the McColl School of Business, the Wayland H. Cato, Jr. School of Education, the James L. Knight School of Communication, Hayworth College of Graduate and Continuing Studies and the Andrew Blair College of Health which features the Presbyterian School of Nursing. The university today offers 39 undergraduate majors and 19 graduate programs. There are many unique opportunities for engagement at Queens, including the Core Program in the Liberal Arts which received accolades from the National Endowment for the Humanities. Our required internship program has been recognized as among the best in the nation. And, because Queens believes so strongly in the importance of a global perspective, all students have the opportunity to access funding in support of an international experience. This commitment has routinely placed Queens among the top institutions in the country for percentage of graduates who study abroad. Our low student-to-professor ratio fosters meaningful student-teacher relationships. In all of our programs, we emphasize active and collaborative learning, a creative synthesis of the liberal arts with the world of work, and the value of lifelong learning. We value the factors which foster student success: an intimate learning environment, excellence in teaching, intellectual curiosity and an education grounded in the liberal arts tradition which develops critical thinking, creativity, communication, commitment to ethical behavior and responsible citizenship, and which serves as a foundation for successful and fulfilling lives. We also value responsibility and service to society in keeping with our Presbyterian heritage and as expressed in our motto, "Not to be served, but to serve." There are 5 undergraduate schools and one graduate school. In addition to regional accreditation, Queens has baccalaureate program accreditation with AACSB, ACBSP, NASM, NCATE, NLN, AMTA, CCNE, NASM, and SACS-COC. The 30-acre campus is in a suburban area 2 miles south of uptown Charlotte. Including any residence halls, there are 38 buildings.

STUDENT LIFE: 59% of undergraduates are from North Carolina. Others are from 36 states, 21 foreign countries, and Canada. 80% are from public schools. 59% are White; 13% African American; 12% race unknown. 17% are Protestant; 13% Catholic. The average age of freshmen is 18; all undergraduates, 20. 30% do not continue beyond their first year; 52% remain to graduate. **Housing:** 916 students can be accommodated in college housing, which includes coed dorms and off-campus apartments. On-campus housing is guaranteed for all 4 years, is available on a first-come, first-served basis, and is available on a lottery system for upperclassmen. 83% of students live on campus. All students may keep cars.

FACULTY/CLASSROOMS: 33% of faculty are male; 67% are female. All teach undergraduates. No introductory courses are taught by graduate students. The average class size in an introductory lecture is 15; in a laboratory is 10; and in a regular course is 15.

PROGRAMS OF STUDY: Queens confers B.A., B.B.A., B.S., B.Mus and B.S.N. degrees. Master's degrees are also awarded. Bachelor's degrees are awarded in AGRICULTURE (environmental studies), BIOLOGICAL SCIENCE (biochemistry and biology/biological science), BUSINESS (accounting, business administration and management, finance, and sports management), COMMUNICATIONS AND THE ARTS (art, communications, creative writing, digital communications, dramatic arts, English literature, French, graphic design, music, romance languages and literature, and Spanish), COMPUTER AND PHYSICAL SCIENCE (chemistry and mathematics), EDUCATION (elementary education), ENGINEERING AND ENVIRONMENTAL DESIGN (environmental science and interior design), HEALTH PROFESSIONS (exercise science, music therapy, and nursing), SOCIAL SCIENCE (community services, history, human services, philosophy, political science/government, psychology, religion, and sociology). Liberal arts and sciences, business and nursing are the strongest academically. Business, nursing, and communications have the largest enrollments.

ACTIVITIES: 13% of men belong to 2 national fraternities; 21% of women belong to 5 national sororities. There are 72 groups on campus, including and Rugby club, art, cheerleading, choir, chorale, chorus, dance, drama, environmental, ethnic, gay, honors, interna-

tional, jazz band, literary magazine, musical theater, newspaper, political, professional, religious, social, social service, student government, Triatholon club, and yearbook. Popular campus events include Casino Night, Midnight on Ice, Spring Carnival, Exam Break Breakfast, Homecoming Week, Welcome Back Week, Moravian Love Feast, Boar's Head, International Week, and Queens After Dark. **Sports:** There are 9 intercollegiate sports for men and 11 for women, and 6 intramural sports for men and 6 for women. Facilities include The Sports Complex is home to the lacrosse and soccer teams, multi-sport champion field, cross country, a grass practice field, and a 14,000 square foot Common areas for informal gatherings, as well as meeting spaces, classrooms, offices and on-sight conference center. The Levine Center for Wellness and Recreation is home to the men's and women's basketball teams, as well as the women's volleyball team. It is the on-campus facility for student wellness and includes the following: 5,000-square-foot fitness center, 1/10th mile indoor walking/jogging track, 33-meter competition swimming pool, 3 full-size basketball courts with pull-out bleacher seating for 2,200, dance/yoga studio, locker rooms, and an Einstein Brothers Bagels. **Graduates:** From July 1, 2013 to June 30, 2014, 414 bachelor's degrees were awarded. The most popular majors were health professions and related programs (30%), business (12%), and communications (11%). 325 companies recruited on campus in 2013-2014. In an average class, 44% graduate in 4 years or less, 51% graduate in 5 years or less, and 52% graduate in 6 years or less.

SERVICES: Counseling and information services are available, as is tutoring in most subjects, math, science, social sciences, foreign languages, nursing, and core classes. The Center for Student Success offers free individual peer tutoring, review sessions, knowledge workshops, academic success strategies, individual academic assistance and guidance, access to the writing center, and referrals to the Office of Disability Services. **Library/Resources:** The library contains 42,081 volumes, 97,670 audio/video tapes/CDs/DVDs, and subscribes to 74 periodicals including electronic. Computerized library services include interlibrary loans, database searching, Internet access, and Wi-Fi capability. Special learning facilities include an art gallery, Platiumn LEED Science Building "living" wallrare books and archival collection, photographic lab, ceramics studio, and recital hall. **Physically Challenged Students:** 70% of the campus is accessible. Facilities include wheelchair ramps, special parking, specially equipped restrooms, special class scheduling, lowered drinking fountains. **Special:** Required Internships in all majors, cross-registration with colleges of the Charlotte Area Educational Consortium, dual majors, nondegree study, and pass/fail options are available. The school offers a Washington semester. Study tours in over 14 countries(included in the cost of tuition) may be arranged through the school's John Belk International Program. There are 5 national honor societies and a freshman honors program. **Visiting:** There are regularly scheduled orientations for prospective students, including a sampling of classes, campus tours, a college overview, a question/answer segment, a meet-the-faculty session, and a scholarship/financial aid session. There are guides for informal visits and visitors may sit in on classes. To schedule a visit, contact the Admissions Department. **Campus Safety and Security:** Measures include 24-hour foot and vehicle patrol, emergency notification system, self-defense education, and security escort services. There are shuttle buses, emergency telephones, lighted pathways/sidewalks, and controlled access to dorms/residences.

REQUIREMENTS: The SAT or ACT is required. The ACT Optional Writing test is also required. Applicants should have a college preparatory background in an accredited secondary school. The GED is accepted. High school courses should include 4 years of English, 3 of math, 2 each of history or social studies and a foreign language, and 2 years of science, including 1 of lab science. An interview is recommended. An audition or portfolio is recommended for art and music students. AP and CLEP credits are accepted. Important factors in the admissions decision are recommendations by school officials, advanced placement or honors courses, and leadership record. To graduate, students must complete a total of 122 credit hours with a minimum GPA of 2.0. For the B.A., between 30 and 40 hours are required in the student's major; for the B.S., 32 are required. 2 courses in English composition, 2 in phys ed, and 1 in lab science are required. If entering freshmen do not pass the placement exams given in math and a foreign language, additional courses will be required.

Some majors require a thesis or research project. **Procedure:** Freshmen are admitted fall, spring, and summer. Entrance exams should be taken in the junior year or as early as possible in the senior year. There are early admissions, deferred admissions, and rolling admissions plans. Application deadlines are open. Application fee is $40. Notifications are sent September 15. Applications are accepted online. Application fees are waived if application is completed on-line. **Transfer Students:** 163 transfer students enrolled in 2013-2014. Transfer students are accepted in all but the senior class. A College GPA of 2.0 is required for all previous college-level work. 45 of 122 credits required for the bachelor's degree must be completed at Queens. **International Students:** They must take the TOEFL with a minimum score of 550 on the paper-based TOEFL (PBT), SAT or ACT Scores accepted if submitted by applicant. They must also take the SAT or ACT.

ADMISSIONS: 77% of the 2014-2015 applicants were accepted. The SAT scores for the 2014-2015 freshman class were: Critical Reading--41% below 500, 44% between 500 and 599, 11% between 600 and 699, and 3% between 700 and 800; Math--39% below 500, 43% between 500 and 599, 17% between 600 and 699, and 1% between 700 and 800; Writing--45% below 500, 37% between 500 and 599, 15% between 600 and 699, and 3% between 700 and 800. The ACT scores were 22% below 21, 26% between 21 and 23, 29% between 24 and 26, 13% between 27 and 28, and 10% above 28. 32% of the current freshmen were in the top fifth of their class; 64% were in the top two fifths. **Admissions Contact:** Woody O'Cain, Assoc. Vice President, Dean of Admission. E-Mail: *admissions@queens.edu* Web: *www.queens.edu*

FINANCIAL AID: In 2014-2015, 97% of all full-time freshmen and continuing full-time students received some form of financial aid. 58% of all full-time freshmen and continuing full-time students received need-based aid. The average freshman award was $26,550. Need-based scholarships or need-based grants averaged $9,074 ($24,446 maximum); need-based self-help aid (loans and jobs) averaged $4,763 ($8,732 maximum); non-need-based athletic scholarships averaged $9,839 ($33,800 maximum); and other non-need-based awards and non-need-based scholarships averaged $12,377 ($28,800 maximum). 15% of undergraduate students work part-time. Average annual earnings from campus work are $1700. The average financial indebtedness of the 2014 graduate was $28,507. Queens is a member of CSS. The FAFSA is required. The priority date for freshman financial aid applications for fall entry is March 1.

SAINT AUGUSTINE'S UNIVERSITY   **D-2**
www.st-aug.edu

Raleigh, NC 27610	**(919) 516-4000**
	(919) 516-5805
Fax: (919) 516-4415	**Email:** admissions@st.aug.edu
Full-time: 505 men, 705 women	**Faculty:** 87
Part-time: 50 men, 100 women	**Ph.D.s:** 59%
Graduate: n/av	**Student/Faculty:** 16 to 1
Year: semesters, summer session	**Tuition:** $10,000
Room & Board: $5000	**Freshman Class:** n/av
SAT or ACT: required	**CEEB CODE:** 5596
Application Deadline: n/av	**COMPETITIVE**

Saint Augustine's College, founded in 1867, is a historically Black Liberal Arts institution affiliated with the Episcopal Church. Figures in the above capsule and in this profile are approximate. The 110-acre campus is in an urban area 1 mile northeast of downtown Raleigh. Including any residence halls, there are 37 buildings. **STUDENT LIFE:** 51% of undergraduates are from North Carolina. Others are from 34 states, 16 foreign countries, and Canada. 99% are from public schools. 90% are African American. 58% are Protestant; 39% claim no religious affiliation. The average age of freshmen is 18; all undergraduates, 22. 38% do not continue beyond their first year; 27% remain to graduate. **Housing:** 1143 students can be accommodated in college housing, which includes single-sex dorms. In addition, there are honors houses. On-campus housing is guaranteed for all 4 years. 62% of students live on campus; of those, 75% remain on

campus on weekends. Alcohol is not permitted. All students may keep cars.

FACULTY/CLASSROOMS: 60% of faculty are male; 40% are female. All teach undergraduates. No introductory courses are taught by graduate students. The average class size in an introductory lecture is 22; in a laboratory is 13; and in a regular course is 14.

PROGRAMS OF STUDY: Saint Augustine confers B.A., and B.S. degrees. Bachelor's degrees are awarded in BIOLOGICAL SCIENCE (biology/biological science), BUSINESS (accounting, business administration and management, and international business management), COMMUNICATIONS AND THE ARTS (communications, English, fine arts, French, music, music business management, Spanish, and visual and performing arts), COMPUTER AND PHYSICAL SCIENCE (applied mathematics, chemistry, computer science, information sciences and systems, and mathematics), EDUCATION (business education, education of the exceptional child, elementary education, English education, mathematics education, music education, physical education, science education, and social studies education), ENGINEERING AND ENVIRONMENTAL DESIGN (industrial administration/management and industrial engineering), HEALTH PROFESSIONS (industrial hygiene, medical laboratory technology, and premedicine), SOCIAL SCIENCE (African American studies, criminal justice, history, physical fitness/movement, political science/government, prelaw, psychology, sociology, and urban studies). Engineering, math, premedicine, and chemistry are the strongest academically. Computer science, business administration and communications have the largest enrollments.

ACTIVITIES: 6% of men belong to 5 national fraternities; 12% of women belong to 4 national sororities. There are 20 groups on campus, including band, cheerleading, chorale, dance, drama, ethnic, honors, international, newspaper, photography, professional, radio and TV, religious, social service, student government, and yearbook. Popular campus events include Opening Convocation each Semester, CIAA Tournament, and Career/Job Fairs. **Sports:** There are 5 intercollegiate sports for men and 4 for women, and 4 intramural sports for men and 3 for women. Facilities include a 1700-seat gym, a track, baseball fields, and tennis and basketball courts. **Graduates:** From July 1, 2013 to June 30, 2014, 242 bachelor's degrees were awarded. The most popular majors were business (28%), psychology (12%), and criminal justice (8%). 25 companies recruited on campus in 2013-2014. In an average class, 1% graduate in 3 years or less, 12% graduate in 4 years or less, 25% graduate in 5 years or less, and 27% graduate in 6 years or less. Of the 2013 graduating class, 23% were enrolled in graduate school within 6 months of graduation, and 60% were employed.

SERVICES: There is remedial math, reading, and writing. Help with writing and test-taking skills is available. **Library/Resources:** Computerized library services include database searching. Special learning facilities include a radio station. **Physically Challenged Students:** 64% of the campus is accessible. Facilities include wheelchair ramps, elevators, special parking, and specially equipped restrooms. **Special:** Students may cross-register at any of 5 area colleges, study abroad, or pursue a 3-2 engineering program with North Carolina State University. There is an accelerated degree program in organizational management for adult learners. Field experience programs, nondegree study, internships, work-study, cooperative programs, and credit for military service are offered. There are 1 national honor societies and a freshman honors program. **Visiting:** There are guides for informal visits and visitors may sit in on classes. To schedule a visit, contact the Admissions Office. **Campus Safety and Security:** Measures include 24-hour foot and vehicle patrol. There are emergency telephones and lighted pathways/sidewalks.

REQUIREMENTS: The SAT or ACT is required. Applicants must be graduates of an accredited secondary school with a C+ average in at least 18 academic units, including 4 in English, 3 in math, and 2 each in social studies and science. AP credits are accepted. Important factors in the admissions decision are geographical diversity, evidence of special talent, and leadership record.Students must complete at least 120 hours with a minimum 2.0 GPA for graduation. All students must complete a 50 to 55 credit core curriculum that includes courses in reading and communication, foreign language, science, math, philosophy, ethics, humanities, world civilization, psychology, and phys ed. Seniors must pass written and oral examinations in their major fields. Total credit hours required for a degree in offered majors range from 124 to 154. **Procedure:** Freshmen are admitted to all sessions. There are deferred admissions and rolling admissions plans. Check with the school for current application deadlines. The fall 2014 application fee was $25. **Transfer Students:** 43 transfer students enrolled in 2013-2014. Transfers must submit high school and college transcripts and must be eligible to reenter the last institution attended. 30 of 124 credits required for the bachelor's degree must be completed at SAU . **International Students:** There are 133 international students enrolled. The school actively recruits these students. They must take the TOEFL. They must also take the SAT or ACT.

ADMISSIONS: Tim Chapman, Interim Director of Admissions. E-Mail: *admissions@es.st.aug.edu* Web: *www.st-aug.edu*

FINANCIAL AID: In 2014-2015, 95% of all full-time freshmen and 90% of continuing full-time students received some form of financial aid. 87% of all full-time freshmen and 80% of continuing full-time students received need-based aid. The average freshman award was $10,474. 69% of undergraduate students work part-time. Average annual earnings from campus work are $1572. The average financial indebtedness of the 2014 graduate was $12,850. is a member of CSS. The FAFSA is required. The deadline for filing freshman financial aid applications for fall entry is April 15.

SALEM COLLEGE C-2
www.salem.edu

Winston-Salem, NC 27101	(336) 721-2600
	(800) 327-2536
Fax: (336) 917-5572	Email: admissions@salem.edu
Full-time: 10 men, 695 women	Faculty: 58; IIB, --$
Part-time: 12 men, 154 women	Ph.D.s: 86%
Graduate: 15 men, 226 women	Student/Faculty: 12 to 1
Year: 4-1-4, summer session	Tuition: $22,860
Room & Board: $12,264	Freshman Class: 387 applied, 267 accepted, 127 enrolled
SAT: required ACT: 28	CEEB CODE: 5607
Application Deadline: open	VERY COMPETITIVE

Salem College, traces its roots back to 1772, when it was begun as a school for girls by the Moravians, an early Protestant denomination. Today the private college, which retains a historical relationship with the church, offers a liberal arts education primarily for women. Figures in the above capsule and in this profile are approximate. There is one graduate school. In addition to regional accreditation, Salem has baccalaureate program accreditation with NASM and NCATE. The 64-acre campus is in an urban area in the center of Old Salem, a restored 18th-century village. Including any residence halls, there are 17 buildings.

STUDENT LIFE: 51% of undergraduates are from North Carolina. Others are from 23 states, and 17 foreign countries. 80% are from public schools. 65% are White; 18% African American. The average age of freshmen is 18; all undergraduates, 27. 25% do not continue beyond their first year; 55% remain to graduate. **Housing:** 488 students can be accommodated in college housing, which includes single-sex dorms, on-campus apartments, and off-campus apartments. On-campus housing is guaranteed for all 4 years. 86% of students live on campus; of those, 55% remain on campus on weekends. All students may keep cars.

FACULTY/CLASSROOMS: 47% of faculty are male; 53% are female. All teach and do research. No introductory courses are taught by graduate students. The average class size in an introductory lecture is 18; in a laboratory is 15; and in a regular course is 15.

PROGRAMS OF STUDY: Salem confers B.A., B.S., B.M. and B.S.B.A. degrees. Master's degrees are also awarded. Bachelor's degrees are awarded in BIOLOGICAL SCIENCE (biology/biological science), BUSINESS (accounting, business administration and management, and international business management), COMMUNICATIONS AND THE ARTS (art history and appreciation, arts administration/management, communications, English, French, German, music, Spanish, and studio art), COMPUTER AND PHYSI-

CAL SCIENCE (chemistry and mathematics), ENGINEERING AND ENVIRONMENTAL DESIGN (interior design), HEALTH PROFESSIONS (medical laboratory technology), SOCIAL SCIENCE (American studies, economics, history, international relations, philosophy, psychology, religion, and sociology). Sociology, business, and communication have the largest enrollments.

ACTIVITIES: There are 41 groups on campus, including band, chorale, chorus, dance, drama, ethnic, gay, honors, international, literary magazine, marching band, musical theater, newspaper, orchestra at Wake Forest University., political, professional, radio and TV, religious, social, social service, student government, and yearbook. Popular campus events include Fall Fest, April Arts, and Dance Weekends. **Sports:** There are 7 intercollegiate sports for women, and 7 intramural sports for women. Facilities include an multiple athletic fields, a swimming pool, 2 gyms (1 practice, 1 regular), tennis courts, a dance studio,a softball field, and a universal weight room. **Graduates:** From July 1, 2013 to June 30, 2014, 189 bachelor's degrees were awarded. The most popular majors were business (13%), sociology (13%), and communication (13%). In an average class, 1% graduate in 3 years or less, 52% graduate in 4 years or less, 55% graduate in 5 years or less, and 56% graduate in 6 years or less. Of the 2013 graduating class, 18% were enrolled in graduate school within 6 months of graduation, and 77% were employed.

SERVICES: Counseling and information services are available, as is tutoring in every subject. **Library/Resources:** The 2 libraries contain 135,000 volumes, 302,534 microform items, 13,553 audio/video tapes/CDs/DVDs, and subscribe to 15,000 periodicals including electronic. Computerized library services include interlibrary loans and database searching. Special learning facilities include an art gallery, radio station, a learning lab (computer lab with multimedia capability). **Physically Challenged Students:** 75% of the campus is accessible. Facilities include special parking, specially equipped restrooms, special class scheduling, lowered drinking fountains. Many buildings are historic, so disability access is limited to individual areas that have had recent renovations or were already accessible. **Special:** Salem offers an extensive internship program in all majors, cross-registration with Wake Forest University, and study abroad at various locations, including a summer program in Oxford, England. A Washington semester, student-designed and interdisciplinary majors, B.A.-B.S. degrees, nondegree study, and pass/fail options during the January term are available. A 3-2 engineering degree is available with Duke and Vanderbilt Universities. Students may participate in a model U.N. program directed by Drew University in Madison, New Jersey. Interdisciplinary majors are offered in American studies, arts management, and international relations. There are 9 national honor societies and a freshman honors program. **Visiting:** There are regularly scheduled orientations for prospective students. There are guides for informal visits, visitors may sit in on classes, and stay overnight. To schedule a visit, contact the Admissions Office. **Campus Safety and Security:** Measures include 24-hour foot and vehicle patrol and security escort services. There are emergency telephones and lighted pathways/sidewalks.

REQUIREMENTS: The SAT or ACT is required. Graduation from an accredited secondary school or the GED is needed. Students must have 12 academic credits plus electives, including 4 years of high school English, 3 each of math and science, and 2 each of a foreign language and history. An essay is required for all students. Music students must audition. AP and CLEP credits are accepted. Important factors in the admissions decision are advanced placement or honors courses, leadership record, and evidence of special talent. To graduate, students must complete a total of 36 courses, or 144 semester hours, with a minimum GPA of 2.0 both cumulative and in the major. All traditional students must complete 4 January-term courses and 2 terms of phys ed. Bachelor of arts degree students must complete the following general ed courses: 3 in a modern foreign language, 3 in math/science (including at least 1 math and at least 1 lab science), 2 each in English, social science, and history, and 1 each in fine arts and philosophy/religion. **Procedure:** Freshmen are admitted fall and spring. Entrance exams should be taken by January of the senior year. There are early admissions, deferred admissions, and rolling admissions plans. Application deadlines are open. Application fee is $30. Applications are accepted on-line. **Transfer Students:** 17 transfer students enrolled in 2013-2014. Applicants must have a minimum GPA of 2.0 in all previous college work and must submit a statement of good standing from the Dean of Students of the college previously attended, 2 letters of recommendation from teachers, a high school transcript, and a transcript and catalog from each college attended. SAT or ACT scores may be required on an individual basis. An interview is recommended. 36 of 144 credits required for the bachelor's degree must be completed at Salem. **International Students:** There are 70 international students enrolled. The school actively recruits these students. They must take the TOEFL. They must also take the SAT or ACT.

ADMISSIONS: 69% of the 2014-2015 applicants were accepted. 2 freshmen graduated first in their class. **Admissions Contact:** Dama E. Evans, Dean of Admissions and Financial Aid. E-Mail: *admissions@salem.edu* Web: *www.salem.edu*

FINANCIAL AID: In 2014-2015, 73% of all full-time freshmen and 64% of continuing full-time students received some form of financial aid. 71% of all full-time freshmen and 62% of continuing full-time students received need-based aid. The average freshman award was $14,500. 66% of undergraduate students work part-time. Average annual earnings from campus work are $1600. The average financial indebtedness of the 2014 graduate was $14,500. The FAFSA and the college's own financial statement are required. The deadline for filing freshman financial aid applications for fall entry is March 15.

SHAW UNIVERSITY D-2
www.shawuniversity.edu

Raleigh, NC 27601

(919) 546-8275
(800) 214-6683

Fax: (919) 546-8271

Email: admissions@shaw.edu

Full-time: 870 men, 1420 women

Faculty: n/av

Part-time: 93 men, 189 women

Ph.D.s: n/av

Graduate: 94 men, 103 women

Student/Faculty: 26 to 1

Year: semesters, summer session

Tuition: $12,676

Room & Board: $8000

Freshman Class: 4226 applied, 2728 accepted, 601 enrolled

SAT or ACT: required

CEEB CODE: 5612

Application Deadline: July 30

COMPETITIVE

Shaw University, founded in 1865, is a private liberal arts university affiliated with the Baptist Church. The figures in the above capsule and in this profile are approximate. There is one graduate school. In addition to regional accreditation, Shaw has baccalaureate program accreditation with NCATE and CAAHEP. The 30-acre campus is in an urban area in downtown Raleigh. Including any residence halls, there are 23 buildings.

STUDENT LIFE: 73% of undergraduates are from North Carolina. Others are from 32 states, and 10 foreign countries. 94% are African American. The average age of freshmen is 24; all undergraduates, 28. **Housing:** 1293 students can be accommodated in college housing, which includes single-sex dorms. On-campus housing is available on a first-come and first-served basis. 62% of students commute. Alcohol is not permitted. Upperclassmen may keep cars.

FACULTY/CLASSROOMS: 94% teach undergraduates. No introductory courses are taught by graduate students. The average class size in a laboratory is 8 and in a regular course is 13.

PROGRAMS OF STUDY: Shaw confers B.A., and B.S. degrees. Associate and Master's degrees are also awarded. Bachelor's degrees are awarded in BIOLOGICAL SCIENCE (biology/biological science), BUSINESS (accounting, business administration and management, and recreation and leisure services), COMMUNICATIONS AND THE ARTS (broadcasting, English, and visual and performing arts), COMPUTER AND PHYSICAL SCIENCE (chemistry, computer science, mathematics, and physics), EDUCATION (athletic training, elementary education, English education, mathematics education, physical education, science education, secondary education, social studies education, and special education), ENGINEERING AND ENVIRONMENTAL DESIGN (environmental science and preengineering), HEALTH PROFESSIONS (recreation therapy, rehabilitation therapy, and speech pathology/audiology), SOCIAL SCIENCE

(African studies, criminal justice, gerontology, international relations, international studies, liberal arts/general studies, political science/government, psychology, public administration, religion, social work, and sociology). Business administration/management, criminal justice, and sociology have the largest enrollments.

ACTIVITIES: 4% of men belong to 4 national fraternities; 5% of women belong to 4 national sororities. There are 30 groups on campus, including band, cheerleading, choir, chorus, criminal justice and business, dance, drama, ethnic, honors, international, jazz band, marching band, musical theater, newspaper, pep band, professional, radio and TV, religious, social, social service, student government, and yearbook. Popular campus events include Career Day, Awards Day, and Religious Emphasis Week. **Sports:** There are 7 intercollegiate sports for men and 7 for women, and 5 intramural sports for men and 4 for women. **Graduates:** From July 1, 2013 to June 30, 2014, 367 bachelor's degrees were awarded. The most popular majors were business (24%), criminal justice (14%), and sociology (11%). In an average class, 26% graduate in 4 years or less, 34% graduate in 5 years or less, and 38% graduate in 6 years or less.

SERVICES: Counseling and information services are available, as is tutoring in some subjects, English, math, biology, chemistry, physical science, statistics, and social science. There is remedial math, reading, and writing. There is peer tutoring in accounting. **Library/Resources:** The library contains 153,304 volumes, 138,950 microform items, 1,306 audio/video tapes/CDs/DVDs, and subscribes to 15,357 periodicals including electronic. Computerized library services include interlibrary loans, database searching, and Internet access. Special learning facilities include a radio station, a praxis lab, Academic Assessment and Achievement Center (AAA), and kinesiotherapy clinic. **Physically Challenged Students:** Facilities include wheelchair ramps, elevators, special parking, specially equipped restrooms, lowered drinking fountains, and labels in braille. **Special:** Shaw offers cross-registration with 4 other North Carolina colleges, internships, a work-study program, a 3-2 engineering degree with North Carolina State University and North Carolina Agricultural and Technical State University, dual and student-designed majors, independent study, and an external degree program for working adults. There are 4 national honor societies and a freshman honors program. **Visiting:** There are regularly scheduled orientations for prospective students, consisting of parent visitation, tours, general administration, and registration. There are guides for informal visits and visitors may sit in on classes. To schedule a visit, contact the Admissions Office. **Campus Safety and Security:** Measures include 24-hour foot and vehicle patrol, self-defense education, and security escort services. There are lighted pathways/sidewalks, and 24-hour electronic surveillance.

REQUIREMENTS: The SAT or ACT is required. Applicants must be graduates of an accredited secondary school or have a GED certificate. They should have completed 3 units of English, 2 each of math, natural science (with 1 in a lab course), and social science, and 4 of academic electives. Admission to the Teacher Education Program follows separate guidelines. AP and CLEP credits are accepted. Important factors in the admissions decision are advanced placement or honors courses, personality/intangible qualities, and recommendations by school officials. To graduate (in most majors), students must earn 120 credits, maintain a minimum GPA of 2.0, and successfully complete competency exams in math and English. The general core curriculum includes a total of 54 credits in college orientation, English, math, ethics, humanities, natural sciences, and social sciences. **Procedure:** Freshmen are admitted to all sessions. Entrance exams should be taken prior to enrollment. There are deferred admissions and rolling admissions plans. Applications should be filed by July 30 for fall entry; November 30 for spring entry. The fall 2014 application fee was $25. Applications are accepted on-line. **Transfer Students:** 246 transfer students enrolled in 2013-2014. Applicants must submit official transcripts from all colleges attended. Transfer credit is given only for course work of grade C or better completed at an accredited degree-granting institution. 30 of 120 credits required for the bachelor's degree must be completed at Shaw. **International Students:** There are 73 international students enrolled. The school actively recruits these students. They must also take the SAT or ACT.

ADMISSIONS: 65% of the 2014-2015 applicants were accepted.

Admissions Contact: Sandy Clifton, Interim Director of Admissions and Recruitment. E-Mail: *sclifton@shaw.edu* Web: *www.shawuniversity.edu*

FINANCIAL AID: The FAFSA is required. The deadline for filing freshman financial aid applications for fall entry is open.

ST. ANDREWS UNIVERSITY *(The complete profile is made available exclusively on our website, www.barronspac.com)*

THE UNIVERSITY OF NORTH CAROLINA AT GREENSBORO   D-2
www.uncg.edu

Greensboro, NC 27412	**(336) 334-5000**
	(336) 334-5243
Fax: (336) 334-4180	**Email: admissions@uncg.edu**
Full-time: 4349 men, 8277 women	**Faculty:** I, +$
Part-time: 798 men, 1599 women	**Ph.D.s:** 81%
Graduate: 1079 men, 2379 women	**Student/Faculty:** n/av
Year: semesters, summer session	**Tuition:** $6442 ($21,304)
Room & Board: $7688	**Freshman Class:** n/av
	CEEB CODE: 5913
Application Deadline: March 1	**COMPETITIVE**

The University of North Carolina at Greensboro, founded in 1891, is a publicly funded liberal arts institution in the University of North Carolina system. There are 7 undergraduate schools and 7 graduate schools. In addition to regional accreditation, UNCG has baccalaureate program accreditation with AACSB, ABET, ADA, NASAD, NASM, NCATE, CACREP, CEPH, and NLNAC. The 210-acre campus is in an urban area in central Greensboro. Including any residence halls, there are 111 buildings.

STUDENT LIFE: 91% of undergraduates are from North Carolina. Others are from 48 states, 27 foreign countries, and Canada. 56% are White; 25% African American. The average age of freshmen is 18; all undergraduates, 22. 26% do not continue beyond their first year; 55% remain to graduate. **Housing:** 5014 students can be accommodated in college housing, which includes coed dorms, on-campus apartments, and off-campus apartments. In addition, there are special-interest houses, an international house, and a residential college program. On-campus housing is guaranteed for all 4 years, is available on a first-come, and first-served basis. 70% of students commute. All students may keep cars.

FACULTY/CLASSROOMS: 47% of faculty are male; 53% are female. No introductory courses are taught by graduate students. The average class size in an introductory lecture is 27; in a laboratory is 19; and in a regular course is 21.

PROGRAMS OF STUDY: UNCG confers B.A., B.S., B.F.A., B.M., B.S.N. and B.S.W. degrees. Master's and Doctoral degrees are also awarded. Bachelor's degrees are awarded in BIOLOGICAL SCIENCE (biochemistry, biology/biological science, and nutrition), BUSINESS (accounting, apparel and accessories marketing, banking and finance, business administration and management, business economics, entrepreneurial studies, finance, hospitality management services, international business management, and marketing/retailing/merchandising), COMMUNICATIONS AND THE ARTS (art, classical languages, communications, dance, dramatic arts, English, fine arts, French, German, information technology, jazz, media arts, music, music performance, music theory and composition, and Spanish), COMPUTER AND PHYSICAL SCIENCE (chemistry, computer science, mathematics, and physics), EDUCATION (art education, dance education, drama education, early childhood education, education of the deaf and hearing impaired, elementary education, English education, foreign languages education, mathematics education, middle school education, music education, physical education, science education, social science education, social studies education, and special education), ENGINEERING AND ENVIRONMENTAL DESIGN (interior design), HEALTH PROFESSIONS (exercise science, nursing, public health, and speech pathology/audiology), SOCIAL SCIENCE (African American studies, anthropology, child care/child and family studies, economics, geography, history, human development, liberal arts/general studies, parks and recreation management, philosophy, political science/government, psychology, religion, social work, sociology, and women's studies). Business administration, elementary education (K-6), and psychology have the largest enrollments.

ACTIVITIES: 4% of men belong to 10 national fraternities; 4% of women belong to 9 national sororities. There are 192 groups on campus, including art, band, chess, choir, chorale, chorus, communications, dance, drama, ethnic, film, gay, honors, international, jazz band, literary magazine, musical theater, newspaper, opera, orchestra, pep band, photography, political, professional, radio and TV, religious, social, social service, student government, and symphony. Popular campus events include Spring Fling, Fall Kickoff, and a International Festival. **Sports:** There are 8 intercollegiate sports for men and 9 for women, and 12 intramural sports for men and 10 for women. Facilities include Baseball Stadium, softball stadium, soccer stadium, gymnasium, tennis courts, campus recreation center, and the 44-acre Piney Lake Field Campus, which includes 2 lakes for swimming, boating, and fishing. **Graduates:** From July 1, 2013 to June 30, 2014, 3038 bachelor's degrees were awarded. The most popular majors were health professions and related programs (21%), business school/marketing (20%), and education (8%). In an average class, 1% graduate in 3 years or less, 28% graduate in 4 years or less, 49% graduate in 5 years or less, and 54% graduate in 6 years or less.

SERVICES: Counseling and information services are available, as is tutoring in most subjects. There is a reader service for the blind. **Library/Resources:** The 2 libraries contain 1.1 million volumes, 324,773 microform items, 52,507 audio/video tapes/CDs/DVDs, and subscribe to 50,646 periodicals including electronic. Computerized library services include interlibrary loans, database searching, Internet access, and Wi-Fi capability. Special learning facilities include an art gallery and radio station. **Physically Challenged Students:** 80% of the campus is accessible. Facilities include wheelchair ramps, elevators, special parking, specially equipped restrooms, special class scheduling, special housing. **Special:** Internships, and accelerated degree programs can be arranged in all majors. Cross-registration is offered with the Greater Greensboro Consortium. Students may study abroad in more than 40 countries. Dual and student-designed majors are also available. The Residential College, a 2-year program for freshmen and sophomores, offers an interdisciplinary curriculum, with faculty and students living in the same residence. Students in this program participate in independent study, community work, and workshops. There is a chapter of Phi Beta Kappa and a freshman honors program. **Visiting:** There are regularly scheduled orientations for prospective students, Spartan Orientation, Advising and Registration programs are offered by Student Affairs for new freshmen and new transfer student. There are guides for informal visits. To schedule a visit, contact the Office of Undergraduate Admissions. **Campus Safety and Security:** Measures include 24-hour foot and vehicle patrol, emergency notification system, self-defense education, and security escort services. There are shuttle buses, emergency telephones, lighted pathways/sidewalks, and controlled access to dorms/residences.

REQUIREMENTS: The SAT is required. The ACT Optional Writing test is also required. Graduation from an accredited secondary school or the GED is required. High school courses must include 4 credits each of English, and math, 3 credits of science, 2 of a foreign language, 1 each of U.S. history and social studies, and an elective. A portfolio or audition is required of art and music students. AP and CLEP credits are accepted. Important factors in the admissions decision are advanced placement or honors courses, leadership record, and evidence of special talent. In order to graduate, students must complete a minimum of 122 credit hours with a GPA of at least 2.0. Major requirements vary from a minimum of 12 credit hours. The general education curriculum for all students requires at least 36 to 37 credit hours chosen from specified courses in the humanities, math and physical sciences, social and behavioral sciences, and a foreign language. Students must take 36 hours at the upper-division level and earn 31 hours of resident credit. **Procedure:** Freshmen are admitted to all sessions. Entrance exams should be taken in June of the junior year or in the fall of the senior year. There is a rolling admissions plan. Applications should be filed by March 1 for fall entry; December 1 for spring entry, along with a $55 fee. Notification is sent on a rolling basis. Applications are accepted on-line. **Transfer Students:** 1687 transfer students enrolled in 2013-2014. Transfer students must have a minimum GPA of 2.0. Students having fewer than 30 semester hours from a regionally accredited institution must meet requirements under both transfer and freshman admissions programs. 31 of 122 credits required for the bachelor's degree must be completed at UNCG. **International Students:** There are 218 international students enrolled. They must take the TOEFL with a minimum score of 550 on the paper-based TOEFL (PBT) or 79 on the Internet-based version (iBT) or take the MELAB, or take the IELTS. They must also take the SAT or ACT.

ADMISSIONS: 40% of the current freshmen were in the top fifth of their class; 70% were in the top two fifths. **Admissions Contact:** Lise Keller, Director, Undergraduate Admissions. E-Mail: *admissions@uncg.edu* Web: *www.uncg.edu*

FINANCIAL AID: In 2014-2015, 72% of all full-time freshmen and 70% of continuing full-time students received some form of financial aid. 77% of all full-time freshmen and 73% of continuing full-time students received need-based aid. The average freshman award was $9,665. Need-based scholarships or need-based grants averaged $5,850 ($16,650 maximum); need-based self-help aid (loans and jobs) averaged $3,229 ($9,500 maximum); non-need-based athletic scholarships averaged $16,225 ($29,675 maximum); and other non-need-based awards and non-need-based scholarships averaged $4,600 ($15,000 maximum). The average financial indebtedness of the 2014 graduate was $24,199. The FAFSA is required. The priority date for freshman financial aid applications for fall entry is March 1.

THE UNIVERSITY OF NORTH CAROLINA AT PEMBROKE *(The complete profile is made available exclusively on our website, www.barronspac.com)*

UNIVERSITY OF MOUNT OLIVE   E-3
www.umo.edu

Mount Olive, NC 28365	(919) 658-2502
	(800) 653-0854
Fax: (919) 658-7180	Email: admissions@moc.edu
Full-time: 816 men, 1660 women	Faculty: 85
Part-time: 227 men, 413 women	Ph.D.s: 39%
Graduate: n/av	Student/Faculty: 29 to 1
Year: semesters, summer session	Tuition: $15,000
Room & Board: $6100	Freshman Class: 975 applied, 654 accepted, 404 enrolled
SAT or ACT: required	CEEB CODE: 5435
Application Deadline: n/av	COMPETITIVE

University of Mount Olive, founded in 1951, is a private liberal arts institution affiliated with the Original Free Will Baptist Church. Figures in the above capsule and in this profile are approximate. The 123-acre campus is in a small town 65 miles southeast of Raleigh. Including any residence halls, there are 16 buildings.

STUDENT LIFE: 92% of undergraduates are from North Carolina. Others are from 21 states, 7 foreign countries, and Canada. 93% are from public schools. 55% are White; 32% African American. The average age of freshmen is 22; all undergraduates, 33. 36% do not continue beyond their first year. **Housing:** 306 students can be accommodated in college housing, which includes single-sex dorms and on-campus apartments. On-campus housing is guaranteed for the freshman year only. 90% of students commute. Alcohol is not permitted. All students may keep cars.

FACULTY/CLASSROOMS: 58% of faculty are male; 42% are female. All teach undergraduates, 14% do research, and 86% do both. No introductory courses are taught by graduate students.

PROGRAMS OF STUDY: Mount Olive confers B.A., B.S. and B.Applied Sc. degrees. Associate degrees are also awarded. Bachelor's degrees are awarded in BIOLOGICAL SCIENCE (biology/biological science), BUSINESS (accounting, business administration and management, human resources, and recreation and leisure services), COMMUNICATIONS AND THE ARTS (art, communications, English, fine arts, and music), COMPUTER AND PHYSICAL SCIENCE (computer management, information sciences and systems, and mathematics), EDUCATION (middle school education and secondary education), ENGINEERING AND ENVIRONMENTAL DESIGN (environmental science), SOCIAL SCIENCE (criminal justice, history, human services, liberal arts/general studies, ministries, psychology, and religion). Business, accounting, and psychology are the strongest academically. Business, psychology, and recreation have the largest enrollments.

ACTIVITIES: There are 20 groups on campus, including art, cheerleading, choir, chorale, chorus, drama, honors, international, literary magazine, newspaper, orchestra, pep band, photography, political, professional, religious, and student government. Popular campus events include Founders Day, Pickle Classic Weekend, and the North Carolina Pickle Festival. **Sports:** There are 6 intercollegiate sports for men and 6 for women, and 10 intramural sports for men and 8 for women. Facilities include a 2000-seat gym, racquetball and tennis courts, a track, wrestling/gymnastics and weight rooms, an athletic field, outdoor basketball areas, a student center, and baseball, softball, and soccer fields. **Graduates:** From July 1, 2013 to June 30, 2014, 629 bachelor's degrees were awarded. The most popular majors were business (52%), criminal justice administration (15%), and education (12%).

SERVICES: Counseling and information services are available, as is tutoring in most subjects, math, English, and science There is remedial math and reading. **Library/Resources:** The 2 libraries contain 77,545 volumes, 48,735 microform items, 2,005 audio/video tapes/CDs/DVDs, and subscribe to 5,979 periodicals including electronic. Computerized library services include interlibrary loans and database searching. Special learning facilities include an art gallery, a church archives collection. **Physically Challenged Students:** 90% of the campus is accessible. Facilities include wheelchair ramps, elevators, special parking, specially equipped restrooms, and special class scheduling. **Special:** Mount Olive offers co-op programs and internships in all majors, work-study, B.A.-B.S. degrees, dual majors, and accelerated degree programs in business, accounting, and criminal justice administration. Cross-registration with James Sprunt Community College and Wayne Community College, study abroad, and credit for life, military, and work experience are also possible. Professional degree completion programs run continuously for 55 to 57 weeks. There is 1 national honor society and a freshman honors program. **Visiting:** There are regularly scheduled orientations for prospective students, consisting of 2 days of advising, sports, and entertainment. There are guides for informal visits and visitors may sit in on classes. To schedule a visit, contact the Admissions Office at (800) 653-0854. **Campus Safety and Security:** There are lighted pathways/sidewalks, evening and weekend patrols.

REQUIREMENTS: The SAT or ACT is required. A satisfactory minimum SAT composite score or ACT score of 16 is recommended. Applicants must be graduates of an accredited secondary school or have a GED certificate. They must have completed 4 units of English, 3 each of math and science, and 2 of history. An essay and interview are suggested. AP and CLEP credits are accepted.To graduate, students must have completed a total of 126 credit hours, with a minimum 2.0 overall GPA in 63 credit hours for the B.A. or B.S. or in 53 hours for the B. Applied Sc. Distribution requirements include 30 to 36 hours in humanities, 18 in science/math/and 12 in social science. Specific course work includes 6 hours of religion, 4 of phys ed, and 3 hours of computer competency. **Procedure:** Freshmen are admitted to all sessions. Entrance exams should be taken in the junior or senior year. There are deferred admissions and rolling admissions plans. Application deadlines are open. Application fee is $20. Notification is sent on a rolling basis. Applications are accepted on-line. **Transfer Students:** 548 transfer students enrolled in 2013-2014. Applicants must have a minimum GPA of 2.0 and submit an official transcript from the previous institution. An interview may be required. 32 of 126 credits required for the bachelor's degree must be completed at Mount Olive. **International Students:** The school actively recruits these students. They must take the TOEFL with a minimum score of 513 on the paper-based TOEFL (PBT) or 65 on the Internet-based version (iBT). They must also take the SAT or ACT.

ADMISSIONS: 67% of the 2014-2015 applicants were accepted. **Admissions Contact:** Tim Woodard, Director of Admissions. E-Mail: *admissions@moc.edu* Web: *www.moc.edu*

FINANCIAL AID: In 2014-2015, 83% of all full-time freshmen and 79% of continuing full-time students received some form of financial aid. 89% of all full-time freshmen and 77% of continuing full-time students received need-based aid. The average freshman award was $8,679. Need-based scholarships or need-based grants averaged $7,351; need-based self-help aid (loans and jobs) averaged $2,210; non-need-based athletic scholarships averaged $3,689; and other non-need-based awards and non-need-based scholarships averaged $4,976. The average financial indebtedness of the 2014 graduate was $12,450. The FAFSA and the college's own financial statement are required. The priority date for freshman financial aid applications for fall entry is March 15.

UNIVERSITY OF NORTH CAROLINA SYSTEM

The University of North Carolina System, established in 1931, is a public system in North Carolina. It is governed by the University of North Carolina board of governors, whose chief administrator is the president. The primary goal of the system is to discover, create, transmit, and apply knowledge to address the needs of North Carolina and its people. The main priorities are teaching/instruction, research/scholarship/creative activities, public service (solving societal problems and enriching quality of life). The student enrollment for all 16 campuses is usually 220,000, with 9000 faculty members. Altogether there are 647 baccalaureate, 451 master's, and 138 doctoral programs offered in the University of North Carolina System. Profiles of the 4-year campuses are included in this section.

UNIVERSITY OF NORTH CAROLINA AT ASHEVILLE   B-2
www.unca.edu

Asheville, NC 28804	(828) 251-6600
	(800) 531-9842
Fax: (828) 251-6482	Email: admissions@unca.edu
Full-time: 1316 men, 1738 women	Faculty: 213; IIB, av$
Part-time: 234 men, 405 women	Ph.D.s: 84%
Graduate: 20 men, 38 women	Student/Faculty: 14 to 1
Year: semesters, summer session	Tuition: $5916 ($19,732)
Room & Board: $7584	Freshman Class: 3018 applied, 1926 accepted, 553 enrolled
SAT CR/M/W: 600/590/570 ACT: 25	CEEB CODE: 5013
Application Deadline: February 15	VERY COMPETITIVE

The University of North Carolina at Asheville is the designated public liberal arts university in the UNC system. Figures in the above capsule and in this profile are approximate. There is one graduate school. In addition to regional accreditation, UNC Asheville has baccalaureate program accreditation with AACSB and NCATE. The 365-acre campus is in an urban area approximately 1 mile north of downtown Asheville. Including any residence halls, there are 34 buildings.

STUDENT LIFE: 88% of undergraduates are from North Carolina. Others are from 40 states, 23 foreign countries, and Canada. 85% are White. The average age of freshmen is 18; all undergraduates, 23. 22% do not continue beyond their first year; 55% remain to graduate.

Housing: 1266 students can be accommodated in college housing, which includes single-sex and coed dorms. In addition, there are honors houses, quiet dorms, and substance-free housing. On-campus housing is guaranteed for the freshman year only. 62% of students commute. Upperclassmen may keep cars.

FACULTY/CLASSROOMS: 55% of faculty are male; 45% are female. All teach undergraduates. No introductory courses are taught by graduate students. The average class size in an introductory lecture is 22; in a laboratory is 18; and in a regular course is 17.

PROGRAMS OF STUDY: UNC Asheville confers B.A., B.S. and B.F.A. degrees. Master's degrees are also awarded. Bachelor's degrees are awarded in BIOLOGICAL SCIENCE (biology/biological science), BUSINESS (accounting and business administration and management), COMMUNICATIONS AND THE ARTS (art, classics, communications, dramatic arts, fine arts, French, German, literature, multimedia, music, music technology, and Spanish), COMPUTER AND PHYSICAL SCIENCE (atmospheric sciences and meteorology, chemistry, computer science, mathematics, and physics), ENGINEERING AND ENVIRONMENTAL DESIGN (engineering, engineering management, environmental science, and industrial administration/management), HEALTH PROFESSIONS (health and health promotion), SOCIAL SCIENCE (anthropology, economics, history, liberal arts/general studies, philosophy, political science/government, psychology, religion, sociology, and women's studies). Psychology, environmental studies, and literature have the largest enrollments.

ACTIVITIES: 3% of men belong to 2 national fraternities; 3% of women belong to 2 national sororities. There are 66 groups on campus, including art, as well as each departmental club, band, cheerleading, choir, chorus, computers, dance, drama, environmental, ethnic, gay, honors, international, jazz band, literary magazine, newspaper, pep band, political, professional, religious, social, social service, and student government. Popular campus events include Homecoming, Lawn Party, Family Weekend and Rockypalooza. **Sports:** There are 8 intercollegiate sports for men and 8 for women, and 17 intramural sports for men and 18 for women. Facilities include a sports and health complex with a state-of-the-art weight/cardio room, educational kitchen, Wellness Café, 4 basketball courts, volleyball and racquetball courts, multiple dance and group exercise studios, an indoor swimming pool, basketball arena, indoor and outdoor tracks, soccer and baseball fields, and disc golf course. Campus Recreation Department also hosts outings for mountain biking, paddling, hiking and other outdoor activities. The campus features more than 5 miles of wooded hiking/walking trails. **Graduates:** From July 1, 2013 to June 30, 2014, 713 bachelor's degrees were awarded. The most popular majors were psychology (15%), health & wellness promotion (7%), and literature (7%). 130 companies recruited on campus in 2013-2014. In an average class, 38% graduate in 4 years or less, 53% graduate in 5 years or less, and 58% graduate in 6 years or less. Of the 2013 graduating class, 19% were enrolled in graduate school within 6 months of graduation.

SERVICES: Counseling and information services are available, as is tutoring in most subjects. There is a reader service for the blind. **Library/Resources:** The library contains 280,449 volumes, 182,062 microform items, 8,494 audio/video tapes/CDs/DVDs, and subscribes to 78,979 periodicals including electronic. Computerized library services include interlibrary loans, database searching, Internet access, and Wi-Fi capability. Special learning facilities include an art gallery, Bob Moog Electric Music Studio (Dr. Moog, inventor of the Moog Synthesizer, was Research Professor of Music at UNC Asheville); N.C. Center for Health and Wellness, including BodPod, Balance Lab, Biofeedback Lab, Meditation Space; NEMAC (National Environmental Modeling and Analysis Center and (RENCI) Renaissance Computing Institute; Pisgah Astronomical Research Institute (radio telescopes), optical telescope observatory, and Botanical Gardens. **Physically Challenged Students:** 97% of the campus is accessible. Facilities include wheelchair ramps, elevators, special parking, specially equipped restrooms, special class scheduling, lowered drinking fountains, lowered telephones, special housing. **Special:** UNC Asheville participates in a consortium with Warren Wilson and Mars Hill Colleges, and there is cross-registration with a number of North Carolina universities and colleges. Study-abroad programs are available in 46 countries. The school offers internships, dual majors, student-designed interdisciplinary majors, and a 2-2 engineering degree and joint engineering degree with North Carolina State University. Nondegree study is available. There are 16 national honor societies, a freshman honors program, and 13 departmental honors programs. **Visiting:** There are regularly scheduled orientations for prospective students, including meetings with admissions counselors, faculty, or other departments, information session for students and families, and a campus tour. Preregistration is prior to fall enrollment during the summer months. There are guides for informal visits, visitors may sit in on classes, and stay overnight. To schedule a visit, contact the Office of Admissions, Visit Coordinator at (828) 350-4553. **Campus Safety and Security:** Measures include 24-hour foot and vehicle patrol, emergency notification system, self-defense education, and security escort services. There are shuttle buses, emergency telephones, lighted pathways/sidewalks, and controlled access to dorms/residences.

REQUIREMENTS: The SAT or ACT is required. The ACT Optional Writing test is also required. In addition, graduation from an accredited secondary school is required. UNC Asheville requires a minimum of 16 high school academic units, including 4 of English, 4 of math (algebra I, geometry, algebra II, and a class beyond algebra II), 3 science (biology, physical science, and a lab course), 2 of social studies/history, and 2 of a foreign language which needs to be a sequence (Spanish I & II, French I & II, etc). Applicants are evaluated primarily on their academic achievement record, extracurricular activities that support academic achievement, and SAT or ACT scores. AP and CLEP credits are accepted. Important factors in the admissions decision are advanced placement or honors courses, leadership record, and evidence of special talent. To graduate, students must complete a minimum of 120 credit hours, including at least 27 hours in the major, to include a senior capstone experience. The core curriculum requires a 3 hour Liberal Studies Introductory Colloquium; 12 hours of humanities; 3 hours of interdisciplinary arts; a minimum of 7 hours of natural science including lab; 3 hours of social science; up to 6 hours of foreign language; 4 hours of math; 4 hours of academic writing; 2 hours of health and wellness; and a 4 hour Liberal Studies Senior Colloquium. Students take their non-lab natural science and social science courses with an additional liberal arts elective, within an integrative topical cluster. In addition, students are required to do intensive course work in writing, information literacy quantitative reasoning, and diversity: these courses can be taken in the major, in general education, or in electives, and need not add credit hours to the students program. **Procedure:** Freshmen are admitted fall and spring. Entrance exams should be taken at the end of the junior year or the beginning of the senior year. There are early decision, early admissions, deferred admissions, and rolling admissions plans. Early decision applications should be filed by November 15; regular applications, by February 15 for fall entry; and October 15 for spring entry, along with a $50 fee. Notification of early decision is sent December 15; regular decision, on a rolling basis. Applications are accepted on-line. **Transfer Students:** 325 transfer students enrolled in 2013-2014. Applicants under 24 years of age or with fewer than 24 semester or 36 quarter credit hours must submit high school transcripts and SAT or ACT scores. *We do not need SAT scores if transferring in -unless you have not received grades from present institutions... (ex. a students first semester at school & submits an application in October for spring semester... no grades to submit so we look at HS record and test scores). 30 of 120 credits required for the bachelor's degree must be completed at UNC Asheville. **International Students:** There are 41 international students enrolled. The school actively recruits these students. They must take the TOEFL with a minimum score of 550 on the paper-based TOEFL (PBT) or 79 on the Internet-based version (iBT). They must also take the SAT or ACT. The SAT or ACT is required for international athletes.

ADMISSIONS: 64% of the 2014-2015 applicants were accepted. The SAT scores for the 2014-2015 freshman class were: Critical Reading--7% below 500, 41% between 500 and 599, 42% between 600 and 699, and 11% between 700 and 800; Math--5% below 500, 46% between 500 and 599, 42% between 600 and 699, and 7% between 700 and 800; Writing--15% below 500, 47% between 500 and 599, 31% between 600 and 699, and 6% between 700 and 800. The ACT scores were 5% below 21, 22% between 21 and 23, 39% between 24 and 26, 17% between 27 and 28, and 18% above 28. 46% of the current freshmen were in the top fifth of their class; 82% were in the top two fifths. 4 freshmen graduated first in their class. **Admissions Contact:** Shannon Earle, Director of Admissions. E-Mail: *admissions@ unca.edu* Web: *www.unca.edu/admissions*

FINANCIAL AID: In 2014-2015, 74% of all full-time freshmen and 71% of continuing full-time students received some form of financial aid. 62% of all full-time freshmen and continuing full-time students received need-based aid. The average freshman award was $9,522. Need-based scholarships or need-based grants averaged $5,687 ($17,227 maximum); need-based self-help aid (loans and jobs) averaged $4,032 ($21,100 maximum); non-need-based athletic scholarships averaged $9,007 ($28,509 maximum); and other non-need-based awards and non-need-based scholarships averaged $3,153 ($9,500 maximum). 17% of undergraduate students work part-time. Average annual earnings from campus work are $2600. The average

financial indebtedness of the 2014 graduate was $17,600. The FAFSA is required. The priority date for freshman financial aid applications for fall entry is March 1.

UNIVERSITY OF NORTH CAROLINA AT CHAPEL HILL D-2
www.unc.edu

Chapel Hill, NC 27599	(919) 962-2211
	(919) 966-3621
Fax: (919) 962-3045	Email: unchelp@admissions.unc.edu
Full-time: 7355 men, 10215 women	Faculty: 1044; I, +$
Part-time: 408 men, 372 women	Ph.D.s: 90%
Graduate: 4891 men, 5894 women	Student/Faculty: 14 to 1
Year: semesters, summer session	Tuition: $8336 ($33,418)
Room & Board: $10,592	Freshman Class: 31332 applied, 8929 accepted, 3976 enrolled
SAT CR/M/W: 640/660/640 ACT: 29	CEEB CODE: 5816
Application Deadline: January 10	MOST COMPETITIVE

Carolina's vibrant people and programs attest to the University's long-standing place among leaders in higher education since it was chartered in 1789 and opened its doors for students in 1795 as the nation's first public university. UNC has earned a reputation as one of the best universities in the world. Carolina prides itself on a strong, diverse student body, academic opportunities not found anywhere else, and a value unmatched by any public university in the nation. UNC-Chapel Hill, the nation's first public university, ranks among the world's leading research universities. A member of the prestigious Association of American Universities, Carolina regularly ranks as the best value for academic quality in U.S. public higher education. Now in its third century, the University offers 78 bachelor's, 112 master's, 68 doctorate and seven professional degree programs through 14 schools and the College of Arts and Sciences. Every day, faculty, staff and students shape their teaching, research and public service to meet North Carolina's most pressing needs in all 100 counties. There are 9 undergraduate schools and 13 graduate schools. In addition to regional accreditation, UNC-Chapel Hill has baccalaureate program accreditation with AACSB, ACEJMC, ACPE, ADA, APTA, CSWE, NCATE, NLN, CCNE, CEPA, and URTA. The 729-acre campus is in a suburban area 25 miles west of Raleigh. Including any residence halls, there are 683 buildings.

STUDENT LIFE: 81% of undergraduates are from North Carolina. Others are from 50 states, 106 foreign countries, and Canada. 82% are from public schools. 65% are White. The average age of freshmen is 17; all undergraduates, 19. 3% do not continue beyond their first year; 90% remain to graduate. **Housing:** 10505 students can be accommodated in college housing, which includes single-sex and coed dorms, on-campus apartments, off-campus apartments, and married student housing. In addition, there are honors houses, language houses, special-interest houses, fraternity houses, sorority houses, substance-free housing. On-campus housing is guaranteed for the freshman year only and is available on a lottery system for upperclassmen. 53% of students live on campus; of those, 80% remain on campus on weekends. Upperclassmen may keep cars.

FACULTY/CLASSROOMS: 57% of faculty are male; 43% are female. 58% teach undergraduates. Graduate students teach 42% of introductory courses. The average class size in an introductory lecture is 46; in a laboratory is 20; and in a regular course is 36.

PROGRAMS OF STUDY: UNC-Chapel Hill confers B.A., B.S., B.A.E.D., B.A.J.M.C., B.F.A., B.M.U.S., B.S.B.A., B.S.N., B.S.P.H., B.S.Ph.S. and B.S.I.S. degrees. Master's and doctoral degrees are also awarded. Bachelor's degrees are awarded in AGRICULTURE (environmental studies), BIOLOGICAL SCIENCE (biology/biological science, biometrics and biostatistics, and nutrition), BUSINESS (business administration and management, management science, and recreational facilities management), COMMUNICATIONS AND THE ARTS (art history and appreciation, classics, communications, comparative literature, dramatic arts, English, German, journalism, linguistics, music, music performance, romance languages and literature, Russian, and studio art), COMPUTER AND PHYSICAL SCIENCE (applied mathematics, applied science, chemistry, computer science, geology, information sciences and systems, mathematics, and physics), EDUCATION (elementary education and middle school education), ENGINEERING AND ENVIRONMENTAL DESIGN (environmental science), HEALTH PROFESSIONS (clinical science, dental hygiene, environmental health science, exercise science, health care administration, nursing, pharmaceutical science, and radiological science), SOCIAL SCIENCE (African American studies, American studies, anthropology, archeology, Asian/Oriental studies, child care/child and family studies, economics, European studies, geography, history, interdisciplinary studies, international studies, Latin American studies, peace studies, philosophy, political science/government, psychology, public affairs, religion, Russian and Slavic studies, sociology, and women's studies). Psychology, biology, journalism/mass communication and business administration have the largest enrollments.

ACTIVITIES: 17% of men belong to 32 national fraternities; 17% of women belong to 23 national sororities. There are 671 groups on campus, including and public/community service, games/e-sports, Greek alliance council, panhellenic council, academic, art, band, cheerleading, chess, choir, chorale, chorus, computers, dance, debate, drama, drill team, environmental, ethnic, film, forensics, gay, honors, international, jazz band, literary magazine, marching band, musical theater, newspaper, opera, orchestra, pep band, photography, political, professional, radio and TV, religious, social, social service, student government, symphony, and yearbook. Popular campus events include FallFest, SpringFest, Derby Days, Homecoming, Unity Conference and Midnight Madness Basketball. **Sports:** There are 13 intercollegiate sports for men and 15 for women, and 38 intramural sports for men and 34 for women. Facilities include a 60,000-seat football stadium, 3 swimming pools, a 21,000-seat sports and student activities center, tennis courts, lacrosse and soccer fields, golf course, boathouse, gym facilities, softball fields, and a student recreation center with aerobics, weights, and wellness programs. **Graduates:** From July 1, 2013 to June 30, 2014, 4566 bachelor's degrees were awarded. The most popular majors were psychology (10%), biology (10%), and journalism and mass communication (8%). 216 companies recruited on campus in 2013-2014. In an average class, 2% graduate in 3 years or less, 81% graduate in 4 years or less, 89% graduate in 5 years or less, and 90% graduate in 6 years or less. Of the 2013 graduating class, 26% were enrolled in graduate school within 6 months of graduation, and 60% were employed.

SERVICES: Counseling and information services are available, as is tutoring in most subjects. There is a reader service for the blind. **Library/Resources:** The 15 libraries contain 7.6 million volumes, 5.3 million microform items, 476,644 audio/video tapes/CDs/DVDs, and subscribe to 113,065 periodicals including electronic. Computerized library services include interlibrary loans, database searching, Internet access, and Wi-Fi capability. Special learning facilities include an art gallery, planetarium, radio station, TV station, an botanical garden and theater. **Physically Challenged Students:** 97% of the campus is accessible. Facilities include wheelchair ramps, elevators, special parking, lowered drinking fountains, and special housing. **Special:** Students may participate in joint programs with Duke University, North Carolina State University, and the National University of Singapore (NUS). Internships at home and abroad, a Washington semester focusing on international affairs, study abroad in 70 countries, B.A.-B.S. degrees, a sea semester, and student-designed majors are available. There are pass/fail options and non-degree study. There are 28 national honor societies, including Phi Beta Kappa, a freshman honors program, and 53 departmental honors programs. **Visiting:** There are regularly scheduled orientations for prospective students, including campus tours and information sessions, offered twice each weekday. Visitors may sit in on classes. To schedule a visit, contact the Office of Undergraduate Admissions. **Campus Safety and Security:** Measures include 24-hour foot and vehicle patrol, emergency notification system, self-defense education, and security escort services. There are shuttle buses, emergency telephones, lighted pathways/sidewalks, controlled access to dorms/residences, and building security surveys.

REQUIREMENTS: The SAT or ACT is required. The ACT Optional Writing test is also required. Applicants should present a minimum of 16 units of high school coursework within the 5 traditional academic areas (literature, math, physical and biological sciences, social sciences, and foreign languages), including 4 units of English; at least 4 units of college preparatory mathematics (2 algebra, 1 geometry, and a higher level math course for which algebra II is a prerequisite); at least 2 units of a single foreign language; 3 units in science, including at least 1 unit in a life or biological science and at least 1 in a physical science, and including at least 1 lab course; and 2 units of social science, including United States history. AP credits are accepted. To graduate, students must complete 120 credits (more for some B.S. degrees) with a 2.0 GPA. The general education requirements fall under 3 categories: Foundations, Approaches, and Connections. B.A. degree candidates must satisfy a supplemental education requirement by completing a second major or a minor, by completing - in addition to a student's major requirements - 9 credit hours outside the home department of the major, or by completing a concentration outside a professional school as part of the degree requirements for graduating from that school. **Procedure:** Freshmen are admitted fall. Entrance exams should be taken in the junior or senior year. There are early admissions and deferred admissions plans. Early decision applications should be filed by October 15; regular applications, by January 10 for fall entry, along with a $80 fee. Notification of early decision is sent January 30; regular decision, March 20. 3154 applicants were on the 2014 waiting list; 31 were admitted. Applications are accepted on-line. **Transfer Students:** 845 transfer students enrolled in 2013-2014. Sophomore transfers need at least 30 credit hours and a minimum GPA of 2.0; junior transfers need at least 60 credit hours and a minimum GPA of 2.0. High school diploma or equivalent, meeting minimum course requirements, also required. 45 of 120 credits required for the bachelor's degree must be completed at UNC-Chapel Hill. **International Students:** There are 474 international students enrolled. The school actively recruits these students. They must also take the SAT or ACT.

ADMISSIONS: 28% of the 2014-2015 applicants were accepted. The SAT scores for the 2014-2015 freshman class were: Critical Reading--2% below 500, 21% between 500 and 599, 52% between 600 and 699, and 24% between 700 and 800; Math--1% below 500, 16% between 500 and 599, 50% between 600 and 699, and 32% between 700 and 800; Writing--4% below 500, 23% between 500 and 599, 48% between 600 and 699, and 25% between 700 and 800. The ACT scores were 1% below 21, 6% between 21 and 23, 17% between 24 and 26, 18% between 27 and 28, and 58% above 28. 94% of the current freshmen were in the top fifth of their class; 99% were in the top two fifths. There were 99 National Merit finalists. 220 freshmen graduated first in their class. **Admissions Contact:** Office of Undergraduate Admisstions E-Mail: *unchelp@admissions.unc.edu* Web: *www.admissions.unc.edu*

FINANCIAL AID: In 2014-2015, 69% of all full-time freshmen and 63% of continuing full-time students received some form of financial aid. 41% of all full-time freshmen and 42% of continuing full-time students received need-based aid. The average freshman award was $13,995. Need-based scholarships or need-based grants averaged $12,428 ($51,640 maximum); need-based self-help aid (loans and jobs) averaged $3,459 ($9,271 maximum); non-need-based athletic scholarships averaged $21,365 ($48,628 maximum); other non-need-based awards and non-need-based scholarships averaged $4,672 ($44,726 maximum); and $5,742 from other forms of aid. Average annual earnings from campus work are $1839. The average financial indebtedness of the 2014 graduate was $16,983. UNC-Chapel Hill is a member of CSS. The CSS/Profile and FAFSA are required. The priority date for freshman financial aid applications for fall entry is March 1.

UNIVERSITY OF NORTH CAROLINA AT CHARLOTTE   C-3
www.uncc.edu

Charlotte, NC 28223	**(704) 687-8622**
	(704) 687-5507
Fax: (704) 687-1664	**Email:** admissions@uncc.edu
Full-time: 9972 men, 9011 women	**Faculty:** I, --$
Part-time: 1601 men, 1632 women	**Ph.Ds:** n/av
Graduate: 2188 men, 2834 women	**Student/Faculty:** n/av
Year: semesters, summer session	**Tuition:** $6277 ($19,448)
Room & Board: $9270	**Freshman Class:** 15610 applied, 10004 accepted, 3319 enrolled
SAT CR/M/W: 530/560/520 **ACT:** 23	**CEEB CODE:** 5105
Application Deadline: July 1	**COMPETITIVE**

University of North Carolina at Charlotte, founded in 1946, is the largest institution of higher education in the Charlotte region and the fourth largest of the 16 institutions within the University of North Carolina system. UNC Charlotte offers 7 colleges with 79 programs leading to Bachelor's degrees, 65 programs leading to Master's degrees and 21 programs leading to Doctoral degrees. As an urban research university, we are frequently recognized for our contributions to higher education and to the region. We're proud of the many programs and services we offer on and off campus to support students by fostering a fundamental understanding of diversity and community. The Charlotte 49ers compete in 17 varsity sports on the NCAA Division I level and are a member of Conference USA. Ultimately, the true foundation of a university is the great minds and enthusiasm of its students and faculty. There are 7 undergraduate schools and one graduate school. In addition to regional accreditation, UNC-Charlotte has baccalaureate program accreditation with AACSB, ABET, CSWE, NAAB, NCATE, CAAHEP, CACREP, CCNE, COA, CAATE, CAHME, CEPH, NCDPI, NASPAA, and ACS. The 1000-acre campus is in a suburban area 8 miles north of uptown Charlotte, North Carolina. Including any residence halls, there are 102 buildings.

STUDENT LIFE: 94% of undergraduates are from North Carolina. Others are from 45 states, 59 foreign countries, and Canada. 60% are White; 17% African American. The average age of freshmen is 18; all undergraduates, 21. 18% do not continue beyond their first year; 55% remain to graduate. **Housing:** 5363 students can be accommodated in college housing, which includes single-sex and coed dorms and on-campus apartments. In addition, there are honors houses, special-interest houses, fraternity houses, sorority houses, Learning communities. On-campus housing is available on a first-come, first-served basis, and is available on a lottery system for upperclassmen. 76% of students commute. All students may keep cars.

FACULTY/CLASSROOMS: No introductory courses are taught by graduate students.

PROGRAMS OF STUDY: UNC-Charlotte confers B.A., B.S., B.Arch., B.F.A., B.M., B.S.B.A, B.S.C.E., B.S.Cp.E, B.S.C.M., B.S.E.E., B.S.S.E., B.S.E.T., B.S.P.H. B.S.R.T., B.S.M.E., B.S.N. and B.S.W. degrees. Master's and Doctoral degrees are also awarded. Bachelor's degrees are awarded in BIOLOGICAL SCIENCE (biology/biological science), BUSINESS (accounting, banking and finance, business administration and management, business economics, finance, international business management, management information systems, marketing, marketing/retailing/merchandising, real estate, and supply chain management), COMMUNICATIONS AND THE ARTS (art, art history and appreciation, communications, dance, English, fine arts, French, German, music, music performance, Spanish, and theatre arts), COMPUTER AND PHYSICAL SCIENCE (atmospheric sciences and meteorology, chemistry, computer science, earth science, geology, mathematics, physics, and software engineering), EDUCATION (athletic training, elementary education, English education, foreign languages education, mathematics education, middle school education, social studies education, and special education), ENGINEERING AND ENVIRONMENTAL DESIGN (architecture, civil engineering, civil engineering technology, computer engineering, construction management, electrical/electronics engineering,

electrical/electronics engineering technology, engineering technology, industrial administration/management, mechanical engineering, mechanical engineering technology, and systems engineering), HEALTH PROFESSIONS (exercise science, medical technology, nursing, public health, and respiratory therapy), SOCIAL SCIENCE (Africana studies, anthropology, child care/child and family studies, child psychology/development, criminal justice, economics, fire control and safety technology, geography, history, international studies, Japanese studies, Latin American studies, liberal arts/general studies, philosophy, physical fitness/movement, political science/government, psychology, religious studies, social work, and sociology). Engineering, business, and education are the strongest academically. Psychology, mechanical engineering, and computer science have the largest enrollments.

ACTIVITIES: 2% of men belong to 21 national fraternities; 5% of women belong to 17 national sororities. There are 328 groups on campus, including art, cheerleading, chess, choir, chorale, chorus, communications, computers, dance, debate, drama, environmental, ethnic, film, forensics, gay, honors, international, jazz band, literary magazine, marching band, musical theater, newspaper, opera, pep band, photography, political, professional, radio and TV, religious, social, social service, and student government. Popular campus events include Week of Welcome, Greek Week, International Festival and Homecoming. **Sports:** There are 9 intercollegiate sports for men and 8 for women, and 16 intramural sports for men and 16 for women. Facilities include The Belk Gymnasium has multiple basketball courts, two racquetball courts, three squash courts, and a Olympic-size swimming pool. The James H. Barnhardt Student Activity Center contains a jogging track, recreational courts, climbing wall, weight room, group fitness room, training center and a 10,000 seat event arena. There are also 8 outdoor recreational fields along with tennis, sand volleyball,basketball courts, fitness/biking trails, and ropes courses. **Graduates:** From July 1, 2013 to June 30, 2014, 4362 bachelor's degrees were awarded. The most popular majors were business (18%), social sciences (9%), and engineering (8%). 125 companies recruited on campus in 2013-2014. In an average class, 1% graduate in 3 years or less, 26% graduate in 4 years or less, 49% graduate in 5 years or less, and 55% graduate in 6 years or less. Of the 2013 graduating class, 20% were enrolled in graduate school within 6 months of graduation, and 74% were employed.

SERVICES: Counseling and information services are available, as is tutoring in some subjects. There is a reader service for the blind. **Library/Resources:** The library contains 1.2 million volumes, 2.2 million microform items, 23,002 audio/video tapes/CDs/DVDs, and subscribes to 4,872 periodicals including electronic. Computerized library services include interlibrary loans, database searching, Internet access, and Wi-Fi capability. Special learning facilities include an art gallery, radio station, TV station, NC Motorsports and Automotive Research Center, Charlotte Visualization Center, eBusiness Technology Institute, Center for Applied Geographic Information Science, Center for Precision Metrology, Center for Optoelectronics and Optical Communications, Bioinformatics Research Center, IDEAS Center, Center for Biomedical Engineering Systems, Center for Global Public Relations, Center for Professional and Applied Ethics, Multicultural Resource Center, UNC Charlotte Botanical Gardens and McMillan Greenhouse, which includes a tropical rain forest. **Physically Challenged Students:** 90% of the campus is accessible. Facilities include wheelchair ramps, elevators, special parking, specially equipped restrooms, special class scheduling, lowered drinking fountains, lowered telephones, special housing. The Disability Services Office assists students with all academic and physical accommodations. **Special:** Cross-registration is available through the Charlotte Area Educational Consortium. Also available are cooperative programs in numerous majors and internships of 1 semester arranged with public and private community organizations. There are 20 national honor societies, a freshman honors program, and 18 departmental honors programs. **Visiting:** There are regularly scheduled orientations for prospective students, including tours. There are guides for informal visits, visitors may sit in on classes, and stay overnight. To schedule a visit, contact the Undergraduate Admissions Office. **Campus Safety and Security:** Measures include 24-hour foot and vehicle patrol, emergency notification system, self-defense education, and security escort services. There are shuttle buses, emergency telephones, and lighted pathways/sidewalks.

REQUIREMENTS: The SAT or ACT is required. Graduation from an accredited secondary school or the GED is required. The school requires 14 academic credits, including 4 years each of English, and math, 3 of science (including 1 of physical science), 2 of a foreign language, and 2 of social studies, including 1 of U.S. history. Seniors should select a challenging academic schedule that includes English, math, science, social studies or history and foreign language. A portfolio and interview are required for art and architecture students only. AP and CLEP credits are accepted. Important factors in the admissions decision are advanced placement or honors courses, leadership record, and recommendations by school officials. Students must complete a minimum of 120 credit hours with an overall minimum GPA of 2.0. Between 30 and 42 hours are required in the major with a minimum GPA of 2.0 in major and minor courses. All students must complete core requirements in the 6 interrelated areas of communication, problem solving, values, science and technology, arts, literature and ideas, and the individual, society, and culture. **Procedure:** Freshmen are admitted fall, spring, and summer. Entrance exams should be taken end of the junior year or by December of the senior year. There are early admissions and rolling admissions plans. Applications should be filed by July 1 for fall entry; November 15 for spring entry; and May 1 for summer entry, along with a $60 fee. Notifications are sent December 15. Applications are accepted on-line. **Transfer Students:** 2407 transfer students enrolled in 2013-2014. Transfer students must have a minimum GPA of 2.0 on all college courses attempted. Certain majors have limited space and require a higher GPA and/or prerequisites. Applicants with fewer than 24 hours of transferable credit must meet both transfer and freshman admissions requirements. An interview is required only for architecture students. 30 of 120 credits required for the bachelor's degree must be completed at UNC-Charlotte. **International Students:** There are 464 international students enrolled. They must take the TOEFL with a minimum score of 507 on the paper-based TOEFL (PBT) or 64 on the Internet-based version (iBT) or take the MELAB. They must also take the SAT or ACT. Students with a score of 450 or higher on the verbal part of the SAT are not required to take the TOEFL or other English Proficiency exam.

ADMISSIONS: 64% of the 2014-2015 applicants were accepted. The SAT scores for the 2014-2015 freshman class were: Critical Reading--26% below 500, 57% between 500 and 599, 16% between 600 and 699, and 1% between 700 and 800; Math--17% below 500, 57% between 500 and 599, 23% between 600 and 699, and 3% between 700 and 800; Writing--35% below 500, 52% between 500 and 599, 12% between 600 and 699, and 1% between 700 and 800. The ACT scores were 17% below 21, 43% between 21 and 23, 26% between 24 and 26, 8% between 27 and 28, and 6% above 28. **Admissions Contact:** Claire Kirby, Director of Admissions. E-Mail: *admissions@uncc .edu* Web: *www.uncc.edu*

FINANCIAL AID: UNC-Charlotte is a member of CSS. The FAFSA is required. The priority date for freshman financial aid applications for fall entry is March 1.

UNIVERSITY OF NORTH CAROLINA AT WILMINGTON   E-4
www.uncw.edu

Wilmington, NC 28403	(910) 962-3000
	(910) 962-3243
Fax: (910) 962-3038	Email: admissions@uncw.edu
Full-time: 4346 men, 6314 women	Faculty: 588; IIA, --$
Part-time: 388 men, 722 women	Ph.D.s: 86%
Graduate: 488 men, 813 women	Student/Faculty: 16 to 1
Year: semesters, summer session	Tuition: $5672 ($17,492)
Room & Board: $7900	Freshman Class: 11397 applied, 5457 accepted, 1981 enrolled
SAT CR/M/W: 592/605/561 ACT: 26	CEEB CODE: 5907
Application Deadline: February 1	VERY COMPETITIVE

The University of North Carolina Wilmington, founded in 1947, is a publicly funded institution offering programs in the liberal arts and sciences, education, and business. It is a part of the University of

North Carolina System. Figures in the above capsule and in this profile are approximate. There are 4 undergraduate schools and 1 graduate school. In addition to regional accreditation, UNCW has baccalaureate program accreditation with NCATE and NLN. The 660-acre campus is in a suburban area 125 miles southeast of Raleigh. Including any residence halls, there are 127 buildings.

STUDENT LIFE: 82% of undergraduates are from North Carolina. Others are from 42 states, 53 foreign countries, and Canada. 86% are White. The average age of freshmen is 18; all undergraduates, 22. 13% do not continue beyond their first year; 67% remain to graduate. **Housing:** 4143 students can be accommodated in college housing, which includes single-sex and coed dorms and on-campus apartments. In addition, there are honors houses, special-interest houses, fraternity houses, sorority houses, and an international student dorm. On-campus housing is guaranteed for all 4 years, is available on a first-come, and first-served basis. 61% of students commute. All students may keep cars.

FACULTY/CLASSROOMS: 53% of faculty are male; 47% are female. 96% teach undergraduates, 62% do research, and 60% do both. No introductory courses are taught by graduate students. The average class size in a regular course is 21.

PROGRAMS OF STUDY: UNCW confers B.A., B.S., B.F.A., B.S.W. and B.A. in Music. degrees. Master's and Doctoral degrees are also awarded. Bachelor's degrees are awarded in BIOLOGICAL SCIENCE (biochemistry, biology/biological science, marine biology, and marine science), BUSINESS (accounting, banking and finance, business administration and management, business economics, business systems analysis, and marketing/retailing/merchandising), COMMUNICATIONS AND THE ARTS (art, art history and appreciation, communications, creative writing, dramatic arts, English, film arts, French, German, music, music performance, Spanish, speech/debate/rhetoric, studio art, and theater design), COMPUTER AND PHYSICAL SCIENCE (chemistry, computer science, geology, mathematics, physics, and statistics), EDUCATION (athletic training, early childhood education, elementary education, middle school education, music education, physical education, secondary education, and special education), ENGINEERING AND ENVIRONMENTAL DESIGN (environmental science and preengineering), HEALTH PROFESSIONS (clinical science, nursing, physical therapy, predentistry, premedicine, preoptometry, prepharmacy, prephysical therapy, prepodiatry, preveterinary science, and recreation therapy), SOCIAL SCIENCE (anthropology, criminal justice, economics, geography, German area studies, history, parks and recreation management, philosophy and religion, political science/government, prelaw, psychology, religion, social work, and sociology).

ACTIVITIES: 6% of men belong to 14 national fraternities; 4% of women belong to 13 national sororities. There are 200 groups on campus, including art, band, cheerleading, choir, chorale, chorus, computers, dance, debate, drama, environmental, ethnic, film, forensics, gay, honors, international, jazz band, literary magazine, musical theater, newspaper, orchestra, pep band, photography, political, professional, radio and TV, religious, social, social service, student government, and symphony. Popular campus events include Business Week, Greek Week, and Spring Week. **Sports:** There are 10 intercollegiate sports for men and 11 for women, and 47 intramural sports for men and 47 for women. Facilities include a 6000-seat coliseum, an collegiate-size swimming pool and separate diving tank, a track and field complex, and basketball, tennis, and volleyball courts. A Student Recreation Center with basketball courts, exercise equipment and exercise classes, indoor track, and a rock climbing wall. As well, each of our upperclassmen apartment complexes have a recreational outdoor pool and clubhouse. **Graduates:** From July 1, 2013 to June 30, 2014, 2628 bachelor's degrees were awarded. 153 companies recruited on campus in 2013-2014. In an average class, 45% graduate in 4 years or less and 67% graduate in 6 years or less.

SERVICES: Counseling and information services are available, as is tutoring in most subjects. There is a reader service for the blind, and remedial math, reading, and writing, and a supplemental instruction program. **Library/Resources:** The library contains 1.0 million volumes, 1.0 million microform items, 82,023 audio/video tapes/CDs/DVDs, and subscribes to 24,081 periodicals including electronic. Computerized library services include interlibrary loans, database searching, Internet access, and Wi-Fi capability. Special learning facilities include an art gallery, radio station, TV station, wildflower preserve, nature preserve, museum of world cultures, and the research vessel Cape Fear, used for a marine biology labs and for research out of the Center for Marine Science, the University's privately owned and operated research center. **Physically Challenged Students:** 98% of the campus is accessible. Facilities include wheelchair ramps, elevators, special parking, specially equipped restrooms, special class scheduling, lowered drinking fountains, lowered telephones, special housing. **Special:** UNC Wilmington offer internships, over 500 study abroad programs in 50 different countries, mentored research, and work-study programs. Dual majors may be pursued if requirements are met, and credit is given for military experience. There is a chapter of Phi Beta Kappa and a freshman honors program. **Visiting:** There are regularly scheduled orientations for prospective students. There are guides for informal visits. To schedule a visit, contact the Admissions Office. **Campus Safety and Security:** Measures include 24-hour foot and vehicle patrol, emergency notification system, self-defense education, and security escort services. There are shuttle buses, emergency telephones, lighted pathways/sidewalks, controlled access to dorms/residences, rape awareness defense (RAD) training, counseling services and the university police are available.

REQUIREMENTS: The SAT or ACT is required. The ACT Optional Writing test is also required. Graduation from an accredited secondary school or the GED is required for admission. High school courses must include 4 years of English, 4 years of math (algebra I, II, and geometry),and a math beyond Algebra II, 3 units of science (1 year each of biology, physical science, and a lab course), 2 years of social studies including 1 year of U.S. history and 2 years of a foreign language. AP and CLEP credits are accepted.Students may qualify for the bachelor's degree by successfully completing the university studies requirements, an approved course of study in an academic major, a minimum of 124 semester hours of credit, and a minimum quality point average of 2.0. The final 31 semester hours of course credit, including the final 15 semester hours in the major, must be completed at the University of North Carolina at Wilmington. **Procedure:** Freshmen are admitted fall and summer. Entrance exams should be taken during the junior or senior year. There are early admissions and deferred admissions plans. Early decision applications should be filed by November 1; regular applications, by February 1 for fall entry. The fall 2014 application fee was $60. Notification of early decision is sent January 20; regular decision, April 1. Applications are accepted online. **Transfer Students:** 1280 transfer students enrolled in 2013-2014. Transfer students must have a minimum GPA of 2.5 and be eligible to return to the institution last attended. Prior to admission, transfer applicants must have successfully completed 1 year of freshman-level English, 1 unit of college-level math and have completed at least 24 semesters or 36 quarter hours of credit. 31 of 124 credits required for the bachelor's degree must be completed at UNCW. **International Students:** There are 211 international students enrolled. The school actively recruits these students. They must take the TOEFL with a minimum score of 525 on the paper-based TOEFL (PBT) or 71 on the Internet-based version (iBT), or the IELTS (minimum score- 6.5). They must also take the SAT or ACT. The SAT/ACT with acceptable scores (minimum 450 SAT writing, 20 ACT writing) is accepted if the TOEFL is not available.

ADMISSIONS: 48% of the 2014-2015 applicants were accepted. The SAT scores for the 2014-2015 freshman class were: Critical Reading--6% below 500, 56% between 500 and 599, 35% between 600 and 699, and 3% between 700 and 800; Math--4% below 500, 50% between 500 and 599, 42% between 600 and 699, and 4% between 700 and 800; Writing--16% below 500, 56% between 500 and 599, 26% between 600 and 699, and 2% between 700 and 800. The ACT scores were 10% below 21, 30% between 21 and 23, 39% between 24 and 26, 14% between 27 and 28, and 8% above 28. 44% of the current freshmen were in the top fifth of their class; 70% were in the top two fifths. **Admissions Contact:** Janice Rockwell, Director of Admissions. E-Mail: *admissions@uncw.edu* Web: *www.uncw.edu*

FINANCIAL AID: In 2014-2015, 60% of all full-time freshmen and 67% of continuing full-time students received some form of financial aid. 53% of all full-time freshmen and 58% of continuing full-time students received need-based aid. The average freshman award was $8,896. Need-based scholarships or need-based grants averaged $6,692; need-based self-help aid (loans and jobs) averaged $3,121;

non-need-based athletic scholarships averaged $7,219; and other non-need-based awards and non-need-based scholarships averaged $2,211. 9% of undergraduate students work part-time. Average annual earnings from campus work are $1017. The average financial indebtedness of the 2014 graduate was $16,980. The FAFSA is required. The priority date for freshman financial aid applications for fall entry is March 1. The deadline for filing freshman financial aid applications for fall entry is December 31.

UNIVERSITY OF NORTH CAROLINA SCHOOL OF THE ARTS
(The complete profile is made available exclusively on our website, www.barronspac.com)

WAKE FOREST UNIVERSITY   C-2
www.wfu.edu

Winston-Salem, NC 27109	(336) 758-5201
	(336) 758-5000
Fax: 336) 716-0185	Email: admissions@wfu.edu
Full-time: 2264 men, 2488 women	Faculty: 461; IIA, ++$
Part-time: 40 men, 20 women	Ph.D.s: 87%
Graduate: 1464 men, 1294 women	Student/Faculty: 11 to 1
Year: semesters, summer session	Tuition: $46,200
Room & Board: $12,638	Freshman Class: 11407 applied, 3875 accepted, 1234 enrolled
SAT CR/M: 650/675 ACT: 29	CEEB CODE: 5885
Application Deadline: January 15	MOST COMPETITIVE

Wake Forest University, established in 1834, is a private institution offering undergraduate programs in the liberal arts and sciences, education, and preprofessional fields. Figures in the above capsule and in this profile are approximate. There are 2 undergraduate schools and 6 graduate schools. In addition to regional accreditation, Wake Forest has baccalaureate program accreditation with AACSB and NCATE. The 340-acre campus is in a suburban area 4 miles northwest of Winston-Salem. Including any residence halls, there are 47 buildings.

STUDENT LIFE: 77% of undergraduates are from out of state, mostly the South. Students are from 48 states, 28 foreign countries, and Canada. 60% are from public schools. 76% are White. 40% are Protestant; 28% Muslim, Hindu, Buddhist, Mormon and Greek Orthodox.; 25% Catholic. The average age of freshmen is 19; all undergraduates, 20. 6% do not continue beyond their first year; 86% remain to graduate. **Housing:** 3380 students can be accommodated in college housing, which includes coed dorms and on-campus apartments. In addition, there are special-interest houses, fraternity houses, sorority houses, theme and wellness housing and accomodations for disabled students. On-campus housing is guaranteed for all 4 years. 68% of students live on campus; of those, 70% remain on campus on weekends. Upperclassmen may keep cars.

FACULTY/CLASSROOMS: 57% of faculty are male; 43% are female. 86% teach undergraduates, and 73% do research. No introductory courses are taught by graduate students. The average class size in a regular course is 21.

PROGRAMS OF STUDY: Wake Forest confers B.A., and B.S. degrees. Master's and Doctoral degrees are also awarded. Bachelor's degrees are awarded in BIOLOGICAL SCIENCE (biology/biological science), BUSINESS (accounting, banking and finance, and business administration and management), COMMUNICATIONS AND THE ARTS (art history, art, Chinese, classics, communications, English, French, German, Greek, Japanese, Latin, music, Russian, Spanish, studio art, and theatre studies), COMPUTER AND PHYSICAL SCIENCE (chemistry, computer science, mathematics, mathematics – economics, and physics), EDUCATION (education), HEALTH PROFESSIONS (exercise science), SOCIAL SCIENCE (anthropology, economics, history, philosophy, political science/government, psychology, religion, and sociology). Business and enterprise management, psychology, political science, communication, and finance have the largest enrollments.

ACTIVITIES: 39% of men belong to 16 national fraternities; 58% of

women belong to 11 national sororities. There are 160 groups on campus, including art, band, cheerleading, choir, chorale, chorus, computers, dance, debate, drama, drill team, environmental, ethnic, film, gay, honors, international, jazz band, literary magazine, marching band, newspaper, orchestra, pep band, photography, political, professional, radio and TV, religious, social, social service, student government, symphony, women's and environmental, and yearbook. Popular campus events include Project Pumpkin, Springfest and President's Ball. **Sports:** There are 8 intercollegiate sports for men and 8 for women, and 18 intramural sports for men and 15 for women. Facilities include indoor sports are played at Reynolds Gym and outdoor sports are played on Water Tower Field, Water Tower Courts, and Leighton Tennis Courts. **Graduates:** From July 1, 2013 to June 30, 2014, 1111 bachelor's degrees were awarded. The most popular majors were social science (20%), business/marketing (18%), and communication/journalism (9%). In an average class, 85% graduate in 4 years or less, 90% graduate in 5 years or less, and 88% graduate in 6 years or less. Of the 2013 graduating class, 26% were enrolled in graduate school within 6 months of graduation, and 68% were employed.

SERVICES: Counseling and information services are available, as is tutoring in some subjects, primarily in the sciences, math, and foreign languages. There is also a reader service for the blind. The Learning Assistance Center offers instructional support and skill development in writing, reading, and study strategies. **Library/Resources:** The 3 libraries contain 2.1 million volumes, 2.2 million microform items, 38,265 audio/video tapes/CDs/DVDs, and subscribe to 51,262 periodicals including electronic. Computerized library services include interlibrary loans, database searching, Internet access, and Wi-Fi capability. Special learning facilities include an art gallery, radio station, TV station, fine arts center, anthropology museum, and laser research facility. **Physically Challenged Students:** 85% of the campus is accessible. Facilities include wheelchair ramps, elevators, special parking, specially equipped restrooms, special class scheduling, lowered drinking fountains, lowered telephones, and special housing. **Special:** Wake Forest offers cooperative programs in engineering with any other schools of engineering accredited by ABET; political science majors who minor in Latin American studies have the opportunity to pursue a 5-year cooperative B.A./M.A. program with Georgetown University. Cross-registration with Salem College is available for full-time students. Wake Forest sponsors study-abroad semester programs in 13 countries. Other special opportunities include internships, work-study programs, dual majors, and a minor in entrepreneurship and social enterprise. Students can also be certified in Spanish language translation and interpreting. An accelerated degree program may be arranged in medical technology. Interdisciplinary honors courses and the Open Curriculum program are available for selected students. Wake Forest owns residences in London, Venice, and Vienna where students and professors attend semester-long courses in a variety of disciplines. A semester-long program in Washington, D.C., is also offered. There are 11 national honor societies, including Phi Beta Kappa, a freshman honors program, and 23 departmental honors programs. **Visiting:** There are regularly scheduled orientations for prospective students, including group information sessions and tours by appointment. There are guides for informal visits, visitors may sit in on classes, and stay overnight. To schedule a visit, contact the Admissions Office. **Campus Safety and Security:** Measures include 24-hour foot and vehicle patrol, emergency notification system, self-defense education, and security escort services. There are shuttle buses, emergency telephones, lighted pathways/sidewalks, There are gatehouses at 2 of the university's 3 entrances that operate from 6 p.m. to 6 a.m.

REQUIREMENTS: SAT Subject Tests, are considered if submitted. Graduation from an accredited secondary school or the GED is required. The school requires 16 academic credits, including 4 credits of English, 3 of math, 2 each of a foreign language, history, and social studies, and 1 of science. 1 credit each of art and music is recommended. All students must submit an essay. AP and CLEP credits are accepted. Important factors in the admissions decision are recommendations by school officials, leadership record, and advanced placement or honors courses. To graduate, students must complete a total of 120 credits with a minimum GPA of 2.0. The number of hours required in the major varies. All students must take 1 semester

of a writing seminar, a first-year seminar, and 1 course in foreign language literature. In addition, students must complete 2 courses each in natural sciences and math, social and behavioral sciences, and history, religion, and philosophy; 1 course in literature; and 1 course in fine arts. **Procedure:** Freshmen are admitted fall and spring. There are early decision and deferred admissions plans. Early decision applications should be filed by November 15; regular applications, by January 15 for fall entry; and November 15 for spring entry, along with a $50 fee. Notification of early decision is sent December 15; regular decision, April 1. 337 early decision candidates were accepted for the 2014-2015 class. Applications are accepted on-line. **Transfer Students:** 35 transfer students enrolled in 2013-2014. Transfer students must have a minimum GPA of 2.0 on all college work attempted. 60 of 120 credits required for the bachelor's degree must be completed at Wake Forest. **International Students:** There are 143 international students enrolled. The school actively recruits these students. They must take the TOEFL. They must also take the SAT or ACT.

ADMISSIONS: 34% of the 2014-2015 applicants were accepted. The SAT scores for the 2014-2015 freshman class were: Critical Reading--3% below 500, 19% between 500 and 599, 49% between 600 and 699, and 29% between 700 and 800; Math--2% below 500, 13% between 500 and 599, 49% between 600 and 699, and 36% between 700 and 800. The ACT scores were 1% below 21, 4% between 21 and 23, 45% between 27 and 28, and 50% above 28. 94% of the current freshmen were in the top fifth of their class; 98% were in the top two fifths. 35 freshmen graduated first in their class. **Admissions Contact:** Martha B. Allman, Director of Admissions. E-Mail: *admissions@wfu .edu* Web: *www.wfu.edu*

FINANCIAL AID: In 2014-2015, 39% of all full-time freshmen and 41% of continuing full-time students received some form of financial aid. 33% of all full-time freshmen and 38% of continuing full-time students received need-based aid. The average freshman award was $36,002. Need-based scholarships or need-based grants averaged $35,029; need-based self-help aid (loans and jobs) averaged $6,254; non-need-based athletic scholarships averaged $42,982; other non-need-based awards and non-need-based scholarships averaged $18,529; and $17,809 from other forms of aid. 44% of undergraduate students work part-time. Average annual earnings from campus work are $1267. The average financial indebtedness of the 2014 graduate was $35,902. Wake Forest is a member of CSS. The CSS/Profile, FAFSA, and the state aid form, and noncustodial profile are required. The priority date for freshman financial aid applications for fall entry is February 15. The deadline for filing freshman financial aid applications for fall entry is March 1.

WARREN WILSON COLLEGE — B-2
www.warren-wilson.edu

Asheville, NC 28815	(828) 771-2073
	(800) 934-3536
Fax: (828) 298-1440	Email: admit@warren-wilson.edu
Full-time: 312 men, 505 women	Faculty: 66
Part-time: 5 men, 2 women	Ph.D.s: 92%
Graduate: 20 men, 42 women	Student/Faculty: 13 to 1
Year: semesters, summer session	Tuition: $30,462
Room & Board: $9280	Freshman Class: 1173 applied, 838 accepted, 234 enrolled
SAT CR/M: 580/540 ACT: 26	CEEB CODE: 5886
Application Deadline: February 1	VERY COMPETITIVE

Warren Wilson College, founded in 1894, is the country's only liberal arts college with a national student body and integrated work and service programs. The college calls its blend of academics, work and service the Triad. Students graduate not only with a rigorous liberal arts education, but also with skills such as problem-solving and team leadership that equip them for life. Warren Wilson is a learning community where people don't just take; they give back. There is 1 undergraduate school and 1 graduate school. In addition to regional accreditation, Warren has baccalaureate program accreditation with CSWE. The 1135-acre campus is in a suburban area 5 miles east of Asheville, North Carolina, in the Swannanoa Valley of the Blue Ridge Mountains. Including any residence halls, there are 110 buildings.

STUDENT LIFE: 76% of undergraduates are from out of state, mostly the Middle Atlantic. Students are from 45 states, and 15 foreign countries. 74% are from public schools. 85% are White. 63% claim no religious affiliation; 18% Protestant. The average age of freshmen is 18; all undergraduates, 20. 31% do not continue beyond their first year; 51% remain to graduate. **Housing:** 820 students can be accommodated in college housing, which includes single-sex and coed dorms. In addition, there are special-interest houses, A wellness dorm, and an eco-dorm. On-campus housing is guaranteed for the freshman year only, is available on a first-come, first-served basis, and is available on a lottery system for upperclassmen. Priority is given to out-of-town students. 90% of students live on campus; of those, 95% remain on campus on weekends. Upperclassmen may keep cars.

FACULTY/CLASSROOMS: 52% of faculty are male; 48% are female. All teach and do research. No introductory courses are taught by graduate students. The average class size in an introductory lecture is 16; in a laboratory is 15; and in a regular course is 11.

PROGRAMS OF STUDY: Warren Wilson confers B.A., and B.S. degrees. Master's degrees are also awarded. Bachelor's degrees are awarded in AGRICULTURE (environmental studies), BIOLOGICAL SCIENCE (biology/biological science), COMMUNICATIONS AND THE ARTS (art, creative writing, English, English literature, English Writing, modern language, and theatre arts), COMPUTER AND PHYSICAL SCIENCE (chemistry and mathematics), HEALTH PROFESSIONS (biology), SOCIAL SCIENCE (anthropology, (Social Science) Global Studies, history, interdisciplinary studies, philosophy, political science/government, psychology, religion, social work, and sociology). Undergraduate: biology, Graduate: master of fine arts in creative writing are the strongest academically. Environmental studies, biology, and art have the largest enrollments.

ACTIVITIES: Groups on campus include peace and social justice, art, band, choir, chorale, chorus, computers, dance, debate, drama, environmental, ethnic, film, gay, honors, international, jazz band, literary magazine, musical theater, newspaper, outdoor activities, photography, political, professional, religious, social, student government, and yearbook. Popular campus events include Homecoming, Family Weekend, Work Day, Service Day, and Circus. **Sports:** There are 7 intercollegiate sports for men and 7 for women, and 5 intramural sports for men and 5 for women. Facilities include 2 gyms, weight and fitness rooms, tennis courts, playing fields, 25 miles of hiking/biking trails, kayak slalom gates, alpine climbing/challenge tower, mountain bike skills area, and outdoor basketball court. **Graduates:** From July 1, 2013 to June 30, 2014, 168 bachelor's degrees were awarded. The most popular majors were environmental studies (24%), psychology (10%), and creative writing (8%). In an average class, 40% graduate in 4 years or less, 51% graduate in 5 years or less, and 51% graduate in 6 years or less.

SERVICES: Counseling and information services are available, as is tutoring in most subjects. Tutoring is available through the Academic Support Center and the Writing Center. ESL tutoring is also available. **Library/Resources:** The library contains 403,500 volumes, 4,400 audio/video tapes/CDs/DVDs, and subscribes to 42,000 periodicals including electronic. Computerized library services include interlibrary loans, database searching, Internet access, and Wi-Fi capability. Special learning facilities include an art gallery, an outdoor adventure learning lab, GIS lab, 276-acre working farm, 5-acre garden, and 776-acre managed forest. **Physically Challenged Students:** 90% of the campus is accessible. Facilities include wheelchair ramps, elevators, special parking, specially equipped restrooms, and special housing. **Special:** Cross-registration is offered with Mars Hill College and the University of North Carolina at Asheville via the Asheville Area Educational Consortium. Students may apply for one of many internship experiences in various disciplines. Students may participate in a semester or year of study abroad in Asia, Latin America, Africa, or Europe, or in one of the College's short-term Study Abroad Courses with on-campus study and travel to places such as Chile, Costa Rica, England, Ghana, Greece, Ireland, Italy, Micronesia, New Zealand, Thailand, China, and Nicaragua. The college offers student-designed majors, non-degree study, and pass/fail options. Students may choose to "double-major" by completing the requirements for more than one major program at a time. Warren Wilson College participates in the Cooperative College Program with the Nicolas School of the Environment at Duke University in a combined program of liberal arts and professional education in environmental resource management. There are 4 departmental honors programs. **Visiting:** There are guides for informal visits, visitors may sit in on classes, and stay overnight. To schedule a visit, contact Monique Cote at mcote@warren-wilson.edu. **Campus Safety and Security:** Measures include 24-hour foot and vehicle patrol, emergency notification system, and security escort services. There are emergency telephones, lighted pathways/sidewalks, and controlled access to dorms/residences.

REQUIREMENTS: The SAT or ACT is required. High school diploma and completion of a college preparatory curriculum, including the following classes is required: four years of English, Algebra I, Algebra II, Geometry, two years of laboratory sciences, and three years of social sciences. Foreign language and AP courses are strongly recommended. Applicants must submit the Common Application, the Common App School Report Form, SAT or ACT scores, and official high school transcripts. Interview is recommended. AP credits are accepted. In order to graduate, baccalaureate students must complete all the requirements of the Triad Educational Program, which includes components in academics, work, and service. All students must complete a total of 128 credit hours with a minimum GPA of 2.0. This must include 32 hours in liberal arts area courses (4 hours in each of 8 areas), a first-year seminar, and college composition. Between 32 and 40 credit hours are required in the student's major, and most majors require a culminating or capstone experience. All residential students must work on campus 240 hours per semester (usually 15 hours per week). Students must have worked a minimum of 480 hours in Warren Wilson College's Work Program in order to graduate. All students must also complete a community engagement commitment, demonstrating learning in four different Points of Engagement and Growth (PEGs). Finally, each candidate for a baccalaureate degree must write a "Senior Letter" addressed to the faculty and staff of the College, which includes an evaluation of his/her experiences at the College and reflections on the college career. **Procedure:** Freshmen are admitted fall and winter. There are early decision, early admissions, and deferred admissions plans. Early decision applications should be filed by November 15; regular applications, by February 1 for fall entry, along with a $50 fee. Notification of early decision is sent December 1; regular decision, April 1. Applications are accepted on-line. **Transfer Students:** 71 transfer students enrolled in 2013-2014. Transfer applicants must have a minimum college GPA of 2.5. Applicants must have left their previous institutions in good standing, and be eligible to return. Transfer applicants must submit the Common application, high school transcript, all college transcripts, SAT or ACT scores, and the Common Application's Registrar Report Form from the most recent institution. 32 of 128 credits required for the bachelor's degree must be completed at Wilson. **International Students:** There are 21 international students enrolled. The school actively recruits these students. They must take the TOEFL with a minimum score of 550 on the paper-based TOEFL (PBT). They must also take the SAT or ACT.

ADMISSIONS: 71% of the 2014-2015 applicants were accepted. The SAT scores for the 2014-2015 freshman class were: Critical Reading--15% below 500, 39% between 500 and 599, 35% between 600 and 699, and 11% between 700 and 800; Math--32% below 500, 46% between 500 and 599, 20% between 600 and 699, and 2% between 700 and 800. The ACT scores were 8% below 21, 21% between 21 and 23, 32% between 24 and 26, 17% between 27 and 28, and 22% above 28. 46% of the current freshmen were in the top fifth of their class; 64% were in the top two fifths. 1 freshman graduated first in the class. **Admissions Contact:** Sharon Lytle, Senior Associate Admission Counselor. E-Mail: *admit@warren-wilson.edu* Web: *www.warren-wilson.edu*

FINANCIAL AID: The FAFSA and the college's own financial statement are required. The priority date for freshman financial aid applications for fall entry is March 15.

WESTERN CAROLINA UNIVERSITY — A-3

www.wcu.edu

Cullowhee, NC 28723

Fax: (828) 227-7319

Full-time: 3216 men, 3579 women
Part-time: 504 men, 680 women
Graduate: 543 men, 1086 women
Year: semesters, summer session
Room & Board: $7477

SAT CR/M/W: 515/526/486 ACT: 22
Application Deadline: March 1

(828) 227-7317
(877) WCU4YOU
Email: admiss@wcu.edu
Faculty: 420; IIA, -$
Ph.D.s: 70%
Student/Faculty: 16 to 1
Tuition: $6479 ($16,076)
Freshman Class: 15234 applied, 5739 accepted, 1560 enrolled
CEEB CODE: 5897
COMPETITIVE

Western Carolina University, founded in 1889 and part of the University of North Carolina system, is a public-funded institution offering undergraduate programs in the arts, sciences, technology, business, and humanities. There are 7 undergraduate schools and 1 graduate school. In addition to regional accreditation, WCU has baccalaureate program accreditation with AACSB, ABET, ACCE, ADA, APTA, CSWE, FIDER, NASM, NCATE, NLN, ACS, AANA, CAATE, CAAHEP, CCNE, EHAC, NAACLS, NCTE, and NASSM. The 682-acre campus is in a rural area 150 miles northeast of Atlanta, Georgia, and 50 miles west of Asheville. Including any residence halls, there are 91 buildings.

STUDENT LIFE: 93% of undergraduates are from North Carolina. Others are from 40 states, 13 foreign countries, and Canada. 95% are from public schools. 83% are White. The average age of freshmen is 18; all undergraduates, 23. 16% do not continue beyond their first year; 48% remain to graduate. **Housing:** 4023 students can be accommodated in college housing, which includes single-sex and coed dorms, on-campus apartments, and married student housing. In addition, there are honors houses, language houses, fraternity houses, and sorority houses. On-campus housing is guaranteed for all 4 years. 51% of students commute. All students may keep cars.

FACULTY/CLASSROOMS: 51% of faculty are male; 49% are female. 81% teach undergraduates. Graduate students teach 5% of introductory courses.

PROGRAMS OF STUDY: WCU confers B.A., B.S., B.F.A., B.M., B.S.B.A., B.S.Ed., B.S.E.E., B.S.N. and B.S.W. degrees. Master's and Doctoral degrees are also awarded. Bachelor's degrees are awarded in AGRICULTURE (natural resource management), BIOLOGICAL SCIENCE (biology/biological science), BUSINESS (accounting, banking and finance, business law, entrepreneurial studies, hospitality management services, international business management, management science, marketing and distribution, and sports management), COMMUNICATIONS AND THE ARTS (art, communications, dramatic arts, English, French, German, music, Spanish, and speech/debate/rhetoric), COMPUTER AND PHYSICAL SCIENCE (chemistry, computer science, geology, and mathematics), EDUCATION (art education, early childhood education, elementary education, English education, foreign languages education, mathematics education, middle school education, music education, physical education, science education, secondary education, social science education, special education, speech correction, and teaching English as a second/foreign language (TESOL/TEFOL)), ENGINEERING AND ENVIRONMENTAL DESIGN (construction management, electrical/electronics engineering, electrical/electronics engineering technology, emergency/disaster science, engineering technology, interior design, manufacturing technology, and preengineering), HEALTH PROFESSIONS (emergency medical technologies, environmental health science, health care administration, medical laboratory science, medical records administration/services, nursing, predentistry, premedicine, preoptometry, prepharmacy, prephysical therapy, preveterinary science, recreation therapy, and sports medicine), SOCIAL SCIENCE (anthropology, criminal justice, dietetics, forensic studies, geography, history, liberal arts/general studies, parks and recreation management, philosophy, political science/government, prelaw, psychology, social science, social work, and sociology). Elementary and Middle School ducation, criminal justice, and nursing have the largest enrollments.

ACTIVITIES: 9% of men belong to 13 national fraternities; 7% of women belong to 9 national sororities. There are 150 groups on campus, including art, band, cheerleading, choir, chorale, chorus, computers, dance, debate, drama, drill team, environmental, ethnic, film, gay, honors, international, jazz band, literary magazine, marching band, musical theater, newspaper, pep band, photography, political, professional, radio and TV, religious, social, social service, and student government. Popular campus events include Mountain Heritage Day, Greek Week, and Fine and Performing Arts Season. **Sports:** There are 6 intercollegiate sports for men and 8 for women, and 33 intramural sports for men and 34 for women. Facilities include a football stadium, baseball diamond, track/tennis complex, 2 intramural softball fields, 2 intramural flag football fields, disc golf course, soccer field, 5 gyms, field house, jogging trails, picnic areas, game rooms, weight training room, swimming pool, golf driving range, golf putting green, and a 73,000-sq-ft student recreation center with 2 multipurpose courts, climbing wall, 9800-sq-ft area for strength training, cardiovascular equipment, 3-lane indoor track, 2500-sq-ft group exercise studio, fitness assessment rooms, and locker rooms. **Graduates:** From July 1, 2013 to June 30, 2014, 1783 bachelor's degrees were awarded. The most popular majors were criminal justice (10%), nursing (7%), and elementary and middle grades education (7%). 300 companies recruited on campus in 2013-2014. In an average class, 1% graduate in 3 years or less, 28% graduate in 4 years or less, 44% graduate in 5 years or less, and 48% graduate in 6 years or less.

SERVICES: Counseling and information services are available, as is tutoring in most subjects. There is a reader service for the blind, and remedial math, reading, and writing. **Library/Resources:** The library contains 626,918 volumes, 1.6 million microform items, 17,043 audio/video tapes/CDs/DVDs, and subscribes to 12,465 periodicals including electronic. Computerized library services include interlibrary loans, database searching, Internet access, and Wi-Fi capability. Special learning facilities include an art gallery, natural history museum, radio station, TV station, the Mountain Heritage Center, the Fine and Performing Arts Center, and the Center for Applied Technology. **Physically Challenged Students:** 90% of the campus is accessible. Facilities include wheelchair ramps, elevators, special parking, specially equipped restrooms, special class scheduling, lowered drinking fountains, lowered telephones, and special housing. **Special:** WCU offers cooperative education programs in most majors, extensive internship opportunities, an accelerated degree in nursing, B.A.-B.S. degrees, dual and student designed majors, nondegree study, pass/fail options in designated courses, and credit for life experience. Study-abroad programs may be arranged in 14 countries and a Washington internship is available to a select few junior- or senior-level students each semester. A joint degree program in electrical engineering with the University of North Carolina-Charlotte is offered. There are 12 national honor societies and a freshman honors program. **Visiting:** There are regularly scheduled orientations for prospective students, consisting of 6 open houses and 8 regional tour events annually and twice-daily campus tours every Monday, Tuesday, Thursday, and Friday. There are guides for informal visits, visitors may sit in on classes, and stay overnight. To schedule a visit, contact the Admissions Office at (877) 928-4968. **Campus Safety and Security:** Measures include 24-hour foot and vehicle patrol and emergency notification system. There are shuttle buses, emergency telephones, lighted pathways/sidewalks, controlled access to dorms/residences, crime-prevention education programs.

REQUIREMENTS: The SAT is required, with the SAT preferred. Graduation from an accredited secondary school or the GED is required. High school courses must include 4 units of English, 4 units of math, 3 units of lab science, 2 of social studies, including 1 of U.S. history, and 2 units of a foreign language. 5 units of academic electives are also required. AP and CLEP credits are accepted. Important factors in the admissions decision are advanced placement or honors courses, recommendations by school officials, and evidence of special talent. In order to graduate, students must complete a total of 120 to 128 credit hours with a minimum GPA of 2.0. Between 27 and 64 hours are required in the major. All students must fulfill liberal studies requirements in writing, oral communication, wellness, social sciences, physical and biological sciences, math, humanities, history, fine and performing arts, world cultures, the freshman seminar, and 1 course in upper-level perspectives outside the major. Most degree plans include a minimum of 12 hours of free electives. **Procedure:** Freshmen are admitted fall, spring, and summer. Entrance exams should be taken during the spring of the junior year or the fall of the senior year. There are early decision, early admissions, and rolling admissions plans. Early decision applications should be filed by November 15; regular applications, by March 1 for fall entry; November 15 for spring entry; and April 15 for summer entry, along with a $55 fee. Notification of early decision is sent December 15; regular decision, on a rolling basis. Applications are accepted on-line. **Transfer Students:** 784 transfer students enrolled in 2013-2014. Transfer students must have a minimum GPA of 2.0 and meet freshman admissions requirements 32 of 128 credits required for the bachelor's degree must be completed at WCU. **International Students:** There are 81 international students enrolled. The school actively recruits these students. They must take the TOEFL with a minimum score of 550 on the paper-based TOEFL (PBT) or 79 on the Internet-based version (iBT). They must also take the SAT.

ADMISSIONS: 38% of the 2014-2015 applicants were accepted. The SAT scores for the 2014-2015 freshman class were: Critical Reading--43% below 500, 43% between 500 and 599, 13% between 600 and 699, and 1% between 700 and 800; Math--36% below 500, 47% between 500 and 599, 16% between 600 and 699, and 1% between 700 and 800; Writing--60% below 500, 32% between 500 and 599, 7% between 600 and 699, and 1% between 700 and 800. The ACT scores were 34% below 21, 38% between 21 and 23, 16% between 24 and 26, 6% between 27 and 28, and 6% above 28. 28% of the current freshmen were in the top fifth of their class; 62% were in the top two fifths. **Admissions Contact:** Undergraduate Admissions E-Mail: *admiss@wcu.edu* Web: *www.wcu.edu/admissions/*

FINANCIAL AID: In 2014-2015, 66% of all full-time freshmen and continuing full-time students received some form of financial aid. 65% of all full-time freshmen and 64% of continuing full-time students received need-based aid. The average freshman award was $8,551. Need-based scholarships or need-based grants averaged $6,214; need-based self-help aid (loans and jobs) averaged $3,386; non-need-based athletic scholarships averaged $9,802; and other non-need-based awards and non-need-based scholarships averaged $3,071. 15% of undergraduate students work part-time. Average annual earnings from campus work are $4350. The average financial indebtedness of the 2014 graduate was $22,608. The FAFSA and the college's own financial statement are required. The priority date for freshman financial aid applications for fall entry is March 15.

WILLIAM PEACE UNIVERSITY (*The complete profile is made available exclusively on our website, www.barronspac.com*)

WINGATE UNIVERSITY	C-3
www.wingate.edu	

Wingate, NC 28174	(704) 233-8000
	(800) 755-5550
Fax: (704) 233-8110	Email: admit@wingate.edu
Full-time: 713 men, 1001 women	Faculty: 87
Part-time: 23 men, 36 women	Ph.D.s: 94%
Graduate: 395 men, 480 women	Student/Faculty: 14 to 1
Year: semesters, summer session	Tuition: $25,040
Room & Board: $9950	Freshman Class: 4862 applied, 3933 accepted, 548 enrolled
SAT CR/M/W: 500/520/490 ACT: 22	CEEB CODE: 5908
Application Deadline: n/av	COMPETITIVE

Wingate University, founded in 1896, is a private liberal arts institution. Figures in the above capsule and in this profile are approximate. There are 4 undergraduate schools and 4 graduate schools. In addition to regional accreditation, Wingate has baccalaureate program accreditation with ACBSP, ACPE, NASM, NCATE, CAATE, NASPE, and NASSM. The 330-acre campus is in a small town 25 miles east of Charlotte. Including any residence halls, there are 35 buildings.

STUDENT LIFE: 80% of undergraduates are from North Carolina. Others are from 33 states, 17 foreign countries, and Canada. 90% are from public schools. 61% are White; 15% African American; 11%

race unknown. 75% are Protestant; 15% Catholic. The average age of freshmen is 18; all undergraduates, 20. 25% do not continue beyond their first year; 52% remain to graduate. **Housing:** 1560 students can be accommodated in college housing, which includes single-sex dorms, on-campus apartments, and married student housing. In addition, there are fraternity houses and sorority houses. On-campus housing is guaranteed for all 4 years. 80% of students live on campus; of those, 60% remain on campus on weekends. All students may keep cars.

FACULTY/CLASSROOMS: 48% of faculty are male; 52% are female. 70% teach undergraduates. No introductory courses are taught by graduate students. The average class size in an introductory lecture is 26; in a laboratory is 15; and in a regular course is 16.

PROGRAMS OF STUDY: Wingate confers B.A., B.S., B.F.A., B.S.N., B.L.S. and B.M.E. degrees. Master's and Doctoral degrees are also awarded. Bachelor's degrees are awarded in BIOLOGICAL SCIENCE (biology/biological science and environmental biology), BUSINESS (accounting, business administration and management, finance, marketing management, and sports management), COMMUNICATIONS AND THE ARTS (communications, English, fine arts, journalism, music, and public relations), COMPUTER AND PHYSICAL SCIENCE (chemistry and mathematics), EDUCATION (athletic training, elementary education, English education, mathematics education, middle school education, music education, physical education, reading education, science education, and social science education), ENGINEERING AND ENVIRONMENTAL DESIGN (preengineering), HEALTH PROFESSIONS (nursing, predentistry, premedicine, prepharmacy, and preveterinary science), SOCIAL SCIENCE (criminal justice, history, human services, liberal arts/general studies, parks and recreation management, philosophy, political science/government, prelaw, psychology, religion, and sociology). Communications, management, education, biology, psychology, marketing, and sport management have the largest enrollments.

ACTIVITIES: 4% of men belong to 4 national fraternities; 10% of women belong to 4 national sororities. There are 53 groups on campus, including art, band, cheerleading, choir, chorale, chorus, computers, ethnic, honors, international, jazz band, literary magazine, musical theater, newspaper, opera, pep band, photography, political, professional, radio and TV, religious, social, social service, and student government. Popular campus events include Spring Fling and Fall Festival at Campus Lake and Name-band Concerts. **Sports:** There are 10 intercollegiate sports for men and 10 for women, and 13 intramural sports for men and 13 for women. Facilities include Wingate has an athletic complex with a gym, swimming pool, racquetball courts, weight room, and tennis courts. The student center has an exercise room, table tennis, pool, and a game room. The university also has a football stadium, and baseball, soccer, and softball fields. **Graduates:** From July 1, 2013 to June 30, 2014, 276 bachelor's degrees were awarded. The most popular majors were business/marketing (22%), sport management (14%), and biology (12%). 50 companies recruited on campus in 2013-2014. In an average class, 38% graduate in 4 years or less, 43% graduate in 5 years or less, and 45% graduate in 6 years or less. Of the 2013 graduating class, 20% were enrolled in graduate school within 6 months of graduation, and 80% were employed.

SERVICES: Counseling and information services are available, as is tutoring in every subject. Additional academic support is available for students with learning disabilities. **Library/Resources:** The library contains 103,397 volumes, 7,024 microform items, 9,317 audio/video tapes/CDs/DVDs, and subscribes to 28,532 periodicals including electronic. Computerized library services include interlibrary loans, database searching, Internet access, and Wi-Fi capability. Special learning facilities include an art gallery, radio station, TV station, student newspaper and a fine arts center. **Physically Challenged Students:** 95% of the campus is accessible. Facilities include wheelchair ramps, elevators, special parking, specially equipped restrooms, special class scheduling, and lowered drinking fountains. **Special:** Cross-registration through the Charlotte Area Education Consortium, in Army and Air Force ROTC programs, internships, a liberal studies degree, B.A.-B.S. degrees, and nondegree study are available. Wingate conducts foreign study semesters in London, Denmark, and China. The school also sponsors Winternational, a semester seminar with a 10-day trip to a foreign country for which students earn academic credit at little personal cost. Dual majors are offered in biology and education, history and education, art and education, English and education, math and education, and chemistry and business.Students can earn a B.S. in biology and pharm.D. through a 3 + 1 program. There are 11 national honor societies and a freshman honors program. **Visiting:** There are regularly scheduled orientations for prospective students, Saturday preview day 4 times a year, campus tours and presentations of travel programs, academic life, athletics, and student life. New student orientation takes place during one of several summer session according to student's declared major. There are guides for informal visits, visitors may sit in on classes, and stay overnight. To schedule a visit, contact the Admissions Office. **Campus Safety and Security:** Measures include 24-hour foot and vehicle patrol, emergency notification system, self-defense education, and security escort services. There are emergency telephones, lighted pathways/sidewalks, and controlled access to dorms/residences.

REQUIREMENTS: Graduation from an accredited secondary school or the GED is required. High school curriculum must include 4 courses in English, 3 in math, 2 each in history and science, and 1 in social studies. 2 courses in a foreign language are recommended. An essay is required of all applicants, and an interview is recommended in some cases. The SAT or ACT is also required. AP and CLEP credits are accepted. Important factors in the admissions decision are advanced placement or honors courses, leadership record, and recommendations by school officials.To graduate, students must complete a minimum of 125 credit hours with a GPA of 2.0. At least 30 hours must be completed in the student's major. All students must complete the Core Curriculum, which includes 24 hours of Global Perspectives. **Procedure:** Freshmen are admitted fall, spring, and summer. Entrance exams should be taken In spring of the junior year or fall of the senior year. There is a rolling admissions plan. Application deadlines are open. The fall 2014 application fee was $30. Applications are accepted on-line. **Transfer Students:** 90 transfer students enrolled in 2013-2014. Applicants must have a minimum GPA of 2.0 and must be eligible to return to the institution last attended. The SAT or ACT is required if a student has been out of high school for less than 5 years or has fewer than 24 transferable hours. An interview may be recommended in some cases. 30 of 125 credits required for the bachelor's degree must be completed at Wingate. **International Students:** There are 65 international students enrolled. They must take the TOEFL with a minimum score of 550 on the paper-based TOEFL (PBT). They must also take the SAT and ACT.

ADMISSIONS: 81% of the 2014-2015 applicants were accepted. The SAT scores for the 2014-2015 freshman class were: Critical Reading--49% below 500, 39% between 500 and 599, 11% between 600 and 699, and 1% between 700 and 800; Math--37% below 500, 42% between 500 and 599, 21% between 600 and 699, and 1% between 700 and 800; Writing--53% below 500, 37% between 500 and 599, 9% between 600 and 699, and 1% between 700 and 800. The ACT scores were 34% below 21, 35% between 21 and 23, 19% between 24 and 26, 6% between 27 and 28, and 6% above 28. 40% of the current freshmen were in the top fifth of their class; 73% were in the top two fifths. 6 freshmen graduated first in their class. **Admissions Contact:** Gabe Hollingsworth, Director of Admissions. E-Mail: *admit@wingate .edu* Web: *www.wingate.edu*

FINANCIAL AID: In 2014-2015, 79% of all full-time freshmen and 83% of continuing full-time students received some form of financial aid. 79% of all full-time freshmen and 82% of continuing full-time students received need-based aid. The average freshman award was $22,406. Need-based scholarships or need-based grants averaged $19,076; need-based self-help aid (loans and jobs) averaged $4,233; non-need-based athletic scholarships averaged $8,428; and other non-need-based awards and non-need-based scholarships averaged $3,822. 20% of undergraduate students work part-time. Average annual earnings from campus work are $1200. The average financial indebtedness of the 2014 graduate was $24,785. The FAFSA is required. The deadline for filing freshman financial aid applications for fall entry is May 1.

WINSTON-SALEM STATE UNIVERSITY (*The complete profile is made available exclusively on our website, www.barronspac.com*)

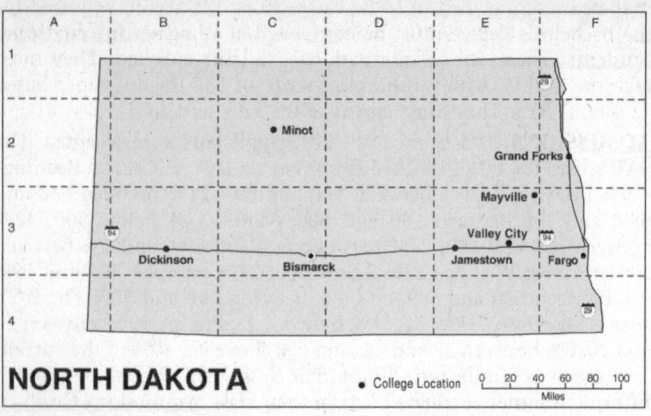

NORTH DAKOTA

● College Location 0 20 40 60 80 100
Miles

DICKINSON STATE UNIVERSITY *(The complete profile is made available exclusively on our website, www.barronspac.com)*

MAYVILLE STATE UNIVERSITY *(The complete profile is made available exclusively on our website, www.barronspac.com)*

MINOT STATE UNIVERSITY   C-2
www.minotstateu.edu

Minot, ND 58707	(701) 858-4347
	(800) 777-0750
Fax: (701) 839-6933	Email: alexis@minotstateu.edu
Full-time: 840 men, 1338 women	Faculty: 159; IIA, --$
Part-time: 438 men, 682 women	Ph.D.s: 60%
Graduate: 77 men, 185 women	Student/Faculty: 16 to 1
Year: semesters, summer session	Tuition: $5921
Room & Board: $4994	Freshman Class: 1003 applied, 538 accepted, 399 enrolled
SAT or ACT: required	CEEB CODE: 6479
Application Deadline: n/av	COMPETITIVE

Minot State University, founded in 1913, is a public institution offering undergraduate and graduate programs in arts and sciences, education, business, nursing, and human services. Figures in the above capsule and in this profile are approximate. There are 3 undergraduate schools and 1 graduate school. In addition to regional accreditation, MSU has baccalaureate program accreditation with CSWE, NASM, NCATE, and NLN. The 103-acre campus is in a small town. Including any residence halls, there are 21 buildings.

STUDENT LIFE: 83% of undergraduates are from North Dakota. Others are from 44 states, 18 foreign countries, and Canada. 95% are from public schools. 84% are White. The average age of freshmen is 19; all undergraduates, 21. 36% do not continue beyond their first year; 32% remain to graduate. **Housing:** 643 students can be accommodated in college housing, which includes single-sex and coed dorms, on-campus apartments, and married student housing. In addition, there are language houses and special-interest houses. On-campus housing is guaranteed for the freshman year only, is available on a first-come, first-served basis, and is available on a lottery system for upperclassmen. 88% of students commute. Alcohol is not permitted. All students may keep cars.

FACULTY/CLASSROOMS: 49% of faculty are male; 51% are female. All teach undergraduates, and 20% do research. No introductory courses are taught by graduate students. The average class size in an introductory lecture is 60; in a laboratory is 20; and in a regular course is 16.

PROGRAMS OF STUDY: MSU confers B.A., B.S., B.A.S., B.G.S., B.S. Ed., B.S.N. and B.S.W. degrees. Associate and Master's degrees are also awarded. Bachelor's degrees are awarded in BIOLOGICAL SCIENCE (biology/biological science), BUSINESS (accounting, banking and finance, international business management, management information systems, management science, and marketing/retailing/

merchandising), COMMUNICATIONS AND THE ARTS (art, broadcasting, communications, English, French, German, multimedia, music, and Spanish), COMPUTER AND PHYSICAL SCIENCE (chemistry, computer science, earth science, geology, mathematics, physical sciences, physics, and radiological technology), EDUCATION (business education, drama education, education of the deaf and hearing impaired, education of the exceptional child, education of the mentally handicapped, elementary education, English education, foreign languages education, mathematics education, music education, physical education, and science education), HEALTH PROFESSIONS (dental laboratory technology, nursing, and speech pathology/audiology), SOCIAL SCIENCE (addiction studies, criminal justice, economics, history, liberal arts/general studies, physical fitness/movement, psychology, social science, social work, and sociology). Communication disorders, special education, and elementary education are the strongest academically. Business, criminal justice, and education have the largest enrollments.

ACTIVITIES: There are no fraternities or sororities. There are 60 groups on campus, including art, band, campus Ministries, choir, chorale, chorus, drama, ethnic, honors, international, marching band, musical theater, newspaper, orchestra, pep band, political, professional, radio and TV, religious, social service, student government, and symphony. Popular campus events include Welcome Week, Final Frenzy and Native American Awareness Week. **Sports:** There are 6 intercollegiate sports for men and 6 for women, and 4 intramural sports for men and 4 for women. Facilities include a 10,000-seat field house, a 2800-seat football stadium, and a 3000-seat gym. **Graduates:** From July 1, 2013 to June 30, 2014, 740 bachelor's degrees were awarded. The most popular majors were business/marketing (31%), health professions and related sciences (19%), and education (15%). 105 companies recruited on campus in 2013-2014. In an average class, 37% graduate in 6 years or less. Of the 2013 graduating class, 11% were enrolled in graduate school within 6 months of graduation, and 89% were employed.

SERVICES: Counseling and information services are available, as is tutoring in most subjects. Special services are offered for disabled students on request. **Library/Resources:** The library contains 411,678 volumes, 687,708 microform items, 12,722 audio/video tapes/CDs/DVDs, and subscribes to 802 periodicals including electronic. Computerized library services include interlibrary loans and database searching. Special learning facilities include an art gallery, natural history museum, radio station, and TV station. **Physically Challenged Students:** 99% of the campus is accessible. Facilities include wheelchair ramps, elevators, special parking, specially equipped restrooms, special class scheduling, lowered drinking fountains, lowered telephones, and special housing. **Special:** A general studies degree, independent research, internships, work-study, and unique programs of study, including student-designed majors, are available. Cross-registration through the North Dakota University system, co-op programs in all majors, and study abroad in 3 countries also are offered. Preliminary programs are available in dental hygiene, dentistry, engineering, law, medicine, and many other areas. There is a freshman honors program. **Visiting:** There are regularly scheduled orientations for prospective students prior to the beginning of the fall term. There are guides for informal visits and visitors may sit in on classes. To schedule a visit, contact the Enrollment Services. **Campus Safety and Security:** Measures include self-defense education. There are emergency telephones and lighted pathways/sidewalks.

REQUIREMENTS: The SAT or ACT is required. Applicants must submit a high school diploma or GED certificate. Core course requirements include 4 years of English and 3 each of math, social studies, and science. AP and CLEP credits are accepted. Students must take a number of general education courses in humanities, history, communication, math, natural sciences, social and behavorial sciences, and leisure-time education. They must complete at least 128 semester hours, with 30 to 37 in the major and a minimum GPA of 2.0. **Procedure:** Freshmen are admitted to all sessions. Entrance exams should be taken any time. There are deferred admissions and rolling admissions plans. Application deadlines are open. Application fee is $35. Applications are accepted on-line. **Transfer Students:** 291 transfer students enrolled in 2013-2014. Transfers must submit transcripts from each college attended. 30 of 128 credits required for the bachelor's degree must be completed at MSU. **International Students:** There are 41 international students enrolled. The school actively recruits these students. They must take the TOEFL.

ADMISSIONS: 54% of the 2014-2015 applicants were accepted. **Admissions Contact:** Alexis Hendricks, Enrollment Services Representative. E-Mail: *alexis@minotstateu.edu* Web: *www.minotstateu.edu*

FINANCIAL AID: In 2014-2015, 67% of all full-time freshmen and 66% of continuing full-time students received some form of financial aid. 64% of all full-time freshmen and 66% of continuing full-time students received need-based aid. 1% of undergraduate students work part-time. Average annual earnings from campus work are $1260. The average financial indebtedness of the 2014 graduate was $25,117. The FAFSA is required. The priority date for freshman financial aid applications for fall entry is March 15. The deadline for filing freshman financial aid applications for fall entry is October 15.

NORTH DAKOTA STATE UNIVERSITY   F-3
www.ndsu.edu

Fargo, ND 58102	(701) 231-8643
	(800) 488-NDSU
Fax: (701) 231-8802	Email: ndsu.admission@ndsu.edu
Full-time: 6129 men, 4736 women	Faculty: I, --$
Part-time: 593 men, 666 women	Ph.D.s: n/av
Graduate: 1239 men, 1384 women	Student/Faculty: n/av
Year: semesters, summer session	Tuition: $7540 ($18,122)
Room & Board: $7102	Freshman Class: 5018 applied, 4727 accepted, 2469 enrolled
SAT: required ACT: 24	CEEB CODE: 6474
Application Deadline: August 1	COMPETITIVE

North Dakota is a student-focused, land grant, research university   an economic engine that educates students, conducts primary research, creates new knowledge, and advances technology. We provide affordable access to an excellent education at a top-ranked research institution that combines teaching and research in a rich learning environment, educating future leaders who will create solutions to national and global challenges that will shape a better world. There are 8 undergraduate schools and 1 graduate school. In addition to regional accreditation, NDSU has baccalaureate program accreditation with AACSB, ABET, ACCE, ACPE, ADA, AHEA, CAHEA, CSAB, FIDER, NAAB, NASAD, NASM, NCATE, and ACS. The 258-acre campus is in an urban area 229 miles northwest of Minneapolis-St. Paul. Including any residence halls, there are 97 buildings.

STUDENT LIFE: 57% of undergraduates are from out of state, mostly the Mid-West. Students are from 48 states, 69 foreign countries, and Canada. 86% are White. The average age of freshmen is 18; all undergraduates, 21. 20% do not continue beyond their first year; 50% remain to graduate. **Housing:** 4996 students can be accommodated in college housing, which includes single-sex and coed dorms, on-campus apartments, married student housing, learning communities and first-year student halls. On-campus housing is guaranteed for the freshman year only. 66% of students commute. Alcohol is not permitted. All students may keep cars.

FACULTY/CLASSROOMS: No introductory courses are taught by graduate students.

PROGRAMS OF STUDY: NDSU confers B.A., B.F.A., B.L.A., B.Mus., B.S., B.S.A.B.En., B.S.Arch., B.S.C.E., B.S.Cpr.E., B.S.Con.E., B.S.Cons.M., B.S.E.E., B.S.I.E.Mgt., B.S.Mfg.E., B.S.M.E., B.S.N. and B.U.S. degrees. Master's and doctoral degrees are also awarded. Bachelor's degrees are awarded in AGRICULTURE (agricultural business management, agricultural communications, agricultural economics, agricultural mechanics, agriculture, animal science, equine science, horticulture, natural resource management, plant protection (pest management), plant science, range/farm management, and soil science), BIOLOGICAL SCIENCE (biochemistry, biology/biological science, biotechnology, botany, microbiology, nutrition, and zoology), BUSINESS (accounting, business administration and management, finance, hospitality management services, hotel and restaurant administration, hotel/motel and restaurant management, management information systems, management science, marketing, recreation and leisure services, and sports management), COMMUNICATIONS AND THE ARTS (apparel design, art, communications, dramatic arts, English, French, instrumental music education, journalism - news and information, music, performing arts, public relations, Spanish, and theatre arts), COMPUTER AND PHYSICAL SCIENCE (actuarial science, chemistry, computer science, earth science, geology, mathematics, physics, radiological technology, and statistics), EDUCATION (agricultural education, athletic training, elementary education, health education, home economics education, music education, physical education, secondary education, and social science education), ENGINEERING AND ENVIRONMENTAL DESIGN (agricultural engineering, agricultural engineering technology, architecture, biomedical engineering, civil engineering, computer engineering, construction engineering, construction management, electrical/electronics engineering, emergency/disaster science, engineering management, environmental design, industrial engineering, interior design, landscape architecture/design, manufacturing engineering, and mechanical engineering), HEALTH PROFESSIONS (clinical science, health communication, nursing, pharmacy, preveterinary science, respiratory therapy, and veterinary science), SOCIAL SCIENCE (anthropology, child care/child and family studies, criminal justice, dietetics, economics, food science, history, human development, humanities, international studies, philosophy and religion, physical fitness/movement, political science/government, psychology, social science, sociology, textiles and clothing, women and gender studies). Biotechnology, pharmacy, nursing, and engieering are the strongest academically. Sciences, engineering, and human development have the largest enroffllments.

ACTIVITIES: 2% of men belong to 11 national fraternities. Groups on campus include, art, band, cheerleading, choir, chorus, computers, dance, debate, drama, drill team, ethnic, forensics, gay, honors, international, jazz band, marching band, musical theater, newspaper, pep band, political, professional, radio and TV, recreational, religious, social, social service, and student government. Popular campus events include International Students' Week, Spring Blast and multicultural activities. **Sports:** There are 8 intercollegiate sports for men and 8 for women, and 11 intramural sports for men and 10 for women. Facilities include a sports arena, indoor and outdoor tracks, baseball and softball fields, wrestling and weight rooms, a multipurpose fitness room, volleyball, tennis, basketball, and racquetball courts, and a wellness center. **Graduates:** From July 1, 2013 to June 30, 2014, 2308 bachelor's degrees were awarded. The most popular majors were business (15%), engineering (13%), health professions, and related sciences (11%). In an average class, 25% graduate in 4 years or less, 49% graduate in 5 years or less, and 56% graduate in 6 years or less.

SERVICES: Counseling and information services are available, as is tutoring in most subjects. There is a reader service for the blind, and remedial math, reading, and writing. **Library/Resources:** The 5 libraries contain 784,978 volumes, 444,951 microform items, 2,873 audio/video tapes/CDs/DVDs, and subscribe to 5,090 periodicals including electronic. Computerized library services include interlibrary loans, database searching, Internet access, and Wi-Fi capability. Special learning facilities include an art gallery, radio station, and TV station. **Physically Challenged Students:** All of the campus is accessible. Facilities include wheelchair ramps, elevators, special parking, specially equipped restrooms, special class scheduling, lowered drinking fountains, and lowered telephones. **Special:** Special academic programs include cooperative work programs and internships. There is cross-registration with the Tri-college Consortium and all North Dakota State institutions. Student-designed and dual majors, study abroad, a B.A.-B.S. degree, nondegree study, and pass/fail options are possible. There are 22 national honor societies and a freshman honors program. **Visiting:** There are regularly scheduled orientations for prospective students, including tours of the campus, academic appointments, and meetings with admissions counselors and financial aid counselors. There are guides for informal visits and visitors may sit in on classes. To schedule a visit, contact the Office of Admission at ndsu.admission@ndsu.edu. **Campus Safety and Security:** Measures include 24-hour foot and vehicle patrol, emergency notification system, self-defense education, and security escort services. There are shuttle buses, emergency telephones, lighted pathways/sidewalks, and controlled access to dorms/residences.

REQUIREMENTS: The SAT or ACT is required. Applicants must have completed 4 units of English, and 3 each of math (algebra I or above), lab science, and social science. The GED is accepted, with a minimum score of 45 and no subject score lower than 40. A GPA of 2.5 is required. AP and CLEP credits are accepted. Students must complete at least 122 semester credits, with at least 24 in the major, and maintain at least a 2.0 GPA. General education requirements include 10 credits in science and technology, including a 1-credit lab course, 12 credits in communication, which includes freshman English and public speaking, 6 credits each in humanities and fine arts and in social and behavioral science, 3 credits in quantitative reasoning, at least 2 credits in a wellness course, and a first-year experience course. Included in these courses must be 1 course designated as a cultural diversity course and 1 designated as a global perspectives course. **Procedure:** Freshmen are admitted to all sessions. Entrance exams should be taken in the spring of the junior year or in the fall of the senior year. There are deferred admissions and rolling admissions plans. Applications should be filed by August 1 for fall entry; December 1 for spring entry; and May 20 for summer entry, along with a $35 fee. Applications are accepted on-line. **Transfer Students:** Transfer students must have a minimum GPA of 2.0; ACT or SAT scores are required if the applicant has fewer than 24 semester credits. 36 of 122 credits required for the bachelor's degree must be completed at NDSU. **International Students:** There are 1059 international students enrolled. The school actively recruits these students. They must take the TOEFL with a minimum score of 525 on the paper-based TOEFL (PBT) or 70 on the Internet-based version (iBT).

ADMISSIONS: 94% of the 2014-2015 applicants were accepted. The SAT scores for the 2014-2015 freshman class were: Critical Reading--32% below 500, 33% between 500 and 599, 15% between 600 and 699, and 20% between 700 and 800; Math--22% below 500, 34% between 500 and 599, 22% between 600 and 699, and 22% between 700 and 800; Writing--41% below 500, 30% between 500 and 599, 25% between 600 and 699, and 4% between 700 and 800. There were 12 National Merit finalists. **Admissions Contact:** Jobey Lichtblau, Director of Admission. E-Mail: *ndsu.admission@ndsu.edu* Web: *www.ndsu.edu*

FINANCIAL AID: The average financial indebtedness of the 2014 graduate was $30,274. The FAFSA is required. The priority date for freshman financial aid applications for fall entry is March 15.

UNIVERSITY OF JAMESTOWN   E-3
www.jc.edu

Jamestown, ND 58405	**(701) 252-3467, ext. 5415**
	(800) 336-2554
Fax: (701) 253-4318	Email: admissions@jc.edu
Full-time: 416 men, 466 women	Faculty: 57; IIB, --$
Part-time: 25 men, 31 women	Ph.D.s: 54%
Graduate: 17 men, 25 women	Student/Faculty: 13 to 1
Year: semesters, summer session	Tuition: $18,494
Room & Board: $6244	Freshman Class: 898 applied, 602 accepted, 233 enrolled
SAT CR/M: 498/495 ACT: 22	CEEB CODE: 6318
Application Deadline: open	COMPETITIVE

University of Jamestown, founded in 1883, is a private, institution founded by the Presbyterian Church. It's emphases are on the liberal arts, business, arts, health science, music, religious studies, and teacher preparation. Figures in the above capsule and in this profile are approximate. There is 1 undergraduate school and 2 graduate schools. In addition to regional accreditation, has baccalaureate program accreditation with NLN and IACBE. The 110-acre campus is in a small town 100 miles west of Fargo, 350 miles west of Minneapolis. Including any residence halls, there are 25 buildings.

STUDENT LIFE: 55% of undergraduates are from out of state, mostly the Mid-West. Students are from 37 states, 15 foreign coun-

tries, and Canada. 83% are White. 50% are Protestant; 27% claim no religious affiliation; 19% Catholic. The average age of freshmen is 18; all undergraduates, 21. 39% do not continue beyond their first year; 52% remain to graduate. **Housing:** 744 students can be accommodated in college housing, which includes coed dorms, on-campus apartments, off-campus apartments, and married student housing. On-campus housing is guaranteed for the freshman year only, is available on a first-come, first-served basis, and is available on a lottery system for upperclassmen. 65% of students live on campus; of those, 65% remain on campus on weekends. Alcohol is not permitted. All students may keep cars.

FACULTY/CLASSROOMS: 54% of faculty are male; 46% are female. All teach undergraduates. No introductory courses are taught by graduate students. The average class size in an introductory lecture is 26; in a laboratory is 15; and in a regular course is 20.

PROGRAMS OF STUDY: confers B.A., B.S. and B.S.N. degrees. Master's and Doctoral degrees are also awarded. Bachelor's degrees are awarded in BIOLOGICAL SCIENCE (biochemistry and biology/biological science), BUSINESS (accounting, business administration and management, and management information systems), COMMUNICATIONS AND THE ARTS (communications, English, fine arts, French, German, music, and Spanish), COMPUTER AND PHYSICAL SCIENCE (chemistry, computer science, information sciences and systems, mathematics, and radiological technology), EDUCATION (elementary education and physical education), HEALTH PROFESSIONS (clinical science, exercise science, and nursing), SOCIAL SCIENCE (criminal justice, history, history of science, psychology, religion, and religious education). Business, nursing, and physical sciences are the strongest academically. Business, nursing, and education have the largest enrollments.

ACTIVITIES: There are no fraternities or sororities. There are 35 groups on campus, including art, band, choir, chorale, chorus, computers, drama, environmental, film, honors, international, jazz band, literary magazine, musical theater, newspaper, orchestra, pep band, political, professional, radio and TV, religious, social, social service, and student government. Popular campus events include Jimmie Jive Week, Homecoming, and Character in Leadership Fall Conference. **Sports:** There are 8 intercollegiate sports for men and 8 for women, and 6 intramural sports for men and 6 for women. Facilities include an athletics center with a basketball court and wrestling and volleyball practice and composition area; a football stadium with an all-weather track; a soccer field; and a sports center with a swimming pool, weight room, running track, YMCA, and basketball, handball, and racquetball courts. Nearby facilities include a civic arena, softball field, baseball stadium, swimming pool, tennis courts, municipal golf course, and winter sports complex. **Graduates:** From July 1, 2013 to June 30, 2014, 154 bachelor's degrees were awarded. The most popular majors were nursing (19%), business (12%), and elementry education (9%). 25 companies recruited on campus in 2013-2014. In an average class, 34% graduate in 4 years or less, 50% graduate in 5 years or less, and 52% graduate in 6 years or less. Of the 2013 graduating class, 13% were enrolled in graduate school within 6 months of graduation, and 80% were employed.

SERVICES: Counseling and information services are available, as is tutoring in most subjects. There is remedial math, reading, and writing. **Library/Resources:** The library contains 112,169 volumes, 9,000 microform items, 5,518 audio/video tapes/CDs/DVDs, and subscribes to 18,610 periodicals including electronic. Computerized library services include interlibrary loans, database searching, and Internet access. Special learning facilities include an art gallery, radio station, and TV station. **Physically Challenged Students:** 51% of the campus is accessible. Facilities include wheelchair ramps, elevators, special parking, specially equipped restrooms, special class scheduling, lowered drinking fountains, lowered telephones, and special housing. **Special:** Special academic options include co-op programs in business, nursing, computer science, and criminal justice, on-campus work-study, internships, study abroad, dual majors within any of the concentrations, and student-designed majors. There is a 3-2 engineering program with North Dakota State University. There are 5 national honor societies and 10 departmental honors programs. **Visiting:** There are regularly scheduled orientations for prospective students, including a campus tour and faculty visits. There are guides for informal visits, visitors may sit in on classes, and stay overnight.

To schedule a visit, contact the Admissions Office. **Campus Safety and Security:** Measures include emergency notification system, self-defense education, and security escort services. There are lighted pathways/sidewalks and controlled access to dorms/residences.

REQUIREMENTS: The ACT is recommended. Other admissions requirements include graduation from an accredited secondary school; the GED is also accepted. An interview is highly recommended. A GPA of 2.5 is required. AP and CLEP credits are accepted. Important factors in the admissions decision are evidence of special talent, extracurricular activities record, and leadership record. To graduate, students must have a minimum of 128 semester credits, at least 48 of which must be at the upper-division level, with an average of 48 semester credits in the major, and maintain at least a 2.0 GPA. **Procedure:** Freshmen are admitted to all sessions. Entrance exams should be taken before or during the fall of the senior year. There is a rolling admissions plan. Application deadlines are open. Applications are accepted on-line. **Transfer Students:** 50 transfer students enrolled in 2013-2014. Applicants must have at least a 2.0 GPA and be in good standing with their previous college. Applicants are required to submit official high school and college transcripts. 35 of 128 credits required for the bachelor's degree must be completed at Jamestown. **International Students:** There are 43 international students enrolled. The school actively recruits these students. They must take the TOEFL with a minimum score of 525 on the paper-based TOEFL (PBT) or 70 on the Internet-based version (iBT), or take the MELAB.

ADMISSIONS: 67% of the 2014-2015 applicants were accepted. The SAT scores for the 2014-2015 freshman class were: Critical Reading--55% below 500, 28% between 500 and 599, 13% between 600 and 699, and 2% between 700 and 800; Math--57% below 500, 28% between 500 and 599, 11% between 600 and 699, and 2% between 700 and 800. The ACT scores were 32% below 21, 32% between 21 and 23, 24% between 24 and 26, 8% between 27 and 28, and 4% above 28. 42% of the current freshmen were in the top fifth of their class; 67% were in the top two fifths. 17 freshmen graduated first in their class. **Admissions Contact:** Tena Lawrence, Dean of Enrollment Management. E-Mail: *admissions@jc.edu* Web: *www.jc.edu*

FINANCIAL AID: In 2014-2015, 100% of all full-time freshmen and continuing full-time students received some form of financial aid. 57% of all full-time freshmen and 52% of continuing full-time students received need-based aid. The average freshman award was $18,372. Need-based scholarships or need-based grants averaged $4,040 ($7,993 maximum); need-based self-help aid (loans and jobs) averaged $3,700 ($11,000 maximum); non-need-based athletic scholarships averaged $4,136 ($14,974 maximum); and other non-need-based awards and non-need-based scholarships averaged $7,940 ($17,974 maximum). 24% of undergraduate students work part-time. Average annual earnings from campus work are $550. The average financial indebtedness of the 2014 graduate was $25,785. The FAFSA is required. The priority date for freshman financial aid applications for fall entry is March 15.

studies, and teacher preparation. The figures in the above capsule and in this profile are approximate. There are 8 undergraduate schools and 4 graduate schools. In addition to regional accreditation, Mary has baccalaureate program accreditation with CAHEA, CSWE, CCNE, ACOTE, CAPTE, and CAATE. The 107-acre campus is in a suburban area 7 miles south of Bismarck. Including any residence halls, there are 13 buildings.

STUDENT LIFE: 70% of undergraduates are from North Dakota. Others are from 33 states, 23 foreign countries, and Canada. 95% are from public schools. 87% are White. 60% are Catholic; 30% Protestant. The average age of freshmen is 18; all undergraduates, 25. 26% do not continue beyond their first year; 51% remain to graduate. **Housing:** 791 students can be accommodated in college housing, which includes single-sex dorms and on-campus apartments. On-campus housing is guaranteed for all 4 years. 61% of students commute. Alcohol is not permitted. All students may keep cars.

FACULTY/CLASSROOMS: 48% of faculty are male; 52% are female. 95% teach undergraduates, and 15% do both. No introductory courses are taught by graduate students. The average class size in an introductory lecture is 15; in a laboratory is 20; and in a regular course is 20.

PROGRAMS OF STUDY: Mary confers B.A., B.S., and B.Univ.Studies degrees. Master's degrees are also awarded. Bachelor's degrees are awarded in BIOLOGICAL SCIENCE (biology/biological science), BUSINESS (accounting, business administration and management, business communications, and management information systems), COMMUNICATIONS AND THE ARTS (communications, English, and music), COMPUTER AND PHYSICAL SCIENCE (information sciences and systems, mathematics, and radiological technology), EDUCATION (athletic training, early childhood education, elementary education, English education, mathematics education, music education, physical education, social science education, and special education), ENGINEERING AND ENVIRONMENTAL DESIGN (engineering and applied science), HEALTH PROFESSIONS (exercise science, nursing, occupational therapy, physical therapy, premedicine, and respiratory therapy), SOCIAL SCIENCE (addiction studies, behavioral science, criminal justice, liberal arts/general studies, ministries, pastoral studies, prelaw, psychology, social science, social work, and theological studies). Business administration, education, and nursing are the strongest academically. Business, nursing, and elementary education have the largest enrollments.

ACTIVITIES: There are no fraternities or sororities. There are 22 groups on campus, including band, cheerleading, choir, chorale, chorus, computers, drama, drill team, environmental, ethnic, forensics, jazz band, musical theater, newspaper, orchestra, pep band, photography, political, professional, radio and tv, religious, social, social service, student government, and symphony. Popular campus events include intramural sports and the convocation series. **Sports:** There are 8 intercollegiate sports for men and 7 for women, and 10 intramural sports for men and 10 for women. Facilities include an activity center housing a 1200-seat gym, basketball and racquetball courts, wrestling and weight rooms, and a swimming pool. The field house includes an indoor track, 3 basketball/volleyball/tennis courts, and a climbing wall. There are also track/football, intramural, and softball fields, tennis courts, a fitness center, and a 1200-seat stadium. **Graduates:** From July 1, 2013 to June 30, 2014, 502 bachelor's degrees were awarded. The most popular majors were business (40%), nursing (19%), and education (10%). 30 companies recruited on campus in 2013-2014. In an average class, 5% graduate in 3 years or less, 39% graduate in 4 years or less, 50% graduate in 5 years or less, and 1% graduate in 6 years or less. Of the 2013 graduating class, 17% were enrolled in graduate school within 6 months of graduation, and 80% were employed.

SERVICES: Counseling and information services are available, as is tutoring in every subject. There is a reader service for the blind, and remedial math, reading, and writing. **Library/Resources:** The library contains 78,137 volumes, 2 microform items, 7,866 audio/video tapes/CDs/DVDs, and subscribes to 6,997 periodicals including electronic. Computerized library services include interlibrary loans, database searching, Internet access, and Wi-Fi capability. Special learning facilities include an art gallery and radio station. **Physically Challenged Students:** All of the campus is accessible. Facilities include wheelchair ramps, elevators, special parking, specially equipped rest-

---

UNIVERSITY OF MARY   C-3
www.umary.edu

Bismarck, ND 58504	**(701) 355-8190**
	(800) 288-6279
Fax: (701) 255-7687	Email: heringer@umary.edu
Full-time: 647 men, 998 women	Faculty: 95
Part-time: 187 men, 228 women	Ph.D.s: 36%
Graduate: 272 men, 451 women	Student/Faculty: 18 to 1
Year: semesters, summer session	Tuition: $13,700
Room & Board: $7500	Freshman Class: 1010 applied, 855 accepted, 367 enrolled
SAT: recommended ACT: 23	CEEB CODE: 6428
Application Deadline: August 15	COMPETITIVE

The University of Mary, founded in 1959, is a private institution affiliated with the Roman Catholic Church. Undergraduate and graduate programs emphasize liberal arts, humanities, social sciences, business, health science, music, professional training, philosophy and religious rooms, special class scheduling, lowered drinking fountains, lowered telephones, and special housing. **Special:** A co-op program in engineering is available as is cross-registration with the University of Minnesota. Special academic programs include internships in all fields and all programs, study abroad in France, Germany, and Spain, on-campus work-study, and a general studies degree. Dual majors include elementary education/early childhood, elementary education/special education, athletic training/biology, athletic training/phys ed, business/accounting, and business/computer information systems. There are accelerated degree programs in several majors, and a 3-2 engineering program with the University of Minnesota. There are 3 national honor societies, a freshman honors program, and 2 departmental honors programs. **Visiting:** There are regularly scheduled orientations for prospective students, including a campus tour and meetings with individual professors, coaches, students, and music instructors. There are guides for informal visits, visitors may sit in on classes, and stay overnight. To schedule a visit, contact the Admissions Office. **Campus Safety and Security:** Measures include emergency notification system and security escort services. There are emergency telephones, lighted pathways/sidewalks, and controlled access to dorms/residences.

REQUIREMENTS: The SAT or ACT and ACT Writing Test are recommended. Applicants should be graduates of an accredited secondary school; the GED is accepted. For automatic acceptance, 3 requirements must be met: a minimum 2.5 GPA; an 18 or higher score on the ACT; and rank in the upper half of the graduating class. The school's own testing can also be used to determine acceptance. A recommendation from a school counselor, teacher, or employer is requested. AP and CLEP credits are accepted. Important factors in the admissions decision are evidence of special talent, leadership record, and advanced placement or honors courses. To graduate, students must complete 128 semester hours, with 32 to 56 in the major and 44 at the 300-400 level, and have a minimum GPA of 2.0. At least 56 semester hours must be in liberal arts courses. In addition, a B.A. degree requires 16 semester hours of a foreign language or 20 semester hours of philosophy/theology, with 12 such hours at the 300-400 level. All students must take 3 courses each in humanities, math/science, philosophy/theology, and social sciences. **Procedure:** Freshmen are admitted fall and spring. Entrance exams should be taken in the fall of the senior year. There are early admissions, deferred admissions, and rolling admissions plans. Applications should be filed by August 15 for fall entry; December 15 for spring entry, along with a $25 fee. Applications are accepted on-line. **Transfer Students:** 259 transfer students enrolled in 2013-2014. Transfer students should have a 2.0 minimum GPA and should present a recommendation from a school counselor, instructor, or employer. 32 of 128 credits required for the bachelor's degree must be completed at Mary. **International Students:** There are 25 international students enrolled. The school actively recruits these students. They must take the TOEFL with a minimum score of 500 on the paper-based TOEFL (PBT).

ADMISSIONS: 85% of the 2014-2015 applicants were accepted. The ACT scores were 27% below 21, 33% between 21 and 23, 27% between 24 and 26, 8% between 27 and 28, and 5% above 28. 37% of the current freshmen were in the top fifth of their class; 69% were in the top two fifths. 20 freshmen graduated first in their class. **Admissions Contact:** Dave Heringer, Vice President For Enrollment. E-Mail: *heringer@umary.edu* Web: *www.umary.edu*

FINANCIAL AID: In 2014-2015, 100% of all full-time freshmen and 85% of continuing full-time students received some form of financial aid. 85% of all full-time freshmen and 75% of continuing full-time students received need-based aid. 70% of undergraduate students work part-time. Average annual earnings from campus work are $1000. The average financial indebtedness of the 2014 graduate was $15,500. The FAFSA is required. The priority date for freshman financial aid applications for fall entry is March 15. The deadline for filing freshman financial aid applications for fall entry is August 1.

www.barronspac.com

UNIVERSITY OF NORTH DAKOTA   E-2
www.go.und.edu

Grand Forks, ND 58202

701-777 3000
1-800-CALL-UND

Fax: (701) 777-2721
Full-time: 4882 men, 4197 women
Part-time: 1637 men, 821 women
Graduate: 1325 men, 2044 women
Year: semesters, summer session
Room & Board: $6810

Email: und.admissions@und.edu
Faculty: 672; I, --$
Ph.D.s: 94%
Student/Faculty: 20 to 1
Tuition: $7741 ($18,409)
Freshman Class: 4642 applied, 3992 accepted, 1906 enrolled

SAT: required **ACT:** 23
Application Deadline: July 1

CEEB CODE: 6878
COMPETITIVE

University of North Dakota, founded in 1883, enrolls students from every state, and in more than 225 fields of study, from baccalaureate through doctoral and professional degrees, including law and medicine. In addition, the University offers more than 40 degree and graduate certificate programs through distance education. Each year, the university has more than 21,000 registrations in online academic courses and other non-academic activities, including workforce development, conferences, professional certificates, teacher workshops, and lifelong learning courses. There are 8 undergraduate schools and 3 graduate schools. In addition to regional accreditation, UND has baccalaureate program accreditation with ABET, ADA, CSWE, NASAD, NASM, NCATE, AABI, ABET, AMTA, ATMAE, NAST, CAATE, CCNE, CAC, and COA. The 548-acre campus is in an urban area 4 hours from Minneapolis, St. Paul and 2 hours from Winnipeg, Manitoba. Including any residence halls, there are 243 buildings.

STUDENT LIFE: 63% of undergraduates are from out of state, mostly the Midwest. Students are from 50 states, 85 foreign countries, and Canada. 95% are from public schools. 80% are White. The average age of freshmen is 18; all undergraduates, 23. 20% do not continue beyond their first year; 80% remain to graduate. **Housing:** 4267 students can be accommodated in college housing, which includes single-sex and coed dorms, on-campus apartments, and married student housing. In addition, there are special-interest houses. On-campus housing is guaranteed for all 4 years. 69% of students commute. Alcohol is not permitted. All students may keep cars.

FACULTY/CLASSROOMS: 57% of faculty are male; 43% are female. 90% teach undergraduates. No introductory courses are taught by graduate students. The average class size in an introductory lecture is 32; in a laboratory is 17; and in a regular course is 28.

PROGRAMS OF STUDY: UND confers B.A., B.Acc., B.B.A., B.F.A., B.G.S., B.M., B.S., B.S.A., B.S.A.T., B.S.AtSc, B.S.C.E., B.S.C.H.E., B.S.Chem., B.S.C.J.S., B.S.C.N., B.S.C.S.C.I., B.S.Cyto., B.S.D., B.S.E.E., B.S.E.D., B.S.E.G., B.S.F.W.B., B.S.G.D.T., B.S.G.E., B.S.Geol., B.S.I.T., B.S.M.E., B.S.M.L.S., B.S.N., B.S.O.S.E.H., B.S.P.A., B.S.P.X.W., B.S.R.T.S., B.S.R.H.S., B.S.S.W., B.S.K.I.N. and B.S.PTE degrees. Master's and Doctoral degrees are also awarded. Bachelor's degrees are awarded in AGRICULTURE (environmental studies and fishing and fisheries), BIOLOGICAL SCIENCE (biology/biological science), BUSINESS (accounting, banking and finance, business economics, human resources, investments and securities, marketing management, and operations management), COMMUNICATIONS AND THE ARTS (Chinese, classical languages, communications, English, French, German, graphic design, music, music performance, musical theater, Norwegian, Spanish, and visual and performing arts), COMPUTER AND PHYSICAL SCIENCE (atmospheric sciences and meteorology, chemistry, computer science, geology, information sciences and systems, mathematics, natural sciences, physics, and science), EDUCATION (athletic training, business education, early childhood education, elementary education, middle school education, music education, and physical education), ENGINEERING AND ENVIRONMENTAL DESIGN (air traffic control, aviation maintenance management, chemical engineering, civil engineering, electrical/electronics engineering, geological engineering, industrial engineering technology, mechanical engineering, occupational safety and health, and petroleum/natural gas engineering), HEALTH PROFESSIONS (clinical science, cytotechnology, medical laboratory science, music therapy, nursing, and physical therapy), SOCIAL SCIENCE (American Indian studies, anthropology, criminal justice, dietetics, early childhood studies, economics, forensic studies, geography, history, interdisciplinary studies, international studies, philosophy, political science/government, psychology, public administration, religion, social science, social work, and sociology). Philosophy Religion, and mathematics are the strongest academically. Health professions, engineering, and business have the largest enrollments.

ACTIVITIES: 9% of men belong to 13 national fraternities; 11% of women belong to 6 national sororities. There are 275 groups on campus, including and special interest, art, band, cheerleading, chess, choir, chorale, chorus, computers, dance, debate, departmental, drama, drill team, ethnic, film, gay, honors, international, jazz band, literary magazine, marching band, musical theater, newspaper, opera, orchestra, pep band, photography, political, professional, radio and tV, religious, social, social service, student government, and symphony. Popular campus events include The Big Event, athletic events and Potato Bowl, Homecoming, Time Out and Wacipi. **Sports:** There are 9 intercollegiate sports for men and 10 for women, and 8 intramural sports for men and 4 for women. Facilities include a golf course, 15,000-seat stadium, 11,700-seat hockey arena, 6,100-seat basketball center, sports/field house with racquetball and basketball courts, weight rooms and a dance studio. The wellness center houses a three-court gymnasium, multiactivity court, cardiovascular, and weight rooms, a 200-meter running track, and 28-foot-high rock-climbing wall. **Graduates:** From July 1, 2013 to June 30, 2014, 1987 bachelor's degrees were awarded. The most popular majors were nursing (7%), psychology (6%), and commercial aviation (5%). 254 companies recruited on campus in 2013-2014. In an average class, 1% graduate in 3 years or less, 24% graduate in 4 years or less, 47% graduate in 5 years or less, and 55% graduate in 6 years or less. Of the 2013 graduating class, 16% were enrolled in graduate school within 6 months of graduation, and 81% were employed.

SERVICES: Counseling and information services are available, as is tutoring in every subject. There is a reader service for the blind. **Library/Resources:** The 2 libraries contain 1.7 million volumes, 902,476 microform items, 20,148 audio/video tapes/CDs/DVDs, and subscribe to 62,663 periodicals including electronic. Computerized library services include interlibrary loans, database searching, Internet access, and Wi-Fi capability. Special learning facilities include an art gallery, natural history museum, planetarium, radio station, TV station, an entrepreneur center, atmospherium, art museum, gallery, and one stop student services. **Physically Challenged Students:** 99% of the campus is accessible. Facilities include wheelchair ramps, elevators, special parking, specially equipped restrooms, special class scheduling, lowered drinking fountains, lowered telephones, special housing, accessible transportation, and academic and personal support services. **Special:** Special academic programs include cooperative programs, accelerated degree programs in most majors, internships in many majors, study abroad in at least 20 countries, work-study, and dual majors in all areas. Also offered are a general studies degree, honors programs, student-designed majors, B.A.-B.S. degrees, non-

degree study, and pass/fail options. Alternative academic programs include the Division of Continuing Education's correspondence study, the Integrated Studies Program, which offers a means of fulfilling general education requirements by a semester of related course work, and study via telecommunications. Cross-registration with all North Dakota 2- and 4-year public institutions is possible. There are 28 national honor societies, including Phi Beta Kappa, a freshman honors program, and 1 departmental honors program. **Visiting:** There are regularly scheduled orientations for prospective students, including a visit with an admissions counselor, a campus tour, an academic appointment, and an athletic appointment (if applicable). There are guides for informal visits, visitors may sit in on classes, and stay overnight. To schedule a visit, contact the Office of Admissions. **Campus Safety and Security:** Measures include 24-hour foot and vehicle patrol, emergency notification system, self-defense education, and security escort services. There are shuttle buses, emergency telephones, lighted pathways/sidewalks, and emergency phones throughout the campus.

REQUIREMENTS: The SAT or ACT is required. Applicants must be graduates of an accredited secondary school or have passed the GED with an average of 50. A GPA of 2.5 is required. AP and CLEP credits are accepted. To graduate, students must complete at least 125 credit hours, 30 in the major, with a minimum GPA of 2.0. At least 36 credits must be numbered 300 or above, and at least 60 credits must be from a 4-year institution. Distribution requirements include 12 credits of math, science, and technology, 9 each of social sciences and arts, and humanities, and 6 of English composition. One course in social science or arts and humanities must meet the world cultures designation. **Procedure:** Freshmen are admitted to all sessions. Entrance exams should be taken in spring of the junior year or fall of the senior year. There are early decision and rolling admissions plans. Applications should be filed by July 1 for fall entry. The fall 2014 application fee was $35. Notification is sent on a rolling basis. **Transfer Students:** 702 transfer students enrolled in 2013-2014. Transfer students must have a minimum GPA of 2.0 and be in good academic standing. A higher GPA may be required in specific programs. 30 of 125 credits required for the bachelor's degree must be completed at UND. **International Students:** There are 355 international students enrolled. They must take the TOEFL. They must also take the SAT or ACT.

ADMISSIONS: 86% of the 2014-2015 applicants were accepted. The ACT scores were 18% below 21, 30% between 21 and 23, 27% between 24 and 26, 10% between 27 and 28, and 11% above 28. 32% of the current freshmen were in the top fifth of their class; 63% were in the top two fifths. There was 1 National Merit finalist. 72 freshmen graduated first in their class. **Admissions Contact:** Jason Trainer, Director of Admissions. E-Mail: *und.admissions@und.edu* Web: *www.go.und.edu*

FINANCIAL AID: UND is a member of CSS. The FAFSA is required. Check with the school for current application deadlines.

VALLEY CITY STATE UNIVERSITY (*The complete profile is made available exclusively on our website, www.barronspac.com*)

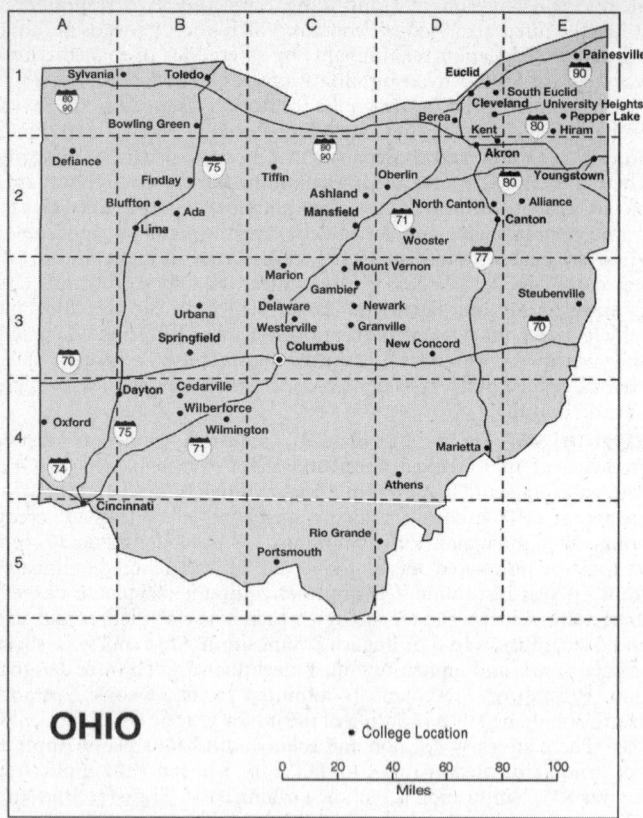

OHIO

• College Location

0 20 40 60 80 100
Miles

ART ACADEMY OF CINCINNATI (*The complete profile is made available exclusively on our website, www.barronspac.com*)

ASHLAND UNIVERSITY   C-2
www.ashland.edu

Ashland, OH 44805   (419) 289-5052
                                     (800) 882-1548
Fax: (419) 289-5333   Email: enrollme@ashland.edu
Full-time: 1000 men, 1450 women   Faculty: n/av; IIA, --$
Part-time: 100 men, 275 women   Ph.D.s: n/av
Graduate: 1475 men, 2480 women   Student/Faculty: n/av
Year: semesters, summer session   Tuition: $28,154
Room & Board: $9852   Freshman Class: n/av
SAT or ACT: required   CEEB CODE: 1021
Application Deadline: open   COMPETITIVE

Ashland University, founded in 1878, is a private liberal arts institution affiliated with the Brethren Church and offering undergraduate and graduate programs in the arts and sciences, business, education, and health services. The figures in the above capsule and in this profile are approximate. There are 3 undergraduate schools and 3 graduate schools. In addition to regional accreditation, AU has baccalaureate program accreditation with AACSB, AHEA, CSWE, NASM, NCATE, and NLN. The 2 libraries contain 270,000 volumes, 250,000 microform items, 8800 audio/video tapes/CDs/DVDs, and subscribe to 700 periodicals including electronic. Computerized library services include interlibrary loans and database searching. Special learning facilities include a learning resource center, art gallery, radio station, TV station, writing center, media center, and theater. The 150-acre campus is in a small town midway between Cleveland and Columbus. Including any residence halls, there are 38 buildings.

STUDENT LIFE: 94% of undergraduates are from Ohio. Others are from 29 states, 13 foreign countries, and Canada. 86% are white. 46% claim no religious affiliation; 34% Protestant; 14% Catholic. The average age of freshmen is 18; all undergraduates, 23. 42% do not continue beyond their first year; 58% remain to graduate.

FACULTY/CLASSROOMS: 61% of faculty are male; 39% are female. 81% teach undergraduates. No introductory courses are taught by graduate students. The average class size in an introductory lecture is 20, in a laboratory, 11, and in a regular course, 18.

PROGRAMS OF STUDY: AU confers B.A., B.S., B.M., B.S.B.A., B.S.Ed., B.S.N., and B.S.W. degrees. Associates, master's, and doctoral degrees are also awarded. Bachelor's degrees are awarded in BIOLOGICAL SCIENCE (biology/biological science and toxicology), BUSINESS (accounting, banking and finance, business administration and management, business economics, fashion merchandising, hotel/motel and restaurant management, management information systems, marketing/retailing/merchandising, and recreational facilities management), COMMUNICATIONS AND THE ARTS (art, broadcasting, communications, creative writing, dramatic arts, English, fine arts, French, journalism, media arts, music, musical theater, Spanish, and speech/debate/rhetoric), COMPUTER AND PHYSICAL SCIENCE (chemistry, computer science, geology, mathematics, and physics), EDUCATION (art education, athletic training, early childhood education, education administration, education of the exceptional child, elementary education, English education, foreign languages education, health education, home economics education, music education, physical education, science education, and secondary education), ENGINEERING AND ENVIRONMENTAL DESIGN (commercial art and environmental science), HEALTH PROFESSIONS (predentistry, premedicine, preoptometry, preveterinary science, and recreation therapy), SOCIAL SCIENCE (American studies, child care/child and family studies, criminal justice, economics, food science, history, international studies, philosophy, physical fitness/movement, political science/government, prelaw, psychology, religion, social science, social work, and sociology). Preprofessional science is the strongest academically. Business and teacher education have the largest enrollments.

ACTIVITIES: 14% of men belong to 4 national fraternities; 22% of women belong to 5 national sororities. There are 100 groups on campus, including art, band, cheerleading, choir, chorus, dance, drama, drill team, ethnic, health and environmental, honors, international, jazz band, literary magazine, marching band, musical theater, newspaper, orchestra, pep band, photography, political, professional, radio and TV, religious, social, social service, student government, symphony, and yearbook. Popular campus events include Spectrum Series, Plays, and Little Sibs Weekend.

SERVICES: Counseling and information services are available, as is tutoring in every subject. There is a reader service for the blind. The 2 libraries contain 270,000 volumes, 250,000 microform items, 8800 audio/video tapes/CDs/DVDs, and subscribe to 700 periodicals including electronic. Computerized library services include interlibrary loans and database searching. Special learning facilities include a learning resource center, art gallery, radio station, TV station, writing center, media center, and theater.

REQUIREMENTS: The SAT or ACT is required. Applicants must be graduates of an accredited secondary school. The GED is accepted. The recommended preparatory program includes 4 units of English, 3 each of science, social studies, and math, and 2 of foreign language. An interview is recommended. A GPA of 2.5 is required. AP and CLEP credits are accepted. Important factors in the admissions decision are advanced placement or honors courses, evidence of special talent, and leadership record.

FINANCIAL AID: The FAFSA, the college's own financial statement, and federal tax returns are required. Check with the school for current application deadlines.

BALDWIN WALLACE UNIVERSITY — D-1
www.bw.edu

Berea, OH 44017	**(440) 826-8002**
	1-877-292-7759
Fax: (440) 826-3830	Email: wgerhard@bw.edu
Full-time: 1361 men, 1608 women	Faculty: 178; IIB, av$
Part-time: 135 men, 258 women	Ph.D.s: 75%
Graduate: 268 men, 349 women	Student/Faculty: 17 to 1
Year: semesters, summer session	Tuition: $28,814
Room & Board: $9504	Freshman Class: 4224 applied, 2702 accepted, 717 enrolled
SAT CR/M/W: 540/540/530 ACT: 23	CEEB CODE: 1050
Application Deadline: n/av	COMPETITIVE

Baldwin Wallace University, established in 1845, is an independent liberal arts institution that blends the hallmarks of the liberal arts with an emphasis on professional and career preparation through undergraduate and graduate degree programs. There is 1 undergraduate school and 2 graduate schools. In addition to regional accreditation, BW has baccalaureate program accreditation with NASM, NCATE, CAATE, CCNE, and ARC-PA (Provisional). The 120-acre campus is in a suburban area 14 miles southwest of Cleveland, OH. Including any residence halls, there are 78 buildings.

STUDENT LIFE: 83% of undergraduates are from Ohio. Others are from 44 states, 24 foreign countries, and Canada. 79% are from public schools. 80% are White. 45% are Protestant; 32% Catholic; 15% Baha'i, Buddhist, Hindu, Mormon, Muslim, Orthodox, Unitarian. The average age of freshmen is 18; all undergraduates, 20. 19% do not continue beyond their first year; 92% remain to graduate.

Housing: 1876 students can be accommodated in college housing, which includes coed dorms and on-campus apartments. In addition, there are honors houses, special-interest houses, student-directed learning comm, themed housing, special housing-disabled and international students, fraternities/sororities. On-campus housing is available on a first-come, first-served basis, and is available on a lottery system for upperclassmen. 63% of students live on campus; of those, 50% remain on campus on weekends. All students may keep cars.

FACULTY/CLASSROOMS: 52% of faculty are male; 48% are female. 93% teach undergraduates. No introductory courses are taught by graduate students. The average class size in an introductory lecture is 20; in a laboratory is 17; and in a regular course is 17.

PROGRAMS OF STUDY: BW confers B.A., B.S., B.M., B.M.E, B.S.Ed. and B.S.N degrees. Master's degrees are also awarded. Bachelor's degrees are awarded in BIOLOGICAL SCIENCE (biology/biological science and neurosciences), BUSINESS (accounting, business administration and management, entrepreneurial studies, finance, human resources, international business, international security/conflict resolution mgmt, marketing, organizational leadership and management, sports management, and sustainable management), COMMUNICATIONS AND THE ARTS (acting, applied music, art history, broadcasting, communication studies, creative writing, digital communications, English, film, television and digital media, French, German, graphic design & media, instrumental performance, keyboard - piano concentration, music, music composition, music history and appreciation, music performance, music theory and composition, musical theater, public relations, Spanish, studio art, theatre acting, theater design, theater management, and voice), COMPUTER AND PHYSICAL SCIENCE (chemistry, computer science, computer security and information assurance, digital arts/technology, mathematics, mathematics – economics, physics, software engineering, and systems analysis), EDUCATION (art education, athletic training, early childhood education, health and physical education, middle school education, music education, physical education, science education, and specific learning disabilities), ENGINEERING AND ENVIRONMENTAL DESIGN (preengineering), HEALTH PROFESSIONS (exercise science, health care administration, health promotion, music therapy, nursing, predentistry, premedicine, prepharmacy, prephysical therapy, preveterinary science, and public health), SOCIAL SCIENCE (communication sciences and disorders, criminal justice, economics, history, industrial and organizational psychology, international studies, philosophy, political science/government, psychology, public administration, public history/archives, religion, and sociology). Business administration, biology, and psychology have the largest enrollments.

ACTIVITIES: 13% of men belong to 7 national fraternities; 20% of women belong to 7 national sororities. There are 130 groups on campus, including art, band, cheerleading, choir, chorale, chorus, computers, dance, drama, drill team, environmental, ethnic, film, forensics, gay, honors, international, jazz band, literary magazine, marching band, musical theater, newspaper, opera, orchestra, pep band, political, professional, radio and TV, religious, social, social service, student government, symphony, and yearbook. Popular campus events include Culture Night, Dance Marathon and April Reign. **Sports:** There are 12 intercollegiate sports for men and 11 for women, and 28 intramural sports for men and 28 for women. Facilities include an 8,000-seat stadium with polyturf and all-weather track, a 3,000-seat gym, new athletic field (Tressel Field), baseball fields, and a 6-court tennis complex. The recreation center houses a 200-meter track, swimming pool, dance studio, athletic training/rehab facility, wrestling/gymnastics/weight rooms, fitness complex, and facilities for basketball, racquetball, tennis,volleyball, and a fitness and wellness programs/activities. **Graduates:** From July 1, 2013 to June 30, 2014, 746 bachelor's degrees were awarded. The most popular majors were accounting (6%), psychology (5%), and early childhood education (5%). 133 companies recruited on campus in 2013-2014. In an average class, 3% graduate in 3 years or less, 51% graduate in 4 years or less, 66% graduate in 5 years or less, and 68% graduate in 6 years or less. Of the 2013 graduating class, 19% were enrolled in graduate school within 6 months of graduation, and 61% were employed.

SERVICES: Counseling and information services are available, as is tutoring in most subjects. There is a reader service for the blind, and remedial math, reading, and writing. Software for students who have difficulty reading or with visual impairments; access to Learning Ally ND Bookshare which both come with a downloadable reader. **Library/Resources:** The 3 libraries contain 305,596 volumes, 21,367 audio/video tapes/CDs/DVDs, and subscribe to 45,000 periodicals including electronic. Computerized library services include interlibrary loans, database searching, and Internet access. Special learning facilities include an art gallery, radio station, a neuroscience lab, and an observatory. **Physically Challenged Students:** 80% of the campus is accessible. Facilities include wheelchair ramps, elevators, special parking, specially equipped restrooms, special class scheduling, lowered telephones, special housing. **Special:** Special academic programs include internships that can qualify for credit, work-study programs and study abroad. There is cross-registration with 7 participating institutions within the Greater Cleveland area, as well as a 3-2 program in social work with Case Western Reserve University, 3-2 master's program in accounting, human resources, computer science/information systems, 3-2 program in engineering with Case Western Reserve and Columbia University. BW also offers the Consortium for Music Therapy, accelerated degree programs, a B.A.-B.S. degree, dual and student-designed majors, credit for life, military, work experience, and pass/fail options. The Adult and Continuing Education Program offers degrees through evening and weekend colleges. 3+1 or 4+1 medical technology-based affiliation with Southwest General Health Center. Pre-professional programs are available in dentistry, law, medicine, pharmacy, and veterinary. Study abroad in Argentina, Australia, Austria, China, Costa Rica, Ecuador, England, France, Germany, Ghana, India, Ireland, Italy, Japan, Mexico, Morocco, Scotland, South Korea, Spain, Sweden and Switzerland. There are 24 national honor societies and a freshman honors program. **Visiting:** There are regularly scheduled orientations for prospective students, student visits include an interview, a tour, and classroom visits. There are guides for informal visits, visitors may sit in on classes, and stay overnight. To schedule a visit, contact the Admission Office. **Campus Safety and Security:** Measures include 24-hour foot and vehicle patrol, emergency notification system, self-defense education, and security escort services. There are emergency telephones, lighted pathways/sidewalks, controlled access to dorms/residences, more than 100 exterior/interior security cameras.

REQUIREMENTS: The SAT or ACT is recommended. Applicants must be graduates of an accredited secondary school or have earned a GED. Applicants must have completed 16 academic credits, including 4 in English, 3 each in math, natural science, and social science, 2 in a foreign language; however, alternative distributions are considered. A teacher's recommendation is required. BW does not require students to submit test scores for admission consideration. BW requires applicants to be in the upper 50% of their class. A GPA of 2.8 is required. AP and CLEP credits are accepted. Important factors in the admissions decision are advanced placement or honors courses, extracurricular activities record, and recommendations by school officials.All students must complete 124 semester hours, and have at least a 2.0 GPA. A total of 43 semester hours must be taken in the liberal arts core, including 14 in humanities, 8 in social science, 7 in natural science, 6 in liberal arts, and sciences, 3 each in math and English, 2 in health and phys ed. All students must complete a minor and coursework in International Studies, Diversity Studies, Experiential Learning. Common courses all students must take include: Liberal Arts and Sciences (LAS 200), English 111, 131 (Composition), a math requirement and HPE-110W (Wellness). Comprehensive exams are required in some majors. **Procedure:** Freshmen are admitted fall and spring. Entrance exams should be taken during junior year or early in senior year. There are deferred admissions and rolling admissions plans. Application deadlines are open. Applications are accepted on-line. **Transfer Students:** 258 transfer students enrolled in 2013-2014. Students must be in good academic and social standing at prior institution(s). 32 of 124 credits required for the bachelor's degree must be completed at BW. **International Students:** There are 44 international students enrolled. The school actively recruits these students. They must take the TOEFL with a minimum score of 550 on the paper-based TOEFL (PBT) or 79 on the Internet-based version (iBT) and the college's own test, or take the IELTS, or ELS Language Centers Level 12. They must also take the SAT or ACT, scoring SAT Critical Reading - 500 min; ACT English 22 min.

ADMISSIONS: 64% of the 2014-2015 applicants were accepted. The SAT scores for the 2014-2015 freshman class were: Critical Reading--28% below 500, 48% between 500 and 599, 19% between 600 and 699, and 5% between 700 and 800; Math--27% below 500, 47% between 500 and 599, 23% between 600 and 699, and 3% between 700 and 800; Writing--33% below 500, 46% between 500 and 599, 18% between 600 and 699, and 3% between 700 and 800. The ACT scores were 30% below 21, 28% between 21 and 23, 25% between 24 and 26, 11% between 27 and 28, and 6% above 28. 39% of the current freshmen were in the top fifth of their class; 68% were in the top two fifths. 17 freshmen graduated first in their class. **Admissions Contact:** Winnie W. Gerhardt, Interim VP for Enrollment Management. E-Mail: *wgerhard@bw.edu* Web: *www.bw.edu*

FINANCIAL AID: In 2014-2015, 100% of all full-time freshmen and 97% of continuing full-time students received some form of financial aid. 100% of all full-time freshmen and continuing full-time students received need-based aid. The average freshman award was $24,907. Need-based scholarships or need-based grants averaged $20,203 ($28,814 maximum); need-based self-help aid (loans and jobs) averaged $4,704 ($12,900 maximum); and other non-need-based awards and non-need-based scholarships averaged $13,440 ($28,814 maximum). 32% of undergraduate students work part-time. Average annual earnings from campus work are $1273. The average financial indebtedness of the 2014 graduate was $27,593. The FAFSA is required. The priority date for freshman financial aid applications for fall entry is May 1. The deadline for filing freshman financial aid applications for fall entry is September 1.

BLUFFTON UNIVERSITY   B-2
www.bluffton.edu

Bluffton, OH 45817   (419) 358-3257
                                               (800) 488-3257
Fax: (419) 358-3232   Email: admissions@bluffton.edu
Full-time: 418 men, 378 women   **Faculty:** 54
Part-time: 81 men, 120 women   **Ph.D.s:** 82%
Graduate: 41 men, 56 women   **Student/Faculty:** 14 to 1
Year: semesters, summer session   **Tuition:** $29,316
Room & Board: $9632   **Freshman Class:** 2315
                                         applied, 1297 accepted,
                                         224 enrolled
SAT CR/M: 495/510 **ACT:** 22   **CEEB CODE:** 1067
Application Deadline: May 31   **COMPETITIVE**

Bluffton University, founded in 1899, is a private, Christian, liberal arts institution affiliated with the Mennonite Church. There is one graduate school. In addition to regional accreditation, Bluffton has baccalaureate program accreditation with ADA, CSWE, NASM, and NCATE. The 65-acre campus is in a small town 60 miles south of Toledo and 75 miles north of Dayton. Including any residence halls, there are 27 buildings.

STUDENT LIFE: 87% of undergraduates are from Ohio. Others are from 23 states, 6 foreign countries, and Canada. 91% are from public schools. 86% are White. 54% are Protestant; 32% unknown religion; 13% Catholic. The average age of freshmen is 18; all undergraduates, 21. 31% do not continue beyond their first year; 61% remain to graduate. **Housing:** 732 students can be accommodated in college housing, which includes single-sex and coed dorms. In addition, there are special-interest houses, All full-time students must live in residence halls unless commuting from the home of their parents. On-campus housing is guaranteed for all 4 years. 84% of students live on campus; of those, 60% remain on campus on weekends. Alcohol is not permitted. All students may keep cars.

FACULTY/CLASSROOMS: 62% of faculty are male; 38% are female. 97% teach undergraduates. No introductory courses are taught by graduate students. The average class size in an introductory lecture is 23; in a laboratory is 8; and in a regular course is 20.

PROGRAMS OF STUDY: Bluffton confers B.A. degrees. Master's degrees are also awarded. Bachelor's degrees are awarded in BIOLOGICAL SCIENCE (biology/biological science), BUSINESS (accounting, business administration and management, human resources, information and communication technology, marketing/retailing/merchandising, organizational leadership and management, recreational facilities management, and sports management), COMMUNICATIONS AND THE ARTS (art, broadcasting, communications, creative writing, English, graphic design and media, music, public relations, and Spanish), COMPUTER AND PHYSICAL SCIENCE (chemistry, computer science, mathematics, physical sciences, and physics), EDUCATION (early childhood education, health information management, home economics education, middle school education, music education, physical education, and special education), HEALTH PROFESSIONS (premedicine and public health), SOCIAL SCIENCE (biblical studies, child psychology/development, criminal justice, early childhood studies, economics, family/consumer studies, food science, history, ministries, psychology, social science, social studies, social work, sociology, and youth ministry). Social work, education, and business have the largest enrollments.

ACTIVITIES: There are 40 groups on campus, including Youth Ministries, student senate, art, band, cheerleading, choir, chorale, chorus, dance, drama, ethnic, gay, honors, international, International Connection, jazz band, literary magazine, musical theater, newspaper, pep band, political, professional, radio and TV, religious, social, social service, student government, and yearbook. Popular campus events include International Week, Spiritual Emphasis Weeks, and Artist Series. **Sports:** There are 7 intercollegiate sports for men and 7 for women, and 8 intramural sports for men and 8 for women. Facilities include a recreation and fitness center that includes a basketball/volleyball court, an athletic complex with baseball, softball, soccer and 2600 seat football stadium. Another building for indoor sports and intramurals. **Graduates:** From July 1, 2013 to June 30, 2014, 307 bachelor's degrees were awarded. The most popular majors were business/marketing (39%), education (16%), and social work (10%). 57 companies recruited on campus in 2013-2014. In an average class, 1% graduate in 3 years or less, 52% graduate in 4 years or less, 58% graduate in 5 years or less, and 60% graduate in 6 years or less.

SERVICES: Counseling and information services are available, as is tutoring in every subject. There is a reader service for the blind, and remedial math, reading, and writing. Tutoring is available for most students, as are classes at the student's request and/or faculty designation. **Library/Resources:** The library contains 397,269 volumes, 83,822 microform items, 7,286 audio/video tapes/CDs/DVDs, and subscribes to 21,931 periodicals including electronic. Computerized library services include interlibrary loans, database searching, Internet access, and Wi-Fi capability. Special learning facilities include an art gallery, radio station, the Lion and Lamb Peace Arts Center, and a Nature Preserve. **Physically Challenged Students:** 75% of the campus is accessible. Facilities include wheelchair ramps, elevators, special parking, specially equipped restrooms, special class scheduling, lowered drinking fountains, lowered telephones. special computers for visually impaired students. **Special:** Special arrangements include internships in business, recreation, social work, and education, a Washington semester through the Council for Christian Colleges and Universities, and study abroad. Student-designed majors and independent study are possible, as is credit for prior learning and for learning in voluntary service. There is an accelerated degree program in organizational management. Nondegree study and pass/fail options are offered. There are 2 national honor societies, a freshman honors program, and 14 departmental honors programs. **Visiting:** There are regularly scheduled orientations for prospective students, Personal visits are scheduled according to students' specific interests and may include obsesrving a class, visit with faculty and a tour of campus. Group visits are scheduled regularly throughout the year. Listed on website with online registration. There are guides for informal visits, visitors may sit in on classes, and stay overnight. To schedule a visit, contact Rachel Hunter at (800) 488-3257. **Campus Safety and Security:** Measures include emergency notification system and self-defense education. There are emergency telephones, lighted pathways/sidewalks, controlled access to dorms/residences, village police cruisers regularly patrol the campus during night hours. There are also 2 night security officers who communicate directly with village police and routinely patrol campus at night.

REQUIREMENTS: The SAT or ACT is required. To be considered for regular admission to Bluffton University as an undergraduate student, you need to have earned a score of 920 on the SAT (critical reading plus math) or 19 on the ACT. Other admissions requirements include graduation from an accredited secondary school with a 2.3 GPA or class rank above 50%. Recommended courses include 4 units of English and 3 units each of math, science, social studies, and a foreign language. The GED is accepted. A personal campus visit and an interview are strongly recommended. Music students must audition and art students submit a portfolio. Bluffton requires applicants to be in the upper 50% of their class. A GPA of 2.3 is required. AP and CLEP credits are accepted. Important factors in the admissions decision are leadership record, recommendations by school officials, and extracurricular activities record.To graduate, students must complete 124 semester hours with 40 to 60 in the major and have a minimum GPA of 2.0. The general education requirements must be met, and satisfactory achievement in departmental senior comprehensives demonstrated. Distribution requirements are approximately one third for general education requirements, including 6 hours of religion, and one third to one half for the major. **Procedure:** Freshmen are admitted to all sessions. Entrance exams should be taken in the spring of the junior year or fall of the senior year. There are deferred admissions and rolling admissions plans. Applications should be filed by May 31 for fall entry, along with a $20 fee. Applications are accepted on-line. **Transfer Students:** 111 transfer students enrolled in 2013-2014. Transfer students must have a minimum college GPA of 2.0, meet eligibility criteria from previous institutions, and have met their financial obligations at the former institution. A signed transfer recommendation must be submitted from each college attended. 30 of 124 credits required for the bachelor's degree must be completed at Bluffton. **International Students:** There are 11 international students enrolled. The school actively recruits these students. They must take the TOEFL with a minimum score of 500 on the paper-based TOEFL (PBT) or 64 on the Internet-based version (iBT). They must also take the SAT, scoring 920, and the college's own entrance exam. The SAT can substitute for the TOEFL.

ADMISSIONS: 56% of the 2014-2015 applicants were accepted. The SAT scores for the 2014-2015 freshman class were: Critical Reading--44% below 500, 40% between 500 and 599, 12% between 600 and 699, and 4% between 700 and 800; Math--48% below 500, 36% between 500 and 599, 8% between 600 and 699, and 8% between 700 and 800. The ACT scores were 37% below 21, 22% between 21 and 23, 24% between 24 and 26, 11% between 27 and 28, and 6% above 28. 28% of the current freshmen were in the top fifth of their class; 56% were in the top two fifths. 9 freshmen graduated first in their class. **Admissions Contact:** Derek Stemen, Director of Admissions. E-Mail: *admissions@bluffton.edu* Web: *www.bluffton.edu/admissions*

FINANCIAL AID: In 2014-2015, 100% of all full-time freshmen and continuing full-time students received some form of financial aid.

94% of all full-time freshmen and 82% of continuing full-time students received need-based aid. The average freshman award was $27,971. Need-based scholarships or need-based grants averaged $22,697 ($28,866 maximum); need-based self-help aid (loans and jobs) averaged $6,344 ($11,570 maximum); and other non-need-based awards and non-need-based scholarships averaged $12,912 ($24,890 maximum). 65% of undergraduate students work part-time. Average annual earnings from campus work are $2400. The average financial indebtedness of the 2014 graduate was $35,883. The FAFSA is required. The priority date for freshman financial aid applications for fall entry is May 1. The deadline for filing freshman financial aid applications for fall entry is October 1.

BOWLING GREEN STATE UNIVERSITY   B-1
www.bgsu.edu

Bowling Green, OH 43403	(419) 372-BGSU 1-866-CHOOSE BGSU
Fax: (419) 372-6955	Email: choosebgsu@bgsu.edu
Full-time: 5608 men, 7385 women	Faculty: 655; I
Part-time: 579 men, 527 women	Ph.D.s: 82%
Graduate: 979 men, 1476 women	Student/Faculty: 19 to 1
Year: semesters, summer session	Tuition: $10,726 ($18,034)
Room & Board: $8244	Freshman Class: 14509 applied, 7743 accepted, 3030 enrolled
SAT CR/M/W: 520/520/490 ACT: 22	CEEB CODE: 1069
Application Deadline: July 15	COMPETITIVE

Bowling Green State University, founded in 1910, is a public institution. There are 7 undergraduate schools and 1 graduate school. In addition to regional accreditation, BGSU has baccalaureate program accreditation with AACSB, ACCE, ACEJMC, ADA, CSWE, NASAD, NASM, NCATE, NRPA, ACS, and NAST. The 1338-acre campus is in a small town 23 miles south of Toledo, adjacent to Interstate 75 Including any residence halls, there are 119 buildings.

STUDENT LIFE: 86% of undergraduates are from Ohio. Others are from 50 states, 41 foreign countries, and Canada. 76% are White. **Male To Female Ratio:** 1.3:1. The average age of freshmen is 19; all undergraduates, 21. 30% do not continue beyond their first year; 58% remain to graduate. **Housing:** 6638 students can be accommodated in college housing, which includes single-sex and coed dorms and on-campus apartments. In addition, there are honors houses, language houses, special-interest houses, fraternity houses, sorority houses, no-alcohol wings, residential/theme communities, and gender-neutral housing. 58% of students commute. All students may keep cars.

FACULTY/CLASSROOMS: 47% of faculty are male; 53% are female. No introductory courses are taught by graduate students. The average class size in an introductory lecture is 26; in a laboratory is 17; and in a regular course is 25.

PROGRAMS OF STUDY: BGSU confers B.A., B.A.C., B.F.A., B.L.S., B.S., B.S.J., B.S.F.A., B.S.B.A., B.S.Econ., B.S.A.M.P.D., B.S.Diet., B.S.Ed., B.S.H.D.F.S., B.S.I.D., B.S.N.S., B.A.H.S., B.S.Comm., B.S.C.J., B.S.Gero., B.S.M.L.S., B.S.Nur., B.S.S.W., B.Mus., B.M.Art., B.S.Tech., B.S.Arch., B.S.C.M. and B.S.E.C.E.T. degrees. Master's and doctoral degrees are also awarded. Bachelor's degrees are awarded in AGRICULTURE (environmental studies), BIOLOGICAL SCIENCE (avian sciences, life science, neurosciences, and nutrition), BUSINESS (accounting, business administration and management, management information systems, marketing, sports management, and tourism), COMMUNICATIONS AND THE ARTS (apparel design, art history, art, classics, communication, creative writing, dance, design, English, English literature, film arts, fine arts, foreign language, French, German, graphic design, instrumental performance, jazz, journalism, Latin, music, music history and appreciation, Technical Communication, music performance, music theory and composition, performing arts, romance languages and literature, Russian, Spanish, telecommunications, theatre studies, and visual and performing arts), COMPUTER AND PHYSICAL SCIENCE (chemistry, computer science, digital arts/technology, earth science, geology, mathematics, physics, science, and statistics), EDUCATION (art education, athletic training, business education, early childhood education, education, education of the deaf and hearing impaired, education of the multiply handicapped, elementary education, foreign languages education, learner designed area of study, mathematics education, middle school education, music education, physical education, science education, secondary education, social science education, special education, and technical education), ENGINEERING AND ENVIRONMENTAL DESIGN (construction management, electrical and computer engineering, electrical/electronics engineering technology, engineering technology, environmental science, and interior design), HEALTH PROFESSIONS (biology, exercise science, health science, nursing, and public health), SOCIAL SCIENCE (African studies, American studies, architectural studies, Asian/Oriental studies, criminal justice, dietetics, economics, ethnic studies, family/consumer studies, fire services administration, geography, gerontology, history, human development, interdisciplinary studies, international studies, liberal arts/general studies, philosophy, political science/government, psychology, social science, social work, sociology, and women's studies). Biology, middle childhood education, and adolescence to young adult education have the largest enrollments.

ACTIVITIES: 12% of men belong to 20 national fraternities; 13% of women belong to 19 national sororities. There are 326 groups on campus, including art, band, cheerleading, chess, choir, chorale, chorus, communications, computers, dance, debate, drama, drill team, environmental, ethnic, film, gay, honors, international, jazz band, literary magazine, marching band, musical theater, newspaper, opera, pep band, photography, political, professional, radio and TV, religious, social, social service, student government, symphony, and yearbook. Popular campus events include Homecoming, Campus Fest, Move-in Weekend and Week of Welcome. **Sports:** There are 7 intercollegiate sports for men and 10 for women, and 13 intramural sports for men and 15 for women. **Graduates:** From July 1, 2013 to June 30, 2014, 2959 bachelor's degrees were awarded. The most popular majors were early childhood education (5%), liberal studies (4%), and adolescence to young adult education (4%). 2031 companies recruited on campus in 2013-2014. In an average class, 1% graduate in 3 years or less, 32% graduate in 4 years or less, 50% graduate in 5 years or less, and 54% graduate in 6 years or less.

SERVICES: Counseling and information services are available, as is tutoring in some subjects, writing, math and stats, and any subject that has been requested by students. There is a reader service for the blind, and remedial math, reading, and writing. **Library/Resources:** The library contains 2.2 million volumes, 2.7 million microform items, 275,189 audio/video tapes/CDs/DVDs, and subscribes to 1,475 periodicals including electronic. Computerized library services include interlibrary loans, database searching, Internet access, and Wi-Fi capability. Special learning facilities include an art gallery, planetarium, radio station, and TV station. **Physically Challenged Students:** 92% of the campus is accessible. Facilities include wheelchair ramps, elevators, special parking, specially equipped restrooms, special class scheduling, lowered drinking fountains, lowered telephones, special housing. **Special:** Special academic programs include co-op programs in all majors with the National Student Exchange, internships, a Washington semester, work-study, and study abroad. Dual majors are available in all programs, and a B.A.-B.S. degree is offered in computer science, geology, math, psychology, statistics, scientific and technical communication, and individualized planned program. Student-designed majors, independent study, credit for experience, nondegree study, and pass/fail options are possible. There are Phi Beta Kappa and a freshman honors program. **Visiting:** There are regularly scheduled orientations for prospective students. There are guides for informal visits and visitors may sit in on classes. To schedule a visit, contact the Office of Admissions. **Campus Safety and Security:** Measures include 24-hour foot and vehicle patrol, emergency notification system, self-defense education, and security escort services. There are shuttle buses, emergency telephones, lighted pathways/sidewalks, controlled access to dorms/residences, in-room safes.

REQUIREMENTS: The ACT is required. The SAT is recommended. AP and CLEP credits are accepted. A minimum of 122 semester hours of credit and at least 30 credit hours must be BGSU courses; earn an accumulative grade point average of at least 2.0 ("C" average) for all coursework attempted; complete the BG Perspective requirements; complete at least 40 hours of credit in courses numbered 3000 and

above; Satisfy all college requirements for a degree; file an application for graduation. **Procedure:** Freshmen are admitted fall, spring, and summer. Entrance exams should be taken in the junior year. There are deferred admissions and rolling admissions plans. Applications should be filed by July 15 for fall entry; December 15 for spring entry; and May 15 for summer entry, along with a $45 fee. Notifications are sent August 1. Applications are accepted on-line. **Transfer Students:** 813 transfer students enrolled in 2013-2014. 30 of 122 credits required for the bachelor's degree must be completed at BGSU. **International Students:** There are 301 international students enrolled. The school actively recruits these students. They must take the TOEFL with a minimum score of 500 on the paper-based TOEFL (PBT) or 71 on the Internet-based version (iBT) or take the MELAB. SAT and ACT scores are considered if submitted.

ADMISSIONS: 53% of the 2014-2015 applicants were accepted. The SAT scores for the 2014-2015 freshman class were: Critical Reading--39% below 500, 40% between 500 and 599, 18% between 600 and 699, and 3% between 700 and 800; Math--36% below 500, 43% between 500 and 599, 18% between 600 and 699, and 3% between 700 and 800; Writing--53% below 500, 34% between 500 and 599, 12% between 600 and 699, and 1% between 700 and 800. The ACT scores were 31% below 21, 30% between 21 and 23, 23% between 24 and 26, 8% between 27 and 28, and 8% above 28. 27% of the current freshmen were in the top fifth of their class; 57% were in the top two fifths. 41 freshmen graduated first in their class. **Admissions Contact:** Castellano, Cecilia Ann, Director, Admissions. E-Mail: *choosebgsu@bgsu.edu* Web: *http://www.bgsu.edu/admissions.html*

FINANCIAL AID: In 2014-2015, 95% of all full-time freshmen and 89% of continuing full-time students received some form of financial aid. 58% of all full-time freshmen and 59% of continuing full-time students received need-based aid. The average freshman award was $15,082. Need-based scholarships or need-based grants averaged $5,226 ($11,278 maximum); need-based self-help aid (loans and jobs) averaged $3,629 ($7,500 maximum); non-need-based athletic scholarships averaged $15,908 ($36,348 maximum); other non-need-based awards and non-need-based scholarships averaged $7,616 ($33,630 maximum); and $13,683 from other forms of aid. 19% of undergraduate students work part-time. Average annual earnings from campus work are $2000. The average financial indebtedness of the 2014 graduate was $29,681. BGSU is a member of CSS. The FAFSA is required. Check with the school for current application deadlines.

CAPITAL UNIVERSITY	**C-3**
www.capital.edu	

Columbus, OH 43209	
	(614) 236-6101
	866-544-6175
Fax: (614) 236-6926	**Email: admission@capital.edu**
Full-time: 1071 men, 1383 women	**Faculty:** 141; IIA, +$
Part-time: 85 men, 203 women	**Ph.D.s:** 78%
Graduate: 359 men, 393 women	**Student/Faculty:** 18 to 1
Year: semesters, summer session	**Tuition:** $31,990
Room & Board: $9060	**Freshman Class:** 3654 applied, 2666 accepted, 710 enrolled
SAT CR/M/W: 537/548/537 **ACT:** 24	**CEEB CODE:** 1099
Application Deadline: May 1	**VERY COMPETITIVE**

Capital University, established in 1830, is a private institution affiliated with the Evangelical Lutheran Church in America. Its undergraduate and graduate programs emphasize the liberal arts and sciences, music, and nursing along with professional studies such as business. There are 5 undergraduate schools and 3 graduate schools. In addition to regional accreditation, Capital has baccalaureate program accreditation with ACBSP, CSWE, NASM, NCATE, ABA, ACS, and CCNE. The 48-acre campus is in a suburban area 5 miles east of downtown Columbus. Including any residence halls, there are 24 buildings.

STUDENT LIFE: 90% of undergraduates are from Ohio. Others are from 38 states, 14 foreign countries, and Canada. 77% are White. 30% are Protestant; 20% Catholic; 14% claim no religious affiliation.

The average age of freshmen is 18; all undergraduates, 22. 24% do not continue beyond their first year; 59% remain to graduate. **Housing:** 1629 students can be accommodated in college housing, which includes coed dorms, on-campus apartments, and off-campus apartments. In addition, there are honors houses, special-interest floors, substance-free floors, Greek organization floors, and a self-governing unit. On-campus housing is guaranteed for all 4 years and is available on a lottery system for upperclassmen. 57% of students live on campus; of those, 50% remain on campus on weekends. All students may keep cars.

FACULTY/CLASSROOMS: 53% of faculty are male; 47% are female. 81% teach undergraduates. No introductory courses are taught by graduate students. The average class size in an introductory lecture is 30; in a laboratory is 12; and in a regular course is 17.

PROGRAMS OF STUDY: Capital confers B.A., B.M., B.S.N. and B.S.W. degrees. Master's and Doctoral degrees are also awarded. Bachelor's degrees are awarded in BIOLOGICAL SCIENCE (biochemistry and biology/biological science), BUSINESS (accounting and business administration and management), COMMUNICATIONS AND THE ARTS (art, communications, creative writing, dramatic arts, English, French, music, public relations, Spanish, speech/debate/rhetoric, and theatre studies), COMPUTER AND PHYSICAL SCIENCE (chemistry, computer science, and mathematics), EDUCATION (art education, athletic training, elementary education, middle school education, physical education, and secondary education), ENGINEERING AND ENVIRONMENTAL DESIGN (environmental science), HEALTH PROFESSIONS (art therapy, exercise science, nursing, predentistry, premedicine, and sports medicine), SOCIAL SCIENCE (behavioral science, criminal justice, economics, history, international relations, philosophy, physical fitness/movement, political science/government, prelaw, psychology, religion, social work, and sociology). Nursing, business, education have the largest enrollments.

ACTIVITIES: 3% of men belong to 5 local and 5 national fraternities; 3% of women belong to 6 local and 6 national sororities. There are 63 groups on campus, including art, band, cheerleading, choir, chorale, chorus, communications, dance, debate, drama, environmental, ethnic, gay, honors, international, jazz band, literary magazine, musical theater, newspaper, opera, orchestra, political, professional, radio and TV, religious, social, social service, student government, and symphony. Popular campus events include Symposium on Undergraduate Scholarship, Honors Convocation, Greek Week, Martin Luther King Jr. Day of Learning, and Kids and Sibs Weekend. **Sports:** There are 10 intercollegiate sports for men and 10 for women, and 9 intramural sports for men and 9 for women. Facilities include a 2500-seat football stadium, a 2400-seat gym, tennis courts, and weight and game rooms. The recreation center offers bowling, billiards, and other game facilities. **Graduates:** From July 1, 2013 to June 30, 2014, 606 bachelor's degrees were awarded. The most popular majors were nursing (18%), education (14%), and business (14%). 27 companies recruited on campus in 2013-2014. In an average class, 51% graduate in 4 years or less, 58% graduate in 5 years or less, and 59% graduate in 6 years or less. Of the 2013 graduating class, 20% were enrolled in graduate school within 6 months of graduation, and 69% were employed.

SERVICES: Counseling and information services are available, as is tutoring in most subjects. There is remedial math and writing. **Library/Resources:** The library contains 225,644 volumes, 148,096 microform items, 103,078 audio/video tapes/CDs/DVDs, and subscribes to 156,739 periodicals including electronic. Computerized library services include interlibrary loans, database searching, Internet access, and Wi-Fi capability. Special learning facilities include an art gallery, radio station, and TV station. **Physically Challenged Students:** All of the campus is accessible. Facilities include wheelchair ramps, elevators, special parking, specially equipped restrooms, and special housing. **Special:** Special academic programs include cross-registration with the Higher Education Council of Columbus, semester internships in most majors, and a Washington semester. Study abroad in 21 countries on 5 continents includes opportunities in Jamaica and at the Kodaly Institute of Music in Hungary. Also possible are a general studies degree and student-designed majors. A dual degree in engineering is offered with Case Western Reserve University and Washington University in St. Louis. Credit for life, military, and work experience may be granted, and nondegree study and pass/fail options are offered. There are 17 national honor societies and a freshman honors program. **Visiting:** There are regularly scheduled orientations for prospective students, including an interview with a counselor and a campus tour. There are guides for informal visits, visitors may sit in on classes, and stay overnight. To schedule a visit, contact the Admissions Office. **Campus Safety and Security:** Measures include 24-hour foot and vehicle patrol, emergency notification system, self-defense education, and security escort services. There are shuttle buses, emergency telephones, lighted pathways/sidewalks, and controlled access to dorms/residences.

REQUIREMENTS: The SAT or ACT is required. Admissions requirements include graduation from an accredited secondary school with 16 academic credits, including 4 units of English, 3 each of math, science, and social science, 2 units of a foreign language, and 1 of electives; nursing applicants need chemistry. The GED is accepted. High school students must submit recommendations from their guidance counselor. An interview is recommended. Students must audition for entry to the Conservatory of Music. A GPA of 2.6 is required. AP and CLEP credits are accepted. Important factors in the admissions decision are advanced placement or honors courses, recommendations by school officials, and evidence of special talent. To graduate, all students must complete at least 124 semester hours, with a varying number of hours in the major, and maintain a minimum 2.0 GPA. The university core, 36 semester hours, must be followed in an ordered sequence throughout the 4 years; considered an assessment program, it includes specific courses in reading and writing, communication, health, art, science, social science, the humanities, ethics, and religion. **Procedure:** Freshmen are admitted fall, spring, and summer. Entrance exams should be taken by December of the senior year. There are deferred admissions and rolling admissions plans. Applications should be filed by May 1 for fall entry, along with a $25 fee. Notifications are sent September 30. Applications are accepted on-line. **Transfer Students:** 75 transfer students enrolled in 2013-2014. Transfer students must have a minimum college GPA of 2.25. The SAT or ACT is recommended, as is an interview. 30 of 124 credits required for the bachelor's degree must be completed at Capital. **International Students:** There are 42 international students enrolled. The school actively recruits these students. They must take the TOEFL with a minimum score of 500 on the paper-based TOEFL (PBT) or 61 on the Internet-based version (iBT).

ADMISSIONS: 73% of the 2014-2015 applicants were accepted. The SAT scores for the 2014-2015 freshman class were: Critical Reading--32% below 500, 44% between 500 and 599, 19% between 600 and 699, and 5% between 700 and 800; Math--35% below 500, 38% between 500 and 599, 25% between 600 and 699, and 2% between 700 and 800; Writing--43% below 500, 40% between 500 and 599, 16% between 600 and 699, and 1% between 700 and 800. The ACT scores were 19% below 21, 25% between 21 and 23, 29% between 24 and 26, 12% between 27 and 28, and 15% above 28. 37% of the current freshmen were in the top fifth of their class; 67% were in the top two fifths. 13 freshmen graduated first in their class. **Admissions Contact:** Amanda Sohl, Director of Admission. E-Mail: *admission@ capital.edu* Web: *www.capital.edu*

FINANCIAL AID: In 2014-2015, 91% of all full-time freshmen and 93% of continuing full-time students received some form of financial aid. 76% of all full-time freshmen and 75% of continuing full-time students received need-based aid. The average freshman award was $25,942. 33% of undergraduate students work part-time. Average annual earnings from campus work are $3400. The average financial indebtedness of the 2014 graduate was $33,200. The FAFSA is required. The priority date for freshman financial aid applications for fall entry is February 28.

CASE WESTERN RESERVE UNIVERSITY   D-1
www.case.edu

Cleveland, OH 44106   (216) 368-4450
                                                                      n/av
Fax: (216) 368-5111   Email: admission@case.edu
Full-time: 2591 men, 2175 women   Faculty: 615; I, +$
Part-time: 73 men, 72 women   Ph.D.s: 91%
Graduate: 2727 men, 3133 women   Student/Faculty: 10 to 1
Year: semesters, summer session   Tuition: $43,158
Room & Board: $13,376   Freshman Class: 21733
                                             applied, 8326 accepted,
                                             1282 enrolled
SAT CR/M/W: 670/710/670 ACT: 31   CEEB CODE: 1105
Application Deadline: January 15   MOST COMPETITIVE

Case Western Reserve University, founded in 1826, is a private institution offering undergraduate, graduate, and professional programs in arts and sciences, dentistry, engineering, law, management, medicine, nursing, and social work. Figures in the above capsule and in this profile are approximate. There are 4 undergraduate schools and 8 graduate schools. In addition to regional accreditation, Case has baccalaureate program accreditation with AACSB, ABET, CSAB, NASM, NLN, and TEAC. The 185-acre campus is in an urban area 4 miles east of downtown Cleveland, OH. Including any residence halls, there are 183 buildings.

STUDENT LIFE: 59% of undergraduates are from out of state, mostly the Middle Atlantic. Students are from 48 states, 37 foreign countries, and Canada. 70% are from public schools. 53% are White; 19% Asian American. The average age of freshmen is 18; all undergraduates, 20. 7% do not continue beyond their first year; 81% remain to graduate. **Housing:** 4126 students can be accommodated in college housing, which includes coed dorms and on-campus apartments. In addition, there are special-interest houses, fraternity houses, sorority houses, Recovery house, and residential colleges for first year students. On-campus housing is guaranteed for the freshman year only, is available on a first-come, first-served basis, and is available on a lottery system for upperclassmen. 82% of students live on campus; of those, 82% remain on campus on weekends. All students may keep cars.

FACULTY/CLASSROOMS: 57% of faculty are male; 43% are female. 75% teach undergraduates, 95% do research, and 77% do both. Graduate students teach 6% of introductory courses. The average class size in an introductory lecture is 35; in a laboratory is 23; and in a regular course is 28.

PROGRAMS OF STUDY: Case confers B.A., B.S., B.S.E. B.S.Mgt., and B.S.N. degrees. Master's and Doctoral degrees are also awarded. Bachelor's degrees are awarded in BIOLOGICAL SCIENCE (biochemistry, biology/biological science, evolutionary biology, and nutrition), BUSINESS (accounting, business administration and management, finance, and marketing management), COMMUNICATIONS AND THE ARTS (art history and appreciation, classics, comparative literature, dance, dramatic arts, English, French, German, music, and Spanish), COMPUTER AND PHYSICAL SCIENCE (applied mathematics, astronomy, chemistry, chemistry / chemical biology, computer science, fluid and thermal science, geology, mathematics, natural sciences, physics, polymer science, and statistics), EDUCATION (art education, education, and music education), ENGINEERING AND ENVIRONMENTAL DESIGN (aeronautical engineering, architecture, biomedical engineering, chemical engineering, civil engineering, computer engineering, electrical/electronics engineering, engineering, engineering physics, environmental science, materials science, mechanical engineering, and systems engineering), HEALTH PROFESSIONS (nursing and speech pathology/audiology), SOCIAL SCIENCE (American studies, anthropology, Asian/Oriental studies, cognitive science, economics, French studies, German area studies, gerontology, history, history of science, international studies, Japanese studies, philosophy, political science/government, psychology, religion, sociology, systems science, and women's studies). Engineering, biology, management, and music are the strongest academically. Engineering, psychology, and biology have the largest enrollments.

ACTIVITIES: 33% of men belong to 17 national fraternities; 33% of women belong to 9 national sororities. There are 201 groups on campus, including symphonic winds ensemble and percussion ensemble, art, band, cheerleading, chess, choir, chorale, chorus, communications, computers, dance, debate, drama, environmental, ethnic, film, gay, honors, international, jazz band, literary magazine, marching band, musical theater, newspaper, orchestra, pep band, photography, political, professional, radio, religious, social, social service, student government, and symphony. Popular campus events include Hudson Relays, Relay-for-Life, Thwing Study Over and Springfest. **Sports:** There are 10 intercollegiate sports for men and 9 for women, and 30 intramural sports for men and 14 for women. Facilities include a gym with multipurpose courts and rock climbing wall, football and soccer fields, baseball/softball ballpark, indoor and all-weather tracks, softball diamonds, 2 swimming pools, weight, and wrestling rooms, basketball, badminton, volleyball, squash, tennis, and racquetball courts, a multipurpose aerobics room, cardio exercise room, rock climbing wall, and an archery range. **Graduates:** From July 1, 2013 to June 30, 2014, 898 bachelor's degrees were awarded. The most popular majors were biomedical engineering (10%), biology (9%), and psychology (7%). 205 companies recruited on campus in 2013-2014. In an average class, 2% graduate in 3 years or less, 64% graduate in 4 years or less, 78% graduate in 5 years or less, and 81% graduate in 6 years or less.

SERVICES: Counseling and information services are available, as is tutoring in every subject. There is a reader service for the blind. In addition, supplemental instruction is available in designated courses in biology, chemistry, math, and physics, and the writing resource center. **Library/Resources:** The 7 libraries contain 2.9 million volumes, 2.2 million microform items, 28,771 audio/video tapes/CDs/DVDs, and subscribe to 111,270 periodicals including electronic. Computerized library services include interlibrary loans, database searching, Internet access, and Wi-Fi capability. Special learning facilities include an art gallery, natural history museum, planetarium, a biology field station. **Physically Challenged Students:** 90% of the campus is accessible. Facilities include wheelchair ramps, elevators, special parking, specially equipped restrooms, special class scheduling, lowered drinking fountains, lowered telephones. TDD, special testing arrangements, note-taking assistance, individualized academic counseling and planning, adaptive equipment, interpreters, and access to audiotaped text materials. **Special:** Case offers co-op programs with nearly 200 employers, and students may alternate classroom study with full-time employment. Cross-registration with 13 institutions in the Cleveland area is available, as well as internships in government, corporations, and nonprofit agencies. Students may participate in study abroad, a Washington semester, work-study programs, and accelerated-degree programs. B.A.-B.S. degrees, dual and student-designed majors, 3-2 engineering degrees, non-degree study, independent study, and pass/fail options are possible. There are extensive opportunities for undergraduates to work with faculty on research projects. Pre-professional Scholars Programs in medicine, dental medicine, social work, and law are available. Interdisciplinary majors, such as environmental geology, and intradisciplinary majors, such as nutritional biochemistry and metabolism, are available. There are 8 national honor societies, including Phi Beta Kappa, and 16 departmental honors programs. **Visiting:** There are regularly scheduled orientations for prospective students. There are guides for informal visits, visitors may sit in on classes, and stay overnight. To schedule a visit, contact the Office of Undergraduate Admission. **Campus Safety and Security:** Measures include 24-hour foot and vehicle patrol, emergency notification system, self-defense education, and security escort services. There are shuttle buses, emergency telephones, lighted pathways/sidewalks, controlled access to dorms/residences, property crime prevention programs, bicycle lock rental, vehicle ID etching, and equipment bolting.

REQUIREMENTS: The SAT or ACT is required. The ACT Optional Writing test is also required. SAT Subject tests in writing plus 2 others of the student's choice are strongly recommended for students who take the SAT. Applicants must be graduates of an accredited secondary school. However, the GED is accepted. 16 high school academic credits are required, including 4 years of English, 3 of math, (4 for science, math, and engineering majors), and 2 of lab science (3 for science and math majors and premedical students). 2 to 4 years of foreign language are strongly recommended. Engineering, math, and science students should take the SAT: Subject tests in math I/IC of IIC and physics and/or chemistry. A writing sample of the student's choice is required, and an interview is recommended. AP credits are accepted. Important factors in the admissions decision are advanced placement or honors courses, leadership record, and recommendations by school officials. To graduate, students must complete a minimum of 120 semester hours, with at least 30 hours in the major, and maintain a minimum GPA of 2.0. Students must complete the SAGES (Seminar Approach to General Education and Scholarship) core curriculum and two semesters of physical education. **Procedure:** Freshmen are admitted fall, spring, and summer. Entrance exams should be taken by the fall of the senior year. There are early decision and deferred admissions plans. Early decision applications should be filed by November 1; regular applications, by January 15 for fall entry. Notification of early decision is sent December 15; regular decision, March 20. 4670 applicants were on the 2014 waiting list; 792 were admitted. Applications are accepted on-line. **Transfer Students:** 38 transfer students enrolled in 2013-2014. Transfer students should have a minimum GPA of 3.2 and meet all high school requirements. Grades of C or better transfer for credit. 60 of 120 credits required for the bachelor's degree must be completed at Case. **International Students:** There are 438 international students enrolled. The school actively recruits these students. They must take the TOEFL with a minimum score of 577 on the paper-based TOEFL (PBT) or 90 on the Internet-based version (iBT), or take the International English Language Testing System. They must also take the SAT or ACT.

ADMISSIONS: 38% of the 2014-2015 applicants were accepted. The SAT scores for the 2014-2015 freshman class were: Critical Reading--1% below 500, 11% between 500 and 599, 53% between 600 and 699, and 35% between 700 and 800; Math--7% between 500 and 599, 37% between 600 and 699, and 56% between 700 and 800; Writing--1% below 500, 17% between 500 and 599, 47% between 600 and 699, and 35% between 700 and 800. The ACT scores were 1% between 21 and 23, 8% between 24 and 26, 10% between 27 and 28, and 81% above 28. 88% of the current freshmen were in the top fifth of their class; 97% were in the top two fifths. 45 freshmen graduated first in their class. **Admissions Contact:** Robert McCullough, Director of Undergraduate Admissions. E-Mail: *admission@case.edu* Web: *www.case.edu*

FINANCIAL AID: Case is a member of CSS. The CSS/Profile, FAFSA, and the college's own financial statement are required. The priority date for freshman financial aid applications for fall entry is February 15.

CEDARVILLE UNIVERSITY   **B-4**
www.cedarville.edu

Cedarville, OH 45314

(937) 766-7700
(800) CEDARVILLE

Fax: (937) 766-2760   Email: admissions@cedarville.edu

Full-time: 1452 men, 1576 women	**Faculty:** 222
Part-time: 131 men, 148 women	**Ph.D.s:** 65%
Graduate: 100 men, 182 women	**Student/Faculty:** 13 to 1
Year: semesters, summer session	**Tuition:** $26,400
Room & Board: $6460	**Freshman Class:** 3005 applied, 2237 accepted, 787 enrolled
SAT CR/M/W: 590/590/570 **ACT:** 26	**CEEB CODE:** 1151
Application Deadline: open	**VERY COMPETITIVE**

Cedarville University, founded in 1887, is a private Baptist college of arts and sciences offering programs in engineering, nursing, accounting, computer information systems, and education. The school is known for its religious commitment, conservative values, and community outreach programs. There are 15 undergraduate schools and 4 graduate schools. In addition to regional accreditation, Cedarville has baccalaureate program accreditation with ABET, ACBSP, ACPE, CSWE, NASM, NCATE, NLN, CCNE, and CAAHEP. The 410-acre campus is in a small town 12 miles south of Springfield. Including any residence halls, there are 47 buildings.

STUDENT LIFE: 60% of undergraduates are from out of state, mostly the Midwest. Students are from 49 states, 33 foreign countries, and Canada. 50% are from public schools. 87% are White. 99% are Protestant. The average age of freshmen is 18; all undergraduates, 20. 12% do not continue beyond their first year; 70% remain to graduate. **Housing:** 2647 students can be accommodated in college housing, which includes single-sex dorms, on-campus apartments, and married student housing. On-campus housing is guaranteed for all 4 years. 78% of students live on campus; of those, 83% remain on campus on weekends. Alcohol is not permitted. All students may keep cars.

FACULTY/CLASSROOMS: 64% of faculty are male; 36% are female. 88% teach undergraduates. No introductory courses are taught by graduate students. The average class size in an introductory lecture is 22; in a laboratory is 22; and in a regular course is 22.

PROGRAMS OF STUDY: Cedarville confers B.A., B.S., B.M., B.M.E., B.S.E.E., B.S.M.E., B.S.N., B.S.Cp.E. and B.S.P.S. degrees. Master's and Doctoral degrees are also awarded. Bachelor's degrees are awarded in BIOLOGICAL SCIENCE (biology/biological science and molecular biology), BUSINESS (accounting, business administration and management, finance, management information systems, marketing/retailing/merchandising, and sports management), COMMUNICATIONS AND THE ARTS (broadcasting, church music, communications, English, graphic design, industrial design, information technology, journalism, keyboard - piano concentration, multimedia, music, music composition, Technical Communication, Spanish, technical and business writing, and theatre arts), COMPUTER AND PHYSICAL SCIENCE (chemistry, computer science, geology, geoscience, information sciences and systems, mathematics, and physics), EDUCATION (athletic training, Christian education, early childhood education, elementary education, English education, foreign languages education, mathematics education, middle school education, music education, physical education, science education, social studies education, and special education), ENGINEERING AND ENVIRONMENTAL DESIGN (computer engineering, electrical/electronics engineering, engineering, environmental science, and mechanical engineering), HEALTH PROFESSIONS (allied health, exercise science, nursing, and pharmacy), SOCIAL SCIENCE (American studies, applied psychology, biblical studies, criminal justice, forensic studies, history, international studies, liberal arts/general studies, missions, pastoral studies, philosophy, political science/government, prelaw, psychology, public administration, social work, sociology, and youth ministry). Nursing, mechanical engineering, and early childhood education have the largest enrollments.

ACTIVITIES: There are 116 groups on campus, including art, band, cheerleading, chess, choir, chorale, chorus, dance, debate, drama, environmental, ethnic, forensics, honors, international, jazz band, musical theater, newspaper, orchestra, pep band, photography, political, professional, radio and TV, religious, social, social service, student government, and yearbook. Popular campus events include Junior and Senior Banquet, Lil' Sibs Weekend, and Campus Christmas. **Sports:** There are 8 intercollegiate sports for men and 8 for women, and 24 intramural sports for men and 23 for women. Facilities include a 2500-seat gym, 5 volleyball and badminton courts, fitness center with 3 racquetball courts, climbing wall, an exercise studio, free weight room, Nautilus strength training areas and cardiovascular areas, field house with a 200-meter track, basketball, volleyball, tennis, and indoor soccer courts, indoor batting cages, training room, outdoor facilities including tennis and sand volleyball courts, a track, soccer, baseball, softball fields, golf driving range, and intramural sports playing fields. **Graduates:** From July 1, 2013 to June 30, 2014, 722 bachelor's degrees were awarded. The most popular majors were nursing (12%), mechanical engineering (5%), and early childhood education (5%). 318 companies recruited on campus in 2013-2014. In an average class, 4% graduate in 3 years or less, 58% graduate in 4 years or less, 69% graduate in 5 years or less, and 70% graduate in 6 years or less. Of the 2013 graduating class, 22% were enrolled in graduate school within 6 months of graduation, and 72% were employed.

SERVICES: Counseling and information services are available, as is tutoring in every subject. There is a reader service for the blind, and remedial math, reading, and writing. In addition to tutoring, we have academic peer coaches, tutoring labs, and mentors. **Library/Resources:** The library contains 239,169 volumes, 16,862 microform items, 9,254 audio/video tapes/CDs/DVDs, and subscribes to 9,094 periodicals including electronic. Computerized library services include interlibrary loans, database searching, Internet access, and Wi-Fi capability. Special learning facilities include a radio station, a media resource center, observatory, state-of-the-art simulation labs for nursing and pharmacy students. **Physically Challenged Students:** 90% of the campus is accessible. Facilities include wheelchair ramps, elevators, special parking, specially equipped restrooms, special class scheduling, lowered drinking fountains, lowered telephones, special housing. We provide academic accommodations for students with disabilities as per ADAA, which includes private room, extended time, scribe, reader, CART services, alternative texts, and more. **Special:** Internships, study abroad in 97 countries, a Washington semester, dual majors, student-designed majors, B.A.-B.S. degrees in biology, chemistry, and math, and work-study programs with the college are available. Cross-registration with the Southwest Ohio Consortium for Higher Education is possible. Cooperative Learning Agreement with the International Center for Creativity for the Industrial and Innovative Design major. There are 5 national honor societies, a freshman honors program, and 1 departmental honors programs. **Visiting:** There are regularly scheduled orientations for prospective students, including campus tours, chapel services, class visits, and meetings with faculty, coaches, and admissions counselors. There are guides for informal visits, visitors may sit in on classes, and stay overnight. To schedule a visit, contact the Admissions Office. **Campus Safety and Security:** Measures include 24-hour foot and vehicle patrol, emergency notification system, self-defense education, and security escort services. There are emergency telephones, lighted pathways/sidewalks, and controlled access to dorms/residences.

REQUIREMENTS: The SAT or ACT is required. The SAT or ACT is required, with scores above the national average preferred. The college recommends that applicants have 4 years of English, 3 to 4 of math, and 3 each of social studies, math, science, and a foreign language. The GED is accepted. Recommendation from a local pastor is required. An interview is recommended. Cedarville requires applicants to be in the upper 50% of their class. AP and CLEP credits are accepted. Important factors in the admissions decision are personality/intangible qualities, recommendations by school officials, and advanced placement or honors courses. To graduate, all students must maintain a minimum GPA of 2.0 while taking 128 semester hours, with a minimum of 32 in specific disciplines, 52 in core curriculum, and 36 in major. Specific courses required include English Composition, Fundamentals of Speech, Politics and American Culture, Introduction to Humanities, and Physical Activity and the Christian life. **Procedure:** Freshmen are admitted to all sessions. Entrance exams should be taken by late junior year or early senior year. There are early admissions, deferred admissions, and rolling admissions plans. Application deadlines are open. Application fee is $30. Applications are accepted on-line. **Transfer Students:** 78 transfer students enrolled in 2013-2014. Applicants must have a minimum college GPA of 3.0. The SAT or ACT (preferred) is strongly recommended. 32 of 128 credits required for the bachelor's degree must be completed at Cedarville. **International Students:** There are 50 international students enrolled. The school actively recruits these students. They must take the TOEFL with a minimum score of 80 on the Internet-based version (iBT). They must also take the SAT or ACT, scoring 22.

ADMISSIONS: 74% of the 2014-2015 applicants were accepted. The SAT scores for the 2014-2015 freshman class were: Critical Reading--11% below 500, 41% between 500 and 599, 37% between 600 and 699, and 11% between 700 and 800; Math--11% below 500, 39% between 500 and 599, 39% between 600 and 699, and 11% between 700 and 800; Writing--16% below 500, 46% between 500 and 599, 31% between 600 and 699, and 7% between 700 and 800. The ACT scores were 6% below 21, 20% between 21 and 23, 27% between 24 and 26, 20% between 27 and 28, and 27% above 28. 56% of the current freshmen were in the top fifth of their class; 81% were in the top two fifths. There were 1 National Merit finalists. 39 freshmen graduated first in their class. **Admissions Contact:** Roscoe Smith, Assoc VP for University Admissions. E-Mail: *admissions@cedarville.edu* Web: *www.cedarville.edu*

FINANCIAL AID: In 2014-2015, 99% of all full-time freshmen and 94% of continuing full-time students received some form of financial aid. 70% of all full-time freshmen and 63% of continuing full-time students received need-based aid. The average freshman award was $25,576. Need-based scholarships or need-based grants averaged $7,762 ($31,770 maximum); need-based self-help aid (loans and jobs) averaged $5,612 ($13,500 maximum); non-need-based athletic scholarships averaged $7,497 ($33,500 maximum); and other non-need-based awards and non-need-based scholarships averaged $19,268 ($37,772 maximum). 50% of undergraduate students work part-time. Average annual earnings from campus work are $1040. The average financial indebtedness of the 2014 graduate was $21,970. The FAFSA and the college's own financial statement are required. Check with the school for current application deadlines.

CENTRAL STATE UNIVERSITY

B-4

www.centralstate.edu

Wilberforce, OH 45384	(937) 376-6348
	(800) 388-CSU1
Fax: (937) 376-6648	Email: admissions@csu.ces.edu
Full-time: 565 men, 655 women	Faculty: n/av
Part-time: 60 men, 75 women	Ph.Ds: n/av
Graduate: 35 men, 60 women	Student/Faculty: n/av
Year: trimesters, summer session	Tuition: $6172 ($13,148)
Room & Board: $8984	Freshman Class: n/av
ACT: required	CEEB CODE: 1107
Application Deadline: see profile	COMPETITIVE

Central State University, founded in 1887, is a public institution offering programs in liberal arts, business, engineering, teacher preparation, and professional training. The figures in the above capsule and in this profile are approximate. There are 3 undergraduate schools and 1 graduate school. In addition to regional accreditation, Central State has baccalaureate program accreditation with ABET and NASM. The 60-acre campus is in a rural area 18 miles east of Dayton. Including any residence halls, there are 34 buildings.

STUDENT LIFE: 77% of undergraduates are from Ohio. Others are from 24 states and 2 foreign countries. 96% are African American. The average age of freshmen is 18; all undergraduates, 22. 42% do not continue beyond their first year; 23% remain to graduate.

FACULTY/CLASSROOMS: 77% of faculty are male; 23% are female. All teach undergraduates, and 75% teach and do research. No introductory courses are taught by graduate students. The average class size in an introductory lecture is 25, in a laboratory, 20, and in a regular course, 15.

PROGRAMS OF STUDY: Central State confers B.A., B.S., B.M., B.S.Ed., and B.S.M.E. degrees. Master's degrees are also awarded. Bachelor's degrees are awarded in BIOLOGICAL SCIENCE (biology/biological science), BUSINESS (accounting, banking and finance, business administration and management, and marketing/retailing/merchandising), COMMUNICATIONS AND THE ARTS (advertising, broadcasting, English, journalism, and music), COMPUTER AND PHYSICAL SCIENCE (chemistry, computer science, and mathematics), EDUCATION (art education, elementary education, health education, music education, physical education, secondary education, and special education), ENGINEERING AND ENVIRONMENTAL DESIGN (graphic arts technology and manufacturing engineering), SOCIAL SCIENCE (economics, history, political science/government, psychology, public administration, social work, sociology, and water resources). Communication, music, and education are the strongest academically. Business administration has the largest enrollment.

ACTIVITIES: 1% of men belong to 2 national fraternities; 1% of women belong to 2 national sororities. There are 30 groups on campus, including art, band, cheerleading, choir, chorale, chorus, communications, drama, drill team, ethnic, honors, jazz band, marching band, pep band, political, professional, radio and TV, religious, social, and student government. Popular campus events include Career Day and May Week.

SERVICES: Counseling and information services are available, as is tutoring in most subjects. **Library/Resources:** The library contains 179,241 volumes, 622,727 microform items, 500 audio/video tapes/

CDs/DVDs, and subscribes to 26,316 periodicals including electronic. Computerized library services include interlibrary loans and database searching. Special learning facilities include an art gallery, radio station, and the National Afro-American Museum and Cultural Center. **Physically Challenged Students:** All of the campus is accessible. Facilities include wheelchair ramps, elevators, special parking, specially equipped restrooms, lowered drinking fountains, and lowered telephones. **Special:** Central State offers co-op programs in all majors, cross-registration with 15 area colleges, study abroad in 3 countries, internships, on-campus work-study programs, and B.A.-B.S. degrees. There are a freshman honors program. **Visiting:** There are regularly scheduled orientations for prospective students. There are guides for informal visits and visitors may sit in on classes. To schedule a visit, contact the Admissions Office. **Campus Safety and Security:** Measures include 24-hour foot and vehicle patrol. There are lighted pathways/sidewalks.

REQUIREMENTS: The ACT is required; the SAT is accepted. Applicants must be graduates of an accredited secondary school. The GED is accepted. Students should have completed 4 years of high school English, 3 years each of math, science, and social studies, and 2 years of the same foreign language. Ohio applicants should have a GPA of 2.0 and a minimum ACT composite score of 15 or SAT score of 720. Criteria are higher for out-of-state applicants. A GPA of 2.0 is required. AP and CLEP credits are accepted.

FINANCIAL AID: The FAFSA and the college's own financial statement are required. Check with the school for current application deadlines.

CHANCELLOR UNIVERSITY   D-1
www.chancellor.edu

Cleveland, OH 44114	(216) 432-8992
	(888) 316-9377
Fax: (216) 696-6430	Email: cuadmissions@chancellor.edu
Full-time: 135 men, 450 women	Faculty: n/av
Part-time: 200 men, 340 women	Ph.D.s: 23%
Graduate: 55 men, 40 women	Student/Faculty: n/av
Year: semesters, summer session	Tuition: $12,500
Room & Board: n/app	Freshman Class: n/av
SAT or ACT: required	CEEB CODE: 1178
Application Deadline: open	**COMPETITIVE**

Chancellor University, founded in 1848, is a private institution offering undergraduate programs in business to commuting students. The figures in the above capsule and in this profile are approximate. The 2-acre campus is in an urban area in Cleveland. There is 1 building. **STUDENT LIFE:** 45% of students are African American; 42% white. The average age of all undergraduates is 26.

FACULTY/CLASSROOMS: 72% of faculty are male; 28% are female. All teach undergraduates. No introductory courses are taught by graduate students. The average class size in an introductory lecture is 11; in a laboratory, 16; and in a regular course, 11.

PROGRAMS OF STUDY: Chancellor confers B.S. degrees. Associates and master's degrees are also awarded. Bachelor's degrees are awarded in BUSINESS (accounting, business administration and management, marketing/retailing/merchandising, office supervision and management, real estate, retailing, and secretarial studies/office management), COMPUTER AND PHYSICAL SCIENCE (information sciences and systems), ENGINEERING AND ENVIRONMENTAL DESIGN (industrial administration/management), HEALTH PROFESSIONS (health care administration), SOCIAL SCIENCE (economics, paralegal studies, public administration, and social science).

ACTIVITIES: There are no fraternities or sororities. Groups on campus include chorale, student government, and yearbook.

SERVICES: Counseling and information services are available, as is tutoring in most subjects. There is a reader service for the blind, and remedial math, reading, and writing. **Library/Resources:** The library contains 13,250 volumes, 616 microform items, 471 audio/video tapes/CDs/DVDs, and subscribes to 140 periodicals including elec-

---

tronic. Computerized library services include interlibrary loans and database searching. Special learning facilities include a **Physically Challenged Students:** All of the campus is accessible. Facilities include wheelchair ramps, elevators, specially equipped restrooms, special class scheduling, lowered drinking fountains, and lowered telephones. **Special:** The external degree program enables working adults to earn a bachelor's degree in a nontraditional manner, including credit by exam and credit for life/work experience. Work-study programs, co-op programs in 7 majors, internships, dual majors, pass/fail options, and cross-registration with other area colleges are offered. Evening and Saturday classes are also available. **Visiting:** There are guides for informal visits and visitors may sit in on classes. To schedule a visit, contact the Admissions Office. **Campus Safety and Security:**

REQUIREMENTS: The SAT or ACT is required for recent high school graduates. Applicants should have completed 19 Carnegie units, including 4 years of high school English, 3 each of math and science, and 2 each of social studies and history. The GED is accepted. An interview is recommended. AP and CLEP credits are accepted. Important factors in the admissions decision are ability to finance college education, advanced placement or honors courses, and recommendations by school officials.

FINANCIAL AID: Chancellor is a member of CSS. The FAFSA is required. Check with the school for current application deadlines.

CLEVELAND INSTITUTE OF ART *(The complete profile is made available exclusively on our website, www.barronspac.com)*

CLEVELAND INSTITUTE OF MUSIC *(The complete profile is made available exclusively on our website, www.barronspac.com)*

CLEVELAND STATE UNIVERSITY   D-1
www.csuohio.edu

Cleveland, OH 44115	(216) 523-7284
	1 (800) CSU-OHIO
Fax: (216) 687-9210	Email: admissions@csuohio.edu
Full-time: 4124 men, 4550 women	Faculty: 511; I, --$
Part-time: 1543 men, 1977 women	Ph.D.s: 84%
Graduate: 2168 men, 2939 women	Student/Faculty: 20 to 1
Year: semesters, summer session	Tuition: $9686 ($12,928)
Room & Board: $12,090	Freshman Class: 6191 applied, 4225 accepted, 1572 enrolled
SAT CR/M: 510/520 ACT: 22	CEEB CODE: 1221
Application Deadline: n/av	**COMPETITIVE**

Cleveland State University, founded in 1964, is a primarily commuter public institution offering undergraduate and graduate programs through the colleges of arts and sciences, business administration, education, engineering, law, urban affairs, and the school of nursing. There are 8 undergraduate schools and 8 graduate schools. In addition to regional accreditation, CSU has baccalaureate program accreditation with AACSB, ABET, CSWE, NCATE, NLN, CCNE, APA, and ASHA. The 85-acre campus is in an urban area in downtown Cleveland, Ohio. Including any residence halls, there are 48 buildings.

STUDENT LIFE: 91% of undergraduates are from Ohio. Others are from 33 states, 7 foreign countries, and Canada. 61% are White; 17% African American. The average age of freshmen is 23; all undergraduates, 25. 33% do not continue beyond their first year; 34% remain to graduate. **Housing:** 1186 students can be accommodated in college housing, which includes coed dorms, on-campus apartments, and off-campus apartments. Including law, quiet study, and first-year experience floors. On-campus housing is available on a first-come and first-served basis. 92% of students commute. All students may keep cars.

FACULTY/CLASSROOMS: 53% of faculty are male; 47% are female. No introductory courses are taught by graduate students.

PROGRAMS OF STUDY: CSU confers B.A., B.S., B.B.A., B.C.E., B.Ch.E., B.E.E., B.M., B.M.E., B.S.C.I.S., B.S.Ed., B.S.I.E., B.S.N. and

B.S.T. degrees. Master's and Doctoral degrees are also awarded. Bachelor's degrees are awarded in BIOLOGICAL SCIENCE (biology/biological science), BUSINESS (accounting, business economics, finance, labor studies, management information systems, management science, and marketing/retailing/merchandising), COMMUNICATIONS AND THE ARTS (art, communications, dramatic arts, English, film, television and digital media, French, linguistics, music, and Spanish), COMPUTER AND PHYSICAL SCIENCE (chemistry, computer science, geology, information sciences and systems, mathematics, and physics), EDUCATION (early childhood education, elementary education, health education, physical education, secondary education, and special education), ENGINEERING AND ENVIRONMENTAL DESIGN (chemical engineering, civil engineering, electrical/electronics engineering, electrical/electronics engineering technology, environmental science, mechanical engineering, and mechanical engineering technology), HEALTH PROFESSIONS (exercise science, health science, medical technology, nursing, occupational therapy, pharmaceutical science, physical therapy, premedicine, speech pathology/audiology, and speech therapy), SOCIAL SCIENCE (anthropology, classical/ancient civilization, criminology, economics, history, international relations, liberal arts/general studies, philosophy, political science/government, psychology, religion, social science, social studies, social work, sociology, urban studies, and women's studies). Business, communications, and psychology have the largest enrollments.

ACTIVITIES: 1% of men belong to 6 local and 4 national fraternities; 1% of women belong to 3 local and 7 national sororities. There are 234 groups on campus, including art, cheerleading, chess, choir, chorale, chorus, computers, dance, drama, environmental, ethnic, film, gay, honors, international, jazz band, literary magazine, musical theater, newspaper, opera, orchestra, pep band, photography, political, professional, radio and TV, religious, social, social service, student government, and symphony. Popular campus events include Weeks of Welcome, Homecoming, and Springfest. **Sports:** There are 7 intercollegiate sports for men and 9 for women, and 5 intramural sports for men and 5 for women. Facilities include a new recreation center, complete with a gym, gymnastics and weight rooms, dance studio, swimming pool, fitness trail, an indoor track, handball and squash courts, 2500-seat soccer stadium, and a convocation center. **Graduates:** From July 1, 2013 to June 30, 2014, 2219 bachelor's degrees were awarded. The most popular majors were business (18%), health professions/related (10%), and psychology (10%). 50 companies recruited on campus in 2013-2014. In an average class, 8% graduate in 4 years or less, 23% graduate in 5 years or less, and 32% graduate in 6 years or less.

SERVICES: Counseling and information services are available, as is tutoring in most subjects. There is a reader service for the blind, and remedial math, reading, and writing. **Library/Resources:** The 2 libraries contain 1.3 million volumes, 225,046 microform items, 38,974 audio/video tapes/CDs/DVDs, and subscribe to 11,364 periodicals including electronic. Computerized library services include interlibrary loans, database searching, Internet access, and Wi-Fi capability. Special learning facilities include an art gallery and radio station. **Physically Challenged Students:** All of the campus is accessible. Facilities include wheelchair ramps, elevators, special parking, specially equipped restrooms, lowered drinking fountains, and special housing. **Special:** CSU offers a developmental program for Ohio students not qualified for regular freshman admission. There are also cooperative education programs, nondegree study, work-study programs, accelerated degree programs, internships, pass/fail options, and cross-registration at other Cleveland area colleges. Student-designed and dual majors, study abroad in 10 countries, and volunteer opportunities are available, as well as a combined liberal arts and engineering degree and a 3-2 engineering degree. There are 6 national honor societies, a freshman honors program, and 38 departmental honors programs. **Visiting:** There are regularly scheduled orientations for prospective students, Including general visitation days for the university (in the fall) and each of the colleges (in the spring). There are guides for informal visits, visitors may sit in on classes, and stay overnight. To schedule a visit, contact the Office of Undergraduate Admissions. **Campus Safety and Security:** Measures include 24-hour foot and vehicle patrol, emergency notification system, and security escort services. There are emergency telephones, lighted pathways/sidewalks, A campus watch organization for faculty and staff.

REQUIREMENTS: The SAT or ACT is required. In addition, a high school diploma is required or the GED is accepted. Students should have completed the following academic credits: 4 years of English, 3 of math, social studies, and science (1 must be a lab), and 2 of a foreign language. A general college-preparatory program is recommended. A GPA of 2.3 is required. AP and CLEP credits are accepted.Students must complete at least 120 semester hours with a minimum 2.0 GPA for graduation. Requirements include a core curriculum containing courses in English composition, arts and humanities, social science, natural sciences, math and logic, non-Western culture and civilization, Western culture and civilization, and human diversity and the African American experience. **Procedure:** Freshmen are admitted to all sessions. Entrance exams should be taken prior to application. There are deferred admissions and rolling admissions plans. Check with the school for current application deadlines. The application fee is $30. Notification is sent on a rolling basis. Applications are accepted on-line. **Transfer Students:** 7128 transfer students enrolled in 2013-2014. Applicants must have a minimum GPA of 2.0 and submit previous college transcripts. Transfer students entering with fewer than 24 semester hours must submit official high school transcripts and test scores if they have been out of high school less than 5 years. 30 of 120 credits required for the bachelor's degree must be completed at CSU. **International Students:** There are 534 international students enrolled. They must take the TOEFL with a minimum score of 525 on the paper-based TOEFL (PBT) or 65 on the Internet-based version (iBT).

ADMISSIONS: 68% of the 2014-2015 applicants were accepted. The SAT scores for the 2014-2015 freshman class were: Critical Reading--42% below 500, 34% between 500 and 599, 21% between 600 and 699, and 3% between 700 and 800; Math--42% below 500, 36% between 500 and 599, 17% between 600 and 699, and 5% between 700 and 800. The ACT scores were 39% below 21, 29% between 21 and 23, 20% between 24 and 26, 7% between 27 and 28, and 5% above 28. **Admissions Contact:** Rob Spademan, Interim Director, Undergrad. Admissions. E-Mail: *admissions@csuohio.edu* Web: *http://www.engagecsu.com/*

FINANCIAL AID: In 2014-2015, 72% of all full-time freshmen and 75% of continuing full-time students received some form of financial aid. 60% of all full-time freshmen and 58% of continuing full-time students received need-based aid. The average freshman award was $9,168. Need-based scholarships or need-based grants averaged $6,904; need-based self-help aid (loans and jobs) averaged $4,329; non-need-based athletic scholarships averaged $11,488; and other non-need-based awards and non-need-based scholarships averaged $4,430. The FAFSA is required. The priority date for freshman financial aid applications for fall entry is February 15.

COLLEGE OF MOUNT SAINT JOSEPH A-5
www.msj.edu

Cincinnati, OH 45233	**(513) 244-4531**
	(800) 654-9314
Fax: (513) 244-4851	Email: admission@mail.msj.edu
Full-time: 548 men, 675 women	Faculty: IIA, --$
Part-time: 114 men, 458 women	Ph.D.s: 71%
Graduate: 136 men, 395 women	Student/Faculty: 11 to 1
Year: semesters, summer session	Tuition: $25,800
Room & Board: $8080	Freshman Class: 1180 applied, 1036 accepted, 321 enrolled
SAT CR/M: 475/468 ACT: 22	CEEB CODE: 1129
Application Deadline: n/av	COMPETITIVE

The College of Mount St. Joseph, founded in 1920, is a private Catholic college offering 34 undergraduate and 5 graduate degree programs. Figures in the above capsule and in this profile are approximate. There is graduate school. In addition to regional accreditation, the Mount has baccalaureate program accreditation with CSWE, NASM, NLN, TEAC, ABA, ACS, and CAPTE. The 92-acre campus is in a suburban area 7 miles west of downtown Cincinnati. Including any residence halls, there are 9 buildings.

STUDENT LIFE: 85% of undergraduates are from Ohio. Others are from 25 states, and 4 foreign countries. 68% are from public schools. 76% are White. The average age of freshmen is 19; all undergraduates, 26. 31% do not continue beyond their first year; 69% remain to graduate. **Housing:** 537 students can be accommodated in college housing, which includes coed dorms. On-campus housing is guaranteed for all 4 years. 79% of students commute. All students may keep cars.

FACULTY/CLASSROOMS: 36% of faculty are male; 65% are female. No introductory courses are taught by graduate students. The average class size in an introductory lecture is 23; in a laboratory is 19; and in a regular course is 19.

PROGRAMS OF STUDY: the Mount confers B.A., B.S., B.F.A. and B.S.N. degrees. Associate, Master's, and Doctoral degrees are also awarded. Bachelor's degrees are awarded in BIOLOGICAL SCIENCE (biochemistry, biology/biological science, and neurosciences), BUSINESS (accounting, business administration and management, organizational leadership and management, and sports management), COMMUNICATIONS AND THE ARTS (art history, art, communications, English, fine arts, graphic design, and music), COMPUTER AND PHYSICAL SCIENCE (chemistry and mathematics), EDUCATION (art education, athletic training, early childhood education, elementary education, general studies, health information management, middle school education, and special education), HEALTH PROFESSIONS (nursing), SOCIAL SCIENCE (criminology, history, liberal arts/general studies, paralegal studies, psychology, religion, religious education, social work, and sociology). Nursing, business administration, and sport management are the strongest academically. Business administration, nursing, and graphic design have the largest enrollments.

ACTIVITIES: There are no fraternities or sororities. There are 46 groups on campus, including art, band, cheerleading, choir, chorale, chorus, computers, dance, departmental clubs, drama, ethnic, gay, honors, international, jazz band, literary magazine, marching band, musical theater, newspaper, orchestra, pep band, photography, professional, religious, social, social service, and student government. Popular campus events include MLK Luncheon, Spring Formal, Homecoming Pep Rally, and Little Sibs Weekend. **Sports:** There are 10 intercollegiate sports for men and 9 for women, and 7 intramural sports for men and 7 for women. Facilities include a sports complex and field for football, soccer, lacrosse, and track and field with an 8-lane track and athletic training facilities. The student center houses 2 gyms used for basketball, volleyball, and wrestling and includes a running track, handball/racquetball courts, a fitness center, an athletic training center, and a wellness center. Facilities also include tennis courts, a softball field, and practice fields for soccer, lacrosse, and baseball. **Graduates:** From July 1, 2013 to June 30, 2014, 380 bachelor's degrees were awarded. The most popular majors were nursing (23%), general studies (9%), and business administration (8%). 75 companies recruited on campus in 2013-2014. In an average class, 57% graduate in 6 years or less. Of the 2013 graduating class, 17% were enrolled in graduate school within 6 months of graduation, and 82% were employed.

SERVICES: Counseling and information services are available, as is tutoring in every subject. There is remedial math and writing. Peer tutoring, services to students with learning disabilities, and math and writing centers are also available. **Library/Resources:** The library contains 95,428 volumes, 340,000 microform items, 4,149 audio/video tapes/CDs/DVDs, and subscribes to 3,906 periodicals including electronic. Computerized library services include interlibrary loans, database searching, Internet access, and Wi-Fi capability. Special learning facilities include an art gallery. **Physically Challenged Students:** 95% of the campus is accessible. Facilities include wheelchair ramps, elevators, special parking, specially equipped restrooms, special class scheduling, lowered drinking fountains, lowered telephones, special housing. Special door openings for wheelchair access, and a chairlift between levels where the science building and classroom building meet. **Special:** The college offers co-op programs in all majors, cross-registration with the Greater Cincinnati Consortium of Colleges and Universities, internships, credit for experiential learning, and study abroad in 3 countries. Also available are work-study programs, accelerated degree programs in 11 majors, dual majors, cultural immersion courses in the United States and abroad, a dual enrollment program (for transfer students), service learning, and off-

campus study for RNs in area hospitals. The Mount also has a program for students with learning disabilities (Project EXCEL). There are 14 national honor societies, a freshman honors program, and 13 departmental honors programs. **Visiting:** There are regularly scheduled orientations for prospective students, including a meeting with an admissions counselor, a student-guided tour, a visit to financial aid, and a meeting with a faculty member and/or athletic coach, if requested. There are guides for informal visits, visitors may sit in on classes, and stay overnight. To schedule a visit, contact the Office of Admission. **Campus Safety and Security:** Measures include 24-hour foot and vehicle patrol, emergency notification system, and security escort services. There are emergency telephones, lighted pathways/sidewalks, crime prevention programs, assistance with vehicle trouble and first aid.

REQUIREMENTS: The SAT or ACT is required. The College of Mount St. Joseph conducts a comprehensive and individualized review of every candidate's credentials for admission including but not limited to the following: a college prep high school curriculum, strong GPA, standardized test scores, evidence of leadership, and extracurricular involvement. An ACT score at or above the national average is recommended. In addition, students' personal background, attributes, and individual life circumstances are taken into consideration. AP and CLEP credits are accepted.To graduate, students must complete a minimum of 120 credits with a minimum GPA of 2.0 overall and in the major. 46-49 core curriculum total hours are required. All students must take 12-15 credit hours on the common good, and 34 credit hours of a discipline-specific core, and a capstone synthesis reflection. **Procedure:** Freshmen are admitted to all sessions. There is a rolling admissions plan. Check with the school for current application deadlines. The application fee is $25. Notification is sent on a rolling basis. Applications are accepted on-line. **Transfer Students:** 97 transfer students enrolled in 2013-2014. Transfer students must have a college GPA of 2.0 or better in a minimum of 12 semester or 18 quarter hours. All college hours must be presented. 30 of 120 credits required for the bachelor's degree must be completed at the Mount. **International Students:** There are 4 international students enrolled. They must also take the SAT or ACT.

ADMISSIONS: 88% of the 2014-2015 applicants were accepted. The SAT scores for the 2014-2015 freshman class were: Critical Reading--62% below 500, 30% between 500 and 599, 7% between 600 and 699, and 1% between 700 and 800; Math--61% below 500, 30% between 500 and 599, 9% between 600 and 699, and % between 700 and 800. The ACT scores were 40% below 21, 29% between 21 and 23, 22% between 24 and 26, 6% between 27 and 28, and 3% above 28. 23% of the current freshmen were in the top fifth of their class; 51% were in the top two fifths. 3 freshmen graduated first in their class. **Admissions Contact:** Peggy Minnich, Director of Admission. E-Mail: *admission@mail.msj.edu* Web: *www.msj.edu*

FINANCIAL AID: In 2014-2015, 100% of all full-time freshmen and 98% of continuing full-time students received some form of financial aid. 84% of all full-time freshmen and 81% of continuing full-time students received need-based aid. The average freshman award was $20,218. Need-based scholarships or need-based grants averaged $16,336 ($32,485 maximum); need-based self-help aid (loans and jobs) averaged $4,969 ($7,000 maximum); and other non-need-based awards and non-need-based scholarships averaged $12,022 ($27,400 maximum). 16% of undergraduate students work part-time. The FAFSA is required. The priority date for freshman financial aid applications for fall entry is March 1.

COLLEGE OF WOOSTER   D-2
www.wooster.edu

Wooster, OH 44691   (330) 263-2322
     (800) 877-9905

Fax: (330) 263-2621	Email: admissions@wooster.edu
Full-time: 865 men, 955 women	Faculty: n/av; IIB, -$
Part-time: 10 men, 10 women	Ph.D.s: 91%
Graduate: n/av	Student/Faculty: n/av
Year: semesters, summer session	Tuition: $38,790
Room & Board: $9810	Freshman Class: n/av
SAT or ACT: required	CEEB CODE: 1134
Application Deadline: see profile	**VERY COMPETITIVE**

The College of Wooster, founded in 1866, is a private liberal arts college. The figures in the above capsule and in this profile are approximate. In addition to regional accreditation, Wooster has baccalaureate program accreditation with NASM. The 240-acre campus is in a suburban area 55 miles southwest of Cleveland. Including any residence halls, there are 37 buildings.

STUDENT LIFE: 52% of undergraduates are from Ohio. Others are from 44 states, 35 foreign countries, and Canada. 74% are from public schools. 76% are white. The average age of freshmen is 19; all undergraduates, 20. 12% do not continue beyond their first year; 68% remain to graduate.

FACULTY/CLASSROOMS: 55% of faculty are male; 45% are female. All teach and do research. The average class size in an introductory lecture is 15 and in a regular course is 20.

PROGRAMS OF STUDY: Wooster confers B.A., B.Mus., and B.Mus.Ed. degrees. Bachelor's degrees are awarded in BIOLOGICAL SCIENCE (biochemistry and biology/biological science), BUSINESS (business economics), COMMUNICATIONS AND THE ARTS (communications, comparative literature, dramatic arts, English, fine arts, French, German, Greek (classical), Latin, music, and Spanish), COMPUTER AND PHYSICAL SCIENCE (chemistry, computer science, geology, mathematics, and physics), SOCIAL SCIENCE (African American studies, anthropology, archeology, area studies, economics, history, interdisciplinary studies, international relations, philosophy, political science/government, psychology, religion, Russian and Slavic studies, sociology, urban studies, and women's studies). Chemistry, history, and English are the strongest academically. History, English, and sociology have the largest enrollments.

ACTIVITIES: 10% of men belong to 3 local fraternities; 17% of women belong to 6 local sororities. There are 11 groups on campus, including art, bagpipe, band, cheerleading, chess, choir, chorale, chorus, dance, debate, drama, ethnic, film, forensics, gay, honors, international, jazz band, literary magazine, marching band, musical theater, newspaper, orchestra, pep band, photography, political, religious, social service, student government, symphony, and yearbook. Popular campus events include Party on the Green, Winter Gala, and Scot Spirit Day.

SERVICES: Counseling and information services are available, as is tutoring in every subject. There is a reader service for the blind, and remedial math, reading, and writing. **Library/Resources:** The 3 libraries contain 622,672 volumes, 210,094 microform items, 24,149 audio/video tapes/CDs/DVDs, and subscribe to 6,696 periodicals including electronic. Computerized library services include interlibrary loans and database searching. Special learning facilities include an art gallery. **Physically Challenged Students:** 95% of the campus is accessible. Facilities include wheelchair ramps, elevators, special parking, specially equipped restrooms, special class scheduling, and lowered drinking fountains. **Special:** A 3-2 engineering degree is offered in conjunction with Case Western Reserve and Washington Universities. A B.A.-B.S. degree is offered in music/music education. Cross-registration is possible with off-campus programs of the Great Lakes Colleges Association. Internships are available in American politics in Washington, D.C., the Ohio State Legislature, and the U.S. State Department, as well as in professional theater and economics. Student-designed majors, dual majors, study abroad in 50 countries, a Washington semester, accelerated degree programs, nondegree study, and pass/fail options for a limited number of courses are available. All seniors participate in a 2-term independent-study project in the major. The student chooses the topic and works on a one-to-one basis with a faculty mentor. A sophomore research program is available by application. There are 12 national honor societies, including Phi Beta Kappa. **Visiting:** There are regularly scheduled orientations for prospective students, including an interview, tour, class visits, and meetings with faculty and coaches. There are guides for informal visits, visitors may sit in on classes, and stay overnight. To schedule a visit, contact the Admissions Office. **Campus Safety and Security:** Measures include 24-hour foot and vehicle patrol and security escort services. There are emergency telephones and lighted pathways/sidewalks.

REQUIREMENTS: The SAT or ACT is required. In addition, applicants should be graduates of an accredited secondary school. The GED is accepted. Students should have completed a minimum of 17 high school academic credits. The school also requires an essay and recommends an interview. AP credits are accepted. Important factors in the admissions decision are advanced placement or honors courses, recommendations by school officials, and leadership record.

FINANCIAL AID: Wooster is a member of CSS. The CSS/Profile, FAFSA, and the college's own financial statement are required. Check with the school for current application deadlines.

COLUMBUS COLLEGE OF ART AND DESIGN (*The complete profile is made available exclusively on our website, www.barronspac.com*)

DEFIANCE COLLEGE	A-2
www.defiance.edu	

Defiance, OH 43512	(419) 783-2365
	(800) 520-GODC
Fax: (419) 783-2468	Email: admissions@defiance.edu
Full-time: 410 men, 355 women	Faculty: n/av; IIB, --$
Part-time: 60 men, 150 women	Ph.D.s: 60%
Graduate: 40 men, 80 women	Student/Faculty: n/av
Year: semesters, summer session	Tuition: $25,800
Room & Board: $8950	Freshman Class: n/av
SAT or ACT: required	CEEB CODE: 1162
Application Deadline: open	COMPETITIVE

Defiance College is an independent, coeducational institution affiliated with the United Church of Christ and home to the McMaster School for Advancing Humanity. The figures in the above capsule and in this profile are approximate. There is 1 graduate school. In addition to regional accreditation, Defiance has baccalaureate program accreditation with CSWE and NCATE. The 150-acre campus is in a small town 55 miles southwest of Toledo and 50 miles east of Fort Wayne. Including any residence halls, there are 24 buildings.

STUDENT LIFE: 85% of undergraduates are from Ohio. Others are from 15 states and 3 foreign countries. 97% are from public schools. 86% are white. 23% are Protestant; 23% claim no religious affiliation; 15% Catholic. The average age of freshmen is 18. 32% do not continue beyond their first year; 50% remain to graduate.

FACULTY/CLASSROOMS: 61% of faculty are male; 39% are female. All teach undergraduates, and 30% both teach and do research. No introductory courses are taught by graduate students. The average class size in an introductory lecture is 22; in a laboratory, 18; and in a regular course, 16.

PROGRAMS OF STUDY: Defiance confers B.A. and B.S. degrees. Associate and master's degrees are also awarded. Bachelor's degrees are awarded in BIOLOGICAL SCIENCE (biology/biological science and ecology), BUSINESS (accounting, banking and finance, business administration and management, human resources, management science, marketing/retailing/merchandising, organizational leadership and management, and sports management), COMMUNICATIONS AND THE ARTS (art, communications, and graphic design), COMPUTER AND PHYSICAL SCIENCE (information sciences and systems and mathematics), EDUCATION (art education, athletic training, Christian education, early childhood education, elementary education, health education, mathematics education, physical education, reading education, science education, secondary education, and social studies education), ENGINEERING AND ENVIRONMENTAL DESIGN (environmental science), HEALTH PROFESSIONS (medical laboratory technology and nursing), SOCIAL SCIENCE (criminal justice, forensic studies, history, humanities, international studies, physical fitness/movement, psychology, religion, and social work). Education and sciences are the strongest academically. Business, forensic sciences, and education have the largest enrollments.

ACTIVITIES: 6% of men belong to 1 national fraternity; 6% of women belong to 2 national sororities. There are 33 groups on campus, including academic, art, band, choir, chorale, chorus, dance, drama, ethnic, gay, honors, international, literary magazine, musical theater, newspaper, pep band, political, professional, religious, social, social service, student government, and yearbook. Popular campus events include Freshman Service Day, Arts on the Quad, and Thanksgiving Dinner.

SERVICES: Counseling and information services are available, as is

tutoring in every subject. There is a reader service for the blind. **Library/Resources:** The library contains 182,812 volumes, 7,387 microform items, 3,336 audio/video tapes/CDs/DVDs, and subscribes to 7,673 periodicals including electronic. Computerized library services include interlibrary loans, database searching, Internet access, and Wi-Fi capability. Special learning facilities include an art gallery, Thoreau Wildlife Sanctuary, a greenhouse, and a learning commons. **Physically Challenged Students:** 80% of the campus is accessible. Facilities include wheelchair ramps, elevators, special parking, specially equipped restrooms, special class scheduling, lowered drinking fountains, and lowered telephones. **Special:** Co-op programs and internships are available in all majors, as are B.A.-B.S. degrees and dual majors. Work study and student-designed majors are also available. The McMaster School for Advancing Humanity allows students and faculty to more closely examine global issues and how they affect the human condition. There are 1 national honor societies, a freshman honors program, and 4 departmental honors programs. **Visiting:** There are regularly scheduled orientations for prospective students, including admissions, financial aid, and special interest sessions, a campus tour, complimentary lunch, meetings with faculty, and observing a class in session. Interested applicants can meet with a coach. There are guides for informal visits, visitors may sit in on classes, and stay overnight. To schedule a visit, contact the Office of Admission. **Campus Safety and Security:** Measures include emergency notification system and security escort services. There are lighted pathways/sidewalks, nighttime security guards in residence halls, security cameras in residence hall entrances, and a security guard on the grounds from dusk to dawn.

REQUIREMENTS: The ACT is required. The SAT is recommended. Applicants should be graduates of an accredited secondary school or have a GED, with 15 Carnegie units completed, including 4 in English, 3 each in math, science, and social studies, and 2 in foreign language. An essay and an interview are recommended. A GPA of 2.3 is required. AP and CLEP credits are accepted. Important factors in the admissions decision are personality/intangible qualities, advanced placement or honors courses, and leadership record.

FINANCIAL AID: The FAFSA and the college's own financial statement are required. Check with the school for current application deadlines.

DENISON UNIVERSITY   **C-3**
www.denison.edu

Granville, OH 43023	(740) 587-6276
	(800) DENISON
Fax: (740) 587-6306	Email: admissions@denison.edu
Full-time: 971 men, 1334 women	Faculty: 230; IIB, av$
Part-time: 11 men, 20 women	Ph.D.s: 99%
Graduate: n/av	Student/Faculty: 10 to 1
Year: semesters	Tuition: $43,910
Room & Board: $10,760	Freshman Class: 4757 applied, 2355 accepted, 629 enrolled
SAT CR/M: 647/639 ACT: 29	CEEB CODE: 1164
Application Deadline: January 15	HIGHLY COMPETITIVE+

Denison University, founded in 1831, is a private independent institution of liberal arts and sciences. The 900-acre campus is in a small town 25 miles east of Columbus. Including any residence halls, there are 62 buildings.

STUDENT LIFE: 70% of undergraduates are from out of state, mostly the Mid-West. Students are from 48 states, 29 foreign countries, and Canada. 70% are from public schools. 71% are White. 36% are Protestant; 30% Catholic; 28% Muslim, Hindu, Buddhist, and Nondenominational. The average age of freshmen is 19; all undergraduates, 21. 8% do not continue beyond their first year; 80% remain to graduate.

FACULTY/CLASSROOMS: 55% of faculty are male; 45% are female. All teach and do research. No introductory courses are taught by graduate students. The average class size in an introductory lecture is 18; in a laboratory is 21; and in a regular course is 20.

PROGRAMS OF STUDY: Denison confers B.A., B.F.A. and B.S.

degrees. Bachelor's degrees are awarded in AGRICULTURE (environmental studies), BIOLOGICAL SCIENCE (biochemistry and biology/biological science), COMMUNICATIONS AND THE ARTS (art history and appreciation, communications, dance, dramatic arts, English, film arts, fine arts, French, German, languages, Latin, media arts, music, Spanish, speech/debate/rhetoric, and studio art), COMPUTER AND PHYSICAL SCIENCE (chemistry, computer science, geology, mathematics, and physics), EDUCATION (education and physical education), SOCIAL SCIENCE (African American studies, anthropology, classical/ancient civilization, East Asian studies, economics, history, international studies, Latin American studies, philosophy, political science/government, psychology, religion, sociology, Western European studies, and women's studies). Psychology, biology, and sociology/anthropology are the strongest academically. Communication, biology, psychology and economics have the largest enrollments.

ACTIVITIES: 35% of men belong to 10 national fraternities; 41% of women belong to 8 national sororities. There are 180 groups on campus, including art, cheerleading, choir, chorale, chorus, communications, computers, dance, drama, ethnic, film, gay, honors, international, jazz band, literary magazine, musical theater, newspaper, orchestra, pep band, photography, political, professional, religious, social, social service, student government, and symphony. Popular campus events include Community Picnic and Fair, Gala, Academic Awards Convocation and Vail Series.

SERVICES: Counseling and information services are available, as is tutoring in most subjects. There is a reader service for the blind. A reading and writing center is available, as are study sessions for math, chemistry, and some languages, reduced course loads, special counselor services, note-taking services, oral tests, extended time for tests, untimed tests, talking books, tape recorders, and readers. **Library/ Resources:** The library contains 1.3 million volumes, 128,175 microform items, 37,365 audio/video tapes/CDs/DVDs, and subscribes to 21,805 periodicals including electronic. Computerized library services include interlibrary loans, database searching, Internet access, and Wi-Fi capability. Special learning facilities include an art gallery, planetarium, TV station, an observatory, a multimedia MIX lab, a field research station in a 350-acre biological reserve, a high-resolution spectrometer, economics computer labs, and a modern languages lab. **Physically Challenged Students:** 70% of the campus is accessible. Facilities include wheelchair ramps, elevators, special parking, specially equipped restrooms, special class scheduling, lowered drinking fountains, and lowered telephones. **Special:** Work-study programs, a Washington semester, study-abroad programs in more than 35 countries, student-designed majors, a dual major in education and various other majors, a philosophy, political science, and economics interdisciplinary major, and pass/fail options are available. A 3-2 engineering program is offered with Rensselaer Polytechnic Institute and Case Western Reserve, Columbia, and Washington Universities. A May-term internship is available at more than 200 U.S. locations. A B.A.-B.S. degree, accelerated degree programs, a media technology and arts interdisciplinary major, and nondegree study are possible. There are 15 national honor societies and including Phi Beta Kappa. **Visiting:** There are regularly scheduled orientations for prospective students, including orientation programs, class visits, tours, and interviews. There are guides for informal visits, visitors may sit in on classes, and stay overnight. To schedule a visit, contact the Admissions Office at (740) 587-6276. **Campus Safety and Security:** Measures include 24-hour foot and vehicle patrol, emergency notification system, self-defense education, and security escort services. There are emergency telephones, lighted pathways/sidewalks, Residence halls are locked 24 hours a day with entry through a card access system.

REQUIREMENTS: The SAT or ACT is recommended. Denison operates under a test optional admissions policy. Applicants should have completed 19 Carnegie units, including 4 each in English, math, and science, 3 in foreign language, 2 in social studies, and 1 each in history and academic electives. An essay is part of the application process. An interview is advised, and a portfolio or an audition is recommended for art and music majors, respectively. AP and CLEP credits are accepted. Important factors in the admissions decision are personality/intangible qualities, evidence of special talent, and advanced placement or honors courses.

ADMISSIONS: 50% of a recent year applicants were accepted. The

SAT scores for a recent year freshman class were: Critical Reading--3% below 500, 22% between 500 and 599, 44% between 600 and 699, and 31% between 700 and 800; Math--37% between 500 and 599, 42% between 600 and 699, and 21% between 700 and 800. The ACT scores were 1% below 21, 1% between 21 and 23, 13% between 24 and 26, 36% between 27 and 28, and 49% above 28. 83% of the current freshmen were in the top fifth of their class; 100% were in the top two fifths. There were 25 National Merit finalists. 15 freshmen graduated first in their class.

FINANCIAL AID: In a recent year, 97% of all full-time freshmen and 96% of continuing full-time students received some form of financial aid. 56% of all full-time freshmen and 52% of continuing full-time students received need-based aid. The average freshman award was $37,445. Need-based scholarships or need-based grants averaged $32,388; need-based self-help aid (loans and jobs) averaged $5,154; and other non-need-based awards and non-need-based scholarships averaged $23,165. 45% of undergraduate students work part-time. Average annual earnings from campus work are $2430. The average financial indebtedness of the 2013 graduate was $20,162. Denison is a member of CSS. The FAFSA is required. The deadline for filing freshman financial aid applications for fall entry is February 15.

FRANCISCAN UNIVERSITY OF STEUBENVILLE   E-3
www.franciscan.edu

Steubenville, OH 43952-1763	(740) 283-6226
	(800) 783-6220
Fax: (740) 284-5456	Email: admissions@franciscan.edu
Full-time: 765 men, 1140 women	Faculty: n/av; IIA, --$
Part-time: 65 men, 90 women	Ph.Ds: 71%
Graduate: 170 men, 245 women	Student/Faculty: n/av
Year: semesters, summer session	Tuition: $21,720
Room & Board: $7600	Freshman Class: n/av
SAT or ACT: required	CEEB CODE: 1133
Application Deadline: open	VERY COMPETITIVE

Franciscan University of Steubenville, founded in 1946 by the Franciscan Friars, is a private liberal arts institution committed to the Catholic Church and its renewal. The figures in the above capsule and in this profile are approximate. There are 7 graduate schools. In addition to regional accreditation, Franciscan University has baccalaureate program accreditation with CSWE and NLN. The 220-acre campus is in a small town 40 miles west of Pittsburgh. Including any residence halls, there are 25 buildings.

STUDENT LIFE: 78% of undergraduates are from out of state, mostly the Midwest. Others are from 50 states, 18 foreign countries, and Canada. 59% are from public schools. 86% are white. 97% are Catholic. The average age of freshmen is 19; all undergraduates, 21. 13% do not continue beyond their first year; 70% remain to graduate.

FACULTY/CLASSROOMS: 65% of faculty are male; 35% are female. 94% teach undergraduates. No introductory courses are taught by graduate students. The average class size in an introductory lecture is 28; in a laboratory, 15; and in a regular course, 21.

PROGRAMS OF STUDY: Franciscan University confers B.A., B.S., and B.S.N. degrees. Associates and master's degrees are also awarded. Bachelor's degrees are awarded in BIOLOGICAL SCIENCE (biology/biological science), BUSINESS (accounting and business administration and management), COMMUNICATIONS AND THE ARTS (classics, communications, dramatic arts, English, French, German, and Spanish), COMPUTER AND PHYSICAL SCIENCE (chemistry, computer science, information sciences and systems, and mathematics), EDUCATION (elementary education), HEALTH PROFESSIONS (mental health/human services and nursing), SOCIAL SCIENCE (anthropology, economics, history, humanities and social science, law, philosophy, political science/government, psychology, religious music, social work, sociology, and theological studies). Theology, catechesis, and nursing are the strongest academically and have the largest enrollments.

ACTIVITIES: There are no fraternities; there is 1 national sorority. There are 35 groups on campus, including choir, chorale, chorus, computers, drama, ethnic, honors, international, literary magazine, newspaper, orchestra, political, pro-life, professional, radio and TV, religious, social, social service, student government, and yearbook. Popular campus events include the Feast of St. Francis, Pro-Life Rally, and all-school Evangelism events.

SERVICES: Counseling and information services are available, as is tutoring in most subjects. There is a reader service for the blind, and remedial reading and writing. Tutoring and counseling are available for learning-disabled students. Tutoring is also available for students on academic probation. **Library/Resources:** The library contains 235,387 volumes, 250,968 microform items, 892 audio/video tapes/CDs/DVDs, and subscribes to 5,874 periodicals including electronic. Computerized library services include interlibrary loans, database searching, and Internet access. Special learning facilities include an art gallery and radio station. **Physically Challenged Students:** 80% of the campus is accessible. Facilities include wheelchair ramps, elevators, special parking, specially equipped restrooms, special class scheduling, lowered drinking fountains, lowered telephones. **Special:** Dual majors and internships for up to 6 credit hours are available in most majors. A humanities and Catholic culture major in Western tradition and minors in human life studies, film studies, Franciscan studies, and music are offered. Study abroad is offered through the university's course location in Gaming, Austria, where students spend a semester studying humanities as well as traveling through Europe. There are 5 national honor societies, a freshman honors program, and 25 departmental honors programs. **Visiting:** There are regularly scheduled orientations for prospective students, including tours, interviews with professors, admissions, and financial aid officers, and class scheduling. There are guides for informal visits, visitors may sit in on classes, and stay overnight. To schedule a visit, contact the Admissions Office. **Campus Safety and Security:** Measures include 24-hour foot and vehicle patrol, emergency notification system, self-defense education, and security escort services. There are shuttle buses, emergency telephones, lighted pathways/sidewalks, and controlled access to dorms/residences.

REQUIREMENTS: The SAT or ACT is required. Applicants should have completed 15 academic high school units, including 10 in 4 of the 5 following areas: English, foreign language, social science, math, and natural sciences. The GED is accepted. An essay is required and an interview is recommended. A GPA of 2.4 is required. AP and CLEP credits are accepted. Important factors in the admissions decision are advanced placement or honors courses, evidence of special talent, and leadership record.

FINANCIAL AID: The FAFSA is required. Check with the school for current application deadlines.

FRANKLIN UNIVERSITY *(The complete profile is made available exclusively on our website, www.barronspac.com)*

HEIDELBERG UNIVERSITY   C-2
www.heidelberg.edu

Tiffin, OH 44883-2434	(419) 448-2330
	n/av
Fax: (419) 448-2334	Email: adminfo@l.heidelberg.edu
Full-time: 630 men, 555 women	Faculty: n/av; IIB, --$
Part-time: 10 men, 25 women	Ph.Ds: 82%
Graduate: 65 men, 150 women	Student/Faculty: n/av
Year: semesters, summer session	Tuition: $28,500
Room & Board: $9208	Freshman Class: n/av
SAT or ACT: required	CEEB CODE: 1292
Application Deadline: see profile	COMPETITIVE

Heidelberg University was founded in 1850 by the German Reformed Church (now United Church of Christ) and is a private liberal arts institution offering undergraduate and graduate degrees. The figures in the above capsule and in this profile are approximate. There is 1 graduate school. In addition to regional accreditation, Heidelberg has baccalaureate program accreditation with NASM. The 120-acre campus is in a small town 50 miles south of Toledo. Including any residence halls, there are 27 buildings.

STUDENT LIFE: 90% of undergraduates are from Ohio. Others are from 27 states, 6 foreign countries, and Canada. 61% are from public schools. 84% are white. 61% are Protestant; 33% Catholic. The average age of freshmen is 18; all undergraduates, 23. 20% do not continue beyond their first year; 56% remain to graduate.

FACULTY/CLASSROOMS: 57% of faculty are male; 43% are female. 97% teach undergraduates. No introductory courses are taught by graduate students. The average class size in an introductory lecture is 20; in a laboratory, 15; and in a regular course, 15.

PROGRAMS OF STUDY: Heidelberg confers B.A., B.S., and B.Mus. degrees. Master's degrees are also awarded. Bachelor's degrees are awarded in BIOLOGICAL SCIENCE (biochemistry, biology/biological science, and environmental biology), BUSINESS (accounting, business administration and management, business economics, management science, and sports management), COMMUNICATIONS AND THE ARTS (communications, dramatic arts, English, German, music, public relations, and Spanish), COMPUTER AND PHYSICAL SCIENCE (chemistry, computer science, information sciences and systems, mathematics, and physics), EDUCATION (athletic training, elementary education, foreign languages education, middle school education, music education, physical education, science education, and secondary education), ENGINEERING AND ENVIRONMENTAL DESIGN (preengineering), HEALTH PROFESSIONS (predentistry and premedicine), SOCIAL SCIENCE (anthropology, criminal justice, economics, forensic studies, history, international studies, philosophy, political science/government, prelaw, psychology, public administration, religion, social science, and water resources). Business administration, education, and sciences are the strongest academically. Business administration, physical sciences, and education have the largest enrollments.

ACTIVITIES: 30% of men belong to 5 local fraternities; 36% of women belong to 4 local sororities. There are 73 groups on campus, including art, band, cheerleading, chess, choir, chorale, chorus, computers, dance, drama, drill team, environmental, ethnic, film, forensics, gay, honors, international, jazz band, literary magazine, musical theater, newspaper, opera, orchestra, pep band, political, professional, radio and TV, religious, social, social service, student government, symphony, and yearbook. Popular campus events include Greek Sing, Battle of the Bands, and T-Bridge.

SERVICES: Counseling and information services are available, as is tutoring in most subjects. There is remedial math and reading. **Library/Resources:** The library contains 260,055 volumes, 108,640 microform items, 8,300 audio/video tapes/CDs/DVDs, and subscribes to 829 periodicals including electronic. Computerized library services include interlibrary loans, database searching, Internet access, and Wi-Fi capability. Special learning facilities include a radio station, TV station, a media center, an anthropology museum, human cadaver lab, water quality lab, an archeology lab, a physiology lab, and a computer-assisted writing classroom. **Physically Challenged Students:** 20% of the campus is accessible. Facilities include wheelchair ramps, elevators, special parking, specially equipped restrooms, special class scheduling, and lowered drinking fountains. **Special:** Cross-registration with Terra Community College and North Central Community College and a 3-4 degree in osteopathic medicine with Lake Erie College of Osteopathic Medicine are offered. Study abroad is possible at the University of Heidelberg, Germany, Seville, Spain, and in Mexico, UK, and others. A Washington semester is available at American University. Dual majors in any combination, an honors program, credit for life experience, internships, and pass/fail options are possible. There are 10 national honor societies, a freshman honors program, and 15 departmental honors programs. **Visiting:** There are regularly scheduled orientations for prospective students, including coach and faculty sessions; academic overview, student panel, admissions; and financial aid presentations; a tour of the college; and lunch. There are guides for informal visits, visitors may sit in on classes, and stay overnight. To schedule a visit, contact the Office of Admission. **Campus Safety and Security:** Measures include 24-hour foot and vehicle patrol, emergency notification system, self-defense education, and security escort services. There are emergency telephones and lighted pathways/sidewalks.

REQUIREMENTS: The SAT or ACT is required. Applicants should have completed 22 high school academic credits, including 4 years each of English and social studies, 3 each of math and science, and 2 of a foreign language. An audition is required for music majors.

Recommendations and an interview are recommended. A GPA of 2.5 is required. AP and CLEP credits are accepted. Important factors in the admissions decision are recommendations by school officials, extracurricular activities record, and advanced placement or honors courses.

FINANCIAL AID: 98% of all full-time freshmen and 99% of continuing full-time students received some form of financial aid. 90% of all full-time freshmen and 61% of continuing full-time students received need-based aid. 65% of undergraduate students worked part-time. Average annual earnings from campus work were $850. The FAFSA is required. Check with the school for current application deadlines.

HIRAM COLLEGE — E-1
www.hiram.edu

Hiram, OH 44234	(330) 569-5169
	(800) 362-5280
Fax: (330) 569-5944	Email: admission@hiram.edu
Full-time: 560 men, 635 women	Faculty: n/av; IIB, --$
Part-time: 55 men, 125 women	Ph.D.s: 92%
Graduate: 10 men, 25 women	Student/Faculty: n/av
Year: see profile, summer session	Tuition: $28,500
Room & Board: $9960	Freshman Class: n/av
SAT or ACT: required	CEEB CODE: 1297
Application Deadline: open	VERY COMPETITIVE

Hiram College, founded in 1850, is a private, residential liberal arts and sciences institution. The figures in the above capsule and in this profile are approximate. In addition to regional accreditation, Hiram has baccalaureate program accreditation with NASM. The 110-acre campus is in a rural area 35 miles southeast of Cleveland. Including any residence halls, there are 39 buildings.

STUDENT LIFE: 75% of undergraduates are from Ohio. Others are from 33 states, 19 foreign countries, and Canada. 62% are white. The average age of freshmen is 18; all undergraduates, 20. 22% do not continue beyond their first year.

FACULTY/CLASSROOMS: 54% of faculty are male; 46% are female. All teach undergraduates. No introductory courses are taught by graduate students. The average class size in an introductory lecture is 19; in a laboratory, 11; and in a regular course, 13.

PROGRAMS OF STUDY: Hiram confers B.A., and B.S.N. degrees. Master's degrees are also awarded. Bachelor's degrees are awarded in BIOLOGICAL SCIENCE (biochemistry, biology/biological science, and neurosciences), BUSINESS (accounting and management science), COMMUNICATIONS AND THE ARTS (art, communications, creative writing, dramatic arts, English, French, music, Spanish, and studio art), COMPUTER AND PHYSICAL SCIENCE (chemistry, computer science, mathematics, and physics), EDUCATION (education), ENGINEERING AND ENVIRONMENTAL DESIGN (environmental science), HEALTH PROFESSIONS (biomedical science and nursing), SOCIAL SCIENCE (economics, history, philosophy, political science/government, psychology, religion, social studies, and sociology). Management, accounting, and biology have the largest enrollments.

ACTIVITIES: There are 90 groups on campus, including art, band, cheerleading, choir, chorale, chorus, computers, dance, drama, ethnic, gay, honors, international, jazz band, literary magazine, marching band, musical theater, newspaper, opera, orchestra, photography, political, professional, radio and TV, religious, social, social service, student government, and yearbook. Popular campus events include Campus Days, Springfest, and Madrigal Revels.

SERVICES: Counseling and information services are available, as is tutoring in every subject. There is a reader service for the blind. Note takers are available for most classes. **Library/Resources:** The library contains 506,792 volumes, 131 microform items, and 22,786 audio/video tapes/CDs/DVDs, and subscribes to 8,890 periodicals including electronic. Computerized library services include interlibrary loans, database searching, and Internet access. Special learning facilities include an art gallery, planetarium, radio station, a 260-acre biological field station, and a field station in the Upper Peninsula of Michigan. **Physically Challenged Students:** 55% of the campus is accessible. Facilities include wheelchair ramps, elevators, special parking, and specially equipped restrooms. **Special:** There is cross-registration through the Cleveland Commission on Higher Education and a 3-2 engineering program with Case Western Reserve and Washington Universities. There is a Washington semester and study abroad in many countries with courses taught by Hiram faculty. Double majors and individually arranged internships in all fields, student-designed majors, and pass/no credit options are possible. An accelerated degree program in biomedical humanities is possible. There are 6 national honor societies and including Phi Beta Kappa. **Visiting:** There are regularly scheduled orientations for prospective students, consisting of campus day visits and prospective student overnights while school is still in session. There are guides for informal visits, visitors may sit in on classes, and stay overnight. To schedule a visit, contact the Admissions Office. **Campus Safety and Security:** Measures include 24-hour foot and vehicle patrol, emergency notification system, self-defense education, and security escort services. There are emergency telephones and lighted pathways/sidewalks.

REQUIREMENTS: The SAT or ACT is required. In addition, applicants should have completed 16 academic units or the GED equivalent. An essay is required. A portfolio, audition, and interview are recommended. A GPA of 2.6 is required. AP and CLEP credits are accepted.

FINANCIAL AID: 94% of all full-time freshmen and 93% of continuing full-time students received some form of financial aid. 82% of all full-time students received need-based aid. Hiram is a member of CSS. The FAFSA is required. Check with the school for current application deadlines.

JOHN CARROLL UNIVERSITY   D-1
www.jcu.edu

| University Heights, OH 44118 | (216) 397-4294 |
| | (888) 335-6800 |

Fax: (216) 397-4981	Email: enrollment@jcu.edu
Full-time: 1587 men, 1433 women	Faculty: 188; IIA, av$
Part-time: 61 men, 44 women	Ph.D.s: 96%
Graduate: 174 men, 401 women	Student/Faculty: 13 to 1
Year: semesters, summer session	Tuition: $35,650
Room & Board: $10,500	Freshman Class: 3873 applied, 3211 accepted, 798 enrolled
SAT CR/M/W: 540/560/530 ACT: 24	CEEB CODE: 1342
Application Deadline: February 1	COMPETITIVE+

John Carroll is a private, coeducational, Jesuit Catholic university providing programs in the liberal arts, sciences, and business at the undergraduate and master's levels. As a Jesuit Catholic university, John Carroll inspires its students to excel in learning, leadership, and service in the region and in the world. Our unique size, structure, culture, and environment make us very successful at providing an outstanding education for our students and helping them become John Carroll graduates in four years. As evidence of that commitment John Carroll students who do not graduate after four years are eligible for full tuition scholarship consideration for their fifth year (view details on the website under Admission). There are 2 undergraduate schools and 2 graduate schools. In addition to regional accreditation, John Carroll has baccalaureate program accreditation with AACSB, NCATE, HLC, CACREP, and NASP. The 62-acre campus is in a suburban area in University Heights, Ohio, 10 miles east of Cleveland. Including any residence halls, there are 21 buildings.

STUDENT LIFE: 68% of undergraduates are from Ohio. Others are from 36 states, and 24 foreign countries. 57% are from public schools. 85% are White. 67% are Catholic; 12% claim no religious affiliation; 11% Protestant. The average age of freshmen is 18; all undergraduates, 20. 14% do not continue beyond their first year; 71% remain to graduate. **Housing:** 1832 students can be accommodated in college housing, which includes coed dorms and off-campus apartments. In addition, there are honors houses, fraternity/sorority, healthy living, special housing for disabled students. On-campus housing is guaranteed for the freshman year only and is available on a lottery system

for upperclassmen. 58% of students live on campus; of those, 60% remain on campus on weekends. Some may keep cars.

FACULTY/CLASSROOMS: 53% of faculty are male; 47% are female. 97% teach undergraduates, 95% do research, and 95% do both. Graduate students teach 1% of introductory courses. The average class size in an introductory lecture is 19; in a laboratory is 15; and in a regular course is 19.

PROGRAMS OF STUDY: John Carroll confers B.A., B.S., B.A.Classics, B.S.B.A. and B.S.Econ. degrees. Master's degrees are also awarded. Bachelor's degrees are awarded in BIOLOGICAL SCIENCE (biochemistry, biology/biological science, cell biology, molecular biology, and (Biological) Pre-Health Studies), BUSINESS (accounting, banking and finance, business administration and management, business (dual major program), entrepreneurial studies, finance, human resources, international business management, logistics, management information systems, and marketing/retailing/merchandising), COMMUNICATIONS AND THE ARTS (art history, art history and appreciation, classical languages, classics, communications, English, French, German, Greek, Latin, literature, modern language, Spanish, theatre arts, and theatre studies), COMPUTER AND PHYSICAL SCIENCE (chemistry, computer science, mathematics, natural sciences, and physics), EDUCATION (early childhood education, education, health information management, mathematics education, middle school education, physical education, secondary education, and sports studies), ENGINEERING AND ENVIRONMENTAL DESIGN (engineering physics and environmental science), HEALTH PROFESSIONS (exercise science and health services technology), SOCIAL SCIENCE (Asian/Oriental studies, criminal justice, criminology, East Asian studies, economics, European studies, gender studies, history, humanities, liberal arts/general studies, peace studies, philosophy, political science/government, psychology, religion, sociology, theological studies, and women's studies). Accounting, biology, education, and communication are the strongest academically. Communication and theatre arts, accountancy, and psychology have the largest enrollments.

ACTIVITIES: 6% of men belong to 4 national fraternities; 11% of women belong to 5 national sororities. There are 110 groups on campus, including band, cheerleading, chess, choir, chorale, chorus, communications, computers, dance, debate, drama, drill team, environmental, ethnic, film, forensics, gay, honors, international, jazz band, literary magazine, musical theater, newspaper, pep band, photography, political, professional, radio and TV, religious, social, social service, student government, symphony, and yearbook. Popular campus events include Celebration of Scholarship, Winter Formal, Christmas Carroll Eve, Relay for Life, Carroll Fest (concert), Homecoming, Senior Week, Greek Week, Grad Fair and Spring Concert. **Sports:** There are 11 intercollegiate sports for men and 11 for women, and 7 intramural sports for men and 6 for women. Facilities include a swimming pool and diving well, a 3,800-seat football stadium and track, a baseball stadium, soccer and softball fields, an indoor track, tennis, volleyball, racquetball, and basketball courts, wrestling room, weight room, and a fitness center, hockey, rugby, lacrosse, field hockey, crew, women's basketball, ultimate frisbee, volleyball and sailing. **Graduates:** From July 1, 2013 to June 30, 2014, 627 bachelor's degrees were awarded. The most popular majors were communications (13%), psychology (10%), and marketing (8%). 795 companies recruited on campus in 2013-2014. In an average class, 1% graduate in 3 years or less, 63% graduate in 4 years or less, 72% graduate in 5 years or less, and 74% graduate in 6 years or less.

SERVICES: Counseling and information services are available, as is tutoring in some subjects, accounting, biology, chemistry, economics, finance, physics, psychology. Chinese, French, German, Spanish,and Theology/Religion. There is a reader service for the blind, and remedial writing. **Library/Resources:** The library contains 442,990 volumes, 701,000 microform items, 10,643 audio/video tapes/CDs/DVDs, and subscribes to 9,444 periodicals including electronic. Computerized library services include interlibrary loans, database searching, Internet access, and Wi-Fi capability. Special learning facilities include a radio station, TV station, a learning commons/academic resource center, computer commons, a digital media center, and group study rooms. **Physically Challenged Students:** 96% of the campus is accessible. Facilities include wheelchair ramps, elevators, special parking, specially equipped restrooms, special class scheduling, lowered drinking fountains, lowered telephones, and special housing. **Special:** Cross-registration is offered with 9 area colleges, universities, and institutes. Study abroad is possible in 16 countries. Joint engineering degrees are offered with Case Western Reserve University or the University of Detroit Mercy. Other dual-degree options: after two years of study at JCU students can enter the University of Toledo College of Medicine MEDStart program; Biology majors can spend 3 years at JCU and then enroll in the Bolton School of Nursing at Case Western Reserve University towards a Doctor of Nursing Practice. Work-study programs with local corporations, internships, a Washington semester, student-designed majors, dual majors, and some pass/fail options are available. We offer 32 Study Abroad programs in the following countries: Australia, China, Costa Rica, Denmark, El Salvador, France, Germany, Ghana, Ireland, Italy, Japan, South Africa, South Korea, spain, Turkey, United Kingdom. There are 15 national honor societies and a freshman honors program. **Visiting:** There are regularly scheduled orientations for prospective students, consisting of open houses, admission and financial aid presentations, campus and Cleveland tours, and opportunities to meet faculty, coaches, and other campus officials. There are guides for informal visits and visitors may sit in on classes. To schedule a visit, contact the Office of Admission. **Campus Safety and Security:** Measures include 24-hour foot and vehicle patrol, emergency notification system, self-defense education, and security escort services. There are shuttle buses, emergency telephones, lighted pathways/sidewalks, and controlled access to dorms/residences.

REQUIREMENTS: The ACT is required. Applicants should be graduates of an accredited secondary school with a minimum of 16 academic credits, including 4 in English, 3 in math, 2 each in foreign language, lab science, and social studies, and 3 in electives. An essay is part of the application process, and an interview is highly encouraged for students concerned about admissions standards. We accept either the ACT or SAT. AP and CLEP credits are accepted. Important factors in the admissions decision are advanced placement or honors courses, extracurricular activities record, and recommendations by school officials. Beginning of 2015, first-year students will participate in a new core curriculum that has a distinctive, integrative framework. In addition to courses in oral and written expression, quantitative analysis, and foreign language, students will choose five courses that will include at least one science, one social science and a humanities, four of which will be linked with another course, offering multiple cross-disciplinary experiences. The core also includes student selection of: two philosophy courses, two theology and religious studies courses, one social justice course, and one arts course. A capstone course in the major, and 120 credit hours with a minimum GPA of 2.0, are required for graduation. **Procedure:** Freshmen are admitted fall, spring, and summer. Entrance exams should be taken in the spring of the junior year or the fall of the senior year. There are deferred admissions and rolling admissions plans. Applications should be filed by February 1 for fall entry. Notification is sent on a rolling basis. Applications are accepted on-line. **Transfer Students:** 135 transfer students enrolled in 2013-2014. Students must be in good standing at the time of application. The most recent term average and the cumulative average at the home school must be 2.0 or better to be considered for admission, and the cumulative average for all schools attended must be 2.0 or better. A GPA of at least 2.5 is preferred. 33 of 128 credits required for the bachelor's degree must be completed at John Carroll. **International Students:** There are 66 international students enrolled. The school actively recruits these students. They must also take the SAT or ACT.

ADMISSIONS: 83% of the 2014-2015 applicants were accepted. The SAT scores for the 2014-2015 freshman class were: Critical Reading--22% below 500, 53% between 500 and 599, 27% between 600 and 699, and 2% between 700 and 800; Math--21% below 500, 50% between 500 and 599, 27% between 600 and 699, and 3% between 700 and 800; Writing--29% below 500, 47% between 500 and 599, 20% between 600 and 699, and 4% between 700 and 800. The ACT scores were 14% below 21, 28% between 21 and 23, 29% between 24 and 26, 13% between 27 and 28, and 16% above 28. 9% of the current freshmen were in the top fifth of their class; 32% were in the top two fifths. 10 freshmen graduated first in their class. **Admissions Contact:** Steven P. Vitatoe, Executive Director of Enrollment. E-Mail: *http://sites.jcu.edu/admission/* Web: *www.jcu.edu*

FINANCIAL AID: The FAFSA is required. The priority date for freshman financial aid applications for fall entry is March 15. The deadline for filing freshman financial aid applications for fall entry is August 1.

KENT STATE UNIVERSITY D-2
www.kent.edu

Kent, OH 44242 — (330) 672-2444 / (800) 988-KENT

Fax: (330) 672-2499
Full-time: 8328 men, 12006 women
Part-time: 1224 men, 1770 women
Graduate: 2284 men, 3865 women
Year: semesters, summer session
Room & Board: $9908

Email: kentadm@kent.edu
Faculty: I, --$
Ph.D.s: 71%
Student/Faculty: 21 to 1
Tuition: $10,012 ($17,972)
Freshman Class: 16156 applied, 13616 accepted, 4292 enrolled

SAT CR/M/W: 520/520/510 ACT: 23
Application Deadline: n/av

CEEB CODE: 1367
COMPETITIVE

Kent State University, founded in 1910, is a public university offering degree programs in liberal and fine arts, business, health science, public health, teacher and professional training, and aviation. Figures in the above capsule and in this profile are approximate. There are 11 undergraduate schools and 11 graduate schools. In addition to regional accreditation, KSU has baccalaureate program accreditation with AACSB, ABET, ACEJMC, CAHEA, FIDER, NAAB, NASAD, NASM, NCATE, NLN, NRPA, CPME, FAA, and CACREP. The 946-acre campus is in a suburban area 45 miles southeast of Cleveland. Including any residence halls, there are 136 buildings.

STUDENT LIFE: 80% of undergraduates are from Ohio. Others are from 49 states, 76 foreign countries, and Canada. 74% are White. The average age of freshmen is 19; all undergraduates, 22. 18% do not continue beyond their first year; 55% remain to graduate. **Housing:** 6200 students can be accommodated in college housing, which includes single-sex and coed dorms, on-campus apartments, and married student housing. In addition, there are honors houses and special-interest houses. On-campus housing is available on a first-come and first-served basis. 73% of students commute. Alcohol is not permitted. All students may keep cars.

FACULTY/CLASSROOMS: 45% of faculty are male; 55% are female. Graduate students teach 5% of introductory courses. The average class size in an introductory lecture is 35 and in a laboratory is 20.

PROGRAMS OF STUDY: KSU confers B.A., B.S., B.B.A., B.F.A, B.A.H., B.S.E., B.S.P.H., B.S.N., B.M., B.G.S., B.I.S., B.R.I.T. and B.T.A.S. degrees. Associate, Master's, and Doctoral degrees are also awarded. Bachelor's degrees are awarded in AGRICULTURE (agricultural business management, conservation and regulation, and horticulture), BIOLOGICAL SCIENCE (biochemistry, biology/biological science, biotechnology, botany, environmental biology, life science, life science secondary school education, molecular biology, nutrition, physiology, and zoology), BUSINESS (accounting, banking and finance, business administration and management, electronic business, entrepreneurial studies, entrepreneurial studies, fashion merchandising, finance, hospitality management services, insurance, marketing, marketing and distribution, marketing management, operations management, recreation and leisure services, recreational facilities management, sports management, tourism, and product design), COMMUNICATIONS AND THE ARTS (advertising, American Sign Language, apparel design, art history and appreciation, ceramic art and design, choral music, classics, communication studies, communications, crafts, dance, dramatic arts, drawing, English, French, game design and development, french and francophone studies, German, Germanic languages and literature, glass, Greek, instrumental performance, journalism, language arts, Latin, multimedia, music, music composition, music production/recording technology, musical theater, painting, photography, physical activity, piano/organ, printmaking, public relations, recreation administration, Russian languages and literature, sculpture, Spanish, theatre acting, visual and performing arts, and visual design), COMPUTER AND PHYSICAL SCIENCE (applied mathematics, chemistry, Computer Engineering Technology, computer game design/development, computer science, computer security and information assurance, earth science, geology, mathematics, mathematics - actuarial concentration, physical chemistry, physical sciences, physics, radiological technology, science, and statistics), EDUCATION (art education, athletic training, early childhood education, general studies, health education, mathematics education, middle school education, music education, physical education, physical science secondary school education, social science education, social studies education, social studies secondary school education, special education, teaching English as a second/foreign language (TESOL/TEFOL), technical education, and trade and industrial education), ENGINEERING AND ENVIRONMENTAL DESIGN (aeronautical science, aeronautical technology, air traffic control, architecture, computational sciences, computational sciences, computer technology, electrical/electronics engineering technology, industrial engineering technology, interior design, manufacturing technology, materials science, mechanical engineering technology, and Mechatronics Engineering), HEALTH PROFESSIONS (allied health, community health work, environmental health science, health care administration, health science, medical laboratory technology, nuclear medicine, nursing, nursing home administration, nutrition and dietetics, predentistry, premedicine, preosteopathy, preveterinary science, public health, radiological science, and speech pathology/audiology), SOCIAL SCIENCE (African studies, American studies, anthropology, archeology, architectural studies, classical/ancient civilization, corrections, criminal justice, criminology, Eastern European studies, economics, ethnic studies, fashion design and technology, geography, gerontology, history, human development, human services, international relations, Latin American studies, law enforcement and corrections, paralegal studies, parks and recreation management, philosophy, political science/government, psychology, Russian and Slavic studies, social science, social studies, sociology, and textiles and clothing). Architecture, education, and fashion design and merchandising are the strongest academically. Business, psychology, and fashion merchandising have the largest enrollments.

ACTIVITIES: 8% of men belong to 21 national fraternities; 9% of women belong to 11 national sororities. There are 330 groups on campus, including academic, art, band, cheerleading, chess, choir, chorale, chorus, communications, computers, dance, drama, environmental, ethnic, film, gay, honors, international, jazz band, literary magazine, marching band, musical theater, newspaper, opera, orchestra, pep band, photography, political, professional, radio and TV, religious, social, social service, and student government. Popular campus events include Black Squirrel Festival, Folk Festival, FlashFest and Back to School Blastoff. **Sports:** There are 8 intercollegiate sports for men and 10 for women, and 23 intramural sports for men and 22 for women. Facilities include a gym, recreation and wellness center, football stadium, field house, 2 fitness circuits, a golf course, bowling alley, tennis courts, lighted basketball courts, an ice arena, a pool, weight room, soccer, lacrosse, rugby, baseball, softball, and field hockey fields, an indoor track, and outdoor track, and a wrestling room. **Graduates:** From July 1, 2013 to June 30, 2014, 4683 bachelor's degrees were awarded. The most popular majors were nursing (11%), psychology (6%), and business management (6%). In an average class, 32% graduate in 4 years or less, 51% graduate in 5 years or less, and 55% graduate in 6 years or less.

SERVICES: Counseling and information services are available, as is tutoring in some subjects. There is a reader service for the blind, and remedial math, reading, and writing. Math, writing, foreign languages, chemistry, biology, academic coaching, and study skills **Library/Resources:** The 5 libraries contain 3.0 million volumes, 1.3 million microform items, 10,400 audio/video tapes/CDs/DVDs, and subscribe to 12,000 periodicals including electronic. Computerized library services include interlibrary loans, database searching, Internet access, and Wi-Fi capability. Special learning facilities include an art gallery, planetarium, radio station, TV station, fashion museum, liquid crystal institute, and May 4 visitor's center. **Physically Challenged Students:** Facilities include wheelchair ramps, elevators, special parking, specially equipped restrooms, special class scheduling, lowered drinking fountains, lowered telephones, special housing. **Special:** Cross-registration is available with the University of Akron, Cleveland State University, Youngstown State University, and Northeastern Ohio Medical University (NEOMED). Work-study programs and internships are offered, and co-op programs are available in several programs. Study abroad in 52 countries, a Washington semester, an accelerated medical degree program, B.A.-B.S. degrees, dual majors, a general studies degree, an integrative studies degree, student-designed majors, credit for military education, nondegree study, and pass/fail options are also possible. The Honors College provides honors course work in all majors. Dual admission with Cuyahoga Community, Lakeland Community, NEOMED, and Lorain County Commmunity Colleges is available. Kent is a member of the national student exchange program. There are 16 national honor societies, including Phi Beta Kappa, and a freshman honors program. **Visiting:** There are regularly scheduled orientations for prospective students, including information sessions (financial aid, residence halls, student panel), a campus tour, and meetings with academic representatives. There are guides for informal visits. To schedule a visit, contact The Admissions Office. **Campus Safety and Security:** Measures include 24-hour foot and vehicle patrol, emergency notification system, self-defense education, and security escort services. There are shuttle buses, emergency telephones, lighted pathways/sidewalks, controlled access to dorms/residences, 24-hour campus police department, overnight security guards, and a 2-key system for residence halls.

REQUIREMENTS: The ACT is required. Applicants most likely to be admitted will have at least a 2.5 cumulative GPA (on a 4.0 scale) in a solid college-preparatory program and an ACT composite score of at least 21. AP and CLEP credits are accepted. Students are required to complete 120 credit hours, of which 39 must be upper division. Distribution requirements are encompassed in the Kent Core general education requirements, a minimum of 36 credit hours, including 9 credit hours in humanities/fine arts, 6 credit hours each in basic sciences (including one laboratory course), composition, and social sciences, 3 hours in mathematics/critical reasoning, and an additional 6 credit hours. Students must also satisfy an experiential learning requirement, a writing-intensive course requirement, and a diversity course requirement. Students must maintain an overall GPA of 2.0. **Procedure:** Freshmen are admitted fall, spring, and summer. Entrance exams should be taken in the spring of the junior year or the fall of the senior year. There is a rolling admissions plan. Application deadlines are open. Application fee is $40. Notification is sent on a rolling basis. Applications are accepted on-line. **Transfer Students:** 1059 transfer students enrolled in 2013-2014. Applicants must present a minimum GPA of 2.0 on completed college course work. For students with fewer than 24 semester hours or 36 quarter hours, a high school transcript and ACT or SAT scores are also required. 30 of 120 credits required for the bachelor's degree must be completed at KSU. **International Students:** There are 1536 international students enrolled. The school actively recruits these students. They must take the TOEFL with a minimum score of 525 on the paper-based TOEFL (PBT) or 71 on the Internet-based version (iBT) or take the MELAB, or take the IELTS.

ADMISSIONS: 84% of the 2014-2015 applicants were accepted. The SAT scores for the 2014-2015 freshman class were: Critical Reading--36% below 500, 46% between 500 and 599, 17% between 600 and 699, and 2% between 700 and 800; Math--36% below 500, 44% between 500 and 599, 18% between 600 and 699, and 3% between 700 and 800; Writing--45% below 500, 40% between 500 and 599, 14% between 600 and 699, and 2% between 700 and 800. The ACT scores were 25% below 21, 35% between 21 and 23, 23% between 24 and 26, 9% between 27 and 28, and 7% above 28. 31% of the current freshmen were in the top fifth of their class; 65% were in the top two fifths. 46 freshmen graduated first in their class. **Admissions Contact:** Nancy Dellavecchia, Director of Admissions. E-Mail: *kentadm@kent .edu* Web: *www.kent.edu/admissions*

FINANCIAL AID: In 2014-2015, 71% of all full-time freshmen students received some form of financial aid. The average freshman award was $9,571. Need-based scholarships or need-based grants averaged $5,292; need-based self-help aid (loans and jobs) averaged $4,414; non-need-based athletic scholarships averaged $16,283; and other non-need-based awards and non-need-based scholarships averaged $5,274. The average financial indebtedness of the 2014 graduate was $32,393. The FAFSA is required. The priority date for freshman financial aid applications for fall entry is March 15.

KENYON COLLEGE
C-3

www.kenyon.edu

Gambier, OH 43022

(740) 427-5776
(800) 848-2468

Fax: (740) 427-5770
Email: admissions@kenyon.edu

Full-time: 751 men, 899 women
Faculty: 159

Part-time: 3 men, 9 women
Ph.D.s: 99%

Graduate: n/av
Student/Faculty: 10 to 1

Year: semesters
Tuition: $47,330

Room & Board: $11,560
Freshman Class: 6635 applied, 1663 accepted, 448 enrolled

SAT CR/M/W: 670/650/660 ACT: 30
CEEB CODE: 1370

Application Deadline: January 15
MOST COMPETITIVE

Kenyon College, among the nation's finest liberal arts institutions, takes pride in its exceptionally strong academic programs, especially in English (Kenyon is the home of the internationally known Kenyon Review), the sciences, and fine arts. Student-faculty interaction, both in and out of the classroom, and a strong sense of community are hallmarks of the Kenyon experience. Kenyon students, who come from all 50 states and 40 countries, enjoy an active extracurricular life, with more than 150 student organizations. The Kenyon campus is known for its beauty and the quality of its facilities, including a new science center, studio art center, art gallery, and top-rated recreation/ athletic center. There is one undergraduate school. The 1000-acre campus is in a rural area 50 miles northeast of Columbus, OH. Including any residence halls, there are 142 buildings.

STUDENT LIFE: 84% of undergraduates are from out of state, mostly the Middle Atlantic. Students are from 50 states, 44 foreign countries, and Canada. 50% are from public schools. 74% are White. The average age of freshmen is 18; all undergraduates, 20. 5% do not continue beyond their first year; 89% remain to graduate. **Housing:** 1772 students can be accommodated in college housing, which includes single-sex and coed dorms and on-campus apartments. In addition, there are special-interest houses, Special interest floors, including community service or social group halls, a substance-free hall, a wellness hall, an international wing, Kosher living, and Township Fire Department. On-campus housing is guaranteed for all 4 years. All students may keep cars.

FACULTY/CLASSROOMS: 55% of faculty are male; 45% are female. All teach undergraduates and all do research. No introductory courses are taught by graduate students. The average class size in an introductory lecture is 14 and in a regular course is 14.

PROGRAMS OF STUDY: Kenyon confers A.B. degrees. Bachelor's degrees are awarded in BIOLOGICAL SCIENCE (biochemistry, biology/biological science, molecular biology, and neurosciences), COMMUNICATIONS AND THE ARTS (art history, art, classics, dance, dramatic arts, English, film arts, French, German, Greek (classical), Latin, modern language, music, and Spanish), COMPUTER AND PHYSICAL SCIENCE (chemistry, mathematics, and physics), SOCIAL SCIENCE (American studies, anthropology, asian studies, economics, history, international studies, philosophy, political science/government, psychology, religious studies, sociology, women and gender studies). English, economics, and political science have the largest enrollments.

ACTIVITIES: 22% of men belong to 2 local and 7 national fraternities; 13% of women belong to 4 local and 1 national sororities. There are 128 groups on campus, including sports clubs, student lectureships, art, band, chess, choir, chorale, chorus, dance, debate, drama, environmental, environmental/conservation, ethnic, film, gay, honors, international, jazz band, literary magazine, musical theater, newspaper, opera, orchestra, pep band, photography, political, professional, radio and TV, religious, social, social service, student government, and symphony. Popular campus events include Founder's Day/Matriculation, Convocation, Summer Send-Off, Fandango, Honors Day, Family Weekend, and Martin Luther King, Jr. Day. **Sports:** There are 11 intercollegiate sports for men and 11 for women, and 9 intramural sports for men and 9 for women. Facilities include an athletic/recreation/fitness center, 70 acres of playing, football, softball, and soccer fields, a 50-yard pool, field house, Nautilus center and

weight rooms, basketball, tennis, squash, and racquetball courts. **Graduates:** From July 1, 2013 to June 30, 2014, 429 bachelor's degrees were awarded. The most popular majors were economics (14%), English (13%), and political science (12%). In an average class, 1% graduate in 3 years or less, 87% graduate in 4 years or less, 89% graduate in 5 years or less, and 90% graduate in 6 years or less.

SERVICES: Counseling and information services are available, as is tutoring in some subjects. There is a reader service for the blind, and remedial writing. Peer note-taking services, oral test option, extended time on tests, use of computer for essay based tests or notes, advance syllabus access, priority registration, priority seating, permission to use digital audio recordings, digital text format and content specific tutors are provided. **Library/Resources:** The library contains 543,882 volumes, 149,554 microform items, 31,028 audio/video tapes/CDs/ DVDs, and subscribes to 7,836 periodicals including electronic. Computerized library services include interlibrary loans, database searching, Internet access, and Wi-Fi capability. Special learning facilities include an art gallery, radio station, an observatory and an environmental center. **Physically Challenged Students:** 70% of the campus is accessible. Facilities include wheelchair ramps, elevators, special parking, specially equipped restrooms, special class scheduling, lowered drinking fountains, lowered telephones, and special housing. **Special:** Kenyon offers more than 200 off-campus study programs. The college also offers dual and student-designed majors, pass/fail options, internships, winter and/or spring break externship programs, a Washington semester consisting of apprenticeships in any of several U.S. programs, and a 3-2 engineering degree with Case Western Reserve, Washington University in St. Louis, and Rensselaer Polytechnic Institute, as well as a 3-2 environmental studies program with Duke University. 3-2 or 4-1 master's (certification) programs with The Bank Street College of Education are also possible. There is a Phi Beta Kappa and 24 departmental honors programs. **Visiting:** There are regularly scheduled orientations for prospective students, consisting of interviews with staff, a campus tour, and a class visit. Students may also request to meet with faculty and coaches. Kenyon students are also available to host a prospective student overnight in the dorm. There are guides for informal visits, visitors may sit in on classes, and stay overnight. To schedule a visit, contact the Admissions Office. **Campus Safety and Security:** Measures include 24-hour foot and vehicle patrol, emergency notification system, self-defense education, and security escort services. There are emergency telephones, lighted pathways/sidewalks, controlled access to dorms/ residences, Formal safety awareness events, and student patrols.

REQUIREMENTS: The SAT or ACT is required. Applicants should be graduates of an accredited secondary school. Candidates are encouraged to exceed the minimum requirements (4 units of English and math, 3 units of science, foreign language and social studies), especially in math and science, and to take advance placement or honors work in at least 2 subjects. Kenyon recommends 4 units each of English, math, foreign language, science, and 3 units of social studies. An interview is important criteria in the admissions decision. Talent in music, theater, art, writing, and athletics is given extra consideration. AP credits are accepted. Important factors in the admissions decision are advanced placement or honors courses, evidence of special talent, and leadership record. Students are required to complete a total of 16 units, including 4 to 7 units in the major, 1 unit in each of 4 divisions representing the arts, humanities, natural sciences, and social sciences, 1 unit of foreign language, and 1/2 unit of quantitative reasoning. Students must maintain a minimum GPA of 2.0 and complete the senior exercise in their major. A thesis is required for honor students. **Procedure:** Freshmen are admitted fall. Entrance exams should be taken in the fall of the senior year. There are early decision, early admissions, and deferred admissions plans. Early decision applications should be filed by November 15; regular applications, by January 15 for fall entry. The fall 2014 application fee was $50. Notification of early decision is sent February 1; regular decision, April 1. 226 early decision candidates were accepted for the 2014-2015 class. 642 applicants were on the 2014 waiting list; 38 were admitted. Applications are accepted on-line. Application fees are waived if application is completed on-line. **Transfer Students:** 13 transfer students enrolled in 2013-2014. Transfer applicants must have a minimum college GPA of 3.0 and a high school record suggesting ability and potential. In addition, Kenyon requires a letter of recommendation from a professor, the Transfer Common Application, and the Transfer Supplement. 8 of 16 credits required for the bachelor's degree must be completed at Kenyon. **International Students:** There are 73 international students enrolled. The school actively recruits these students. They must take the TOEFL with a minimum score of 600 on the paper-based TOEFL (PBT) or 100 on the Internet-based version (iBT). They must also take the SAT or ACT.

ADMISSIONS: 25% of the 2014-2015 applicants were accepted. The SAT scores for the 2014-2015 freshman class were: Critical Reading--1% below 500, 14% between 500 and 599, 51% between 600 and 699, and 35% between 700 and 800; Math--1% below 500, 16% between 500 and 599, 59% between 600 and 699, and 24% between 700 and 800; Writing--1% below 500, 15% between 500 and 599, 52% between 600 and 699, and 32% between 700 and 800. The ACT scores were 2% between 21 and 23, 9% between 24 and 26, 17% between 27 and 28, and 72% above 28. 80% of the current freshmen were in the top fifth of their class; 96% were in the top two fifths. There were 11 National Merit finalists. 16 freshmen graduated first in their class. **Admissions Contact:** Darryl Uy, Interim Dean of Admissions & Fin.Aid. E-Mail: *admissions@kenyon.edu* Web: *www.kenyon.edu*

FINANCIAL AID: In 2014-2015, 49% of all full-time freshmen and 42% of continuing full-time students received some form of financial aid. 47% of all full-time freshmen and 49% of continuing full-time students received need-based aid. The average freshman award was $39,738. Need-based scholarships or need-based grants averaged $37,450; need-based self-help aid (loans and jobs) averaged $3,975; other non-need-based awards and non-need-based scholarships averaged $12,884; and $2,712 from other forms of aid. The average financial indebtedness of the 2014 graduate was $15,705. Kenyon is a member of CSS. The CSS/Profile and FAFSA, and tax returns and non-custodial parent income are required. The priority date for freshman financial aid applications for fall entry is February 15. The deadline for filing freshman financial aid applications for fall entry is February 15.

LAKE ERIE COLLEGE   **E-1**
www.lec.edu

Painesville, OH 44077	(855) GOSTORM
	(855) GOSTORM
Fax: (440) 375-7005	Email: admissions@lec.edu
Full-time: 421 men, 381 women	Faculty: 41
Part-time: 35 men, 66 women	Ph.D.s: 71%
Graduate: 102 men, 109 women	Student/Faculty: 22 to 1
Year: semesters, summer session	Tuition: $28,354
Room & Board: $8912	Freshman Class: 906 applied, 568 accepted, 186 enrolled
SAT CR/M/W: 485/510/460 ACT: 21	CEEB CODE: 1391
Application Deadline: August 1	COMPETITIVE

Lake Erie College, founded in 1856, is a private liberal arts institution offering 33 undergraduate majors and master's degrees in business administration, education and physician assistant studies. The college is nationally recognized for its equine studies programs. There are 5 undergraduate schools and 3 graduate schools. In addition to regional accreditation, LEC has baccalaureate program accreditation with TEAC, IACBE, and ARC-PA. The 270-acre campus is in a small town 30 miles east of Cleveland. Including any residence halls, there are 21 buildings.

STUDENT LIFE: 73% of undergraduates are from Ohio. Others are from 26 states, 13 foreign countries, and Canada. 77% are White; 12% African American. 100% are unknown denomination. The average age of freshmen is 19; all undergraduates, 21. 33% do not continue beyond their first year; 47% remain to graduate. **Housing:** 530 students can be accommodated in college housing, which includes single-sex and coed dorms and off-campus apartments. On-campus housing is guaranteed for the freshman year only, is available on a first-come, first-served basis, and is available on a lottery system for upperclassmen. Priority is given to out-of-town students. 58% of students live on campus; of those, 45% remain on campus on weekends. All students may keep cars.

FACULTY/CLASSROOMS: 50% of faculty are male; 50% are female.

92% teach undergraduates. No introductory courses are taught by graduate students. The average class size in an introductory lecture is 15; in a laboratory is 12; and in a regular course is 15.

PROGRAMS OF STUDY: LEC confers B.A., B.S. and B.F.A. degrees. Master's degrees are also awarded. Bachelor's degrees are awarded in AGRICULTURE (equine science and range/farm management), BIOLOGICAL SCIENCE (biology/biological science), BUSINESS (accounting, business administration and management, entrepreneurial studies, finance, human resources, international business management, marketing and distribution, and sports management), COMMUNICATIONS AND THE ARTS (communications, English, fine arts, language arts, and media arts), COMPUTER AND PHYSICAL SCIENCE (chemistry, digital arts/technology, and mathematics), EDUCATION (early childhood education, middle school education, special education, and sports studies), SOCIAL SCIENCE (criminal justice, French studies, German area studies, history, interdisciplinary studies, Italian studies, paralegal studies, political science/government, psychology, social science, and Spanish studies). Biology, equine studies, and business are the strongest academically. Biology, business administration, and equine studies have the largest enrollments.

ACTIVITIES: There are 31 groups on campus, including art, cheerleading, chorus, dance, drama, environmental, equestrian., ethnic, gay, honors, international, musical theater, political, professional, religious, social, social service, and student government. Popular campus events include Prix de Ville of North America, Class Receptions, and Mountain Day. **Sports:** There are 11 intercollegiate sports for men and 10 for women, and 6 intramural sports for men and 6 for women. Facilities include on campus soccer and softball fields, a nearby off-campus baseball field and an 85-acre equestrian center, including a competition arena. The college also has an athletic and wellness center with an indoor basketball/volleyball arena, a multipurpose practice/intramural and recreational gym with a suspended indoor jogging track, and a 4000-square foot fitness center and weight room. Football, tennis, and baseball may be played at nearby Paineville Park. **Graduates:** From July 1, 2013 to June 30, 2014, 175 bachelor's degrees were awarded. The most popular majors were biology (18%), business administration (10%), and psychology (6%). In an average class, 35% graduate in 4 years or less, 46% graduate in 5 years or less, and 47% graduate in 6 years or less. Of the 2013 graduating class, 23% were enrolled in graduate school within 6 months of graduation, and 25% were employed.

SERVICES: Counseling and information services are available, as is tutoring in most subjects. There is a reader service for the blind, and remedial math, reading, and writing. **Library/Resources:** The library contains 66,900 volumes, and 1,824 audio/video tapes/CDs/DVDs. Computerized library services include interlibrary loans, database searching, Internet access, and Wi-Fi capability. Special learning facilities include an art gallery, a fine arts theater, equestrian center, music hall, and athletic trainng facilities. **Physically Challenged Students:** 45% of the campus is accessible. Facilities include wheelchair ramps, elevators, special parking, specially equipped restrooms, special class scheduling, lowered drinking fountains, and lowered telephones. **Special:** Students may choose either national or international internships or study abroad in the Netherlands, France, Germany, Spain, England, Italy, or another country, as arranged by the student, B.A.-B.S. degrees, including a B.F.A. in fine arts, music, dance, or an individual major, student-designed majors, and potential credit for life, military, or work experience are offered. Cross-registration is available with the Northeast Ohio Commission on Higher Education. 128 credits are required. There are 2 national honor societies and a freshman honors program. **Visiting:** There are regularly scheduled orientations for prospective students, including a campus tour, a financial aid information session, classroom observation, and faculty or department head interviews. There are guides for informal visits, visitors may sit in on classes, and stay overnight. To schedule a visit, contact the Admissions Office. **Campus Safety and Security:** Measures include 24-hour foot and vehicle patrol, emergency notification system, and security escort services. There are emergency telephones, lighted pathways/sidewalks, and controlled access to dorms/residences.

REQUIREMENTS: The SAT or ACT is required. Applicants should be graduates of an accredited secondary school with a minimum GPA of 2.5. The high school program should include 4 years each of English, 3 years each of math and science (including 2 years of lab science), and 3 years each of history and social studies, with 2 years of a foreign language. Two letters of recommendation are required, with at least one being from a guidance counselor or teacher. A 500-word essay is required. A GED is required for home-schooled students. A campus visit is strongly encouraged. A GPA of 2.5 is required. AP and CLEP credits are accepted. Important factors in the admissions decision are leadership record, advanced placement or honors courses, and geographical diversity. General education requirements include 4 hours each of math, English, 8 hours of a foreign language, and 2 hours of public speaking. A computer literacy course is required. There are specific core requirements for 25 additional semester hours. Students must complete 128 credits, including an average of 64 in the major, with a minimum GPA of 2.0. **Procedure:** Freshmen are admitted fall, spring, and summer. Entrance exams should be taken by November of the senior year. There are deferred admissions and rolling admissions plans. Early decision applications should be filed by May 1; regular applications, by August 1 for fall entry; and January 1 for spring entry, along with a $30 fee. Notification is sent on a rolling basis. Applications are accepted on-line. Application fees are waived if application is completed on-line. **Transfer Students:** 57 transfer students enrolled in 2013-2014. Applicants should submit transcripts from all schools attended and show a GPA of 2.5 in all college work, plus 2 letters of recommendation and proof of high school graduation (copy of diploma or transcripts). 32 of 128 credits required for the bachelor's degree must be completed at LEC. **International Students:** There are 35 international students enrolled. The school actively recruits these students. They must take the TOEFL with a minimum score of 550 on the paper-based TOEFL (PBT) and the Comprehensive English Language Test. They must also take the SAT or ACT, and the college's own entrance exam.

ADMISSIONS: 63% of the 2014-2015 applicants were accepted. The SAT scores for the 2014-2015 freshman class were: Critical Reading--63% below 500, 27% between 500 and 599, and 10% between 600 and 699; Math--47% below 500, 41% between 500 and 599, 8% between 600 and 699, and 4% between 700 and 800; Writing--71% below 500, 20% between 500 and 599, and 10% between 600 and 699. The ACT scores were 53% below 21, 26% between 21 and 23, 11% between 24 and 26, 4% between 27 and 28, and 6% above 28. **Admissions Contact:** Will Brown, Associate Director of Recruitment. E-Mail: *wbrown1@lec.edu; admissions@lec.edu* Web: *http:/www.lec.edu/admissions*

FINANCIAL AID: In 2014-2015, 89% of all full-time freshmen and 83% of continuing full-time students received some form of financial aid. 89% of all full-time freshmen and 82% of continuing full-time students received need-based aid. The average freshman award was $22,717. Need-based scholarships or need-based grants averaged $18,788; need-based self-help aid (loans and jobs) averaged $4,508; non-need-based athletic scholarships averaged $14,898; and other non-need-based awards and non-need-based scholarships averaged $12,738. Average annual earnings from campus work are $2000. The FAFSA is required. The priority date for freshman financial aid applications for fall entry is March 1. The deadline for filing freshman financial aid applications for fall entry is August 1.

LOURDES UNIVERSITY *(The complete profile is made available exclusively on our website, www.barronspac.com)*

MALONE UNIVERSITY — D-2
www.malone.edu

Canton, OH 44709

(330) 471-8145
(800) 521-1146

Fax: (330) 471-8149

Email: admissions@malone.edu

Full-time: 571 men, 761 women

Faculty: 90; IIA

Part-time: 84 men, 172 women

Ph.D.s: 78%

Graduate: 135 men, 280 women

Student/Faculty: 18 to 1

Year: semesters, summer session

Tuition: $26,416

Room & Board: $8948

Freshman Class: 1327 applied, 952 accepted, 314 enrolled

SAT CR/M: 525/500 ACT: 23

CEEB CODE: 1439

Application Deadline: n/av

COMPETITIVE

Malone University, founded in 1892, is a private Christian university for the arts, sciences, and professions in the liberal arts tradition. The mission of Malone University is to provide students with an education based on biblical faith in order to develop men and women in intellectual maturity, wisdom, and Christian faith who are committed to serving the church, community, and world. There are 4 undergraduate schools and 4 graduate schools. In addition to regional accreditation, Malone has baccalaureate program accreditation with ACBSP, CSWE, NCATE, CCNE, and CACREP. The 96-acre campus is in a suburban area 56 miles southeast of Cleveland. Including any residence halls, there are 22 buildings.

STUDENT LIFE: 86% of undergraduates are from Ohio. Others are from 32 states, 13 foreign countries, and Canada. 80% are from public schools. 84% are White. 78% are Protestant; 14% claim no religious affiliation. The average age of freshmen is 18; all undergraduates, 24. 28% do not continue beyond their first year; 57% remain to graduate. **Housing:** 1009 students can be accommodated in college housing, which includes single-sex dorms. Special topic/discipleship floors for upperclassmen. On-campus housing is guaranteed for the freshman year only, is available on a first-come, first-served basis, and is available on a lottery system for upperclassmen. 53% of students live on campus; of those, 40% remain on campus on weekends. Alcohol is not permitted. All students may keep cars.

FACULTY/CLASSROOMS: 45% of faculty are male; 55% are female. 80% teach undergraduates. No introductory courses are taught by graduate students. The average class size in an introductory lecture is 27; in a laboratory is 14; and in a regular course is 19.

PROGRAMS OF STUDY: Malone confers B.A., B.S.Ed. and B.S.N. degrees. Master's degrees are also awarded. Bachelor's degrees are awarded in BIOLOGICAL SCIENCE (biology/biological science, life science, and zoology), BUSINESS (accounting, business administration and management, and sports management), COMMUNICATIONS AND THE ARTS (art, broadcasting, communications, creative writing, English, language arts, music, music technology, public relations, and theatre studies), COMPUTER AND PHYSICAL SCIENCE (chemistry, computer science, mathematics, and physical sciences), EDUCATION (Christian education, early childhood education, middle school education, music education, science education, secondary education, social studies education, and special education), HEALTH PROFESSIONS (community health work, exercise science, medical laboratory technology, nursing, and public health), SOCIAL SCIENCE (biblical studies, history, international studies, liberal arts/general studies, ministries, philosophy, political science/government, psychology, religious music, social work, theological studies, and youth ministry). Nursing, social work, and history are the strongest academically. Nursing, business administration, and communication arts have the largest enrollments.

ACTIVITIES: There are 60 groups on campus, including art, band, cheerleading, chess, choir, chorale, communications, computers, drama, drill team, environmental, ethnic, film, honors, international, jazz band, literary magazine, marching band, musical theater, newspaper, opera, photography, political, professional, radio and TV, religious, social, social service, and student government. Popular campus events include Little Sibs Weekend, Christmas Celebration and Worldview Forums. **Sports:** There are 9 intercollegiate sports for men and 9 for women, and 9 intramural sports for men and 9 for women. Facilities include a gym, a wellness center with a strength room and a cardio room, an outdoor track, baseball, softball, and soccer fields, practice soccer and football fields, intramural fields, a cross-country course, and outdoor volleyball and basketball courts. . **Graduates:** From July 1, 2013 to June 30, 2014, 427 bachelor's degrees were awarded. The most popular majors were business administration/management (27%), nursing and other health professions and related programs (22%), and education (13%). In an average class, 2% graduate in 3 years or less, 44% graduate in 4 years or less, 56% graduate in 5 years or less, and 58% graduate in 6 years or less.

SERVICES: Counseling and information services are available, as is tutoring in most subjects. There is a reader service for the blind, and remedial math, reading, and writing. There are also disability support services such as a distraction-reduced testing room. **Library/Resources:** The library contains 172,046 volumes, 653,741 microform items, 11,693 audio/video tapes/CDs/DVDs, and subscribes to 33,896 periodicals including electronic. Computerized library services include interlibrary loans, database searching, Internet access, and Wi-Fi capability. Special learning facilities include an art gallery, radio/TV station, a writing lab; subject area tutoring; a TV production studio, a radio producing studio and a number of other production spaces in the Student Media Center. **Physically Challenged Students:** Facilities include wheelchair ramps, elevators, special parking, specially equipped restrooms, special class scheduling, lowered drinking fountains, lowered telephones, and special housing. **Special:** Students may participate in co-op programs and internships in many majors and may cross-register within the Christian College Consortium. Malone offers study abroad in England, China, Costa Rica, Israel, India, Australia, Uganda, and Kenya as well as Hollywood (Film Studies), Nashville (Contemporary Music), or Washington semesters through the Council for Christian Colleges and Universities. Approximately 20 other study abroad opportunities are available through Brethren Colleges Abroad (BCA). A liberal arts degree, dual and student-designed majors, and credit for life, military, or work experience are also available. The Malone Management Program(M-MP)offers accelerated degree completion for students with 5 years of work experience and 40 to 88 transfer hours. MMP offers 4 majors: Organizational Management, Project Management, Business Accounting Management, and Health Services Management. The School of Nursing and Health Sciences offers a traditional BSN program and a degree-completion BSN program for RNs. There are 10 national honor societies and a freshman honors program. **Visiting:** There are regularly scheduled orientations for prospective students, including Discover Day: a tour of campus, a chance to meet with faculty, a community worship service, a class visit, a parent session, a student panel, an activity fair and lunch on us!. There are guides for informal visits, visitors may sit in on classes, and stay overnight. To schedule a visit, contact Jody Dimit at (330) 471-8147. **Campus Safety and Security:** Measures include 24-hour foot and vehicle patrol, emergency notification system, and security escort services. There are emergency telephones, lighted pathways/sidewalks, and controlled access to dorms/residences.

REQUIREMENTS: The ACT is preferred; the SAT is accepted. Applicants should be graduates of an accredited secondary school with a minimum GPA of 2.5. The GED is accepted. AP and CLEP credits are accepted. Important factors in the admissions decision are advanced placement or honors courses, personality/intangible qualities, and extracurricular activities record. Students must maintain a GPA of 2.0 overall and 2.25 to 2.75 in the major, depending upon the major. At least 30 hours in the major and 39 hours at the 300 or 400 level are required. To graduate, all students must complete at least 124 credit hours. The 41- to 43-hour general education curriculum includes 10 hours of Faith Learning courses, 9 hours of Foundational Skills courses, 9 hours of Engaging in Human Experience courses, 7-9 hours in Engaging Cultures and Institutions courses, 3 hours in Engaging the Created Order (one course) and 3 hours in Faith in the World (one course). **Procedure:** Freshmen are admitted fall, spring, and summer. Entrance exams should be taken in the junior year. There are early admissions, deferred admissions, and rolling admissions plans. Application deadlines are open. Application fee is $20. Notifications are sent September 1. Applications are accepted on-line. **Transfer Students:** 68 transfer students enrolled in 2013-2014. Applicants must submit a transfer reference form from the last institution attended. 30 of 124 credits required for the bachelor's degree must be completed at Malone. **International Students:** There are 20 international students enrolled. They must take the TOEFL with a minimum score of 550 on the paper-based TOEFL (PBT) or 79 on the Internet-based version (iBT). They must also take the SAT or ACT, scoring 860-SAT or18-ACT. not required of all international students; but definitely athletes due to NCAA requirements.

ADMISSIONS: 72% of the 2014-2015 applicants were accepted. The SAT scores for the 2014-2015 freshman class were: Critical Reading--33% below 500, 54% between 500 and 599, and 13% between 600 and 699; Math--48% below 500, 35% between 500 and 599, and 17% between 600 and 699. The ACT scores were 31% below 21, 25% between 21 and 23, 27% between 24 and 26, 9% between 27 and 28, and 7% above 28. 37% of the current freshmen were in the top fifth of their class; 65% were in the top two fifths. 10 freshmen graduated first in their class. **Admissions Contact:** Linda Kurtz Hoffman, Director of Admissions. E-Mail: *admissions@malone.edu* Web: *www.malone.edu*

FINANCIAL AID: In 2014-2015, 100% of all full-time freshmen and 91% of continuing full-time students received some form of financial aid. 77% of all full-time freshmen and 70% of continuing full-time students received need-based aid. The average freshman award was $28,310. Need-based scholarships or need-based grants averaged $9,717 ($25,560 maximum); need-based self-help aid (loans and jobs) averaged $5,783 ($9,500 maximum); non-need-based athletic scholarships averaged $13,044 ($30,364 maximum); other non-need-based awards and non-need-based scholarships averaged $13,116 ($40,000 maximum); and $11,294 from other forms of aid. 23% of undergraduate students work part-time. Average annual earnings from campus work are $1950. The average financial indebtedness of the 2014 graduate was $30,679. The FAFSA, and verification documents if chosen is required. The priority date for freshman financial aid applications for fall entry is March 1. The deadline for filing freshman financial aid applications for fall entry is July 31.

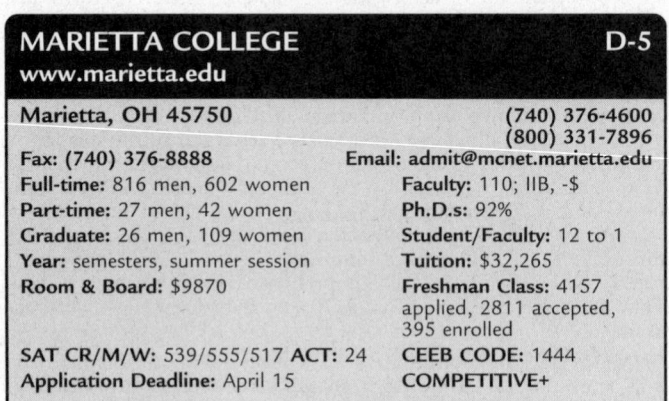

MARIETTA COLLEGE **D-5**
www.marietta.edu

Marietta, OH 45750 (740) 376-4600
(800) 331-7896

Fax: (740) 376-8888 Email: admit@mcnet.marietta.edu
Full-time: 816 men, 602 women Faculty: 110; IIB, -$
Part-time: 27 men, 42 women Ph.D.s: 92%
Graduate: 26 men, 109 women Student/Faculty: 12 to 1
Year: semesters, summer session Tuition: $32,265
Room & Board: $9870 Freshman Class: 4157 applied, 2811 accepted, 395 enrolled
SAT CR/M/W: 539/555/517 ACT: 24 CEEB CODE: 1444
Application Deadline: April 15 COMPETITIVE+

Marietta College, founded in 1835, is a private liberal arts college. There is 1 undergraduate school and 4 graduate schools. In addition to regional accreditation, Marietta has baccalaureate program accreditation with ABET, NASM, NCATE, CAAHEP, ACS, and ARC-PA. The 90-acre campus is in a small town 115 miles southeast of Columbus. Including any residence halls, there are 40 buildings.

STUDENT LIFE: 64% of undergraduates are from Ohio. Others are from 40 states, 15 foreign countries, and Canada. 89% are from public schools. 71% are White. **Male To Female Ratio:** 1.2:1. The average age of freshmen is 18; all undergraduates, 20. 22% do not continue beyond their first year; 56% remain to graduate. **Housing:** 1276 students can be accommodated in college housing, which includes single-sex and coed dorms and on-campus apartments. In addition, there are honors houses, special-interest houses, fraternity houses, and sorority houses. On-campus housing is guaranteed for all 4 years. 76% of students live on campus; of those, 80% remain on campus on weekends. All students may keep cars.

FACULTY/CLASSROOMS: 51% of faculty are male; 49% are female. All teach undergraduates. No introductory courses are taught by graduate students. The average class size in an introductory lecture is 19; in a laboratory is 13; and in a regular course is 16.

PROGRAMS OF STUDY: Marietta confers B.A., B.S. and B.F.A. degrees. Associate and master's degrees are also awarded. Bachelor's degrees are awarded in AGRICULTURE (environmental studies), BIOLOGICAL SCIENCE (biochemistry and biology/biological science), BUSINESS (accounting, banking and finance, business administration and management, human resources, international business management, management information systems, marketing/retailing/merchandising, and sports management), COMMUNICATIONS AND THE ARTS (advertising, broadcasting, communications, dramatic arts, English, graphic design, journalism, music, public relations, Spanish, speech/debate/rhetoric, and studio art), COMPUTER AND PHYSICAL SCIENCE (applied physics, chemistry, computer science, geology, information sciences and systems, mathematics, and physics), EDUCATION (athletic training, early childhood education, and music education), ENGINEERING AND ENVIRONMENTAL DESIGN (environmental science and petroleum/natural gas engineering), HEALTH PROFESSIONS (health science and physician's assistant), SOCIAL SCIENCE (Asian/

Oriental studies, economics, history, interdisciplinary studies, political science/government, and psychology). Petroleum engineering is the strongest academically. Petroleum engineering, advertising public relations, and psychology are the largest.

ACTIVITIES: 23% of men belong to 3 national fraternities; 41% of women belong to 3 national sororities. There are 80 groups on campus, including and arts and humanities, Circle K, art, athletic training, band, cheerleading, choir, chorale, chorus, computers, dance, debate, drama, drill team, environmental, ethnic, film, forensics, gay, honors, international, jazz band, literary magazine, musical theater, newspaper, orchestra, pep band, photography, political, professional, radio and TV, religious, social, social service, student government, and yearbook. Popular campus events include DooDah Day, Little Sibs Weekend and Welcome Back Bash. **Sports:** There are 9 intercollegiate sports for men and 9 for women, and 12 intramural sports for men and 12 for women. Facilities include a 7000-seat stadium, a 1500-seat performance gym, a 3500-seat field house, baseball, softball, and soccer fields, a boat house, a cross-country course, tennis courts, and a recreational center housing a 200-meter track, multipurpose and racquetball courts, an ergometer training room, cardio equipment, and a climbing wall. **Graduates:** From July 1, 2013 to June 30, 2014, 222 bachelor's degrees were awarded. The most popular majors were petroleum engineering (7%), advertising/public relations (7%), and psychology (6%). 60 companies recruited on campus in 2013-2014. In an average class, 3% graduate in 3 years or less, 46% graduate in 4 years or less, 55% graduate in 5 years or less, and 56% graduate in 6 years or less. Of the 2013 graduating class, 24% were enrolled in graduate school within 6 months of graduation, and 95% were employed.

SERVICES: Counseling and information services are available, as is tutoring in most subjects. There is a reader service for the blind, and remedial math and writing. Peer tutoring program. **Library/ Resources:** The library contains 449,123 volumes, 146,583 microform items, 5,031 audio/video tapes/CDs/DVDs, and subscribes to 13,557 periodicals including electronic. Computerized library services include interlibrary loans, database searching, and Internet access. Special learning facilities include an art gallery, planetarium, radio station, TV station, an observatory, a greenhouse, and a geology annex. **Physically Challenged Students:** 90% of the campus is accessible. Facilities include wheelchair ramps, elevators, special parking, specially equipped restrooms, special class scheduling, lowered drinking fountains, lowered telephones, and special housing. **Special:** There are 3-2 binary engineering programs with Case Western Reserve, Columbia, and Ohio Universities. Internships are available in many majors, and students may study abroad in numerous countries and participate in a Washington semester through American University. Work-study programs, B.A.-B.S. degrees in all majors, and student-designed majors are also available. There are 23 national honor societies, including Phi Beta Kappa, a freshman honors program, and 17 departmental honors programs. **Visiting:** There are regularly scheduled orientations for prospective students, including fall and spring open houses, tours, and meetings with faculty, coaches, and financial aid representatives. There are guides for informal visits, visitors may sit in on classes, and stay overnight. To schedule a visit, contact the Office of Admissions. **Campus Safety and Security:** Measures include 24-hour foot and vehicle patrol, emergency notification system, self-defense education, and security escort services. There are shuttle buses, emergency telephones, lighted pathways/sidewalks, controlled access to dorms/residences, Airport shuttles available upon request.

REQUIREMENTS: The SAT or ACT is required. In addition, Students seeking admission should have completed 4 years of English and 3 of history, math, and science; 2 years of a foreign language is also recommended. An interview is strongly recommended. AP and CLEP credits are accepted. Important factors in the admissions decision are advanced placement or honors courses, evidence of special talent, and leadership record. To graduate, students must complete at least 120 total credit hours, with general education requirements. The minimum number of hours required for a major is 36. A minimum GPA of 2.0 must be maintained. Seniors must complete a capstone project in their major. **Procedure:** Freshmen are admitted fall and spring. Entrance exams should be taken no later than February of the senior year. There is a rolling admissions plan. Applications

should be filed by April 15 for fall entry, along with a $25 fee. Notification is sent on a rolling basis. Applications are accepted on-line. **Transfer Students:** 46 transfer students enrolled in 2013-2014. A minimum GPA of 2.5, a recommendation, and an essay are required. 36 of 120 credits required for the bachelor's degree must be completed at Marietta. **International Students:** There are 155 international students enrolled. The school actively recruits these students. They must take the TOEFL with a minimum score of 550 on the paper-based TOEFL (PBT) or 79 on the Internet-based version (iBT) and the college's own test, or take the IELTS. They must also take the SAT or ACT.

ADMISSIONS: 68% of the 2014-2015 applicants were accepted. The SAT scores for the 2014-2015 freshman class were: Critical Reading-- 33% below 500, 40% between 500 and 599, 25% between 600 and 699, and 2% between 700 and 800. Math-- 27% below 500, 36% between 500 and 599, 34% between 600 and 699, and 3% between 700 and 800. Writing-- 40% below 500, 42% between 500 and 599, 17% between 600 and 699, and 1% between 700 and 800. The ACT scores were 23% below 21, 27% between 21 and 23, 23% between 24 and 26, 13% between 27 and 28, and 15% above 28. 49% of the current freshmen were in the top fifth of their class; 79% were in the top two fifths. 9 freshmen graduated first in their class. **Admissions Contact:** Jason Turley, Dean of Admission. E-Mail: *admit@ mcnet.marietta.edu* Web: *www.marietta.edu*

FINANCIAL AID: In 2014-2015, 96% of all full-time freshmen and 93% of continuing full-time students received some form of financial aid. 84% of all full-time freshmen and 79% of continuing full-time students received need-based aid. The average freshman award was $27,091. Need-based scholarships or need-based grants averaged $9,561 ($19,220 maximum); need-based self-help aid (loans and jobs) averaged $3,602 ($7,500 maximum); and other non-need-based awards and non-need-based scholarships averaged $8,650 ($35,112 maximum). 30% of undergraduate students work part-time. Average annual earnings from campus work are $2000. The average financial indebtedness of the 2014 graduate was $20,911. The FAFSA is required. The deadline for filing freshman financial aid applications for fall entry is March 1.

MIAMI UNIVERSITY   A-4
www.MiamiOH.edu

Oxford, OH 45056	**(513) 529-2531**
	n/av
Fax: (513) 529-1550	**Email: admission@MiamiOH.edu**
Full-time: 7017 men, 7640 women	**Faculty:** 841; I, --$
Part-time: 215 men, 209 women	**Ph.D.s:** 89%
Graduate: 783 men, 1819 women	**Student/Faculty:** 17 to 1
Year: semesters, summer session	**Tuition:** $13,595 ($29,159)
Room & Board: $10,596	**Freshman Class:** 20314 applied, 14788 accepted, 3734 enrolled
SAT CR/M: 580/610 **ACT:** 27	**CEEB CODE:** 1463
Application Deadline: February 1	**VERY COMPETITIVE**

Miami University, founded in 1909, provides a rigorous academic experience in the quintessential collegiate setting of Oxford, Ohio. Here, the best and brightest students prepare for success as they are given the opportunities of a large university while experiencing the personalized teaching, attention, and sense of community found in the best small colleges. A public university, Miami offers a wide range of academic programs. The bachelor's degree is offered in more than 100 areas of study, the master's degree in more than 50 and doctoral programs in 10 disciplines. Dedicated to fostering an environment of teaching for more than 200 years, Miami faculty guide both undergraduates and graduate students in conducting significant research, completing projects with real-world clients, and fostering leadership skills. With a long-standing dedication to global learning, complete with a European center in Luxembourg, Miami ranks first among public colleges nationwide for the rate of undergraduate students who study abroad. Miami students and faculty have an intense appreciation for a global view and multicultural approaches to learning. Retention and graduation rates are some of the highest in NCAA

Division I schools, as is our students' successful entry into top graduate programs and professional schools. As a result, Miami is regularly cited by national publications as a best value in higher education. The university is located in the Miami Valley region of Ohio. There are 5 undergraduate schools and 1 graduate school. In addition to regional accreditation, has baccalaureate program accreditation with AACSB, ABET, CSAB, CSWE, FIDER, NAAB, NASAD, NCATE, and NLN. The 2138-acre campus is in a small town 35 miles north of Cincinnati, OH. Including any residence halls, there are 119 buildings.

STUDENT LIFE: 70% of undergraduates are from Ohio. Others are from 50 states, 73 foreign countries, and Canada. 74% are from public schools. 82% are White. 38% are Protestant; 36% Catholic; 19% claim no religious affiliation. The average age of freshmen is 18; all undergraduates, 20. 11% do not continue beyond their first year; 80% remain to graduate. **Housing:** 7138 students can be accommodated in college housing, which includes single-sex and coed dorms, on-campus apartments, and married student housing. In addition, there are honors houses, language houses, special-interest houses, sorority houses, international housing and first-year only housing. On-campus housing is guaranteed for the freshman year only and is available on a lottery system for upperclassmen. 52% of students commute. All students may keep cars.

FACULTY/CLASSROOMS: 56% of faculty are male; 44% are female. All teach undergraduates. No introductory courses are taught by graduate students. The average class size in a regular course is 32.

PROGRAMS OF STUDY: confers A.B., B.S., B.F.A., B.Mus., A.B.Arc., A.B.Art., A.B.The., B.I.S., B.S.Aps., B.S.Art., B.S.AT., B.S.Bus., B.S.Cj., B.S.Cs., B.S.Ed., B.S.Egr., B.S.Ff., B.S.IT., B.S.Knh., B.W.Se. and B.S.Swk. degrees. Associate, master's, and doctoral degrees are also awarded. Bachelor's degrees are awarded in BIOLOGICAL SCIENCE (biochemistry, botany, microbiology, nutrition, and zoology), BUSINESS (accounting, banking and finance, business economics, management information systems, management science, marketing/retailing/merchandising, sports management, sports marketing, and supply chain management), COMMUNICATIONS AND THE ARTS (art, art history and appreciation, classical languages, classics, communications, dramatic arts, East Asian languages and literature, English, French, German, graphic design, journalism, linguistics, media arts, music, music performance, Russian, Spanish, and speech/debate/rhetoric), COMPUTER AND PHYSICAL SCIENCE (chemistry, computer science, earth science, geology, mathematics, physics, software engineering, and statistics), EDUCATION (art education, athletic training, early childhood education, elementary education, foreign languages education, health information management, middle school education, music education, science education, secondary education, special education, and sports studies), ENGINEERING AND ENVIRONMENTAL DESIGN (architectural history, architecture, bioengineering, chemical engineering, computer engineering, electrical/electronics engineering, engineering, engineering management, engineering physics, engineering technology, environmental science, interior design, manufacturing engineering, mechanical engineering, and paper and pulp science), HEALTH PROFESSIONS (clinical science, health promotion, nursing, and speech pathology/audiology), SOCIAL SCIENCE (African American studies, American studies, anthropology, criminal justice, economics, family/consumer studies, geography, gerontology, history, interdisciplinary studies, international relations, international studies, Italian studies, Latin American studies, philosophy, physical fitness/movement, political science/government, psychology, public administration, religion, social work, sociology, urban studies, and women's studies). Marketing, finance, accountancy, zoology and psychology have the largest enrollments.

ACTIVITIES: 24% of men belong to 29 national fraternities; 25% of women belong to 21 national sororities. There are 344 groups on campus, including art, bagpipe, band, cheerleading, chess, choir, chorale, chorus, communications, computers, dance, debate, drama, drill team, environmental, ethnic, film, forensics, gay, honors, international, jazz band, literary magazine, marching band, musical theater, newspaper, opera, orchestra, pep band, photography, political, professional, radio and TV, religious, social, social service, student government, symphony, and yearbook. Popular campus events include Parents Weekend, Kidsfest Weekend, and Unity Fest. **Sports:** There are 8 intercollegiate sports for men and 10 for women, and 17 intra-

mural sports for men and 16 for women. Facilities include a 25,000-seat football stadium, a 170,000 sf ice arena, 70 acres of playing fields, 30 outdoor tennis courts, a recreational sports center, 10 indoor basketball/volleyball courts, racquetball, handball, and squash courts, a floor hockey/indoor soccer court, a climbing wall, equestrian stables and dressage course, a world-class aquatic center containing 3 indoor swimming pools, jogging paths, a par course, sand volleyball courts, aerobics and weight rooms, and a Frisbee golf course. **Graduates:** From July 1, 2013 to June 30, 2014, 4121 bachelor's degrees were awarded. The most popular majors were finance (7%), accountancy (6%), and marketing (6%). 336 companies recruited on campus in 2013-2014. In an average class, 68% graduate in 4 years or less, 79% graduate in 5 years or less, and 80% graduate in 6 years or less.

SERVICES: Counseling and information services are available, as is tutoring in most subjects. Assistance in study skills is available. **Library/Resources:** The 4 libraries contain 4.2 million volumes, 276,385 microform items, 2.2 million audio/video tapes/CDs/DVDs, and subscribe to 109,477 periodicals including electronic. Computerized library services include interlibrary loans, database searching, Internet access, and Wi-Fi capability. Special learning facilities include an art gallery, natural history museum, radio station, and TV station. **Physically Challenged Students:** All of the campus is accessible. Facilities include wheelchair ramps, elevators, special parking, specially equipped restrooms, special class scheduling, lowered drinking fountains, lowered telephones, and special housing. **Special:** The university offers cross-registration with Cincinnati area colleges, study abroad in multiple countries, co-op programs in the School of Applied Science, internships in health and sport studies and applied science, a 3-2 engineering degree with Case Western Reserve and Columbia Universities, and a 3-2 forestry degree with Duke University. Students may pursue student-designed majors through the Western Program or interdisciplinary majors. There are 21 national honor societies, including Phi Beta Kappa, and a freshman honors program. **Visiting:** There are regularly scheduled orientations for prospective students. Information sessions and guided tours are available throughout the year. . There are guides for informal visits and visitors may sit in on classes. To schedule a visit, contact the Office of Admissions at visitcoor@MiamiOH.edu. **Campus Safety and Security:** Measures include 24-hour foot and vehicle patrol, emergency notification system, self-defense education, and security escort services. There are shuttle buses, emergency telephones, lighted pathways/sidewalks, and controlled access to dorms/residences.

REQUIREMENTS: Applicants must complete either the ACT or the SAT. Candidates for admission must ordinarily be graduates of accredited secondary schools or hold the GED. Students should have completed 4 units of English, 3 each of math, science, and social studies/history, 2 of a foreign language, and 1 of fine arts. An audition, a portfolio, or an interview are required for direct admission to majors in the School of Fine Arts. AP and CLEP credits are accepted. To graduate students must complete 128 semester hours, with a minimum 2.0 GPA. At least 32 semester hours must be from Miami University. Students must fulfill all requirements for either the Miami Plan (i.e., liberal education requirements) or the Honors Plan. The Miami plan includes 36 semester hours of foundation courses, 9 semester hours in a thematic sequence, and a 3 hour capstone experience. **Procedure:** Freshmen are admitted to all sessions. Entrance exams should be taken by December of the senior year. There are early decision and deferred admissions plans. Early decision applications should be filed by November 15; regular applications, by February 1 for fall entry; and November 1 for spring entry. The fall 2014 application fee was $50. Notification of early decision is sent December 15; regular decision, March 15. 692 early decision candidates were accepted for the 2014-2015 class. 629 applicants were on the 2014 waiting list; 6 were admitted. Applications are accepted on-line. **Transfer Students:** 224 transfer students enrolled in 2013-2014. A limited number of transfer students will be accepted. A GPA of 2.00 or higher is necessary. 32 of 128 credits required for the bachelor's degree must be completed at Miami. **International Students:** There are 827 international students enrolled. The school actively recruits these students. They must take the TOEFL with a minimum score of 550 on the paper-based TOEFL (PBT) or 80 on the Internet-based version (iBT) or take the MELAB, or take the IELTS or alternative proof of English language proficiency. They must also take the SAT or ACT. The SAT or ACT is required only for Canadian applicants, athletes, and those students who have followed a U.S. high school curriculum.

ADMISSIONS: 73% of the 2014-2015 applicants were accepted. The SAT scores for the 2014-2015 freshman class were: Critical Reading--11% below 500, 46% between 500 and 599, 34% between 600 and 699, and 9% between 700 and 800; Math--7% below 500, 35% between 500 and 599, 45% between 600 and 699, and 13% between 700 and 800. The ACT scores were 3% below 21, 13% between 21 and 23, 33% between 24 and 26, 21% between 27 and 28, and 29% above 28. 59% of the current freshmen were in the top fifth of their class; 89% were in the top two fifths. 69 freshmen graduated first in their class. **Admissions Contact:** Ann Larson, Director of Admissions. E-Mail: *admission@MiamiOH.edu* Web: *www.MiamiOH.edu/apply*

FINANCIAL AID: In 2014-2015, 71% of all full-time freshmen and 66% of continuing full-time students received some form of financial aid. 42% of all full-time freshmen and 41% of continuing full-time students received need-based aid. The average freshman award was $10,647. Need-based scholarships or need-based grants averaged $7,326; need-based self-help aid (loans and jobs) averaged $3,741; non-need-based athletic scholarships averaged $19,975; and other non-need-based awards and non-need-based scholarships averaged $6,673. 38% of undergraduate students work part-time. Average annual earnings from campus work are $4320. The average financial indebtedness of the 2014 graduate was $22,579. The FAFSA is required. The priority date for freshman financial aid applications for fall entry is February 15.

MOUNT VERNON NAZARENE UNIVERSITY   C-3
www.mvnu.edu

Mount Vernon, OH 43050	**(740) 392-6868 ext. 4511**
	(866) 462-MVNU
Fax: (740) 393-0511	**Email:** admissions@mvnu.edu
Full-time: 522 men, 926 women	**Faculty:** 82; IIA, --$
Part-time: 96 men, 212 women	**Ph.D.s:** 62%
Graduate: 172 men, 339 women	**Student/Faculty:** 18 to 1
Year: 4-1-4, summer session	**Tuition:** $22,890
Room & Board: $6700	**Freshman Class:** 1000 applied, 733 accepted, 290 enrolled
SAT CR/M: 493/524 **ACT:** 23	**CEEB CODE:** 1531
Application Deadline: May 1	**COMPETITIVE**

Mount Vernon Nazarene University, founded in 1968, is a private liberal arts college affiliated with the Church of the Nazarene. There are 6 undergraduate schools and 3 graduate schools. In addition to regional accreditation, MVNU has baccalaureate program accreditation with ACBSP, CSWE, NASM, and NCATE. The 406-acre campus is in a small town 45 miles northeast of Columbus. Including any residence halls, there are 51 buildings.

STUDENT LIFE: 92% of undergraduates are from Ohio. Others are from 33 states, 5 foreign countries, and Canada. 74% are from public schools. 85% are White. 50% are Unknown Religious Affiliation. The average age of freshmen is 18; all undergraduates, 25. 24% do not continue beyond their first year; 76% remain to graduate.

FACULTY/CLASSROOMS: 58% of faculty are male; 42% are female. 85% teach undergraduates. No introductory courses are taught by graduate students. The average class size in an introductory lecture is 20; in a laboratory is 16; and in a regular course is 16.

PROGRAMS OF STUDY: MVNU confers B.A., B.S., B.S.W. and B.B.A. degrees. Associate and master's degrees are also awarded. Bachelor's degrees are awarded in BIOLOGICAL SCIENCE (biology/biological science and life science), BUSINESS (accounting, business administration and management, business data processing, finance, international business management, management information systems, management science, marketing/retailing/merchandising, and sports management), COMMUNICATIONS AND THE ARTS (art, broadcasting, communications, dramatic arts, English, graphic design, journalism, music, public relations, and Spanish), COM-

PUTER AND PHYSICAL SCIENCE (chemistry, Computer Engineering Technology, computer science, and mathematics), EDUCATION (art education, business education, early childhood education, English education, mathematics education, middle school education, music education, physical education, science education, social studies education, and special education), ENGINEERING AND ENVIRONMENTAL DESIGN (preengineering), HEALTH PROFESSIONS (exercise science, medical technology, nursing, premedicine, prepharmacy, and prephysical therapy), SOCIAL SCIENCE (biblical studies, criminal justice, family/consumer studies, history, ministries, missions, pastoral studies, philosophy, political science/government, prelaw, psychology, religion, religious education, religious music, social work, sociology, theological studies, and youth ministry). Biology, nursing, and education are the strongest academically. Nursing, business, and education have the largest enrollments.

ACTIVITIES: There are 55 groups on campus, including art, band, cheerleading, choir, chorale, chorus, communications, computers, drama, environmental, ethnic, honors, international, jazz band, literary magazine, musical theater, newspaper, orchestra, pep band, photography, political, professional, radio and TV, religious, social, social service, student government, symphony, and yearbook. Popular campus events include Friday Night Live, Battle of the Bands, Sonfest, Annual Luau and all Cougars Sporting Events.

SERVICES: Counseling and information services are available, as is tutoring in most subjects. There is a reader service for the blind, and remedial math, reading, and writing. Students in the at-risk program are required to take University Success Strategies. **Library/Resources:** The library contains 107,246 volumes, 11,439 microform items, 6,212 audio/video tapes/CDs/DVDs, and subscribes to 17,411 periodicals including electronic. Computerized library services include interlibrary loans, database searching, Internet access, and Wi-Fi capability. Special learning facilities include an art gallery, radio station, an academic support center and a nature center. **Physically Challenged Students:** 95% of the campus is accessible. Facilities include wheelchair ramps, elevators, special parking, specially equipped restrooms, special class scheduling, lowered drinking fountains, lowered telephones, and special housing. **Special:** MVNU offers internships with local businesses and organizations, on-campus work-study programs, study abroad in 20 countries, dual majors, a general studies degree, and nondegree study. Cross-registration is available with Nazarene Universities, and the Council for Christian College and Universities program. There are 5 national honor societies, a freshman honors program, and 21 departmental honors programs. **Visiting:** There are regularly scheduled orientations for prospective students, MVNYou Visit Days - held throughout the year. There are guides for informal visits, visitors may sit in on classes, and stay overnight. To schedule a visit, contact the Admissions Office at (866) 462-6868. **Campus Safety and Security:** Measures include 24-hour foot and vehicle patrol, emergency notification system, self-defense education, and security escort services. There are shuttle buses, emergency telephones, lighted pathways/sidewalks, controlled access to dorms/residences, fire safety training with student leadership, and bloodborne pathogen seminars. Campus-wide sexual harassment training is required of all faculty, staff, and students. There is a Campus Safety and Security Review Committee.

REQUIREMENTS: The ACT is required. Applicants should be graduates of an accredited high school or home-school program and have ACT composite and subscores of 19 or above, or comparable SAT scores. Recommended preparatory courses include 4 units in English and 4 units each in math (algebra I and II, geometry, other), social studies, science, lab science, and 3 foreign language. An essay is required. Applicants not meeting minimum academic standards may be granted conditional admission with additional course requirements. A GPA of 2.5 is required. AP and CLEP credits are accepted. Important factors in the admissions decision are recommendations by school officials, personality/intangible qualities, and leadership record.

ADMISSIONS: 73% of a recent year applicants were accepted. The SAT scores for a recent year freshman class were: Critical Reading--34% below 500, 39% between 500 and 599, 20% between 600 and 699, and 6% between 700 and 800; Math--39% below 500, 37% between 500 and 599, and 24% between 600 and 699. The ACT scores were 26% below 21, 28% between 21 and 23, 20% between 24 and

26, 15% between 27 and 28, and 12% above 28. 32% of the current freshmen were in the top fifth of their class; 53% were in the top two fifths. 10 freshmen graduated first in their class.

FINANCIAL AID: In a recent year, 100% of all full-time freshmen and 99% of continuing full-time students received some form of financial aid. 96% of all full-time freshmen and 96% of continuing full-time students received need-based aid. The average freshman award was $19,942. Need-based scholarships or need-based grants averaged $12,919 ($29,590 maximum); need-based self-help aid (loans and jobs) averaged $7,107 ($18,054 maximum); non-need-based athletic scholarships averaged $6,701 ($14,950 maximum); and other non-need-based awards and non-need-based scholarships averaged $5,753 ($15,250 maximum). 46% of undergraduate students work part-time. Average annual earnings from campus work are $1800. The average financial indebtedness of the 2013 graduate was $25,313. The FAFSA and the college's own financial statement are required. The priority date for freshman financial aid applications for fall entry is March 15. The deadline for filing freshman financial aid applications for fall entry is August 8.

MUSKINGUM UNIVERSITY　　　　　D-3
www.muskingum.edu

New Concord, OH 43762　　　　(740) 826-8137
　　　　　　　　　　　　　　　(800) 752-6082
Fax: (740) 826-8100　　　Email: adminfo@muskingum.edu
Full-time: 802 men, 771 women　　Faculty: 99; IIB, -$
Part-time: 44 men, 132 women　　Ph.D.s: 87%
Graduate: 146 men, 395 women　　Student/Faculty: 14 to 1
Year: semesters, summer session　　Tuition: $22,462
Room & Board: $8940　　Freshman Class: 2134 applied, 1656 accepted, 438 enrolled
SAT CR/M: 491/513 ACT: 22　　CEEB CODE: 1496
Application Deadline: n/av　　COMPETITIVE

Muskingum University, founded in 1837, is a private liberal arts and sciences institution affiliated with the Presbyterian Church. There is one graduate school. In addition to regional accreditation, Muskingum has baccalaureate program accreditation with NASM and NCATE. The 245-acre campus is in a small town 9 miles west of Cambridge and 50 miles east of Columbus. Including any residence halls, there are 35 buildings.

STUDENT LIFE: 86% of undergraduates are from Ohio. Others are from 28 states, and 10 foreign countries. 85% are from public schools. 87% are White. 42% are Protestant; 30% claim no religious affiliation; 16% Catholic. The average age of freshmen is 18; all undergraduates, 20. 33% do not continue beyond their first year; 55% remain to graduate.

FACULTY/CLASSROOMS: 56% of faculty are male; 44% are female. 98% teach undergraduates, and 85% do both. No introductory courses are taught by graduate students. The average class size in an introductory lecture is 25; in a laboratory is 16; and in a regular course is 22.

PROGRAMS OF STUDY: Muskingum confers B.A., and B.S. degrees. Master's degrees are also awarded. Bachelor's degrees are awarded in AGRICULTURE (conservation and regulation), BIOLOGICAL SCIENCE (biology/biological science, molecular biology, and neurosciences), BUSINESS (accounting, business administration and management, and international business management), COMMUNICATIONS AND THE ARTS (art, communications, digital communications, dramatic arts, English, French, German, journalism, music, Spanish, and speech/debate/rhetoric), COMPUTER AND PHYSICAL SCIENCE (chemistry, computer science, earth science, geology, mathematics, and physics), EDUCATION (Christian education, early childhood education, elementary education, foreign languages education, music education, physical education, reading education, science education, secondary education, and special education), ENGINEERING AND ENVIRONMENTAL DESIGN (engineering and environmental science), HEALTH PROFESSIONS (nursing), SOCIAL SCIENCE (American studies, criminal justice,

economics, history, international relations, philosophy, political science/government, psychology, public affairs, religion, religious education, social science, and sociology). Sciences and education is the strongest academically. Education, business, psychology, and nursing have the largest enrollments.

ACTIVITIES: 24% of men belong to 3 local and 2 national fraternities; 37% of women belong to 4 local and 2 national sororities. There are 90 groups on campus, including and dance team, art, band, cheerleading, choir, chorus, computers, dance, debate, drama, environmental, ethnic, forensics, gay, honors, international, jazz band, literary magazine, marching band, musical theater, newspaper, orchestra, pep band, political, professional, radio and TV, religious, social, social service, student government, symphony, and yearbook. Popular campus events include Li'l Sibs Weekend and Muskiepalooza.

SERVICES: Counseling and information services are available, as is tutoring in every subject. There is a reader service for the blind. The PLUS program is available for learning-disabled and disabled students. **Library/Resources:** The library contains 209,220 volumes, 171,964 microform items, 3,471 audio/video tapes/CDs/DVDs, and subscribes to 14,127 periodicals including electronic. Computerized library services include interlibrary loans, database searching, and Internet access. Special learning facilities include an art gallery, radio station, TV station, a greenhouse. **Physically Challenged Students:** 40% of the campus is accessible. Facilities include wheelchair ramps, elevators, special parking, specially equipped restrooms, and lowered drinking fountains. **Special:** Internships, both national and regional, work-study programs, study abroad in 13 countries, and a Washington semester are possible. Dual and student-designed majors, nondegree study, pass/fail options, and credit for life, military, or work experience are also available. There are 18 national honor societies. **Visiting:** There are regularly scheduled orientations for prospective students, consisting of an admission presentation, faculty panel, student panel, and class attendance. There are guides for informal visits, visitors may sit in on classes, and stay overnight. To schedule a visit, contact the Admission Office. **Campus Safety and Security:** Measures include 24-hour foot and vehicle patrol, emergency notification system, and security escort services. There are emergency telephones, lighted pathways/sidewalks, and controlled access to dorms/residences.

REQUIREMENTS: The SAT or ACT is required. Candidates for admission must have a high school diploma or its equivalent and should have 4 years of English, 3 years of college preparatory math, and 2 years each of science, social science, and foreign language. A GPA of 2.0 is required. AP and CLEP credits are accepted. Important factors in the admissions decision are advanced placement or honors courses, extracurricular activities record, and leadership record.

ADMISSIONS: 78% of a recent year applicants were accepted. The SAT scores for a recent year freshman class were: Critical Reading--50% below 500, 43% between 500 and 599, 5% between 600 and 699, and 2% between 700 and 800; Math--45% below 500, 36% between 500 and 599, 14% between 600 and 699, and 5% between 700 and 800. The ACT scores were 40% below 21, 28% between 21 and 23, 19% between 24 and 26, 6% between 27 and 28, and 6% above 28. 39% of the current freshmen were in the top fifth of their class; 59% were in the top two fifths. 11 freshmen graduated first in their class.

FINANCIAL AID: In a recent year, 99% of all full-time freshmen and 98% of continuing full-time students received some form of financial aid. 84% of all full-time freshmen and 82% of continuing full-time students received need-based aid. The average freshman award was $19,518. Need-based scholarships or need-based grants averaged $15,314 ($30,500 maximum); and need-based self-help aid (loans and jobs) averaged $4,204 ($8,500 maximum). 45% of undergraduate students work part-time. Average annual earnings from campus work are $1000. The average financial indebtedness of the 2013 graduate was $34,207. Muskingum is a member of CSS. The FAFSA is required. The priority date for freshman financial aid applications for fall entry is March 1.

NOTRE DAME COLLEGE · D-1
www.notredamecollege.com

South Euclid, OH 44121	(216) 373-5351
	(800) NDC-OHIO
Fax: (216) 937-0357	Email: admissions@ndc.edu
Full-time: n/av	Faculty: n/av
Part-time: n/av	Ph.Ds: n/av
Graduate: n/av	Student/Faculty: n/av
Year: semesters, summer session	Tuition: $26,344
Room & Board: $8598	Freshman Class: n/av
SAT or ACT: required	CEEB CODE: 1566
Application Deadline: August	VERY COMPETITIVE

Notre Dame College, founded in 1922, is a private liberal arts and sciences college affiliated with the Roman Catholic Church. There is 1 undergraduate school and 1 graduate school. In addition to regional accreditation, NDC has baccalaureate program accreditation with ADA and NCATE. The 53-acre campus is in a suburban area Off of the 271 Cedar/Brainard Exit just past Beachwood Mall and Legacy Village. It is located 13 miles east of Cleveland. Including any residence halls, there are 10 buildings.

STUDENT LIFE: Students are from 20 states, 12 foreign countries, and Canada. 65% are from public schools. 65% are White; 23% African American. 55% are Catholic; 20% Baptist, and Muslim; 15% Protestant. The average age of freshmen is 18; all undergraduates, 26. 34% do not continue beyond their first year; 52% remain to graduate.

FACULTY/CLASSROOMS: All teach undergraduates. No introductory courses are taught by graduate students. The average class size in an introductory lecture is 16.

PROGRAMS OF STUDY: NDC confers B.A., and B.S. degrees. Associate and master's degrees are also awarded. Bachelor's degrees are awarded in BIOLOGICAL SCIENCE (biology/biological science), BUSINESS (accounting, business economics, human resources, management science, and marketing/retailing/merchandising), COMMUNICATIONS AND THE ARTS (art, communications, English, graphic design, public relations, studio art, and visual and performing arts), COMPUTER AND PHYSICAL SCIENCE (chemistry, information sciences and systems, and mathematics), EDUCATION (early childhood education, elementary education, middle school education, secondary education, and special education), ENGINEERING AND ENVIRONMENTAL DESIGN (environmental science), HEALTH PROFESSIONS (nursing and physical therapy), SOCIAL SCIENCE (economics, history, ministries, political science/government, psychology, and theological studies). Business, education, and science are the strongest academically. Business administration, education, and sciences have the largest enrollments.

ACTIVITIES: There are 32 groups on campus, including indoor colorguard, indoor percussions ensemble, art, band, cheerleading, choir, chorus, computers, dance, drama, ethnic, gay, honors, international, jazz band, literary magazine, marching band, marching band, newspaper, pep band, political, professional, religious, social, social service, and student government. Popular campus events include Founders Weekend, Welcome Weekend and Spring Fest Week.

SERVICES: Counseling and information services are available, as is tutoring in every subject, Notre Dame offers free peer tutoring within our Dwyer Learning Center. We also have an Academic Support Center for Students with Learning Differences. There is remedial math, reading, and writing. **Library/Resources:** The library contains 89,292 volumes, 14,200 microform items, 1,768 audio/video tapes/CDs/DVDs, and subscribes to 300 periodicals including electronic. Computerized library services include interlibrary loans and database searching. Special learning facilities include an art gallery, Tolerance Resource Center, Academic Support Center for Students with Learning Disabilities. **Physically Challenged Students:** 75% of the campus is accessible. Facilities include wheelchair ramps, elevators, special parking, specially equipped restrooms, lowered drinking fountains, and lowered telephones. **Special:** There are a freshman honors program. **Visiting:** There are regularly scheduled orientations for prospective students, students and their families will meet with an admissions counselor individually to discuss admissions, financial aid, and any other questions they may have. They also have the

options of taking a tour of campus or meeting with a professor. There are guides for informal visits, visitors may sit in on classes, and stay overnight. To schedule a visit, contact The Admissions Office at (216) 373-5355. **Campus Safety and Security:** Measures include 24-hour foot and vehicle patrol, emergency notification system, self-defense education, and security escort services. There are emergency telephones, lighted pathways/sidewalks, controlled access to dorms/residences, Notre Dame offers 24/7 campus security that work hand in had with the South Euclid Police Department.

REQUIREMENTS: The SAT or ACT is required. Applicants should be graduates of an accredited secondary school with 15 academic credits, including 4 of English, 2 of foreign language, 1 each of math, social studies, and science, plus 5 electives. The GED is accepted. An interview is recommended. A GPA of 2.5 is required. AP and CLEP credits are accepted.

FINANCIAL AID: In a recent year, 99% of all full-time freshmen received some form of financial aid. The FAFSA is required. Check with the school for current application deadlines.

OBERLIN COLLEGE · D-2
www.oberlin.edu

Oberlin, OH 44074	(440) 775-8411
	(800) 622-6243
Fax: (440) 775-6905	Email: college.admissions@oberlin.edu
Full-time: 1297 men, 1623 women	Faculty: 345; IIB, +$
Part-time: 22 men, 19 women	Ph.Ds: 96%
Graduate: 12 men, 5 women	Student/Faculty: 10 to 1
Year: 4-1-4	Tuition: $48,682
Room & Board: $13,106	Freshman Class: 7227 applied, 2365 accepted, 797 enrolled
SAT CR/M/W: 690/671/683 ACT: 30	CEEB CODE: 1587
Application Deadline: January 15	MOST COMPETITIVE

Oberlin College, founded in 1833, is a private institution offering degree programs in the liberal arts and sciences, as well as music. There are 2 undergraduate schools and 1 graduate school. In addition to regional accreditation, Oberlin has baccalaureate program accreditation with NASM. The 440-acre campus is in a small town 35 miles southwest of Cleveland, OH. Including any residence halls, there are 68 buildings.

STUDENT LIFE: 92% of undergraduates are from out of state, mostly the Middle Atlantic. Students are from 48 states, 45 foreign countries, and Canada. 63% are from public schools. 70% are White. The average age of freshmen is 18; all undergraduates, 20. 6% do not continue beyond their first year; 88% remain to graduate. **Housing:** 2700 students can be accommodated in college housing, which includes single-sex and coed dorms and on-campus apartments. In addition, there are language houses, special-interest houses, Including co-ops. On-campus housing is guaranteed for all 4 years. 87% of students live on campus; of those, 99% remain on campus on weekends. All students may keep cars.

FACULTY/CLASSROOMS: 62% of faculty are male; 38% are female. All teach and do research. No introductory courses are taught by graduate students. The average class size in a laboratory is 14 and in a regular course is 20.

PROGRAMS OF STUDY: Oberlin confers B.A., and B.Mus. degrees. Master's degrees are also awarded. Bachelor's degrees are awarded in AGRICULTURE (environmental studies), BIOLOGICAL SCIENCE (biochemistry, biology/biological science, and neurosciences), COMMUNICATIONS AND THE ARTS (acting, art history, art, art/visual culture, classics, composition, comparative literature, conducting, creative writing, dance, dramatic arts, English, film arts, fine arts, French, German, Germanic languages and literature, music, music composition, music history and appreciation, music performance, music theory and composition, painting, performing arts, photography, piano/organ, romance languages and literature, Russian, Russian languages and literature, Spanish, strings, studio art, studio art painting, theatre acting, theater design, theatre studies, and winds), COMPUTER AND PHYSICAL SCIENCE (applied mathematics, astronomy, astronomy and physics, chemistry, computer science, geology, mathematics, and physics), EDUCATION (music education), HEALTH PROFESSIONS (biology and premedicine), SOCIAL SCIENCE (africana studies, African American studies, American studies, anthropology, archeology, East Asian studies, Eastern European studies, economics, gender studies, history, humanities, international studies, Judaic studies, Latin American studies, law, Near Eastern studies, philosophy, political science/government, prelaw, psychology, religion, Russian and Slavic studies, sociology, spanish and hispanic studies, women & gender studies, and women's studies). Sciences, art, and humanities are the strongest academically. English, biology, history and politics have the largest enrollments.

ACTIVITIES: There are 200 groups on campus, including art, band, chess, choir, chorale, chorus, communications, computers, dance, debate, drama, environmental, ethnic, film, forensics, gay, honors, international, jazz band, literary magazine, marching band, musical theater, newspaper, opera, orchestra, photography, political, professional, radio and TV, religious, social, social service, student government, and symphony. Popular campus events include Big Parade, Earth Day, and Art Rental. **Sports:** There are 11 intercollegiate sports for men and 11 for women, and 10 intramural sports for men and 10 for women. Facilities include an all-weather multi-purpose field with artificial turf and lights, field house, indoor 6-lane, 200-meter track, 8-lane outdoor track, 12 outdoor and 4 indoor tennis courts, cross-country course, fitness trail, swimming pool, nautilus center, free-weight room, 22 practice/play fields, indoor space for football, soccer, and lacrosse practice, and a climbing wall. **Graduates:** From July 1, 2013 to June 30, 2014, 693 bachelor's degrees were awarded. The most popular majors were politics (10%), biology (8%), and history (7%). In an average class, 1% graduate in 3 years or less, 76% graduate in 4 years or less, 86% graduate in 5 years or less, and 88% graduate in 6 years or less.

SERVICES: Counseling and information services are available, as is tutoring in every subject. There is a reader service for the blind, and remedial math, reading, and writing. Computer-assisted services for hearing and visually impaired students. **Library/Resources:** The 4 libraries contain 1.5 million volumes, 330,900 microform items, 158,661 audio/video tapes/CDs/DVDs, and subscribe to 173,245 periodicals including electronic. Computerized library services include interlibrary loans, database searching, and Internet access. Special learning facilities include an art gallery, radio station, an observatory, art museum, art library, arboretum, a conservatory of music, a music library, science library, and a learning center specializing in foreign language education. **Physically Challenged Students:** 90% of the campus is accessible. Facilities include wheelchair ramps, elevators, special parking, specially equipped restrooms, special class scheduling, lowered drinking fountains, lowered telephones, special housing. An indoor/outdoor lift. **Special:** Internships are available through the Business Initiatives Program. Students may study abroad in 38 countries. Three-quarters of Oberlin students spend time abroad for study or service. The college offers independent and dual majors, 3-2 engineering programs with other institutions, non-degree study for special and visiting students, and a 5-year B.A.-B.Mus. double degree. Pass/no credit options are available to all students. There are 4 national honor societies, including Phi Beta Kappa, and 25 departmental honors programs. **Visiting:** There are regularly scheduled orientations for prospective students, consisting of campus tour, information session, class visits, interview, and an overnight stay in the dorm. There are guides for informal visits, visitors may sit in on classes, and stay overnight. To schedule a visit, contact the Campus Visit Office. **Campus Safety and Security:** Measures include 24-hour foot and vehicle patrol, emergency notification system, self-defense education, and security escort services. There are emergency telephones, lighted pathways/sidewalks, controlled access to dorms/residences, Full-time crime prevention officer, a 24-hour headquarters facility staffed by professional dispatchers, and an electronic card-access system in all dorms.

REQUIREMENTS: The SAT or ACT is required. The ACT Optional Writing test is also required. Candidates for admission should have completed 4 years each of English and math, and 3 each of science, social studies, and a foreign language. Either the SAT or ACT Plus Writing is required. International students must also submit TOEFL or IELTS exam scores. AP credits are accepted. Important factors in the admissions decision are leadership record, personality/intangible qualities, and advanced placement or honors courses. Students are required to complete 32 full courses, including 2 in each of the 3 academic divisions (arts/humanities, social/behavioral sciences, natural science/math), 3 courses dealing with cultural diversity, plus 3 winter term projects. In addition, they must earn a writing and quantitative proficiency certification. **Procedure:** Freshmen are admitted in fall. Entrance exams should be taken in the junior year or early in the senior year. There are early decision, early admissions, and deferred admissions plans. Early decision applications should be filed by November 15; regular applications, by January 15 for fall entry; and November 15 for spring entry. Notification of early decision is sent December 15; regular decision, April 1. 269 early decision candidates were accepted for the 2014-2015 class. Applications are accepted online. Application fees are waived if application is completed on-line. **Transfer Students:** 29 transfer students enrolled in 2013-2014. Applicants should submit official transcripts of all college work completed, plus a list of current courses and midterm grades. An average of B or better should be presented. A high school transcript, recommendations, and standardized test scores are also required. 16 of 32 credits required for the bachelor's degree must be completed at Oberlin. **International Students:** There are 197 international students enrolled. The school actively recruits these students. They must take the TOEFL with a minimum score of 600 on the paper-based TOEFL (PBT) or 100 on the Internet-based version (iBT), or take the IELTS. They must also take the SAT or ACT. International students whose native language is English must take the SAT or ACT Plus Writing.

ADMISSIONS: 33% of the 2014-2015 applicants were accepted. The SAT scores for the 2014-2015 freshman class were: Critical Reading--1% below 500, 9% between 500 and 599, 47% between 600 and 699, and 43% between 700 and 800; Math--2% below 500, 13% between 500 and 599, 50% between 600 and 699, and 35% between 700 and 800; Writing--1% below 500, 10% between 500 and 599, 48% between 600 and 699, and 41% between 700 and 800. The ACT scores were % below 21, 2% between 21 and 23, % between 24 and 26, 38% between 27 and 28, and 60% above 28. 91% of the current freshmen were in the top fifth of their class; 100% were in the top two fifths. **Admissions Contact:** Debra Chermonte, VP/Dean of Admissions & Financial Aid. E-Mail: *college.admissions@oberlin.edu* Web: *www.oberlin.edu*

FINANCIAL AID: In 2014-2015, 86% of all full-time freshmen and 85% of continuing full-time students received some form of financial aid. 47% of all full-time freshmen and 48% of continuing full-time students received need-based aid. The average freshman award was $37,344. Need-based scholarships or need-based grants averaged $32,992; need-based self-help aid (loans and jobs) averaged $5,445; and other non-need-based awards and non-need-based scholarships averaged $13,380. 59% of undergraduate students work part-time. Average annual earnings from campus work are $2100. The average financial indebtedness of the 2014 graduate was $23,814. Oberlin is a member of CSS. The CSS/Profile, FAFSA, and the college's own financial statement are required. The deadline for filing freshman financial aid applications for fall entry is February 15.

OHIO DOMINICAN UNIVERSITY C-3
www.ohiodominican.edu

Columbus, OH 43219

(614) 251-4500
(800) 955-OHIO

Fax: (614) 252-0776   Email: admissions@ohiodominican.edu

Full-time: 611 men, 780 women	Faculty: n/av
Part-time: 239 men, 375 women	Ph.D.s: 91%
Graduate: 178 men, 390 women	Student/Faculty: 12 to 1
Year: semesters, summer session	Tuition: $28,402
Room & Board: $9978	Freshman Class: 2652 applied, 1310 accepted
ACT: required	CEEB CODE: 1131
Application Deadline: open	COMPETITIVE+

Ohio Dominican University, founded in 1911 by the Dominican Sisters of St. Mary of the Springs, is a private liberal arts university affiliated with the Roman Catholic Church. There are 2 undergraduate schools and 1 graduate school. In addition to regional accreditation, ODU has baccalaureate program accreditation with ACBSP, CSWE, and NCATE. The 98-acre campus is in an urban area 5 miles from downtown Columbus. Including any residence halls, there are 16 buildings.

STUDENT LIFE: 96% of undergraduates are from Ohio. Others are from 16 states, 12 foreign countries, and Canada. 82% are from public schools. 67% are White; 23% African American. 37% are Catholic; 34% Protestant. The average age of freshmen is 18; all undergraduates, 24. 34% do not continue beyond their first year; 66% remain to graduate.

FACULTY/CLASSROOMS: 54% of faculty are male; 46% are female. All teach undergraduates. No introductory courses are taught by graduate students. The average class size in an introductory lecture is 20 and in a regular course is 20.

PROGRAMS OF STUDY: ODU confers B.A., B.S. and B.S.Ed. degrees. Associate and master's degrees are also awarded. Bachelor's degrees are awarded in AGRICULTURE (environmental studies), BIOLOGICAL SCIENCE (biology/biological science), BUSINESS (accounting, banking and finance, business administration and management, international business management, management information systems, and sports management), COMMUNICATIONS AND THE ARTS (art, communications, English, graphic design, and public relations), COMPUTER AND PHYSICAL SCIENCE (chemistry, computer science, and mathematics), EDUCATION (early childhood education, middle school education, and special education), HEALTH PROFESSIONS (exercise science), SOCIAL SCIENCE (criminal justice, economics, history, interdisciplinary studies, liberal arts/general studies, peace studies, philosophy, political science/government, psychology, social work, sociology, and theological studies). Business, education, and psychology have the largest enrollments.

ACTIVITIES: There are 40 groups on campus; including academic, black student union, commuter, religious clubs, student government PhiAlpha club, art, association of resident students, band, cheerleading, choir, dance, drama, drill team, environmental, ethnic, honors, international, literary magazine, newspaper, panther players, pep band, political, professional, radio and TV, religious, social, social service, social work, St. Alberts club, and student government. Popular campus events include Black History Week, International Student Week, and ODU Day in the Spring.

SERVICES: Counseling and information services are available, as is tutoring in most subjects. There is remedial math, reading, and writing. The Academic Center is a support unit designed to help all students meet their academic commitment and improve their learning skills. The staff offers workshops in study-related topics, and provides professional and peer tutoring. **Library/Resources:** The library contains 161,704 volumes, 10,878 microform items, and 4,422 audio/video tapes/CDs/DVDs, and subscribes to 13,282 periodicals including electronic. Computerized library services include interlibrary loans, database searching, Internet access, and Wi-Fi capability. Special learning facilities include an art gallery and radio station. **Physically Challenged Students:** 90% of the campus is accessible. Facilities include wheelchair ramps, elevators, special parking, specially equipped restrooms, special class scheduling, and lowered drinking fountains. **Special:** Students may cross-register with members of the Higher Education Council of Columbus Consortium, study abroad in various countries, and participate in a Washington semester. Internships are required in some majors. ODU offers dual majors and pass/fail options in some courses. Nondegree study and credit for life, military, and work experience are available. There is an accelerated degree program in business administration. There are 2 national honor societies and a freshman honors program. **Visiting:** There are regularly scheduled orientations for prospective students, including an August orientation for fall entry and a January orientation for the second semester. Individual appointments can be arranged. There are guides for informal visits, visitors may sit in on classes, and stay overnight. To schedule a visit, contact the Director of Admissions.

Campus Safety and Security: Measures include 24-hour foot and vehicle patrol, emergency notification system, and security escort services. There are shuttle buses, emergency telephones, and lighted pathways/sidewalks.

REQUIREMENTS: The ACT is required. Candidates for admission should have completed 4 units of English and 3 units each of a foreign language, math, science, and social studies. The freshman applicant is required to submit a completed application and transcripts of secondary courses and grades. An essay and an interview (in-state applicants) are required. A GPA of 2.0 is required. AP and CLEP credits are accepted.

ADMISSIONS: 49% of a recent year applicants were accepted. The SAT scores for a recent year freshman class were: Critical Reading--53% below 500, 28% between 500 and 599, 14% between 600 and 699, and 5% between 700 and 800; Math--35% below 500, 42% between 500 and 599, and 23% between 600 and 699. The ACT scores were 33% below 21, 33% between 21 and 23, 22% between 24 and 26, 7% between 27 and 28, and 4% above 28. 36% of the current freshmen were in the top fifth of their class; 68% were in the top two fifths. 7 freshmen graduated first in their class.

FINANCIAL AID: In a recent year, 100% of all full-time freshmen and 98% of continuing full-time students received some form of financial aid. 88% of all full-time freshmen and 87% of continuing full-time students received need-based aid. The average freshman award was $23,000. Need-based scholarships or need-based grants averaged $4,200 ($6,000 maximum); need-based self-help aid (loans and jobs) averaged $5,200 ($8,000 maximum); and other non-need-based awards and non-need-based scholarships averaged $7,000 ($13,000 maximum). 35% of undergraduate students work part-time. Average annual earnings from campus work are $1500. The FAFSA is required. Check with the school for current application deadlines.

OHIO NORTHERN UNIVERSITY   B-2
www.onu.edu

Ada, OH 45810

(419) 772-2260
(800) 408-4668

Fax: (419) 772-2313
Email: admissions-ug@onu.edu

Full-time: 1190 men, 1055 women	**Faculty:** IIB, av$
Part-time: 40 men, 35 women	**Ph.D.s:** 82%
Graduate: 425 men, 580 women	**Student/Faculty:** n/av
Year: trimesters, summer session	**Tuition:** $34,640
Room & Board: $10,344	**Freshman Class:** n/av
SAT or ACT: required	**CEEB CODE:** 1591
Application Deadline: see profile	**VERY COMPETITIVE**

Ohio Northern University, founded in 1871, is a private institution affiliated with the United Methodist Church. Undergraduate programs are offered in arts and sciences, business administration, engineering, and pharmacy. The figures in the above capsule and in this profile are approximate. There are 4 undergraduate schools and 1 graduate school. In addition to regional accreditation, ONU has baccalaureate program accreditation with ABET, ACPE, NASM, and NCATE. The 285-acre campus is in a small town about 75 miles south of Toledo. Including any residence halls, there are 39 buildings.

STUDENT LIFE: 86% of undergraduates are from Ohio. Others are from 42 states, 17 foreign countries, and Canada. 82% are from public schools. 95% are white. 43% are Baptist, Muslim, Lutheran, Presbyterian, United Church of Christ; 26% Catholic; 12% claim no religious affiliation. The average age of freshmen is 18; all undergraduates, 20. 18% do not continue beyond their first year; 66% remain to graduate.

FACULTY/CLASSROOMS: 67% of faculty are male; 33% are female. 90% teach undergraduates. No introductory courses are taught by graduate students. The average class size in an introductory lecture is 29; in a laboratory, 14; and in a regular course, 25.

PROGRAMS OF STUDY: ONU confers B.A., B.S., B.F.A., B.M., B.S.B.A., B.S.C.E., B.S.C.P.E., B.S.E.E., B.S.M.E., B.S.M.T., and B.S.Ph. degrees. Doctoral degrees are also awarded. Bachelor's degrees are awarded in AGRICULTURE (environmental studies), BIOLOGICAL SCIENCE (biochemistry, biology/biological science, and molecular biology), BUSINESS (accounting, business administration and management, business economics, international business management, management science, and sports management), COMMUNICATIONS AND THE ARTS (broadcasting, ceramic art and design, communications, creative writing, dramatic arts, English, fine arts, French, graphic design, journalism, language arts, literature, music, music business management, music performance, music theory and composition, public relations, and Spanish), COMPUTER AND PHYSICAL SCIENCE (chemistry, computer science, mathematics, physics, and statistics), EDUCATION (athletic training, early childhood education, health education, middle school education, music education, and physical education), ENGINEERING AND ENVIRONMENTAL DESIGN (civil engineering, computer engineering, electrical/electronics engineering, mechanical engineering, and technological management), HEALTH PROFESSIONS (health, medical technology, and pharmacy), SOCIAL SCIENCE (criminal justice, history, international studies, philosophy, political science/government, psychology, religion, social studies, sociology, and youth ministry). Chemistry, engineering, and pharmacy are the strongest academically. Pharmacy, engineering, and biology have the largest enrollments.

ACTIVITIES: 25% of men belong to 8 national fraternities; 22% of women belong to 4 national sororities. There are 170 groups on campus, including art, band, cheerleading, chess, choir, chorale, chorus, computers, dance, debate, drama, drill team, ethnic, honors, international, jazz band, literary magazine, marching band, musical theater, newspaper, orchestra, pep band, political, professional, radio and TV, religious, social, social service, student government, symphony, and yearbook. Popular campus events include Tunes on the Tundra, International Week, and Little Sibs Weekend.

SERVICES: Counseling and information services are available, as is tutoring in most subjects. There is a reader service for the blind, and remedial math and writing. **Library/Resources:** The 2 libraries contain 250,518 volumes, 72,067 microform items, and 10,815 audio/video tapes/CDs/DVDs, and subscribe to 1,038 periodicals including electronic. Computerized library services include interlibrary loans and database searching. Special learning facilities include an art gallery, radio station, TV station, pharmacy museum. **Physically Challenged Students:** 95% of the campus is accessible. Facilities include wheelchair ramps, elevators, special parking, specially equipped restrooms, special class scheduling, lowered drinking fountains, and lowered telephones. **Special:** Co-op programs are available in civil, electrical, computer, and mechanical engineering and technology, computer science, and math. Students may take internships in pharmacy, engineering, and business and may study abroad in 15 countries. B.A.-B.S. degrees and dual majors are available in arts/engineering, arts/pharmacy, and arts/business. The university also offers pass/fail options and work-study programs. There are 38 national honor societies, a freshman honors program, and 21 departmental honors programs. **Visiting:** There are regularly scheduled orientations for prospective students, including a tour, lunch, and appointments in academics, admissions, and financial aid. A meeting with a coach can also be arranged. There are guides for informal visits, visitors may sit in on classes, and stay overnight. To schedule a visit, contact the Admissions Office. **Campus Safety and Security:** Measures include 24-hour foot and vehicle patrol, self-defense education, and security escort services. There are emergency telephones and lighted pathways/sidewalks.

REQUIREMENTS: The SAT or ACT is required. In addition, the preparatory program should include 4 years of English, 3 of math, and 2 each of science, social studies, art, history, and music; 2 years of foreign language are recommended. ONU requires applicants to be in the upper 50% of their class. A GPA of 2.5 is required. AP and CLEP credits are accepted. Important factors in the admissions decision are advanced placement or honors courses, leadership record, and extracurricular activities record.

FINANCIAL AID: ONU is a member of CSS. The FAFSA and the college's own financial statement are required. Check with the school for current application deadlines.

OHIO STATE UNIVERSITY SYSTEM

The Ohio State University System, established in 1963, is a land-grant system in Ohio. It is governed by the Ohio Board of Regents, whose chief administrator is the president. The primary goal of the system is teaching, research, and public service. The main priorities are to enhance the quality of human life by developing individual capacity for understanding, thinking, and acting; to serve as a natural

resource; and to shape society for the common good. The total student enrollment is usually about 527,000 with 4558 faculty members. Altogether there are 220 baccalaureate, 132 master's, and 100 doctoral programs offered in the Ohio State University System. Profiles of the 4-year campuses are included in this section.

OHIO STATE UNIVERSITY AT LIMA   B-2
www.lima.osu.edu

Lima, OH 45804	**(419) 995-8600**
	(419) 995-8391
Fax: (419) 995-8483	**Email:** lima-askabuckeye@osu.edu
Full-time: 401 men, 473 women	**Faculty:** I, +$
Part-time: 72 men, 95 women	**Ph.D.s:** 97%
Graduate: 1 men, 14 women	**Student/Faculty:** n/av
Year: semesters, summer session	**Tuition:** $7140 ($22,860)
Room & Board: n/a	**Freshman Class:** 1257 applied, 1244 accepted, 432 enrolled
SAT CR/M/W: 550/565/515 **ACT:** 22	**CEEB CODE:** 1541
Application Deadline: June 1	**COMPETITIVE**

Ohio State University at Lima, founded in 1960, is a regional commuter campus in the Ohio State University system. At Lima, students may earn a bachelor's degree in education, English, and psychology as well as 1 to 3 years of credit toward any degree conferred by OSU. The student may finish the degree at the Columbus campus or transfer to another institution. In addition to regional accreditation, Ohio State Lima has baccalaureate program accreditation with AACSB, ABET, ACPE, ADA, AHEA, APTA, ASLA, CSAB, CSWE, FIDER, NAAB, NASAD, NASM, and NCATE. The 562-acre campus is in a suburban area 3 miles east of Lima, OH. Including any residence halls, there are 13 buildings.

STUDENT LIFE: 100% of undergraduates are from Ohio. Others are from 5 states, and 1 foreign country. 95% are from public schools. 86% are White. **Male To Female Ratio:** 1.2:1. The average age of freshmen is 18; all undergraduates, 21. 36% do not continue beyond their first year; 64% remain to graduate. Alcohol is not permitted. All students commute. All students may keep cars.

FACULTY/CLASSROOMS: 51% of faculty are male; 49% are female. No introductory courses are taught by graduate students.

PROGRAMS OF STUDY: Ohio State Lima confers B.A., B.S. and B.S.Ed. degrees. Associate and Master's degrees are also awarded. Bachelor's degrees are awarded in BIOLOGICAL SCIENCE (biology/biological science), BUSINESS (business administration and management), COMMUNICATIONS AND THE ARTS (English), EDUCATION (education and health information management), HEALTH PROFESSIONS (dental hygiene and nursing), SOCIAL SCIENCE (family/consumer resource management, history, and psychology). Biology, psychology, and early childhood education have the largest enrollments.

ACTIVITIES: Groups on campus include art, choir, chorale, chorus, dance, drama, drill team, film, forensics, honors, international, literary magazine, musical theater, newspaper, political, professional, radio and TV, social, social service, student government, and yearbook. **Sports:** There are 3 intercollegiate sports for men and 2 for women, and 5 intramural sports for men and 5 for women. Facilities include Cook Hall gymnasium (The Hanger) 634 seating; Baron's baseball field, five indoor facilities and over 70 acres of outdoor parks. **Graduates:** In an average class, 1% graduate in 3 years or less, 21% graduate in 4 years or less, 29% graduate in 5 years or less, and 33% graduate in 6 years or less.

SERVICES: **Library/Resources:** Computerized library services include interlibrary loans, database searching, Internet access, and Wi-Fi capability. Special learning facilities include a radio station, including a Greenhouse, and a Geology Museum. **Physically Challenged Students:** All of the campus is accessible. **Special:** Cross-registration is possible with Ohio State Main Campus and there is work-study with Ohio State. There are co-op programs, extensive study abroad in about 40 countries, work-study programs, dual and student-designed majors, a general degree, an accelerated degree, credit by exam, nondegree study, and pass/fail options. There is a freshman honors program and 4 departmental honors programs. **Visiting:** There are regularly scheduled orientations for prospective students. There are guides for informal visits and visitors may sit in on classes. To schedule a visit, contact the Office of Admissions.

REQUIREMENTS: Open admission policy for in-state students. Applicants must complete high school and should have 4 credits in English, 3 each in math and science, 2 each in foreign language and history or social studies, and 1 in art or music. The GED is accepted. AP and CLEP credits are accepted.To graduate, all students must complete an average of 120 semester hours, with a minimum GPA of 2.0, and fulfill the general education curriculum requirements. **Procedure:** Freshmen are admitted fall, spring, and summer. Entrance exams should be taken October of Senior Year. There is a rolling admissions plan. Application deadlines are open. Application fee is $60. Applications are accepted on-line. **Transfer Students:** 111 transfer students enrolled in 2013-2014. 2.0 or 45+ quarter hours; applicants with less than 45 qtr hrs considered for admission based on college and/or high school performance where the criteria vary by hours earned 30 of 120 credits required for the bachelor's degree must be completed at Ohio State Lima. **International Students:** There are 1 international students enrolled. They must take the TOEFL. They must also take the SAT or ACT.

ADMISSIONS: 99% of the 2014-2015 applicants were accepted. The SAT scores for the 2014-2015 freshman class were: Critical Reading--9% below 500, 59% between 500 and 599, 27% between 600 and 699, and 5% between 700 and 800; Math--32% below 500, 32% between 500 and 599, and 36% between 600 and 699; Writing--23% below 500, 59% between 500 and 599, 14% between 600 and 699, and 4% between 700 and 800. The ACT scores were 35% below 21, 29% between 21 and 23, 22% between 24 and 26, 9% between 27 and 28, and 5% above 28. 8% of the current freshmen were in the top fifth of their class; 30% were in the top two fifths. 3 freshmen graduated first in their class. **Admissions Contact:** Beth Keehn, MBA, Associate Director of Enrollment Service. Web: *www.lima.osu.edu*

FINANCIAL AID: In 2014-2015, 93% of all full-time freshmen and 87% of continuing full-time students received some form of financial aid. 70% of all full-time freshmen and 70% of continuing full-time students received need-based aid. The average freshman award was $8,893. Need-based scholarships or need-based grants averaged $4,593 ($6,230 maximum); need-based self-help aid (loans and jobs) averaged $3,666 ($6,500 maximum); and other non-need-based awards and non-need-based scholarships averaged $4,409 ($21,500 maximum). The FAFSA is required. The priority date for freshman financial aid applications for fall entry is February 15.

OHIO STATE UNIVERSITY AT MANSFIELD   C-2
www.mansfield.osu.edu

Mansfield, OH 44906	419-755-4317
	Email: elliot.625@osu.edu
Full-time: 434 men, 526 women	**Faculty:** IIB, av$
Part-time: 81 men, 114 women	**Ph.D.s:** 99%
Graduate: 5 men, 28 women	**Student/Faculty:** n/av
Year: quarters, summer session	**Tuition:** $7140 ($22,860)
Room & Board: $6020	**Freshman Class:** 1626 applied, 1610 accepted, 477 enrolled
SAT CR/M/W: 520/560/480 **ACT:** 23	**CEEB CODE:** 0744
Application Deadline: June 1	**COMPETITIVE**

Ohio State University at Mansfield, founded in 1958, is a regional commuter campus of the Ohio State University system. At Mansfield, students may earn an undergraduate degree in elementary education. In addition to regional accreditation, OSU Mansfield has baccalaureate program accreditation with AACSB, ABET, ACPE, ADA, AHEA, APTA, CSAB, CSWE, FIDER, NAAB, NASM, NCATE, and NCA-HLC. The 620-acre campus is in an urban area 2 miles from Mansfield, OH. Including any residence halls, there are 29 buildings. **STUDENT LIFE:** 100% of undergraduates are from Ohio. Others are

from 3 states. 90% are from public schools. 81% are White. The average age of freshmen is 18; all undergraduates, 22. 33% do not continue beyond their first year; 67% remain to graduate. **Housing:** 197 students can be accommodated in college housing, which includes coed on-campus apartments. Apartments for single students. On-campus housing is guaranteed for the freshman year only, is available on a first-come, first-served basis, and is available on a lottery system for upperclassmen. 72% of students commute. All students may keep cars.

FACULTY/CLASSROOMS: 42% of faculty are male; 58% are female. No introductory courses are taught by graduate students.

PROGRAMS OF STUDY: OSU Mansfield confers B.A., and B.S.Ed degrees. Associate and Master's degrees are also awarded. Bachelor's degrees are awarded in BUSINESS (business administration and management), COMMUNICATIONS AND THE ARTS (English), EDUCATION (elementary education), HEALTH PROFESSIONS (nursing), SOCIAL SCIENCE (history and psychology). Psychology, biology, and English are the strongest academically. Early and middle childhood education, psychology, and English have the largest enrollments.

ACTIVITIES: Groups on campus include cheerleading. **Sports:** There are 3 intercollegiate sports for men and 3 for women, and 10 intramural sports for men and 11 for women. Facilities include a gym and a weight room. **Graduates:** In an average class, 1% graduate in 3 years or less, 23% graduate in 4 years or less, 36% graduate in 5 years or less, and 42% graduate in 6 years or less.

SERVICES: Counseling and information services are available, as is tutoring in most subjects. There is a reader service for the blind, and remedial math, reading, and writing. **Library/Resources:** Computerized library services include interlibrary loans, database searching, Internet access, and Wi-Fi capability. Special learning facilities include a TV station. **Physically Challenged Students:** All of the campus is accessible. Facilities include wheelchair ramps, elevators, special parking, specially equipped restrooms, special class scheduling, lowered drinking fountains, lowered telephones, and special housing. **Special:** OSU Mansfield offers co-op programs, study abroad, internships, a general studies degree (no major), nondegree study, pass/fail options, and work-study programs. There are 3 national honor societies, a freshman honors program, and 2 departmental honors programs. **Visiting:** There are regularly scheduled orientations for prospective students. There are guides for informal visits, visitors may sit in on classes, and stay overnight. To schedule a visit, contact Pamela Leonard, Coordinator at (419) 755-4317.

REQUIREMENTS: There is an open admission policy for in-state students. Applicants must complete high school and should have 4 credits in English, 3 each in math and science, 2 each in foreign language and history or social studies, and 1 in art or music. The GED is accepted. AP and CLEP credits are accepted. To graduate, all students must complete 181 to 220 quarter hours, with a minimum GPA of 2.0. General education curriculum requirements must be met. **Procedure:** Freshmen are admitted fall, spring, and summer. Entrance exams should be taken Spring of the junior year or early Fall of the senior year. There is a rolling admissions plan. Application deadlines are open. Application fee is $60. Applications are accepted on-line. **Transfer Students:** 98 transfer students enrolled in 2013-2014. 2.0 on 30+ semester hours; applicants with less than 30 sem. hrs considered for admission based on college and/or high school performance where the criteria vary by hours earned. 30 of 120 credits required for the bachelor's degree must be completed at OSU Mansfield. **International Students:** They must also take the SAT or ACT.

ADMISSIONS: 99% of the 2014-2015 applicants were accepted. The SAT scores for the 2014-2015 freshman class were: Critical Reading--42% below 500, 51% between 500 and 599, 5% between 600 and 699, and 2% between 700 and 800; Math--33% below 500, 39% between 500 and 599, 26% between 600 and 699, and 2% between 700 and 800; Writing--54% below 500, 37% between 500 and 599, and 9% between 600 and 699. The ACT scores were 30% below 21, 30% between 21 and 23, 23% between 24 and 26, 9% between 27 and 28, and 8% above 28. 24% of the current freshmen were in the top fifth of their class; 57% were in the top two fifths. 6 freshmen graduated first in their class. **Admissions Contact:** Office of Admission E-Mail: *galat.12@osu.edu* Web: *http://mansfield.osu.edu/HTML/admissions/admissions.html*

FINANCIAL AID: In 2014-2015, 94% of all full-time freshmen and 87% of continuing full-time students received some form of financial aid. 70% of all full-time freshmen and 73% of continuing full-time students received need-based aid. The average freshman award was $10,511. Need-based scholarships or need-based grants averaged $4,959 ($6,778 maximum); need-based self-help aid (loans and jobs) averaged $3,971 ($6,500 maximum); and other non-need-based awards and non-need-based scholarships averaged $5,336 ($22,894 maximum). OSU Mansfield is a member of CSS. The FAFSA and CCS/Profile, or FAFSA, or FFS, or SFS are required. The priority date for freshman financial aid applications for fall entry is February 15.

OHIO STATE UNIVERSITY AT MARION — C-3
www.marion.osu.edu

Marion, OH 43302	(740) 725-6242
Fax: (740) 725-6258	Email: moreau.1@osu.edu
Full-time: 20,989 men, 19,031 women	Faculty: IIB, av$
	Ph.D.s: 99%
Part-time: 2293 men, 1888 women	Student/Faculty: 19 to 1
Graduate: 6139 men, 7126 women	Tuition: $9850 ($22,860)
Year: quarters, summer session	Freshman Class: 31359 applied, 48772 accepted, 7130 enrolled
Room & Board: n/av	
SAT CR/M/W: 600/665/605 ACT: 29	CEEB CODE: 0751
Application Deadline: n/av	MOST COMPETITIVE

Ohio State University at Marion, founded in 1957, is a commuter campus of the Ohio State University system. At Marion, students may earn a bachelor's degree in elementary education, English, history, business management, and psychology as well as 1 to 3 years of credit applicable to any other degree, including more than 170 academic programs, conferred by OSU, provided the program is completed at the main campus in Columbus. In addition to regional accreditation, OSU Marion has baccalaureate program accreditation with AACSB, ABET, ACPE, ADA, AHEA, APTA, CSAB, CSWE, FIDER, NAAB, NASM, and NCATE. The 188-acre campus is in a rural area 45 miles north of Columbus, OH. Including any residence halls, there are 9 buildings.

STUDENT LIFE: 100% of undergraduates are from Ohio. Others are from 5 states, and 1 foreign countries. 93% are from public schools. 82% are White. The average age of freshmen is 18; all undergraduates, 21. 33% do not continue beyond their first year; 67% remain to graduate.

FACULTY/CLASSROOMS: 52% of faculty are male; 48% are female. No introductory courses are taught by graduate students.

PROGRAMS OF STUDY: OSU Marion confers B.A., B.S. and B.S.Ed. degrees. Associate and master's degrees are also awarded. Bachelor's degrees are awarded in BUSINESS (business administration and management), COMMUNICATIONS AND THE ARTS (English), EDUCATION (education and elementary education), HEALTH PROFESSIONS (nursing), SOCIAL SCIENCE (history and psychology). Psychology, English, and history have the largest enrollments.

ACTIVITIES: There are no fraternities or sororities. There are 25 groups on campus, including art, choir, chorus, dance, drama, ethnic, honors, international, jazz band, literary magazine, musical theater, newspaper, political, professional, religious, social, social service, and student government. Popular campus events include Buckeye Week, May Day and Cultural Events.

SERVICES: Counseling and information services are available, as is tutoring in most subjects. There is a reader service for the blind, and remedial math, reading, and writing. **Library/Resources:** Computerized library services include interlibrary loans, database searching, Internet access, and Wi-Fi capability. Special learning facilities include an art gallery, planetarium, TV station, natural reconstructed prairie site, greenhouse, psychology lab, and early childhood education center. **Physically Challenged Students:** All of the campus is accessible. Facilities include wheelchair ramps, elevators, special parking, specially equipped restrooms, special class scheduling, lowered drinking fountains, and lowered telephones. **Special:** OSU Marion

offers cross-registration with Ohio State University Columbus, various co-op and work-study programs, nondegree study in continuing education, and pass/fail options. There are a freshman honors program and 3 departmental honors programs. **Visiting:** There are regularly scheduled orientations for prospective students. There are guides for informal visits and visitors may sit in on classes. To schedule a visit, contact the Office of Admissions at (740) 725-6242. **Campus Safety and Security:** Measures include emergency notification system and security escort services. There are shuttle buses, emergency telephones, and lighted pathways/sidewalks.

REQUIREMENTS: The SAT or ACT is required. OSU Marion follows an open admissions policy for in-state students. Applicants should be high school graduates with 4 units of English, 3 of math, 2 each of foreign language, history or social studies, and science, and 1 of art or music. AP and CLEP credits are accepted. Important factors in the admissions decision are advanced placement or honors courses, evidence of special talent, and extracurricular activities record.

ADMISSIONS: The SAT scores for a recent year freshman class were: Critical Reading--13% below 500, 32% between 500 and 599, 41% between 600 and 699, and 14% between 700 and 800; Math--2% below 500, 18% between 500 and 599, 46% between 600 and 699, and 34% between 700 and 800; Writing--9% below 500, 35% between 500 and 599, 44% between 600 and 699, and 12% between 700 and 800. The ACT scores were 6% between 21 and 23, and 94% above 28. 28% of the current freshmen were in the top fifth of their class; 70% were in the top two fifths.

FINANCIAL AID: In a recent year, 67% of all full-time freshmen and 70% of continuing full-time students received some form of financial aid. 70% of all full-time freshmen and 68% of continuing full-time students received need-based aid. The average freshman award was $12,183. Need-based scholarships or need-based grants averaged $9,032; need-based self-help aid (loans and jobs) averaged $5,107; non-need-based athletic scholarships averaged $22,992; other non-need-based awards and non-need-based scholarships averaged $6,027; and $5,443 from other forms of aid. The average financial indebtedness of the 2013 graduate was $22,472. The FAFSA is required. The priority date for freshman financial aid applications for fall entry is February 15.

OHIO STATE UNIVERSITY AT NEWARK — C-3
www.newark.osu.edu

Newark, OH 43055	(740) 366-3321 (800) 963-9275
Fax: (740) 366-9460	Email: askabuckeye@osu.edu
Full-time: 974 men, 1019 women	Faculty: IIB, +$
Part-time: 206 men, 185 women	Ph.D.s: 99%
Graduate: 1 men, 11 women	Student/Faculty: n/av
Year: semesters, summer session	Tuition: $7140 ($22,860)
Room & Board: $10,373	Freshman Class: 3105 applied, 3078 accepted, 1234 enrolled
SAT CR/M/W: 530/530/490 ACT: 22	CEEB CODE: 0824
Application Deadline: June 1	COMPETITIVE

The Ohio State University at Newark, founded in 1957, is a regional public commuter campus of the Ohio State University system. At Newark, students may earn a bachelor's degree in elementary education, psychology, history, or English as well as 1 to 3 years of credit applicable to any other degree, including 219 academic programs, conferred by OSU, provided the program is completed at the main campus in Columbus. In addition to regional accreditation, OSU Newark has baccalaureate program accreditation with AACSB, ABET, ACPE, ADA, AHEA, APTA, CSAB, CSWE, FIDER, NAAB, NASM, and NCATE. The 111-acre campus is in a suburban area 40 miles east of Columbus, OH. Including any residence halls, there are 18 buildings.

STUDENT LIFE: 100% of undergraduates are from Ohio. Others are from 11 states, and 1 foreign countries. 90% are from public schools. 73% are White; 13% African American. The average age of freshmen is 18; all undergraduates, 21. 37% do not continue beyond their first year; 63% remain to graduate. **Housing:** 180 students can be accommodated in college housing, which includes coed dorms and on-campus apartments. On-campus housing is available on a first-come and first-served basis. 93% of students commute. All students may keep cars.

FACULTY/CLASSROOMS: 50% of faculty are male; 50% are female. No introductory courses are taught by graduate students.

PROGRAMS OF STUDY: OSU Newark confers B.A., and B.S.Ed. degrees. Associate and Master's degrees are also awarded. Bachelor's degrees are awarded in BUSINESS (business administration and management), COMMUNICATIONS AND THE ARTS (English), EDUCATION (elementary education), HEALTH PROFESSIONS (nursing), SOCIAL SCIENCE (history and psychology). Biology, social work, and psychology have the largest enrollments.

ACTIVITIES: There are 30 groups on campus, including cheerleading, choir, chorale, chorus, drama, ethnic, gay, honors, professional, religious, social, social service, and student government. Popular campus events include Movies, Ice Skating, Family and Friends Day, and Halloween Boogie. **Sports:** There are 3 intercollegiate sports for men and 4 for women, and 10 intramural sports for men and 10 for women. Facilities include a cardio room, weight room, a gym with open gym times. In addition, a baseball field and outdoor areas that we utilize for intramurals. **Graduates:** In an average class, 1% graduate in 3 years or less, 20% graduate in 4 years or less, 35% graduate in 5 years or less, and 39% graduate in 6 years or less.

SERVICES: Counseling and information services are available, as is tutoring in most subjects. There is a reader service for the blind, and remedial math and writing. **Library/Resources:** Computerized library services include interlibrary loans, database searching, Internet access, and Wi-Fi capability. Special learning facilities include an art gallery. **Physically Challenged Students:** All of the campus is accessible. Facilities include wheelchair ramps, elevators, special parking, specially equipped restrooms, special class scheduling, and lowered drinking fountains. **Special:** Co-op programs and internships are available in some majors, and study abroad is available in some departments. Cross-registration is possible with Central Ohio Technical College and HECC member schools, and there is work-study with Ohio State. B.A.-B.S. degrees are offered in elementary education, general business, English, history, and psychology. Dual and student-designed majors and nondegree study are possible, and pass/fail options are available. There are 4 national honor societies, a freshman honors program, and 4 departmental honors programs. **Visiting:** There are regularly scheduled orientations for prospective students, visits include a campus tour, meeting with faculty, financial aid, and student services, a placement test, and class scheduling. There are guides for informal visits, visitors may sit in on classes, and stay overnight. To schedule a visit, contact the Office of Admissions - Newark at (740) 366-9333. **Campus Safety and Security:** Measures include 24-hour foot and vehicle patrol, emergency notification system, self-defense education, and security escort services. There are emergency telephones.

REQUIREMENTS: OSU Newark follows an open admissions policy for in-state students. Applicants should be high school graduates with 4 units of English, 3 of math, 2 each of science, foreign language, and history or social studies, and 1 of visual or performing arts. OSU Newark follows an open admissions policy for Ohio resident applicants. AP and CLEP credits are accepted.To graduate, students must complete on average 120 semester hours, with a minimum GPA of 2.0. The core curriculum consists of courses in writing skills, quantitative and logical skills, foreign language, the sciences, math, and the arts. Distribution requirements include 5 courses in arts and humanities, 4 to 5 courses in natural science, and 3 in social science. **Procedure:** Freshmen are admitted fall and spring. Entrance exams should be taken October of Senior Year. There is a rolling admissions plan. Applications should be filed by June 1 for fall entry; October 1 for winter entry; and March 1 for spring entry, along with a $60 fee. Notifications are sent in November. Applications are accepted on-line. **Transfer Students:** 266 transfer students enrolled in 2013-2014. A GPA of 2.0 is required. 30 of 120 credits required for the bachelor's degree must be completed at OSU Newark.

ADMISSIONS: 99% of the 2014-2015 applicants were accepted. The SAT scores for the 2014-2015 freshman class were: Critical Reading--40% below 500, 40% between 500 and 599, 17% between 600 and 699, and 3% between 700 and 800; Math--38% below 500, 39% between 500 and 599, and 21% between 600 and 699; Writing--53% below 500, 37% between 500 and 599, 9% between 600 and 699, and 1% between 700 and 800. The ACT scores were 31% below 21, 31% between 21 and 23, 28% between 24 and 26, 7% between 27 and 28, and 3% above 28. 14% of the current freshmen were in the top fifth of their class; 44% were in the top two fifths. 3 freshmen graduated first in their class. **Admissions Contact:** Ann Donahue, Director of Enrollment. E-Mail: *donahue.5@osu.edu* Web: *www.newark.osu.edu*

FINANCIAL AID: In 2014-2015, 85% of all full-time freshmen and 82% of continuing full-time students received some form of financial aid. 63% of all full-time freshmen and 66% of continuing full-time students received need-based aid. The average freshman award was $9,696. Need-based scholarships or need-based grants averaged $4,832 ($10,028 maximum); need-based self-help aid (loans and jobs) averaged $3,672 ($6,500 maximum); and other non-need-based awards and non-need-based scholarships averaged $5,215 ($22,894 maximum). OSU Newark is a member of CSS. The FAFSA is required. The priority date for freshman financial aid applications for fall entry is February 15.

OHIO UNIVERSITY   D-4
www.ohio.edu

Athens, OH 45701

(740) 593-4100
(740) 593-1000

Fax: (740) 593-0560
Email: admissions@ohio.edu

Full-time: 8168 men, 8875 women
Faculty: 889; I, -$

Part-time: 1275 men, 5206 women
Ph.D.s: 80%

Graduate: 2762 men, 2832 women
Student/Faculty: 18 to 1

Year: semesters, summer session
Tuition: $10,602 ($19,566)

Room & Board: $10,478
Freshman Class: 20935 applied, 15548 accepted, 4378 enrolled

SAT CR/M/W: 540/550/520 **ACT:** 24
CEEB CODE: 1593

Application Deadline: February 1
COMPETITIVE

Ohio University, founded in 1804, is a public university offering more than 250 areas of undergraduate study. On the graduate level, the university grants master's degrees in nearly all of its major academic divisions and doctoral degrees in selected departments. The university strives to be a "home away from home" for its students, with a welcoming atmosphere and supportive professors who are both teachers and mentors. There are 9 undergraduate schools and 11 graduate schools. In addition to regional accreditation, Ohio has baccalaureate program accreditation with AACSB, ABET, ACEJMC, CSWE, NASAD, NASM, NCATE, NRPA, AAFCS, ACEN, ACEND, ACS, APA, ATMAE, CAAHEP, CAPTE, CCA, CCNE, CEPH, COAPRT, COCA, CORE, COSMA, EHAC, NAB, NASD, NAST, NARHA, NLNAC, and OBN. The 1774-acre campus is in a small town 75 miles southeast of Columbus. Including any residence halls, there are 209 buildings.

STUDENT LIFE: 86% of undergraduates are from Ohio. Others are from 48 states, 65 foreign countries, and Canada. 82% are from public schools. 83% are White. 47% are Protestant; 34% Catholic; 14% claim no religious affiliation. The average age of freshmen is 18; all undergraduates, 20. 20% do not continue beyond their first year; 67% remain to graduate. **Housing:** 8100 students can be accommodated in college housing, which includes single-sex and coed dorms. In addition, there are honors houses, special-interest houses, fraternity houses, and sorority houses. On-campus housing is guaranteed for the freshman year only and is available on a lottery system for upperclassmen. 60% of students commute. Upperclassmen may keep cars.

FACULTY/CLASSROOMS: 56% of faculty are male; 44% are female. All teach and do research. Graduate students teach 12% of introductory courses. The average class size in an introductory lecture is 48; in a laboratory is 21; and in a regular course is 32.

PROGRAMS OF STUDY: Ohio confers A.B., B.A., B.A.H.C.S.,

B.B.A., B.C.J., B.F.A., B.Mus., B.S., B.S.A., B.S.A.M., B.S.A.T., B.S.C., B.S.C.E., B.S.C.F.S., B.S.Ch.E., B.S.C.S., B.S.C.S.D., B.S.Ed., B.S.E.E., B.S.E.H., B.S.E.N.E.N.G., B.S.E.T.M, B.S.F.N.S., B.S.H., B.S.H.C.S., B.S.I.S.E., B.S.J., B.S.M.E., B.S.N., B.S.O.H.S., B.S.T.O.M., B.S.P.E., B.S.P.E.X., B.S.R.S., B.S.S., B.S.S.L.S., B.S.S.P.S., B.S.V.C., B.S.W., B.T.A.S. and B.F.A.-DA. degrees. Associate, master's, and doctoral degrees are also awarded. Bachelor's degrees are awarded in BIO- LOGICAL SCIENCE (biochemistry, biology/biological science, bio- technology, botany, cell biology, customer service, ecology, environmental biology, life science, marine biology, microbiology, molecular biology, neurosciences, nutrition, wildlife biology, and zoology), BUSINESS (accounting, applied management, banking and finance, business administration and management, business econom- ics, business law, entrepreneurial studies, fashion merchandising, finance, hotel/motel and restaurant management, international busi- ness management, management information systems, management science, management & strategic leadership, marketing management, recreation and leisure services, recreational facilities management, retailing, sports management, and tourism), COMMUNICATIONS AND THE ARTS (acting, advertising, applied communication, art history, art, audio technology, broadcasting, ceramic art and design, choral music, classics, communications, communications technol- ogy, creative writing, dance, design, digital communications, digital media, dramatic arts, English, film arts, French, German, graphic design, Greek, Greek (classical), illustration, journalism, journalism - magazine journalism, journalism - news and information, journal- ism - newswriting /edit, language arts, Latin, linguistics, literature, media arts, media management, modern language, multimedia, music, music composition, music history and appreciation, music performance, music theory and composition, painting, performing arts, photography, piano/organ, playwriting/screenwriting, print- making, public relations, radio/television technology, Russian, sculp- ture, Spanish, speech/debate/rhetoric, stage management, sports administration, sport and lifestyle studies, studio art, telecommunica- tions, theater design, theater management, video, visual and perform- ing arts, and voice), COMPUTER AND PHYSICAL SCIENCE (actuarial science, applied mathematics, applied physics, astrophysics, atmospheric sciences and meteorology, chemistry, computer science, digital arts/technology, earth science, environmental geology, geol- ogy, geoscience, mathematics, physics, and statistics), EDUCATION (athletic training, business education, early childhood education, global studies, mathematics education, music education, nutrition education, physical education, science education, social studies edu- cation, special education, and technical and applied studies), ENGI- NEERING AND ENVIRONMENTAL DESIGN (airline piloting and navigation, aviation administration/management, bioengineering, chemical engineering, civil engineering, computer engineering, electrical/electronics engineering, energy management technology, engineering physics, engineering technology, environmental engi- neering, industrial engineering technology, interior design, materials engineering, mechanical engineering, and technical operations man- agement), HEALTH PROFESSIONS (applied nutrition, community health work, environmental health science, exercise science, health care administration, human biology, industrial hygiene, music ther- apy, nursing, nursing home administration, occupational hygiene and safety, physical therapy, predentistry, premedicine, prepharmacy, public health, and sports medicine), SOCIAL SCIENCE (African American studies, anthropology, Asian/American studies, child care/ child and family studies, classical/ancient civilization, communica- tion sciences and disorders, community services, criminal justice, criminology, Eastern European studies, economics, European studies, family and community services, family/consumer resource manage- ment, family/consumer studies, forensic studies, gender studies, geography, geography information science, history, human develop- ment, international studies, Latin American studies, parks and recre- ation management, philosophy, political science/government, prelaw, psychology, public administration, religion, social work, sociology, urban studies, have the largest enrollments.

ACTIVITIES: 10% of men belong to 20 national fraternities; 15% of women belong to 12 national sororities. There are 443 groups on campus, including art, band, cheerleading, chess, choir, chorale, chorus, computers, dance, drama, environmental, ethnic, film, foren- sics, gay, honors, international, jazz band, literary magazine, march-

ing band, musical theater, newspaper, opera, orchestra, pep band, photography, political, professional, radio and TV, religious, social, social service, student government, symphony, and yearbook. Popu- lar campus events include Performing Arts Series, Kennedy Lecture Series, and University Program Council (UPC). **Sports:** There are 6 intercollegiate sports for men and 10 for women, and 25 intramural sports for men and 25 for women. Facilities include a recreation center, a football stadium with artificial turf, fieldhouse, convocation center (accommodating basketball, volleyball, and wrestling), an aquatic center, ice rink, tennis courts, golf course, intramural gym, running track, fitness and aerobic center, baseball, softball, and soccer fields, a hockey field with a track, and 2 large outdoor recreation facil- ities (one can accommodate 4 flag football fields or 3 slow-pitch soft- ball fields and the other can accommodate 2 full-size soccer or rugby fields). **Graduates:** From July 1, 2013 to June 30, 2014, 6341 bache- lor's degrees were awarded. The most popular majors were nursing (35%), health administration (6%), and communication studies (4%). 382 companies recruited on campus in 2013-2014. In an aver- age class, 48% graduate in 4 years or less, 64% graduate in 5 years or less, and 67% graduate in 6 years or less. Of the 2013 graduating class, 24% were enrolled in graduate school within 6 months of graduation, and 82% were employed.

SERVICES: Counseling and information services are available, as is tutoring in most subjects. There is remedial math, reading, and writ- ing. **Library/Resources:** The 3 libraries contain 3.4 million volumes, 2.0 million microform items, and 233,896 audio/video tapes/CDs/ DVDs, and subscribe to 76,648 periodicals including electronic. Computerized library services include interlibrary loans, database searching, Internet access, and Wi-Fi capability. Special learning facil- ities include an art gallery, radio station, TV station, a quarterly mag- azine, an accelerator lab, a hearing and speech and other wellness (physical & mental) clinics, integrated technology labs, specialized academic labs within buildings, land labs, recreational facilities and fields, and a 3D printer. **Physically Challenged Students:** 89% of the campus is accessible. Facilities include wheelchair ramps, elevators, special parking, specially equipped restrooms, special class schedul- ing, lowered drinking fountains, lowered telephones, and special housing. **Special:** The University offers co-op programs in engineer- ing and computer science, internships, study abroad, work-study programs, and an accelerated degree program for students in the Honors Tutorial College. Students may earn a B.A. - B.S. degree in most arts and sciences majors, or a general studies degree. Dual and student-designed majors, non-degree study, limited pass/fail options, and credit for life, military, or work experience are also available. There are 23 national honor societies and a freshman honors pro- gram. **Visiting:** There are regularly scheduled orientations for pro- spective students, including information sessions and campus tours conducted daily Monday through Friday and Saturday by appoint- ment. Visitors may sit in on classes. To schedule a visit, contact the Undergraduate Admissions at (740) 593-4100. **Campus Safety and Security:** Measures include 24-hour foot and vehicle patrol, emer- gency notification system, self-defense education, and security escort services. There are shuttle buses, emergency telephones, lighted pathways/sidewalks, and controlled access to dorms/residences.

REQUIREMENTS: The SAT or ACT is required. Applicants should graduate with 4 units each of English and math, 3 each of science and social studies, 2 of foreign language, and 5 academic electives (which includes 1 unit of visual/performing arts). Ohio University operates on holistic review and rolling admissions. AP and CLEP credits are accepted. Important factors in the admissions decision are advanced placement or honors courses, recommendations by school officials, and extracurricular activities record. Ohio University has two sets of graduation requirements: University-wide requirements, which all students must complete, and college-level requirements, which include the requirements for completing a major or minor. In gen- eral, you must have a minimum of 120 semester hours of credit for a bachelor's degree, with all other requirements met. All baccalaure- ate students (except Honors Tutorial College students) also must complete Ohio University's General Education requirements. Ohio University believes that, as an educated person, you need certain intellectual skills in order to participate effectively in society. These include the following: the ability to communicate effectively through the written word and the ability to use quantitative or symbolic reasoning, broad knowledge of the major fields of learning and a capacity for evaluation and synthesis. **Procedure:** Freshmen are admitted fall, spring, and summer. Entrance exams should be taken in spring of the junior year or fall of the senior year. There are deferred admissions and rolling admissions plans. Applications should be filed by February 1 for fall entry; December 1 for spring entry; and February 1 for summer entry, along with a $45 fee. Notifications are sent September 15. Applications are accepted on-line. **Transfer Students:** 545 transfer students enrolled in 2013-2014. Transfer students are evaluated individually, but must have a GPA of at least 2.0 and 20 semester hours of transferable college credit. Business and journalism majors usually require a GPA of 3.0 or higher. 30 of 120 credits required for the bachelor's degree must be completed at Ohio. **International Students:** There are 1047 international students enrolled. The school actively recruits these students. They must take the TOEFL, or take the IELTS.

ADMISSIONS: 74% of the 2014-2015 applicants were accepted. The SAT scores for the 2014-2015 freshman class were: Critical Reading--26% below 500, 49% between 500 and 599, 21% between 600 and 699, and 4% between 700 and 800; Math--27% below 500, 48% between 500 and 599, 23% between 600 and 699, and 3% between 700 and 800; Writing--34% below 500, 46% between 500 and 599, 17% between 600 and 699, and 3% between 700 and 800. The ACT scores were 16% below 21, 33% between 21 and 23, 30% between 24 and 26, 11% between 27 and 28, and 10% above 28. 34% of the current freshmen were in the top fifth of their class; 69% were in the top two fifths. There were 6 National Merit finalists. 63 freshmen graduated first in their class. **Admissions Contact:** Candace Boeninger, A.V. Provost for Enroll Mgmt & Dir of Ad. E-Mail: *admissions@ohio .edu* Web: *www.ohio.edu*

FINANCIAL AID: In 2014-2015, 89% of all full-time freshmen and 79% of continuing full-time students received some form of financial aid. 55% of all full-time freshmen and 51% of continuing full-time students received need-based aid. The average freshman award was $14,037. Need-based scholarships or need-based grants averaged $6,038 ($12,428 maximum); need-based self-help aid (loans and jobs) averaged $3,695 ($7,600 maximum); non-need-based athletic scholarships averaged $18,655 ($38,704 maximum); and other non-need-based awards and non-need-based scholarships averaged $10,106 ($35,352 maximum). 32% of undergraduate students work part-time. Average annual earnings from campus work are $1900. The average financial indebtedness of the 2014 graduate was $27,645. The FAFSA is required. The priority date for freshman financial aid applications for fall entry is March 15.

OHIO WESLEYAN UNIVERSITY C-3
choose.owu.edu

Delaware, OH 43015	**(740) 368-3020**
	(800) 922-8953
Fax: (740) 368-3314	**Email:** owuadmit@owu.edu
Full-time: 816 men, 990 women	**Faculty:** 142; IIB, +$
Part-time: 8 men, 7 women	**Ph.D.s:** 100%
Graduate: n/av	**Student/Faculty:** 12 to 1
Year: semesters, summer session	**Tuition:** $39,150
Room & Board: $10,310	**Freshman Class:** 3030 applied, 2823 accepted, 541 enrolled
SAT CR/M: 569/581 **ACT:** 26	**CEEB CODE:** 1594
Application Deadline: March 1	**COMPETITIVE+**

Ohio Wesleyan University, founded in 1842, is an independent liberal arts institution affiliated with the United Methodist Church. There is one undergraduate school. In addition to regional accreditation, OWU has baccalaureate program accreditation with NASM, NCATE, and ACS. The 200-acre campus is in a small town 20 miles north of Columbus. Including any residence halls, there are 55 buildings.

STUDENT LIFE: 53% of undergraduates are from Ohio. Others are from 41 states, 45 foreign countries, and Canada. 76% are White. The average age of freshmen is 18; all undergraduates, 20. 16% do not continue beyond their first year; 68% remain to graduate. **Housing:** 1720 students can be accommodated in college housing, which includes single-sex and coed dorms and on-campus apartments. In addition, there are honors houses, language houses, special-interest houses, fraternity houses. Students are invited to submit theme proposals to run a residential house for 10 to 15 students. On-campus housing is guaranteed for all 4 years. 90% of students live on campus. All students may keep cars.

FACULTY/CLASSROOMS: 60% of faculty are male; 40% are female. All teach undergraduates, all do research, and all teach and do research. No introductory courses are taught by graduate students. The average class size in an introductory lecture is 30; in a laboratory is 19; and in a regular course is 16.

PROGRAMS OF STUDY: OWU confers B.A., B.F.A. and B.M. degrees. Bachelor's degrees are awarded in BIOLOGICAL SCIENCE (biochemistry, biology/biological science, botany, genetics, microbiology, and zoology), BUSINESS (accounting, business economics, and international business management), COMMUNICATIONS AND THE ARTS (dramatic arts, English, fine arts, French, German, journalism, music, and Spanish), COMPUTER AND PHYSICAL SCIENCE (chemistry, computer science, earth science, geology, mathematics, and physics), EDUCATION (art education, early childhood education, elementary education, foreign languages education, middle school education, music education, physical education, and science education), ENGINEERING AND ENVIRONMENTAL DESIGN (environmental science), HEALTH PROFESSIONS (predentistry, premedicine, and preveterinary science), SOCIAL SCIENCE (African American studies, anthropology, economics, geography, history, international relations, philosophy, political science/government, prelaw, psychology, religion, social science, sociology, and women's studies). Economics and business, biological sciences, and psychology have the largest enrollments.

ACTIVITIES: 40% of men belong to 8 national fraternities; 32% of women belong to 5 national sororities. There are 100 groups on campus, including art, cheerleading, chess, choir, chorale, chorus, communications, computers, dance, drama, ethnic, gay, honors, international, jazz band, literary magazine, musical theater, newspaper, opera, orchestra, pep band, political, professional, radio and TV, religious, social, social service, student government, symphony, and yearbook. Popular campus events include Sagan National Colloquium Fallfest, Black Family, and Alumni Weekend Celebration. **Sports:** There are 11 intercollegiate sports for men and 11 for women, and 17 intramural sports for men and 17 for women. Facilities include a gym, football and lacrosse stadium, field hockey and soccer fields, practice fields, a weight room, indoor and outdoor tracks, handball and squash courts, indoor pool, an exercise facility, and weight resistance equipment. **Graduates:** From July 1, 2013 to June 30, 2014, 471 bachelor's degrees were awarded. The most popular majors were biological science (12%), psychology (10%), and economics management (9%). In an average class, 1% graduate in 3 years or less, 61% graduate in 4 years or less, 67% graduate in 5 years or less, and 68% graduate in 6 years or less.

SERVICES: Counseling and information services are available, as is tutoring in most subjects. Students with learning disabilities may receive special help in writing and organization and in quantitive areas. **Library/Resources:** The 3 libraries contain 545,863 volumes, 72,358 microform items, 11,249 audio/video tapes/CDs/DVDs, and subscribe to 66,994 periodicals including electronic. Computerized library services include interlibrary loans, database searching, Internet access, and Wi-Fi capability. Special learning facilities include an art gallery, radio station, an astronomical observatory. **Physically Challenged Students:** 60% of the campus is accessible. Facilities include wheelchair ramps, elevators, special parking, specially equipped restrooms, special class scheduling, lowered drinking fountains, lowered telephones, and special housing. **Special:** Cross-registration is available with members of the Great Lakes Colleges Association. Students may study abroad in 20 countries or participate in a Washington semester or a departmental internship. Students may also take dual majors in any combination, design their own majors, or pursue a 3-2 engineering degree in conjunction with 4 major universities. Nondegree study and pass/fail options are available. There are 27 national honor societies, including Phi Beta Kappa, a freshman honors program, and 22 departmental honors programs. **Visiting:** There are regularly scheduled orientations for prospective students, the visit is approximately two hours and 15 minutes and includes a short presentation, a walking/riding tour of campus, and a conversation with an admission counselor. Optional class visit, meet professor or coach, and/or lunch on campus available. There are guides for informal visits, visitors may sit in on classes, and stay overnight. To schedule a visit, contact the Office of Admission. **Campus Safety and Security:** Measures include 24-hour foot and vehicle patrol, emergency notification system, self-defense education, and security escort services. There are emergency telephones and lighted pathways/sidewalks.

REQUIREMENTS: The SAT or ACT is required. Candidates for admission should complete a recommended 4 units of English and 3 each of math, foreign language, social studies, and science. AP credits are accepted. Important factors in the admissions decision are advanced placement or honors courses, extracurricular activities record, and recommendations by school officials. Students are required to complete at least 34 units, including 3 units each of humanities/English, social sciences, and science, 2 units of foreign languages, and 1 unit of fine or performing arts. Each unit equals a full course and 3.75 semester hours. All students must also take 8 to 12 units in the major, maintain a minimum GPA of 2.0, and satisfy the university writing skills requirements. **Procedure:** Freshmen are admitted fall and spring. Entrance exams should be taken in the spring of the junior year or fall of the senior year. There are early decision, early admissions, deferred admissions, and rolling admissions plans. Early decision applications should be filed by November 15; regular applications, by March 1 for fall entry. Notification of early decision is sent November 30; regular decision, on a rolling basis. 182 applicants were on the 2014 waiting list; 77 were admitted. Applications are accepted on-line. **Transfer Students:** 29 transfer students enrolled in 2013-2014. Applicants should have better than a 2.5 college GPA. High school and college transcripts and an essay are required, along with a statement of good standing from the previous institution. An interview is recommended. 16 of 34 credits required for the bachelor's degree must be completed at OWU. **International Students:** There are 142 international students enrolled. The school actively recruits these students. They must take the TOEFL with a minimum score of 550 on the paper-based TOEFL (PBT) or 80 on the Internet-based version (iBT), or take the IELTS. They must also take the SAT or ACT.

ADMISSIONS: 93% of the 2014-2015 applicants were accepted. The SAT scores for the 2014-2015 freshman class were: Critical Reading--20% below 500, 44% between 500 and 599, 26% between 600 and 699, and 10% between 700 and 800; Math--13% below 500, 41% between 500 and 599, 36% between 600 and 699, and 10% between 700 and 800. The ACT scores were 11% below 21, 23% between 21 and 23, 26% between 24 and 26, 19% between 27 and 28, and 25% above 28. 29% of the current freshmen were in the top fifth of their class; 42% were in the top two fifths. 20 freshmen graduated first in their class. **Admissions Contact:** Alisha Couch, Director of Admission. E-Mail: *owuadmit@owu.edu* Web: *choose.owu.edu*

FINANCIAL AID: In 2014-2015, 99% of all full-time freshmen and 98% of continuing full-time students received some form of financial aid. 59% of all full-time freshmen and 63% of continuing full-time students received need-based aid. The average freshman award was $32,580. Need-based scholarships or need-based grants averaged $28,175; and need-based self-help aid (loans and jobs) averaged $5,065. 45% of undergraduate students work part-time. Average annual earnings from campus work are $2366. The average financial indebtedness of the 2014 graduate was $31,489. OWU is a member of CSS. The FAFSA is required. The priority date for freshman financial aid applications for fall entry is February 15. The deadline for filing freshman financial aid applications for fall entry is May 1.

Otterbein College, founded in 1847, is an independent institution affiliated with the United Methodist Church. The college provides a solid liberal arts education combined with professional/career preparation. There are 4 graduate schools. The figures in the above capsule and in this profile are approximate. In addition to regional accreditation, Otterbein has baccalaureate program accreditation with NASM, NCATE, and NLN. The 142-acre campus is in a suburban area 12 miles northeast of Columbus. Including any residence halls, there are 28 buildings.

STUDENT LIFE: 91% of undergraduates are from Ohio. Others are from 29 states, 28 foreign countries, and Canada. 87% are white. 26% claim no religious affiliation; 22% Catholic. The average age of freshmen is 18; all undergraduates, 22. 27% do not continue beyond their first year; 73% remain to graduate.

FACULTY/CLASSROOMS: 52% of faculty are male; 48% are female. All teach undergraduates. No introductory courses are taught by graduate students. The average class size in an introductory lecture is 20; in a laboratory, 10; and in a regular course, 20.

PROGRAMS OF STUDY: Otterbein confers B.A., B.S., B.F.A., B.M., B.Mus.Ed., B.S.E., and B.S.N. degrees. Master's degrees are also awarded. Bachelor's degrees are awarded in AGRICULTURE (equine science), BIOLOGICAL SCIENCE (biochemistry, life science, and molecular biology), BUSINESS (accounting and business administration and management), COMMUNICATIONS AND THE ARTS (art, broadcasting, communications, dramatic arts, English, French, journalism, music, music performance, musical theater, public relations, Spanish, speech/debate/rhetoric, and visual and performing arts), COMPUTER AND PHYSICAL SCIENCE (chemistry, computer science, mathematics, and physics), EDUCATION (athletic training, elementary education, health education, music education, and physical education), HEALTH PROFESSIONS (nursing), SOCIAL SCIENCE (economics, history, international studies, liberal arts/general studies, philosophy, political science/government, psychology, religion, and sociology). Life science, chemistry, and athletic training are the strongest academically. Business, education, and communications have the largest enrollments.

ACTIVITIES: 28% of men belong to 7 local and 1 national fraternity; 28% of women belong to 6 local sororities. There are 90 groups on campus, including art, band, cheerleading, choir, chorale, chorus, communications, dance, debate, drama, drill team, equestrian, ethnic, forensics, gay, honors, international, jazz band, literary magazine, marching band, musical theater, newspaper, opera, orchestra, pep band, photography, political, professional, radio and TV, religious, social, social service, student government, symphony, and yearbook.

SERVICES: Counseling and information services are available, as is tutoring in every subject. There is a reader service for the blind, and remedial math, reading, and writing. **Library/Resources:** The library contains 300,000 volumes. Computerized library services include interlibrary loans and database searching. Special learning facilities include an art gallery, planetarium, radio station, TV station, an equine facility, 2 theaters, and a recital hall. **Physically Challenged Students:** 81% of the campus is accessible. Facilities include wheelchair ramps, elevators, special parking, specially equipped restrooms, special class scheduling, lowered drinking fountains, and lowered telephones. **Special:** Students may cross-register with members of the Higher Education Council of Columbus, study abroad in 9 countries, have an internship in most majors, or participate in a Washington semester. B.A.-B.S. degrees, 3-2 engineering degrees with Case Western Reserve and Washington Universities, credit for military experience, student-designed majors, nondegree study, and limited pass/fail options are also available. There are 9 national honor societies and a freshman honors program. **Visiting:** There are regularly scheduled orientations for prospective students, including a conference with an admissions counselor and a campus tour. There are guides for informal visits, visitors may sit in on classes, and stay overnight.. **Campus Safety and Security:** Measures include 24-hour foot and vehicle patrol, self-defense education, and security escort services. There are emergency telephones, lighted pathways/sidewalks, controlled access to dorms/residences, 24-hour locked dorm facilities.

REQUIREMENTS: The SAT or ACT is required. Applicants should be graduates of an accredited secondary school. The recommended

OTTERBEIN COLLEGE	C-3
www.otterbein.edu	
Westerville, OH 43081	
	(614) 823-1500
	(800) 488-8144
Fax: (614) 823-1200	Email: uotterb@otterbein.edu
Full-time: 830 men, 1470 women	Faculty: IIB, -$
Part-time: 135 men, 310 women	Ph.Ds: n/av
Graduate: 80 men, 325 women	Student/Faculty: n/av
Year: trimesters, summer session	Tuition: $30,050
Room & Board: $8752	Freshman Class: n/av
SAT or ACT: required	CEEB CODE: 1597
Application Deadline: see profile	COMPETITIVE

preparatory program includes 4 units of English, 3 to 4 units each of math, science, and social studies, 2 to 3 units of foreign language, and 1 to 2 units of performing arts. A high school GPA of 2.5 or better is recommended. Otterbein requires applicants to be in the upper 50% of their class. AP and CLEP credits are accepted. Important factors in the admissions decision are advanced placement or honors courses, evidence of special talent, and recommendations by school officials.

FINANCIAL AID: The FAFSA is required. Check with the school for current application deadlines.

SHAWNEE STATE UNIVERSITY C-5
www.shawnee.edu

Portsmouth, OH 45662 (740) 351-2778
(800) 959-2778

Fax: (740) 351-3111 Email: info@shawnee.edu
Full-time: 1502 men, 1807 women Faculty: 145; IIB, -$
Part-time: 287 men, 518 women Ph.D.s: 59%
Graduate: 35 men, 98 women Student/Faculty: 18 to 1
Year: semesters, summer session Tuition: $7364 ($12,617)
Room & Board: $9552 Freshman Class: 3686 applied, 2733 accepted, 955 enrolled
SAT CR/M/W: 525/570/490 ACT: 21 CEEB CODE: 1790
Application Deadline: n/av **COMPETITIVE**

Shawnee State University, founded in 1975, is a public institution offering programs in arts and sciences, business, engineering, health sciences, and education. There are 2 undergraduate schools and 1 graduate school. In addition to regional accreditation, Shawnee has baccalaureate program accreditation with ADA, NCATE, NLN, AOTA, CoARC, CAATE, CAPTA, JRCERT, and NAACLS. The 50-acre campus is in a small town 90 miles south of Columbus. Including any residence halls, there are 30 buildings.

STUDENT LIFE: 89% of undergraduates are from Ohio. Others are from 25 states, and 20 foreign countries. 85% are White. The average age of freshmen is 20; all undergraduates, 23. 43% do not continue beyond their first year; 26% remain to graduate. **Housing:** 960 students can be accommodated in college housing, which includes coed on-campus apartments. In addition, there are special-interest houses, gaming dorm. On-campus housing is available on a first-come, first-served basis. 76% of students commute. Alcohol is not permitted. All students may keep cars.

FACULTY/CLASSROOMS: 59% of faculty are male; 41% are female. All teach undergraduates. No introductory courses are taught by graduate students.

PROGRAMS OF STUDY: Shawnee State confers B.A., B.S., B.F.A., B.I.S., B.S.E., B.S.S.S. and B.S.N. degrees. Associate and Master's degrees are also awarded. Bachelor's degrees are awarded in BIOLOGICAL SCIENCE (biology/biological science), BUSINESS (business administration and management and sports management), COMMUNICATIONS AND THE ARTS (English and fine arts), COMPUTER AND PHYSICAL SCIENCE (chemistry, Computer Engineering Technology, computer game design/development, mathematics, and natural sciences), EDUCATION (athletic training, early childhood education, education, elementary education, and special education), ENGINEERING AND ENVIRONMENTAL DESIGN (engineering technology, environmental engineering technology, and plastics technology), HEALTH PROFESSIONS (nursing and premedicine), SOCIAL SCIENCE (history, humanities, interdisciplinary studies, international relations, philosophy and religion, prelaw, psychology, social science, and sociology). Nursing is the strongest academically. Psychology and business administration have the largest enrollments.

ACTIVITIES: 1% of men belong to 2 national fraternities; 1% of women belong to 1 local and 1 national sororities. There are 31 groups on campus, including academic club, art, cheerleading, choir, chorus, computers, drama, ethnic, gay, honors, international, literary magazine, musical theater, newspaper, pep band, photography, political, professional, religious, social, social service, and student govern-

ment. Popular campus events include Fall Fest, Spring Fest and Scare Week. **Sports:** There are 5 intercollegiate sports for men and 6 for women, and 9 intramural sports for men and 9 for women. Facilities include a soccer field, an activities center with basketball and volleyball courts, sports center with racquetball courts, Nautilus and weight rooms, pool, sauna, and a whirlpool. **Graduates:** From July 1, 2013 to June 30, 2014, 422 bachelor's degrees were awarded. The most popular majors were business administration (22%), fine art (9%), and psychology (8%). In an average class, 13% graduate in 4 years or less, 23% graduate in 5 years or less, and 26% graduate in 6 years or less.

SERVICES: Counseling and information services are available, as is tutoring in most subjects. There is a reader service for the blind, and remedial math, reading, and writing. **Library/Resources:** The library contains 156,346 volumes, 266,229 microform items, 7,081 audio/video tapes/CDs/DVDs, and subscribes to 78,847 periodicals including electronic. Computerized library services include interlibrary loans, database searching, Internet access, and Wi-Fi capability. Special learning facilities include an art gallery and planetarium. **Physically Challenged Students:** All of the campus is accessible. Facilities include wheelchair ramps, elevators, special parking, specially equipped restrooms, lowered drinking fountains, and lowered telephones. **Special:** Study abroad available in several countries, internships in sports studies, business, psychology, and health management, and student-designed programs are available. Cross-registration with Miami University, a Washington semester, and 2+2 programs are also possible as well as a 3+2 program in psychology and occupational therapy. There are 1 national honor society and a freshman honors program. **Visiting:** There are regularly scheduled orientations for prospective students, including fall and spring visitation days, which consist of small sessions with deans and faculty, orientation by student affairs offices, and tours with current college students. There are guides for informal visits and visitors may sit in on classes. To schedule a visit, contact the Office of Admissions. **Campus Safety and Security:** Measures include 24-hour foot and vehicle patrol and emergency notification system. There are emergency telephones and lighted pathways/sidewalks.

REQUIREMENTS: Applicants must graduate from an accredited high school or have a GED. AP and CLEP credits are accepted. To graduate, students must complete a general education program of at least 34 semester hours and a senior seminar. A total of 120 to 135 semester hours including 40 hours in the major is required along with a 2.0 GPA in all course work and in the major. **Procedure:** Freshmen are admitted to all sessions. Entrance exams should be taken in late spring or early summer. There is a rolling admissions plan. Application deadlines are open. Applications are accepted on-line. **Transfer Students:** 230 transfer students enrolled in 2013-2014. A completed application and college and high school transcripts sent directly to SSU from previous institutions are required. 45 of 120 credits required for the bachelor's degree must be completed at Shawnee State. **International Students:** There are 63 international students enrolled. The school actively recruits these students. They must take the TOEFL with a minimum score of 500 on the paper-based TOEFL (PBT) or 60 on the Internet-based version (iBT) or take the MELAB.

ADMISSIONS: 74% of the 2014-2015 applicants were accepted. The SAT scores for the 2014-2015 freshman class were: Critical Reading--44% below 500, 34% between 500 and 599, 20% between 600 and 699, and 2% between 700 and 800; Math--30% below 500, 32% between 500 and 599, 34% between 600 and 699, and 4% between 700 and 800; Writing--55% below 500, 36% between 500 and 599, and 9% between 600 and 699. The ACT scores were 49% below 21, 26% between 21 and 23, 16% between 24 and 26, 5% between 27 and 28, and 4% above 28. 25% of the current freshmen were in the top fifth of their class; 53% were in the top two fifths. 15 freshmen graduated first in their class. **Admissions Contact:** Rick Merb, Interim Director of Admissions. E-Mail: To_SSU@shawnee.edu Web: www.shawnee.edu

FINANCIAL AID: The average financial indebtedness of the 2014 graduate was $24,054. Shawnee State is a member of CSS. The FAFSA is required. Check with the school for current application deadlines.

THE OHIO STATE UNIVERSITY-COLUMBUS CAMPUS
www.osu.edu

C-3

Columbus, OH 43210   **(614) 292-3980**

Fax: (614) 292-4818
Full-time: 21205 men, 19408 women
Part-time: 2265 men, 1863 women
Graduate: 6194 men, 7387 women
Year: semesters, summer session
Room & Board: $9850

Email: askabuckeye@osu.edu
Faculty: n/av
Ph.D.s: 99%
Student/Faculty: n/av
Tuition: $10,037 ($25,537)
Freshman Class: 36788 applied, 19484 accepted, 7079 enrolled

SAT CR/M/W: 630/620/600 **ACT:** 29
Application Deadline: February 1

CEEB CODE: 1152
HIGHLY COMPETITIVE+

The Ohio State University is one of America's largest and most comprehensive academic institutions. Columbus campus select from 14 colleges, 200 undergraduate majors and 240 master's, doctoral and professional degree programs. More than 6,500 additional students attend Ohio State's regional campuses in Lima, Mansfield, Marion and Newark, and the Agricultural Technical Institute in Wooster. As Ohio's best and one of the nation's top-20 public universities, Ohio State is further recognized by a top-rated academic medical center and a premier cancer hospital and research center. Its legacy extends to more than half a million living alumni. There are 16 undergraduate schools and 1 graduate school. In addition to regional accreditation, Ohio State, OSU has baccalaureate program accreditation with AACSB, ABET, ACPE, ADA, ASLA, CSWE, FIDER, NAAB, NASAD, and NCATE. The 1904-acre campus is in an urban area 2 miles north of downtown Columbus, OH. Including any residence halls, there are 697 buildings.

STUDENT LIFE: 85% of undergraduates are from Ohio. Others are from 50 states, 109 foreign countries, and Canada. 85% are from public schools. 72% are White. The average age of freshmen is 18; all undergraduates, 21. 6% do not continue beyond their first year; 94% remain to graduate. **Housing:** 10,855 students can be accommodated in college housing, which includes single-sex and coed dorms, on-campus apartments, off-campus apartments, and married student housing. In addition, there are honors houses, language houses, special-interest houses, Veterans house, international houses, language floors, and an alumnae scholarship house. On-campus housing is guaranteed for the freshman year only, is available on a first-come, and first-served basis. 75% of students commute. All students may keep cars.

FACULTY/CLASSROOMS: 58% of faculty are male; 42% are female. 75% teach undergraduates, 98% do research, and 74% do both. No introductory courses are taught by graduate students.

PROGRAMS OF STUDY: Ohio State, OSU confers B.A., B.S., B.A.E., B.F.A., B.Mus. and B.Mus.Ed. degrees. Associate, Master's, and Doctoral degrees are also awarded. Bachelor's degrees are awarded in AGRICULTURE (agricultural business management, agricultural economics, animal science, fishing and fisheries, forestry and related sciences, natural resource management, and plant science), BIOLOGICAL SCIENCE (avian sciences, biochemistry, biology/biological science, ecology, entomology, evolutionary biology, microbiology, molecular biology, neurosciences, nutrition, plant physiology, and zoology), BUSINESS (accounting, banking and finance, business administration and management, fashion merchandising, hospitality management services, human resources, insurance and risk management, international business management, logistics, management information systems, marketing and distribution, operations management, real estate, and transportation management), COMMUNICATIONS AND THE ARTS (Arabic, art, Chinese, classics, communications, dance, English, fine arts, French, German, Germanic languages and literature, Greek, Hebrew, industrial design, Italian, Japanese, jazz, journalism, Korean, linguistics, music, music history and appreciation, music performance, music theory and composition, piano/organ, Portuguese, Russian, Spanish, theatre arts, theater design, and visual design), COMPUTER AND PHYSICAL SCIENCE (actuarial science, astronomy, astrophysics, atmospheric sciences and meteorology, chemistry, computer science, earth science, geology, information sciences and systems, mathematics, and physics), EDUCATION (agricultural education, art education, athletic training, dance education, education, environmental education, health information management, middle school education, music education, physical education, and technical education), ENGINEERING AND ENVIRONMENTAL DESIGN (aeronautical engineering, architecture, biomedical engineering, chemical engineering, city/community/regional planning, civil engineering, computer engineering, construction management, electrical/electronics engineering, engineering physics, environmental engineering, environmental science, industrial engineering, interior design, landscape architecture/design, materials engineering, materials science, mechanical engineering, and welding engineering), HEALTH PROFESSIONS (biomedical science, dental hygiene, exercise science, health science, medical laboratory science, medical technology, nursing, occupational therapy, pharmaceutical science, physical therapy, radiograph medical technology, respiratory therapy, speech pathology/audiology, and speech therapy), SOCIAL SCIENCE (African American studies, anthropology, community services, criminal justice, criminology, economics, family/consumer resource management, family/consumer studies, French studies, geography, history, human development, human ecology, industrial and organizational psychology, international studies, Islamic studies, Judaic studies, medieval studies, philosophy, physical fitness/movement, political science/government, psychology, public affairs, social work, sociology, and women's studies). Biology, psychology and finance have the largest enrollments.

ACTIVITIES: There are 916 groups on campus, including art, band, cheerleading, chess, choir, chorale, chorus, communications, computers, dance, debate, drama, environmental, ethnic, film, forensics, gay, honors, international, jazz band, literary magazine, marching band, musical theater, newspaper, opera, orchestra, pep band, photography, political, professional, radio and TV, religious, social, social service, student government, symphony, and yearbook. Popular campus events include OSU, African American Heritage Festival, Greek Week and May Week. **Sports:** There are 17 intercollegiate sports for men and 18 for women, and 16 intramural sports for men and 16 for women. Facilities include a 100,000-seat football stadium, 17,500-to-21,000-seat multipurpose event center, 13,000-seat arena, an archery range, a running track, sand volleyball courts, cricket field, an in-line hockey rink, weight rooms, swimming pools, basketball, volleyball, and racquetball courts, field houses for tennis, volleyball, basketball, and soccer, and baseball and softball fields. **Graduates:** From July 1, 2013 to June 30, 2014, 10195 bachelor's degrees were awarded. The most popular majors were psychology (6%), communication (4%), and finance (4%). 1000 companies recruited on campus in 2013-2014. In an average class, 3% graduate in 3 years or less, 61% graduate in 4 years or less, 80% graduate in 5 years or less, and 84% graduate in 6 years or less.

SERVICES: Counseling and information services are available, as is tutoring in most subjects. There is a reader service for the blind, and remedial math, reading, and writing. **Library/Resources:** The 21 libraries contain 7.0 million volumes, 600,296 audio/video tapes/CDs/DVDs, and subscribe to 26,297 periodicals including electronic. Computerized library services include interlibrary loans, database searching, Internet access, and Wi-Fi capability. Special learning facilities include an art gallery, planetarium, radio/TV station, the Museum of Biological Diversity, the John Glenn Institute for Public Service and Public Policy, and the Cartoon Research Library. **Physically Challenged Students:** 96% of the campus is accessible. Facilities include wheelchair ramps, elevators, special parking, specially equipped restrooms, special class scheduling, lowered drinking fountains, lowered telephones, special housing. Accessible rooms are intergrated across residential options. Campus bus system is fully lift equipted and suplemented by paratransit. Adaptive recreation facilites are available. **Special:** Students may cross-register with all central Ohio colleges. OSU offers internships, co-op programs, extensive study abroad in about 40 countries, work-study programs, dual and student-designed majors, a general degree, an accelerated degree, credit by exam, nondegree study, and pass/fail options. There are 39 national honor societies, Phi Beta Kappa, a freshman honors program, and 15 departmental honors programs. **Visiting:** There are regularly scheduled orientations for prospective students, including campus tours, placement tests, course scheduling, and special sessions designed for parents. There are guides for informal visits, visitors may sit in on classes, and stay overnight. To schedule a visit, contact the Student Visitor Center at campusvisit.osu.edu. **Campus Safety and Security:** Measures include 24-hour foot and vehicle patrol, emergency notification system, self-defense education, and security escort services. There are shuttle buses, emergency telephones, lighted pathways/sidewalks, Including crisis action teams, and off-campus patrols in cooperation with the city police.

REQUIREMENTS: The SAT or ACT is required. Applicants must complete high school with at least 19 academic credits, including 4 in English, 3 in math, 2 each in foreign language, science, and history or social studies, and 1 in art or music. The GED is accepted. AP and CLEP credits are accepted. Important factors in the admissions decision are advanced placement or honors courses, evidence of special talent, and extracurricular activities record. To graduate, students must complete 120 or more semester hours, depending on major, including 30 to 40 in the major, with a minimum GPA of 2.0. The core curriculum consists of courses in writing skills, quantitative and logical skills, foreign language, the sciences, math, and the arts. Distribution requirements include 5 courses in arts and humanities, 4 to 5 courses in natural science, and 3 in social science. **Procedure:** Freshmen are admitted fall, spring, and summer. Entrance exams should be taken by October of the senior year. There is a rolling admissions plan. Applications should be filed by February 1 for fall entry; October 1 for spring entry; and March 1 for summer entry, along with a $60 fee. Notifications are sent in 3/31. 239 applicants were on the 2014 waiting list; 239 were admitted. Applications are accepted on-line. **Transfer Students:** 3501 transfer students enrolled in 2013-2014. High school graduates with 30 hours of college credit and a minimum GPA of 2.0 are admitted for transfer. Those with fewer than 30 hours apply on a competitive basis. 30 of 120 credits required for the bachelor's degree must be completed at Ohio State, OSU. **International Students:** There are 3266 international students enrolled. The school actively recruits these students. They must take the TOEFL with a minimum score of 550 on the paper-based TOEFL (PBT) or 79 on the Internet-based version (iBT). They must also take the SAT or ACT.

ADMISSIONS: 53% of the 2014-2015 applicants were accepted. The SAT scores for the 2014-2015 freshman class were: Critical Reading--4% below 500, 29% between 500 and 599, 52% between 600 and 699, and 15% between 700 and 800; Math--2% below 500, 18% between 500 and 599, 56% between 600 and 699, and 24% between 700 and 800; Writing--2% below 500, 4% between 500 and 599, 14% between 600 and 699, and 25% between 700 and 800. The ACT scores were 2% below 21, 4% between 21 and 23, 14% between 24 and 26, 25% between 27 and 28, and 55% above 28. 90% of the current freshmen were in the top fifth of their class; 98% were in the top two fifths. There were 86 National Merit finalists. 350 freshmen graduated first in their class. **Admissions Contact:** Undergraduate Admissions and First Year Experience E-Mail: askabuckeye@osu.edu Web: http://undergrad.osu.edu/contact-us/index.html

FINANCIAL AID: In 2014-2015, 89% of all full-time freshmen and 80% of continuing full-time students received some form of financial aid. 42% of all full-time freshmen and 46% of continuing full-time students received need-based aid. The average freshman award was $15,384. Need-based scholarships or need-based grants averaged $7,767 ($23,633 maximum); need-based self-help aid (loans and jobs) averaged $3,700 ($9,000 maximum); non-need-based athletic scholarships averaged $19,419 ($58,835 maximum); and other non-need-based awards and non-need-based scholarships averaged $11,457 ($44,193 maximum). The average financial indebtedness of the 2014 graduate was $26,830. Ohio State, OSU is a member of CSS. The FAFSA is required. The priority date for freshman financial aid applications for fall entry is February 15.

TIFFIN UNIVERSITY (*The complete profile is made available exclusively on our website, www.barronspac.com*)

UNION INSTITUTE & UNIVERSITY (*The complete profile is made available exclusively on our website, www.barronspac.com*)

UNIVERSITY OF AKRON   D-2
www.uakron.edu

Akron, OH 44325   (330) 972-7100
                                       (800) 655-4884
Fax: (330) 972-7022   Email: admissions@uakron.edu
Full-time: 8258 men, 7254 women   Faculty: 718; I, -$
Part-time: 2137 men, 2161 women   Ph.D.s: 81%
Graduate: 1920 men, 2337 women   Student/Faculty: 21 to 1
Year: semesters, summer session   Tuition: $10,054 ($18,418)
Room & Board: $10,382   Freshman Class: 13109
                                   applied, 12645 accepted,
                                   3605 enrolled
SAT CR/M: 520/540 ACT: 22   CEEB CODE: 1829
Application Deadline: August 11   COMPETITIVE

The University of Akron is the public research university for northern Ohio. Home to the nation's largest academic program for polymer science and polymer engineering, The University of Akron also earned national recognition in several other undergraduate and graduate degree programs. The university offers more than 300 associate, bachelor's, master's, doctoral, and law degree programs and 100 certificate programs at sites in Summit, Wayne, Holmes, Medina and Cuyahoga counties. There are 8 undergraduate schools and 8 graduate schools. In addition to regional accreditation, UA has baccalaureate program accreditation with AACSB, ABET, ADA, CSWE, NASAD, NASM, NCATE, APA, ABA, and AAFCS. The 223-acre campus is in an urban area in downtown Akron, 40 miles south of Cleveland. Including any residence halls, there are 89 buildings.

STUDENT LIFE: 94% of undergraduates are from Ohio. Others are from 45 states, 86 foreign countries, and Canada. 72% are White; 12% African American. The average age of freshmen is 19; all undergraduates, 23. 26% do not continue beyond their first year; 40% remain to graduate. **Housing:** 2888 students can be accommodated in college housing, which includes single-sex and coed dorms and on-campus apartments. In addition, there are honors houses, special-interest houses, fraternity houses, sorority houses, private apartment-type halls and private residence halls. On-campus housing is available on a first-come and first-served basis. Priority is given to out-of-town students. 86% of students commute. Alcohol is not permitted. All students may keep cars.

FACULTY/CLASSROOMS: 51% of faculty are male; 49% are female. 95% teach undergraduates. Graduate students teach 8% of introductory courses. The average class size in an introductory lecture is 26; in a laboratory is 24; and in a regular course is 26.

PROGRAMS OF STUDY: UA confers B.A., B.A.E., B.A.S.W., B.B.A., B.F.A., B.M., B.S., B.S.A., B.S.A.T., B.S.B.A, B.S.C.S., B.S.E., B.S.N. and B.S.T. degrees. Associate, Master's, and Doctoral degrees are also awarded. Bachelor's degrees are awarded in BIOLOGICAL SCIENCE (biology/biological science), BUSINESS (accounting, banking and finance, business administration and management, business communications, fashion merchandising, international business management, labor studies, management science, and marketing/retailing/merchandising), COMMUNICATIONS AND THE ARTS (art, classics, dance, English, French, media arts, music, music history and appreciation, music performance, music theory and composition, musical theater, public relations, Spanish, studio art, and theater management), COMPUTER AND PHYSICAL SCIENCE (applied mathematics, chemistry, computer science, computer security and information assurance, environmental geology, geology, geophysics and seismology, mathematics, natural sciences, physics, and statistics), EDUCATION (art education, athletic training, early childhood education, education, home economics education, middle school education, music education, physical education, special education, and technical education), ENGINEERING AND ENVIRONMENTAL DESIGN (automotive technology, biomedical engineering, chemical engineering, civil engineering, computer engineering, construction technology, electrical/electronics engineering, electrical/electronics engineering technology, emergency/disaster science, engineering, geological engineering, interior design, mechanical engineering, mechanical engineering technology, and survey and mapping technology), HEALTH PROFESSIONS (exercise science, nursing, physical therapy, respiratory therapy, and speech pathology/

audiology), SOCIAL SCIENCE (anthropology, child psychology/ development, criminal justice, criminology, dietetics, economics, family/consumer studies, family/juvenile justice, geography, history, interdisciplinary studies, philosophy, political science/government, psychology, social science, social work, and sociology). Engineering, nursing, and business are the strongest academically. Engineering, business and nursing have the largest enrollments.

ACTIVITIES: 4% of men belong to 1 local and 13 national fraternities; 4% of women belong to 9 national sororities. There are 300 groups on campus, including art, band, cheerleading, chess, choir, chorale, chorus, computers, dance, drama, ethnic, gay, honors, international, jazz band, marching band, musical theater, newspaper, opera, orchestra, pep band, photography, political, professional, radio and TV, religious, social, social service, student government, and symphony. Popular campus events include Celebrating Akron Traditions and Zips Fest. **Sports:** There are 8 intercollegiate sports for men and 10 for women, and 12 intramural sports for men and 12 for women. Facilities include a recreation and wellness center with features that include a 56-foot rock climbing wall and aerobics/dance studio, a natatorium with an Olympic-sized pool, and the athletic fieldhouse and indoor varsity golf practice facility, which includes a 120-yard football field and a 6-lane, 300 meter track. Facilities include a 5500-seat basketball/volleyball an arena, 30,000-seat on-campus weight room and athletic training room, outdoor 100-yard astro play practice field, 8-lane outdoor track, outdoor soccer field, and a baseball field. **Graduates:** From July 1, 2013 to June 30, 2014, 3027 bachelor's degrees were awarded. The most popular majors were nursing (8%), organizational supervision (4%), and psychology (4%). 300 companies recruited on campus in 2013-2014. In an average class, 16% graduate in 4 years or less, 34% graduate in 5 years or less, and 41% graduate in 6 years or less. Of the 2013 graduating class, 20% were enrolled in graduate school within 6 months of graduation, and 81% were employed.

SERVICES: Counseling and information services are available, as is tutoring in most subjects. There is a reader service for the blind, and remedial math, reading, and writing. TDDs are available. **Library/Resources:** The 3 libraries contain 1.6 million volumes, 1.6 million microform items, 104,537 audio/video tapes/CDs/DVDs, and subscribe to 475,145 periodicals including electronic. Computerized library services include interlibrary loans, database searching, Internet access, and Wi-Fi capability. Special learning facilities include an art gallery, radio station, TV station, a nursing center, speech and hearing center, dance institute, educational media lab, and synchro hours learning classrooms. **Physically Challenged Students:** 90% of the campus is accessible. Facilities include wheelchair ramps, elevators, special parking, specially equipped restrooms, special class scheduling, lowered drinking fountains, lowered telephones, special housing. city/campus bus service, residence hall accommodations, and priority registration for disabled students. **Special:** UA offers co-op programs with local and out-of-state employers, study abroad in 22 countries, internships and work-study opportunities with community employers, a 6-year accelerated B.S.-M.D. program, B.A.-B.S. degrees in 10 majors, credit for military experience, nondegree study, and pass/fail options. There are 26 national honor societies, a freshman honors program, and 46 departmental honors programs. **Visiting:** There are regularly scheduled orientations for prospective students, including small groups for information on financial aid, student organizations, campus tours, and meetings with college faculty. There are guides for informal visits, visitors may sit in on classes, and stay overnight. To schedule a visit, contact the Office of Undergraduate Admissions. **Campus Safety and Security:** Measures include 24-hour foot and vehicle patrol, emergency notification system, self-defense education, and security escort services. There are shuttle buses, emergency telephones, lighted pathways/sidewalks, controlled access to dorms/residences, in-room safes, Including security cameras.

REQUIREMENTS: The SAT or ACT is required. Admission to the University of Akron is competitive. Students who demonstrate outstanding college preparation through completion of a college prep curriculum may be admitted directly to a specific academic program. Criteria considered include high school GPA, test scores, class rank, and some majors/programs additional information is reviewed, such as activities, leadership, recommendations, essays, portfolios, and

auditions. AP and CLEP credits are accepted. Important factors in the admissions decision are advanced placement or honors courses, leadership record, and evidence of special talent. To graduate, all students must complete at least 120 credits, with a varying number of hours in the major, and maintain a GPA of 2.0. Specific course requirements include English composition, oral communications, Western cultural traditions, math, natural science, social science, humanities, speech, cultural diversity, and phys ed. **Procedure:** Freshmen are admitted to all sessions. Entrance exams should be taken received by November 1 for scholarship consideration. There are deferred admissions and rolling admissions plans. Applications should be filed by August 11 for fall entry, along with a $45 fee. Notification is sent on a rolling basis. Applications are accepted on-line. **Transfer Students:** 1126 transfer students enrolled in 2013-2014. Applicants should present a minimum college GPA of 2.0. There are other requirements for direct admission to specific academic programs. 32 of 120 credits required for the bachelor's degree must be completed at UA. **International Students:** There are 437 international students enrolled. The school actively recruits these students. They must take the TOEFL with a minimum score of 71 on the Internet-based version (iBT), the International English Language Testing System (IELTS). They must also take the SAT or ACT. The English proficiency tests are in lieu of the SAT or ACT unless they are interested in scholarships and the scholarships requires it.

ADMISSIONS: 96% of the 2014-2015 applicants were accepted. The SAT scores for the 2014-2015 freshman class were: Critical Reading--43% below 500, 34% between 500 and 599, 19% between 600 and 699, and 5% between 700 and 800; Math--36% below 500, 32% between 500 and 599, 23% between 600 and 699, and 9% between 700 and 800. The ACT scores were 37% below 21, 24% between 21 and 23, 18% between 24 and 26, 10% between 27 and 28, and 11% above 28. 28% of the current freshmen were in the top fifth of their class; 55% were in the top two fifths. There were 2 National Merit finalists. 51 freshmen graduated first in their class. **Admissions Contact:** Diane Raybuck, Director of Admissions. E-Mail: *admissions@uakron.edu* Web: *www.uakron.edu*

FINANCIAL AID: In 2014-2015, 79% of all full-time freshmen and 72% of continuing full-time students received some form of financial aid. 58% of all full-time freshmen and 61% of continuing full-time students received need-based aid. The average freshman award was $7,825. Need-based scholarships or need-based grants averaged $5,996; need-based self-help aid (loans and jobs) averaged $4,104; non-need-based athletic scholarships averaged $13,996; and other non-need-based awards and non-need-based scholarships averaged $4,629. 11% of undergraduate students work part-time. Average annual earnings from campus work are $4800. The average financial indebtedness of the 2014 graduate was $18,515. The FAFSA is required. The priority date for freshman financial aid applications for fall entry is February 1. The deadline for filing freshman financial aid applications for fall entry is June 30.

UNIVERSITY OF CINCINNATI A-5
www.uc.edu

Cincinnati, OH 45221	(513) 556-1100 n/av
Fax: (513) 556-1105	Email: admissions@uc.edu
Full-time: 10939 men, 9849 women	Faculty: 1192; I, --$
Part-time: 1188 men, 2431 women	Ph.D.s: 76%
Graduate: 4328 men, 6686 women	Student/Faculty: 17 to 1
Year: semesters, summer session	Tuition: $11,010 ($26,334)
Room & Board: $10,496	Freshman Class: 16593 applied, 12611 accepted, 4578 enrolled
SAT CR/M/W: 565/590/550 ACT: 25	CEEB CODE: 1833
Application Deadline: March 1	VERY COMPETITIVE

University of Cincinnati, founded in 1819, is a state-supported institution offering undergraduate programs in art and architecture, business, engineering, health science, liberal arts and sciences, music, and technical training. There are 8 undergraduate schools and 11 graduate schools. In addition to regional accreditation, UC has baccalaureate program accreditation with AACSB, ABET, CSWE, NASAD, NASM, NCATE, and NLN. The 270-acre campus is in an urban area in downtown Cincinnati. Including any residence halls, there are 90 buildings.

STUDENT LIFE: 84% of undergraduates are from Ohio. Others are from 50 states, 118 foreign countries, and Canada. 71% are White. The average age of freshmen is 18; all undergraduates, 22. 14% do not continue beyond their first year. **Housing:** 5172 students can be accommodated in college housing, which includes coed dorms and on-campus apartments. In addition, there are honors houses. On-campus housing is guaranteed for the freshman year only. Priority is given to out-of-town students. 81% of students commute. Alcohol is not permitted. All students may keep cars.

FACULTY/CLASSROOMS: 57% of faculty are male; 43% are female. No introductory courses are taught by graduate students.

PROGRAMS OF STUDY: UC confers B.A., B.S., B.F.A., B.M., B.S.Des., B.U.P., B.S.M.E., B.S.N., B.S.I.M., B.S.Ed., B.A.Art His., B.S.Ch.E., B.S.C.E., B.S.E.E., B.S.Comp.E., B.S.Aero.E., B.S.Arch., B.S.Int.Des, B.S.H.S., B.I.S., B.S.Bm.E., B.R.S.T., B.S.Mat.E., B.B.A., B.S.C.S., B.S.A.E.T., B.S.C.E.T., B.S.C.M., B.S.E.E.T., B.S.M.E.T., B.S.W., B.S.F.S.E.T., B.S.A.E., B.S.E.V.E., B.S.I.T. and B.T.A.S. degrees. Associate, master's, and doctoral degrees are also awarded. Bachelor's degrees are awarded in AGRICULTURE (environmental studies and horticulture), BIOLOGICAL SCIENCE (biochemistry, biology/biological science, and neurosciences), BUSINESS (accounting, banking and finance, business administration and management, finance, insurance, international business, management science, marketing/retailing/merchandising, operations management, organizational behavior, real estate, and sports management), COMMUNICATIONS AND THE ARTS (Arabic, art history, broadcasting, communications, communication science, comparative literature, creative writing, dance, design, digital communications, dramatic arts, English, fine arts, French, German, graphic design, Hebrew, information technology, jazz, journalism, keyboard - piano concentration, linguistics, music, music history and appreciation, music performance, music theory and composition, piano/organ, radio/tv, Spanish, speech/debate/rhetoric, theater design, visual and performing arts, and voice), COMPUTER AND PHYSICAL SCIENCE (astrophysics, chemical technology, chemistry, Computer Engineering Technology, computer information technology, computer science, geology, information sciences and systems, mathematics, physics, and quantitative methods), EDUCATION (art education, athletic training, business education, early childhood education, elementary education, foreign languages education, guidance education, health education, health information management, industrial arts education, middle school education, music education, nutrition education, science education, secondary education, and special education), ENGINEERING AND ENVIRONMENTAL DESIGN (aeronautical engineering, architectural engineering, architectural technology, bioengineering, biomedical engineering, chemical engineering, city/community/regional planning, civil engineering, computer engineering, construction management, electrical/electronics engineering, electrical/electronics engineering technology, engineering, engineering mechanics, engineering technology, industrial administration/management, industrial engineering technology, interior design, materials engineering, mechanical engineering, mechanical engineering technology, metallurgical engineering, and nuclear engineering), HEALTH PROFESSIONS (medical laboratory technology, nuclear medical technology, nursing, predentistry, premedicine, prepharmacy, respiratory therapy, and speech pathology/audiology), SOCIAL SCIENCE (addiction studies, African American studies, anthropology, archeology, Asian/Oriental studies, classical/ancient civilization, criminal justice, dietetics, economics, fashion design and technology, geography, history, international studies, Judaic studies, Latin American studies, liberal arts/general studies, philosophy, political science/government, prelaw, psychology, social science, social work, sociology, urban studies, and women's studies). Architecture, music, and engineering are the strongest academically. Marketing, psychology, and criminal justice have the largest enrollments.

ACTIVITIES: 10% of men belong to 24 national fraternities; 11% of women belong to 15 national sororities. There are 416 groups on campus, including art, band, cheerleading, chess, choir, chorale, chorus, computers, dance, drama, environmental, ethnic, gay, honors, international, jazz band, literary magazine, marching band, musical theater, newspaper, opera, orchestra, pep band, photography, political, professional, radio and TV, religious, social, social service, student government, and symphony. Popular campus events include College Conservatory of Music Productions. **Sports:** There are 8 intercollegiate sports for men and 9 for women, and 14 intramural sports for men and 14 for women. Facilities include an athletic and recreation, a 30,000-seat stadium, a field house, a 13,000-seat gym, indoor and outdoor tracks, a climbing wall, recreation center with cardiovascular and weight equipment, three swimming pools, tennis courts, and athletic fields. **Graduates:** From July 1, 2013 to June 30, 2014, 5022 bachelor's degrees were awarded. The most popular majors were business/marketing (16%), health professions and related programs (15%), and engineering (10%). In an average class, 2% graduate in 3 years or less, 28% graduate in 4 years or less, 60% graduate in 5 years or less, and 65% graduate in 6 years or less.

SERVICES: Counseling and information services are available, as is tutoring in most subjects. There is a reader service for the blind, and remedial math, reading, and writing. Other services offered include interpreting services for the hearing impaired and note taking and reading services for the blind. **Library/Resources:** Computerized library services include interlibrary loans, database searching, Internet access, and Wi-Fi capability. Special learning facilities include an art gallery and radio station. **Physically Challenged Students:** 95% of the campus is accessible. Facilities include wheelchair ramps, elevators, special parking, specially equipped restrooms, special class scheduling, lowered drinking fountains, and lowered telephones. **Special:** The Professional Practice Program, a 5-year cooperative plan offering alternate work in academic subjects and industry, is available for students in engineering, business, arts and sciences, design, architecture, and art. Study abroad is available in 29 countries. Non-degree study is possible. There are including Phi Beta Kappa and a freshman honors program. **Visiting:** There are regularly scheduled orientations for prospective students. There are guides for informal visits, visitors may sit in on classes, and stay overnight. To schedule a visit, contact the Admissions Office. **Campus Safety and Security:** Measures include emergency notification system and security escort services. There are shuttle buses, emergency telephones, and lighted pathways/sidewalks.

REQUIREMENTS: The ACT Optional Writing test is also required. In addition, ACT and SAT are accepted, with the ACT preferred. Applicants should be graduates of an accredited secondary school with 4 units of high school English, 3 of math, 2 each of science, social science, foreign language, and electives, and 1 of fine arts. A GPA of 2.0 is required. AP and CLEP credits are accepted.The General Education Core has a firm foundation in UC's Academic Plan, to reaffirm liberal education as the core to preparing students as life-long learners. Our General Education course requirements are purposefully designed to strengthen four important learning outcomes or competencies throughout the student's progress toward their degree. Undergraduate courses at the University of Cincinnati promote development of four Baccalaureate Competencies: Critical Thinking, Knowledge Integration, Effective Communication, and Social Responsibility. Students must complete coursework in English Composition and Quantitative Reasoning. Students must complete at least 120 semester credit hours in order to earn a baccalaureate degree. **Procedure:** Freshmen are admitted to all sessions. Entrance exams should be taken in May of the junior year or January or March of the senior year. There is a rolling admissions plan. Applications should be filed by March 1 for fall entry, along with a $50 fee. Notifications are sent October 1. **Transfer Students:** 1165 transfer students enrolled in 2013-2014. A minimum college GPA of 2.0 is required. Specific programs may have higher GPA and requirements and prerequisite courses. **International Students:** There are 350 international students enrolled. The school actively recruits these students. They must take the TOEFL with a minimum score of 517 on the paper-based TOEFL (PBT) or 66 on the Internet-based version (iBT), or take the IELTS or SAT.

ADMISSIONS: 76% of the 2014-2015 applicants were accepted. The SAT scores for the 2014-2015 freshman class were: Critical Reading--21% below 500, 42% between 500 and 599, 29% between 600 and 699, and 8% between 700 and 800; Math--14% below 500, 37% between 500 and 599, 37% between 600 and 699, and 12% between

700 and 800; Writing--26% below 500, 44% between 500 and 599, 25% between 600 and 699, and 5% between 700 and 800. The ACT scores were 8% below 21, 22% between 21 and 23, 32% between 24 and 26, 17% between 27 and 28, and 21% above 28. 40% of the current freshmen were in the top fifth of their class; 71% were in the top two fifths. There were 45 National Merit finalists. 74 freshmen graduated first in their class. **Admissions Contact:** Tom Canepa, Assistant Vice President of Admissions. E-Mail: *admissions@uc.edu* Web: *www.uc.edu*

FINANCIAL AID: In 2014-2015, 80% of all full-time freshmen and 66% of continuing full-time students received some form of financial aid. 64% of all full-time freshmen and 66% of continuing full-time students received need-based aid. The average freshman award was $8,662. Need-based scholarships or need-based grants averaged $6,107 need-based self-help aid (loans and jobs) averaged $4,092; and non-need-based athletic scholarships averaged $12,019. The CSS/Profile and FAFSA are required. Check with the school for current application deadlines.

UNIVERSITY OF DAYTON   B-4
www.udayton.edu

Dayton, OH 45469	(937) 229-4411
	(800) 837-7433
Fax: (937) 229-4729	Email: admission@udayton.edu
Full-time: 4147 men, 3771 women	Faculty: 463; IIA, +$
Part-time: 381 men, 255 women	Ph.D.s: 88%
Graduate: 1429 men, 1385 women	Student/Faculty: 15 to 1
Year: semesters, summer session	Tuition: $37,230
Room & Board: $11,840	Freshman Class: 16968 applied, 9982 accepted, 2164 enrolled
SAT CR/M: 561/582 ACT: 27	CEEB CODE: 1834
Application Deadline: March 1	VERY COMPETITIVE

The University of Dayton, founded in 1850, is a private comprehensive institution affiliated with the Roman Catholic Church. University of Dayton is part of the Southwestern Ohio Council for Higher Education, it has undergraduate and graduate programs emphasizing the arts and sciences, business administration, engineering, education, health sciences, and law. There are 4 undergraduate schools and 5 graduate schools. In addition to regional accreditation, UD has baccalaureate program accreditation with AACSB, ABET, NASAD, NASM, NCATE, ACEND, HLC, and MPAC. The 388-acre campus is in a suburban area 2 miles south of downtown Dayton. Including any residence halls, there are 58 buildings.

STUDENT LIFE: 52% of undergraduates are from out of state, mostly the Midwest. Students are from 45 states, 42 foreign countries, and Canada. 46% are from public schools. 77% are White; 11% Foreign. 40% are Catholic. The average age of freshmen is 18; all undergraduates, 20. 9% do not continue beyond their first year; 77% remain to graduate. **Housing:** 6600 students can be accommodated in college housing, which includes coed dorms and on-campus apartments. In addition, there are honors houses, special-interest houses, fraternity houses, and sorority houses. On-campus housing is available on a first-come, first-served basis, and is available on a lottery system for upperclassmen. 74% of students live on campus; of those, 100% remain on campus on weekends. Upperclassmen may keep cars.

FACULTY/CLASSROOMS: 60% of faculty are male; 40% are female. 88% teach undergraduates. No introductory courses are taught by graduate students. The average class size in an introductory lecture is 28; in a laboratory is 20; and in a regular course is 27.

PROGRAMS OF STUDY: UD confers B.A., B.S., B.C.E., B.Ch.E., B.E.E., B.F.A., B.G.S., B.M.E. and B.Mus. degrees. Master's and doctoral degrees are also awarded. Bachelor's degrees are awarded in BIOLOGICAL SCIENCE (biochemistry, biology/biological science, environmental biology, and nutrition), BUSINESS (accounting, banking and finance, business administration and management, business economics, entrepreneurial studies, international business management, management information systems, marketing/retailing/merchandising, operations research, and sports management), COMMUNICATIONS AND THE ARTS (art, art history and appreciation, communications, dramatic arts, English, fine arts, French, German, music, music performance, music theory and composition, photography, Spanish, and visual design), COMPUTER AND PHYSICAL SCIENCE (chemistry, computer science, environmental geology, geology, information sciences and systems, mathematics, mathematics economics, physical sciences, and physics), EDUCATION (art education, early childhood education, elementary education, music education, secondary education, and special education), ENGINEERING AND ENVIRONMENTAL DESIGN (chemical engineering, civil engineering, computer engineering, computer technology, electrical/electronics engineering, electrical/electronics engineering technology, engineering technology, industrial engineering technology, manufacturing technology, mechanical engineering, and mechanical engineering technology), HEALTH PROFESSIONS (exercise science, music therapy, pharmaceutical chemistry, predentistry, premedicine, and prephysical therapy), SOCIAL SCIENCE (American studies, criminal justice, dietetics, early childhood studies, economics, ethics, politics, and social policy, history, international studies, liberal arts/general studies, philosophy, political science/government, psychology, religion, religious education, sociology, and women's studies). Engineering, business, and education are the strongest academically. Business/marketing and engineering/engineering technologies have the largest enrollments.

ACTIVITIES: 13% of men belong to 1 local and 10 national fraternities; 20% of women belong to 10 national sororities. There are 244 groups on campus, including art, band, cheerleading, chess, choir, chorale, chorus, computers, dance, debate, drama, drill team, environmental, ethnic, film, gay, honors, international, jazz band, literary magazine, marching band, musical theater, newspaper, orchestra, pep band, photography, political, professional, radio and TV, religious, social, social service, student government, symphony, and yearbook. Popular campus events include Christmas on Campus, Green Sweep and Weekend Scene. **Sports:** There are 7 intercollegiate sports for men and 9 for women, and 12 intramural sports for men and 12 for women. Facilities include a 13,455-seat arena, an 11,000-seat football stadium with a track, a 2000-seat soccer field, a 5000-seat volleyball facility, a baseball stadium, a softball stadium, and a state-of-the-art recreational sports facility containing a 4-court main gym, an aquatic center, a climbing wall, a 2-court MAC gym, a juice bar, 3 racquetball courts, classrooms, fitness studios, a fitness center, and an indoor track. **Graduates:** From July 1, 2013 to June 30, 2014, 1953 bachelor's degrees were awarded. The most popular majors were marketing (8%), communication (7%), and finance (6%). 200 companies recruited on campus in 2013-2014. In an average class, 60% graduate in 4 years or less, 76% graduate in 5 years or less, and 77% graduate in 6 years or less.

SERVICES: Counseling and information services are available, as is tutoring in some subjects. (SI) are available for many entry-level courses and some high-attrition upper level courses. Curricular and tutorial support is available for writing at all levels. **Library/Resources:** The 3 libraries contain 1.2 million volumes, 747,670 microform items, and 47,901 audio/video tapes/CDs/DVDs, and subscribe to 76,020 periodicals including electronic. Computerized library services include interlibrary loans, database searching, Internet access, and Wi-Fi capability. Special learning facilities include an art gallery, radio station, TV station, UD Research Institute, Bombeck Family Learning Center, a learning teaching center, and Davis Center for Portfolio Management. **Physically Challenged Students:** Facilities include wheelchair ramps, elevators, special parking, specially equipped restrooms, special class scheduling, lowered drinking fountains, special housing. The university provides access to programs and services through the Office of Learning Resources. **Special:** Traditional co-op programs are available in the School of Engineering; however, any student in any discipline may co-op, and qualification is determined on a case-by-case basis. Internships are available in all majors. Cross-registration is available with the Southwestern Ohio Council for Higher Education. Study abroad, work-study programs, a Washington semester, accelerated degree programs, and B.A.-B.S. degrees in chemistry, math, economics, and psychology are available. For students who wish to have a dual major, almost all programs may be combined. Student-designed majors include general studies and interdisciplinary studies. An engineering curriculum agreement exists with Sinclair Community College. There are a freshman honors program. **Visiting:** There are regularly scheduled orientations for prospective students, including an admission interview, financial aid consultation, campus tour, residence hall tour, and faculty or class visit. High school seniors who have been accepted to the university may participate in an overnight visit during the winter semester. There are guides for informal visits, visitors may sit in on classes, and stay overnight. To schedule a visit, contact the Office of Admission. **Campus Safety and Security:** Measures include 24-hour foot and vehicle patrol, emergency notification system, and security escort services. There are shuttle buses, emergency telephones, lighted pathways/sidewalks, controlled access to dorms/residences, a bike patrol, electronic access control for residence hall access, about 1000 video cameras, an on-campus ambulance service, automated external debrillators in residence halls and key facilities, centrally monitored fire alarm systems in all residential facilities, and fire suppression in high-density residential facilities.

REQUIREMENTS: The SAT or ACT is required. Applicants should be graduates of an accredited secondary school with 16 units in English, math, science, social studies, and academic electives. In addition, 2 units of foreign language are required for admission to the College of Arts and Sciences. The GED is accepted. High school transcripts must be submitted. An essay or personal statement, a recommendation from the high school guidance counselor, and an interview are recommended. Music students must audition. AP and CLEP credits are accepted. Important factors in the admissions decision are personality/intangible qualities, recommendations by school officials, and leadership record.To graduate, all students must complete a minimum of 120 semester hours with at least 30 hours of residence, and maintain a minimum GPA of 2.0. The curricula must include general education requirements, including 4 classes in religious studies and philosophy as well as basic skills requirements. Departmental requirements vary. **Procedure:** Freshmen are admitted fall, winter, and summer. Entrance exams should be taken by December of the senior year. There are deferred admissions and rolling admissions plans. Applications should be filed by March 1 for fall entry. Notification is sent on a rolling basis. Applications are accepted on-line. **Transfer Students:** 184 transfer students enrolled in 2013-2014. Attention is directed to college and high school GPA and course selection. The minimum grade point average is 2.0. The School of Education and Allied Professions requires a minimum 2.5 GPA in previous college work. Achievement of the minimum GPA does not guarantee admission. For students under 21 years of age, results of the SAT or ACT are required. All students applying to the School of Education and Allied Professions must submit SAT or ACT and Praxis I scores. 30 of 120 credits required for the bachelor's degree must be completed at UD. **International Students:** There are 903 international students enrolled. The school actively recruits these students. They must take the TOEFL with a minimum score of 523 on the paper-based TOEFL (PBT) or 70 on the Internet-based version (iBT), or English Language Proficiency Test, or Advanced Placement International English Language Examination.

ADMISSIONS: 59% of the 2014-2015 applicants were accepted. The SAT scores for the 2014-2015 freshman class were: Critical Reading--19% below 500, 50% between 500 and 599, 26% between 600 and 699, and 5% between 700 and 800; Math--14% below 500, 44% between 500 and 599, 34% between 600 and 699, and 9% between 700 and 800. The ACT scores were 4% below 21, 15% between 21 and 23, 31% between 24 and 26, 20% between 27 and 28, and 30% above 28. 44% of the current freshmen were in the top fifth of their class; 75% were in the top two fifths. There were 7 National Merit finalists. 11 freshmen graduated first in their class. **Admissions Contact:** Robert F. Durkle, Director of Admission. E-Mail: *admission@udayton .edu* Web: *www.udayton.edu*

FINANCIAL AID: In 2014-2015, 88% of all full-time freshmen and 72% of continuing full-time students received some form of financial aid. 62% of all full-time freshmen and 52% of continuing full-time students received need-based aid. The average freshman award was $28,419. Need-based scholarships or need-based grants averaged $23,610; need-based self-help aid (loans and jobs) averaged $3,722; non-need-based athletic scholarships averaged $16,351; and other non-need-based awards and non-need-based scholarships averaged

$13,572. 35% of undergraduate students work part-time. Average annual earnings from campus work are $1970. The average financial indebtedness of the 2014 graduate was $21,096. UD is a member of CSS. The FAFSA is required. The priority date for freshman financial aid applications for fall entry is March 31.

UNIVERSITY OF FINDLAY B-2
www.findlay.edu

Findlay, OH 45840	(419) 424-4732
	(800) 548-0932
Fax: (419) 424-4822	Email: admissions@findlay.edu
Full-time: 1055 men, 1810 women	Faculty: IIA, --$
Part-time: 480 men, 660 women	Ph.D.s: n/av
Graduate: 610 men, 710 women	Student/Faculty: n/av
Year: semesters, summer session	Tuition: $27,590
Room & Board: $9570	Freshman Class: n/av
SAT or ACT: required	CEEB CODE: 1223
Application Deadline: see profile	COMPETITIVE

The University of Findlay, founded in 1882, is a private, independent institution affiliated with the Churches of God, General Conference, offering liberal arts and sciences and career preparation programs. The figures in the above capsule and in this profile are approximate. There are 4 undergraduate schools and 1 graduate school. In addition to regional accreditation, Findlay has baccalaureate program accreditation with NCATE. The library contains 135,000 volumes, 90,000 microform items, 1200 audio/video tapes/CDs/DVDs, and subscribes to 2500 periodicals including electronic. Computerized library services include interlibrary loans, database searching, Internet access, and laptop Internet portals. Special learning facilities include a learning resource center, art gallery, planetarium, radio station, TV station, university-owned farm, equine facility, and emergency response training center. The 250-acre campus is in a small town 45 miles south of Toledo and 100 miles northwest of Columbus. Including any residence halls, there are 55 buildings.

STUDENT LIFE: 80% of undergraduates are from Ohio. Others are from 45 states, 30 foreign countries, and Canada. 80% are from public schools. 85% are white. 60% are Protestant; 35% Catholic. The average age of freshmen is 18; all undergraduates, 22. 25% do not continue beyond their first year; 55% remain to graduate.

FACULTY/CLASSROOMS: 53% of faculty are male; 47% are female. All teach undergraduates. No introductory courses are taught by graduate students. The average class size in an introductory lecture is 23; in a laboratory, 15; and in a regular course, 22.

PROGRAMS OF STUDY: Findlay confers B.A., B.S., B.S.B.M., B.S.C.J., and B.S.E.M. degrees. Associate, Master's, and Doctoral degrees are also awarded. Bachelor's degrees are awarded in AGRICULTURE (equine science), BIOLOGICAL SCIENCE (biology/ biological science), BUSINESS (accounting, banking and finance, business administration and management, business economics, business systems analysis, hospitality management services, human resources, international business management, and marketing/ retailing/merchandising), COMMUNICATIONS AND THE ARTS (arts administration/management, broadcasting, communications, dramatic arts, English, English as a second/foreign language, illustration, Japanese, Spanish, studio art, and technical and business writing), COMPUTER AND PHYSICAL SCIENCE (chemistry, computer science, mathematics, and science), EDUCATION (art education, bilingual/bicultural education, elementary education, foreign languages education, middle school education, physical education, and secondary education), ENGINEERING AND ENVIRONMENTAL DESIGN (environmental science, occupational safety and health, and technological management), HEALTH PROFESSIONS (health science, nuclear medical technology, nursing, occupational therapy, physician's assistant, premedicine, and preveterinary science), SOCIAL SCIENCE (criminal justice, economics, forensic studies, history, international studies, philosophy, political science/government, prelaw, psychology, religion, social work, and sociology). Business administration, preveterinary medicine, and education are the strongest academically. Business administration, equestrian studies, and education have the largest enrollments.

ACTIVITIES: 4% of men belong to 3 national fraternities; 1% of women belong to 2 national sororities. There are 40 groups on campus, including art, band, cheerleading, choir, chorale, chorus, computers, drama, drum and bugle corps, equestrian, ethnic, honors, international, jazz band, literary magazine, marching band, musical theater, newspaper, pep band, political, preveterinary, professional, radio and TV, religious, social, social service, and student government. Popular campus events include International Night and Spring Bash.

SERVICES: Counseling and information services are available, as is tutoring in most subjects. There is a reader service for the blind, and remedial math, reading, and writing. Other services include assistance with note taking, test taking, and study skills, and assistive technology per student need. **Library/Resources:** The library contains 135,000 volumes, 90,000 microform items, and 1,200 audio/video tapes/CDs/DVDs, and subscribes to 2,500 periodicals including electronic. Computerized library services include interlibrary loans, database searching, Internet access, and Wi-Fi capability. Special learning facilities include an art gallery, planetarium, radio station, TV station, university-owned farm, equine facility, and emergency response training center. **Physically Challenged Students:** 90% of the campus is accessible. Facilities include wheelchair ramps, elevators, special parking, specially equipped restrooms, special class scheduling, lowered drinking fountains. **Special:** Co-op programs are available in accounting and occupational health and safety. There is cross-registration with Mount Carmel College of Nursing and Lourdes College. The field experience program provides up to 20 semester hours in field placement. Internships are available for many majors, including business, business education, communication, hazardous materials management, and theater majors. Through the College Consortium for International Studies, study abroad is possible in 16 countries. Work-study, a Washington semester, dual and student-designed majors, a general studies degree, pass/fail options, and credit for life experience are offered. Nondegree study is possible. There are a freshman honors program. **Visiting:** There are regularly scheduled orientations for prospective students, including a tour, interview, and coach/faculty visits. There are guides for informal visits, visitors may sit in on classes, and stay overnight. To schedule a visit, contact the Admissions Office. **Campus Safety and Security:** Measures include 24-hour foot and vehicle patrol, emergency notification system, self-defense education, and security escort services. There are emergency telephones and lighted pathways/sidewalks.

REQUIREMENTS: The SAT or ACT is required. The ACT Optional Writing test is also required. Applicants should have completed 16 high school credits or GED equivalents, including 4 years of English, 2 years of social studies/history, 3 to 4 math courses, and 2 to 3 science courses. A letter of recommendation and an essay are required for all applicants. A GPA of 2.3 is required. AP and CLEP credits are accepted. Important factors in the admissions decision are advanced placement or honors courses, evidence of special talent, and extracurricular activities record.

FINANCIAL AID: Findlay is a member of CSS. The FAFSA is required. Check with the school for current deadlines.

UNIVERSITY OF MOUNT UNION   E-2
www.mountunion.edu

Alliance, OH 44601	(330) 821-5320
	(800) 992-6682
Fax: (330) 823-3457	Email: admission@mountunion.edu
Full-time: 1095 men, 1053 women	Faculty: 124
Part-time: 14 men, 13 women	Ph.D.s: 87%
Graduate: 18 men, 60 women	Student/Faculty: 17 to 1
Year: semesters, summer session	Tuition: $26,650
Room & Board: $8480	Freshman Class: 2333 applied, 2071 accepted, 705 enrolled
ACT: 22	CEEB CODE: 1492
Application Deadline: open	COMPETITIVE

University of Mount Union, founded in 1846, is a private, liberal arts college affiliated with the United Methodist Church. In addition to regional accreditation, Mount Union has baccalaureate program accreditation with NASM and NCATE. The 2 libraries contain 230,000 volumes, 43,000 microform items, 35,700 audio/video tapes/CDs/DVDs, and subscribe to 950 periodicals including electronic. Computerized library services include interlibrary loans, database searching, Internet access, and Wi-Fi capability. Special learning facilities include an art gallery, radio station, An astronomical observatory, a university theater, a playhouse, and a nature center. The 115-acre campus is in a suburban area 20 miles east of Canton. Including any residence halls, there are 37 buildings.

STUDENT LIFE: 84% of undergraduates are from Ohio. Others are from 27 states, 17 foreign countries, and Canada. 89% are from public schools. 85% are White. 42% are Protestant; 29% claim no religious affiliation; 28% Catholic. The average age of freshmen is 18; all undergraduates, 20. 22% do not continue beyond their first year; 65% remain to graduate.

FACULTY/CLASSROOMS: 59% of faculty are male; 41% are female. All teach undergraduates. No introductory courses are taught by graduate students. The average class size in an introductory lecture is 19; in a laboratory is 15; and in a regular course is 18.

PROGRAMS OF STUDY: Mount Union confers B.A., B.S., B.Mus. and B.Mus.Ed. degrees. Master's degrees are also awarded. Bachelor's degrees are awarded in BIOLOGICAL SCIENCE (biochemistry, biology/biological science, and environmental biology), BUSINESS (accounting, business administration and management, human resources, international business management, and sports management), COMMUNICATIONS AND THE ARTS (art, communications, creative writing, dramatic arts, English, French, German, Japanese, media arts, music, music performance, and Spanish), COMPUTER AND PHYSICAL SCIENCE (astronomy, chemistry, computer science, geology, information sciences and systems, mathematics, and physics), EDUCATION (athletic training, early childhood education, elementary education, middle school education, music education, and physical education), ENGINEERING AND ENVIRONMENTAL DESIGN (civil engineering, environmental science, and mechanical engineering), HEALTH PROFESSIONS (exercise science, health, and medical technology), SOCIAL SCIENCE (American studies, cognitive science, criminal justice, economics, history, international studies, Near Eastern studies, philosophy, political science/government, psychology, religion, social science, and sociology). Business, early childhood education, and sports management have the largest enrollments.

ACTIVITIES: 21% of men belong to 4 national fraternities; 43% of women belong to 1 local and 3 national sororities. There are 80 groups on campus, including art, band, cheerleading, chess, choir, chorale, chorus, computers, dance, debate, drama, drill team, environmental, ethnic, forensics, gay, honors, international, jazz band, literary magazine, marching band, musical theater, newspaper, orchestra, pep band, political, professional, radio and TV, religious, social, social service, student government, and symphony. Popular campus events include Spring Fest, Greek Week and Schooler Lecture series.

SERVICES: Counseling and information services are available, as is tutoring in most subjects, general education courses and most introductory courses There is a reader service for the blind, and remedial writing. Facilitated study groups for most general education courses that meet once a week. **Library/Resources:** The 2 libraries contain 230,000 volumes, 43,000 microform items, and 35,700 audio/video tapes/CDs/DVDs, and subscribe to 950 periodicals including electronic. Computerized library services include interlibrary loans, database searching, Internet access, and Wi-Fi capability. Special learning facilities include an art gallery, radio station, an astronomical observatory, university theater, playhouse, and a nature center. **Physically Challenged Students:** 98% of the campus is accessible. Facilities include wheelchair ramps, elevators, special parking, specially equipped restrooms, special class scheduling, lowered drinking fountains, and special housing. **Special:** Mount Union offers internships for credit in many majors, study abroad in 26 countries, co-op programs in business, work-study programs with various employers, student-designed majors, and pass/fail options. Adults in the nontraditional study program may receive credit for life, military, or work experience. There are 18 national honor societies, a freshman honors program, and 19 departmental honors programs. **Visiting:**

There are regularly scheduled orientations for prospective students, including interviews, a campus tour, meetings with faculty, and classroom visits. There are guides for informal visits, visitors may sit in on classes, and stay overnight. To schedule a visit, contact The Office of Admissions at (800) 992-6682. **Campus Safety and Security:** Measures include 24-hour foot and vehicle patrol, emergency notification system, self-defense education, and security escort services. There are emergency telephones and lighted pathways/sidewalks.

REQUIREMENTS: The ACT is required. Preference is given to high school graduates who have completed a minimum of 15 academic units, including 4 in English, 3 each in math, social science, and lab science, and 2 in foreign language. A GPA of 2.0 is required. AP and CLEP credits are accepted. Important factors in the admissions decision are advanced placement or honors courses, recommendations by school officials, and personality/intangible qualities.

ADMISSIONS: 89% of a recent year applicants were accepted. The ACT scores were 30% below 21, 34% between 21 and 23, 18% between 24 and 26, 11% between 27 and 28, and 7% above 28. 31% of the current freshmen were in the top fifth of their class; 59% were in the top two fifths. 8 freshmen graduated first in their class.

FINANCIAL AID: 94% of all full-time freshmen and 96% of continuing full-time students received some form of financial aid. 80% of all full-time freshmen and 82% of continuing full-time students received need-based aid. The average freshman award was $20,644. Need-based scholarships or need-based grants averaged $14,651 ($26,350 maximum); need-based self-help aid (loans and jobs) averaged $5,734 ($6,900 maximum); and other non-need-based awards and non-need-based scholarships averaged $9,883 ($26,350 maximum). 39% of undergraduate students work part-time. Average annual earnings from campus work are $1350. The average financial indebtedness of the 2013 graduate was $27,862. Mount Union is a member of CSS. The FAFSA is required. The priority date for freshman financial aid applications for fall entry is March 1. The deadline for filing freshman financial aid applications for fall entry is September 1.

UNIVERSITY OF RIO GRANDE *(The complete profile is made available exclusively on our website, www.barronspac.com)*

UNIVERSITY OF TOLEDO   B-1
www.utoledo.edu

Toledo, OH 43606-3398	(419) 530-5704
	(800) 5TOLEDO
Fax: (419) 530-1202	Email: enroll@utoledo.edu
Full-time: 7355 men, 7162 women	Faculty: I, --$
Part-time: 1611 men, 1716 women	Ph.D.s: n/av
Graduate: 2132 men, 2634 women	Student/Faculty: n/av
Year: semesters, summer session	Tuition: $9288 ($18,408)
Room & Board: $10,176	Freshman Class: 11633 applied, 11131 accepted, 3837 enrolled
SAT: recommended ACT: 22	CEEB CODE: 1845
Application Deadline: open	COMPETITIVE

The University of Toledo, founded in 1872, is a public comprehensive institution emphasizing undergraduate degree programs in the liberal arts and sciences, business, engineering, teacher preparation, and health professions. Many graduate and professional degree programs, including medicine, are also offered. There are 12 undergraduate schools and 10 graduate schools. In addition to regional accreditation, UT has baccalaureate program accreditation with AACSB, ABET, ACPE, APTA, NASM, and NCATE. The 813-acre campus is in a suburban area 6 miles northwest of downtown Toledo. Including any residence halls, there are 107 buildings.

STUDENT LIFE: 84% of undergraduates are from Ohio. Others are from 47 states, 92 foreign countries, and Canada. 67% are white; 21% African American. The average age of freshmen is 19; all undergraduates, 22. 32% do not continue beyond their first year; 45% remain to graduate.

FACULTY/CLASSROOMS: 57% of faculty are male; 43% are female.

No introductory courses are taught by graduate students. The average class size in an introductory lecture is 38; in a laboratory is 18; and in a regular course is 31.

PROGRAMS OF STUDY: UT confers B.A., B.A.Env.Studies, B.A. in Africana Studies, B.B.A., B.Ed., B.E.T., B.F.A., B.M., B.S.Admin.Svcs., B.S.C.E., B.S.Chem.Eng., B.S.Comp.Sci. and Eng., B.S.Const.Eng., B.S.Crim.Just., B.S.C.S.E., B.S.E., B.S.E.E., B.S.El.Eng.Tech., B.S.Eng.Phys., B.S.Env.Sci., B.S.Exer.Sci., B.S.Health Care Spvsn., B.S.I.E., B.S. in Bioeng., B.S. in Comp.Sci. and Eng.Tech., B.S.M.E., B.S.Med.Tech., B.S.N., B.S.Pharm., B.S.P.T., B.S.Rad.Sci., B.S.Resp.Care, B.S.W., and B.Voc.Ed. degrees. Associate, master's, and doctoral degrees are also awarded. Bachelor's degrees are awarded in BIOLOGICAL SCIENCE (biology/biological science), BUSINESS (accounting, banking and finance, business administration and management, marketing/retailing/merchandising, and recreation and leisure services), COMMUNICATIONS AND THE ARTS (art history and appreciation, communications, dramatic arts, English, film arts, fine arts, French, German, linguistics, music, and Spanish), COMPUTER AND PHYSICAL SCIENCE (chemistry, computer science, geology, information sciences and systems, mathematics, and physics), EDUCATION (art education, business education, early childhood education, elementary education, foreign languages education, health education, music education, physical education, science education, secondary education, special education, and vocational education), ENGINEERING AND ENVIRONMENTAL DESIGN (bioengineering, chemical engineering, civil engineering, computer engineering, electrical/electronics engineering, electromechanical technology, engineering, engineering technology, environmental science, industrial engineering, and mechanical engineering), HEALTH PROFESSIONS (nursing, pharmacy, physical therapy, and speech pathology/audiology), SOCIAL SCIENCE (anthropology, community services, criminal justice, economics, geography, history, humanities, international relations, philosophy, physical fitness/movement, political science/government, psychology, social work, sociology, and women's studies). Engineering, pharmacy, and business are the strongest academically. Pharmacy, nursing, and business have the largest enrollments.

ACTIVITIES: 5% of men belong to 17 local and 7 national fraternities; 4% of women belong to 13 local and 7 national sororities. There are 200 groups on campus, including art, band, cheerleading, chess, choir, chorale, chorus, computers, dance, drama, drill team, ethnic, film, gay, honors, international, jazz band, literary magazine, marching band, musical theater, newspaper, orchestra, pep band, photography, political, professional, radio and TV, religious, social, social service, student government, and symphony. Popular campus events include Songfest and Greek Week.

SERVICES: Counseling and information services are available, as is tutoring in most subjects. There is a reader service for the blind, and remedial math, reading, and writing. **Library/Resources:** The 3 libraries contain 2.1 million volumes, 1.8 million microform items, and 42,941 audio/video tapes/CDs/DVDs, and subscribe to 0 periodicals including electronic. Computerized library services include interlibrary loans, database searching, Internet access, and Wi-Fi capability. Special learning facilities include an art gallery, planetarium, and radio station. **Physically Challenged Students:** 96% of the campus is accessible. Facilities include wheelchair ramps, elevators, special parking, specially equipped restrooms, special class scheduling, lowered drinking fountains, and lowered telephones. **Special:** Special academic programs include internships in most majors, study abroad in 25 countries, and on-campus employment through the Financial Aid Office. There is a co-op program with the College of Engineering and cross-registration with Bowling Green State University. The B.A.-B.S. degree and dual majors are available in many areas of study. A general studies degree, student-designed majors, an accelerated degree, credit for life, military, and work experience, nondegree study, and pass/fail options are also offered. There are 56 national honor societies, a freshman honors program, and 21 departmental honors programs. **Visiting:** There are regularly scheduled orientations for prospective students, including an interview with an admissions representative and a student-guided campus tour. Academic appointments are available by request. There are guides for informal visits, visitors may sit in on classes, and stay overnight. To schedule a visit, contact the Office of Undergraduate Admissions at enroll@utoledo.edu. **Campus Safety and Security:** Measures include 24-hour foot and vehicle patrol, emergency notification system, self-defense education, and security escort services. There are shuttle buses, emergency telephones, lighted pathways/sidewalks, and controlled access to dorms/residences.

REQUIREMENTS: The SAT or ACT and ACT Writing Test are recommended. In addition, the university follows an open admissions policy for Ohio applicants. Students should be graduates of an accredited secondary school or hold the GED. The preparatory program should include 4 years of English, 3 each of math, natural science, and social studies, and 2 of a foreign language. A GPA of 2.0 is required. AP and CLEP credits are accepted.

ADMISSIONS: 96% of a recent year applicants were accepted. The ACT scores were 47% below 21, 25% between 21 and 23, 17% between 24 and 26, 6% between 27 and 28, and 5% above 28. 30% of the current freshmen were in the top fifth of their class; 56% were in the top two fifths.

FINANCIAL AID: In a recent year, 81% of all full-time freshmen and 71% of continuing full-time students received some form of financial aid. 65% of all full-time freshmen and 64% of continuing full-time students received need-based aid. The average freshman award was $11,006. Need-based scholarships or need-based grants averaged $8,377; need-based self-help aid (loans and jobs) averaged $3,661; non-need-based athletic scholarships averaged $15,697; and other non-need-based awards and non-need-based scholarships averaged $4,781. The average financial indebtedness of a recent year graduate was $27,378. UT is a member of CSS. The FAFSA is required. The priority date for freshman financial aid applications for fall entry is April 1.

URBANA UNIVERSITY   **B-3**
www.urbana.edu

Urbana, OH 43078   (937) 484-1356
                                              800 - 7 -URBANA
Fax: (937) 484-1322   Email: admissions@urbana.edu
Full-time: 500 men, 420 women   Faculty: 55
Part-time: 191 men, 346 women   Ph.D.s: 74%
Graduate: 32 men, 58 women   Student/Faculty: 17 to 1
Year: semesters, summer session Tuition: $22,012
Room & Board: $8808   Freshman Class: n/av
SAT or ACT: required   CEEB CODE: 1847
Application Deadline: open   COMPETITIVE

Urbana University, founded in 1850. Known for innovative academic programs that feature personal attention from faculty, the University offers more than 30 undergraduate programs and several graduate degrees, delivering course work in class, online, or a combination of both. Urbana University was the first college in the state to offer a nontraditional degree completion program and the second institution of higher education in Ohio to admit women. Founded by the Swedenborgian friends of John Chapman, the famous frontiersman called "Johnny Appleseed," the campus is home to the Johnny Appleseed Museum, a rich collection of the personal artifacts and history of this 19th century American hero. There are 3 undergraduate schools and one graduate school. In addition to regional accreditation, Urbana has baccalaureate program accreditation with NCATE, CCNE, and IACBE. The 128-acre campus is in a small town 40 miles west of Columbus and 50 miles north of Dayton. Including any residence halls, there are 30 buildings.

STUDENT LIFE: 90% of undergraduates are from Ohio. Others are from 5 states, and 5 foreign countries. 95% are from public schools. 79% are White; 17% African American. The average age of freshmen is 20; all undergraduates, 24. 23% do not continue beyond their first year; 35% remain to graduate. **Housing:** 500 students can be accommodated in college housing, which includes single-sex and coed dorms. In addition, there are honors houses. On-campus housing is guaranteed for all 4 years, is guaranteed for the freshman year only, and is available on a lottery system for upperclassmen. Priority is given to out-of-town students. 54% of students commute. All students may keep cars.

FACULTY/CLASSROOMS: 60% of faculty are male; 40% are female.

All teach undergraduates. No introductory courses are taught by graduate students. The average class size in an introductory lecture is 18; in a laboratory is 7; and in a regular course is 19.

PROGRAMS OF STUDY: Urbana confers B.A., B.S., and B.S.N. degrees. Associate and master's degrees are also awarded. Bachelor's degrees are awarded in AGRICULTURE (agricultural business management), BIOLOGICAL SCIENCE ((Biological) Pre-Health Studies), BUSINESS (business administration and management, business administration marketing, and sports management), COMMUNICATIONS AND THE ARTS (communications and English), COMPUTER AND PHYSICAL SCIENCE (mathematics and science), EDUCATION (early childhood education, education of the mentally handicapped, elementary education, English education, middle school education, and secondary education), HEALTH PROFESSIONS (exercise science, nursing, and premedicine), SOCIAL SCIENCE (criminal justice, family/consumer studies, history, liberal arts/general studies, philosophy and religion, prelaw, psychology, and sociology). Business, education, exercise science, criminal justice, and sport management are the strongest academically. Business, education, and sport studies have the largest enrollments.

ACTIVITIES: There are 30 groups on campus, including art, band, cheerleading, choir, chorus, dance, drama, environmental, ethnic, gay, Honor societies, honors, international, literary magazine, marching band, musical theater, newspaper, pep band, political, professional, religious, social, social service, and student government. Popular campus events include Spring Week, Founders Day, and Activities Fair. **Sports:** There are 11 intercollegiate sports for men and 12 for women, and 6 intramural sports for men and 6 for women. Facilities include a community center with a 3500-seat gym, a pool, handball and racquetball courts, a weight room, outdoor sand volleyball court, and outdoor tennis courts.

SERVICES: Counseling and information services are available, as is tutoring in most subjects. There is remedial math, reading, and writing. Taped textbooks, reading and writing labs, and study skills seminars are also available. **Library/Resources:** The library contains 316,000 volumes, 1,000 audio/video tapes/CDs/DVDs, and subscribes to 6,000 periodicals including electronic. Computerized library services include interlibrary loans, database searching, Internet access, and Wi-Fi capability. Special learning facilities include a **Physically Challenged Students:** 70% of the campus is accessible. Facilities include wheelchair ramps, elevators, special parking, and special class scheduling. **Special:** Special academic programs include internships, cross-registration with the Southwestern Ohio Council for Higher Education, study abroad, and accelerated degree programs in teacher certification. B.A.-B.S. degrees, dual and student-designed majors, credit for life, military, and work experience, and nondegree study are also available. There are 5 national honor societies, a freshman honors program, and 3 departmental honors programs. **Visiting:** There are regularly scheduled orientations for prospective students, consisting of a campus tour, admissions, financial aid, student life, meetings with coaches, attending classes. There are guides for informal visits, visitors may sit in on classes, and stay overnight. To schedule a visit, contact the Admissions Office at admissions@urbana.edu. **Campus Safety and Security:** Measures include 24-hour foot and vehicle patrol, emergency notification system, self-defense education, and security escort services. There are emergency telephones, lighted pathways/sidewalks, and controlled access to dorms/residences.

REQUIREMENTS: The SAT or ACT is required. An applicant must present evidence of high school completion in the form of a high school diploma or GED Certificate. The recommended high school curriculum includes 4 units of English, 3 units of mathematics, 2 units of science, 2 units of social science and one additional unit in English, mathematics, or science, and 4 additional units from English, mathematics, science, social science, foreign language or philosophy. ACT scores are preferred. A GPA of 2.0 is required. AP and CLEP credits are accepted. Important factors in the admissions decision are advanced placement or honors courses, evidence of special talent, and extracurricular activities record.To graduate, all students must complete 126 semester credits, with a minimum overall GPA of 2.0 and 2.5 in the major. Distribution requirements in a 47-49 credit core curriculum include 12 to 13 credit hours in math and science, 12 credits social sciences, 13 credits in humanities, 9 in communications, and 2-3 in health and physical education. The number of credits required per major varies. **Procedure:** Freshmen are admitted to all sessions. Entrance exams should be taken during the junior or senior year. There are deferred admissions and rolling admissions plans. Application deadlines are open. The fall 2014 application fee was $25. Applications are accepted on-line. **Transfer Students:** 50 transfer students enrolled in 2013-2014. Applicants must have a cumulative GPA of 2.0. 30 of 126 credits required for the bachelor's degree must be completed at Urbana. **International Students:** There are 4 international students enrolled. The school actively recruits these students. They must take the TOEFL.

ADMISSIONS: Melissa Tolle, Director of Admissions. Web: *www.urbana.edu*

FINANCIAL AID: The FAFSA, the state aid form, and the college's own financial statement, and the state aid form for residents are required. Check with the school for current application deadlines.

URSULINE COLLEGE (*The complete profile is made available exclusively on our website, www.barronspac.com*)

WALSH UNIVERSITY D-2
www.walsh.edu

North Canton, OH 44720	**(330) 490-7172**
	(800) 362-9846
Fax: (330) 490-7165	Email: admissions@walsh.edu
Full-time: 781 men, 1135 women	**Faculty:** 118; IIB, -$
Part-time: 143 men, 326 women	**Ph.D.s:** 65%
Graduate: 166 men, 412 women	**Student/Faculty:** 13 to 1
Year: semesters, summer session	**Tuition:** $25,840
Room & Board: $9260	**Freshman Class:** 1317 applied, 1194 accepted, 447 enrolled
SAT CR/M: 500/540 **ACT:** 22	**CEEB CODE:** 1926
Application Deadline: August 25	**COMPETITIVE**

Walsh University, was established in 1958 by the Brothers of Christian Instruction, a religious order of the Roman Catholic Church. The private institution offers undergraduate programs in liberal arts, business, communication, education, professional training, and nursing. There are 9 undergraduate schools and 6 graduate schools. In addition to regional accreditation, Walsh has baccalaureate program accreditation with NCATE, NLN, and CACREP. The 143-acre campus is in a small town 20 miles south of Akron. Including any residence halls, there are 24 buildings.

STUDENT LIFE: 94% of undergraduates are from Ohio. Others are from 18 states, 20 foreign countries, and Canada. 70% are from public schools. 78% are White. 43% are Catholic; 30% claim no religious affiliation; 26% Protestant. The average age of freshmen is 18; all undergraduates, 24. 25% do not continue beyond their first year; 65% remain to graduate. **Housing:** 1050 students can be accommodated in college housing, which includes single-sex and coed dorms and on-campus apartments. In addition, there are honors houses, special-interest houses, Study floors, and substance-free floors. On-campus housing is guaranteed for all 4 years. 56% of students commute. All students may keep cars.

FACULTY/CLASSROOMS: 45% of faculty are male; 55% are female. 90% teach undergraduates, 37% do research, and 20% do both. No introductory courses are taught by graduate students. The average class size in an introductory lecture is 15; in a laboratory is 14; and in a regular course is 16.

PROGRAMS OF STUDY: Walsh confers B.A., B.S., B.S.Ed. and B.S.N. degrees. Associate, Master's, and Doctoral degrees are also awarded. Bachelor's degrees are awarded in BIOLOGICAL SCIENCE (biochemistry, bioinformatics, and biology/biological science), BUSINESS (accounting, business administration and management, business communications, international business management, and marketing management), COMMUNICATIONS AND THE ARTS (communications, English, French, graphic design, and Spanish), COMPUTER AND PHYSICAL SCIENCE (chemistry, computer science, mathematics, and science), EDUCATION (early childhood education, education of the emotionally handicapped, education of the exceptional child, education of the mentally handicapped, education of the physically handicapped, elementary education, middle school education, museum studies, physical education, secondary education, and special education), ENGINEERING AND ENVIRONMENTAL DESIGN (environmental science), HEALTH PROFESSIONS (clinical science, exercise science, nursing, physical therapy, predentistry, premedicine, preoptometry, prepharmacy, prephysical therapy, and preveterinary science), SOCIAL SCIENCE (criminal justice, family/consumer studies, history, international relations, international studies, liberal arts/general studies, philosophy, political science/government, prelaw, psychology, science and society, sociology, and theological studies). Biology, nursing, and business are the strongest academically. Biology, nursing, and management have the largest enrollments.

ACTIVITIES: There are 40 groups on campus, including and special interest, art, band, cheerleading, choir, chorale, chorus, dance, drama, environmental, ethnic, honors, international, leadership honor societies, literary magazine, marching band, newspaper, pep band, political, professional, radio and TV, religious, social, social service, student government, and yearbook. Popular campus events include Walshfest, Spring Formal, and Improv. **Sports:** There are 9 intercollegiate sports for men and 9 for women, and 10 intramural sports for men and 9 for women. Facilities include 2 gymnasiums, 1200-seat and 2,000 seat, outdoor basketball and tennis courts, a track, softball and baseball fields, practice and intramural fields, a lighted soccer field, a game room, student exercise and weight rooms, located around campus, including in the residence halls, and an all-purpose artifical practice field. Intercollegiate football games are played at Fawcett Stadium, next door to the National Pro Football Hall of Fame and site of the annual Hall of Fame game. **Graduates:** From July 1, 2013 to June 30, 2014, 451 bachelor's degrees were awarded. The most popular majors were nursing (24%), management (19%), and biology (12%). 98 companies recruited on campus in 2013-2014. In an average class, 52% graduate in 4 years or less, 62% graduate in 5 years or less, and 64% graduate in 6 years or less. Of the 2013 graduating class, 23% were enrolled in graduate school within 6 months of graduation, and 70% were employed.

SERVICES: Counseling and information services are available, as is tutoring in every subject. There is remedial math, reading, and writing. One-on-one and group tutoring and a study skills course are available. **Library/Resources:** The library contains 299,111 volumes, 16,133 audio/video tapes/CDs/DVDs, and subscribes to 87,434 periodicals including electronic. Computerized library services include interlibrary loans, database searching, Internet access, and Wi-Fi capability. Special learning facilities include an art gallery, radio station, a child development center, a corporate museum, Hoover Park, which includes trails and recreation facilities, bioinformatics lab, and a community clinic with counseling and wellness programs for the underserved. **Physically Challenged Students:** All of the campus is accessible. Facilities include wheelchair ramps, elevators, special parking, specially equipped restrooms, special class scheduling, lowered drinking fountains, lowered telephones, and special housing. **Special:** Work-study programs are available to students having financial need. Walsh offers internships for most majors; study abroad in 14 countries, with a campus outside Rome, Italy and a partner school in Kisubi, Uganda; accelerated degree programs in nursing, business and management; pre-medical, pre-dental, pre-pharmacy, preveterinary, pre-physical therapy, graduate programs in business, physial therapy, education, counseling, theology, and nursing; evening and continuing education programs; and credit for life experience. Reduced core for transfer students. There are 11 national honor societies, a freshman honors program, and 11 departmental honors programs. **Visiting:** There are regularly scheduled orientations for prospective students, consisting of a campus tour, a session with financial aid and admissions staff, and an opportunity to meet with faculty, coaches, and other personnel. There are guides for informal visits, visitors may sit in on classes, and stay overnight. To schedule a visit, contact the Admissions Office. **Campus Safety and Security:** Measures include 24-hour foot and vehicle patrol, emergency notification system, self-defense education, and security escort services. There are emergency telephones, lighted pathways/sidewalks, and controlled access to dorms/residences.

REQUIREMENTS: The ACT is required. The SAT is recommended.

In addition, the applicant must be a graduate of an accredited secondary school; the GED is accepted. Walsh recommends completion of 4 units of English, 3 each of math, science, and social studies, 2 of foreign language, and 1 of fine or performing arts. An essay and an interview are recommended. A GPA of 2.4 is required. AP and CLEP credits are accepted. Important factors in the admissions decision are recommendations by school officials, leadership record, and extracurricular activities record. To graduate, students must complete 125 semester hours with a minimum 2.0 GPA. The number of hours required in the major varies. A core curriculum of 37 hours is required, including courses in English, art or music, science, social science, math, humanities, theology, philosophy, service learning, diversity, and a foreign language. **Procedure:** Freshmen are admitted to all sessions. Entrance exams should be taken during the junior year. There are deferred admissions and rolling admissions plans. Applications should be filed by August 25 for fall entry; January 1 for spring entry; and April 29 for summer entry, along with a $25 fee. Notification is sent on a rolling basis. Applications are accepted online. **Transfer Students:** 213 transfer students enrolled in 2013-2014. Applicants must have a minimum GPA of 2.0 from previous colleges attended. 32 of 125 credits required for the bachelor's degree must be completed at Walsh. **International Students:** There are 80 international students enrolled. The school actively recruits these students. They must take the TOEFL with a minimum score of 500 on the paper-based TOEFL (PBT) or 61 on the Internet-based version (iBT), or take the STEP.

ADMISSIONS: 91% of the 2014-2015 applicants were accepted. The SAT scores for the 2014-2015 freshman class were: Critical Reading--47% below 500, 40% between 500 and 599, 12% between 600 and 699, and 1% between 700 and 800; Math--34% below 500, 48% between 500 and 599, 17% between 600 and 699, and 1% between 700 and 800. The ACT scores were 31% below 21, 31% between 21 and 23, 23% between 24 and 26, 10% between 27 and 28, and 5% above 28. 35% of the current freshmen were in the top fifth of their class; 67% were in the top two fifths. 4 freshmen graduated first in their class. **Admissions Contact:** Brett Freshhour, Vice President for Enrollment Management. E-Mail: *admissions@walsh.edu* Web: *www. walsh.edu*

FINANCIAL AID: In 2014-2015, 99% of all full-time freshmen and 97% of continuing full-time students received some form of financial aid. 81% of all full-time freshmen and 78% of continuing full-time students received need-based aid. The average freshman award was $24,987. Need-based scholarships or need-based grants averaged $7,349 ($13,234 maximum); need-based self-help aid (loans and jobs) averaged $4,319 ($7,500 maximum); non-need-based athletic scholarships averaged $7,566 ($32,790 maximum); and other non-need-based awards and non-need-based scholarships averaged $9,358 ($25,350 maximum). 90% of undergraduate students work part-time. Average annual earnings from campus work are $1257. The average financial indebtedness of the 2014 graduate was $24,987. Walsh is a member of CSS. The FAFSA and the college's own financial statement are required. The priority date for freshman financial aid applications for fall entry is February 14. The deadline for filing freshman financial aid applications for fall entry is rolling.

WILBERFORCE UNIVERSITY (*The complete profile is made available exclusively on our website, www.barronspac.com*)

WILMINGTON COLLEGE   B-4
www.wilmington.edu

Wilmington, OH 45177	(937) 382-6661, ext. 260
	(800) 341-9318
Fax: (937) 382-7077	Email: admissions@wilmington.edu
Full-time: 530 men, 635 women	Faculty: IIB, --$
Part-time: 90 men, 150 women	Ph.D.s: 69%
Graduate: n/av	Student/Faculty: n/av
Year: semesters, summer session	Tuition: $26,840
Room & Board: $9370	Freshman Class: n/av
SAT or ACT: required	CEEB CODE: 0909
Application Deadline: open	COMPETITIVE

Wilmington College, established in 1870, is a private institution sponsored by the Society of Friends. The college offers programs in the liberal arts, business, health science, teacher preparation, agricultural studies, religious studies, and athletic training. There is 1 graduate school. In addition to regional accreditation, Wilmington has baccalaureate program accreditation with NCATE. The 65-acre campus is in a small town 50 miles from Cincinnati. Including any residence halls, there are 21 buildings.

STUDENT LIFE: 98% of undergraduates are from Ohio. Others are from 13 states and 4 foreign countries. 67% are white; 11% African American. 40% claim no religious affiliation; 17% Catholic. The average age of freshmen is 18; all undergraduates, 21. 31% do not continue beyond their first year.

FACULTY/CLASSROOMS: 65% of faculty are male; 57% are female. All teach undergraduates. The average class size in an introductory lecture is 25 and in a regular course is 19.

PROGRAMS OF STUDY: Wilmington confers B.A. and B.S. degrees. Master's degrees are also awarded. Bachelor's degrees are awarded in AGRICULTURE (agricultural business management, agronomy, animal science, equine science, and range/farm management), BIOLOGICAL SCIENCE (bacteriology, biochemistry, biology/biological science, and environmental biology), BUSINESS (accounting, business administration and management, management science, marketing and distribution, marketing management, and sports management), COMMUNICATIONS AND THE ARTS (advertising, art, communications, dramatic arts, English, journalism, music, public relations, Spanish, and speech/debate/rhetoric), COMPUTER AND PHYSICAL SCIENCE (astronomy, chemistry, computer science, geology, information sciences and systems, mathematics, and planetary and space science), EDUCATION (agricultural education, athletic training, early childhood education, education, elementary education, English education, health education, mathematics education, middle school education, physical education, science education, secondary education, social science education, and social studies education), HEALTH PROFESSIONS (premedicine and preveterinary science), SOCIAL SCIENCE (criminal justice, economics, history, liberal arts/general studies, philosophy, political science/government, prelaw, psychology, religion, social science, social work, and sociology). Chemistry, biology, and athletic training are the strongest academically. Business, agriculture, and athletic training have the largest enrollments.

ACTIVITIES: 8% of men belong to 4 local and 1 national fraternities; 8% of women belong to 4 local sororities. There are 63 groups on campus, including band, cheerleading, choir, chorale, drama, ethnic, gay, honors, international, literary magazine, musical theater, newspaper, orchestra, photography, political, professional, religious, social, social service, student government, and yearbook. Popular campus events include Community Day, Westheimer Peace Symposium, and Fall Fest.

SERVICES: Counseling and information services are available, as is tutoring in every subject. There is remedial math, reading, and writing. **Library/Resources:** The library contains 110,000 volumes, 42,000 microform items, and 1,400 audio/video tapes/CDs/DVDs, and subscribes to 400 periodicals including electronic. Computerized library services include interlibrary loans, database searching, Internet access, and Wi-Fi capability. Special learning facilities include an art gallery, a Peace Resource Center, Quaker museum, greenhouse, and academic farm. **Physically Challenged Students:** 20% of the campus is accessible. Facilities include wheelchair ramps, elevators, special parking, specially equipped restrooms, and special class scheduling. **Special:** Special academic programs include work-study, internships, a Washington semester, and cross-registration with the Southwest Ohio Consortium. Study abroad may be arranged in Mexico, Austria, France, and other countries. Dual majors in any subject and student-designed majors are offered. Credit for experience, nondegree study, and pass/fail options are possible. There are 5 national honor societies, a freshman honors program, and 3 departmental honors programs. **Visiting:** There are regularly scheduled orientations for prospective students, including meetings with faculty and a tour of the campus. There are guides for informal visits, visitors may sit in on classes, and stay overnight. To schedule a visit, contact the Admissions Office. **Campus Safety and Security:** Measures include 24-hour foot and vehicle patrol and security escort services. There are emergency telephones and lighted pathways/sidewalks.

REQUIREMENTS: The SAT or ACT is required. Applicants must be graduates of an accredited secondary school, with 4 units of English, 2 units each of math, science, and social studies, and a recommended 2 units of a foreign language. An additional 6 units is required in other areas. The GED is accepted. An interview is recommended. An essay may be required. A GPA of 3.0 is required. AP and CLEP credits are accepted. Important factors in the admissions decision are recommendations by school officials, parents or siblings who attended the school, and recommendations by alumni.

FINANCIAL AID: The FAFSA is required. Check with the school for current application deadlines.

WITTENBERG UNIVERSITY   B-3
www.wittenberg.edu

Springfield, OH 45501

(937) 327-6377
(877) 206-0332

Fax: (937) 327-6379   Email: admission@wittenberg.edu

Full-time: 807 men, 1043 women   Faculty: IIB, -$

Part-time: 37 men, 61 women   Ph.D.s: n/av

Graduate: 2 men, 14 women   Student/Faculty: n/av

Year: semesters, summer session   Tuition: $38,030

Room & Board: $9932   Freshman Class: 4850 applied, 4432 accepted, 516 enrolled

SAT CR/M: 580/540 ACT: 25   CEEB CODE: 1922

Application Deadline: March 15   COMPETITIVE+

Wittenberg University, founded in 1845, is a private liberal arts and sciences institution affiliated with the Evangelical Lutheran Church in America. In addition to regional accreditation, Wittenberg has baccalaureate program accreditation with NASM, NCATE, and ACS. The 114-acre campus is in a suburban area 25 miles east of Dayton, 40 miles west of Columbus, and 75 miles from Cincinnati. Including any residence halls, there are 26 buildings.

STUDENT LIFE: 73% of undergraduates are from Ohio. Others are from 38 states, 25 foreign countries, and Canada. 76% are from public schools. 80% are White. 32% are Protestant; 28% claim no religious affiliation; 16% Catholic. The average age of freshmen is 18; all undergraduates, 21. 20% do not continue beyond their first year; 65% remain to graduate. **Housing:** 1583 students can be accommodated in college housing, which includes single-sex and coed dorms, on-campus apartments, off-campus apartments, and married student housing. In addition, there are honors houses, language houses, special-interest houses, fraternity houses, sorority houses, a substance-free residence hall, and an international awareness house. On-campus housing is guaranteed for the freshman year only and is available on a lottery system for upperclassmen. 86% of students live on campus; of those, 84% remain on campus on weekends. All students may keep cars.

FACULTY/CLASSROOMS: All teach undergraduates. No introductory courses are taught by graduate students. The average class size in an introductory lecture is 25; in a laboratory is 20; and in a regular course is 18.

PROGRAMS OF STUDY: Wittenberg confers B.A., B.F.A., B.M.E. and B.S. degrees. Master's degrees are also awarded. Bachelor's degrees are awarded in BIOLOGICAL SCIENCE (biology/biological science), BUSINESS (business administration and management), COMMUNICATIONS AND THE ARTS (communications, dramatic arts, English, fine arts, French, German, music, Russian, and Spanish), COMPUTER AND PHYSICAL SCIENCE (chemistry, computer science, geology, mathematics, and physics), EDUCATION (elementary education, foreign languages education, middle school education, music education, science education, secondary education, and special education), ENGINEERING AND ENVIRONMENTAL DESIGN (environmental science), SOCIAL SCIENCE (American studies, East Asian studies, economics, history, international relations, philosophy, political science/government, psychology, religion, and sociology). Biology, communication, and psychology are the strongest academically. Business, education, and biology have the largest enrollments.

ACTIVITIES: 26% of men belong to 6 national fraternities; 33% of women belong to 5 national sororities. There are 125 groups on campus, including and mock trail association, caving club, fishing club, outdoor club, anime club, art, band, cheerleading, choir, chorale, computers, dance, debate, drama, ethnic, gay, honors, international, jazz band, literary magazine, musical theater, newspaper, opera, orchestra, pep band, photography, political, professional, radio and TV, religious, social, social service, and student government. Popular campus events include Wittenberg Series, International Festival and Wittfest. **Sports:** There are 11 intercollegiate sports for men and 12 for women, and 12 intramural sports for men and 12 for women. Facilities include a multipurpose field house, a swimming pool, 6 racquetball/handball courts, a cardio fitness center, a strength center, and sports medicine rooms. There is also a 3,200-seat gym, a 3,200-seat stadium, 12 acres of playing fields, a 1,000-seat baseball stadium, a 120-seat softball field and rugby playing field, a 400-meter track, and 12 tennis courts. **Graduates:** From July 1, 2013 to June 30, 2014, 393 bachelor's degrees were awarded. The most popular majors were business (13%), psychology (12%), and biology (11%). 125 companies recruited on campus in 2013-2014. In an average class, 61% graduate in 4 years or less, 65% graduate in 5 years or less, and 65% graduate in 6 years or less.

SERVICES: Counseling and information services are available, as is tutoring in most subjects. There is also a math workshop and writing and oral communication center. **Library/Resources:** The library contains 517,199 volumes, 82,936 microform items, and 21,633 audio/video tapes/CDs/DVDs, and subscribes to 13,664 periodicals including electronic. Computerized library services include interlibrary loans, database searching, Internet access, and Wi-Fi capability. Special learning facilities include an art gallery, radio station, a geology museum, an observatory, a GIS lab with supercomputer, and a parallel processing lab. **Physically Challenged Students:** 81% of the campus is accessible. Facilities include wheelchair ramps, elevators, special parking, specially equipped restrooms, special class scheduling, lowered drinking fountains, and lowered telephones. **Special:** Special academic programs include internships, cross-registration through the Southwest Ohio Consortium, a Washington semester, work-study programs, study-abroad opportunities in many countries, accelerated degree programs, dual and student-designed majors, nondegree study, and pass/fail options. A 3-2 engineering degree is offered through Washington, Columbia, and Case Western Reserve Universities and Georgia Institute of Technology. There is also a 3-2 nursing program with Johns Hopkins University and an occupational therapy program with Washington University. There are 11 national honor societies, including Phi Beta Kappa, a freshman honors program, and 19 departmental honors programs. **Visiting:** There are regularly scheduled orientations for prospective students, including a tour and interview. . There are guides for informal visits, visitors may sit in on classes, and stay overnight. To schedule a visit, contact the Admissions Office at (877) 206-0332. **Campus Safety and Security:** Measures include 24-hour foot and vehicle patrol, emergency notification system, self-defense education, and security escort services. There are emergency telephones, lighted pathways/sidewalks, a bicycle patrol, and various prevention programs. City police support campus police during the evening. There is also a student Eyes and Ears Program and a campus security committee made up of students and faculty.

REQUIREMENTS: Students should have graduated from an accredited secondary school with 16 academic credits, including 4 units of English and 3 each of a foreign language, math, science, and social studies, which includes history. An essay is required and an interview advised. Art students must present a portfolio, and music students must audition. Wittenberg is test score optional. AP credits are accepted. Important factors in the admissions decision are advanced placement or honors courses, evidence of special talent, and extracurricular activities record. To graduate, students must complete at least 130 credits and have a minimum GPA of 2.0. The required minimum GPA and number of hours in the major vary by department. All Wittenberg students complete a program of general education built on 16 learning goals. These include acquisition of foundations skills in writing, math, foreign language, speaking, research, and computing, the understanding of the different arts and sciences disciplines and their distinct methodological approaches to knowledge, and an introduction to non-Western culture, the diversity of human experience, and inter- and transdisciplinary knowledge. Students achieve each general education learning goal by completing 1 to 2 courses. As part of general education, students perform 30 hours of community service. **Procedure:** Freshmen are admitted to all sessions. Entrance exams should be taken by the fall of the senior year, but as early as possible. There are early decision, early admissions, deferred admissions, and rolling admissions plans. Early decision applications should be filed by November 15; regular applications, by March 15 for fall entry; and December 1 for spring entry, along with a $40 fee. Notification of early decision is sent January 1; regular decision, on a rolling basis. 301 early decision candidates were accepted for the 2014-2015 class. applicants were on the 2014 waiting list; were admitted. Applications are accepted on-line. **Transfer Students:** 38 transfer students enrolled in 2013-2014. Applicants should have a minimum GPA of 2.0 at an accredited college and be in good academic and social standing. High school transcripts are required in some cases. An interview is recommended. 50 of 130 credits required for the bachelor's degree must be completed at Wittenberg. **International Students:** There are 47 international students enrolled. The school actively recruits these students. They must take the TOEFL with a minimum score of 550 on the paper-based TOEFL (PBT) or 79 on the Internet-based version (iBT), or take the SAT or ACT. Institutions math and language placement tests.

ADMISSIONS: 91% of the 2014-2015 applicants were accepted. The SAT scores for the 2014-2015 freshman class were: Critical Reading--13% below 500, 50% between 500 and 599, 31% between 600 and 699, and 6% between 700 and 800; Math--29% below 500, 43% between 500 and 599, 22% between 600 and 699, and 6% between 700 and 800; Writing--5% below 500, 25% between 500 and 599, 44% between 600 and 699, and 26% between 700 and 800. The ACT scores were 13% below 21, 23% between 21 and 23, 25% between 24 and 26, 17% between 27 and 28, and 22% above 28. 40% of the current freshmen were in the top fifth of their class; 66% were in the top two fifths. **Admissions Contact:** Karen Hunt, Director of Admissions. E-Mail: *admission@wittenberg.edu* Web: *www.wittenberg.edu*

FINANCIAL AID: In 2014-2015, 99% of all full-time freshmen and 98% of continuing full-time students received some form of financial aid. 86% of all full-time freshmen and 77% of continuing full-time students received need-based aid. The average freshman award was $36,285. Need-based scholarships or need-based grants averaged $27,454; need-based self-help aid (loans and jobs) averaged $6,163; and other non-need-based awards and non-need-based scholarships averaged $9,233. 46% of undergraduate students work part-time. Average annual earnings from campus work are $2400. The average financial indebtedness of the 2014 graduate was $30,442. The FAFSA is required. The deadline for filing freshman financial aid applications for fall entry is March 15.

WRIGHT STATE UNIVERSITY   **B-4**
www.wright.edu

Dayton, OH 45435	(937) 775-5700
	(800) 247-1770
Fax: (937) 775-4410	Email: admissions@wright.edu
Full-time: 4882 men, 5055 women	Faculty: I, --$
Part-time: 1304 men, 1441 women	Ph.D.s: n/av
Graduate: 1969 men, 2191 women	Student/Faculty: n/av
Year: semesters, summer session	Tuition: $8354 ($16,182)
Room & Board: $8629	Freshman Class: 5237 applied, 5067 accepted, 2359 enrolled
SAT CR/M/W: 520/520/490 **ACT:** 22	CEEB CODE: 1179
Application Deadline: open	**COMPETITIVE**

Wright State University, founded in 1964, is a state-supported institution offering undergraduate programs in business and administration, education and human services, engineering and computer science, liberal arts, math and science, and nursing and health. There are 6 undergraduate schools and 8 graduate schools. In addition to regional accreditation, Wright State has baccalaureate program accreditation with AACSB, ABET, CAHEA, CSWE, NASM, NCATE, and NLN. The 557-acre campus is in a suburban area 10 miles northeast of Dayton. Including any residence halls, there are 60 buildings.

STUDENT LIFE: 90% of undergraduates are from Ohio. Others are from 49 states, 69 foreign countries, and Canada. 85% are from public schools. 68% are White; 12% African American; 11% Foreign. The average age of freshmen is 18; all undergraduates, 23. 44% do not continue beyond their first year; 40% remain to graduate. **Housing:** 3000 students can be accommodated in college housing, which includes coed dorms, on-campus apartments, and married student housing. In addition, there are honors houses and special-interest houses. On-campus housing is available on a first-come, first-served basis, and is available on a lottery system for upperclassmen. 81% of students commute. Alcohol is not permitted. All students may keep cars.

FACULTY/CLASSROOMS: No introductory courses are taught by graduate students.

PROGRAMS OF STUDY: Wright State confers B.A., B.A.C.S., B.A.Mus., B.F.A., B.S., B.S.B., B.S.B.E., B.S.C.E., B.S.C.L.S., B.S.C.S., B.S.Ed., B.S.E.E., B.S.E.P., B.S.I.S.E., B.S.M.E., B.S.M.S.E., B.S.N., and B.T.A.S. degrees. Associate, master's, and doctoral degrees are also awarded. Bachelor's degrees are awarded in BIOLOGICAL SCIENCE (biology/biological science and life science), BUSINESS (accounting, banking and finance, business economics, management information systems, management science, marketing/retailing/merchandising, nonprofit/public organization management, organizational leadership and management, real estate finance, and supply chain management), COMMUNICATIONS AND THE ARTS (American Sign Language, art history, art, art history and appreciation, arts administration/management, classical languages, communications, creative writing, dance, dramatic arts, English, film arts, fine arts, French, German, Greek, guitar, instrumental performance, language arts, Latin, literature, modern language, music, music history and appreciation, music theory and composition, musical theater, organ performance, percussion, Spanish, strings, studio art, theatre acting, theater design, theatre studies, theater management, vocal performance, and winds), COMPUTER AND PHYSICAL SCIENCE (applied mathematics, chemistry, computer science, geology, geophysics and seismology, mathematics, physics, and statistics), EDUCATION (art education, athletic training, business education, (Education) Childhood Education, career, technical education & training, early childhood education, education, elementary education, foreign languages education, mathematics education, middle school education, music education, physical education, science education, secondary education, social science education, and special education), ENGINEERING AND ENVIRONMENTAL DESIGN (biomedical engineering, computer engineering, electrical/electronics engineering, engineering physics, environmental science, industrial engineering, materials engineering, mechanical engineering, systems engineering, and water and wastewater technology), HEALTH PROFESSIONS (clinical science, community health work, environmental health science, exercise science, medical laboratory technology, nursing, predentistry, premedicine, and rehabilitation therapy), SOCIAL SCIENCE (African American studies, anthropology, applied psychology, cognitive science, criminal justice, economics, geography, history, humanities, international relations, liberal arts/general studies, philosophy, political science/government, prelaw, psychology, religion, social work, sociology, and urban studies). Business education, theater arts, and engineering are the strongest academically. Nursing, mechanical engineering, and biological sciences have the largest enrollments.

ACTIVITIES: 3% of men belong to 11 local fraternities; 4% of women belong to 11 local sororities. There are 200 groups on campus, including band, cheerleading, chess, choir, chorale, chorus, computers, dance, drill team, ethnic, film, gay, honors, international, jazz band, literary magazine, newspaper, orchestra, pep band, political, professional, radio and TV, religious, social, social service, and student government. Popular campus events include Fall Fest, April Craze, Lunar New Year Celebration and Madrigal Dinner. **Sports:** There are 7 intercollegiate sports for men and 8 for women, and 26 intramural sports for men and 23 for women. Facilities include an athletic and entertainment center with an arena seating 13,000 spectators, break-off rooms, an auxiliary gym, and baseball and practice fields. The student union houses a natatorium, climbing wall, weight rooms, workout center, game rooms, and playing courts. **Graduates:** From July 1, 2013 to June 30, 2014, 2374 bachelor's degrees were awarded. The most popular majors were nursing (10%), organizational leadership (8%), and psychology (7%). In an average class, 1% graduate in 3 years or less, 21% graduate in 4 years or less, 33% graduate in 5 years or less, and 38% graduate in 6 years or less.

SERVICES: Counseling and information services are available, as is tutoring in most subjects. There is a reader service for the blind, and remedial math, reading, and writing. **Library/Resources:** The library contains 842,026 volumes, 1.4 million microform items, and 20,738 audio/video tapes/CDs/DVDs, and subscribes to 5,700 periodicals including electronic. Computerized library services include interlibrary loans, database searching, Internet access, and Wi-Fi capability. Special learning facilities include an art gallery, radio station, TV station, TV production studio. The Department of Archives and Special Collections houses one of the most complete depositories of information on the Wright Brothers in the world. **Physically Challenged Students:** All of the campus is accessible. Facilities include wheelchair ramps, elevators, special parking, specially equipped restrooms, lowered drinking fountains, lowered telephones, special housing. An underground tunnel system connects all academic buildings. Adaptive technology is available. **Special:** B.A.-B.S. degrees are offered in computer science, geography, urban affairs, biological sciences, chemistry, geological sciences, math, and psychology. Cross-registration with other area colleges is available through the Southwestern Ohio Council for Higher Education. Dual majors, co-op programs, internships, study abroad, work-study programs, student-designed majors, nondegree study, and credit for military experience are available. There are 3 national honor societies, a freshman honors program, and 32 departmental honors programs. **Visiting:** There are regularly scheduled orientations for prospective students, including a campus tour and information on academic and student services. There are guides for informal visits and visitors may sit in on classes. To schedule a visit, contact the Office of Undergraduate Admissions. **Campus Safety and Security:** Measures include 24-hour foot and vehicle patrol, emergency notification system, self-defense education, and security escort services. There are shuttle buses, emergency telephones, and lighted pathways/sidewalks.

REQUIREMENTS: The SAT or ACT is required. Applicants should be graduates of an accredited secondary school and have 4 units in English, 3 units each in math, science, and social studies, 2 units in a foreign language, and 1 unit in the arts. A portfolio is required for art majors, an audition for theater and music majors. The GED is accepted. A GPA of 2.0 is required. AP and CLEP credits are accepted. To graduate, students must complete 183 quarter hours, with a minimum GPA of 2.0. All students are required to take 56 credit hours of general education courses in 4 areas: communication and math skills, the Western experience, the non-Western world, and understanding the contemporary world. **Procedure:** Freshmen are admitted to all sessions. Entrance exams should be taken in the spring of the junior year. There are deferred admissions and rolling admissions plans. Application deadlines are open. Application fee is $30. Applications are accepted on-line. **Transfer Students:** 2031 transfer students enrolled in 2013-2014. Applicants must have a 2.0 GPA. 45 of 183 credits required for the bachelor's degree must be completed at Wright State. **International Students:** There are 671 international students enrolled. The school actively recruits these students. They must take the TOEFL with a minimum score of 500 on the paper-based TOEFL (PBT) or 61 on the Internet-based version (iBT).

ADMISSIONS: 97% of the 2014-2015 applicants were accepted. The SAT scores for the 2014-2015 freshman class were: Critical Reading--40% below 500, 36% between 500 and 599, 21% between 600 and 699, and 3% between 700 and 800; Math--40% below 500, 39% between 500 and 599, 18% between 600 and 699, and 3% between 700 and 800; Writing--54% below 500, 33% between 500 and 599, 11% between 600 and 699, and 1% between 700 and 800. The ACT scores were 40% below 21, 25% between 21 and 23, 18% between 24 and 26, 9% between 27 and 28, and 8% above 28. 31% of the current freshmen were in the top fifth of their class; 57% were in the top two fifths. **Admissions Contact:** Cathy Davis, Assistant VP for Undergraduate Admission. E-Mail: *admissions@wright.edu* Web: *www.wright.edu*

FINANCIAL AID: In 2014-2015, 83% of all full-time freshmen and 78% of continuing full-time students received some form of financial aid. 71% of all full-time freshmen and 69% of continuing full-time

students received need-based aid. The average freshman award was $8,912. Need-based scholarships or need-based grants averaged $5,937; need-based self-help aid (loans and jobs) averaged $4,370; non-need-based athletic scholarships averaged $10,010; and other non-need-based awards and non-need-based scholarships averaged $3,132. 14% of undergraduate students work part-time. The average financial indebtedness of the 2014 graduate was $28,349. Wright State is a member of CSS. The FAFSA is required. The priority date for freshman financial aid applications for fall entry is March 1.

XAVIER UNIVERSITY A-5
www.xavier.edu

Cincinnati, OH 45207

	(513) 745-3301
	(877) 982-3648
Fax: (513) 745-4319	**Email:** xuadmit@xavier.edu
Full-time: 1948 men, 2322 women	**Faculty:** 323
Part-time: 183 men, 180 women	**Ph.D.s:** 76%
Graduate: 706 men, 1199 women	**Student/Faculty:** 12 to 1
Year: semesters, summer session	**Tuition:** $33,960
Room & Board: $11,020	**Freshman Class:** 11607 applied, 8489 accepted, 1215 enrolled
SAT CR/M: 540/550 **ACT:** 25	**CEEB CODE:** 1965
Application Deadline: February 1	**VERY COMPETITIVE**

Xavier University, founded in 1831, is a comprehensive Jesuit institution affiliated with the Roman Catholic Church. There are 3 undergraduate schools and 10 graduate schools. In addition to regional accreditation, XU has baccalaureate program accreditation with AACSB, CSWE, NASM, NCATE, TEAC, ACS, CEA, ACOTE, CAHME, CACREP, CCNE, JRCERT, MACTE, APA, CAATE, and CELP. The 189-acre campus is in a small town 5 miles northeast of the center of Cincinnati in a residential area. Including any residence halls, there are 52 buildings.

STUDENT LIFE: 51% of undergraduates are from out of state, mostly the Midwest. Students are from 47 states, 47 foreign countries, and Canada. 52% are from public schools. 71% are White. 65% are Catholic; 27% Protestant. The average age of freshmen is 18; all undergraduates, 21. 15% do not continue beyond their first year; 76% remain to graduate. **Housing:** 2480 students can be accommodated in college housing, which includes coed dorms, on-campus apartments, and off-campus apartments. In addition, there are honors houses, and living-learning communities. On-campus housing is guaranteed for the freshman year only, is available on a first-come, first-served basis, and is available on a lottery system for upperclassmen. 52% of students live on campus; of those, 75% remain on campus on weekends. All students may keep cars.

FACULTY/CLASSROOMS: 47% of faculty are male; 53% are female. 84% teach undergraduates. No introductory courses are taught by graduate students. The average class size in an introductory lecture is 22; in a laboratory is 17; and in a regular course is 22.

PROGRAMS OF STUDY: XU confers B.A., B.S., Honors A.B., B.F.A., B.L.A., B.D.U., B.S.B.A., B.S.N. and B.S.W. degrees. Associate, master's, and doctoral degrees are also awarded. Bachelor's degrees are awarded in AGRICULTURE (agriculture), BIOLOGICAL SCIENCE (biology/biological science, biophysics, and life science), BUSINESS (accounting, banking and finance, business administration and management, business economics, entrepreneurial studies, human resources, international business management, management science, marketing/retailing/merchandising, purchasing/inventory management, sports management, sports marketing, and sustainable management), COMMUNICATIONS AND THE ARTS (advertising, art, classics, communication rhetoric/communication, design, English, fine arts, French, German, media arts, modern language, music, public relations, Spanish, theatre arts, and theatre studies), COMPUTER AND PHYSICAL SCIENCE (actuarial science, applied physics, chemistry, computer science, information sciences and systems, mathematics, natural sciences, physics, radiological technology, and Urban Ecology), EDUCATION (athletic training, early childhood education, education, health information management, middle school education, music education, science education, and special education), ENGINEERING AND ENVIRONMENTAL DESIGN (engineering physics and environmental science), HEALTH PROFESSIONS (health administration and policy, health care administration, medical laboratory science, nursing, preallied health, and prepharmacy), SOCIAL SCIENCE (counseling/psychology, criminal justice, economics, gender studies, history, humanities, international studies, liberal arts/general studies, philosophy, political science/government, psychology, social work, sociology, and theological studies). Natural sciences; and the philosophy, politics, and the public honors program are the strongest academically. Nursing, biology, and business have the largest enrollments.

ACTIVITIES: There are 152 groups on campus, including art, band, cheerleading, choir, chorale, chorus, communications, computers, drama, drill team, environmental, ethnic, film, gay, honors, international, jazz band, literary magazine, musical theater, newspaper, orchestra, pep band, photography, political, professional, radio and TV, religious, social, social service, student government, and symphony. Popular campus events include Family Weekend, Academic Day and Spirit Celebration. **Sports:** There are 8 intercollegiate sports for men and 8 for women, and 12 intramural sports for men and 12 for women. Facilities include a field house, sports center, basketball and volleyball courts, baseball, soccer, and softball fields, rifle range, and tennis courts. **Graduates:** From July 1, 2013 to June 30, 2014, 907 bachelor's degrees were awarded. The most popular majors were liberal arts (12%), nursing (9%), and marketing (7%). 283 companies recruited on campus in 2013-2014. In an average class, 1% graduate in 3 years or less, 67% graduate in 4 years or less, 75% graduate in 5 years or less, and 76% graduate in 6 years or less.

SERVICES: Counseling and information services are available, as is tutoring in every subject. There is a reader service for the blind, remedial math, reading, and writing. Xavier has a Learning Assistance Center which provides individual and small group tutoring in almost all subjects and study skills assistance, a math lab, and a writing center. There is also an efficient reading and study skills course. **Library/Resources:** The library contains 793,003 volumes, 13,628 microform items, 27,828 audio/video tapes/CDs/DVDs, and subscribes to 144,186 periodicals including electronic. Computerized library services include interlibrary loans, database searching, Internet access, and Wi-Fi capability. Special learning facilities include an art gallery, radio station, TV station, an observatory and a financial trading room. **Physically Challenged Students:** 99% of the campus is accessible. Facilities include wheelchair ramps, elevators, special parking, specially equipped restrooms, special class scheduling, lowered drinking fountains, lowered telephones, and special housing. **Special:** Xavier offers internships related to some majors, cross-registration through the Greater Cincinnati Consortium, and co-op programs in business and computer science. Students may study abroad in over 100 countries through Xavier's network of program providers. A Washington semester and nondegree study are available. A 3-2 engineering degree is offered with the University of Cincinnati, and a 3-2 applied biology degree is offered with Duke University. A professional accountancy B.S.B.A and M.B.A program is also offered. There are 10 national honor societies, including Phi Beta Kappa, a freshman honors program, and 2 departmental honors programs. **Visiting:** There are regularly scheduled orientations for prospective students, including an interview and a tour of the campus. There are guides for informal visits and visitors may sit in on classes. To schedule a visit, contact Office of Undergraduate Admission. **Campus Safety and Security:** Measures include 24-hour foot and vehicle patrol, emergency notification system, self-defense education, and security escort services. There are shuttle buses, emergency telephones, lighted pathways/sidewalks, controlled access to dorms/residences, Alcohol awareness, drug awareness, sexual assault programs, security camera system for certain areas on campus, and presence of a Title IX Coordinator.

REQUIREMENTS: The SAT or ACT is required. Graduation from an accredited secondary school or satisfactory scores on the GED are required for admission. The school requires 21 academic credits, including 4 years of English, 3 each of math, social studies, and science, 2 of foreign language, and 1 of health/phys ed, plus 5 electives, one essay no fewer than 250 words, at least one recommendation from a high school counselor (preferred) or teacher, satisfactory results on the ACT or the SAT, and a resume or list of activities. AP

and CLEP credits are accepted. Important factors in the admissions decision are advanced placement or honors courses, leadership record, and extracurricular activities record.To graduate, students must complete a minimum of 120 credit hours with a minimum GPA of 2.0. The total number of hours required in the major varies. All students must take core curriculum courses in English composition, cultural diversity, math, science, social science, history, theology, philosophy, a foreign language, literature, fine arts, and an ethics/religion and society focus. **Procedure:** Freshmen are admitted fall, spring, and summer. Entrance exams should be taken by fall of the senior year. There are deferred admissions and rolling admissions plans. Applications should be filed by February 1 for fall entry; December 1 for spring entry; and May 10 for summer entry, along with a $35 fee. Notifications are sent April 15. 103 applicants were on the 2014 waiting list; 9 were admitted. Applications are accepted on-line. Application fees are waived if application is completed on-line. **Transfer Students:** 104 transfer students enrolled in 2013-2014. Transfer students must have a minimum GPA of 2.0 in all college-level work. An interview is also recommended. Students who transfer to Xavier with 30 or more semester hours are not required to submit results of the ACT or SAT tests, an essay, or a counselor recommendation. 30 of 120 credits required for the bachelor's degree must be completed at XU. **International Students:** There are 119 international students enrolled. The school actively recruits these students. They must take the TOEFL with a minimum score of 550 on the paper-based TOEFL (PBT) or 79 on the Internet-based version (iBT). They must also take the SAT or ACT or TOEFL.

ADMISSIONS: 73% of the 2014-2015 applicants were accepted. The SAT scores for the 2014-2015 freshman class were: Critical Reading--27% below 500, 48% between 500 and 599, 20% between 600 and 699, and 5% between 700 and 800; Math--26% below 500, 46% between 500 and 599, 24% between 600 and 699, and 4% between 700 and 800; Writing--34% below 500, 43% between 500 and 599, 19% between 600 and 699, and 4% between 700 and 800. The ACT scores were 10% below 21, 26% between 21 and 23, 32% between 24 and 26, 15% between 27 and 28, and 17% above 28. 39% of the current freshmen were in the top fifth of their class; 71% were in the top two fifths. 12 freshmen graduated first in their class. **Admissions Contact:** Aaron Meis, Dean of Undergraduate Admissions. E-Mail: *xuadmit@xavier.edu* Web: *www.xavier.edu*

FINANCIAL AID: In 2014-2015, 99% of all full-time freshmen and 95% of continuing full-time students received some form of financial aid. 67% of all full-time freshmen and 60% of continuing full-time students received need-based aid. The average freshman award was $20,000. Need-based scholarships or need-based grants averaged $15,000 ($20,000 maximum); need-based self-help aid (loans and jobs) averaged $2,500 ($4,500 maximum); non-need-based athletic scholarships averaged $18,700 ($48,000 maximum); and other non-need-based awards and non-need-based scholarships averaged $16,000 ($34,000 maximum). 35% of undergraduate students work part-time. Average annual earnings from campus work are $2000. The average financial indebtedness of the 2014 graduate was $23,000. XU is a member of CSS. The FAFSA is required. The priority date for freshman financial aid applications for fall entry is February 15. The deadline for filing freshman financial aid applications for fall entry is February 15.

YOUNGSTOWN STATE UNIVERSITY   E-2
www.ysu.edu

Youngstown, OH 44555

(330) 941-2000
(877) 468-6978

Fax: (330) 941-3674

Email: enroll@ysu.edu

Full-time: 4246 men, 4564 women	Faculty: 426; IIA, av$
Part-time: 1124 men, 1414 women	Ph.D.s: 90%
Graduate: 495 men, 702 women	Student/Faculty: 21 to 1
Year: semesters, summer session	Tuition: $8087 ($14,087)
Room & Board: $8645	Freshman Class: 3870 applied, 3243 accepted, 1842 enrolled
SAT CR/M/W: 470/480/450 ACT: 21	CEEB CODE: 1975
Application Deadline: August 1	COMPETITIVE

Youngstown State University, founded in 1908, is a publicly funded, primarily commuter institution offering undergraduate and graduate programs in education, business, creative arts and communication, health and human services, liberal arts and social sciences, science, technology, engineering, and mathematics. There are 6 undergraduate schools and 1 graduate school. In addition to regional accreditation, YSU has baccalaureate program accreditation with AACSB, ABET, ADA, CSWE, NASAD, NASM, NCATE, NLN, ACS, ACEND, AAFS, AAFCS, CoARC, NAACLS, NAST, ETAC-ABET, and ACTFL. The 278-acre campus is in an urban area 65 miles southeast of Cleveland. Including any residence halls, there are 53 buildings.

STUDENT LIFE: 88% of undergraduates are from Ohio. Others are from 38 states, 34 foreign countries, and Canada. 75% are White; 13% African American. The average age of freshmen is 19; all undergraduates, 24. 30% do not continue beyond their first year; 33% remain to graduate. **Housing:** 1381 students can be accommodated in college housing, which includes single-sex and coed dorms, on-campus apartments, and off-campus apartments. In addition, there are honors houses, fraternity houses, and sorority houses. On-campus housing is guaranteed for all 4 years. 90% of students commute. All students may keep cars.

FACULTY/CLASSROOMS: 56% of faculty are male; 44% are female. All teach undergraduates. No introductory courses are taught by graduate students.

PROGRAMS OF STUDY: YSU confers B.A., B.S., B.E., B.F.A., B.G.S., B.M., B.S., B.S.A.S., B.S.B.A., B.S.Ed., B.S.N., B.S.R.C. and B.S.W degrees. Associate, Master's, and Doctoral degrees are also awarded. Bachelor's degrees are awarded in AGRICULTURE (environmental studies), BIOLOGICAL SCIENCE (biology/biological science and nutrition), BUSINESS (accounting, apparel and accessories marketing, banking and finance, business administration and management, business economics, fashion merchandising, hospitality management services, hotel/motel and restaurant management, human resources, management information systems, marketing management, marketing/retailing/merchandising, and retailing), COMMUNICATIONS AND THE ARTS (advertising, applied music, art history, art, art history and appreciation, broadcasting, communications, dance, design, digital media, dramatic arts, English, English literature, French, graphic design, information technology, Italian, jazz, journalism, keyboard - piano concentration, literature, music, music composition, music history and appreciation, music performance, music theory and composition, musical theater, painting, percussion, performing arts, photography, piano/organ, piano performance, printmaking, public relations, Spanish, spanish / adolescence education, strings, studio art, technical and business writing, telecommunications, theatre acting, theatre arts, theatre production, theatre studies, vocal performance, voice, vocal music education, and winds), COMPUTER AND PHYSICAL SCIENCE (actuarial mathematics, applied mathematics, astronomy and physics, chemistry, computer programming, computer science, computer security and information assurance, digital arts/technology, geology, information sciences and systems, mathematics, physical sciences, physics, and statistics), EDUCATION (art education, (Education) Childhood Education, computer education, early childhood education, education, English education, general studies, health education, mathematics education, middle school education, music education, physical education, physical science secondary school education, science education, secondary education, social science education, social studies education, social studies secondary school education, special education, and vocational education), ENGINEERING AND ENVIRONMENTAL DESIGN (chemical engineering, civil engineering, civil engineering technology, computer technology, electrical/electronics engineering, electrical/electronics engineering technology, engineering, graphic and printing production, industrial engineering, mechanical engineering, and mechanical engineering technology), HEALTH PROFESSIONS (allied health, clinical science, dental hygiene, exercise science, nursing, nursing home administration, predentistry, premedicine, preoptometry, preosteopathy, preveterinary science, public health, and respiratory therapy), SOCIAL SCIENCE (African studies, American studies, anthropology, child care/child and family studies, criminal justice, dietetics, early childhood studies, economics, family/consumer studies, food science, forensic studies, French studies, geography, gerontology, history, Italian studies, law enforcement and corrections, philosophy, philosophy and religion, political science/government, prelaw, psychology, religion, social studies, social work, sociology, and Spanish studies). Nursing, criminal justice, and early childhood education have the largest enrollments.

ACTIVITIES: 2% of men belong to 6 national fraternities; 3% of women belong to 5 national sororities. There are 173 groups on campus, including and education, art, band, cheerleading, choir, chorale, chorus, computers, dance, drama, engineering, environmental, ethnic, film, forensics, gay, honors, international, jazz band, literary magazine, marching band, musical theater, newspaper, opera, orchestra, pep band, photography, political, professional, radio and TV, religious, social, social service, student government, and symphony. Popular campus events include Organizational Fair, Greek Sing, Homecoming and Welcome Week, Martin Luther King Jr. Breakfast and Cinco de Mayo. **Sports:** There are 8 intercollegiate sports for men and 10 for women, and 9 intramural sports for men and 9 for women. Facilities include The Department of Campus Recreation is located in the Andrews Student Recreation and Wellness Center. This state-of-the art facility contains more than 140 pieces of strength and conditioning equipment. Located near the free-weight and cardio area is the Center's impressive rock wall, at 53 feet Ohio's tallest. Volleyball, basketball, and other activities are situated within the multi-purpose sports forum, which contains four courts. The spacious aerobic studios are home to many group exercise classes and are adjacent to the 1/8-mile indoor track, both on the top floor of the facility. The Andrews Center also includes a tranquil meditation studio, full-functioning locker rooms, and the Wellness Resource Center. In addition to the Andrews Student Recreation and Wellness Center, the Department supervises programs in Beeghly Physical Education Center, Stambaugh Stadium, and the outdoor complex. Located on an 18-acre site adjacent to Beeghly Physical Education Center, the All-Sports Complex includes Arnold D. Stambaugh Stadium and Beede Field, an artificial-turf sports field for football and soccer, with seating for more than 20,630 spectators; officials' dressing rooms; varsity athletic offices; classrooms, racquetball courts, gymnasiums, weight rooms and facilities for various other health and physical education activities. The Watson and Tressel Training Site, one of the more eye-popping buildings on campus, the WATTS is an indoor athletic facility containing a 300-meter competition track, a full-Ylength football field, batting cages, a putting green, protective netting and locker room facilities. This facility allows for year-round training for all athletic programs, as well as a competition site for the track and field teams. Students are permitted in the facility at most times and in the winter, the WATTS is open for public use in the evening. **Graduates:** From July 1, 2013 to June 30, 2014, 1557 bachelor's degrees were awarded. The most popular majors were criminal justice (6%), general studies (6%), and nursing (6%). 233 companies recruited on campus in 2013-2014. In an average class, 1% graduate in 3 years or less, 9% graduate in 4 years or less, 25% graduate in 5 years or less, and 33% graduate in 6 years or less. Of the 2013 graduating class, 74% were employed within 6 months of graduation.

SERVICES: Counseling and information services are available, as is tutoring in most subjects. There is a reader service for the blind, remedial math, reading, and writing. A foreign language lab is also available. **Library/Resources:** The library contains 758,645 volumes, 1.0 million microform items, and 20,132 audio/video tapes/CDs/DVDs, and subscribes to 39,135 periodicals including electronic. Computerized library services include interlibrary loans, database searching, Internet access, and Wi-Fi capability. Special learning facilities include an art gallery, natural history museum, planetarium, radio station, a center for historic preservation, university archives and special collections, and the Rose Melnick medical museum. **Physically Challenged Students:** 98% of the campus is accessible. Facilities include wheelchair ramps, elevators, special parking, specially equipped restrooms, special class scheduling, lowered drinking fountains, special housing. **Special:** YSU offers co-op programs in a variety of majors, as well as internships, work study, dual majors, credit for military experience, nondegree study, honors degree programs, distance learning,accelerated degrees, and pass/fail options. Student-designed majors are available through the Individualized Curriculum Program, Washington Semester, study abroad in a variety of countries and cross registration opportunities and accelerated degree program, partnerships with community colleges, The English Language

Institute, off-site degree programs, University honors program, 4+1 program Economics, combined BS/MS program in chemistry, online programs. There are 19 national honor societies and a freshman honors program. **Visiting:** There are regularly scheduled orientations for prospective students, including an official academic advising session, registration for classes, and complete overview of the university resources and services. There are guides for informal visits and visitors may sit in on classes. To schedule a visit, contact the Office of Admissions at (330) 941-2000. **Campus Safety and Security:** Measures include 24-hour foot and vehicle patrol, emergency notification system, self-defense education, and security escort services. There are shuttle buses, emergency telephones, lighted pathways/sidewalks, controlled access to dorms/residences, Night security posts in dorms, and concentrated security in parking and other critical areas.

REQUIREMENTS: The SAT or ACT is required. In state students may be admitted conditionally who do not meet minimum standards. Students who have been out of school for 2 or more years and who are not pursuing a restricted program of study are exempt from test requirements. Graduation from an accredited secondary school or satisfactory scores on the GED are required for all applicants. High school courses recommended are 4 units of English, 4 of math, 3 of science, and 3 of social studies, 2 of foreign language, and 1 of fine or performing arts. A GPA of 2.0 is required. AP and CLEP credits are accepted. A minimum of 124 semester hours must be successfully completed to earn a bachelor's degree, with a minimum GPA of 2.0. At least 60 semester hours must be completed in courses numbered 2600 or higher; at least 48 of these 60 hours must be in courses numbered 3700 or higher. All students must fulfill core requirements including requirements in English, speech, and math. **Procedure:** Freshmen are admitted fall, spring, and summer. Entrance exams should be taken during spring of the junior year or fall of the senior year. There are deferred admissions and rolling admissions plans. Early decision applications should be filed by February 15; regular applications, by August 1 for fall entry; December 1 for spring entry; and April 15 for summer entry, along with a $45 fee. Notification is sent on a rolling basis. Applications are accepted on-line. **Transfer Students:** 1083 transfer students enrolled in 2013-2014. Transfer applicants in good standing at the last institution attended with an aggregate cumulative point average of 2.0 or higher for all courses taken at other colleges or universities are admitted in good standing. Those with an aggregate cumulative point average of less than 2.0 or on probation may be considered for probationary transfer if their overall academic record, including high school grades and test scores, indicate potential success. Applicants suspended or dismissed from other institutions are not eligible for consideration (without appeal to the Office of Undergraduate Admission) until at least 1 semester has passed following the term in which the suspension occurred. 30 of 124 credits required for the bachelor's degree must be completed at YSU. **International Students:** There are 111 international students enrolled. The school actively recruits these students. They must take the TOEFL with a minimum score of 500 on the paper-based TOEFL (PBT) or 61 on the Internet-based version (iBT) or take the MELAB, Minimum score of 80 is required on the MELAB.

ADMISSIONS: 84% of the 2014-2015 applicants were accepted. The SAT scores for the 2014-2015 freshman class were: Critical Reading--63% below 500, 23% between 500 and 599, 11% between 600 and 699, and 3% between 700 and 800; Math--54% below 500, 27% between 500 and 599, 15% between 600 and 699, and 4% between 700 and 800; Writing--66% below 500, 21% between 500 and 599, 12% between 600 and 699, and 1% between 700 and 800. The ACT scores were 47% below 21, 25% between 21 and 23, 14% between 24 and 26, 7% between 27 and 28, and 7% above 28. 23% of the current freshmen were in the top fifth of their class; 47% were in the top two fifths. 44 freshmen graduated first in their class. **Admissions Contact:** Sue Davis, Director, Admissions. E-Mail: *enroll@ysu.edu* Web: *www.ysu.edu*

FINANCIAL AID: In 2014-2015, 93% of all full-time freshmen and 91% of continuing full-time students received some form of financial aid. 77% of all full-time freshmen and 72% of continuing full-time students received need-based aid. The average freshman award was $9,411. 12% of undergraduate students work part-time. Average annual earnings from campus work are $2710. The average financial indebtedness of the 2014 graduate was $21,387. YSU is a member of CSS. The FAFSA and the college's own financial statement are required. The deadline for filing freshman financial aid applications for fall entry is February 15.

OKLAHOMA

• College Location

0 20 40 60 80 100
Miles

CAMERON UNIVERSITY (*The complete profile is made available exclusively on our website, www.barronspac.com*)

EAST CENTRAL UNIVERSITY (*The complete profile is made available exclusively on our website, www.barronspac.com*)

LANGSTON UNIVERSITY   D-3
www.lunet.edu

Langston, OK 73050	**(405) 466-3224**
	n/av
Fax: (405) 466-3381	Email: gtrobertson@lunet.edu
Full-time: 1290 men, 1920 women	Faculty: 105
Part-time: 290 men, 520 women	Ph.D.s: 50%
Graduate: 20 men, 40 women	Student/Faculty: 31 to 1
Year: semesters, summer session	Tuition: $4618 ($10,808)
Room & Board: $8002	Freshman Class: n/av
SAT or ACT: required	CEEB CODE: 6361
Application Deadline: n/av	**COMPETITIVE**

Langston University founded in 1897, is a multiracial, public institution offering programs in liberal arts, business, allied health, and teacher preparation. The figures in above capsule and in this profile are approximate. In addition to regional accreditation, Langston has baccalaureate program accreditation with ADA, APTA, NCATE, and NLN. The 40-acre campus is in a rural area 45 miles from Oklahoma City. Including any residence halls, there are 20 buildings.

STUDENT LIFE: 66% of undergraduates are from Oklahoma. Others are from states. 98% are from public schools. 50% are White; 50% African American. 65% remain to graduate. **Housing:** 676 students can be accommodated in college housing, which includes dorms and married student housing. Alcohol is not permitted. All students may keep cars.

FACULTY/CLASSROOMS: All teach undergraduates. No introductory courses are taught by graduate students.

PROGRAMS OF STUDY: Langston confers B.A., B.B.A., B.S.,

B.S.Ed. and B.S.N. degrees. Associate and Master's degrees are also awarded. Bachelor's degrees are awarded in AGRICULTURE (agricultural economics and animal science), BIOLOGICAL SCIENCE (biology/biological science and nutrition), BUSINESS (accounting, business administration and management, and management science), COMMUNICATIONS AND THE ARTS (dramatic arts, English, music, and speech/debate/rhetoric), COMPUTER AND PHYSICAL SCIENCE (chemistry, computer science, and mathematics), EDUCATION (business education, elementary education, home economics education, industrial arts education, mathematics education, physical education, and science education), ENGINEERING AND ENVIRONMENTAL DESIGN (industrial engineering technology), HEALTH PROFESSIONS (health care administration, medical laboratory technology, nursing, and physical therapy), SOCIAL SCIENCE (criminal justice, early childhood studies, economics, gerontology, history, home economics, psychology, social science, sociology, and urban studies).

ACTIVITIES: 25% of men belong to 4 national fraternities; 30% of women belong to 4 national sororities. There are 30 groups on campus, including band, cheerleading, choir, drama, ethnic, international, jazz band, marching band, newspaper, professional, religious, social service, student government, and yearbook. Popular campus events include Student Theater Productions, and a Performing Arts Series. **Sports:** There are 4 intercollegiate sports for men and 2 for women, and 6 intramural sports for men and 5 for women. Facilities include a gym, tennis courts, a baseball field, and a track.

SERVICES: Counseling and information services are available, as is tutoring in some subjects. There is remedial math, reading, and writing. **Library/Resources:** The 6 libraries contain 110,248 volumes, 465,319 microform items, and subscribe to 80 periodicals including electronic. Computerized library services include interlibrary loans. **Physically Challenged Students:** 70% of the campus is accessible. Facilities include wheelchair ramps, elevators, special parking, specially equipped restrooms, and special class scheduling. **Special:** Work-study programs, internships, and nondegree and noncredit study are available. There are 6 national honor societies and a freshman honors program. **Visiting:** There are regularly scheduled orientations for prospective students. There are guides for informal visits, visitors may sit in on classes, and stay overnight.

REQUIREMENTS: The SAT or ACT is required. In general, test scores should place students in the upper 60 percent of Oklahoma high school seniors. Applicants should be graduates of accredited high schools with at least a C average (2.7 on a 4.0 scale) and rank in the upper 60 percent of their graduating classes. Required secondary preparation includes 4 years of English, 3 years of math, and 2 years each of lab science and history, including 1 year of American history. 4 additional academic units, including a foreign language, are strongly recommended. There are alternative admission programs for students with varying backgrounds. AP and CLEP credits are accepted. To graduate, students must complete a total of 124 semester hours, with a GPA of 2.0. The required general education core consists of 50 credits in English, math, computer science, biological and physical sciences, social science, and health and phys ed. 6 credits are required in American history and government, and all students must complete an internship or field experience. **Procedure:** Freshmen are admitted to all sessions. There is a rolling admissions plan. Application deadlines are open. The fall 2014 application fee was $15. **Transfer Students:** Applicants should be in good standing and have earned at least a C average in previous college work. 30 of 124 credits required for the bachelor's degree must be completed at Langston.

ADMISSIONS: Gayle T. Robertson, Driector of Admissions and Enrollment Management. E-Mail: *gtrobertson@lunet.edu* Web: *www.lunet.edu*

FINANCIAL AID: In 2014-2015, 70% of all full-time freshmen and 70% of continuing full-time students received some form of financial aid. 65% of all full-time freshmen and 60% of continuing full-time students received need-based aid. The average freshman award was $2,800. The CSS/Profile, FFS, SFS, or FAFSA is required. The deadline for filing freshman financial aid applications for fall entry is March 1.

NORTHEASTERN STATE UNIVERSITY   F-3
www.nsuok.edu

Tahlequah, OK 74464

Fax: (918) 458-2342

Full-time: 2700 men, 3850 women
Part-time: 716 men, 1393 women
Graduate: 334 men, 743 women
Year: semesters, summer session
Room & Board: $5800

ACT: 24
Application Deadline: open

(918) 456-5511, ext. 2200
n/av
Email: nsuinfo@nsuok.edu
Faculty: 314
Ph.D.s: 72%
Student/Faculty: 21 to 1
Tuition: $5500 ($11,500)
Freshman Class: 1651 accepted, 1102 enrolled
CEEB CODE: 6485
VERY COMPETITIVE

Northeastern State University, founded in 1846, is a public institution offering programs in arts and sciences, professional training, teacher preparation, and business. Figures in the above capsule and in this profile are approximate. There are 4 undergraduate schools and 5 graduate schools. In addition to regional accreditation, NSU has baccalaureate program accreditation with ACBSP, ADA, ASLA, CSWE, NASM, NCATE, and NLN. The 200-acre campus is in a small town 70 miles from Tulsa. Including any residence halls, there are 51 buildings.

STUDENT LIFE: 94% of undergraduates are from Oklahoma. Others are from 34 states, 47 foreign countries, and Canada. 61% are White; 28% American Indian/Alaska Native. The average age of freshmen is 19; all undergraduates, 26. 30% do not continue beyond their first year. **Housing:** 1653 students can be accommodated in college housing, which includes single-sex and coed dorms, on-campus apartments, and married student housing. In addition, there are special-interest houses. On-campus housing is available on a first-come, first-served basis. 80% of students commute. Alcohol is not permitted. All students may keep cars.

FACULTY/CLASSROOMS: 56% of faculty are male; 44% are female. 90% teach undergraduates. Graduate students teach 5% of introductory courses. The average class size in an introductory lecture is 60; in a laboratory is 24; and in a regular course is 20.

PROGRAMS OF STUDY: NSU confers B.A., B.S., B.A.Ed., B.B.A., B.S.Ed., B.S.Sci.Ed., B.S.N. and B.S.W. degrees. Master's and Doctoral degrees are also awarded. Bachelor's degrees are awarded in BIOLOGICAL SCIENCE (biology/biological science), BUSINESS (accounting, banking and finance, business administration and management, and marketing/retailing/merchandising), COMMUNICATIONS AND THE ARTS (advertising, communications, English, fine arts, journalism, music, Spanish, and speech/debate/rhetoric), COMPUTER AND PHYSICAL SCIENCE (chemistry, computer science, information sciences and systems, and mathematics), EDUCATION (art education, early childhood education, elementary education, health education, industrial arts education, music education, science education, secondary education, and special education), HEALTH PROFESSIONS (medical laboratory technology and nursing), SOCIAL SCIENCE (criminal justice, geography, history, political science/government, social science, social work, and sociology). Elementary education, early childhood education, and business are the strongest academically. Administration, psychology, and criminal justice have the largest enrollments.

ACTIVITIES: 5% of men belong to 7 national fraternities; 2% of women belong to 5 national sororities. There are 80 groups on campus, including art, band, cheerleading, choir, chorus, dance, drama, drill team, ethnic, film, gay, honors, international, jazz band, literary magazine, marching band, musical theater, newspaper, orchestra, pep band, photography, political, professional, radio and TV, religious, social service, student government, and symphony. Popular campus events include Cherokee Seminaries, Symposium on the American Indian, and Sequoyah Institute Shows. **Sports:** There are 5 intercollegiate sports for men and 5 for women, and 16 intramural sports for men and 16 for women. Facilities include a 12,500 seat football stadium, indoor practice facility, exercise/fitness track, baseball field, softball field, tennis courts, soccer fields, baseball field house, soccer/softball field house, and a 1,200 seat basketball gymnasium and basketball court. **Graduates:** From July 1, 2013 to June 30, 2014, 1404 bachelor's degrees were awarded. 254 companies recruited on campus in 2013-2014.

SERVICES: Counseling and information services are available, as is tutoring in most subjects. There is remedial math, reading, and writing. **Library/Resources:** The library contains 400,000 volumes, 766,300 microform items, 8,659 audio/video tapes/CDs/DVDs, and subscribes to 15,000 periodicals including electronic. Computerized library services include interlibrary loans, database searching, Internet access, and Wi-Fi capability. Special learning facilities include a radio station. **Physically Challenged Students:** 70% of the campus is accessible. Facilities include wheelchair ramps, elevators, special parking, specially equipped restrooms, special class scheduling, lowered drinking fountains, lowered telephones, and special housing. **Special:** Internships are offered in business, mass communications, and education. There are 10 national honor societies, a freshman honors program, and 5 departmental honors programs. **Visiting:** There are regularly scheduled orientations for prospective students, including a general campus visit with highlights presented by trained tour guides. Visitors may sit in on classes and stay overnight. To schedule a visit, contact High School and College Relations. **Campus Safety and Security:** Measures include 24-hour foot and vehicle patrol, self-defense education, and security escort services. There are shuttle buses, emergency telephones, lighted pathways/sidewalks, and a campus security police department.

REQUIREMENTS: The ACT is required, with a minimum composite score on the ACT of 20. Applicants should be high school graduates or have a GED. Students should have completed 4 years of English, 3 of math, and 2 each of history and science. NSU requires applicants to be in the upper 50% of their class. A GPA of 2.7 is required. AP and CLEP credits are accepted. To graduate, students must complete at least 124 credit hours, with 24 to 50 in the major. General education requirements include 40 hours in language arts, social science, natural science, humanities, and phys ed. Freshman orientation and English proficiency are required. **Procedure:** Freshmen are admitted to all sessions. There is a rolling admissions plan. Application deadlines are open. Notification is sent on a rolling basis. **Transfer Students:** 1404 transfer students enrolled in 2013-2014. Transfer applicants must have a minimum GPA of 2.0, with 24 transfer hours completed, and be in good standing at the last institution attended. 30 of 124 credits required for the bachelor's degree must be completed at NSU. **International Students:** There are 252 international students enrolled. They must take the TOEFL.

ADMISSIONS: Dawn Cain, Director of Admissions. E-Mail: *nsuinfo@nsuok.edu* Web: *www.nsuok.edu*

FINANCIAL AID: In 2014-2015, 86% of all full-time freshmen and 85% of continuing full-time students received some form of financial aid. 67% of all full-time freshmen and 63% of continuing full-time students received need-based aid. 7% of undergraduate students work part-time. Average annual earnings from campus work are $2850. The average financial indebtedness of the 2014 graduate was $17,824. The FAFSA and the college's own financial statement are required. The priority date for freshman financial aid applications for fall entry is March 1.

NORTHWESTERN OKLAHOMA STATE UNIVERSITY *(The complete profile is made available exclusively on our website, www. barronspac.com)*

OKLAHOMA BAPTIST UNIVERSITY   E-3
www.okbu.edu

Shawnee, OK 74804

(405) 585-5120
(800) 654-3285

Fax: (405) 585-5105

Email: admissions@okbu.edu

Full-time: 731 men, 1137 women	Faculty: n/av
Part-time: 88 men, 63 women	Ph.D.s: n/av
Graduate: 34 men, 44 women	Student/Faculty: 15 to 1
Year: 4-1-4, summer session	Tuition: $21,842
Room & Board: $6360	Freshman Class: 6560 applied, 3704 accepted, 580 enrolled
SAT CR/M: 536/536 ACT: 24	CEEB CODE: 6541
Application Deadline: August 1	COMPETITIVE

Oklahoma Baptist University, founded in 1910, is a liberal arts institution affiliated with the Southern Baptist Convention. OBU offers degrees in Christian service, business, nursing, fine arts, telecommunications, teacher education, and the traditional liberal arts areas. Figures in the above capsule and in this profile are approximate. There are 6 undergraduate schools and 1 graduate school. In addition to regional accreditation, OBU has baccalaureate program accreditation with ACBSP, NASM, NCATE, and NLN. The 189-acre campus is in a small town 30 miles east of Oklahoma City and 90 miles southwest of Tulsa. Including any residence halls, there are 54 buildings.

STUDENT LIFE: 70% of undergraduates are from Oklahoma. Others are from 34 states, 31 foreign countries, and Canada. 84% are from public schools. 70% are White. 93% are Protestant; 15% claim no religious affiliation. The average age of freshmen is 18; all undergraduates, 20. 26% do not continue beyond their first year; 56% remain to graduate. **Housing:** 1391 students can be accommodated in college housing, which includes single-sex dorms, on-campus apartments, and married student housing. On-campus housing is guaranteed for all 4 years. 63% of students live on campus; of those, 75% remain on campus on weekends. Alcohol is not permitted. All students may keep cars.

FACULTY/CLASSROOMS: 55% of faculty are male; 45% are female. All teach undergraduates. No introductory courses are taught by graduate students. The average class size in an introductory lecture is 25; in a laboratory is 19; and in a regular course is 15.

PROGRAMS OF STUDY: OBU confers B.A., B.S., B.B.A., B.F.A., B.Hum., B.M., B.M.A., B.Mus.Ed. and B.S.E. degrees. Associate and Master's degrees are also awarded. Bachelor's degrees are awarded in BIOLOGICAL SCIENCE (biology/biological science), BUSINESS (accounting, banking and finance, business administration and management, and marketing/retailing/merchandising), COMMUNICATIONS AND THE ARTS (broadcasting, communications, dramatic arts, English, fine arts, French, German, journalism, music, Spanish, speech/debate/rhetoric, and telecommunications), COMPUTER AND PHYSICAL SCIENCE (chemistry, computer science, information sciences and systems, mathematics, and physics), EDUCATION (art education, early childhood education, elementary education, for-

eign languages education, music education, physical education, science education, and secondary education), HEALTH PROFESSIONS (nursing, physical therapy, predentistry, and premedicine), SOCIAL SCIENCE (history, political science/government, prelaw, psychology, religion, social science, social work, and sociology). Teacher education, biology, and religion are the strongest academically. Elementary education and nursing have the largest enrollments.

ACTIVITIES: 1% of men belong to 1 local fraternity; 10% of women belong to 4 local sororities. There are 85 groups on campus, including art, band, cheerleading, choir, chorale, chorus, computers, drama, environmental, ethnic, film, honors, international, jazz band, literary magazine, marching band, musical theater, newspaper, opera, orchestra, pep band, photography, political, professional, radio and TV, religious, social, social service, student government, and yearbook. Popular campus events include Stampede of Stars, International Awareness Day and Hanging of the Green. **Sports:** There are 10 intercollegiate sports for men and 12 for women, and 14 intramural sports for men and 14 for women. Facilities include a sports complex, which houses a 2500-seat arena; a 60,000-sqare-foot recreation and wellness center, which includes 3 basketball/volleyball courts, a 2-story rock climbing wall, state-of-the-art exercise and fitness equipment, weight rooms, a swimming pool, a walking track on the top floor; an all-weather track; and baseball, softball, soccer, and sand volleyball facilities. **Graduates:** From July 1, 2013 to June 30, 2014, 302 bachelor's degrees were awarded. The most popular majors were health profession & related programs (19%), education (18%), and business/marketing (8%). In an average class, 41% graduate in 4 years or less and 56% graduate in 6 years or less.

SERVICES: Counseling and information services are available, as is tutoring in most subjects. There is a reader service for the blind, and remedial math, reading, and writing. **Library/Resources:** The library contains 290,000 volumes, 230,000 microform items, 1,500 audio/video tapes/CDs/DVDs, and subscribes to 600 periodicals including electronic. Computerized library services include interlibrary loans, database searching, Internet access, and Wi-Fi capability. Special learning facilities include an art gallery, planetarium, radio station, TV station, a language lab, and a Biblical research library. **Physically Challenged Students:** 95% of the campus is accessible. Facilities include wheelchair ramps, elevators, special parking, specially equipped restrooms, lowered drinking fountains, lowered telephones, and special housing. **Special:** OBU offers co-op programs in business, and a 3-2 engineering degree with Oklahoma State University. Students may study abroad in 15 countries in Europe, Central and South America, Asia, and Africa. Internships in several fields, student-designed majors, including an interdisciplinary program in humanities, and pass/fail options are available. There are 4 national honor societies and a freshman honors program. **Visiting:** There are regularly scheduled orientations for prospective students, including tours, faculty visits, and general information sessions. There are guides for informal visits, visitors may sit in on classes, and stay overnight. To schedule a visit, contact the OBU Admissions Office. **Campus Safety and Security:** Measures include 24-hour foot and vehicle patrol, emergency notification system, self-defense education, and security escort services. There are emergency telephones, lighted pathways/sidewalks, and controlled access to dorms/residences.

REQUIREMENTS: The SAT or ACT is required, Admission is granted to students with composite scores of 950 on the SAT or 20 on the ACT, with a 3.0 GPA. Graduation from an accredited secondary school or satisfactory scores on the GED are required for admission. The recommended high school courses should include 4 units of English, 3 units of math, and 2 units each of social studies, lab science, and a foreign language. OBU requires applicants to be in the upper 50% of their class. AP and CLEP credits are accepted. Important factors in the admissions decision are advanced placement or honors courses, recommendations by school officials, and leadership record. To graduate, students must complete a total of 128 credit hours, including 30 to 48 hours in the major, with a 2.0 GPA. Students are also required to complete 6 credits each of English, literature, history, science, Bible, social sciences, and language; 3 each in math, fine arts, and comparative civilization; 2 each in speech, philosophy, and phys ed; and 1 in computer literacy. **Procedure:** Freshmen are admitted to all sessions. Entrance exams should be taken during the spring of the junior year. There are deferred admissions and rolling admissions plans. Applications should be filed by August 1 for fall entry; December 15 for winter entry; January 15 for spring entry; and May 15 for summer entry. Applications are accepted on-line. **Transfer Students:** 98 transfer students enrolled in 2013-2014. Transfer students must have a GPA of 2.5 for all college work attempted. 32 of 128 credits required for the bachelor's degree must be completed at OBU. **International Students:** There are 90 international students enrolled. The school actively recruits these students. They must take the TOEFL with a minimum score of 550 on the paper-based TOEFL (PBT) or 61 on the Internet-based version (iBT), or take the MELAB. They must also take the SAT or ACT, scoring 20.

ADMISSIONS: 56% of the 2014-2015 applicants were accepted. The SAT scores for the 2014-2015 freshman class were: Critical Reading--32% below 500, 40% between 500 and 599, 23% between 600 and 699, and 5% between 700 and 800; Math--25% below 500, 47% between 500 and 599, 25% between 600 and 699, and 3% between 700 and 800. The ACT scores were 21% below 21, 27% between 21 and 23, 25% between 24 and 26, 12% between 27 and 28, and 15% above 28. 51% of the current freshmen were in the top fifth of their class; 78% were in the top two fifths. 28 freshmen graduated first in their class. **Admissions Contact:** Bruce Perkins, Dean of Enrollment Management. E-Mail: *admissions@okbu.edu* Web: *www.okbu.edu*

FINANCIAL AID: In 2014-2015, 99% of all full-time freshmen and continuing full-time students received some form of financial aid. 75% of all full-time freshmen and 60% of continuing full-time students received need-based aid. The average freshman award was $19,681. Need-based scholarships or need-based grants averaged $5,846; need-based self-help aid (loans and jobs) averaged $3,223; non-need-based athletic scholarships averaged $5,551; and other non-need-based awards and non-need-based scholarships averaged $10,419. 95% of undergraduate students work part-time. Average annual earnings from campus work are $2000. The average financial indebtedness of the 2014 graduate was $26,557. The FAFSA is required. The priority date for freshman financial aid applications for fall entry is April 1.

OKLAHOMA CHRISTIAN UNIVERSITY   D-3
www.oc.edu

Oklahoma City, OK 73136	(405) 425-5050
	(800) 877-5010
Fax: (405) 425-5069	Email: info@oc.edu
Full-time: 982 men, 910 women	Faculty: 111
Part-time: 38 men, 43 women	Ph.D.s: 68%
Graduate: 310 men, 190 women	Student/Faculty: 14 to 1
Year: semesters, summer session	Tuition: $19,120
Room & Board: $6750	Freshman Class: 2178 applied, 1369 accepted, 507 enrolled
SAT CR/M/W: 540/540/510 ACT: 25	CEEB CODE: 6086
Application Deadline: open	VERY COMPETITIVE

Oklahoma Christian University, founded in 1950, is a private, liberal arts institution affiliated with Churches of Christ. Oklahoma Christian, ranked as one of the best universities in the western region of the United States offers undergraduate programs in more than 60 fields of study, an undergraduate Honors Program, ABET accredited programs in mechanical, electrical and computer engineering, and graduate programs in accountancy, business administration, engineering, Christian ministry, divinity and theological studies. There are 5 undergraduate schools and 3 graduate schools. In addition to regional accreditation, OC has baccalaureate program accreditation with ABET, ACBSP, NASM, NCATE, CIDA, and CCNE. The 200-acre campus is in a suburban area on the north side of Oklahoma City. Including any residence halls, there are 33 buildings. **STUDENT LIFE:** 58% of undergraduates are from out of state, mostly the Midwest. Students are from 41 states, 49 foreign countries, and Canada. 66% are White; 16% Foreign; 13% African American. 26% are Protestant. The average age of freshmen is 18; all undergraduates, 20. 24% do not continue beyond their first year; 50% remain to graduate. **Housing:** 1730 students can be accommodated in college housing, which includes single-sex dorms, on-campus apartments,

and married student housing. In addition, there are honors houses. On-campus housing is guaranteed for all 4 years. 80% of students live on campus. Alcohol is not permitted. All students may keep cars.
FACULTY/CLASSROOMS: 67% of faculty are male; 33% are female. All teach undergraduates. No introductory courses are taught by graduate students. The average class size in an introductory lecture is 19; in a laboratory is 15; and in a regular course is 21.
PROGRAMS OF STUDY: OC confers B.A., B.S., B.B.A., B.F.A., B.M.E., B.S.C.E., B.S.E., B.S.E.E., B.S.N. and B.S.M.E. degrees. Master's degrees are also awarded. Bachelor's degrees are awarded in BIOLOGICAL SCIENCE (biochemistry, biology/biological science, and forensic science), BUSINESS (accounting, banking and finance, business administration and management, business administration -international, business administration, mgmt, operations, business administration marketing, finance, international business management, marketing management, and marketing/retailing/merchandising), COMMUNICATIONS AND THE ARTS (advertising, art, broadcasting, communications, creative writing, design, English, English Writing, game design and development, instrumental performance, journalism, music, photography, public relations, Spanish, visual design, vocal performance, and writing), COMPUTER AND PHYSICAL SCIENCE (chemistry, computer game design/development, computer science, information sciences and systems, and mathematics), EDUCATION (early childhood education, elementary education, English education, mathematics education, middle school education, music education, physical education, science education, social science education, social studies education, sports and wellness studies, and teaching English as a second/foreign language (TESOL/TEFOL)), ENGINEERING AND ENVIRONMENTAL DESIGN (computer engineering, electrical and computer engineering, electrical/electronics engineering, interior design, and mechanical engineering), HEALTH PROFESSIONS (biology, medical laboratory technology, and nursing), SOCIAL SCIENCE (biblical studies, child care/child and family studies, history, history and political science, interdisciplinary studies, liberal arts/general studies, ministries, missions, prelaw, psychology, religious education, social studies, and youth ministry). Engineering, gaming and animation history and political science are the strongest academically. Business, education, and engineering have the largest enrollments.
ACTIVITIES: 31% of men belong to 5 local fraternities; 35% of women belong to 6 local sororities. There are 56 groups on campus, including band, cheerleading, choir, chorale, chorus, communications, computers, drama, ethnic, honors, international, jazz band, literary magazine, musical theater, newspaper, opera, orchestra, pep band, photography, political, professional, radio and TV, religious, social service, student government, symphony, and yearbook. Popular campus events include Spring Sing, Homecoming, Winter Wonderland Week, Earn Your Wings, and McGaw Lecture Series. **Sports:** There are 7 intercollegiate sports for men and 7 for women, and 10 intramural sports for men and 10 for women. Facilities include basketball courts, a 25-meter six-lane swimming pool for recreational swimming, on campus baseball, softball, intramural football, and soccer fields, a track and field facility, tennis courts, 4,000-square-foot fitness center, and an auxiliary gym. **Graduates:** From July 1, 2013 to June 30, 2014, 377 bachelor's degrees were awarded. The most popular majors were business (18%), engineering (13%), and health (7%). 50 companies recruited on campus in 2013-2014. In an average class, 29% graduate in 4 years or less, 45% graduate in 5 years or less, and 47% graduate in 6 years or less.
SERVICES: Counseling and information services are available, as is tutoring in some subjects. There is remedial math, reading, and writing. **Library/Resources:** The library contains 185,522 volumes, 682,861 microform items, 6,673 audio/video tapes/CDs/DVDs, and subscribes to 41,949 periodicals including electronic. Computerized library services include interlibrary loans, database searching, Internet access, and Wi-Fi capability. Special learning facilities include an art gallery, radio station, TV station, a journalism lab. **Physically Challenged Students:** 98% of the campus is accessible. Facilities include wheelchair ramps, elevators, special parking, specially equipped restrooms, special class scheduling, lowered drinking fountains, lowered telephones, and special housing. **Special:** OC offers a wide range of undergraduate degrees and many graduate programs in accounting, business, theology, ministry, and engineering. Our

ABET accredited engineering complements a full spectrum of majors across the arts, sciences, and humanities. Internships and practice are commonly required or offered in the nearby city. Students may study abroad in Austria, Japan, and China. Major-minor combinations and interdisciplinary studies options help students combine fields such as business, mass communications, family life, prelaw, advertising design, speech communication, education, English, music, math and others. An interdisciplinary Honors program serves students with high ACT/SAT scores. Cross-registration can be offered with the University of Central Oklahoma. There are 8 national honor societies, a freshman honors program, and 16 departmental honors programs. **Visiting:** There are regularly scheduled orientations for prospective students, consisting of a comprehensive campus overview including academic conversations. There are guides for informal visits, visitors may sit in on classes, and stay overnight. To schedule a visit, contact Michael Mitchell at info@oc.edu. **Campus Safety and Security:** Measures include 24-hour foot and vehicle patrol, emergency notification system, and security escort services. There are emergency telephones, lighted pathways/sidewalks, and campus police.

REQUIREMENTS: The SAT or ACT is required. High school graduation with college prep courses or satisfactory scores on the GED are required for admission AP and CLEP credits are accepted. To graduate, students must have a minimum of 126 credit hours, including 30 to 104 in the major, with a GPA of 2.0. All students must complete 55 hours in our general education area, which includes courses in American history, behavioral science, Bible, communication, English, fine arts, foreign language, liberal arts, literature, mathematics, music, non-western civilization, political science, science, social science, and Western civilization. **Procedure:** Freshmen are admitted to all sessions. There are deferred admissions and rolling admissions plans. Application deadlines are open. Application fee is $25. Notification is sent on a rolling basis. Applications are accepted on-line. **Transfer Students:** 134 transfer students enrolled in 2013-2014. Applicants must be eligible to return to the school from which they are transferring. 30 of 126 credits required for the bachelor's degree must be completed at OC. **International Students:** There are 196 international students enrolled. The school actively recruits these students. They must take the TOEFL with a minimum score of 500 on the paper-based TOEFL (PBT) or 61 on the Internet-based version (iBT). They must also take the SAT or ACT.

ADMISSIONS: 63% of the 2014-2015 applicants were accepted. The SAT scores for the 2014-2015 freshman class were: Critical Reading--30% below 500, 37% between 500 and 599, 26% between 600 and 699, and 7% between 700 and 800; Math--36% below 500, 33% between 500 and 599, 21% between 600 and 699, and 9% between 700 and 800; Writing--42% below 500, 37% between 500 and 599, 14% between 600 and 699, and 7% between 700 and 800. The ACT scores were 16% below 21, 20% between 21 and 23, 26% between 24 and 26, 16% between 27 and 28, and 21% above 28. There were 11 National Merit finalists. **Admissions Contact:** Michael Mitchell, Director of Admissions. E-Mail: *info@oc.edu* Web: *www.oc.edu*

FINANCIAL AID: In 2014-2015, 99% of all full-time freshmen and 97% of continuing full-time students received some form of financial aid. 32% of all full-time freshmen and 50% of continuing full-time students received need-based aid. The average freshman award was $17,201. Need-based scholarships or need-based grants averaged $2,852; need-based self-help aid (loans and jobs) averaged $2,116; non-need-based athletic scholarships averaged $857; other non-need-based awards and non-need-based scholarships averaged $9,453; and $1,923 from other forms of aid. 37% of undergraduate students work part-time. Average annual earnings from campus work are $1597. The average financial indebtedness of the 2014 graduate was $26,578. The FAFSA is required. The priority date for freshman financial aid applications for fall entry is March 15. The deadline for filing freshman financial aid applications for fall entry is April 15.

OKLAHOMA CITY UNIVERSITY D-3
www.okcu.edu

Oklahoma City, OK 73106

Fax: (405) 208-5916
Full-time: 584 men, 994 women
Part-time: 69 men, 134 women
Graduate: 598 men, 635 women
Year: semesters, summer session
Room & Board: $9750

SAT: required ACT: 25
Application Deadline: rolling

(405) 208-5055
(800) 633-7242
Email: uadmissions@okcu.edu
Faculty: 194; IIA, -$
Ph.D.s: 76%
Student/Faculty: 11 to 1
Tuition: $30,726
Freshman Class: 1505 applied, 1020 accepted, 297 enrolled
CEEB CODE: 6543
VERY COMPETITIVE

Oklahoma City University, founded in 1904, is a private, comprehensive university affiliated with the United Methodist Church, offering undergraduate and graduate programs in arts and sciences, business, music and performing arts, religion and church vocations, nursing, and law. There are 7 undergraduate schools and 6 graduate schools. In addition to regional accreditation, OCU has baccalaureate program accreditation with AACSB, NASM, NCATE, NLN, AAPL, ACEN, and Oklahoma Commission for Teacher Preparation. The 104-acre campus is in an urban area within Oklahoma City. Including any residence halls, there are 37 buildings.

STUDENT LIFE: 53% of undergraduates are from Oklahoma. Others are from 46 states, 41 foreign countries, and Canada. 88% are from public schools. 61% are White; 13% Foreign. 54% are Protestant; 29% claim no religious affiliation; 13% Catholic. The average age of freshmen is 18.3; all undergraduates, 22.3. 20% do not continue beyond their first year; 60% remain to graduate. **Housing:** 1270 students can be accommodated in college housing, which includes single-sex and coed dorms, on-campus apartments, and married student housing. In addition, there are honors houses, special-interest houses, fraternity houses, and learning communities. On-campus housing is guaranteed for all 4 years. 53% of students live on campus. Alcohol is not permitted. All students may keep cars.

FACULTY/CLASSROOMS: 52% of faculty are male; 48% are female. 80% teach undergraduates. No introductory courses are taught by graduate students. The average class size in an introductory lecture is 16 and in a laboratory is 13.

PROGRAMS OF STUDY: OCU confers B.A., B.S., B.F.A., B.M., B.Perf.Arts, B.S.B., B.B.A., B.M., B.M.E. and B.S.N. degrees. Master's and Doctoral degrees are also awarded. Bachelor's degrees are awarded in AGRICULTURE (environmental studies), BIOLOGICAL SCIENCE (biochemistry and cell biology), BUSINESS (accounting, banking and finance, business administration and management, management science, and marketing), COMMUNICATIONS AND THE ARTS (acting, advertising, art, broadcasting, church music, communications, dance, English, film arts, French, guitar, instrumental performance, instrumental music education, instrumental music education, music, music composition, photography, piano/organ, piano pedagogy, piano performance, public relations, Spanish, studio art, theatre acting, theatre arts, theater design, theatre production, and vocal performance), COMPUTER AND PHYSICAL SCIENCE (chemistry, mathematics, physics, science, and software engineering), EDUCATION (early childhood education, education, elementary education, music education, and secondary education), HEALTH PROFESSIONS (biology, biomedical science, exercise science, health care administration, nursing, Pre-Health Studies, and premedicine), SOCIAL SCIENCE (addiction studies, behavioral science, economics, history, humanities, liberal arts/general studies, philosophy, philosophy and religion, political science/government, prelaw, psychology, religion, religious education, and sociology). Nursing, business, and performing arts are the strongest academically. Sciences, performing arts, and liberal arts have the largest enrollments.

ACTIVITIES: 25% of men belong to 3 national fraternities; 14% of women belong to 4 national sororities. There are 87 groups on campus, including art, band, cheerleading, choir, chorus, computers, dance, debate, drama, environmental, ethnic, film, gay, honors, international, jazz band, literary magazine, musical theater, newspaper, opera, orchestra, pep band, photography, political, professional, radio and TV, religious, social, social service, student government, symphony, and yearbook. Popular campus events include Midnight Breakfast, Movie Night, Oozeball, Homecoming, and Relay for Life. **Sports:** There are 9 intercollegiate sports for men and 11 for women, and 7 intramural sports for men and 7 for women. Facilities include a baseball, softball, and soccer fields, a wellness and activity center which houses basketball, volleyball, and wrestling. **Graduates:** From July 1, 2013 to June 30, 2014, 594 bachelor's degrees were awarded. The most popular majors were liberal arts and sciences (34%), nursing (30%), and business (9%). 102 companies recruited on campus in 2013-2014. In an average class, 49% graduate in 4 years or less, 58% graduate in 5 years or less, and 59% graduate in 6 years or less. **SERVICES:** Counseling and information services are available, as is tutoring in most subjects. There is a reader service for the blind, and remedial math, reading, and writing. There are writing and learning enhancement centers and a math lab. **Library/Resources:** The 2 libraries contain 327,229 volumes, 635,725 microform items, 16,618 audio/video tapes/CDs/DVDs, and subscribe to 10,976 periodicals including electronic. Computerized library services include interlibrary loans, database searching, Internet access, and Wi-Fi capability. Special learning facilities include an art gallery, radio station, and TV station. **Physically Challenged Students:** 98% of the campus is accessible. Facilities include wheelchair ramps, elevators, special parking, specially equipped restrooms, lowered drinking fountains, and lowered telephones. **Special:** OCU offers internships, a Washington semester, work-study programs, a general studies degree, dual and student-designed majors, credit for life experience, and study-abroad programs in many countries. B.A.-B.S. degrees and an accelerated degree program in nursing and law are also available. There are 8 national honor societies, a freshman honors program, and 10 departmental honors programs. **Visiting:** There are regularly scheduled orientations for prospective students, consisting of a 9 am and 1 pm informational presentation, and a campus tour. There are guides for informal visits and visitors may sit in on classes. To schedule a visit, contact Tasha Casey-Loveless at tasha.loveless@okcu.edu. **Campus Safety and Security:** Measures include 24-hour foot and vehicle patrol, emergency notification system, and security escort services. There are emergency telephones, lighted pathways/sidewalks, controlled access to dorms/residences, and an inner-campus bicycle patrol.

REQUIREMENTS: The SAT or ACT is required. Graduation from an accredited secondary school or satisfactory scores on the GED is required for admission. High school courses must include 4 units of English, 2-3 units each of science (at least one should be lab), 1 unit of world history, 1 unit of state history and civics, 1 unit of US History, 2 units math, and 2 units of a foreign language. OCU looks for a 3.0 unweighted GPA and 22 on the ACT or 1020 on the SAT. Additionally, OCU reviews the essay, letter of recommendation, and application materials. Dance and arts management, music, and theatre all require an audition. Studio art and photography require portfolio review. AP and CLEP credits are accepted. Important factors in the admissions decision are evidence of special talent, advanced placement or honors courses, and leadership record. To graduate, students must complete a total of 124 credit hours, including 30 to 80 in the major, with a minimum GPA of 2.0. Students must complete their last 15 hours, including the last 6 in the major, at OCU with a minimum GPA of 2.0. All students must take 43 hours in the core curriculum as specified by their college or department. **Procedure:** Freshmen are admitted to all sessions. Entrance exams should be taken by February of the senior year. There are deferred admissions and rolling admissions plans. Application deadlines are open. The fall 2014 application fee was $55. Notification is sent on a rolling basis. Applications are accepted on-line. **Transfer Students:** 252 transfer students enrolled in 2013-2014. Applicants must submit a transcript from each college attended and must have a minimum cumulative GPA of 2.0 from an accredited institution. Applicants having fewer than 29 credit hours must submit a high school transcript and ACT or SAT scores. The application also requires an essay and recommendation from their Dean of Students. 30 of 124 credits required for the bachelor's degree must be completed at OCU. **International Students:** There are 13 international students enrolled. The school actively recruits

these students. They must take the TOEFL with a minimum score of 550 on the paper-based TOEFL (PBT) or 80 on the Internet-based version (iBT), or take the IELTS.

ADMISSIONS: 68% of the 2014-2015 applicants were accepted. The ACT scores were 13% below 21, 20% between 21 and 23, 32% between 24 and 26, 12% between 27 and 28, and 23% above 28. 56% of the current freshmen were in the top fifth of their class; 82% were in the top two fifths. There were 4 National Merit finalists. 14 freshmen graduated first in their class. **Admissions Contact:** Michelle Cook, Director of Admissions Operations . E-Mail: *uadmissions@okcu .edu* Web: *www.okcu.edu*

FINANCIAL AID: In 2014-2015, 97% of all full-time freshmen and 80% of continuing full-time students received some form of financial aid. 82% of all full-time freshmen and 58% of continuing full-time students received need-based aid. The average freshman award was $26,609. Need-based scholarships or need-based grants averaged $16,681 ($38,836 maximum); need-based self-help aid (loans and jobs) averaged $2,348 ($12,000 maximum); non-need-based athletic scholarships averaged $7,398 ($20,000 maximum); and other non-need-based awards and non-need-based scholarships averaged $19,120 ($44,851 maximum). 31% of undergraduate students work part-time. Average annual earnings from campus work are $2749. The average financial indebtedness of the 2014 graduate was $24,237. OCU is a member of CSS. The FAFSA and tax returns, if selected for verifications are required. The priority date for freshman financial aid applications for fall entry is March 1. The deadline for filing freshman financial aid applications for fall entry is June 30.

OKLAHOMA PANHANDLE STATE UNIVERSITY   B-2
www.opsu.edu

Goodwell, OK 73939	**(580) 349-1376** **(800) 664-6778**
Fax: (580) 349-1371	Email: bjenkins@opsu.edu
Full-time: 615 men, 501 women	Faculty: 65; IIB
Part-time: 82 men, 189 women	Ph.D.s: 32%
Graduate: n/av	Student/Faculty: 15 to 1
Year: semesters, summer session	Tuition: $5844 ($11,403)
Room & Board: $4152	Freshman Class: 316 applied, 316 accepted, 286 enrolled
SAT CR/M: 525/520 ACT: 22	CEEB CODE: 6571
Application Deadline: open	COMPETITIVE

Oklahoma Panhandle State University, founded in 1909, is a publicly funded institution offering undergraduate programs in the liberal arts, business and technology, education, agriculture, mathematics, sciences, and nursing. Figures in the above capsule and in this profile are approximate. There are 5 undergraduate schools. In addition to regional accreditation, OPSU has baccalaureate program accreditation with NCATE and NLN. The 120-acre campus is in a rural area 100 miles north of Amarillo, Texas. Including any residence halls, there are 29 buildings.

STUDENT LIFE: 50% of undergraduates are from out of state, mostly the Midwest. Students are from 35 states, 15 foreign countries, and Canada. 98% are from public schools. 65% are White; 18% Hispanic. The average age of freshmen is 20; all undergraduates, 24. 42% do not continue beyond their first year; 38% remain to graduate. **Housing:** 613 students can be accommodated in college housing, which includes single-sex and coed dorms, on-campus apartments, and married student housing. On-campus housing is guaranteed for the freshman year only, and is available on a first-come, first-served basis. 60% of students commute. Alcohol is not permitted. All students may keep cars. **FACULTY/CLASSROOMS:** 58% of faculty are male; 42% are female. All teach undergraduates. No introductory courses are taught by graduate students. The average class size in an introductory lecture is 30; in a laboratory is 20; and in a regular course is 20.

PROGRAMS OF STUDY: OPSU confers B.A., B.S., B.B.A., B.F.A., B.I.T., B.M., B.S.N. and B.T. degrees. Associate degrees are also awarded. Bachelor's degrees are awarded in AGRICULTURE (agricultural business management, agronomy, animal science, and equine science), BIOLOGICAL SCIENCE (biology/biological science), BUSINESS (accounting and business administration and management), COMMUNICATIONS AND THE ARTS (English, fine arts, and music), COMPUTER AND PHYSICAL SCIENCE (chemistry, information sciences and systems, mathematics, and physical sciences), EDUCATION (agricultural education, business education, and physical education), ENGINEERING AND ENVIRONMENTAL DESIGN (industrial engineering technology and technological management), HEALTH PROFESSIONS (nursing), SOCIAL SCIENCE (history, psychology, and social studies). Biology, business administration, and nursing have the largest enrollments.

ACTIVITIES: 5% of men belong to 1 local fraternity. There are 40 groups on campus, including art, band, cheerleading, choir, chorale, computers, dance, drama, drill team, ethnic, honors, international, jazz band, marching band, musical theater, newspaper, pep band, photography, professional, radio and TV, religious, Rodeo Club, student government, and yearbook. Popular campus events include Mardi Gras, Talent Show, and Holiday Dinner. **Sports:** There are 10 intercollegiate sports for men and 8 for women, and Facilities include a field house, an athletic field, a golf course, tennis courts, a gym, and an activity center. Water skiing and fishing spots are nearby. **Graduates:** From July 1, 2013 to June 30, 2014, 198 bachelor's degrees were awarded. The most popular majors were business administration (16%), registered nursing (12%), and biology (12%). In an average class, 38% graduate in 6 years or less.

SERVICES: There is remedial math, reading, and writing. Free tutoring is provided through the peer counseling center. **Library/ Resources:** The library contains 123,026 volumes, 12,764 microform items, 7,159 audio/video tapes/CDs/DVDs, and subscribes to 275 periodicals including electronic. Computerized library services include interlibrary loans, database searching, and Internet access. Special learning facilities include a radio station, a writing lab, academic support lab, farm lab, children's collection library, and 2 instructional ITV facilities. **Physically Challenged Students:** 97% of the campus is accessible. Facilities include wheelchair ramps, elevators, special parking, specially equipped restrooms, and special class scheduling. **Special:** The university offers dual majors and B.A.-B.S. degrees in several majors. There is 1 national honor society and 1 departmental honors program. **Visiting:** There are regularly scheduled orientations for prospective students. There are guides for informal visits, visitors may sit in on classes, and stay overnight. To schedule a visit, contact High School and Community Relations. **Campus Safety and Security:** Measures include emergency notification system. There are lighted pathways/sidewalks.

REQUIREMENTS: The SAT or ACT is recommended, with a minimum composite score of 19 on the ACT. Graduation from an accredited secondary school or satisfactory scores on the GED are required. High school courses must include 4 units of English, 3 units of math (beginning with Algebra I), 3 units of other courses such as foreign language or computer application courses, 2 units each of history (including 1 unit of American history) and lab science, and 1 unit of citizenship (for example, government, or civics). AP and CLEP credits are accepted. To graduate, students must complete a total of 124 semester hours with a minimum GPA of 2.0. The number of hours required in the major varies. All students must complete 45 hours of general education courses, with at least 1 course at the upper-division level. Students must complete 40 upper-level hours and must have completed 60 hours at a 4-year institution. **Procedure:** Freshmen are admitted to all sessions. There is a rolling admissions plan. Application deadlines are open. **Transfer Students:** An application for admission, a medical history form, college transcripts, high school transcripts, and ACT scores are required. If students are transferring in with a GPA below 2.0, they come in on academic probation. 30 of 124 credits required for the bachelor's degree must be completed at OPSU. **International Students:** There are 42 international students enrolled. The school actively recruits these students. They must take the TOEFL with a minimum score of 500 on the paper-based TOEFL (PBT). They must also take the SAT or ACT, scoring 19.

ADMISSIONS: 100% of the 2014-2015 applicants were accepted. The SAT scores for the 2014-2015 freshman class were: Critical Reading--16% below 500, 67% between 500 and 599, and 7% between 600 and

699; Math--33% below 500, 50% between 500 and 599, and 17% between 600 and 699. The ACT scores were 25% below 21, 35% between 21 and 23, 28% between 24 and 26, 11% between 27 and 28, and 1% above 28. **Admissions Contact:** Bobby Jenkins, Registrar and Director of Admissions. E-Mail: *bjenkins@opsu.edu* Web: *www.opsu .edu*

FINANCIAL AID: The FAFSA and the college's own financial statement are required. Check with the school for current application deadlines.

OKLAHOMA STATE SYSTEM OF HIGHER EDUCATION

The Oklahoma State System of Higher Education, established in 1941, is a public system in Oklahoma. It is governed by the Oklahoma State Regents for Higher Education, whose chief administrator is the chancellor. The primary mission of the system is to set academic standards, approve courses of study and grant degrees for all public colleges and universities, as well as recommend budget allocations and approve tuition and fees. The main priorities are to increase the number of college graduates, assure access to higher education, and achieve increasingly higher-quality education for students. The total student enrollment is usually about 207,905 with 5000 faculty members. Altogether there are 659 baccalaureate, 319 master's, and 110 doctoral programs offered in the Oklahoma State System of Higher Education. Profiles of the 4-year campuses are included in this section.

OKLAHOMA STATE UNIVERSITY E-2
www.okstate.edu

Stillwater, OK 74078	**(405) 744-5358**
	(800) 223-5019, ext.1
Fax: (405) 744-7092	**Email:** admission@okstate.edu
Full-time: 9057 men, 8492 women	**Faculty:** 808; I, --$
Part-time: 1381 men, 1124 women	**Ph.D.s:** 91%
Graduate: 2981 men, 2433 women	**Student/Faculty:** 20 to 1
Year: semesters, summer session	**Tuition:** $7942 ($19,957)
Room & Board: $7368	**Freshman Class:** 12056 applied, 9351 accepted, 4289 enrolled
SAT CR/M: 540/560 **ACT:** 25	**CEEB CODE:** 6546
Application Deadline: n/av	**VERY COMPETITIVE**

Oklahoma State University, founded in 1890, is a publicly funded land-grant institution, offering undergraduate programs in agricultural sciences and natural resources, arts and sciences, business, education, engineering, architecture, technology, and human environmental resources. Figures in the above capsule and in this profile are approximate. There are 6 undergraduate schools and 1 graduate school. In addition to regional accreditation, OSU has baccalaureate program accreditation with AACSB, ABET, ACEJMC, ADA, AHEA, ASLA, FIDER, NAAB, NASM, NCATE, NRPA, SAF, ACS, APA, ASLHA, and NAACLS. The 840-acre campus is in a small town 65 miles north of Oklahoma City.

STUDENT LIFE: 74% of undergraduates are from Oklahoma. Others are from 48 states, 128 foreign countries, and Canada. 70% are White. The average age of freshmen is 19; all undergraduates, 22. 21% do not continue beyond their first year; 79% remain to graduate. **Housing:** College-sponsored housing includes single-sex and coed dorms, on-campus apartments, off-campus apartments, and married student housing. In addition, there are honors houses, language houses, special-interest houses, fraternity houses, and sorority houses. On-campus housing is guaranteed for the freshman year only, and is available on a first-come, first-served basis. 55% of students commute. Alcohol is not permitted. All students may keep cars.

FACULTY/CLASSROOMS: 63% of faculty are male; 37% are female. Graduate students teach 19% of introductory courses. The average class size in an introductory lecture is 30 and in a laboratory is 21.

PROGRAMS OF STUDY: OSU confers B.A., B.S., B.Arch.,B.E.N., B.F.A., B.Land.Arch., B.M., B.S.A.E., B.S.A.G., B.S.B.A., B.S.B.E., B.S.C.H., B.S.C.P., B.S.C.V., B.S.E.E., B.S.E.T., B.S.I.E., B.S.M.E. and

B.U.S. degrees. Master's and Doctoral degrees are also awarded. Bachelor's degrees are awarded in AGRICULTURE (agricultural business management, agricultural communications, agricultural economics, animal science, horticulture, natural resource management, plant science, and soil science), BIOLOGICAL SCIENCE (biochemistry, biology/biological science, botany, cell biology, entomology, microbiology, molecular biology, nutrition, physiology, and zoology), BUSINESS (accounting, banking and finance, business administration and management, entrepreneurial studies, hotel/motel and restaurant management, international business management, management information systems, marketing/retailing/merchandising, and recreation and leisure services), COMMUNICATIONS AND THE ARTS (art, broadcasting, design, dramatic arts, English, French, German, journalism, music, Russian languages and literature, and Spanish), COMPUTER AND PHYSICAL SCIENCE (chemistry, computer science, geology, mathematics, physics, and statistics), EDUCATION (agricultural education, athletic training, education, elementary education, health education, music education, physical education, secondary education, and vocational education), ENGINEERING AND ENVIRONMENTAL DESIGN (aerospace studies, architectural engineering, architecture, bioengineering, chemical engineering, civil engineering, computer engineering, construction management, construction technology, electrical/electronics engineering, electrical/electronics engineering technology, environmental science, industrial administration/management, industrial engineering, landscape architecture/design, mechanical engineering, and mechanical engineering technology), HEALTH PROFESSIONS (speech pathology/audiology), SOCIAL SCIENCE (American studies, child care/child and family studies, economics, fire control and safety technology, food science, geography, history, human development, liberal arts/general studies, philosophy, political science/government, psychology, and sociology).

ACTIVITIES: There are 400 groups on campus, including art, band, cheerleading, choir, chorale, chorus, computers, dance, drama, environmental, ethnic, gay, honors, international, jazz band, literary magazine, marching band, musical theater, newspaper, opera, orchestra, pep band, political, professional, radio and TV, religious, social, social service, student government, and symphony. Popular campus events include Freshmen Follies, Salsa Ball, and African Night. **Sports:** There are 8 intercollegiate sports for men and 8 for women. Facilities include an recreation center, 10 basketball-volleyball courts, a large multipurpose court, 30,000 square feet of weight and fitness equipment, cardio-theater, indoor climbing wall, golf practice area including 2 golf simulators, a 3-lane jogging track, indoor and outdoor swimming pools, and 12 racquetball-handball courts. **Graduates:** From July 1, 2013 to June 30, 2014, 3775 bachelor's degrees were awarded. In an average class, 2% graduate in 3 years or less, 32% graduate in 4 years or less, 55% graduate in 5 years or less, and 61% graduate in 6 years or less.

SERVICES: Counseling and information services are available, as is tutoring in most subjects. There is a reader service for the blind, and remedial math, reading, and writing. Academic assessment and minority programs are also available. **Library/Resources:** The 5 libraries contain 3.5 million volumes, 4.6 million microform items, and 445,551 audio/video tapes/CDs/DVDs. Computerized library services include interlibrary loans, database searching, Internet access, and Wi-Fi capability. Special learning facilities include an art gallery and radio station. **Physically Challenged Students:** 99% of the campus is accessible. Facilities include wheelchair ramps, elevators, special parking, specially equipped restrooms, special class scheduling, lowered drinking fountains, lowered telephones, special housing. **Special:** OSU offers cross-registration with Northern Oklahoma College and Tulsa Community College, a Washington semester, and an internship program. A B.A.-B.S. degree, dual majors, an individualized university studies degree, multidisciplinary majors in biosystems engineering and in cell and molecular biology, nondegree study, and pass/fail options are available. Students may study abroad in several countries. The school also sponsors Semester at Sea, a 1-semester program of study on a ship traveling to ports throughout the world. There is a freshman honors program. **Visiting:** There are regularly scheduled orientations for prospective students, including personal meetings and tours. Appointments are scheduled with other campus departments, as needed, to assist prospective students. There are guides for informal visits, visitors may sit in on classes, and stay overnight. To schedule a visit, contact the Undergraduate Admissions Office. **Campus Safety and Security:** Measures include 24-hour foot and vehicle patrol, emergency notification system, self-defense education, and security escort services. There are shuttle buses, emergency telephones, lighted pathways/sidewalks, and controlled access to dorms/residences.

REQUIREMENTS: The SAT or ACT is required. Freshman applicants must have a cumulative high school GPA of 3.0 and rank in the upper third of their graduating class; or achieve at least a 24 composite score on the ACT or 1090 on the SAT; or have a 3.0 GPA in the required 15 curricular units, which include 4 years of English, 3 of math (algebra I and above), 2 each of history and lab science, 1 of citizenship skills, and 3 more from any of the above or computer science or foreign language, along with an ACT score of 21 or SAT score of 980. AP and CLEP credits are accepted. Important factors in the admissions decision are advanced placement or honors courses, evidence of special talent, and recommendations by school officials. To graduate, students must have a minimum GPA of 2.0 and at least 120 hours, including a minimum of 30 hours in the major for most programs. A higher GPA may be required in some majors. All students must take a minimum of 40 credit hours of core courses, including 6 each of English, humanities, analytical and quantitative thought, natural sciences, and social and behavioral sciences, 3 each of American history and government, and 1 each of scientific investigation and international studies. **Procedure:** Freshmen are admitted fall, spring, and summer. Entrance exams should be taken during the junior or senior year. There is a rolling admissions plan. Application deadlines are open. Application fee is $40. Applications are accepted on-line. **Transfer Students:** 1779 transfer students enrolled in 2013-2014. Applicants must submit official transcripts from all colleges attended. Students having fewer than 24 credit hours must also meet the requirements for entering freshmen and have a 2.25 GPA. Students that have earned 24-59 hours of college credit must achieve a minimum transfer GPA of 2.25 or higher in all college-level course work attempted. Students that have earned 60 or more hours of college credit must achieve a minimum transfer GPA of 2.0 or higher in all college-level course work attempted. 30 of 120 credits required for the bachelor's degree must be completed at OSU. **International Students:** There are 757 international students enrolled. The school actively recruits these students. They must take the TOEFL with a minimum score of 500 on the paper-based TOEFL (PBT) or 61 on the Internet-based version (iBT). They must also take the SAT or ACT, scoring 24.

ADMISSIONS: 78% of the 2014-2015 applicants were accepted. The SAT scores for the 2014-2015 freshman class were: Critical Reading--27% below 500, 48% between 500 and 599, 21% between 600 and 699, and 4% between 700 and 800; Math--19% below 500, 42% between 500 and 599, 33% between 600 and 699, and 6% between 700 and 800. The ACT scores were 13% below 21, 23% between 21 and 23, 31% between 24 and 26, 14% between 27 and 28, and 19% above 28. 48% of the current freshmen were in the top fifth of their class; 78% were in the top two fifths. There were 16 National Merit finalists. **Admissions Contact:** Christine Crenshaw, Director Undergraduate Admissions. E-Mail: *admission@okstate.edu* Web: *www.okstate.edu*

FINANCIAL AID: The FAFSA and the college's own financial statement are required. The priority date for freshman financial aid applications for fall entry is February 1. The deadline for filing freshman financial aid applications for fall entry is rolling.

OKLAHOMA WESLEYAN UNIVERSITY E-1
www.okwu.edu

Bartlesville, OK 74006	(918) 335-6219
	(866) 222-8226
Fax: (918) 335-6229	Email: admissions@okwu.edu
Full-time: 278 men, 290 women	Faculty: 31
Part-time: 163 men, 328 women	Ph.D.s: 48%
Graduate: n/av	Student/Faculty: 18 to 1
Year: semesters, summer session	Tuition: $20,160
Room & Board: $6874	Freshman Class: n/av
SAT or ACT: recommended	CEEB CODE: 6135
Application Deadline: n/av	COMPETITIVE

Oklahoma Wesleyan University, founded in 1909, is a private liberal arts institution affiliated with the Wesleyan Church. Figures in the above capsule and in this profile are approximate. There are 5 undergraduate schools and 1 graduate school. In addition to regional accreditation, OWU has baccalaureate program accreditation with NCATE, CCNE, and IACBE. The 101-acre campus is in a suburban area 40 miles north of Tulsa. Including any residence halls, there are 15 buildings.

STUDENT LIFE: 73% of undergraduates are from Oklahoma. Others are from 33 states and 9 foreign countries. 80% are from public schools. 83% are White. 74% are Protestant; 23% claim no religious affiliation. The average age of freshmen is 18; all undergraduates, 26. 20% do not continue beyond their first year; 60% remain to graduate. **Housing:** 315 students can be accommodated in college housing, which includes single-sex dorms. In addition, there are honors houses. On-campus housing is guaranteed for all 4 years. 69% of students commute. Alcohol is not permitted. All students may keep cars.

FACULTY/CLASSROOMS: 65% of faculty are male; 35% are female. All teach undergraduates. No introductory courses are taught by graduate students. The average class size in an introductory lecture is 20; in a laboratory is 20; and in a regular course is 20.

PROGRAMS OF STUDY: OWU confers B.A. and B.S. degrees. Associate and Master's degrees are also awarded. Bachelor's degrees are awarded in BIOLOGICAL SCIENCE (biology/biological science), BUSINESS (accounting, business administration and management, and human resources), COMMUNICATIONS AND THE ARTS (communications, English, and music), COMPUTER AND PHYSICAL SCIENCE (chemistry, mathematics, and science), EDUCATION (business education, elementary education, English education, mathematics education, middle school education, music education, physical education, science education, secondary education, and social studies education), HEALTH PROFESSIONS (predentistry and premedicine), SOCIAL SCIENCE (behavioral science, history, liberal arts/general studies, pastoral studies, political science/government, prelaw, religion, religious music, social studies, sociology, and youth ministry). Business and education are the strongest academically and have the largest enrollments.

ACTIVITIES: There are no fraternities or sororities. There are 10 groups on campus, including band, cheerleading, choir, chorale, chorus, computers, drama, ethnic, honors, international, musical theater, photography, political, professional, religious, social service, and student government. Popular campus events include Spiritual Emphasis Week and Youth Conference. **Sports:** There are 7 intercollegiate sports for men and 7 for women, and 10 intramural sports for men and 10 for women. Facilities include a 2000-seat indoor gym and an 8-acre athletic field. **Graduates:** The most popular majors were business/marketing (19%), biological/life science (18%), and parks/recreation (10%).

SERVICES: Counseling and information services are available, as is tutoring in most subjects. There is remedial math, reading, and writing. **Library/Resources:** The library contains 120,000 volumes, 20,000 microform items, 500 audio/video tapes/CDs/DVDs, and subscribes to 18,000 periodicals including electronic. Computerized library services include interlibrary loans and database searching. **Physically Challenged Students:** 73% of the campus is accessible. Facilities include wheelchair ramps, elevators, special parking, and specially equipped restrooms. **Special:** OWU offers cross-registration with Tri-County Tech, a Washington semester, a co-op program, internships, general studies degree, credit for life experience, and an accelerated degree program in business and the B.S.N. **Visiting:** There are regularly scheduled orientations for prospective students. There are guides for informal visits, visitors may sit in on classes, and stay overnight. To schedule a visit, contact the Enrollment Services Office. **Campus Safety and Security:** There are lighted pathways/sidewalks, and an evening patrol by a security guard.

REQUIREMENTS: The SAT or ACT is recommended. Graduation from an accredited secondary school or satisfactory scores on the GED are required for admission. 18 academic credits must be completed, including 4 credits of English and 2 credits each of history, math, science, and social studies. AP and CLEP credits are accepted. To graduate, students must complete a total of 126 credit hours with a minimum GPA of 2.0. About 40 hours are required in the major.

All students must take 9 hours of religion and a writing proficiency exam. **Procedure:** Freshmen are admitted to all sessions. Entrance exams should be taken during the senior year. There is a rolling admissions plan. Application deadlines are open. Application fee is $25. Applications are accepted on-line. **Transfer Students:** 54 transfer students enrolled in 2013-2014. Applicants must have a minimum GPA of 2.0. 24 of 126 credits required for the bachelor's degree must be completed at OWU. **International Students:** There are 16 international students enrolled. They must take the TOEFL or MELAB.

ADMISSIONS: Audrey Kelleher, Associate Vice President for Enrollment. E-Mail: *admissions@okwu.edu* Web: *www.okwu.edu*

FINANCIAL AID: In 2014-2015, 98% of all full-time freshmen and continuing full-time students received some form of financial aid. 90% of all full-time freshmen and continuing full-time students received need-based aid. 60% of undergraduate students work part-time. The average financial indebtedness of the 2014 graduate was $20,000. The FAFSA and the college's own financial statement are required. The deadline for filing freshman financial aid applications for fall entry is open.

ORAL ROBERTS UNIVERSITY E-2
www.oru.edu

Tulsa, OK 74171	**(918) 495-6529**
	(800) 678-8876
Fax: (918) 495-6222	**Email: admission@oru.edu**
Full-time: 1102 men, 1443 women	**Faculty:** 135; I
Part-time: 86 men, 151 women	**Ph.D.s:** 3%
Graduate: 249 men, 304 women	**Student/Faculty:** 15 to 1
Year: semesters, summer session	**Tuition:** $22,438
Room & Board: $9296	**Freshman Class:** 1557 applied, 811 accepted, 480 enrolled
SAT CR/M: 530/510 **ACT:** 22	**CEEB CODE:** 6552
Application Deadline: open	**COMPETITIVE**

Oral Roberts University, founded in 1963, is a private, Christian University located in Tulsa, Oklahoma. ORU offer more than 60 undergraduate degree programs, 13 master's degree programs and 2 doctoral degree programs. Figures in the above capsule and in this profile are approximate. There are 6 undergraduate schools and 3 graduate schools. In addition to regional accreditation, ORU has baccalaureate program accreditation with ABET, ACBSP, CSWE, NASM, NCATE, CCNE, ATS, and OCTP. The 400-acre campus is in an urban area in Tulsa, Oklahoma. Including any residence halls, there are 29 buildings.

STUDENT LIFE: 62% of undergraduates are from out of state, mostly the Mid-West. Students are from 48 states, 62 foreign countries, and Canada. 75% are from public schools. 42% are White; 11% African American. 98% are Protestant. The average age of freshmen is 19; all undergraduates, 22. 8% do not continue beyond their first year; 54% remain to graduate. **Housing:** 2218 students can be accommodated in college housing, which includes single-sex dorms and honors wings of several dorms. On-campus housing is available on a first-come, first-served basis. 75% of students live on campus; of those, 99% remain on campus on weekends. Alcohol is not permitted. All students may keep cars.

FACULTY/CLASSROOMS: 56% of faculty are male; 44% are female. And 84% do research. No introductory courses are taught by graduate students. The average class size in an introductory lecture is 30; in a laboratory is 20; and in a regular course is 20.

PROGRAMS OF STUDY: ORU confers B.A., B.S., B.M., B.Mus.Ed., B.S.E., B.S.N. and B.S.W. degrees. Master's and Doctoral degrees are also awarded. Bachelor's degrees are awarded in BIOLOGICAL SCIENCE (biology/biological science), BUSINESS (accounting, banking and finance, business administration and management, international business management, management information systems, management science, marketing/retailing/merchandising, organizational behavior, and recreation and leisure services), COMMUNICATIONS AND THE ARTS (applied art, broadcasting, communications, dance, dramatic arts, English, English literature, film arts, French, German, literature, music, music performance, music theory and composition, Spanish, speech/debate/rhetoric, and studio art), COMPUTER AND PHYSICAL SCIENCE (chemistry, computer science, mathematics, and physics), EDUCATION (art education, business education, drama education, early childhood education, elementary education, English education, foreign languages education, health education, mathematics education, music education, physical education, recreation education, science education, social studies education, and special education), ENGINEERING AND ENVIRONMENTAL DESIGN (bioengineering, commercial art, computer engineering, electrical/electronics engineering, engineering, engineering management, mechanical engineering, and preengineering), HEALTH PROFESSIONS (biomedical science, health science, medical laboratory technology, nursing, optometry, predentistry, and premedicine), SOCIAL SCIENCE (biblical studies, history, international relations, international studies, liberal arts/general studies, ministries, philosophy, political science/government, prelaw, psychology, religion, religious education, religious music, and social work). All science programs, music and theology are the strongest academically. Nursing, media, business, psychology, ministry and leadership have the largest enrollments.

ACTIVITIES: There are no fraternities or sororities. There are 40 groups on campus, including leadership, art, band, cheerleading, choir, chorale, chorus, computers, dance, debate, drama, environmental, ethnic, film, honors, international, jazz band, musical theater, newspaper, opera, pep band, photography, political, professional, radio and TV, religious, social, social service, student government, symphony, and yearbook. **Sports:** There are 8 intercollegiate sports for men and 8 for women, and 20 intramural sports for men and 20 for women. Facilities include a physical fitness center, track, tennis, racquetball, squash, volleyball, and basketball courts, and baseball and soccer fields. **Graduates:** From July 1, 2013 to June 30, 2014, 470 bachelor's degrees were awarded. The most popular majors were business marketing, theology and religious vocations, and communication/journalism.

SERVICES: Counseling and information services are available, as is tutoring in most subjects. There is a reader service for the blind, and remedial math, reading, and writing. **Library/Resources:** The library contains 487,000 volumes, 50,000 microform items, 18,000 audio/video tapes/CDs/DVDs, and subscribes to 65 periodicals including electronic. Computerized library services include interlibrary loans, database searching, Internet access, and Wi-Fi capability. Special learning facilities include a natural history museum, radio station, TV station, and a TV production studio. **Physically Challenged Students:** 90% of the campus is accessible. Facilities include wheelchair ramps, elevators, special parking, specially equipped restrooms, special class scheduling, lowered drinking fountains, and lowered telephones. **Special:** ORU offers combined B.A.-B.S. degrees, internships, 3-2 programs, a Washington semester, work-study programs, dual and student-designed majors, study abroad in 5 countries, independent study, nondegree study, an accelerated degree in business and education, and a liberal arts degree. An honors program/leadership academy is also offered. There are 4 national honor societies, a freshman honors program, and 12 departmental honors programs. **Visiting:** There are regularly scheduled orientations for prospective students, including College Weekend, which consists of visiting classes, meeting with faculty and staff, attending chapel services, and attending student life events. Visitors may sit in on classes and stay overnight. To schedule a visit, contact the Admissions Office at campusvisits@oru.edu. **Campus Safety and Security:** Measures include 24-hour foot and vehicle patrol, emergency notification system, self-defense education, and security escort services. There are shuttle buses, lighted pathways/sidewalks, and controlled access to dorms/residences.

REQUIREMENTS: The SAT or ACT is required. Students should be graduates of an accredited secondary school or hold a GED. High school preparation should include 4 years of English, 2 of math, including algebra and geometry or 2 years of algebra, and 2 each of foreign language, social studies, and science, including lab science. A recommendation from the student's minister is required. An academic recommendation and an interview are recommended. ORU requires applicants to be in the upper 40% of their class. A GPA of 2.6 is required. AP and CLEP credits are accepted. Important factors

in the admissions decision are advanced placement or honors courses, evidence of special talent, and leadership record. A minimum of 128 credit hours, with a minimum of 30 hours in the major, and a 2.0 GPA are required to graduate. All students must complete specific courses in the Bible, theology, and English, plus 12 hours in social sciences, 11 in biological, physical, and mathematical sciences, 6 to 7 in a modern foreign language, 3 in communication arts, and 2 in fine arts. 1 physical activity course is required per semester, along with regular, semiweekly chapel attendance. A senior paper must be completed in most majors. **Procedure:** Freshmen are admitted to all sessions. Entrance exams should be taken the last semester of the junior year or during senior year. There are deferred admissions and rolling admissions plans. Application deadlines are open. Application fee is $35. Applications are accepted on-line. **Transfer Students:** 238 transfer students enrolled in 2013-2014. An official transcript showing honorable dismissal from each previous institution is required. 30 of 128 credits required for the bachelor's degree must be completed at ORU. **International Students:** There are 167 international students enrolled. They must take the TOEFL with a minimum score of 500 on the paper-based TOEFL (PBT) or 61 on the Internet-based version (iBT). They must also take the SAT or ACT.

ADMISSIONS: 52% of the 2014-2015 applicants were accepted. The SAT scores for the 2014-2015 freshman class were: Critical Reading--32% below 500, 43% between 500 and 599, 19% between 600 and 699, and 7% between 700 and 800; Math--44% below 500, 33% between 500 and 599, 18% between 600 and 699, and 5% between 700 and 800. The ACT scores were 35% below 21, 28% between 21 and 23, 21% between 24 and 26, 9% between 27 and 28, and 8% above 28. 36% of the current freshmen were in the top fifth of their class; 64% were in the top two fifths. There were 7 National Merit finalists. 21 freshmen graduated first in their class. **Admissions Contact:** Chris Belcher, Admissions. E-Mail: *admission@oru.edu* Web: *www.oru.edu*

FINANCIAL AID: In 2014-2015, 75% of all full-time freshmen and 69% of continuing full-time students received some form of financial aid. 74% of all full-time freshmen and 66% of continuing full-time students received need-based aid. The average freshman award was $15,320. Need-based scholarships or need-based grants averaged $9,759; need-based self-help aid (loans and jobs) averaged $6,443; non-need-based athletic scholarships averaged $19,354; other non-need-based awards and non-need-based scholarships averaged $6,871; and $6,534 from other forms of aid. 101% of undergraduate students work part-time. Average annual earnings from campus work are $840. The average financial indebtedness of the 2014 graduate was $34,555. The FAFSA, and the federal income tax return are required. The priority date for freshman financial aid applications for fall entry is March 15. The deadline for filing freshman financial aid applications for fall entry is July 30.

SOUTHEASTERN OKLAHOMA STATE UNIVERSITY (*The complete profile is made available exclusively on our website, www. barronspac.com*)

SOUTHERN NAZARENE UNIVERSITY   D-3
www.snu.edu

Bethany, OK 73008	**(405) 491-6324**
	(800) 648-9899
Fax: (405) 491-6320	Email: admiss@snu.edu
Full-time: 759 men, 843 women	**Faculty:** 74
Part-time: 23 men, 28 women	**Ph.D.s:** 74%
Graduate: 178 men, 279 women	**Student/Faculty:** 15 to 1
Year: semesters, summer session	**Tuition:** $17,664
Room & Board: $6690	**Freshman Class:** 852 applied, 852 accepted, 284 enrolled
SAT: required **ACT:** 23	**CEEB CODE:** 6036
Application Deadline: August 10	**COMPETITIVE**

Southern Nazarene University, founded in 1899, is a private institution affiliated with the Church of the Nazarene. It offers programs in liberal arts and sciences, health fields, business, and education. Figures in the above capsule and in this profile are approximate. There are 3 undergraduate schools and 1 graduate school. In addition to regional accreditation, SNU has baccalaureate program accreditation with NASM, NCATE, and NLN. The 40-acre campus is in a suburban area 10 miles northwest of Oklahoma City. Including any residence halls, there are 20 buildings.

STUDENT LIFE: 70% of undergraduates are from Oklahoma. Others are from 36 states, 34 foreign countries, and Canada. 73% are White; 11% African American. 45% are Protestant; 19% claim no religious affiliation. The average age of freshmen is 18; all undergraduates, 22. 12% do not continue beyond their first year; 49% remain to graduate.

Housing: 800 students can be accommodated in college housing, which includes single-sex dorms and on-campus apartments. On-campus housing is guaranteed for all 4 years. 68% of students live on campus; of those, 80% remain on campus on weekends. Alcohol is not permitted. All students may keep cars.

FACULTY/CLASSROOMS: 50% of faculty are male; 50% are female. All teach undergraduates. No introductory courses are taught by graduate students. The average class size in an introductory lecture is 20 and in a laboratory is 15.

PROGRAMS OF STUDY: SNU confers A.B., B.Mus.Ed. and B.S. degrees. Associate and Master's degrees are also awarded. Bachelor's degrees are awarded in AGRICULTURE (environmental studies), BIOLOGICAL SCIENCE (biochemistry, biology/biological science, and biophysics), BUSINESS (accounting, banking and finance, business administration and management, management information systems, management science, marketing/retailing/merchandising, sports management, and sports marketing), COMMUNICATIONS AND THE ARTS (communications, English, graphic design, journalism, music, music business management, music performance, Spanish, speech/debate/rhetoric, and sports media), COMPUTER AND PHYSICAL SCIENCE (chemistry, computer science, mathematics, physics, and science), EDUCATION (athletic training, Christian education, early childhood education, education, elementary education, English education, mathematics education, music education, physical education, science education, social studies education, and sports studies), ENGINEERING AND ENVIRONMENTAL DESIGN (aviation administration/management and systems engineering), HEALTH PROFESSIONS (exercise science and nursing), SOCIAL SCIENCE (American studies, history, human development, international studies, Latin American studies, missions, philosophy, physical fitness/movement, political science/government, psychology, religious music, sociology, Spanish studies, theological studies, urban studies, and youth ministry). Premedicine, physics, and theology are the strongest academically. Business and education have the largest enrollments.

ACTIVITIES: There are no fraternities or sororities. There are 40 groups on campus, including band, cheerleading, choir, chorale, chorus, computers, drama, drum and bugle corps, honors, international, jazz band, literary magazine, musical theater, newspaper, opera, orchestra, pep band, photography, political, professional, religious, social, social service, student government, symphony, and yearbook. Popular campus events include Valentine Banquet, Fall Fest, and Yule Feast. **Sports:** There are 7 intercollegiate sports for men and 7 for women, and 3 intramural sports for men and 3 for women. Facilities include an 1,824-seat phys ed center, gyms, a soccer complex, tennis courts, and a new athletic convocation center that seats 4,000. **Graduates:** From July 1, 2013 to June 30, 2014, 540 bachelor's degrees were awarded. The most popular majors were organizational leadership (36%), business administration (11%), and nursing (10%). In an average class, 2% graduate in 3 years or less, 31% graduate in 4 years or less, 42% graduate in 5 years or less, and 49% graduate in 6 years or less.

SERVICES: Counseling and information services are available, as is tutoring in most subjects. There is remedial math, reading, and writing. Services may be arranged for deaf or learning-disabled students. **Library/Resources:** The library contains 101,901 volumes, 332,461 microform items, and 4,360 audio/video tapes/CDs/DVDs. Computerized library services include interlibrary loans, database searching, Internet access, and Wi-Fi capability. **Physically Challenged Students:** All of the campus is accessible. Facilities include wheelchair ramps, elevators, special parking, specially equipped restrooms, special class scheduling, lowered drinking fountains, lowered telephones.

Dorm rooms may be adapted for disabled students. **Special:** Cross-registration and co-op programs are available through the Southwestern Colleges of Christian Ministry. Internships may be arranged in the major. A Washington semester, accelerated degree programs, study abroad in England, Russia, Costa Rica, Australia, China, and Egypt through the Council of Christian Colleges and Universities, work-study programs in sociology, and dual and student-designed majors are available. SNU offers nondegree study for life/military/work experience. There are 6 national honor societies, including Phi Beta Kappa, and a freshman honors program. **Visiting:** There are regularly scheduled orientations for prospective students, including visits with faculty and students and seminars on financial aid and admissions. There are campus tours, group social activities, and small group mentoring throughout the fall semester. There are guides for informal visits, visitors may sit in on classes, and stay overnight. To schedule a visit, contact the Office of Admissions. **Campus Safety and Security:** Measures include 24-hour foot and vehicle patrol, emergency notification system, self-defense education, and security escort services. There are lighted pathways/sidewalks, 24-hour controlled access into dorms.

REQUIREMENTS: The SAT or ACT is required. Applicants must be graduates of an accredited secondary school or have a GED. AP and CLEP credits are accepted. Important factors in the admissions decision are advanced placement or honors courses, extracurricular activities record, and leadership record. A total of 124 semester hours, including at least 32 hours in the major, with a minimum GPA of 2.0, is required to graduate. All students must complete 53 hours of general education requirements covering core areas of self and identity, faith and tradition, and service and society. Skills courses must be taken in computer science, composition, speech communication, math, natural science, citizenship, foreign language, and phys ed. **Procedure:** Freshmen are admitted fall and spring. Entrance exams should be taken by April of the senior year or at orientation. There are early admissions, deferred admissions, and rolling admissions plans. Applications should be filed by August 10 for fall entry. **Transfer Students:** 92 transfer students enrolled in 2013-2014. Transfer applicants must have a 2.0 GPA and be in good standing at their previous college. 30 of 124 credits required for the bachelor's degree must be completed at SNU. **International Students:** There are 52 international students enrolled. They must take the TOEFL with a minimum score of 500 on the paper-based TOEFL (PBT) or 61 on the Internet-based version (iBT).

ADMISSIONS: 100% of the 2014-2015 applicants were accepted. The ACT scores were 36% below 21, 26% between 21 and 23, 18% between 24 and 26, 8% between 27 and 28, and 12% above 28. 32% of the current freshmen were in the top fifth of their class; 53% were in the top two fifths. There were 3 National Merit finalists. **Admissions Contact:** Todd Brant, Director of Recruitment. E-Mail: admiss@snu.edu Web: www.snu.edu

FINANCIAL AID: In 2014-2015, 90% of all full-time freshmen and 90% of continuing full-time students received some form of financial aid. The FAFSA is required. Check with the school for current application deadlines.

SOUTHWESTERN OKLAHOMA STATE UNIVERSITY

D-3

www.swosu.edu

Weatherford, OK 73096	**(580) 774-3009**
	n/av
Fax: (580) 774-3795	**Email:** phillic@swosu.edu
Full-time: 1655 men, 2044 women	**Faculty:** 184; IIA
Part-time: 256 men, 562 women	**Ph.D.s:** 62%
Graduate: 362 men, 461 women	**Student/Faculty:** 20 to 1
Year: semesters, summer session	**Tuition:** $5300 ($11,360)
Room & Board: $4860	**Freshman Class:** 1717 applied, 1585 accepted, 986 enrolled
ACT: 21	**CEEB CODE:** 6673
Application Deadline: n/av	**COMPETITIVE**

Southwestern Oklahoma State University, founded in 1901, is a public institution offering programs in education, arts and sciences, business, health sciences, and pharmacy. Figures in the above capsule and in this profile are approximate. There are 4 undergraduate schools and 3 graduate schools. In addition to regional accreditation, SWOSU has baccalaureate program accreditation with ABET, ABHES, ACBSP, ACPE, APTA, CAHEA, CSWE, NASM, NCATE, NLN, ACS, CAAHEP, ACOTE, JRCERT, and NAMT. The 73-acre campus is in a small town 70 miles west of Oklahoma City. Including any residence halls, there are 30 buildings.

STUDENT LIFE: 11% of undergraduates are from out of state, mostly the Southwest. Students are from 37 states, 36 foreign countries, and Canada. 98% are from public schools. 79% are White. The average age of freshmen is 19; all undergraduates, 23. 36% do not continue beyond their first year; 32% remain to graduate. **Housing:** 1255 students can be accommodated in college housing, which includes single-sex dorms and married student housing. On-campus housing is guaranteed for all 4 years. 75% of students commute. Alcohol is not permitted. All students may keep cars.

FACULTY/CLASSROOMS: 58% of faculty are male; 42% are female. All teach undergraduates, 10% do research, and 10% do both. Graduate students teach 1% of introductory courses. The average class size in a laboratory is 15 and in a regular course is 27.

PROGRAMS OF STUDY: SWOSU confers B.A., B.S., B.A.Ed., B.Art, B.B.A., B.Comm.Art, B.Gen.Tech., B.M., B.M.Ed., B.Rec., B.S.Ed., B.S.Eng.Tech., B.S.H.I.M., B.S.M.T., B.S.N. and B.S.P. degrees. Associate, Master's, and doctoral degrees are also awarded. Bachelor's degrees are awarded in BIOLOGICAL SCIENCE (biology/biological science and biophysics), BUSINESS (accounting, banking and finance, business administration and management, management information systems, management science, marketing/retailing/merchandising, and recreational facilities management), COMMUNICATIONS AND THE ARTS (communications, English, and graphic design), COMPUTER AND PHYSICAL SCIENCE (chemistry, computer programming, computer science, information sciences and systems, mathematics, natural sciences, and physics), EDUCATION (art education, athletic training, education administration, elementary education, English education, health education, industrial arts education, mathematics education, music education, physical education, school psychology, science education, secondary education, social science education, special education, and technical education), ENGINEERING AND ENVIRONMENTAL DESIGN (computer engineering, electrical/electronics engineering technology, engineering physics, engineering technology, environmental engineering technology, industrial administration/management, industrial engineering technology, manufacturing engineering, and manufacturing technology), HEALTH PROFESSIONS (health care administration, health science, medical records administration/services, medical technology, music therapy, and nursing), SOCIAL SCIENCE (community psychology, criminal justice, history, political science/government, psychology, and social work). Chemistry is the strongest academically. Business and education have the largest enrollments.

ACTIVITIES: 7% of men belong to 2 local and 1 national fraternities; 5% of women belong to 3 local sororities. There are 66 groups on campus, including art, band, cheerleading, choir, chorale, chorus, computers, debate, drama, drill team, ethnic, forensics, honors, international, jazz band, marching band, musical theater, newspaper, opera, orchestra, pep band, political, professional, religious, social, social service, student government, and symphony. Popular campus events include Howdy Week, Miss Southwestern Pageant, and Panorama Series. **Sports:** There are 6 intercollegiate sports for men and 6 for women, and 8 intramural sports for men and 8 for women. Facilities include a weight room, an indoor pool, outdoor track, tennis courts, outdoor football field and baseball diamond, 2 football practice fields, a rodeo arena, an exercise equipment room, ropes course, and a lake. A soccer practice field, sand volleyball courts, and outdoor basketball courts are also available. **Graduates:** From July 1, 2013 to June 30, 2014, 629 bachelor's degrees were awarded. The most popular majors were business/marketing (22%), health professions and related sciences (20%), and education (17%).

SERVICES: Counseling and information services are available, as is tutoring in some subjects. There is remedial math, reading, and writing. A student development center offers counseling and tutoring on an individual basis. **Library/Resources:** The library contains 287,572 volumes, 1.2 million microform items, 872 audio/video tapes/CDs/DVDs, and subscribes to 1,551 periodicals including electronic. Computerized library services include interlibrary loans and database searching. **Physically Challenged Students:** 98% of the campus is accessible. Facilities include wheelchair ramps, elevators, special parking, specially equipped restrooms, special class scheduling, lowered drinking fountains, and lowered telephones. **Special:** SWOSU offers work-study programs and a program allowing high school seniors to earn college credits. Preprofessional curricula are offered in numerous areas including medicine, law, engineering, and allied health professions. There are 4 national honor societies. **Visiting:** There are regularly scheduled orientations for prospective students, including counseling sessions on careers, financial aid, social activities, and enrollment procedures. There are guides for informal visits, visitors may sit in on classes, and stay overnight. To schedule a visit, contact the Director of High School and College. **Campus Safety and Security:** Measures include 24-hour foot and vehicle patrol and self-defense education. There are emergency telephones and lighted pathways/sidewalks.

REQUIREMENTS: The ACT is required. Applicants must have a minimum composite score of 19. Applicants should be graduates of an accredited secondary school. The GED is accepted. Students should present at least 15 academic credits, including 4 in English, 3 in math, 2 each in history and lab science, 1 in citizenship, and 3 additional units in computer science or foreign language. A GPA of 2.7 is required. AP and CLEP credits are accepted. To graduate, students must complete 124 semester hours with a minimum GPA of 2.0. Distribution requirements include 8 hours in communication and natural sciences, 6 each in history and government, fine arts and humanities, and international and cultural studies, 3 each in economics, health and phys ed, behavioral/social science, and math, and 2 in computer applications. **Procedure:** Freshmen are admitted to all sessions. Entrance exams should be taken during the senior year. There is a rolling admissions plan. Check with the school for current application deadlines. The fall 2014 application fee was $15. Notification is sent on a rolling basis. **Transfer Students:** Applicants must have a minimum college GPA of 2.0 and submit official transcripts from all institutions attended. 30 of 124 credits required for the bachelor's degree must be completed at SWOSU. **International Students:** They must take the TOEFL. They must also take the SAT or ACT, scoring 19.

ADMISSIONS: 92% of the 2014-2015 applicants were accepted. **Admissions Contact:** Connie Phillips, Admissions Coordinator. E-Mail: *phillic@swosu.edu* Web: *www.swosu.edu*

FINANCIAL AID: The FAFSA and the college's own financial statement are required. Check with the school for current application deadlines.

ST. GREGORY'S UNIVERSITY (*The complete profile is made available exclusively on our website, www.barronspac.com*)

THE UNIVERSITY OF OKLAHOMA	D-3
www.ou.edu	
Norman, OK 73019	**(405) 325-0311**
	(405) 325-2252
Fax: (405) 325-7124	Email: admrec@ou.edu
Full-time: 9168 men, 8817 women	Faculty: 1123
Part-time: 1636 men, 1390 women	Ph.D.s: 85%
Graduate: 3134 men, 3116 women	Student/Faculty: 18 to 1
Year: semesters, summer session	Tuition: $9495 ($22,269)
Room & Board: $9126	Freshman Class: 11331 applied, 9216 accepted, 4176 enrolled
SAT CR/M: 590/608 ACT: 26	CEEB CODE: 6879
Application Deadline: April 1	VERY COMPETITIVE

The University of Oklahoma, founded in 1890, is a comprehensive research university offering 160 different majors for undergraduate study. There are 13 undergraduate schools and 13 graduate schools.

In addition to regional accreditation, OU has baccalaureate program accreditation with AACSB, ABET, ACCE, ACEJMC, CSWE, NAAB, NASM, NCATE, NAST, EAC, and APA. The 3304-acre campus is in a suburban area 20 miles south of Oklahoma City. Including any residence halls, there are 257 buildings.

STUDENT LIFE: 66% of undergraduates are from Oklahoma. Others are from 50 states, 122 foreign countries, and Canada. 62% are White. The average age of freshmen is 18; all undergraduates, 22. 16% do not continue beyond their first year; 66% remain to graduate. **Housing:** 5940 students can be accommodated in college housing, which includes single-sex and coed dorms, on-campus apartments, and married student housing. In addition, there are honors houses, international floors, honors house, cultural housing, national merit, scholastic and quiet lifestyle floors. On-campus housing is guaranteed for the freshman year only, and is available on a first-come, first-served basis. 67% of students commute. Alcohol is not permitted. All students may keep cars.

FACULTY/CLASSROOMS: 62% of faculty are male; 38% are female. Graduate students teach 36% of introductory courses. The average class size in an introductory lecture is 42; in a laboratory is 21; and in a regular course is 38.

PROGRAMS OF STUDY: OU confers B.A., B.S., B.Arch., B.B.A., B.F.A., B.Int.Des., B.Mus.Arts, B.Mus.Ed. and B.Mus. degrees. Master's and Doctoral degrees are also awarded. Bachelor's degrees are awarded in AGRICULTURE (environmental studies), BIOLOGICAL SCIENCE (biochemistry, botany, microbiology, and zoology), BUSINESS (accounting, business administration and management, business economics, finance, human resources, management information systems, marketing, and organizational behavior), COMMUNICATIONS AND THE ARTS (advertising, Arabic, art, art history and appreciation, broadcasting, Chinese, classical languages, classics, communications, dance, dramatic arts, English, film arts, French, German, Italian, journalism, language arts, languages, linguistics, literature, music, music performance, musical theater, Russian languages and literature, Spanish, and video), COMPUTER AND PHYSICAL SCIENCE (astronomy, astrophysics, atmospheric sciences and meteorology, chemistry, computer science, environmental geology, geology, geophysics and seismology, information sciences and systems, mathematics, and physics), EDUCATION (early childhood education, elementary education, foreign languages education, mathematics education, music education, science education, social studies education, and special education), ENGINEERING AND ENVIRONMENTAL DESIGN (aeronautical engineering, architectural engineering, architecture, aviation administration/management, chemical engineering, civil engineering, computer engineering, construction management, electrical/electronics engineering, engineering, engineering physics, environmental design, environmental engineering, environmental science, geological engineering, geophysical engineering, industrial engineering, interior design, mechanical engineering, and petroleum/natural gas engineering), HEALTH PROFESSIONS (exercise science and health care administration), SOCIAL SCIENCE (African American studies, anthropology, area studies, criminal justice, economics, geography, geography information science, history, history of science, humanities, interdisciplinary studies, international studies, Judaic studies, liberal arts/general studies, Native American studies, philosophy, political science/government, psychology, public administration, religion, social work, sociology, and women's studies). Chemistry, finance and accounting, meteorology, petroleum and geology have the largest enrollments.

ACTIVITIES: 27% of men belong to 1 local and 29 national fraternities; 32% of women belong to 1 local and 19 national sororities. There are 397 groups on campus, including art, band, cheerleading, chess, choir, chorale, chorus, computers, dance, debate, drama, drill team, environmental, ethnic, film, forensics, gay, honors, international, jazz band, literary magazine, marching band, musical theater, newspaper, opera, orchestra, pep band, photography, political, professional, radio and TV, religious, social, social service, student government, symphony, and yearbook. Popular campus events include CAC Homecoming, Eve of Nations, Pink and Black Ball, and CAC Soonerthon. **Sports:** There are 10 intercollegiate sports for men and 11 for women, and 25 intramural sports for men and 25 for women. Facilities include a golf course, field house, arena, gymnastics center, tennis courts, swimming pool complex, fitness center, football stadium, track and field facilities, baseball, soccer, and softball fields, 25 acres of turf grass maintained for intramural and recreational use and an indoor rowing facility. **Graduates:** From July 1, 2013 to June 30, 2014, 4063 bachelor's degrees were awarded. The most popular majors were multidisciplinary studies (11%), psychology (4%), and finance (3%). 2602 companies recruited on campus in 2013-2014. In an average class, 2% graduate in 3 years or less, 35% graduate in 4 years or less, 60% graduate in 5 years or less, and 66% graduate in 6 years or less.

SERVICES: Counseling and information services are available, as is tutoring in some subjects. There is a reader service for the blind, and remedial math, reading, and writing. There are also volunteer note takers, interpreter and real-time reporting services for the deaf or hearing impaired, and alternative testing services. **Library/Resources:** The 9 libraries contain 5.4 million volumes, 3.6 million microform items, 12,911 audio/video tapes/CDs/DVDs, and subscribe to 158,361 periodicals including electronic. Computerized library services include interlibrary loans, database searching, Internet access, and Wi-Fi capability. Special learning facilities include an art gallery, natural history museum, radio station, TV station, an observatory. **Physically Challenged Students:** 95% of the campus is accessible. Facilities include wheelchair ramps, elevators, special parking, specially equipped restrooms, special class scheduling, lowered drinking fountains, lowered telephones, special housing. **Special:** Co-op programs are available in Arts and Sciences, Business, and Engineering. A variety of voluntary and required internships is available in more than 50 fields of study. OU offers study abroad in over 50 countries, work-study programs, a Washington semester, a general studies degree, dual and student-designed majors, nondegree study, pass/fail options, and credit for life experience. B.A.-B.S. degrees are offered in many subjects and an accelerated degree is offered in 15 majors. The interdisciplinary major in Letters combines the classics, history, philosophy, and languages. There are 17 national honor societies, including Phi Beta Kappa, and a freshman honors program. **Visiting:** There are regularly scheduled orientations for prospective students, consisting of sessions tailored to individual needs and interests. There are guides for informal visits, visitors may sit in on classes, and stay overnight. To schedule a visit, contact the Prospective Student Services. **Campus Safety and Security:** Measures include 24-hour foot and vehicle patrol, emergency notification system, self-defense education, and security escort services. There are shuttle buses, emergency telephones, lighted pathways/sidewalks, controlled access to dorms/residences, a bicycle patrol, and safe ride program.

REQUIREMENTS: The SAT or ACT is required. Applicants will be considered for admission using a holistic review and selection process which considers several factors that predict academic success (i.e. high school grade point average, high school course rigor, academic engagement, writing ability, leadership and ACT/SAT scores). Students must have a total of 15 curricular units, including 4 units of English, 3 units of math, 3 units of lab science, 1 unit of American history, 2 units of citizenship skills, and 2 elective units from areas previously mentioned or computer science or foreign language. AP and CLEP credits are accepted. To graduate, students must have a minimum 2.0 GPA, depending on the major, and complete a minimum of 120 semester hours, the last 30 hours of which must be in residence. The number of hours required in the major varies. A 40-hour general education core includes courses in arts and humanities, oral and symbolic communication, natural science, and social science. Seniors must take a 3-credit-hour capstone experience course integrating their undergraduate studies, and it must include writing. **Procedure:** Freshmen are admitted to all sessions. Entrance exams should be taken during the junior year or the first part of the senior year. There is a rolling admissions plan. Applications should be filed by April 1 for fall entry; November 1 for spring entry; and March 1 for summer entry, along with a $40 fee. Notification is sent on a rolling basis. 897 applicants were on the 2014 waiting list; 221 were admitted. Applications are accepted on-line. **Transfer Students:** 1147 transfer students enrolled in 2013-2014. Applicants with 60 or more semester hours attempted must have a minimum GPA of 2.00. The College of Architecture, College of Atmospheric and Geographic Sciences, College of Business, College of Earth and Energy and College of Fine Arts require a 2.5. The College of Education and College of Journalism and Mass Communication require a 2.75. Nonresident engineering applicants must have a minimum GPA of 3.0. Applicants with fewer than 24 semester hours of college-level work must also meet freshman admission requirements. Applicants must be in good standing at the last institution attended. 30 of 120 credits required for the bachelor's degree must be completed at OU. **International Students:** There are 1119 international students enrolled. The school actively recruits these students. They must take the TOEFL with a minimum score of 79 on the Internet-based version (iBT).

ADMISSIONS: 81% of the 2014-2015 applicants were accepted. The SAT scores for the 2014-2015 freshman class were: Critical Reading--18% below 500, 39% between 500 and 599, 24% between 600 and 699, and 19% between 700 and 800; Math--11% below 500, 35% between 500 and 599, 35% between 600 and 699, and 19% between 700 and 800. The ACT scores were 6% below 21, 21% between 21 and 23, 29% between 24 and 26, 14% between 27 and 28, and 30% above 28. 56% of the current freshmen were in the top fifth of their class; 84% were in the top two fifths. There were 311 National Merit finalists. 305 freshmen graduated first in their class. **Admissions Contact:** Jeffrey Blahnik, Director of Admissions. E-Mail: *admrec@ou.edu* Web: *www.ou.edu*

FINANCIAL AID: 15% of undergraduate students work part-time. Average annual earnings from campus work are $7491. The average financial indebtedness of the 2014 graduate was $22,274. OU is a member of CSS. The FAFSA is required. The priority date for freshman financial aid applications for fall entry is March 1.

UNIVERSITY OF CENTRAL OKLAHOMA   D-2
www.uco.edu

Edmond, OK 73034	**(405) 974-2000**
	(405) 944-2727
Fax: 405-974-3841	Email: 4ucoinfo@uco.edu
Full-time: 4782 men, 6199 women	Faculty: 466; IIA, --$
Part-time: 1862 men, 2524 women	Ph.D.s: 75%
Graduate: 526 men, 1324 women	Student/Faculty: 21 to 1
Year: semesters, summer session	Tuition: $5437 ($13,552)
Room & Board: $6856	Freshman Class: 4939 applied, 3945 accepted, 2223 enrolled
ACT: 21	CEEB CODE: 6091
Application Deadline: n/av	COMPETITIVE

University of Central Oklahoma, founded in 1890, is a state-supported institution offering undergraduate and graduate programs in the liberal arts and sciences, education, business, and music. There are 5 undergraduate schools and 1 graduate school. In addition to regional accreditation, UCO has baccalaureate program accreditation with ABET, ABFSE, ACBSP, ADA, NASM, NCATE, and NLN. The 200-acre campus is in a suburban area north of Oklahoma City. Including any residence halls, there are 51 buildings.

STUDENT LIFE: 88% of undergraduates are from Oklahoma. Others are from 46 states, 86 foreign countries, and Canada. 83% are from public schools. 59% are White. The average age of freshmen is 20; all undergraduates, 24. 35% do not continue beyond their first year; 36% remain to graduate.

FACULTY/CLASSROOMS: 46% of faculty are male; 54% are female. Graduate students teach 2% of introductory courses. The average class size in an introductory lecture is 31 and in a laboratory is 26.

PROGRAMS OF STUDY: UCO confers B.A., B.S., B.A.Ed., B.B.A., B.F.A., B.F.A.Ed., B.M.Ed., B.Mus., B.A.T., and B.S.Ed. degrees. Master's degrees are also awarded. Bachelor's degrees are awarded in BIOLOGICAL SCIENCE (biology/biological science, forensic psychology, forensic science, and nutrition), BUSINESS (accounting, banking and finance, business administration and management, fashion merchandising, finance, funeral home services, human resources, insurance, management information systems, and marketing/retailing/merchandising), COMMUNICATIONS AND THE ARTS (advertising, art history, art, broadcasting, communications, creative writing, dance, English, English as a second/foreign language, French, German, graphic design, journalism, music, photography, piano performance, public relations, Spanish, theatre acting, theatre arts, the-

ater design, and theatre studies), COMPUTER AND PHYSICAL SCIENCE (actuarial science, applied mathematics, chemistry, computer science, and mathematics), EDUCATION (art education, athletic training, bilingual/bicultural education, dance education, early childhood education, elementary education, English education, foreign languages education, general studies, mathematics education, museum studies, music education, physical education, science education, secondary education, social studies education, and special education), ENGINEERING AND ENVIRONMENTAL DESIGN (biomedical engineering, electrical/electronics engineering, engineering, engineering physics, and interior design), HEALTH PROFESSIONS (allied health, art therapy, community health work, exercise science, industrial hygiene, nursing, predentistry, premedicine, preoptometry, and speech pathology/audiology), SOCIAL SCIENCE (addiction studies, child psychology/development, criminal justice, economics, family/consumer studies, forensic studies, geography, gerontology, history, humanities, legal studies, liberal arts/general studies, philosophy, physical fitness/movement, political science/government, psychology, public administration, and sociology). Nursing, speech/language pathology, educational leadership, and forensic science are the strongest academically. Nursing, accounting, and psychology have the largest enrollments.

ACTIVITIES: 6% of men belong to 11 national fraternities; 6% of women belong to 8 national sororities. There are 200 groups on campus, including art, band, cheerleading, choir, chorus, communications, computers, dance, debate, drama, drum and bugle corps, ethnic, film, gay, honors, international, jazz band, literary magazine, marching band, musical theater, newspaper, opera, orchestra, pep band, photography, political, professional, radio and TV, religious, social, student government, and yearbook. Popular campus events include Homecoming, Earth Day, May Day, The Big Event, Winterglow, International Festival, Big Pink Volleyball, and Miss UCO.

SERVICES: Counseling and information services are available, as is tutoring in some subjects. There is a reader service for the blind, and remedial math. **Library/Resources:** The library contains 526,153 volumes, 578,619 microform items, 39,845 audio/video tapes/CDs/DVDs, and subscribes to 29,549 periodicals including electronic. Computerized library services include interlibrary loans, database searching, Internet access, and Wi-Fi capability. Special learning facilities include an art gallery, radio station, and TV station. **Physically Challenged Students:** Facilities include wheelchair ramps, elevators, special parking, specially equipped restrooms, special class scheduling, and lowered drinking fountains. **Special:** There is cross-registration with the Downtown Consortium. Opportunities are provided for internships, B.A.-B.S. degrees, dual majors, a general studies degree, credit by exam, nondegree study, and credit for military experience. Work-study programs may be arranged through the Federal College Work-Study Program. There are 6 national honor societies. **Visiting:** There are regularly scheduled orientations for prospective students, including a brief tour, a question-and-answer period, and access to an information booth. There are guides for informal visits. To schedule a visit, contact Gina Hickey at ghickey@uco.edu. **Campus Safety and Security:** Measures include 24-hour foot and vehicle patrol, emergency notification system, and security escort services. There are emergency telephones, lighted pathways/sidewalks, crime and terrorism tip line.

REQUIREMENTS: The ACT is required. Graduation from an accredited secondary school is required and a GED is accepted. The applicant's academic record should include 4 units of English; 3 units of math (first-year algebra and beyond); 3 units of lab science; and 3 units of history, of which 1 year must be in American history. UCO requires applicants to be in the upper 50% of their class. A GPA of 2.7 is required. AP and CLEP credits are accepted. Important factors in the admissions decision are evidence of special talent, extracurricular activities record, and leadership record.

ADMISSIONS: 80% of a recent year applicants were accepted. The ACT scores were 35% below 21, 33% between 21 and 23, 19% between 24 and 26, 7% between 27 and 28, and 6% above 28. 29% of the current freshmen were in the top fifth of their class; 59% were in the top two fifths.

FINANCIAL AID: In a recent year, 82% of all full-time freshmen and 71% of continuing full-time students received some form of financial aid. 55% of all full-time freshmen and 53% of continuing full-time students received need-based aid. The average freshman award was $6,970. Need-based scholarships or need-based grants averaged $2,832; need-based self-help aid (loans and jobs) averaged $2,289; and non-need-based athletic scholarships averaged $197. 13% of undergraduate students work part-time. Average annual earnings from campus work are $3046. The average financial indebtedness of the 2013 graduate was $22,665. The CSS/Profile, FFS, and the college's own financial statement are required. The priority date for freshman financial aid applications for fall entry is May 31. The deadline for filing freshman financial aid applications for fall entry is May 31.

UNIVERSITY OF SCIENCE AND ARTS OF OKLAHOMA   D-3
www.usao.edu

Chickasha, OK 73018	(405) 224-3141
	(800) 933-8726
Fax: (405) 574-1220	Email: admissions@usao.edu
Full-time: 299 men, 564 women	Faculty: 55; IIB, --$
Part-time: 45 men, 75 women	Ph.D.s: 85%
Graduate: n/av	Student/Faculty: 13 to 1
Year: trimesters, summer session	Tuition: $5400 ($12,720)
Room & Board: $5160	Freshman Class: 597 applied, 230 accepted, 187 enrolled
ACT: 24	CEEB CODE: 6544
Application Deadline: May 8	VERY COMPETITIVE

The University of Science and Arts of Oklahoma, founded in 1908, is Oklahoma's only publicly funded liberal arts college, providing interdisciplinary learning opportunities. There is 1 undergraduate school. In addition to regional accreditation, USAO has baccalaureate program accreditation with NASM and NCATE. The 75-acre campus is in a small town 40 miles southwest of Oklahoma City. Including any residence halls, there are 14 buildings.

STUDENT LIFE: 86% of undergraduates are from Oklahoma. Others are from 24 states, 19 foreign countries, and Canada. 95% are from public schools. 70% are White; 13% American Indian/Alaska Native. The average age of freshmen is 19; all undergraduates, 24. 39% do not continue beyond their first year; 41% remain to graduate.

FACULTY/CLASSROOMS: 49% of faculty are male; 51% are female. All teach undergraduates, 55% do research, and 55% do both. No introductory courses are taught by graduate students. The average class size in an introductory lecture is 20; in a laboratory is 20; and in a regular course is 17.

PROGRAMS OF STUDY: USAO confers B.A., B.S. and B.F.A. degrees. Bachelor's degrees are awarded in BIOLOGICAL SCIENCE (biology/biological science), BUSINESS (business administration and management), COMMUNICATIONS AND THE ARTS (art, communications, dramatic arts, English, fine arts, and music), COMPUTER AND PHYSICAL SCIENCE (chemistry, mathematics, natural sciences, and physics), EDUCATION (early childhood education, education of the deaf and hearing impaired, elementary education, and physical education), HEALTH PROFESSIONS (speech pathology/audiology), SOCIAL SCIENCE (American Indian studies, economics, history, political science/government, psychology, and sociology). Humanities and physical science is the strongest academically. Business administration, psychology and art have the largest enrollments.

ACTIVITIES: 1% of men belong to 1 national fraternity; 1% of women belong to 1 national sorority. There are 45 groups on campus, including art, band, cheerleading, choir, chorale, chorus, computers, dance, drama, drill team, ethnic, gay, honors, international, jazz band, literary magazine, musical theater, newspaper, opera, orchestra, pep band, photography, political, professional, radio and TV, religious, social, social service, and student government. Popular campus events include Montmartre Art Festival/Droverstock, Festival of Arts and Ideas and Drover Difference Day.

SERVICES: Counseling and information services are available, as is tutoring in some subjects. There is remedial math, reading, and writ-

ing. Tutors and interpreters are available for hearing-impaired students. **Library/Resources:** The library contains 69,605 volumes, 214 microform items, and 3,562 audio/video tapes/CDs/DVDs, and subscribes to 55,000 periodicals including electronic. Computerized library services include interlibrary loans, database searching, and Internet access. Special learning facilities include an art gallery, radio station, a commercial art computer lab, TV studio, a child development center, herbarium, art gallery and a speech pathology clinic. **Physically Challenged Students:** 95% of the campus is accessible. Facilities include wheelchair ramps, elevators, special parking, specially equipped restrooms, special class scheduling, lowered drinking fountains, and lowered telephones. **Special:** USAO offers dual majors, accelerated degree programs in all majors through year-round study, work-study programs, internship placement in community institutions, a Tutorial Scholars Program for student-designed majors, an interdisciplinary studies program, and a limited number of pass/fail options. There are 7 national honor societies, a freshman honors program, and 1 departmental honors program. **Visiting:** There are guides for informal visits, visitors may sit in on classes, and stay overnight. To schedule a visit, contact the Admissions Office at (800) 933-8726. **Campus Safety and Security:** Measures include 24-hour foot and vehicle patrol and emergency notification system. There are lighted pathways/sidewalks, security cameras near housing and parking lots.

REQUIREMENTS: The ACT is required. Applicants must meet one of the following 3 (1) have a minimum score of 24 on the ACT or 1090 on the SAT (3.0 GPA or top 50% of high school class); (2) have a high school GPA of 3.0 and be in the top 25% of their high school class; or (3) have a minimum GPA of 3.0 in their high school core courses and a minimum score of 22 on the ACT or 1020 on the SAT. AP and CLEP credits are accepted. Important factors in the admissions decision are evidence of special talent, leadership record, and personality/intangible qualities.

ADMISSIONS: 39% of a recent year applicants were accepted. The ACT scores were 18% below 21, 29% between 21 and 23, 28% between 24 and 26, 16% between 27 and 28, and 9% above 28. 57% of the current freshmen were in the top fifth of their class; 85% were in the top two fifths.

FINANCIAL AID: In a recent year, 90% of all full-time freshmen and 83% of continuing full-time students received some form of financial aid. 66% of all full-time freshmen and 64% of continuing full-time students received need-based aid. The average freshman award was $9,174. Need-based scholarships or need-based grants averaged $7,452; need-based self-help aid (loans and jobs) averaged $3,367; non-need-based athletic scholarships averaged $10,594; and other non-need-based awards and non-need-based scholarships averaged $3,376. 20% of undergraduate students work part-time. Average annual earnings from campus work are $2180. The average financial indebtedness of the 2013 graduate was $18,378. The FAFSA, the college's own financial statement, and institution information sheet are required. The priority date for freshman financial aid applications for fall entry is March 15. The deadline for filing freshman financial aid applications for fall entry is rolling.

UNIVERSITY OF TULSA   E-2
www.utulsa.edu

Tulsa, OK 74104	(918) 631-2307
	(800) 331-3050
Fax: (918) 631-5003	Email: admission@utulsa.edu
Full-time: 1951 men, 1411 women	Faculty: 316; IIA, ++$
Part-time: 65 men, 46 women	Ph.D.s: 96%
Graduate: 676 men, 533 women	Student/Faculty: 11 to 1
Year: semesters, summer session	Tuition: $35,855
Room & Board: $10,476	Freshman Class: 7636 applied, 3074 accepted, 764 enrolled
SAT CR/M: 620/640 ACT: 29	CEEB CODE: 6883
Application Deadline: n/av	MOST COMPETITIVE

The University of Tulsa, was founded in 1894, and is a private comprehensive institution offering over 60 undergraduate major areas of study through its programs in liberal arts and social sciences, engineering and natural sciences, business and finance, and health sciences. A number of interdisciplinary programs are also available and students are encouraged to participate in individual research, scholarship, and creative endeavors beginning in their freshman year. The University also offers a number of combined undergraduate/graduate degree programs which allow interested and qualified students to earn an undergraduate and graduate degree in less time than would normally be required to earn both degrees. There are 4 undergraduate schools and 2 graduate schools. In addition to regional accreditation, TU has baccalaureate program accreditation with AACSB, ABET, CSAB, NASM, TEAC, CED, NLNAC, and CAATE. The 209-acre campus is in an urban area in the city of Tulsa. Including any residence halls, there are 93 buildings.

STUDENT LIFE: 55% of undergraduates are from out of state, mostly the Southwest. Students are from 41 states, 58 foreign countries, and Canada. 67% are from public schools. 55% are White; 27% Foreign. 41% claim no religious affiliation; 37% Protestant; 15% Catholic. The average age of freshmen is 18; all undergraduates, 21. 11% do not continue beyond their first year; 70% remain to graduate.

Housing: 2684 students can be accommodated in college housing, which includes single-sex and coed dorms, on-campus apartments, off-campus apartments, and married student housing. In addition, there are honors houses, language houses, special-interest houses, fraternity houses, and sorority houses. On-campus housing is guaranteed for the freshman year only, is available on a first-come, first-served basis, and is available on a lottery system for upperclassmen. 73% of students live on campus; of those, 95% remain on campus on weekends. All students may keep cars.

FACULTY/CLASSROOMS: 66% of faculty are male; 34% are female. All teach and do research. Graduate students teach 5% of introductory courses. The average class size in an introductory lecture is 20; in a laboratory is 17; and in a regular course is 20.

PROGRAMS OF STUDY: TU confers B.A., B.F.A., B.A.D.E., B.M., B.M.E., B.S., B.S.A.M., B.S.A.T., B.S.B., B.S.B.A., B.S.Ch.E., B.S.C., B.S.C.S., B.S.D.E., B.S.S.P., B.S.E.C.E., B.S.I.T., B.S.E.E., B.S.E.P., B.S.E.S.S., B.S.G.S., B.S.I.B.L., B.S.M.E., B.S.N., B.S.P.E., B.S.E.P., B.S.B.G. and B.S.G.P. degrees. Master's and doctoral degrees are also awarded. Bachelor's degrees are awarded in AGRICULTURE (environmental studies), BIOLOGICAL SCIENCE (biochemistry and biology/biological science), BUSINESS (accounting, accounting/CPA, banking and finance, business administration and management, business (dual major program), international business management, management information systems, management science, marketing/retailing/merchandising, organizational behavior, and sports management), COMMUNICATIONS AND THE ARTS (art history, art, arts administration/management, communications, English, film arts, French, German, music, music performance, musical theater, piano/organ, Spanish, theatre arts, and voice), COMPUTER AND PHYSICAL SCIENCE (applied mathematics, chemistry, computer science, geology, geophysics and seismology, geoscience, information sciences and systems, mathematics, and physics), EDUCATION (athletic training, education, education of the deaf and hearing impaired, elementary education, and music education), ENGINEERING AND ENVIRONMENTAL DESIGN (chemical engineering, computer engineering, electrical/electronics engineering, energy management technology, engineering physics, mechanical engineering, and petroleum/natural gas engineering), HEALTH PROFESSIONS (biology, exercise science, nursing, premedicine, and speech pathology/audiology), SOCIAL SCIENCE (anthropology, archeology, communication sciences & disorders, economics, history, philosophy, political science/government, prelaw, psychology, religion, Russian and Slavic studies, sociology, women and gender studies). Petroleum engineering, mechanical engineering, English, psychology, energy management, and accounting are the strongest academically. Petroleum engineering, psychology, and finance have the largest enrollments.

ACTIVITIES: 21% of men belong to 7 national fraternities; 23% of women belong to 8 national sororities. There are 172 groups on campus, including art, band, cheerleading, chess, choir, chorale, chorus, communications, computers, dance, debate, drama, drill team, environmental, ethnic, film, forensics, gay, honors, international, jazz band, literary magazine, marching band, musical theater, newspaper, orchestra, pep band, photography, political, professional, radio and TV, religious, social, social service, student government, symphony, and yearbook. Popular campus events include Homecoming, Springfest, Black Heritage Month, and International Education Week. **Sports:** There are 8 intercollegiate sports for men and 10 for women, and 22 intramural sports for men and 22 for women. Facilities include a 30,000-seat stadium, 8,355-seat basketball arena, a gym, athletic field, indoor racquetball courts, basketball and tennis courts, handball court, weight room, dance studio, student fitness center, soccer fields, softball field, track, multipurpose recreational field, and outdoor track. **Graduates:** From July 1, 2013 to June 30, 2014, 724 bachelor's degrees were awarded. The most popular majors were petroleum engineering (10%), finance (7%), and psychology (5%). 246 companies recruited on campus in 2013-2014. In an average class, 52% graduate in 4 years or less, 68% graduate in 5 years or less, and 70% graduate in 6 years or less. Of the 2013 graduating class, 15% were enrolled in graduate school within 6 months of graduation, and 82% were employed.

SERVICES: Counseling and information services are available, as is tutoring in most subjects. There is a reader service for the blind. Special labs are available to students in need of assistance in math and writing. **Library/Resources:** The 2 libraries contain 1.5 million volumes, 2.6 million microform items, 26,890 audio/video tapes/CDs/DVDs, and subscribe to 58,011 periodicals including electronic. Computerized library services include interlibrary loans, database searching, Internet access, and Wi-Fi capability. Special learning facilities include an art gallery, radio station, and TV station. **Physically Challenged Students:** 94% of the campus is accessible. Facilities include wheelchair ramps, elevators, special parking, specially equipped restrooms, special class scheduling, lowered drinking fountains, lowered telephones, special housing. **Special:** Internships are available in the Tulsa area during the school year and in cities throughout the United States during the summer. Students are encouraged to participate in study abroad, with more than 50 study-abroad programs in countries across the entire globe available. TU offers B.A.-B.S. degrees, combined bachelors/master's degree programs in a variety of majors, dual and student-designed majors, accelerated degree programs, non-degree study, work-study programs, and pass/fail options. There are 34 national honor societies, including Phi Beta Kappa, and a freshman honors program. **Visiting:** There are regularly scheduled orientations for prospective students, including a one hour walking tour of campus; an admission presentation and interview, appointments with relevant faculty members, classroom visits, lunch with current students. There are guides for informal visits, visitors may sit in on classes, and stay overnight. To schedule a visit, contact the Office of Admission. **Campus Safety and Security:** Measures include 24-hour foot and vehicle patrol, emergency notification system, self-defense education, and security escort services. There are shuttle buses, emergency telephones, lighted pathways/sidewalks, and controlled access to dorms/residences.

REQUIREMENTS: The SAT or ACT is required. Graduation from an accredited secondary school or satisfactory scores on the GED are also required for admission. The school recommends a minimum of 18 academic credits, including 4 years of English, 4 years of math, 3 years of science and social studies (including history), 2 years of a single foreign language and 1 year of fine arts and humanities. Computer competency is also expected. An essay and an interview are highly recommended. An audition or a portfolio is required for students applying for music, theater, or art scholarships. AP credits are accepted. Important factors in the admissions decision are advanced placement or honors courses, leadership record, and extracurricular activities record. To graduate, students must complete 124 to 134 credit hours, including 24 to 51 in the major, with a minimum GPA determined by the major. Freshmen in liberal arts and business administration must complete a First Seminar. All students must complete the core curriculum, which includes 2 writing courses and at least 1 course in math. All students must also complete the general curriculum, which requires 25 credit hours in 3 categories (aesthetic inquiry and creative expression; historical and social interpretation; and scientific investigation). A foreign language requirement of 2 years for liberal arts and sciences students and 1 year for business majors must be completed. **Procedure:** Freshmen are admitted fall and spring. Entrance exams should be taken during spring of the junior year or fall of the senior year. There are early admissions, deferred admissions, and rolling admissions plans. Application deadlines are open. Application fee is $50. Notification is sent on a rolling basis. Applications are accepted on-line. **Transfer Students:** 141 transfer students enrolled in 2013-2014. Transfer students must submit official transcripts from all colleges attended and should have a minimum GPA of 2.75 for all college and high school work. Applicants with fewer than 30 credit hours must submit ACT or SAT scores. Those with fewer than 60 credit hours must submit an official high school transcript. Applicants 25 years of age or older are exempt from submitting ACT or SAT scores unless requested to do so by the Admission Office. 45 of 126 credits required for the bachelor's degree must be completed at TU. **International Students:** There are 922 international students enrolled. The school actively recruits these students. They must take the TOEFL with a minimum score of 550 on the paper-based TOEFL (PBT) or 80 on the Internet-based version (iBT).

ADMISSIONS: 40% of the 2014-2015 applicants were accepted. The SAT scores for the 2014-2015 freshman class were: Critical Reading--15% below 500, 29% between 500 and 599, 31% between 600 and 699, and 26% between 700 and 800; Math--12% below 500, 20% between 500 and 599, 39% between 600 and 699, and 29% between 700 and 800. The ACT scores were 4% below 21, 8% between 21 and 23, 15% between 24 and 26, 16% between 27 and 28, and 57% above 28. 86% of the current freshmen were in the top fifth of their class; 97% were in the top two fifths. There were 36 National Merit finalists. 26 freshmen graduated first in their class. **Admissions Contact:** Barbara Adkins, Dean of Admission. E-Mail: *admission@utulsa.edu* Web: *www.utulsa.edu*

FINANCIAL AID: In 2014-2015, 91% of all full-time freshmen and 86% of continuing full-time students received some form of financial aid. 29% of all full-time freshmen and 25% of continuing full-time students received need-based aid. The average freshman award was $27,137. Need-based scholarships or need-based grants averaged $5,778 ($12,410 maximum); need-based self-help aid (loans and jobs) averaged $4,520 ($8,600 maximum); non-need-based athletic scholarships averaged $27,372 ($46,331 maximum); and other non-need-based awards and non-need-based scholarships averaged $21,316 ($46,331 maximum). 22% of undergraduate students work part-time. Average annual earnings from campus work are $5000. The average financial indebtedness of the 2014 graduate was $24,625. The FAFSA is required. Check with the school for current application deadlines.

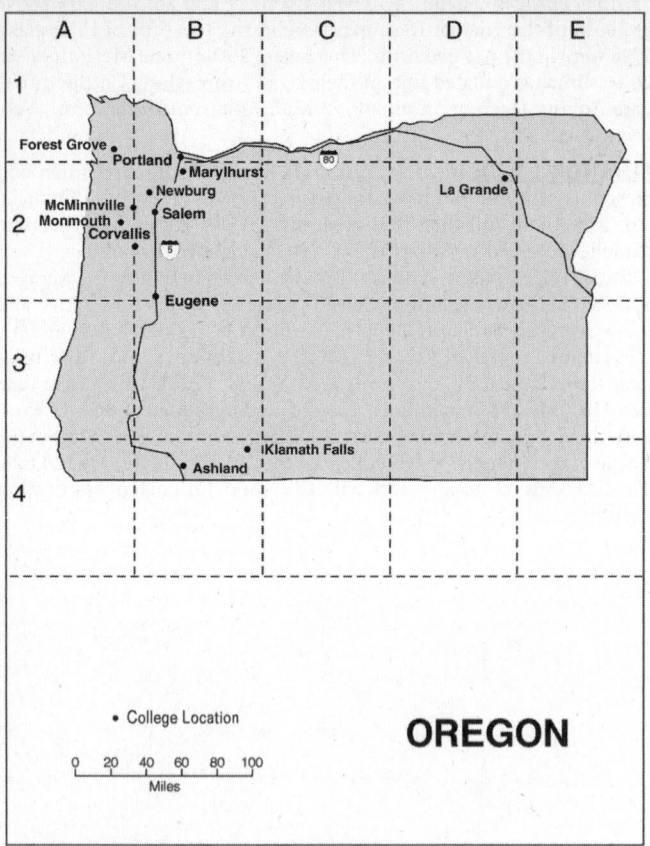

A B C D E

1
Forest Grove
Portland
Marylhurst
Newburg
La Grande
McMinnville
Monmouth Salem
Corvallis
2
Eugene
3
Klamath Falls
Ashland
4

• College Location

OREGON

0 20 40 60 80 100
Miles

ART INSTITUTE OF PORTLAND (*The complete profile is made available exclusively on our website, www.barronspac.com*)

CONCORDIA UNIVERSITY   B-1
www.cu-portland.edu

Portland, OR 97211	**(503) 280-8501** **(800) 321-9371**
Fax: (503) 280-8531	**Email: admission@cu-portland.edu**
Full-time: 462 men, 938 women	**Faculty:** 40
Part-time: 73 men, 125 women	**Ph.D.s:** 57%
Graduate: 179 men, 321 women	**Student/Faculty:** 20 to 1
Year: semesters, summer session	**Tuition:** $26,900
Room & Board: $8100	**Freshman Class:** 804 applied, 532 accepted, 201 enrolled
SAT CR/M: 500/500 **ACT:** 21	**CEEB CODE:** 4079
Application Deadline: open	**COMPETITIVE**

Concordia University, founded in 1905, is a private liberal arts institution affiliated with the Lutheran Church Missouri Synod and is 1 of 10 institutions of the Concordia University System. There are 4 undergraduate schools and 3 graduate schools. In addition to regional accreditation, Concordia has baccalaureate program accreditation with NWCCU. The 24-acre campus is in an urban area in Portland. Including any residence halls, there are 20 buildings.
STUDENT LIFE: 65% of undergraduates are from Oregon. Others are from 14 states, 18 foreign countries, and Canada. 75% are White. 59% are Protestant; 30% claim no religious affiliation. The average age of freshmen is 19; all undergraduates, 25. 25% do not continue beyond their first year; 45% remain to graduate. **Housing:** 500 students can be accommodated in college housing, which includes single-sex and coed dorms, on-campus apartments, and married student housing. On-campus housing is guaranteed for the freshman year only, is available on a first-come, first-served basis, and is available on a lottery system for upperclassmen. 59% of students live on

campus; of those, 95% remain on campus on weekends. Alcohol is not permitted. All students may keep cars.
FACULTY/CLASSROOMS: 67% of faculty are male; 33% are female. All teach undergraduates, and 5% do research. No introductory courses are taught by graduate students. The average class size in an introductory lecture is 19; in a laboratory is 19; and in a regular course is 17.
PROGRAMS OF STUDY: Concordia confers B.A., and B.S. degrees. Associate, Master's, and Doctoral degrees are also awarded. Bachelor's degrees are awarded in BIOLOGICAL SCIENCE (biology/biological science), BUSINESS (business administration and management), COMMUNICATIONS AND THE ARTS (English), COMPUTER AND PHYSICAL SCIENCE (chemistry), EDUCATION (early childhood education, elementary education, and secondary education), ENGINEERING AND ENVIRONMENTAL DESIGN (environmental science), HEALTH PROFESSIONS (health care administration, nursing, and premedicine), SOCIAL SCIENCE (humanities, psychology, social work, theological studies, and youth ministry). Nursing, biology, business administration, education, and psychology are the strongest academically. Nursing, business, and education have the largest enrollments.
ACTIVITIES: There are 14 groups on campus, including handbell, brass ensemble, cheerleading, choir, chorus, communications, drama, environmental, honors, international, literary magazine, newspaper, orchestra, professional, religious, social, social service, and student government. **Sports:** There are 6 intercollegiate sports for men and 7 for women, and 10 intramural sports for men and 10 for women. Facilities include a weight room, 1200-seat gym, and baseball/soccer stadium. **Graduates:** From July 1, 2013 to June 30, 2014, 219 bachelor's degrees were awarded. The most popular majors were business administration (36%), education (34%), and nursing . 35 companies recruited on campus in 2013-2014. In an average class, 30% graduate in 4 years or less, 39% graduate in 5 years or less, and 43% graduate in 6 years or less.
SERVICES: Counseling and information services are available, as is tutoring in most subjects. There is remedial math, reading, and writing. There is also student-supported individual help and media resources. **Library/Resources:** The library contains 70,000 volumes, 56,706 microform items, 2,888 audio/video tapes/CDs/DVDs, and subscribes to 424 periodicals including electronic. Computerized library services include interlibrary loans, database searching, and Internet access. **Physically Challenged Students:** 80% of the campus is accessible. Facilities include wheelchair ramps, elevators, special parking, specially equipped restrooms, special class scheduling, and lowered telephones. **Special:** Cross-registration may be arranged through the Concordia University System and with Oregon Independent. There is a dual enrollment program with Portland Community College. There are also internships, study abroad in more than 20 countries, and an accelerated degree program in business, health care administration, and social work. There are 1 national honor society, a freshman honors program, and 1 departmental honors program. **Visiting:** There are regularly scheduled orientations for prospective students, including class visitations and meetings with program deans and faculty. There are guides for informal visits, visitors may sit in on classes, and stay overnight. To schedule a visit, contact the Admissions Office at admissions@cu-portland.edu. **Campus Safety and Security:** Measures include 24-hour foot and vehicle patrol, self-defense education, and security escort services. There are emergency telephones, lighted pathways/sidewalks, controlled access to dorms/residences, and emergency cell phone available 24 hours.
REQUIREMENTS: The SAT or ACT is required, with satisfactory SAT verbal scores recommended. Graduation from an accredited secondary school or satisfactory scores on the GED are required. The school recommends that high school courses include 4 units of English, 3 units each of social studies, math, and science, 2 units of a foreign language, and 1 unit of art and music. An interview is recommended. A GPA of 2.5 is required. AP and CLEP credits are accepted. Important factors in the admissions decision are recommendations by school officials, leadership record, and personality/intangible qualities. To graduate, students must complete a total of 124 semester hours, with a minimum GPA of 2.0. General education

requirements total 48 semester hours. All students must take freshman composition and courses in math, phys ed, humanities, religion, science, writing, fine arts, and social sciences. In the major, 45 hours of 300-400 level courses must be taken. **Procedure:** Freshmen are admitted fall, spring, and summer. Entrance exams should be taken during the junior year or early in the senior year. There is a rolling admissions plan. Early decision applications should be filed by March 1. The fall 2014 application fee was $20. Notification is sent on a rolling basis. Applications are accepted on-line. **Transfer Students:** 141 transfer students enrolled in 2013-2014. Transfer students must have a minimum GPA of 2.0. 45 of 124 credits required for the bachelor's degree must be completed at Concordia. **International Students:** There are 15 international students enrolled. The school actively recruits these students. They must take the TOEFL. They must also take the SAT or ACT.

ADMISSIONS: 66% of the 2014-2015 applicants were accepted. The ACT scores were 40% below 21, 35% between 21 and 23, 16% between 24 and 26, 9% between 27 and 28, and 2% above 28. 42% of the current freshmen were in the top fifth of their class; 69% were in the top two fifths. **Admissions Contact:** Office of Admission E-Mail: *admission@cu-portland.edu* Web: *www.cu-portland.edu*

FINANCIAL AID: The average freshman award was $13,000. The FAFSA is required. Check with the school for current application deadlines.

CORBAN UNIVERSITY — B-2
www.corban.edu

Salem, OR 97317

(503) 375-8180
(800) 845-3005

Fax: (503) 375-7042

Email: admissions@corban.edu

Full-time: 334 men, 521 women

Faculty: 45

Part-time: 38 men, 40 women

Ph.D.s: 68%

Graduate: 21 men, 34 women

Student/Faculty: 14 to 1

Year: semesters, summer session

Tuition: $28,640

Room & Board: $8740

Freshman Class: 2678 applied, 1001 accepted, 220 enrolled

SAT CR/M/W: 518/500/495 ACT: 22

CEEB CODE: 4956

Application Deadline: August 1

COMPETITIVE+

Corban University is a Christian university offering degrees in biblical-theological studies, business administration, education, humanities, math, phys ed, social sciences, psychology, intercultural studies, and youth work. There are 5 undergraduate schools and 4 graduate schools. The 142-acre campus is in a suburban area in Salem, Oregon. Including any residence halls, there are 28 buildings.

STUDENT LIFE: 53% of undergraduates are from Oregon. Others are from 29 states, 11 foreign countries, and Canada. 60% are from public schools. 78% are White. 96% are Protestant. The average age of freshmen is 18; all undergraduates, 20. 24% do not continue beyond their first year; 53% remain to graduate. **Housing:** 547 students can be accommodated in college housing, which includes single-sex dorms, on-campus apartments, and married student housing. On-campus housing is guaranteed for the freshman year only, and is available on a first-come, first-served basis. 65% of students live on campus; of those, 90% remain on campus on weekends. Alcohol is not permitted. All students may keep cars.

FACULTY/CLASSROOMS: 76% of faculty are male; 24% are female. 90% teach undergraduates, 10% do research, and 95% do both. No introductory courses are taught by graduate students. The average class size in a regular course is 15.

PROGRAMS OF STUDY: Corban confers B.A. and B.S. degrees. Associate, Master's, and Doctoral degrees are also awarded. Bachelor's degrees are awarded in BUSINESS (accounting, business administration and management, marketing, marketing management, and sports management), COMMUNICATIONS AND THE ARTS (communications, creative writing, English, journalism, music, and music performance), COMPUTER AND PHYSICAL SCIENCE (information sciences and systems and mathematics), EDUCATION (business education, education, elementary education, mathematics education, music education, physical education, social studies education, and sports and wellness studies), HEALTH PROFESSIONS (exercise science, health care administration, health science, predentistry, premedicine, preoptometry, prepharmacy, prephysical therapy, and preveterinary science), SOCIAL SCIENCE (biblical studies, counseling/psychology, criminal justice, crosscultural studies, history, humanities, interdisciplinary studies, ministries, pastoral studies, political science/government, prelaw, psychology, social science, and youth ministry). Education and business is the strongest academically. Psychology, business, and education have the largest enrollments.

ACTIVITIES: There are no fraternities or sororities. There are 16 groups on campus, including art, band, choir, chorale, chorus, drama, film, honors, jazz band, literary magazine, musical theater, newspaper, orchestra, radio and TV, religious, social, social service, student government, and yearbook. Popular campus events include Sports Weekends, Chapel Services, International Fair, Various Student Led Activities and Contests. **Sports:** There are 6 intercollegiate sports for men and 7 for women, and 12 intramural sports for men and 12 for women. Facilities include a sports center with a gym, soccer fields, baseball fields and the student fitness center. **Graduates:** From July 1, 2013 to June 30, 2014, 216 bachelor's degrees were awarded. The most popular majors were psychology (27%), business/marketing (21%), and education (17%). 10 companies recruited on campus in 2013-2014. In an average class, 10% graduate in 3 years or less, 49% graduate in 4 years or less, and 53% graduate in 6 years or less.

SERVICES: Counseling and information services are available, as is tutoring in most subjects. **Library/Resources:** The library contains 85,000 volumes, 2,000 microform items, 3,000 audio/video tapes/CDs/DVDs, and subscribes to 552 periodicals including electronic. Computerized library services include interlibrary loans, database searching, Internet access, and Wi-Fi capability. Special learning facilities include an art gallery, radio station, an archaeological museum. **Physically Challenged Students:** 95% of the campus is accessible. Facilities include wheelchair ramps, elevators, special parking, specially equipped restrooms, and lowered telephones. **Special:** Corban offers a pre-seminary co-op program, cross-registration with Oregon Independent Colleges, study abroad in 4 countries, a Washington semester, internships with the approval of a program adviser, accelerated programs in management and communication and in family studies, and student-designed majors with adviser approval. Also, Corban offers a fast-track B.S./M.Div. degree, and AMBEX Study Abroad in Germany. There is a freshman honors program. **Visiting:** There are regularly scheduled orientations for prospective students, including a campus tour, classroom visit, and activities with the student body. There are guides for informal visits, visitors may sit in on classes, and stay overnight. To schedule a visit, contact the Admissions Office at admissions@corban.edu. **Campus Safety and Security:** Measures include 24-hour foot and vehicle patrol, emergency notification system, self-defense education, and security escort services. There are emergency telephones, lighted pathways/sidewalks, controlled access to dorms/residences, 24 hour emergency response patrol.

REQUIREMENTS: The SAT or ACT is required. Corban University requires a statement of faith essay. A GPA of 2.7 is required. AP and CLEP credits are accepted. Important factors in the admissions decision are extracurricular activities record, recommendations by school officials, leadership record, personality/intangible qualities, and recommendations by alumni. To graduate, students must complete 128 credits with 40 to 74 in the major. The minimum required GPA is 2.0 for most programs; the education major requires a 3.0 GPA. The general education core consists of 68 credits. Courses must be taken in Bible, humanities, social sciences, math, science, and phys ed. **Procedure:** Freshmen are admitted fall and spring. There is a rolling admissions plan. Applications should be filed by August 1 for fall entry; December 1 for spring entry, along with a $35 fee. Notification is sent on a rolling basis. Applications are accepted on-line. **Transfer Students:** 43 transfer students enrolled in 2013-2014. Transfer applicants are required to have a minimum 2.0 cumulative college GPA and submit the college transcript and 3 references. 30 of 128 credits required for the bachelor's degree must be completed at Corban. **International Students:** There are 23 international students enrolled.

The school actively recruits these students. They must take the TOEFL with a minimum score of 500 on the paper-based TOEFL (PBT) or 61 on the Internet-based version (iBT). They must also take the SAT or ACT.

ADMISSIONS: 37% of the 2014-2015 applicants were accepted. The SAT scores for the 2014-2015 freshman class were: Critical Reading--38% below 500, 37% between 500 and 599, 19% between 600 and 699, and 5% between 700 and 800; Math--46% below 500, 37% between 500 and 599, and 16% between 600 and 699; Writing--78% below 500, 38% between 500 and 599, 13% between 600 and 699, and 2% between 700 and 800. 27% of the current freshmen were in the top fifth of their class; 41% were in the top two fifths. There was 1 National Merit finalist. 15 freshmen graduated first in their class. **Admissions Contact:** Chris Vetter, Associate Provost of Enrollment Services. E-Mail: *admissions@corban.edu* Web: *www.corban.edu*

FINANCIAL AID: In 2014-2015, 99% of all full-time freshmen and 99% of continuing full-time students received some form of financial aid, 80% of all full-time freshmen and 83% of continuing full-time students received need-based aid. The average freshman award was $21,012. Need-based scholarships or need-based grants averaged $18,547; need-based self-help aid (loans and jobs) averaged $3,821; non-need-based athletic scholarships averaged $14,135; and $8,470 from other forms of aid. 37% of undergraduate students work part-time. Average annual earnings from campus work are $1721. The average financial indebtedness of the 2014 graduate was $26,407. The FAFSA is required. The priority date for freshman financial aid applications for fall entry is February 15. The deadline for filing freshman financial aid applications for fall entry is September 1.

EASTERN OREGON UNIVERSITY   D-2
www.eou.edu

La Grande, OR 97850-2807	(541) 962-3393
	(800) 452-8639
Fax: (541) 962-3418	Email: admissions@eou.edu
Full-time: 850 men, 2000 women	Faculty: IIB, --$
Part-time: 420 men, 680 women	Ph.D.s: n/av
Graduate: 60 men, 190 women	Student/Faculty: n/av
Year: varies, summer session	Tuition: $7046
Room & Board: $8289	Freshman Class: n/av
SAT or ACT: required	CEEB CODE: 4300
Application Deadline: see profile	COMPETITIVE

Eastern Oregon University, founded in 1929, is a public institution that is part of the Oregon University System. It offers programs in liberal and fine arts, agriculture, business, health science, and teacher preparation. There are 3 undergraduate schools and 1 graduate school. The figures in the above capsule and in this profile are approximate. Beginning with the 2012-13 award year, EOU will charge nonresident tuition. In addition to regional accreditation, EOU has baccalaureate program accreditation with NCATE. The 121-acre campus is in a rural area 260 miles east of Portland. Including any residence halls, there are 13 buildings.

STUDENT LIFE: 70% of undergraduates are from Oregon. Others are from 42 states, 25 foreign countries, and Canada. 96% are from public schools. 82% are white. The average age of freshmen is 19; all undergraduates, 27. 32% do not continue beyond their first year; 37% remain to graduate.

FACULTY/CLASSROOMS: No introductory courses are taught by graduate students. The average class size in an introductory lecture is 60; in a laboratory, 20; and in a regular course, 35.

PROGRAMS OF STUDY: EOU confers B.A. and B.S degrees. Master's degrees are also awarded. Bachelor's degrees are awarded in AGRICULTURE (agricultural business management, agricultural economics, forestry and related sciences, range/farm management, and soil science), BIOLOGICAL SCIENCE (biology/biological science), BUSINESS (accounting and business administration and management), COMMUNICATIONS AND THE ARTS (art, dramatic arts, English, and music), COMPUTER AND PHYSICAL SCIENCE (chemistry, computer science, mathematics, and physics), EDUCATION (education and physical education), HEALTH PROFESSIONS

(health and nursing), SOCIAL SCIENCE (anthropology, history, liberal arts/general studies, psychology, and sociology).

ACTIVITIES: There are no fraternities or sororities. There are 44 groups on campus, including art, band, cheerleading, choir, chorale, chorus, communications, computers, dance, drama, ethnic, international, jazz band, literary magazine, musical theater, newspaper, orchestra, pep band, photography, professional, radio and TV, religious, social, student government, symphony, and yearbook. Popular campus events include Casino Night, Spring Fling, and Spring Symposium.

SERVICES: Counseling and information services are available, as is tutoring in most subjects. There is a reader service for the blind, and remedial math, reading, and writing. **Library/Resources:** The library contains 335,455 volumes, 250,834 microform items, 34,176 audio/video tapes/CDs/DVDs, and subscribes to 893 periodicals including electronic. Computerized library services include interlibrary loans, database searching, and Internet access. Special learning facilities include an art gallery, natural history museum, and radio station. **Physically Challenged Students:** 80% of the campus is accessible. Facilities include wheelchair ramps, elevators, special parking, and specially equipped restrooms. **Special:** There are cooperative and 3-2 engineering degree programs with Oregon State University. The university offers internships, work-study with federal agencies, accelerated degree program, student-designed and dual majors, study abroad in 8 countries, a general studies degree, B.A.-B.S. degrees, a multidisciplinary degree, numerous preprofessional programs, credit by exam, and for life/military/work experience, external degrees, and pass/fail options. The university also serves students with course work via telecommunications and video, and with a weekend University. There are 6 national honor societies, including Phi Beta Kappa, and 6 departmental honors programs. **Visiting:** There are regularly scheduled orientations for prospective students, including a campus tour, academic advising, and information sessions on financial aid and residence life. There are guides for informal visits, visitors may sit in on classes, and stay overnight. To schedule a visit, contact Admissions/New Student Programs at admissions@eou.edu. **Campus Safety and Security:** Measures include 24-hour foot and vehicle patrol and security escort services. There are emergency telephones and lighted pathways/sidewalks.

REQUIREMENTS: The SAT or ACT is required. A GED is accepted. Applicants must complete 14 academic credits, including 4 years of English, 3 each of math and social studies, and 2 of science. A GPA of 3.0 is required. AP and CLEP credits are accepted. Important factors in the admissions decision are extracurricular activities record and geographical diversity.

FINANCIAL AID: EOU is a member of CSS. The FAFSA is required. Check with the school for application deadlines.

GEORGE FOX UNIVERSITY   B-2
www.georgefox.edu

Newberg, OR 97132	(503) 554-2240
	(800) 765-4369
Fax: (503) 554-3110	Email: admissions@georgefox.edu
Full-time: 919 men, 1189 women	Faculty: 110; IIA, --$
Part-time: 104 men, 171 women	Ph.D.s: 75%
Graduate: 594 men, 708 women	Student/Faculty: 14 to 1
Year: semesters, summer session	Tuition: $31,120
Room & Board: $9630	Freshman Class: 2432 applied, 1830 accepted, 619 enrolled
SAT CR/M/W: 540/530/520 ACT: 23	CEEB CODE: 4325
Application Deadline: February 1	COMPETITIVE+

George Fox University, founded in 1891, is a Christian university of the humanities, sciences and professional studies. It offers bachelor's degrees in more than 40 majors, adult degree programs, five seminary degrees, and 12 master's and doctoral degrees at its main campus in Newberg, Oregon, and at teaching centers in Portland and Salem, Oregon. There are 6 undergraduate schools and 4 graduate schools. In addition to regional accreditation, George Fox has baccalaureate program accreditation with ABET, ACBSP, CSWE, NASM, and NCATE. The 85-acre campus is in a small town 23 miles southwest of Portland. Including any residence halls, there are 80 buildings.

STUDENT LIFE: 65% of undergraduates are from Oregon. Others are from 27 states, 17 foreign countries, and Canada. 72% are from public schools. 71% are White. 82% are Protestant; 14% claim no religious affiliation. The average age of freshmen is 18; all undergraduates, 21. 18% do not continue beyond their first year; 62% remain to graduate.

FACULTY/CLASSROOMS: 55% of faculty are male; 45% are female. 64% teach undergraduates. No introductory courses are taught by graduate students. The average class size in an introductory lecture is 36; in a laboratory is 17; and in a regular course is 20.

PROGRAMS OF STUDY: George Fox confers B.A., B.S., B.S.A.T. and B.S.W. degrees. Master's and Doctoral degrees are also awarded. Bachelor's degrees are awarded in BIOLOGICAL SCIENCE (biology/biological science), BUSINESS (accounting, business administration and management, business communications, management information systems, management science, and organizational leadership and management), COMMUNICATIONS AND THE ARTS (art, communications, creative writing, dramatic arts, film arts, literature, multimedia, music, and Spanish), COMPUTER AND PHYSICAL SCIENCE (chemistry, computer science, information sciences and systems, and mathematics), EDUCATION (athletic training, elementary education, and music education), ENGINEERING AND ENVIRONMENTAL DESIGN (engineering and applied science), HEALTH PROFESSIONS (allied health, health, health care administration, nursing, predentistry, premedicine, and preveterinary science), SOCIAL SCIENCE (behavioral science, biblical studies, cognitive science, economics, family/consumer studies, history, international studies, ministries, philosophy, political science/government, prelaw, psychology, religion, social science, social work, and sociology). Business, nursing, and elementary education have the largest enrollments.

ACTIVITIES: There are no fraternities or sororities. There are 20 groups on campus, including art, band, choir, chorale, chorus, computers, debate, drama, ethnic, film, forensics, honors, international, jazz band, literary magazine, musical theater, newspaper, orchestra, outdoor club, pep band, political, professional, radio and TV, religious, social, social service, student government, symphony, and yearbook. Popular campus events include Serve Day, Juniors Abroad, and Cultural Celebration Week.

SERVICES: Counseling and information services are available, as is tutoring in most subjects. There is a reader service for the blind, and remedial math, reading, and writing. **Library/Resources:** The 2 libraries contain 174,988 volumes, 210,708 microform items, 5,372 audio/video tapes/CDs/DVDs, and subscribe to 60,000 periodicals including electronic. Computerized library services include interlibrary loans, database searching, Internet access, and Wi-Fi capability. Special learning facilities include an art gallery, radio station, a television production studio; a pottery kiln; physical therapy, nursing and engineering labs. **Physically Challenged Students:** All of the campus is accessible. Facilities include wheelchair ramps, elevators, special parking, specially equipped restrooms, special class scheduling, lowered drinking fountains, lowered telephones, and special housing. **Special:** Half of George Fox students participate in study abroad programs, which include a three-week faculty-led, subsidized trip in the spring of a student's junior year. The university offers a dual-degree 3/2 program through its applied science major, enabling students to pursue engineering in a discipline such as chemical, environmental or aerospace engineering. Students can complete a semester at the Contemporary Music Center in Martha's Vineyard or the Los Angeles Film Studies Center. George Fox offers internships with area companies, study abroad, and a Washington semester through the Council of Christian Colleges and Universities. Work-study programs, accelerated degrees, dual and student-designed interdisciplinary majors, and pass/fail options in upper-division courses outside of the major also are offered. There are 3 national honor societies, a freshman honors program, and 1 departmental honors program. **Visiting:** There are regularly scheduled orientations for prospective students, including observation of classes and talking with professors. There are guides for informal visits, visitors may sit in on classes, and stay overnight. To schedule a visit, contact the Office of Admissions at (800) 765-4369, ext. 2249. **Campus Safety and Security:** Measures include

24-hour foot and vehicle patrol, emergency notification system, self-defense education, and security escort services. There are emergency telephones, lighted pathways/sidewalks, controlled access to dorms/residences, parking lot cameras, and video surveillance of key buildings.

REQUIREMENTS: The SAT or ACT is required. Applicants need 16 academic credits or 14 Carnegie units, including a suggested 4 units of English, 3 units of social studies, 2 units each of a foreign language, math, and science, and 1 unit of health and physical education. An essay and 2 personal recommendations are required; a portfolio, audition, and interview are recommended in certain majors. A GPA of 2.6 is required. AP and CLEP credits are accepted. Important factors in the admissions decision are advanced placement or honors courses, extracurricular activities record, and leadership record.

ADMISSIONS: 75% of a recent year applicants were accepted. The SAT scores for a recent year, freshman class were: Critical Reading--27% below 500, 37% between 500 and 599, 21% between 600 and 699, and 5% between 700 and 800; Math--33% below 500, 40% between 500 and 599, 23% between 600 and 699, and 4% between 700 and 800; Writing--40% below 500, 37% between 500 and 599, 20% between 600 and 699, and 3% between 700 and 800. The ACT scores were 35% below 21, 21% between 21 and 23, 22% between 24 and 26, 8% between 27 and 28, and 13% above 28. 49% of the current freshmen were in the top fifth of their class; 77% were in the top two fifths. 36 freshmen graduated first in their class.

FINANCIAL AID: In 2013-2014, 100% of all full-time freshmen and 98% of continuing full-time students received some form of financial aid. 81% of all full-time freshmen and 71% of continuing full-time students received need-based aid. The average freshman award was $28,270. Need-based scholarships or need-based grants averaged $9,606; need-based self-help aid (loans and jobs) averaged $3,704; and other non-need-based awards and non-need-based scholarships averaged $14,960. George Fox is a member of CSS. The FAFSA and the state aid form are required. The priority date for freshman financial aid applications for fall entry is February 1.

LEWIS & CLARK COLLEGE B-1
www.lclark.edu

Portland, OR 97219

(503) 768-7040
(800) 444-4111

Fax: (503) 768-7055

Email: admissions@lclark.edu

Full-time: 879 men, 1277 women

Faculty: 129

Part-time: 14 men, 9 women

Ph.D.s: 95%

Graduate: 507 men, 818 women

Student/Faculty: 12 to 1

Year: semesters, summer session

Tuition: $43,382

Room & Board: $11,000

Freshman Class: 3291 applied, 4207 accepted, 564 enrolled
CEEB CODE: 4384

Application Deadline: January 15

MOST COMPETITIVE

Lewis and Clark College, founded in 1867, is a private, independent liberal arts and sciences institution with a global reach. There is 1 undergraduate school and 2 graduate schools. In addition to regional accreditation, L & C has baccalaureate program accreditation with NCATE, ABA, CACREP, and COAMFTE. The 137-acre campus is in a suburban area 6 miles south of downtown Portland. Including any residence halls, there are 58 buildings.

STUDENT LIFE: 88% of undergraduates are from out of state, mostly the West. Students are from 48 states, 53 foreign countries, and Canada. 76% are from public schools. 64% are White. The average age of freshmen is 18; all undergraduates, 20. 15% do not continue beyond their first year; 74% remain to graduate. **Housing:** 1394 students can be accommodated in college housing, which includes single-sex and coed dorms and on-campus apartments. In addition, there are language houses, special-interest houses, theme communities. On-campus housing is guaranteed for the freshman year only and is available on a lottery system for upperclassmen. 65% of students live on campus; of those, 95% remain on campus on weekends. Upperclassmen may keep cars.

FACULTY/CLASSROOMS: 50% of faculty are male; 50% are female.

No introductory courses are taught by graduate students. The average class size in a regular course is 20.

PROGRAMS OF STUDY: L & C confers B.A. degrees. Master's and doctoral degrees are also awarded. Bachelor's degrees are awarded in AGRICULTURE (environmental studies), BIOLOGICAL SCIENCE (biochemistry and biology/biological science), COMMUNICATIONS AND THE ARTS (art history and appreciation, classics, communications, dramatic arts, English, fine arts, languages, music, and studio art), COMPUTER AND PHYSICAL SCIENCE (chemistry, computer mathematics, computer science, mathematics, and physics), SOCIAL SCIENCE (anthropology, East Asian studies, economics, French studies, German area studies, Hispanic American studies, history, interdisciplinary studies, international relations, philosophy, political science/government, psychology, religion, and sociology). Psychology, biology, and sociology/anthropology have the largest enrollments.

ACTIVITIES: There are no fraternities or sororities. There are 70 groups on campus, including art, band, choir, chorale, chorus, computers, dance, debate, drama, ethnic, film, forensics, gay, honors, international, jazz band, literary magazine, meridian journal of international and cross-cultural perspectives; college outdoors, newspaper, orchestra, photography, political, professional, radio and TV, religious, social, social service, student government, and symphony. Popular campus events include Gender Studies Symposium, International Affairs Symposium, and Environmental Studies Symposium, Day of Service, Alternative Breaks. **Sports:** There are 9 intercollegiate sports for men and 10 for women, and 19 intramural sports for men and 19 for women. Facilities include 3 full basketball courts which also serve as volleyball courts and indoor practice facilities for several intercollegiate teams. The gym has padded bleachers, 3,600-square-foot, fully equipped weight room, and a state-of-the art Astro-Turf Game Day 3D Synthetic surface. The Zehntbauer Swimming Pavilion, houses an eight-lane, 25-yard pool with one and three-meter diving boards. The pavilion, with its fully automatic Colorado timing system, has been the site of an NAIA National Swimming Championship meet. **Graduates:** From July 1, 2013 to June 30, 2014, 459 bachelor's degrees were awarded. The most popular majors were social sciences (21%), psychology (17%), and visual and performing arts (9%). 100 companies recruited on campus in 2013-2014. In an average class, 1% graduate in 3 years or less, 68% graduate in 4 years or less, 75% graduate in 5 years or less, and 76% graduate in 6 years or less.

SERVICES: Counseling and information services are available, as is tutoring in every subject. There is a reader service for the blind. There are mentors, note takers, books on tape, and math and writing skills centers. **Library/Resources:** The 2 libraries contain 586,144 volumes, 1.5 million microform items, 23,851 audio/video tapes/CDs/DVDs, and subscribe to 42,560 periodicals including electronic. Computerized library services include interlibrary loans, database searching, Internet access, and Wi-Fi capability. Special learning facilities include an art gallery, radio station, telescope, research astronomical observatory, language lab, greenhouse, and adaptive technology lab. **Physically Challenged Students:** 80% of the campus is accessible. Facilities include wheelchair ramps, elevators, special parking, specially equipped restrooms, special class scheduling, lowered drinking fountains, and lowered telephones. **Special:** L & C offers internships; study-abroad programs in 60 countries; semesters in Washington and New York City; dual and student-designed majors; and cross-registration with schools that are part of the Oregon Independent College Association. A 3-2 engineering program is available with Columbia University, Washington University, and the University of Southern California. There are 5 national honor societies, including Phi Beta Kappa. **Visiting:** There are regularly scheduled orientations for prospective students. There are information sessions and campus tours daily; class visits, interviews, special-interest appointments are available. Visitors may sit in on classes and stay overnight. To schedule a visit, contact the Office of Admissions. **Campus Safety and Security:** Measures include 24-hour foot and vehicle patrol, emergency notification system, self-defense education, and security escort services. There are shuttle buses, emergency telephones, lighted pathways/sidewalks, controlled access to dorms/residences, and card key locks in all residence halls.

REQUIREMENTS: When admitting new students, the admissions staff looks for individuals from diverse backgrounds, with diverse talents and interests – students who will not only meet the rigorous academic challenges of a Lewis and Clark education, but will also take full advantage of the opportunities for individual achievement and growth offered here. Academic Preparation: the high school course load (grades 9-12) should include a minimum of: 4 years of English, 4 years of mathematics, 3-4 years of history and social sciences, 2-3 years of a foreign language, 3 years of lab sciences, 1 year of creative arts. Advanced Placement, International Baccalaureate, or honors courses are viewed as further evidence of serious preparation for college-level studies. Successful candidates have taken some of these advanced courses if they are offered at their schools. We look not only at your performance in a challenging curriculum, but at the following criteria as well: SAT or ACT scores (unless applying through the Portfolio Path), counselor report (first-year students only). Teacher recommendation, personal essay, leadership, community service and work experience, and extracurricular involvements, expressed interest in the College or personal interview (interviews are optional, not required). A GPA of 2.0 is required. AP credits are accepted. To graduate, students must complete a total of 128 semester hours with a 2.0 GPA. A third of this total generally falls in the major program, a third in electives, and a third in general requirements, which includes a required first-year course, 12 hours in scientific and quantitative reasoning, 8 hours in international studies, 3 semesters of a foreign language, 2 semesters of phys ed, and 1 course in creative arts. Certain majors require a thesis or a senior project/recital. **Procedure:** Freshmen are admitted fall and spring. Entrance exams should be taken during spring of the junior year or fall of the senior year. There is an early decision plan. Early decision applications should be filed by November 1; regular applications, by January 15 for fall entry. Notification of early decision is sent December 31; regular decision, April 1. 146 applicants were on the 2014 waiting list; 21 were admitted. Applications are accepted on-line. Application fees are waived if application is completed on-line. **Transfer Students:** 59 transfer students enrolled in 2013-2014. Applicants must submit high school and college transcripts, and 2 essays. SAT or ACT scores are required for transfers with fewer than 2 years of transferable credit (60 semester units). 60 of 128 credits required for the bachelor's degree must be completed at L & C. **International Students:** There are 207 international students enrolled. The school actively recruits these students. They must take the TOEFL with a minimum score of 575 on the paper-based TOEFL (PBT) or 91 on the Internet-based version (iBT), or take the MELAB, or take the ELPT, or IB English. They must also take the SAT or ACT.

ADMISSIONS: 28% of the 2014-2015 applicants were accepted. There were 3 National Merit finalists. 12 freshmen graduated first in their class. **Admissions Contact:** Erica Johnson, Director of Admissions. E-Mail: *admissions@lclark.edu* Web: *www.lclark.edu*

FINANCIAL AID: In 2014-2015, 95% of all full-time freshmen and 86% of continuing full-time students received some form of financial aid. 64% of all full-time freshmen and 59% of continuing full-time students received need-based aid. The average freshman award was $34,253. Need-based scholarships or need-based grants averaged $31,120; need-based self-help aid (loans and jobs) averaged $9,551; and other non-need-based awards and non-need-based scholarships averaged $17,355. The average financial indebtedness of the 2014 graduate was $26,759. The CSS/Profile and FAFSA are required. The priority date for freshman financial aid applications for fall entry is February 15.

LINFIELD COLLEGE-MCMINNVILLE CAMPUS   B-2

www.linfield.edu

McMinnville, OR 97128	(503) 883-2213
	(800) 640-2287
Fax: (503) 883-2472	Email: admission@linfield.edu
Full-time: 629 men, 1015 women	Faculty: 119; IIB, .av$
Part-time: 16 men, 23 women	Ph.D.s: 91%
Graduate: n/av	Student/Faculty: 14 to 1
Year: 4-1-4, summer session	Tuition: $37,346
Room & Board: $10,330	Freshman Class: 2054 applied, 1926 accepted, 463 enrolled
SAT CR/M/W: 530/540/520 ACT: 24	CEEB CODE: 4387
Application Deadline: February 15	COMPETITIVE

Linfield College is dedicated exclusively to undergraduate education, and is home to a vibrant community of engaged students. There are 3 undergraduate schools. In addition to regional accreditation, Linfield College has baccalaureate program accreditation with NASM, CCNE, CAATE, and NAEYC. The 189-acre campus is in a small town 40 miles southwest of Portland. Including any residence halls, there are 78 buildings.

STUDENT LIFE: 50% of undergraduates are from out of state, mostly the Northwest. Students are from 23 states, 25 foreign countries, and Canada. 90% are from public schools. 62% are White; 11% two or more races. The average age of freshmen is 18; all undergraduates, 20. 12% do not continue beyond their first year; 71% remain to graduate. **Housing:** 1367 students can be accommodated in college housing, which includes single-sex and coed dorms and on-campus apartments. In addition, there are special-interest houses. On-campus housing is guaranteed for all 4 years. 78% of students live on campus; of those, 80% remain on campus on weekends. All students may keep cars.

FACULTY/CLASSROOMS: 53% of faculty are male; 47% are female. All teach and do research. No introductory courses are taught by graduate students. The average class size in a laboratory is 16 and in a regular course is 17.

PROGRAMS OF STUDY: Linfield College confers B.A., B.S. and B.S.N. degrees. Bachelor's degrees are awarded in AGRICULTURE (environmental studies), BIOLOGICAL SCIENCE (biochemistry and biology/biological science), BUSINESS (accounting, banking and finance, business administration and management, international business management, and marketing management), COMMUNICATIONS AND THE ARTS (art, communications, creative writing, dramatic arts, English, French, french and francophone studies, German, Japanese, journalism, literature, music, Spanish, studio art, and theatre arts), COMPUTER AND PHYSICAL SCIENCE (applied physics, chemistry, computer science, mathematics, and physics), EDUCATION (athletic training, elementary education, health education, music education, and physical education), HEALTH PROFESSIONS (exercise science and nursing), SOCIAL SCIENCE (African studies, anthropology, crosscultural studies, economics, German area studies, history, international relations, Japanese studies, Latin American studies, philosophy, political science/government, psychology, religion, and sociology). Nursing, accounting, exercise science, and the basic sciences are the strongest academically. Nursing, finance, and exercise science have the largest enrollments.

ACTIVITIES: 26% of men belong to 1 local and 3 national fraternities; 23% of women belong to 1 local and 3 national sororities. There are 40 groups on campus, including ultimate frisbee, the Hawaiian club, art, ASL, band, cheerleading, choir, chorale, chorus, computers, dance, debate, drama, environmental, ethnic, forensics, gay, honors, international, jazz band, literary magazine, musical theater, newspaper, opera, orchestra, pep band, photography, political, professional, radio and TV, religious, social, social service, student government, and symphony. Popular campus events include Wildstock, Luau, Hispanic Heritage Day and Homecoming. **Sports:** There are 9 intercollegiate sports for men and 10 for women, and 6 intramural sports for men and 6 for women. Facilities include a football stadium with turf field, all-weather track, soccer field with lights, indoor complex with 2,200-seat gym, 3 basketball courts, 25-yard swimming pool, 2 racquetball courts, 6,000-square-foot weight room, baseball stadium with turf infield and lights, softball stadium with lights, field house with 3 tennis courts and 4 hitting cages, wellness trail, bike Co-op, and a campus garden. **Graduates:** From July 1, 2013 to June 30, 2014, 320 bachelor's degrees were awarded. The most popular majors were business/marketing (22%), social sciences (15%), parks, recreation, leisure, and and fitness studies (8%). In an average class, 1% graduate in 3 years or less, 61% graduate in 4 years or less, 69% graduate in 5 years or less, and 71% graduate in 6 years or less. Of the 2013 graduating class, 12% were enrolled in graduate school within 6 months of graduation, and 75% were employed.

SERVICES: Counseling and information services are available, as is tutoring in every subject. There is a reader service for the blind. There is also the Linfield Speaking Center and Linfield Writing Lab. **Library/Resources:** The library contains 185,062 volumes, 17,491 microform items, 38,437 audio/video tapes/CDs/DVDs, and subscribes to 989 periodicals including electronic. Computerized library services include interlibrary loans, database searching, Internet access, and Wi-Fi capability. Special learning facilities include an art gallery, radio station, Linfield Center for the Northwest, Delkin Recital Hall, Ford Theatre, Linfield Research Institute, Linfield Art Gallery, Linfield Anthropology Museum, Writing Center, Career Development Center, Speaking Center, Academic Advising Office, Multimedia Studio, Science and Computer Labs. **Physically Challenged Students:** 85% of the campus is accessible. Facilities include wheelchair ramps, elevators, special parking, specially equipped restrooms, special class scheduling, lowered drinking fountains, lowered telephones, and special housing. **Special:** Through Linfield's January Term and Semester Abroad programs, students study in 30 locations around the globe, including China, Africa, Europe and Southeast Asia. During the past five years, almost 700 students completed internships off campus, many in the industry of their choice. Some students intern abroad through the IE3 Global Internships program, and others take advantage of off-campus work-study programs that target literacy and disadvantaged youth. In addition to Linfield's campus-based programs, online degrees and certificates are available, including accelerated degrees. Students are also offered a 3-2 engineering degree as part of a collaboration with the University of Southern California and Oregon and Washington State Universities. Students partner with more than 100 community-based organizations for service learning, sponsored through Linfield's Community Engagement and Service Office. Many outreach projects lead to job opportunities. New students are introduced to college with rich immersion experiences that include First CLAS (Community, Leadership, Action, and Service) and iFocus (for those interested in the sciences) as well as Colloquium and Inquiry Seminars for all. Many also choose to get to know their faculty through the "Take a Professor to Lunch" program. There are 19 national honor societies and 13 departmental honors programs. **Visiting:** There are regularly scheduled orientations for prospective students, consisting of tours and interviews. There are guides for informal visits and visitors may sit in on classes. To schedule a visit, contact the Office of Admission. **Campus Safety and Security:** Measures include 24-hour foot and vehicle patrol, emergency notification system, self-defense education, and security escort services. There are emergency telephones, lighted pathways/sidewalks, and controlled access to dorms/residences.

REQUIREMENTS: The SAT or ACT is required. Applicants should have 4 years each of English and math, 3 to 4 years each of natural science and social studies, and 2 to 4 years of a foreign language. An essay is required, and an interview is recommended. The GED is accepted. AP and CLEP credits are accepted. Important factors in the admissions decision are advanced placement or honors courses, evidence of special talent, and recommendations by school officials. To graduate, students must maintain 2.0 cumulative GPA and complete 125 credit hours, including 35 to 45 in the major. Core requirements include courses from the sciences, literature, fine arts, religion or philosophy, the social sciences, history, and quantitative reasoning. An inquiry seminar in critical thinking and writing is also required. Students must also take courses in American pluralism and global diversity and also 3 credits of activity courses (phys ed, music, or community service). **Procedure:** Freshmen are admitted fall and spring. Entrance exams should be taken during the fall of the senior year of high school. There are early admissions and deferred admissions plans. Applications should be filed by February 15 for fall entry; December 1 for spring entry. Notifications are sent April 1. Applications are accepted on-line. Application fees are waived if application is completed on-line. **Transfer Students:** 75 transfer students enrolled in 2013-2014. Applicants must have a minimum 2.0 GPA from an accredited institution to be considered. An interview is also recommended. 30 of 125 credits required for the bachelor's degree must be completed at Linfield College. **International Students:** There are 93 international students enrolled. The school actively recruits these students. They must take the TOEFL with a minimum score of 550 on the paper-based TOEFL (PBT) or 80 on the Internet-based version (iBT), or take the MELAB and the college's own test.

ADMISSIONS: 94% of the 2014-2015 applicants were accepted. The SAT scores for the 2014-2015 freshman class were: Critical Reading--32% below 500, 41% between 500 and 599, 23% between 600 and 699, and 4% between 700 and 800; Math--29% below 500, 43% between 500 and 599, 25% between 600 and 699, and 2% between

700 and 800; Writing--39% below 500, 39% between 500 and 599, 18% between 600 and 699, and 3% between 700 and 800. The ACT scores were 31% below 21, 18% between 21 and 23, 26% between 24 and 26, 11% between 27 and 28, and 14% above 28. 48% of the current freshmen were in the top fifth of their class; 81% were in the top two fifths. 8 freshmen graduated first in their class. **Admissions Contact:** Lisa Knodle-Bragiel, Director of Admission. E-Mail: *admission@linfield.edu* Web: *www.linfield.edu*

FINANCIAL AID: In 2014-2015, 92% of all full-time freshmen and 98% of continuing full-time students received some form of financial aid. 79% of all full-time freshmen and 76% of continuing full-time students received need-based aid. The average freshman award was $32,134. Need-based scholarships or need-based grants averaged $26,477; need-based self-help aid (loans and jobs) averaged $5,641; and other non-need-based awards and non-need-based scholarships averaged $15,900. 16% of undergraduate students work part-time. Average annual earnings from campus work are $1369. The average financial indebtedness of the 2014 graduate was $28,697. Linfield College is a member of CSS. The FAFSA, (FAFSA forecaster for early action) only is required. The priority date for freshman financial aid applications for fall entry is February 1.

MARYLHURST UNIVERSITY (*The complete profile is made available exclusively on our website, www.barronspac.com*)

NORTHWEST CHRISTIAN UNIVERSITY	B-2
www.nwcu.edu	

Eugene, OR 97401-3727	(541) 343-1641
	(877) 463-6622
Fax: (541) 349-5281	Email: admissions@nwcu.edu
Full-time: 150 men, 250 women	Faculty: n/av
Part-time: 10 men, 20 women	Ph.D.s: n/av
Graduate: 50 men, 50 women	Student/Faculty: n/av
Year: trimesters, summer session	Tuition: $24,100
Room & Board: $7900	Freshman Class: n/av
SAT or ACT: required	CEEB CODE: 4543
Application Deadline: see profile	COMPETITIVE

Northwest Christian University was founded in 1895 and is a private institution affiliated with the Christian Church, offering programs in the arts and sciences, business, education, and ministries. The figures in the above capsule and figures in this profile are approximate. The 8-acre campus is in an urban area 125 miles south of Portland. Including any residence halls, there are 14 buildings.

STUDENT LIFE: 92% of undergraduates are from Oregon. Others are from 8 states. 94% are from public schools. 70% are white. 64% claim no religious affiliation; 35% Protestant. The average age of freshmen is 18; all undergraduates, 30.

FACULTY/CLASSROOMS: No introductory courses are taught by graduate students. The average class size in an introductory lecture is 40 and in a regular course, 25.

PROGRAMS OF STUDY: NCU confers B.A. and B.S. degrees. Associate and Master's degrees are also awarded. Bachelor's degrees are awarded in BUSINESS (accounting, business administration and management, and management information systems), COMMUNICATIONS AND THE ARTS (communications and music), COMPUTER AND PHYSICAL SCIENCE (computer science), EDUCATION (education and elementary education), HEALTH PROFESSIONS (exercise science and health care administration), SOCIAL SCIENCE (human services, humanities, interdisciplinary studies, international studies, ministries, psychology, and social science).

ACTIVITIES: There are 15 groups on campus, including cheerleading, choir, chorale, debate, drama, forensics, literary magazine, musical theater, newspaper, religious, social service, student government, and yearbook. Popular campus events include Annual Musical, Spirit Week, and Wellness Week.

SERVICES: Counseling and information services are available, as is tutoring in most subjects. There is remedial math, reading, and writing. **Library/Resources:** The library contains 60,250 volumes, 766 microform items, 10,367 audio/video tapes/CDs/DVDs, and subscribes to 261 periodicals including electronic. Computerized library services include interlibrary loans, database searching, and Internet access. **Physically Challenged Students:** 60% of the campus is accessible. Facilities include wheelchair ramps, elevators, special parking, specially equipped restrooms, special class scheduling, lowered drinking fountains, and lowered telephones. **Special:** NCC offers internships, study abroad in 4 countries, a Washington semester, work study, accelerated degree programs, and student-designed majors. **Visiting:** There are regularly scheduled orientations for prospective students. There are guides for informal visits, visitors may sit in on classes, and stay overnight. To schedule a visit, contact the Admissions Office at (541) 684-7209. **Campus Safety and Security:** Measures include 24-hour foot and vehicle patrol and security escort services. There are emergency telephones and lighted pathways/sidewalks.

REQUIREMENTS: The SAT or ACT is required. Students are required to submit a completed admission application, high school transcripts, and 2 references. An interview is recommended. A GPA of 2.5 is required. AP and CLEP credits are accepted. Important factors in the admissions decision are advanced placement or honors courses, recommendations by school officials, and extracurricular activities record.

FINANCIAL AID: NCU is a member of CSS. The FAFSA and the college's own financial statement are required. Check with the school for current application deadlines.

OREGON INSTITUTE OF TECHNOLOGY	B-4
www.oit.edu	

Klamath Falls, OR 97601-8801	(541) 885-1000
	(800) 422-2017
Fax: (541) 885-1024	Email: oit@oit.edu
Full-time: 1120 men, 850 women	Faculty: n/av
Part-time: 575 men, 560 women	Ph.D.s: n/av
Graduate: 15 men, 5 women	Student/Faculty: n/av
Year: trimesters, summer session	Tuition: $7052 ($19,976)
Room & Board: $8900	Freshman Class: n/av
SAT or ACT: required	CEEB CODE: 4587
Application Deadline: see profile	COMPETITIVE

Oregon Institute of Technology provides degree programs in engineering and health technologies, management, communications, and applied sciences. There are 3 undergraduate schools and 1 graduate school. The figures in the above capsule and in this profile are approximate. In addition to regional accreditation, OIT has baccalaureate program accreditation with ABET and NLN. The 173-acre campus is in a small town 60 miles east of Medford in south central Oregon. Including any residence halls, there are 12 buildings.

STUDENT LIFE: 85% of undergraduates are from Oregon. Others are from 35 states and 17 foreign countries. 95% are from public schools. 80% are white. The average age of freshmen is 23; all undergraduates, 26. 26% do not continue beyond their first year; 29% remain to graduate.

FACULTY/CLASSROOMS: No introductory courses are taught by graduate students. The average class size in an introductory lecture is 30; in a laboratory, 18; and in a regular course, 30.

PROGRAMS OF STUDY: OIT confers B.S. degrees. Associate and Master's degrees are also awarded. Bachelor's degrees are awarded in BUSINESS (management information systems), ENGINEERING AND ENVIRONMENTAL DESIGN (civil engineering, computer technology, electrical/electronics engineering technology, engineering technology, environmental science, industrial administration/management, laser electro-optics technology, manufacturing technology, mechanical engineering technology, and surveying engineering), HEALTH PROFESSIONS (dental hygiene, health science, radiograph medical technology, and ultrasound technology), SOCIAL SCIENCE (industrial and organizational psychology).

ACTIVITIES: 3% of men belong to 1 local and 1 national fraternities; 3% of women belong to 1 local and 1 national sororities. There are 37 groups on campus, including cheerleading, communications, computers, ethnic, honors, international, newspaper, outdoor, pep band, professional, radio and TV, religious, social, and student government. Popular campus events include Tech Challenge, Family Weekend Tech Fest, and a skills contest for business and math students.

SERVICES: Counseling and information services are available, as is tutoring in some subjects, math, sciences, and computers. There is a reader service for the blind, and remedial math, reading, and writing. **Library/Resources:** The library contains 145,988 volumes, 158,278 microform items, and 2,069 audio/video tapes/CDs/DVDs, subscribes to 1,815 periodicals including electronic. Computerized library services include interlibrary loans and database searching. Special learning facilities include an art gallery and radio station. **Physically Challenged Students:** 90% of the campus is accessible. Facilities include wheelchair ramps, elevators, special parking, specially equipped restrooms, and special class scheduling. **Special:** Cross-registration with Klamath Community College, internships in all majors, and co-op programs in all engineering technologies are available. OIT also offers advanced degree programs in software engineering technology and vascular imaging. There are 2 national honor societies. **Visiting:** There are regularly scheduled orientations for prospective students, including tours and meetings with admissions counselors, faculty, and students. There are guides for informal visits, visitors may sit in on classes, and stay overnight. To schedule a visit, contact the Admissions Office at oit@oit.edu. **Campus Safety and Security:** Measures include 24-hour foot and vehicle patrol and security escort services. There are lighted pathways/sidewalks.

REQUIREMENTS: The SAT or ACT is required for placement purposes; however, a satisfactory composite score on the SAT or 21 on the ACT is required for applicants who do not meet the minimum GPA requirement. Applicants must have 14 academic units, including 4 years of English, 3 each of math and social sciences, and 2 each of science and a foreign language. The GED is accepted. A GPA of 2.5 is required. AP and CLEP credits are accepted.

FINANCIAL AID: The FAFSA is required. Check with the school for current application deadlines.

OREGON STATE UNIVERSITY　　　　　　B-2
www.oregonstate.edu

Corvallis, OR 97331　　　　　　　(541) 737-4411
　　　　　　　　　　　　　　　　　　　(800) 291-4192
Fax: n/av　　　　　　　Email: osuadmit@oregonstate.edu
Full-time: 10018 men, 8459 women　　**Faculty:** 1111; I, --$
Part-time: 2856 men, 2570 women　　**Ph.D.s:** 85%
Graduate: 2592 men, 2391 women　　**Student/Faculty:** 17 to 1
Year: quarters, summer session　　**Tuition:** $9122 ($26,354)
Room & Board: $11,151　　**Freshman Class:** 14395 applied, 11192 accepted, 3857 enrolled
SAT CR/M/W: 540/560/520 **ACT:** 24　　**CEEB CODE:** 4586
Application Deadline: September 1　　**VERY COMPETITIVE**

Oregon State, founded in 1868, is the state's Land Grant university and is one of only two universities in the U.S. to have Sea Grant, Space Grant and Sun Grant designations. Oregon State is also the only university in Oregon to hold both the Carnegie Foundation's top designation for research institutions and its prestigious Community Engagement classification. There are 10 undergraduate schools and 12 graduate schools. In addition to regional accreditation, Oregon State has baccalaureate program accreditation with AACSB, ABET, ACCE, ACPE, AHEA, CSAB, NASM, NCATE, and SAF. The 400-acre campus is in a small town 90 miles south of Portland and an hour from the Cascades or the Pacific Coast. Including any residence halls, there are 203 buildings.

STUDENT LIFE: 73% of undergraduates are from Oregon. Others are from 50 states, 64 foreign countries, and Canada. 68% are White. **Male To Female Ratio:** 0.9:1. The average age of freshmen is 19; all undergraduates, 23. 16% do not continue beyond their first year; 63% remain to graduate. **Housing:** 4641 students can be accommodated in college housing, which includes coed dorms and married student

housing. In addition, there are honors houses, special-interest houses, fraternity houses, sorority houses, housing for international students and housing for entrepreneurship majors. On-campus housing is guaranteed for the freshman year only, and is available on a first-come, first-served basis. 78% of students commute. Alcohol is not permitted. All students may keep cars.

FACULTY/CLASSROOMS: 60% of faculty are male; 40% are female. No introductory courses are taught by graduate students. The average class size in an introductory lecture is 60; in a laboratory is 26; and in a regular course is 38.

PROGRAMS OF STUDY: Oregon State confers B.A., B.S. and B.F.A. degrees. Master's and doctoral degrees are also awarded. Bachelor's degrees are awarded in AGRICULTURE (agricultural business management, agricultural economics, agriculture, agronomy, animal science, fishing and fisheries, forest engineering, forestry production and processing, forestry and related sciences, horticulture, natural resource management, range/farm management, wildlife management, and wood science), BIOLOGICAL SCIENCE (biochemistry, biology/biological science, biotechnology, botany, ecology, microbiology, nutrition, wildlife biology, and zoology), BUSINESS (accounting, business administration and management, business systems analysis, management information systems, management science, marketing management, marketing/retailing/merchandising, and recreational facilities management), COMMUNICATIONS AND THE ARTS (apparel design, applied art, art, English, French, German, music, Spanish, speech/debate/rhetoric, and visual and performing arts), COMPUTER AND PHYSICAL SCIENCE (chemistry, computer science, earth science, mathematics, medical physics, natural sciences, physics, and science), EDUCATION (education), ENGINEERING AND ENVIRONMENTAL DESIGN (agricultural engineering, bioengineering, chemical engineering, civil engineering, computer engineering, construction management, electrical/electronics engineering, engineering physics, environmental engineering, environmental science, geological engineering, geophysical engineering, industrial engineering, interior design, manufacturing engineering, mechanical engineering, metallurgical engineering, and nuclear engineering), HEALTH PROFESSIONS (exercise science, health, health care administration, medical technology, predentistry, premedicine, preoptometry, prepharmacy, prephysical therapy, prepodiatry, public health, and radiation therapy), SOCIAL SCIENCE (American studies, anthropology, economics, ethnic studies, family/consumer studies, food science, history, human development, international studies, liberal arts/general studies, parks and recreation management, philosophy, political science/government, psychology, sociology, and women's studies). Engineering, agricultural sciences, and forestry are the strongest academically. Business, exercise and sports science, human development and family sciences are the largest.

ACTIVITIES: 13% of men belong to 23 national fraternities; 18% of women belong to 20 national sororities. There are 360 groups on campus, including and adventure club, art, band, cheerleading, chess, choir, chorale, chorus, communications, computers, dance, debate, drama, drill team, drum and bugle corps, environmental, ethnic, film, forensics, gay, honors, international, jazz band, literary magazine, marching band, musical theater, newspaper, orchestra, pep band, photography, political, professional, radio and TV, religious, social, social service, student government, student sustainability initiative, symphony, and yearbook. Popular campus events include Connect Week, Dads Weekend, Civil War, Moms Weekend, Battle of the Bands and Bard in the Quad. **Sports:** There are 7 intercollegiate sports for men and 10 for women, and 19 intramural sports for men and 17 for women. Facilities include two cardio rooms, two weight rooms, two gyms, six racquetball courts, three squash courts, three multipurpose rooms, a 42 ft tall climbing wall, 1/10 mile indoor track, 25-yard pool, a dive well, a hot tub, three sand volleyball courts, and the Adventure Leadership Institute, in Dixon Center a fieldhouse with indoor multipurpose court, turf field, and rock climbing wall, multiple artificial and natural terf fields around campus, tennis courts, and basketball courts. **Graduates:** From July 1, 2013 to June 30, 2014, 4157 bachelor's degrees were awarded. The most popular majors were engineering (14%), business (13%), and human development and family studies (11%). In an average class, 31% graduate in 4 years or less, 56% graduate in 5 years or less, and 63% graduate in 6 years or less.

SERVICES: Counseling and information services are available, as is tutoring in most subjects. There is a reader service for the blind, and remedial math, reading, and writing. Facilities include a communication skills center and a math sciences learning center. **Library/ Resources:** The 4 libraries contain 2.0 million volumes, 2.2 million microform items, 27,256 audio/video tapes/CDs/DVDs, and subscribe to 107,975 periodicals including electronic. Computerized library services include interlibrary loans, database searching, Internet access, and Wi-Fi capability. Special learning facilities include an art gallery, natural history museum, radio station, TV station, an arboretum, a wave research lab, a research farm, research vessel, and the Linus Pauling Collection. **Physically Challenged Students:** 92% of the campus is accessible. Facilities include wheelchair ramps, elevators, special parking, specially equipped restrooms, special class scheduling, lowered drinking fountains, lowered telephones. **Special:** Oregon State University offers a double degree in education, where a student has a primary degree in any field and then also earns an education degree. With the education degree the student also earns an Oregon teaching license. The university began a program in the fall of 2012 offering a double degree in sustainability, students take an additional 36 credits beyond their primary degree. The Sustainability degree is interdisciplinary drawing on courses from many disciplines in the university. OSU has a list of over 200 approved study abroad programs in 77 different countries. There are 14 national honor societies, a freshman honors program, and 40 departmental honors programs. **Visiting:** There are regularly scheduled orientations for prospective students. There are guides for informal visits, visitors may sit in on classes, and stay overnight. To schedule a visit, contact the Visitor Center. **Campus Safety and Security:** Measures include 24-hour foot and vehicle patrol, emergency notification system, and security escort services. There are shuttle buses, emergency telephones, lighted pathways/sidewalks, and controlled access to dorms/residences.

REQUIREMENTS: The SAT or ACT is required. Applicants should be high school graduates or hold the GED. Required high school preparation includes 4 years of English; 3 years of math, including algebra II; 3 years of science; 3 years of social science; and 2 years of foreign language. Some subject requirements may be fulfilled by test scores. A GPA of 3.0 is required. AP and CLEP credits are accepted.To graduate, students must complete at least 180 quarter credits with a GPA of 2.0. The required core curriculum includes writing, mathematics, speech, physical science, biological science, culture, difference and power, technology and society, global issues, and fitness. Students must also take a writing-intensive course in their major field and meet additional distribution requirements. **Procedure:** Freshmen are admitted to all sessions. Entrance exams should be taken during the junior or senior year. There are early admissions, deferred admissions, and rolling admissions plans. Early decision applications should be filed by February 1; regular applications, by September 1 for fall entry; December 8 for winter entry; March 2 for spring entry; and June 22 for summer entry, along with a $60 fee. Notification of early decision is sent March 15. Applications are accepted on-line. **Transfer Students:** 1854 transfer students enrolled in 2013-2014. Applicants must present a GPA of at least 2.25 in previous college work. Students should have completed at least 36 hours of college credit, and must have a C- or better in English Composition and College Algebra. Transfer students must show two years of foreign language in high school or two semesters of foreign language. Either SAT I or ACT scores must be submitted. 45 of 180 credits required for the bachelor's degree must be completed at Oregon State. **International Students:** There are 1201 international students enrolled. The school actively recruits these students. They must take the TOEFL with a minimum score of 80 on the Internet-based version (iBT).

ADMISSIONS: 78% of the 2014-2015 applicants were accepted. The SAT scores for the 2014-2015 freshman class were: Critical Reading--30% below 500, 41% between 500 and 599, 23% between 600 and 699, and 6% between 700 and 800; Math--25% below 500, 39% between 500 and 599, 27% between 600 and 699, and 9% between 700 and 800; Writing--37% below 500, 40% between 500 and 599, 20% between 600 and 699, and 3% between 700 and 800. The ACT scores were 20% below 21, 25% between 21 and 23, 24% between 24 and 26, 14% between 27 and 28, and 17% above 28. 47% of the current freshmen were in the top fifth of their class; 80% were in the top

two fifths. 166 freshmen graduated first in their class. **Admissions Contact:** Noah Buckley, Director of Admissions. E-Mail: *osuadmit@ oregonstate.edu* Web: *http:/oregonstate.edu/admissions/*

FINANCIAL AID: Oregon State is a member of CSS. The FAFSA is required. The priority date for freshman financial aid applications for fall entry is February 28.

OREGON UNIVERSITY SYSTEM

The Oregon University System, established in 1929, is a public system in Oregon. It is governed by the Oregon state board of higher education, whose chief administrator is the chancellor. The primary goals of the system are teaching at the undergraduate, graduate, and professional levels, both basic and applied research, and public service to the state and nation. The main priorities are to insure that students are liberally educated, to advance understanding in the areas of arts and sciences, and to be responsive to the particular circumstances of the people of Oregon. The total student enrollment is usually about 69,000 with 4000 faculty members. Altogether there are 182 baccalaureate, 116 master's, and 63 doctoral programs offered in the Oregon University System. Profiles of the 4-year campuses are included in this section.

PACIFIC NORTHWEST COLLEGE OF ART (*The complete profile is made available exclusively on our website, www.barronspac.com*)

PACIFIC UNIVERSITY	A-1
www.pacificu.edu	

Forest Grove, OR 97116	(503) 359-2218
	(800) 677-6712
Fax: n/av	Email: admissions@pacificu.edu
Full-time: 720 men, 995 women	Faculty: 87
Part-time: 6 men, 9 women	Ph.D.s: 78%
Graduate: 393 men, 1193 women	Student/Faculty: 12 to 1
Year: 4-1-4, summer session	Tuition: $38,510
Room & Board: $11,116	Freshman Class: 2658 applied, 2291 accepted, 421 enrolled
SAT CR/M: 545/555 ACT: 24	CEEB CODE: 4601
Application Deadline: February 15	COMPETITIVE+

Pacific University, founded in 1849, is an independent institution affiliated with the Congregational Church (United Church of Christ), offering degree programs in liberal arts, science, business, education, and health professions. There are 6 graduate schools. In addition to regional accreditation, Pacific has baccalaureate program accreditation with NASM. The 55-acre campus is in a small town 25 miles west of Portland. Including any residence halls, there are 18 buildings.

STUDENT LIFE: 50% of undergraduates are from out of state, mostly the West. Students are from 31 states, 7 foreign countries, and Canada. 91% are from public schools. 64% are White; 17% Asian American. The average age of freshmen is 18; all undergraduates, 21. 22% do not continue beyond their first year; 54% remain to graduate.

FACULTY/CLASSROOMS: 52% of faculty are male; 48% are female. All teach and do research. No introductory courses are taught by graduate students. The average class size in an introductory lecture is 35; in a laboratory is 20; and in a regular course is 19.

PROGRAMS OF STUDY: Pacific confers B.A., B.S. and B.M. degrees. Master's and Doctoral degrees are also awarded. Bachelor's degrees are awarded in BIOLOGICAL SCIENCE (biology/biological science), BUSINESS (business administration and management), COMMUNICATIONS AND THE ARTS (creative writing, dramatic arts, Japanese, literature, music, and Spanish), COMPUTER AND PHYSICAL SCIENCE (chemistry, computer science, mathematics, and physics), SOCIAL SCIENCE (economics, history, humanities, philosophy, political science/government, psychology, social work, and sociology). Natural sciences, literature, and creative writing are the strongest academically. Business administration, English and psychology have the largest enrollments.

ACTIVITIES: 6% of men belong to 3 local fraternities; 9% of women belong to 3 local sororities. There are 35 groups on campus, including art, band, cheerleading, choir, chorale, chorus, computers, dance, debate, drama, ethnic, forensics, gay, honors, international, jazz band, literary magazine, musical theater, newspaper, opera, orchestra, pep band, photography, political, professional, radio and TV, religious, social, social service, student government, and yearbook. Popular campus events also include Hawaiian Club Luau, International Club Banquet, and Japan Day.

SERVICES: Counseling and information services are available, as is tutoring in most subjects. There is a reader service for the blind. **Library/Resources:** The library contains 152,060 volumes, 76,609 microform items, 3,708 audio/video tapes/CDs/DVDs, and subscribes to 945 periodicals including electronic. Computerized library services include interlibrary loans and database searching. Special learning facilities include an art gallery, radio station, TV station, and museum of the history of the university. **Physically Challenged Students:** 80% of the campus is accessible. Facilities include wheelchair ramps, elevators, special parking, specially equipped restrooms, and lowered drinking fountains. **Special:** Cross-registration is available with Oregon Independent Colleges and Oregon Graduate Institute of Science and Technology (OGIST). The university also offers cooperative programs with Washington University in St. Louis, OGIST, and Oregon School of Arts and Crafts, as well as study abroad in 13 countries. Full-time, semester-long internships, including one in Washington D.C., are possible. Dual majors, a general studies degree in humanities, nondegree study, 3-2 engineering programs with Washington University in St. Louis and OGIST, and an interdisciplinary program in peace and conflict studies are available. There are 2 national honor societies, a freshman honors program, and 1 departmental honors programs. **Visiting:** There are regularly scheduled orientations for prospective students, including overnight housing with current students, a campus tour, classroom visitations, and meetings with faculty and coaches. There are guides for informal visits, visitors may sit in on classes, and stay overnight. To schedule a visit, contact the Admissions Office. **Campus Safety and Security:** Measures include 24-hour foot and vehicle patrol and security escort services. There are emergency telephones and lighted pathways/sidewalks.

REQUIREMENTS: The SAT or ACT is required. Applicants are expected to be high school graduates or to hold the GED. A personal essay is required, and an interview is recommended. On-line applications are available on Pacific's Web pages. A GPA of 3.0 is required. AP and CLEP credits are accepted. Important factors in the admissions decision are advanced placement or honors courses, recommendations by school officials, and extracurricular activities record.

ADMISSIONS: 86% of a recent year's applicants were accepted. The SAT scores for a recent year, freshman class were: Critical Reading--26% below 500, 48% between 500 and 599, 22% between 600 and 699, and 4% between 700 and 800; Math--24% below 500, 45% between 500 and 599, 26% between 600 and 699, and 5% between 700 and 800. The ACT scores were 4% below 21, 49% between 21 and 23, 36% between 24 and 26, % between 27 and 28, and 11% above 28. 18 freshmen graduated first in their class.

FINANCIAL AID: In 2014-2015, 80% of all full-time freshmen students received some form of financial aid. 80% of all full-time freshmen students received need-based aid. The average freshman award was $32,087. Need-based scholarships or need-based grants averaged $24,105; need-based self-help aid (loans and jobs) averaged $24,105; other non-need-based awards and non-need-based scholarships averaged $6,182; and $18,078 from other forms of aid. 54% of undergraduate students work part-time. Average annual earnings from campus work are $823. The average financial indebtedness of the 2013 graduate was $27,945. Pacific is a member of CSS. The FAFSA is required. Check with the school for current application deadlines.

PORTLAND STATE UNIVERSITY   B-1
www.pdx.edu

Portland, OR 97207	503-725-5504
	(800) 547-8887
Fax: 503-725-5525	Email: mtrifi@pdx.edu
Full-time: 6935 men, 7582 women	Faculty: I, --$
Part-time: 4074 men, 4579 women	Ph.D.s: n/av
Graduate: 2237 men, 3324 women	Student/Faculty: 18 to 1
Year: quarters, summer session	Tuition: $7653 ($22,863)
Room & Board: $11,019	Freshman Class: n/av
SAT CR/M: 520/510 ACT: 22	CEEB CODE: 4610
Application Deadline: open	COMPETITIVE

Portland State University (PSU), is a nationally acclaimed leader in sustainability and community-based learning. The University's position in the heart of Oregon's economic and cultural center enables PSU students and faculty to apply scholarly theory to the real-world problems of business and community organizations. Portland State offers more than 220 undergraduate, master's, and doctoral degree options, as well as graduate certificates and continuing education programs. PSU is Oregon's largest and most diverse university, with some 30,000 students who come from all 50 states and from nearly 100 nations around the world. There are 8 undergraduate schools. In addition to regional accreditation, PSU has baccalaureate program accreditation with AACSB, ABET, ASLA, CSWE, NASAD, NASM, and NCATE. The 50-acre campus is in an urban area in the center of Portland. Including any residence halls, there are 56 buildings.

STUDENT LIFE: 89% of undergraduates are from Oregon. 65% are White. The average age of all undergraduates is 27. 26% do not continue beyond their first year; 74% remain to graduate.

FACULTY/CLASSROOMS: 50% of faculty are male; 50% are female. No introductory courses are taught by graduate students.

PROGRAMS OF STUDY: PSU confers B.A., B.S. and B.M. degrees. Master's and Doctoral degrees are also awarded. Bachelor's degrees are awarded in BIOLOGICAL SCIENCE (biochemistry and biology/biological science), BUSINESS (accounting, business administration and management, management science, marketing/retailing/merchandising, and personnel management), COMMUNICATIONS AND THE ARTS (advertising, art history and appreciation, Chinese, dramatic arts, English, fine arts, French, German, Japanese, languages, music, Russian, Spanish, and speech/debate/rhetoric), COMPUTER AND PHYSICAL SCIENCE (chemistry, computer science, geology, information sciences and systems, mathematics, and physics), EDUCATION (health education), ENGINEERING AND ENVIRONMENTAL DESIGN (architecture, civil engineering, computer engineering, electrical/electronics engineering, and environmental science), SOCIAL SCIENCE (anthropology, child care/child and family studies, community services, economics, geography, history, international studies, law enforcement and corrections, liberal arts/general studies, philosophy, political science/government, psychology, social work, sociology, and women's studies). Electrical engineering, environmental science, and physics are the strongest academically. Psychology, business administration, and art have the largest enrollments.

ACTIVITIES: There are 246 groups on campus, including art, band, cheerleading, chess, choir, chorale, chorus, communications, computers, dance, debate, drama, drill team, environmental, ethnic, film, forensics, gay, honors, international, jazz band, literary magazine, musical theater, newspaper, opera, orchestra, outdoor, pep band, photography, political, professional, radio and TV, religious, social, social service, student government, and symphony. Popular campus events include Portland State of Mind, International Student Cultural Night, Friends of Chamber Music and LunchBox Theater.

SERVICES: Counseling and information services are available, as is tutoring in most subjects. There is a reader service for the blind, and remedial math and writing. Student Support Services provides assistance to students who are low-income, who have a physical disability, or whose parents did not graduate from college. **Library/Resources:** Computerized library services include interlibrary loans, database searching, and Internet access. Special learning facilities include an art gallery, radio station, a multicultural center and a Native American center. **Physically Challenged Students:** 95% of the campus is accessible. Facilities include wheelchair ramps, elevators, special parking, specially equipped restrooms, special class scheduling, lowered drinking fountains, lowered telephones, and special housing. **Special:** Students may study abroad in 59 countries. Numerous internships, co-op programs, a Washington semester, and work-study programs are available. Most undergraduate programs may be taken on an accelerated basis, and students in all programs may undertake dual majors or design their own majors. A general studies program is available in arts and letters, science, or social science. Nondegree study and pass/fail grading options are possible. Students may enroll for 7 or fewer credits per term without formal admission. There are 8 national honor societies and a freshman honors program. **Visiting:** There are regularly scheduled orientations for prospective students, including daily campus tours led by student guides and opportunities for prospective students to meet with faculty, staff, and advisers. There are guides for informal visits, visitors may sit in on classes, and stay overnight. To schedule a visit, contact Campus Tour Coordinator at (503) 725-5555. **Campus Safety and Security:** Measures include 24-hour foot and vehicle patrol, emergency notification system, self-defense education, and security escort services. There are emergency telephones, lighted pathways/sidewalks, A campus watch newsletter, information lectures, and community liaison.

REQUIREMENTS: The SAT or ACT is required. Various combination of test scores and GPA may qualify for admissions under special action by the admissions committee. Applicants should be high school graduates or have earned the GED. Secondary preparation should include 4 years of English, 3 years of math, and 2 years each of science a foreign language and social studies and 1 year of history. In addition, one unit of laboratory science is recommended. A GPA of 3.0 is required. AP and CLEP credits are accepted.

ADMISSIONS: The SAT scores for a recent year freshman class were: Critical Reading--39% below 500, 39% between 500 and 599, 19% between 600 and 699, and 3% between 700 and 800; Math--42% below 500, 4% between 500 and 599, 16% between 600 and 699, and 1% between 700 and 800; Writing--50% below 500, 36% between 500 and 599, 13% between 600 and 699, and 1% between 700 and 800. The ACT scores were 38% below 21, 26% between 21 and 23, 20% between 24 and 26, 10% between 27 and 28, and 6% above 28.

FINANCIAL AID: In a recent year, 73% of all full-time freshmen and 87% of continuing full-time students received some form of financial aid. 58% of all full-time freshmen and 77% of continuing full-time students received need-based aid. The average freshman award was $11,540. Need-based scholarships or need-based grants averaged $5,350 ($18,500 maximum); need-based self-help aid (loans and jobs) averaged $6,916 ($27,661 maximum); non-need-based athletic scholarships averaged $14,168 ($28,610 maximum); and other non-need-based awards and non-need-based scholarships averaged $3,589 ($33,152 maximum). 80% of undergraduate students work part-time. Average annual earnings from campus work are $1716. The FAFSA and the college's own financial statement are required. Check with the school for current application deadlines.

REED COLLEGE   **B-1**
www.reed.edu

Portland, OR 97202   (503) 777-7511
                                          (800) 547-4750
Fax: (503) 777-7553   Email: admission@reed.edu
Full-time: 646 men, 711 women   Faculty: 153; IIB, +$
Part-time: 18 men, 21 women   Ph.D.s: 96%
Graduate: 7 men, 9 women   Student/Faculty: 9 to 1
Year: semesters   Tuition: $46,010
Room & Board: $11,770   Freshman Class: 2893
                                 applied, 1404 accepted,
                                 356 enrolled
SAT CR/M/W: 710/670/680   CEEB CODE: 4654
Application Deadline: January 15   **MOST COMPETITIVE**

Reed College, founded in 1908, is a private, nonsectarian institution offering programs in liberal arts and sciences, and emphasizing instruction through small conference-style classes. There is 1 undergraduate school and 1 graduate school. The 116-acre campus is in an urban area in Portland. Including any residence halls, there are 43 buildings.

STUDENT LIFE: 87% of undergraduates are from out of state, mostly the Southwest. Students are from 47 states, 45 foreign countries, and Canada. 56% are from public schools. 59% are White; 11% Hispanic. The average age of freshmen is 18; all undergraduates, 20. 4% do not continue beyond their first year; 82% remain to graduate.

FACULTY/CLASSROOMS: 56% of faculty are male; 44% are female. All teach and do research. No introductory courses are taught by graduate students.

PROGRAMS OF STUDY: Reed confers B.A. degrees. Master's degrees are also awarded. Bachelor's degrees are awarded in AGRICULTURE (environmental studies), BIOLOGICAL SCIENCE (bio-

chemistry and biology/biological science), COMMUNICATIONS AND THE ARTS (art, Chinese, classics, dramatic arts, English literature, Germanic languages and literature, linguistics, literature, music, and Russian languages and literature), COMPUTER AND PHYSICAL SCIENCE (chemical physics, chemistry, mathematics, mathematics – economics, and physics), SOCIAL SCIENCE (American studies, anthropology, economics, French studies, history, international political science, philosophy, political science/government, psychology, religion, sociology, and Spanish studies). English, biology, and psychology have the largest enrollments.

ACTIVITIES: There are 104 groups on campus, including art, chess, choir, chorus, computers, dance, debate, drama, environmental, ethnic, gay, international, jazz band, literary magazine, musical theater, newspaper, orchestra, photography, radio and TV, religious, social service, student government, and symphony. Popular campus events include Performing Arts Festival, Campus Clean Up Day (Canyon Day), and Reed Arts Week (RAW).

SERVICES: Counseling and information services are available, as is tutoring in every subject. There is a reader service for the blind, and remedial math, reading, and writing. **Library/Resources:** The 2 libraries contain 629,871 volumes, 180,996 microform items, and 31,456 audio/video tapes/CDs/DVDs, and subscribe to 17,169 periodicals including electronic. Computerized library services include interlibrary loans, database searching, Internet access, and Wi-Fi capability. Special learning facilities include an art gallery, radio station, a reactor, and centers for bio science, math, quantitative skills, science, and writing. **Physically Challenged Students:** Facilities include wheelchair ramps, elevators, special parking, specially equipped restrooms, special class scheduling, lowered drinking fountains, and lowered telephones. **Special:** Cross-registration is available through the Oregon Independent Colleges organization and Pacific Northwest College of Art. 3-2 programs are available for computer science with University of Washington and for engineering with CalTech, Columbia University, and Rensselaer Polytechnic Institute. Also available are combined programs with the Pacific Northwest College of Art for Visual Arts. Study abroad in 18 countries, a domestic exchange program with Howard University in Washington, D.C., Sarah Lawrence College, and Sea Education Association (SEA), accelerated degree programs, dual majors, student-designed majors, numerous interdisciplinary majors, nondegree study, and pass/fail options are also offered. There is a chapter of Phi Beta Kappa. **Visiting:** There are regularly scheduled orientations for prospective students, including an information session, campus tour, and an admission interview. Visitors may sit in on classes and stay overnight. To schedule a visit, contact the Office of Admission at admission@reed.edu. **Campus Safety and Security:** Measures include 24-hour foot and vehicle patrol, emergency notification system, self-defense education, and security escort services. There are shuttle buses, emergency telephones, lighted pathways/sidewalks, and controlled access to dorms/residences.

REQUIREMENTS: SAT or ACT are required. Reed strongly recommends that applicants have 4 years of English, 3 each of math and science, and 2 each of foreign language, history, and social studies. An essay is required, and an interview is recommended. The GED is accepted. AP credits are accepted. Important factors in the admissions decision are advanced placement or honors courses, personality/intangible qualities, and evidence of special talent.

ADMISSIONS: 49% of a recent year applicants were accepted. The SAT scores for a recent year freshman class were: Critical Reading--5% between 500 and 599, 36% between 600 and 699, and 59% between 700 and 800; Math--16% between 500 and 599, 49% between 600 and 699, and 35% between 700 and 800; Writing--1% below 500, 8% between 500 and 599, 52% between 600 and 699, and 39% between 700 and 800. The ACT scores were 2% between 21 and 23, 7% between 24 and 26, 18% between 27 and 28, and 73% above 28. 84% of the current freshmen were in the top fifth of their class; 94% were in the top two fifths. 13 freshmen graduated first in their class.

FINANCIAL AID: In a recent year, 50% of all full-time freshmen and 46% of continuing full-time students received some form of financial aid. 49% of all full-time freshmen and 46% of continuing full-time students received need-based aid. The average freshman award was $44,328. Need-based scholarships or need-based grants averaged

$41,510; and need-based self-help aid (loans and jobs) averaged $3,895. 39% of undergraduate students work part-time. The average financial indebtedness of the 2013 graduate was $20,079. Reed is a member of CSS. The CSS/Profile, FAFSA, the college's own financial statement, and parent and student federal tax forms are required. The deadline for filing freshman financial aid applications for fall entry is March 1.

SOUTHERN OREGON UNIVERSITY   B-4
www.sou.edu

Ashland, OR 97520   (541) 552-6411
   n/av

Fax: (541) 552-8403
Full-time: 1655 men, 2071 women
Part-time: 656 men, 1032 women
Graduate: 216 men, 374 women
Year: quarters, summer session
Room & Board: $10,080

Email: admissions@sou.edu
Faculty: 199; IIA, --$
Ph.D.s: 93%
Student/Faculty: 20 to 1
Tuition: $7794 ($21,276)
Freshman Class: 1985 applied, 1837 accepted, 637 enrolled

SAT CR/M/W: 510/500/480 ACT: 22
Application Deadline: September 9

CEEB CODE: 4702
COMPETITIVE

Southern Oregon University, founded in 1882, is a public comprehensive university providing undergraduate and graduate programs in humanities, science, business, fine and performing arts, social sciences, and teacher education. There are 3 undergraduate schools and 1 graduate school. In addition to regional accreditation, Southern has baccalaureate program accreditation with ACBSP, NASM, and NCATE. The 175-acre campus is in a small town 10 miles southeast of Medford. Including any residence halls, there are 40 buildings.

STUDENT LIFE: 69% of undergraduates are from Oregon. Others are from 44 states, 17 foreign countries, and Canada. 85% are from public schools. 54% are White; 28% race unknown. The average age of freshmen is 19; all undergraduates, 25. 30% do not continue beyond their first year; 35% remain to graduate.

FACULTY/CLASSROOMS: 55% of faculty are male; 45% are female. All teach undergraduates. No introductory courses are taught by graduate students. The average class size in a regular course is 25.

PROGRAMS OF STUDY: Southern confers B.A., B.S. and B.F.A. degrees. Master's degrees are also awarded. Bachelor's degrees are awarded in AGRICULTURE (environmental studies and natural resource management), BIOLOGICAL SCIENCE (biology/biological science), BUSINESS (accounting, business administration and management, business (dual major program), hospitality management services, hotel and restaurant administration, marketing, and marketing/retailing/merchandising), COMMUNICATIONS AND THE ARTS (art history, art, communication, dramatic arts, English, English Writing, film, television and digital media, fine arts, foreign language, graphic design, graphic design and media, languages, music, music business management, music composition, music performance, Spanish, studio art, theatre arts, theatre production, theatre studies, and visual and performing arts), COMPUTER AND PHYSICAL SCIENCE (chemistry, computer mathematics, computer programming, computer information systems, computer science, digital arts/technology, mathematics, mathematics – economics, physics, and science), EDUCATION (early childhood education, education, elementary education, English education, environmental education, physical education, and recreation education), ENGINEERING AND ENVIRONMENTAL DESIGN (environmental science and preengineering), HEALTH PROFESSIONS (biology, biomedical science, health, mental health/human services, nursing, premedicine, prepharmacy, prephysical therapy, and sports medicine), SOCIAL SCIENCE (American Indian studies, anthropology, criminal justice, criminology, economics, gender studies, geography, history, human services, interdisciplinary studies, international studies, liberal arts/general studies, Native American studies, philosophy, political science/government, prelaw, psychology, social science, sociology, and women & gender studies). Fine and performing arts, psychology, criminology/criminal justice, sciences, and social sciences are the strongest academically. Business, psychology, communica-

tion, education, and criminology/criminal justice have the largest enrollments.

ACTIVITIES: There are no fraternities or sororities. There are 125 groups on campus, including art, band, cheerleading, chess, choir, chorale, chorus, communications, computers, dance, drama, environmental, ethnic, film, forensics, gay, honors, international, jazz band, literary magazine, musical theater, newspaper, pep band, photography, political, professional, radio and TV, religious, social, social service, student government, and symphony. Popular campus events include Raider Orientation, Convocation, Southern Oregon Arts and Research Symposium, Commencement Weekend, International Week and One World Series.

SERVICES: Counseling and information services are available, as is tutoring in some subjects. There is a reader service for the blind, remedial math and writing. Program design is offered for students with learning disabilities. **Library/Resources:** The library contains 336,000 volumes, 807,000 microform items, and 90,000 audio/video tapes/CDs/DVDs, and subscribes to 4,300 periodicals including electronic. Computerized library services include interlibrary loans, database searching, Internet access, and Wi-Fi capability. Special learning facilities include an art gallery, radio station, TV station, a center for the visual arts, an art museum, and art galleries, a wildlife forensics lab, a music recital hall, 2 theaters, a greenhouse, and an ecology center. **Physically Challenged Students:** 95% of the campus is accessible. Facilities include wheelchair ramps, elevators, special parking, specially equipped restrooms, special class scheduling, lowered drinking fountains, lowered telephones, special housing. **Special:** Cross-registration through the National Student and Western Student Exchanges, study abroad in 23 countries, internships, and federal work-study are all available. Accelerated degrees in business, communication, computer science, economics, geography, math, political science, foreign languages and literature, and sociology; dual majors in business and chemistry, physics, math, or music, and in math and computer science; and interdisciplinary majors in environmental or international studies are all offered. There are 13 national honor societies, a freshman honors program, and 10 departmental honors programs. **Visiting:** There are regularly scheduled orientations for prospective students, includes tours of the campus and residence halls and a meeting with an admissions representative. Appointments with faculty and class visits can be arranged. There are guides for informal visits, visitors may sit in on classes, and stay overnight. To schedule a visit, contact The Admissions Office at (800) 482-7672 Ext. 6411. **Campus Safety and Security:** Measures include 24-hour foot and vehicle patrol, emergency notification system, self-defense education, and security escort services. There are emergency telephones, lighted pathways/sidewalks, controlled access to dorms/residences, Loud speaker public address system for emergencies.

REQUIREMENTS: The SAT or ACT is required. A satisfactory score on the SAT is needed if the high school GPA is less than 2.75. Applicants need 14 academic credits, including 4 years of English, 3 each of math and social studies, 2 of science, and 2 years of 1 foreign language. The GED is accepted. A GPA of 2.8 is required. AP and CLEP credits are accepted.

ADMISSIONS: 93% of a recent year applicants were accepted. The SAT scores for a recent year freshman class were: Critical Reading--45% below 500, 36% between 500 and 599, 16% between 600 and 699, and 3% between 700 and 800; Math--49% below 500, 38% between 500 and 599, 11% between 600 and 699, and 2% between 700 and 800; Writing--56% below 500, 32% between 500 and 599, 10% between 600 and 699, and 2% between 700 and 800. The ACT scores were 46% below 21, 26% between 21 and 23, 16% between 24 and 26, 9% between 27 and 28, and 3% above 28.

FINANCIAL AID: In a recent year, 75% of all full-time freshmen and 81% of continuing full-time students received some form of financial aid. 56% of all full-time freshmen and 54% of continuing full-time students received need-based aid. The average freshman award was $8,440. Need-based scholarships or need-based grants averaged $6,370; need-based self-help aid (loans and jobs) averaged $3,087; non-need-based athletic scholarships averaged $1,787; and other non-need-based awards and non-need-based scholarships averaged $1,210. 50% of undergraduate students work part-time. Average annual earnings from campus work are $1500. The average financial indebtedness of the 2013 graduate was $29,000. The FAFSA is required. The priority date for freshman financial aid applications for fall entry is March 1.

UNIVERSITY OF OREGON   B-2
www.uoregon.edu

Eugene, OR 97403

(541) 346-3201
(800) 232-3825

Fax: (541) 346-5815

Email: uoadmit@uoregon.edu

Full-time: 8849 men, 9824 women

Faculty: 1048; I, -$

Part-time: 975 men, 911 women

Ph.D.s: 98%

Graduate: 1675 men, 1862 women

Student/Faculty: 18 to 1

Year: quarters, summer session

Tuition: $9918 ($30,888)

Room & Board: $11,442

Freshman Class: 21145 applied, 15908 accepted, 3895 enrolled

SAT CR/M/W: 550/560/540 ACT: 25

CEEB CODE: 4846

Application Deadline: January 15

COMPETITIVE+

The University of Oregon, founded in 1876, is a public liberal arts institution. There are 7 undergraduate schools and 9 graduate schools. In addition to regional accreditation, UO has baccalaureate program accreditation with AACSB, ACEJMC, ASLA, FIDER, NAAB, NASM, ACS, APA, and ASLA. The 295-acre campus is in a suburban area 110 miles south of Portland. Including any residence halls, there are 80 buildings.

STUDENT LIFE: 52% of undergraduates are from Oregon. Others are from 50 states, 75 foreign countries, and Canada. 62% are White; 13% Foreign. The average age of freshmen is 19; all undergraduates, 22. 13% do not continue beyond their first year; 69% remain to graduate. **Housing:** 4552 students can be accommodated in college housing, which includes single-sex and coed dorms, on-campus apartments, off-campus apartments, and married student housing. On-campus housing is available on a first-come, first-served basis. 81% of students commute. All students may keep cars.

FACULTY/CLASSROOMS: 55% of faculty are male; 45% are female. 96% teach undergraduates, all do research, and 96% do both. Graduate students teach 31% of introductory courses. The average class size in an introductory lecture is 40; in a laboratory is 17; and in a regular course is 42.

PROGRAMS OF STUDY: UO confers B.A., B.S., B.Arch., B.Ed., B.F.A., B.I.Arch., B.L.A., B.Mus. and B.Mme degrees. Master's and Doctoral degrees are also awarded. Bachelor's degrees are awarded in AGRICULTURE (environmental studies), BIOLOGICAL SCIENCE (biochemistry, biology/biological science, marine biology, and physiology), BUSINESS (accounting and business administration and management), COMMUNICATIONS AND THE ARTS (advertising, art, art history and appreciation, ceramic art and design, Chinese, classics, communications, communication science, comparative literature, creative writing, dance, design, digital communications, dramatic arts, English, fiber/textiles/weaving, film arts, fine arts, folklore and mythology, French, German, Greek, Italian, Japanese, jazz, journalism, Latin, linguistics, metal/jewelry, music, music performance, music theory and composition, painting, photography, printmaking, public relations, romance languages and literature, Russian, sculpture, Spanish, and theatre arts), COMPUTER AND PHYSICAL SCIENCE (chemistry, computer science, digital arts/technology, geology, mathematics, physics, and science), EDUCATION (education and music education), ENGINEERING AND ENVIRONMENTAL DESIGN (architecture, environmental science, and landscape architecture/design), HEALTH PROFESSIONS (speech pathology/audiology), SOCIAL SCIENCE (anthropology, Asian/Oriental studies, classical/ancient civilization, economics, ethnic studies, family and community services, geography, history, humanities, international studies, Judaic studies, Latin American studies, medieval studies, philosophy, political science/government, psychology, public administration, religion, social science, sociology, and women's studies). Pre-business administration, psychology, and human physiology have the largest enrollments.

ACTIVITIES: 14% of men belong to 20 national fraternities; 19% of women belong to 1 local and 13 national sororities. There are 250 groups on campus, including art, band, cheerleading, chess, choir, chorale, chorus, communications, computers, dance, debate, drama, drill team, environmental, ethnic, film, forensics, gay, honors, international, jazz band, literary magazine, marching band, musical theater, newspaper, pep band, photography, political, professional, radio and TV, religious, social, social service, and student government. Popular campus events include University Day, Family Weekends, and Convocation. **Sports:** There are 7 intercollegiate sports for men and 11 for women, and 18 intramural sports for men and 18 for women. Facilities include a 59,796 seat football stadium with 40 private suites, a 12,500-seat basketball arena, an 8-lane 400-meter track and field complex with seating for 10,500 spectators, a baseball stadium that seats 2,500 and includes a player development area, 12 tennis courts six indoor/6 outdoors, an artificial field used for soccer and lacrosse with seating for 1,500, and an indoor practice facility for athletic teams. The student recreation center, includes 40,000 square feet of fitness space, exercise and yoga studios, a cycling studio, 3-court gym (more capacity for basketball, volleyball and badminton), 12-lane lap pool (used for lap swimming, water polo, water aerobics, instructional classes), 3-lane recreational pool (water volleyball, basketball instructional classes), a whirlpool spa, 2-story locker rooms with private showers, and social and lounge spaces. **Graduates:** From July 1, 2013 to June 30, 2014, 4654 bachelor's degrees were awarded. The most popular majors were business administration (14%), psychology (8%), and general social science (6%). In an average class, 2% graduate in 3 years or less, 46% graduate in 4 years or less, 66% graduate in 5 years or less, and 69% graduate in 6 years or less.

SERVICES: Counseling and information services are available, as is tutoring in some subjects. There is a reader service for the blind. Private tutoring is available for many courses, small group tutoring for some courses. Math and Writing Labs that offer free drop in support. **Library/Resources:** The 6 libraries contain 3.2 million volumes, 3.0 million microform items, 113,578 audio/video tapes/CDs/DVDs, and subscribe to 72,037 periodicals including electronic. Computerized library services include interlibrary loans, database searching, Internet access, and Wi-Fi capability. Special learning facilities include an art gallery, natural history museum, radio station, TV station, an art museum, a natural and cultural history museum, centers for sports marketing, entrepreneurship, a green chemistry lab, and a longhouse. **Physically Challenged Students:** 95% of the campus is accessible. Facilities include wheelchair ramps, elevators, special parking, specially equipped restrooms, lowered drinking fountains. An adviser is available for students with disabilities. Other accommodations are made upon request. **Special:** Matriculation agreements with more than 30 Oregon and Washington community colleges, dual enrollment with Lane and Southwestern Oregon Community Colleges, study abroad in more than 90 countries, pre-engineering in conjunction with Lane Community College, and a 3-2 engineering degree with Oregon State University are available. In addition, numerous internship opportunities, dual majors, and pass/fail options are available. There are 21 national honor societies, including Phi Beta Kappa, and 42 departmental honors programs. **Visiting:** There are regularly scheduled orientations for prospective students, including IntroDUCKtion, a 2-day program scheduled for late July that includes both advising and Web-based registration. There are guides for informal visits and visitors may sit in on classes. **Campus Safety and Security:** Measures include 24-hour foot and vehicle patrol, emergency notification system, self-defense education, and security escort services. There are shuttle buses, emergency telephones, lighted pathways/sidewalks, controlled access to dorms/residences. The university has a campus-wide emergency management program, campus emergency operations, and mitigation plans.

REQUIREMENTS: The SAT or ACT is required. The ACT Optional Writing test is also required. Standard freshman admission requirements include graduation from a standard or regionally accredited high school, and C- or higher in 15 college preparatory courses. Applications are evaluated based on strength of academic course work, grades earned, grade trends, senior year course load, standardized test scores, academic motivation as demonstrated in the application essay, academic potential, special talents, extracurricular activities, including community service or the need to work to assist your family, and ability to enhance the diversity of the university. AP and CLEP credits are accepted. For graduation, at least 180 quarter credits are required of all students, with a minimum GPA of 2.0 and a minimum of 62 credits upper division. A minimum of 36 credits must be in the major, including 24 in upper-division work. Basic courses vary by major, but all students must complete 12 to 16 credits each in the areas of arts and letters, social science, and science, as well as 2 courses in written English and 2 courses in multicultural studies. A bachelor of science requires one year college level or equivalent mathematics or computer science or combination of the two. A bachelor of arts requires two years college level or equivalent of a second language. **Procedure:** Freshmen are admitted to all sessions. There is a rolling admissions plan. Applications should be filed by January 15 for fall entry; October 15 for winter entry; February 1 for spring entry; and March 1 for summer entry, along with a $50 fee. Notification is sent on a rolling basis. 441 applicants were on the 2014 waiting list; 300 were admitted. Applications are accepted on-line. **Transfer Students:** 1289 transfer students enrolled in 2013-2014. If transfer students have completed 35 or fewer transferable quarter credits (23 semester credits), they must meet admission requirements for both freshmen and transfer students. If transfer students have completed 36 or more quarter credits (24 of which must be graded), admission will be based on college-level course work only. Transfer students must be eligible to return to their most recent institution and have completed 1 college-level composition course and 1 college-level mathematics course with grades of C- or better. They must have earned a minimum GPA of 2.25 if they are Oregon residents or 2.5 if they are nonresidents, and they must demonstrate second-language proficiency. 45 of 180 credits required for the bachelor's degree must be completed at UO. **International Students:** There are 2575 international students enrolled. The school actively recruits these students. They must take the TOEFL with a minimum score of 500 on the paper-based TOEFL (PBT) or 61 on the Internet-based version (iBT). SAT/ACT scores are not required for international students unless they are applying to the architecture program.

ADMISSIONS: 75% of the 2014-2015 applicants were accepted. The SAT scores for the 2014-2015 freshman class were: Critical Reading--25% below 500, 43% between 500 and 599, 27% between 600 and 699, and 5% between 700 and 800; Math--22% below 500, 45% between 500 and 599, 28% between 600 and 699, and 5% between 700 and 800; Writing--28% below 500, 44% between 500 and 599, 23% between 600 and 699, and 5% between 700 and 800. The ACT scores were 16% below 21, 22% between 21 and 23, 30% between 24 and 26, 15% between 27 and 28, and 17% above 28. 57% of the current freshmen were in the top fifth of their class; 85% were in the top two fifths. There were 9 National Merit finalists. 129 freshmen graduated first in their class. **Admissions Contact:** Jim Rawlins, Director of Admissions. E-Mail: *uoadmit@uoregon.edu* Web: *www.admissions.uoregon.edu*

FINANCIAL AID: 14% of undergraduate students work part-time. Average annual earnings from campus work are $3160. The average financial indebtedness of the 2014 graduate was $24,508. The FAFSA is required. The deadline for filing freshman financial aid applications for fall entry is March 1.

UNIVERSITY OF PORTLAND   B-1
www.up.edu

Portland, OR 97203	(503) 943-7147
	(888) 627-5601
Fax: (503) 943-7315	Email: admissio@up.edu
Full-time: 1057 men, 1469 women	Faculty: 214; IIA, -$
Part-time: 21 men, 25 women	Ph.D.s: 92%
Graduate: 101 men, 146 women	Student/Faculty: 14 to 1
Year: semesters, summer session	Tuition: $38,520
Room & Board: $11,444	Freshman Class: 11099 applied, 6986 accepted, 1082 enrolled
SAT CR/M: 600/595 ACT: required	CEEB CODE: 4847
Application Deadline: February 1	VERY COMPETITIVE

The University of Portland, founded in 1901, is an independent institution affiliated with the Roman Catholic Church. It offers degree programs in the arts and sciences, business administration, education, engineering, and nursing. There are 5 undergraduate schools and 1 graduate school. In addition to regional accreditation, UP has baccalaureate program accreditation with AACSB, ABET, CSWE, NASM, NCATE, CCNE, and NAST. The 155-acre campus is in an urban area 4 miles north of downtown Portland. Including any residence halls, there are 30 buildings.

STUDENT LIFE: 67% of undergraduates are from out of state, mostly the Northwest. Students are from 44 states, 37 foreign countries, and Canada. 67% are from public schools. 66% are White; 12% Asian American. 45% are Catholic; 18% claim no religious affiliation. The average age of freshmen is 18; all undergraduates, 20. 10% do not continue beyond their first year; 79% remain to graduate. **Housing:** 2100 students can be accommodated in college housing, which includes single-sex and coed dorms and on-campus apartments. In addition, there are honors houses, language houses, special-interest houses, university-owned rental houses, and theme housing. On-campus housing is guaranteed for the freshman year only and is available on a lottery system for upperclassmen. 55% of students live on campus; of those, 85% remain on campus on weekends. Upperclassmen may keep cars.

FACULTY/CLASSROOMS: 56% of faculty are male; 44% are female. All teach undergraduates. No introductory courses are taught by graduate students. The average class size in an introductory lecture is 25; in a laboratory is 20; and in a regular course is 20.

PROGRAMS OF STUDY: UP confers B.A., B.S., B.A.Ed., B.B.A., B.M.Ed., B.S.C.E., B.S.E.E., B.S.E.M., B.S.E.S., B.S.M.E. and B.S.N. degrees. Master's and Doctoral degrees are also awarded. Bachelor's degrees are awarded in BIOLOGICAL SCIENCE (biology/biological science), BUSINESS (accounting, banking and finance, entrepreneurial studies, international business management, marketing/retailing/merchandising, and operations management), COMMUNICATIONS AND THE ARTS (communications, dramatic arts, English, music, and Spanish), COMPUTER AND PHYSICAL SCIENCE (chemistry, computer science, mathematics, and physics), EDUCATION (elementary education and secondary education), ENGINEERING AND ENVIRONMENTAL DESIGN (civil engineering, electrical/electronics engineering, engineering, environmental science, and mechanical engineering), HEALTH PROFESSIONS (nursing), SOCIAL SCIENCE (economics, French studies, German area studies, history, interdisciplinary studies, philosophy, political science/government, psychology, social work, sociology, and theological studies). Engineering, nursing, and biology are the strongest academically. Nursing, biology, and mechanical engineering have the largest enrollments.

ACTIVITIES: There are no fraternities or sororities. There are 62 groups on campus, including art, band, cheerleading, choir, chorale, chorus, computers, dance, debate, drama, environmental, ethnic, film, gay, honors, international, jazz band, literary magazine, musical theater, newspaper, orchestra, pep band, photography, political, professional, radio station, religious, social, social service, student government, symphony, and yearbook. Popular campus events include Dance of the Decade, International Night, Pilotpalooza and Luau. **Sports:** There are 6 intercollegiate sports for men and 6 for women, and 20 intramural sports for men and 20 for women. Facilities include weight rooms, an indoor track, a gym, a swimming pool, and a 5000-seat athletic and convocation center. Rental equipment is available for biking and camping activities. **Graduates:** From July 1, 2013 to June 30, 2014, 895 bachelor's degrees were awarded. The most popular majors were health professions and related programs (18%), business/marketing (17%), and engineering (6%). 85 companies recruited on campus in 2013-2014. In an average class, 75% graduate in 4 years or less, 77% graduate in 5 years or less, and 80% graduate in 6 years or less. Of the 2013 graduating class, 12% were enrolled in graduate school within 6 months of graduation.

SERVICES: Counseling and information services are available, as is tutoring in most subjects, including English and math. The faculty is available for individual assistance. **Library/Resources:** The library contains 220,340 volumes, 41,624 microform items, 15,002 audio/video tapes/CDs/DVDs, and subscribes to 6,830 periodicals including electronic. Computerized library services include interlibrary loans, database searching, Internet access, and Wi-Fi capability. Special learning facilities include an art gallery. **Physically Challenged Stu-**

dents: All of the campus is accessible. Facilities include wheelchair ramps, elevators, special parking, specially equipped restrooms, special class scheduling, lowered drinking fountains, and lowered telephones. **Special:** UP offers internships through individual departments, cross-registration with members of the Oregon Independent College Association, dual and interdisciplinary majors, including engineering chemistry and organizational communications, work-study programs, and pass/fail options. Study abroad may be arranged in Japan, Mexico, Australia, Chile, and several European countries. There are 9 national honor societies and a freshman honors program. **Visiting:** There are regularly scheduled orientations for prospective students, including a campus tour, class attendance, and a meeting with an admissions counselor. There are guides for informal visits, visitors may sit in on classes, and stay overnight. To schedule a visit, contact the Office of Admissions. **Campus Safety and Security:** Measures include 24-hour foot and vehicle patrol, emergency notification system, self-defense education, and security escort services. There are shuttle buses, emergency telephones, lighted pathways/sidewalks, and controlled access to dorms/residences.

REQUIREMENTS: The SAT or ACT is required, with a minimum score of 550 on each section of the SAT or a composite of 19 on the ACT. Graduation from an accredited secondary school or satisfactory scores on the GED are required. The high school curriculum should include courses in English composition, math, social studies, science, and a foreign language. 2 essays are required, as is a letter of recommendation from the high school counselor or principal. UP requires applicants to be in the upper 50% of their class. A GPA of 3.0 is required. AP and CLEP credits are accepted. To graduate, students must complete 120 credit hours, including at least 24 upper-division classes in the major, with a minimum GPA of 2.0. Required courses include 9 hours each of philosophy and theology, 6 each of science, social sciences, and electives, and 3 each of fine arts, history, math, and literature. Some majors may require a comprehensive exam and/or thesis. **Procedure:** Freshmen are admitted to all sessions. Entrance exams should be taken preferably before February 1 but no later than June 1 of the senior year. There are deferred admissions and rolling admissions plans. Applications should be filed by February 1 for fall entry, along with a $50 fee. Notification is sent on a rolling basis. Applications are accepted on-line. **Transfer Students:** 75 transfer students enrolled in 2013-2014. Applicants with 26 or more credits must have a minimum GPA of 2.5 and be in good standing at their previous school. Students with fewer credits may need to meet freshman requirements. 30 of 120 credits required for the bachelor's degree must be completed at UP. **International Students:** There are 109 international students enrolled. The school actively recruits these students. They must take the TOEFL with a minimum score of 71 on the Internet-based version (iBT).

ADMISSIONS: 63% of the 2014-2015 applicants were accepted. The SAT scores for the 2014-2015 freshman class were: Critical Reading--9% below 500, 43% between 500 and 599, 33% between 600 and 699, and 14% between 700 and 800; Math--9% below 500, 38% between 500 and 599, 41% between 600 and 699, and 10% between 700 and 800. **Admissions Contact:** Jason McDonald, Dean of Admissions. E-Mail: *admissio@up.edu* Web: *www.up.edu*

FINANCIAL AID: In 2014-2015, 97% of all full-time freshmen and 94% of continuing full-time students received some form of financial aid. 67% of all full-time freshmen and 64% of continuing full-time students received need-based aid. The average freshman award was $28,258. Need-based scholarships or need-based grants averaged $24,569; need-based self-help aid (loans and jobs) averaged $4,559; non-need-based athletic scholarships averaged $26,183; other non-need-based awards and non-need-based scholarships averaged $3,653; and $17,275 from other forms of aid. 36% of undergraduate students work part-time. Average annual earnings from campus work are $2325. The average financial indebtedness of the 2014 graduate was $26,490. The FAFSA is required. The priority date for freshman financial aid applications for fall entry is February 1. The deadline for filing freshman financial aid applications for fall entry is March 1.

WARNER PACIFIC COLLEGE   B-1
www.warnerpacific.edu

Portland, OR 97215

(503) 517-1020
(800) 804-1510

Fax: (503) 517-1540   Email: admissions@warnerpacific.edu

Full-time: 532 men, 956 women	**Faculty:** 34
Part-time: 19 men, 43 women	**Ph.D.s:** 50%
Graduate: 49 men, 80 women	**Student/Faculty:** 14 to 1
Year: semesters, summer session	**Tuition:** $18,290
Room & Board: $7260	**Freshman Class:** n/av
SAT or ACT: required	**CEEB CODE:** 4595
Application Deadline: open	**COMPETITIVE**

Warner Pacific College, founded in 1937, is a private Christian liberal arts college affiliated with the Church of God. There is 1 undergraduate school and 1 graduate school. The 14-acre campus is in an urban area 5 miles east of downtown Portland. Including any residence halls, there are 30 buildings.

STUDENT LIFE: 71% of undergraduates are from Oregon. Others are from 18 states, 2 foreign countries, and Canada. 78% are from public schools. 78% are White. 51% claim no religious affiliation; 42% Protestant. The average age of freshmen is 27; all undergraduates, 31. 25% do not continue beyond their first year; 45% remain to graduate.

FACULTY/CLASSROOMS: 62% of faculty are male; 38% are female. All teach undergraduates, and 40% do research. No introductory courses are taught by graduate students. The average class size in an introductory lecture is 15; in a laboratory is 10; and in a regular course is 15.

PROGRAMS OF STUDY: Warner Pacific confers B.A., and B.S degrees. Associate degrees are also awarded. Bachelor's degrees are awarded in BIOLOGICAL SCIENCE (biology/biological science), BUSINESS (business administration and management), COMMUNICATIONS AND THE ARTS (English and music), EDUCATION (music education and physical education), SOCIAL SCIENCE (American studies, history, human development, liberal arts/general studies, ministries, religious music, social science, and sociology). Biological science and business administration is the strongest academically. Business administration, human development, education, and Christian ministries have the largest enrollments.

ACTIVITIES: Thhere are 11 groups on campus, including spiritual growth groups, art, band, Bible study, choir, chorale, chorus, dance, debate, drama, environmental, ethnic, international, jazz band, literary magazine, newspaper, orchestra, professional, religious, social, social service, student government, and yearbook. Popular campus events include Winter Banquet and Spring Banquet.

SERVICES: Counseling and information services are available, as is tutoring in most subjects, math, writing. There is remedial math, reading, and writing. Testing and study skills workshops. **Library/Resources:** The library contains 67,948 volumes, 2,093 microform items, and 2,899 audio/video tapes/CDs/DVDs, and subscribes to 27,038 periodicals including electronic. Computerized library services include interlibrary loans, database searching, and Internet access. **Physically Challenged Students:** 75% of the campus is accessible. Facilities include wheelchair ramps, elevators, special parking, specially equipped restrooms, special class scheduling, lowered drinking fountains. **Special:** Warner Pacific offers cross-registration through OICA, a Washington semester, a co-op nursing program, 27 majors, accelerated degree programs in human development and business administration, and study abroad in Latin America, the Middle East, and Russia. Internships, work-study programs, double majors, individualized majors, independent study credit for life and military experience, and pass/fail options are available. **Visiting:** There are regularly scheduled orientations for prospective students, including 2 campus preview days, 2 knight life visit weekends, academic fairs, and scholarship days. There are guides for informal visits, visitors may sit in on classes, and stay overnight. To schedule a visit, contact the Office of Enrollment. **Campus Safety and Security:** Measures include 24-hour foot and vehicle patrol, emergency notification system, self-defense education, and security escort services. There are emergency telephones, lighted pathways/sidewalks, and controlled access to dorms/residences.

REQUIREMENTS: The SAT or ACT is required. Applicants must be graduates of an accredited secondary school. The GED is accepted. High school preparation should include 4 years of English, 3 of social studies, and 2 each of math and lab science. A GPA of 2.3 is required. AP and CLEP credits are accepted. Important factors in the admissions decision are evidence of special talent, leadership record, and advanced placement or honors courses.

FINANCIAL AID: In 2014-2015, 98% of all full-time freshmen and continuing full-time students received some form of financial aid. 97% of all full-time freshmen and continuing full-time students received need-based aid. The average freshman award was $15,003. 5% of undergraduate students work part-time. Average annual earnings from campus work are $2000. The average financial indebtedness of the 2013 graduate was $27,000. Warner Pacific is a member of CSS. The FAFSA is required. Check with the school for current application deadlines.

WESTERN OREGON UNIVERSITY   A-2
www.wou.edu

Monmouth, OR 97361	(503) 838-8211
	(877) 877-1593
Fax: (503) 838-8067	Email: wolfgram@wou.edu
Full-time: 1820 men, 2450 women	Faculty: 209; IIA, --$
Part-time: 250 men, 350 women	Ph.Ds: 72%
Graduate: 240 men, 540 women	Student/Faculty: n/av
Year: quarters, summer session	Tuition: $7928 ($19,905)
Room & Board: $9122	Freshman Class: n/av
SAT or ACT: required	CEEB CODE: 4585
Application Deadline: open	COMPETITIVE

Western Oregon University, founded in 1856, is a publicly funded institution and a member of the Oregon University System. WOU offers undergraduate programs through the Colleges of Education and Liberal Arts and Sciences. There are 2 undergraduate schools and 1 graduate school. In addition to regional accreditation, WOU has baccalaureate program accreditation with NASM and NCATE. The 157-acre campus is in a rural area 15 miles west of Salem. Including any residence halls, there are 36 buildings.

STUDENT LIFE: 89% of undergraduates are from Oregon. Others are from 27 states, 22 foreign countries, and Canada. 99% are from public schools. 73% are white. The average age of freshmen is 18; all undergraduates, 22. 30% do not continue beyond their first year; 50% remain to graduate.

FACULTY/CLASSROOMS: 52% of faculty are male; 48% are female. No introductory courses are taught by graduate students. The average class size in an introductory lecture is 40; in a laboratory is 25; and in a regular course is 30.

PROGRAMS OF STUDY: WOU confers B.A., B.S., and B.Mus. degrees. Associate and Master's degrees are also awarded. Bachelor's degrees are awarded in BIOLOGICAL SCIENCE (biology/biological science), BUSINESS (business administration and management), COMMUNICATIONS AND THE ARTS (American Sign Language, art, dance, dramatic arts, English, music, Spanish, and speech/debate/rhetoric), COMPUTER AND PHYSICAL SCIENCE (chemistry, computer science, earth science, information sciences and systems, mathematics, and natural sciences), EDUCATION (education and health education), SOCIAL SCIENCE (anthropology, corrections, economics, fire protection, geography, history, humanities, interdisciplinary studies, international studies, interpreter for the deaf, law enforcement and corrections, philosophy, political science/government, psychology, public administration, social science, and sociology). Education, business, and psychology are the strongest academically. Education, criminal justice, and business have the largest enrollments.

ACTIVITIES: There are no fraternities or sororities. There are 50 groups on campus, including art, band, cheerleading, chess, choir, chorale, chorus, computers, dance, debate, drama, drill team, ethnic, gay, honors, international, jazz band, literary magazine, marching band, Model UN, musical theater, newspaper, orchestra, pep band, political, professional, radio and TV, religious, social, social service,

and student government. Popular campus events include Annual Christmas Tree Lighting, Alcohol Awareness Week, and Family Day.

SERVICES: Counseling and information services are available, as is tutoring in most subjects. There is a reader service for the blind, and remedial math, reading, and writing. There is also a student support and services program for first-generation, low-income, and physically disabled students. **Library/Resources:** Computerized library services include interlibrary loans, database searching, Internet access, and Wi-Fi capability. Special learning facilities include an art gallery, radio station, TV station, the Paul Jensen Arctic Museum. **Physically Challenged Students:** 95% of the campus is accessible. Facilities include wheelchair ramps, elevators, special parking, specially equipped restrooms, special class scheduling, lowered drinking fountains, lowered telephones, special housing. **Special:** Most academic majors in liberal arts and sciences offer a B.A.-B.S degree option. Dual majors, internships, study abroad through international exchange programs and the Oregon University System, and student-designed majors in interdisciplinary studies are available. Nondegree study and pass/fail options are possible. There are 7 national honor societies, a freshman honors program, and 5 departmental honors programs. **Visiting:** There are regularly scheduled orientations for prospective students, including seveal spring and summer orientation programs for students and a parent program. All newly admitted students should register during orientation to reserve their enrollment slot; new students can register until the first week of school. There are guides for informal visits and visitors may sit in on classes. To schedule a visit, contact the Admissions Office. **Campus Safety and Security:** Measures include 24-hour foot and vehicle patrol, self-defense education, and security escort services. There are emergency telephones, lighted pathways/sidewalks, WOU's Safe Ride provides a free and reliable shuttle service to students who would otherwise walk alone at night and risk their safety or possible assault.

REQUIREMENTS: The SAT or ACT is required. Graduation from an accredited secondary school or satisfactory scores on the GED are required. Students must have 14 academic credits or Carnegie units. High school courses must include 4 years of English, 3 each of math and social studies, and 2 each of science and a foreign language. A GPA of 2.8 is required. AP and CLEP credits are accepted. Important factors in the admissions decision are evidence of special talent, advanced placement or honors courses, and extracurricular activities record.

ADMISSIONS: 89% of a recent year applicants were accepted.

FINANCIAL AID: 83% of all full-time freshmen and 75% of continuing full-time students received some form of financial aid. 61% of all full-time freshmen and 58% of continuing full-time students received need-based aid. The FAFSA, is required. Some campus-based scholarships have separate applications. Check with the school for current application deadlines.

WILLAMETTE UNIVERSITY   B-2
www.willamette.edu

Salem, OR 97301	(503) 370-6300
	(503) 370-6303
Fax: (503) 375-5363	Email: bearcat@willamette.edu
Full-time: 881 men, 1139 women	Faculty: 167; IIA, +$
Part-time: 104 men, 105 women	Ph.Ds: 95%
Graduate: 439 men, 357 women	Student/Faculty: 11 to 1
Year: semesters	Tuition: $40,874
Room & Board: $10,380	Freshman Class: 6462 applied, 5370 accepted, 525 enrolled
SAT CR/M/W: 610/600/600 ACT: 27	CEEB CODE: 4954
Application Deadline: February 1	VERY COMPETITIVE+

Willamette University, founded in 1842, is an independent liberal arts institution affiliated with the Methodist Church. There are 3 graduate schools. In addition to regional accreditation, Willamette has baccalaureate program accreditation with NASM. The 72-acre campus is in an urban area 50 minutes south of Portland. Including any residence halls, there are 45 buildings.

STUDENT LIFE: 79% of undergraduates are from out of state, mostly the West. Students are from 42 states, 19 foreign countries, and Canada. 69% are from public schools. 63% are White. 50% claim no religious affiliation; 27% Protestant; 12% Catholic. The average age of freshmen is 18; all undergraduates, 20. 12% do not continue beyond their first year; 78% remain to graduate.

FACULTY/CLASSROOMS: 54% of faculty are male; 46% are female. All teach and do research. No introductory courses are taught by graduate students. The average class size in an introductory lecture is 30; in a laboratory is 14; and in a regular course is 16.

PROGRAMS OF STUDY: Willamette confers B.A. and B.M. degrees. Master's and Doctoral degrees are also awarded. Bachelor's degrees are awarded in BIOLOGICAL SCIENCE (biology/biological science), COMMUNICATIONS AND THE ARTS (art history and appreciation, comparative literature, dramatic arts, English, French, German, music, music performance, music theory and composition, Spanish, speech/debate/rhetoric, and studio art), COMPUTER AND PHYSICAL SCIENCE (chemistry, computer science, mathematics, physics, and science), EDUCATION (music education), ENGINEERING AND ENVIRONMENTAL DESIGN (environmental science), HEALTH PROFESSIONS (exercise science), SOCIAL SCIENCE (American studies, anthropology, Asian/Oriental studies, classical/ancient civilization, economics, history, humanities, international studies, Japanese studies, Latin American studies, philosophy, political science/government, psychology, religion, sociology, and women's studies). Politics, biology, and economics have the largest enrollments.

ACTIVITIES: 18% of men belong to 5 national fraternities; 12% of women belong to 3 national sororities. There are 105 groups on campus, including art, band, cheerleading, choir, chorale, chorus, computers, dance, debate, drama, ethnic, film, forensics, gay, honors, international, jazz band, literary magazine, musical theater, newspaper, orchestra, pep band, photography, political, professional, radio and TV, religious, social, social service, student government, and symphony. Popular campus events include Lu'au, Black Tie Affair, and Wulapalooza.

SERVICES: Counseling and information services are available, as is tutoring in most subjects. There is a reader service for the blind. Therapists are available for students on an individual need basis. **Library/Resources:** The 2 libraries contain 403,135 volumes, 290,140 microform items, and 13,425 audio/video tapes/CDs/DVDs, and subscribe to 26,430 periodicals including electronic. Computerized library services include interlibrary loans, database searching, and Internet access. Special learning facilities include an art gallery, natural history museum, radio station, botanical and Japanese gardens, multimedia center, and "smart" classrooms. **Physically Challenged Students:** 90% of the campus is accessible. Facilities include wheelchair ramps, elevators, special parking, specially equipped restrooms, special class scheduling, lowered drinking fountains, lowered telephones. **Special:** Willamette offers internships with the state and city

governments, a Chicago semester, a Washington semester, and a 3-2 engineering degree with Washington University, University of Southern California, and Columbia University. Nondegree study, B.A.-B.S. degrees, dual majors, work-study programs with numerous employers in the Salem area and at the university, and credit/no-credit options are also available. Study abroad programs are available in 14 countries. There are 3-2 degrees in management, forestry, and computer science. There are 7 national honor societies including Phi Beta Kappa. **Visiting:** There are regularly scheduled orientations for prospective students, consisting of fall and spring campus preview days, tours, and faculty and student presentations. There are guides for informal visits, visitors may sit in on classes, and stay overnight. To schedule a visit, contact Sue Corner at (877) LIBARTS. **Campus Safety and Security:** Measures include 24-hour foot and vehicle patrol, emergency notification system, self-defense education, and security escort services. There are emergency telephones, lighted pathways/sidewalks, Formal programs and education, and a weekly published campus safety report.

REQUIREMENTS: The SAT or ACT is required. The ACT Optional Writing test is also required. Graduation from an accredited secondary school or satisfactory scores on the GED are required. Institutional preferences include 4 years each of English and math, and 3 years each of foreign language, lab science, and social studies or history. 2 essays are required, and an interview is recommended. Portfolios or auditions are recommended for art and music students. A GPA of 2.0 is required. AP credits are accepted. Important factors in the admissions decision are advanced placement or honors courses, recommendations by school officials, parents or siblings attended your school, evidence of special talent, personality/intangible qualities, extracurricular activities record, and geographical diversity.

ADMISSIONS: 83% of a recent year applicants were accepted. The SAT scores for a recent year freshman class were: Critical Reading--11% below 500, 38% between 500 and 599, 39% between 600 and 699, and 13% between 700 and 800; Math--9% below 500, 46% between 500 and 599, 34% between 600 and 699, and 12% between 700 and 800; Writing--12% below 500, 42% between 500 and 599, 39% between 600 and 699, and 7% between 700 and 800. The ACT scores were 2% below 21, 9% between 21 and 23, 35% between 24 and 26, 19% between 27 and 28, and 35% above 28. 38 freshmen graduated first in their class.

FINANCIAL AID: 99% of all full-time freshmen and 95% of continuing full-time students received some form of financial aid. 71% of all full-time freshmen and 61% of continuing full-time students received need-based aid. The average freshman award was $33,644. Need-based scholarships or need-based grants averaged $26,888; and need-based self-help aid (loans and jobs) averaged $6,516. The average financial indebtedness of the 2013 graduate was $28,849. Willamette is a member of CSS. The FAFSA is required. The priority date for freshman financial aid applications for fall entry is February 1.

PENNSYLVANIA

• College Location

0 20 40 60 80 100
Miles

ALBRIGHT COLLEGE   E-3
www.albright.edu

Reading, PA 19612	**(610) 921-2381**
	(800) 252-1856
Fax: (610) 921-7294	Email: admission@alb.edu
Full-time: 747 men, 970 women	Faculty: 113; IIB, -$
Part-time: 16 men, 18 women	Ph.D.s: 58%
Graduate: n/av	Student/Faculty: 13 to 1
Year: 4-1-4, summer session	Tuition: $36,660
Room & Board: $10,000	Freshman Class: 6060
	applied, 3776 accepted,
	655 enrolled
SAT CR/M: 510/520	CEEB CODE: 2004
Application Deadline: n/av	**COMPETITIVE**

Albright College, founded in 1856, is a private liberal arts institution affiliated with the United Methodist Church. Figures in the above capsule and in this profile are approximate. There is 1 undergraduate school and 1 graduate school. The 118-acre campus is in a suburban area 55 miles west of Philadelphia. Including any residence halls, there are 47 buildings.

STUDENT LIFE: 60% of undergraduates are from Pennsylvania. Others are from 24 states, and 18 foreign countries. 84% are from public schools. 61% are White; 18% African American. 52% claim no religious affiliation; 23% Unknown Religious affiliation; 22% Catholic. The average age of freshmen is 18; all undergraduates, 20. 25% do not continue beyond their first year; 62% remain to graduate.

Housing: 1192 students can be accommodated in college housing, which includes single-sex and coed dorms. In addition, there are honors houses, special-interest houses, Theme housing. On-campus housing is guaranteed for the freshman year only. 69% of students live on campus; of those, 80% remain on campus on weekends. All students may keep cars.

FACULTY/CLASSROOMS: 46% of faculty are male; 54% are female. All teach undergraduates. No introductory courses are taught by graduate students. The average class size in an introductory lecture is 25; in a laboratory is 15; and in a regular course is 18.

PROGRAMS OF STUDY: Albright confers B.A., and B.S. degrees. Master's degrees are also awarded. Bachelor's degrees are awarded in BIOLOGICAL SCIENCE (biochemistry and biology/biological science), BUSINESS (accounting, business administration and management, and fashion merchandising), COMMUNICATIONS AND THE ARTS (art, communications, digital communications, dramatic arts, English, French, music business management, and Spanish), COMPUTER AND PHYSICAL SCIENCE (chemistry, computer science, information sciences and systems, mathematics, and physics), EDUCATION (elementary education, secondary education, and special education), ENGINEERING AND ENVIRONMENTAL DESIGN (environmental science), SOCIAL SCIENCE (American studies, child care/child and family studies, criminal justice, economics, history, Latin American studies, philosophy, political science/government, psychobiology, psychology, religion, sociology, textiles and clothing, and women's studies). Visual and performing arts, business, and social sciences have the largest enrollments.

ACTIVITIES: 14% of men belong to 4 national fraternities; 19% of

women belong to 3 national sororities. There are 72 groups on campus, including band, cheerleading, chess, choir, chorus, computers, dance, debate, drama, environmental, ethnic, film, gay, honors, international, jazz band, literary magazine, musical theater, newspaper, orchestra, pep band, photography, political, professional, radio and TV, religious, social, social service, student government, and yearbook. Popular campus events include Greek Weekend, and Spring Fever Weekend. **Sports:** There are 11 intercollegiate sports for men and 12 for women, and 5 intramural sports for men and 3 for women. Facilities include a 5,000-seat stadium, 2,000-seat gymnasium, baseball, softball, and soccer fields, fitness center, weight room, indoor track, bowling alley, a swimming pool, spin bikes, and racquetball courts. **Graduates:** From July 1, 2013 to June 30, 2014, 353 bachelor's degrees were awarded. The most popular majors were visual and performing arts (18%), social sciences (16%), and business/marketing (16%). 25 companies recruited on campus in 2013-2014. In an average class, 54% graduate in 6 years or less. Of the 2013 graduating class, 28% were enrolled in graduate school within 6 months of graduation, and 61% were employed.

SERVICES: Counseling and information services are available, as is tutoring in most subjects. There is a reader service for the blind. An academic learning center, a writing center, and an ESL program are available. **Library/Resources:** The library contains 224,174 volumes, and subscribes to 37,520 periodicals including electronic. Computerized library services include interlibrary loans, database searching, Internet access, and Wi-Fi capability. Special learning facilities include an art gallery, a center for business, civic and global leadership, including a 30,000 square feet of state-of-the-art classrooms, offices and meeting spaces, a radio station offers first-hand opportunities for students to learn about marketing, public relations and communications, as well as the delivery side of the music business industry. Including a satellite dish for foreign language program, transmission and scanning electron microscopes, Holocaust resource center, center for excellence in local government, center for cultural ecology, center for Latin American studies, and an community garden. **Physically Challenged Students:** 75% of the campus is accessible. Facilities include wheelchair ramps, elevators, special parking, specially equipped restrooms, and special class scheduling. **Special:** The school offers credit and noncredit internships, a Washington center, an accelerated degree program for working adults, cross-registration, dual majors, student-designed majors, non-degree study, and pass/fail options. Study abroad may be arranged in any country. There are 11 national honor societies and a freshman honors program. **Visiting:** There are regularly scheduled orientations for prospective students, including an interview with a counselor and a tour of the campus with a currently enrolled student. There are guides for informal visits, visitors may sit in on classes, and stay overnight. To schedule a visit, contact the Admissions Office. **Campus Safety and Security:** Measures include 24-hour foot and vehicle patrol, emergency notification system, self-defense education, and security escort services. There are shuttle buses, emergency telephones, lighted pathways/sidewalks, controlled access to dorms/residences, comprehensive crisis action plan, and a bicycle patrol.

REQUIREMENTS: Graduation from an accredited secondary school or satisfactory scores on the GED are required for admission. Students must have a total of 16 Carnegie units, including 4 years of English, 3 in both math and science, including 1 lab, 2 years each of a foreign language and social studies, and 1 year of both history and visual/performing arts. An essay is required, and an interview recommended. Submission of test scores is optional for admission. Students applying test optional must complete an on-campus admission interview. AP and CLEP credits are accepted. Important factors in the admissions decision are advanced placement or honors courses, leadership record, and recommendations by school officials. To graduate, students must complete 32 courses, including 13 to 14 in the major, with a minimum GPA of 2.0. All students take one interdisciplinary/synthesis course, one First Year Seminar and they must fulfill the cultural experience requirement. General studies requirements include 11 to 15 courses in English composition, a foreign language, natural science, quantitative reasoning, social science, the arts, and humanities (literature, history, philosophy and religion). **Procedure:** Freshmen are admitted fall, spring, and summer. Entrance exams should be taken during the spring of the junior year or the fall of the senior

year. There are early admissions, deferred admissions, and rolling admissions plans. Application deadlines are open. Application fee is $25. Applications are accepted on-line. **Transfer Students:** 20 transfer students enrolled in 2013-2014. Transfer students must have a minimum GPA of 2.5 and be in good standing. 64 of 128 credits required for the bachelor's degree must be completed at Albright. **International Students:** There are 72 international students enrolled. The school actively recruits these students. They must take the TOEFL with a minimum score of 520 on the paper-based TOEFL (PBT) or 68 on the Internet-based version (iBT) or take the MELAB. SAT or ACT considered if submitted.

ADMISSIONS: 62% of the 2014-2015 applicants were accepted. The SAT scores for the 2014-2015 freshman class were: Critical Reading--42% below 500, 43% between 500 and 599, 14% between 600 and 699, and 1% between 700 and 800; Math--36% below 500, 48% between 500 and 599, 14% between 600 and 699, and 2% between 700 and 800. 49% of the current freshmen were in the top fifth of their class; 69% were in the top two fifths. 4 freshmen graduated first in their class. **Admissions Contact:** Gregory E. Eichhorn, Vice President for Enrollment Management and Dean of Admission. E-Mail: *albright@alb.edu* Web: *www.albright.edu*

FINANCIAL AID: In 2014-2015, 97% of all full-time freshmen and 79% of continuing full-time students received some form of financial aid. 89% of all full-time freshmen and 93% of continuing full-time students received need-based aid. The average freshman award was $35,065. Need-based scholarships or need-based grants averaged $29,190; need-based self-help aid (loans and jobs) averaged $6,281; and other non-need-based awards and non-need-based scholarships averaged $4,708. 40% of undergraduate students work part-time. Average annual earnings from campus work are $1825. The average financial indebtedness of the 2014 graduate was $26,252. Albright is a member of CSS. The FAFSA is required. The priority date for freshman financial aid applications for fall entry is March 1.

ALLEGHENY COLLEGE   B-1
www.allegheny.edu

Meadville, PA 16335

	(814) 332-4351
	(800) 521-5293
Fax: (814) 337-0431	Email: admissions@allegheny.edu
Full-time: 903 men, 1076 women	Faculty: 171; IIB, +$
Part-time: 14 men, 30 women	Ph.D.s: 92%
Graduate: n/av	Student/Faculty: 11 to 1
Year: semesters	Tuition: $40,660
Room & Board: $10,320	Freshman Class: 3857 applied, 2768 accepted, 473 enrolled
SAT CR/M/W: 600/590/580 ACT: 26	CEEB CODE: 2006
Application Deadline: February 15	HIGHLY COMPETITIVE

Allegheny College has been the premiere college in the country for students with "Unusual Combinations" of interests and talents for nearly 200 years. Because of the academic rigor, experiential focus, and strong reputation behind an Allegheny degree, graduates are well prepared for extraordinary outcomes. The 565-acre campus is in a suburban area 90 miles north of Pittsburgh, 35 miles south of Erie. Including any residence halls, there are 41 buildings.

STUDENT LIFE: 55% of undergraduates are from Pennsylvania. Others are from 43 states, 47 foreign countries, and Canada. 80% are from public schools. 77% are White. 42% claim no religious affiliation; 25% Catholic; 20% Protestant. **Male To Female Ratio:** 1.2:1. The average age of freshmen is 19; all undergraduates, 20. 14% do not continue beyond their first year; 78% remain to graduate. **Housing:** 1901 students can be accommodated in college housing, which includes single-sex and coed dorms, on-campus apartments, and off-campus apartments. In addition, there are language houses, special-interest houses, fraternity houses, wellness community, quiet study floors, townhouses, ADA accessible, gender neutral, living and learning residential communities. On-campus housing is guaranteed for all 4 years and is available on a lottery system for upperclassmen. 90% of students live on campus; of those, 80% remain on campus on weekends. All students may keep cars.

FACULTY/CLASSROOMS: 53% of faculty are male; 47% are female.

All teach undergraduates, 81% do research, and 81% do both. No introductory courses are taught by graduate students. The average class size in an introductory lecture is 19; in a laboratory is 17; and in a regular course is 16.

PROGRAMS OF STUDY: Allegheny confers B.A., and B.S. degrees. Bachelor's degrees are awarded in AGRICULTURE (environmental studies), BIOLOGICAL SCIENCE (biochemistry, biology/biological science, and neurosciences), COMMUNICATIONS AND THE ARTS (art, art history and appreciation, communications, dramatic arts, English, French, German, music, Spanish, and studio art), COMPUTER AND PHYSICAL SCIENCE (chemistry, computer science, environmental geology, geology, mathematics, physics, and software engineering), ENGINEERING AND ENVIRONMENTAL DESIGN (environmental science), HEALTH PROFESSIONS (public health), SOCIAL SCIENCE (economics, history, international studies, philosophy, political science/government, psychology, religion, and women and gender studies). Physical and biological sciences, economics, international studies, psychology and environmental science are the strongest academically. Biology, economics, psychology, political science and English have the largest enrollments.

ACTIVITIES: 27% of men belong to 5 national fraternities; 30% of women belong to 5 national sororities. There are 129 groups on campus, including coffee house, music ensembles, outdoor programs, student programming board, academic, art, band, cheerleading, chess, choir, chorale, chorus, computers, dance, drama, environmental, ethnic, gay, honors, international, jazz band, literary magazine, musical theater, newspaper, orchestra, political, professional, radio and TV, religious, social, social service, student government, symphony, and yearbook. Popular campus events include Homecoming, Orchesis Dance Performance, Make A Difference Day, Springfest, Black Heritage month, Celebrate Asia, International month, Wingfest, Late Night Events, Relay For Life, and Coming Out Week.

Sports: There are 10 intercollegiate sports for men and 11 for women, and 6 intramural sports for men and 6 for women. Facilities include a comprehensive sports and fitness center that includes a 200 meter training track, weight rooms, cardio machines, 4 multipurpose indoor courts (volleyball, basketball, tennis, badminton, putting green, batting cage), a natatorium, a dance studio, 3 racquetball courts. Outdoor sports complex with a stadium, stadium lights, field turf playing surface, LED graphic display scoreboard, championship style cross-country course, 12 lighted tennis courts, baseball, softball, soccer and rugby grass fields, field for shot put, discuss and hammer throw and a 400 meter double bend 8-lane competition track. In addition, there are 80 wooded acres for mountain biking, hiking, and cross-country skiing. **Graduates:** From July 1, 2013 to June 30, 2014, 491 bachelor's degrees were awarded. The most popular majors were psychology (13%), biology (12%), and English (9%). 87 companies recruited on campus in 2013-2014. In an average class, 70% graduate in 4 years or less, 77% graduate in 5 years or less, and 78% graduate in 6 years or less. Of the 2013 graduating class, 28% were enrolled in graduate school within 6 months of graduation, and 66% were employed.

SERVICES: Counseling and information services are available, as is tutoring in some subjects, biology, chemistry, economics, geology, mathematics, modern languages, physics, psychology. Other support services available for study skills, technology assistance, time management, a speech consultation, a learning center, writing consultants, note-taking scribe services, tape recorders, and books on tape. **Library/Resources:** The library contains 914,276 volumes, 222,469 microform items, 146,673 audio/video tapes/CDs/DVDs, and subscribes to 21,603 periodicals including electronic. Computerized library services include interlibrary loans, database searching, and Internet access. Special learning facilities include an art gallery, planetarium, radio station, TV station, an observatory, 283-acre experimental research reserve, art studio, 80-acre protected forest, dance studio, geographic information systems learning laboratory, language learning center, science complex, seismographic network station, center for political participation, theater and communication arts center, living and learning residential communities, environmental roof garden, Richard J. Cook center for environmental science, Allegheny gateway to communities, cultures and careers. **Physically Challenged Students:** 42% of the campus is accessible. Facilities include wheelchair ramps, elevators, special parking, specially equipped restrooms, special class scheduling, lowered drinking fountains, special housing. Reasonable accommodations are made for special needs. **Special:** Allegheny offers domestic off campus semesters in 7 programs - New York Arts, Oak Ridge Science Center, Philadelphia Center, Washington semester, Duke Marine Lab NC, Ecosystems Center MA, Newberry Seminar Research in the Humanities IL; internships; double majors; independent study; student-designed majors; study abroad in 15 countries; work study. A 3-2 engineering degree is available with Case Western Reserve, Columbia, Duke, University of Pittsburgh, and Washington University. Accelerated masters in public policy and management, occupational therapy, and physician assistant. Accelerated doctorates in nursing, physical therapy, and osteopathic medicine. Preprofessional programs, graduate school partnerships, and an experiential learning term are also available. There are 15 national honor societies, including Phi Beta Kappa, and 18 departmental honors programs. **Visiting:** There are regularly scheduled orientations for prospective students, consisting of tours, panels, presentations on academic programs, student life, admissions, and financial aid. There are guides for informal visits, visitors may sit in on classes, and stay overnight. To schedule a visit, contact the Office of Admissions. **Campus Safety and Security:** Measures include 24-hour foot and vehicle patrol, emergency notification system, self-defense education, and security escort services. There are shuttle buses, emergency telephones, lighted pathways/sidewalks, controlled access to dorms/residences, TTY phones, emergency medical dispatching, motorist assistance, property engraving, on-campus sworn police officers, compliance program, CCTV cameras.

REQUIREMENTS: The SAT or ACT is required. Graduation from an accredited secondary school is required for admission. The GED is accepted. Students must have 16 Carnegie units, including 4 years of English, 3 years each of math, science, and social studies, and 2 years of a foreign language. An essay is required, and an interview is recommended. A college prep program and 2 letters of recommendation are required. AP and CLEP credits are accepted. Important factors in the admissions decision are advanced placement or honors courses, extracurricular activities record, and leadership record. To graduate, students must complete 128 credit hours with a minimum GPA of 2.0 in both the major and a minor. Between 36 and 64 hours are required in the major, including the junior seminar and senior research project. All students must fulfill liberal arts studies requirements of 8 credits in the division least represented in the major and minor and a laboratory course is required for non-natural science majors or minors. Additional required courses include freshman first seminar, freshman second seminar, a sophomore writing and speaking seminar. All graduating seniors complete an independent research project and an oral defense of the project. **Procedure:** Freshmen are admitted fall and spring. Entrance exams should be taken by January of the senior year. There are early decision, early admissions, and deferred admissions plans. Early decision applications should be filed by November 1; regular applications, by February 15 for fall entry; and November 1 for spring entry. Notification of early decision is sent December 15; regular decision, April 1. 60 early decision candidates were accepted for the 2014-2015 class. 134 applicants were on the 2014 waiting list; 12 were admitted. Applications are accepted online. Application fees are waived if application is completed on-line. **Transfer Students:** 25 transfer students enrolled in 2013-2014. Transfer applicants must submit a transcript of all college courses, a high school transcript, standardized test scores, college official's report from prior institutions, essay/personal statement, a letter describing reasons for transfer, and one recommendation from college official. A minimum GPA of 2.5 from college and high school is required, with 3.0 from college recommended. An interview is recommended. 64 of 128 credits required for the bachelor's degree must be completed at Allegheny. **International Students:** There are 85 international students enrolled. The school actively recruits these students. They must take the TOEFL with a minimum score of 550 on the paper-based TOEFL (PBT) or 80 on the Internet-based version (iBT). They must also take the SAT or ACT. SAT or ACT can be submitted in place of TOEFL.

ADMISSIONS: 72% of the 2014-2015 applicants were accepted. The SAT scores for the 2014-2015 freshman class were: Critical Reading--13% below 500, 37% between 500 and 599, 40% between 600 and 699, and 10% between 700 and 800; Math--13% below 500, 40%

between 500 and 599, 41% between 600 and 699, and 6% between 700 and 800; Writing--17% below 500, 37% between 500 and 599, 36% between 600 and 699, and 10% between 700 and 800. The ACT scores were 6% below 21, 18% between 21 and 23, 30% between 24 and 26, 16% between 27 and 28, and 30% above 28. 68% of the current freshmen were in the top fifth of their class; 90% were in the top two fifths. There were 1 National Merit finalists. 14 freshmen graduated first in their class. **Admissions Contact:** Brian Dalton, V.P. of Enrollment & College Relations. E-Mail: *admissions@allegheny.edu* Web: *www.allegheny.edu/admissions/*

FINANCIAL AID: In 2014-2015, 100% of all full-time freshmen and 99% of continuing full-time students received some form of financial aid. 80% of all full-time freshmen and 71% of continuing full-time students received need-based aid. The average freshman award was $34,700. Need-based scholarships or need-based grants averaged $29,200 ($50,980 maximum); need-based self-help aid (loans and jobs) averaged $5,700 ($10,500 maximum); other non-need-based awards and non-need-based scholarships averaged $17,275 ($36,180 maximum); and $35,800 from other forms of aid. 66% of undergraduate students work part-time. Average annual earnings from campus work are $1350. The FAFSA is required. The priority date for freshman financial aid applications for fall entry is February 15.

ALVERNIA UNIVERSITY (*The complete profile is made available exclusively on our website, www.barronspac.com*)

ARCADIA UNIVERSITY	F-3
www.arcadia.edu	

Glenside, PA 19038	(215) 572-2910
	(877) 272-2342
Fax: (215) 572-4049	Email: admiss@arcadia.edu
Full-time: 480 men, 1270 women	Faculty: 103; IIA, -$
Part-time: 71 men, 136 women	Ph.D.s: 89%
Graduate: 353 men, 1095 women	Student/Faculty: 17 to 1
Year: semesters, summer session	Tuition: $27,440
Room & Board: $9300	Freshman Class: 2432 applied, 2056 accepted, 440 enrolled
SAT: required ACT: 25	CEEB CODE: 2039
Application Deadline: open	COMPETITIVE+

Arcadia University, founded in 1853, is a private institution offering undergraduate and graduate degrees in the fine arts, sciences, business, education, and pre-professional fields. In addition to regional accreditation, Arcadia has a baccalaureate program accreditation with ACBSP, APTA, CAHEA, and NASAD. The 76-acre campus is in a suburban area 10 miles north of Philadelphia. Including any residence halls, there are 21 buildings.

STUDENT LIFE: 68% of undergraduates are from Pennsylvania. Others are from 24 states, and 12 foreign countries. 70% are from public schools. 70% are White. 77% claim no religious affiliation; 13% Catholic. The average age of freshmen is 18; all undergraduates, 22. 19% do not continue beyond their first year; 64% remain to graduate. **Housing:** 1284 students can be accommodated in college housing, which includes single-sex and coed dorms, on-campus apartments, and off-campus apartments. There is a living and learning community in Grey Towers Castle. On-campus housing is guaranteed for all 4 years. 68% of students live on campus. Upperclassmen may keep cars.

FACULTY/CLASSROOMS: 44% of faculty are male; 56% are female. And all do research. No introductory courses are taught by graduate students. The average class size in an introductory lecture is 28; in a laboratory is 20; and in a regular course is 16.

PROGRAMS OF STUDY: Arcadia confers B.A., B.S., and B.F.A. degrees. Master's and Doctoral degrees are also awarded. Bachelor's degrees are awarded in BIOLOGICAL SCIENCE (biology/biological science), BUSINESS (accounting, banking and finance, business administration and management, international business management, marketing/retailing/merchandising, and personnel management), COMMUNICATIONS AND THE ARTS (art history and

appreciation, communications, dramatic arts, English, fine arts, graphic design, illustration, photography, and theater design), COMPUTER AND PHYSICAL SCIENCE (chemistry, computer science, mathematics, and science), EDUCATION (art education, early childhood education, elementary education, music education, secondary education, and special education), ENGINEERING AND ENVIRONMENTAL DESIGN (engineering, environmental science, and interior design), HEALTH PROFESSIONS (art therapy, health care administration, predentistry, premedicine, preoptometry, and preveterinary science), SOCIAL SCIENCE (criminal justice, history, international studies, liberal arts/general studies, philosophy, political science/government, prelaw, psychobiology, psychology, and sociology). Biology, psychology, and math are the strongest academically. Fine arts, business, and education have the largest enrollments.

ACTIVITIES: There are 40 groups on campus, including art, cheerleading, choir, chorale, chorus, communications, computers, dance, drama, ethnic, gay, honors, international, literary magazine, musical theater, newspaper, photography, political, professional, radio and TV, religious, social, social service, student government, and yearbook. Popular campus events include Mr. Beaver Contest, Woodstock Weekend, and International Festival. **Sports:** There are 6 intercollegiate sports for men and 9 for women, and 5 intramural sports for men and 5 for women. Facilities include a softball field, outdoor tennis and basketball courts, field hockey and soccer/lacrosse fields, and an athletic and recreation center with a 1500-seat gym for basketball and volleyball, an indoor track, an indoor NCAA regulation swimming pool, an aerobics and dance studio, and fitness and training rooms. **Graduates:** From July 1, 2013 to June 30, 2014, 381 bachelor's degrees were awarded. The most popular majors were business (15%), education (15%), and psychology (11%).

SERVICES: Counseling and information services are available, as is tutoring in every subject. There is a reader service for the blind, remedial math, reading, and writing. **Library/Resources:** The library contains 148,271 volumes, 50,301 microform items, 3,236 audio/video tapes/CDs/DVDs, and subscribes to 7,832 periodicals including electronic. Computerized library services include interlibrary loans, database searching, Internet access, and Wi-Fi capability. Special learning facilities include an art gallery, radio station, observatory, theater, computer graphics and communication labs, and multimedia classrooms. **Physically Challenged Students:** 70% of the campus is accessible. Facilities include wheelchair ramps, elevators, special parking, specially equipped restrooms, special class scheduling, lowered drinking fountains, and lowered telephones. **Special:** Internships are encouraged in all majors. There are study-abroad programs in 13 countries and co-op programs in business, computer science, chemistry, actuarial science, and accounting. There is a 3+2 engineering program with Columbia University or Washington University in St. Louis, as well as a 3+4 optometry program with Salus University. Arcadia also offers work study, student-designed majors, and credit by exam. There are 13 national honor societies and a freshman honors program. **Visiting:** There are regularly scheduled orientations for prospective students, including personal interviews Monday through Saturday, open houses, and opportunities to dine on campus and to meet with faculty, financial aid officers, and current students. There are guides for informal visits, visitors may sit in on classes, and stay overnight. To schedule a visit, contact the Office of Enrollment Management. **Campus Safety and Security:** Measures include 24-hour foot and vehicle patrol, self-defense education, and security escort services. There are shuttle buses, emergency telephones, lighted pathways/sidewalks, alarmed doors, night receptionists, and card access to residence halls.

REQUIREMENTS: The SAT is required. The ACT and ACT Writing Test are recommended. Applicants must be graduates of an accredited secondary school or have a GED. A total of 16 academic credits is required, including 4 years of English, 3 each of math and social studies, and 2 each of a foreign language and science. An essay is required. All art and illustration majors (except art education) must submit a portfolio. AP and CLEP credits are accepted. Important factors in the admissions decision are advanced placement or honors courses, recommendations by school officials, and extracurricular activities record.Students must take English composition, math, and two semesters each of a lab science and a foreign language. They must also fulfill 24 credits of distribution requirements in the arts, humanities, and social sciences; core courses in American pluralism and non-Western cultures; and a final project or thesis. 128 credit hours are required to graduate, including 40 to 52 in the major, with a minimum GPA of 2.0. **Procedure:** Freshmen are admitted fall and spring. Entrance exams should be taken during orientation. There are early decision, early admissions, deferred admissions, and rolling admissions plans. Application deadlines are open. Application fee is $30. Notification of early decision is sent December 1; regular decision, on a rolling basis. 12 early decision candidates were accepted for the 2014-2015 class. Applications are accepted on-line. **Transfer Students:** 167 transfer students enrolled in 2013-2014. Applicants must have a GPA of 2.5. Art majors must submit a portfolio. The SAT or the ACT is required if the student has earned less than 1 year of college credit. An interview is encouraged. 32 of 128 credits required for the bachelor's degree must be completed at . **International Students:** There are 41 international students enrolled. The school actively recruits these students. They must take the TOEFL, or take the IELTS.

ADMISSIONS: 85% of the 2014-2015 applicants were accepted. 51% of the current freshmen were in the top fifth of their class; 86% were in the top two fifths. 4 freshmen graduated first in their class. **Admissions Contact:** Office of Enrollment Management E-Mail: *admiss@arcadia.edu* Web: *www.arcadia.edu*

FINANCIAL AID: In 2014-2015, 99% of all full-time freshmen and 94% of continuing full-time students received some form of financial aid. 77% of all full-time freshmen and continuing full-time students received need-based aid. 30% of undergraduate students work part-time. Average annual earnings from campus work are $709. The average financial indebtedness of the 2014 graduate was $31,923. The FAFSA and the college's own financial statement, and PHEAA, and parent and student tax returns are required. The priority date for freshman financial aid applications for fall entry is March 1.

BLOOMSBURG UNIVERSITY OF PENNSYLVANIA   E-2
www.bloomu.edu

Bloomsburg, PA 17815	(570) 389-4000
Fax: (570) 389-4741	Email: buadmiss@bloomu.edu
Full-time: 3430 men, 4675 women	Faculty: 387; IIA, +$
Part-time: 190 men, 310 women	Ph.D.s: 92%
Graduate: 280 men, 630 women	Student/Faculty: n/av
Year: semesters, summer session	Tuition: $8582 ($17,942)
Room & Board: $7716	Freshman Class: n/av
SAT or ACT: required	CEEB CODE: 2646
Application Deadline: open	COMPETITIVE

Bloomsburg University of Pennsylvania, founded in 1839, is a public institution offering undergraduate programs in the liberal arts, sciences, business, teacher education, technology, and health professions. There are 4 undergraduate schools and 1 graduate school. Some figures in the above capsule and in this profile are approximate. In addition to regional accreditation, BU has baccalaureate program accreditation with AACSB, ABET, CAAHEP, CCNE, CSWE, NASM, NAST, and NCATE. The library contains 489,636 volumes, 2.1 million microform items, 13,502 audio/video tapes/CDs/DVDs, and subscribes to 1710 periodicals including electronic. Computerized library services include interlibrary loans, database searching, Internet access, and laptop Internet portals. Special learning facilities include a learning resource center, art gallery, radio station, and TV station. The 282-acre campus is in a small town 80 miles northeast of Harrisburg. Including any residence halls, there are 72 buildings.

STUDENT LIFE: 89% of undergraduates are from Pennsylvania. Others are from 22 states, 23 foreign countries, and Canada. 88% are from public schools. 77% are white. The average age of freshmen is 18; all undergraduates, 21. 19% do not continue beyond their first year; 63% remain to graduate.

FACULTY/CLASSROOMS: 53% of faculty are male; 47% are female. 87% teach undergraduates. No introductory courses are taught by graduate students. The average class size in a laboratory is 16; in a regular course, 31.

PROGRAMS OF STUDY: BU confers B.A., B.S., B.S.Ed., B.S.N., and B.S.W. degrees. Associate, Master's, and Doctoral degrees are also awarded. Bachelor's degrees are awarded in BIOLOGICAL SCIENCE (biology/biological science), BUSINESS (accounting, business administration and management, and business economics), COMMUNICATIONS AND THE ARTS (American Sign Language, art history and appreciation, communications, dramatic arts, English, French, German, music, Spanish, speech/debate/rhetoric, and studio art), COMPUTER AND PHYSICAL SCIENCE (chemistry, computer science, geoscience, mathematics, physics, and radiological technology), EDUCATION (business education, early childhood education, middle school education, secondary education, social studies education, and special education), ENGINEERING AND ENVIRONMENTAL DESIGN (electrical/electronics engineering), HEALTH PROFESSIONS (exercise science, health science, medical laboratory technology, nursing, and speech pathology/audiology), SOCIAL SCIENCE (anthropology, criminal justice, economics, geography, history, philosophy, political science/government, psychology, social work, and sociology). Elementary education, business administration, and special education have the largest enrollments.

ACTIVITIES: 7% of men belong to 3 local and 12 national fraternities; 9% of women belong to 5 local and 8 national sororities. There are 237 groups on campus, including art, band, cheerleading, chess, choir, chorale, chorus, computers, dance, drama, drill team, ethnic, film, forensics, gay, honors, international, jazz band, literary magazine, marching band, musical theater, newspaper, orchestra, pep band, political, professional, radio and TV, religious, social, social service, student government, and yearbook. Popular campus events include Renaissance Jamboree and Siblings and Children Weekend.

SERVICES: Counseling and information services are available, as is tutoring in some subjects. There is a reader service for the blind, remedial math, reading, and writing.

REQUIREMENTS: The SAT or ACT is required. Applicants must be graduates of an accredited secondary school. To be competitive, a student should also rank in the top 30% of the high school class with a B average. The GED is accepted. Applicants should complete 4 years each of English and social studies, 3 each of math and science, and 2 of a foreign language. An interview is recommended. AP and CLEP credits are accepted.

ADMISSIONS: 64% of a recent year's applicants were accepted. 28% of a recent year's freshmen were in the top fifth of their class; 62% were in the top two fifths. 12 freshmen graduated first in their class.

FINANCIAL AID: In a recent year, 82% of all full-time freshmen and 80% of continuing full-time students received some form of financial aid. 62% of all full-time freshmen and 60% of continuing full-time students received need-based aid. The average freshman award was $11,880. Need-based scholarships or need-based grants averaged $6609; need-based self-help aid (loans and jobs) averaged $4122; non-need-based athletic scholarships averaged $2867; and other non-need-based awards and non-need-based scholarships averaged $2025. The FAFSA and PHEAA Aid Information Request (PAIR) are required. Check with the school for current application deadlines.

BRYN ATHYN COLLEGE   F-3
www.brynathyn.edu

Bryn Athyn, PA 19009	(267) 502-6000
	(800) 767-9552
Fax: (267) 502-2593	Email: admissions@brynathyn.edu
Full-time: 93 men, 109 women	Faculty: 32
Part-time: 6 men, 5 women	Ph.D.s: 56%
Graduate: 12 men, 5 women	Student/Faculty: 7 to 1
Year: trimesters	Tuition: $17,724
Room & Board: $10,260	Freshman Class: 396 applied, 207 accepted, 80 enrolled
SAT CR/M/W: 510/510/470 ACT: 22	CEEB CODE: 2002
Application Deadline: February 1	COMPETITIVE

Bryn Athyn College, founded in 1877, is a private, independent, liberal arts institution affiliated with the General Church of the New Jerusalem. There is one undergraduate school and one graduate school. The 2 libraries contain 144,475 volumes, 3,593 microform items, 2,017 audio/video tapes/CDs/DVDs, and subscribe to 8,497 periodicals including electronic. Computerized library services include interlibrary loans, database searching, Internet access, and Wi-Fi capability. Special learning facilities include a The 130-acre campus is in a suburban area 15 miles northeast of Philadelphia, PA. Including any residence halls, there are 13 buildings.

STUDENT LIFE: 71% of undergraduates are from Pennsylvania. Others are from 16 states, 21 foreign countries, and Canada. 39% are from public schools. 67% are White; 19% Foreign. The average age of freshmen is 18; all undergraduates, 21. 9% do not continue beyond their first year; 91% remain to graduate.

FACULTY/CLASSROOMS: 50% of faculty are male; 50% are female. All teach undergraduates, 24% do research, and 24% do both. No introductory courses are taught by graduate students. The average class size in a regular course is 12.

PROGRAMS OF STUDY: Bryn Athyn College confers B.A., and B.S. degrees. Associate and Master's degrees are also awarded. Bachelor's degrees are awarded in BIOLOGICAL SCIENCE (biology/biological science), COMMUNICATIONS AND THE ARTS (English), EDUCATION (education), SOCIAL SCIENCE (history, interdisciplinary studies, psychology, and religion). Interdisciplinary studies, history, and education have the largest enrollments.

ACTIVITIES: There are 18 groups on campus, including and college games club, business club, psychology club, chorale, chorus, dance, drama, international, newspaper, outing club, social, social service, and student government. Popular campus events include Charter Day, Service Day, and Alumni Weekend.

SERVICES: Counseling and information services are available, as is tutoring in most subjects.

REQUIREMENTS: The SAT or ACT is required. Applicants' SAT or ACT scores must reflect promise of success in college work. Applicants must complete and essay. Applicants must be graduates of an accredited secondary school or achieve satisfactory scores on the GED. An interview is recommended. A GPA of 2.2 is required. AP and CLEP credits are accepted. Important factors in the admissions decision are recommendations by school officials, personality/intangible qualities, and advanced placement or honors courses.

ADMISSIONS: 52% of a recent year applicants were accepted. The SAT scores for a recent year freshman class were: Critical Reading--44% below 500, 27% between 500 and 599, 25% between 600 and 699, and 4% between 700 and 800; Math--44% below 500, 35% between 500 and 599, 18% between 600 and 699, and 3% between 700 and 800; Writing--56% below 500, 26% between 500 and 599, 12% between 600 and 699, and 6% between 700 and 800. The ACT scores were 11% below 21, 56% between 21 and 23, 11% between 24 and 26, and 22% above 28.

FINANCIAL AID: In a recent year, 96% of all full-time freshmen and 98% of continuing full-time students received some form of financial aid. 79% of all full-time freshmen and 63% of continuing full-time students received need-based aid. The average freshman award was $17,130. Need-based scholarships or need-based grants averaged $9,656; need-based self-help aid (loans and jobs) averaged $4,718; and other non-need-based awards and non-need-based scholarships averaged $4,868. 59% of undergraduate students work part-time. Average annual earnings from campus work are $1850. The average financial indebtedness of the 2013 graduate was $17,988. The FAFSA is required. The priority date for freshman financial aid applications for fall entry is February 15. The deadline for filing freshman financial aid applications for fall entry is June 1.

Bryn Mawr College, founded in 1885, is an independent liberal arts institution, primarily for women. The Graduate School of Social Work and Research, the Graduate School of the Arts and Sciences, and the postbaccalaureate premedical programs are coed. There is 1 undergraduate school and 2 graduate schools. The 135-acre campus is in a suburban area 11 miles west of Philadelphia. Including any residence halls, there are 40 buildings.

STUDENT LIFE: 81% of undergraduates are from out of state, mostly the Middle Atlantic. Students are from 44 states, 57 foreign countries, and Canada. 64% are from public schools. 36% are White; 25% Foreign; 12% Asian American. The average age of freshmen is 18; all undergraduates, 20. 9% do not continue beyond their first year; 82% remain to graduate. **Housing:** 1247 students can be accommodated in college housing, which includes single-sex and coed dorms and off-campus apartments. In addition, there are language houses, special-interest houses, Students may live at Haverford. Foreign language houses available to students studying Chinese, French, German, Hebrew, Italian, Russian or Spanish. Coed housing is available. Special housing available for non-traditional-aged students. Co-ops, such as Vegan House, are available as well. On-campus housing is guaranteed for all 4 years. 91% of students live on campus; of those, 90% remain on campus on weekends. Upperclassmen may keep cars.

FACULTY/CLASSROOMS: 43% of faculty are male; 57% are female. All teach and do research. No introductory courses are taught by graduate students. The average class size in an introductory lecture is 25; in a laboratory is 15; and in a regular course is 16.

PROGRAMS OF STUDY: Bryn Mawr confers A.B. degrees. Master's and Doctoral degrees are also awarded. Bachelor's degrees are awarded in BIOLOGICAL SCIENCE (biology/biological science), COMMUNICATIONS AND THE ARTS (art history and appreciation, classical languages, classics, comparative literature, English, fine arts, French, German, Greek, Italian, Latin, linguistics, music, romance languages and literature, Russian, and Spanish), COMPUTER AND PHYSICAL SCIENCE (astronomy, chemistry, computer science, geology, mathematics, and physics), SOCIAL SCIENCE (anthropology, archeology, East Asian studies, economics, history, international studies, philosophy, political science/government, psychology, religion, sociology, and urban studies). English, psychology, and math have the largest enrollments.

ACTIVITIES: There are 100 groups on campus, including girl scouts, investing, media, model UN, art, business, chess, choir, chorale, chorus, computers, dance, drama, environmental, ethnic, forensics, gay, honors, international, literary magazine, musical theater, orchestra, photography, political, professional, religious, social, social service, and student government. Popular campus events include May Day, Lantern Night and Fall Frolic. **Sports:** There are 12 intercollegiate sports for women, and 10 intramural sports for women. Facilities include 3 playing fields with access to an indoor track, a gym with an 8-lane pool and diving well, basketball, badminton, and volleyball courts, a gymnastics room and dance studio, a weight-training and fitness room, a 1,000-seat auditorium, and a student center. **Graduates:** From July 1, 2013 to June 30, 2014, 333 bachelor's degrees were awarded. The most popular majors were mathematics (13%), psychology (10%), and English (10%). In an average class, 2% graduate in 3 years or less, 78% graduate in 4 years or less, 84% graduate in 5 years or less, and 84% graduate in 6 years or less.

SERVICES: Counseling and information services are available, as is tutoring in every subject. There is a reader service for the blind. **Library/Resources:** The 4 libraries contain 951,791 volumes, 18,726 microform items, 10,352 audio/video tapes/CDs/DVDs, and subscribe to 102,519 periodicals including electronic. Computerized library services include interlibrary loans, database searching, Internet access, and Wi-Fi capability. Special learning facilities include an art gallery, an archeological museum, and a language learning center with audio, video, and computer technology. **Physically Challenged Students:** Facilities include wheelchair ramps, elevators, special parking, specially equipped restrooms, special class scheduling, lowered drinking fountains, lowered telephones, and special housing. **Special:** Students may cross-register with Haverford and Swarthmore Colleges and the University of Pennsylvania. Bryn Mawr sponsors more than 100 grants and internships for summer study in a wide range of disciplines and sponsors/cosponsors study abroad in 27 countries. Student-designed and dual majors are possible. Pass/fail options, work-

BRYN MAWR COLLEGE   **F-3**
www.brynmawr.edu

Bryn Mawr, PA 19010	(610) 526-5152
	(800) 262-1885
Fax: (610) 526-7471	Email: admissions@brynmawr.edu
Full-time: 1291 women	Faculty: 161; IIA, ++$
Part-time: 17 women	Ph.D.s: 93%
Graduate: 80 men, 321 women	Student/Faculty: 8 to 1
Year: semesters, summer session	Tuition: $45,540
Room & Board: $14,350	Freshman Class: 2706 applied, 1095 accepted, 351 enrolled
SAT CR/M/W: 660/650/670 ACT: 29	CEEB CODE: 2049
Application Deadline: January 15	MOST COMPETITIVE

study programs, a 3-2 degree in engineering with the California Institute of Technology, and a 3-2 degree in city and regional planning with the University of Pennsylvania are offered. **Visiting:** There are regularly scheduled orientations for prospective students, including student-guided campus tours and interviews can be arranged. There are guides for informal visits, visitors may sit in on classes, and stay overnight. To schedule a visit, contact the Office of Admissions. **Campus Safety and Security:** Measures include 24-hour foot and vehicle patrol, emergency notification system, self-defense education, and security escort services. There are shuttle buses, emergency telephones, lighted pathways/sidewalks, controlled access to dorms/residences, a web page, bicycle registration, and personal safety education (road safety, car maintenance).

REQUIREMENTS: Requirements for admission are 4 years of English, at least 3 years of math (2 of algebra and 1 of geometry), 3 years of a foreign language or 2 years of 2 languages, and 1 year each of science and history. Most applicants have taken at least 3 lab science courses and trigonometry. An essay is required. An interview is strongly recommended. Submission of standardized test scores (SAT or ACT) is optional for US citizens and US permanent residents. Non-US citizens and Non-US permanent residents are required to submit standardized test scores (SAT I or ACT) as well as either the TOEFL or IELTS if their primary language is not English and/or their language of instruction over the past four years has not been English. AP credits are accepted. Important factors in the admissions decision are advanced placement or honors courses, evidence of special talent, and extracurricular activities record. To graduate, students must complete 128 semester hours, with 40 to 60 in the major and a minimum GPA of 2.0. All students must complete 2 courses each in the social sciences, the humanities, and natural sciences or math, including 1 lab science. Additional required courses include 1 college seminar and 1 quantitative skills course. Students must be able to demonstrate proficiency in 1 foreign language. **Procedure:** Freshmen are admitted fall. Entrance exams should be taken in the spring of the junior year or the fall of the senior year. There are early decision and deferred admissions plans. Early decision applications should be filed by November 15; regular applications, by January 15 for fall entry, along with a $50 fee. Notification of early decision is sent December 15; regular decision, in April. 118 early decision candidates were accepted for the 2014-2015 class. 696 applicants were on the 2014 waiting list; 33 were admitted. Applications are accepted on-line. Application fees are waived if application is completed on-line. **Transfer Students:** 46 transfer students enrolled in 2013-2014. Applicants for transfer must be in good academic standing at their current institutions. An official SAT score report or ACT score report (for international students only), 2 professor recommendations, a school official's report, high school transcripts, college transcripts, and the Bryn Mawr Supplement to the College Application for Transfers must be submitted. 96 of 128 credits required for the bachelor's degree must be completed at Bryn Mawr. **International Students:** There are 377 international students enrolled. The school actively recruits these students. They must take the TOEFL with a minimum score of 600 on the paper-based TOEFL (PBT) or 90 on the Internet-based version (iBT), or a score of 7 or above on the IELTS. They must also take the SAT or ACT.

ADMISSIONS: 40% of the 2014-2015 applicants were accepted. The SAT scores for the 2014-2015 freshman class were: Critical Reading--2% below 500, 20% between 500 and 599, 47% between 600 and 699, and 31% between 700 and 800; Math--1% below 500, 24% between 500 and 599, 41% between 600 and 699, and 34% between 700 and 800; Writing--2% below 500, 13% between 500 and 599, 51% between 600 and 699, and 35% between 700 and 800. The ACT scores were 3% below 21, 6% between 21 and 23, 14% between 24 and 26, 25% between 27 and 28, and 52% above 28. 83% of the current freshmen were in the top fifth of their class; 96% were in the top two fifths. 5 freshmen graduated first in their class. **Admissions Contact:** Peaches Valdes, Director of Admissions. E-Mail: *admissions@brynmawr.edu* Web: *www.brynmawr.edu*

FINANCIAL AID: In 2014-2015, 75% of all full-time freshmen and 75% of continuing full-time students received some form of financial aid. 50% of all full-time freshmen and 52% of continuing full-time students received need-based aid. The average freshman award was $42,724. Need-based scholarships or need-based grants averaged $36,525; and need-based self-help aid (loans and jobs) averaged $5,490. 63% of undergraduate students work part-time. Average annual earnings from campus work are $2000. The average financial indebtedness of the 2014 graduate was $24,675. Bryn Mawr is a member of CSS. The CSS/Profile and FAFSA, and the prior year's tax returns, the noncustodial parent statement, and the business/farm supplement are required. The deadline for filing freshman financial aid applications for fall entry is March 1.

BUCKNELL UNIVERSITY   D-2
www.bucknell.edu

Lewisburg, PA 17837	(570) 577-2000
	(570) 577-3000
Fax: (570) 577-3538	Email: admissions@bucknell.edu
Full-time: 1702 men, 1836 women	Faculty: 372; IIB, ++$
Part-time: 12 men, 15 women	Ph.D.s: 97%
Graduate: 27 men, 32 women	Student/Faculty: 10 to 1
Year: semesters, summer session	Tuition: $48,498
Room & Board: $11,642	Freshman Class: 7864 applied, 2416 accepted, 939 enrolled
SAT CR/M/W: 640/670/650 ACT: 30	CEEB CODE: 2050
Application Deadline: January 15	MOST COMPETITIVE

Bucknell University, established in 1846, is a private independent institution offering undergraduate and graduate programs in arts, music, education, humanities, management, engineering, sciences, and social sciences. There are 3 undergraduate schools and one graduate school. In addition to regional accreditation, Bucknell has baccalaureate program accreditation with AACSB, ABET, NASM, CAC, and ACS. The 450-acre campus is in a small town 75 miles north of Harrisburg. Including any residence halls, there are 128 buildings.

STUDENT LIFE: 78% of undergraduates are from out of state, mostly the Middle Atlantic. Students are from 44 states, 45 foreign countries, and Canada. 63% are from public schools. 78% are White. 34% are Catholic; 28% Protestant; 26% claim no religious affiliation. **Male To Female Ratio:** 1.1:1. The average age of freshmen is 18; all undergraduates, 21. 7% do not continue beyond their first year; 89% remain to graduate. **Housing:** 3039 students can be accommodated in college housing, which includes single-sex and coed dorms and on-campus apartments. In addition, there are special-interest houses, fraternity houses, Sustainable living, substance-free housing. There are also 7 residential colleges for the first year (arts, discovery, environmental, humanities, global, science and technology, languages and cultures and social justice). On-campus housing is guaranteed for all 4 years and is available on a lottery system for upperclassmen. 86% of students live on campus; of those, 85% remain on campus on weekends. Upperclassmen may keep cars.

FACULTY/CLASSROOMS: 59% of faculty are male; 41% are female. All teach undergraduates and do research. No introductory courses are taught by graduate students. The average class size in an introductory lecture is 22; in a laboratory is 13; and in a regular course is 18.

PROGRAMS OF STUDY: Bucknell confers B.A., B.S., B.S.B.A., B.E.V.E., B.S.B.E., B.S.C.E., B.S.C.M., B.S.C.S., B.S.E.D., B.S.E.E., B.S.M.E., B.C.E.N. and B.M.U.S. degrees. Master's degrees are also awarded. Bachelor's degrees are awarded in AGRICULTURE (animal science), BIOLOGICAL SCIENCE (biochemistry, biology/biological science, cell biology, and neurosciences), BUSINESS (accounting and business administration and management), COMMUNICATIONS AND THE ARTS (art, art history and appreciation, classics, dramatic arts, English, fine arts, French, German, linguistics, music, music history and appreciation, music performance, music theory and composition, Russian, Spanish, and visual and performing arts), COMPUTER AND PHYSICAL SCIENCE (applied mathematics, chemistry, computer science, geology, mathematics, physics, and quantitative methods), EDUCATION (early childhood education, education, educational statistics and research, elementary education, music education, and secondary education), ENGINEERING AND ENVIRONMENTAL DESIGN (biomedical engineering, chemical engineering, civil engineering, computer engineering, electrical/electronics engineering, engineering, environmental engineering, environmental science, and mechanical engineering), SOCIAL SCIENCE (anthropology, East Asian studies, economics, geography, history, humanities, interdisciplinary studies, international relations, Latin American studies, philosophy, political science/government, psychology, religion, sociology, and women's studies). Humanities, biology, engineering and English are the strongest academically. Economics, biology, mechanical engineering have the largest enrollments.

ACTIVITIES: 44% of men belong to 11 national fraternities; 41% of women belong to 8 national sororities. There are 150 groups on campus, including art, band, cheerleading, chess, choir, chorale, chorus, communications, computers, dance, debate, drama, environmental, ethnic, film, forensics, gay, honors, international, jazz band, literary magazine, musical theater, newspaper, opera, orchestra, pep band, photography, political, professional, radio station, religious, social, social service, student government, symphony, and yearbook. Popular campus events include Celebration for the Arts, Chrysalis Ball, Family Weekend, Christy's (a capella concert) and Christmas Candlelight Service. **Sports:** There are 13 intercollegiate sports for men and 14 for women, and 10 intramural sports for men and 14 for women. Facilities include an athletic and recreation center with an Olympic-size pool, a 16,000-sq.-foot fitness center, a 4,000-seat basketball arena, a 13,000-seat stadium with 8-lane track, hockey and lacrosse fields, baseball fields, and recreational fields for soccer, softball, and other activities, a field house with a 4-lane track, tennis, squash, and racquetball courts, climbing wall, and dance studio, an 18-hole golf course with a training facility, tennis courts and a high-ropes course. **Graduates:** From July 1, 2013 to June 30, 2014, 853 bachelor's degrees were awarded. The most popular majors were management (10%), economics (8%), and biology (8%). 862 companies recruited on campus in 2013-2014. In an average class, 85% graduate in 4 years or less, 88% graduate in 5 years or less, and 89% graduate in 6 years or less. Of the 2013 graduating class, 21% were enrolled in graduate school within 6 months of graduation, and 71% were employed.

SERVICES: Counseling and information services are available, as is tutoring in some subjects, biology, chemistry, physics, math, and writing across the curriculum. **Library/Resources:** The library contains 1.0 million volumes, 20,157 microform items, 42,107 audio/video tapes/CDs/DVDs, and subscribes to 40,261 periodicals including electronic. Computerized library services include interlibrary loans, database searching, Internet access, and Wi-Fi capability. Special learning facilities include an art gallery, an outdoor natural area, greenhouse, primate facility, observatory, photography lab, race and gender resource center, library resources training lab, electronic classroom, multimedia lab, conference center, performing arts center, and multicultural, writing, craft, environmental, public policy and poetry centers, herbarium, and engineering structural test lab. **Physically Challenged Students:** 75% of the campus is accessible. Facilities include wheelchair ramps, elevators, special parking, specially equipped restrooms, special class scheduling, lowered drinking fountains, lowered telephones, and special housing. **Special:** Bucknell offers internships, study abroad in more than 60 countries, a Washington semester, a 5-year B.A.-B.S. degree in arts and engineering, a 3-2 engineering degree, and dual and student-designed majors. An interdisciplinary major in animal behavior is offered through the biology and psychology departments as well as an interdisciplinary studies major in economics and mathematics. Non-degree study is possible, and a pass/fail grading option is offered in some courses. The Residential College program offers opportunities for an academic-residential mix and faculty-student collaborative learning. Undergraduate research opportunities are available in the humanities/social sciences and the sciences and engineering. There are 27 national honor societies, including Phi Beta Kappa, a freshman honors program, and 55 departmental honors programs. **Visiting:** There are regularly scheduled orientations for prospective students. There are guides for informal visits and visitors may sit in on classes. To schedule a visit, contact the Admissions Office. **Campus Safety and Security:** Measures include 24-hour foot and vehicle patrol, emergency notification system, self-defense education, and security escort services. There are shuttle buses, emergency telephones, lighted pathways/sidewalks, controlled access to dorms/residences, campus safety alerts and intrusion alarms in residence halls.

REQUIREMENTS: The SAT or ACT is required. The ACT Optional Writing test is also required. Applicants must graduate from an accredited secondary school or have a GED. 16 Sixteen units must be earned, including 4 in English, 3 in math, and 2 each in history, science, social studies, and a foreign language. An essay is required, and a campus visit is recommended. Music applicants are required to audition. A portfolio is recommended for art applicants. AP and CLEP credits are accepted. Important factors in the admissions decision are advanced placement or honors courses, evidence of special talent, and extracurricular activities record. The College Core Curriculum is based on an interrelated set of principles that emphasize intellectual and practical skills, transferable tools for integrative learning, and disciplinary perspectives. It recognizes writing, oral communication, and information literacy as central tools for learning and disseminating new knowledge that permeate the entirety of the learning experience. The curriculum is intended to help students understand the synergistic, and complementary relationships among academic disciplines and their varied approaches to describing, analyzing, comprehending, interpreting, and critiquing a range of phenomena in both human cultures, and the physical and natural world. In doing so, it will prepare students to apply the skills, knowledge and sense of responsibility they have gained to new settings and complex problems as engaged citizens in an interconnected world. Although students will satisfy the requirements in different ways, each student must devise a program in accordance with the College Core Curriculum, and the University Writing Requirement. AP credit will not count toward any of the requirements that have defined learning goals. AP courses may count for Disciplinary Perspectives courses without defined learning goals. **Procedure:** Freshmen are admitted fall. Entrance exams should be taken before January 1. There are early decision and deferred admissions plans. Early decision applications should be filed by November 15; regular applications, by January 15 for fall entry, along with a $40 fee. Notification of early decision is sent December 15; regular decision, April 1. 458 early decision candidates were accepted for the 2014-2015 class. 1822 applicants were on the 2014 waiting list; 57 were admitted. Applications are accepted online. **Transfer Students:** 30 transfer students enrolled in 2013-2014. Transfer students must have a minimum GPA of 2.5 in courses comparable to those offered at Bucknell. The SAT or ACT is required. A minimum of 16 credit hours must have been earned; 32 are recommended. Students are accepted on a space-available basis. 48 of 128 credits required for the bachelor's degree must be completed at Bucknell. **International Students:** There are 204 international students enrolled. The school actively recruits these students. They must take the TOEFL with a minimum score of 600 on the paper-based TOEFL (PBT) or 100 on the Internet-based version (iBT). They must also take the SAT or ACT.

ADMISSIONS: 31% of the 2014-2015 applicants were accepted. The SAT scores for the 2014-2015 freshman class were: Critical Reading--1% below 500, 24% between 500 and 599, 57% between 600 and 699, and 18% between 700 and 800; Math--1% below 500, 11% between 500 and 599, 54% between 600 and 699, and 34% between 700 and 800; Writing--3% below 500, 16% between 500 and 599, 56% between 600 and 699, and 25% between 700 and 800. The ACT scores were 2% between 21 and 23, 10% between 24 and 26, 21% between 27 and 28, and 67% above 28. 89% of the current freshmen were in the top fifth of their class; 95% were in the top two fifths. There were 5 National Merit finalists. 31 freshmen graduated first in their class. **Admissions Contact:** Robert G. Springall, Dean of Admissions. E-Mail: *admissions@bucknell.edu* Web: *www.bucknell.edu*

FINANCIAL AID: In 2014-2015, 62% of all full-time freshmen and 61% of continuing full-time students received some form of financial aid. 44% of all full-time freshmen and 43% of continuing full-time students received need-based aid. The average freshman award was $31,500. Need-based scholarships or need-based grants averaged $26,700 ($60,140 maximum); need-based self-help aid (loans and jobs) averaged $4,200 ($7,300 maximum); non-need-based athletic scholarships averaged $33,629 ($60,140 maximum); and other non-need-based awards and non-need-based scholarships averaged $11,668 ($48,498 maximum). 35% of undergraduate students work part-time. Average annual earnings from campus work are $1500. The average financial indebtedness of the 2014 graduate was $22,500. Bucknell is a member of CSS. The CSS/Profile and FAFSA, and non-custodial parent's statement are required. The deadline for filing freshman financial aid applications for fall entry is January 15.

CABRINI COLLEGE (*The complete profile is made available exclusively on our website, www.barronspac.com*)

CAIRN UNIVERSITY   **F-3**
www.cairn.edu

Langhorne, PA 19047   (215) 752-5800
                                            (800) 366-0049
Fax: (215) 702-4248   Email: admissions@cairn.edu
Full-time: 348 men, 423 women   Faculty: 47; IIB, --$
Part-time: 26 men, 20 women   Ph.D.s: 70%
Graduate: 106 men, 139 women   Student/Faculty: 13 to 1
Year: semesters, summer session   Tuition: $23,920
Room & Board: $9350   Freshman Class: 318
                                  applied, 311 accepted, 159
                                  enrolled
SAT CR/M: 520/480 ACT: 21   CEEB CODE: 2661
Application Deadline: open   COMPETITIVE

Cairn University, founded in 1913, is a private institution offering instruction in the Bible, liberal arts and professional theory. Figures in the above capsule and in this profile are approximate. There are 5 undergraduate schools and 4 graduate schools. In addition to regional accreditation, Cairn University has baccalaureate program accreditation with CSWE, NASM, ABHE, IACBE, and ACSI. The 115-acre campus is in a suburban area 30 miles north of Philadelphia. Including any residence halls, there are 26 buildings.

STUDENT LIFE: 57% of undergraduates are from Pennsylvania. Others are from 32 states, 29 foreign countries, and Canada. 66% are from public schools. 74% are White; 12% African American. 99% are Protestant. The average age of freshmen is 18; all undergraduates, 23. 26% do not continue beyond their first year; 73% remain to graduate.

Housing: 662 students can be accommodated in college housing, which includes single-sex dorms, on-campus apartments, and married student housing. On-campus housing is guaranteed for all 4 years. 60% of students live on campus. Alcohol is not permitted. All students may keep cars.

FACULTY/CLASSROOMS: 64% of faculty are male; 36% are female. 87% teach undergraduates. No introductory courses are taught by graduate students. The average class size in an introductory lecture is 18 and in a regular course is 17.

PROGRAMS OF STUDY: Cairn University confers B.A., B.S., BSB, B.Mus., B.S.B.A., B.S.Ed. and B.S.W. degrees. Master's degrees are also awarded. Bachelor's degrees are awarded in BUSINESS (accounting and business administration and management), COMMUNICATIONS AND THE ARTS (English, music, music composition, and music performance), EDUCATION (education, education administration, and music education), SOCIAL SCIENCE (biblical studies, history, liberal arts/general studies, psychology, social work, and youth ministry). Biblical studies is the strongest academically. Teacher education, and social work have the largest enrollments.

ACTIVITIES: There are 21 groups on campus, including art, band, choir, chorale, chorus, drama, honors, international, musical theater, newspaper, opera, orchestra, professional, religious, social, student government, symphony, and yearbook. Popular campus events include Homecoming, Hoedown and Christmas Celebration. **Sports:** There are 6 intercollegiate sports for men and 6 for women, and 8 intramural sports for men and 7 for women. Facilities include a gym, baseball diamond, soccer, hockey, softball fields, sand volleyball court, lighted tennis courts, fitness circuit, and weight room. **Graduates:** From July 1, 2013 to June 30, 2014, 300 bachelor's degrees were awarded. The most popular majors were Bible (69%), teacher education (13%), and social work (9%). 900 companies recruited on campus in 2013-2014. In an average class, 14% graduate in 4 years or less, 60% graduate in 5 years or less, and 64% graduate in 6 years or less. Of the 2013 graduating class, 33% were enrolled in graduate school within 6 months of graduation, and 82% were employed.

SERVICES: Counseling and information services are available, as is tutoring in most subjects. **Library/Resources:** The library contains 121,023 volumes, 63,817 microform items, 10,423 audio/video tapes/CDs/DVDs, and subscribes to 35,197 periodicals including electronic.

Computerized library services include interlibrary loans, database searching, Internet access, and Wi-Fi capability. **Physically Challenged Students:** All of the campus is accessible. Facilities include wheelchair ramps, elevators, special parking, specially equipped restrooms, lowered drinking fountains, and special housing. **Special:** Cairn University offers an accelerated degree program in Biblical Studies, along with multiple internship and study abroad opportunities in the traditional undergraduate programs. There are double degree programs in social work, music, education, and business administration. There are 1 national honor society and a freshman honors program. **Visiting:** There are regularly scheduled orientations for prospective students, including class and chapel visits, a meal in the dining room, and an interview with a counselor. There are guides for informal visits, visitors may sit in on classes, and stay overnight. To schedule a visit, contact Kristina O'Connell at (215) 702-4235. **Campus Safety and Security:** Measures include 24-hour foot and vehicle patrol, emergency notification system, and security escort services. There are shuttle buses, emergency telephones, lighted pathways/sidewalks, and controlled access to dorms/residences.

REQUIREMENTS: The SAT or ACT is required. A GPA of 2.0 is required. AP and CLEP credits are accepted. Important factors in the admissions decision are advanced placement or honors courses, personality/intangible qualities, and leadership record.Students must complete 30 credits in Biblical Studies. At least 121 credits, with a minimum GPA of 2.0, is required. Approximately 30% of the students are enrolled in dual degree programs and receive the BS in Bible degree plus a baccalaureate or masters in their professional area. **Procedure:** Freshmen are admitted fall and spring. Entrance exams should be taken Junior or senior year of high school. There are deferred admissions and rolling admissions plans. Application deadlines are open. Application fee is $25. Notification is sent on a rolling basis. Applications are accepted on-line. **Transfer Students:** 86 transfer students enrolled in 2013-2014. Transfers must submit an application, a pastor's reference, college transcripts, and a health form. SAT scores and high school transcripts are also required if the student has fewer than 60 college credit hours. 60 of 121 credits required for the bachelor's degree must be completed at Cairn University. **International Students:** There are 16 international students enrolled. The school actively recruits these students. They must take the TOEFL with a minimum score of 520 on the paper-based TOEFL (PBT) or 68 on the Internet-based version (iBT).

ADMISSIONS: 98% of the 2014-2015 applicants were accepted. The SAT scores for the 2014-2015 freshman class were: Critical Reading--42% below 500, 42% between 500 and 599, 12% between 600 and 699, and 4% between 700 and 800; Math--58% below 500, 32% between 500 and 599, 10% between 600 and 699, and 1% between 700 and 800. The ACT scores were 46% below 21, 29% between 21 and 23, 8% between 24 and 26, 4% between 27 and 28, and 13% above 28. 27% of the current freshmen were in the top fifth of their class; 58% were in the top two fifths. **Admissions Contact:** Eric Rivera, Dir. of Undergrad Admissions. E-Mail: *admissions@cairn.edu* Web: *www.cairn.edu*

FINANCIAL AID: In 2014-2015, 99% of all full-time freshmen and 94% of continuing full-time students received some form of financial aid. 79% of all full-time freshmen and continuing full-time students received need-based aid. The average freshman award was $20,728. Need-based scholarships or need-based grants averaged $16,454; need-based self-help aid (loans and jobs) averaged $4,723; and other non-need-based awards and non-need-based scholarships averaged $11,200. 55% of undergraduate students work part-time. The average financial indebtedness of the 2014 graduate was $33,016. The FAFSA is required. Check with the school for current application deadlines.

CALIFORNIA UNIVERSITY OF   **B-3**
PENNSYLVANIA
www.cup.edu

California, PA 15419-1394   (724) 938-4404
                                            (888) 412-0479
Fax: (724) 938-4564   Email: inquiry@cup.edu
Full-time: 2600 men, 2700 women   Faculty: 266; IIA, +$
Part-time: 250 men, 420 women   Ph.D.s: 55%
Graduate: 490 men, 760 women   Student/Faculty: n/av
Year: semesters, summer session   Tuition: $9412 ($13,156)
Room & Board: $10,434   Freshman Class: n/av
SAT or ACT: required   CEEB CODE: 2647
Application Deadline: open   COMPETITIVE

California University of Pennsylvania, founded in 1852, is a state-supported institution offering degree programs in the arts and sciences, engineering, and education. There are 3 undergraduate schools and 1 graduate school. Some figures in the above capsule and in this profile are approximate. In addition to regional accreditation, the university has baccalaureate program accreditation with CSWE, NCATE, and NLN. The 148-acre campus is in a small town 35 miles south of Pittsburgh. Including any residence halls, there are 38 buildings.

STUDENT LIFE: 95% of undergraduates are from Pennsylvania. Others are from 35 states, 21 foreign countries, and Canada. 95% are from public schools. 93% are white. The average age of freshmen is 19; all undergraduates, 23. 25% do not continue beyond their first year; 50% remain to graduate.

FACULTY/CLASSROOMS: 58% of faculty are male; 42% are female. All teach undergraduates. No introductory courses are taught by graduate students. The average class size in an introductory lecture is 30; in a laboratory, 24; and in a regular course, 30.

PROGRAMS OF STUDY: The university confers B.A., B.S., B.S.Ed., and B.S.N. degrees. Associate and Master's degrees are also awarded. Bachelor's degrees are awarded in BIOLOGICAL SCIENCE (biology/biological science), BUSINESS (accounting, business administration and management, management science, and sports management), COMMUNICATIONS AND THE ARTS (art, dramatic arts, English, French, graphic design, Spanish, and speech/debate/rhetoric), COMPUTER AND PHYSICAL SCIENCE (chemistry, geology, information sciences and systems, mathematics, physical sciences, and physics), EDUCATION (athletic training, early childhood education, education, elementary education, guidance education, reading education, school psychology, secondary education, and special education), ENGINEERING AND ENVIRONMENTAL DESIGN (commercial art, computer technology, electrical/electronics engineering technology, engineering technology, environmental science, and industrial engineering technology), HEALTH PROFESSIONS (medical laboratory technology, mental health/human services, nursing, and physical therapy assistant), SOCIAL SCIENCE (criminal justice, geography, gerontology, history, liberal arts/general studies, parks and recreation management, philosophy, political science/government, psychology, social science, and social work).

ACTIVITIES: 10% of men belong to 7 national fraternities; 6% of women belong to 7 national sororities. There are 78 groups on campus, including art, band, cheerleading, chess, choir, chorale, chorus, computers, dance, debate, drama, drill team, ethnic, forensics, honors, international, jazz band, literary magazine, marching band, musical theater, newspaper, pep band, professional, radio and TV, religious, student government, and yearbook.

SERVICES: Counseling and information services are available, as is tutoring in most subjects. There is a reader service for the blind, remedial math, reading, and writing. **Library/Resources:** The library contains 451,382 volumes, 830,298 microform items, 60,416 audio/video tapes/CDs/DVDs, and subscribes to 822 periodicals including electronic. Computerized library services include interlibrary loans and database searching. Special learning facilities include an art gallery, natural history museum, radio station, and TV station. **Physically Challenged Students:** 95% of the campus is accessible. Facilities include wheelchair ramps, elevators, special parking, specially equipped restrooms, special class scheduling, lowered drinking fountains, and lowered telephones. **Special:** Cooperative programs are available in all academic areas when eligibility requirements have been met. Opportunities are provided for internships, and an accelerated degree program in justice studies is also available. There are 25 national honor societies and a freshman honors program. **Visiting:** There are regularly scheduled orientations for prospective students. There are guides for informal visits, visitors may sit in on classes, and stay overnight. To schedule a visit, contact the Admissions Office. **Campus Safety and Security:** Measures include 24-hour foot and vehicle patrol, self-defense education, and security escort services. There are shuttle buses and lighted pathways/sidewalks.

REQUIREMENTS: The SAT or ACT is required. Graduation from an accredited secondary school is required; a GED will be accepted. Applicants should submit an academic record that includes 4 credits each in English and history, 3 each in math and academic electives,

2 in science, and 1 each in social studies and a foreign language. An essay and an interview are recommended. A GPA of 2.5 is required. AP and CLEP credits are accepted.

ADMISSIONS: 78% of a recent year's applicants were accepted. 17% of a recent year's freshmen were in the top fifth of their class; 44% were in the top two fifths. 3 freshmen graduated first in their class.

FINANCIAL AID: The FAFSA is required. Check with the school for current application deadlines.

CARLOW UNIVERSITY   B-3
www.carlow.edu

Pittsburgh, PA 15213	(412) 578-6059
	(800) 333-CARLOW
Fax: (412) 578-6668	**Email:** admissions@carlow.edu
Full-time: 74 men, 1043 women	**Faculty:** 82
Part-time: 124 men, 577 women	**Ph.D.s:** 72%
Graduate: 77 men, 707 women	**Student/Faculty:** 14 to 1
Year: semesters, summer session	**Tuition:** $21,720 ($19,514)
Room & Board: $8552	**Freshman Class:** 1205 applied, 743 accepted, 257 enrolled
SAT CR/M/W: 480/470/475 **ACT:** 21	**CEEB CODE:** 2421
Application Deadline: July 1	**COMPETITIVE**

Carlow University, founded in 1929, is the first women-centered, liberal arts university in Pennsylvania, prepares students, primarily women, for leadership and service in personal and professional life. There are 6 undergraduate schools and 5 graduate schools. In addition to regional accreditation, Carlow has baccalaureate program accreditation with CSWE. The 15-acre campus is in an urban area in the Oakland section of Pittsburgh. Including any residence halls, there are 14 buildings.

STUDENT LIFE: 98% of undergraduates are from Pennsylvania. Others are from 11 states, and 7 foreign countries. 90% are from public schools. 56% are White; 14% African American. 43% are Catholic; 17% claim no religious affiliation. The average age of freshmen is 18; all undergraduates, 26. 31% do not continue beyond their first year; 47% remain to graduate.

FACULTY/CLASSROOMS: 24% of faculty are male; 76% are female. 79% teach undergraduates. No introductory courses are taught by graduate students. The average class size in an introductory lecture is 13; in a laboratory is 10; and in a regular course is 7.

PROGRAMS OF STUDY: Carlow confers B.A., B.S., B.S.N. and B.S.W. degrees. Master's and doctoral degrees are also awarded. Bachelor's degrees are awarded in BIOLOGICAL SCIENCE (biology/biological science), BUSINESS (accounting, business administration and management, business communications, and human resources), COMMUNICATIONS AND THE ARTS (art, art history and appreciation, communications, creative writing, English, media arts, Spanish, and technical and business writing), COMPUTER AND PHYSICAL SCIENCE (chemistry, information sciences and systems, and mathematics), EDUCATION (art education, early childhood education, elementary education, journalism education, middle school education, secondary education, and special education), HEALTH PROFESSIONS (art therapy, health care administration, nursing, and scientific/medical marketing), SOCIAL SCIENCE (forensic studies, history, liberal arts/general studies, philosophy, political science/government, psychology, public administration, social work, sociology, and theological studies). Nursing, creative writing, and education are the strongest academically. Nursing, psychology, and business management have the largest enrollments.

ACTIVITIES: There are 23 groups on campus, including and campus activities board, students in the natural sciences, band, choir, chorale, chorus, communications, dance, drama, ethnic, honors, literary magazine, musical theater, newspaper, pep band, political, professional, social, social service, student education association, and student government. Popular campus events include Constitution Day, Halloween, and Spring Carnival.

SERVICES: Counseling and information services are available, as is tutoring in most subjects. There is remedial math, reading, and writing. Professional tutoring is available for reading, writing, study skills, math, and sciences. Peer tutoring is available in other subject areas. **Library/Resources:** The library contains 133,864 volumes, 11,712 microform items, 5,113 audio/video tapes/CDs/DVDs, and subscribes to 14,784 periodicals including electronic. Computerized library services include interlibrary loans, database searching, Internet access, and Wi-Fi capability. Special learning facilities include a **Physically Challenged Students:** 30% of the campus is accessible. Facilities include wheelchair ramps, elevators, special parking, specially equipped restrooms, special class scheduling, lowered drinking fountains, lowered telephones. 6 power doors, and 1 doorbell. **Special:** Carlow offers cross-registration to member institutions of the Pittsburgh Council for Higher Education, internships in all areas, and work-study. There are accelerated degree programs, and dual majors are possible in most majors, as are student-designed majors. There are 3-2 engineering programs with Carnegie Mellon University and a 3-2 biology/environmental science and management program with Duquesne University. Students can study abroad in all countries deemed by the government to be safe for travel. There are 4 national honor societies, a freshman honors program, and 31 departmental honors programs. **Visiting:** There are regularly scheduled orientations for prospective students, including a campus tour, information sessions on admission and financial aid, and interaction with faculty and students regarding academic and student life. There are guides for informal visits, visitors may sit in on classes, and stay overnight. To schedule a visit, contact the Admissions Office. **Campus Safety and Security:** Measures include 24-hour foot and vehicle patrol, emergency notification system, self-defense education, and security escort services. There are emergency telephones, lighted pathways/sidewalks, an electronically secured dorm entrance and most doors on campus are secured electronically and require an ID badge to enter.

REQUIREMENTS: The SAT or ACT is required. The minimum scores depend on the major selected. Candidates must be graduates of an accredited secondary school. 18 Carnegie units are required, including 4 each in English and arts/humanities, 3 each in math and science, and 4 in electives. Applicants for nursing must have completed a minimum 4 units in English, 3 in social sciences, and 2 each in math (including algebra) and lab science (including chemistry), as required by the State Board of Nursing. The GED is accepted. An essay and/or interview are recommended. A GPA of 2.0 is required. AP and CLEP credits are accepted.

ADMISSIONS: 62% of a recent year applicants were accepted. The SAT scores for the 2013-2014 freshman class were: Critical Reading--58% below 500, 32% between 500 and 599, 8% between 600 and 699, and 2% between 700 and 800; Math--65% below 500, 32% between 500 and 599, and 3% between 600 and 699; Writing--60% below 500, 30% between 500 and 599, 9% between 600 and 699, and 1% between 700 and 800. The ACT scores were 46% below 21, 32% between 21 and 23, 15% between 24 and 26, 3% between 27 and 28, and 4% above 28. 27% of the current freshmen were in the top fifth of their class; 60% were in the top two fifths.

FINANCIAL AID: In a recent year, 100% of all full-time freshmen students received some form of financial aid. 86% of all full-time freshmen students received need-based aid. The average freshman award was $25,093. Need-based scholarships or need-based grants averaged $3,381 ($15,352 maximum); need-based self-help aid (loans and jobs) averaged $2,706 ($3,500 maximum); non-need-based athletic scholarships averaged $6,600 ($10,000 maximum); and other non-need-based awards and non-need-based scholarships averaged $4,398 ($20,854 maximum). Carlow is a member of CSS. The FAFSA, and Verification worksheets and tax returns when applicable is required. The priority date for freshman financial aid applications for fall entry is April 1. The deadline for filing freshman financial aid applications for fall entry is rolling.

CARNEGIE MELLON UNIVERSITY B-3
www.cmu.edu

Pittsburgh, PA 15213	(412) 268-2082
	(412) 268-2000
Fax: (412) 268-7838	Email: undergraduate-admissions+@
	andrew.cmu.edu

Full-time: 3430 men, 2430 women	**Faculty:** I, +$
Part-time: 70 men, 40 women	**Ph.D.s:** 96%
Graduate: 3790 men, 1630 women	**Student/Faculty:** n/av
Year: semesters, summer session	**Tuition:** $44,520
Room & Board: $11,610	**Freshman Class:** n/av
SAT or ACT: required	**CEEB CODE:** 2074
Application Deadline: see profile	**MOST COMPETITIVE**

Carnegie Mellon University, established in 1900, is a private nonsectarian institution offering undergraduate programs in liberal arts and science and technology. There are 6 undergraduate schools and 7 graduate schools. The figures in the above capsule and in this profile are approximate. In addition to regional accreditation, Carnegie Mellon has baccalaureate program accreditation with AACSB, ABET, NAAB, NASAD, and NASM. The 145-acre campus is in a suburban area 4 miles from downtown Pittsburgh. Including any residence halls, there are 80 buildings.

STUDENT LIFE: 81% of undergraduates are from out of state, mostly the Middle Atlantic. Students are from 49 states, 65 foreign countries, and Canada. 40% are white; 24% Asian American; 15% foreign nationals. The average age of freshmen is 18; all undergraduates, 20. 5% do not continue beyond their first year; 85% remain to graduate.

FACULTY/CLASSROOMS: 72% of faculty are male; 28% are female. All teach and do research. No introductory courses are taught by graduate students.

PROGRAMS OF STUDY: Carnegie Mellon confers B.A., B.S., B.A.H., B.Arch., B.F.A., and B.S.A. degrees. Master's and doctoral degrees are also awarded. Bachelor's degrees are awarded in BIOLOGICAL SCIENCE (biology/biological science), BUSINESS (business administration and management, business economics, and marketing/retailing/merchandising), COMMUNICATIONS AND THE ARTS (communications, design, dramatic arts, English, fine arts, French, German, journalism, languages, music, and Spanish), COMPUTER AND PHYSICAL SCIENCE (chemistry, computer programming, computer science, information sciences and systems, mathematics, physics, and statistics), EDUCATION (music education), ENGINEERING AND ENVIRONMENTAL DESIGN (chemical engineering, civil engineering, computer engineering, electrical/electronics engineering, engineering, and mechanical engineering), SOCIAL SCIENCE (economics, history, philosophy, political science/government, psychology, public administration, social science, and urban studies). Computer science, engineering, and business administration are the strongest academically. Engineering has the largest enrollments.

ACTIVITIES: 15% of men belong to 16 national fraternities; 10% of women belong to 7 national sororities. There are 225 groups on campus, including art, bagpipe, band, cheerleading, chess, choir, chorale, chorus, computers, debate, drama, ethnic, film, gay, honors, international, jazz band, literary magazine, marching band, musical theater, newspaper, opera, orchestra, pep band, photography, political, professional, radio and TV, religious, social, social service, student government, and symphony. Popular campus events include Spring Carnival, International Festival, and Watson Arts Festival.

SERVICES: Counseling and information services are available, as is tutoring in most subjects. There is a reader service for the blind. **Library/Resources:** The 4 libraries contain 1.1 million volumes, 1.1 million microform items, and 30,729 audio/video tapes/CDs/DVDs, and subscribe to 1,955 periodicals including electronic. Computerized library services include interlibrary loans, database searching, Internet access, and Wi-Fi capability. Special learning facilities include an art gallery, radio station, and TV station. **Physically Challenged Students:** 98% of the campus is accessible. Facilities include wheelchair ramps, elevators, special parking, specially equipped restrooms, special class scheduling, lowered drinking fountains, and lowered telephones. **Special:** Students may cross-register with other Pittsburgh Council of Higher Education institutions. Also available are internships, work-study programs, study abroad in 49 countries, a Washington semester, accelerated degrees, B.A.-B.S. degrees, co-op programs, dual majors, and limited student-designed majors. There are 10 national honor societies, including Phi Beta Kappa, and a freshman honors program. **Visiting:** There are regularly scheduled orientations for prospective students, including Saturday group sessions in September, October, November, and April. There are guides for informal visits, visitors may sit in on classes, and stay overnight. To schedule a visit, contact the Admissions Office. **Campus Safety and Security:** Measures include 24-hour foot and vehicle patrol, emergency notification system, self-defense education, and security escort services. There are shuttle buses, emergency telephones, lighted pathways/sidewalks, SafeWalk Program.

REQUIREMENTS: The SAT or ACT is required. SAT subject tests are not required for drama, design, art, or music applicants. All other applicants must take appropriate tests, preferably by December but no later than January. Applicants must graduate from an accredited secondary school or have a GED. They must earn 16 Carnegie units and must have completed 4 years of English. Applicants to the Carnegie Institute of Technology and the Mellon College of Science must take 4 years of math and 1 year each of biology, chemistry, and physics. Essays are required, and interviews are recommended. Art and design applicants must submit a portfolio. Drama and music applicants must audition. AP credits are accepted.

ADMISSIONS: 36% of a recent year's applicants were accepted. 88% of a recent year's freshmen were in the top fifth of their class; 97% were in the top two fifths. 69 freshmen graduated first in their class.

FINANCIAL AID: In a recent year, 76% of all full-time freshmen and 67% of continuing full-time students received some form of financial aid. 53% of all full-time freshmen and 47% of continuing full-time students received need-based aid. The average freshman award was $28,678. 31% of undergraduate students work part-time. The average financial indebtedness of a recent year's graduate was $29,546. Carnegie Mellon is a member of CSS. The FAFSA, the college's own financial statement, and parent and student federal tax returns and W-2 forms are required. Check with the school for current application deadlines.

CEDAR CREST COLLEGE   E-3
www.cedarcrest.edu

Allentown, PA 18104	(610) 740-3780
	(800) 360-1222
Fax: (610) 606-4647	Email: admissions@cedarcrest.edu
Full-time: 33 men, 607 women	Faculty: 73; IIB, -$
Part-time: 57 men, 589 women	Ph.D.s: 73%
Graduate: 19 men, 181 women	Student/Faculty: 9 to 1
Year: semesters, summer session	Tuition: $33,550
Room & Board: $9690	Freshman Class: 1063 applied, 625 accepted, 141 enrolled
SAT CR/M/W: 460/470/460 ACT: 22	CEEB CODE: 2079
Application Deadline: open	COMPETITIVE

Cedar Crest College, founded in 1867, was one of the first women's colleges in the nation. Today it remains an independent, comprehensive liberal arts college for women that combines excellence in scholarship and undergraduate education with an extensive School of Adult and Graduate Education (SAGE) program and growing graduate programs that serve women and men in the surrounding region. There is 1 undergraduate school and 1 graduate school. In addition to regional accreditation, Cedar Crest has baccalaureate program accreditation with ACBSP and CSWE. The 84-acre campus is in a suburban area 55 miles north of Philadelphia and 90 miles west of New York City. Including any residence halls, there are 20 buildings.

STUDENT LIFE: 67% of undergraduates are from Pennsylvania. Others are from 21 states, and 27 foreign countries. 95% are from public schools. 69% are White; 12% Hispanic. The average age of freshmen is 18; all undergraduates, 28. 33% do not continue beyond their first year; 60% remain to graduate.

FACULTY/CLASSROOMS: 32% of faculty are male; 68% are female. All teach undergraduates. No introductory courses are taught by graduate students. The average class size in an introductory lecture is 20; in a laboratory is 13; and in a regular course is 14.

PROGRAMS OF STUDY: Cedar Crest confers B.A., and B.S degrees. Master's degrees are also awarded. Bachelor's degrees are awarded in BIOLOGICAL SCIENCE (biochemistry, biology/biological science, environmental biology, genetics, neurosciences, and nutrition), BUSINESS (accounting, business administration and management, and marketing/retailing/merchandising), COMMUNICATIONS AND THE ARTS (art, communications, dance, dramatic arts, English, fine arts, and music), COMPUTER AND PHYSICAL SCIENCE (chemistry, computer science, information sciences and systems, mathematics, and science), EDUCATION (early childhood education, education, and elementary education), HEALTH PROFESSIONS (nuclear medical technology and nursing), SOCIAL SCIENCE (criminal justice, history, industrial and organizational psychology, political science/government, psychology, social work, and Spanish studies). Sciences, and nursing are the strongest academically. Nursing, social work, and business have the largest enrollments.

ACTIVITIES: There are 51 groups on campus, including art, band, cheerleading, choir, chorus, computers, dance, drama, ethnic, forensics, gay, honors, international, literary magazine, musical theater, newspaper, political, professional, radio and TV, religious, social, social service, student government, and yearbook. Popular campus events include Student Faculty Frolic, Midnight Breakfast and Ring Ceremony.

SERVICES: Counseling and information services are available, as is tutoring in most subjects. There is remedial math and writing. Computer software skills program for underprepared students. **Library/Resources:** Computerized library services include interlibrary loans, database searching, Internet access, and Wi-Fi capability. Special learning facilities include an art gallery, radio station, an arboretum, theaters, and a sculpture garden. **Physically Challenged Students:** 35% of the campus is accessible. Facilities include wheelchair ramps, elevators, special parking, specially equipped restrooms, special class scheduling, lowered drinking fountains, and lowered telephones. **Special:** Cross-registration is available through the Lehigh Valley Association of Independent Colleges and Online Consortium. Also available are internships, work-study programs, an accelerated degree program in business, and B.A.-B.S. degrees in math, biology, and psychology. Dual majors, student-designed majors, pass/fail options, and credit for life, military, and work experience are offered. There are 15 national honor societies, a freshman honors program, and 1 departmental honors programs. **Visiting:** There are regularly scheduled orientations for prospective students. There are guides for informal visits, visitors may sit in on classes, and stay overnight. To schedule a visit, contact the Admissions Office at admissions@cedarcrest.edu. **Campus Safety and Security:** Measures include 24-hour foot and vehicle patrol, emergency notification system, self-defense education, and security escort services. There are emergency telephones, lighted pathways/sidewalks, Residence halls are equipped with fire/intrusion alarms, which are monitored 24 hours a day. A keyless access system is in place; exterior doors are locked 24 hours a day.

REQUIREMENTS: The SAT is required. Applicants must be graduates of an accredited secondary school. The GED is accepted. Students should have completed 16 high school academic credits, including 4 years of English, 3 of math, 2 each of science, history, and foreign language, and 1 each of art, music, and social studies. An essay is required. Cedar Crest requires applicants to be in the upper 50% of their class. A GPA of 2.0 is required. AP and CLEP credits are accepted. Important factors in the admissions decision are advanced placement or honors courses, leadership record, and evidence of special talent.

ADMISSIONS: 59% of a recent year applicants were accepted. The SAT scores for the 2013-2014 freshman class were: Critical Reading--64% below 500, 30% between 500 and 599, and 6% between 600 and 699; Math--57% below 500, 38% between 500 and 599, and 5% between 600 and 699; Writing--70% below 500, 23% between 500 and 599, and 7% between 600 and 699. 55% of the current freshmen were in the top fifth of their class; 92% were in the top two fifths.

FINANCIAL AID: In a recent year, 97% of all full-time freshmen and

99% of continuing full-time students received some form of financial aid. 94% of all full-time freshmen and 95% of continuing full-time students received need-based aid. The average freshman award was $26,840. Need-based scholarships or need-based grants averaged $23,477; need-based self-help aid (loans and jobs) averaged $3,787; and other non-need-based awards and non-need-based scholarships averaged $3,497. Cedar Crest is a member of CSS. The FAFSA is required. The deadline for filing freshman financial aid applications for fall entry is May 1.

CHATHAM UNIVERSITY   B-3
www.chatham.edu

Pittsburgh, PA 15232	(412) 365-1139
	(800) 837-1290
Fax: (412) 365-1609	Email: admission@chatham.edu
Full-time: 27 men, 535 women	Faculty: 45
Part-time: 71 men, 299 women	Ph.D.s: 88%
Graduate: 236 men, 966 women	Student/Faculty: 22 to 1
Year: 4-1-4, summer session	Tuition: $33,429
Room & Board: $10,368	Freshman Class: 596 applied, 342 accepted, 104 enrolled
SAT CR/M: 530/500 ACT: 22	CEEB CODE: 2081
Application Deadline: open	COMPETITIVE

Chatham University, formerly Chatham College and founded in 1869, is a private university, of the Falk School of Sustainability, the School of Health Sciences, the School of Arts, Science and Business, and the College for Continuing and Professional Studies. Chatham offers undergraduate and graduate degrees in more than 60 programs, on campus and online. There is 1 undergraduate school and 2 graduate schools. In addition to regional accreditation, Chatham has baccalaureate program accreditation with ACS. The 35-acre campus is in an urban area 5 miles east of downtown Pittsburgh. Including any residence halls, there are 33 buildings.

STUDENT LIFE: 76% of undergraduates are from Pennsylvania. Others are from 47 states, 31 foreign countries, and Canada. 96% are from public schools. 46% are White; 28% race unknown; 12% Foreign. The average age of freshmen is 19; all undergraduates, 24.2. 23% do not continue beyond their first year; 61% remain to graduate. **Housing:** 499 students can be accommodated in college housing, which includes single-sex and coed dorms, on-campus apartments, and off-campus apartments. In addition, there are special-interest houses, Intercultural residence hall. On-campus housing is available on a lottery system for upperclassmen. 50% of students commute. Upperclassmen may keep cars.

FACULTY/CLASSROOMS: 28% of faculty are male; 72% are female. All teach undergraduates. No introductory courses are taught by graduate students. The average class size in an introductory lecture is 11; in a laboratory is 12; and in a regular course is 11.

PROGRAMS OF STUDY: Chatham confers B.A., B.S., B.S.N. and B.S.W. degrees. Master's and Doctoral degrees are also awarded. Bachelor's degrees are awarded in AGRICULTURE (environmental studies), BIOLOGICAL SCIENCE (biochemistry and biology/biological science), BUSINESS (accounting, business administration and management, international business management, management information systems, marketing management, and sustainable management), COMMUNICATIONS AND THE ARTS (art history and appreciation, arts administration/management, communications, creative writing, English, English literature, film, television and digital media, media arts, music, Spanish, theatre studies, and visual and performing arts), COMPUTER AND PHYSICAL SCIENCE (chemistry, mathematics, and physics), EDUCATION (early childhood education, education, and elementary education), ENGINEERING AND ENVIRONMENTAL DESIGN (environmental science and interior design), HEALTH PROFESSIONS (exercise science and physical therapy), SOCIAL SCIENCE (crosscultural studies, economics, forensic studies, history, interdisciplinary studies, international relations, political science/government, psychology, public affairs, social work, and women's studies). Nursing, psychology, and biology have the largest enrollments.

ACTIVITIES: There are 67 groups on campus, including choir, dance, drama, environmental, ethnic, feminist club, film, gay, honors, international, literary magazine, newspaper, photography, political, professional, religious, social service, and student government. Popular campus events include Fall Festival, Spring Fling and Air Band Contest. **Sports:** There are 9 intercollegiate sports for women, and 5 intramural sports for women. Facilities include The Athletic and Fitness Center is an advanced four-level athletic facility designed by the St. Louis, Missouri firm of Hastings and Chivetta. On the lower level is an eight-lane competition swimming pool, whirlpool/sauna/steam room, squash courts, and rock-climbing wall. The athletic training room contains a hydrotherapy room and complete line of rehabilitation equipment. The second level has a smart classroom with an adjoining human performance laboratory. The fitness and cardiovascular rooms contain treadmills, elliptical machines, bikes, free weights, and circuit strength machines. The dance and aerobics studio is a multi-function space that houses Pilates, martial arts, aerobic classes, and dance courses. On the third level, the gymnasium seats 600 spectators for athletic events and up to 1,000 for other events. Finally, the fourth level offers a three-lane walking track and smoothie bar where students may purchase healthy snacks and beverages. There is a out-door field for both soccer and softball. **Graduates:** From July 1, 2013 to June 30, 2014, 187 bachelor's degrees were awarded. The most popular majors were nursing (28%), psychology (12%), and interior architecture (11%). In an average class, 5% graduate in 3 years or less, 47% graduate in 4 years or less, 55% graduate in 5 years or less, and 56% graduate in 6 years or less. Of the 2013 graduating class, 17% were enrolled in graduate school within 6 months of graduation.

SERVICES: Counseling and information services are available, as is tutoring in every subject. There is a reader service for the blind, remedial math, reading, and writing. One-on-one and group tutoring are available by both students and professional specialists, and there is also computer-aided tutoring and an organized study group. **Library/Resources:** The library contains 117,630 volumes, 22,450 microform items, 1,677 audio/video tapes/CDs/DVDs, and subscribes to 273,313 periodicals including electronic. Computerized library services include interlibrary loans, database searching, Internet access, and Wi-Fi capability. Special learning facilities include an art gallery, theaters, a media center, and an arboretum. **Physically Challenged Students:** 75% of the campus is accessible. Facilities include wheelchair ramps, elevators, special parking, specially equipped restrooms, and special class scheduling. **Special:** Chatham offers a study-abroad program in 12 countries, cross-registration with other Pittsburgh Council on Higher Education institutions, co-op programs in all majors, internships in the public and private sectors, and a Washington semester in conjunction with American University and the Public Leadership Education Network. Accelerated degree programs, work-study, combined B.A.-B.S. degrees, multidisciplinary majors, and dual and student-designed majors are available. There are 3-2 engineering degrees with Carnegie Mellon and Penn State Universities and the University of Pittsburgh, dual degree programs, and an accelerated Master's program with Carnegie Mellon's Heinz School. There are 11 national honor societies, including Phi Beta Kappa, a freshman honors program, and 30 departmental honors programs. **Visiting:** There are regularly scheduled orientations for prospective students, including campus tours, student and faculty panels, financial aid presentations, and athletic coach meetings. There are guides for informal visits, visitors may sit in on classes, and stay overnight. To schedule a visit, contact the Admissions Office. **Campus Safety and Security:** Measures include 24-hour foot and vehicle patrol, emergency notification system, self-defense education, and security escort services. There are shuttle buses, emergency telephones, and lighted pathways/sidewalks.

REQUIREMENTS: Applicants who choose not to submit the SAT or ACT will be required instead to submit a graded writing sample and resume or list of curricular and cocurricular activities. Applicants will also have the option to submit a portfolio or special project or activity. These materials may also be applied toward Chatham's scholarship review process upon acceptance. AP and CLEP credits are accepted. Important factors in the admissions decision are recommendations by school officials, leadership record, and extracurricular activities record. To graduate, students must complete 120 credit hours, including a general education curriculum of 7 courses and a senior tutorial, with a minimum GPA of 2.0. Students must also demonstrate proficiencies in writing, math, and computer literacy. **Procedure:** Freshmen are admitted fall and spring. Entrance exams should be taken by fall of the senior year. There are deferred admissions and rolling admissions plans. Application deadlines are open. Application fee is $35. Notification is sent on a rolling basis. Applications are accepted on-line. Application fees are waived if application is completed on-line. **Transfer Students:** 83 transfer students enrolled in 2013-2014. Applicants must present college transcripts 45 of 120 credits required for the bachelor's degree must be completed at Chatham. **International Students:** There are 98 international students enrolled. The school actively recruits these students. They must take the TOEFL with a minimum score of 550 on the paper-based TOEFL (PBT) or 79 on the Internet-based version (iBT) or take the MELAB, or take the IELTS. The SAT is required if no TOEFL score is available.

ADMISSIONS: 57% of the 2014-2015 applicants were accepted. The SAT scores for the 2014-2015 freshman class were: Critical Reading--31% below 500, 42% between 500 and 599, 21% between 600 and 699, and 6% between 700 and 800; Math--46% below 500, 37% between 500 and 599, 13% between 600 and 699, and 4% between 700 and 800. The ACT scores were 37% below 21, 17% between 21 and 23, 20% between 24 and 26, 14% between 27 and 28, and 11% above 28. 50% of the current freshmen were in the top fifth of their class; 84% were in the top two fifths. 3 freshmen graduated first in their class. **Admissions Contact:** Amy Becher, Vice President for Enrollment Management. E-Mail: *admission@chatham.edu* Web: *www.chatham.edu*

FINANCIAL AID: In 2014-2015, 74% of all full-time freshmen and 81% of continuing full-time students received some form of financial aid. 69% of all full-time freshmen and 64% of continuing full-time students received need-based aid. The average freshman award was $30,217. Need-based scholarships or need-based grants averaged $8,628; and need-based self-help aid (loans and jobs) averaged $4,796. The FAFSA, and None are required, but students need to complete the FAFSA in order to be considered for need-based grants from the Univ is required. The priority date for freshman financial aid applications for fall entry is March 1. The deadline for filing freshman financial aid applications for fall entry is Rolling.

CHESTNUT HILL COLLEGE (*The complete profile is made available exclusively on our website, www.barronspac.com*)

CHEYNEY UNIVERSITY OF PENNSYLVANIA (*The complete profile is made available exclusively on our website, www.barronspac.com*)

CLARION UNIVERSITY OF PENNSYLVANIA (*The complete profile is made available exclusively on our website, www.barronspac.com*)

CURTIS INSTITUTE OF MUSIC (*The complete profile is made available exclusively on our website, www.barronspac.com*)

DE SALES UNIVERSITY   F-3
www.desales.edu

Center Valey, PA 18034	**(610) 282-1100, ext. 1475**
	(877) 433-7253
Fax: **(610) 282-0131**	Email: **admiss@desales.edu**
Full-time: 760 men, 1024 women	Faculty: 100; IIA, -$
Part-time: 189 men, 408 women	Ph.D.s: 84%
Graduate: 309 men, 498 women	Student/Faculty: 16 to 1
Year: semesters, summer session	Tuition: $32,350
Room & Board: $11,620	Freshman Class: 2658 applied, 2117 accepted, 406 enrolled
SAT: required	CEEB CODE: 2021
Application Deadline: n/av	**COMPETITIVE**

DeSales University is a medium-sized, private, four-year Catholic university with a Salesian mission administered by the Oblates of St. Francis de Sales. Our priority is to give our students a quality, broad-based liberal arts and career-centered education. Students are exposed to Catholic teachings but are also afforded the luxury of exploring in an atmosphere of intellectual freedom. Everyone is treated with the dignity of the human person that they deserve. In addition to regional accreditation, DSU has baccalaureate program accreditation with ACBSP, NLN, ARC-PA, CAPTE, and ACEN. The 480-acre campus is in a suburban area 50 miles north of Philadelphia. Including any residence halls, there are 33 buildings.

STUDENT LIFE: 68% of undergraduates are from Pennsylvania. Others are from 18 states, and 5 foreign countries. 93% are White. The average age of freshmen is 18. 15% do not continue beyond their first year; 70% remain to graduate. **Housing:** 1192 students can be accommodated in college housing, which includes single-sex dorms and on-campus apartments. In addition, there are special-interest houses. On-campus housing is guaranteed for all 4 years, is available on a first-come, first-served basis, and is available on a lottery system for upperclassmen. 65% of students live on campus. All students may keep cars.

FACULTY/CLASSROOMS: 42% of faculty are male; 58% are female. 85% teach undergraduates, all do research, and 85% do both. No introductory courses are taught by graduate students.

PROGRAMS OF STUDY: DSU confers B.A., B.S. and B.S.N. degrees. Master's and Doctoral degrees are also awarded. Bachelor's degrees are awarded in BIOLOGICAL SCIENCE (biochemistry and biology/biological science), BUSINESS (accounting, business administration and management, finance, human resources, management information systems, marketing/retailing/merchandising, and sports management), COMMUNICATIONS AND THE ARTS (communications, dance, dramatic arts, English, film arts, media arts, performing arts, radio/television technology, Spanish, theatre acting, theater design, theatre production, and theater management), COMPUTER AND PHYSICAL SCIENCE (chemistry, computer game design/development, computer science, and mathematics), EDUCATION (early childhood education and elementary education), HEALTH PROFESSIONS (exercise science, nursing, pharmaceutical science, physical therapy, and physician's assistant), SOCIAL SCIENCE (criminal justice, history, liberal arts/general studies, philosophy, political science/government, psychology, and theological studies). Physician assistant, physical thearpy, and theatre are the strongest academically. Biology, physician assistant, and nursing have the largest enrollments.

ACTIVITIES: There are 50 groups on campus, including band, cheerleading, choir, chorale, chorus, communications, computers, dance, debate, drama, ethnic, film, honors, international, literary magazine, marching band, musical theater, newspaper, pep band, political, professional, radio and TV, religious, social, social service, student government, and yearbook. **Sports:** There are 7 intercollegiate sports for men and 7 for women, and 9 intramural sports for men and 9 for women. Facilities include Facilities for soccer, baseball, softball, tennis, basketball, lacrosse, track, cross country, volleyball, and a sports and recreation facility featuring a fitness center, and multipurpose athletic courts. Club sports include: ice hockey, rugby, swimming, tennis and volleyball. **Graduates:** From July 1, 2013 to June 30, 2014, 557 bachelor's degrees were awarded. The most popular majors were business (23%), health professions and related fields (23%), and visual and performing arts (11%). In an average class, 64% graduate in 4 years or less, 69% graduate in 5 years or less, and 70% graduate in 6 years or less.

SERVICES: Counseling and information services are available, as is tutoring in most subjects. There is a reader service for the blind, remedial math, reading, and writing. The Academic Resource Center (ARC) provides services (including tutoring) for students. **Library/Resources:** The library contains 388,812 volumes, 373,050 microform items, 4,464 audio/video tapes/CDs/DVDs, and subscribes to 23,000 periodicals including electronic. Computerized library services include interlibrary loans, database searching, Internet access, and Wi-Fi capability. Special learning facilities include a radio station, TV station, The Gambet Building for Business and Healthcare is a 77,000 sq. ft. facility includes state-of-the-science simulation laboratories to replicate clinical scenarios specific to adult, pediatric and birthing care, as well as globally integrated classrooms and administrative operations for undergraduate and graduate health care and business degree programs. The center is a showcase of green architecture featuring environmentally advanced design consistent with the Leadership in Energy and Environmental Design (LEED) certification standards of the U.S. Green Building Council. The Priscilla Payne Hurd Science Center provides state-of-the-art teaching and research laboratories in chemistry, biology, biotechnology, environmental, and human performance. The Labuda Center for the Performing Arts is home to most Act 1 events. It is completely handicapped accessible. The Trexler Library collection includes a diverse range of American and international films as well as a current collection of reference materials related to film, television, and media studies. Our total volumes 388,812 consists of 168,812 paper volumes and 120,000 electronic books. **Physically Challenged Students:** 99% of the campus is accessible. Facilities include wheelchair ramps, elevators, special parking, specially equipped restrooms, special class scheduling, lowered drinking fountains, lowered telephones, and special housing. **Special:** Students may cross-register with schools in the Lehigh Valley Association of Independent Colleges (LVAIC). Internships are strongly encouraged in all majors, and study abroad in seven countries is possible. Dual majors, a Washington semester, pass/fail options, accelerated degree programs, and credit for life, military, and work experience are offered. 5 Year BA/MACJ, 4 1/2 Year BS/MBA, and 5 Year Medical Studies/Physician Assistant Programs. There are 11 national honor societies and a freshman honors program. **Visiting:** There are regularly scheduled orientations for prospective students, including meetings with faculty advisers and social activities. There are guides for informal visits, visitors may sit in on classes, and stay overnight. To schedule a visit, contact Mr. Derrick Wetzel at (610) 282-4443. **Campus Safety and Security:** Measures include 24-hour foot and vehicle patrol, emergency notification system, self-defense education, and security escort services. There are emergency telephones, lighted pathways/sidewalks, and controlled access to dorms/residences.

REQUIREMENTS: The SAT is required. Applicants must be graduates of an accredited secondary school. The GED is accepted. Applicants should have completed 17 college preparatory courses including 4 years each of English, history, and math, 3 years of science, and 2 years of foreign language. The school will accept an essay but strongly recommends an interview. For theater students, a performance appraisal is required. For dance students an audition is required. AP and CLEP credits are accepted. Important factors in the admissions decision are advanced placement or honors courses, leadership record, recommendations by school officials, and evidence of special talent. For graduation, students must complete a minimum of 120 credit hours including a maximum of 48 in the major with a minimum GPA of 2.0 overall and in the major. Liberal arts distribution requirements consist of 12 to 16 courses including cultural literacy, modes of thinking, and Christian values and theology, as well as 3 courses in phys ed (one-credit courses). Internships are strongly encouraged for most majors. **Procedure:** Freshmen are admitted fall and spring. Entrance exams should be taken during the junior or senior year. There are deferred admissions and rolling admissions plans. Application deadlines are open. Application fee is $30. Notification is sent on a rolling basis. Applications are accepted on-line. **Transfer Students:** 72 transfer students enrolled in 2013-2014. Applicants for transfer should have completed a minimum of 24 college credit hours with a GPA of 2.5. An interview is recommended. 45 of 120 credits required for the bachelor's degree must be completed at DSU. **International Students:** The school actively recruits these students. They must take the TOEFL with a minimum score of 550 on the paper-based TOEFL (PBT) or 100 on the Internet-based version (iBT). They must also take the SAT or ACT or the IELTS could be required.

ADMISSIONS: 80% of the 2014-2015 applicants were accepted. The SAT scores for the 2014-2015 freshman class were: Critical Reading--44% below 500, 37% between 500 and 599, 15% between 600 and 699, and 5% between 700 and 800; Math--46% below 500, 36% between 500 and 599, 15% between 600 and 699, and 3% between 700 and 800; Writing--48% below 500, 34% between 500 and 599, 15% between 600 and 699, and 3% between 700 and 800. **Admissions Contact:** Mrs. Mary Birkhead, Dean of Enrollment Management. E-Mail: *admiss@desales.edu* Web: *www.desales.edu*

FINANCIAL AID: In 2014-2015, 86% of all full-time freshmen and 79% of continuing full-time students received some form of financial aid. 86% of all full-time freshmen and 76% of continuing full-time students received need-based aid. The average freshman award was $25,787. Need-based scholarships or need-based grants averaged $20,398; need-based self-help aid (loans and jobs) averaged $5,097; and other non-need-based awards and non-need-based scholarships averaged $13,014. The average financial indebtedness of the 2014 graduate was $25,875. DSU is a member of CSS. The FAFSA, the state aid form, and the college's own financial statement are required. The deadline for filing freshman financial aid applications for fall entry is February 1.

DELAWARE VALLEY COLLEGE F-3
www.devalcol.edu

Doylestown, PA 18901-2697	(215) 489-2211
	(800) 2DELVAL
Fax: (215) 230-2968	Email: admitme@devalcol.edu
Full-time: 700 men, 900 women	Faculty: 79; IIB, -$
Part-time: 210 men, 190 women	Ph.D.s: 62%
Graduate: 30 men, 40 women	Student/Faculty: n/av
Year: semesters, summer session	Tuition: $29,896
Room & Board: $11,242	Freshman Class: n/av
SAT or ACT: required	CEEB CODE: 2510
Application Deadline: open	COMPETITIVE

Delaware Valley College, founded in 1896, is a private institution offering undergraduate programs in specialized fields of agriculture, business administration, English, the sciences, math, criminal justice administration, and secondary education. The college also offers graduate programs in educational leadership and in food and agribusiness. Some figures in the above capsule and in this profile are approximate. The 550-acre campus is in a suburban area 20 miles north of Philadelphia. Including any residence halls, there are 36 buildings.

STUDENT LIFE: 67% of undergraduates are from Pennsylvania. Students are from 22 states, 1 foreign country, and Canada. 85% are from public schools. 80% are white. 35% are Catholic; 32% Protestant; 16% claim no religious affiliation; 14% Buddhist, Seventh-day Adventist, and others. The average age of freshmen is 18; all undergraduates, 21. 26% do not continue beyond their first year; 75% remain to graduate.

FACULTY/CLASSROOMS: 66% of faculty are male; 34% are female. All teach undergraduates. No introductory courses are taught by graduate students. The average class size in an introductory lecture is 24; in a laboratory, 21; and in a regular course, 20.

PROGRAMS OF STUDY: DVC confers B.A. and B.S. degrees. Associate and Master's degrees are also awarded. Bachelor's degrees are awarded in AGRICULTURE (agronomy, animal science, dairy science, equine science, horticulture, and wildlife management), BIOLOGICAL SCIENCE (biology/biological science and zoology), BUSINESS (accounting, business administration and management, marketing/retailing/merchandising, and sports management), COMMUNICATIONS AND THE ARTS (English), COMPUTER AND PHYSICAL SCIENCE (chemistry and computer science), EDUCATION (secondary education), ENGINEERING AND ENVIRONMENTAL DESIGN (environmental science and food services technology), SOCIAL SCIENCE (criminal justice, food production/management/services, and food science). Physical and biological science and animal science are the strongest academically. Business administration and animal science have the largest enrollments.

ACTIVITIES: 4% of men belong to 5 national fraternities; 5% of women belong to 3 national sororities. There are 40 groups on campus, including art, band, cheerleading, chess, choir, chorale, chorus, computers, dance, drama, ethnic, honors, international, literary magazine, newspaper, pep band, photography, professional, radio and TV, religious, social, social service, student government, and yearbook. Popular campus events include A-Day, Parents Day, and Family Weekend.

SERVICES: Counseling and information services are available, as is tutoring in most subjects. There is a reader service for the blind, and remedial math, reading, and writing. **Library/Resources:** The library contains 70,000 volumes, 162,914 microform items, and 0 audio/

video tapes/CDs/DVDs, and subscribes to 728 periodicals including electronic. Computerized library services include interlibrary loans, database searching, Internet access, and Wi-Fi capability. Special learning facilities include a radio station, TV station, a dairy science center, a livestock farm, horse facilities, an apiary, a small animal lab, a tissue culture lab, an arboretum, and greenhouses. **Physically Challenged Students:** 85% of the campus is accessible. Facilities include wheelchair ramps, elevators, special parking, specially equipped restrooms, special class scheduling, and lowered drinking fountains. **Special:** DVC offers a specialized methods and techniques program that enables students to learn lab techniques and gain experience in the practical aspects of their majors. There is a zoo science major that prepares students for careers in zoo management and animal conservation. There are co-op programs in all majors, dual majors, study abroad in England, internships, and work-study programs in a wide variety of employment and research settings. Cross-registration is available with Rutgers University and Middle Bucks Technical Institute. Nondegree study and pass/fail options are also available. There are 3 national honor societies, a freshman honors program, and 2 departmental honors programs. **Visiting:** There are regularly scheduled orientations for prospective students, consisting of a student panel, meetings with department chairs, and general information sessions. There are guides for informal visits, visitors may sit in on classes, and stay overnight. To schedule a visit, contact the Admissions Department. **Campus Safety and Security:** Measures include 24-hour foot and vehicle patrol, self-defense education, and security escort services. There are shuttle buses, emergency telephones, and lighted pathways/sidewalks.

REQUIREMENTS: The SAT or ACT is required. Applicants must be graduates of accredited secondary schools or have earned a GED. The college requires 15 academic units, including 6 in electives, 3 in English, and 2 each in math, science, and social studies. An interview is recommended. DVC requires applicants to be in the upper 50% of their class. A GPA of 2.8 is required. AP and CLEP credits are accepted. Important factors in the admissions decision are leadership record, personality/intangible qualities, and extracurricular activities record.

ADMISSIONS: 79% of a recent year's applicants were accepted. 25% of a recent year's freshmen were in the top fifth of their class; 49% were in the top two fifths. 1 freshman graduated first in the class.

FINANCIAL AID: In a recent year, 98% of all full-time freshmen and 94% of continuing full-time students received some form of financial aid. 78% of all full-time students received need-based aid. The average freshman award was $16,050. 20% of undergraduate students work part-time. Average annual earnings from campus work are $1600. The average financial indebtedness of a recent year's graduate was $17,760. The FAFSA is required. Check with the school for current application deadlines.

DICKINSON COLLEGE   D-3
www.dickinson.edu

Carlisle, PA 17013	(717) 245-1231
	(800) 644-1773
Fax: (717) 245-1442	Email: admit@dickinson.edu
Full-time: 1031 men, 1308 women	Faculty: 216; IIB, +$
Part-time: 6 men, 7 women	Ph.D.s: 95%
Graduate: n/av	Student/Faculty: 11 to 1
Year: semesters, summer session	Tuition: $46,094
Room & Board: $11,568	Freshman Class: 5827 applied, 2590 accepted, 626 enrolled
SAT CR/M/W: 640/640/635 **ACT:** 29	CEEB CODE: 2186
Application Deadline: February 1	**HIGHLY COMPETITIVE+**

Dickinson College is a nationally recognized liberal-arts institution chartered in 1783. Devoted to its revolutionary roots, the college maintains the mission of founder Benjamin Rush to provide a useful education in the liberal arts and sciences. Known for its global curriculum, Dickinson offers more than 40 study-abroad programs in 24 countries on six continents. The college is a leader among educational institutions committed to environmental sustainability and green ini-

tiatives. The 180-acre campus is in a suburban area about 20 miles west of Harrisburg, PA and 2 hours from Washington, D.C. Including any residence halls, there are 146 buildings.

STUDENT LIFE: 77% of undergraduates are from out of state, mostly the Middle Atlantic. Students are from 42 states, and 44 foreign countries. 60% are from public schools. 76% are White. 26% are Catholic; 25% Protestant; 19% claim no religious affiliation; 12% Jewish. The average age of freshmen is 18; all undergraduates, 20. 10% do not continue beyond their first year; 83% remain to graduate.

FACULTY/CLASSROOMS: 53% of faculty are male; 47% are female. All teach and do research. No introductory courses are taught by graduate students. The average class size in an introductory lecture is 35 and in a laboratory is 17.

PROGRAMS OF STUDY: Dickinson confers B.A. and B.S. degrees. Bachelor's degrees are awarded in AGRICULTURE (environmental studies), BIOLOGICAL SCIENCE (biochemistry, biology/biological science, and neurosciences), BUSINESS (international business management), COMMUNICATIONS AND THE ARTS (art history, classical languages, dance, English, French, German, Greek, Latin, music, Russian, Spanish, and theatre arts), COMPUTER AND PHYSICAL SCIENCE (chemistry, computer science, earth science, mathematics, and physics), ENGINEERING AND ENVIRONMENTAL DESIGN (environmental science), SOCIAL SCIENCE (African studies, American studies, anthropology, archeology, classical/ancient civilization, East Asian studies, economics, history, international studies, Italian studies, Judaic studies, Latin American studies, law, medieval studies, Middle Eastern studies, philosophy, political science/government, psychology, public affairs, religion, sociology, and women's studies). International education/foreign languages, sciences, sustainability education and preprofessional programs are the strongest academically. International business and management/international studies, biology, and political science have the largest enrollments.

ACTIVITIES: 12% of men belong to 4 national fraternities; 20% of women belong to 1 local and 5 national sororities. There are 122 groups on campus, including art, band, cheerleading, chess, choir, chorale, chorus, computers, dance, debate, drama, environmental, ethnic, film, gay, honors, international, jazz band, literary magazine, musical theater, newspaper, orchestra, photography, political, professional, radio and TV, religious, social, social service, student government, symphony, and yearbook. Popular campus events include Public Affairs Symposium, and Clarke Forum Events.

SERVICES: Counseling and information services are available, as is tutoring in every subject, services are provided as necessary on a case-by-case basis. There is a reader service for the blind. There also is a Writing Center **Library/Resources:** The library contains 547,711 volumes, 168,703 microform items, 86,231 audio/video tapes/CDs/DVDs, and subscribes to 5,192 periodicals including electronic. Computerized library services include interlibrary loans, database searching, Internet access, and Wi-Fi capability. Special learning facilities include an art gallery, planetarium, radio station, fiber-optic and satellite telecommunications networks, a telescope observatory, scanning electron microscope, research-quality greenhouse and an archival collection. **Physically Challenged Students:** 68% of the campus is accessible. Facilities include wheelchair ramps, elevators, special parking, specially equipped restrooms, special class scheduling, lowered drinking fountains, lowered telephones, and special housing. **Special:** Students may cross-register with Central Pennsylvania Consortium Colleges. Instruction in 13 languages is available. Internships are available on and off campus. Dickinson now sponsors more than 40 programs on six continents in 24 countries. These options include academic year programs, semester programs, summer programs, globally-integrated courses that include a January international field experience and specialized programs which combine domestic study with international study. A Washington semester, work-study, and accelerated degree programs are available, as are dual majors, student-designed majors, non-degree study, pass/fail options, and a 3-3 law degree with the Dickinson School of Law of Pennsylvania State University. There are 3-2 engineering degrees offered with Case Western Reserve University, Rensselaer Polytechnic Institute, the University of Pennsylvania and with Columbia University. Graduate school agreements are currently in place for: Medicine/Health programs with The Johns Hopkins University School of Nursing; Jefferson School of Population Health at the Jefferson Medical

College; Law with The Pennsylvania State University Dickinson School of Law (3-3 Program); Business with The Thunderbird School of Global Management; William E. Simon Graduate School of Business Administration at The University of Rochester; Engineering with Rensselaer Polytechnic Institute (3-2 Program) and Case Western Reserve University (3-2 Program); Columbia University (3-2 Program); International Graduate Education with The Network of Autonomous Schools of the Lombardy Region (Italy); University of Bremen (Bremen, Germany); University of East Anglia (Norwich, England); University of Maine; University of Malaga (Malaga, Spain), and the University of Queensland (Queensland, Australia). There are 16 national honor societies, including Phi Beta Kappa, and 34 departmental honors programs. **Visiting:** There are regularly scheduled orientations for prospective students, prospective students can participate in campus tours, individual interviews, group information sessions, class visits, overnight stays in residence halls, and open houses. There are guides for informal visits, visitors may sit in on classes, and stay overnight. To schedule a visit, contact the Admissions Office at (800) 644-1773. **Campus Safety and Security:** Measures include 24-hour foot and vehicle patrol, emergency notification system, self-defense education, and security escort services. There are shuttle buses, emergency telephones, lighted pathways/sidewalks, controlled access to dorms/residences, Electronic access to residence halls, and required electronic access for on campus administrative and academic buildings.

REQUIREMENTS: The SAT or ACT and ACT Writing Test are recommended. The SAT and ACT Subject Tests are optional submissions. The GED is accepted. Applicants should have completed 16 academic credits, including 4 years of English, 3 each of math and science, 2 (preferably 3) of foreign language, 2 of social studies, and 2 additional courses drawn from the above areas. An essay is required, and an interview is recommended. AP credits are accepted. Important factors in the admissions decision are advanced placement or honors courses, extracurricular activities record, and recommendations by school officials.

ADMISSIONS: 44% of a recent year applicants were accepted. The SAT scores for the 2013-2014 freshman class were: Critical Reading--3% below 500, 25% between 500 and 599, 53% between 600 and 699, and 18% between 700 and 800; Math--3% below 500, 20% between 500 and 599, 55% between 600 and 699, and 22% between 700 and 800; Writing--4% below 500, 22% between 500 and 599, 57% between 600 and 699, and 17% between 700 and 800. The ACT scores were 2% below 21, 2% between 21 and 23, 11% between 24 and 26, 31% between 27 and 28, and 55% above 28. 70% of the current freshmen were in the top fifth of their class; 92% were in the top two fifths.

FINANCIAL AID: In a recent year, 76% of all full-time freshmen and 74% of continuing full-time students received some form of financial aid. 58% of all full-time freshmen and 56% of continuing full-time students received need-based aid. The average freshman award was $32,929. Need-based scholarships or need-based grants averaged $30,591 ($57,230 maximum); need-based self-help aid (loans and jobs) averaged $6,790 ($10,000 maximum); other non-need-based awards and non-need-based scholarships averaged $10,031 ($53,594 maximum); and $8,815 from other forms of aid. 49% of undergraduate students work part-time. Average annual earnings from campus work are $1133. The average financial indebtedness of the 2013 graduate was $24,739. Dickinson is a member of CSS. The CSS/Profile, FAFSA, and the state aid form, and noncustodial parent statement are required. The priority date for freshman financial aid applications for fall entry is November 15. The deadline for filing freshman financial aid applications for fall entry is February 1.

Drexel is a comprehensive national research university ranked among the top 100 in the United States. The University has built its global reputation on core achievements that include: leadership in experiential learning through its cooperative education program; a history of academic technology firsts; and recognition as a model of best practices in translational research initiatives. Founded in 1891, Drexel now engages with students and communities around the world via three Philadelphia campuses and other regional sites, Drexel University Sacramento, Academy of Natural Sciences of Drexel University and international research partnerships in several countries around the globe. Drexel Online is one of the oldest and most successful providers of online degree programs. There are 12 undergraduate schools and 14 graduate schools. In addition to regional accreditation, Drexel has baccalaureate program accreditation with AACSB, ABET, ACCE, ADA, CSAB, FIDER, NAAB, and NASAD. The 109-acre campus is in an urban area in the University City neighborhood of Philadelphia. Including any residence halls, there are 111 buildings.

STUDENT LIFE: 58% of undergraduates are from out of state, mostly the Middle Atlantic. Students are from 47 states, 132 foreign countries, and Canada. 56% are White; 13% Foreign; 12% Asian American. The average age of freshmen is 18; all undergraduates, 23. 16% do not continue beyond their first year; 68% remain to graduate. **Housing:** College-sponsored housing includes coed dorms, on-campus apartments, and off-campus apartments. In addition, there are fraternity houses, sorority houses, Honors floors in residence halls and international student housing. On-campus housing is guaranteed for the freshman year only, is available on a first-come, first-served basis, and is available on a lottery system for upperclassmen. 75% of students commute. All students may keep cars.

FACULTY/CLASSROOMS: No introductory courses are taught by graduate students.

PROGRAMS OF STUDY: Drexel confers B.A., BACS, B.A.Arch., B.S., B.S.A.E., B.S.B.A., BSBA, B.S.Bus.Ed., BSCA, B.S.C.E., B.S.ChE., BSCIV, B.S.CMGT., B.S.Comp.Sci., B.S.E., B.S.Econ., B.S.E.E., BSENE, B.S.E.T., B.S.H.M., B.S.I., B.S.I.S., B.S.I.T., B.S.M.E., BSMSE, B.S.N., and BSSM degrees. Associate, Master's, and Doctoral degrees are also awarded. Bachelor's degrees are awarded in AGRICULTURE (environmental studies), BIOLOGICAL SCIENCE (biology/biological science and nutrition), BUSINESS (accounting, business administration and management, business economics, entrepreneurial studies, fashion merchandising, hotel/motel and restaurant management, marketing/retailing/merchandising, and sports management), COMMUNICATIONS AND THE ARTS (animation, communications, design, film arts, graphic design, music industry, photography, and video), COMPUTER AND PHYSICAL SCIENCE (chemistry, computer science, digital arts/technology, information sciences and systems, mathematics, physics, science, software engineering, and web technology), EDUCATION (education and elementary education), ENGINEERING AND ENVIRONMENTAL DESIGN (architectural engineering, architecture, biomedical engineering, chemical engineering, civil engineering, computer engineering, construction management, electrical/electronics engineering, engineering, environmental engineering, environmental science, interior design, materials engineering, and mechanical engineering), HEALTH PROFESSIONS (biology, nursing, and premedicine), SOCIAL SCIENCE (anthropology, criminal justice, criminology, culinary arts, economics, fashion design and technology, history, international studies, philosophy, political science/government, psychology, and sociology). Engineering, business, and design arts are the strongest academically. Mechanical engineering, biological sciences, and nursing have the largest enrollments.

ACTIVITIES: There are 340 groups on campus, including art, band, cheerleading, chess, choir, chorus, computers, dance, drama, environmental, ethnic, film, forensics, gay, honors, international, jazz band, literary magazine, musical theater, newspaper, orchestra, pep band, photography, political, professional, radio and TV, religious, social, social service, student government, and yearbook. Popular campus events include Musical, Cultural, and Art Events. **Sports:** There are 10 intercollegiate sports for men and 10 for women, and 11 intramural sports for men and 11 for women. Facilities include an athletic center with 3 gyms, 5 squash courts, a 25-yard swimming pool, a diving well, 4 exercise rooms, and 1 wrestling room; a recreation center with 2 gyms, 2 floors of fitness (18,000 square feet), 2

DREXEL UNIVERSITY　　　　　　　　　　　　　　　**F-3**
www.drexel.edu

Philadelphia, PA 19104	**(215) 895-2400**
	(800) 2-DREXEL
Fax: (215) 895-5939	Email: enroll@drexel.edu
Full-time: 8110 men, 6255 women	Faculty: n/av
Part-time: 825 men, 1706 women	Ph.Ds: n/av
Graduate: 3591 men, 5872 women	Student/Faculty: n/av
Year: quarters, summer session	Tuition: $47,051
Room & Board: $14,367	Freshman Class: 47477 applied, 36088 accepted, 2928 enrolled
SAT CR/M/W: 580/620/570 ACT: 26	CEEB CODE: 2149
Application Deadline: January 13	VERY COMPETITIVE+

exercise studios, 2 squash courts, a climbing wall, and an indoor track; and an armory with 3 multipurpose courts. **Graduates:** From July 1, 2013 to June 30, 2014, 3083 bachelor's degrees were awarded. The most popular majors were nursing (15%), mechanical engineering (5%), and biological sciences (5%). In an average class, 70% graduate in 6 years or less.

SERVICES: Counseling and information services are available, as is tutoring in most subjects. There is remedial math, reading, and writing. **Library/Resources:** The 2 libraries contain 609,339 volumes, 18,133 microform items, 10,923 audio/video tapes/CDs/DVDs, and subscribe to 36,584 periodicals including electronic. Computerized library services include interlibrary loans, database searching, Internet access, and Wi-Fi capability. Special learning facilities include an art gallery, natural history museum, radio station, and TV station. **Physically Challenged Students:** 98% of the campus is accessible. Facilities include wheelchair ramps, elevators, special parking, specially equipped restrooms, special class scheduling, lowered drinking fountains, and special housing. **Special:** The Drexel Plan of Cooperative Education enables students to alternate periods of full-time classroom studies and full-time employment with university-approved employers. Participation in cooperative education is mandatory for most students. Cross-registration is available with Indiana University of Pennsylvania and Lincoln University. Drexel also offers study abroad, internships, accelerated degrees, 3-3 engineering degrees, dual majors, nondegree study, and credit/no credit options. There are 1 national honor society and a freshman honors program. **Visiting:** There are regularly scheduled orientations for prospective students, consisting of a 2-day program for new freshmen and their parents in late July. There are guides for informal visits, visitors may sit in on classes, and stay overnight. To schedule a visit, contact the Admissions Office. **Campus Safety and Security:** Measures include 24-hour foot and vehicle patrol, emergency notification system, self-defense education, and security escort services. There are shuttle buses, emergency telephones, lighted pathways/sidewalks, controlled access to dorms/residences, Residential and commuter safety and security programs.

REQUIREMENTS: The SAT is required. Applicants must be graduates of an accredited secondary school. The GED is accepted. A GPA of 2.0 is required. AP and CLEP credits are accepted. To graduate, students must complete 180 to 192 term credits with a minimum GPA of 2.0 and must earn the number of Drexel Co-op Units determined by the major. There are requirements in math, computer literacy, English, lab science, humanities, and history. **Procedure:** Freshmen are admitted fall. There are early admissions and deferred admissions plans. Applications should be filed by January 13 for fall entry, along with a $50 fee. Notifications are sent April 1. Applications are accepted on-line. Application fees are waived if application is completed on-line. **Transfer Students:** Applicants must have a minimum GPA of 2.5. Other requirements vary among the individual colleges within the university. 45 of 180 credits required for the bachelor's degree must be completed at Drexel. **International Students:** There are 2161 international students enrolled. The school actively recruits these students. They must take the TOEFL with a minimum score of 550 on the paper-based TOEFL (PBT) or 79 on the Internet-based version (iBT), or take the IELTS.

ADMISSIONS: 76% of the 2014-2015 applicants were accepted. The SAT scores for the 2014-2015 freshman class were: Critical Reading--11% below 500, 49% between 500 and 599, 32% between 600 and 699, and 8% between 700 and 800; Math--5% below 500, 34% between 500 and 599, 45% between 600 and 699, and 16% between 700 and 800; Writing--15% below 500, 45% between 500 and 599, 33% between 600 and 699, and 7% between 700 and 800. The ACT scores were 3% below 21, 17% between 21 and 23, 34% between 24 and 26, 19% between 27 and 28, and 27% above 28. 50% of the current freshmen were in the top fifth of their class; 81% were in the top two fifths. 16 freshmen graduated first in their class. **Admissions Contact:** Director of Admissions E-Mail: *enroll@drexel.edu* Web: *www.drexel.edu*

FINANCIAL AID: Drexel is a member of CSS. The FAFSA is required. The priority date for freshman financial aid applications for fall entry is January 28.

DUQUESNE UNIVERSITY   B-3
www.duq.edu

Pittsburgh, PA 15282   (412) 396-6222
                                                   (800) 456-0590
Fax: (412) 396-5644   Email: admissions@duq.edu
Full-time: 2217 men, 3530 women   Faculty: 453; I, -$
Part-time: 126 men, 122 women   Ph.D.s: 94%
Graduate: 1455 men, 2198 women   Student/Faculty: 14 to 1
Year: semesters, summer session   Tuition: $32,636
Room & Board: $11,084   Freshman Class: 6534
                                       applied, 4774 accepted,
                                       1343 enrolled
SAT CR/M/W: 560/570/560 ACT: 25   CEEB CODE: 2196
Application Deadline: July 1   VERY COMPETITIVE

Duquesne University, founded in 1878 by the Spiritan Congregation, is a private Roman Catholic institution offering programs in liberal arts, natural and environmental sciences, nursing, health sciences, pharmacy, business, music, teacher preparation, preprofessional training, law, and leadership and professional development. There are 9 undergraduate schools and 10 graduate schools. In addition to regional accreditation, Duquesne has baccalaureate program accreditation with AACSB, NASM, NCATE, AMTA, CCNE, and CAATE. The 50-acre campus is in an urban area on a private, self-contained campus in the center of Pittsburgh. Including any residence halls, there are 43 buildings.

STUDENT LIFE: 73% of undergraduates are from Pennsylvania. Others are from 45 states, 49 foreign countries, and Canada. 83% are White. 54% are Catholic; 26% claim no religious affiliation; 15% Protestant. The average age of freshmen is 18; all undergraduates, 21. 10% do not continue beyond their first year; 76% remain to graduate. **Housing:** 3887 students can be accommodated in college housing, which includes coed dorms and on-campus apartments. In addition, there are honors houses, special-interest houses, Fraternity and sorority wings, international wings, and club wings. On-campus housing is available on a first-come, first-served basis, and is available on a lottery system for upperclassmen. 58% of students live on campus; of those, 70% remain on campus on weekends. Some may keep cars.

FACULTY/CLASSROOMS: 52% of faculty are male; 48% are female. 94% teach undergraduates. No introductory courses are taught by graduate students. The average class size in an introductory lecture is 28; in a laboratory is 30; and in a regular course is 28.

PROGRAMS OF STUDY: Duquesne confers B.A., B.S., B.M., B.S.A.T., B.S.B.A., B.S.Ed., B.S.H.M.S., B.S.H.S., B.S.N., B.S.P.S. and B.M.E degrees. Master's and Doctoral degrees are also awarded. Bachelor's degrees are awarded in BIOLOGICAL SCIENCE (biochemistry, biology/adolescence education, and biology/biological science), BUSINESS (accounting, banking and finance, business administration and management, business communications, business economics, entrepreneurial studies, international business management, management information systems, management science, marketing/retailing/merchandising, nonprofit/public organization management, sports marketing, and supply chain management), COMMUNICATIONS AND THE ARTS (advertising, art history and appreciation, classical languages, communications, dramatic arts, English, Greek (classical), journalism, Latin, literature, modern language, multimedia, music performance, music technology, public relations, Spanish, and speech/debate/rhetoric), COMPUTER AND PHYSICAL SCIENCE (chemistry, chemistry/adolescence education, computer science, mathematics, and physics), EDUCATION (athletic training, computer education, early childhood education, education, English education, foreign languages education, health information management, mathematics education, middle school education, music education, physical science secondary school education, and social studies education), ENGINEERING AND ENVIRONMENTAL DESIGN (biomedical engineering, computer technology, and environmental science), HEALTH PROFESSIONS (health care administration, music therapy, nursing, occupational therapy, pharmaceutical science, pharmacy, physical therapy, physician's assistant, and speech pathology/audiology), SOCIAL SCIENCE (behavioral science, classical/ancient civilization, economics, history, humanities, international relations, liberal arts/general studies, philosophy, political science/government, psychology, sociology, theological studies, and women and gender studies). Pharmacy, nursing, and accounting have the largest enrollments.

ACTIVITIES: 18% of men belong to 1 local and 10 national fraternities; 19% of women belong to 9 national sororities. There are 200 groups on campus, including and social programming, art, band, cheerleading, chess, choir, chorale, chorus, computers, dance, debate, drama, drill team, environmental, ethnic, film, forensics, gay, honors, international, jazz band, literary magazine, marching band, musical theater, newspaper, opera, orchestra, pep band, photography, political, professional, radio and TV, religious, social, social service, student government, symphony, and yearbook. Popular campus events include Orientation, Carnival, International Student Organization Week, Christmas Ball, Family Weekend, Greek Week, Trivia Nights, Multi-Cultural Unity Banquet, Commuter Family Day, Spotlight Musical Theater Shows, DUQ 'n Roll Battle of the BandsL. **Sports:** There are 6 intercollegiate sports for men and 10 for women, and 6 intramural sports for men and 6 for women. Facilities include The Power Center is a 130,000-square-foot multipurpose facility; 80,000-square-feet is dedicated to athletic and recreation facilities which feature separate student and staff locker facilities, aerobics space, three big-screen plasma TVs and 50 cardio fitness machines with personal viewing screens, basketball/volleyball courts, walking/running track, free weight room, and racquetball courts. The A.J. Palumbo Center houses the main arena, two regulation-sized basketball courts, a new athletic training room, weight training and cardiovascular areas and locker room facilities for student athletes. McCloskey Field is the center for outdoor intramural activity. The field is made up of artificial turf and is surrounded by a four-lane all-weather track. Rooney Athletic Field is home to Duquesne University's football, men's and women's soccer, and women's lacrosse teams. Other facilities include a six-lane swimming pool, a tennis court and an outdoor basketball/deck hockey court. **Graduates:** From July 1, 2013 to June 30, 2014, 1292 bachelor's degrees were awarded. The most popular majors were nursing (12%), biology (7%), and psychology (5%). 128 companies recruited on campus in 2013-2014. In an average class, 66% graduate in 4 years or less, 74% graduate in 5 years or less, and 76% graduate in 6 years or less.

SERVICES: Counseling and information services are available, as is tutoring in every subject. There is a reader service for the blind, and remedial math, reading, and writing. **Library/Resources:** The 2 libraries contain 749,297 volumes, 247,120 microform items, and 89,994 audio/video tapes/CDs/DVDs, and subscribe to 116,321 periodicals including electronic. Computerized library services include interlibrary loans, database searching, Internet access, and Wi-Fi capability. Special learning facilities include an art gallery, radio station, TV station, 274 multimedia-enhanced teaching facilities; 224 classrooms, 24 labs, and 26 others. **Physically Challenged Students:** 95% of the campus is accessible. Facilities include wheelchair ramps, elevators, special parking, specially equipped restrooms, special class scheduling, lowered drinking fountains, lowered telephones, and special housing. **Special:** The university offers cross-registration through the Pittsburgh Council on Higher Education, internships, study abroad in 23 countries, and a Washington semester. Also available are B.A.-B.S. degrees, accelerated degree programs, dual and student-designed majors, a 3-2 engineering program with Case Western Reserve University and University of Pittsburgh, the nation's first dual degree in biomedical engineering and nursing (BME-BSN), a 3-3 law degree and a 3-2 business degree, pass/fail options, and evaluation credit for life, military, and work experience. There are 20 national honor societies and a freshman honors program. **Visiting:** There are regularly scheduled orientations for prospective students, consisting of a campus tour and individual interviews with counselors and professors. There are guides for informal visits and visitors may sit in on classes. To schedule a visit, contact Robbyn Snyder at (412) 396-6222. **Campus Safety and Security:** Measures include 24-hour foot and vehicle patrol, emergency notification system, self-defense education, and security escort services. There are shuttle buses, emergency telephones, lighted pathways/sidewalks, controlled access to dorms/residences, There are security cameras throughout campus that monitor exterior areas 24 hours a day.

REQUIREMENTS: The SAT or ACT is required. Liberal Arts applicants meeting select criteria can choose to apply as standardized test-optional candidates. Students should have either a high school diploma or the GED. Applicants are required to have 16 academic credits, including 4 each in English and academic electives, and 8 combined in social studies, language, math, and science. An essay is required, and an interview is recommended. An audition is required for music majors. 40 hours shadowing for physical therapy (prior to enrollment). A GPA of 3.0 is required. AP and CLEP credits are accepted. Important factors in the admissions decision are advanced placement or honors courses, leadership record, recommendations by school officials, and extracurricular activities record.To graduate, students are required to complete at least 120 credit hours, including a specified number in the major (varies by program), with a minimum 2.0 GPA. General requirements vary by department, but there is a 33 credit liberal arts core curriculum. **Procedure:** Freshmen are admitted to all sessions. Entrance exams should be taken during the spring of the junior year or the fall of the senior year. There are early decision, early admissions, deferred admissions, and rolling admissions plans. Early decision applications should be filed by November 1; regular applications, by July 1 for fall entry; December 1 for spring entry; and April 1 for summer entry, along with a $50 fee. Notification of early decision is sent December 15; regular decision, on a rolling basis. 173 early decision candidates were accepted for the 2014-2015 class. Applications are accepted on-line. **Transfer Students:** 209 transfer students enrolled in 2013-2014. Applicants must submit complete high school and college transcripts. Students should have a minimum GPA of 2.5 for the university, but some schools require a higher average. A minimum of 12 credits earned is required, and an interview is recommended. 30 of 120 credits required for the bachelor's degree must be completed at Duquesne. **International Students:** There are 183 international students enrolled. The school actively recruits these students. They must take the MELAB and the college's own test, students are required to sit for ENG language placement tests as part of their arrival program.

ADMISSIONS: 73% of the 2014-2015 applicants were accepted. The SAT scores for the 2014-2015 freshman class were: Critical Reading--13% below 500, 57% between 500 and 599, 27% between 600 and 699, and 3% between 700 and 800; Math--11% below 500, 54% between 500 and 599, 31% between 600 and 699, and 4% between 700 and 800; Writing--20% below 500, 50% between 500 and 599, 26% between 600 and 699, and 4% between 700 and 800. The ACT scores were 3% below 21, 22% between 21 and 23, 35% between 24 and 26, 20% between 27 and 28, and 20% above 28. 48% of the current freshmen were in the top fifth of their class; 80% were in the top two fifths. 20 freshmen graduated first in their class. **Admissions Contact:** Debra Zugates, Director, Admissions. E-Mail: *admissions@duq.edu* Web: *www.duq.edu*

FINANCIAL AID: 13% of undergraduate students work part-time. The FAFSA and the college's own financial statement are required. The priority date for freshman financial aid applications for fall entry is May 1. The deadline for filing freshman financial aid applications for fall entry is May 1.

EAST STROUDSBURG UNIVERSITY OF PENNSYLVANIA *(The complete profile is made available exclusively on our website, www.barronspac.com)*

EASTERN UNIVERSITY   E-3
www.eastern.edu

St. Davids, PA 19087	(610) 241-5800
	(800) 732-7669
Fax: (610) 225-5601	Email: ugadm@eastern.edu
Full-time: 705 men, 1474 women	Faculty: n/av
Part-time: 131 men, 391 women	Ph.D.s: 69%
Graduate: 534 men, 1028 women	Student/Faculty: 11 to 1
Year: semesters, summer session	Tuition: $28,090
Room & Board: $9614	Freshman Class: n/av
	CEEB CODE: 2220
Application Deadline: n/av	COMPETITIVE

Eastern University, founded in 1932, is a private liberal arts institution affiliated with the American Baptist Church. There are 2 graduate schools. In addition to regional accreditation, Eastern has baccalaureate program accreditation with CSWE and NLN. The 114-acre campus is in a suburban area 20 miles northwest of Philadelphia. Including any residence halls, there are 23 buildings.

STUDENT LIFE: 56% of undergraduates are from Pennsylvania. Others are from 38 states, 22 foreign countries, and Canada. 53% are White; 23% African American; 11% Hispanic. 77% are unknown denominations; 15% claim no religious affiliation. The average age of freshmen is 18; all undergraduates, 21. 20% do not continue beyond their first year; 60% remain to graduate.

FACULTY/CLASSROOMS: 49% of faculty are male; 51% are female. No introductory courses are taught by graduate students.

PROGRAMS OF STUDY: Eastern confers B.A., B.S., B.S.N. and B.S.W. degrees. Associate, Master's, and Doctoral degrees are also awarded. Bachelor's degrees are awarded in AGRICULTURE (environmental studies), BIOLOGICAL SCIENCE (biochemistry and biology/biological science), BUSINESS (accounting, business administration and management, entrepreneurial studies, marketing/retailing/merchandising, and organizational leadership and management), COMMUNICATIONS AND THE ARTS (communications, dance, English, music, and Spanish), COMPUTER AND PHYSICAL SCIENCE (chemistry and mathematics), EDUCATION (athletic training, early childhood education, and middle school education), HEALTH PROFESSIONS (exercise science and nursing), SOCIAL SCIENCE (biblical studies, history, missions, philosophy, political science/government, psychology, social work, sociology, theological studies, and youth ministry). Biblical/theological studies is the strongest academically. Education, and business have the largest enrollments.

ACTIVITIES: There are 70 groups on campus, including band, cheerleading, choir, chorale, chorus, communications, computers, dance, drama, drill team, ethnic, honors, international, jazz band, literary magazine, musical theater, newspaper, orchestra, pep band, political, professional, radio and TV, religious, social, social service, student government, and yearbook. Popular campus events include Homecoming, Spring Banquet and World Culture Day.

SERVICES: Counseling and information services are available, as is tutoring in every subject. There is a reader service for the blind, and remedial math, reading, and writing. Summer skills workshop **Library/Resources:** The 4 libraries contain 473,190 volumes, 869,487 microform items, and 17,421 audio/video tapes/CDs/DVDs. Computerized library services include interlibrary loans, database searching, and Internet access. Special learning facilities include a planetarium and radio station. **Physically Challenged Students:** 75% of the campus is accessible. Facilities include wheelchair ramps, elevators, special parking, specially equipped restrooms, special class scheduling, lowered drinking fountains, lowered telephones, and special housing. **Special:** The college offers cross-registration with Cabrini and Rosemont Colleges, Valley Forge Military Academy, and Villanova University, internships, a Washington semester in the American studies program, and student-designed majors. Also available are accelerated degree programs in organizational management and management of information systems, credit for experience, non-degree study, and pass/fail options. There is a different calendar for the organizational management program. There are 10 national honor societies, a freshman honors program, and 1 departmental honors programs. **Visiting:** There are regularly scheduled orientations for prospective students. There are guides for informal visits, visitors may sit in on classes, and stay overnight. To schedule a visit, contact the Admissions Office at (800) 452-0996. **Campus Safety and Security:** Measures include 24-hour foot and vehicle patrol, emergency notification system, self-defense education, and security escort services. There are shuttle buses, emergency telephones, lighted pathways/sidewalks, and controlled access to dorms/residences.

REQUIREMENTS: The SAT or ACT is required. A GPA of 2.0 is required. AP and CLEP credits are accepted. Important factors in the admissions decision are advanced placement or honors courses and recommendations by school officials.

FINANCIAL AID: Eastern is a member of CSS. The FAFSA and the college's own financial statement are required. Check with the school for current application deadlines.

EDINBORO UNIVERSITY OF PENNSYLVANIA (*The complete profile is made available exclusively on our website, www.barronspac.com*)

ELIZABETHTOWN COLLEGE   D-3
www.etown.edu

Elizabethtown, PA 17022   (717) 361-1000
                                               (717) 361-1400
Fax: (717) 361-1365   Email: admissions@etown.edu
Full-time: 645 men, 1104 women   Faculty: 137; IIB, +$
Part-time: 21 men, 18 women   Ph.D.s: 100%
Graduate: no men, 34 women   Student/Faculty: 13 to 1
Year: semesters, summer session   Tuition: $39,920
Room & Board: $9820   Freshman Class: n/av
                                      CEEB CODE: 2225
Application Deadline: n/av   VERY COMPETITIVE

Elizabethtown College is a community of learners dedicated to educating students intellectually, socially, aesthetically and ethically for lives of service and leadership as citizens of the world. We offer more than four dozen degrees in liberal arts, fine and performing arts, science and engineering, business, communications and education. Through personal attention, creative inspiration and academic challenge, Elizabethtown students are encouraged to expand their intellectual curiosity. Our students become a bigger part of the world through Real-World Learning opportunities which include: collaborative research with faculty mentors, study-abroad experiences in more than 70 locations around the world, civic-engagement outreach, and internships offerings. There are 2 undergraduate schools. In addition to regional accreditation, E-town has baccalaureate program accreditation with ABET, ACBSP, CSWE, NASM, ACOTE, ACS, and ACBSP. The 201-acre campus is in a small town in Lancaster County, PA. It is 10 minutes from Hershey and 25 minutes from Lancaster and Harrisburg. Including any residence halls, there are 52 buildings.

STUDENT LIFE: 65% of undergraduates are from Pennsylvania. Others are from 26 states, and 21 foreign countries. 84% are from public schools. 86% are White. 34% are Protestant; 28% Catholic. The average age of freshmen is 18; all undergraduates, 20. 20% do not continue beyond their first year; 70% remain to graduate. **Housing:** 1494 students can be accommodated in college housing, which includes coed dorms, on-campus apartments, and off-campus apartments. In addition, there are honors houses, special-interest houses, Substance free and quiet study. On-campus housing is guaranteed for all 4 years. 87% of students live on campus; of those, 85% remain on campus on weekends. All students may keep cars.

FACULTY/CLASSROOMS: 49% of faculty are male; 51% are female. All teach and do research. No introductory courses are taught by graduate students. The average class size in an introductory lecture is 21; in a laboratory is 19; and in a regular course is 17.

PROGRAMS OF STUDY: E-town confers B.A., B.S., B.S.W. and B.Mus. degrees. Master's degrees are also awarded. Bachelor's degrees are awarded in AGRICULTURE (forestry and related sciences), BIOLOGICAL SCIENCE (biochemistry, biology/adolescence education, biology/biological science, and biotechnology), BUSINESS (accounting, business administration and management, business economics, business systems analysis, international business management, and marketing management), COMMUNICATIONS AND THE ARTS (art history and appreciation, communications, dramatic arts, English, English literature, English Writing, fine arts, French, German, Japanese, modern language, music, performing arts, Spanish, and studio art), COMPUTER AND PHYSICAL SCIENCE (actuarial science, applied mathematics, chemistry, chemistry/adolescence education, computer science, earth science / adolescence education, information sciences and systems, mathematics, and physics), EDUCATION (art education, early childhood education, education, elementary education, English education, mathematics education, music education, science education, secondary education, social studies education, and social studies secondary school education), ENGINEERING AND ENVIRONMENTAL DESIGN (computer engineering, electrical/electronics engineering, engineering, environmental science, industrial engineering, mechanical engineering, and preengineering), HEALTH PROFESSIONS (music therapy, occupational therapy, predentistry, premedicine, and prephysical therapy), SOCIAL SCIENCE (criminal justice, economics, history, legal studies, philosophy, political science/government, psychology, public administration, religion, social work, and sociology). Business administration, occupational therapy, and biology have the largest enrollments.

ACTIVITIES: There are 80 groups on campus, including residential, learning communities, academic, art, band, cheerleading, choir, chorale, chorus, computers, dance, drama, environmental, ethnic, forensics, gay, honors, international, jazz band, literary magazine, musical theater, newspaper, orchestra, photography, political, professional, radio and TV, religious, social, social service, student government, and yearbook. Popular campus events include Scholarship and Creative Arts Day, Martin Luther king Celebration Week, Hispanic Heritage Month and Into the Streets. **Sports:** There are 11 intercollegiate sports for men and 11 for women, and 7 intramural sports for men and 7 for women. Facilities include A 2,200-seat soccer stadium, 2,000-seat gymnasium, swimming pool, track and field complex, fitness center, racquetball and tennis courts, sand volleyball courts and baseball, softball, lacrosse, and field hockey fields. **Graduates:** From July 1, 2013 to June 30, 2014, 417 bachelor's degrees were awarded. The most popular majors were health and occupation (pre-occupational therapy) (8%), business administration (8%), and early childhood education (7%). 60 companies recruited on campus in 2013-2014. In an average class, 69% graduate in 4 years or less, 77% graduate in 5 years or less, and 70% graduate in 6 years or less. Of the 2013 graduating class, 26% were enrolled in graduate school within 6 months of graduation, and 58% were employed.

SERVICES: Counseling and information services are available, as is tutoring in most subjects. There is a reader service for the blind, remedial math, reading, and writing. Workshops and individual help with study skills as well as assistive technology is also available. **Library/Resources:** The library contains 260,258 volumes, 24,078 microform items, 9,750 audio/video tapes/CDs/DVDs, and subscribes to 96,260 periodicals including electronic. Computerized library services include interlibrary loans, database searching, Internet access, and Wi-Fi capability. Special learning facilities include an art gallery, radio station, TV station, the Young Center for Anabaptist and Pietist Studies, a nationally unique academic research facility, and mineral gallery. **Physically Challenged Students:** 75% of the campus is accessible. Facilities include wheelchair ramps, elevators, special parking, specially equipped restrooms, special class scheduling, lowered drinking fountains, lowered telephones, special housing. **Special:** Students can participate in short-term, semester-long, and year-long study-abroad experiences in 26 different locations worldwide. Also available are work-study programs, internships, a Washington semester, and dual majors, including sociology and anthropology. There is a 5-year cooperative engineering degree where the student will participate in two 7-month co-op rotations; a 3-3 allied health degree and a 3-3 physical therapy degree with Thomas Jefferson University and Widener University; a Premedical Primary Care Program with Penn State University College of Medicine; Biotechnology (B.S.) and Molecular Medicine (M.S.) with Drexel University College of Medicine; a 3-4 B.S. in biology/D.M.D. program with Temple University; a Cardiovascular Invasive Specialty program with Lancaster General College of Nursing and Health Sciences; and a D.O program with Philadelphia College of Osteopathic Medicine. There are 22 national honor societies, a freshman honors program, and 14 departmental honors programs. **Visiting:** There are regularly scheduled orientations for prospective students, including 5 open houses and weekday appointments throughout the year. Special academic department days are also hosted. There are guides for informal visits, visitors may sit in on classes, and stay overnight. To schedule a visit, contact the Admissions. **Campus Safety and Security:** Measures include 24-hour foot and vehicle patrol, emergency notification system, self-defense education, and security escort services. There are shuttle buses, emergency telephones, lighted pathways/sidewalks, controlled access to dorms/residences, crime prevention program.

REQUIREMENTS: The SAT or ACT is required. Recommended composite scores for the SAT range from 1030 to 1230; for the ACT, 21 to 27. Applicants must be graduates of an accredited secondary school or have earned a GED. The college encourages completion of 18 academic credits, based on 4 years of English, 3 of math, 2 each of lab science, social studies, and consecutive foreign language, and 5 additional college preparatory units. An audition is required for music majors and an interview is required for occupational therapy

majors. AP credits are accepted. Important factors in the admissions decision are advanced placement or honors courses, recommendations by school officials, and extracurricular activities record. The core curriculum includes a first-year seminar and courses in math, language, creative expression, western cultural heritage, non-western cultural heritage, the natural and social sciences, and humanities. Distribution requirements include 40 hours in 8 areas of understanding. Students must complete a minimum of 125 credit hours and maintain a GPA of 2.0 overall and in their major. Additional requirements are dependent on the enrolled major. **Procedure:** Freshmen are admitted to all sessions. Entrance exams should be taken in spring of the junior year or fall of the senior year. There are deferred admissions and rolling admissions plans. Application deadlines are open. Application fee is $30. 77 applicants were on the 2014 waiting list; 42 were admitted. Applications are accepted on-line. **Transfer Students:** 33 transfer students enrolled in 2013-2014. Applicants should present a minimum GPA of 3.0 in at least 15 credit hours earned from a community college, or 2.5 from a 4-year institution. 30 of 125 credits required for the bachelor's degree must be completed at E-town. **International Students:** There are 68 international students enrolled. The school actively recruits these students. They must take the TOEFL with a minimum score of 525 on the paper-based TOEFL (PBT) or 75 on the Internet-based version (iBT). They must also take the SAT or ACT.

ADMISSIONS: 55% of the current freshmen were in the top fifth of their class; 85% were in the top two fifths. 7 freshmen graduated first in their class. **Admissions Contact:** Paul Cramer, Vice President for Enrollment. E-Mail: *admissions@etown.edu* Web: *http://www.etown.edu/admissions/*

FINANCIAL AID: In 2014-2015, 99% of all full-time freshmen and continuing full-time students received some form of financial aid. 79% of all full-time freshmen and 75% of continuing full-time students received need-based aid. The average freshman award was $28,192. Need-based scholarships or need-based grants averaged $24,506 ($39,920 maximum); and need-based self-help aid (loans and jobs) averaged $4,863 ($8,000 maximum). 63% of undergraduate students work part-time. Average annual earnings from campus work are $1192. E-town is a member of CSS. The FAFSA and the college's own financial statement, and family federal tax returns are required. The deadline for filing freshman financial aid applications for fall entry is March 15.

Elizabethtown College School of Continuing and Professional Studies, is a community of learners dedicated to educating students intellectually, socially, aesthetically and ethically for lives of service and leadership as citizens of the world. We offer more than four dozen degrees in liberal arts, fine and perfoming arts, science and engineering, business, communications and education. Through personal attention, creative inspiration and academic challenge, Elizabethtown students are encouraged to expand their intellectual curiosity. They also are given an opportunity to be a bigger part of the world through experiential learning-collaborative research with caring faculty mentors, study-abroad and civic engagement opportunities, and internships. Figures in the above capsule and in this profile are approximate. The 201-acre campus is in a small town 10 minutes from Hershey and 25 minutes from Lancaster and Harrisburg. Including any residence halls, there are 52 buildings.

STUDENT LIFE: 98% of undergraduates are from Pennsylvania.

Others are from 3 states, and 2 foreign countries. 85% are White. The average age of all undergraduates is 37. **Housing:** College-sponsored housing includes All students commute. All students may keep cars.

FACULTY/CLASSROOMS: 63% of faculty are male; 37% are female. All teach undergraduates. No introductory courses are taught by graduate students. The average class size in an introductory lecture is 20.

PROGRAMS OF STUDY: Elizabethtown College Adult Degrees confers B.A., B.S., and B.P.S. degrees. Associate and Master's degrees are also awarded. Bachelor's degrees are awarded in BUSINESS (accounting, business administration and management, human resources, and marketing/retailing/merchandising), COMMUNICATIONS AND THE ARTS (communications and information technology), SOCIAL SCIENCE (addiction studies, behavioral science, criminal justice, human services, public administration, and religion). Business administration, accounting, and human services have the largest enrollments.

ACTIVITIES: Sports: There is no sports program at Elizabethtown College Adult Degrees. **Graduates:** From July 1, 2013 to June 30, 2014, 128 bachelor's degrees were awarded. The most popular majors were business administration (38%), accounting (17%), and corporate communications (12%).

SERVICES: Library/Resources: The library contains 262,101 volumes, 24,078 microform items, 9,750 audio/video tapes/CDs/DVDs, and subscribes to 96,260 periodicals including electronic. Computerized library services include interlibrary loans, database searching, Internet access, and Wi-Fi capability. Special learning facilities include an art gallery, TV station, the Young Center for Anabaptist and Pietist Studies, a nationally unique academic research facility, and mineral gallery. **Physically Challenged Students:** 75% of the campus is accessible. Facilities include wheelchair ramps, elevators, special parking, specially equipped restrooms, special class scheduling, lowered drinking fountains, and lowered telephones. **Campus Safety and Security:** Measures include 24-hour foot and vehicle patrol, emergency notification system, self-defense education, and security escort services. There are shuttle buses, emergency telephones, lighted pathways/sidewalks, controlled access to dorms/residences, and crime prevention programs.

REQUIREMENTS: Procedure: Freshmen are admitted to all sessions. There is a rolling admissions plan. Application deadlines are open. Applications are accepted on-line. **Transfer Students:** 65 transfer students enrolled in 2013-2014.

ADMISSIONS: Barbara Randazzo, Asst. Dean of Enrollment Management. E-Mail: *randazzob@etown.edu* Web: *http://www.etowndegrees.com*

FINANCIAL AID: Check with the school for current application deadlines.

FRANKLIN AND MARSHALL COLLEGE   E-3
www.fandm.edu

Lancaster, PA 17604	(717) 291-3953
	(877) 678-9111
Fax: (717) 291-4389	Email: admission@fandm.edu
Full-time: 1077 men, 1097 women	Faculty: 226; IIB, +$
Part-time: 14 men, 21 women	Ph.D.s: 88%
Graduate: n/av	Student/Faculty: 9 to 1
Year: semesters, summer session	Tuition: $48,514
Room & Board: $12,285	Freshman Class: 5472 applied, 2130 accepted, 592 enrolled
SAT CR/M: 637/675 ACT: 29	CEEB CODE: 2261
Application Deadline: January 15	MOST COMPETITIVE

Franklin and Marshall College, founded in 1787, is a private liberal arts institution. There is one undergraduate school. The 209-acre campus is in a suburban area 60 miles west of Philadelphia. Including any residence halls, there are 45 buildings.

STUDENT LIFE: 76% of undergraduates are from out of state, mostly the Middle Atlantic. Students are from 42 states, 52 foreign countries, and Canada. 63% are from public schools. 60% are White;

14% Foreign. The average age of freshmen is 18; all undergraduates, 20. 9% do not continue beyond their first year; 87% remain to graduate. **Housing:** 2318 students can be accommodated in college housing, which includes single-sex and coed dorms, on-campus apartments, and off-campus apartments. In addition, there are language houses, special-interest houses, including a French house, an arts house, an international living center, and a community outreach house. On-campus housing is guaranteed for all 4 years, is guaranteed for the freshman year only, and is available on a lottery system for upperclassmen. 99% of students live on campus. Upperclassmen may keep cars.

FACULTY/CLASSROOMS: 54% of faculty are male; 46% are female. All teach undergraduates, and all teach and do research. No introductory courses are taught by graduate students. The average class size in an introductory lecture is 23; in a laboratory is 19; and in a regular course is 17.

PROGRAMS OF STUDY: F & M confers B.A. degrees. Bachelor's degrees are awarded in AGRICULTURE (environmental studies), BIOLOGICAL SCIENCE (biochemistry, biology/biological science, and neurosciences), BUSINESS (business administration and management), COMMUNICATIONS AND THE ARTS (art history and appreciation, classics, dramatic arts, English, fine arts, French, German, Greek, Latin, music, Spanish, and studio art), COMPUTER AND PHYSICAL SCIENCE (astronomy, astrophysics, chemistry, geology, mathematics, and physics), ENGINEERING AND ENVIRONMENTAL DESIGN (environmental science), SOCIAL SCIENCE (African studies, American studies, anthropology, economics, history, interdisciplinary studies, philosophy, political science/government, psychology, religion, and sociology). Chemistry, geosciences, and psychology are the strongest academically. Government, business, organizations and society have the largest enrollments.

ACTIVITIES: 24% of men belong to 7 national fraternities; 36% of women belong to 3 national sororities. There are 120 groups on campus, including (a student-run club/restaurant), art, band, Ben's Underground, cheerleading, chess, choir, chorale, chorus, communications, computers, dance, debate, drama, environmental, ethnic, film, forensics, gay, honors, international, jazz band, literary magazine, musical theater, newspaper, opera, orchestra, photography, political, professional, radio and TV, religious, social, social service, student government, symphony, and yearbook. Popular campus events include Spring Arts Weekend. **Sports:** There are 13 intercollegiate sports for men and 13 for women, and 12 intramural sports for men and 12 for women. Facilities include a 3000-seat gym, 4 squash courts, a wrestling room, 54 acres of playing fields, a 400-meter all-weather track, a wellness/aerobic center, a strength training center, and tennis courts. A sports center features a fitness center, 5 multipurpose courts, 2 jogging tracks, and an Olympic-size pool. **Graduates:** From July 1, 2013 to June 30, 2014, 603 bachelor's degrees were awarded. The most popular majors were business, organizations, and society (14%), government (12%), and English (7%). In an average class, 82% graduate in 4 years or less, 86% graduate in 5 years or less, and 87% graduate in 6 years or less.

SERVICES: Counseling and information services are available, as is tutoring in every subject. **Library/Resources:** The 2 libraries contain 577,462 volumes, 22,894 microform items, 13,061 audio/video tapes/CDs/DVDs, and subscribe to 2,317 periodicals including electronic. Computerized library services include interlibrary loans, database searching, and Internet access. Special learning facilities include an art gallery, natural history museum, planetarium, radio station, TV station, academic technology services, writing center, and student newspaper. **Physically Challenged Students:** 80% of the campus is accessible. Facilities include wheelchair ramps, elevators, special parking, specially equipped restrooms, special class scheduling, lowered drinking fountains, lowered telephones, and special housing. **Special:** There is a 3-2 degree program in forestry and environmental studies with Duke University as well as 3-2 degree programs in engineering with the Pennsylvania State University College of Engineering, Columbia University, Rensselaer Polytechnic Institute, Case Western Reserve, and Washington University at St. Louis. Cross-registration is possible with the Lancaster Theological Seminary, the Central Pennsylvania Consortium, and Millersville University allows students to study at nearby Dickinson College or Gettysburg College. Students may also study architecture and urban planning at Columbia University, studio art at the School of Visual Arts in New York City, theater in Connecticut, oceanography in Massachusetts, and American studies at American University. There are study-abroad programs in England, France, Germany, Greece, Italy, Denmark, India, Japan, and other countries. There are internships for credit, joint majors, many minors, dual majors, student-designed majors, independent study, interdisciplinary studies, optional first-year seminars, collaborative projects, pass/fail options, and nondegree study. There are 12 national honor societies including Phi Beta Kappa. **Visiting:** There are regularly scheduled orientations for prospective students, including a campus tour, an interview, and a class visit. There are guides for informal visits and visitors may sit in on classes. To schedule a visit, contact the Admission Office. **Campus Safety and Security:** Measures include 24-hour foot and vehicle patrol, emergency notification system, self-defense education, and security escort services. There are shuttle buses, emergency telephones, lighted pathways/ sidewalks, controlled access to dorms/residences, regular fire safety drills are held in residence halls, academic buildings and residence hall.

REQUIREMENTS: Standardized tests are optional for students; if this option is selected, 2 recent graded writing samples are required. Applicants must be graduates of accredited secondary schools. Recommended college preparatory study includes 4 years each of English and math, 3 or 4 of foreign language, 3 each of lab science and history/social studies, and 1 or 2 courses in art or music. All students must also submit their high school transcripts, recommendations from a teacher and a counselor, and a personal essay. An interview is recommended. AP and CLEP credits are accepted. Important factors in the admissions decision are advanced placement or honors courses, recommendations by school officials, and extracurricular activities record.General education requirements proceed from 2 Connections courses and a distribution requirement to a major. Students must take at least 1 course in arts, humanities, social science, non-Western cultures, and 1 natural science (including a lab) and a second lab course or natural science in perspective course. 3 semesters of language study are required. The bachelor's degree requires completion of 32 courses, including a minimum of 8 in the major, with a minimum GPA of 2.0. **Procedure:** Freshmen are admitted fall and spring. Entrance exams should be taken by December of the senior year. There are early decision and deferred admissions plans. Early decision applications should be filed by November 15; regular applications, by January 15 for fall entry, along with a $60 fee. Notification of early decision is sent December 15; regular decision, April 1. 289 early decision candidates were accepted for the 2014-2015 class. 411 applicants were on the 2014 waiting list; 76 were admitted. Applications are accepted on-line. **Transfer Students:** 21 transfer students enrolled in 2013-2014. Applicants must present a minimum of 4 course credits (16 semester hours) completed at an accredited college. An interview, SAT or ACT scores, college and secondary school transcripts, a dean's form, recommendations from 2 professors, and a letter explaining the reason for transfer are also required. 16 of 32 credits required for the bachelor's degree must be completed at F & M. **International Students:** There are 298 international students enrolled. The school actively recruits these students. They must take the TOEFL. They must also take the SAT or ACT.

ADMISSIONS: 39% of the 2014-2015 applicants were accepted. The SAT scores for the 2014-2015 freshman class were: Critical Reading--1% below 500, 24% between 500 and 599, 57% between 600 and 699, and 17% between 700 and 800; Math--8% between 500 and 599, 59% between 600 and 699, and 32% between 700 and 800. **Admissions Contact:** Daniel Lugo, Vice President for Enrollment Management and Dean of Admissions. E-Mail: *admission@fandm.edu* Web: *www.fandm.edu*

FINANCIAL AID: In 2014-2015, 58% of all full-time freshmen and 70% of continuing full-time students received some form of financial aid. 56% of all full-time freshmen and 50% of continuing full-time students received need-based aid. The average freshman award was $45,769. Need-based scholarships or need-based grants averaged $41,770; need-based self-help aid (loans and jobs) averaged $4,935; and other non-need-based awards and non-need-based scholarships averaged $2,375. The average financial indebtedness of the 2014 graduate was $27,474. F & M is a member of CSS. The CSS/Profile, FAFSA, and the college's own financial statement, and if applicable,

the business/farm supplement and noncustodial parents statement are required. are required. The deadline for filing freshman financial aid applications for fall entry is February 1.

GANNON UNIVERSITY B-1
www.gannon.edu

Erie, PA 16541	(814) 871-7000
	1-800-426-6668
Fax: n/av	**Email:** admissions@gannon.edu
Full-time: 1142 men, 1451 women	**Faculty:** 177; IIA, -$
Part-time: 252 men, 360 women	**Ph.D.s:** 74%
Graduate: 596 men, 609 women	**Student/Faculty:** 15 to 1
Year: semesters, summer session	**Tuition:** $28,368
Room & Board: $11,240	**Freshman Class:** 4097 applied, 3183 accepted, 593 enrolled
SAT CR/M: 510/520 **ACT:** 22	**CEEB CODE:** 2270
Application Deadline: open	**COMPETITIVE**

Gannon is a Catholic, Diocesan university dedicated to excellence in teaching, scholarship and service. Our faculty and staff prepare students to be global citizens through programs grounded in the liberal arts and sciences and professional specializations. Inspired by the Catholic Intellectual Tradition, we offer a comprehensive, values-centered learning experience that emphasizes faith, leadership, inclusiveness and social responsibility. There are 3 undergraduate schools and 1 graduate school. In addition to regional accreditation, Gannon has baccalaureate program accreditation with ABET, ACBSP, APTA, CSWE, ACOTE, ARC-PA, CoARC, CAAHEP, CCNE, PDE, and JRCERT. The 37-acre campus is in an urban area downtown Erie, Pennsylvania; 128 miles north of Pittsburgh, 99 miles east of Cleveland, and 106 miles southwest of Buffalo. Including any residence halls, there are 47 buildings.

STUDENT LIFE: 72% of undergraduates are from Pennsylvania. Others are from 36 states, 27 foreign countries, and Canada. 80% are White. 38% are Catholic; 38% claim no religious affiliation; 16% Protestant. The average age of freshmen is 18; all undergraduates, 21. 17% do not continue beyond their first year; 83% remain to graduate. **Housing:** 1456 students can be accommodated in college housing, which includes coed dorms, on-campus apartments, and off-campus apartments. In addition, there are language houses, special-interest houses, fraternity houses, and sorority houses. On-campus housing is guaranteed for all 4 years. Priority is given to out-of-town students. 63% of students commute. Upperclassmen may keep cars.

FACULTY/CLASSROOMS: 51% of faculty are male; 49% are female. 80% teach undergraduates. Graduate students teach 2% of introductory courses. The average class size in an introductory lecture is 22 and in a laboratory is 21.

PROGRAMS OF STUDY: Gannon confers B.A., B.S., B.S.E., B.S.M., B.S.B.A. and B.S.N. degrees. Associate, Master's, and Doctoral degrees are also awarded. Bachelor's degrees are awarded in BIOLOGICAL SCIENCE (bioinformatics, biology/adolescence education, biology/biological science, and nutrition), BUSINESS (accounting, banking and finance, business administration and management, entrepreneurial studies, funeral home services, insurance and risk management, international business management, management science, marketing/retailing/merchandising, sports management, and supply chain management), COMMUNICATIONS AND THE ARTS (advertising, communications, dramatic arts, English, foreign language, and journalism), COMPUTER AND PHYSICAL SCIENCE (chemistry, computer science, information sciences and systems, mathematics, science, and software engineering), EDUCATION (early childhood education, English education, health information management, mathematics education, middle school education, social studies education, and special education), ENGINEERING AND ENVIRONMENTAL DESIGN (biomedical engineering, chemical engineering, electrical/electronics engineering, environmental engineering, environmental science, and mechanical engineering), HEALTH PROFESSIONS (health science, kinesiology, medical technology, nursing, nutrition and wellness, occupational therapy, physical therapy, physician's assistant, predentistry, premedicine, preoptometry, prepodiatry, preveterinary science, and respiratory therapy), SOCIAL SCIENCE (criminal justice, history, interdisciplinary studies, international studies, philosophy, political science/government, psychology, social work, and theological studies). Health professions is the strongest academically. Nursing, physician's assistant, sport and exercise science have the largest enrollments.

ACTIVITIES: 18% of men belong to 7 national fraternities, 19% of women belong to 5 national sororities. There are 92 groups on campus, including activities programming board and a radio station, band, cheerleading, choir, chorus, computers, dance, drama, environmental, ethnic, honors, international, literary magazine, newspaper, pep band, political, professional, radio and TV, religious, social, social service, and student government. Popular campus events include Family Weekend, GIVE Day, Home Coming Weekend, Day of Caring and Springtopia. **Sports:** There are 9 intercollegiate sports for men and 9 for women, and 12 intramural sports for men and 12 for women. Facilities include a 16000 square-foot multi-purpose athletic field that includes five NCAA regulation fields, and seats 2500, a collegiate-sized swimming pool, six regulation racquetball courts, an indoor running track, weight machines and cardio equipment, a 3000 seat basketball and volleyball venue, a 14,000-square-foot locker rooms, areas for wrestling, and a acrobatics and tumbling program, a 51,300-square-foot indoor field house that features an 80-yard indoor field that allows for year-round practice and increased intramural and club sports programs. Including is a Human Performance Laboratory that includes motion analysis and human performance and testing laboratories where faculty and students in the physical therapy, sport and exercise science, occupational therapy, biomedical engineering and Doctor of Nursing Practice (DNP) programs can collaborate on learning and research projects. **Graduates:** From July 1, 2013 to June 30, 2014, 511 bachelor's degrees were awarded. The most popular majors were health sciences (19%), nursing (12%), and biology (9%). 16 companies recruited on campus in 2013-2014. In an average class, 50% graduate in 4 years or less, 63% graduate in 5 years or less, and 65% graduate in 6 years or less.

SERVICES: Counseling and information services are available, as is tutoring in most subjects. There is a reader service for the blind, remedial math, reading, and writing. There are math, writing, and advising centers. **Library/Resources:** The library contains 258,190 volumes, 79 microform items, 4,977 audio/video tapes/CDs/DVDs, and subscribes to 56,251 periodicals including electronic. Computerized library services include interlibrary loans, database searching, Internet access, and Wi-Fi capability. Special learning facilities include an art gallery, radio station, an environaut research vessel, patient simulation center, human performance center, and archaeology museum. **Physically Challenged Students:** 70% of the campus is accessible. Facilities include wheelchair ramps, elevators, special parking, specially equipped restrooms, special class scheduling, lowered drinking fountains, and special housing. **Special:** The university offers study abroad in more than 15 countries, co-op programs, dual majors, summer internships, pass/fail options, work-study programs, a general studies program, accelerated degree programs in law, medicine, optometry, podiatry, veterinary, and pharmacy. Gannon University offers several programs that work in conjunction with other Colleges and Universities such as Charleston School of Pharmacy, LECOM, PCOM, PCO, Ross University School of Medicine, and Duquesne toward degree completion. Gannon also provides students with numerous service and experiential learning opportunities. There are 16 national honor societies, a freshman honors program, and 12 departmental honors programs. **Visiting:** There are regularly scheduled orientations for prospective students, consisting of open houses for prospective students in the fall and spring. Students may meet with faculty, tour the campus, meet with financial aid advisors, and sit in on a variety of presentations. There are guides for informal visits and visitors may stay overnight. To schedule a visit, contact Kristin Manczka at (814) 871-7407. **Campus Safety and Security:** Measures include 24-hour foot and vehicle patrol, emergency notification system, and security escort services. There are shuttle buses, emergency telephones, lighted pathways/sidewalks, controlled access to dorms/residences, security cameras in buildings, card access systems to residential hall, fire alarm systems in all building, fire suppression systems in all residential halls, card access for after hour access in educational buildings.

REQUIREMENTS: The SAT or ACT is required. Candidates should have completed 16 academic units including 4 in English and 12 in social sciences, foreign languages, math, and science, depending on the degree sought. Specific courses in math and science are required for some majors in health sciences and engineering. Essays are required for some programs and encouraged for the general population. The same is true for letters of recommendation. Credits may be earned for those that complete AP exams and IB exams. Gannon accepts the GED in replacement of a high school diploma with appropriate scores earned overall and in each subject matter. AP and CLEP credits are accepted. Important factors in the admissions decision are advanced placement or honors courses, recommendations by school officials, parents or siblings attended your school, personality/intangible qualities, and extracurricular activities record.Students must complete at least 128 hours of academic work. Each academic program has specific course requirements. Students must have a cumulative GPA of at least 2.0 overall and in the area of concentration. **Procedure:** Freshmen are admitted fall, spring, and summer. Entrance exams should be taken at the end of the junior year or the beginning of the senior year. There are deferred admissions and rolling admissions plans. Application deadlines are open. Application fee is $25. Notification is sent on a rolling basis. Applications are accepted on-line. **Transfer Students:** 133 transfer students enrolled in 2013-2014. Transfer students should be in good standing at their previous institution with at least a 2.0 GPA. They must submit a college clearance from the college most recently attended and transcripts from all institutions attended. A high school transcript is required from transfer students with fewer than 30 credits or for those pursuing a health related field. Some health profession programs offer limited seating. 40 of 128 credits required for the bachelor's degree must be completed at Gannon. **International Students:** There are 225 international students enrolled. The school actively recruits these students. They must take the TOEFL with a minimum score of 550 on the paper-based TOEFL (PBT) or 79 on the Internet-based version (iBT).

ADMISSIONS: 78% of the 2014-2015 applicants were accepted. The SAT scores for the 2014-2015 freshman class were: Critical Reading--41% below 500, 46% between 500 and 599, 12% between 600 and 699, and 1% between 700 and 800; Math--35% below 500, 48% between 500 and 599, 15% between 600 and 699, and 2% between 700 and 800. The ACT scores were 25% below 21, 38% between 21 and 23, 21% between 24 and 26, 10% between 27 and 28, and 6% above 28. 38% of the current freshmen were in the top fifth of their class; 69% were in the top two fifths. 8 freshmen graduated first in their class. **Admissions Contact:** Patricia Maughn, Coordinator, Admissions Inquiries. E-Mail: *admissions@gannon.edu* Web: *www.gannon.edu*

FINANCIAL AID: In 2014-2015, 98% of all full-time freshmen and 97% of continuing full-time students received some form of financial aid. 84% of all full-time freshmen and 78% of continuing full-time students received need-based aid. The average freshman award was $24,660. Need-based scholarships or need-based grants averaged $20,887; need-based self-help aid (loans and jobs) averaged $4,090; non-need-based athletic scholarships averaged $12,529; and other non-need-based awards and non-need-based scholarships averaged $12,710. 22% of undergraduate students work part-time. Average annual earnings from campus work are $1800. The average financial indebtedness of the 2014 graduate was $27,560. Gannon is a member of CSS. The FAFSA is required. The priority date for freshman financial aid applications for fall entry is March 15.

GENEVA COLLEGE   A-3
www.geneva.edu

Beaver Falls, PA 15010   (724) 847-6500
                                                    (800) 847-8255
Fax: (724) 847-6776   Email: admissions@geneva.edu
Full-time: 600 men, 730 women   Faculty: 75; IIB, -$
Part-time: 30 men, 30 women   Ph.D.s: 76%
Graduate: 120 men, 180 women   Student/Faculty: n/av
Year: semesters, summer session   Tuition: $23,330
Room & Board: $8560   Freshman Class: n/av
SAT or ACT: required   CEEB CODE: 2273
Application Deadline: open   COMPETITIVE

Geneva College, founded in 1848, is a private institution affiliated with the Reformed Presbyterian Church of North America. The college offers undergraduate programs in the arts and sciences, business, education, health science, biblical and religious studies, engineering, and preprofessional training. Some figures in the above capsule and in this profile are approximate. There are approximately 450 nontraditional undergraduates. In addition to regional accreditation, Geneva has baccalaureate program accreditation with ABET and ACBSP. The 50-acre campus is in a small town 35 miles northwest of Pittsburgh. Including any residence halls, there are 30 buildings.

STUDENT LIFE: 73% of undergraduates are from Pennsylvania. Students are from 37 states, 19 foreign countries, and Canada. 87% are from public schools. 91% are white. 89% are Protestant. The average age of freshmen is 19; all undergraduates, 26. 23% do not continue beyond their first year; 55% remain to graduate.

FACULTY/CLASSROOMS: 76% of faculty are male; 24% are female. 95% teach undergraduates. No introductory courses are taught by graduate students. The average class size in an introductory lecture is 135; in a laboratory, 22; and in a regular course, 20.

PROGRAMS OF STUDY: Geneva confers B.A., B.S., B.S.B.A., B.S.E., and B.S.Ed. degrees. Associate and Master's degrees are also awarded. Bachelor's degrees are awarded in BIOLOGICAL SCIENCE (biology/biological science), BUSINESS (accounting and business administration and management), COMMUNICATIONS AND THE ARTS (applied music, broadcasting, communications, creative writing, English, music, music business management, Spanish, and speech/debate/rhetoric), COMPUTER AND PHYSICAL SCIENCE (applied mathematics, chemistry, computer science, and physics), EDUCATION (elementary education, mathematics education, and music education), ENGINEERING AND ENVIRONMENTAL DESIGN (aviation administration/management, chemical engineering, and engineering), HEALTH PROFESSIONS (speech pathology/audiology), SOCIAL SCIENCE (biblical studies, counseling/psychology, history, human services, interdisciplinary studies, ministries, philosophy, political science/government, psychology, and sociology). Engineering, business administration, and education are the strongest academically. Elementary education, business administration, and psychology have the largest enrollments.

ACTIVITIES: There are 50 groups on campus, including band, cheerleading, chess, choir, chorale, chorus, computers, drama, ethnic, forensics, honors, international, literary magazine, marching band, newspaper, photography, political, professional, radio, religious, social, social service, student government, and yearbook. Popular campus events include International Day, Fall Fest, and The Big Event.

SERVICES: Counseling and information services are available, as is tutoring in most subjects. There is remedial math, reading, and writing. **Library/Resources:** The library contains 167,206 volumes, 198,624 microform items, 12,901 audio/video tapes/CDs/DVDs, and subscribes to 879 periodicals including electronic. Computerized library services include interlibrary loans, database searching, and Internet access. Special learning facilities include a TV station, an observatory. **Physically Challenged Students:** 90% of the campus is accessible. Facilities include wheelchair ramps, elevators, special parking, specially equipped restrooms, special class scheduling, lowered drinking fountains, and lowered telephones. **Special:** Cross-registration is offered in conjunction with Pennsylvania State University/Beaver Campus and Community College of Beaver County. There is a 3-1 degree program in cardiovascular technology, and an accelerated degree programs in human resources and community ministry. Off-campus study includes programs at the Philadelphia Center for Urban Theological Studies, a Washington semester, a summer program at AuSable, Institute of Environmental Studies in Michigan, art studies in Pittsburgh, CCCU music program in Martha's Vineyard, film studies in Los Angeles, and study abroad in Costa Rica, Egypt, China, England, Russia, and Israel. Geneva also offers internships, independent study, and credit by proficiency exam. Nondegree study is available through adult education programs. There are 2 national honor societies, a freshman honors program, and 1 departmental honors program. **Visiting:** There are regularly scheduled orientations for prospective students, including class visits, a campus tour, meetings with faculty, admissions, and financial aid counselors, and meetings with coaches. There are guides

for informal visits, visitors may sit in on classes, and stay overnight. To schedule a visit, contact Campus Visit Coordinator. **Campus Safety and Security:** Measures include security escort services. There are emergency telephones, lighted pathways/sidewalks, off-duty city policemen on campus from 4:30 p.m. to 7 a.m. daily and a full-time Director of Campus Security.

REQUIREMENTS: The SAT or ACT is required. Applicants must be graduates of an accredited secondary school or have earned a GED. Geneva requires 16 academic units, based on 4 each of English and electives, 3 of social studies, 2 each of math and foreign language, and 1 of science. An essay is required and an interview is recommended. A GPA of 2.5 is required. AP and CLEP credits are accepted. Important factors in the admissions decision are recommendations by school officials, advanced placement or honors courses, and leadership record.

FINANCIAL AID: In a recent year, 90% of all full-time students received some form of financial aid. 70% of all full-time students received need-based aid. The average freshman award was $13,785. Need-based scholarships or need-based grants averaged $10,241 ($22,000 maximum); need-based self-help aid (loans and jobs) averaged $4212 ($5625 maximum); and non-need-based athletic scholarships averaged $2542 ($14,980 maximum). 75% of undergraduate students work part-time. Average annual earnings from campus work are $1000. The average financial indebtedness of a recent year's graduate was $20,000. Geneva is a member of CSS. The FAFSA is required. Check with the school for current application deadlines.

GETTYSBURG COLLEGE   D-4
www.gettysburg.edu

Gettysburg, PA 17325	(717) 337-6100
	(800) 431-0803
Fax: (717) 337-6145	Email: admiss@gettysburg.edu
Full-time: 1155 men, 1274 women	Faculty: 225; IIB, +$
Part-time: 10 men, 12 women	Ph.D.s: 95%
Graduate: n/av	Student/Faculty: 10 to 1
Year: semesters	Tuition: $47,480
Room & Board: $11,340	Freshman Class: 4915 applied, 2233 accepted, 745 enrolled
SAT or ACT: required	CEEB CODE: 2275
Application Deadline: January 15	HIGHLY COMPETITIVE

Gettysburg College, founded in 1832, is a nationally ranked college offering programs in the liberal arts and sciences. There is one undergraduate school. The 200-acre campus is in a suburban area 30 miles south of Harrisburg, 55 miles from Baltimore, MD, and 80 miles from Washington, D.C. Including any residence halls, there are 81 buildings.

STUDENT LIFE: 73% of undergraduates are from out of state, mostly the Middle Atlantic. Students are from 36 states, 28 foreign countries, and Canada. 65% are from public schools. 80% are White. 35% are Protestant; 341% Catholic. The average age of freshmen is 18; all undergraduates, 20. 11% do not continue beyond their first year; 80% remain to graduate. **Housing:** 2389 students can be accommodated in college housing, which includes single-sex and coed dorms, on-campus apartments, and off-campus apartments. In addition, there are honors houses, language houses, special-interest houses, fraternity houses, and theme housing. On-campus housing is guaranteed for all 4 years and is available on a lottery system for upperclassmen. Upperclassmen may keep cars.

FACULTY/CLASSROOMS: 60% of faculty are male; 40% are female. All teach and do research. No introductory courses are taught by graduate students. The average class size in an introductory lecture is 19; in a laboratory is 15; and in a regular course is 18.

PROGRAMS OF STUDY: Gettysburg confers B.A., B.S. and B.M.(Performance and Music) degrees. Bachelor's degrees are awarded in BIOLOGICAL SCIENCE (biochemistry and biology/biological science), BUSINESS (business administration and management), COMMUNICATIONS AND THE ARTS (art history and appreciation, classics, dramatic arts, English, French, German, Greek,

Latin, music, Spanish, and studio art), COMPUTER AND PHYSICAL SCIENCE (chemistry, computer science, mathematics, mathematics – economics, and physics), EDUCATION (elementary education, foreign languages education, music education, science education, and secondary education), ENGINEERING AND ENVIRONMENTAL DESIGN (environmental science), HEALTH PROFESSIONS (health science, predentistry, and premedicine), SOCIAL SCIENCE (anthropology, Caribbean studies, economics, gender studies, history, international relations, Islamic studies, Japanese studies, Judaic studies, Latin American studies, Middle Eastern studies, philosophy, political science/government, prelaw, psychology, religion, sociology, and women's studies). Sciences, psychology, history, management, and political science are the strongest academically. Management, political science, and psychology have the largest enrollments.

ACTIVITIES: 31% of men belong to 9 national fraternities; 31% of women belong to 5 national sororities. There are 120 groups on campus, including dance ensemble, campus activities board, art, band, cheerleading, choir, chorale, chorus, communications, computers, dance, drama, environmental, ethnic, film, gay, honors, international, jazz band, literary magazine, marching band, musical theater, newspaper, opera, orchestra, outdoor recreation program, pep band, photography, political, professional, radio and TV, religious, social, social service, student government, symphony, and yearbook. Popular campus events include Thanksgiving Dinner, Oceanfest, Snowball and Springfest. **Sports:** There are 11 intercollegiate sports for men and 11 for women, and 10 intramural sports for men and 10 for women. Facilities include state-of-the-art center for athletics, recreation, and fitness facility, a natatorium, rock walls, basketball courts, indoor and outdoor tennis courts, several tracks and fields, 2 outdoor turf fields, a field house. **Graduates:** From July 1, 2013 to June 30, 2014, 750 bachelor's degrees were awarded. The most popular majors were organization and management studies (8%), psychology (8%), and political science (8%). 160 companies recruited on campus in 2013-2014. In an average class, 80% graduate in 4 years or less, 84% graduate in 5 years or less, and 84% graduate in 6 years or less. Of the 2013 graduating class, 24% were enrolled in graduate school within 6 months of graduation, and 70% were employed.

SERVICES: Counseling and information services are available, as is tutoring in most subjects. **Library/Resources:** The library contains 409,241 volumes, 71,368 microform items, 182,931 audio/video tapes/CDs/DVDs, subscribes to 53,181 periodicals including electronic. Computerized library services include interlibrary loans, database searching, Internet access, and Wi-Fi capability. Special learning facilities include an art gallery, planetarium, radio station, TV station, electron microscopes, spectrometers, an optics lab, plasma physics lab, greenhouse, observatory, child study lab, fine and performing arts facilities, and a state-of-the-art athletic facility. **Physically Challenged Students:** 90% of the campus is accessible. Facilities include wheelchair ramps, elevators, special parking, specially equipped restrooms, special class scheduling, lowered drinking fountains, and special housing. **Special:** The college offers an extensive global education (study abroad) program and has special centers worldwide. There are summer internships and a Washington semester with American University. Cross-registration is possible with members of the Central Pennsylvania Consortium. There is a United Nations semester at Drew University, and a 3-2 engineering program with Columbia University, Rensselaer Polytechnic, and Washington University in St. Louis. There are also joint programs in optometry with the Pennsylvania College of Optometry, and forestry and environmental studies with Duke University. The college offers double majors, student-designed majors, and B.A.-B.S. degrees in biology, chemistry, physics, biochemistry, and molecular biology, environmental studies and health and exercise sciences. Education certification is also available. There are 29 national honor societies, and a chapter of Phi Beta Kappa. **Visiting:** There are regularly scheduled orientations for prospective students, including interviews, tours, day visits, open houses, and group information sessions. There are guides for informal visits and visitors may sit in on classes. To schedule a visit, contact The Admissions Office. **Campus Safety and Security:** Measures include 24-hour foot and vehicle patrol, emergency notification system, self-defense education, and security escort services. There are emergency

telephones, lighted pathways/sidewalks, and controlled access to dorms/residences.

REQUIREMENTS: The SAT or ACT is required. An essay is required. Students planning to major in music must audition and art students can submit a portfolio. An interview and SAT Subject tests are recommended. AP credits are accepted. Important factors in the admissions decision are evidence of special talent, recommendations by school officials, and advanced placement or honors courses. All students must complete 32 courses including a concentration in a major field of study culminating with a capstone experience; 1 course each in the arts, humanities, social sciences, quantitative reasoning, diversity: non-western culture; first-year writing; 2 courses in natural sciences and in a foreign language. The minimum GPA is 2.0. **Procedure:** Freshmen are admitted fall and spring. Entrance exams should be taken by the January testing date of the senior year. There are early decision and deferred admissions plans. Early decision applications should be filed by November 15; regular applications, by January 15 for fall entry, along with a $60 fee. Notification of early decision is sent December 15; regular decision, April 1. 330 early decision candidates were accepted for the 2014-2015 class. 558 applicants were on the 2014 waiting list. Applications are accepted on-line. **Transfer Students:** 16 transfer students enrolled in 2013-2014. Transfer applicants must have a GPA of at least 2.5. An interview is recommended. The high school record, test scores, college official's report and transcript from college(s) attended are also required. 16 of 32 credits required for the bachelor's degree must be completed at Gettysburg. **International Students:** There are 94 international students enrolled. The school actively recruits these students. They must take the TOEFL. They must also take the SAT or ACT.

ADMISSIONS: 45% of the 2014-2015 applicants were accepted. The SAT scores for the 2014-2015 freshman class were: Critical Reading--23% between 500 and 599, 63% between 600 and 699, and 13% between 700 and 800; Math--17% between 500 and 599, 68% between 600 and 699, and 15% between 700 and 800. 88% of the current freshmen were in the top fifth of their class; 99% were in the top two fifths. **Admissions Contact:** Gail Sweezey, Director of Admissions. E-Mail: *admiss@gettysburg.edu* Web: *www.gettysburg.edu*

FINANCIAL AID: In 2014-2015, 60% of all full-time freshmen and continuing full-time students received some form of financial aid. 58% of all full-time freshmen and 59% of continuing full-time students received need-based aid. The average freshman award was $36,825. 46% of undergraduate students work part-time. Average annual earnings from campus work are $1500. The average financial indebtedness of the 2014 graduate was $22,212. Gettysburg is a member of CSS. The CSS/Profile and FAFSA are required. The deadline for filing freshman financial aid applications for fall entry is February 1.

GROVE CITY COLLEGE
B-2
www.gcc.edu

Grove City, PA 16127
(724) 458-2100
(724) 458-2000

Fax: (724) 458-3395	Email: admissions@gcc.edu
Full-time: 1221 men, 1244 women	Faculty: 150
Part-time: 19 men, 25 women	Ph.D.s: 80%
Graduate: n/av	Student/Faculty: 16 to 1
Year: semesters, summer session	Tuition: $15,550
Room & Board: $8472	Freshman Class: 1492 applied, 1306 accepted, 637 enrolled
SAT CR/M: 603/600 ACT: 26	CEEB CODE: 2277
Application Deadline: February 1	VERY COMPETITIVE

Grove City College, founded in 1876, is a private, liberal arts and science Christian college that is committed to providing rigorous academics within a Christian environment at an amazing value. There are 2 undergraduate schools. In addition to regional accreditation, Grove City has baccalaureate program accreditation with ABET, CAAHEP, and ACS. The 180-acre campus is in a small town 60 miles north of Pittsburgh. Including any residence halls, there are 30 buildings.

STUDENT LIFE: 51% of undergraduates are from Pennsylvania.

Others are from 41 states, 11 foreign countries, and Canada. 60% are from public schools. 93% are White. 62% claim no religious affiliation; 21% Protestant. The average age of freshmen is 18; all undergraduates, 20. 9% do not continue beyond their first year; 82% remain to graduate. **Housing:** 2333 students can be accommodated in college housing, which includes single-sex dorms and on-campus apartments. On-campus housing is guaranteed for all 4 years and is available on a lottery system for upperclassmen. 95% of students live on campus; of those, 85% remain on campus on weekends. Alcohol is not permitted. Upperclassmen may keep cars.

FACULTY/CLASSROOMS: 62% of faculty are male; 38% are female. All teach undergraduates, and 30% do both. No introductory courses are taught by graduate students. The average class size in an introductory lecture is 24; in a laboratory is 21; and in a regular course is 25.

PROGRAMS OF STUDY: Grove City confers B.A., B.S., B.Mus., B.S.E.E. and B.S.M.E. degrees. Bachelor's degrees are awarded in BIOLOGICAL SCIENCE (biochemistry and biology/biological science), BUSINESS (accounting, business administration and management, business economics, entrepreneurial studies, finance, international business management, and marketing management), COMMUNICATIONS AND THE ARTS (communications, English, French, music, music business management, music performance, and Spanish), COMPUTER AND PHYSICAL SCIENCE (chemistry, computer information technology, computer science, mathematics, and physics), EDUCATION (early childhood education, elementary education, middle school education, music education, and special education), ENGINEERING AND ENVIRONMENTAL DESIGN (electrical/electronics engineering, industrial administration/management, and mechanical engineering), HEALTH PROFESSIONS (exercise science), SOCIAL SCIENCE (biblical studies, economics, history, philosophy, political science/government, psychology, religious music, and sociology). Engineering, computer science, biology, communication studies, business, and education are the strongest academically. Mechanical engineering, biology, and communication studies have the largest enrollments.

ACTIVITIES: 17% of men belong to 10 local fraternities; 17% of women belong to 8 local sororities. There are 145 groups on campus, including art, band, cheerleading, chess, choir, chorale, chorus, computers, dance, debate, drama, drill team, environmental, ethnic, film, forensics, honors, international, jazz band, literary magazine, marching band, musical theater, newspaper, opera, orchestra, pep band, photography, political, professional, radio and TV, religious, social, social service, student government, symphony, and yearbook. Popular campus events include Family Weekend, Christmas Candlelight Service, Homecoming, and President's Gala. **Sports:** There are 9 intercollegiate sports for men and 10 for women, and 13 intramural sports for men and 14 for women. Facilities include a field house, 2 indoor pools, indoor running track, an intramural room with 4 basketball, volleyball, or tennis courts, 3 racquetball courts, a bowling alley, 2 fitness rooms, 10 outdoor tennis courts, turf football stadium with an all-weather track, baseball, soccer, and softball fields, and 3 intramural fields. **Graduates:** From July 1, 2013 to June 30, 2014, 584 bachelor's degrees were awarded. The most popular majors were English (7%), communication studies (7%), and mechanical engineering (6%). 219 companies recruited on campus in 2013-2014. In an average class, 77% graduate in 4 years or less, 82% graduate in 5 years or less, and 83% graduate in 6 years or less.

SERVICES: Counseling and information services are available, as is tutoring in most subjects. A student peer tutoring program is available for a small fee. **Library/Resources:** The library contains 162,000 volumes, 4,000 microform items, 3,600 audio/video tapes/CDs/DVDs, and subscribes to 84,000 periodicals including electronic. Computerized library services include interlibrary loans, database searching, Internet access, and Wi-Fi capability. Special learning facilities include an art gallery, radio station, TV station, an off-site research grade observatory. **Physically Challenged Students:** 10% of the campus is accessible. Facilities include wheelchair ramps, elevators, special parking, specially equipped restrooms, special class scheduling, lowered drinking fountains, and special housing. **Special:** The college offers study abroad; accelerated and double major degrees; semester and summer internships; and a Washington, DC semester. There are 18 national honor societies and 15 departmental honors programs. **Visiting:** There are regularly scheduled orientations for prospective students, daily interviews and tours; high school visitation days: 5 in the fall and 2 in the spring. There are various department-specific open houses throughout the year as well. There are guides for informal visits, visitors may sit in on classes, and stay overnight. To schedule a visit, contact the Admissions Office. **Campus Safety and Security:** Measures include 24-hour foot and vehicle patrol, emergency notification system, and security escort services. There are emergency telephones, lighted pathways/sidewalks, controlled access to dorms/residences, An emergency response program is in place, which includes a public warning siren and cell phone call/text message system.

REQUIREMENTS: The SAT or ACT is required. An academic or college preparatory curriculum is highly recommended, including 4 units of English; 3 units each of math, science, and a foreign language; and 2 units of history. Two essays are required of all applicants, and an audition is required of music students. An interview is highly recommended. AP and CLEP credits are accepted. Important factors in the admissions decision are extracurricular activities record, personality/intangible qualities, and parents or siblings attended your school.Students are required to complete a minimum of 128 credit hours. All students must complete the 40-46 semester-hour general education curriculum, which includes 18 hours of humanities; 8 hours of natural science; 3 hours of science, faith, and technology; 3 hours of social science; and 6 hours of quantitative and logical reasoning. Specific courses required include 2 hours of physical/wellness education and 2 years demonstrated proficiency in a foreign language. A minimum GPA of 2.0 is required. **Procedure:** Freshmen are admitted fall and spring. Entrance exams should be taken Spring of the junior year or the fall of the senior year. There are early decision, early admissions, and deferred admissions plans. Early decision applications should be filed by November 1; regular applications, by February 1 for fall entry; and December 15 for spring entry, along with a $50 fee. Notification of early decision is sent December 15; regular decision, March 15. 352 early decision candidates were accepted for the 2014-2015 class. 60 applicants were on the 2014 waiting list; 24 were admitted. Applications are accepted on-line. **Transfer Students:** 42 transfer students enrolled in 2013-2014. Either the SAT or the ACT is required as well as two letters of recommendation, official high school and college transcripts, and two essays. An interview is highly recommended. 64 of 128 credits required for the bachelor's degree must be completed at Grove City. **International Students:** There are 21 international students enrolled. The school actively recruits these students. They must take the TOEFL with a minimum score of 550 on the paper-based TOEFL (PBT) or 79 on the Internet-based version (iBT). They must also take the SAT or ACT. If the TOEFL is not available, either the SAT or the ACT is required.

ADMISSIONS: 88% of the 2014-2015 applicants were accepted. The SAT scores for the 2014-2015 freshman class were: Critical Reading--10% below 500, 39% between 500 and 599, 37% between 600 and 699, and 14% between 700 and 800; Math--9% below 500, 38% between 500 and 599, 41% between 600 and 699, and 12% between 700 and 800. The ACT scores were 6% below 21, 17% between 21 and 23, 26% between 24 and 26, 20% between 27 and 28, and 31% above 28. 37% of the current freshmen were in the top fifth of their class; 50% were in the top two fifths. There were 7 National Merit finalists. 32 freshmen graduated first in their class. **Admissions Contact:** Sarah E. Gibbs, Director of Admissions. E-Mail: *admissions@gcc.edu* Web: *www.gcc.edu*

FINANCIAL AID: In 2014-2015, 70% of all full-time freshmen and 74% of continuing full-time students received some form of financial aid. 47% of all full-time freshmen and 41% of continuing full-time students received need-based aid. The average freshman award was $12,954. Need-based scholarships or need-based grants averaged $6,958; need-based self-help aid (loans and jobs) averaged $7,246; and other non-need-based awards and non-need-based scholarships averaged $4,370. 40% of undergraduate students work part-time. Average annual earnings from campus work are $1100. The average financial indebtedness of the 2014 graduate was $31,634. The college's own financial statement is required. The deadline for filing freshman financial aid applications for fall entry is April 15.

GWYNEDD-MERCY COLLEGE F-4
www.gmc.edu

Gwynedd Valley, PA 19437	(215) 641-5510
	(800) DIAL-GMC
Fax: (215) 641-5556	Email: admissions@gmc.edu
Full-time: 420 men, 1080 women	Faculty: 69
Part-time: 170 men, 540 women	Ph.Ds: 63%
Graduate: 110 men, 320 women	Student/Faculty: n/av
Year: semesters, summer session	Tuition: $28,370
Room & Board: $10,525	Freshman Class: n/av
SAT or ACT: required	CEEB CODE: 2278
Application Deadline: see profile	COMPETITIVE

Gwynedd-Mercy College, founded in 1948, is a private institution affiliated with the Roman Catholic Church and offering degree programs in the arts and sciences, business, education, and health fields. There are 5 undergraduate schools and 2 graduate schools. The figures in the above capsule and in this profile are approximate. In addition to regional accreditation, Gwynedd-Mercy has baccalaureate program accreditation with NLN. The 170-acre campus is in a suburban area 20 miles northwest of Philadelphia. Including any residence halls, there are 21 buildings.

STUDENT LIFE: 92% of undergraduates are from Pennsylvania. Others are from 14 states and 38 foreign countries. 59% are from public schools. 69% are white; 20% African American. 54% are Catholic; 13% Protestant. The average age of freshmen is 25; all undergraduates, 28. 24% do not continue beyond their first year; 69% remain to graduate.

FACULTY/CLASSROOMS: 29% of faculty are male; 71% are female. 92% teach undergraduates. No introductory courses are taught by graduate students. The average class size in an introductory lecture, 24; in a laboratory, 15; and in a regular course, 17.

PROGRAMS OF STUDY: Gwynedd-Mercy confers B.A., B.S., and B.H.S. degrees. Associate and Master's degrees are also awarded. Bachelor's degrees are awarded in BIOLOGICAL SCIENCE (biology/biological science), BUSINESS (accounting, banking and finance, business administration and management, human resources, international business management, management science, marketing and distribution, and sports management), COMMUNICATIONS AND THE ARTS (communications, English, and public relations), COMPUTER AND PHYSICAL SCIENCE (computer science, information sciences and systems, mathematics, natural sciences, and radiological technology), EDUCATION (business education, elementary education, mathematics education, science education, secondary education, social studies education, and special education), HEALTH PROFESSIONS (clinical science, health care administration, medical laboratory technology, medical technology, nursing, radiation therapy, and respiratory therapy), SOCIAL SCIENCE (criminal justice, gerontology, history, human services, psychology, social work, and sociology). Nursing, biology, and medical technology are the strongest academically. Nursing, business, and education have the largest enrollments.

ACTIVITIES: There are 21 groups on campus, including choir, chorus, drama, ethnic, honors, international, literary magazine, newspaper, professional, religious, social, social service, and student government. Popular campus events include Fall Fest, Carol Night, and International Night.

SERVICES: Counseling and information services are available, as is tutoring in most subjects. There is remedial math, reading, and writing. Tutoring is made available in conjunction with student needs.

Library/Resources: The library contains 104,899 volumes, and 11,775 audio/video tapes/CDs/DVDs. Computerized library services include interlibrary loans, database searching, Internet access, and Wi-Fi capability. Special learning facilities include a **Physically Challenged Students:** 75% of the campus is accessible. Facilities include wheelchair ramps, elevators, special parking, specially equipped restrooms, and special class scheduling. **Special:** The college offers co-op programs in computer science, business administration, and accounting, as well as internships, dual majors, accelerated degree programs, B.A.-B.S. degrees, and pass/fail options. Cross-registration is offered with South Eastern Pennsylvania Consortium for Higher Education.

All programs require or have the option for hands-on experience. There is a 3-1 program in medical technology available wherein the last year is a hospital rotation. There are 4 national honor societies, a freshman honors program, and 1 departmental honors programs.

Visiting: There are regularly scheduled orientations for prospective students, consisting of open houses with formal presentations and campus tours, and class days with class visitations and campus tours. There are guides for informal visits, visitors may sit in on classes, and stay overnight. To schedule a visit, contact the Admissions Office.

Campus Safety and Security: Measures include 24-hour foot and vehicle patrol, emergency notification system, and security escort services. There are shuttle buses, emergency telephones, and lighted pathways/sidewalks.

REQUIREMENTS: The SAT or ACT is required. Candidates for admission must be graduates of accredited secondary schools and have completed 16 academic credits/Carnegie units, including 4 credits in English, 3 each in math, science, and college preparatory electives, 2 in a foreign language, and 1 in history. The GED is accepted. An interview is recommended for all candidates and is required for some programs. A GPA of 2.0 is required. AP and CLEP credits are accepted. Important factors in the admissions decision are advanced placement or honors courses, parents or siblings attended your school, and recommendations by alumni.

ADMISSIONS: 60% of a recent year's applicants were accepted. 18% of a recent year's freshmen were in the top fifth of their class; 42% were in the top two fifths.

FINANCIAL AID: In a recent year, 73% of all full-time freshmen and 74% of continuing full-time students received some form of financial aid. 72% of all full-time freshmen and 73% of continuing full-time students received need-based aid. The average freshman award was $14,349. The average financial indebtedness of a recent year's graduate was $20,636. The FAFSA, the college's own financial statement, and federal income tax returns are required. Check with the school for current application deadlines.

HAVERFORD COLLEGE E-4
www.haverford.edu

Haverford, PA 19041	(610) 896-1000
	(610) 896-1350
Fax: (610) 896-1338	Email: admission@haverford.edu
Full-time: 560 men, 629 women	Faculty: 122; IIB, ++$
Part-time: 4 men, 1 women	Ph.Ds: 98%
Graduate: n/av	Student/Faculty: 9 to 1
Year: semesters	Tuition: $47,214
Room & Board: $14,350	Freshman Class: 3496 applied, 863 accepted, 338 enrolled
SAT CR/M/W: 710/700/700 ACT: 32	CEEB CODE: 2289
Application Deadline: January 15	MOST COMPETITIVE

Haverford College, founded in 1833, is a private liberal arts college. There is one undergraduate school. The 200-acre campus is in a suburban area 10 miles west of Philadelphia, PA. Including any residence halls, there are 87 buildings.

STUDENT LIFE: 88% of undergraduates are from out of state, mostly the Middle Atlantic. Students are from 42 states, 35 foreign countries, and Canada. 54% are from public schools. 64% are White. The average age of freshmen is 18; all undergraduates, 20. 3% do not continue beyond their first year; 94% remain to graduate. **Housing:** 1236 students can be accommodated in college housing, which includes coed dorms and on-campus apartments. In addition, there are language houses, special-interest houses, Haverford students may live at Bryn Mawr College through a dorm exchange program. On-campus housing is guaranteed for all 4 years and is available on a lottery system for upperclassmen. 98% of students live on campus; of those, 90% remain on campus on weekends. Upperclassmen may keep cars.

FACULTY/CLASSROOMS: 54% of faculty are male; 46% are female. All teach undergraduates. No introductory courses are taught by graduate students. The average class size in a regular course is 20.

PROGRAMS OF STUDY: Haverford confers B.A., and B.S. degrees.

Bachelor's degrees are awarded in BIOLOGICAL SCIENCE (biology/ biological science), COMMUNICATIONS AND THE ARTS (art history and appreciation, classics, comparative literature, English, fine arts, French, German, Greek, Italian, Latin, linguistics, music, romance languages and literature, Russian, Spanish, and visual and performing arts), COMPUTER AND PHYSICAL SCIENCE (astronomy, astrophysics, chemistry, computer science, geology, information sciences and systems, mathematics, and physics), SOCIAL SCIENCE (anthropology, archeology, East Asian studies, economics, history, interdisciplinary studies, liberal arts/general studies, philosophy, political science/government, psychology, religion, sociology, and urban studies). Natural sciences is the strongest academically. English, biology and psychology have the largest enrollments.

ACTIVITIES: There are 229 groups on campus, including art, chess, choir, chorale, computers, dance, debate, drama, environmental, ethnic, film, gay, international, literary magazine, musical theater, newspaper, photography, political, religious, social, social service, student government, and yearbook. Popular campus events include Haverfest, Snowball, and Haverford vs Swarthmore Athletic Events. **Sports:** There are 11 intercollegiate sports for men and 13 for women, and 3 intramural sports for men and 3 for women. Facilities include Integrated Athletic Center: 102,000 square foot, basketball, volleyball and fitness center, cybex exercise equipment, Dana Swan multipurpose room for dance, martial arts, recreational activities, five international squash courts, sports medicine, locker room, and a conference/AV room. **Graduates:** From July 1, 2013 to June 30, 2014, 304 bachelor's degrees were awarded. The most popular majors were biology (13%), psychology (12%), and English (10%). 267 companies recruited on campus in 2013-2014. In an average class, 88% graduate in 4 years or less, 93% graduate in 5 years or less, and 94% graduate in 6 years or less. Of the 2013 graduating class, 18% were enrolled in graduate school within 6 months of graduation, and 60% were employed.

SERVICES: Counseling and information services are available, as is tutoring in every subject. There is a reader service for the blind. **Library/Resources:** The 4 libraries contain 592,984 volumes, 8,039 microform items, 16,280 audio/video tapes/CDs/DVDs, and subscribe to 14,775 periodicals including electronic. Computerized library services include interlibrary loans, database searching, Internet access, and Wi-Fi capability. Special learning facilities include an art gallery, planetarium, an observatory, and an arboretum. **Physically Challenged Students:** 60% of the campus is accessible. Facilities include wheelchair ramps, elevators, special parking, specially equipped restrooms, special class scheduling, lowered drinking fountains, lowered telephones. **Special:** Haverford offers internship programs, cross-registration with Bryn Mawr and Swarthmore Colleges, study abroad in 38 countries, dual majors, and student-designed majors. Pass/fail options are limited to 4 in 4 years. Haverford offers a 3-2 program in engineering with the California Institute of Technology and a 4-1 program in engineering with the University of Pennsylvania. **Visiting:** There are guides for informal visits, visitors may sit in on classes, and stay overnight. To schedule a visit, contact the Admissions Office. **Campus Safety and Security:** Measures include 24-hour foot and vehicle patrol, emergency notification system, self-defense education, and security escort services. There are shuttle buses, emergency telephones, lighted pathways/sidewalks, controlled access to dorms/residences, and a fire safety program.

REQUIREMENTS: The SAT or ACT is required. First-year applicants must take the SAT (all 3 tests, including Writing) or the ACT and 2 SAT subject tests before the deadline for the decision plan chosen. Candidates for admission must be graduates of an accredited secondary school and have taken 4 courses in English, 3 each in a foreign language and math, 2 in social studies, and 1 each in science. The GED is accepted. An essay is required, and an interview is recommended. AP credits are accepted. Important factors in the admissions decision are advanced placement or honors courses, leadership record, and recommendations by school officials.All students must take a minimum of 32 course credits, including freshman writing and 3 courses each in social science, natural science, and the humanities. Students must also take 3 semesters of phys ed and demonstrate proficiency in a foreign language. Students must take a minimum of 6 courses in the major and 6 in related fields. Each major includes a capstone experience. **Procedure:** Freshmen are admitted fall.

Entrance exams should be taken by January 15. There are early decision, early admissions, and deferred admissions plans. Early decision applications should be filed by November 15; regular applications, by January 15 for fall entry, along with a $60 fee. Notification of early decision is sent December 15; regular decision, April 1. 141 early decision candidates were accepted for the 2014-2015 class. 831 applicants were on the 2014 waiting list; 5 were admitted. Applications are accepted on-line. **Transfer Students:** 5 transfer students enrolled in 2013-2014. Transfer students must be able to enter the sophomore or junior class. Admission depends mainly on the strength of college grades. A minimum GPA of 3.0 is necessary and the SAT is recommended. The equivalent of 1 year of courses must have been earned. A liberal arts curriculum is also recommended. 64 of 128 credits required for the bachelor's degree must be completed at Haverford. **International Students:** There are 66 international students enrolled. The school actively recruits these students. They must take the TOEFL with a minimum score of 600 on the paper-based TOEFL (PBT) or 100 on the Internet-based version (iBT). They must also take the SAT or ACT. Haverford requires the SAT (all 3 tests, including Writing) or the ACT plus 2 SAT subject tests.

ADMISSIONS: 25% of the 2014-2015 applicants were accepted. The SAT scores for the 2014-2015 freshman class were: Critical Reading--6% between 500 and 599, 37% between 600 and 699, and 57% between 700 and 800; Math--6% between 500 and 599, 40% between 600 and 699, and 54% between 700 and 800; Writing--5% between 500 and 599, 39% between 600 and 699, and 56% between 700 and 800. The ACT scores were 13% between 27 and 28, and 87% above 28. 98% of the current freshmen were in the top fifth of their class; 100% were in the top two fifths. **Admissions Contact:** Jess Lord, Dean of Admission & Financial Aid. E-Mail: *admission@haverford.edu* Web: *www.haverford.edu*

FINANCIAL AID: In 2014-2015, 52% of all full-time freshmen and 51% of continuing full-time students received some form of financial aid. 50% of all full-time freshmen and 49% of continuing full-time students received need-based aid. The average freshman award was $43,864. Need-based scholarships or need-based grants averaged $40,607; and need-based self-help aid (loans and jobs) averaged $3,620. 64% of undergraduate students work part-time. Haverford is a member of CSS. The CSS/Profile and FAFSA are required. The priority date for freshman financial aid applications for fall entry is February 1. The deadline for filing freshman financial aid applications for fall entry is February 1.

HOLY FAMILY UNIVERSITY (*The complete profile is made available exclusively on our website, www.barronspac.com*)

IMMACULATA UNIVERSITY	E-4
www.immaculata.edu	
Immaculata, PA 19345	**(610) 647-4400, ext. 3015**
	(877) IC-TODAY
Fax: **(610) 640-0836**	Email: **admiss@immaculata.edu**
Full-time: 327 men, 848 women	**Faculty:** 100; IIA, --$
Part-time: 284 men, 1424 women	**Ph.D.s:** 74%
Graduate: 330 men, 904 women	**Student/Faculty:** 10 to 1
Year: semesters, summer session	**Tuition:** $30,740
Room & Board: $12,260	**Freshman Class:** 1650 applied, 1314 accepted, 243 enrolled
SAT or ACT: required	**CEEB CODE:** 2320
Application Deadline: March 1	**COMPETITIVE**

Immaculata University, founded in 1920, is a private Catholic, primarily women's liberal arts and career preparation college. There is one graduate school. In addition to regional accreditation, Immaculata has baccalaureate program accreditation with ADA, AHEA, NASM, and NLN. The library contains 130,000 volumes, 1,373 microform items, 1,500 audio/video tapes/CDs/DVDs, and subscribes to 760 periodicals including electronic. Computerized library services include interlibrary loans, database searching, and Internet access. The 400-acre campus is in a suburban area 20 miles west of Philadelphia. Including any residence halls, there are 13 buildings.

STUDENT LIFE: 69% of undergraduates are from Pennsylvania.

Others are from states. 38% are from public schools. 75% are White. 76% are Catholic; 16% Protestant. The average age of freshmen is 18; all undergraduates, 22. 30% do not continue beyond their first year; 55% remain to graduate.

FACULTY/CLASSROOMS: 40% of faculty are male; 60% are female. 92% teach undergraduates. No introductory courses are taught by graduate students.

PROGRAMS OF STUDY: Immaculata confers B.A., B.S., B.Mus. and B.S.N. degrees. Associate, Master's, and Doctoral degrees are also awarded. Bachelor's degrees are awarded in BIOLOGICAL SCIENCE (biochemistry and biology/biological science), BUSINESS (accounting, banking and finance, business administration and management, and fashion merchandising), COMMUNICATIONS AND THE ARTS (English, French, music, and Spanish), COMPUTER AND PHYSICAL SCIENCE (information sciences and systems and mathematics), EDUCATION (early childhood education, elementary education, foreign languages education, home economics education, middle school education, music education, science education, and secondary education), HEALTH PROFESSIONS (music therapy, nursing, and premedicine), SOCIAL SCIENCE (dietetics, economics, experimental psychology, food science, history, international relations, prelaw, psychology, social science, sociology, and theological studies). Premedicine, education, and dietetics are the strongest academically. Education, business, and music therapy have the largest enrollments.

ACTIVITIES: There are 32 groups on campus, including art, band, choir, chorale, chorus, computers, dance, debate, drama, ethnic, honors, international, jazz band, literary magazine, musical theater, newspaper, orchestra, photography, political, professional, religious, social, social service, and student government. Popular campus events include Rose Arbor Dinner, Class Proms, and Friday's Pub.

SERVICES: Counseling and information services are available, as is tutoring in most subjects. There is a reader service for the blind, remedial math, reading, and writing.

REQUIREMENTS: The SAT or ACT is required. Candidates for admission should be graduates of an accredited secondary school with a minimum of 16 academic credits including 4 in English, 2 each in a foreign language, math, science, and social studies, 1 in history, and 4 more in college preparatory courses. The GED is accepted. An audition is required for music students, and an essay and an interview are recommended for all. A GPA of 2.0 is required. AP and CLEP credits are accepted. Important factors in the admissions decision are advanced placement or honors courses, recommendations by school officials, and extracurricular activities record.

ADMISSIONS: 80% of the 2013-2014 applicants were accepted.

FINANCIAL AID: In a recent year, 81% of all full-time freshmen and 68% of continuing full-time students received some form of financial aid. 74% of all full-time freshmen and 61% of continuing full-time students received need-based aid. The average freshman award was $16,122. Need-based scholarships or need-based grants averaged $5,907; need-based self-help aid (loans and jobs) averaged $4,274; and other non-need-based awards and non-need-based scholarships averaged $6,457. Immaculata is a member of CSS. The FAFSA is required. The priority date for freshman financial aid applications for fall entry is February 15. The deadline for filing freshman financial aid applications for fall entry is April 15.

INDIANA UNIVERSITY OF PENNSYLVANIA (*The complete profile is made available exclusively on our website, www.barronspac.com*)

JUNIATA COLLEGE   D-3
www.juniata.edu

Huntingdon, PA 16652	(814) 641-3420
	(877) JUNIATA
Fax: (814) 641-3100	Email: admissions@juniata.edu
Full-time: 713 men, 839 women	Faculty: 99; IIB, +$
Part-time: 29 men, 39 women	Ph.D.s: 95%
Graduate: 7 men, 10 women	Student/Faculty: 13 to 1
Year: semesters, summer session	Tuition: $38,630
Room & Board: $10,710	Freshman Class: 2207 applied, 1637 accepted, 423 enrolled
SAT CR/M: 570/580 ACT: recommended	
	CEEB CODE: 2341
Application Deadline: June 15	VERY COMPETITIVE

Juniata College, founded in 1876, is an independent liberal arts college. Figures in the above capsule and in this profile are approximate. In addition to regional accreditation, Juniata has baccalaureate program accreditation with CSWE and ACS. The 110-acre campus is in a small town 31 miles south of State College, in the heart of rural Pennsylvania. Including any residence halls, there are 43 buildings.

STUDENT LIFE: 59% of undergraduates are from Pennsylvania. Others are from 32 states, 44 foreign countries, and Canada. 78% are from public schools. 72% are White. 56% are Protestant; 32% Catholic. The average age of freshmen is 18; all undergraduates, 20. 12% do not continue beyond their first year; 88% remain to graduate.

Housing: 1274 students can be accommodated in college housing, which includes single-sex and coed dorms, on-campus apartments, and off-campus apartments. In addition, there are special-interest houses, and international housing. On-campus housing is guaranteed for all 4 years. 82% of students live on campus; of those, 75% remain on campus on weekends. All students may keep cars.

FACULTY/CLASSROOMS: 59% of faculty are male; 41% are female. All teach undergraduates. No introductory courses are taught by graduate students. The average class size in an introductory lecture is 19.

PROGRAMS OF STUDY: Juniata confers B.A., and B.S. degrees. Master's degrees are also awarded. Bachelor's degrees are awarded in AGRICULTURE (environmental studies), BIOLOGICAL SCIENCE (biochemistry and biology/biological science), BUSINESS (accounting, banking and finance, business administration and management, human resources, international business management, and marketing/retailing/merchandising), COMMUNICATIONS AND THE ARTS (art history and appreciation, communications, digital communications, dramatic arts, English, French, German, Russian, Spanish, and studio art), COMPUTER AND PHYSICAL SCIENCE (chemistry, computer science, geology, information sciences and systems, mathematics, and physics), EDUCATION (early childhood education, elementary education, English education, foreign languages education, mathematics education, museum studies, science education, secondary education, social studies education, and special education), ENGINEERING AND ENVIRONMENTAL DESIGN (engineering physics and environmental science), SOCIAL SCIENCE (anthropology, economics, history, international studies, peace studies, philosophy, political science/government, psychology, public administration, social work, sociology, and theological studies). Biology, psychology, and business are the strongest academically. Biology, business, and environmental studies/science have the larges enrollments.

ACTIVITIES: There are 93 groups on campus, including art, band, cheerleading, chess, choir, chorale, chorus, computers, dance, drama, environmental, ethnic, gay, honors, international, jazz band, literary magazine, musical theater, newspaper, orchestra, outing and Model UN club, photography, political, professional, radio and TV, religious, social, social service, student government, and symphony. Popular campus events include Mountain Day, Madrigal Dinner and Dance, and Spring Fest and Relay for Life. **Sports:** There are 9 intercollegiate sports for men and 10 for women, and 8 intramural sports for men and 8 for women. Facilities include 2 gyms, a swimming pool, a fitness center, 4 racquetball courts, a multipurpose fitness/dance room, a varsity football field and stadium, baseball, soccer, softball, and hockey fields, an outdoor running track, 7 tennis courts, and 1 outdoor basketball court. **Graduates:** From July 1, 2013 to June 30, 2014, 326 bachelor's degrees were awarded. The most popular majors were biology/prehealth (15%), business/accounting (12%), and psychology (10%). 122 companies recruited on campus in 2013-2014. In an average class, 72% graduate in 4 years or less, 71% graduate in 5 years or less, and 78% graduate in 6 years or less. Of the 2013 graduating class, 39% were enrolled in graduate school within 6 months of graduation, and 61% were employed.

SERVICES: Counseling and information services are available, as is tutoring in most subjects. There is a reader service for the blind. Juniata also offers courses and workshops in study, reading, and writing skills. **Library/Resources:** The library contains 505,000 volumes, 400 microform items, 2,800 audio/video tapes/CDs/DVDs, and subscribes to 11,000 periodicals including electronic. Computerized library services include interlibrary loans, database searching, Internet access, and Wi-Fi capability. Special learning facilities include an art gallery, radio station, an observatory, an environmental studies field station, a nature preserve, an early childhood education center, and a ceramics studio. **Physically Challenged Students:** 75% of the campus is accessible. Facilities include wheelchair ramps, elevators, special parking, specially equipped restrooms, and lowered drinking fountains. **Special:** Juniata offers cooperative programs in marine science, cytogenetics, cytotechnology, marine biology, biotechnology, nursing, medical technology, diagnostic imaging, occupational and physical therapy, dentistry, medicine, optometry, and podiatry. Internships, study abroad in 26 countries, Washington and Philadelphia semesters, and nondegree study are also offered. There are 3-2 engineering degrees with Columbia, Clarkson, Washington, and Pennsylvania State Universities, a 3-3 law program with Duquesne University, and various preprofessional programs, including optometry, chiropractic, medicine, dentistry, pharmacy, physician assistant, and podiatry. With the assistance of faculty advisers, most students design their own majors to meet their individual goals. There are 15 national honor societies, a freshman honors program, and 16 departmental honors programs. **Visiting:** There are regularly scheduled orientations for prospective students, including a campus tour, interviews, attend classes, meet with faculty, coaches, and, members of the financial planning staff. There are guides for informal visits, visitors may sit in on classes, and stay overnight. To schedule a visit, contact Pam Zilch, Campus Visit Coordinator at (814) 641-3428. **Campus Safety and Security:** Measures include 24-hour foot and vehicle patrol, emergency notification system, self-defense education, and security escort services. There are emergency telephones, awareness programs, fire safety training, weather alerts, terror alerts, an emergency operation plan, a firearms storage vault, vehicle lockout service, identification processing, and evacuation mapping.

REQUIREMENTS: The SAT or ACT is recommended. Candidates for admission should be graduates of an accredited secondary school and have completed 16 academic credits, including 4 in English, 2 in a foreign language, and a combination of 10 in math, social studies, and lab science. The GED is accepted, and homeschoolers are encouraged to apply. An essay is required, and an interview is recommended. A GPA of 3.0 is required. AP credits are accepted. Important factors in the admissions decision are advanced placement or honors courses, leadership record, and recommendations by school officials.Students are required to complete a minimum of 120 credit hours, including courses in fine arts, international studies, social sciences, humanities, and natural sciences, as well as 4 communications-based courses, 2 cultural analysis courses, a math and statistics course, and the college writing seminar. The total number of hours required for the program of emphasis varies from 45 to 60; majors do not exist as such, and students must develop a program of emphasis and complete it to obtain their degree. Students must have a minimum GPA of 2.0. **Procedure:** Freshmen are admitted fall and spring. Entrance exams should be taken by the January test date of the year of admission for fall entry. There are early decision, deferred admissions, and rolling admissions plans. Early decision applications should be filed by November 15; regular applications, by June 15 for fall entry; and December 1 for spring entry. Notification of early decision is sent December 23; regular decision, on a rolling basis. 79 early decision candidates were accepted for the 2014-2015 class. 40 applicants were on the 2014 waiting list; 8 were admitted. Applications are accepted on-line. Application fees are waived if application is completed online. **Transfer Students:** 23 transfer students enrolled in 2013-2014. A GPA of 2.5 is required. Applicants must submit a high school transcript, a college transcript, and an essay. SAT scores are required of some students. 30 of 120 credits required for the bachelor's degree must be completed at Juniata. **International Students:** There are 155 international students enrolled. The school actively recruits these students. They must take the TOEFL with a minimum score of 550 on the paper-based TOEFL (PBT) or 79 on the Internet-based version (iBT).

ADMISSIONS: 74% of the 2014-2015 applicants were accepted. The SAT scores for the 2014-2015 freshman class were: Critical Reading--15% below 500, 45% between 500 and 599, 31% between 600 and 699, and 10% between 700 and 800; Math--14% below 500, 48% between 500 and 599, 32% between 600 and 699, and 6% between 700 and 800. 59% of the current freshmen were in the top fifth of their class; 89% were in the top two fifths. There were 9 National

Merit finalists. 6 freshmen graduated first in their class. **Admissions Contact:** Michelle Bartol, Office of Enrollment. E-Mail: *admissions@ juniata.edu* Web: *www.juniata.edu*

FINANCIAL AID: In 2014-2015, 100% of all full-time freshmen and continuing full-time students received some form of financial aid. 86% of all full-time freshmen and 81% of continuing full-time students received need-based aid. The average freshman award was $31,877. Need-based scholarships or need-based grants averaged $26,934 ($44,750 maximum); and need-based self-help aid (loans and jobs) averaged $4,558 ($11,000 maximum). 53% of undergraduate students work part-time. Average annual earnings from campus work are $680. The average financial indebtedness of the 2014 graduate was $33,421. The FAFSA is required. The priority date for freshman financial aid applications for fall entry is February 15. The deadline for filing freshman financial aid applications for fall entry is February 15.

KEYSTONE COLLEGE (*The complete profile is made available exclusively on our website, www.barronspac.com*)

KING'S COLLEGE E-2
www.kings.edu

Wilkes Barre, PA 18711 (570) 208-5858
(888) 546-4772

Fax: (570) 208-5971	Email: admissions@kings.edu
Full-time: 975 men, 836 women	Faculty: 138; IIB, av$
Part-time: 71 men, 112 women	Ph.D.s: 86%
Graduate: 83 men, 195 women	Student/Faculty: 13 to 1
Year: semesters, summer session	Tuition: $31,816
Room & Board: $11,686	Freshman Class: 3150 applied, 2119 accepted, 484 enrolled
SAT CR/M/W: 530/490/500 ACT: 23	CEEB CODE: 2353
Application Deadline: n/av	COMPETITIVE

King's College, founded in 1946, is a private institution affiliated with the Roman Catholic Church. The college offers 35 undergraduate majors plus master's degree programs in health care administration, education with a concentration in reading, curriculum and instruction, and special education. A 5-year physician assistant program is also offered. In addition, King's College offers a 3-2 engineering degree with the University of Notre Dame. There is one graduate school. In addition to regional accreditation, King's has baccalaureate program accreditation with AACSB, NCATE, ACS, ARC-PA, and CAATE. The 48-acre campus is in an urban area in northeastern Pennsylvania 19 miles south of Scranton. Including any residence halls, there are 30 buildings.

STUDENT LIFE: 71% of undergraduates are from Pennsylvania. Others are from 20 states, and 4 foreign countries. 74% are from public schools. 79% are White. 52% are Catholic. The average age of freshmen is 18; all undergraduates, 20. 25% do not continue beyond their first year; 65% remain to graduate. **Housing:** 1121 students can be accommodated in college housing, which includes single-sex and coed dorms and on-campus apartments. On-campus housing is guaranteed for all 4 years. 51% of students live on campus; of those, 80% remain on campus on weekends. All students may keep cars.

FACULTY/CLASSROOMS: 55% of faculty are male; 45% are female. 98% teach undergraduates. No introductory courses are taught by graduate students. The average class size in an introductory lecture is 20; in a laboratory is 14; and in a regular course is 17.

PROGRAMS OF STUDY: King's confers B.A., B.S. and B.S.B.A degrees. Associate and Master's degrees are also awarded. Bachelor's degrees are awarded in AGRICULTURE (environmental studies), BIOLOGICAL SCIENCE (biology/biological science and neurosciences), BUSINESS (accounting, banking and finance, business administration and management, international business management, marketing/retailing/merchandising, and personnel management), COMMUNICATIONS AND THE ARTS (communications, dramatic arts, English, French, and Spanish), COMPUTER AND PHYSICAL SCIENCE (chemistry, computer science, information sciences and systems, mathematics, physics, and science), EDUCATION (early childhood education, elementary education, foreign languages education, middle school education, science education, secondary education, and special education), HEALTH PROFESSIONS (exercise science, medical laboratory technology, physician's assistant, predentistry, premedicine, and sports medicine), SOCIAL SCIENCE (criminal justice, economics, history, philosophy, political science/government, prelaw, psychology, sociology, and theological studies). Accounting, English, and biology are the strongest academically. Physician assistant, criminal justice, and accounting have the largest enrollments.

ACTIVITIES: There are no fraternities or sororities. There are 50 groups on campus, including art, cheerleading, choir, chorale, chorus, computers, dance, drama, environmental, ethnic, film, honors, international, jazz band, literary magazine, musical theater, newspaper, pep band, photography, political, professional, radio and TV, religious, social, social service, student government, and yearbook. Popular campus events include All College Ball, Student Activities Fair and Spring Fling. **Sports:** There are 10 intercollegiate sports for men and 9 for women, and 6 intramural sports for men and 6 for women. Facilities include a phys ed center, three multipurpose courts, fitness center, wrestling room, racquetball courts, swimming pool, multipurpose area, 2800-seat gym, free weight area, an outdoor athletic complex with a field house, multi-purpose turf for football, field hockey, soccer, and women's and men's lacrosse, grass soccer and field hockey fields as well as baseball and softball fields. **Graduates:** From July 1, 2013 to June 30, 2014, 442 bachelor's degrees were awarded. The most popular majors were education (11%), criminal justice (9%), and accounting (8%). 43 companies recruited on campus in 2013-2014. In an average class, 60% graduate in 4 years or less, 64% graduate in 5 years or less, and 65% graduate in 6 years or less. Of the 2013 graduating class, 30% were enrolled in graduate school within 6 months of graduation, and 59% were employed.

SERVICES: Counseling and information services are available, as is tutoring in every subject. The academic skills center provides a writing center, learning skills workshops, a tutoring program, and learning disability services. **Library/Resources:** The library contains 186,860 volumes, 15,920 microform items, 2,943 audio/video tapes/CDs/DVDs, and subscribes to 15,165 periodicals including electronic. Computerized library services include interlibrary loans, database searching, Internet access, and Wi-Fi capability. Special learning facilities include an art gallery, radio station, a TV studio. **Physically Challenged Students:** 99% of the campus is accessible. Facilities include wheelchair ramps, elevators, special parking, specially equipped restrooms, special class scheduling, lowered drinking fountains, lowered telephones, and special housing. **Special:** Cross-registration with Wilkes University and College Misericordia are offered. The Experiential Learning Program provides internship opportunities in all majors with a variety of employers. King's also offers study-abroad through an agreement with Webster University and John Cabot University, a Washington semester, study-abroad programs in 30 countries, an accelerated degree program in healthcare administration, B.A.-B.S. degrees in psychology, dual majors, credit for life experience, and pass/fail options on a few courses. Student-designed majors are available through the King's honors program. In addition, King's College offers a 3-2 engineering degree with the University of Notre Dame. There are 11 national honor societies and a freshman honors program. **Visiting:** There are regularly scheduled orientations for prospective students, consisting of interviews, financial aid presentations, faculty one-on-one meetings, and campus tours. There are guides for informal visits, visitors may sit in on classes, and stay overnight. To schedule a visit, contact the Admissions Office. **Campus Safety and Security:** Measures include 24-hour foot and vehicle patrol, emergency notification system, self-defense education, and security escort services. There are shuttle buses, emergency telephones, lighted pathways/sidewalks, and controlled access to dorms/residences.

REQUIREMENTS: The SAT is recommended. King's requires 16 academic credits, although 24 are recommended, including 4 in English, 3 each in science, math, and social studies, and 2 in foreign language. A GPA of 2.0 is required. AP and CLEP credits are accepted. Important factors in the admissions decision are extracurricular activities record, recommendations by school officials, and leadership

record. All students must earn a minimum of 120 credits and maintain a GPA of 2.0. The core requirements represent between 52 and 59 credits. The major comprises a maximum of 60 credits, of which up to 40 can be specified in the major department, with the balance designated for related fields. **Procedure:** Freshmen are admitted fall, spring, and summer. Entrance exams should be taken so that scores are received by April 1. There are deferred admissions and rolling admissions plans. Application deadlines are open. Application fee is $30. Notification is sent on a rolling basis. Applications are accepted on-line. **Transfer Students:** 59 transfer students enrolled in 2013-2014. Applicants must present a minimum GPA of 2.0 to 3.0. Students must have earned at least 12 credit hours at another college. An interview is recommended. 60 of 120 credits required for the bachelor's degree must be completed at King's. **International Students:** There are 13 international students enrolled. The school actively recruits these students. They must take the TOEFL with a minimum score of 530 on the paper-based TOEFL (PBT) or 71 on the Internet-based version (iBT). They must also take the SAT or ACT.

ADMISSIONS: 67% of the 2014-2015 applicants were accepted. The SAT scores for the 2014-2015 freshman class were: Critical Reading--46% below 500, 43% between 500 and 599, 10% between 600 and 699, and 1% between 700 and 800; Math--36% below 500, 42% between 500 and 599, 21% between 600 and 699, and 1% between 700 and 800; Writing--50% below 500, 39% between 500 and 599, and 12% between 600 and 699. The ACT scores were 25% below 21, 34% between 21 and 23, 23% between 24 and 26, 14% between 27 and 28, and 4% above 28. 29% of the current freshmen were in the top fifth of their class; 56% were in the top two fifths. **Admissions Contact:** James Anderson, Director of Admissions. E-Mail: *admissions@kings.edu* Web: *www.kings.edu*

FINANCIAL AID: In 2014-2015, 99% of all full-time freshmen and continuing full-time students received some form of financial aid. 88% of all full-time freshmen and 85% of continuing full-time students received need-based aid. The average freshman award was $23,692. Need-based scholarships or need-based grants averaged $17,373 ($31,416 maximum); need-based self-help aid (loans and jobs) averaged $6,076 ($10,700 maximum); and other non-need-based awards and non-need-based scholarships averaged $10,653 ($31,416 maximum). 34% of undergraduate students work part-time. Average annual earnings from campus work are $1200. The average financial indebtedness of the 2014 graduate was $33,765. King's is a member of CSS. The FAFSA and the college's own financial statement are required. The priority date for freshman financial aid applications for fall entry is February 15.

KUTZTOWN UNIVERSITY OF PENNSYLVANIA *(The complete profile is made available exclusively on our website, www.barronspac.com)*

LA ROCHE COLLEGE *(The complete profile is made available exclusively on our website, www.barronspac.com)*

LA SALLE UNIVERSITY F-3
www.lasalle.edu

Philadelphia, PA 19141	**(215) 951-1500**
	(800) 328-1910
Fax: (215) 951-1656	Email: admiss@lasalle.edu
Full-time: 1363 men, 2179 women	**Faculty:** n/av; IIA, +$
Part-time: 195 men, 672 women	**Ph.D.s:** 81%
Graduate: 620 men, 1419 women	**Student/Faculty:** 12 to 1
Year: semesters, summer session	**Tuition:** $38,200
Room & Board: $12,070	**Freshman Class:** 5405 applied, 4370 accepted, 876 enrolled
SAT CR/M: 510/510 **ACT:** 21	**CEEB CODE:** 2363
Application Deadline: April 1	**COMPETITIVE**

La Salle University is inspired by St. John Baptist de La Salle, the patron saint of teachers, and shaped by Lasallian and Catholic values. The La Salle University experience prepares students for a lifetime of personal development, service and success. La Salle University puts theory into practice by guiding each student's intellectual and spiritual development. There are 4 undergraduate schools and 24 graduate schools. In addition to regional accreditation, La Salle has baccalaureate program accreditation with AACSB, CSWE, and NLN. The 133-acre campus is in an urban area 8 miles northwest of Center City, Philadelphia. Including any residence halls, there are 55 buildings.

STUDENT LIFE: 67% of undergraduates are from Pennsylvania. Others are from 37 states, 29 foreign countries, and Canada. 50% are from public schools. 61% are White; 17% African American. 72% are Catholic; 21% Christian. The average age of freshmen is 18; all undergraduates, 21. 18% do not continue beyond their first year; 65% remain to graduate.

FACULTY/CLASSROOMS: 47% of faculty are male; 53% are female. No introductory courses are taught by graduate students. The average class size in an introductory lecture is 23; in a laboratory is 14; and in a regular course is 19.

PROGRAMS OF STUDY: La Salle confers B.A., B.S., B.S.N. and B.S.W. degrees. Associate, Master's, and Doctoral degrees are also awarded. Bachelor's degrees are awarded in BIOLOGICAL SCIENCE (biochemistry, biology/biological science, and nutrition), BUSINESS (accounting, banking and finance, business administration and management, international economics, management information systems, marketing/retailing/merchandising, and organizational behavior), COMMUNICATIONS AND THE ARTS (classical languages, communications, English, fine arts, French, German, Italian, multimedia, music, Russian, and Spanish), COMPUTER AND PHYSICAL SCIENCE (chemistry, computer science, geology, information sciences and systems, mathematics, and science), EDUCATION (elementary education, foreign languages education, science education, secondary education, social studies education, and special education), ENGINEERING AND ENVIRONMENTAL DESIGN (computer graphics and environmental science), HEALTH PROFESSIONS (nursing, preallied health, predentistry, premedicine, and speech pathology/audiology), SOCIAL SCIENCE (criminal justice, economics, history, philosophy, political science/government, prelaw, psychology, public administration, religion, social work, and sociology). Accounting, education, speech-language and hearing, and biology are the strongest academically. Nursing, communication, and biology have the largest enrollments.

ACTIVITIES: 6% of men belong to 1 local and 4 national fraternities; 18% of women belong to 1 local and 3 national sororities. There are 121 groups on campus, including art, band, cheerleading, choir, chorus, computers, dance, drama, drill team, environmental, ethnic, film, forensics, gay, honors, international, jazz band, literary magazine, musical theater, newspaper, orchestra, pep band, photography, political, professional, radio and TV, religious, social, social service, student government, and yearbook.

SERVICES: Counseling and information services are available, as is tutoring in most subjects. There is a reader service for the blind, and remedial writing. A writing center is also available. **Library/Resources:** The library contains 404,300 volumes, 9,350 microform items, and 15,800 audio/video tapes/CDs/DVDs, and subscribes to 7,450 periodicals including electronic. Computerized library services include interlibrary loans, database searching, Internet access, and Wi-Fi capability. Special learning facilities include an art gallery, radio station, TV station, La Salle University Art Museum: a collection of European and American since the Middle Ages. In addition to paintings, the Museum has a collection of Old Master prints and drawings from the 19th and 20th centuries. Collections include: illustrated rare Bibles, Japanese prints, Indian miniatures, African tribal art, pre-Columbian pottery and ancient Greek cotta pottery. La Salle 56 is a cable television station housed in the University's Communication Center. **Physically Challenged Students:** 95% of the campus is accessible. Facilities include wheelchair ramps, elevators, special parking, specially equipped restrooms, special class scheduling, lowered drinking fountains, and special housing. **Special:** Cross-registration is offered in conjunction with Chestnut Hill College, and there is a 2-2 program in allied health with Thomas Jefferson University. La Salle also offers travel study courses, study abroad in Ireland, Australia, Rome, Mexico and more, co-op programs, work-study programs, internships in most majors, dual majors, an university-honors program for gifted students, as well as a business scholars co-op program. An integrated science, business, and technology pro-

gram is offered. La Salle offers a 4-year BS/MBA in Accounting, a 5-year BA/BS/MS in Computer Science, a 5-year BA/MA in History, and a 5-year BS/MA in Speech Language Hearing Science. There are 16 national honor societies, including Phi Beta Kappa, a freshman honors program, and 2 departmental honors programs. **Visiting:** There are regularly scheduled orientations for prospective students, group Information sessions and tours are scheduled 5 days a week. Open Houses in September, October, and February. There are guides for informal visits and visitors may sit in on classes. To schedule a visit, contact the Office of Undergraduate Admissions at (215) 951-1500. **Campus Safety and Security:** Measures include 24-hour foot and vehicle patrol, emergency notification system, and security escort services. There are shuttle buses, emergency telephones, lighted pathways/sidewalks, controlled access to dorms/residences, magnetic card access to residence facilities.

REQUIREMENTS: The SAT is required. The ACT is recommended. In addition, the SAT: Subject Test in math is recommended. Applicants must be graduates of accredited secondary schools or have earned a GED. La Salle requires 16 academic units, based on 4 years of English, 3 of math, 2 of foreign language, and 1 of history, with the remaining 5 units in academic electives; science and math majors must have an additional one-half unit of math. An essay is required, and an interview is recommended. AP and CLEP credits are accepted. Important factors in the admissions decision are advanced placement or honors courses, leadership record, and recommendations by school officials.

ADMISSIONS: 81% of a recent year applicants were accepted. The SAT scores for the 2013-2014 freshman class were: Critical Reading--41% below 500, 44% between 500 and 599, 13% between 600 and 699, and 2% between 700 and 800; Math--42% below 500, 40% between 500 and 599, 14% between 600 and 699, and 3% between 700 and 800. The ACT scores were 42% below 21, 31% between 21 and 23, 13% between 24 and 26, 7% between 27 and 28, and 7% above 28. 29% of the current freshmen were in the top fifth of their class; 59% were in the top two fifths. 8 freshmen graduated first in their class.

FINANCIAL AID: In a recent year, 99% of all full-time freshmen and 96% of continuing full-time students received some form of financial aid. 85% of all full-time freshmen and 79% of continuing full-time students received need-based aid. The average freshman award was $28,841. Need-based scholarships or need-based grants averaged $26,749 ($51,670 maximum); need-based self-help aid (loans and jobs) averaged $3,967 ($6,800 maximum); and non-need-based athletic scholarships averaged $16,610 ($50,270 maximum). 7% of undergraduate students work part-time. Average annual earnings from campus work are $4000. The average financial indebtedness of the 2013 graduate was $37,903. The FAFSA is required. The deadline for filing freshman financial aid applications for fall entry is February 15.

LAFAYETTE COLLEGE

F-3

www.lafayette.edu

Easton, PA 18042	
	(610) 330-5000
	(610) 330-5100
Fax: (610) 330-5355	Email: hydem@lafayette.edu
Full-time: 1293 men, 1153 women	Faculty: 224; IIB, ++$
Part-time: 37 men, 20 women	Ph.D.s: 96%
Graduate: n/av	Student/Faculty: 10 to 1
Year: semesters, summer session	Tuition: $45,635
Room & Board: $13,520	Freshman Class: 7796 applied, 2319 accepted, 648 enrolled
SAT CR/M/W: 630/670/635 ACT: 29	CEEB CODE: 2361
Application Deadline: January 15	HIGHLY COMPETITIVE+

Lafayette College, founded in 1826, is a highly selective private, exclusively undergraduate college, emphasizing the liberal arts, sciences, and engineering. Figures in the above capsule and in this profile are approximate. In addition to regional accreditation, Lafayette has baccalaureate program accreditation with ABET and ACS. The 342-acre campus is in a suburban area 70 miles west of New York City, off

Interstate 78 and US 22. Including any residence halls, there are 81 buildings.

STUDENT LIFE: 80% of undergraduates are from out of state, mostly the Middle Atlantic. Students are from 45 states, 47 foreign countries, and Canada. 62% are from public schools. 68% are White. 33% are Catholic; 20% Protestant; 18% claim no religious affiliation. The average age of freshmen is 18; all undergraduates, 20. 7% do not continue beyond their first year; 90% remain to graduate. **Housing:** 2308 students can be accommodated in college housing, which includes single-sex and coed dorms, on-campus apartments, and off-campus apartments. In addition, there are honors houses, special-interest houses, fraternity houses, sorority houses, Diversity-oriented houses, arts houses, a black cultural center, and language and special-interest floors. On-campus housing is guaranteed for all 4 years. 93% of students live on campus; of those, 98% remain on campus on weekends. Upperclassmen may keep cars.

FACULTY/CLASSROOMS: 63% of faculty are male; 37% are female. All teach and do research. No introductory courses are taught by graduate students. The average class size in a laboratory is 12 and in a regular course is 17.

PROGRAMS OF STUDY: Lafayette confers A.B., and B.S. degrees. Bachelor's degrees are awarded in BIOLOGICAL SCIENCE (biochemistry, biology/biological science, and neurosciences), BUSINESS (business economics and international economics), COMMUNICATIONS AND THE ARTS (art, English, French, German, music, and Spanish), COMPUTER AND PHYSICAL SCIENCE (chemistry, computer science, geology, mathematics, and physics), ENGINEERING AND ENVIRONMENTAL DESIGN (chemical engineering, civil engineering, electrical/electronics engineering, engineering, and mechanical engineering), SOCIAL SCIENCE (African studies, American studies, anthropology, Asian/Oriental studies, economics, history, interdisciplinary studies, international relations, philosophy, political science/government, prelaw, psychology, religion, Russian and Slavic studies, and sociology). Social sciences, engineering, and biological life sciences are the strongest academically. Economics, mechanical engineering, and biology have the largest enrollments.

ACTIVITIES: 17% of men belong to 4 national fraternities; 35% of women belong to 6 national sororities. There are 250 groups on campus, including art, band, cheerleading, chess, choir, chorale, chorus, computers, dance, debate, drama, environmental, ethnic, film, forensics, gay, honors, international, jazz band, literary magazine, musical theater, newspaper, orchestra, pep band, photography, political, professional, radio and TV, religious, social, social service, and student government. Popular campus events include 1,000 Nights, Block pARTy, Rivalry Week, Earth Day, International Extravaganza, and Presidential Ball. **Sports:** There are 11 intercollegiate sports for men and 11 for women, and 18 intramural sports for men and 18 for women. Facilities include an 14,000-seat stadium, sports center containing a 2644-seat arena, a field house, varsity house, a natatorium, fitness center, 2 exercise rooms, weight training room, outdoor track, indoor track, climbing wall, 6 racquet courts, and 3 multipurpose courts. In addition, there is a 230-acre athletic complex for outdoor track lacrosse, field hockey, soccer, and baseball. **Graduates:** From July 1, 2013 to June 30, 2014, 614 bachelor's degrees were awarded. The most popular majors were social sciences (34%), engineering (16%), and biological life sciences (10%). 83 companies recruited on campus in 2013-2014. In an average class, 88% graduate in 4 years or less, 90% graduate in 5 years or less, and 90% graduate in 6 years or less. Of the 2013 graduating class, 22% were enrolled in graduate school within 6 months of graduation, and 72% were employed.

SERVICES: Counseling and information services are available, as is tutoring in most subjects, most 100-level and many 200-level classes. **Library/Resources:** The 2 libraries contain 510,000 volumes, 120,000 microform items, and subscribe to 2,600 periodicals including electronic. Computerized library services include interlibrary loans, database searching, Internet access, and Wi-Fi capability. Special learning facilities include an art gallery, radio station, a geological museum, foreign languages lab, and calculus lab. **Physically Challenged Students:** 95% of the campus is accessible. Facilities include wheelchair ramps, elevators, special parking, specially equipped restrooms, special class scheduling, lowered drinking fountains, and lowered telephones. **Special:** Cross-registration is available through the Lehigh

Valley Association of Independent Colleges, internships in all academic departments, study abroad in 3 countries as well as through other individually arranged plans, a Washington semester at American University, and work-study programs with area employers are possible. An accelerated degree plan in all majors, dual and student-designed majors, 5-year dual-degree programs, and pass/fail options in any non major subject also are available. There are 12 national honor societies, including Phi Beta Kappa, and 24 departmental honors programs. **Visiting:** There are regularly scheduled orientations for prospective students, student visits include student/faculty panel discussions, tours, and departmental open houses. There are guides for informal visits, visitors may sit in on classes, and stay overnight. To schedule a visit, contact Patricia Lorenz at (610) 330-5100. **Campus Safety and Security:** Measures include 24-hour foot and vehicle patrol, emergency notification system, self-defense education, and security escort services. There are shuttle buses, emergency telephones, lighted pathways/sidewalks, controlled access to dorms/residences, Advisers in all residence halls, residence hall lock down from 8 p.m. to 7 a.m.

REQUIREMENTS: The SAT or ACT is required. The ACT Optional Writing test is also required. Applicants should have taken 4 years of English, 3 of math (4 for science or engineering majors), 2 each of a foreign language and lab science (with physics and chemistry for science or engineering students), and at least an additional 5 units in academic subjects. An essay is required and an interview recommended. Evaluations from the secondary school counselor and a teacher are required. The GED is accepted. AP credits are accepted. Important factors in the admissions decision are advanced placement or honors courses, leadership record, evidence of special talent, extracurricular activities record, ability to finance college education, parents or siblings attended your school, personality/intangible qualities, and geographical diversity.To graduate, students must maintain a GPA of 2.0, and take a minimum of 32 to 36 courses (36 for engineering). The common course of study, designed to build a background in the liberal arts and sciences includes interdisciplinary seminars, a course in humanities, social science, natural science with a lab,and quantitative reasoning. Students must take 2 courses dealing with global and multicultural issues, and must demonstrate elementary proficiency in a foreign language (typically 2 courses). A Science and Technology in a Social Context requirement can be met by taking two classes designated as STSC outside of the student's home division. Finally, student must take one course that explores values in society and four writing intensive courses. **Procedure:** Freshmen are admitted fall. Entrance exams should be taken by January of the senior year. There are early decision, early admissions, and deferred admissions plans. Early decision applications should be filed by November 15; regular applications, by January 15 for fall entry, along with a $65 fee. Notification of early decision is sent December 15; regular decision, April 1. 323 early decision candidates were accepted for the 2014-2015 class. 464 applicants were on the 2014 waiting list; 37 were admitted. Applications are accepted on-line. **Transfer Students:** 11 transfer students enrolled in 2013-2014. Acceptance usually depends on college-level performance and achievements. An interview is required if the student lives within 200 miles of the college. No minimum GPA is required, and neither the SAT nor the ACT is needed. The number of credit hours required varies with the program, but usually enough for freshman status with advanced standing is needed. Typically, Lafayette will enroll about 20 transfers in the fall and about 5 in the spring of each year. 16 of 32 credits required for the bachelor's degree must be completed at Lafayette. **International Students:** There are 196 international students enrolled. The school actively recruits these students. They must take the TOEFL with a minimum score of 513 on the paper-based TOEFL (PBT) or 80 on the Internet-based version (iBT) and the Comprehensive English Language Test. They must also take the SAT or ACT.

ADMISSIONS: 30% of the 2014-2015 applicants were accepted. The SAT scores for the 2014-2015 freshman class were: Critical Reading--4% below 500, 28% between 500 and 599, 52% between 600 and 699, and 16% between 700 and 800; Math--1% below 500, 16% between 500 and 599, 51% between 600 and 699, and 32% between 700 and 800; Writing--4% below 500, 21% between 500 and 599, 55% between 600 and 699, and 20% between 700 and 800. The ACT scores were 3% below 21, % between 21 and 23, % between 24 and 26, %

between 27 and 28, and 43% above 28. 88% of the current freshmen were in the top fifth of their class; 97% were in the top two fifths. There were 2 National Merit finalists. 12 freshmen graduated first in their class. **Admissions Contact:** Matthew Hyde, Director of Admissions. E-Mail: *hydem@lafayette.edu* Web: *www.lafayette.edu*

FINANCIAL AID: In 2014-2015, 55% of all full-time freshmen and 62% of continuing full-time students received some form of financial aid. 35% of all full-time freshmen and 43% of continuing full-time students received need-based aid. The average freshman award was $42,316. Need-based scholarships or need-based grants averaged $35,381 ($63,100 maximum); need-based self-help aid (loans and jobs) averaged $5,107 ($7,000 maximum); non-need-based athletic scholarships averaged $36,274 ($60,738 maximum); other non-need-based awards and non-need-based scholarships averaged $12,991 ($45,230 maximum); and $11,114 from other forms of aid. 47% of undergraduate students work part-time. Average annual earnings from campus work are $1468. The average financial indebtedness of the 2014 graduate was $27,497. Lafayette is a member of CSS. The CSS/Profile, FAFSA, and the college's own financial statement, and the Business/Farm supplement, and Divorce/Separation parent statement (if applicable) are required. are required. The priority date for freshman financial aid applications for fall entry is January 15. The deadline for filing freshman financial aid applications for fall entry is March 1.

LEBANON VALLEY COLLEGE E-3
www.lvc.edu

Annville, PA 17003	(717) 867-6181
	(866) LVC-4ADM
Fax: (717) 867-6026	Email: admission@lvc.edu
Full-time: 699 men, 883 women	Faculty: 100; IIB, av$
Part-time: 63 men, 102 women	Ph.D.s: 88%
Graduate: 126 men, 172 women	Student/Faculty: 16 to 1
Year: semesters, summer session	Tuition: $30,490
Room & Board: $8080	Freshman Class: 1698 applied, 1368 accepted, 378 enrolled
SAT CR/M/W: 540/560/530 ACT: 22	CEEB CODE: 2364
Application Deadline: n/av	COMPETITIVE

Founded in 1866, Lebanon Valley College is a private institution that offers 34 major fields of study, where students can develop their own individualized major. LVC offers graduate programs in physical therapy, business, music education, and science education. Figures in the above capsule and in this profile are approximate. There are no undergraduate schools. In addition to regional accreditation, LVC has baccalaureate program accreditation with NASM and CAPTE. The 340-acre campus is in a small town 6 miles east of Hershey, PA. Including any residence halls, there are 53 buildings.

STUDENT LIFE: 80% of undergraduates are from Pennsylvania. Others are from 23 states, 3 foreign countries, and Canada. 94% are from public schools. 92% are White. **Female To Male Ratio:** 1.3:1. The average age of freshmen is 18; all undergraduates, 20. 14% do not continue beyond their first year; 71% remain to graduate. **Housing:** 1292 students can be accommodated in college housing, which includes single-sex and coed dorms and on-campus apartments. In addition, there are special-interest houses. On-campus housing is guaranteed for all 4 years. 74% of students live on campus; of those, 60% remain on campus on weekends. All students may keep cars.

FACULTY/CLASSROOMS: 63% of faculty are male; 37% are female. 90% teach undergraduates. No introductory courses are taught by graduate students. The average class size in an introductory lecture is 23; in a laboratory is 14; and in a regular course is 19.

PROGRAMS OF STUDY: LVC confers B.A., B.S., B.M., B.S.Ch. and B.S.Med.Tech. degrees. Associate, master's, and doctoral degrees are also awarded. Bachelor's degrees are awarded in BIOLOGICAL SCIENCE (biochemistry and biology/biological science), BUSINESS (accounting and business administration and management), COMMUNICATIONS AND THE ARTS (art, audio technology, communications technology, English, French, German, music, music business

management, and Spanish), COMPUTER AND PHYSICAL SCIENCE (actuarial science, chemistry, computer science, mathematics, and physics), EDUCATION (early childhood education, elementary education, music education, and special education), HEALTH PROFESSIONS (health, health care administration, and medical laboratory technology), SOCIAL SCIENCE (American studies, criminal justice, economics, history, philosophy, political science/government, psychobiology, psychology, religion, and sociology). Actuarial science, natural sciences, and education are the strongest academically. Education, business, and natural sciences are the largest.

ACTIVITIES: 9% of men and 1 of women belong to 2 local and 2 national fraternities; 9% of women belong to 1 local and 3 national sororities. There are 85 groups on campus, including and music ensembles., art, band, cheerleading, choir, chorus, concert band, drama, ethnic, gay, honors, international, jazz band, literary magazine, marching band, musical theater, newspaper, orchestra, political, professional, radio and TV, religious, social, social service, student government, and symphony. Popular campus events include Christmas at the Valley, Valley Festival, and Dutchmen Day. **Sports:** There are 12 intercollegiate sports for men and 11 for women, and 12 intramural sports for men and 12 for women. Facilities include a 3000-seat stadium, a sports center, more than 60 acres of athletic fields, indoor and outdoor tracks, a 1660 seat gym, playing courts for basketball, handball, squash, and tennis, a 500-seat baseball grandstand, and a football field. **Graduates:** From July 1, 2013 to June 30, 2014, 424 bachelor's degrees were awarded. The most popular majors were education (17%), business administration (14%), and social science (11%). 65 companies recruited on campus in 2013-2014. In an average class, 68% graduate in 4 years or less, 75% graduate in 5 years or less, and 76% graduate in 6 years or less. Of the 2013 graduating class, 26% were enrolled in graduate school within 6 months of graduation, and 82% were employed.

SERVICES: Counseling and information services are available, as is tutoring in every subject. There is a reader service for the blind. **Library/Resources:** The library contains 203,335 volumes, 15,485 microform items, and 17,827 audio/video tapes/CDs/DVDs, and subscribes to 792 periodicals including electronic. Computerized library services include interlibrary loans, database searching, Internet access, and Wi-Fi capability. Special learning facilities include an art gallery and radio station. **Physically Challenged Students:** 80% of the campus is accessible. Facilities include wheelchair ramps, elevators, special parking, specially equipped restrooms, special class scheduling, lowered drinking fountains, lowered telephones, and special housing. **Special:** Study abroad opportunities are available in Argentina, Australia, England, France, Italy, Germany, Greece, Sweden, Spain, the Netherlands, and New Zealand. There are also 2 off-campus domestic programs in Philadelphia and Washingtgon, D.C. There are 3-2 degree programs in engineering with Penn State University and Case Western Reserve, and in forestry with Duke University. There is also a 2-2 degree program in allied health sciences with Thomas Jefferson University. LVC offers internships in a number of areas. There are 6 national honor societies and 11 departmental honors programs. **Visiting:** There are regularly scheduled orientations for prospective students, visiting students can take tours, and schedule interviews and meetings with professors. There are guides for informal visits and visitors may sit in on classes. To schedule a visit, contact the Director of Admission. **Campus Safety and Security:** Measures include 24-hour foot and vehicle patrol, self-defense education, and security escort services. There are emergency telephones and lighted pathways/sidewalks.

REQUIREMENTS: The SAT is required. The ACT Optional Writing test is also required. In addition, Applicants must be graduates of an accredited secondary school or have earned a GED. LVC requires 16 academic units or 16 Carnegie units, including 4 in English, 2 each in math and foreign language, and 1 each in science and social studies. An interview is recommended. Students applying as music majors must audition. AP and CLEP credits are accepted. Important factors in the admissions decision are advanced placement or honors courses, leadership record, and personality/intangible qualities.The general education program consists of course work in these areas: communications, liberal studies, foreign studies, social diversity studies, and disciplinary perspectives. Students are required to complete 3 writing process courses, and be proficient in computer applications and modes of information access and retrieval. To graduate, students must complete at least 120 credit hours, 2 units of phys ed, and the requirements for the major with a minimum cumulative GPA of 2.0. **Procedure:** Freshmen are admitted fall and spring. There is a rolling admissions plan. Application deadlines are open. Application fee is $30. Notifications are sent October 15. Applications are accepted on-line. **Transfer Students:** 49 transfer students enrolled in 2013-2014. Requirements for transfer applicants include a minimum GPA of 2.0, SAT scores, and an interview. 30 of 120 credits required for the bachelor's degree must be completed at LVC. **International Students:** There are 9 international students enrolled. They must take the TOEFL with a minimum score of 550 on the paper-based TOEFL (PBT) or 80 on the Internet-based version (iBT).

ADMISSIONS: 81% of the 2014-2015 applicants were accepted. The SAT scores for the 2014-2015 freshman class were: Critical Reading--31% below 500, 48% between 500 and 599, 19% between 600 and 699, and 3% between 700 and 800; Math--24% below 500, 41% between 500 and 599, 32% between 600 and 699, and 4% between 700 and 800; Writing--36% below 500, 43% between 500 and 599, 20% between 600 and 699, and 1% between 700 and 800. The ACT scores were 35% below 21, 23% between 21 and 23, 28% between 24 and 26, 8% between 27 and 28, and 6% above 28. 54% of the current freshmen were in the top fifth of their class; 75% were in the top two fifths. 9 freshmen graduated first in their class. **Admissions Contact:** Susan Jones, Director of Admission. E-Mail: *admission@lvc.edu* Web: *www.lvc.edu*

FINANCIAL AID: In 2014-2015, 99% of all full-time freshmen and 98% of continuing full-time students received some form of financial aid. 85% of all full-time freshmen and 80% of continuing full-time students received need-based aid. The average freshman award was $24,801. Need-based scholarships or need-based grants averaged $20,015 ($22,945 maximum); need-based self-help aid (loans and jobs) averaged $5,597 ($9,250 maximum); and other non-need-based awards and non-need-based scholarships averaged $12,684 ($29,780 maximum). 48% of undergraduate students work part-time. Average annual earnings from campus work are $1071. The average financial indebtedness of the 2014 graduate was $27,319. LVC is a member of CSS. The FAFSA and the college's own financial statement are required. The priority date for freshman financial aid applications for fall entry is March 1.

LEHIGH UNIVERSITY   F-3
www.lehigh.edu

Bethlehem, PA 18015   (610) 758-3000

Fax: (610) 758-4361   Email: admissions@lehigh.edu
Full-time: 2752 men, 2232 women   Faculty: 473; I, +$
Part-time: 50 men, 28 women   Ph.D.s: 96%
Graduate: 1138 men, 919 women   Student/Faculty: 10 to 1
Year: semesters, summer session   Tuition: $44,890
Room & Board: $11,880   Freshman Class: 11512
                                   applied, 3945 accepted,
                                   1299 enrolled
SAT CR/M: 630/680 ACT: 30   CEEB CODE: 2365
Application Deadline: January 1   **MOST COMPETITIVE**

Lehigh University, founded in 1865, is a private research university offering both undergraduate and graduate programs in liberal arts, sciences, business, education, and engineering. Our students experience interesting, independent research, and work closely with faculty who offer their time and attention to hands-on projects, internships, and innovative studies. There are 3 undergraduate schools and 4 graduate schools. In addition to regional accreditation, Lehigh has baccalaureate program accreditation with AACSB, ABET, and NCATE. The 2355-acre campus is in a suburban area 50 miles north of Philadelphia and 75 miles southwest of New York City. Including any residence halls, there are 169 buildings.

STUDENT LIFE: 73% of undergraduates are from out of state, mostly the Middle Atlantic. Students are from 48 states, 63 foreign countries, and Canada. 67% are White. The average age of freshmen is 18; all undergraduates, 20. 4% do not continue beyond their first year; 86% remain to graduate. **Housing:** 3317 students can be accommodated in college housing, which includes coed dorms, on-campus apartments, and married student housing. In addition, there are special-interest houses, fraternity houses, sorority houses, Substance free housing, UMOJA house, and an ROTC house. On-campus housing is guaranteed for the freshman year only, is available on a first-come, first-served basis, and is available on a lottery system for upperclassmen. 67% of students live on campus; of those, 85% remain on campus on weekends. Upperclassmen may keep cars.

FACULTY/CLASSROOMS: 64% of faculty are male; 36% are female. All teach and do research. No introductory courses are taught by graduate students. The average class size in a regular course is 28.

PROGRAMS OF STUDY: Lehigh confers B.A., and B.S. degrees. Master's and Doctoral degrees are also awarded. Bachelor's degrees are awarded in AGRICULTURE (environmental studies), BIOLOGICAL SCIENCE (biochemistry, biology/biological science, and molecular biology), BUSINESS (accounting, business economics, business information systems, finance, marketing, management & strategic leadership, and supply chain management), COMMUNICATIONS AND THE ARTS (art, art history and appreciation, Chinese, classics, design, English, French, German, journalism, music, music theory and composition, Spanish, and theater design), COMPUTER AND PHYSICAL SCIENCE (applied mathematics, applied science, astronomy, astrophysics, chemistry, computer science, earth science, mathematics, physics, science technology, and statistics), ENGINEERING AND ENVIRONMENTAL DESIGN (architecture, bioengineering, chemical engineering, civil engineering, computer engineering, electrical/electronics engineering, engineering mechanics, engineering physics, environmental engineering, environmental science, industrial engineering, materials science and engineering, and mechanical engineering), HEALTH PROFESSIONS (pharmaceutical chemistry, predentistry, premedicine, and preoptometry), SOCIAL SCIENCE (African studies, anthropology, Asian/Oriental studies, behavioral science, classical/ancient civilization, cognitive science, economics, (Social Science) Global Studies, history, interdisciplinary studies, international relations, philosophy, political science/government, psychology, religion, social psychology, sociology, and women's studies). Finance, mechanical engineering, and marketing have the largest enrollments.

ACTIVITIES: 40% of men belong to 20 national fraternities; 45% of women belong to 11 national sororities. There are 150 groups on campus, including art, band, cheerleading, chess, choir, chorale, chorus, computers, dance, debate, drama, environmental, ethnic, gay, honors, international, jazz band, literary magazine, marching band, musical theater, newspaper, orchestra, pep band, photography, political, professional, radio and TV, religious, social, social service, student government, symphony, and yearbook. Popular campus events include Spirit Week, Spring Fling, International Week, Move Out Collection Drive, and Great South Side Sale. **Sports:** There are 12 intercollegiate sports for men and 13 for women, and 14 intramural sports for men and 14 for women. Facilities include a 16,000-seat stadium, 6500-seat arena, a gym, champion cross-country course, field house with basketball, tennis courts, swimming pools, a track, indoor squash and racquetball courts, playing fields including astro-turf for field hockey, football, lacrosse, and soccer, weight rooms, fitness center, climbing wall, indoor tennis center, and golf range (driving/chipping/putting). **Graduates:** From July 1, 2013 to June 30, 2014, 1172 bachelor's degrees were awarded. The most popular majors were finance (12%), mechanical engineering (9%), and marketing (5%). 260 companies recruited on campus in 2013-2014. In an average class, 1% graduate in 3 years or less, 76% graduate in 4 years or less, 86% graduate in 5 years or less, and 87% graduate in 6 years or less. Of the 2013 graduating class, 29% were enrolled in graduate school within 6 months of graduation, and 66% were employed.

SERVICES: Counseling and information services are available, as is tutoring in most subjects, including calculus, physics, English, accounting, finance, and economics. There is a reader service for the blind. Tutoring is available upon request. Also, there are special programs for students with learning disabilities and English as a second language. **Library/Resources:** The 2 libraries contain 1.2 million volumes, 1.6 million microform items, 12,543 audio/video tapes/CDs/DVDs, and subscribe to 54,969 periodicals including electronic. Computerized library services include interlibrary loans, database searching, Internet access, and Wi-Fi capability. Special learning facilities include an art gallery, radio station, TV station, special collections/rare book reading room, digital media studio, financial services lab, and international multimedia resource center. **Physically Challenged Students:** Facilities include wheelchair ramps, elevators, special parking, specially equipped restrooms, special class scheduling, lowered drinking fountains, lowered telephones, and special housing. **Special:** Lehigh offers many interdisciplinary programs including Integrated Product Development, Computer Science and Business, Integrated Business and Engineering, Integrated Degree in Engineering, Arts and Sciences, Global Citizenship, Lehigh Earth Observatory, and South Mountain College, Lehigh's residential academic program. The university offers co-op programs, cross-registration with the Lehigh Valley Association of Independent Colleges, many combinations of dual majors, study abroad programs in 40 countries, internships, a Washington semester, work-study, a 7-year BA/MD program with Drexel University College of Medicine, a 7-year BA/OD program with SUNY Optometry and a 7-year BA/DMD program with the School of Dental Medicine at the University of Pennsylvania. There are 18 national honor societies, including Phi Beta Kappa, and a freshman honors program. **Visiting:** There are regularly scheduled orientations for prospective students, including group information sessions and tours scheduled Monday through Friday, and some Saturdays, as well as special events and open houses. There are guides for informal visits, visitors may sit in on classes, and stay overnight. To schedule a visit, contact the Office of Admissions. **Campus Safety and Security:** Measures include 24-hour foot and vehicle patrol, emergency notification system, self-defense education, and security escort services. There are shuttle buses, emergency telephones, lighted pathways/sidewalks, controlled access to dorms/residences, and LU-alert text messaging system.

REQUIREMENTS: The SAT or ACT is required. The ACT Optional Writing test is also required. Candidates for admission should have completed 4 years of English, 3 years of math and electives, and 2 years each of a foreign language, science, and social science. Most students present 4 years each of science, math, and English. Opportunities for an on-campus interview are made available to prospective students but are not required. Interviews are by appointment only. AP credits are accepted. Important factors in the admissions decision are advanced placement or honors courses, recommendations by school officials, evidence of special talent, and extracurricular activities record. Graduation requirements vary by degree sought, but all students must complete 2 semesters of English, at least 30 credits in the chosen major, and a minimum of 121 credit hours. Students must also maintain a minimum GPA of 2.0. **Procedure:** Freshmen are admitted fall and spring. Entrance exams should be taken by the January test date. There are early decision, early admissions, and deferred admissions plans. Early decision applications should be filed by November 15; regular applications, by January 1 for fall entry; and November 1 for spring entry. The fall 2014 application fee was $70. Notification of early decision is sent December 15; regular decision, April 1. 614 early decision candidates were accepted for the 2014-2015 class. 1296 applicants were on the 2014 waiting list; 2 were admitted. Applications are accepted on-line. **Transfer Students:** 29 transfer students enrolled in 2013-2014. Transfer candidates should have a minimum GPA of 3.25 and submit high school and college transcripts, an essay, and a statement of good standing from previous institutions. 30 of 121 credits required for the bachelor's degree must be completed at Lehigh. **International Students:** There are 376 international students enrolled. The school actively recruits these students. They must take the TOEFL with a minimum score of 570 on the paper-based TOEFL (PBT) or 90 on the Internet-based version (iBT). They must also take the SAT or ACT.

ADMISSIONS: 34% of the 2014-2015 applicants were accepted. The SAT scores for the 2014-2015 freshman class were: Critical Reading--3% below 500, 27% between 500 and 599, 56% between 600 and 699, and 14% between 700 and 800; Math--1% below 500, 11% between 500 and 599, 44% between 600 and 699, and 44% between 700 and 800. 85% of the current freshmen were in the top fifth of their class; 96% were in the top two fifths. 29 freshmen graduated first in their class. **Admissions Contact:** Bruce Bunnick, Director of Admissions. E-Mail: *admissions@lehigh.edu* Web: *www.lehigh.edu*

FINANCIAL AID: In 2014-2015, 40% of all full-time freshmen and

41% of continuing full-time students received some form of financial aid. 39% of all full-time freshmen and 40% of continuing full-time students received need-based aid. The average freshman award was $36,551. Need-based scholarships or need-based grants averaged $31,819; need-based self-help aid (loans and jobs) averaged $5,270; non-need-based athletic scholarships averaged $40,409; and other non-need-based awards and non-need-based scholarships averaged $15,235. 32% of undergraduate students work part-time. Average annual earnings from campus work are $1267. The average financial indebtedness of the 2014 graduate was $31,877. Lehigh is a member of CSS. The CSS/Profile and FAFSA, and noncustodial profile, and business/farm supplement are required. The deadline for filing freshman financial aid applications for fall entry is February 15.

LOCK HAVEN UNIVERSITY OF PENNSYLVANIA *(The complete profile is made available exclusively on our website, www. barronspac.com)*

LYCOMING COLLEGE D-2
www.lycoming.edu

| Williamsport, PA 17701 | (570) 321-4026 |
| | (800) 345-3920 |

Fax: (570) 321-4317	Email: admissions@lycoming.edu
Full-time: 621 men, 710 women	Faculty: 82; IIB, -$
Part-time: 9 men, 17 women	Ph.D.s: 95%
Graduate: n/av	Student/Faculty: 14 to 1
Year: semesters, summer session	Tuition: $34,706
Room & Board: $10,376	Freshman Class: 1782 applied, 1287 accepted, 394 enrolled
SAT CR/M/W: 520/520/490 ACT: 22	CEEB CODE: 2372
Application Deadline: March 1	COMPETITIVE

Lycoming College, established in 1812, is a private, residential, liberal arts institution affiliated with the United Methodist Church. In addition to regional accreditation, Lycoming has baccalaureate program accreditation with AACSB. The 35-acre campus is in a small town in north central Pennsylvania. Including any residence halls, there are 25 buildings.

STUDENT LIFE: 66% of undergraduates are from Pennsylvania. Others are from 27 states, and 16 foreign countries. 81% are from public schools. 76% are White. 26% are Protestant; 20% Catholic. The average age of freshmen is 18; all undergraduates, 20. 18% do not continue beyond their first year; 64% remain to graduate. **Housing:** 1201 students can be accommodated in college housing, which includes single-sex and coed dorms, on-campus apartments, and off-campus apartments. In addition, there are special-interest houses, and nonsmoking and Greek floors. On-campus housing is guaranteed for all 4 years. 87% of students live on campus; of those, 75% remain on campus on weekends. All students may keep cars.

FACULTY/CLASSROOMS: 56% of faculty are male; 44% are female. All teach undergraduates. No introductory courses are taught by graduate students. The average class size in an introductory lecture is 24 and in a laboratory is 16.

PROGRAMS OF STUDY: Lycoming confers B.A., and B.S. degrees. Bachelor's degrees are awarded in BIOLOGICAL SCIENCE (biology/biological science), BUSINESS (accounting and business administration and management), COMMUNICATIONS AND THE ARTS (art, art history and appreciation, communications, digital communications, dramatic arts, English, French, German, literature, music, Spanish, studio art, and theatre acting), COMPUTER AND PHYSICAL SCIENCE (actuarial mathematics, astronomy, astrophysics, chemistry, mathematics, and physics), SOCIAL SCIENCE (American studies, anthropology, archeology, criminal justice, criminology, economics, history, international studies, philosophy, political science/government, psychology, religion, sociology, women and gender studies). Archaeology, creative writing, and astrophysics are the strongest academically. Business, psychology, and biology have the largest enrollments.

ACTIVITIES: 12% of men belong to 5 national fraternities; 20% of

women belong to 3 local and 2 national sororities. There are 62 groups on campus, including art, band, cheerleading, choir, chorus, computers, dance, drama, environmental, ethnic, film, gay, honors, international, jazz band, literary magazine, musical theater, newspaper, orchestra, pep band, photography, political, professional, radio and TV, religious, social, social service, student government, and yearbook. Popular campus events include Campus Carnival, Annual Christmas Candlelight Service and Choir Concert. **Sports:** There are 9 intercollegiate sports for men and 8 for women, and 7 intramural sports for men and 5 for women. Facilities include an outdoor softball, football, soccer, and lacrosse complex, indoor basketball courts, weight and exercise rooms, indoor pool, and intramural fields. **Graduates:** From July 1, 2013 to June 30, 2014, 268 bachelor's degrees were awarded. The most popular majors were business/marketing (19%), social sciences (13%), and biological/life sciences (12%). 9 companies recruited on campus in 2013-2014. In an average class, 52% graduate in 4 years or less, 61% graduate in 5 years or less, and 62% graduate in 6 years or less. Of the 2013 graduating class, 20% were enrolled in graduate school within 6 months of graduation.

SERVICES: Counseling and information services are available, as is tutoring in every subject. There is remedial math, reading, and writing. **Library/Resources:** The library contains 325,211 volumes, 201,601 microform items, 1,200 audio/video tapes/CDs/DVDs, and subscribes to 53,000 periodicals including electronic. Computerized library services include interlibrary loans, database searching, Internet access, and Wi-Fi capability. Special learning facilities include an art gallery, planetarium, radio station, and TV station. **Physically Challenged Students:** 85% of the campus is accessible. Facilities include wheelchair ramps, elevators, special parking, specially equipped restrooms, special class scheduling, lowered drinking fountains, lowered telephones, and special housing. **Special:** Cooperative programs are available with the Ohio and Pennsylvania Colleges of Podiatric Medicine, Pennsylvania College of Optometry, and Penn State and Duke Universities. Cross-registration is available with the Pennsylvania College of Technology. More than 200 internships, including teacher programs, study abroad in 7 countries, and a Washington semester at American University are available. Lycoming offers work-study programs, dual and student-designed majors, and an accelerated degree program in conjunction with the college's Scholar Program in optometry, podiatric medicine, and dentistry. Nondegree study and pass/fail grading options are available. There are 24 national honor societies, a freshman honors program, and 35 departmental honors programs. **Visiting:** There are regularly scheduled orientations for prospective students, consisting of a student-guided tour of campus and an interview with an admissions counselor. Meetings with professors and coaches and attending a class are possible upon request. There are guides for informal visits, visitors may sit in on classes, and stay overnight. To schedule a visit, contact Barb Carlin at admissions@lycoming.edu. **Campus Safety and Security:** Measures include 24-hour foot and vehicle patrol, emergency notification system, self-defense education, and security escort services. There are emergency telephones, lighted pathways/sidewalks, and controlled access to dorms/residences.

REQUIREMENTS: The SAT or ACT is recommended. Applicants must graduate from an accredited secondary school or have a GED. They must have earned 16 academic units including a minimum of 4 years of English, 3 each of math and social studies, and 2 each of lab science, a foreign language, and academic electives. 2 personal letters of recommendation are required. Admissions interview is recommended. Portfolios and auditions may be required for students seeking scholarships in the arts. A GPA of 2.3 is required. AP and CLEP credits are accepted. Important factors in the admissions decision are advanced placement or honors courses, leadership record, and evidence of special talent.To graduate, students must complete 128 credits with a minimum overall GPA of 2.0 and a minimum GPA of 2.0 within the major. Distribution requirements include 4 courses in humanities and 2 each in math, fine arts, natural science, and social science, one in English and cultural diversity. Foreign language requirements include a course numbered 101 (unless exempted on the basis of placement) and a course numbered above 101 in the same language. Students must also complete 3 writing intensive courses (1 in major, 1 outside the major, and 1 additional) and 2 semesters of phys ed, wellness, or community service. Several majors offer a cap-

stone course for which a major research paper or project is completed. **Procedure:** Freshmen are admitted fall and spring. Entrance exams should be taken during the junior year or by January of the senior year. There are early admissions, deferred admissions, and rolling admissions plans. Applications should be filed by March 1 for fall entry; December 1 for spring entry, along with a $35 fee. Notification is sent on a rolling basis. Applications are accepted on-line. Application fees are waived if application is completed on-line. **Transfer Students:** 24 transfer students enrolled in 2013-2014. Applicants must submit appropriate transcripts and have a minimum GPA of 2.0 in transferable courses. Students who have completed 24 transferable semester hours are not required to submit SAT I or ACT results. 32 of 128 credits required for the bachelor's degree must be completed at Lycoming. **International Students:** There are 61 international students enrolled. The school actively recruits these students. They must take the TOEFL with a minimum score of 525 on the paper-based TOEFL (PBT) or 70 on the Internet-based version (iBT), or take the IELTS.

ADMISSIONS: 72% of the 2014-2015 applicants were accepted. The SAT scores for the 2014-2015 freshman class were: Critical Reading--42% below 500, 44% between 500 and 599, 13% between 600 and 699, and 2% between 700 and 800; Math--38% below 500, 40% between 500 and 599, 20% between 600 and 699, and 2% between 700 and 800; Writing--53% below 500, 36% between 500 and 599, 9% between 600 and 699, and 2% between 700 and 800. The ACT scores were 32% below 21, 34% between 21 and 23, 10% between 24 and 26, 12% between 27 and 28, and 12% above 28. 37% of the current freshmen were in the top fifth of their class; 70% were in the top two fifths. 3 freshmen graduated first in their class. **Admissions Contact:** Mike Konopski, VP for Enrollment Management. E-Mail: *admissions@lycoming.edu* Web: *www.lycoming.edu*

FINANCIAL AID: In 2014-2015, 100% of all full-time freshmen and 99% of continuing full-time students received some form of financial aid. 83% of all full-time freshmen and 86% of continuing full-time students received need-based aid. The average freshman award was $38,542. Need-based scholarships or need-based grants averaged $13,670 ($28,000 maximum); need-based self-help aid (loans and jobs) averaged $3,711 ($7,000 maximum); and other non-need-based awards and non-need-based scholarships averaged $25,019 ($44,179 maximum). 50% of undergraduate students work part-time. Average annual earnings from campus work are $1305. Lycoming is a member of CSS. The FAFSA and the college's own financial statement are required. The priority date for freshman financial aid applications for fall entry is May 1. The deadline for filing freshman financial aid applications for fall entry is May 15.

MANSFIELD UNIVERSITY (*The complete profile is made available exclusively on our website, www.barronspac.com*)

MARYWOOD UNIVERSITY — E-2
www.marywood.edu

Scranton, PA 18509	**(570) 348-6234**
	(866) 279-9663
Fax: (570) 961-4763	Email: yourfuture@marywood.edu
Full-time: 633 men, 1238 women	Faculty: IIA, av$
Part-time: 50 men, 117 women	Ph.D.s: 87%
Graduate: 263 men, 790 women	Student/Faculty: 11 to 1
Year: semesters, summer session	Tuition: $31,695
Room & Board: $13,900	Freshman Class: 2111 applied, 1566 accepted, 373 enrolled
SAT CR/M/W: 510/520/500 **ACT:** recommended	
	CEEB CODE: 2407
Application Deadline: open	COMPETITIVE

Marywood University is a comprehensive, Catholic university with 99 undergraduate, graduate and doctoral degree programs. Established in 1915 by the Sisters, Servants of the Immaculate Heart of Mary. In 1996, Marywood University offered the region's first doctoral degree program and is a leading provider of graduate education in the region, with 36 master's degree programs and 37 certificate offerings.

Marywood University includes four Colleges and three Schools: The Insalaco College of Creative and Performing Arts, The Reap College of Education and Human Development, The College of Health and Human Services, The Munley College of Liberal Arts and Sciences, The School of Architecture, The School of Business, The School of Social Work and the Center for Interdisciplinary Studies. Committed to enriching human lives through ethical and religious values and a tradition of service, and motivated by a pioneering, progressive spirit, Marywood provides a framework for educational excellence that enables students to develop fully as persons and to master professional and leadership skills necessary for meeting human needs. There are 7 undergraduate schools and 7 graduate schools. In addition to regional accreditation, Marywood has baccalaureate program accreditation with ACBSP, ADA, CSWE, NASAD, NASM, NCATE, NLN, AATA, AMTA, APA, ACEN, ARC-PA, ASHA, CAATE, and CACREP. The 123-acre campus is in a suburban area 120 miles west of New York City and 115 miles north of Philadelphia. Including any residence halls, there are 33 buildings.

STUDENT LIFE: 68% of undergraduates are from Pennsylvania. Others are from 21 states, and 10 foreign countries. 74% are White; 11% race unknown. The average age of freshmen is 18; all undergraduates, 21. 20% do not continue beyond their first year; 69% remain to graduate. **Housing:** 1004 students can be accommodated in college housing, which includes single-sex and coed dorms and on-campus apartments. Themed interest communities located within the residence halls. On-campus housing is guaranteed for all 4 years. 57% of students commute. Alcohol is not permitted. All students may keep cars.

FACULTY/CLASSROOMS: 44% of faculty are male; 56% are female. No introductory courses are taught by graduate students.

PROGRAMS OF STUDY: Marywood confers B.A., B.Arch., B.E.D.A., B.S., B.B.A., B.F.A., B.M., B.S.N. and B.S.W. degrees. Master's and Doctoral degrees are also awarded. Bachelor's degrees are awarded in BIOLOGICAL SCIENCE (biology/biological science and biotechnology), BUSINESS (accounting, banking and finance, business administration and management, hospitality management services, information and communication technology, international business management, marketing/retailing/merchandising, and retailing), COMMUNICATIONS AND THE ARTS (advertising, arts administration/management, broadcasting, ceramic art and design, communications, digital communications, dramatic arts, English, French, graphic design, illustration, music business management, music performance, musical theater, painting, photography, sculpture, Spanish, studio art, and theater management), COMPUTER AND PHYSICAL SCIENCE (information sciences and systems, mathematics, and science), EDUCATION (art education, athletic training, dance education, early childhood education, education of the deaf and hearing impaired, elementary education, English education, foreign languages education, mathematics education, music education, physical education, science education, secondary education, social science education, and special education), ENGINEERING AND ENVIRONMENTAL DESIGN (architecture, aviation administration/management, environmental design, environmental science, and interior design), HEALTH PROFESSIONS (art therapy, health care administration, health science, medical technology, music therapy, nursing, physician's assistant, premedicine, preosteopathy, and speech pathology/audiology), SOCIAL SCIENCE (clinical psychology, communication sciences and disorders, criminal justice, dietetics, family/consumer studies, gerontology, history, industrial and organizational psychology, philosophy, physical fitness/movement, political science/government, prelaw, psychology, religion, social science, and social work). Architecture, Pre-physician and communication sciences and disorders are the strongest academically. Environmental design (architecture), nutrition and dietetics, and Pre-physician studies have the largest enrollments.

ACTIVITIES: 9% of women belong to 2 local sororities. There are 60 groups on campus, including film club, art, band, cheerleading, choir, chorus, dance, drama, environmental, ethnic, gay, honors, international, jazz band, literary magazine, musical theater, newspaper, orchestra, photography, political, professional, radio and TV, religious, social, social service, student government, symphony, and volunteer. Popular campus events include Spring Fling, Homecoming formal, Flapjack Fest and Midnight Madness. **Sports:** There are

9 intercollegiate sports for men and 10 for women, and 22 intramural sports for men and 22 for women. Facilities include The Center for Athletics and Wellness is a state-of-the-art facility with a fitness center, climbing wall, an elevated running track, a dance/aerobics studio, a 1500 seat arena and high tech athletic training areas. The Aquatics Center, features eight lanes, one meter and three meter diving boards, spectator seating and team rooms. This major expansion of the university's athletics and recreation facilities was designed to complement the outdoor facilities that include a lighted multipurpose turf field, tennis courts, sand volleyball court, basketball courts and three grass fields. **Graduates:** From July 1, 2013 to June 30, 2014, 506 bachelor's degrees were awarded. The most popular majors were health professions and related programs (22%), business/marketing (12%), and visual and performing arts (12%). 89 companies recruited on campus in 2013-2014. In an average class, 1% graduate in 3 years or less, 54% graduate in 4 years or less, 69% graduate in 5 years or less, and 69% graduate in 6 years or less. Of the 2013 graduating class, 60% were enrolled in graduate school within 6 months of graduation.

SERVICES: Counseling and information services are available, as is tutoring in most subjects. There is a reader service for the blind. **Library/Resources:** The library contains 220,273 volumes, 24,568 audio/video tapes/CDs/DVDs, and subscribes to 35,169 periodicals including electronic. Computerized library services include interlibrary loans, database searching, Internet access, and Wi-Fi capability. Special learning facilities include an art gallery, radio station, TV station, the University's facilities include a fully-equipped conference center accommodating groups up to 1,200 (summer conference overnight capacity: 950); an academic excellence center; a student counseling center; a human physiology lab; human development (counseling, psychology) laboratories; biotechnology lab; a communication sciences and disorders clinic; a nutrition and dietetics lab; an assistive technology center; an outpatient mental health clinic; multiple "smart" classrooms, multiple computer labs, a full-service library, a center for architectural studies studios; a television studio and editing suites, a radio station and studio; a 60,000-square-foot studio art center (including ceramic, painting, drawing/foundation, sculpture, glass, metal, clay, wood, photography, fabric, jewelry, and printmaking studios), a 15,000-square foot visual arts center (including graphic design and interior architecture computer labs, two art exhibit galleries, the Maslow Collection of Contemporary Art and Maslow Study Gallery), 1,100-seat performance theater, a black box theater, 1,500 seat arena accommodating more than 2,500 for major speakers, concerts and other events, 5,000 square-foot fully-equipped fitness center with a climbing wall; an NCAA regulation competition pool and aquatics center; basketball, volleyball and tennis courts, 1,200-square foot dance/aerobics studio, hydro-therapy room, separate team and student locker rooms. **Physically Challenged Students:** 95% of the campus is accessible. Facilities include wheelchair ramps, elevators, special parking, specially equipped restrooms, special class scheduling, lowered drinking fountains. **Special:** Marywood offers cross-registration with the University of Scranton, internships, and study abroad (Argentina, Austria, Brazil, China, England, France, Greece Ireland, Italy, Japan, New Zealand, Portugal, South Africa, South Korea, Spain, Taiwan, Turkey, Wales). Also offered are accelerated degree programs in dietetics and social work, dual majors, and student-designed majors. Students may earn credit for life, military and work experience. There are 23 national honor societies, a freshman honors program, and 18 departmental honors programs. **Visiting:** There are regularly scheduled orientations for prospective students, including a presentation/overview of Marywood University, talking with academic department faculty members and meeting and talking with current students. There are guides for informal visits, visitors may sit in on classes, and stay overnight. To schedule a visit, contact the Office of University Admissions. **Campus Safety and Security:** Measures include 24-hour foot and vehicle patrol, emergency notification system, self-defense education, and security escort services. There are emergency telephones, lighted pathways/sidewalks, controlled access to dorms/residences, Night security in dorms, card access to dorm floors, and transportation on request.

REQUIREMENTS: The SAT is required. The ACT is recommended. Applicants are expected to be graduates of an accredited secondary school or have the GED. A minimum of 17 academic credits is required, including 4 in English, 3 each in social studies and science

(1 as lab), 2 in math and 6 academic electives. A letter of support is required in selected majors, as is a portfolio or an audition where appropriate. A personal interview is strongly recommended. AP and CLEP credits are accepted. Important factors in the admissions decision are advanced placement or honors courses, leadership record, and recommendations by school officials. To graduate, students must complete a liberal arts core consisting of religious studies, philosophy, math, science, history, social science, literature, writing, foreign language and fine arts. Additional course requirements include a first-year experience course for new undergraduate students who have not transferred from another post-secondary institution and one course with a global studies perspective. **Procedure:** Freshmen are admitted fall and spring. Entrance exams should be taken in the junior and senior year before graduation. There are deferred admissions and rolling admissions plans. Application deadlines are open. Application fee is $35. Notification of early decision is sent September 1; regular decision, Applications are accepted on-line. Application fees are waived if application is completed on-line. **Transfer Students:** 115 transfer students enrolled in 2013-2014. SAT or ACT scores are required of transfer applicants who have earned fewer then 12 college credits; both secondary school and college transcripts are required. Transfer students are required to have earned a minimum GPA of 2.25 at the college most recently attended (3.0 minimum for some majors). A grade of C is the minimum requirement for transfer of academic credit. The SAT is required for nursing transfer students. 60 of 126 credits required for the bachelor's degree must be completed at Marywood. **International Students:** There are 78 international students enrolled. The school actively recruits these students. They must take the TOEFL with a minimum score of 71 on the Internet-based version (iBT), or take the IELTS score band of 5.5 minimum. They must also take the SAT or ACT, scoring 19 ACT/900 SAT. **ADMISSIONS:** 74% of the 2014-2015 applicants were accepted. The SAT scores for the 2014-2015 freshman class were: Critical Reading--43% below 500, 43% between 500 and 599, 12% between 600 and 699, and 2% between 700 and 800; Math--40% below 500, 46% between 500 and 599, and 14% between 600 and 699; Writing--43% below 500, 42% between 500 and 599, 13% between 600 and 699, and 2% between 700 and 800. 36% of the current freshmen were in the top fifth of their class; 74% were in the top two fifths. 1 freshman graduated first in the class. **Admissions Contact:** Christian DiGregorio, Director of University Admissions. E-Mail: *yourfuture@marywood.edu* Web: *www.marywood.edu*

FINANCIAL AID: In 2014-2015, 87% of all full-time freshmen and 84% of continuing full-time students received some form of financial aid. 69% of all full-time freshmen and 70% of continuing full-time students received need-based aid. The average freshman award was $26,647. Need-based scholarships or need-based grants averaged $23,630 ($37,990 maximum); and need-based self-help aid (loans and jobs) averaged $4,708 ($11,000 maximum). 33% of undergraduate students work part-time. Average annual earnings from campus work are $2000. The average financial indebtedness of the 2014 graduate was $27,290. The FAFSA and the state aid form are required. The priority date for freshman financial aid applications for fall entry is February 15.

MERCYHURST UNIVERSITY   **B-1**
Mercyhurst College
www.mercyhurst.edu

Erie, PA 16546	(814) 824-2980
	(800) 825-1926
Fax: (814) 824-2071	Email: admug@mercyhurst.edu
Full-time: 1390 men, 1988 women	Faculty: n/av; IIB, --$
Part-time: 129 men, 333 women	Ph.D.s: 60%
Graduate: 140 men, 140 women	Student/Faculty: n/av
Year: 4-1-4, summer session	Tuition: $30,300
Room & Board: $10,400	Freshman Class: 3000 applied, 1900 accepted, 650 enrolled
SAT CR/M/W: 550/530/510 ACT: 23	CEEB CODE: 2410
Application Deadline: open	COMPETITIVE

Mercyhurst University, established in 1926, is a private, nonprofit institution affiliated with the Roman Catholic Church. The college offers undergraduate degrees in the arts, business, health science, liberal arts, religious studies, and teacher preparation as well as a degree-directed program for the learning disabled. There is 1 graduate school. In addition to regional accreditation, Mercyhurst has baccalaureate program accreditation with ADA and CSWE. The 88-acre campus is in a suburban area within Erie, PA. Including any residence halls, there are 44 buildings.

STUDENT LIFE: 60% of undergraduates are from Pennsylvania. Others are from 37 states, 14 foreign countries, and Canada. 76% are from public schools. 91% are White. 53% are Catholic; 21% Protestant; 18% claim no religious affiliation. The average age of freshmen is 18; all undergraduates, 26. 20% do not continue beyond their first year; 62% remain to graduate.

FACULTY/CLASSROOMS: 57% of faculty are male; 43% are female. All teach undergraduates, and 30% do research. No introductory courses are taught by graduate students. The average class size in an introductory lecture is 35; in a laboratory is 12; and in a regular course is 25.

PROGRAMS OF STUDY: Mercyhurst confers B.A., B.S. and B.M. degrees. Associate, Master's, and Doctoral degrees are also awarded. Bachelor's degrees are awarded in BIOLOGICAL SCIENCE (biochemistry and biology/biological science), BUSINESS (accounting, banking and finance, business administration and management, fashion merchandising, hotel/motel and restaurant management, insurance and risk management, management information systems, and marketing/retailing/merchandising), COMMUNICATIONS AND THE ARTS (advertising, broadcasting, communications, dance, English, graphic design, journalism, languages, music, musical theater, public relations, and studio art), COMPUTER AND PHYSICAL SCIENCE (chemistry, earth science, geology, mathematics, web services, and web technology), EDUCATION (art education, athletic training, business education, early childhood education, elementary education, home economics education, mathematics education, music education, science education, secondary education, social science education, and special education), ENGINEERING AND ENVIRONMENTAL DESIGN (environmental science and interior design), HEALTH PROFESSIONS (art therapy, medical laboratory technology, predentistry, premedicine, preosteopathy, prepharmacy, preveterinary science, and sports medicine), SOCIAL SCIENCE (anthropology, archeology, criminal justice, family/consumer studies, forensic studies, history, philosophy, political science/government, prelaw, psychology, religion, religious education, social work, and sociology). Archeology/anthropology, intelligence studies, and sports medicine are the strongest academically. Business, education, and sports medicine have the largest enrollments.

ACTIVITIES: There are 49 groups on campus, including art, band, cheerleading, choir, chorus, communications, computers, dance, debate, drama, ethnic, film, gay, honors, international, jazz band, literary magazine, musical theater, newspaper, opera, orchestra, pep band, photography, political, professional, radio and TV, religious, social, social service, and student government. Popular campus events include Activities Day, Parents Weekend, and Winter and Spring Formals.

SERVICES: Counseling and information services are available, as is tutoring in every subject. There is remedial math, reading, and writing. **Library/Resources:** The library contains 165,644 volumes, 50,631 microform items, and 9,309 audio/video tapes/CDs/DVDs, and subscribes to 848 periodicals including electronic. Computerized library services include interlibrary loans and database searching. Special learning facilities include an art gallery, planetarium, radio station, TV station, Northwestern Pennsylvania historical archives, and archeological institute. **Physically Challenged Students:** 90% of the campus is accessible. Facilities include wheelchair ramps, elevators, special parking, specially equipped restrooms, and lowered drinking fountains. **Special:** Mercyhurst offers cross-registration with Gannon University, internships in all majors through the co-op office, and study abroad in London and Dublin. Dual and student-designed majors, credit for life, military, or work experience, nondegree study, work-study, and a pass/fail grading option are also available. There are 7 national honor societies, a freshman honors program, and 4 departmental honors programs. **Visiting:** There are regularly scheduled orientations for prospective students, including tours, class visits, faculty meetings, and interviews with financial aid and admissions counselors. There are guides for informal visits, visitors may sit in on classes, and stay overnight. To schedule a visit, contact the Admissions Office at admug@mercyhurst.edu. **Campus Safety and Security:** Measures include 24-hour foot and vehicle patrol, emergency notification system, and self-defense education. There are shuttle buses, emergency telephones, lighted pathways/sidewalks, controlled access to dorms/residences, 24-hour security camera surveillance system.

REQUIREMENTS: The SAT or ACT is required. Applicants must graduate from an accredited secondary school or have a GED. 16 academic credits are required, including 4 years of English, 3 each of math and social studies, and 2 each of history, science, and a foreign language. Interviews are recommended. Art applicants must submit portfolios; auditions are required of music and dance applicants. Mercyhurst requires applicants to be in the upper 50% of their class. A GPA of 2.8 is required. AP and CLEP credits are accepted. Important factors in the admissions decision are recommendations by alumni, evidence of special talent, and personality/intangible qualities.

ADMISSIONS: 63% of a recent year applicants were accepted. The ACT scores were 21% below 21, 46% between 21 and 23, 33% between 24 and 26, 79% were in the top two fifths. 20 freshmen graduated first in their class.

FINANCIAL AID: In a recent year, 95% of all full-time freshmen students received some form of financial aid. 76% of all full-time freshmen students received need-based aid. The average freshman award was $15,000. Need-based scholarships or need-based grants averaged $8,000. 60% of undergraduate students work part-time. Average annual earnings from campus work are $1200. The average financial indebtedness of the 2013 graduate was $27,000. Mercyhurst is a member of CSS. The FAFSA is required. The priority date for freshman financial aid applications for fall entry is May 1. The deadline for filing freshman financial aid applications for fall entry is August.

MESSIAH COLLEGE — D-3
www.messiah.edu

Mechanicsburg, PA 17055

(717) 691-6000
(800) 233-4220

Fax: (717) 796-5374
Email: admiss@messiah.edu

Full-time: 1067 men, 1613 women
Faculty: 167; IIB, av$

Part-time: 41 men, 68 women
Ph.D.s: 85%

Graduate: 115 men, 330 women
Student/Faculty: 13 to 1

Year: semesters, summer session
Tuition: $31,340

Room & Board: $9350
Freshman Class: 2472 applied, 1977 accepted, 696 enrolled

SAT CR/M/W: 560/560/530 **ACT:** 25
CEEB CODE: 2411

Application Deadline: open
COMPETITIVE+

Messiah College, founded in 1909, is a private Christian college of the liberal and applied arts and sciences. The college is committed to the evangelical spirit rooted in the Anabaptist, Pietist, and Wesleyan traditions. There are 4 undergraduate schools and 1 graduate school. In addition to regional accreditation, Messiah has baccalaureate program accreditation with ABET, ACBSP, ADA, CSWE, NASAD, NASM, CAAHEP, CCNE, and ACEND. The 471-acre campus is in a small town 12 miles southwest of Harrisburg. Including any residence halls, there are 53 buildings.

STUDENT LIFE: 63% of undergraduates are from Pennsylvania. Others are from 38 states, 23 foreign countries, and Canada. 73% are from public schools. 84% are White. 88% are Protestant. The average age of freshmen is 19; all undergraduates, 20. 12% do not continue beyond their first year; 80% remain to graduate. **Housing:** 2383 students can be accommodated in college housing, which includes single-sex and coed dorms, on-campus apartments, and off-campus apartments. In addition, there are special-interest houses. On-campus housing is guaranteed for all 4 years. 86% of students live on campus; of those, 70% remain on campus on weekends. Alcohol is not permitted. Upperclassmen may keep cars.

FACULTY/CLASSROOMS: 59% of faculty are male; 41% are female. 92% teach undergraduates. No introductory courses are taught by graduate students. The average class size in an introductory lecture is 27; in a laboratory is 18; and in a regular course is 24.

PROGRAMS OF STUDY: Messiah confers B.A., B.S., B.M., B.S.E., B.S.N., B.S.W. and B.F.A. degrees. Master's degrees are also awarded. Bachelor's degrees are awarded in BIOLOGICAL SCIENCE (biochemistry, biology/adolescence education, biology/biological science, molecular biology, and nutrition), BUSINESS (accounting, business administration and management, international business management, management information systems, marketing/retailing/merchandising, sports management, and sustainable management), COMMUNICATIONS AND THE ARTS (art history and appreciation, arts administration/management, communications, dance, dramatic arts, English, film, television and digital media, French, German, journalism, media arts, media management, music, music business management, music ministry, music performance, musical theater, public relations, Spanish, spanish / adolescence education, studio art, and theater management), COMPUTER AND PHYSICAL SCIENCE (applied science, chemistry, chemistry/adolescence education, computer science, digital arts/technology, mathematics, and physics), EDUCATION (art education, athletic training, early childhood education, elementary education, English education, environmental education, foreign languages education, mathematics education, music education, physical education, recreation education, science education, and social studies education), ENGINEERING AND ENVIRONMENTAL DESIGN (engineering and environmental science), HEALTH PROFESSIONS (exercise science, nursing, and Pre-Health Studies), SOCIAL SCIENCE (biblical studies, biopsychology, child care/child and family studies, Chinese Studies, criminal justice, dietetics, economics, ethnic studies, family/consumer studies, history, human development, interdisciplinary studies, ministries, peace studies, philosophy, political science/government, psychology, social work, sociology, Spanish studies, and theological studies). Engineering, nursing, and business administration have the largest enrollments.

ACTIVITIES: There are 81 groups on campus, including art, band, choir, chorale, chorus, dance, debate, drama, environmental, ethnic, film, honors, international, jazz band, literary magazine, musical theater, newspaper, orchestra, pep band, political, professional, radio and TV, religious, social, social service, student government, symphony, and yearbook. Popular campus events include Cultural Series, Traveling Music Ensembles, and Theater Productions. **Sports:** There are 10 intercollegiate sports for men and 10 for women, and 5 intramural sports for men and 5 for women. Facilities include indoor and outdoor tracks, pool with separate diving well, wrestling and gymnastics areas, weight room, numerous playing fields, and courts for racquetball, basketball, and tennis. The campus center provides additional recreational facilities. **Graduates:** From July 1, 2013 to June 30, 2014, 652 bachelor's degrees were awarded. The most popular majors were nursing (8%), psychology (6%), and business administration (6%). 558 companies recruited on campus in 2013-2014. In an average class, 72% graduate in 4 years or less, 76% graduate in 5 years or less, and 80% graduate in 6 years or less. Of the 2013 graduating class, 14% were enrolled in graduate school within 6 months of graduation, and 81% were employed.

SERVICES: Counseling and information services are available, as is tutoring in most subjects. There is a reader service for the blind, remedial math, reading, and writing. **Library/Resources:** The library contains 254,862 volumes, 6 microform items, 20,583 audio/video tapes/CDs/DVDs, and subscribes to 107,565 periodicals including electronic. Computerized library services include interlibrary loans, database searching, Internet access, and Wi-Fi capability. Special learning facilities include an art gallery, natural history museum, and radio station. **Physically Challenged Students:** 80% of the campus is accessible. Facilities include wheelchair ramps, elevators, special parking, specially equipped restrooms, special class scheduling, lowered drinking fountains, and special housing. **Special:** Off-campus study is available through over 30 carefully selected programs on every continent (except Antarctica) and in a variety of major metropolitan cities around the world, including Paris, London, and Barcelona, and in such diverse counties as Chile, China, India, and Lithuania. Off-campus options within the United States include the

Contemporary Music Center in Nashville, the American Studies Program in Washington DC, the AuSable Institute of Environmental Studies, Los Angeles Film Studies, Oregon Extension, and others. Students may also spend a semester or year at any of 12 other Christian Consortium Colleges in a student exchange program. Numerous internships, practicum, and service opportunities are also available both domestically and around the globe, with an average of over 600 students traveling around the world each year through Messiah College. There are 7 national honor societies, a freshman honors program, and 17 departmental honors programs. **Visiting:** There are regularly scheduled orientations for prospective students, including a campus tour, academic and career advising, and a financial aid information session. There are guides for informal visits, visitors may sit in on classes, and stay overnight. To schedule a visit, contact the Admissions Office. **Campus Safety and Security:** Measures include 24-hour foot and vehicle patrol, emergency notification system, self-defense education, and security escort services. There are emergency telephones, lighted pathways/sidewalks, controlled access to dorms/residences, and text messaging alert system.

REQUIREMENTS: The SAT or ACT is required. Applicants must have graduated from an accredited high school or the equivalent. Secondary preparation of students who enroll usually includes 4 units in English, 2 or 3 in math, 2 or 3 in natural science, 2 or more in both social studies and foreign languages, and 4 in academic electives. Students who enroll are usually in the top one third of their class and have a B average or better. A campus visit with an information session is recommended. Potential music majors must audition. AP and CLEP credits are accepted. Important factors in the admissions decision are advanced placement or honors courses, recommendations by school officials, and leadership record.All students must complete at least 123 credits with a minimum GPA of 2.0. The last 30 credits must be taken at Messiah College and a minimum of 12 credits must be in the major. **Procedure:** Freshmen are admitted fall and spring. Entrance exams should be taken in the spring of the junior year. There is a rolling admissions plan. Application deadlines are open. Application fee is $20. Notification is sent on a rolling basis. 0 applicants were on the 2014 waiting list; were admitted. Applications are accepted on-line. **Transfer Students:** 81 transfer students enrolled in 2013-2014. Transfer applicants should have earned a 2.5 GPA in at least 12 college credits. The college prefers that applicants also have composite SAT or ACT scores and that they seek a campus visit. Students with fewer than 30 credits in college should submit a high school transcript as well. 30 of 123 credits required for the bachelor's degree must be completed at Messiah. **International Students:** There are 89 international students enrolled. The school actively recruits these students. They must take the TOEFL. They must also take the SAT or ACT.

ADMISSIONS: 80% of the 2014-2015 applicants were accepted. The SAT scores for the 2014-2015 freshman class were: Critical Reading--23% below 500, 44% between 500 and 599, 27% between 600 and 699, and 6% between 700 and 800; Math--20% below 500, 44% between 500 and 599, 29% between 600 and 699, and 8% between 700 and 800; Writing--29% below 500, 45% between 500 and 599, 20% between 600 and 699, and 5% between 700 and 800. The ACT scores were 24% below 21, 26% between 21 and 23, 36% between 24 and 26, 14% between 27 and 28, and 20% above 28. 53% of the current freshmen were in the top fifth of their class; 79% were in the top two fifths. There were 2 National Merit finalists. 9 freshmen graduated first in their class. **Admissions Contact:** John Chopka, Vice President for Enrollment Management. E-Mail: *admiss@messiah.edu* Web: *www.messiah.edu*

FINANCIAL AID: In 2014-2015, 100% of all full-time freshmen and 99% of continuing full-time students received some form of financial aid. 63% of all full-time freshmen and 64% of continuing full-time students received need-based aid. The average freshman award was $15,056. 58% of undergraduate students work part-time. Average annual earnings from campus work are $2175. The average financial indebtedness of the 2014 graduate was $34,301. Messiah is a member of CSS. The FAFSA is required. The priority date for freshman financial aid applications for fall entry is April 1.

MILLERSVILLE UNIVERSITY OF PENNSYLVANIA

E-4

www.millersville.edu

Millersville, PA 17551

(717) 871-4625
n/av

Fax: (717) 871-2147   Email: admissions@millersville.edu

Full-time: 2829 men, 3529 women	Faculty: 281; IIA, +$
Part-time: 368 men, 445 women	Ph.D.s: 97%
Graduate: 231 men, 645 women	Student/Faculty: 22 to 1
Year: 4-1-4, summer session	Tuition: $10,268 ($23,868)
Room & Board: $11,380	Freshman Class: 6184 applied, 4249 accepted, 1357 enrolled
SAT CR/M/W: 500/510/480 ACT: 21	CEEB CODE: 2656
Application Deadline: rolling	COMPETITIVE

Millersville University of Pennsylvania, founded as a teaching college in 1855, is one of the most highly regarded universities in the northeast region of the United States. Millersville recognizes excellence in teaching and learning as its reason for being and is committed to offering students a high quality, comprehensive university experience of exceptional value. Dedicated to providing nationally recognized programs that embrace the liberal arts, Millersville provides academic opportunities which are supported by outstanding faculty who are accomplished scholars, artists and practitioners. Millersville is one of 14 comprehensive universities within the PA State System of Higher Education. Millersville University is proud to provide rigorous academic programs and rich cultural offerings. Deeply rooted in the history of Lancaster County, Millersville's commitment to excellence began in the 1850s and continues today through nationally recognized teacher education programs, strong science and technology programs, ample service learning opportunities, and a strong liberal arts-based curriculum. With more than 55 majors to choose from, students select Millersville based on its academic reputation, finding opportunities to explore an amazing array of academic programs supported by state-of-the-art science and industrial technology laboratories, art studios, writing and language laboratories. Emphasizing holistic development, these academic programs are complemented by countless co-curricular opportunities, such as intercollegiate (NCAA Division II) and intramural athletics, and the University's emphasis on community engagement and civic responsibility. There are 3 undergraduate schools and 1 graduate school. In addition to regional accreditation, Millersville, MU has baccalaureate program accreditation with ABET, ACBSP, CSWE, NASAD, NASM, NCATE, NLN, AACTE, ACEN, ACS, ATMAE, CoARC, ITEEA, and NASP. The 250-acre campus is in a small town 5 miles southwest of Lancaster. Including any residence halls, there are 91 buildings.

STUDENT LIFE: 96% of undergraduates are from Pennsylvania. Others are from 23 states, 57 foreign countries, and Canada. 77% are White. The average age of freshmen is 18; all undergraduates, 21. 23% do not continue beyond their first year; 77% remain to graduate. **Housing:** 2340 students can be accommodated in college housing, which includes coed dorms, on-campus apartments, and off-campus apartments. In addition, there are honors houses, special-interest houses, coed dorms, apartments for single students, special housing for disabled students and international students, theme and wellness housing, academic interest housing for several subject areas, University-affiliated apartments and dormitory for single students adjacent to campus. On-campus housing is available on a first-come, first-served basis, and is available on a lottery system for upperclassmen. 67% of students commute. Alcohol is not permitted. Upperclassmen may keep cars.

FACULTY/CLASSROOMS: 49% of faculty are male; 51% are female. All teach undergraduates. No introductory courses are taught by graduate students. The average class size in an introductory lecture is 29; in a laboratory is 21; and in a regular course is 29.

PROGRAMS OF STUDY: Millersville, MU confers B.A., B.S., B.F.A., B.S.Ed. and B.S.N. degrees. Associate and Master's degrees are also awarded. Bachelor's degrees are awarded in AGRICULTURE (animal science), BIOLOGICAL SCIENCE (biochemistry, biology/biological science, biotechnology, botany, and environmental biology), BUSI-

NESS (accounting, business administration and management, business administration - international, business administration marketing, and finance), COMMUNICATIONS AND THE ARTS (art, broadcasting, communication studies, communications, English, English as a second/foreign language, English literature, English Writing, French, German, graphic communications, journalism, linguistics, music, public relations, Spanish, and theatre acting), COMPUTER AND PHYSICAL SCIENCE (actuarial science, applied mathematics, atmospheric sciences and meteorology, chemistry, computer science, earth science, environmental chemistry, environmental geology, geology, mathematics, oceanography, physics, polymer science, and statistics), EDUCATION (art education, early childhood education, elementary education, English education, middle school education, music education, social studies education, special education, and technical education), ENGINEERING AND ENVIRONMENTAL DESIGN (construction technology, industrial engineering technology, manufacturing technology, nuclear medicine technology, and occupational safety and health), HEALTH PROFESSIONS (allied health, medical technology, nursing, preoptometry, prepharmacy, prepodiatry, and respiratory therapy), SOCIAL SCIENCE (anthropology, archeology, criminology, economics, geography, history, interdisciplinary studies, international studies, philosophy, political science/government, psychology, social studies, social work, and sociology). Special education, foreign language, and nursing are the strongest academically. Business administration, biology, and psychology have the largest enrollments.

ACTIVITIES: 2% of men belong to 8 national fraternities; 4% of women belong to 1 local and 9 national sororities. There are 190 groups on campus, including art, band, cheerleading, chess, choir, chorale, chorus, communications, computers, dance, drama, environmental, ethnic, film, gay, honors, jazz band, literary magazine, marching band, musical theater, newspaper, orchestra, pep band, photography, political, professional, radio and TV, religious, social, social service, student government, and symphony. Popular campus events include Organizational Outbreak, Superfest, Wellness Fair, Homecoming, Greek Week, Into the Streets, and Spring Concert. **Sports:** There are 7 intercollegiate sports for men and 12 for women, and 11 intramural sports for men and 11 for women. Facilities include a football stadium, 2 pools, 2 gyms, 2 fitness centers, dance studio, ropes course, wrestling and weight rooms, basketball, volleyball, tennis, and badminton courts, indoor and outdoor running track, baseball and softball stadiums, and a golf course. **Graduates:** From July 1, 2013 to June 30, 2014, 1545 bachelor's degrees were awarded. The most popular majors were business administration (10%), psychology (9%), and biology (8%). 245 companies recruited on campus in 2013-2014. In an average class, 38% graduate in 4 years or less, 60% graduate in 5 years or less, and 64% graduate in 6 years or less.

SERVICES: Counseling and information services are available, as is tutoring in most subjects. There is a reader service for the blind, and remedial math. Every effort is made to tailor tutoring services to individual needs. **Library/Resources:** The library contains 360,544 volumes, 81,518 microform items, 5,665 audio/video tapes/CDs/DVDs, and subscribes to 201,739 periodicals including electronic. Computerized library services include interlibrary loans, database searching, Internet access, and Wi-Fi capability. Special learning facilities include an art gallery, radio station, TV station, Recording studio, teleconferencing center, weather information center, foreign language lab, two performing arts centers, Winter and Ware, Atmospheric Research and Aerostat Facility, Center for Disaster Research and Education, Foucault Pendulum, Marine Science Consortium (Field Station at Wallops Island, VA), Service members Opportunity Colleges Consortium (SOCC). **Physically Challenged Students:** 85% of the campus is accessible. Facilities include wheelchair ramps, elevators, special parking, specially equipped restrooms, special class scheduling, lowered drinking fountains, lowered telephones, and special housing. **Special:** Numerous co-op and internship programs, including student teaching opportunities, are available. Millersville has exchange agreements with Franklin and Marshall College, Lancaster Theological Seminary, and Wallops Island Consortium, as well as 3-2 chemical and physical engineering programs with Pennsylvania State University. Study abroad is offered in Australia, Chile, China, England, France, Germany, Japan, Northern Island, Iceland, South

Africa, Spain. Dual majors and accelerated degrees are possible in most disciplines. There are 18 national honor societies, a freshman honors program, and 15 departmental honors programs. **Visiting:** There are regularly scheduled orientations for prospective students, Campus information sessions and tours are offered to prospective students on a daily basis. Additionally, departmental information sessions, open houses, admitted student expos, transfer sessions, and junior preview days are offered throughout the yr. There are guides for informal visits and visitors may sit in on classes. To schedule a visit, contact the Office of Admissions. **Campus Safety and Security:** Measures include 24-hour foot and vehicle patrol, emergency notification system, self-defense education, and security escort services. There are shuttle buses, emergency telephones, lighted pathways/sidewalks, controlled access to dorms/residences, student patrols, crime awareness programs and timely warning alerts.

REQUIREMENTS: The SAT is required. To be considered for admission, one must be a graduate of an approved secondary school or hold a GED high school equivalency diploma. Generally, the student's academic program should include 4 units of academic English in addition to 3 units or more of academic mathematics, science, and social science course work. Also required are satisfactory scores on the SAT or ACT. Finally, auditions are required for music majors and portfolios are required for art majors. Millersville, MU requires applicants to be in the upper 40% of their class. AP and CLEP credits are accepted. Important factors in the admissions decision are leadership record, extracurricular activities record, and advanced placement or honors courses. All students must complete at least 120 hours, demonstrating proficiency in mathematics and English and maintaining a minimum 2.0 GPA. Students must complete the general education program and complete specific courses in physical education and fundamentals of speech. **Procedure:** Freshmen are admitted to all sessions. Entrance exams should be taken during spring of the junior year. There are early admissions, deferred admissions, and rolling admissions plans. Application deadlines are open. Application fee is $50. Notification is sent on a rolling basis. 465 applicants were on the 2014 waiting list; 244 were admitted. Applications are accepted online. **Transfer Students:** 693 transfer students enrolled in 2013-2014. All transfer applicants must submit high school transcript, college transcript, essay or personal statement, and a statement of good standing. Review based on course selection and performance at previous college. Preference given to students with 2.5 GPA or higher. Preference given to graduates of in-state community colleges and students transferring from other PA State System of Higher Education Schools. 30 of 120 credits required for the bachelor's degree must be completed at Millersville, MU. **International Students:** There are 48 international students enrolled. The school actively recruits these students. They must take the TOEFL with a minimum score of 550 on the paper-based TOEFL (PBT) or 79 on the Internet-based version (iBT). They must also take the SAT or ACT.

ADMISSIONS: 69% of the 2014-2015 applicants were accepted. The SAT scores for the 2014-2015 freshman class were: Critical Reading--47% below 500, 41% between 500 and 599, 11% between 600 and 699, and 2% between 700 and 800; Math--43% below 500, 42% between 500 and 599, 15% between 600 and 699, and 1% between 700 and 800; Writing--58% below 500, 34% between 500 and 599, 8% between 600 and 699, and 1% between 700 and 800. The ACT scores were 44% below 21, 32% between 21 and 23, 14% between 24 and 26, 6% between 27 and 28, and 4% above 28. 21% of the current freshmen were in the top fifth of their class; 44% were in the top two fifths. **Admissions Contact:** Ms. Katy Ferrier, Director of Admissions. E-Mail: *admissions@millersville.edu* Web: *www.millersville.edu/admissions/undergrad/index.php*

FINANCIAL AID: In 2014-2015, 86% of all full-time freshmen and 83% of continuing full-time students received some form of financial aid. 63% of all full-time freshmen and 64% of continuing full-time students received need-based aid. The average freshman award was $12,698. Need-based scholarships or need-based grants averaged $5,822 ($16,860 maximum); need-based self-help aid (loans and jobs) averaged $3,273 ($6,584 maximum); non-need-based athletic scholarships averaged $4,153 ($29,000 maximum); and other non-need-based awards and non-need-based scholarships averaged $5,980 ($28,878 maximum). Average annual earnings from campus work are $1718. The average financial indebtedness of the 2014 graduate was

$29,791. The FAFSA is required. The priority date for freshman financial aid applications for fall entry is March 15.

MISERICORDIA UNIVERSITY — E-2
www.misericordia.edu

Dallas, PA 18612

(570) 674-6400
(866) 262-6363

Fax: (570) 675-2441
Email: admiss@misericordia.edu

Full-time: 616 men, 1157 women
Faculty: 103; IIB, av$

Part-time: 164 men, 528 women
Ph.D.s: 78%

Graduate: 211 men, 520 women
Student/Faculty: 16 to 1

Year: semesters, summer session
Tuition: $29,010

Room & Board: $12,050
Freshman Class: 2050 applied, 1465 accepted, 438 enrolled

SAT CR/M: 530/540 ACT: 23
CEEB CODE: 2087

Application Deadline: n/av
COMPETITIVE

Misericordia University, founded in 1924 by the Sisters of Mercy, is a private liberal arts institution affiliated with the Roman Catholic Church and offers professional programs in health-related fields. There are 3 undergraduate schools. In addition to regional accreditation, has baccalaureate program accreditation with APTA, ASLA, CAHEA, CSWE, ACOTE, CCNE, JRCERT, IACBE, and JRCENMT. The 120-acre campus is in a suburban area 9 miles north of Wilkes-Barre. Including any residence halls, there are 22 buildings.

STUDENT LIFE: 77% of undergraduates are from Pennsylvania. Others are from 23 states, and 1 foreign countries. 84% are from public schools. 94% are White. 47% are Catholic; 20% Protestant; 17% claim no religious affiliation; 14% Christian, Buddhist, and Hindu. The average age of freshmen is 18; all undergraduates, 24. 20% do not continue beyond their first year; 69% remain to graduate.

Housing: 1024 students can be accommodated in college housing, which includes coed dorms. In addition, there are special-interest houses. On-campus housing is guaranteed for the freshman year only, is available on a first-come, first-served basis, and is available on a lottery system for upperclassmen. 57% of students live on campus; of those, 50% remain on campus on weekends. Upperclassmen may keep cars.

FACULTY/CLASSROOMS: 41% of faculty are male; 59% are female. 85% teach undergraduates. No introductory courses are taught by graduate students. The average class size in an introductory lecture is 23; in a laboratory is 14; and in a regular course is 20.

PROGRAMS OF STUDY: confers B.A., B.S., B.S.N. and B.S.W. degrees. Master's and Doctoral degrees are also awarded. Bachelor's degrees are awarded in BIOLOGICAL SCIENCE (biochemistry and biology/biological science), BUSINESS (accounting, business administration and management, marketing/retailing/merchandising, and sports management), COMMUNICATIONS AND THE ARTS (communications and English), COMPUTER AND PHYSICAL SCIENCE (chemistry, computer science, information sciences and systems, and mathematics), EDUCATION (elementary education), HEALTH PROFESSIONS (health care administration, medical laboratory technology, nursing, occupational therapy, physical therapy, radiograph medical technology, and speech therapy), SOCIAL SCIENCE (history, liberal arts/general studies, philosophy, psychology, and social work). Occupational therapy, physical therapy, speech language pathology are the strongest academically. Nursing, business, occupational therapy have the largest enrollments.

ACTIVITIES: There are no fraternities or sororities. There are 32 groups on campus, including art, cheerleading, choir, chorale, chorus, drama, ethnic, honors, international, literary magazine, musical theater, newspaper, political, professional, radio and TV, religious, social service, and student government. Popular campus events include Winter Snowball Dance, Homecoming and Spring Fest. **Sports:** There are 10 intercollegiate sports for men and 11 for women, and 14 intramural sports for men and 14 for women. Facilities include The athletics facilities at Misericordia University recently underwent major renovations which provide MU's student-athletes with some of the finest competition venues in the region. The facilities all located on campus, include the Anderson Center, Mangelsdorf Field at the Anderson Outdoor Athletics Complex, Tambur Field, Metz Field House, McGeehan Field, Anderson Softball Field and six tennis courts. The Anderson Center has provided a home for the Cougars basketball, volleyball and swim teams, and features a six-lane swimming pool, indoor track, racquetball courts, fitness center and an aerobic/dance studio, football, soccer, field hockey, lacrosse, track and field programs, a synthetic grass field and a six-lane synthetic track, with an eight-lane straightaway. **Graduates** From July 1, 2013 to June 30, 2014, 502 bachelor's degrees were awarded. The most popular majors were nursing (14%), business (10%), and health care management (8%). In an average class, 64% graduate in 4 years or less, 68% graduate in 5 years or less, and 69% graduate in 6 years or less. Of the 2013 graduating class, 26% were enrolled in graduate school within 6 months of graduation, and 82% were employed.

SERVICES: Counseling and information services are available, as is tutoring in every subject. There is a reader service for the blind. Services for students with disabilities are provided through the Alternative Learners Program. **Library/Resources:** The library contains 80,572 volumes, 4,219 microform items, 7,911 audio/video tapes/CDs/DVDs, and subscribes to 178 periodicals including electronic. Computerized library services include interlibrary loans, database searching, Internet access, and Wi-Fi capability. Special learning facilities include an art gallery and radio station. **Physically Challenged Students:** 95% of the campus is accessible. Facilities include wheelchair ramps, elevators, special parking, specially equipped restrooms, special class scheduling, and lowered drinking fountains. **Special:** Students may cross-register with King's College and Wilkes University. The college offers internships, work-study programs, study abroad, an accelerated degree program in Business, Govt Law and National Security, Applied Behavioral Science, and Nursing for adult students, and a student-designed major. Credit may be granted for life, military, and work experience through prior learning assessment. Nondegree study is also available. The college offers an alternative learner's project, which accepts a limited number of learning disabled students each year. There are 10 national honor societies, a freshman honors program, and 3 departmental honors programs. **Visiting:** There are regularly scheduled orientations for prospective students, meetings with admissions and financial aid counselors, a tour of the campus, and optional meetings with faculty and coaches. There are guides for informal visits, visitors may sit in on classes, and stay overnight. To schedule a visit, contact Glenn Bozinski at (570) 675-6264. **Campus Safety and Security:** Measures include 24-hour foot and vehicle patrol, emergency notification system, and security escort services. There are shuttle buses, emergency telephones, lighted pathways/sidewalks, and controlled access to dorms/residences.

REQUIREMENTS: The SAT is required. Applicants must graduate from an accredited secondary school or have a GED. 16 Carnegie units must be earned, and students must complete 3 years each in English, math, history, and science, and 2 to 3 years in social studies. Misericordia requires applicants to be in the upper 50% of their class. AP and CLEP credits are accepted. Important factors in the admissions decision are extracurricular activities record, advanced placement or honors courses, and leadership record. To graduate, students must earn a minimum of 120 credits. The required core curriculum includes courses in behavioral science, English literature, fine arts, history, math, philosophy, religious studies, and natural science. Within the core curriculum, students must complete one Unviersity Writing Seminar, and two additional courses that are writing intensive. A minimum GPA of 2.0 is required. **Procedure:** Freshmen are admitted fall and spring. Entrance exams should be taken during the junior year. There are deferred admissions and rolling admissions plans. Application deadlines are open. Application fee is $35. 70 applicants were on the 2014 waiting list; 5 were admitted. Applications are accepted on-line. **Transfer Students:** 104 transfer students enrolled in 2013-2014. Applicants must have a minimum GPA of 2.0. Requirements may be higher for selected majors. 30 of 120 credits required for the bachelor's degree must be completed at Misericordia. **International Students:** There are 3 international students enrolled. The school actively recruits these students. They must take the TOEFL with a minimum score of 500 on the paper-based TOEFL (PBT) or 75 on the Internet-based version (iBT).

ADMISSIONS: 71% of the 2014-2015 applicants were accepted. The

SAT scores for the 2014-2015 freshman class were: Critical Reading--30% below 500, 52% between 500 and 599, 17% between 600 and 699, and 1% between 700 and 800; Math--26% below 500, 50% between 500 and 599, 22% between 600 and 699, and 2% between 700 and 800. The ACT scores were 16% below 21, 43% between 21 and 23, 18% between 24 and 26, 10% between 27 and 28, and 13% above 28. 51% of the current freshmen were in the top fifth of their class; 77% were in the top two fifths. 8 freshmen graduated first in their class. **Admissions Contact:** Glenn Bozinski, Director of Admissions. E-Mail: *admiss@misericordia.edu* Web: *www.misericordia.edu*

FINANCIAL AID: In 2014-2015, 99% of all full-time freshmen and continuing full-time students received some form of financial aid. 67% of all full-time freshmen and 70% of continuing full-time students received need-based aid. The average freshman award was $27,895. Need-based scholarships or need-based grants averaged $2,989 ($20,235 maximum); need-based self-help aid (loans and jobs) averaged $2,509 ($7,500 maximum); other non-need-based awards and non-need-based scholarships averaged $12,058 ($29,010 maximum); and $10,339 from other forms of aid. The average financial indebtedness of the 2014 graduate was $33,270. is a member of CSS. The FAFSA and the college's own financial statement are required. The priority date for freshman financial aid applications for fall entry is March 1. The deadline for filing freshman financial aid applications for fall entry is May 1.

MOORE COLLEGE OF ART AND DESIGN (*The complete profile is made available exclusively on our website, www.barronspac.com*)

MORAVIAN COLLEGE   F-3
www.moravian.edu

Bethlehem, PA 18018	(610) 861-1320
	(800) 441-3191
Fax: (610) 625-7930	Email: admissions@moravian.edu
Full-time: 670 men, 875 women	Faculty: n/av; IIB, av$
Part-time: 65 men, 140 women	Ph.D.s: n/av
Graduate: 50 men,100 women	Student/Faculty: n/av
Year: semesters, summer session	Tuition: $34,086
Room & Board: $9782	Freshman Class: n/av
SAT or ACT: required	CEEB CODE: 2418
Application Deadline: see profile	VERY COMPETITIVE

Moravian College, founded in 1742, is a private, liberal arts institution affiliated with the Moravian Church. There are 2 undergraduate schools and 1 graduate school. Figures in the above capsule and figures in this profile are approximate. In addition to regional accreditation, Moravian has baccalaureate program accreditation with CAHEA and NASM. The 80-acre campus is in a suburban area 60 miles north of Philadelphia and 90 miles west of New York City. Including any residence halls, there are 127 buildings.

STUDENT LIFE: 63% of undergraduates are from Pennsylvania. Others are from 20 states and 15 foreign countries. 79% are from public schools. 90% are white. 40% are Catholic; 27% Protestant; 12% claim no religious affiliation. The average age of freshmen is 18; all undergraduates, 20. 14% do not continue beyond their first year; 75% remain to graduate.

FACULTY/CLASSROOMS: 51% of faculty are male; 49% are female. All teach and do research. No introductory courses are taught by graduate students. The average class size in an introductory lecture is 19; in a laboratory, 15; and in a regular course, 17.

PROGRAMS OF STUDY: Moravian confers B.A., B.S., and B.Mus. degrees. Master's degrees are also awarded. Bachelor's degrees are awarded in BIOLOGICAL SCIENCE (biochemistry, biology/biological science, and neurosciences), BUSINESS (accounting, business administration and management, business economics, and international business management), COMMUNICATIONS AND THE ARTS (art history and appreciation, classics, dramatic arts, English, French, German, graphic design, music, Spanish, and studio art), COMPUTER AND PHYSICAL SCIENCE (chemistry, computer science, mathematics, and physics), EDUCATION (art education, elementary education, music education, and secondary education),

HEALTH PROFESSIONS (nursing), SOCIAL SCIENCE (criminal justice, economics, German area studies, history, philosophy, political science/government, psychology, religion, social science, and sociology). Physics, chemistry, and computer science are the strongest academically. Psychology, management, and sociology have the largest enrollments.

ACTIVITIES: 10% of men belong to 1 local and 2 national fraternities; 22% of women belong to 4 national sororities. There are 77 groups on campus, including alumni, art, band, cheerleading, choir, chorale, chorus, communications, computers, dance, debate, drama, environmental, ethnic, gay, honors, international, jazz band, literary magazine, marching band, newspaper, orchestra, outdoor recreation, pep band, photography, political, professional, radio, religious, social, social service, and student government. Popular campus events include Arts and Lecture series, Christmas Vesper services, and Mardi Gras Dance.

SERVICES: Counseling and information services are available, as is tutoring in most subjects. There is a reader service for the blind, including peer assistance, and a writing center. **Library/Resources:** The library contains 263,000 volumes, 11,000 microform items, 5,385 audio/video tapes/CDs/DVDs, and subscribes to 15,415 periodicals including electronic. Computerized library services include interlibrary loans, database searching, and Internet access. Special learning facilities include an art gallery. **Physically Challenged Students:** Facilities include wheelchair ramps, elevators, special parking, specially equipped restrooms, special class scheduling, lowered drinking fountains, lowered telephones, and special housing. **Special:** The college offers 3-2 engineering degrees in conjunction with Washington University and a 4-1 engineering program with Lehigh University. Moravian also offers cooperative programs in allied health, natural resource management, and geology with Lehigh, Duke, and Thomas Jefferson Universities. Cross-registration is available with Lehigh and DeSales Universities and Lafayette, Muhlenberg, and Cedar Crest Colleges. Internships, study abroad in many countries, a Washington semester, and student-designed majors may be pursued. There are 17 national honor societies and 30 departmental honors programs. **Visiting:** There are regularly scheduled orientations for prospective students, including information sessions, tours and interviews with admissions staff. There are guides for informal visits, visitors may sit in on classes, and stay overnight. To schedule a visit, contact the Office of Admission. **Campus Safety and Security:** Measures include 24-hour foot and vehicle patrol, emergency notification system, self-defense education, and security escort services. There are shuttle buses, emergency telephones, lighted pathways/sidewalks, an ongoing crime prevention program supervised by a crime prevention officer.

REQUIREMENTS: The SAT or ACT is required. Applicants must graduate from an accredited secondary school or have a GED. Moravian requires 16 Carnegie units, based on 4 years each of English and social science, 3 to 4 of math, and 2 each of lab science, a foreign language, and electives. Essays are required and interviews are recommended. For music students, auditions are required; for art students, portfolios are required. AP and CLEP credits are accepted. Important factors in the admissions decision are advanced placement or honors courses, recommendations by school officials, and leadership record.

FINANCIAL AID: Moravian is a member of CSS. The CSS/Profile and FAFSA are required. Check with the school for current deadlines.

MOUNT ALOYSIUS COLLEGE   C-3
www.mtaloy.edu

Cresson, PA 16630	(814) 886-6383
	(888) 823-2220
Fax: (814) 886-6441	Email: admissions@mtaloy.edu
Full-time: 385 men, 881 women	Faculty: 68
Part-time: 78 men, 267 women	Ph.D.s: 44%
Graduate: 11 men, 27 women	Student/Faculty: 18 to 1
Year: semesters, summer session	Tuition: $20,790
Room & Board: $9186	Freshman Class: 1189 applied, 850 accepted, 338 enrolled
SAT or ACT: required	CEEB CODE: 2420
Application Deadline: rolling	COMPETITIVE

Mount Aloysius College, a comprehensive, private, Catholic, co-educational, liberal arts and sciences based college offering undergraduate and graduate education emphasizing career preparation and Mercy values. Our campus overlooks the Allegheny Mountains in the Laurel Highlands of west central Pennsylvania. There are 3 undergraduate schools and 1 graduate school. In addition to regional accreditation, Mount Aloysius College has baccalaureate program accreditation with APTA, NLN, CAPTE, CAAHEP, and NAACLS. The 220-acre campus is in a small town in the southern Allegheny Mountains between Altoona and Johnstown. Including any residence halls, there are 14 buildings.

STUDENT LIFE: 90% of undergraduates are from Pennsylvania. Others are from 20 states, 15 foreign countries, and Canada. 80% are from public schools. 94% are White. 40% are Catholic; 35% Protestant. The average age of freshmen is 19; all undergraduates, 25. 30% do not continue beyond their first year; 60% remain to graduate. **Housing:** 545 students can be accommodated in college housing, which includes single-sex and coed dorms, on-campus apartments, and off-campus apartments. In addition, there are special-interest houses, Christian Living Community. On-campus housing is guaranteed for all 4 years, and is available on a first-come, first-served basis. Priority is given to out-of-town students. 60% of students commute. Alcohol is not permitted. All students may keep cars.

FACULTY/CLASSROOMS: 39% of faculty are male; 61% are female. All teach and do research. No introductory courses are taught by graduate students. The average class size in an introductory lecture is 17; in a laboratory is 12; and in a regular course is 17.

PROGRAMS OF STUDY: Mount Aloysius College confers B.A., and B.S. degrees. Associate and Master's degrees are also awarded. Bachelor's degrees are awarded in BIOLOGICAL SCIENCE (biology/biological science, biotechnology, and environmental biology), BUSINESS (accounting, business administration and management, business economics, entrepreneurial studies, human resources, management information systems, management science, marketing management, nonprofit/public organization management, organizational leadership and management, and small business management), COMMUNICATIONS AND THE ARTS (American Sign Language, choral music, English, and voice), COMPUTER AND PHYSICAL SCIENCE (computer security and information assurance, information sciences and systems, radiological technology, science, and web technology), EDUCATION ((Education) Childhood Education, early childhood education, education, elementary education, English education, middle school education, science education, secondary education, and social studies education), ENGINEERING AND ENVIRONMENTAL DESIGN (computational sciences and environmental science), HEALTH PROFESSIONS (allied health, chiropractic, health care administration, medical laboratory technology, medical technology, nuclear medical technology, nursing, nursing home administration, occupational therapy, physical therapy, physical therapy assistant, physician's assistant, preallied health, predentistry, premedicine, preoptometry, preosteopathy, prepharmacy, prephysical therapy, prepodiatry, preventive/wellness health care, preveterinary science, radiation therapy, radiograph medical technology, radiological science, and ultrasound technology), SOCIAL SCIENCE (behavioral science, child care/child and family studies, community psychology, criminal justice, criminology, history, humanities, humanities and social science, interpreter for the deaf, law, law enforcement and corrections, liberal arts/general studies, paralegal studies, political science/government, prelaw, psychology, public administration, religion, social studies, and women's studies). Nursing, medical imaging, and allied health sciences are the strongest academically. Nursing, medical imaging, and business have the largest enrollments.

ACTIVITIES: There are 100 groups on campus, including art, band, campus ministry (community service organization) and all academic majors have a club, cheerleading, choir, chorale, chorus, computers, dance, drama, environmental, ethnic, forensics, honors, international, musical theater, newspaper, photography, political, professional, religious, social, social service, student government, and yearbook. Popular campus events include Madrigal Dinner, Heritage days, Mountie Madness, and Christmas at MAC. **Sports:** There are 6 intercollegiate sports for men and 8 for women, and 13 intramural sports for men and 12 for women. Facilities include a 3500-seat athletic convocation and wellness center with floating gym floor, auxiliary gym, 2 weight-and-exercise rooms, and 6 locker rooms. **Graduates:** From July 1, 2013 to June 30, 2014, 176 bachelor's degrees were awarded. The most popular majors were nursing (28%), business administration (14%), and criminology (10%). 200 companies recruited on campus in 2013-2014. In an average class, 27% graduate in 3 years or less, 45% graduate in 4 years or less, 50% graduate in 5 years or less, and 51% graduate in 6 years or less. Of the 2013 graduating class, 22% were enrolled in graduate school within 6 months of graduation, and 97% were employed.

SERVICES: Counseling and information services are available, as is tutoring in every subject. There is remedial math, reading, and writing. **Library/Resources:** The library contains 77,186 volumes, 4,680 microform items, 2,431 audio/video tapes/CDs/DVDs, and subscribes to 275 periodicals including electronic. Computerized library services include interlibrary loans, database searching, Internet access, and Wi-Fi capability. Special learning facilities include an art gallery. **Physically Challenged Students:** All of the campus is accessible. Facilities include wheelchair ramps, elevators, special parking, specially equipped restrooms, special class scheduling, lowered drinking fountains, lowered telephones, and special housing. **Special:** The Professional Studies curriculum provides a student-designed course of study, with an emphasis in behavior and social science, humanities, math/science/computer science, or prelaw. B.A.-B.S. degrees are offered, as are internships in nursing, business, criminology, and student teaching. Our education department offers Early Level Pre K-4/Middle Level 4-8, and secondary education. There are 3 national honor societies, a freshman honors program, and 1 departmental honors program. **Visiting:** There are regularly scheduled orientations for prospective students, on the hour and select Saturdays. There are guides for informal visits, visitors may sit in on classes, and stay overnight. To schedule a visit, contact the Admissions Office at admissions@mtaloy.edu. **Campus Safety and Security:** Measures include 24-hour foot and vehicle patrol, emergency notification system, self-defense education, and security escort services. There are shuttle buses, emergency telephones, lighted pathways/sidewalks, and controlled access to dorms/residences.

REQUIREMENTS: The SAT or ACT is required. Applicants must graduate from an accredited high school or have the GED. A placement test and any necessary developmental studies classes may need to be taken. Science classes and an interview are required of some allied health programs. AP and CLEP credits are accepted. Important factors in the admissions decision are recommendations by school officials, advanced placement or honors courses, and leadership record. Baccalaureate-level students are required during their final semester of study to complete 2 3-credit courses designed to integrate and synthesize scientific, behavioral, and moral concepts. Students in allied health programs must complete an approved clinical experience. Courses in research writing and speech are required. A total of 120 credits is required with an overall 2.0 GPA, including a C average in all core courses. **Procedure:** Freshmen are admitted fall and spring. Entrance exams should be taken as early as possible. There is a rolling admissions plan. Check with the school for current application deadlines. The application fee is $30. Notifications are sent in weekly. 7 applicants were on the 2014 waiting list. Applications are accepted on-line. **Transfer Students:** 250 transfer students enrolled in 2013-2014. Transfer students must have a 2.0 GPA. Only courses with a C or better will be considered for transfer; all other requirements are the same as for freshmen. 30 of 120 credits required for the bachelor's degree must be completed at Mount Aloysius College. **International Students:** There are 23 international students enrolled. The school actively recruits these students. They must take the TOEFL with a minimum score of 500 on the paper-based TOEFL (PBT) or 61 on the Internet-based version (iBT) and the Comprehensive English Language Test. They must also take the SAT or ACT. Student must also take the New Jersey Basic Skills Test.

ADMISSIONS: 71% of the 2014-2015 applicants were accepted. 5 freshmen graduated first in their class. **Admissions Contact:** Francis Crouse, Vice President for Enrollment Management. E-Mail: *admissions@mtaloy.edu* Web: *www.mtaloy.edu*

FINANCIAL AID: In 2014-2015, 94% of all full-time freshmen and 95% of continuing full-time students received some form of financial aid. 85% of all full-time freshmen and 86% of continuing full-time

students received need-based aid. The average freshman award was $11,000. Need-based scholarships or need-based grants averaged $3,000 ($5,000 maximum); need-based self-help aid (loans and jobs) averaged $3,000 ($5,000 maximum); and other non-need-based awards and non-need-based scholarships averaged $3,000 ($7,000 maximum). 65% of undergraduate students work part-time. Average annual earnings from campus work are $750. The average financial indebtedness of the 2014 graduate was $17,125. Mount Aloysius College is a member of CSS. The FAFSA, and Affidavit for International Students is required. The priority date for freshman financial aid applications for fall entry is April 1. The deadline for filing freshman financial aid applications for fall entry is May 1.

MUHLENBERG COLLEGE — E-3
www.muhlenberg.edu

Allentown, PA 18104   (484) 664-3200

Fax: (484) 664-3234   Email: admissions@muhlenberg.edu
Full-time: 948 men, 1375 women   Faculty: 173; IIB, av$
Part-time: 61 men, 64 women   Ph.D.s: 88%
Graduate: n/av   Student/Faculty: 11 to 1
Year: semesters, summer session   Tuition: $42,755
Room & Board: $10,080   Freshman Class: 5152 applied, 2378 accepted, 579 enrolled
   CEEB CODE: 2424
Application Deadline: February 15   **HIGHLY COMPETITIVE**

Muhlenberg College, established in 1848, is a private liberal arts institution affiliated with the Lutheran Church. The 82-acre campus is in a suburban area 50 miles north of Philadelphia and 90 miles west of New York City. Including any residence halls, there are 91 buildings. **STUDENT LIFE:** 79% of undergraduates are from out of state, mostly the Middle Atlantic. Students are from 39 states, and 15 foreign countries. 70% are from public schools. 77% are White; 32% are Jewish; 30% Catholic; 12% Protestant. The average age of freshmen is 18; all undergraduates, 21. 10% do not continue beyond their first year; 86% remain to graduate.

FACULTY/CLASSROOMS: 50% of faculty are male; 50% are female. All teach undergraduates, and 84% do both. No introductory courses are taught by graduate students. The average class size in an introductory lecture is 26; in a laboratory is 16; and in a regular course is 19.

PROGRAMS OF STUDY: Muhlenberg confers B.A., and B.S. degrees. Associate degrees are also awarded. Bachelor's degrees are awarded in BIOLOGICAL SCIENCE (biochemistry, biology/biological science, and neurosciences), BUSINESS (accounting, banking and finance, and business administration and management), COMMUNICATIONS AND THE ARTS (art, communications, dance, dramatic arts, English, film arts, French, German, music, and Spanish), COMPUTER AND PHYSICAL SCIENCE (chemistry, computer science, mathematics, natural sciences, physical sciences, and physics), ENGINEERING AND ENVIRONMENTAL DESIGN (environmental science), SOCIAL SCIENCE (American studies, anthropology, economics, German area studies, history, international studies, philosophy, political science/government, psychology, religion, Russian and Slavic studies, and sociology). Biology, theatre, and psychology are the strongest academically. Biology, business administration, and psychology have the largest enrollments.

ACTIVITIES: 14% of men belong to 4 national fraternities; 17% of women belong to 1 local and 4 national sororities. There are 126 groups on campus, including step team, human rights, art, band, cheerleading, chess, choir, chorale, chorus, computers, dance, drama, environmental, ethnic, film, gay, honors, international, jazz band, literary magazine, musical theater, newspaper, opera, orchestra, pep band, photography, political, professional, radio and TV, religious, social, social service, student government, and yearbook. Popular campus events include Spring Fling Weekend, Candlelight Carols and Jefferson Field Day.

SERVICES: Counseling and information services are available, as is tutoring in every subject. There is a reader service for the blind. There

is also a writing center. **Library/Resources:** The library contains 338,859 volumes, 359,462 microform items, and 12,836 audio/video tapes/CDs/DVDs, and subscribes to 39,453 periodicals including electronic. Computerized library services include interlibrary loans, database searching, Internet access, and Wi-Fi capability. Special learning facilities include an art gallery, natural history museum, radio station, TV station, 2 environmental field stations. **Physically Challenged Students:** 95% of the campus is accessible. Facilities include wheelchair ramps, elevators, special parking, specially equipped restrooms, special class scheduling, lowered drinking fountains, lowered telephones, special housing. **Special:** Students may cross-register with Lehigh, Lafayette, Cedar Crest, Moravian, and Allentown Colleges. Internships, work-study programs, B.A.-B.S. degrees, study abroad in Asia, Australia, Latin America, Russia, and Europe, and a Washington semester are available. Dual majors and student-designed majors may be pursued. A 3-2 engineering degree is available in cooperation with Columbia and Washington Universities, a 4-4 assured admission medical program is offered with Drexel University College of Medicine, a 3-4 dental program is offered with University of Pennsylvania, and a 3-2 forestry degree is offered in cooperation with Duke University. An army ROTC program is also available. Nondegree study and a pass/fail grading option are also offered. There are 14 national honor societies, including Phi Beta Kappa, a freshman honors program, and 8 departmental honors programs. **Visiting:** There are regularly scheduled orientations for prospective students, consisting of a tour of the campus and a personal interview. There are 2 open houses in the fall and 1 in the spring. There are guides for informal visits, visitors may sit in on classes, and stay overnight.. **Campus Safety and Security:** Measures include 24-hour foot and vehicle patrol, self-defense education, and security escort services. There are shuttle buses, emergency telephones, and lighted pathways/sidewalks.

REQUIREMENTS: Applicants must graduate from an accredited secondary school or have a GED. 16 Carnegie units are required, and students must complete 4 courses in English, 3 in math, and 2 each in history, science, and a foreign language. All students must submit essays. Interviews are recommended and are required for those who do not submit SAT scores. AP and CLEP credits are accepted. Important factors in the admissions decision are geographical diversity, evidence of special talent, personality/intangible qualities, parents or siblings attended your school, extracurricular activities record, recommendations by alumni, recommendations by school officials, ability to finance college education, leadership record, and advanced placement or honors courses.

ADMISSIONS: 46% of a recent year applicants were accepted. The SAT scores for the 2013-2014 freshman class were: Critical Reading--3% below 500, 35% between 500 and 599, 45% between 600 and 699, and 17% between 700 and 800; Math--4% below 500, 33% between 500 and 599, 52% between 600 and 699, and 11% between 700 and 800; Writing--3% below 500, 36% between 500 and 599, 45% between 600 and 699, and 16% between 700 and 800. The ACT scores were 23% above 28.

FINANCIAL AID: In a recent year, 90% of all full-time freshmen and 82% of continuing full-time students received some form of financial aid. 53% of all full-time freshmen and 51% of continuing full-time students received need-based aid. The average freshman award was $24,762. Need-based scholarships or need-based grants averaged $25,175 ($46,700 maximum); need-based self-help aid (loans and jobs) averaged $5,119 ($9,300 maximum); and other non-need-based awards and non-need-based scholarships averaged $12,215 ($26,000 maximum). Muhlenberg is a member of CSS. The CSS/Profile, FAFSA, and the college's own financial statement, and parent and student tax returns and W-2 forms are required. The priority date for freshman financial aid applications for fall entry is February 15. The deadline for filing freshman financial aid applications for fall entry is February 15.

NEUMANN UNIVERSITY (*The complete profile is made available exclusively on our website, www.barronspac.com*)

PEIRCE COLLEGE (*The complete profile is made available exclusively on our website, www.barronspac.com*)

PENN STATE ERIE/THE BEHREND COLLEGE   B-1
www.psbehrend.psu.edu

Erie, PA 16563	(814) 898-6100
	(866) 374-3378
Fax: (814) 898-6044	Email: behrend.admissions@psu.edu
Full-time: 2473 men, 1358 women	Faculty: 204; IIB, av$
Part-time: 103 men, 81 women	Ph.D.s: 61%
Graduate: 81 men, 26 women	Student/Faculty: 16 to 1
Year: semesters, summer session	Tuition: $11,500 ($16,500)
Room & Board: $6730	Freshman Class: 2590 applied, 2092 accepted, 854 enrolled
SAT or ACT: required	CEEB CODE: 2660
Application Deadline: open	COMPETITIVE

Penn State Erie/The Behrend College, founded in 1948, offers 34 baccalaureate programs as well as the first 2 years of most Penn State University Park baccalaureate programs. It offers courses in business, humanities, social sciences, science, engineering technology, and engineering. There are 5 undergraduate schools and 1 graduate school. In addition to regional accreditation, Penn State Erie has baccalaureate program accreditation with AACSB, ABET, and NLN. The 840-acre campus is in a suburban area 5 miles east of Erie. Including any residence halls, there are 45 buildings.

STUDENT LIFE: 92% of undergraduates are from Pennsylvania. Others are from 28 states, 23 foreign countries, and Canada. 86% are white. The average age of freshmen is 18; all undergraduates, 22. 9% do not continue beyond their first year; 61% remain to graduate.

FACULTY/CLASSROOMS: 70% of faculty are male; 30% are female. All teach and do research. No introductory courses are taught by graduate students. The average class size in an introductory lecture is 35; in a laboratory is 18; and in a regular course is 29.

PROGRAMS OF STUDY: Penn State Erie confers B.A., B.S., B.F.A. degrees. Associate and Master's degrees are also awarded. Bachelor's degrees are awarded in BIOLOGICAL SCIENCE (biology/biological science), BUSINESS (accounting, banking and finance, business administration and management, business economics, management information systems, and marketing management), COMMUNICATIONS AND THE ARTS (communications and English), COMPUTER AND PHYSICAL SCIENCE (chemistry, computer science, mathematics, physics, and science), ENGINEERING AND ENVIRONMENTAL DESIGN (computer engineering, engineering, engineering technology, mechanical engineering technology, and plastics technology), SOCIAL SCIENCE (economics, history, political science/government, and psychology). Management information systems, psychology, and math are the strongest academically. Engineering, business, and psychology have the largest enrollments.

ACTIVITIES: 5% of men belong to 3 national fraternities; 16% of women belong to 3 national sororities. There are 80 groups on campus, including band, cheerleading, chess, choir, computers, dance, drama, ethnic, gay, honors, international, jazz band, literary magazine, newspaper, pep band, political, professional, radio and TV, religious, social, social service, student government, and yearbook. Popular campus events include a speaker series, parents events, and black cultural awareness month.

SERVICES: Counseling and information services are available, as is tutoring in every subject. There is a reader service for the blind, and remedial math, reading, and writing. **Library/Resources:** Computerized library services include interlibrary loans, database searching, Internet access, and Wi-Fi capability. Special learning facilities include a radio station, engineering workstation labs, media labs, and an observatory. **Physically Challenged Students:** 90% of the campus is accessible. Facilities include wheelchair ramps, elevators, special parking, specially equipped restrooms, special class scheduling, lowered drinking fountains, and lowered telephones. **Special:** Internships, study abroad in 14 countries, work-study programs, and accelerated degree programs are available. In addition, a B.A.-B.S. degree in psychology, a 3-2 engineering degree with Edinboro University, dual majors, a general studies degree, and student-designed majors in business and general arts and sciences are offered. Nonde-

gree study and up to 12 credits of pass/fail options are possible. There are 4 national honor societies and a freshman honors program. **Visiting:** There are regularly scheduled orientations for prospective students, including meetings with a counselor and faculty, a campus tour, and a class visit. There are guides for informal visits, visitors may sit in on classes, and stay overnight. To schedule a visit, contact the Admissions Office. **Campus Safety and Security:** Measures include 24-hour foot and vehicle patrol, self-defense education, and security escort services. There are emergency telephones and lighted pathways/sidewalks.

REQUIREMENTS: The SAT or ACT is required. Candidates for admission must have 15 academic credits or 15 Carnegie units, including 5 in social studies, 4 in English, 3 each in math and science, and 2 in foreign language. The GED is accepted. AP and CLEP credits are accepted.

ADMISSIONS: 81% of a recent year applicants were accepted. 25% of the current freshmen were in the top fifth of their class; 40% were in the top two fifths. 12 freshmen graduated first in their class.

FINANCIAL AID: The FAFSA is required. The priority date for freshman financial aid applications for fall entry is February 15. Check with the school for application deadlines and fees.

PENN STATE UNIVERSITY/ALTOONA   C-3
www.altoona.psu.edu

Altoona, PA 16601	(814) 949-5466
	(800) 848-9843
Fax: n/av	Email: aaadmit@psu.edu
Full-time: 1955 men, 1815 women	Faculty: n/av
Part-time: 115 men, 178 women	Ph.D.s: n/av
Graduate: 5 men, 5 women	Student/Faculty: n/av
Year: semesters, summer session	Tuition: $15,624 ($27,706)
Room & Board: $10,500	Freshman Class: n/av
SAT or ACT: required	CEEB CODE: 2660
Application Deadline: open	COMPETITIVE

Penn State Altoona, founded in 1939, offers 18 baccalaureate degree programs, 8 associate degrees, and 19 minors. There are 17 undergraduate schools and 1 graduate school. Figures in the above capsule and in this profile are approximate. In addition to regional accreditation, Penn State Altoona has baccalaureate program accreditation with ABET, NASAD, NCATE, and NRPA. The library contains 90,000 audio/video tapes/CDs/DVDs, and subscribes to 500 periodicals including electronic. Computerized library services include interlibrary loans, database searching, Internet access, and laptop Internet portals. Special learning facilities include a learning resource center, art gallery, Pic-Tel teleconferencing, 5 state-of-the-art engineering labs, and CAD/CAM computer lab facilities. The 150-acre campus is in a suburban area. Including any residence halls, there are 33 buildings.

STUDENT LIFE: 85% of undergraduates are from Pennsylvania. Others are from 28 states, 20 foreign countries, and Canada. 84% are white. The average age of freshmen is 18; all undergraduates, 22. 12% do not continue beyond their first year; 65% remain to graduate.

FACULTY/CLASSROOMS: No introductory courses are taught by graduate students. The average class size in an introductory lecture is 50; in a laboratory, 24; and in a regular course, 28.

PROGRAMS OF STUDY: Penn State Altoona confers B.A. and B.S. degrees. Associates and Master's degrees are also awarded. Bachelor's degrees are awarded in AGRICULTURE (environmental studies), BIOLOGICAL SCIENCE (biology/biological science), BUSINESS (business administration and management), COMMUNICATIONS AND THE ARTS (communications, English, and visual and performing arts), COMPUTER AND PHYSICAL SCIENCE (mathematics and science), EDUCATION (elementary education), ENGINEERING AND ENVIRONMENTAL DESIGN (electromechanical technology), HEALTH PROFESSIONS (nursing), SOCIAL SCIENCE (criminal justice, history, human development, and liberal arts/general studies). Engineering and education are the strongest academically. Business, criminal justice, and elementary education have the largest enrollments.

ACTIVITIES: There are 5 local fraternities and 2 local sororities.

There are 70 groups on campus, including cheerleading, choir, communications, dance, drama, ethnic, gay, honors, horticulture, international, jazz band, literary magazine, martial arts, newspaper, pep band, political, professional, religious, social, social service, STEP team, student government, and yearbook. Popular campus events include Distinguished Speaker Series, Hoops Hysteria, and Black History and Women's History Month events. **SERVICES:** Counseling and information services are available, as is tutoring in most subjects. There is remedial math, reading, and writing. **Library/Resources:** The library contains 90,000 audio/video tapes/CDs/DVDs, and subscribes to 500 periodicals including electronic. Computerized library services include interlibrary loans, database searching, Internet access, and Wi-Fi capability. Special learning facilities include an art gallery, Pic-Tel teleconferencing, 5 state-of-the-art engineering labs, and CAD/CAM computer lab facilities. **Physically Challenged Students:** 95% of the campus is accessible. Facilities include wheelchair ramps, elevators, special parking, specially equipped restrooms, special class scheduling, lowered drinking fountains, and lowered telephones. **Special:** Internships, study abroad in 5 countries, work-study programs, B.A.-B.S. degrees, accelerated degree programs, and dual and student-designed majors are available. There is an integrative arts major, which allows students to pursue interest across artistic boundaries. There is a Phi Beta Kappa and a freshman honors program. **Visiting:** There are regularly scheduled orientations for prospective students, including campus tours and meetings with academic counselors and faculty. There are guides for informal visits, visitors may sit in on classes, and stay overnight. To schedule a visit, contact the Admissions Office - Altoona campus. **Campus Safety and Security:** Measures include 24-hour foot and vehicle patrol, emergency notification system, self-defense education, and security escort services. There are shuttle buses, emergency telephones, and lighted pathways/sidewalks.

REQUIREMENTS: The SAT or ACT is required. Applicants should have 15 academic or Carnegie units, including 4 in English, 3 each in math, science, and social studies, and 2 in foreign language (required for some majors). The GED is accepted. AP and CLEP credits are accepted.

FINANCIAL AID: Some academic scholarships require a specific application, which varies according to the college/major. Check with the school for current deadlines.

PENNSYLVANIA COLLEGE OF TECHNOLOGY *(The complete profile is made available exclusively on our website, www. barronspac.com)*

PENNSYLVANIA STATE SYSTEM OF HIGHER EDUCATION

The Pennsylvania State System of Higher Education, established in 1983, is a public system in Pennsylvania. It is governed by a board of governors, whose chief administrator is the chancellor. The primary goal of the system is to provide high-quality liberal arts education at an affordable cost with a central mission of teaching and service. The main priorities are capital facilities matters of maintenance and funding, social equity, and tuition stabilization through appropriate funding. The total student enrollment is usually about 100,000 with 5500 faculty members. Altogether there are 217 baccalaureate, 107 master's, and 6 doctoral programs offered in the Pennsylvania State System of Higer Education. Profiles of the 4-year campuses are included in this section.

PHILADELPHIA UNIVERSITY	F-3
www.philau.edu	

Philadelphia, PA 19144	(215) 951-2700
	(800) 951-7287
Fax: (215) 951-2907	Email: admissions@philau.edu
Full-time: 940 men, 1739 women	Faculty: 110; IIA, av$
Part-time: 60 men, 149 women	Ph.Ds: 83%
Graduate: 208 men, 444 women	Student/Faculty: 24 to 1
Year: semesters, summer session	Tuition: $33,590
Room & Board: $10,660	Freshman Class: 3602 applied, 2590 accepted, 604 enrolled
SAT or ACT: required	CEEB CODE: 2666
Application Deadline: n/av	COMPETITIVE

Philadelphia University, founded in 1884, is a private institution offering preprofessional programs in architecture, design, business, sciences, textiles, fashion, and health. There are 6 undergraduate schools and 1 graduate school. In addition to regional accreditation, PhilaU has baccalaureate program accreditation with ABET, FIDER, NAAB, and NASAD. The 100-acre campus is in a suburban area 10 minutes west of metropolitan Philadelphia. Including any residence halls, there are 56 buildings.

STUDENT LIFE: 52% of undergraduates are from Pennsylvania. Others are from 37 states, 24 foreign countries, and Canada. 65% are from public schools. 72% are White. 18% claim no religious affiliation The average age of freshmen is 23; all undergraduates, 20. 20% do not continue beyond their first year; 56% remain to graduate.

FACULTY/CLASSROOMS: 58% of faculty are male; 42% are female. All teach undergraduates, and 50% do both. No introductory courses are taught by graduate students. The average class size in an introductory lecture is 25; in a laboratory is 14; and in a regular course is 17.

PROGRAMS OF STUDY: PhilaU confers B.S., and B.Arch. degrees. Associate, Master's, and Doctoral degrees are also awarded. Bachelor's degrees are awarded in BIOLOGICAL SCIENCE (biochemistry and biology/biological science), BUSINESS (accounting, banking and finance, fashion merchandising, international business management, management information systems, management science, and marketing/retailing/merchandising), COMMUNICATIONS AND THE ARTS (graphic design and industrial design), COMPUTER AND PHYSICAL SCIENCE (chemistry, digital arts/technology, and science and management), ENGINEERING AND ENVIRONMENTAL DESIGN (architecture, engineering, environmental science, industrial engineering, interior design, landscape architecture/design, textile engineering, and textile technology), HEALTH PROFESSIONS (physician's assistant and premedicine), SOCIAL SCIENCE (biopsychology, fashion design and technology, and psychology). Physician's assistant, architecture, and engineering are the strongest academically. Architecture, fashion merchandising, and fashion design have the largest enrollments.

ACTIVITIES: There are 30 groups on campus, including cheerleading, choir, dance, drama, ethnic, gay, honors, international, newspaper, professional, religious, social, social service, and student government. Popular campus events include Annual Fashion Show and Design Competition, Welcome Week, and Spring Weekend.

SERVICES: Counseling and information services are available, as is tutoring in every subject. There is a reader service for the blind, and remedial math, reading, and writing. Study skills workshops, course-related workshops, math review sessions, writing review sessions, time management and stress reduction workshops. **Library/Resources:** The library contains 109,235 volumes, 125,000 microform items, and 50,630 audio/video tapes/CDs/DVDs, and subscribes to 1,011 periodicals including electronic. Computerized library services include interlibrary loans and database searching. Special learning facilities include an art gallery, the Design Center at Philadelphia University. **Physically Challenged Students:** 85% of the campus is accessible. Facilities include wheelchair ramps, elevators, special parking, specially equipped restrooms, special class scheduling, lowered drinking fountains, and lowered telephones. **Special:** Internships in all academic majors, study abroad, a dual major in international business, an accelerated business administration degree program, and an integrated major in business and science are available. There are a freshman honors program. **Visiting:** There are regularly scheduled orientations for prospective students, including an interview and a campus tour. There are guides for informal visits, visitors may sit in on classes, and stay overnight. To schedule a visit, contact the Admissions Office at colemanp@philau.edu. **Campus Safety and Security:** Measures include 24-hour foot and vehicle patrol, self-defense education, and security escort services. There are shuttle buses, emergency telephones, and lighted pathways/sidewalks.

REQUIREMENTS: The SAT or ACT is required. Applicants should be high school graduates or have earned the GED. Recommended secondary preparation includes 4 years each of English and history, 3 years of math which must include algebra II and geometry, and 3 years of science and 2 years of social studies, and 1 year of history. Potential science majors are strongly urged to take 4 years of math and science. A GPA of 2.5 is required. AP and CLEP credits are accepted. Important factors in the admissions decision are evidence of special talent, extracurricular activities record, and leadership record.

ADMISSIONS: 72% of a recent year applicants were accepted. 31% of the current freshmen were in the top fifth of their class; 65% were in the top two fifths.

FINANCIAL AID: In a recent year, 78% of all full-time freshmen and 71% of continuing full-time students received some form of financial aid. 78% of all full-time freshmen and 69% of continuing full-time students received need-based aid. The average freshman award was $24,833. Need-based scholarships or need-based grants averaged $20,708; need-based self-help aid (loans and jobs) averaged $5,834; other non-need-based awards and non-need-based scholarships averaged $15,475, The FAFSA is required. The deadline for filing freshman financial aid applications for fall entry is April 15. Check with the school for current applications deadline.

POINT PARK UNIVERSITY   **B-3**
www.pointpark.edu

Pittsburgh, PA 15222	(412) 392-3430
	n/av
Fax: (412) 392-3902	Email: enroll@pointpark.edu
Full-time: 1070 men, 1481 women	Faculty: n/av; IIA, -$
Part-time: 313 men, 362 women	Ph.D.s: 75%
Graduate: 273 men, 342 women	Student/Faculty: 19 to 1
Year: semesters, summer session	Tuition: $26,170
Room & Board: $10,220	Freshman Class: 3237 applied, 2393 accepted, 548 enrolled
SAT or ACT: required	CEEB CODE: 2676
Application Deadline: open	COMPETITIVE

Point Park is a comprehensive, master's-level university with a strong liberal arts tradition. Point Park offers programs through its School of Arts and Sciences, School of Business, School of Communication, and Conservatory of Performing Arts. The University's students represent 44 states and 56 countries. There are 4 undergraduate schools and 4 graduate schools. In addition to regional accreditation, Point Park has baccalaureate program accreditation with ABET. The campus is in an urban area in Downtown Pittsburgh. Including any residence halls, there are 15 buildings.

STUDENT LIFE: 79% of undergraduates are from Pennsylvania. Others are from 49 states, 25 foreign countries, and Canada. 72% are White; 16% African American. The average age of freshmen is 18; all undergraduates, 24. 26% do not continue beyond their first year; 50% remain to graduate.

FACULTY/CLASSROOMS: No introductory courses are taught by graduate students.

PROGRAMS OF STUDY: Point Park confers B.A., B.S. and B.F.A. degrees. Associate and Master's degrees are also awarded. Bachelor's degrees are awarded in AGRICULTURE (environmental studies), BIOLOGICAL SCIENCE (biology/biological science, biotechnology, and forensic science), BUSINESS (accounting, business administration and management, finance, funeral home services, human resources, management science, organizational leadership and management, and sports management), COMMUNICATIONS AND THE ARTS (advertising, applied art, arts administration/management, broadcasting, communications, dance, dramatic arts, English, film arts, journalism, media arts, performing arts, photography, public relations, theatre arts, and video), COMPUTER AND PHYSICAL SCIENCE (computer science, digital arts/technology, earth science, and information sciences and systems), EDUCATION ((Education) Childhood Education, dance education, drama education, early childhood education, education, elementary education, secondary education, and special education), ENGINEERING AND ENVIRONMENTAL DESIGN (civil engineering, civil engineering technology, electrical/electronics engineering, electrical/electronics engineering technology, engineering management, engineering technology, environmental science, mechanical engineering, mechanical engineering technology, and systems engineering), HEALTH PRO-FESSIONS (environmental health science, health care administration, Pre-Health Studies, premedicine, and respiratory therapy), SOCIAL SCIENCE (behavioral science, criminal justice, early childhood studies, history, international studies, law enforcement and corrections, legal studies, liberal arts/general studies, paralegal studies, political science/government, psychology, and public administration). Business, dance, and theater have the largest enrollments.

ACTIVITIES: There are 34 groups on campus, including choir, chorale, computers, dance, drama, ethnic, film, gay, honors, international, literary magazine, musical theater, newspaper, photography, political, professional, radio and TV, religious, social, social service, and student government.

SERVICES: Counseling and information services are available, as is tutoring in some subjects, Learning-disabled services are available on a case-by-case basis. There is a reader service for the blind, and remedial math, reading, and writing. **Library/Resources:** The library contains 82,565 volumes, 16,275 microform items, and 6,831 audio/video tapes/CDs/DVDs, and subscribes to 77,064 periodicals including electronic. Computerized library services include interlibrary loans, database searching, Internet access, and Wi-Fi capability. Special learning facilities include an art gallery, radio station, TV station, natural sciences labs; engineering technology labs; forensic crime scene house; computer newsrooms; MAC and PC multimedia labs; black/white and color photography darkrooms; digital photography lab; radio station, TV studio/newsroom; cinema production and editing suites; performance and dance studios; performing arts center/theaters; and art galleries. **Physically Challenged Students:** 95% of the campus is accessible. Facilities include wheelchair ramps, elevators, specially equipped restrooms, special class scheduling, lowered drinking fountains, lowered telephones, and special housing. **Special:** Cross-registration is available through the Pittsburgh Council on Higher Education. The university offers internships, work study, dual and student-designed majors, credit by exam and for life/military/work experience, and nondegree study. Capstone programs are available for students with associate degrees. Accelerated degree programs are available. There are 2 national honor societies and a freshman honors program. **Visiting:** There are regularly scheduled orientations for prospective students. There are guides for informal visits and visitors may sit in on classes. To schedule a visit, contact the Office of Admissions at (412) 392-3430. **Campus Safety and Security:** Measures include 24-hour foot and vehicle patrol, emergency notification system, self-defense education, and security escort services. There are shuttle buses, emergency telephones, and lighted pathways/sidewalks.

REQUIREMENTS: The SAT or ACT is required. Students should have completed 12 academic credits or 16 Carnegie units consisting of 4 in English, 3 in history, science, and math, and 2 years of foreign language. The GED is accepted. Theater and dance students must audition, and an interview is requested for all candidates. A GPA of 2.0 is required. AP and CLEP credits are accepted.

ADMISSIONS: 74% of a recent year applicants were accepted. The SAT scores for a recent year freshman class were: Critical Reading--45% below 500, 39% between 500 and 599, 14% between 600 and 699, and 2% between 700 and 800; Math--57% below 500, 34% between 500 and 599, 8% between 600 and 699, and 1% between 700 and 800; Writing--52% below 500, 35% between 500 and 599, 12% between 600 and 699, and 2% between 700 and 800. The ACT scores were 34% below 21, 22% between 21 and 23, 25% between 24 and 26, 20% between 27 and 28, and 6% above 28.

FINANCIAL AID: In a recent year, 99% of all full-time freshmen and continuing full-time students received some form of financial aid. 75% of all full-time freshmen and 76% of continuing full-time students received need-based aid. The average freshman award was $29,218. Need-based scholarships or need-based grants averaged $5,664 ($16,000 maximum); need-based self-help aid (loans and jobs) averaged $5,788 ($7,000 maximum); non-need-based athletic scholarships averaged $5,335 ($14,000 maximum); and other non-need-based awards and non-need-based scholarships averaged $11,086 ($31,540 maximum). 16% of undergraduate students work part-time. Average annual earnings from campus work are $2173. The average financial indebtedness of the 2013 graduate was $21,838. The FAFSA is required. The priority date for freshman financial aid applications for fall entry is March 15. The deadline for filing freshman financial aid applications for fall entry is August 15.

ROBERT MORRIS UNIVERSITY   A-3
www.rmu.edu

| Moon Township, PA 15108 | (800) 762-0097 |
| | (412) 397-3000 |

Fax: (412) 397-5915   Email: admissionsoffice@rmu.edu

Full-time: 2343 men, 1625 women   **Faculty:** 214; IIA, +$

Part-time: 239 men, 367 women   **Ph.D.s:** 82%

Graduate: 491 men, 490 women   **Student/Faculty:** 15 to 1

Year: semesters, summer session   **Tuition:** $26,054

Room & Board: $11,810   **Freshman Class:** 6123 applied, 4664 accepted, 888 enrolled

SAT CR/M/W: 517/535/494 **ACT:** 22   **CEEB CODE:** 2769

Application Deadline: May 1   **COMPETITIVE**

Robert Morris University, founded in 1921, is a private institution offering 50 undergraduate degree programs, 34 master's and doctoral degree programs, as well as 23 fully online degree programs. There are 5 undergraduate schools and 5 graduate schools. In addition to regional accreditation, RMU has baccalaureate program accreditation with AACSB, ABET, TEAC, CCNE, Society of Actuaries, and JRC on Educational Programs in Nuclear Medicine. The 230-acre campus is in a suburban area 17 miles southwest of downtown Pittsburgh. Including any residence halls, there are 25 buildings.

STUDENT LIFE: 83% of undergraduates are from Pennsylvania. Others are from 43 states, 41 foreign countries, and Canada. 90% are from public schools. 75% are White. 41% are Catholic; 35% Protestant. The average age of freshmen is 18; all undergraduates, 22. 17% do not continue beyond their first year; 63% remain to graduate. **Housing:** 2015 students can be accommodated in college housing, which includes single-sex and coed dorms and on-campus apartments. On-campus housing is available on a first-come and first-served basis. 53% of students live on campus; of those, 60% remain on campus on weekends. Alcohol is not permitted. All students may keep cars.

FACULTY/CLASSROOMS: 46% of faculty are male; 44% are female. 99% teach undergraduates, 80% do research, and 80% do both. No introductory courses are taught by graduate students. The average class size in an introductory lecture is 22; in a laboratory is 12; and in a regular course is 22.

PROGRAMS OF STUDY: RMU confers B.A., B.S., B.F.A., B.S.B.A. and B.S.N. degrees. Master's and Doctoral degrees are also awarded. Bachelor's degrees are awarded in BIOLOGICAL SCIENCE (biology/biological science), BUSINESS (accounting, banking and finance, business administration and management, hospitality management services, marketing/retailing/merchandising, organizational behavior, and sports management), COMMUNICATIONS AND THE ARTS (communications, English, and media arts), COMPUTER AND PHYSICAL SCIENCE (actuarial science, applied mathematics, and information sciences and systems), EDUCATION (business education and elementary education), ENGINEERING AND ENVIRONMENTAL DESIGN (engineering, environmental science, and manufacturing engineering), HEALTH PROFESSIONS (health care administration, nuclear medical technology, and nursing), SOCIAL SCIENCE (economics, psychology, and social science). Actuarial science and engineering is the strongest academically. Accounting, nursing and engineering have the largest enrollments.

ACTIVITIES: 14% of men belong to 8 national fraternities; 18% of women belong to 6 national sororities. There are 131 groups on campus, including band, cheerleading, choir, chorus, computers, dance, drama, environmental, ethnic, film, gay, honors, international, jazz band, literary magazine, marching band, musical theater, newspaper, pep band, photography, political, professional, radio and TV, religious, social, social service, student government, and yearbook. Popular campus events include Homecoming, Prom and Dances. **Sports:** There are 6 intercollegiate sports for men and 9 for women, and 11 intramural sports for men and 11 for women. Facilities include RMU's Moon Campus offers a field house, gym, health club, and 11 athletic fields. The RMU Island Sports Center (4 miles away) has 2 hockey rinks, golf dome, batting cages, health club, and an 8-lane track. Extensive club sport and intramural programs in addi-

tion to 15 NCAA sports. **Graduates:** From July 1, 2013 to June 30, 2014, 867 bachelor's degrees were awarded. The most popular majors were management (11%), accounting (11%), and communications (9%). 140 companies recruited on campus in 2013-2014. In an average class, 46% graduate in 4 years or less, 61% graduate in 5 years or less, and 63% graduate in 6 years or less. Of the 2013 graduating class, 7% were enrolled in graduate school within 6 months of graduation, and 85% were employed.

SERVICES: Counseling and information services are available, as is tutoring in most subjects. There is a reader service for the blind, and remedial math, reading, and writing. **Library/Resources:** The library contains 106,862 volumes, 7,054 microform items, 3,210 audio/video tapes/CDs/DVDs, and subscribes to 242 periodicals including electronic. Computerized library services include interlibrary loans, database searching, and Internet access. Special learning facilities include an art gallery, radio station, TV station, a manufacturing lab for engineering and other students. Nursing Students also learn to care for patients in state-of-the-art nursing laboratory, where bedside computers and patient simulators assist in developing clinical decision-making skills. **Physically Challenged Students:** 75% of the campus is accessible. Facilities include wheelchair ramps, elevators, special parking, specially equipped restrooms, special class scheduling, lowered drinking fountains, lowered telephones, and special housing. **Special:** The university offers internship programs in most majors, cross-registration with the 9 colleges of the Pittsburgh Council of Higher Education, work-study programs, study abroad in 12 countries, and non-degree study. Credit by exam and pass/fail options are available. There are 9 national honor societies, a freshman honors program, and 1 departmental honors program. **Visiting:** There are regularly scheduled orientations for prospective students, consisting of placement testing, orientation, and academic advising. There are guides for informal visits, visitors may sit in on classes, and stay overnight. To schedule a visit, contact the Admissions Office. **Campus Safety and Security:** Measures include 24-hour foot and vehicle patrol, emergency notification system, and security escort services. There are shuttle buses, emergency telephones, lighted pathways/sidewalks, and controlled access to dorms/residences.

REQUIREMENTS: The SAT is required. Applicants should be graduates of an accredited secondary school or hold a GED diploma. They must have completed 16 Carnegie units, including 4 in English and Social Studies, 3 in math and 2 in science. An interview is required for some and recommended for all others. A GPA of 2.0 is required. AP and CLEP credits are accepted. Important factors in the admissions decision are advanced placement or honors courses, leadership record, and personality/intangible qualities.All candidates must complete 126 to 135 credit hours, including 24 to 31 in the major, with a 2.0 GPA overall and a 2.5 in the major. A core curriculum varies with each major and consists of humanities, communication skills, social sciences, computing, and math. All students must demonstrate competency in computer software applications. **Procedure:** Freshmen are admitted fall, spring, and summer. Entrance exams should be taken by fall or late winter of the senior year. There are deferred admissions and rolling admissions plans. Applications should be filed by May 1 for fall entry; December 1 for spring entry, along with a $30 fee. Notification is sent on a rolling basis. 111 applicants were on the 2014 waiting list; 27 were admitted. Applications are accepted online. **Transfer Students:** 347 transfer students enrolled in 2013-2014. Students must have a minimum 2.0 GPA in nondevelopmental academic courses. Those with fewer than 30 earned credits must also submit an official high school transcript and test results of the SAT or ACT. An interview is recommended. 30 of 126 credits required for the bachelor's degree must be completed at RMU. **International Students:** There are 475 international students enrolled. The school actively recruits these students. They must take the TOEFL with a minimum score of 500 on the paper-based TOEFL (PBT) or 61 on the Internet-based version (iBT).

ADMISSIONS: 76% of the 2014-2015 applicants were accepted. The SAT scores for the 2014-2015 freshman class were: Critical Reading--41% below 500, 45% between 500 and 599, 13% between 600 and 699, and 1% between 700 and 800; Math--33% below 500, 45% between 500 and 599, 22% between 600 and 699, and 1% between 700 and 800; Writing--54% below 500, 35% between 500 and 599, 10% between 600 and 699, and 1% between 700 and 800. 12 freshmen graduated first in their class. **Admissions Contact:** Kellie Laurenzi, Dean of Admissions. E-Mail: *admissionsoffice@rmu.edu* Web: *www.rmu.edu*

FINANCIAL AID: In 2014-2015, 99% of all full-time freshmen and 90% of continuing full-time students received some form of financial aid. 99% of all full-time freshmen and 95% of continuing full-time students received need-based aid. The average freshman award was $22,315. Need-based scholarships or need-based grants averaged $16,939; need-based self-help aid (loans and jobs) averaged $6,089; and non-need-based athletic scholarships averaged $19,763. 100% of undergraduate students work part-time. The average financial indebtedness of the 2014 graduate was $37,531. RMU is a member of CSS. The FAFSA, and PHEAA is required. The deadline for filing freshman financial aid applications for fall entry is May 1.

ROSEMONT COLLEGE   F-4
www.rosemont.edu

Rosemont, PA 19010	(610) 527-0200
	(800) 331-0708
Fax: (610) 520-4399	Email: admissions@rosemont.edu
Full-time: 143 men, 283 women	Faculty: 28
Part-time: 24 men, 74 women	Ph.D.s: 90%
Graduate: 80 men, 304 women	Student/Faculty: 8 to 1
Year: semesters	Tuition: $30,450
Room & Board: $12,380	Freshman Class: 941 applied, 470 accepted, 75 enrolled
SAT CR/M/W: 504/493/500 ACT: 23	CEEB CODE: 2763
Application Deadline: open	COMPETITIVE

Rosemont College, founded in 1921, is an independent coeducational liberal arts and sciences college affiliated with the Roman Catholic Church. Accelerated degree and graduate programs are offered in the School of Graduate and Professional Studies. There are 2 undergraduate schools and 1 graduate school. The 56-acre campus is in a suburban area 11 miles west of Philadelphia. Including any residence halls, there are 15 buildings.

STUDENT LIFE: 75% of undergraduates are from Pennsylvania. Others are from 11 states, and 14 foreign countries. 40% are White; 35% African American. 60% are Catholic; 17% Protestant; 15% Muslim, and Quaker. The average age of freshmen is 18; all undergraduates, 23. 8% do not continue beyond their first year; 72% remain to graduate.

FACULTY/CLASSROOMS: 40% of faculty are male; 60% are female. All teach undergraduates. No introductory courses are taught by graduate students. The average class size in an introductory lecture is 20; in a laboratory is 10; and in a regular course is 12.

PROGRAMS OF STUDY: Rosemont confers B.A., B.F.A. and B.S. degrees. Master's degrees are also awarded. Bachelor's degrees are awarded in BIOLOGICAL SCIENCE (biochemistry and biology/biological science), BUSINESS (accounting and business administration and management), COMMUNICATIONS AND THE ARTS (communications, English, fine arts, French, German, and Spanish), COMPUTER AND PHYSICAL SCIENCE (chemistry and mathematics), EDUCATION (art education, education, foreign languages education, and secondary education), ENGINEERING AND ENVIRONMENTAL DESIGN (environmental science), HEALTH PROFESSIONS (predentistry and premedicine), SOCIAL SCIENCE (economics, history, humanities, Italian studies, liberal arts/general studies, philosophy, political science/government, prelaw, psychology, religion, social science, sociology, and women's studies). Biology, chemstry, and liberal arts are the strongest academically. Biology, psychology, business, English literature, and studio art have the largest enrollments.

ACTIVITIES: There are 23 groups on campus, including art, band, choir, chorus, dance, drama, ethnic, gay, honors, international, jazz band, literary magazine, marching band, musical theater, newspaper, orchestra, photography, political, professional, religious, social service, student government, symphony, and yearbook. Popular campus events include Oktoberfest, Founders Day, and International/Multi-Cultural Festival and Petaltones Concert.

SERVICES: Counseling and information services are available, as is tutoring in every subject. A writing and learning resource center **Library/Resources:** The library contains 165,425 volumes, 22,908 microform items, and 3,425 audio/video tapes/CDs/DVDs, and subscribes to 16,370 periodicals including electronic. Computerized library services include interlibrary loans, database searching, Internet access, and Wi-Fi capability. Special learning facilities include an art gallery. **Physically Challenged Students:** 20% of the campus is accessible. Facilities include wheelchair ramps, elevators, special parking, specially equipped restrooms, special class scheduling, lowered drinking fountains, and lowered telephones. **Special:** Cross-registration opportunities are available with Villanova, Arcadia, Eastern, Holy Family, Immaculata, and Neumann Universities; Cabrini, Gwynedd-Mercy, and Chestnut Hill Colleges; and the Art Institute International Exchange Program. There is a joint admission program with Temple University School of Dentistry and Drexel University College of Medicine. Internships, study abroad, a Washington semester, dual and student-designed majors, and accelerated degree programs are also available. There are 6 national honor societies and a freshman honors program. **Visiting:** There are regularly scheduled orientations for prospective students, including a campus tour and meetings with financial aid advisers, faculty, and student life representatives. There are guides for informal visits, visitors may sit in on classes, and stay overnight. To schedule a visit, contact the Admissions Office at (610) 527-0200 x2966. **Campus Safety and Security:** Measures include 24-hour foot and vehicle patrol, emergency notification system, self-defense education, and security escort services. There are shuttle buses, emergency telephones, lighted pathways/sidewalks, Electronically operated residence hall entrances activated by security cards.

REQUIREMENTS: The SAT is required. The GED is accepted. Applicants must complete 16 academic units, including 4 in English and 2 each in foreign language, history, math, and science. An interview is recommended. A GPA of 2.0 is required. AP and CLEP credits are accepted. Important factors in the admissions decision are advanced placement or honors courses, leadership record, and recommendations by school officials.

ADMISSIONS: 50% of a recent year applicants were accepted. The SAT scores for the 2013-2014 freshman class were: Critical Reading--52% below 500, 33% between 500 and 599, 13% between 600 and 699, and 2% between 700 and 800; Math--50% below 500, 41% between 500 and 599, 5% between 600 and 699, and 4% between 700 and 800; Writing--58% below 500, 32% between 500 and 599, 6% between 600 and 699, and 4% between 700 and 800. The ACT scores were 8% below 21, 10% between 21 and 23, 57% between 24 and 26, 18% between 27 and 28, and 7% above 28.

FINANCIAL AID: In a recent year, 99% of all full-time freshmen and 95% of continuing full-time students received some form of financial aid. 93% of all full-time freshmen and 86% of continuing full-time students received need-based aid. The average freshman award was $25,744. Need-based scholarships or need-based grants averaged $26,427 ($36,530 maximum); and need-based self-help aid (loans and jobs) averaged $3,562 ($11,000 maximum). 27% of undergraduate students work part-time. Average annual earnings from campus work are $805. The average financial indebtedness of the 2013 graduate was $21,622. The FAFSA is required. The priority date for freshman financial aid applications for fall entry is February 15. The deadline for filing freshman financial aid applications for fall entry is March 15.

SAINT FRANCIS UNIVERSITY *(The complete profile is made available exclusively on our website, www.barronspac.com)*

SAINT JOSEPH'S UNIVERSITY   F-3
www.sju.edu

Philadelphia, PA 19131	(610) 660-1300
	(888) BE-A-HAWK
Fax: (610) 660-1314	Email: admit@sju.edu
Full-time: 2208 men, 2463 women	Faculty: 287; IIA, ++$
Part-time: 339 men, 502 women	Ph.D.s: 89%
Graduate: 1344 men, 2118 women	Student/Faculty: 16 to 1
Year: semesters, summer session	Tuition: $40,580
Room & Board: $14,426	Freshman Class: 8432 applied, 7160 accepted, 1353 enrolled
SAT CR/M/W: 550/570/560 ACT: 25	CEEB CODE: 2801
Application Deadline: February 1	VERY COMPETITIVE

Saint Joseph's University, founded by the Society of Jesus in 1851, advances the professional and personal ambitions of men and women by providing a demanding, yet supportive, educational experience. Saint Joseph's has three principal academic colleges – the College of Arts and Sciences, the Erivan K. Haub School of Business and the College of Professional and Liberal Studies/Haub Degree Completion. In total, Saint Joseph's University offers over 55 undergraduate day majors and 50 minors and over 30 degree completion and certificate programs including online options. There are 3 undergraduate schools and 2 graduate schools. In addition to regional accreditation, Saint Joseph's has baccalaureate program accreditation with AACSB. The 114-acre campus is in a suburban area on the western edge of Philadelphia and eastern Montgomery County. Including any residence halls, there are 82 buildings.

STUDENT LIFE: 52% of undergraduates are from out of state, mostly the Middle Atlantic. Students are from 42 states, 34 foreign countries, and Canada. 50% are from public schools. 79% are White. 78% are Catholic; 16% Protestant. The average age of freshmen is 18; all undergraduates, 21. 10% do not continue beyond their first year; 73% remain to graduate. **Housing:** 2928 students can be accommodated in college housing, which includes single-sex and coed dorms, on-campus apartments, and off-campus apartments. In addition, there are honors houses, special-interest houses, Special interest floors. On-campus housing is available on a lottery system for upperclassmen. 59% of students live on campus. Upperclassmen may keep cars.

FACULTY/CLASSROOMS: 58% of faculty are male; 42% are female. No introductory courses are taught by graduate students. The average class size in an introductory lecture is 27; in a laboratory is 17; and in a regular course is 26.

PROGRAMS OF STUDY: Saint Joseph's confers B.A., and B.S. degrees. Associate, Master's, and Doctoral degrees are also awarded. Bachelor's degrees are awarded in BIOLOGICAL SCIENCE (biochemistry and biology/biological science), BUSINESS (accounting, business administration and management, entrepreneurial studies, finance, human resources, insurance and risk management, international business management, investments and securities, management information systems, marketing management, marketing/retailing/merchandising, organizational leadership and management, and sports marketing), COMMUNICATIONS AND THE ARTS (art, art/art studies, communications, English, French, German, Italian, Latin, music, Spanish, and theatre arts), COMPUTER AND PHYSICAL SCIENCE (actuarial science, chemistry, computer science, information sciences and systems, mathematics, and physics), EDUCATION (art education, early childhood education, elementary education, and special education), ENGINEERING AND ENVIRONMENTAL DESIGN (environmental science), HEALTH PROFESSIONS (health care administration and health science), SOCIAL SCIENCE (Asian studies, criminal justice, economics, European studies, French studies, history, international relations, liberal arts/general studies, philosophy, political science/government, psychology, public administration, religious studies, sociology, and theological studies). Biology and accounting is the strongest academically. Food marketing, finance, and biology have the largest enrollments.

ACTIVITIES: 6% of men belong to 3 national fraternities; 15% of women belong to 5 national sororities. There are 100 groups on campus, including art, cheerleading, choir, chorale, dance, debate, drama, ethnic, forensics, gay, honors, international, jazz band, literary magazine, musical theater, newspaper, pep band, political, professional, radio club, religious, social, social service, and student government. Popular campus events include Community Day, Spring Concert and Hawk-A-Palooza. **Sports:** There are 10 intercollegiate sports for men and 10 for women. Facilities include All Saint Joseph's University students are encouraged to participate in intercollegiate, club and intramural activities as well as in the numerous recreational and fitness opportunities that are available. The Athletic Center and the O'Pake Recreation Center, along with Sweeney Field and fields on the Maguire Campus, provide indoor and outdoor locations for athletic and recreational events. These facilities are utilized to enhance the students' physical development under the supervision of Saint Joseph's staff. **Graduates:** From July 1, 2013 to June 30, 2014, 1168 bachelor's degrees were awarded. The most popular majors were food marketing (10%), marketing (9%), and finance (8%). 385 companies recruited on campus in 2013-2014. In an average class, 67% graduate in 4 years or less, 73% graduate in 5 years or less, and 73% graduate in 6 years or less. Of the 2013 graduating class, 21% were enrolled in graduate school within 6 months of graduation, and 73% were employed.

SERVICES: Counseling and information services are available, as is tutoring in most subjects. There is a reader service for the blind. In addition to tutoring, there are study and life skills workshops, supplemental instruction, a writing center, and other educational support services to help students. **Library/Resources:** The library contains 353,500 volumes, 860,000 microform items, 4,000 audio/video tapes/CDs/DVDs, and subscribes to 67,400 periodicals including electronic. Computerized library services include interlibrary loans, database searching, Internet access, and Wi-Fi capability. Special learning facilities include an art gallery, an instructional media center, foreign language labs, Mandeville Hall Wall Street Trading Room, and Claver Honors House, Post Learning Commons. **Physically Challenged Students:** 85% of the campus is accessible. Facilities include wheelchair ramps, elevators, special parking, specially equipped restrooms, special class scheduling, lowered drinking fountains, lowered telephones, special housing. Automatic eye doors, curb cuts, a specially equipped van for wheelchairs, a pool lift, and a bell system at major road crossings. **Special:** The University offers internships, a Washington semester, 5-year combined Bachelors/Masters degree programs, dual majors, minor concentrations, and study abroad. There are co-op programs for business majors. There are 23 national honor societies, including Phi Beta Kappa, a freshman honors program, and 16 departmental honors programs. **Visiting:** There are regularly scheduled orientations for prospective students, consisting of open houses, tours, and information sessions. There are guides for informal visits and visitors may sit in on classes. To schedule a visit, contact the Admissions Office at (610) 660-1300. **Campus Safety and Security:** Measures include 24-hour foot and vehicle patrol, emergency notification system, self-defense education, and security escort services. There are shuttle buses, emergency telephones, lighted pathways/sidewalks, controlled access to dorms/residences, and bicycle patrol.

REQUIREMENTS: Beginning with the incoming class of 2014, the submission of the SAT and ACT standardized test scores is optional for admission. Academic information, recommendations, and the record of extracurricular involvement and evidence of special talent, leadership and service will be reviewed. Students will continue to have the option to submit an SAT or ACT score if they want additional representation presented to the admissions committee. A variety of factors are considered during the application process including, but not limited to strength of high school, rigor of academic curriculum, service, and overall academic achievement and community involvement. AP and CLEP credits are accepted. Important factors in the admissions decision are advanced placement or honors courses, recommendations by school officials, and leadership record. A new General Education Program (GEP) has been implemented beginning with the Fall 2010 freshman. GEP consists of 6 signature core courses; up to 10 variable courses(AP and transfer credits may be accepted); 3 integrative learning courses; and 3 overlay courses focusing on the areas of diversity/globalization, ethics,and writing-intensive. **Procedure:** Freshmen are admitted fall and spring. Entrance exams should be taken in the spring of the junior year and/or the fall of the senior year. There are early admissions and deferred admissions plans. Applications should be filed by February 1 for fall entry; November 15 for spring entry, along with a $60 fee. Notification of early decision is sent December 25; regular decision, March 15. Applications are accepted on-line. **Transfer Students:** 87 transfer students enrolled in 2013-2014. Transfer students requirements include a minimum of 12 transferable credits. Typically, students with a 2.5 cumulative GPA or higher are considered for admission. Transfer applicants must submit high school and college transcripts. 60 of 120 credits required for the bachelor's degree must be completed at Saint Joseph's. **International Students:** There are 100 international students enrolled. The school actively recruits these students. They must take the TOEFL with a minimum score of 550 on the paper-based TOEFL (PBT) or 80 on the Internet-based version (iBT). They must also take the SAT or ACT, scoring 450. or the TOEFL.

ADMISSIONS: 85% of the 2014-2015 applicants were accepted. The SAT scores for the 2014-2015 freshman class were: Critical Reading- -17% below 500, 55% between 500 and 599, 25% between 600 and 699, and 3% between 700 and 800; Math--14% below 500, 50% between 500 and 599, 32% between 600 and 699, and 4% between 700 and 800; Writing--17% below 500, 51% between 500 and 599, 28% between 600 and 699, and 4% between 700 and 800. The ACT scores were 9% below 21, 24% between 21 and 23, 34% between 24 and 26, 15% between 27 and 28, and 17% above 28. **Admissions Contact:** Maureen Mathis, Assistant Provost. E-Mail: *admit@sju.edu* Web: *www.sju.edu*

FINANCIAL AID: In 2014-2015, 95% of all full-time freshmen and 90% of continuing full-time students received some form of financial aid. The average freshman award was $28,300. Average annual earnings from campus work are $1500. Saint Joseph's is a member of CSS. The FAFSA is required. The priority date for freshman financial aid applications for fall entry is February 15. The deadline for filing freshman financial aid applications for fall entry is May 1.

SAINT VINCENT COLLEGE   B-3
www.stvincent.edu

Latrobe, PA 15650	(724) 805-2500
	(800) SVC-5549
Fax: (724) 532-5069	**Email:** admission@stvincent.edu
Full-time: 790 men, 742 women	**Faculty:** 99
Part-time: 32 men, 32 women	**Ph.Ds:** 91%
Graduate: 87 men, 130 women	**Student/Faculty:** 16 to 1
Year: semesters, summer session	**Tuition:** $30,350
Room & Board: $9894	**Freshman Class:** 2035 applied, 1399 accepted, 472 enrolled
SAT CR/M/W: 510/520/520 **ACT:** 22	**CEEB CODE:** 2808
Application Deadline: April 1	**COMPETITIVE**

Saint Vincent College, founded in 1846, is a private Catholic college of liberal arts and sciences sponsored by Benedictine monks. There are 4 undergraduate schools and 3 graduate schools. In addition to regional accreditation, Saint Vincent has baccalaureate program accreditation with ACBSP. The 200-acre campus is in a suburban area 35 miles east of Pittsburgh. Including any residence halls, there are 22 buildings.

STUDENT LIFE: 82% of undergraduates are from Pennsylvania. Others are from 27 states, 9 foreign countries, and Canada. 85% are White. 57% are Catholic; 20% Protestant; 11% Unknown denominations. The average age of freshmen is 18; all undergraduates, 20. 15% do not continue beyond their first year; 70% remain to graduate.

FACULTY/CLASSROOMS: 60% of faculty are male; 40% are female. All teach and do research. No introductory courses are taught by graduate students. The average class size in an introductory lecture is 20; in a laboratory is 20; and in a regular course is 25.

PROGRAMS OF STUDY: Saint Vincent confers B.A., and B.S. degrees. Master's and Doctoral degrees are also awarded. Bachelor's degrees are awarded in BIOLOGICAL SCIENCE (biochemistry, bioinformatics, and biology/biological science), BUSINESS (accounting, banking and finance, business administration and management,

international business management, and marketing/retailing/merchandising), COMMUNICATIONS AND THE ARTS (art, art history and appreciation, arts administration/management, communications, English, fine arts, French, music, music performance, Spanish, studio art, and visual and performing arts), COMPUTER AND PHYSICAL SCIENCE (chemistry, computer science, mathematics, and physics), EDUCATION (art education, business education, early childhood education, middle school education, psychology education, and science education), ENGINEERING AND ENVIRONMENTAL DESIGN (engineering and environmental science), HEALTH PROFESSIONS (occupational therapy, physical therapy, physician's assistant, predentistry, premedicine, prepharmacy, and preveterinary science), SOCIAL SCIENCE (anthropology, economics, history, liberal arts/general studies, philosophy, political science/government, prelaw, psychology, public affairs, sociology, and theological studies). Biology, economics, and psychology are the strongest academically. Biology, psychology, and management have the largest enrollments.

ACTIVITIES: There are 63 groups on campus, including art, band, cheerleading, choir, chorus, dance, drama, environmental, ethnic, honors, international, literary magazine, marching band, musical theater, newspaper, pep band, political, professional, radio and TV, religious, social, social service, student government, and yearbook. Popular campus events include Founders' Day, Threshold Lecture Series, and Pittsburgh Steelers Training Camp.

SERVICES: Counseling and information services are available, as is tutoring in most subjects. The Opportunity Office provides individual counseling and a study skills class, for first-year students. **Library/Resources:** The library contains 287,678 volumes, 99,223 microform items, and 7,000 audio/video tapes/CDs/DVDs, and subscribes to 418 periodicals including electronic. Computerized library services include interlibrary loans, database searching, Internet access, and Wi-Fi capability. Special learning facilities include an art gallery, planetarium, radio station, TV station, an observatory, a radio telescope, and a small-business development center. **Physically Challenged Students:** 95% of the campus is accessible. Facilities include wheelchair ramps, elevators, special parking, specially equipped restrooms, lowered drinking fountains, special housing. **Special:** There is cross-registration with Seton Hill University, co-op programs, internships, study abroad in Europe and Asia, a work-study program, dual majors, a general studies degree, credit by exam and for life/military/work experience, nondegree study, and pass/fail options. There is a 3-2 engineering option with Boston University, Pennsylvania State University, the University of Pittsburgh, and the Catholic University of America. The college offers teacher certificate courses in early childhood (K-12) and secondary education. There are 16 national honor societies, a freshman honors program, and 13 departmental honors programs. **Visiting:** There are regularly scheduled orientations for prospective students, consisting of a general information session, an informal meeting with faculty, and campus tours. There are guides for informal visits, visitors may sit in on classes, and stay overnight. To schedule a visit, contact the Admission and Financial Aid Office. **Campus Safety and Security:** Measures include 24-hour foot and vehicle patrol, emergency notification system, and security escort services. There are emergency telephones, lighted pathways/sidewalks, and controlled access to dorms/residences.

REQUIREMENTS: The SAT or ACT is required. Applicants must complete 15 academic credits, including 4 of English, 3 each of social studies and math, 2 of foreign language, and 1 of a lab science. Art students must submit a portfolio, and music and theater students must audition. An essay is required. A GED is accepted. A GPA of 3.2 is required. AP and CLEP credits are accepted. Important factors in the admissions decision are advanced placement or honors courses, evidence of special talent, and recommendations by school officials.

ADMISSIONS: 69% of a recent year applicants were accepted. The SAT scores for a recent year freshman class were: Critical Reading- -36% below 500, 45% between 500 and 599, 16% between 600 and 699, and 2% between 700 and 800; Math--28% below 500, 49% between 500 and 599, 21% between 600 and 699, and 2% between 700 and 800; Writing--42% below 500, 42% between 500 and 599, 15% between 600 and 699, and 1% between 700 and 800. The ACT scores were 29% below 21, 30% between 21 and 23, 22% between 24 and 26, 11% between 27 and 28, and 6% above 28. 48% of the current freshmen were in the top fifth of their class; 75% were in the top two fifths. 7 freshmen graduated first in their class.

FINANCIAL AID: In a recent year, 100% of all full-time freshmen and 93% of continuing full-time students received some form of financial aid. 64% of all full-time freshmen and 77% of continuing full-time students received need-based aid. The average freshman award was $19,800. Need-based scholarships or need-based grants averaged $5,690 ($10,807 maximum); need-based self-help aid (loans and jobs) averaged $6,891 ($7,820 maximum); and other non-need-based awards and non-need-based scholarships averaged $19,168 ($39,078 maximum). 44% of undergraduate students work part-time. Average annual earnings from campus work are $1680. The average financial indebtedness of the 2013 graduate was $22,350. The FAFSA is required. The priority date for freshman financial aid applications for fall entry is March 1. The deadline for filing freshman financial aid applications for fall entry is April 1.

SETON HILL UNIVERSITY   B-4
www.setonhill.edu

Greensburg, PA 15601-1599	(724) 838-4255
	(800) 826-6234
Fax: (724) 830-1294	Email: admit@setonhill.edu
Full-time: 535 men, 815 women	Faculty: n/av; IIB, -$
Part-time: 65 men, 135 women	Ph.D.s: 88%
Graduate: 100 men, 310 women	Student/Faculty: n/av
Year: semesters, summer session	Tuition: $28,154
Room & Board: $9626	Freshman Class: n/av
SAT or ACT: recommended	CEEB CODE: 2812
Application Deadline: open	COMPETITIVE

Seton Hill University, founded in 1883, is a private university affiliated with the Roman Catholic Church and offers programs in liberal arts and career preparation. The figures in the above capsule and in this profile are approximate. There is 1 graduate school. In addition to regional accreditation, Seton Hill has baccalaureate program accreditation with ADA, CSWE, and NASM. The 200-acre campus is in a small town 35 miles east of Pittsburgh. Including any residence halls, there are 19 buildings.

STUDENT LIFE: 79% of undergraduates are from Pennsylvania. Others are from 32 states, 16 foreign countries, and Canada. 80% are white. The average age of freshmen is 18; all undergraduates, 21. 19% do not continue beyond their first year; 64% remain to graduate.

FACULTY/CLASSROOMS: 40% of faculty are male; 60% are female. 87% teach undergraduates, and 60% do research. No introductory courses are taught by graduate students. The average class size in an introductory lecture is 25; in a laboratory, 16; and in a regular course, 17.

PROGRAMS OF STUDY: Seton Hill confers B.A., B.S., B.F.A., B.Mus., B.S.Med.Tech., and B.S.W. degrees. Master's degrees are also awarded. Bachelor's degrees are awarded in BIOLOGICAL SCIENCE (biochemistry and biology/biological science), BUSINESS (accounting, business administration and management, business economics, entrepreneurial studies, human resources, international business management, management information systems, marketing/retailing/merchandising, personnel management, sports management, and tourism), COMMUNICATIONS AND THE ARTS (art history and appreciation, arts administration/management, communications, creative writing, dramatic arts, English, fine arts, graphic design, journalism, music, musical theater, performing arts, Spanish, studio art, theater design, and theater management), COMPUTER AND PHYSICAL SCIENCE (actuarial science, chemistry, computer science, mathematics, and physics), EDUCATION (art education, early childhood education, elementary education, English education, foreign languages education, home economics education, mathematics education, music education, science education, secondary education, social science education, and special education), ENGINEERING AND ENVIRONMENTAL DESIGN (engineering), HEALTH PROFESSIONS (art therapy, medical laboratory technol-

ogy, music therapy, pharmacy, physician's assistant, predentistry, premedicine, preosteopathy, and preveterinary science), SOCIAL SCIENCE (child care/child and family studies, criminal justice, dietetics, economics, family/consumer resource management, family/consumer studies, food production/management/services, forensic studies, history, human services, international studies, liberal arts/general studies, political science/government, prelaw, psychology, religion, religious music, social work, and sociology). Sciences, education, and fine arts are the strongest academically. Psychology, art, and business have the largest enrollments.

ACTIVITIES: There are 40 groups on campus, including art, bagpipe, band, cheerleading, choir, chorale, chorus, dance, drama, entrepreneurial, environmental, ethnic, gay, honors, international, jazz band, literary magazine, marching band, musical theater, newspaper, orchestra, pep band, political, professional, religious, social, social service, student government, and symphony. Popular campus events include Christmas on the Hill, Family Weekend, and President's Reception.

SERVICES: Counseling and information services are available, as is tutoring in most subjects. There is a reader service for the blind, and remedial math and writing. **Library/Resources:** The library contains 123,538 volumes, 5,403 microform items, 6,684 audio/video tapes/CDs/DVDs, and subscribes to 423 periodicals including electronic. Computerized library services include interlibrary loans, database searching, and Internet access. Special learning facilities include an art gallery, TV station, a nursery school that functions as laboratory school for education students, a performing arts center, a visual arts center, and technology wing. **Physically Challenged Students:** 95% of the campus is accessible. Facilities include wheelchair ramps, elevators, special parking, specially equipped restrooms, special class scheduling, lowered drinking fountains, and lowered telephones. **Special:** There are cooperative programs in all majors and cross-registration with St. Vincent College, the University of Pittsburgh at Greensburg, and Westmoreland County Community College. Internships are encouraged. Seton Hill offers study abroad, a Washington semester, work-study, dual and student-designed majors, accelerated degree programs, a 3-2 engineering program with Pennsylvania State University and Georgia Institute of Technology, a 2-2 nursing program with Catholic University of America, a 3-2 or 3-1 medical technology program with area hospitals, credit by exam and for life/military/work experience, nondegree study, and pass/fail options. There are 5 national honor societies and a freshman honors program. **Visiting:** There are regularly scheduled orientations for prospective students, consisting of an introduction, an address by the president or dean, an open reception with faculty, a financial aid session, a student panel, and a campus tour. There are guides for informal visits, visitors may sit in on classes, and stay overnight. To schedule a visit, contact the Campus Visit Coordinator. **Campus Safety and Security:** Measures include 24-hour foot and vehicle patrol, emergency notification system, self-defense education, and security escort services. There are shuttle buses, emergency telephones, and lighted pathways/sidewalks.

REQUIREMENTS: The SAT or ACT is recommended. Including 2 graded writing samples are accepted in place of SAT or ACT scores. A total of 15 Carnegie units is required, including 4 each of English and electives, 2 each of math, social studies, and foreign language, and 1 of a lab science. Art students must submit a portfolio; music and theater students must audition. An interview is recommended. The GED is accepted with supporting recommendations. A GPA of 2.5 is required. AP and CLEP credits are accepted. Important factors in the admissions decision are advanced placement or honors courses, evidence of special talent, and leadership record.

FINANCIAL AID: The FAFSA and the college's own financial statement are required. Check with school for current application deadlines.

SHIPPENSBURG UNIVERSITY OF PENNSYLVANIA
D-3
www.ship.edu

Shippensburg, PA 17257	(717) 477-1231
	n/av
Fax: (717) 477-4016	Email: admiss@ship.edu
Full-time: 3033 men, 2923 women	Faculty: n/av
Part-time: 176 men, 173 women	Ph.D.s: n/av
Graduate: 406 men, 644 women	Student/Faculty: n/av
Year: semesters, summer session	Tuition: $9774 ($18,520)
Room & Board: $11,160	Freshman Class: 6319 applied, 5253 accepted, 1484 enrolled
SAT CR/M/W: 500/500/480 ACT: 21	CEEB CODE: 2657
Application Deadline: n/av	COMPETITIVE

Shippensburg University, founded in 1871, is a public university that is part of the Pennsylvania State System of Higher Education offering undergraduate and graduate degree programs in the College of Arts and Sciences, College of Business, and College of Education and Human Services. There are 4 undergraduate schools and 1 graduate school. In addition to regional accreditation, Ship has baccalaureate program accreditation with AACSB, ABET, CSWE, NCATE, ACS, CACREP, and IACS. The 200-acre campus is in a rural area 40 miles southwest of Harrisburg. Including any residence halls, there are 50 buildings.

STUDENT LIFE: 92% of undergraduates are from Pennsylvania. Others are from 25 states, 24 foreign countries, and Canada. 90% are from public schools. 79% are White. **Male To Female Ratio:** 1.0:1. The average age of freshmen is 18; all undergraduates, 21. 29% do not continue beyond their first year; 55% remain to graduate. **Housing:** 2364 students can be accommodated in college housing, which includes coed dorms, on-campus apartments, and off-campus apartments. Living Learning Communities provide the opportunity to live together with those who have similar academic, personal, or social interests. Academic Communities include: First-year Biology Interest Groups, Honors Programs, and Discover SU for first-year undeclared majors. Interest Communities include the following: Engaging Services through Action, Healthy Living Community, and Shippensburg Leadership Academy. On-campus housing is guaranteed for the freshman year only and is available on a lottery system for upperclassmen. 64% of students commute. Alcohol is not permitted. All students may keep cars.

FACULTY/CLASSROOMS: No introductory courses are taught by graduate students.

PROGRAMS OF STUDY: Ship confers B.A., B.S., B.S.B.A., B.S.Ed. and B.S.W. degrees. Master's degrees are also awarded. Bachelor's degrees are awarded in BIOLOGICAL SCIENCE (biology/biological science and (Biological) Pre-Health Studies), BUSINESS (accounting, banking and finance, business administration and management, management information systems, marketing management, supply chain management, and professional studies), COMMUNICATIONS AND THE ARTS (art, communications, English, French, journalism, Spanish, and speech/debate/rhetoric), COMPUTER AND PHYSICAL SCIENCE (applied physics, chemistry, computer science, earth science, geoenvironmental studies, mathematics, physics, and software engineering), EDUCATION (art education, business education, early childhood education, elementary education, English education, foreign languages education, mathematics education, middle school education, secondary education, social studies education, and special education), ENGINEERING AND ENVIRONMENTAL DESIGN (computer engineering, electrical/electronics engineering, and environmental science), HEALTH PROFESSIONS (exercise science and health care administration), SOCIAL SCIENCE (criminal justice, early childhood studies, economics, geography, history, interdisciplinary studies, international studies, political science/government, psychology, public administration, social work, and sociology). Psychology, criminal justice, and management have the largest enrollments.

ACTIVITIES: 8% of men belong to 12 national fraternities; 11% of women belong to 10 national sororities. There are 90 groups on campus, including a vet's club, big brother/big sister, a ROTC ranger challenge team, activities program board, art, band, cheerleading, choir, chorale, chorus, computers, dance, debate, drama, environmental, ethnic, gay, honors, international, jazz band, literary magazine, marching band, musical theater, newspaper, orchestra, pep band, photography, political, professional, radio and TV, religious, social, social service, student government, and yearbook. Popular campus events include Planetarium Shows, Senior Olympics and Summer Music Festival. **Sports:** There are 8 intercollegiate sports for men and 10 for women, and 5 intramural sports for men and 5 for women. Facilities include a 7700-seat stadium for football and track-and-field events and complexes for varsity baseball, softball, and tennis. There is a 450-seat stadium with an artificial turf surface for soccer, field hockey, and lacrosse. Basketball, volleyball, and wrestling competitions are conducted within a 2700-seat facility, with swimming facilities. Outdoor recreational facilities include a 12-acre sports complex. Students also have access to a 64,000-square-foot recreational building. **Graduates:** From July 1, 2013 to June 30, 2014, 1421 bachelor's degrees were awarded. The most popular majors were psychology (9%), pk-4 (7%), and criminal justice (7%). 127 companies recruited on campus in 2013-2014. In an average class, 37% graduate in 4 years or less, 53% graduate in 5 years or less, and 55% graduate in 6 years or less.

SERVICES: Counseling and information services are available, as is tutoring in most subjects, most general education courses and writing. JAWS and Zoom Text for the blind and visually impaired. There is remedial math, reading, and writing. Individual meetings with Learning Specialists who are available to help students interested in developing individual strategies and group study. **Library/Resources:** The library contains 358,330 volumes, 1.2 million microform items, and 70,723 audio/video tapes/CDs/DVDs, and subscribes to 19,517 periodicals including electronic. Computerized library services include interlibrary loans, database searching, Internet access, and Wi-Fi capability. Special learning facilities include an art gallery, planetarium, radio/TV station, a closed-circuit television, fashion archives center, vertebrate museum, women's center, on-campus elementary school, electron microscope, greenhouse, and herbarium. **Physically Challenged Students:** 92% of the campus is accessible. Facilities include wheelchair ramps, elevators, special parking, specially equipped restrooms, special class scheduling, lowered drinking fountains, lowered telephones, special housing. Enlarged printing, extended time for tests, classroom accessibility, note taking, reader and scribe services for exams, alternative testing sites, priority scheduling, including a tech room in the library that has the following software: Kurzweil Reader, Text Help, JAWS, and Zoom Text. **Special:** There are 26 national honor societies, a freshman honors program, and 1 departmental honors programs. **Visiting:** There are regularly scheduled orientations for prospective students, including daily academic group meetings, campus tours, and 5 weekend open house programs per year. There are guides for informal visits and visitors may sit in on classes. To schedule a visit, contact the Admissions Office. **Campus Safety and Security:** Measures include 24-hour foot and vehicle patrol, emergency notification system, self-defense education, and security escort services. There are shuttle buses, emergency telephones, lighted pathways/sidewalks, controlled access to dorms/residences, residence halls are equipped with an automatic heat/smoke detection sprinkler system monitored 24 hours a day by police. A strobe light unit notifies students who are hearing impaired. Residence hall doors are locked 24 hours a day. There are digital cameras at the main entrance to residence halls, computer labs, and other buildings, as well as many exterior cameras covering parking lots and other campus areas. A text emergency message system has also been implemented. Additional cameras and card swipes to gain floor entry into the residence halls.

REQUIREMENTS: The SAT is required. Applicants are urged to pursue a typical college preparatory program, which should include 4 units of English, 3 social sciences, 3 math, and 3 lab science, and 3 foreign language. A GED is accepted. AP and CLEP credits are accepted. Important factors in the admissions decision are advanced placement or honors courses, recommendations by school officials, and evidence of special talent. General education courses include English composition, oral communications, math, and history, as well as courses in logic and numbers for rational thinking; linguistic, literary, artistic, and cultural traditions; lab science; biological and physical science; political, economic, and geographic sciences; and social and behavioral sciences. The core curriculum varies for degree programs. Most degree programs require 120 credit hours, with 22 to 30 hours in the major, and a 2.0 minimum GPA for graduation. **Procedure:** Freshmen are admitted fall, winter, and spring. Entrance exams should be taken in the junior year and senior year. There are early admissions, deferred admissions, and rolling admissions plans. Application deadlines are open. The fall 2014 application fee was $45. Notification is sent on a rolling basis. Applications are accepted online. **Transfer Students:** 387 transfer students enrolled in 2013-2014. Applicants must provide high school and college transcripts and SAT or ACT scores if they have fewer than 30 college credits. 45 of 120 credits required for the bachelor's degree must be completed at Ship. **International Students:** There are 45 international students enrolled. They must take the TOEFL with a minimum score of 500 on the paper-based TOEFL (PBT) or 66 on the Internet-based version (iBT), Students whose native language is English must submit SAT scores instead of TOEFL. They must also take the SAT or ACT.

ADMISSIONS: 83% of the 2014-2015 applicants were accepted. The SAT scores for the 2014-2015 freshman class were: Critical Reading--48% below 500, 42% between 500 and 599, 9% between 600 and 699, and 1% between 700 and 800; Math--44% below 500, 44% between 500 and 599, 11% between 600 and 699, and 1% between 700 and 800; Writing--63% below 500, 31% between 500 and 599, and 6% between 600 and 699. The ACT scores were 49% below 21, 30% between 21 and 23, 12% between 24 and 26, 8% between 27 and 28, and 1% above 28. 17% of the current freshmen were in the top fifth of their class; 45% were in the top two fifths. 6 freshmen graduated first in their class. **Admissions Contact:** Angelo Lee, Dean of Admissions. E-Mail: *admiss@ship.edu* Web: *www.ship.edu*

FINANCIAL AID: Ship is a member of CSS. The FAFSA, and PHEAA is required. The deadline for filing freshman financial aid applications for fall entry is May 1.

SLIPPERY ROCK UNIVERSITY OF PENNSYLVANIA
B-2

www.sru.edu

Slippery Rock, PA 16057	(724) 738-2015
	(800) 929-4778
Fax: (724) 738-2913	Email: asktherock@sru.edu
Full-time: 2860 men, 3565 women	Faculty: 366; IIA, +$
Part-time: 225 men, 415 women	Ph.D.s: 78%
Graduate: 235 men, 510 women	Student/Faculty: 18 to 1
Year: semesters, summer session	Tuition: $6619 ($9302)
Room & Board: $4550	Freshman Class: 4310 applied, 3481 accepted, 1491 enrolled
SAT: required	CEEB CODE: 2658
Application Deadline: n/av	COMPETITIVE

Slippery Rock University of Pennsylvania, founded in 1889, is a public institution that is part of the Pennsylvania State System of Higher Education. It offers programs in business, information, social sciences, education, health, environment, science, humanities, and fine and performing arts. There are 4 undergraduate schools and one graduate school. In addition to regional accreditation, The Rock has baccalaureate program accreditation with ACBSP, APTA, CSWE, NASAD, NASM, NCATE, NLN, NRPA, and CAAHEP. The 600-acre campus is in a small town 50 miles north of Pittsburgh. Including any residence halls, there are 60 buildings.

STUDENT LIFE: 96% of undergraduates are from Pennsylvania. Others are from 35 states, 47 foreign countries, and Canada. 70% are from public schools. 87% are White. The average age of freshmen is 18; all undergraduates, 22. 22% do not continue beyond their first year; 49% remain to graduate. **Housing:** 2810 students can be accommodated in college housing, which includes single-sex and coed dorms, on-campus apartments, off-campus apartments, and married student housing. In addition, there are honors houses, language houses, special-interest houses, fraternity houses, and sorority houses.

On-campus housing is guaranteed for the freshman year only, is available on a first-come, and first-served basis. 62% of students commute. Alcohol is not permitted. All students may keep cars. **FACULTY/CLASSROOMS:** 53% of faculty are male; 47% are female. All teach undergraduates. No introductory courses are taught by graduate students. The average class size in an introductory lecture is 33; in a laboratory is 20; and in a regular course is 25.

PROGRAMS OF STUDY: The Rock confers B.A., B.S., B.F.A., B.Mus., B.Mus.Ed., B.S.B.A., B.S.Ed. and B.S.N. degrees. Master's and Doctoral degrees are also awarded. Bachelor's degrees are awarded in BIOLOGICAL SCIENCE (biology/biological science), BUSINESS (accounting, business administration and management, international business management, and marketing/retailing/merchandising), COMMUNICATIONS AND THE ARTS (communications, dance, English, fine arts, French, German, music, and Spanish), COMPUTER AND PHYSICAL SCIENCE (chemistry, computer science, earth science, geology, information sciences and systems, mathematics, and physics), EDUCATION (early childhood education, elementary education, foreign languages education, health education, music education, science education, secondary education, and special education), HEALTH PROFESSIONS (community health work, medical laboratory technology, and nursing), SOCIAL SCIENCE (anthropology, economics, geography, history, parks and recreation management, philosophy, political science/government, psychology, public administration, social science, social work, and sociology). Business, education, and health science areas have the largest enrollments.

ACTIVITIES: 7% of men belong to 11 national fraternities; 6% of women belong to 9 national sororities. There are 100 groups on campus, including art, band, cheerleading, chess, choir, chorale, chorus, communications, computers, dance, drama, ethnic, film, gay, honors, international, jazz band, literary magazine, marching band, musical theater, newspaper, orchestra, pep band, photography, political, professional, radio and TV, religious, social, social service, student government, symphony, and yearbook. Popular campus events include Spring Weekend. **Sports:** There are 12 intercollegiate sports for men and 12 for women, and 7 intramural sports for men and 7 for women. Facilities include a field house, a gym, and a fitness center. The campus stadium seats 10,000, the indoor gym seats 3000, and the largest auditorium/arena seats 1000. **Graduates:** From July 1, 2013 to June 30, 2014, 1190 bachelor's degrees were awarded. The most popular majors were education (23%), marketing (15%), and parks and recreation (13%). 260 companies recruited on campus in 2013-2014. In an average class, 24% graduate in 4 years or less, 46% graduate in 5 years or less, and 49% graduate in 6 years or less. Of the 2013 graduating class, 12% were enrolled in graduate school within 6 months of graduation, and 81% were employed.

SERVICES: Counseling and information services are available, as is tutoring in some subjects. There is a reader service for the blind, remedial math and writing. **Library/Resources:** The library contains 502,974 volumes, 1.5 million microform items, 22,707 audio/video tapes/CDs/DVDs, and subscribes to 1,300 periodicals including electronic. Computerized library services include interlibrary loans, database searching, and Internet access. Special learning facilities include an art gallery, natural history museum, planetarium, radio/TV station, and wellness center. **Physically Challenged Students:** 80% of the campus is accessible. Facilities include wheelchair ramps, elevators, special parking, specially equipped restrooms, special class scheduling, lowered drinking fountains, lowered telephones, and special housing. **Special:** Study abroad is available in 16 countries. Internships are offered in most majors, and international internships are available in Scotland and England. There is a 3-2 engineering program with Pennsylvania State University. The dual major is an option, and credit is given for military experience. Pass/fail options also are available. There are 26 national honor societies, a freshman honors program, and 33 departmental honors programs. **Visiting:** There are regularly scheduled orientations for prospective students, including a meeting with faculty, an information fair, and a campus tour. There are guides for informal visits, visitors may sit in on classes, and stay overnight. To schedule a visit, contact the Admissions Office. **Campus Safety and Security:** Measures include 24-hour foot and vehicle patrol, self-defense education, and security escort services. There are shuttle buses, emergency telephones, lighted pathways/sidewalks, The university maintains its own police department.

REQUIREMENTS: The SAT is required. The ACT is recommended. Students should graduate from an accredited secondary school or have a GED. A total of 16 academic credits is required. The recommended college preparatory program includes 4 years of English and social studies, 3 each of science and math, and 2 of a foreign language. An interview is recommended. AP and CLEP credits are accepted. Important factors in the admissions decision are advanced placement or honors courses, extracurricular activities record, and evidence of special talent.B.A. students must demonstrate proficiency in a foreign language, and all must complete 42 to 53 credits in a 7-part liberal studies program, including basic competencies, arts, cultural diversity/global perspective, human institutions, science and math, natural experience, and modern age. Specific requirements include public speaking, college writing, algebra, and phys ed. A minimum of 120 credit hours, with at least 30 in the major, is required for graduation. **Procedure:** Freshmen are admitted fall, spring, and summer. Entrance exams should be taken in the junior year or fall of the senior year. There are deferred admissions and rolling admissions plans. Check with the school for current application deadlines. The fall 2014 application fee was $25. Notification is sent on a rolling basis. Applications are accepted on-line. **Transfer Students:** 559 transfer students enrolled in 2013-2014. Applicants should have completed at least 24 credit hours with a GPA of 2.5. The SAT I or ACT, as well as an interview, are recommended. 36 of 120 credits required for the bachelor's degree must be completed at The Rock. **International Students:** There are 130 international students enrolled. The school actively recruits these students. They must take the TOEFL.

ADMISSIONS: 81% of the 2014-2015 applicants were accepted. 10 freshmen graduated first in their class. **Admissions Contact:** Jim Barrett, Director of Admissions. E-Mail: *asktherock@sru.edu* Web: *www. sru.edu*

FINANCIAL AID: In 2014-2015, 64% of all full-time freshmen and 58% of continuing full-time students received some form of financial aid. 51% of all full-time freshmen and 43% of continuing full-time students received need-based aid. The average freshman award was $6,074. Need-based scholarships or need-based grants averaged $2,907 ; need-based self-help aid (loans and jobs) averaged $2,437; non-need-based athletic scholarships averaged $2,507; and other non-need-based awards and non-need-based scholarships averaged $3,590. 30% of undergraduate students work part-time. Average annual earnings from campus work are $1000. The average financial indebtedness of the 2014 graduate was $19,195. The Rock is a member of CSS. The FAFSA is required. The priority date for freshman financial aid applications for fall entry is May 1.

SUSQUEHANNA UNIVERSITY   D-3
www.susqu.edu

Selinsgrove, PA 17870

(570) 372-4260
(800) 326-9672

Fax: (570) 372-2722   Email: suadmiss@susqu.edu

Full-time: 902 men, 1106 women	Faculty: 140; IIB, +$
Part-time: 37 men, 39 women	Ph.D.s: 92%
Graduate: 3 men, 6 women	Student/Faculty: 12 to 1
Year: semesters, summer session	Tuition: $40,350
Room & Board: $10,800	Freshman Class: 4013 applied, 3527 accepted, 575 enrolled
SAT or ACT: recommended	CEEB CODE: 2820
Application Deadline: February 15	COMPETITIVE

Susquehanna University, founded in 1858, is an independent, selective, residential institution affiliated with the Lutheran Church. It offers programs through schools of arts, sciences, and business. There are 2 undergraduate schools. In addition to regional accreditation, S.U. has baccalaureate program accreditation with AACSB, NASM, and ACS. The 325-acre campus is in a small town 50 miles north of Harrisburg. Including any residence halls, there are 94 buildings.

STUDENT LIFE: 51% of undergraduates are from out of state, mostly the Middle Atlantic. Students are from 35 states, and 22 foreign countries. 79% are from public schools. 80% are White. 33% are Catholic; 32% Protestant; 17% claim no religious affiliation; 16%

Buddhist, Muslim, Hindu, Mormon, Eastern and Orthodox. The average age of freshmen is 18; all undergraduates, 20. 17% do not continue beyond their first year; 83% remain to graduate. **Housing:** 2023 students can be accommodated in college housing, which includes coed dorms, on-campus apartments, and off-campus apartments. In addition, there are honors houses, special-interest houses, fraternity houses, and sorority houses. On-campus housing is guaranteed for all 4 years and is available on a lottery system for upperclassmen. 90% of students live on campus; of those, 85% remain on campus on weekends. All students may keep cars.

FACULTY/CLASSROOMS: 54% of faculty are male; 46% are female. All teach and do research. No introductory courses are taught by graduate students. The average class size in a laboratory is 18 and in a regular course is 19.

PROGRAMS OF STUDY: S.U. confers B.A., B.S. and B.M. degrees. Bachelor's degrees are awarded in BIOLOGICAL SCIENCE (biochemistry, biology/biological science, and ecology), BUSINESS (accounting and business administration and management), COMMUNICATIONS AND THE ARTS (art history and appreciation, communications, English, French, German, graphic design, Italian, music, music performance, Spanish, studio art, and visual and performing arts), COMPUTER AND PHYSICAL SCIENCE (chemistry, computer science, earth science, information sciences and systems, mathematics, and physics), EDUCATION (early childhood education and music education), ENGINEERING AND ENVIRONMENTAL DESIGN (environmental science), SOCIAL SCIENCE (anthropology, economics, history, international studies, liberal arts/general studies, philosophy, political science/government, psychology, religion, and sociology). Business, communications, and biology have the largest enrollments.

ACTIVITIES: 19% of men belong to 6 national fraternities; 14% of women belong to 5 national sororities. There are 143 groups on campus, including academic clubs (by major/discipline), Asian student coalition, Big brothers/Big sisters, black student union, equestrian, Habitat for Humanity, Hillel, Hispanic organization for student awareness, honor societies, national organization of women, rugby), sports/athletics (Ice hockey, student awareness of the value of the environment, ultimate frisbee, art, band, cheerleading, chess, choir, chorale, chorus, communications, computers, dance, drama, environmental, ethnic, film, gay, honors, international, jazz band, literary magazine, musical theater, newspaper, opera, orchestra, outdoors club, pep band, photography, political, professional, radio and TV, religious, social, social service, student government, and yearbook. Popular campus events include Thanksgiving Dinner, Spring Weekend, Candlelight Christmas Service, Homecomimg Semi-Formal Ball, Annual Concert and Fall Frenzy. **Sports:** There are 11 intercollegiate sports for men and 12 for women, and 7 intramural sports for men and 7 for women. Facilities include a field house with indoor track, tennis, basketball courts, football stadium and track, soccer, baseball, lacrosse, rugby, hockey fields, basketball, tennis courts, swimming pool, racquetball courts, weight training room, and a fitness center. **Graduates:** From July 1, 2013 to June 30, 2014, 509 bachelor's degrees were awarded. The most popular majors were business/marketing (22%), communications (13%), and psychology (8%). 50 companies recruited on campus in 2013-2014. In an average class, 70% graduate in 4 years or less, 71% graduate in 5 years or less, and 76% graduate in 6 years or less.

SERVICES: Counseling and information services are available, as is tutoring in some subjects, writing, math, foreign languages, and study skills. Academic departments also provide tutoring. **Library/ Resources:** The library contains 575,133 volumes, 122,376 microform items, 9,703 audio/video tapes/CDs/DVDs, and subscribes to 42,596 periodicals including electronic. Computerized library services include interlibrary loans, database searching, Internet access, and Wi-Fi capability. Special learning facilities include an art gallery, radio station, multimedia classrooms, video studios, a campus wide telecommunications network, satellite dishes and distribution system for foreign-language broadcasts, video conferencing facility, an ecological field station, and observatory, a child development center, and an electronic music lab. **Physically Challenged Students:** 95% of the campus is accessible. Facilities include wheelchair ramps, elevators, special parking, specially equipped restrooms, special class scheduling, lowered drinking fountains, and lowered telephones. **Special:**

78% of Susquehanna students get professional experience before graduation in the form of internships and research opportunities. The Global Opportunities (GO) program places students in short-term or semester-long study with programs in 75 countries on 6 continents. The School of Business offers a semester in London specifically for junior business majors. The university offers dual and student-designed majors, work-study programs, credit by examination, non-degree study, and pass/fail options. The B.A.-B.S. degree is available in 34 majors. In addition, the university offers a 2-2 program in allied health with Thomas Jefferson University, and a 3-2 program in dentistry with Temple University. Highly motivated students have the option of earning their baccalaureate degree in three years. There are 22 national honor societies and a freshman honors program. **Visiting:** There are regularly scheduled orientations for prospective students, special visiting days for prospective students and their parents held in the spring, fall, and summer. These events include sessions with faculty, admissions, financial aid, and placement staff and tours of the campus. There are guides for informal visits, visitors may sit in on classes, and stay overnight. To schedule a visit, contact J. Scott Myers at (570) 372-4260. **Campus Safety and Security:** Measures include 24-hour foot and vehicle patrol, emergency notification system, self-defense education, and security escort services. There are emergency telephones, lighted pathways/sidewalks, controlled access to dorms/residences, closed circuit TV cameras in common exterior areas on campus.

REQUIREMENTS: The SAT or ACT is recommended. Either the Susquehanna Application or Common Application, along with an official high school transcript, school report, and SAT/ACT scores or a graded writing sample under our Test Score Optional plan. Students should be graduates of an accredited high school. Academic preparation should include 4 years of English and math, 3 to 4 years of science, and 2 to 3 years each of social studies and foreign language. In addition, 1 unit of art or music is recommended. An essay is required, as are, for relevant fields, a music audition or writing or graphic design portfolio. An interview is strongly recommended. AP and CLEP credits are accepted. Important factors in the admissions decision are advanced placement or honors courses, evidence of special talent, and recommendations by school officials. The Central Curriculum is at the heart of a Susquehanna education. The diverse courses in the Central Curriculum comprise 40 percent of the graduation requirement, and are divided into five complementary sections: Richness of Thought, Natural World, Human Interactions, Intellectual Skills, and Connections. All students at Susquehanna are required to participate in a unique, nationally recognized cross-cultural program, Global Opportunities (GO). Students study in the U.S. or abroad, for at least two weeks or as long as a semester, in a culture different from their own. They take a two-semester-hour reflection course after their return to campus. **Procedure:** Freshmen are admitted fall and spring. Entrance exams should be taken by January of the senior year. There are early decision, early admissions, deferred admissions, and rolling admissions plans. Early decision applications should be filed by November 15; regular applications, by February 15 for fall entry; and January 1 for spring entry. Notification of early decision is sent November 15; regular decision, March 15. 75 early decision candidates were accepted for the 2014-2015 class. 377 applicants were on the 2014 waiting list; 5 were admitted. Applications are accepted on-line. Application fees are waived if application is completed on-line. **Transfer Students:** 29 transfer students enrolled in 2013-2014. Applicants must submit high school and college transcripts, test scores, and a recommendation from a dean. An interview is strongly recommended. A music audition or writing portfolio is required for relevant fields. 65 of 130 credits required for the bachelor's degree must be completed at S.U.. **International Students:** There are 34 international students enrolled. The school actively recruits these students. They must take the TOEFL with a minimum score of 550 on the paper-based TOEFL (PBT) or 80 on the Internet-based version (iBT), or take the IELTS.

ADMISSIONS: 88% of the 2014-2015 applicants were accepted. The SAT scores for the 2014-2015 freshman class were: Critical Reading--22% below 500, 48% between 500 and 599, 26% between 600 and 699, and 4% between 700 and 800; Math--14% below 500, 54% between 500 and 599, 30% between 600 and 699, and 2% between 700 and 800; Writing--26% below 500, 46% between 500 and 599,

25% between 600 and 699, and 3% between 700 and 800. 44% of the current freshmen were in the top fifth of their class; 77% were in the top two fifths. 6 freshmen graduated first in their class. **Admissions Contact:** J. Scott Myers, Director of Admissions. E-Mail: *suadmiss@susqu.edu* Web: *www.susqu.edu*

FINANCIAL AID: In 2014-2015, 98% of all full-time freshmen and 97% of continuing full-time students received some form of financial aid. 80% of all full-time freshmen and 76% of continuing full-time students received need-based aid. The average freshman award was $30,922. Need-based scholarships or need-based grants averaged $27,465 ($49,570 maximum); need-based self-help aid (loans and jobs) averaged $4,369 ($9,950 maximum); and other non-need-based awards and non-need-based scholarships averaged $16,381 ($39,830 maximum). 58% of undergraduate students work part-time. Average annual earnings from campus work are $973. The average financial indebtedness of the 2014 graduate was $29,734. S.U. is a member of CSS. The CSS/Profile and FAFSA, and prior year federal tax return for parents and students are required. The priority date for freshman financial aid applications for fall entry is March 1. The deadline for filing freshman financial aid applications for fall entry is May 1.

SWARTHMORE COLLEGE E-3
www.swarthmore.edu

Swarthmore, PA 19081

(610) 328-8300
(800) 667-3110

Fax: (610) 328-8580
Email: admissions@swarthmore.edu

Full-time: 751 men, 775 women
Faculty: 178; IIB, ++$

Part-time: 2 men, 6 women
Ph.D.s: 98%

Year: semesters
Student/Faculty: 8 to 1

Room & Board: $13,152
Tuition: $44,718

Freshman Class: 6615 applied, 947 accepted, 388 enrolled

SAT CR/M/W: 730/720/730 **ACT:** 32
CEEB CODE: 2821

Application Deadline: January 1
MOST COMPETITIVE

Swarthmore College, founded in 1864, is a highly selective college of liberal arts and engineering, celebrates the life of the mind. Swarthmore has given students the knowledge, insight, skills, and experience to become leaders for the common good. The College is private, yet open to all regardless of financial need; and decidedly global in outlook, drawing students from around the world and all 50 states. So much of what Swarthmore stands for, from its commitment to curricular breadth and rigor to its demonstrated interest in facilitating discovery and fostering civic engagement, lies in the quality and passion of its faculty. In addition to regional accreditation, Swarthmore has baccalaureate program accreditation with ABET. The 425-acre campus is in a suburban area 11 miles southwest of Philadelphia. Including any residence halls, there are 56 buildings.

STUDENT LIFE: 87% of undergraduates are from out of state, mostly the Middle Atlantic. Students are from 50 states, 44 foreign countries, and Canada. 57% are from public schools. 43% are White; 15% Asian American; 14% Hispanic. The average age of freshmen is 18; all undergraduates, 20. 4% do not continue beyond their first year; 93% remain to graduate.

FACULTY/CLASSROOMS: 57% of faculty are male; 43% are female. All teach and do research. No introductory courses are taught by graduate students. The average class size in a laboratory is 12 and in a regular course is 16.

PROGRAMS OF STUDY: Swarthmore confers B.A., and B.S. degrees. Bachelor's degrees are awarded in BIOLOGICAL SCIENCE (biochemistry, biology/biological science, and neurosciences), COMMUNICATIONS AND THE ARTS (art, art history and appreciation, Chinese, classics, comparative literature, dance, dramatic arts, English literature, film arts, French, German, Greek, Latin, linguistics, literature, media arts, music, Russian, Spanish, and theatre arts), COMPUTER AND PHYSICAL SCIENCE (astronomy, astrophysics, chemical physics, chemistry, computer science, mathematics, and physics), EDUCATION (education), ENGINEERING AND ENVIRONMENTAL DESIGN (engineering), SOCIAL SCIENCE (anthropology, Asian/Oriental studies, Chinese Studies, classical/ancient civilization, economics, gender studies, German area studies, history, Japanese studies, medieval studies, peace studies, philosophy, political science/government, psychobiology, psychology, religion, and sociology). Economics, biology, and political science have the largest enrollments.

ACTIVITIES: There are 150 groups on campus, including cappella groups, drama board, art, band, chess, choir, chorus, club sports, computers, dance, debate, environmental, ethnic, film, gay, honors, international, jazz band, literary magazine, musical theater, newspaper, orchestra, photography, political, radio and TV, religious, social, social service, student government, and yearbook. Popular campus events also include Large Scale Event, Midnight Breakfast, Worthstock and the Crum Regatta.

SERVICES: Counseling and information services are available, as is tutoring in most subjects. There is a reader service for the blind. The campus writing center, Student Academic Mentors, Science Associates, and Math Associates provide academic support to students. **Library/Resources:** The 7 libraries contain 849,268 volumes, 197,650 microform items, and 31,176 audio/video tapes/CDs/DVDs, and subscribe to 17,484 periodicals including electronic. Computerized library services include interlibrary loans, database searching, Internet access, and Wi-Fi capability. Special learning facilities include an art gallery, radio station, the College's LEED-certified integrated science center includes an observatory and robotics and solar energy labs. Arts resources include two galleries, one of which is curated by students, dance studios, cinema, and theater. Research facilities include a music and dance library, a science library, the Friends Historical Library, and the Swarthmore Peace Collection. Students interested in community-based learning are supported by the Lang Center for Civic and Social Responsibility. **Physically Challenged Students:** 85% of the campus is accessible. Facilities include wheelchair ramps, elevators, special parking, specially equipped restrooms, special class scheduling, lowered drinking fountains, lowered telephones, and special housing. **Special:** Special educational opportunities at the College include the Honors Program which features small groups of students working closely with faculty and peers; an emphasis on independent learning; and a final examination by outside scholars. Swarthmore offers an engineering major and a program leading toward Teacher Certification. Students may cross-register for courses at Bryn Mawr and Haverford Colleges and the University of Pennsylvania. The Off-Campus Study Office supports students who wish to study abroad, opportunities are widely available and off campus study is encouraged. There are 3 national honor societies, including Phi Beta Kappa, and 31 departmental honors programs. **Visiting:** There are regularly scheduled orientations for prospective students, Tours, information sessions, and interviews are offered throughout the year. . There are guides for informal visits, visitors may sit in on classes, and stay overnight. To schedule a visit, contact the Admissions Office at (610) 328-8300. **Campus Safety and Security:** Measures include 24-hour foot and vehicle patrol, emergency notification system, self-defense education, and security escort services. There are shuttle buses, emergency telephones, lighted pathways/sidewalks, and controlled access to dorms/residences.

REQUIREMENTS: The SAT or ACT is required. The ACT Optional Writing test is also required. Swarthmore does not require a specific high school curriculum. We do, however, recommend the inclusion of four years of English and at least three years each of mathematics, the sciences, history and social studies; the study of one or two foreign languages; and coursework in art and music. Applicants are required to submit scores for either the SAT and any two SAT Subject tests; or the ACT with writing; or the SAT and the ACT (with or without writing). Two essays are required. Interviews are recommended, though not required for first-year applicants. AP credits are accepted.

ADMISSIONS: 14% of a recent year applicants were accepted. The SAT scores for a recent year freshman class were: Critical Reading--3% between 500 and 599, 31% between 600 and 699, and 66% between 700 and 800; Math--3% between 500 and 599, 31% between 600 and 699, and 66% between 700 and 800; Writing--4% between 500 and 599, 26% between 600 and 699, and 70% between 700 and 800. The ACT scores were 5% between 24 and 26, 9% between 27 and 28, and 86% above 28. 76% of the current freshmen were in the top fifth of their class; 99% were in the top two fifths. 30 freshmen graduated first in their class.

FINANCIAL AID: In a recent year, 52% of all full-time freshmen and 50% of continuing full-time students received some form of financial aid. 52% of all full-time freshmen and 50% of continuing full-time students received need-based aid. The average freshman award was $41,766. Need-based scholarships or need-based grants averaged $40,076 ($58,000 maximum); and need-based self-help aid (loans and jobs) averaged $1,690 ($1,840 maximum). 81% of undergraduate students work part-time. Average annual earnings from campus work are $1890. Swarthmore is a member of CSS. The CSS/Profile, FAFSA, the state aid form, and the college's own financial statement, and tax returns, W-2 statements, and year-end paycheck stubs are required. The priority date for freshman financial aid applications for fall entry is February 15.

TEMPLE UNIVERSITY
F-3
www.temple.edu

Philadelphia, PA 19122

(215) 204-7200
(888) 340-2222

Fax: n/av	Email: tuadm@temple.edu
Full-time: 12116 men, 12800 women	Faculty: 1343; 1, av$
	Ph.D.s: 76%
Part-time: 1749 men, 1578 women	Student/Faculty: 18 to 1
Graduate: 4204 men, 5174 women	Tuition: $14,096 ($24,122)
Year: semesters, summer session	Freshman Class: 18813 applied, 12016 accepted, 4390 enrolled
Room & Board: $10,296	
SAT CR/M/W: 558/571/553 ACT: 24	CEEB CODE: 2906
Application Deadline: March 1	VERY COMPETITIVE

Temple University, founded in 1888, is part of the Commonwealth System of Higher Education in Pennsylvania. It offers programs in the liberal arts, science and technology, health professions and social work, education, engineering, art, business and management, environmental design, media and communication, music and dance, theater, film and media arts, and tourism and hospitality. Temple has 9 campuses, including 1 in Rome and 1 in Tokyo. There are 17 undergraduate schools. In addition to regional accreditation, Temple has baccalaureate program accreditation with AACSB, ABET, ACEJMC, ACPE, ADA, APTA, ASLA, CSWE, NAAB, NASAD, NASM, NRPA, TEAC, ACS, APA-COA, AOTA, NATA, CAAHEP, COAPRT, ABA, ASHA, NASP, CAHIIM, CAATE, AMTA, U/RTA, PDE, UCEA, NAST, CAHME, CCNE, CEPH, NASD, APMA, and LCME. The 330-acre campus is in an urban area approximately 1.5 miles from downtown Philadelphia. Including any residence halls, there are 211 buildings.

STUDENT LIFE: 79% of undergraduates are from Pennsylvania. Others are from 50 states, 96 foreign countries, and Canada. 56% are White; 12% African American. The average age of freshmen is 18; all undergraduates, 22. 11% do not continue beyond their first year; 66% remain to graduate. **Housing:** 5506 students can be accommodated in college housing, which includes coed dorms, on-campus apartments, and off-campus apartments. In addition, there are honors houses, special-interest houses, and living-learning communities. On-campus housing is guaranteed for the freshman year only. 86% of students commute. Alcohol is not permitted. All students may keep cars.

FACULTY/CLASSROOMS: 61% of faculty are male; 39% are female. No introductory courses are taught by graduate students.

PROGRAMS OF STUDY: Temple confers B.A., B.F.A., B.B.A., B.MUS, B.S., B.S. BioE, B.S. Arch, B.S.A.T., B.S.C.E., B.S. Ed., B.S.E.E., B.S.E.T., B.S.M.E., B.S.N. and B.S.W. degrees. Associate, Master's, and Doctoral degrees are also awarded. Bachelor's degrees are awarded in AGRICULTURE (environmental studies and horticulture), BIOLOGICAL SCIENCE (biochemistry, biology/adolescence education, biology/biological science, and biophysics), BUSINESS (accounting, banking and finance, business administration and management, entrepreneurial studies, finance, international business management, management information systems, marketing/retailing/merchandising, real estate, sports management, and tourism), COMMUNICATIONS AND THE ARTS (advertising, art, art history and appreciation, broadcasting, ceramic art and design, classics, communications, dance, English, fiber/textiles/weaving, film arts, French, German, glass, graphic design, Italian, jazz, journalism, linguistics, media arts, metal/jewelry, music, music composition, music history and appreciation, music performance, music theory and composition, painting, performing arts, photography, piano/organ, printmaking, public relations, sculpture, Spanish, speech/debate/rhetoric, telecommunications, theater design, theater management, and visual and performing arts), COMPUTER AND PHYSICAL SCIENCE (actuarial science, applied mathematics, chemistry, chemistry/adolescence education, computer science, earth science / adolescence education, geology, information sciences and systems, mathematics, mathematics/computational, mathematics – economics, and physics), EDUCATION (art education, athletic training, technical education and training, early childhood education, elementary education, health information management, mathematics education, music education, physical education, secondary education, and technical education), ENGINEERING AND ENVIRONMENTAL DESIGN (architecture, city/community/regional planning, civil engineering, construction management, electrical/electronics engineering, engineering, engineering technology, environmental science, landscape architecture/design, and mechanical engineering), HEALTH PROFESSIONS (music therapy, nursing, predentistry, premedicine, public health, recreation therapy, and speech therapy), SOCIAL SCIENCE (African American studies, American studies, anthropology, Asian/Oriental studies, criminal justice, economics, geography, history, Latin American studies, legal studies, philosophy, physical fitness/movement, political science/government, prelaw, psychology, religion, social science, social work, sociology, and women's studies). Art, journalism, and business are the strongest academically. Biology, psychology, and accounting have the largest enrollments.

ACTIVITIES: 4% of men belong to 19 national fraternities; 4% of women belong to 15 national sororities. There are 329 groups on campus, including art, band, cheerleading, chess, choir, chorale, chorus, communications, computers, dance, debate, drama, drill team, environmental, ethnic, film, forensics, gay, honors, international, jazz band, literary magazine, marching band, musical theater, newspaper, opera, orchestra, pep band, photography, political, professional, radio and TV, religious, social, social service, student government, symphony, and yearbook. Popular campus events include Homecoming, Cherry and White Day. **Sports:** There are 12 intercollegiate sports for men and 13 for women, and 14 intramural sports for men and 14 for women. Facilities include Pearson McGonigle Halls is home to several campus recreation facilities, including the climbing wall, fitness mezzanine, and the 3rd floor courts. Temple University Fitness (TUF) is a campus recreation fitness facility with nearly 16,000-square feet of space that includes: cardio machines, selectorized machines, and areas designated for circuit training, light weights, and stretch/abs/core. Other fitness facilities include: men's and women's basketball, football, volleyball, men's and women's gymnastics, fencing, men's and women's basketball practice facility, field hockey and women's lacrosse, men's and women's tennis, baseball, softball stadium, men's and women's soccer, and the Independence Blue Cross recreation center. **Graduates:** From July 1, 2013 to June 30, 2014, 6080 bachelor's degrees were awarded. The most popular majors were business/marketing (20%), visual and performing arts (11%), and communication/journalism (11%). In an average class, 38% graduate in 4 years or less, 61% graduate in 5 years or less, and 66% graduate in 6 years or less.

SERVICES: Counseling and information services are available, as is tutoring in most subjects. There is a reader service for the blind, and remedial math, reading, and writing. **Library/Resources:** The 14 libraries contain 4.1 million volumes, 3.4 million microform items, and 45,385 audio/video tapes/CDs/DVDs, and subscribe to 67,942 periodicals including electronic. Computerized library services include interlibrary loans, database searching, Internet access, and Wi-Fi capability. Special learning facilities include an art gallery, planetarium, radio station, and TV station. **Physically Challenged Students:** All of the campus is accessible. Facilities include wheelchair ramps, elevators, special parking, specially equipped restrooms, special class scheduling, lowered drinking fountains, lowered telephones, special housing. Additional services may be arranged through the Disabled Student Services Office. **Special:** Temple offers co-op programs in business/marketing, computer/information sciences, and engineering, internships, study abroad in 15 countries, an extern program in which participating students receive 2 or 3 academic credits, dual majors, distance learning, dual enrollment, ESL, domestic exchange, independent study, and a teacher certification program. There are 3 national honor societies, including Phi Beta Kappa, and a freshman honors program. **Visiting:** There are regularly scheduled orientations for prospective students. There are guides for informal visits and visitors may sit in on classes. To schedule a visit, contact the Office of Undergraduate Admissions. **Campus Safety and Security:** Measures include 24-hour foot and vehicle patrol, emergency notification system, self-defense education, and security escort services. There are shuttle buses, emergency telephones, lighted pathways/sidewalks, controlled access to dorms/residences, 24-hour security in residence halls.

REQUIREMENTS: The SAT or ACT is required. Applicants should complete 16 academic credits/Carnegie units, including 4 years of English, 3 of math, 2 each of social studies, foreign language, and science, including 1 of lab science, and 1 each of history and an academic elective. A GED is accepted. A portfolio and audition are required in relevant fields. AP and CLEP credits are accepted. Important factors in the admissions decision are advanced placement or honors courses, parents or siblings attended your school, evidence of special talent, and recommendations by school officials. The required core curriculum includes nine areas of learning and a total of eleven courses. Areas include: Diversity, World Society, Science and Technology, and U.S. Society. All GenEd courses must be completed with a grade of C- or higher to satisfy a GenEd requirement. **Procedure:** Freshmen are admitted fall and spring. Entrance exams should be taken by March of the junior year or April of the senior year. There is a rolling admissions plan. Applications should be filed by March 1 for fall entry; November 15 for spring entry. The fall 2014 application fee was $55. Notification is sent on a rolling basis. applicants were on the 2014 waiting list; were admitted. Applications are accepted on-line. **Transfer Students:** 3847 transfer students enrolled in 2013-2014. Applicants must have earned at least 15 college credit hours with at least a 2.5 GPA and must submit official high school and college transcripts. 30 of 124 credits required for the bachelor's degree must be completed at Temple. **International Students:** There are 1022 international students enrolled. The school actively recruits these students. They must take the TOEFL with a minimum score of 550 on the paper-based TOEFL (PBT) or 79 on the Internet-based version (iBT). They must also take the SAT or ACT.

ADMISSIONS: 64% of the 2014-2015 applicants were accepted. The SAT scores for the 2014-2015 freshman class were: Critical Reading--22% below 500, 48% between 500 and 599, 25% between 600 and 699, and 5% between 700 and 800; Math--17% below 500, 46% between 500 and 599, 30% between 600 and 699, and 7% between 700 and 800; Writing--24% below 500, 46% between 500 and 599, 25% between 600 and 699, and 5% between 700 and 800. The ACT scores were 16% below 21, 27% between 21 and 23, 28% between 24 and 26, 12% between 27 and 28, and 17% above 28. 42% of the current freshmen were in the top fifth of their class; 77% were in the top two fifths. 13 freshmen graduated first in their class. **Admissions Contact:** Karin Mormando, Director of Undergraduate Admissions. E-Mail: *kmormando@temple.edu* Web: *www.temple.edu*

FINANCIAL AID: The average freshman award was $15,200. Need-based scholarships or need-based grants averaged $6,193; need-based self-help aid (loans and jobs) averaged $3,518; non-need-based athletic scholarships averaged $17,929; and other non-need-based awards and non-need-based scholarships averaged $5,192. The average financial indebtedness of the 2014 graduate was $34,382. The FAFSA and the college's own financial statement, and and the PHEAA (Pennsylvania residents) are required. The priority date for freshman financial aid applications for fall entry is March 1.

THE LINCOLN UNIVERSITY (*The complete profile is made available exclusively on our website, www.barronspac.com*)

THE PENNSYLVANIA STATE UNIVERSITY - C-3
UNIVERSITY PARK
www.psu.edu/

University Park, PA 16802	(814) 863-4700

Fax: (814) 863-7590	Email: admissions@psu.edu
Full-time: 20898 men, 18179 women	Faculty: n/av
	Ph.D.s: 76%
Part-time: 517 men, 364 women	Student/Faculty: 16 to 1
Graduate: 3563 men, 2936 women	Tuition: $17,502 ($30,452)
Year: semesters, summer session	Freshman Class: 50299
Room & Board: $10,520	applied, 25295 accepted, 8183 enrolled
SAT CR/M/W: 580/610/590 ACT: 27	CEEB CODE: 2660
Application Deadline: November 30	VERY COMPETITIVE+

The Pennsylvania State University - University Park Campus, founded in 1855, is a public institution that is the oldest and largest of 24 campuses in the Penn State system. The university offers undergraduate and graduate degrees in agricultural sciences, arts and architecture, business, earth and mineral sciences, education, engineering, health and human development, liberal arts, science, communications, and information sciences and technology. Penn State also offers graduate and first professional degrees in medicine and law. There are 14 undergraduate schools and 1 graduate school. In addition to regional accreditation, Penn State has baccalaureate program accreditation with AACSB, ABET, ACEJMC, APTA, ASLA, NAAB, NASAD, NASM, NCATE, NLN, and SAF. The 8556-acre campus is in a suburban area 90 miles west of Harrisburg, PA. Including any residence halls, there are 933 buildings.

STUDENT LIFE: 62% of undergraduates are from Pennsylvania. Others are from 50 states, 131 foreign countries, and Canada. 67% are White; 14% Foreign. The average age of freshmen is 18; all undergraduates, 20. 7% do not continue beyond their first year; 93% remain to graduate. **Housing:** 13628 students can be accommodated in college housing, which includes single-sex and coed dorms, on-campus apartments, and married student housing. In addition, there are honors houses, language houses, special-interest houses, fraternity houses, and sorority houses. On-campus housing is guaranteed for the freshman year only and is available on a lottery system for upperclassmen. 65% of students commute. Upperclassmen may keep cars.

FACULTY/CLASSROOMS: 63% of faculty are male; 37% are female. No introductory courses are taught by graduate students.

PROGRAMS OF STUDY: Penn State confers B.A., B.S., B.A.E., B.Arch., B.Des., B.Eled., B.F.A., B.Hum., B.L.A., B.M., B.M.A., B.M.E., B.Ph. and B.Sosc. degrees. Associate, Master's, and Doctoral degrees are also awarded. Bachelor's degrees are awarded in AGRICULTURE (agricultural business management, agricultural sciences, agriculture, animal science, environmental studies, forestry and related sciences, natural resources, natural resource management, plant science, and turfgrass and landscape management), BIOLOGICAL SCIENCE (biochemistry, biology/biological science, biotechnology, microbiology, nutrition, nutritional sciences, and toxicology), BUSINESS (accounting, business administration and management, business administration marketing, finance, hospitality management services, industrial and labor relations, management information systems, marketing, marketing management, organizational behavior, organizational leadership and management, and supply chain management), COMMUNICATIONS AND THE ARTS (acting, advertising, art history, art/art studies, Chinese, classical languages, communication science, comparative literature, design, English, English literature, film arts, French, German, graphic design, Italian, Japanese, journalism, journalism & technical communications, music, music performance, musical theater, Russian languages and literature, Spanish, speech/debate/rhetoric, theatre arts, theater design, and visual and performing arts), COMPUTER AND PHYSICAL SCIENCE (astronomy, atmospheric sciences and meteorology, chemistry, Computer Engineering Technology, computer science, earth science, geology, geoscience, information science, mathematics, physics, science technology, and statistics), EDUCATION (agricultural education, art education, athletic training, childhood education:

1-6, early childhood education, educational statistics and research, elementary education, foreign languages education, global studies, music education, secondary education, and special education), ENGINEERING AND ENVIRONMENTAL DESIGN (aerospace engineering, agricultural engineering, architectural engineering, architecture, biomedical engineering, chemical engineering, civil engineering, electrical and computer engineering, electrical/electronics engineering technology, engineering, engineering science, environmental engineering, industrial engineering, landscape architecture, landscape architecture/design, materials science, mechanical engineering, mining and mineral engineering, nuclear engineering, and petroleum/natural gas engineering), HEALTH PROFESSIONS (biomedical science, health administration and policy, health care administration, kinesiology, nursing, premedicine, preveterinary science, rehabilitation therapy, and veterinary science), SOCIAL SCIENCE (African studies, African American studies, anthropology, archeology, asian studies, communication sciences and disorders, criminal justice, criminology, economics, food science, forensic studies, geography, history, homeland security, human development, international relations, Judaic studies, Latin American studies, medieval studies, parks and recreation management, philosophy, political science/government, psychology, sociology, and women's studies). Business and marketing, engineering, communications and journalism have the largest enrollments.

ACTIVITIES: 17% of men belong to 1 local and 59 national fraternities; 19% of women belong to 28 national sororities. There are 980 groups on campus, including art, band, cheerleading, chess, choir, chorale, chorus, computers, dance, debate, drama, drill team, environmental, ethnic, film, forensics, gay, honors, international, jazz band, literary magazine, marching band, musical theater, newspaper, opera, orchestra, pep band, photography, political, professional, radio and TV, religious, social, social service, student government, symphony, and yearbook. Popular campus events include Late Night Penn State, Dance Marathon, Penn State football, and Distinguished Speaker Series. **Sports:** There are 15 intercollegiate sports for men and 14 for women, and 18 intramural sports for men and 18 for women. Facilities include a 107,282-seat football stadium, baseball field with seating for 6,000, 15,000-seat basketball center, 2 golf courses, an ice skating pavilion, indoor track/multipurpose field, outdoor track, soccer field with seating for 5,000, indoor and outdoor swimming pools, bowling lanes, tennis center, 4 fitness facilities, Shaver's Creek Environmental Center, Stone Valley Recreation Center (fishing, swimming, canoeing, sailing, and kayaking), a rifle range, facilities for gymnastics, volleyball, field hockey, lacrosse, fencing, wrestling, 1,084-seat softball field, and a 6,000 plus seat ice arena. **Graduates:** From July 1, 2013 to June 30, 2014, 11390 bachelor's degrees were awarded. The most popular majors were business (15%), engineering (15%), and communications/journalism (9%). 910 companies recruited on campus in 2013-2014. In an average class, 68% graduate in 4 years or less, 83% graduate in 5 years or less, and 86% graduate in 6 years or less. Of the 2013 graduating class, 24% were enrolled in graduate school within 6 months of graduation, and 58% were employed.

SERVICES: Counseling and information services are available, as is tutoring in most subjects. There is a reader service for the blind, remedial math, reading, and writing. **Library/Resources:** The 28 libraries contain 7.3 million volumes, 4.0 million microform items, 137,140 audio/video tapes/CDs/DVDs, and subscribe to 146,804 periodicals including electronic. Computerized library services include interlibrary loans, database searching, Internet access, and Wi-Fi capability. Special learning facilities include an art gallery, planetarium, radio/TV station, 6 major museums at University Park house, significant research and educational collections in the fields of agriculture, anthropology, entomology, earth and mineral sciences, and the fine arts. **Physically Challenged Students:** 95% of the campus is accessible. Facilities include wheelchair ramps, elevators, special parking, specially equipped restrooms, special class scheduling, lowered drinking fountains, lowered telephones, special housing. Reasonable accommodations are available to provide access to all campus services, programs, and activities. **Special:** Co-op programs, internships, study-abroad in more than 45 countries, and work-study programs are available. Dual majors and student-designed majors are possible. Accelerated degree programs, and a 3-2 engineering degree are also offered. There are 30 national honor societies and a freshman honors program. **Visiting:** There are regularly scheduled orientations for prospective students. There are guides for informal visits and visitors may stay overnight. To schedule a visit, contact the Undergraduate Admissions Office. **Campus Safety and Security:** Measures include 24-hour foot and vehicle patrol, emergency notification system, self-defense education, and security escort services. There are shuttle buses, emergency telephones, lighted pathways/sidewalks, and controlled access to dorms/residences.

REQUIREMENTS: The SAT or ACT is required. The ACT Optional Writing test is also required. Applicants may submit SAT or ACT scores. Admissions decisions for first-year students are made on the basis of several combined factors. Approximately two thirds of the decision for each student is based upon the high school GPA. The remaining one third of the decision is based on the factors, which may include standardized critical reading and math test scores, class rank, personal statement, and activities list. Weighted average or class rank for students who have taken AP/Honors courses are considered. AP and CLEP credits are accepted.The typical baccalaureate Penn State academic program requires the completion of between 120 and 130 credits. The General Education requirements are common to all degree programs and compose about one third of the course work (45 credits). All students must also complete a Writing-Across-The-Curriculum course (3 credits), a first-year seminar (1 credit), United States Culture (3 credits), and International Cultures (3 credits) as part of their degree program. **Procedure:** Freshmen are admitted fall, spring, and summer. Entrance exams should be taken In the junior year. There are early admissions, deferred admissions, and rolling admissions plans. Applications should be filed by November 30 for fall entry, along with a $50 fee. Notification is sent on a rolling basis. applicants were on the 2014 waiting list; were admitted. Applications are accepted on-line. **Transfer Students:** 464 transfer students enrolled in 2013-2014. Transfer applicants need a minimum GPA of 2.0 and good academic standing. 36 of 120 credits required for the bachelor's degree must be completed at Penn State. **International Students:** There are 4056 international students enrolled. The school actively recruits these students. They must take the TOEFL with a minimum score of 550 on the paper-based TOEFL (PBT) or 80 on the Internet-based version (iBT). Students whose native language is English or if U.S. citizen or permanent resident must submit SAT or ACT scores; others submit TOEFL.

ADMISSIONS: 50% of the 2014-2015 applicants were accepted. The SAT scores for the 2014-2015 freshman class were: Critical Reading--12% below 500, 49% between 500 and 599, 33% between 600 and 699, and 6% between 700 and 800; Math--5% below 500, 34% between 500 and 599, 45% between 600 and 699, and 16% between 700 and 800; Writing--11% below 500, 43% between 500 and 599, 38% between 600 and 699, and 8% between 700 and 800. **Admissions Contact:** David Kuskowski, Interim Director of Admissions. E-Mail: *admissions@psu.edu* Web: *http:/admissions.psu.edu/*

FINANCIAL AID: The FAFSA is required. The priority date for freshman financial aid applications for fall entry is February 15.

THIEL COLLEGE (*The complete profile is made available exclusively on our website, www.barronspac.com*)

UNIVERSITY OF PENNSYLVANIA   F-3
www.upenn.edu

Philadelphia, PA 19104

(215) 898-7507
(215) 598-5000

Fax: (215) 898-9670   Email: info@admissions.upenn.edu

Full-time: 4703 men, 4704 women	Faculty: 1456; I, ++$
Part-time: 169 men, 136 women	Ph.D.s: 100%
Graduate: 5455 men, 6191 women	Student/Faculty: 6 to 1
Year: semesters, summer session	Tuition: $47,668
Room & Board: $13,464	Freshman Class: 35866 applied, 3718 accepted, 2425 enrolled
SAT or ACT: required	CEEB CODE: 2926
Application Deadline: January 1	MOST COMPETITIVE

The University of Pennsylvania, a member of the Ivy League. Penn's 4 undergraduate schools--the College, Engineering, Nursing and the Wharton School, pursuing interdisciplinary study within the schools and across the University's 12 graduate schools, and engaged in learning in our 165 research centers. There are 4 undergraduate schools and 13 graduate schools. In addition to regional accreditation, Penn has baccalaureate program accreditation with AACSB, ABET, CCNE, and ACNM. The 302-acre campus is in an urban area in Philadelphia. Including any residence halls, there are 187 buildings.

STUDENT LIFE: 82% of undergraduates are from out of state, mostly the Middle Atlantic. Students are from 50 states, 103 foreign countries, and Canada. 59% are from public schools. 46% are White; 19% Asian American; 11% Foreign. 29% claim no religious affiliation; 26% Protestant; 19% Catholic; 19% Jewish. The average age of freshmen is 18; all undergraduates, 20. 2% do not continue beyond their first year; 96% remain to graduate. **Housing:** 6850 students can be accommodated in college housing, which includes coed dorms, on-campus apartments, off-campus apartments, and married student housing. In addition, there are language houses, special-interest houses, fraternity houses, There are over 40 academic residence programs, including the areas of: arts; entrepreneurship; politics, law & society; international studies; media; visual arts; women in science. On-campus housing is guaranteed for the freshman year only, is available on a first-come, first-served basis, and is available on a lottery system for upperclassmen. All students may keep cars.

FACULTY/CLASSROOMS: 63% of faculty are male; 37% are female. All teach and do research. No introductory courses are taught by graduate students.

PROGRAMS OF STUDY: Penn confers B.A., B.S., B.Applied Sc., B.B.A., B.F.A., B.S.E. and B.S.N. degrees. Associate, Master's, and Doctoral degrees are also awarded. Bachelor's degrees are awarded in AGRICULTURE (environmental studies), BIOLOGICAL SCIENCE (biochemistry, biology/biological science, and biophysics), BUSINESS (accounting, business administration and management, entrepreneurial studies, human resources, insurance and risk management, logistics, management information systems, marketing/retailing/merchandising, operations management, real estate, retailing, and transportation management), COMMUNICATIONS AND THE ARTS (art history and appreciation, classics, communications, comparative literature, design, dramatic arts, English, fine arts, folklore and mythology, French, German, linguistics, music, Russian, and visual and performing arts), COMPUTER AND PHYSICAL SCIENCE (actuarial science, applied science, chemistry, computer science, digital arts/technology, geology, information sciences and systems, mathematics, physics, science technology, and statistics), EDUCATION (elementary education), ENGINEERING AND ENVIRONMENTAL DESIGN (architecture, bioengineering, chemical engineering, civil engineering, computer engineering, electrical/electronics engineering, and materials engineering), HEALTH PROFESSIONS (health, health care administration, and nursing), SOCIAL SCIENCE (African studies, African American studies, American studies, anthropology, Asian/Oriental studies, cognitive science, economics, gender studies, Hispanic American studies, history, history of science, international relations, international studies, Italian studies, Judaic studies, Latin American studies, law, Middle Eastern studies, Near Eastern studies, philosophy, political science/government, psychology, public administration, religion, sociology, South Asian studies, urban studies, and women's studies). Finance, economics, nursing, political science, and history have the largest enrollments.

ACTIVITIES: 30% of men belong to 36 national fraternities; 17% of women belong to 13 national sororities. There are 450 groups on campus, including art, band, cheerleading, chess, choir, chorale, chorus, computers, dance, debate, drama, environmental, ethnic, film, forensics, gay, honors, international, jazz band, literary magazine, marching band, musical theater, newspaper, opera, orchestra, pep band, photography, political, professional, radio and TV, religious, social, social service, student government, and symphony. **Sports:** There are 17 intercollegiate sports for men and 16 for women, and 11 intramural sports for men and 11 for women. Facilities include 4 gyms, 1 swimming pool, squash courts, indoor and outdoor tennis courts, 7 playing fields, an indoor ice rink, rowing tanks, saunas, weight rooms, exercise facilities, a boathouse, and a stadium.

Graduates: From July 1, 2013 to June 30, 2014, 2848 bachelor's degrees were awarded. The most popular majors were finance (14%), nursing (6%), and economics (5%). 601 companies recruited on campus in 2013-2014. In an average class, 88% graduate in 4 years or less and 96% graduate in 6 years or less. Of the 2013 graduating class, 20% were enrolled in graduate school within 6 months of graduation, and 60% were employed.

SERVICES: Counseling and information services are available, as is tutoring in most subjects. There is a reader service for the blind. The WHEEL academic support program is available in all residences.

Library/Resources: The 15 libraries contain 5.9 million volumes, 4.2 million microform items, 121,233 audio/video tapes/CDs/DVDs, and subscribe to 98,145 periodicals including electronic. Computerized library services include interlibrary loans, database searching, Internet access, and Wi-Fi capability. Special learning facilities include an art gallery, natural history museum, planetarium, radio station, TV station, Museum of Archaeology and Anthropology, Institute of Contemporary Art (ICA), Morris Arboretum, Annenberg Center (Theater), Astronomical observatory, Large Animal Research Center, Equine Sports Medicine and Imaging Center, Women's center, Undergraduate Research Center, Wind Tunnel, Cyclotron Facility, Marshak Dairy, Arthur Ross Gallery, Galleries in Van Pelt Library, Galleries in Inn@Penn, Charles Addams Gallery, Kroiz Gallery in Architectural Archives, Kelly Writer's House, ENIAC Museum, Hillel Foundation, Center for Advanced Judaic Studies, LRSM material testing equipment. **Physically Challenged Students:** 93% of the campus is accessible. Facilities include wheelchair ramps, elevators, special parking, specially equipped restrooms, special class scheduling, lowered drinking fountains, lowered telephones, special housing. **Special:** Cross-registration is permitted with Haverford, Swarthmore, and Bryn Mawr Colleges and through the Quaker Consortium. Opportunities are provided for internships, a Washington semester, accelerated degree programs, joint degree programs, preprofessional programs, B.A.-B.S. degrees, dual and student-designed majors, credit by exam, limited pass/fail options, and study abroad in 39 countries. Through the "one university" concept, students in one undergraduate school may study in any of the other three. There are 11 national honor societies, a freshman honors program, and 27 departmental honors programs. **Visiting:** There are regularly scheduled orientations for prospective students, including an information session by the Admissions Office and a tour of the campus led by current students. There are guides for informal visits, visitors may sit in on classes, and stay overnight. To schedule a visit, contact the Admissions Office. **Campus Safety and Security:** Measures include 24-hour foot and vehicle patrol, emergency notification system, self-defense education, and security escort services. There are shuttle buses, emergency telephones, lighted pathways/sidewalks, controlled access to dorms/residences, a bicycle patrol, police officers, victim support and special services, Students Together Against Acquaintance Rape, Penn watch, student walking escort, and security guard personnel, many on public patrol.

REQUIREMENTS: The SAT or ACT is required. Graduation from an accredited secondary school is not required. Recommended preparation includes 4 years of high school English, 3 or 4 each of a foreign language and math, and 3 each of history and social science. An essay is required. A portfolio is recommended for prospective art majors. AP credits are accepted. The bachelor's degree requires completion of 32 to 40 course units, depending on the student's major, with 12 to 18 of these units in the major and a GPA of 2.0. **Procedure:** Freshmen are admitted fall. Entrance exams should be taken by December of the senior year. There are early decision and deferred admissions plans. Early decision applications should be filed by November 1; regular applications, by January 1 for fall entry, along with a $75 fee. Notification of early decision is sent December 15; regular decision, April 1. 1299 early decision candidates were accepted for the 2014-2015 class. 1600 applicants were on the 2014 waiting list; 136 were admitted. Applications are accepted on-line. **Transfer Students:** 170 transfer students enrolled in 2013-2014. Applicants must provide college and high school transcripts, essays, and 2 recommendations. SAT or ACT scores are required for transfer students. 16 of 32 credits required for the bachelor's degree must be completed at Penn. **International Students:** There are 1077 international students enrolled. The school actively recruits these students. They must take the

TOEFL. They must also take the SAT, and SAT: Subject tests or the ACT with writing.

ADMISSIONS: 10% of the 2014-2015 applicants were accepted. The SAT scores for the 2014-2015 freshman class were: Critical Reading--5% between 500 and 599, 31% between 600 and 699, and 64% between 700 and 800; Math--2% between 500 and 599, 24% between 600 and 699, and 74% between 700 and 800; Writing--% below 500, 3% between 500 and 599, 22% between 600 and 699, and 75% between 700 and 800; 100% were in the top two fifths. **Admissions Contact:** E-Mail: *info@admissions.upenn.edu* Web: *http://www.admissionsug.upenn.edu/request/*

FINANCIAL AID: In 2014-2015, 50% of all full-time freshmen and 47% of continuing full-time students received some form of financial aid. 50% of all full-time freshmen and 47% of continuing full-time students received need-based aid. The average freshman award was $41,713. Need-based scholarships or need-based grants averaged $39,459; and need-based self-help aid (loans and jobs) averaged $2,890. 44% of undergraduate students work part-time. Average annual earnings from campus work are $1835. The average financial indebtedness of the 2014 graduate was $19,798. Penn is a member of CSS. The CSS/Profile, FAFSA, and the college's own financial statement, and Parents' and student's most recently completed income tax returns are required. The priority date for freshman financial aid applications for fall entry is February 15.

UNIVERSITY OF PITTSBURGH SYSTEM

The University of Pittsburgh System, established in 1787, is a public system in Pennsylvania. It is governed by the board of trustees of the University of Pittsburgh, whose chief administrator is the chancellor. The primary goal of the system is enhancing educational opportunities for the citizens of Pennsylvania and contributing to the state's social, intellectual, and economic development. The main priorities are to engage in research, artistic, and scholarly activities, to provide high-quality undergraduate, graduate, and professional programs, and to offer expertise and educational services to meet the needs of the region and state. The total student enrollment of all 5 campuses is usually 35,581 with 5210 faculty members. Altogether there are 203 baccalaureate, 131 master's, and 94 doctoral programs offered in University of Pittsburgh System. 4-year campuses are located in Pittsburgh, Bradford, Greensburg, and Johnstown. Profiles of the 4-year campuses are included in this section.

UNIVERSITY OF PITTSBURGH AT BRADFORD   C-1
www.upb.pitt.edu

Bradford, PA 16701	(814) 362-7500
	(800) 872-1787
Fax: (814) 362-7578	Email: admissions@upb.pitt.edu
Full-time: 648 men, 736 women	Faculty: 69; IIB, av$
Part-time: 41 men, 74 women	Ph.D.s: 39%
Graduate: n/av	Student/Faculty: 18 to 1
Year: semesters, summer session	Tuition: $13,322 ($24,138)
Room & Board: $8480	Freshman Class: 1720 applied, 449 accepted, 398 enrolled
SAT CR/M/W: 480/500/455 ACT: 21	CEEB CODE: 2935
Application Deadline: n/av	COMPETITIVE

The University of Pittsburgh at Bradford, established in 1963, is a public, state-related for students who want to earn a world-renowned education in a personalized environment. There is one undergraduate school. In addition to regional accreditation, Pitt-Bradford has baccalaureate program accreditation with NLN and CAATE. The 317-acre campus is in a small town 160 miles northeast of Pittsburgh and 80 miles south of Buffalo. Including any residence halls, there are 32 buildings.

STUDENT LIFE: 84% of undergraduates are from Pennsylvania. Others are from 26 states, and 11 foreign countries. 89% are from public schools. 73% are White. 42% are Protestant; 29% claim no religious affiliation; 25% Catholic. The average age of freshmen is 18; all undergraduates, 21. 31% do not continue beyond their first year; 52% remain to graduate. **Housing:** 1047 students can be accommodated in college housing, which includes single-sex and coed on-campus apartments. On-campus housing is available on a first-come and first-served basis. 67% of students live on campus; of those, 38% remain on campus on weekends. All students may keep cars.

FACULTY/CLASSROOMS: 48% of faculty are male; 52% are female. All teach undergraduates. No introductory courses are taught by graduate students. The average class size in an introductory lecture is 22; in a laboratory is 14; and in a regular course is 19.

PROGRAMS OF STUDY: Pitt-Bradford confers B.A., B.S. and B.S.N. degrees. Associate degrees are also awarded. Bachelor's degrees are awarded in AGRICULTURE (environmental studies), BIOLOGICAL SCIENCE (biology/biological science), BUSINESS (accounting, business administration and management, hospitality management services, and sports management), COMMUNICATIONS AND THE ARTS (communications, English, and public relations), COMPUTER AND PHYSICAL SCIENCE (applied mathematics, chemistry, mathematics, and physical sciences), EDUCATION (athletic training, business education, elementary education, English education, environmental education, health education, mathematics education, science education, and social studies education), ENGINEERING AND ENVIRONMENTAL DESIGN (engineering), HEALTH PROFESSIONS (nursing, radiological science, and sports medicine), SOCIAL SCIENCE (criminal justice, economics, history, human development, interdisciplinary studies, liberal arts/general studies, psychology, social science, and sociology). Engineering, nursing, and biology are the strongest academically. Business administration, criminal justice, and biology have the largest enrollments.

ACTIVITIES: 5% of men belong to 5 local fraternities; 4% of women belong to 4 local sororities. There are 63 groups on campus, including art, cheerleading, choir, chorale, computers, dance, drama, environmental, ethnic, gay, honors, international, literary magazine, newspaper, political, professional, radio and TV, religious, social, social service, and student government. Popular campus events include Winter Weekend, Spring Fling, and Alumni Weekend. **Sports:** There are 6 intercollegiate sports for men and 7 for women, and 15 intramural sports for men and 15 for women. Facilities include a sport and fitness center that includes a 1200-seat performance arena for basketball, volleyball, and general recreation; a fitness center with physical conditioning equipment; and an exercise arts studio for dance, martial arts, and aerobics. There is also an auxiliary gym for recreated and intramurals, phys ed classes, and other events, and a 6-lane swimming pool. Outdoor facilities include a lighted softball field, a baseball field, tennis courts, 2 handball courts, several basketball courts, football/softball fields, and a sand volleyball court. **Graduates:** From July 1, 2013 to June 30, 2014, 228 bachelor's degrees were awarded. The most popular majors were business management (17%), sports medicine (8%), and biology (8%). 47 companies recruited on campus in 2013-2014. In an average class, 33% graduate in 4 years or less, 51% graduate in 5 years or less, and 54% graduate in 6 years or less. Of the 2013 graduating class, 21% were enrolled in graduate school within 6 months of graduation, and 75% were employed.

SERVICES: Counseling and information services are available, as is tutoring in most subjects. There is remedial math, reading, and writing. **Library/Resources:** The library contains 103,121 volumes, 1,055 microform items, 4,076 audio/video tapes/CDs/DVDs, and subscribes to 91 periodicals including electronic. Computerized library services include interlibrary loans, database searching, and Internet access. Special learning facilities include an art gallery, radio station, The university also has a crime scene investigation house, a nursing suite with computerized mannequins, psychology lab, human performance lab, and athletic training facilities. **Physically Challenged Students:** 99% of the campus is accessible. Facilities include elevators, special parking, specially equipped restrooms, lowered drinking fountains, lowered telephones, and special housing. **Special:** Students may cross-register with colleges in the University of Pittsburgh system. Internships are required or strongly recommended for all majors. The school offers study abroad, dual majors, nondegree study, and a 3-2 engineering degree with the University of Pittsburgh (Oakland campus). Interdisciplinary majors are offered in human relations combining anthropology, psychology, and sociology; social

sciences, combining anthropology, economics, history, political science, and sociology; and in interdisciplinary arts, combining art, music, and theater. Professional preparation is available in many areas including premedicine, prelaw, preveterinary science, prepharmacy, and predentistry. Teacher certification is also offered. There are 7 national honor societies. **Visiting:** There are regularly scheduled orientations for prospective students, programs throughout the year, offering a workshop with admissions representatives on academics, admissions, guidance, standardized tests, the application process, and financial aid. Tours led by students, a financial aid presentation , and a special campus event are also offered. There are guides for informal visits and visitors may sit in on classes. To schedule a visit, contact Alexander Nazemetz at (800) 872-1787. **Campus Safety and Security:** Measures include 24-hour foot and vehicle patrol, emergency notification system, and security escort services. There are shuttle buses, emergency telephones, and lighted pathways/sidewalks.

REQUIREMENTS: The SAT or ACT is required. Students must be graduates of an accredited secondary school with 16 Carnegie units, including 4 in English, 3 in history or social studies, and 3 each in science and math. The GED is accepted. Also used in the admissions decision are standardized test scores, rank in class, extracurricular activities, and recommendations. An essay is strongly recommended, as is an interview. A GPA of 2.0 is required. AP and CLEP credits are accepted. Important factors in the admissions decision are advanced placement or honors courses, extracurricular activities record, and leadership record. To graduate, students must complete a minimum of 120 credits with 30 to 76 in the major, and maintain a minimum GPA of 2.0. At least 30 should be upper-level courses. The core curriculum varies from 12 to 30 credits and distribution requirements from 56 to 59. English, math competency, and phys ed courses are required. **Procedure:** Freshmen are admitted fall, spring, and summer. Entrance exams should be taken during the junior year or the fall of the senior year. There are deferred admissions and rolling admissions plans. Application deadlines are open. Application fee is $45. Notifications are sent October 16. Applications are accepted online. **Transfer Students:** 100 transfer students enrolled in 2013-2014. A GPA of 2.0 or higher is required. 30 of 120 credits required for the bachelor's degree must be completed at Pitt-Bradford. **International Students:** There are 55 international students enrolled. They must take the TOEFL with a minimum score of 550 on the paper-based TOEFL (PBT) or 80 on the Internet-based version (iBT) or the IELTS, scoring 6.5.

ADMISSIONS: 26% of the 2014-2015 applicants were accepted. The SAT scores for the 2014-2015 freshman class were: Critical Reading--57% below 500, 36% between 500 and 599, 6% between 600 and 699, and 1% between 700 and 800; Math--49% below 500, 36% between 500 and 599, 12% between 600 and 699, and 3% between 700 and 800; Writing--70% below 500, 26% between 500 and 599, and 4% between 600 and 699. The ACT scores were 43% below 21, 24% between 21 and 23, 25% between 24 and 26, 5% between 27 and 28, and 3% above 28. 25% of the current freshmen were in the top fifth of their class; 52% were in the top two fifths. 2 freshmen graduated first in their class. **Admissions Contact:** Alexander P. Nazemetz, Director of Admissions. E-Mail: *admissions@upb.pitt.edu* Web: *www.upb.pitt.edu/Admissions/*

FINANCIAL AID: In 2014-2015, 98% of all full-time freshmen and 94% of continuing full-time students received some form of financial aid. 93% of all full-time freshmen and 85% of continuing full-time students received need-based aid. The average freshman award was $9,318. Need-based scholarships or need-based grants averaged $4,725 ($12,700 maximum); need-based self-help aid (loans and jobs) averaged $4,672 ($14,871 maximum); and other non-need-based awards and non-need-based scholarships averaged $4,168 ($18,920 maximum). 11% of undergraduate students work part-time. Average annual earnings from campus work are $1740. The average financial indebtedness of the 2014 graduate was $36,720. The FAFSA is required. The priority date for freshman financial aid applications for fall entry is March 1.

UNIVERSITY OF PITTSBURGH AT GREENSBURG — B-3
www.upg.pitt.edu

Greensburg, PA 15601-5898	(724) 836-9880 n/av
Fax: (724) 836-7160	Email: upgadmit@pitt.edu
Full-time: 810 men, 855 women	Faculty: n/av; IIB, --$
Part-time: 85 men, 85 women	Ph.D.s: n/av
Graduate: n/av	Student/Faculty: n/av
Year: semesters, summer session	Tuition: $12,626 ($22,818)
Room & Board: $8410	Freshman Class: n/av
SAT or ACT: required	CEEB CODE: 2936
Application Deadline: open	COMPETITIVE

The University of Pittsburgh at Greensburg, established in 1963, is a public state-related institution, offering undergraduate majors that can be completed at Pitt-Greensburg, as well as relocation programs that are begun at Greensburg and completed at another Pitt campus. The figures in the above capsule and in this profile are approximate. The 219-acre campus is in a suburban area 33 miles southeast of Pittsburgh. Including any residence halls, there are 25 buildings.

STUDENT LIFE: 99% of undergraduates are from Pennsylvania. Others are from 5 states, 1 foreign country, and Canada. 94% are white. The average age of freshmen is 18; all undergraduates, 21. 25% do not continue beyond their first year; 55% remain to graduate.

FACULTY/CLASSROOMS: 52% of faculty are male; 48% are female. All teach undergraduates, and 50% do research. No introductory courses are taught by graduate students. The average class size in an introductory lecture is 30; in a laboratory, 15; and in a regular course, 25.

PROGRAMS OF STUDY: Pitt-Greensburg confers B.A. and B.S. degrees. Bachelor's degrees are awarded in BIOLOGICAL SCIENCE (biology/biological science), BUSINESS (accounting and management science), COMMUNICATIONS AND THE ARTS (communications, creative writing, and English literature), COMPUTER AND PHYSICAL SCIENCE (applied mathematics and natural sciences), SOCIAL SCIENCE (American studies, anthropology, humanities, political science/government, psychology, and social science). Management and psychology are the strongest academically. Management and administration of justice have the largest enrollments.

ACTIVITIES: There are 44 groups on campus, including academic, band, cheerleading, chess, choir, chorale, chorus, computers, dance, debate, drama, ethnic, honors, literary magazine, newspaper, pep band, political, religious, social, social service, and student government. Popular campus events include a La Cultura study of a different historically significant era each year, the St. Clair history lecture, and Westmoreland Forum on a topic of countywide significance.

SERVICES: Counseling and information services are available, as is tutoring in most subjects, math, computer science, and English. There is remedial math, reading, and writing. **Library/Resources:** The library contains 75,000 volumes, 9,458 microform items, and 1,280 audio/video tapes/CDs/DVDs, and subscribes to 0 periodicals including electronic. Computerized library services include interlibrary loans, database searching, Internet access, and Wi-Fi capability. **Physically Challenged Students:** 95% of the campus is accessible. Facilities include wheelchair ramps, elevators, special parking, specially equipped restrooms, special class scheduling, lowered drinking fountains, lowered telephones, and special housing. **Special:** Pitt-Greensburg offers cross-registration with the Pittsburgh and Johnstown campuses of the university system and with Seton Hill College and Westmoreland County Community College. Internships are available in all majors and required for English writing and criminology. Double majors, student-designed majors, a Washington semester, nondegree study, and pass/fail options are available. There are 2 national honor societies and including Phi Beta Kappa. **Visiting:** There are regularly scheduled orientations for prospective students, including Open House, Preview Day, and Junior Jump Start, weekday visits that include campus tours and information sessions. There are guides for informal visits and visitors may sit in on classes. To schedule a visit, contact the Admissions Office. **Campus Safety and Security:** Measures include 24-hour foot and vehicle patrol and security

escort services. There are emergency telephones and lighted pathways/sidewalks.

REQUIREMENTS: The SAT or ACT is required, including the writing test. Students must be graduates of an accredited secondary school. The GED is also accepted. Students must complete 15 college-preparatory high school units, including 4 each of English and academic electives, 3 of a single foreign language (recommended), 2 of math, and 1 each of history and a lab science; additional units in all but English are recommended. An essay is optional; an interview is recommended. GPA and class rank are also considered heavily. Pitt-Greensburg requires applicants to be in the upper 60% of their class. A GPA of 2.0 is required. AP and CLEP credits are accepted. Important factors in the admissions decision are advanced placement or honors courses, recommendations by school officials, and leadership record.

FINANCIAL AID: The FAFSA and the college's own financial statement are required. Check with the school for current deadlines.

UNIVERSITY OF PITTSBURGH AT JOHNSTOWN *(The complete profile is made available exclusively on our website, www.barronspac.com)*

UNIVERSITY OF PITTSBURGH AT PITTSBURGH — B-3
www.pitt.edu

Pittsburgh, PA 15260	(412) 624-4141 (412) 624-7488
Fax: (412) 624-4138	Email: oafa@pitt.edu
Full-time: 8691 men, 8792 women	Faculty: I
Part-time: 571 men, 561 women	Ph.D.s: 91%
Graduate: 4611 men, 5423 women	Student/Faculty: 14 to 1
Year: semesters, summer session	Tuition: $17,772 ($28,168)
Room & Board: $10,800	Freshman Class: 30629 applied, 16271 accepted, 3852 enrolled
SAT CR/M/W: 629/647/623 ACT: 29	CEEB CODE: 2927
Application Deadline: open	HIGHLY COMPETITIVE+

The University of Pittsburgh, founded in 1787, is a state-related, public research university with programs in arts and sciences, education, engineering, law, social work, business, health and rehabilitation sciences, nursing, pharmacy, dental medicine, public health, medicine, information sciences, and public and international affairs. There are 9 undergraduate schools and 6 graduate schools. In addition to regional accreditation, Pitt has baccalaureate program accreditation with AACSB, ABET, ADA, and CSWE. The 145-acre campus is in a suburban area 3 miles east of downtown Pittsburgh. Including any residence halls, there are 131 buildings.

STUDENT LIFE: 71% of undergraduates are from Pennsylvania. Others are from 50 states, 45 foreign countries, and Canada. 76% are White. The average age of all undergraduates is 21. 7% do not continue beyond their first year; 82% remain to graduate. **Housing:** 7851 students can be accommodated in college housing, which includes single-sex and coed dorms, on-campus apartments, and off-campus apartments. In addition, there are honors houses, language houses, special-interest houses, fraternity houses, sorority houses, emerging leaders, engineering, nursing, business, international living, health sciences, healthy U, honors college, ROTC, service to others, and appreciation of the arts. On-campus housing is guaranteed for the freshman year only, is available on a first-come, first-served basis, and is available on a lottery system for upperclassmen. 57% of students commute. All students may keep cars.

FACULTY/CLASSROOMS: 60% of faculty are male; 40% are female. No introductory courses are taught by graduate students.

PROGRAMS OF STUDY: Pitt confers B.A., B.S., B.A.S.W., B.Phil., B.S.B.A., B.S.E., B.S.N. and B.S.P.S. degrees. Master's and Doctoral degrees are also awarded. Bachelor's degrees are awarded in AGRICULTURE (environmental studies), BIOLOGICAL SCIENCE (bioinformatics, biology/biological science, ecology, microbiology, molecular biology, and neurosciences), BUSINESS (accounting, banking and finance, business administration and management, business (dual major program), business information systems, economics –statistics, finance, global/general management, human resources, international business management, marketing/retailing/merchandising, and supply chain management), COMMUNICATIONS AND THE ARTS (Chinese, classics, communications, communication rhetoric/communication, communication science, English literature, English Writing, film arts, French, German, Germanic languages and literature, Italian, Japanese, linguistics, media arts, music, physical activity, Polish, Russian, Slavic languages, Spanish, studio art, and theatre arts), COMPUTER AND PHYSICAL SCIENCE (actuarial mathematics, applied mathematics, astronomy, chemistry, computer science, environmental geology, geology, information sciences and systems, mathematics, mathematics – economics, natural sciences, physics, and statistics), EDUCATION (athletic training and health information management), ENGINEERING AND ENVIRONMENTAL DESIGN (bioengineering, chemical engineering, civil engineering, computer engineering, electrical/electronics engineering, engineering physics, industrial engineering, materials engineering, materials science, and mechanical engineering), HEALTH PROFESSIONS (dental hygiene, emergency medical technologies, health services technology, nursing, occupational therapy, pharmaceutical science, and rehabilitation therapy), SOCIAL SCIENCE (administration of justice , africana studies, anthropology, applied psychology, architectural studies, economics, history, history of philosophy, humanities, interdisciplinary studies, international studies, legal studies, liberal arts/general studies, philosophy, political science/government, prelaw, psychology, public administration, public affairs, religion, social science, social work, sociology, and urban studies). Engineering, psychology, and nursing have the largest enrollments.

ACTIVITIES: 11% of men belong to 20 national fraternities; 10% of women belong to 16 national sororities. There are 528 groups on campus, including art, band, cheerleading, chess, choir, chorale, chorus, communications, dance, debate, drama, ethnic, film, gay, honors, international, jazz band, literary magazine, marching band, musical theater, newspaper, pep band, political, professional, radio and TV, religious, social, social service, student government, symphony, and yearbook. Popular campus events include Lantern Night, Fall Fest and Bigelow Bash. **Sports:** There are 8 intercollegiate sports for men and 9 for women, and 12 intramural sports for men and 11 for women. Facilities include Petersen Events Center -a 12,000-seat field house for hosting basketball games and concerts; the complex also has a fitness center for student use as well as a food court and shops; a field house with volleyball, gymnastics, wrestling, and an indoor track and field; a pool, and a gymnastics training center. The Petersen Sports Complex has a baseball stadium, a soccer stadium, and a softball stadium. There are billiard tables, table tennis, video games, and televisions in the student union. **Graduates:** From July 1, 2013 to June 30, 2014, 4346 bachelor's degrees were awarded. The most popular majors were business (15%), engineering (11%), and English language and literature (8%). 734 companies recruited on campus in 2013-2014. In an average class, 82% graduate in 6 years or less.

SERVICES: Counseling and information services are available, as is tutoring in some subjects, many lower-level undergraduate science and humanities courses. There is remedial math and writing. **Library/Resources:** The 19 libraries contain 6.8 million volumes, 5.6 million microform items, 1.2 million audio/video tapes/CDs/DVDs, and subscribe to 186,012 periodicals including electronic. Computerized library services include interlibrary loans, database searching, Internet access, and Wi-Fi capability. Special learning facilities include an art gallery, radio station, international classrooms, located in the 42-story Cathedral of Learning, an observatory, music hall, and a natural history museum very near campus. **Physically Challenged Students:** 90% of the campus is accessible. Facilities include wheelchair ramps, elevators, special parking, specially equipped restrooms, lowered drinking fountains, lowered telephones, and special housing. **Special:** Students may cross-register with 9 neighboring colleges and universities. Internships, unlimited study abroad, work-study programs, a dual major in business and any other subject in arts and sciences, and student-designed majors are available. There is a 5-year joint degree in arts and sciences/engineering. There are co-op programs in engineering, computer science, and chemistry. An accelerated second degree B.S.N. program is available as well as a 3-2 engineering degree. There are 20 national honor societies, including Phi Beta Kappa, and a freshman honors program. **Visiting:** There are regularly scheduled orientations for prospective students, including information sessions, student-guided tours, and class attendance. . There are guides for informal visits and visitors may sit in on classes. To schedule a visit, contact the Office of Admissions and Financial Aid at 1-877-SEE-PITT. **Campus Safety and Security:** Measures include 24-hour foot and vehicle patrol, emergency notification system, self-defense education, and security escort services. There are shuttle buses, emergency telephones, lighted pathways/sidewalks, and controlled access to dorms/residences.

REQUIREMENTS: The SAT or ACT is required. The ACT Optional Writing test is also required. Applicants for admission to the Kenneth P. Dietrich School of Arts and Sciences must be graduates of an accredited secondary school. Students must have 17 high school academic credits, including 4 units of English, 3 to 4 each of math and lab science, 2-3 of social studies, plus 3 to 5 units in academic electives. Pitt recommends that the student have 3 or more years of a single foreign language. An essay is recommended if the student is seeking scholarship consideration. AP and CLEP credits are accepted. Important factors in the admissions decision are advanced placement or honors courses, leadership record, and evidence of special talent. All students in the Kenneth P. Dietrich School of Arts and Sciences must take a minimum of 120 credits. Skills and general education requirements vary but include course work in the humanities, social and natural sciences, and foreign culture. A 2.0 GPA are required. Students must earn their last 30 credits while enrolled in Arts and Sciences and earn at least half of the credits for their majors while enrolled in Arts and Sciences. Requirements for other schools may vary. **Procedure:** Freshmen are admitted to all sessions. Entrance exams should be taken preferably by January for September admission. There are deferred admissions and rolling admissions plans. Application deadlines are open. Application fee is $45. Notification is sent on a rolling basis. 2492 applicants were on the 2014 waiting list; 289 were admitted. Applications are accepted on-line. **Transfer Students:** 762 transfer students enrolled in 2013-2014. Applicants for transfer to the Kenneth P. Dietrich School of Arts and Sciences must supply transcripts of all secondary school and college course work and have a minimum GPA of 3.0. An interview is recommended. Grades of C or better transfer for credit. Application deadlines vary by school. 30 of 120 credits required for the bachelor's degree must be completed at Pitt. **International Students:** There are 703 international students enrolled. The school actively recruits these students. They must take the TOEFL with a minimum score of 600 on the paper-based TOEFL (PBT) or 100 on the Internet-based version (iBT), or take the IELTS. They must also take the SAT or ACT.

ADMISSIONS: 53% of the 2014-2015 applicants were accepted. The SAT scores for the 2014-2015 freshman class were: Critical Reading--2% below 500, 30% between 500 and 599, 53% between 600 and 699, and 15% between 700 and 800; Math--1% below 500, 19% between 500 and 599, 57% between 600 and 699, and 23% between 700 and 800; Writing--2% below 500, 34% between 500 and 599, 48% between 600 and 699, and 16% between 700 and 800. The ACT scores were 1% below 21, 4% between 21 and 23, 23% between 24 and 26, 21% between 27 and 28, and 51% above 28. 81% of the current freshmen were in the top fifth of their class; 98% were in the top two fifths. **Admissions Contact:** Mr. Marc L. Harding, Chief Enrollment Officer. E-Mail: *oafa@pitt.edu* Web: *www.pitt.edu*

FINANCIAL AID: In 2014-2015, 64% of all full-time freshmen and 58% of continuing full-time students received some form of financial aid. 56% of all full-time freshmen and 54% of continuing full-time students received need-based aid. The average freshman award was $14,031. Need-based scholarships or need-based grants averaged $9,457; need-based self-help aid (loans and jobs) averaged $5,872; and non-need-based athletic scholarships averaged $16,044. The average financial indebtedness of the 2014 graduate was $36,466. The FAFSA is required. The priority date for freshman financial aid applications for fall entry is March 1.

UNIVERSITY OF SCRANTON — E-2
www.scranton.edu

Scranton, PA 18510

(570) 941-7540
(888) SCRANTON

Fax: (570) 941-5928   Email: admissions@scranton.edu

Full-time: 1735 men, 2112 women   Faculty: n/av; IIA, +$

Part-time: 88 men, 106 women   Ph.D.s: 85%

Graduate: 755 men, 1102 women   Student/Faculty: n/av

Year: semesters, summer session   Tuition: $38,754

Room & Board: $13,186   Freshman Class: 9672 applied, 6655 accepted, 971 enrolled

SAT or ACT: required   CEEB CODE: 2929

Application Deadline: March 1   **VERY COMPETITIVE**

The University of Scranton, founded in 1888, is a private institution operated by the Jesuit order of the Roman Catholic Church. It offers programs in business, behavioral sciences, education, health science, humanities, math, science, and social science. There are 4 undergraduate schools and 1 graduate school. In addition to regional accreditation, the University has baccalaureate program accreditation with AACSB, ABET, APTA, CSAB, NCATE, and NLN. The 58-acre campus is in an urban area 125 miles north of Philadelphia. Including any residence halls, there are 67 buildings.

STUDENT LIFE: 60% of undergraduates are from out of state, mostly the Middle Atlantic. Students are from 24 states, and 12 foreign countries. 81% are White. 75% are Catholic. The average age of freshmen is 19; all undergraduates, 21. 12% do not continue beyond their first year; 83% remain to graduate.

FACULTY/CLASSROOMS: 59% of faculty are male; 41% are female. No introductory courses are taught by graduate students. The average class size in a regular course is 20.

PROGRAMS OF STUDY: the University confers B.A., and B.S. degrees. Associate, Master's, and Doctoral degrees are also awarded. Bachelor's degrees are awarded in BIOLOGICAL SCIENCE (biochemistry, biology/biological science, biomathematics, biophysics, and neurosciences), BUSINESS (accounting, banking and finance, business administration and management, business economics, electronic business, human resources, information and communication technology, international business management, marketing/retailing/merchandising, and operations management), COMMUNICATIONS AND THE ARTS (communications, English, French, German, Greek, Latin, Spanish, and theatre arts), COMPUTER AND PHYSICAL SCIENCE (chemistry, computer science, information sciences and systems, mathematics, and physics), EDUCATION (early childhood education, elementary education, and secondary education), ENGINEERING AND ENVIRONMENTAL DESIGN (computer engineering, electrical/electronics engineering, and environmental science), HEALTH PROFESSIONS (community health work, exercise science, health care administration, medical laboratory technology, nursing, and occupational therapy), SOCIAL SCIENCE (criminal justice, economics, forensic studies, history, human services, international studies, philosophy, political science/government, psychology, sociology, theological studies, and women's studies). Chemistry, biology, and nursing are the strongest academically. Biology, communication, and nursing have the largest enrollments.

ACTIVITIES: There are no fraternities or sororities. There are 80 groups on campus, including art, band, cheerleading, chess, choir, chorale, chorus, communications, computers, dance, debate, drama, environmental, ethnic, film, forensics, honors, international, jazz band, literary magazine, musical theater, newspaper, orchestra, photography, political, professional, radio and TV, religious, social, social service, student government, symphony, and yearbook. Popular campus events include Spring Fest, Senior Formal, Royal Ball, Shamrockin' Eve, IGNITE Leadershop Conference and Relay for Life.

SERVICES: Counseling and information services are available, as is tutoring in most subjects. There is a reader service for the blind. **Library/Resources:** The library contains 486,650 volumes, 26,241 microform items, 21,285 audio/video tapes/CDs/DVDs, and subscribes to 75,198 periodicals including electronic. Computerized

library services include interlibrary loans, database searching, Internet access, and Wi-Fi capability. Special learning facilities include an art gallery, radio station, TV station, the University offers a number of unique facilities including: Hope Horn Gallery in Hyland Hall for paintings and sculpture; the Royal Theater and Studio Theater in the McDade Center for Literary and Performing Arts for University Players productions; television studio and broadcast FM-radio station; 700-seat performance hall in the Houlihan-McLean Center; and the Institute of Molecular Biology and Medicine offering proteomics, genomics and PCR equipment. **Physically Challenged Students:** All of the campus is accessible. Facilities include wheelchair ramps, elevators, special parking, specially equipped restrooms, special class scheduling, lowered drinking fountains, lowered telephones, and special housing. **Special:** The university also offers dual, student-designed, and interdisciplinary majors, including chemistry-business, chemistry-computers, electronics-business, and international language-business, credit by exam and for life/military/work experience, work-study, nondegree study, and pass/fail options. There are 32 national honor societies. **Visiting:** There are regularly scheduled orientations for prospective students, group information sessions and tours are available most weekdays and Saturdays throughout the year. There are also personal appointments available with admissions counselors by appointment. There are guides for informal visits and visitors may sit in on classes. To schedule a visit, contact the Office of Admissions at 1-888-SCRANTON. **Campus Safety and Security:** Measures include 24-hour foot and vehicle patrol, emergency notification system, self-defense education, and security escort services. There are emergency telephones, lighted pathways/sidewalks, and controlled access to dorms/residences.

REQUIREMENTS: The SAT or ACT is required. Applicants should be graduates of an accredited secondary school, though in some cases a GED may be accepted. They should complete 18 academic or Carnegie units, including 4 years of high school English, 3 each of math, science, history, and social studies, and 2 of foreign language. 2 letters of reference/recommendation are required. Essays are required. AP and CLEP credits are accepted. Important factors in the admissions decision are advanced placement or honors courses, leadership record, and extracurricular activities record.

ADMISSIONS: 69% of a recent year applicants were accepted. The SAT scores for the 2013-2014 freshman class were: Critical Reading--15% below 500, 56% between 500 and 599, 25% between 600 and 699, and 4% between 700 and 800; Math--12% below 500, 51% between 500 and 599, 31% between 600 and 699, and 5% between 700 and 800. 11 freshmen graduated first in their class.

FINANCIAL AID: In a recent year, 90% of all full-time freshmen and 89% of continuing full-time students received some form of financial aid. 69% of all full-time freshmen and 66% of continuing full-time students received need-based aid. The average freshman award was $25,338. The University is a member of CSS. The FAFSA is required. The priority date for freshman financial aid applications for fall entry is February 15.

UNIVERSITY OF THE ARTS (*The complete profile is made available exclusively on our website, www.barronspac.com*)

UNIVERSITY OF THE SCIENCES — F-3
www.usciences.edu

Philadelphia, PA 19104

(215) 596-8815
(888) 996-8747

Fax: (215) 596-8821   Email: admit@usciences.edu

Full-time: 927 men, 1474 women   Faculty: 182

Part-time: 12 men, 25 women   Ph.D.s: 84%

Graduate: 146 men, 196 women   Student/Faculty: 10 to 1

Year: semesters, summer session   Tuition: $34,742

Room & Board: $13,578   Freshman Class: 4099 applied, 2500 accepted, 440 enrolled

SAT CR/M/W: 557/603/567 ACT: 25   CEEB CODE: 2663

Application Deadline: n/av   **VERY COMPETITIVE+**

University of the Sciences founded in 1821, when the institution was founded as America's first pharmacy college, the Philadelphia College of Pharmacy. USciences has 25 undergraduate and 25 graduate programs in five colleges. There are 4 undergraduate schools and 4 graduate schools. In addition to regional accreditation, Usciences has baccalaureate program accreditation with ACPE and APTA. The 35-acre campus is in an urban area Philadelphia. Including any residence halls, there are 17 buildings.

STUDENT LIFE: 58% of undergraduates are from out of state, mostly the Middle Atlantic. Students are from 40 states, 19 foreign countries, and Canada. 46% are White; 36% Asian American. The average age of freshmen is 18; all undergraduates, 21. 12% do not continue beyond their first year; 80% remain to graduate.

FACULTY/CLASSROOMS: 46% of faculty are male; 54% are female. 99% teach undergraduates. No introductory courses are taught by graduate students. The average class size in an introductory lecture is 100; in a laboratory is 28; and in a regular course is 25.

PROGRAMS OF STUDY: Usciences confers B.S., and B.S.H.S. degrees. Master's and Doctoral degrees are also awarded. Bachelor's degrees are awarded in BIOLOGICAL SCIENCE (biochemistry, bioinformatics, biology/biological science, microbiology, and toxicology), BUSINESS (marketing management and recreational facilities management), COMPUTER AND PHYSICAL SCIENCE (chemistry, computer science, and physics), ENGINEERING AND ENVIRONMENTAL DESIGN (environmental science), HEALTH PROFESSIONS (health science, medical technology, mental health/human services, occupational therapy, pharmaceutical chemistry, pharmaceutical science, pharmacology, pharmacy, physical therapy, and physician's assistant), SOCIAL SCIENCE (humanities and social science, interdisciplinary studies, and psychology). Pharmacy, physical therapy, physician assistant studies, and occupational therapy are the strongest academically. Pharmacy, physical therapy, and biology have the largest enrollments.

ACTIVITIES: 7% of men belong to 3 local and 7 national fraternities; 7% of women belong to 3 local and 5 national sororities. There are 83 groups on campus, including band, cheerleading, chess, chorale, chorus, computers, dance, drama, ethnic, gay, honors, international, literary magazine, martial arts, musical theater, newspaper, orchestra, political, professional, religious, social, social service, and student government. Popular campus events include Student Appreciation Weekend, Founder's Day, Usciences Scholarly Day, and Convocation.

SERVICES: Counseling and information services are available, as is tutoring in every subject. There is remedial math and writing. **Library/Resources:** The library contains 82,380 volumes, 24,485 microform items, and 1,790 audio/video tapes/CDs/DVDs, and subscribes to 22,634 periodicals including electronic. Computerized library services include interlibrary loans, database searching, Internet access, and Wi-Fi capability. **Physically Challenged Students:** 90% of the campus is accessible. Facilities include wheelchair ramps, elevators, special parking, specially equipped restrooms, special class scheduling. Individual student accommondation available. **Special:** USciences offers 5- and 6-year integrated professional programs in occupational therapy, physical therapy, and physician's assistant studies. Internships are required in all health science disciplines. Study abroad is available in Asia, Africa, and Europe through the NYU Study Abroad program. A 1-year undeclared major program is offered, as is a program of curriculum and advisement to prepare students to enter medical school. Students may elect dual majors or a minor in communications, economics, psychology, sociology, math, physics, computer science, biochemistry, biology, chemistry, forensic science, humanities, math, microbiology, social sciences, and writing. There are 5 national honor societies. **Visiting:** There are regularly scheduled orientations for prospective students, student visits consist of summer open houses for rising seniors, campus day visits, campus tours, and meetings with faculty members. There are guides for informal visits and visitors may sit in on classes. To schedule a visit, contact the Admission Office. **Campus Safety and Security:** Measures include 24-hour foot and vehicle patrol, self-defense education, and security escort services. There are shuttle buses, emergency telephones, lighted pathways/sidewalks, controlled access to dorms/residences, required key and student identification for dorm entry; id access only to campus buildings in the evenings.

REQUIREMENTS: The SAT or ACT is required. Applicants must be high school graduates or hold the GED. Minimum academic requirements include 4 credits in English, 1 credit each in American history and social science, and 4 credits in academic electives. Math requirements include 2 years of algebra and 1 year of geometry. The university strongly recommends an additional year of higher-level math, such as pre-calculus or calculus. In addition, 3 science credits are required, and the university strongly recommends that students have 1 credit each in biology, chemistry, and physics. A strong background in English, science, and math is recommended. Usciences requires applicants to be in the upper 50% of their class. AP and CLEP credits are accepted. Important factors in the admissions decision are extracurricular activities record, leadership record, and advanced placement or honors courses.

ADMISSIONS: 61% of a recent year applicants were accepted. The SAT scores for the 2013-2014 freshman class were: Critical Reading--15% below 500, 61% between 500 and 599, 21% between 600 and 699, and 3% between 700 and 800; Math--6% below 500, 43% between 500 and 599, 40% between 600 and 699, and 11% between 700 and 800; Writing--16% below 500, 52% between 500 and 599, 26% between 600 and 699, and 6% between 700 and 800. The ACT scores were 3% below 21, 34% between 21 and 23, 31% between 24 and 26, 16% between 27 and 28, and 16% above 28. 71% of the current freshmen were in the top fifth of their class; 93% were in the top two fifths. 3 freshmen graduated first in their class.

FINANCIAL AID: The FAFSA is required. Check with the school for freshman financial aid applications deadlines.

URSINUS COLLEGE E-3
www.ursinus.edu

Collegeville, PA 19426	**(610) 409-3000**
	(610) 409-3200
Fax: n/av	Email: admission@ursinus.edu
Full-time: 796 men, 866 women	**Faculty:** 123; IIB, +$
Part-time: 11 men, 8 women	**Ph.D.s:** 92%
Graduate: n/av	**Student/Faculty:** 12 to 1
Year: semesters	**Tuition:** $46,080
Room & Board: $11,500	**Freshman Class:** 2672 applied, 2222 accepted, 497 enrolled
	CEEB CODE: 2931
Application Deadline: February 15	**VERY COMPETITIVE**

Ursinus College, founded in 1869, is a private residential college offering programs in the liberal arts. In addition to regional accreditation, Ursinus has baccalaureate program accreditation with ACS. The 170-acre campus is in a suburban area 25 miles west of Philadelphia. Including any residence halls, there are 65 buildings.

STUDENT LIFE: 54% of undergraduates are from Pennsylvania. Others are from 31 states, 16 foreign countries, and Canada. 75% are from public schools. 75% are White. The average age of freshmen is 18; all undergraduates, 20. 8% do not continue beyond their first year; 80% remain to graduate. **Housing:** 1542 students can be accommodated in college housing, which includes single-sex and coed dorms, on-campus apartments, and off-campus apartments. In addition, there are special-interest houses, muticultural, wellness, art, physical sciences, community service, literary, international, coed dorms, theme and wellness housing, and quiet houses. On-campus housing is guaranteed for all 4 years. 96% of students live on campus; of those, 90% remain on campus on weekends. Upperclassmen may keep cars.

FACULTY/CLASSROOMS: 49% of faculty are male; 51% are female. All teach and do research. No introductory courses are taught by graduate students. The average class size in an introductory lecture is 40; in a laboratory is 22; and in a regular course is 18.

PROGRAMS OF STUDY: Ursinus confers B.A., and B.S. degrees. Bachelor's degrees are awarded in BIOLOGICAL SCIENCE (biochemistry, biology/biological science, and neurosciences), BUSINESS (business economics), COMMUNICATIONS AND THE ARTS (art, classics, communications, dance, dramatic arts, English, French, German, and Spanish), COMPUTER AND PHYSICAL SCIENCE (chemistry, computer science, mathematics, and physics), ENGINEERING AND ENVIRONMENTAL DESIGN (environmental science), HEALTH PROFESSIONS (exercise science), SOCIAL SCIENCE (American studies, anthropology, East Asian studies, history, international relations, philosophy, political science/government, psychology, and sociology). Biology, chemistry, and politics are the strongest academically. Economics, biology, and psychology have the largest enrollments.

ACTIVITIES: 18% of men belong to 5 local and 2 national fraternities; 24% of women belong to 5 local and 1 national sororities. There are 100 groups on campus, including gospel choir, campus ministries, fencing, folk music, men's chorus, art, band, cheerleading, chess, choir, chorale, chorus, computers, dance, debate, drama, environmental, ethnic, forensics, gay, honors, international, jazz band, literary magazine, newspaper, pep band, photography, political, professional, radio and TV, religious, social, social service, student government, UCEMS (student EMT group), and yearbook. Popular campus events include Air Band Competition, Relay for Life, and Family Day. **Sports:** There are 12 intercollegiate sports for men and 13 for women, and 14 intramural sports for men and 12 for women. Facilities include Racquetball and squash courts, a dance studio, tennis courts, field house, fitness center, and all types of playing fields. **Graduates:** From July 1, 2013 to June 30, 2014, 367 bachelor's degrees were awarded. The most popular majors were biology/life sciences (27%), social sciences (22%), and psychology (11%). 60 companies recruited on campus in 2013-2014. In an average class, 79% graduate in 4 years or less, 80% graduate in 5 years or less, and 80% graduate in 6 years or less. Of the 2013 graduating class, 27% were enrolled in graduate school within 6 months of graduation, and 65% were employed.

SERVICES: Counseling and information services are available, as is tutoring in every subject. There is a reader service for the blind. The college provides appropriate services on an as-needed basis. **Library/Resources:** The library contains 420,000 volumes, 201,995 microform items, 32,000 audio/video tapes/CDs/DVDs, and subscribes to 25,883 periodicals including electronic. Computerized library services include interlibrary loans, database searching, Internet access, and Wi-Fi capability. Special learning facilities include an art gallery, planetarium, radio station, TV station, an observatory. **Physically Challenged Students:** 95% of the campus is accessible. Facilities include wheelchair ramps, elevators, special parking, specially equipped restrooms, special class scheduling, lowered drinking fountains, lowered telephones, and special housing. **Special:** The college offers study abroad, student-designed majors, internships, a Washington semester, dual majors, and a 3-2 engineering degree with Columbia University. Ursinus offers an international studies certificate in addition to a degree in international relations. There are 17 national honor societies, including Phi Beta Kappa, and 27 departmental honors programs. **Visiting:** There are regularly scheduled orientations for prospective students, including a campus interview and a tour. There are guides for informal visits, visitors may sit in on classes, and stay overnight. To schedule a visit, contact the Admissions Office at admission@ursinus.edu. **Campus Safety and Security:** Measures include 24-hour foot and vehicle patrol, emergency notification system, self-defense education, and security escort services. There are emergency telephones and lighted pathways/sidewalks.

REQUIREMENTS: The SAT or ACT and ACT Writing Test are recommended. SAT Subject Tests are recommended. Applicants should prepare with 16 academic credits, including 4 years of English, 3 of math, 2 of foreign language, and 1 each of science and social studies. An interview is recommended. A GPA of 2.0 is required. AP credits are accepted. Important factors in the admissions decision are advanced placement or honors courses, recommendations by school officials, and leadership record.All students must fulfill requirements in the common intellectual experience, math or logic, foreign language, humanities, and natural and social science, including an independent learning experience. A total of 128 semester hours, with 32 to 40 in the major, is required, as is a GPA of at least 2.0. **Procedure:** Freshmen are admitted fall and spring. Entrance exams should be taken in the junior or senior year. There are early decision, early admissions, deferred admissions, and rolling admissions plans. Early decision applications should be filed by January 15; regular applications, by February 15 for fall entry; and December 1 for spring entry.

Notification of early decision is sent January 15; regular decision, April 1. 49 early decision candidates were accepted for the 2014-2015 class. 6 applicants were on the 2014 waiting list; 2 were admitted. Applications are accepted on-line. **Transfer Students:** 9 transfer students enrolled in 2013-2014. Transfer applicants must submit transcripts from all institutions attended. 64 of 128 credits required for the bachelor's degree must be completed at Ursinus. **International Students:** There are 45 international students enrolled. The school actively recruits these students. They must take the TOEFL with a minimum score of 80 on the Internet-based version (iBT). They must also take the SAT or ACT.

ADMISSIONS: 83% of the 2014-2015 applicants were accepted. There were 42 National Merit finalists. 6 freshmen graduated first in their class. **Admissions Contact:** E-Mail: *admission@ursinus.edu* Web: *www.ursinus.edu*

FINANCIAL AID: In 2014-2015, 90% of all full-time freshmen and 90% of continuing full-time students received some form of financial aid. 95% of all full-time freshmen and 69% of continuing full-time students received need-based aid. The average freshman award was $32,560. Need-based scholarships or need-based grants averaged $29,16; need-based self-help aid (loans and jobs) averaged $4,243; other non-need-based awards and non-need-based scholarships averaged $19,412; and $3,366 from other forms of aid. 69% of undergraduate students work part-time. Average annual earnings from campus work are $1404. The average financial indebtedness of the 2014 graduate was $35,360. Ursinus is a member of CSS. The CSS/Profile and FAFSA are required. The deadline for filing freshman financial aid applications for fall entry is February 15.

VILLANOVA UNIVERSITY E-3
www.villanova.edu

Villanova, PA 19085	(610) 519-4500
	(610) 519-4000
Fax: (610) 519-6450	Email: gotovu@villanova.edu
Full-time: 3145 men, 3408 women	Faculty: IIA, ++$
Part-time: 255 men, 310 women	Ph.D.s: 90%
Graduate: 1792 men, 1825 women	Student/Faculty: 12 to 1
Year: semesters, summer session	Tuition: $46,116
Room & Board: $12,278	Freshman Class: n/av
SAT CR/M/W: 640/670/640 **ACT:** 30	CEEB CODE: 2959
Application Deadline: January 15	**MOST COMPETITIVE**

Villanova University's, founded in 1842, Augustinian Catholic intellectual tradition has been the cornerstone of an academic community in which students learn to think critically, act compassionately and succeed while serving others. There are more than 10,000 undergraduate, graduate and law students in the University's five colleges – the College of Liberal Arts and Sciences, the Villanova School of Business, the College of Engineering, the College of Nursing and the Villanova University School of Law. As students grow intellectually, Villanova prepares them to become ethical leaders who create positive change everywhere life takes them. There are 5 undergraduate schools and 6 graduate schools. In addition to regional accreditation, Villanova has baccalaureate program accreditation with AACSB, ABET, NLN, and ABA. The 260-acre campus is in a suburban area 12 miles west of Philadelphia. Including any residence halls, there are 69 buildings.

STUDENT LIFE: 81% of undergraduates are from out of state, mostly the Middle Atlantic. Students are from 46 states, 50 foreign countries, and Canada. 51% are from public schools. 74% are White. 70% are Catholic; 12% Protestant. The average age of freshmen is 18; all undergraduates, 20. 6% do not continue beyond their first year; 94% remain to graduate. **Housing:** 4500 students can be accommodated in college housing, which includes single-sex and coed dorms and on-campus apartments. In addition, there are honors houses, learning communities for freshmen and special sophomore residence hall, a service learning community, and 24-hour quiet study hall. On-campus housing is available on a lottery system for upperclassmen. 70% of students live on campus; of those, 85% remain on campus on weekends. Upperclassmen may keep cars.

FACULTY/CLASSROOMS: 58% of faculty are male; 42% are female.

90% teach undergraduates, 74% do research, and 74% do both. Graduate students teach 1% of introductory courses. The average class size in a regular course is 22.

PROGRAMS OF STUDY: Villanova confers B.A., B.S., B.B.A., B.S.N. and B.I.S. degrees. Associate, Master's, and Doctoral degrees are also awarded. Bachelor's degrees are awarded in AGRICULTURE (environmental studies), BIOLOGICAL SCIENCE (biochemistry and biology/biological science), BUSINESS (accounting, banking and finance, business administration and management, business economics, international business management, management information systems, marketing/retailing/merchandising, and real estate), COMMUNICATIONS AND THE ARTS (art history and appreciation, classics, communications, English, French, Italian, and Spanish), COMPUTER AND PHYSICAL SCIENCE (astronomy, astrophysics, chemistry, computer science, information sciences and systems, mathematics, physics, and science), EDUCATION (secondary education), ENGINEERING AND ENVIRONMENTAL DESIGN (chemical engineering, civil engineering, computer engineering, electrical/electronics engineering, environmental science, and mechanical engineering), HEALTH PROFESSIONS (nursing), SOCIAL SCIENCE (criminal justice, crosscultural studies, economics, gender studies, geography, history, humanities, interdisciplinary studies, Latin American studies, liberal arts/general studies, philosophy, political science/government, psychology, religion, sociology, and theological studies). Nursing, engineering, and business have the largest enrollments.

ACTIVITIES: 19% of men belong to 13 national fraternities; 41% of women belong to 14 national sororities. There are 265 groups on campus, including day of service, multicultural; service and advocacy, art, band, cheerleading, choir, chorale, chorus, communications, computers, dance, debate, drama, drill team, environmental, ethnic, film, forensics, gay, honors, international, jazz band, literary magazine, marching band, musical theater, newspaper, pep band, photography, political, professional, radio and TV, religious, social, social service, student government, university service blue key ambassadors; special olympics, and yearbook. Popular campus events include Special Olympics, Hoops Mania, and Diwahni, Diwali, and Holi. **Sports:** There are 11 intercollegiate sports for men and 13 for women, and 13 intramural sports for men and 13 for women. Facilities include a 400-meter outdoor track, 1 swimming pool, weight rooms, field house, basketball and volleyball courts, softball field, 2 soccer fields and tennis courts. The football stadium seats 12,500, the pavilion, 6500. The soocer complex seats 1000, the softball field seats 250. **Graduates:** From July 1, 2013 to June 30, 2014, 1790 bachelor's degrees were awarded. The most popular majors were business/marketing (29%), nursing (11%), and social sciences (10%). 261 companies recruited on campus in 2013-2014. In an average class, 86% graduate in 4 years or less, 90% graduate in 5 years or less, and 90% graduate in 6 years or less.

SERVICES: Counseling and information services are available, as is tutoring in some subjects. There is a reader service for the blind. Tutoring is open to all students and is not particular to students with disabilities. Some tutoring is offered through individual departments and colleges for first and second year courses. There is a writing center and Math Center for all students. Study skills and academic coaching is available to all students. **Library/Resources:** The 2 libraries contain 1.3 million volumes, 700,000 microform items, 10,000 audio/video tapes/CDs/DVDs, and subscribe to 16,720 periodicals including electronic. Computerized library services include interlibrary loans, database searching, Internet access, and Wi-Fi capability. Special learning facilities include an art gallery, radio station, TV station, 1 observatory. **Physically Challenged Students:** 90% of the campus is accessible. Facilities include wheelchair ramps, elevators, special parking, specially equipped restrooms, special class scheduling, lowered drinking fountains, lowered telephones. Specially equipped van for campus transportation, and proximity card readers for several buildings with automatic doors. **Special:** Internships are available for each college in the Philadelphia area as well as in New York City and Washington D.C. Students may study abroad worldwide. Villanova offers a Washington semester, an accelerated degree program in biology for allied health program, dual majors, a general studies degree, and credit by exam. There are 36 national honor societies, including Phi Beta Kappa, and a freshman honors program. **Visiting:** There are regularly scheduled orientations for prospective

students, consisting of group admission presentations, and campus tours are conducted throughout the year. Please consult our admission web site for a calendar and to register for a visitca. There are guides for informal visits and visitors may sit in on classes. To schedule a visit, contact the Office of University Admission. **Campus Safety and Security:** Measures include 24-hour foot and vehicle patrol, emergency notification system, self-defense education, and security escort services. There are shuttle buses, emergency telephones, lighted pathways/sidewalks, and controlled access to dorms/residences.

REQUIREMENTS: The SAT or ACT is required. The ACT Optional Writing test is also required. Applicants must be graduates of an accredited secondary school and should have completed 16 academic units. The specific courses required vary according to college. A GED is accepted. An essay is required. AP and CLEP credits are accepted. Important factors in the admissions decision are leadership record, advanced placement or honors courses, and evidence of special talent.All students are required to take core courses in humanities, Augustine and culture, social science, religious studies, natural sciences, philosophy, and math. Students must complete a minimum of 122 credit hours and achieve at least a 2.0 overall G.P.A. **Procedure:** Freshmen are admitted fall. Entrance exams should be taken by December of the senior year. There is a deferred admissions plan. Early decision applications should be filed by November 1; regular applications, by January 15 for fall entry. The fall 2014 application fee was $80. Notification of early decision is sent December 20; regular decision, April 1. 1943 applicants were on the 2014 waiting list; 464 were admitted. Applications are accepted on-line. **Transfer Students:** 54 transfer students enrolled in 2013-2014. 60 of 122 credits required for the bachelor's degree must be completed at Villanova. **International Students:** There are 128 international students enrolled. The school actively recruits these students. They must take the TOEFL with a minimum score of 550 on the paper-based TOEFL (PBT) or 85 on the Internet-based version (iBT). They must also take the SAT or ACT.

ADMISSIONS: The SAT scores for the 2014-2015 freshman class were: Critical Reading--2% below 500, 22% between 500 and 599, 55% between 600 and 699, and 20% between 700 and 800; Math--1% below 500, 14% between 500 and 599, 52% between 600 and 699, and 33% between 700 and 800; Writing--3% below 500, 20% between 500 and 599, 50% between 600 and 699, and 26% between 700 and 800. The ACT scores were 2% between 24 and 26, 36% between 27 and 28, and 62% above 28. **Admissions Contact:** Michael Gaynor, Director of Admission. E-Mail: *gotovu@villanova.edu* Web: *www.admission.villanova.edu*

FINANCIAL AID: In 2014-2015, 50% of all full-time freshmen and 48% of continuing full-time students received some form of financial aid. 47% of all full-time freshmen and 44% of continuing full-time students received need-based aid. The average freshman award was $35,413. Need-based scholarships or need-based grants averaged $31,227; need-based self-help aid (loans and jobs) averaged $6,218; non-need-based athletic scholarships averaged $39,408; and other non-need-based awards and non-need-based scholarships averaged $13,589. 16% of undergraduate students work part-time. The average financial indebtedness of the 2014 graduate was $35,122. Villanova is a member of CSS. The CSS/Profile, FAFSA, the state aid form, and the college's own financial statement, and parent and student federal income tax return and W2s are required. The deadline for filing freshman financial aid applications for fall entry is February 7.

WASHINGTON & JEFFERSON COLLEGE   A-3
www.washjeff.edu

Washington, PA 15301

(724) 223-6025
(888) 926-3529

Fax: (724) 223-6534
Email: admission@washjeff.edu

Full-time: 688 men, 666 women
Faculty: 109; IIB, av$

Part-time: 4 men, 4 women
Ph.D.s: 94%

Graduate: n/av
Student/Faculty: 11 to 1

Year: 4-1-4, summer session
Tuition: $41,282

Room & Board: $10,666
Freshman Class: 7094 applied, 2955 accepted, 399 enrolled

SAT CR/M: 560/570 **ACT:** 25
CEEB CODE: 2967

Application Deadline: March 1
VERY COMPETITIVE

Washington and Jefferson College, founded in 1781, is a highly selective, residential, private liberal arts and sciences college. There are no undergraduate schools. In addition to regional accreditation, W & J has baccalaureate program accreditation with ACS. The 60-acre campus is in a small town 27 miles southwest of Pittsburgh, PA. Including any residence halls, there are 53 buildings.

STUDENT LIFE: 72% of undergraduates are from Pennsylvania. Others are from 33 states, and 18 foreign countries. 86% are from public schools. 81% are White. The average age of freshmen is 18; all undergraduates, 20. 14% do not continue beyond their first year; 76% remain to graduate. **Housing:** 1366 students can be accommodated in college housing, which includes single-sex and coed dorms and on-campus apartments. In addition, there are special-interest houses, fraternity houses, sorority houses, On-campus suites, special housing for international students, wellness housing, civics house, pet dorm, quiet house and green house. On-campus housing is guaranteed for all 4 years. 94% of students live on campus; of those, 85% remain on campus on weekends. All students may keep cars.

FACULTY/CLASSROOMS: 54% of faculty are male; 46% are female. All teach and do research. No introductory courses are taught by graduate students. The average class size in an introductory lecture is 16; in a laboratory is 15; and in a regular course is 16.

PROGRAMS OF STUDY: W & J confers B.A. degrees. Bachelor's degrees are awarded in AGRICULTURE (environmental studies), BIOLOGICAL SCIENCE (biochemistry, biology/biological science, biophysics, cell biology, and neurosciences), BUSINESS (accounting, business administration and management, and international business management), COMMUNICATIONS AND THE ARTS (art, communication rhetoric/communication, English, French, German, music, and Spanish), COMPUTER AND PHYSICAL SCIENCE (chemistry, computer information technology, mathematics, and physics), EDUCATION (art education and education), SOCIAL SCIENCE (economics, history, interdisciplinary studies, international studies, philosophy, political science/government, psychology, and sociology). Biology, chemistry, and political science are the strongest academically. Business/accounting, psychology, and English have the largest enrollments.

ACTIVITIES: 37% of men belong to 6 national fraternities; 40% of women belong to 4 national sororities. There are 71 groups on campus, including improv, yoga and zumba, young entrepreneurs society, art, band, cheerleading, chess, choir, chorale, chorus, computers, dance, debate, drama, environmental, equestrian, ethnic, film, gay, honors, international, jazz band, literary magazine, musical theater, newspaper, pep band, photography, political, professional, radio and TV, religious, social, social service, student government, and yearbook. Popular campus events include International Week, Street Fair, Holiday Light-up Night, Involvement Expo and the Spring Concert. **Sports:** There are 12 intercollegiate sports for men and 12 for women, and 22 intramural sports for men and 22 for women. Facilities include swimming and diving pools, an all-weather track, weight room, football, baseball, softball, soccer/lacrosse fields, and basketball, volleyball, squash, racquetball courts and fitness center. The stadium seats 3500, the gymnasium seats 2388. **Graduates:** From July 1, 2013 to June 30, 2014, 307 bachelor's degrees were awarded. The most popular majors were business administration/accounting (24%), psychology (12%), and English (5%). 40 companies recruited on campus in 2013-2014. In an average class, 1% graduate in 3 years or less, 71% graduate in 4 years or less, 75% graduate in 5 years or less, and 76% graduate in 6 years or less. Of the 2013 graduating class, 39% were enrolled in graduate school within 6 months of graduation, and 69% were employed.

SERVICES: Counseling and information services are available, as is tutoring in most subjects, accounting, biology, chemistry, computing and information studies, economics, logic, mathematics, modern languages, oral communication, physics, psychology, quantitative reasoning, sociology and writing. **Library/Resources:** The 4 libraries contain 188,718 volumes, 15,655 microform items, 9,360 audio/video tapes/CDs/DVDs, and subscribe to 44,818 periodicals including electronic. Computerized library services include interlibrary loans, database searching, Internet access, and Wi-Fi capability. Special learning facilities include an art gallery, radio station, biological field station, microplate reader, cell culture labs, isolator lab, X-ray diffraction unit, neuropsychology lab, atomic absorption unit, nuclear magnetic resonance lab, refrigerated centrifuge, global learning unit, language lab, spectrometers, and laser scanning confocal microscope facility. **Physically Challenged Students:** 48% of the campus is accessible. Facilities include wheelchair ramps, elevators, special parking, specially equipped restrooms, special class scheduling, lowered drinking fountains, and special housing. **Special:** The college offers semester-long off-campus study in 23 countries (Australia, Austria, Chile, China, Denmark, Ecuador and the Galapagos Islands, Egypt, France, the Gambia, Germany, Hong Kong, Ireland, Italy, Japan, Mexico, Netherlands, Norway, Russia, South Africa, South Korea, Spain, United Kingdom and the United States), internships in all majors, dual and student-designed majors, credit by exam, and pass/fail options. Concentrations are offered in conflict and resolution studies, entrepreneurial studies, graphic design, and professional writing. Special programs are offered in education, biological physics, engineering, mind, brain, and behavior, pre-law, ROTC and pre-health professions (pre-physical therapy, pre-occupational therapy, pre-pharmacy, pre-veterinary and pre-dentistry). The college also offers emphasis in film studies, financial economics, human resource management, public relations, rhetoric, and theatre. The BA in financial economics is recognized by the CFA Institute, one of only 77 programs in the U.S. to have been awarded this recognition. Students can take electives in Arabic, Chinese, earth and space science, physical education, Russian, and interdisciplinary courses. There is a 3-3 law program with Duquesne University and the University of Pittsburgh, medicine program with Temple University School of Medicine, optometry program with Pennsylvania College of Optometry at Salus University, physician assistant program with Saint Francis University and Chatham University and a physical therapy program with Chatham University. In addition, there is 3-2 engineering program with Case Western Reserve University, Washington University and Columbia University. A Washington semester is available with American University. W&J's proprietary Magellan Project provides financial support for students who wish to pursue summer internships or independent study abroad, making these opportunities available to every W&J student. There are 23 national honor societies, including Phi Beta Kappa, a freshman honors program, and 18 departmental honors programs. **Visiting:** There are regularly scheduled orientations for prospective students, student visits include a general session, departmental meetings, preprofessional meetings, a financial aid meeting, and class scheduling. There are guides for informal visits, visitors may sit in on classes, and stay overnight. To schedule a visit, contact Erin McGarry at (724) 223-6025. **Campus Safety and Security:** Measures include 24-hour foot and vehicle patrol, emergency notification system, self-defense education, and security escort services. There are emergency telephones, lighted pathways/sidewalks, controlled access to dorms/residences, Blue light emergency phones; security cameras monitored 24/7.

REQUIREMENTS: The SAT or ACT is recommended. Applicants must complete 15 academic credits or Carnegie units, including 3 credits of English and math, 2 of foreign language, 1 of history, social science, or nautural science and 6 or more academic courses from the aforementioned areas. An essay is required and interviews are recommended. A GED is accepted. AP credits are accepted. Important factors in the admissions decision are advanced placement or honors courses, evidence of special talent, and personality/intangible qualities. Students must complete the general education requirement of at least 8 courses in 4 divisions. Other requirements include phys ed, first-year seminar, freshman composition, foreign language, cultural diversity, oral communication, quantitative reasoning, academic skills, and 8 to 10 elective courses. A total of 34 courses, with 8 to 10 courses in the major, is required for graduation, as is a 2.0 GPA. **Procedure:** Freshmen are admitted fall, winter, and spring. Entrance exams should be taken junior or senior year. There are early decision, early admissions, deferred admissions, and rolling admissions plans. Early decision applications should be filed by December 1; regular applications, by March 1 for fall entry; December 15 for winter entry; and January 15 for spring entry, along with a $25 fee. Notification of early decision is sent December 15; regular decision, April 1. 13 early decision candidates were accepted for the 2014-2015 class. 14 applicants were on the 2014 waiting list. Applications are accepted on-line. Application fees are waived if application is completed on-line. **Transfer Students:** 19 transfer students enrolled in 2013-2014.

Transfer students are required to submit an official high school transcript with standardized test results from the SAT or ACT unless they are applying score optional. 64 of 136 credits required for the bachelor's degree must be completed at W & J. **International Students:** There are 60 international students enrolled. The school actively recruits these students. They must take the TOEFL with a minimum score of 563 on the paper-based TOEFL (PBT) or 85 on the Internet-based version (iBT).

ADMISSIONS: 42% of the 2014-2015 applicants were accepted. The SAT scores for the 2014-2015 freshman class were: Critical Reading--16% below 500, 54% between 500 and 599, 27% between 600 and 699, and 3% between 700 and 800; Math--14% below 500, 48% between 500 and 599, 33% between 600 and 699, and 5% between 700 and 800. The ACT scores were 10% below 21, 23% between 21 and 23, 29% between 24 and 26, 16% between 27 and 28, and 22% above 28. 53% of the current freshmen were in the top fifth of their class; 82% were in the top two fifths. 16 freshmen graduated first in their class. **Admissions Contact:** Robert J. Gould, Vice President for Enrollment . E-Mail: *admission@washjeff.edu* Web: *www.washjeff.edu*

FINANCIAL AID: In 2014-2015, 100% of all full-time freshmen and 99% of continuing full-time students received some form of financial aid. 74% of all full-time freshmen and 71% of continuing full-time students received need-based aid. The average freshman award was $33,543. Need-based scholarships or need-based grants averaged $11,069; need-based self-help aid (loans and jobs) averaged $3,019; and other non-need-based awards and non-need-based scholarships averaged $19,455. 46% of undergraduate students work part-time. Average annual earnings from campus work are $1150. The average financial indebtedness of the 2014 graduate was $26,100. The FAFSA is required. The priority date for freshman financial aid applications for fall entry is February 15.

WAYNESBURG UNIVERSITY   B-4
www.waynesburg.edu

Waynesburg, PA 15370

(724) 852-3248
(800) 225-7393

Fax: n/av
Email: admissions@waynesburg.edu

Full-time: 582 men, 832 women
Faculty: IIB, -$

Part-time: 17 men, 97 women
Ph.D.s: n/av

Graduate: 168 men, 343 women
Student/Faculty: n/av

Year: semesters, summer session
Tuition: $21,290

Room & Board: $8860
Freshman Class: 1506 applied, 1257 accepted, 366 enrolled

SAT or ACT: required
CEEB CODE: 2969

Application Deadline: open
COMPETITIVE

Waynesburg University, founded in 1849 by the Cumberland Presbyterian Church, is a private, comprehensive Christian university offering doctoral, graduate and undergraduate programs in more than 70 academic concentrations. The University has three adult centers located in the Pittsburgh region in addition to its main campus in Waynesburg. The University is a member of the Council for Christian Colleges and Universities and is 1 of only 27 schools in the country to offer the Bonner Scholarship that affords local, regional and international opportunities to touch the lives of others through service. There is 1 graduate school. In addition to regional accreditation, Waynesburg has baccalaureate program accreditation with TEAC, CCNE, CACREP, and PA Dept. of Education. The 30-acre campus is in a small town 50 miles south of Pittsburgh. Including any residence halls, there are 40 buildings.

STUDENT LIFE: 80% of undergraduates are from Pennsylvania. Others are from 30 states, and 4 foreign countries. 90% are from public schools. 89% are White. 62% are Protestant; 22% Catholic; 14% Unknown, Agnostic, and Jehovah Witness. The average age of freshmen is 18; all undergraduates, 22. 19% do not continue beyond their first year; 53% remain to graduate. **Housing:** 1066 students can be accommodated in college housing, which includes single-sex and coed dorms. On-campus housing is guaranteed for all 4 years. 67% of students live on campus. Alcohol is not permitted. Upperclassmen may keep cars.

FACULTY/CLASSROOMS: No introductory courses are taught by graduate students.

PROGRAMS OF STUDY: Waynesburg confers B.A., B.S., B.M.L., B.S.B.A., B.S.M.B. and B.S.N. degrees. Master's and Doctoral degrees are also awarded. Bachelor's degrees are awarded in BIOLOGICAL SCIENCE (biology/biological science, forensic science, and marine biology), BUSINESS (accounting, entrepreneurial studies, finance, international business management, management science, and marketing/retailing/merchandising), COMMUNICATIONS AND THE ARTS (advertising, art, arts administration/management, broadcasting, communication rhetoric/communication, creative writing, English, graphic design, literature, multimedia, and public relations), COMPUTER AND PHYSICAL SCIENCE (chemistry, computer science, information sciences and systems, and mathematics), EDUCATION (athletic training, early childhood education, elementary education, middle school education, and special education), ENGINEERING AND ENVIRONMENTAL DESIGN (engineering and environmental science), HEALTH PROFESSIONS (exercise science, nursing, predentistry, premedicine, prephysical therapy, and preveterinary science), SOCIAL SCIENCE (biblical studies, criminal justice, history, human services, ministries, prelaw, psychology, social science, and sociology). Nursing, business, and education are the strongest academically. Nursing, business, and criminal justice have the largest enrollments.

ACTIVITIES: There are no fraternities or sororities. There are 53 groups on campus, including band, cheerleading, choir, chorale, chorus, drama, environmental, ethnic, film, honors, jazz band, literary magazine, marching band, musical theater, newspaper, orchestra, pep band, photography, professional, radio and TV, religious, social, social service, student government, and yearbook. Popular campus events include Spring Weekend Formal, VIP Forum and Fine Arts Series. **Sports:** There are 9 intercollegiate sports for men and 9 for women, and 7 intramural sports for men and 7 for women. Facilities include a 1500-seat stadium, 1500-seat gym, 250-seat arena, fitness center, basketball and racquetball courts, wrestling and weight rooms, golf driving net, 3 all-weather tennis courts, and table tennis and billiards tables. **Graduates:** From July 1, 2013 to June 30, 2014, 383 bachelor's degrees were awarded. The most popular majors were registered nurse (28%), business administration (13%), and education (8%). In an average class, 45% graduate in 4 years or less, 52% graduate in 5 years or less, and 53% graduate in 6 years or less. Of the 2013 graduating class, 16% were enrolled in graduate school within 6 months of graduation, and 70% were employed.

SERVICES: Counseling and information services are available, as is tutoring in every subject. There is remedial writing. **Library/Resources:** Computerized library services include interlibrary loans, database searching, and Internet access. Special learning facilities include an art gallery, natural history museum, radio station and TV station. **Physically Challenged Students:** All of the campus is accessible. Facilities include wheelchair ramps, elevators, special parking, specially equipped restrooms, special class scheduling, and lowered drinking fountains. **Special:** The college offers internships, an accelerated degree program in marketing and business management, dual majors, a student-designed interdisciplinary major, credit for experience, non-degree study, and pass/fail options. There is a 3-2 engineering degree program with Washington University and Penn State University and a 3-1 in marine biology with Florida Institute of Technology or University of North Carolina Wilmington. A variety of study abroad experiences are available in countries around the world. There are 16 national honor societies and a freshman honors program. **Visiting:** There are regularly scheduled orientations for prospective students, including visits with faculty, students, administrators, and financial aid officers, and a tour of the campus. There are guides for informal visits, visitors may sit in on classes, and stay overnight. To schedule a visit, contact the Admissions Office. **Campus Safety and Security:** Measures include 24-hour foot and vehicle patrol, emergency notification system, and security escort services. There are emergency telephones, lighted pathways/sidewalks, 24-hour security access.

REQUIREMENTS: The SAT or ACT is required. Applicants must be graduates of an accredited secondary school or have a GED certificate and have completed 16 academic credits, including 4 in English, 3 in math, and 2 in sciences, history, or social studies. A GPA of 2.8 is required. AP and CLEP credits are accepted. Important factors in the admissions decision are advanced placement or honors courses, recommendations by school officials, and extracurricular activities record.To graduate, students must complete a minimum of 124 semester hours, including at least 30 in the major, with a minimum 2.0 GPA. Requirements include 15 credits of humanities and social and behavioral sciences, 8 of natural and physical sciences, 6 each of English and literature/arts, 3 credits each in math and computer science and 1 each of life skills, service learning, and Fiat Lux. Students must also pass an English usage and written competency test as well as a math test. **Procedure:** Freshmen are admitted to all sessions. Entrance exams should be taken in April of the junior year or December of the senior year. There is a rolling admissions plan. Application deadlines are open. Application fee is $20. Applications are accepted on-line. **Transfer Students:** 28 transfer students enrolled in 2013-2014. Students must submit a high school transcript and complete transcripts from all colleges previously attended. 45 of 124 credits required for the bachelor's degree must be completed at Waynesburg. **International Students:** There are 4 international students enrolled. The school actively recruits these students. They must take the TOEFL with a minimum score of 80 on the Internet-based version (iBT).

ADMISSIONS: 83% of the 2014-2015 applicants were accepted. **Admissions Contact:** Robin L. King, Sr. V.P. Enrollment and Univ Relation. E-Mail: *admissions@waynesburg.edu* Web: *www.waynesburg.edu*

FINANCIAL AID: In 2014-2015, 98% of all full-time freshmen and 94% of continuing full-time students received some form of financial aid. 91% of all full-time freshmen and 87% of continuing full-time students received need-based aid. The average freshman award was $20,500. Need-based scholarships or need-based grants averaged $6,500 ($30,150 maximum); need-based self-help aid (loans and jobs) averaged $5,500 ($32,600 maximum); and other non-need-based awards and non-need-based scholarships averaged $7,000 ($30,150 maximum). 27% of undergraduate students work part-time. Average annual earnings from campus work are $1500. The average financial indebtedness of the 2014 graduate was $21,500. The FAFSA is required. The deadline for filing freshman financial aid applications for fall entry is rolling.

WEST CHESTER UNIVERSITY OF PENNSYLVANIA   E-3
www.wcupa.edu

West Chester, PA 19383	**(610) 436-1000**
	(610) 436-3411
Fax: (610) 436-2907	Email: ugadmiss@wcupa.edu
Full-time: 4991 men, 7591 women	Faculty: IIA, +$
Part-time: 556 men, 706 women	Ph.Ds: n/av
Graduate: 711 men, 1521 women	Student/Faculty: n/av
Year: semesters, summer session	Tuition: $9144 ($19,594)
Room & Board: $8042	Freshman Class: 13291 applied, 7108 accepted, 2351 enrolled
SAT CR/M/W: 530/540/520	CEEB CODE: 2959
Application Deadline: open	**COMPETITIVE**

West Chester University, founded in 1871, is a public institution that is part of the Pennsylvania State System of Higher Education. It offers programs through the Colleges of Arts and Sciences, Business and Public Affairs, Education, Health Sciences, and Visual and Performing Arts. There are 5 undergraduate schools and 5 graduate schools. In addition to regional accreditation, West Chester University has baccalaureate program accreditation with AACSB, ABET, CSWE, NASAD, NASM, NCATE, ACCME, ACS, AOSA, ASHA, CAAHEP, CAATE, CACREP, CADE, CCNE, CEPH, CoARC, FEPAC, EHAC, IRA, MSCHE, NAST, OAKE, and PDE. The 409-acre campus is in a suburban area 25 miles west of Philadelphia. Including any residence halls, there are 115 buildings.

STUDENT LIFE: 88% of undergraduates are from Pennsylvania. Others are from 28 states, 72 foreign countries, and Canada. 83% are from public schools. 80% are White. The average age of freshmen is 18; all undergraduates, 21. 12% do not continue beyond their first year; 67% remain to graduate. **Housing:** 5078 students can be accommodated in college housing, which includes coed dorms and on-campus apartments. In addition, there are special-interest houses, International student sections, and disabled students. On-campus housing is available on a first-come and first-served basis. 64% of students commute. Alcohol is not permitted. Upperclassmen may keep cars.

FACULTY/CLASSROOMS: No introductory courses are taught by graduate students.

PROGRAMS OF STUDY: West Chester University confers B.A., B.S., B.F.A., B.Mus., B.S.Ed., B.S.N. and B.S.W. degrees. Master's and Doctoral degrees are also awarded. Bachelor's degrees are awarded in AGRICULTURE (environmental studies), BIOLOGICAL SCIENCE (biochemistry, biology/biological science, cell biology, ecology, environmental biology, marine science, microbiology, molecular biology, and nutrition), BUSINESS (accounting, banking and finance, business administration and management, and marketing management), COMMUNICATIONS AND THE ARTS (art, communications, dance, dramatic arts, English, French, German, Latin, literature, music, music history and appreciation, music performance, music theory and composition, musical theater, performing arts, piano performance, Russian, Spanish, studio art, visual and performing arts, and voice), COMPUTER AND PHYSICAL SCIENCE (actuarial science, chemistry, computer science, earth science, geology, geoscience, mathematics, mathematics - actuarial concentration, mathematics/computational, physics, and statistics), EDUCATION (athletic training, early childhood education, elementary education, English education, health education, mathematics education, middle school education, music education, physical education, science education, secondary education, social studies education, and special education), ENGINEERING AND ENVIRONMENTAL DESIGN (engineering physics and urban planning technology), HEALTH PROFESSIONS (exercise science, health, health science, medical technology, nursing, pharmaceutical science, predentistry, premedicine, prephysical therapy, public health, respiratory therapy, and speech pathology/audiology), SOCIAL SCIENCE (American studies, anthropology, criminal justice, dietetics, economics, forensic studies, geography, history, international relations, liberal arts/general studies, philosophy, philosophy and religion, political science/government, prelaw, psychology, social work, sociology, and women's studies). Premedical is the strongest academically. PK-4 early grades prep, psychology, nutrition and dietetics have the largest enrollments.

ACTIVITIES: 12% of men belong to 15 national fraternities; 16% of women belong to 17 national sororities. There are 260 groups on campus, including art, band, cheerleading, chess, choir, chorale, chorus, communications, computers, dance, debate, drama, drill team, drum and bugle corps, environmental, ethnic, film, forensics, gay, honors, international, jazz band, literary magazine, marching band, musical theater, newspaper, opera, orchestra, pep band, photography, political, professional, radio and TV, religious, social, social service, student government, symphony, and yearbook. Popular campus events include Martin Luther King Day, University Fesitval, Student Involvement Fair, Homecoming, Greek Week and Spring Weekend. **Sports:** There are 10 intercollegiate sports for men and 14 for women, and 16 intramural sports for men and 18 for women. Facilities include a 2500-seat field house, gymnastics room, six gyms, 2 swimming pools and diving well, several practice and game fields, softball complex, 12 tennis courts, 2,500 seat basketball facility, a 500-seat baseball stadium, 7500-seat stadium, 500 seat field hockey/lacrosse complex two fitness centers, fi mile track, climbing wall, two recreational outdoor pursuits education (ROPE) course. **Graduates:** From July 1, 2013 to June 30, 2014, 3232 bachelor's degrees were awarded. The most popular majors were liberal studies (7%), psychology (6%), early grades prep, and PK-4 (6%). 169 companies recruited on campus in 2013-2014. In an average class, 45% graduate in 4 years or less, 66% graduate in 5 years or less, and 67% graduate in 6 years or less.

SERVICES: Counseling and information services are available, as is tutoring in some subjects, 100- and - 200 level general education courses There is a reader service for the blind, and remedial math, reading, and writing. **Library/Resources:** The library contains 1.6 million volumes, 926,596 microform items, 68,886 audio/video tapes/CDs/DVDs, and subscribes to 90,417 periodicals including electronic.

Computerized library services include interlibrary loans, database searching, Internet access, and Wi-Fi capability. Special learning facilities include an art gallery, planetarium, radio station, TV station, art gallery, radio station, TV station, planetarium, observatory, an herbarium, a speech and hearing clinic, an autism clinic, a center for government and community affairs, a 151-acre natural area for environmental studies, mineral museum, music library, fully-equipped food preparation laboratory for nutrition and dietetics program, state-of-the-art nursing skills laboratory, athletic training rooms, HEAT (Heat Illness Evaluation Avoidance and Treatment) institute, dance studio, poetry center, outdoor classroom, native plant, ornithology, microsoft demonstration and application center. **Physically Challenged Students:** 95% of the campus is accessible. Facilities include wheelchair ramps, elevators, special parking, specially equipped restrooms, special class scheduling, lowered drinking fountains, and lowered telephones. **Special:** There is cross-registration with Cheyney University and a 3-2 engineering program with Pennsylvania State University and Philadelphia University. The university offers some accelerated degree programs, a Washington semester, some student-designed majors, credit by examination for life, military, and work experience, and pass/fail options. Students arrange study-abroad programs through a third party. There are also several faculty-led study programs. There are 29 national honor societies and a freshman honors program. **Visiting:** There are regularly scheduled orientations for prospective students, campus tours offered four times daily and on selected dates we offer admissions information sessions. During the fall we host two preview days on Saturdays for prospective students and accepted student days on Saturdays in March and April. Our large. There are guides for informal visits and visitors may sit in on classes. To schedule a visit, contact the Office of Admissions. **Campus Safety and Security:** Measures include 24-hour foot and vehicle patrol, emergency notification system, self-defense education, and security escort services. There are shuttle buses, emergency telephones, lighted pathways/sidewalks, controlled access to dorms/residences, bike patrol, card access/security alarms, in all resident halls and resident security officers are posted in residence halls over night and crime prevention programming and alcohol-free alternative events.

REQUIREMENTS: The SAT is required. A college preparatory curriculum in high school, standardized test scores from the SAT or ACT, and a personal statement are required. An interview is required for athletic training, premedical, pharmaceutical product development and respiratory care programs. An audition is required for music applicants and portfolio for art applicants. Specific course prerequisites depend on major selection. Additional documentation is required of candidates for the summer academic development program. The GED is acceptable. West Chester University requires applicants to be in the upper 60% of their class. A GPA of 3.0 is required. AP and CLEP credits are accepted.All students must satisfy requirements in English composition, math, interdisciplinary study. Distribution requirements include 9 hours each of science, behavioral and social science, and humanities, and 3 hours in the arts. A total of 120 (126 or 124 for some degrees) credit hours and a 2.0 GPA are required. **Procedure:** Freshmen are admitted fall and spring. Entrance exams should be taken in spring of the junior year or fall of the senior year. There is a rolling admissions plan. Application deadlines are open. Application fee is $45. Notification is sent on a rolling basis. 462 applicants were on the 2014 waiting list. Applications are accepted on-line. **Transfer Students:** 1331 transfer students enrolled in 2013-2014. Applicants must submit official copies of college transcripts for every institution attended. In some cases students will be required to submit a midterm progress report. If a transfer applicant has completed less than 30 credits they must submit a high school transcript and standardized test scores if they have been out of high school for less than 5 years. Audition is required for music applicants, portfolio for art applicants, and interview for Pre-Med, Pharmaceutical Product Development, and Respiratory Care. 30 of 120 credits required for the bachelor's degree must be completed at West Chester University. **International Students:** There are 42 international students enrolled. The school actively recruits these students. They must take the TOEFL with a minimum score of 550 on the paper-based TOEFL (PBT) or 80 on the Internet-based version (iBT) and the college's own test, or the IELTS. The SAT is recommended. **ADMISSIONS:** 53% of the 2014-2015 applicants were accepted. The

SAT scores for the 2014-2015 freshman class were: Critical Reading--27% below 500, 56% between 500 and 599, 16% between 600 and 699, and 1% between 700 and 800. Math--22% below 500, 57% between 500 and 599, 20% between 600 and 699, and 1% between 700 and 800. Writing--31% below 500, 54% between 500 and 599, 14% between 600 and 699, and 1% between 700 and 800. 22% of the current freshmen were in the top fifth of their class; 41% were in the top two fifths. 2 freshmen graduated first in their class. **Admissions Contact:** Marsha Haug, Director of Admissions. E-Mail: *ugadmiss@wcupa.edu* Web: *www.wcupa.edu*

FINANCIAL AID: In 2014-2015, 81% of all full-time freshmen and 73% of continuing full-time students received some form of financial aid. 62% of all full-time freshmen and 58% of continuing full-time students received need-based aid. The average freshman award was $7,385. Need-based scholarships or need-based grants averaged $5,863 ($39,367 maximum); need-based self-help aid (loans and jobs) averaged $3,347 ($11,480 maximum); non-need-based athletic scholarships averaged $2,413 ($8,000 maximum); and other non-need-based awards and non-need-based scholarships averaged $4,758. 7% of undergraduate students work part-time. Average annual earnings from campus work are $3500. The average financial indebtedness of the 2014 graduate was $30,881. West Chester University is a member of CSS. The FAFSA is required. The priority date for freshman financial aid applications for fall entry is March 1.

WESTMINSTER COLLEGE   B-2
www.westminster.edu

New Wilmington, PA 16172

(724) 946-7100
(800) 942-8033

Fax: (724) 946-6171
Full-time: 510 men, 905 women
Part-time: 20 men, 34 women
Graduate: 43 men, 86 women
Year: semesters, summer session
Room & Board: $7070

Email: admis@westminster.edu
Faculty: 100; IIB, --$
Ph.D.s: 83%
Student/Faculty: 14 to 1
Tuition: $24,220
Freshman Class: 1302 applied, 1006 accepted, 359 enrolled

SAT: required ACT: 24
Application Deadline: open

CEEB CODE: 2975
COMPETITIVE+

Westminster College, founded in 1852, is a private liberal arts institution related to the Presbyterian Church. In addition to regional accreditation, Westminster has baccalaureate program accreditation with NASM. The 350-acre campus is in a rural area 60 miles north of Pittsburgh. Including any residence halls, there are 25 buildings.

STUDENT LIFE: 79% of undergraduates are from Pennsylvania. Others are from 23 states, and 1 foreign countries. 90% are from public schools. 97% are White. 56% are Protestant; 34% Catholic. The average age of freshmen is 18; all undergraduates, 20. 11% do not continue beyond their first year; 76% remain to graduate.

FACULTY/CLASSROOMS: 53% of faculty are male; 47% are female. All teach undergraduates. No introductory courses are taught by graduate students. The average class size in an introductory lecture is 20; in a laboratory is 20; and in a regular course is 22.

PROGRAMS OF STUDY: Westminster confers B.A., B.S. and B.M. degrees. Master's degrees are also awarded. Bachelor's degrees are awarded in BIOLOGICAL SCIENCE (biology/biological science and molecular biology), BUSINESS (accounting, banking and finance, business administration and management, international business management, and marketing/retailing/merchandising), COMMUNICATIONS AND THE ARTS (art, broadcasting, communications, dramatic arts, English, fine arts, French, German, Latin, music, music performance, music theory and composition, public relations, and Spanish), COMPUTER AND PHYSICAL SCIENCE (chemistry, computer science, mathematics, and physics), EDUCATION (Christian education, elementary education, guidance education, music education, and secondary education), HEALTH PROFESSIONS (predentistry and premedicine), SOCIAL SCIENCE (criminal justice, economics, history, international relations, philosophy, political science/government, prelaw, psychology, religion, religious music, social science, and sociology). Sciences, business, and education are the strongest academically and have the largest enrollments.

ACTIVITIES: 33% of men belong to 5 national fraternities; 34% of women belong to 5 national sororities. There are 60 groups on campus, including band, cheerleading, choir, chorale, chorus, communications, dance, debate, drama, drill team, ethnic, forensics, gay, honors, jazz band, literary magazine, marching band, musical theater, newspaper, orchestra, pep band, political, radio and TV, religious, social, social service, student government, and symphony. Popular campus events include Mock Conventions, Mardi Gras, and Volleyrock.

SERVICES: Counseling and information services are available, as is tutoring in most subjects, through the learning center There is a reader service for the blind, and remedial math, reading, and writing. **Library/Resources:** The 2 libraries contain 283,070 volumes, 9,737 microform items, and 14,251 audio/video tapes/CDs/DVDs, and subscribe to 848 periodicals including electronic. Computerized library services include interlibrary loans, database searching, Internet access, and Wi-Fi capability. Special learning facilities include an art gallery, planetarium, radio station, TV station, electron microscope labs in the science center, and a graphics computer center. **Physically Challenged Students:** 50% of the campus is accessible. Facilities include wheelchair ramps, elevators, special parking, specially equipped restrooms, and special class scheduling. **Special:** The college offers internships, study abroad in many countries, a Washington semester, various dual and student-designed majors, a 3-2 engineering degree with Case Western Reserve, Pennsylvania State, and Washington Universities, London study at Regent's College, a 3-3 J.D. program with Duquesne, and nondegree study. There are 12 national honor societies and a freshman honors program. **Visiting:** There are regularly scheduled orientations for prospective students, consisting of an introduction, a student panel, a financial aid workshop, a campus tour, a faculty fair, and a lunch. Optional activities include a tour of residence halls and radio and TV stations and a football game. There are 2 visitation days in the fall and 2 in the spring. There are guides for informal visits, visitors may sit in on classes, and stay overnight. To schedule a visit, contact the Office of Admissions. **Campus Safety and Security:** Measures include 24-hour foot and vehicle patrol, self-defense education, and security escort services. There are shuttle buses, emergency telephones, and lighted pathways/sidewalks.

REQUIREMENTS: The SAT or ACT is required, with a minimum recommended composite score of 900 on the SAT or 20 on the ACT. Applicants must be graduates of an accredited secondary school and have a minimum of 16 academic credits, including 4 units in English, 3 in math, and 2 each in foreign language, science, and social studies. The GED will be considered with a minimum composite score of 270. A portfolio, audition, and interview are recommended. An essay is required. Applications are accepted on-line. Westminster requires applicants to be in the upper 50% of their class. A GPA of 2.5 is required. AP and CLEP credits are accepted. Important factors in the admissions decision are advanced placement or honors courses, leadership record, and recommendations by school officials.

ADMISSIONS: 77% of a recent year applicants were accepted. The ACT scores were 73% below 21, 13% between 21 and 23, 8% between 24 and 26, 2% between 27 and 28, and 3% above 28. 48% of the current freshmen were in the top fifth of their class; 80% were in the top two fifths. 8 freshmen graduated first in their class.

FINANCIAL AID: In a recent year, 98% of all full-time freshmen and 97% of continuing full-time students received some form of financial aid. 81% of all full-time freshmen and 78% of continuing full-time students received need-based aid. The average freshman award was $16,427. 40% of undergraduate students work part-time. Average annual earnings from campus work are $1650. The average financial indebtedness of the 2013 graduate was $20,386. Westminster is a member of CSS. The FAFSA and the college's own financial statement are required. The deadline for filing freshman financial aid applications for fall entry is May 1.

WIDENER UNIVERSITY   F-4
www.widener.edu

Chester, PA 19013   (888)-WIDENER
    (610) 499-4126

Fax: (610) 499-4676   Email: admissions.office@widener.edu
Full-time: 1337 men, 1546 women   Faculty: 217; IIA, +$
Part-time: 167 men, 387 women   Ph.D.s: 84%
Graduate: 849 men, 1699 women   Student/Faculty: 12 to 1
Year: semesters, summer session   Tuition: $39,830
Room & Board: $12,588   Freshman Class: 5501 applied, 3576 accepted, 733 enrolled
SAT CR/M: 490/510   CEEB CODE: 2642
Application Deadline: February 15   COMPETITIVE

Widener University, founded in 1821, is a private liberal arts institution offering undergraduate programs in the arts and sciences, business administration, engineering, nursing, and hospitality management. Other campuses are in Harrisburg and Wilmington, Delaware. Figures in the above capsule and in this profile are approximate. There are 7 undergraduate schools and 8 graduate schools. In addition to regional accreditation, Widener has baccalaureate program accreditation with AACSB, ABET, APTA, CSWE, NCATE, ABA, and CCNE. The 105-acre campus is in a suburban area 12 miles south of Philadelphia. Including any residence halls, there are 89 buildings.

STUDENT LIFE: 64% of undergraduates are from Pennsylvania. Others are from 21 states, and 15 foreign countries. 70% are White; 14% African American. The average age of freshmen is 18; all undergraduates, 20. 28% do not continue beyond their first year; 55% remain to graduate. **Housing:** 1670 students can be accommodated in college housing, which includes single-sex and coed dorms and on-campus apartments. In addition, there are honors houses, special-interest houses, fraternity houses, sorority houses, Substance-free housing, affinity housing, wellness housing, and quiet/study wings. On-campus housing is guaranteed for all 4 years and is available on a lottery system for upperclassmen. 52% of students commute. All students may keep cars.

FACULTY/CLASSROOMS: 46% of faculty are male; 54% are female. 82% teach undergraduates, 70% do research, and 70% do both. No introductory courses are taught by graduate students. The average class size in an introductory lecture is 30; in a laboratory is 14; and in a regular course is 24.

PROGRAMS OF STUDY: Widener confers B.A., B.S., B.S.B., B.S.C.E., B.S.Ch.E., B.S.E.E., B.S. in H.M., B.S.M.E., B.S.N., and B.S.W. degrees. Associate, Master's, and Doctoral degrees are also awarded. Bachelor's degrees are awarded in BIOLOGICAL SCIENCE (biochemistry and biology/biological science), BUSINESS (accounting, business administration and management, business economics, finance, hospitality management services, international business management, and management information systems), COMMUNICATIONS AND THE ARTS (art, communications, creative writing, English, fine arts, French, media arts, modern language, and Spanish), COMPUTER AND PHYSICAL SCIENCE (chemistry, computer science, information sciences and systems, mathematics, physics, and science), EDUCATION (early childhood education, elementary education, mathematics education, science education, and special education), ENGINEERING AND ENVIRONMENTAL DESIGN (biomedical engineering, chemical engineering, civil engineering, electrical/electronics engineering, engineering, environmental science, mechanical engineering, and preengineering), HEALTH PROFESSIONS (nursing and prephysical therapy), SOCIAL SCIENCE (anthropology, behavioral science, criminal justice, economics, gender studies, history, humanities, international relations, political science/government, psychology, social work, sociology, and women's studies). Computer science, biology, and psychology are the strongest academically. Nursing, psychology, and management have the largest enrollments.

ACTIVITIES: 10% of men belong to 6 national fraternities; 9% of women belong to 5 national sororities. There are 106 groups on campus, including men's hockey club, video, outdoor, ice hockey, model UN, rugby, ski and snowboard, art, cheerleading, chess, choir, chorale, chorus, computers, dance, drama, environmental, ethnic, film, gay, honors, international, jazz band, literary magazine, musical theater, pep band, photography, political, professional, radio and TV, religious, social, social service, student government, and yearbook. Popular campus events include Greek Week, Hundredth Night and Honors Week. **Sports:** There are 10 intercollegiate sports for men and 10 for women, and 7 intramural sports for men and 7 for women. Facilities include a 4000-seat stadium, an 1800-seat basketball gym, a field house, a championship pool, a weight training room, an exercise room, tennis courts, outdoor game and practice fields, and an 8-lane, all-weather championship track. **Graduates:** The most popular majors were business/marketing (24%), nursing/health professions (20%), and engineering (12%). In an average class, 40% graduate in 4 years or less, 54% graduate in 5 years or less, and 56% graduate in 6 years or less. Of the 2013 graduating class, 20% were enrolled in graduate school within 6 months of graduation, and 70% were employed.

SERVICES: Counseling and information services are available, as is tutoring in every subject. There is a reader service for the blind. Academic support is offered as needed for all students. **Library/Resources:** Computerized library services include interlibrary loans, database searching, and Internet access. Special learning facilities include an art gallery, radio station, TV station, a child development center, and a wireless accessible library. **Physically Challenged Students:** All of the campus is accessible. Facilities include wheelchair ramps, elevators, special parking, specially equipped restrooms, special class scheduling, lowered drinking fountains, and lowered telephones. **Special:** Widener offers internships, study abroad in 12 countries, a Washington semester, accelerated degree programs, dual, student-designed, and interdisciplinary majors, including chemistry management, nondegree study, and pass/fail options. Co-op programs are available in business administration, computer science, and engineering and are required in hospitality management. There are 26 national honor societies, a freshman honors program, and 8 departmental honors programs. **Visiting:** There are regularly scheduled orientations for prospective students. There are guides for informal visits, visitors may sit in on classes, and stay overnight. To schedule a visit, contact the Office of Admissions at office.admissions@widener.edu. **Campus Safety and Security:** Measures include 24-hour foot and vehicle patrol, emergency notification system, self-defense education, and security escort services. There are shuttle buses, emergency telephones, lighted pathways/sidewalks, controlled access to dorms/residences, residence hall briefings on personal safety, housing security, and enforcement procedures. There are bike patrols.

REQUIREMENTS: The SAT is required. Applicants must be graduates of an accredited secondary school and have completed 4 units each of English and social studies, 3 units each of math and science, and 1 unit each of art, history, and music. The GED is accepted under limited circumstances. An interview is recommended. A GPA of 3.0 is required. AP credits are accepted. Important factors in the admissions decision are advanced placement or honors courses, recommendations by school officials, and extracurricular activities record. All students must complete 12 credits each in humanities, social sciences, and science/math, and 1 credit in phys ed. For graduation, students must have 121 credit hours and a GPA of 2.0. Hours in the major vary by program. There is a university-wide writing requirement for all students. **Procedure:** Freshmen are admitted fall and spring. Entrance exams should be taken in the junior year and November or December of the senior year. There are early admissions, deferred admissions, and rolling admissions plans. Applications should be filed by February 15 for fall entry; January 3 for spring entry, along with a $35 fee. Notification of early decision is sent December 15; regular decision, February 15. 17 applicants were on the 2014 waiting list; 4 were admitted. Applications are accepted online. **Transfer Students:** 138 transfer students enrolled in 2013-2014. Applicants must have at least 12 college credits with a minimum GPA of 2.0 (2.5 for nursing students). An associate's degree and an interview are recommended. 45 of 121 credits required for the bachelor's degree must be completed at Widener. **International Students:** There are 98 international students enrolled. The school actively recruits these students. They must take the TOEFL.

ADMISSIONS: 65% of the 2014-2015 applicants were accepted. The SAT scores for the 2014-2015 freshman class were: Critical Reading--44% below 500, 42% between 500 and 599, 8% between 600 and 699, and 2% between 700 and 800; Math--39% below 500, 40% between 500 and 599, 18% between 600 and 699, and 3% between 700 and 800. 26% of the current freshmen were in the top fifth of their class; 56% were in the top two fifths. 5 freshmen graduated first in their class. **Admissions Contact:** Ed Wright, Director of Admissions. E-Mail: *admissions.office@widener.edu* Web: *www.widener.edu*

FINANCIAL AID: In 2014-2015, 99% of all full-time freshmen and 79% of continuing full-time students received some form of financial aid. 75% of all full-time freshmen and 64% of continuing full-time students received need-based aid. The average freshman award was $40,200. Need-based scholarships or need-based grants averaged $8,200; need-based self-help aid (loans and jobs) averaged $6,390; and other non-need-based awards and non-need-based scholarships averaged $21,230. 45% of undergraduate students work part-time. Average annual earnings from campus work are $944. Widener is a member of CSS. The FAFSA is required. The deadline for filing freshman financial aid applications for fall entry is February 15.

WILKES UNIVERSITY   E-2
www.wilkes.edu

Wilkes Barre, PA 18766

(800) WILKESU
(570) 408-4400

Fax: (570) 408-4904

Email: admissions@wilkes.edu

Full-time: 1173 men, 1044 women

Faculty: IIA, av$

Part-time: 69 men, 74 women

Ph.D.s: 89%

Graduate: 704 men, 1498 women

Student/Faculty: 15 to 1

Year: semesters, summer session

Tuition: $31,262

Room & Board: $12,808

Freshman Class: 2812 applied, 2211 accepted, 559 enrolled

SAT CR/M/W: 510/530/500 **ACT:** required

CEEB CODE: 2977

Application Deadline: open

COMPETITIVE

Wilkes University, founded in 1933, is an independent comprehensive university offering undergraduate programs in 40 fields, including the arts and sciences, business, and engineering. There are 6 undergraduate schools and one graduate school. In addition to regional accreditation, Wilkes has baccalaureate program accreditation with ABET, ACBSP, ACPE, and CCNE. The 27-acre campus is in an urban area 120 miles west of New York City. Including any residence halls, there are 53 buildings.

STUDENT LIFE: 83% of undergraduates are from Pennsylvania. Others are from 22 states, 11 foreign countries, and Canada. 80% are from public schools. 73% are White. The average age of freshmen is 19; all undergraduates, 21. 21% do not continue beyond their first year; 56% remain to graduate. **Housing:** 1102 students can be accommodated in college housing, which includes single-sex and coed dorms and on-campus apartments. On-campus housing is guaranteed for all 4 years and is available on a lottery system for upperclassmen. 59% of students commute. Alcohol is not permitted. All students may keep cars.

FACULTY/CLASSROOMS: 53% of faculty are male; 47% are female. No introductory courses are taught by graduate students. The average class size in an introductory lecture is 24; in a laboratory is 16; and in a regular course is 21.

PROGRAMS OF STUDY: Wilkes confers B.A., B.S. and B.B.A. degrees. Master's and Doctoral degrees are also awarded. Bachelor's degrees are awarded in BIOLOGICAL SCIENCE (biochemistry and biology/biological science), BUSINESS (accounting, business administration and management, entrepreneurial studies, marketing and distribution, and sports management), COMMUNICATIONS AND THE ARTS (communications, dramatic arts, English, media arts, musical theater, and Spanish), COMPUTER AND PHYSICAL SCIENCE (chemistry, computer science, earth science, information sciences and systems, mathematics, and physics), EDUCATION (elementary education and middle school education), ENGINEERING AND ENVIRONMENTAL DESIGN (electrical/electronics engineering, engineering and applied science, engineering management, environmental engineering, and mechanical engineering), HEALTH PROFESSIONS (medical technology, nursing, and prepharmacy), SOCIAL SCIENCE (criminology, history, international studies, liberal arts/general studies, philosophy, political science/government, psychology, and sociology). Pre-pharmacy, biology, and engineering are the strongest academically. Nursing, biology, and mechanical engineering have the largest enrollments.

ACTIVITIES: There are 80 groups on campus, including art, band, cheerleading, choir, chorus, computers, dance, debate, drama, environmental, ethnic, gay, honors, international, jazz band, literary magazine, marching band, musical theater, newspaper, orchestra, pep band, political, professional, radio and TV, religious, social, social service, and student government. Popular campus events include Casino Night, Junior-Senior Dinner Dance and Winter Weekend. **Sports:** There are 10 intercollegiate sports for men and 10 for women. Facilities include tennis courts, a 5,000-seat stadium, a 3,500-seat gym, a game room, weight and exercise rooms, and an indoor recreation and athletic center. **Graduates:** From July 1, 2013 to June 30, 2014, 463 bachelor's degrees were awarded. The most popular majors were business (17%), nursing (15%), and engineering (9%). In an average class, 45% graduate in 4 years or less, 55% graduate in 5 years or less, and 56% graduate in 6 years or less. Of the 2013 graduating class, 23% were enrolled in graduate school within 6 months of graduation, and 72% were employed.

SERVICES: Counseling and information services are available, as is tutoring in every subject. There is remedial math, reading, and writing. The Learning Center also provides individual tutoring, group study sessions, and small-group supplemental instruction seminars. **Library/Resources:** The library contains 212,700 volumes, 16,000 microform items, and 2,100 audio/video tapes/CDs/DVDs. Computerized library services include interlibrary loans, database searching, Internet access, and Wi-Fi capability. Special learning facilities include an art gallery, radio station, and TV station. **Physically Challenged Students:** All of the campus is accessible. Facilities include wheelchair ramps, elevators, special parking, specially equipped restrooms, special class scheduling, lowered drinking fountains, and lowered telephones. **Special:** Wilkes offers cooperative education, cross-registration with King's College and Misericordia, internships, and study abroad. Dual majors in all disciplines, credit for military experience, and nondegree study are also offered. There are 19 national honor societies and 3 departmental honors programs. **Visiting:** There are regularly scheduled orientations for prospective students, including a general orientation session, a tour of the campus, and a meeting with faculty from the department of the student's intended major. There are guides for informal visits, visitors may sit in on classes, and stay overnight. To schedule a visit, contact the Admissions Office. **Campus Safety and Security:** Measures include 24-hour foot and vehicle patrol, emergency notification system, and security escort services. There are shuttle buses, emergency telephones, lighted pathways/sidewalks, controlled access to dorms/residences, personal alarm devices for students who wish to carry one, and engraving of personal belongings. Students and others may contact security anonymously.

REQUIREMENTS: The SAT or ACT is required. Applicants must be graduates of an accredited secondary school or have the GED. Secondary-school preparation should include 4 years of English, 3 years each of math and social studies, and 2 years of science. Theater majors must audition. Wilkes requires applicants to be in the upper 50% of their class. A GPA of 2.5 is required. AP and CLEP credits are accepted. Important factors in the admissions decision are recommendations by school officials, advanced placement or honors courses, and leadership record. To graduate, all students must complete at least 120 credit hours, with a minimum of 30 in the major, and a cumulative GPA of at least 2.0 overall and in the major. Students must demonstrate competency in written communication, computer literacy, oral communication, and qualitative reasoning. General education requirements consist of 12 to 15 credits in humanities, 9 to 12 in sciences, 6 to 9 in social sciences, and 3 in fine arts. **Procedure:** Freshmen are admitted fall, spring, and summer. Entrance exams should be taken before the second semester of the senior year in high school. There are early admissions, deferred admissions, and rolling admissions plans. Application deadlines are open. Application fee is $40. Notification is sent on a rolling basis.

Applications are accepted on-line. **Transfer Students:** 182 transfer students enrolled in 2013-2014. Applicants must have a minimum college GPA of 2.0 and at least 30 earned credits. A GPA of 2.5 is required for engineering majors. Students with fewer than 30 credits must submit official high school transcripts and SAT or ACT scores. An interview is recommended. 60 of 120 credits required for the bachelor's degree must be completed at Wilkes. **International Students:** There are 202 international students enrolled. The school actively recruits these students. They must take the TOEFL with a minimum score of 500 on the paper-based TOEFL (PBT) or 60 on the Internet-based version (iBT). They must also take the SAT or ACT.

ADMISSIONS: 79% of the 2014-2015 applicants were accepted. The SAT scores for the 2014-2015 freshman class were: Critical Reading--42% below 500, 43% between 500 and 599, 14% between 600 and 699, and 1% between 700 and 800; Math--33% below 500, 43% between 500 and 599, 22% between 600 and 699, and 2% between 700 and 800; Writing--50% below 500, 37% between 500 and 599, 12% between 600 and 699, and 1% between 700 and 800. 45% of the current freshmen were in the top fifth of their class; 72% were in the top two fifths. **Admissions Contact:** Melanie Wade, Vice President for Enrollment Services. E-Mail: *melanie.wade@wilkes.edu* Web: *www.wilkes.edu*

FINANCIAL AID: In 2014-2015, 96% of all full-time freshmen and 89% of continuing full-time students received some form of financial aid. 30% of undergraduate students work part-time. Average annual earnings from campus work are $800. The average financial indebtedness of the 2014 graduate was $38,082. The FAFSA is required. The deadline for filing freshman financial aid applications for fall entry is March 1.

WILSON COLLEGE   D-3
www.wilson.edu

Chambersburg, PA 17201

	(717) 262-4141
	(800) 421-8402
Fax: n/av	Email: admissions@wilson.edu
Full-time: 38 men, 327 women	Faculty: 40
Part-time: 50 men, 192 women	Ph.D.s: 78%
Graduate: 32 men, 120 women	Student/Faculty: 9 to 1
Year: 4-1-4, summer session	Tuition: $24,380
Room & Board: $10,700	Freshman Class: 472 applied, 407 accepted, 141 enrolled
ACT: 22	CEEB CODE: 2979
Application Deadline: open	COMPETITIVE

Wilson College, founded in 1869, is a private, coeducational liberal arts college offering bachelor's degrees in 29 majors and master's degrees in education, the humanities, accountancy and nursing. Wilson is committed to providing an affordable education that offers value to its students beyond graduation. There is 1 undergraduate school and 1 graduate school. In addition to regional accreditation, Wilson has baccalaureate program accreditation with AVMA. The 300-acre campus is in a small town 55 miles south of Harrisburg, 76 miles west of Baltimore, 90 miles west of Washington, D.C. Including any residence halls, there are 34 buildings.

STUDENT LIFE: 83% of undergraduates are from Pennsylvania. Others are from 19 states, 10 foreign countries, and Canada. 91% are from public schools. 85% are White. 51% claim no religious affiliation; 31% Protestant; 11% Catholic. The average age of freshmen is 18; all undergraduates, 30. 33% do not continue beyond their first year; 48% remain to graduate. **Housing:** 473 students can be accommodated in college housing, which includes single-sex and coed dorms and on-campus apartments. Including single-mother housing for women with children. On-campus housing is guaranteed for all 4 years. 59% of students commute. All students may keep cars.

FACULTY/CLASSROOMS: 47% of faculty are male; 53% are female. All teach undergraduates. No introductory courses are taught by graduate students. The average class size in an introductory lecture is 20; in a laboratory is 14; and in a regular course is 14.

PROGRAMS OF STUDY: Wilson confers B.A., and B.S. degrees.

Associate and Master's degrees are also awarded. Bachelor's degrees are awarded in AGRICULTURE (animal science, environmental studies, and equine science), BIOLOGICAL SCIENCE (biochemistry and biology/biological science), BUSINESS (accounting, business economics, and sports management), COMMUNICATIONS AND THE ARTS (communications, creative writing, English, fine arts, French, graphic design, graphic design & media, languages, and Spanish), COMPUTER AND PHYSICAL SCIENCE (actuarial mathematics, chemistry, and mathematics), EDUCATION (early childhood education, elementary education, English education, foreign languages education, mathematics education, physical education, secondary education, and social studies education), ENGINEERING AND ENVIRONMENTAL DESIGN (environmental science), HEALTH PROFESSIONS (biology, exercise science, Pre-Health Studies, predentistry, premedicine, preoptometry, preosteopathy, prepharmacy, prephysical therapy, preveterinary science, and veterinary science), SOCIAL SCIENCE (economics, (Social Science) Global Studies, history, international relations, international studies, law, liberal arts/general studies, liberal arts, sciences, general studies, humanities, philosophy, philosophy and religion, political science/government, prelaw, psychobiology, psychology, religion, sociology, and therapeutic riding). Biology, and veterinary medical technology are the strongest academically. Business and economics, education, and veterinary medical technology have the largest enrollments.

ACTIVITIES: There are 28 groups on campus, including Spanish, business, math, veterinary, art, cheerleading, choir, chorale, dance, drama, environmental, equestrian, ethnic, gay, honors, international, literary magazine, newspaper, photography, political, professional, radio and TV, religious, social, social service, student government, and yearbook. Popular campus events include May Weekend and Thanksgiving, Christmas, and Muhibbah International Dinners. **Sports:** There are 5 intercollegiate sports for men and 5 for women, and 3 intramural sports for men and 3 for women. Facilities include a 400-seat gym, a field house, a pool, a gymnastics gym, an archery range, a hockey field, a softball field, tennis courts, a 2-lane bowling alley, an equestrian center (indoor and outdoor arena), a soccer field, and a fitness center. **Graduates:** From July 1, 2013 to June 30, 2014, 95 bachelor's degrees were awarded. The most popular majors were veterinary medical (21%), elementary education (13%), and business economics (10%). In an average class, 58% graduate in 4 years or less, 59% graduate in 5 years or less, and 62% graduate in 6 years or less.

SERVICES: Counseling and information services are available, as is tutoring in every subject. There is remedial math, reading, and writing including a study skills workshops **Library/Resources:** The library contains 175,000 volumes, 10,933 microform items, 2,007 audio/video tapes/CDs/DVDs, and subscribes to 293 periodicals including electronic. Computerized library services include interlibrary loans, database searching, and Internet access. Special learning facilities include an art gallery, natural history museum, radio station, a veterinary technology center, transmission electron microscope, classics collection, stables, center for sustainable living with USDA-certified organic farm, and an on-campus equestrian center. **Physically Challenged Students:** 55% of the campus is accessible. Facilities include wheelchair ramps, elevators, special parking, specially equipped restrooms, and special class scheduling. **Special:** Cross-registration is available with Shippensburg University and Gettysburg College. Wilson offers internships, a Washington semester, student-designed majors, B.A.-B.S. degree in psychology and sociology credit by exam, pass/fail options, and credit for noncollegiate learning. Students may participate in study-abroad programs sponsored by other colleges. Army ROTC is available through Shippensburg University There are 2 national honor societies, including Phi Beta Kappa, and a freshman honors program. **Visiting:** There are regularly scheduled orientations for prospective students, campus tour, meetings with faculty, students, or administration, and an interview with an admissions counselor and financial aid. There are guides for informal visits, visitors may sit in on classes, and stay overnight. To schedule a visit, contact the Office of Admissions. **Campus Safety and Security:** Measures include 24-hour foot and vehicle patrol and emergency notification system. There are shuttle buses, emergency telephones, lighted pathways/sidewalks, and controlled access to dorms/residences.

REQUIREMENTS: Wilson is test-optional for applicants with a 3.0 unweighted GPA who have completed a college prep curriculum including 4 years each of English and social studies/history, 3 of math, and 2 of science with a lab and a foreign language. A graded English paper and at least one academic reference are required, with an interview is recommended. Wilson requires applicants to be in the upper 50% of their class. A GPA of 2.5 is required. AP and CLEP credits are accepted. Important factors in the admissions decision are personality/intangible qualities, advanced placement or honors courses, and leadership record.To graduate, students must complete a minimum of 120 credits, with a minimum GPA of 2.0. At least half of the credits must be outside any single discipline. **Procedure:** Freshmen are admitted fall and spring. Entrance exams should be taken in the spring of the junior year. There are deferred admissions and rolling admissions plans. Application deadlines are open. Notification is sent on a rolling basis. Applications are accepted on-line. **Transfer Students:** 22 transfer students enrolled in 2013-2014. Applicants must have a college GPA of at least 2.0. The SAT I or ACT may be waived after discussion with the Admissions Office 73 of 120 credits required for the bachelor's degree must be completed at Wilson. **International Students:** There are 31 international students enrolled. The school actively recruits these students. They must take the TOEFL with a minimum score of 500 on the paper-based TOEFL (PBT) or 61 on the Internet-based version (iBT), or IELTS, or STEP. They must also take the SAT or ACT. The SAT is recommended.

ADMISSIONS: 86% of the 2014-2015 applicants were accepted. The ACT scores were 50% below 21, 10% between 21 and 23, 30% between 24 and 26, % between 27 and 28, and 10% above 28. 21% of the current freshmen were in the top fifth of their class; 43% were in the top two fifths. 1 freshman graduated first in the class. **Admissions Contact:** Patricia Beidel, Director of Admissions. E-Mail: *admissions @wilson.edu* Web: *www.wilson.edu*

FINANCIAL AID: In 2014-2015, 99% of all full-time freshmen and ontinuing full-time students received some form of financial aid. 77% of all full-time freshmen and 71% of continuing full-time students received need-based aid. The average freshman award was $15,469. Need-based scholarships or need-based grants averaged $12,411; need-based self-help aid (loans and jobs) averaged $3,855; and other non-need-based awards and non-need-based scholarships averaged $11,381. 40% of undergraduate students work part-time. Average annual earnings from campus work are $1340. The average financial indebtedness of the 2014 graduate was $32,540. The FAFSA and the college's own financial statement are required. The priority date for freshman financial aid applications for fall entry is April 30.

YORK COLLEGE OF PENNSYLVANIA D-4
www.ycp.edu

York, PA 17403

(717) 846-7788
(800) 455-8018

Fax: (717) 849-1607

Email: admissions@ycp.edu

Full-time: 2052 men, 2410 women
Part-time: 213 men, 342 women
Graduate: 91 men, 149 women
Year: semesters, summer session
Room & Board: $9580

Faculty: 164; IIA, +$
Ph.Ds: 87%
Student/Faculty: 28 to 1
Tuition: $14,460
Freshman Class: 9934 applied, 7302 accepted, 1064 enrolled

SAT CR/M/W: 510/520/500 **ACT:** 22
Application Deadline: open

CEEB CODE: 2991
COMPETITIVE

York College of Pennsylvania, founded in 1787, is a private institution offering undergraduate programs in the liberal arts and sciences, as well as professional programs. In addition to regional accreditation, YCP has baccalaureate program accreditation with ABET, ACBSP, NASM, NLN, and NRPA. The 190-acre campus is in a suburban area 45 miles north of Baltimore. Including any residence halls, there are 46 buildings.

STUDENT LIFE: 58% of undergraduates are from Pennsylvania. Others are from 32 states, and 7 foreign countries. 85% are from public schools. 83% are White. 36% claim no religious affiliation; 25% Protestant; 24% Catholic; 13% Unknown denominations, and Muslim. The average age of freshmen is 19; all undergraduates, 21. 25% do not continue beyond their first year; 58% remain to graduate.

FACULTY/CLASSROOMS: 57% of faculty are male; 43% are female.

All teach undergraduates. No introductory courses are taught by graduate students. The average class size in an introductory lecture is 22; in a laboratory is 17; and in a regular course is 19.

PROGRAMS OF STUDY: YCP confers B.A. and B.S. degrees. Associate, Master's, and Doctoral degrees are also awarded. Bachelor's degrees are awarded in BIOLOGICAL SCIENCE (biology/biological science), BUSINESS (accounting, banking and finance, business administration and management, entrepreneurial studies, management information systems, marketing/retailing/merchandising, recreation and leisure services, and sports management), COMMUNICATIONS AND THE ARTS (broadcasting, communications, creative writing, dramatic arts, English, English literature, fine arts, graphic design, music, music technology, public relations, and Spanish), COMPUTER AND PHYSICAL SCIENCE (chemistry, computer science, and mathematics), EDUCATION (education, elementary education, English education, mathematics education, music education, science education, secondary education, social studies education, and special education), ENGINEERING AND ENVIRONMENTAL DESIGN (computer engineering, electrical/electronics engineering, engineering, engineering management, and mechanical engineering), HEALTH PROFESSIONS (medical laboratory science, nuclear medical technology, nursing, and respiratory therapy), SOCIAL SCIENCE (behavioral science, criminal justice, economics, history, humanities, parks and recreation management, philosophy, political science/government, psychology, and sociology). Electrical, computer, mechanical engineering, nursing, business, criminal justice and education are the strongest academically. Nursing, education, and criminal justice have the largest enrollments.

ACTIVITIES: 10% of men belong to 8 national fraternities; 10% of women belong to 6 national sororities. There are 80 groups on campus, including band, cheerleading, chess, choir, chorale, chorus, computers, debate, drama, environmental, ethnic, film, forensics, gay, honors, international, jazz band, literary magazine, musical theater, newspaper, orchestra, photography, political, professional, radio and TV, religious, social, social service, student government, and symphony. Popular campus events include Fall Weekend, Spring Weekend and Spartalooza.

SERVICES: Counseling and information services are available, as is tutoring in most subjects. There is remedial math and writing. There is also an education learning resource center. **Library/Resources:** The library contains 300,000 volumes, 500,000 microform items, 11,000 audio/video tapes/CDs/DVDs, and subscribes to 1,500 periodicals including electronic. Computerized library services include interlibrary loans, database searching, and Internet access. Special learning facilities include an art gallery, radio station, TV station, a telecommunications center, Abraham Lincoln artifacts collection, rare books collection, oral history room, and a nursing education center. **Physically Challenged Students:** 90% of the campus is accessible. Facilities include wheelchair ramps, elevators, special parking, specially equipped restrooms, special class scheduling, lowered drinking fountains, and lowered telephones. **Special:** YCP offers internships for upper-division students and a co-op program in mechanical engineering. Study abroad is offered in England, Mexico, Japan, Puerto Rico, Korea, and other countries. Dual majors in any combination, nondegree study, and pass/fail options are available. There are 6 national honor societies. **Visiting:** There are regularly scheduled orientations for prospective students, including 2 open houses in October/November; 1 junior open house in April; and 2 spring orientation programs in April/May, featuring a general orientation, academic and support services sessions, and campus tours. There are guides for informal visits and visitors may sit in on classes. To schedule a visit, contact the Admissions Office. **Campus Safety and Security:** Measures include 24-hour foot and vehicle patrol, emergency notification system, and security escort services. There are shuttle buses, emergency telephones, lighted pathways/sidewalks, safety seminars, crime prevention speakers, a desk monitor in residence halls, and a personal property engraving program.

REQUIREMENTS: The SAT or ACT is required. The ACT Optional Writing test is also required. Applicants must be graduates of an accredited secondary school or have a GED certificate. 15 academic credits are required, including 4 units in English, 3 or 4 in math, 2 or 3 in science, 2 in history, and 1 in social studies. Music students must audition. A GPA of 2.5 is required. AP and CLEP credits are accepted. Important factors in the admissions decision are advanced placement or honors courses, leadership record, and extracurricular activities record.

ADMISSIONS: 74% of a recent year applicants were accepted. The SAT scores for a recent year freshman class were: Critical Reading--41% below 500, 46% between 500 and 599, 12% between 600 and 699, and 1% between 700 and 800; Math--32% below 500, 50% between 500 and 599, 16% between 600 and 699, and 2% between 700 and 800; Writing--47% below 500, 45% between 500 and 599, and 8% between 600 and 699. The ACT scores were 31% below 21, 32% between 21 and 23, 21% between 24 and 26, 12% between 27 and 28, and 4% above 28. 4 freshmen graduated first in their class.

FINANCIAL AID: In a recent year, 90% of all full-time freshmen and 83% of continuing full-time students received some form of financial aid. 74% of all full-time freshmen and 58% of continuing full-time students received need-based aid. The average freshman award was $13,498. Need-based scholarships or need-based grants averaged $1,961 ($15,100 maximum); need-based self-help aid (loans and jobs) averaged $3,132 ($5,700 maximum); and other non-need-based awards and non-need-based scholarships averaged $5,363 ($27,340 maximum). 20% of undergraduate students work part-time. Average annual earnings from campus work are $1500. The average financial indebtedness of the 2013 graduate was $35,604. YCP is a member of CSS. The FAFSA is required. The priority date for freshman financial aid applications for fall entry is March 1.

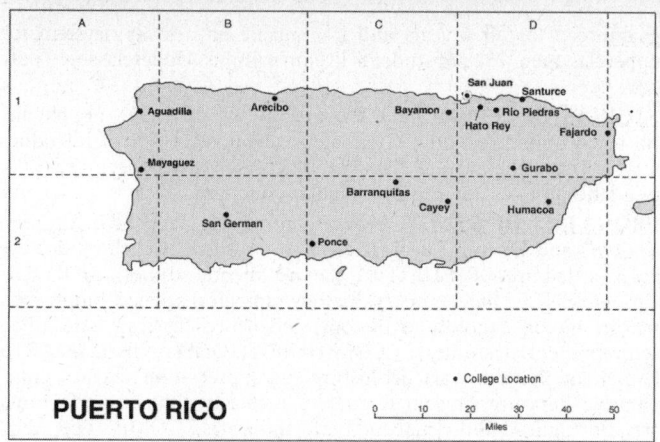

PUERTO RICO

College Location

0   10   20   30   40   50
Miles

CARIBBEAN UNIVERSITY (*The complete profile is made available exclusively on our website, www.barronspac.com*)

CENTRAL UNIVERSITY OF BAYAMON (*The complete profile is made available exclusively on our website, www.barronspac.com*)

CONSERVATORY OF MUSIC OF PUERTO RICO (*The complete profile is made available exclusively on our website, www.barronspac.com*)

ESCUELA DE ARTES PLASTICAS DE PUERTO RICO (*The complete profile is made available exclusively on our website, www.barronspac.com*)

INTER-AMERICAN UNIVERSITY OF PUERTO RICO SYSTEM

The Inter-American University of Puerto Rico System, established in 1912, is a private system in Puerto Rico. It is governed by a board of trustees, whose chief administrator is the president. The primary goal of the system is teaching. The main priorities are to provide quality education and public service, and to devote attention to students' needs. The total student enrollment is usually about 43,937, with 874 faculty members. Altogether there are 35 baccalaureate, 28 master's, and 1 doctoral program offered in Inter-American University of Puerto Rico System. Profiles of the 4-year colleges are available exclusively on our website, barronspac.com.

INTER-AMERICAN UNIVERSITY OF PUERTO RICO/ AGUADILLA CAMPUS (*The complete profile is made available exclusively on our website, www.barronspac.com*)

INTER-AMERICAN UNIVERSITY OF PUERTO RICO/ARECIBO CAMPUS (*The complete profile is made available exclusively on our website, www.barronspac.com*)

INTER-AMERICAN UNIVERSITY OF PUERTO RICO/ BARRANQUITAS (*The complete profile is made available exclusively on our website, www.barronspac.com*)

INTER-AMERICAN UNIVERSITY OF PUERTO RICO/BAYAMON UNIVERSITY COLLEGE (*The complete profile is made available exclusively on our website, www.barronspac.com*)

INTER-AMERICAN UNIVERSITY OF PUERTO RICO/FAJARDO CAMPUS (*The complete profile is made available exclusively on our website, www.barronspac.com*)

INTER-AMERICAN UNIVERSITY OF PUERTO RICO/ METROPOLITAN CAMPUS (*The complete profile is made available exclusively on our website, www.barronspac.com*)

INTER-AMERICAN UNIVERSITY OF PUERTO RICO/PONCE (*The complete profile is made available exclusively on our website, www.barronspac.com*)

INTER-AMERICAN UNIVERSITY OF PUERTO RICO/SAN GERMÁN (*The complete profile is made available exclusively on our website, www.barronspac.com*)

PONTIFICAL CATHOLIC UNIVERSITY OF PUERTO RICO (*The complete profile is made available exclusively on our website, www.barronspac.com*)

UNIVERSIDAD ADVENTISTA DE LAS ANTILLAS (*The complete profile is made available exclusively on our website, www.barronspac.com*)

UNIVERSIDAD DE PUERTO/ARECIBO (*The complete profile is made available exclusively on our website, www.barronspac.com*)

UNIVERSIDAD DEL TURABO (*The complete profile is made available exclusively on our website, www.barronspac.com*)

UNIVERSIDAD METROPOLITANA (*The complete profile is made available exclusively on our website, www.barronspac.com*)

UNIVERSIDAD POLITECNICA DE PUERTO RICO (*The complete profile is made available exclusively on our website, www.barronspac.com*)

UNIVERSITY OF PUERTO RICO SYSTEM

The University of Puerto Rico System, established in 1903, is a public system in Puerto Rico. It is governed by the Puerto Rico council on higher education, whose chief administrator is the president. The primary goal of the system is to serve as a center for scholarly research, to develop academic excellence, and to capitalize on its location as a focal point of the Caribbean region and the international community by developing programs germane to the residents of the region. The main priorities are to improve academic programs in key areas, to strengthen research and research training, and to upgrade physical facilities. The total student enrollment for all eleven campuses is usually 56,000 with 4,500 faculty members. Altogether there are 194 baccalaureate, 97 master's, and 15 doctoral programs offered in the University of Puerto Rico System. Profiles of the 4-year colleges are available exclusively on our website, barronspac.com.

UNIVERSITY OF PUERTO RICO RECINTO DE RIO PIEDRAS (*The complete profile is made available exclusively on our website, www.barronspac.com*)

UNIVERSITY OF PUERTO RICO/BAYAMON (*The complete profile is made available exclusively on our website, www.barronspac.com*)

UNIVERSITY OF PUERTO RICO/CAYEY (*The complete profile is made available exclusively on our website, www.barronspac.com*)

UNIVERSITY OF PUERTO RICO/HUMACAO (*The complete profile is made available exclusively on our website, www.barronspac.com*)

UNIVERSITY OF PUERTO RICO/MAYAGUEZ (*The complete profile is made available exclusively on our website, www.barronspac.com*)

UNIVERSITY OF THE SACRED HEART (*The complete profile is made available exclusively on our website, www.barronspac.com*)

RHODE ISLAND

• College Location

0   5   10   15   20
Miles

BROWN UNIVERSITY   C-2
www.brown.edu

Providence, RI 02912   (401) 863-1000

Fax: (401) 863-9300   Email: admission@brown.edu
Full-time: 3041 men, 3200 women   Faculty: 871; I, ++$
Part-time: 16 men, 7 women   Ph.D.s: 100%
Graduate: 1099 men, 995 women   Student/Faculty: 8 to 1
Year: semesters, summer session   Tuition: $47,434
Room & Board: $11,994   Freshman Class: 30431
                                     applied, 2660 accepted,
                                     1561 enrolled
SAT CR/M/W: 730/730/730 ACT: 31   CEEB CODE: 3094
Application Deadline: January 1   MOST COMPETITIVE

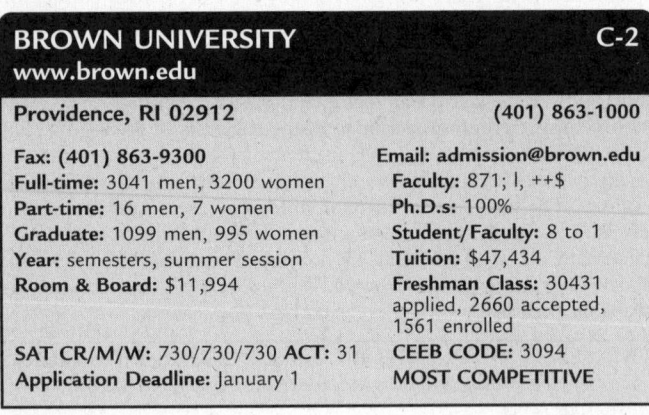

Rhode Island, Brown University is the seventh-oldest college in the United States founded in 1764. Brown is an independent Ivy League institution comprised of undergraduate and graduate programs, plus the Alpert Medical School, School of Public Health, School of Engineering, and School of Professional Studies. There is one undergraduate school and one graduate school. In addition to regional accreditation, Brown has baccalaureate program accreditation with ABET. The 140-acre campus is in an urban area 45 miles south of Boston, MA. Including any residence halls, there are 243 buildings.

STUDENT LIFE: 95% of undergraduates are from out of state, mostly the Northeast. Students are from 50 states, 81 foreign countries, and Canada. 60% are from public schools. 44% are White; 13% Asian American; 12% Foreign; 11% Hispanic. The average age of freshmen is 18; all undergraduates, 20. 3% do not continue beyond their first year; 95% remain to graduate. **Housing:** 4858 students can be accommodated in college housing, which includes single-sex and coed dorms, on-campus apartments, and off-campus apartments. In addition, there are language houses, special-interest houses, fraternity houses, sorority houses, international house, technology house, environmental studies house, and cooperatives. On-campus housing is guaranteed for all 4 years and is available on a lottery system for upperclassmen. 78% of students live on campus. Upperclassmen may keep cars.

FACULTY/CLASSROOMS: 67% of faculty are male; 33% are female. All teach undergraduates. Graduate students teach 5% of introductory courses. The average class size in an introductory lecture is 200; in a laboratory is 20; and in a regular course is 40.

PROGRAMS OF STUDY: Brown confers A.B., and Sc.B. degrees. Master's and Doctoral degrees are also awarded. Bachelor's degrees are awarded in AGRICULTURE (environmental studies), BIOLOGICAL SCIENCE (biochemistry, biology/biological science, biophysics, marine biology, molecular biology, and neurosciences), BUSINESS (entrepreneurial studies), COMMUNICATIONS AND THE ARTS (American literature, art, art history and appreciation, classics, comparative literature, English, linguistics, media arts, music, performing arts, Portuguese, and visual and performing arts), COMPUTER AND PHYSICAL SCIENCE (applied mathematics, chemical physics, chemistry, computer science, geology, mathematics, physics, and statistics), EDUCATION (education), ENGINEERING AND ENVIRONMENTAL DESIGN (architectural history, architectural technology, architecture, computational sciences, engineering, and environmental science), HEALTH PROFESSIONS (biomedical science and community health work), SOCIAL SCIENCE (African studies, African American studies, American studies, anthropology, archeology, classical/ancient civilization, cognitive science, developmental psychology, East Asian studies, economics, ethnic studies, French studies, gender studies, German area studies, Hispanic American studies, history, human development, international relations, Italian studies, Judaic studies, Latin American studies, medieval studies, Middle Eastern studies, philosophy, political science/government, psychology, public administration, religion, Russian and Slavic studies, science and society, sociology, South Asian studies, and urban studies). Biological Sciences, Economics, and History have the largest enrollments.

ACTIVITIES: 18% of men belong to 11 national fraternities; 8% of women belong to 4 national sororities. There are 400 groups on campus, including ethnic groups, volunteer, art, band, cheerleading, chess, choir, chorale, chorus, computers, dance, debate, drama, environmental, ethnic, film, gay, honors, international, jazz band, literary magazine, marching band, musical theater, newspaper, opera, orchestra, photography, political, professional, public service, radio and TV, religious, social, social service, student government, symphony, and yearbook. Popular campus events include Commencement, Spring Weekend, and Family Weekend. **Sports:** There are 17 intercollegiate sports for men and 21 for women, and 19 intramural sports for men and 19 for women. Facilities include a 25,000-seat stadium, Olympic-size pool, 6-lane track, hockey rink, playing fields, weight-training rooms, facilities for wrestling, and courts for squash, handball, racquetball, tennis, basketball, and volleyball. **Graduates:** From July 1, 2013 to June 30, 2014, 1594 bachelor's degrees were awarded. The most popular majors were economics (10%), biological sciences (10%), and history (4%). In an average class, 83% graduate in 4 years or less, 94% graduate in 5 years or less, and 95% graduate in 6 years or less. Of the 2013 graduating class, 22% were enrolled in graduate school within 6 months of graduation, and 65% were employed.

SERVICES: Counseling and information services are available, as is tutoring in most subjects. There is a reader service for the blind. Other services include class note taking, books on tape, diagnostic testing services, oral tests, tutors, and untimed tests. **Library/Resources:** The 6 libraries contain 4.2 million volumes, 2.0 million microform items, 98,000 audio/video tapes/CDs/DVDs, and subscribe to 123,540 periodicals including electronic. Computerized library services include interlibrary loans, database searching, Internet access, and Wi-Fi capability. Special learning facilities include an art gallery, planetarium, radio station, TV station, an anthropology museum. **Physically Challenged Students:** Facilities include wheelchair ramps, elevators, special parking, specially equipped restrooms, special class scheduling, lowered drinking fountains, and special housing. **Special:** Students may cross-register with Rhode Island School of Design (RISD) or study abroad in any of 120 programs in 11 countries. A combined A.B. - S.C.B. degree is possible in any major field with five years of study. Dual and student-designed majors and community internships are available. Students may pursue five year programs in the arts or sciences, or the eight year Program in the Liberal Medical Education continuum or the five year Brown/RISD dual degree program. There are 3 national honor societies, including Phi Beta Kappa, and 45 departmental honors programs. **Visiting:** There are regularly scheduled orientations for prospective students, including Group Information Sessions are usually conducted Monday through Friday at 10:15 a.m. and 2:15 p.m. from mid-February through November and on Saturday mornings from mid-September to mid-November. There are guides for informal visits and visitors may sit in on classes. **Campus Safety and Security:** Measures include 24-hour foot and vehicle patrol, emergency notification system, self-defense education, and security escort services. There are shuttle buses, emergency telephones, lighted pathways/sidewalks, controlled access to dorms/residences, SafeWALK and SafeRIDE programs.

REQUIREMENTS: The SAT or ACT is required. The ACT Optional Writing test is also required. Applicants must be graduates of accredited high schools. Preparation is expected to include courses in English, foreign language, math, lab science, the arts (music or art), and history. A personal essay is required, as are two teacher recommendations. Students must take either the SAT or the ACT. They may submit the SAT along with any 2 SAT Subject tests or they may submit the ACT with Writing. The high school transcript is the central criterion for admission. AP credits are accepted. Important factors in the admissions decision are advanced placement or honors courses, evidence of special talent, and personality/intangible qualities.To graduate, students must pass 30 courses in eight semesters, including 8 to 21 courses in the major. Students must also demonstrate writing proficiency. With the exception of required courses in the major, there are no distribution requirements or specific required courses. **Procedure:** Freshmen are admitted fall. Entrance exams should be taken in the junior or senior year. There are early decision and deferred admissions plans. Early decision applications should be filed by November 1; regular applications, by January 1 for fall entry, along with a $75 fee. Notification of early decision is sent December 15; regular decision, March 31. 583 early decision candidates were accepted for the 2014-2015 class. Applications are accepted on-line. **Transfer Students:** 116 transfer students enrolled in 2013-2014. Transfer applicants must submit high school and college transcripts, two recommendations from college professors, scores on the ACT or on the SAT and any two SAT Subject tests, a letter of good standing, and a personal essay. 15 of 30 credits required for the bachelor's degree must be completed at Brown. **International Students:** There are 794 international students enrolled. The school actively recruits these students. They must take the TOEFL with a minimum score of 100 on the Internet-based version (iBT), If a student receives at least a 600 on their SAT Critical Reading, they need not take the TOEFL. They must also take the SAT or ACT. Brown requires the SAT and two subjects, or the ACT with writing.

ADMISSIONS: 9% of the 2014-2015 applicants were accepted. The SAT scores for the 2014-2015 freshman class were: Critical Reading--6% between 500 and 599, 28% between 600 and 699, and 66% between 700 and 800; Math--5% between 500 and 599, 28% between 600 and 699, and 67% between 700 and 800; Writing--5% between 500 and 599, 27% between 600 and 699, and 68% between 700 and 800. The ACT scores were 3% between 21 and 23, 10% between 24 and 26, 12% between 27 and 28, and 74% above 28. 97% of the current freshmen were in the top fifth of their class; 100% were in the top two fifths. 155 freshmen graduated first in their class. **Admissions Contact:** James S. Miller, Dean of Admission. E-Mail: *admission@brown.edu* Web: *www.brown.edu*

FINANCIAL AID: In 2014-2015, 65% of all full-time freshmen and 57% of continuing full-time students received some form of financial aid. 48% of all full-time freshmen and 46% of continuing full-time students received need-based aid. The average freshman award was $44,268. Need-based scholarships or need-based grants averaged $40,005 ($65,919 maximum); and need-based self-help aid (loans and jobs) averaged $4,251 ($7,750 maximum). 52% of undergraduate students work part-time. Average annual earnings from campus work are $1400. The average financial indebtedness of the 2014 graduate was $24,301. Brown is a member of CSS. The CSS/Profile and FAFSA, and some state forms are required. The deadline for filing freshman financial aid applications for fall entry is January 1.

BRYANT UNIVERSITY C-2
www.bryant.edu

Smithfield, RI 02917

Fax: (401) 232-6741
Full-time: 1324 men, 1876 women
Part-time: 41 men, 46 women
Graduate: 75 men, 92 women
Year: semesters, summer session
Room & Board: $13,240

SAT CR/M/W: 550/585/545 ACT: 25
Application Deadline: n/av

(401) 232-6100
(800) 622-7001
Email: admission@bryant.edu
Faculty: n/av; IIB, ++$
Ph.D.s: 82%
Student/Faculty: 18 to 1
Tuition: $35,939
Freshman Class: 6013 applied, 4603 accepted, 890 enrolled
CEEB CODE: 3095
VERY COMPETITIVE

Bryant University has earned a distinguished reputation for innovative academic programs and technology that are marketplace driven and highly attuned to the emerging needs of industry and society. Bryant's close-knit, student-centered community of scholars delivers challenging academic programs that integrate business and the arts and sciences, with an emphasis on real-world application and a global perspective. Abundant co-curricular opportunities, service learning programs, internships, and practicums allow students to put theory into practice while building character and leadership skills. There are 2 undergraduate schools and 3 graduate schools. In addition to regional accreditation, Bryant has baccalaureate program accreditation with AACSB. The library contains 256,241 volumes, 14,541 microform items, 2,293 audio/video tapes/CDs/DVDs, and subscribes to 70,129 periodicals including electronic. Computerized library services include interlibrary loans, database searching, Internet access, and Wi-Fi capability. Special learning facilities include a radio station, TV station, information and technology, C.V. Star Financial Markets center, Stepan Grand Hall, Cerce Multi Media Wall; Douglas and Judith Krupp Library, Mahre Periodical Center; Koffler Technology Center and Communications Complex, Janikies Memorial Auditiorium; Koffler Rotunda multimedia student exhibition space; John H. Chafee Center for International Business; Center for Global and Regional Economic Studies; Intercultural Center; Gertrude Meth Hochberg Women's Center; Ronald K. and Kati C. Machtley Interfaith Center; Center for Student Invovlement. The 428-acre campus is in a suburban area 10 miles northwest of Providence, 45 miles southwest of Boston, 190 miles from New York City. Including any residence halls, there are 54 buildings.

STUDENT LIFE: 85% of undergraduates are from out of state, mostly the Northeast. Students are from 31 states, 65 foreign countries, and Canada. 73% are from public schools. 83% are White. The average age of freshmen is 18; all undergraduates, 20. 13% do not continue beyond their first year; 76% remain to graduate.

FACULTY/CLASSROOMS: 58% of faculty are male; 42% are female. 99% teach undergraduates, 55% do research, and 55% do both. No introductory courses are taught by graduate students. The average class size in an introductory lecture is 26; in a laboratory is 12; and in a regular course is 24.

PROGRAMS OF STUDY: Bryant confers B.A, B.S., B.S.B.A., B.S.I.B. and B.Sc.I.T. degrees. Master's degrees are also awarded. Bachelor's degrees are awarded in BIOLOGICAL SCIENCE (biology/biological science and forensic science), BUSINESS (accounting, applied economics / management, banking and finance, business administration and management, business communications, business data processing, business economics, business information systems, business intelligence and analytics, business law, business statistics, business systems analysis, economics – statistics, entrepreneurial studies, finance, financial services, global/general management, global management, human resources, international accounting, international business, international business information systems, international business management, international economics, investments and securities, international entrepreneurial management, international finance, international marketing, international supply and value chain management, logistics, management information systems, management science, marketing, marketing and distribution, marketing management, marketing/retailing/merchandising, nonprofit/public organization management, and supply chain management),

COMMUNICATIONS AND THE ARTS (art and design, art/visual culture, Chinese, communication design , communication, communication studies, communications, communication rhetoric/communication, communication science, comparative literature, English, foreign language, French, information technology, literature, modern language, and Spanish), COMPUTER AND PHYSICAL SCIENCE (actuarial science, actuarial mathematics, applied mathematics, computer management, computer information technology, computer information systems, information sciences and systems, information science, informatics and computer science, mathematics, mathematics - actuarial concentration, mathematics/computational, mathematics – economics, and statistics), EDUCATION (business education, education, education administration, educational statistics and research, English education, foreign languages education, mathematics education, and sports studies), ENGINEERING AND ENVIRONMENTAL DESIGN (computational sciences and environmental science), HEALTH PROFESSIONS (biology), SOCIAL SCIENCE (American studies, applied psychology, applied social science, community services, economics, feminist, gender, sexuality studies, forensic studies, gender studies, (Social Science) Global Studies, history, international studies, law, legal studies, political science/government, prelaw, psychology, public affairs, and sociology). Accounting, finance, international business, marketing, actuarial math, communications, and entrepreneurship have the largest enrollments.

ACTIVITIES: 6% of men belong to 5 national fraternities; 7% of women belong to 5 national sororities. There are 111 groups on campus, including cultural, sports and recreation, art, band, cheerleading, chess, choir, chorale, chorus, communications, computers, dance, debate, drama, drill team, environmental, ethnic, film, forensics, gay, honors, international, jazz band, literary magazine, media, musical theater, newspaper, orchestra, pep band, photography, political, professional, radio and TV, religious, social, social service, student government, and yearbook. Popular campus events include Reunion at Homecoming, Spring Weekend, Festival of Lights, REDay, International Education Week, SASS, RI Special Olympics, Women's Summit, i2i Cultural Fashion Show and Up 'Til Dawn Benefit.

SERVICES: Counseling and information services are available, as is tutoring in most subjects. The Academic Center for Excellence offers tutoring for all currently enrolled students at Bryant and is certified by the College Reading and Learning Association.

REQUIREMENTS: Accredited high school diploma or GED. High school general college prepatory program. Academic units: 4 English, 4 Math, 2 Lab Science, 2 Foreign Language, 2 History. Very important: rigor of high school record, GPA. Important: class rank, standardized test scores, application essay, recommendations. AP and CLEP credits are accepted.

ADMISSIONS: 77% of a recent year applicants were accepted. The SAT scores for a recent year freshman class were: Critical Reading--18% below 500, 59% between 500 and 599, 20% between 600 and 699, and 3% between 700 and 800; Math--8% below 500, 48% between 500 and 599, 37% between 600 and 699, and 7% between 700 and 800; Writing--22% below 500, 53% between 500 and 599, 23% between 600 and 699, and 2% between 700 and 800. The ACT scores were 26% between 21 and 23, and 74% above 28. 43% of the current freshmen were in the top fifth of their class; 77% were in the top two fifths. 1 freshman graduated first in the class.

FINANCIAL AID: The average freshman award was $23,109. Need-based scholarships or need-based grants averaged $11,816; need-based self-help aid (loans and jobs) averaged $5,005; non-need-based athletic scholarships averaged $17,835; other non-need-based awards and non-need-based scholarships averaged $3,862; and $12,412 from other forms of aid. The average financial indebtedness of the 2013 graduate was $44,580. Bryant is a member of CSS. The FAFSA is required. Check with the school for current application deadlines.

JOHNSON & WALES UNIVERSITY/ PROVIDENCE CAMPUS

C-2

www.jwu.edu/providence

Providence, RI 02903	(401) 598-1000
	(800) 342-5598
Fax: (401) 598-1171	**Email:** admissions.pvd@jwu.edu
Full-time: 3333 men, 4913 women	**Faculty:** 264
Part-time: 230 men, 370 women	**Ph.D.s:** 25%
Graduate: 291 men, 491 women	**Student/Faculty:** 15 to 1
Year: trimesters, summer session	**Tuition:** $29,576
Room & Board: n/app	**Freshman Class:** 11899 applied, 9656 accepted, 1952 enrolled
	CEEB CODE: 3465
Application Deadline: n/av	**COMPETITIVE**

Johnson & Wales University/Providence Campus, founded in 1914, is the largest of the JWU campuses and offers more than 50 majors in business, hospitality, culinary arts, technology, and graduate programs. There are 4 undergraduate schools and 2 graduate schools. The 166-acre campus is in a small town in Providence, 45 minutes from Boston, Cape Cod, and Newport and 3 hours from New York. Including any residence halls, there are 38 buildings.

STUDENT LIFE: 81% of undergraduates are from out of state, mostly the Northeast. Students are from 50 states, 91 foreign countries, and Canada. 58% are White. **Female To Male Ratio:** 1.5:1. The average age of freshmen is 18; all undergraduates, 21. **Housing:** College-sponsored housing includes coed dorms and on-campus apartments, apartments for single students, special housing for disabled, and wellness housing. On-campus housing is available on a lottery system for upperclassmen. 70% of students commute. Alcohol is not permitted. All students may keep cars.

FACULTY/CLASSROOMS: 56% of faculty are male; 44% are female. 95% teach undergraduates. No introductory courses are taught by graduate students.

PROGRAMS OF STUDY: JWU confers B.S. degrees. Associate, master's, and doctoral degrees are also awarded. Bachelor's degrees are awarded in AGRICULTURE (equine science), BUSINESS (accounting, business administration and management, entrepreneurial studies, fashion merchandising, hospitality management services, hotel/motel and restaurant management, international business management, management information systems, marketing and distribution, marketing management, marketing/retailing/merchandising, office supervision and management, recreation and leisure services, recreational facilities management, retailing, secretarial studies/office management, small business management, sports management, tourism, and transportation and travel marketing), COMMUNICATIONS AND THE ARTS (advertising), COMPUTER AND PHYSICAL SCIENCE (computer management, computer science, information sciences and systems, systems analysis, and web services), EDUCATION (marketing and distribution education), ENGINEERING AND ENVIRONMENTAL DESIGN (electrical/electronics engineering, food services technology, and technological management), SOCIAL SCIENCE (clothing and textiles management/production/services, criminal justice, food production/management/services, paralegal studies, parks and recreation management, and systems science). Culinary arts, hotel/restaurant management, and marketing are the strongest academically. Culinary arts, hotel/restaurant management, and sports entertainment event management have the largest enrollments.

ACTIVITIES: 2% of men belong to 9 national fraternities; 2% of women belong to 7 national sororities. There are 65 groups on campus, including cheerleading, computers, dance, debate, drama, environmental, ethnic, gay, honors, international, Multicultural clubs, musical theater, newspaper, pep band, political, professional, religious, social, social service, student government, and yearbook. **Sports:** There is no sports program at JWU. Facilities include state-of-the-art exercise machines and numerous programs, including weight management, personal exercise, wellness programs, body composition analysis, strength training, physical fitness testing, nutritional analysis, physical fitness assessments, life saving, and stress relief days. **Graduates:** From July 1, 2013 to June 30, 2014, 1884 bachelor's degrees were awarded. The most popular majors were business/marketing (42%), family and consumer sciences (24%), and parks and recreation (10%).

SERVICES: Counseling and information services are available, as is tutoring in every subject. Workshops in stress and time management and wellness and learning centers are available. **Library/Resources:** The 2 libraries contain 108,706 volumes, 439,822 microform items, and 3,832 audio/video tapes/CDs/DVDs, and subscribe to 26,160 periodicals including electronic. Computerized library services include interlibrary loans, database searching, Internet access, and Wi-Fi capability. Special learning facilities include a **Physically Challenged Students:** All of the campus is accessible. Facilities include wheelchair ramps, elevators, special parking, specially equipped restrooms, special class scheduling, lowered drinking fountains, and lowered telephones. **Special:** The university offers 11-week internships in most majors, study abroad in 19 countries, work-study programs, accelerated degree programs, and dual majors. Students have the opportunity to receive hands-on experience through 2 JWU programs: Summer Work Experience (SWEP) and Cooperative Education. There is 1 national honor society, a freshman honors program, and 5 departmental honors programs. **Visiting:** There are regularly scheduled orientations for prospective students, including tours conducted by JWU students. These tours include an introduction to the academic and social aspects of the campus experience through interactive sessions. There are guides for informal visits, visitors may sit in on classes, and stay overnight. To schedule a visit, contact the Admissions Office. **Campus Safety and Security:** Measures include 24-hour foot and vehicle patrol and security escort services. There are shuttle buses, emergency telephones, lighted pathways/sidewalks, 24-hour dorm coverage, a phone hot line for campus emergencies, and crime alerts in the student weekly newspaper.

REQUIREMENTS: Although SAT and ACT scores are required only for students applying for honors admissions, students who have taken these tests are encouraged to submit their scores. GED is accepted. Applicants must complete 4 years of English, 3 years each of Mathematics and Science, and 2 years of social studies. AP and CLEP credits are accepted. Important factors in the admissions decision are advanced placement or honors courses, extracurricular activities record, evidence of special talent, personality/intangible qualities, recommendations by alumni, and recommendations by school officials. To graduate, students must complete 180 quarter credit hours, including at least 36 in the major, with a minimum GPA of 2.0. Required classes include English, math, history, economics, science, psychology, sociology, and professional development. **Procedure:** There are deferred admissions and rolling admissions plans. Application deadlines are open. **Transfer Students:** Applicants are required to submit official high school and college transcripts and must have earned a minimum college GPA of 2.0. 45 of 180 credits required for the bachelor's degree must be completed at JWU. **International Students:** There are 949 international students enrolled. The school actively recruits these students.

ADMISSIONS: 81% of the 2014-2015 applicants were accepted. **Admissions Contact:** William Priante, Dean of Admissions. E-Mail: *admissions.pvd@jwu.edu* Web: *www.jwu.edu/providence*

FINANCIAL AID: Check with the school for current application deadlines.

PROVIDENCE COLLEGE · C-2
www.providence.edu

Providence, RI 02918	
	(401) 865-1000
	(800) 721-6444
Fax: (401) 865-2826	Email: pcadmiss@providence.edu
Full-time: 1671 men, 2195 women	Faculty: 296
Part-time: 137 men, 173 women	Ph.D.s: 94%
Graduate: 231 men, 280 women	Student/Faculty: 13 to 1
Year: semesters, summer session	Tuition: $44,323
Room & Board: $13,060	Freshman Class: 8973 applied, 5657 accepted, 1030 enrolled
SAT CR/M/W: 560/580/580 ACT: 25	CEEB CODE: 3693
Application Deadline: January 15	VERY COMPETITIVE

Providence College is a primarily undergraduate, liberal arts, independent, not-for-profit, Catholic institution of higher education. Committed to fostering academic excellence through the sciences and humanities, the college provides a variety of opportunities for intellectual, social, moral, and spiritual growth in a supportive environment. There are 4 undergraduate schools and 3 graduate schools. In addition to regional accreditation, PC has baccalaureate program accreditation with AACSB, CSWE, NASM, and ACS. The 105-acre campus is in a suburban area 50 miles south of Boston. Including any residence halls, there are 46 buildings.

STUDENT LIFE: 87% of undergraduates are from out of state, mostly the Northeast. Students are from 41 states, 27 foreign countries, and Canada. 77% are White. 71% are Catholic; 16% claim no religious affiliation. The average age of freshmen is 18; all undergraduates, 20. 8% do not continue beyond their first year; 86% remain to graduate. **Housing:** 2975 students can be accommodated in college housing, which includes single-sex and coed dorms and on-campus apartments. Housing for freshman and sophomore years only. On-campus housing is available on a first-come, first-served basis, and is available on a lottery system for upperclassmen. 72% of students live on campus; of those, 90% remain on campus on weekends. Upperclassmen may keep cars.

FACULTY/CLASSROOMS: 59% of faculty are male; 41% are female. All teach undergraduates. No introductory courses are taught by graduate students. The average class size in an introductory lecture is 20; in a laboratory is 18; and in a regular course is 20.

PROGRAMS OF STUDY: PC confers B.A., and B.S. degrees. Associate and Master's degrees are also awarded. Bachelor's degrees are awarded in BIOLOGICAL SCIENCE (biochemistry and biology/biological science), BUSINESS (accounting, business administration and management, business economics, finance, management and strategic leadership, marketing management, and organizational leadership and management), COMMUNICATIONS AND THE ARTS (art history, dramatic arts, English, French, German, Italian, music, painting, photography, printmaking, sculpture, Spanish, studio art, and theatre arts), COMPUTER AND PHYSICAL SCIENCE (applied physics, chemistry, computer science, and mathematics), EDUCATION (elementary education, English education, foreign languages education, global studies, mathematics education, music education, secondary education, social studies education, and special education), ENGINEERING AND ENVIRONMENTAL DESIGN (preengineering), HEALTH PROFESSIONS (health administration and policy), SOCIAL SCIENCE (American studies, community services, economics, fire science, history, humanities, liberal arts/general studies, philosophy, political science/government, psychology, social science, social work, sociology, theological studies, and women's studies). Biology, business and chemistry are the strongest academically. Marketing, finance, and biology have the largest enrollments.

ACTIVITIES: There are 120 groups on campus, including club and intramural sports, art, band, cheerleading, chess, chorale, dance, debate, drama, environmental, ethnic, film, gay, honors, international, jazz band, literary magazine, mock trial, musical theater, newspaper, pep band, political, professional, radio and TV, religious, social, social service, student government, and yearbook. Popular campus events include Late Night Madness, Clam Jam and Provapalooza. **Sports:** There are 7 intercollegiate sports for men and 10 for women, and 15 intramural sports for men and 15 for women. Facilities include an ice arena, indoor track, tennis courts, basketball courts, volleyball court, pool, two intercollegiate strength and conditioning facilities, softball field, outdoor track, 2 outdoor artificial fields, and 1 outdoor grass field. **Graduates:** From July 1, 2013 to June 30, 2014, 1100 bachelor's degrees were awarded. The most popular majors were marketing (11%), accountancy (9%), and finance (9%). 349 companies recruited on campus in 2013-2014. In an average class, 83% graduate in 4 years or less, 86% graduate in 5 years or less, and 86% graduate in 6 years or less. Of the 2013 graduating class, 20% were enrolled in graduate school within 6 months of graduation, and 53% were employed.

SERVICES: Counseling and information services are available, as is tutoring in most subjects. Assistance with time management and study skills **Library/Resources:** The library contains 410,012 volumes, 199,683 microform items, 3,126 audio/video tapes/CDs/DVDs, and subscribes to 52,681 periodicals including electronic. Computerized library services include interlibrary loans, database searching, Internet access, and Wi-Fi capability. Special learning facilities include an art gallery, radio station, TV station, Blackfriars Theater, Smith Center for the Arts, Science Center Complex, Ruane Center for the Humanities, Smith Hill Annex- a community learning space, computer and language labs. **Physically Challenged Students:** 90% of the campus is accessible. Facilities include wheelchair ramps, elevators, special parking, specially equipped restrooms, lowered drinking fountains, and special housing. **Special:** Providence College offers internships in a variety of fields, including politics, broadcasting, journalism and business. Study abroad is available to students in every major. PC approves over 350 study abroad program options in more than 50 different countries. Also available are student-designed majors, a 3-2 engineering program with Columbia University or Washington University in St. Louis, non-degree study, a Washington semester, work-study, B.A.-B.S. degrees and pass/fail options. There are 21 national honor societies, a freshman honors program, and 16 departmental honors programs. **Visiting:** There are regularly scheduled orientations for prospective students, including campus tours and information sessions. Visitors may sit in on classes. To schedule a visit, contact the Admissions Office at pcadmiss@providence.edu. **Campus Safety and Security:** Measures include 24-hour foot and vehicle patrol, emergency notification system, self-defense education, and security escort services. There are shuttle buses, emergency telephones, lighted pathways/sidewalks, and controlled access to dorms/residences.

REQUIREMENTS: Applicants must be graduates of an accredited secondary school. An unweighted GPA of 3.25 in a rigorous curriculum is recommended. High school preparation should include 4 years of English, 4 years of math, 3 years of 1 foreign language, 3 years of science with at least 2 years of lab science, 2 years of history/social studies, and 2 other academic subjects. An essay and 2 academic letters of recommendation are required. Submission of standardized tests is optional. AP credits are accepted. Important factors in the admissions decision are advanced placement or honors courses, extracurricular activities record, and personality/intangible qualities.To graduate, all students must complete at least 120 credit hours including all requirements for the student's major, and maintain an overall and major GPA of at least 2.0. Students must also meet all core requirements, including 16 credits in Development of Western Civilization, 6 credits in theology, 6 credits in philosophy (3 in ethics and 3 in a non-ethics philosophy course), 3 credits each in natural science, social science, fine arts and quantitative reasoning. Courses in the major or elective courses must include two intensive writing courses, as well as courses which address oral communication skills, diversity and civic engagement, and a set of two linked courses outside the major. **Procedure:** Freshmen are admitted fall and spring. Entrance exams should be taken by February 15. There are early decision, early admissions, and deferred admissions plans. Early decision applications should be filed by December 1; regular applications, by January 15 for fall entry; and December 1 for spring entry, along with a $65 fee. Notifications are sent April 1. 135 early decision candidates were accepted for the 2014-2015 class. 1936 applicants were on the 2014 waiting list; 163 were admitted. Applications are accepted on-line. **Transfer Students:** 68 transfer students enrolled in 2013-2014. Students must complete the Common Application and forms for Transfer students, and submit a final official high school transcript, college transcript(s), essay, statement of good standing from prior institution(s) and a minimum college grade point average of 3.0 on a 4.0 scale. Submission of standardized tests is optional. Class syllabi should be sent to syllabi@providence.edu for transfer credit evaluation. Transfer student policies listed apply to our traditional undergraduate day school only. However, we also have a School of Continuing Education that enrolls transfer students and they are included in our above transfer student totals. The School of Continuing Education has a variety of different transfer credit policies and requirements. If applying to our School of Continuing Education program, please contact them directly for guidelines. 60 of 120 credits required for the bachelor's degree must be completed at PC. **International Students:** There are 81 international students enrolled. The school actively recruits these students. They must take the TOEFL with a minimum score of 90 on the Internet-based version (iBT), or take the IELTS.

ADMISSIONS: 63% of the 2014-2015 applicants were accepted. The SAT scores for the 2014-2015 freshman class were: Critical Reading--18% below 500, 49% between 500 and 599, 29% between 600 and 699, and 5% between 700 and 800; Math--16% below 500, 40% between 500 and 599, 38% between 600 and 699, and 6% between 700 and 800; Writing--15% below 500, 41% between 500 and 599, 37% between 600 and 699, and 8% between 700 and 800. The ACT scores were 9% below 21, 21% between 21 and 23, 34% between 24 and 26, 15% between 27 and 28, and 22% above 28. 52% of the current freshmen were in the top fifth of their class; 85% were in the top two fifths. 15 freshmen graduated first in their class. **Admissions Contact:** Raul A. Fonts, Dean of Admission. E-Mail: *pcadmiss@ providence.edu* Web: *www.providence.edu*

FINANCIAL AID: In 2014-2015, 81% of all full-time freshmen and 80% of continuing full-time students received some form of financial aid. 56% of all full-time freshmen and 55% of continuing full-time students received need-based aid. Average annual earnings from campus work are $2075. The average financial indebtedness of the 2014 graduate was $32,475. PC is a member of CSS. The CSS/Profile and FAFSA, and In lieu of Business/Farm supplement business tax returns (schedules) are required. are required. The priority date for freshman financial aid applications for fall entry is February 1. The deadline for filing freshman financial aid applications for fall entry is February 1.

RHODE ISLAND COLLEGE *(The complete profile is made available exclusively on our website, www.barronspac.com)*

RHODE ISLAND SCHOOL OF DESIGN   C-2
www.risd.edu

Providence, RI 02903	(401) 454-6100
	(800) 364-7473
Fax: (401) 454-6309	Email: admissions@risd.edu
Full-time: 671 men, 1343 women	Faculty: 155
Part-time: n/av	Ph.D.s: 72%
Graduate: 151 men, 284 women	Student/Faculty: 13 to 1
Year: 4-1-4	Tuition: $44,594
Room & Board: $12,640	Freshman Class: 3047 applied, 827 accepted, 465 enrolled
	CEEB CODE: 3726
Application Deadline: February 1	MOST COMPETITIVE

Each year students from around the world pursue a creative, studio-based education at RISD, which offers rigorous bachelor's and master's degree programs in 19 architecture, design, fine arts and art education majors. There is 1 undergraduate school and 1 graduate school. In addition to regional accreditation, RISD has baccalaureate program accreditation with NAAB, NASAD, NEASC, and LAAB. The 18-acre campus is in an urban area 52 miles south of Boston and 180 miles from New York City. Including any residence halls, there are 51 buildings.

STUDENT LIFE: 96% of undergraduates are from out of state, mostly the Northeast. Students are from 44 states, 47 foreign countries, and Canada. 55% are from public schools. 32% are White; 26% Foreign; 18% Asian American. The average age of freshmen is 18; all undergraduates, 20. 6% do not continue beyond their first year; 88% remain to graduate. **Housing:** 1528 students can be accommodated in college housing, which includes coed dorms, on-campus apartments, and married student housing. On-campus housing is guaranteed for the freshman year only and is available on a lottery system for upperclassmen. 60% of students live on campus; of those, 99% remain on campus on weekends. Alcohol is not permitted. No one may keep cars.

FACULTY/CLASSROOMS: 55% of faculty are male; 45% are female. All teach undergraduates. No introductory courses are taught by graduate students. The average class size in an introductory lecture is 20 and in a laboratory is 17.

PROGRAMS OF STUDY: RISD confers B.Arch., and B.F.A. degrees. Master's degrees are also awarded. Bachelor's degrees are awarded in COMMUNICATIONS AND THE ARTS (apparel design, ceramic art and design, film arts, glass, graphic design, illustration, industrial design, metal/jewelry, painting, photography, printmaking, and sculpture), ENGINEERING AND ENVIRONMENTAL DESIGN (architecture, furniture design, and interior design), SOCIAL SCIENCE (textiles and clothing). Fine arts and design is the strongest academically. Illustration, Industrial Design and Graphic Design have the largest enrollments.

ACTIVITIES: There are 73 groups on campus, including design guild, E-ship, expose, programming board, STEAM, art, chorale, computers, dance, drama, environmental, ethnic, film, gay, international, literary magazine, musical theater, newspaper, photography, political, professional, professional orgs: 2nd life, religious, social, social service, student government, and yearbook. Popular campus events include Student and Alumni Sale, Artists Ball, RISD By Design, Take-A-Break, RISD LEADS, MLK Week, and ReDesign Thanksgiving. **Sports:** There is 1 intercollegiate sports for men and 1 for women, and 1 intramural sports for men and 1 for women. Facilities include RISD's Catanzaro Student Fitness Center has areas and equipment for dance, aerobics, weight and fitness training. Students may also enroll in activity classes at Brown University and use its athletic complex which includes a swimming pool, an ice skating rink, a track, weight training equipment, and courts for basketball, tennis, and squash. The Brown University facilities are utilized by RISD students and student clubs, and some of their clubs and organizations also have Brown/RISD student members. Tillinghast Farm provides over 34 acres of open space on Narragansett Bay for members of the RISD community interested in fresh air, quiet spaces, pick-up games, swimming, picnics and more. **Graduates:** From July 1, 2013 to June 30, 2014, 519 bachelor's degrees were awarded. The most popular majors were illustration (14%), industrial design (14%), and architecture (11%). 257 companies recruited on campus in 2013-2014. In an average class, 88% graduate in 6 years or less.

SERVICES: There is a reader service for the blind. The RISD Writing Center provides free peer tutoring in writing to all RISD students **Library/Resources:** The library contains 153,693 volumes, 1,855 microform items, 5,290 audio/video tapes/CDs/DVDs, and subscribes to 981 periodicals including electronic. Computerized library services include interlibrary loans, database searching, Internet access, and Wi-Fi capability. Special learning facilities include an art gallery, The Edna Lawrence Nature Lab has more than 80,000 specimens and other items of natural history. The RISD Museum of Art is an integral part of the institution and the principal art museum for the city, state, and southeastern New England. There are student and department galleries throughout the school. **Physically Challenged Students:** 23% of the campus is accessible. Facilities include wheelchair ramps, elevators, special parking, specially equipped restrooms, special class scheduling, and special housing. **Special:** RISD offers cross-registration with Brown University, as well as a Brown/RISD Dual Degree Program. Study off-campus is available in the U.S. through the AICAD mobility program; abroad at 75 institutions in 25 countries throughout Europe, Asia and South and Central America; our own European Honors Program in Rome; and travel courses during RISD's mid-year Wintersession. Students may elect a concentration in one of the Liberal Arts departments (History of Art and Visual Culture, Literary Arts and Studies, or History, Philosophy and the Social Sciences); or a new cross-divisional concentration, Nature-Culture Sustainability Studies. Credit-bearing internships are available during Wintersession, Summer and, in some departments, during Fall and Spring semesters. **Visiting:** There are regularly scheduled orientations for prospective students, Presentation by members of admissions staff and a student-guided tour of campus. Visitors may sit in on classes. To schedule a visit, contact the Admissions Office at admissions@risd.edu. **Campus Safety and Security:** Measures include 24-hour foot and vehicle patrol, emergency notification system, self-defense education, and security escort services. There are shuttle buses, lighted pathways/sidewalks, controlled access to dorms/residences, Security escort on a case-by-case basis, and building access cards.

REQUIREMENTS: SAT or ACT scores must be submitted. Applicants must be graduates of an accredited secondary school or have a GED. Academic transcripts, writing samples, assigned drawings, a portfolio, and a statement of purpose are also required. Up to 3 letters of recommendation are recommended. All applicants who speak English as a second language, including US citizens, must submit results from either TOEFL or IELTS. AP credits are accepted. Important factors in the admissions decision are evidence of special talent.To graduate, all students must complete at least 126 credit hours, including 54 in the major, 42 in Liberal Arts, 18 in the freshman Foundation program, and 12 in non-major, art department electives. Liberal Arts credits must include 12 each in History of Art and Visual Culture and electives, and 9 each in Literary Arts and Sciences and History/Philosophy/Social Science. Core courses include 2 semesters each of Foundation Drawing, Design, and Spatial Dynamics. A minimum GPA of 2.0 and, for many majors, completion of the final-year degree project are required. **Procedure:** Freshmen are admitted fall and spring. Entrance exams should be taken at least 6 weeks before the application deadline. There are early decision, early admissions, and deferred admissions plans. Early decision applications should be filed by November 1; regular applications, by February 1 for fall entry, along with a $60 fee. Notification of early decision is sent December 1; regular decision, March 15. Applications are accepted on-line. **Transfer Students:** 64 transfer students enrolled in 2013-2014. Applicants must have at least 27 college credits and should submit an essay along with academic transcripts from the previous 3 years. All students must submit a portfolio and complete a drawing assignment. Letters of recommendation are recommended. The SAT or ACT is required for architecture and industrial design applicants. 66 of 126 credits required for the bachelor's degree must be completed at RISD. **International Students:** There are 519 international students enrolled. The school actively recruits these students. They must take the TOEFL with a minimum score of 93 on the Internet-based version (iBT), or take the IELTS. They must also take the SAT or ACT.

ADMISSIONS: 27% of the 2014-2015 applicants were accepted. The SAT scores for the 2014-2015 freshman class were: Critical Reading--13% below 500, 29% between 500 and 599, 41% between 600 and 699, and 17% between 700 and 800; Math--5% below 500, 25% between 500 and 599, 38% between 600 and 699, and 31% between 700 and 800; Writing--8% below 500, 27% between 500 and 599, 45% between 600 and 699, and 20% between 700 and 800. The ACT scores were 5% between 21 and 23, 25% between 24 and 26, 18% between 27 and 28, and 53% above 28. **Admissions Contact:** Edward Newhall, Associate Vice President for Enrollment. E-Mail: *admissions@risd.edu* Web: *www.risd.edu*

FINANCIAL AID: 60% of undergraduate students work part-time. Average annual earnings from campus work are $1131. The average financial indebtedness of the 2014 graduate was $31,000. RISD is a member of CSS. The CSS/Profile and FAFSA, and parents' income tax returns are required. The deadline for filing freshman financial aid applications for fall entry is February 15.

ROGER WILLIAMS UNIVERSITY   D-3
www.rwu.edu

Bristol, RI 02809

(401) 254-1040
(401) 254-3500

Fax: (401) 254-3557

Email: admit@rwu.edu

Full-time: 1977 men, 2053 women
Part-time: 306 men, 274 women
Graduate: 131 men, 143 women
Year: semesters, summer session
Room & Board: $14,546

Faculty: 207; IIB, ++$
Ph.D.s: 90%
Student/Faculty: 19 to 1
Tuition: $31,750
Freshman Class: 9913 applied, 7727 accepted, 1152 enrolled
CEEB CODE: 3729

Application Deadline: February 1

VERY COMPETITIVE

Roger Williams University, founded in 1956, is a leading independent, coeducational university with programs in arts and sciences, professional studies, architecture, and law. At RWU, students become community- and globally-minded citizens through project-based, experiential learning. Offering 43 majors and a plethora of co-curricular activities as well as study abroad options, RWU is dedicated to the success of students, commitment to a set of core values, the pursuit of affordable excellence and to providing a relevant, world-class education above all else. There are 8 undergraduate schools and 6 graduate schools. In addition to regional accreditation, RWU has baccalaureate program accreditation with AACSB, ABET, ACCE, NAAB, NASDTEC, ABA, and NASDTEC. The 140-acre campus is in a small town 18 miles southeast of Providence. Including any residence halls, there are 42 buildings.

STUDENT LIFE: 81% of undergraduates are from out of state, mostly the Northeast. Students are from 44 states, 62 foreign countries, and Canada. 72% are White; 12% race unknown. The average age of freshmen is 18; all undergraduates, 22. 21% do not continue beyond their first year; 62% remain to graduate. **Housing:** 3050 students can be accommodated in college housing, which includes single-sex and coed dorms, on-campus apartments, off-campus apartments, and married student housing. In addition, there are honors houses, special-interest houses, academic major living learning communities. On-campus housing is guaranteed for the freshman year only and is available on a lottery system for upperclassmen. 67% of students live on campus; of those, 70% remain on campus on weekends. Upperclassmen may keep cars.

FACULTY/CLASSROOMS: 57% of faculty are male; 43% are female. All teach undergraduates. No introductory courses are taught by graduate students.

PROGRAMS OF STUDY: RWU confers B.A., B.S., B.Arch., B.F.A. and B.G.S degrees. Associate and Master's degrees are also awarded. Bachelor's degrees are awarded in BIOLOGICAL SCIENCE (biochemistry, biology/biological science, and marine biology), BUSINESS (accounting, banking and finance, business administration and management, business law, international business management, management science, and marketing/retailing/merchandising), COMMUNICATIONS AND THE ARTS (art history and appreciation, communications, creative writing, dance, dramatic arts, English, graphic design, historic preservation, journalism, languages, media arts, music, theatre arts, and visual and performing arts), COMPUTER AND PHYSICAL SCIENCE (chemistry, computer science, computer security and information assurance, mathematics, web services, and web technology), EDUCATION (education, elementary education, and secondary education), ENGINEERING AND ENVIRONMENTAL DESIGN (architecture, construction management, engineering, environmental science, industrial engineering technology, and technological management), HEALTH PROFESSIONS (health care administration), SOCIAL SCIENCE (American studies, anthropology, community services, criminal justice, economics, history, humanities, international relations, legal studies, paralegal studies, philosophy, political science/government, psychology, public administration, social science, and sociology). Architecture and engineering is the strongest academically. Architecture, psychology, and criminal justice have the largest enrollments.

ACTIVITIES: There are 70 groups on campus, including art, band, cheerleading, chess, choir, chorale, chorus, communications, computers, dance, drama, environmental, ethnic, film, gay, honors, international, jazz band, literary magazine, musical theater, newspaper, orchestra, photography, political, professional, radio and TV, religious, social service, student government, and yearbook. Popular campus events include Spring Weekend, International Dinner, and Campus Entertainment Network. **Sports:** There are 11 intercollegiate sports for men and 11 for women, and 17 intramural sports for men and 16 for women. Facilities include an athletic facilities, 8,500 square-foot fitness center, aquatic center, dance studios also home to exercise classes, 2 convertible racquetball/squash courts, and 1 regulation squash court. The campus' athletic facilities extend outdoors, including: RWU Waterfront, sailing and kayaking, including soccer and lacrosse, softball and baseball, outdoor tennis, volleyball, and basketball courts. **Graduates:** From July 1, 2013 to June 30, 2014, 884 bachelor's degrees were awarded. The most popular majors were business/marketing (24%), architecture (10%), and justice studies (9%). 80 companies recruited on campus in 2013-2014. In an average class, 50% graduate in 4 years or less, 58% graduate in 5 years or less, and 62% graduate in 6 years or less. Of the 2013 graduating class, 13% were enrolled in graduate school within 6 months of graduation.

SERVICES: Counseling and information services are available, as is tutoring in every subject. There is a reader service for the blind, remedial math, reading, and writing. **Library/Resources:** The 3 libraries contain 499,355 volumes, 140,689 microform items, 5,347 audio/video tapes/CDs/DVDs, and subscribe to 50,391 periodicals including electronic. Computerized library services include interlibrary loans, database searching, Internet access, and Wi-Fi capability. Special learning facilities include an art gallery, radio station, RWU marine and natural sciences building is home to a marine biology wet-lab and shellfish hatchery. The University also accesses an 80 acre field site on nearby Prudence Island, which includes Jenny's Creek Salt Marsh and the Oyster Nursey Pond. **Physically Challenged Students:** Facilities include wheelchair ramps, elevators, special parking, specially equipped restrooms, special class scheduling, lowered drinking fountains, and lowered telephones. **Special:** RWU offers co-op programs, internships, accelerated degree programs, study abroad in 30 countries, work-study, individualized majors, and dual majors. There are 16 national honor societies and a freshman honors program. **Visiting:** There are regularly scheduled orientations for prospective students. There are guides for informal visits and visitors may sit in on classes. To schedule a visit, contact the Office of Admission. **Campus Safety and Security:** Measures include 24-hour foot and vehicle patrol, emergency notification system, and security escort services. There are shuttle buses, emergency telephones, lighted pathways/sidewalks, and controlled access to dorms/residences.

REQUIREMENTS: Applicants should be graduates of an accredited secondary school with a minimum GPA of 2.0. The GED is accepted. Students should have 4 years of English, 3 years of math, 3 years of social sciences, 3 years of natural sciences (of which 2 must be lab units), 2 years of history and 4 to 6 electives, for a total of 16 Carnegie units. Art and architecture students must submit portfolios. An essay is required, and an interview is recommended. AP and CLEP credits are accepted. Important factors in the admissions decision are recommendations by school officials, leadership record, and advanced placement or honors courses. All students must: Earn a minimum cumulative grade point average (GPA) of 2.0 in order to graduate. Each college or school may also require a minimum GPA in the major. Successfully complete a minimum of 30 credits of course work in a major, all University Core Curriculum requirements and the Service Learning Requirement. Complete 45 of the last 60 credits at RWU or at an RWU Semester Abroad program. All financial obligations must be satisfied. **Procedure:** Freshmen are admitted fall and spring. Entrance exams should be taken September or October of the senior year. There are early admissions, deferred admissions, and rolling admissions plans. Applications should be filed by February 1 for fall entry, along with a $50 fee. Notification of early decision is sent December 15; regular decision, March 15. 164 applicants were on the 2014 waiting list; 56 were admitted. Applications are accepted online. **Transfer Students:** 184 transfer students enrolled in 2013-2014. Applicants need a minimum college GPA of 2.5, college transcripts, an essay or personal statement and a statement of good standing from the prior institution. 45 of 120 credits required for the bachelor's degree must be completed at RWU. **International Students:** There are 229 international students enrolled. The school actively recruits these students. They must take the TOEFL with a minimum score of 85 on the Internet-based version (iBT) and the college's own test. SAT scores are required for all education majors.

ADMISSIONS: 78% of the 2014-2015 applicants were accepted. 44% of the current freshmen were in the top fifth of their class; 81% were in the top two fifths. **Admissions Contact:** Amanda Marsili, Director of Admissions Operations. E-Mail: *admit@rwu.edu* Web: *http://www.rwu.edu/admission-financial-aid/undergraduate-admission*

FINANCIAL AID: In 2014-2015, 66% of all full-time freshmen and 60% of continuing full-time students received some form of financial aid. 50% of all full-time freshmen and 40% of continuing full-time students received need-based aid. The average freshman award was $20,071. Need-based scholarships or need-based grants averaged $14,310; need-based self-help aid (loans and jobs) averaged $5,761; and other non-need-based awards and non-need-based scholarships averaged $11,831. 35% of undergraduate students work part-time. Average annual earnings from campus work are $2000. RWU is a member of CSS. The CSS/Profile and FAFSA are required. The priority date for freshman financial aid applications for fall entry is February 1. The deadline for filing freshman financial aid applications for fall entry is February 1.

SALVE REGINA UNIVERSITY D-4
www.salve.edu

Newport, RI 02840

(401) 847-6650
(401) 341-2908

Fax: (401) 341-2996

Email: sruadmis@salve.edu

Full-time: 610 men, 1349 women

Faculty: 119; IIA, av$

Part-time: 26 men, 136 women

Ph.D.s: 82%

Graduate: 233 men, 385 women

Student/Faculty: 16 to 1

Year: semesters, summer session

Tuition: $35,690

Room & Board: $12,860

Freshman Class: 4812 applied, 3413 accepted, 624 enrolled

SAT CR/M/W: 550/548/548 ACT: 24

CEEB CODE: 3759

Application Deadline: February 1

VERY COMPETITIVE

Salve Regina University, founded in 1934 and sponsored by the Sisters of Mercy, is an independent institution affiliated with the Roman Catholic Church. The university offers programs in liberal arts, business, health science, and professional training. There is 1 undergraduate school and 1 graduate school. In addition to regional accreditation, Salve has baccalaureate program accreditation with CSWE, NASAD, IACBE, CORE, and AACN. The 80-acre campus is in a suburban area is 35 south of Providence and 60 miles south of Boston with an off-site location in Warwick, Rhode Island. Including any residence halls, there are 51 buildings.

STUDENT LIFE: 77% of undergraduates are from out of state, mostly the Northeast. Students are from 31 states, 18 foreign countries, and Canada. 72% are from public schools. 77% are White. The average age of freshmen is 18; all undergraduates, 21. 16% do not continue beyond their first year; 70% remain to graduate. **Housing:** 1307 students can be accommodated in college housing, which includes single-sex and coed dorms, on-campus apartments, and off-campus apartments. living/learning dorms. On-campus housing is guaranteed for the freshman year only, is available on a first-come, first-served basis, and is available on a lottery system for upperclassmen. 60% of students live on campus; of those, 75% remain on campus on weekends. Upperclassmen may keep cars.

FACULTY/CLASSROOMS: 43% of faculty are male; 57% are female. All teach undergraduates. No introductory courses are taught by graduate students. The average class size in an introductory lecture is 22; in a laboratory is 17; and in a regular course is 18.

PROGRAMS OF STUDY: Salve confers B.A., B.S. and B.A.S. degrees. Associate, Master's, and Doctoral degrees are also awarded. Bachelor's degrees are awarded in BIOLOGICAL SCIENCE (biology/biological science), BUSINESS (accounting, business administration and management, international business management, management science, and marketing and distribution), COMMUNICATIONS AND THE ARTS (art history and appreciation, communications, communications technology, dramatic arts, English, French, historic preservation, media arts, music, Spanish, and studio art), COMPUTER AND PHYSICAL SCIENCE (chemistry, information sciences and systems, and mathematics), EDUCATION (early childhood education, elementary education, secondary education, and special education), HEALTH PROFESSIONS (nursing), SOCIAL SCIENCE (American studies, criminal justice, economics, history, international studies, philosophy, political science/government, psychology, religion, social work, and sociology). Social work, nursing, and accounting are the strongest academically. Business, administration of justice, and teacher education have the largest enrollments.

ACTIVITIES: There are 42 groups on campus, including art, band, cheerleading, choir, chorus, computers, dance, drama, environmental, ethnic, film, gay, honors, international, jazz band, literary magazine, musical theater, newspaper, outdoor, pep band, photography, political, professional, radio and TV, religious, social, social service, student government, and yearbook. Popular campus events include September Welcome-Back Weekend, Octoberfest Weekend, and New Year's Eve Ball. **Sports:** There are 8 intercollegiate sports for men and 10 for women, and 8 intramural sports for men and 9 for women. Facilities include an recreation center, tennis courts, outdoor basketball courts, weight room, fitness center, soccer, baseball, and softball fields. **Graduates:** From July 1, 2013 to June 30, 2014, 431 bachelor's

degrees were awarded. The most popular majors were nursing (15%), administration of justice (9%), and marketing (8%). 105 companies recruited on campus in 2013-2014. In an average class, 1% graduate in 3 years or less, 64% graduate in 4 years or less, 66% graduate in 5 years or less, and 67% graduate in 6 years or less. Of the 2013 graduating class, 20% were enrolled in graduate school within 6 months of graduation, and 85% were employed.

SERVICES: Counseling and information services are available, as is tutoring in most subjects. There is remedial math, reading, and writing. There also is a writing center and a computer-based tutorial program. **Library/Resources:** The library contains 139,161 volumes, 43,146 microform items, 19,420 audio/video tapes/CDs/DVDs, and subscribes to 1,041 periodicals including electronic. Computerized library services include interlibrary loans, database searching, Internet access, and Wi-Fi capability. Special learning facilities include an art gallery, radio station, biology, chemistry and nursing labs, graphic design and studio art facilities, information systems and computer science labs. **Physically Challenged Students:** 75% of the campus is accessible. Facilities include wheelchair ramps, elevators, special parking, specially equipped restrooms, special class scheduling, lowered drinking fountains, and lowered telephones. **Special:** Salve offers internships in most academic disciplines as well as work-study programs on campus. Study abroad in 18 countries, a Washington semester, B.A.-B.S. degrees in biology, business, and economics, dual majors in many programs, and accelerated degree programs in administration of justice, business, international relations, holistic counseling leadership, and rehabilitation counseling are available. A liberal studies degree, credit for life, military, and work experience, non degree study, and pass/fail options are also offered. There are 15 national honor societies, a freshman honors program, and 10 departmental honors programs. **Visiting:** There are regularly scheduled orientations for prospective students, including information sessions led by an admissions professional with question/answer sessions and a student-led campus tour. There are guides for informal visits, visitors may sit in on classes, and stay overnight. To schedule a visit, contact the Admissions Office at sruadmis@salve.edu. **Campus Safety and Security:** Measures include 24-hour foot and vehicle patrol, emergency notification system, self-defense education, and security escort services. There are shuttle buses, emergency telephones, lighted pathways/sidewalks, and controlled access to dorms/residences.

REQUIREMENTS: Applicants must be high school graduates or hold a GED. Students should have 16 Carnegie units, consisting of 4 each in English, 3 each in math including algebra and geometry, 2 each in science and foreign language, and 1 in history, and electives. An essay is required. The submission of standardized test scores is optional at Salve Regina unless you are considering a major in education or nursing. Students who decide not to submit scores will not be at any disadvantage during the admission process. A GPA of 2.7 is required. AP and CLEP credits are accepted. Important factors in the admissions decision are advanced placement or honors courses, recommendations by school officials, and leadership record. To graduate, students must have 120 credit hours, with about 36 in the major, and must maintain a minimum GPA of 2.0. Distribution requirements include 9 credit hours in social science, 6 each in religious studies, science, English, and a foreign language, and 3 each in visual and performing arts, philosophy, and math. **Procedure:** Freshmen are admitted fall and spring. Entrance exams should be taken as early as possible. There are early admissions and deferred admissions plans. Applications should be filed by February 1 for fall entry; December 1 for spring entry, along with a $50 fee. Notifications are sent March 1. Applications are accepted on-line. **Transfer Students:** 34 transfer students enrolled in 2013-2014. Applicants must have a college GPA of 2.7 or better. 36 of 120 credits required for the bachelor's degree must be completed at Salve. **International Students:** There are 27 international students enrolled. The school actively recruits these students. They must take the TOEFL with a minimum score of 80 on the Internet-based version (iBT). The submission of standardized test scores is optional unless you are considering a major in education or nursing.

ADMISSIONS: 71% of the 2014-2015 applicants were accepted. The SAT scores for the 2014-2015 freshman class were: Critical Reading-19% below 500, 59% between 500 and 599, 21% between 600 and 699, and 1% between 700 and 800; Math--20% below 500, 57%

between 500 and 599, 22% between 600 and 699, and 1% between 700 and 800; Writing--22% below 500, 54% between 500 and 599, 22% between 600 and 699, and 2% between 700 and 800. The ACT scores were 8% below 21, 35% between 21 and 23, 32% between 24 and 26, 15% between 27 and 28, and 10% above 28. 35% of the current freshmen were in the top fifth of their class; 70% were in the top two fifths. 2 freshmen graduated first in their class. **Admissions Contact:** Colleen Emerson, Dean of Admissions. E-Mail: *sruadmis@salve .edu* Web: *www.salve.edu*

FINANCIAL AID: In 2014-2015, 97% of all full-time freshmen and 92% of continuing full-time students received some form of financial aid. 80% of all full-time freshmen and 77% of continuing full-time students received need-based aid. The average freshman award was $27,418. Need-based scholarships or need-based grants averaged $22,985; and need-based self-help aid (loans and jobs) averaged $5,157. 25% of undergraduate students work part-time. Average annual earnings from campus work are $745. Salve is a member of CSS. The FAFSA is required. The priority date for freshman financial aid applications for fall entry is March 1.

UNIVERSITY OF RHODE ISLAND   C-4
www.uri.edu

Kingston, RI 02881	(401) 874-1000
	(401) 874-7100
Fax: (401) 874-5523	Email: admission@uri.edu
Full-time: 5591 men, 6548 women	Faculty: I, -$
Part-time: 692 men, 758 women	Ph.D.s: 83%
Graduate: 1211 men, 1771 women	Student/Faculty: 16 to 1
Year: semesters, summer session	Tuition: $12,506 ($28,072)
Room & Board: $11,496	Freshman Class: 20928 applied, 15846 accepted, 3390 enrolled
SAT CR/M/W: 540/560/530 ACT: 24	CEEB CODE: 3919
Application Deadline: February 1	COMPETITIVE

The University of Rhode Island, founded in 1892, is a land-grant, sea-grant, and urban-grant institution offering programs in liberal arts, business, engineering, human services, nursing, and pharmacy. Located near the ocean and the bay, the university has strong marine and environmental programs. There are satellite campuses in Providence, West Greenwich, and Narragansett. We are the largest university in the nation's smallest state, but with 13,500 undergraduates and 2,500 graduate students, URI is small enough to be friendly, intimate, safe, and student-centered. Our Students come from most states in the U.S. and dozens of countries all over the world. More than 100 undergraduate and 80 graduate degree programs, plus more than 100 student clubs and activities spark creativity and inspire our students' pioneering spirit. There are 8 undergraduate schools and 3 graduate schools. In addition to regional accreditation, URI has baccalaureate program accreditation with AACSB, ABET, ACPE, ADA, ASLA, NASM, NCATE, and NLN. The 1245-acre campus is in a small town 6 miles from Rhodes Island's coastal beaches and easy driving distances from Providence, Boston, and New York. Including any residence halls, there are 155 buildings.

STUDENT LIFE: 56% of undergraduates are from Rhode Island. Others are from 44 states, 68 foreign countries, and Canada. 70% are White. The average age of freshmen is 18; all undergraduates, 20. 18% do not continue beyond their first year; 59% remain to graduate. **Housing:** 6759 students can be accommodated in college housing, which includes single-sex and coed dorms, on-campus apartments, off-campus apartments, and married student housing. In addition, there are language houses, special-interest houses, fraternity houses, sorority houses, First year focused residence halls, living learning communities by academic college and program. On-campus housing is guaranteed for the freshman year only and is available on a lottery system for upperclassmen. 55% of students commute. All students may keep cars.

FACULTY/CLASSROOMS: 48% of faculty are male; 52% are female. No introductory courses are taught by graduate students.

PROGRAMS OF STUDY: URI confers B.A., B.S., B.F.A., B.G.S.,

B.L.A. and B.M. degrees. Master's and Doctoral degrees are also awarded. Bachelor's degrees are awarded in AGRICULTURE (animal science and technology, aquaculture and fishery technology, and environmental horticulture and turf management), BIOLOGICAL SCIENCE (biological sciences, cell and molecular biology, marine affairs, and wildlife conservation biology), BUSINESS (business institutions, coastal marine policy management, coastal marine policy standards, environment and natural resource economics, resource economy and commerce, and production and operations management), COMMUNICATIONS AND THE ARTS (writing and rhetoric), COMPUTER AND PHYSICAL SCIENCE (chemistry/forensic chemistry, geology and geology oceanography, and physics and physical oceanography), EDUCATION (classical studies), ENGINEERING AND ENVIRONMENTAL DESIGN (industry and systems engineering, textile marketing, textile, and fashion merchandising and design), HEALTH PROFESSIONS (communicative disorders, health services administration, and human studies), SOCIAL SCIENCE (human development and family studies). Pharmacy, engineering, and biology are the strongest academically. Nursing, psychology, and kinesiology have the largest enrollments.

ACTIVITIES: 5% of men belong to 17 national fraternities; 7% of women belong to 10 national sororities. There are 100 groups on campus, including music ensembles, band, cheerleading, chess, choir, chorale, chorus, computers, concert band, dance, drama, ethnic, gay, honors, international, jazz band, literary magazine, marching band, musical theater, newspaper, pep band, photography, political, professional, radio and TV, religious, social, social service, student government, and yearbook. Popular campus events include First Night, Welcome Week, and Wintefest. **Sports:** There are 8 intercollegiate sports for men and 11 for women. Facilities include a 8000-seat area, 10,000-seat stadium, 3 pools, multipurpose field house with an indoor 2 betrack, fitness center, 3 fitness rooms, courts for basketball, tennis, and volleyball. There are also outdoor tennis courts, an all-weather track, and varsity and practice fields. **Graduates:** From July 1, 2013 to June 30, 2014, 2798 bachelor's degrees were awarded. The most popular majors were nusrsing (8%), psychology (7%), and communication studies (7%). In an average class, 39% graduate in 4 years or less, 55% graduate in 5 years or less, and 59% graduate in 6 years or less.

SERVICES: Counseling and information services are available, as is tutoring in some subjects, ELS and popular freshman courses, including math, physics, chemistry, and biology There is a reader service for the blind, remedial math, reading, and writing. **Library/Resources:** The 3 libraries contain 1.8 million volumes, 1.7 million microform items, and 1,200 audio/video tapes/CDs/DVDs, and subscribe to 248,194 periodicals including electronic. Computerized library services include interlibrary loans, database searching, Internet access, and Wi-Fi capability. Special learning facilities include an art gallery, planetarium, radio station, TV station, a historic textile collection, and early childhood education center. **Physically Challenged Students:** 90% of the campus is accessible. Facilities include wheelchair ramps, elevators, special parking, specially equipped restrooms, special class scheduling, lowered drinking fountains, lowered telephones, special housing. **Special:** Cross-registration is available with Rhode Island College and Community College of Rhode Island. URI also offers a Washington semester as well as semester-long internships with businesses and state agencies, study abroad in 40 countries, a B.A.-B.S. degree in German and engineering and in languages and business, a general studies degree, dual majors, pass/fail options, and credit for life, military, and work experience. The College of Engineering offers co-op programs and an international internship. There are 30 national honor societies, including Phi Beta Kappa, and a freshman honors program. **Visiting:** There are regularly scheduled orientations for prospective students, including campus tours and information sessions. Visitors may sit in on classes. To schedule a visit, contact the Admission Office at admission@uri.edu. **Campus Safety and Security:** Measures include 24-hour foot and vehicle patrol, emergency notification system, self-defense education, and security escort services. There are shuttle buses, emergency telephones, lighted pathways/sidewalks, and controlled access to dorms/residences.

REQUIREMENTS: The SAT or ACT is required. Applicants should be high school graduates, having completed 18 courses, including 4

of English, 3 to 4 of math, and 2 each of science (chemistry and physics for engineering majors), foreign language, and history or social studies. Remaining units should be college preparatory. Music majors must audition. AP and CLEP credits are accepted. Important factors in the admissions decision are parents or siblings attended your school, extracurricular activities record, geographical diversity, and recommendations by school officials. To graduate, the student must earn 120 to 150 credit hours, at least 30 in the major, with a GPA of 2.0. Distribution requirements include 6 credits each in English communication, fine arts and literature, foreign language or culture, letters, natural science, and social sciences, as well as 3 credits in math and quantitative reasoning. **Procedure:** Freshmen are admitted fall and spring. Entrance exams should be taken during the spring of the junior year or fall of the senior year. There are early admissions, deferred admissions, and rolling admissions plans. Applications should be filed by February 1 for fall entry; December 1 for spring entry, along with a $65 fee. Notification is sent on a rolling basis. 1452 applicants were on the 2014 waiting list; 457 were admitted. Applications are accepted on-line. **Transfer Students:** 505 transfer students enrolled in 2013-2014. Applicants must submit transcripts from high school and all colleges or universities attended. A minimum GPA of 2.5 is required; many programs require higher. An essay or personal statement is required and a statement of good standing from prior institutions. 24 of 120 credits required for the bachelor's degree must be completed at URI. **International Students:** There are 45 international students enrolled. The school actively recruits these students. They must take the TOEFL with a minimum score of 550 on the paper-based TOEFL (PBT) or 79 on the Internet-based version (iBT), or the English proficiency test administered by the American Consulate. They must also take the SAT or ACT.

ADMISSIONS: 76% of the 2014-2015 applicants were accepted. The SAT scores for the 2014-2015 freshman class were: Critical Reading--24% below 500, 53% between 500 and 599, 21% between 600 and 699, and 2% between 700 and 800; Math--20% below 500, 51% between 500 and 599, 26% between 600 and 699, and 3% between 700 and 800; Writing--27% below 500, 52% between 500 and 599, 19% between 600 and 699, and 2% between 700 and 800. 49% of the current freshmen were in the top fifth of their class; 86% were in the top two fifths. **Admissions Contact:** Cynthia Bonn, Dean of Admissions. E-Mail: *admission@uri.edu* Web: *www.uri.edu/admission*

FINANCIAL AID: In 2014-2015, 62% of all full-time freshmen and 76% of continuing full-time students received some form of financial aid. 55% of all full-time freshmen and 70% of continuing full-time students received need-based aid. The average freshman award was $16,091. Need-based scholarships or need-based grants averaged $10,183 ($18,730 maximum); need-based self-help aid (loans and jobs) averaged $5,142 ($6,700 maximum); and non-need-based athletic scholarships averaged $912 ($45,025 maximum). 23% of undergraduate students work part-time. Average annual earnings from campus work are $1500. The average financial indebtedness of the 2014 graduate was $26,894. The FAFSA is required. The priority date for freshman financial aid applications for fall entry is March 1.

ALLEN UNIVERSITY *(The complete profile is made available exclusively on our website, www.barronspac.com)*

BENEDICT COLLEGE *(The complete profile is made available exclusively on our website, www.barronspac.com)*

CHARLESTON SOUTHERN UNIVERSITY   D-4
www.csuniv.edu

Charleston, SC 29423-8087	(843) 863-7000
	(800) 947-7474
Fax: (843) 863-7070	Email: enroll@csuniv.edu
Full-time: 821 men, 1236 women	Faculty: 93; IIB, --$
Part-time: 160 men, 320 women	Ph.D.s: 71%
Graduate: 100 men, 140 women	Student/Faculty: n/av
Year: semesters, summer session	Tuition: $21,100
Room & Board: $8500	Freshman Class: n/av
SAT or ACT: recommended	CEEB CODE: 5079
Application Deadline: open	COMPETITIVE

Charleston Southern University, founded in 1964, is a private liberal arts institution affiliated with the South Carolina Baptist Convention. There are 4 undergraduate schools and 3 graduate schools. The figures in the above capsule and in this profile are approximate. In addition to regional accreditation, CSU has baccalaureate program accreditation with NASDTEC, NASM, and NLN. The 500-acre campus is in a suburban area 20 miles west of Charleston. Including any residence halls, there are 16 buildings.

STUDENT LIFE: 81% of undergraduates are from South Carolina. Others are from 45 states, 35 foreign countries, and Canada. 85% are from public schools. 47% are white; 27% African American. 50% claim no religious affiliation; 42% Protestant. The average age of freshmen is 18; all undergraduates, 25. 28% do not continue beyond their first year; 31% remain to graduate.

FACULTY/CLASSROOMS: 55% of faculty are male; 45% are female. All teach undergraduates. No introductory courses are taught by graduate students. The average class size in an introductory lecture is 40; in a laboratory, 15; and in a regular course, 25.

PROGRAMS OF STUDY: CSU confers B.A., B.S., and B.Tech. degrees. Associate and Master's degrees are also awarded. Bachelor's degrees are awarded in BIOLOGICAL SCIENCE (biochemistry and biology/biological science), BUSINESS (business administration and management), COMMUNICATIONS AND THE ARTS (dramatic arts, English, fine arts, music, Spanish, and speech/debate/rhetoric), COMPUTER AND PHYSICAL SCIENCE (chemistry, computer science, geology, mathematics, and natural sciences), EDUCATION (early childhood education, elementary education, music education, physical education, and science education), ENGINEERING AND ENVIRONMENTAL DESIGN (environmental science), HEALTH PROFESSIONS (music therapy and nursing), SOCIAL SCIENCE (criminal justice, economics, geography, history, humanities, political science/government, psychology, religion, religious music, social science, sociology, and youth ministry).

ACTIVITIES: There are 20 groups on campus, including art, band, cheerleading, choir, chorus, drama, honors, jazz band, literary magazine, marching band, newspaper, religious, social service, student government, and yearbook.

SERVICES: Counseling and information services are available, as is tutoring in most subjects. There is remedial math, reading, and writing. **Library/Resources:** The library contains 212,666 volumes, 212,539 microform items, 7,527 audio/video tapes/CDs/DVDs, and subscribes to 9,788 periodicals including electronic. Computerized library services include database searching. Special learning facilities include a **Physically Challenged Students:** All of the campus is accessible. Facilities include wheelchair ramps, elevators, special parking, specially equipped restrooms, and lowered drinking fountains. **Special:** CSU offers internships, cross-registration through the Trident Area Consortium, work-study programs, dual majors, and nondegree study. Nonmajor preprofessional programs are available in dentistry, engineering, law, medicine, and ministry. There are 5 national honor societies, a freshman honors program, and 100 departmental honors programs. **Visiting:** There are regularly scheduled orientations for prospective students, consisting of orientation for students, orientation for parents, placement testing for students, a tour, and lunch. There are guides for informal visits and visitors may sit in on classes. To schedule a visit, contact the Office of Enrollment Services. **Campus Safety and Security:** Measures include 24-hour foot and vehicle patrol and security escort services. There are emergency telephones and lighted pathways/sidewalks.

REQUIREMENTS: The SAT or ACT is recommended. Applicants must be graduates of an accredited secondary school. The GED is accepted. Character references are preferred. An English proficiency exam is required for all entering students. A GPA of 2.0 is required. AP and CLEP credits are accepted. Important factors in the admissions decision are evidence of special talent, leadership record, and advanced placement or honors courses.

FINANCIAL AID: CSU is a member of CSS. The CSS/Profile and FAFSA are required. Check with the school for current deadlines.

CITADEL, THE   D-4
www.citadel.edu

Charleston, SC 29409	(843) 225-3294
	(800) 868-1842
Fax: (843) 953-7036	Email: admissions@citadel.edu
Full-time: 2353 men, 164 women	Faculty: n/av; IIA, -$
Part-time: 129 men, 89 women	Ph.D.s: 92%
Graduate: 370 men, 493 women	Student/Faculty: 14 to 1
Year: semesters, summer session	Tuition: $12,237 ($31,038)
Room & Board: $6265	Freshman Class: 2765 applied, 2116 accepted, 645 enrolled
SAT CR/M: 538/549 ACT: 23	CEEB CODE: 5108
Application Deadline: n/av	COMPETITIVE

The Citadel, established in 1842 by the South Carolina legislature, is a liberal arts military college supported by the state and offers degrees in the humanities, business, math, science, engineering, and education. The figures for students in the Corps of Cadets include charges for lab fees, athletic fees, most books, school supplies, uniforms, alterations, and laundry and dry cleaning. There are 5 undergraduate schools and 1 graduate school. In addition to regional accreditation, The Citadel has baccalaureate program accreditation with AACSB, ABET, and NCATE. The 300-acre campus is in a suburban area in Charleston, SC. Including any residence halls, there are 69 buildings.

STUDENT LIFE: 58% of undergraduates are from South Carolina. Others are from 43 states, and 12 foreign countries. 79% are White. The average age of freshmen is 18; all undergraduates, 20. 15% do not continue beyond their first year; 85% remain to graduate.

FACULTY/CLASSROOMS: 65% of faculty are male; 35% are female. All teach and do research. No introductory courses are taught by graduate students. The average class size in an introductory lecture is 25 and in a regular course is 20.

PROGRAMS OF STUDY: The Citadel confers B.A., B.S., B.S.B.A., B.S.C.E. and B.S.E.E. degrees. Master's degrees are also awarded. Bachelor's degrees are awarded in BIOLOGICAL SCIENCE (biology/biological science), BUSINESS (business administration and management), COMMUNICATIONS AND THE ARTS (English, French, German, and Spanish), COMPUTER AND PHYSICAL SCIENCE (chemistry, computer science, mathematics, and physics), EDUCATION (health education, physical education, and secondary education), ENGINEERING AND ENVIRONMENTAL DESIGN (civil engineering and electrical/electronics engineering), SOCIAL SCIENCE (criminal justice, history, political science/government, and psychology). Engineering is the strongest academically. Business administration has the largest enrollment.

ACTIVITIES: There are 100 groups on campus, including bagpipe, band, cheerleading, choir, chorale, debate, drill team, ethnic, honors, literary magazine, marching band, newspaper, pep band, political, professional, religious, student government, and yearbook. Popular campus events include Parents Weekend, Corps Day, and Parades most Friday afternoons during Fall and Spring semesters.

SERVICES: Counseling and information services are available, as is tutoring in every subject. **Library/Resources:** The library contains 193,992 volumes, 1.2 million microform items, and 5,538 audio/video tapes/CDs/DVDs, and subscribes to 1,260 periodicals including electronic. Computerized library services include interlibrary loans, database searching, Internet access, and Wi-Fi capability. Special learning facilities include a **Physically Challenged Students:** 80% of the campus is accessible. Facilities include wheelchair ramps, elevators, special parking, and specially equipped restrooms. **Special:** Work-study programs, internships, dual majors, independent study, and study abroad are available. Qualified students may enroll in a separate honors program. There is a teacher certification program. There are 8 national honor societies, including Phi Beta Kappa, a freshman honors program, and 1 departmental honors programs. **Visiting:** There are regularly scheduled orientations for prospective students, including an interview with an admissions counselor and a campus tour guided by a cadet. There are guides for informal visits, visitors may sit in on classes, and stay overnight. To schedule a visit, contact the Admissions Office. **Campus Safety and Security:** Measures include 24-hour foot and vehicle patrol, emergency notification system, and security escort services. There are emergency telephones, lighted pathways/sidewalks, and controlled access to dorms/residences.

REQUIREMENTS: The SAT or ACT is required. High school diploma is required and GED is accepted. Applicants must be between 17 and 22, unmarried, and must meet certain physical requirements. High school preparation should include 4 units in English; 4 in math, 3 in lab science: biology, chemistry, or physics; 2 each in foreign language and social science; 1 academic elective; 1 in visual/perfoming arts; 1 in phys ed or ROTC; and 1 in American history. AP and CLEP credits are accepted. Important factors in the admissions decision are advanced placement or honors courses, extracurricular activities record, and leadership record.

ADMISSIONS: 77% of a recent year applicants were accepted. The SAT scores for the recent year freshman class were: Critical Reading--36% below 500, 46% between 500 and 599, 15% between 600 and 699, and 3% between 700 and 800; Math--23% below 500, 51% between 500 and 599, 23% between 600 and 699, and 3% between 700 and 800. The ACT scores were 22% below 21, 35% between 21 and 23, 27% between 24 and 26, 7% between 27 and 28, and 9% above 28. 30% of the current freshmen were in the top fifth of their class; 59% were in the top two fifths.

FINANCIAL AID: In a recent year, 84% of all full-time freshmen and 78% of continuing full-time students received some form of financial aid. 61% of all full-time freshmen and 46% of continuing full-time students received need-based aid. 2% of undergraduate students work part-time. Average annual earnings from campus work are $1325. The average financial indebtedness of a recent year graduate was $33,998. The FAFSA is required. The priority date for freshman financial aid applications for fall entry is March 1.

CLAFLIN UNIVERSITY (*The complete profile is made available exclusively on our website, www.barronspac.com*)

CLEMSON UNIVERSITY   A-2
www.clemson.edu

Clemson, SC 29634-5124   (864) 656-2287

Fax: (864) 656-0622	Email: cuadmissions@clemson.edu
Full-time: 7947 men, 6887 women	Faculty: n/av; I, --$
Part-time: 626 men, 376 women	Ph.D.s: 88%
Graduate: 2235 men, 1843 women	Student/Faculty: 16 to 1
Year: semesters, summer session	Tuition: $12,408 ($27,920)
Room & Board: $7728	Freshman Class: 16282 applied, 10224 accepted, 3386 enrolled
SAT CR/M/W: 600/630/540 ACT: 27	CEEB CODE: 5111
Application Deadline: May 1	HIGHLY COMPETITIVE

Clemson University, founded in 1889, is a public institution with programs in agriculture, architecture, commerce and industry, education, engineering, forest and recreation resources, liberal arts, nursing, and sciences. There are 5 undergraduate schools and 1 graduate school. The figures in the above capsule and in this profile are approximate. In addition to regional accreditation, Clemson has baccalaureate program accreditation with AACSB, ABET, CSAB, NAAB, NCATE, NLN, and NRPA. The 1400-acre campus is in a small town 32 miles west of Greenville. Including any residence halls, there are 587 buildings.

STUDENT LIFE: 69% of undergraduates are from South Carolina. Others are from 50 states, 96 foreign countries, and Canada. 81% are from public schools. 78% are white. The average age of freshmen is 18; all undergraduates, 21. 10% do not continue beyond their first year; 80% remain to graduate.

FACULTY/CLASSROOMS: 66% of faculty are male; 34% are female. 99% teach undergraduates, 73% do research, and 72% do both. Graduate students teach 18% of introductory courses. The average class size in an introductory lecture is 45; in a laboratory is 19; and in a regular course is 29.

PROGRAMS OF STUDY: Clemson confers B.A., B.S., B.F.A., and B.L.A. degrees. Master's and Doctoral degrees are also awarded. Bachelor's degrees are awarded in AGRICULTURE (agriculture, animal science, forestry production and processing, forestry and related sciences, horticulture, and soil science), BIOLOGICAL SCIENCE (biochemistry, biology/biological science, and microbiology), BUSINESS (accounting, banking and finance, business administration and management, management science, and marketing/retailing/merchandising), COMMUNICATIONS AND THE ARTS (communications, design, English, fine arts, French, German, modern language, and Spanish), COMPUTER AND PHYSICAL SCIENCE (chemistry, computer science, geology, information sciences and systems, mathematics, and physics), EDUCATION (agricultural education, early childhood education, elementary education, industrial arts education, secondary education, and special education), ENGINEERING AND ENVIRONMENTAL DESIGN (agricultural engineering, ceramic engineering, chemical engineering, civil engineering, computer engineering, construction management, electrical/electronics engineering, graphic arts technology, industrial administration/management, industrial engineering, landscape architecture/design, mechanical engineering, and textile technology), HEALTH PROFESSIONS (medical laboratory technology, nursing, predentistry, premedicine, prepharmacy, preveterinary science, and speech pathology/audiology), SOCIAL SCIENCE (economics, food science, history, parks and recreation management, philosophy, political science/government, prelaw, psychology, and sociology). Engineering, architecture, and biological sciences are the strongest academically. Marketing has the largest enrollment.

ACTIVITIES: 18% of men belong to 18 national fraternities; 24% of women belong to 17 national sororities. There are 350 groups on campus, including art, bagpipe, band, cheerleading, choir, chorus, computers, dance, debate, drama, drill team, ethnic, gay, honors, international, jazz band, literary magazine, marching band, musical theater, newspaper, orchestra, pep band, photography, political, professional, radio and TV, religious, social, social service, student government, symphony, and yearbook. Popular campus events include First Friday Parade, Tigerama, Welcome Back Festival, and Annual Shakespeare.

SERVICES: Counseling and information services are available, as is tutoring in most subjects. There is a reader service for the blind. Other services include textbooks, testing modifications, library assistance, interpreters, note takers, and letters to faculty members. **Library/Resources:** The 3 libraries contain 1.2 million volumes, 1.2 million microform items, and 140,000 audio/video tapes/CDs/DVDs, and subscribe to 11,400 periodicals including electronic. Computerized library services include interlibrary loans, database searching, Internet access, and Wi-Fi capability. Special learning facilities include an art gallery, natural history museum, planetarium, radio station, TV station, a geology museum, experimental forest, research park, and state botanical gardens. **Physically Challenged Students:** 75% of the campus is accessible. Facilities include wheelchair ramps, elevators, special parking, specially equipped restrooms, special class scheduling, lowered drinking fountains, lowered telephones, and special housing. **Special:** Co-op programs are available in all majors except nursing. Work-study programs and study abroad in 39 countries are offered. There are 24 national honor societies, including Phi Beta Kappa, a freshman honors program, and 40 departmental honors programs. **Visiting:** There are regularly scheduled orientations for prospective students, including a series of 2-day summer programs of advisement, student services presentations, and registration for the fall semester. There are guides for informal visits and visitors may sit in on classes. To schedule a visit, contact the Visitor's Center at (864) 656-4789. **Campus Safety and Security:** Measures include 24-hour foot and vehicle patrol, emergency notification system, self-defense education, and security escort services. There are shuttle buses, emergency telephones, lighted pathways/sidewalks, Electronic card access to residence halls, and limited outdoor surveillance cameras.

REQUIREMENTS: The SAT or ACT is required. The ACT Optional Writing test is also required. In addition, applicants should be graduates of an accredited secondary school. The GED is accepted. AP and CLEP credits are accepted. Important factors in the admissions decision are advanced placement or honors courses, parents or siblings attended your school, and evidence of special talent.

ADMISSIONS: 63% of a recent year applicants were accepted. The SAT scores for the recent year freshman class were: Critical Reading--8% below 500, 41% between 500 and 599, 42% between 600 and 700, and 9% above 700; Math--4% below 500, 25% between 500 and 599, 54% between 600 and 700, and 17% above 700; Writing--24% below 500, 49% between 500 and 599, 23% between 600 and 700, and 2% above 700. The ACT scores were 8% below 21, 15% between 21 and 23, 31% between 24 and 26, 15% between 27 and 28, and 31% above 28. 69% of the current freshmen were in the top fifth of their class; 97% were in the top two fifths. There were 24 National Merit finalists. 179 freshmen graduated first in their class.

FINANCIAL AID: In a recent year, 87% of all full-time freshmen and 71% of continuing full-time students received some form of financial aid. 28% of all full-time freshmen and 31% of continuing full-time students received need-based aid. The average freshman award was $9,147. Need-based scholarships or need-based grants averaged $4,680 ($7,500 maximum); need-based self-help aid (loans and jobs) averaged $4,113 ($7,125 maximum); non-need-based athletic scholarships averaged $17,653 ($25,390 maximum); and other non-need-based awards and non-need-based scholarships averaged $6,971 ($26,990 maximum). 57% of undergraduate students work part-time. Average annual earnings from campus work are $3353. The average financial indebtedness of a recent graduate was $14,382. The FAFSA is required. The priority date for freshman financial aid applications for fall entry is April 1.

COASTAL CAROLINA UNIVERSITY E-3
www.coastal.edu

Conway, SC 29528

(843) 347-3161
(800) 277-7000

Fax: (843) 349-6436

Email: admissions@coastal.edu

Full-time: 3941 men, 4561 women
Part-time: 344 men, 518 women
Graduate: 196 men, 416 women
Year: semesters, summer session
Room & Board: $8440

Faculty: 387; IIB, -$
Ph.D.s: 81%
Student/Faculty: 22 to 1
Tuition: $10,140 ($23,480)
Freshman Class: 14799 applied, 9412 accepted, 2375 enrolled

SAT CR/M: 490/500 ACT: 21
Application Deadline: June 1

CEEB CODE: 5837
COMPETITIVE

Coastal Carolina University, established in 1954, is a public liberal arts institution offering undergraduate programs through the colleges of business, science, education, humanities, fine arts and university college. Graduate programs are offered through the colleges of education, humanities and fine arts, science, and the college of business. There are 5 undergraduate schools and 1 graduate school. In addition to regional accreditation, Coastal Carolina has baccalaureate program accreditation with AACSB, ABET, NASAD, NASM, and NCATE. The 630-acre campus is in a suburban area 9 miles west of Myrtle Beach. Including any residence halls, there are 101 buildings.

STUDENT LIFE: 50% of undergraduates are from out of state, mostly the Northeast. Students are from 45 states, 58 foreign countries, and Canada. 92% are from public schools. 70% are White; 19% African American. The average age of freshmen is 18; all undergraduates, 21. 33% do not continue beyond their first year; 45% remain to graduate. **Housing:** 3715 students can be accommodated in college housing, which includes coed dorms and off-campus apartments. In addition, there are honors houses and special-interest houses. On-campus housing is available on a first-come, first-served basis, and is available on a lottery system for upperclassmen. 61% of students commute. Alcohol is not permitted. All students may keep cars.

FACULTY/CLASSROOMS: 59% of faculty are male; 41% are female. 97% teach undergraduates, and 50% do both. No introductory courses are taught by graduate students. The average class size in an introductory lecture is 25; in a laboratory is 20; and in a regular course is 20.

PROGRAMS OF STUDY: Coastal Carolina confers B.A., B.F.A., B.S., BSN, B.A.Ed., B.A.I.S., B.S.B.A., B.S.Ed., B.S.I.S. and B.S.P.E. degrees. Master's and Doctoral degrees are also awarded. Bachelor's degrees are awarded in BIOLOGICAL SCIENCE (biochemistry, biology/biological science, and marine science), BUSINESS (accounting, banking and finance, business administration and management, information & communication technology, marketing/retailing/merchandising, sports management, and tourism), COMMUNICATIONS AND THE ARTS (communications, dramatic arts, English, fine arts, graphic design, music, musical theater, Spanish, and studio art), COMPUTER AND PHYSICAL SCIENCE (chemistry, computer science, information sciences and systems, mathematics, and physics), EDUCATION (early childhood education, elementary education, middle school education, physical education, and special education), HEALTH PROFESSIONS (exercise science, health, health care administration, and nursing), SOCIAL SCIENCE (economics, history, interdisciplinary studies, philosophy, political science/government, psychology, and sociology). Accounting, finance, and management are the strongest academically. marine science, management, exercise and sport science have the largest enrollments.

ACTIVITIES: 2% of men belong to 10 national fraternities; 5% of women belong to 7 national sororities. There are 153 groups on campus, including art, band, cheerleading, chess, choir, chorale, chorus, computers, dance, drama, environmental, ethnic, gay, honors, international, jazz band, literary magazine, marching band, musical theater, newspaper, pep band, political, professional, radio and TV, religious, social, social service, and student government. Popular campus events include CINO Day, Cultural Celebration, Club Recruitment Day, and Homecoming. **Sports:** There are 8 intercollegiate sports for men and 9 for women, and 14 intramural sports for men and 14 for women. Facilities include HTC Student Recreation and Convocation Center, a gym, a football stadium, baseball, soccer, and softball fields, tennis, basketball, volleyball, and racquetball courts, an indoor Olympic-size swimming pool, an aerobic dance room, weight rooms, and a track. **Graduates:** From July 1, 2013 to June 30, 2014, 1553 bachelor's degrees were awarded. The most popular majors were management (9%), communication (8%), and interdisciplinary studies (6%). 316 companies recruited on campus in 2013-2014. In an average class, 26% graduate in 4 years or less, 43% graduate in 5 years or less, and 45% graduate in 6 years or less.

SERVICES: Counseling and information services are available, as is tutoring in some subjects, English, foreign languages, math and statistics There is a reader service for the blind. **Library/Resources:** The library contains 127,601 volumes, 4,658 microform items, 6,726 audio/video tapes/CDs/DVDs, and subscribes to 52,430 periodicals including electronic. Computerized library services include interlibrary loans, database searching, Internet access, and Wi-Fi capability. Special learning facilities include an art gallery, radio station, a marine science research center. **Physically Challenged Students:** 95% of the campus is accessible. Facilities include wheelchair ramps, elevators, special parking, specially equipped restrooms, special class scheduling, lowered drinking fountains, and special housing. **Special:** Internships are offered in most majors, as well as study abroad in 15 countries. Interdisciplinary studies and a 3-2 engineering degree with Clemson University are available. There are 15 national honor societies and a freshman honors program. **Visiting:** There are regularly scheduled orientations for prospective students, including sessions for academic requirements, housing, financial aid, and student life, parents' orientation, tours, cookouts, and entertainment. Visitors may sit in on classes. To schedule a visit, contact Holley Aufdemorte at admissions@coastal.edu. **Campus Safety and Security:** Measures include 24-hour foot and vehicle patrol, emergency notification system, self-defense education, and security escort services. There are shuttle buses, emergency telephones, and lighted pathways/sidewalks.

REQUIREMENTS: The SAT or ACT is required. Graduation from an accredited secondary or homeschool program is required; a GED will be accepted with appropriate scores. Applicants are required to submit complete specific high school credits, including 4 years of college prep English, 4 units of mathematics (algebra ll required), 3 units of lab science, 3 units of social sciences (U.S. history required), 2 units of the same foreign language, 1 advanced electives (from computer science, math, additional science, foreign language, social science, humanities, and arts), 1 unit of visual/performing arts, and 1 unit of physical education or ROTC. An interview is recommended. AP and CLEP credits are accepted. Important factors in the admissions decision are advanced placement or honors courses, recommendations by school officials, and evidence of special talent. Students must successfully complete a minimum of 120 credits, varying with major department requirements, and must maintain a minimum GPA of 2.0. A 4-year core curriculum of 34 to 41 hours is required for proficiency in the broad areas of writing, library research, a foreign language, and computer usage. **Procedure:** Freshmen are admitted to all sessions. Entrance exams should be taken in spring of the junior year or fall of the senior year. There are deferred admissions and rolling admissions plans. Applications should be filed by June 1 for fall entry; December 1 for spring entry, along with a $45 fee. Notification is sent on a rolling basis. Applications are accepted on-line. **Transfer Students:** 834 transfer students enrolled in 2013-2014. A minimum GPA of 2.0 is required. Transfers with fewer than 30 hours earned must also meet freshman admission requirements. Students must submit college transcripts and be eligible to return to the last institution attended. 30 of 120 credits required for the bachelor's degree must be completed at Coastal Carolina. **International Students:** There are 144 international students enrolled. They must take the TOEFL with a minimum score of 527 on the paper-based TOEFL (PBT) or 71 on the Internet-based version (iBT). They must also take the SAT or ACT for first-time freshmen.

ADMISSIONS: 64% of the 2014-2015 applicants were accepted. The SAT scores for the 2014-2015 freshman class were: Critical Reading--51% below 500, 40% between 500 and 599, 8% between 600 and 699, and 1% between 700 and 800; Math--48% below 500, 42% between 500 and 599, 9% between 600 and 699, and 1% between 700 and 800. The ACT scores were 49% below 21, 26% between 21 and 23, 15% between 24 and 26, 7% between 27 and 28, and 3% above 28. 29% of the current freshmen were in the top fifth of their class; 67% were in the top two fifths. **Admissions Contact:** Amanda Craddock, Director of Admissions. E-Mail: *admissions@coastal.edu* Web: *www.coastal.edu/admissions/*

FINANCIAL AID: In 2014-2015, 54% of all full-time freshmen and 53% of continuing full-time students received some form of financial aid. 36% of all full-time freshmen and continuing full-time students received need-based aid. The average freshman award was $19,015. Need-based scholarships or need-based grants averaged $3,491; need-based self-help aid (loans and jobs) averaged $3,957; non-need-based athletic scholarships averaged $8,507; other non-need-based awards and non-need-based scholarships averaged $3,385; and $7,143 from other forms of aid. 2% of undergraduate students work part-time. Average annual earnings from campus work are $3000. The average financial indebtedness of the 2014 graduate was $33,453. The FAFSA and the college's own financial statement are required. The priority date for freshman financial aid applications for fall entry is March 1.

COKER COLLEGE *(The complete profile is made available exclusively on our website, www.barronspac.com)*

COLLEGE OF CHARLESTON D-4
www.cofc.edu

Charleston, SC 29424	(843) 805-5507
	(843) 953-5670
Fax: (843) 953-6322	Email: admissions@cofc.edu
Full-time: 3502 men, 6106 women	Faculty: 569; IIA, av$
Part-time: 384 men, 448 women	Ph.Ds: 77%
Graduate: 241 men, 775 women	Student/Faculty: 15 to 1
Year: semesters, summer session	Tuition: $11,018 ($28,008)
Room & Board: $11,127	Freshman Class: 11179 applied, 8722 accepted, 2166 enrolled
SAT CR/M: 560/570 ACT: 25	CEEB CODE: 5113
Application Deadline: April 1	VERY COMPETITIVE

College of Charleston is a nationally recognized public liberal arts and sciences university, founded in 1770, the College is among the nation's top universities for quality education, student life and affordability. The College offers the distinctive combination of a beautiful and historic campus, modern facilities and cutting-edge programs. The College provides a creative and intellectually stimulating environment where students are challenged by a committed and caring faculty of distinguished teacher-scholars, all in an incomparable setting. The City of Charleston, world-renowned for its history, culture, architecture and coastal environment, for experiences in business, science, teaching, the humanities, languages and the arts. At the same time, students and faculty are engaged with the community in partnerships to improve education, enhance the business environment and enrich the overall quality of life in the region. There are 6 undergraduate schools and one graduate school. In addition to regional accreditation, C of C has baccalaureate program accreditation with AACSB, ABET, NASM, NCATE, NAST, CAATE, and NCTE. The 52-acre campus is in an urban area in the historic city center of Charleston, SC. Including any residence halls, there are 146 buildings.

STUDENT LIFE: 64% of undergraduates are from South Carolina. Others are from 49 states, 55 foreign countries, and Canada. 78% are from public schools. 80% are White. The average age of freshmen is 18; all undergraduates, 21. 21% do not continue beyond their first year; 79% remain to graduate. **Housing:** 3221 students can be accommodated in college housing, which includes single-sex and coed dorms and on-campus apartments. In addition, there are honors houses, language houses, special-interest houses, fraternity houses, sorority houses, Restored old Charleston houses used as residence halls, some with kitchen facilities in suites. On-campus housing is available on a first-come and first-served basis. 69% of students commute. Upperclassmen may keep cars.

FACULTY/CLASSROOMS: 51% of faculty are male; 49% are female. 97% teach undergraduates. No introductory courses are taught by graduate students. The average class size in an introductory lecture is 30; in a laboratory is 19; and in a regular course is 22.

PROGRAMS OF STUDY: C of C confers B.A., B.S. and A.B. degrees. Master's degrees are also awarded. Bachelor's degrees are awarded in BIOLOGICAL SCIENCE (biochemistry, biology/biological science, and marine biology), BUSINESS (accounting, business administration and management, finance, hospitality management services, international business management, marketing, and professional studies), COMMUNICATIONS AND THE ARTS (art history, arts administration/management, classics, communications, dance, English, German, historic preservation, music, Spanish, studio art, and theatre arts), COMPUTER AND PHYSICAL SCIENCE (astronomy, astrophysics, chemistry, computer information systems, computer science, geology, mathematics, and physics), EDUCATION (athletic training, early childhood education, elementary education, foreign languages education, middle school education, physical education, secondary education, and special education), HEALTH PROFESSIONS (exercise science and public health), SOCIAL SCIENCE (African American studies, anthropology, archeology, economics, French studies, history, international studies, Latin American studies, philosophy, political science/government, psychology, religious studies, sociology, urban studies, and women's studies). Business, biology, and psychology have the largest enrollemnts.

ACTIVITIES: 19% of men belong to 14 national fraternities; 23% of women belong to 12 national sororities. There are 200 groups on campus, including art, band, chess, choir, chorale, chorus, computers, dance, drama, ethnic, film, forensics, gay, honors, international, jazz band, literary magazine, musical theater, newspaper, opera, orchestra, pep band, political, professional, radio and TV, religious, social, social service, student government, and symphony. Popular campus events include Pep Supper, Homecoming Spirit Cup Competition, Georgestock, Welcome Week and Cougarpalooza. **Sports:** There are 8 intercollegiate sports for men and 13 for women, and 30 intramural sports for men and 30 for women. Facilities include basketball and volleyball courts, racquetball and squash courts, a running track, and a multi-purpose room, fitness center houses the cardio and resistance training equipment, and a 12 acre site serves the outdoor sport clubs and intramural sport leagues. **Graduates:** From July 1, 2013 to June 30, 2014, 2375 bachelor's degrees were awarded. The most popular majors were business administration (23%), communication (12%), and biology (10%). 161 companies recruited on campus in 2013-2014. In an average class, 54% graduate in 4 years or less, 66% graduate in 5 years or less, and 67% graduate in 6 years or less.

SERVICES: Counseling and information services are available, as is tutoring in every subject. There is a reader service for the blind, and remedial math, reading, and writing. **Library/Resources:** The library contains 1.0 million volumes, 881,864 microform items, 12,932 audio/video tapes/CDs/DVDs, and subscribes to 107,354 periodicals including electronic. Computerized library services include interlibrary loans, database searching, Internet access, and Wi-Fi capability. Special learning facilities include an art gallery, natural history museum, radio station, an observatory, a communications museum, a marine lab, an African American history and culture research center, and a bronze sculpture foundry. **Physically Challenged Students:** 70% of the campus is accessible. Facilities include wheelchair ramps, elevators, special parking, specially equipped restrooms, special class scheduling, lowered drinking fountains, and lowered telephones. **Special:** Cross-registration is possible with the Medical University of South Carolina and Trident Technical College. Co-op programs and internships in all majors, a Washington semester, study abroad in 36 countries, work-study programs, B.A.-B.S. degrees, and dual majors are offered. A 2-2 program in allied health, biometry or nursing is offered with the Medical University of South Carolina. The college's 3-week Maymester session offers unconventional courses and programs using alternative methods of instruction. There is an interdisciplinary honors program available to talented students. There are 15 national honor societies, a freshman honors program, and 3 departmental honors programs. **Visiting:** There are regularly scheduled orientations for prospective students, consisting of 1-day open houses throughout the year and 10 2-day orientation sessions throughout the summer, including a family session. Academic requirements and expectations, services offered, placement testing,

individual academic advising. There are guides for informal visits and visitors may sit in on classes. To schedule a visit, contact the Admissions Office. **Campus Safety and Security:** Measures include 24-hour foot and vehicle patrol, emergency notification system, self-defense education, and security escort services. There are emergency telephones, lighted pathways/sidewalks, and controlled access to dorms/residences.

REQUIREMENTS: The SAT or ACT is required. The admissions committee carefully weighs the student's academic preparation (which includes grades, rank in class, and rigor of courses taken), SAT/ACT results, personal statements and essays, leadership qualification, and special talents. Applicants should have completed the following high school units: 4 units of English, 4 units of Math, 3 units of lab science, 3 units of foreign language, 2 units of social studies, 1 unit of history (2 recommended), 3 units of academic electives. 1 unit of computer science (advanced math, computer science or a combination of the two will fulfill this) and 1 unit of fine arts are recommended. The GED is accepted. AP and CLEP credits are accepted. Important factors in the admissions decision are advanced placement or honors courses, leadership record, and recommendations by school officials.In order to graduate with a BA or a BS degree, a student must satisfy the General Education requirement, select and complete the requirements for a major academic program, and complete elective coursework such that the total credit hours reach 122 with a minimum grade point average of 2.0 in all courses taken at the College. All students, regardless of major, must satisfy General Education requirements by completing approved courses distributed across seven areas: Writing, Foreign Languages, History, Humanities, Natural Science, Mathematics or Logic, and Social Science. All students entering the College of Charleston with less than one year of college experience are also required to complete a First Year Experience by selecting a First Year Seminar course or two courses organized into a Learning Community. **Procedure:** Freshmen are admitted fall and spring. Entrance exams should be taken by March 1. There are early admissions, deferred admissions, and rolling admissions plans. Early decision applications should be filed by November 1; regular applications, by April 1 for fall entry; and November 1 for spring entry, along with a $50 fee. Notification of early decision is sent December 15; regular decision, May 15. 537 applicants were on the 2014 waiting list; 55 were admitted. Applications are accepted on-line. **Transfer Students:** 690 transfer students enrolled in 2013-2014. Applicants must have 24 hours and must have a 2.6 GPA for in-state residents and 3.0 for out-of-state residents. 30 of 122 credits required for the bachelor's degree must be completed at C of C. **International Students:** There are 154 international students enrolled. They must take the TOEFL with a minimum score of 570 on the paper-based TOEFL (PBT) or 80 on the Internet-based version (iBT). They must also take the SAT or ACT.

ADMISSIONS: 78% of the 2014-2015 applicants were accepted. The SAT scores for the 2014-2015 freshman class were: Critical Reading--16% below 500, 50% between 500 and 599, 29% between 600 and 699, and 5% between 700 and 800; Math--15% below 500, 53% between 500 and 599, 28% between 600 and 699, and 3% between 700 and 800. The ACT scores were 8% below 21, 26% between 21 and 23, 32% between 24 and 26, 17% between 27 and 28, and 17% above 28. 44% of the current freshmen were in the top fifth of their class; 80% were in the top two fifths. There were 4 National Merit finalists. 11 freshmen graduated first in their class. **Admissions Contact:** Suzette Stille, Director of Undergraduate Admissions. E-Mail: *admissions@cofc.edu* Web: *www.cofc.edu*

FINANCIAL AID: The FAFSA is required. The priority date for freshman financial aid applications for fall entry is March 1.

COLUMBIA COLLEGE   C-3
www.columbia.edu

Columbia, SC 29203	(803) 786-3871
	(800) 277-1301
Fax: (803) 786-3674	Email: admissions@columbiasc.edu
Full-time: 6 men, 978 women	Faculty: n/av; IIB, --$
Part-time: 24 men, 231 women	Ph.D.s: 80%
Graduate: 17 men, 255 women	Student/Faculty: n/av
Year: semesters, summer session	Tuition: $21,650
Room & Board: $6232	Freshman Class: 1097 applied, 833 accepted, 271 enrolled
SAT CR/M: 500/500 ACT: recommended	CEEB CODE: 5117
Application Deadline: August 1	COMPETITIVE

Columbia College, founded in 1854, is a private primarily women's liberal arts college affiliated with the United Methodist Church. The figures in the above capsule and in this profile are approximate. There is one graduate school. In addition to regional accreditation, has baccalaureate program accreditation with CSWE, NASAD, NASDTEC, NASM, and NCATE. The 53-acre campus is in an urban area in the northern section of Columbia. Including any residence halls, there are 26 buildings.

STUDENT LIFE: 90% of undergraduates are from South Carolina. Others are from 23 states, and 10 foreign countries. 52% are White; 39% African American. 84% are Protestant; 17% claim no religious affiliation. The average age of freshmen is 18; all undergraduates, 23. 30% do not continue beyond their first year; 70% remain to graduate.

FACULTY/CLASSROOMS: 36% of faculty are male; 64% are female. 95% teach undergraduates. No introductory courses are taught by graduate students. The average class size in an introductory lecture is 20 and in a laboratory is 20.

PROGRAMS OF STUDY: confers B.A., B.F.A. and B.Mus. degrees. Master's degrees are also awarded. Bachelor's degrees are awarded in BIOLOGICAL SCIENCE (biology/biological science), BUSINESS (accounting and business administration and management), COMMUNICATIONS AND THE ARTS (communications, dance, English, French, languages, music, music performance, performing arts, piano/organ, Spanish, and studio art), COMPUTER AND PHYSICAL SCIENCE (chemistry, information sciences and systems, and mathematics), EDUCATION (Christian education, dance education, early childhood education, elementary education, music education, special education, and speech correction), HEALTH PROFESSIONS (medical laboratory technology), SOCIAL SCIENCE (history, political science/government, psychology, public affairs, religion, religious music, social work, and sociology). Education, sciences, and performing arts have the largest enrollments.

ACTIVITIES: There are no fraternities or sororities. There are 57 groups on campus, including art, band, choir, chorus, computers, dance, drama, ethnic, honors, international, literary magazine, musical theater, newspaper, opera, photography, political, professional, radio and TV, religious, social, social service, and student government. Popular campus events include Fine Arts Series, Follies, and Ludy Bowl.

SERVICES: Counseling and information services are available. Peer tutoring and remedial instruction are offered in some subjects. **Library/Resources:** The library contains 170,000 volumes, 8,353 microform items, and 29,834 audio/video tapes/CDs/DVDs, and subscribes to 633 periodicals including electronic. Computerized library services include interlibrary loans, database searching, Internet access, and Wi-Fi capability. Special learning facilities include an art gallery, radio station, women's leadership center, and a science and technology center. **Physically Challenged Students:** 90% of the campus is accessible. Facilities include wheelchair ramps, elevators, special parking, specially equipped restrooms, and special class scheduling. **Special:** The Center for Contractual Studies allows qualified students to pursue individualized programs through independent study, practicums, and a senior project. The college also offers internships, study abroad, a Washington semester, dual majors, and credit for life, military, and work experience. Nondegree study and pass/fail

options are available. There are a freshman honors program. **Visiting:** There are regularly scheduled orientations for prospective students, consisting of meetings with faculty advisers, classroom visits, campus tours, lunch, and student life and financial aid presentations. There are guides for informal visits and visitors may sit in on classes. To schedule a visit, contact the Admissions Office. **Campus Safety and Security:** Measures include 24-hour foot and vehicle patrol, self-defense education, and security escort services. There are emergency telephones and lighted pathways/sidewalks.

REQUIREMENTS: The SAT is required. The ACT is recommended. Applicants must be graduates of an accredited secondary school or have earned a GED. They should complete 16 Carnegie units, including 4 years of English, 3 of math, and 2 each of foreign language and lab science, as well as courses in history and social studies. An essay and an interview are recommended, as is a portfolio or an audition for fine or performing arts students. AP and CLEP credits are accepted. Important factors in the admissions decision are recommendations by school officials, advanced placement or honors courses, and leadership record.

ADMISSIONS: 76% of a recent year applicants were accepted. The SAT scores for a recent year freshman class were: Critical Reading--49% below 500, 32% between 500 and 599, 16% between 600 and 699, and 3% between 700 and 800; Math--50% below 500, 36% between 500 and 599, 13% between 600 and 699, and 1% between 700 and 800.

FINANCIAL AID: 34% of undergraduate students work part-time. Average annual earnings from campus work are $700. The FAFSA is required. Check with the school for current application deadlines.

CONVERSE COLLEGE   B-1
www.converse.edu

Spartanburg, SC 29302	(864) 596-9000
	(864) 596-9040
Fax: n/av	Email: admissions@converse.edu
Full-time: 608 women	Faculty: 76; IIB, --$
Part-time: 82 women	Ph.D.s: 89%
Graduate: 120 men, 411 women	Student/Faculty: 11 to 1
Year: 4-1-4, summer session	Tuition: $28,276
Room & Board: $8854	Freshman Class: 1383 applied, 710 accepted, 183 enrolled
SAT CR/M: 530/520 ACT: 23	CEEB CODE: 5121
Application Deadline: n/av	COMPETITIVE

Converse College, founded in 1889, is a private women's liberal arts college. Men are admitted to the graduate programs. There are 3 undergraduate schools and 2 graduate schools. In addition to regional accreditation, has baccalaureate program accreditation with NASAD, NASM, and NCATE. The 72-acre campus is in an urban area 80 miles southwest of Charlotte. Including any residence halls, there are 27 buildings.

STUDENT LIFE: 65% of undergraduates are from South Carolina. Others are from 27 states, 11 foreign countries, and Canada. 70% are from public schools. 45% are White. The average age of freshmen is 18; all undergraduates, 20. 26% do not continue beyond their first year; 54% remain to graduate.

FACULTY/CLASSROOMS: 46% of faculty are male; 54% are female. All teach undergraduates, and 50% do both. No introductory courses are taught by graduate students. The average class size in an introductory lecture is 20; in a laboratory is 15; and in a regular course is 11.

PROGRAMS OF STUDY: Converse confers B.A., B.S., B.F.A. and B.Mus. degrees. Master's degrees are also awarded. Bachelor's degrees are awarded in BIOLOGICAL SCIENCE (biology/biological science), BUSINESS (accounting and business administration and management), COMMUNICATIONS AND THE ARTS (English, fine arts, French, languages, modern language, music, and Spanish), COMPUTER AND PHYSICAL SCIENCE (chemistry, computer science, and mathematics), EDUCATION (art education, early childhood education, elementary education, foreign languages education, music education, science education, and secondary education), ENGI-

NEERING AND ENVIRONMENTAL DESIGN (interior design), HEALTH PROFESSIONS (art therapy, predentistry, and premedicine), SOCIAL SCIENCE (economics, history, political science/government, prelaw, psychology, and religion). English, politics, and biology are the strongest academically. Music, education, and business have the largest enrollments.

ACTIVITIES: There are 50 groups on campus, including art, cheerleading, choir, chorale, chorus, computers, dance, debate, drama, ethnic, gay, honors, international, literary magazine, musical theater, newspaper, opera, orchestra, photography, political, professional, religious, social service, student government, symphony, and yearbook. Popular campus events include Founders Day, May Day, and Family Weekend.

SERVICES: Counseling and information services are available, as is tutoring in most subjects. There is a reader service for the blind.

REQUIREMENTS: The SAT or ACT is recommended. Applicants should be graduates of an accredited secondary school, having completed 20 Carnegie units, including 4 years of English, 3 of math, 2 each of foreign language, science, and social studies, and 1 of history. The GED is accepted. An interview is recommended for all students and an audition is recommended for music students. A GPA of 2.0 is required. AP and CLEP credits are accepted. Important factors in the admissions decision are advanced placement or honors courses, recommendations by school officials, and leadership record.

ADMISSIONS: 51% of a recent year applicants were accepted. The SAT scores for a recent year freshman class were: Critical Reading--29% below 500, 43% between 500 and 599, 25% between 600 and 699, and 3% between 700 and 800; Math--35% below 500, 50% between 500 and 599, 14% between 600 and 699, and 1% between 700 and 800. The ACT scores were 32% below 21, 25% between 21 and 23, 25% between 24 and 26, 13% between 27 and 28, and 6% above 28. 5 freshmen graduated first in their class.

FINANCIAL AID: In a recent year, 100% of all full-time freshmen and 99% of continuing full-time students received some form of financial aid. 86% of all full-time freshmen and 90% of continuing full-time students received need-based aid. The average freshman award was $23,916. Need-based scholarships or need-based grants averaged $20,717; need-based self-help aid (loans and jobs) averaged $4,043; non-need-based athletic scholarships averaged $5,504; and other non-need-based awards and non-need-based scholarships averaged $13,105. The average financial indebtedness of the 2013 graduate was $28,986. The FAFSA is required. The deadline for filing freshman financial aid applications for fall entry is March 15.

ERSKINE COLLEGE B-2
www.erskine.edu

Due West, SC 29639	**(864) 379-8838**
	(864) 359-4358
Fax: n/av	**Email: admissions@erskine.edu**
Full-time: 250 men, 291 women	Faculty: 41; IIB, --$
Part-time: 9 men, 3 women	Ph.D.s: 85%
Graduate: n/av	Student/Faculty: 11 to 1
Year: semesters, summer session	Tuition: $28,160
Room & Board: $9200	Freshman Class: 500 applied, 373 accepted, 144 enrolled
SAT CR/M: 531/543 **ACT:** required	**CEEB CODE:** 5188
Application Deadline: open	**COMPETITIVE**

Erskine College, founded in 1839, is a private liberal arts college affiliated with the Associate Reformed Presbyterian Church. There is 1 undergraduate school and 1 graduate school. In addition to regional accreditation, Erskine has baccalaureate program accreditation with NCATE. The 85-acre campus is in a rural area 90 miles west of Columbia. Including any residence halls, there are 30 buildings.

STUDENT LIFE: 76% of undergraduates are from South Carolina. Others are from 19 states, 8 foreign countries, and Canada. 85% are from public schools. 72% are white. The average age of freshmen is 18; all undergraduates, 20. 23% do not continue beyond their first year; 69% remain to graduate.

FACULTY/CLASSROOMS: 61% of faculty are male; 39% are female.

All teach undergraduates. No introductory courses are taught by graduate students. The average class size in an introductory lecture is 22; in a laboratory is 25; and in a regular course is 14.

PROGRAMS OF STUDY: Erskine confers A.B. and B.S. degrees. Master's and Doctoral degrees are also awarded. Bachelor's degrees are awarded in BIOLOGICAL SCIENCE (biology/biological science), BUSINESS (business administration and management and sports management), COMMUNICATIONS AND THE ARTS (art, English, music, and visual and performing arts), COMPUTER AND PHYSICAL SCIENCE (chemistry, mathematics, natural sciences, and physics), EDUCATION (athletic training, Christian education, early childhood education, elementary education, foreign languages education, physical education, and special education), SOCIAL SCIENCE (American studies, behavioral science, history, philosophy, psychology, religion, and social studies). Mathematics, chemistry, philosophy, and Spanish are the strongest academically. Business administration and biology have the largest enrollments.

ACTIVITIES: There are no fraternities or sororities. There are 51 groups on campus, including art, cheerleading, choir, chorale, chorus, computers, dance, drama, ethnic, honors, jazz band, literary magazine, newspaper, pep band, political, professional, radio and TV, religious, social, social service, student government, and yearbook. Popular campus events include Spring Fling, Back to School Bash, and Freshman Follies.

SERVICES: Counseling and information services are available, as is tutoring in every subject. There is a reader service for the blind.

Library/Resources: The library contains 217,947 volumes, 63,064 microform items, 2,979 audio/video tapes/CDs/DVDs, and subscribes to 1,125 periodicals including electronic. Computerized library services include interlibrary loans, database searching, Internet access, and Wi-Fi capability. Special learning facilities include an art gallery and radio station. **Physically Challenged Students:** 75% of the campus is accessible. Facilities include wheelchair ramps, elevators, special parking, specially equipped restrooms, and special class scheduling. **Special:** Externships are available during the January term. Study abroad in 5 countries, 3-2 engineering degrees with Clemson University, the University of Tennessee at Knoxville, and Medical University of South Carolina, and pass/fail options are offered. There are 7 national honor societies and 10 departmental honors programs. **Visiting:** There are guides for informal visits, visitors may sit in on classes, and stay overnight. To schedule a visit, contact the Admissions Office at admissions@erskine.edu. **Campus Safety and Security:** Measures include emergency notification system and security escort services. There are lighted pathways/sidewalks.

REQUIREMENTS: The SAT or ACT is required. In addition, grades from college preparatory courses are weighed twice as heavily as the SAT or ACT scores. Applicants must be graduates of an accredited secondary school. The GED is accepted. Applicants should have a minimum of 14 high school academic credits, including 4 credits of English and 2 credits each of math, science, and history. AP and CLEP credits are accepted. Important factors in the admissions decision are advanced placement or honors courses, recommendations by school officials, and extracurricular activities record.

ADMISSIONS: 75% of a recent applicants were accepted. The SAT scores for a recent freshman class were: Critical Reading--40% below 500, 36% between 500 and 599, 19% between 600 and 700, and 5% above 700; Math--37% below 500, 35% between 500 and 599, 23% between 600 and 700, and 5% above 700. 65% of the current freshmen were in the top fifth of their class; 87% were in the top two fifths.

FINANCIAL AID: The FAFSA and the college's own financial statement are required. The deadline for filing freshman financial aid applications for fall entry is April 1.

FRANCIS MARION UNIVERSITY (*The complete profile is made available exclusively on our website, www.barronspac.com*)

FURMAN UNIVERSITY — B-1
www.furman.edu

Greenville, SC 29613	(864) 294-2000
	(864) 294-2034
Fax: (864) 294-2018	Email: admission@furman.edu
Full-time: 1139 men, 1536 women	Faculty: 239; IIB, +$
Part-time: 50 men, 73 women	Ph.D.s: 96%
Graduate: 37 men, 118 women	Student/Faculty: 11 to 1
Year: semesters, summer session	Tuition: $43,164
Room & Board: $10,842	Freshman Class: 5935 applied, 3802 accepted, 756 enrolled
SAT CR/M/W: 610/620/610 ACT: 28	CEEB CODE: 5222
Application Deadline: January 15	HIGHLY COMPETITIVE

Founded in 1826, Furman University is an independent liberal arts institution offering undergraduate and graduate programs. In addition to regional accreditation, Furman has baccalaureate program accreditation with NASM and NCATE. The 750-acre campus is in a suburban area 5 miles north of Greenville. Including any residence halls, there are 69 buildings.

STUDENT LIFE: 72% of undergraduates are from out of state, mostly the South. Students are from 46 states, 53 foreign countries, and Canada. 52% are from public schools. 84% are White. 73% are Protestant; 15% Catholic. The average age of freshmen is 18; all undergraduates, 20. 11% do not continue beyond their first year; 84% remain to graduate.

FACULTY/CLASSROOMS: 62% of faculty are male; 38% are female. All teach undergraduates. No introductory courses are taught by graduate students. The average class size in an introductory lecture is 19; in a laboratory is 10; and in a regular course is 16.

PROGRAMS OF STUDY: Furman confers B.A., B.S., B.L.A. and B.M. degrees. Master's degrees are also awarded. Bachelor's degrees are awarded in BIOLOGICAL SCIENCE (biology/biological science and neurosciences), BUSINESS (accounting and business administration and management), COMMUNICATIONS AND THE ARTS (art, classics, communications, dramatic arts, English, French, German, Greek, Latin, music, music performance, music theory and composition, and Spanish), COMPUTER AND PHYSICAL SCIENCE (chemistry, computer science, information sciences and systems, mathematics, and physics), EDUCATION (education, elementary education, and music education), ENGINEERING AND ENVIRONMENTAL DESIGN (environmental science and preengineering), HEALTH PROFESSIONS (exercise science and health science), SOCIAL SCIENCE (Asian/Oriental studies, economics, history, philosophy, political science/government, psychology, religion, religious music, sociology, and urban studies). Chemistry, biology, and music are the strongest academically. Political Science, Health Sciences and Business Administration have the largest enrollments.

ACTIVITIES: 31% of men belong to 7 national fraternities; 54% of women belong to 7 national sororities. There are 150 groups on campus, including art, band, cheerleading, chess, choir, chorale, chorus, computers, dance, debate, drama, drill team, environmental, ethnic, film, forensics, gay, honors, international, jazz band, literary magazine, marching band, musical theater, newspaper, opera, orchestra, pep band, photography, political, professional, radio and TV, religious, social, social service, student government, symphony, and yearbook. Popular campus events also include Beach Weekend and Mountain Weekend.

SERVICES: Counseling and information services are available, as is tutoring in every subject. There is a reader service for the blind. **Library/Resources:** The 3 libraries contain 526,690 volumes, 862,324 microform items, and 9,200 audio/video tapes/CDs/DVDs, and subscribe to 13,200 periodicals including electronic. Computerized library services include interlibrary loans, database searching, Internet access, and Wi-Fi capability. Special learning facilities include an art gallery, planetarium, radio station, an observatory, and cable TV with on-campus broadcasting. **Physically Challenged Students:** 99% of the campus is accessible. Facilities include wheelchair ramps, elevators, special parking, specially equipped restrooms, special class

scheduling, lowered drinking fountains, lowered telephones, and special housing. **Special:** A 3-2 engineering degree is offered with the Georgia Institute of Technology, Clemson, North Carolina State, and Auburn and Washington Universities. Internships, study abroad in at least 17 countries, a Washington semester with an internship in a government agency or political organization, and work-study programs are offered. B.A.-B.S. degrees, dual majors, interdisciplinary majors such as computer science-math, math-economics, and computing-business, and student-designed majors are available. A bachelor of general studies degree is granted in the evening division. Nondegree study and pass/fail options are possible. Furman features student/faculty research programs. There are 20 national honor societies and including Phi Beta Kappa. **Visiting:** There are regularly scheduled orientations for prospective students, consisting of an individual or group session with an admissions officer and a campus tour. There are guides for informal visits, visitors may sit in on classes, and stay overnight. To schedule a visit, contact the Admissions Office at admissions@furman.edu. **Campus Safety and Security:** Measures include 24-hour foot and vehicle patrol, emergency notification system, self-defense education, and security escort services. There are shuttle buses, emergency telephones, lighted pathways/sidewalks, and controlled access to dorms/residences.

REQUIREMENTS: The SAT or ACT and ACT Writing Test are recommended. Applicants must be high school graduates or hold a GED. Students should have earned at least 20 units in high school, including 4 of English, 3 each of history, math, and science, and 2 each of social studies and foreign language. A portfolio or an audition, where appropriate, is required. AP credits are accepted. Important factors in the admissions decision are advanced placement or honors courses, evidence of special talent, personality/intangible qualities, extracurricular activities record, leadership record, and parents or siblings attended your school.

ADMISSIONS: 64% of a recent year applicants were accepted. The SAT scores for a recent year freshman class were: Critical Reading--7% below 500, 35% between 500 and 599, 42% between 600 and 699, and 16% between 700 and 800; Math--5% below 500, 28% between 500 and 599, 50% between 600 and 699, and 17% between 700 and 800; Writing--10% below 500, 33% between 500 and 599, 42% between 600 and 699, and 15% between 700 and 800. The ACT scores were 3% below 21, 11% between 21 and 23, 22% between 24 and 26, 26% between 27 and 28, and 38% above 28. 64% of the current freshmen were in the top fifth of their class; 86% were in the top two fifths.

FINANCIAL AID: In a recent year, 94% of all full-time freshmen and 85% of continuing full-time students received some form of financial aid. 52% of all full-time freshmen and 40% of continuing full-time students received need-based aid. The average freshman award was $27,940. 47% of undergraduate students work part-time. Average annual earnings from campus work are $2400. The average financial indebtedness of the 2013 graduate was $27,511. Furman is a member of CSS. The CSS/Profile, FAFSA, and the state aid form are required. The deadline for filing freshman financial aid applications for fall entry is February 15.

LANDER UNIVERSITY — B-2
www.lander.edu

Greenwood, SC 29649	(864) 388-8307
	(888) 4LANDER
Fax: (864) 388-8125	Email: admissions@lander.edu
Full-time: 740 men, 1360 women	Faculty: 137; IIB, --$
Part-time: 80 men, 190 women	Ph.D.s: 63%
Graduate: 5 men, 40 women	Student/Faculty: n/av
Year: semesters, summer session	Tuition: $9504 ($17,976)
Room & Board: $7456	Freshman Class: n/av
SAT or ACT: required	CEEB CODE: 5363
Application Deadline: open	COMPETITIVE+

Lander University, founded in 1872, is a state-supported institution offering undergraduate programs in liberal arts, science and math, business, education, nursing, and phys ed and exercise studies. The figures in the above capsule and in this profile are approximate. There are 10 undergraduate schools and 1 graduate school. In addition to regional accreditation, Lander has baccalaureate program accreditation with AACSB, NASAD, NASM, and NCATE. The 100-acre campus is in a small town 75 miles west of Columbia. Including any residence halls, there are 33 buildings.

STUDENT LIFE: 92% of undergraduates are from South Carolina. Others are from 23 states, 21 foreign countries, and Canada. 67% are white; 24% African American. The average age of freshmen is 19; all undergraduates, 26. 38% do not continue beyond their first year; 62% remain to graduate.

FACULTY/CLASSROOMS: 47% of faculty are male; 53% are female. All teach undergraduates. No introductory courses are taught by graduate students. The average class size in a regular course is 22.

PROGRAMS OF STUDY: Lander confers B.A., B.S., and B.M.Ed. degrees. Master's degrees are also awarded. Bachelor's degrees are awarded in BIOLOGICAL SCIENCE (biology/biological science), BUSINESS (business administration and management), COMMUNICATIONS AND THE ARTS (communications, dramatic arts, English, music, Spanish, speech/debate/rhetoric, and visual and performing arts), COMPUTER AND PHYSICAL SCIENCE (chemistry, computer science, and mathematics), EDUCATION (early childhood education, elementary education, music education, physical education, and special education), ENGINEERING AND ENVIRONMENTAL DESIGN (environmental science), HEALTH PROFESSIONS (exercise science, nursing, and sports medicine), SOCIAL SCIENCE (history, interdisciplinary studies, political science/government, psychology, and sociology). Premedical and dual engineering are the strongest academically. Business administration, education, and behavioral science have the largest enrollments.

ACTIVITIES: 11% of men belong to 5 national fraternities; 12% of women belong to 5 national sororities. There are 65 groups on campus, including art, band, cheerleading, choir, chorale, chorus, computers, dance, drama, ethnic, honors, international, jazz band, literary magazine, musical theater, newspaper, orchestra, pep band, political, professional, religious, social, social service, and student government. Popular campus events include the Greenwood Performing Arts Series.

SERVICES: Counseling and information services are available, as is tutoring in most subjects. There is a reader service for the blind, and remedial math, reading, and writing. **Library/Resources:** The library contains 174,624 volumes, 157,707 microform items, and 2,592 audio/video tapes/CDs/DVDs, and subscribes to 656 periodicals including electronic. Computerized library services include interlibrary loans, database searching, and Internet access. Special learning facilities include an art gallery, a media center. **Physically Challenged Students:** All of the campus is accessible. Facilities include wheelchair ramps, elevators, special parking, specially equipped restrooms, special class scheduling, lowered drinking fountains, and lowered telephones. **Special:** Lander offers internships, co-op and work-study programs, accelerated degrees, B.A.-B.S. degrees, dual engineering degree's with Clemson University, student-designed majors in interdisciplinary studies, credit for military experience, and nondegree study. Students in the Honors International Program study abroad in England for 1 semester during their sophomore year. There are 7 national honor societies and a freshman honors program. **Visiting:** There are regularly scheduled orientations for prospective students, consisting of open houses. There are guides for informal visits and visitors may sit in on classes. To schedule a visit, contact the Admissions Office at admissions@lander.edu. **Campus Safety and Security:** Measures include 24-hour foot and vehicle patrol, emergency notification system, self-defense education, and security escort services. There are emergency telephones, lighted pathways/sidewalks, and controlled access to dorms/residences.

REQUIREMENTS: The SAT or ACT is required. Applicants must be high school graduates with 20 credits, including 4 each of English and academic electives, 3 each of math and lab science, 2 each of foreign language and social studies, and 1 each of American history and phys ed or ROTC. An interview and a portfolio or an audition, if appropriate, are recommended. A GPA of 2.0 is required. AP and CLEP credits are accepted.

FINANCIAL AID: The FAFSA is required. Check with the school for current deadlines.

LIMESTONE COLLEGE B-1
www.limestone.edu

Gaffney, SC 29340 (864) 489-7151
(800) 795-7151
Fax: (864) 487-8706 Email: admissions@limestone.edu
Full-time: 717 men, 454 women Faculty: 81
Part-time: 6 men, 11 women Ph.D.s: 79%
Graduate: 30 men, 45 women Student/Faculty: 13 to 1
Year: semesters, summer session Tuition: $23,000
Room & Board: $7800 Freshman Class: 2623
applied, 1397 accepted,
410 enrolled
SAT CR/M: 500/510 ACT: 21 CEEB CODE: 5366
Application Deadline: August 27 COMPETITIVE

Limestone College, founded in 1845, is a private, accredited, coeducational, Christian non-denominational, four-year liberal arts College offering programs in the arts, sciences, business, and teacher preparation. Its programs lead to the Bachelor of Arts, Bachelor of Fine Arts, Bachelor of Science, Bachelor of Social Work, Associate of Arts, and Associate of Science degrees. At the graduate level, a Master of Business Administration is offered. There is 1 undergraduate school and 1 graduate school. In addition to regional accreditation, has baccalaureate program accreditation with CSWE, NASM, NCATE, CAATE, and SACS. The 125-acre campus is in a suburban area 50 miles south of Charlotte, NC and 25 miles north of Spartanburg, SC. Including any residence halls, there are 33 buildings.

STUDENT LIFE: 57% of undergraduates are from South Carolina. Others are from 33 states, 19 foreign countries, and Canada. 51% are White; 32% African American. The average age of freshmen is 19; all undergraduates, 20. 39% do not continue beyond their first year; 72% remain to graduate. **Housing:** 539 students can be accommodated in college housing, which includes single-sex dorms, on-campus apartments, and off-campus apartments. On-campus housing is guaranteed for the freshman year only, is available on a first-come, and first-served basis. 58% of students live on campus; of those, 55% remain on campus on weekends. Alcohol is not permitted. All students may keep cars.

FACULTY/CLASSROOMS: 53% of faculty are male; 47% are female. All teach undergraduates. No introductory courses are taught by graduate students. The average class size in an introductory lecture is 22; in a laboratory is 16; and in a regular course is 14.

PROGRAMS OF STUDY: confers B.A., B.S., B.F.A. and B.S.W. degrees. Associate and Master's degrees are also awarded. Bachelor's degrees are awarded in BIOLOGICAL SCIENCE (biology/biological science), BUSINESS (accounting, business administration and management, business economics, electronic business, finance, human resources, management science, marketing, marketing and distribution, personnel management, and sports management), COMMUNICATIONS AND THE ARTS (communications, English, English Writing, graphic design, jazz, music, musical theater, studio art, and theatre arts), COMPUTER AND PHYSICAL SCIENCE (chemistry, computer programming, computer information technology, computer science, computer security and information assurance, information sciences and systems, mathematics, web services, and web technology), EDUCATION (athletic training, early childhood education, elementary education, English education, mathematics education, music education, and physical education), ENGINEERING AND ENVIRONMENTAL DESIGN (computer technology), HEALTH PROFESSIONS (health care administration), SOCIAL SCIENCE (criminal justice, economics, history, liberal arts/general studies, physical fitness/movement, prelaw, psychology, and social work). Business administration, sport management, and criminal justice have the largest enrollments.

ACTIVITIES: There are 22 groups on campus, including art, band, cheerleading, choir, chorus, computers, dance, drama, gay, honors, international, jazz band, literary magazine, marching band, musical theater, pep band, professional, religious, social, social service, student government, symphony, and yearbook. Popular campus events include Christmas on Campus, Homecoming and Saints Festival. **Sports:** There are 13 intercollegiate sports for men and 12 for women, and 28 intramural sports for men and 28 for women. Facilities include an 1,500-seat gym, Olympic-size indoor pool, 8 lighted tennis courts, baseball, softball, soccer, field hockey, and lacrosse fields, 4 practice fields, student center with game room, physical education center, fitness center, Timken East gym and facilities. **Graduates:** From July 1, 2013 to June 30, 2014, 133 bachelor's degrees were awarded. The most popular majors were sports management (12%), elementary education (11%), and social work (9%). In an average class, 13% graduate in 4 years or less, 26% graduate in 5 years or less, and 27% graduate in 6 years or less. Of the 2013 graduating class, 19% were enrolled in graduate school within 6 months of graduation. **SERVICES:** Counseling and information services are available, as is tutoring in every subject. There is remedial math, reading, and writing. Special assistance is also available to students with documented learning disabilities through the Program for Alternative Learning Styles (PALS) Program. **Library/Resources:** The library contains 207,115 volumes, 2,924 microform items, 21,408 audio/video tapes/ CDs/DVDs, and subscribes to 37,246 periodicals including electronic. Computerized library services include interlibrary loans, database searching, Internet access, and Wi-Fi capability. Special learning facilities include an art gallery, Student Success Center with computer workstations, writing center, math lab, computer graphics art lab, testing center, monitored study halls, and tutorial services. Online math and writing labs. Winnie Davis Hall of Southern History Museum. **Physically Challenged Students:** 75% of the campus is accessible. Facilities include wheelchair ramps, elevators, special parking, specially equipped restrooms, special class scheduling, lowered drinking fountains, special housing. Individual accommodations are made on an as-needed basis. **Special:** The College offers senior internships in public and private organizations for 3 to 6 semester credit hours, as well as a work-study program, on- and off-campus evening courses, and courses on the Internet. The College confers a liberal studies degree and may grant credit for military experience. Double majors are possible; however, granting of 2 baccalaureate degrees requires an additional 31 semester hours. There are 5 national honor societies, a freshman honors program, and 4 departmental honors programs. **Visiting:** There are regularly scheduled orientations for prospective students, Open House: November 15, 2013; February 21, 2014; and April 11, 2014, or by appointment with Admissions Office. Agenda: President's address, campus tour, science/ business faculty teaching demonstrations, lunch, & tour of athletics & residence halls. There are guides for informal visits, visitors may sit in on classes, and stay overnight. To schedule a visit, contact Jennifer Ledbetter at (864) 488-4552. **Campus Safety and Security:** Measures include 24-hour foot and vehicle patrol, emergency notification system, and security escort services. There are emergency telephones, lighted pathways/sidewalks, and controlled access to dorms/residences.

REQUIREMENTS: The SAT or ACT is required. SAT combined score (critical reading and math) of 910 or ACT combined score (English and math) of 19. The College recommends that students present 4 units of English, 3 each of math and social science, and 2 of lab science. The GED is accepted. An interview is recommended. A GPA of 2.0 is required. AP and CLEP credits are accepted. Important factors in the admissions decision are advanced placement or honors courses, leadership record, and evidence of special talent. To graduate a student must complete a minimum of 123 credit hours for a baccalaureate degree or 62 credit hours for an associate degree with a minimum overall GPA of 2.0, including within their major. **Procedure:** Freshmen are admitted fall and spring. Entrance exams should be taken during fall of the senior year of high school. There are deferred admissions and rolling admissions plans. Application deadlines are open. Application fee is $25. Notification is sent on a rolling basis. Applications are accepted on-line. Application fees are waived if application is completed on-line. **Transfer Students:** 131 transfer students enrolled in 2013-2014. Applicants must have a minimum GPA of 2.0 and be in good standing at their previous school. 31 of 123 credits required for the bachelor's degree must be completed at Limestone. **International Students:** There are 97 international students enrolled. The school actively recruits these students. They must take the TOEFL with a minimum score of 500 on the paper-based TOEFL (PBT) or 75 on the Internet-based version (iBT). They must also take the SAT or ACT, scoring 910.

ADMISSIONS: 53% of the 2014-2015 applicants were accepted. The SAT scores for the 2014-2015 freshman class were: Critical Reading--46% below 500, 45% between 500 and 599, and 7% between 600 and 699; Math--31% below 500, 54% between 500 and 599, and 14% between 600 and 699. The ACT scores were 43% below 21, 37% between 21 and 23, 12% between 24 and 26, 3% between 27 and 28, and 5% above 28. 13% of the current freshmen were in the top fifth of their class; 38% were in the top two fifths. **Admissions Contact:** Chris Phenicie, Vice President for Enrollment Services. E-Mail: *cphenicie@limestone.edu* Web: *www.limestone.edu*

FINANCIAL AID: In 2014-2015, 91% of all full-time freshmen and 94% of continuing full-time students received some form of financial aid. 91% of all full-time freshmen and 92% of continuing full-time students received need-based aid. The average freshman award was $16,350. Need-based scholarships or need-based grants averaged $5,623 ($9,745 maximum); need-based self-help aid (loans and jobs) averaged $6,562 ($12,500 maximum); non-need-based athletic scholarships averaged $6,940 ($24,380 maximum); other non-need-based awards and non-need-based scholarships averaged $4,660 ($28,760 maximum); and $1,445 from other forms of aid. 31% of undergraduate students work part-time. Average annual earnings from campus work are $1565. The average financial indebtedness of the 2014 graduate was $30,580. is a member of CSS. The FAFSA is required. The priority date for freshman financial aid applications for fall entry is February 1. The deadline for filing freshman financial aid applications for fall entry is July 1.

MORRIS COLLEGE (*The complete profile is made available exclusively on our website, www.barronspac.com*)

NEWBERRY COLLEGE (*The complete profile is made available exclusively on our website, www.barronspac.com*)

PRESBYTERIAN COLLEGE B-2
www.presby.edu

Clinton, SC 29325

(864) 833-8258
(800) 960-7583

Fax: (864) 833-8195
Email: admissions@presby.edu

Full-time: 490 men, 597 women
Faculty: 77

Part-time: 16 men, 20 women
Ph.D.s: 96%

Graduate: 92 men, 218 women
Student/Faculty: 14 to 1

Year: semesters, summer session
Tuition: $33,650

Room & Board: $9028
Freshman Class: 1650 applied, 1089 accepted, 296 enrolled

SAT CR/M: 550/550 **ACT:** 24
CEEB CODE: 5540

Application Deadline: February 1
COMPETITIVE+

Presbyterian College, founded in 1880, is a private liberal arts institution affiliated with the Presbyterian Church. PC also has a school of pharmacy that offers a doctorate in pharmacy. There is 1 undergraduate school and 1 graduate school. In addition to regional accreditation, PC has baccalaureate program accreditation with NASM, NCATE, and SACS. The 240-acre campus is in a small town 40 miles south of Greenville. Including any residence halls, there are 74 buildings.

STUDENT LIFE: 65% of undergraduates are from South Carolina. Others are from 33 states, and 23 foreign countries. 80% are White; 11% African American. 80% are Protestant. The average age of freshmen is 18; all undergraduates, 20. 14% do not continue beyond their first year; 68% remain to graduate. **Housing:** 1151 students can be accommodated in college housing, which includes single-sex and coed dorms, on-campus apartments, and off-campus apartments. In addition, there are special-interest houses, fraternity houses, Carol International House serves as housing for international students and students with an interest in studying abroad or experiencing international cultures. On-campus housing is guaranteed for all 4 years. 100% of students live on campus; of those, 75% remain on campus on weekends. All students may keep cars.

FACULTY/CLASSROOMS: 59% of faculty are male; 41% are female. All teach undergraduates, all do research, and all teach and do research. No introductory courses are taught by graduate students. The average class size in an introductory lecture is 20; in a laboratory is 15; and in a regular course is 15.

PROGRAMS OF STUDY: PC confers B.A., and B.S. degrees. Doctoral degrees are also awarded. Bachelor's degrees are awarded in BIOLOGICAL SCIENCE (biochemistry and biology/biological science), BUSINESS (business administration and management and business economics), COMMUNICATIONS AND THE ARTS (art, art history and appreciation, dramatic arts, English, French, modern language, music, Spanish, and visual and performing arts), COMPUTER AND PHYSICAL SCIENCE (chemistry, mathematics, medical physics, and physics), EDUCATION (early childhood education, middle school education, and music education), HEALTH PROFESSIONS (pharmacy), SOCIAL SCIENCE (history, international studies, political science/government, psychology, religion, religious education, and sociology). All majors are academically strong. is the strongest academically. Business administration, biology, and history have the largest enrollments.

ACTIVITIES: 38% of men belong to 6 national fraternities; 47% of women belong to 3 national sororities. There are 85 groups on campus, including art, band, cheerleading, choir, chorale, chorus, computers, dance, drama, environmental, ethnic, gay, honors, international, jazz band, literary magazine, newspaper, orchestra, pep band, photography, political, professional, religious, social, social service, student government, and yearbook. Popular campus events include Fall Fling, Spring Swing, and Greek Week. **Sports:** There are 7 intercollegiate sports for men and 8 for women, and 9 intramural sports for men and 9 for women. Facilities include an physical education center, tennis courts, soccer stadium, baseball complex, softball complex, and two additional stadiums. Springs Campus Center contains a canteen, table tennis and pool tables, a fitness center, aerobics room, and a gym. **Graduates:** From July 1, 2013 to June 30, 2014, 266 bachelor's degrees were awarded. The most popular majors were business administration (18%), biology (14%), and English (11%). 60 companies recruited on campus in 2013-2014. In an average class, 60% graduate in 4 years or less, 68% graduate in 5 years or less, and 68% graduate in 6 years or less. Of the 2013 graduating class, 40% were enrolled in graduate school within 6 months of graduation, and 54% were employed.

SERVICES: Counseling and information services are available, as is tutoring in every subject. There is a reader service for the blind. **Library/Resources:** The library contains 121,499 volumes, 6,866 microform items, 12,866 audio/video tapes/CDs/DVDs, and subscribes to 8,134 periodicals including electronic. Computerized library services include interlibrary loans, database searching, Internet access, and Wi-Fi capability. Special learning facilities include an art gallery. **Physically Challenged Students:** 95% of the campus is accessible. Facilities include wheelchair ramps, elevators, special parking, specially equipped restrooms, lowered drinking fountains, and special housing. **Special:** Educational internships, study abroad in 25 countries, and a Washington semester are available. Dual majors, work-study programs, accelerated degree programs, B.A.-B.S. degrees, and a 3-2 engineering degree with Auburn, Clemson, and Vanderbilt Universities are offered. There is a forestry environmental studies program with Duke University. Credit for military experience, auditing courses, and pass/fail options are possible. There are 10 national honor societies, a freshman honors program, and 17 departmental honors programs. **Visiting:** There are regularly scheduled orientations for prospective students, including academics, student activity, financial aid information, tour, and lunch. There are guides for informal visits, visitors may sit in on classes, and stay overnight. To schedule a visit, contact the Office of Admissions. **Campus Safety and Security:** Measures include 24-hour foot and vehicle patrol, emergency notification system, and security escort services. There are shuttle buses, emergency telephones, lighted pathways/sidewalks, controlled access to dorms/residences, and 24-hour key card dorm locks.

REQUIREMENTS: Applicants must be graduates of an accredited secondary school with 18 academic credits, including 4 years of English, 3 of math, and 2 or more each of foreign language, history, science, and social studies. The GED is accepted. An essay is required. For music scholarships, an audition is required. Depending on high school GPA, some students will be required to submit either SAT or ACT scores. A GPA of 2.0 is required. AP and CLEP credits are accepted. Important factors in the admissions decision are advanced placement or honors courses, recommendations by school officials, and leadership record.To graduate, students must complete a minimum of 122 semester hours, including 30 to 48 in the major, with a minimum GPA of 2.0. Distribution requirements include 8 hours of natural science, 6 each of English, history, social science, and religion, 4 to 6 of intercultural experience, 3 each of math and fine arts, 2 to 3 of phys ed, 1 to 3 each of freshman experience and senior capstone, and 0 to 7 of foreign language. **Procedure:** Freshmen are admitted to all sessions. Entrance exams should be taken during the spring of the junior year. There are early decision, early admissions, deferred admissions, and rolling admissions plans. Early decision applications should be filed by November 1; regular applications, by February 1 for fall entry; and December 1 for spring entry. Notification of early decision is sent December 1; regular decision, March 15. 35 early decision candidates were accepted for the 2014-2015 class. Applications are accepted on-line. Application fees are waived if application is completed on-line. **Transfer Students:** 12 transfer students enrolled in 2013-2014. 48 of 122 credits required for the bachelor's degree must be completed at PC. **International Students:** There are 44 international students enrolled. The school actively recruits these students. They must take the TOEFL with a minimum score of 550 on the paper-based TOEFL (PBT) or 80 on the Internet-based version (iBT). They must also take the SAT or ACT.

ADMISSIONS: 66% of the 2014-2015 applicants were accepted. The SAT scores for the 2014-2015 freshman class were: Critical Reading--27% below 500, 46% between 500 and 599, 24% between 600 and 699, and 3% between 700 and 800; Math--18% below 500, 50% between 500 and 599, 28% between 600 and 699, and 4% between 700 and 800. The ACT scores were 16% below 21, 26% between 21 and 23, 24% between 24 and 26, 15% between 27 and 28, and 19% above 28. 52% of the current freshmen were in the top fifth of their class; 84% were in the top two fifths. **Admissions Contact:** Brian J. Fortman, Dean of Enrollment Management. E-Mail: *admissions@ presby.edu* Web: *www.presby.edu*

FINANCIAL AID: In 2014-2015, 85% of all full-time freshmen students received some form of financial aid. 95% of all full-time freshmen and 85% of continuing full-time students received need-based aid. The average freshman award was $31,000. Need-based scholarships or need-based grants averaged $30,263; need-based self-help aid (loans and jobs) averaged $3,438; and non-need-based athletic scholarships averaged $18,000. 41% of undergraduate students work part-time. Average annual earnings from campus work are $1004. The average financial indebtedness of the 2014 graduate was $21,211. PC is a member of CSS. The FAFSA and the college's own financial statement are required. The priority date for freshman financial aid applications for fall entry is March 15. The deadline for filing freshman financial aid applications for fall entry is June 30.

SOUTH CAROLINA STATE UNIVERSITY (*The complete profile is made available exclusively on our website, www.barronspac.com*)

SOUTHERN WESLEYAN UNIVERSITY A-2
www.swu.edu

Central, SC 29630-1020	(864) 644-5000
	(864) 644-5556
Fax: n/av	Email: admissions@swu.edu
Full-time: 615 men, 1030 women	Faculty: 44
Part-time: 10 men, 20 women	Ph.Ds: 75%
Graduate: 200 men, 510 women	Student/Faculty: n/av
Year: semesters, summer session	Tuition: $20,550
Room & Board: $8050	Freshman Class: n/av
SAT or ACT: required	CEEB CODE: 5896
Application Deadline: see profile	COMPETITIVE

Southern Wesleyan University, founded in 1906 and affiliated with the Wesleyan Church, is a private liberal arts institution that is a part of the Council for Christian Colleges and Universities. There are 3 undergraduate schools and 3 graduate schools. In addition to regional accreditation, SWU has baccalaureate program accreditation with NASDTEC and NCATE. The 325-acre campus is in a small town 30 miles southwest of Greenville and 5 miles from Clemson. Including any residence halls, there are 30 buildings.

STUDENT LIFE: 83% of undergraduates are from South Carolina. Students are from 23 states, 18 foreign countries, and Canada. 78% are white; 13% African American. 82% are Protestant. The average age of freshmen is 18; all undergraduates, 21. 33% do not continue beyond their first year; 46% remain to graduate.

FACULTY/CLASSROOMS: 62% of faculty are male; 38% are female. All teach and do research. No introductory courses are taught by graduate students. The average class size in an introductory lecture is 22 and in a laboratory is 18.

PROGRAMS OF STUDY: SWU confers B.A. and B.S. degrees. Associate and Master's degrees are also awarded. Bachelor's degrees are awarded in BIOLOGICAL SCIENCE (biology/biological science), BUSINESS (business administration and management, recreation and leisure services, and sports management), COMMUNICATIONS AND THE ARTS (communications, English, and music), COMPUTER AND PHYSICAL SCIENCE (chemistry, computer science, and mathematics), EDUCATION (early childhood education, elementary education, English education, mathematics education, music education, physical education, and special education), ENGINEERING AND ENVIRONMENTAL DESIGN (computer technology), HEALTH PROFESSIONS (medical laboratory technology), SOCIAL SCIENCE (criminal justice, forensic studies, history, human services, psychology, religion, and social studies). Education, business, and biology have the largest enrollments.

ACTIVITIES: There are 15 groups on campus, including band, cheerleading, choir, chorale, chorus, computers, drama, ethnic, honors, jazz band, literary magazine, musical theater, orchestra, professional, religious, social, social service, student government, and yearbook. Popular campus events include Christmas Banquet, Junior/Senior Banquet, and Coffee House.

SERVICES: Counseling and information services are available, as is tutoring in most subjects. There is a reader service for the blind, remedial math, reading, and writing. Supplemental instruction is available for biology. The library contains 116,200 volumes, 2160 microform items, 5755 audio/video tapes/CDs/DVDs, and subscribes to 510 periodicals including electronic. Computerized library services include interlibrary loans, database searching, and Internet access. Special learning facilities include a learning resource center, electron microscope lab, genealogical research collection, and Freedom's Hill Historic Site.

REQUIREMENTS: The SAT or ACT is required. Applicants should complete 16 Carnegie units, including 4 credits of English and 2 each of math, science, and social studies, as well as 6 electives. The GED is accepted. SWU requires applicants to be in the upper 50% of their class. A GPA of 2.3 is required. AP and CLEP credits are accepted.

ADMISSIONS: 94% of a recent year's applicants were accepted. 22 freshmen graduated first in their class.

FINANCIAL AID: In a recent year, 94% of all full-time freshmen and 93% of continuing full-time students received some form of financial aid, including need-based aid. 76% of undergraduate students work part-time. The average financial indebtedness of a recent year's graduate was $23,055. The FAFSA and the college's own financial statement are required. Check with the school for current application deadlines.

UNIVERSITY OF SOUTH CAROLINA SYSTEM

The University of South Carolina System, established in 1801, is a private system in South Carolina. It is governed by a board of trustees, whose chief administrator is the president. The primary goal of the system is to prepare informed and productive citizens in order to adapt to an increasingly complex environment. The main priorities are to foster excellence in undergraduate and graduate education, research, and service programs. The total student enrollment for all 8 campuses is usually 31,964 with 2500 faculty members. Altogether there are 76 baccalaureate, 105 master's, and 56 doctoral programs offered in the University of South Carolina System. Profiles of the 4-year campuses are included in this section.

UNIVERSITY OF SOUTH CAROLINA AIKEN	C-3
www.usca.edu	

Aiken, SC 29801	(803) 648-6851
	(803) 641-3366
Fax: (803) 641-3727	Email: admit@usca.edu
Full-time: 914 men, 1580 women	Faculty: 149; IIB, --$
Part-time: 301 men, 444 women	Ph.D.s: 75%
Graduate: 42 men, 140 women	Student/Faculty: 17 to 1
Year: semesters, summer session	Tuition: $9602 ($18,926)
Room & Board: $7110	Freshman Class: 2103 applied, 1448 accepted, 635 enrolled
SAT CR/M/W: 480/480/460 ACT: 21	CEEB CODE: 5840
Application Deadline: open 1	COMPETITIVE

The University of South Carolina Aiken, founded in 1961 is a comprehensive liberal arts institution committed to active learning through teaching, faculty and student scholarship, research, creative activities and service. The university offers degrees in the arts and sciences and in the professional disciplines of business, education, and nursing. There are 5 undergraduate schools and 2 graduate schools. In addition to regional accreditation, USCA has baccalaureate program accreditation with AACSB, ABET, NASM, NCATE, and CCNE. The 453-acre campus is in a suburban area 14 miles east of Augusta, Georgia. Including any residence halls, there are 25 buildings.

STUDENT LIFE: 86% of undergraduates are from South Carolina. Others are from 29 states, and 24 foreign countries. 91% are from public schools. 61% are White; 25% African American. The average age of freshmen is 18; all undergraduates, 22. 34% do not continue beyond their first year; 43% remain to graduate. **Housing:** 950 students can be accommodated in college housing, which includes coed dorms and on-campus apartments. On-campus housing is available on a first-come, first-served basis, and is available on a lottery system for upperclassmen. 71% of students commute. All students may keep cars.

FACULTY/CLASSROOMS: 48% of faculty are male; 52% are female. All teach undergraduates. No introductory courses are taught by graduate students. The average class size in an introductory lecture is 17 and in a laboratory is 15.

PROGRAMS OF STUDY: USCA confers B.A., B.S., B.S.(in Business Administration), B.A.Ed, B.S.Ed, B.A.Spec.Ed, B.A.I.S, B.S.N. and B.S.I.S. degrees. Master's degrees are also awarded. Bachelor's degrees are awarded in BIOLOGICAL SCIENCE (biology/biological science), BUSINESS (business administration and management), COMMUNICATIONS AND THE ARTS (communications, English, and fine arts), COMPUTER AND PHYSICAL SCIENCE (applied mathematics, chemistry, and computer mathematics), EDUCATION (early childhood education, elementary education, middle school education, music education, secondary education, and special education), HEALTH PROFESSIONS (exercise science and nursing), SOCIAL SCIENCE (history, interdisciplinary studies, political science/government, psychology, and sociology). Special education, early childhood education, nursing, and secondary education are the strongest academically. Business, exercise and sports science, and nursing have the largest enrollments.

ACTIVITIES: There are 78 groups on campus, including and veterans, band, cheerleading, choir, chorus, computers, dance, drama, ethnic, gay, honors, international, jazz band, literary magazine, musical theater, newspaper, nontraditional students, pep band, photography, political, professional, religious, social, social service, and student government. Popular campus events include Waterfest, Homecoming, Greek Life Recruitment Week, Dance Marathon, and Relay for Life. **Sports:** There are 5 intercollegiate sports for men and 6 for women, and 6 intramural sports for men and 6 for women. Facilities include an activities center, the Roberto Hernandez baseball stadium, a soccer/intramural/softball field, tennis courts, and a wellness/exercise center. **Graduates:** From July 1, 2013 to June 30, 2014, 516 bachelor's degrees were awarded. The most popular majors were business (23%), nursing (13%), and education (12%). 296 companies recruited on campus in 2013-2014. In an average class, 24%

graduate in 4 years or less, 35% graduate in 5 years or less, and 43% graduate in 6 years or less.

SERVICES: Counseling and information services are available, as is tutoring in most subjects. There is a reader service for the blind. Individual subject tutoring available upon request **Library/Resources:** The library contains 174,413 volumes, 79,876 microform items, 309,706 audio/video tapes/CDs/DVDs, and subscribes to 30,188 periodicals including electronic. Computerized library services include interlibrary loans, database searching, Internet access, and Wi-Fi capability. Special learning facilities include an art gallery, planetarium, a science education center, and a language lab. **Physically Challenged Students:** All of the campus is accessible. Facilities include wheelchair ramps, elevators, special parking, specially equipped restrooms, lowered drinking fountains, lowered telephones. **Special:** Cross-registration is permitted with other schools in the University of South Carolina system. Co-op programs,internships, study abroad, student-designed majors, and work-study programs are offered. B.A.-B.S. degrees in Interdisciplinary Studies, nondegree study, and pass/fail options are possible. There are 13 national honor societies, a freshman honors program, and 10 departmental honors programs. **Visiting:** There are regularly scheduled orientations for prospective students, including regularly scheduled 3-day orientations for prospective students. There are guides for informal visits and visitors may sit in on classes. To schedule a visit, contact the Admissions Office at admit@usca.edu. **Campus Safety and Security:** Measures include 24-hour foot and vehicle patrol, emergency notification system, self-defense education, and security escort services. There are emergency telephones, lighted pathways/sidewalks, and controlled access to dorms/residences.

REQUIREMENTS: The SAT is required. The ACT and ACT Writing Test are recommended. Admission is based on a combination of an applicant's scores on college entrance exams and high school GPA. Applicants are required to submit 21 academic credits, including 4 years of high school English, 3 units of math, 3 units of social studies, 2 units of foreign language, 3 units of a lab science, 1 of US history, and 1 year of phys ed or ROTC, and 4 electives from 3 different areas such as computer science, English, fine arts, foreign language, humanities, certain lab sciences, a math above algebra II, and social science. It is strongly suggested that 1 be in computer science programming. AP and CLEP credits are accepted. Important factors in the admissions decision are advanced placement or honors courses, recommendations by school officials, and leadership record. Students must complete a minimum of 120 credit hours, with at least a 2.0 GPA. USC Aiken has a strong liberal arts emphasis. General education requirements include courses in English, math, applied speech, natural science, social and behavioral sciences, humanities, nonwestern studies course, and history. In addition, students must complete a critical inquiry course, a prescribed number of writing intensive courses and inter-curricular enrichment events. **Procedure:** Freshmen are admitted to all sessions. Entrance exams should be taken by the fall of the senior year. There are early admissions, deferred admissions, and rolling admissions plans. Application deadlines are open. The fall 2014 application fee was $45. Notification is sent on a rolling basis. Applications are accepted on-line. **Transfer Students:** The college GPA is considered. A high school transcript is required of applicants with fewer than 30 semester hours. 30 of 120 credits required for the bachelor's degree must be completed at USCA. **International Students:** There are 96 international students enrolled. They must take the TOEFL with a minimum score of 550 on the paper-based TOEFL (PBT) or 80 on the Internet-based version (iBT). They must also take the SAT or ACT.

ADMISSIONS: 69% of the 2014-2015 applicants were accepted. The SAT scores for the 2014-2015 freshman class were: Critical Reading--57% below 500, 33% between 500 and 599, and 10% between 600 and 699; Math--55% below 500, 34% between 500 and 599, and 11% between 600 and 699; Writing--68% below 500, 27% between 500 and 599, and 5% between 600 and 699. The ACT scores were 38% below 21, 27% between 21 and 23, 20% between 24 and 26, 10% between 27 and 28, and 5% above 28. 33% of the current freshmen were in the top fifth of their class; 67% were in the top two fifths. 9 freshmen graduated first in their class. **Admissions Contact:** Andrew Hendrix, Director of Admissions.

FINANCIAL AID: The FAFSA is required. The priority date for freshman financial aid applications for fall entry is February 15. The deadline for filing freshman financial aid applications for fall entry is March 15.

UNIVERSITY OF SOUTH CAROLINA AT BEAUFORT (*The complete profile is made available exclusively on our website, www. barronspac.com*)

UNIVERSITY OF SOUTH CAROLINA AT COLUMBIA   C-3
www.sc.edu

Columbia, SC 29208	(803) 777-7700
	(800) 868-5872
Fax: (803) 777-0101	Email: admissions-ugrad@sc.edu
Full-time: 9849 men, 11797 women	Faculty: 854; I, -$
Part-time: 898 men, 819 women	Ph.D.s: 84%
Graduate: 3268 men, 4657 women	Student/Faculty: 25 to 1
Year: semesters, summer session	Tuition: $10,816 ($28,528)
Room & Board: $8909	Freshman Class: 23429 applied, 14199 accepted, 4625 enrolled
SAT CR/M: 590/610 ACT: 27	CEEB CODE: 5818
Application Deadline: December 1	VERY COMPETITIVE+

The University of South Carolina at Columbia, founded in 1801, is a publicly assisted institution serving the entire state of South Carolina. In addition to the main campus at Columbia, there are 3 senior campuses at Aiken, Beaufort, and Upstate, and 4 regional campuses at Lancaster, Salkehatchie, Sumter, and Union. There are 11 undergraduate schools and 12 graduate schools. In addition to regional accreditation, USC has baccalaureate program accreditation with AACSB, ABET, ACEJMC, ACPE, CSAB, NASM, NCATE, and NLN. The 444-acre campus is in an urban area in the downtown area of Columbia. Including any residence halls, there are 181 buildings.

STUDENT LIFE: 65% of undergraduates are from South Carolina. Others are from 50 states, 115 foreign countries, and Canada. 77% are White; 11% African American. The average age of freshmen is 18; all undergraduates, 21. 13% do not continue beyond their first year; 72% remain to graduate. **Housing:** 6838 students can be accommodated in college housing, which includes single-sex and coed dorms, on-campus apartments, and married student housing. In addition, there are honors houses, special-interest houses, fraternity houses, sorority houses, Honors, wellness, residential college, Pre-medical, Pre-law, French, Spanish, Journalism, Engineering, Athletic, Music, Global, Common Courses Programs and Environmentally Friendly. On-campus housing is guaranteed for the freshman year only and is available on a lottery system for upperclassmen. 64% of students commute. All students may keep cars.

FACULTY/CLASSROOMS: 59% of faculty are male; 41% are female. All do research. No introductory courses are taught by graduate students. The average class size in an introductory lecture is 30; in a laboratory is 23; and in a regular course is 29.

PROGRAMS OF STUDY: USC confers B.A., B.A.I.S., B.A.I.S., B.A.J.M.C., B.F.A., B.M., B.S., B.S.B.A., B.S.C., B.S.C.S., B.S.E., B.S.I.S., B.S.N., B.S.P.E., B.S.W. and BarSc. degrees. Associate, Master's, and Doctoral degrees are also awarded. Bachelor's degrees are awarded in BIOLOGICAL SCIENCE (biology/biological science and marine science), BUSINESS (accounting, banking and finance, business administration and management, business economics, hotel/motel and restaurant management, insurance, management science, marketing/retailing/merchandising, office supervision and management, real estate, retailing, and sports management), COMMUNICATIONS AND THE ARTS (advertising, art history and appreciation, broadcasting, classics, communications, comparative literature, dance, dramatic arts, English, fine arts, French, German, journalism, media arts, music, public relations, Russian, Spanish, speech/debate/rhetoric, and studio art), COMPUTER AND PHYSICAL SCIENCE (chemistry, computer science, geology, geophysics and seismology, mathematics, physics, and statistics), EDUCATION (art education, early childhood education, elementary education, middle school education, music education, and physical education), ENGINEERING AND ENVIRONMENTAL DESIGN (biomedical engineering, chemical engineering, civil engineering, computer engineering, electrical/electronics engineering, environmental science, and mechanical engineering), HEALTH PROFESSIONS (exercise science, nursing, and public health), SOCIAL SCIENCE (African American studies, anthropology, criminal justice, economics, European studies, experimental psychology, geography, history, interdisciplinary studies, Latin American studies, philosophy, political science/government, psychology, religion, social work, sociology, and women's studies). engineering, business, and nursing are the strongest academically. biology, nursing, experimental psychology, exercise science, and criminology/criminal justice have the largest enrollments.

ACTIVITIES: 13% of men belong to 22 national fraternities; 28% of women belong to 16 national sororities. There are 387 groups on campus, including art, band, cheerleading, chess, choir, chorale, chorus, computers, dance, debate, drama, drill team, ethnic, film, forensics, gay, honors, international, jazz band, literary magazine, marching band, musical theater, newspaper, opera, orchestra, pep band, photography, political, professional, radio and TV, religious, social, social service, student government, symphony, and yearbook. Popular campus events include First-Year Reading Experience, Civil Rights Tour, Parents Weekend, Alternative Spring and Fall Break Trips, Homecoming Week and Carolina Cares. **Sports:** There are 9 intercollegiate sports for men and 11 for women, and 29 intramural sports for men and 29 for women. Facilities include football and soccer stadiums, a basketball coliseum, a field house, a volleyball and basketball practice facility, baseball, softball, and practice fields, and an all-weather track. There is also a recreation center with badminton, basketball, handball/racquetball, an aquatics center, climbing wall, and weight room. **Graduates:** From July 1, 2013 to June 30, 2014, 7162 bachelor's degrees were awarded. The most popular majors were experimental psychology (6%), integrated IT (6%), and biology (5%). 900 companies recruited on campus in 2013-2014. In an average class, 56% graduate in 4 years or less, 70% graduate in 5 years or less, and 72% graduate in 6 years or less. Of the 2013 graduating class, 23% were enrolled in graduate school within 6 months of graduation.

SERVICES: Counseling and information services are available, as is tutoring in every subject, reader services for LD students. There is a reader service for the blind. **Library/Resources:** The 7 libraries contain 4.5 million volumes, and 5.5 million microform items. Computerized library services include interlibrary loans, database searching, Internet access, and Wi-Fi capability. Special learning facilities include an art gallery, natural history museum, planetarium, radio station, and TV station. **Physically Challenged Students:** 85% of the campus is accessible. Facilities include wheelchair ramps, elevators, special parking, specially equipped restrooms, special class scheduling, lowered drinking fountains, special housing. Listening devices, sign language interpreting, and adapted transportation and computers. **Special:** USC transmits live interactive televised instruction to more than 20 locations in the state. Cross-registration is offered with the National Technological University in Engineering and through the National Student Exchange. Internships in many fields, study abroad in many countries through the Byrnes International Center, co-op programs, and work-study programs are available. Double majors through the colleges of humanities and social sciences and science and math, student-designed majors, an interdisciplinary studies degree, and a 3-2 engineering degree with the College of Charleston are offered. Credit for military experience, nondegree study, and pass/fail options also are possible. There are 28 national honor societies, including Phi Beta Kappa, and a freshman honors program. **Visiting:** There are regularly scheduled orientations for prospective students, students take placement tests, are advised and register for classes. There are guides for informal visits. To schedule a visit, contact the USC Visitor's Center. **Campus Safety and Security:** Measures include 24-hour foot and vehicle patrol, emergency notification system, self-defense education, and security escort services. There are shuttle buses, emergency telephones, lighted pathways/sidewalks, controlled access to dorms/residences.

REQUIREMENTS: The SAT or ACT is required. Admission as a freshman into the University is primarily based upon a combination of grades earned in specific high-school courses and official SAT or ACT scores. Additional factors may be taken into consideration, such as extraordinary personal circumstances, special talents, outstanding extracurricular activities, and evidence of leadership. AP and CLEP credits are accepted. All students must maintain a GPA of 2.0 in 120 semester hours including 24 in their major. Distribution requirements include 6 hours in English, 6 in Numerical/Analytical Reasoning, 12 in Liberal Arts, 7 in Natural Sciences, and Foreign Language demonstrated proficiency. **Procedure:** Freshmen are admitted to all sessions. Entrance exams should be taken during spring of the junior year and fall of the senior year, if necessary. There is a rolling admissions plan. Applications should be filed by December 1 for fall entry; November 1 for spring entry; and May 1 for summer entry, along with a $50 fee. Applications are accepted on-line. **Transfer Students:** 1961 transfer students enrolled in 2013-2014. Cumulative GPA of 2.25 from all regionally accredited colleges (remedial courses are not included in the GPA computation). Must meet freshman requirements if the student has attempted fewer than 30 semester hours. 30 of 120 credits required for the bachelor's degree must be completed at USC. **International Students:** There are 390 international students enrolled. The school actively recruits these students. They must take the TOEFL with a minimum score of 550 on the paper-based TOEFL (PBT) or 77 on the Internet-based version (iBT). The SAT and ACT are recommended.

ADMISSIONS: 61% of the 2014-2015 applicants were accepted. The SAT scores for the 2014-2015 freshman class were: Critical Reading--10% below 500, 45% between 500 and 599, 36% between 600 and 699, and 10% between 700 and 800; Math--5% below 500, 37% between 500 and 599, 48% between 600 and 699, and 11% between 700 and 800. The ACT scores were 3% below 21, 17% between 21 and 23, 29% between 24 and 26, 22% between 27 and 28, and 29% above 28. 57% of the current freshmen were in the top fifth of their class; 88% were in the top two fifths. There were 47 National Merit finalists. 66 freshmen graduated first in their class. **Admissions Contact:** R. Scott Verzyl, Associate Vice President for Enrollment.

FINANCIAL AID: In 2014-2015, 96% of all full-time freshmen and 87% of continuing full-time students received some form of financial aid. 47% of all full-time freshmen and 46% of continuing full-time students received need-based aid. The average freshman award was $13,526. Need-based scholarships or need-based grants averaged $7,116 ($27,912 maximum); need-based self-help aid (loans and jobs) averaged $2,358 ($15,500 maximum); non-need-based athletic scholarships averaged $11,747; and other non-need-based awards and non-need-based scholarships averaged $5,304. 15% of undergraduate students work part-time. Average annual earnings from campus work are $2396. USC is a member of CSS. The FAFSA is required. The deadline for filing freshman financial aid applications for fall entry is April 15.

UNIVERSITY OF SOUTH CAROLINA UPSTATE *(The complete profile is made available exclusively on our website, www.barronspac.com)*

VOORHEES COLLEGE   C-3
www.voorhees.edu

Denmark, SC 29042	(803) 780-1234
	(866) 685-9904
Fax: (803) 780-1430	Email: info@voorhees.edu
Full-time: 231 men, 288 women	Faculty: 40
Part-time: 4 men, 10 women	Ph.D.s: 40%
Graduate: n/av	Student/Faculty: 14 to 1
Year: semesters, summer session	Tuition: $10,780
Room & Board: $7346	Freshman Class: n/av
SAT or ACT: required	CEEB CODE: 5863
Application Deadline: n/av	COMPETITIVE

Voorhees College, founded in 1897, is a historically black liberal arts college affiliated with the Protestant Episcopal Church. The 342-acre campus is in a small town 50 miles south of Columbia. Including any residence halls, there are 25 buildings.

STUDENT LIFE: 68% of undergraduates are from South Carolina.

Others are from 16 states, and 1 foreign countries. 80% are from public schools. 95% are African American. 98% are Protestant. The average age of freshmen is 17; all undergraduates, 23. 40% remain to graduate. **Housing:** 537 students can be accommodated in college housing, which includes single-sex dorms. On-campus housing is guaranteed for all 4 years. 75% of students live on campus; of those, 50% remain on campus on weekends. Alcohol is not permitted. All students may keep cars.

FACULTY/CLASSROOMS: All teach undergraduates. No introductory courses are taught by graduate students. The average class size in an introductory lecture is 30; in a laboratory is 20; and in a regular course is 25.

PROGRAMS OF STUDY: Voorhees confers B.A., and B.S. degrees. Bachelor's degrees are awarded in BIOLOGICAL SCIENCE (biology/biological science), BUSINESS (accounting, business administration and management, organizational leadership and management, and recreation and leisure services), COMMUNICATIONS AND THE ARTS (communications and English), COMPUTER AND PHYSICAL SCIENCE (computer science and mathematics), HEALTH PROFESSIONS (health), SOCIAL SCIENCE (criminal justice and sociology). Biology and business administration is the strongest academically. Business and organizational management has the largest enrollment.

ACTIVITIES: 20% of men belong to 4 national fraternities; 20% of women belong to 4 national sororities. There are 20 groups on campus, including cheerleading, choir, computers, dance, drama, honors, newspaper, political, professional, radio and TV, religious, social, student government, and yearbook. Popular campus events include Career Awareness Week, Black History Month, Religious Emphasis Week, National Women's History Month, Business Week, National Library Week, Founders Day Week. **Sports:** There are 3 intercollegiate sports for men and 4 for women, and 4 intramural sports for men and 4 for women. Facilities include a gym, swimming pool, tennis and basketball courts, baseball and softball fields, track field, a weight room, a dance studio, and a student center. **Graduates:** From July 1, 2013 to June 30, 2014, 131 bachelor's degrees were awarded. The most popular majors were organizational management (28%), criminal justice (11%), and biology (8%). In an average class, 40% graduate in 4 years or less.

SERVICES: Counseling and information services are available, as is tutoring in most subjects. There is remedial math, reading, and writing. 24 hour campus-wide video surveillance system **Library/Resources:** The library contains 309,479 volumes, 26,010 microform items, 298 audio/video tapes/CDs/DVDs, and subscribes to 14,522 periodicals including electronic. Computerized library services include interlibrary loans, database searching, Internet access, and Wi-Fi capability. Special learning facilities include a radio station, an academic success center and a writing center. **Physically Challenged Students:** 90% of the campus is accessible. Facilities include wheelchair ramps, elevators, special parking, specially equipped restrooms, lowered drinking fountains. **Special:** Voorhees offers cooperative education, internships in some programs, work-study, an evening/Saturday program, off-campus summer study, dual majors, credit by exam, and a degree completion program. Cross-registration with Denmark Technical College and interdisciplinary majors, such as health and recreation, are possible. There are 3 national honor societies and 1 departmental honors program. **Visiting:** There are regularly scheduled orientations for prospective students, consisting of senior visitation days held January through April. There are guides for informal visits, visitors may sit in on classes, and stay overnight. To schedule a visit, contact Adrian West at west@voorhees.edu. **Campus Safety and Security:** Measures include 24-hour foot and vehicle patrol and emergency notification system. There are lighted pathways/sidewalks.

REQUIREMENTS: The SAT or ACT is required. In addition, with a satisfactory minimum score of 600 on the SAT or 16 on the ACT. Applicants must be high school graduates or hold a GED. Students should have earned 24 academic credits in high school, including 4 units of English, 4 units of math, 3 units of science, 1 unit of foreign language (optional), and 1 each of history, social studies, economics/government, 1 unit of physical education, 1 unit of computer science/keyboarding and 7 electives. Letters of recommendation and a campus visit are advised. A GPA of 2.0 is required. AP and CLEP

credits are accepted. Important factors in the admissions decision are advanced placement or honors courses, recommendations by school officials, and recommendations by alumni.To graduate, students must earn at least 122 credit hours, with at least 30 in the major, and have a minimum GPA of 2.0. The 50-hour general education requirement includes 12 hours of English/Speech, 5 hours of Humanities, 3 hours of foreign language, 1 hour of freshmen orientation, 2 hours of physical fitness, 12 hours of economics and history and 15 hours of mathematics, science and technology. A number of free electives and a senior seminar are also required. An English proficiency exam and an exit exam must be passed. **Procedure:** Freshmen are admitted to all sessions. Entrance exams should be taken in the senior year. There are deferred admissions and rolling admissions plans. Applications should be filed by December 15 for spring entry, along with a $25 fee. Notification of early decision is sent August 15; regular decision, December 15. **Transfer Students:** 35 transfer students enrolled in 2013-2014. Transfer students must submit complete records, including a confidential report from each college attended. The confidential report form is provided by the Office of Admission and Recruitment. Students with fewer than 30 semester hours must submit their high school record with rank in class and GPA. The SAT is recommended; a satisfactory composite score is expected. An interview is advised. 30 of 122 credits required for the bachelor's degree must be completed at Voorhees. **International Students:** They must take the TOEFL. They must also take the SAT or ACT.

ADMISSIONS: Paula Payton, Director of Admissions and Recruitment. E-Mail: *ppayton@voorhees.edu* Web: *www.voorhees.edu*

FINANCIAL AID: The average freshman award was $13,967. Need-based self-help aid (loans and jobs) averaged $5,500. Voorhees is a member of CSS. The FAFSA and the college's own financial statement, and or SAR. The FAFSA is preferred. are required. The priority date for freshman financial aid applications for fall entry is April 15.

WINTHROP UNIVERSITY   **C-1**
www.winthrop.edu

Rock Hill, SC 29733	**(803) 323-2211**
	(800) 946-8476
Fax: (803) 323-2137	**Email: admissions@winthrop.edu**
Full-time: n/av	**Faculty:** 281; IIA, --$
Part-time: n/av	**Ph.D.s:** 87%
Graduate: n/av	**Student/Faculty:** 15 to 1
Year: semesters, summer session	**Tuition:** $13,430 ($26,000)
Room & Board: $7690	**Freshman Class:** 4316 applied, 3051 accepted, 1143 enrolled
SAT CR/M: 525/525 **ACT:** 23	**CEEB CODE:** 5910
Application Deadline: May 1	**COMPETITIVE**

Nationally recognized for quality and value, Winthrop University, a public, comprehensive institution in Rock Hill, S.C., blends liberal arts, professional programs, global awareness and civic engagement. No matter what students study at Winthrop, they are prepared for successful careers, engaged in our democratic society, responsive to local and global concerns, and grounded in values that give meaning to their lives. These outcomes reflect the university's commitment to be among the very best institutions of its kind in the nation. Winthrop embodies the characteristics essential to being one of the best – a high-achieving, diverse student body; a national caliber curriculum; an undergraduate residential experience emphasizing community; and institutional values centered around global learning, undergraduate research, and engaged public service. Bolstered by a nationally acclaimed faculty and staff, Winthrop students learn that to be a person of success, they must first be a person of value. As a result, they develop the integrity that makes them stand out as leaders in their communities and in their chosen professions. There are 4 undergraduate schools and 4 graduate schools. In addition to regional accreditation, Winthrop has baccalaureate program accreditation with AACSB, ABET, ACEJMC, CSAB, CSWE, NASAD, NASM, and NCATE. The 445-acre campus is in a small town 23 miles south of Charlotte, NC. Including any residence halls, there are 75 buildings.
STUDENT LIFE: Students are from 34 states, 37 foreign countries,

and Canada. 62% are White; 28% African American. The average age of freshmen is 18; all undergraduates, 21. 27% do not continue beyond their first year; 58% remain to graduate.

FACULTY/CLASSROOMS: 42% of faculty are male; 58% are female. 98% teach undergraduates. No introductory courses are taught by graduate students. The average class size in an introductory lecture is 32; in a laboratory is 19; and in a regular course is 24.

PROGRAMS OF STUDY: Winthrop confers B.A., B.S., B.F.A., B.M., B.M.E. and B.S.W. degrees. Master's degrees are also awarded. Bachelor's degrees are awarded in AGRICULTURE (environmental studies), BIOLOGICAL SCIENCE (biology/biological science and nutrition), BUSINESS (business administration and management, electronic business, and sports management), COMMUNICATIONS AND THE ARTS (art, art history and appreciation, communications, dance, English, English literature, fine arts, French, German, modern language, music, music performance, public relations, Spanish, technical and business writing, and theatre arts), COMPUTER AND PHYSICAL SCIENCE (chemistry, computer science, and mathematics), EDUCATION (athletic training, early childhood education, elementary education, middle school education, music education, physical education, secondary education, special education, and sports and wellness studies), ENGINEERING AND ENVIRONMENTAL DESIGN (environmental science and interior design), HEALTH PROFESSIONS (exercise science and medical laboratory technology), SOCIAL SCIENCE (economics, history, philosophy, philosophy and religion, political science/government, psychology, religion, social work, sociology, and Spanish studies). Business administration, biology, psychology and fine arts have the largest enrollments.

ACTIVITIES: 4% of men belong to 7 national fraternities; 9% of women belong to 9 national sororities. There are 160 groups on campus, including art, band, cheerleading, chess, choir, chorale, chorus, computers, dance, drama, environmental, ethnic, gay, honors, international, jazz band, literary magazine, musical theater, newspaper, opera, pep band, political, professional, radio and TV, religious, social, social service, and student government. Popular campus events include Welcome Week, Convocation and Picnic, Basketball Game Tailgaiting, Homecoming Talent Show, and Movies at DiGiorgio Campus Center.

SERVICES: Counseling and information services are available, as is tutoring in some subjects, math and writing center, as well as any subjects tutoring program within Residence Halls. There is a reader service for the blind. Academic Success Center focuses on helping students achieve academic excellence and earn their college degree. This program provides tutoring opportunities and tools to excel in their classes.

REQUIREMENTS: The SAT or ACT is required. Graduation from an accredited secondary school is required; a GED will be accepted. Applicants must have successfully completed 4 credits in high school English, 3 in math, 3 in lab science, 2 each in social studies and foreign language, 1 in United States history, and 4 in Electives that must be taken from at least three different fields selected from among Computer Science, English, Fine Arts, Foreign Languages, Humanities, Laboratory Science (excluding earth science, general physical science, general environmental science, or other introductory science courses for which biology and/or chemistry is not a prerequisite), Mathematics above the level of Algebra II, and Social Sciences. It is suggested that one unit be in Computer Science which includes programming (not just keyboarding) and one unit in Fine Arts (i.e. appreciation of, history, or performance). A GPA of 3.0 is required. AP and CLEP credits are accepted. Important factors in the admissions decision are advanced placement or honors courses, evidence of special talent, and geographical diversity.

ADMISSIONS: 71% of a recent year applicants were accepted. The SAT scores for a recent year freshman class were: Critical Reading--37% below 500, 39% between 500 and 599, 18% between 600 and 699, and 3% between 700 and 800; Math--37% below 500, 43% between 500 and 599, 17% between 600 and 699, and 1% between 700 and 800. The ACT scores were 36% below 21, 28% between 21 and 23, 17% between 24 and 26, 13% between 27 and 28, and 9% above 28. 43% of the current freshmen were in the top fifth of their class; 76% were in the top two fifths.

FINANCIAL AID: In a recent year, 79% of all full-time freshmen and 70% of continuing full-time students received some form of financial aid. 67% of all full-time freshmen and 60% of continuing full-time students received need-based aid. The average freshman award was $13,298. Need-based scholarships or need-based grants averaged $9,179 ($10,154 maximum); need-based self-help aid (loans and jobs) averaged $3,577 ($4,700 maximum); non-need-based athletic scholarships averaged $9,761 ($28,466 maximum); and other non-need-based awards and non-need-based scholarships averaged $4,262 ($14,006 maximum). 18% of undergraduate students work part-time. Average annual earnings from campus work are $1600. The average financial indebtedness of the 2013 graduate was $22,521. Winthrop is a member of CSS. The FAFSA is required. The priority date for freshman financial aid applications for fall entry is March 1.

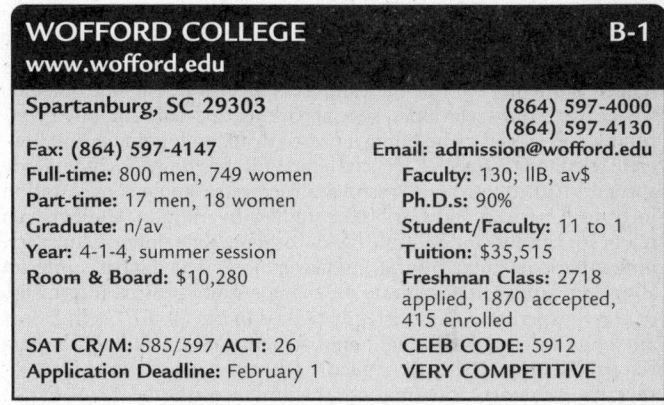

WOFFORD COLLEGE   **B-1**
www.wofford.edu

Spartanburg, SC 29303	(864) 597-4000 / (864) 597-4130
Fax: (864) 597-4147	Email: admission@wofford.edu
Full-time: 800 men, 749 women	Faculty: 130; IIB, av$
Part-time: 17 men, 18 women	Ph.D.s: 90%
Graduate: n/av	Student/Faculty: 11 to 1
Year: 4-1-4, summer session	Tuition: $35,515
Room & Board: $10,280	Freshman Class: 2718 applied, 1870 accepted, 415 enrolled
SAT CR/M: 585/597 ACT: 26	CEEB CODE: 5912
Application Deadline: February 1	VERY COMPETITIVE

Wofford College, founded in 1854, is a private four-year institution affiliated with the United Methodist Church, offering programs in liberal arts and preprofessional studies. In addition to regional accreditation, Wofford has baccalaureate program accreditation with NASDTEC. The 170-acre campus is in an urban area 70 miles southwest of Charlotte. Including any residence halls, there are 72 buildings.

STUDENT LIFE: 56% of undergraduates are from South Carolina. Others are from 37 states, and 12 foreign countries. 67% are from public schools. 80% are White. 67% are Protestant; 18% Unknown Religious affiliation; 12% Catholic. The average age of freshmen is 18; all undergraduates, 20. 10% do not continue beyond their first year; 82% remain to graduate.

FACULTY/CLASSROOMS: 60% of faculty are male; 40% are female. All teach undergraduates. No introductory courses are taught by graduate students. The average class size in an introductory lecture is 21; in a laboratory is 21; and in a regular course is 17.

PROGRAMS OF STUDY: Wofford confers B.A., and B.S. degrees. Bachelor's degrees are awarded in AGRICULTURE (environmental studies), BIOLOGICAL SCIENCE (biology/biological science), BUSINESS (accounting, banking and finance, business economics, and finance), COMMUNICATIONS AND THE ARTS (art history, Chinese, creative writing, dramatic arts, English, French, German, Spanish, studio art, and theatre arts), COMPUTER AND PHYSICAL SCIENCE (applied mathematics, chemistry, computer science, mathematics, and physics), SOCIAL SCIENCE (African American studies, crosscultural studies, economics, gender studies, history, humanities, Latin American studies, philosophy, political science/government, psychology, religion, and sociology). Biology, foreign languages, finance/accounting are the strongest academically. Biology, business economics and Spanish have the largest enrollments.

ACTIVITIES: 43% of men belong to 8 national fraternities; 55% of women belong to 4 national sororities. There are 98 groups on campus, including and the interfaith youth core, band, cheerleading, choir, chorale, chorus, college bowl team, computers, dance, drama, environmental, ethnic, gay, international, jazz band, literary magazine, newspaper, orchestra, pep band, photography, political, professional, religious, social, social service, student government, and yearbook. Popular campus events include Phi Beta Kappa Day, Honors Day, Novel Experience, and Winter Lighting.

SERVICES: Counseling and information services are available, as is

tutoring in every subject. There is a reader service for the blind. **Library/Resources:** The library contains 184,715 volumes, 21,150 microform items, 3,866 audio/video tapes/CDs/DVDs, and subscribes to 47,528 periodicals including electronic. Computerized library services include interlibrary loans, database searching, Internet access, and Wi-Fi capability. Special learning facilities include an art gallery, international studies, arboretum, greenhouse, the Goodall environmental studies, and The Space in The Mungo Center that houses several programs: The Space to: Prepare (houses the Career Services office, the Sophomore Experience and the Institute); The Space to: Impact (a competitive four-year program teaching design thinking, entrepreneurship, project management and the consultative approach to problem solving.; The Space to:Launch (supports students in the concept, development and launch of a business idea.); The Space to:Consult (student consulting group providing business and organizations strategies to improve performance.); The Space to:Explore (helps make the Wofford liberal arts degree global-ready by providing internship and travel opportunities); . **Physically Challenged Students:** 95% of the campus is accessible. Facilities include wheelchair ramps, elevators, special parking, specially equipped restrooms, special class scheduling, lowered drinking fountains, and lowered telephones. **Special:** Special academic programs include study abroad in 70 countries, a Washington semester, and a concentration in Latin American and Caribbean studies. In addition, students can major or minor in multiple fields or complete interdisciplinary, humanities, or intercultural studies majors. The January interim allows students to concentrate on a single study project, internship, or travel experience. (Consistently ranked in top 10, IIE Open Doors Survey) There are 9 national honor societies and including Phi Beta Kappa. **Visiting:** There are regularly scheduled orientations for prospective students, information sessions are offered Mon-Fri at 10:00am and 2:00pm. A visit consists of an information session with an admission counselor and campus tour. There are guides for informal visits, visitors may sit in on classes, and stay overnight. To schedule a visit, contact the Director of Admission at admission@wofford .edu. **Campus Safety and Security:** Measures include 24-hour foot and vehicle patrol, emergency notification system, self-defense education, and security escort services. There are emergency telephones, lighted pathways/sidewalks, and controlled access to dorms/residences.

REQUIREMENTS: The SAT or ACT is required. The ACT Optional Writing test is also required. In addition, applicants must be graduates of an accredited secondary school. The GED is accepted. Students should have completed 4 years each of high school English and math, 3 of lab science, and 3 each of a foreign language and social studies. An essay is required and an interview is strongly recommended. AP and CLEP credits are accepted. Important factors in the admissions decision are advanced placement or honors courses, leadership record, and personality/intangible qualities.

ADMISSIONS: 69% of the 2013-2014 applicants were accepted. The SAT scores for the 2013-2014 freshman class were: Critical Reading--12% below 500, 40% between 500 and 599, 42% between 600 and 699, and 6% between 700 and 800; Math--11% below 500, 35% between 500 and 599, 42% between 600 and 699, and 11% between 700 and 800; Writing--21% below 500, 38% between 500 and 599, 37% between 600 and 699, and 4% between 700 and 800. The ACT scores were 3% below 21, 15% between 21 and 23, 27% between 24 and 26, 23% between 27 and 28, and 32% above 28. 69% of the current freshmen were in the top fifth of their class; 96% were in the top two fifths. 7 freshmen graduated first in their class.

FINANCIAL AID: In a recent year, 93% of all full-time freshmen and 94% of continuing full-time students received some form of financial aid. 65% of all full-time freshmen and 58% of continuing full-time students received need-based aid. The average freshman award was $27,649. Need-based scholarships or need-based grants averaged $28,257; need-based self-help aid (loans and jobs) averaged $3,312; non-need-based athletic scholarships averaged $21,855; and other non-need-based awards and non-need-based scholarships averaged $14,262. 19% of undergraduate students work part-time. Average annual earnings from campus work are $1014. The average financial indebtedness of the 2013 graduate was $24,721. Wofford is a member of CSS. The FAFSA is required. The deadline for filing freshman financial aid applications for fall entry is March 15.

SOUTH DAKOTA

• College Location

0 20 40 60 80 100
Miles

AUGUSTANA COLLEGE — F-3
www.augie.edu

Sioux Falls, SD 57197

	(605) 274-0770
	(800) 727-2844
Fax: (605) 274-5518	Email: admission@augie.edu
Full-time: 644 men, 948 women	Faculty: 127
Part-time: 36 men, 43 women	Ph.D.s: 83%
Graduate: 32 men, 120 women	Student/Faculty: 12 to 1
Year: 4-1-4, summer session	Tuition: $29,214
Room & Board: $7286	Freshman Class: 1545 applied, 947 accepted, 396 enrolled
SAT: required ACT: 26	CEEB CODE: 6015
Application Deadline: n/av	VERY COMPETITIVE

Augustana College, founded in 1860, is a comprehensive (liberal arts and professional) private college of the Lutheran church. In addition to regional accreditation, has baccalaureate program accreditation with NASM, NCATE, NCA, DECA, CED, CCNE, CAATE, ACS, SDBN, and NAACLS. The 100-acre campus is in an urban area Sioux Falls, SD. Including any residence halls, there are 47 buildings.

STUDENT LIFE: 55% of undergraduates are from out of state, mostly the Mid-West. Students are from 30 states, and 40 foreign countries. 85% are from public schools. 87% are White. 47% are Protestant; 20% Catholic; 16% claim no religious affiliation. The average age of freshmen is 18; all undergraduates, 20. 19% do not continue beyond their first year; 66% remain to graduate. **Housing:** 1225 students can be accommodated in college housing, which includes coed dorms, on-campus apartments, off-campus apartments, and married student housing. In addition, there are special-interest houses, Theme houses. On-campus housing is guaranteed for all 4 years. 71% of students live on campus; of those, 70% remain on campus on weekends. Alcohol is not permitted. All students may keep cars.

FACULTY/CLASSROOMS: 54% of faculty are male; 46% are female. All teach undergraduates, 95% do research, and all teach and do research. No introductory courses are taught by graduate students.

The average class size in an introductory lecture is 32; in a laboratory is 18; and in a regular course is 20.

PROGRAMS OF STUDY: Augustana confers B.A. degrees. Master's degrees are also awarded. Bachelor's degrees are awarded in BIOLOGICAL SCIENCE (biochemistry and biology/biological science), BUSINESS (accounting, business administration and management, business communications, and sports management), COMMUNICATIONS AND THE ARTS (American Sign Language, art, classics, communications, dramatic arts, English, French, German, journalism, modern language, music, Spanish, and theatre arts), COMPUTER AND PHYSICAL SCIENCE (chemical physics, chemistry, computer science, information sciences and systems, mathematics, and physics), EDUCATION (athletic training, drama education, elementary education, middle school education, music education, physical education, social studies education, and special education), ENGINEERING AND ENVIRONMENTAL DESIGN (engineering physics), HEALTH PROFESSIONS (exercise science, medical laboratory science, and nursing), SOCIAL SCIENCE (American studies, anthropology, economics, history, interdisciplinary studies, international studies, philosophy, philosophy and religion, physical fitness/movement, political science/government, psychology, religion, and sociology). Nursing, biology, physics, mathematics, business and education are the strongest academically. Nursing, biology, business and education have the largest enrollments.

ACTIVITIES: There are 100 groups on campus, including art, band, cheerleading, chess, choir, chorale, chorus, computers, dance, drama, drill team, environmental, ethnic, gay, honors, international, jazz band, literary magazine, musical theater, newspaper, opera, orchestra, pep band, photography, political, professional, religious, social, social service, student government, symphony, and yearbook. Popular campus events include Christmas at Augustana, Viking Days, Boe Forum on Public Affairs and Semester Shutdown. **Sports:** There are 9 intercollegiate sports for men and 9 for women, and 18 intramural sports for men and 18 for women. Facilities include a 3600-seat athletic facility, 2 practice gyms, football complex with new stadium, softball and baseball complexes, soccer, baseball, and softball fields, a pool, weight/cardio work-out room, and a health, phys ed, and recreation center. **Graduates:** From July 1, 2013 to June 30, 2014, 361 bachelor's degrees were awarded. The most popular majors were education (16%), business administration (16%), and nursing/health professions (13%). 35 companies recruited on campus in 2013-2014. In an average class, 1% graduate in 3 years or less, 52% graduate in 4 years or less, 65% graduate in 5 years or less, and 66% graduate in 6 years or less. Of the 2013 graduating class, 21% were enrolled in graduate school within 6 months of graduation, and 98% were employed.

SERVICES: Counseling and information services are available, as is tutoring in most subjects. There is a reader service for the blind, remedial reading and writing center. **Library/Resources:** The library contains 233,000 volumes, 8,100 microform items, 7,300 audio/video tapes/CDs/DVDs, and subscribes to 6,150 periodicals including electronic. Computerized library services include interlibrary loans, database searching, Internet access, and Wi-Fi capability. Special learning facilities include an art gallery, including a center for Western studies. **Physically Challenged Students:** 75% of the campus is accessible. Facilities include wheelchair ramps, elevators, special parking, specially equipped restrooms, special class scheduling, lowered drinking fountains, lowered telephones, special housing. Arkenstone reader, Dragon Dictate, TTYs, and doorbell lights. **Special:** Cross-registration with Upper Midwest Association for Intercultural Education and Higher Education Consortium for Urban Affairs is available. Internships (both national and local), study abroad in unlimited countries, and a 3-2 engineering degree with Washington University in St. Louis, University of Minnesota, and Columbia University are offered. A Washington semester with Lutheran College Washington Consortium or American University is offered. Credit for life experience is possible. There are 12 national honor societies, a freshman honors program, and 21 departmental honors programs. **Visiting:** There are regularly scheduled orientations for prospective students, a campus tour, visits with professors, current students, and coaches. There are guides for informal visits, visitors may sit in on classes, and stay overnight. To schedule a visit, contact Jenn Henson at (605) 274-5516. **Campus Safety and Security:** Measures include 24-hour foot and vehicle patrol, emergency notification system, self-defense education, and security escort services. There are emergency telephones, lighted pathways/sidewalks, and controlled access to dorms/residences.

REQUIREMENTS: The SAT or ACT is required. Applicants may present either ACT or SAT scores. Applicants should have completed 4 years of high school English, math, and science, 2 of a foreign language and 3 of history. An essay, a transcript, and a recommendation are required. AP and CLEP credits are accepted. Important factors in the admissions decision are advanced placement or honors courses, extracurricular activities record, leadership record, and personality/intangible qualities. Students must complete 124 semester hours, with a minimum GPA of 2.0. General education requirements total 59 semester hours, including component courses in writing for graduation. 2 physical education activity courses are required, religion, and a capstone course. **Procedure:** Freshmen are admitted to all sessions. Entrance exams should be taken in the spring of the junior year or early fall of the senior. There are deferred admissions and rolling admissions plans. Application deadlines are open. Notification is sent on a rolling basis. Applications are accepted on-line. **Transfer Students:** 50 transfer students enrolled in 2013-2014. Applicants must have a 2.25 GPA in previous college work. 30 of 124 credits required for the bachelor's degree must be completed at Augustana. **International Students:** There are 139 international students enrolled. The school actively recruits these students. They must take the TOEFL with a minimum score of 550 on the paper-based TOEFL (PBT) or 79 on the Internet-based version (iBT). They must also take the SAT or ACT, scoring 20.

ADMISSIONS: 61% of the 2014-2015 applicants were accepted. The ACT scores were 3% below 21, 21% between 21 and 23, 29% between 24 and 26, 27% between 27 and 28, and 20% above 28. 63% of the current freshmen were in the top fifth of their class; 75% were in the top two fifths. 15 freshmen graduated first in their class. **Admissions Contact:** Nancy L. Davidson, Vice President of Enrollment. E-Mail: *admission@augie.edu* Web: *www.augie.edu*

FINANCIAL AID: In 2014-2015, 100% of all full-time freshmen and continuing full-time students received some form of financial aid. 67% of all full-time freshmen and 60% of continuing full-time students received need-based aid. The average freshman award was $25,651. Need-based scholarships or need-based grants averaged $22,028; need-based self-help aid (loans and jobs) averaged $5,364; non-need-based athletic scholarships averaged $11,000; and other non-need-based awards and non-need-based scholarships averaged $15,959. 31% of undergraduate students work part-time. Average annual earnings from campus work are $1657. The average financial indebtedness of the 2014 graduate was $26,428. The FAFSA is required. The priority date for freshman financial aid applications for fall entry is March 1.

BLACK HILLS STATE UNIVERSITY A-2
www.bhsu.edu

Spearfish, SD 57799	(605) 642-6343
	(800) ALL-BHSU
Fax: (605) 642-6022	Email: admissions@bhsu.edu
Full-time: 859 men, 1420 women	Faculty: 231
Part-time: 601 men, 1140 women	Ph.D.s: n/a
Graduate: 113 men, 356 women	Student/Faculty: 20 to 1
Year: semesters, summer session	Tuition: $7617 ($10,097)
Room & Board: $6330	Freshman Class: 1355 applied, 1267 accepted, 507 enrolled
ACT: 21	CEEB CODE: 003459
Application Deadline: n/av	COMPETITIVE

Black Hills State University is a master's level university that promotes excellence in teaching and learning; supports research, creative and scholarly activities and provides service to the state, region, nation and global community. BHSU provides innovative, high quality undergraduate (associate and baccalaureate) programs in the arts, humanities, education, behavioral sciences, mathematics, social sciences, natural sciences, business and technology as well as selected disciplines of strength at the graduate level. Black Hills State University is the only comprehensive University in western South Dakota. There are 3 undergraduate schools and 1 graduate school. In addition to regional accreditation, BHSU has baccalaureate program accreditation with AACSB, NASM, NCATE, CAEP, and South Dakota Department of Education. The 123-acre campus is in a small town 45 miles northwest of Rapid City, South Dakota. Including any residence halls, there are 18 buildings.

STUDENT LIFE: 74% of undergraduates are from South Dakota. Others are from 45 states, and 22 foreign countries. 82% are White. The average age of freshmen is 19; all undergraduates, 24. 37% do not continue beyond their first year; 31% remain to graduate. **Housing:** 840 students can be accommodated in college housing, which includes single-sex and coed dorms, on-campus apartments, and married student housing. On-campus housing is guaranteed for the freshman year only. 79% of students commute. Alcohol is not permitted. All students may keep cars.

FACULTY/CLASSROOMS: 95% teach undergraduates. No introductory courses are taught by graduate students.

PROGRAMS OF STUDY: BHSU confers B.A., B.G.S., B.A.T.S., B.S., and B.S.Ed degrees. Associate and Master's degrees are also awarded. Bachelor's degrees are awarded in BIOLOGICAL SCIENCE (biology/adolescence education and biology/biological science), BUSINESS (accounting, business administration and management, business administration, mgmt, operations, business administration marketing, entrepreneurial studies, human resources, human resources/organizational mgmt, tourism, and professional program in accounting), COMMUNICATIONS AND THE ARTS (art, art/art studies, communication, communication studies, English, graphic communications management, graphic design, English and Professional Communication, music, Spanish, speech/debate/rhetoric, and communication arts - speech), COMPUTER AND PHYSICAL SCIENCE (applied science, chemistry, chemistry/adolescence education, industrial technology, mathematics, physical sciences, and science), EDUCATION (business education, early childhood education, elementary education, English education, general studies, mathematics education, outdoor leadership/education, physical education, reading education, science education, social science education, Spanish education K-12, and special education), ENGINEERING AND ENVI-

RONMENTAL DESIGN (construction technology and manufacturing technology), HEALTH PROFESSIONS (biology and exercise science), SOCIAL SCIENCE (economics, history, history and political science, human services, Native American studies, political science/government, psychology, social science, and sociology). Elementary education, biology, and business administration are the strongest academically and have the largest enrollments are the strongest academically.

ACTIVITIES: Groups on campus include art, band, cheerleading, choir, chorale, chorus, computers, dance, debate, drama, drill team, environmental, ethnic, forensics, gay, honors, international, jazz band, musical theater, newspaper, pep band, photography, political, professional, radio and TV, religious, social, social service, student government, and yearbook. Popular campus events include Swarm Week. **Sports:** There are 5 intercollegiate sports for men and 7 for women. Facilities include a stadium, gymnasium (with basketball and volleyball courts), tennis courts, swimming pools, indoor and outdoor tracks, golf course, baseball and softball complex.

SERVICES: Counseling and information services are available, as is tutoring in most subjects. There is remedial math, reading, and writing. **Library/Resources:** Computerized library services include interlibrary loans, database searching, Internet access, and Wi-Fi capability. Special learning facilities include an art gallery, radio station, TV station, a gymnasium, and theater. **Physically Challenged Students:** Facilities include wheelchair ramps, elevators, special parking, specially equipped restrooms, lowered drinking fountains, and special housing. **Special:** High School Dual Credit. There are Phi Beta Kappa and a freshman honors program. **Visiting:** There are regularly scheduled orientations for prospective students, consisting of open houses, receptions, green and gold days. There are guides for informal visits, visitors may sit in on classes, and stay overnight. To schedule a visit, contact Beth Oaks at Beth.Oaks@BHSU.edu. **Campus Safety and Security:** Measures include 24-hour foot and vehicle patrol, emergency notification system, and security escort services. There are lighted pathways/sidewalks and controlled access to dorms/residences.

REQUIREMENTS: The ACT is required. Admitted to Black Hills State University, you must have the following credentials: ACT Composite Score of 18 or above or Rank in the top 60 percent of your graduating class or High School GPA of 2.60 on a 4.00 scale. All baccalaureate or general studies students under 24 years of age, including students transferring with fewer than 24 credit hours, must meet the following minimum high school course requirements with an overall grade point average of "C" or higher: 4 years of English, or an ACT English subtest score of 18 or above, or an Advanced Placement Language and Composition or Literature and Composition score of 3 or above. 3 years of Advanced Math (algebra and above) or an ACT mathematics subtest score of 20 or above; or an Advanced Placement Calculus AB or Calculus BC score of 3 or above. 3 years of Laboratory Science (biology, chemistry, or physics, or approved physical science or earth science), or an ACT science reasoning subtest score of 17 or above, or and Advanced Placement Biology, Chemistry, or Physics B score of 3 or above. 3 years of Social Sciences, or an ACT social studies subtest score of 17 or above, or an Advanced Placement Microeconomics, Macroeconomics, Comparative or United States Government and Policies, European or United States History, or Psychology score of 3 or above. 1 year of Fine Arts. Applications received from students with deficiencies will be reviewed on an individual basis. AP and CLEP credits are accepted. Depending on Catalog year, 120/128 minimum hours (baccalaureate degrees) (150 minimum semester hours for Professional Accountancy). Depending on Catalog year, 60/64 minimum hours (associate degrees). All major, minor, and professional education requirements must be met. 2.0 minimum institutional and cumulative grade point average (non-teaching degrees). 2.6 minimum cumulative grade point average (teaching degrees). 2.6 minimum grade point average in teaching major, teaching minor and professional education core (teaching degrees). Thirty-six minimum upper division hours (courses numbered 300/400) (baccalaureate degrees). System and Institutional general education requirements must be met. Must take and pass the CAAP Proficiency Exam. Must take exit examination for each major (baccalaureate degrees). No more than sixteen hours of internship will be counted toward a major or a degree. No more than thirty-two hours can be

earned by special examinations, correspondence, extension courses from other colleges and/or non-collegiate courses, other than military courses. No more than six hours will be accepted toward graduation or final GPA for participation in the following activities: physical education activities, wind ensemble, choir, small ensembles, jazz ensemble, forensics, theatre, yearbook or newspaper unless such participation is a requirement for a major or minor. Depending on Catalog year, a minimum of 30/32 hours (baccalaureate degrees) and 15/16 semester hours (associate degrees) must be earned from Black Hills State University. Depending on Catalog year, 15/16 hours (baccalaureate degrees) of the last 30/32 hours and 6/8 hours (associate degrees) of the last 15/16 hours preceding the completion of a degree must be earned from Black Hills State University. Minimum number of credit hours in the major or minor that must be completed from Black Hills State University: fifty percent (50%). Composite majors do not need to complete a minor. Degree seeking students may complete requirements for a minor at any Regental University that has been approved to grant that minor. This minor will be recorded on the transcript in conjunction with a degree/major at that university or a degree/major at any other Regental University. A minor will only be recorded on the transcript in conjunction with a degree and major. Non-teaching, regular majors must complete a minor OR a second major. Bachelor of Arts candidates must complete twelve hours of a foreign language (Minimum of 4 courses of Beginning I & II and Intermediate I & II). Remedial Courses (courses numbered below 100) will not be counted toward graduation. Coursework taken for graduate credit will not apply toward a baccalaureate degree. *In addition to the BHSU cumulative GPA requirement, transfer students must have a BHSU and transfer combined GPA of 2.0 for non-teaching programs and 2.6 for teaching programs. **Procedure:** Freshmen are admitted to all sessions. Entrance exams should be taken during the senior year of high school. There are early admissions and rolling admissions plans. Application deadlines are open. Application fee is $20. Applications are accepted on-line. **Transfer Students:** 313 transfer students enrolled in 2013-2014. Transfer to Baccalaureate Program - Students who are under the age of 24 at the start of the term, and who are transferring into baccalaureate degree programs with fewer than 24 transfer credit hours may be required to fulfill the baccalaureate degree admission requirements. Students with 24 or more transfer credit hours with a cumulative GPA of at least 2.0 may transfer into baccalaureate degree programs. Specific degree programs may include additional admissions requirements. If students are applying for federal financial aid, they must meet federal guidelines for transfer students. Transfer to Associate Degree Program - Students who are under the age of 24 at the start of the term and who are transferring into associate degree programs with fewer than 12 transfer credit hours must meet the associate degree admission requirements. Students with 12 or more transfer credit hours with a cumulative GPA of at least 2.0 may transfer into associate degree programs. Specific degree programs may include additional admissions requirements. Non-Regental Accredited Colleges or Universities – Transfer students may be accepted from other non-Regental universities outside of the SD system; preferential consideration will be given to applicants from institutions which are accredited by their respective regional accrediting association. Non-Accredited Colleges – BHSU is not required to accept credits from a non-accredited college or university. The university may admit the applicant on a provisional basis and provide a means for the evaluation of some or all of the credits. Credits from colleges or universities which are not accredited by a regional accrediting association may be considered for transfer, subject to all other provisions of these guidelines and any conditions for validation which may be set by BHSU. Students on Suspension/Probation – Transfer student who have not maintained a cumulative grade point average of 2.00 may appeal for admissions. If admitted, such students are on academic probation. If the last institution attended was outside the Regental system, and the transfer applicant left under academic suspension, the applicant will not be considered for admission during the period of suspension or, if suspended for an indefinite period, until one semester has passed since the last date of attendance at the previous school. Students on academic suspension from a Regental university will not be allowed to register for any coursework at any Regental university except when an appeal has been approved by the Regental university from which the student is pursuing a degree. An approved appeal granted by one

Regental university will be honored by all Regental universities. Application Procedure: Transfer applicants should submit a completed admission application, a $20 non-refundable application fee, a current complete official transcript sent directly from each college, school or institution attended since high school, and an official high school transcript. The application fee is not charged to students who transfer from other South Dakota Regental schools. Applicant who are 21 years of age or younger must submit Enhanced ACT (or SAT-I) results. Applicants who are over 21 need to submit their scores if they have taken the test within the last five years. Students transferring from a degree seeking program at one Regental university to a degree seeking program at BHSU are required to apply for admission. Note: Transfer students applying for federal financial aid must meet federal guidelines for transfer students. **International Students:** The school actively recruits these students. They must take the TOEFL. They must also take the ACT, scoring 18.

ADMISSIONS: 94% of the 2014-2015 applicants were accepted. **Admissions Contact:** Admissions Officer, Enrollment Services Center. E-Mail: *admissions@bhsu.edu* Web: *www.bhsu.edu*

FINANCIAL AID: The FAFSA, and state aid form is required. Check with the school for current application deadlines.

DAKOTA STATE UNIVERSITY   E-3
www.dsu.edu

Madison, SD 57042	**(605) 256-5139**
	(888) 378-9988
Fax: (605) 256-5020	**Email: admissions@dsu.edu**
Full-time: n/av	**Faculty:** IIB, av$
Part-time: n/av	**Ph.D.s:** n/av
Graduate: n/av	**Student/Faculty:** n/av
Year: semesters, summer session	**Tuition:** $8286 ($10,286)
Room & Board: $5525	**Freshman Class:** 600 accepted, 360 enrolled
SAT or ACT: required	**CEEB CODE:** 6247
Application Deadline: open	**COMPETITIVE**

Dakota State University, founded in 1881, is a public institution offering undergraduate programs through the Colleges of Business and Information Systems, Education, and Arts and Sciences. There are 3 undergraduate schools and 1 graduate school. In addition to regional accreditation, DSU has baccalaureate program accreditation with ACBSP, AHEA, NCATE, AHIMA, and CoARC. The 56-acre campus is in a rural area 45 miles northwest of Sioux Falls. Including any residence halls, there are 22 buildings.

STUDENT LIFE: Housing: 659 students can be accommodated in college housing, which includes single-sex and coed dorms and on-campus apartments. On-campus housing is guaranteed for the freshman year only, is available on a first-come, first-served basis, and is available on a lottery system for upperclassmen. Alcohol is not permitted. All students may keep cars.

FACULTY/CLASSROOMS: No introductory courses are taught by graduate students.

PROGRAMS OF STUDY: DSU confers B.S., B.B.A., B.G.S. and B.S.Ed. degrees. Associate, Master's, and Doctoral degrees are also awarded. Bachelor's degrees are awarded in BIOLOGICAL SCIENCE (biology/biological science), BUSINESS (business administration and management), COMMUNICATIONS AND THE ARTS (communications technology, English, and information technology), COMPUTER AND PHYSICAL SCIENCE (computer programming, computer game design/development, computer science, computer security and information assurance, digital arts/technology, information sciences and systems, mathematics, and physical sciences), EDUCATION (business education, computer education, elementary education, English education, health education, health information management, marketing and distribution education, mathematics education, and secondary education), ENGINEERING AND ENVIRONMENTAL DESIGN (computer graphics), HEALTH PROFESSIONS (medical records administration/services, premedicine, and respiratory therapy).

ACTIVITIES: There are 36 groups on campus, including art, band, cheerleading, choir, chorale, chorus, computers, dance, drama, ethnic, honors, international, literary magazine, musical theater, newspaper, pep band, political, professional, radio and TV, religious, social, and student government. Popular campus events include Homecoming, Convocation and Frost Bites Week. **Sports:** There are 6 intercollegiate sports for men and 6 for women, and 3 intramural sports for men and 3 for women. Facilities include courts for basketball and racquetball, a football field, a weight room, and a swimming pool. **Graduates:** From July 1, 2013 to June 30, 2014, 145 bachelor's degrees were awarded. 25 companies recruited on campus in 2013-2014. In an average class, 24% graduate in 4 years or less, 42% graduate in 5 years or less, and 15% graduate in 6 years or less. Of the 2013 graduating class, 1% were enrolled in graduate school within 6 months of graduation, and 96% were employed.

SERVICES: Counseling and information services are available, as is tutoring in every subject. There is a reader service for the blind, remedial math, reading, and writing. **Library/Resources:** The library contains 177,454 volumes, 3,669 microform items, 3,426 audio/video tapes/CDs/DVDs, and subscribes to 350 periodicals including electronic. Computerized library services include interlibrary loans, database searching, Internet access, and Wi-Fi capability. Special learning facilities include an art gallery, natural history museum, and radio station. **Physically Challenged Students:** 80% of the campus is accessible. Facilities include wheelchair ramps, elevators, special parking, specially equipped restrooms, special class scheduling, and lowered drinking fountains. **Special:** The university offers co-op programs with South Dakota State University, internships, study abroad in London, and on-campus work-study programs. Also available are the general studies degree, a 3-2 engineering degree with the University of Minnesota/Twin Cities, credit for life, military, and work experience, nondegree study, and pass/fail options. There are 2 national honor societies and a freshman honors program. **Visiting:** There are regularly scheduled orientations for prospective students, including general information and academic sessions, a campus tour, and financial aid information. There are guides for informal visits, visitors may sit in on classes, and stay overnight. To schedule a visit, contact the Admissions Office. **Campus Safety and Security:** Measures include self-defense education and security escort services. There are emergency telephones, lighted pathways/sidewalks, controlled access to dorms/residences, and a foot patrol.

REQUIREMENTS: The SAT or ACT is required, with a minimum composite score of 18 on the ACT. Applicants must be graduates of an accredited secondary school or have a GED certificate, and have completed 4 years of English, 3 years each of math, science, and social studies, and 1/2 year of computer science and the fine arts. AP and CLEP credits are accepted. All students seeking a bachelor's degree are required to complete 30 credit hours of general education coursework (math, English, science, humanities) as well as 11 credit hours of institutional specific coursework (information technology and personal health). Associate's degree seeking students are required to complete 18 credit hours of general education coursework as well as 6 credit hours of institutional specific coursework. Graduates must have a 2.0 GPA. A general education assessment exam and exit assessment are required of all students. **Procedure:** Freshmen are admitted to all sessions. Entrance exams should be taken before students register for classes. There is a rolling admissions plan. Application deadlines are open. Application fee is $20. Notification is sent on a rolling basis. Applications are accepted on-line. **Transfer Students:** 67 transfer students enrolled in 2013-2014. Transfer applicants must have a minimum 2.0 GPA. 32 of 128 credits required for the bachelor's degree must be completed at DSU. **International Students:** There are 120 international students enrolled. The school actively recruits these students. They must take the TOEFL.

ADMISSIONS: 9 freshmen graduated first in their class. **Admissions Contact:** Amy Crissinger, Director of Admission. E-Mail: *admissions@dsu.edu* Web: *www.dsu.edu*

FINANCIAL AID: In 2014-2015, 88% of continuing full-time students received some form of financial aid. The average freshman award was $5,836. 50% of undergraduate students work part-time. Average annual earnings from campus work are $1405. The average financial indebtedness of the 2014 graduate was $16,588. The FAFSA is required. The deadline for filing freshman financial aid applications for fall entry is March 1.

DAKOTA WESLEYAN UNIVERSITY — E-3

www.dwu.edu

Mitchell, SD 57301	(605) 995-2600
	(800) 333-8506
Fax: (605) 995-2699	Email: admissionsk@dwu.edu
Full-time: 680 men and women	Faculty: 51
Part-time: 90 men and women	Ph.Ds: 68%
Graduate: 30 men and women	Student/Faculty: n/av
Year: semesters, summer session	Tuition: $21,310
Room & Board: $7200	Freshman Class: n/av
SAT or ACT: required	CEEB CODE: 6155
Application Deadline: see profile	COMPETITIVE

Dakota Wesleyan University, founded in 1885, is a private liberal arts institution affiliated with the United Methodist Church. The figures in the above capsule and in this profile are approximate. There is 1 graduate school. In addition to regional accreditation, DWU has baccalaureate program accreditation with NLN. The 50-acre campus is in a small town 70 miles west of Sioux Falls. Including any residence halls, there are 18 buildings.

STUDENT LIFE: 69% of undergraduates are from South Dakota. Others are from 27 states, 3 foreign countries, and Canada. 99% are from public schools. 86% are white. 50% are Protestant; 24% Catholic. The average age of freshmen is 19; all undergraduates, 23. 32% do not continue beyond their first year.

FACULTY/CLASSROOMS: 45% of faculty are male; 55% are female. All teach undergraduates. No introductory courses are taught by graduate students. The average class size in an introductory lecture is 20; in a laboratory, 17; and in a regular course, 17.

PROGRAMS OF STUDY: DWU confers B.A. degrees. Associate and Master's degrees are also awarded. Bachelor's degrees are awarded in AGRICULTURE (wildlife management), BIOLOGICAL SCIENCE (biology/biological science), BUSINESS (accounting, business administration and management, and sports management), COMMUNICATIONS AND THE ARTS (art, communications, dramatic arts, English, multimedia, and music), COMPUTER AND PHYSICAL SCIENCE (mathematics), EDUCATION (athletic training, elementary education, physical education, special education, and sports and wellness studies), HEALTH PROFESSIONS (nursing), SOCIAL SCIENCE (behavioral science, criminal justice, history, human services, philosophy and religion, psychology, public administration, and sociology). Biochemistry is the strongest academically. Nursing and business have the largest enrollments.

ACTIVITIES: There are 30 groups on campus, including academic, art, band, bell choir, brass and woodwind ensembles, cheerleading, choir, chorale, chorus, dance, drama, drill team, ethnic, forensics, honors, international, literary magazine, musical theater, newspaper, political, professional, religious, social, social service, student government, and yearbook. Popular campus events include Spring Week and Family Life Conference.

SERVICES: Counseling and information services are available, as is tutoring in every subject. There is a reader service for the blind, remedial math, reading, and writing. The library contains 62,500 volumes, 72,500 microform items, 3700 audio/video tapes/CDs/DVDs, and subscribes to 620 periodicals including electronic. Computerized library services include interlibrary loans, database searching, and Internet access. Special learning facilities include a learning resource center and observatory as well as a history museum with art gallery.

REQUIREMENTS: The SAT or ACT is required. Applicants must be graduates of an accredited secondary school or have a GED certificate. An interview is recommended. A GPA of 2.0 is required. AP and CLEP credits are accepted. Important factors in the admissions decision are advanced placement or honors courses, extracurricular activities record, and parents or siblings attended the school.

FINANCIAL AID: DWU is a member of CSS. The FAFSA is required. Check with the school for current application deadlines.

MOUNT MARTY COLLEGE — E-4

www.mtmc.edu

Yankton, SD 57078	(605) 668-1545
	(855) MT-MARTY
Fax: (605) 668-1508	Email: mmcadmit@mtmc.edu
Full-time: 215 men, 500 women	Faculty: 35; IIB, --$
Part-time: 76 men, 301 women	Ph.Ds: 64%
Graduate: 50 men, 50 women	Student/Faculty: 20 to 1
Year: semesters, summer session	Tuition: $22,992
Room & Board: $6646	Freshman Class: 397
	accepted, 190 enrolled
ACT: required	CEEB CODE: 6416
Application Deadline: open	COMPETITIVE

Mount Marty College is a private, Catholic Benedictine liberal arts college, open to students of all faiths and backgrounds. Mount Marty prepares students for a contemporary world of work, service to the human community, and personal growth. There are 2 undergraduate schools and 3 graduate schools. In addition to regional accreditation, Mount Marty has baccalaureate program accreditation with ADA and NLN. The 80-acre campus is in a small town 60 miles northwest of Sioux City, Iowa, and 80 miles southwest of Sioux Falls. Including any residence halls, there are 11 buildings.

STUDENT LIFE: 60% of undergraduates are from South Dakota. Others are from 25 states, and 5 foreign countries. 79% are from public schools. 94% are White. 42% are Catholic; 36% claim no religious affiliation. The average age of freshmen is 19; all undergraduates, 26. 22% do not continue beyond their first year; 61% remain to graduate.

FACULTY/CLASSROOMS: 54% of faculty are male; 46% are female. All teach undergraduates. No introductory courses are taught by graduate students. The average class size in an introductory lecture is 30; in a laboratory is 15; and in a regular course is 20.

PROGRAMS OF STUDY: Mount Marty confers B.A., B.S. and B.S.N. degrees. Associate and Master's degrees are also awarded. Bachelor's degrees are awarded in BIOLOGICAL SCIENCE (biology/biological science), BUSINESS (accounting and business administration and management), COMMUNICATIONS AND THE ARTS (English, journalism, and music), COMPUTER AND PHYSICAL SCIENCE (chemistry, computer science, mathematics, and radiological technology), EDUCATION (athletic training, elementary education, physical education, secondary education, and special education), ENGINEERING AND ENVIRONMENTAL DESIGN (environmental science), HEALTH PROFESSIONS (health care administration, medical technology, and nursing), SOCIAL SCIENCE (behavioral science, criminal justice, food production/management/services, history, religion, and social science). Nursing, business, and teacher education are the strongest academically.

ACTIVITIES: There are 50 groups on campus, including art, band, choir, chorus, computers, drama, ethnic, forensics, honors, jazz band, literary magazine, musical theater, newspaper, pep band, photography, political, professional, religious, social, social service, and student government. Popular campus events include Blue and Gold Days, Formal Dances, and Benedictine Lecture Series.

SERVICES: Counseling and information services are available, as is tutoring in most subjects. There is remedial math, reading, and writing. **Library/Resources:** The library contains 79,228 volumes, 11,624 microform items, and 8,465 audio/video tapes/CDs/DVDs, and subscribes to 439 periodicals including electronic. Computerized library services include interlibrary loans, database searching, Internet access, and Wi-Fi capability. Special learning facilities include an art gallery. **Physically Challenged Students:** All of the campus is accessible. Facilities include wheelchair ramps, elevators, special parking, specially equipped restrooms, special class scheduling, lowered drinking fountains, and lowered telephones. **Special:** Mount Marty offers co-op programs, internships, student-designed majors in selected studies, an accelerated degree program in business administration, credit for work, life, and military experience, and pass/fail options. There are 8 national honor societies, a freshman honors program, and 7 departmental honors programs. **Visiting:** There are regularly scheduled orientations for prospective students, including campus tours, faculty appointments, and admission and financial aid information. There are guides for informal visits, visitors may sit in on classes, and stay overnight. To schedule a visit, contact the Director of Admissions. **Campus Safety and Security:** Measures include 24-hour foot and vehicle patrol and security escort services. There are emergency telephones and lighted pathways/sidewalks.

REQUIREMENTS: The ACT is required. Applicants must be graduates of an accredited secondary school or have a GED certificate. An audition and an interview are recommended. A GPA of 2.0 is required. AP and CLEP credits are accepted.

ADMISSIONS: The ACT scores were 10% below 21, 50% between 21 and 23, 30% between 24 and 26, 5% between 27 and 28, and 5% above 28. 10% of the current freshmen were in the top fifth of their class; 56% were in the top two fifths. 5 freshmen graduated first in their class.

FINANCIAL AID: In a recent year, 99% of all full-time freshmen and continuing full-time students received some form of financial aid. 84% of all full-time freshmen and continuing full-time students received need-based aid. The average freshman award was $12,343. 60% of undergraduate students work part-time. Average annual earnings from campus work are $1500. The average financial indebtedness of the 2013 graduate was $17,407. The FAFSA is required. The deadline for filing freshman financial aid applications for fall entry is March 1.

NORTHERN STATE UNIVERSITY - ABERDEEN   D-1
www.northern.edu

Aberdeen, SD 57401	(605) 626-3011
	(605) 626-2544
Fax: n/av	Email: admissions@northern.edu
Full-time: 666 men, 811 women	Faculty: 90
Part-time: 597 men, 927 women	Ph.D.s: 86%
Graduate: 121 men, 409 women	Student/Faculty: 21 to 1
Year: semesters, summer session	Tuition: $7563 ($10,042)
Room & Board: $6942	Freshman Class: 1379 applied, 1143 accepted, 363 enrolled
ACT: 22	CEEB CODE: 6487
Application Deadline: n/av	COMPETITIVE

Northern State University, established in 1901, is a state-supported institution offering undergraduate and graduate programs in the liberal arts and sciences, business, and education. Distance delivery technology is a core mission in all programs, especially all levels of teacher preparation. There are 4 undergraduate schools and 1 graduate school. In addition to regional accreditation, NSU has baccalaureate program accreditation with NASM and NCATE. The 72-acre campus is in an urban area one-half mile south of Aberdeen's city center. Including any residence halls, there are 21 buildings.

STUDENT LIFE: 77% of undergraduates are from South Dakota. Others are from 41 states, 36 foreign countries, and Canada. 87% are White. The average age of freshmen is 18; all undergraduates, 22. 30% do not continue beyond their first year; 70% remain to graduate. **Housing:** 850 students can be accommodated in college housing, which includes coed dorms, on-campus apartments, and married student housing. Learning communities. On-campus housing is guaranteed for all 4 years. 59% of students commute. Alcohol is not permitted. All students may keep cars.

FACULTY/CLASSROOMS: 50% of faculty are male; 50% are female. All teach and do research. No introductory courses are taught by graduate students. The average class size in an introductory lecture is 25 and in a laboratory is 18.

PROGRAMS OF STUDY: NSU confers B.A., B.S., B.M.E., B.G.S. and B.S.Ed. degrees. Associate and Master's degrees are also awarded. Bachelor's degrees are awarded in BIOLOGICAL SCIENCE (biology/biological science), BUSINESS (accounting, banking and finance, business administration and management, business economics, international business management, marketing/retailing/merchandising, and personnel management), COMMUNICATIONS AND THE ARTS (English, fine arts, French, German, music, and Spanish), COMPUTER AND PHYSICAL SCIENCE (chemistry and mathematics), EDUCATION (art education, business education, early childhood education, elementary education, foreign languages education, health education, middle school education, music education, physical education, science education, secondary education, and special education), ENGINEERING AND ENVIRONMENTAL DESIGN (environmental science), HEALTH PROFESSIONS (medical laboratory technology, predentistry, premedicine, and speech pathology/audiology), SOCIAL SCIENCE (community services, criminal justice, economics, history, human services, physical fitness/movement, political science/government, prelaw, psychology, social science, and sociology). Business and education is the strongest academically.

ACTIVITIES: There are no fraternities or sororities. There are 100 groups on campus, including art, band, cheerleading, chess, choir, chorale, chorus, computers, dance, debate, drama, drill team, drum and bugle corps, environmental, ethnic, forensics, gay, honors, international, jazz band, literary magazine, marching band, musical theater, newspaper, orchestra, pep band, photography, political, professional, radio and TV, religious, social, social service, student government, and symphony. Popular campus events include Gypsy Day, Gypsy Week, and I Hate Winter Weekend. **Sports:** There are 6 intercollegiate sports for men and 7 for women, and 11 intramural sports for men and 11 for women. Facilities include a sports complex; football stadium and an all-weather track, a 160-meter track, an Olympic-size pool, weight room, 3 racquetball courts, human performance lab, 2 basketball courts, and an 8300-seat arena. **Graduates:** From July 1, 2013 to June 30, 2014, 300 bachelor's degrees were awarded. The most popular majors were business (33%), education (20%), and social sciences (10%). 37 companies recruited on campus in 2013-2014. Of the 2013 graduating class, 33% were enrolled in graduate school within 6 months of graduation, and 99% were employed.

SERVICES: Counseling and information services are available, as is tutoring in most subjects. There is remedial math, reading, and writing. There is an educational media center, a math lab, an ASL interpreter for the deaf, and a speech, language, and hearing clinic. **Library/Resources:** The library contains 179,721 volumes, 381,874 microform items, 10,092 audio/video tapes/CDs/DVDs, and subscribes to 45,379 periodicals including electronic. Computerized library services include interlibrary loans, database searching, Internet access, and Wi-Fi capability. Special learning facilities include an art gallery, radio station, TV station, and a fine arts center. **Physically Challenged Students:** 90% of the campus is accessible. Facilities include wheelchair ramps, elevators, special parking, specially equipped restrooms, lowered drinking fountains. **Special:** Opportunities are provided for internships, a Washington semester, work-study programs, a B.A.-B.S. degree, dual majors, a general studies degree, credit by exam, and nondegree study. Study abroad and a co-op program in international business are available. Technology proficiency certification is available with a diverse selection of certifications. There are 4 national honor societies, including Phi Beta Kappa, a freshman honors program, and 4 departmental honors programs. **Visiting:** There are regularly scheduled orientations for prospective students, consisting of a welcome presentation, registration, refreshments, an academic visit, a campus tour, lunch, a financial aid presentation, a student panel, and a cost and scholarship presentation. There are guides for informal visits, visitors may sit in on classes, and stay overnight. To schedule a visit, contact the Admissions Office. **Campus Safety and Security:** Measures include emergency notification system, self-defense education, and security escort services. There are emergency telephones, lighted pathways/sidewalks, and controlled access to dorms/residences.

REQUIREMENTS: The ACT is required. Minimum ACT composite score of 18, or students must earn a high school GPA of at least 2.6 on a 4.0 scale, or rank in the top 60% of their graduating class. Graduation from an accredited secondary school is required; a GED will be accepted. Applicants should submit a minimum academic record distributed as follows: 4 years of English, 3 each of math, science, and social studies, and one year of fine arts. AP and CLEP credits are accepted. Important factors in the admissions decision are evidence of special talent, advanced placement or honors courses, and extracurricular activities record. Students must complete a minimum of

120 semester hours, with 27 to 36 in the major, and must maintain a 2.0 minimum GPA. The core curriculum consists of courses in English, history, fine arts, science, math, and psychology. In addition, there are specific course requirements. All students must pass a comprehensive exam. **Procedure:** Freshmen are admitted fall, spring, and summer. Entrance exams should be taken during the summer before the senior year. There are early admissions, deferred admissions, and rolling admissions plans. Check with the school for current application deadlines. The application fee is $20. Notification is sent on a rolling basis. **Transfer Students:** 119 transfer students enrolled in 2013-2014. Applicants must submit official transcripts from all previous colleges attended. D grades do not transfer. If the applicant has not maintained a C average, an ACT score that places the applicant in the upper 50% of college-bound freshmen may be submitted for consideration. 24 of 120 credits required for the bachelor's degree must be completed at NSU. **International Students:** There are 107 international students enrolled. The school actively recruits these students. They must take the TOEFL with a minimum score of 525 on the paper-based TOEFL (PBT) or 61 on the Internet-based version (iBT).

ADMISSIONS: 83% of the 2014-2015 applicants were accepted. The SAT scores for the 2014-2015 freshman class were: Critical Reading--58% below 500, 30% between 500 and 599, 8% between 600 and 699, and 4% between 700 and 800; Math--47% below 500, 38% between 500 and 599, 12% between 600 and 699, and 3% between 700 and 800. The ACT scores were 42% below 21, 26% between 21 and 23, 115% between 24 and 26, 14% between 27 and 28, and 3% above 28. **Admissions Contact:** JoEllen Lindner, VP Student Affairs & Enrollment Mgt. E-Mail: *admission2@northern.edu* Web: *www.northern.edu*

FINANCIAL AID: In 2014-2015, 95% of all full-time freshmen and 90% of continuing full-time students received some form of financial aid. NSU is a member of CSS. The CCS/Profile, or FAFSA, or FFS, or SFS is required. The priority date for freshman financial aid applications for fall entry is March 1.

OGLALA LAKOTA COLLEGE (*The complete profile is made available exclusively on our website, www.barronspac.com*)

PRESENTATION COLLEGE (*The complete profile is made available exclusively on our website, www.barronspac.com*)

SINTE GLESKA UNIVERSITY (*The complete profile is made available exclusively on our website, www.barronspac.com*)

SOUTH DAKOTA BOARD OF REGENTS

The South Dakota Board of Regents, established in 1890, is a public system in South Dakota. It is governed by a Board of Regents, whose chief administrator is the executive director. The primary goal of the system is to provide high quality, diverse educational opportunities and services to the people of South Dakota. The main priorities are excellence in academic programs, diverse campus communities, and resources for economic development efforts. The total student enrollment is usually 32,500, with 1600 faculty members. Altogether there are approximate 437 baccalaureate, 94 master's, and 31 doctoral programs offered in the South Dakota Board of Regents. Profiles of the 4-year campuses are included in this section.

SOUTH DAKOTA SCHOOL OF MINES AND TECHNOLOGY
B-3
www.sdsmt.edu

Rapid City, SD 57701

	(605) 394-2511
	(800) 544-8162
Fax: n/av	Email: admissions@sdsmt.edu
Full-time: 1350 men, 370 women	Faculty: 143
Part-time: 223 men, 158 women	Ph.D.s: 88%
Graduate: 243 men, 80 women	Student/Faculty: 13 to 1
Year: semesters, summer session	Tuition: $9370 ($11,310)
Room & Board: $5890	Freshman Class: 1127 applied, 991 accepted, 454 enrolled
SAT CR/M/W: 560/600/500 **ACT:** 26	CEEB CODE: 6652
Application Deadline: August 15	VERY COMPETITIVE

South Dakota School of Mines and Technology, founded in 1885, is a public university offering undergraduate and graduate programs in engineering, science, and mathematics. There is 1 undergraduate school and 1 graduate school. In addition to regional accreditation, SDSM&T has baccalaureate program accreditation with ABET and CSAB. The 120-acre campus is in a suburban area 350 miles northeast of Denver. Including any residence halls, there are 21 buildings.

STUDENT LIFE: 55% of undergraduates are from South Dakota. Others are from 40 states, 24 foreign countries, and Canada. 82% are White. The average age of freshmen is 19; all undergraduates, 22. 20% do not continue beyond their first year; 55% remain to graduate.

FACULTY/CLASSROOMS: 76% of faculty are male; 24% are female. All teach undergraduates, and 31% do research. Graduate students teach 4% of introductory courses. The average class size in an introductory lecture is 38; in a laboratory is 17; and in a regular course is 21.

PROGRAMS OF STUDY: South Dakota School of Mines and Technology, confers B.S. degrees. Associate, Master's, and Doctoral degrees are also awarded. Bachelor's degrees are awarded in COMPUTER AND PHYSICAL SCIENCE (chemistry, computer science, geology, mathematics, and physics), ENGINEERING AND ENVIRONMENTAL DESIGN (chemical engineering, civil engineering, computer engineering, electrical/electronics engineering, environmental engineering, geological engineering, industrial engineering, mechanical engineering, metallurgical engineering, and mining and mineral engineering), SOCIAL SCIENCE (interdisciplinary studies). Engineering is the strongest academically. Mechanical engineering, civil engineering, and electrical engineering have the largest enrollments.

ACTIVITIES: 8% of men belong to 4 national fraternities; 9% of women belong to 2 national sororities. There are 135 groups on campus, including ski club and biking, art, band, cheerleading, choir, chorale, chorus, circle K, computers, dance, drama, drill team, environmental, ethnic, film, gay, honors, international, jazz band, newspaper, orchestra, pep band, political, professional, radio and TV, religious, social, social service, and student government. Popular campus events include M-Week, Christmas Chorale Concert, International Cultural Exposition and Engineers Week.

SERVICES: Counseling and information services are available, as is tutoring in most subjects. There is a reader service for the blind, and remedial math. **Library/Resources:** The library contains 172,180 volumes, 18,958 microform items, 10,357 audio/video tapes/CDs/DVDs, and subscribes to 7,364 periodicals including electronic. Computerized library services include interlibrary loans, database searching, Internet access, and Wi-Fi capability. Special learning facilities include an art gallery, natural history museum, planetarium, radio station, an Geology and Paleontology Museum, and a Apex Gallery. **Physically Challenged Students:** 81% of the campus is accessible. Facilities include wheelchair ramps, elevators, special parking, specially equipped restrooms, special class scheduling, lowered drinking fountains, special housing. ADA lab with specialized workstations, software, and hardware to aid students with visual, auditory, and mobility impairments and dyslexia. **Special:** Opportunities are provided for study abroad, co-op programs, internships, dual degrees, undergraduate research experiences, interdisciplinary design teams, credit by exam, and nondegree study. There are 5 national honor societies and including Phi Beta Kappa. **Visiting:** There are regularly scheduled orientations for prospective students, including a campus tour, discussions, training, and a meal. There are guides for informal visits, visitors may sit in on classes, and stay overnight. To schedule a visit, contact the Admissions Office. **Campus Safety and Security:** Measures include 24-hour foot and vehicle patrol, emergency notification system, self-defense education, and security escort services. There are emergency telephones, lighted pathways/sidewalks, and controlled access to dorms/residences.

REQUIREMENTS: The ACT is required. The SAT is accepted. The ACT is preferred, with a minimum composite score of 920 (420 critical reading/writing and 500 math) on the SAT, or a minimum composite score of 18 on the ACT. Graduation from an accredited secondary school is required. A GED is accepted. Applicants must submit high school credits, distributed as follows: 4 years of English, 3 each of math, lab science, and social studies, and 1/2 year each of fine arts and computer science. A GPA of 2.8 is required. AP and CLEP credits are accepted.

ADMISSIONS: 88% of a recent year applicants were accepted. The SAT scores for a recent year freshman class were: Critical Reading--31% below 500, 40% between 500 and 599, 22% between 600 and 699, and 7% between 700 and 800; Math--12% below 500, 40% between 500 and 599, 29% between 600 and 699, and 19% between 700 and 800; Writing--42% below 500, 40% between 500 and 599, 16% between 600 and 699, and 2% between 700 and 800. The ACT scores were 4% below 21, 17% between 21 and 23, 35% between 24 and 26, 20% between 27 and 28, and 24% above 28. 39% of the current freshmen were in the top fifth of their class; 65% were in the top two fifths. There were 6 National Merit finalists. 24 freshmen graduated first in their class.

FINANCIAL AID: In a recent year, 60% of all full-time freshmen and 56% of continuing full-time students received some form of financial aid. 44% of all full-time freshmen and 34% of continuing full-time students received need-based aid. The average freshman award was $13,258. Need-based scholarships or need-based grants averaged $4,115; need-based self-help aid (loans and jobs) averaged $3,646; non-need-based athletic scholarships averaged $3,868; and other non-need-based awards and non-need-based scholarships averaged $2,799. 16% of undergraduate students work part-time. Average annual earnings from campus work are $1286. The average financial indebtedness of the 2013 graduate was $18,331. The FAFSA is required. The deadline for filing freshman financial aid applications for fall entry is March 15.

SOUTH DAKOTA STATE UNIVERSITY   **F-3**
www.sdstate.edu

Brookings, SD 57007   (605) 688-4121
                                        (800) 952-3541
Fax: (605) 688-6891   Email: sdsu.admissions@sdstate.edu

Full-time: n/av	Faculty: n/av
Part-time: n/av	Ph.D.s: n/av
Graduate: n/av	Student/Faculty: n/av
Year: semesters, summer session	Tuition: $7713 ($9795)
Room & Board: $6583	Freshman Class: 4851 applied, 4458 accepted, 2306 enrolled
ACT: required	CEEB CODE: 6653
Application Deadline: open	COMPETITIVE

South Dakota State University, founded in 1881, is a public land-grant institution, that offers undergraduate programs in agriculture and biological sciences, arts and sciences, engineering, education and human sciences, nursing, pharmacy, and general studies. There are 8 undergraduate schools and 1 graduate school. In addition to regional accreditation, SDSU has baccalaureate program accreditation with ABET, ACCE, ACEJMC, ACPE, NASM, NCATE, and NLN. The 275-acre campus is in a small town 50 miles north of Sioux Falls, 200 miles west of Minneapolis. Including any residence halls, there are 172 buildings.

STUDENT LIFE: 87% are White.

FACULTY/CLASSROOMS: No introductory courses are taught by graduate students.

PROGRAMS OF STUDY: SDSU confers B.A., B.G.S., B.S. and B.M.E. degrees. Associate, Master's, and Doctoral degrees are also awarded. Bachelor's degrees are awarded in AGRICULTURE (agricultural business management, agricultural communications, agricultural economics, agriculture, agronomy, animal science, dairy science, fish and game management, forestry and related sciences, horticulture, natural resource management, plant science, and range/farm management), BIOLOGICAL SCIENCE (biochemistry, biology/biological science, biotechnology, ecology, environmental biology, microbiology, nutrition, and wildlife biology), BUSINESS (apparel and accessories marketing, entrepreneurial studies, and hotel/motel and restaurant management), COMMUNICATIONS AND THE ARTS (art, communications, dramatic arts, English, German, graphic design, journalism, music, and Spanish), COMPUTER AND PHYSI-

CAL SCIENCE (chemistry, computer science, geoscience, mathematics, physics, and software engineering), EDUCATION (agricultural education, art education, athletic training, early childhood education, education, health education, home economics education, music education, physical education, secondary education, technical education, and vocational education), ENGINEERING AND ENVIRONMENTAL DESIGN (agricultural engineering, agricultural engineering technology, architecture, aviation administration/management, aviation maintenance management, civil engineering, construction management, electrical/electronics engineering, electrical/electronics engineering technology, engineering, engineering physics, engineering technology, environmental engineering, industrial administration/management, interior design, landscape architecture/design, manufacturing technology, and mechanical engineering), HEALTH PROFESSIONS (clinical science, exercise science, medical laboratory science, nursing, pharmaceutical science, and pharmacy), SOCIAL SCIENCE (consumer services, early childhood studies, economics, family/consumer resource management, family/consumer studies, food production/management/services, food science, French studies, geography, history, human development, liberal arts/general studies, parks and recreation management, philosophy and religion, political science/government, psychology, rural sociology, safety management, and sociology).

ACTIVITIES: 4% of men belong to 6 national fraternities; 2% of women belong to 3 national sororities. There are 207 groups on campus, including art, band, cheerleading, chess, choir, chorale, chorus, computers, dance, debate, drama, drill team, environmental, ethnic, film, forensics, gay, honors, international, jazz band, literary magazine, marching band, musical theater, newspaper, opera, orchestra, pep band, photography, political, professional, radio and TV, religious, social, social service, student government, and symphony. Popular campus events include Little International, Engineering Exploration Days, Capers, Cavorts, and Hobo Days.

SERVICES: Counseling and information services are available, as is tutoring in most subjects, accounting, biology, chemistry, economics, physics, and history There is a reader service for the blind, and remedial math, reading, and writing. **Library/Resources:** The library contains 897,150 volumes, 88,489 microform items, and 4,682 audio/video tapes/CDs/DVDs, and subscribes to 57,010 periodicals including electronic. Computerized library services include interlibrary loans, database searching, Internet access, and Wi-Fi capability. Special learning facilities include an art gallery, radio station, an Arboretum, Agricultural Heritage Museum, Northern Plains Biostress Lab, Animal Disease Research and Diagnostic Lab, and South Dakota Art Museum. **Physically Challenged Students:** 99% of the campus is accessible. Facilities include wheelchair ramps, elevators, special parking, specially equipped restrooms, special class scheduling, lowered drinking fountains, lowered telephones, special housing. All academic programs can be made accessible. **Special:** Co-op programs in elementary education and social work, internships, work-study programs, B.A.-B.S. degrees, and interdisciplinary majors including agricultural journalism, environmental management, and wildlife and fisheries science, are available. SDSU offers cross-registration with Dakota State University, Black Hills State University, and the University of South Dakota, Northern State University and South Dakota School of Mines and Technology. Opportunities are provided for dual majors, study abroad in more than 50 countries, credit by examination, student-designed majors, credit for military experience, nondegree study, a general studies degree, and pass/fail options. There are 33 national honor societies and a freshman honors program. **Visiting:** There are regularly scheduled orientations for prospective students, student orientation sessions which are offered each June. Students become acquainted with the university and student resources. They also meet with an academic adviser and register for fall semester classes. Information is sent to all admitted students. There are guides for informal visits, visitors may sit in on classes, and stay overnight. To schedule a visit, contact the Admissions Office at SDSU_Admissions@sdstate.edu. **Campus Safety and Security:** Measures include 24-hour foot and vehicle patrol, emergency notification system, self-defense education, and security escort services. There are emergency telephones, lighted pathways/sidewalks, and controlled access to dorms/residences.

REQUIREMENTS: The ACT is required. Students must have an 18

ACT composite score, or be in the top 60% of their class, or have a 2.6 GPA in required classes. Graduation from an accredited secondary school is required. A GED will be accepted. Applicants must submit 4 years of English, 3 years each of social studies, math, and science, and 1 year of fine arts and have a GPA of 2.0 in the required courses. SDSU requires applicants to be in the upper 60% of their class. A GPA of 2.6 is required. AP and CLEP credits are accepted. Important factors in the admissions decision are advanced placement or honors courses, evidence of special talent, and extracurricular activities record.

ADMISSIONS: 92% of a recent year applicants were accepted.

FINANCIAL AID: SDSU is a member of CSS. The FAFSA is required. The priority date for freshman financial aid applications for fall entry is March 20.

UNIVERSITY OF SIOUX FALLS F-3
www.usiouxfalls.edu

Sioux Falls, SD 57105	(605) 331-5000
	(800) 888-1047
Fax: (605) 331-6615	Email: admissions@usiouxfalls.edu
Full-time: 490 men, 550 women	Faculty: n/av; IIB; $--
Part-time: 110 men, 130 women	Ph.D.s: 75%
Graduate: 140 men, 230 women	Student/Faculty: n/av
Year: semesters, summer session	Tuition: $23,350
Room & Board: $7080	Freshman Class: n/av
SAT or ACT: required	CEEB CODE: 6651
Application Deadline: open	COMPETITIVE

University of Sioux Falls, founded in 1883, is a private liberal arts institution affiliated with the American Baptist Churches. Some figures in the above capsule and in this profile are approximate. In addition to regional accreditation, USF has baccalaureate program accreditation with CSWE and NCATE. The 22-acre campus is in a suburban area 250 miles from Minneapolis/St. Paul, Minnesota, and 180 miles from Omaha, Nebraska. Including any residence halls, there are 15 buildings.

STUDENT LIFE: 67% of undergraduates are from South Dakota. Others are from 28 states, 5 foreign countries, and Canada. 95% are from public schools. 94% are white. 73% are Protestant; 14% Catholic; 13% claim no religious affiliation. The average age of freshmen is 18; all undergraduates, 21. 32% do not continue beyond their first year; 68% remain to graduate.

FACULTY/CLASSROOMS: 69% of faculty are male; 31% are female. All teach undergraduates, and 60% do research. No introductory courses are taught by graduate students. The average class size in an introductory lecture is 40; in a laboratory, 15; and in a regular course, 20.

PROGRAMS OF STUDY: USF confers B.A. and B.S. degrees. Associate and Master's degrees are also awarded. Bachelor's degrees are awarded in BIOLOGICAL SCIENCE (biology/biological science), BUSINESS (accounting, business administration and management, business economics, and marketing/retailing/merchandising), COMMUNICATIONS AND THE ARTS (communications, English, music, and speech/debate/rhetoric), COMPUTER AND PHYSICAL SCIENCE (chemistry, computer science, and mathematics), EDUCATION (art education, early childhood education, elementary education, middle school education, music education, science education, and secondary education), HEALTH PROFESSIONS (medical laboratory technology and premedicine), SOCIAL SCIENCE (history, philosophy, political science/government, prelaw, psychology, religion, social work, and sociology). Business and elementary education are the strongest academically and have the largest enrollments.

ACTIVITIES: There are 35 groups on campus, including art, band, cheerleading, choir, chorale, chorus, computers, drama, ethnic, honors, international, jazz band, musical theater, newspaper, opera, orchestra, pep band, photography, political, professional, radio and TV, religious, social, social service, and student government. Popular campus events include Spring Formal and Madrigals.

SERVICES: Counseling and information services are available, as is

tutoring in most subjects. There is remedial math, reading, and writing. The library contains 78,000 volumes, 4600 audio/video tapes/CDs/DVDs, and subscribes to 450 periodicals including electronic. Computerized library services include interlibrary loans and database searching. Special learning facilities include a learning resource center, radio station, and TV station.

REQUIREMENTS: The SAT or ACT is required, with a minimum score for the critical reading and math section of the SAT of 1050 or a 22 on the ACT. Applicants must be graduates of an accredited secondary school or have a GED certificate. Students should have completed 4 years each of English and math and 2 years each of foreign language, science, and social studies. USF requires applicants to be in the upper 50% of their class. A GPA of 2.5 is required. AP and CLEP credits are accepted. Important factors in the admissions decision are advanced placement or honors courses, evidence of special talent, and leadership record.

ADMISSIONS: 96% of the 2014-2015 applicants were accepted. The SAT scores for the 2014-2015 freshman class were: Critical Reading-- 44% below 500, 33% between 500 and 599, and 23% between 700 and 800. Math-- 55% below 500, 34% between 500 and 599, and 11% between 700 and 800. The ACT scores were 36% below 21, 24% between 21 and 23, 27% between 24 and 26, 5% between 27 and 28, and 8% above 28. There were 1 National Merit finalists. **Admissions Contact:** Greg Fritz, Vice President for Enrollment Management. E-Mail: *greg.fritz@usiouxfalls.edu* Web: *www.usiouxfalls.edu*

FINANCIAL AID: USF is a member of CSS. The FAFSA, FFS, CCS/Profile, or SFS is required. Check with the school for current application deadlines.

UNIVERSITY OF SOUTH DAKOTA F-4
www.usd.edu

Vermillion, SD 57069	(877) 269-6837
	(877) COYOTES
Fax: (605) 677-6323	Email: admission@usd.edu
Full-time: 1927 men, 2805 women	Faculty: 383; I, --$
Part-time: 895 men, 2006 women	Ph.D.s: 85%
Graduate: 1125 men, 1477 women	Student/Faculty: 17 to 1
Year: semesters, summer session	Tuition: $8022 ($10,104)
Room & Board: $7089	Freshman Class: 3606 applied, 3469 accepted, 1342 enrolled
SAT CR/M: 509/527 ACT: 23	CEEB CODE: 6681
Application Deadline: open	COMPETITIVE

The University of South Dakota, founded in 1862, is a public institution with undergraduate programs in arts and sciences, education, fine arts, business, health sciences and professional schools of law, medicine, audiology and physcial therapy. There are 6 undergraduate schools and 7 graduate schools. In addition to regional accreditation, USD has baccalaureate program accreditation with AACSB, APTA, CSWE, NASAD, NASM, NCATE, and NLN. The 284-acre campus is in a small town between Sioux City, Iowa and Sioux Falls, South Dakota. Including any residence halls, there are 69 buildings.

STUDENT LIFE: 69% of undergraduates are from South Dakota. Others are from 48 states, 27 foreign countries, and Canada. 86% are White. The average age of freshmen is 18; all undergraduates, 22. 25% do not continue beyond their first year; 56% remain to graduate.

FACULTY/CLASSROOMS: 50% of faculty are male; 50% are female. 95% teach undergraduates and 5% do research. Graduate students teach 8% of introductory courses. The average class size in an introductory lecture is 29; in a laboratory is 19; and in a regular course is 23.

PROGRAMS OF STUDY: USD confers B.A., B.S., B.B.A., B.F.A., B.G.S., B.M., B.S.Ed, B.S.N. and B.S.R. degrees. Associate, Master's, and Doctoral degrees are also awarded. Bachelor's degrees are awarded in BIOLOGICAL SCIENCE (biology/biological science), BUSINESS (accounting, banking and finance, management science, and recreation and leisure services), COMMUNICATIONS AND THE ARTS (art, communications technology, dramatic arts, English, German, journalism, music, music performance, and Spanish),

COMPUTER AND PHYSICAL SCIENCE (chemistry, computer science, earth science, mathematics, and physics), EDUCATION (art education, elementary education, music education, physical education, secondary education, and special education), HEALTH PROFESSIONS (dental hygiene, health care administration, medical technology, and speech pathology/audiology), SOCIAL SCIENCE (addiction studies, American Indian studies, anthropology, criminal justice, economics, French studies, history, international studies, liberal arts/general studies, philosophy, political science/government, psychology, social work, and sociology). Business, biology, and chemistry are the strongest academically. Business, psychology, and biology have the largest enrollments.

ACTIVITIES: 18% of men belong to 7 national fraternities; 11% of women belong to 8 national sororities. There are 140 groups on campus, including art, band, cheerleading, chess, choir, chorale, chorus, computers, dance, debate, drama, drill team, ethnic, forensics, gay, honors, international, jazz band, literary magazine, marching band, musical theater, newspaper, opera, orchestra, pep band, photography, political, professional, radio and TV, religious, social, social service, student government, and symphony. Popular campus events include Dakota Days, Strollers (a variety production), and Rockfest.

SERVICES: Counseling and information services are available, as is tutoring in most subjects. There is a reader service for the blind, remedial math, reading, and writing. There is an academic advising and testing center. **Library/Resources:** The library contains 863,292 volumes, 740,454 microform items, 15,185 audio/video tapes/CDs/DVDs, and subscribes to 64,575 periodicals including electronic. Computerized library services include interlibrary loans, database searching, Internet access, and Wi-Fi capability. Special learning facilities include an art gallery, natural history museum, radio station, TV station, music museum, historical study center, institutes of American Indian studies, social science research, child welfare training, business and governmental research bureaus, centers for speech and hearing, international studies, fine arts, and telecommunications, natural sciences field station, and archeology and human factors labs. **Physically Challenged Students:** 95% of the campus is accessible. Facilities include wheelchair ramps, elevators, special parking, specially equipped restrooms, special class scheduling, lowered drinking fountains, and lowered telephones. **Special:** USD offers internships, study abroad in 7 countries, and work-study programs. B.A.-B.S. degrees in 34 majors, a student-designed liberal studies major, dual majors, nondegree study, and pass/fail options are available. The Arts

Outreach program provides arts activities and noncredit classes. There are 16 national honor societies, including Phi Beta Kappa, a freshman honors program, and 19 departmental honors programs. **Visiting:** There are regularly scheduled orientations for prospective students, student visits include an introductory session with an admission counselor, academic department visits, a campus tour with a student guide, and any other requested units. There are guides for informal visits, visitors may sit in on classes, and stay overnight.. **Campus Safety and Security:** Measures include 24-hour foot and vehicle patrol, emergency notification system, self-defense education, and security escort services. There are shuttle buses, emergency telephones, and lighted pathways/sidewalks.

REQUIREMENTS: The ACT is required. Applicants must have earned a 2.0 GPA in 4 years of English, 3 years each of lab science, math, and social studies, and 2 semesters of fine arts. They must also rank in the top 60% of their graduation class, have an ACT score of 18, or have a high school GPA of 2.6. A GPA of 2.0 is required. AP and CLEP credits are accepted.

ADMISSIONS: 96% of a recent year applicants were accepted. The SAT scores for a recent year freshman class were: Critical Reading--46% below 500, 34% between 500 and 599, 18% between 600 and 699, and 2% between 700 and 800; Math--39% below 500, 32% between 500 and 599, 25% between 600 and 699, and 4% between 700 and 800. The ACT scores were 24% below 21, 31% between 21 and 23, 26% between 24 and 26, 11% between 27 and 28, and 8% above 28. 31% of the current freshmen were in the top fifth of their class; 60% were in the top two fifths. 66 freshmen graduated first in their class.

FINANCIAL AID: In a recent year, 95% of all full-time freshmen and 88% of continuing full-time students received some form of financial aid. 59% of all full-time freshmen and 62% of continuing full-time students received need-based aid. The average freshman award was $10,479. Need-based scholarships or need-based grants averaged $1,389 ($14,150 maximum); need-based self-help aid (loans and jobs) averaged $2,148 ($10,150 maximum); non-need-based athletic scholarships averaged $609 ($18,818 maximum); and other non-need-based awards and non-need-based scholarships averaged $2,992 ($19,856 maximum). 15% of undergraduate students work part-time. Average annual earnings from campus work are $2007. The average financial indebtedness of the 2013 graduate was $26,629. The FAFSA is required. The priority date for freshman financial aid applications for fall entry is March 15.

TENNESSEE

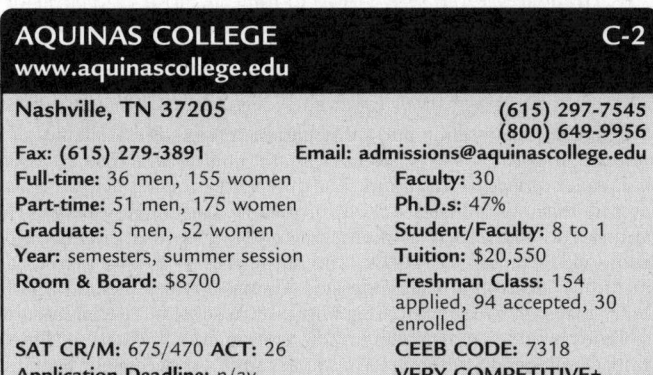

AQUINAS COLLEGE   C-2
www.aquinascollege.edu

Nashville, TN 37205

(615) 297-7545
(800) 649-9956

Fax: (615) 279-3891   Email: admissions@aquinascollege.edu

Full-time: 36 men, 155 women   Faculty: 30
Part-time: 51 men, 175 women   Ph.D.s: 47%
Graduate: 5 men, 52 women   Student/Faculty: 8 to 1
Year: semesters, summer session   Tuition: $20,550
Room & Board: $8700   Freshman Class: 154
    applied, 94 accepted, 30
    enrolled

SAT CR/M: 675/470 ACT: 26   CEEB CODE: 7318
Application Deadline: n/av   VERY COMPETITIVE+

Aquinas College, is a Catholic community of learning in the Dominican Tradition with Christ at its center. The College directs all its efforts to the intellectual, moral, spiritual, and professional formation of the human person in wisdom. Students are formed individually and in Christian community so that the harmonious integration between faith and reason can permeate every dimension of their lives. Immersed in exploring the relationship between human civilization and the message of salvation, the college community embraces the Dominican imperative to preach the Gospel, serve others, and engage culture in truth and charity. There are 4 undergraduate schools. In addition to regional accreditation, has baccalaureate program accreditation with ACEN. The 83-acre campus is in an urban area in the western section of metropolitan Nashville, four miles from downtown. Including any residence halls, there are 6 buildings.

STUDENT LIFE: 84% of undergraduates are from Tennessee. Others are from 24 states. 74% are White. 46% are Catholic. The average age of freshmen is 20; all undergraduates, 27. 24% do not continue beyond their first year; 76% remain to graduate. **Housing:** 92 students can be accommodated in college housing, which includes single-sex dorms. On-campus housing is available on a first-come, first-served basis. Priority is given to out-of-town students. 88% of students commute. Alcohol is not permitted. All students may keep cars.

FACULTY/CLASSROOMS: 29% of faculty are male; 71% are female. 97% teach undergraduates. No introductory courses are taught by graduate students. The average class size in a laboratory is 9 and in a regular course is 13.

PROGRAMS OF STUDY: Aquinas confers B.A., B.B.A., B.S. and B.S.N. degrees. Associate and Master's degrees are also awarded. Bachelor's degrees are awarded in BUSINESS (business administration and management and finance), COMMUNICATIONS AND THE ARTS (English), EDUCATION (elementary education, nursing education, and secondary education), HEALTH PROFESSIONS (nursing), SOCIAL SCIENCE (history, interdisciplinary studies, liberal arts/general studies, philosophy, and theological studies). Nursing, education, and management have the largest enrollments.

ACTIVITIES: There are 11 groups on campus, including socratic club, student activities board, synaxis of St. John, literary magazine, professional, religious, social, social service, and student ambassadors. Popular campus events include Semi-annual Table Tennis and Pool Tournaments, Drive-In-Movie Nights, Fall and Spring Festivals, and St. Thomas Aquinas Feast Day. **Sports:** There is no sports program at Aquinas. **Graduates:** From July 1, 2013 to June 30, 2014, 33 bachelor's degrees were awarded. The most popular majors were nursing (42%), education (39%), and business (9%).

SERVICES: Counseling and information services are available, as is tutoring in some subjects, nursing, theology, philosophy, math, writing, and biology. There is remedial math and writing. Write Reason writing center is available to all students for assistance with writing assignments for any course. **Library/Resources:** The library contains 73,394 volumes, 162,805 microform items, 2,187 audio/video tapes/CDs/DVDs, subscribes to 374 periodicals including electronic. Computerized library services include interlibrary loans, database searching, Internet access, and Wi-Fi capability. **Physically Challenged Students:** 75% of the campus is accessible. Facilities include wheelchair ramps, special parking, specially equipped restrooms, special class scheduling, and lowered drinking fountains. **Special:** The RN-BSN program is offered in an accelerated format. Also, students of the School of Business must complete an internship as a component of their program of study. A study abroad program (in Bracciano, Italy) is currently in the development phase. There are 3 national honor societies. **Visiting:** There are regularly scheduled orientations for prospective students, including campus tours and information on admissions, financial aid, student life, and degree programs. There are guides for informal visits and visitors may sit in on classes. To schedule a visit, contact Connie Hansom at admissions@aquinascollege.edu. **Campus Safety and Security:** Measures include 24-hour foot and vehicle patrol, emergency notification system, and self-defense education. There are lighted pathways/sidewalks and controlled access to dorms/residences.

REQUIREMENTS: The SAT or ACT is required. The GED is accepted. A GPA of 2.4 is required. AP and CLEP credits are accepted. Courses in theology and philosophy are required in every undergraduate curriculum. **Procedure:** Freshmen are admitted to all sessions. There is a rolling admissions plan. Application deadlines are open. The fall 2014 application fee was $25. Applications are accepted online. **Transfer Students:** 122 transfer students enrolled in 2013-2014. Transfer applicants must have a 2.4 GPA in previous college work. Transfer students with less than 30 semester hours of college-level course work must also submit their high school transcripts and SAT/ACT scores. 30 of 120 credits required for the bachelor's degree must be completed at Aquinas. **International Students:** There are 13 international students enrolled. They must take the TOEFL with a minimum score of 525 on the paper-based TOEFL (PBT) or 70 on the Internet-based version (iBT). They must also take the SAT or ACT, scoring 21.

ADMISSIONS: 61% of the 2014-2015 applicants were accepted. The SAT scores for the 2014-2015 freshman class were: Critical Reading-

-10% below 500, 20% between 500 and 599, 40% between 600 and 699, and 30% between 700 and 800; Math--60% below 500, 20% between 500 and 599, 10% between 600 and 699, and 10% between 700 and 800. The ACT scores were 25% below 21, 20% between 21 and 23, 10% between 24 and 26, 20% between 27 and 28, and 25% above 28. **Admissions Contact:** Connie Hansom, Director of Admissions. E-Mail: *admissions@aquinascollege.edu* Web: *http://www.aquinascollege.edu/admissions/*

FINANCIAL AID: In 2014-2015, 90% of all full-time freshmen and 81% of continuing full-time students received some form of financial aid. 53% of all full-time freshmen and 60% of continuing full-time students received need-based aid. The average freshman award was $7,316. Need-based scholarships or need-based grants averaged $1,103; need-based self-help aid (loans and jobs) averaged $750; and other non-need-based awards and non-need-based scholarships averaged $5,571. 4% of undergraduate students work part-time. Average annual earnings from campus work are $2364. is a member of CSS. The FAFSA and the college's own financial statement are required. The priority date for freshman financial aid applications for fall entry is February 15. The deadline for filing freshman financial aid applications for fall entry is February 15.

AUSTIN PEAY STATE UNIVERSITY   C-1
www.apsu.edu

Clarksville, TN 37044

	(931) 221-7011
	(877) 861-2778
Fax: (931) 221-6168	Email: admission@.apsu.edu
Full-time: 2769 men, 4097 women	Faculty: 360; IIA, --$
Part-time: 1078 men, 1606 women	Ph.D.s: n/av
Graduate: 226 men, 623 women	Student/Faculty: 18 to 1
Year: semesters, summer session	Tuition: $7164 ($21,664)
Room & Board: $8106	Freshman Class: 3551 applied, 3054 accepted, 1582 enrolled
ACT: 22	CEEB CODE: 1028
Application Deadline: August 5	COMPETITIVE

Austin Peay State University, established in 1927, is a public institution offering undergraduate degrees in the liberal arts and sciences and professional preparation. Figures in the above capsule and in this profile are aproximate. There are 6 undergraduate schools and 1 graduate school. In addition to regional accreditation, APSU has baccalaureate program accreditation with CSWE, NASAD, NASM, NCATE, NLN, ACS, and NAALS. The 182-acre campus is in an urban area 47 miles from Nashville. Including any residence halls, there are 58 buildings.

STUDENT LIFE: 89% of undergraduates are from Tennessee. Others are from 44 states, 23 foreign countries, and Canada. 66% are White; 19% African American. The average age of freshmen is 19; all undergraduates, 25. 34% do not continue beyond their first year; 37% remain to graduate. **Housing:** 1818 students can be accommodated in college housing, which includes single-sex and coed dorms, on-campus apartments, and married student housing. In addition, there are honors houses. On-campus housing is available on a first-come and first-served basis. 85% of students commute. Alcohol is not permitted. All students may keep cars.

FACULTY/CLASSROOMS: 47% of faculty are male; 53% are female. All teach undergraduates. No introductory courses are taught by graduate students. The average class size in an introductory lecture is 24; in a laboratory is 16; and in a regular course is 25.

PROGRAMS OF STUDY: APSU confers B.A., B.S., B.B.A., B.F.A., B.P.S. and B.S.N. degrees. Associate and Master's degrees are also awarded. Bachelor's degrees are awarded in AGRICULTURE (agriculture), BIOLOGICAL SCIENCE (biology/biological science), BUSINESS (business administration and management), COMMUNICATIONS AND THE ARTS (art, communications, English, languages, and music), COMPUTER AND PHYSICAL SCIENCE (chemistry, computer science, geoscience, mathematics, physics, and radiological technology), EDUCATION (health education and special education), ENGINEERING AND ENVIRONMENTAL DESIGN (engineering technology), HEALTH PROFESSIONS (medical technology and nursing), SOCIAL SCIENCE (criminal justice, history, interdisciplinary studies, liberal arts/general studies, philosophy, political science/government, psychology, public administration, social work, and sociology). Biology, nursing, and physics are the strongest academically. General business has the largest enrollment.

ACTIVITIES: 12% of men belong to 9 national fraternities; 11% of women belong to 6 national sororities. There are 86 groups on campus, including art, band, cheerleading, choir, chorus, debate, drama, ethnic, gay, honors, international, jazz band, literary magazine, marching band, newspaper, orchestra, pep band, political, professional, radio and TV, religious, social, social service, student government, and yearbook. Popular campus events include Graduation, Parents Day and Mud Bowl. **Sports:** There are 6 intercollegiate sports for men and 9 for women, and 12 intramural sports for men and 12 for women. Facilities include a recreation complex that houses 3 multipurpose courts, 4 fully-enclosed racquetball courts, an indoor track, a dynamic climbing area, an expanded fitness area, 2 modern fitness studios, a dedicated indoor cycling studio, and spacious locker rooms. A fitness center and outdoor recreation fields are also available. **Graduates:** From July 1, 2013 to June 30, 2014, 1546 bachelor's degrees were awarded. The most popular majors were general business (11%), nursing (8%), and communications (8%). In an average class, 1% graduate in 3 years or less, 16% graduate in 4 years or less, 32% graduate in 5 years or less, and 37% graduate in 6 years or less.

SERVICES: Counseling and information services are available, as is tutoring in some subjects, sciences, math, English, and history. There is a reader service for the blind. The university provides help with academic, learning, and test-taking problems. **Library/Resources:** The library contains 225,117 volumes, 672,421 microform items, 7,143 audio/video tapes/CDs/DVDs, and subscribes to 81,782 periodicals including electronic. Computerized library services include interlibrary loans, database searching, and Internet access. Special learning facilities include an art gallery, radio station, and TV station. **Physically Challenged Students:** 95% of the campus is accessible. Facilities include wheelchair ramps, elevators, special parking, specially equipped restrooms, special class scheduling, lowered drinking fountains, and lowered telephones. **Special:** APSU offers cooperative programs in nuclear medicine with Vanderbilt University and a pre-engineering (2-year transfer) program in which a student will earn a degree in physics and an engineering degree from one of Tennessee's colleges of engineering. Credit may be granted for military experience. Pass/fail grading options and work-study programs are available. There are 11 national honor societies and a freshman honors program. **Visiting:** There are regularly scheduled orientations for prospective students. There are guides for informal visits. To schedule a visit, contact the Admissions Office at (800) 844-2778. **Campus Safety and Security:** Measures include 24-hour foot and vehicle patrol, emergency notification system, self-defense education, and security escort services. There are shuttle buses, emergency telephones, lighted pathways/sidewalks, and controlled access to dorms/residences.

REQUIREMENTS: Applicants must be graduates of an accredited secondary school or have a GED. 14 academic units are required, including 4 units of English, 3 units of mathematics, 2 units each of natural/physical science, and a foreign language, and 1 unit each of visual and/or performing arts, social studies, and U.S. history. Applicants who do not meet these requirements may be considered for admission. A GPA of 2.8 is required. AP and CLEP credits are accepted.To graduate, students must earn a minimum of 120 semester hours, of which 39 hours are in upper division elective courses, earn a cumulative GPA of 2.00, complete a Common General Education Core, and complete the First Year Experience Course. **Procedure:** Freshmen are admitted fall, spring, and summer. There is a rolling admissions plan. Applications should be filed by August 5 for fall entry; December 19 for spring entry; and May 19 for summer entry. The fall 2014 application fee was $15. Applications are accepted online. **Transfer Students:** 900 transfer students enrolled in 2013-2014. Applicants must have a 2.0 GPA and be in good standing with the last institution attended. Grades of D or better will be considered for credit. Application deadlines are the same as those for freshmen. Transfer students having attended only non-regionally accredited institutions are considered new students. 30 of 120 credits required for the bachelor's degree must be completed at APSU. **International Students:** There are 35 international students enrolled. They must take the TOEFL with a minimum score of 500 on the paper-based TOEFL (PBT) or 61 on the Internet-based version (iBT).

ADMISSIONS: 86% of the 2014-2015 applicants were accepted. The ACT scores were 43% below 21, 30% between 21 and 23, 16% between 24 and 26, 5% between 27 and 28, and 6% above 28. 30% of the current freshmen were in the top fifth of their class; 58% were in the top two fifths. **Admissions Contact:** Amy Deaton, Director of Admissions. E-Mail: *admission@apsu.edu* Web: *www.apsu.edu*

FINANCIAL AID: In 2014-2015, 96% of all full-time freshmen and 98% of continuing full-time students received some form of financial aid. 69% of all full-time freshmen and 81% of continuing full-time students received need-based aid. The FAFSA is required. The priority date for freshman financial aid applications for fall entry is February 3. The deadline for filing freshman financial aid applications for fall entry is August 5.

BELMONT UNIVERSITY — C-2
www.belmont.edu

Nashville, TN 37212

(615) 460-6785
(800) 460-6000

Fax: (615) 460-5434 — Email: buadmission@belmont.edu

Full-time: 2095 men, 3345 women	**Faculty:** IIA, +$
Part-time: 160 men, 237 women	**Ph.D.s:** 82%
Graduate: 511 men, 896 women	**Student/Faculty:** 13 to 1
Year: semesters, summer session	**Tuition:** $28,660
Room & Board: $10,530	**Freshman Class:** 5665 applied, 4686 accepted, 1392 enrolled
SAT CR/M: 580/570 **ACT:** 26	**CEEB CODE:** 1058
Application Deadline: August 1	**VERY COMPETITIVE+**

Belmont University, founded in 1890, is a private, Christian liberal arts university. Figures in the above capsule and in this profile are approximate. There are 7 undergraduate schools and 6 graduate schools. In addition to regional accreditation, Belmont has baccalaureate program accreditation with AACSB, CSWE, NASAD, NASM, NCATE, NLN, MACTE, and NAST. The 69-acre campus is in an urban area in Nashville, TN. Including any residence halls, there are 37 buildings.

STUDENT LIFE: 67% of undergraduates are from out of state, mostly the South. Students are from 49 states, 27 foreign countries, and Canada. 81% are White. The average age of freshmen is 18; all undergraduates, 21. 17% do not continue beyond their first year; 70% remain to graduate. **Housing:** College-sponsored housing includes single-sex dorms and on-campus apartments. On-campus housing is guaranteed for the freshman year only, and is available on a first-come, first-served basis. 50% of students commute. Alcohol is not permitted. All students may keep cars.

FACULTY/CLASSROOMS: 45% of faculty are male; 55% are female. No introductory courses are taught by graduate students. The average class size in a regular course is 20.

PROGRAMS OF STUDY: Belmont confers B.A., B.S., B.B.A., B.F.A., B.M., B.S.W. and B.S.N. degrees. Master's and Doctoral degrees are also awarded. Bachelor's degrees are awarded in BIOLOGICAL SCIENCE (biochemistry, biology/biological science, environmental biology, and neurosciences), BUSINESS (accounting, business administration and management, entrepreneurial studies, finance, international business management, international economics, management science, and marketing/retailing/merchandising), COMMUNICATIONS AND THE ARTS (art history, audio technology, classics, communications, design, English, French, German, journalism, multimedia, music, music business management, music performance, music theory and composition, musical theater, public relations, Spanish, studio art, theatre arts, theater design, and visual and performing arts), COMPUTER AND PHYSICAL SCIENCE (applied mathematics, chemistry, computer science, mathematics, medical physics, physics, and web technology), EDUCATION (early childhood education, elementary education, middle school educa-

tion, and physical education), ENGINEERING AND ENVIRONMENTAL DESIGN (engineering physics), HEALTH PROFESSIONS (exercise science, medical technology, nursing, and pharmaceutical science), SOCIAL SCIENCE (Asian/Oriental studies, biblical languages, biblical studies, Christian studies, economics, European studies, history, liberal arts/general studies, ministries, philosophy, political science/government, psychology, religion, social work, and sociology). Music, business, and humanities are the strongest academically. Business, music, nursing, and music business management have the largest enrollments.

ACTIVITIES: There are 73 groups on campus, including art, band, cheerleading, choir, chorale, chorus, computers, dance, debate, drama, environmental, ethnic, film, forensics, gay, honors, international, jazz band, literary magazine, marching band, musical theater, newspaper, orchestra, pep band, photography, political, professional, radio and TV, religious, social, social service, student government, and symphony. **Sports:** There are 7 intercollegiate sports for men and 7 for women, and 8 intramural sports for men and 8 for women. Facilities include 3 full-size basketball courts and 8 suites, and men's golf. **Graduates:** From July 1, 2013 to June 30, 2014, 1145 bachelor's degrees were awarded. The most popular majors were music business, nursing, and audio engineering technology. 113 companies recruited on campus in 2013-2014. In an average class, 59% graduate in 4 years or less, 68% graduate in 5 years or less, and 70% graduate in 6 years or less. Of the 2013 graduating class, 8% were enrolled in graduate school within 6 months of graduation, and 92% were employed.

SERVICES: Counseling and information services are available, as is tutoring in some subjects. Writing and computer labs are available. **Library/Resources:** The 2 libraries contain 232,140 volumes, 29,999 microform items, 34,506 audio/video tapes/CDs/DVDs, and subscribe to 788 periodicals including electronic. Computerized library services include interlibrary loans, database searching, and Internet access. Special learning facilities include an art gallery, radio station, TV station, including an 19th century antebellum mansion. **Physically Challenged Students:** 98% of the campus is accessible. Facilities include wheelchair ramps, elevators, special parking, specially equipped restrooms, special class scheduling, and lowered drinking fountains. **Special:** Belmont offers study abroad, student-designed majors, dual majors in math, physics, and chemistry. Dual degree programs are available with Auburn University and the University of Tennessee at Knoxville. Programs require 3 years of study at Belmont followed by 2 years at the other institution. There are 11 national honor societies, a freshman honors program, and 1 departmental honors program. **Visiting:** There are regularly scheduled orientations for prospective students, consisting of a 2-day program in summer and a 4-day program right before classes begin. There are guides for informal visits, visitors may sit in on classes, and stay overnight. To schedule a visit, contact the Admissions Office at buadmissions@belmont.edu. **Campus Safety and Security:** Measures include 24-hour foot and vehicle patrol, emergency notification system, self-defense education, and security escort services. There are shuttle buses, emergency telephones, lighted pathways/sidewalks, and controlled access to dorms/residences.

REQUIREMENTS: The ACT is required. The SAT is recommended. Applicants should be high school graduates or hold the GED. Secondary preparation should include 4 units of English, 3 of math, and 2 each of a foreign language, history, science, and social studies. Potential music majors must audition. AP and CLEP credits are accepted. Important factors in the admissions decision are advanced placement or honors courses, recommendations by school officials, and evidence of special talent. All students must complete at least 128 hours with a C average, including 22 to 24 hours in the major field. B.A. candidates are required to pursue a minor field. All programs except the B.B.A. require a core curriculum, which includes courses in language and literature, humanities (including religion), social sciences, science, math, and phys ed. **Procedure:** Freshmen are admitted fall, spring, and summer. Entrance exams should be taken during the junior or senior year. There are early admissions and rolling admissions plans. Applications should be filed by August 1 for fall entry; December 1 for spring entry, along with a $50 fee. Notification is sent on a rolling basis. Applications are accepted on-line. **Transfer Students:** 466 transfer students enrolled in 2013-2014. Applicants should present an above average GPA in previous college work and be able to meet freshman entrance requirements. Those with fewer than 64 credit hours must also submit SAT or ACT scores. 32 of 128 credits required for the bachelor's degree must be completed at Belmont. **International Students:** There are 72 international students enrolled. The school actively recruits these students. They must take the TOEFL with a minimum score of 550 on the paper-based TOEFL (PBT) or 80 on the Internet-based version (iBT).

ADMISSIONS: 83% of the 2014-2015 applicants were accepted. The SAT scores for the 2014-2015 freshman class were: Critical Reading--10% below 500, 50% between 500 and 599, 34% between 600 and 699, and 6% between 700 and 800; Math--13% below 500, 47% between 500 and 599, 34% between 600 and 699, and 6% between 700 and 800. The ACT scores were 6% below 21, 20% between 21 and 23, 28% between 24 and 26, 20% between 27 and 28, and 25% above 28. 62% of the current freshmen were in the top fifth of their class; 91% were in the top two fifths. **Admissions Contact:** Mary Lucus, Director, Institutional Research. E-Mail: *buadmission@belmont.edu* Web: *www.belmont.edu*

FINANCIAL AID: 58% of all full-time freshmen and 53% of continuing full-time students received need-based aid. The FAFSA is required. The deadline for filing freshman financial aid applications for fall entry is March 1.

BETHEL UNIVERSITY B-2
www.bethelu.edu

McKenzie, TN 38201	(731) 352-4000
	n/av
Fax: (731) 352-4069	Email: admission@bethelu.edu
Full-time: 738 men, 996 women	Faculty: 80
Part-time: 147 men, 351 women	Ph.D.s: 35%
Graduate: 190 men, 309 women	Student/Faculty: 16 to 1
Year: semesters, summer session	Tuition: $12,902
Room & Board: $13,552	Freshman Class: 598 applied, 317 accepted, 198 enrolled
	CEEB CODE: 1063
Application Deadline: August 30	COMPETITIVE

Bethel University, established in 1842, is a private institution affiliated with the Cumberland Presbyterian Church. The 3 colleges of Bethel University offer undergraduate degrees through a variety of traditional and nontraditional programs. There is 1 graduate school. The 100-acre campus is in a small town 120 miles northeast of Memphis. Including any residence halls, there are 18 buildings.
STUDENT LIFE: 89% of undergraduates are from Tennessee. Others are from 26 states, 25 foreign countries, and Canada. 99% are from public schools. 49% are white; 33% African American. 72% are Protestant. The average age of freshmen is 26; all undergraduates, 31. 38% do not continue beyond their first year; 37% remain to graduate.
FACULTY/CLASSROOMS: 54% of faculty are male; 46% are female. All teach undergraduates. No introductory courses are taught by graduate students. The average class size in an introductory lecture, 25, in a laboratory, 15, and in a regular course, 12.
PROGRAMS OF STUDY: Bethel confers B.A., B.S., B.S.N. degrees. Master's degrees are also awarded. Bachelor's degrees are awarded in BIOLOGICAL SCIENCE (biology/biological science), BUSINESS (business administration and management and management science), COMMUNICATIONS AND THE ARTS (English, music, music business management, and theater management), COMPUTER AND PHYSICAL SCIENCE (chemistry and mathematics), EDUCATION (education of the exceptional child, music education, and physical education), HEALTH PROFESSIONS (nursing and pre-medicine), SOCIAL SCIENCE (child psychology/development, history, human services, psychology, and sociology). Education, physicians assistant studies, and nursing are the strongest academically. Education and organizational management have the largest enrollments.
ACTIVITIES: 25% of men belong to 5 local fraternities; 25% of women belong to 5 local sororities. There are 25 groups on campus, including art, band, cheerleading, choir, chorale, chorus, drama,

honors, marching band, musical theater, pep band, political, professional, religious, social, social service, student government, and yearbook.
SERVICES: Counseling and information services are available, as is tutoring in every subject. There is remedial math, reading, and writing. Tutoring is available free of charge to students. **Library/Resources:** The library contains 79,164 volumes, 185 microform items, 2,166 audio/video tapes/CDs/DVDs, and subscribes to 1,208 periodicals including electronic. Computerized library services include interlibrary loans, database searching, Internet access, and Wi-Fi capability. Special learning facilities include a **Physically Challenged Students:** 75% of the campus is accessible. Facilities include wheelchair ramps, elevators, special parking, specially equipped restrooms, special class scheduling, and lowered drinking fountains. **Special:** Bethel offers evening classes for adults, in-service training for teachers, off-site classes, an accelerated degree program in organizational management, student-designed majors, internships, work-study, non-degree study, a pass/fail option, and portfolio credit for prior learning and work experience. There is 1 national honor society, a freshman honors program, and 11 departmental honors programs.
Visiting: There are regularly scheduled orientations for prospective students, including about the college, dorms, and the lap-top program; they meet advisers, register for classes, and meet with the financial aid and business office. There are guides for informal visits, visitors may sit in on classes, and stay overnight. To schedule a visit, contact the Admissions Office at hodgest@bethel-college.edu.
Campus Safety and Security: Measures include 24-hour foot and vehicle patrol, self-defense education, and security escort services. There are lighted pathways/sidewalks, controlled access to dorms/residences, and security cameras are in some buildings.
REQUIREMENTS: Applicants must graduate from an accredited secondary school. Those ranking in the upper half of their class or scoring a satisfactory score on the SAT or ACT are granted regular acceptance. Other applicants may be admitted conditionally. Other factors in the admission procedure are standardized test scores, an interview, evidence of special talent, and personality. Open admission is available for the nontraditional bachelor of science in the Management and Organizational Development program. Admission for all other programs is competitive. Bethel requires applicants to be in the upper 50% of their class. A GPA of 2.0 is required. AP and CLEP credits are accepted. Important factors in the admissions decision are advanced placement or honors courses, leadership record, and evidence of special talent.
ADMISSIONS: In a recent year, 53% applicants were accepted.
FINANCIAL AID: In a recent year, 95% of all full-time freshmen and 90% of continuing full-time students received some form of financial aid. 67% of all full-time freshmen and 51% of continuing full-time students received need-based aid. 14% of undergraduate students work part-time. Average annual earnings from campus work are $1187. The FAFSA and the college's own financial statement are required. The deadline for filing freshman financial aid applications for fall entry is March 15.

BRYAN COLLEGE D-3
www.bryan.edu

Dayton, TN 37321-7000	(423) 775-2041
	(800) 277-9522
Fax: (423) 775-7100	Email: admissions@bryan.edu
Full-time: 453 men, 521 women	Faculty: n/av
Part-time: 17 men, 20 women	Ph.D.s: 81%
Graduate: 48 men, 24 women	Student/Faculty: n/av
Year: semesters, summer session	Tuition: $18,740
Room & Board: $5454	Freshman Class: 459 applied, 344 accepted, 192 enrolled
SAT or ACT: required	CEEB CODE: 1908
Application Deadline: open	COMPETITIVE

Bryan College, founded in 1930, is a private, Christian institution that is evangelical and interdenominational. Its emphases are on the liberal arts, business, health science, fine arts, Bible and religious studies, music, and teacher preparation. There is 1 undergraduate school. The 130-acre campus is in a small town 40 miles north of Chattanooga. Including any residence halls, there are 28 buildings.

STUDENT LIFE: 55% of undergraduates are from out of state, mostly the South. Students are from 39 states, 6 foreign countries, and Canada. 89% are white. 99% are Protestant. The average age of freshmen is 18; all undergraduates, 20. 24% do not continue beyond their first year; 56% remain to graduate.

FACULTY/CLASSROOMS: 81% of faculty are male; 18% are female. All teach undergraduates. No introductory courses are taught by graduate students. The average class size in an introductory lecture is 27; in a laboratory, 13; and in a regular course, 16.

PROGRAMS OF STUDY: Bryan confers B.A. and B.S. degrees. Associate and Master's degrees are also awarded. Bachelor's degrees are awarded in BIOLOGICAL SCIENCE (biology/biological science), BUSINESS (business administration and management), COMMUNICATIONS AND THE ARTS (communications, English, music, and Spanish), COMPUTER AND PHYSICAL SCIENCE (computer science and mathematics), EDUCATION (elementary education, physical education, and science education), HEALTH PROFESSIONS (exercise science), SOCIAL SCIENCE (Christian studies, history, liberal arts/general studies, psychology, and religion). Communication studies and business administration have the largest enrollment.

ACTIVITIES: There are 17 groups on campus, including art, choir, chorale, computers, drama, honors, international, literary magazine, musical theater, newspaper, orchestra, pep band, photography, religious, social, social service, student government, and yearbook. Popular campus events include a fine arts series.

SERVICES: Counseling and information services are available, as is tutoring in some subjects. There is also remedial math, reading, and writing. **Library/Resources:** The library contains 150,000 volumes, 13,489 microform items, 3,015 audio/video tapes/CDs/DVDs, and subscribes to 10,000 periodicals including electronic. Computerized library services include interlibrary loans, database searching, Internet access, and Wi-Fi capability. **Physically Challenged Students:** All of the campus is accessible. Facilities include wheelchair ramps, elevators, special parking, specially equipped restrooms, and lowered drinking fountains. **Special:** Special academic programs include practicum's in business and psychology, and psychology internships. An American Studies Program in Washington and a study-abroad Latin American Studies Program are offered through the Christian College Coalition. There is a freshman honors program. **Visiting:** There are regularly scheduled orientations for prospective students, consisting of college visitation weekends, which include a tour of the campus, sitting in on classes and chapel, meeting with professors in the area of academic interest, staying with current students in residence halls, and eating meals in the dining room. There are guides for informal visits, visitors may sit in on classes, and stay overnight.. **Campus Safety and Security:** Measures include self-defense education and security escort services. There are lighted pathways/sidewalks, and a night security patrol.

REQUIREMENTS: The SAT or ACT is required. The ACT Optional Writing test is also required. Clear admission is granted to applicants who have graduated from an approved high school and who have a minimum GPA of 2.5 with a minimum composite score of 18 on the ACT or 860 on the SAT; clear admission is also granted to applicants with a minimum GPA of 2.0 and a composite score of 20 on the ACT or 920 on the SAT. The high school record should include a minimum of 18 academic credits with a recommended distribution of 4 units of English, 3 each of math, science, and social science/humanities, and 2 of a foreign language. The GED is also accepted. References are required, and an interview is recommended. A GPA of 2.0 is required. AP and CLEP credits are accepted.

FINANCIAL AID: In a recent year, 78% of all full-time freshmen and 75% of continuing full-time students received some form of financial aid. At least 74% of all full-time freshmen and at least 66% of continuing full-time students received need-based aid. The average freshman award was $17,870. Need-based scholarships or need-based grants averaged $11,374; need-based self-help aid (loans and jobs) averaged $3734; institutional non-need-based athletic scholarships

averaged $6699; and other institutional non-need-based awards and non-need-based scholarships averaged $5307. 45% of undergraduate students work part-time. Average annual earnings from campus work are $1500. The FAFSA and the college's own financial statement are required. The priority date for freshman financial aid applications for fall entry is February 15.

CARSON-NEWMAN UNIVERSITY   E-2
www.cn.edu

Jefferson City, TN 37760	(865) 471-2000
	(800) 678-9061
Fax: (865) 471-4817	Email: admitme@cn.edu
Full-time: 735 men, 838 women	Faculty: n/av; IIB, --$
Part-time: 33 men, 40 women	Ph.D.s: 77%
Graduate: 105 men, 216 women	Student/Faculty: 12 to 1
Year: semesters, summer session	Tuition: $22,652
Room & Board: $6406	Freshman Class: 2917 applied, 1913 accepted, 453 enrolled
SAT CR/M: 455/520 ACT: 23	CEEB CODE: 1102
Application Deadline: August 15	COMPETITIVE+

Carson-Newman, founded in 1851, is a private liberal arts college affiliated with the Tennessee Baptist Convention. There are 2 graduate schools. In addition to regional accreditation, Carson-Newman has baccalaureate program accreditation with ADA, AHEA, NASAD, NASM, NCATE, and NLN. The 100-acre campus is in a small town 27 miles northeast of Knoxville, TN. Including any residence halls, there are 27 buildings.

STUDENT LIFE: 86% of undergraduates are from Tennessee. Others are from 29 states, 17 foreign countries, and Canada. 92% are from public schools. 81% are White. 84% are Protestant. The average age of freshmen is 18; all undergraduates, 22. 25% do not continue beyond their first year; 60% remain to graduate.

FACULTY/CLASSROOMS: 53% of faculty are male; 47% are female. All teach undergraduates, and 40% do research. No introductory courses are taught by graduate students. The average class size in an introductory lecture is 25; in a laboratory is 16; and in a regular course is 17.

PROGRAMS OF STUDY: Carson-Newman confers B.A., B.S., B.M., B.S.M. and B.S.N. degrees. Associate and Master's degrees are also awarded. Bachelor's degrees are awarded in BIOLOGICAL SCIENCE (biology/biological science), BUSINESS (accounting, business administration and management, and business economics), COMMUNICATIONS AND THE ARTS (communications, English, fine arts, French, languages, music, and Spanish), EDUCATION (art education, early childhood education, elementary education, foreign languages education, health education, home economics education, middle school education, music education, science education, and secondary education), HEALTH PROFESSIONS (nursing and physical therapy), SOCIAL SCIENCE (economics, history, philosophy, psychology, religion, social science, and sociology). Nursing, music, and biology are the strongest academically. Nursing, business, and education have the largest enrollments.

ACTIVITIES: 20% of men belong to 2 local and 1 national fraternity; 20% of women belong to 2 local and 1 national sorority. There are 55 groups on campus, including art, band, cheerleading, chess, choir, chorale, chorus, computers, dance, debate, drama, drill team, ethnic, film, forensics, honors, international, jazz band, literary magazine, marching band, musical theater, newspaper, orchestra, pep band, photography, political, professional, radio and TV, religious, social, social service, student government, and yearbook. Popular campus events include Spring Fest, Fall Formal and Honors Convocation.

SERVICES: Counseling and information services are available, as is tutoring in most subjects, English, math, and science. There is remedial math, reading, and writing. **Library/Resources:** The library contains 300,000 volumes, 221,960 microform items, and 15,000 audio/video tapes/CDs/DVDs, and subscribes to 2,000 periodicals including electronic. Computerized library services include interlibrary loans, database searching, and Internet access. Special learning facilities include an art gallery, natural history museum, radio station, and TV station. **Physically Challenged Students:** 10% of the campus is accessible. Facilities include wheelchair ramps, elevators, special parking, and special class scheduling. **Special:** The college offers internships, study in England, France, Japan, Hong Kong, and Spain, a Washington semester, on-campus work-study programs, B.A.-B.S. degrees, dual majors, a general studies degree, student-designed majors, and pass/fail options. Students may receive credit for life, military, or work experience. There is 1 national honor society, a freshman honors program, and 16 departmental honors programs. **Visiting:** There are regularly scheduled orientations for prospective students, including information sessions, meetings with advisers, and preregistration. There are guides for informal visits, visitors may sit in on classes, and stay overnight. To schedule a visit, contact the Admissions Office at admitme@cn.edu. **Campus Safety and Security:** Measures include 24-hour foot and vehicle patrol, self-defense education, and security escort services. There are lighted pathways/sidewalks.

REQUIREMENTS: The SAT or ACT is required. Students must have a minimum composite score of 19 on the ACT or a satisfactory score on the SAT. Applicants should be graduates of an accredited secondary school. The GED is accepted. 20 academic credits are required, including 4 units of English and 2 units each of history, math, science, and social studies. An essay, a portfolio, an audition, and an interview are recommended. A GPA of 2.3 is required. AP and CLEP credits are accepted. Important factors in the admissions decision are advanced placement or honors courses, leadership record, and parents or siblings attended your school.

ADMISSIONS: 66% of a recent year applicants were accepted. The ACT scores were 35% below 21, 30% between 21 and 23, 20% between 24 and 26, 7% between 27 and 28, and 8% above 28. There were 3 National Merit finalists. 10 freshmen graduated first in their class.

FINANCIAL AID: Carson-Newman is a member of CSS. The FAFSA and the college's own financial statement are required. The deadline for filing freshman financial aid applications for fall entry is March 1.

CHRISTIAN BROTHERS UNIVERSITY   A-3
www.cbu.edu

Memphis, TN 38104	**(901) 321-4213**
	(800) 288-7576
Fax: (901) 321-3202	Email: admissions@cbu.edu
Full-time: 564 men, 631 women	Faculty: 94
Part-time: 52 men, 104 women	Ph.D.s: 87%
Graduate: 222 men, 255 women	Student/Faculty: 13 to 1
Year: semesters, summer session	Tuition: $28,600
Room & Board: $3070	Freshman Class: 1853 applied, 889 accepted, 290 enrolled
ACT: 25	CEEB CODE: 1121
Application Deadline: August 1	HIGHLY COMPETITIVE

Christian Brothers University, founded in 1871, is a private Catholic university providing undergraduate educational opportunities in the arts, business, engineering, the sciences, and teacher education, and specialized graduate programs. There are 4 undergraduate schools and 4 graduate schools. In addition to regional accreditation, CBU has baccalaureate program accreditation with ABET, NCATE, and CCNE. The 75-acre campus is in a small town in Memphis, about 4 miles east of downtown. Including any residence halls, there are 27 buildings.

STUDENT LIFE: 79% of undergraduates are from Tennessee. Others are from 23 states, 26 foreign countries, and Canada. 70% are from public schools. 48% are White; 30% African American. 50% are Protestant; 41% Buddhist, Muslim and unknown; 29% claim no religious affiliation; 21% Catholic. The average age of freshmen is 18; all undergraduates, 23. 26% do not continue beyond their first year; 56% remain to graduate. **Housing:** 576 students can be accommodated in college housing, which includes single-sex and coed dorms and on-campus apartments. Quiet floors in residence halls and a living/

learning community dorm. On-campus housing is available on a first-come, first-served basis, and is available on a lottery system for upperclassmen. Priority is given to out-of-town students. 67% of students live on campus; of those, 50% remain on campus on weekends. All students may keep cars.

FACULTY/CLASSROOMS: 56% of faculty are male; 44% are female. 83% teach undergraduates. No introductory courses are taught by graduate students. The average class size in an introductory lecture is 17; in a laboratory is 12; and in a regular course is 17.

PROGRAMS OF STUDY: CBU confers B.A., B.F.A. and B.S. degrees. Master's degrees are also awarded. Bachelor's degrees are awarded in BIOLOGICAL SCIENCE (biochemistry and biology/biological science), BUSINESS (accounting and business administration and management), COMMUNICATIONS AND THE ARTS (English and studio art), COMPUTER AND PHYSICAL SCIENCE (chemistry, computer science, mathematics, natural sciences, and physics), EDUCATION (early childhood education and special education), ENGINEERING AND ENVIRONMENTAL DESIGN (chemical engineering, civil engineering, electrical/electronics engineering, engineering management, engineering physics, and mechanical engineering), HEALTH PROFESSIONS (biomedical science), SOCIAL SCIENCE (applied psychology, history, liberal arts/general studies, philosophy and religion, and psychology). Engineering and biology is the strongest academically. Psychology, business, and electrical have the largest enrollments.

ACTIVITIES: 25% of men belong to 5 national fraternities; 19% of women belong to 6 national sororities. There are 37 groups on campus, including art, chess, chorale, chorus, computers, drama, ethnic, gay, honors, international, literary magazine, musical theater, political, professional, religious, social, social service, student government, and yearbook. Popular campus events include Bacchus, Sofapalooza, and Up Til Dawn. **Sports:** There are 5 intercollegiate sports for men and 6 for women, and 10 intramural sports for men and 10 for women. Facilities include a swimming pool, gym, theater, multimedia auditorium, batting cage, jogging track, basketball/volleyball and handball/racquetball courts, baseball and soccer fields, tennis courts, cross-country and weight-training facilities. **Graduates:** From July 1, 2013 to June 30, 2014, 257 bachelor's degrees were awarded. The most popular majors were business (41%), psychology (15%), and engineering (15%). In an average class, 39% graduate in 4 years or less, 54% graduate in 5 years or less, and 55% graduate in 6 years or less.

SERVICES: Counseling and information services are available, as is tutoring in most subjects. CBU also has centers for math and writing. **Library/Resources:** The library contains 165,796 volumes, 61,523 microform items, 2,004 audio/video tapes/CDs/DVDs. Computerized library services include interlibrary loans, database searching, Internet access, and Wi-Fi capability. Special learning facilities include an art gallery. **Physically Challenged Students:** 90% of the campus is accessible. Facilities include wheelchair ramps, elevators, special parking, specially equipped restrooms, lowered drinking fountains, and lowered telephones. **Special:** Special academic programs include on-campus work-study, study abroad in 4 countries, and internships for all juniors and seniors. There is cross-registration with the Greater Memphis Consortium, Rhodes College, and the University of Memphis. An accelerated degree program is available to all business and psychology majors through the professional studies program, and a general studies degree is offered. Up to 36 hours of nondegree study is possible, as are dual majors, an honors program, and pass/fail options. Numerous teacher licensure programs are also offered. There are 9 national honor societies and a freshman honors program. **Visiting:** There are regularly scheduled orientations for prospective students, including attendance at classes, meetings with professors and students, a campus tour, and meetings with admissions and financial aid representatives. There are guides for informal visits, visitors may sit in on classes, and stay overnight. To schedule a visit, contact the Dean of Admissions. **Campus Safety and Security:** Measures include 24-hour foot and vehicle patrol, emergency notification system, and security escort services. There are emergency telephones, lighted pathways/sidewalks, and controlled access to dorms/residences.

REQUIREMENTS: The ACT is required, with a score of 21 on the ACT and a high school GPA of at least 2.5. Other admissions requirements include graduation from an accredited secondary school, with a college-preparatory curriculum recommended. The GED is also accepted. An interview is advised. ACT scores between 18 and 20 with a high school GPA of 3.0 or better are considered. A GPA of 2.5 is required. AP and CLEP credits are accepted. Important factors in the admissions decision are advanced placement or honors courses, leadership record, and recommendations by school officials.In addition to meeting degree requirements for a particular major, a student at CBU is required to have a broad understanding of self, others, and the contemporary world. The graduate of CBU shall have cultivated, through the arts and sciences, the necessary skills of inquiry, reasoning, and communication, and shall have developed an awareness of the religious dimension of human existence. All students take a broad range of courses; common requirements are 9 hours of English, 3 hours of math, 4 hours of natural and physical sciences, 6 hours of religious studies, 3 hours of moral values, and 6 hours of social science/history for a total of 31 general education hours. Students must take a minimum of 30 hours of general education courses. **Procedure:** Freshmen are admitted to all sessions. Entrance exams should be taken by the end of the junior year. There are deferred admissions and rolling admissions plans. Applications should be filed by August 1 for fall entry; December 1 for spring entry; and May 1 for summer entry, along with a $25 fee. Notifications are sent December 1. Applications are accepted on-line. **Transfer Students:** 41 transfer students enrolled in 2013-2014. Transfer students should have a minimum GPA of 2.5 and be in good academic and disciplinary standing. 35 of 122 credits required for the bachelor's degree must be completed at CBU. **International Students:** There are 35 international students enrolled. The school actively recruits these students. They must take the TOEFL with a minimum score of 500 on the paper-based TOEFL (PBT).

ADMISSIONS: 48% of the 2014-2015 applicants were accepted. The ACT scores were 4% below 21, 42% between 21 and 23, 28% between 24 and 26, 11% between 27 and 28, and 15% above 28. 68% of the current freshmen were in the top fifth of their class; 84% were in the top two fifths. 4 freshmen graduated first in their class. **Admissions Contact:** Dr. Anne Kenworthy, Dean of Admissions. E-Mail: *admissions@cbu.edu*

FINANCIAL AID: In 2014-2015, 95% of all full-time freshmen and continuing full-time students received some form of financial aid. The average freshman award was $21,283. Need-based scholarships or need-based grants averaged $24,188; and non-need-based athletic scholarships averaged $8,937. 91% of undergraduate students work part-time. Average annual earnings from campus work are $2400. The average financial indebtedness of the 2014 graduate was $29,207. The FAFSA is required. Check with the school for current application deadlines.

CUMBERLAND UNIVERSITY   C-2
www.cumberland.edu

Lebanon, TN 37087

	(615) 547-1290
	(800) 467-0562
Fax: (615) 444-2569	Email: admissions@cumberland.edu
Full-time: 983 women	Faculty: n/av
Part-time: 372 men, and women	Ph.D.s: 49%
Graduate: 80 men, 185 women	Student/Faculty: 16 to 1
Year: semesters, summer session	Tuition: $18,700
Room & Board: $6500	Freshman Class: n/av
SAT: recommended ACT: required	CEEB CODE: 1146
Application Deadline: open	COMPETITIVE

Cumberland University, founded in 1842, is a private institution offering undergraduate and graduate degrees in business, education, and social sciences. The figures in the above capsule are approximate. There are 4 graduate schools. In addition to regional accreditation, Cumberland has baccalaureate program accreditation with AACSB and NLN. The 44-acre campus is in a small town 28 miles east of Nashville. Including any residence halls, there are 17 buildings.

STUDENT LIFE: 87% of undergraduates are from Tennessee. Others are from 29 states, 29 foreign countries, and Canada. 89% are from

public schools. 72% are white; 14% African American. The average age of freshmen is 18; all undergraduates, 22. 44% do not continue beyond their first year; 35% remain to graduate.

FACULTY/CLASSROOMS: 52% of faculty are male; 48% are female. 82% teach undergraduates. No introductory courses are taught by graduate students. The average class size in an introductory lecture is 20; in a laboratory, 20; and in a regular course, 20.

PROGRAMS OF STUDY: Cumberland confers B.A., B.S., B.B.A., and B.S.N. degrees. Associates and Master's degrees are also awarded. Bachelor's degrees are awarded in BIOLOGICAL SCIENCE (biology/biological science), BUSINESS (accounting, business administration and management, management science, marketing management, and recreation and leisure services), COMMUNICATIONS AND THE ARTS (English, fine arts, and music), COMPUTER AND PHYSICAL SCIENCE (mathematics), EDUCATION (elementary education, middle school education, music education, physical education, secondary education, and special education), HEALTH PROFESSIONS (nursing), SOCIAL SCIENCE (American studies, criminal justice, history, political science/government, psychology, social science, and sociology). Business, education, and nursing have the largest enrollments.

ACTIVITIES: 17% of men belong to 3 national fraternities; 7% of women belong to 2 national sororities. There are 15 groups on campus, including art, band, cheerleading, chorale, chorus, computers, dance, drama, honors, international, jazz band, marching band, musical theater, newspaper, pep band, political, professional, religious, social, social service, and student government. Popular campus events include Fall Frolic, Halloween at CU, and Fall and Spring Preview Days.

SERVICES: Counseling and information services are available, as is tutoring in most subjects. There is remedial math, reading, and writing. **Library/Resources:** The library contains 37,056 volumes, 590 microform items, 1,260 audio/video tapes/CDs/DVDs, and subscribes to 357 periodicals including electronic. Computerized library services include interlibrary loans, database searching, and Internet access. Special learning facilities include an Art Gallery and a Natural History Museum. **Physically Challenged Students:** All of the campus is accessible. Facilities include wheelchair ramps, special parking, and lowered telephones. **Special:** Internships with local businesses and with the state legislature are available. Nondegree study, pass/fail options, and an accelerated degree program in general business are offered. There are 13 national honor societies, a freshman honors program, and 5 departmental honors programs. **Visiting:** There are regularly scheduled orientations for prospective students, consisting of campus tours, testing, information sessions pertaining to college life, and academic advising. A parent orientation is provided in conjunction with student orientation programs. There are guides for informal visits and visitors may sit in on classes. To schedule a visit, contact the Admissions Office. **Campus Safety and Security:** Measures include 24-hour foot and vehicle patrol and emergency notification system. There are emergency telephones, lighted pathways/sidewalks. The outside entrances of the dorms are always secured; only residents have keys.

REQUIREMENTS: The ACT is required. The SAT and ACT Writing Test are recommended. A minimum composite ACT score of 19 and a GPA of 2.5 are expected. Applicants must be high school graduates or have earned the GED with a composite 50 score. A GPA of 2.5 is required. AP and CLEP credits are accepted.

FINANCIAL AID: In a recent year, 95% of all students received some form of financial aid. 33% of students received need-based aid. The average freshmen award was $6133, with $5191 ($9972 maximum) from need-based scholarships or need-based grants; $2800 ($11,500 maximum) from need-based self-help aid (loans and jobs); $7899 ($20,020 maximum) from non-need-based athletic scholarships; and $3212 ($14,710 maximum) from other non-need-based awards and non-need-based scholarships. Average annual earnings from campus work are $1000. The FAFSA and the college's own financial statement are required. Check with the school for current application deadlines.

EAST TENNESSEE STATE UNIVERSITY   F-1
www.etsu.edu

Johnson City, TN 37614	(423) 439-1000
	(800) 462-3878
Fax: (423) 439-4630	Email: go2etsu@etsu.edu
Full-time: 3400 men, 4550 women	Faculty: n/av; IIA, --$
Part-time: 650 men, 980 women	Ph.D.s: 75%
Graduate: 620 men, 1225 women	Student/Faculty: n/av
Year: semesters, summer session	Tuition: $5500 ($14,500)
Room & Board: $5500	Freshman Class: n/av
SAT or ACT: required	CEEB CODE: 1198
Application Deadline: open	COMPETITIVE

East Tennessee State University, founded in 1911, is a public institution that is part of the State University and Community College System of Tennessee. ETSU's undergraduate and graduate programs stress the liberal arts, business, art, fine arts, professional training, music, teacher preparation, technical studies, and health science. The figures in the above capsule and in this profile are approximate. There are 6 undergraduate schools and 2 graduate schools. In addition to regional accreditation, ETSU has baccalaureate program accreditation with AACSB, ABET, ACEJMC, ADA, CSAB, CSWE, NASAD, NASM, NCATE, and NLN. The 366-acre campus is in a small town 90 miles northeast of Knoxville. Including any residence halls, there are 68 buildings.

STUDENT LIFE: 89% of undergraduates are from Tennessee. Others are from 38 states, 46 foreign countries, and Canada. 97% are from public schools. 91% are white. The average age of freshmen is 19; all undergraduates, 23. 33% do not continue beyond their first year; 38% remain to graduate.

FACULTY/CLASSROOMS: 55% of faculty are male; 45% are female. 85% teach undergraduates. No introductory courses are taught by graduate students. The average class size in an introductory lecture is 30; in a laboratory, 15; and in a regular course, 25.

PROGRAMS OF STUDY: ETSU confers B.A., B.S., B.A.S., B.B.A., B.F.A, B.G.S., B.M., B.S.D.H., B.S.Ed., B.S.E.H., B.S.M.T., B.S.N., and B.S.W. degrees. Associates, master's, and doctoral degrees are also awarded. Bachelor's degrees are awarded in BIOLOGICAL SCIENCE (biology/biological science), BUSINESS (accounting, management science, and marketing/retailing/merchandising), COMMUNICATIONS AND THE ARTS (art, communications, English, fine arts, music, and speech/debate/rhetoric), COMPUTER AND PHYSICAL SCIENCE (chemistry, computer science, information sciences and systems, mathematics, and physics), EDUCATION (foreign languages education, physical education, and special education), ENGINEERING AND ENVIRONMENTAL DESIGN (engineering technology and survey and mapping technology), HEALTH PROFESSIONS (allied health, dental hygiene, environmental health science, health science, nursing, and public health), SOCIAL SCIENCE (child psychology/development, criminal justice, economics, geography, history, human development, interdisciplinary studies, liberal arts/general studies, philosophy, political science/government, psychology, social work, and sociology). Engineering technology, computer science, and nursing have the largest enrollments.

ACTIVITIES: 4% of men belong to 8 national fraternities; 4% of women belong to 1 local and 6 national sororities. There are 200 groups on campus, including art, band, cheerleading, choir, chorale, chorus, computers, dance, drama, drill team, ethnic, forensic, gay, honors, international, jazz band, literary magazine, newspaper, pep band, photography, political, professional, radio and TV, religious, residence hall, social, social service, and student government. Popular campus events include Leadership Retreat, National Clean Up for Hunger, and Winter Cruise.

SERVICES: Counseling and information services are available, as is tutoring in most subjects. There is a reader service for the blind, remedial math, reading, and writing. **Library/Resources:** The library contains 1.1 million volumes, 1.7 million microform items, and 23,658 audio/video tapes/CDs/DVDs, and subscribes to 3,714 periodicals including electronic. Computerized library services include interlibrary loans, database searching, and Internet access. Special learning facilities include an art gallery, planetarium, radio station,

TV station, a regional art and history museum. **Physically Challenged Students:** 75% of the campus is accessible. Facilities include wheelchair ramps, elevators, special parking, specially equipped restrooms, special class scheduling, lowered drinking fountains, lowered telephones, special housing. Adaptive computer equipment. **Special:** Special academic programs include cooperative education programs, cross-registration with Milligan College, internships in political science, applied human sciences, and management,and dual majors study abroad in Scotland, England, France, and Spain, and B.A.-B.S. degrees and dual majors in most arts and sciences undergraduate majors. A general studies degree is offered. Credit for military experience may be granted, and nondegree study and pass/fail options are possible. There are 19 national honor societies, a freshman honors program, and 12 departmental honors programs. **Visiting:** There are regularly scheduled orientations for prospective students, including 5; 2-day orientation programs held during spring and summer for new students admitted to fall term. There are guides for informal visits, visitors may sit in on classes, and stay overnight. To schedule a visit, contact the Admissions Office. **Campus Safety and Security:** Measures include 24-hour foot and vehicle patrol, self-defense education, and security escort services. There are shuttle buses, emergency telephones, lighted pathways/sidewalks, and engravers available to identify personal property.

REQUIREMENTS: The SAT or ACT is required. Other admissions requirements include graduation from an accredited secondary school, with 20 Carnegie units and 14 academic credits, including 4 of English, 3 of math, 2 each of a foreign language and science, and 1 each of history, social studies, and art. In-state students who pass the Tennessee State Proficiency Test are eligible to apply for admission. Applicants whose ACT/SAT is below a certain score must complete the Academic Assessment Placement Program (AAPP) test battery before registration for classes. The GED is also accepted. A GPA of 2.3 is required. AP and CLEP credits are accepted.

FINANCIAL AID: The FAFSA is required. Check with the school for current application deadlines.

FISK UNIVERSITY   C-2
www.fisk.edu

Nashville, TN 37208-3051	(615) 329-8550
	(888) 702-0022
Fax: (615) 329-8774	Email: admit@fisk.edu
Full-time: 245 men, 575 women	Faculty: 66
Part-time: 20 men, 30 women	Ph.D.s: 76%
Graduate: 20 men, 40 women	Student/Faculty: 12 to 1
Year: semesters	Tuition: $18,452
Room & Board: $12,472	Freshman Class: n/av
SAT or ACT: required	CEEB CODE: 1224
Application Deadline: open	COMPETITIVE

Fisk University, founded in 1866, is a private, nonsectarian, liberal arts institution. Established as a college for African Americans, Fisk accepts students regardless of race. The figures in the above capsule and in this profile are approximate. There is 1 graduate school. In addition to regional accreditation, Fisk has baccalaureate program accreditation with NASM. The 40-acre campus is in an urban area. Including any residence halls, there are 21 buildings.

STUDENT LIFE: 69% of undergraduates are from out of state, mostly the South. Students are from 39 states and 6 foreign countries. 87% are from public schools. 92% are African American. The average age of freshmen is 18; all undergraduates, 20. 16% do not continue beyond their first year; 68% remain to graduate.

FACULTY/CLASSROOMS: 61% of faculty are male; 39% are female. All teach undergraduates, 22% do research, and 24% do both. No introductory courses are taught by graduate students. The average class size in an introductory lecture is 30; in a laboratory, 15; and in a regular course, 19.

PROGRAMS OF STUDY: Fisk confers B.A., B.S., and B.M. degrees. Master's degrees are also awarded. Bachelor's degrees are awarded in BIOLOGICAL SCIENCE (biology/biological science), BUSINESS (business administration and management), COMMUNICATIONS

AND THE ARTS (dramatic arts, English, fine arts, French, music, Spanish, and speech/debate/rhetoric), COMPUTER AND PHYSICAL SCIENCE (chemistry, computer science, mathematics, and physics), EDUCATION (art education and music education), SOCIAL SCIENCE (economics, history, philosophy, political science/government, psychology, religion, and sociology). Biology, chemistry, and physics are the strongest academically. Biology has the largest enrollment.

ACTIVITIES: 25% of men belong to 4 national fraternities; 20% of women belong to 4 national sororities. There are 102 groups on campus, including cheerleading, choir, dance, drama, honors, international, literary magazine, newspaper, political, professional, radio and TV, religious, social, student government, and yearbook. Popular campus events include Jubilee Day.

SERVICES: Counseling and information services are available, as is tutoring in every subject. There is remedial math, reading, and writing. **Library/Resources:** The library contains 210,000 volumes, 114,998 microform items, 3,880 audio/video tapes/CDs/DVDs, and subscribes to 844 periodicals including electronic. Computerized library services include database searching, Internet access, and Wi-Fi capability. Special learning facilities include an art gallery and radio station. **Physically Challenged Students:** 80% of the campus is accessible. Facilities include wheelchair ramps and elevators. **Special:** Fisk offers cross-registration with Vanderbilt University, study abroad, dual majors in engineering and pharmacy, student-designed majors, and campus work-study. Students may take a 5-year B.S.-B.E. program or a combined B.S.-M.B.A. program with Vanderbilt University. There are 8 national honor societies, including Phi Beta Kappa, and 6 departmental honors programs. **Visiting:** There are guides for informal visits, visitors may sit in on classes, and stay overnight. To schedule a visit, contact the Admissions Office. **Campus Safety and Security:** Measures include 24-hour foot and vehicle patrol and security escort services. There are lighted pathways/sidewalks.

REQUIREMENTS: The SAT or ACT is required. Applicants should be high school graduates with 14 academic credits. A GPA of 2.5 is required. AP credits are accepted. Important factors in the admissions decision are advanced placement or honors courses, leadership record, and evidence of special talent.

FINANCIAL AID: The FAFSA and the college's own financial statement are required. Check with the school for current application deadlines.

FREED-HARDEMAN UNIVERSITY B-3
www.fhu.edu

Henderson, TN 38340	(731) 989-6651
	(800) 348-3481
Fax: (731) 989-6047	Email: admissions@fhu.edu
Full-time: 653 men, 837 women	Faculty: n/av; IIA, --$
Part-time: n/av	Ph.D.s: 69%
Graduate: 482	Student/Faculty: 15 to 1
Year: semesters, summer session	Tuition: $25,000
Room & Board: $7500	Freshman Class: n/av
ACT: required	CEEB CODE: 1230
Application Deadline: open	VERY COMPETITIVE

Freed-Hardeman University, founded in 1869, is a private, liberal arts institution associated with Churches of Christ. The figures in the above capsule and in this profile are approximate. There are 6 undergraduate schools and 4 graduate schools. In addition to regional accreditation, FHU has baccalaureate program accreditation with ACBSP, CSWE, and NCATE. The 120-acre campus is in a small town 85 miles east of Memphis and 13 miles south of Jackson. Including any residence halls, there are 39 buildings.

STUDENT LIFE: 52% of undergraduates are from out of state, mostly the South. Students are from 38 states, 25 foreign countries, and Canada. 75% are from public schools. 91% are white. 99% are Protestant. The average age of freshmen is 19; all undergraduates, 21. 26% do not continue beyond their first year; 57% remain to graduate.

FACULTY/CLASSROOMS: 68% of faculty are male; 32% are female. 91% teach undergraduates. No introductory courses are taught by graduate students. The average class size in a laboratory is 22 and in a regular course, 20.

PROGRAMS OF STUDY: FHU confers B.A., B.S., B.B.A., and B.S.W. degrees. Associates and Master's degrees are also awarded. Bachelor's degrees are awarded in BIOLOGICAL SCIENCE (biochemistry and biology/biological science), BUSINESS (accounting, banking and finance, and business administration and management), COMMUNICATIONS AND THE ARTS (art, broadcasting, communications, dramatic arts, English, fine arts, journalism, public relations, and speech/debate/rhetoric), COMPUTER AND PHYSICAL SCIENCE (chemistry, computer programming, computer science, information sciences and systems, mathematics, and physical sciences), EDUCATION (art education, early childhood education, elementary education, health education, middle school education, music education, physical education, science education, secondary education, and special education), ENGINEERING AND ENVIRONMENTAL DESIGN (preengineering), HEALTH PROFESSIONS (predentistry, premedicine, preoptometry, prepharmacy, and preveterinary science), SOCIAL SCIENCE (biblical studies, child care/child and family studies, criminal justice, family/consumer studies, history, ministries, psychology, and social work). Premedicine, preengineering, and business are the strongest academically. Business, Bible, and elementary education have the largest enrollments.

ACTIVITIES: There are 52 groups on campus, including art, band, cheerleading, choir, chorus, communications, computers, drama, drum and bugle corps, ethnic, honors, international, jazz band, musical theater, newspaper, orchestra, pep band, photography, political, professional, radio and TV, religious, social, social service, student government, and yearbook. Popular campus events include Makin' Music and Annual Bible Lectureship.

SERVICES: Counseling and information services are available, as is tutoring in most subjects. **Library/Resources:** The library contains 175,748 volumes, 240,000 microform items, 43,000 audio/video tapes/CDs/DVDs, and subscribes to 1,650 periodicals including electronic. Computerized library services include interlibrary loans, database searching, and Internet access. Special learning facilities include an art gallery, radio station, TV station, and an undergraduate research center. **Physically Challenged Students:** 70% of the campus is accessible. Facilities include wheelchair ramps, elevators, special parking, specially equipped restrooms, special class scheduling, lowered drinking fountains, and lowered telephones. **Special:** FHU offers study abroad in Belgium and Italy, a B.A.-B.S. degree in Bible, biology, communication, and arts and humanities, co-op programs, a dual major, field practicum opportunities in several majors, student-designed majors, 3-2 engineering degrees with 6 universities, and nondegree study. There are 4 national honor societies, a freshman honors program, and 13 departmental honors programs. **Visiting:** There are regularly scheduled orientations for prospective students, including an orientation during the 5 days prior to classes beginning in the fall. There are guides for informal visits, visitors may sit in on classes, and stay overnight. **Campus Safety and Security:** Measures include 24-hour foot and vehicle patrol, emergency notification system, and security escort services. There are lighted pathways/sidewalks.

REQUIREMENTS: The ACT is required. Candidates for admission should be graduates of an accredited secondary school. An interview is recommended. A GPA of 2.25 is required. AP and CLEP credits are accepted. Important factors in the admissions decision are personality/intangible qualities, recommendations by school officials, and leadership record.

FINANCIAL AID: The FAFSA is required. Check with the school for current application deadlines.

KING UNIVERSITY F-1
www.king.edu

Bristol, TN 37620	(423) 652-4861
	(800) 362-0014
Fax: (423) 652-4727	Email: admissions@king.edu
Full-time: 646 men, 1197 women	Faculty: 58; IIB, --$
Part-time: 52 men, 68 women	Ph.D.s: 81%
Graduate: 141 men, 238 women	Student/Faculty: 20 to 1
Year: semesters, summer session	Tuition: $24,960
Room & Board: $8180	Freshman Class: 856 applied, 184 accepted, 221 enrolled
SAT CR/M: 485/509 ACT: 23	CEEB CODE: 1371
Application Deadline: open	COMPETITIVE

King University, is a Presbyterian, master's-level comprehensive university offering more than 80 majors, minors, pre-professional degrees and concentrations in fields such as business, digital media, nursing, forensic science, education, and humanities. Graduate programs are offered in business administration, nursing, and education. A number of off-campus learning opportunities and travel destinations are also available. King University has 6 academic schools of learning: King College of Arts and Sciences, King School of Business and Economics, King School of Education, King School of Graduatie and Professional Studies and Online Programs, King School of Nursing, and Peeke School of Christian Mission. There are 5 undergraduate schools and 3 graduate schools. The 135-acre campus is in a small town 2 miles east of Bristol, VA. Including any residence halls, there are 20 buildings.

STUDENT LIFE: 65% of undergraduates are from Tennessee. Others are from 31 states, 29 foreign countries, and Canada. 89% are from public schools. 77% are White. 68% are Protestant; 18% claim no religious affiliation. The average age of freshmen is 18; all undergraduates, 28.

FACULTY/CLASSROOMS: 37% of faculty are male; 46% are female. All teach undergraduates. No introductory courses are taught by graduate students. The average class size in an introductory lecture is 30 and in a laboratory is 30.

PROGRAMS OF STUDY: King confers B.A., B.S., B.B.A., B.Chem., B.S.Med.Tech. and B.S.N. degrees. Master's degrees are also awarded. Bachelor's degrees are awarded in BIOLOGICAL SCIENCE (biochemistry, biology/biological science, and neurosciences), BUSINESS (accounting, business administration and management, business economics, international business management, management information systems, marketing management, and sports management), COMMUNICATIONS AND THE ARTS (digital communications, English, French, modern language, photography, Spanish, technical and business writing, theatre arts, and visual and performing arts), COMPUTER AND PHYSICAL SCIENCE (chemistry, mathematics, and physics), EDUCATION (athletic training, elementary education, music education, physical education, and secondary education), HEALTH PROFESSIONS (health science and nursing), SOCIAL SCIENCE (biblical studies, economics, forensic studies, history, interdisciplinary studies, philosophy, political science/government, psychology, and youth ministry). Business and economics, English, and natural sciences are the strongest academically. Business and economics, nursing, and social sciences have the largest enrollments.

ACTIVITIES: There are 36 groups on campus, including art, band, cheerleading, choir, chorale, chorus, dance, debate, drama, environmental, honors, international, jazz band, literary magazine, musical theater, newspaper, pep band, photography, political, professional, religious, social service, student government, and yearbook. Popular campus events include International Fair, Fall Ball and Dogwood Ball.

SERVICES: Counseling and information services are available, as is tutoring in most subjects. The Academic Center for Excellence (ACE) includes a writing center, math center, and speaking center. **Library/ Resources:** The library contains 104,697 volumes, 62,173 microform items, 7,009 audio/video tapes/CDs/DVDs, and subscribes to 349 periodicals including electronic. Computerized library services include interlibrary loans, database searching, Internet access, and Wi-Fi capability. Special learning facilities include a **Physically Challenged Students:** 80% of the campus is accessible. Facilities include wheelchair ramps, elevators, special parking, and specially equipped restrooms. **Special:** King offers internships, study abroad in approximately 50 countries, a Washington semester, and work-study programs. There are 3-2 engineering degrees available with Vanderbilt University and University of Tennessee. Dual degrees in pharmacy, engineering, and physical therapy are offered. Nondegree study and pass/fail options for special students are available. There is 1 national honor society, a freshman honors program, and 1 departmental honors program. **Visiting:** There are regularly scheduled orientations for prospective students, including a campus tour, financial aid seminar, faculty sessions, and admissions counseling. There are guides for informal visits and visitors may sit in on classes. To schedule a visit, contact The Admissions Office. **Campus Safety and Security:** Measures include 24-hour foot and vehicle patrol, emergency notification system, and security escort services. There are emergency telephones,

lighted pathways/sidewalks, 24-hour foot and vehicle patrol on weekends, and 12-hour patrol Monday through Friday.

REQUIREMENTS: The SAT or ACT is required. Graduation from an accredited or recognized secondary institution is required, with a minimum of 16 academic units, distributed as follows: 4 of English; 2 of algebra (Algebra I and II); 1 of geometry; 2 of foreign language; 2 of history and social studies; 1 of natural science; and 4 of other academic electives. A GPA of 2.6 is required. AP and CLEP credits are accepted. Important factors in the admissions decision are advanced placement or honors courses, extracurricular activities record, and leadership record.

ADMISSIONS: 21% of a recent year applicants were accepted. The SAT scores for the recent year freshman class were: Critical Reading--47% below 500, 47% between 500 and 599, 6% between 600 and 699; Math--36% below 500, 51% between 500 and 599, 12% between 600 and 699, and 1% between 700 and 800. The ACT scores were 6% below 21, 47% between 21 and 23, 43% between 24 and 26, and 4% above 28. 37% of the current freshmen were in the top fifth of their class; 66% were in the top two fifths. 6 freshmen graduated first in their class.

FINANCIAL AID: In a recent year, 83% of all full-time freshmen and 69% of continuing full-time students received some form of financial aid. 80% of all full-time freshmen and 60% of continuing full-time students received need-based aid. The average freshman award was $16,442. Need-based scholarships or need-based grants averaged $14,147; need-based self-help aid (loans and jobs) averaged $4,010; non-need-based athletic scholarships averaged $5,961; and other non-need-based awards and non-need-based scholarships averaged $12,206. 30% of undergraduate students work part-time. Average annual earnings from campus work are $962. The average financial indebtedness of a recent year graduate was $9,998. King is a member of CSS. The FAFSA and the college's own financial statement are required. The priority date for freshman financial aid applications for fall entry is March 1. The deadline for filing freshman financial aid applications for fall entry is rolling.

LANE COLLEGE   B-3
www.lanecollege.edu

Jackson, TN 38301-4598	(731) 426-7533
	(800) 960-7533
Fax: (731) 426-7559	Email: ebrown@lanecollege.edu
Full-time: 2,200 men, and women	Faculty: 17:1
Part-time: n/av	Ph.Ds: 60%
Graduate: n/av	Student/Faculty: n/av
Year: semesters, summer session	Tuition: $8290 ($8500)
Room & Board: $5700	Freshman Class: n/av
SAT or ACT: required	CEEB CODE: 1395
Application Deadline: see profile	**COMPETITIVE**

Lane College, founded in 1882, is a private liberal arts institution affiliated with the Christian Methodist Episcopal Church. The figures in the above capsule and in this profile are approximate. The library contains 98,619 volumes, 53,125 microform items, 820 audio/video tapes/CDs/DVDs, and subscribes to 226 periodicals including electronic. Computerized library services include interlibrary loans, database searching, and Internet access. Special learning facilities include a learning resource center, a media center, several computer labs for students majoring in education and other areas, a curriculum lab, a video teleconferencing center, a math lab, a writing center, and a mass communications lab. The 25-acre campus is in a small town 79 miles from Memphis and 122 miles from Nashville. Including any residence halls, there are 23 buildings.

STUDENT LIFE: 57% of undergraduates are from Tennessee. Others are from 30 states, and 1 foreign country. 85% are from public schools. 99% are African American. 95% are Protestant. The average age of freshmen is 19; all undergraduates, 21. 20% do not continue beyond their first year; 65% remain to graduate.

FACULTY/CLASSROOMS: 72% of faculty are male; 28% are female. All teach undergraduates. The average class size in an introductory lecture is 25; in a laboratory, 16; and in a regular course, 16.

PROGRAMS OF STUDY: Lane confers B.A. and B.S. degrees. Bachelor's degrees are awarded in BIOLOGICAL SCIENCE (biology/biological science), BUSINESS (business administration and management), COMMUNICATIONS AND THE ARTS (communications, English, French, and music), COMPUTER AND PHYSICAL SCIENCE (chemistry, computer science, mathematics, and physics), EDUCATION (physical education), SOCIAL SCIENCE (criminal justice, history, interdisciplinary studies, religion, and sociology). Business, education, and criminal justice are the strongest academically. Education, business, and sociology have the largest enrollments.

ACTIVITIES: 3% of men belong to 2 local and 2 national fraternities; 9% of women belong to 4 local and 4 national sororities. There are 21 groups on campus, including band, cheerleading, chess, choir, chorus, computers, debate, drama, honors, marching band, newspaper, pep band, religious, social, social service, student government, and yearbook. Popular campus events include Founders Day, Fine Arts Week, and Religious Emphasis Week.

SERVICES: Counseling and information services are available, as is tutoring in most subjects. The writing center provides tutoring in writing and the math lab offers tutoring in math. Student Support Services provides tutoring in English, math, reading, computer science, computer literacy, test-taking, and study skills.

REQUIREMENTS: The ACT or SAT is required. Graduation from an accredited secondary school is required; a GED will be accepted. Applicants' academic record must include 16 credits, including 4 credits in English and 2 credits each in math, science, and social studies. An additional 2 credits in a foreign language is recommended. An interview is also recommended. A GPA of 2.0 is required. AP and CLEP credits are accepted. Important factors in the admissions decision are evidence of special talent, recommendations by school officials, and ability to finance college education.

FINANCIAL AID: The CCS/Profile, or FAFSA, or FFS, or SFS is required. Check with the school for current application deadlines.

LEE UNIVERSITY   D-3
www.leeuniversity.edu

Cleveland, TN 37311	(423) 614-8000
	(800) 533-9930
Fax: (423) 614-8533	Email: admissions@leeuniversity.edu
Full-time: 1459 men, 2095 women	Faculty: 158; IIB, --$
Part-time: 211 men, 251 women	Ph.D.s: 73%
Graduate: 143 men, 252 women	Student/Faculty: 23 to 1
Year: semesters, summer session	Tuition: $12,680
Room & Board: $6010	Freshman Class: 1777 applied, 1088 accepted, 875 enrolled
SAT CR/M: 550/530 ACT: 24	CEEB CODE: 1401
Application Deadline: September 1	COMPETITIVE+

Lee University, founded in 1918, is a private liberal arts institution affiliated with the Church of God. There are 4 undergraduate schools and 4 graduate schools. In addition to regional accreditation, Lee has baccalaureate program accreditation with NASM. The 120-acre campus is in a suburban area 20 miles north of Chattanooga. Including any residence halls, there are 50 buildings.

STUDENT LIFE: 55% of undergraduates are from out of state, mostly the South. Students are from 49 states, 50 foreign countries, and Canada. 83% are White. The average age of freshmen is 18; all undergraduates, 20. 29% do not continue beyond their first year; 48% remain to graduate.

FACULTY/CLASSROOMS: 63% of faculty are male; 37% are female. All teach undergraduates. No introductory courses are taught by graduate students. The average class size in an introductory lecture is 25; in a laboratory is 15; and in a regular course is 28.

PROGRAMS OF STUDY: Lee confers B.A., B.S., B.C.M., B.M. and B.M.E. degrees. Master's degrees are also awarded. Bachelor's degrees are awarded in BIOLOGICAL SCIENCE (biochemistry and biology/biological science), BUSINESS (accounting and business administration and management), COMMUNICATIONS AND THE ARTS (communications, dramatic arts, English, French, music, music business management, music performance, public relations, Spanish, and telecommunications), COMPUTER AND PHYSICAL SCIENCE (chemistry, information sciences and systems, mathematics, and science), EDUCATION (athletic training, business education, elementary education, health education, mathematics education, middle school education, music education, physical education, and special education), HEALTH PROFESSIONS (health care administration, health science, and medical laboratory technology), SOCIAL SCIENCE (anthropology, biblical studies, crosscultural studies, history, human development, humanities, interdisciplinary studies, ministries, political science/government, psychology, religious music, sociology, and youth ministry). Business administration, communication, human development are the strongest academically. Education, business, and psychology have the largest enrollments.

ACTIVITIES: 10% of men belong to 5 local fraternities; 10% of women belong to 5 local sororities. There are 95 groups on campus, including art, band, cheerleading, choir, chorale, chorus, computers, debate, drama, ethnic, film, honors, international, jazz band, literary magazine, musical theater, newspaper, opera, orchestra, pep band, photography, political, professional, radio and TV, religious, social, social service, student government, and symphony. Popular campus events include Lee Day, Parade of Favorites, and Dorm Wars.

SERVICES: Counseling and information services are available, as is tutoring in every subject. There is a reader service for the blind, and remedial math, reading, and writing. **Library/Resources:** The 2 libraries contain 271,897 volumes, 51,385 microform items, and 1,671 audio/video tapes/CDs/DVDs, and subscribe to 34,881 periodicals including electronic. Computerized library services include interlibrary loans, database searching, Internet access, and Wi-Fi capability. Special learning facilities include a radio station, an audiovisual center. **Physically Challenged Students:** 73% of the campus is accessible. Facilities include wheelchair ramps, elevators, special parking, specially equipped restrooms, special class scheduling, lowered drinking fountains, and lowered telephones. **Special:** Lee offers internships, cross-registration with the Coalition for Christian Colleges and Universities, study abroad in 25 countries, a Washington semester, numerous work-study programs, an accelerated degree program in Christian leadership, dual and student-designed majors, nondegree study, and limited pass/fail options. Every student completes a minor in religion. There are 16 national honor societies, a freshman honors program, and 6 departmental honors programs. **Visiting:** There are regularly scheduled orientations for prospective students, a complete campus tour upon request. There are guides for informal visits and visitors may sit in on classes. To schedule a visit, contact the Admissions Office. **Campus Safety and Security:** Measures include 24-hour foot and vehicle patrol, emergency notification system, and security escort services. There are shuttle buses, emergency telephones, and lighted pathways/sidewalks.

REQUIREMENTS: The SAT or ACT is recommended. Students must be graduates of accredited secondary schools. The GED is accepted. A portfolio is recommended. A GPA of 2.0 is required. AP and CLEP credits are accepted. Important factors in the admissions decision are advanced placement or honors courses, leadership record, and recommendations by school officials.

ADMISSIONS: 61% of a recent year applicants were accepted. The SAT scores for the recent year freshman class were: Critical Reading--34% below 500, 37% between 500 and 599, 23% between 600 and 699, and 6% between 700 and 800; Math--37% below 500, 34% between 500 and 599, 26% between 600 and 699, and 3% between 700 and 800. The ACT scores were 25% below 21, 18% between 21 and 23, 23% between 24 and 26, 18% between 27 and 28, and 16% above 28. 43% of the current freshmen were in the top fifth of their class; 68% were in the top two fifths.

FINANCIAL AID: In a recent year, 96% of all full-time freshmen and 92% of continuing full-time students received some form of financial aid. 68% of all full-time freshmen and 62% of continuing full-time students received need-based aid. The average financial indebtedness of a recent year graduate was $27,213. The FAFSA and the college's own financial statement are required. The deadline for filing freshman financial aid applications for fall entry is March 15.

LEMOYNE-OWEN COLLEGE — A-3
www.loc.edu

Memphis, TN 38126	**(901) 435-1528**
	(800) 737-7778
Fax: (901) 435-1524	**Email:** admissions@loc.edu
Full-time: 640 men and women	**Faculty:** n/av
Part-time: 145 men and women	**Ph.D.s:** 80%
Graduate: n/av	**Student/Faculty:** n/av
Year: semesters, summer session	**Tuition:** $10,598
Room & Board: $5500	**Freshman Class:** n/av
SAT or ACT: required	**CEEB CODE:** 1403
Application Deadline: see profile	**COMPETITIVE**

LeMoyne-Owen College, established in 1872, is a private, liberal arts college affiliated with the United Church of Christ and the Tennessee Baptist, Missionary and Educational Convention, offering degrees in the liberal arts and sciences and business administration. The figures in the above capsule and in this profile are approximate. In addition to regional accreditation, LOC has baccalaureate program accreditation with NCATE. The 15-acre campus is in an urban area. Including any residence halls, there are 18 buildings.

STUDENT LIFE: 86% of undergraduates are from Tennessee. Others are from 20 states and 3 foreign countries. 95% are from public schools. 94% are African American. 90% are Protestant. The average age of all undergraduates is 23. 30% do not continue beyond their first year; 20% remain to graduate.

FACULTY/CLASSROOMS: The average class size in an introductory lecture is 15; in a laboratory, 15; and in a regular course, 12.

PROGRAMS OF STUDY: LOC confers B.A., B.S., and B.B.A. degrees. Bachelor's degrees are awarded in BIOLOGICAL SCIENCE (biology/biological science), BUSINESS (accounting and business administration and management), COMMUNICATIONS AND THE ARTS (art, English, language arts, and music), COMPUTER AND PHYSICAL SCIENCE (chemistry, computer science, mathematics, natural sciences, and science), EDUCATION (early childhood education and special education), SOCIAL SCIENCE (criminal justice, history, humanities, political science/government, social science, social work, and sociology). Business, biology, and education are the strongest academically. Business and biology have the largest enrollments.

ACTIVITIES: 20% of men belong to 4 local and 4 national fraternities; 20% of women belong to 4 local and 4 national sororities. There are 15 groups on campus, including cheerleading, choir, chorus, community outreach, computers, drama, ethnic, math, newspaper, photography, professional, religious, social service, student government, and yearbook.

SERVICES: Counseling and information services are available, as is tutoring in every subject. There is remedial math, reading, and writing. **Library/Resources:** The library contains 90,000 volumes, 1,000 audio/video tapes/CDs/DVDs, and subscribes to 300 periodicals including electronic. Computerized library services include interlibrary loans, database searching, and Internet access. Special learning facilities include an art gallery. **Physically Challenged Students:** 80% of the campus is accessible. Facilities include wheelchair ramps and elevators. **Special:** Students may cross-register with other institutions of the Greater Memphis Consortium. The college offers a work-study program, dual and student-designed majors, internships, nondegree study, and a pass/fail grading option. There are dual-degree programs in pharmacy with Xavier School of Pharmacy, in optometry with Southern College of Optometry, and in engineering with Christian Brothers University. There is 1 national honor society, a freshman honors program, and 100 departmental honors programs. **Visiting:** There are regularly scheduled orientations for prospective students. There are guides for informal visits and visitors may sit in on classes. **Campus Safety and Security:** Measures include 24-hour foot and vehicle patrol and security escort services. There are emergency telephones and lighted pathways/sidewalks.

REQUIREMENTS: The SAT or ACT is required. Applicants must graduate from an accredited secondary school having completed 20 high school units. The college recommends 4 years of English, 2 each of math, science, and social studies, and 1 of a foreign language.

Applicants must submit 2 letters of recommendation. Students 23 or older may be admitted to the division of lifelong learning, which accepts the GED. A GPA of 2.0 is required. AP and CLEP credits are accepted. Important factors in the admissions decision are advanced placement or honors courses, evidence of special talent, and parents or siblings attended the school.

FINANCIAL AID: LOC is a member of CSS. The FAFSA and the college's own financial statement are required. Check with the school for current application deadlines.

LINCOLN MEMORIAL UNIVERSITY — E-1
www.lmunet.edu

Harrogate, TN 37752-0901	**(423) 869-3611**
	(800) 325-0900
Fax: (423) 869-6444	**Email:** admissions@lmunet.edu
Full-time: 350 men, 1000 women	**Faculty:** n/av
Part-time: 85 men, 220 women	**Ph.D.s:** 85
Graduate: 410 men, 1080 women	**Student/Faculty:** n/av
Year: semesters, summer session	**Tuition:** $18,740
Room & Board: $6,980	**Freshman Class:** n/av
SAT or ACT: required	**CEEB CODE:** 1408
Application Deadline: open	**COMPETITIVE**

Lincoln Memorial University, founded in 1897, is an independent institution offering degree programs in the arts and sciences, business, education, and preprofessional training. The figures in the above capsule are and in this profile are approximate. There are 4 undergraduate schools and 2 graduate schools. In addition to regional accreditation, LMU has baccalaureate program accreditation with CAHEA and NLN. The 1000-acre campus is in a rural area 55 miles north of Knoxville. Including any residence halls, there are 32 buildings.

STUDENT LIFE: 67% of undergraduates are from Tennessee. Others are from 25 states, 22 foreign countries, and Canada. 89% are from public schools. 94% are white. The average age of freshmen is 19; all undergraduates, 23. 20% do not continue beyond their first year; 50% remain to graduate.

FACULTY/CLASSROOMS: 49% of faculty are male; 51% are female. 80% teach undergraduates. No introductory courses are taught by graduate students. The average class size in an introductory lecture is 20; in a laboratory, 25; and in a regular course, 20.

PROGRAMS OF STUDY: LMU confers B.A., B.S., B.B.A., B.S.N., and B.S.W. degrees. Associates and Master's degrees are also awarded. Bachelor's degrees are awarded in AGRICULTURE (wildlife management), BIOLOGICAL SCIENCE (biology/biological science), BUSINESS (accounting and business administration and management), COMMUNICATIONS AND THE ARTS (broadcasting, communications, English, and fine arts), COMPUTER AND PHYSICAL SCIENCE (chemistry, information sciences and systems, and mathematics), EDUCATION (athletic training, business education, early childhood education, elementary education, health education, middle school education, science education, and secondary education), ENGINEERING AND ENVIRONMENTAL DESIGN (environmental science), HEALTH PROFESSIONS (medical laboratory technology, nursing, predentistry, premedicine, and veterinary science), SOCIAL SCIENCE (history, prelaw, psychology, social science, and social work). Nursing, business, and education have the largest enrollments.

ACTIVITIES: There are 3 local fraternities and 3 local sororities. There are 26 groups on campus, including art, cheerleading, choir, chorus, computers, drama, drill team, honors, international, literary magazine, newspaper, photography, radio and TV, religious, social service, student government, and yearbook. Popular campus events include Lincoln Day.

SERVICES: Counseling and information services are available, as is tutoring in most subjects. There is remedial math, reading, and writing. **Library/Resources:** The library contains 200,000 volumes, 160,506 microform items, 254 audio/video tapes/CDs/DVDs, and subscribes to 893 periodicals including electronic. Computerized library services include interlibrary loans, database searching, and

Internet access. Special learning facilities include a radio station, TV station, the Lincoln Museum. **Physically Challenged Students:** 60% of the campus is accessible. Facilities include wheelchair ramps, elevators, special parking, and special class scheduling. **Special:** LMU offers pass/fail options and credit for life, military, and work experience. Some internships are available. **Visiting:** There are regularly scheduled orientations for prospective students, including introductory sessions for both students and their parents and opportunities for advising, and registration sessions. There are guides for informal visits, visitors may sit in on classes, and stay overnight. To schedule a visit, contact the Office of Admissions and Recruitment. **Campus Safety and Security:** Measures include 24-hour foot and vehicle patrol, lighted pathways and sidewalks.

REQUIREMENTS: The SAT or ACT is required. Applicants must score 18 on the ACT or 850 on the SAT or graduate with a GPA of at least 3.2. Candidates for admission should be graduates of accredited secondary schools or have the GED. Students should have completed 4 years of English, 2 each of math and science, and 1 each of history and social studies. LMU requires applicants to be in the upper 50% of their class. AP and CLEP credits are accepted. Important factors in the admissions decision are recommendations by school officials, personality and intangible qualities, and leadership record.

FINANCIAL AID: LMU is a member of CSS. The CCS/Profile, FAFSA, FFS, or SFS is required. Check with the school for current application deadlines.

LIPSCOMB UNIVERSITY   C-2
www.lipscomb.edu

Nashville, TN 37204	(615) 966-1000
	(800) 333-4358
Fax: (615) 966-1804	Email: admissions@lipscomb.edu
Full-time: 1013 men, 1570 women	Faculty: 158; IIA, av$
Part-time: 121 men, 179 women	Ph.D.s: 84%
Graduate: 565 men, 1041 women	Student/Faculty: 16 to 1
Year: semesters, summer session	Tuition: $27,390
Room & Board: $10,100	Freshman Class: 3699 applied, 2056 accepted, 630 enrolled
SAT CR/M: 580/570 ACT: 24	CEEB CODE: 1161
Application Deadline: open	VERY COMPETITIVE

Lipscomb University is a private coeducational institution whose principal focus is undergraduate education in the liberal arts and sciences, combined with a number of undergraduate professional and pre-professional fields, master's and doctoral degree programs. Its primary mission is to integrate Christian faith and practice with academic excellence. This mission is carried out not only in the classroom but also by involvement in numerous services to the church and the larger community. There are 8 undergraduate schools and 15 graduate schools. In addition to regional accreditation, Lipscomb has baccalaureate program accreditation with ABET, ACBSP, ACPE, ADA, CSWE, NASM, NCATE, NLN, CAAHEP, ACS, and ATS. The 75-acre campus is in a suburban area 2 miles south of downtown Nashville. Including any residence halls, there are 25 buildings.

STUDENT LIFE: 66% of undergraduates are from Tennessee. Others are from 40 states, 37 foreign countries, and Canada. 56% are from public schools. 77% are White. 76% are Protestant; 14% claim no religious affiliation. The average age of freshmen is 19; all undergraduates, 22. 20% do not continue beyond their first year; 62% remain to graduate. **Housing:** 1450 students can be accommodated in college housing, which includes single-sex dorms and on-campus apartments. On-campus housing is guaranteed for the freshman year only, and is available on a first-come, first-served basis. 50% of students commute. Alcohol is not permitted. All students may keep cars.

FACULTY/CLASSROOMS: 53% of faculty are male; 47% are female. 75% teach undergraduates, and 2% do research. No introductory courses are taught by graduate students.

PROGRAMS OF STUDY: Lipscomb confers B.A., B.S., B.B.A., B.F.A., B.M., B.S.N. and B.S.W. degrees. Associate, Master's, and Doctoral degrees are also awarded. Bachelor's degrees are awarded in AGRICULTURE (conservation and regulation), BIOLOGICAL SCIENCE (biochemistry, biology/adolescence education, biology/biological science, biophysics, and molecular biology), BUSINESS (accounting, business administration and management, entrepreneurial studies, fashion merchandising, finance, human resources/organizational mgmt, international business management, management information systems, marketing management, marketing/retailing/merchandising, sports management, supply chain management, and sustainable management), COMMUNICATIONS AND THE ARTS (acting, art, communications, English, French, German, graphic design, journalism, music, music composition, music ministry, music performance, musical theater, Spanish, studio art, theatre arts, and visual and performing arts), COMPUTER AND PHYSICAL SCIENCE (applied mathematics, chemistry, chemistry/adolescence education, computer science, mathematics, physics, software engineering, and web services), EDUCATION (art education, drama education, early childhood education, education, elementary education, English education, foreign languages education, health education, mathematics education, middle school education, music education, and physical education), ENGINEERING AND ENVIRONMENTAL DESIGN (civil engineering, computer engineering, electrical/electronics engineering, environmental science, mechanical engineering, and preengineering), HEALTH PROFESSIONS (art therapy, exercise science, medical technology, nursing, predentistry, premedicine, preoptometry, prepharmacy, prephysical therapy, and preveterinary science), SOCIAL SCIENCE (American studies, biblical languages, biblical studies, dietetics, economics, European studies, family/consumer studies, food production/management/services, history, interdisciplinary studies, international studies, legal studies, liberal arts/general studies, missions, philosophy, political science/government, prelaw, psychology, social work, textiles and clothing, urban studies, and youth ministry). Biology, education, and engineering are the strongest academically. Business, biology, and nursing have the largest enrollments.

ACTIVITIES: 16% of men belong to 6 local fraternities; 17% of women belong to 7 local sororities. There are 55 groups on campus, including art, band, cheerleading, choir, chorale, chorus, computers, drama, environmental, ethnic, honors, international, jazz band, musical theater, newspaper, orchestra, pep band, photography, political, professional, radio and TV, religious, social, social service, student government, and yearbook. Popular campus events include Singarama, Annual Service Day, International Square Fair, StompFest, Anteater's Ball, Paint the Herd, and Battle of the Boulevard. **Sports:** There are 7 intercollegiate sports for men and 8 for women, and 13 intramural sports for men and 13 for women. Facilities include Allen Arena with a basketball/multi-purpose court; Student Activity Center with 2 full-size basketball courts, 4 racquetball courts, a jogging course, and weight, aerobics, spinning, and recreation rooms for both men and women. **Graduates:** From July 1, 2013 to June 30, 2014, 525 bachelor's degrees were awarded. The most popular majors were business administration and marketing (18%), health professions and related programs (14%), and biological/life sciences (12%). 70 companies recruited on campus in 2013-2014. In an average class, 45% graduate in 4 years or less, 60% graduate in 5 years or less, and 62% graduate in 6 years or less. Of the 2013 graduating class, 30% were enrolled in graduate school within 6 months of graduation, and 60% were employed.

SERVICES: Counseling and information services are available, as is tutoring in some subjects, math, English, biology, chemistry. There is a reader service for the blind, and remedial math, reading, and writing. **Library/Resources:** The library contains 184,759 volumes, 401,791 microform items, 5,740 audio/video tapes/CDs/DVDs, and subscribes to 825 periodicals including electronic. Computerized library services include interlibrary loans, database searching, Internet access, and Wi-Fi capability. Special learning facilities include an art gallery, radio station, a multimedia production studio. **Physically Challenged Students:** All of the campus is accessible. Facilities include wheelchair ramps, elevators, special parking, specially equipped restrooms, special class scheduling, and lowered drinking fountains. **Special:** Some majors require an internship. There are study-abroad options through Lipscomb programs in Austria, Chile, and England, as well as a cooperative with the Council for Christian Colleges and Universities (CCCU) that allows students to choose from multiple countries. Several degree programs can be completed in an accelerated three-year format. A B.A.-B.S. option is available in music, and a B.F.A. option is available in art and theatre. Students can pursue an integrated studies major that allows them to custom design a course of study to match their personal and professional interests and goals. There are dual bachelor's/master's degree options available in accounting, biology, and information technology. There are 5 national honor societies and a freshman honors program. **Visiting:** There are regularly scheduled orientations for prospective students. There are guides for informal visits, visitors may sit in on classes, and stay overnight. To schedule a visit, contact Dana Anderson at (615) 966-1776. **Campus Safety and Security:** Measures include 24-hour foot and vehicle patrol, emergency notification system, self-defense education, and security escort services. There are shuttle buses, emergency telephones, lighted pathways/sidewalks, controlled access to dorms/residences, and residence hall security systems.

REQUIREMENTS: The SAT or ACT is required. Candidates for admission should be graduates of accredited secondary schools. The GED is accepted. 14 academic units are required. Students should have completed 4 units of English and 2 units each of history, math, and science. 2 units of a foreign language are highly recommended. 2 additional units from the areas of English, foreign language, history, math, science, and social studies are also required. AP and CLEP credits are accepted. All students must take 18 hours of Bible/theology courses. Other general education requirements include Lipscomb Seminar (freshman seminar class), 6 semester hours each in communications, humanities, science, history, and social science, 3 in math, 2 physical education, and 2 service learning experiences. Students must complete a total of 126 semester hours and have a minimum GPA of 2.0. At least 25% of credit hours must be earned at Lipscomb. Students are required to take and pass a proficiency test of basic computer concepts. **Procedure:** Freshmen are admitted to all sessions. There is a rolling admissions plan. Application deadlines are open. Application fee is $50. Applications are accepted on-line. **Transfer Students:** 154 transfer students enrolled in 2013-2014. College transcripts, an interview, and a statement of good standing from prior institutions are required. 32 of 126 credits required for the bachelor's degree must be completed at Lipscomb. **International Students:** There are 60 international students enrolled. The school actively recruits these students. They must take the TOEFL with a minimum score of 550 on the paper-based TOEFL (PBT) or 80 on the Internet-based version (iBT) or take the MELAB. They must also take the SAT or ACT.

ADMISSIONS: 56% of the 2014-2015 applicants were accepted. The SAT scores for the 2014-2015 freshman class were: Critical Reading--22% below 500, 38% between 500 and 599, 32% between 600 and 699, and 9% between 700 and 800; Math--19% below 500, 42% between 500 and 599, 30% between 600 and 699, and 9% between 700 and 800. The ACT scores were 12% below 21, 21% between 21 and 23, 26% between 24 and 26, 15% between 27 and 28, and 26% above 28. 46% of the current freshmen were in the top fifth of their class; 71% were in the top two fifths. There were 11 National Merit finalists. 12 freshmen graduated first in their class. **Admissions Contact:** Director of Admissions. Web: *www.lipscomb.edu*

FINANCIAL AID: In 2014-2015, 99% of all full-time freshmen and 90% of continuing full-time students received some form of financial aid. 108% of undergraduate students work part-time. Average annual earnings from campus work are $3500. The FAFSA is required. The priority date for freshman financial aid applications for fall entry is January 31.

Maryville College, founded in 1819, is a private liberal arts college affiliated with the Presbyterian Church. The figures in the above capsule and in this profile are approximate. In addition to regional accreditation, Maryville has baccalaureate program accreditation with NASM. The 350-acre campus is in a suburban area 15 miles south of Knoxville. Including any residence halls, there are 22 buildings.

STUDENT LIFE: 76% of undergraduates are from Tennessee. Others are from 32 states, 20 foreign countries, and Canada. 87% are from public schools. 85% are white. 64% are Protestant. The average age of freshmen is 18; all undergraduates, 21. 28% do not continue beyond their first year; 52% remain to graduate.

FACULTY/CLASSROOMS: 45% of faculty are male; 55% are female. All teach and do research. The average class size in an introductory lecture is 28; in a laboratory, 15; and in a regular course, 16.

PROGRAMS OF STUDY: Maryville confers B.A. and B.Mus. degrees. Bachelor's degrees are awarded in AGRICULTURE (environmental studies), BIOLOGICAL SCIENCE (biochemistry and biology/biological science), BUSINESS (business administration and management and recreation and leisure services), COMMUNICATIONS AND THE ARTS (American Sign Language, art, art history and appreciation, creative writing, dramatic arts, English, English as a second/foreign language, music, music performance, and Spanish), COMPUTER AND PHYSICAL SCIENCE (chemical physics, chemistry, computer science, and mathematics), EDUCATION (elementary education, music education, physical education, science education, and secondary education), ENGINEERING AND ENVIRONMENTAL DESIGN (engineering and preengineering), HEALTH PROFESSIONS (nursing, predentistry, and premedicine), SOCIAL SCIENCE (economics, history, international relations, interpreter for the deaf, political science/government, prelaw, psychology, religion, social science, and sociology). Biology, chemistry, and English are the strongest academically. Business, biology, and psychology have the largest enrollments.

ACTIVITIES: There are 53 groups on campus, including art, band, cheerleading, choir, chorus, computers, dance, drama, equestrian, ethnic, gay, gospel music, honors, international, jazz band, literary magazine, musical theater, newspaper, orchestra, pep band, photography, political, professional, radio and TV, religious, social service, student government, and symphony. Popular campus events include Dogwood Arts Festival, Blister-in-the-Sun, and Spring Fling.

SERVICES: Counseling and information services are available, as is tutoring in every subject. There is a reader service for the blind, and remedial math. Sign language interpreters for deaf students **Library/Resources:** The 2 libraries contain 133,686 volumes, 8,263 microform items, and 0 audio/video tapes/CDs/DVDs, and subscribe to 16,525 periodicals including electronic. Computerized library services include interlibrary loans, database searching, Internet access, and Wi-Fi capability. Special learning facilities include an art gallery, radio station, a greenhouse, and college woods. **Physically Challenged Students:** 75% of the campus is accessible. Facilities include wheelchair ramps, elevators, special parking, specially equipped restrooms, special class scheduling, lowered drinking fountains, lowered telephones, and special housing. **Special:** Maryville offers cross-registration with the University of Tennessee and Vanderbilt University, internships, study abroad in 9 countries, a Washington semester, accelerated degree programs, a B.A.-B.S. degree in engineering, and dual and student-designed majors. There are 3-2 engineering degrees offered with regional universities. Nondegree study and pass/fail options are possible. There are 6 national honor societies, a freshman honors program, and 100 departmental honors programs. **Visiting:** There are regularly scheduled orientations for prospective students, including an overnight in a residence hall, class attendance, meeting with students and faculty, a campus tour, and an interview. There are guides for informal visits, visitors may sit in on classes, and stay overnight. To schedule a visit, contact the Admissions Office. **Campus Safety and Security:** Measures include 24-hour foot and vehicle patrol and security escort services. There are lighted pathways/sidewalks.

REQUIREMENTS: The SAT or ACT is required. Candidates should be graduates of accredited secondary schools or have the GED. They should also have 15 academic credits with 4 years of English, 3 each

---

MARYVILLE COLLEGE

E-2

www.maryvillecollege.edu

Maryville, TN 37804

(865) 981-8206
(800) 597-2687

Fax: (865) 981-8005   Email: admissions@maryvillecollege.edu

Full-time: 518 men, 644 women	**Faculty:** 78; IIB, av$
Part-time: 8 men, 6 women	**Ph.D.s:** 91%
Graduate: n/av	**Student/Faculty:** 15 to 1
Year: semesters, summer session	**Tuition:** $ ($25,850)
Room & Board: $8300	**Freshman Class:** 1584 applied, 1203 accepted, 317 enrolled
SAT CR/M/W: 537/535/528 **ACT:** 24	**CEEB CODE:** 1454
Application Deadline: March 1	**COMPETITIVE+**

of math and science, 2 years of foreign language, and 2 of history or social studies. An essay, portfolio, audition, and interview are all recommended. A GPA of 2.5 is required. AP and CLEP credits are accepted. Important factors in the admissions decision are advanced placement or honors courses, extracurricular activities record, and leadership record.

ADMISSIONS: 5 freshmen graduated first in their class in a recent year.

FINANCIAL AID: In a recent year, 100% of all full-time freshmen and 98% of continuing full-time students received some form of financial aid. 82% of all full-time freshmen and 79% of continuing full-time students received need-based aid. The average freshmen award was $26,518, with $17,728 ($36,610 maximum) from need-based scholarships or need-based grants; $2859 ($7500 maximum) from need-based self-help aid (loans and jobs); and $1947 ($23,000 maximum) from other non-need-based awards and non-need-based scholarships. 49% of undergraduate students work part-time. Average annual earnings from campus work are $1559. The average financial indebtedness of a recent graduate was $14,344. Maryville is a member of CSS. The FAFSA is required. Check with the school for current application deadlines.

MEMPHIS COLLEGE OF ART (*The complete profile is made available exclusively on our website, www.barronspac.com*)

MIDDLE TENNESSEE STATE UNIVERSITY   C-2
www.mtsu.edu

Murfreesboro, TN 37132	(615) 898-2300
	(800) 433-MTSU
Fax: (615) 898-5478	Email: admissions@mtsu.edu
Full-time: 9204 men, 9708 women	Faculty: n/av
Part-time: 1577 men, 1810 women	Ph.D.s: 68%
Graduate: 963 men, 1926 women	Student/Faculty: n/av
Year: semesters, summer session	Tuition: $4000 ($11,900)
Room & Board: $4650	Freshman Class: 9431 applied, 6616 accepted, 1758 enrolled
SAT: required ACT: 22	CEEB CODE: 1466
Application Deadline: July 1	COMPETITIVE

Middle Tennessee State University, founded in 1911, is a comprehensive public university that offers undergraduate and graduate programs reflecting an emphasis on research, creative arts, and public and professional service activities. There are 7 undergraduate schools and 1 graduate school. In addition to regional accreditation, MTSU has baccalaureate program accreditation with AACSB, ABET, ACEJMC, ADA, CSAB, CSWE, FIDER, NASAD, NASM, NCATE, NLN, and NRPA. The 500-acre campus is in an urban area 32 miles southeast of Nashville, TN. Including any residence halls, there are 159 buildings.

STUDENT LIFE: 93% of undergraduates are from Tennessee. Others are from 47 states, 70 foreign countries, and Canada. 80% are White; 14% African American. 45% are Protestant; 43% claim no religious affiliation. The average age of freshmen is 18; all undergraduates, 19.

FACULTY/CLASSROOMS: 53% of faculty are male; 47% are female. No introductory courses are taught by graduate students. The average class size in an introductory lecture is 24; in a laboratory is 18; and in a regular course is 23.

PROGRAMS OF STUDY: MTSU confers B.A., B.S., B.B.A., B.F.A., B.Mus., B.S.N., B.S.W. and B.U.S. degrees. Master's and Doctoral degrees are also awarded. Bachelor's degrees are awarded in AGRICULTURE (agricultural business management, animal science, and plant science), BIOLOGICAL SCIENCE (biology/biological science and nutrition), BUSINESS (accounting, banking and finance, business administration and management, entrepreneurial studies, marketing/retailing/merchandising, office supervision and management, and recreation and leisure services), COMMUNICATIONS AND THE ARTS (communications, English, French, German, graphic design, music, music business management, public relations, Spanish, and studio art), COMPUTER AND PHYSICAL SCIENCE

(chemistry, computer science, information sciences and systems, mathematics, physics, and science), EDUCATION (art education, athletic training, business education, early childhood education, health education, physical education, and special education), ENGINEERING AND ENVIRONMENTAL DESIGN (engineering technology, environmental science, industrial engineering technology, and interior design), HEALTH PROFESSIONS (health science and nursing), SOCIAL SCIENCE (anthropology, criminal justice, economics, family/consumer studies, geography, history, interdisciplinary studies, international relations, philosophy, political science/government, prelaw, psychology, public administration, social work, sociology, and textiles and clothing). Nursing and science are the strongest academically. Recording industry has the largest enrollment.

ACTIVITIES: 9% of men belong to 16 national fraternities; 11% of women belong to 1 local and 11 national sororities. There are 153 groups on campus, including art, band, cheerleading, chess, choir, chorale, chorus, computers, dance, debate, drama, drill team, ethnic, film, gay, honors, international, jazz band, literary magazine, marching band, Model UN, musical theater, newspaper, pep band, photography, political, professional, radio and TV, religious, social, social service, student government, and symphony. Popular campus events include Founders Day, Family Day, and African American History Month.

SERVICES: Counseling and information services are available, as is tutoring in most subjects. There is a reader service for the blind, and remedial math, reading, and writing. **Library/Resources:** The library contains 702,764 volumes, 1.3 million microform items, and subscribes to 3,798 periodicals including electronic. Computerized library services include interlibrary loans, database searching, and Internet access. Special learning facilities include an art gallery, planetarium, radio station, TV station, numerous research centers. **Physically Challenged Students:** All of the campus is accessible. Facilities include wheelchair ramps, elevators, special parking, specially equipped restrooms, special class scheduling, lowered drinking fountains, and lowered telephones. **Special:** MTSU offers co-op programs in aerospace, computer science, math, engineering technology, and industrial studies, cross-registration with Tennessee State University, internships, study abroad, work-study, double majors, a general studies degree, student-designed majors, nondegree study, and pass/fail options. Credit for life, military, and work experience may be granted. There are 2 national honor societies, a freshman honors program, and 25 departmental honors programs. **Visiting:** There are regularly scheduled orientations for prospective students, including campus tours and meeting with a departmental adviser. There are guides for informal visits and visitors may sit in on classes. To schedule a visit, contact the Office of Admissions. **Campus Safety and Security:** Measures include 24-hour foot and vehicle patrol, self-defense education, and security escort services. There are shuttle buses, emergency telephones, and lighted pathways/sidewalks.

REQUIREMENTS: The SAT or ACT is required. Applicants must have a minimum composite score of 22 on the ACT if the GPA is less than 3.0. A high school diploma is required, the GED is accepted. The number of academic credits required is 14, including 4 years of English, 3 of math, 2 each of a foreign language and science, and 1 each of social studies, U.S. history, and visual and/or performance arts, with an additional unit of math, language, or art recommended. A GPA of 3.0 is required. AP and CLEP credits are accepted.

ADMISSIONS: 70% of a recent year applicants were accepted. The ACT scores were 32% below 21, 35% between 21 and 23, 20% between 24 and 26, 7% between 27 and 28, and 5% above 28. There were 2 National Merit finalists. 31 freshmen graduated first in their class.

FINANCIAL AID: In a recent year, 35% of all full-time freshmen and 52% of continuing full-time students received some form of financial aid. 19% of all full-time freshmen and 29% of continuing full-time students received need-based aid. The average freshman award was $6,265. Need-based scholarships or need-based grants averaged $2,295 ($6,150 maximum); need-based self-help aid (loans and jobs) averaged $1,589 ($10,500 maximum); non-need-based athletic scholarships averaged $11,180 ($9,500 maximum); and other non-need-based awards and non-need-based scholarships averaged $4,057 ($5,000 maximum). 84% of undergraduate students work part-time.

The FAFSA is required. Check with the school for current application deadlines.

MILLIGAN COLLEGE   **F-1**
www.milligan.edu

Milligan College, TN 37682	(423) 461-8700
	(800) 262-8337
Fax: (423) 461-8982	Email: admissions@milligan.edu
Full-time: 338 men, 473 women	Faculty: 68; IIB, --$
Part-time: 34 men, 58 women	Ph.D.s: 75%
Graduate: 60 men, 137 women	Student/Faculty: 12 to 1
Year: semesters, summer session	Tuition: $21,860
Room & Board: $5650	Freshman Class: 643 applied, 438 accepted, 218 enrolled
SAT CR/M/W: 530/520/510 ACT: 23	CEEB CODE: 1469
Application Deadline: August 15	COMPETITIVE

Milligan College, founded in 1866, is a private institution affiliated with the Christian Church and Churches of Christ. Its degree programs stress the liberal arts and biblical studies. The figures in the above capsule and in this profile are approximate. There are 3 graduate schools. In addition to regional accreditation, Milligan has baccalaureate program accreditation with NCATE, ACOTE, and CCNE. The 181-acre campus is in a suburban area 4 miles south of Johnson City, TN. Including any residence halls, there are 23 buildings.

STUDENT LIFE: 59% of undergraduates are from Tennessee. Others are from 36 states, 15 foreign countries, and Canada. 80% are from public schools. 87% are White. 83% are Protestant. The average age of freshmen is 18; all undergraduates, 22. 23% do not continue beyond their first year; 54% remain to graduate. **Housing:** 572 students can be accommodated in college housing, which includes single-sex dorms, on-campus apartments, and married student housing. On-campus housing is guaranteed for all 4 years. 74% of students live on campus; of those, 85% remain on campus on weekends. Alcohol is not permitted. All students may keep cars.

FACULTY/CLASSROOMS: 49% of faculty are male; 51% are female. 96% teach undergraduates. No introductory courses are taught by graduate students. The average class size in an introductory lecture is 50; in a laboratory is 15; and in a regular course is 15.

PROGRAMS OF STUDY: Milligan confers B.A., B.S. and B.S.N. degrees. Master's degrees are also awarded. Bachelor's degrees are awarded in BIOLOGICAL SCIENCE (biology/biological science), BUSINESS (accounting and business administration and management), COMMUNICATIONS AND THE ARTS (communications, English, fine arts, and music), COMPUTER AND PHYSICAL SCIENCE (chemistry, information sciences and systems, and mathematics), EDUCATION (early childhood education and music education), HEALTH PROFESSIONS (exercise science, nursing, and premedicine), SOCIAL SCIENCE (biblical studies, history, humanities, psychology, religious music, and sociology). Business, nursing, and Bible have the largest enrollments.

ACTIVITIES: There are 40 groups on campus, including art, band, cheerleading, choir, chorus, drama, film, honors, jazz band, literary magazine, musical theater, newspaper, orchestra, pep band, photography, political, professional, radio and TV, religious, social, social service, student government, and symphony. Popular campus events include Wonderful Wednesday, Campus Theater Productions, and a Faculty Auction. **Sports:** There are 6 intercollegiate sports for men and 6 for women, and 7 intramural sports for men and 7 for women. Facilities include a 25-meter swimming pool, basketball court, 500-seat stadium, 1500-seat gym, tennis courts, baseball, softball, and soccer fields. **Graduates:** From July 1, 2013 to June 30, 2014, 187 bachelor's degrees were awarded. The most popular majors were business administration (20%), communications (13%), and psychology (8%). 9 companies recruited on campus in 2013-2014. In an average class, 2% graduate in 3 years or less, 49% graduate in 4 years or less, 59% graduate in 5 years or less, and 59% graduate in 6 years or less.

SERVICES: Counseling and information services are available, as is tutoring in most subjects. There is remedial math, reading, and writing. **Library/Resources:** The library contains 212,861 volumes, 493,520 microform items, and 3,767 audio/video tapes/CDs/DVDs, and subscribes to 79,750 periodicals including electronic. Computerized library services include interlibrary loans, database searching, Internet access, and Wi-Fi capability. Special learning facilities include an art gallery, radio station, TV station, editing rooms, and darkroom. **Physically Challenged Students:** 80% of the campus is accessible. Facilities include wheelchair ramps, elevators, special parking, specially equipped restrooms, and lowered drinking fountains. **Special:** Milligan offers a Washington semester, study abroad in England, Australia, China, Costa Rica, Egypt, Russia, and Uganda, co-op programs and internships in several majors, cross-registration with East Tennessee State University and Emmanuel School of Religion, work-study, nondegree study, and dual majors. 3 credits are offered for students participating in the annual summer tour of Europe. There are 5 national honor societies. **Visiting:** There are regularly scheduled orientations for prospective students, consisting of 1-day open houses in November and March that include a campus tour, a financial aid workshop, a meal in the cafeteria, and the opportunity to meet faculty and to learn about student life. There are new student orientation weekends in April, June, and August. There are guides for informal visits, visitors may sit in on classes, and stay overnight. To schedule a visit, contact the Campus Visits Coordinator. **Campus Safety and Security:** There are emergency telephones, lighted pathways/sidewalks, and an evening vehicle patrol.

REQUIREMENTS: The SAT or ACT is required. Students must be graduates of an accredited secondary school, with 18 Carnegie units and 18 academic credits, including courses in English, math, science, history and social studies, and speech, music, or art, along with 2 years of a foreign language. Music students must audition. The GED is accepted. Other factors in the admission decision include character, recommendations by school officials, advanced placement or honor courses, ability, preparation, and Christian commitment. AP and CLEP credits are accepted. Important factors in the admissions decision are leadership record, recommendations by school officials, and personality/intangible qualities. Students must complete at least 128 semester hours, including 24 to 62 in the major, and 59 to 71 in the general education core, with a minimum GPA of 2.0. Required disciplines include 24 credit hours of humanities, 9 of Bible studies, 8 of lab science, 6 of social science, 3 each of math, speech, and ethnic studies, 2 of phys ed, and 1 of introduction to college; B.A. candidates must also complete 6 to 12 in foreign language. All students must demonstrate computer literacy and attend all required chapel/convocation sessions. Measures of Academic Proficiency and Progress and an exam in the major are also required. **Procedure:** Freshmen are admitted to all sessions. Entrance exams should be taken beginning in the spring of the junior year. There are deferred admissions and rolling admissions plans. Applications should be filed by August 15 for fall entry; December 15 for spring entry, along with a $30 fee. Notification is sent on a rolling basis. Applications are accepted on-line. **Transfer Students:** 70 transfer students enrolled in 2013-2014. A minimum GPA of 2.5 is preferred. Applicants must submit transcripts of all previous college work. 45 of 128 credits required for the bachelor's degree must be completed at Milligan. **International Students:** There are 18 international students enrolled. They must take the TOEFL with a minimum score of 550 on the paper-based TOEFL (PBT) or 79 on the Internet-based version (iBT) or take the MELAB. They must also take the SAT or ACT.

ADMISSIONS: 68% of the 2014-2015 applicants were accepted. The SAT scores for the 2014-2015 freshman class were: Critical Reading--34% below 500, 45% between 500 and 599, 18% between 600 and 699, and 3% between 700 and 800; Math--38% below 500, 43% between 500 and 599, 15% between 600 and 699, and 3% between 700 and 800; Writing--39% below 500, 44% between 500 and 599, 10% between 600 and 699, and 7% between 700 and 800. The ACT scores were 26% below 21, 30% between 21 and 23, 26% between 24 and 26, 7% between 27 and 28, and 11% above 28. **Admissions Contact:** Director of Enrollment Management. E-Mail: *admissions@milligan.edu* Web: *www.milligan.edu*

FINANCIAL AID: In 2014-2015, 96% of all full-time freshmen and 99% of continuing full-time students received some form of financial aid. 48% of all full-time freshmen and 56% of continuing full-time

students received need-based aid. The average freshman award was $18,709. Need-based scholarships or need-based grants averaged $5,005 ($7,500 maximum); need-based self-help aid (loans and jobs) averaged $4,295 ($7,140 maximum); non-need-based athletic scholarships averaged $7,499 ($22,000 maximum); other non-need-based awards and non-need-based scholarships averaged $9,598 ($20,000 maximum); and $17,745 from other forms of aid. 39% of undergraduate students work part-time. Average annual earnings from campus work are $1443. The average financial indebtedness of the 2014 graduate was $17,224. The FAFSA and the college's own financial statement are required. The priority date for freshman financial aid applications for fall entry is March 1.

RHODES COLLEGE   A-3
www.rhodes.edu

Memphis, TN 38112   (901) 843-3000
                                             (800) 844-5969
Fax: (901) 843-3631   Email: adminfo@rhodes.edu
Full-time: 846 men, 1170 women   Faculty: 174; IIB, +$
Part-time: 6 men, 9 women   Ph.D.s: 92%
Graduate: 13 men, 10 women   Student/Faculty: 11 to 1
Year: semesters, summer session   Tuition: $41,572
Room & Board: $10,328   Freshman Class: 3382
                                  applied, 2029 accepted,
                                  507 enrolled
SAT CR/M/W: 630/630/620 ACT: 28   CEEB CODE: 1730
Application Deadline: January 15   HIGHLY COMPETITIVE+

Rhodes College, founded in 1848, is a private, church-affiliated college of arts and sciences. The campus is in a Gothic architectural style, and 13 of its buildings are listed on the National Register of Historic Places. There is one graduate school. The 100-acre campus is in an urban area Memphis, TN. Including any residence halls, there are 45 buildings.

STUDENT LIFE: 74% of undergraduates are from out of state, mostly the South. Students are from 47 states, and 15 foreign countries. 53% are from public schools. 75% are White. The average age of freshmen is 18; all undergraduates, 20. 11% do not continue beyond their first year; 80% remain to graduate. **Housing:** 1488 students can be accommodated in college housing, which includes single-sex and coed dorms and on-campus apartments. learning communities. On-campus housing is guaranteed for the freshman year only and is available on a lottery system for upperclassmen. 71% of students live on campus; of those, 90% remain on campus on weekends. All students may keep cars.

FACULTY/CLASSROOMS: 52% of faculty are male; 48% are female. All teach and do research. No introductory courses are taught by graduate students. The average class size in an introductory lecture is 14; in a laboratory is 14; and in a regular course is 14.

PROGRAMS OF STUDY: Rhodes confers B.A., and B.S. degrees. Master's degrees are also awarded. Bachelor's degrees are awarded in AGRICULTURE (environmental studies), BIOLOGICAL SCIENCE (biochemistry, biology/biological science, molecular biology, and neurosciences), BUSINESS (business administration and management), COMMUNICATIONS AND THE ARTS (art, English, French, German, music, Spanish, and theatre arts), COMPUTER AND PHYSICAL SCIENCE (chemistry, computer science, mathematics, and physics), ENGINEERING AND ENVIRONMENTAL DESIGN (environmental science), SOCIAL SCIENCE (anthropology, classical/ancient civilization, economics, history, interdisciplinary studies, international studies, Latin American studies, philosophy, political science/government, psychology, religion, Russian and Slavic studies, sociology, and urban studies). Business administration, biology, psychology and English are the strongest academically and have the largest enrollments.

ACTIVITIES: 35% of men belong to 8 national fraternities; 65% of women belong to 7 national sororities. There are 103 groups on campus, including Black Student association, club sports, contents under pressure (comedy improv troupe), mock trial team, Model UN, art, cheerleading, chess, choir, chorale, chorus, computers,

dance, debate, drama, environmental, ethnic, gay, Honor Council, honors, international, literary magazine, musical theater, newspaper, orchestra, pep band, photography, political, professional, religious, social, social service, student government, symphony, and yearbook. Popular campus events include Rites of Spring, All-Sing, and Hunger for Homelessness. **Sports:** There are 11 intercollegiate sports for men and 12 for women, and 16 intramural sports for men and 16 for women. Facilities include a campus life center, which includes a performance gym, a 3-court multi-use gym, racquetball, and squash courts, a fitness center, and an indoor jogging track. Outdoor facilities include a pool, 10 lighted tennis courts, 2 soccer fields, a football field, a track, and baseball, softball and intramural fields. **Graduates:** From July 1, 2013 to June 30, 2014, 433 bachelor's degrees were awarded. The most popular majors were business (15%), english, and psychology (9%), biology, and and history (8%). 100 companies recruited on campus in 2013-2014. In an average class, 76% graduate in 4 years or less, 80% graduate in 5 years or less, and 80% graduate in 6 years or less.

SERVICES: Counseling and information services are available, as is tutoring in some subjects, including math, writing, modern languages, biology, chemistry, economics, business, computer science and physics. There is a reader service for the blind. **Library/Resources:** The library contains 304,512 volumes, 110,513 microform items, 14,017 audio/video tapes/CDs/DVDs, and subscribes to 7,355 periodicals including electronic. Computerized library services include interlibrary loans, database searching, Internet access, and Wi-Fi capability. Special learning facilities include an art gallery, an art gallery, MRI, electron microscopes, astronomical observatory, GIS and archeology labs, and a modern languages lab. **Physically Challenged Students:** 90% of the campus is accessible. Facilities include wheelchair ramps, elevators, special parking, specially equipped restrooms, special class scheduling, lowered drinking fountains, lowered telephones, and an infrared hearing system in 1 of the auditoriums. **Special:** More than half of Rhodes students have an internship experience, in which off-campus work and significant academic work are combined for credit. Study abroad in 11 countries, a Washington semester, cross-registration with Memphis College of Art and Christian Brothers University, and a science semester at Oak Ridge National Laboratory are offered. A 3-2 engineering degree with Washington University is available. The B.A.-B.S. degree and dual majors are offered in any combination, and student-designed majors can be arranged. Nondegree study and pass/fail options are possible. There are 20 national honor societies and Phi Beta Kappa. **Visiting:** There are regularly scheduled orientations for prospective students, including class visits, meetings with students and faculty, tours, and an overnight stay with students if desired. Interviews also are available. There are guides for informal visits, visitors may sit in on classes, and stay overnight. To schedule a visit, contact the Admissions Office. **Campus Safety and Security:** Measures include 24-hour foot and vehicle patrol, emergency notification system, self-defense education, and security escort services. There are emergency telephones, lighted pathways/sidewalks, controlled access to dorms/residences, 24/7 staffed guard house, electronic readers on all gate entrances and residential dorms, security cameras monitored 24 hours a day, a fenced campus, and city cab service billed to student accounts.

REQUIREMENTS: The SAT or ACT is required. Graduation from an accredited secondary school is required, with 16 or more academic credits, including 4 years of English, 3 of math, and 2 each of a foreign language, science, and social studies/history. The GED is accepted. An essay is required; an interview is recommended. AP credits are accepted. Important factors in the admissions decision are advanced placement or honors courses, recommendations by school officials, and extracurricular activities record.To graduate, students must complete 128 credit hours with a variable number of hours in the major, and maintain a minimum GPA of 2.0. There is a basic degree requirement in 12 foundation areas. Students must complete 3 courses examining questions of meaning and value; 2 courses in writing; 1 course in each of literature, art, math, natural science, human interaction and contemporary institutions, and cultural perspective. Students must further demonstrate intermediate proficiency with a second language, engage in 1 for-credit activity broadening connections between the classroom and the world, participate in three half-semesters of physical education, and complete a senior seminar in the major. **Procedure:** Freshmen are admitted fall and spring. Entrance exams should be taken prior to December of the senior year. There are early decision, early admissions, and deferred admissions plans. Early decision applications should be filed by November 1; regular applications, by January 15 for fall entry; and December 1 for spring entry. Notification of early decision is sent December 1; regular decision, April 1. 75 early decision candidates were accepted for the 2014-2015 class. 738 applicants were on the 2014 waiting list; 52 were admitted. Applications are accepted on-line. **Transfer Students:** 15 transfer students enrolled in 2013-2014. Applicants must submit all high school and college transcripts, as well as SAT or ACT scores, and must be in good standing at the last institution they attended. 64 of 128 credits required for the bachelor's degree must be completed at Rhodes. **International Students:** There are 47 international students enrolled. The school actively recruits these students. They must take the TOEFL with a minimum score of 550 on the paper-based TOEFL (PBT) or 80 on the Internet-based version (iBT). They must also take the SAT or ACT.

ADMISSIONS: 60% of the 2014-2015 applicants were accepted. The SAT scores for the 2014-2015 freshman class were: Critical Reading--3% below 500, 20% between 500 and 599, 53% between 600 and 699, and 24% between 700 and 800; Math--2% below 500, 22% between 500 and 599, 56% between 600 and 699, and 20% between 700 and 800. The ACT scores were % below 21, 4% between 21 and 23, 22% between 24 and 26, 24% between 27 and 28, and 46% above 28. **Admissions Contact:** Carey Thompson, VP of Enrollment and Communications. E-Mail: *adminfo@rhodes.edu* Web: *www.rhodes.edu*

FINANCIAL AID: In 2014-2015, 95% of all full-time freshmen and 93% of continuing full-time students received some form of financial aid. 52% of all full-time freshmen and 41% of continuing full-time students received need-based aid. The average freshman award was $34,061. 26% of undergraduate students work part-time. Average annual earnings from campus work are $2000. The average financial indebtedness of the 2014 graduate was $27,077. Rhodes is a member of CSS. The CSS/Profile and FAFSA are required. The deadline for filing freshman financial aid applications for fall entry is March 1.

SEWANEE: THE UNIVERSITY OF THE SOUTH
D-3

www.sewanee.edu

Sewanee, TN 37383	**(931) 598-1000**
	(800) 522-2234
Fax: (931) 598-3248	**Email:** admiss@sewanee.edu
Full-time: 786 men, 834 women	**Faculty:** 138; IIB, +$
Part-time: 5 men, 6 women	**Ph.D.s:** 97%
Graduate: 46 men, 37 women	**Student/Faculty:** 11 to 1
Year: semesters, summer session	**Tuition:** $37,100
Room & Board: $10,600	**Freshman Class:** 2978 applied, 1927 accepted, 466 enrolled
SAT CR/M/W: 630/620/630 **ACT:** 29	**CEEB CODE:** 1842
Application Deadline: February 1	**HIGHLY COMPETITIVE+**

The University of the South, founded in 1857, is an independent liberal arts institution affiliated with the Episcopal Church. There is 1 undergraduate school and 2 graduate schools. The 13000-acre campus is in a small town 45 miles northwest of Chattanooga. Including any residence halls, there are 102 buildings.

STUDENT LIFE: 74% of undergraduates are from out of state, mostly the South. Students are from 46 states, 24 foreign countries, and Canada. 43% are from public schools. 82% are White. 61% are Protestant; 22% claim no religious affiliation; 14% Catholic. The average age of freshmen is 18; all undergraduates, 20. 12% do not continue beyond their first year; 79% remain to graduate. **Housing:** 1602 students can be accommodated in college housing, which includes single-sex and coed dorms, on-campus apartments, and married student housing. In addition, there are language houses, special-interest houses, fraternity houses, sorority houses, substance-free housing. On-campus housing is guaranteed for all 4 years. 96% of

students live on campus; of those, 98% remain on campus on weekends. All students may keep cars.

FACULTY/CLASSROOMS: 59% of faculty are male; 41% are female. All teach undergraduates. No introductory courses are taught by graduate students. The average class size in an introductory lecture is 20; in a laboratory is 16; and in a regular course is 16.

PROGRAMS OF STUDY: Sewanee confers B.A. and B.S. degrees. Master's and Doctoral degrees are also awarded. Bachelor's degrees are awarded in AGRICULTURE (environmental studies, forestry and related sciences, and natural resources), BIOLOGICAL SCIENCE (biochemistry, biology/biological science, and environmental biology), COMMUNICATIONS AND THE ARTS (art history, classical languages, English, fine arts, French, German, Greek, Latin, music, Russian, Spanish, and theatre arts), COMPUTER AND PHYSICAL SCIENCE (chemistry, computer science, geology, mathematics, and physics), SOCIAL SCIENCE (American studies, anthropology, Asian/Oriental studies, economics, French studies, history, international studies, medieval studies, philosophy, political science/government, psychology, and religion). English, international and global studies, and environmental studies are the strongest academically. English, economics, and history have the largest enrollments.

ACTIVITIES: 67% of men belong to 2 local and 10 national fraternities; 71% of women belong to 8 local and 1 national sororities. There are 100 groups on campus, including art, cheerleading, choir, chorale, chorus, communications, computers, dance, drama, environmental, ethnic, film, gay, honors, international, jazz band, literary magazine, musical theater, newspaper, orchestra, pep band, photography, political, professional, radio and TV, religious, social, social service, student government, symphony, and yearbook. Popular campus events include spring festival weekend, perpetual motion dance performances, and performing arts series. **Sports:** There are 11 intercollegiate sports for men and 12 for women, and 13 intramural sports for men and 13 for women. Facilities include a sport and fitness center with multipurpose volleyball and basketball courts, an indoor pool with diving well, indoor track, batting cage, racquetball, squash courts, indoor and outdoor tennis courts, dance and fitness studios, a golf course, a multiweather track, an equestrian center and stables, 15 playing fields, a lake, and areas for rappelling, mountain biking, caving, hiking, and rock climbing. **Graduates:** From July 1, 2013 to June 30, 2014, 384 bachelor's degrees were awarded. The most popular majors were English (10%), psychology (10%), and economics (9%). 30 companies recruited on campus in 2013-2014. In an average class, 76% graduate in 4 years or less, 79% graduate in 5 years or less, and 79% graduate in 6 years or less. Of the 2013 graduating class, 28% were enrolled in graduate school within 6 months of graduation, and 53% were employed.

SERVICES: Counseling and information services are available, as is tutoring in most subjects. There is a reader service for the blind. Study skills training is also offered. **Library/Resources:** The library contains 775,511 volumes, 331,879 microform items, and 26,289 audio/video tapes/CDs/DVDs, and subscribes to 6,033 periodicals including electronic. Computerized library services include interlibrary loans, database searching, Internet access, and Wi-Fi capability. Special learning facilities include an art gallery, radio station, an observatory, materials analysis lab with an electron scanning microscope, rare books collection, archives, and a music listening room and library. **Physically Challenged Students:** 90% of the campus is accessible. Facilities include wheelchair ramps, elevators, special parking, specially equipped restrooms, special class scheduling, lowered drinking fountains, special housing. Special administrative services, and a telecommunications device for the deaf are available. **Special:** Sewanee offers internships in economics and public affairs, study abroad in 13 countries, a Washington semester, and student-designed majors. Teacher certification and Peace Corps, medical, law, and veterinary preparation are available. A 3-2 engineering degree is offered with Columbia, Washington, and Vanderbilt Universities, and Georgia Institute of Technology. Pass/fail options are possible. There are 10 national honor societies, including Phi Beta Kappa. **Visiting:** There are regularly scheduled orientations for prospective students, include a tour, an interview, class visits, and a meeting with an admission counselor. There are guides for informal visits, visitors may sit in on classes, and stay overnight. To schedule a visit, contact the Office of Admission at (931) 598-1238. **Campus Safety and Security:**

Measures include 24-hour foot and vehicle patrol, emergency notification system, self-defense education, and security escort services. There are shuttle buses, emergency telephones, lighted pathways/sidewalks, and controlled access to dorms/residences.

REQUIREMENTS: Candidates for admission should have 15 secondary school academic credits, including 4 years of English, 3 of math, and 2 each of lab science, a foreign language, and history or social science. An essay and recommendation are required and an interview is recommended. AP credits are accepted. Important factors in the admissions decision are advanced placement or honors courses, leadership record, and evidence of special talent.To graduate, students must complete at least 32 full courses (128 semester hours) with a minimum GPA of 2.0. The core curriculum includes 4 courses in language and literature, 3 in math and natural science, 2 each in social science and phys ed, and 1 each in the arts and in religion or philosophy. Comprehensive exams in the major field of study are required. **Procedure:** Freshmen are admitted fall. Entrance exams should be taken by December of the senior year. There are early decision, early admissions, and deferred admissions plans. Early decision applications should be filed by November 15; regular applications, by February 1 for fall entry. Notification of early decision is sent December 15; regular decision, April 1. 103 early decision candidates were accepted for the 2014-2015 class. 77 applicants were on the 2014 waiting list; 6 were admitted. Applications are accepted on-line. Application fees are waived if application is completed on-line. **Transfer Students:** 21 transfer students enrolled in 2013-2014. Applicants should have a minimum GPA of 3.0 and take the SAT or ACT. They must submit official transcripts from all previous colleges attended and 2 letters of recommendation from college instructors, and they must be eligible to continue in their present school. An interview is recommended. 64 of 130 credits required for the bachelor's degree must be completed at Sewanee. **International Students:** There are 52 international students enrolled. The school actively recruits these students. They must take the TOEFL with a minimum score of 550 on the paper-based TOEFL (PBT) or 80 on the Internet-based version (iBT).

ADMISSIONS: 65% of the 2014-2015 applicants were accepted. The SAT scores for the 2014-2015 freshman class were: Critical Reading--4% below 500, 30% between 500 and 599, 41% between 600 and 699, and 24% between 700 and 800; Math--5% below 500, 32% between 500 and 599, 48% between 600 and 699, and 15% between 700 and 800; Writing--6% below 500, 29% between 500 and 599, 50% between 600 and 699, and 15% between 700 and 800. The ACT scores were 1% below 21, 8% between 21 and 23, 15% between 24 and 26, 22% between 27 and 28, and 54% above 28. 10 freshmen graduated first in their class. **Admissions Contact:** Lee Ann Backlund, Dean of Admission and Financial Aid. E-Mail: *admiss@sewanee.edu* Web: *www.sewanee.edu*

FINANCIAL AID: In 2014-2015, 85% of all full-time freshmen and 76% of continuing full-time students received some form of financial aid. 50% of all full-time freshmen and 48% of continuing full-time students received need-based aid. The average freshman award was $26,097. Need-based scholarships or need-based grants averaged $19,894 ($48,200 maximum); need-based self-help aid (loans and jobs) averaged $3,043 ($23,486 maximum); other non-need-based awards and non-need-based scholarships averaged $1,319 ($28,422 maximum); and $1,841 from other forms of aid. 36% of undergraduate students work part-time. Average annual earnings from campus work are $1519. The average financial indebtedness of the 2014 graduate was $8,344. Sewanee is a member of CSS. The CSS/Profile and FAFSA are required. The priority date for freshman financial aid applications for fall entry is February 1. The deadline for filing freshman financial aid applications for fall entry is February 1.

SOUTHERN ADVENTIST UNIVERSITY   D-3
www.southern.edu

Collegedale, TN 37315
(423) 236-2835
(800) 768-8437

Fax: (423) 236-1835
Email: admissions@southern.edu

Full-time: 985 men, 1172 women   **Faculty:** 132
Part-time: 130 men, 190 women   **Ph.D.s:** 64%
Graduate: 56 men, 107 women   **Student/Faculty:** 16 to 1
Year: semesters, summer session   **Tuition:** $21,610
Room & Board: $5,580   **Freshman Class:** 1513 applied, 1074 accepted, 603 enrolled

SAT: recommended **ACT:** 22   **CEEB CODE:** 1727
Application Deadline: open   **COMPETITIVE**

Southern Adventist University, founded in 1892, is a private liberal arts institution affiliated with the Seventh-day Adventist Church. The figures in the above capsule and in this profile are approximate. There are 9 undergraduate schools. In addition to regional accreditation, Southern has baccalaureate program accreditation with CSWE, NASM, NCATE, and NLN. The 1000-acre campus is in a small town 18 miles southeast of Chattanooga, TN. Including any residence halls, there are 17 buildings.

STUDENT LIFE: 78% of undergraduates are from out of state, mostly the South. Students are from 46 states, 42 foreign countries, and Canada. 16% are from public schools. 63% are white; 15% Hispanic; 11% African American. 97% are Protestant. The average age of freshmen is 19; all undergraduates, 21. 31% do not continue beyond their first year; 45% remain to graduate.

FACULTY/CLASSROOMS: 60% of faculty are male; 40% are female. 98% teach undergraduates. No introductory courses are taught by graduate students. The average class size in an introductory lecture is 40; in a laboratory is 25; and in a regular course is 13.

PROGRAMS OF STUDY: Southern confers B.A., B.S., B.B.A., B.F.A., B.Mus., and B.S.W. degrees. Associates and Master's degrees are also awarded. Bachelor's degrees are awarded in BIOLOGICAL SCIENCE (biology/biological science), BUSINESS (accounting, banking and finance, business administration and management, entrepreneurial studies, international business management, marketing/retailing/merchandising, and nonprofit/public organization management), COMMUNICATIONS AND THE ARTS (animation, art, broadcasting, communications, English, film arts, fine arts, graphic design, journalism, music, and public relations), COMPUTER AND PHYSICAL SCIENCE (chemistry, computer management, computer science, information sciences and systems, mathematics, physics, and web services), EDUCATION (elementary education, music education, physical education, and recreation education), HEALTH PROFESSIONS (health care administration, health science, medical technology, and nursing), SOCIAL SCIENCE (behavioral science, history, international studies, psychology, public administration, religious education, social work, and theological studies). Business, nursing, and education are the strongest academically. Nursing and business have the largest enrollments.

ACTIVITIES: There are 30 groups on campus, including band, choir, chorus, drama, ethnic, honors, international, jazz band, newspaper, orchestra, professional, radio and TV, religious, social, student government, symphony, and yearbook. Popular campus events include Alumni Weekend, Strawberry Festival, and Week of Spiritual Emphasis.

SERVICES: Counseling and information services are available, as is tutoring in most subjects. There is remedial math, reading, and writing. **Library/Resources:** The library contains 166,905 volumes, 410,551 microform items, and 6,666 audio/video tapes/CDs/DVDs, and subscribes to 2,123 periodicals including electronic. Computerized library services include interlibrary loans, database searching, Internet access, and Wi-Fi capability. Special learning facilities include an art gallery and radio station. **Physically Challenged Students:** 70% of the campus is accessible. Facilities include wheelchair ramps, elevators, special parking, specially equipped restrooms, and special class scheduling. **Special:** Internships are available in long-term care, nursing, and journalism. A social work practicum, an accelerated degree program in nursing, and study abroad in Austria, Spain, Argentina, Italy, Germany, Mexico, and France are offered. The B.A.-B.S. degree and dual majors in any combination including business administration and automotive service and business administration and public relations, and interdisciplinary student-designed majors are available. Credit may be granted for 4 years of military experience. Pass/fail options are possible only for phys ed activity classes. There are paraprofessional and pre-professional programs in dentistry and medicine, and various other health-related fields, as well as law. There are 9 national honor societies. **Visiting:** There are regularly scheduled orientations for prospective students, visiting students can take a tour of the campus and dorms, schedule appointments with academic departments, and interview with an admissions officer. There are guides for informal visits, visitors may sit in on classes, and stay overnight. To schedule a visit, contact the Admissions Office. **Campus Safety and Security:** Measures include 24-hour foot and vehicle patrol, emergency notification system, and security escort services. There are emergency telephones and lighted pathways/sidewalks.

REQUIREMENTS: The ACT is required. The SAT is recommended. Applicants must have a minimum composite score of 22 on the ACT. Students must graduate from an accredited secondary school with 14 academic credits, including 4 units of English and 2 each of a foreign language, math, science, social studies, and history. The GED is accepted. An essay must be submitted if home schooled. A GPA of 2.0 is required. AP and CLEP credits are accepted. Important factors in the admissions decision are advanced placement or honors courses, recommendations by school officials, and leadership record.

ADMISSIONS: In a recent year, 71% of applicants were accepted. The ACT scores were 34% below 21, 27% between 21 and 23, 21% between 24 and 26, 10% between 27 and 28, and 8% above 28. There were 2 National Merit finalists.

FINANCIAL AID: In a recent year, 93% of all full-time freshmen and 90% of continuing full-time students received some form of financial aid. 77% of all full-time freshmen and 76% of continuing full-time students received need-based aid. The average freshmen award was $20,130, with $4,697 ($10,000 maximum) from need-based scholarships or need-based grants; $3,740 ($5,800 maximum) from need-based self-help aid (loans and jobs); and $2,290 ($16,205 maximum) from other non-need-based awards and non-need-based scholarships. 43% of undergraduate students work part-time. Average annual earnings from campus work are $3000. The FAFSA is required. The priority date for freshman financial aid applications for fall entry is March 1.

STATE UNIVERSITY AND COMMUNITY COLLEGE SYSTEM OF TENNESSEE

The State University and Community College System of Tennessee, established in 1972, is a private system in Tennessee. It is governed by the Tennessee Board of Regents, whose chief administrator is the chancellor. The primary goal of the system is teaching, research, and public service. The main priorities are to provide quality programs accessible to state residents with equal opportunity in education and employment. In a recent year, the total enrollment was 135,500 with 4200 faculty members. Altogether there are approximately 359 baccalaureate, 195 master's, and 29 doctoral programs offered by the State University and Community College System of Tennessee. Profiles of the 4-year campuses are included in this section.

TENNESSEE STATE UNIVERSITY　　　　　　　　**C-2**
www.tnstate.edu

Nashville, TN 37209-1561	(615) 963-5000
	(888) 463-6878
	n/av
Fax: (615) 963-5108	
Full-time: 2000 men, 3750 women	**Faculty:** 450;IIA, --$
Part-time: 415 men, 760 women	**Ph.D.s:** 80%
Graduate: 625 men, 1280 women	**Student/Faculty:** 16 to 1
Year: semesters, summer session	**Tuition:** $6100 ($18,50)
Room & Board: $5900	**Freshman Class:** n/av
SAT or ACT: required	**CEEB CODE:** 1803
Application Deadline: see profile	**COMPETITIVE**

Tennessee State University, founded in 1912, is a state-supported land-grant institution offering undergraduate and graduate programs in arts and sciences, agriculture, health professions, business, education, engineering and technology, and nursing. The figures in the above capsule and in this profile are approximate. There are 7 undergraduate schools and 1 graduate school. In addition to regional accreditation, TSU has baccalaureate program accreditation with AACSB, ABET, AHEA, CSWE, NASAD, NASM, NCATE, and NLN. The 450-acre campus is in an urban area in Nashville. Including any residence halls, there are 66 buildings.

STUDENT LIFE: 67% of undergraduates are from Tennessee. Others are from 44 states, 42 foreign countries, and Canada. 90% are from public schools. 74% are African American; 21% white. The average age of freshmen is 18; all undergraduates, 25.

FACULTY/CLASSROOMS: 55% of faculty are male; 45% are female. 90% teach undergraduates, 20% do research, and 85% do both. No introductory courses are taught by graduate students. The average class size in an introductory lecture is 30; in a laboratory, 35; and in a regular course, 30.

PROGRAMS OF STUDY: TSU confers B.A., B.S., B.B.A., and B.S.N. degrees. Associates, Master's, and Doctoral degrees are also awarded. Bachelor's degrees are awarded in AGRICULTURE (agriculture), BIOLOGICAL SCIENCE (biology/biological science), BUSINESS (accounting, business administration and management, business economics, and hotel/motel and restaurant management), COMMUNICATIONS AND THE ARTS (art, dramatic arts, English, languages, music, and speech/debate/rhetoric), COMPUTER AND PHYSICAL SCIENCE (chemistry, computer science, mathematics, and physics), EDUCATION (early childhood education, health education, and special education), ENGINEERING AND ENVIRONMENTAL DESIGN (aeronautical technology, architectural engineering, civil engineering, electrical/electronics engineering, and mechanical engineering), HEALTH PROFESSIONS (dental hygiene, health care administration, medical records administration/services, medical technology, nursing, occupational therapy, physical therapy, respiratory therapy, and speech pathology/audiology), SOCIAL SCIENCE (African studies, criminal justice, family/consumer studies, history, interdisciplinary studies, political science/government, psychology, social work, and sociology). Engineering, allied health professions, and nursing are the strongest academically. Allied health, nursing, and engineering have the largest enrollments.

ACTIVITIES: 1% of men belong to 4 national fraternities; 2% of women belong to 4 national sororities. There are 63 groups on campus, including band, cheerleading, choir, chorale, computers, dance, drama, forensics, honors, jazz band, literary magazine, marching band, newspaper, pep band, professional, radio and TV, religious, social, social service, and student government. Popular campus events include Miss TSU Pageant and Inauguration, Greek Show, and Christmas Tree Lighting Ceremony.

SERVICES: Counseling and information services are available, as is tutoring in some subjects. There is a reader service for the blind, and remedial math, reading, and writing. A writing clinic, math lab, and reading center provide individualized assistance. **Library/Resources:** The 2 libraries contain 463,621 volumes, 754,955 microform items, and 5,125 audio/video tapes/CDs/DVDs, and subscribe to 1,272 periodicals including electronic. Computerized library services include interlibrary loans and database searching. Special learning facilities include an art gallery and radio station. **Physically Challenged Students:** 90% of the campus is accessible. Facilities include wheelchair ramps, elevators, special parking, specially equipped restrooms, lowered drinking fountains, A campus improvement program makes all new and renovated buildings accessible. **Special:** Opportunities are provided for co-op programs in business and engineering, cross-registration with Middle Tennessee State University and Meharry Medical College, a B.A.-B.S. degree in interdisciplinary studies, credit by exam, and nondegree study. There are 19 national honor societies, a freshman honors program, and 5 departmental honors programs. **Visiting:** There are guides for informal visits, visitors may sit in on classes, and stay overnight. To schedule a visit, contact the Recruiting Staff. **Campus Safety and Security:** Measures include 24-hour foot and vehicle patrol. There are shuttle buses, emergency telephones, and lighted pathways/sidewalks.

REQUIREMENTS: The SAT or ACT is required, with a minimum score of 900 on the SAT or 19 on the ACT. Graduation from an accredited secondary school is required; the GED is accepted. Applicants should have 4 credits in English, 3 in math, 2 each in science and a foreign language, and 1 each in history, social studies, and art. A GPA of 2.3 is required. AP and CLEP credits are accepted.

FINANCIAL AID: The FAFSA is required. Check with the school for current application deadlines.

Tennessee Technological University, founded in 1915 and a member of the state university and community college system of Tennessee, is a public institution offering undergraduate and graduate programs in the liberal arts, business, engineering, agriculture studies, art and fine arts, music, professional training, teacher preparation, nursing, home economics, and crafts. The figures in the above capsule and in this profile are approximate. There are 8 undergraduate schools and 5 graduate schools. In addition to regional accreditation, Tennessee Tech has baccalaureate program accreditation with AACSB, ABET, NASAD, NASM, NCATE, and NLN. The 235-acre campus is in a small town 78 miles east of Nashville. Including any residence halls, there are 97 buildings.

STUDENT LIFE: 93% of undergraduates are from Tennessee. Others are from 41 states, 55 foreign countries, and Canada. 88% are white. 55% claim no religious affiliation The average age of freshmen is 19; all undergraduates, 22. 27% do not continue beyond their first year; 44% remain to graduate.

FACULTY/CLASSROOMS: 64% of faculty are male; 36% are female. 99% teach undergraduates, 73% do research, and 70% do both. Graduate students teach 5% of introductory courses. The average class size in an introductory lecture is 27; in a laboratory, 30; and in a regular course, 26.

PROGRAMS OF STUDY: Tennessee Tech confers B.A., B.S., B.F.A., B.M., B.S.Agr., B.S.B.A., B.S.C.E., B.S.Ch.E., B.S.Ed., B.S.E.E., B.S.H.E., B.S.I.E., B.S.Ind.Tech., B.S.M.E., and B.S.N. degrees. Master's and Doctoral degrees are also awarded. Bachelor's degrees are awarded in AGRICULTURE (agricultural economics, agriculture, animal science, fish and game management, plant science, soil science, and wildlife management), BIOLOGICAL SCIENCE (biochemistry and biology/biological science), BUSINESS (accounting, banking and finance, business administration and management, management science, and marketing/retailing/merchandising), COMMUNICATIONS AND THE ARTS (English, fine arts, French, German, journalism, Spanish, and technical and business writing), COMPUTER AND PHYSICAL SCIENCE (chemistry, computer science, geology, mathematics, physics, and web technology), EDUCATION (agricultural education, art education, home economics education, music education, physical education, secondary education, and special education), ENGINEERING AND ENVIRONMENTAL DESIGN (chemical engineering, civil engineering, electrical/electronics engineering, engineering, environmental engineering, industrial engineering, industrial engineering technology, manufacturing engineering, and mechanical engineering), HEALTH PROFESSIONS (nursing), SOCIAL SCIENCE (child care/child and family studies, economics, history, human ecology, political science/government, psychology, and sociology). Engineering, business, and education are the strongest academically. Engineering has the largest enrollment.

ACTIVITIES: 10% of men belong to 13 national fraternities; 10% of women belong to 9 national sororities. There are 178 groups on campus, including art, band, cheerleading, chess, choir, chorale, chorus, communications, computers, dance, debate, drama, drill team, ethnic, forensics, gay, honors, international, jazz band, literary magazine, marching band, musical theater, newspaper, opera, orchestra, pep band, photography, political, professional, radio and TV, religious, social, social service, student government, symphony, and yearbook. Popular campus events include intramural events, Greek Week, and Parents Day.

SERVICES: Counseling and information services are available, as is tutoring in some subjects, English and lower levels of mathematics. There is a reader service for the blind, and remedial math, reading, and writing. **Library/Resources:** The library contains 365,000 volumes, 1,000,000 microform items, and 38,000 audio/video tapes/CDs/DVDs, and subscribes to 3,800 periodicals including electronic. Computerized library services include interlibrary loans, database searching, and Internet access. Special learning facilities include an art gallery, radio station, and TV station. **Physically Challenged Students:** 95% of the campus is accessible. Facilities include wheelchair ramps, elevators, special parking, specially equipped restrooms, special class scheduling, lowered drinking fountains, lowered telephones, and special housing. **Special:** Co-op programs in most academic areas, internships in community-based programs, study abroad, a Washington semester, multidisciplinary majors and work-study programs are available. Accelerated degree programs are offered in all specified majors with 3 calendar years of continuous studies. A B.A.-B.S. degree is available, as are dual majors in all areas. Credit may be granted for military experience, and nondegree study and pass/fail options are offered. There are 29 national honor societies and a freshman honors program. **Visiting:** There are regularly scheduled orientations for prospective students, including visits either morning or afternoon each weekday and meetings with an admission officer, faculty member in student's major, and a campus tour. There are guides for informal visits and visitors may sit in on classes. To schedule a visit, contact the Admissions Office. **Campus Safety and Security:** Measures include 24-hour foot and vehicle patrol, self-defense education, and security escort services. There are emergency telephones, lighted pathways/sidewalks, and student safety organization.

REQUIREMENTS: The ACT is required. Applicants must have a minimum composite score of 19 on the ACT (17 if GPA is 2.5 or higher). Other admissions requirements include graduation from an accredited secondary school with 14 academic credits, including 4 of English, 3 of math, 2 each in science and a single foreign language, 1 in American history, 1 in world history, ancient history, modern history, world geography or European history, and 1 in music/art. The GED is also accepted. A GPA of 2.0 is required. AP and CLEP credits are accepted.

ADMISSIONS: There were 4 National Merit finalists in a recent year.

FINANCIAL AID: In a recent year, 91% of all full-time freshmen and 89% of continuing full-time students received some form of financial aid. 87% of all full-time freshmen and 83% of continuing full-time students received need-based aid. The average freshmen award was $8120. The average financial indebtedness of a recent graduate was $14,478. The FAFSA is required. Check with the school for current application deadlines.

Tennessee Wesleyan College, founded in 1857, is a private institution affiliated with the United Methodist Church. Its undergraduate programs stress the liberal arts, teacher preparation, business, and nursing. The 40-acre campus is in a small town 55 miles south of Knoxville, TN. Including any residence halls, there are 21 buildings.

STUDENT LIFE: 91% of undergraduates are from Tennessee. Students are from 22 states, and 11 foreign countries. 77% are white. 51% are Protestant. The average age of freshmen is 18; all undergraduates, 33. 38% do not continue beyond their first year; 44% remain to graduate.

FACULTY/CLASSROOMS: 49% of faculty are male; 51% are female. All teach undergraduates. No introductory courses are taught by graduate students. The average class size in an introductory lecture is 14; in a laboratory is 15; and in a regular course is 15.

PROGRAMS OF STUDY: TWC confers B.A., B.S., B.Applied Sc., B.Mus.Ed., and B.S.N. degrees. Bachelor's degrees are awarded in AGRICULTURE (environmental studies), BIOLOGICAL SCIENCE (biology/biological science), BUSINESS (accounting, banking and finance, business administration and management, human resources, management information systems, and sports management), COMMUNICATIONS AND THE ARTS (English and music), COMPUTER AND PHYSICAL SCIENCE (chemistry and mathematics), EDUCATION (early childhood education, elementary education, physical education, and secondary education), HEALTH PROFESSIONS (exercise science, health, and nursing), SOCIAL SCIENCE (behavioral science, history, human development, human services, interdisciplinary studies, international studies, ministries, pastoral studies, and psychology). Business administration, education, and nursing have the largest enrollments.

ACTIVITIES: 7% of men belong to 1 local fraternity; 6% of women belong to 1 local and 1 national sororities. There are 22 groups on campus, including art, band, cheerleading, choir, chorale, computers, dance, drama, ethnic, honors, international, literary magazine, musical theater, newspaper, professional, religious, social, social service, student government, and yearbook. Popular campus events include skiing trips and the annual spring Dodge Ball Tournament.

SERVICES: Testing accommodations for learning disabled students are offered in the Academic Success Center. **Library/Resources:** The library contains 153,505 volumes, 9,668 microform items, and 3,558 audio/video tapes/CDs/DVDs, and subscribes to 9,663 periodicals including electronic. Computerized library services include interlibrary loans, database searching, and Internet access. Special learning facilities include an art gallery, an education technology lab. **Physically Challenged Students:** 30% of the campus is accessible. Facilities include wheelchair ramps, elevators, special parking, specially equipped restrooms, and special class scheduling. **Special:** The college offers for credit internships in most majors, study abroad, an accelerated degree program, B.A.-B.S. degrees, and dual and student-designed majors. Students in natural science programs may take summer courses offered by the Gulf Coast Research Laboratory of the University of Southern Mississippi Institute of Marine Sciences. TWC also holds an ambassadorial agreement with the University of St. Augustine for health sciences. There are 5 national honor societies and a freshman honors program. **Visiting:** There are regularly scheduled orientations for prospective students. There are guides for informal visits, visitors may sit in on classes, and stay overnight. To schedule a visit, contact the Office of Admissions. **Campus Safety and Security:** Measures include 24-hour foot and vehicle patrol, emergency notification system, self-defense education, and security escort services. There are lighted pathways/sidewalks and controlled access to dorms/residences.

REQUIREMENTS: The ACT is required. The SAT is recommended. Other admission requirements include graduation from an accredited secondary school, with 16 academic credits, including 4 units in English, 2 each in math and science, and 1 each in social studies and history. Foreign language is recommended. The GED is also accepted in lieu of a high school diploma and test scores. A GPA of 2.5 is required. AP and CLEP credits are accepted. Important factors in the admissions decision are evidence of special talent and personality/intangible qualities.

ADMISSIONS: 44% of the current freshmen were in the top fifth of their class; 75% were in the top two fifths. 18 freshmen graduated first in their class.

FINANCIAL AID: The FAFSA and the college's own financial statement are required. The priority date for freshman financial aid applications for fall entry is March 1.

THE UNIVERSITY OF MEMPHIS   A-3
www.memphis.edu

Memphis, TN 38152   (901) 678-2000
    (800) 669-2678

Fax: (901) 648-3053	Email: admissions@memphis.edu
Full-time: 5185 men, 7543 women	Faculty: n/av; I, av$
Part-time: 1760 men, 3159 women	Ph.D.s: 80%
Graduate: 1826 men, 2666 women	Student/Faculty: n/av
Year: semesters, summer session	Tuition: $8234 ($23,684)
Room & Board: $6860	Freshman Class: 6798 applied, 4243 accepted, 2252 enrolled
ACT: 23	CEEB CODE: 1459
Application Deadline: July 1	COMPETITIVE

The University of Memphis, founded in 1912, is a public metropolitan research university and is part of the Tennessee Board of Regents. There are 7 undergraduate schools and 4 graduate schools. In addition to regional accreditation, U of M has baccalaureate program accreditation with AACSB, ABET, ACEJMC, ADA, ASLA, CAHEA, CSWE, FIDER, NASAD, NASM, NCATE, and NLN. The 1607-acre campus is in an urban area in a residential area of Memphis. Including any residence halls, there are 239 buildings.

STUDENT LIFE: 90% of undergraduates are from Tennessee. Others are from 44 states, 54 foreign countries, and Canada. 50% are White; 39% African American. The average age of freshmen is 18; all undergraduates, 24.

FACULTY/CLASSROOMS: 53% of faculty are male; 47% are female. No introductory courses are taught by graduate students.

PROGRAMS OF STUDY: U of M confers B.A., B.S., B.B.A., B.F.A., B.L.S., B.M., B.P.S., B.S.B.E., B.S.C.E., B.S.Ch., B.S.C.P., B.S.Ed., B.S.E.E., B.S.E.T., B.S.M.E. and B.S.N. degrees. Master's and Doctoral degrees are also awarded. Bachelor's degrees are awarded in BIOLOGICAL SCIENCE (biology/biological science and microbiology), BUSINESS (accounting, banking and finance, business economics, hospitality management services, international business management, logistics, management information systems, management science, marketing management, and recreation and leisure services), COMMUNICATIONS AND THE ARTS (art, art history and appreciation, communications, dramatic arts, English, journalism, languages, music, and music business management), COMPUTER AND PHYSICAL SCIENCE (chemistry, computer science, earth science, mathematics, and physics), EDUCATION (physical education and special education), ENGINEERING AND ENVIRONMENTAL DESIGN (architecture, biomedical engineering, civil engineering, computer engineering, computer technology, electrical/electronics engineering, electrical/electronics engineering technology, engineering technology, manufacturing engineering, and mechanical engineering), HEALTH PROFESSIONS (health science and nursing), SOCIAL SCIENCE (African American studies, anthropology, criminal justice, criminology, economics, geography, history, human development, interdisciplinary studies, international studies, liberal arts/general studies, philosophy, political science/government, psychology, social work, and sociology). Nursing, professional studies, psychology, accounting, teaching all learners, criminology and criminal justice have the largest enrollments.

ACTIVITIES: There are 140 groups on campus, including art, band, cheerleading, chess, choir, chorale, chorus, computers, dance, drama, drill team, environmental, ethnic, film, gay, honors, international, jazz band, literary magazine, marching band, musical theater, newspaper, opera, orchestra, pep band, photography, political, professional, radio and TV, religious, social, social service, student government, and symphony. Popular campus events include Black History Month, Step Shows by Greek organizations, and International Night.

SERVICES: Counseling and information services are available, as is

tutoring in most subjects. There is a reader service for the blind, and remedial math, reading, and writing. **Library/Resources:** Computerized library services include interlibrary loans, database searching, Internet access, and Wi-Fi capability. Special learning facilities include an art gallery, radio station, TV station, an earthquake research center, a center for electron microscopy, Chucalissa Indian Village and Museum, a speech and hearing center, Center for the Humanities, Institute for Intelligent Systems, Institute of Egyptian Art and Archaeology, Ecological Research Center, and Biological Station. **Physically Challenged Students:** 95% of the campus is accessible. Facilities include wheelchair ramps, elevators, special parking, specially equipped restrooms, special class scheduling, lowered drinking fountains, lowered telephones, special housing, A transportation service. **Special:** The university offers co-op programs, dual enrollment, internships, study abroad and domestic student exchange, accelerated degree programs, double and student-designed majors, independent study, distance learning, an external degree program, preprofessional and professional studies programs, teacher certification, ESL, nondegree study, and pass/fail options. Students may receive credit for life, military, and work experience. There are 20 national honor societies, a freshman honors program, and 17 departmental honors programs. **Visiting:** There are regularly scheduled orientations for prospective students, including daily campus tour programs Monday-Friday and the first Saturday of the month. There are guides for informal visits, visitors may sit in on classes, and stay overnight. To schedule a visit, contact Recruitment and Orientation Services at (800) 669-2678. **Campus Safety and Security:** Measures include 24-hour foot and vehicle patrol, emergency notification system, and security escort services. There are shuttle buses, emergency telephones, lighted pathways/sidewalks, controlled access to dorms/residences, digital video cameras, a computerized entry system, a gated parking lot, parking lot fences, parking lot security towers, campus safety forums, and a personal safety program.

REQUIREMENTS: The ACT is required, with a minimum acceptable composite score of 20. Candidates for admission should be graduates of an accredited secondary school and have 15 academic credits or 20 Carnegie units. The GED is accepted. Academic preparation should include 4 units in English, 3 in math, 2 each in science, social studies, and foreign language, 1 in history, and 1 in visual and performing arts. An interview is required for University College applicants, a portfolio is required for art program applicants, and an audition is required for music applicants. A GPA of 2.0 is required. AP and CLEP credits are accepted. Important factors in the admissions decision are advanced placement or honors courses, evidence of special talent, and recommendations by school officials.

ADMISSIONS: 62% of a recent year applicants were accepted.

FINANCIAL AID: In a recent year, 72% of all full-time freshmen and 69% of continuing full-time students received some form of financial aid. 51% of all full-time freshmen and 56% of continuing full-time students received need-based aid. The FAFSA is required. The priority date for freshman financial aid applications for fall entry is March 1. The deadline for filing freshman financial aid applications for fall entry is June 1.

grams in liberal and fine arts, business, engineering, health science, and teacher preparation. There are 4 undergraduate schools and 1 graduate school. In addition to regional accreditation, UTC has baccalaureate program accreditation with AACSB, ABET, ACEJMC, AHEA, APTA, CSWE, NASAD, NASM, NCATE, and NLN. The 417-acre campus is in an urban area 120 miles north of Atlanta. Including any residence halls, there are 85 buildings.

STUDENT LIFE: 94% of undergraduates are from Tennessee. Others are from 43 states, 40 foreign countries, and Canada. 75% are from public schools. 74% are White; 11% African American. The average age of freshmen is 19; all undergraduates, 22. 31% do not continue beyond their first year; 67% remain to graduate.

FACULTY/CLASSROOMS: 52% of faculty are male; 48% are female. 95% teach undergraduates, 2% do research, and 98% do both. Graduate students teach 1% of introductory courses. The average class size in an introductory lecture is 25 and in a laboratory is 10.

PROGRAMS OF STUDY: UTC confers B.A., B.S., B.F.A., B.M., B.S.E., B.S.E.E., B.S.M.E., B.S.N., B.S.W., B.S.ChE. and B.S.C.E. degrees. Master's and Doctoral degrees are also awarded. Bachelor's degrees are awarded in BIOLOGICAL SCIENCE (biology/biological science), BUSINESS (business administration and management and recreation and leisure services), COMMUNICATIONS AND THE ARTS (art, communications, dramatic arts, English, fine arts, French, Greek, Latin, music, and Spanish), COMPUTER AND PHYSICAL SCIENCE (applied mathematics, chemistry, computer science, geology, mathematics, and physics), EDUCATION (art education, early childhood education, education, education of the exceptional child, English education, music education, secondary education, and special education), ENGINEERING AND ENVIRONMENTAL DESIGN (chemical engineering, civil engineering, construction management, electrical/electronics engineering, engineering, engineering management, environmental engineering, environmental science, industrial engineering, interior design, mechanical engineering, and nuclear engineering), HEALTH PROFESSIONS (medical laboratory technology, nursing, and rehabilitation therapy), SOCIAL SCIENCE (criminal justice, economics, history, humanities, paralegal studies, philosophy, political science/government, psychology, social work, and sociology). Education, physical therapy and engineering are the strongest academically. Business, health and human performance, and biology have the largest enrollments.

ACTIVITIES: 8% of men belong to 14 national fraternities; 18% of women belong to 10 national sororities. There are 130 groups on campus, including band, cheerleading, chess, choir, chorale, chorus, communications, computers, dance, debate, drama, drill team, environmental, ethnic, film, gay, honors, international, jazz band, literary magazine, marching band, musical theater, newspaper, opera, orchestra, pep band, photography, political, professional, radio and TV, religious, social, social service, student government, and symphony. Popular campus events include Homecoming and Welcome Week.

SERVICES: Counseling and information services are available, as is tutoring in most subjects. There is a reader service for the blind, and remedial math, reading, and writing. **Library/Resources:** The library contains 613,906 volumes, 111 microform items, and 22,619 audio/video tapes/CDs/DVDs, and subscribes to 49,911 periodicals including electronic. Computerized library services include interlibrary loans, database searching, Internet access, and Wi-Fi capability. Special learning facilities include an art gallery, radio station, an observatory, and challenger center. **Physically Challenged Students:** 95% of the campus is accessible. Facilities include wheelchair ramps, elevators, special parking, specially equipped restrooms, special class scheduling, lowered drinking fountains, and lowered telephones. **Special:** Cooperative programs are offered in accounting, business systems, chemistry, communications, engineering, environmental studies, nursing, and psychology. UTC offers internships, study abroad in England, work-study and accelerated degree programs, B.A.-B.S. degrees, dual majors, interdisciplinary majors, including theater and speech, 3-2 engineering degrees, and nondegree study. Credit is given for life, military, or work experience. There are 33 national honor societies, a freshman honors program, and 29 departmental honors programs. **Visiting:** There are regularly scheduled orientations for prospective students. There are guides for informal visits, visitors may sit in on classes, and stay overnight. To schedule a visit, contact the Admissions Office at utcmocs@utc.edu. **Campus**

THE UNIVERSITY OF TENNESSEE AT CHATTANOOGA   **D-3**
www.utc.edu

Chattanooga, TN 37403	(423) 425-4111
Fax: (423) 425-4157	Email: info@utc.edu
Full-time: 4029 men, 5037 women	Faculty: 453; IIA, --$
Part-time: 586 men, 645 women	Ph.D.s: 75%
Graduate: 622 men, 755 women	Student/Faculty: 18 to 1
Year: semesters, summer session	Tuition: $7554 ($22,760)
Room & Board: $9329	Freshman Class: n/av
SAT CR/M: 530/530 ACT: 23	CEEB CODE: 1831
Application Deadline: May 1	COMPETITIVE

The University of Tennessee at Chattanooga, founded in 1886, is a public institution. Part of the state's university system, it offers pro-

Safety and Security: Measures include 24-hour foot and vehicle patrol, emergency notification system, self-defense education, and security escort services. There are shuttle buses, emergency telephones, lighted pathways/sidewalks, and controlled access to dorms/residences.

REQUIREMENTS: The SAT or ACT is required. Secondary school credits should include 4 in English, 4 in math, 3 in Science with labs, 2 in a consecutive foreign language, and 1 each in social studies, history, and fine arts. The GED is accepted. Applications are accepted on-line at the school's web site. AP and CLEP credits are accepted.

ADMISSIONS: The SAT scores for a recent year freshman class were: Critical Reading--36% below 500, 40% between 500 and 599, 17% between 600 and 699, and 7% between 700 and 800; Math--38% below 500, 40% between 500 and 599, 20% between 600 and 699, and 2% between 700 and 800. The ACT scores were 21% below 21, 37% between 21 and 23, 26% between 24 and 26, 10% between 27 and 28, and 6% above 28.

FINANCIAL AID: In a recent year, 65% of all full-time freshmen and 62% of continuing full-time students received some form of financial aid. 63% of all full-time freshmen and 53% of continuing full-time students received need-based aid. The average freshman award was $8,765. Need-based scholarships or need-based grants averaged $8,713; need-based self-help aid (loans and jobs) averaged $3,238; non-need-based athletic scholarships averaged $20,128; and other non-need-based awards and non-need-based scholarships averaged $2,857. The FAFSA is required. The priority date for freshman financial aid applications for fall entry is April 1. The deadline for filing freshman financial aid applications for fall entry is April 1.

TREVECCA NAZARENE UNIVERSITY   C-2
www.trevecca.edu

Nashville, TN 37210

(615) 248-1320
(888) 210-4TNU

Fax: (615) 248-7406   Email: admissions_und@trevecca.edu

Full-time: 505 men, 671 women	Faculty: IIA, --$
Part-time: 237 men, 264 women	Ph.D.s: 90%
Graduate: 295 men, 634 women	Student/Faculty: 18 to 1
Year: semesters, summer session	Tuition: $23,126
Room & Board: $8060	Freshman Class: 1029 applied, 752 accepted, 320 enrolled
SAT CR/M: 530/520 ACT: 23	CEEB CODE: 1809
Application Deadline: August 1	COMPETITIVE

Trevecca Nazarene University, founded in 1901, is a private institution affiliated with the Church of the Nazarene. Trevecca offers programs in liberal arts and sciences and a number of professional content areas. The university also provides a variety of nontraditional continuing education professional programs at the undergraduate and graduate levels. There are 4 undergraduate schools and 4 graduate schools. In addition to regional accreditation, TNU has baccalaureate program accreditation with NASM, NCATE, CCNE, and ARC-PA. The 80-acre campus is in an urban area. Including any residence halls, there are 26 buildings.

STUDENT LIFE: 62% of undergraduates are from Tennessee. Others are from 42 states, 15 foreign countries, and Canada. 71% are White; 11% race unknown. 51% are Protestant; 15% claim no religious affiliation. The average age of freshmen is 19; all undergraduates, 26. 21% do not continue beyond their first year; 51% remain to graduate.

Housing: 759 students can be accommodated in college housing, which includes single-sex dorms, on-campus apartments, off-campus apartments, and married student housing. On-campus housing is guaranteed for all 4 years. 53% of students commute. Alcohol is not permitted. All students may keep cars.

FACULTY/CLASSROOMS: 63% of faculty are male; 37% are female. No introductory courses are taught by graduate students.

PROGRAMS OF STUDY: TNU confers B.A., B.S., B.B.A., B.S.N. and B.S.S.W. degrees. Associate, Master's, and Doctoral degrees are also awarded. Bachelor's degrees are awarded in BIOLOGICAL SCIENCE (biology/biological science), BUSINESS (accounting, business administration and management, business administration - international, electronic business, management science, marketing, marketing/retailing/merchandising, and sports management), COMMUNICATIONS AND THE ARTS (communication studies, digital communications, dramatic arts, English, journalism, music, and music business management), COMPUTER AND PHYSICAL SCIENCE (chemistry, chemistry/adolescence education, computer information technology, information sciences and systems, mathematics, physics, and science), EDUCATION (business education, drama education, early childhood education, education, English education, mathematics education, music education, physical education, science education, secondary education, and special education), HEALTH PROFESSIONS (biology, exercise science, and nursing), SOCIAL SCIENCE (behavioral science, criminal justice, history, pastoral studies, political science/government, psychology, religion, social work, and sociology). Management and human relations, religion, and biology have the largest enrollments.

ACTIVITIES: There are 23 groups on campus, including art, band, cheerleading, choir, chorale, chorus, drama, environmental, forensics, honors, international, jazz band, literary magazine, marching band, musical theater, newspaper, orchestra, pep band, professional, religious, social service, student government, symphony, and yearbook. Popular campus events include Drama Productions and Athletic Events. **Sports:** There are 6 intercollegiate sports for men and 7 for women, and 10 intramural sports for men and 10 for women. Facilities include a gym, a jogging track, handball, racquetball, and tennis courts, exercise and weight rooms, and playing fields. **Graduates:** From July 1, 2013 to June 30, 2014, 353 bachelor's degrees were awarded. The most popular majors were business/management (42%), religion/christian ministry (6%), and psychology (5%). In an average class, 39% graduate in 4 years or less, 49% graduate in 5 years or less, and 51% graduate in 6 years or less.

SERVICES: Counseling and information services are available, as is tutoring in every subject. There is a reader service for the blind, remedial math, reading, and writing. An academic enrichment program for students scoring below 19 on the ACT provides tutoring in math, reading, writing, and study skills. **Library/Resources:** The library contains 183,605 volumes. Computerized library services include interlibrary loans, database searching, Internet access, and Wi-Fi capability. **Physically Challenged Students:** Facilities include wheelchair ramps, elevators, special parking, specially equipped restrooms, special class scheduling, and lowered drinking fountains. **Special:** 1) cross registration with other Nazarene colleges and universities in the United States, 2)internships, 3) practicums 4)a Washington semester and study abroad through Council of Christian Colleges and Universities. Three adult degree-completion programs leading to bachelor degrees. A 3-2 nursing program is offered with Belmont University. There is 1 national honor society. **Visiting:** There are regularly scheduled orientations for prospective students, including a tour and meetings with admissions and financial aid personnel and faculty. There are guides for informal visits, visitors may sit in on classes, and stay overnight. To schedule a visit, contact the Admissions Office at (888) 210-4TNU. **Campus Safety and Security:** Measures include 24-hour foot and vehicle patrol and emergency notification system. There are lighted pathways/sidewalks, weekend and evening foot and vehicle patrols.

REQUIREMENTS: The SAT or ACT is required. The ACT is preferred, with a composite score of at least 18. Candidates should have completed at least 15 academic secondary credits, including 4 units in English, 2 each in math, foreign language, and social science, and 1 in natural science. A GED of at least 45 is also accepted. The teacher education program has special admission requirements. A GPA of 2.5 is required. AP and CLEP credits are accepted.To graduate, students must complete at least 120 semester hours with a minimum 2.0 GPA. The required 54-hour general education curriculum includes courses in English, communications, religion and philosophy, fine arts, history and social science (including foreign language), science, math, financial stewardship and health and wellness. **Procedure:** Freshmen are admitted fall, spring, and summer. Entrance exams should be taken in the junior or senior year. There are deferred admissions and rolling admissions plans. Applications should be filed by August 1 for fall entry, along with a $25 fee. Applications are accepted on-line. Application fees are waived if application is completed on-line.

Transfer Students: 87 transfer students enrolled in 2013-2014. Transfer applicants must present official transcripts and recommendations from a regionally accredited institution. 30 of 120 credits required for the bachelor's degree must be completed at TNU. **International Students:** There are 18 international students enrolled. They must take the TOEFL with a minimum score of 500 on the paper-based TOEFL (PBT) or 61 on the Internet-based version (iBT). They must also take the SAT or ACT, scoring 18.

ADMISSIONS: 73% of the 2014-2015 applicants were accepted. The SAT scores for the 2014-2015 freshman class were: Critical Reading--31% below 500, 44% between 500 and 599, 15% between 600 and 699, and 10% between 700 and 800; Math--37% below 500, 41% between 500 and 599, 18% between 600 and 699, and 4% between 700 and 800. The ACT scores were 28% below 21, 29% between 21 and 23, 22% between 24 and 26, 8% between 27 and 28, and 13% above 28. **Admissions Contact:** Melinda Miller, Director Undergraduate Admissions. E-Mail: *admissions_und@trevecca.edu* Web: *www.trevecca.edu*

FINANCIAL AID: In 2014-2015, 94% of all full-time freshmen students received some form of financial aid. The FAFSA is required. The priority date for freshman financial aid applications for fall entry is Feb 1.

TUSCULUM COLLEGE — F-2
www.tusculum.edu

Greeneville, TN 37743
(423) 636-7300
(800) 729-0256

Fax: (423) 638-7166 — Email: admissions@tusculum.edu

Full-time: 915 men, 1460 women	Faculty: n/av
Part-time: 35 men, 45 women	Ph.D.s: n/av
Graduate: 40 men, 115 women	Student/Faculty: 16 to 1
Year: see profile, summer session	Tuition: $20,500
Room & Board: $8500	Freshman Class: n/av
SAT or ACT: required	CEEB CODE: 1812
Application Deadline: open	COMPETITIVE

Tusculum College, a civic arts institution chartered in 1794, is the oldest college in Tennessee and the oldest coeducational college affiliated with the Presbyterian Church. The figures in the above capsule and in this profile are approximate. There is 1 graduate school. The 142-acre campus is in a small town 30 miles south of Johnson City, in the foothills of the Great Smoky Mountains. Including any residence halls, there are 21 buildings.

STUDENT LIFE: 80% of undergraduates are from Tennessee. Others are from 31 states, 22 foreign countries, and Canada. 97% are from public schools. 87% are white. The average age of freshmen is 19; all undergraduates, 28. 40% do not continue beyond their first year; 43% remain to graduate.

FACULTY/CLASSROOMS: 67% of faculty are male; 33% are female. 89% teach undergraduates. No introductory courses are taught by graduate students. The average class size in an introductory lecture is 25; in a laboratory, 20; and in a regular course, 15.

PROGRAMS OF STUDY: Tusculum confers B.A. and B.S. degrees. Master's degrees are also awarded. Bachelor's degrees are awarded in BIOLOGICAL SCIENCE (biology/biological science), BUSINESS (management science, small business management, and sports management), COMMUNICATIONS AND THE ARTS (design, English, and fine arts), COMPUTER AND PHYSICAL SCIENCE (computer science, information sciences and systems, and mathematics), EDUCATION (athletic training, early childhood education, education, elementary education, middle school education, museum studies, physical education, and special education), ENGINEERING AND ENVIRONMENTAL DESIGN (environmental science), HEALTH PROFESSIONS (medical technology, premedicine, and sports medicine), SOCIAL SCIENCE (history, political science/government, and psychology). Management, education, and biology are the strongest academically. Management and education have the largest enrollments.

ACTIVITIES: There are 21 groups on campus, including art, cheerleading, chorale, dance, drama, ethnic, honors, international, news-paper, pep band, photography, professional, radio and TV, religious, social service, student government, and yearbook. Popular campus events include McCormick Day, Opening Convocation, and Honors Convocation.

SERVICES: Counseling and information services are available, as is tutoring in most subjects. There is a reader service for the blind, and remedial math, reading, and writing. Math and English tutoring are available on a limited basis through the College Learning Center. **Library/Resources:** The 2 libraries contain 67,202 volumes, 210,798 microform items, and 966 audio/video tapes/CDs/DVDs, and subscribe to 300 periodicals including electronic. Computerized library services include interlibrary loans, database searching, and Internet access. Special learning facilities include an art gallery, radio station, TV station, and a President Andrew Johnson Museum. **Physically Challenged Students:** 50% of the campus is accessible. Facilities include wheelchair ramps, elevators, special parking, specially equipped restrooms, special class scheduling, lowered drinking fountains, lowered telephones, and special housing. Classes and activities are scheduled in accessible areas. **Special:** Each semester is divided into four 3 1/2-week blocks, with 1 course taken per block. Internships, practicums, and student-teaching opportunities are offered in business administration, professional and special education, social services, psychology, biology, chemistry, and medical technology. The B.S. in applied organizational management is designed for adult students with previous training and work experience. The medical technology program is offered in cooperation with a medical center in Kingsport. Study abroad, independent majors, non-degree study, an accelerated degree program in applied organizational management, work-study programs, student-designed majors, and pass/fail options are available. There is an accelerated evening program for working adults. There is 1 national honor society. There is a fall and spring open house during which students are given campus tours, financial aid information, and application materials. There are guides for informal visits, visitors may sit in on classes, and stay overnight. To schedule a visit, contact the Admissions Office. **Campus Safety and Security:** Measures include 24-hour foot and vehicle patrol and security escort services. There are emergency telephones and lighted pathways/sidewalks.

REQUIREMENTS: The SAT or ACT is required. Applicants should be high school graduates or have the GED. Secondary school preparation should include 4 units of English, 2 units each of foreign language, math, and science, and 1 unit of history. A personal essay is also required and an interview may be necessary. Tusculum requires applicants to be in the upper 50% of their class. A GPA of 2.0 is required. AP and CLEP credits are accepted. Important factors in the admissions decision are advanced placement or honors courses, leadership record, and evidence of special talent.

FINANCIAL AID: The FAFSA is required. Check with the school for current application deadlines.

UNION UNIVERSITY — B-2
www.uu.edu

Jackson, TN 38305
(731) 668-1818
(800) 33-UNION

Fax: (731) 661-5017 — Email: info@uu.edu

Full-time: 803 men, 1369 women	Faculty: 239
Part-time: 303 men, 354 women	Ph.D.s: 80%
Graduate: 428 men, 739 women	Student/Faculty: 11 to 1
Year: 4-1-4, summer session	Tuition: $22,390
Room & Board: $5870	Freshman Class: 1930 applied, 1432 accepted, 452 enrolled
SAT CR/M: 590/590 ACT: 25	CEEB CODE: 1826
Application Deadline: open	VERY COMPETITIVE

Union University, founded in 1823, is a private, nonprofit institution affiliated with the Southern Baptist Convention. The university offers programs in arts and sciences, education, business, and nursing. There are 5 undergraduate schools and 3 graduate schools. In addition to regional accreditation, Union has baccalaureate program accreditation with AACSB, ABET, CSWE, NASAD, NASM, NCATE, and NLN. The 360-acre campus is in a suburban area 80 miles east of Memphis. Including any residence halls, there are 40 buildings.

STUDENT LIFE: 69% of undergraduates are from Tennessee. Others are from 44 states, 35 foreign countries, and Canada. 75% are from public schools. 75% are White; 14% African American. 94% are Protestant. The average age of freshmen is 18; all undergraduates, 20. 7% do not continue beyond their first year; 64% remain to graduate.

FACULTY/CLASSROOMS: 53% of faculty are male; 47% are female. All teach undergraduates, and 25% do research. No introductory courses are taught by graduate students. The average class size in an introductory lecture is 25; in a laboratory is 18; and in a regular course is 15.

PROGRAMS OF STUDY: Union confers B.A., B.S., B.M., B.S.B.A., B.S.M.T. and B.S.N. degrees. Associate, Master's, and Doctoral degrees are also awarded. Bachelor's degrees are awarded in BIOLOGICAL SCIENCE (biology/biological science), BUSINESS (accounting, banking and finance, business administration and management, management science, marketing management, marketing/retailing/merchandising, and sports management), COMMUNICATIONS AND THE ARTS (advertising, art, broadcasting, communications, dramatic arts, English, English as a second/foreign language, English literature, French, graphic design, Greek, journalism, music, music performance, music theory and composition, piano/organ, public relations, Spanish, and voice), COMPUTER AND PHYSICAL SCIENCE (chemistry, computer science, mathematics, physical chemistry, physical sciences, and physics), EDUCATION (education, elementary education, middle school education, music education, physical education, secondary education, special education, and teaching English as a second/foreign language (TESOL/TEFOL)), ENGINEERING AND ENVIRONMENTAL DESIGN (preengineering), HEALTH PROFESSIONS (medical laboratory technology, nursing, predentistry, premedicine, prepharmacy, and sports medicine), SOCIAL SCIENCE (biblical languages, biblical studies, Christian studies, economics, family and community services, history, ministries, missions, pastoral studies, philosophy, political science/government, prelaw, psychology, religion, religious music, social work, sociology, and youth ministry). Business, nursing, and education have the largest enrollments.

ACTIVITIES: 27% of men belong to 3 national fraternities; 23% of women belong to 3 national sororities. There are 73 groups on campus, including music ensembles, art, band, cheerleading, choir, chorus, computers, concert band, debate, drama, ethnic, film, honors, international, jazz band, literary magazine, musical theater, newspaper, opera, orchestra, photography, political, professional, radio and TV, religious, social, social service, student government, and symphony. Popular campus events include Campus Day, Parents Weekend, and Variety Show.

SERVICES: Counseling and information services are available, as is tutoring in most subjects. There is also assistance with study skills, time management, note taking, reading comprehension, and writing. **Library/Resources:** The 2 libraries contain 146,055 volumes, 479,357 microform items, and 11,088 audio/video tapes/CDs/DVDs, and subscribe to 705 periodicals including electronic. Computerized library services include interlibrary loans, database searching, and Internet access. Special learning facilities include an art gallery, radio station, a radio and TV lab facilities. **Physically Challenged Students:** 98% of the campus is accessible. Facilities include wheelchair ramps, elevators, special parking, specially equipped restrooms, special class scheduling, lowered drinking fountains, lowered telephones, and special housing. **Special:** Cooperative and accelerated degree programs are available in business department majors. Cross-registration with Freed-Hardeman Universities, internships, study abroad in 7 countries, a Washington semester, work-study programs, composite majors in religion and church ministry, religion and Greek, and religion and philosophy, dual and student-designed majors, 3-2 engineering degrees, and nondegree study are also offered. There are 15 national honor societies, a freshman honors program, and 14 departmental honors programs. **Visiting:** There are regularly scheduled orientations for prospective students, including campus tours, class visits, and appointments with counselors. There are guides for informal visits, visitors may sit in on classes, and stay overnight. To schedule a visit, contact Robbie Graves at (731) 661-5590. **Campus Safety and Security:** Measures include 24-hour foot and vehicle patrol,

emergency notification system, self-defense education, and security escort services. There are emergency telephones and lighted pathways/sidewalks.

REQUIREMENTS: The SAT or ACT is required. The ACT is preferred. A minimum composite score of 20 on the ACT or 820 on the SAT I is recommended. Candidates must be graduates of an accredited secondary school or have the GED. A minimum of 20 academic credits is required, including at least 14 in English, math, foreign language, and social and natural sciences. An interview is also recommended. Union requires applicants to be in the upper 50% of their class. A GPA of 2.5 is required. AP and CLEP credits are accepted. Important factors in the admissions decision are leadership record, advanced placement or honors courses, and recommendations by school officials.

ADMISSIONS: 74% of a recent year applicants were accepted. The SAT scores for the recent year freshman class were: Critical Reading--13% below 500, 23% between 500 and 599, 30% between 600 and 699, and 23% between 700 and 800; Math--13% below 500, 35% between 500 and 599, 36% between 600 and 699, and 10% between 700 and 800. The ACT scores were 16% below 21, 21% between 21 and 23, 22% between 24 and 26, 12% between 27 and 28, and 29% above 28. 66% of the current freshmen were in the top fifth of their class; 89% were in the top two fifths. There were 6 National Merit finalists. 44 freshmen graduated first in their class.

FINANCIAL AID: 65% of all full-time freshmen and 63% of continuing full-time students received need-based aid. 35% of undergraduate students work part-time. Average annual earnings from campus work are $1000. The FAFSA and the college's own financial statement are required. Check with the school for current application deadlines.

UNIVERSITY OF TENNESSEE SYSTEM

The University of Tennessee System, established in 1794, is a landgrand system in Tennessee. It is governed by a board of trustees, whose chief administrator is the president. The primary goal of the system is to provide a full range of teaching, research, and service programs at all levels. The main priorities are to provide quality learning and research opportunities for students from Tennessee and throughout the country. The total student enrollment for all four campuses is usually 38,500 with 3150 faculty members. Altogether there are 182 baccalaureate, 123 master's, and 62 doctoral programs offered in the University of Tennessee System. Profiles of the 4-year campuses are included in this section.

UNIVERSITY OF TENNESSEE AT KNOXVILLE
E-2
www.utk.edu

Knoxville, TN 37996

	(865) 974-1000
	(865) 974-2184
Fax: n/av	Email: admissions@utk.edu
Full-time: 10013 men, 9648 women	Faculty: 1324; I, --$
Part-time: 712 men, 660 women	Ph.D.s: 85%
Graduate: 2938 men, 3200 women	Student/Faculty: 17 to 1
Year: semesters, summer session	Tuition: $11,194 ($29,684)
Room & Board: $9170	Freshman Class: 14398 applied, 9693 accepted, 4207 enrolled
SAT CR/M: 580/590 ACT: 27	CEEB CODE: 1843
Application Deadline: December 1	VERY COMPETITIVE+

The University of Tennessee is the state's flagship, land grant public research university. Founded as a private college in 1794, it became the first campus of the University of Tennessee in 1879. Programs are offered through the colleges of Agricultural Sciences and Natural Resources; Architecture and Design; Arts and Sciences; Business Administration; Communication and Information; Education, Health, and Human Sciences; Engineering; Law; Nursing; Social Work; and Veterinary Medicine. There are 9 undergraduate schools and 11 graduate schools. In addition to regional accreditation, UT Knoxville has baccalaureate program accreditation with AACSB,

ABET, ACEJMC, ACPE, ADA, ASLA, CAHEA, CSWE, FIDER, NAAB, NASAD, NASM, NCATE, NLN, NRPA, and SAF. The 561-acre campus is in an urban area in Knoxville, TN, Including any residence halls, there are 236 buildings.

STUDENT LIFE: 89% of undergraduates are from Tennessee. Others are from 50 states, 113 foreign countries, and Canada. 81% are White. The average age of freshmen is 18; all undergraduates, 21. 15% do not continue beyond their first year; 85% remain to graduate.

FACULTY/CLASSROOMS: 58% of faculty are male; 42% are female. 76% teach undergraduates. No introductory courses are taught by graduate students.

PROGRAMS OF STUDY: UT Knoxville confers B.A., B.S., B.Arch., B.F.A., B.M., B.S.ArtEd., B.S.Ag.E., BSAN, BSFS, B.S.F., B.S.P.S., BSID, B.S.C., B.S.B.A., B.A.C., B.S.H.S., B.S.Ed., B.S.Ch.E., B.S.C.E., BSCOME, B.S.C.S., B.S.E.E., B.S.I.E., B.S.A.E., BSBME, B.S.M.E., B.S.N. and B.S.S.W. degrees. Master's and Doctoral degrees are also awarded. Bachelor's degrees are awarded in AGRICULTURE (agricultural economics, agriculture, animal science, forestry and related sciences, natural resources, plant science, and soil science), BIOLOGICAL SCIENCE (biology/biological science, nutrition, and wildlife biology), BUSINESS (accounting, business systems analysis, finance, hotel/motel and restaurant management, human resources, logistics, management science, retailing, and sports management), COMMUNICATIONS AND THE ARTS (advertising, art history, art, classics, communications, English, French, German, graphic design, Italian, journalism, music, public relations, Russian, studio art, and theatre arts), COMPUTER AND PHYSICAL SCIENCE (chemistry, computer science, geology, mathematics, physics, and statistics), EDUCATION (education, health information management, marketing and distribution education, recreation education, and special education), ENGINEERING AND ENVIRONMENTAL DESIGN (aerospace studies, architecture, biomedical engineering, chemical engineering, civil engineering, computer engineering, electrical/electronics engineering, environmental science, industrial engineering, interior design, materials engineering, mechanical engineering, and nuclear engineering), HEALTH PROFESSIONS (clinical science, dental hygiene, medical technology, nursing, predentistry, premedicine, prepharmacy, and preveterinary science), SOCIAL SCIENCE (anthropology, child care/child and family studies, economics, food science, geography, Hispanic American studies, history, interdisciplinary studies, philosophy, political science/government, psychology, public administration, religion, social work, and sociology). Engineering, business, nursing, and education are the strongest academically. Logistics, accounting, and psychology have the largest enrollments.

ACTIVITIES: 14% of men belong to 24 national fraternities; 21% of women belong to 18 national sororities. There are 296 groups on campus, including art, band, cheerleading, chess, choir, chorale, chorus, computers, dance, debate, drama, environmental, Environmental Law Association, ethnic, film, gay, honors, international, jazz band, literary magazine, marching band, musical theater, newspaper, opera, orchestra, pep band, photography, political, professional, radio and TV, religious, social, social service, student government, symphony, and yearbook. Popular campus events include All-Sing, Torch Night, International Festival, Volapalooza, Vol Night Long, Dance Marathon, Carnius, and Football and Basketball Games.

SERVICES: Counseling and information services are available, as is tutoring in some subjects. There is a reader service for the blind. Supplemental instruction in math and chemistry, tutoring in English, math, chemistry and most lower division courses. **Library/Resources:** The 5 libraries contain 3.1 million volumes, 4.7 million microform items, and 80,122 audio/video tapes/CDs/DVDs, and subscribe to 58,765 periodicals including electronic. Computerized library services include interlibrary loans, database searching, Internet access, and Wi-Fi capability. Special learning facilities include an art gallery, natural history museum, radio station, TV station, communications students are able to use the Scripps Laboratory, an emergent communications technology facility with workstations and facilities to conduct focus-group research. Communications students also get hands-on media experience at WUTK, a student-run radio station and UTTV, a television production facility on campus. Business students have access to the Masters Investment Learning Center, a finance laboratory with real-time stock quotes from the world's financial markets, and the Anderson Center for Entrepreneurship and Innovation, a learning environment for those interested in starting and growing new businesses. The Clarence Brown Theatre produces plays and musicals featuring nationally renowned guest artists. Home to the Clarence Brown Theatre Professional Company, the University Company, and the undergraduate performance group, the theatre also provides students with space to rehearse and perform experimental stage plays. The University of Tennessee is one of only twenty-seven universities nationwide that is affiliated with the League of Resident Theatres (LORT). This professional theatre affiliation allows students regular opportunities to work alongside professional actors, directors, designers, and production artists. Campus is also home to the McClung Museum of Natural History and Culture, which is accredited by the American Association of Museums. The McClung Museum is one of only thirteen AAM-accredited museums in Tennessee, which puts it in the top four percent of museums nationwide. The Ewing Gallery of Art and Architecture emphasizes historic and current trends in art and architecture and supports creative works by students in these areas. The Commons in Hodges Library is a learning environment designed to meet the changing needs of students with the latest technological advances in a private yet collaborative workspace. The Commons provides its users with the tools, information, and adaptability they need to be successful learners and teachers in the 21st century. The Humanities and Social Sciences Building is one of the first higher-education facilities in the country to transform its classrooms into student-centric collaborative teaching and learning centers. **Physically Challenged Students:** 95% of the campus is accessible. Facilities include wheelchair ramps, elevators, special parking, specially equipped restrooms, special class scheduling, lowered drinking fountains, lowered telephones, special housing. **Special:** Students can design a wide variety of interdisciplinary majors through the College of Arts and Sciences. Honors programs exist within several colleges. University-wide honors programs include the Baker Scholars, Haslam Scholars and Chancellor's Honors Programs. The university offers many dual graduate and professional degrees that include law and business, public administration and law, business and engineering, and recreation and sport management and business. New graduate programs include a master's in landscape architecture, a master's in public health, a master's in business analytics, a doctorate in energy science and engineering, a doctorate of nursing practice, and a doctorate in social work. Study-abroad programs are offered in more than fifty-nine countries. There are 27 national honor societies, including Phi Beta Kappa, and a freshman honors program. **Visiting:** There are regularly scheduled orientations for prospective students, including 2 open houses yearly where prospective students can meet with faculty, administrators, and students to discuss admissions, housing, financial aid, and student activities. There are guides for informal visits and visitors may sit in on classes.. **Campus Safety and Security:** Measures include 24-hour foot and vehicle patrol, emergency notification system, self-defense education, and security escort services. There are shuttle buses, emergency telephones, lighted pathways/sidewalks, campus safety educational programs.

REQUIREMENTS: The SAT or ACT is required. Applicants should be high school graduates or have the GED. Required secondary school courses include 4 credits in English, 4 in math, 3 in science, and 2 foreign language, 1 each in history, social studies, and visual/performing arts. A GPA of 2.0 is required. AP and CLEP credits are accepted. Important factors in the admissions decision are advanced placement or honors courses, evidence of special talent, and extracurricular activities record.

ADMISSIONS: 67% of a recent year applicants were accepted. The SAT scores for a recent year freshman class were: Critical Reading--12% below 500, 46% between 500 and 599, 32% between 600 and 699, and 10% between 700 and 800; Math--12% below 500, 39% between 500 and 599, 38% between 600 and 699, and 10% between 700 and 800. The ACT scores were 12% between 21 and 23, 22% between 24 and 26, 9% between 27 and 28, and 22% above 28. There were 20 National Merit finalists.

FINANCIAL AID: In a recent year, 61% of all full-time freshmen and 58% of continuing full-time students received some form of financial aid. 59% of all full-time freshmen and 52% of continuing full-time students received need-based aid. The average freshman award was $12,866. Need-based scholarships or need-based grants averaged $10,391 ($40,196 maximum); need-based self-help aid (loans and jobs) averaged $4,705 ($40,196 maximum); non-need-based athletic scholarships averaged $12,747 ($42,055 maximum); and other non-need-based awards and non-need-based scholarships averaged $2,783 ($14,850 maximum). 15% of undergraduate students work part-time. Average annual earnings from campus work are $7063. The average financial indebtedness of a recent year graduate was $22,860. The FAFSA is required. The priority date for freshman financial aid applications for fall entry is March 1.

UNIVERSITY OF TENNESSEE AT MARTIN   B-1
www.utm.edu

Martin, TN 38238	(731) 881-7000
	(800) 829-8861
Fax: (731) 881-7029	Email: admitme@utm.edu
Full-time: 2437 men, 3301 women	Faculty: 295; IIA, --$
Part-time: 345 men, 594 women	Ph.D.s: 73%
Graduate: 107 men, 258 women	Student/Faculty: 17 to 1
Year: semesters, summer session	Tuition: $8024 ($21,968)
Room & Board: $5786	Freshman Class: 3526 applied, 2586 accepted, 1181 enrolled
ACT: 22	CEEB CODE: 1844
Application Deadline: open	COMPETITIVE

UT Martin is a primary campus in the University of Tennessee System and is known for providing high-quality undergraduate and graduate academic programs. From the founding in 1900 of Hall-Moody Institute, through the establishment in 1927 of UT Junior College, to today's status as a comprehensive public university, UT Martin remains committed to preparing students for success in the global economy. UT Martin serves students by offering more than 100 different areas of study at the undergraduate and graduate levels. Figures in the above capsule and in this profile are approximate. There are 5 undergraduate schools and 4 graduate schools. In addition to regional accreditation, UT Martin has baccalaureate program accreditation with AACSB, ABET, ACEJMC, ADA, AHEA, CSWE, NASM, NCATE, NLN, and ACS. The 250-acre campus is in a rural area 125 miles northeast of Memphis and 150 miles northwest of Nashville. Including any residence halls, there are 49 buildings.

STUDENT LIFE: 93% of undergraduates are from Tennessee. Others are from 38 states, 19 foreign countries, and Canada. 91% are from public schools. 77% are White; 15% African American. 73% are Protestant. The average age of freshmen is 19; all undergraduates, 23. 29% do not continue beyond their first year; 47% remain to graduate.

Housing: 2382 students can be accommodated in college housing, which includes single-sex and coed dorms, on-campus apartments, and married student housing. In addition, there are honors houses and special-interest houses. On-campus housing is guaranteed for all 4 years, and is available on a first-come, first-served basis. 70% of students commute. Alcohol is not permitted. All students may keep cars.

FACULTY/CLASSROOMS: 56% of faculty are male; 44% are female. All teach undergraduates, 84% do research, and 84% do both. No introductory courses are taught by graduate students. The average class size in an introductory lecture is 23; in a laboratory is 16; and in a regular course is 17.

PROGRAMS OF STUDY: UT Martin confers B.A., B.S., B.A.Mus., B.F.A., B.Mus., B.S.Agri., B.S.Bus.Admn., B.S.Chem., B.S.Crim.Just., B.S.Ed., B.S.Eng., B.S.Fam.C.S., B.S.Health/HP., B.S.N.R.M., B.S.N., B.S.S.W. and B.U.S. degrees. Master's degrees are also awarded. Bachelor's degrees are awarded in AGRICULTURE (agricultural business management, agriculture, animal science, natural resource management, and plant science), BIOLOGICAL SCIENCE (biology/biological science and nutrition), BUSINESS (accounting, business administration and management, business economics, management science, and marketing/retailing/merchandising), COMMUNICATIONS AND THE ARTS (communications, English, fine arts, French, music, performing arts, and Spanish), COMPUTER AND PHYSICAL SCIENCE (chemistry, computer science, geology, information sciences and systems, and mathematics), EDUCATION (education administration, elementary education, secondary education, and special education), ENGINEERING AND ENVIRONMENTAL

DESIGN (engineering), HEALTH PROFESSIONS (health science and nursing), SOCIAL SCIENCE (child care/child and family studies, criminal justice, economics, geography, history, international studies, philosophy, political science/government, psychology, public administration, social work, and sociology). Preprofessional health programs, biology, and engineering are the strongest academically. Agriculture, health and human performance, and integrated studies have the largest enrollments.

ACTIVITIES: 5% of men belong to 12 national fraternities; 10% of women belong to 1 local and 9 national sororities. There are 175 groups on campus, including art, band, cheerleading, choir, chorale, chorus, computers, dance, drama, drill team, environmental, ethnic, film, gay, honors, international, jazz band, literary magazine, marching band, musical theater, newspaper, opera, pep band, photography, political, professional, radio and TV, religious, social, social service, student government, and yearbook. Popular campus events include Greekfest, Homecoming and Pyramid. **Sports:** There are 7 intercollegiate sports for men and 10 for women, and 11 intramural sports for men and 11 for women. Facilities include an Olympic-size swimming pool, 7 racquetball courts, a running/walking track, weight room, 6 basketball, volleyball, badminton and tennis court combinations, and outdoor: a 1.5 mile fitness track, 16 tennis courts, a soccer field, and lighted intramural playing fields. **Graduates:** From July 1, 2013 to June 30, 2014, 1224 bachelor's degrees were awarded. The most popular majors were business/marketing (18%), interdisciplinary studies (13%), and education (12%). 62 companies recruited on campus in 2013-2014. In an average class, 21% graduate in 4 years or less, 40% graduate in 5 years or less, and 46% graduate in 6 years or less. Of the 2013 graduating class, 25% were enrolled in graduate school within 6 months of graduation, and 68% were employed.

SERVICES: Counseling and information services are available, as is tutoring in some subjects, astronomy, biology, chemistry, computer science, English, French, geography, geology, German, history, Japanese, math, psychology, and Spanish. **Library/Resources:** The library contains 379,072 volumes, 709,966 microform items, and 17,122 audio/video tapes/CDs/DVDs. Computerized library services include interlibrary loans, database searching, Internet access, and Wi-Fi capability. Special learning facilities include a natural history museum, radio station, TV station, a teacher resource center, 680-acre agriculture and natural resources teaching and demonstration complex, teaching/research facility at Reelfoot Lake State resort, and a center for global studies and international education. **Physically Challenged Students:** All of the campus is accessible. Facilities include wheelchair ramps, elevators, special parking, specially equipped restrooms, special class scheduling, lowered drinking fountains, lowered telephones, and special housing. **Special:** UTM offers co-op programs in engineering, agriculture, computer science, business, and chemistry, for-credit internships, cross-registration through the Gulf Coast consortium, study abroad, B.A.-B.S. degrees, dual and student-designed majors, and pass/fail options. There are 11 national honor societies, a freshman honors program, and 6 departmental honors programs. **Visiting:** There are regularly scheduled orientations for prospective students, Campus visits include Summer Orientation and Registration (SOAR); 4 sessions conducted for students and parents that include information sessions and class registration. There are guides for informal visits, visitors may sit in on classes, and stay overnight. To schedule a visit, contact the Admissions Office. **Campus Safety and Security:** Measures include 24-hour foot and vehicle patrol, emergency notification system, and self-defense education. There are emergency telephones, lighted pathways/sidewalks, bicycle patrol, security cameras in residence halls, auto dialer alert system, text messaging alert system, and severe weather siren alert system.

REQUIREMENTS: The ACT is required. Students should have a minimum composite score of 21 on the ACT with a 2.5 minimum GPA, or 18 on the ACT with a minimum 2.85 GPA. Candidates for admission should be graduates of an accredited secondary school with 14 academic credits. The GED is accepted with a score of 500. Secondary school units should include 4 of English, 3 of math, 2 of a foreign language, and 1 each of science, history, social studies, and fine and performing arts. A GPA of 2.7 is required. AP and CLEP credits are accepted. The number of credit hours required for graduation ranges from 120 to 134 (based on degree). All students must have at least a 2.0 GPA. Specific courses and major requirements vary by the program selected. There is a 1 year or 30 hour UTM residency requirement. The general education core curriculum is 38 hours; English and communications courses are required. Major field and general education tests are required. **Procedure:** Freshmen are admitted to all sessions. Entrance exams should be taken by the spring of the junior year. There are deferred admissions and rolling admissions plans. Application deadlines are open. Application fee is $30. Notification is sent on a rolling basis. Applications are accepted on-line. **Transfer Students:** 543 transfer students enrolled in 2013-2014. Transfer students should have a minimum GPA of 2.0. 30 of 120 credits required for the bachelor's degree must be completed at UT Martin. **International Students:** There are 140 international students enrolled. The school actively recruits these students. They must take the TOEFL with a minimum score of 500 on the paper-based TOEFL (PBT) or 61 on the Internet-based version (iBT), and a writing proficiency exam.

ADMISSIONS: 73% of the 2014-2015 applicants were accepted. The ACT scores were 34% below 21, 28% between 21 and 23, 19% between 24 and 26, 6% between 27 and 28, and 12% above 28. 49% of the current freshmen were in the top fifth of their class; 80% were in the top two fifths. 21 freshmen graduated first in their class. **Admissions Contact:** Brandy Cartmell, Int Exec Dir Student Engagement. E-Mail: *admitme@utm.edu* Web: *www.utm.edu*

FINANCIAL AID: In 2014-2015, 78% of all full-time freshmen and 75% of continuing full-time students received some form of financial aid. 52% of all full-time freshmen and 54% of continuing full-time students received need-based aid. The average freshman award was $13,655. Need-based scholarships or need-based grants averaged $6,695 ($10,039 maximum); need-based self-help aid (loans and jobs) averaged $3,376; non-need-based athletic scholarships averaged $10,506; and other non-need-based awards and non-need-based scholarships averaged $2,046 ($2,956 maximum). 39% of undergraduate students work part-time. Average annual earnings from campus work are $2147. The average financial indebtedness of the 2014 graduate was $27,147. The FAFSA is required. The priority date for freshman financial aid applications for fall entry is March 1.

VANDERBILT UNIVERSITY C-2
www.vanderbilt.edu

Nashville, TN 37203

(615) 322-7311
(800) 288-0432

Fax: (615) 343-7765   Email: admissions@vanderbilt.edu

Full-time: 3383 men, 3395 women	Faculty: I, +$
Part-time: 35 men, 38 women	Ph.D.s: 96%
Graduate: 2475 men, 3360 women	Student/Faculty: 8 to 1
Year: semesters, summer session	Tuition: $43,838
Room & Board: $14,382	Freshman Class: 29518 applied, 3865 accepted, 1605 enrolled
SAT or ACT: required	CEEB CODE: 1871
Application Deadline: January 3	MOST COMPETITIVE

Vanderbilt University, founded in 1873, is a private university offering programs in liberal and fine arts, business, engineering, health science, religion, law, music, and teacher preparation. There are 4 undergraduate schools and 8 graduate schools. In addition to regional accreditation, Vanderbilt has baccalaureate program accreditation with AACSB, ABET, CAHEA, and NCATE. The 330-acre campus is in an urban area in Nashville. Including any residence halls, there are 227 buildings.

STUDENT LIFE: 89% of undergraduates are from out of state, mostly the South. Students are from 50 states, 49 foreign countries, and Canada. 65% are from public schools. 58% are White. The average age of freshmen is 18; all undergraduates, 20. 3% do not continue beyond their first year; 93% remain to graduate. **Housing:** 6041 students can be accommodated in college housing, which includes single-sex and coed dorms, on-campus apartments, and married student housing. In addition, there are language houses, special-interest houses, fraternity houses, and sorority houses. On-campus housing is guaranteed for the freshman year only, is available on a first-come,

first-served basis, and is available on a lottery system for upperclassmen. Priority is given to out-of-town students. 86% of students live on campus. Upperclassmen may keep cars.

FACULTY/CLASSROOMS: 63% of faculty are male; 37% are female. No introductory courses are taught by graduate students. The average class size in an introductory lecture is 20; in a laboratory is 31; and in a regular course is 19.

PROGRAMS OF STUDY: Vanderbilt confers B.A., B.S., B.E. and B.Mu degrees. Master's and Doctoral degrees are also awarded. Bachelor's degrees are awarded in BIOLOGICAL SCIENCE (biology/biological science, ecology, molecular biology, and neurosciences), COMMUNICATIONS AND THE ARTS (art, classical languages, classics, communications, composition, English, fine arts, French, German, music history and appreciation, music performance, music theory and composition, Russian, Spanish, and theatre arts), COMPUTER AND PHYSICAL SCIENCE (chemistry, computer science, earth science, mathematics, and physics), EDUCATION (childhood education: 1-6, early childhood education, education, elementary education, music education, secondary education, and special education), ENGINEERING AND ENVIRONMENTAL DESIGN (bioengineering, biomedical engineering, chemical engineering, civil engineering, computer engineering, electrical/electronics engineering, engineering and applied science, and mechanical engineering), SOCIAL SCIENCE (African American studies, American studies, anthropology, Asian studies, child psychology/development, cognitive science, East Asian studies, economics, European studies, history, human development, interdisciplinary studies, Italian studies, Judaic studies, Latin American studies, philosophy, political science/government, psychology, public affairs, religion, sociology, and women and gender studies). Social science, engineering, and education have the largest enrollemnts.

ACTIVITIES: 32% of men belong to 18 national fraternities; 54% of women belong to 16 national sororities. There are 705 groups on campus, including art, band, cheerleading, chess, choir, chorale, chorus, computers, dance, debate, drama, drill team, environmental, ethnic, film, gay, honors, international, jazz band, literary magazine, marching band, musical theater, newspaper, opera, orchestra, pep band, photography, political, professional, radio and TV, religious, social, social service, student government, symphony, video production., and yearbook. Popular campus events include Rites of Spring, International Lens Film Series, Diwali Festival and IMPACT Speakers Series. **Sports:** There are 6 intercollegiate sports for men and 9 for women, and 45 intramural sports for men and 44 for women. Facilities include a gym, pool, football and intramural fields, indoor football field, student recreation and tennis centers, basketball and racquetball courts, a suspended indoor track, and a climbing wall. **Graduates:** From July 1, 2013 to June 30, 2014, 1663 bachelor's degrees were awarded. The most popular majors were social sciences (28%), engineering (13%), and interdisciplinary studies (10%). 205 companies recruited on campus in 2013-2014. In an average class, 88% graduate in 4 years or less, 92% graduate in 5 years or less, and 93% graduate in 6 years or less.

SERVICES: Counseling and information services are available, as is tutoring in most subjects. There is a reader service for the blind. **Library/Resources:** The 9 libraries contain 4.6 million volumes, 3.1 million microform items, 64,912 audio/video tapes/CDs/DVDs, and subscribe to 95,722 periodicals including electronic. Computerized library services include interlibrary loans, database searching, Internet access, and Wi-Fi capability. Special learning facilities include an art gallery, radio station, TV station, 2 observatories, and a TV news archive. **Physically Challenged Students:** 90% of the campus is accessible. Facilities include wheelchair ramps, elevators, special parking, specially equipped restrooms, special class scheduling, lowered drinking fountains, and lowered telephones. **Special:** Vanderbilt offers cross-registration with Fisk and Howard Universities and Meharry Medical College, study abroad in 18 countries, a Washington semester, a work-study program, B.A.-B.S. degrees, dual and student-designed majors, accelerated degree programs, nondegree study, and pass/fail options. Internships, required for human development majors, are available in human service agencies, city and state government, and businesses. A 3-2 engineering degree is offered with Fisk University. The school belongs to NASA's Tennessee Space Grant Consortium, and the Intercollegiate Center for Classical Studies in

Rome. There are 19 national honor societies, including Phi Beta Kappa, a freshman honors program, and 21 departmental honors programs. **Visiting:** There are regularly scheduled orientations for prospective students, including group information sessions and campus tours available Monday through Saturday during the academic year and Monday through Friday during the summer. Schedules vary, so visitors must call in advance. There are guides for informal visits, visitors may sit in on classes, and stay overnight. To schedule a visit, contact the Office of Undergraduate Admissions. **Campus Safety and Security:** Measures include 24-hour foot and vehicle patrol, emergency notification system, self-defense education, and security escort services. There are shuttle buses, emergency telephones, lighted pathways/sidewalks, a bicycle patrol, and student dorm monitors.

REQUIREMENTS: The SAT or ACT is required. SAT Subject tests are recommended in math level I, II, or IIc, writing, and foreign language. Admission requirements vary by school. Candidates should be graduates of an accredited secondary school with a minimum of 15 academic credits. Most programs require 4 years of English, 3 of math, and 2 of a foreign language and recommend 2 of history and 1 of social studies. An essay is required. An audition is required for Blair School of Music. AP credits are accepted. Important factors in the admissions decision are advanced placement or honors courses, extracurricular activities record, and evidence of special talent. All students must take at least 120 total credit hours. General requirements vary, as do specific major requirements, depending on the chosen program. A minimum GPA of 2.0 is usually needed. There is a mandatory writing requirement. Students majoring in human development must complete an internship in the fall semester of the senior year. **Procedure:** Freshmen are admitted fall. Entrance exams should be taken Spring of the junior year or the fall of the senior year. There are early decision and deferred admissions plans. Early decision applications should be filed by November 1; regular applications, by January 3 for fall entry, along with a $50 fee. Notification of early decision is sent December 15; regular decision, April 1. 687 early decision candidates were accepted for the 2014-2015 class. 4536 applicants were on the 2014 waiting list; 210 were admitted. Applications are accepted on-line. **Transfer Students:** 206 transfer students enrolled in 2013-2014. Transfers must take the SAT or the ACT. A minimum of 12 hours of college credit must have been earned. Students must meet all freshman requirements and be in good standing at the previous institution attended. Applicants must submit high school and college transcripts and an essay or personal statement. 60 of 120 credits required for the bachelor's degree must be completed at Vanderbilt. **International Students:** There are 427 international students enrolled. The school actively recruits these students. They must take the TOEFL. They must also take the SAT or ACT.

ADMISSIONS: 13% of the 2014-2015 applicants were accepted. The SAT scores for the 2014-2015 freshman class were: Critical Reading--1% below 500, 5% between 500 and 599, 16% between 600 and 699, and 78% between 700 and 800; Math--1% below 500, 3% between 500 and 599, 14% between 600 and 699, and 82% between 700 and 800; Writing--2% below 500, 3% between 500 and 599, 26% between 600 and 699, and 69% between 700 and 800. The ACT scores were 1% below 21, 1% between 21 and 23, 1% between 24 and 26, 4% between 27 and 28, and 93% above 28. 96% of the current freshmen were in the top fifth of their class; 99% were in the top two fifths. There were 273 National Merit finalists. 118 freshmen graduated first in their class. **Admissions Contact:** Admissions Officer E-Mail: *admissions@vanderbilt.edu* Web: *www.vanderbilt.edu*

FINANCIAL AID: In 2014-2015, 69% of all full-time freshmen and 65% of continuing full-time students received some form of financial aid. 47% of all full-time freshmen and 45% of continuing full-time students received need-based aid. The average freshman award was $46,023. Need-based scholarships or need-based grants averaged $40,201 ($63,523 maximum); need-based self-help aid (loans and jobs) averaged $2,396 ($5,500 maximum); non-need-based athletic scholarships averaged $46,385 ($59,754 maximum); and other non-need-based awards and non-need-based scholarships averaged $7,814 ($46,722 maximum). The average financial indebtedness of the 2014 graduate was $20,790. The CSS/Profile and FAFSA, and tax return information are required. The priority date for freshman financial aid applications for fall entry is February 2.

TEXAS

• College Location

0 40 80 120 160
Miles

ABILENE CHRISTIAN UNIVERSITY   C-2
www.acu.edu

Abilene, TX 79699

(325) 674-2000
(800) 460-6228

Fax: (325) 674-2130
Email: info@admissions.acu.edu

Full-time: 1500 men, 2010 women
Part-time: 99 men, 118 women
Graduate: 294 men, 440 women
Year: semesters, summer session
Room & Board: $8800

Faculty: 222; IIA, -$
Ph.D.s: 79%
Student/Faculty: 14 to 1
Tuition: $28,350
Freshman Class: 10188 applied, 4986 accepted, 1030 enrolled

SAT CR/M/W: 532/547/511 ACT: 24
Application Deadline: February 15

CEEB CODE: 6001
COMPETITIVE+

Abilene Christian University, is a selective four-year private Christian university, ACU is the best at providing exceptional academics in a Christ-centered community. It includes the colleges of Arts and Sciences, Biblical Studies, Business Administration, Education, Human Services, and Honors. The Graduate Schools of Theology, Information Technology and Computing, Social Work and the School of Nursing. ACU is affiliated with the Churches of Christ and is one of the largest private universities in the Southwest. There are 8 undergraduate schools and 6 graduate schools. In addition to regional accreditation, ACU has baccalaureate program accreditation with AACSB, ACEJMC, CSWE, FIDER, NASM, TEAC, and ACEND. The 250-acre campus is in a small town 180 miles west of the Dallas-Fort Worth metroplex. Including any residence halls, there are 46 buildings.

STUDENT LIFE: 84% of undergraduates are from Texas. Others are from 49 states, 43 foreign countries, and Canada. 64% are from public schools. 69% are White; 11% Hispanic. 48% are Protestant. **Female To Male Ratio:** 1.4:1. The average age of freshmen is 18; all undergraduates, 20. 25% do not continue beyond their first year; 60% remain to graduate. **Housing:** 1856 students can be accommodated in college housing, which includes single-sex dorms, on-campus

apartments, and married student housing. On-campus housing is available on a first-come, first-served basis, and is available on a lottery system for upperclassmen. 52% of students commute. Alcohol is not permitted. All students may keep cars.

FACULTY/CLASSROOMS: 59% of faculty are male; 41% are female. 92% teach undergraduates. Graduate students teach 1% of introductory courses. The average class size in an introductory lecture is 29; in a laboratory is 17; and in a regular course is 24.

PROGRAMS OF STUDY: ACU confers B.A., B.S., B.B.A., B.F.A., B.M., B.S.E. and B.S.N. degrees. Associate, Master's, and Doctoral degrees are also awarded. Bachelor's degrees are awarded in AGRICULTURE (agricultural business management and animal science), BIOLOGICAL SCIENCE (biochemistry, biology/biological science, and nutrition), BUSINESS (accounting, finance, information and communication technology, management science, and marketing/retailing/merchandising), COMMUNICATIONS AND THE ARTS (advertising, art, communications, communication science, dramatic arts, English, fine arts, game design and development, graphic design, journalism, multimedia, music, public relations, and Spanish), COMPUTER AND PHYSICAL SCIENCE (chemistry, computer game design/development, computer science, information sciences and systems, mathematics, mathematics/computational, and physics), EDUCATION (art education, early childhood education, elementary education, foreign languages education, music education, secondary education, and special education), ENGINEERING AND ENVIRONMENTAL DESIGN (engineering, environmental science, and interior design), HEALTH PROFESSIONS (exercise science and nursing), SOCIAL SCIENCE (biblical studies, criminal justice, family/consumer studies, history, international relations, liberal arts/general studies, ministries, political science/government, psychology, social work, and sociology). Accounting, music, biology, psychology, and English are the strongest academically. Management, biology, and nursing have the largest enrollments.

ACTIVITIES: 24% of men belong to 6 local fraternities; 24% of women belong to 5 local sororities. There are 95 groups on campus, including art, band, cheerleading, chess, choir, chorale, chorus, computers, debate, drama, environmental, ethnic, film, forensics, gay, honors, international, jazz band, literary magazine, marching band, musical theater, newspaper, opera, orchestra, photography, political, professional, radio and TV, religious, social, social service, steel drum band, student government, and symphony. Popular campus events include Sing Song Festival, Bible Lectures and Freshman Follies. **Sports:** There are 7 intercollegiate sports for men and 7 for women, and 12 intramural sports for men and 12 for women. Facilities include an student recreation and wellness center with fitness center, indoor track, group exercise studios, bouldering wall, indoor swimming pools, gyms, racquetball courts. Also have a coliseum, track, baseball and softball stadiums, soccer field, tennis courts, and a disc golf course. **Graduates:** From July 1, 2013 to June 30, 2014, 698 bachelor's degrees were awarded. The most popular majors were accounting, management, and and family studies (7%). 163 companies recruited on campus in 2013-2014. In an average class, 2% graduate in 3 years or less, 42% graduate in 4 years or less, 57% graduate in 5 years or less, and 58% graduate in 6 years or less. Of the 2013 graduating class, 28% were enrolled in graduate school within 6 months of graduation, and 53% were employed.

SERVICES: There is a reader service for the blind, and remedial math and writing. A sign language interpreter. **Library/Resources:** The library contains 558,009 volumes, 1.2 million microform items, and 66,358 audio/video tapes/CDs/DVDs, and subscribes to 42,083 periodicals including electronic. Computerized library services include interlibrary loans, database searching, Internet access, and Wi-Fi capability. Special learning facilities include an art gallery, planetarium, radio station, TV station, a learning commons, writing center, speaking center, AT&T learning studio, maker lab, center for Christian service and leadership, a converged media newsroom, demonstration farm and ranch, and center for restoration studies. **Physically Challenged Students:** 95% of the campus is accessible. Facilities include wheelchair ramps, elevators, special parking, specially equipped restrooms, special class scheduling, lowered drinking fountains, and lowered telephones. **Special:** A cooperative engineering degree is offered with the University of Texas at Arlington and an admissions agreement with Texas Tech for applied physics MS program. ACU also offers a Health Professions Cooperative Degree. ACU offers cross-registration with Hardin-Simmons and McMurry Universities and study abroad in 3 countries. Double majors are available; internships are possible in most majors, as are B.A.-B.S. degrees in biology, bio-chemistry, communication, and mathematics. Student designed majors (interdisciplinary studies) are available. There are 14 national honor societies and a freshman honors program. **Visiting:** There are regularly scheduled orientations for prospective students, consisting of academic department, attend chapel, financial aid and admission information, and special interest sessions. There are guides for informal visits and visitors may sit in on classes. To schedule a visit, contact the Director of Campus Visits at (800) 460-6228. **Campus Safety and Security:** Measures include 24-hour foot and vehicle patrol, emergency notification system, self-defense education, and security escort services. There are shuttle buses, emergency telephones, lighted pathways/sidewalks, and fire safety discussions.

REQUIREMENTS: The SAT or ACT is required. The ACT Optional Writing test is also required. Applicants must be graduates of an accredited secondary school or have the GED and have completed 12 academic credits, including 4 in English, 3 each in math and science, and 2 years of the same foreign language. Art majors need to submit a portfolio, and music and theater majors must audition. ACU requires applicants to be in the upper 50% of their class. AP and CLEP credits are accepted. Important factors in the admissions decision are leadership record, recommendations by alumni, and advanced placement or honors courses. To graduate, students must complete courses in Bible (15 hours), English, communication, science, mathematics, social science/fine arts/humanities, kinesiology (3 hours), foreign language and cultural awareness. 33 semester hours of advanced work must be taken and a minimum 2.0 GPA maintained. A minimum of 128 credit hours is needed (more in some programs) and 30 to 64 hours of that is in the major, 18 of which must be upper division. **Procedure:** Freshmen are admitted to all sessions. Entrance exams should be taken by February of the senior year. There is an early admissions plan. Applications should be filed by February 15 for fall entry, along with a $50 fee. Notification of early decision is sent November 1; regular decision, February 15. Applications are accepted on-line. **Transfer Students:** 116 transfer students enrolled in 2013-2014. Transfer students are evaluated for admission on the basis of their college GPA. Entrance exam scores and high school transcripts will be reviewed for students with GPA's below 2.5. 40 of 128 credits required for the bachelor's degree must be completed at ACU. **International Students:** There are 146 international students enrolled. The school actively recruits these students. They must take the TOEFL with a minimum score of 400 on the paper-based TOEFL (PBT) or 80 on the Internet-based version (iBT). They must also take the SAT or ACT.

ADMISSIONS: 49% of the 2014-2015 applicants were accepted. The SAT scores for the 2014-2015 freshman class were: Critical Reading-36% below 500, 43% between 500 and 599, 15% between 600 and 699, and 6% between 700 and 800; Math--27% below 500, 45% between 500 and 599, 24% between 600 and 699, and 4% between 700 and 800; Writing--46% below 500, 39% between 500 and 599, 13% between 600 and 699, and 2% between 700 and 800. The ACT scores were 18% below 21, 27% between 21 and 23, 26% between 24 and 26, 12% between 27 and 28, and 17% above 28. 49% of the current freshmen were in the top fifth of their class; 78% were in the top two fifths. There were 7 National Merit finalists. 16 freshmen graduated first in their class. **Admissions Contact:** Tamera Long, Director of Admissions. E-Mail: *info@admissions.acu.edu* Web: *www.acu.edu*

FINANCIAL AID: In 2014-2015, 100% of all full-time freshmen and 99% of continuing full-time students received some form of financial aid. 76% of all full-time freshmen and 66% of continuing full-time students received need-based aid. The average freshman award was $12,350. Need-based scholarships or need-based grants averaged $20,397; need-based self-help aid (loans and jobs) averaged $5,163; non-need-based athletic scholarships averaged $16,512; and other non-need-based awards and non-need-based scholarships averaged $11,053. 28% of undergraduate students work part-time. Average annual earnings from campus work are $4800. The average financial indebtedness of the 2014 graduate was $42,585. The FAFSA is required. The deadline for filing freshman financial aid applications for fall entry is March 1.

ANGELO STATE UNIVERSITY (*The complete profile is made available exclusively on our website, www.barronspac.com*)

AUSTIN COLLEGE   **D-2**
www.austincollege.edu

| Sherman, TX 75090 | (903) 813-2000 |
| | (800) 526-4276 |

Fax: (903) 813-3198   Email: admission@austincollege.edu

Full-time: 616 men, 655 women	**Faculty:** 123; IIB, av$
Part-time: 2 men, 5 women	**Ph.D.s:** 95%
Graduate: 10 men, 13 women	**Student/Faculty:** 12 to 1
Year: 4-1-4, summer session	**Tuition:** $34,840
Room & Board: $11,035	**Freshman Class:** 3044 applied, 1657 accepted, 357 enrolled
SAT CR/M: 601/604 **ACT:** 26	**CEEB CODE:** 6016
Application Deadline: March 1	**HIGHLY COMPETITIVE**

Austin College is a private, residential, co-educational college dedicated to educating undergraduate students in the liberal arts and sciences while also offering select pre-professional programs and a graduate teacher education program. Founded by the Presbyterian Church in 1849, Austin College continues its relationship with the church and its commitment to a heritage that values personal growth, justice, community, and service. There is 1 undergraduate school and 1 graduate school. The 70-acre campus is in a rural area 60 miles north of Dallas. Including any residence halls, there are 34 buildings.

STUDENT LIFE: 91% of undergraduates are from Texas. Others are from 32 states, 17 foreign countries, and Canada. 85% are from public schools. 56% are White; 20% Hispanic; 14% Asian American. 44% are Protestant; 18% claim no religious affiliation; 17% Catholic. The average age of freshmen is 18; all undergraduates, 20. 13% do not continue beyond their first year; 68% remain to graduate. **Housing:** 1072 students can be accommodated in college housing, which includes single-sex and coed dorms and on-campus apartments. In addition, there are language houses, and a suite-style residence hall. On-campus housing is available on a lottery system for upperclassmen. 81% of students live on campus; of those, 35% remain on campus on weekends. All students may keep cars.

FACULTY/CLASSROOMS: 63% of faculty are male; 37% are female. All teach and do research. No introductory courses are taught by graduate students. The average class size in an introductory lecture is 19; in a laboratory is 16; and in a regular course is 20.

PROGRAMS OF STUDY: AC confers B.A. degrees. Master's degrees are also awarded. Bachelor's degrees are awarded in AGRICULTURE (natural resources), BIOLOGICAL SCIENCE (biochemistry and biology/biological science), BUSINESS (business administration and management and international economics), COMMUNICATIONS AND THE ARTS (art history, art, classical languages, classics, communications, East Asian languages and literature, English, French, German, Latin, music, and Spanish), COMPUTER AND PHYSICAL SCIENCE (chemistry, computer science, mathematics, and physics), SOCIAL SCIENCE (American studies, economics, history, interdisciplinary studies, international studies, Latin American studies, philosophy, political science/government, psychology, religion, sociology, and women and gender studies). Biology, psychology, and political science are the strongest academically. Business administration has the larges enrollment.

ACTIVITIES: 20% of men belong to 10 local fraternities; 11% of women belong to 5 local sororities. There are 55 groups on campus, including art, cheerleading, choir, chorale, chorus, communications, dance, drama, ethnic, film, gay, honors, international, jazz band, literary magazine, model UN and international student organizations, musical theater, newspaper, orchestra, pep band, photography, political, professional, religious, social, social service, student government, symphony, and yearbook. Popular campus events include Christmas Pops, Kangapalooza (spring concert), Great Day of Service, Film

Series and Diwali Dinner. **Sports:** There are 7 intercollegiate sports for men and 7 for women, and 8 intramural sports for men and 8 for women. Facilities include an athletic/recreation complex that includes 2 gyms, a natatorium, a fitness pavilion, tennis stadium, soccer and baseball fields. **Graduates:** From July 1, 2013 to June 30, 2014, 246 bachelor's degrees were awarded. The most popular majors were business administration (17%), psychology (14%), and biology (10%). 43 companies recruited on campus in 2013-2014. In an average class, 67% graduate in 4 years or less, 73% graduate in 5 years or less, and 77% graduate in 6 years or less. Of the 2013 graduating class, 44% were enrolled in graduate school within 6 months of graduation, and 47% were employed.

SERVICES: Counseling and information services are available, as is tutoring in some subjects. Individual and group assistance to strengthen reading, writing, and study skills is available. **Library/ Resources:** The library contains 227,019 volumes, 120,808 microform items, 6,393 audio/video tapes/CDs/DVDs, and subscribes to 5,727 periodicals including electronic. Computerized library services include interlibrary loans, database searching, Internet access, and Wi-Fi capability. **Physically Challenged Students:** All of the campus is accessible. Facilities include wheelchair ramps, elevators, special parking, specially equipped restrooms, special class scheduling, and lowered drinking fountains. **Special:** AC offers study abroad in 58 countries, internships during the January and summer terms, and fall, spring, and summer internships in Washington, D.C. Work-study, accelerated degree programs in all majors, and dual and student-designed majors are available. There is a 3-2 engineering degree program in conjunction with the University of Texas at Dallas and Washington University in St. Louis, as well as cooperative agreements with Columbia University and Texas A&M University. There are 14 national honor societies including Phi Beta Kappa. **Visiting:** There are regularly scheduled orientations for prospective students, 1-day and 2-day preview programs held for high school juniors, seniors and parents. Individual appointments may be made as well. There are guides for informal visits, visitors may sit in on classes, and stay overnight. To schedule a visit, contact the Admissions Office. **Campus Safety and Security:** 24-hour foot and vehicle patrol, emergency notification system, self-defense education, and security escort services. There are emergency telephones and lighted pathways/sidewalks.

REQUIREMENTS: The SAT or ACT is required. Applicants must be graduates of an accredited secondary school, home schooled, or have a GED. The minimum recommended academic requirements are 4 credits in English, 3 each in math and science, 2 each in social studies and foreign language, and 1 in art/music/theater. An essay and recommendation are required. AP and CLEP credits are accepted. Important factors in the admissions decision are advanced placement or honors courses, leadership record, and extracurricular activities record. Core requirements for graduation include completion of the Foundation Dimension, the Breadth Dimension, and 1 course in Lifetime Sports. To graduate, students must have a minimum 2.0 GPA and a total of 34 course credits (136 semester hours). Students must demonstrate an ability in a modern or classical language other than their own, quantitative competency with an approved course or test, and the required skills in written communication with approved course work. A minor or a 2nd major is required. **Procedure:** Freshmen are admitted fall and summer. Entrance exams should be taken by the junior year or the fall of the senior year. There are deferred admissions and rolling admissions plans. Applications should be filed by March 1 for fall entry. Notifications are sent April 1. 12 applicants were on the 2014 waiting list; 6 were admitted. Applications are accepted on-line. **Transfer Students:** 46 transfer students enrolled in 2013-2014. Applicants must have a minimum 3.0 GPA, submit official college transcripts and 2 recommendations, and be in good standing at most recently attended schools. Students with fewer than 30 credit hours must submit SAT or ACT scores and their high school transcript or GED. 17 of 34 credits required for the bachelor's degree must be completed at AC. **International Students:** There are 39 international students enrolled. The school actively recruits these students. They must take the TOEFL with a minimum score of 550 on the paper-based TOEFL (PBT) or 80 on the Internet-based version (iBT). They must also take the SAT or ACT.

ADMISSIONS: 54% of the 2014-2015 applicants were accepted. The SAT scores for the 2014-2015 freshman class were: Critical Reading--14% below 500, 30% between 500 and 599, 42% between 600 and 699, and 14% between 700 and 800; Math--8% below 500, 34% between 500 and 599, 41% between 600 and 699, and 17% between 700 and 800; Writing--15% below 500, 40% between 500 and 599, 34% between 600 and 699, and 11% between 700 and 800. The ACT scores were 13% below 21, 20% between 21 and 23, 55% between 24 and 26, 12% between 27 and 28, and 20% above 28. 72% of the current freshmen were in the top fifth of their class; 96% were in the top two fifths. **Admissions Contact:** Nan Davis, VP for Institutional Enrollment. E-Mail: *admission@austincollege.edu* Web: *www. austincollege.edu*

FINANCIAL AID: In 2014-2015, 93% of all full-time freshmen and 96% of continuing full-time students received some form of financial aid. 68% of all full-time freshmen and 61% of continuing full-time students received need-based aid. 30% of undergraduate students work part-time. Average annual earnings from campus work are $1700. The average financial indebtedness of the 2014 graduate was $34,744. AC is a member of CSS. The FAFSA is required. The priority date for freshman financial aid applications for fall entry is March 1. The deadline for filing freshman financial aid applications for fall entry is April 1.

BAYLOR UNIVERSITY D-3
www.baylor.edu

Waco, TX 76798

(800) 229-5678
(254) 710-3435
Fax: (254) 710-3436
Email: admissions@baylor.edu

Full-time: 5700 men, 7913 women	Faculty: I, -$
Part-time: 116 men, 130 women	Ph.D.s: 83%
Graduate: 1295 men, 1109 women	Student/Faculty: 15 to 1
Year: semesters, summer session	Tuition: $38,120
Room & Board: $12,209	Freshman Class: n/av
	CEEB CODE: 6032
Application Deadline: February 1	HIGHLY COMPETITIVE

Baylor University, is a private Christian university, founded in 1845, by the Republic of Texas. Baylor offers undergraduate programs in liberal arts and sciences, business, computer science, education, engineering, health and human services, music, nursing, social work, and an honors college. There are 8 undergraduate schools and 10 graduate schools. In addition to regional accreditation, Baylor has baccalaureate program accreditation with AACSB, ABET, ACEJMC, ADA, CSWE, FIDER, NASM, NCATE, NAST, AAFCS, and ACS. The 1000-acre campus is in a small town 100 miles south of Dallas/Fort Worth. Including any residence halls, there are 127 buildings.

STUDENT LIFE: 74% of undergraduates are from Texas. Others are from 50 states, 54 foreign countries, and Canada. 63% are White; 14% Hispanic. 77% are Protestant; 16% Catholic. The average age of freshmen is 19; all undergraduates, 20. 14% do not continue beyond their first year; 73% remain to graduate. **Housing:** 5402 students can be accommodated in college housing, which includes single-sex and coed dorms, on-campus apartments, off-campus apartments, and married student housing. In addition, there are honors houses, language houses, special-interest houses. On-campus housing is guaranteed for the freshman year only, and is available on a first-come, first-served basis. 62% of students commute. Alcohol is not permitted. All students may keep cars.

FACULTY/CLASSROOMS: 58% of faculty are male; 42% are female. No introductory courses are taught by graduate students. The average class size in a regular course is 28.

PROGRAMS OF STUDY: Baylor confers B.A., B.S., B.B.A., B.F.A., B.M., B.M.E., B.S.Av.Sc., B.S.C., B.S.C.S., B.S.E., B.S.E.C.E., B.S.Ed., B.S.F.C.S., B.S.I., B.S.M.E., B.S.N. and B.S.W. degrees. Master's and Doctoral degrees are also awarded. Bachelor's degrees are awarded in BIOLOGICAL SCIENCE (biochemistry, bioinformatics, biology/biological science, life science, neurosciences, and nutrition), BUSINESS (accounting, apparel and accessories marketing, apparel and textiles, banking and finance, business administration and management, business economics, business statistics, business systems analysis, entrepreneurial studies, fashion merchandising, human resources, insurance, international business management, management information systems, marketing/retailing/merchandising, personnel management, real estate, and sports marketing), COMMUNICATIONS AND THE ARTS (acting, apparel design, applied music, art history, art, art history and appreciation, broadcasting, choral music, classics, communications, creative writing, dramatic arts, English, French, German, Greek (classical), journalism, languages, Latin, literature, music, music history and appreciation, music performance, music theory and composition, performing arts, Russian, Spanish, speech/debate/rhetoric, studio art, telecommunications, theater design, and theatre studies), COMPUTER AND PHYSICAL SCIENCE (applied mathematics, chemistry, computer science, earth science, geology, geophysics and seismology, information sciences and systems, mathematics, and physics), EDUCATION (art education, athletic training, business education, computer education, drama education, elementary education, English education, foreign languages education, health education, home economics education, journalism education, mathematics education, museum studies, music education, physical education, reading education, recreation education, science education, secondary education, social science education, social studies education, and special education), ENGINEERING AND ENVIRONMENTAL DESIGN (airline piloting and navigation, computer engineering, electrical/electronics engineering, engineering, environmental science, interior design, and mechanical engineering), HEALTH PROFESSIONS (community health work, health science, medical laboratory technology, nursing, optometry, predentistry, premedicine, speech pathology/audiology, and speech therapy), SOCIAL SCIENCE (American studies, anthropology, area studies, Asian/Oriental studies, biblical languages, child care/child and family studies, dietetics, economics, family/consumer studies, fashion design and technology, forensic studies, history, interdisciplinary studies, international public service, Latin American studies, Middle Eastern studies, philosophy, physical fitness/movement, political science/government, psychology, public administration, religion, religious education, religious music, Russian and Slavic studies, social work, sociology, and urban studies). Business, biology, and psychology have the largest enrollments.

ACTIVITIES: 15% of men belong to 2 local and 19 national fraternities; 28% of women belong to 1 local and 16 national sororities. There are 290 groups on campus, including art, band, cheerleading, chess, choir, chorale, chorus, computers, dance, debate, drama, ethnic, film, forensics, honors, international, jazz band, literary magazine, marching band, musical theater, newspaper, opera, orchestra, pep band, photography, political, professional, radio and TV, religious, social, social service, student government, symphony, and yearbook. Popular campus events include Dia del Oso (Day of the Bear), Campus Sing and Pigskin Review. **Sports:** There are 8 intercollegiate sports for men and 10 for women, and 17 intramural sports for men and 17 for women. Facilities include a 45,000-seat, on-campus, riverfront football stadium with features that include a 106-feet-wide by 45-feet-tall video board, a canopy to provide shade for spectators, high density Wi-Fi, wide concourses and docks for sailgaters. The stadium's 93-acre site, including 10 acres for the soon-to-be completed track stadium, connects to campus via a 35-feet-wide by 775-feet-long pedestrian bridge across the Brazos River. The track stadium will hold 5,000 spectators plus offer a team building and an indoor practice facility. Other on-campus athletic facilities include a student-athlete services and administration building, an indoor practice facility, softball stadium, baseball stadium, soccer complex, outdoor and indoor tennis facilities, a basketball practice facility and a 10,000-plus center for basketball and volleyball. An equestrian center and golf center are close to campus. Students have access to gyms, intramural fields, tennis courts, a marina, and a 158,000-square-foot student life center that offers a 53-feet-tall climbing rock plus a separate bouldering area, a fitness center, aerobics room, racquetball/squash courts, basketball courts, a pool, an indoor walking/jogging track, and an outdoor sand volleyball court. **Graduates:** From July 1, 2013 to June 30, 2014, 2848 bachelor's degrees were awarded. The most popular majors were biology (8%), nursing (7%), and accounting (5%). In an average class, 2% graduate in 3 years or less, 56% graduate in 4 years or less, 71% graduate in 5 years or less, and 73% graduate in 6 years or less.

SERVICES: Counseling and information services are available, as is

tutoring in some subjects. There is a reader service for the blind. **Library/Resources:** The 7 libraries contain 2.6 million volumes, 2.3 million microform items, and 99,615 audio/video tapes/CDs/DVDs. Computerized library services include interlibrary loans, database searching, and Internet access. Special learning facilities include an art gallery, natural history museum, radio station, TV station, a speech/hearing clinic. **Physically Challenged Students:** 95% of the campus is accessible. Facilities include wheelchair ramps, elevators, special parking, specially equipped restrooms, and lowered drinking fountains. **Special:** Baylor offers internships in each school, study abroad and student exchange in more than 30 countries, and pass/fail options. There are also honors and university scholars programs and faculty exchange with 4 schools in China and 1 each in Japan, Thailand, and Russia. There are 36 national honor societies, including Phi Beta Kappa, and a freshman honors program. **Visiting:** There are regularly scheduled orientations for prospective students, including day-and-a-half sessions in June and a Welcome Week in August. There are guides for informal visits, visitors may sit in on classes, and stay overnight. To schedule a visit, contact Campus Visitation Program at (254) 710-2407. **Campus Safety and Security:** Measures include 24-hour foot and vehicle patrol, emergency notification system, and security escort services. There are shuttle buses, emergency telephones, lighted pathways/sidewalks, and controlled access to dorms/residences.

REQUIREMENTS: The SAT or ACT is required. The ACT Optional Writing test is also required. Applicants must be graduates of an accredited secondary school. An interview is recommended. Baylor requires applicants to be in the upper 50% of their class. AP and CLEP credits are accepted. All degree programs require a minimum of 124 hours and a 2.0 GPA to graduate. Requirements for the B.A. degree include 18 semester hours of social science, 12 each of English and science, 6 to 9 of fine arts, 6 of religion, 4 of phys ed, 3 to 16 of foreign language, 3 of math, and 2 semesters of chapel forum. Requirements for other degrees vary. **Procedure:** Freshmen are admitted fall, spring, and summer. Entrance exams should be taken in spring of the junior year or fall of the senior year. There is an early admissions plan. Early decision applications should be filed by November 1; regular applications, by February 1 for fall entry, along with a $50 fee. Notification of early decision is sent January 15; regular decision, March 15. 1766 applicants were on the 2014 waiting list; 49 were admitted. Applications are accepted on-line. Application fees are waived if application is completed on-line. **Transfer Students:** 454 transfer students enrolled in 2013-2014. Transfer students should begin studies no later than the end of the sophomore year because of the 60-semester-hour residence requirement for a bachelor's degree. A minimum 2.5 GPA is required. Students with fewer than 30 credit hours earned must meet the entrance requirements for freshmen. 60 of 124 credits required for the bachelor's degree must be completed at Baylor. **International Students:** There are 458 international students enrolled. The school actively recruits these students. They must take the TOEFL with a minimum score of 540 on the paper-based TOEFL (PBT) or 76 on the Internet-based version (iBT). They must also take the SAT or ACT.

ADMISSIONS: 65% of the current freshmen were in the top fifth of their class; 91% were in the top two fifths. There were 83 National Merit finalists. **Admissions Contact:** Jennifer Carron, Director of Undergraduate Admissions. E-Mail: *admissions@baylor.edu* Web: *www.baylor.edu*

FINANCIAL AID: The FAFSA, and if awarded state aid (gift or loan), student must complete a residency affirmation. The priority date for freshman financial aid applications for fall entry is February 15. The deadline for filing freshman financial aid applications for fall entry is May 1.

CONCORDIA UNIVERSITY TEXAS D-3
www.concordia.edu

Austin, TX 78705-2799

(512) 486-3000
(512) 313-3000

Fax: (512) 313-4639

Email: admissions@concordia.edu

Full-time: 360 men, 420 women

Faculty: n/av

Part-time: 100 men, 200 women

Ph.D.s: 74%

Graduate: 25 men, 75 women

Student/Faculty: n/av

Year: semesters, summer session

Tuition: $23,420

Room & Board: $8960

Freshman Class: n/av

SAT or ACT: required

CEEB CODE: 6127

Application Deadline: see profile

COMPETITIVE

Concordia University Texas, was founded in 1926 and is a private college affiliated with the Lutheran Church-Missouri Synod. The school offers undergraduate programs in liberal arts, behavioral science, business, communication, education, environmental science, and church music. The figures in the above capsule and in this profile are approximate. There are 4 undergraduate schools. The 20-acre campus is in an urban area in the heart of Austin. Including any residence halls, there are 20 buildings.

STUDENT LIFE: 93% of undergraduates are from Texas. Others are from 21 states and 13 foreign countries. 89% are from public schools. 63% are white; 16% Hispanic. 78% are Protestant; 16% Catholic. The average age of freshmen is 19; all undergraduates, 25. 40% do not continue beyond their first year; 35% remain to graduate.

FACULTY/CLASSROOMS: 69% of faculty are male; 31% are female. All teach undergraduates. No introductory courses are taught by graduate students. The average class size in a laboratory is 16 and in a regular course is 21.

PROGRAMS OF STUDY: Concordia confers B.A. degrees. Associates and Master's degrees are also awarded. Bachelor's degrees are awarded in BUSINESS (accounting and business administration and management), COMMUNICATIONS AND THE ARTS (communications, English, music, and Spanish), COMPUTER AND PHYSICAL SCIENCE (computer science), EDUCATION (elementary education and secondary education), ENGINEERING AND ENVIRONMENTAL DESIGN (environmental science), SOCIAL SCIENCE (behavioral science, history, liberal arts/general studies, Mexican-American/Chicano studies, and religious music). Education is the strongest academically. Business management, education, and communication have the largest enrollments.

ACTIVITIES: There are 9 groups on campus, including band, choir, chorus, dance, drama, ethnic, religious, social, and student government. Popular campus events include Fall Festival Weekend, Parents Day, and Founders Day.

SERVICES: Counseling and information services are available, as is tutoring in most subjects. **Library/Resources:** The library contains 56,146 volumes, 8,504 microform items, and 3,213 audio/video tapes/CDs/DVDs, and subscribes to 514 periodicals including electronic. Computerized library services include interlibrary loans and database searching. **Physically Challenged Students:** 75% of the campus is accessible. Facilities include wheelchair ramps, elevators, special parking, specially equipped restrooms, and lowered drinking fountains. **Special:** Concordia offers internships in communications, behavioral science, business, environmental science, and Mexican-American studies, study abroad in Mexico, an accelerated degree program in business management, dual majors, credit for prior experiential learning, nondegree study, pass/fail options, and a preseminary program. There are 1 national honor societies. **Visiting:** There are regularly scheduled orientations for prospective students, consisting of placement exams, scheduling and registration of classes, and information sessions for parents with faculty and administrators. There are guides for informal visits, visitors may sit in on classes, and stay overnight. To schedule a visit, contact the Admissions Office. **Campus Safety and Security:** Measures include 24-hour foot and vehicle patrol and security escort services. There are lighted pathways/sidewalks.

REQUIREMENTS: The SAT or ACT is required. The recommended minimum composite score is 860 on the SAT or 17 on the ACT. Applicants must be graduates of an accredited secondary school or have the GED. A GPA of 2.5 is required. AP and CLEP credits are accepted.

FINANCIAL AID: The FAFSA and the college's own financial statement are required. Check with the school for current application deadlines.

DALLAS BAPTIST UNIVERSITY D-2
www.dbu.edu

Dallas, TX 75211

(214) 333-7100
(800) 460-1328

Fax: (214) 333-5536
Email: admiss@dbu.edu

Full-time: 1045 men, 1352 women
Faculty: 102

Part-time: 404 men, 656 women
Ph.D.s: 80%

Graduate: 753 men, 1235 women
Student/Faculty: 13 to 1

Year: 4-1-4, summer session
Tuition: $23,650

Room & Board: $6930
Freshman Class: 2787 applied, 1288 accepted, 494 enrolled

SAT CR/M: 560/557 ACT: 22
CEEB CODE: 6159

Application Deadline:
VERY COMPETITIVE

Dallas Baptist University is a Christ-centered comprehensive, liberal arts university offering 69 Bachelor programs, 32 Accelerated Bachelor/Master programs, 25 Master programs, 49 Dual Master programs, and 2 Doctoral degree programs. DBU integrates faith and academic learning, giving students freedom to explore their faith in the classroom and the encouragement to live out their faith as servant leaders in the world. With online classes as well as weekend and evening classes at locations throughout the Dallas/Fort Worth Metroplex, DBU offers working adults the convenience and flexibility they need to complete their degree. There are 7 undergraduate schools and 25 graduate schools. In addition to regional accreditation, DBU has baccalaureate program accreditation with ACBSP, NASM, and Texas Education Agency. The 293-acre campus is in a suburban area 13 miles from downtown Dallas and 29 miles from downtown Fort Worth. Including any residence halls, there are 43 buildings.

STUDENT LIFE: 90% of undergraduates are from Texas. Others are from 44 states, 42 foreign countries, and Canada. 60% are White; 15% African American; 14% Hispanic. 91% are Protestant. The average age of freshmen is 18; all undergraduates, 25. 28% do not continue beyond their first year; 55% remain to graduate. **Housing:** 1916 students can be accommodated in college housing, which includes single-sex dorms, on-campus apartments, off-campus apartments, and married student housing. On-campus housing is available on a first-come and first-served basis. 55% of students live on campus; of those, 80% remain on campus on weekends. Alcohol is not permitted. All students may keep cars.

FACULTY/CLASSROOMS: 58% of faculty are male; 42% are female. 78% teach undergraduates. No introductory courses are taught by graduate students. The average class size in a regular course is 12.

PROGRAMS OF STUDY: DBU confers B.A., B.S., B.A.S., B.B.A., B.B.S., B.M. and B.M.E. degrees. Associate, Master's, and Doctoral degrees are also awarded. Bachelor's degrees are awarded in BIOLOGICAL SCIENCE (biology/biological science and cell biology), BUSINESS (accounting, banking and finance, business administration and management, finance, hospitality management services, management information systems, marketing/retailing/merchandising, and sports management), COMMUNICATIONS AND THE ARTS (applied music, art, choral music, communication design , communication, communications, English, fine arts, graphic design, music, music business management, music performance, music theory and composition, piano performance, and vocal performance), COMPUTER AND PHYSICAL SCIENCE (computer science, mathematics, and natural sciences), EDUCATION (education, elementary education, and physical education), ENGINEERING AND ENVIRONMENTAL DESIGN (environmental science), HEALTH PROFESSIONS (biology and health care administration), SOCIAL SCIENCE (biblical studies, Christian studies, counseling/psychology, criminal justice, cultural studies/critical theory and analysis, history, interdisciplinary studies, liberal arts/general studies, ministries, pastoral studies, philosophy, physical fitness/movement, political science/government, psychology, religious education, religious studies, religious music, and sociology). Education, business, and music are the strongest academically. Business administration/management, psychology, and music have the largest enrollments.

ACTIVITIES: 10% of men belong to 5 local fraternities; 15% of women belong to 6 local sororities. There are 52 groups on campus, including civil service, community outreach, art, cheerleading, choir, chorale, chorus, communications, dance, drama, drill team, ethnic, honors, international, leadership/mission work, musical theater, opera, pep band, political, professional, religious, social, social service, student government, and yearbook. Popular campus events include Family Weekend, Homecoming, Midnight Madness, Mr. Big Chief, Spring Sing, and SWAT (Student Welcome and Transition). **Sports:** There are 8 intercollegiate sports for men and 7 for women, and 13 intramural sports for men and 13 for women. Facilities include a fitness center, tennis courts, baseball field, ballpark, visitor guesthouse, soccer field, 2 pools, sand volleyball courts, indoor/outdoor basketball courts, visitor locker rooms, ping pong, billiards, and football tables, intramural fields, and athletic training center. **Graduates:** From July 1, 2013 to June 30, 2014, 728 bachelor's degrees were awarded. The most popular majors were business administration (16%), multi/interdisciplinary studies (14%), and psychology (11%). 199 companies recruited on campus in 2013-2014. In an average class, 43% graduate in 4 years or less, 53% graduate in 5 years or less, and 55% graduate in 6 years or less.

SERVICES: Counseling and information services are available, as is tutoring in most subjects, math, science, writing, and English. There is a reader service for the blind, and remedial math. **Library/Resources:** The library contains 300,104 volumes, 521,429 microform items, 8,362 audio/video tapes/CDs/DVDs, and subscribes to 31,859 periodicals including electronic. Computerized library services include interlibrary loans, database searching, Internet access, and Wi-Fi capability. Special learning facilities include a **Physically Challenged Students:** 90% of the campus is accessible. Facilities include wheelchair ramps, elevators, special parking, specially equipped restrooms, special class scheduling, lowered drinking fountains, lowered telephones, and special housing. **Special:** Study abroad programs are available in Australia, China, Costa Rica, England, India, Israel, and Uganda. National programs are available through American Studies Program in Washington, D.C., Contemporary Music Center in Nashville, Los Angeles Film Studies Center, and Washington Journalism Center, in Washington D.C. There are 5 national honor societies and a freshman honors program. **Visiting:** There are regularly scheduled orientations for prospective students, Patriot Preview days each fall, spring, and summer semesters provide parents and students information about life at DBU. Campus tours, visits with faculty and administration, information about admissions, financial aid, and campus life are included. There are guides for informal visits and visitors may sit in on classes. To schedule a visit, contact the Undergraduate Admissions Office. **Campus Safety and Security:** Measures include 24-hour foot and vehicle patrol, emergency notification system, self-defense education, and security escort services. There are shuttle buses, emergency telephones, lighted pathways/sidewalks, and controlled access to dorms/residences.

REQUIREMENTS: The SAT or ACT is required. The ACT Optional Writing test is also required. Applicants must be graduates, or expect to graduate, from an accredited secondary school, home school, or have a GED. A composite SAT score of at least 1020 (Critical Reading and Math sections) or a composite ACT score of at least 21 is required, along with a minimum high school GPA of 2.5. An essay is required, and an interview is encouraged. Recommended high school courses should include 4 years each of English and history or social studies, 3 years of math, and 2 to 3 years of a foreign language and science. DBU requires applicants to be in the upper 50% of their class. AP and CLEP credits are accepted. Important factors in the admissions decision are leadership record, personality/intangible qualities, and extracurricular activities record. To graduate with a bachelor degree, students must have a minimum GPA of 2.0 and complete a minimum of 120 credit hours, including 24 hours in the major and 42 upper-level hours. Chapel attendance is required. At least 12 credit hours in the major program must be completed at DBU, including 9 upper-level credits. Students must complete a minimum of 25% of credit hours in residence at DBU; complete 30 of the last 36 credit hours with courses offered by DBU; and complete the General Studies requirements including English, history, religion, fine arts, computer science, math, kinesiology, natural science, and social science. **Procedure:** Freshmen are admitted to all sessions. Entrance exams should be taken during the spring of the junior year

or the fall of the senior year. There are deferred admissions and rolling admissions plans. Application deadlines are open. Application fee is $25. Application fees are waived if application is completed on-line. **Transfer Students:** 489 transfer students enrolled in 2013-2014. Applicants must submit an essay along with their application and fee, and transcripts of all previous college work, and should have a cumulative GPA of 2.5 or higher. Students with fewer than 30 credit hours must furnish high school transcripts and ACT or SAT scores. 32 of 120 credits required for the bachelor's degree must be completed at DBU. **International Students:** There are 181 international students enrolled. The school actively recruits these students. They must take the TOEFL with a minimum score of 525 on the paper-based TOEFL (PBT) or 71 on the Internet-based version (iBT). Student must take the IELTS, or complete the DBU intensive English program.

ADMISSIONS: 46% of the 2014-2015 applicants were accepted. The SAT scores for the 2014-2015 freshman class were: Critical Reading--14% below 500, 55% between 500 and 599, 27% between 600 and 699, and 4% between 700 and 800; Math--17% below 500, 53% between 500 and 599, 28% between 600 and 699, and 2% between 700 and 800. The ACT scores were 46% below 21, 25% between 21 and 23, 18% between 24 and 26, 7% between 27 and 28, and 4% above 28. 5 freshmen graduated first in their class. **Admissions Contact:** Bobby Soto, Director of Undergraduate Admissions. E-Mail: *admiss@dbu.edu* Web: *www.dbu.edu*

FINANCIAL AID: In 2014-2015, 97% of all full-time freshmen and 86% of continuing full-time students received some form of financial aid. 64% of all full-time freshmen and 55% of continuing full-time students received need-based aid. The average freshman award was $19,886. Need-based scholarships or need-based grants averaged $5,895 ($12,605 maximum); need-based self-help aid (loans and jobs) averaged $3,277 ($9,500 maximum); non-need-based athletic scholarships averaged $14,896 ($33,600 maximum); other non-need-based awards and non-need-based scholarships averaged $11,673 ($28,250 maximum); and $10,565 from other forms of aid. 20% of undergraduate students work part-time. Average annual earnings from campus work are $3200. The average financial indebtedness of the 2014 graduate was $18,719. The FAFSA and the college's own financial statement are required. The priority date for freshman financial aid applications for fall entry is March 1.

EAST TEXAS BAPTIST UNIVERSITY *(The complete profile is made available exclusively on our website, www.barronspac.com)*

HARDIN-SIMMONS UNIVERSITY	C-2
www.hsutx.edu	

Abilene, TX 79698	(325) 670-1000
	(877) 464-7889
Fax: (325) 671-2115	Email: enroll@hsutx.edu
Full-time: 800 men, 1000 women	Faculty: n/av; IIA, --$
Part-time: 100 men, 175 women	Ph.D.s: 77%
Graduate: 200 men, 230 women	Student/Faculty: n/av
Year: semesters, summer session	Tuition: $22,500
Room & Board: $7000	Freshman Class: n/av
SAT or ACT: required	CEEB CODE: 6268
Application Deadline: open	COMPETITIVE+

Hardin-Simmons University, founded in 1891, is a private liberal arts institution affiliated with the Baptist General Convention of Texas. The figures in the above capsule and in this profile are approximate. There are 7 undergraduate schools and 1 graduate school. In addition to regional accreditation, HSU has baccalaureate program accreditation with ACBSP, CSWE, and NASM. The 209-acre campus is in an urban area 150 miles west of Fort Worth. Including any residence halls, there are 44 buildings.

STUDENT LIFE: 96% of undergraduates are from Texas. Others are from 23 states, 19 foreign countries, and Canada. 88% are from public schools. 74% are white. 66% are Protestant; 15% unknown; 13% claim no religious affiliation. The average age of freshmen is 18; all undergraduates, 21. 34% do not continue beyond their first year; 49% remain to graduate.

FACULTY/CLASSROOMS: 64% of faculty are male; 36% are female.

87% teach undergraduates. No introductory courses are taught by graduate students. The average class size in an introductory lecture is 23; in a laboratory, 15; and in a regular course, 17.

PROGRAMS OF STUDY: HSU confers B.A., B.S., B.B.A., B.B.S., B.Mus., and B.S.N. degrees. Master's and Doctoral degrees are also awarded. Bachelor's degrees are awarded in AGRICULTURE (agricultural business management, agriculture, and animal science), BIOLOGICAL SCIENCE (biochemistry, biology/biological science, and molecular biology), BUSINESS (accounting, banking and finance, business administration and management, management science, and marketing management), COMMUNICATIONS AND THE ARTS (art, broadcasting, communications, dramatic arts, English, graphic design, music, music business management, music history and appreciation, music performance, music theory and composition, piano/organ, public relations, radio/television technology, Spanish, speech/debate/rhetoric, strings, and voice), COMPUTER AND PHYSICAL SCIENCE (chemistry, computer science, geology, mathematics, and physics), EDUCATION (art education, athletic training, business education, computer education, drama education, early childhood education, education, elementary education, English education, foreign languages education, mathematics education, middle school education, music education, physical education, reading education, science education, secondary education, and social studies education), ENGINEERING AND ENVIRONMENTAL DESIGN (environmental science), HEALTH PROFESSIONS (exercise science, health science, nursing, predentistry, premedicine, and speech pathology/audiology), SOCIAL SCIENCE (biblical studies, corrections, criminal justice, economics, history, ministries, missions, philosophy, political science/government, prelaw, psychology, religious music, social work, sociology, theological studies, and youth ministry). English, speech pathology, and music are the strongest academically. Education, biology, and nursing have the largest enrollments.

ACTIVITIES: 5% of men belong to 4 local fraternities; 16% of women belong to 4 local sororities. There are 57 groups on campus, including art, band, cheerleading, choir, chorale, computers, debate, drama, drill team, ethnic, honors, international, literary magazine, marching band, musical theater, newspaper, opera, orchestra, pep band, photography, political, professional, radio and TV, religious, six white horse program, social, social service, student government, and symphony. Popular campus events include Western Heritage Day, All-School SING!, and Founders Day.

SERVICES: Counseling and information services are available, as is tutoring in most subjects. There is remedial math, reading, and writing. **Library/Resources:** The 2 libraries contain 262,599 volumes, 23,734 microform items, and 12,013 audio/video tapes/CDs/DVDs, and subscribe to 33,942 periodicals including electronic. Computerized library services include interlibrary loans, database searching, Internet access, and Wi-Fi capability. Special learning facilities include an art gallery, radio station, an observatory. **Physically Challenged Students:** All of the campus is accessible. Facilities include wheelchair ramps, elevators, special parking, specially equipped restrooms, special class scheduling, lowered drinking fountains, lowered telephones and special housing. **Special:** Cross-registration may be arranged with Abilene Christian and McMurry Universities. HSU offers cooperative programs, internships, dual majors, credit by exam, nondegree study, and pass/fail options. Students may study abroad in England, Austria, China, Spain, Italy and Israel, where HSU is involved in an ongoing archeological excavation of early Christian sites. There are 9 national honor societies and a freshman honors program. **Visiting:** There are regularly scheduled orientations for prospective students, including Cowboy Fridays, plus Fall and Winter preview and Spring Round-Up. There are guides for informal visits and visitors may sit in on classes. To schedule a visit, contact the Visitor Coordinator at (325) 670-5890. **Campus Safety and Security:** Measures include 24-hour foot and vehicle patrol. There are emergency telephones and lighted pathways/sidewalks.

REQUIREMENTS: The SAT or ACT is required. The ACT Optional Writing test is also required. Graduation from an accredited secondary school is required; a GED will be accepted. Applicants should submit an academic record of at least 16 units, distributed as follows: 3 units of English, 2 units each of math, science, and social studies, and 7 units of electives, with a GPA of 2.0 or above. 3 letters of recommendation are also required. HSU requires applicants to be in the upper 75% of their class. AP and CLEP credits are accepted.

FINANCIAL AID: The FAFSA is required. Check with the school for current application deadlines.

HOUSTON BAPTIST UNIVERSITY E-3
www.hbu.edu

Houston, TX 77074

(281) 649-3000
(281) 649-3211

Fax: (281) 649-3217
Full-time: 839 men, 1298 women
Part-time: 111 men, 199 women
Graduate: 238 men, 602 women
Year: semesters, summer session
Room & Board: $7650

Email: admissions@hbu.edu
Faculty: 118
Ph.Ds: 69%
Student/Faculty: 15 to 1
Tuition: $28,800
Freshman Class: 6519 applied, 4562 accepted, 615 enrolled

SAT CR/M/W: 530/540/520 ACT: 22
Application Deadline: open

CEEB CODE: 6282
COMPETITIVE

Houston Baptist University, founded in 1960, is a private institution affiliated with the Baptist General Convention of Texas and offering undergraduate programs in nursing, arts and science, music, and business administration. There are 8 undergraduate schools and 4 graduate schools. In addition to regional accreditation, HBU has baccalaureate program accreditation with ACBSP and NLN. The 100-acre campus is in an urban area in southwest Houston. Including any residence halls, there are 29 buildings.

STUDENT LIFE: 95% of undergraduates are from Texas. Others are from 32 states, 27 foreign countries, and Canada. 28% are White; 24% African American; 23% Hispanic; 11% Asian American. 49% are Protestant; 31% claim no religious affiliation; 11% Catholic. The average age of freshmen is 19; all undergraduates, 21. 30% do not continue beyond their first year; 70% remain to graduate. **Housing:** 568 students can be accommodated in college housing, which includes single-sex dorms and on-campus apartments. On-campus housing is available on a first-come, first-served basis, and is available on a lottery system for upperclassmen. Priority is given to out-of-town students. 61% of students commute. Alcohol is not permitted. All students may keep cars.

FACULTY/CLASSROOMS: 45% of faculty are male; 55% are female. 94% teach undergraduates. No introductory courses are taught by graduate students. The average class size in a laboratory is 14 and in a regular course is 10.

PROGRAMS OF STUDY: HBU confers B.A., B.S., B.B.A., B.M. and B.S.N. degrees. Master's degrees are also awarded. Bachelor's degrees are awarded in BIOLOGICAL SCIENCE (biology/biological science and molecular biology), BUSINESS (accounting, banking and finance, business administration and management, and entrepreneurial studies), COMMUNICATIONS AND THE ARTS (art, communications, English, French, music, music performance, music theory and composition, and Spanish), COMPUTER AND PHYSICAL SCIENCE (chemistry, information sciences and systems, mathematics, and physics), EDUCATION (art education, early childhood education, elementary education, mathematics education, music education, physical education, reading education, secondary education, special education, and teaching English as a second/foreign language (TESOL/TEFOL)), HEALTH PROFESSIONS (nursing), SOCIAL SCIENCE (biblical languages, Christian studies, economics, history, liberal arts/general studies, physical fitness/movement, political science/government, psychology, religious music, and sociology). Premedical studies, health professions, nursing and education are the strongest academically. Biology, nursing, and business administration have the largest enrollments.

ACTIVITIES: 3% of men belong to 1 local and 1 national fraternities; 5% of women belong to 3 national sororities. There are 51 groups on campus, including art, band, cheerleading, choir, chorale, chorus, computers, debate, drama, ethnic, forensics, honors, international, jazz band, newspaper, opera, pep band, photography, political, professional, radio and TV, religious, social service, student government, and symphony. Popular campus events include Welcome Days for New Students, Husky Fest Fall Festival, and Winter Formal. **Sports:**

There are 6 intercollegiate sports for men and 7 for women, and 12 intramural sports for men and 12 for women. Facilities include volleyball, basketball, and tennis courts, an indoor track, softball, baseball, and soccer fields, and areas for track. **Graduates:** From July 1, 2013 to June 30, 2014, 365 bachelor's degrees were awarded. The most popular majors were nursing (21%), biology (10%), and psychology (8%). In an average class, 24% graduate in 4 years or less, 40% graduate in 5 years or less, and 44% graduate in 6 years or less. **SERVICES:** Counseling and information services are available, as is tutoring in most subjects. There is remedial math and writing. **Library/Resources:** The library contains 235,026 volumes, 98,065 microform items, 9,591 audio/video tapes/CDs/DVDs, and subscribes to 29,992 periodicals including electronic. Computerized library services include interlibrary loans, database searching, Internet access, and Wi-Fi capability. Special learning facilities include an art gallery, radio station, TV station, a Museum of American Architecture and Decorative Arts, Dunham Family Bible in America Museum, Museum of Southern History, and Morris Cultural Arts Center. **Physically Challenged Students:** 90% of the campus is accessible. Facilities include wheelchair ramps, elevators, special parking, specially equipped restrooms, lowered drinking fountains, lowered telephones, and special housing. **Special:** HBU offers internships through its academic colleges, B.A.-B.S. degrees, and dual majors in most areas, work-study programs, credit for military experience, and pass/fail options. There is a freshman honors program. **Visiting:** There are guides for informal visits, visitors may sit in on classes, and stay overnight. To schedule a visit, contact the Office of Admissions at admissions@hbu.edu. **Campus Safety and Security:** Measures include 24-hour foot and vehicle patrol, emergency notification system, and security escort services. There are emergency telephones and lighted pathways/sidewalks.

REQUIREMENTS: The SAT or ACT is required. The ACT Optional Writing test is also required. In addition, with a recommended satisfactory score on the SAT or ACT composite score of 20. One counselor or teacher written recommendation, and an official high school transcript or GED scores are also required. AP and CLEP credits are accepted. Important factors in the admissions decision are recommendations by school officials, personality/intangible qualities, and advanced placement or honors courses. To graduate, students must complete a minimum of 130 semester hours, including at least 48 semester hours of upper-level courses and 24 to 36 hours in the major. They must complete courses in Christianity, written and oral communications, math, lab science, computer, kinetics, social and behavioral sciences, humanities, and fine arts. No grade below "C" within majors and program requirements and a cumulative GPA of 2.0 is required. Proficiency is required in reading, computer, communication, and math. Spiritual Life Program participation is also a graduation requirement. **Procedure:** Freshmen are admitted to all sessions. Entrance exams should be taken in the fall of the senior year. There are early decision and rolling admissions plans. Application deadlines are open. Application fee is $25. Applications are accepted on-line. **Transfer Students:** 334 transfer students enrolled in 2013-2014. Applicants with fewer than 30 semester hours earned must submit high school and college transcripts and SAT or ACT scores. All students must have a minimum 2.0 GPA and submit all previous college transcripts. 32 of 130 credits required for the bachelor's degree must be completed at HBU. **International Students:** There are 110 international students enrolled. They must take the TOEFL with a minimum score of 550 on the paper-based TOEFL (PBT) or 80 on the Internet-based version (iBT). Student must take the IELTS. **ADMISSIONS:** The SAT scores for the 2014-2015 freshman class were: Critical Reading--37% below 500, 38% between 500 and 599, 22% between 600 and 699, and 3% between 700 and 800; Math--35% below 500, 41% between 500 and 599, 22% between 600 and 699, and 2% between 700 and 800; Writing--39% below 500, 40% between 500 and 599, 17% between 600 and 699, and 4% between 700 and 800. The ACT scores were 40% below 21, 30% between 21 and 23, 16% between 24 and 26, 8% between 27 and 28, and 6% above 28. 38% of the current freshmen were in the top fifth of their class; 67% were in the top two fifths. **Admissions Contact:** Eduardo Borges, Director of Admissions. E-Mail: *admissions@hbu.edu* Web: *www.hbu.edu*

FINANCIAL AID: In 2014-2015, 90% of all full-time freshmen and 79% of continuing full-time students received some form of financial aid. 27% of all full-time freshmen and 27% of continuing full-time students received need-based aid. The average freshman award was $14,957. Need-based scholarships or need-based grants averaged $9,941 ($22,941 maximum); need-based self-help aid (loans and jobs) averaged $5,352 ($9,000 maximum); non-need-based athletic scholarships averaged $13,994 ($25,671 maximum); and other non-need-based awards and non-need-based scholarships averaged $7,613 ($23,203 maximum). 100% of undergraduate students work part-time. Average annual earnings from campus work are $867. The average financial indebtedness of the 2014 graduate was $23,000. The FAFSA and the college's own financial statement are required. The priority date for freshman financial aid applications for fall entry is March 1. The deadline for filing freshman financial aid applications for fall entry is April 15.

HOWARD PAYNE UNIVERSITY   C-3
www.hputx.edu

Brownwood, TX 76801-2794	(325) 649-8020
	(800) 880-4478
Fax: n/av	Email: enroll@hputx.edu
Full-time: 515 men, 545 women	Faculty: n/av
Part-time: 165 men, 170 women	Ph.D.s: 49%
Graduate: n/av	Student/Faculty: n/av
Year: semesters, summer session	Tuition: $22,200
Room & Board: $6622	Freshman Class: n/av
SAT or ACT: required	CEEB CODE: 6278
Application Deadline: see profile	COMPETITIVE

Howard Payne University, founded in 1889, and affiliated with the Baptist General Convention of Texas, offers undergraduate programs in the arts and sciences, business administration, education, Christianity, music, and social sciences. The figures in the above capsule and in this profile are approximate. There are 6 undergraduate schools. In addition to regional accreditation, HPU has baccalaureate program accreditation with CSWE and NASM. The 29-acre campus is in a small town 120 miles southwest of Dallas/Fort Worth. Including any residence halls, there are 31 buildings.

STUDENT LIFE: 96% of undergraduates are from Texas. Others are from 18 states and 2 foreign countries. 93% are from public schools. 74% are white; 14% Hispanic. 85% are Protestant. The average age of freshmen is 18; all undergraduates, 22. 40% do not continue beyond their first year; 33% remain to graduate.

FACULTY/CLASSROOMS: 64% of faculty are male; 36% are female. All teach undergraduates. No introductory courses are taught by graduate students. The average class size in an introductory lecture is 22; in a laboratory, 20; and in a regular course, 18.

PROGRAMS OF STUDY: HPU confers B.A., B.S., B.A.A.S., B.B.A., and B.M. degrees. Associates degrees are also awarded. Bachelor's degrees are awarded in BIOLOGICAL SCIENCE (biology/biological science), BUSINESS (accounting and business administration and management), COMMUNICATIONS AND THE ARTS (art, communications, dramatic arts, English, multimedia, music, and Spanish), COMPUTER AND PHYSICAL SCIENCE (chemistry, computer science, and mathematics), EDUCATION (athletic training, elementary education, secondary education, and teaching English as a second/foreign language (TESOL/TEFOL)), ENGINEERING AND ENVIRONMENTAL DESIGN (occupational safety and health), HEALTH PROFESSIONS (exercise science), SOCIAL SCIENCE (Christian studies, history, liberal arts/general studies, political science/government, psychology, social work, and sociology). Biology, chemistry, and political science are the strongest academically. Business management, elementary education, and exercise and sports science have the largest enrollments.

ACTIVITIES: 14% of men belong to 5 local fraternities; 16% of women belong to 6 local sororities. There are 33 groups on campus, including art, band, cheerleading, choir, chorus, drama, drill team, ethnic, honors, jazz band, literary magazine, marching band, musical theater, newspaper, photography, professional, radio and TV, religious, social, social service, student government, and yearbook. Popular campus events include Christian concerts and college preview weekends.

SERVICES: Counseling and information services are available, as is tutoring in some subjects. There is remedial math, reading, and writing. A writing lab and computer lab are available for English, math, and computer science. **Library/Resources:** The library contains 118,825 volumes, 271,542 microform items, and subscribes to 30,598 periodicals including electronic. Computerized library services include interlibrary loans, database searching, Internet access, and Wi-Fi capability. Special learning facilities include a radio station, a children's literature center, audio production facility, TV production studio, and video editing facility. **Physically Challenged Students:** 90% of the campus is accessible. Facilities include wheelchair ramps, elevators, special parking, specially equipped restrooms, special class scheduling, and lowered drinking fountains. **Special:** Cross-registration is offered with several hospitals, and internships are available in many fields. HPU offers credit for experience for B.A.A.S. candidates only, study abroad in Israel and England, pass/fail options, and work-study programs. Special programs include the Douglas MacArthur Academy of Freedom, an interdisciplinary honors program in the social sciences; a chemistry honors program; and a provisional program for underprepared students. There are 4 national honor societies, a freshman honors program, and 1 departmental honors program. **Visiting:** There are regularly scheduled orientations for prospective students, including college preview weekends in the fall and spring. There are guides for informal visits, visitors may sit in on classes, and stay overnight. To schedule a visit, contact the Enrollment Services Office. **Campus Safety and Security:** There are emergency telephones, lighted pathways/sidewalks, In addition, there are 12-hour foot patrols, monthly dorm meetings, 2 security seminars for the entire campus, and 24-hour telephone availability with on-duty officers carrying cell phones.

REQUIREMENTS: The SAT or ACT is required. Applicants must be graduates of an accredited secondary school or have a GED. It is recommended that they have completed 4 credits of English, 3 of math including algebra I, 2 1/2 of social studies, 2 of science, 1 1/2 of phys ed, and 1 each of technology applications and a science/social studies elective, along with courses in economics, health, and speech; the remaining credits should be earned in courses approved by the Texas Board of Education. Graduates of high schools or home study programs that are not accredited by a regional or state accrediting agency will have their work reviewed by the admissions committee on an individual basis. A GPA of 3.0 is required. AP and CLEP credits are accepted. Important factors in the admissions decision are recommendations by school officials, leadership record, and personality/intangible qualities.

FINANCIAL AID: The FAFSA is required. Check with the school for current application deadlines.

HUSTON-TILLOTSON UNIVERSITY   D-3
www.htu.edu

Austin, TX 78702	(512) 505-3000
	(512) 505-3028
Fax: (512) 505-3190	Email: admission@htu.edu
Full-time: 400 men, 420 women	Faculty: 40
Part-time: 15 men, 25 women	Ph.D.s: 75%
Graduate: 20 men, 25 women	Student/Faculty: 16 to 1
Year: semesters, summer session	Tuition: $24,860
Room & Board: $6946	Freshman Class: n/av
SAT or ACT: required	CEEB CODE: 6280
Application Deadline: see profile	COMPETITIVE+

Huston-Tillotson University, founded in 1952, is a private liberal arts institution affiliated with the United Church of Christ and the United Methodist Church. The figures in the above capsule and in this profile are approximate. There are 2 undergraduate schools. The 23-acre campus is in an urban area downtown Austin. Including any residence halls, there are 12 buildings.

STUDENT LIFE: 91% of undergraduates are from Texas. Others are from 24 states, and 10 foreign countries. 85% are from public schools. 76% are African American; 13% Hispanic. 64% are Protestant. The average age of freshmen is 19; all undergraduates, 23. 45% do not continue beyond their first year; 29% remain to graduate.

FACULTY/CLASSROOMS: 50% of faculty are male; 50% are female. All teach undergraduates, and 4% do research. No introductory courses are taught by graduate students. The average class size in an introductory lecture, 16, in a laboratory, 16, and in a regular course, 20.

PROGRAMS OF STUDY: HT confers B.A. and B.S. degrees. Bachelor's degrees are awarded in BIOLOGICAL SCIENCE (biology/biological science), BUSINESS (business administration and management and marketing/retailing/merchandising), COMMUNICATIONS AND THE ARTS (English and music), COMPUTER AND PHYSICAL SCIENCE (chemistry, computer science, and mathematics), EDUCATION (education, elementary education, and physical education), SOCIAL SCIENCE (criminal justice, history, interdisciplinary studies, political science/government, psychology, and sociology). Biology, computer science, and education are the strongest academically. Business administration and criminal justice have the largest enrollments.

ACTIVITIES: 3% of men belong to 4 national fraternities; 8% of women belong to 4 local and 4 national sororities. There are 35 groups on campus, including band, cheerleading, choir, chorus, drill team, honors, international, jazz band, newspaper, professional, radio and TV, religious, social, social service, and student government. Popular campus events include Charter Day, Miss UNCF Contest, and the President's Masked Ball.

SERVICES: Counseling and information services are available, as is tutoring in every subject. There is remedial math, reading, and writing. **Library/Resources:** The library contains 93,034 volumes, 69,945 microform items, and 49,619 audio/video tapes/CDs/DVDs, and subscribes to 2,353 periodicals including electronic. Computerized library services include interlibrary loans, database searching, and Internet access. Special learning facilities include a radio station. **Physically Challenged Students:** 82% of the campus is accessible. Facilities include wheelchair ramps, elevators, special parking, and specially equipped restrooms. **Special:** The university offers co-op programs, internships, study abroad in 3 countries, work-study programs, and dual majors. A 3-2 engineering degree with Prairie View A&M University is also available. There are 4 national honor societies, a freshman honors program, and 2 departmental honors programs. **Visiting:** There are guides for informal visits, visitors may sit in on classes, and stay overnight. To schedule a visit, contact the Director of Admission. **Campus Safety and Security:** Measures include 24-hour foot and vehicle patrol and security escort services. There are lighted pathways/sidewalks.

REQUIREMENTS: The SAT or ACT is required. The ACT Optional Writing test is also required. Applicants must be graduates of any accredited high school with a minimum 2.0 GPA, with a satisfactory score on the SAT or 18 on the ACT, with specific academic credits, including 3 credits each in math, English, and science. AP and CLEP credits are accepted. Important factors in the admissions decision are advanced placement or honors courses, extracurricular activities record, and parents or siblings that attended your school.

FINANCIAL AID: The FAFSA and the college's own financial statement are required. Check with the school for current application deadlines.

JARVIS CHRISTIAN COLLEGE (*The complete profile is made available exclusively on our website, www.barronspac.com*)

LAMAR UNIVERSITY (*The complete profile is made available exclusively on our website, www.barronspac.com*)

LETOURNEAU UNIVERSITY   E-2
www.letu.edu

Longview, TX 75607	(800) 759-8811
	(903) 233-4300
Fax: (903) 233-4301	Email: admissions@letu.edu
Full-time: 918 men, 422 women	Faculty: n/av
Part-time: 285 men, 625 women	Ph.D.s: 71%
Graduate: 91 men, 326 women	Student/Faculty: 13 to 1
Year: semesters, summer session	Tuition: $26,910
Room & Board: $9300	Freshman Class: n/av
SAT CR/M/W: 576/591/555 ACT: 26	CEEB CODE: 6365
Application Deadline: n/av	VERY COMPETITIVE

LeTourneau University graduates are professionals of ingenuity and Christ-like character who see life's work as a holy calling with eternal impact. From nationally acclaimed academics in fields like engineering and aeronautical science, to excellent programs in business, computer science, education, health care, the humanities, kinesiology, liberal arts, the natural sciences and psychology. LETU students have participated in ground-breaking research, including biomedical engineering in Africa, visual literacy in Kenya, micro-finance in Ethiopia, or macroeconomics in South America. Students co-author and present research at international conferences. Undergraduate and graduate programs for working adults are offered online and at educational centers in Longview, Dallas, and Houston. LETU's Paul and Betty Abbott Aviation Center at East Texas Regional Airport features a fleet of 12 airplanes, a 10,000-square foot hangar, classrooms and laboratories equipped with state-of-the-art technology for students majoring in flight science, aircraft systems and an FAA-approved program in air traffic control. Students regularly compete with large public and private schools and take top honors at regional and national competitions in many fields, especially electrical, mechanical and aeronautical design. Life on campus is biblically based, with chapel services, professor-led devotionals, student-led praise and worship and Bible study and prayer times. Students attend weekly chapel services in the state-of-the-art S.E. Belcher Jr. Chapel and Performance center that attracts world-class entertainment. There are 6 undergraduate schools and 1 graduate school. In addition to regional accreditation, LeTourneau has baccalaureate program accreditation with ABET, IACBE, FAA, and SBEC. The 162-acre campus is in a small town 60 miles west of Shreveport, Louisiana, and 120 miles east of the Dallas/Fort Worth metroplex. Including any residence halls, there are 56 buildings.

STUDENT LIFE: Students are from 49 states, 37 foreign countries, and Canada. 58% are White; 16% race unknown. 23% are non-denominational. The average age of freshmen is 18. **Housing:** College-sponsored housing includes single-sex dorms, on-campus apartments, and married student housing. In addition, there are special-interest houses. On-campus housing is guaranteed for all 4 years. Alcohol is not permitted. All students may keep cars.

FACULTY/CLASSROOMS: 65% of faculty are male; 35% are female. No introductory courses are taught by graduate students.

PROGRAMS OF STUDY: LeTourneau confers B.A., B.S. and B.B.A. degrees. Associate and Master's degrees are also awarded. Bachelor's degrees are awarded in BIOLOGICAL SCIENCE (biology/biological science), BUSINESS (accounting, business administration and management, management information systems, marketing management, and marketing/retailing/merchandising), COMMUNICATIONS AND THE ARTS (English), COMPUTER AND PHYSICAL SCIENCE (chemistry, computer mathematics, computer science, and mathematics), EDUCATION (business education, elementary education, physical education, science education, and secondary education), ENGINEERING AND ENVIRONMENTAL DESIGN (aeronautical science, aeronautical technology, computer engineering, computer technology, electrical/electronics engineering, engineering, engineering technology, industrial administration/management, mechanical engineering, and welding engineering), HEALTH PROFESSIONS (health, premedicine, and preveterinary science), SOCIAL SCIENCE (biblical studies, history, interdisciplinary studies, prelaw, psychology, and public administration).

ACTIVITIES: There are no fraternities or sororities. Groups on campus include chorale, drama, film, honors, international, jazz band, literary magazine, newspaper, religious, student government, and yearbook. **Sports:** There are 6 intercollegiate sports for men and 7 for women. **Graduates:** From July 1, 2013 to June 30, 2014, 570 bachelor's degrees were awarded. The most popular majors were business (33%), education (16%), and engineering (14%).

SERVICES: Counseling and information services are available, as is tutoring in most subjects. There is remedial math and writing. **Library/Resources:** The library contains 86,676 volumes, 310 microform items, and 263 audio/video tapes/CDs/DVDs. Computerized library services include interlibrary loans, database searching, Internet access, and Wi-Fi capability. **Physically Challenged Students:** Facilities include wheelchair ramps, elevators, special parking, specially equipped restrooms, special class scheduling, lowered drinking fountains, lowered telephones, special housing, and automated doors.

Special: Le Tourneau offers co-op programs in engineering, business, accounting, computer science, biology, design technology, and others, internships through business and liberal arts programs, an American studies program with the Council for Christian Colleges and Universities, credit for experience, and study abroad. There is a freshman honors program. **Visiting:** There are regularly scheduled orientations for prospective students, visits are individualized and may include touring the school, attending classes, special events, or chapel, meeting with faculty and financial aid personnel, and staying in a dorm. There are guides for informal visits, visitors may sit in on classes, and stay overnight. **Campus Safety and Security:** Measures include 24-hour foot and vehicle patrol, emergency notification system, self-defense education, and security escort services. There are lighted pathways/sidewalks and controlled access to dorms/residences.

REQUIREMENTS: AP and CLEP credits are accepted. All students must fulfill general curricula requirements, including 12 hours of biblical studies, 9 of English, 3 each of lab science, math, history, and humanities and social science, as well as 2 of kiniesology and 1 of introduction to the university. A minimum of 126 semester credit hours, including at least 24 in the major, with a minimum GPA of 2.0 is required to graduate. **Procedure:** Freshmen are admitted to all sessions. Entrance exams should be taken by the fall of the senior year. There are deferred admissions and rolling admissions plans. Applications are accepted on-line. **Transfer Students:** 149 transfer students enrolled in 2013-2014. **International Students:** The school actively recruits these students. They must take the TOEFL with a minimum score of 525 on the paper-based TOEFL (PBT) or 80 on the Internet-based version (iBT). They must also take the SAT or ACT.

ADMISSIONS: The SAT scores for the 2014-2015 freshman class were: Critical Reading--21% below 500, 35% between 500 and 599, 32% between 600 and 699, and 12% between 700 and 800; Math--13% below 500, 40% between 500 and 599, 35% between 600 and 699, and 12% between 700 and 800; Writing--25% below 500, 39% between 500 and 599, 30% between 600 and 699, and 6% between 700 and 800. **Admissions Contact:** Mike VanBrocklin, Director of Admissions. E-Mail: *admissions@letu.edu* Web: *www.letu.edu*

FINANCIAL AID: LeTourneau is a member of CSS. The FAFSA is required. Check with the school for current application deadlines.

LUBBOCK CHRISTIAN UNIVERSITY   B-2
www.lcu.edu

Lubbock, TX 79407

(806) 720-7151
(800) 933-7601

Fax: (806) 720-7162
Full-time: 482 men, 740 women
Part-time: 81 men, 136 women
Graduate: 105 men, 358 women
Year: semesters, summer session
Room & Board: $6908

Email: admissions@lcu.edu
Faculty: 88; IIB, --$
Ph.D.s: 71%
Student/Faculty: 12 to 1
Tuition: $19,400
Freshman Class: 828 applied, 781 accepted, 264 enrolled

SAT CR/M/W: 502/510/473 **ACT:** 22
Application Deadline: open

CEEB CODE: 6378
COMPETITIVE

Lubbock Christian University, founded in 1957 in affiliation with the Churches of Christ, offers undergraduate degrees in liberal arts and professional studies, and graduate degrees in Biblical studies and education, behavioral sciences and nursing. There are 3 undergraduate schools and 2 graduate schools. In addition to regional accreditation, LCU has baccalaureate program accreditation with CSWE and NLN. The 65-acre campus is in a suburban area 350 miles from Dallas and 325 miles from Albuquerque. Including any residence halls, there are 24 buildings.

STUDENT LIFE: 87% of undergraduates are from Texas. Others are from 39 states, 16 foreign countries, and Canada. 87% are from public schools. 68% are White; 21% Hispanic. 50% are Protestant; 11% Catholic. The average age of freshmen is 18; all undergraduates, 23. 28% do not continue beyond their first year; 43% remain to graduate. **Housing:** 589 students can be accommodated in college housing, which includes single-sex dorms, on-campus apartments, and married student housing. On-campus housing is guaranteed for the freshman year only, is available on a first-come, and first-served basis. 64% of students commute. Alcohol is not permitted. All students may keep cars.

FACULTY/CLASSROOMS: 57% of faculty are male; 43% are female. All teach undergraduates. No introductory courses are taught by graduate students. The average class size in an introductory lecture is 17; in a laboratory is 14; and in a regular course is 13.

PROGRAMS OF STUDY: LCU confers B.A., B.S., B.B.A., B.M., B.S.I.S., B.S.N. and B.S.W. degrees. Associate and Master's degrees are also awarded. Bachelor's degrees are awarded in AGRICULTURE (agriculture, animal science, and natural resource management), BIOLOGICAL SCIENCE (biochemistry and biology/biological science), BUSINESS (accounting, banking and finance, business administration and management, finance, marketing, organizational leadership and management, personal financial planning, and sports management), COMMUNICATIONS AND THE ARTS (communications, communications technology, creative writing, journalism, literature, music, music business management, and theatre arts), COMPUTER AND PHYSICAL SCIENCE (chemistry, digital arts/technology, information sciences and systems, and mathematics), EDUCATION (art education, athletic training, early childhood education, elementary education, middle school education, music education, physical education, school psychology, science education, secondary education, and spanish education K-12), ENGINEERING AND ENVIRONMENTAL DESIGN (engineering), HEALTH PROFESSIONS (exercise science, health promotion, medical technology, music therapy, nursing, premedicine, prepharmacy, prephysical therapy, and sports psychology), SOCIAL SCIENCE (biblical studies, criminal justice, economics, family/consumer studies, history, humanities, ministries, missions, physical fitness/movement, prelaw, psychology, social work, and youth ministry). Education, business administration, and social work are the strongest academically. Early childhood education, nursing, and secondary education have the largest enrollments.

ACTIVITIES: 21% of men belong to 4 local fraternities; 18% of women belong to 3 local sororities. There are 32 groups on campus, including art, band, cheerleading, chorus, drama, ethnic, honors, international, jazz band, musical theater, newspaper, pep band, professional, radio and TV, religious, social, social service, student government, symphony, and yearbook. Popular campus events include Master Follies, Family Weekend and Spiritual Renewal Week. **Sports:** There are 5 intercollegiate sports for men and 5 for women, and 7 intramural sports for men and 8 for women. Facilities include the Rip Griffin center, which serves as the home for the university's intercollegiate teams. The Rhodes Perrin Recreation center is the center for intramural and phys ed activities with an indoor track, a rock wall, basketball courts, volleyball, futsball, ping pong, and a fitness center. **Graduates:** From July 1, 2013 to June 30, 2014, 369 bachelor's degrees were awarded. The most popular majors were nursing (14%), early childhood education (8%), and secondary education (4%). In an average class, 4% graduate in 3 years or less, 28% graduate in 4 years or less, 39% graduate in 5 years or less, and 43% graduate in 6 years or less.

SERVICES: Counseling and information services are available, as is tutoring in every subject. There is a reader service for the blind, remedial math, reading, and writing. **Library/Resources:** The library contains 125,184 volumes, 172 audio/video tapes/CDs/DVDs, and subscribes to 404 periodicals including electronic. Computerized library services include interlibrary loans, database searching, Internet access, and Wi-Fi capability. Special learning facilities include an art gallery and radio station. **Physically Challenged Students:** Facilities include wheelchair ramps, elevators, special parking, specially equipped restrooms, special class scheduling, and lowered drinking fountains. **Special:** LCU offers co-op programs in engineering, medical technology, and criminal justice, internships in several fields, and cross-registration with Texas Tech University and other regional schools. A general studies degree, nondegree study, and pass/fail options are also available. A 3-2 engineering degree with Texas Tech University is offered. There are 3 national honor societies, a freshman honors program, and 1 departmental honors program. **Visiting:**

There are regularly scheduled orientations for prospective students. There are guides for informal visits, visitors may sit in on classes, and stay overnight. To schedule a visit, contact the LCU Admissions.

Campus Safety and Security: Measures include 24-hour foot and vehicle patrol, emergency notification system, and security escort services. There are lighted pathways/sidewalks and controlled access to dorms/residences.

REQUIREMENTS: The SAT or ACT is required. Applicants must be graduates of an accredited secondary school or have a GED certificate. Unconditional admission is granted to freshmen who score 18 or higher on the ACT or 860 or higher on the SAT and who meet all other admission requirements. AP and CLEP credits are accepted. Important factors in the admissions decision are personality/intangible qualities, parents or siblings attended your school, and geographical diversity. To graduate, students must complete 120 credit hours, including at least 39 in upper-division courses, 18 in the major, and 15 in residence after achieving senior status, with a minimum GPA of 2.25 overall and 2.5 in the major. All students must fulfill general education and biblical studies course requirements, including courses in English, math, history, science, communication, computer science, and exercise science. The core curriculum totals 45 hours. **Procedure:** Freshmen are admitted fall, spring, and summer. Entrance exams should be taken before registration. There are deferred admissions and rolling admissions plans. Application deadlines are open. Application fee is $25. Applications are accepted online. **Transfer Students:** 191 transfer students enrolled in 2013-2014. Transfer students with fewer than 16 hours of college credit must meet freshman admission requirements. All transfers must submit an official transcript from previously attended colleges or universities and be in good academic standing. Only courses with a grade of C or above are transferred from another institution. 30 of 126 credits required for the bachelor's degree must be completed at LCU. **International Students:** There are 29 international students enrolled. They must take the TOEFL with a minimum score of 525 on the paper-based TOEFL (PBT) or 71 on the Internet-based version (iBT) or take the MELAB. They must also take the SAT or ACT, scoring 18.

ADMISSIONS: 94% of the 2014-2015 applicants were accepted. The SAT scores for the 2014-2015 freshman class were: Critical Reading--47% below 500, 35% between 500 and 599, 16% between 600 and 699, and 2% between 700 and 800; Math--49% below 500, 29% between 500 and 599, 19% between 600 and 699, and 3% between 700 and 800; Writing--61% below 500, 31% between 500 and 599, and 8% between 600 and 699. The ACT scores were 41% below 21, 24% between 21 and 23, 21% between 24 and 26, 6% between 27 and 28, and 8% above 28. 30% of the current freshmen were in the top fifth of their class; 64% were in the top two fifths. 3 freshmen graduated first in their class. **Admissions Contact:** Mondy Brewer, Director of Admissions. E-Mail: *mondy.brewer@lcu.edu* Web: *www.lcu.edu*

FINANCIAL AID: In 2014-2015, 65% of all full-time freshmen and 63% of continuing full-time students received some form of financial aid. 65% of all full-time freshmen and 60% of continuing full-time students received need-based aid. The average freshman award was $14,336. Need-based scholarships or need-based grants averaged $10,014; need-based self-help aid (loans and jobs) averaged $5,281; non-need-based athletic scholarships averaged $10,070; and other non-need-based awards and non-need-based scholarships averaged $4,470. 100% of undergraduate students work part-time. Average annual earnings from campus work are $967. The average financial indebtedness of the 2014 graduate was $25,291. The FAFSA and the college's own financial statement are required. The priority date for freshman financial aid applications for fall entry is June 1.

MCMURRY UNIVERSITY (*The complete profile is made available exclusively on our website, www.barronspac.com*)

MIDWESTERN STATE UNIVERSITY D-2
www.mwsu.edu

Wichita Falls, TX 76308-2099	(940) 397-4000
	(800) 842-1922
Fax: (940) 397-4672	Email: admissions@mwsu.edu
Full-time: 1,885 men, 2,401 women	Faculty: 332
Part-time: 565 men, 860 women	Ph.D.s: 68%
Graduate: 234 men, 480 women	Student/Faculty: 19 to 1
Year: semesters, summer session	Tuition: $11,390
Room & Board: $6300	Freshman Class: n/av
SAT or ACT: required	CEEB CODE: 6408
Application Deadline: see profile	COMPETITIVE

Midwestern State University, founded in 1922, is a public liberal arts institution offering courses in business administration, education, fine arts, health sciences, humanities, math and science, political science and public administration, and social and behavioral sciences. The figures in the above capsule and in this profile are approximate. There are 6 undergraduate schools and 5 graduate schools. In addition to regional accreditation, MSU has baccalaureate program accreditation with ABET, ACBSP, ADA, NASM, NCATE, and NLN. The 172-acre campus is in an urban area 135 miles northwest of Dallas. Including any residence halls, there are 31 buildings.

STUDENT LIFE: 94% of undergraduates are from Texas. Others are from 50 states, 40 foreign countries, and Canada. 67% are white; 13% African American. The average age of freshmen is 18; all undergraduates, 25. 28% do not continue beyond their first year; 30% remain to graduate.

FACULTY/CLASSROOMS: 50% of faculty are male; 50% are female. All teach undergraduates. Graduate students teach 10% of introductory courses. The average class size in an introductory lecture is 25; in a laboratory, 20; and in a regular course, 25.

PROGRAMS OF STUDY: MSU confers B.A., B.S., B.A.A.S., B.B.A., B.F.A., B.M., B.S.C.J., B.S.D.H., B.S.I.S., B.S.M.T., B.S.N., B.S.R.C., B.S.R.S., and B.S.W. degrees. Associates and Master's degrees are also awarded. Bachelor's degrees are awarded in BIOLOGICAL SCIENCE (biology/biological science), BUSINESS (accounting, banking and finance, business administration and management, business economics, international economics, management science, and marketing/retailing/merchandising), COMMUNICATIONS AND THE ARTS (communications, dramatic arts, English, fine arts, music, and Spanish), COMPUTER AND PHYSICAL SCIENCE (chemical technology, chemistry, computer science, geology, information sciences and systems, and mathematics), EDUCATION (music education and physical education), ENGINEERING AND ENVIRONMENTAL DESIGN (engineering technology, environmental science, manufacturing engineering, and preengineering), HEALTH PROFESSIONS (dental hygiene, health care administration, health science, medical laboratory technology, nursing, predentistry, premedicine, prepharmacy, preveterinary science, radiological science, and respiratory therapy), SOCIAL SCIENCE (criminal justice, economics, history, humanities, interdisciplinary studies, political science/government, prelaw, psychology, social work, and sociology). Business and nursing have the largest enrollments.

ACTIVITIES: 13% of men belong to 6 national fraternities; 11% of women belong to 6 national sororities. There are 102 groups on campus, including art, band, cheerleading, choir, chorale, chorus, computers, dance, drama, environmental, ethnic, honors, international, jazz band, literary magazine, marching band, newspaper, pep band, political, professional, radio and TV, religious, social, social service, student government, and symphony. Popular campus events include Family Day, Spirit Days, and College Day Preview.

SERVICES: Counseling and information services are available, as is tutoring in some subjects, including algebra, sciences, and history. There is a reader service for the blind and remedial math, reading, and writing.

REQUIREMENTS: The SAT or ACT is required. The minimum required composite score on the SAT or ACT is dependent on class rank. For students in the top quarter of the class, there is no minimum requirement. High school credits should include 4 years of English, 3 years of math, 2 years of science, and 6 units of electives. The GED is accepted. AP and CLEP credits are accepted.

FINANCIAL AID: MSU is a member of CSS. The FAFSA and the college's own financial statement are required. Check with the school for current application deadlines.

NORTHWOOD UNIVERSITY (*The complete profile is made available exclusively on our website, www.barronspac.com*)

OUR LADY OF THE LAKE UNIVERSITY (*The complete profile is made available exclusively on our website, www.barronspac.com*)

PAUL QUINN COLLEGE (*The complete profile is made available exclusively on our website, www.barronspac.com*)

PRAIRIE VIEW A&M UNIVERSITY (*The complete profile is made available exclusively on our website, www.barronspac.com*)

RICE UNIVERSITY E-3
www.rice.edu

Houston, TX 77251-1892	(713) 348-7423
	(713) 348-0000
Fax: (713) 348-5323	Email: admission@rice.edu
Full-time: 1600 men, 1475 women	Faculty: 670; I, +$
Part-time: 25 men, 15 women	Ph.D.s: 96%
Graduate: 1430 men, 810 women	Student/Faculty: 6 to 1
Year: semesters, summer session	Tuition: $33,620
Room & Board: $12,250	Freshman Class: n/av
SAT or ACT: required	CEEB CODE: 6609
Application Deadline: see profile	MOST COMPETITIVE

Rice University, founded in 1912, is a comprehensive research university offering undergraduate and graduate programs through its schools of Engineering, Natural Sciences, Humanities, Social Sciences, Music, and Architecture; Rice's School of Business offers graduate degrees and an undergraduate minor. The figures in the above capsule and in this profile are approximate. There are 6 undergraduate schools and 7 graduate schools. In addition to regional accreditation, Rice has baccalaureate program accreditation with ABET and NAAB. The 300-acre campus is in an urban area 3 miles southwest of downtown Houston. Including any residence halls, there are 75 buildings.

STUDENT LIFE: 55% of undergraduates are from Texas. Others are from 50 states, 44 foreign countries, and Canada. 48% are white; 21% Asian American; 12% Hispanic. 33% are Protestant; 32% claim no religious affiliation; 18% Catholic. The average age of freshmen is 18; all undergraduates, 20. 3% do not continue beyond their first year; 93% remain to graduate.

FACULTY/CLASSROOMS: 69% of faculty are male; 31% are female. All teach undergraduates and do research. No introductory courses are taught by graduate students. The average class size in a regular course is 14.

PROGRAMS OF STUDY: Rice confers B.A., B.S., B.Arch., B.F.A., B.Mus., and B.S.E degrees. Master's and Doctoral degrees are also awarded. Bachelor's degrees are awarded in BIOLOGICAL SCIENCE (biology/biological science), BUSINESS (management science), COMMUNICATIONS AND THE ARTS (art history and appreciation, classics, English, linguistics, music, music history and appreciation, music performance, music theory and composition, and visual and performing arts), COMPUTER AND PHYSICAL SCIENCE (applied mathematics, chemistry, computer science, earth science, geology, geophysics and seismology, mathematics, physics, and statistics), ENGINEERING AND ENVIRONMENTAL DESIGN (architectural engineering, architecture, bioengineering, chemical engineering, civil engineering, electrical/electronics engineering, environmental engineering, and mechanical engineering), HEALTH PROFESSIONS (exercise science), SOCIAL SCIENCE (anthropology, Asian/Oriental studies, classical/ancient civilization, cognitive science, economics, French studies, German area studies, Hispanic American studies, history, medieval studies, philosophy, political science/government, psychology, public affairs, religion, sociology, and women's studies). Biochemistry and cell biology, mechanical engineering, and political science have the largest enrollments.

ACTIVITIES: There are 225 groups on campus, including academic, art, band, cheerleading, chess, choir, chorale, chorus, computers, dance, debate, drama, environmental, ethnic, film, forensics, gay, honors, international, jazz band, literary magazine, marching band, musical theater, newspaper, opera, orchestra, pep band, photography, political, professional, radio and TV, religious, social, social service, student government, symphony, and yearbook. Popular campus events include Baker Shakespeare Festival, Biking Relay Race, Archi Arts, and Costume Ball.

SERVICES: Counseling and information services are available, as is tutoring in every subject. **Library/Resources:** The library contains 2.6 million volumes, 3.3 million microform items, and 62,279 audio/video tapes/CDs/DVDs, and subscribes to 72,352 periodicals including electronic. Computerized library services include interlibrary loans, database searching, Internet access, and Wi-Fi capability. Special learning facilities include an art gallery, radio station, TV station, a media center, and an observatory. **Physically Challenged Students:** 90% of the campus is accessible. Facilities include wheelchair ramps, elevators, special parking, specially equipped restrooms, special class scheduling, lowered drinking fountains, lowered telephones, special housing, a stair lift. **Special:** An 8-year guaranteed medical school program with the Baylor College of Medicine; a 5-year joint degree program for the B.S.E./M.S.E. in engineering; a 5-year joint degree for the B.S.E./M.B.A. in engineering and business; and a 3-2 engineering degree are possible, as are cross-registration, internships, study abroad, work-study, dual majors, and student-designed majors. There are 10 national honor societies, including Phi Beta Kappa, and 9 departmental honors programs. **Visiting:** There are regularly scheduled orientations for prospective students, consisting of information sessions and tours available year-round. There are guides for informal visits, visitors may sit in on classes, and stay overnight. To schedule a visit, contact the Office of Admissions. **Campus Safety and Security:** Measures include 24-hour foot and vehicle patrol, emergency notification system, self-defense education, and security escort services. There are shuttle buses, emergency telephones, lighted pathways/sidewalks, controlled access to dorms/residences, a campus police department with a variety of outreach programs.

REQUIREMENTS: The SAT or ACT is required. The ACT Optional Writing test is also required. In addition, official high school transcripts, 1 counselor recommendation, and 1 teacher recommendation are required. To satisfy the testing requirement, students must submit either (a) the SAT plus 2 SAT subject tests or (b) the ACT with the Writing Test. Music students must arrange an audition. Architecture students must submit a portfolio. An interview is recommended but not required. Candidates should have completed 16 college preparatory units, including 4 years of English, 3 of math, and 2 each of social studies, foreign language, and lab science. AP credits are accepted.

FINANCIAL AID: In a recent year, all full-time students received some form of financial aid. 35% of all full-time freshmen and 37% of continuing full-time students received need-based aid. Need-based scholarships or need-based grants averaged $28,392; need-based self-help aid (loans and jobs) averaged $1624; non-need-based athletic scholarships averaged $16,276; and other non-need-based awards and non-need-based scholarships averaged $9589. Rice is a member of CSS. The CSS/Profile, the FAFSA, and parent and student tax returns are required. Check with the school for current application deadlines.

SAINT MARY'S UNIVERSITY   D-4
www.stmarytx.edu

San Antonio, TX 78228

(210) 436-3011
(800) 367-7868

Fax: (210) 431-6742

Email: uadm@stmarytx.edu

Full-time: 1000 men, 1284 women

Faculty: 162; IIA, +$

Part-time: 50 men, 57 women

Ph.D.s: 93%

Graduate: 777 men, 698 women

Student/Faculty: 12 to 1

Year: semesters, summer session

Tuition: $25,188

Room & Board: $8666

Freshman Class: 5147 applied, 2997 accepted, 596 enrolled

SAT CR/M/W: 510/530/490 **ACT:** 22

CEEB CODE: 6637

Application Deadline: open

COMPETITIVE

Saint Mary's University, established in 1852, is a private Roman Catholic institution in the Marianist tradition, offering undergraduate programs in humanities and social sciences, business and administration, science, engineering, and technology. There are 3 undergraduate schools and 2 graduate schools. In addition to regional accreditation, St. Mary's has baccalaureate program accreditation with AACSB and ABET. The 135-acre campus is in a suburban area 5 miles northwest of downtown San Antonio. Including any residence halls, there are 45 buildings.

STUDENT LIFE: 7% of undergraduates are from out of state, mostly the Southwest. Students are from 32 states, 36 foreign countries, and Canada. 68% are from public schools. 72% are Hispanic; 14% White. 41% are Catholic; 15% Baptist, Buddhist, Eastern Orthodox, Episcopal and Hindu. The average age of freshmen is 18; all undergraduates, 21. 27% do not continue beyond their first year; 64% remain to graduate.

FACULTY/CLASSROOMS: 63% of faculty are male; 37% are female. 75% teach undergraduates. No introductory courses are taught by graduate students. The average class size in an introductory lecture is 30; in a laboratory is 60; and in a regular course is 25.

PROGRAMS OF STUDY: St. Mary's confers B.A., B.S. and B.B.A. degrees. Master's and Doctoral degrees are also awarded. Bachelor's degrees are awarded in BIOLOGICAL SCIENCE (biochemistry and biology/biological science), BUSINESS (accounting, banking and finance, business administration and management, human resources, international business management, and marketing/retailing/merchandising), COMMUNICATIONS AND THE ARTS (communications, English, French, German, music, Spanish, and speech/debate/rhetoric), COMPUTER AND PHYSICAL SCIENCE (chemistry, computer science, earth science, mathematics, and physics), EDUCATION (business education, elementary education, science education, and secondary education), ENGINEERING AND ENVIRONMENTAL DESIGN (computer engineering, electrical/electronics engineering, engineering, environmental science, industrial engineering, and mechanical engineering), HEALTH PROFESSIONS (predentistry and premedicine), SOCIAL SCIENCE (criminal justice, economics, history, international relations, international studies, Latin American studies, philosophy, political science/government, prelaw, psychology, sociology, and theological studies). Biology, accounting, and political science are the strongest academically. Biology, business, and political science have the largest enrollments.

ACTIVITIES: 15% of men belong to 1 local and 4 national fraternities; 13% of women belong to 1 local and 3 national sororities. There are 55 groups on campus, including art, band, cheerleading, choir, chorale, dance, drama, ethnic, honors, international, jazz band, newspaper, pep band, photography, political, professional, religious, social, social service, and student government. Popular campus events include Campus Ministry Retreat, Hunger Awareness Week, Fiesta Oyster Bake, President's Peace Commision, and Lin Great Speaker.

SERVICES: Counseling and information services are available, as is tutoring in most subjects, Biology, chemistry, physics, psychology, languages, math, writing, accounting, statistics, English, and engineering There is remedial math, reading, and writing. Biochemistry, organic chemistry, programming, macro/micro economics, philosphy, electronics **Library/Resources:** The 2 libraries contain 222,220 volumes, 367,294 microform items, and 5,741 audio/video tapes/CDs/DVDs, and subscribe to 36,954 periodicals including electronic. Computerized library services include interlibrary loans, database searching, Internet access, and Wi-Fi capability. Special learning facilities include an art gallery, natural history museum, the learning assistance center is a learner-oriented service that provides academic support and instructional resources to the students, staff and faculty of St. Mary's University. **Physically Challenged Students:** 80% of the campus is accessible. Facilities include wheelchair ramps, elevators, special parking, specially equipped restrooms, special class scheduling, lowered drinking fountains, and special housing. **Special:** St. Mary's offers cooperative programs and internships in all majors, depending on the student's needs. Students may cross-register at any of the United Colleges of San Antonio, spend a semester in Washington, D.C., or study in England, Austria, or Mexico. Dual majors are possible in computer science and engineering and public justice and

sociology, political science, or psychology. Accelerated degree programs are offered in law, and dentistry. Required theology courses may be taken on a pass/fail basis. There are 10 national honor societies, a freshman honors program, and 3 departmental honors programs. **Visiting:** There are regularly scheduled orientations for prospective students, consisting of a campus tour, admissions/financial aid session, overnight stay, student only activities, parent only activities, and placement testing. There are guides for informal visits, visitors may sit in on classes, and stay overnight. To schedule a visit, contact Undergraduate Admissions Office at (800) 367-7868.
Campus Safety and Security: Measures include 24-hour foot and vehicle patrol, emergency notification system, self-defense education, and security escort services. There are emergency telephones, lighted pathways/sidewalks, controlled access to dorms/residences, a crime prevention awareness program each semester.
REQUIREMENTS: The SAT or ACT is required. All applicants must be high school graduates or have the GED, rank in the upper half of their graduating classes, and score in the 50th percentile on SAT I or ACT. Secondary school preparation should include 4 units of English, 3 each of math and academic electives, and 3 each of social science, natural science, and foreign language. Potential science and engineering majors should have 4 units of math and 3 of lab science, including chemistry or physics. AP and CLEP credits are accepted. Important factors in the admissions decision are leadership record, advanced placement or honors courses, and personality/intangible qualities.
ADMISSIONS: 58% of a recent year applicants were accepted. The SAT scores for the recent year freshman class were: Critical Reading--43% below 500, 42% between 500 and 599, 12% between 600 and 699, and 2% between 700 and 800; Math--31% below 500, 51% between 500 and 599, 17% between 600 and 699, and 1% between 700 and 800; Writing--52% below 500, 38% between 500 and 599, 9% between 600 and 699, and 1% between 700 and 800. The ACT scores were 25% below 21, 42% between 21 and 23, 21% between 24 and 26, 6% between 27 and 28, and 6% above 28. 3 freshmen graduated first in their class.
FINANCIAL AID: St. Mary's is a member of CSS. The CSS/Profile is required. The deadline for filing freshman financial aid applications for fall entry is April 1.

SAM HOUSTON STATE UNIVERSITY D-3
www.shsu.edu

Huntsville, TX 77341	**(936) 294-1111**
	(936) 294-1828
Fax: (936) 294-3758	Email: admissions@shsu.edu
Full-time: 5429 men, 7010 women	Faculty: 582; IIA, -$
Part-time: 1041 men, 1515 women	Ph.D.s: 95%
Graduate: 911 men, 1711 women	Student/Faculty: 20 to 1
Year: semesters, summer session	Tuition: $9938 ($19,083)
Room & Board: $8144	Freshman Class: 7070 applied, 5473 accepted, 2069 enrolled
SAT or ACT: required	CEEB CODE: 6643
Application Deadline: open	COMPETITIVE

Sam Houston University, founded in 1879, is a public institution offering programs in fine arts and mass communication, applied sciences, business administration, criminal justice, education, and humanities and social sciences. There are 6 undergraduate schools and 6 graduate schools. In addition to regional accreditation, Sam Houston State has baccalaureate program accreditation with AACSB, ABET, ADA, NASM, and NCATE. The 1256-acre campus is in a small town 70 miles north of Houston. Including any residence halls, there are 228 buildings.
STUDENT LIFE: 98% of undergraduates are from Texas. Others are from 48 states, 59 foreign countries, and Canada. 71% are white; 14% African American; 12% Hispanic. The average age of freshmen is 18; all undergraduates, 22. 31% do not continue beyond their first year; 40% remain to graduate.
FACULTY/CLASSROOMS: 53% of faculty are male; 47% are female. All teach and do research. Graduate students teach 5% of introductory courses.

PROGRAMS OF STUDY: Sam Houston State confers B.A., B.S., B.A.A.S., B.B.A., B.F.A., and B.M. degrees. Master's and Doctoral degrees are also awarded. Bachelor's degrees are awarded in AGRICULTURE (agriculture, animal science, and horticulture), BIOLOGICAL SCIENCE (biology/biological science), BUSINESS (accounting, banking and finance, business administration and management, and marketing/retailing/merchandising), COMMUNICATIONS AND THE ARTS (art, dance, dramatic arts, English, French, German, graphic design, journalism, music, music performance, music theory and composition, musical theater, photography, Spanish, and speech/debate/rhetoric), COMPUTER AND PHYSICAL SCIENCE (chemistry, computer science, geology, mathematics, and physics), EDUCATION (physical education), ENGINEERING AND ENVIRONMENTAL DESIGN (environmental science), HEALTH PROFESSIONS (health, medical technology, and music therapy), SOCIAL SCIENCE (criminal justice, economics, geography, history, law enforcement and corrections, philosophy, physical fitness/movement, political science/government, psychology, and sociology). Criminal justice, general business, and psychology have the largest enrollments.
ACTIVITIES: 9% of men belong to 15 local fraternities; 5% of women belong to 13 local sororities. There are 235 groups on campus, including art, band, cheerleading, choir, chorale, chorus, computers, dance, drama, drill team, environmental, ethnic, film, forensics, gay, honors, international, jazz band, marching band, musical theater, newspaper, orchestra, pep band, photography, political, professional, radio and TV, religious, social, social service, student government, and symphony. Popular campus events include Organization Fair, Greek Week, and Welcome Week.
SERVICES: Counseling and information services are available, as is tutoring in every subject. There is a reader service for the blind, and remedial math, reading, and writing. **Library/Resources:** The library contains 1.3 million volumes, and 3,744 audio/video tapes/CDs/DVDs, and subscribes to 7,175 periodicals including electronic. Computerized library services include interlibrary loans, database searching, Internet access, and Wi-Fi capability. Special learning facilities include a planetarium, radio station, TV station, the Sam Houston Museum. **Physically Challenged Students:** 90% of the campus is accessible. Facilities include wheelchair ramps, elevators, special parking, specially equipped restrooms, lowered drinking fountains, closed-circuit television (CCTV), computer workstations with large print and speech output capabilities, and telecommunication devices for the disabled. **Special:** Work-study programs with the university, study abroad in 6 countries, second degrees, and B.A.-B.S. degrees are available. There are 10 national honor societies and a freshman honors program. **Visiting:** There are regularly scheduled orientations for prospective students, including a tour of the campus, dorms, and departments. There are guides for informal visits. To schedule a visit, contact the Visitor Center at visitsam@shsu.edu. **Campus Safety and Security:** Measures include 24-hour foot and vehicle patrol, emergency notification system, and security escort services. There are emergency telephones and lighted pathways/sidewalks.
REQUIREMENTS: The SAT or ACT is required. Applicants must have secondary school credits as follows: 4 of English, 2 each of math, history, and science, 1 1/2 of phys ed, and a half credit each of social studies and health education. The GED is accepted. A GPA of 2.0 is required. AP and CLEP credits are accepted.
ADMISSIONS: 77% of a recent year, applicants were accepted. 32% of the current freshmen were in the top fifth of their class; 67% were in the top two fifths. 10 freshmen graduated first in their class.
FINANCIAL AID: In a recent year, 61% of continuing full-time students received some form of financial aid. 45% of continuing full-time students received need-based aid. 5% of undergraduate students work part-time. The average financial indebtedness of a recent graduate was $19,188. The FAFSA is required. The priority date for freshman financial aid applications for fall entry is March 31. The deadline for filing freshman financial aid applications for fall entry is May 31.

SCHREINER UNIVERSITY (*The complete profile is made available exclusively on our website, www.barronspac.com*)

SOUTHERN METHODIST UNIVERSITY   D-2
www.smu.edu

Dallas, TX 75275	**(214) 768-2000**
	(800) 323-0672
Fax: (214) 768-0103	Email: ugadmission@smu.edu
Full-time: 3057 men, 3136 women	Faculty: I, +$
Part-time: 107 men, 91 women	Ph.D.s: 84%
Graduate: 2703 men, 2178 women	Student/Faculty: n/av
Year: semesters, summer session	Tuition: $45,940
Room & Board: $14,645	Freshman Class: n/av
	CEEB CODE: 6660
Application Deadline: January 15	**MOST COMPETITIVE**

Southern Methodist University, founded in 1911, is a private nonsectarian institution affiliated with the United Methodist Church. SMU offers undergraduate and graduate programs in humanities and sciences, business, arts, education, engineering and applied sciences. Figures in the above capsule and in this profile are approximate. There are 5 undergraduate schools and 7 graduate schools. In addition to regional accreditation, SMU has baccalaureate program accreditation with AACSB, ABET, NASAD, NASM, ACS, NASD, and NAST. The 234-acre campus is in an urban area 5 miles north of downtown Dallas. Including any residence halls, there are 101 buildings.

STUDENT LIFE: 51% of undergraduates are from out of state, mostly the South. Students are from 49 states, 101 foreign countries, and Canada. 59% are from public schools. 62% are White; 11% Foreign. 18% are Protestant; 15% Catholic. The average age of freshmen is 18; all undergraduates, 20. 11% do not continue beyond their first year; 77% remain to graduate. **Housing:** 2000 students can be accommodated in college housing, which includes coed dorms, on-campus apartments, and married student housing. In addition, there are honors houses, special-interest houses, fraternity houses, sorority houses, living-learning communities with some classes taught in residence hall classrooms. On-campus housing is available on a first-come and first-served basis. 53% of students live on campus; of those, 85% remain on campus on weekends. Alcohol is not permitted. All students may keep cars.

FACULTY/CLASSROOMS: 60% of faculty are male; 40% are female. No introductory courses are taught by graduate students.

PROGRAMS OF STUDY: SMU confers B.A., B.S., B.B.A., B.F.A., B.M., B.S.C.P.E., B.S.C.E., B.S.E.E., B.S.Env.E. and B.S.M.E. degrees. Master's and Doctoral degrees are also awarded. Bachelor's degrees are awarded in AGRICULTURE (environmental studies), BIOLOGICAL SCIENCE (biochemistry and biology/biological science), BUSINESS (accounting, business administration and management, economics – statistics, finance, finance (financial planning), insurance and risk management, management science, marketing/retailing/merchandising, real estate, and real estate finance), COMMUNICATIONS AND THE ARTS (advertising, art history and appreciation, broadcasting, communications, creative writing, dance, dramatic arts, English, film arts, fine/studio arts, general, French, German, journalism, languages, media arts, music performance, music theory and composition, performing arts, piano/organ, public relations, Spanish, sports administration, and studio art), COMPUTER AND PHYSICAL SCIENCE (chemistry, computer science, environmental geology, geology, geophysics and seismology, mathematics, physics, and statistics), EDUCATION (health education and music education), ENGINEERING AND ENVIRONMENTAL DESIGN (civil engineering, computer engineering, electrical/electronics engineering, environmental engineering, environmental science, and mechanical engineering), HEALTH PROFESSIONS (music therapy), SOCIAL SCIENCE (African American studies, anthropology, economics, history, humanities, Iberian studies, international relations, international studies, Italian studies, Latin American studies, liberal arts/general studies, medieval studies, Mexican-American/Chicano studies, philosophy, physical fitness/movement, political science/government, psychology, public affairs, religion, and sociology). Economics, finance, accounting, psychology and advertising have the largest enrollments.

ACTIVITIES: 32% of men belong to 15 national fraternities; 48% of women belong to 14 national sororities. There are 180 groups on campus, including art, band, cheerleading, choir, chorale, chorus, computers, dance, drama, drill team, ethnic, forensics, gay, honors, international, jazz band, literary magazine, marching band, musical theater, opera, orchestra, pep band, photography, political, professional, religious, social, social service, student government, and symphony. Popular campus events include Celebration of Lights and Community Service Day. **Sports:** There are 6 intercollegiate sports for men and 11 for women, and 20 intramural sports for men and 20 for women. Facilities include gymnastic and weight rooms, a dance studio, indoor and outdoor jogging tracks, indoor and outdoor pools, 2400-seat outdoor stadium, 6500-seat indoor stadium, and courts for basketball, volleyball, tennis, badminton, and racquetball. **Graduates:** From July 1, 2013 to June 30, 2014, 1712 bachelor's degrees were awarded. The most popular majors were economics (9%), finance (8%), and accounting (6%). In an average class, 2% graduate in 3 years or less, 67% graduate in 4 years or less, 76% graduate in 5 years or less, and 77% graduate in 6 years or less.

SERVICES: Counseling and information services are available, as is tutoring in most subjects. There is a reader service for the blind, remedial reading and writing. The Learning Enhancement Center provides study skills workshops, note-taking techniques, and time management skills seminars. **Library/Resources:** The 8 libraries contain 3.1 million volumes, 2.0 million microform items, 58,145 audio/video tapes/CDs/DVDs, and subscribe to 29,852 periodicals including electronic. Computerized library services include interlibrary loans, database searching, Internet access, and Wi-Fi capability. Special learning facilities include an art gallery, natural history museum, TV station, Meadows Museum houses one of the finest Spanish art collections outside Spain; SMU's engineering school is the nation's first to host a Lockheed Martin Skunk Works Lab modeled after the California research facility; performance facilities include theatres with classical thrust stage, proscenium stage and black box area; journalism complex includes digital newsroom and TV studio. **Physically Challenged Students:** 95% of the campus is accessible. Facilities include wheelchair ramps, elevators, special parking, specially equipped restrooms, special class scheduling, lowered drinking fountains, and lowered telephones. Automatic doors. **Special:** SMU offers a co-op program in engineering, work-study programs, B.A.-B.S. degrees, study abroad in 50 countries with 150 programs, dual majors in any combination, student-designed majors, numerous internships, and interdisciplinary majors, including economics with finance applications and economics with systems analysis. A 3-2 advanced degree in business is available, as are evening degree programs in humanities and social sciences, and teacher certification programs. There are 30 national honor societies, including Phi Beta Kappa, and a freshman honors program. **Visiting:** There are regularly scheduled orientations for prospective students, including information about academic studies, financial aid sessions, discussions with current students, lunch with faculty and students, and a tour of the campus. There is also a Spring Fest visitation in March for high school sophomores and juniors. There are guides for informal visits, visitors may sit in on classes, and stay overnight. To schedule a visit, contact the Undergraduate Admissions Office. **Campus Safety and Security:** Measures include 24-hour foot and vehicle patrol, emergency notification system, self-defense education, and security escort services. There are shuttle buses, emergency telephones, lighted pathways/sidewalks, controlled access to dorms/residences. Card-key devices are issued to all students living in residence halls, must be used to enter these buildings.

REQUIREMENTS: The SAT or ACT is recommended. Applicants should graduate from an accredited high school with a minimum of 15 academic credits: 4 in English, 3 in higher math, including algebra I, II, and plane geometry, 3 each in natural science and social science, and 2 in a foreign language. Home School Certificate applicants may qualify with the SAT or ACT and 3 SAT Subject Tests in math, literature, and science. Performing arts majors must audition. AP and CLEP credits are accepted. Important factors in the admissions decision are advanced placement or honors courses, leadership record, and recommendations by school officials. Basic requirements consist of 122 semester hours, including the major requirements for one of SMU's over 100 majors, as well as the University Curriculum (UC), which consists of three, main course-based components: Foundations, Pillars and Capstone. The Foundations emphasize reading and writing, quantitative reasoning, applied critical thinking, and wellness. The five UC Pillars cover the natural sciences, the arts and humanities, and the social and behavioral sciences. The Capstone completes each student's general education. In addition to the three core components, there are eight proficiencies and experiences that can be satisfied through coursework or out-of-class activities. For more detailed information about the SMU University Curriculum. **Procedure:** Freshmen are admitted to all sessions. Entrance exams should be taken by December of the senior year. There are early decision, deferred admissions, and rolling admissions plans. Early decision applications should be filed by November 1; regular applications, by January 15 for fall entry, along with a $60 fee. Notification of early decision is sent April 1; regular decision, on a rolling basis. 209 early decision candidates were accepted for the 2014-2015 class. 476 applicants were on the 2014 waiting list; 98 were admitted. Applications are accepted on-line. **Transfer Students:** 337 transfer students enrolled in 2013-2014. A minimum 2.5 GPA is generally required for transfer, but specific requirements vary according to the program of study. Candidates must demonstrate math proficiency. A foreign language requirement may be met through high school or college work. 60 of 122 credits required for the bachelor's degree must be completed at SMU. **International Students:** There are 453 international students enrolled. The school actively recruits these students. They must take the TOEFL with a minimum score of 550 on the paper-based TOEFL (PBT) or 80 on the Internet-based version (iBT), or the IELTS, with a minimum score of 6.5. SAT or ACT are not required for non-US citizens attending high school outside of the US, but are required for US citizens.

ADMISSIONS: 52% of the 2014-2015 applicants were accepted. 70% of the current freshmen were in the top fifth of their class; 91% were in the top two fifths. **Admissions Contact:** Wes Waggoner, Dean, Undergraduate Admission. E-Mail: *enrol_serv@mail.smu.edu* Web: *www.smu.edu/admissions*

FINANCIAL AID: In 2014-2015, 75% of all full-time freshmen and continuing full-time students received some form of financial aid. 70% of all full-time freshmen and continuing full-time students received need-based aid. The average freshman award was $38,600. Need-based scholarships or need-based grants averaged $19,444; need-based self-help aid (loans and jobs) averaged $6,054; non-need-based athletic scholarships averaged $47,655; and other non-need-based awards and non-need-based scholarships averaged $19,568. The average financial indebtedness of the 2014 graduate was $34,671. SMU is a member of CSS. The CSS/Profile and FAFSA are required. The priority date for freshman financial aid applications for fall entry is February 15.

SOUTHWESTERN ADVENTIST UNIVERSITY (*The complete profile is made available exclusively on our website, www.barronspac.com*)

SOUTHWESTERN UNIVERSITY	D-3
www.southwestern.edu	
Georgetown, TX 78626	**(512) 863-6511**
	(800) 252-3166
Fax: (512) 863-9601	Email: admission@southwestern.edu
Full-time: 652 men, 867 women	Faculty: 116; IIB, av$
Part-time: 3 men, 13 women	Ph.D.s: 100%
Graduate: none	Student/Faculty: 13 to 1
Year: semesters, summer session	Tuition: n/av
Room & Board: $10,420	Freshman Class: 3546 applied, 1850 accepted, 491 enrolled
SAT CR/M: 590/580 ACT: 26	CEEB CODE: 6674
Application Deadline: February 1	**VERY COMPETITIVE**

Southwestern University, founded in 1840, is a private, national liberal arts institution affiliated with the United Methodist Church. There are 2 undergraduate schools. In addition to regional accreditation, Southwestern has baccalaureate program accreditation with NASM, SACS, University Senate of United Methodist Church, and Texas Education Agency. The 700-acre campus is in a suburban area 28 miles north of Austin. Including any residence halls, there are 36 buildings.

STUDENT LIFE: 88% of undergraduates are from Texas. Others are from 36 states, and 9 foreign countries. 81% are from public schools. 67% are White; 19% Hispanic. 68% are Protestant; 25% Catholic. The average age of freshmen is 18; all undergraduates, 20. 13% do not continue beyond their first year; 75% remain to graduate. **Housing:** 1108 students can be accommodated in college housing, which includes single-sex and coed dorms and on-campus apartments. In addition, there are fraternity houses. On-campus housing is available on a first-come, first-served basis, and is available on a lottery system for upperclassmen. 77% of students live on campus; of those, 80% remain on campus on weekends. All students may keep cars.

FACULTY/CLASSROOMS: 50% of faculty are male; 50% are female. All teach undergraduates, and 68% do both. No introductory courses are taught by graduate students. The average class size in an introductory lecture is 19; in a laboratory is 18; and in a regular course is 13.

PROGRAMS OF STUDY: Southwestern confers B.A., B.S., B.F.A., B.Ed., and B.Mus. degrees. Bachelor's degrees are awarded in AGRICULTURE (animal science and environmental studies), BIOLOGICAL SCIENCE (biochemistry and biology/biological science), BUSINESS (accounting and business administration and management), COMMUNICATIONS AND THE ARTS (art history, art, classics, communications, dramatic arts, English, French, German, Greek, Latin, music, and Spanish), COMPUTER AND PHYSICAL SCIENCE (applied science, chemistry, mathematics, mathematics/computational, and physics), EDUCATION (education), HEALTH PROFESSIONS (exercise science), SOCIAL SCIENCE (anthropology, economics, history, international studies, Latin American studies, philosophy, political science/government, psychology, religion, sociology, and women's studies). biology, business, and communication have the largest enrollments.

ACTIVITIES: 29% of men belong to 4 national fraternities; 20% of women belong to 4 national sororities. There are 99 groups on campus, including art, band, cheerleading, choir, chorale, chorus, computers, dance, debate, drama, environmental, ethnic, film, gay, honors, international, jazz band, literary magazine, musical theater, newspaper, opera, orchestra, pep band, political, professional, radio and TV, religious, social, social service, and student government. Popular campus events include Homecoming, Sing, ClusterFest Musical Festival and Brown Symposium. **Sports:** There are 10 intercollegiate sports for men and 10 for women, and 20 intramural sports for men and 20 for women. Facilities include a 2000-seat performance gym, a recreation gym, locker rooms, indoor jogging track, racquetball and handball courts, indoor swimming pool, a weight room and fitness area. Outdoor facilities: baseball, softball, soccer and lacrosse fields, tennis courts, and recreational fields. An athletic field house with locker room, weight room, athletic training center, offices and meeting rooms, football practice fields, outdoor track and field complex, sand volleyball and cove with food, billiards, and Friday night live. **Graduates:** From July 1, 2013 to June 30, 2014, 338 bachelor's degrees were awarded. The most popular majors were biology (10%), psychology (9%), and business (9%). 5 companies recruited on campus in 2013-2014. In an average class, 2% graduate in 3 years or less, 67% graduate in 4 years or less, 73% graduate in 5 years or less, and 75% graduate in 6 years or less.

SERVICES: Counseling and information services are available, as is tutoring in some subjects. There is a reader service for the blind, and remedial writing. **Library/Resources:** The library contains 391,040 volumes, 65,316 microform items, 21,371 audio/video tapes/CDs/DVDs, and subscribes to 1,578 periodicals including electronic. Computerized library services include interlibrary loans, database searching, Internet access, and Wi-Fi capability. Special learning facilities include an art gallery, radio station, observatory. **Physically Challenged Students:** 90% of the campus is accessible. Facilities include wheelchair ramps, elevators, special parking, specially equipped restrooms, special class scheduling, lowered drinking fountains, lowered telephones, and special housing. **Special:** Students may study abroad in a multitude of countries. The university offers a Fall London semester, Washington semester, dual, student-designed, and independent majors, and internships in government, fine arts, psychology, sociology, science, and other fields, including those in the New York Arts Program. A Physical Science major allows students to spend several years at Southwestern, then finish their SU degree with a year's qualifying engineering coursework at another university. There are 7 national honor societies, including Phi Beta Kappa, and 37 departmental honors programs. **Visiting:** There are regularly scheduled orientations for prospective students, including 3 or 4 group overnight options and individually arranged visits throughout the year. All visits typically include tours, faculty appointments and interview, and may also include an overnight on campus and class visit. There are guides for informal visits, visitors may sit in on classes, and stay overnight. To schedule a visit, contact the Admission Office.

Campus Safety and Security: Measures include 24-hour foot and vehicle patrol, emergency notification system, self-defense education, and security escort services. There are emergency telephones, lighted pathways/sidewalks, and controlled access to dorms/residences.

REQUIREMENTS: The SAT or ACT is required. Applicants should be graduates of an accredited high school or have the GED. Secondary preparation should include, at a minimum, 4 years each of English and math, 3 each of science and social science or history, 2 of a foreign language, and 1 of an academic elective. An essay, an SAT or ACT score and a counselor recommendation are required, and an interview is recommended. AP and CLEP credits are accepted. Important factors in the admissions decision are advanced placement or honors courses, recommendations by school officials, and leadership record. All degrees require a 2.0 or higher GPA in 127 or more credits. Each requires a First Year Seminar, 2 Fitness and Recreational Activity Credits, at least 1 course (3-4 credits) tagged for each of Social Justice, Intercultural Perspectives, Math or Computer Science, Fine Arts Performance, Fine Arts Lecture, and Natural Science with lab. Two tagged courses in both Humanities and Social Science are required, as is 4th semester proficiency in a foreign language. Major requirements vary, but require a minimum of 30 credits, including a capstone. **Procedure:** Freshmen are admitted fall. Entrance exams should be taken in the fall or early spring of the senior year. There are early admissions and deferred admissions plans. Applications should be filed by February 1 for fall entry. Notifications are sent April 15. 7 applicants were on the 2014 waiting list; 0 were admitted. Applications are accepted on-line. **Transfer Students:** 65 transfer students enrolled in 2013-2014. Preference is given to students having a 3.0 in all college work. 64 of 127 credits required for the bachelor's degree must be completed at Southwestern. **International Students:** There are 22 international students enrolled. The school actively recruits these students. They must take the TOEFL with a minimum score of 570 on the paper-based TOEFL (PBT) or 88 on the Internet-based version (iBT). Student must take the IELTS. They must also take the SAT or ACT.

ADMISSIONS: 52% of the 2014-2015 applicants were accepted. The SAT scores for the 2014-2015 freshman class were: Critical Reading--16% below 500, 39% between 500 and 599, 35% between 600 and 699, and 10% between 700 and 800; Math--7% below 500, 44% between 500 and 599, 37% between 600 and 699, and 9% between 700 and 800. The ACT scores were 9% below 21, 20% between 21 and 23, 28% between 24 and 26, 16% between 27 and 28, and 26% above 28. 65% of the current freshmen were in the top fifth of their class; 90% were in the top two fifths. There were 2 National Merit finalists. 11 freshmen graduated first in their class. **Admissions Contact:** Christine Bowman, Director of Admissions. E-Mail: *admission@ southwestern.edu* Web: *www.southwestern.edu/admission/*

FINANCIAL AID: In 2014-2015, 99% of all full-time freshmen and 95% of continuing full-time students received some form of financial aid. 68% of all full-time freshmen and 63% of continuing full-time students received need-based aid. The average freshman award was $30,216. Need-based scholarships or need-based grants averaged $25,793; need-based self-help aid (loans and jobs) averaged $4,863; and other non-need-based awards and non-need-based scholarships averaged $18,874. 53% of undergraduate students work part-time. Average annual earnings from campus work are $1301. The average financial indebtedness of the 2014 graduate was $34,997. Southwestern is a member of CSS. The FAFSA is required. The priority date for freshman financial aid applications for fall entry is March 1. The deadline for filing freshman financial aid applications for fall entry is March 1.

ST. EDWARD'S UNIVERSITY   D-3
www.stedwards.edu

Austin, TX 78704 (512) 448-8400 / (855) 468-6738

Fax: (512) 464-8877	Email: seu.admit@stedwards.edu
Full-time: 1346 men, 2090 women	Faculty: IIA, av$
Part-time: 214 men, 353 women	Ph.D.s: 89%
Graduate: 248 men, 435 women	Student/Faculty: n/av
Year: semesters, summer session	Tuition: $36,550
Room & Board: $11,234	Freshman Class: n/av
SAT CR/M/W: 560/550/550 ACT: 24	CEEB CODE: 6619
Application Deadline: May 1	COMPETITIVE

St. Edward's University is an independent, Catholic, liberal arts university, founded by the Congregation of the Holy Cross in 1885. Students at St. Edward's are part of a small yet diverse community that provides a global perspective. Students learn to think critically and creatively, make ethical decisions, solve problems rationally and lead effectively. Through hands-on service projects and internships, students develop a deeper understanding of their role in the world and gain the confidence to excel and make a difference in the community. There are 6 undergraduate schools and 3 graduate schools. In addition to regional accreditation, SEU has baccalaureate program accreditation with CSWE. The 160-acre campus is in an urban area in Austin. Including any residence halls, there are 59 buildings.

STUDENT LIFE: 78% of undergraduates are from Texas. Others are from 45 states, 54 foreign countries, and Canada. 74% are from public schools. 40% are Hispanic; 37% White. 38% are Catholic; 37% 2% Muslim, 1% Buddhist, 6% Christian and Unknown. The average age of freshmen is 18; all undergraduates, 21. 17% do not continue beyond their first year; 67% remain to graduate. **Housing:** 1383 students can be accommodated in college housing, which includes coed dorms and on-campus apartments. Community style living (casas/casitas) and 10 living learning communities. On-campus housing is guaranteed for the freshman year only, is available on a first-come, first-served basis, and is available on a lottery system for upperclassmen. 61% of students commute. All students may keep cars.

FACULTY/CLASSROOMS: 51% of faculty are male; 49% are female. No introductory courses are taught by graduate students.

PROGRAMS OF STUDY: SEU confers B.A., B.S., B.B.A., B.F.A., B.A.A.S. and B.L.S. degrees. Master's degrees are also awarded. Bachelor's degrees are awarded in BIOLOGICAL SCIENCE (biochemistry, bioinformatics, and biology/biological science), BUSINESS (accounting, banking and finance, business administration and management, entrepreneurial studies, international business management, and marketing management), COMMUNICATIONS AND THE ARTS (acting, art, communications, digital communications, English literature, English Writing, French, game design and development, graphic design, photography, Spanish, and theatre arts), COMPUTER AND PHYSICAL SCIENCE (chemistry, computer information technology, computer science, environmental chemistry, information sciences and systems, and mathematics), EDUCATION (art education, athletic training, drama education, English education, foreign languages education, global studies, mathematics education, physical education, science education, social studies education, and special education), ENGINEERING AND ENVIRONMENTAL DESIGN (environmental science and preengineering), HEALTH PROFESSIONS (medical laboratory science, predentistry, premedicine, and prephysical therapy), SOCIAL SCIENCE (criminal justice, criminology, economics, forensic studies, history, interdisciplinary studies, international relations, Latin American studies, liberal arts/general studies, philosophy, physical fitness/movement, political science/government, prelaw, psychology, religion, social work, and sociology). Psychology, biology, and communication have the largest enrollments.

ACTIVITIES: There are 114 groups on campus, including art, cheerleading, choir, chorale, chorus, computers, dance, debate, drama, drill team, environmental, ethnic, film, forensics, gay, honors, international, jazz band, literary magazine, musical theater, newspaper, orchestra, pep band, photography, political, professional, radio and TV, religious, social, social service, sports clubs, and student government. Popular campus events include Homecoming, Hip Hop on the

Hilltop, Involvement Fair, Hillfest, Casino Night, Leadershape, Festival of Lights, MAC Lead, Anchors, Legacy Walk, and Medalion Ceremony. **Sports:** There are 7 intercollegiate sports for men and 8 for women, and 9 intramural sports for men and 9 for women. Facilities include 2 gyms, baseball and softball fields, soccer field, tennis, basketball, racquetball/handball, and volleyball courts, indoor pool, fitness center, sand volleyball courts, recreation multipurpose field and a fitness studio. **Graduates:** From July 1, 2013 to June 30, 2014, 914 bachelor's degrees were awarded. The most popular majors were psychology (11%), communication (8%), and global studies (5%). 200 companies recruited on campus in 2013-2014. In an average class, 4% graduate in 3 years or less, 52% graduate in 4 years or less, 61% graduate in 5 years or less, and 67% graduate in 6 years or less.

SERVICES: Counseling and information services are available, as is tutoring in some subjects. There is a reader service for the blind. **Library/Resources:** The library contains 291,802 volumes, 29,549 audio/video tapes/CDs/DVDs, and subscribes to 2,474 periodicals including electronic. Computerized library services include interlibrary loans, database searching, Internet access, and Wi-Fi capability. Special learning facilities include an art gallery, radio station, an digital photography lab, a theater, natural sciences center, an interdisciplinary research laboratory, and a global digital classroom. **Physically Challenged Students:** 93% of the campus is accessible. Facilities include wheelchair ramps, elevators, special parking, specially equipped restrooms, special class scheduling, lowered drinking fountains, lowered telephones, and special housing. **Special:** Internships and study abroad in a variety of countries through the ISEP, SEU, and other university programs are available. Student-designed majors, nondegree study, and pass/fail options also are possible. A flexible program for working adults is offered through New College. There are 13 national honor societies and a freshman honors program. **Visiting:** There are regularly scheduled orientations for prospective students, including a tour, financial aid session, academic session, class visits, and entertainment. There are guides for informal visits, visitors may sit in on classes, and stay overnight. To schedule a visit, contact Lisa Furler at (512) 448-8500. **Campus Safety and Security:** Measures include 24-hour foot and vehicle patrol, emergency notification system, self-defense education, and security escort services. There are emergency telephones, lighted pathways/sidewalks, and controlled access to dorms/residences.

REQUIREMENTS: The SAT or ACT is required. The ACT Optional Writing test is also required. Successful applicants should be in the top half of their graduating class with testing at or above a combined Critical Reading and Math score of 1000 on the SAT, or a composite score, not including writing, of 21 on the ACT. The GED is accepted. An interview is recommended. An essay is required. SEU requires applicants to be in the upper 50% of their class. AP and CLEP credits are accepted. Important factors in the admissions decision are advanced placement or honors courses, extracurricular activities record, and leadership record.All students must maintain a minimum GPA of 2.0 while taking 120 semester hours, including 36 to 81 in the major. The core curriculum includes courses from Foundational Skills, Cultural Foundations, and Foundations for Values and Decisions. In the required capstone class, seniors identify a problem in society, research it, present their solutions orally and in writing, and perform a civic engagement activity that supports their position. **Procedure:** Freshmen are admitted fall and spring. Entrance exams should be taken in spring of the junior year or in summer or fall of the senior year. There are deferred admissions and rolling admissions plans. Early decision applications should be filed by February 1; regular applications, by May 1 for fall entry; November 15 for spring entry; and May 1 for summer entry, along with a $50 fee. Notification is sent on a rolling basis. Applications are accepted on-line. **Transfer Students:** 239 transfer students enrolled in 2013-2014. Transfer applicants must have a minimum GPA of 2.5. 30 of 120 credits required for the bachelor's degree must be completed at SEU. **International Students:** There are 333 international students enrolled. The school actively recruits these students. They must take the TOEFL with a minimum score of 500 on the paper-based TOEFL (PBT) or 61 on the Internet-based version (iBT). Student must take the IELTS, IB (English Higher Level) or AP (English or English Literature) may be submitted. They must also take the SAT or ACT.

ADMISSIONS: The SAT scores for the 2014-2015 freshman class were: Critical Reading--15% below 500, 50% between 500 and 599, 31% between 600 and 699, and 4% between 700 and 800; Math--19% below 500, 57% between 500 and 599, 22% between 600 and 699, and 2% between 700 and 800; Writing--26% below 500, 47% between 500 and 599, 25% between 600 and 699, and 2% between 700 and 800. The ACT scores were 10% below 21, 32% between 21 and 23, 32% between 24 and 26, 13% between 27 and 28, and 13% above 28. 50% of the current freshmen were in the top fifth of their class; 75% were in the top two fifths. 5 freshmen graduated first in their class. **Admissions Contact:** Tracy Manier, Associate Vice President and Dean of Undergraduate Admission. E-Mail: *seu.admit@stedwards.edu* Web: *www.stedwards.edu*

FINANCIAL AID: In 2014-2015, 91% of all full-time freshmen and 91% of continuing full-time students received some form of financial aid. 84% of all full-time freshmen and 83% of continuing full-time students received need-based aid. The average freshman award was $29,461. Need-based scholarships or need-based grants averaged $19,167; need-based self-help aid (loans and jobs) averaged $3,833; non-need-based athletic scholarships averaged $19,301; and other non-need-based awards and non-need-based scholarships averaged $11,267. 31% of undergraduate students work part-time. Average annual earnings from campus work are $1046. SEU is a member of CSS. The FAFSA is required. The priority date for freshman financial aid applications for fall entry is March 1. The deadline for filing freshman financial aid applications for fall entry is May 1.

STEPHEN F. AUSTIN STATE UNIVERSITY E-3
www.sfasu.edu

Nacogdoches, TX 75962

(936) 468-2504
(936) 468-3401

Fax: (936) 468-3849	Email: admissions@sfasu.edu
Full-time: 3647 men, 5908 women	Faculty: n/av
Part-time: 658 men, 1056 women	Ph.Ds: 73%
Graduate: 617 men, 1068 women	Student/Faculty: n/av
Year: semesters, summer session	Tuition: $7498 ($16,798)
Room & Board: $8170	Freshman Class: 9190 applied, 5993 accepted, 2177 enrolled
SAT CR/M/W: 470/490/460 ACT: 20	CEEB CODE: 6682
Application Deadline: open	COMPETITIVE

Stephen F. Austin State University, founded in 1923, is a public regional university offering undergraduate and graduate degree programs through 6 colleges. There are 6 undergraduate schools and 1 graduate school. In addition to regional accreditation, SFA has baccalaureate program accreditation with AACSB, ABET, ADA, CSWE, FIDER, NASAD, NASM, NCATE, NLN, and SAF. The figures in the above capsule and in this profile are approximate. The 430-acre campus is in a small town 140 miles northeast of Houston. Including any residence halls, there are 120 buildings.

STUDENT LIFE: 98% of undergraduates are from Texas. Others are from 43 states, 34 foreign countries, and Canada. 97% are from public schools. 62% are white; 23% African American. The average age of freshmen is 18; all undergraduates, 22. 36% do not continue beyond their first year; 45% remain to graduate.

FACULTY/CLASSROOMS: 49% of faculty are male; 51% are female. No introductory courses are taught by graduate students. The average class size in an introductory lecture is 36; in a laboratory is 24; and in a regular course is 26.

PROGRAMS OF STUDY: SFA confers B.A., B.A.A.S., B.B.A., B.F.A., B.M., B.S., B.S.A.G., B.S.F., B.S.I.S., B.S.N., B.S.R.H.B., and B.S.W. degrees. Master's and Doctoral degrees are also awarded. Bachelor's degrees are awarded in AGRICULTURE (agricultural business management, agricultural mechanics, agriculture, animal science, fish and game management, forestry production and processing, forestry and related sciences, horticulture, poultry science, and wildlife management), BIOLOGICAL SCIENCE (biology/biological science and nutrition), BUSINESS (accounting, banking and finance, business administration and management, fashion merchandising, hospitality management services, international business management, management information systems, management science, marketing management, and marketing/retailing/merchandising), COMMUNICATIONS AND THE ARTS (art, broadcasting, communications, dance, dramatic arts, English, French, journalism, music, radio/television technology, Spanish, and speech/debate/rhetoric), COMPUTER AND PHYSICAL SCIENCE (chemistry, computer programming, computer science, geology, information sciences and systems, mathematics, and physics), EDUCATION (agricultural education, education of the deaf and hearing impaired, and education of the visually handicapped), ENGINEERING AND ENVIRONMENTAL DESIGN (environmental science and interior design), HEALTH PROFESSIONS (health science, nursing, rehabilitation therapy, and speech therapy), SOCIAL SCIENCE (child psychology/development, corrections, criminal justice, dietetics, economics, family/consumer studies, geography, history, interdisciplinary studies, law enforcement and corrections, paralegal studies, parks and recreation management, philosophy, physical fitness/movement, political science/government, psychology, public administration, social work, and sociology). Interdisciplinary studies, nursing, and kinesiology have the largest enrollements.

ACTIVITIES: 10% of men belong to 24 national fraternities; 9% of women belong to 12 local sororities. There are 211 groups on campus, including art, band, cheerleading, choir, chorale, chorus, computers, dance, debate, drama, drill team, ethnic, film, flag corps, gay, honors, international, jazz band, literary magazine, marching band, musical theater, newspaper, opera, orchestra, pep band, photography, political, professional, radio and TV, religious, social, social service, student government, and symphony. Popular campus events include Showcase Saturday and Big Dip Mentor Ring Ceremony.

SERVICES: Counseling and information services are available, as is tutoring in most subjects. There is a reader service for the blind, and remedial math, reading, and writing. **Library/Resources:** The library contains 741,055 volumes, 854,752 microform items, and 24,256 audio/video tapes/CDs/DVDs, and subscribes to 1,195 periodicals including electronic. Computerized library services include interlibrary loans, database searching, Internet access, and Wi-Fi capability. Special learning facilities include an art gallery, planetarium, radio station, TV station, an arboretum, beef and poultry research centers, experimental forest, biotechnology and environmental science research centers. **Physically Challenged Students:** All of the campus is accessible. Facilities include wheelchair ramps, elevators, special parking, specially equipped restrooms, special class scheduling, lowered drinking fountains, and lowered telephones. **Special:** Internships, dual majors, and dual degrees are possible in some programs. Study abroad is available in more than 40 countries. Preengineering and 3-2 engineering programs with Texas A&M are offered, as are preprofessional programs and a general studies degree. There are a freshman honors program. **Visiting:** There are regularly scheduled orientations for prospective students, including 5; 3-day summer orientations for incoming freshmen and their families and 3 1-day sessions for incoming transfer students. Showcase Saturdays are 1-day open house programs held in the fall and spring for prospective students. There are guides for informal visits and visitors may sit in on classes. To schedule a visit, contact the Office of Admissions. **Campus Safety and Security:** Measures include 24-hour foot and vehicle patrol, emergency notification system, self-defense education, and security escort services. There are shuttle buses, emergency telephones, and lighted pathways/sidewalks.

REQUIREMENTS: The SAT or ACT is required. AP and CLEP credits are accepted.

ADMISSIONS: 65% of a recent year applicants were accepted. The SAT scores for the recent year freshman class were: Critical Reading--62% below 500, 29% between 500 and 599, 8% between 600 and 700, and 1% above 700; Math--55% below 500, 35% between 500 and 599, 10% between 600 and 700, and 1% above 700; Writing--67% below 500, 28% between 500 and 599, 5% between 600 and 700, and 1% above 700. The ACT scores were 52% below 21, 26% between 21 and 23, 16% between 24 and 26, 4% between 27 and 28, and 2% above 28. 31% of the current freshmen were in the top fifth of their class; 68% were in the top two fifths. 19 freshmen graduated first in their class.

FINANCIAL AID: In a recent year, 66% of all full-time freshmen and 62% of continuing full-time students received some form of financial aid. 52% of all full-time freshmen and 51% of continuing full-time students received need-based aid. The FAFSA and the college's own financial statement are required. The priority date for freshman financial aid applications for fall entry is April 1. The deadline for filing freshman financial aid applications for fall entry is rolling.

SUL ROSS STATE UNIVERSITY *(The complete profile is made available exclusively on our website, www.barronspac.com)*

TARLETON STATE UNIVERSITY *(The complete profile is made available exclusively on our website, www.barronspac.com)*

TEXAS A&M UNIVERSITY SYSTEM

The Texas A&M University System, established in 1876, is a public system in Texas. It is governed by a 9-member board of regents, whose chief administrator is the chancellor. The primary goal of the system is teaching, research, and service. The main priorities are to provide undergraduate and graduate students with a quality education, and to be a world leader in the development and dissemination of new knowledge. The total student enrollment for all 8 campuses is usually about 71,500 with 4000 faculty members. Altogether there are 496 baccalaureate, 352 master's, 105 doctoral programs offered in Texas A&M University System. Profiles of the 4-year campuses are included in this section.

TEXAS A&M UNIVERSITY	D-3
www.tamu.edu	
College Station, TX 77843	(979) 845-1060
	(979) 845-3211
Fax: (979) 458-1808	**Email:** admissions@tamu.edu
Full-time: 21587 men, 20572 women	**Faculty:** I, av$
	Ph.D.s: 88%
Part-time: 2637 men, 2328 women	**Student/Faculty:** 14 to 1
Graduate: 8102 men, 6368 women	**Tuition:** $9685 ($26,583)
Year: semesters, summer session	**Freshman Class:** 33451
Room & Board: $9522	applied, 23786 accepted, 10835 enrolled
SAT CR/M/W: 570/600/550 **ACT:** 26	**CEEB CODE:** 6003
Application Deadline: February 15	**VERY COMPETITIVE**

Texas A&M University, founded in 1876, is part of the Texas A&M University system. Undergraduate degrees are offered in agriculture and life sciences, architecture, business administration, education, engineering, geosciences, liberal arts, science, and biomedical science. There are 9 undergraduate schools and 11 graduate schools. In addition to regional accreditation, Texas A&M has baccalaureate program accreditation with AACSB, ABET, ACCE, ACEJMC, ADA, ASLA, CSAB, NAAB, NCATE, and SAF. The 8300-acre campus is in an urban area 90 miles northwest of Houston. Including any residence halls, there are 796 buildings.

STUDENT LIFE: 94% of undergraduates are from Texas. Others are from 50 states, 113 foreign countries, and Canada. 60% are White; 18% Hispanic. The average age of freshmen is 18; all undergraduates, 21. 9% do not continue beyond their first year; 81% remain to graduate. **Housing:** 10433 students can be accommodated in college housing, which includes single-sex and coed dorms, on-campus apartments, off-campus apartments, and married student housing. In addition, there are honors houses, fraternity houses, sorority houses, Honors dorm. On-campus housing is available on a first-come and first-served basis. 76% of students commute. All students may keep cars.

FACULTY/CLASSROOMS: 66% of faculty are male; 34% are female. 55% teach undergraduates, 62% do research, and 35% do both. Graduate students teach 16% of introductory courses. The average class size in an introductory lecture is 79; in a laboratory is 39; and in a regular course is 40.

PROGRAMS OF STUDY: Texas A&M confers B.A., B.S., B.B.A., B.Ed. B.L.A., B.S.I.S. and B.S.N. degrees. Master's and Doctoral degrees are also awarded. Bachelor's degrees are awarded in AGRICULTURE (agricultural business management, agricultural communications, agricultural economics, agronomy, animal science, dairy science, fish and game management, fishing and fisheries, forestry and related sciences, horticulture, poultry science, and range/farm management), BIOLOGICAL SCIENCE (biochemistry, biology/biological science, botany, entomology, genetics, microbiology, and zoology), BUSINESS (accounting, banking and finance, business systems analysis, management science, marketing/retailing/merchandising, and personnel management), COMMUNICATIONS AND THE ARTS (English, French, German, journalism, performing arts, Russian, Spanish, and speech/debate/rhetoric), COMPUTER AND PHYSICAL SCIENCE (atmospheric sciences and meteorology, chemistry, computer science, geology, geophysics and seismology, mathematics, and physics), EDUCATION (agricultural education, elementary education, health education, physical education, and secondary education), ENGINEERING AND ENVIRONMENTAL DESIGN (aeronautical engineering, agricultural engineering, bioengineering, biomedical engineering, chemical engineering, civil engineering, computer engineering, construction engineering, electrical/electronics engineering, engineering technology, environmental design, environmental science, industrial engineering technology, landscape architecture/design, mechanical engineering, nuclear engineering, and petroleum/natural gas engineering), HEALTH PROFESSIONS (biomedical science), SOCIAL SCIENCE (anthropology, economics, history, international studies, parks and recreation management, philosophy, political science/government, psychology, and sociology). Biomedical science, business administration, and biology are the strongest academically. Biomedical science, engineering, and business administration have the largest enrollments.

ACTIVITIES: 5% of men belong to 5 local and 15 national fraternities; 10% of women belong to 3 local and 33 national sororities. There are 1024 groups on campus, including art, band, cheerleading, chess, choir, chorale, chorus, computers, dance, drama, drill team, drum and bugle corps, ethnic, film, gay, honors, international, jazz band, literary magazine, marching band, musical theater, newspaper, opera, orchestra, photography, political, professional, radio and TV, religious, social, social service, student government, symphony, and yearbook. Popular campus events include Midnight Yell Practice, Silver Taps and Muster. **Sports:** There are 9 intercollegiate sports for men and 12 for women, and 20 intramural sports for men and 20 for women. Facilities include a coliseum, a natatorium, 12 basketball/volleyball courts, 14 handball/racquetball courts, badminton, weight and activity rooms, jogging trails, 14 tennis courts, a squash court, an 18-hole golf course, a 2500-seat auditorium/arena, a driving range, flag football fields, 4 soccer fields, 3 outdoor basketball courts, and 5 walking trails. Intercollegiate athletic facilities include a 70,210-seat football stadium, a 7200-seat indoor basketball and volleyball coliseum, a 7053-seat baseball stadium, a 1750-seat softball complex, a 1000-seat soccer complex, a 2000-seat natatorium, a 3000-seat track-and-field complex, a 1500-seat tennis center, and an 18,000-square-foot physical strength and conditioning lab. **Graduates:** From July 1, 2013 to June 30, 2014, 9847 bachelor's degrees were awarded. The most popular majors were engineering (19%), agriculture (15%), and business/marketing (14%). 3500 companies recruited on campus in 2013-2014. In an average class, 1% graduate in 3 years or less, 52% graduate in 4 years or less, 77% graduate in 5 years or less, and 81% graduate in 6 years or less.

SERVICES: Counseling and information services are available, as is tutoring in most subjects. There is a reader service for the blind. Workshops in time management, basic study techniques, and test-taking skills are available. **Library/Resources:** The 7 libraries contain 5.2 million volumes, 5.7 million microform items, 129,221 audio/video tapes/CDs/DVDs, and subscribe to 121,838 periodicals including electronic. Computerized library services include interlibrary loans, database searching, Internet access, and Wi-Fi capability. Special learning facilities include an art gallery, radio station, TV station, a weather station, observatory, cyclotron, wind tunnel, visualization lab, nuclear reactor, ocean wave pool, and the Bush Museum and Library. **Physically Challenged Students:** 85% of the campus is accessible. Facilities include wheelchair ramps, elevators, special parking, specially equipped restrooms, special class scheduling, lowered drinking fountains, lowered telephones. Office of support services for students with disabilities. **Special:** The university offers extensive opportunities through the Career Center and Study Abroad Office.

B.A.- B.S. degrees, study abroad in 12 countries, internships, a Washington semester, credit for military experience, nondegree study, co-op programs, dual majors, and pass/fail options are available. A 5-year graduate business/liberal arts program is offered, as well as a 3-2 engineering degree with Sam Houston State University. There are 41 national honor societies, including Phi Beta Kappa, and a freshman honors program. **Visiting:** There are regularly scheduled orientations for prospective students, some 20 new-student conferences are held for students to meet with academic advisers to select courses, become acquainted with student life activities, and tour the campus. There are guides for informal visits and visitors may sit in on classes. To schedule a visit, contact the Aggieland Visitor Center. **Campus Safety and Security:** Measures include 24-hour foot and vehicle patrol, emergency notification system, self-defense education, and security escort services. There are shuttle buses, emergency telephones, lighted pathways/sidewalks, a security awareness committee, and crime-watch and safety tip lines, and crime bulletins are available on the university police web site.

REQUIREMENTS: The SAT or ACT is required. The ACT Optional Writing test is also required. Secondary school graduation is a condition of freshman admission. Required high school courses include 4 credits in English, 3 1/2 credits in math, 3 credits in science (2 from biology, chemistry, or physics), 2 credits of social studies and the same foreign language, and 1 of history. AP and CLEP credits are accepted. Important factors in the admissions decision are leadership record, evidence of special talent, and extracurricular activities record. To graduate, students must complete at least 128 credit hours, including 30 to 33 in the major. A minimum 2.0 GPA is required. Students must complete a core curriculum of 48 hours in 8 subject areas, including courses in American history and government, phys ed, computers, foreign language, speech and writing skills, math/logical reasoning, science, humanities, and social science. Requirements in the major vary. **Procedure:** Freshmen are admitted fall, spring, and summer. Entrance exams should be taken during the spring of the junior year or by December of the senior year. There is a rolling admissions plan. Applications should be filed by February 15 for fall entry; October 15 for spring entry; and February 15 for summer entry, along with a $60 fee. Applications are accepted online. **Transfer Students:** 2769 transfer students enrolled in 2013-2014. Applicants must submit transcripts from previously attended colleges. Requirements vary, depending on how many semester hours were attempted and the grades for those hours. Transfer applicants must submit high school transcripts and, if they have fewer than 12 graded semester hours, SAT or ACT scores. 30 of 128 credits required for the bachelor's degree must be completed at Texas A&M. **International Students:** There are 721 international students enrolled. They must take the TOEFL with a minimum score of 550 on the paper-based TOEFL (PBT) or 80 on the Internet-based version (iBT). The SAT or ACT is required for graduates of U.S. high schools only.

ADMISSIONS: 71% of the 2014-2015 applicants were accepted. The SAT scores for the 2014-2015 freshman class were: Critical Reading--17% below 500, 39% between 500 and 599, 35% between 600 and 699, and 9% between 700 and 800; Math--8% below 500, 34% between 500 and 599, 43% between 600 and 699, and 15% between 700 and 800; Writing--26% below 500, 42% between 500 and 599, 26% between 600 and 699, and 5% between 700 and 800. The ACT scores were 7% below 21, 10% between 21 and 23, 22% between 24 and 26, 11% between 27 and 28, and 50% above 28. 84% of the current freshmen were in the top fifth of their class; 98% were in the top two fifths. There were 162 National Merit finalists. 327 freshmen graduated first in their class. **Admissions Contact:** Admissions Counseling E-Mail: *admissions@tamu.edu* Web: *www.tamu.edu*

FINANCIAL AID: In 2014-2015, 71% of all full-time freshmen and 59% of continuing full-time students received some form of financial aid. 58% of all full-time freshmen and 51% of continuing full-time students received need-based aid. The average freshman award was $5,960. Need-based scholarships or need-based grants averaged $3,834 ($25,700 maximum); need-based self-help aid (loans and jobs) averaged $5,179 ($35,399 maximum); non-need-based athletic scholarships averaged $3,939 ($17,806 maximum); other non-need-based awards and non-need-based scholarships averaged $2,261 ($18,625 maximum); and $4,026 from other forms of aid. 20% of undergraduate students work part-time. Average annual earnings from campus work are $3100. The average financial indebtedness of the 2014 graduate was $26,599. The FAFSA is required. The priority date for freshman financial aid applications for fall entry is March 15.

TEXAS A&M UNIVERSITY AT COMMERCE　　D-2
www.tamu-commerce.edu

Commerce, TX 75429-3011	(903) 886-5000
	(888) 868-2682
Fax: (903) 468-8685	Email: admissions@tamuc.edu
Full-time: 1575 men, 2475 women	Faculty: n/av; I, -$
Part-time: 445 men, 735 women	Ph.D.s: 65%
Graduate: 1420 men, 2430 women	Student/Faculty: n/av
Year: semesters, summer session	Tuition: $6628 ($16,647)
Room & Board: $6750	Freshman Class: n/av
SAT or ACT: required	CEEB CODE: 6205
Application Deadline: see profile	COMPETITIVE

Texas A&M University at Commerce, founded in 1889, offers undergraduate and graduate programs in business and technology, arts and sciences, and education. The figures in the above capsule and this profile are approximate. There are 3 undergraduate schools and 1 graduate school. In addition to regional accreditation, TAMU-C has baccalaureate program accreditation with AACSB, CSWE, NASM, and NCATE. The 1883-acre campus is in a small town 65 miles northeast of Dallas. Including any residence halls, there are 121 buildings.

STUDENT LIFE: 97% of undergraduates are from Texas. Others are from 30 states, 21 foreign countries, and Canada. 98% are from public schools. 65% are white; 17% African American. The average age of freshmen is 19; all undergraduates, 25. 42% do not continue beyond their first year; 57% remain to graduate.

FACULTY/CLASSROOMS: 53% of faculty are male; 47% are female. 77% teach undergraduates, 46% do research, and 37% do both. Graduate students teach 21% of introductory courses. The average class size in an introductory lecture is 30; in a laboratory, 20; and in a regular course, 25.

PROGRAMS OF STUDY: TAMU-C confers B.A., B.S., B.A.C.J., B.B.A., B.F.A., B.G.S., B.M., B.M.Ed., B.S.C.J., B.S.Lib.Sci., and B.S.W. degrees. Master's and Doctoral degrees are also awarded. Bachelor's degrees are awarded in AGRICULTURE (agricultural economics, agriculture, animal science, and wildlife management), BIOLOGICAL SCIENCE (biology/biological science and botany), BUSINESS (accounting, banking and finance, business administration and management, and marketing/retailing/merchandising), COMMUNICATIONS AND THE ARTS (advertising, broadcasting, dramatic arts, English, fine arts, French, German, journalism, languages, music, photography, printmaking, and Spanish), COMPUTER AND PHYSICAL SCIENCE (chemistry, computer science, earth science, geology, mathematics, and physics), EDUCATION (agricultural education, business education, early childhood education, elementary education, guidance education, health education, industrial arts education, music education, science education, and secondary education), ENGINEERING AND ENVIRONMENTAL DESIGN (engineering technology and preengineering), HEALTH PROFESSIONS (predentistry, premedicine, and prepharmacy), SOCIAL SCIENCE (anthropology, criminal justice, economics, geography, history, political science/government, prelaw, psychology, religion, social work, and sociology). Education, computer science, and business administration are the strongest academically and has the largest enrollments.

ACTIVITIES: 15% of men belong to 9 national fraternities; 12% of women belong to 7 national sororities. There are 96 groups on campus, including art, band, cheerleading, chess, choir, chorale, chorus, dance, drama, ethnic, film, gay, honors, international, jazz band, literary magazine, marching band, musical theater, newspaper, orchestra, pep band, photography, political, professional, radio and TV, religious, social, social service, and student government. Popular campus events include Sam Rayburn Symposium, Christmas Feast of Carols, and Springfest.

SERVICES: Counseling and information services are available, as is tutoring in some subjects, math and writing There is remedial math, reading, and writing. **Library/Resources:** The library contains 1.2 million volumes, 1.2 million microform items, and subscribes to 16,222 periodicals including electronic. Computerized library services include interlibrary loans, database searching, Internet access, and Wi-Fi capability. Special learning facilities include a planetarium, radio station, TV station, performing arts center, and farm. **Physically Challenged Students:** All of the campus is accessible. Facilities include wheelchair ramps, elevators, special parking, and specially equipped restrooms. **Special:** TAMU-C offers co-op programs with E-Systems Inc. and numerous other firms, cross-registration by independent arrangement, study abroad in England, and work-study programs. B.A.-B.S. degrees, second degrees, dual majors, a general studies degree, credit for life experience, internships, nondegree study, and pass/fail options are also available. There are 18 national honor societies, a freshman honors program, and 26 departmental honors programs. **Visiting:** There are regularly scheduled orientations for prospective students. There are guides for informal visits and visitors may sit in on classes. To schedule a visit, contact the Admissions Office. **Campus Safety and Security:** Measures include 24-hour foot and vehicle patrol, self-defense education, and security escort services. There are emergency telephones, lighted pathways/sidewalks, a victim assistance officer, a police service for special and social events, crime and date-rape prevention presentations, and motorist assistance.

REQUIREMENTS: The SAT or ACT is required, with a minimum recommended composite score of 800 or 20, respectively. Applicants need not be graduates of an accredited secondary school, although high school graduation is required. The GED is also accepted. A GPA of 2.0 is required. AP and CLEP credits are accepted.

FINANCIAL AID: The FAFSA and the college's own financial statement are required. Check with the school for current application deadlines.

TEXAS A&M UNIVERSITY AT CORPUS CHRISTI *(The complete profile is made available exclusively on our website, www. barronspac.com)*

TEXAS A&M UNIVERSITY AT GALVESTON　　E-4
www.tamug.edu

Galveston, TX 77553-1675	(409) 740-4414
	(877) 322-4443
Fax: (409) 740-4731	Email: seaaggie@tamug.edu
Full-time: 875 men, 600 women	Faculty: n/av
Part-time: 65 men, 60 women	Ph.D.s: 40%
Graduate: 20 men, 50 women	Student/Faculty: n/av
Year: semesters, summer session	Tuition: $9500 ($18,500)
Room & Board: $7500	Freshman Class: n/av
SAT or ACT: required	CEEB CODE: 6835
Application Deadline: open	COMPETITIVE

Texas A&M University at Galveston, founded in 1962, is a public institution that offers marine and maritime-related programs. It is part of the Texas A&M University system. The figures in the above capsule and this profile are approximate. There are 9 undergraduate schools and 1 graduate school. In addition to regional accreditation, TAMUG has baccalaureate program accreditation with ABET. The library contains 43,000 volumes 52,984 microform items, and subscribes to 970 periodicals including electronic. Computerized library services include interlibrary loans and database searching. Special learning facilities include a learning resource center and a training ship, the T/S Texas Clipper, used for an annual summer training cruise. The 120-acre campus is in a suburban area 50 miles south of Houston on the Gulf of Mexico. Including any residence halls, there are 14 buildings.

STUDENT LIFE: 81% of undergraduates are from Texas. Others are from 43 states and 8 foreign countries. 94% are from public schools. 85% are white. The average age of freshmen is 18; all undergraduates, 20. 28% do not continue beyond their first year; 52% remain to graduate.

FACULTY/CLASSROOMS: 65% of faculty are male; 35% are female.

All teach undergraduates. No introductory courses are taught by graduate students. The average class size in an introductory lecture is 48; in a laboratory, 14; and in a regular course, 24.

PROGRAMS OF STUDY: TAMUG confers B.A., B.S. degrees. Master's degrees are also awarded. Bachelor's degrees are awarded in AGRICULTURE (environmental studies, fishing and fisheries, and natural resource management), BIOLOGICAL SCIENCE (biology/biological science, environmental biology, marine biology, and marine science), BUSINESS (international business management, recreation and leisure services, and transportation management), COMPUTER AND PHYSICAL SCIENCE (earth science, geoscience, hydrology, natural sciences, oceanography, and science and management), ENGINEERING AND ENVIRONMENTAL DESIGN (civil engineering, electrical/electronics engineering technology, electromechanical technology, environmental science, land use management and reclamation, marine engineering, maritime science, mechanical engineering technology, naval architecture and marine engineering, ocean engineering, systems engineering, and transportation engineering), SOCIAL SCIENCE (archeology, geography, humanities and social science, liberal arts/general studies, and water resources). Marine systems engineering is the strongest academically. Marine biology has the largest enrollment.

ACTIVITIES: There are no fraternities or sororities. There are 39 groups on campus, including chorale, drama, ethnic, international, literary magazine, newspaper, political, professional, religious, social, social service, student government, and yearbook. Popular campus events include Springfest, Mardi Grass, and Maritime Ball.

SERVICES: Counseling and information services are available, as is tutoring in most subjects. There is a reader service for the blind and remedial math, reading, and writing.

REQUIREMENTS: The SAT or ACT is required. Acceptable test scores depend on high school rank, with minimum composite scores of 1000 for the SAT and 24 for the ACT. Applicants must be graduates of an accredited high school or hold a GED. A minimum of 16 academic credits is required, including 4 units of English, 3 1/2 units of math, 2 1/2 units of either history or social studies, 2 units each of a foreign language and science, and the rest in electives. AP and CLEP credits are accepted. Important factors in the admissions decision are leadership record, extracurricular activities record, and recommendations by school officials.

FINANCIAL AID: The FAFSA is required. Check with the school for current application deadlines.

TEXAS A&M UNIVERSITY AT KINGSVILLE (*The complete profile is made available exclusively on our website, www.barronspac.com*)

TEXAS CHRISTIAN UNIVERSITY	**D-2**
www.tcu.edu	

Fort Worth, TX 76129	(817) 257-7000
	(800) 828-3764
Fax: (817) 257-7268	Email: frogmail@tcu.edu
Full-time: 3320 men, 5018 women	Faculty: 602
Part-time: 153 men, 156 women	Ph.D.s: 83%
Graduate: 620 men, 766 women	Student/Faculty: 14 to 1
Year: semesters, summer session	Tuition: $38,600
Room & Board: $11,380	Freshman Class: 17029 applied, 8322 accepted, 1891 enrolled
	CEEB CODE: 6820
Application Deadline: February 15	HIGHLY COMPETITIVE

Texas Christian University, founded in 1873, is a private university affiliated with the Christian Church (Disciples of Christ). TCU is a teaching and research institution offering undergraduate programs in arts, sciences, business, education, fine arts, communications, nursing, and engineering. There are 8 undergraduate schools and 8 graduate schools. In addition to regional accreditation, TCU has baccalaureate program accreditation with AACSB, ABET, ACEJMC, CSWE, NASAD, NASM, ACS, ASHA, CAATE, CIDA, COA, AACN, ACEND, CCNE, NASD, BON, TEA, NAEYC, SACS CASI, UCIEP,

NASD, SAIS, TANS, and AAIEP. The 278-acre campus is in a suburban area 5 miles southwest of downtown Fort Worth. Including any residence halls, there are 114 buildings.

STUDENT LIFE: 55% of undergraduates are from Texas. Others are from 50 states, 70 foreign countries, and Canada. 61% are from public schools. 74% are White; 11% Hispanic. 50% are Protestant; 25% Catholic; 20% claim no religious affiliation. The average age of freshmen is 18; all undergraduates, 20. 10% do not continue beyond their first year; 76% remain to graduate. **Housing:** 4042 students can be accommodated in college housing, which includes single-sex and coed dorms and on-campus apartments. In addition, there are honors houses, language houses, fraternity houses, and sorority houses. On-campus housing is available on a lottery system for upperclassmen. 52% of students commute. All students may keep cars.

FACULTY/CLASSROOMS: 52% of faculty are male; 48% are female. All teach and do research. No introductory courses are taught by graduate students. The average class size in an introductory lecture is 33 and in a laboratory is 20.

PROGRAMS OF STUDY: TCU confers B.A., B.B.A., B.F.A., B.G.S., B.Mus., B.S., B.S.Ed., B.S.N., B.S.W., B.C.J., B.Mus.Ed., B.Ath.Trng. and B.C.S. degrees. Master's and Doctoral degrees are also awarded. Bachelor's degrees are awarded in AGRICULTURE (ranch management), BIOLOGICAL SCIENCE (biochemistry, biology/biological science, neurosciences, and nutrition), BUSINESS (accounting, business information systems, entrepreneurial studies, fashion merchandising, finance, international accounting, international business information systems, international economics, international entrepreneurial management, international finance, international real estate finance, international marketing, international supply and value chain management, marketing, real estate finance, supply chain management, and professional program in accounting), COMMUNICATIONS AND THE ARTS (art history, ballet, ballet modern dance, church music, communications, English, film, television and digital media, French, German, graphic design, instrumental performance, instrumental music education, journalism, keyboard - piano concentration, modern dance, music, music theory and composition, musical theater, organ performance, photography, piano pedagogy, printmaking, sculpture, Spanish, sports media, strategic communication, strings, studio art, studio art ceramics, studio art painting, theatre acting, theatre arts, theater design, theatre production, theatre studies, vocal performance, vocal music education, and writing), COMPUTER AND PHYSICAL SCIENCE (applied geoscience, astronomy and physics, chemistry, combined science, computer information technology, computer science, geology, mathematics, mathematics - actuarial concentration, and physics), EDUCATION (art education, athletic training, bilingual early childhood education, early childhood education, educational studies, general studies, middle school education, physical education, and secondary education), ENGINEERING AND ENVIRONMENTAL DESIGN (electrical/electronics engineering, engineering, engineering/ele emphasis/energy sys focus, engineering/mechanical emp/energy sys focus, environmental science, interior design, and mechanical engineering), HEALTH PROFESSIONS (habilitation of the deaf, health, movement science, nursing, Pre-Health Studies, speech pathology/audiology, and sports psychology), SOCIAL SCIENCE (anthropology, child psychology/development, criminal justice, dietetics, economics, food production/management/services, geography, history, international political science, philosophy, political science/government, psychology, religion, social work, and sociology). General business, nursing, and liberal arts pre-major are the largest.

ACTIVITIES: 56% of women belong to 2 local and 19 national sororities. There are 240 groups on campus, including art, band, cheerleading, choir, chorale, chorus, communications, computers, dance, debate, drama, drill team, environmental, ethnic, film, forensics, gay, honors, international, jazz band, literary magazine, marching band, musical theater, newspaper, opera, orchestra, pep band, photography, political, professional, radio and TV, religious, social, social service, student government, symphony, and yearbook. Popular campus events include Frog Camp, Frogs First Weekend, Family Weekend, Second Year Pinning, Homecoming, Christmas Tree Lighting, Carols by Candlelight, and Senior Fiesta. **Sports:** There are 8 intercollegiate sports for men and 11 for women, and 22 intramural sports for men and 22 for women. Facilities include a 232,000 square foot recreation facility includes a natatorium, outdoor swimming pool, racquetball courts, squash court, track, two multi-use gymnasiums sports, weight training, a cardiovascular fitness area, multi-purpose exercise studios, and a climbing wall. **Graduates:** From July 1, 2013 to June 30, 2014, 1965 bachelor's degrees were awarded. The most popular majors were nursing (10%), strategic communication (6%), and psychology (6%). In an average class, 2% graduate in 3 years or less, 59% graduate in 4 years or less, 74% graduate in 5 years or less, and 76% graduate in 6 years or less. Of the 2013 graduating class, 29% were enrolled in graduate school within 6 months of graduation, and 73% were employed.

SERVICES: Library/Resources: The library contains 1.4 million volumes, 512,185 microform items, 68,524 audio/video tapes/CDs/DVDs, and subscribes to 97,281 periodicals including electronic. Computerized library services include interlibrary loans, database searching, Internet access, and Wi-Fi capability. Special learning facilities include an art gallery, natural history museum, radio station, TV station, an observatory, speech and hearing clinic, energy institute, behavioral research institute, laboratory schools and various other centers within each college. **Physically Challenged Students:** All of the campus is accessible. Facilities include wheelchair ramps, elevators, special parking, specially equipped restrooms, lowered drinking fountains, and lowered telephones. **Special:** A general studies degree and a combined B.A.-B.S. degree in numerous majors are offered. TCU also accepts credit by exam and credit for life, military, and work experience. 4-1 programs are available in education. Internships are available in almost all major areas. The university also offers a Washington semester, student exchange programs, and study abroad in 26 countries. TCU also offers study at its London Center and study through the American Airlines Leadership for the Americas program. An accelerated degree program in nursing is also offered. TCU also offers a B.S.W. and B.S.C.J. There are 36 national honor societies, including Phi Beta Kappa, and a freshman honors program. **Visiting:** There are regularly scheduled orientations for prospective students, including student-led campus tours, group information sessions, optional personal interviews, and departmental visits. There are guides for informal visits, visitors may sit in on classes, and stay overnight. To schedule a visit, contact TCU Admissions Office at (800) 828-3764. **Campus Safety and Security:** Measures include 24-hour foot and vehicle patrol, emergency notification system, self-defense education, and security escort services. There are shuttle buses, emergency telephones, lighted pathways/sidewalks, controlled access to dorms/residences, bike patrol, and video monitoring of some parking lots.

REQUIREMENTS: Either the SAT or the ACT is required. Candidates should be graduates of an accredited secondary school and have completed 15 Carnegie units, including 4 years of English, 3 years each of math, science, and social studies, and 2 each of the same foreign language and of academic electives. TCU also requires an essay, a counselor's recommendation and a teacher's recommendation. A personal interview is optional. AP and CLEP credits are accepted. Important factors in the admissions decision are advanced placement or honors courses, leadership record, and extracurricular activities record. TCU requires completion of university curriculum requirements, which are divided into foundations (composition, mathematics, oral communication, and advanced writing) and explorations (humanities, fine arts, social sciences and natural sciences). These are normally satisfied with 15 to 18 courses. At least 124 credit hours (58 of which must be in residence) with a 2.0 GPA; 42 hours of upper division work; at least the last 30 hours in residence; a major or concentration. **Procedure:** Freshmen students are admitted fall, spring, and summer. Entrance exams should be taken during or before the fall semester of the senior year. There are early decision, early admissions, and deferred admissions plans. Early decision applications should be filed by November 1; regular applications, by February 15 for fall entry, along with a $40 fee. Notification of early decision is sent January 1; regular decision, April 1. 276 early decision candidates were accepted for the 2014-2015 class. 1236 applicants were on the 2014 waiting list; 64 were admitted. Applications are accepted online. **Transfer Students:** 374 transfer students enrolled in 2013-2014. The recommended GPA is 2.7 and a minimum GPA of 2.0 is required. Applicants must complete an application form and submit official transcripts from each college attended. If fewer than 24 semester hours of transferable work have been completed at the time of application, SAT or ACT scores and secondary school transcripts are required. 58 credits required for the bachelor's degree must be completed at TCU. **International Students:** There are 422 international students enrolled. The school actively recruits these students. They must take the TOEFL with a minimum score of 550 on the paper-based TOEFL (PBT) or 80 on the Internet-based version (iBT). Student must take the SAT, ACT, or IELTS. SAT or ACT required for freshmen whose high school was taught in English or who want to be considered for scholarship.

ADMISSIONS: 49% of the 2014-2015 applicants were accepted. 66% of the current freshmen were in the top fifth of their class; 90% were in the top two fifths. **Admissions Contact:** Ray Brown, Dean of Admissions. E-Mail: *frogmail@tcu.edu* Web: *www.tcu.edu*

FINANCIAL AID: In 2014-2015, 75% of all full-time freshmen and 66% of continuing full-time students received some form of financial aid. 37% of all full-time freshmen and 39% of continuing full-time students received need-based aid. The average freshman award was $25,746. Need-based scholarships or need-based grants averaged $15,541 ($51,030 maximum); need-based self-help aid (loans and jobs) averaged $2,781 ($9,000 maximum); non-need-based athletic scholarships averaged $38,488 ($63,148 maximum); and other non-need-based awards and non-need-based scholarships averaged $14,327 ($55,480 maximum). 28% of undergraduate students work part-time. Average annual earnings from campus work are $3168. The average financial indebtedness of the 2014 graduate was $39,584. TCU is a member of CSS. The CSS/Profile and FAFSA are required. The priority date for freshman financial aid applications for fall entry is March 15. The deadline for filing freshman financial aid applications for fall entry is March 15.

TEXAS LUTHERAN UNIVERSITY D-4
www.tlu.edu

Seguin, TX 78155

(830) 372-8000
(800) 771-8521

Fax: (830) 372-8096 — Email: admissions@tlu.edu

Full-time: 589 men, 640 women	Faculty: 81; IIB, -$
Part-time: 33 men, 44 women	Ph.D.s: 84%
Graduate: 10 men, 8 women	Student/Faculty: 15 to 1
Year: semesters, summer session	Tuition: $26,800
Room & Board: $9240	Freshman Class: 1516 applied, 847 accepted, 309 enrolled
SAT CR/M/W: 500/520/470 ACT: 21	CEEB CODE: 6823
Application Deadline: June 1	COMPETITIVE

Texas Lutheran University, founded in 1891, is an exclusively undergraduate university of the liberal arts, sciences, and professional studies. The university's mission is to prepare students academically, spiritually, and socially for lives of leadership and service. There is 1 undergraduate school and 1 graduate school. In addition to regional accreditation, TLU has baccalaureate program accreditation with ACBSP, NASM, TEAC, and CAATE. The 184-acre campus is in a small town 37 miles east of San Antonio and 50 miles south of Austin. Including any residence halls, there are 37 buildings.

STUDENT LIFE: 97% of undergraduates are from Texas. Others are from 33 states, 2 foreign countries, and Canada. 94% are from public schools. 55% are White; 31% Hispanic. 28% claim no religious affiliation; 20% Protestant; 18% Catholic. The average age of freshmen is 18; all undergraduates, 21. 30% do not continue beyond their first year; 44% remain to graduate. **Housing:** 861 students can be accommodated in college housing, which includes single-sex and coed dorms, on-campus apartments, and married student housing. On-campus housing is guaranteed for all 4 years, is guaranteed for the freshman year only, and is available on a first-come, first-served basis. 59% of students live on campus; of those, 70% remain on campus on weekends. All students may keep cars.

FACULTY/CLASSROOMS: 50% of faculty are male; 50% are female. All teach undergraduates. No introductory courses are taught by graduate students. The average class size in an introductory lecture is 20; in a laboratory is 20; and in a regular course is 12.

PROGRAMS OF STUDY: TLU confers B.A., B.S., B.B.A., BSN and B.M.MAacy degrees. Master's degrees are also awarded. Bachelor's degrees are awarded in BIOLOGICAL SCIENCE (biochemistry and biology/biological science), BUSINESS (accounting and business administration and management), COMMUNICATIONS AND THE ARTS (art, communications, dramatic arts, English, music, and Spanish), COMPUTER AND PHYSICAL SCIENCE (applied science, chemistry, computer science, information sciences and systems, mathematics, and physics), EDUCATION (athletic training, education, and physical education), HEALTH PROFESSIONS (nursing), SOCIAL SCIENCE (economics, history, international studies, philosophy, political science/government, psychology, sociology, and theological studies). Business, biology, and psychology are the strongest academically. Business, kinesiology, and psychology have the largest enrollments.

ACTIVITIES: 7% of men belong to 3 local and 1 national fraternities; 10% of women belong to 3 local sororities. There are 52 groups on campus, including art, band, cheerleading, choir, chorus, computers, dance, drama, environmental, ethnic, forensics, gay, honors, international, jazz band, literary magazine, musical theater, newspaper, orchestra, pep band, political, professional, religious, science, social, social service, student government, and symphony. Popular campus events include Christmas Vespers, Spring Fling and Student Academic Symposium. **Sports:** There are 8 intercollegiate sports for men and 8 for women, and 14 intramural sports for men and 14 for women. Facilities include a football and track stadium, a 2,200-seat gym, fitness center, an 8-lane swimming pool, softball, baseball, and soccer fields, intramural/recreation fields, golf practice greens, a lighted walking track, practice gym, lighted sand volleyball courts, tennis courts, and racquetball courts. **Graduates:** From July 1, 2013 to June 30, 2014, 198 bachelor's degrees were awarded. The most popular majors were business administration (22%), kinesiology (17%), and education (8%). 29 companies recruited on campus in 2013-2014. In an average class, 31% graduate in 4 years or less, 43% graduate in 5 years or less, and 44% graduate in 6 years or less.

SERVICES: Counseling and information services are available, as is tutoring in most subjects. There is a reader service for the blind. Assistance with writing assignments is also available. **Library/Resources:** The library stocks 157,116 volumes, 118,272 microform items, 2,913 audio/video tapes/CDs/DVDs, and subscribes to 62,350 periodicals including electronic. Computerized library services include interlibrary loans, database searching, Internet access, and Wi-Fi capability. Special learning facilities include an art gallery and a natural history museum. **Physically Challenged Students:** 90% of the campus is accessible. Facilities include wheelchair ramps, elevators, special parking, specially equipped restrooms, special class scheduling, lowered drinking fountains, and special housing. **Special:** Internships are available in most majors. Study abroad in all countries affiliated with ISEP, Augsburg College, Central College, Equador Exchange, and Kansai Gaidai, a Washington semester with American University, and work-study programs are available. The college offers student-designed majors and dual majors. There is a 3-2 engineering program with Texas A&M, Baylor University and Southern Methodist University. There are 11 national honor societies, a freshman honors program, and 20 departmental honors programs. **Visiting:** There are regularly scheduled orientations for prospective students, including a campus tour, classroom visits, a financial aid presentation, a study abroad session, an athlete session, and a student panel. There are guides for informal visits, visitors may sit in on classes, and stay overnight. To schedule a visit, contact the Admissions Office. **Campus Safety and Security:** Measures include 24-hour foot and vehicle patrol, self-defense education, and security escort services. There are lighted pathways/sidewalks, and coded locks in residence halls.

REQUIREMENTS: The SAT or ACT is required. Applicants must have 16 Carnegie units, including a recommended 4 years in English, 3 each of social studies, math, and science, and 2 in foreign language. The GED is accepted. AP and CLEP credits are accepted. Important factors in the admissions decision are advanced placement or honors courses, recommendations by school officials, and extracurricular activities record.All students must complete 124 semester hours,

including 24 to 54 in their major, with a 2.0 GPA. Between 45 and 49 hours of distribution courses are required. A senior seminar, project, or concert is required in all majors. **Procedure:** Freshmen are admitted fall and spring. Entrance exams should be taken in the spring of the junior year or the summer before the senior year. There is a rolling admissions plan. Applications should be filed by June 1 for fall entry; December 1 for spring entry, along with a $40 fee. Notification is sent on a rolling basis. Applications are accepted on-line. **Transfer Students:** 54 transfer students enrolled in 2013-2014. Applicants for transfer must have a GPA of at least 2.25 and be in good academic standing. 33 of 124 credits required for the bachelor's degree must be completed at TLU. **International Students:** There are 2 international students enrolled. The school actively recruits these students. They must take the TOEFL with a minimum score of 550 on the paper-based TOEFL (PBT) or 79 on the Internet-based version (iBT). They must also take the SAT or ACT, scoring 960.

ADMISSIONS: 56% of the 2014-2015 applicants were accepted. The SAT scores for the 2014-2015 freshman class were: Critical Reading--50% below 500, 37% between 500 and 599, 12% between 600 and 699, and 1% between 700 and 800; Math--38% below 500, 45% between 500 and 599, 16% between 600 and 699, and 1% between 700 and 800; Writing--61% below 500, 33% between 500 and 599, 5% between 600 and 699, and 1% between 700 and 800. The ACT scores were 42% below 21, 28% between 21 and 23, 21% between 24 and 26, 7% between 27 and 28, and 2% above 28. 41% of the current freshmen were in the top fifth of their class; 72% were in the top two fifths. 2 freshmen graduated first in their class. **Admissions Contact:** Adam Navarro-Jusino, Director of Admissions. E-Mail: *admissions@ tlu.edu* Web: *www.tlu.edu*

FINANCIAL AID: In 2014-2015, 100% of all full-time freshmen and 99% of continuing full-time students received some form of financial aid. 96% of all full-time freshmen and 95% of continuing full-time students received need-based aid. The average freshman award was $26,803. Need-based scholarships or need-based grants averaged $18,750 ($32,400 maximum); need-based self-help aid (loans and jobs) averaged $4,355 ($8,500 maximum); and other non-need-based awards and non-need-based scholarships averaged $7,407 ($28,500 maximum). 9% of undergraduate students work part-time. Average annual earnings from campus work are $1282. The average financial indebtedness of the 2014 graduate was $26,410. The FAFSA is required. The priority date for freshman financial aid applications for fall entry is March 1. The deadline for filing freshman financial aid applications for fall entry is April 1.

TEXAS SOUTHERN UNIVERSITY (*The complete profile is made available exclusively on our website, www.barronspac.com*)

TEXAS STATE UNIVERSITY SYSTEM

The Texas State University System, established in 1911, is a public system in Texas. It is governed by a 9-member board of regents, whose chief administrator is the chancellor. The primary mission of the system is teaching. The main priorities are the teacher education, business and liberal arts. The total student enrollment for all 12 campuses is usually about 80,000 with 15,000 faculty members. Altogether there are 325 baccalaureate programs, 200 master's, 1 doctoral programs offered in Texas State University System. Profiles of the 4-year campuses are included in this section.

TEXAS STATE UNIVERSITY   D-3
www.txstate.edu

San Marcos, TX 78666	(512) 245-2111
	(512) 245-2364
Fax: (512) 245-8100	Email: admissions@txstate.edu
Full-time: 11591 men, 15060 women	Faculty: 978
	Ph.D.s: 77%
Part-time: 2581 men, 2983 women	Student/Faculty: 22 to 1
Graduate: 1731 men, 2844 women	Tuition: $9516 ($20,376)
Year: semesters, summer session	Freshman Class: 18413
Room & Board: $7612	applied, 13423 accepted, 5357 enrolled
SAT CR/M/W: 500/520/490 ACT: 22	CEEB CODE: 6667
Application Deadline: May 1	COMPETITIVE

Texas State University was founded in 1899 and is part of the Texas State University System. Texas State offers programs in general studies, applied arts, business, education, fine arts, health professions, liberal arts, science, engineering and technology. Texas State offers 97 Bachelor degrees, 88 Master degrees, 11 Doctoral degrees and 1 Special Professional degree. There are 8 undergraduate schools and 1 graduate school. In addition to regional accreditation, Texas State has baccalaureate program accreditation with AACSB, ABET, ACCE, ACEJMC, ADA, AHEA, CSAB, CSWE, FIDER, NASM, NRPA, NAACLS, CAAHEP, and Texas State Board for Education Certification/TEA. The 456-acre campus is in a suburban area 30 miles south of Austin and 45 miles northeast of San Antonio. Including any residence halls, there are 265 buildings.

STUDENT LIFE: 98% of undergraduates are from Texas. Others are from 48 states, 40 foreign countries, and Canada. 98% are from public schools. 51% are White; 33% Hispanic. The average age of freshmen is 18; all undergraduates, 22. 23% do not continue beyond their first year; 57% remain to graduate. **Housing:** 6723 students can be accommodated in college housing, which includes single-sex and coed dorms, on-campus apartments, and married student housing. In addition, there are honors houses, special-interest houses, special residences for international students, single parents, upper-division students, and freshmen experience housing. On-campus housing is guaranteed for the freshman year only, and is available on a first-come, first-served basis. 79% of students commute. All students may keep cars.

FACULTY/CLASSROOMS: 49% of faculty are male; 51% are female. 87% teach undergraduates, and 10% do research. Graduate students teach 6% of introductory courses. The average class size in an introductory lecture is 48; in a laboratory is 21; and in a regular course is 36.

PROGRAMS OF STUDY: Texas State confers B.A., B.A.A.S., B.A.I.S., B.B.A., B.E.S.S., B.F.A., B.G.S., B.H.A., B.H.W.P., B.M., B.P.A., B.S., B.S.A.G., B.S.A.S., B.S.C.L.S., B.S.C.D., B.S.C.J., B.S.F.C.S., B.S.H.I.M., B.S.H.P., B.S.N, B.S.R.A., B.S.R.C., B.S.R.T., B.S.T. and B.S.W. degrees. Master's and Doctoral degrees are also awarded. Bachelor's degrees are awarded in AGRICULTURE (agricultural business management, agriculture, and animal science), BIOLOGICAL SCIENCE (biochemistry, biology/biological science, marine biology, microbiology, nutrition, physiology, wildlife biology, and zoology), BUSINESS (accounting, banking and finance, business administration and management, business economics, fashion merchandising, finance, management science, marketing/retailing/merchandising, recreational facilities management, and tourism), COMMUNICATIONS AND THE ARTS (advertising, applied art, art, art history and appreciation, audio technology, broadcasting, communication design , communication studies, communications, dance, dramatic arts, English, French, German, jazz, journalism, music, music performance, musical theater, photography, public relations, Spanish, studio art, and theatre arts), COMPUTER AND PHYSICAL SCIENCE (chemistry, computer information systems, computer science, mathematics, and physics), EDUCATION (athletic training, education, health education, health information management, physical education, special education, and technical education), ENGINEERING AND ENVIRONMENTAL DESIGN (cartography, city/community/regional planning, construction management, construction technology, electrical/electronics engineering, engineering technology, environmental science, industrial engineering, industrial engineering technology, interior design, land use management and reclamation, manufacturing engineering, manufacturing technology, urban planning technology, and water and waste-water technology), HEALTH PROFESSIONS (clinical science, exercise science, health and physical activity, health care administration, medical records administration/services, nursing, radiation therapy, respiratory therapy, and speech pathology/audiology), SOCIAL SCIENCE (American studies, anthropology, Asian/Oriental studies, child care/child and family studies, communication sciences and disorders, corrections, criminal justice, economics, European studies, family/consumer studies, geography, history, interdisciplinary studies, international relations, international studies, law enforcement and corrections, liberal arts/general studies, Middle Eastern studies, philosophy, political science/government, psychology, public administration, social work, and sociology). Geography, education,

nursing, anthropology, and engineering are the strongest academically. Education, business, psychology, exercise and sports science are the largest.

ACTIVITIES: 5% of men belong to 6 local and 15 national fraternities; 5% of women belong to 12 national sororities. There are 329 groups on campus, including art, band, cheerleading, chess, choir, chorale, chorus, computers, dance, debate, drama, drill team, ethnic, gay, honors, international, jazz band, literary magazine, marching band, musical theater, newspaper, nontraditional students, opera, orchestra, pep band, photography, political, professional, radio and TV, religious, social, social service, student government, symphony, and yearbook. Popular campus events include University Common Experience, Welcome Week, Trade Up Days, Moonlight Breakfast, Philosophy Dialogues Series, Encore Series of Music and Theatrical Performances. **Sports:** There are 5 intercollegiate sports for men and 7 for women, and 10 intramural sports for men and 10 for women. Facilities include a 30,000-seat stadium, a 7200-seat gym, 2000-seat baseball stadium, and 1000-seat softball stadium. There are tennis courts, a spring-fed pool, an aquatic sports center. A student recreation center with basketball and volleyball courts, racquetball courts, an indoor jogging/walking track, weight-lifting equipment, exercise machines, and rooms for fitness, dance, and aerobics. **Graduates:** From July 1, 2013 to June 30, 2014, 6020 bachelor's degrees were awarded. The most popular majors were Interdisciplinary studies (education) (7%), psychology (6%), and management (6%). 889 companies recruited on campus in 2013-2014. In an average class, 2% graduate in 3 years or less, 28% graduate in 4 years or less, 49% graduate in 5 years or less, and 56% graduate in 6 years or less. Of the 2013 graduating class, 22% were enrolled in graduate school within 6 months of graduation, and 83% were employed.

SERVICES: Counseling and information services are available, as is tutoring in most subjects. There is a reader service for the blind, remedial math, reading, and writing. Tutoring is available for all core curriculum classes. **Library/Resources:** The library contains 4.2 million volumes, 2.0 million microform items, 116,439 audio/video tapes/CDs/DVDs, and subscribes to 14,762 periodicals including electronic. Computerized library services include interlibrary loans, database searching, Internet access, and Wi-Fi capability. Special learning facilities include an art gallery, planetarium, radio station, recording studio, a telescope, clean room for manufacturing micro chips, anthropology forensics laboratory. **Physically Challenged Students:** 88% of the campus is accessible. Facilities include wheelchair ramps, elevators, special parking, specially equipped restrooms, special class scheduling, lowered drinking fountains, lowered telephones, special housing, curb cuts, pay TTY text telephones, adaptive computer technology, sign language interpreter, and reading recorder services for the visually impaired. **Special:** Co-op programs in medicine, dentistry, engineering, architecture, law, pharmacy, nursing, occupational therapy, and veterinary medicine, internships in many departments, study abroad in 26 countries, and Washington semesters are available. Dual majors, credit for life experience, and non-degree study also are possible. Two summer sessions are offered in most programs. A 3-2 engineering degree is possible with the University of Texas, Texas A&M, Texas Tech University, and University of Texas at San Antonio. There are 24 national honor societies, a freshman honors program, and 1 departmental honors program. **Visiting:** There are regularly scheduled orientations for prospective students, a 2-day event, with registration required. First-time freshmen parents may attend. Students receive registration instructions, academic advising, and information concerning Texas State's academic policies, procedures, and student services. Time is allotted to register for classes. There are guides for informal visits and visitors may sit in on classes. To schedule a visit, contact the Admissions Office. **Campus Safety and Security:** Measures include 24-hour foot and vehicle patrol, emergency notification system, self-defense education, and security escort services. There are shuttle buses, emergency telephones, and lighted pathways/sidewalks.

REQUIREMENTS: The SAT or ACT is required. The ACT Optional Writing test is also required. Minimum test scores are determined by high school class rank. Applicants need 24 academic credits, including 4 units in English, 3.5 in social science and electives, 3 in math and science, 2 in foreign language, 1.5 in physical education, 1 in technology applications and fine arts and .5 in speech, economics, health education, and 3.5 in electives. The GED is accepted; applicants with a GED are treated as though they were in the 4th quarter of their graduating class. AP and CLEP credits are accepted. Important factors in the admissions decision are advanced placement or honors courses, leadership record, and extracurricular activities record.All students must earn a minimum GPA of 2.0 while taking at least 120 semester hours, including 30 SCH in their major. The core curriculum includes basic skills, history and political science, natural science, social science, philosophy, international perspectives, literature, fine arts, and physical fitness. **Procedure:** Freshmen are admitted to all sessions. Entrance exams should be taken at the end of the junior year. There is a rolling admissions plan. Applications should be filed by May 1 for fall entry; December 1 for spring entry; and May 1 for summer entry, along with a $75 fee. Applications are accepted on-line. **Transfer Students:** 3735 transfer students enrolled in 2013-2014. Transfer students with 29 or fewer credits must meet freshman requirements; those with 30 or more credits must submit official transcripts to verify a minimum 2.25 GPA. 30 of 120 credits required for the bachelor's degree must be completed at Texas State. **International Students:** There are 145 international students enrolled. They must take the TOEFL with a minimum score of 550 on the paper-based TOEFL (PBT) or 78 on the Internet-based version (iBT). They must also take the SAT or ACT.

ADMISSIONS: 73% of the 2014-2015 applicants were accepted. The SAT scores for the 2014-2015 freshman class were: Critical Reading--45% below 500, 44% between 500 and 599, 10% between 600 and 699, and 1% between 700 and 800; Math--37% below 500, 51% between 500 and 599, 11% between 600 and 699, and 1% between 700 and 800; Writing--54% below 500, 40% between 500 and 599, 5% between 600 and 699, and 1% between 700 and 800. The ACT scores were 25% below 21, 37% between 21 and 23, 23% between 24 and 26, 9% between 27 and 28, and 6% above 28. 34% of the current freshmen were in the top fifth of their class; 76% were in the top two fifths. There were 1 National Merit finalists. 22 freshmen graduated first in their class. **Admissions Contact:** Stephanie Anderson, Assistant VP for Enrollment Management. E-Mail: *admissions@txstate.edu* Web: *www.txstate.edu*

FINANCIAL AID: In 2014-2015, 84% of all full-time freshmen and 75% of continuing full-time students received some form of financial aid. 59% of all full-time freshmen and 51% of continuing full-time students received need-based aid. The average freshman award was $8,429. Need-based scholarships or need-based grants averaged $4,066 ($9,055 maximum); need-based self-help aid (loans and jobs) averaged $1,987 ($5,631 maximum); non-need-based athletic scholarships averaged $9,205 ($19,297 maximum); other non-need-based awards and non-need-based scholarships averaged $7,087 ($21,260 maximum); and $4,562 from other forms of aid. 56% of undergraduate students work part-time. Average annual earnings from campus work are $5444. The average financial indebtedness of the 2014 graduate was $16,723. The FAFSA is required. The priority date for freshman financial aid applications for fall entry is April 1.

TEXAS TECH UNIVERSITY   B-2
www.ttu.edu

Lubbock, TX 79409-5005	(806) 742-2011
	(806) 742-1480
Fax: (806) 742-0062	Email: admissions@ttu.edu
Full-time: 11,700 men, 9450 women	Faculty: n/av; I, --$
Part-time: 1200 men, 800 women	Ph.D.s: 92%
Graduate: 2760 men, 2500 women	Student/Faculty: n/av
Year: semesters, summer session	Tuition: $10,500 ($18,155)
Room & Board: $8095	Freshman Class: n/av
SAT or ACT: required	CEEB CODE: 6827
Application Deadline: see profile	COMPETITIVE

Texas Tech University, founded in 1923, is a large, comprehensive public university offering undergraduate and graduate programs in a variety of professional fields. The figures in the above capsule and this profile are approximate. There are 10 undergraduate schools and 1 graduate school. In addition to regional accreditation, Texas Tech has baccalaureate program accreditation with AACSB, ABET,

ACEJMC, ASLA, CSWE, NAAB, NASAD, NASM, and NCATE. The 1839-acre campus is in an urban area in Lubbock. Including any residence halls, there are 138 buildings.

STUDENT LIFE: 93% of undergraduates are from Texas. Others are from 47 states, 121 foreign countries, and Canada. 75% are white; 12% Hispanic. The average age of freshmen is 19; all undergraduates, 21. 17% do not continue beyond their first year; 56% remain to graduate.

FACULTY/CLASSROOMS: 62% of faculty are male; 38% are female. All teach undergraduates, 46% do research, and 46% do both. No introductory courses are taught by graduate students. The average class size in an introductory lecture is 45; in a laboratory, 21; and in a regular course, 35.

PROGRAMS OF STUDY: Texas Tech confers B.A., B.S., B.F.A., B.G.S., B.I.D., B.Land.Arch., B.M., B.S.ARCH., B.S.C.E., B.S.Ch.E., B.S.E.E., B.S. Eng. Physics, B.S. Eng. Tech., B.S.Envir. Eng., B.S. in Family and Consumer Sciences, B.S. Home Eco., B.S. Indust. Eng., B.S. Int'l Eco., B.S in Community, Family, and Addiction Services, B.S.M.E., B.S.P.E., and B.S.R.H.I.M degrees. Master's and doctoral degrees are also awarded. Bachelor's degrees are awarded in AGRICULTURE (agricultural business management, agricultural communications, agricultural economics, agronomy, animal science, conservation and regulation, fish and game management, horticulture, plant protection (pest management), range/farm management, and wildlife management), BIOLOGICAL SCIENCE (biochemistry, biology/biological science, cell biology, microbiology, molecular biology, nutrition, and zoology), BUSINESS (banking and finance, business administration and management, business economics, hotel/motel and restaurant management, international business management, international economics, management information systems, marketing and distribution, and retailing), COMMUNICATIONS AND THE ARTS (advertising, apparel design, art history and appreciation, broadcasting, classics, communications, dance, design, dramatic arts, English, French, German, journalism, music, music performance, music theory and composition, performing arts, photography, public relations, Spanish, studio art, telecommunications, theater design, and visual and performing arts), COMPUTER AND PHYSICAL SCIENCE (chemistry, computer science, geology, geophysics and seismology, geoscience, mathematics, and physics), EDUCATION (early childhood education, middle school education, and science education), ENGINEERING AND ENVIRONMENTAL DESIGN (architecture, chemical engineering, civil engineering, construction technology, electrical/electronics engineering, electrical/electronics engineering technology, energy management technology, engineering, engineering physics, engineering technology, environmental engineering, industrial engineering, interior design, landscape architecture/design, mechanical engineering, and mechanical engineering technology), HEALTH PROFESSIONS (exercise science and health), SOCIAL SCIENCE (addiction studies, anthropology, child psychology/development, clothing and textiles management/production/services, dietetics, economics, family/consumer resource management, family/consumer studies, food production/management/services, food science, geography, history, home economics, human development, Latin American studies, liberal arts/general studies, philosophy, political science/government, psychology, Russian and Slavic studies, social work, and sociology). Business, exercise and sports sciences, and mechanical engineering have the largest enrollments.

ACTIVITIES: 14% of men belong to 25 national fraternities; 18% of women belong to 1 local and 17 national sororities. There are 400 groups on campus, including art, band, cheerleading, chess, choir, chorale, chorus, communications, computers, dance, debate, drama, drill team, drum and bugle corps, environmental, ethnic, film, forensics, gay, honors, international, jazz band, literary magazine, marching band, musical theater, newspaper, opera, orchestra, pep band, photography, political, professional, radio and TV, religious, social, social service, student government, symphony, and yearbook. Popular campus events include Parents Day, Carol of the Lights, and Madrigal Dinner.

SERVICES: Counseling and information services are available, as is tutoring in every subject. There is a reader service for the blind, remedial math, reading, and writing. Books on tape, note taking services, tape recorders, a learning center which provides peer tutoring, a computer video lab, academic skills assessments, and testing accommodations for students with disabilities. **Library/Resources:** The 5 libraries contain 4.9 million volumes, 2.3 million microform items, and 85,909 audio/video tapes/CDs/DVDs, and subscribe to 22,717 periodicals including electronic. Computerized library services include interlibrary loans, database searching, Internet access, and Wi-Fi capability. Special learning facilities include an art gallery, natural history museum, planetarium, radio station, TV station, a ranching heritage center, an international cultural center, an international textile center, and a Southwest collection. **Physically Challenged Students:** All of the campus is accessible. Facilities include wheelchair ramps, elevators, special parking, specially equipped restrooms, special class scheduling, lowered drinking fountains, lowered telephones, special housing. **Special:** Texas Tech offers many bachelor-to-masters accelerated degree programs, internships, study abroad, dual degrees, dual majors, extended studies, and pass/fail options. There are 20 national honor societies, including Phi Beta Kappa, and a freshman honors program. **Visiting:** There are regularly scheduled orientations for prospective students, including summer orientation conferences offering new students an opportunity to meet with advisers, register early for the fall semester, and get acquainted with the campus. There are guides for informal visits. To schedule a visit, contact Visitor Center at (806) 742-1299. **Campus Safety and Security:** Measures include 24-hour foot and vehicle patrol and emergency notification system. There are shuttle buses, emergency telephones, lighted pathways/sidewalks, and presentations on crime prevention.

REQUIREMENTS: The SAT or ACT is required. Applicants should be graduates of an accredited high school or have the GED. The university requires 11 credits of academic work in high school, including 4 credits in English, 3 in math, 2 in lab sciences, and 2 in foreign language. AP and CLEP credits are accepted.

FINANCIAL AID: The FAFSA is required. Check with the school for current application deadlines.

TEXAS WESLEYAN UNIVERSITY   D-2
www.txwes.edu

Fort Worth, TX 76105	(817) 531-4444
	(800) 580-8980
Fax: (817) 531-7515	Email: admissions@txwes.edu
Full-time: 768 men, 656 women	Faculty: 112
Part-time: 188 men, 305 women	Ph.D.s: 87%
Graduate: 256 men, 433 women	Student/Faculty: 15 to 1
Year: semesters, summer session	Tuition: $23,144
Room & Board: $8238	Freshman Class: 1027 applied, 706 accepted, 313 enrolled
SAT CR/M/W: 490/500/460 ACT: 21	CEEB CODE: 6828
Application Deadline: open	COMPETITIVE

Texas Wesleyan University, founded in 1890, is a liberal arts institution affiliated with the United Methodist Church. There are 4 undergraduate schools and 3 graduate schools. In addition to regional accreditation, Texas Wesleyan has baccalaureate program accreditation with AACSB, ACBSP, NASM, and CAATE. The 79-acre campus is in an urban area 2 miles east of downtown Fort Worth. Including any residence halls, there are 37 buildings.

STUDENT LIFE: 74% of undergraduates are from Texas. Others are from 26 states, 45 foreign countries, and Canada. 95% are from public schools. 33% are White; 22% Foreign; 21% Hispanic; 13% African American. 48% claim no religious affiliation; 39% Protestant. The average age of freshmen is 19; all undergraduates, 23. 49% do not continue beyond their first year; 51% remain to graduate. **Housing:** 467 students can be accommodated in college housing, which includes single-sex and coed dorms and on-campus apartments. On-campus housing and is available on a first-come, first-served basis. 79% of students commute. Alcohol is not permitted. All students may keep cars.

FACULTY/CLASSROOMS: 45% of faculty are male; 55% are female. 89% teach undergraduates. No introductory courses are taught by graduate students. The average class size in an introductory lecture is 15.

PROGRAMS OF STUDY: Texas Wesleyan confers B.A., B.B.A., B.F.A., B.M. and B.S. degrees. Master's and Doctoral degrees are also awarded. Bachelor's degrees are awarded in BIOLOGICAL SCIENCE (biochemistry and biology/biological science), BUSINESS (accounting, business administration and management, business economics, management information systems, marketing management, marketing/retailing/merchandising, and sports management), COMMUNICATIONS AND THE ARTS (advertising, art, broadcasting, dramatic arts, English, journalism, music, Spanish, and theater design), COMPUTER AND PHYSICAL SCIENCE (chemistry, computer science, and mathematics), EDUCATION (athletic training, education, elementary education, foreign languages education, mathematics education, physical education, social science education, social studies education, and teaching English as a second/foreign language (TESOL/TEFOL)), HEALTH PROFESSIONS (exercise science), SOCIAL SCIENCE (criminal justice, economics, history, industrial and organizational psychology, interdisciplinary studies, international relations, paralegal studies, political science/government, prelaw, psychology, religion, religious education, and sociology). Computer science, psychology and general business have the largest enrollments.

ACTIVITIES: 3% of men belong to 1 local and 1 national fraternities; 3% of women belong to 1 local and 2 national sororities. There are 23 groups on campus, including art, band, cheerleading, choir, chorale, computers, drama, ethnic, forensics, gay, honors, international, jazz band, literary magazine, musical theater, newspaper, opera, political, professional, radio and TV, religious, social, social service, and student government. Popular campus events include We Are Wesleyan Concert, RAM JAM and University College Day. **Sports:** There are 8 intercollegiate sports for men and 10 for women, and 7 intramural sports for men and 7 for women. Facilities include a 1,500-seat athletic center, 2 tennis courts, an off-campus baseball park, softball and soccer fields. **Graduates:** From July 1, 2013 to June 30, 2014, 290 bachelor's degrees were awarded. The most popular majors were liberal studies (13%), education (12%), and criminal justice (8%). 62 companies recruited on campus in 2013-2014. In an average class, 1% graduate in 3 years or less, 16% graduate in 4 years or less, 32% graduate in 5 years or less, and 39% graduate in 6 years or less.

SERVICES: Counseling and information services are available, as is tutoring in most subjects. There is remedial math, reading, and writing. **Library/Resources:** The library contains 194,022 volumes, 20,397 microform items, 6,259 audio/video tapes/CDs/DVDs, and subscribes to 1,710 periodicals including electronic. Computerized library services include interlibrary loans, database searching, Internet access, and Wi-Fi capability. Special learning facilities include an art gallery, radio station, and a theater. **Physically Challenged Students:** Facilities include wheelchair ramps, elevators, special parking, specially equipped restrooms, special class scheduling, and lowered telephones. **Special:** Study abroad is offered in more than 25 countries. A 3-2 engineering degree is offered in conjunction with a number of universities. Pass/fail options are available, as are B.A.-B.S. degrees and internships in sports management, business, psychology, mass communication, and sociology. A predentistry program is available. There are 15 national honor societies and 8 departmental honors programs. **Visiting:** There are regularly scheduled orientations for prospective students. There are guides for informal visits, visitors may sit in on classes, and stay overnight. To schedule a visit, contact the Office of Admissions. **Campus Safety and Security:** Measures include 24-hour foot and vehicle patrol, emergency notification system, self-defense education, and security escort services. There are emergency telephones, lighted pathways/sidewalks, controlled access to dorms/residences, and residence hall programs.

REQUIREMENTS: The SAT or ACT is required. Applicants must be graduates of an accredited secondary school or have a GED equivalent, with satisfactory of 19 ACT composite score or 920 SAT combined score in critical reading and math only. Texas Wesleyan requires applicants to be in the upper 50% of their class. A GPA of 2.5 is required. AP and CLEP credits are accepted. Important factors in the admissions decision are leadership record, extracurricular activities record, and recommendations by alumni. A minimum GPA of 2.0 and a minimum of 124 credit hours are required to graduate. All students must complete a general education requirement of 51 credits, including courses in writing, literature, religion, lab science, history, math, political or economic systems, fine arts, humanities, phys ed, and social science, philosophy, or psychology. The total number of hours in the major varies. **Procedure:** Freshmen are admitted to all sessions. Entrance exams should be taken as early as possible. There is a rolling admissions plan. Application deadlines are open. Applications are accepted on-line. **Transfer Students:** 287 transfer students enrolled in 2013-2014. Applicants with fewer than 30 credit hours must submit a high school transcript and the results of either the SAT or the ACT. A minimum GPA of 2.0 is required. 45 of 124 credits required for the bachelor's degree must be completed at Texas Wesleyan. **International Students:** There are 406 international students enrolled. The school actively recruits these students. They must take the TOEFL with a minimum score of 520 on the paper-based TOEFL (PBT) or 68 on the Internet-based version (iBT).

ADMISSIONS: 69% of the 2014-2015 applicants were accepted. The SAT scores for the 2014-2015 freshman class were: Critical Reading--56% below 500, 38% between 500 and 599, and 6% between 600 and 699; Math--42% below 500, 53% between 500 and 599, and 5% between 600 and 699; Writing--60% below 500, 33% between 500 and 599, 7% between 600 and 699, and 1% between 700 and 800. The ACT scores were 44% below 21, 36% between 21 and 23, 12% between 24 and 26, 7% between 27 and 28, and 1% above 28. 1 freshman graduated first in the class. **Admissions Contact:** Chadd Bridwell, Enrollment Services Assistant V.P.. E-Mail: *cbridwell@txwes .edu* Web: *www.txwes.edu*

FINANCIAL AID: In 2014-2015, 90% of all full-time freshmen and continuing full-time students received some form of financial aid. 90% of all full-time freshmen and continuing full-time students received need-based aid. The average freshman award was $21,919. Need-based scholarships or need-based grants averaged $8,500 ($12,000 maximum); need-based self-help aid (loans and jobs) averaged $3,658 ($5,000 maximum); non-need-based athletic scholarships averaged $3,700 ($4,700 maximum); and other non-need-based awards and non-need-based scholarships averaged $2,850 ($6,000 maximum). 7% of undergraduate students work part-time. Average annual earnings from campus work are $3100. The average financial indebtedness of the 2014 graduate was $33,333. The FAFSA and the college's own financial statement are required. The priority date for freshman financial aid applications for fall entry is March 1. The deadline for filing freshman financial aid applications for fall entry is March 1.

TEXAS WOMAN'S UNIVERSITY (*The complete profile is made available exclusively on our website, www.barronspac.com*)

TRINITY UNIVERSITY   D-4
www.trinity.edu

San Antonio, TX 78212	**(210) 999-7011**
	1-800-TRINITY
Fax: (210) 999-8164	**Email:** admissions@trinity.edu
Full-time: 1071 men, 1184 women	**Faculty:** 244; IIA, ++$
Part-time: 19 men, 19 women	**Ph.D.s:** 98%
Graduate: 62 men, 129 women	**Student/Faculty:** 9 to 1
Year: semesters, summer session	**Tuition:** $36,214
Room & Board: $11,936	**Freshman Class:** 5502 applied, 2664 accepted, 655 enrolled
SAT CR/M/W: 631/639/607 **ACT:** 29	**CEEB CODE:** 6831
Application Deadline: February 1	**HIGHLY COMPETITIVE+**

Trinity University, founded in 1869, is a private liberal arts university. There is 1 undergraduate school and 1 graduate school. In addition to regional accreditation, Trinity has baccalaureate program accreditation with AACSB, ABET, NASM, and NCATE. The 117-acre campus is in an urban area 3 miles north of downtown San Antonio. Including any residence halls, there are 45 buildings.

STUDENT LIFE: 68% of undergraduates are from Texas. Others are from 45 states, 72 foreign countries, and Canada. 63% are from public schools. 56% are White; 18% Hispanic. 31% claim no religious affiliation; 29% Unknown Religious affiliation; 21% Catholic; 11%

Protestant. The average age of freshmen is 18; all undergraduates, 20. 12% do not continue beyond their first year; 88% remain to graduate. **Housing:** 1816 students can be accommodated in college housing, which includes coed dorms. In addition, there are language houses and special-interest houses. On-campus housing is guaranteed for all 4 years. 75% of students live on campus. All students may keep cars. **FACULTY/CLASSROOMS:** 59% of faculty are male; 41% are female. All teach undergraduates, all do research. No introductory courses are taught by graduate students. The average class size in an introductory lecture is 21; in a laboratory is 25; and in a regular course is 21.

PROGRAMS OF STUDY: Trinity confers B.A., B.S. and B.M. degrees. Master's degrees are also awarded. Bachelor's degrees are awarded in AGRICULTURE (environmental studies), BIOLOGICAL SCIENCE (biochemistry and biology/biological science), BUSINESS (business administration and management), COMMUNICATIONS AND THE ARTS (art history, art, Chinese, classics, communications, dramatic arts, English, French, German, Greek, Latin, music, Russian, and Spanish), COMPUTER AND PHYSICAL SCIENCE (chemistry, computer science, geoscience, mathematics, and physics), ENGINEERING AND ENVIRONMENTAL DESIGN (engineering and applied science), SOCIAL SCIENCE (anthropology, economics, history, international relations, philosophy, political science/government, psychology, religion, sociology, and urban studies). Business, communication, and modern languages and literatures have the largest enrollments.

ACTIVITIES: 22% of men belong to 8 local fraternities; 29% of women belong to 7 local sororities. There are 146 groups on campus, including art, band, cheerleading, chess, choir, chorale, chorus, communications, computers, dance, debate, drama, drill team, environmental, ethnic, film, forensics, gay, honors, international, jazz band, literary magazine, musical theater, newspaper, opera, orchestra, pep band, photography, political, professional, radio and TV, religious, social, social service, student government, symphony, wind ensemble and gaming, and yearbook. Popular campus events include Chocolate Festival, TigerFest Gala, and the Tower Climb. **Sports:** There are 9 intercollegiate sports for men and 9 for women, and 20 intramural sports for men and 20 for women. Facilities include an indoor Olympic pool and diving center, a 5000-seat stadium, and a 3000-seat auditorium/arena. **Graduates:** From July 1, 2013 to June 30, 2014, 517 bachelor's degrees were awarded. The most popular majors were business administration (21%), communication (7%), and modern languages and literature (6%). 83 companies recruited on campus in 2013-2014. In an average class, 72% graduate in 4 years or less, 80% graduate in 5 years or less, and 81% graduate in 6 years or less. Of the 2013 graduating class, 26% were enrolled in graduate school within 6 months of graduation, and 64% were employed.

SERVICES: Counseling and information services are available, as is tutoring in most subjects. **Library/Resources:** The library contains 911,530 volumes, 307,774 microform items, 35,315 audio/video tapes/CDs/DVDs, and subscribes to 2,444 periodicals including electronic. Computerized library services include interlibrary loans, database searching, Internet access, and Wi-Fi capability. Special learning facilities include an art gallery, radio station, and TV station. **Physically Challenged Students:** Facilities include wheelchair ramps, elevators, special parking, specially equipped restrooms, special class scheduling, lowered drinking fountains, lowered telephones and special housing. Accommodations for students with disabilities are determined through the office of Disability Services for Students. **Special:** The university offers student-designed interdisciplinary majors, double majors, significant opportunities for undergraduate research in the humanities and sciences, an entrepreneurship minor and program, a robust business curriculum, study abroad in 35 countries, and internship experiences outside the normal classroom for credit, as well as teacher certification. There are 21 national honor societies, including Phi Beta Kappa, and 14 departmental honors programs. **Visiting:** There are regularly scheduled orientations for prospective students, campus tour, information session, and meetings with current students, faculty, or staff. There are guides for informal visits, visitors may sit in on classes, and stay overnight. To schedule a visit, contact The Admissions Office at 1 (800) TRINITY . **Campus Safety and Security:** Measures include 24-hour foot and vehicle patrol, emergency notification system, self-defense education, and security escort services. There are emergency telephones, lighted pathways/sidewalks, controlled access to dorms/residences, and shuttle carts.

REQUIREMENTS: The SAT or ACT is required. Applicants are expected to have completed 4 years of English, 3 of math, 3 each of lab science and social studies, and 2 foreign language. A personal essay, standardized test scores, an official high school transcript, high school counselor recommendation, and teacher evaluation are required. A campus visit is also recommended. AP credits are accepted. Important factors in the admissions decision are advanced placement or honors courses, recommendations by school officials, and extracurricular activities record. To graduate, students must satisfy the common curriculum, complete at least one major, the residency requirements, and complete a minimum of 124 credit hours (129 for B.S. in engineering science and 141 for a B.M. in performance and composition). Students must take at least 60 hours outside the major and 30 hours in upper-division courses. A minimum 2.0 GPA is required. **Procedure:** Freshmen are admitted fall, spring, and summer. Entrance exams should be taken late in the junior year or early in the senior year. There are early decision, early admissions, and deferred admissions plans. Early decision applications should be filed by November 1; regular applications, by February 1 for fall entry; and November 15 for spring entry. Notification of early decision is sent December 15; regular decision, April 1. 102 early decision candidates were accepted for the 2014-2015 class. 196 applicants were on the 2014 waiting list; 23 were admitted. Applications are accepted online. Application fees are waived if application is completed on-line. **Transfer Students:** 23 transfer students enrolled in 2013-2014. Transcripts for all colleges attended or attending, high school transcripts, an essay, standardized test scores, and a statement of good standing from the prior institution are required. An interview and visit to campus is recommended. 60 of 124 credits required for the bachelor's degree must be completed at Trinity. **International Students:** There are 170 international students enrolled. The school actively recruits these students. They must take the TOEFL. They must also take the SAT or ACT.

ADMISSIONS: 48% of the 2014-2015 applicants were accepted. The SAT scores for the 2014-2015 freshman class were: Critical Reading--3% below 500, 29% between 500 and 599, 48% between 600 and 699, and 19% between 700 and 800; Math--1% below 500, 25% between 500 and 599, 53% between 600 and 699, and 22% between 700 and 800; Writing--8% below 500, 32% between 500 and 599, 48% between 600 and 699, and 11% between 700 and 800. The ACT scores were % below 21, 2% between 21 and 23, 23% between 24 and 26, 20% between 27 and 28, and 55% above 28. 63% of the current freshmen were in the top fifth of their class; 87% were in the top two fifths. There were 10 National Merit finalists. 11 freshmen graduated first in their class. **Admissions Contact:** Office of Admissions E-Mail: *admissions@trinity.edu* Web: *www.trinity.edu*

FINANCIAL AID: In 2014-2015, 97% of all full-time freshmen and 91% of continuing full-time students received some form of financial aid. 46% of all full-time freshmen and 44% of continuing full-time students received need-based aid. The average freshman award was $29,622. Need-based scholarships or need-based grants averaged $6,664; need-based self-help aid (loans and jobs) averaged $2,148; other non-need-based awards and non-need-based scholarships averaged $18,733; and $2,077 from other forms of aid. The average financial indebtedness of the 2014 graduate was $35,318. Trinity is a member of CSS. The CSS/Profile and FAFSA are required. The priority date for freshman financial aid applications for fall entry is February 15.

The University of Dallas, founded in 1955, is a private Catholic liberal arts institution. The university includes four schools: Constantin College of Liberal Arts (undergraduates), Braniff Graduate School of Liberal Arts, Satish and Yasmin Gupta College of Business and School of Ministry. There are 4 undergraduate schools and 3 graduate schools. In addition to regional accreditation, UD has baccalaureate program accreditation with AACSB and IACBE. The 750-acre campus is in an urban area Irving, Texas, 10 miles west of Dallas, 30 miles east of Fort Worth. Including any residence halls, there are 33 buildings.

STUDENT LIFE: 52% of undergraduates are from out of state, mostly the Midwest. Students are from 50 states, 15 foreign countries, and Canada. 45% are from public schools. 69% are White; 17% Hispanic. 84% are Catholic. The average age of freshmen is 18; all undergraduates, 20. 20% do not continue beyond their first year; 73% remain to graduate. **Housing:** 838 students can be accommodated in college housing, which includes single-sex and coed dorms and on-campus apartments. On-campus housing is guaranteed for the freshman year only, and is available on a first-come, first-served basis. 65% of students live on campus; of those, 90% remain on campus on weekends. All students may keep cars.

FACULTY/CLASSROOMS: 64% of faculty are male; 36% are female. 90% teach undergraduates. No introductory courses are taught by graduate students. The average class size in an introductory lecture is 22; in a laboratory is 16; and in a regular course is 19.

PROGRAMS OF STUDY: UD confers B.A., and B.S. degrees. Master's and Doctoral degrees are also awarded. Bachelor's degrees are awarded in BIOLOGICAL SCIENCE (biochemistry and biology/biological science), BUSINESS (business administration and management), COMMUNICATIONS AND THE ARTS (art history and appreciation, ceramic art and design, classics, dramatic arts, English, French, German, painting, printmaking, sculpture, and Spanish), COMPUTER AND PHYSICAL SCIENCE (chemistry, computer science, mathematics, and physics), EDUCATION (art education, education, and elementary education), ENGINEERING AND ENVIRONMENTAL DESIGN (electrical/electronics engineering technology), HEALTH PROFESSIONS (nursing), SOCIAL SCIENCE (economics, history, pastoral studies, philosophy, political science/government, psychology, and theological studies). Biology, classics, English, and politics are the strongest academically. Business, biology, English and psychology have the largest enrollments.

ACTIVITIES: There are 50 groups on campus, including intramural sports, ultimate, art, chess, choir, chorale, chorus, club Rugby, computers, dance, debate, drama, ethnic, film, honors, international, literary magazine, musical theater, newspaper, opera, photography, political, professional, religious, social, social service, student government, symphony, and yearbook. Popular campus events include Charity Week, Groundhog Celebration, Lazy Faire, Mallapalooza, Winter Cotillion, Battle of the Bands, Alumni and Family Weekend, TGIT and Spring Formal. **Sports:** There are 7 intercollegiate sports for men and 8 for women, and 6 intramural sports for men and 3 for women. Facilities include an athletic center with a gym, weight room, aerobics equipment and locker facilities. An outdoor pool and outdoor tennis courts. A collegiate soccer field, a baseball field, a multipurpose field, and 5 miles of jogging trails are also available. **Graduates:** From July 1, 2013 to June 30, 2014, 310 bachelor's degrees were awarded. The most popular majors were social science (16%), business (14%), and English (12%). In an average class, 66% graduate in 4 years or less and 73% graduate in 6 years or less. Of the 2013 graduating class, 21% were enrolled in graduate school within 6 months of graduation.

SERVICES: Counseling and information services are available, as is tutoring in most subjects. There is remedial math and writing. There are writing and math labs, an academic success office, and department sponsored tutoring in nearly every subject. **Library/Resources:** The library contains 364,691 volumes, 4,526 microform items, 432 audio/video tapes/CDs/DVDs, and subscribes to 64,000 periodicals including electronic. Computerized library services include interlibrary loans, database searching, Internet access, and Wi-Fi capability. Special learning facilities include an art gallery, a 80-seat theater, a performance lab and an observatory. **Physically Challenged Students:** 70% of the campus is accessible. Facilities include wheelchair ramps, elevators, special parking, specially equipped restrooms, spe-

---

UNIVERSITY OF DALLAS   D-2
www.udallas.edu

Irving, TX 75062

(972) 721-5000
(972) 721-5266

Fax: (972) 721-5017   Email: crusader@udallas.edu

Full-time: 641 men, 739 women   Faculty: 81; IIA, -$

Part-time: 15 men, 9 women   Ph.D.s: 88%

Graduate: 731 men, 489 women   Student/Faculty: 11 to 1

Year: semesters, summer session   Tuition: $34,430

Room & Board: $11,070   Freshman Class: 1426 applied, 1212 accepted, 353 enrolled

SAT CR/M/W: 615/595/595 ACT: 27   CEEB CODE: 6868

Application Deadline: March 1   VERY COMPETITIVE+

cial class scheduling, and lowered drinking fountains. **Special:** UD offers internships in field experience or an off-campus research semester. The majority of students participate in the Rome Program, a semester-long experience on the UD Rome campus, and summer programs are available in Rome, as well. 3-2 electrical engineering degree (UT-Arlington) and 3-2 nursing degree (Texas Woman's University) are available. There are myriad opportunities for on-campus work-study programs. B.A.-B.S. degrees and double majors are available, as well. 33 concentrations are offered to combine with any major. There are 5 national honor societies, including Phi Beta Kappa, and 4 departmental honors programs. **Visiting:** There are regularly scheduled orientations for prospective students, including a campus tour, meeting with admission counselor, scholarship competition, tour of residence halls, sitting in on classes, lunch with students in the cafeteria, mass and one-on-one meetings with professors. There are guides for informal visits, visitors may sit in on classes, and stay overnight. To schedule a visit, contact the Office of Admission. **Campus Safety and Security:** Measures include 24-hour foot and vehicle patrol, emergency notification system, self-defense education, and security escort services. There are emergency telephones, lighted pathways/sidewalks, and controlled access to dorms/residences.

REQUIREMENTS: The SAT or ACT is required. The university seeks high school students who have pursued a curriculum of college preparatory courses including English, social science, math, science, and a foreign language. Applicants pursuing a discipline in the sciences should have 4 years of math. Depth in a foreign language is advised. Although the university is flexible in its admission requests, applicants should be in the upper third of their graduating class and should present satisfactory SAT or ACT scores. AP and CLEP credits are accepted. Important factors in the admissions decision are leadership record, extracurricular activities record, and advanced placement or honors courses. To graduate with a B.A., students must complete at least 120 credits, including 38 in advanced credits, which included 12 in the major, with a 2.0 GPA. Completion of the 60-credit-hour Core curriculum as well as major requirements is required. To graduate with a B.S degree, students must complete the above requirements for a B.A. plus 12 additional hours in the major. Seniors must pass a comprehensive exam, write a thesis or complete a research or capstone project in their major. **Procedure:** Freshmen are admitted fall and spring. Entrance exams should be taken during the junior year or by the fall of the senior year. There are early admissions, deferred admissions, and rolling admissions plans. Early decision applications should be filed by November 1; regular applications, by March 1 for fall entry; and December 1 for spring entry, along with a $50 fee. Notification is sent on a rolling basis. Applications are accepted on-line. **Transfer Students:** 38 transfer students enrolled in 2013-2014. Applicants must have a minimum 2.5 GPA from an accredited college or university. Official transcripts from all previous colleges attended, a writing sample, a personal statement, and an academic letter of recommendation are required. Students with fewer than 30 transferable credits must also submit SAT or ACT scores and an official high school transcript. 60 of 120 credits required for the bachelor's degree must be completed at UD. **International Students:** There are 34 international students enrolled. The school actively recruits these students. They must take the TOEFL with a minimum score of 79 on the Internet-based version (iBT). SAT or ACT scores may be submitted in place of the TOEFL.

ADMISSIONS: 85% of the 2014-2015 applicants were accepted. The SAT scores for the 2014-2015 freshman class were: Critical Reading--7% below 500, 36% between 500 and 599, 39% between 600 and 699, and 18% between 700 and 800; Math--12% below 500, 44% between 500 and 599, 29% between 600 and 699, and 15% between 700 and 800; Writing--13% below 500, 40% between 500 and 599, 30% between 600 and 699, and 17% between 700 and 800. The ACT scores were 4% below 21, 22% between 21 and 23, 29% between 24 and 26, 14% between 27 and 28, and 31% above 28. 68% of the current freshmen were in the top fifth of their class; 80% were in the top two fifths. There were 14 National Merit finalists. **Admissions Contact:** Elizabeth Griffin Smith, Director of Admission. E-Mail: *crusader@udallas.edu* Web: *www.udallas.edu*

FINANCIAL AID: In 2014-2015, 96% of all full-time freshmen and 94% of continuing full-time students received some form of financial aid. 68% of all full-time freshmen and 58% of continuing full-time students received need-based aid. The average freshman award was $26,613. Need-based scholarships or need-based grants averaged $22,328; need-based self-help aid (loans and jobs) averaged $5,208; and other non-need-based awards and non-need-based scholarships averaged $14,168. 15% of undergraduate students work part-time. Average annual earnings from campus work are $1650. The average financial indebtedness of the 2014 graduate was $31,446. The FAFSA is required. The priority date for freshman financial aid applications for fall entry is January 15.

UNIVERSITY OF HOUSTON SYSTEM

The University of Houston System, established in 1977, is a private system in Texas. It is governed by a 9-member board of regents, whose chief administrator is the chancellor. The primary goal of the system is the overall coordination of teaching, research, and service. The main priorities are long-range planning, governmental and private representation, and overall executive management. The total student enrollment for all four campuses is usually 66,000 with 3,680 faculty members. Altogether there are 180 baccalaureate, 163 master's, and 51 doctural programs offered in the University of Houston System. Profiles of the 4-year campuses are included in this section.

UNIVERSITY OF HOUSTON	E-3
www.uh.edu	

Houston, TX 77004	**(713) 743-2255**
	(713) 743-1010
Fax: n/av	Email: admissions@uh.edu
Full-time: 11963 men, 12010 women	**Faculty:** 938; I, av$
	Ph.D.s: 85%
Part-time: 4696 men, 4246 women	**Student/Faculty:** 25 to 1
Graduate: 4071 men, 3928 women	**Tuition:** $10,518 ($24,378)
Year: semesters, summer session	**Freshman Class:** 17328
Room & Board: $9278	applied, 10915 accepted, 4048 enrolled
SAT CR/M: 554/588 **ACT:** 25	**CEEB CODE:** 6870
Application Deadline: August 1	**VERY COMPETITIVE**

University of Houston, founded in 1927, is a Carnegie-designated Tier-One public research university located the nation's fourth largest city. The University offers 120 undergraduate majors and minors, 139 master's programs and 54 doctoral programs. UH is a global research leader in a variety of disciplines including energy, health and the humanities. It hosts a range of nationally-ranked programs including the acclaimed Creative Writing Program and the Cyvia and the Melvyn Wolff Center for Entrepreneurship. The University also is home to 40 research centers including the pioneering Texas Center for Superconductivity at UH. There are 8 undergraduate schools and 4 graduate schools. In addition to regional accreditation, UH has baccalaureate program accreditation with AACSB, ABET, ACCE, ACPE, NAAB, NASM, NCATE, ACS, CSAC, and ACCE. The 594-acre campus is in an urban area 3 miles from downtown Houston, Texas . Including any residence halls, there are 157 buildings.

STUDENT LIFE: 93% of undergraduates are from Texas. Others are from 48 states, 105 foreign countries, and Canada. 93% are from public schools. 28% are White; 27% Hispanic; 20% Asian American. The average age of freshmen is 18; all undergraduates, 22. 14% do not continue beyond their first year; 48% remain to graduate. **Housing:** 8008 students can be accommodated in college housing, which includes coed dorms, on-campus apartments, off-campus apartments, and married student housing. In addition, there are honors houses, special-interest houses, fraternity houses, and sorority houses. On-campus housing is available on a first-come, first-served basis. 81% of students commute. All students may keep cars.

FACULTY/CLASSROOMS: 61% of faculty are male; 39% are female. 56% teach undergraduates. Graduate students teach 17% of introductory courses. The average class size in an introductory lecture is 76; in a laboratory is 26; and in a regular course is 9.

PROGRAMS OF STUDY: UH confers B.A., B.S., B.A.C.Y., B.Arch., B.B.A., B.F.A., B.M., B.S.C.E., B.S.Ch.E., B.S.C.P.E., B.S.E.E., B.S.I.E.,

B.S.M.E., B.S.B.E. and B.S.P.E.T.E. degrees. Master's and Doctoral degrees are also awarded. Bachelor's degrees are awarded in BIOLOGICAL SCIENCE (biology/biological science), BUSINESS (accounting, hotel/motel and restaurant management, management information systems, marketing and distribution, and supply chain management), COMMUNICATIONS AND THE ARTS (American Sign Language, applied music, art, Chinese, communications, dance, English, French, industrial design, Spanish, and studio art), COMPUTER AND PHYSICAL SCIENCE (chemistry, geology, mathematics, and physics), ENGINEERING AND ENVIRONMENTAL DESIGN (architecture, biomedical engineering, chemical engineering, civil engineering, computer engineering, construction management, electrical/electronics engineering, environmental design, environmental science, industrial engineering, mechanical engineering, mechanical engineering technology, and petroleum/natural gas engineering), HEALTH PROFESSIONS (health and pharmaceutical science), SOCIAL SCIENCE (anthropology, interdisciplinary studies, Italian studies, liberal arts/general studies, and philosophy). Business, and engineering are the strongest academically. Business, biology and psychology have the largest enrollments.

ACTIVITIES: There are 412 groups on campus, including art, band, cheerleading, chess, choir, chorale, chorus, computers, dance, debate, drama, drill team, environmental, ethnic, film, forensics, gay, honors, international, jazz band, literary magazine, marching band, musical theater, newspaper, opera, orchestra, pep band, photography, political, professional, radio and TV, religious, social, social service, student government, symphony, and yearbook. Popular campus events include Frontier Fiesta, Homecoming and Cat's Back. **Sports:** There are 7 intercollegiate sports for men and 10 for women, and 23 intramural sports for men and 23 for women. Facilities include 8 athletics facilities for nearly 400 student-athletes to train and compete — baseball, softball, men's and women's basketball, volleyball, indoor men's and women's track, women's soccer, men's and women's outdoor track, women's tennis and football practice fields. Athletics partners with the University for its women's swimming and diving program to train and compete in the Campus Recreation and Wellness Center Natatorium. **Graduates:** From July 1, 2013 to June 30, 2014, 6372 bachelor's degrees were awarded. The most popular majors were psychology (8%), interdisciplinary studies - general (6%), and accounting (5%). 382 companies recruited on campus in 2013-2014. In an average class, 2% graduate in 3 years or less, 18% graduate in 4 years or less, 39% graduate in 5 years or less, and 48% graduate in 6 years or less.

SERVICES: Counseling and information services are available, as is tutoring in most subjects. There is a reader service for the blind, remedial math, reading, and writing. Accommodation assistance for students taking exams, tutors assisting with course work, and other accommodations are available. **Library/Resources:** The 5 libraries contain 2.8 million volumes, 6.0 million microform items, and 35,117 audio/video tapes/CDs/DVDs, and subscribe to 66,859 periodicals including electronic. Computerized library services include interlibrary loans, database searching, Internet access, and Wi-Fi capability. Special learning facilities include an art gallery, radio station, TV station, and an observatory. **Physically Challenged Students:** 98% of the campus is accessible. Facilities include wheelchair ramps, elevators, special parking, specially equipped restrooms, special class scheduling, lowered drinking fountains, lowered telephones, and special housing. **Special:** Many colleges at the University of Houston offer internships and cooperative education opportunities in areas such as business, engineering, government/policy, education, hospitality, research, healthcare/health education, communications/media, sports, and science, math and technology. UH also offers a 3-2 program with the School of Nursing at the University of Texas Health Science Center. Partnering with The University of Texas Health Science Center at Houston (UTHealth) and The University of Texas Medical Branch at Galveston (UTMB), UH will allow entering students to earn credit hours toward both a Bachelor of Science (B.S.) degree from UH and a Doctor of Medicine (M.D.) from either UTHealth or UTMB in seven years. Study abroad programs include Faculty-Led programs, such as those offered through the Department of Modern and Classical Languages to China and France, and through the African American Studies Program to Africa; Special Programs under the direction of the Department of Hispanic Studies to Latin America and Spain; Affiliated Programs through organizations such as the Council on International Education and Exchange (CIEE), and the University Study Abroad Consortium (USAC), which have established programs all over the world; and Reciprocal Exchange Studies. There are 18 national honor societies, a freshman honors program, and 40 departmental honors programs. **Visiting:** There are regularly scheduled orientations for prospective students, consisting of a tour, information sessions that help with the transition from high school to college and have scheduled time with an academic advisor. There are guides for informal visits and visitors may stay overnight. To schedule a visit, contact the Admissions Staff at the Welcome Center at vc@uh.edu. **Campus Safety and Security:** Measures include 24-hour foot and vehicle patrol, emergency notification system, self-defense education, and security escort services. There are shuttle buses, emergency telephones, lighted pathways/sidewalks, controlled access to dorms/residences, Community dialogues, and assistance with disabled vehicles.

REQUIREMENTS: The SAT or ACT is required. Automatic enrollment granted to applicants who rank in top-tenth of secondary school class and submit a completed application by August 1st. All other students are reviewed using a holistic administration process. A GPA of 2.0 is required. AP and CLEP credits are accepted. Important factors in the admissions decision are evidence of special talent, advanced placement or honors courses, and recommendations by school officials. To graduate, student must complete 120 semester credit hours, including at least 36 in advance-level courses, with a minimum GPA of 2.0. Core Curriculum requirements include 6 hours each in communication, history, government, life and physical sciences; also 3 hours each in math, math/reasoning, language, philosophy and culture, creative arts, social/behavioral sciences, and writing in the disciplines courses. **Procedure:** Freshmen are admitted to all sessions. Entrance exams should be taken priority deadline of December 1st. There is a rolling admissions plan. Early decision applications should be filed by December 1; regular applications, by August 1 for fall entry; January 5 for spring entry; and April 1 for summer entry, along with a $50 fee. Notifications are sent April 15. Applications are accepted on-line. **Transfer Students:** 4674 transfer students enrolled in 2013-2014. Applicants must be eligible to return to their last college. A 2.0 GPA is required for students with 30 or more semester hours of college credit, a 2.5 GPA for those with 15 to 29. 30 of 120 credits required for the bachelor's degree must be completed at UH. **International Students:** There are 1254 international students enrolled. The school actively recruits these students. They must take the TOEFL with a minimum score of 550 on the paper-based TOEFL (PBT) or 79 on the Internet-based version (iBT). They must also take the SAT or ACT.

ADMISSIONS: 63% of the 2014-2015 applicants were accepted. The SAT scores for the 2014-2015 freshman class were: Critical Reading--22% below 500, 49% between 500 and 599, 25% between 600 and 699, and 4% between 700 and 800; Math--10% below 500, 44% between 500 and 599, 38% between 600 and 699, and 8% between 700 and 800. The ACT scores were 12% below 21, 28% between 21 and 23, 33% between 24 and 26, 15% between 27 and 28, and 12% above 28. 55% of the current freshmen were in the top fifth of their class. There were 32 National Merit finalists. 29 freshmen graduated first in their class. **Admissions Contact:** Djuana Young, Admissions Director. E-Mail: *admissions@uh.edu* Web: *http://www.uh.edu/admissions/*

FINANCIAL AID: In 2014-2015, 85% of all full-time freshmen and 73% of continuing full-time students received some form of financial aid. 54% of all full-time freshmen and 55% of continuing full-time students received need-based aid. The average freshman award was $12,641. Need-based scholarships or need-based grants averaged $8,485 ($17,730 maximum); need-based self-help aid (loans and jobs) averaged $3,562 ($8,500 maximum); non-need-based athletic scholarships averaged $18,822 ($29,450 maximum); and other non-need-based awards and non-need-based scholarships averaged $5,993 ($41,960 maximum). 7% of undergraduate students work part-time. The average financial indebtedness of the 2014 graduate was $18,453. UH is a member of CSS. The FAFSA is required. The priority date for freshman financial aid applications for fall entry is April 1. The deadline for filing freshman financial aid applications for fall entry is May 1.

UNIVERSITY OF HOUSTON-DOWNTOWN (*The complete profile is made available exclusively on our website, www.barronspac.com*)

UNIVERSITY OF MARY HARDIN-BAYLOR D-3
www.umhb.edu

Belton, TX 76513	**(254) 295-8642** **(254) 295-4520**
Fax: (254) 295-5049	**Email: admission@umhb.edu**
Full-time: 1058 men, 1731 women	**Faculty:** n/av
Part-time: 104 men, 163 women	**Ph.D.s:** 72%
Graduate: 184 men, 252 women	**Student/Faculty:** 16 to 1
Year: semesters, summer session	**Tuition:** $25,200
Room & Board: $6750	**Freshman Class:** 5540 applied, 4691 accepted, 675 enrolled
SAT CR/M/W: 516/530/485 **ACT:** 24	**CEEB CODE:** 6396
Application Deadline: n/av	**COMPETITIVE+**

The University of Mary Hardin-Baylor, founded in 1845, is a private facility affiliated with the Baptist General Convention of Texas. It offers undergraduate degrees in liberal arts, fine arts, music, business, education, nursing, and social work, as well as graduate degrees in business, information systems, education, psychology/counseling, and nursing, and a doctorate in educational administration. The figures in the above capsule and in this profile are approximate. There are 7 undergraduate schools and 7 graduate schools. In addition to regional accreditation, UMHB has baccalaureate program accreditation with CSWE. The 170-acre campus is in a small town in central Texas halfway between San Antonio and Dallas/Fort Worth. Including any residence halls, there are 71 buildings.

STUDENT LIFE: 98% of undergraduates are from Texas. Others are from 29 states, 14 foreign countries, and Canada. 60% are White; 17% Hispanic; 14% African American. 20% claim no religious affiliation; 13% Catholic. The average age of freshmen is 18; all undergraduates, 22. 34% do not continue beyond their first year; 47% remain to graduate.

FACULTY/CLASSROOMS: 43% of faculty are male; 57% are female. No introductory courses are taught by graduate students. The average class size in an introductory lecture is 25; in a laboratory is 20; and in a regular course is 17.

PROGRAMS OF STUDY: UMHB confers B.A., B.S., B.B.A., B.C.M., B.F.A., B.G.S., B.M., B.S.N. and B.S.W. degrees. Master's and doctoral degrees are also awarded. Bachelor's degrees are awarded in BIOLOGICAL SCIENCE (biology/adolescence education and biology/biological science), BUSINESS (accounting, business administration and management, finance, international business, marketing/retailing/merchandising, and sports management), COMMUNICATIONS AND THE ARTS (art, church music, communications, English, journalism, multimedia, music, music performance, performing arts, Spanish, speech/debate/rhetoric, and visual design), COMPUTER AND PHYSICAL SCIENCE (chemistry, chemistry/adolescence education, clinical laboratory science, computer science, information sciences and systems, and mathematics), EDUCATION (art education, early childhood education, elementary education, English education, foreign languages education, mathematics education, middle school education, music education, physical education, reading education, science education, secondary education, social studies education, and special education), ENGINEERING AND ENVIRONMENTAL DESIGN (computer graphics and engineering science), HEALTH PROFESSIONS (exercise science and nursing), SOCIAL SCIENCE (biblical studies, Christian studies, criminal justice, economics, history, ministries, political science/government, psychology, religion, social work, and sociology). Education, business, and nursing are the strongest academically. Nursing has the largest enrollment.

ACTIVITIES: There are 59 groups on campus, including art, band, cheerleading, chess, choir, chorale, chorus, computers, debate, drama, drill team, ethnic, forensics, honors, international, jazz band, literary magazine, marching band, musical theater, newspaper, opera, orchestra, pep band, photography, political, professional, religious, social service, student government, symphony, and yearbook. Popular campus events include Miss UMHB Pageants, Mr. Crusader Knights, Play Day, and Easter Pageant.

SERVICES: Counseling and information services are available, as is tutoring in most subjects. There is a reader service for the blind, remedial math, reading, and writing. **Library/Resources:** The library contains 206,617 volumes, 5,317 microform items, and 8,679 audio/video tapes/CDs/DVDs, and subscribes to 80,733 periodicals including electronic. Computerized library services include interlibrary loans, database searching, Internet access, and Wi-Fi capability. Special learning facilities include an art gallery, a nature walk. **Physically Challenged Students:** 85% of the campus is accessible. Facilities include wheelchair ramps, elevators, special parking, specially equipped restrooms, special class scheduling, lowered drinking fountains, lowered telephones, and special housing. **Special:** Study abroad in 5 countries, internships, a work-study program, dual majors, a professional studies degree, an applied science bachelor's degree, post-baccalaureate certification in education, and a 5-year B.B.A./M.B.A. accounting specialization are offered. There are 7 national honor societies and a freshman honors program. **Visiting:** There are regularly scheduled orientations for prospective students, consisting of campus tours and visits with counselors to discuss admissions, financial aid, housing, and degree plans. There are guides for informal visits, visitors may sit in on classes, and stay overnight. To schedule a visit, contact the Admissions Office at admissions@umhb.edu. **Campus Safety and Security:** Measures include 24-hour foot and vehicle patrol, emergency notification system, self-defense education, and security escort services. There are emergency telephones, lighted pathways/sidewalks, and a campus police force.

REQUIREMENTS: Students who rank in the top half of their high school graduating class must score a minimum of 950 on the SAT or 20 on the ACT. Those who graduate in the lower half of their class must score a minimum of 990 on the SAT or 21 on the ACT. There is no minimum test score for students who rank in the top 10% of their high school graduating class. All students should be graduates of an accredited high school and have 22 units of credit, including 4 in English, 3 in math, and 2.5 in social science. AP and CLEP credits are accepted. Important factors in the admissions decision are advanced placement or honors courses, recommendations by school officials, and extracurricular activities record.

ADMISSIONS: 85% of a recent year applicants were accepted. The SAT scores for the recent year freshman class were: Critical Reading--42% below 500, 44% between 500 and 599, 12% between 600 and 699, and 2% between 700 and 800; Math--34% below 500, 49% between 500 and 599, 16% between 600 and 699, and 1% between 700 and 800; Writing--60% below 500, 32% between 500 and 599, 7% between 600 and 699, and 1% between 700 and 800. The ACT scores were 28% below 21, 30% between 21 and 23, 22% between 24 and 26, 11% between 27 and 28, and 9% above 28.

FINANCIAL AID: In a recent year, 78% of all full-time freshmen and 81% of continuing full-time students received some form of financial aid. 78% of all full-time freshmen and 80% of continuing full-time students received need-based aid. The average freshman award was $16,940. Need-based scholarships or need-based grants averaged $13,883 ($19,537 maximum); need-based self-help aid (loans and jobs) averaged $3,971 ($6,300 maximum); and other non-need-based awards and non-need-based scholarships averaged $7,926 ($20,000 maximum). 15% of undergraduate students work part-time. Average annual earnings from campus work are $2300. The FAFSA and the college's own financial statement are required. The priority date for freshman financial aid applications for fall entry is March 1. The deadline for filing freshman financial aid applications for fall entry is September 1.

UNIVERSITY OF NORTH TEXAS D-2
www.unt.edu

Denton, TX 76203	**(940) 565-2000** **(800) 868-8211**
Fax: n/av	**Email: unt.freshman@abn.unt.edu**
Full-time: 10503 men, 11964 women	**Faculty:** 613; I, --$
Part-time: 2925 men, 2829 women	**Ph.D.s:** 80%
Graduate: 3065 men, 4719 women	**Student/Faculty:** 28 to 1
Year: semesters, summer session	**Tuition:** $8842 ($18,232)
Room & Board: $7392	**Freshman Class:** 13737 applied, 8969 accepted, 3746 enrolled
SAT CR/M/W: 540/550/520 **ACT:** 23	**CEEB CODE:** 6481
Application Deadline: August 1	**COMPETITIVE**

The University of North Texas, founded in 1890, is a public institution offering students 12 undergraduate schools and 1 graduate school. In addition to regional accreditation, UNT has baccalaureate program accreditation with AACSB, ABET, ACCE, ACEJMC, CSAB, CSWE, FIDER, NASM, NCATE, and NRPA. The 875-acre campus is in a suburban area 35 miles north of Dallas/Fort Worth. Including any residence halls, there are 165 buildings. The figures in the above capsule and in this profile are approximate.

STUDENT LIFE: 97% of undergraduates are from Texas. Others are from 50 states, 139 foreign countries, and Canada. 60% are white; 14% Hispanic; 12% African American. The average age of freshmen is 18; all undergraduates, 22. 22% do not continue beyond their first year; 48% remain to graduate.

FACULTY/CLASSROOMS: 55% of faculty are male; 45% are female. 80% teach undergraduates. Graduate students teach 34% of introductory courses. The average class size in an introductory lecture is 52 and in a laboratory is 51.

PROGRAMS OF STUDY: UNT confers B.A., B.A.A.S., B.B.A., B.F.A., B.M., B.S., B.S.B.C., B.S.Bio, B.S.Chem., B.S.Eco., B.S.E.P., B.S.E.T., B.S.Math., B.S.M.T., B.S.Phy., and B.S.W. degrees. Master's and Doctoral degrees are also awarded. Bachelor's degrees are awarded in BIOLOGICAL SCIENCE (biochemistry and biology/biological science), BUSINESS (accounting, banking and finance, business administration and management, electronic business, entrepreneurial studies, hospitality management services, human resources, insurance, investments and securities, logistics, management information systems, management science, marketing/retailing/merchandising, operations management, organizational behavior, organizational leadership and management, purchasing/inventory management, real estate, and recreation and leisure services), COMMUNICATIONS AND THE ARTS (applied art, art, art history and appreciation, broadcasting, choral music, communications, dance, design, dramatic arts, English, French, German, jazz, journalism, music, music history and appreciation, music performance, music theory and composition, musical theater, performing arts, radio/television technology, Spanish, studio art, telecommunications, theater design, theater management, and visual and performing arts), COMPUTER AND PHYSICAL SCIENCE (chemistry, computer science, information sciences and systems, mathematics, and physics), ENGINEERING AND ENVIRONMENTAL DESIGN (aviation administration/management, commercial art, computer engineering, construction engineering, electrical/electronics engineering, electrical/electronics engineering technology, emergency/disaster science, engineering physics, engineering technology, interior design, manufacturing engineering, mechanical engineering, mechanical engineering technology, and nuclear engineering technology), HEALTH PROFESSIONS (cytotechnology, health, medical laboratory technology, rehabilitation therapy, and speech pathology/audiology), SOCIAL SCIENCE (anthropology, applied psychology, child care/child and family studies, criminal justice, economics, fashion design and technology, geography, history, home furnishings and equipment management/production/services, human services, interdisciplinary studies, international studies, liberal arts/general studies, philosophy, physical fitness/movement, political science/government, psychology, social science, social work, and sociology). Jazz studies, public administration, and accounting are the strongest academically. Biology, psychology, and interdisciplinary studies have the largest enrollments.

ACTIVITIES: 4% of men belong to 25 national fraternities; 5% of women belong to 16 national sororities. There are 440 groups on campus, including band, cheerleading, chess, choir, chorale, chorus, computers, dance, debate, drama, ethnic, film, gay, honors, international, jazz band, literary magazine, marching band, musical theater, newspaper, opera, orchestra, pep band, photography, political, professional, radio and TV, religious, social, social service, student government, and symphony. Popular campus events include Howdy Week, Taste of North Texas, Union Day, and Earth Day.

SERVICES: Counseling and information services are available, as is tutoring in most subjects. There is a reader service for the blind, remedial math, reading, and writing. **Library/Resources:** The 5 libraries contain 2.3 million volumes, 3.9 million microform items, and 232,620 audio/video tapes/CDs/DVDs, and subscribe to 95,958 periodicals including electronic. Computerized library services

include interlibrary loans, database searching, Internet access, and Wi-Fi capability. Special learning facilities include an art gallery, planetarium, radio station, TV station, an observatory, and a TV and film production unit. **Physically Challenged Students:** 90% of the campus is accessible. Facilities include wheelchair ramps, elevators, special parking, specially equipped restrooms, special class scheduling, lowered drinking fountains, lowered telephones, and dorm rooms adapted for disabled students. **Special:** UNT offers co-op programs, internships, and work-study programs with the university. Students may study abroad in several locations. An accelerated degree program in math and science allows Texas high school students to obtain 2 years of college credit during their last 2 years in high school. Dual degrees, a general studies degree, and pass/fail options are also offered. There are 42 national honor societies and a freshman honors program. **Visiting:** There are regularly scheduled orientations for prospective students, including 3-day, 2-night sessions throughout the summer. There are guides for informal visits, visitors may sit in on classes, and stay overnight. **Campus Safety and Security:** Measures include 24-hour foot and vehicle patrol, emergency notification system, self-defense education, and security escort services. There are shuttle buses, emergency telephones, lighted pathways/sidewalks, controlled access to dorms/residences, sexual assault information services, and a full-time crime prevention officer on duty.

REQUIREMENTS: The SAT or ACT is required. Applicants must be graduates of an accredited high school and submit a high school transcript. The required minimum score for entrance exams is determined by high school class rank. AP and CLEP credits are accepted.

ADMISSIONS: 65% of a recent year, applicants were accepted. The SAT scores for a recent freshman class were: Critical Reading--29% below 500, 44% between 500 and 599, 23% between 600 and 700, and 4% above 700; Math--23% below 500, 45% between 500 and 599, 25% between 600 and 700, and 6% above 700; Writing--39% below 500, 42% between 500 and 599, 17% between 600 and 700, and 2% above 700. The ACT scores were 21% below 21, 31% between 21 and 23, 25% between 24 and 26, 13% between 27 and 28, and 11% above 28. 40% of the current freshmen were in the top fifth of their class; 75% were in the top two fifths. There were 9 National Merit finalists.

FINANCIAL AID: 7% of undergraduate students work part-time. The FAFSA is required. The priority date for freshman financial aid applications for fall entry is March 31. The deadline for filing freshman financial aid applications for fall entry is June 1.

UNIVERSITY OF ST. THOMAS - HOUSTON E-3
www.stthom.edu

Houston, TX 77006	**(713) 522-7911** **(800) 856-8565**
Fax: (713) 525-3558	**Email:** admissions@stthom.edu
Full-time: 456 men, 818 women	**Faculty:** 131; IIA, -$
Part-time: 185 men, 186 women	**Ph.D.s:** 93%
Graduate: 543 men, 1334 women	**Student/Faculty:** 10 to 1
Year: semesters, summer session	**Tuition:** $29,440
Room & Board: $8250	**Freshman Class:** 795 applied, 628 accepted, 227 enrolled
SAT CR/M/W: 530/560/530 **ACT:** 23	**CEEB CODE:** 6880
Application Deadline: May 1	**COMPETITIVE**

University of St. Thomas in Houston offers a Catholic liberal arts education for a lifetime of opportunities, committed to educating leaders of faith and character. Liberal arts degrees provide invaluable training to a range of careers including business, teaching and health. UST offers 33 undergraduate and 15 graduate degree programs. There are 4 undergraduate schools and 6 graduate schools. In addition to regional accreditation, UST has baccalaureate program accreditation with AACSB, TEAC, ATS, and CCNE. The 23-acre campus is in an urban area 3 miles from Downtown Houston. Including any residence halls, there are 67 buildings.

STUDENT LIFE: 96% of undergraduates are from Texas. Others are from 26 states, 38 foreign countries, and Canada. 74% are from public schools. 37% are Hispanic; 30% White; 12% Asian American.

61% are Catholic; 14% claim no religious affiliation; 13% Buddhist, Muslim, Hindu, Orthodox, Unitarian and Mormon; 11% Protestant. The average age of freshmen is 18; all undergraduates, 25. 12% do not continue beyond their first year; 52% remain to graduate. **Housing:** 326 students can be accommodated in college housing, which includes coed dorms and on-campus apartments. In addition, there are special-interest houses, residents are grouped by classification. On-campus housing is available on a first-come, first-served basis. Priority is given to out-of-town students. 81% of students commute. All students may keep cars.

FACULTY/CLASSROOMS: 51% of faculty are male; 49% are female. 66% teach undergraduates. No introductory courses are taught by graduate students. The average class size in an introductory lecture is 17 and in a laboratory is 16.

PROGRAMS OF STUDY: UST confers B.A., B.F.A., B.S., B.S.N., B.B.A. and B.I.B. degrees. Master's and doctoral degrees are also awarded. Bachelor's degrees are awarded in AGRICULTURE (environmental studies), BIOLOGICAL SCIENCE (biochemistry, bioinformatics, and biology/biological science), BUSINESS (accounting, banking and finance, business administration and management, finance, international business management, marketing, and marketing/retailing/merchandising), COMMUNICATIONS AND THE ARTS (communications, dramatic arts, English, French, music, Spanish, and studio art), COMPUTER AND PHYSICAL SCIENCE (applied mathematics, chemistry, computer science, mathematics, and physics), EDUCATION (business education, education, music education, and nursing education), ENGINEERING AND ENVIRONMENTAL DESIGN (environmental science), HEALTH PROFESSIONS (nursing), SOCIAL SCIENCE (economics, history, international studies, liberal arts/general studies, philosophy, political science/government, psychology, religion, and theological studies). Biology is the strongest academically. Biology, finance, and psychology have the largest enrollments.

ACTIVITIES: There are 80 groups on campus, including art, cheerleading, choir, communications, dance, drama, environmental, ethnic, film, forensics, honors, international, jazz band, literary magazine, musical theater, newspaper, orchestra, political, professional, religious, social, social service, and student government. Popular campus events include Research Symposium, Mass of Holy Spirit, Mass of St. Thomas Aquinas, Family and Alumni Weekend, President's Day of Service, and Deck the Mall. **Sports:** There are 3 intercollegiate sports for men and 4 for women, and 12 intramural sports for men and 12 for women. Facilities include a gym, 3 racquetball courts, a weight room, fitness room, dance room, swimming pool, 2 tennis courts, sand volleyball court, men's and women's locker rooms. Outdoor facilities include 2 lighted playing fields, 2 batting cages, pitching machine, half basketball court and soccer goals. **Graduates:** From July 1, 2013 to June 30, 2014, 304 bachelor's degrees were awarded. The most popular majors were psychology (9%), nursing (9%), and finance (8%). In an average class, 34% graduate in 4 years or less, 48% graduate in 5 years or less, and 52% graduate in 6 years or less.

SERVICES: Counseling and information services are available, as is tutoring in most subjects. There is remedial math, reading, and writing. Kurzweil Educational software for the visually impaired. **Library/ Resources:** The 4 libraries contain 325,445 volumes, 608,296 microform items, 4,011 audio/video tapes/CDs/DVDs, and subscribe to 78,832 periodicals including electronic. Computerized library services include interlibrary loans, database searching, and Internet access. Special learning facilities include an art gallery, and a meditation garden. **Physically Challenged Students:** 90% of the campus is accessible. Facilities include wheelchair ramps, elevators, special parking, specially equipped restrooms, lowered drinking fountains, lowered telephones, special housing. **Special:** UST has a cooperative 3-2 engineering program with the University of Houston, Texas A&M University, University of Notre Dame and Catholic University of America. Internships in the major field of study and study abroad in 11 countries are also available. Dual and joint majors and 5 year joint bachelor's and master's degree programs, combining BBA/MBA are available. There are 23 national honor societies, a freshman honors program, and 1 departmental honors program. **Visiting:** There are regularly scheduled orientations for prospective students, tours, class visitations, introductions to faculty, administrative members, and currently enrolled students, financial aid sessions and social activities.

There are guides for informal visits, visitors may sit in on classes, and stay overnight. To schedule a visit, contact the Admissions Counselor. **Campus Safety and Security:** Measures include 24-hour foot and vehicle patrol, emergency notification system, self-defense education, and security escort services. There are shuttle buses, emergency telephones, lighted pathways/sidewalks, controlled access to dorms/ residences, fire suppression system, fire extinguishers and smoke detectors, annual fire drills; and IP security cameras.

REQUIREMENTS: The SAT or ACT is required. The ACT Optional Writing test is also required. Applicants must graduate from an accredited secondary school, home school program or successfully complete the GED. Additionally, applicants should have competitive grades (minimum high school GPA of 2.80 on a 4.0 scale) in a minimum of 18 college preparatory high school units: including 4 units of English, 3 units of social science, 3 units of mathematics, 3 units of science, 2 units of the same classical or modern language other than English, and 3 units of electives in college preparatory classes. Applicants should also have competitive official SAT or ACT scores and competitive class rank if high school ranks graduates. If appropriate, applicants should submit official transcripts of home school coursework. Home schooled students may also need to submit course descriptions, reading lists, or other information if requested. UST requires applicants to be in the upper 50% of their class. A GPA of 2.5 is required. AP and CLEP credits are accepted. Important factors in the admissions decision are advanced placement or honors courses, recommendations by school officials, and extracurricular activities record. To graduate, students must complete the core curriculum and 30 to 48 hours in their selected majors. In some cases, students need to complete special projects according to the requirements of specific majors. Students must have a minimum 2.0 GPA in a total of 126 credit hours, including 36 hours of upper-division credits and the final 36 hours competed in residence at the University. **Procedure:** Freshmen are admitted fall, spring, and summer. Entrance exams should be taken as early as possible. There are early admissions and deferred admissions plans. Early decision applications should be filed by December 1; regular applications, by May 1 for fall entry; December 1 for spring entry; and May 1 for summer entry. Notification of early decision is sent 12 15; regular decision, on a rolling basis. Applications are accepted on-line. Application fees are waived if application is completed on-line. **Transfer Students:** 253 transfer students enrolled in 2013-2014. Transfer students must have a minimum 2.50 GPA college GPA a minimum high school GPA of 2.80 and have a high school diploma or GED. 36 of 126 credits required for the bachelor's degree must be completed at UST. **International Students:** There are 153 international students enrolled. The school actively recruits these students. They must take the TOEFL with a minimum score of 550 on the paper-based TOEFL (PBT) or 79 on the Internet-based version (iBT). They must also take the SAT or ACT, scoring 23.

ADMISSIONS: 79% of the 2014-2015 applicants were accepted. The SAT scores for the 2014-2015 freshman class were: Critical Reading--27% below 500, 46% between 500 and 599, 20% between 600 and 699, and 7% between 700 and 800; Math--23% below 500, 43% between 500 and 599, 29% between 600 and 699, and 6% between 700 and 800; Writing--33% below 500, 50% between 500 and 599, 13% between 600 and 699, and 4% between 700 and 800. The ACT scores were 12% below 21, 30% between 21 and 23, 30% between 24 and 26, 7% between 27 and 28, and 22% above 28. 45% of the current freshmen were in the top fifth of their class; 65% were in the top two fifths. 3 freshmen graduated first in their class. **Admissions Contact:** Arthur Ortiz, Assistant Vice President for Enrollment. E-Mail: *admissions@stthom.edu* Web: *www.stthom.edu*

FINANCIAL AID: In 2014-2015, 91% of all full-time freshmen and 84% of continuing full-time students received some form of financial aid. 72% of all full-time freshmen and 60% of continuing full-time students received need-based aid. The average freshman award was $23,773. Need-based scholarships or need-based grants averaged $18,997; need-based self-help aid (loans and jobs) averaged $5,371; non-need-based athletic scholarships averaged $4,654; and other non-need-based awards and non-need-based scholarships averaged $11,794. 17% of undergraduate students work part-time. Average annual earnings from campus work are $2367. The average financial indebtedness of the 2014 graduate was $36,497. The FAFSA is required. The priority date for freshman financial aid applications for fall entry is April 15.

UNIVERSITY OF TEXAS - PAN AMERICAN (*The complete profile is made available exclusively on our website, www.barronspac.com*)

UNIVERSITY OF TEXAS AT ARLINGTON (*The complete profile is made available exclusively on our website, www.barronspac.com*)

UNIVERSITY OF TEXAS AT AUSTIN   D-3
www.utexas.edu

Austin, TX 78712   (512) 471-3434
                                             (512) 475-7440
                                                        n/av

Fax: (512) 475-7478
Full-time: 16,500 men, 18,110   **Faculty:** 1100; I, avg$
women   **Ph.D.s:** 84%
Part-time: 1480 men, 1375 women   **Student/Faculty:** 13 to 1
Graduate: 5685 men, 5230 women   **Tuition:** $9500 ($35,000)
Year: semesters, summer session   **Freshman Class:** n/av
Room & Board: $9500
SAT or ACT: required   **CEEB CODE:** 6882
Application Deadline: see profile   **HIGHLY COMPETITIVE**

University of Texas at Austin, founded in 1883, is a major research institution within the University of Texas System and provides a broad range of degree programs. There are 12 undergraduate schools and 15 graduate schools. The figures in the above capsule and this profile are approximate. In addition to regional accreditation, UT has baccalaureate program accreditation with AACSB, ABET, ACEJMC, ACPE, ADA, CSWE, FIDER, NAAB, NASAD, and NASM. The 350-acre campus is in an urban area near downtown Austin, just off the interstate. Including any residence halls, there are 120 buildings.

STUDENT LIFE: 92% of undergraduates are from Texas. Others are from 50 states, 125 foreign countries, and Canada. 56% are white; 18% Hispanic; 17% Asian American. The average age of freshmen is 18; all undergraduates, 21. 8% do not continue beyond their first year; 78% remain to graduate.

FACULTY/CLASSROOMS: 64% of faculty are male; 36% are female. All teach and do research. No introductory courses are taught by graduate students.

PROGRAMS OF STUDY: UT confers B.A., B.S., B.Arch., B.B.A., B.F.A., B.M., B.J., and B.S.W. degrees. Master's and Doctoral degrees are also awarded. Bachelor's degrees are awarded in BIOLOGICAL SCIENCE (biochemistry, biology/biological science, microbiology, molecular biology, and nutrition), BUSINESS (accounting, banking and finance, business administration and management, management information systems, management science, and marketing management), COMMUNICATIONS AND THE ARTS (advertising, applied music, Arabic, art history and appreciation, classics, dance, design, dramatic arts, English, film arts, French, German, Greek, Hebrew, Italian, journalism, Latin, linguistics, music, music theory and composition, Portuguese, public relations, Russian, Scandinavian languages, Slavic languages, Spanish, speech/debate/rhetoric, studio art, and visual and performing arts), COMPUTER AND PHYSICAL SCIENCE (astronomy, chemistry, computer science, geology, geophysics and seismology, mathematics, and physics), ENGINEERING AND ENVIRONMENTAL DESIGN (aerospace studies, architectural engineering, architecture, biomedical engineering, chemical engineering, civil engineering, electrical/electronics engineering, geophysical engineering, interior design, landscape architecture/design, mechanical engineering, and petroleum/natural gas engineering), HEALTH PROFESSIONS (medical technology, nursing, pharmacy, and speech pathology/audiology), SOCIAL SCIENCE (American studies, anthropology, archeology, Asian/Oriental studies, child care/child and family studies, classical/ancient civilization, dietetics, Eastern European studies, economics, ethnic studies, geography, history, human ecology, humanities, Islamic studies, Judaic studies, Latin American studies, liberal arts/general studies, Middle Eastern studies, philosophy, physical fitness/movement, political science/government, psy-

chology, religion, Russian and Slavic studies, social work, sociology, textiles and clothing, and urban studies). Biological sciences, electrical, computer engineering, and government have the largest enrollments.

ACTIVITIES: 9% of men belong to 27 national fraternities; 14% of women belong to 23 national sororities. There are 100 groups on campus, including art, band, cheerleading, chess, choir, chorale, chorus, computers, dance, drama, ethnic, film, forensics, gay, honors, international, jazz band, literary magazine, marching band, musical theater, newspaper, opera, orchestra, pep band, photography, political, professional, radio and TV, religious, social, social service, student government, and symphony. Popular campus events include Gone to Texas, Cinco de Mayo, and Texas Revue.

SERVICES: Counseling and information services are available, as is tutoring in most subjects. There is a reader service for the blind, and remedial math, reading, and writing. **Library/Resources:** The 17 libraries contain 10.2 million volumes, 6.7 million microform items, and 14.1 million audio/video tapes/CDs/DVDs, and subscribe to 103,589 periodicals including electronic. Computerized library services include interlibrary loans, database searching, Internet access, and Wi-Fi capability. Special learning facilities include an art gallery, natural history museum, radio station, TV station, observatory, marine science institute, fusion reactor, and Lyndon Baines Johnson Library and Museum. **Physically Challenged Students:** 98% of the campus is accessible. Facilities include wheelchair ramps, elevators, special parking, specially equipped restrooms, lowered drinking fountains, lowered telephones. specially equipped reading rooms, a speech and hearing center, academic accommodations specific to the student's disability, and interpreters for the hearing impaired. **Special:** Cooperative programs are available in most engineering courses, microbiology, chemistry, computer science, geology, and actuarial studies. Cross-registration is provided in pharmacy with the University of Texas at San Antonio. Internships, study abroad, B.A.-B.S. degrees, dual majors, student-designed majors for humanities students, and pass/fail options are offered. There are 45 national honor societies, including Phi Beta Kappa, a freshman honors program, and 50 departmental honors programs. **Visiting:** There are regularly scheduled orientations for prospective students. There are guides for informal visits and visitors may sit in on classes. To schedule a visit, contact the Office of Admissions. **Campus Safety and Security:** Measures include 24-hour foot and vehicle patrol, self-defense education, and security escort services. There are shuttle buses, emergency telephones, lighted pathways/sidewalks, There is also a crime prevention unit and closed-circuit TV covering some parking areas and offices.

REQUIREMENTS: The SAT or ACT is required. The ACT Optional Writing test is also required. All students graduating in the top 10% of their class from an accredited Texas high school are eligible for admission. Applicants not meeting that requirement are reviewed based on SAT or ACT scores, class rank, writing samples, and related factors; consideration may be given to socioeconomic and geographic information. In addition, applicants need 15.5 academic credits, including 4 in English, 3 each in math and social studies, 2 each in science and foreign language, and 1.5 in electives. An audition is required for applied music majors. The GED is accepted, with supportive information. Home-schooled students are required to submit the results of either the SAT: Subject tests or AP exams in English, math, and a third subject of the student's choosing. AP and CLEP credits are accepted. Important factors in the admissions decision are leadership record, evidence of special talent, and extracurricular activities record.

FINANCIAL AID: UT is a member of CSS. The FAFSA is required. Check with the school for current application deadlines.

UNIVERSITY OF TEXAS AT DALLAS   D-2
www.utdallas.edu

Richardson, TX 75080   (972) 883-2270
                                            (800) 889-2443
Fax: (972) 883-2599   Email: interest@utdallas.edu
Full-time: 6614 men, 5016 women   Faculty: 535; I, ++$
Part-time: 1489 men, 1781 women   Ph.D.s: 94%
Graduate: 5001 men, 3794 women   Student/Faculty: 21 to 1
Year: semesters, summer session   Tuition: $11,806 ($31,328)
Room & Board: $9542   Freshman Class: 9587
                                    applied, 5938 accepted,
                                    2520 enrolled
SAT CR/M/W: 610/650/590 ACT: 28   CEEB CODE: 6897
Application Deadline: July 1   HIGHLY COMPETITIVE+

The University of Texas at Dallas, founded in 1969 as part of the University of Texas system, offers undergraduate and graduate programs in the liberal arts and sciences, business, engineering, computer science, cognitive science, and neuroscience. There are 7 undergraduate schools and 7 graduate schools. In addition to regional accreditation, UTD has baccalaureate program accreditation with AACSB, ABET, ACS, and NASPAA. The 550-acre campus is in a suburban area 18 miles north of downtown Dallas. Including any residence halls, there are 140 buildings.

STUDENT LIFE: 93% of undergraduates are from Texas. Others are from 50 states, 76 foreign countries, and Canada. 91% are from public schools. 33% are White; 24% Foreign; 20% Asian American; 13% Hispanic. The average age of freshmen is 18; all undergraduates, 23. 13% do not continue beyond their first year; 71% remain to graduate. **Housing:** 5754 students can be accommodated in college housing, which includes coed dorms, on-campus apartments, and married student housing. privately owned campus apartments, students can request to be assigned to a living learning group. On-campus housing is available on a first-come, first-served basis. 74% of students commute. All students may keep cars.

FACULTY/CLASSROOMS: 66% of faculty are male; 34% are female. 52% teach undergraduates, 21% do research, and 27% do both. Graduate students teach 9% of introductory courses. The average class size in an introductory lecture is 48; in a laboratory is 29; and in a regular course is 43.

PROGRAMS OF STUDY: UTD confers B.A., B.S., B.S.E.E. and B.S.T.E. degrees. Master's and Doctoral degrees are also awarded. Bachelor's degrees are awarded in BIOLOGICAL SCIENCE (biochemistry, biology/biological science, molecular biology, and neurosciences), BUSINESS (accounting, banking and finance, business administration and management, international business management, and marketing management), COMMUNICATIONS AND THE ARTS (fine arts, literature, media arts, telecommunications, Telecommunications Engineering Technology, and visual and performing arts), COMPUTER AND PHYSICAL SCIENCE (actuarial science, chemistry, computer science, geoscience, information sciences and systems, mathematics, physics, and software engineering), ENGINEERING AND ENVIRONMENTAL DESIGN (biomedical engineering, computer engineering, electrical/electronics engineering, and mechanical engineering), HEALTH PROFESSIONS (speech pathology/audiology), SOCIAL SCIENCE (American studies, child psychology/development, cognitive science, criminology, economics, geography, history, humanities, interdisciplinary studies, international public service, political science/government, psychology, public administration, and sociology). Electrical engineering, biological sciences, arts and technology are the strongest academically. Business administration, biology, and computer science have the largest enrollments.

ACTIVITIES: 3% of men belong to 12 national fraternities; 2% of women belong to 8 national sororities. There are 301 groups on campus, including art, band, cheerleading, chess, choir, chorale, chorus, computers, dance, debate, drama, drill team, environmental, ethnic, film, forensics, gay, honors, international, jazz band, literary magazine, musical theater, newspaper, opera, orchestra, pep band, photography, political, professional, radio and TV, religious, social, social service, and student government. Popular campus events include Welcome Week, Homecoming, Holiday Sing, Oozeball and Green Lecture Series. **Sports:** There are 6 intercollegiate sports for men and 7 for women, and 16 intramural sports for men and 14 for women. Facilities include 4 racquetball courts, 3 squash courts, 10 lighted tennis courts, indoor and outdoor basketball courts, a sand volleyball court, a 1-mile gravel track, 4 soccer fields, 4 softball fields, a junior Olympic pool/natatorium, and a 4000-seat gym, a basketball court and a weight room. **Graduates:** From July 1, 2013 to June 30, 2014, 2800 bachelor's degrees were awarded. The most popular majors were accounting (9%), business administration (8%), and biology (8%). 1250 companies recruited on campus in 2013-2014. In an average class, 6% graduate in 3 years or less, 51% graduate in 4 years or less, 66% graduate in 5 years or less, and 71% graduate in 6 years or less. Of the 2013 graduating class, 31% were enrolled in graduate school within 6 months of graduation, and 52% were employed.

SERVICES: Counseling and information services are available, as is tutoring in most subjects. There is a reader service for the blind, and remedial math, reading, and writing. **Library/Resources:** The library contains 2.5 million volumes, 641,413 microform items, 15,527 audio/video tapes/CDs/DVDs, and subscribes to 74,360 periodicals including electronic. Computerized library services include interlibrary loans, database searching, and Internet access. Special learning facilities include an art gallery, radio station, TV station, a center for communications disorders, a rare books library, and special library collections on aviation history, geophysics, philatelic research, and botanicals. **Physically Challenged Students:** All of the campus is accessible. Facilities include wheelchair ramps, elevators, special parking, specially equipped restrooms, lowered drinking fountains, and lowered telephones. **Special:** Cross-registration is available with other University of Texas campuses. Accelerated degree programs and B.A.-B.S. degrees are offered in several majors, as is a 3-2 engineering degree. Co-op programs, internships, work-study programs with several major corporations, dual majors, student-designed majors and Washington semester are also possible. In addition, students may study abroad in Europe, Asia, Mexico and New Zealand. There are 5 national honor societies, a freshman honors program, and 16 departmental honors programs. **Visiting:** There are regularly scheduled orientations for prospective students, including meetings with faculty and an admissions counselor, and a campus tour. There are guides for informal visits and visitors may sit in on classes. To schedule a visit, contact the Office of Enrollment Services at (972) 883-2270. **Campus Safety and Security:** Measures include 24-hour foot and vehicle patrol, emergency notification system, self-defense education, and security escort services. There are emergency telephones, lighted pathways/sidewalks, controlled access to dorms/residences, campus crime watch bulletins, bicycle patrols, crime prevention programs, ID engraving, police liaison who works with students on security issues.

REQUIREMENTS: The SAT or ACT is required. The ACT Optional Writing test is also required. Applicants should be graduates of an accredited secondary school. In-state students who rank in the top 10% of their class gain automatic admission to UTD. Credentials for other students must include completion of 4 units of English, 3.5 of math, 3 each of social science and lab science, 2 of a foreign language, and course work in fine arts and electives, with health and phys ed courses recommended. AP and CLEP credits are accepted. Important factors in the admissions decision are advanced placement or honors courses, leadership record, and evidence of special talent. To graduate, students must complete at least 120 credit hours, including 30 in the major and 51 in upper-division courses, with a minimum GPA of 2.0. Core courses include 15 credits in social science (with 6 each in U.S./Texas government and U.S./Texas history), 9 in natural science, and 6 each in communications, math, and humanities/fine arts. Magna and Summa cum Laude graduates must complete a thesis. **Procedure:** Freshmen are admitted to all sessions. Entrance exams should be taken at the end of the junior year or beginning of the senior year. There are deferred admissions and rolling admissions plans. Applications should be filed by July 1 for fall entry; November 1 for spring entry; and April 1 for summer entry, along with a $50 fee. Applications are accepted on-line. **Transfer Students:** 1941 transfer students enrolled in 2013-2014. Sophomore applicants must present a GPA of 3.0 and 12 credits in the general education core. Upper-division applicants should have a GPA of 2.5 and be in good standing at the last school attended. 30 of 120 credits required for the bachelor's degree must be completed at UTD. **International Students:** There are 500 international students enrolled. They must take the TOEFL with a minimum score of 550 on the paper-based TOEFL (PBT) or 80 on the Internet-based version (iBT). They must also take the SAT or ACT.

ADMISSIONS: 62% of the 2014-2015 applicants were accepted. The SAT scores for the 2014-2015 freshman class were: Critical Reading--9% below 500, 33% between 500 and 599, 41% between 600 and 699, and 16% between 700 and 800; Math--3% below 500, 22% between 500 and 599, 46% between 600 and 699, and 29% between 700 and 800; Writing--14% below 500, 38% between 500 and 599, 34% between 600 and 699, and 14% between 700 and 800. The ACT scores were 3% below 21, 10% between 21 and 23, 23% between 24 and 26, 17% between 27 and 28, and 47% above 28. 62% of the current freshmen were in the top fifth of their class; 86% were in the top two fifths. There were 100 National Merit finalists. 50 freshmen graduated first in their class. **Admissions Contact:** Matthew Sanchez, Director, Enrollment Services. E-Mail: *interest@utdallas.edu* Web: *www.utdallas.edu*

FINANCIAL AID: In 2014-2015, 51% of all full-time freshmen and 53% of continuing full-time students received some form of financial aid. 47% of all full-time freshmen and continuing full-time students received need-based aid. The average freshman award was $15,466. Need-based scholarships or need-based grants averaged $11,961; need-based self-help aid (loans and jobs) averaged $4,785; and other non-need-based awards and non-need-based scholarships averaged $11,142. 10% of undergraduate students work part-time. Average annual earnings from campus work are $3058. The average financial indebtedness of the 2014 graduate was $20,504. The FAFSA is required. The priority date for freshman financial aid applications for fall entry is March 31. The deadline for filing freshman financial aid applications for fall entry is April 15.

UNIVERSITY OF TEXAS AT EL PASO (*The complete profile is made available exclusively on our website, www.barronspac.com*)

UNIVERSITY OF TEXAS AT SAN ANTONIO   D-4

www.utsa.edu

San Antonio, TX 78249	(210) 458-4011
	(210) 458-8000
Fax: (210) 458-7857	Email: prospects@utsa.edu
Full-time: 10455 men, 9578 women	Faculty: 784; IIA, av$
Part-time: 2359 men, 1950 women	Ph.D.s: 74%
Graduate: 1909 men, 2372 women	Student/Faculty: 23 to 1
Year: semesters, summer session	Tuition: $8737 ($19,455)
Room & Board: $9635	Freshman Class: n/av
	CEEB CODE: 6919
Application Deadline: July 1	COMPETITIVE

The University of Texas at San Antonio is dedicated to the advancement of knowledge through research and discovery, teaching and learning, community engagement and public service. There are 9 undergraduate schools and 7 graduate schools. In addition to regional accreditation, UTSA has baccalaureate program accreditation with AACSB, ABET, NASAD, and NASM. The 725-acre campus is in a suburban area approximately 18 miles northwest of downtown San Antonio. Including any residence halls, there are 121 buildings.

STUDENT LIFE: 98% of undergraduates are from Texas. Others are from 50 states, 96 foreign countries, and Canada. 47% are Hispanic; 29% White. The average age of freshmen is 18; all undergraduates, 23. 37% do not continue beyond their first year; 34% remain to graduate.

FACULTY/CLASSROOMS: 58% of faculty are male; 42% are female. 81% teach undergraduates. Graduate students teach 13% of introductory courses. The average class size in an introductory lecture is 55 and in a laboratory is 21.

PROGRAMS OF STUDY: UTSA confers B.A., B.S., B.A.A.S., B.B.A.,

B.F.A., B.M., B.S.C.E., B.S.E.E., B.P.A. and B.S.M.E. degrees. Master's and Doctoral degrees are also awarded. Bachelor's degrees are awarded in BIOLOGICAL SCIENCE (biochemistry and biology/biological science), BUSINESS (accounting, business administration and management, business statistics, finance, human resources, management science, and marketing management), COMMUNICATIONS AND THE ARTS (art, art history and appreciation, classics, communications, English, modern language, music, and Spanish), COMPUTER AND PHYSICAL SCIENCE (actuarial science, actuarial mathematics, chemistry, computer science, computer security and information assurance, geology, information sciences and systems, mathematics, physics, and statistics), EDUCATION ((Education) Childhood Education, early childhood education, and education), ENGINEERING AND ENVIRONMENTAL DESIGN (architecture, biomedical engineering, civil engineering, computer engineering, construction management, electrical/electronics engineering, engineering, environmental science, interior design, and mechanical engineering), HEALTH PROFESSIONS (health), SOCIAL SCIENCE (American studies, anthropology, child care/child and family studies, criminal justice, economics, geography, history, humanities, interdisciplinary studies, Mexican-American/Chicano studies, philosophy, philosophy and religion, political science/government, public administration, sociology, and women's studies). Honors college, business, engineering and sciences are the strongest academically. Business, biology, psychology and kinesiology have the largest enrollments.

ACTIVITIES: 3% of men belong to 12 national fraternities; 3% of women belong to 10 national sororities. There are 217 groups on campus, including art, band, cheerleading, chess, choir, chorale, chorus, computers, dance, debate, drama, environmental, ethnic, film, forensics, gay, honors, international, jazz band, marching band, newspaper, orchestra, pep band, political, professional, religious, social, social service, student government, and symphony. Popular campus events include Fiesta UTSA, Best Fest and Rowdy Rampage Fireworks Spectacular.

SERVICES: Counseling and information services are available, as is tutoring in some subjects. There is a reader service for the blind, and remedial math, reading, and writing. The 3 libraries contain 1.9 million volumes, 2.9 million microform items, 3.6 million audio/video tapes/CDs/DVDs, and subscribe to 70,467 periodicals including electronic. Computerized library services include interlibrary loans, database searching, Internet access, and Wi-Fi capability. Special learning facilities include an art gallery, and the Institute of Texan Cultures.

REQUIREMENTS: The SAT or ACT is required. Admission is based on a formula derived from high school class rank and SAT or ACT scores. Applicants must be graduates of accredited high schools or have earned the GED. AP and CLEP credits are accepted.

ADMISSIONS: 62% of a recent year applicants were accepted. The SAT scores for the recent year freshman class were: Critical Reading--49% below 500, 36% between 500 and 599, 13% between 600 and 699, and 2% between 700 and 800; Math--35% below 500, 45% between 500 and 599, 18% between 600 and 699, and 2% between 700 and 800. The ACT scores were 38% below 21, 29% between 21 and 23, 21% between 24 and 26, 7% between 27 and 28, and 5% above 28. 23 freshmen graduated first in their class.

FINANCIAL AID: In a recent year, 46% of all full-time freshmen and 53% of continuing full-time students received some form of financial aid. 45% of all full-time freshmen and 52% of continuing full-time students received need-based aid. The average freshman award was $10,434. Need-based scholarships or need-based grants averaged $7,557; need-based self-help aid (loans and jobs) averaged $3,301; non-need-based athletic scholarships averaged $8,557; and other non-need-based awards and non-need-based scholarships averaged $1,518. 7% of undergraduate students work part-time. Average annual earnings from campus work are $5855. The average financial indebtedness of a recent graduate was $25,140. The FAFSA and the college's own financial statement are required. The priority date for freshman financial aid applications for fall entry is March 15. The deadline for filing freshman financial aid applications for fall entry is June 30.

UNIVERSITY OF THE INCARNATE WORD (*The complete profile is made available exclusively on our website, www.barronspac.com*)

WAYLAND BAPTIST UNIVERSITY (*The complete profile is made available exclusively on our website, www.barronspac.com*)

WEST TEXAS A&M UNIVERSITY B-1
www.wtamu.edu

Canyon, TX 79016	(806) 651-0000
	(800) 99-WTAMU
Fax: (806) 651-5285	Email: admissions@wtamu.edu
Full-time: 1900 men, 2450 women	Faculty: 252, IIA, --$
Part-time: 550 men, 700 women	Ph.D.s: 70%
Graduate: 550 men, 900 women	Student/Faculty: 252
Year: semesters, summer session	Tuition: $6430 ($15,820)
Room & Board: $6000	Freshman Class: n/av
SAT or ACT: required	CEEB CODE: 6938
Application Deadline: open	COMPETITIVE

West Texas A&M University, a member of the Texas A&M University System and founded in 1910, is a public institution offering programs in the liberal arts and sciences, fine arts, agriculture, nursing, and education. There are 4 undergraduate schools and 1 graduate school. Figures in the above capsule and this profile are approximate. In addition to regional accreditation, WTAMU has baccalaureate program accreditation with ACBSP, CSWE, and NASM. The 135-acre campus is in a small town 17 miles south of Amarillo. Including any residence halls, there are 82 buildings.

STUDENT LIFE: 90% of undergraduates are from Texas. Others are from 39 states, 26 foreign countries, and Canada. 93% are from public schools. 76% are white; 14% Hispanic. The average age of freshmen is 18; all undergraduates, 24. 36% do not continue beyond their first year; 66% remain to graduate.

FACULTY/CLASSROOMS: 56% of faculty are male; 44% are female. 95% teach undergraduates, 47% do research, and 44% do both. Graduate students teach 16% of introductory courses. The average class size in an introductory lecture is 28; in a laboratory, 23; and in a regular course, 26.

PROGRAMS OF STUDY: WTAMU confers B.A., B.S., B.A.A.S., B.B.A., B.F.A., B.G.S., B.M., B.S.M.T., and B.S.N. degrees. Master's and Doctoral degrees are also awarded. Bachelor's degrees are awarded in AGRICULTURE (agricultural business management, agricultural economics, agriculture, animal science, plant protection (pest management), plant science, and soil science), BIOLOGICAL SCIENCE (biology/biological science, biotechnology, and wildlife biology), BUSINESS (accounting, banking and finance, business administration and management, business economics, management science, and marketing/retailing/merchandising), COMMUNICATIONS AND THE ARTS (applied art, art, broadcasting, dance, dramatic arts, English, graphic design, music, music theory and composition, musical theater, performing arts, public relations, publishing, Spanish, speech/debate/rhetoric, and studio art), COM-PUTER AND PHYSICAL SCIENCE (chemistry, computer science, geology, information sciences and systems, mathematics, and physics), EDUCATION (art education, athletic training, business education, drama education, English education, foreign languages education, mathematics education, music education, physical education, reading education, science education, social studies education, and special education), ENGINEERING AND ENVIRONMENTAL DESIGN (emergency/disaster science, engineering technology, environmental science, mechanical engineering, and preengineering), HEALTH PROFESSIONS (allied health, exercise science, medical technology, music therapy, nursing, predentistry, premedicine, prepharmacy, preveterinary science, and speech pathology/audiology), SOCIAL SCIENCE (criminal justice, economics, geography, history, interdisciplinary studies, liberal arts/general studies, political science/government, prelaw, psychology, public administration, social science, social work, and sociology). Education and music are the strongest academically. Education has the largest enrollment.

ACTIVITIES: 4% of men belong to 1 local and 4 national fraternities; 4% of women belong to 2 local and 3 national sororities. There are 97 groups on campus, including academic, art, band, cheerleading, choir, chorale, chorus, computers, dance, debate, drama, ethnic, film, forensics, honors, international, jazz band, literary magazine, marching band, musical theater, newspaper, opera, orchestra, photography, political, professional, radio and TV, religious, social, social service, student government, and symphony. Popular campus events include Workathon, RHA Mud Pull, and Buffalo Branding.

SERVICES: Counseling and information services are available, as is tutoring in most subjects, including core curriculum courses. There is a reader service for the blind and remedial math, reading, and writing. The 2 libraries contain 1.1 million volumes, 1.3 million microform items, 1555 audio/video tapes/CDs/DVDs, and subscribe to 16,973 periodicals including electronic. Computerized library services include interlibrary loans, database searching, Internet access, and laptop Internet portals. Special learning facilities include a learning resource center, art gallery, natural history museum, radio station, alternative energy institute, electronic learning center, communications disorders center, and nursing learning center.

REQUIREMENTS: The SAT or ACT is required. Applicants should have graduated from an accredited secondary school or have a GED. Admission requires graduation in the top 50% of the student's high school class or a minimum composite score of 20 on the ACT or 950 on the SAT. AP and CLEP credits are accepted.

FINANCIAL AID: The FAFSA is required. Check with the school for current application deadlines.

WILEY COLLEGE (*The complete profile is made available exclusively on our website, www.barronspac.com*)

UTAH

0 20 40 60 80 100
Miles

● College Location

BRIGHAM YOUNG UNIVERSITY   C-2
www.byu.edu

Provo, UT 84602	**(801) 422-4636**
	(801) 422-1211
Fax: (801) 422-0005	**Email: admissions@byu.edu**
Full-time: 13,536 men, 11,550 women	**Faculty:** n/av
	Ph.D.s: 98%
Part-time: 1422 men, 1259 women	**Student/Faculty:** 23 to 1
Graduate: 2021 men, 1335 women	**Tuition:** $5350
Year: quarters, summer session	**Freshman Class:** 12557 applied, 6895 accepted, 5526 enrolled
Room & Board: $7750	
ACT: required	**CEEB CODE:** 4019
Application Deadline: February 15	**HIGHLY COMPETITIVE**

Brigham Young University, founded in 1875, is a private university affiliated with the Church of Jesus Christ of Latter-day Saints. The university follows a semester calendar with spring and summer terms. Tuition figures in this profile are for members of the church. Students who are not members of the Church of Jesus Christ of Latter-day Saints pay twice the tuition amount listed. Living costs are identical for members and non-members. There are 10 undergraduate schools and 1 graduate school. In addition to regional accreditation, BYU has baccalaureate program accreditation with AACSB, ABET, ACCE, ACEJMC, ADA, ASLA, CSAB, CSWE, NASAD, NASDTEC, NASM, NCATE, NLN, and NRPA. The 557-acre campus is in a suburban area 45 miles south of Salt Lake City. Including any residence halls, there are 330 buildings.

STUDENT LIFE: 71% of undergraduates are from out of state, mostly the West. Students are from 50 states, 121 foreign countries, and Canada. 86% are White. The average age of freshmen is 19; all undergraduates, 22. 11% do not continue beyond their first year; 77% remain to graduate.

FACULTY/CLASSROOMS: 72% of faculty are male; 28% are female. No introductory courses are taught by graduate students.

PROGRAMS OF STUDY: BYU confers B.A., B.S., B.F.A., B.G.S.,

B.M. and B.Mus. degrees. Master's and Doctoral degrees are also awarded. Bachelor's degrees are awarded in AGRICULTURE (agricultural business management, environmental studies, plant science, and wildlife management), BIOLOGICAL SCIENCE (biochemistry, bioinformatics, biology/biological science, biophysics, biotechnology, botany, microbiology, molecular biology, neurosciences, nutrition, physiology, plant genetics, and plant physiology), BUSINESS (accounting, business administration and management, management information systems, management science, marketing management, recreation and leisure services, and tourism), COMMUNICATIONS AND THE ARTS (advertising, animation, art, art history and appreciation, audio technology, Chinese, classical languages, classics, communications, comparative literature, dance, dramatic arts, English, fine arts, French, German, graphic design, Greek, illustration, industrial design, Italian, Japanese, jazz, Korean, Latin, linguistics, literature, media arts, music, music performance, music technology, music theory and composition, musical theater, performing arts, photography, Portuguese, public relations, Russian, Spanish, studio art, and visual and performing arts), COMPUTER AND PHYSICAL SCIENCE (actuarial science, astronomy, chemistry, computer science, geology, information sciences and systems, mathematics, physics, and statistics), EDUCATION (art education, dance education, drama education, early childhood education, elementary education, English education, home economics education, mathematics education, music education, science education, social science education, special education, and technical education), ENGINEERING AND ENVIRONMENTAL DESIGN (chemical engineering, city/community/regional planning, civil engineering, computer engineering, construction management, electrical/electronics engineering, electrical/electronics engineering technology, environmental design, food services technology, landscape architecture/design, manufacturing engineering, manufacturing technology, and mechanical engineering), HEALTH PROFESSIONS (clinical science, exercise science, health science, nursing, and speech pathology/audiology), SOCIAL SCIENCE (American studies, anthropology, archeology, Asian/American studies, Asian/Oriental studies, classical/ancient civilization, dietetics, economics, family/consumer studies, food science, geography, history, human development, humanities, international relations, Latin American studies, Middle Eastern studies, Near Eastern studies, philosophy, political science/government, psychology, social work, and sociology). Engineering, accounting and business are the strongest academically. Business, communications and exercise science have the largest enrollments.

ACTIVITIES: There are 390 groups on campus, including art, band, cheerleading, chess, choir, chorale, chorus, computers, dance, debate, drama, drill team, environmental, ethnic, film, honors, international, jazz band, literary magazine, marching band, musical theater, newspaper, opera, orchestra, pep band, photography, political, professional, radio and TV, religious, social, social service, student government, and symphony. Popular campus events include Fall and Spring Fling and Preference Dances.

SERVICES: Counseling and information services are available, as is tutoring in most subjects. There is a reader service for the blind, remedial math, reading, and writing. Counseling and information services are available, as is tutoring in most subjects. There is a reader service for the blind, remedial math, reading, and writing. **Library/Resources:** The 2 libraries contain 4.0 million volumes, 3.5 million microform items, 304,688 audio/video tapes/CDs/DVDs, and subscribes to 198,871 periodicals including electronic. Computerized library services include interlibrary loans, database searching, Internet access, and Wi-Fi capability. Special learning facilities include an art gallery, natural history museum, planetarium, radio station, TV station, an archeological museum, an earth science museum, reading and writing labs, math, language, and computer labs. **Physically Challenged Students:** Facilities include wheelchair ramps, elevators, special parking, specially equipped restrooms, special class scheduling, lowered drinking fountains, lowered telephones, and special housing. **Special:** SUU offers co-op programs with Weber State University, work-study programs, study abroad, dual majors, student-designed majors leading to a B.I.S. degree, and internships

REQUIREMENTS: Applicants must be graduates of an accredited secondary school. Either the ACT or SAT is required. The GED is accepted. The school recommends that applicants complete 4 years of English, 3 years of math, and 2 courses in foreign language, lab science, history, and literature or writing. Essays and letters of recommendation are required with the application. AP and CLEP credits are accepted. Important factors in the admissions decision are advanced placement or honors courses, recommendations by school officials, and evidence of special talent.

ADMISSIONS: 55% of the 2013-2014 applicants were accepted. The SAT scores for the 2013-2014 freshman class were: Critical Reading--6% below 500, 28% between 500 and 599, 43% between 600 and 699, and 23% between 700 and 800; Math--4% below 500, 24% between 500 and 599, 50% between 600 and 699, and 22% between 700 and 800; Writing--10% below 500, 37% between 500 and 599, 41% between 600 and 699, and 12% between 700 and 800. The ACT scores were 2% below 21, 6% between 21 and 23, 20% between 24 and 26, 25% between 27 and 28, and 47% above 28. 80% of the current freshmen were in the top fifth of their class.

FINANCIAL AID: In a recent year, 63% of all full-time freshmen and 69% of continuing full-time students received some form of financial aid. 19% of all full-time freshmen and 42% of continuing full-time students received need-based aid. The average freshman award was $4,990. Need-based scholarships or need-based grants averaged $4,515; need-based self-help aid (loans and jobs) averaged $3,249; non-need-based athletic scholarships averaged $5,168; and other non-need-based awards and non-need-based scholarships averaged $3,641. 44% of undergraduate students work part-time. The FAFSA is required. The deadline for filing freshman financial aid applications for fall entry is June 30.

SOUTHERN UTAH UNIVERSITY   B-4
www.suu.edu

Cedar City, UT 84720	**(435) 586-7700**
	(435) 586-7740
Fax: (435) 865-8223	Email: adminfo@suu.edu
Full-time: 2428 men, 2703 women	Faculty: 283; IIA, --$
Part-time: 720 men, 1102 women	Ph.D.s: 69%
Graduate: 283 men, 420 women	Student/Faculty: n/av
Year: semesters, summer session	Tuition: $6138 ($18,596)
Room & Board: $6890	Freshman Class: 8268 applied, 5046 accepted, 1195 enrolled
SAT or ACT: required	CEEB CODE: 4092
Application Deadline: May 1	COMPETITIVE

Southern Utah University, founded in 1897, is part of the Utah System of Higher Education and offers undergraduate degrees in arts and letters, science, education, and business. There are 7 undergraduate schools and 4 graduate schools. In addition to regional accreditation, SUU has baccalaureate program accreditation with AACSB, ABET, ACBSP, NASAD, NASM, TEAC, NASD, CCNE, and AACN. The 133-acre campus is in a small town Cedar City, Utah, 170 miles north of Las Vegas.

STUDENT LIFE: 74% of undergraduates are from Utah. Others are from 50 states, 28 foreign countries, and Canada. 79% are White. The average age of freshmen is 23; all undergraduates, 24. **Housing:** 599 students can be accommodated in college housing, which includes single-sex and coed dorms and on-campus apartments. Special housing for disabled students and international students. On-campus housing is available on a first-come and first-served basis. 90% of students commute. Alcohol is not permitted. All students may keep cars.

FACULTY/CLASSROOMS: No introductory courses are taught by graduate students.

PROGRAMS OF STUDY: SUU confers B.A., B.F.A., B.M.U., B.S.N., B.S. and B.I.S. degrees. Associate and Master's degrees are also awarded. Bachelor's degrees are awarded in Business, science, and education are the strongest academically. Education, business, and psychology have the largest enrollments.

ACTIVITIES: Groups on campus include art, band, cheerleading, choir, chorus, communications, computers, dance, drama, ethnic,

film, gay, honors, international, jazz band, literary magazine, musical theater, newspaper, opera, pep band, political, professional, radio and TV, religious, social, social service, student government, and symphony. Popular campus events include Homecoming, Founders Day, Dances, and Service Programs. **Sports:** Facilities include a 10,000-seat stadium for football and for track and field, a baseball field, recreation grounds, a 5300-seat special events facility for basketball, volleyball, and gymnastics, tennis and racquetball courts, and large, all-weather practice areas. SUU owns and operates a 1000-acre farm and a 3700-acre ranch. **Graduates:** From July 1, 2013 to June 30, 2014, 954 bachelor's degrees were awarded. The most popular majors were education (21%), business/marketing (12%), and psychology (8%).

SERVICES: Counseling and information services are available, as is tutoring in most subjects. There is a reader service for the blind, remedial math, reading, and writing. **Library/Resources:** The library contains 289,486 volumes, 28,525 microform items, 10,821 audio/video tapes/CDs/DVDs, and subscribes to 749 periodicals including electronic. Computerized library services include interlibrary loans, database searching, and Internet access. Special learning facilities include an art gallery, natural history museum, planetarium, radio station, and TV station. **Physically Challenged Students:** Facilities include wheelchair ramps, elevators, special parking, specially equipped restrooms, special class scheduling, lowered drinking fountains, lowered telephones, and special housing. **Special:** SUU offers co-op programs with Weber State University, work-study programs, study abroad, dual majors, student-designed majors leading to a B.I.S. degree, and internships with government officials in Washington, D.C. Other programs offered include distance learning, ESL, independent study, liberal arts/career combinations, a teacher certification program, and weekend college. **Visiting:** There are regularly scheduled orientations for prospective students, including campus tours, which can be arranged by appointment. There are guides for informal visits, visitors may sit in on classes, and stay overnight. To schedule a visit, contact the Admissions Welcome Center. **Campus Safety and Security:** Measures include self-defense education and security escort services. There are emergency telephones and lighted pathways/sidewalks.

REQUIREMENTS: The SAT or ACT is required. The ACT is recommended. Applicants should be graduates of an accredited secondary school or have a GED, and should have completed 4 years of English, (composition and literature emphasis), 3 of math, at least 2 of which are elementary algebra or beyond, 3 each of biological/physical sciences (1 with a lab) and social studies including U.S. history/government, and 2 years of a foreign language. AP and CLEP credits are accepted. To graduate, all students must complete at least 122 credit hours with a minimum 2.0 GPA. Students must satisfy general education, major, minor, and basic skills requirements, including 4 courses each in social and physical sciences, 2 each in English, fine arts, and humanities, 1 each in math, phys ed, and communications, and a course in either history, political science, or economics to fulfill the U.S. government requirement. Other courses required for graduation include computer literacy and philosophy. **Procedure:** Freshmen are admitted fall, spring, and summer. There are deferred admissions and rolling admissions plans. Applications should be filed by May 1 for fall entry; December 1 for spring entry. The fall 2014 application fee was $50. Applications are accepted on-line. **Transfer Students:** 330 transfer students enrolled in 2013-2014. Applicants must submit transcripts from previously attended colleges and have a minimum 2.0 GPA in college courses and a 2.0 high school GPA. ACT scores as well as high school transcripts are required from students who have not completed English or math courses at another institution or who have not completed a minimum of 24 credit hours at an institution of higher education. 30 of 120 credits required for the bachelor's degree must be completed at SUU. **International Students:** There are 287 international students enrolled. The school actively recruits these students. They must take the TOEFL with a minimum score of 525 on the paper-based TOEFL (PBT) or 71 on the Internet-based version (iBT), or take the IELTS.

ADMISSIONS: 61% of the 2014-2015 applicants were accepted. The SAT scores for the 2014-2015 freshman class were: Critical Reading--39% below 500, 43% between 500 and 599, 16% between 600 and 699, and 2% between 700 and 800; Math--44% below 500, 42% between 500 and 599, 11% between 600 and 699, and 3% between

700 and 800; Writing--50% below 500, 36% between 500 and 599, 12% between 600 and 699, and 2% between 700 and 800. **Admissions Contact:** Christine Proctor, Associate Director of Admissions. E-Mail: *adminfo@suu.edu* Web: *www.suu.edu*

FINANCIAL AID: The FAFSA and the college's own financial statement are required. The priority date for freshman financial aid applications for fall entry is December 1.

THE UNIVERSITY OF UTAH   C-2
www.utah.edu

Salt Lake City, UT 84112   (801) 581-7200
                                                 (800) 581-8761

Fax: (801) 585-3257   Email: admissions@utah.edu
Full-time: 9445 men, 7692 women   Faculty: 867; I, -$
Part-time: 3776 men, 2994 women   Ph.D.s: 81%
Graduate: 4266 men, 3342 women   Student/Faculty: 17 to 1
Year: semesters, summer session   Tuition: $7935 ($25,267)
Room & Board: $8528   Freshman Class: 10991
                                  applied, 8949 accepted,
                                  3158 enrolled
SAT CR/M/W: 570/585/550 ACT: 25   CEEB CODE: 4853
Application Deadline: April 1   **VERY COMPETITIVE**

The University of Utah, founded in 1850, part of the Utah System of Higher Education, and offers graduate and undergraduate programs in various disciplines. There are 12 undergraduate schools and 16 graduate schools. In addition to regional accreditation, U of U has baccalaureate program accreditation with AACSB, ABET, ACPE, ADA, APTA, CAHEA, CSWE, NAAB, NRPA, TEAC, CCNE, and CAPTE. The 1535-acre campus is in an urban area in Salt Lake City. Including any residence halls, there are 375 buildings.

STUDENT LIFE: 80% of undergraduates are from Utah. Others are from 50 states, 94 foreign countries, and Canada. 94% are from public schools. 69% are White. The average age of freshmen is 19; all undergraduates, 24. 89% do not continue beyond their first year; 60% remain to graduate. **Housing:** 4873 students can be accommodated in college housing, which includes single-sex and coed dorms, on-campus apartments, off-campus apartments, and married student housing. In addition, there are honors houses, special-interest houses, fraternity houses, sorority houses, theme houses, limited visitation and 24-hour quiet housing. On-campus housing is available on a first-come and first-served basis. 87% of students commute. Alcohol is not permitted. All students may keep cars.

FACULTY/CLASSROOMS: 58% of faculty are male; 42% are female. No introductory courses are taught by graduate students.

PROGRAMS OF STUDY: U of U confers B.A., B.F.A., B.Mus., B.S., B.S.W. and B.U.S. degrees. Master's and Doctoral degrees are also awarded. Bachelor's degrees are awarded in AGRICULTURE (environmental studies), BIOLOGICAL SCIENCE (biology/biological science), BUSINESS (accounting, business administration and management, entrepreneurial studies, finance, management information systems, management science, marketing management, marketing/retailing/merchandising, operations management, and recreation and leisure services), COMMUNICATIONS AND THE ARTS (animation, Arabic, art history, art, art history and appreciation, ballet, Chinese, classics, communications, comparative literature, dance, design, dramatic arts, English, film arts, film, television and digital media, fine arts, French, German, Hebrew, Japanese, linguistics, media arts, music, Russian, Spanish, theatre arts, visual and performing arts, and writing), COMPUTER AND PHYSICAL SCIENCE (applied mathematics, atmospheric sciences and meteorology, chemistry, computer science, earth science, environmental geology, geology, geophysics and seismology, geoscience, information sciences and systems, mathematics, and physics), EDUCATION (art education, athletic training, elementary education, English education, health education, social science education, special education, and teaching English as a second/foreign language (TESOL/TEFOL)), ENGINEERING AND ENVIRONMENTAL DESIGN (architecture, bioengineering, biomedical engineering, chemical engineering, civil engineering, computer engineering, electrical/electronics engineer-

ing, engineering, geological engineering, materials engineering, materials science, mechanical engineering, metallurgical engineering, mining and mineral engineering, and urban planning technology), HEALTH PROFESSIONS (exercise science, medical laboratory science, medical laboratory technology, medical science, nursing, occupational therapy, pharmacy, physical therapy, public health, and speech pathology/audiology), SOCIAL SCIENCE (anthropology, architectural studies, Asian/Oriental studies, behavioral science, consumer services, economics, ethnic studies, family/consumer studies, gender studies, geography, history, human development, humanities, international studies, Latin American studies, Middle Eastern studies, parks and recreation management, peace studies, philosophy, political science/government, psychology, social science, social work, sociology, urban studies, and women's studies). Biology, business administration, exercise and sport science, communication, and economics have the largest enrollments.

ACTIVITIES: 5% of men belong to 10 national fraternities; 7% of women belong to 7 national sororities. There are 500 groups on campus, including art, band, cheerleading, chess, choir, chorale, chorus, computers, dance, debate, drama, drill team, drum and bugle corps, environmental, ethnic, film, forensics, gay, honors, international, jazz band, marching band, musical theater, newspaper, opera, orchestra, pep band, photography, political, professional, radio and TV, religious, social, social service, student government, and symphony. Popular campus events include Redfest, Plazafest, and Welcome Week. **Sports:** There are 81 intercollegiate sports for men and 19 for women, and 84 intramural sports for men and 16 for women. Facilities include a 45,635-seat stadium, 15,500-seat basketball arena, 6 indoor gyms, indoor tennis courts, sand volleyball court, 3 indoor swimming pools, gymnastics room, 5 weight rooms, 19 handball/racquetball/squash courts, 200-meter indoor track, 400-meter outdoor track, disc golf course, 3 outdoor playing fields, and a 10-lane bowling alley. **Graduates:** From July 1, 2013 to June 30, 2014, 5092 bachelor's degrees were awarded. The most popular majors were psychology (6%), communication (6%), and human development and family studies (4%). 230 companies recruited on campus in 2013-2014. In an average class, 24% graduate in 4 years or less, 49% graduate in 5 years or less, and 62% graduate in 6 years or less.

SERVICES: Counseling and information services are available, as is tutoring in most subjects. There is a reader service for the blind, and remedial math, reading, and writing. There are also support services for the deaf, including readers, scribes, tutors, and interpreters. The on-campus Center for Disability Services directs students to on-campus services for people with disabilities and provides a supportive environment so they can achieve their academic goals. **Library/Resources:** The 3 libraries contain 4.2 million volumes, 3.0 million microform items, 96,897 audio/video tapes/CDs/DVDs, and subscribe to 86,266 periodicals including electronic. Computerized library services include interlibrary loans, database searching, Internet access, and Wi-Fi capability. Special learning facilities include an art gallery, natural history museum, radio station, TV station, an arboretum. **Physically Challenged Students:** All of the campus is accessible. Facilities include wheelchair ramps, elevators, special parking, specially equipped restrooms, special class scheduling, lowered drinking fountains, lowered telephones, and special housing. **Special:** The university offers numerous opportunities for cooperative programs, cross-registration through the Western Undergraduate Exchange (WUC) as part of the Western Interstate Commission for Higher Education (WICHE), study abroad in more than 30 countries, internships, work-study and accelerated degree programs, and B.A.-B.S. degrees. Also available are the general studies degree, a Washington semester, student-designed and dual majors, credit for telecourses and military experience, nondegree study, and pass/fail options. There are 40 national honor societies, including Phi Beta Kappa, a freshman honors program, and 27 departmental honors programs. **Visiting:** There are regularly scheduled orientations for prospective students, including an information session with an admissions counselor to discuss academic and student involvement opportunities, scholarships, financial aid, admissions requirements, and deadlines, along with a campus tour and tour of residence halls. If time permits, prospective students are encouraged to meet with academic advisers on various majors, visit classrooms, and stay overnight in a residence hall. There are guides for informal visits, visitors

may sit in on classes, and stay overnight. To schedule a visit, contact the Office of Admissions, Welcome Center at (801) 581-6295.
Campus Safety and Security: Measures include 24-hour foot and vehicle patrol, emergency notification system, self-defense education, and security escort services. There are shuttle buses, emergency telephones, lighted pathways/sidewalks, and controlled access to dorms/residences.

REQUIREMENTS: The ACT is required. The SAT is accepted. Applicants must be graduates of an accredited secondary school or have the GED. Academic credits required include 4 years each of English and electives, 2 years each of foreign language and math, 3 years of biological and/or physical science, and 1 year of history. AP and CLEP credits are accepted. Important factors in the admissions decision are advanced placement or honors courses, leadership record, and personality/intangible qualities. To graduate, all students must satisfy requirements in the general education and intellectual exploration programs. General education requirements include 1 course each in American institutions and lower-division writing; 2 in quantitative reasoning; and 2 each in fine arts, humanities, physical science, and social science, excluding the major area. Students must complete at least 122 credit hours, with 45 to 60 in the major. A minimum 2.0 GPA is required. **Procedure:** Freshmen are admitted fall, spring, and summer. Entrance exams should be taken in the junior year of high school. There are deferred admissions and rolling admissions plans. Applications should be filed by April 1 for fall entry; November 1 for spring entry; and March 15 for summer entry, along with a $45 fee. Notification is sent on a rolling basis. Applications are accepted online. **Transfer Students:** 1709 transfer students enrolled in 2013-2014. Transfer students must have completed at least 45 quarter (30 semester) hours with a minimum 2.6 GPA. 30 of 122 credits required for the bachelor's degree must be completed at U of U. **International Students:** There are 1576 international students enrolled. They must take the TOEFL with a minimum score of 550 on the paper-based TOEFL (PBT) or 80 on the Internet-based version (iBT). They must also take the SAT or ACT.

ADMISSIONS: 81% of the 2014-2015 applicants were accepted. The SAT scores for the 2014-2015 freshman class were: Critical Reading--23% below 500, 38% between 500 and 599, 30% between 600 and 699, and 9% between 700 and 800; Math--19% below 500, 36% between 500 and 599, 34% between 600 and 699, and 11% between 700 and 800; Writing--28% below 500, 41% between 500 and 599, 27% between 600 and 699, and 4% between 700 and 800. The ACT scores were 19% below 21, 22% between 21 and 23, 24% between 24 and 26, 13% between 27 and 28, and 22% above 28. 41% of the current freshmen were in the top fifth of their class; 72% were in the top two fifths. **Admissions Contact:** Matthew Lopez, Director of Admissions. E-Mail: *admissions@utah.edu* Web: *www.admissions.utah.edu*

FINANCIAL AID: In 2014-2015, 79% of all full-time freshmen and 55% of continuing full-time students received some form of financial aid. 51% of all full-time freshmen and 49% of continuing full-time students received need-based aid. The average freshman award was $11,317. Need-based self-help aid (loans and jobs) averaged $6,703 ($40,512 maximum); non-need-based athletic scholarships averaged $21,037 ($41,688 maximum); and other non-need-based awards and non-need-based scholarships averaged $6,947 ($46,000 maximum). 6% of undergraduate students work part-time. Average annual earnings from campus work are $3500. The average financial indebtedness of the 2014 graduate was $34,066. The FAFSA and the college's own financial statement are required. The priority date for freshman financial aid applications for fall entry is March 15.

UTAH STATE UNIVERSITY C-1
www.usu.edu

Logan, UT 84322

(435) 797-1000
(800) 488-8108

Fax: (435) 797-3708

Email: admit@usu.edu

Full-time: 7760 men, 8063 women

Faculty: 880; I, --$

Part-time: 3404 men, 5044 women

Ph.D.s: 83%

Graduate: 1540 men, 1851 women

Student/Faculty: 21 to 1

Year: semesters, summer session

Tuition: $6384 ($18,491)

Room & Board: $5680

Freshman Class: 10935 applied, 10768 accepted, 3970 enrolled

ACT: 23

CEEB CODE: 4857

Application Deadline: April 1

COMPETITIVE

Utah State University, founded in 1888, is a public institution that offers degree programs in the liberal arts and sciences, agriculture and natural resources, engineering, business, education, fine arts, music, family life, and the sciences. The figures in the above capsule and in this profile are approximate. There are 8 undergraduate schools and 1 graduate school. In addition to regional accreditation, USU has baccalaureate program accreditation with AACSB, ABET, ADA, AHEA, ASLA, CSWE, FIDER, NASM, NCATE, NRPA, and SAF. The 332-acre campus is in a small town 86 miles north of Salt Lake City. Including any residence halls, there are 104 buildings.

STUDENT LIFE: 74% of undergraduates are from Utah. Others are from 50 states, 87 foreign countries, and Canada. 79% are White. The average age of freshmen is 21; all undergraduates, 23. 34% do not continue beyond their first year; 65% remain to graduate. **Housing:** 3297 students can be accommodated in college housing, which includes single-sex dorms, on-campus apartments, and married student housing. In addition, there are honors houses, special-interest houses, fraternity houses, and sorority houses. On-campus housing is available on a first-come and first-served basis. Alcohol is not permitted. All students may keep cars.

FACULTY/CLASSROOMS: 63% of faculty are male; 37% are female. Graduate students teach 5% of introductory courses. The average class size in an introductory lecture is 35; in a laboratory is 20; and in a regular course is 25.

PROGRAMS OF STUDY: USU confers B.A., B.S., B.F.A., B.I.D., B.L.A. and B.M. degrees. Associate, Master's, and Doctoral degrees are also awarded. Bachelor's degrees are awarded in AGRICULTURE (agricultural business management, agricultural economics, animal science, dairy science, forestry and related sciences, international agriculture, natural resource management, plant science, range/farm management, soil science, and wildlife management), BIOLOGICAL SCIENCE (biochemistry, biology/biological science, and microbiology), BUSINESS (accounting, banking and finance, business administration and management, business economics, fashion merchandising, international business management, management information systems, marketing/retailing/merchandising, and personnel management), COMMUNICATIONS AND THE ARTS (dance, dramatic arts, English, fine arts, French, German, journalism, music, and Spanish), COMPUTER AND PHYSICAL SCIENCE (chemistry, computer science, earth science, geology, information sciences and systems, mathematics, physics, and statistics), EDUCATION (agricultural education, art education, business education, early childhood education, elementary education, foreign languages education, health education, home economics education, industrial arts education, mathematics education, music education, physical education, science education, secondary education, and special education), ENGINEERING AND ENVIRONMENTAL DESIGN (agricultural engineering, civil engineering, electrical/electronics engineering, engineering, environmental science, industrial engineering, industrial engineering technology, interior design, landscape architecture/design, and mechanical engineering), HEALTH PROFESSIONS (medical laboratory technology, music therapy, predentistry, premedicine, public health, speech pathology/audiology, and veterinary science), SOCIAL SCIENCE (American studies, child care/child and family studies, economics, food science, geography, history, home economics, human development, international relations, liberal arts/general studies, parks and recreation management, philosophy, political science/government, prelaw, psychology, social work, and sociology). Natural resources, engineering, and special education are the strongest academically. Humanities, business, and education have the largest enrollments.

ACTIVITIES: 2% of men belong to 1 local and 5 national fraternities; 2% of women belong to 1 local and 3 national sororities. There are 230 groups on campus, including art, bagpipe, band, cheerleading, choir, chorale, chorus, computers, dance, drama, drill team, environmental, ethnic, film, gay, honors, international, jazz band, literary magazine, marching band, musical theater, newspaper, opera, orchestra, pep band, photography, political, professional, radio and TV, religious, social, social service, student government, and symphony. Popular campus events include Festival of the American West, Halloween Howl, Homecoming, and A-Day. **Sports:** There are 7 intercollegiate sports for men and 9 for women, and 20 intramural sports for men and 20 for women. Facilities include 5 gyms, indoor and outdoor tennis courts, 2 swimming pools, 40 acres of grass for outdoor sports, a field house, and golf and skiing areas. The campus stadium seats 30,257, and the largest auditorium seats 10,000. **Graduates:** From July 1, 2013 to June 30, 2014, 3548 bachelor's degrees were awarded. The most popular majors were communicative disorders and deaf education (9%), economics (8%), and human movement science (4%). 230 companies recruited on campus in 2013-2014. In an average class, 54% graduate in 6 years or less.

SERVICES: Counseling and information services are available, as is tutoring in most subjects. There is a reader service for the blind, and remedial math, reading, and writing. There is also a writing lab and a tutor room. **Library/Resources:** The 3 libraries contain 1.5 million volumes, 2.7 million microform items, 18,027 audio/video tapes/CDs/DVDs, and subscribe to 10,281 periodicals including electronic. Computerized library services include interlibrary loans, database searching, Internet access, and Wi-Fi capability. Special learning facilities include an art gallery, natural history museum, radio station, a laboratory school, a historical farm, a fine arts center, and a developmental center for people who are disabled. **Physically Challenged Students:** 97% of the campus is accessible. Facilities include wheelchair ramps, elevators, special parking, specially equipped restrooms, special class scheduling, lowered drinking fountains, lowered telephones. special phones to receive calls from the deaf, and a disability resource center. **Special:** Internships are available in most departments through the Cooperative Education Program. The National Student Exchange Program allows students to cross-register in designated institutions and programs, and the International Student Exchange Program enables students to study abroad. There is also cross-registration with the University of the Americas of Mexico. A general studies degree and student-designed majors are available. Nondegree study, work-study programs, co-op programs, B.A.-B.S. degrees, pass/fail options, and credit for military experience are offered. There are 11 national honor societies, a freshman honors program, and 35 departmental honors programs. **Visiting:** There are regularly scheduled orientations for prospective students, consisting of a campus tour, including a meeting with an academic adviser, lunch, and a housing tour, available at 10:30 a.m. and 1:30 p.m., September to May, and 1:30 p.m., June to August. There are guides for informal visits, visitors may sit in on classes, and stay overnight. To schedule a visit, contact the Admissions Office at admit@usu.edu. **Campus Safety and Security:** Measures include 24-hour foot and vehicle patrol, emergency notification system, self-defense education, and security escort services. There are shuttle buses, emergency telephones, lighted pathways/sidewalks, and campus police.

REQUIREMENTS: USU requires that either the SAT or ACT be provided. The ACT has been the preferred choice, but either is accepted. In addition, students should graduate from an accredited secondary school with 15 academic units, including 4 in English, 3 each in math and science, and 1 in social sciences. GED equivalency is accepted, provided ACT scores are 19 or higher. Students not meeting entrance requirements may be considered for admission on a provisional basis. A GPA of 2.7 is required. AP and CLEP credits are accepted. Important factors in the admissions decision are evidence of special talent, parents or siblings attended your school, and recommendations by school officials.The core curriculum of 30 semester credits includes at least 6 of writing; the total number of credits required for graduation is 120. Students must maintain a minimum GPA of 2.5. The number of credits required in the major varies, but there is a minimum of 40 in major classes. **Procedure:** Freshmen are admitted to all sessions. Entrance exams should be taken in the spring of the junior year. There are deferred admissions and rolling admissions plans. Applications should be filed by April 1 for fall entry; October 1 for spring entry; and April 1 for summer entry, along with a $40 fee. Applications are accepted on-line. **Transfer Students:** 1769 transfer students enrolled in 2013-2014. A minimum 2.2 GPA, higher for some majors, is required for transfer students. Those applicants with fewer than 45 credits must also submit ACT scores. 30 of 120 credits required for the bachelor's degree must be completed at USU. **International Students:** There are 379 international students enrolled. They must take the TOEFL with a minimum score of 525 on the paper-based TOEFL (PBT) or 71 on the Internet-based version (iBT) or take the MELAB, the TOEFL is preferred.

ADMISSIONS: 98% of the 2014-2015 applicants were accepted. The ACT scores were 23% below 21, 27% between 21 and 23, 23% between 24 and 26, 11% between 27 and 28, and 16% above 28. 37% of the current freshmen were in the top fifth of their class; 74% were in the top two fifths. 168 freshmen graduated first in their class. **Admissions Contact:** Katie Nielsen, Director of Admissions Office. E-Mail: *admit@usu.edu* Web: *www.usu.edu*

FINANCIAL AID: In 2014-2015, 81% of all full-time freshmen and 59% of continuing full-time students received some form of financial aid. 49% of all full-time freshmen and 45% of continuing full-time students received need-based aid. The average freshman award was $8,450. Need-based scholarships or need-based grants averaged $7,676; need-based self-help aid (loans and jobs) averaged $3,400; non-need-based athletic scholarships averaged $13,200; and other non-need-based awards and non-need-based scholarships averaged $3,100. 21% of undergraduate students work part-time. Average annual earnings from campus work are $3200. The average financial indebtedness of the 2014 graduate was $18,990. The FAFSA is required. The priority date for freshman financial aid applications for fall entry is March 1.

UTAH SYSTEM OF HIGHER EDUCATION

The Utah System of Higher Education, established in 1969, is a private system in Utah. It is governed by a state board of regents, whose chief administrator is the commissioner of higher education. The primary goal of the system is teaching, research, and public service. The main priorities are to provide a high-quality, efficient, and economical public system of higher education, to coordinate, consolidate, and avoid unnecessary duplication, and to systematically develop the role of each institution within the system. The total student enrollment for all nine campuses is usually 79,790 with 3200 faculty members. Profiles of the 4-year campuses are included in this section.

WEBER STATE UNIVERSITY   C-1
weber.edu

Ogden, UT 84408

(801) 626-6000
(801) 626-6743

Fax: (801) 626-6747

Email: admissions@weber.edu

Full-time: 5774 men, 6010 women	**Faculty:** 439; IIA, --$
Part-time: 6407 men, 7677 women	**Ph.D.s:** 82%
Graduate: 365 men, 299 women	**Student/Faculty:** 22 to 1
Year: semesters, summer session	**Tuition:** $4761 ($12,858)
Room & Board: $6600	**Freshman Class:** 5561 applied, 5561 accepted, 2954 enrolled
ACT: 21	**CEEB CODE:** 4941
Application Deadline: August 21	**COMPETITIVE**

Weber State University provides associate, baccalaureate and master degree programs in liberal arts, sciences, technical and professional fields. Encouraging freedom of expression and valuing diversity, the university provides excellent educational experiences for students through extensive personal contact among faculty, staff and students in and out of the classroom. Through academic programs, research, artistic expression, public service and community-based learning, the university serves as an educational, cultural and economic leader for the region. There are 7 undergraduate schools and 11 graduate schools. In addition to regional accreditation, WSU has baccalaureate program accreditation with AACSB, ABET, ACCE, ADA, CSWE, NASAD, NASM, NCATE, and NLN.

STUDENT LIFE: 92% of undergraduates are from Utah. Others are from 50 states, 45 foreign countries, and Canada. 99% are from public schools. 54% are White; 32% race unknown. The average age of freshmen is 23; all undergraduates, 26. 26% do not continue beyond their first year. *Housing:* 864 students can be accommodated in college housing, which includes single-sex and coed dorms, on-campus apartments, and married student housing. On-campus housing is guaranteed for all 4 years, is available on a first-come, first-served basis. 97% of students commute. Alcohol is not permitted. All students may keep cars. The 526-acre campus is in an urban area located in the foothills of the Wasatch Mountains, 33 miles north of Salt Lake City. Including any residence halls, there are 61 buildings.

FACULTY/CLASSROOMS: 53% of faculty are male; 47% are female. All teach undergraduates. No introductory courses are taught by graduate students. The average class size in an introductory lecture is 34 and in a laboratory is 26.

PROGRAMS OF STUDY: WSU confers B.A., B.S., B.F.A., B.I.S., B.M. and B.M.E. degrees. Associate and master's degrees are also awarded. Bachelor's degrees are awarded in BIOLOGICAL SCIENCE (biology/biological science, botany, microbiology, and zoology), BUSINESS (accounting, banking and finance, business administration and management, business economics, human resources, international economics, management information systems, marketing management, personnel management, purchasing/inventory management, and supply chain management), COMMUNICATIONS AND THE ARTS (art, communications, dance, dramatic arts, English, fine arts, French, German, graphic design, journalism, media arts, music, music performance, musical theater, photography, piano/organ, public relations, Spanish, theatre arts, visual and performing arts, and voice), COMPUTER AND PHYSICAL SCIENCE (chemistry, computer programming, computer science, earth science, geology, information sciences and systems, mathematics, physical sciences, and physics), EDUCATION (art education, athletic training, business education, early childhood education, education, elementary education, English education, foreign languages education, health education, mathematics education, music education, physical education, science education, secondary education, social science education, special education, and teaching English as a second/foreign language (TESOL/TEFOL)), ENGINEERING AND ENVIRONMENTAL DESIGN (automotive technology, computer engineering, construction management, electrical/electronics engineering, electrical/electronics engineering technology, environmental science, interior design, manufacturing engineering, manufacturing technology, mechanical engineering technology, plastics engineering, and plastics technology), HEALTH PROFESSIONS (clinical science, dental hygiene, health care administration, nursing, radiation therapy, radiograph medical technology, radiological science, and respiratory therapy), SOCIAL SCIENCE (anthropology, child care/child and family studies, criminal justice, early childhood studies, economics, family/consumer studies, geography, gerontology, history, interdisciplinary studies, liberal arts/general studies, philosophy, political science/government, psychology, social work, and sociology). Keyboard performance/pedagogy, master of taxation, and vocal performance/pedagogy are the strongest academically. Nursing, business administration, and accounting have the largest enrollments.

ACTIVITIES: There are 229 groups on campus, including art, band, cheerleading, chess, choir, chorale, chorus, communications, computers, dance, debate, drama, drill team, drum and bugle corps, environmental, ethnic, forensics, gay, honors, international, jazz band, literary magazine, marching band, musical theater, newspaper, opera, orchestra, pep band, photography, political, professional, radio and TV, religious, social, social service, student government, symphony, and The Latter-day Saint Student Association (LDSSA) is established by the Ogden Institute of Religion to help students attending a Weber State University have a balanced secular and spiritual educational experience during their years of formal education. Popular campus events include homecoming, graduation, and student elections. **Sports:** There are 5 intercollegiate sports for men and 7 for women, and 8 intramural sports for men and 8 for women. Facilities include Weber State University is home to many athletic and recreation facilities including: an indoor track, a strength-training center, indoor basketball and volleyball courts, group fitness areas, the Swenson Pool, racquetball and tennis courts, the 17,000-seat Wildcat Stadium, the 11,592-seat Dee Events Center, the 7,800-seat Val A. Browning Center for the Performing Arts, outdoor playing fields, fitness centers located at University Village and Davis Campus, a 1-mile jogging trail, and the Weber Rocks Climbing Wall. **Graduates:** In a recent year, 2157 bachelor's degrees were awarded. The most popular majors were teacher education (8%), sales and service technology (7%), and nursing (5%). In an average class, 8% graduate in 4 years or less, 23% graduate in 5 years or less, and 43% graduate in 6 years or less.

SERVICES: Counseling and information services are available, as is tutoring in every subject. There is a reader service for the blind, and remedial math, reading, and writing. Translators are offered for the hearing impaired. **Library/Resources:** The library contains 708,606 volumes, 623,973 microform items, and 22,957 audio/video tapes/CDs/DVDs, and subscribes to 793 periodicals including electronic. Computerized library services include interlibrary loans, database searching, and Internet access. Special learning facilities include an art gallery, natural history museum, planetarium, radio station, TV station, and a working crime lab. **Physically Challenged Students:** 99% of the campus is accessible. Facilities include wheelchair ramps, elevators, special parking, specially equipped restrooms, special class scheduling, lowered drinking fountains, lowered telephones, and special housing. **Special:** Weber State University offers co-op programs and internships in many majors, a Washington semester, study abroad in Mexico and England, work-study programs with community businesses, B.A.-B.S. degrees, dual majors in many combinations, student-designed majors resulting in a B.I.S. degree, a general studies degree, credit for military experience, non-degree study, and pass/fail options. There are 20 national honor societies, a freshman honors program, and 17 departmental honors programs. **Visiting:** There are regularly scheduled orientations for prospective students. There are guides for informal visits, visitors may sit in on classes, and stay overnight. To schedule a visit, contact Laura Albright at (801) 626-6050. **Campus Safety and Security:** Measures include self-defense education, and security escort services. There are shuttle buses, emergency telephones, and lighted pathways/sidewalks.

REQUIREMENTS: The ACT is recommended. Applicants must be graduates of an accredited secondary school or have a GED. Other requirements vary by department. Out-of-state residents must have a minimum high school GPA of 2.0. AP and CLEP credits are accepted. To graduate, students must demonstrate math competency and complete courses in government/history, English, humanities, math, biological/physical sciences, and social sciences. At least 120 semester credit hours, with 45 at the upper-division level, and a minimum GPA of 2.0 are required. Hours in the major and distribution requirements vary with the degree. **Procedure:** Freshmen are admitted to all sessions. Entrance exams should be taken Junior or senior year of high school. There are early admissions, deferred admissions, and rolling admissions plans. Applications should be filed by August 21 for fall entry, along with a $30 fee. Applications are accepted online. **Transfer Students:** 1249 transfer students enrolled in 2012-2013. Transfer students must submit official transcripts from previously attended colleges or universities and have a minimum GPA of 2.0. 30 of 120 credits required for the bachelor's degree must be completed at WSU. **International Students:** There are 441 international students enrolled. The school actively recruits these students.

ADMISSIONS: 100% of the 2013-2014 applicants were accepted. The ACT scores were 46% below 21, 25% between 21 and 23, 18% between 24 and 26, 7% between 27 and 28, and 5% above 28. **Admissions Contact:** Scott Teichert, Director of Admissions. E-Mail: *ScottTeichert@weber.edu* Web: *www.weber.edu*

FINANCIAL AID: In a recent year, 77% of all full-time freshmen and 72% of continuing full-time students received some form of financial aid. 47% of all full-time freshmen and 55% of continuing full-time students received need-based aid. The average freshman award was $6,154. Need-based scholarships or need-based grants averaged $3,999 ($9,273 maximum); need-based self-help aid (loans and jobs) averaged $3,492 ($18,647 maximum); non-need-based athletic scholarships averaged $8,403 ($20,024 maximum); and other non-need-based awards and non-need-based scholarships averaged $3,601 ($26,483 maximum). 1% of undergraduate students work part-time. Average annual earnings from campus work are $8514. The FAFSA and the college's own financial statement are required. The deadline for filing freshman financial aid applications for fall entry is March 1.

WESTMINSTER COLLEGE   C-2
www.westminstercollege.edu

Salt Lake City, UT 84105

(801) 832-2200
(800) 484-7651

Fax: (801) 832-3101   Email: admission@westminstercollege.edu

Full-time: 932 men, 1143 women	Faculty: 161; IIB, +$
Part-time: 87 men, 71 women	Ph.D.s: 82%
Graduate: 343 men, 415 women	Student/Faculty: 13 to 1
Year: 4-1-4, summer session	Tuition: $29,500
Room & Board: $8208	Freshman Class: 1784 applied, 1737 accepted, 485 enrolled

SAT CR/M: 560/560 **ACT:** 24   **CEEB CODE:** 4948
Application Deadline: rolling   **COMPETITIVE+**

Westminster College, founded in 1875, is a private, comprehensive, liberal arts institution offering undergraduate programs through the Bill and Vieve Gore school of business, the St. Mark's Westminster school of nursing and health sciences, the school of arts and sciences and education. There are 4 undergraduate schools and 4 graduate schools. In addition to regional accreditation, has baccalaureate program accreditation with ACBSP, NLN, TEAC, AABI, AANA, and CEPH. The 27-acre campus is in an urban area 6 miles southeast of downtown Salt Lake City. Including any residence halls, there are 31 buildings.

STUDENT LIFE: 57% of undergraduates are from Utah. Others are from 48 states, 23 foreign countries, and Canada. 80% are from public schools. 71% are White. The average age of freshmen is 18; all undergraduates, 22. 72% remain to graduate. **Housing:** 809 students can be accommodated in college housing, which includes coed dorms, on-campus apartments, and off-campus apartments. On-campus housing is guaranteed for the freshman year only, is available on a first-come, first-served basis, and is available on a lottery system for upperclassmen. Priority is given to out-of-town students. 68% of students commute. All students may keep cars.

FACULTY/CLASSROOMS: 42% of faculty are male; 58% are female. All teach undergraduates. No introductory courses are taught by graduate students.

PROGRAMS OF STUDY: confers B.A., B.S. and B.F.A. degrees. Master's degrees are also awarded. Bachelor's degrees are awarded in AGRICULTURE (environmental studies), BIOLOGICAL SCIENCE (biology/biological science and neurosciences), BUSINESS (accounting, banking and finance, business administration and management, international business management, investments and securities, and marketing/retailing/merchandising), COMMUNICATIONS AND THE ARTS (art, arts administration/management, communications, dramatic arts, English, fine arts, and music), COMPUTER AND PHYSICAL SCIENCE (chemistry, computer science, information sciences and systems, mathematics, and physics), EDUCATION (early childhood education, elementary education, and special education), ENGINEERING AND ENVIRONMENTAL DESIGN (aviation administration/management and aviation computer technology), HEALTH PROFESSIONS (nursing), SOCIAL SCIENCE (criminal justice, economics, gender studies, history, homeland security, philosophy, political science/government, prelaw, psychology, social science, sociology, and Spanish studies). Nursing, business, communication, education, and social science are the strongest academically. Business, nursing, biology, and psychology have the largest enrollments.

ACTIVITIES: There are no fraternities or sororities. There are 42 groups on campus, including art, choir, chorale, chorus, computers, dance, debate, drama, environmental, ethnic, film, gay, honors, international, jazz band, literary magazine, musical theater, newspaper, orchestra, photography, political, professional, religious, social service, student government, and symphony. Popular campus events include Westminster Welcome Week, Pizza Tasting, Halloween Dance, Documentary Film and Lecture Series, Homecoming Week, and Late Night Breakfast. **Sports:** There are 8 intercollegiate sports for men and 10 for women, and 13 intramural sports for men and 13 for women. Facilities include a health and wellness recreation center, including basketball courts, weight room, lap pool, racquet-

ball courts, dance studio, two floors of cardio equipment, and a climbing wall. **Graduates:** From July 1, 2013 to June 30, 2014, 556 bachelor's degrees were awarded. The most popular majors were business (23%), health professions (20%), and psychology (7%). 60 companies recruited on campus in 2013-2014. In an average class, 49% graduate in 4 years or less, 60% graduate in 5 years or less, and 61% graduate in 6 years or less.

SERVICES: Counseling and information services are available, as is tutoring in most subjects. There is a reader service for the blind, and remedial math, reading, and writing. **Library/Resources:** The 2 libraries contain 261,854 volumes, 237,930 microform items, 6,147 audio/video tapes/CDs/DVDs, and subscribe to 40,938 periodicals including electronic. Computerized library services include interlibrary loans, database searching, Internet access, and Wi-Fi capability. Special learning facilities include a **Physically Challenged Students:** 99% of the campus is accessible. Facilities include wheelchair ramps, elevators, special parking, specially equipped restrooms, special class scheduling, lowered drinking fountains, lowered telephones, and special housing. **Special:** The college offers internships in every major, study abroad, dual and student-designed majors, an accelerated degree, co-op, work-study, independent study, weekend college, and freshman seminar courses. A 3-2 engineering degree with USC in Los Angeles or Washington University in St. Louis, Missouri, is also possible. There are 2 national honor societies, a freshman honors program, and 1 departmental honors programs. **Visiting:** There are regularly scheduled orientations for prospective students, including a welcome program, lunch, various workshops, a campus tour, and meetings with faculty. There are guides for informal visits, visitors may sit in on classes, and stay overnight. To schedule a visit, contact Darlene Dilley at admission@westminstercollege.edu. **Campus Safety and Security:** Measures include 24-hour foot and vehicle patrol, emergency notification system, self-defense education, and security escort services. There are emergency telephones, lighted pathways/sidewalks, controlled access to dorms/residences, and a separate dorm security.

REQUIREMENTS: The SAT or ACT is required. Applicants must be graduates of an accredited secondary school or have a GED certificate. College preparatory work should include 4 units of English, 3 of science, 2 each of math, foreign language, social studies, and electives, and 1 of history. An interview is recommended. AP and CLEP credits are accepted. Important factors in the admissions decision are evidence of special talent, extracurricular activities record, and advanced placement or honors courses. To be eligible for a bachelor's degree, students must satisfy the following requirements: complete a minimum of 124 semester credit hours, 30 of which must be upper division courses numbered 300 or above from a four-year institution fulfill all liberal education requirements; maintain an overall grade point average of 2.00 or above; meet all course requirements and grade point average requirements in the major; fulfill the residency requirements in their governing academic catalog. **Procedure:** Freshmen are admitted to all sessions. Entrance exams should be taken in the junior or senior year of high school. There are deferred admissions and rolling admissions plans. Application deadlines are open. The fall 2014 application fee was $50. Notifications are sent September 1. Applications are accepted on-line. **Transfer Students:** 181 transfer students enrolled in 2013-2014. Transfer students must have a minimum 2.5 GPA and be in good standing at all previously attended institutions. They must provide college transcripts and submit an essay. An interview is recommended. Some students may need to present standardized test scores and high school transcripts. 36 of 124 credits required for the bachelor's degree must be completed at Westminster. **International Students:** There are 119 international students enrolled. The school actively recruits these students. They must take the TOEFL with a minimum score of 550 on the paper-based TOEFL (PBT) or 79 on the Internet-based version (iBT). They must also take the SAT or ACT.

ADMISSIONS: 97% of the 2014-2015 applicants were accepted. The SAT scores for the 2014-2015 freshman class were: Critical Reading--25% below 500, 41% between 500 and 599, 30% between 600 and 699, and 4% between 700 and 800; Math--25% below 500, 41% between 500 and 599, 30% between 600 and 699, and 5% between 700 and 800. The ACT scores were 15% below 21, 26% between 21 and 23, 26% between 24 and 26, 17% between 27 and 28, and 16%

above 28. 43% of the current freshmen were in the top fifth of their class; 85% were in the top two fifths. 13 freshmen graduated first in their class. **Admissions Contact:** Darlene Dilley, Director of Admissions. E-Mail: *admission@westminstercollege.edu* Web: *www. westminstercollege.edu*

FINANCIAL AID: In 2014-2015, 98% of all full-time freshmen and 93% of continuing full-time students received some form of financial aid. 66% of all full-time freshmen and 58% of continuing full-time students received need-based aid. The average freshman award was $26,092. Need-based scholarships or need-based grants averaged $18,786 ($29,856 maximum); need-based self-help aid (loans and jobs) averaged $5,518 ($12,500 maximum); non-need-based athletic scholarships averaged $5,043 ($20,268 maximum); and other non-need-based awards and non-need-based scholarships averaged $15,372 ($29,856 maximum). 27% of undergraduate students work part-time. Average annual earnings from campus work are $2950. The average financial indebtedness of the 2014 graduate was $27,523. is a member of CSS. The FAFSA is required. The priority date for freshman financial aid applications for fall entry is April 15. The deadline for filing freshman financial aid applications for fall entry is rolling.

Craftsbury

Johnson

Colchester

Lyndonville

Burlington

Plainfield
Montpelier

Middlebury

Northfield

Randolph Center

Castleton

Rutland

Poultney

VERMONT

Bennington
Marlboro

• College Location

0 10 20 30 40 50
Miles

BENNINGTON COLLEGE · A-6
www.bennington.edu

Bennington, VT 05201

(802) 442-5401
(800) 833-6845

Fax: (802) 440-4320 · Email: admissions@bennington.edu

Full-time: 244 men, 440 women	Faculty: 64
Part-time: 1 men, 3 women	Ph.D.s: 70%
Graduate: 27 men, 111 women	Student/Faculty: 11 to 1
Year: other	Tuition: $44,220
Room & Board: $12,770	Freshman Class: 1236 applied, 779 accepted, 197 enrolled
SAT CR/M/W: 690/610/660 ACT: 29	CEEB CODE: 3080
Application Deadline: January 3	HIGHLY COMPETITIVE+

Bennington College, founded in 1932, is a private liberal arts institution characterized by cross-disciplinary learning, a close working relationship between student and teacher, a self-directed academic planning process, and a connection to the world through it's winter internship term. There are 4 graduate schools. The 440-acre campus is in a small town in the southwestern corner of Vermont, 160 miles north of New York City and 150 miles west of Boston. Including any residence halls, there are 70 buildings.

STUDENT LIFE: 96% of undergraduates are from out of state, mostly the Middle Atlantic. Students are from 46 states, 35 foreign countries, and Canada. 57% are from public schools. 77% are White. The average age of freshmen is 18; all undergraduates, 20. 17% do not continue beyond their first year; 64% remain to graduate.

FACULTY/CLASSROOMS: 51% of faculty are male; 49% are female. All teach undergraduates, all do research, and all teach and do research. No introductory courses are taught by graduate students. The average class size in an introductory lecture is 16; in a laboratory is 15; and in a regular course is 10.

PROGRAMS OF STUDY: Bennington confers B.A. degrees. Master's degrees are also awarded. Bachelor's degrees are awarded in AGRI-

CULTURE (environmental studies), BIOLOGICAL SCIENCE (biology/biological science, botany, ecology, environmental biology, evolutionary biology, and zoology), COMMUNICATIONS AND THE ARTS (American literature, animation, art, ceramic art and design, Chinese, comparative literature, creative writing, dance, design, digital communications, dramatic arts, drawing, English, English literature, film arts, fine arts, French, Germanic languages and literature, illustration, Italian, Japanese, jazz, journalism, languages, literature, multimedia, music, music performance, music theory and composition, painting, performing arts, photography, piano/organ, playwriting/screenwriting, printmaking, sculpture, Spanish, strings, studio art, theater design, video, visual and performing arts, and voice), COMPUTER AND PHYSICAL SCIENCE (astronomy, chemistry, computer science, digital arts/technology, mathematics, physical sciences, physics, and science), EDUCATION (drama education, early childhood education, education, elementary education, foreign languages education, mathematics education, middle school education, and secondary education), ENGINEERING AND ENVIRONMENTAL DESIGN (architecture and environmental science), HEALTH PROFESSIONS (premedicine), SOCIAL SCIENCE (American studies, anthropology, child psychology/development, European studies, fashion design and technology, history, humanities, humanities and social science, interdisciplinary studies, international relations, international studies, Judaic studies, Latin American studies, liberal arts/general studies, philosophy, political science/government, prelaw, psychology, social psychology, social science, sociology, and women's studies). Literature, languages, and visual and performing arts are the strongest academically. Literature, and interdisciplinary studies have the largest enrollments.

ACTIVITIES: There are 37 groups on campus, including campus activities board, student educational policies committee, student endowment for the arts, sustainability committee, art, chess, choir, chorale, chorus, computers, dance, debate, drama, environmental, ethnic, film, gay, international, jazz band, literary magazine, musical theater, newspaper, opera, outing club, photography, political, radio and TV, religious, social, social service, student government, and symphony. Popular campus events include Sunfest, Faculty Concerts, and Student-Work Performances.

SERVICES: Counseling and information services are available, as is tutoring in some subjects. There is remedial writing. Tutoring for learning disabilities is available in the town of Bennington at a cost to the student. **Library/Resources:** The 2 libraries contain 125,000 volumes, 6,000 audio/video tapes/CDs/DVDs, and subscribe to 14,500 periodicals including electronics. Computerized library services include interlibrary loans, database searching, Internet access, and Wi-Fi capability. Special learning facilities include an art gallery, radio station, Center for the Advancement of Public Action with unique tiered symposium space for U.N.-style dialogue and webcasting; observatory; greenhouse; digital arts lab; art gallery; architecture, drawing, painting, printmaking, and sculpture studios; ceramic studio and kilns; photography darkrooms; film and video editing studio; several fully equipped theaters; dance studios; scripts library; costume shop; electronic music and sound recording studios; music practice rooms and music library; student-run cafe and bar; and 440 acres of forest, ponds, wetlands and fields for recreation and scientific study.

REQUIREMENTS: Bennington admits students who have demonstrated a passion for learning and academic excellence. The Common Application as well as the Bennington Supplement are required. Submission of standardized test scores is optional. A majority of applicants are interviewed in person or by phone.

ADMISSIONS: 63% of a recent year applicants were accepted. The SAT scores for the recent year freshman class were: Critical Reading--13% between 500 and 599, 46% between 600 and 699, and 41% between 700 and 800; Math--2% below 500, 38% between 500 and 599, 48% between 600 and 699, and 13% between 700 and 800; Writing--2% below 500, 21% between 500 and 599, 51% between 600 and 699, and 27% between 700 and 800. The ACT scores were 5% below 21, 23% between 24 and 26, 23% between 27 and 28, and 50% above 28. 56% of the current freshmen were in the top fifth of their class; 84% were in the top two fifths.

FINANCIAL AID: In a recent year, 95% of all full-time freshmen and

90% of continuing full-time students received some form of financial aid. 58% of all full-time freshmen and 63% of continuing full-time students received need-based aid. The average freshman award was $33,336. Need-based scholarships or need-based grants averaged $23,448; need-based self-help aid (loans and jobs) averaged $4,696; and other non-need-based awards and non-need-based scholarships averaged $13,019. 20% of undergraduate students work part-time. Average annual earnings from campus work are $2214. The average financial indebtedness of the 2013 graduate was $25,716. Bennington is a member of CSS. The CSS/Profile, FAFSA, the college's own financial statement, and student and parent tax returns and W-2s are required. The priority date for freshman financial aid applications for fall entry is February 1. The deadline for filing freshman financial aid applications for fall entry is February 15.

BURLINGTON COLLEGE (*The complete profile is made available exclusively on our website, www.barronspac.com*)

CASTLETON STATE COLLEGE		B-4
www.castleton.edu		

Castleton, VT 05735	(802) 468-1213
	(800) 639-8521
Fax: (802) 468-1476	Email: info@castleton.edu
Full-time: 859 men, 861 women	Faculty: 102; IIB, --$
Part-time: 97 men, 168 women	Ph.D.s: 99%
Graduate: 49 men, 150 women	Student/Faculty: 14 to 1
Year: semesters, summer session	Tuition: $10,772 ($25,436)
Room & Board: $9414	Freshman Class: 2397 applied, 1868 accepted, 382 enrolled
SAT or ACT: required	CEEB CODE: 3765
Application Deadline: open	COMPETITIVE

Castleton State College, founded in 1787, is the oldest institution of higher learning in Vermont. As part of the Vermont State Colleges system, it offers a state-supported undergraduate and graduate program in liberal arts, teacher preparation, and professional studies. There is 1 undergraduate school and 1 graduate school. In addition to regional accreditation, Castleton has baccalaureate program accreditation with CSWE and NLN. The 165-acre campus is in a rural area 12 miles west of Rutland. Including any residence halls, there are 24 buildings.

STUDENT LIFE: 85% are White. The average age of freshmen is 18; all undergraduates, 21. **Housing:** 1100 students can be accommodated in college housing, which includes single-sex and coed dorms. Including wellness housing. On-campus housing is guaranteed for the freshman year only and is available on a lottery system for upperclassmen. 54% of students live on campus; of those, 70% remain on campus on weekends. All students may keep cars.

FACULTY/CLASSROOMS: 50% of faculty are male; 50% are female. All teach undergraduates, and 50% do both. No introductory courses are taught by graduate students. The average class size in an introductory lecture is 25; in a laboratory is 14; and in a regular course is 18.

PROGRAMS OF STUDY: Castleton confers B.A., B.S., B.M. and B.S.W. degrees. Associate and Master's degrees are also awarded. Bachelor's degrees are awarded in BIOLOGICAL SCIENCE (biology/biological science and ecology), BUSINESS (business administration and management and sports management), COMMUNICATIONS AND THE ARTS (art, communications, English, literature, music, Spanish, and theatre arts), COMPUTER AND PHYSICAL SCIENCE (chemistry, computer science, geology, mathematics, and natural sciences), EDUCATION (athletic training, education, global studies, health education, music education, and physical education), ENGINEERING AND ENVIRONMENTAL DESIGN (environmental science), HEALTH PROFESSIONS (exercise science, health science, and nursing), SOCIAL SCIENCE (criminal justice, economics, history, liberal arts/general studies, philosophy, political science/government, psychology, social science, social work, sociology, and women and gender studies). Business, nursing, and teacher preparation havee the largest enrollments.

ACTIVITIES: There are 40 groups on campus, including art, band,

cheerleading, choir, chorale, chorus, computers, dance, drama, drill team, environmental, ethnic, film, gay, honors, international, jazz band, literary magazine, marching band, musical theater, newspaper, pep band, photography, political, professional, radio and TV, religious, social, social service, and student government. Popular campus events include Spring, Winter, and Alumni Weekends. **Sports:** There are 10 intercollegiate sports for men and 10 for women, and 10 intramural sports for men and 10 for women. Facilities include 2 full-size gymnasiums, a 6-lane swimming pool, 2 racquetball courts, 3 fitness centers, a recreation gym, an ice hockey rink, an outdoor skating facility, multi-purpose turf field, baseball and softball fields, 3 additional full size grass fields, 2 athletic training rooms, a rock climbing wall, and an extensive trail system for hiking, running, and X-C skiing. **Graduates:** From July 1, 2013 to June 30, 2014, 372 bachelor's degrees were awarded. The most popular majors were health professions and related programs (20%), business/marketing (13%), and communication/journalism (10%). 63 companies recruited on campus in 2013-2014. In an average class, 34% graduate in 4 years or less, 47% graduate in 5 years or less, and 51% graduate in 6 years or less.

SERVICES: Counseling and information services are available, as is tutoring in every subject. There is a reader service for the blind, remedial math, reading, and writing. **Library/Resources:** The library contains 272,223 volumes, 626,965 microform items, 22,349 audio/video tapes/CDs/DVDs, and subscribes to 67,896 periodicals including electronic. Computerized library services include interlibrary loans, database searching, Internet access, and Wi-Fi capability. Special learning facilities include an art gallery, radio station, TV studio, observatory, and theater. **Physically Challenged Students:** 95% of the campus is accessible. Facilities include wheelchair ramps, elevators, special parking, specially equipped restrooms, special class scheduling, lowered drinking fountains, and lowered telephones. **Special:** Cross-registration with other Vermont State Colleges, co-op programs, internships, study abroad, and work-study programs are available. In addition, B.A.-B.S. degrees, dual majors, student-designed majors in history, math, and social sciences, credit for life experience, nondegree study, and pass/fail options are offered. There are 8 national honor societies, a freshman honors program, and 4 departmental honors programs. **Visiting:** There are regularly scheduled orientations for prospective students, including meetings with admissions counselors, faculty, and coaches as well as a campus tour. There are guides for informal visits and visitors may sit in on classes. To schedule a visit, contact the Admissions Office. **Campus Safety and Security:** Measures include 24-hour foot and vehicle patrol, emergency notification system, self-defense education, and security escort services. There are emergency telephones, lighted pathways/sidewalks, and controlled access to dorms/residences.

REQUIREMENTS: The SAT or ACT is required. The college requires that candidates have 4 years of English, 3 year of math, 3 years of social studies or history, 3 years of sciences (two of which must be a lab). The college recommends 2 years of a foreign language. The GED is accepted. An interview is recommended. AP and CLEP credits are accepted. Important factors in the admissions decision are advanced placement or honors courses, leadership record, and recommendations by school officials. All students must maintain a GPA of 2.0 while taking 122 semester hours, including 30 or more in their major. Distribution requirements include 3 courses each in literature and the arts, 2 each in math and natural sciences, and 1 each in foreign cultures, history, philosophy and psychology, and social analysis. Specific courses include computers, communication, and an introduction to liberal arts. **Procedure:** Freshmen are admitted fall and spring. Entrance exams should be taken during the spring of the junior year or fall of the senior year. There are early admissions, deferred admissions, and rolling admissions plans. Application deadlines are open. Application fee is $40. Applications are accepted online. **Transfer Students:** 183 transfer students enrolled in 2013-2014. All transfer applicants must have a 2.0 GPA and submit both previous college transcripts and an essay/personal statement. Some transfer applicants will be asked to submit high school transcripts, standardized test scores, and a statement of good standing from the prior institution. An interview may also be required of some transfer students. 30 of 122 credits required for the bachelor's degree must be completed at Castleton. **International Students:** There are 27 international students enrolled. The school actively recruits these students. They must take the TOEFL with a minimum score of 550 on the paper-based TOEFL (PBT) or 80 on the Internet-based version (iBT). They must also take the SAT or ACT.

ADMISSIONS: 78% of the 2014-2015 applicants were accepted. 3 freshmen graduated first in their class. **Admissions Contact:** Maurice Ouimet, Dean of Enrollment. E-Mail: *info@castleton.edu* Web: *www.castleton.edu*

FINANCIAL AID: Castleton is a member of CSS. The FAFSA is required. The deadline for filing freshman financial aid applications for fall entry is April 1.

CHAMPLAIN COLLEGE A-2
www.champlain.edu

Burlington, VT 05402
(802) 860-2700
(800) 570-5858

Fax: n/av   Email: admission@champlain.edu
Full-time: 1357 men, 827 women   Faculty: 97
Part-time: 26 men, 16 women   Ph.D.s: 69%
Graduate: 205 men, 256 women   Student/Faculty: 22 to 1
Year: semesters, summer session Tuition: $32,900
Room & Board: $13,750   Freshman Class: 5600
                                 applied, 3596 accepted,
                                 637 enrolled
SAT CR/M/W: 570/565/550 ACT: 26 CEEB CODE: 3291
Application Deadline: February 1 VERY COMPETITIVE+

Champlain College, founded in 1878, is a leading private college overlooking Lake Champlain in Burlington Vermont, with additional campuses in Montreal, Quebec and Dublin, Ireland. Our career-driven approach to education prepares students for their professional life beginning with their very first semester. Students choose from more than 80 subject areas, including undergraduate majors, minors, specializations, graduate degrees, and certificate programs. Champlain also boasts over 50 student clubs and organizations, exceptional study abroad opportunities, and a strong internship program. There is one undergraduate school and 5 graduate schools. In addition to regional accreditation, Champlain has baccalaureate program accreditation with CSWE, ASCLD, and JRCERT. The 22-acre campus is in an urban area just up the hill from the city's downtown area and Lake Champlain, and at the edge of Vermont's Green Mountains and within sight of New York's Adirondack Mountains. Including any residence halls, there are 46 buildings.

STUDENT LIFE: 76% of undergraduates are from out of state, mostly the Northeast. Students are from 45 states, 23 foreign countries, and Canada. 70% are White; 18% race unknown. The average age of freshmen is 18; all undergraduates, 20. 19% do not continue beyond their first year. **Housing:** 1422 students can be accommodated in college housing, which includes single-sex and coed dorms and off-campus apartments. In addition, there are special-interest houses, including international student housing, and sophmore housing. On-campus housing is guaranteed for the freshman year only, is available on a first-come, first-served basis, and is available on a lottery system for upperclassmen. 62% of students live on campus; of those, 90% remain on campus on weekends. Alcohol is not permitted. No one may keep cars.

FACULTY/CLASSROOMS: 58% of faculty are male; 42% are female. All teach undergraduates. No introductory courses are taught by graduate students. The average class size in a laboratory is 10 and in a regular course is 17.

PROGRAMS OF STUDY: Champlain confers B.S., B.F.A., B.S.W. and B.S.B.A. degrees. Associate and Master's degrees are also awarded. Bachelor's degrees are awarded in AGRICULTURE (environmental studies), BUSINESS (accounting, business administration and management, finance, international business management, management science, marketing, and marketing management), COMMUNICATIONS AND THE ARTS (advertising, broadcasting, communications, communications technology, film arts, fine arts, game design and development, game art, game programming, graphic design, graphic design & media, information technology,

media arts, multimedia, public relations, and writing), COMPUTER AND PHYSICAL SCIENCE (computer game design/development, computer information technology, computer science, computer security and information assurance, cyber intelligence/security studies, information sciences and systems, radiological technology, and web services), EDUCATION (early childhood education, elementary education, health information management, middle school education, and secondary education), ENGINEERING AND ENVIRONMENTAL DESIGN (computational sciences), SOCIAL SCIENCE (criminal justice, forensic studies, legal studies, liberal arts/general studies, psychology, and social work). Game design and programming, graphic design and digital media are the strongest academically. Business administration, game design, and graphic design have the largest enrollments.

ACTIVITIES: There are 50 groups on campus, including art, chess, chorale, computers, dance, debate, drama, environmental, ethnic, forensics, gay, honors, international, literary magazine, musical theater, newspaper, photography, professional, radio and TV, religious, ski and ride, sailing, social, social service, and student government. Popular campus events include Skiing, Snowboarding Trips and Spring Meltdown. **Sports:** There are 16 intramural sports for men and 16 for women. Facilities include a wellness and fitness center, a gym, and game centers. **Graduates:** From July 1, 2013 to June 30, 2014, 580 bachelor's degrees were awarded. The most popular majors were cyber/computer forensics (9%), graphic design (8%), and business administration and management (8%). 1003 companies recruited on campus in 2013-2014. In an average class, 52% graduate in 4 years or less, 55% graduate in 5 years or less, and 57% graduate in 6 years or less. Of the 2013 graduating class, 2% were enrolled in graduate school within 6 months of graduation, and 80% were employed.

SERVICES: Counseling and information services are available, as is tutoring in some subjects, math, accounting, and writing. Peer tutoring is available. **Library/Resources:** The library contains 200,994 volumes, 767 audio/video tapes/CDs/DVDs, and subscribes to 59,499 periodicals including electronic. Computerized library services include interlibrary loans, database searching, Internet access, and Wi-Fi capability. Special learning facilities include a radio station, Champlain College offers on-campus learning centers in studio-like environments in which students across majors work on professional projects that put Champlain students' classroom knowledge to the test through practical application on real projects. These Centers include; EMC, (Emergent Media Center), BYOBiz, (Build Your Own Business), LCDI (Leahy Center for Digital Investigation) and the Publishing Initiative. A video production studio, broadcasting studio, several multimedia and graphic design studio and game design and production studio. **Physically Challenged Students:** 79% of the campus is accessible. Facilities include wheelchair ramps, elevators, special parking, specially equipped restrooms, special class scheduling, lowered drinking fountains, and lowered telephones. **Special:** Champlain College offers Bachelor of Science (BS)degrees in various fields of study in the areas of business, communication and creative media, education, human studies, and computer and information technology. We also offer the Bachelor of Social Work degree (BSW), the Bachelor of Fine Arts (BFA)degrees in creative media, filemaking and graphic design; and the Bachelor of Business Administration (BSBA). The College also offers study abroad opportunities with campuses in Dublin, Ireland and Montreal, Canada in addition to global partnerships with institutions around the world. The courses offered at the Champlain Abroad campuses fit across majors with a variety of professional, liberal arts, and interdisciplinary options that provide students with an understanding of culture and global perspective. Located in Burlington, Vermont, the College is accredited by the New England Association of Schools and Colleges (NEASC), which allows the credit transfer process to be seamless! We also prioritize creating internship opportunities! As a professionally focused institution, Champlain emphasizes the value of getting as much time in the field as possible. We go to great lengths to create the best options for our students to do so. If you have the drive, we will work with you extensively to help you find or create an internship that will give you a chance to really dig into the work of your profession, build up your professional portfolio and capture impressive credentials for your resume. Champlain has established close ties with the local business community, and Champlain students are the interns of choice at numerous businesses in and around Vermont. The College has developed a relationship with other area schools that allows students to take classes at their campuses as part of their regular class load. Champlain students can register for select classroom courses offered during the academic year at St. Michaels's College or Burlington College. The agreement does not apply to summer session or online courses. The College maintains guaranteed admissions arrangements with NYU's School of Continuing and Professional Studies and the Vermont Law School. Students who meet the G.P.A. and other admission requirements of the programs are guaranteed admission into one of 14 Masters programs offered through NYU including an M.S. in Management and Systems and an M.S. in Global Affairs or into the J.D. program at Vermont Law School. An additional agreement with Clarkson University for a 4+1 graduate program allows students to complete the M.B.A. or M.S. in Management in one additional year. Through a special agreement with the prestigious Thunderbird School of Global Management, Champlain students may be able to pursue a Certificate of Advanced Global Studies during the Fall of the fourth year, and upon successful completion, have those credits apply towards one of Thunderbird's masters programs. Students are also eligible for a 15% reduction in price per credit hour for certain Thunderbird Master's programs. **Visiting:** There are regularly scheduled orientations for prospective students, including a group information session followed by a tour. Personal interviews are also available with an admissions counselor. There are guides for informal visits and visitors may sit in on classes. To schedule a visit, contact the Admissions Office. **Campus Safety and Security:** Measures include 24-hour foot and vehicle patrol, emergency notification system, self-defense education, and security escort services. There are shuttle buses, emergency telephones, lighted pathways/sidewalks, and controlled access to dorms/residences.

REQUIREMENTS: The SAT or ACT is required. Applicants must be graduates of an accredited high school or the equivalent. AP and CLEP credits are accepted. Important factors in the admissions decision are extracurricular activities record, recommendations by school officials, and advanced placement or honors courses. Traditional Student: A GPA of 2.0 and 120 credits are required for Baccalaureate degrees. Students must take between 40 and 60 hours in the major. Every undergraduate takes Champlain's Core Curriculum, a four-year course of interdisciplinary study that cultivates the intellectual leadership prized by a complex economy and a rapidly changing world. All undergraduate students also participate in LEAD (Life Experience and Action Dimension),a four-year program designed to help develop life skills that are practical, meaningful and useful and that will serve graduates throughout their entire lifetime. CPS Student: Adult undergraduate students complete a professionally focused general education curriculum intentionally designed to support courses in the major. **Procedure:** Freshmen are admitted fall and spring. Entrance exams should be taken prior to applying. There are early decision and deferred admissions plans. Early decision applications should be filed by November 15; regular applications, by February 1 for fall entry; and December 1 for spring entry. Notification of early decision is sent December 15; regular decision, March 15. 369 early decision candidates were accepted for the 2014-2015 class. 100 applicants were on the 2014 waiting list; 5 were admitted. Applications are accepted on-line. **Transfer Students:** 128 transfer students enrolled in 2013-2014. High school and college transcripts are required. 45 of 120 credits required for the bachelor's degree must be completed at Champlain. **International Students:** There are 23 international students enrolled. The school actively recruits these students. They must take the TOEFL with a minimum score of 550 on the paper-based TOEFL (PBT) or 79 on the Internet-based version (iBT). They must also take the SAT or ACT. for students whose high school was conducted in English.

ADMISSIONS: 64% of the 2014-2015 applicants were accepted. The SAT scores for the 2014-2015 freshman class were: Critical Reading-15% below 500, 44% between 500 and 599, 33% between 600 and 699, and 8% between 700 and 800; Math--20% below 500, 43% between 500 and 599, 31% between 600 and 699, and 6% between 700 and 800; Writing--26% below 500, 47% between 500 and 599, 24% between 600 and 699, and 3% between 700 and 800. The ACT scores were 7% below 21, 25% between 21 and 23, 30% between 24

and 26, 11% between 27 and 28, and 27% above 28. **Admissions Contact:** Sarah Andriano, Director of Admissions. E-Mail: *admission@champlain.edu* Web: *www.champlain.edu*

FINANCIAL AID: In 2014-2015, 95% of all full-time freshmen and 93% of continuing full-time students received some form of financial aid. 71% of all full-time freshmen and 75% of continuing full-time students received need-based aid. The average freshman award was $25,238. Need-based scholarships or need-based grants averaged $8,657 ($42,410 maximum); need-based self-help aid (loans and jobs) averaged $6,845 ($11,500 maximum); and other non-need-based awards and non-need-based scholarships averaged $12,200 ($43,246 maximum). 24% of undergraduate students work part-time. Average annual earnings from campus work are $1433. The average financial indebtedness of the 2014 graduate was $26,840. The FAFSA is required. The priority date for freshman financial aid applications for fall entry is February 15.

COLLEGE OF ST JOSEPH *(The complete profile is made available exclusively on our website, www.barronspac.com)*

GODDARD COLLEGE	C-3
www.goddard.edu	
Plainfield, VT 05667	(800) 906-8312
	(800) 468-4888
Fax: (802) 454-1029	**Email:** admissions@.goddard.edu
Full-time: 73 men, 136 women	**Faculty:** 16
Part-time: n/av	**Ph.D.s:** 87%
Graduate: 108 men, 274 women	**Student/Faculty:** n/av
Year: semesters	**Tuition:** $14,930
Room & Board: $1488	**Freshman Class:** n/av
	CEEB CODE: 3416
Application Deadline: open	**VERY COMPETITIVE**

Goddard College, founded in 1863, is a private college that stresses progressive, individualized education for personal and community transformation, based on John Dewey's learning-by-engagement philosophy. There is 1 undergraduate school and 1 graduate school. The 200-acre campus is in a rural area 10 miles from Montpelier, and 45 miles from Burlington, Vermont. Including any residence halls, there are 28 buildings.

STUDENT LIFE: 85% of undergraduates are from out of state, mostly the Northeast. 73% are White; 13% race unknown. **Housing:** 175 students can be accommodated in college housing, which includes single-sex and coed dorms. In addition, there are special-interest houses, family-friendly dorm, substance-free (i.e. no perfumes, etc.) dorm. 100% of students commute. All students commute. All students may keep cars.

FACULTY/CLASSROOMS: 23% of faculty are male; 77% are female. No introductory courses are taught by graduate students.

PROGRAMS OF STUDY: Goddard confers B.A., B.F.A. degrees. Master's degrees are also awarded. Bachelor's degrees are awarded in AGRICULTURE (environmental studies), BIOLOGICAL SCIENCE (nutrition), BUSINESS (sustainable management), COMMUNICATIONS AND THE ARTS (applied art, art, comparative literature, creative writing, dramatic arts, English, English Writing, fine arts, folklore and mythology, intermedia/multimedia, literature, media arts, photography, playwriting/screenwriting, and visual and performing arts), EDUCATION (art education, collaborative education, early childhood education, education, elementary education, English education, health education, learner designed area of study, middle school education, and secondary education), HEALTH PROFESSIONS (health, health promotion, and health science), SOCIAL SCIENCE (addiction studies, clinical psychology, counseling/psychology, crosscultural studies, cultural studies/critical theory and analysis, ethics, politics, and social policy, history, human development, human ecology, humanities and social science, industrial and organizational psychology, interdisciplinary studies, justice and society, liberal arts/general studies, psychology, social psychology, social science, and women and gender studies). Creative writing, interdisciplinary arts, and psychology are the strongest academically. Psychology and counseling and creative writing have the largest enrollments.

ACTIVITIES: There are 9 groups on campus, including art, drama, environmental, literary magazine, radio and TV, and student government. **Sports:** There is no sports program at Goddard. Facilities include an workout room, hiking and cross-country ski trails. **Graduates:** From July 1, 2013 to June 30, 2014, 92 bachelor's degrees were awarded.

SERVICES: There is remedial writing. **Library/Resources:** The library contains 142,241 volumes, 397 audio/video tapes/CDs/DVDs, and subscribes to 10,000 periodicals including electronic. Computerized library services include interlibrary loans, database searching, Internet access, and Wi-Fi capability. Special learning facilities include a radio station. **Physically Challenged Students:** 60% of the campus is accessible. Facilities include wheelchair ramps, elevators, special parking, and specially equipped restrooms. **Special:** The BA/MA Fast Track in Psychology saves students a semester toward earning an MA while completing their bachelor's degree. All programs entail students designing their own studies. The B.A. in Sustainability, B.A. in Education, B.A. in Health Arts and Sciences, and B.F.A. in Creative Writing are upper-division programs, requiring 60 prior credits. The main undergraduate program encompasses both lower and upper divisions. **Visiting:** There are regularly scheduled orientations for prospective students, One Discover Goddard Day held each fall and spring, one visiting day during every residency, and individual meetings by appointment. There are guides for informal visits and visitors may sit in on classes. To schedule a visit, contact Respective admissions counselor for the program.. **Campus Safety and Security:** Measures include 24-hour foot and vehicle patrol. There are lighted pathways/sidewalks and controlled access to dorms/residences.

REQUIREMENTS: Goddard admits students who can contribute to its learning community and who will thrive in a self-directed degree program. The admission decision is based on the application, including essays, letters of recommendation, transcripts, samples of the student's creative or academic work, and an interview. Standardized test scores are unhelpful and not required. Homeschooled students are welcome to apply. AP and CLEP credits are accepted. Important factors in the admissions decision are personality/intangible qualities, recommendations by alumni, and evidence of special talent.Students come to campus for eight days at the beginning of each semester, then study independently the rest of the term, at home or elsewhere. Collaborating with a faculty advisor, students design and carry out programs of study specifically tailored to their own personal and professional interests and goals. Assessment takes the form of narrative evaluations rather than letter grades; students must pass comprehensive reviews of performance and progress. There are no declared majors, but in the last semester of enrollment, all students must complete a culminating senior study or project that may be multidisciplinary and requires foundation work comparable to a major. A total of 120 credits is required to graduate. Students must conduct, or transfer in, substantive studies in the arts, humanities, social sciences, natural sciences, and quantitative reasoning. **Procedure:** Freshmen are admitted to all sessions. There are deferred admissions and rolling admissions plans. Check with the school for current application deadlines. The application fee is $40. Notification is sent on a rolling basis. Applications are accepted on-line. **Transfer Students:** Official transcripts from previous institutions, writing samples, personal statements, letters of recommendation, and interviews are required. 45 of 120 credits required for the bachelor's degree must be completed at Goddard. **International Students:** There are 2 international students enrolled.

ADMISSIONS: Jen Morin, Admissions Counselor. E-Mail: *admissions@goddard.edu* Web: *www.goddard.edu*

FINANCIAL AID: The average freshman award was $9,515. Need-based scholarships or need-based grants averaged $5,662; and need-based self-help aid (loans and jobs) averaged $3,853. The FAFSA is required. Check with the school for current application deadlines.

GREEN MOUNTAIN COLLEGE (*The complete profile is made available exclusively on our website, www.barronspac.com*)

JOHNSON STATE COLLEGE	B-2
www.jsc.edu	

Johnson, VT 05656	(802) 635-1219
	(800) 635-2356
Fax: (802) 635-1230	Email: jscadmissions@jsc.edu
Full-time: 550 men, 660 women	Faculty: n/av; IIB, -$
Part-time: 100 men, 375 women	Ph.D.s: 90%
Graduate: 75 men, 225 women	Student/Faculty: n/av
Year: semesters, summer session	Tuition: $9400 ($19,500)
Room & Board: $8700	Freshman Class: n/av
SAT or ACT: required	CEEB CODE: 3766
Application Deadline: open	COMPETITIVE

Johnson State College, founded in 1828, is a public liberal arts and science college, offering more than 30 academic and professional degree programs. There is 1 graduate school. Figures in the above capsule and this profile are approximate. The 350-acre campus is in a small town 45 miles northeast of Burlington. Including any residence halls, there are 12 buildings.

STUDENT LIFE: 63% of undergraduates are from Vermont. Others are from 23 states, 6 foreign countries, and Canada. 90% are white. The average age of freshmen is 19; all undergraduates, 21. 30% do not continue beyond their first year; 45% remain to graduate.

FACULTY/CLASSROOMS: 58% of faculty are male; 42% are female. All teach undergraduates. No introductory courses are taught by graduate students.

PROGRAMS OF STUDY: Johnson State confers B.A., B.S., and B.F.A. degrees. Associate and Master's degrees are also awarded. Bachelor's degrees are awarded in AGRICULTURE (natural resource management), BIOLOGICAL SCIENCE (biology/biological science and cell biology), BUSINESS (business administration and management, business systems analysis, hospitality management services, recreational facilities management, small business management, and tourism), COMMUNICATIONS AND THE ARTS (art, creative writing, English, fine arts, jazz, journalism, music, music business management, music history and appreciation, music performance, performing arts, studio art, theater design, theater management, and visual and performing arts), COMPUTER AND PHYSICAL SCIENCE (mathematics), EDUCATION (art education, athletic training, education, elementary education, English education, environmental education, mathematics education, middle school education, music education, physical education, recreation education, science education, and secondary education), ENGINEERING AND ENVIRONMENTAL DESIGN (environmental science), HEALTH PROFESSIONS (allied health, health science, and premedicine), SOCIAL SCIENCE (anthropology, behavioral science, history, humanities, liberal arts/general studies, physical fitness/movement, political science/government, prelaw, psychology, and sociology). Environmental science, elementary/secondary/middle school education, and wellness and alternative medicine have the largest enrollments.

ACTIVITIES: There are 35 groups on campus, including art, band, choir, chorus, dance, debate, drama, environmental, gay, hospitality, jazz band, leadership, literary magazine, musical theater, newspaper, outdoor, photography, political, professional, radio and TV, religious, social, social service, and student government. Popular campus events include Winter Carnival and Coffee House (weekly live entertainment).

SERVICES: Counseling and information services are available, as is tutoring in most subjects. There is a reader service for the blind, and remedial math, reading, and writing. The Academic Support Services Department provides accommodations for students with a documented learning disability. **Library/Resources:** The library contains 96,584 volumes, 180,158 microform items, and 7,200 audio/video tapes/CDs/DVDs, and subscribes to 631 periodicals including electronic. Computerized library services include interlibrary loans, database searching, Internet access, and Wi-Fi capability. Special learning facilities include an art gallery, radio station, a 24-hour study room. **Physically Challenged Students:** 60% of the campus is accessible. Facilities include wheelchair ramps, elevators, special parking, specially equipped restrooms, special class scheduling, and lowered drinking fountains. **Special:** All students are encouraged to complete an internship. Through the National Student Exchange Program, students may study at another institution or abroad for a semester or a year. Co-op programs are offered in business, tourism, hospitality management, and education, and cross-registration is available with other Vermont state colleges. There are 1 national honor societies. **Visiting:** There are regularly scheduled orientations for prospective students, including a campus tour and an admission interview. Students may request to meet with a faculty member. There are guides for informal visits and visitors may sit in on classes. To schedule a visit, contact the Admissions Office. **Campus Safety and Security:** Measures include 24-hour foot and vehicle patrol, self-defense education, and security escort services. There are shuttle buses, emergency telephones, and lighted pathways/sidewalks.

REQUIREMENTS: The SAT or ACT is required. Successful candidates for admission have generally completed a college preparatory curriculum consisting of 4 years of English, 3 of math (2 of algebra, 1 of geometry), 3 of social sciences, and 2 of science (including 1 lab science). An official high school transcript or GED test score must be submitted with the application. In addition, 1 letter of recommendation, preferably from a guidance counselor, and SAT or ACT scores should be sent with the application or under separate cover. A GPA of 2.3 is required. AP and CLEP credits are accepted. Important factors in the admissions decision are advanced placement or honors courses, recommendations by school officials, and extracurricular activities record.

FINANCIAL AID: Johnson State is a member of CSS. The FAFSA is required. Check with the school for current application deadlines.

LYNDON STATE COLLEGE · D-2
www.lyndonstate.edu

Lyndonville, VT 05851	(802) 626-6413
	(800) 225-1998
Fax: n/av	Email: admissions@lyndonstate.edu
Full-time: 560 men, 570 women	Faculty: n/av; IIB, --$
Part-time: 70 men, 230 women	Ph.D.s: 60%
Graduate: 1 men, 5 women	Student/Faculty: n/av
Year: semesters, summer session	Tuition: $19,856
Room & Board: $8946	Freshman Class: n/av
SAT or ACT: required	CEEB CODE: 3767
Application Deadline: see profile	COMPETITIVE

Lyndon State College, founded in 1911 as a teachers' college, became a liberal arts school in 1962, offering undergraduate and graduate courses. There is 1 graduate school. Figures in the above capsule and this profile are approximate. In addition to regional accreditation, LSC has baccalaureate program accreditation with NRPA. The 175-acre campus is in a small town in northeastern Vermont, 184 miles north of Boston. Including any residence halls, there are 17 buildings. **STUDENT LIFE:** 60% of undergraduates are from Vermont. Others are from 24 states, 12 foreign countries, and Canada. 99% are white. The average age of freshmen is 18; all undergraduates, 24. 33% do not continue beyond their first year; 41% remain to graduate.

FACULTY/CLASSROOMS: 66% of faculty are male; 34% are female. All teach undergraduates. No introductory courses are taught by graduate students. The average class size in an introductory lecture is 20; in a laboratory, 16; and in a regular course, 16.

PROGRAMS OF STUDY: LSC confers B.A. and B.S. degrees. Associate and Master's degrees are also awarded. Bachelor's degrees are awarded in BUSINESS (accounting, business administration and management, recreation and leisure services, and sports management), COMMUNICATIONS AND THE ARTS (communications, English, graphic design, journalism, multimedia, and radio/television technology), COMPUTER AND PHYSICAL SCIENCE (atmospheric sciences and meteorology, mathematics, natural sciences, and science), EDUCATION (early childhood education, elementary education, English education, physical education, recreation education, and science education), SOCIAL SCIENCE (human services, interdisciplinary studies, psychology, and social science). Meteorology, natural science, and math are the strongest academically. Education, communications, and business have the largest enrollments.

ACTIVITIES: There are 22 groups on campus, including cheerleading, choir, chorale, chorus, communications, dance, drama, film, gay, honors, international, jazz band, literary magazine, newspaper, photography, political, professional, radio and TV, religious, social, social service, student government, and yearbook. Popular campus events include Family Weekend, Alumni Weekend, and a concert series.

SERVICES: Counseling and information services are available, as is tutoring in every subject. There is remedial math, reading, and writing. A math lab and a writing center are available for student use. **Library/Resources:** The library contains 100,000 volumes, 10,000 microform items, and 3,600 audio/video tapes/CDs/DVDs, and subscribes to 545 periodicals including electronic. Computerized library services include interlibrary loans, database searching, and Internet access. Special learning facilities include an art gallery, radio station, TV station, a founder's museum, and meteorology lab. **Physically Challenged Students:** 70% of the campus is accessible. Facilities include wheelchair ramps, elevators, special parking, specially equipped restrooms, and lowered drinking fountains. **Special:** Cooperative programs in a variety of businesses, including local ski areas, social agencies, and radio and TV stations, internships in recreation programs and communications, and study abroad in Nova Scotia and England are available. B.A.-B.S. degrees, work-study, a general studies degree, dual and student-designed majors, a 3-2 engineering degree with Norwich University in Vermont, credit for life experience, non-degree study, cross-registration, work study, accelerated degree programs and pass/fail options also are offered. There are 1 national honor societies, a freshman honors program, and 1 departmental honors programs. **Visiting:** There are regularly scheduled orientations for prospective students, including a tour, an information session, and faculty presentations. There are guides for informal visits, visitors may sit in on classes, and stay overnight. To schedule a visit, contact the Admissions Office. **Campus Safety and Security:** Measures include 24-hour foot and vehicle patrol, self-defense education, and security escort services. There are emergency telephones, lighted pathways/sidewalks, A security and safety service on campus as well as a 24-hour emergency rescue squad.

REQUIREMENTS: The SAT or ACT is required. LSC recommends that applicants have 4 years of English and 2 each of math, foreign language, history, and science. An essay is required, as is a recommendation from the high school principal or guidance counselor. An interview is recommended. The GED is accepted. A GPA of 2.0 is required. AP and CLEP credits are accepted. Important factors in the admissions decision are advanced placement or honors courses, recommendations by school officials, and leadership record.

FINANCIAL AID: LSC is a member of CSS. The FAFSA and parent and student income tax forms, if requested, are required. Check with the school for current application deadlines.

MARLBORO COLLEGE · B-6
www.marlboro.edu

Marlboro, VT 05344	(802) 257-4333
	(800) 343-0049
Fax: (802) 451-7555	Email: admissions@marlboro.edu
Full-time: 126 men, 201 women	Faculty: 35
Part-time: 4 men, 5 women	Ph.D.s: 77%
Graduate: n/av	Student/Faculty: 9 to 1
Year: semesters	Tuition: $37,060
Room & Board: $10,140	Freshman Class: n/av
SAT or ACT: required	CEEB CODE: 3509
Application Deadline: February 15	VERY COMPETITIVE

Marlboro College, established in 1946, is a small private institution offering degrees in the liberal and fine arts and humanities, and employing self-designed programs of study. The figures in the above capsule and in this profile are approximate. There is 1 graduate school. The 366-acre campus is in a rural area 9 miles west of Brattleboro, 2 1/2 hours from Boston. Including any residence halls, there are 36 buildings. **STUDENT LIFE:** 89% of undergraduates are from out of state, mostly the Northeast. Students are from 36 states, 5 foreign countries, and Canada. 70% are from public schools. 83% are White. The average age of freshmen is 19; all undergraduates, 21. 28% do not continue beyond their first year; 48% remain to graduate.

FACULTY/CLASSROOMS: 62% of faculty are male; 38% are female. All teach undergraduates. No introductory courses are taught by graduate students. The average class size in an introductory lecture is 10; in a laboratory is 8; and in a regular course is 8.

PROGRAMS OF STUDY: Marlboro confers B.A., and B.S. degrees. Master's degrees are also awarded. Bachelor's degrees are awarded in BIOLOGICAL SCIENCE (biochemistry, biology/biological science, botany, and microbiology), COMMUNICATIONS AND THE ARTS (creative writing, dance, dramatic arts, English, fine arts, French, German, Greek, Italian, Latin, linguistics, music, photography, Russian, and Spanish), COMPUTER AND PHYSICAL SCIENCE (chemistry, computer science, mathematics, and physics), HEALTH PROFESSIONS (premedicine), SOCIAL SCIENCE (anthropology, economics, history, interdisciplinary studies, international studies, philosophy, political science/government, prelaw, psychology, social science, and sociology). Sciences, humanities, and world studies are the strongest academically. Literature, biology, and sociology have the largest enrollments.

ACTIVITIES: There are 25 groups on campus, including art, chess, chorus, communications, computers, dance, drama, film, gay, international, jazz band, literary magazine, musical theater, newspaper, photography, political, social, social service, and student government. Popular campus events include Green-up Day, Creativity Lecture Series, and Visiting Writers Series.

SERVICES: Counseling and information services are available, as is tutoring in some subjects, including writing, languages, math, and organic chemistry. **Library/Resources:** The library contains 65,216 volumes, 5,799 microform items, 2,990 audio/video tapes/CDs/DVDs, and subscribes to 188 periodicals including electronic. Computerized library services include interlibrary loans, database searching, Internet access, and Wi-Fi capability. Special learning facilities include an art gallery, planetarium, observatory.

REQUIREMENTS: The SAT or ACT is required. Applicants typically graduate from an accredited secondary school or have a GED. They are encouraged to earn 16 Carnegie units and complete 4 years of English and 3 years each of math, science, history, and a foreign language. Essays and interviews are required. AP and CLEP credits are accepted. Important factors in the admissions decision are advanced placement or honors courses, evidence of special talent, and extracurricular activities record.

ADMISSIONS: 78% of a recent year applicants were accepted. The ACT scores were 35% between 21 and 23, 29% between 24 and 26, 29% between 27 and 28, and 7% above 28. 46% of the current freshmen were in the top fifth of their class; 82% were in the top two fifths. 2 freshmen graduated first in their class.

FINANCIAL AID: In a recent year, 85% of all full-time freshmen and continuing full-time students received some form of financial aid. 68% of all full-time freshmen and 80% of continuing full-time students received need-based aid. The average freshman award was $20,907. Need-based scholarships or need-based grants averaged $15,969 ($24,250 maximum); need-based self-help aid (loans and jobs) averaged $4,289 ($4,555 maximum); and other non-need-based awards and non-need-based scholarships averaged $11,723 ($20,950 maximum). 68% of undergraduate students work part-time. Average annual earnings from campus work are $1118. Marlboro is a member of CSS. The CSS/Profile and FAFSA are required. The priority date for freshman financial aid applications for fall entry is February 15. The deadline for filing freshman financial aid applications for fall entry is March 1.

MIDDLEBURY COLLEGE A-3
www.middlebury.edu

Middlebury, VT 05753

(802) 443-3000
(802) 443-5000

Fax: (802) 443-2056   Email: admissions@middlebury.edu

Full-time: 1211 men, 1281 women   Faculty: 270; IIB, ++$
Part-time: 11 men, 23 women   Ph.D.s: 92%
Graduate: n/av   Student/Faculty: 9 to 1
Year: 4-1-4   Tuition: $46,044
Room & Board: $13,116   Freshman Class: 8195 applied, 1407 accepted, 580 enrolled

SAT CR/M/W: 679/684/689 **ACT:** 31   CEEB CODE: 3526
Application Deadline: January 1   **MOST COMPETITIVE**

Middlebury College, founded in 1800, is a small, private liberal arts institution offering degree programs in languages, humanities, social and natural sciences. There is 1 undergraduate school and 3 graduate schools. The 355-acre campus is in a small town 35 miles south of Burlington. Including any residence halls, there are 115 buildings.

STUDENT LIFE: 94% of undergraduates are from out of state, mostly the Northeast. Students are from 52 states, 74 foreign countries, and Canada. 65% are White; 11% Foreign. The average age of freshmen is 18; all undergraduates, 20. 4% do not continue beyond their first year; 96% remain to graduate. **Housing:** 2435 students can be accommodated in college housing, which includes single-sex and coed dorms, on-campus apartments, and married student housing. In addition, there are language houses, special-interest houses, Coed social, multicultural and environmental houses. On-campus housing is guaranteed for all 4 years and is available on a lottery system for upperclassmen. 96% of students live on campus. All students may keep cars.

FACULTY/CLASSROOMS: 56% of faculty are male; 44% are female. All teach undergraduates. No introductory courses are taught by graduate students. The average class size in an introductory lecture is 18 and in a regular course is 18.

PROGRAMS OF STUDY: Midd confers A.B. degrees. Master's and doctoral degrees are also awarded. Bachelor's degrees are awarded in AGRICULTURE (environmental studies), BIOLOGICAL SCIENCE (biochemistry, biology/biological science, molecular biology, and neurosciences), BUSINESS (international economics), COMMUNICATIONS AND THE ARTS (Arabic, Chinese, classics, comparative literature, dance, dramatic arts, English, film arts, French, German, Italian, Japanese, music, Russian, Spanish, and studio art), COMPUTER AND PHYSICAL SCIENCE (chemistry, computer science, geology, mathematics, and physics), ENGINEERING AND ENVIRONMENTAL DESIGN (architectural history), SOCIAL SCIENCE (African American studies, American studies, anthropology, East Asian studies, economics, European studies, geography, history, Latin American studies, liberal arts/general studies, Middle Eastern studies, philosophy, political science/government, psychology, religion, Russian and Slavic studies, sociology, South Asian studies, and women's studies). Foreign languages, international studies, and sciences are the strongest academically. Economics, environmental studies, and political science have the largest enrollments.

ACTIVITIES: There are 178 groups on campus, including art, band, cheerleading, chess, choir, chorus, communications, computers, dance, debate, drama, environmental, ethnic, film, gay, honors, international, jazz band, literary magazine, Middlebury Mountain Club, musical theater, newspaper, orchestra, pep band, photography, political, professional, radio and TV, religious, social, social service, student government, and yearbook. Popular campus events include Winter Carnival, Student Concert Series, and Clifford Symposium. **Sports:** There are 12 intercollegiate sports for men and 11 for women, and 16 intramural sports for men and 16 for women. Facilities include Middlebury's well-maintained playing fields and outstanding athletic facilities rank among the best in the country. Facilities include a 3,500-seat football and lacrosse complex, baseball and softball fields, 18-hole golf course, 3.5-km cross country trail, 2,200-seat hockey arena, Olympic-size natatorium, squash courts, tennis courts, climbing wall, gymnasium, 6,500-square-foot fitness center, astro-turf fields, and all-weather outdoor track.

Graduates: From July 1, 2013 to June 30, 2014, 645 bachelor's degrees were awarded. The most popular majors were economics (15%), political science (9%), and environmental studies (8%). In an average class, 89% graduate in 4 years or less, 94% graduate in 5 years or less, and 94% graduate in 6 years or less. Of the 2013 graduating class, 12% were enrolled in graduate school within 6 months of graduation, and 46% were employed.

SERVICES: Counseling and information services are available, as is tutoring in every subject. There is a reader service for the blind. **Library/Resources:** The 2 libraries contain 809,865 volumes, 620 microform items, 48,888 audio/video tapes/CDs/DVDs, and subscribe to 181,350 periodicals including electronic. Computerized library services include interlibrary loans, database searching, Internet access, and Wi-Fi capability. Special learning facilities include an art gallery, planetarium, and radio station. **Physically Challenged Students:** 65% of the campus is accessible. Facilities include wheelchair ramps, elevators, special parking, specially equipped restrooms, special class scheduling, lowered drinking fountains, lowered telephones, and special housing. **Special:** In addition to extensive study abroad opportunities, Middlebury College offers Pre-Professional Combined Programs as well as Washington Semester, Maritime Studies, and Exchange Programs with Spelman and Swarthmore Colleges and the Association of Vermont Independent Colleges. Other opportunities include a semester at Woods Hole Marine Biological Laboratory and Dual-Degree Engineering Programs with Dartmouth and Columbia. There are Phi Beta Kappa and 36 departmental honors programs. **Visiting:** There are regularly scheduled orientations for prospective students, including campus tours and a group or individual interview. There are guides for informal visits and visitors may sit in on classes. To schedule a visit, contact the Admissions Office. **Campus Safety and Security:** Measures include 24-hour foot and vehicle patrol, emergency notification system, self-defense education, and security escort services. There are shuttle buses, emergency telephones, lighted pathways/sidewalks, controlled access to dorms/residences, a paid student patrol, a ski patrol at the snow bowl, and a special events staff.

REQUIREMENTS: The SAT or ACT is required. AP credits are accepted. Important factors in the admissions decision are leadership record, advanced placement or honors courses, evidence of special talent, personality/intangible qualities, extracurricular activities record, geographical diversity, recommendations by school officials, and parents or siblings attended your school. Candidates for the Bachelor of Arts degree must complete 36 courses. At least 18 of these courses must be Middlebury courses. Courses taken at Middlebury summer Language Schools or at the Middlebury Schools Abroad will count in the 18-course total and the grades will count in the undergraduate grade point average. **Procedure:** Freshmen are admitted fall and spring. Entrance exams should be taken by December of the senior year. There are early decision, early admissions, and deferred admissions plans. Early decision applications should be filed by November 1; regular applications, by January 1 for fall entry, along with a $65 fee. Notification of early decision is sent January 1; regular decision, March 30. 307 early decision candidates were accepted for the 2014-2015 class. 663 applicants were on the 2014 waiting list; 1 was admitted. Applications are accepted on-line. **Transfer Students:** 10 transfer students enrolled in 2013-2014. Transfer students must have the strongest academic record possible through high school and a minimum 3.0 average in college. 18 of 36 credits required for the bachelor's degree must be completed at Middlebury. **International Students:** There are 250 international students enrolled. The school actively recruits these students. They must take the TOEFL. They must also take the SAT or ACT, and fulfill the same requirements as first-year applicants.

ADMISSIONS: 17% of the 2014-2015 applicants were accepted. The SAT scores for the 2014-2015 freshman class were: Critical Reading--1% below 500, 14% between 500 and 599, 40% between 600 and 699, and 45% between 700 and 800; Math--12% between 500 and 599, 40% between 600 and 699, and 48% between 700 and 800; Writing--1% below 500, 12% between 500 and 599, 34% between 600 and 699, and 53% between 700 and 800. The ACT scores were 22% between 24 and 26, and 77% above 28. **Admissions Contact:** Greg Buckles, Dean of Admissions. E-Mail: *admissions@middlebury.edu* Web: *www.middlebury.edu*

FINANCIAL AID: In 2014-2015, 48% of all full-time freshmen and

43% of continuing full-time students received some form of financial aid. 48% of all full-time freshmen and 42% of continuing full-time students received need-based aid. The average freshman award was $40,926. Need-based scholarships or need-based grants averaged $39,238; and need-based self-help aid (loans and jobs) averaged $3,232. The average financial indebtedness of the 2014 graduate was $17,975. Midd is a member of CSS. The CSS/Profile and FAFSA, and federal tax forms, non-custodial profile are required. The priority date for freshman financial aid applications for fall entry is November 15. The deadline for filing freshman financial aid applications for fall entry is February 1.

NORWICH UNIVERSITY — C-3
www.norwich.edu

Northfield, VT 05663

(802) 485-2000
(800) 468-6679

Fax: (802) 485-2032
Full-time: 1360 men, 502 women
Part-time: 34 men, 7 women
Graduate: 537 men, 211 women
Year: semesters, summer session
Room & Board: $7374

Email: nuadm@norwich.edu
Faculty: 117; IIA, -$
Ph.Ds: 85%
Student/Faculty: 16 to 1
Tuition: $21,000
Freshman Class: 1899 applied, 1470 accepted, 578 enrolled

SAT: required ACT: 22
Application Deadline: n/av

CEEB CODE: 3669
COMPETITIVE

Norwich University, founded in 1819, is the oldest private military college in the country and the birthplace of the Reserve Officers' Training Corps (ROTC). Norwich is a coeducational, four-year university where students choose either a military or civilian lifestyle. Norwich offers both undergraduate and graduate programs. There are 6 undergraduate schools and 2 graduate schools. In addition to regional accreditation, Norwich has baccalaureate program accreditation with ABET, ACBSP, NLN, and CAAHEP. The 1125-acre campus is in a rural area 11 miles south of Montpelier. Including any residence halls, there are 36 buildings.

STUDENT LIFE: 80% of undergraduates are from out of state, mostly the Northeast. Students are from 39 states, 13 foreign countries, and Canada. 82% are White. The average age of freshmen is 18; all undergraduates, 21. 25% do not continue beyond their first year; 52% remain to graduate. **Housing:** 1598 students can be accommodated in college housing, which includes single-sex and coed dorms. On-campus housing is guaranteed for the freshman year only and is available on a lottery system for upperclassmen. Priority is given to out-of-town students. 83% of students live on campus; of those, 85% remain on campus on weekends. Alcohol is not permitted. Upperclassmen may keep cars.

FACULTY/CLASSROOMS: 74% of faculty are male; 26% are female. 82% teach undergraduates. No introductory courses are taught by graduate students. The average class size in an introductory lecture is 20; in a laboratory is 13; and in a regular course is 18.

PROGRAMS OF STUDY: Norwich confers B.A., B.S. and B.Arch. degrees. Associate degrees are also awarded. Bachelor's degrees are awarded in BIOLOGICAL SCIENCE (biochemistry and biology/biological science), BUSINESS (accounting, business administration and management, and business economics), COMMUNICATIONS AND THE ARTS (communications and English), COMPUTER AND PHYSICAL SCIENCE (chemistry, computer science, computer security and information assurance, geology, information sciences and systems, mathematics, and physics), EDUCATION (physical education), ENGINEERING AND ENVIRONMENTAL DESIGN (architecture, civil engineering, computer engineering, electrical/electronics engineering, environmental science, mechanical engineering, and military science), HEALTH PROFESSIONS (medical laboratory technology, nursing, and sports medicine), SOCIAL SCIENCE (criminal justice, history, international studies, liberal arts/general studies, peace studies, political science/government, and psychology). Engineering and architecture is the strongest academically. Criminal justice and nursing have the largest enrollments.

ACTIVITIES: There are 75 groups on campus, including band, cheerleading, chess, choir, chorus, communications, computers, drama, drill team, ethnic, honors, international, jazz band, literary magazine, marching band, musical theater, newspaper, orchestra, pep band, photography, political, professional, radio and TV, religious, social service, and student government. Popular campus events include Regimental Ball, Winter Carnival, and Junior Weekend. **Sports:** There are 12 intercollegiate sports for men and 7 for women, and 8 intramural sports for men and 8 for women. Facilities include an ice hockey arena, field house with an indoor track, indoor swimming pool, aerobics room, weight and wrestling rooms, playing fields and an outdoor track, 1200-seat basketball arena, and a 1000-seat hockey arena. **Graduates:** From July 1, 2013 to June 30, 2014, 269 bachelor's degrees were awarded. The most popular majors were criminal justice (18%), management (12%), and nursing/civil engineering (7%). 25 companies recruited on campus in 2013-2014. In an average class, 37% graduate in 4 years or less, 49% graduate in 5 years or less, and 52% graduate in 6 years or less.

SERVICES: Counseling and information services are available, as is tutoring in most subjects. There is remedial math, reading, and writing. **Library/Resources:** The library contains 245,931 volumes, 90,435 microform items, 2,872 audio/video tapes/CDs/DVDs, and subscribes to 815 periodicals including electronic. Computerized library services include interlibrary loans, database searching, Internet access, and Wi-Fi capability. Special learning facilities include an art gallery, natural history museum, radio station, a greenhouse, and 5 computer labs. **Physically Challenged Students:** Facilities include wheelchair ramps, elevators, special parking, specially equipped restrooms, and lowered drinking fountains. **Special:** Norwich offers internships, a Washington semester, work-study on-and-off-campus for service organizations and criminal justice programs, a B.A.-B.S. degree in communications, and study abroad in 15 countries through other schools and organizations and through the Vermont Overseas Studies Program. International studies majors must study abroad in a country whose language they are studying. There are 5 national honor societies, including Phi Beta Kappa, and 5 departmental honors programs. **Visiting:** There are regularly scheduled orientations for prospective students, including meetings with representatives from admissions, financial aid, academic offices, including Dean of Students or Commandant's Office, athletics (if desired), and a campus tour. There are guides for informal visits, visitors may sit in on classes, and stay overnight. To schedule a visit, contact the Admissions, Main Office. **Campus Safety and Security:** Measures include 24-hour foot and vehicle patrol. There are lighted pathways/sidewalks.

REQUIREMENTS: The SAT or ACT is required. Applicants should graduate from an accredited secondary school with 18 academic credits or achieve the GED equivalent. Applications are accepted on IBM/Windows formatted computer disks. AP and CLEP credits are accepted. Important factors in the admissions decision are leadership record, extracurricular activities record, and evidence of special talent.The total number of required credits and courses vary by program. All students are required to complete 3 credit hours in history and English 101-102, and 2 semesters in phys ed. A 2.0 GPA is required to graduate. **Procedure:** Freshmen are admitted fall and spring. Entrance exams should be taken starting with spring of the junior year. There is a rolling admissions plan. Application deadlines are open. Application fee is $35. 60 early decision candidates were accepted for the 2014-2015 class. Applications are accepted on-line. **Transfer Students:** 91 transfer students enrolled in 2013-2014. Transfer students should present a 2.0 GPA and meet all standards for entering freshmen. 60 of 116 credits required for the bachelor's degree must be completed at Norwich. **International Students:** There are 39 international students enrolled. They must take the TOEFL.

ADMISSIONS: 77% of the 2014-2015 applicants were accepted. The ACT scores were 40% below 21, 28% between 21 and 23, 20% between 24 and 26, 7% between 27 and 28, and 5% above 28. 30% of the current freshmen were in the top fifth of their class; 58% were in the top two fifths. 3 freshmen graduated first in their class. **Admissions Contact:** Karen McGarth, Dean of Enrollment Management. E-Mail: *nuadm@norwich.edu* Web: *www.norwich.edu*

FINANCIAL AID: In 2014-2015, 97% of all full-time freshmen and 96% of continuing full-time students received some form of financial aid. 90% of all full-time freshmen and 89% of continuing full-time students received need-based aid. 50% of undergraduate students work part-time. Average annual earnings from campus work are $990. The average financial indebtedness of the 2014 graduate was $26,072. Norwich is a member of CSS. The CSS/Profile and FAFSA are required. The priority date for freshman financial aid applications for fall entry is March 1.

SAINT MICHAEL'S COLLEGE A-2
www.smcvt.edu

Colchester, VT 05439

(802) 654-2000
(800) 762-8000

Fax: (802) 654-2906
Full-time: 976 men, 1138 women
Part-time: 42 men, 17 women
Graduate: 106 men, 388 women
Year: semesters, summer session
Room & Board: $10,600

Email: admission@smcvt.edu
Faculty: 141; IIB, +$
Ph.D.s: 84%
Student/Faculty: 14 to 1
Tuition: $39,375
Freshman Class: 4299 applied, 3459 accepted, 574 enrolled

SAT CR/M/W: 585/568/572 **ACT:** 26
Application Deadline: February 1

CEEB CODE: 3757
VERY COMPETITIVE

Saint Michael's College, was founded in 1904 by the Society of Saint Edmund. We are a selective Catholic liberal arts college, with a community of 2,000 students in residence and over 150 full-time faculty members. We are located on a 440 acre campus overlooking the Green Mountains and Burlington, Vermont. There is 1 undergraduate school and 1 graduate school. In addition to regional accreditation, Saint Michael's has baccalaureate program accreditation with ACS, ROPA, and CELPA. The 440-acre campus is in a suburban area 2 miles east of Burlington, Vermont. Including any residence halls, there are 52 buildings.

STUDENT LIFE: 81% of undergraduates are from out of state, mostly the Northeast. Students are from 35 states, 46 foreign countries, and Canada. 70% are from public schools. 86% are White. 46% are Catholic; 32% claim no religious affiliation. The average age of freshmen is 18; all undergraduates, 20. 9% do not continue beyond their first year; 79% remain to graduate. **Housing:** 2077 students can be accommodated in college housing, which includes single-sex and coed dorms and on-campus apartments. In addition, there are honors houses, special-interest houses, theme housing, substance-free housing, ambassador housing (opportunity to live with international students). On-campus housing is guaranteed for all 4 years. 95% of students live on campus; of those, 90% remain on campus on weekends. All students may keep cars.

FACULTY/CLASSROOMS: 54% of faculty are male; 46% are female. All teach and do research. No introductory courses are taught by graduate students. The average class size in an introductory lecture is 24; in a laboratory is 16; and in a regular course is 18.

PROGRAMS OF STUDY: Saint Michael's confers B.A., and B.S. degrees. Master's degrees are also awarded. Bachelor's degrees are awarded in AGRICULTURE (environmental studies), BIOLOGICAL SCIENCE (biochemistry and biology/biological science), BUSINESS (accounting and business administration and management), COMMUNICATIONS AND THE ARTS (dramatic arts, English, fine arts, French, journalism, music, and Spanish), COMPUTER AND PHYSICAL SCIENCE (chemistry, computer science, information sciences and systems, mathematics, physical sciences, and physics), EDUCATION (art education, elementary education, foreign languages education, science education, and secondary education), ENGINEERING AND ENVIRONMENTAL DESIGN (preengineering), HEALTH PROFESSIONS (preallied health and prepharmacy), SOCIAL SCIENCE (American studies, anthropology, economics, gender studies, history, international relations, philosophy, political science/government, prelaw, psychology, religion, and sociology). Business administration, biology, and psychology have the largest enrollments.

ACTIVITIES: There are 50 groups on campus, including Mobilization of Volunteer Efforts (MOVE), cycling, skiing, wilderness program, art, band, choir, chorale, chorus, communications, dance, drama, environmental, ethnic, film, fire and rescue, gay, honors, international, jazz band, literary magazine, musical theater, newspaper, photography, political, professional, radio and TV, religious, social, social service, student government, and yearbook. Popular campus events include Family Weekend, Homecoming, Martin Luther King, Jr. Convocation, research Symposium, and Jib Fest. **Sports:** There are 10 intercollegiate sports for men and 11 for women, and 15 intramural sports for men and 15 for women. Facilities include a 2,500-seat gym and field house with basketball, volleyball, tennis, and badminton courts, 4 multipurpose courts, a 6-lane swimming pool, fitness center, training room, weight room, climbing wall, pool, table tennis, suspended track, soccer, racquetball and squash courts, field hockey, lacrosse, baseball, and softball fields. **Graduates:** From July 1, 2013 to June 30, 2014, 484 bachelor's degrees were awarded. The most popular majors were business administration and accounting (17%), biological/life sciences (12%), and psychology (10%). 72 companies recruited on campus in 2013-2014. In an average class, 74% graduate in 4 years or less, 78% graduate in 5 years or less, and 79% graduate in 6 years or less. Of the 2013 graduating class, 14% were enrolled in graduate school within 6 months of graduation, and 87% were employed.

SERVICES: Counseling and information services are available, as is tutoring in every subject. Tutoring can be arranged on an individual basis. The following are available: peer tutoring, writing center, quantitative skills, study skills, and research help. **Library/Resources:** The library contains 469,578 volumes, 137,000 microform items, 12,984 audio/video tapes/CDs/DVDs, and subscribes to 13,000 periodicals including electronic. Computerized library services include interlibrary loans, database searching, Internet access, and Wi-Fi capability. Special learning facilities include an art gallery, radio station, an observatory, and McCarthy Arts Center. **Physically Challenged Students:** 75% of the campus is accessible. Facilities include wheelchair ramps, elevators, special parking, specially equipped restrooms, special class scheduling, lowered drinking fountains, lowered telephones, and special housing. Other accommodations are provided on an individual basis. **Special:** A variety of special academic programs and enriching academic experiences are available at Saint Michael's College. During the most recent academic year over 40% of our graduates participated in a "for credit" internship, most of which were associated with the student's major. On-campus work-study opportunities are available in departments and offices throughout the College. Students can choose from more than 100 study abroad programs in countries spanning the globe (see our website for specific destinations). There are also opportunities for semester long domestic "study away" programs including a Washington semester with American University. Student-designed majors may be pursued and nearly 20% of our most recent graduating class completed a double major. During the last four years an average of nearly 40% of the graduating classes participated in "for credit" study abroad experiences including summer and winter sessions as well as short term faculty led programs. The college offers a 3-2 engineering degree program in cooperation with Clarkson University and the University of Vermont and a 4+1 graduate business program is available with Clarkson University. A B.S./Pharm.D. degree is also available with the Albany College of Pharmacy and Health Services. Non-degree study and pass/fail grading options are offered on a limited basis. Independent research and undergraduate research opportunities with faculty are available through many departments. There are 11 national honor societies, including Phi Beta Kappa, a freshman honors program, and 1 departmental honors program. **Visiting:** There are regularly scheduled orientations for prospective students, a campus visit begins with a group information session led by an admission counselor, which includes information about admission criteria and financial aid. It is followed by a student-led tour. There are guides for informal visits, visitors may sit in on classes, and stay overnight. To schedule a visit, contact the Admissions Office. **Campus Safety and Security:** Measures include 24-hour foot and vehicle patrol, emergency notification system, self-defense education, and security escort services. There are shuttle buses, emergency telephones, lighted pathways/sidewalks, controlled access to dorms/residences, a campus fire and rescue squad.

REQUIREMENTS: The SAT or ACT and ACT Writing Test are recommended. Applicants must graduate from an accredited secondary school or have a GED. They must complete 16 Carnegie units. The college requires 4 credits in English, 3 to 4 credits in math and science, and 3 each in history (social studies) and a foreign language. An essay is required and an interview is recommended. Stanardized tests are optional. There are three application deadlines: Early Action 1-(November 1st), Early Action 2-(December 1st), Regular Decision-(February 1st). AP and CLEP credits are accepted. Important factors in the admissions decision are advanced placement or honors courses, evidence of special talent, and recommendations by school officials.To earn the degree of Bachelor of Arts or the degree of Bachelor of Science a student must: Complete a minimum of 128 credit hours (equivalent to 32 full-courses). Complete the degree requirements of one of the established majors or a self-designated major approved by the Curriculum and Education Policy Committee. Complete the Liberal Studies Curriculum requirements (see below). Achieve a minimum cumulative quality point average of 2.0 and a minimum of a 2.0 average in courses taken in the major. Complete a minimum of twenty-four of the last thirty-two credits at Saint Michael's. Transfer students, must earn a minimum of sixty four credits at Saint Michael's College. The Liberal Studies Curriculum (LSC) is fulfilled through specific course requirement options and courses within the student's major field. Areas of study within the LSC include: Fundamental Philosophical Questions, Study of Christian Traditions and Thought, Ethical Decision Making, Global Issues that Impact the Common Good, Historical Studies, Literary Studies, Processes of Scientific Reasoning, Quantitative Reasoning, Second Language (depending on placement), Social and Institutional Dimensions of Human Behavior, Artistic Experience, Experiential Learning, Oral and Written Communication. **Procedure:** Freshmen are admitted fall and spring. Entrance exams should be taken in the fall of the senior year. There are early admissions and deferred admissions plans. Applications should be filed by February 1 for fall entry; December 1 for winter entry; and November 1 for spring entry, along with a $50 fee. Notifications are sent April 1. 75 applicants were on the 2014 waiting list; were admitted. Applications are accepted online. **Transfer Students:** 29 transfer students enrolled in 2013-2014. Transfer applicants must have a minimum GPA of 3.0; generally. The SAT is optional. An interview is recommended. 64 of 128 credits required for the bachelor's degree must be completed at Saint Michael's. **International Students:** There are 88 international students enrolled. The school actively recruits these students. They must take the TOEFL with a minimum score of 550 on the paper-based TOEFL (PBT) or 79 on the Internet-based version (iBT) and the college's own test, . The SAT or ACT is optional for international students but recommended. The TOEFL may be used in place of the SAT.

ADMISSIONS: 80% of the 2014-2015 applicants were accepted. The SAT scores for the 2014-2015 freshman class were: Critical Reading--11% below 500, 46% between 500 and 599, 36% between 600 and 699, and 8% between 700 and 800; Math--15% below 500, 49% between 500 and 599, 32% between 600 and 699, and 4% between 700 and 800; Writing--15% below 500, 47% between 500 and 599, 32% between 600 and 699, and 5% between 700 and 800. The ACT scores were 5% below 21, 16% between 21 and 23, 36% between 24 and 26, 22% between 27 and 28, and 21% above 28. 44% of the current freshmen were in the top fifth of their class; 71% were in the top two fifths. 9 freshmen graduated first in their class. **Admissions Contact:** Jacqueline Murphy, Director of Office of Admission. E-Mail: *admission@smcvt.edu* Web: *www.smcvt.edu*

FINANCIAL AID: In 2014-2015, 99% of all full-time freshmen and 98% of continuing full-time students received some form of financial aid. 75% of all full-time freshmen and 69% of continuing full-time students received need-based aid. The average freshman award was $30,604. Need-based scholarships or need-based grants averaged $23,557 ($39,050 maximum); need-based self-help aid (loans and jobs) averaged $6,488 ($13,250 maximum); non-need-based athletic scholarships averaged $48,137 ($49,975 maximum); and other non-need-based awards and non-need-based scholarships averaged $15,974 ($39,050 maximum). 37% of undergraduate students work part-time. Average annual earnings from campus work are $1700. The average financial indebtedness of the 2014 graduate was $36,967. Saint Michael's is a member of CSS. The FAFSA, and federal tax forms from both student and parents, and W-2 forms is required. The deadline for filing freshman financial aid applications for fall entry is February 1.

SOUTHERN VERMONT COLLEGE *(The complete profile is made available exclusively on our website, www.barronspac.com)*

STERLING COLLEGE   B-1
www.sterlingcollege.edu

Craftsbury Common, VT 05827	(802) 586-7711
	(800) 648-3591
Fax: (802) 586-2596	Email: admission@sterlingcollege.edu
Full-time: 57 men, 46 women	Faculty: 14
Part-time: 1 men, 1 women	Ph.D.s: 29%
Graduate: n/av	Student/Faculty: 7 to 1
Year: semesters	Tuition: $25,500
Room & Board: $8500	Freshman Class: 97 applied, 74 accepted, 30 enrolled
SAT or ACT: recommended	CEEB CODE: 3752
Application Deadline: February 15	COMPETITIVE

Sterling College offers a liberal arts curriculum with an environmental focus. It combines traditional and experiential academics and offers internships and global field studies. The 430-acre campus is in a rural area 40 miles north of Montpelier and 60 miles from Burlington. Including any residence halls, there are 16 buildings. **STUDENT LIFE:** 82% of undergraduates are from out of state, mostly the Northeast. Students are from 22 states. 70% are white. The average age of freshmen is 19; all undergraduates, 21. 33% do not continue beyond their first year; 60% remain to graduate. **FACULTY/CLASSROOMS:** 50% of faculty are male; 50% are female. All teach undergraduates. No introductory courses are taught by graduate students. The average class size in an introductory lecture is 12; in a laboratory is 12; and in a regular course is 12. **PROGRAMS OF STUDY:** Sterling confers B.A. degrees. Bachelor's degrees are awarded in AGRICULTURE (agriculture, conservation and regulation, natural resource management, and wildlife management), EDUCATION (recreation education), SOCIAL SCIENCE (area studies). Conservation ecology, northern studies, and sustainable agriculture are the strongest academically. **ACTIVITIES:** Groups on campus include activism theater, diversity, folk music, art, dance, environmental, film, literary magazine, outing, photography, student government, and yearbook. Popular campus events include All-College Work Days, Earth Day, and Annual Wood-Projects show. **SERVICES:** Counseling and information services are available, as is tutoring in every subject. There is remedial math. Students seek assistance directly from faculty or teacher assistants. In addition, there is a learning support coordinator as well as a writing center. **Library/ Resources:** The 2 libraries contain 13,630 volumes, 0 microform items, and 600 audio/video tapes/CDs/DVDs, and subscribe to 127 periodicals including electronic. Computerized library services include interlibrary loans, database searching, Internet access, and Wi-Fi capability. Special learning facilities include an art gallery, a woodshop, darkroom, managed woodlot, organic garden, working livestock farm, 30-foot-tall climbing wall, challenge course, greenhouse, blacksmith shop, sugar house, and a 300-acre boreal forest/ wetland research area. **Physically Challenged Students:** Facilities include wheelchair ramps and specially equipped restrooms. **Special:** Internships are required. Study abroad, work study, and student-designed majors are available. We are the only federally recognized Work College in the Northeast; all students, regardless of financial aid, must work on campus. **Visiting:** There are regularly scheduled orientations for prospective students, including a student-led campus tour, an interview with admissions, and a meal in the dining hall. Weekend Open Houses offer a more comprehensive view of the college. There are 2 open houses per year. Monday Visit Days are similar to open houses, but students may sit in on classes. There are guides for informal visits and visitors may sit in on classes. To schedule a visit, contact Tim Patterson at tpatterson@sterlingcollege.edu.

Campus Safety and Security: Measures include emergency notification system.

REQUIREMENTS: The SAT or ACT is recommended. In addition, essays, quality of the interview, and the comments provided by references are equal to the value of high school and college transcripts. Home-schooled students are strongly encouraged to contact the admissions office to discuss their particular needs and interests. A GPA of 2.0 is required. AP credits are accepted. Important factors in the admissions decision are advanced placement or honors courses, recommendations by school officials, and leadership record. **ADMISSIONS:** 76% of a recent year applicants were accepted. 20% of the current freshmen were in the top fifth of their class; 40% were in the top two fifths. **FINANCIAL AID:** 90% of undergraduate students work part-time. Average annual earnings from campus work are $1500. The FAFSA and the college's own financial statement are required. The priority date for freshman financial aid applications for fall entry is March 1.

UNIVERSITY OF VERMONT   A-2
www.uvm.edu

Burlington, VT 05401	(802) 656-3370
	(802) 656-3131
Fax: (802) 656-8611	Email: admissions@uvm.edu
Full-time: 4310 men, 5454 women	Faculty: I, -$
Part-time: 461 men, 687 women	Ph.D.s: 77%
Graduate: 779 men, 1032 women	Student/Faculty: 16 to 1
Year: semesters, summer session	Tuition: $16,196 ($37,844)
Room & Board: $10,810	Freshman Class: 24234 applied, 17793 accepted, 2310 enrolled
SAT CR/M/W: 592/595/591 ACT: 27	CEEB CODE: 3920
Application Deadline: January 15	VERY COMPETITIVE+

The University of Vermont, established in 1791, is a public, land-grant, comprehensive institution with a dual focus on teaching and research. Its undergraduate and graduate offerings include the liberal arts, business administration, engineering, math, natural resources, agricultural studies, fine arts, teacher preparation, social services, environmental studies, and health science, including nursing. There are 7 undergraduate schools and 2 graduate schools. In addition to regional accreditation, UVM has baccalaureate program accreditation with AACSB, ABET, APTA, ASLA, CAHEA, CSWE, NCATE, and CCNE. The 460-acre campus is in a suburban area 90 miles south of Montreal, 200 miles north of Boston, campus is located between the shore of Lake Champlain and the Green Mountains. Including any residence halls, there are 119 buildings. **STUDENT LIFE:** 69% of undergraduates are from out of state, mostly the Northeast. Students are from 48 states, 50 foreign countries, and Canada. 88% are White. 40% claim no religious affiliation. The average age of freshmen is 18; all undergraduates, 20. 13% do not continue beyond their first year; 75% remain to graduate. **Housing:** 5500 students can be accommodated in college housing, which includes coed dorms, on-campus apartments, off-campus apartments, and married student housing. There are honors houses, language houses, special-interest houses, fraternity houses, sorority houses. In addition, the living/learning center provides an integrated, theme-based academic and residential option. On-campus housing is guaranteed for all 4 years and is available on a lottery system for upperclassmen. 50% of students commute. Upperclassmen may keep cars. **FACULTY/CLASSROOMS:** 58% of faculty are male; 42% are female. Graduate students teach 2% of introductory courses. The average class size in a regular course is 31. **PROGRAMS OF STUDY:** UVM confers B.A., B.S., B.Mus., B.S.A.E., B.S.B.A., B.S.Ed., B.S.C.E., B.S.C.S., B.S.E.E., B.S.E.M., B.S.M., B.S.M.E. and B.S.M.S. degrees. Master's and Doctoral degrees are also awarded. Bachelor's degrees are awarded in AGRICULTURE (agriculture, animal science, environmental studies, fishing and fisheries, forestry and related sciences, horticulture, natural resource management, and plant science), BIOLOGICAL SCIENCE (biochemistry, biology/biological science, botany, genetics, microbiology, molecular biology, neurosciences, nutrition, wildlife biology, and zoology), BUSINESS (business administration and management, entrepreneurial studies, and international economics), COMMUNICATIONS AND THE ARTS (art, art history and appreciation, Chinese, classics, communications, dramatic arts, English, film arts, French, German, Greek, Japanese, Latin, linguistics, music, Russian, and Spanish), COMPUTER AND PHYSICAL SCIENCE (chemistry, computer science, geology, information sciences and systems, mathematics, physics, and statistics), EDUCATION (art education, athletic training, early childhood education, education, elementary education, English education, foreign languages education, mathematics education, middle school education, music education, physical education, science education, secondary education, social studies education, and special education), ENGINEERING AND ENVIRONMENTAL DESIGN (civil engineering, electrical/electronics engineering, engineering, engineering management, environmental engineering, environmental science, landscape architecture/design, and mechanical engineering), HEALTH PROFESSIONS (biomedical science, exercise science, medical laboratory science, nuclear medical technology, nursing, radiation therapy, and speech pathology/audiology), SOCIAL SCIENCE (anthropology, area studies, Asian/Oriental studies, child care/child and family studies, dietetics, economics, ethnic studies, European studies, food science, gender studies, geography, history, human development, Italian studies, Latin American studies, parks and recreation management, philosophy, political science/government, psychology, religion, Russian and Slavic studies, social work, and sociology). Business administration, psychology, and biology/biological science have the largest enrollments.

ACTIVITIES: 6% of men belong to 9 national fraternities; 6% of women belong to 6 national sororities. There are 170 groups on campus, including environmental clubs, an outing club, art, band, cheerleading, chess, choir, chorale, chorus, communications, community service, computers, dance, debate, drama, environmental, ethnic, gay, honors, international, jazz band, literary magazine, musical theater, newspaper, orchestra, pep band, photography, political, professional, radio and TV, religious, social, social service, and student government. Popular campus events include Winterfest, Community Serve-a-thon, and Sugar on Snow day. **Sports:** There are 8 intercollegiate sports for men and 10 for women, and 24 intramural sports for men and 24 for women. Facilities include a 3228-seat gym, 4000-seat ice hockey stadium, turffield, a field house, soccer and baseball fields, fitness center, indoor and outdoor tracks, a natatorium, indoor tennis courts, racquetball court, climbing facility, dance studio, and a gymnastics facility. **Graduates:** From July 1, 2013 to June 30, 2014, 2319 bachelor's degrees were awarded. The most popular majors were business (8%), psychology (5%), and English (4%). 170 companies recruited on campus in 2013-2014. In an average class, 62% graduate in 4 years or less, 75% graduate in 5 years or less, and 75% graduate in 6 years or less. Of the 2013 graduating class, 24% were enrolled in graduate school within 6 months of graduation, and 85% were employed.

SERVICES: Counseling and information services are available, as is tutoring in most subjects. There is a reader service for the blind. There is also supplemental instruction, note-taking and test-taking seminars, time management instruction, outreach programs, exam proctoring, and writing tutors, as well as support for ESL students. **Library/Resources:** The 2 libraries contain 2.5 million volumes, 2.0 million microform items, 55,310 audio/video tapes/CDs/DVDs, and subscribe to 30,000 periodicals including electronic. Computerized library services include interlibrary loans, database searching, Internet access, and Wi-Fi capability. Special learning facilities include an art gallery, radio station, TV station, a health care center (the University of Vermont Medical Center), 4 research farms, the Fleming Museum, geology museum, 9 natural areas (in state), lakeshore science center, and aquatic research vessel. **Physically Challenged Students:** 90% of the campus is accessible. Facilities include wheelchair ramps, elevators, special parking, specially equipped restrooms, special class scheduling, lowered drinking fountains, lowered telephones. First-priority routes in poor weather, a TTY phone system for hearing-impaired students, and closed-caption video decoders. **Special:** Special academic programs include co-op programs, internships in every discipline, study abroad in 110 countries, a Washington semes-

ter, work-study, an accelerated degree program in computer science, secondary education, and public administration, RN-BS-MS, dual majors, and student-designed majors. In addition, a 3-4 veterinary medicine degree is offered with Tufts University. There are 25 national honor societies, including Phi Beta Kappa, a freshman honors program, and 14 departmental honors programs. **Visiting:** There are regularly scheduled orientations for prospective students, group information sessions and tours most weekdays and many Saturdays year round. Visitors may sit in on classes. To schedule a visit, contact The Admissions Office. **Campus Safety and Security:** Measures include 24-hour foot and vehicle patrol, emergency notification system, self-defense education, and security escort services. There are shuttle buses, emergency telephones, lighted pathways/sidewalks, controlled access to dorms/residences, bike registration, identification of property, and 18 fully certified police officers.

REQUIREMENTS: The SAT or ACT is required. The ACT Optional Writing test is also required. Including graduation from an accredited secondary school with 16 Carnegie units. Required high school course work includes 4 years of English, 3 years each of social science and math, including algebra I and II and geometry, and 2 years each of the same foreign language and science (one of which must be a lab science). Some academic units require additional course work. An essay must be submitted. The GED is also accepted. AP and CLEP credits are accepted. Important factors in the admissions decision are advanced placement or honors courses, extracurricular activities record, and recommendations by school officials. Degree requirements vary among the individual colleges, but all require at least a 2.0 GPA and 122 credit hours to graduate. Most students must enroll in at least 30 distribution credits (approximately 10 courses) in the arts, humanities, social sciences, languages, literature, math, and the sciences. All academic units require 2 courses in Race and Culture. **Procedure:** Freshmen are admitted fall and spring. Entrance exams should be taken by November of the senior year. There are early admissions and deferred admissions plans. Early decision applications should be filed by November 1; regular applications, by January 15 for fall entry; and November 1 for spring entry, along with a $55 fee. Notification of early decision is sent December 15; regular decision, March 15. 3094 applicants were on the 2014 waiting list; 103 were admitted. Applications are accepted on-line. **Transfer Students:** 600 transfer students enrolled in 2013-2014. Successful transfer students have a cumulative grade point average of at least 2.8 in credited courses and meet the same entrance requirements as first-year applicants. Considerations include the college and high school records, the major indicated, and availability of space at UVM. 30 of 122 credits required for the bachelor's degree must be completed at UVM. **International Students:** There are 268 international students enrolled. The school actively recruits these students. They must take the TOEFL with a minimum score of 90 on the Internet-based version (iBT), or take the IELTS. They must also take the SAT or ACT.

ADMISSIONS: 73% of the 2014-2015 applicants were accepted. The SAT scores for the 2014-2015 freshman class were: Critical Reading--8% below 500, 42% between 500 and 599, 41% between 600 and 699, and 9% between 700 and 800; Math--8% below 500, 42% between 500 and 599, 41% between 600 and 699, and 9% between 700 and 800; Writing--10% below 500, 42% between 500 and 599, 41% between 600 and 699, and 7% between 700 and 800. The ACT scores were 5% below 21, 12% between 21 and 23, 29% between 24 and 26, 23% between 27 and 28, and 31% above 28. 55% of the current freshmen were in the top fifth of their class; 88% were in the top two fifths. There were 2 National Merit finalists. **Admissions Contact:** Dr. Beth A. Wiser, Director of Admission. E-Mail: *admissions@uvm.edu* Web: *www.uvm.edu*

FINANCIAL AID: In 2014-2015, 94% of all full-time freshmen and 84% of continuing full-time students received some form of financial aid. 62% of all full-time freshmen and 56% of continuing full-time students received need-based aid. The average freshman award was $18,810. Need-based scholarships or need-based grants averaged $16,621 ($52,299 maximum). The average financial indebtedness of the 2014 graduate was $25,783. The FAFSA is required. The priority date for freshman financial aid applications for fall entry is February 10.

VERMONT STATE COLLEGES

The Vermont State Colleges, established in 1962, is a public system in Vermont. It is governed by a board of trustees, whose chief administrator is the chancellor. The primary goal of the system is teaching. The main priorities are to insure all citizens have access to higher education and continuous learning opportunities, and to provide educational programs that are affordable, high quality, student centered and accessible to maintain the quality of cultural, social, and economic life in Vermont. The total student enrollment of all 5 campuses was 9,050 with 285 faculty members. Altogether there are 60 baccalaureate, and 5 master's programs offered in the Vermont State Colleges. Profiles of the 4-year campuses are included in this section.

VERMONT TECHNICAL COLLEGE   C-4
www.vtc.edu

Randolph Center, VT 05061	(802) 728-1000
	(800) 442-8821
Fax: (802) 728-1321	Email: admissions@vtc.edu
Full-time: 655 men, 380 women	Faculty: n/av; III, --$
Part-time: 165 men, 160 women	Ph.D.s: 54%
Graduate: n/av	Student/Faculty: n/av
Year: semesters	Tuition: $12,500 ($21,500)
Room & Board: $8500	Freshman Class: n/av
SAT or ACT: required	CEEB CODE: 3941
Application Deadline: open	COMPETITIVE

Vermont Technical College, founded in 1910, is one of the 5 institutions in the Vermont State Colleges System and is the state's only public technical college. The figures in the above capsule and this profile are approximate. In addition to regional accreditation, VTC has baccalaureate program accreditation with ABET. The 544-acre campus is in a rural area. Including any residence halls, there are 19 buildings.

STUDENT LIFE: 60% of undergraduates are from Vermont. Others are from 12 states and 2 foreign countries. 90% are from public schools. 94% are white. The average age of freshmen is 25; all undergraduates, 26. 25% do not continue beyond their first year; 55% remain to graduate.

FACULTY/CLASSROOMS: 58% of faculty are male; 42% are female. All teach undergraduates. The average class size in an introductory lecture is 28; in a laboratory, 16; and in a regular course, 32.

PROGRAMS OF STUDY: VTC confers B.S. degrees. Associates degrees are also awarded. Bachelor's degrees are awarded in COMPUTER AND PHYSICAL SCIENCE (information sciences and systems and software engineering), EDUCATION (business education), ENGINEERING AND ENVIRONMENTAL DESIGN (architectural engineering, computer engineering, and electromechanical technology). Electromechanical engineering technology is the strongest academically. Architectural engineering technology and business have the largest enrollments.

ACTIVITIES: There are no fraternities or sororities. Groups on campus include chess, computers, drama, ethnic, gay, international, photography, professional, radio and TV, religious, social, social service, and student government. Popular campus events include Harvest Days, Winter Carnival, and Spring Fling.

SERVICES: Counseling and information services are available, as is tutoring in every subject. **Library/Resources:** The library contains 59,480 volumes, 5,920 microform items, and 4,122 audio/video tapes/CDs/DVDs, and subscribes to 348 periodicals including electronic. Computerized library services include interlibrary loans, database searching, and Internet access. Special learning facilities include a radio station, Vermont Interactive Technologies and Anaerobic Digester. **Physically Challenged Students:** All of the campus is accessible. Facilities include wheelchair ramps, elevators, special parking, specially equipped restrooms, special class scheduling, lowered drinking fountains, and lowered telephones. **Special:** Cross-registration, internships, work-study programs, and dual majors are offered. There are 2 national honor societies, a freshman honors program, and 2 departmental honors programs. **Visiting:** There are regularly scheduled orientations for prospective students. There are guides for informal visits, visitors may sit in on classes, and stay overnight. To schedule a visit, contact the Admissions Office. **Campus Safety and Security:** Measures include 24-hour foot and vehicle patrol, self-defense education, and security escort services. There are emergency telephones and lighted pathways/sidewalks.

REQUIREMENTS: The SAT or ACT is required. AP and CLEP credits are accepted.

FINANCIAL AID: The FAFSA is required. Check with the school for current application deadlines.

WOODBURY INSTITUTE OF CHAMPLAIN COLLEGE (*The complete profile is made available exclusively on our website, www. barronspac.com*)

VIRGINIA

- College Location

0   20   40   60   80   100
            Miles

AVERETT UNIVERSITY *(The complete profile is made available exclusively on our website, www.barronspac.com)*

BLUEFIELD COLLEGE   B-3
www.bluefield.edu

Bluefield, VA 24605	**(276) 326-3682**
	(800) 872-0176
Fax: (276) 326-4395	
Full-time: 287 men, 405 women	**Faculty:** 33; IIB, --$
Part-time: 27 men, 57 women	**Ph.D.s:** 61%
Graduate: n/av	**Student/Faculty:** 21 to 1
Year: semesters, summer session	**Tuition:** $12,000
Room & Board: $5800	**Freshman Class:** 731 applied, 358 accepted, 110 enrolled
SAT: required **ACT:** 21	**CEEB CODE:** 1523
Application Deadline: open	**COMPETITIVE+**

Bluefield College is a Christ-centered liberal arts college in covenant with the Baptist General Association of Virginia. We offer a challenging academic experience within a diverse Christian environment. Our academic and co-curricular programs transform students' lives by integrating liberal arts with career-oriented studies and service to God and the global community. We are committed to graduating students who think critically, communicate effectively, and adapt readily to a changing world. There is 1 undergraduate school. In addition to regional accreditation, BC has baccalaureate program accreditation with TEAC. The 82-acre campus is in a small town 100 miles west of Roanoke on the Virginia-West Virginia state line. Including any residence halls, there are 26 buildings.

STUDENT LIFE: 80% of undergraduates are from Virginia. Others are from 19 states, and 2 foreign countries. 79% are White; 18% African American.

FACULTY/CLASSROOMS: 70% of faculty are male; 30% are female. All teach undergraduates, 30% do research, and 30% do both. No introductory courses are taught by graduate students. The average class size in an introductory lecture is 17; in a laboratory is 12; and in a regular course is 10.

PROGRAMS OF STUDY: BC confers B.A., and B.S. degrees. Bachelor's degrees are awarded in BIOLOGICAL SCIENCE (biology/biological science), BUSINESS (business administration and management), COMMUNICATIONS AND THE ARTS (communications, English, fine arts, and music), COMPUTER AND PHYSICAL SCIENCE (chemistry and mathematics), EDUCATION (middle school education and secondary education), HEALTH PROFESSIONS (exercise science), SOCIAL SCIENCE (Christian studies, criminal justice, history, interdisciplinary studies, psychology, religion, and

social studies). Business, teacher education, and biology are the strongest academically. Business, organizational management and development, and criminal justice have the largest enrollments.

ACTIVITIES: 5% of men belong to 2 local fraternities; 10% of women belong to 2 local sororities. There are 15 groups on campus, including art, cheerleading, choir, chorale, chorus, communications, dance, drama, honors, literary magazine, musical theater, newspaper, orchestra, professional, religious, social, and student government. Popular campus events include Homecoming and Mud Pig Day.

SERVICES: Counseling and information services are available, as is tutoring in most subjects. There is remedial math and writing. **Library/Resources:** The library contains 47,000 volumes, 3,477 audio/video tapes/CDs/DVDs, and subscribes to 70,000 periodicals including electronic. Computerized library services include interlibrary loans, database searching, and Internet access. **Physically Challenged Students:** 95% of the campus is accessible. Facilities include wheelchair ramps, elevators, special parking, specially equipped restrooms, and lowered drinking fountains. **Special:** The college offers credit for life/military/work experience, nondegree study through the Fine Arts Community School, study abroad in England, an accelerated degree program in organizational management and development and in criminal justice, and internships in criminal justice, psychology, and recreation. There are 4 national honor societies, a freshman honors program, and 7 departmental honors programs. **Visiting:** There are regularly scheduled orientations for prospective students, including campus tours, opportunities to develop class schedules, and financial aid workshops. Visitors may sit in on classes and stay overnight. To schedule a visit, contact the Admissions Office. **Campus Safety and Security:** Measures include 24-hour foot and vehicle patrol, emergency notification system, and security escort services. There are lighted pathways/sidewalks and controlled access to dorms/residences.

REQUIREMENTS: The SAT or ACT is required. Applicants must be graduates of an accredited secondary school or have a GED certificate, and have completed 4 years of English, 2 of social sciences, 1 of science, and 5 of electives. A GPA of 2.0 is required. AP and CLEP credits are accepted. Important factors in the admissions decision are leadership record, advanced placement or honors courses, and recommendations by school officials.

ADMISSIONS: 49% of the 2013-2014 applicants were accepted. The ACT scores were 57% below 21, 20% between 21 and 23, 13% between 24 and 26, 3% between 27 and 28, and 7% above 28. 38% of the current freshmen were in the top fifth of their class; 64% were in the top two fifths.

FINANCIAL AID: The FAFSA and the college's own financial statement are required. The deadline for filing freshman financial aid applications for fall entry is March 10.

BRIDGEWATER COLLEGE   D-2
www.bridgewater.edu

Bridgewater, VA 22812-1599	**(540) 828-8000**
	(800) 759-8328
Fax: (540) 828-5481	**Email:** admissions@bridgewater.edu
Full-time: 815 men, 951 women	**Faculty:** 111; IIB, --$
Part-time: 8 men, 11 women	**Ph.D.s:** 80%
Graduate: n/av	**Student/Faculty:** 16 to 1
Year: 4-1-4, summer session	**Tuition:** $30,380
Room & Board: $11,070	**Freshman Class:** 6169 applied, 2950 accepted, 488 enrolled
SAT CR/M/W: 510/520/490 **ACT:** 24	**CEEB CODE:** 5069
Application Deadline: May 1	**COMPETITIVE**

Bridgewater College, founded in 1880, is a private liberal arts institution affiliated with the Church of the Brethren. In addition to regional accreditation, Bridgewater has baccalaureate program accreditation with CAATE. The 300-acre campus is in a small town 2 hours southwest of Washington D.C., and 8 miles south of Harrisonburg, Virginia. Including any residence halls, there are 44 buildings.

STUDENT LIFE: 75% of undergraduates are from Virginia. Others are from 26 states, 11 foreign countries, and Canada. 93% are from public schools. 75% are White. 56% are Protestant; 23% claim no religious affiliation; 12% Catholic. The average age of freshmen is 18; all undergraduates, 20. 26% do not continue beyond their first year; 61% remain to graduate. **Housing:** 1484 students can be accommodated in college housing, which includes single-sex and coed dorms and on-campus apartments. In addition, there are honors houses. On-campus housing is guaranteed for all 4 years. 80% of students live on campus; of those, 60% remain on campus on weekends. Alcohol is not permitted. All students may keep cars.

FACULTY/CLASSROOMS: 54% of faculty are male; 46% are female. All teach undergraduates, 50% do research, and 50% do both. No introductory courses are taught by graduate students. The average class size in an introductory lecture is 22; in a laboratory is 16; and in a regular course is 18.

PROGRAMS OF STUDY: Bridgewater confers B.A., B.S. and B.G.S. degrees. Bachelor's degrees are awarded in BIOLOGICAL SCIENCE (biology/biological science), BUSINESS (business administration and management and management information systems), COMMUNICATIONS AND THE ARTS (art, communications, English, French, music, and Spanish), COMPUTER AND PHYSICAL SCIENCE (applied chemistry, applied physics, chemistry, computer science, mathematics, physics and mathematics, and physics), EDUCATION (athletic training and health and physical education), ENGINEERING AND ENVIRONMENTAL DESIGN (environmental science), HEALTH PROFESSIONS (exercise science and nutrition and wellness), SOCIAL SCIENCE (economics, family/consumer studies, history, history and political science, international relations, liberal arts/general studies, philosophy and religion, political science/government, psychology, and sociology). Biology, chemistry, and English are the strongest academically. Biology, business administration, and health/exercise science have the largest enrollments.

ACTIVITIES: There are 71 groups on campus, including art, band, cheerleading, choir, chorale, chorus, communications, dance, drama, environmental, ethnic, gay, honors, international, jazz band, literary magazine, musical theater, newspaper, pep band, professional, radio and TV, religious, social, social service, student government, and yearbook. Popular campus events include Homecoming, Welcome Week Activities, and Spring Fest Concert. **Sports:** There are 9 intercollegiate sports for men and 11 for women, and 24 intramural sports for men and 24 for women. Facilities include a gym, 2500-seat football stadium, swimming pool, tennis courts, an all-weather track, playing fields for baseball, lacrosse, softball, football, field hockey, and soccer, 34,000-square-foot fitness center with basketball, volleyball, racquetball courts, indoor track, cardiac and weight-training center, aerobics/dance rooms, a 75-acre equestrian center that includes 2 barns with 50 stalls in total, fully equipped classrooms and offices, and 1 indoor and 2 outdoor arenas. **Graduates:** From July 1, 2013 to June 30, 2014, 379 bachelor's degrees were awarded. The most popular majors were business administration (17%), biology (12%), and health and exercise science (10%). In an average class, 53% graduate in 4 years or less, 57% graduate in 5 years or less, and 60% graduate in 6 years or less.

SERVICES: Counseling and information services are available, as is tutoring in every subject. There is a reader service for the blind. The academic support center provides students with academic assistance through an academic coach program, departmental help sessions, learning strategy workshops, transition program, tutoring services, learning skill websites, and support for students with learning disabilities. **Library/Resources:** The library contains 152,808 volumes, 2,163 microform items, and 5,992 audio/video tapes/CDs/DVDs, and subscribes to 47,649 periodicals including electronic. Computerized library services include interlibrary loans, database searching, Internet access, and Wi-Fi capability. Special learning facilities include an art gallery, radio station, a museum of the Shenandoah Valley and Church of the Brethren. **Physically Challenged Students:** 95% of the campus is accessible. Facilities include wheelchair ramps, elevators, special parking, specially equipped restrooms, lowered drinking fountains, lowered telephones, special housing. **Special:** Bridgewater offers internships to junior and seniors; study abroad in over 50

countries; participation in the Smithsonian-Mason Semester for Conservation Studies; and a teacher certification program in elementary and secondary education. Interdisciplinary majors include environmental science, history and political science, global studies, liberal studies, nutrition and wellness, philosophy and religion, and physics and math. Dual-degree programs are offered in engineering with George Washington University (3-2) and Virginia Tech (3-2), in physical therapy with Shenandoah University (3-4), and in nursing with Vanderbilt University (3-2). There are 8 national honor societies, a freshman honors program, and 16 departmental honors programs. **Visiting:** There are regularly scheduled orientations for prospective students, including a meeting with a faculty adviser, course scheduling and registration, and social activities. There are guides for informal visits and visitors may sit in on classes. To schedule a visit, contact the Admissions Office. **Campus Safety and Security:** Measures include 24-hour foot and vehicle patrol, emergency notification system, and self-defense education. There are emergency telephones, lighted pathways/sidewalks, and controlled access to dorms/residences.

REQUIREMENTS: The SAT or ACT is required. SAT is preferred, an interview is recommended. Applicants must be graduates of an accredited secondary school or have a GED certificate, and have completed 17 units, including 4 in English, 3 in math, 2 in science, 2 in history and social studies, and 6 in electives (recommend 2 academic electives are in a foreign language; preferably French, German, or Spanish). AP credits are accepted. Important factors in the admissions decision are advanced placement or honors courses, recommendations by school officials, and leadership record.To graduate, all students must complete a minimum of 123 credit hours, with a minimum of 48 credit hours chosen from junior/senior level courses. A major consists of 32 to 54 credit hours. A minimum 2.0 GPA is required, overall and in the major. The BA and BS degrees are awarded as defined by the chosen major. Students must complete a course in Critical Inquiry in the Liberal Arts and a e-senior portfolio requirement. Other general education requirements include core skill courses in writing, oral communication, math, and exercise science; courses for a global society in world languages, world cultures, and global dynamics; courses across the disciplines in fine arts and music, literature, history, philosophy or religion, social sciences, and natural and physical sciences; and courses integrating skills of writing intensive, ethical reasoning, and experiential learning. A minimum of 33 credit hours with 30 of the last 33 credits hours earned in residence at the college. **Procedure:** Freshmen are admitted fall and spring. Entrance exams should be taken in spring of the junior year or fall of the senior year. There are deferred admissions and rolling admissions plans. Application deadlines are open. 135 applicants were on the 2014 waiting list; 80 were admitted. Applications are accepted on-line. Application fees are waived if application is completed on-line. **Transfer Students:** 52 transfer students enrolled in 2013-2014. A degree from an accredited high school and a 2.2 GPA in all undergraduate work are required. 33 of 123 credits required for the bachelor's degree must be completed at Bridgewater. **International Students:** There are 16 international students enrolled. The school actively recruits these students. They must take the TOEFL with a minimum score of 550 on the paper-based TOEFL (PBT) or 79 on the Internet-based version (iBT), The SAT may replace the TOEFL. Most international students take the SAT rather than TOEFL. They must also take the ACT.

ADMISSIONS: 48% of the 2014-2015 applicants were accepted. The SAT scores for the 2014-2015 freshman class were: Critical Reading--40% below 500, 41% between 500 and 599, 16% between 600 and 699, and 3% between 700 and 800; Math--37% below 500, 47% between 500 and 599, 15% between 600 and 699, and 1% between 700 and 800; Writing--53% below 500, 36% between 500 and 599, 10% between 600 and 699, and 1% between 700 and 800. The ACT scores were 18% below 21, 30% between 21 and 23, 25% between 24 and 26, 13% between 27 and 28, and 14% above 28. 42% of the current freshmen were in the top fifth of their class; 75% were in the top two fifths. 4 freshmen graduated first in their class. **Admissions Contact:** Jarret L. Smith, Director of Admissions. E-Mail: *admissions@bridgewater.edu* Web: *www.bridgewater.edu*

FINANCIAL AID: In 2014-2015, 99% of all full-time freshmen and continuing full-time students received some form of financial aid.

85% of all full-time freshmen and 81% of continuing full-time students received need-based aid. The average freshman award was $27,710. Need-based scholarships or need-based grants averaged $24,595 ($36,610 maximum); need-based self-help aid (loans and jobs) averaged $4,770 ($7,200 maximum); and other non-need-based awards and non-need-based scholarships averaged $18,243 ($33,480 maximum). 25% of undergraduate students work part-time. Average annual earnings from campus work are $726. The average financial indebtedness of the 2014 graduate was $33,326. Bridgewater is a member of CSS. The FAFSA and the state aid form are required. The priority date for freshman financial aid applications for fall entry is March 1.

CHRISTENDOM COLLEGE   D-2
www.christendom.edu

Front Royal, VA 22630	**(540) 636-2900**
	(800) 877-5456
Fax: (540) 636-1655	Email: admissions@christendom.edu
Full-time: 177 men, 255 women	Faculty: 32
Part-time: 1 men	Ph.D.s: 65%
Graduate: n/av	Student/Faculty: 15 to 1
Year: semesters	Tuition: $23,900
Room & Board: $8700	Freshman Class: 228 applied, 211 accepted, 104 enrolled
SAT CR/M/W: 632/570/616 ACT: 25	CEEB CODE: 5691
Application Deadline: March 1	VERY COMPETITIVE

Christendom College, founded in 1977, is a private liberal arts institution affiliated with the Roman Catholic Church. Figures in the above capsule and in this profile are approximate. There is 1 graduate school. In addition to regional accreditation, Christendom has baccalaureate program accreditation with SACS. The 120-acre campus is in a rural area 65 miles west of Washington, D.C. Including any residence halls, there are 21 buildings.

STUDENT LIFE: 74% of undergraduates are from out of state, mostly the Middle Atlantic. Students are from 43 states, 2 foreign countries, and Canada. 91% are White. 100% are Catholic. The average age of freshmen is 18; all undergraduates, 20. 7% do not continue beyond their first year; 70% remain to graduate. **Housing:** College-sponsored housing includes single-sex dorms and on-campus apartments. On-campus housing is guaranteed for all 4 years. 95% of students live on campus; of those, 100% remain on campus on weekends. Alcohol is not permitted. All students may keep cars.

FACULTY/CLASSROOMS: 79% of faculty are male; 21% are female. All teach undergraduates. No introductory courses are taught by graduate students. The average class size in an introductory lecture is 22 and in a regular course is 20.

PROGRAMS OF STUDY: Christendom confers B.A. degrees. Associate and Master's degrees are also awarded. Bachelor's degrees are awarded in COMMUNICATIONS AND THE ARTS (English), SOCIAL SCIENCE (classical/ancient civilization, history, philosophy, political science/government, and theological studies). Philosophy is the strongest academically, and has the largest enrollment.

ACTIVITIES: There are no fraternities or sororities. There are 15 groups on campus, including chess, choir, chorale, computers, debate, drama, film, literary magazine, musical theater, newspaper, photography, political, professional, radio and TV, religious, social, social service, student government, and yearbook. Popular campus events include Christmas Dinner Dance, Coffee House, and St. Patrick's Day. **Sports:** There are 4 intercollegiate sports for men and 3 for women, and 7 intramural sports for men and 7 for women. Facilities include an indoor basketball and volleyball courts, racquetball courts, playing fields, table games, a recreation center, and an outdoor swimming pool. **Graduates:** From July 1, 2013 to June 30, 2014, 69 bachelor's degrees were awarded. 8 companies recruited on campus in 2013-2014. In an average class, 70% graduate in 4 years or less and 70% graduate in 6 years or less. Of the 2013 graduating class, 12% were enrolled in graduate school within 6 months of graduation, and 80% were employed.

SERVICES: Library/Resources: The library contains 90,000 volumes,

860 microform items, 1,345 audio/video tapes/CDs/DVDs, and subscribes to 279 periodicals including electronic. Computerized library services include interlibrary loans and database searching. Special learning facilities include a radio station, a writing center. **Physically Challenged Students:** 60% of the campus is accessible. Facilities include wheelchair ramps, elevators, special parking, and specially equipped restrooms. **Special:** Christendom offers summer internships in Washington, D.C. for political science students and also sponsors a semester in Rome during the junior year. Students may pursue dual majors. There is a work-study program with the college. There are 5 departmental honors programs. **Visiting:** There are guides for informal visits, visitors may sit in on classes, and stay overnight. To schedule a visit, contact the Admissions Counselor at admission@christendom.edu. **Campus Safety and Security:** Measures include 24-hour foot and vehicle patrol and security escort services. There are emergency telephones and lighted pathways/sidewalks.

REQUIREMENTS: The SAT or ACT is required, the SAT is preferred. A minimum composite score of 1500 on the newest SAT or 21 on the ACT is required. Applicants need not be graduates of an accredited secondary school. GED certificates are accepted. Essays and letters of recommendation are required. A campus visit and a meeting with the Admissions Director are highly recommended. Christendom requires applicants to be in the upper 50% of their class. A GPA of 3.0 is required. AP credits are accepted. To graduate, all students must complete a total of 126 credit hours, including a 30-hour major and an 86-credit core curriculum, which includes 18 hours each in theology and philosophy. All students must demonstrate proficiency in a foreign language and complete a thesis. **Procedure:** Freshmen are admitted fall and spring. Entrance exams should be taken in the spring of the junior year or fall of the senior year. There is an early admissions plan. Early decision applications should be filed by December 1; regular applications, by March 1 for fall entry; and January 2 for spring entry, along with a $25 fee. Notification of early decision is sent December 15; regular decision, April 1. Applications are accepted on-line. **Transfer Students:** 9 transfer students enrolled in 2013-2014. Students must have a minimum 2.0 GPA and meet all other applicable standard admissions requirements. The SAT or ACT is recommended. 36 of 126 credits required for the bachelor's degree must be completed at Christendom. **International Students:** There are 7 international students enrolled. They must take the TOEFL.

ADMISSIONS: 93% of the 2014-2015 applicants were accepted. The SAT scores for the 2014-2015 freshman class were: Critical Reading--5% below 500, 33% between 500 and 599, 33% between 600 and 699, and 29% between 700 and 800; Math--20% below 500, 46% between 500 and 599, 24% between 600 and 699, and 10% between 700 and 800; Writing--11% below 500, 24% between 500 and 599, 43% between 600 and 699, and 22% between 700 and 800. The ACT scores were 3% below 21, 28% between 21 and 23, 50% between 24 and 26, 12% between 27 and 28, and 7% above 28. 40% of the current freshmen were in the top fifth of their class; 85% were in the top two fifths. **Admissions Contact:** Samuel J. Phillips, Director of Admissions . E-Mail: *admissions@christendom.edu* Web: *www.christendom .edu*

FINANCIAL AID: In 2014-2015, 69% of all full-time freshmen and 56% of continuing full-time students received some form of financial aid. 56% of all full-time freshmen and 54% of continuing full-time students received need-based aid. The average freshman award was $17,236. Need-based scholarships or need-based grants averaged $6,270; need-based self-help aid (loans and jobs) averaged $7,530; and other non-need-based awards and non-need-based scholarships averaged $8,183. 40% of undergraduate students work part-time. Average annual earnings from campus work are $2000. The average financial indebtedness of the 2014 graduate was $28,084. The the college's own financial statement is required. Check with the school for current application deadlines.

CHRISTOPHER NEWPORT UNIVERSITY   F-3
www.cnu.edu

Newport News, VA 23606	(757) 594-7000
	(757) 594-7015
Fax: (757) 594-7333	Email: admit@cnu.edu
Full-time: 2123 men, 2867 women	Faculty: 274; IIB, av$
Part-time: 54 men, 52 women	Ph.D.s: 87%
Graduate: 47 men, 78 women	Student/Faculty: 15 to 1
Year: semesters, summer session	Tuition: $11,646 ($21,974)
Room & Board: $10,314	Freshman Class: 7366 applied, 4116 accepted, 1228 enrolled
SAT CR/M: 570/570 ACT: 25	CEEB CODE: 5128
Application Deadline: February 1	VERY COMPETITIVE

Christopher Newport University, is a public school offering a private school experience great teaching, small classes and a safe, vibrant campus. A "student-first, teaching-first" community, CNU is dedicated to the ideals of scholarship, leadership and service. We celebrate the values inherent in the liberal arts and sciences and live as a community of honor transforming hearts and minds. We offer outstanding academics; promote service, honor and leadership; and provide rich opportunities for undergraduate research a rare occurrence at many schools. Superb teaching, personal attention and faculty-student mentorship allow creativity and excellence to flourish. CNU students develop the qualities of mind and spirit to lead lives of significance, thanks to a curriculum that stimulates intellectual inquiry and fosters civic responsibility. Through the four-year Honors Program, academically talented students enjoy a rich educational experience, participating in challenging courses and cultural/intellectual activities. Additional signature programs prepare students for career success. Through the Pre-Med and Pre-Health Program, qualified students may apply for early acceptance to Eastern Virginia Medical School (EVMS). Students successful in this competitive process receive, before the end of their sophomore year, guaranteed admission to EVMS after graduating from CNU (without having to take the MCAT). The Master of Arts in Teaching allows students to earn a graduate degree with just one additional year of study beyond the bachelor's degree. Courses are based on an academic interest, satisfy graduation requirements and smooth the transition into college by connecting like-minded students. All freshmen are assigned a core faculty advisor who mentors them for two years, provides academic support, helps with course selection, and introduces campus resources and engagement opportunities. The University promotes study abroad for all students, sponsoring international study programs for cross-cultural education and growth. This includes a permanent relationship with the University of Oxford and dozens of smaller, faculty-led programs. There are 3 undergraduate schools and 1 graduate school. In addition to regional accreditation, CNU has baccalaureate program accreditation with AACSB, ABET, CSWE, NASM, and NAST. The 260-acre campus is in a suburban area in the heart of Newport News, Virginia. Three hours south of Washington, D.C. Including any residence halls, there are 42 buildings.

STUDENT LIFE: 93% of undergraduates are from Virginia. Others are from 30 states, 32 foreign countries, and Canada. 75% are White. The average age of freshmen is 18; all undergraduates, 20. 13% do not continue beyond their first year; 68% remain to graduate. **Housing:** 3718 students can be accommodated in college housing, which includes coed dorms and on-campus apartments. In addition, there are fraternity houses, sorority houses, learning communities. On-campus housing is available on a lottery system for upperclassmen. 74% of students live on campus; of those, 75% remain on campus on weekends. Alcohol is not permitted. All students may keep cars.

FACULTY/CLASSROOMS: 54% of faculty are male; 46% are female. All teach undergraduates. No introductory courses are taught by graduate students.

PROGRAMS OF STUDY: CNU confers B.A., B.S., B.M., B.S.B.A. and B.S.I.S. degrees. Master's degrees are also awarded. Bachelor's degrees are awarded in AGRICULTURE (environmental studies), BIOLOGICAL SCIENCE (biochemistry, biology/biological science, environmental biology, and neurosciences), BUSINESS (accounting, business administration and management, finance, and marketing), COM-MUNICATIONS AND THE ARTS (classical languages, communications, English, fine arts, French, German, music, romance languages and literature, Spanish, and theatre arts), COMPUTER AND PHYSICAL SCIENCE (applied mathematics, applied physics, chemistry, computer science, information sciences and systems, and mathematics), ENGINEERING AND ENVIRONMENTAL DESIGN (computer engineering and electrical and computer engineering), HEALTH PROFESSIONS (predentistry, premedicine, preoptometry, prepharmacy, prephysical therapy, and preveterinary science), SOCIAL SCIENCE (American studies, economics, history, interdisciplinary studies, philosophy, political science/government, prelaw, psychology, social work, and sociology). Psychology, biology, and communications have the largest enrollments.

ACTIVITIES: 21% of men belong to 10 national fraternities; 26% of women belong to 8 national sororities. There are 225 groups on campus, including art, band, cheerleading, chess, choir, chorale, chorus, communications, computers, dance, drama, environmental, ethnic, film, gay, honors, international, jazz band, literary magazine, marching band, musical theater, newspaper, opera, orchestra, pep band, political, professional, radio and TV, religious, social, social service, student government, and symphony. Popular campus events include Campus Tie Dye, Candelight Ceremony, Captain's Ball, Club Fair, Day of Service, FallFest, Family Weekend, Ferguson Center for the Arts Concerts Performances, Food 4 Thought, Glow in the Dar-Capella, and Spectrum Drag Ball. **Sports:** There are 12 intercollegiate sports for men and 12 for women, and 7 intramural sports for men and 7 for women. Facilities include 200-meter indoor track, 5 basketball courts, a 13,500 square foot fitness pavilion with state of the art fitness equipment, football stadium which includes a 400-meter track, 6 outdoor tennis courts, individual state of the art fields for soccer, field hockey, baseball and softball. **Graduates:** From July 1, 2013 to June 30, 2014, 1060 bachelor's degrees were awarded. The most popular majors were psychology (13%), communications (12%), and political science (7%). 743 companies recruited on campus in 2013-2014. In an average class, 2% graduate in 3 years or less, 63% graduate in 4 years or less, 69% graduate in 5 years or less, and 68% graduate in 6 years or less.

SERVICES: Counseling and information services are available, as is tutoring in most subjects. **Library/Resources:** The library contains 244,487 volumes, 199,387 microform items, 10,248 audio/video tapes/CDs/DVDs, and subscribes to 59,906 periodicals including electronic. Computerized library services include interlibrary loans, database searching, Internet access, and Wi-Fi capability. Special learning facilities include an art gallery, radio station, TV station, Ferguson Center for the Arts, and the Mariner's Museum Library at Christopher Newport University. **Physically Challenged Students:** 96% of the campus is accessible. Facilities include wheelchair ramps, elevators, special parking, specially equipped restrooms, special class scheduling, lowered drinking fountains, and special housing. **Special:** CNU offers cross-registration, dual majors, a student-designed interdisciplinary studies major, internships, and study abroad. Special course offerings: Honors Program, the President's Leadership Program and Freshman Learning Communities. There are 15 national honor societies and a freshman honors program. **Visiting:** There are regularly scheduled orientations for prospective students, Information sessions and walking campus tours are available Monday through Friday at 10 a.m. & 2 p.m.; Saturday information session and tour at 11 a.m. Special on and off campus events and receptions as scheduled annually. Visitors may sit in on classes and stay overnight. To schedule a visit, contact the Admission Office. **Campus Safety and Security:** Measures include 24-hour foot and vehicle patrol, emergency notification system, self-defense education, and security escort services. There are emergency telephones, lighted pathways/sidewalks, controlled access to dorms/residences, campus police department, and a full time communication center for emergency radio and telephone communications.

REQUIREMENTS: CNU requires Virginia's Advanced Studies Diploma (ASD) or similar college preparatory diploma from an accredited high school with a satisfactory score on the SAT verbal and math or ACT composite. The GED is not accepted in lieu of a final high school transcript for freshman admission, as GED recipients do not meet ASD requirements. A total of 24 academic credits are recommended, including 4 units of English, 4 each of social science, math, and science and either 3 units of 1 foreign language (preferred) or 2 years of 2 foreign languages. An essay and a personal statement are required. SAT or ACT scores are not required for students with a 3.5 or higher high school GPA in a rigorous curriculum that includes college level work. Letters of recommendation and interviews are strongly recommended but not required. AP and CLEP credits are accepted. Important factors in the admissions decision are recommendations by school officials, extracurricular activities record, and evidence of special talent. To graduate, all students must fulfill the liberal learning core, including mathematics, second language literacy, written communication (with minimum grades of C- or better), logical reasoning, economic modeling and analysis, civic and democratic engagement, global and multicultural perspectives, creative expressions, science lecture with laboratory, western traditions, two writing intensive designated courses, with a minimum of 120 semester hours and with 45 credits in residence, and 30 of the last 36 credit hours, including last 12 credit hours within the major in residence. In addition, students must complete all requirements specific to the major, and present an overall and an 'in-major' GPA of at least 2.0, and required enrollment of at least one CNU course during the semester of the degree conferral. **Procedure:** Freshmen are admitted fall and spring. Entrance exams should be taken before the senior year. There are early decision, early admissions, and deferred admissions plans. Early decision applications should be filed by November 15; regular applications, by February 1 for fall entry; and October 1 for spring entry. The fall 2014 application fee was $50. Notification of early decision is sent December 15; regular decision, March 15. 366 early decision candidates were accepted for the 2014-2015 class. 513 applicants were on the 2014 waiting list; 66 were admitted. Applications are accepted on-line. **Transfer Students:** 167 transfer students enrolled in 2013-2014. Applicants must present a minimum 3.0 GPA, and be academically eligible to return to the most recently attended college or university. All transfer applicants must submit official college and high school transcripts. SAT or ACT scores are required if high school graduation is within the last five years. In addition, transfer applicants must submit the Transfer College Report certified from each college or university attended. 45 of 120 credits required for the bachelor's degree must be completed at CNU. **International Students:** There are 11 international students enrolled. The school actively recruits these students. They must take the TOEFL with a minimum score of 530 on the paper-based TOEFL (PBT) or 71 on the Internet-based version (iBT), or take the IELTS, or the iTep. They must also take the SAT or ACT.

ADMISSIONS: 56% of the 2014-2015 applicants were accepted. The SAT scores for the 2014-2015 freshman class were: Critical Reading--10% below 500, 51% between 500 and 599, 33% between 600 and 699, and 6% between 700 and 800; Math--10% below 500, 54% between 500 and 599, 32% between 600 and 699, and 4% between 700 and 800. The ACT scores were 8% below 21, 27% between 21 and 23, 33% between 24 and 26, 17% between 27 and 28, and 15% above 28. 44% of the current freshmen were in the top fifth of their class; 79% were in the top two fifths. 8 freshmen graduated first in their class. **Admissions Contact:** Rob Lange, Dean of Admissions. E-Mail: admit@cnu.edu Web: www.cnu.edu

FINANCIAL AID: In 2014-2015, 74% of all full-time freshmen and 65% of continuing full-time students received some form of financial aid. 41% of all full-time freshmen and 40% of continuing full-time students received need-based aid. The average freshman award was $11,801. Need-based scholarships or need-based grants averaged $6,069 ($6,930 maximum); need-based self-help aid (loans and jobs) averaged $3,417 ($5,500 maximum); and other non-need-based awards and non-need-based scholarships averaged $8,094 ($29,000 maximum). 27% of undergraduate students work part-time. Average annual earnings from campus work are $2133. The average financial indebtedness of the 2014 graduate was $23,118. The FAFSA is required. The priority date for freshman financial aid applications for fall entry is March 1. The deadline for filing freshman financial aid applications for fall entry is June 30.

COLLEGE OF WILLIAM & MARY   E-3
www.wm.edu

Williamsburg, VA 23187

(757) 221-4000
(757) 221-4223

Fax: (757) 221-1242
Full-time: 2712 men, 3502 women
Part-time: 44 men, 41 women
Graduate: 982 men, 1156 women
Year: semesters, summer session
Room & Board: $10,344

Email: admission@wm.edu
Faculty: I, av$
Ph.D.s: n/av
Student/Faculty: n/av
Tuition: $17,656 ($39,916)
Freshman Class: n/av
CEEB CODE: 5115

Application Deadline: January 1   **MOST COMPETITIVE**

College of William & Mary, founded by Royal Charter in 1693, is the second-oldest college in the country. It has a long history of liberal arts education and a growing research and science curriculum that demonstrates a strong commitment to undergraduate research. The figures in the above capsule and in this profile are approximate. There are 3 undergraduate schools and 5 graduate schools. In addition to regional accreditation, William & Mary has baccalaureate program accreditation with AACSB and NCATE. The 1200-acre campus is in a small town 50 miles southeast of Richmond. Including any residence halls, there are 183 buildings.

STUDENT LIFE: 66% of undergraduates are from Virginia. Others are from 56 states, 60 foreign countries, and Canada. 59% are White. The average age of freshmen is 18; all undergraduates, 20. 5% do not continue beyond their first year; 90% remain to graduate. **Housing:** 5000 students can be accommodated in college housing, which includes single-sex and coed dorms and on-campus apartments. In addition, there are honors houses, language houses, special-interest houses, fraternity houses, sorority houses, An international studies hall; smoke-free and multicultural housing; and Africana, community scholars, and Eco house. On-campus housing is guaranteed for the freshman year only and is available on a lottery system for upperclassmen. 74% of students live on campus; of those, 80% remain on campus on weekends. Upperclassmen may keep cars.

FACULTY/CLASSROOMS: No introductory courses are taught by graduate students.

PROGRAMS OF STUDY: William & Mary confers B.A., B.S. and B.B.A. degrees. Master's and Doctoral degrees are also awarded. Bachelor's degrees are awarded in BIOLOGICAL SCIENCE (neurosciences), BUSINESS (accounting, banking and finance, business administration and management, entrepreneurial studies, and marketing management), COMMUNICATIONS AND THE ARTS (art history, art, Chinese, English, French, German, linguistics, music, and theatre arts), COMPUTER AND PHYSICAL SCIENCE (chemistry, computer science, geology, mathematics, and physics), HEALTH PROFESSIONS (biology and health science), SOCIAL SCIENCE (Africana studies, American studies, anthropology, classical/ancient civilization, economics, gender studies, history, interdisciplinary studies, international relations, Latin American studies, medieval studies, philosophy, political science/government, psychology, public affairs, religion, sociology, Spanish studies, and women's studies). Biology, government, and economics have the larges enrollments.

ACTIVITIES: 27% of men belong to 20 national fraternities; 32% of women belong to 12 national sororities. There are 380 groups on campus, including art, band, cheerleading, chess, choir, chorale, chorus, computers, dance, debate, drama, drill team, environmental, ethnic, film, gay, honors, international, jazz band, literary magazine, musical theater, newspaper, opera, orchestra, pep band, photography, political, professional, radio and TV, religious, social, social service, student government, symphony, and yearbook. Popular campus events include Yule Log Ceremony, Raft Debate and Senior Walk Across Campus (Commencement). **Sports:** There are 10 intercollegiate sports for men and 11 for women, and 28 intramural sports for men and 26 for women. Facilities include football stadium, football center, basketball arena, lighted baseball facility, natural grass field for lacrosse and soccer, tennis center with six indoor tennis courts, hockey field, gymnasium with a 25 yard, 6-lane pool, a basketball court, and two volleyball courts, strength training center, recreation center with a 25 yard, a fitness room, two weight rooms, five racquetball courts, two squash courts, and a host of other amenities. **Graduates:** From July 1, 2013 to June 30, 2014, 1517 bachelor's degrees were awarded. The most popular majors were business administration (13%), government (9%), and psychology (8%). 171 companies recruited on campus in 2013-2014. In an average class, 90% graduate in 6 years or less. Of the 2013 graduating class, 56% were enrolled in graduate school within 6 months of graduation, and 29% were employed.

SERVICES: Counseling and information services are available, as is tutoring in most subjects. There is a reader service for the blind. **Library/Resources:** The 5 libraries contain 2.2 million volumes, 2.5 million microform items, 41,029 audio/video tapes/CDs/DVDs, and subscribe to 170,658 periodicals including electronic. Computerized library services include interlibrary loans, database searching, Internet access, and Wi-Fi capability. Special learning facilities include an art gallery, radio station, an anthropology museum, an art studio, a greenhouse, the center for Archaeological Research, and the Omohundro Institute of Early American History and Culture. **Physically Challenged Students:** 95% of the campus is accessible. Facilities include wheelchair ramps, elevators, special parking, specially equipped restrooms, special class scheduling, lowered drinking fountains. Modified recreational facilities, braille signage, Kurzweil reader, and a special learning lab for the visually impaired. Individual accommodations are made on a case-by-case basis. **Special:** William and Mary has various special academic programs available to students: Study abroad in 23 countries over the world; Work-study programs with various employer including campus departments and off-campus community agencies; Washington Program which is open to students in all majors and disciplines; Accelerated degree program in Computer Science and Public Policy with an option whereby a small number of current W&M undergraduates will be able to earn both a Bachelor's degree and a Master degree in a total of five years of coursework; Student Self-designed majors in Interdisciplinary Studies; Combined Degree Programs with engineering schools of Columbia University; Joint degree program with University of St Andrews in Scotland; The Department Honors programs administered by the Roy R. Charles Center; Internships for credit; and Dual major in all majors. There are 29 national honor societies, including Phi Beta Kappa, a freshman honors program, and 27 departmental honors programs. **Visiting:** There are regularly scheduled orientations for prospective students, group information session followed by a student-led tour. There are guides for informal visits and visitors may sit in on classes. To schedule a visit, contact the Office of Admissions at admission@wm.edu. **Campus Safety and Security:** Measures include 24-hour foot and vehicle patrol, emergency notification system, self-defense education, and security escort services. There are shuttle buses, emergency telephones, lighted pathways/sidewalks, controlled access to dorms/residences, crime prevention programs.

REQUIREMENTS: The SAT or ACT is required. The Common Application, William & Mary Supplement to the Common Application, Secondary School Report form complete with a high school transcript and counselor letter of recommendation, Midyear School Report form, and official report of standardized test scores, application fee, or a fee waiver request. AP and CLEP credits are accepted. Important factors in the admissions decision are advanced placement or honors courses, extracurricular activities record, and leadership record. To graduate, students must demonstrate proficiencies in foreign language, writing, and computing. Freshman seminars are required. Students must complete 120 credit hours, with 33 to 48 in the major, a minimum 2.0 GPA, and a minimum of 60 credit hours in residence at the College. Distribution requirements include courses in math and quantitative reasoning, natural sciences, social sciences, world cultures and history, literature and history of the arts, and philosophical, religious, and social thought. **Procedure:** Freshmen are admitted fall. Entrance exams should be taken in spring of the junior year or fall of the senior year. There are early decision and deferred admissions plans. Early decision applications should be filed by November 1; regular applications, by January 1 for fall entry; and November 1 for spring entry. The fall 2014 application fee was $70. Notification of early decision is sent December 1; regular decision, April 1. 603 early decision candidates were accepted for the 2014-2015 class. 3603 applicants were on the 2014 waiting list; 1526 were admitted. Applications are accepted on-line. **Transfer Students:** 185

transfer students enrolled in 2013-2014. William & Mary recommends that students interested in transferring to the College take challenging courses in the liberal arts and sciences. Typically, competitive transfer applicants have a GPA of 3.5 or higher at their current institution. Additional application requirements include: official transcripts from all colleges and universities attended, and official high school transcript or copy of GED certificate. If you have completed less than a full year of college coursework when you apply, you must submit SAT or ACT scores. If you have been out of high school for more than five years, SAT or ACT scores are not required. Test scores listed on the high school transcript will be accepted. Midterm grades are due November 22 for students applying for Spring and March 28 for students applying for the Fall. Student must use the Midterm Report form to submit current grades. 60 of 120 credits required for the bachelor's degree must be completed at William & Mary. **International Students:** There are 343 international students enrolled. The school actively recruits these students. They must take the TOEFL with a minimum score of 600 on the paper-based TOEFL (PBT) or 100 on the Internet-based version (iBT), or take the IELTS. They must also take the SAT or ACT. SAT II: Subject tests are considered if they are submitted.

ADMISSIONS: 94% of the current freshmen were in the top fifth of their class; 99% were in the top two fifths. **Admissions Contact:** Deborah Basket, Associate Dean. E-Mail: *admission@wm.edu* Web: *www.wm.edu/admission*

FINANCIAL AID: The FAFSA and the college's own financial statement, and the CSS Profile is required for early decision enrollees. are required. The priority date for freshman financial aid applications for fall entry is March 1. The deadline for filing freshman financial aid applications for fall entry is March 1.

EASTERN MENNONITE UNIVERSITY   D-2
www.emu.edu

Harrisonburg, VA 22802	(540) 432-4000
	(800) 368-2665
Fax: (540) 432-4444	Email: admiss@emu.edu
Full-time: n/av	Faculty: 89; IIA
Part-time: 15 men, 15 women	Ph.D.s: 78%
Graduate: 81 men, 265 women	Student/Faculty: 10 to 1
Year: semesters, summer session	Tuition: $30,800
Room & Board: $9860	Freshman Class: 1723 applied, 1053 accepted, 243 enrolled
SAT CR/M: 502/498 ACT: 23	CEEB CODE: 5181
Application Deadline: open	COMPETITIVE

Eastern Mennonite University, founded in 1917, is a private Christian liberal arts university affiliated with the Mennonite Church. The university offers programs in the arts and sciences, education, biology, and nursing. EMU also offers master's degrees in several areas. EMU's Lancaster site provides some programs in Lancaster, Pennsylvania. There are 7 graduate schools. In addition to regional accreditation, EMU has baccalaureate program accreditation with ACPE, CSWE, NCATE, and NLN. The 97-acre campus is in a small town Harrisonburg, VA., 110 miles southwest of Washington, D.C. Including any residence halls, there are 44 buildings.

STUDENT LIFE: 57% of undergraduates are from out of state, mostly the Middle Atlantic. Students are from 32 states, 19 foreign countries, and Canada. 58% are from public schools. 76% are White. 91% are Protestant. The average age of freshmen is 18; all undergraduates, 21. 23% do not continue beyond their first year; 62% remain to graduate. **Housing:** 683 students can be accommodated in college housing, which includes single-sex and coed dorms, on-campus apartments, off-campus apartments, and married student housing, and an intentional community. On-campus housing is guaranteed for all 4 years. 57% of students live on campus; of those, 75% remain on campus on weekends. Alcohol is not permitted. All students may keep cars.

FACULTY/CLASSROOMS: 58% of faculty are male; 42% are female. 75% teach undergraduates, 38% do research, and 35% do both. No introductory courses are taught by graduate students. The average class size in an introductory lecture is 40; in a laboratory is 17; and in a regular course is 18.

PROGRAMS OF STUDY: EMU confers B.A., and B.S. degrees. Associate and Master's degrees are also awarded. Bachelor's degrees are awarded in AGRICULTURE (international agriculture), BIOLOGICAL SCIENCE (biochemistry and biology/biological science), BUSINESS (accounting, business administration and management, international business management, and recreational facilities management), COMMUNICATIONS AND THE ARTS (art, communications, dramatic arts, English, French, German, music, and Spanish), COMPUTER AND PHYSICAL SCIENCE (chemistry, computer management, computer science, and mathematics), EDUCATION (early childhood education, elementary education, physical education, secondary education, and special education), ENGINEERING AND ENVIRONMENTAL DESIGN (environmental science), HEALTH PROFESSIONS (medical laboratory technology and nursing), SOCIAL SCIENCE (biblical studies, development economics, economics, history, liberal arts/general studies, ministries, peace studies, philosophy, psychology, religion, social science, social work, sociology, and theological studies). Biology/pre-med, education, and nursing are the strongest academically. Business, education, and nursing have the largest enrollments.

ACTIVITIES: There are 51 groups on campus, including art, chess, choir, chorale, chorus, computers, dance, drama, environmental, ethnic, film, honors, international, jazz band, literary magazine, musical theater, newspaper, orchestra, pep band, photography, political, professional, radio and TV, religious, social, social service, student government, student women's association and peace fellowship, and yearbook. Popular campus events include Spring Fling, Fall Festival, and Multicultural Week. **Sports:** There are 7 intercollegiate sports for men and 8 for women, and 15 intramural sports for men and 15 for women. Facilities include a fitness center, aerobics room, indoor track, and climbing wall. The gym includes 1 regular varsity court and 2 courts for team practice. Outside facilities include a lighted artificial turf playing field, lighted tennis courts, baseball, softball, and soccer fields, a rubberized outdoor track, as well as basketball and sand volleyball courts. **Graduates:** From July 1, 2013 to June 30, 2014, 315 bachelor's degrees were awarded. The most popular majors were business (30%), nursing (16%), and education (9%). 15 companies recruited on campus in 2013-2014. In an average class, 45% graduate in 4 years or less, 59% graduate in 5 years or less, and 62% graduate in 6 years or less. Of the 2013 graduating class, 8% were enrolled in graduate school within 6 months of graduation, and 90% were employed.

SERVICES: Counseling and information services are available, as is tutoring in most subjects. There is a reader service for the blind, and remedial reading and writing. EMU owns technology, such as the ability to burn textbooks onto CD's, for visually impaired students and those with other special learning needs. Technology for the hearing impaired will be provided as needed. **Library/Resources:** The library contains 167,242 volumes, 92,096 microform items, 3,723 audio/video tapes/CDs/DVDs, and subscribes to 1,056 periodicals including electronic. Computerized library services include interlibrary loans, database searching, Internet access, and Wi-Fi capability. Special learning facilities include an art gallery, natural history museum, planetarium, radio station, an arboretum and greenhouse, nursing laboratory, and a cadaver laboratory. **Physically Challenged Students:** 75% of the campus is accessible. Facilities include wheelchair ramps, elevators, special parking, specially equipped restrooms, special class scheduling, lowered drinking fountains, special housing. Some buildings on campus have accessible telephones. **Special:** EMU offers study-abroad programs each semester and during the summer at a variety of locations around the world. Students may also choose to study 1 or 2 semesters in Washington, D.C. There are internships in a variety of majors, dual majors, a student-designed major, and a 2 year general studies degree. There are 1 national honor society and a freshman honors program. **Visiting:** There are regularly scheduled orientations for prospective students, including an address by the president, a financial aid seminar, a review of general education, and attendance at a chapel; the opportunity to sit in on classes, meet with professors and admissions representatives, sleep in residence halls, and eat in the cafeteria; and attendance at special campus events.

There are guides for informal visits. To schedule a visit, contact the Admissions Office. **Campus Safety and Security:** Measures include self-defense education and security escort services. There are emergency telephones, lighted pathways/sidewalks. There is a 12-hour foot or vehicle watchman.

REQUIREMENTS: The SAT or ACT is required. Applicants must be graduates of an accredited secondary school or have a GED certificate. The university recommends that students have completed 4 credits of English, 3 each of math, science, and social studies, 2 or more of foreign language and chemistry for nursing majors. A personal reference is required and an interview is recommended. A GPA of 2.6 is required. AP and CLEP credits are accepted. Important factors in the admissions decision are leadership record, extracurricular activities record, and recommendations by school officials.To graduate, students must complete interdisciplinary core courses, courses in Bible and religion, cross-cultural study, writing, speech, and math, a major (minors are optional), and a variety of electives for a minimum of 128 semester hours. A minimum cumulative GPA of 2.0 is required while some majors require a higher GPA in the major or overall. **Procedure:** Freshmen are admitted fall and spring. Entrance exams should be taken in the spring of the junior year or the fall of the senior year. There are deferred admissions and rolling admissions plans. Application deadlines are open. The fall 2014 application fee was $25. Applications are accepted on-line. **Transfer Students:** 77 transfer students enrolled in 2013-2014. Transfer students must have a minimum college GPA of 2.0. 32 of 128 credits required for the bachelor's degree must be completed at EMU. **International Students:** There are 86 international students enrolled. The school actively recruits these students. They must take the TOEFL. They must also take the SAT or ACT, scoring 920.

ADMISSIONS: 61% of the 2014-2015 applicants were accepted. The ACT scores were 17% below 21, 21% between 21 and 23, 30% between 24 and 26, 9% between 27 and 28, and 23% above 28. 36% of the current freshmen were in the top fifth of their class; 65% were in the top two fifths. 7 freshmen graduated first in their class. **Admissions Contact:** Bonnie Lofton E-Mail: *admiss@emu.edu* Web: *www.emu.edu*

FINANCIAL AID: In 2014-2015, 97% of all full-time freshmen and 96% of continuing full-time students received some form of financial aid. 89% of all full-time freshmen and 87% of continuing full-time students received need-based aid. The average freshman award was $25,000. 35% of undergraduate students work part-time. Average annual earnings from campus work are $1500. The average financial indebtedness of the 2014 graduate was $18,208. EMU is a member of CSS. The FAFSA and the state aid form are required. The deadline for filing freshman financial aid applications for fall entry is April 15.

EMORY AND HENRY COLLEGE   B-4
www.ehc.edu

Emory, VA 24327   (276) 944-4121
                                             (276) 944-6133
Fax: (276) 944-6935   Email: ehadmiss@ehc.edu
Full-time: 464 men, 410 women   Faculty: 72; IIB, --$
Part-time: 12 men, 11 women   Ph.Ds: n/av
Graduate: 14 men, 34 women   Student/Faculty: 10 to 1
Year: semesters, summer session   Tuition: $28,966
Room & Board: $9780   Freshman Class: n/av
SAT or ACT: required   CEEB CODE: 5185
Application Deadline: April 15   COMPETITIVE

Emory and Henry College, founded in 1836, is a private liberal arts institution affiliated with the United Methodist Church. The 331-acre campus is in a rural area in Emory, southwest Virginia.

STUDENT LIFE: 64% of undergraduates are from Virginia. Others are from 26 states, 5 foreign countries, and Canada. 99% are from public schools. 80% are White. The average age of freshmen is 18; all undergraduates, 20.

FACULTY/CLASSROOMS: 59% of faculty are male; 41% are female. All teach undergraduates. No introductory courses are taught by graduate students. The average class size in an introductory lecture is 25; in a laboratory is 13; and in a regular course is 22.

PROGRAMS OF STUDY: E and H confers B.A., and B.S. degrees. Master's degrees are also awarded. Bachelor's degrees are awarded in BIOLOGICAL SCIENCE (biology/biological science), BUSINESS (business administration and management), COMMUNICATIONS AND THE ARTS (art, communications, creative writing, dramatic arts, English literature, journalism, literature, modern language, music performance, and music theory and composition), COMPUTER AND PHYSICAL SCIENCE (chemistry, computer management, computer science, mathematics, and physics), EDUCATION (English education, mathematics education, and physical education), ENGINEERING AND ENVIRONMENTAL DESIGN (environmental science), SOCIAL SCIENCE (community services, East Asian studies, economics, European studies, geography, history, interdisciplinary studies, international studies, Middle Eastern studies, philosophy, political science/government, psychology, public affairs, religion, and sociology).

ACTIVITIES: 15% of men belong to 9 local fraternities; 30% of women belong to 6 local sororities. There are 50 groups on campus, including art, band, cheerleading, choir, chorus, dance, debate, drama, ethnic, gay, international, literary magazine, musical theater, newspaper, opera, pep band, photography, political, professional, radio and TV, religious, social, social service, student government, and yearbook. Popular campus events include Homecoming, Founder's Day, Martin Luther King Junior Day, Fall Formals, Parents Day, Greek Air Band, and the Literary Festival.

SERVICES: Counseling and information services are available, as is tutoring in most subjects. There is a reader service for the blind, and remedial math and writing. **Library/Resources:** The library contains 271,209 volumes, 207,000 microform items, 7,950 audio/video tapes/CDs/DVDs, and subscribes to 352 periodicals including electronic. Computerized library services include interlibrary loans, database searching, and Internet access. Special learning facilities include an art gallery, radio station, and TV station. **Physically Challenged Students:** 50% of the campus is accessible. Facilities include wheelchair ramps, elevators, special parking, specially equipped restrooms, special class scheduling, lowered drinking fountains, and special housing. **Special:** A cooperative program in medical technology and 2-2, 4-1, and 3-2 engineering degrees are available. Dual and student-designed majors, an interdisciplinary English major, combined B.A.-B.S. degrees, internships, a Washington Semester, work-study, nondegree study, and pass/fail options are also available. There are 10 national honor societies and 8 departmental honors programs. **Visiting:** There are regularly scheduled orientations for prospective students, including a program for students to meet faculty and staff and to attend education sessions on college life. There are guides for informal visits, visitors may sit in on classes, and stay overnight. To schedule a visit, contact the Admissions Office. **Campus Safety and Security:** Measures include 24-hour foot and vehicle patrol, self-defense education, and security escort services. There are lighted pathways/sidewalks.

REQUIREMENTS: The SAT or ACT is required. Applicants should be high school graduates. High school courses required include 4 years of English, 3 or more units of math including algebra I, algebra II, and geometry, 2 or more units of lab science, 2 units of a single foreign language, and 2 or more units of social studies and history. One additional unit in fine arts is strongly recommended. A personal essay is required. AP credits are accepted. Important factors in the admissions decision are advanced placement or honors courses, recommendations by school officials, and evidence of special talent.

FINANCIAL AID: The FAFSA, the state aid form, and the college's own financial statement are required. The priority date for freshman financial aid applications for fall entry is April 1. The deadline for filing freshman financial aid applications for fall entry is August 1.

FERRUM COLLEGE *(The complete profile is made available exclusively on our website, www.barronspac.com)*

GEORGE MASON UNIVERSITY   E-2
www.gmu.edu

Fairfax, VA 22030

(703) 993-1000
(703) 993-2400

Fax: (703) 993-4622
Full-time: 7147 men, 8042 women
Part-time: 2203 men, 2310 women
Graduate: 5117 men, 7248 women
Year: semesters, summer session
Room & Board: $7700

Email: admissions@gmu.edu
Faculty: 1041; I, -$
Ph.D.s: 90%
Student/Faculty: 15 to 1
Tuition: $8024 ($24,008)
Freshman Class: 13732 applied, 8691 accepted, 2656 enrolled

SAT CR/M: 560/570 ACT: 25
Application Deadline: January 15

CEEB CODE: 5827
VERY COMPETITIVE

George Mason University, founded in 1972, is an entrepreneurial public institution with national distinction in a range of academic fields. The university has undergraduate and graduate degree programs in engineering, information technology, biotechnology, and health care. The figures in the above capsule and in this profile are approximate. There are 8 undergraduate schools and 11 graduate schools. In addition to regional accreditation, Mason has baccalaureate program accreditation with AACSB, ABET, CSAB, CSWE, NASM, NCATE, ACS, CAAHEP, and CCNE. The 806-acre campus is in a suburban area in the Greater Washington Metropolitan area, 21 miles southwest of Washington, D.C. Including any residence halls, there are 115 buildings.

STUDENT LIFE: 88% of undergraduates are from Virginia. Others are from 50 states, 131 foreign countries, and Canada. 86% are from public schools. 59% are White; 16% Asian American. The average age of freshmen is 18; all undergraduates, 23. 15% do not continue beyond their first year; 69% remain to graduate. **Housing:** 5057 students can be accommodated in college housing, which includes single-sex and coed dorms, on-campus apartments, and off-campus apartments. In addition, there are honors houses and special-interest houses. On-campus housing is guaranteed for all 4 years, is available on a first-come, and first-served basis. 74% of students commute. All students may keep cars.

FACULTY/CLASSROOMS: 55% of faculty are male; 45% are female. 84% teach undergraduates. Graduate students teach 12% of introductory courses. The average class size in an introductory lecture is 43; in a laboratory is 23; and in a regular course is 25.

PROGRAMS OF STUDY: Mason confers B.A., B.S., B.F.A., B.I.S., B.S.E.D. and B.S.N. degrees. Master's and Doctoral degrees are also awarded. Bachelor's degrees are awarded in AGRICULTURE (environmental studies), BIOLOGICAL SCIENCE (biology/biological science and neurosciences), BUSINESS (accounting, banking and finance, business administration and management, marketing/retailing/merchandising, operations management, and tourism), COMMUNICATIONS AND THE ARTS (art history and appreciation, communications, communications technology, dance, dramatic arts, English, film arts, French, music, Spanish, video, and visual and performing arts), COMPUTER AND PHYSICAL SCIENCE (astronomy, chemistry, computer science, earth science, geology, information sciences and systems, mathematics, physics, science and management, and software engineering), EDUCATION (athletic training and physical education), ENGINEERING AND ENVIRONMENTAL DESIGN (civil engineering, computational sciences, computer engineering, electrical/electronics engineering, industrial engineering, and systems engineering), HEALTH PROFESSIONS (community health work, health science, medical technology, and nursing), SOCIAL SCIENCE (anthropology, criminal justice, economics, geography, history, interdisciplinary studies, international relations, Latin American studies, parks and recreation management, philosophy, political science/government, psychology, public administration, religion, Russian and Slavic studies, social work, and sociology). Accounting, biology, and psychology have the largest enrollments.

ACTIVITIES: 7% of men belong to 23 national fraternities; 6% of women belong to 15 national sororities. There are 255 groups on campus, including art, band, cheerleading, chess, choir, chorale, chorus, computers, dance, drama, environmental, ethnic, film, forensics, gay, honors, international, jazz band, literary magazine, musical theater, newspaper, opera, orchestra, pep band, photography, political, professional, radio and TV, religious, social, social service, student government, symphony, and yearbook. Popular campus events include Welcome Week, Mason Day, and Patriot Day. **Sports:** There are 11 intercollegiate sports for men and 11 for women, and 11 intramural sports for men and 11 for women. Facilities include a 10,000-seat arena for basketball, indoor soccer, and concerts; a sports and recreation complex that includes a 200-meter track, basketball, handball/racquetball, tennis, and volleyball courts, baseball and softball diamonds, batting cages, a weight room, saunas, and a golf and archery net; a 400-meter outdoor track; and playing fields. The aquatic and fitness center offers a 2-story fitness area with 3000-sq-ft of cardio and 5000-sq-ft of weight training equipment, a recreational pool, an Olympic-size competition pool and diving well, a hot tub, and a dry sauna. **Graduates:** From July 1, 2013 to June 30, 2014, 4009 bachelor's degrees were awarded. The most popular majors were business/marketing (22%), social sciences (14%), and English (9%). 546 companies recruited on campus in 2013-2014. In an average class, 2% graduate in 3 years or less, 39% graduate in 4 years or less, 58% graduate in 5 years or less, and 63% graduate in 6 years or less.

SERVICES: Counseling and information services are available, as is tutoring in most subjects. There is a reader service for the blind. Additional tutoring is offered for a fee. **Library/Resources:** The 5 libraries contain 1.9 million volumes, 3.2 million microform items, 43,289 audio/video tapes/CDs/DVDs, and subscribe to 56,433 periodicals including electronic. Computerized library services include interlibrary loans, database searching, Internet access, and Wi-Fi capability. Special learning facilities include an art gallery, radio station, TV station, an astronomy observatory, and the Smithsonian Conservation and Research Center. **Physically Challenged Students:** 95% of the campus is accessible. Facilities include wheelchair ramps, elevators, special parking, specially equipped restrooms, special class scheduling, lowered drinking fountains, lowered telephones, special housing. Special arrangements can be made for testing, readers, note takers, and interpreters. **Special:** Mason offers internships through academic departments and on-campus work-study programs. Also available are dual and student-designed majors, accelerated degrees, non-degree study, and pass/fail options. New Century College is an integrated program of study that emphasizes collaboration, experimental learning, and self-reflection. Mason also offers the Smithsonian Semester, a 16-credit resident program in conservation studies at the Smithsonian Conservation and Research Center in Front Royal, Virginia. There are 4 national honor societies, a freshman honors program, and 1 departmental honors program. **Visiting:** There are regularly scheduled orientations for prospective students, including campus tours and an information session. There are guides for informal visits and visitors may sit in on classes. To schedule a visit, contact the Admissions Office. **Campus Safety and Security:** Measures include 24-hour foot and vehicle patrol, emergency notification system, self-defense education, and security escort services. There are shuttle buses, lighted pathways/sidewalks, controlled access to dorms/residences, and security call boxes located throughout the campus.

REQUIREMENTS: The ACT is recommended. A score-optional review of applications allows applicants to be considered for admission without submitting test scores. Applicants must be graduates of an accredited secondary school or have a GED certificate. A minimum high school GPA of 3.5 is recommended. A minimum of 18 academic credits is required, including 4 years of English, 3 each of math, science, lab science, social studies, and academic electives, and 2 of foreign language. An written personal statement is required. A GPA of 2.0 is required. AP and CLEP credits are accepted. Important factors in the admissions decision are advanced placement or honors courses, evidence of special talent, and recommendations by school officials. To graduate, all students must complete a core of study that includes 6 credits written communication, 3 to 4 credits information technology, 4 credits lab science, 3 credits each oral communication, quantitative reasoning, literature, arts, Western civilization/world history, social and behavioral science, natural science, and global understanding, and 1 to 6 credits synthesis as well as at least 45 hours of upper-division work. Hours in the major vary. A minimum 2.0 GPA is required and a total of 120 to 133 credit hours must be completed. **Procedure:** Freshmen are admitted fall, spring, and summer. Entrance exams should be taken during the spring of the junior year. There is a deferred admissions plan. Applications should be filed by January 15 for fall entry; October 15 for spring entry. The fall 2014 application fee was $75. Notifications are sent April 1. applicants were on the 2014 waiting list; were admitted. Applications are accepted online. **Transfer Students:** 2600 transfer students enrolled in 2013-2014. Applicants must have a minimum 2.0 GPA and generally have completed 30 or more transferable credits from an accredited college or university. Official transcripts (including high school if 30 credits or less have been completed) are required. SAT or ACT scores must be submitted if 30 credits or less have been completed unless applicant graduated from high school more than 5 years before application. 30 of 120 credits required for the bachelor's degree must be completed at Mason. **International Students:** There are 488 international students enrolled. The school actively recruits these students. They must take the TOEFL with a minimum score of 570 on the paper-based TOEFL (PBT) or 88 on the Internet-based version (iBT). They must also take the SAT or ACT.

ADMISSIONS: 63% of the 2014-2015 applicants were accepted. The SAT scores for the 2014-2015 freshman class were: Critical Reading--15% below 500, 52% between 500 and 599, 28% between 600 and 699, and 6% between 700 and 800; Math--12% below 500, 49% between 500 and 599, 34% between 600 and 699, and 5% between 700 and 800. The ACT scores were 4% below 21, 30% between 21 and 23, 37% between 24 and 26, 15% between 27 and 28, and 14% above 28. 44% of the current freshmen were in the top fifth of their class; 83% were in the top two fifths. **Admissions Contact:** Andrew Flagel, Dean of Undergraduate Admissions. E-Mail: *admissions@gmu.edu* Web: *www.gmu.edu*

FINANCIAL AID: In 2014-2015, 67% of all full-time freshmen and 61% of continuing full-time students received some form of financial aid. 43% of all full-time freshmen and 44% of continuing full-time students received need-based aid. The average freshman award was $12,012. Need-based scholarships or need-based grants averaged $7,182 ($24,800 maximum); need-based self-help aid (loans and jobs) averaged $3,660 ($8,500 maximum); non-need-based athletic scholarships averaged $16,156 ($36,533 maximum); and other non-need-based awards and non-need-based scholarships averaged $5,940 ($33,540 maximum). The average financial indebtedness of the 2014 graduate was $19,582. The FAFSA is required. The priority date for freshman financial aid applications for fall entry is March 1.

HAMPDEN-SYDNEY COLLEGE D-3

www.hsc.edu

Hampden-Sydney, VA 23943	(434) 223-6120
	(800) 755-0733
Fax: (434) 223-6346	Email: hsapp@hsc.edu
Full-time: 1069 men, 1 women	Faculty: 85; IIB, av$
Part-time: n/av	Ph.D.s: 84%
Graduate: n/av	Student/Faculty: 11 to 1
Year: semesters, summer session	Tuition: $39,604
Room & Board: $12,312	Freshman Class: 3639 applied, 1720 accepted, 322 enrolled
SAT CR/M/W: 554/555/513 ACT: 23	CEEB CODE: 5291
Application Deadline: March 1	COMPETITIVE

Hampden-Sydney College, founded in 1775, is a private men's liberal arts institution affiliated with the Presbyterian Church. There is one undergraduate school. The 1340-acre campus is in a rural area 60 miles southwest of Richmond. Including any residence halls, there are 118 buildings.

STUDENT LIFE: 70% of undergraduates are from Virginia. Others are from 32 states, 15 foreign countries, and Canada. 66% are from public schools. 82% are White. 56% are Protestant; 17% claim no religious affiliation; 16% Catholic. The average age of freshmen is 18; all undergraduates, 20. 20% do not continue beyond their first year; 68% remain to graduate. **Housing:** 1122 students can be accommodated in college housing, which includes single-sex dorms, on-campus apartments, off-campus apartments, and married student housing. In addition, there are honors houses, language houses, special-interest houses, fraternity houses, minority student house, and International student house. On-campus housing is guaranteed for all 4 years. 95% of students live on campus; of those, 60% remain on campus on weekends. All students may keep cars.

FACULTY/CLASSROOMS: 70% of faculty are male; 30% are female. All teach and do research. No introductory courses are taught by graduate students. The average class size in an introductory lecture is 13; in a laboratory is 13; and in a regular course is 14.

PROGRAMS OF STUDY: Hampden-Sydney confers B.A., and B.S. degrees. Bachelor's degrees are awarded in BIOLOGICAL SCIENCE (biology/biological science), BUSINESS (business economics), COMMUNICATIONS AND THE ARTS (classics, English, fine arts, French, German, Greek, Latin, and Spanish), COMPUTER AND PHYSICAL SCIENCE (applied mathematics, chemistry, computer science, mathematics, and physics), SOCIAL SCIENCE (economics, history, humanities, philosophy, political science/government, psychology, and religion). Sciences, economics, and rhetoric are the strongest academically. Economics, history, and biology have the largest enrollments.

ACTIVITIES: 30% of men belong to 8 national fraternities. There are no sororities. There are 83 groups on campus, including art, band, chess, choir, chorale, chorus, computers, debate, drama, environmental, ethnic, gay, honors, international, literary magazine, newspaper, pep band, photography, political, professional, radio and TV, religious, social, social service, student government, and yearbook. Popular campus events include Greek Week, Macon Week, and Midwinters CAC events. **Sports:** There are 9 intercollegiate sports for men, and 8 intramural sports for men. Facilities include a field house with 3 basketball courts, 5 racquetball/handball courts, an outdoor track, a pool, squash courts, weight room, gym, tennis courts, and many playing fields. Gammon gym is now Snyder Hall, and also includes an Athletic Hall of Fame. **Graduates:** From July 1, 2013 to June 30, 2014, 206 bachelor's degrees were awarded. The most popular majors were economics (30%), history (19%), and psychology (10%). 123 companies recruited on campus in 2013-2014. In an average class, 66% graduate in 4 years or less, 67% graduate in 5 years or less, and 68% graduate in 6 years or less. Of the 2013 graduating class, 20% were enrolled in graduate school within 6 months of graduation, and 42% were employed.

SERVICES: Counseling and information services are available, as is tutoring in every subject. **Library/Resources:** The library contains 269,245 volumes, 4,545 microform items, 7,064 audio/video tapes/CDs/DVDs, and subscribes to 140 periodicals including electronic. Computerized library services include interlibrary loans, database searching, Internet access, and Wi-Fi capability. Special learning facilities include an art gallery, planetarium, radio station, an international communications center, college history museum, and observatory, men's studies, and the Wilcon Center for Leadership. **Physically Challenged Students:** 80% of the campus is accessible. Facilities include wheelchair ramps, elevators, special parking, specially equipped restrooms, special class scheduling, and lowered telephones. **Special:** The college offers co-op programs with Longwood, Randolph-Macon, Randolph College, Hollins, and Mary Baldwin Colleges and Washington and Lee University. Cross-registration with Longwood College, internships, study abroad, a 3-2 engineering program with the University of Virginia, dual-degree program in Physics and Engineering from Hampden-Sydney College and Old Dominion University, Eastern Virginaia Medical School Joint program, The George Washington University School of Medicine Ealry Selection program, the VCU-MCV early slection program, Duke University Fuqua School of Business Early Admission program - Master of Management Studies, The UVA Darden School of Business preferred consideration program - Master of Business Administration, Washington semester, work-study programs, B.A.-B.S. degree, and dual majors are available. There is a public service concentration in all majors. There are 15 national honor societies, including Phi Beta Kappa, a freshman honors program, and 10 departmental honors programs. **Visiting:** There are regularly scheduled orientations for prospective students, consisting of lectures, information sessions, tours, lunch, and an athletic event. There are guides for informal visits, visitors may sit in on classes, and stay overnight. To schedule a visit, contact Mary Brooks at (434) 223-6123. **Campus Safety and Security:** Measures include 24-hour foot and vehicle patrol, emergency notification system, and self-defense education. There are emergency telephones, lighted pathways/sidewalks, controlled access to dorms/residences, There also is a fire department on campus and a first responder unit for emergency medical assistance. The dorm phone lines are hooked into 911.

REQUIREMENTS: The SAT or ACT is required. The school recommends the SAT. Applicants must be graduates of an accredited secondary school and have completed 16 high school academic credits, including 4 of English, 3 of math, 2 each of foreign language and science, and 1 of social studies. An essay is required and an interview is recommended. The GED is accepted. A GPA of 2.5 is required. AP credits are accepted. Important factors in the admissions decision are advanced placement or honors courses, recommendations by school officials, and leadership record. To graduate, students must complete 120 credit hours with a minimum GPA of 2.0. Distribution requirements include 7 courses in humanities, 4 in math and natural sciences, and 3 in social sciences. All students must also take rhetoric and foreign language and pass a rhetoric exam. **Procedure:** Freshmen are admitted fall and spring. Entrance exams should be taken during the junior or senior year of high school. There are early decision and early admissions plans. Early decision applications should be filed by November 15; regular applications, by March 1 for fall entry; and December 1 for spring entry, along with a $30 fee. Notification of early decision is sent December 15; regular decision, April 15. 55 early decision candidates were accepted for the 2014-2015 class. Applications are accepted on-line. **Transfer Students:** 21 transfer students enrolled in 2013-2014. Applicants must have a minimum GPA of 2.5 and must take either the SAT or the ACT. An interview is recommended. 60 of 120 credits required for the bachelor's degree must be completed at Hampden-Sydney. **International Students:** There are 15 international students enrolled. They must take the TOEFL with a minimum score of 114 on the Internet-based version (iBT).

ADMISSIONS: 47% of the 2014-2015 applicants were accepted. The SAT scores for the 2014-2015 freshman class were: Critical Reading--25% below 500, 48% between 500 and 599, 22% between 600 and 699, and 5% between 700 and 800; Math--21% below 500, 46% between 500 and 599, 28% between 600 and 699, and 5% between 700 and 800. 28% of the current freshmen were in the top fifth of their class; 85% were in the top two fifths. 4 freshmen graduated first in their class. **Admissions Contact:** Anita H. Garland, Dean of Admissions. E-Mail: *hsapp@hsc.edu* Web: *www.hsc.edu*

FINANCIAL AID: In 2014-2015, 100% of all full-time freshmen and 98% of continuing full-time students received some form of financial aid. 69% of all full-time freshmen and 63% of continuing full-time students received need-based aid. The average freshman award was $33,393. Need-based scholarships or need-based grants averaged $27,644 ($38,000 maximum); need-based self-help aid (loans and jobs) averaged $4,519 ($11,000 maximum); and other non-need-based awards and non-need-based scholarships averaged $15,151 ($52,000 maximum). 27% of undergraduate students work part-time. Average annual earnings from campus work are $1398. The average financial indebtedness of the 2014 graduate was $26,811. The FAFSA is required. The deadline for filing freshman financial aid applications for fall entry is March 1.

HAMPTON UNIVERSITY F-3
www.hamptonu.edu

Hampton, VA 23668	**(757) 727-5000**
	(757) 727-5328
Fax: (757) 727-5095	Email: helpdesk@hamptonu.edu
Full-time: 1242 men, 2222 women	**Faculty:** 323
Part-time: 151 men, 236 women	**Ph.Ds:** 74%
Graduate: 314 men, 589 women	**Student/Faculty:** 10 to 1
Year: semesters, summer session	**Tuition:** $19,738
Room & Board: $8790	**Freshman Class:** n/av
SAT CR/M: 514/517 **ACT:** 20	**CEEB CODE:** 5292
Application Deadline: March 1	**COMPETITIVE**

Hampton University, founded in 1868, is a multicultural, historically-black, private university. Programs are offered through the following schools: business, engineering and technology, liberal arts, nursing, pharmacy, science, education and human development, and university college and graduate college. Hampton offers associates, bachelors, masters, doctoral, professional and research program opportunities. The campus, including buildings are listed with the National Register of Historic Places. There are 8 undergraduate schools and 1 graduate school. In addition to regional accreditation, HU has baccalaureate program accreditation with ABET, ACEJMC, ASLA, CSAB, NAAB, NASM, NCATE, NLN, and ACS. The 314-acre campus is in an urban area 15 miles west of Norfolk. Including any residence halls, there are 125 buildings.

STUDENT LIFE: 67% of undergraduates are from out of state, mostly the Middle Atlantic. Students are from 44 states, 27 foreign countries, and Canada. 92% are from public schools. 89% are African American. The average age of freshmen is 18; all undergraduates, 20. 22% do not continue beyond their first year; 78% remain to graduate. **Housing:** 3066 students can be accommodated in college housing, which includes single-sex and coed dorms and off-campus apartments. In addition, there are honors houses, student cottages. On-campus housing is available on a first-come, first-served basis, and is available on a lottery system for upperclassmen. 53% of students live on campus; of those, 65% remain on campus on weekends. Alcohol is not permitted. Upperclassmen may keep cars.

FACULTY/CLASSROOMS: 49% of faculty are male; 51% are female. 90% teach undergraduates, and 10% do research. No introductory courses are taught by graduate students. The average class size in an introductory lecture is 50; in a laboratory is 20; and in a regular course is 25.

PROGRAMS OF STUDY: HU confers B.A., B.S. and B.S.Nurs. degrees. Associate, Master's, and Doctoral degrees are also awarded. Bachelor's degrees are awarded in BIOLOGICAL SCIENCE (biology/biological science), BUSINESS (accounting, banking and finance, business administration and management, marketing/retailing/merchandising, and sports management), COMMUNICATIONS AND THE ARTS (art, communications, dramatic arts, English, and music), COMPUTER AND PHYSICAL SCIENCE (chemistry, computer science, information sciences and systems, mathematics, and physics), EDUCATION (physical education), ENGINEERING AND ENVIRONMENTAL DESIGN (architecture, chemical engineering, and electrical/electronics engineering), HEALTH PROFESSIONS (nursing, recreation therapy, and speech pathology/audiology), SOCIAL SCIENCE (economics, history, political science/government, psychology, and sociology). Architecture, biology, and physics are the strongest academically. Biology, psychology, business management, nursing and journalism have the largest enrollments.

ACTIVITIES: 5% of men belong to 6 national fraternities; 4% of women belong to 3 national sororities. There are 110 groups on campus, including art, band, cheerleading, choir, chorale, chorus, communications, dance, debate, drama, drill team, ethnic, honors, international, jazz band, marching band, newspaper, orchestra, pep band, photography, political, radio and TV, religious, social service, student government, symphony, and yearbook. Popular campus events include Career Day, High School Day, Parents' Weekend, Homecoming, Founder's Day and Convocation. **Sports:** There are 5 intercollegiate sports for men and 6 for women, and 2 intramural sports for men and 1 for women. Facilities include an football stadium, a convocation center, 12 outdoor tennis courts, open fields for intramural sports, 2 basketball courts, 2 swimming pools, volleyball court, exercise and training room, a student center with a health center, bowling alley, movie theater, indoor track, and restaurants. **Graduates:** From July 1, 2013 to June 30, 2014, 830 bachelor's degrees were awarded. The most popular majors were psychology (13%), nursing (8%), and biology (7%). 376 companies recruited on campus in 2013-2014. In an average class, 43% graduate in 4 years or less, 50% graduate in 5 years or less, and 65% graduate in 6 years or less. Of the 2013 graduating class, 26% were enrolled in graduate school within 6 months of graduation, and 93% were employed.

SERVICES: Counseling and information services are available, as is tutoring in most subjects. There is remedial math, reading, and writing. **Library/Resources:** The 4 libraries contain 526,154 volumes, 1.1 million microform items, 5,835 audio/video tapes/CDs/DVDs, and subscribe to 32,187 periodicals including electronic. Computerized library services include interlibrary loans, database searching, and Internet access. Special learning facilities include an art gallery, natural history museum, radio station, TV station, an academic technology mall. **Physically Challenged Students:** 90% of the campus is accessible. Facilities include wheelchair ramps, elevators, special parking, specially equipped restrooms, lowered drinking fountains, and lowered telephones. **Special:** The college offers co-op programs in most majors, cross-registration with 6 schools, internships, and student-designed majors. Work study, study abroad, and dual majors are also available. Students may receive credit for life, military, and work experience. There are pass/fail options. There are 15 national honor societies and a freshman honors program. **Visiting:** There are regularly scheduled orientations for prospective students, including years of academic tradition and success are here to greet you. We invite you to visit the campus and experience our diverse culture, beautiful scenery, and meet future classmates through group, personal, online, or virtual tour options. There are guides for informal visits and visitors may sit in on classes. To schedule a visit, contact the Office of Admission. **Campus Safety and Security:** Measures include 24-hour foot and vehicle patrol and self-defense education. There are emergency telephones, lighted pathways/sidewalks, bike patrols, on-campus police officers, video cameras, gated campus, identification of valuables, limited access to campus, smoke detectors in residence halls, motorist assistance, and civilian support team.

REQUIREMENTS: Applicants must be graduates of an accredited secondary school, or the GED is accepted. Students should complete 17 Carnegie units, including 4 units of English, 3 units of math, (algebra I and II and geometry), 2 years of science (chemistry and biology), 2 years of social studies, and 6 academic electives. An interview is recommended. Additional important factors that may be considered into the admissions decision are demonstrated leadership qualities, essays, and extracurricular activities. A GPA of 2.5 is required. AP and CLEP credits are accepted. Important factors in the admissions decision are advanced placement or honors courses, personality/intangible qualities, leadership record, extracurricular activities record, recommendations by school officials, and recommendations by alumni. To graduate, students must complete 120 credit hours, with 74 hours in the major, related subjects, and free electives, and a GPA of 2.0.(The average GPA of the graduating class is 3.1.) There is a 44 to 48 hour distribution requirement in freshman studies, history, language, arts and humanities, English, social sciences, math, pure and applied sciences, speech, and health and phys ed. **Procedure:** Freshmen are admitted fall and spring. Entrance exams should be taken during the junior year or fall of the senior year. There are early admissions, deferred admissions, and rolling admissions plans. Early decision applications should be filed by November 1; regular applications, by March 1 for fall entry; and November 1 for spring entry; along with a $35 fee. Notification of early decision is sent December 31; regular decision; on a rolling basis. Applications are accepted on-line. **Transfer Students:** 183 transfer students enrolled in 2013-2014. Applicants for transfer must have a minimum GPA of 2.5 and 15 transferable hours. Students must have at least 60 semester or 90 quarter hours. 30 of 120 credits required for the bachelor's degree must be completed at HU. **International Students:** There are 58 international students enrolled. The school actively recruits these students. They must take the TOEFL with a minimum score of 550 on the paper-based TOEFL (PBT).

ADMISSIONS: The SAT scores for the 2014-2015 freshman class were: Critical Reading--45% below 500, 43% between 500 and 599, 10% between 600 and 699, and 2% between 700 and 800; Math--44% below 500, 44% between 500 and 599, 12% between 600 and 699, and 1% between 700 and 800. The ACT scores were 40% below 21, 34% between 21 and 23, 15% between 24 and 26, 1% between 27 and 28, and 1% above 28. 45% of the current freshmen were in the top fifth of their class; 45% were in the top two fifths. There were 224 National Merit finalists. 49 freshmen graduated first in their class. **Admissions Contact:** Angela Boyd, Director of Admission. E-Mail: *angela.boyd@hamptonu.edu* Web: *www.hamptonu.edu*

FINANCIAL AID: In 2014-2015, 58% of all full-time freshmen and 54% of continuing full-time students received some form of financial aid. 56% of all full-time freshmen and 51% of continuing full-time students received need-based aid. The average freshman award was $5,045. Need-based scholarships or need-based grants averaged

$5,424; need-based self-help aid (loans and jobs) averaged $5,291; non-need-based athletic scholarships averaged $24,257; and other non-need-based awards and non-need-based scholarships averaged $12,047. Average annual earnings from campus work are $1400. The average financial indebtedness of the 2014 graduate was $15,374. The FAFSA is required. The deadline for filing freshman financial aid applications for fall entry is February 15.

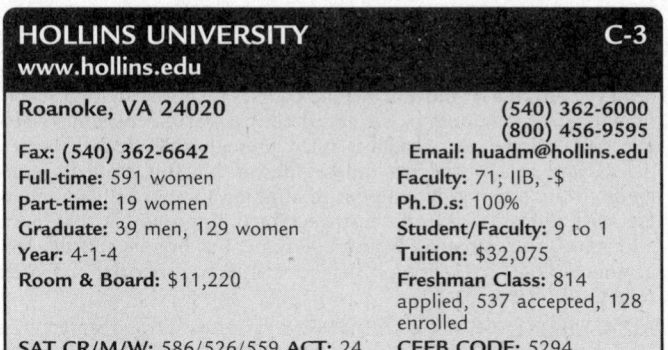

HOLLINS UNIVERSITY	C-3
www.hollins.edu	

Roanoke, VA 24020	(540) 362-6000
	(800) 456-9595
Fax: (540) 362-6642	Email: huadm@hollins.edu
Full-time: 591 women	Faculty: 71; IIB, -$
Part-time: 19 women	Ph.D.s: 100%
Graduate: 39 men, 129 women	Student/Faculty: 9 to 1
Year: 4-1-4	Tuition: $32,075
Room & Board: $11,220	Freshman Class: 814 applied, 537 accepted, 128 enrolled
SAT CR/M/W: 586/526/559 ACT: 24	CEEB CODE: 5294
Application Deadline: May 1	VERY COMPETITIVE

Founded in 1842 and Virginia's first chartered women's college, Hollins offers a broad liberal arts curriculum. There is 1 undergraduate school and 1 graduate school. In addition to regional accreditation, Hollins has baccalaureate program accreditation with TEAC. The 475-acre campus is in a suburban area in Roanoke County. Including any residence halls, there are 73 buildings.

STUDENT LIFE: 57% of undergraduates are from Virginia. Others are from 42 states, and 13 foreign countries. 80% are from public schools. 72% are White; 11% African American. 43% are Agnostic, Buddhist, Hindu, Muslim, Wicca and Unitarian; 28% Protestant; 16% Catholic; 12% claim no religious affiliation. The average age of freshmen is 19; all undergraduates, 22. 30% do not continue beyond their first year; 70% remain to graduate.

FACULTY/CLASSROOMS: 41% of faculty are male; 64% are female. All teach undergraduates. Graduate students teach 1% of introductory courses. The average class size in an introductory lecture is 11; in a laboratory is 11; and in a regular course is 14.

PROGRAMS OF STUDY: Hollins confers B.A., B.S., and B.A./B.F.A. degrees. Master's degrees are also awarded. Bachelor's degrees are awarded in AGRICULTURE (environmental studies), BIOLOGICAL SCIENCE (biology/biological science), BUSINESS (business administration and management), COMMUNICATIONS AND THE ARTS (art history and appreciation, communications, dance, dramatic arts, English, film arts, French, music, Spanish, and studio art), COMPUTER AND PHYSICAL SCIENCE (chemistry, mathematics, and physics), SOCIAL SCIENCE (classical/ancient civilization, economics, gender studies, history, interdisciplinary studies, international studies, philosophy, political science/government, psychology, religion, and sociology). Art history, classical studies, French, and theatre are the strongest academically. English/creative writing, psychology, studio art, and biology have the largest enrollments.

ACTIVITIES: There are 36 groups on campus, including art, choir, chorale, dance, drama, environmental, ethnic, film, gay, honors, international, literary magazine, musical theater, newspaper, political, radio and TV, religious, social, social service, student government, and yearbook. Popular campus events include Literary Festival, Classics Symposium, Tinker Day, Ring Night, Holiday Tea, Dance and Theatre Productions.

SERVICES: Counseling and information services are available, as is tutoring in most subjects. There is a reader service for the blind, and remedial writing. A writing center and a quantitative reasoning center. **Library/Resources:** The library contains 626,085 volumes, 12,985 microform items, and 13,796 audio/video tapes/CDs/DVDs, and subscribes to 38,349 periodicals including electronic. Computerized library services include interlibrary loans, database searching, Internet access, and Wi-Fi capability. Special learning facilities include an art gallery, radio station, and TV station. **Physically Chal-**

lenged Students: 42% of the campus is accessible. Facilities include wheelchair ramps, elevators, special parking, specially equipped restrooms, special class scheduling, lowered drinking fountains, special housing. **Special:** Hollins offers internships during the January term, dual majors, student-designed majors, accelerated degrees, and study abroad in 16 countries. There is cross-registration with the Virginia Seven College Exchange and Roanoke College. A Washington Semester is availalbe through The American University. There are 16 national honor societies, including Phi Beta Kappa, and 22 departmental honors programs. **Visiting:** There are regularly scheduled orientations for prospective students, includes 2 open houses for Seniors, 1 in October and 1 in November. Sophomores and Juniors are invited to Spring Visit Days in March and May. Admitted students are invited to visit the campus in April. There are guides for informal visits, visitors may sit in on classes, and stay overnight. To schedule a visit, contact the Campus Visit Coordinator at (540) 362-6401. **Campus Safety and Security:** Measures include 24-hour foot and vehicle patrol, emergency notification system, self-defense education, and security escort services. There are emergency telephones, lighted pathways/sidewalks, emergency buttons located along walkways and in labs.

REQUIREMENTS: The SAT or ACT is required. Applicants must be graduates of an accredited secondary school. With proper documentation, the GED and home-schooled students are accepted. Applicants should complete 16 high school academic credits, including 4 credits of English and 3 credits each of foreign language, math, science, and social studies. Official high school transcripts and letters of recommendation are required. An essay is also required, and an interview is recommended. AP credits are accepted. Important factors in the admissions decision are advanced placement or honors courses, recommendations by school officials, and parents or siblings attended the school.

ADMISSIONS: 66% of a recent year applicants were accepted. The SAT scores for the 2013-2014 freshman class were: Critical Reading--19% below 500, 33% between 500 and 599, 34% between 600 and 699, and 14% between 700 and 800; Math--33% below 500, 45% between 500 and 599, 20% between 600 and 699, and 2% between 700 and 800; Writing--32% below 500, 33% between 500 and 599, 25% between 600 and 699, and 10% between 700 and 800. The ACT scores were 20% below 21, 26% between 21 and 23, 16% between 24 and 26, 23% between 27 and 28, and 15% above 28. 48% of the current freshmen were in the top fifth of their class; 83% were in the top two fifths. 1 freshman graduated first in the class.

FINANCIAL AID: In a recent year, 100% of all full-time freshmen and 98% of continuing full-time students received some form of financial aid. 75% of all full-time freshmen and 76% of continuing full-time students received need-based aid. The average freshman award was $29,987. Need-based scholarships or need-based grants averaged $9,806 ($31,490 maximum); need-based self-help aid (loans and jobs) averaged $4,315 ($8,000 maximum); other non-need-based awards and non-need-based scholarships averaged $21,450 ($36,990 maximum); and $4,516 from other forms of aid. The average financial indebtedness of a recent graduate was $29,576. The FAFSA and the state aid form are required. The priority date for freshman financial aid applications for fall entry is February 15.

JAMES MADISON UNIVERSITY	D-2
www.jmu.edu	

Harrisonburg, VA 22807	(540) 568-6211
	(540) 568-5681
Fax: (540) 568-3332	Email: admissions@jmu.edu
Full-time: 6999 men, 10330 women	Faculty: 840; IIA, -$
Part-time: 400 men, 378 women	Ph.D.s: 78%
Graduate: 559 men, 1261 women	Student/Faculty: 20 to 1
Year: semesters, summer session	Tuition: $9176 ($23,654)
Room & Board: $8873	Freshman Class: 22648 applied, 14392 accepted, 4325 enrolled
SAT CR/M/W: 570/580/565 ACT: required	
	CEEB CODE: 5392
Application Deadline: January 15	VERY COMPETITIVE

James Madison University, founded in 1908, is a public institution with programs in science and math, business, education, arts and letters, visual and performing arts, and integrated science and technology. There are 7 undergraduate schools and 1 graduate school. In addition to regional accreditation, JMU has baccalaureate program accreditation with AACSB, ABET, ADA, AHEA, CSWE, FIDER, NASAD, NASM, and NCATE. The 712-acre campus is in a small town 123 miles southwest of Washington, D.C. Including any residence halls, there are 111 buildings.

STUDENT LIFE: 71% of undergraduates are from Virginia. Others are from 45 states, 55 foreign countries, and Canada. 81% are White. 32% are Catholic; 26% Protestant; 23% claim no religious affiliation. The average age of freshmen is 18; all undergraduates, 21. 8% do not continue beyond their first year; 81% remain to graduate.

FACULTY/CLASSROOMS: 52% of faculty are male; 48% are female. 92% teach undergraduates. Graduate students teach 1% of introductory courses. The average class size in an introductory lecture is 39; in a laboratory is 22; and in a regular course is 31.

PROGRAMS OF STUDY: JMU confers B.A., B.S., B.B.A., B.F.A., B.I.S., B.M., B.S.N. and B.S.W. degrees. Master's and Doctoral degrees are also awarded. Bachelor's degrees are awarded in BIOLOGICAL SCIENCE (biology/biological science and biotechnology), BUSINESS (accounting, banking and finance, business administration and management, business economics, hospitality management services, international business management, marketing/retailing/merchandising, recreation and leisure services, and tourism), COMMUNICATIONS AND THE ARTS (art, art history and appreciation, communications, communications technology, dance, dramatic arts, English, fine arts, media arts, modern language, music, and speech/debate/rhetoric), COMPUTER AND PHYSICAL SCIENCE (chemistry, computer science, geology, information sciences and systems, mathematics, physics, quantitative methods, science technology, and statistics), EDUCATION (athletic training), ENGINEERING AND ENVIRONMENTAL DESIGN (engineering), HEALTH PROFESSIONS (health care administration, health science, nursing, and speech pathology/audiology), SOCIAL SCIENCE (anthropology, criminal justice, dietetics, economics, geography, history, international studies, liberal arts/general studies, philosophy, physical fitness/movement, political science/government, psychology, public administration, religion, social science, social work, and sociology). Interdisciplinary liberal studies, health science, and kinesiology have the largest enrollments.

ACTIVITIES: 12% of men belong to 15 national fraternities; 12% of women belong to 9 national sororities. There are 298 groups on campus, including art, band, cheerleading, chess, choir, chorale, chorus, computers, dance, drama, environmental, ethnic, gay, honors, international, jazz band, literary magazine, marching band, musical theater, newspaper, opera, orchestra, pep band, photography, political, professional, radio and TV, religious, social, social service, student government, symphony, and yearbook. Popular campus events include Madison Symposium, James Madison Week, and International Week.

SERVICES: Counseling and information services are available, as is tutoring in every subject, through various learning centers There is a reader service for the blind. Support is also available in time management, organization, test preparation, and test taking. **Library/Resources:** The 3 libraries contain 645,740 volumes, 1.1 million microform items, and 42,676 audio/video tapes/CDs/DVDs, and subscribe to 12,662 periodicals including electronic. Computerized library services include interlibrary loans, database searching, and Internet access. Special learning facilities include an art gallery, planetarium, radio station, an arboretum, a music library, CISAT library services, a mineral museum, and science on a sphere. **Physically Challenged Students:** 90% of the campus is accessible. Facilities include wheelchair ramps, elevators, special parking, specially equipped restrooms, special class scheduling, lowered drinking fountains, lowered telephones, special housing. **Special:** JMU offers internships, work-study programs, a Washington semester, and study abroad in London, Antwerp, Florence, and Salamanca. There is a combined program in forestry with Virginia Tech. An individualized study degree, nondegree study, pass/fail options, and credit for life, military, and work experience are available. There are 28 national honor societies, including Phi Beta Kappa, a freshman honors pro-

gram, and 82 departmental honors programs. **Visiting:** There are regularly scheduled orientations for prospective students, including daily campus tours during the week and on Saturdays, and tours following group conferences with admissions counselors. There are guides for informal visits. To schedule a visit, contact the Admissions Office. **Campus Safety and Security:** Measures include 24-hour foot and vehicle patrol, emergency notification system, self-defense education, and security escort services. There are emergency telephones, lighted pathways/sidewalks, controlled access to dorms/residences, public bus transportation routes through the campus.

REQUIREMENTS: The SAT or ACT is required. Applicants must be graduates of an accredited secondary school. They must show solid achievement in 4 or more academic courses each year of high school including some honors or advanced course work. A personal statement is optional. Art students must present a portfolio. Theater, dance, and music students must audition. Nursing students must apply to the nursing department in addition to applying for undergraduate admission. AP credits are accepted. Important factors in the admissions decision are advanced placement or honors courses, recommendations by school officials, and extracurricular activities record.

ADMISSIONS: 64% of a recent year applicants were accepted. The SAT scores for the recent year freshman class were: Critical Reading--13% below 500, 52% between 500 and 599, 31% between 600 and 699, and 4% between 700 and 800; Math--10% below 500, 47% between 500 and 599, 39% between 600 and 699, and 4% between 700 and 800; Writing--14% below 500, 51% between 500 and 599, 31% between 600 and 699, and 4% between 700 and 800. 21 freshmen graduated first in their class.

FINANCIAL AID: In a recent year, 32% of all full-time freshmen and 33% of continuing full-time students received some form of financial aid. 35% of all full-time freshmen and 31% of continuing full-time students received need-based aid. Need-based scholarships or need-based grants averaged $7,560; need-based self-help aid (loans and jobs) averaged $4,736; non-need-based athletic scholarships averaged $18,500; other non-need-based awards and non-need-based scholarships averaged $4,695; and $3,384 from other forms of aid. The average financial indebtedness of a recent year graduate was $23,562. The FAFSA is required. The deadline for filing freshman financial aid applications for fall entry is March 1.

LIBERTY UNIVERSITY — D-3
www.liberty.edu

Lynchburg, VA 24502

	(434) 582-2000
	(800) 543-5317
Fax: n/av	Email: admissions@liberty.edu
Full-time: 2800 men, 3300 women	Faculty: 200
Part-time: 110 men, 120 women	Ph.D.s: 67%
Graduate: n/av	Student/Faculty: 31 to 1
Year: semesters, summer session	Tuition: $14,000
Room & Board: $5401	Freshman Class: n/av
SAT or ACT: required	CEEB CODE: 5385
Application Deadline: n/av	COMPETITIVE

Liberty University, founded in 1971, is a private liberal arts institution affiliated with the Baptist Church. The figures in the above capsule and in this profile are approximate. There are 6 undergraduate schools and 5 graduate schools. In addition to regional accreditation, Liberty has baccalaureate program accreditation with NASM and NLN. The 160-acre campus is in a suburban area 45 miles east of Roanoke. Including any residence halls, there are 73 buildings.

STUDENT LIFE: 60% of undergraduates are from out of state, mostly the Middle Atlantic. Students are from 48 states, 76 foreign countries, and Canada. 78% are White; 11% African American. 89% are Protestant. The average age of freshmen is 19; all undergraduates, 21. **Housing:** 4303 students can be accommodated in college housing, which includes single-sex dorms and on-campus apartments. On-campus housing is guaranteed for all 4 years. 64% of students live on campus; of those, 90% remain on campus on weekends. Alcohol is not permitted. All students may keep cars.

FACULTY/CLASSROOMS: 67% of faculty are male; 33% are female.

90% teach undergraduates. No introductory courses are taught by graduate students. The average class size in an introductory lecture is 43; in a laboratory is 22; and in a regular course is 23.

PROGRAMS OF STUDY: Liberty confers B.A., B.S., B.M. and B.S.N. degrees. Associate, Master's, and Doctoral degrees are also awarded. Bachelor's degrees are awarded in BIOLOGICAL SCIENCE (biology/biological science), BUSINESS (accounting, business administration and management, management information systems, and sports management), COMMUNICATIONS AND THE ARTS (communications, English, English as a second/foreign language, music, and Spanish), COMPUTER AND PHYSICAL SCIENCE (computer science and mathematics), EDUCATION (athletic training, elementary education, and physical education), HEALTH PROFESSIONS (community health work, exercise science, and nursing), SOCIAL SCIENCE (family/consumer studies, history, interdisciplinary studies, international studies, liberal arts/general studies, political science/government, psychology, religion, and social science). Education, psychology, and business are the strongest academically. Business, psychology, and education have the largest enrollments.

ACTIVITIES: There are no fraternities or sororities. There are 40 groups on campus, including band, cheerleading, choir, chorale, chorus, communications, computers, debate, drama, drill team, ethnic, honors, international, marching band, musical theater, newspaper, opera, orchestra, pep band, political, professional, radio and TV, religious, social service, student government, and yearbook. Popular campus events include Super Conference and Missions Emphasis Week. **Sports:** There are 9 intercollegiate sports for men and 8 for women, and 16 intramural sports for men and 16 for women. Facilities include an 11000-seat football stadium, 8000-seat basketball arena/convention center, baseball and soccer fields, a track complex and a tennis center. **Graduates:** From July 1, 2013 to June 30, 2014, 945 bachelor's degrees were awarded. The most popular majors were psychology (17%), business (16%), and religion (14%).

SERVICES: Counseling and information services are available, as is tutoring in every subject. There is remedial math, reading, and writing. **Library/Resources:** The library contains 211,092 volumes, 95,329 microform items, 7,149 audio/video tapes/CDs/DVDs, and subscribes to 10,806 periodicals including electronic. Computerized library services include interlibrary loans, database searching, and Internet access. Special learning facilities include a radio station and TV station. **Physically Challenged Students:** 90% of the campus is accessible. Facilities include wheelchair ramps, elevators, special parking, specially equipped restrooms, special class scheduling, lowered drinking fountains, lowered telephones, and special housing. **Special:** Liberty offers internships, B.A.-B.S. degrees, and student-designed majors in interdisciplinary and general studies. There are 8 national honor societies, including Phi Beta Kappa, and a freshman honors program. **Visiting:** There are regularly scheduled orientations for prospective students, including College for a Weekend, a 2-day program offering a chance to attend classes and special meetings. There are guides for informal visits, visitors may sit in on classes, and stay overnight. To schedule a visit, contact the Visitor's Center at visitorscenter@liberty.edu. **Campus Safety and Security:** Measures include 24-hour foot and vehicle patrol, self-defense education, and security escort services. There are shuttle buses and lighted pathways/sidewalks.

REQUIREMENTS: The SAT or ACT is required. Applicants must have completed 16 high school academic credits. The GED is accepted. An essay is required. A GPA of 2.0 is required. AP and CLEP credits are accepted. Important factors in the admissions decision are ability to finance college education, recommendations by school officials, and advanced placement or honors courses. Students must complete 120 to 123 credit hours to graduate, with a minimum GPA of 2.0. With few exceptions, by major, all must complete 18 hours of foundational studies in English, math, speech communications, and general education. An additional 42 credits of investigative studies are required; these vary according to the degree sought, either B.A. or B.S., but include English, natural sciences, history, arts, music, languages, government, social sciences, philosophy, theology, Bible studies, and integrated studies. **Procedure:** Freshmen are admitted to all sessions. Entrance exams should be taken during the junior year. There are early decision, early admissions, deferred admissions, and rolling admissions plans. Application deadlines are open. Application

fee is $35. Notification is sent on a rolling basis. Applications are accepted on-line. **Transfer Students:** 743 transfer students enrolled in 2013-2014. Applicants for transfer must have a GPA of 2.0. If transferring fewer than 60 hours, a high school transcript and test scores are required. 30 of 120 credits required for the bachelor's degree must be completed at Liberty. **International Students:** There are 238 international students enrolled. The school actively recruits these students. They must take the TOEFL or MELAB. They must also take the SAT or ACT.

ADMISSIONS: There were 5 National Merit finalists. **Admissions Contact:** David Hart, Associate Director of Admissions. E-Mail: *admissions@liberty.edu* Web: *www.liberty.edu*

FINANCIAL AID: In 2014-2015, 98% of all full-time freshmen and 88% of continuing full-time students received some form of financial aid. 64% of all full-time freshmen and continuing full-time students received need-based aid. The average freshman award was $8,506. Need-based scholarships or need-based grants averaged $1,800 ($4,000 maximum); need-based self-help aid (loans and jobs) averaged $3,725 ($3,940 maximum); non-need-based athletic scholarships averaged $8,172 ($18,850 maximum); and other non-need-based awards and non-need-based scholarships averaged $4,667 ($15,220 maximum). 15% of undergraduate students work part-time. Average annual earnings from campus work are $2500. The average financial indebtedness of the 2014 graduate was $15,619. The FAFSA, and Singlefile Form (preferred) is required. The deadline for filing freshman financial aid applications for fall entry is March 1.

LONGWOOD UNIVERSITY D-3
www.longwood.edu

Farmville, VA 23909

(434) 395-2060
(800) 281-4677

Fax: (434) 395-2332

Email: admissions@longwood.edu

Full-time: 540 men, 2733 women	**Faculty:** 238; IIA, --$
Part-time: 144 men, 1080 women	**Ph.D.s:** 77%
Graduate: 154 men, 309 women	**Student/Faculty:** 18 to 1
Year: semesters, summer session	**Tuition:** $11,340 ($24,210)
Room & Board: $9584	**Freshman Class:** 4055 applied, 3299 accepted, 1111 enrolled
SAT CR/M: 500/500 **ACT:** 21	**CEEB CODE:** 5368
Application Deadline: March 1	**COMPETITIVE**

Longwood University, founded in 1839, is a state-supported institution with programs in liberal arts, business, and teacher preparation. There are 3 undergraduate schools and 1 graduate school. In addition to regional accreditation, Longwood has baccalaureate program accreditation with AACSB, CSWE, NASM, NCATE, and NRPA. The library contains 362,151 volumes, 667,409 microform items, and 23,331 audio/video tapes/CDs/DVDs. Computerized library services include interlibrary loans, database searching, Internet access, and Wi-Fi capability. Special learning facilities include an art gallery, radio station, a greenhouse, a language lab, 6 computer labs, and a psychology lab. The 160-acre campus is in a small town 60 miles west of Richmond and 60 miles south of Charlottesville. Including any residence halls, there are 44 buildings.

STUDENT LIFE: 96% of undergraduates are from Virginia. Others are from 22 states, 19 foreign countries, and Canada. 93% are from public schools. 82% are White. The average age of freshmen is 18; all undergraduates, 19. 20% do not continue beyond their first year; 60% remain to graduate.

FACULTY/CLASSROOMS: 45% of faculty are male; 55% are female. All teach undergraduates, and 50% do both. No introductory courses are taught by graduate students. The average class size in an introductory lecture is 21 and in a regular course is 21.

PROGRAMS OF STUDY: Longwood confers B.A., B.S., B.F.A., B.M. and B.S.B.A. degrees. Master's degrees are also awarded. Bachelor's degrees are awarded in BIOLOGICAL SCIENCE (biology/biological science), BUSINESS (business administration and management), COMMUNICATIONS AND THE ARTS (art, communications, English, modern language, music, and visual and performing arts),

COMPUTER AND PHYSICAL SCIENCE (chemistry, computer science, mathematics, and physics), EDUCATION (art education, athletic training, elementary education, music education, physical education, and special education), HEALTH PROFESSIONS (community health work, nursing, and recreation therapy), SOCIAL SCIENCE (anthropology, criminal justice, criminology, economics, history, liberal arts/general studies, political science/government, psychology, social work, and sociology). Natural sciences and secondary education are the strongest academically. Business, biology and elementary education have the largest enrollments.

ACTIVITIES: 22% of men belong to 12 national fraternities; 22% of women belong to 10 national sororities. There are 176 groups on campus, including art, band, cheerleading, chess, choir, chorus, computers, dance, drama, ethnic, gay, honors, international, jazz band, musical theater, newspaper, pep band, photography, political, professional, radio and TV, religious, social, social service, and student government. Popular campus events include Spring Weekend, and Oktoberfest.

SERVICES: Counseling and information services are available, as is tutoring in some subjects, learning strategies, study skills, organizational skills and time management. There is a reader service for the blind, and remedial writing. There is also assistance in study skills, learning strategies, advocacy training, and compensatory strategy instruction. **Library/Resources:** The library contains 362,151 volumes, 667,409 microform items, and 23,331 audio/video tapes/CDs/DVDs. Computerized library services include interlibrary loans, database searching, Internet access, and Wi-Fi capability. Special learning facilities include an art gallery, radio station, a greenhouse, a language lab, 6 computer labs, and a psychology lab. **Physically Challenged Students:** Facilities include wheelchair ramps, elevators, special parking, special class scheduling, lowered drinking fountains, lowered telephones, special housing. The campus is mostly accessible with continuous monitoring for accessibility. **Special:** Longwood offers internships or directed research projects in all majors, study abroad in 15 countries, and B.A.-B.S. degrees in many majors. Cross-registration is possible with Hampden-Sydney College, as are 3-2 engineering degrees with several regional universities. Also, there is a 3-3 preprofessional program in physical therapy with University of Virginia, Old Dominion, and Virginia Commonwealth Universities. There are 10 national honor societies and a freshman honors program. **Visiting:** There are regularly scheduled orientations for prospective students, including informational and tour programs, and open houses September - December and March - May. Visitors may sit in on classes and stay overnight. To schedule a visit, contact the Admissions Office at admissions@longwood.edu. **Campus Safety and Security:** Measures include 24-hour foot and vehicle patrol, emergency notification system, self-defense education, and security escort services. There are shuttle buses, emergency telephones, lighted pathways/sidewalks, controlled access to dorms/residences, Electronic card key entry into dorms, and video cameras.

REQUIREMENTS: The SAT or ACT is required. Applicants must be graduates of an accredited secondary school; the GED is accepted. Students should complete 4 years of high school English, 2 years each of foreign language and 3 years science (including 2 lab courses), 2 years of history, and algebra I, II, and geometry. A personal statement is required. An audition is required for music students. AP and CLEP credits are accepted. Important factors in the admissions decision are advanced placement or honors courses, leadership record, and evidence of special talent.

ADMISSIONS: 81% of a recent year applicants were accepted. The SAT scores for the recent year freshman class were: Critical Reading--43% below 500, 44% between 500 and 599, 10% between 600 and 699, and 1% between 700 and 800; Math--44% below 500, 45% between 500 and 599, and 9% between 600 and 699.

FINANCIAL AID: The FAFSA is required. The priority date for freshman financial aid applications for fall entry is March 1.

LYNCHBURG COLLEGE   **D-3**
www.lynchburg.edu

Lynchburg, VA 24501	(800) 426-8101
	(434) 544-8300
Fax: (434) 544-8653	Email: admissions@lynchburg.edu
Full-time: 842 men, 1247 women	Faculty: n/av; IIA, --$
Part-time: 31 men, 58 women	Ph.D.s: 82%
Graduate: 192 men, 343 women	Student/Faculty: 12 to 1
Year: semesters, summer session	Tuition: $33,565
Room & Board: $9080	Freshman Class: 5695 applied, 3627 accepted, 512 enrolled
SAT CR/M/W: 500/500/490 ACT: 21	CEEB CODE: 5372
Application Deadline: open	COMPETITIVE

Lynchburg College, established in 1903, is a private institution affiliated with the Christian Church (Disciples of Christ). LC offers bachelor's degrees in 39 majors, master's degrees in 12 programs, and 2 doctoral degrees (Physical Therapy & Leadership Studies). There are 6 undergraduate schools and 1 graduate school. In addition to regional accreditation, L.C. has baccalaureate program accreditation with ACBSP. The 250-acre campus is in a suburban area 180 miles southwest of Washington, D.C., and 120 west of Richmond. Including any residence halls, there are 40 buildings.

STUDENT LIFE: 68% of undergraduates are from Virginia. Others are from 39 states, and 9 foreign countries. 77% are White; 11% African American. The average age of freshmen is 18; all undergraduates, 21. 22% do not continue beyond their first year; 57% remain to graduate.

FACULTY/CLASSROOMS: 44% of faculty are male; 56% are female. 95% teach undergraduates. No introductory courses are taught by graduate students.

PROGRAMS OF STUDY: L.C. confers B.A., and B.S. degrees. Master's and Doctoral degrees are also awarded. Bachelor's degrees are awarded in AGRICULTURE (environmental studies), BIOLOGICAL SCIENCE (biology/biological science), BUSINESS (accounting, business administration and management, human resources, management science, marketing/retailing/merchandising, and sports management), COMMUNICATIONS AND THE ARTS (art, communications, English, French, music, Spanish, and theatre arts), COMPUTER AND PHYSICAL SCIENCE (chemistry, computer science, mathematics, and physics), EDUCATION (athletic training, education, and elementary education), ENGINEERING AND ENVIRONMENTAL DESIGN (environmental science), HEALTH PROFESSIONS (biomedical science, exercise science, health promotion, and nursing), SOCIAL SCIENCE (criminology, economics, history, international relations, philosophy, physical fitness/movement, political science/government, psychology, religion, and sociology). Communication studies, nursing, elementary education, business administration have the largest enrollments.

ACTIVITIES: 11% of men belong to 5 national fraternities; 14% of women belong to 5 national sororities. There are 80 groups on campus, including art, cheerleading, choir, chorus, communications, computers, dance, drama, environmental, ethnic, gay, honors, international, jazz band, literary magazine, musical theater, newspaper, orchestra, political, professional, religious, social, social service, and student government. Popular campus events include Homecoming, Turkey Bowl and Campus Days.

SERVICES: Counseling and information services are available, as is tutoring in most subjects, Tutoring is available in most freshman and sophomore subjects, some upperclass subjects, and in math and writing. **Library/Resources:** The library contains 379,947 volumes, 466,605 microform items, 7,994 audio/video tapes/CDs/DVDs, and subscribes to 38,522 periodicals including electronic. Computerized library services include interlibrary loans, database searching, and Internet access. Special learning facilities include an art gallery, an astronomical observatory, Claytor nature center (470 acre farm used for science classes), a theatre, and cadaver lab. **Physically Challenged Students:** 95% of the campus is accessible. Facilities include wheelchair ramps, elevators, special parking, specially equipped restrooms, special class scheduling, lowered drinking fountains, lowered telephones, and special housing. **Special:** There is a Washington semester available, B.A.-B.S. degrees in chemistry, internships, and a work-study program. A 3-2 engineering degree is available in cooperation with Old Dominion University and the University of Virginia. There are 14 national honor societies and a freshman honors program. **Visiting:** There are regularly scheduled orientations for prospective students, including individual appointments. There are guides for informal visits, visitors may sit in on classes, and stay overnight. To schedule a visit, contact the Admissions Office at admissions@lynchburg.edu. **Campus Safety and Security:** Measures include 24-hour foot and vehicle patrol, emergency notification system, and security escort services. There are emergency telephones, lighted pathways/sidewalks, controlled access to dorms/residences, all residence halls are locked 24 hours a day admission is only by scanning an ID card.

REQUIREMENTS: The SAT or ACT is required. SAT: Subject Tests are recommended. GED's are reviewed on a case-by-case basis. Applicants should have earned between 16 to 20 academic high school credits in English, math and social science, lab science, and foreign language. AP and CLEP credits are accepted. Important factors in the admissions decision are advanced placement or honors courses, leadership record, and recommendations by school officials.

ADMISSIONS: 64% of a recent year applicants were accepted. The SAT scores for the 2013-2014 freshman class were: Critical Reading--50% below 500, 38% between 500 and 599, 10% between 600 and 699, and 2% between 700 and 800; Math--49% below 500, 36% between 500 and 599, 14% between 600 and 699, and 1% between 700 and 800; Writing--54% below 500, 36% between 500 and 599, and 10% between 600 and 699. The ACT scores were 41% below 21, 28% between 21 and 23, 17% between 24 and 26, 8% between 27 and 28, and 6% above 28.

FINANCIAL AID: In a recent year, 82% of all full-time freshmen and 76% of continuing full-time students received some form of financial aid. 82% of all full-time freshmen and 76% of continuing full-time students received need-based aid. Need-based scholarships or need-based grants averaged $23,105; and need-based self-help aid (loans and jobs) averaged $4,570. 37% of undergraduate students work part-time. L.C. is a member of CSS. The FAFSA and the state aid form are required. The deadline for filing freshman financial aid applications for fall entry is March 1.

MARY BALDWIN COLLEGE — D-2
www.mbc.edu

Staunton, VA 24401	(540) 887-7019
	(800) 468-2262
Fax: (540) 887-7292	Email: admit@mbc.edu
Full-time: 37 men, 953 women	Faculty: 75; IIB, -$
Part-time: 62 men, 362 women	Ph.D.s: 84%
Graduate: 44 men, 287 women	Student/Faculty: 10 to 1
Year: 4-1-4, summer session	Tuition: $29,595
Room & Board: $8650	Freshman Class: 3088 applied, 2996 accepted, 294 enrolled
SAT CR/M/W: 500/480/480 ACT: 21	CEEB CODE: 5397
Application Deadline: April 15	COMPETITIVE

Mary Baldwin College, since its founding as Augusta Female Seminary in 1842. Empowered with an education that is personalized, experiential, and relevant, MBC students have the confidence to lead, the compassion to serve others, and the courage to make a positive difference in the world. The master's level university serves students in the Residential College for Women, which includes the Virginia Women's Institute for Leadership (the nation's only all-female cadet corps) and the Program for the Exceptionally Gifted on its historic main campus near downtown Staunton, Virginia. Its Adult Degree Program serves men and women on campus and at regional centers throughout Virginia. Master's and doctoral degrees are offered through the College of Education, the Murphy Deming College of Health Sciences, and the Shakespeare and Performance program. There are 2 undergraduate schools and 3 graduate schools. In addition to regional accreditation, MBC has baccalaureate program

accreditation with CSWE, TEAC, and SACS. The 54-acre campus is in a small town in downtown Staunton, Virginia. Including any residence halls, there are 40 buildings.

STUDENT LIFE: 60% of undergraduates are from Virginia. Others are from 37 states, and 7 foreign countries. 89% are from public schools. 42% are White; 32% African American; 11% Hispanic. 78% are Unknown denomination. The average age of freshmen is 18; all undergraduates, 19. 31% do not continue beyond their first year; 48% remain to graduate. **Housing:** 775 students can be accommodated in college housing, which includes single-sex dorms and on-campus apartments. In addition, there are honors houses, special-interest houses, lofts and suites. On-campus housing is guaranteed for all 4 years. 82% of students live on campus; of those, 70% remain on campus on weekends. All students may keep cars.

FACULTY/CLASSROOMS: 36% of faculty are male; 64% are female. 87% teach undergraduates. No introductory courses are taught by graduate students. The average class size in an introductory lecture is 21; in a laboratory is 14; and in a regular course is 19.

PROGRAMS OF STUDY: MBC confers B.A., B.S. and B.S.W. degrees. Master's and Doctoral degrees are also awarded. Bachelor's degrees are awarded in BIOLOGICAL SCIENCE (biology/biological science), BUSINESS (business administration and management, international economics, and marketing management), COMMUNICATIONS AND THE ARTS (art, art history and appreciation, arts administration/management, English, music, studio art, and theatre arts), COMPUTER AND PHYSICAL SCIENCE (applied mathematics, chemistry, mathematics, and physics), HEALTH PROFESSIONS (clinical science and health care administration), SOCIAL SCIENCE (American studies, anthropology, Asian/Oriental studies, criminal justice, East Asian studies, economics, history, international relations, philosophy, political science/government, psychology, religion, social work, and sociology). Psychology, business, biology, and chemistry are the strongest academically. Education, psychology, and history have the largest enrollments.

ACTIVITIES: There are 60 groups on campus, including academic honor societies, event planning, civic engagement, leadership, wellness, art, choir, chorale, chorus, dance, drama, drill team, drum and bugle corps, environmental, ethnic, film, gay, hiking, honors, international, literary magazine, marching band, musical theater, orchestra, photography, political, professional, religious, social, social service, student government, and yearbook. Popular campus events include Apple Day, Junior Dads, Family Weekend, Signature Ball, Halloween pumpkin carving, Las Posadas, Kwanzaa, International Festival, Capstone Festival. **Sports:** There are 6 intercollegiate sports for women, and 6 intramural sports for women. Facilities include Students practice and play on facilities in and around the Physical Activities Center, known as PAC. The 40,000-square-foot building houses a main gym for basketball and volleyball practice and competition; a studio used for dance, fencing, and aerobics and other group fitness classes; a cardio and weight room; a climbing wall; racquetball courts; and staff offices. Surrounding facilities include a track, tennis courts, and fields for softball, soccer, field hockey, lacrosse. **Graduates:** From July 1, 2013 to June 30, 2014, 259 bachelor's degrees were awarded. The most popular majors were psychology (16%), business (12%), and history (10%). 17 companies recruited on campus in 2013-2014. In an average class, 2% graduate in 3 years or less, 42% graduate in 4 years or less, 47% graduate in 5 years or less, and 49% graduate in 6 years or less. Of the 2013 graduating class, 23% were enrolled in graduate school within 6 months of graduation, and 84% were employed.

SERVICES: Counseling and information services are available, as is tutoring in most subjects. There is a reader service for the blind, and remedial math and writing. **Library/Resources:** The library contains 147,624 volumes, 65,502 microform items, 7,907 audio/video tapes/CDs/DVDs, and subscribes to 36,606 periodicals including electronic. Computerized library services include interlibrary loans, database searching, Internet access, and Wi-Fi capability. Special learning facilities include an art gallery. The campus is also home to the Staunton Military Academy/Virginia Women's Institute for Leadership Museum, dedicated to preserving local military history while inspiring future service members. In addition, the Spencer Center for Civic and Global Engagement at the heart of campus provides connections to local and regional service organizations, coordinates study abroad and international visitors, and offers meeting and event space. **Physically Challenged Students:** 30% of the campus is accessible. Facilities include wheelchair ramps, elevators, special parking, and specially equipped restrooms. **Special:** Study abroad locations vary from year to year, and can include: Costa Rica, Mexico, New Zealand, Japan, China, England, South Korea, Italy, Bermuda, Wales, The Netherlands, France, and Peru; cadets in the Virginia Women's Institute for Leadership are eligible for special study opportunities in India and at Norwich University in Connecticut. Dual-degree programs in education (BA/MAT and BA/MEd) and Shakespeare studies (BA/MLitt) through Mary Baldwin; 3-2 program in engineering (BS/MS) in partnership with the University of Virginia; 3-2 program in nursing (BS/MSN) with Vanderbilt University. Virginia State Teacher Licensure via the College of Education in undergraduate, Master of Arts in Teaching, and post-baccalaureate teacher Licensure programs. MBC and six other private colleges in Virginia (Hampden-Sydney College, Hollins University, Randolph-Macon College, Randolph College, and Washington and Lee University) form a consortium through which students may attend another of the participating colleges for a semester or a year. An agreement with the Virginia Community College System provides that a student with a transfer-oriented degree may qualify for guaranteed admission. Minor in public history through a partnership with the nearby Woodrow Wilson Presidential Library. Accelerated degree program, double majors, and student-designed major, Non-degree study, and pass/fail grading options. There are 18 national honor societies, including Phi Beta Kappa, a freshman honors program, and 29 departmental honors programs. **Visiting:** There are regularly scheduled orientations for prospective students, consisting of a tour, an interview, meet faculty, attend class, eat in dining hall, student events, athletic tours, and other activities as requested or available. There are guides for informal visits, visitors may sit in on classes, and stay overnight. To schedule a visit, contact the MBC Admissions Office at admit@mbc.edu. **Campus Safety and Security:** Measures include 24-hour foot and vehicle patrol, emergency notification system, self-defense education, and security escort services. There are emergency telephones, lighted pathways/sidewalks, controlled access to dorms/residences, 24-hour locked residence halls, video surveillance in all-night computer labs and access areas, and video surveillance in the program for the exceptionally gifted center.

REQUIREMENTS: Applicants must graduate from an accredited secondary school, have a GED, or meet state equivalency requirements for homeschooling. A minimum of 16 academic units are required, including 4 in English, 3 in math, 2 to 3 in social studies, and 2 each in a foreign language and science. Either the SAT or the ACT (not both) is required. Essays and interviews are recommended. A GPA of 2.0 is required. AP and CLEP credits are accepted. Important factors in the admissions decision are extracurricular activities record, leadership record, and advanced placement or honors courses. To graduate, students must complete a minimum of 126 semester hours, including at least 18 in the major. The Common Curriculum, which is organized by three learning outcomes (understanding of the liberal arts and sciences, understanding of the self in relationship to the broader community, and the capacity to make a positive difference in the world), includes 6 hours or more each in natural sciences, social sciences, arts, and humanities and history; 6 hours each in courses focused on writing, quantitative reasoning, and diverse cultures in a global context (foreign language, cross-cultural studies, and/or study abroad); 3 hours each in courses emphasizing oral communication, role of race and ethnicity, role of gender, and research and information literacy; 2 hours of health and physical education; and 1 hour of community involvement credit. A minimum GPA of 2.0 is required. Additional requirements for the Bachelor of Science (offered in biology, business, chemistry, economics, mathematics, physics, policy analysis, psychology) are 6 semester hours in mathematics at the 200-level or above, three hours emphasizing quantitative reasoning/data analysis, and at least two 200-level lab science courses. All graduates must complete a senior requirement for a minimum of 3 and a maximum of 6 semester hours of credit. The purpose of the senior requirement is to serve as a context within which students may establish themselves as capable of independent scholarship on a significant level. **Procedure:** Freshmen are admitted fall and spring. Entrance exams should be taken in the junior or senior year. There are early admissions, deferred admissions, and rolling admissions plans. Applications should be filed by April 15 for fall entry; December 15 for spring entry. Applications are accepted on-line. Application fees are waived if application is completed on-line. **Transfer Students:** 31 transfer students enrolled in 2013-2014. Transfer applicants must have at least a 2.0 GPA at the institution where they are currently enrolled. 66 of 126 credits required for the bachelor's degree must be completed at MBC. **International Students:** There are 11 international students enrolled. The school actively recruits these students. They must take the TOEFL with a minimum score of 500 on the paper-based TOEFL (PBT) or 61 on the Internet-based version (iBT).

ADMISSIONS: 97% of the 2014-2015 applicants were accepted. The SAT scores for the 2014-2015 freshman class were: Critical Reading--46% below 500, 38% between 500 and 599, 13% between 600 and 699, and 3% between 700 and 800; Math--63% below 500, 30% between 500 and 599, and 7% between 600 and 699; Writing--58% below 500, 29% between 500 and 599, and 13% between 600 and 699. The ACT scores were 34% below 21, 44% between 21 and 23, 10% between 24 and 26, 5% between 27 and 28, and 7% above 28. 20% of the current freshmen were in the top fifth of their class; 81% were in the top two fifths. **Admissions Contact:** Roberta Palmer, Director of Admissions. E-Mail: *admit@mbc.edu* Web: *www.mbc.edu*

FINANCIAL AID: In 2014-2015, 92% of all full-time freshmen and 90% of continuing full-time students received some form of financial aid. 90% of all full-time freshmen and 88% of continuing full-time students received need-based aid. The average freshman award was $22,529. Need-based scholarships or need-based grants averaged $7,592 ($20,322 maximum); need-based self-help aid (loans and jobs) averaged $9,780 ($19,900 maximum); and other non-need-based awards and non-need-based scholarships averaged $15,716 ($29,595 maximum). 20% of undergraduate students work part-time. Average annual earnings from campus work are $1400. The average financial indebtedness of the 2014 graduate was $30,340. The FAFSA and the state aid form are required. The priority date for freshman financial aid applications for fall entry is February 15. The deadline for filing freshman financial aid applications for fall entry is May 1.

MARYMOUNT UNIVERSITY E-2
www.marymount.edu

Arlington, VA 22207	(703) 522-5600
	(800) 548-7638

Fax: (703) 522-0349	**Email:** admissions@marymount.edu
Full-time: 737 men, 1390 women	**Faculty:** 127; IIA, av$
Part-time: 82 men, 154 women	**Ph.D.s:** 85%
Graduate: 271 men, 807 women	**Student/Faculty:** 17 to 1
Year: semesters, summer session	**Tuition:** $27,470
Room & Board: $12,010	**Freshman Class:** 1976 applied, 1659 accepted, 353 enrolled
SAT CR/M/W: 500/490/480 **ACT:** 21	**CEEB CODE:** 5405
Application Deadline: rolling	**COMPETITIVE**

Marymount, founded in 1950, is a Catholic-affiliated, comprehensive university. Undergraduate and graduate programs are offered through the Schools of Arts and Sciences, Business Administration, Education, Human Services, and Health Professions. There are 4 undergraduate schools and 4 graduate schools. In addition to regional accreditation, Marymount has baccalaureate program accreditation with ACBSP, NCATE, CACREP, CCNE, and CIDA. The 21-acre campus is in a suburban area 6 miles southwest of Washington, D.C. Including any residence halls, there are 15 buildings.

STUDENT LIFE: 56% of undergraduates are from Virginia. Others are from 40 states, 58 foreign countries, and Canada. 86% are from public schools. 42% are White; 16% Hispanic; 15% African American. 35% are Catholic; 28% claim no religious affiliation; 22% Protestant; 14% Muslim, Orthodox, Hindu, and Buddhist. The average age of freshmen is 18; all undergraduates, 23. 19% do not continue beyond their first year; 58% remain to graduate. **Housing:** 927 students can be accommodated in college housing, which includes single-sex and coed dorms and off-campus apartments. Theme housing, and on-campus housing is available on a lottery system for upperclassmen. 66% of students commute. Upperclassmen may keep cars.

FACULTY/CLASSROOMS: 30% of faculty are male; 70% are female. 77% teach undergraduates. No introductory courses are taught by graduate students. The average class size in an introductory lecture is 21; in a laboratory is 13; and in a regular course is 15.

PROGRAMS OF STUDY: Marymount confers B.A., B.S., B.B.A. and B.S.N. degrees. Master's and Doctoral degrees are also awarded. Bachelor's degrees are awarded in BIOLOGICAL SCIENCE (biochemistry, biology/biological science, and forensic science), BUSINESS (business administration and management and fashion merchandising), COMMUNICATIONS AND THE ARTS (art, communications, English, graphic design, and information technology), COMPUTER AND PHYSICAL SCIENCE (computer science, computer security and information assurance, mathematics, and web services), EDUCATION (art education, English education, health information management, mathematics education, and special education), ENGINEERING AND ENVIRONMENTAL DESIGN (interior design), HEALTH PROFESSIONS (health science, nursing, premedicine, and prephysical therapy), SOCIAL SCIENCE (criminal justice, economics, fashion design and technology, history, liberal arts/general studies, philosophy, political science/government, psychology, sociology, and theological studies). Business administration, nursing, and information technology have the largest enrollments.

ACTIVITIES: There are 39 groups on campus, including art, cheerleading, choir, chorus, communications, dance, drama, ethnic, honors, international, literary magazine, newspaper, political, professional, religious, social, social service, student government, and yearbook. Popular campus events include Portfolio in Motion (Fashion Show), Snowball (Winter Formal Dance), International Week, Saintsfest, Midnight Madness, and Club Fair. **Sports:** There are 9 intercollegiate sports for men and 7 for women, and 6 intramural sports for men and 7 for women. Facilities include an basketball arena, practice field, recreational gymnasium, swimming pool, aerobics and weight rooms, and off-campus baseball field. **Graduates:** From July 1, 2013 to June 30, 2014, 655 bachelor's degrees were awarded. The most popular majors were nursing (26%), business administration (15%), and psychology (7%). In an average class, 44% graduate in 4 years or less, 56% graduate in 5 years or less, and 58% graduate in 6 years or less. Of the 2013 graduating class, 67% were employed within 6 months of graduation.

SERVICES: Counseling and information services are available, as is tutoring in most subjects. There is a reader service for the blind, and remedial math, reading, and writing. **Library/Resources:** The library contains 361,678 volumes, 199,257 microform items, 17,034 audio/video tapes/CDs/DVDs, and subscribes to 12,985 periodicals including electronic. Computerized library services include interlibrary loans, database searching, Internet access, and Wi-Fi capability. Special learning facilities include an art gallery, instructional media center. **Physically Challenged Students:** Facilities include wheelchair ramps, elevators, special parking, specially equipped restrooms, special class scheduling, lowered drinking fountains, lowered telephones, and special housing. **Special:** Students can cross-register with the Consortium of Universities of the Washington Metropolitan Area and participate in short-term and semester-long study abroad in various countries. Marymount offers student-designed majors, an accelerated degree program in nursing, and dual-degree programs in business administration, information technology, and health sciences. An internship, clinical, or student teaching experience is required in all majors except nursing. There are 12 national honor societies and a freshman honors program. **Visiting:** There are regularly scheduled orientations for prospective students, including Campus Visit Days, Information Nights, and new student summer orientation. There are guides for informal visits, visitors may sit in on classes, and stay overnight. To schedule a visit, contact the Admissions Office. **Campus Safety and Security:** Measures include 24-hour foot and vehicle patrol, emergency notification system, and security escort services. There are shuttle buses, emergency telephones, lighted pathways/sidewalks, and controlled access to dorms/residences.

REQUIREMENTS: The SAT or ACT is required. Applicants must graduate from an accredited secondary school or have a GED. Marymount requires 15 academic credits in preparatory courses and

strongly recommends biology and chemistry for Nursing candidates. Average incoming freshman SAT score is 1000. If both SAT and ACT scores are submitted, the highest equivalent test score will be used. A letter of recommendation and writing sample also are required. A GPA of 2.6 is required. AP and CLEP credits are accepted. Important factors in the admissions decision are advanced placement or honors courses, extracurricular activities record, and evidence of special talent.To graduate, students must complete all course requirements with a minimum cumulative grade point average of 2.0. Students must earn 120 credits by completing all liberal arts core requirements, all general education university requirements, and all major requirements. Core curriculum includes courses in humanities, mathematics and sciences, philosophy and theology, written communication, and freshman seminar. **Procedure:** Freshmen are admitted fall, spring, and summer. Entrance exams should be taken scores must be received by August 15 for fall-term admission. There are deferred admissions and rolling admissions plans. Application deadlines are open. Application fee is $40. Notification is sent on a rolling basis. Applications are accepted on-line. **Transfer Students:** 303 transfer students enrolled in 2013-2014. One letter of recommendation required. Transfer applicants with fewer than 30 credits must meet freshman admission requirements. Additional requirements for Nursing and International applicants. 36 of 120 credits required for the bachelor's degree must be completed at Marymount. **International Students:** There are 218 international students enrolled. The school actively recruits these students. They must take the TOEFL with a minimum score of 550 on the paper-based TOEFL (PBT) or 79 on the Internet-based version (iBT), or take the IELTS. They must also take the SAT or ACT, scoring 950.

ADMISSIONS: 84% of the 2014-2015 applicants were accepted. The SAT scores for the 2014-2015 freshman class were: Critical Reading--47% below 500, 43% between 500 and 599, 9% between 600 and 699, and 1% between 700 and 800; Math--50% below 500, 39% between 500 and 599, 10% between 600 and 699, and 1% between 700 and 800; Writing--57% below 500, 34% between 500 and 599, 8% between 600 and 699, and 1% between 700 and 800. The ACT scores were 48% below 21, 24% between 21 and 23, 20% between 24 and 26, 6% between 27 and 28, and 2% above 28. **Admissions Contact:** Heather Renault, Director of Undergraduate Admissions. E-Mail: *admissions@marymount.edu* Web: *www.marymount.edu*

FINANCIAL AID: In 2014-2015, 95% of all full-time freshmen and 85% of continuing full-time students received some form of financial aid. 56% of all full-time freshmen and 59% of continuing full-time students received need-based aid. The average freshman award was $26,301. Need-based scholarships or need-based grants averaged $4,409; need-based self-help aid (loans and jobs) averaged $4,745; and other non-need-based awards and non-need-based scholarships averaged $17,922. 8% of undergraduate students work part-time. Average annual earnings from campus work are $2174. The average financial indebtedness of the 2014 graduate was $27,683. The FAFSA is required. The priority date for freshman financial aid applications for fall entry is March 1.

NORFOLK STATE UNIVERSITY *(The complete profile is made available exclusively on our website, www.barronspac.com)*

OLD DOMINION UNIVERSITY *(The complete profile is made available exclusively on our website, www.barronspac.com)*

RADFORD UNIVERSITY *(The complete profile is made available exclusively on our website, www.barronspac.com)*

RANDOLPH COLLEGE   D-3
www.randolphcollege.edu

Lynchburg, VA 24503

	(434) 947-8000
	(800) 745-7692
Fax: (434) 947-8996	Email: admissions@randolphcollege.edu
Full-time: 234 men, 419 women	Faculty: 69; IIB, av$
Part-time: 1 men, 4 women	Ph.D.s: 96%
Graduate: 5 men, 10 women	Student/Faculty: 9 to 1
Year: semesters	Tuition: $34,010
Room & Board: $11,650	Freshman Class: 1353 applied, 1096 accepted, 191 enrolled
SAT CR/M/W: 540/535/520 ACT: 25	CEEB CODE: 5557
Application Deadline: March 15	VERY COMPETITIVE

Randolph College, founded in 1891, is an independent, coeducational, liberal arts institution. The college's curriculum offers the best feature of an honors education with a global outlook. Students are encouraged to travel, to take on real problems, to pursue and achieve a goal with personal meaning. Embedded within a student's education are opportunities to study abroad, both national and international internships, career guidance, leadership development, and one-on-one faculty advising. There is 1 undergraduate school and 1 graduate school. In addition to regional accreditation, Randolph has baccalaureate program accreditation with NASDTEC and TEAC. The 100-acre campus is in a suburban area within minutes of the Blue Ridge Mountains, 1 hour southwest of Charlottesville. Including any residence halls, there are 18 buildings.

STUDENT LIFE: 59% of undergraduates are from Virginia. Others are from 36 states, 32 foreign countries, and Canada. 72% are from public schools. 67% are White; 13% Foreign. 55% are Protestant; 15% Catholic; 15% claim no religious affiliation; 12% Muslim, Hindu, Buddhist, and Orthodox. The average age of freshmen is 18; all undergraduates, 20. 20% do not continue beyond their first year; 64% remain to graduate. **Housing:** 675 students can be accommodated in college housing, which includes single-sex and coed dorms. In addition, there are special-interest houses, theme housing, and coed dorms. On-campus housing is guaranteed for all 4 years. 90% of students live on campus; of those, 80% remain on campus on weekends. All students may keep cars.

FACULTY/CLASSROOMS: 46% of faculty are male; 54% are female. All teach undergraduates, 58% do research, and 58% do both. No introductory courses are taught by graduate students. The average class size in an introductory lecture is 16; in a laboratory is 11; and in a regular course is 12.

PROGRAMS OF STUDY: Randolph confers B.A., B.S. and B.F.A. degrees. Master's degrees are also awarded. Bachelor's degrees are awarded in AGRICULTURE (environmental studies), BIOLOGICAL SCIENCE (biology/biological science), BUSINESS (business administration and management), COMMUNICATIONS AND THE ARTS (art, classics, communications, dance, dramatic arts, English, French, music, and Spanish), COMPUTER AND PHYSICAL SCIENCE (chemistry, mathematics, and physics), EDUCATION (education and physical education), ENGINEERING AND ENVIRONMENTAL DESIGN (engineering physics and environmental science), HEALTH PROFESSIONS (health science), SOCIAL SCIENCE (economics, history, international studies, philosophy, political science/government, psychology, religion, and sociology). Biology, psychology, political science, and English have the largest enrollments.

ACTIVITIES: There are 35 groups on campus, including campus ministries, environmental, equestrian, Model UN, outdoor adventures, art, chorale, chorus, dance, debate, drama, environmental, ethnic, film, foreign language, gay, honors, international, literary magazine, newspaper, pep band, photography, political, professional, radio and TV, religious, social, social service, student government, and yearbook. Popular campus events include Tacky Party, Never-ending Weekend, Senior Dinner Dance and Dell Parties. **Sports:** There are 6 intercollegiate sports for men and 8 for women, and 6 intramural sports for men and 6 for women. Facilities include a multi-purpose playing field and track, gym, an indoor heated swimming pool, dance studios, aerobic and weight rooms, 8 tennis courts, 2 athletic fields, frisbee golf course, 100-acre riding center with teaching and amphitheater show rings and indoor and outdoor arenas, and a 900-seat auditorium. **Graduates:** From July 1, 2013 to June 30, 2014, 118 bachelor's degrees were awarded. The most popular majors were social sciences (16%), psychology (11%), and history (10%). In an average class, 2% graduate in 3 years or less, 63% graduate in 4 years or less, 64% graduate in 5 years or less, and 64% graduate in 6 years or less. Of the 2013 graduating class, 35% were enrolled in graduate school within 6 months of graduation, and 60% were employed.

SERVICES: Counseling and information services are available, as is tutoring in every subject. Computing and study skills resources, writing lab, science and math center. **Library/Resources:** The library contains 197,332 volumes, 187,000 microform items, 3,600 audio/video tapes/CDs/DVDs, and subscribes to 618 periodicals including electronic. Computerized library services include interlibrary loans, database searching, and Internet access. Special learning facilities include

an art gallery, radio station, an observatory, acclaimed collection of American art housed in the Maier Museum, 2 theaters, recital hall, organic garden, a 100-acre equestrian center, and 3 nature preserves. **Physically Challenged Students:** 50% of the campus is accessible. Facilities include wheelchair ramps, elevators, special parking, specially equipped restrooms, special class scheduling, special housing. **Special:** Randolph offers a spring semester American Culture Program, as well as study abroad in 11 countries, including its own program in England, and both domestic and international internships. A Washington semester at American University is available, as is the Tri-College Consortium with Lynchburg Colleges, and the Seven-College Exchange Program with Hampden-Sydney, Hollins, Mary Baldwin, Randolph-Macon, and Washington and Lee University. There is a 3-2 nursing program with Johns Hopkins University and Vanderbilt University and a 3-2 engineering degree with several institutions. There are 17 national honor societies, including Phi Beta Kappa, and 16 departmental honors programs. **Visiting:** There are regularly scheduled orientations for prospective students, including a campus tour, student panels, faculty panels, class visits, and individual sessions with admissions and financial planning counselor. There are guides for informal visits, visitors may sit in on classes, and stay overnight. To schedule a visit, contact the Admissions Office at admissions@randolphcollegec.edu. **Campus Safety and Security:** Measures include 24-hour foot and vehicle patrol, emergency notification system, self-defense education, and security escort services. There are emergency telephones, lighted pathways/sidewalks, and controlled access to dorms/residences.

REQUIREMENTS: The SAT or ACT is required. Applicants must be graduates of an accredited secondary school with at least 16 academic credits, including 4 units in English, 3 units in math (4 recommended), 3 units in foreign language (recommended), 3 units in science and 2 units with lab, 2 units in history, and 1 in academic electives (3 recommended). An interview is strongly encouraged. AP and CLEP credits are accepted. Important factors in the admissions decision are advanced placement or honors courses, recommendations by school officials, extracurricular activities record, recommendations by alumni, leadership record, parents or siblings attended your school, evidence of special talent, and personality/intangible qualities. To graduate, all students must complete at least 124 credit hours with a minimum GPA of 2.0. Students must satisfy the requirements for the general education and major programs and must have a minimum GPA of 2.0 in the major. **Procedure:** Freshmen are admitted fall and spring. Entrance exams should be taken in the junior or senior year. There are early admissions and deferred admissions plans. Early decision applications should be filed by December 1; regular applications, by March 15 for fall entry; and December 1 for spring entry, along with a $35 fee. Notification of early decision is sent December 15; regular decision, on a rolling basis. Applications are accepted on-line. **Transfer Students:** 26 transfer students enrolled in 2013-2014. Transfer students must submit college and high school transcripts, a letters of recommendation from a college official. An interview is recommended. 62 of 124 credits required for the bachelor's degree must be completed at Randolph. **International Students:** There are 66 international students enrolled. The school actively recruits these students. They must take the TOEFL with a minimum score of 550 on the paper-based TOEFL (PBT) or 79 on the Internet-based version (iBT).

ADMISSIONS: 81% of the 2014-2015 applicants were accepted. The SAT scores for the 2014-2015 freshman class were: Critical Reading-33% below 500, 41% between 500 and 599, 20% between 600 and 699, and 7% between 700 and 800; Math--37% below 500, 38% between 500 and 599, 19% between 600 and 699, and 6% between 700 and 800; Writing--36% below 500, 44% between 500 and 599, 15% between 600 and 699, and 4% between 700 and 800. The ACT scores were 8% below 21, 37% between 21 and 23, 31% between 24, and 25% above 28. 71% of the current freshmen were in the top fifth of their class; 91% were in the top two fifths. **Admissions Contact:** Margaret Blount, Director of Recruitment. E-Mail: *admissions@randolphcollege.edu* Web: *www.randolphcollege.edu*

FINANCIAL AID: In 2014-2015, 99% of all full-time freshmen and continuing full-time students received some form of financial aid. 76% of all full-time freshmen and 74% of continuing full-time students received need-based aid. The average freshman award was

$28,259. Need-based scholarships or need-based grants averaged $24,330; need-based self-help aid (loans and jobs) averaged $4,704; and other non-need-based awards and non-need-based scholarships averaged $27,741. 66% of undergraduate students work part-time. Average annual earnings from campus work are $1100. The average financial indebtedness of the 2014 graduate was $33,854. The FAFSA and the state aid form are required. The priority date for freshman financial aid applications for fall entry is March 1.

RANDOLPH-MACON COLLEGE E-3
www.rmc.edu

Ashland, VA 23005 (804) 752-7200
(800) 888-1762
Fax: (804) 752-4707 Email: admissions@rmc.edu
Full-time: 624 men, 741 women Faculty: 94; IIB, av$
Part-time: 11 men, 18 women Ph.D.s: 99%
Graduate: n/av Student/Faculty: 14 to 1
Year: 4-1-4, summer session Tuition: $36,340
Room & Board: $10,529 Freshman Class: 2955 applied, 1783 accepted, 427 enrolled
SAT CR/M/W: 548/542/528 ACT: 24 CEEB CODE: 5566
Application Deadline: March 1 COMPETITIVE+

The mission of Randolph-Macon College is to develop the mind and the character of its students, which underlies the college's ultimate purpose: to prepare undergraduates for successful lives. Randolph-Macon is a private, coeducational liberal arts and sciences college. There is 1 undergraduate school. In addition to regional accreditation, Randolph-Macon has baccalaureate program accreditation with NCATE and ACS. The 116-acre campus is in a suburban area 15 miles north of Richmond and 90 miles south of Washington, D.C. Including any residence halls, there are 75 buildings.

STUDENT LIFE: 74% of undergraduates are from Virginia. Others are from 29 states, 23 foreign countries, and Canada. 80% are from public schools. 76% are White; 46% are Protestant; 14% Catholic. The average age of freshmen is 18; all undergraduates, 20. 23% do not continue beyond their first year; 61% remain to graduate. **Housing:** 1074 students can be accommodated in college housing, which includes single-sex and coed dorms and on-campus apartments. In addition, there are honors houses, language houses, special-interest houses, fraternity houses, sorority houses, senior apartments, Greek housing, and several college-owned houses. On-campus housing is guaranteed for all 4 years and is available on a lottery system for upperclassmen. 80% of students live on campus; of those, 77% remain on campus on weekends. All students may keep cars.

FACULTY/CLASSROOMS: 56% of faculty are male; 44% are female. All teach and do research. No introductory courses are taught by graduate students. The average class size in an introductory lecture is 15; in a laboratory is 12; and in a regular course is 16.

PROGRAMS OF STUDY: Randolph-Macon confers B.A., and B.S. degrees. Bachelor's degrees are awarded in AGRICULTURE (environmental studies), BIOLOGICAL SCIENCE (biology/biological science and neurosciences), BUSINESS (accounting and business economics), COMMUNICATIONS AND THE ARTS (art history and appreciation, arts administration/management, classics, communications, dramatic arts, English, French, German, Greek, Latin, music, Spanish, and studio art), COMPUTER AND PHYSICAL SCIENCE (chemistry, computer science, mathematics, and physics), ENGINEERING AND ENVIRONMENTAL DESIGN (engineering physics), SOCIAL SCIENCE (archeology, Asian/Oriental studies, economics, history, international studies, philosophy, political science/government, psychology, religion, sociology, and women's studies). Biology, psychology, and economics/business have the largest enrollments.

ACTIVITIES: 31% of men belong to 8 national fraternities; 40% of women belong to 4 national sororities. There are 80 groups on campus, including and diversity council, leadership fellows, art, cheerleading, choir, chorale, chorus, commons activity board, communications, computers, dance, debate, drama, environmental,

ethnic, film, forensics, gay, honors, international, jazz band, literary magazine, musical theater, newspaper, opera, pep band, photography, political, professional, radio and TV, religious, social, social service, and student government. Popular campus events include Cultural Arts Series, Monster Bash and Beat Hampden-Sydney Week. **Sports:** There are 8 intercollegiate sports for men and 9 for women, and 15 intramural sports for men and 15 for women. Facilities include 6 tennis courts; several playing fields for men's and women's sports; 2 gyms; indoor 25-meter pool; lighted, all-weather turf football/lacrosse field; weight room; training room; sports and recreation center includes racquetball and squash courts, aerobics room, 3-lane track, multipurpose gym, and a climbing wall. **Graduates:** From July 1, 2013 to June 30, 2014, 120 bachelor's degrees were awarded. The most popular majors were visual and performing arts (17%), social sciences (14%), and biological/life sciences (13%). 20 companies recruited on campus in 2013-2014. In an average class, 2% graduate in 3 years or less, 56% graduate in 4 years or less, 62% graduate in 5 years or less, and 62% graduate in 6 years or less. Of the 2013 graduating class, 12% were enrolled in graduate school within 6 months of graduation, and 48% were employed.

SERVICES: Counseling and information services are available, as is tutoring in every subject. There is a reader service for the blind. **Library/Resources:** The library contains 173,817 volumes, 337,743 microform items, 6,644 audio/video tapes/CDs/DVDs, and subscribes to 4,892 periodicals including electronic. Computerized library services include interlibrary loans, database searching, Internet access, and Wi-Fi capability. Special learning facilities include an art gallery, radio station, TV station, an observatory, radio telescope, darkroom, and a greenhouse. **Physically Challenged Students:** 90% of the campus is accessible. Facilities include wheelchair ramps, elevators, special parking, specially equipped restrooms, special class scheduling, special housing. advisors for learning-disabled students. **Special:** The College offers special programs in engineering with Columbia University and the University of Virginia, in forestry with Duke University, and in accounting with Virginia Commonwealth University and Union University. The College has a Guaranteed Admission Agreement with the George Washington University School of Nursing. A new Early Assurance Program (EAP) exists with the Eastern Virginia Medical School (EVMS) Physician Assistant program. The College also offers priority acceptance agreements into medical schools with VCU, GWU, and EVMS. There is cross-registration with Hollins, Randolph College, Hampden-Sydney, Washington and Lee, and Mary Baldwin. Study-abroad programs are offered in 45 countries. Internships, dual majors, and a Washington semester are available. B.A.-B.S. degrees are possible in all majors. There are 19 national honor societies, including Phi Beta Kappa, and a freshman honors program. **Visiting:** There are regularly scheduled orientations for prospective students, including interviews, information sessions, tours, open houses, and visitation days. There are guides for informal visits, visitors may sit in on classes, and stay overnight. To schedule a visit, contact the Office of Admissions. **Campus Safety and Security:** Measures include 24-hour foot and vehicle patrol, emergency notification system, self-defense education, and security escort services. There are emergency telephones, lighted pathways/sidewalks, and controlled access to dorms/residences.

REQUIREMENTS: The SAT is required. Applicants must be graduates of an accredited secondary school or have completed their GED. Applicants should complete a minimum of 16 high school academic credits, including 4 years of English, 3 to 4 years each of math and science, and 2 to 3 years of foreign language, history, and social studies. An essay is required, and an interview is recommended. A GPA of 2.0 is required. AP and CLEP credits are accepted. Important factors in the admissions decision are advanced placement or honors courses, recommendations by school officials, and extracurricular activities record. To graduate, students must complete 110 credit hours, with 30 to 42 hours in the major and a minimum GPA of 2.0. All students must complete a Capstone course culminating the academic experience. All students must satisfy requirements in math, social science, lab science, literature, philosophy/theology, phys ed, fine arts, foreign language, history, and writing. There are also requirements for Western, non-Western, computing, multidisciplinary, and experiential courses. All first-year students must complete the First-Year Experience, a yearlong course team-taught by 2 professors in different disciplines. **Procedure:** Freshmen are admitted fall and spring. Entrance exams should be taken by January of the senior year. There are early admissions and deferred admissions plans. Early decision applications should be filed by November 15; regular applications, by March 1 for fall entry; and December 1 for spring entry, along with a $30 fee. Notification of early decision is sent January 1; regular decision, April 1. 65 applicants were on the 2014 waiting list; 15 were admitted. Applications are accepted on-line. Application fees are waived if application is completed on-line. **Transfer Students:** 22 transfer students enrolled in 2013-2014. Applicants must have a minimum GPA of 2.0 and must be eligible to return to their previous institution. They must submit high school and college transcripts and SAT scores (the SAT requirement is waived for students who have earned an associate degree). **International Students:** There are 38 international students enrolled. The school actively recruits these students. They must take the TOEFL with a minimum score of 550 on the paper-based TOEFL (PBT) or 80 on the Internet-based version (iBT), or take the IELTS. Either TOEFL or SAT or ACT is required for non-native English speakers.

ADMISSIONS: 60% of the 2014-2015 applicants were accepted. The SAT scores for the 2014-2015 freshman class were: Critical Reading--26% below 500, 48% between 500 and 599, 22% between 600 and 699, and 4% between 700 and 800; Math--30% below 500, 47% between 500 and 599, 21% between 600 and 699, and 3% between 700 and 800; Writing--35% below 500, 47% between 500 and 599, 16% between 600 and 699, and 2% between 700 and 800. 44% of the current freshmen were in the top fifth of their class; 73% were in the top two fifths. 6 freshmen graduated first in their class. **Admissions Contact:** David Lesesne, VP Enrollment, Dean of Admissions. E-Mail: *admissions@rmc.edu* Web: *www.rmc.edu*

FINANCIAL AID: In 2014-2015, 100% of all full-time freshmen and 99% of continuing full-time students received some form of financial aid. 37% of all full-time freshmen and 42% of continuing full-time students received need-based aid. The average freshman award was $27,792. Need-based scholarships or need-based grants averaged $12,798 ($17,700 maximum); need-based self-help aid (loans and jobs) averaged $4,450 ($5,500 maximum); other non-need-based awards and non-need-based scholarships averaged $19,844 ($31,860 maximum); and $5,934 from other forms of aid. 46% of undergraduate students work part-time. Average annual earnings from campus work are $1500. The average financial indebtedness of the 2014 graduate was $34,930. Randolph-Macon is a member of CSS. The FAFSA, the state aid form, and the college's own financial statement are required. The priority date for freshman financial aid applications for fall entry is February 15. The deadline for filing freshman financial aid applications for fall entry is March 1.

ROANOKE COLLEGE   C-3
www.roanoke.edu

Salem, VA 24153

	(540) 375-2500
	(800) 388-2276
Fax: (540) 375-2267	Email: admissions@roanoke.edu
Full-time: 794 men, 1184 women	Faculty: 164; IIB, av$
Part-time: 34 men, 42 women	Ph.D.s: 85%
Graduate: n/av	Student/Faculty: 12 to 1
Year: semesters, summer session	Tuition: $38,052
Room & Board: $11,924	Freshman Class: 4824 applied, 3344 accepted, 562 enrolled
SAT CR/M/W: 550/550/550 **ACT:** 23	CEEB CODE: 5571
Application Deadline: March 15	**COMPETITIVE**

Roanoke College provides its students with a true classic college experience with a focus on personal connections. Students receive a strong liberal arts foundation through a unique Intellectual Inquiry core curriculum emphasizing learning firsthand through topic based courses where fundamental concepts and skills are taught and then applied to real problems and issues. The college offers undergraduate programs in the arts and sciences and in business administration. There is one undergraduate school. In addition to regional accreditation, Roanoke has baccalaureate program accreditation with ACBSP,

TEAC, CAATE, and ACS. The 80-acre campus is in a suburban area 7 miles west of Roanoke, VA, in the Blue Ridge Mountains. Including any residence halls, there are 69 buildings.

STUDENT LIFE: 52% of undergraduates are from Virginia. Others are from 41 states, 33 foreign countries, and Canada. 81% are from public schools. 82% are White. 37% are Protestant; 24% claim no religious affiliation; 18% Catholic. The average age of freshmen is 18; all undergraduates, 20. 20% do not continue beyond their first year; 64% remain to graduate. **Housing:** 1503 students can be accommodated in college housing, which includes single-sex and coed dorms and on-campus apartments. In addition, there are honors houses, special-interest houses, fraternity houses, sorority houses, and six different living learning communities within residence life. On-campus housing is guaranteed for the freshman year only, is available on a first-come, first-served basis, and is available on a lottery system for upperclassmen. Priority is given to out-of-town students. 76% of students live on campus. All students may keep cars.

FACULTY/CLASSROOMS: 51% of faculty are male; 49% are female. All teach undergraduates, 73% do research, and 73% do both. No introductory courses are taught by graduate students. The average class size in an introductory lecture is 18; in a laboratory is 19; and in a regular course is 19.

PROGRAMS OF STUDY: Roanoke confers B.A., B.S. and B.B.A. degrees. Bachelor's degrees are awarded in AGRICULTURE (environmental studies), BIOLOGICAL SCIENCE (biochemistry and biology/biological science), BUSINESS (business administration and management and sports management), COMMUNICATIONS AND THE ARTS (art, art history and appreciation, communications, creative writing, French, literature, music, Spanish, and theatre arts), COMPUTER AND PHYSICAL SCIENCE (chemistry, computer science, mathematics, and physics), EDUCATION (athletic training and physical education), HEALTH PROFESSIONS (exercise science), SOCIAL SCIENCE (Christian studies, criminal justice, economics, history, international relations, philosophy, political science/ government, psychology, religion, and sociology). Biology, chemistry, philosophy, and Religious studies are the strongest academically. Business administration, biology, and psychology have the largest enrollments.

ACTIVITIES: 22% of men belong to 5 national fraternities; 20% of women belong to 4 national sororities. There are 100 groups on campus, including art, band, cheerleading, choir, chorale, chorus, computers, dance, debate, drama, environmental, ethnic, gay, honors, international, jazz band, literary magazine, newspaper, orchestra, pep band, photography, political, professional, radio and TV, religious, social, social service, and student government. Popular campus events include Family weekend, President's Ball, Fridays on the Quad (FOTQ), Winterfest and Alumni Weekend. **Sports:** There are 9 intercollegiate sports for men and 10 for women, and 14 intramural sports for men and 14 for women. Facilities include a 1400 seat FieldTurf stadium, a 2400-seat gym, lighted turf athletic fields, an all-weather track, practice and playing fields, tennis and racquetball courts, a swimming pool, and a fitness center with weight training and physical conditioning equipment. **Graduates:** From July 1, 2013 to June 30, 2014, 454 bachelor's degrees were awarded. The most popular majors were business administration (16%), psychology (11%), and communications (8%). 122 companies recruited on campus in 2013-2014. In an average class, 1% graduate in 3 years or less, 57% graduate in 4 years or less, 63% graduate in 5 years or less, and 64% graduate in 6 years or less. Of the 2013 graduating class, 31% were enrolled in graduate school within 6 months of graduation, and 93% were employed.

SERVICES: Counseling and information services are available, as is tutoring in every subject. A supervised peer tutoring program is available at no charge to students, as well as a writing center, and the center for learning and teaching. **Library/Resources:** The library contains 222,192 volumes, 142,837 microform items, 7,868 audio/video tapes/CDs/DVDs, and subscribes to 64,189 periodicals including electronic. Computerized library services include interlibrary loans, database searching, Internet access, and Wi-Fi capability. Special learning facilities include an art gallery, radio station, media classrooms, a video production facility, and multimedia computer labs. **Physically Challenged Students:** 85% of the campus is accessible. Facilities include wheelchair ramps, elevators, special parking, specially equipped restrooms, special class scheduling, and special housing. **Special:** We offer cross-registration with Hollins University and study abroad in many countries. Roanoke also offers internships, research with faculty, a Washington semester, the Virginia at Oxford Program, a dual degree engineering degree with Virginia Polytechnic Institute and State University, credit by exam, and pass/fail options. A special May Term offers unique intensive travel and local experiences. Non-degree study is available to those students admitted with special status. There are 28 national honor societies, including Phi Beta Kappa, a freshman honors program, and 15 departmental honors programs. **Visiting:** There are regularly scheduled orientations for prospective students, open houses that provide a sampling of college life at Roanoke as well as discussing financial aid and admissions. Student/Faculty panels answer questions, and campus tours are given. There are guides for informal visits, visitors may sit in on classes, and stay overnight. To schedule a visit, contact the Admissions Office. **Campus Safety and Security:** Measures include 24-hour foot and vehicle patrol, emergency notification system, self-defense education, and security escort services. There are shuttle buses, emergency telephones, lighted pathways/sidewalks, and controlled access to dorms/residences.

REQUIREMENTS: SAT or ACT is required. An essay, and an interview are recommended. Applicants must be graduates of accredited secondary schools or have earned a GED. The college requires 16 (20 recommended) academic units, based on 4 years of English, 3 courses in math, 4 courses in foreign language (recommended), and 2 courses each in lab science and social studies. An audition is also recommended for performing arts majors. AP and CLEP credits are accepted. Important factors in the admissions decision are advanced placement or honors courses, personality/intangible qualities, and leadership record. Requirements for graduation include completion of 33.5 courses, including about 9 to 12 in the major and about 11 to 14 in the Intellectual Inquiry core curriculum. The core consists of 2 first-year seminars; 5 to 7 topical courses drawn from the mathematical and natural sciences, the social sciences, and the humanities; a capstone that addresses a contemporary issue; and an intensive learning course. Students must also demonstrate competency in a foreign language at an intermediate level and complete 2 physical education courses. A 2.0 GPA is required. **Procedure:** Freshmen are admitted fall and spring. Entrance exams should be taken by January of the senior year. There are early decision, deferred admissions, and rolling admissions plans. Early decision applications should be filed by November 1; regular applications, by March 15 for fall entry, along with a $30 fee. Notification of early decision is sent December 1; regular decision, on a rolling basis. 95 early decision candidates were accepted for the 2014-2015 class. 190 applicants were on the 2014 waiting list; 47 were admitted. Applications are accepted on-line. Application fees are waived if application is completed on-line. **Transfer Students:** 78 transfer students enrolled in 2013-2014. Transfers must have a minimum GPA of 2.2. SAT scores and an interview are recommended. Transfers must be in good academic standing with their previous institution. 17 of 34 credits required for the bachelor's degree must be completed at Roanoke. **International Students:** There are 59 international students enrolled. The school actively recruits these students. They must take the TOEFL with a minimum score of 520 on the paper-based TOEFL (PBT) or 68 on the Internet-based version (iBT). They must also take the SAT or ACT.

ADMISSIONS: 69% of the 2014-2015 applicants were accepted. The SAT scores for the 2014-2015 freshman class were: Critical Reading-26% below 500, 42% between 500 and 599, 26% between 600 and 699, and 6% between 700 and 800; Math--30% below 500, 44% between 500 and 599, 24% between 600 and 699, and 1% between 700 and 800; Writing--31% below 500, 46% between 500 and 599, 20% between 600 and 699, and 3% between 700 and 800. The ACT scores were 27% below 21, 26% between 21 and 23, 23% between 24 and 26, 14% between 27 and 28, and 10% above 28. 34% of the current freshmen were in the top fifth of their class; 68% were in the top two fifths. There was 1 National Merit finalist. 4 freshmen graduated first in their class. **Admissions Contact:** Dr. Brenda Poggendorf, Vice President of Enrollment. E-Mail: *admissions@roanoke.edu* Web: *www.roanoke.edu*

FINANCIAL AID: In 2014-2015, 99% of all full-time freshmen and 97% of continuing full-time students received some form of financial

aid. 76% of all full-time freshmen and 72% of continuing full-time students received need-based aid. The average freshman award was $31,039. Need-based scholarships or need-based grants averaged $9,453; need-based self-help aid (loans and jobs) averaged $6,593; and other non-need-based awards and non-need-based scholarships averaged $17,083. 37% of undergraduate students work part-time. Average annual earnings from campus work are $1570. The average financial indebtedness of the 2014 graduate was $34,320. The FAFSA and the state aid form are required. The priority date for freshman financial aid applications for fall entry is March 1.

SAINT PAUL'S COLLEGE *(The complete profile is made available exclusively on our website, www.barronspac.com)*

SHENANDOAH UNIVERSITY D-1
www.su.edu

Winchester, VA 22601	(540) 665-4581
	(800) 432-2266
Fax: (540) 665-4627	Email: admit@su.edu
Full-time: 794 men, 1029 women	Faculty: 140; I
Part-time: 34 men, 35 women	Ph.D.s: 84%
Graduate: 500 men, 1301 women	Student/Faculty: 13 to 1
Year: semesters, summer session	Tuition: $30,188
Room & Board: $9728	Freshman Class: 1907 applied, 1575 accepted, 417 enrolled
SAT CR/M/W: 500/500/490 ACT: 21	CEEB CODE: 5613
Application Deadline: rolling	COMPETITIVE

Shenandoah University, founded in 1875, is a private university, affiliated with the United Methodist Church, offering undergraduate programs in arts and sciences, nursing, respiratory care, business, music, theater, and dance. Graduate programs include: Business, music, performance, pedagogy, music education, education, nursing and pharmacy. Health professions include: athletic training, occupational therapy, physical therapy, and physician assistant studies. There are 4 undergraduate schools and 7 graduate schools. In addition to regional accreditation, Shenandoah, SU has baccalaureate program accreditation with AACSB, ACPE, NASM, NLN, TEAC, CCNE, AMTA, and CoARC. The 315-acre campus is in a small town 72 miles west of Washington, D.C. Including any residence halls, there are 49 buildings.

STUDENT LIFE: 59% of undergraduates are from Virginia. Others are from 37 states, 20 foreign countries, and Canada. 65% are White; 14% African American. 58% are Protestant; 22% Catholic. The average age of freshmen is 18; all undergraduates, 21. 34% do not continue beyond their first year; 37% remain to graduate. **Housing:** 916 students can be accommodated in college housing, which includes coed dorms and off-campus apartments. In addition, there are honors houses, special-interest houses, and honors housing/community service required housing. On-campus housing is guaranteed for the freshman year only, is available on a first-come, first-served basis, and is available on a lottery system for upperclassmen. 54% of students commute. All students may keep cars.

FACULTY/CLASSROOMS: 42% of faculty are male; 58% are female. 63% teach undergraduates. No introductory courses are taught by graduate students. The average class size in an introductory lecture is 16; in a laboratory is 9; and in a regular course is 14.

PROGRAMS OF STUDY: Shenandoah, SU confers B.A., B.S., B.B.A., B.F.A, B.M. and B.M.T. degrees. Master's and Doctoral degrees are also awarded. Bachelor's degrees are awarded in BIOLOGICAL SCIENCE (biology/biological science), BUSINESS (business administration and management, entrepreneurial studies, and sports management), COMMUNICATIONS AND THE ARTS (acting, church music, collaborative piano, communications, composition, costume design, dance, dramatic arts, English, jazz, music, music production/recording technology, music performance, music technology, music theatre accompanying , music theory and composition, musical theater, performing arts, scenic and lighting design, Spanish, theater design, and theatre production), COMPUTER AND PHYSICAL SCIENCE (chemistry and mathematics), EDUCATION (core studies, music education, outdoor leadership/education, and university studies), ENGINEERING AND ENVIRONMENTAL DESIGN (environmental science), HEALTH PROFESSIONS (exercise science, health care administration, kinesiology, music therapy, nursing, public health, and respiratory therapy), SOCIAL SCIENCE (criminal justice, economics, history, political science/government, psychology, public administration, religion, and sociology. Conservatory, nursing, and pharmacy are the strongest academically. Pharmacy, nursing, and education have the largest enrollments.

ACTIVITIES: There are no fraternities or sororities. There are 83 groups on campus, including art, band, cheerleading, choir, chorale, chorus, dance, drama, environmental, ethnic, film, gay, honors, international, jazz band, literary magazine, musical theater, newspaper, Online radio station; Campus Activity Network- a group of students that work with the Office of Student Engagement to provide activities on campus, orchestra, pep band, political, professional, religious, social, social service, student government, and symphony. Popular campus events include Movie Nights, Wine Tasting, Jazz Trio Social, Relay for Life, Welcome Back, Sun Block Party, International Days, Homecoming and Family Weekend. **Sports:** There are 10 intercollegiate sports for men and 11 for women, and 8 intramural sports for men and 8 for women. Facilities include gymnasium for football, volleyball, and men's and women's basketball; seating 600. Stadium for football, men's and women's soccer, field hockey, men's and women's lacrosse; seating 2,500. Baseball, softball, and tennis practice and play at an adjoining community park. Four-lane 400-meter track. One multi-use grass field for practice and intramurals; armory has indoor athletics facility with batting cages. One weight room, one fitness room. The fitness room in the Brandt Center has cardio equipment, dumbbells, and selectorized weights. The weight room in Aikens has racks, weights, benches, and free weights. **Graduates:** From July 1, 2013 to June 30, 2014, 509 bachelor's degrees were awarded. The most popular majors were nursing (28%), kinesiology (10%), and business administration (9%). 62 companies recruited on campus in 2013-2014. In an average class, 36% graduate in 4 years or less, 52% graduate in 5 years or less, and 55% graduate in 6 years or less. Of the 2013 graduating class, 12% were enrolled in graduate school within 6 months of graduation, and 66% were employed.

SERVICES: Counseling and information services are available, as is tutoring in every subject. **Library/Resources:** The 2 libraries contain 130,954 volumes, 56,680 microform items, 24,193 audio/video tapes/CDs/DVDs, and subscribe to 86,490 periodicals including electronic. Computerized library services include interlibrary loans, database searching, Internet access, and Wi-Fi capability. Special learning facilities include an art gallery, Cadaver and nursing simulation labs in Health and Life Sciences Building, Children's Literature Center and Media Center in the Alson H. Smith, Jr. Library, Claude Moore Center for Literacy in the School of Education. The library has a book scan station including Discovery, is an online tool designed to provide a single, unified search interface for nearly all of the university's digital and print library content. The campus has a WEPA (wireless everywhere, print anywhere) system. Pharmacy Apothecary Museum, Feltner museum, Environmental Studies green rooftop garden. In October 2012, SU launched the All Steinway School initiative. When completed, SU will join an elite group of 12 conservatories in the U.S. and 10 international conservatories which bear the coveted "All-Steinway School" status. Our outdoor classroom, The Shenandoah River Campus at Cool Spring Battlefield, is 195 acres of land along the Shenandoah River providing outdoor leadership opportunities; a model computer classroom in the School of Education, as well as the Academic Enrichment Center. Conservatory has three academic observation rooms: recording studio, music therapy clinic, and Ruebush 209, music education. Ruebush 111 is a designated Mac Lab and is a specialized music technology classroom. Two designated classrooms for class piano. Specialized rooms for film and acting, Ruebush 154. Specialized equipment for voice: a voice science lab. **Physically Challenged Students:** 91% of the campus is accessible. Facilities include wheelchair ramps, elevators, special parking, specially equipped restrooms, special class scheduling, lowered drinking fountains, special housing. Electric doors, and 22 defibrillators. **Special:** Internships; dual majors (Pharm-MBA, MSN-MBA, DPT/MSAT); Accelerated degree programs: ASD NUR.BS, 3+2 model with AT, 3+4 model with PharmD; cross-registration consortiums (collaborative

agreements) with James Madison University (Nursing), Johns Hopkins School of Nursing, Marshall University School of Nursing, Old Dominion University School of Nursing, Radford University School of Nursing, West Virginia Wesleyan Department of Nursing, George Washington University (Pharmacy); B.A. interdisciplinary studies. Study abroad: Choice of 166 Global Partner institutions among 55 nations. No work-study programs; non-degree study is possible. Study abroad opportunities with Global Experiential Learning (GEL): short-term, credit-bearing, faculty-led programs offered during winter, spring and summer breaks. We also have the Global Citizenship Project (GCP). Selected students, faculty and staff can travel with their group during spring break to one of five destinations around the world. GCP is an exclusive offering created and funded by Shenandoah University. Applicants are selected according to their application and one-page essay submission. We also participate in the VFIC Foreign Language project. There are 3 national honor societies and 1 departmental honors program. **Visiting:** There are regularly scheduled orientations for prospective students, including information sessions with faculty and staff, student-guided campus tours, and lunch in the dining hall. There are guides for informal visits, visitors may sit in on classes, and stay overnight. To schedule a visit, contact Andrew Woodall at (800) 432-2266. **Campus Safety and Security:** Measures include 24-hour foot and vehicle patrol, emergency notification system, self-defense education, and security escort services. There are shuttle buses, emergency telephones, lighted pathways/sidewalks, controlled access to dorms/residences, lock-out car and dead-car battery jump assistance; online ICE program - In Case of Emergency, online program: Safer in 60 Seconds; orientation attendees get an emergency preparedness list; Emergency Operation Plan Program, each campus building has an emergency coordinator and outfitted with emergency preparedness items. RAD systems self-defense classes (men and women). TIPS - Responsible Alcohol Use and Peer Intervention Training Class. Training of Leesburg and GW campus staff on emergency/safety topics. All residence life staff trained in FEMA Incident Command procedures.

REQUIREMENTS: The SAT is required. The high school transcript should indicate courses pursued, grades earned, grade-point average and credits earned. It is required that the coursework include: four units of English, three units of mathematics (Algebra I, Algebra II and Geometry), two units of social studies, and two units of science (including one laboratory science). Two units of a foreign language are strongly recommended. Other classes may be appropriate for some curricula and will be evaluated on an individual basis by the Office of Admissions. Applicants are strongly recommended to indicate community and extra-curricular involvement. Shenandoah Conservatory applicants are also required to successfully complete an audition or portfolio review. The most heavily weighted factor in the applicant's total profile is actual academic performance, as indicated by the high school transcript. The SAT or the ACT is required. No preference as to which one a student submits. Applicants to music, theatre and dance programs must complete an audition or portfolio review. A GPA of 2.5 is required. AP and CLEP credits are accepted. Important factors in the admissions decision are advanced placement or honors courses, extracurricular activities record, and evidence of special talent.To graduate, all students must have taken the required core curriculum with a cumulative grade-point average of 2.0. Some programs require higher grade-point average in the major. The minimum number of credit hours required for a baccalaureate degree is 120. Other requirements vary depending on the program of study. Candidates for baccalaureate degrees must earn a minimum of 30-credit hours of the 120-credit-hour requirement at Shenandoah University. At least 30-credit hours must be at or above the 300 level. **Procedure:** Freshmen are admitted fall and spring. Entrance exams should be taken by junior year or early in the senior year. There are deferred admissions and rolling admissions plans. Application deadlines are open. Application fee is $30. Notification is sent on a rolling basis. 12 applicants were on the 2014 waiting list; 9 were admitted. Applications are accepted on-line. **Transfer Students:** 130 transfer students enrolled in 2013-2014. Transfer applicants must submit evidence of good standing at the college last attended and an official transcript(s) of credits earned at all institutions previously attended, showing entrance credits accepted and results of standardized tests administered. Minimum cumulative 2.0 GPA with 24 college credits is required. Those with less than 24 college credits earned need to submit high school transcript for review. 30 of 120 credits required for the bachelor's degree must be completed at Shenandoah, SU. **International Students:** There are 98 international students enrolled. The school actively recruits these students. They must take the TOEFL with a minimum score of 527 on the paper-based TOEFL (PBT) or 71 on the Internet-based version (iBT), or take the IELTS (International English Language Testing System) is also accepted. They must also take the SAT.

ADMISSIONS: 83% of the 2014-2015 applicants were accepted. The SAT scores for the 2014-2015 freshman class were: Critical Reading- -48% below 500, 40% between 500 and 599, 10% between 600 and 699, and 2% between 700 and 800; Math--47% below 500, 37% between 500 and 599, 15% between 600 and 699, and 1% between 700 and 800; Writing--55% below 500, 32% between 500 and 599, 11% between 600 and 699, and 2% between 700 and 800. The ACT scores were 46% below 21, 22% between 21 and 23, 20% between 24 and 26, 5% between 27 and 28, and 7% above 28. **Admissions Contact:** Andrew Woodall, Exe Director of Recruitment & Admissions. E-Mail: *admit@su.edu* Web: *www.su.edu*

FINANCIAL AID: In 2014-2015, 96% of all full-time freshmen and 98% of continuing full-time students received some form of financial aid. 76% of all full-time freshmen and 75% of continuing full-time students received need-based aid. The average freshman award was $25,881. Need-based scholarships or need-based grants averaged $6,995 ($10,000 maximum); need-based self-help aid (loans and jobs) averaged $4,273 ($5,500 maximum); and other non-need-based awards and non-need-based scholarships averaged $9,641 ($28,000 maximum). 49% of undergraduate students work part-time. Average annual earnings from campus work are $2300. The average financial indebtedness of the 2014 graduate was $28,738. The FAFSA and the state aid form, and Virginia United Methodist Scholarship application are required. Check with the school for current application deadlines.

THE UNIVERSITY OF VIRGINIA'S COLLEGE AT WISE
A-3

www.uvawise.edu

Wise, VA 24293

(276) 328-0100
(756) 328-0102

Fax: (276) 376-1045
Email: admissions@uvawise.edu

Full-time: 710 men, 735 women	**Faculty:** n/av; IIB, -$
Part-time: 125 men, 335 women	**Ph.D.s:** 70%
Graduate: n/av	**Student/Faculty:** n/av
Year: semesters, summer session	**Tuition:** $7721 ($21,336)
Room & Board: $8000	**Freshman Class:** n/av
SAT or ACT: required	**CEEB CODE:** 5124
Application Deadline: see profile	**COMPETITIVE**

The University of Virginia's College at Wise, founded in 1954, offers undergraduate programs through the departments of business studies, education, languages and literature, behavioral and social sciences, natural sciences, math and computer science, history and philosophy, visual and performing arts, and nursing. The figures in the above capsule and this profile are approximate. In addition to regional accreditation, UVA's College at Wise has baccalaureate program accreditation with NLN. The 396-acre campus is in a small town 60 miles northwest of Bristol. Including any residence halls, there are 42 buildings.

STUDENT LIFE: 95% of undergraduates are from Virginia. Others are from 11 states and 7 foreign countries. 99% are from public schools. 89% are white. The average age of freshmen is 18; all undergraduates, 24. 35% do not continue beyond their first year; 29% remain to graduate.

FACULTY/CLASSROOMS: 60% of faculty are male; 40% are female. All teach undergraduates, 50% do research, and 50% do both. The average class size in an introductory lecture is 20; in a laboratory, 17; and in a regular course, 18.

PROGRAMS OF STUDY: UVA's College at Wise confers B.A., B.S., and B.S.N. degrees. Bachelor's degrees are awarded in BIOLOGICAL SCIENCE (biology/biological science), BUSINESS (accounting and business administration and management), COMMUNICATIONS AND THE ARTS (art, communications, dramatic arts, English, French, and Spanish), COMPUTER AND PHYSICAL SCIENCE (chemistry, information sciences and systems, and mathematics), ENGINEERING AND ENVIRONMENTAL DESIGN (environmental science), HEALTH PROFESSIONS (medical laboratory technology and nursing), SOCIAL SCIENCE (criminal justice, economics, history, international studies, law enforcement and corrections, liberal arts/general studies, political science/government, psychology, and social science). Natural science, accounting, and math are the strongest academically. Business administration, history, and education have the largest enrollments.

ACTIVITIES: 7% of men belong to 1 local and 3 national fraternities; 7% of women belong to 3 local and 1 national sororities. There are 53 groups on campus, including art, band, cheerleading, chess, choir, chorale, chorus, communications, dance, drama, ethnic, film, gay, honor court, honors, inter-Greek council, international, jazz band, literary magazine, musical theater, multicultural alliance, newspaper, pep band, political, professional, radio and TV, religious, resident hall association, social, social service, student activities board, and student government. Popular campus events include the Holly Ball, Jam for Man, and Extramural Flag Football Scramble.

SERVICES: Counseling and information services are available, as is tutoring in every subject. There is a reader service for the blind, and remedial math and writing. Tutoring is free to all registered students. **Library/Resources:** The library contains 143,265 volumes, 66,230 microform items, and 4,786 audio/video tapes/CDs/DVDs, and subscribes to 2,265 periodicals including electronic. Computerized library services include interlibrary loans, database searching, and Internet access. Special learning facilities include a radio station, and observatory. **Physically Challenged Students:** All of the campus is accessible. Facilities include wheelchair ramps, elevators, special parking, specially equipped restrooms, special class scheduling, lowered drinking fountains, and special housing. **Special:** The college offers co-op programs in all majors, internships in education, social sciences, and communication, on-campus work-study programs, B.A.-B.S. degrees in most majors, dual and student-designed majors, and pass/fail options for classes not required for the major. There are 4 national honor societies, a freshman honors program, and 9 departmental honors programs. **Visiting:** There are regularly scheduled orientations for prospective students, including an interview, a campus tour, a meal, and class visitation. There are guides for informal visits and visitors may sit in on classes. To schedule a visit, contact the Admissions Office. **Campus Safety and Security:** Measures include 24-hour foot and vehicle patrol, self-defense education, and security escort services. There are emergency telephones, lighted pathways/sidewalks, and a crime prevention office.

REQUIREMENTS: The SAT or ACT is required. All applicants must be graduates of approved secondary schools or hold a GED. Preference is given to students who earn an Advanced Studies Diploma or its equivalent, rank in the top half of their graduating class, have a satisfactory score on the SAT (18 on the ACT), and complete 4 years of English, 3 or more courses in math, including algebra I and II and a course selected from among geometry, trigonometry, advanced math, or calculus, 2 or more years of natural science beyond general science, 2 or more years of a foreign language, and 1 year each of American history and world history. A GPA of 2.4 is required. AP credits are accepted. Important factors in the admissions decision are advanced placement or honors courses, recommendations by school officials, and leadership record.

FINANCIAL AID: The FAFSA and the college's own financial statement are required. Check with the school for current application deadlines.

UNIVERSITY OF MARY WASHINGTON E-2
www.umw.edu

Fredericksburg, VA 22401   **(540) 654-2000**

Fax: (540) 654-1857	Email: admit@umw.edu
Full-time: 1357 men, 2524 women	Faculty: 244; IIB, av$
Part-time: 244 men, 390 women	Ph.D.s: 89%
Graduate: 176 men, 402 women	Student/Faculty: 14 to 1
Year: semesters, summer session	Tuition: $9546 ($21,560)
Room & Board: $10,238	Freshman Class: 4847 applied, 3724 accepted, 955 enrolled
SAT CR/M/W: 570/560/560 ACT: 25	CEEB CODE: 5398
Application Deadline: February 1	VERY COMPETITIVE

The University of Mary Washington is a premier, selective public liberal arts and sciences university in Virginia, highly respected for its commitment to academic excellence, strong undergraduate liberal arts and sciences program, and dedication to life-long learning. The university features colleges of business, education and arts and sciences, including a residential campus in Fredericksburg, Va., Stafford and Dahlgren, Va., which serves as a center of development of educational and research partnerships between the Navy, higher education institutions and the region's employers. There are 3 undergraduate schools and 2 graduate schools. In addition to regional accreditation, has baccalaureate program accreditation with NASM. The 176-acre campus is in a suburban area 50 miles south of Washington, D.C., and 50 miles north of Richmond. Including any residence halls, there are 48 buildings.

STUDENT LIFE: 87% of undergraduates are from Virginia. Others are from 38 states, 23 foreign countries, and Canada. 87% are from public schools. 64% are White; 14% race unknown. The average age of freshmen is 18; all undergraduates, 22. 17% do not continue beyond their first year; 76% remain to graduate.

FACULTY/CLASSROOMS: 51% of faculty are male; 49% are female. All teach undergraduates. No introductory courses are taught by graduate students. The average class size in an introductory lecture is 27; in a laboratory is 22; and in a regular course is 20.

PROGRAMS OF STUDY: confers B.A., B.S. and B.L.S. degrees. Master's degrees are also awarded. Bachelor's degrees are awarded in BIOLOGICAL SCIENCE (biology/biological science), BUSINESS (business administration and management), COMMUNICATIONS AND THE ARTS (art history and appreciation, classics, dramatic arts, English, French, German, historic preservation, music, Spanish, and studio art), COMPUTER AND PHYSICAL SCIENCE (chemistry, computer science, mathematics, and physics), ENGINEERING AND ENVIRONMENTAL DESIGN (environmental science), SOCIAL SCIENCE (American studies, anthropology, economics, geography, history, international relations, liberal arts/general studies, philosophy, political science/government, psychology, religion, and sociology). Historic preservation, history, political science, international affairs, English, biology, psychology, earth and environmental sciences are the strongest academically. Business administration, psychology, biology, English, and history have the largest enrollments.

ACTIVITIES: There are 140 groups on campus, including Students Helping Honduras, art, bagpipe, cheerleading, choir, chorale, chorus, Class council, computers, dance, debate, drama, environmental, ethnic, film, gay, honors, international, jazz band, literary magazine, musical theater, newspaper, opera, orchestra, pep band, photography, political, professional, radio and TV, religious, social, social service, student government, symphony, and yearbook. Popular campus events include Rocktoberfest, Junior Ring Dance and Multicultural Fair.

SERVICES: Counseling and information services are available, as is tutoring in most subjects. There is a reader service for the blind. A writing center, and a speaking center **Physically Challenged Students:** 75% of the campus is accessible. Facilities include wheelchair ramps, elevators, special parking, specially equipped restrooms, lowered drinking fountains, lowered telephones, and special housing. **Special:** Study abroad anywhere in the world, a Washington semester, and credit for off-campus work experience are available. The univer-

sity offers dual majors, work-study programs, student-designed majors, and pass/fail options. More than 500 internships for credit are also available. Teacher licensure preparation is offered for elementary and secondary education. Elementary education is a 5-year bachelor's-master's degree program. There are 23 national honor societies, including Phi Beta Kappa, and a freshman honors program. **Visiting:** There are regularly scheduled orientations for prospective students, including information sessions, available Monday through Friday at 10:30 a.m. and 2 p.m., followed by a student-guided tour, and 2 Saturday open houses each semester. Visitors may sit in on classes and stay overnight. To schedule a visit, contact the Office of Admissions at (540) 654-2000. **Campus Safety and Security:** Measures include 24-hour foot and vehicle patrol, emergency notification system, self-defense education, and security escort services. There are emergency telephones, lighted pathways/sidewalks, and controlled access to dorms/residences.

REQUIREMENTS: The SAT or ACT and ACT Writing Test are recommended. Applicants must be graduates of an accredited secondary school or hold the GED. The Admissions Committee recommends that applicants complete 4 years of each of math, English, foreign language, science, and social studies. A SAT subject test is strongly recommended. Application essays are required. A counselor or teacher recommendation is also required. AP and CLEP credits are accepted. Important factors in the admissions decision are advanced placement or honors courses, evidence of special talent, and recommendations by school officials.

ADMISSIONS: 77% of the 2013-2014 applicants were accepted. The SAT scores for the 2013-2014 freshman class were: Critical Reading--10% below 500, 42% between 500 and 599, 37% between 600 and 699, and 10% between 700 and 800; Math--14% below 500, 47% between 500 and 599, 34% between 600 and 699, and 4% between 700 and 800; Writing--12% below 500, 45% between 500 and 599, 37% between 600 and 699, and 6% between 700 and 800. The ACT scores were 7% below 21, 24% between 21 and 23, 34% between 24 and 26, 18% between 27 and 28, and 17% above 28. There were 3 National Merit finalists. 5 freshmen graduated first in their class.

FINANCIAL AID: In a recent year, 66% of all full-time freshmen and 63% of continuing full-time students received some form of financial aid. 34% of all full-time freshmen and 32% of continuing full-time students received need-based aid. The average freshman award was $4,800. Need-based scholarships or need-based grants averaged $6,493 ($2,455 maximum); need-based self-help aid (loans and jobs) averaged $3,324 ($7,500 maximum); and other non-need-based awards and non-need-based scholarships averaged $15,423 ($30,371 maximum). 28% of undergraduate students work part-time. Average annual earnings from campus work are $2175. The average financial indebtedness of a recent year graduate was $23,300. The FAFSA and the college's own financial statement are required. The deadline for filing freshman financial aid applications for fall entry is March 1.

UNIVERSITY OF VIRGINIA D-3
www.virginia.edu

Charlottesville, VA 22904   **(434) 982-0311**

Fax: (434) 924-3587	Email: undergradadmission@virginia.edu
Full-time: 6965 men, 8667 women	Faculty: 1187; I, +$
Part-time: 358 men, 493 women	Ph.D.s: 91%
Graduate: 3584 men, 3665 women	Student/Faculty: 15 to 1
Year: semesters, summer session	Tuition: $12,998 ($42,184)
Room & Board: $10,052	Freshman Class: 31021 applied, 8997 accepted, 3709 enrolled
SAT CR/M/W: 680/710/670 ACT: 32	CEEB CODE: 5820
Application Deadline: January 1	MOST COMPETITIVE

The University of Virginia, founded in 1819, is a public institution with undergraduate programs in architecture, arts and sciences, commerce, education, engineering and applied science, and nursing. There are 7 undergraduate schools and 10 graduate schools. In addition to regional accreditation, UVA has baccalaureate program accreditation with AACSB, ABET, ASLA, NAAB, TEAC, ACS, APA,

ASLHA, CCNE, and NAST. The 1167-acre campus is in a suburban area 70 miles northwest of Richmond, VA. Including any residence halls, there are 537 buildings.

STUDENT LIFE: 70% of undergraduates are from Virginia. Others are from 49 states, 121 foreign countries, and Canada. 72% are from public schools. 61% are White; 12% Asian American. The average age of freshmen is 18; all undergraduates, 20. 3% do not continue beyond their first year; 93% remain to graduate. **Housing:** 6213 students can be accommodated in college housing, which includes coed dorms, on-campus apartments, and married student housing. In addition, there are honors houses, language houses, and special-interest houses. On-campus housing is guaranteed for the freshman year only, is available on a first-come, first-served basis, and is available on a lottery system for upperclassmen. 59% of students commute. Upperclassmen may keep cars.

FACULTY/CLASSROOMS: 62% of faculty are male; 38% are female. 89% teach undergraduates, 71% do research, and 62% do both. Graduate students teach 36% of introductory courses. The average class size in an introductory lecture is 44; in a laboratory is 22; and in a regular course is 33.

PROGRAMS OF STUDY: UVA confers B.A., B.S., B.Ar.H., B.I.S., B.S.C., B.S.Ed., B.S.N. and B.U.E.P. degrees. Master's and Doctoral degrees are also awarded. Bachelor's degrees are awarded in BIOLOGICAL SCIENCE (biology/biological science), BUSINESS (business administration and management), COMMUNICATIONS AND THE ARTS (art, classics, comparative literature, dramatic arts, English, French, German, Italian, music, Slavic languages, and Spanish), COMPUTER AND PHYSICAL SCIENCE (astronomy, chemistry, computer science, mathematics, and physics), ENGINEERING AND ENVIRONMENTAL DESIGN (aerospace studies, architectural history, architecture, biomedical engineering, chemical engineering, city/community/regional planning, civil engineering, computer engineering, electrical/electronics engineering, engineering and applied science, environmental science, mechanical engineering, systems engineering, and urban design), HEALTH PROFESSIONS (health care administration, nursing, and speech pathology/audiology), SOCIAL SCIENCE (African American studies, anthropology, area studies, child psychology/development, economics, history, interdisciplinary studies, international relations, philosophy, political science/government, psychology, public administration, religion, and sociology). English, history, and biology are the strongest academically. Commerce, biology, and economics have the largest enrollments.

ACTIVITIES: 23% of men belong to 27 national fraternities; 25% of women belong to 16 national sororities. Groups on campus include and tour guides, art, band, cheerleading, chess, choir, chorale, chorus, computers, dance, debate, drama, environmental, ethnic, film, forensics, gay, honors, international, jazz band, judiciary, literary magazine, marching band, musical theater, newspaper, opera, orchestra, pep band, photography, political, professional, radio and TV, religious, social, social service, student government, symphony, and yearbook. Popular campus events include Culturefest and Family Weekend. **Sports:** There are 11 intercollegiate sports for men and 12 for women, and 18 intramural sports for men and 18 for women. Facilities include a 61,500-seat stadium, 16,000 seat arena, 4 recreation centers including an aquatics and fitness center. **Graduates:** From July 1, 2013 to June 30, 2014, 3697 bachelor's degrees were awarded. The most popular majors were economics (10%), commerce (9%), and psychology (8%). 500 companies recruited on campus in 2013-2014. In an average class, 2% graduate in 3 years or less, 86% graduate in 4 years or less, 92% graduate in 5 years or less, and 93% graduate in 6 years or less.

SERVICES: Counseling and information services are available, as is tutoring in every subject. There is a reader service for the blind. There are transcribers, note takers, and taped readings for disabled students. **Library/Resources:** The 15 libraries contain 5.2 million volumes, 2.1 million microform items, 148,776 audio/video tapes/CDs/DVDs, and subscribe to 152,902 periodicals including electronic. Computerized library services include interlibrary loans, database searching, Internet access, and Wi-Fi capability. Special learning facilities include an art gallery, radio station, TV station, an art museum, and observatory. **Physically Challenged Students:** All of the campus is accessible. Facilities include wheelchair ramps, elevators, special parking, specially equipped restrooms, special class scheduling, lowered drinking fountains, lowered telephones, curb cuts, voice synthesizers, braille printers, and large-screen monitors. **Special:** The college offers internships, study abroad, accelerated degree programs, B.A.-B.S. degrees in biology, environmental sciences, chemistry and physics, co-op programs in engineering, and nondegree study. Dual majors in most arts and sciences programs, student-designed majors, an interdisciplinary major and Echols, and Rodman Scholars program (invited students design own curricula with many requirements waived), and pass/fail options are available. There is a chapter of Phi Beta Kappa, and a freshman honors program, and 35 departmental honors programs. **Visiting:** There are regularly scheduled orientations for prospective students, including visits consist of comprehensive information sessions and campus tours. There are guides for informal visits, visitors may sit in on classes, and stay overnight. To schedule a visit, contact the Monroe Society at (434) 924-3321. **Campus Safety and Security:** Measures include 24-hour foot and vehicle patrol, emergency notification system, self-defense education, and security escort services. There are shuttle buses, emergency telephones, lighted pathways/sidewalks, controlled access to dorms/residences, and bicycle registration.

REQUIREMENTS: Applicants can substitute the ACT for the SAT if the optional ACT Writing Test is also taken. Two SAT subject tests of the student's choosing are strongly recommended. With few exceptions, candidates graduate from accredited secondary schools. While the GED is accepted, it is rare for candidates for first-year admission who have this credential to be competitive in the admissions process. Applicants should complete 16 high school academic courses, including 4 courses of English, 4 courses of math, 2 courses of physics, biology, or chemistry (3 if applying to engineering), 2 years of foreign language, and 1 course of social science. A letter of recommendation (preferably from the secondary school) is required; also, a teacher's recommendation is recommended. AP credits are accepted. To graduate, students must complete 120 credit hours, with 18 to 42 hours in the major and a minimum GPA of 2.0. Distribution requirements include 12 hours of math and science, 6 hours each of humanities, composition, and social sciences, 4 semesters of foreign languages, 3 hours of historical studies, and 3 hours of non-Western perspectives. **Procedure:** Freshmen are admitted fall. Entrance exams should be taken by December of the senior year. There are early admissions and deferred admissions plans. Applications should be filed by January 1 for fall entry, along with a $60 fee. Notifications are sent April 1. 3456 applicants were on the 2014 waiting list; 42 were admitted. Applications are accepted on-line. **Transfer Students:** 671 transfer students enrolled in 2013-2014. For the largest school (Arts and Sciences) an applicant for transfer admission must be in good academic and social standing at any college that he or she is currently attending or has previously attended and must be eligible to return there. To be competitive for admission, we recommend that a transfer student have a cumulative grade point average of B+ or better in all college work attempted. 60 of 120 credits required for the bachelor's degree must be completed at UVA. **International Students:** There are 776 international students enrolled. The school actively recruits these students. They must take the TOEFL, International English Language Testing System (IELTS). They must also take the SAT or ACT, as well as the same tests as all other entering students.

ADMISSIONS: 29% of the 2014-2015 applicants were accepted. The SAT scores for the 2014-2015 freshman class were: Critical Reading--2% below 500, 15% between 500 and 599, 48% between 600 and 699, and 36% between 700 and 800; Math--2% below 500, 12% between 500 and 599, 42% between 600 and 699, and 44% between 700 and 800; Writing--3% below 500, 14% between 500 and 599, 46% between 600 and 699, and 37% between 700 and 800. The ACT scores were 1% below 21, 2% between 21 and 23, 9% between 24 and 26, 13% between 27 and 28, and 75% above 28. 95% of the current freshmen were in the top fifth of their class; 98% were in the top two fifths. **Admissions Contact:** Gregory W. Roberts, Dean of Admissions. E-Mail: *undergradadmission@virginia.edu* Web: *www.virginia.edu*

FINANCIAL AID: In 2014-2015, 56% of all full-time freshmen and 49% of continuing full-time students received some form of financial aid. 34% of all full-time freshmen and 33% of continuing full-time students received need-based aid. The average freshman award was $19,017. The average financial indebtedness of the 2014 graduate was

$22,933. The FAFSA and the college's own financial statement are required. The deadline for filing freshman financial aid applications for fall entry is March 1.

VIRGINIA COMMONWEALTH UNIVERSITY E-3
www.vcu.edu

Richmond, VA 23284

(804) 828-0100
(800) 841-3638

Fax: (804) 828-1899

Email: admissions@vcu.edu

Full-time: 8779 men, 11515 women

Faculty: I, --$

Part-time: 1489 men, 2179 women

Ph.D.s: n/av

Graduate: 2751 men, 4450 women

Student/Faculty: 17 to 1

Year: semesters, summer session

Tuition: $12,398 ($30,459)

Room & Board: $9318

Freshman Class: 13818 applied, 10426 accepted, 3586 enrolled

SAT CR/M/W: 550/540/530 **ACT:** 23

CEEB CODE: 5570

Application Deadline: January 15

COMPETITIVE

Virginia Commonwealth University (VCU)is a major public research university. VCU enrolls more than 31,000 students in 222 degree and certificate programs and encompasses one of the largest academic health centers in the nation. The VCU Health System supports the university's health care education, research and patient care mission. VCU became one of the only 28 public universities in the country with an academic medical center to be designated as a research university with very high research activity as well as a community engaged institution, both by the Carnegie Foundation. A broad array of university-approved centers and institutes of excellence involving faculty from multiple disciplines in public policy, biotechnology and health care discoveries supports the university's research mission. There are 14 undergraduate schools and 1 graduate school. In addition to regional accreditation, VCU has baccalaureate program accreditation with AACSB, ABET, ACEJMC, ACPE, ADA, APTA, CSAB, CSWE, FIDER, NASAD, NASDTEC, NASM, NCATE, NLN, NRPA, CAATE, and CACREP. The 144-acre campus is in an urban area 2 miles west of downtown Richmond and 90 miles from Washington, D.C. Including any residence halls, there are 216 buildings.

STUDENT LIFE: 90% of undergraduates are from Virginia. Others are from 50 states, 106 foreign countries, and Canada. 52% are White; 15% African American; 12% Asian American. The average age of freshmen is 18; all undergraduates, 21. **Housing:** 5857 students can be accommodated in college housing, which includes coed dorms and on-campus apartments. In addition, there are honors houses, ASPIRE- is an innovative and comprehensive community engagement focused living-learning program for sophmores at VCU. On-campus housing is guaranteed for the freshman year only, is available on a first-come, and first-served basis. 77% of students commute. All students may keep cars.

FACULTY/CLASSROOMS: 55% of faculty are male; 45% are female. No introductory courses are taught by graduate students.

PROGRAMS OF STUDY: VCU confers B.A., B.S., B.I.S., B.M., B.S.W. and B.F.A. degrees. Master's and Doctoral degrees are also awarded. Bachelor's degrees are awarded in AGRICULTURE (environmental studies), BIOLOGICAL SCIENCE (bioinformatics and biology/biological science), BUSINESS (accounting, business administration and management, marketing/retailing/merchandising, and sports management), COMMUNICATIONS AND THE ARTS (art history and appreciation, communications, crafts, dance, dramatic arts, English, film arts, graphic design, languages, media arts, music, painting, photography, and sculpture), COMPUTER AND PHYSICAL SCIENCE (chemistry, computer science, information sciences and systems, mathematics, physics, and science), EDUCATION (art education, foreign languages education, and health education), ENGINEERING AND ENVIRONMENTAL DESIGN (bioengineering, biomedical engineering, chemical engineering, computer engineering, electrical/electronics engineering, electrical/electronics engineering technology, interior design, and mechanical engineering), HEALTH PROFESSIONS (clinical science, dental hygiene, and nursing), SOCIAL SCIENCE (African American studies, anthropology, criminal justice, economics, fashion design and technology,

forensic studies, history, homeland security, interdisciplinary studies, international studies, philosophy, philosophy and religion, political science/government, psychology, religion, safety science, social work, sociology, and urban studies). Biology, psychology and mass communication have the largest enrollments.

ACTIVITIES: There are 580 groups on campus, including art, band, cheerleading, chess, choir, chorale, chorus, computers, dance, debate, drama, ethnic, film, forensics, gay, honors, international, jazz band, literary magazine, musical theater, newspaper, opera, pep band, photography, political, professional, radio and TV, religious, social, social service, student government, symphony, and yearbook. Popular campus events include Annual Fall Step Show, Fest, Greek Week, Homecoming International Festival, Spring Fest, and Welcome Week. **Sports:** There are 8 intercollegiate sports for men and 8 for women, and 28 intramural sports for men and 28 for women. Facilities include Facilities include a multipurpose indoor facility for intercollegiate athletics and recreational sports; a 24,495-square-foot recreation space with a fitness center, an activity center, and a wellness resource center; a 3,250-seat stadium for soccer and track and field events; a 250-seat tennis center open year-round, and a 25,990-square-foot recreation complex containing gym, handball/racquetball courts, weight room, and cardiovascular fitness space. Facilities also include a 1,200-seat field and jogging track with artificial turf; a baseball field; and a 42,989-square-foot aquatic and recreational facility with a 6-lane pool and spa, handball/racquetball and squash courts, and gyms. **Graduates:** From July 1, 2013 to June 30, 2014, 4786 bachelor's degrees were awarded. The most popular majors were psychology (7%), business (6%), and nursing (5%). In an average class, 57% graduate in 6 years or less.

SERVICES: Counseling and information services are available, as is tutoring in most subjects. There is a reader service for the blind, remedial math, reading, and writing. **Library/Resources:** The 2 libraries contain 2.5 million volumes, 3.3 million microform items, and 54,177 audio/video tapes/CDs/DVDs. Computerized library services include interlibrary loans, database searching, Internet access, and Wi-Fi capability. Special learning facilities include an art gallery, radio station, and TV station. **Physically Challenged Students:** 90% of the campus is accessible. Facilities include wheelchair ramps, elevators, special parking, specially equipped restrooms, special class scheduling, and lowered drinking fountains. **Special:** The university has these special study options: Accelerated programs, cooperative education program, distance learning, double major, dual enrollment, English as a second language (ESL), Honors program, independent study, internships, student-designed major, study abroad and teacher certification program. There are 21 national honor societies and a freshman honors program. **Visiting:** There are regularly scheduled orientations for prospective students, daily tours every Monday-Saturday except holidays and holiday weekends. The information session is followed by an hour-long guided walk tour of the Monroe Park. Registration is required for attendance at these daily sessions. To schedule a visit, contact the Office of Admissions. **Campus Safety and Security:** Measures include 24-hour foot and vehicle patrol, emergency notification system, self-defense education, and security escort services. There are shuttle buses, emergency telephones, lighted pathways/sidewalks, controlled access to dorms/residences, formal presentations, online crime prevention program, annual security report, crime prevention through environmental design, community police officers/certified prevention specialists, security inspections of facilities, operation ID bike and computer registration, and victim/witness assistance program.

REQUIREMENTS: Candidates for admission to VCU are reviewed base on their academic performance in an accredited high school or on GED scores and either SAT Test or ACT scores. The college preparatory curriculum is highly preferred, and a minimum of 20 units is required for admission to all programs on the Monroe Park Campus. Extracurricular activities and employment experience may strengthen an application. Essays are required for scholarship consideration and for School for the Arts applicants. Freshman also are required to take SATs and have a personal computer. Freshman applicants under 22yrs must submit official SAT or ACT scores. Applicants with native language other than English must submit scores for English as a Foreign Language (TOEFL) in addition to any other required test scores. A GPA of 2.0 is required. AP and CLEP credits are accepted.The total number of semester credits required for graduation depends upon the degree program. Specific information may be found under degree program descriptions. In addition to the specific requirements listed by the college/school/department, the following graduation checklist for undergraduate students summarizes all general requirements for graduation and insurance of a diploma. • Overall undergraduate GPA must be 2.0 or greater. • Student must have completed 25 percent of the semester-hour credits required for the bachelor's degree in residence at VCU, including at least 30 of the last 45 credits. • Student must have earned a minimum of 120 credits, including transfer credits • All grades of Incomplete (I), Continued (CO), Progress (PR), Not Recorded (NR) and No Grade (NG) must be converted to final letter grades no later than the last day of class of the semester in which the candidate plans to graduate. Students are reminded to complete a final check of their academic records before they exit the university to ensure that all temporary grades have been converted, that the record accurately reflects their academic histories and that all degrees have been posted. Requests for changes to the academic record must be made within the first six months following graduation, but this requirement may be superseded by other university-specific deadlines (e.g., those governing requests for a change of grade). Commonwealth of Virginia record-retention requirements may affect the university's ability to address requests for changes to the academic record. Students must settle all financial obligations to the university prior to the issuance of a diploma. **Procedure:** Freshmen are admitted fall and spring. Entrance exams should be taken SAT or ACT scores must be received for fall term admission by March. There are early admissions, deferred admissions, and rolling admissions plans. Applications should be filed by January 15 for fall entry. The fall 2014 application fee was $50. Notifications are sent April 1. Applications are accepted on-line. **Transfer Students:** 2287 transfer students enrolled in 2013-2014. VCU generally accept up to 90 credits from another four-year college or university because most undergraduate degrees require completion of 120 credits and students must complete a minimum of 30 credit hours (called the "residency requirement") at VCU. Because of the upper-level graduation requirement (45 upper-level credits) and since most community college credits transfer as lower-level, we also recommend that students at two-year colleges take no more than 70 credit hours from a community college, and earn a final grade of "C" or better for the course to transfer into VCU from another institution. **International Students:** There are 1047 international students enrolled. The school actively recruits these students. They must take the TOEFL with a minimum score of 550 on the paper-based TOEFL (PBT) or 80 on the Internet-based version (iBT) and the college's own test, or take the IELTS.

ADMISSIONS: 75% of the 2014-2015 applicants were accepted. The SAT scores for the 2014-2015 freshman class were: Critical Reading--21% below 500, 48% between 500 and 599, 26% between 600 and 699, and 5% between 700 and 800; Math--23% below 500, 49% between 500 and 599, 23% between 600 and 699, and 4% between 700 and 800; Writing--30% below 500, 47% between 500 and 599, 20% between 600 and 699, and 3% between 700 and 800. The ACT scores were 20% below 21, 30% between 21 and 23, 23% between 24 and 26, 11% between 27 and 28, and 15% above 28. 27 freshmen graduated first in their class. **Admissions Contact:** E-Mail: *ugrad@vcu.edu* Web: *www.vcu.edu*

FINANCIAL AID: In 2014-2015, 75% of all full-time freshmen and 70% of continuing full-time students received some form of financial aid. The average freshman award was $14,996. Need-based scholarships or need-based grants averaged $8,466 ($30,790 maximum); need-based self-help aid (loans and jobs) averaged $3,747 ($8,771 maximum); non-need-based athletic scholarships averaged $20,924 ($43,668 maximum); and other non-need-based awards and non-need-based scholarships averaged $9,631 ($46,758 maximum). 3% of undergraduate students work part-time. Average annual earnings from campus work are $1803. The average financial indebtedness of the 2014 graduate was $32,411. The FAFSA is required. The priority date for freshman financial aid applications for fall entry is March 1.

Virginia Military Institute, established in 1839, is the nation's first state-supported military college. It offers academic programs in engineering, sciences, and liberal arts. All students are members of the Corps of Cadets, live in barracks, eat together in the mess hall, wear uniforms, and adhere to the honor system. The figures in the above capsule and in this profile are approximate. In addition to regional accreditation, VMI has baccalaureate program accreditation with ABET. The 134-acre campus is in a small town 50 miles north of Roanoke. Including any residence halls, there are 68 buildings.

STUDENT LIFE: 59% of undergraduates are from Virginia. Others are from 45 states, 9 foreign countries, and Canada. 78% are from public schools. 85% are white. 64% are Protestant; 28% Catholic. The average age of freshmen is 18; all undergraduates, 20. 20% do not continue beyond their first year; 74% remain to graduate.

FACULTY/CLASSROOMS: 80% of faculty are male; 20% are female. All teach undergraduates and do research. No introductory courses are taught by graduate students. The average class size in an introductory lecture is 17; in a laboratory is 13; and in a regular course is 12.

PROGRAMS OF STUDY: VMI confers B.A. and B.S. degrees. Bachelor's degrees are awarded in BIOLOGICAL SCIENCE (biology/biological science), BUSINESS (business economics), COMMUNICATIONS AND THE ARTS (English), COMPUTER AND PHYSICAL SCIENCE (chemistry, computer science, mathematics, and physics), ENGINEERING AND ENVIRONMENTAL DESIGN (civil engineering, electrical/electronics engineering, and mechanical engineering), SOCIAL SCIENCE (history, international studies, and psychology). Engineering (civil, electrical, and mechanical) and sciences are the strongest academically. History, business/economics, and civil and mechanical engineering have the largest enrollments.

ACTIVITIES: There are 50 groups on campus, including bagpipe, band, cheerleading, choir, chorus, communications, dance, drama, drill team, ethnic, historical, honors, international, investment, jazz band, literary magazine, marching band, musical theater, newspaper, orchestra, pep band, photography, political, professional, religious, social, social service, and student government. Popular campus events include Ring Figure, Virginia Transportation Conference, and dance and concert weekends.

SERVICES: Counseling and information services are available, as is tutoring in some subjects, French, Spanish, German, Arabic, chemistry, math, physics, economics, business, writing, and most required freshman classes. Tutoring for intercollegiate athletes, paid for by NCAA, also is available. **Library/Resources:** The 2 libraries contain 240,000 volumes, 12,963 microform items, 5,747 audio/video tapes/CDs/DVDs, and subscribe to 26,789 periodicals including electronic. Computerized library services include interlibrary loans, database searching, Internet access, and Wi-Fi capability. **Physically Challenged Students:** 75% of the campus is accessible. Facilities include wheelchair ramps, elevators, special parking, and specially equipped restrooms. **Special:** Study abroad in 14 countries and work-study programs are available, as are for-credit internships in English and international studies and summer internships in foreign countries. VMI offers dual majors in any combination and B.A.-B.S. degrees in liberal arts, physical sciences, and engineering. Minors are offered in each field of study. There are 11 national honor societies, a freshman honors program, and 3 departmental honors programs. **Visiting:** There are regularly scheduled orientations for prospective students, consisting of tours, conferences with academic and ROTC instructors, interaction with current freshmen, and overnight stays. There are guides for informal visits, visitors may sit in on classes, and stay overnight. To schedule a visit, contact the Admissions Office at Admissions@VMI.edu. **Campus Safety and Security:** Measures include 24-hour foot and vehicle patrol and self-defense education. There are emergency telephones, lighted pathways/sidewalks, 24-hour student guard team.

REQUIREMENTS: The SAT or ACT is required. Applicants must be graduates of an accredited secondary school. Applicants should complete 19 to 20 high school academic units, including 4 years of English and math, 3 of science, history, and foreign language, and 2 of social studies. An essay is encouraged and an interview is recommended. A GPA of 2.0 is required. AP credits are accepted. Important factors in the admissions decision are advanced placement or honors courses, extracurricular activities record, and leadership record.

FINANCIAL AID: VMI is a member of CSS. The FAFSA and the college's own financial statement are required. Check with the school for current application deadlines.

VIRGINIA POLYTECHNIC INSTITUTE AND STATE UNIVERSITY   C-3
www.vt.edu

Blacksburg, VA 24061

(540) 231-6267
(540) 231-6000

Fax: (540) 231-3242

Email: admissions@vt.edu

Full-time: 15886 men, 11992 women

Faculty: n/av; I, av$

Ph.D.s: 90%

Part-time: 1689 men, 1288 women

Student/Faculty: n/av

Graduate: 4086 men, 2853 women

Tuition: $9500 ($22,800)

Year: semesters, summer session

Freshman Class: 21201 applied, 12947 accepted, 5177 enrolled

Room & Board: $7000

SAT CR/M/W: 590/621/586 **ACT:** required

Application Deadline: January 15

CEEB CODE: 5859

HIGHLY COMPETITIVE

Virginia Polytechnic Institute and State University, founded in 1872, is a public land-grant institution. It offers a cadet program within the larger, nonmilitary student body. There are 7 undergraduate schools and 2 graduate schools. In addition to regional accreditation, Virginia Tech has baccalaureate program accreditation with AACSB, ABET, ACCE, ADA, AHEA, ASLA, FIDER, NAAB, NCATE, and SAF. The 2600-acre campus is in a rural area 40 miles southwest of Roanoke. Including any residence halls, there are 110 buildings.

STUDENT LIFE: 74% of undergraduates are from Virginia. Others are from 49 states, 77 foreign countries, and Canada. 77% are white. The average age of freshmen is 18; all undergraduates, 20. 11% do not continue beyond their first year; 78% remain to graduate.

FACULTY/CLASSROOMS: 69% of faculty are male; 31% are female. 74% teach undergraduates, and all do research. Graduate students teach 12% of introductory courses. The average class size in an introductory lecture, 46, and in a laboratory, 30.

PROGRAMS OF STUDY: Virginia Tech confers B.A., B.S., B.Arch., B.F.A., B.Land.Arch., B.S.Bus., B.S.E., and B.S.Ed. degrees. Master's and Doctoral degrees are also awarded. Bachelor's degrees are awarded in AGRICULTURE (agricultural economics, animal science, dairy science, forestry and related sciences, horticulture, poultry science, and soil science), BIOLOGICAL SCIENCE (biochemistry, biology/biological science, and nutrition), BUSINESS (accounting, apparel and accessories marketing, banking and finance, business economics, entrepreneurial studies, hotel/motel and restaurant management, management science, marketing management, and tourism), COMMUNICATIONS AND THE ARTS (art, communications, dramatic arts, English, French, German, industrial design, music, and Spanish), COMPUTER AND PHYSICAL SCIENCE (chemistry, computer science, geology, mathematics, physics, planetary and space science, and statistics), EDUCATION (agricultural education, business education, environmental education, foreign languages education, science education, and secondary education), ENGINEERING AND ENVIRONMENTAL DESIGN (aerospace studies, agricultural engineering, architecture, chemical engineering, civil engineering, com-

puter engineering, construction engineering, construction management, electrical/electronics engineering, engineering mechanics, environmental science, industrial engineering, interior design, landscape architecture/design, materials engineering, mechanical engineering, mining and mineral engineering, and ocean engineering), HEALTH PROFESSIONS (physical therapy, predentistry, and premedicine), SOCIAL SCIENCE (dietetics, economics, food science, geography, history, human development, interdisciplinary studies, international studies, interpreter for the deaf, parks and recreation management, philosophy, physical fitness/movement, political science/government, prelaw, psychology, public affairs, sociology, and urban studies). Engineering, architecture, and business are the strongest academically. Engineering, computer science, and biology have the largest enrollments.

ACTIVITIES: 13% of men belong to 43 national fraternities; 19% of women belong to 21 national sororities. There are 600 groups on campus, including art, band, cheerleading, chess, choir, chorale, chorus, computers, dance, drama, drill team, drum and bugle corps, ethnic, film, gay, honors, international, jazz band, literary magazine, marching band, musical theater, newspaper, orchestra, pep band, photography, political, professional, radio and TV, religious, social, social service, student government, and symphony. Popular campus events include Quad Jams, Ring Dance, and German's Mid-Winter Dance.

SERVICES: Counseling and information services are available, as is tutoring in most subjects. There is a reader service for the blind, and remedial reading. **Library/Resources:** The 4 libraries contain 2.3 million volumes, 6.3 million microform items, and 27,574 audio/video tapes/CDs/DVDs, and subscribe to 35,596 periodicals including electronic. Computerized library services include interlibrary loans, database searching, and Internet access. Special learning facilities include an art gallery, natural history museum, radio station, TV station, airport, wind tunnels, agricultural stations, radio/visual observatories, satellite up-link station, multimedia, digital music, writing, and CAD/CAM labs, math emporium, and CAVE (cave automatic virtual environment). **Physically Challenged Students:** 60% of the campus is accessible. Facilities include wheelchair ramps, elevators, special parking, specially equipped restrooms, special class scheduling, lowered drinking fountains, lowered telephones, special housing. Special services library room for the visually impaired. **Special:** Students may cross-register with Miami University in Ohio, Oxford Polytechnic Institute, California Polytechnic Institute, and Florida A & M. Study abroad in 36 countries, internships in nearly every major, a Washington semester, and a wide range of work-study programs are available, as well as co-ops in 48 majors. There are honors options for most majors, B.A.-B.S. degrees, dual and student-designed majors, credit for independent study or research, nondegree study, and pass/fail options. The Corps of Cadets, a militarily structured organization, is open to men and women. Undergraduate advising programs are available to students wishing to prepare for professional school in law, dentistry, medicine, pharmacy, physical therapy, or veterinary medicine. There are 13 national honor societies, including Phi Beta Kappa, and a freshman honors program. **Visiting:** There are regularly scheduled orientations for prospective students, consisting of a Fall Open House Series: half-day on-campus programs that include presentations, tours, and question-and-answer sessions. There are guides for informal visits and visitors may sit in on classes. To schedule a visit, contact the Office of Undergraduate Admissions at admissions@vt.edu. **Campus Safety and Security:** Measures include 24-hour foot and vehicle patrol, emergency notification system, self-defense education, and security escort services. There are shuttle buses, emergency telephones, and lighted pathways/sidewalks.

REQUIREMENTS: The SAT or ACT is required. Applicants must be graduates of an accredited secondary school, or the GED is accepted. Applicants should complete 18 high school academic credits, including 4 years of English, 3 of math, including algebra II and geometry, 2 of lab science, to be chosen from biology, chemistry, or physics, and 1 each of history and social studies. An additional 3 years from college preparatory courses and 4 from any credit course offerings are required. AP and CLEP credits are accepted. Important factors in the admissions decision are advanced placement or honors courses, evidence of special talent, and extracurricular activities record.

ADMISSIONS: 61% of a recent year applicants were accepted. 82%

of the current freshmen were in the top fifth of their class; 97% were in the top two fifths.

FINANCIAL AID: In a recent year, 36% of all full-time freshmen and 35% of continuing full-time students received some form of financial aid. 29% of all full-time freshmen and 28% of continuing full-time students received need-based aid. Need-based scholarships or need-based grants averaged $6,924; need-based self-help aid (loans and jobs) averaged $4,002 and other non-need based awards and non-need based scholarships averaged $2,562. The FAFSA is required. Check with the school for current application deadlines.

VIRGINIA STATE UNIVERSITY   E-3
www.vsu.edu

Petersburg, VA 23806	(804) 524-5902
	(800) 871-7611
Fax: (804) 524-5055	Email: admiss@vsu.edu
Full-time: 1400 men, 1800 women	Faculty: 168; IIA, --$
Part-time: 200 men, 200 women	Ph.D.s: 74%
Graduate: 220 men, 580 women	Student/Faculty: 19 to 1
Year: semesters, summer session	Tuition: $5000 ($13,000)
Room & Board: $6484	Freshman Class: 4138 applied, 2028 accepted, 1011 enrolled
SAT or ACT: required	CEEB CODE: 5860
Application Deadline:	COMPETITIVE+

Virginia State University is a historically black public land-grant institution of higher education providing academic programs that integrate instruction, research, and extension/public service. The figures in the above capsule and in this profile are approximate. There are 4 undergraduate schools and one graduate school. In addition to regional accreditation, VSU has baccalaureate program accreditation with ABET, ADA, CSWE, NASM, and NCATE. The 652-acre campus is in a suburban area 25 miles south of Richmond. Including any residence halls, there are 52 buildings.

STUDENT LIFE: 65% of undergraduates are from Virginia. Others are from 35 states, and 1 foreign countries. 96% are from public schools. 90% are African American. **Female To Male Ratio:** 1.4:1. The average age of freshmen is 18; all undergraduates, 21. 40% do not continue beyond their first year; 18% remain to graduate. **Housing:** 2050 students can be accommodated in college housing, which includes single-sex dorms. In addition, there are honors houses. On-campus housing is guaranteed for the freshman year only, is available on a first-come, and first-served basis. 52% of students live on campus; of those, 20% remain on campus on weekends. Alcohol is not permitted. Upperclassmen may keep cars.

FACULTY/CLASSROOMS: 67% of faculty are male; 33% are female. Graduate students teach 2% of introductory courses.

PROGRAMS OF STUDY: VSU confers B.A., B.S., B.F.A., B.I.S. and B.Mus. degrees. Master's degrees are also awarded. Bachelor's degrees are awarded in AGRICULTURE (agriculture), BIOLOGICAL SCIENCE (biology/biological science), BUSINESS (accounting, business administration and management, hotel/motel and restaurant management, management information systems, and marketing management), COMMUNICATIONS AND THE ARTS (English literature, music performance, and visual and performing arts), COMPUTER AND PHYSICAL SCIENCE (chemistry, mathematics, and physics), EDUCATION (athletic training, business education, physical education, and trade and industrial education), ENGINEERING AND ENVIRONMENTAL DESIGN (engineering technology), SOCIAL SCIENCE (economics, history, home economics, interdisciplinary studies, political science/government, psychology, public administration, social work, and sociology). Business administration, accounting, and business information systems are the largest.

ACTIVITIES: 10% of men belong to 4 national fraternities; 10% of women belong to 4 national sororities. There are 44 groups on campus, including band, cheerleading, chess, choir, chorus, computers, dance, drama, drill team, ethnic, honors, international, jazz band, marching band, musical theater, newspaper, orchestra, pep band, photography, political, professional, radio and TV, religious, social,

student government, symphony, and yearbook. Popular campus events include High School Day, VSU Day, and Commencement. **Sports:** There are 7 intercollegiate sports for men and 6 for women, and 5 intramural sports for men and 6 for women. Facilities include a gym, an Olympic-size pool, dance studio, tennis courts, track field, football field, baseball field, indoor and outdoor basketball courts. **Graduates:** In an average class, 10% graduate in 4 years or less, 26% graduate in 5 years or less, and 33% graduate in 6 years or less.

SERVICES: Counseling and information services are available, as is tutoring in most subjects. There is a reader service for the blind. **Library/Resources:** The library contains 280,599 volumes, 662,075 microform items, and 3,939 audio/video tapes/CDs/DVDs, and subscribes to 1,198 periodicals including electronic. Computerized library services include interlibrary loans and database searching. Special learning facilities include an art gallery, radio station, and TV station. **Physically Challenged Students:** 75% of the campus is accessible. Facilities include wheelchair ramps, elevators, special parking, and specially equipped restrooms. **Special:** VSU offers dual majors, a general studies degree, a 3-2 engineering degree program, nondegree study, and a pass/fail grading option. There are 10 national honor societies, including Phi Beta Kappa, a freshman honors program, and 7 departmental honors programs. **Visiting:** There are regularly scheduled orientations for prospective students. There are guides for informal visits and visitors may sit in on classes. To schedule a visit, contact the Admissions Office. **Campus Safety and Security:** Measures include a 24-hour foot and vehicle patrol. There are emergency telephones and lighted pathways/sidewalks.

REQUIREMENTS: The SAT or ACT is required. In addition, applicants must graduate from an accredited secondary school with 16 academic credits and 12 Carnegie units, or have a GED. Students must take 4 years of English, 2 each of a foreign language, math, and science, and 1 each of history and social studies. Essays, 2 letters of recommendation, evidence of physical condition, interviews, and, if appropriate, auditions are required. AP and CLEP credits are accepted. Important factors in the admissions decision are advanced placement or honors courses, recommendations by school officials, and leadership record. To graduate, students must have a minimum GPA of 2.0. They must earn at least 120 credits, with the last 27 semester hours in residence. Requirements include those in phys ed, freshman writing, math, biology, social or physical science, history, and psychology. Freshman orientation must also be completed. **Procedure:** Freshmen are admitted fall and spring. There are deferred admissions and rolling admissions plans. Check with the school for current application deadlines. Applications are accepted on-line. **Transfer Students:** Applicants must have a minimum GPA of 2.0. Those transferring fewer than 25 semester hours must meet freshman standards. 30 of 120 credits required for the bachelor's degree must be completed at VSU. **International Students:** They must take the TOEFL. They must also take the SAT or ACT.

ADMISSIONS: 49% of the 2014-2015 applicants were accepted. **Admissions Contact:** Irene Logan, Director of Admissions. E-Mail: *ilogan@vsu.edu* Web: *www.vsu.edu*

FINANCIAL AID: In 2014-2015, 95% of all full-time freshmen received some form of financial aid. VSU is a member of CSS. The CSS/Profile and the college's own financial statement are required. Check with the school for current application deadlines.

VIRGINIA UNION UNIVERSITY   E-3
www.vuu.edu

Richmond, VA 23220	(804) 257-5600
	(804) 368-3227
Fax: (804) 342-3511	Email: visitus@vuu.edu
Full-time: 1210 men and women	Faculty: n/av
Part-time: n/av	Ph.D.s: 55%
Graduate: 310 men and women	Student/Faculty: n/av
Year: semesters, summer session	Tuition: $14,000
Room & Board: $7000	Freshman Class: n/av
SAT: required	CEEB CODE: 5862
Application Deadline: see profile	COMPETITIVE

Virginia Union University, established in 1865 and affiliated with the Baptist Church, is a private institution offering undergraduate programs in education and psychology, business, humanities, natural science and math, and social sciences. The figures in the above capsule and in this profile are approximate. There are 2 undergraduate schools and 1 graduate school. In addition to regional accreditation, VUU has baccalaureate program accreditation with ACBSP and CSWE. The 72-acre campus is in an urban area in the city of Richmond. Including any residence halls, there are 18 buildings.

STUDENT LIFE: 52% of undergraduates are from Virginia. Others are from 27 states, and 4 foreign countries. 85% are from public schools. 98% are African American. The average age of freshmen is 18. 31% do not continue beyond their first year; 55% remain to graduate.

FACULTY/CLASSROOMS: 55% of faculty are male; 45% are female. 86% teach undergraduates. No introductory courses are taught by graduate students. The average class size in an introductory lecture is 28; in a laboratory is 20; and in a regular course is 22.

PROGRAMS OF STUDY: VUU confers B.A., B.S., and B.S.W. degrees. Master's and Doctoral degrees are also awarded. Bachelor's degrees are awarded in BIOLOGICAL SCIENCE (biology/biological science), BUSINESS (accounting, banking and finance, and business administration and management), COMMUNICATIONS AND THE ARTS (English, journalism, and music), COMPUTER AND PHYSICAL SCIENCE (chemistry and mathematics), EDUCATION (art education, business education, early childhood education, elementary education, music education, secondary education, and special education), SOCIAL SCIENCE (criminology, history, political science/government, psychology, religion, social work, and sociology). Teacher education, accounting, and history/political science are the strongest academically. Teacher education, criminology, and business administration have the largest enrollments.

ACTIVITIES: There are 32 groups on campus, including cheerleading, drama, international, newspaper, religious, student government, and yearbook. Popular campus events include films, lectures, and concerts.

SERVICES: Counseling and information services are available, as is tutoring in every subject. There is remedial math, reading, and writing. **Library/Resources:** The library contains 145,305 volumes, 62,079 microform items, and 1,523 audio/video tapes/CDs/DVDs, and subscribes to 308 periodicals including electronic. Computerized library services include database searching. Special learning facilities include an art gallery. **Physically Challenged Students:** 90% of the campus is accessible. Facilities include wheelchair ramps, elevators, and special parking. **Special:** The university offers cross-registration with Virginia Commonwealth and Virginia State Universities, and the University of Richmond. Internships, co-op programs, federal work-study programs, a general studies degree, a joint law degree with St. John's University School of Law in New York, a 3-2 degree in engineering with the Universities of Michigan and Iowa and Howard University, and exchange programs are also offered. There are 2 national honor societies and a freshman honors program. **Visiting:** There are guides for informal visits and visitors may sit in on classes. To schedule a visit, contact the Admissions Office. **Campus Safety and Security:** Measures include 24-hour foot and vehicle patrol and security escort services. There are emergency telephones and lighted pathways/sidewalks.

REQUIREMENTS: The SAT is required. Graduation from an accredited secondary school is required; the GED is accepted. Sixteen academic units are required, including 4 of English, 3 each of math and academic electives, and 2 each of foreign language, social science, and natural science. Special consideration is given to disadvantaged students. Children of alumni are given some preference. A GPA of 2.0 is required. AP and CLEP credits are accepted. Important factors in the admissions decision are extracurricular activities record, advanced placement or honors courses, and leadership record.

FINANCIAL AID: VUU is a member of CSS. The CSS/Profile is required. Check with the school for current application deadlines.

VIRGINIA WESLEYAN COLLEGE (*The complete profile is made available exclusively on our website, www.barronspac.com*)

WASHINGTON AND LEE UNIVERSITY C-3
www.wlu.edu

Lexington, VA 24450

(540) 458-8400
(540) 458-8710

Fax: (540) 458-8062
Full-time: 929 men, 906 women
Part-time: 1 men, 2 women
Graduate: 259 men, 205 women
Year: other
Room & Board: $9450

Email: admissions@wlu.edu
Faculty: 209; IIB, ++$
Ph.D.s: 96%
Student/Faculty: 8 to 1
Tuition: $43,362
Freshman Class: 5972 applied, 1163 accepted, 479 enrolled

SAT CR/M/W: 691/693/683 ACT: 30
Application Deadline: January 1

CEEB CODE: 5887
MOST COMPETITIVE

Washington and Lee is a private, highly selective liberal arts university. Founded in 1749. There are 2 undergraduate schools and 1 graduate school. In addition to regional accreditation, Washington and Lee has baccalaureate program accreditation with AACSB, ACEJMC, and ACS. The 430-acre campus is in a small town 50 miles northeast of Roanoke, Virginia and 190 miles southwest of Washington, DC. Including any residence halls, there are 112 buildings.

STUDENT LIFE: 86% of undergraduates are from out of state, mostly the South. Students are from 53 states, 31 foreign countries, and Canada. 55% are from public schools. 83% are White. 50% are Protestant; 22% Catholic; 19% claim no religious affiliation. The average age of freshmen is 18; all undergraduates, 20. 5% do not continue beyond their first year; 90% remain to graduate. **Housing:** 1267 students can be accommodated in college housing, which includes coed dorms and on-campus apartments. In addition, there are language houses, special-interest houses, fraternity houses, and sorority houses. On-campus housing is available on a lottery system for upperclassmen. 59% of students live on campus; of those, 95% remain on campus on weekends. All students may keep cars.

FACULTY/CLASSROOMS: 66% of faculty are male; 34% are female. 86% teach undergraduates, all do research, and 86% do both. No introductory courses are taught by graduate students. The average class size in an introductory lecture is 19; in a laboratory is 17; and in a regular course is 15.

PROGRAMS OF STUDY: Washington and Lee confers B.A., and B.S. degrees. Master's and Doctoral degrees are also awarded. Bachelor's degrees are awarded in BIOLOGICAL SCIENCE (biochemistry, biology/biological science, and neurosciences), BUSINESS (accounting and business administration and management), COMMUNICATIONS AND THE ARTS (art history and appreciation, classics, dramatic arts, English, French, German, Germanic languages and literature, journalism, music, romance languages and literature, Russian languages and literature, Spanish, and studio art), COMPUTER AND PHYSICAL SCIENCE (chemistry, computer science, geology, mathematics, natural sciences, and physics), ENGINEERING AND ENVIRONMENTAL DESIGN (chemical engineering, engineering physics, and environmental science), SOCIAL SCIENCE (anthropology, archeology, East Asian studies, economics, history, interdisciplinary studies, medieval studies, philosophy, political science/government, psychology, public affairs, religion, and sociology). Mass communications, neuroscience, business administration, accounting, and chemistry are the strongest academically. Business administration, economics, politics, accounting, and biology have the largest enrollments.

ACTIVITIES: 81% of men belong to 17 national fraternities; 82% of women belong to 7 national sororities. There are 128 groups on campus, including leadership, Spanish, sports, volunteer, cheerleading, choir, chorale, chorus, communications, dance, debate, drama, environmental, ethnic, film, forensics, gay, honors, international, jazz band, literary magazine, musical theater, newspaper, orchestra, outing, pep band, photography, political, professional, radio and TV, religious, social, social service, student government, symphony, and yearbook. Popular campus events include Presidential Mock Convention, Fancy Dress Ball and NABORS Service Day. **Sports:** There are 12 intercollegiate sports for men and 12 for women, and 19 intramural sports for men and 17 for women. Facilities include a gymnasium,

2400-seat arena, 7000-seat stadium, pool with a 500-seat gallery, fitness center, weight training and exercise rooms, handball, racquetball, squash, and tennis courts, outdoor track, baseball and practice fields, indoor tennis facility, 1000-seat soccer/lacrosse stadium, and a 1000-seat turf field for field hockey and lacrosse. **Graduates:** From July 1, 2013 to June 30, 2014, 421 bachelor's degrees were awarded. The most popular majors were business administration (14%), economics (10%), and politics (10%). 65 companies recruited on campus in 2013-2014. In an average class, 88% graduate in 4 years or less, 90% graduate in 5 years or less, and 90% graduate in 6 years or less. Of the 2013 graduating class, 32% were enrolled in graduate school within 6 months of graduation, and 83% were employed.

SERVICES: Counseling and information services are available, as is tutoring in every subject. There is a reader service for the blind. **Library/Resources:** The 3 libraries contain 973,445 volumes, 1.4 million microform items, and 18,522 audio/video tapes/CDs/DVDs, and subscribe to 11,794 periodicals including electronic. Computerized library services include interlibrary loans, database searching, Internet access, and Wi-Fi capability. Special learning facilities include an art gallery, radio station, TV station, special collections, history, fine arts, and archeological museums including Lee Chapel and museum, Stanier gallery, Lenfest center for the performing arts, Watson Pavilion, the Reeves center with Japanese tea room, and Kamen gallery. Tucker multimedia center for foreign language learning. Instrumental laboratory, seismograph/scanning electron microscope, light microscopy with digital imaging/electrophysiological recording facilities. **Physically Challenged Students:** 55% of the campus is accessible. Facilities include wheelchair ramps, elevators, special parking, specially equipped restrooms, special class scheduling, lowered drinking fountains, and special housing. **Special:** Special academic programs are available throughout The College and The Williams School of Commerce. Internship opportunities include the Washington Term, First-Year Internship Program, and study abroad opportunities in over 50 countries. Students may earn dual degrees and double majors; over 30 departments offer honors programs. Teacher certification is offered in consortium with Virginia Military Institute and Southern Virginia University. There are 17 national honor societies, including Phi Beta Kappa, and 31 departmental honors programs. **Visiting:** There are regularly scheduled orientations for prospective students, including hourly interviews and campus tours, 2 group information sessions daily, seasonal Saturday tours and interviews. There are guides for informal visits and visitors may sit in on classes. To schedule a visit, contact the Admissions Office at (540) 458-8710. **Campus Safety and Security:** Measures include 24-hour foot and vehicle patrol, emergency notification system, self-defense education, and security escort services. There are shuttle buses, emergency telephones, lighted pathways/sidewalks, controlled access to dorms/residences, required safety programs for first-year students.

REQUIREMENTS: The SAT or ACT is required. The ACT Optional Writing test is also required. A high school diploma is not required. Applicants must earn 17 units (24 recommended), including 4 units in English, 3 in math (4 recommended), 3 in a foreign language (4 recommended), and 1 each in history (2 recommended) and natural science (4 recommended with 1 lab science). Course work in social sciences(1) is also required (2 recommended). Essays, test scores, a transcript, and recommendation letters are needed to apply. An interview is recommended. AP credits are accepted. Important factors in the admissions decision are advanced placement or honors courses, leadership record, extracurricular activities record, and recommendations by school officials.To graduate, students must achieve proficiency in a foreign language and English composition and complete at least 1 course in fine arts and humanities, lab science and math, and literature and 2 courses in social sciences. A total of 113 credits, with a minimum GPA of 2.0, is required. All students must take 4 skills courses in physical education and pass a swimming test. **Procedure:** Freshmen are admitted fall. Entrance exams should be taken prior to January of the senior year. There are early decision and deferred admissions plans. Early decision applications should be filed by November 1; regular applications, by January 1 for fall entry. The fall 2014 application fee was $50. Notification of early decision is sent December 21; regular decision, April 1. 261 early decision candidates were accepted for the 2014-2015 class. 2002 applicants were on the 2014 waiting list; 89 were admitted. Applications are accepted online. **Transfer Students:** 1 transfer students enrolled in 2013-2014. Transfer applicants must have a GPA of at least 2.0 (at least 3.5 to be competitive); no more than 56 credits will transfer. There is a 2-year residency requirement. 57 of 113 credits required for the bachelor's degree must be completed at Washington and Lee. **International Students:** There are 79 international students enrolled. The school actively recruits these students. They must take the TOEFL with a minimum score of 600 on the paper-based TOEFL (PBT) or 100 on the Internet-based version (iBT), or take the APIEL or ELPT. They must also take the SAT or ACT.

ADMISSIONS: 19% of the 2014-2015 applicants were accepted. The SAT scores for the 2014-2015 freshman class were: Critical Reading--4% between 500 and 599, 47% between 600 and 699, and 49% between 700 and 800; Math--3% between 500 and 599, 50% between 600 and 699, and 47% between 700 and 800; Writing--10% between 500 and 599, 44% between 600 and 699, and 46% between 700 and 800. The ACT scores were 27% between 27 and 28, and 73% above 28. 96% of the current freshmen were in the top fifth of their class; 100% were in the top two fifths. There were 14 National Merit finalists. 36 freshmen graduated first in their class. **Admissions Contact:** William M. Hartog, Dean of Admissions and Financial Aid. E-Mail: *admissions@wlu.edu* Web: *www.wlu.edu*

FINANCIAL AID: In 2014-2015, 49% of all full-time freshmen and continuing full-time students received some form of financial aid. 44% of all full-time freshmen and 41% of continuing full-time students received need-based aid. The average freshman award was $44,349. Need-based scholarships or need-based grants averaged $39,120; need-based self-help aid (loans and jobs) averaged $2,043; and other non-need-based awards and non-need-based scholarships averaged $44,427. 17% of undergraduate students work part-time. Average annual earnings from campus work are $780. The average financial indebtedness of the 2014 graduate was $23,409. Washington and Lee is a member of CSS. The CSS/Profile and FAFSA, and Federal tax returns for parents and students and business tax returns are required. The priority date for freshman financial aid applications for fall entry is February 1. The deadline for filing freshman financial aid applications for fall entry is February 1.

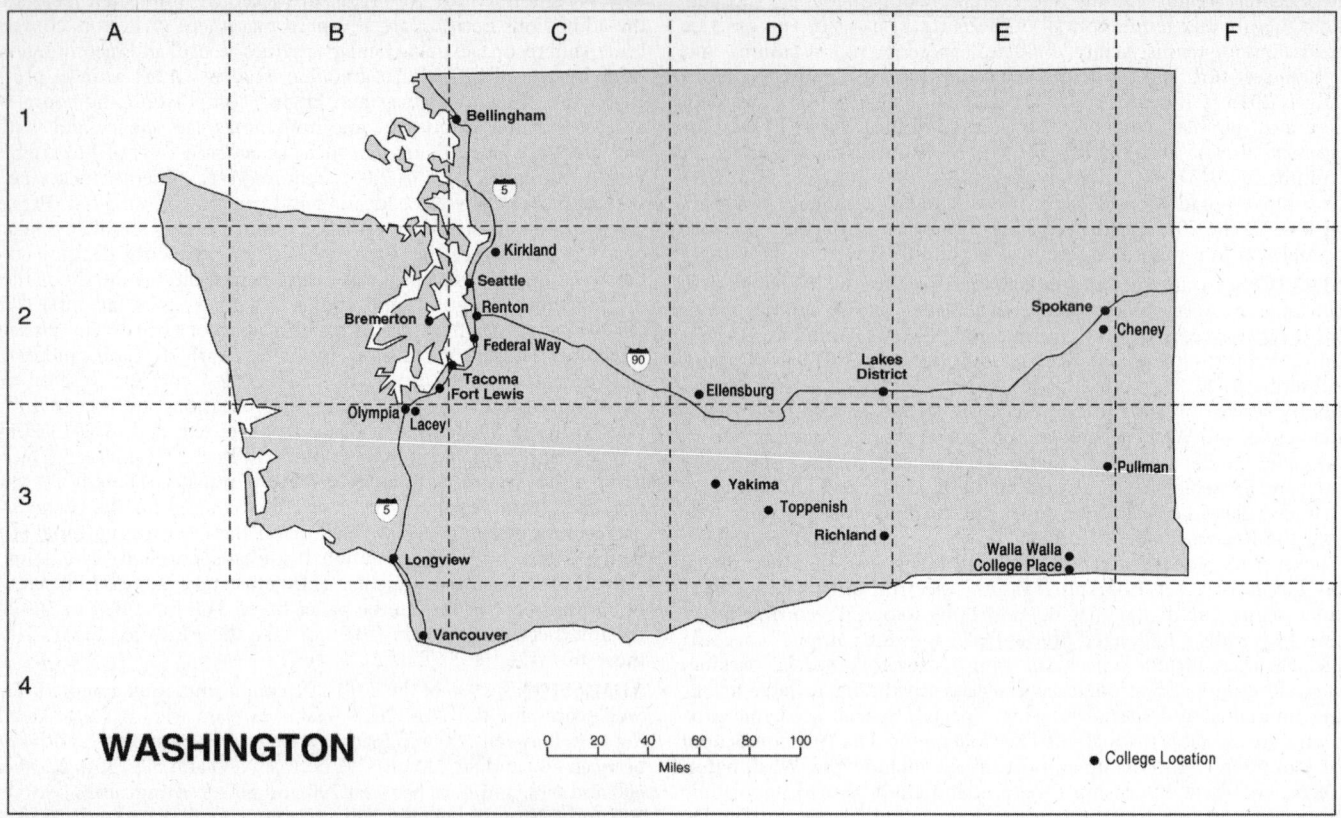

WASHINGTON

CENTRAL WASHINGTON UNIVERSITY D-2
www.cwu.edu

Ellensburg, WA 98926
(509) 963-1111
(866) 298-4968

Fax: (509) 963-3022	Email: cwuadmis@cwu.edu
Full-time: 7500 men and women	Faculty: n/av; IIA, --$
Part-time: n/av	Ph.D.s: 90%
Graduate: 500 men and women	Student/Faculty: n/av
Year: trimesters, summer session	Tuition: $6500 ($15,500)
Room & Board: $7500	Freshman Class: n/av
SAT or ACT: required	CEEB CODE: 4044
Application Deadline: see profile	COMPETITIVE

Central Washington University is a public institution offering undergraduate programs in the arts and sciences, business administration, and education. There are 4 undergraduate schools and 1 graduate school. Figures in the above capsule and in this profile are approximate. In addition to regional accreditation, CWU has baccalaureate program accreditation with ABET, ACCE, ADA, NASM, NCATE, and NRPA. The 380-acre campus is in a rural area 100 miles east of Seattle. Including any residence halls, there are 74 buildings.

STUDENT LIFE: 97% of undergraduates are from Washington. Others are from 35 states, 32 foreign countries, and Canada. 95% are from public schools. 78% are white. The average age of freshmen is 19; all undergraduates, 23. 24% do not continue beyond their first year; 52% remain to graduate.

FACULTY/CLASSROOMS: 58% of faculty are male; 42% are female. All teach and do research. Graduate students teach 7% of introductory courses. The average class size in an introductory lecture is 45; in a laboratory is 20; and in a regular course is 40.

PROGRAMS OF STUDY: CWU confers B.A., B.S., B.A.Ed., B.F.A., and B.M. degrees. Master's degrees are also awarded. Bachelor's degrees are awarded in BIOLOGICAL SCIENCE (biology/biological science), BUSINESS (accounting, banking and finance, business administration and management, business economics, fashion merchandising, international business management, marketing/retailing/merchandising, recreation and leisure services, and tourism), COMMUNICATIONS AND THE ARTS (art, broadcasting, Chinese, communications, dramatic arts, English, fine arts, French, German, guitar, Japanese, journalism, language arts, music, music business management, music theory and composition, percussion, piano/organ, public relations, Russian, Spanish, speech/debate/rhetoric, strings, studio art, visual and performing arts, and voice), COMPUTER AND PHYSICAL SCIENCE (actuarial science, chemistry, computer programming, computer science, earth science, geology, information sciences and systems, mathematics, physics, and software engineering), EDUCATION (art education, business education, early childhood education, elementary education, English education, foreign languages education, health education, home economics education, industrial arts education, marketing and distribution education, mathematics education, middle school education, music education, physical education, science education, secondary education, social studies education, and special education), ENGINEERING AND ENVIRONMENTAL DESIGN (aeronautical technology, aviation administration/management, aviation maintenance management, construction management, electrical/electronics engineering, engineering technology, industrial engineering technology, and mechanical engineering), HEALTH PROFESSIONS (community health work, emergency medical technologies, exercise science, and public health), SOCIAL SCIENCE (anthropology, Asian/Oriental studies, criminal justice, economics, family and community services, family/consumer studies, food science, geography, gerontology, history, liberal arts/general studies, paralegal studies, parks and recreation management, philosophy, political science/government, prelaw, psychology, public administration, safety science, social science, social work, and sociology). Accounting, music, and geology are the strongest academically. Business and education have the largest enrollments.

ACTIVITIES: There are 80 groups on campus, including art, band, cheerleading, chess, choir, chorale, chorus, computers, dance, drama, ethnic, film, gay, honors, international, jazz band, literary magazine, marching band, musical theater, newspaper, opera, orchestra, pep band, photography, political, professional, radio and TV, religious, social, social service, student government, and symphony. Popular campus events include Tower Theater productions and Jazz Night.

1484

SERVICES: Counseling and information services are available, as is tutoring in most subjects. There is a reader service for the blind, and remedial math, reading, and writing. **Library/Resources:** The library contains 546,025 volumes, 1.2 million microform items, 9,500 audio/video tapes/CDs/DVDs. Computerized library services include inter-library loans and database searching. Special learning facilities include an art gallery, natural history museum, planetarium, radio station, an anthropology museum, a botanical greenhouse, and a primate research lab. **Physically Challenged Students:** All of the campus is accessible. Facilities include wheelchair ramps, elevators, special parking, specially equipped restrooms, special class scheduling, lowered drinking fountains, and lowered telephones. **Special:** Students may study abroad; there is a formal exchange program with Japanese universities. There are 3-2 engineering degree programs in conjunction with the University of Puget Sound, the University of Washington, and Washington State University. CWU also offers co-op programs, cross-registration, internships, work-study programs, an accelerated degree program, credit/no credit options, dual and student-designed majors, and credit for military experience. Nondegree study is offered through adult/continuing education programs. There are 11 national honor societies, a freshman honors program, and 12 departmental honors programs. **Visiting:** There are regularly scheduled orientations for prospective students, consisting of an information session, a tour of residence halls, a tour of the campus, prearranged appointments with faculty, and a financial aid presentation. There are guides for informal visits, visitors may sit in on classes, and stay overnight. To schedule a visit, contact the Admissions Office. **Campus Safety and Security:** Measures include 24-hour foot and vehicle patrol, self-defense education, and security escort services. There are shuttle buses, emergency telephones, lighted pathways/sidewalks, and controlled-entry residence halls.

REQUIREMENTS: The SAT or ACT is required. Test scores and GPA are considered in combination according to a sliding scale. Applicants must be graduates of accredited secondary schools or have earned a GED. The university requires 15 academic credits or Carnegie units: 4 years of English, 3 each of math and social studies, 2 of the same foreign language, 2 of science, and 1 of performing arts or an academic elective. A GPA of 2.0 is required. AP and CLEP credits are accepted. Important factors in the admissions decision are leadership record, personality/intangible qualities, and recommendations by school officials.

FINANCIAL AID: The FAFSA is required. Check with the school for current application deadlines.

CITY UNIVERSITY OF SEATTLE (*The complete profile is made available exclusively on our website, www.barronspac.com*)

CORNISH COLLEGE OF THE ARTS (*The complete profile is made available exclusively on our website, www.barronspac.com*)

EASTERN WASHINGTON UNIVERSITY	E-2
www.ewu.edu	
Cheney, WA 99004	(509) 359-6200
	(509) 359-2397
Fax: (509) 359-6692	Email: admissions@ewu.edu
Full-time: 4617 men, 5444 women	Faculty: 462; IIA, -$
Part-time: 1049 men, 1301 women	Ph.D.s: 99%
Graduate: 305 men, 737 women	Student/Faculty: 22 to 1
Year: quarters, summer session	Tuition: $7,972 (21,066)
Room & Board: $9,628	Freshman Class: 4987 applied, 3710 accepted, 1642 enrolled
SAT CR/M/W: 475/485/455 ACT: 20	CEEB CODE: 4301
Application Deadline: February 15	COMPETITIVE

Eastern Washington University, founded in 1882, is a comprehensive public university that provides programs in the arts and sciences, business, health sciences, nursing, and technology. There are 5 undergraduate schools and 1 graduate school. In addition to regional accreditation, EWU has baccalaureate program accreditation with AACSB, ABET, ADA, APTA, ASLA, CSAB, CSWE, NASM, NCATE,

NLN, NRPA, NASP, PAB, and CACREP. The 35-acre campus is in a small town 18 miles southwest of Spokane. Including any residence halls, there are 79 buildings.

STUDENT LIFE: 92% of undergraduates are from Washington. Others are from 45 states, 16 foreign countries, and Canada. 98% are from public schools. 66% are White; 12% Hispanic. The average age of freshmen is 18; all undergraduates, 22. 25% do not continue beyond their first year; 75% remain to graduate. **Housing:** 2250 students can be accommodated in college housing, which includes coed dorms, on-campus apartments, and married student housing. In addition, there are special-interest houses, fraternity houses, sorority houses, living and learning communities, all-male, all-female, academic, music, and drama floors, and floors for older students, theme housing, wellness housing, and special housing for disabled students. On-campus housing is guaranteed for the freshman year only, is available on a first-come, and first-served basis. 81% of students commute. Alcohol is not permitted. All students may keep cars.

FACULTY/CLASSROOMS: 52% of faculty are male; 48% are female. 99% teach undergraduates. No introductory courses are taught by graduate students. The average class size in an introductory lecture is 30; in a laboratory is 20; and in a regular course is 30.

PROGRAMS OF STUDY: EWU confers B.A., B.S., B.A.B., B.A.E., B.D.H., B.F.A., B.Mus. and B.S.N. degrees. Master's degrees are also awarded. Bachelor's degrees are awarded in BIOLOGICAL SCIENCE (biochemistry, biology/biological science, botany, and microbiology), BUSINESS (accounting, banking and finance, business administration and management, management science, marketing/retailing/merchandising, personnel management, and recreation and leisure services), COMMUNICATIONS AND THE ARTS (art, art history and appreciation, broadcasting, communications, creative writing, dance, dramatic arts, English, French, German, graphic design, journalism, literature, music, music performance, Spanish, speech/debate/rhetoric, and studio art), COMPUTER AND PHYSICAL SCIENCE (chemistry, computer science, geology, information sciences and systems, mathematics, and physics), EDUCATION (art education, computer education, elementary education, foreign languages education, guidance education, health education, marketing and distribution education, mathematics education, middle school education, music education, physical education, recreation education, science education, secondary education, and social science education), ENGINEERING AND ENVIRONMENTAL DESIGN (computer technology, engineering, engineering technology, mechanical engineering technology, and military science), HEALTH PROFESSIONS (dental hygiene, health administration and policy, health care administration, medical laboratory technology, nursing, predentistry, premedicine, preveterinary science, recreation therapy, and speech pathology/audiology), SOCIAL SCIENCE (anthropology, criminal justice, economics, geography, history, humanities, international relations, parks and recreation management, philosophy, political science/government, prelaw, psychology, social science, social work, sociology, and urban studies). Health sciences, biology, and computer science are the strongest academically. Business, education, and social science have the largest enrollments.

ACTIVITIES: 5% of men belong to 9 national fraternities; 6% of women belong to 11 national sororities. There are 98 groups on campus, including and sports clubs, art, band, cheerleading, chess, choir, chorale, chorus, computers, dance, debate, drama, environmental, ethnic, film, gay, honors, including outdoor recreation, international, jazz band, literary magazine, marching band, musical theater, newspaper, orchestra, pep band, photography, political, professional, radio and TV, religious, social, social service, student government, symphony, and yearbook. Popular campus events include Cinco de Mayo, Hawaii Luau, Homecoming, Pass Through the Pillars, World Party, Mardi Gras, Greek Week Neighbor Festival, and Day of Silence. **Sports:** There are 6 intercollegiate sports for men and 8 for women, and 13 intramural sports for men and 13 for women. Facilities include a recreation center, 200-meter indoor track, 12 racquetball courts, an indoor swimming pool, wrestling rooms, dance studio, 7000-seat stadium and red turf, 5800-seat indoor gym, a fitness studio, volleyball, baseball, and basketball courts. **Graduates:** From July 1, 2013 to June 30, 2014, 2259 bachelor's degrees were awarded. The most popular majors were business/marketing (17%), health professions and related programs (10%), and social sciences

(9%). 159 companies recruited on campus in 2013-2014. In an average class, 19% graduate in 4 years or less, 38% graduate in 5 years or less, and 45% graduate in 6 years or less.

SERVICES: Counseling and information services are available, as is tutoring in every subject. There is a reader service for the blind, remedial math, reading, and writing. **Library/Resources:** The library contains 858,862 volumes, 792,319 microform items, 56,490 audio/video tapes/CDs/DVDs, and subscribes to 75,183 periodicals including electronic. Computerized library services include interlibrary loans, database searching, Internet access, and Wi-Fi capability. Special learning facilities include an art gallery, planetarium, radio station, Riverpoint Health Sciences complex, Weissenborn Map Library, Indian Education Center, State Digital Archives building, State Crime Lab, and a Turnbull Nature Preserve. **Physically Challenged Students:** 93% of the campus is accessible. Facilities include wheelchair ramps, elevators, special parking, specially equipped restrooms, special class scheduling, lowered drinking fountains, lowered telephones, special housing. **Special:** Cooperative programs in nursing, cross-registration with the Intercollegiate School of Nursing, internships with area businesses, and work-study based on federal financial aid are available. B.A.-B.S. degrees, dual majors in any subject, study abroad in 12 countries, 3 types of general studies degrees, student-designed majors, and a 3-2 engineering degree with Washington State University are offered. Credit for military experience, nondegree study, and pass/fail options for nonmajor or nonminor courses also are possible. There are 9 national honor societies, including Phi Beta Kappa, and a freshman honors program. **Visiting:** There are regularly scheduled orientations for prospective students, consisting of overnight programs for students and parents that present informational sessions on campus life and academic survival skills, academic advising, course registration, and social functions. There are guides for informal visits, visitors may sit in on classes, and stay overnight. To schedule a visit, contact The Visitors Center at (509) 359-6555. **Campus Safety and Security:** Measures include 24-hour foot and vehicle patrol, emergency notification system, self-defense education, and security escort services. There are emergency telephones, lighted pathways/sidewalks, controlled access to dorms/residences, Crisis lines and emergency contact light standards.

REQUIREMENTS: The SAT or ACT is required. Admission is determined by an index coordinating the GPA with entrance exam scores. The GED is accepted. EWU requires 4 years of English, 3 each of math and social science, 2 each of science (including a lab science) and a single foreign language (ASL accepted), and 1 of fine arts or academic electives. A GPA of 2.0 is required. AP and CLEP credits are accepted. Important factors in the admissions decision are advanced placement or honors courses, evidence of special talent, personality/intangible qualities, extracurricular activities record, recommendations by school officials, parents or siblings attended your school, recommendations by alumni, and geographical diversity.All students must complete 180 quarter credits, including 60 to 110 in their major, while earning a minimum GPA of 2.0. Specific requirements include English composition and math courses to demonstrate competency. Distribution requirements include 11 total courses from 3 breadth areas: humanities, natural sciences, math, and social sciences. Seniors must complete a capstone course. **Procedure:** Freshmen are admitted to all sessions. Entrance exams should be taken during the spring of the junior year or fall of the senior year. There are deferred admissions and rolling admissions plans. Applications should be filed by February 15 for fall entry; October 1 for winter entry; and March 1 for spring entry, along with a $50 fee. Notifications are sent November 1. Applications are accepted on-line. **Transfer Students:** 1423 transfer students enrolled in 2013-2014. Applicants with fewer than 40 credits must submit high school and college transcripts and test scores; those with more than 40 credits acceptable by Eastern or who have earned an associate degree from a Washington community college must submit a college transcript. 45 of 180 credits required for the bachelor's degree must be completed at EWU. **International Students:** There are 371 international students enrolled. The school actively recruits these students. They must take the TOEFL with a minimum score of 525 on the paper-based TOEFL (PBT) or 71 on the Internet-based version (iBT). They must also take the SAT or ACT.

ADMISSIONS: 74% of the 2014-2015 applicants were accepted. The

SAT scores for the 2014-2015 freshman class were: Critical Reading--59% below 500, 32% between 500 and 599, 8% between 600 and 699, and 1% between 700 and 800; Math--54% below 500, 36% between 500 and 599, 9% between 600 and 699, and 1% between 700 and 800; Writing--68% below 500, 27% between 500 and 599, 5% between 600 and 699, and % between 700 and 800. **Admissions Contact:** Boubacar Bouaré, Assistant Director of Admissions . E-Mail: *Admissions@ewu.edu* Web: *http://www.ewu.edu/Admissions.xml*

FINANCIAL AID: The FAFSA is required. The priority date for freshman financial aid applications for fall entry is February 15.

EVERGREEN STATE COLLEGE   B-3
www.evergreen.edu

Olympia, WA 98505	(360) 867-6000
	(360) 867-6170
Fax: (360) 867-5114	Email: admissions@evergreen.edu
Full-time: 2176 men, 2618 women	Faculty: 247
Part-time: 510	Ph.Ds: 87%
Graduate: 100 men, 210 women	Student/Faculty: 23 to 1
Year: trimesters, summer session	Tuition: $20,500
Room & Board: $8500	Freshman Class: n/av
SAT or ACT: required	CEEB CODE: 4292
Application Deadline: see profile	COMPETITIVE+

Evergreen State College, founded in 1967, is a public liberal arts and sciences college offering interdisciplinary, collaborative, and team-taught academic programs. There are 3 graduate schools. Figures in the above capsule and in this profile are approximate. The 1000-acre campus is in a small town 7 miles west of Olympia. Including any residence halls, there are 73 buildings.

STUDENT LIFE: 77% of undergraduates are from Washington. Others are from 48 states, 9 foreign countries, and Canada. 69% are white. The average age of freshmen is 19; all undergraduates, 25. 32% do not continue beyond their first year; 57% remain to graduate.

FACULTY/CLASSROOMS: 51% of faculty are male; 49% are female. 91% teach undergraduates. No introductory courses are taught by graduate students. The average class size in an introductory lecture is 50; in a laboratory is 23; and in a regular course is 25.

PROGRAMS OF STUDY: Evergreen confers B.A., B.S., and B.A.S degrees. Master's degrees are also awarded. Bachelor's degrees are awarded in COMPUTER AND PHYSICAL SCIENCE (natural sciences), SOCIAL SCIENCE (liberal arts/general studies).

ACTIVITIES: There are 78 groups on campus, including art, choir, chorale, communications, dance, drama, environmental, ethnic, film, gay, international, literary magazine, newspaper, photography, political, professional, radio and TV, religious, social, social service, and student government. Popular campus events include Super Saturday, Evergreen Expressions Series (performance/media art), and Olympia Film Society.

SERVICES: Counseling and information services are available, as is tutoring in some subjects. The Writing Center offers assistance in writing; the Quantitive and Symbolic Reasoning Center offers assistance with all levels of math, economics, statistics, chemistry, biology, physics, and computer science There is also a reader service for the blind. **Library/Resources:** The library contains 471,406 volumes, 494,714 microform items, 89,195 audio/video tapes/CDs/DVDs, and subscribes to 12,579 periodicals including electronic. Computerized library services include interlibrary loans, database searching, Internet access, and Wi-Fi capability. Special learning facilities include an art gallery, radio station, TV station, organic farm and community gardens, Longhouse education and cultural center, evergreen art galleries, animation and design studio, ceramics studio, metal shop, wood shop, photography studios and darkrooms, science laboratories, access to media equipment, computer labs, and scientific equipment. **Physically Challenged Students:** All of the campus is accessible. Facilities include wheelchair ramps, elevators, special parking, specially equipped restrooms, lowered drinking fountains, and lowered telephones. **Special:** All work at the college is interdisciplinary, and the programs of study change annually. The college's credit-generating options include the comprehensive Coordinated Study

Program, which allows students and faculty to work together intensively. Credits may be earned through cooperative programs, work-study programs, internships, independent contracts, or from prior learning and military experience. **Visiting:** There are regularly scheduled orientations for prospective students, includes an admissions session, a class visit, and a campus tour. There are guides for informal visits, visitors may sit in on classes, and stay overnight. To schedule a visit, contact the Student Visitor Program. **Campus Safety and Security:** Measures include 24-hour foot and vehicle patrol, self-defense education, and security escort services. There are emergency telephones and lighted pathways/sidewalks.

REQUIREMENTS: The SAT or ACT is required. Candidates should be graduates of an accredited secondary school and have completed 15 academic credits, consisting of 4 in English, 3 each in math and social studies, 2 each in foreign language and science (one of which must be a lab science in biology, chemistry, or physics), and 1 in fine, visual, or performing arts or other college preparatory elective from another area mentioned in list. A GED is acceptable. A GPA of 2.0 is required. AP and CLEP credits are accepted. Important factors in the admissions decision are advanced placement or honors courses, evidence of special talent, and ability to finance college education.

FINANCIAL AID: Evergreen is a member of CSS. The FAFSA and the college's own financial statement are required. Check with the school for current application deadlines.

GONZAGA UNIVERSITY

E-2

www.gonzaga.edu

Spokane, WA 99258

(800) 986-9585
(800) 322-2584

Fax: (509) 313-5780

Email: admissions@gonzaga.edu

Full-time: 2205 men, 2547 women

Faculty: 361

Part-time: 36 men, 49 women

Ph.D.s: 83%

Graduate: 961 men, 1554 women

Student/Faculty: 11 to 1

Year: semesters, summer session

Tuition: $36,535

Room & Board: $9906

Freshman Class: 7162 applied, 4835 accepted, 1048 enrolled

SAT CR/M: 590/606 ACT: 27

CEEB CODE: 4330

Application Deadline: February 1

HIGHLY COMPETITIVE

Gonzaga University, founded in 1887, is a private, liberal arts institution affiliated with the Roman Catholic Church and the Society of Jesus (Jesuits). The university offers undergraduate and graduate degrees in arts and sciences, business, education, engineering, nursing, and human physiology. There are 5 undergraduate schools and 7 graduate schools. In addition to regional accreditation, Gonzaga has baccalaureate program accreditation with AACSB, ABET, NCATE, CACREP, NWCCU, and CSLE/ABA. The 131-acre campus is in an urban area alongside the Spokane River, near downtown Spokane. Including any residence halls, there are 105 buildings.

STUDENT LIFE: 52% of undergraduates are from out of state, mostly the West. Students are from 44 states, 26 foreign countries, and Canada. 63% are from public schools. 72% are White. 50% are Catholic; 22% claim no religious affiliation; 15% Protestant. The average age of freshmen is 18; all undergraduates, 20. 8% do not continue beyond their first year; 83% remain to graduate. **Housing:** 3028 students can be accommodated in college housing, which includes single-sex and coed dorms, on-campus apartments, off-campus apartments, and married student housing. In addition, there are special-interest houses, living and learning communities within residence halls. On-campus housing is guaranteed for the freshman year only, is available on a first-come, first-served basis, and is available on a lottery system for upperclassmen. 59% of students live on campus; of those, 75% remain on campus on weekends. All students may keep cars.

FACULTY/CLASSROOMS: 56% of faculty are male; 44% are female. 80% teach undergraduates. No introductory courses are taught by graduate students. The average class size in an introductory lecture is 23; in a laboratory is 18; and in a regular course is 23.

PROGRAMS OF STUDY: Gonzaga confers B.A., B.S., B.B.A., B.Ed., and B.S.N. degrees. Master's and Doctoral degrees are also awarded. Bachelor's degrees are awarded in AGRICULTURE (environmental studies), BIOLOGICAL SCIENCE (biochemistry and biology/biological science), BUSINESS (accounting, business administration and management, business economics, and sports management), COMMUNICATIONS AND THE ARTS (art, broadcasting, classics, communications, dramatic arts, English, French, journalism, literature, music, public relations, Spanish, speech/debate/rhetoric, and theatre acting), COMPUTER AND PHYSICAL SCIENCE (chemistry, computer science, mathematics, and physics), EDUCATION (music education, physical education, and special education), ENGINEERING AND ENVIRONMENTAL DESIGN (civil engineering, computer engineering, electrical/electronics engineering, engineering management, and mechanical engineering), HEALTH PROFESSIONS (exercise science and nursing), SOCIAL SCIENCE (classical/ancient civilization, criminal justice, economics, history, interdisciplinary studies, international studies, Italian studies, philosophy, political science/government, psychology, religion, and sociology). Engineering, biology, and business administration are the strongest academically. Business, engineering, and liberal arts have the largest enrollments.

ACTIVITIES: There are 102 groups on campus, including art, band, cheerleading, chess, choir, chorale, chorus, communications, computers, dance, debate, drama, drill team, environmental, ethnic, gay, honors, international, jazz band, literary magazine, mock trial, musical theater, newspaper, orchestra, pep band, photography, political, professional, radio and TV, religious, social, social service, student government, symphony, and yearbook. Popular campus events include Search and other Spiritual Retreats, GEL Weekend, Charity Ball, Diversity Monologues, and Fall Family Weekend. **Sports:** There are 7 intercollegiate sports for men and 7 for women, and 26 intramural sports for men and 26 for women. Facilities include Basketball arena, 2 basketball/volleyball courts, indoor golf and tennis building (six courts), outdoor grass soccer practice facility adjoined to an outdoor grass game field, outdoor baseball stadium and field, indoor rowing room, athletic weight room, student fitness center with cardiovascular and weight areas, multipurpose synthetic turf field, 3 multipurpose courts, 4 racquetball courts, 2 aerobics rooms, indoor running track, and a 6-lane 25-yard swimming pool. **Graduates:** From July 1, 2013 to June 30, 2014, 1125 bachelor's degrees were awarded. The most popular majors were business and management (23%), social sciences (16%), and engineering (10%). 100 companies recruited on campus in 2013-2014. In an average class, 1% graduate in 3 years or less, 74% graduate in 4 years or less, 81% graduate in 5 years or less, and 83% graduate in 6 years or less. Of the 2013 graduating class, 30% were enrolled in graduate school within 6 months of graduation, and 92% were employed.

SERVICES: Counseling and information services are available, as is tutoring in most subjects. There is a reader service for the blind. Informal peer tutoring in English and math is available. **Library/Resources:** The 2 libraries contain 527,693 volumes, 6,808 audio/video tapes/CDs/DVDs, and subscribe to 48,895 periodicals including electronic. Computerized library services include interlibrary loans, database searching, Internet access, and Wi-Fi capability. Special learning facilities include an art gallery, radio station, and TV station. **Physically Challenged Students:** 90% of the campus is accessible. Facilities include wheelchair ramps, elevators, special parking, specially equipped restrooms, special class scheduling, lowered drinking fountains, lowered telephones. Academic adjustments are provided for students with disabilities who provide appropriate documentation and request services from Disabilities, Resources, Education, and Access Management (DREAM). Accessible rooms exist in some residence halls and apartments. **Special:** Cross-registration with Whitworth University, internships, study abroad in 35 countries (including a Gonzaga-in-Florence campus), a Washington semester, summer faculty-led programs and on- and off-campus work-study programs are offered. High school juniors and seniors may take 6 credits per semester in certain areas. There is a limited pass/fail option, and dual majors are possible. There are 12 national honor societies and a freshman honors program. **Visiting:** There are regularly scheduled orientations for prospective students, day visits are permitted Monday through Friday; overnight visits, Sunday through Thursday (except for holiday periods). There are guides for informal visits, visitors may sit in on classes, and stay overnight. To schedule a visit, contact the Gonzaga Visit Office at (509) 13-6531. **Campus Safety and Security:** Measures include 24-hour foot and vehicle patrol, emergency notification system, self-defense education, and security escort services. There are shuttle buses, emergency telephones, lighted pathways/sidewalks, and controlled access to dorms/residences.

REQUIREMENTS: The SAT or ACT is required. Applicants should be graduates of an accredited secondary school. They must have completed 17 academic credits consisting of 4 years of English, 3 to 4 years of math, 2 to 3 years of the same foreign language; world language preferred, ASL accepted, 3 years of history and/or social science, and 3 to 4 years of natural or physical laboratory science. An essay and letters of recommendation are required. An interview is optional but recommended for students with a GPA lower than 3.2 or SAT score less than 1070 for Verbal/Critical plus Math, or 23 ACT Composite. Gonzaga's Nursing Program accepts first-year applications only. Applicants interested in the Nursing Program must choose "Nursing" on their application to be considered. Students not admitted into the Nursing Program through the application process will not be permitted to change their major to nursing. Applicants interested in pursuing any of the majors in the School of Engineering and Applied Science as a first-year student should be ready for college calculus and (with the exception of computer science applicants) should have completed physics in high school. Students not meeting these criteria are encouraged to consider majors outside the School. AP credits are accepted. Important factors in the admissions decision are advanced placement or honors courses, leadership record, extracurricular activities record, and recommendations by school officials. All students must complete at least 128 credit hours with a minimum 2.0 GPA. The major requirements are 18 hours in upper-division courses and supporting courses required by the major department. Students must complete 9 credits each of philosophy and religious studies, 7 credits in English, speech, and critical thinking, and 3 credits each in math and English literature. **Procedure:** Freshmen are admitted fall and spring. Entrance exams should be taken by time of application. There are early admissions and deferred admissions plans. Early decision applications should be filed by November 15; regular applications, by February 1 for fall entry; and November 15 for spring entry, along with a $50 fee. Notification of early decision is sent January 15; regular decision, April 1. 171 applicants were on the 2014 waiting list; 162 were admitted. Applications are accepted on-line. **Transfer Students:** 138 transfer students enrolled in 2013-2014. A minimum GPA of 2.7 is required. An interview is recommended. 30 of 128 credits required for the bachelor's degree must be completed at Gonzaga. **International Students:** There are 62 international students enrolled. The school actively recruits these students. They must take the TOEFL with a minimum score of 550 on the paper-based TOEFL (PBT) or 80 on the Internet-based version (iBT). Students must take the MELAB, or the ESL Exit Exam, which includes a writing test.

ADMISSIONS: 68% of the 2014-2015 applicants were accepted. The SAT scores for the 2014-2015 freshman class were: Critical Reading--7% below 500, 48% between 500 and 599, 38% between 600 and 699, and 7% between 700 and 800; Math--4% below 500, 42% between 500 and 599, 45% between 600 and 699, and 9% between 700 and 800. The ACT scores were 1% below 21, 15% between 21 and 23, 31% between 24 and 26, 22% between 27 and 28, and 31% above 28. There were 1 National Merit finalists. **Admissions Contact:** Julie McCulloh, Dean of Admissions. E-Mail: *mcculloh@gu.gonzaga.edu* Web: *www.gonzaga.edu*

FINANCIAL AID: In 2014-2015, 97% of all full-time freshmen and 96% of continuing full-time students received some form of financial aid. 63% of all full-time freshmen and 58% of continuing full-time students received need-based aid. The average freshman award was $24,846. Need-based scholarships or need-based grants averaged $19,339; need-based self-help aid (loans and jobs) averaged $5,845; non-need-based athletic scholarships averaged $21,019; and other non-need-based awards and non-need-based scholarships averaged $11,885. 32% of undergraduate students work part-time. Average annual earnings from campus work are $2200. The average financial indebtedness of the 2014 graduate was $25,753. Gonzaga is a member of CSS. The FAFSA, and WASFA for undocumented students from Washington in order to receive State aid is required. The priority date

for freshman financial aid applications for fall entry is February 1. The deadline for filing freshman financial aid applications for fall entry is February 1.

HERITAGE UNIVERSITY *(The complete profile is made available exclusively on our website, www.barronspac.com)*

NORTHWEST UNIVERSITY   C-2
www.northwestu.edu

Kirkland, WA 98033	(425) 882-8266
	(800) 669-3781
Fax: (425) 889-5224	Email: info@ncag.edu
Full-time: 365 men, 610 women	Faculty: n/av; IIB, --$
Part-time: 40 men, 50 women	Ph.D.s: 41%
Graduate: 30 men, 55 women	Student/Faculty: n/av
Year: semesters, summer session	Tuition: $12,000
Room & Board: $8000	Freshman Class: n/av
SAT or ACT: required	CEEB CODE: 4541
Application Deadline: see profile	COMPETITIVE

Northwest University, founded in 1934, is a private institution offering programs in ministry, business, nursing, and education. There are 2 graduate schools. The figures in the above capsule and this profile are approximate. The 56-acre campus is in a suburban area in Kirkland, 10 miles east of Seattle and overlooking Lake Washington. Including any residence halls, there are 27 buildings.

STUDENT LIFE: 79% of undergraduates are from Washington. Others are from 23 states, 15 foreign countries, and Canada. 60% are white. 99% are Protestant. The average age of freshmen is 19; all undergraduates, 25. 34% do not continue beyond their first year; 34% remain to graduate.

FACULTY/CLASSROOMS: 65% of faculty are male; 35% are female. All teach undergraduates. No introductory courses are taught by graduate students. The average class size in an introductory lecture is 30, in a laboratory, 20, and in a regular course, 24.

PROGRAMS OF STUDY: NC confers B.A. degrees. Associates and Master's degrees are also awarded. Bachelor's degrees are awarded in BIOLOGICAL SCIENCE (life science), BUSINESS (business administration and management), COMMUNICATIONS AND THE ARTS (communications, English, journalism, music, and music business management), COMPUTER AND PHYSICAL SCIENCE (computer management), EDUCATION (education, elementary education, middle school education, physical education, secondary education, and special education), ENGINEERING AND ENVIRONMENTAL DESIGN (environmental science), HEALTH PROFESSIONS (nursing), SOCIAL SCIENCE (behavioral science, biblical studies, counseling/psychology, history, interdisciplinary studies, liberal arts/general studies, ministries, missions, pastoral studies, philosophy, psychology, religion, religious education, religious music, theological studies, and youth ministry). Teacher education, business, and psychology are the strongest academically. Teacher education, church ministries, and business have the largest enrollments.

ACTIVITIES: There are 20 groups on campus, including and radio, band, choir, chorale, chorus, communications, debate, drama, forensics, international, jazz band, literary magazine, musical theater, newspaper, orchestra, photography, professional, religious, social, social service, student government, and yearbook. Popular campus events include Christmas Holiday Social, All-School Banquet, and Roomies Night-out.

SERVICES: There is a reader service for the blind, and remedial writing. The Student Success Office provides assistance in most areas, including study skills. **Library/Resources:** The library contains 174,100 volumes, 40,800 microform items, 5,000 audio/video tapes/CDs/DVDs, and subscribes to 900 periodicals including electronic. Computerized library services include interlibrary loans, database searching, and Internet access. **Physically Challenged Students:** 75% of the campus is accessible. Facilities include wheelchair ramps, elevators, special parking and specially equipped restrooms. **Special:** Northwest offers study in several locations in the U.S. and foreign countries through the Council for Christian Colleges and Universities. Dual majors are available. There are 2 national honor societies and 1 departmental honors program. **Visiting:** There are regularly scheduled orientations for prospective students. There are guides for informal visits, visitors may sit in on classes, and stay overnight. **Campus Safety and Security:** Measures include 24-hour foot and vehicle patrol and security escort services. There are shuttle buses, emergency telephones, and lighted pathways/sidewalks.

REQUIREMENTS: The SAT or ACT is required. A GPA of 2.3 is required. AP and CLEP credits are accepted. Important factors in the admissions decision are personality/intangible qualities, recommendations by alumni, and leadership record.

FINANCIAL AID: The FAFSA and the college's own financial statement are required. Check with the school for application deadlines.

PACIFIC LUTHERAN UNIVERSITY   C-2
www.plu.edu

Tacoma, WA 98447

	(253) 535-7411
	(800) 274-6758
Fax: (253) 536-5136	Email: admission@plu.edu
Full-time: 1053 men, 1802 women	Faculty: 254; IIA, -$
Part-time: 48 men, 56 women	Ph.D.s: 88%
Graduate: 99 men, 217 women	Student/Faculty: 15 to 1
Year: 4-1-4, summer session	Tuition: $36,530
Room & Board: $10,230	Freshman Class: 2818 applied, 2643 accepted, 648 enrolled
SAT CR/M/W: 550/540/530 ACT: 25	CEEB CODE: 4597
Application Deadline:	COMPETITIVE+

Pacific Lutheran University offers approximately 3,500 students a blend of academically rigorous liberal arts and professional programs. Founded in 1890 by Norwegian immigrants, PLU is a private university affiliated with the Evangelical Lutheran Church in America. The university offers three pathways to academic distinction: global education and service to the world; robust student-faculty collaborative research and creative projects; helping students discern meaning and purpose in their lives. There are 7 undergraduate schools and 5 graduate schools. In addition to regional accreditation, PLU has baccalaureate program accreditation with AACSB, ABET, CSWE, NASM, NCATE, ACS, and CCNE. The 156-acre campus is in a suburban area 7 miles south of Tacoma, WA. Including any residence halls, there are 41 buildings.

STUDENT LIFE: 75% of undergraduates are from Washington. Others are from 40 states, 28 foreign countries, and Canada. 97% are from public schools. 67% are White. 50% are Protestant; 13% claim no religious affiliation; 11% Catholic. The average age of freshmen is 18; all undergraduates, 21. 18% do not continue beyond their first year; 68% remain to graduate. **Housing:** 1700 students can be accommodated in college housing, which includes single-sex and coed dorms, on-campus apartments, and married student housing. In addition, there are honors houses, language houses, special-interest houses. We have many other living communities including First Year, First in the Family, New Transfer and Upper Division Student. We also have themed communities such as Gender Neutral Housing, Women's Empowerment and Gender Equity, Community for Creative Expression, International Hall and our Social Action and Leadership Wing. On-campus housing is guaranteed for the freshman year only. 57% of students commute. All students may keep cars.

FACULTY/CLASSROOMS: 44% of faculty are male; 56% are female. 99% teach undergraduates, 90% do research, and 90% do both. No introductory courses are taught by graduate students. The average class size in an introductory lecture is 23; in a laboratory is 16; and in a regular course is 17.

PROGRAMS OF STUDY: PLU confers B.A., B.S., B.A.E., B.A.K., B.A.P.E., B.A.Rec., B.B.A., B.F.A., B.M., B.M.A., B.M.Ed., B.S.N. and B.S.P.E. degrees. Master's and Doctoral degrees are also awarded. Bachelor's degrees are awarded in BIOLOGICAL SCIENCE (biology/biological science), BUSINESS (business administration and management and recreation and leisure services), COMMUNICATIONS AND THE ARTS (art, classics, communications, English, fine arts,

French, German, music, music performance, music theory and composition, piano/organ, Scandinavian languages, Spanish, and voice), COMPUTER AND PHYSICAL SCIENCE (applied physics, chemistry, computer programming, computer science, geoscience, mathematics, and physics), EDUCATION (education, music education, and physical education), ENGINEERING AND ENVIRONMENTAL DESIGN (computer engineering, engineering and applied science, and environmental science), HEALTH PROFESSIONS (nursing), SOCIAL SCIENCE (anthropology, Asian/Oriental studies, economics, history, international studies, philosophy, political science/government, psychology, religion, Scandinavian studies, social work, sociology, and women's studies). Business administration, education, and nursing have the largest enrollments.

ACTIVITIES: There are 67 groups on campus, including adult student, advertising, club sports, comedy, commuter, interfaith programs, intramurals, outdoor recreation, art, band, cheerleading, choir, chorale, chorus, computers, dance, debate, drama, environmental, ethnic, film, forensics, gay, honors, international, jazz band, literary magazine, musical theater, newspaper, opera, orchestra, pep band, photography, political, professional, radio and TV, religious, social, social service, student government, Student Leadership Institute, and symphony. Popular campus events include Wang Symposium, EXPLORE! Retreat, Holocaust Education Conference, Relay for Life, unPLUg, Songfest, Family Weekend, Homecoming, PLUtonic concerts, Berry Festival, Clay Crows - improv, and Dance Ensemble. **Sports:** There are 11 intercollegiate sports for men and 10 for women, and 8 intramural sports for men and 8 for women. Facilities include a 3500-seat gym/auditorium, the 800-seat center for the performing arts, a 150-seat black box theatre, concert hall, fitness center, swimming pool, racquetball and tennis courts. Additional recreational space in memorial gym for volleyball and basketball. All weather soccer field, softball and baseball fields, upgraded synthetic surface track and other fields for practice. Access to 4500 seat Sparks stadium for football and indoor tennis center. **Graduates:** From July 1, 2013 to June 30, 2014, 784 bachelor's degrees were awarded. The most popular majors were social sciences (11%), health professions (11%), and business (9%). 53 companies recruited on campus in 2013-2014. In an average class, 58% graduate in 4 years or less, 67% graduate in 5 years or less, and 68% graduate in 6 years or less.

SERVICES: Counseling and information services are available, as is tutoring in most subjects. There is a reader service for the blind. Study groups and pretest and posttest reviews are also available. **Library/Resources:** The library contains 610,134 volumes, 236,411 microform items, 13,521 audio/video tapes/CDs/DVDs, and subscribes to 4,474 periodicals including electronic. Computerized library services include interlibrary loans, database searching, Internet access, and Wi-Fi capability. Special learning facilities include an art gallery, radio station, TV station, W.M. Keck Observatory, Marriage and Family Therapy Center, Rieke Science Center's nuclear magnetic resonance spectrometer, an herbarium, invertebrate and vertebrate museums, a biology field station, Northwest history collections, a Scandinavian history collection, and a language resource center. **Physically Challenged Students:** 90% of the campus is accessible. Facilities include wheelchair ramps, elevators, special parking, specially equipped restrooms, special class scheduling, lowered drinking fountains, and lowered telephones. **Special:** PLU offers 2 different bachelor's degrees simultaneously, 3-2 engineering degrees with Washington University in St. Louis and Columbia University, and accelerated degree programs in most majors. Dual majors and student-designed majors can be arranged. Extensive internships with local businesses and nonprofit organizations, work-study programs, non-degree study, and pass/fail options are also available. The Wang Center for International Programs supports the university's internationally focused academic programs. There are study-abroad programs in 28 countries. There are 6 national honor societies and a freshman honors program. **Visiting:** There are regularly scheduled orientations for prospective students, consisting of activities based on the students' individual interests - tour, class visits, meeting with coaches and/or faculty, overnight stays. There are guides for informal visits, visitors may sit in on classes, and stay overnight. To schedule a visit, contact the Office of Admissions. **Campus Safety and Security:** Measures include 24-hour foot and vehicle patrol, emergency notification system, self-defense education, and security escort services. There are emergency telephones, lighted pathways/sidewalks, controlled access to dorms/residences, and an emergency notification system is automated.

REQUIREMENTS: The SAT or ACT is required. Applicants should be graduates of accredited secondary schools, although GED certificates are accepted. PLU requires 2 years each of college preparatory math and a foreign language and recommends 4 years of English, 2 each of social studies and lab science, 1 of fine or performing arts, and 3 of electives. An essay is required. AP and CLEP credits are accepted. Important factors in the admissions decision are advanced placement or honors courses, leadership record, and evidence of special talent. All students must complete 128 credit hours, with a maximum of 40 in the major. Candidates for degrees in nursing, business administration, and education need a cumulative 2.5 GPA; all others must have a 2.0 GPA. The required curriculum is 36 credit hours of distributive core courses in arts/literature, natural sciences/math, philosophy, religious studies, and social sciences; writing and critical conversation courses; and diversity classes. There is a senior capstone project required. **Procedure:** Freshmen are admitted fall and spring. Entrance exams should be taken by January of the senior year. There are deferred admissions and rolling admissions plans. Application deadlines are open. Application fee is $40. Notification is sent on a rolling basis. Applications are accepted on-line. Application fees are waived if application is completed on-line. **Transfer Students:** 233 transfer students enrolled in 2013-2014. Candidates must be in good academic and personal standing at the institutions last attended full time. Although it does not guarantee admission, a 2.5 GPA in all college work is usually required. For applicants with fewer than 30 semester hours or 45 quarter hours, secondary school records and standardized test scores must be submitted. All students must meet the foreign language and math entrance requirements. 32 of 128 credits required for the bachelor's degree must be completed at PLU. **International Students:** There are 116 international students enrolled. The school actively recruits these students. They must take the TOEFL with a minimum score of 550 on the paper-based TOEFL (PBT) or 79 on the Internet-based version (iBT).

ADMISSIONS: 94% of the 2014-2015 applicants were accepted. The SAT scores for the 2014-2015 freshman class were: Critical Reading--28% below 500, 42% between 500 and 599, 26% between 600 and 699, and 4% between 700 and 800; Math--27% below 500, 46% between 500 and 599, 23% between 600 and 699, and 4% between 700 and 800; Writing--34% below 500, 42% between 500 and 599, 21% between 600 and 699, and 3% between 700 and 800. The ACT scores were 18% below 21, 20% between 21 and 23, 25% between 24 and 26, 12% between 27 and 28, and 24% above 28. 64% of the current freshmen were in the top fifth of their class; 87% were in the top two fifths. **Admissions Contact:** Dave Veazey, Director. E-Mail: *oira@plu.edu* Web: *https://www.plu.edu/institutional-research/*

FINANCIAL AID: In 2014-2015, 99% of all full-time freshmen and 95% of continuing full-time students received some form of financial aid. 81% of all full-time freshmen and 73% of continuing full-time students received need-based aid. The average freshman award was $32,992. Need-based scholarships or need-based grants averaged $22,233 ($42,308 maximum); need-based self-help aid (loans and jobs) averaged $10,608; and other non-need-based awards and non-need-based scholarships averaged $17,076 ($48,308 maximum). 48% of undergraduate students work part-time. Average annual earnings from campus work are $3336. The average financial indebtedness of the 2014 graduate was $26,866. The FAFSA is required. The priority date for freshman financial aid applications for fall entry is January 31.

SAINT MARTIN'S UNIVERSITY   B-3
www.stmartin.edu

Lacey, WA 98503	**(360) 491-4700**
	(800) 368-8803
Fax: (360) 412-6189	Email: admissions@stmartin.edu
Full-time: 538 men, 554 women	Faculty: 72; IIB, --$
Part-time: 195 men, 128 women	Ph.D.s: 85%
Graduate: 124 men, 221 women	Student/Faculty: 12 to 1
Year: semesters, summer session	Tuition: $31,688
Room & Board: $9990	Freshman Class: 680 applied, 604 accepted, 154 enrolled
SAT CR/M/W: 520/526/510 ACT: 23	CEEB CODE: 4674
Application Deadline: March 1	COMPETITIVE

Saint Martin's University, founded in 1895, is a private, non-profit Roman Catholic institution conducted by the Benedictine order, offering undergraduate and graduate programs in liberal arts and sciences, business, education, and engineering. There are 4 undergraduate schools and 4 graduate schools. In addition to regional accreditation, has baccalaureate program accreditation with ABET, TEAC, and CCNE. The 300-acre campus is in a suburban area 3 miles from Olympia and 60 miles south of Seattle. Including any residence halls, there are 17 buildings.

STUDENT LIFE: 75% of undergraduates are from Washington. Others are from 25 states, 13 foreign countries, and Canada. 85% are from public schools. 56% are White. 43% claim no religious affiliation; 23% Catholic. The average age of freshmen is 18; all undergraduates, 24. 26% do not continue beyond their first year; 54% remain to graduate. **Housing:** 630 students can be accommodated in college housing, which includes coed dorms. On-campus housing is guaranteed for the freshman year only, is available on a first-come, and first-served basis. 70% of students commute. Alcohol is not permitted. All students may keep cars.

FACULTY/CLASSROOMS: 55% of faculty are male; 45% are female. 97% teach undergraduates. No introductory courses are taught by graduate students. The average class size in an introductory lecture is 20; in a laboratory is 12; and in a regular course is 12.

PROGRAMS OF STUDY: Saint Martin confers B.A., B.S., B.S.W., B.S.N., B.S.C.E. and B.S.M.E. degrees. Master's degrees are also awarded. Bachelor's degrees are awarded in BIOLOGICAL SCIENCE (biology/biological science), BUSINESS (accounting and business administration and management), COMMUNICATIONS AND THE ARTS (communications, English, music, and theatre arts), COMPUTER AND PHYSICAL SCIENCE (chemistry, computer science, and mathematics), EDUCATION (education, elementary education, and special education), ENGINEERING AND ENVIRONMENTAL DESIGN (civil engineering and mechanical engineering), HEALTH PROFESSIONS (nursing), SOCIAL SCIENCE (community services, criminal justice, history, interdisciplinary studies, political science/government, psychology, religious studies, social work, and sociology). Engineering is the strongest academically. Business administration, mechanical engineering, and biology have the largest enrollments.

ACTIVITIES: There are 30 groups on campus, including band, choir, drama, ethnic, honors, international, jazz band, musical theater, newspaper, pep band, political, religious, social, social service, and student government. Popular campus events include Career Fair, International Day, Capital Food and Wine Festival. **Sports:** There are 6 intercollegiate sports for men and 7 for women, and 9 intramural sports for men and 9 for women. Facilities include a 5300-seat multipurpose pavilion, new recreation center, athletic fields, and nearby golf courses, lakes, and mountains. **Graduates:** From July 1, 2013 to June 30, 2014, 350 bachelor's degrees were awarded. The most popular majors were business (18%), psychology (14%), and engineering (12%). In an average class, 41% graduate in 4 years or less, 46% graduate in 5 years or less, and 48% graduate in 6 years or less.

SERVICES: Counseling and information services are available, as is tutoring in some subjects. There is a reader service for the blind. **Library/Resources:** The library contains 210,081 volumes, 165,488 microform items, 2,459 audio/video tapes/CDs/DVDs, and subscribes to 3,903 periodicals including electronic. Computerized library services include interlibrary loans, database searching, Internet access, and Wi-Fi capability. Special learning facilities include an art gallery. **Physically Challenged Students:** 90% of the campus is accessible. Facilities include wheelchair ramps, elevators, special parking, specially equipped restrooms, lowered drinking fountains, lowered telephones. **Special:** Double majors, work-study with the state of Washington, nonprofit organizations, and Saint Martin's, internships in all disciplines, a Washington semester with American University, and pass/fail options are offered. The FOCUS program offers credit for job experience. Nondegree study and study abroad is possible. There are 2 national honor societies and 2 departmental honors programs. **Visiting:** There are regularly scheduled orientations for prospective students, including a campus tour and faculty, student service, and financial aid presentations. There are guides for informal visits, visitors may sit in on classes, and stay overnight. To schedule a visit, contact the Admissions Office at (800) 368-8803. **Campus**

Safety and Security: Measures include 24-hour foot and vehicle patrol, emergency notification system, and security escort services. There are emergency telephones, lighted pathways/sidewalks, controlled access to dorms/residences, There is a security patrol from dark to dawn.

REQUIREMENTS: The SAT or ACT is required. Applicants must be graduates of an accredited secondary school or have a GED, with a minimum of 16 academic units, including 4 in English, 2 or 3 in math, 2 in history/social science, 1 or 2 each in foreign language and lab science, and 7 in electives. Class standing also is considered. An essay and recommendation from a teacher or counselor are required. Students should have a score of 800 on the SAT I and a 2.5 GPA. AP and CLEP credits are accepted. Important factors in the admissions decision are advanced placement or honors courses, recommendations by school officials, and personality/intangible qualities. All students must complete freshman composition and general education requirements, including 2 courses in social sciences, 1 course each in literature, philosophy, the arts, religious studies, natural science with lab, math (precalculus), U.S. history, and non-U.S. history. A total of 120 semester credits with a 2.0 GPA is required. 1 year of a world language is required if the student did not take 2 years of a single foreign language in high school. **Procedure:** Freshmen are admitted fall, spring, and summer. There is a rolling admissions plan. Applications should be filed by March 1 for fall entry; December 15 for spring entry. Notification is sent on a rolling basis. Applications are accepted on-line. **Transfer Students:** 204 transfer students enrolled in 2013-2014. Transfer applicants must submit transcripts from all colleges previously attended and have a 2.0 GPA. 30 of 120 credits required for the bachelor's degree must be completed at . **International Students:** There are 114 international students enrolled. The school actively recruits these students. They must take the TOEFL with a minimum score of 525 on the paper-based TOEFL (PBT) or 71 on the Internet-based version (iBT).

ADMISSIONS: 89% of the 2014-2015 applicants were accepted. The SAT scores for the 2014-2015 freshman class were: Critical Reading-39% below 500, 46% between 500 and 599, 11% between 600 and 699, and 4% between 700 and 800; Math--36% below 500, 43% between 500 and 599, 19% between 600 and 699, and 2% between 700 and 800; Writing--42% below 500, 42% between 500 and 599, 14% between 600 and 699, and 2% between 700 and 800. The ACT scores were 37% below 21, 18% between 21 and 23, 15% between 24 and 26, 18% between 27 and 28, and 12% above 28. **Admissions Contact:** Sarah Weiss, Director of Admissions. E-Mail: admissions@stmartin.edu Web: www.stmartin.edu

FINANCIAL AID: SMU is a member of CSS. The FAFSA, and INternational Student's Certification of Finances is required. The deadline for filing freshman financial aid applications for fall entry is March 1.

SEATTLE PACIFIC UNIVERSITY C-2
www.spu.edu

Seattle, WA 98119	(206) 281-2000
	(206) 281-2021
Fax: (206) 281-2669	Email: admissions@spu.edu
Full-time: 1102 men, 2146 women	Faculty: n/av; IIA, av$
Part-time: 45 men, 102 women	Ph.D.s: 87%
Graduate: 269 men, 606 women	Student/Faculty: 15 to 1
Year: quarters, summer session	Tuition: $32,067
Room & Board: $9492	Freshman Class: 5165 applied, 3726 accepted, 767 enrolled
SAT CR/M/W: 570/570/550 ACT: 25	CEEB CODE: 4694
Application Deadline: March 1	VERY COMPETITIVE+

Seattle Pacific University, founded in 1891, is a private, institution affiliated with the Free Methodist Church. It offers programs in business and economics, education, fine and performing arts, health science, humanities, natural and mathematical sciences, phys ed and athletics, religion, and social and behavioral sciences. There are 6 undergraduate schools and 6 graduate schools. In addition to regional accreditation, SPU has baccalaureate program accreditation with AACSB, ABET, NASM, NCATE, and NLN. The 35-acre campus is in an urban area seven minutes from downtown Seattle. Including any residence halls, there are 94 buildings.

STUDENT LIFE: 62% of undergraduates are from Washington. Others are from 44 states, 20 foreign countries, and Canada. 65% are White; 11% Asian American. The average age of freshmen is 18; all undergraduates, 21. 15% do not continue beyond their first year; 70% remain to graduate.

FACULTY/CLASSROOMS: 29% of faculty are male; 41% are female. No introductory courses are taught by graduate students. The average class size in a regular course is 18.

PROGRAMS OF STUDY: SPU confers B.A., and B.S. degrees. Master's and Doctoral degrees are also awarded. Bachelor's degrees are awarded in BIOLOGICAL SCIENCE (biochemistry and biology/biological science), BUSINESS (accounting and business administration and management), COMMUNICATIONS AND THE ARTS (art, classics, communications, creative writing, English, fine arts, French, German, language arts, Latin, linguistics, literature, music, Russian, and Spanish), COMPUTER AND PHYSICAL SCIENCE (chemistry, computer science, information sciences and systems, mathematics, and physics), EDUCATION (education, elementary education, home economics education, mathematics education, music education, nursing education, physical education, science education, secondary education, social science education, special education, and teaching English as a second/foreign language (TESOL/TEFOL)), ENGINEERING AND ENVIRONMENTAL DESIGN (electrical/electronics engineering, engineering, engineering and applied science, and interior design), HEALTH PROFESSIONS (exercise science and nursing), SOCIAL SCIENCE (Christian studies, clinical psychology, economics, European studies, family/consumer resource management, family/consumer studies, food science, history, Latin American studies, liberal arts/general studies, philosophy, physical fitness/movement, political science/government, prelaw, psychology, social science, sociology, and theological studies). Education, nursing, and business administration have the largest enrollments.

ACTIVITIES: There are 51 groups on campus, including art, chess, choir, chorale, drama, ethnic, honors, international, jazz band, literary magazine, newspaper, orchestra, pep band, political, professional, radio, religious, social, social service, student government, and symphony. Popular campus events include Family Weekend, Talent Show, and Ivy Cutting at Graduation.

SERVICES: Counseling and information services are available, as is tutoring in most subjects. There is a reader service for the blind, and remedial math and writing. In addition, there is priority registration for disabled students. **Library/Resources:** The library contains 217,369 volumes, 497,248 microform items, 7,414 audio/video tapes/CDs/DVDs, and subscribes to 2,729 periodicals including electronic. Computerized library services include interlibrary loans, database searching, Internet access, and Wi-Fi capability. Special learning facilities include an art gallery, a science center, performing arts theater, a writing lab, and a media center. **Physically Challenged Students:** 70% of the campus is accessible. Facilities include wheelchair ramps, elevators, special parking, specially equipped restrooms, and special class scheduling. **Special:** There is a cooperative program with Fashion Institute of Technology in New York City, Fashion Institute of Design and Merchandising in Los Angeles, and Han Nam University in Korea, cross-registration with the Christian College Consortium and Christian College Coalition, and a Washington semester in American studies through the Christian College Coalition. SPU offers internships, study abroad in more than 5 countries, work-study programs, dual and student-designed majors, interdisciplinary majors such as language arts, and a liberal studies major for associate degree graduates. A general studies degree, pass/no credit options, and non-degree study are available. There are 5 national honor societies, a freshman honors program, and 10 departmental honors programs. **Visiting:** There are regularly scheduled orientations for prospective students. There are guides for informal visits, visitors may sit in on classes, and stay overnight. To schedule a visit, contact the Admissions Office at (206) 281-2021. **Campus Safety and Security:** Measures include 24-hour foot and vehicle patrol, emergency notification system, and security escort services. There are emergency telephones, lighted pathways/sidewalks, controlled access to dorms/residences, Closed-circuit TV monitors.

REQUIREMENTS: The SAT or ACT is required. The SAT I is preferred, with a minimum required composite score of 950. Candidates should be graduates of an accredited secondary school with a minimum high school GPA of 2.5 or hold a GED certificate. A strong college preparatory program in high school is recommended, including 4 years of English, 3 each of math, science, and foreign language, 2 of history, and 1 of social studies. An essay and 2 letters of recommendation are required, and an interview is recommended. AP and CLEP credits are accepted. Important factors in the admissions decision are advanced placement or honors courses, leadership record, and extracurricular activities record.

ADMISSIONS: 72% of a recent year applicants were accepted. The SAT scores for a recent year freshman class were: Critical Reading -16% below 500, 47% between 500 and 599, 28% between 600 and 699, and 9% between 700 and 800; Math--19% below 500, 46% between 500 and 599, 32% between 600 and 699, and 3% between 700 and 800; Writing--23% below 500, 45% between 500 and 599, 27% between 600 and 699, and 5% between 700 and 800. The ACT scores were 9% below 21, 22% between 21 and 23, 30% between 24 and 26, 18% between 27 and 28, and 21% above 28.

FINANCIAL AID: The FAFSA is required. The deadline for filing freshman financial aid applications for fall entry is June 30.

SEATTLE UNIVERSITY C-2
www.seattleu.edu

Seattle, WA 98122	**(206) 296-6000**
	(800) 426-7123
Fax: (206) 296-5656	Email: admissions@seattleu.edu
Full-time: 1762 men, 2524 women	Faculty: 358; IIA, +$
Part-time: 95 men, 130 women	Ph.D.s: 89%
Graduate: 1323 men, 1439 women	Student/Faculty: 12 to 1
Year: quarters, summer session	Tuition: $38,205
Room & Board: $10,830	Freshman Class: 7412 applied, 5438 accepted, 936 enrolled
SAT CR/M/W: 580/580/590 ACT: 27	CEEB CODE: 4695
Application Deadline: January 15	VERY COMPETITIVE+

Seattle University is centralized in an urban location in one of the world's most innovative, vibrant and culturally rich metropolitan cities. Graduates recognize how SU enhances and strengthens abilities that businesses and organizations prize critical thinking, effective communication, global perspectives and solving complex problems across disciplines. Undergraduate, graduate and certificate programs include science and engineering, business, liberal arts, humanities, nursing, education, theology and law. Service is an element of learning that enriches spirituality at SU. It's a free-thinking approach that underscores this independent university's commitment to empower leaders for a just and humane world. There are 5 undergraduate schools and 7 graduate schools. In addition to regional accreditation, Seattle U has baccalaureate program accreditation with AACSB, ABET, CAHEA, NCATE, and NLN. The 46-acre campus is in an urban area east of downtown Seattle in the Capitol Hill neighborhood. Including any residence halls, there are 34 buildings.

STUDENT LIFE: 56% of undergraduates are from out of state, mostly the West. Students are from 48 states, 90 foreign countries, and Canada. 49% are from public schools. 45% are White; 16% Asian American; 11% Foreign. 22% are Catholic. The average age of freshmen is 18; all undergraduates, 20. 88% do not continue beyond their first year; 77% remain to graduate. **Housing:** 2085 students can be accommodated in college housing, which includes coed dorms and on-campus apartments. In addition, there are language houses, and 24-hour quiet floors. On-campus housing is available on a lottery system for upperclassmen. Priority is given to out-of-town students. Some may keep cars.

FACULTY/CLASSROOMS: 48% of faculty are male; 52% are female. No introductory courses are taught by graduate students. The average class size in a regular course is 18.

PROGRAMS OF STUDY: Seattle U confers B.A., B.S., B.A.B.A., B.A.E., B.A.H., B.C.J., B.M., B.F.A., B.S.B., B.S.B.C., B.S.P., B.S.C.E., B.S.C.S., B.S.D.U., B.S.E.E., B.S.E.S., B.S.G.S., B.S.M., B.S.M.E., B.S.N. and B.S.W. degrees. Master's and Doctoral degrees are also awarded. Bachelor's degrees are awarded in AGRICULTURE (environmental studies), BIOLOGICAL SCIENCE (biochemistry, biology/adolescence education, biology/biological science, cell biology, and marine biology), BUSINESS (accounting, business administration and management, business economics, finance, international business management, international economics, and marketing management), COMMUNICATIONS AND THE ARTS (art history, communications, creative writing, English, film arts, fine arts, French, journalism, music, photography, Spanish, strings, theatre arts, and visual and performing arts), COMPUTER AND PHYSICAL SCIENCE (applied mathematics, chemistry, chemistry/adolescence education, computer science, digital arts/technology, mathematics, mathematics - actuarial concentration, mathematics/theoretical, physics, science, and Urban Ecology), EDUCATION (environmental education and mathematics education), ENGINEERING AND ENVIRONMENTAL DESIGN (civil engineering, computer engineering, electrical/electronics engineering, environmental engineering, environmental science, and mechanical engineering), HEALTH PROFESSIONS (exercise science, medical technology, nursing, and ultrasound technology), SOCIAL SCIENCE (anthropology, Asian studies, criminal justice, economics, forensic studies, history, humanities, international studies, liberal arts/general studies, philosophy, political science/government, psychology, public administration, religion, social work, sociology, theological studies, and women & gender studies). Nursing, criminal justice, and business are the strongest academically. Nursing, engineering, and business have the largest enrollments.

ACTIVITIES: There are 61 groups on campus, including art, cheerleading, choir, chorale, communications, dance, debate, drama, environmental, ethnic, forensics, gay, honors, international, jazz band, literary magazine, musical theater, newspaper, photography, political, professional, radio and TV, religious, social, social service, and student government. Popular campus events include Hawaiian Luau, Quad Stock and International Student Dinner. **Sports:** There are 8 intercollegiate sports for men and 10 for women, and 14 intramural sports for men and 14 for women. Facilities include an 180,000 sq. ft of recreational fitness and athletic space center with 2 swimming pools, cardio, weight rooms, group exercise, yoga, artial arts classrooms, racquetball, squash courts, 3 basketball courts, outdoor track, soccer and softball fields, tennis courts, and astroturf gym for indoor soccer/tennis with 2 batting cages. **Graduates:** From July 1, 2013 to June 30, 2014, 1383 bachelor's degrees were awarded. The most popular majors were business/marketing (26%), health professions and related sciences (12%), and engineering (8%). In an average class, 59% graduate in 4 years or less, 74% graduate in 5 years or less, and 77% graduate in 6 years or less.

SERVICES: Counseling and information services are available, as is tutoring in most subjects, math, English, accounting, language and science There is a reader service for the blind. a writing center **Library/Resources:** The 2 libraries contain 591,668 volumes, 1.8 million microform items, 6,358 audio/video tapes/CDs/DVDs, and subscribe to 61,985 periodicals including electronic. Computerized library services include interlibrary loans, database searching, Internet access, and Wi-Fi capability. Special learning facilities include an art gallery, planetarium, radio station, an electron microscope, a recording studio, and MRI. **Physically Challenged Students:** 95% of the campus is accessible. Facilities include wheelchair ramps, elevators, special parking, specially equipped restrooms, special class scheduling, lowered drinking fountains, and lowered telephones. **Special:** Seattle University provides many opportunities for dual majors, local, national and international internships, and on and off-campus work study positions. In addition, distinctive programs include: International Development Internship Program (IDIP) With a goal of instilling in students a lifelong commitment to the Jesuit mission of service and promotion of social justice, IDIP is a 20-credit, three-phase academic program designed for undergraduates. About 500 Seattle University students now participate in educational and service programs in more than 40 countries. Short-term programs at SU are slightly more popular than long-term ones. Developing a long-term relationship with a sister Jesuit school, the University of Central America (UCA) in Nicaragua, also has increased opportunities abroad for SU students. Project Center Seattle University runs one of the oldest and strongest Project Centers in the country. It's a great experiential learning opportunity for students in engineering, computer science and business. Sponsoring companies come back year after year; it's a great way for them to connect with SU and engage with great students. In fact, many students do go on to work for the sponsors of their projects. Albers Mentor Program The Albers Mentor Program is a unique opportunity for graduate-level and senior undergraduate business students to interact with upper level executives from leading Puget Sound companies and organizations. It offers opportunities to develop business contacts, access industry information, and gain valuable insights from experienced and successful professionals. There are a freshman honors program and 8 departmental honors programs. **Visiting:** There are regularly scheduled orientations for prospective students, About an hour of sharing what it's like to live and learn in our distinct urban setting. Get a chance to see classroom spaces, a residence hall room, our award-winning Chapel of St. Ignatius, and the new Lemieux Library among many others. There are guides for informal visits, visitors may sit in on classes, and stay overnight. To schedule a visit, contact the Undergraduate Admissions Office. **Campus Safety and Security:** Measures include 24-hour foot and vehicle patrol, emergency notification system, self-defense education, and security escort services. There are shuttle buses, emergency telephones, lighted pathways/sidewalks, and controlled access to dorms/residences.

REQUIREMENTS: The SAT or ACT is required. Admissions requirements include graduation from an accredited secondary school, with 16 academic credits, including 4 years of English, 3 each of math and social studies, 2 of foreign language, 2 of lab science, and 2 academic electives; 4 years of math and lab physics and chemistry are required of science and engineering students; lab biology and chemistry are needed by nursing students. The GED is also accepted. A GPA of 2.7 is required. AP and CLEP credits are accepted. Students must complete 180 to 192 quarter hours, depending on the degree, with 70 to 90 in the major, and maintain a minimum GPA of 2.25 to 2.5. Core curriculum requirements include 12 courses (60 credits) and a major-specific capstone course divided into four modules: Engaging Academic Inquiry, Exploring the Self and Others, Engaging the World, and Reflection. **Procedure:** Freshmen are admitted to all sessions. Entrance exams should be taken During the fall of the senior year. There are early admissions and deferred admissions plans. Applications should be filed by January 15 for fall entry; November 1 for winter entry; February 15 for spring entry; and May 1 for summer entry, along with a $55 fee. Notifications are sent March 15. 358 applicants were on the 2014 waiting list; 180 were admitted. Applications are accepted on-line. **Transfer Students:** 424 transfer students enrolled in 2013-2014. Generally, transfer students should have a college GPA of at least 2.25. An associate degree is recommended; a 2.75 GPA is required for nursing and business administration students. 45 of 180 credits required for the bachelor's degree must be completed at Seattle U. **International Students:** There are 478 international students enrolled. The school actively recruits these students. They must take the TOEFL with a minimum score of 520 on the paper-based TOEFL (PBT) or 68 on the Internet-based version (iBT).

ADMISSIONS: 73% of the 2014-2015 applicants were accepted. The SAT scores for the 2014-2015 freshman class were: Critical Reading--13% below 500, 41% between 500 and 599, 39% between 600 and 699, and 7% between 700 and 800; Math--12% below 500, 43% between 500 and 599, 36% between 600 and 699, and 9% between 700 and 800; Writing--12% below 500, 45% between 500 and 599, 35% between 600 and 699, and 8% between 700 and 800. The ACT scores were 4% below 21, 21% between 21 and 23, 28% between 24 and 26, 18% between 27 and 28, and 29% above 28. **Admissions Contact:** Melore Nielsen, Dean of Admissions. E-Mail: *admissions@seattleu.edu* Web: *www.seattleu.edu*

FINANCIAL AID: In 2014-2015, 93% of all full-time freshmen and 87% of continuing full-time students received some form of financial aid. 90% of all full-time freshmen and 81% of continuing full-time students received need-based aid. The average freshman award was $26,933. Need-based scholarships or need-based grants averaged $17,794 ($58,315 maximum); need-based self-help aid (loans and jobs) averaged $4,823 ($41,705 maximum); non-need-based athletic scholarships averaged $1,372 ($71,675 maximum); and other non-need-based awards and non-need-based scholarships averaged $731 ($44,485 maximum). The average financial indebtedness of the 2014 graduate was $21,369. The FAFSA is required. The priority date for freshman financial aid applications for fall entry is February 1.

UNIVERSITY OF PUGET SOUND C-2
www.pugetsound.edu

Tacoma, WA 98416	(253) 879-3100
	(253) 879-3211
Fax: (253) 879-3993	Email: jdmiller@pugetsound.edu
Full-time: 1079 men, 1444 women	Faculty: 207; IIB, +$
Part-time: 20 men, 8 women	Ph.D.s: 90%
Graduate: 60 men, 182 women	Student/Faculty: 12 to 1
Year: semesters, summer session	Tuition: $43,428
Room & Board: $11,180	Freshman Class: 5583 applied, 4427 accepted, 663 enrolled
SAT CR/M/W: 620/600/600 ACT: 28	CEEB CODE: 4067
Application Deadline: January 15	HIGHLY COMPETITIVE

University of Puget Sound is a residential national liberal arts college, drawing students and faculty from around the country and throughout the world. Named a "College That Changes Lives," Puget Sound graduates include Rhodes and Fulbright scholars, notables in the arts and culture, entrepreneurs and elected officials, and leaders in business and finance in the U.S. and abroad. A low student-faculty ratio provides Puget Sound students with personal attention from faculty members who have a strong commitment to teaching and offer 1,200 courses each year in more than 50 areas of study. Puget Sound is the only national, independent undergraduate liberal arts college in Western Washington, and one of just five independent colleges in the Pacific Northwest granted a charter by Phi Beta Kappa, the nation's most prestigious academic honor society. The college also offers sought-after graduate programs in education, physical therapy, and occupational therapy. There is one undergraduate school and 3 graduate schools. In addition to regional accreditation, Puget Sound has baccalaureate program accreditation with NASM, ACS, ACOTE, and CAPTE. The 97-acre campus is in an urban area near Commencement Bay in the historic North End neighborhood of Tacoma, Washington. Including any residence halls, there are 135 buildings.

STUDENT LIFE: 76% of undergraduates are from out of state, mostly the West. Students are from 44 states, 11 foreign countries, and Canada. 68% are from public schools. 75% are White. 57% claim no religious affiliation; 24% Protestant. The average age of freshmen is 18; all undergraduates, 20. 13% do not continue beyond their first year; 77% remain to graduate. **Housing:** 1751 students can be accommodated in college housing, which includes single-sex and coed dorms and on-campus apartments. In addition, there are honors houses, language houses, special-interest houses, fraternity houses, and sorority houses. On-campus housing is available on a first-come, first-served basis, and is available on a lottery system for upperclassmen. 65% of students live on campus; of those, 90% remain on campus on weekends. All students may keep cars.

FACULTY/CLASSROOMS: 53% of faculty are male; 47% are female. 89% teach undergraduates. No introductory courses are taught by graduate students. The average class size in an introductory lecture is 18; in a laboratory is 12; and in a regular course is 15.

PROGRAMS OF STUDY: Puget Sound confers B.A., B.M. and B.S. degrees. Master's and Doctoral degrees are also awarded. Bachelor's degrees are awarded in BIOLOGICAL SCIENCE (biochemistry, biology/biological science, cell biology, and molecular biology), BUSINESS (business administration and management and international economics), COMMUNICATIONS AND THE ARTS (art, Chinese, classics, communications, dramatic arts, East Asian languages and literature, English, French, German, Japanese, music, music performance, and Spanish), COMPUTER AND PHYSICAL SCIENCE (chemistry, computer science, geology, mathematics, natural sciences, and physics), EDUCATION (music education), HEALTH PROFESSIONS (exercise science), SOCIAL SCIENCE (Asian/Oriental studies, economics, history, philosophy, political science/government, psychology, religion, science and society, and sociology). Psychology, exercise science, and business have the largest enrollments.

ACTIVITIES: 23% of men belong to 4 national fraternities; 28% of women belong to 4 national sororities. There are 125 groups on campus, including and diversity awareness, health and wellness, sports, art, band, cheerleading, choir, chorale, chorus, computers, dance, debate, drama, environmental, ethnic, forensics, gay, gender, honors, international, jazz band, literary magazine, musical theater, newspaper, opera, orchestra, pep band, photography, political, professional, radio and TV, religious, social, social service, student government, symphony, and yearbook. Popular campus events include Foolish Pleasures (student film festival), Mistletoast Holiday, and Hawaiian Luau, Drag Show. **Sports:** There are 11 intercollegiate sports for men and 12 for women, and 8 intramural sports for men and 8 for women. Facilities include 3,000-seat basketball and volleyball gym; 6-lane pool; 2,488-seat football, soccer, lacrosse, and track stadium; 6 indoor tennis courts; fitness center with free weights and aerobics equipment, dance studio, track, baseball, softball, and intramural fields (one of which is synthetic), indoor climbing wall; auxiliary gym for intramurals and recreation. **Graduates:** From July 1, 2013 to June 30, 2014, 577 bachelor's degrees were awarded. The most popular majors were psychology (12%), business (7%), and biology (6%). In an average class, 68% graduate in 4 years or less, 75% graduate in 5 years or less, and 76% graduate in 6 years or less.

SERVICES: Counseling and information services are available, as is tutoring in most subjects. There is a reader service for the blind.

Library/Resources: The library contains 520,919 volumes, 19,806 microform items, 28,528 audio/video tapes/CDs/DVDs, and subscribes to 68,497 periodicals including electronic. Computerized library services include interlibrary loans, database searching, Internet access, and Wi-Fi capability. Special learning facilities include an art gallery, natural history museum, radio station, sculpture building, theatres, greenhouse, transmission and scanning electron microscopes, confocal microscope, DNA sequencer, NMR, X-ray diffractometer, microcomputer labs, sedimentology lab, stereoscopic and petrographic microscopes, computerized plotting/digitizing board and image analysis system, portable seismograph, gravimeter, proton precession magnetometer, ICP, GPS GIS lab, electronic music composition lab, electronic music keyboard lab with MIDI workstations, three electronic music classrooms, one music v-room. **Physically Challenged Students:** 80% of the campus is accessible. Facilities include wheelchair ramps, elevators, special parking, specially equipped restrooms, special class scheduling, lowered drinking fountains, lowered telephones, and special housing. **Special:** International programs: Include 130 study abroad programs in 45 countries, as well as local, national, and international internships in conjunction with an internship seminar. A curricular strength in Asian studies includes the full academic year Pacific Rim/Asian Study-Travel Program. Interdisciplinary programs: A highly interdisciplinary curriculum includes undergraduate studies in Asian languages and cultures; biochemistry, bioethics, and biophysics; a liberal arts-focused business leadership program; environmental policy and decision making; gender and queer studies; global development studies; international political economy; science, technology, and society; a student-designed interdisciplinary major; and more, including a conservatory quality School of Music and an Honors Program. Many students choose to double major. Internships: Internship programs are available through the Alumni Sharing Knowledge network and Career and Employment Services, with companies such as Amazon, Boeing, Google, and Microsoft. Engineering: A 3-2 engineering degree offered with Washington University in St. Louis, Columbia University, Duke University, and the University of Southern California. Fellowships: Puget Sound is a top producer of Fulbright Scholars; Peace Corps volunteers; graduates who earn doctorates, with high acceptance rates to graduate programs in law and medicine; and prestigious fellowships including the Watson, Boren, and National Science Foundation. There are 15 national honor societies, including Phi Beta Kappa, a freshman honors program, and 13 departmental honors programs.

Visiting: There are regularly scheduled orientations for prospective students, tour of campus, meetings with counselors, faculty, and coaches, classroom visits, overnight stays (if desired). There are guides for informal visits, visitors may sit in on classes, and stay over-

night. To schedule a visit, contact Carolyn Johnson at crjohnson@pugetsound.edu. **Campus Safety and Security:** Measures include 24-hour foot and vehicle patrol, emergency notification system, and security escort services. There are emergency telephones, lighted pathways/sidewalks, controlled access to dorms/residences, 24-hour live dispatch.

REQUIREMENTS: The SAT or ACT is required. Puget Sound only accepts the Common Application for undergraduate admission. Admission requirements include graduation from an accredited secondary school with a recommended 4 years of English, 3 to 4 of mathematics, 3 to 4 years of natural, and/or physical, laboratory science, 3 of social studies or history, 2 to 3 of foreign language, and 1 year of fine, visual, or performing arts. Also required are letters of personal recommendation from a teacher and counselor. An essay must be submitted, and an interview is recommended. The GED is also accepted. AP credits are accepted. Important factors in the admissions decision are advanced placement or honors courses, evidence of special talent, and personality/intangible qualities. In order to receive the baccalaureate degree from the University of Puget Sound, a student must: Earn a minimum of 32 units. The 32 units may include up to 4 academic courses graded pass/fail, up to 2 units in activity courses, and up to 4 units of independent study. Earn a minimum of 16 units, including the last 8, in residence at the University of Puget Sound. Residence requirements also exist in core, majors, minors, and graduation honors. Maintain a minimum GPA of 2.0 in all graded courses, including transfer courses, in the major(s) and the minor(s), if a minor is elected. Successfully complete Puget Sound's core requirements. The faculty of the University of Puget Sound has designed the core curriculum to give undergraduates an integrated and demanding introduction to the life of the mind and to established methods of intellectual inquiry. The Puget Sound undergraduate's core experience begins with two first-year seminars that guide the student through an in-depth exploration of a focused area of interest and that sharpen the student's skills in constructing persuasive arguments. In the first three years of their Puget Sound college career, students also study five "Approaches to Knowing" - Fine Arts, Humanities, Mathematics, Natural Science, and Social Science. These core areas develop the student's understanding of different disciplinary perspectives on society, culture, and the physical world, and explore both the strengths of those disciplinary approaches and their limitations. Connections, an upper-level integrative course, challenges the traditional boundaries of disciplines and examines the benefits and limits of interdisciplinary approaches to knowledge. Further, in accordance with the stated educational goals of the University of Puget Sound, core curriculum requirements have been established: (a) to improve each student's grasp of the intellectual tools necessary for the understanding and communication of ideas; (b) to enable each student to understand herself or himself as a thinking person capable of making ethical and aesthetic choices; (c) to help each student comprehend the diversity of intellectual approaches to understanding human society and the physical world; and (d) to increase each student's awareness of his or her place in those broader contexts. Students choose from a set of courses in eight Core areas, developing over four years an understanding of the liberal arts as the foundation for a lifetime of learning. Satisfy the foreign language graduation requirement in one of the following ways-:(a)Successfully complete 2 semesters of a foreign language at the 101-102 college level, or 1 semester of a foreign language at the 200 level or above (courses taken pass/fail will not fulfill the foreign language graduation requirement); (b)Pass a Puget Sound-approved foreign language proficiency exam at the third-year high school or first-year college level; (c)Receive a score of 4 or 5 on an Advanced Placement foreign language exam or a score of 5, 6, or 7 on an International Baccalaureate Higher Level foreign language exam. **Procedure:** Freshmen are admitted fall and spring. Entrance exams should be taken during the fall of the senior year. There are early decision and deferred admissions plans. Early decision applications should be filed by November 15; regular applications, by January 15 for fall entry; and November 1 for spring entry, along with a $50 fee. Notification of early decision is sent December 15; regular decision, April 1. 100 early decision candidates were accepted for the 2014-2015 class. 463 applicants were on the 2014 waiting list; 11 were admitted. Applications are accepted on-line. **Transfer Students:** 60 transfer students enrolled in 2013-2014. Applicants must have had an honorable dismissal from the institution(s) previously attended and be in good academic standing with a minimum GPA of 2.0. All college transcripts and the rigor of prior course work and resulting grades are evaluated. High school transcripts and SAT or ACT scores are required if less than 1 year of college has been completed. An interview is recommended. An essay is required. Puget Sound only accepts the Common Application for undergraduate transfer admission. 64 of 128 credits required for the bachelor's degree must be completed at Puget Sound. **International Students:** There are 10 international students enrolled. The school actively recruits these students. They must take the TOEFL with a minimum score of 550 on the paper-based TOEFL (PBT) or 80 on the Internet-based version (iBT). They must also take the SAT or ACT. All freshman applicants and transfers with less than 1 full year of college work must take the SAT or ACT.

ADMISSIONS: 79% of the 2014-2015 applicants were accepted. The SAT scores for the 2014-2015 freshman class were: Critical Reading--8% below 500, 31% between 500 and 599, 41% between 600 and 699, and 20% between 700 and 800; Math--9% below 500, 38% between 500 and 599, 43% between 600 and 699, and 10% between 700 and 800; Writing--11% below 500, 35% between 500 and 599, 43% between 600 and 699, and 11% between 700 and 800. The ACT scores were 4% below 21, 10% between 21 and 23, 23% between 24 and 26, 22% between 27 and 28, and 40% above 28. 55% of the current freshmen were in the top fifth of their class; 86% were in the top two fifths. There were 3 National Merit finalists. **Admissions Contact:** Carolyn Johnson, Senior Associate Director of Admission. E-Mail: *admission@pugetsound.edu* Web: *http://www.pugetsound.edu/admission*

FINANCIAL AID: In 2014-2015, 57% of all full-time freshmen and 40% of continuing full-time students received some form of financial aid. 56% of all full-time freshmen and 40% of continuing full-time students received need-based aid. The average freshman award was $28,459. Need-based scholarships or need-based grants averaged $24,168; need-based self-help aid (loans and jobs) averaged $6,945; other non-need-based awards and non-need-based scholarships averaged $5,019; and $13,755 from other forms of aid. 44% of undergraduate students work part-time. Average annual earnings from campus work are $2175. Puget Sound is a member of CSS. The CSS/Profile and FAFSA, and The CSS/Profile is required of early decision candidates. are required. The deadline for filing freshman financial aid applications for fall entry is February 1.

UNIVERSITY OF WASHINGTON C-2
www.washington.edu

Seattle, WA 98195	(206) 543-2100
	(206) 543-9686
Fax: (206) 685-3655	
Full-time: 11612 men, 12597 women	**Faculty:** n/av
	Ph.D.s: 89%
Part-time: 2141 men, 2220 women	**Student/Faculty:** n/av
Graduate: 5354 men, 6294 women	**Tuition:** $12,397 ($31,971)
Year: trimesters, summer session	**Freshman Class:** 17877
Room & Board: $10,752	applied, 11586 accepted, 5338 enrolled
SAT or ACT: required	**CEEB CODE:** 4854
Application Deadline: n/av	**VERY COMPETITIVE**

The University of Washington, founded in 1861, is a public institution offering a broad range of degree programs. There are 12 undergraduate schools and 1 graduate school. In addition to regional accreditation, UW has baccalaureate program accreditation with AACSB, ABET, NCATE, and NLN. The 643-acre campus is in an urban area 5 miles from downtown Seattle. Including any residence halls, there are 279 buildings.

STUDENT LIFE: 80% of undergraduates are from Washington. Others are from 44 states, 107 foreign countries, and Canada. 51% are White; 26% Asian American. The average age of freshmen is 18; all undergraduates, 21. 8% do not continue beyond their first year; 75% remain to graduate.

FACULTY/CLASSROOMS: 62% of faculty are male; 38% are female.

85% do both. No introductory courses are taught by graduate students.

PROGRAMS OF STUDY: UW confers B.A., B.S., B.A.B.A., B.C.H.S., B.L.Arch., B.Mus., B.S.A.&A., B.S.B.C., B.S.Cer.E., B.S.Comp.E., B.S.F., B.S.Fish., B.S.I.E., B.S.M.E., B.S.Med.Tech., B.S.Met.E. and B.S.Nur. degrees. Master's and Doctoral degrees are also awarded. Bachelor's degrees are awarded in AGRICULTURE (fishing and fisheries, forest engineering, and forestry production and processing), BIOLOGICAL SCIENCE (biochemistry, biology/biological science, botany, microbiology, neurosciences, and zoology), BUSINESS (accounting, banking and finance, business administration and management, business economics, international business management, marketing/retailing/merchandising, and personnel management), COMMUNICATIONS AND THE ARTS (art history and appreciation, classics, communications, comparative literature, dance, dramatic arts, English, French, Germanic languages and literature, graphic design, Italian, Japanese, jazz, music history and appreciation, music performance, painting, photography, Scandinavian languages, sculpture, Slavic languages, Spanish, speech/debate/rhetoric, studio art, and technical and business writing), COMPUTER AND PHYSICAL SCIENCE (astronomy, atmospheric sciences and meteorology, computer science, geology, information sciences and systems, mathematics, oceanography, physics, quantitative methods, and statistics), EDUCATION (music education), ENGINEERING AND ENVIRONMENTAL DESIGN (aeronautical engineering, ceramic engineering, chemical engineering, civil engineering, computer engineering, construction engineering, electrical/electronics engineering, engineering, landscape architecture/design, materials science, ocean engineering, and paper and pulp science), HEALTH PROFESSIONS (dental hygiene, environmental health science, health care administration, medical laboratory technology, nursing, and speech pathology/audiology), SOCIAL SCIENCE (African American studies, anthropology, Asian/American studies, Asian/Oriental studies, Canadian studies, economics, ethnic studies, food science, geography, history, international relations, Judaic studies, liberal arts/general studies, Near Eastern studies, philosophy, political science/government, psychology, religion, Russian and Slavic studies, social work, sociology, South Asian studies, and women's studies). Business, political science, and art have the largest enrollments.

ACTIVITIES: 6% of men belong to 27 national fraternities; 5% of women belong to 16 national sororities. There are 550 groups on campus, including band, cheerleading, chess, choir, chorale, chorus, communications, computers, dance, debate, drama, ethnic, film, gay, honors, international, jazz band, literary magazine, marching band, musical theater, newspaper, opera, orchestra, pep band, political, professional, radio and TV, religious, social, social service, student government, and symphony. Popular campus events include Convocation, Dawg Daze, and Washington Weekend.

SERVICES: Counseling and information services are available, as is tutoring in every subject. There is a reader service for the blind, and remedial math, reading, and writing. **Library/Resources:** The 16 libraries contain 7.0 million volumes. Computerized library services include interlibrary loans, database searching, Internet access, and Wi-Fi capability. Special learning facilities include an art gallery, natural history museum, planetarium, radio station, TV station, state museum, full teaching hospital, marine science lab, 200-acre arboretum, and field research forest. **Physically Challenged Students:** 95% of the campus is accessible. Facilities include wheelchair ramps, elevators, special parking, specially equipped restrooms, special class scheduling, lowered drinking fountains, lowered telephones, and special housing. **Special:** A wide variety of internships, including those for minority students in engineering, concurrent dual majors, study abroad in 60 countries, a Washington semester, a general studies degree, and co-op programs are available. Work-study programs, cross-registration with the National Student Exchange, credit/no credit options, student-designed majors, accelerated degree programs, nondegree study, and a 5-year B.A.-B.S. degree also are offered. There are 20 national honor societies, including Phi Beta Kappa, a freshman honors program, and 36 departmental honors programs. **Visiting:** There are regularly scheduled orientations for prospective students, including attending a class, a meeting with an admissions counselor and/or academic advisor, going on a campus tour, and attending information sessions. There are guides for informal visits and visitors may sit in on classes. To schedule a visit, contact the Student Visitation Program at (206) 543-5429. **Campus Safety and Security:** Measures include 24-hour foot and vehicle patrol, emergency notification system, self-defense education, and security escort services. There are shuttle buses, emergency telephones, lighted pathways/sidewalks, Emergency telephone numbers.

REQUIREMENTS: The SAT or ACT is required. The ACT Optional Writing test is also required. Applicants must have completed 15 academic units, including 4 years of English, 3 each of math and social sciences, 2 each of foreign language and science, and 1/2 year each in fine/visual performing arts and electives. Admission is based on a comprehensive review. A GPA of 2.0 is required. AP credits are accepted.

ADMISSIONS: 65% of a recent year applicants were accepted. The SAT scores for a recent year freshman class were: Critical Reading--16% below 500, 36% between 500 and 599, 36% between 600 and 699, and 12% between 700 and 800; Math--9% below 500, 32% between 500 and 599, 44% between 600 and 699, and 16% between 700 and 800; Writing--17% below 500, 42% between 500 and 599, 34% between 600 and 699, and 8% between 700 and 800. The ACT scores were 9% below 21, 16% between 21 and 23, 27% between 24 and 26, 20% between 27 and 28, and 28% above 28. 97% of the current freshmen were in the top fifth of their class; 99% were in the top two fifths. There were 39 National Merit finalists.

FINANCIAL AID: In a recent year, 50% of all full-time freshmen and 45% of continuing full-time students received some form of financial aid. 32% of all full-time freshmen and 37% of continuing full-time students received need-based aid. The FAFSA is required. The priority date for freshman financial aid applications for fall entry is February 28.

WALLA WALLA UNIVERSITY (*The complete profile is made available exclusively on our website, www.barronspac.com*)

WASHINGTON STATE UNIVERSITY   E-3
www.wsu.edu

Pullman, WA 99164	(509) 335-3564
	(888) 468-6978
Fax: (509) 335-4902	Email: admissions@wsu.edu
Full-time: 10195 men, 10117 women	Faculty: I, --$
	Ph.D.s: 90%
Part-time: 1184 men, 1574 women	Student/Faculty: 15 to 1
Graduate: 2228 men, 2344 women	Tuition: $12,428 ($25,510)
Year: semesters, summer session	Freshman Class: n/av
Room & Board: $11,276	
SAT or ACT: required	CEEB CODE: 4705
Application Deadline: January 31	COMPETITIVE

Founded as a land-grant institution in 1890, Washington State University in Pullman is today a major research university. Its undergraduate and graduate offerings span the liberal arts and sciences, business, education, engineering and architecture, agricultural, human and natural resource sciences, and the health sciences, including nursing, pharmacy, and veterinary medicine. There are 12 undergraduate schools and 1 graduate school. In addition to regional accreditation, Washington State has baccalaureate program accreditation with AACSB, ABET, ACCE, ACPE, ADA, ASLA, FIDER, NAAB, NASM, NCATE, NRPA, SAF, AACTE, APA, ASHA, AVMA, CADE, CCNE, and CIDA. The 620-acre campus is in a small town 80 miles south of Spokane, and 285 miles east of Seattle. Including any residence halls, there are 549 buildings.

STUDENT LIFE: 88% of undergraduates are from Washington. Others are from 50 states, 57 foreign countries, and Canada. 69% are White. The average age of freshmen is 19; all undergraduates, 23. 16% do not continue beyond their first year; 72% remain to graduate. **Housing:** 8644 students can be accommodated in college housing, which includes single-sex and coed dorms, on-campus apartments, and married student housing. In addition, there are honors houses, language houses, special-interest houses, fraternity houses, sorority houses, living-learning communities. On-campus housing is guaran-

teed for the freshman year only. 74% of students commute. All students may keep cars.

FACULTY/CLASSROOMS: 58% of faculty are male; 42% are female. Graduate students teach 18% of introductory courses. The average class size in a regular course is 36.

PROGRAMS OF STUDY: Washington State confers B.A., B.S., B.F.A., B.L.A. and B.M. degrees. Master's and Doctoral degrees are also awarded. Bachelor's degrees are awarded in AGRICULTURE (agricultural business management, agricultural communications, agricultural economics, agricultural mechanics, agriculture, agronomy, animal science, horticulture, natural resource management, plant protection (pest management), plant science, range/farm management, soil science, and wildlife management), BIOLOGICAL SCIENCE (biochemistry, biology/biological science, cell biology, entomology, genetics, microbiology, neurosciences, plant genetics, plant pathology, wildlife biology, and zoology), BUSINESS (accounting, business administration and management, business economics, business law, business statistics, entrepreneurial studies, hotel/motel and restaurant management, international business management, management information systems, marketing management, operations management, and sports management), COMMUNICATIONS AND THE ARTS (advertising, broadcasting, Chinese, communications, digital communications, English, fine arts, French, journalism, linguistics, multimedia, music, music performance, music theory and composition, public relations, and Spanish), COMPUTER AND PHYSICAL SCIENCE (applied mathematics, chemistry, computer science, digital arts/technology, geology, mathematics, physical sciences, physics, and science), EDUCATION (agricultural education, athletic training, bilingual/bicultural education, early childhood education, education, English education, foreign languages education, physical education, science education, secondary education, social studies education, and special education), ENGINEERING AND ENVIRONMENTAL DESIGN (agricultural engineering, architecture, bioengineering, biomedical engineering, chemical engineering, civil engineering, computer engineering, construction management, electrical/electronics engineering, environmental science, interior design, landscape architecture/design, manufacturing engineering, materials engineering, and mechanical engineering), HEALTH PROFESSIONS (biomedical science, exercise science, nursing, predentistry, premedicine, preoptometry, prepharmacy, prephysical therapy, preveterinary science, and speech pathology/audiology), SOCIAL SCIENCE (anthropology, Asian/Oriental studies, clothing and textiles management/production/services, criminal justice, crosscultural studies, economics, ethnic studies, family/consumer studies, food science, history, human development, humanities, interdisciplinary studies, liberal arts/general studies, philosophy, political science/government, prelaw, psychology, religion, social science, social studies, sociology, and women's studies). Organic agriculture, interior design, and international business are the strongest academically. Business administration, general social sciences, and nursing have the largest enrollments.

ACTIVITIES: 20% of men belong to 25 national fraternities; 25% of women belong to 14 national sororities. There are 383 groups on campus, including art, band, cheerleading, chess, choir, chorale, chorus, computers, dance, debate, drama, environmental, ethnic, film, forensics, gay, honors, international, jazz band, literary magazine, marching band, musical theater, newspaper, opera, orchestra, pep band, photography, political, professional, radio and TV, religious, social, social service, student government, symphony, and yearbook. Popular campus events include Convocation, All-Campus Picnic, and Civic Engagement Week. **Sports:** There are 7 intercollegiate sports for men and 10 for women, and 12 intramural sports for men and 12 for women. Facilities include a 40,000-seat stadium, a 12,000-seat coliseum, full 200-meter NCAA indoor and outdoor tracks, tennis courts, a 165,500-square-foot student recreation center, an 18-hole championship golf course, an indoor practice facility with roll-out turf system, baseball and soccer fields, indoor swimming pools, racquetball and squash courts, a climbing wall, ballrooms, gyms, an indoor rowing facility, an outdoor recreation center, basketball courts, sand volleyball courts, and intramural playing fields. **Graduates:** From July 1, 2013 to June 30, 2014, 4907 bachelor's degrees were awarded. The most popular majors were business administration (18%), social sciences (13%), and communication

(11%). 275 companies recruited on campus in 2013-2014. In an average class, 38% graduate in 4 years or less, 62% graduate in 5 years or less, and 69% graduate in 6 years or less.

SERVICES: Counseling and information services are available, as is tutoring in most subjects. There is a reader service for the blind. Learning assistance is available in workshops that address study skills, note taking, test preparation, time management, career/major choice, stress management, and life skills **Library/Resources:** The 6 libraries contain 2.2 million volumes, 4.0 million microform items, 424,265 audio/video tapes/CDs/DVDs, and subscribe to 42,987 periodicals including electronic. Computerized library services include interlibrary loans, database searching, Internet access, and Wi-Fi capability. Special learning facilities include an art gallery, natural history museum, planetarium, radio station, TV station, Specialized teaching and research labs for science and engineering, a planetarium and observatory, virtual reality computer-integrated manufacturing lab, fine arts studio facilities with specialized equipment, museums, displays and collections, and art galleries, digital recording studio; music listening library; radio and television studios; livestock centers, labs, and barns, a wildlife center, a bear center (live grizzly bears in captivity for research, education, and conservation), human anatomy lab, greenhouses, vivaria, and an herbarium, financial markets lab (trading room), food sensory evaluation facility, a veterinary teaching hospital, a social and economic sciences research center, a water research center, a laboratory for atmospheric research, nuclear radiation center. **Physically Challenged Students:** Facilities include wheelchair ramps, elevators, special parking, specially equipped restrooms, special class scheduling, lowered drinking fountains, lowered telephones, special housing, and a van to provide transportation to and from classes. **Special:** Undergraduates can become involved in faculty research, internships, study-abroad programs in 95 countries, an Honors College, academic club projects and competitions, civic engagement projects, work-study programs, and co-op programs in numerous majors. Dual majors are available, as are B.A.-B.S. degrees in computer science and psychology and student-designed majors in general studies. Interior design and veterinary medicine programs offer accelerated paths to advanced degrees. Credit may be granted for military service, and nondegree and pass/fail options are offered. Cross-registration is available with the Universities of Idaho and Washington, Eastern Washington University, and Wenatchee Valley College. The WSU College of Nursing is a consortium of Washington State, Eastern Washington, and Whitworth University. There are 34 national honor societies, including Phi Beta Kappa, a freshman honors program, and 100 departmental honors programs. **Visiting:** There are regularly scheduled orientations for prospective students, consisting of a campus tour and a presentation about admissions, financial aid, and scholarship opportunities. There are guides for informal visits and visitors may sit in on classes. **Campus Safety and Security:** Measures include 24-hour foot and vehicle patrol, emergency notification system, self-defense education, and security escort services. There are shuttle buses, emergency telephones, lighted pathways/sidewalks, controlled access to dorms/residences, crime prevention and personal safety education, monitored lighting levels on campus, a women's transit service, residence hall security hours, a police intern program, and housing patrols.

REQUIREMENTS: The SAT or ACT is required. Students should be graduates of an accredited secondary school with 4 years of English, 3 each of math (1 year each of algebra, geometry, and advanced math) and social science, and 2 each of a world language (includes Native American languages and American Sign language), science, and 1 year of fine, visual or performing arts, or elective from any of the other required subjects. A combination of the high school GPA and test scores is considered. The GED is also accepted. A GPA of 2.0 is required. AP and CLEP credits are accepted. Important factors in the admissions decision are advanced placement or honors courses, evidence of special talent, and personality/intangible qualities.Students must complete 120 semester hours, with fulfillment of a major and 40 hours of upper-division work, and maintain a minimum GPA of 2.0. Specific disciplines to be taken vary within majors. General university requirements include 10 hours of science, 9 of arts and humanities and social sciences, 6 of world civilization, 6 of communication, and 3 each of math, intercultural studies, and American diversity. Students must complete a writing portfolio, undergo a mid-

career assessment, and pass a writing qualifying exam prior to graduation. **Procedure:** Freshmen are admitted fall, spring, and summer. Entrance exams should be taken during spring of the junior year or fall of the senior year. Applications should be filed by January 31 for fall entry; November 15 for spring entry, along with a $50 fee. Notifications are sent November 1. Applications are accepted on-line. **Transfer Students:** 1233 transfer students enrolled in 2013-2014. Transfer applicants who have less than a full year of college-level academic work may be required to submit a high school transcript, test scores, and/or a personal statement. 30 of 120 credits required for the bachelor's degree must be completed at Washington State. **International Students:** There are 779 international students enrolled. The school actively recruits these students. They must take the TOEFL with a minimum score of 550 on the paper-based TOEFL (PBT) or 79 on the Internet-based version (iBT) or take the MELAB, or IELTS, IB with a passing score in English, or SAT with a reading/writing score of 500.

ADMISSIONS: Wendy Peterson, Director of Admissions. E-Mail: *admissions@wsu.edu* Web: *www.wsu.edu*

FINANCIAL AID: In 2014-2015, 86% of all full-time freshmen and 76% of continuing full-time students received some form of financial aid. 49% of all full-time freshmen and 53% of continuing full-time students received need-based aid. The average freshman award was $18,745. Need-based scholarships or need-based grants averaged $8,523 ($16,326 maximum); need-based self-help aid (loans and jobs) averaged $3,988 ($10,000 maximum); non-need-based athletic scholarships averaged $19,085 ($34,834 maximum); and other non-need-based awards and non-need-based scholarships averaged $4,077 ($28,750 maximum). 26% of undergraduate students work part-time. Average annual earnings from campus work are $3367. The average financial indebtedness of the 2014 graduate was $20,544. The FAFSA is required. The priority date for freshman financial aid applications for fall entry is February 15.

WESTERN WASHINGTON UNIVERSITY C-1
www.wwu.edu

Bellingham, WA 98225	(360) 650-3000
	(360) 650-3440
Fax: (360) 650-7369	Email: admit@wwu.edu
Full-time: 5689 men, 7226 women	Faculty: n/av; IIA, -$
Part-time: 552 men, 458 women	Ph.D.s: 88%
Graduate: 342 men, 582 women	Student/Faculty: 20 to 1
Year: quarters, summer session	Tuition: $8863 ($19,752)
Room & Board: $9656	Freshman Class: 9791 applied, 7799 accepted, 2688 enrolled
SAT CR/M/W: 550/550/530 ACT: 25	CEEB CODE: 4947
Application Deadline: March 1	VERY COMPETITIVE

Western Washington University, founded in 1893, is a nonprofit, public institution whose emphasis is on the liberal arts and sciences, business and business administration, and economics, art, fine arts, and performing arts, music, teacher preparation, interdisciplinary learning, and environmental studies. There are 7 undergraduate schools and 1 graduate school. In addition to regional accreditation, WWU has baccalaureate program accreditation with AACSB, ABET, ASLA, NASM, NCATE, and NRPA. The 195-acre campus is in a small town 60 miles south of Vancouver, British Columbia and 90 miles north of Seattle. Including any residence halls, there are 80 buildings.

STUDENT LIFE: 91% of undergraduates are from Washington. Others are from states, and Canada. 75% are White. The average age of freshmen is 18; all undergraduates, 21. 15% do not continue beyond their first year; 85% remain to graduate.

FACULTY/CLASSROOMS: 50% of faculty are male; 50% are female. No introductory courses are taught by graduate students.

PROGRAMS OF STUDY: WWU confers B.A., B.S., B.A.E., B.F.A. and B.Mus. degrees. Master's degrees are also awarded. Bachelor's degrees are awarded in AGRICULTURE (environmental studies), BIOLOGICAL SCIENCE (biochemistry, biology/biological science, cell biology, ecology, life science, marine biology, marine science, and molecular biology), BUSINESS (accounting, business administration and management, fashion merchandising, human resources, international business management, international economics, management information systems, management science, marketing/retailing/merchandising, and operations management), COMMUNICATIONS AND THE ARTS (apparel design, art, ceramic art and design, classics, communications, creative writing, dance, design, dramatic arts, English, fine arts, French, German, Japanese, journalism, linguistics, multimedia, music, music history and appreciation, painting, photography, Russian, sculpture, Spanish, theater design, and visual and performing arts), COMPUTER AND PHYSICAL SCIENCE (applied mathematics, applied physics, chemistry, computer science, earth science, geology, mathematics, physics, and polymer science), EDUCATION (art education, early childhood education, education administration, elementary education, foreign languages education, health education, music education, physical education, reading education, recreation education, science education, secondary education, special education, and technical education), ENGINEERING AND ENVIRONMENTAL DESIGN (electrical/electronics engineering, electrical/electronics engineering technology, engineering technology, environmental science, industrial engineering technology, manufacturing technology, mechanical design technology, mechanical engineering technology, plastics engineering, and technology and public affairs), HEALTH PROFESSIONS (nursing, rehabilitation therapy, and speech pathology/audiology), SOCIAL SCIENCE (American studies, anthropology, behavioral science, Canadian studies, child psychology/development, East Asian studies, economics, geography, history, human services, interdisciplinary studies, parks and recreation management, philosophy, political science/government, psychology, public affairs, social studies, and sociology). Industrial technology, materials science, business, and computer science are the strongest academically. Business and marketing, social sciences, visual and performing arts have the largest enrollments.

ACTIVITIES: There are 225 groups on campus, including environmental, art, band, cheerleading, chess, choir, chorale, chorus, computers, dance, debate, drama, environmental, ethnic, film, forensics, gay, honors, international, jazz band, literary magazine, musical theater, newspaper, opera, orchestra, pep band, photography, political, professional, recreational, religious, social, social service, student government, and symphony. Popular campus events include The Western Jam Talent Show, Casino Night and Cinco de Mayo.

SERVICES: Counseling and information services are available, as is tutoring in most subjects, English, humanities, social sciences, math and natural sciences. There is a reader service for the blind. **Library/Resources:** The 2 libraries contain 1.3 million volumes, 1.4 million microform items, and 93,199 audio/video tapes/CDs/DVDs, and subscribe to 129,895 periodicals including electronic. Computerized library services include interlibrary loans, database searching, Internet access, and Wi-Fi capability. Special learning facilities include an art gallery, planetarium, a marine lab, neutron generator lab, motor vehicle research lab, a wind tunnel, air pollution lab, an electronic music studio, and performing arts center. **Physically Challenged Students:** All of the campus is accessible. Facilities include wheelchair ramps, elevators, special parking, specially equipped restrooms, special class scheduling, lowered drinking fountains, lowered telephones. Transcription services. **Special:** Special academic programs include internships through various academic departments and study abroad in 75 countries. Dual majors are available through various departments. There is a general studies degree, and a B.A. in humanities. A 3-2 engineering degree is possible with the University of Washington. WWU is in the process of starting an Engineering Program that will replace the 3-2. Student-designed majors are offered through the liberal studies department in the College of Arts and Sciences and through Fairhaven College, which affords an unusual degree of student involvement in the structure and content of their own programs and which uses faculty narrative for students' academic evaluations. In addition, Huxley College of Environmental Studies provides specialized education and research. Up to 30 credits of electives may be granted for military service, and nondegree study and pass/fail options are possible. There are 12 national honor societies, a freshman honors program, and 12 departmental honors programs. **Visiting:** There are regularly scheduled orientations for prospective students, student visits include tours, class visits and advisement.

There are guides for informal visits, visitors may sit in on classes, and stay overnight. To schedule a visit, contact the STARS Program at (360) 650-3861. **Campus Safety and Security:** Measures include 24-hour foot and vehicle patrol, emergency notification system, self-defense education, and security escort services. There are shuttle buses, emergency telephones, and lighted pathways/sidewalks.

REQUIREMENTS: The SAT or ACT is required. Other admissions requirements include completion of 16 academic units, comprised of 4 years of college preparatory English composition and literature courses; 3 units of college preparatory math, including 2 years of algebra; 3 units of social studies/history; 2 units of science, including 1 unit of a chemistry or physics with an algebra prerequisite; 2 units of the same foreign language; 1 unit of fine and performing arts; and 1 semester in another academic field. Freshman applicants meeting minimum GPA and subject requirements are ranked by an index combining the GPA and a standardized test score. The GED is also accepted. Other factors taken into consideration include curricular rigor (level of difficulty of courses), grade trends, leadership, community involvement, special talent, multicultural experience, and personal hardship or circumstances. A GPA of 2.5 is required. AP credits are accepted. Important factors in the admissions decision are advanced placement or honors courses, leadership record, and personality/intangible qualities.

ADMISSIONS: 80% of a recent year applicants were accepted. The SAT scores for a recent year freshman class were: Critical Reading--25% below 500, 43% between 500 and 599, 27% between 600 and 699, and 5% between 700 and 800; Math--25% below 500, 47% between 500 and 599, 26% between 600 and 699, and 3% between 700 and 800; Writing--32% below 500, 45% between 500 and 599, 21% between 600 and 699, and 2% between 700 and 800. The ACT scores were 13% below 21, 26% between 21 and 23, 28% between 24 and 26, 15% between 27 and 28, and 18% above 28.

FINANCIAL AID: In a recent year, 51% of all full-time freshmen and 48% of continuing full-time students received some form of financial aid. 41% of all full-time freshmen and 42% of continuing full-time students received need-based aid. Need-based scholarships or need-based grants averaged $8,828; and need-based self-help aid (loans and jobs) averaged $4,098. 10% of undergraduate students work part-time. The FAFSA is required. The deadline for filing freshman financial aid applications for fall entry is February 15.

WHITMAN COLLEGE   E-3
www.whitman.edu

Walla Walla, WA 99362

Fax: (509) 527-4967
Full-time: 642 men, 825 women
Part-time: 13 men, 18 women
Graduate: n/av
Year: semesters
Room & Board: $11,228

SAT CR/M/W: 670/660/660 ACT: 30
Application Deadline: January 15

(509) 527-5111
(509) 527-5176
Email: admission@whitman.edu
Faculty: 154; IIB, +$
Ph.D.s: 91%
Student/Faculty: 9 to 1
Tuition: $44,800
Freshman Class: 3653 applied, 1498 accepted, 393 enrolled
CEEB CODE: 4951
MOST COMPETITIVE

Whitman College, founded in 1883, is a nonprofit, private, independent residential liberal arts and sciences college. There is one undergraduate school. In addition to regional accreditation, Whitman has baccalaureate program accreditation with ACS. The 117-acre campus is in a small town 150 miles south of Spokane, 260 miles southeast of Seattle, and 235 miles east of Portland. Including any residence halls, there are 41 buildings.

STUDENT LIFE: 65% of undergraduates are from out of state, mostly the Northwest. Students are from 42 states, 26 foreign countries, and Canada. 71% are from public schools. 72% are White. The average age of freshmen is 18; all undergraduates, 19. 6% do not continue beyond their first year; 87% remain to graduate. **Housing:** 1067 students can be accommodated in college housing, which includes single-sex and coed dorms and off-campus apartments. In addition, there are language houses, special-interest houses, and fraternity houses. On-campus housing is guaranteed for the freshman year only and is available on a lottery system for upperclassmen. All students may keep cars.

FACULTY/CLASSROOMS: 53% of faculty are male; 47% are female. All teach undergraduates, all do research, and all teach and do research. No introductory courses are taught by graduate students. The average class size in an introductory lecture is 23; in a laboratory is 21; and in a regular course is 17.

PROGRAMS OF STUDY: Whitman confers B.A. degrees. Bachelor's degrees are awarded in AGRICULTURE (environmental studies), BIOLOGICAL SCIENCE (biochemistry), COMMUNICATIONS AND THE ARTS (art history, classics, dance, English, film arts, fine arts, French, German, music, Spanish, speech/debate/rhetoric, studio art, and theatre arts), COMPUTER AND PHYSICAL SCIENCE (astronomy, chemistry, geology, mathematics, and physics), ENGINEERING AND ENVIRONMENTAL DESIGN (environmental science), HEALTH PROFESSIONS (biology), SOCIAL SCIENCE (anthropology, Asian/Oriental studies, economics, ethnic studies, history, philosophy, political science/government, psychology, religion, and sociology). Biology, psychology, and biochemistry have the largest enrollments.

ACTIVITIES: 48% of men belong to 4 national fraternities; 44% of women belong to 4 national sororities. There are 136 groups on campus, including art, choir, chorale, chorus, dance, debate, drama, environmental, ethnic, film, forensics, gay, honors, international, jazz band, literary magazine, musical theater, newspaper, opera, orchestra, photography, political, professional, radio and TV, religious, social, social service, student government, symphony, and yearbook. Popular campus events include Renaissance Fair, Choral Contest, and Interest House Block Party. **Sports:** There are 7 intercollegiate sports for men and 8 for women, and 9 intramural sports for men and 9 for women. Facilities include a stadium, two gyms, squash and handball courts, saunas, climbing walls, and an aerobic/dance room. There is an athletics center with a 10,000-square-foot weights/cardiovascular area, 8-lane swimming pool, 6 outdoor tennis courts, 4 indoor tennis courts, soccer field, dance studio, soccer, baseball, and track facilities.
Graduates: From July 1, 2013 to June 30, 2014, 414 bachelor's degrees were awarded. The most popular majors were biology (12%), English (8%), biochemistry, biophysics, and and molecular biology (7%). In an average class, 82% graduate in 4 years or less, 87% graduate in 5 years or less, and 87% graduate in 6 years or less.

SERVICES: Counseling and information services are available, as is tutoring in most subjects. There is a reader service for the blind. There are also centers for study skills and writing. **Library/Resources:** The library contains 572,648 volumes, 7,354 audio/video tapes/CDs/DVDs, and subscribes to 67,230 periodicals including electronic. Computerized library services include interlibrary loans, database searching, Internet access, and Wi-Fi capability. Special learning facilities include an art gallery, natural history museum, planetarium, radio station, an electron microscope lab, an indoor planetarium, an off-campus an observatory and on-campus astronomical telescopes, an Asian art collection, a video-conferencing center, an outdoor sculpture walk, an organic garden, and indoor and outdoor rock climbing walls. **Physically Challenged Students:** 96% of the campus is accessible. Facilities include wheelchair ramps, elevators, special parking, specially equipped restrooms, lowered drinking fountains, lowered telephones. Any modifications necessary for specific cases will be made. **Special:** Special academic programs include more than 500 internships, over 80 semester or year-long study abroad programs in 40 countries, a Washington semester, and study programs in Chicago and Philadelphia. Dual majors are available in any area, and student-designed majors are offered. There is a 3-2 environmental management and forestry program with Duke University and a 3-2 engineering program with Washington University in St. Louis, California Institute of Technology and Applied Science, Columbia and Duke Universities, and University of Washington. A 3-3 law program is offered through Columbia University. A 4-1 education program is available through Bank Street College of Education and University of Puget Sound Cooperative. Certification is offered for elementary and secondary education. A pass-D-fail option is available. A 3-2 program in international studies is available with the Monterey Institute of International Studies. A 3-2 program in ocean-ography is available with University of Washington. There are 3 national honor societies, including Phi Beta Kappa, and a freshman honors program. **Visiting:** There are regularly scheduled orientations for prospective students. There are guides for informal visits, visitors may sit in on classes, and stay overnight.. **Campus Safety and Security:** Measures include emergency notification system, self-defense education, and security escort services. There are emergency telephones, lighted pathways/sidewalks, controlled access to dorms/residences, and 24-hour foot patrol.

REQUIREMENTS: Applicants must submit either ACT or SAT scores. The GED is accepted. 3 essays must be submitted, and an interview is recommended. Credit by challenge examination is accepted. AP credits are accepted. Important factors in the admissions decision are advanced placement or honors courses, personality/intangible qualities, evidence of special talent, recommendations by alumni, recommendations by school officials, and extracurricular activities record.Students must complete 124 credits, with 32 to 36 in the major, and maintain a minimum GPA of 2.0. Distribution requirements include a minimum of 6 credits in social sciences, humanities, fine arts, and science (including 1 course with a lab); 1 course of 3 or more credits in quantitative analysis; and 2 courses that fulfill the alternative voices requirement. Freshman must take the year-long Encounters (great works) course. All majors require an oral exam as well as a thesis project or comprehensive written exam. **Procedure:** Freshmen are admitted fall and spring. Entrance exams should be taken by fall of the senior year. There are early decision and deferred admissions plans. Early decision applications should be filed by November 15; regular applications, by January 15 for fall entry, along with a $50 fee. Notification of early decision is sent December 21; regular decision, April 1. 130 early decision candidates were accepted for the 2014-2015 class. 862 applicants were on the 2014 waiting list; 59 were admitted. Applications are accepted on-line. **Transfer Students:** 21 transfer students enrolled in 2013-2014. Transfer applicants must submit the common application, a transfer supplement, a teacher/counselor recommendation, a statement of good standing from prior institutions, their high school and college transcripts, SAT or ACT scores (required for some), and the application fee. 54 of 124 credits required for the bachelor's degree must be completed at Whitman. **International Students:** There are 57 international students enrolled. The school actively recruits these students. They must take the TOEFL with a minimum score of 560 on the paper-based TOEFL (PBT) or 85 on the Internet-based version (iBT), or, either the APIEL or ELPT. They must also take the SAT or ACT.

ADMISSIONS: 41% of the 2014-2015 applicants were accepted. The SAT scores for the 2014-2015 freshman class were: Critical Reading--4% below 500, 18% between 500 and 599, 45% between 600 and 699, and 33% between 700 and 800; Math--4% below 500, 18% between 500 and 599, 49% between 600 and 699, and 29% between 700 and 800; Writing--3% below 500, 20% between 500 and 599, 46% between 600 and 699, and 31% between 700 and 800. The ACT scores were 2% below 21, 1% between 21 and 23, 10% between 24 and 26, 16% between 27 and 28, and 70% above 28. 80% of the current freshmen were in the top fifth of their class; 96% were in the top two fifths. **Admissions Contact:** Tony Cabasco, Dean of Admission and Financial Aid. E-Mail: *admission@whitman.edu* Web: *www.whitman.edu*

FINANCIAL AID: In 2014-2015, 74% of all full-time freshmen and 77% of continuing full-time students received some form of financial aid. 45% of all full-time freshmen and 44% of continuing full-time students received need-based aid. The average freshman award was $34,801. Need-based scholarships or need-based grants averaged $25,978; need-based self-help aid (loans and jobs) averaged $6,181; and other non-need-based awards and non-need-based scholarships averaged $10,120. The average financial indebtedness of the 2014 graduate was $9,388. is a member of CSS. The CSS/Profile and FAFSA are required. The priority date for freshman financial aid applications for fall entry is November 15. The deadline for filing freshman financial aid applications for fall entry is February 1.

WHITWORTH UNIVERSITY   E-2
www.whitworth.edu

Spokane, WA 99251   (509) 777-1000
                                           (800) 533-4668
Fax: (509) 777-3758   Email: admission@whitworth.edu
Full-time: 938 men, 1381 women   **Faculty:** 150; IIB, -$
Part-time: 26 men, 25 women   **Ph.Ds:** 84%
Graduate: 90 men, 194 women   **Student/Faculty:** 11 to 1
Year: 4-1-4, summer session   **Tuition:** $37,456
Room & Board: $10,278   **Freshman Class:** 3177
                                        applied, 2690 accepted,
                                        619 enrolled
SAT CR/M/W: 600/600/590 **ACT:** 26 **CEEB CODE:** 4953
Application Deadline: March 1   **VERY COMPETITIVE**

Whitworth University, founded in 1890, is an independent, comprehensive institution affiliated with the Presbyterian Church. The emphasis of its undergraduate and graduate programs is on the liberal arts, business, art and fine arts, music, religious studies, and teacher preparation. There are 4 undergraduate schools and 3 graduate schools. In addition to regional accreditation, Whitworth has baccalaureate program accreditation with NASM, NCATE, and NLN. The 200-acre campus is in a suburban area 7 miles north of Spokane. Including any residence halls, there are 40 buildings.

STUDENT LIFE: 61% of undergraduates are from Washington. Others are from 32 states, 38 foreign countries, and Canada. 88% are from public schools. 76% are White. 81% are Protestant. The average age of freshmen is 18; all undergraduates, 21. 14% do not continue beyond their first year; 86% remain to graduate. **Housing:** 1350 students can be accommodated in college housing, which includes single-sex and coed dorms, on-campus apartments, and off-campus apartments. In addition, there are special-interest houses, and theme houses. On-campus housing is guaranteed for all 4 years. 58% of students live on campus; of those, 90% remain on campus on weekends. Alcohol is not permitted. All students may keep cars.

FACULTY/CLASSROOMS: 58% of faculty are male; 42% are female. All teach undergraduates. No introductory courses are taught by graduate students. The average class size in an introductory lecture is 30; in a laboratory is 15; and in a regular course is 19.

PROGRAMS OF STUDY: Whitworth confers B.A. and B.S. degrees. Master's degrees are also awarded. Bachelor's degrees are awarded in BIOLOGICAL SCIENCE (biology/biological science and biophysics), BUSINESS (accounting, business administration and management, international business management, and marketing management), COMMUNICATIONS AND THE ARTS (art, communications, dramatic arts, English, French, journalism, music, Spanish, and speech/debate/rhetoric), COMPUTER AND PHYSICAL SCIENCE (applied physics, chemistry, computer science, mathematics, physics, and quantitative methods), EDUCATION (athletic training, elementary education, English education, foreign languages education, mathematics education, music education, science education, secondary education, and social studies education), ENGINEERING AND ENVIRONMENTAL DESIGN (engineering physics), HEALTH PROFESSIONS (community health work, health science, nursing, predentistry, and premedicine), SOCIAL SCIENCE (American studies, crosscultural studies, economics, history, international studies, peace studies, philosophy, political science/government, prelaw, psychology, sociology, theological studies, and women's studies). Music, sciences, and education are the strongest academically. Biology, health sciences, and psychology have the largest enrollments.

ACTIVITIES: There are 45 groups on campus, including art, band, cheerleading, choir, chorale, chorus, computers, dance, debate, drama, environmental, ethnic, forensics, honors, international, jazz band, literary magazine, musical theater, newspaper, orchestra, photography, political, radio and TV, religious, social, social service, and student government. Popular campus events include Guest Speakers, Student Research Conference, and Community Building Day. **Sports:** There are 9 intercollegiate sports for men and 9 for women, and 10 intramural sports for men and 8 for women. Facilities include an university recreation center complete with climbing walls, a 2000-seat stadium, 1200-seat gym, field house, an aquatic center, and playing

fields. **Graduates:** From July 1, 2013 to June 30, 2014, 539 bachelor's degrees were awarded. The most popular majors were business management (14%), health professions (12%), and social sciences (10%). 60 companies recruited on campus in 2013-2014. In an average class, 4% graduate in 3 years or less, 64% graduate in 4 years or less, 74% graduate in 5 years or less, and 75% graduate in 6 years or less. Of the 2013 graduating class, 20% were enrolled in graduate school within 6 months of graduation, and 72% were employed.

SERVICES: Counseling and information services are available, as is tutoring in most subjects, biology, chemistry, computer science, French, German, Spanish, math, physics, and writing. **Library/Resources:** The 2 libraries contain 286,000 volumes, 10,000 microform items, 9,000 audio/video tapes/CDs/DVDs, and subscribe to 3,000 periodicals including electronic. Computerized library services include interlibrary loans, database searching, Internet access, and Wi-Fi capability. Special learning facilities include an art gallery, radio station, a writing center. **Physically Challenged Students:** 80% of the campus is accessible. Facilities include wheelchair ramps, elevators, special parking, specially equipped restrooms, special class scheduling, lowered drinking fountains, and lowered telephones. **Special:** Special academic programs include many work-study opportunities, 1 to 3 internship course credits that may be earned by juniors and seniors, and a January Washington term. Study abroad is available in 15 countries. There is cross-registration with the Intercollegiate Language Study Consortium. Accelerated degree programs are possible, as is a 3-2 engineering degree, and students may choose to specialize in an area of concentration in lieu of a major. Credit may be granted for life, military, or work experience. Nondegree study is possible for those auditing or in seminars, and there is 1 pass/fail option allowed per year. A special feature of the school is the modified semester calendar, which affords unusual opportunities for internships, study tours, and other activities. There is a freshman honors program. **Visiting:** There are regularly scheduled orientations for prospective students, including a class visit, a tour, and an overnight stay, if desired. There are guides for informal visits, visitors may sit in on classes, and stay overnight. To schedule a visit, contact Megan Thompson at admissions@whitworth.edu. **Campus Safety and Security:** Measures include 24-hour foot and vehicle patrol, emergency notification system, and security escort services. There are emergency telephones, lighted pathways/sidewalks, and controlled access to dorms/residences.

REQUIREMENTS: The ACT is recommended. Admissions criteria include 4 high school credits in English, 3 each in math, science, and history/social studies, and 2 of a foreign language. An essay must be submitted, and an interview is recommended. Music students are advised to audition. AP and CLEP credits are accepted. Important factors in the admissions decision are advanced placement or honors courses, extracurricular activities record, and leadership record. Students must complete 126 credit hours, with about 45 in the major, and maintain a GPA of at least 2.0. The curriculum includes 3 core courses on religious, rationalist, and scientific traditions; distribution requirements are comprised of 3 phys ed activity courses, 2 each in a foreign language and science/math, and 1 course each in biblical literature, oral communication, fine arts, social science, and humanities. Additionally, global perspectives and an American diversity course must be fulfilled. **Procedure:** Freshmen are admitted fall, winter, and spring. Entrance exams should be taken by fall of the senior year, though spring of the junior year is preferred. There are deferred admissions and rolling admissions plans. Early decision applications should be filed by November 30; regular applications, by March 1 for fall entry. Notification of early decision is sent December 20; regular decision, March 15. Applications are accepted on-line. **Transfer Students:** 84 transfer students enrolled in 2013-2014. Transfer students must have a GPA of at least 2.75 and a recommended 45 quarter credits earned. The SAT or ACT is recommended. 32 of 126 credits required for the bachelor's degree must be completed at Whitworth. **International Students:** There are 76 international students enrolled. The school actively recruits these students. They must take the TOEFL.

ADMISSIONS: 85% of the 2014-2015 applicants were accepted. The SAT scores for the 2014-2015 freshman class were: Critical Reading--16% below 500, 42% between 500 and 599, 32% between 600 and 699, and 9% between 700 and 800; Math--13% below 500, 42%

between 500 and 599, 35% between 600 and 699, and 10% between 700 and 800; Writing--20% below 500, 42% between 500 and 599, 32% between 600 and 699, and 6% between 700 and 800. 42 freshmen graduated first in their class. **Admissions Contact:** Greg Orwig, Vice President, Admissions and Fin Aid. E-Mail: *admission@whitworth.edu* Web: *www.whitworth.edu*

FINANCIAL AID: 100% of undergraduate students work part-time.

Average annual earnings from campus work are $1402. The average financial indebtedness of the 2014 graduate was $26,132. The CCS/Profile, or FAFSA, or FFS, or SFS, and the FAFSA is preferred. is required. The deadline for filing freshman financial aid applications for fall entry is March 1.

education, music education, physical education, recreation education, and secondary education), ENGINEERING AND ENVIRONMENTAL DESIGN (environmental science), HEALTH PROFESSIONS (health science, nursing, radiograph medical technology, and recreation therapy), SOCIAL SCIENCE (Christian studies, criminology, family/consumer studies, history, interdisciplinary studies, political science/government, and psychology). Nursing, health sciences, and biology are the strongest academically.

ACTIVITIES: 9% of men belong to 2 local fraternities; 6% of women belong to 3 local sororities. There are 49 groups on campus, including art, band, choir, chorale, chorus, computers, debate, drama, ethnic, forensics, honors, jazz band, musical theater, newspaper, opera, photography, political, professional, radio and TV, religious, social, social service, student government, and yearbook. Popular campus events include Final Fling, Monte Carlo Night, and Spring Festival Weekend.

SERVICES: Counseling and information services are available, as is tutoring in every subject. There is remedial math, reading, and writing. There is also an academic support network. **Library/Resources:** The library contains 60,000 volumes, 40,000 microform items, and 1,500 audio/video tapes/CDs/DVDs, and subscribes to 59,000 periodicals including electronic. Computerized library services include interlibrary loans, database searching, and Internet access. Special learning facilities include an art gallery, radio station, TV station, a gross anatomy lab, a hydrotherapy pool, and a simulation lab. **Physically Challenged Students:** 75% of the campus is accessible. Facilities include wheelchair ramps, elevators, special parking, specially equipped restrooms, special class scheduling, and special housing. **Special:** Internships in numerous majors, study abroad through the college's programs in Austria, and work scholarships at the college are available. In addition, the college offers dual majors, a general studies degree, the B.A.-B.S. degree, nondegree study, and an accelerated B.A. degree in natural science. There are 2 national honor societies, a freshman honors program, and 1 departmental honors programs. **Visiting:** There are regularly scheduled orientations for prospective students, including placement tests and social programs. There are guides for informal visits, visitors may sit in on classes, and stay overnight. To schedule a visit, contact the Admissions Office. **Campus Safety and Security:** Measures include emergency notification system and self-defense education. There are lighted pathways/sidewalks, a foot and vehicle patrol evenings and weekends.

REQUIREMENTS: The SAT or ACT is required. The recommended composite score for the SAT is 950 (critical reading and math); for the ACT, 21. Applicants who are graduates of secondary schools or have passed the GED are considered for admission. An audition for certain majors and an interview are recommended. A GPA of 2.5 is required. AP and CLEP credits are accepted. Important factors in the admissions decision are advanced placement or honors courses, leadership record, and recommendations by school officials.

ADMISSIONS: 74% of the 2013-2014 applicants were accepted. The SAT scores for the 2013-2014 freshman class were: Critical Reading--57% below 500, 38% between 500 and 599, and 5% between 600 and 699; Math--61% below 500, 32% between 500 and 599, and 7% between 600 and 699; Writing--69% below 500, 29% between 500 and 599, and 2% between 600 and 699. The ACT scores were 47% below 21, 29% between 21 and 23, 19% between 24 and 26, 3% between 27 and 28, and 2% above 28. 35% of the current freshmen were in the top fifth of their class; 68% were in the top two fifths. 9 freshmen graduated first in their class.

FINANCIAL AID: In a recent year, 99% of all full-time freshmen students received some form of financial aid. 94% of all full-time freshmen and 92% of continuing full-time students received need-based aid. Need-based scholarships or need-based grants averaged $15,885 ($31,776 maximum); need-based self-help aid (loans and jobs) averaged $5,620 ($6,900 maximum); non-need-based athletic scholarships averaged $1,195 ($19,465 maximum); and other non-need-based awards and non-need-based scholarships averaged $3,690 ($30,900 maximum). 50% of undergraduate students work part-time. The FAFSA and the college's own financial statement are required. The priority date for freshman financial aid applications for fall entry is March 1. The deadline for filing freshman financial aid applications for fall entry is September 1.

ALDERSON BROADDUS UNIVERSITY   C-3
www.ab.edu

Philippi, WV 26416	(304) 457-1700
	(800) 263-1549
Fax: (304) 457-6239	Email: admissions@ab.edu
Full-time: 531 men, 464 women	Faculty: 60
Part-time: 12 men, 45 women	Ph.D.s: 47%
Graduate: 22 men, 43 women	Student/Faculty: 11 to 1
Year: semesters, summer session	Tuition: $21,654
Room & Board: $7002	Freshman Class: 597 applied, 441 accepted, 162 enrolled
SAT CR/M/W: 470/470/470 ACT: 21	CEEB CODE: 5005
Application Deadline: August 1	COMPETITIVE

Alderson-Broaddus University is a private institution, founded in 1871 and affiliated with American Baptist Churches. It offers a strong liberal arts foundation, with selected programs in the health sciences, humanities, natural sciences, and education. The figures in the above capsule and in this profile are approximate. There is 1 undergraduate school and 1 graduate school. In addition to regional accreditation, AB has baccalaureate program accreditation with NLN and TEAC. The 170-acre campus is in a small town 100 miles south of Pittsburgh and 100 miles north of Charleston. Including any residence halls, there are 15 buildings.

STUDENT LIFE: 56% of undergraduates are from out of state, mostly the Middle Atlantic. Students are from 40 states, 13 foreign countries, and Canada. 90% are from public schools. 74% are White; 16% African American. 14% claim no religious affiliation; 11% Catholic. The average age of freshmen is 19; all undergraduates, 21. 29% do not continue beyond their first year; 39% remain to graduate.

FACULTY/CLASSROOMS: 44% of faculty are male; 56% are female. All teach undergraduates. No introductory courses are taught by graduate students. The average class size in an introductory lecture is 40; in a laboratory is 30; and in a regular course is 20.

PROGRAMS OF STUDY: AB confers B.A., and B.S. degrees. Associate and Master's degrees are also awarded. Bachelor's degrees are awarded in BIOLOGICAL SCIENCE (biology/biological science), BUSINESS (accounting, business administration and management, human resources, marketing/retailing/merchandising, organizational leadership and management, and recreational facilities management), COMMUNICATIONS AND THE ARTS (communications, creative writing, music, and visual and performing arts), COMPUTER AND PHYSICAL SCIENCE (chemistry, computer science, mathematics, and natural sciences), EDUCATION (athletic training, elementary

BETHANY COLLEGE (*The complete profile is made available exclusively on our website, www.barronspac.com*)

BLUEFIELD STATE COLLEGE (*The complete profile is made available exclusively on our website, www.barronspac.com*)

CONCORD UNIVERSITY   B-5
www.concord.edu

Athens, WV 24712	(800) 344-6679
	(888) 384-5249
Fax: (304) 384-3218	Email: admissions@concord.edu
Full-time: 1033 men, 1344 women	Faculty: 119
Part-time: 93 men, 182 women	Ph.D.s: 49%
Graduate: 54 men, 182 women	Student/Faculty: 16 to 1
Year: semesters, summer session	Tuition: $5716 ($12,698)
Room & Board: $7386	Freshman Class: 2495 applied, 1224 accepted, 573 enrolled
SAT CR/M: 486/482 ACT: 21	CEEB CODE: 5120
Application Deadline: open	COMPETITIVE

Concord University, founded in 1872, is a public institution with undergraduate programs in liberal arts and professional training. There is 1 undergraduate school and 1 graduate school. In addition to regional accreditation, Concord has baccalaureate program accreditation with CSWE and NCATE. The 123-acre campus is in a small town 85 miles south of Charleston. Including any residence halls, there are 21 buildings.

STUDENT LIFE: 83% of undergraduates are from West Virginia. Others are from 29 states, 22 foreign countries, and Canada. 97% are from public schools. 89% are White. 40% are Protestant; 40% claim no religious affiliation; 15% Catholic. The average age of freshmen is 19; all undergraduates, 23. 38% do not continue beyond their first year; 39% remain to graduate.

FACULTY/CLASSROOMS: 48% of faculty are male; 52% are female. All teach undergraduates, all do research, and all teach and do research. No introductory courses are taught by graduate students. The average class size in an introductory lecture is 23; in a laboratory is 17; and in a regular course is 22.

PROGRAMS OF STUDY: Concord confers B.A., B.S., B.B.A., B.S.C.I.S., B.S.Ed., B.S.Med.Tech. and B.S.W. degrees. Associate and Master's degrees are also awarded. Bachelor's degrees are awarded in BIOLOGICAL SCIENCE (biology/biological science), BUSINESS (accounting, banking and finance, business administration and management, hotel/motel and restaurant management, marketing/retailing/merchandising, office supervision and management, and small business management), COMMUNICATIONS AND THE ARTS (broadcasting, communications, and English), COMPUTER AND PHYSICAL SCIENCE (chemistry, computer programming, computer science, information sciences and systems, and mathematics), EDUCATION (art education, business education, early childhood education, elementary education, middle school education, music education, science education, secondary education, and special education), HEALTH PROFESSIONS (medical laboratory technology, predentistry, premedicine, and prepharmacy), SOCIAL SCIENCE (geography, history, parks and recreation management, political science/government, prelaw, psychology, social science, social work, and sociology). Teacher education, business, and preprofessional biology are the strongest academically. Teacher education, business, biology, psychology have the largest enrollments.

ACTIVITIES: 20% of men belong to 1 local and 4 national fraternities; 20% of women belong to 4 national sororities. There are 70 groups on campus, including art, bagpipe, band, cheerleading, choir, chorale, computers, dance, drama, environmental, film, gay, honors, international, jazz band, literary magazine, marching band, newspaper, pep band, political, professional, radio and TV, religious, social, social service, student government, and yearbook. Popular campus events include Big-name Concerts, Alumni Day, Faculty and Student Plays, Homecoming and Spring Fling.

SERVICES: Counseling and information services are available, as is tutoring in every subject. There is a reader service for the blind, and remedial math, reading, and writing. **Library/Resources:** The library contains 168,164 volumes, 240,089 microform items, and 3,800 audio/video tapes/CDs/DVDs, and subscribes to 140 periodicals including electronic. Computerized library services include interlibrary loans, database searching, Internet access, and Wi-Fi capability. Special learning facilities include an art gallery, radio station, and TV station. **Physically Challenged Students:** 90% of the campus is accessible. Facilities include wheelchair ramps, elevators, special parking, specially equipped restrooms, special class scheduling, lowered drinking fountains, lowered telephones, and special housing. **Special:** Students may serve internships in medical technology, social work, travel industry management, commercial art/advertising, and communications arts. Concord offers a Washington semester, cross-registration with Bluefield State College, dual majors, interdisciplinary student-designed majors, and nondegree study. Credit for life, military, and work experience is granted to adult students through the Regents Bachelor of Arts Degree Program. There are 5 national honor societies and a freshman honors program. **Visiting:** There are regularly scheduled orientations for prospective students. There are guides for informal visits, visitors may sit in on classes, and stay overnight. To schedule a visit, contact the Admissions Office at (888) 384-5249. **Campus Safety and Security:** Measures include 24-hour foot and vehicle patrol, emergency notification system, and security escort services. There are emergency telephones, lighted pathways/sidewalks, controlled access to dorms/residences, foot and vehicle patrol is available 24 hours Monday through Friday and is on call Saturday and Sunday.

REQUIREMENTS: The SAT or ACT is required. The ACT is preferred. Applicants must be high school graduates or hold a GED. Students should present 17 academic credits, including 4 in English, 3 each in social studies and science, 4 in math and 1 each in history and health/phys ed. An interview is recommended and, where appropriate, a portfolio or an audition. A GPA of 2.0 is required. AP and CLEP credits are accepted.

ADMISSIONS: 49% of the 2013-2014 applicants were accepted. The SAT scores for the 2013-2014 freshman class were: Critical Reading-58% below 500, 32% between 500 and 599, and 10% between 600 and 699; Math--58% below 500, 34% between 500 and 599, 7% between 600 and 699, and 1% between 700 and 800; Writing--68% below 500, 23% between 500 and 599, 8% between 600 and 699, and 1% between 700 and 800.

FINANCIAL AID: 93% of all full-time freshmen and 80% of continuing full-time students received some form of financial aid. 41% of all full-time freshmen and 40% of continuing full-time students received need-based aid. The average freshman award was $12,103. 26% of undergraduate students work part-time. Average annual earnings from campus work are $2100. The FAFSA is required. The priority date for freshman financial aid applications for fall entry is March 1. The deadline for filing freshman financial aid applications for fall entry is April 15.

DAVIS & ELKINS COLLEGE   C-3
www.davisandelkins.edu

Elkins, WV 26241	(304) 637-1900
	(800) 624-3157
Fax: (304) 637-1800	Email: admissions@dewv.edu
Full-time: 347 men, 450 women	Faculty: 66; IIB, --$
Part-time: 4 men, 23 women	Ph.D.s: 73%
Graduate: n/av	Student/Faculty: 9 to 1
Year: semesters, summer session	Tuition: $24,992
Room & Board: $8750	Freshman Class: n/av
SAT or ACT: required	CEEB CODE: 8099
Application Deadline: open	COMPETITIVE

Davis & Elkins College, founded in 1904 and affiliated with the Presbyterian Church, offers programs in the liberal arts, business, professional training, teacher preparation, nursing, and recreation management. In addition to regional accreditation, D&E has baccalaureate program accreditation with TEAC. Computerized library services include interlibrary loans, database searching, Internet access, and Wi-Fi capability. The 170-acre campus is in a small town 200 miles west of Washington, D.C. Including any residence halls, there are 22 buildings.

FACULTY/CLASSROOMS: 61% of faculty are male; 39% are female. All teach undergraduates. No introductory courses are taught by graduate students. The average class size in an introductory lecture is 15; in a laboratory is 11; and in a regular course is 11.

PROGRAMS OF STUDY: D&E confers B.A., and B.S. degrees. Associate degrees are also awarded. Bachelor's degrees are awarded in BIOLOGICAL SCIENCE (biology/biological science), BUSINESS (accounting, business administration and management, hospitality management services, management science, and marketing/retailing/merchandising), COMMUNICATIONS AND THE ARTS (art, communications, dramatic arts, English, languages, and music), COMPUTER AND PHYSICAL SCIENCE (chemistry, computer science, and mathematics), EDUCATION (elementary education, physical education, and secondary education), ENGINEERING AND ENVIRONMENTAL DESIGN (environmental science), HEALTH PROFESSIONS (predentistry and premedicine), SOCIAL SCIENCE (economics, history, political science/government, prelaw, psychology, religion, and sociology). Business, psychology, and biology are the strongest academically. Business, nursing, and hospitality management have the largest enrollments.

ACTIVITIES: Groups on campus include art, choir, computers, drama, honors, international, jazz band, musical theater, newspaper, pep band, religious, student government, and yearbook. Popular campus events include Parents Weekend, Deja Vu, and International Week.

SERVICES: Counseling and information services are available, as is tutoring in every subject. There is remedial math, reading, and writing. Learning disabilities services also are available.

REQUIREMENTS: The SAT or ACT is required, with a minimum composite score of 900 on the the SAT I or 19 on the ACT. Applicants should be high school graduates or hold a GED. Students should have earned 16 academic credits, including 4 in English, 3 in social studies, 3 in math, including a minimum of algebra I and geometry, and 3 in natural science, including a lab course. Two years of foreign language is recommended. A GPA of 2.0 is required. AP and CLEP credits are accepted. Important factors in the admissions decision are advanced placement or honors courses, recommendations by school officials, and leadership record.

FINANCIAL AID: 89% of all full-time freshmen and continuing full-time students received some form of financial aid. 69% of all full-time freshmen and 70% of continuing full-time students received need-based aid. The average freshman award was $16,512. Need-based scholarships or need-based grants averaged $2,807 ($5,550 maximum); need-based self-help aid (loans and jobs) averaged $2,587 ($6,125 maximum); non-need-based athletic scholarships averaged $3,402 ($8,000 maximum); and other non-need-based awards and non-need-based scholarships averaged $7,716 ($10,000 maximum). 40% of undergraduate students work part-time. Average annual earnings from campus work are $1200. The FAFSA, is required. Check with the school for current application deadlines.

FAIRMONT STATE UNIVERSITY (*The complete profile is made available exclusively on our website, www.barronspac.com*)

GLENVILLE STATE COLLEGE (*The complete profile is made available exclusively on our website, www.barronspac.com*)

MARSHALL UNIVERSITY A-4
www.marshall.edu

Huntington, WV 25755

	(800) 642-3463
	(800) 642-9842
Fax: n/av	Email: admissions@marshall.edu
Full-time: 3643 men, 4629 women	Faculty: n/av; IIA, --$
Part-time: 605 men, 885 women	Ph.D.s: 77%
Graduate: 1247 men, 2047 women	Student/Faculty: 18 to 1
Year: semesters, summer session	Tuition: $6216 ($14,446)
Room & Board: $8604	Freshman Class: n/av
SAT or ACT: required	CEEB CODE: 5396
Application Deadline: n/av	**COMPETITIVE**

Marshall University, founded in 1837 and part of the University of West Virginia system, is a comprehensive public institution offering programs in Liberal Arts, Science, Business, Education, Journalism and Mass Communications, Arts and Media, Information Technology and Engineering, and Health Professions. There are 10 undergraduate schools and 3 graduate schools. In addition to regional accreditation, Marshall has baccalaureate program accreditation with AACSB, ABET, ACEJMC, CSWE, NASM, NCATE, and NRPA. The 100-acre campus is in an urban area 126 miles east of Lexington, Kentucky, and 50 miles west of Charleston, West Virginia. Including any residence halls, there are 55 buildings.

STUDENT LIFE: 79% of undergraduates are from West Virginia. Others are from 47 states, 51 foreign countries, and Canada. 82% are White. The average age of freshmen is 19; all undergraduates, 23.

FACULTY/CLASSROOMS: 54% of faculty are male; 46% are female. No introductory courses are taught by graduate students. The average class size in a regular course is 22.

PROGRAMS OF STUDY: Marshall confers B.A., B.S., B.B.A., B.F.A., B.S.Cyotech, B.S.Chem, B.S.N., B.S.W. and B.S.E. degrees. Associate, master's, and doctoral degrees are also awarded. Bachelor's degrees are awarded in AGRICULTURE (natural resource management), BIOLOGICAL SCIENCE (anatomy, biochemistry, biology/biological science, biotechnology, cell biology, ecology, evolutionary biology, molecular biology, and nutrition), BUSINESS (accounting, banking and finance, business economics, finance, international business management, management information systems, marketing/retailing/merchandising, and sports management), COMMUNICATIONS AND THE ARTS (advertising, applied art, art, broadcasting, ceramic art and design, classics, communications, communication rhetoric/communication, creative writing, English, English literature, French, German, graphic design, information technology, Japanese, jazz, journalism, literature, music, music performance, music theory and composition, painting, percussion, photography, piano/organ, public relations, radio/television technology, sculpture, Spanish, sports media, strings, theatre arts, theater design, and voice), COMPUTER AND PHYSICAL SCIENCE (applied mathematics, chemistry, computer game design/development, computer science, computer security and information assurance, environmental chemistry, geology, information sciences and systems, mathematics, physics, and science technology), EDUCATION (athletic training, (Education) Childhood Education, early childhood education, education, elementary education, English education, foreign languages education, middle school education, music education, physical education, secondary education, social studies education, and special education), ENGINEERING AND ENVIRONMENTAL DESIGN (civil engineering, engineering, environmental science, occupational safety and health, and preengineering), HEALTH PROFESSIONS (allied health, cytotechnology, exercise science, health science, medical laboratory technology, nursing, Pre-Health Studies, predentistry, premedicine, preoptometry, preosteopathy, prepharmacy, prephysical therapy, prepodiatry, public health, respiratory therapy, and speech pathology/audiology), SOCIAL SCIENCE (criminal justice, dietetics, economics, forensic studies, geography, history, humanities, international relations, parks and recreation management, philosophy, physical fitness/movement, political science/government, prelaw, psychology, safety and security technology, safety management, social work, sociology, and women's studies). Biological science, elementary education, and secondary education have the largest enrollments.

ACTIVITIES: There are 194 groups on campus, including art, band, cheerleading, choir, chorale, chorus, communications, computers, dance, debate, drama, environmental, ethnic, forensics, gay, honors, international, jazz band, literary magazine, marching band, musical theater, newspaper, opera, orchestra, pep band, photography, political, professional, radio and TV, religious, social, social service, student government, symphony, and yearbook. Popular campus events include Week of Welcome, Parents Weekend, Homecoming, Springfest and International Festival.

SERVICES: Counseling and information services are available, as is tutoring in most subjects. There is a reader service for the blind, and remedial math, reading, and writing. Study skills courses, and other services for all students with disabilities. **Library/Resources:** The 2 libraries contain 2.2 million volumes, 1.0 million microform items, and 43,449 audio/video tapes/CDs/DVDs, and subscribe to 45,508 periodicals including electronic. Computerized library services include interlibrary loans, database searching, and Internet access. Special learning facilities include an art gallery, natural history museum, radio station, TV station, a greenhouse. **Physically Challenged Students:** All of the campus is accessible. Facilities include wheelchair ramps, elevators, special parking, specially equipped restrooms, special class scheduling, lowered drinking fountains, lowered telephones, special housing. An attendant care program. **Special:** Many programs require or offer internships. Work-study opportunities are available on campus. Students participate in student exchange and study abroad programs. B.A.-B.S. degrees, dual majors and minors, nondegree study, credit for life experience, and credit/no-credit options are available. There are 20 national honor societies and a freshman honors program. **Visiting:** There are regularly scheduled orientations for prospective students. There are guides for informal visits, visitors may sit in on classes, and stay overnight. To schedule a visit, contact the Office of Recruitment at (304) 696-3646. **Campus Safety and Security:** Measures include 24-hour foot and vehicle patrol, emergency notification system, self-defense education, and security escort services. There are emergency telephones, lighted pathways/sidewalks, and controlled access to dorms/residences.

REQUIREMENTS: The SAT or ACT is required. General freshman admission is open to all applicants with a high school diploma with an overall GPA of 2.00 on a 4.00 scale and an ACT composite score of 19 or a SAT combined score 900 (critical reading + math) or an overall GPA of 3.00 on a 4.00 scale and an ACT composite score of 16 or a SAT combined score 770 (critical reading + math). The GED is also accepted. The following high school units are recommended for admission: 4 years of English (including courses in grammar, composition, literature), 3 years of social studies (including U.S. history), 4 years of math (including Algebra I and at least two higher units), 3 years of laboratory science, 2 years of the same foreign language, 1 year of fine arts. A GPA of 2.0 is required. AP and CLEP credits are accepted.

FINANCIAL AID: In a recent year, 87% of all full-time freshmen and 89% of continuing full-time students received some form of financial aid. 75% of all full-time freshmen and 74% of continuing full-time students received need-based aid. The average freshman award was $10,915. Need-based scholarships or need-based grants averaged $5,260 ($23,172 maximum); need-based self-help aid (loans and jobs) averaged $5,622 ($15,000 maximum); non-need-based athletic scholarships averaged $11,892 ($24,560 maximum); and other non-need-based awards and non-need-based scholarships averaged $5,164 ($25,769 maximum). 3% of undergraduate students work part-time. Average annual earnings from campus work are $1598. The average financial indebtedness of a recent year graduate was $26,727. Marshall is a member of CSS. The FAFSA is required. The priority date for freshman financial aid applications for fall entry is March 1. The deadline for filing freshman financial aid applications for fall entry is March 1.

OHIO VALLEY UNIVERSITY B-2
www.ovu.edu

Vienna, WV 26105	(877) 446-8668 n/av
Fax: n/av	Email: admissions@ovu.edu
Full-time: 250 men, 275 women	Faculty: 21; IIB, --$
Part-time: 12 men, 22 women	Ph.D.s: 75%
Graduate: n/av	Student/Faculty: 18 to 1
Year: semesters, summer session	Tuition: $14,364
Room & Board: $5660	Freshman Class: 304 applied, 170 accepted, 85 enrolled
ACT: 23	CEEB CODE: 5519
Application Deadline: open	COMPETITIVE

Ohio Valley University, founded in 1960, is a liberal arts institution affiliated with the Church of Christ. There are 4 undergraduate schools and 1 graduate school. The 270-acre campus is in a suburban area OVU is located in beautiful Vienna, West Virginia, on the Ohio River in the historic Mid-Ohio Valley. Including any residence halls, there are 9 buildings.

STUDENT LIFE: 65% of undergraduates are from out of state, mostly the Mid-West. Students are from 28 states, 13 foreign countries, and Canada. 97% are from public schools. 88% are White. 97% are Protestant. The average age of freshmen is 18; all undergraduates, 22. 26% do not continue beyond their first year; 35% remain to graduate.

FACULTY/CLASSROOMS: 68% of faculty are male; 32% are female. All teach undergraduates. No introductory courses are taught by graduate students. The average class size in an introductory lecture is 30; in a laboratory is 20; and in a regular course is 15.

PROGRAMS OF STUDY: Ohio Valley confers B.A., and B.S. degrees. Associate degrees are also awarded. Bachelor's degrees are awarded in BIOLOGICAL SCIENCE (biochemistry), BUSINESS (accounting, business administration and management, organizational leadership and management, and sports management), COMMUNICATIONS AND THE ARTS (English), COMPUTER AND PHYSICAL SCIENCE (computer information technology and mathematics), EDUCATION (elementary education, English education, health education, mathematics education, and science education), HEALTH PROFESSIONS (biology and health), SOCIAL SCIENCE (biblical studies, criminal justice, history, humanities, interdisciplinary studies, psychology, and sociology). Business is the strongest academically. Elementary education, psychology, business administration have the largest enrollments.

ACTIVITIES: There are 16 groups on campus, including band, cheerleading, choir, chorale, chorus, communications, drama, jazz band, newspaper, pep band, religious, social, and student government. Popular campus events include Expressions, and a schoolwide musical review.

SERVICES: Counseling and information services are available, as is tutoring in most subjects. There is remedial math, reading, and writing. **Library/Resources:** The library contains 31,750 volumes, 51,530 microform items, and 2,946 audio/video tapes/CDs/DVDs, and subscribes to 165 periodicals including electronic. Computerized library services include interlibrary loans, database searching, Internet access, and Wi-Fi capability. **Physically Challenged Students:** 30% of the campus is accessible. Facilities include wheelchair ramps, elevators, special parking, specially equipped restrooms, special class scheduling, and lowered telephones. **Special:** Ohio Valley offers internships with churches for student ministers. Study abroad programs are frequently offered in England, France and Italy. OVU is also affiliated with the Washington Center for Internships and Academic Seminars. There is 1 national honor society and 1 departmental honors programs. **Visiting:** There are guides for informal visits, visitors may sit in on classes, and stay overnight. To schedule a visit, contact the Office of Admissions. **Campus Safety and Security:** Measures include 24-hour foot and vehicle patrol.

REQUIREMENTS: The ACT is required. Applicants should be graduates of an accredited secondary school or have earned a GED. Ohio Valley requires applicants to be in the upper 50% of their class. A GPA of 2.0 is required. AP and CLEP credits are accepted. Important factors in the admissions decision are recommendations by school officials, personality/intangible qualities, and leadership record.

ADMISSIONS: 56% of the 2013-2014 applicants were accepted. The ACT scores were 75% below 21, 25% between 21 and 23, 9% between 24 and 26, 3% between 27 and 28, and 2% above 28. 10% of the current freshmen were in the top fifth of their class; 32% were in the top two fifths. 10 freshmen graduated first in their class.

FINANCIAL AID: In a recent year, 95% of all full-time freshmen and 98% of continuing full-time students received some form of financial aid. 70% of all full-time freshmen and 65% of continuing full-time students received need-based aid. The average freshman award was $9,768. Need-based scholarships or need-based grants averaged $7,219; need-based self-help aid (loans and jobs) averaged $3,248 ($5,500 maximum); non-need-based athletic scholarships averaged $5,442 ($16,796 maximum); and other non-need-based awards and non-need-based scholarships averaged $7,732 ($15,000 maximum). 44% of undergraduate students work part-time. Average annual earnings from campus work are $800. Ohio Valley is a member of CSS. The FAFSA is required. The priority date for freshman financial aid applications for fall entry is February 14.

SALEM INTERNATIONAL UNIVERSITY (*The complete profile is made available exclusively on our website, www.barronspac.com*)

SHEPHERD UNIVERSITY — E-2
www.shepherd.edu

Shepherdstown, WV 25443   (304) 876-5212
(800) 344-5231

Fax: (304) 876-5165   Email: admissions@shepherd.edu

Full-time: 1253 men, 1840 women   **Faculty:** 135; IIB, -$

Part-time: 302 men, 381 women   **Ph.D.s:** 87%

Graduate: 84 men, 181 women   **Student/Faculty:** 23 to 1

Year: semesters, summer session   **Tuition:** $6570 ($16,628)

Room & Board: $9305   **Freshman Class:** 1817 applied, 1786 accepted, 642 enrolled

SAT CR/M: 500/480 **ACT:** 21   **CEEB CODE:** 5615

Application Deadline: **COMPETITIVE**

Shepherd University, founded in 1871, is a state-supported institution offering programs in the liberal and creative arts, business administration, teacher education, social and natural sciences, health fields, and other career-oriented areas. There are 4 undergraduate schools and 1 graduate school. In addition to regional accreditation, Shepherd has baccalaureate program accreditation with CSWE, NASM, NCATE, CCNE, IACBE, and WVBOERN. The 323-acre campus is in a small town 70 miles northwest of Washington, D.C., and Baltimore. Including any residence halls, there are 52 buildings. **STUDENT LIFE:** 60% of undergraduates are from West Virginia. Others are from 47 states, 15 foreign countries, and Canada. 87% are from public schools. 83% are White. The average age of freshmen is 18; all undergraduates, 23. 32% do not continue beyond their first year; 40% remain to graduate. **Housing:** 1300 students can be accommodated in college housing, which includes coed dorms and on-campus apartments. In addition, there are honors houses and special-interest houses. On-campus housing is guaranteed for all 4 years. 67% of students commute. All students may keep cars.

FACULTY/CLASSROOMS: 54% of faculty are male; 46% are female. 99% teach undergraduates, 81% do research, and 81% do both. No introductory courses are taught by graduate students. The average class size in an introductory lecture is 23; in a laboratory is 20; and in a regular course is 15.

PROGRAMS OF STUDY: Shepherd confers B.A., B.S., B.F.A., B.M.E., B.S.N., B.S.W., B.M.P., and R.B.A. degrees. Master's degrees are also awarded. Bachelor's degrees are awarded in AGRICULTURE (environmental studies), BIOLOGICAL SCIENCE (biology/biological science), BUSINESS (accounting, business administration and management, and recreation and leisure services), COMMUNICATIONS AND THE ARTS (art, communications, English, music, and Spanish), COMPUTER AND PHYSICAL SCIENCE (chemistry, computer science, information sciences and systems, and mathematics), EDUCATION (art education, elementary education, English education, health education, home economics education, mathematics education, music education, physical education, science education, secondary education, and social studies education), ENGINEERING AND ENVIRONMENTAL DESIGN (computer engineering and computer technology), HEALTH PROFESSIONS (nursing), SOCIAL SCIENCE (economics, family/consumer studies, history, political science/government, psychology, social work, and sociology). Biology, education, art, nursing, music, and social work are the strongest academically. Nursing, education, and business have the largest enrollments.

ACTIVITIES: 3% of men and 4% of women belong to 5 national fraternities; 4% of women belong to 3 national sororities. There are 86 groups on campus, including art, band, cheerleading, choir, chorale, chorus, computers, dance, debate, drama, drill team, environmental, ethnic, gay, honors, international, jazz band, literary magazine, marching band, musical theater, newspaper, opera, orchestra, pep band, political, professional, radio and TV, religious, social, social service, student government, and symphony. Popular campus events include Family Day, Midnight Breakfast, Late Night in the Zone, Appalachian Heritage Festival, Appalachian Writer in Residence, and Relay for Life. **Sports:** There are 6 intercollegiate sports for men and 6 for women, and 7 intramural sports for men and 7 for women. Facilities include A 5000-seat football and women's lacrosse field, 2 soccer fields, baseball and softball fields, a 3000-seat gym, 9 outdoor and 2 indoor tennis courts, 2 outdoor sand volleyball courts, and a fitness/wellness center with 2 basketball courts with 6 hoops, 2 racquetball courts, 1/10 of a mile indoor track, cardio area, free weight area, large group exercise studio, and an 8-lane/25-yd indoor swimming pool. **Graduates:** From July 1, 2013 to June 30, 2014, 762 bachelor's degrees were awarded. The most popular majors were regents bachelor of arts (11%), business administration (11%), and education (10%). 89 companies recruited on campus in 2013-2014. In an average class, 20% graduate in 4 years or less, 36% graduate in 5 years or less, and 40% graduate in 6 years or less. Of the 2013 graduating class, 24% were enrolled in graduate school within 6 months of graduation, and 69% were employed.

SERVICES: Counseling and information services are available, as is tutoring in most subjects. There is remedial math, reading, and writing. Tutorial assistance for students with learning disabilities. **Library/Resources:** The library contains 182,885 volumes, 18,500 microform items, 7,180 audio/video tapes/CDs/DVDs, and subscribes to 50,669 periodicals including electronic. Computerized library services include interlibrary loans, database searching, Internet access, and Wi-Fi capability. Special learning facilities include an art gallery, radio station, a nursery school, 3 theaters, the Center for the Study of the Civil War, and the Robert C. Byrd Center for Legislative Studies. **Physically Challenged Students:** 90% of the campus is accessible. Facilities include wheelchair ramps, elevators, special parking, specially equipped restrooms, special class scheduling, lowered drinking fountains, lowered telephones. automatic door openers. **Special:** Shepherd offers study abroad, a B.A.-B.S. degree in communication and new media, and internships and co-op programs that are available in most majors. There is a Washington semester, and dual majors are possible in any 2 majors. Credit by exam, life experience credentialing through the Regents degree, nondegree study, and pass/fail options for electives are offered. There are 9 national honor societies, a freshman honors program, and 19 departmental honors programs. **Visiting:** There are regularly scheduled orientations for prospective students, consisting of 3 fall open houses and 2 spring open houses, and weekday campus tours. There are guides for informal visits, visitors may sit in on classes, and stay overnight. To schedule a visit, contact the Admissions Office at admissions@shepherd.edu. **Campus Safety and Security:** Measures include 24-hour foot and vehicle patrol, emergency notification system, and security escort services. There are shuttle buses, emergency telephones, lighted pathways/sidewalks, and controlled access to dorms/residences.

REQUIREMENTS: The SAT or ACT is required, with a minimum composite score of 820 on the SAT (critical reading and math) or 17 on the ACT. Applicants should be graduates of an accredited secondary school and have earned academic credits including 4 each in English and math, 3 each in history or social science (1 in American history) and lab science, 1 in art, and the rest in computer, foreign language, and other academic electives. Applicants must have a minimum 2.0 academic core GPA. The GED is accepted. AP and CLEP credits are accepted. Important factors in the admissions decision are advanced placement or honors courses, leadership record, and extracurricular activities record.To graduate, students must complete a minimum of 120 semester hours with a 2.0 GPA overall and in the major and minor fields. The core curriculum totals 42: written English, 6; mathematics, 3; history, 3; sciences, 8; first-year experience, 1; arts, 3; humanities, 6; social sciences, 9; and wellness, 3. Students pursuing the Bachelor of Arts degree (not including education) are required to complete 12 semester hours in the same foreign language, except music students whose requirements must be approved by the chairs of the Music and English and Modern Languages departments. Two years of German or French or both are recommended for students who anticipate going to graduate or professional school. The foreign language requirement for the B.A. degree can be satisfied through advanced placement or CLEP tests. **Procedure:** Freshmen are admitted fall, spring, and summer. Entrance exams should be taken during the junior year. There are early decision, early admissions, deferred admissions, and rolling admissions plans. Application deadlines are open. Application fee is $45. Notification is sent on a rolling basis. 47 early decision candidates were accepted for the 2014-2015 class. Applications are accepted on-line. **Transfer Students:** 288 transfer students enrolled in 2013-2014. Applicants must have a 2.0 cumulative GPA in a minimum of 24 semester hours of college-level work completed and must submit a transcript from each college attended. 30 of 120 credits required for the bachelor's degree must be completed at Shepherd. **International Students:** There are 14 international students enrolled. The school actively recruits these students. They must take the TOEFL with a minimum score of 550 on the paper-based TOEFL (PBT) or 79 on the Internet-based version (iBT). They must also take the SAT or ACT, scoring 820.

ADMISSIONS: 98% of the 2014-2015 applicants were accepted. The SAT scores for the 2014-2015 freshman class were: Critical Reading--47% below 500, 41% between 500 and 599, 11% between 600 and 699, and 1% between 700 and 800; Math--58% below 500, 30% between 500 and 599, 11% between 600 and 699, and 1% between 700 and 800. The ACT scores were 44% below 21, 31% between 21 and 23, 17% between 24 and 26, 5% between 27 and 28, and 3% above 28. **Admissions Contact:** Kristen Lorenz, Director of Admissions. E-Mail: *admissions@shepherd.edu* Web: *www.shepherd.edu*

FINANCIAL AID: In 2014-2015, 91% of all full-time freshmen and 81% of continuing full-time students received some form of financial aid. 65% of all full-time freshmen and 63% of continuing full-time students received need-based aid. The average freshman award was $11,733. Need-based scholarships or need-based grants averaged $5,076 ($10,000 maximum); need-based self-help aid (loans and jobs) averaged $4,166 ($5,500 maximum); and non-need-based athletic scholarships averaged $6,021 ($15,702 maximum). 12% of undergraduate students work part-time. Average annual earnings from campus work are $2467. The average financial indebtedness of the 2014 graduate was $23,233. The FAFSA and the state aid form are required. The priority date for freshman financial aid applications for fall entry is March 1.

UNIVERSITY OF CHARLESTON B-4
www.ucwv.edu

Charleston, WV 25304	**(304) 357-4750**
	(800) 995-4682
Fax: (304) 357-4781	**Email:** admissions@ucwv.edu
Full-time: 579 men, 776 women	**Faculty:** 74; IIB, --$
Part-time: 80 men, 114 women	**Ph.D.s:** 56%
Graduate: 293 men, 269 women	**Student/Faculty:** 17 to 1
Year: varies, summer session	**Tuition:** $23,200
Room & Board: $9100	**Freshman Class:** 1632 applied, 997 accepted, 335 enrolled
SAT CR/M: 470/490 **ACT:** 21	**CEEB CODE:** 5419
Application Deadline: n/av	**COMPETITIVE**

The University of Charleston prepares students for a life of productive work, enlightened living and community involvement. UC is a private, non-profit institution with locations in Charleston, Beckley and Martinsburg, West Virginia as well as online. Our nationally recognized outcomes-based curriculum focuses on flexible, learner-centered, and demonstrable learning. Students are prepared to thrive in the real world with skills in Citizenship, Communication, Creativity, Critical Thinking, Ethical Practice, Inquiry, and their chosen career. There are 3 undergraduate schools and 3 graduate schools. In addition to regional accreditation, UC has baccalaureate program accreditation with ACPE, NLN, TEAC, CAATE, JRCERT, and ACOTE. The 40-acre campus is in a small town in Charleston, Beckley, and Martinsburg.

STUDENT LIFE: 67% of undergraduates are from West Virginia. Others are from 31 states, 38 foreign countries, and Canada. 66% are White; 11% race unknown. The average age of freshmen is 18; all undergraduates, 24. 35% do not continue beyond their first year; 44% remain to graduate. **Housing:** 969 students can be accommodated in college housing, which includes coed dorms and married student housing. Housing available on Charleston and Beckley campuses. On-campus housing is guaranteed for the freshman year only, is

available on a first-come, and first-served basis. Priority is given to out-of-town students. 59% of students commute. All students may keep cars.

FACULTY/CLASSROOMS: 68% teach undergraduates. No introductory courses are taught by graduate students. The average class size in an introductory lecture is 24 and in a laboratory is 20.

PROGRAMS OF STUDY: UC confers B.A., B.S. and B.S.N. degrees. Associate, Master's, and Doctoral degrees are also awarded. Bachelor's degrees are awarded in BIOLOGICAL SCIENCE (biology/biological science), BUSINESS (accounting, business administration and management, finance, and sports management), COMMUNICATIONS AND THE ARTS (art and communications), COMPUTER AND PHYSICAL SCIENCE (chemistry), EDUCATION (athletic training, elementary education, English education, physical education, science education, social studies education, and special education), ENGINEERING AND ENVIRONMENTAL DESIGN (interior design), HEALTH PROFESSIONS (diagnostic medical sonography, nursing, and radiological science), SOCIAL SCIENCE (history, liberal arts/general studies, political science/government, psychology, and social work). Biological sciences is the strongest academically. Business, nursing, and biology have the largest enrollments.

ACTIVITIES: Groups on campus include art, cheerleading, chess, choir, chorale, communications, computers, debate, ethnic, film, honors, international, newspaper, pep band, photography, political, professional, religious, social, social service, and student government. Popular campus events include Governor's Cup Regatta, and Worldfest. **Sports:** There are 8 intercollegiate sports for men and 9 for women. Facilities include a gym, game room, a nautilus center, an indoor pool, soccer, softball, baseball fields, racquetball, volleyball, tennis courts, and a fitness center. **Graduates:** From July 1, 2013 to June 30, 2014, 253 bachelor's degrees were awarded. The most popular majors were business/marketing (15%), biological/life studies (11%), and organizational leadership (8%). In an average class, 5% graduate in 3 years or less, 26% graduate in 4 years or less, 32% graduate in 5 years or less, and 36% graduate in 6 years or less.

SERVICES: Counseling and information services are available, as is tutoring in most subjects. There is a reader service for the blind, remedial math, reading, and writing. **Library/Resources:** The library contains 94,267 volumes, 229,551 microform items, 5,000 audio/video tapes/CDs/DVDs, and subscribes to 150 periodicals including electronic. Computerized library services include interlibrary loans, database searching, Internet access, and Wi-Fi capability. Special learning facilities include an art gallery, an academic success center, and a career center. **Physically Challenged Students:** 85% of the campus is accessible. Facilities include wheelchair ramps, elevators, special parking, specially equipped restrooms, lowered drinking fountains, lowered telephones, and special housing. **Special:** The university offers credit by exam and credit for prior learning, self-acquired competency (SAC) credits, and credits for educational experiences in the armed services. Internships, on-campus work-study, and hospital clinical experience in qualified programs are available. There are 6 national honor societies. **Visiting:** There are regularly scheduled orientations for prospective students, including meetings with faculty, financial aid and student life information sessions, a campus tour, and meetings with coaches for athletes. There are guides for informal visits, visitors may sit in on classes, and stay overnight. To schedule a visit, contact the Admissions Office. **Campus Safety and Security:** Measures include 24-hour foot and vehicle patrol, emergency notification system, self-defense education, and security escort services. There are shuttle buses, emergency telephones, lighted pathways/sidewalks, controlled access to dorms/residences, There are burglar alarms in dorms, safety and date-rape seminars, drug awareness programs, surveillance cameras at dorms (used in conjunction with card access), and emergency radio communications.

REQUIREMENTS: The SAT or ACT is required. Six semesters of high school, with a minimum 2.25 academic grade point average (on a 4-point scale), or GED score of 500 (50 if taken prior to 1/1/2003). Minimum composite ACT score of 19 and/or SAT I score of 900 on the re-centered SAT* including a record of active participation in school or community organizations or events throughout high school. A commitment to achieving a college degree. A GPA of 2.3 is required. AP and CLEP credits are accepted. Students must obtain degree objective within 150% of the normal time frame for degree completion. For example, in a baccalaureate program requiring 120 credit hours, students must obtain degrees within 180 attempted credit hours (120 X 1.50 = 180). For associate programs of 60 credit hours, students must complete within 90 attempted hours. Graduate students in master degree programs requiring 68 hours must complete within 102 attempted credit hours. Doctoral students have a maximum of 219 attempted credit hours. This maximum time frame is based upon student classification in the University's academic records. Students who are pursuing a course of study with greater credit hour requirements need to notify the Financial Aid Office in order to have a review done on a case-by-case basis. This request for review will not be considered an appeal. The student is responsible for completing all requirements of his or her major program, including mastery of exit-level outcomes at designated standards, and for meeting all University requirements, including the completion of a comprehensive exit assessment, before they will be allowed to graduate. Students should confer with major advisors and mentors, and refer to the Academic Catalog, to assure satisfactory progress toward graduation. **Procedure:** Freshmen are admitted to all sessions. Entrance exams should be taken by December of the senior year. There are deferred admissions and rolling admissions plans. Application deadlines are open. Application fee is $25. Notification is sent on a rolling basis. Applications are accepted on-line. **Transfer Students:** 345 transfer students enrolled in 2013-2014. Applicants who have earned 12 or more college-level credits (generally, courses numbered 100 and above) at another institution, have a minimum 2.25 grade point average (on a 4.0 point scale) and are in good standing at the institution last attended must submit the following: A completed Undergraduate Application for admission. Official transcript from each college previously attended, and an approved transfer clearance form from most recent institution. **International Students:** There are 115 international students enrolled. The school actively recruits these students. They must take the TOEFL with a minimum score of 500 on the paper-based TOEFL (PBT) or 61 on the Internet-based version (iBT) or take the MELAB and the college's own test, or take the IELTS, or ELS. They must also take the SAT or ACT.

ADMISSIONS: 61% of the 2014-2015 applicants were accepted. The SAT scores for the 2014-2015 freshman class were: Critical Reading--61% below 500, 31% between 500 and 599, 7% between 600 and 699, and 1% between 700 and 800; Math--51% below 500, 35% between 500 and 599, and 14% between 600 and 699. The ACT scores were 46% below 21, 33% between 21 and 23, 15% between 24 and 26, 3% between 27 and 28, and 2% above 28. **Admissions Contact:** Joan Clark, Vice President for Admissions. E-Mail: *admissions@ucwv.edu* Web: *http://www.ucwv.edu/*

FINANCIAL AID: In 2014-2015, 100% of all full-time freshmen and 90% of continuing full-time students received some form of financial aid. The average freshman award was $19,300.. UC is a member of CSS. The FAFSA and the college's own financial statement are required. The priority date for freshman financial aid applications for fall entry is March 1. The deadline for filing freshman financial aid applications for fall entry is September 15.

WEST LIBERTY UNIVERSITY (*The complete profile is made available exclusively on our website, www.barronspac.com*)

WEST VIRGINIA STATE UNIVERSITY (*The complete profile is made available exclusively on our website, www.barronspac.com*)

WEST VIRGINIA UNIVERSITY C-2
www.wvu.edu

Morgantown, WV 26506

(304) 293-0111
(800) 293-2121
Fax: (304) 293-8832   Email: wvuadmissions@mail.wvu.edu

Full-time: 11434 men, 9429 women	Faculty: n/av
Part-time: 817 men, 883 women	Ph.D.s: 83%
Graduate: 2848 men, 3764 women	Student/Faculty: 21 to 1
Year: semesters, summer session	Tuition: $6960 ($20,242)
Room & Board: $9582	Freshman Class: 15601 applied, 13386 accepted, 4868 enrolled
SAT CR/M: 512/533 ACT: 24	CEEB CODE: 5904
Application Deadline: August 1	COMPETITIVE+

West Virginia University, founded in 1867, is a comprehensive, public land-grant research university offering more than 100 undergraduate degrees in liberal arts and sciences, health science, and professional training. The figures in the above capsule and in this profile are approximate. There are 15 undergraduate schools and 13 graduate schools. In addition to regional accreditation, WVU has baccalaureate program accreditation with AACSB, ABET, ACEJMC, ACPE, ADA, APTA, ASLA, CAHEA, CSWE, FIDER, NASAD, NASM, NCATE, NLN, NRPA, and SAF. The 2800-acre campus is in a small town 75 miles south of Pittsburgh, and 200 miles west of Baltimore. Including any residence halls, there are 255 buildings.

STUDENT LIFE: 56% of undergraduates are from West Virginia. Others are from 50 states, 109 foreign countries, and Canada. 81% are White. The average age of freshmen is 19; all undergraduates, 21. 56% remain to graduate. **Housing:** 6475 students can be accommodated in college housing, which includes single-sex and coed dorms, on-campus apartments, off-campus apartments, and married student housing. In addition, there are honors houses, language houses, special-interest houses, fraternity houses, sorority houses, and sections within residence halls designated for special programming. On-campus housing is available on a first-come, first-served basis, and is available on a lottery system for upperclassmen. 76% of students commute. Alcohol is not permitted. All students may keep cars.

FACULTY/CLASSROOMS: 55% of faculty are male; 45% are female. No introductory courses are taught by graduate students.

PROGRAMS OF STUDY: WVU confers B.A., B.S., B.F.A., B.M., B.Md.S., B.S.A.E., B.S.Agr., B.S.B.Ad., B.S.B.S., B.S.C.E., B.S.Ch.E., B.S.Cp.E., B.S.E.E., B.S.F., B.S.C.S., B.S.I.E., B.S.J., B.S.L.A., B.S.M.E., B.S.Min.E., B.S.N., B.S.Pnge., B.S.R., R.B.A. and B.S.W. degrees. Master's and Doctoral degrees are also awarded. Bachelor's degrees are awarded in AGRICULTURE (agriculture, agronomy, animal science, fish and game management, fishing and fisheries, forestry and related sciences, horticulture, natural resource management, and plant science), BIOLOGICAL SCIENCE (biology/biological science and nutrition), BUSINESS (accounting, banking and finance, business administration and management, fashion merchandising, marketing and distribution, recreation and leisure services, sports management, and tourism), COMMUNICATIONS AND THE ARTS (advertising, art, broadcasting, communications, dramatic arts, English, journalism, music, public relations, speech/debate/rhetoric, and visual and performing arts), COMPUTER AND PHYSICAL SCIENCE (chemistry, computer science, geology, geoscience, mathematics, physics, and science), EDUCATION (athletic training, English education, environmental education, foreign languages education, mathematics education, and physical education), ENGINEERING AND ENVIRONMENTAL DESIGN (aeronautical engineering, aerospace studies, chemical engineering, civil engineering, computer engineering, electrical/electronics engineering, engineering, environmental science, interior design, landscape architecture/design, mechanical engineering, mining and mineral engineering, petroleum/natural gas engineering, and systems engineering), HEALTH PROFESSIONS (dental hygiene, medical technology, nursing, occupational therapy, pharmacy, physical therapy, speech pathology/audiology, and veterinary science), SOCIAL SCIENCE (anthropology, child care/child and family studies, economics, family/consumer resource management, geography, history, interdisciplinary studies, international studies, liberal arts/general studies, parks and recreation management, philosophy, political science/government, psychology, social work, and sociology). Engineering and mineral resources, psychology, and political science are the strongest academically. Business and economics, engineering and mineral resources, and health sciences have the largest enrollments.

ACTIVITIES: 7% of men belong to 20 national fraternities; 7% of women belong to 1 local and 8 national sororities. There are 440 groups on campus, including art, band, cheerleading, chess, choir, chorale, chorus, computers, dance, debate, drama, environmental, ethnic, film, forensics, gay, honors, international, jazz band, marching band, newspaper, orchestra, pep band, photography, political, professional, radio and TV, religious, social, social service, student government, and symphony. Popular campus events include Mountaineer Week, Greek Week and Fall Fest. **Sports:** There are 7 intercollegiate sports for men and 9 for women, and 17 intramural sports for men and 17 for women. Facilities include 5 lighted tennis courts, weight and exercise space, jogging track, turf field, lacrosse, frisbee, three swimming pools, 7 basketball courts, a 50 foot high climbing wall. There is a natatorium with swimming and diving pools, rifle facilities, tennis courts, a weight room, indoor/outdoor tracks, a bowling alley, lacrosse, baseball, football, and soccer fields, a 63,500-seat stadium, a 14,000-seat gym, a coliseum offering basketball, wrestling, volleyball, and gymnastics, and a soccer stadium. **Graduates:** From July 1, 2013 to June 30, 2014, 4268 bachelor's degrees were awarded. The most popular majors were engineering (13%), business (12%), and health field (10%). 1200 companies recruited on campus in 2013-2014. In an average class, 34% graduate in 4 years or less, 53% graduate in 5 years or less, and 57% graduate in 6 years or less. **SERVICES:** Counseling and information services are available, as is tutoring in most subjects. There is a reader service for the blind, remedial math, reading, and writing. **Library/Resources:** The 5 libraries contain 2.5 million volumes, 263,203 microform items, 15,663 audio/video tapes/CDs/DVDs, and subscribe to 83,495 periodicals including electronic. Computerized library services include interlibrary loans, database searching, Internet access, and Wi-Fi capability. Special learning facilities include an art gallery, planetarium, radio station, a discovery lab for inventors, coal, mining, and minerals history museum, a pharmacy museum, art museum, and an arboretum. **Physically Challenged Students:** 90% of the campus is accessible. Facilities include wheelchair ramps, elevators, special parking, specially equipped restrooms, special class scheduling, lowered drinking fountains, lowered telephones, special housing. Academic programs are made accessible by transferring class to an architecturally accessible facility. Other facilities include tactile signage, specially designed lab facilities, portable lab stations, a Kurzweil reading machine, and a specially equipped van for inner-city transportation. **Special:** A co-op program in engineering and cross-registration with schools in the Southern Regional Education Board through the Academic Common Market are possible. Internships, study abroad in 25 countries, a Washington semester, student-designed majors, dual majors in business and foreign languages, and B.A.-B.S. degrees in economics, chemistry, physics, biology, math, psychology, and geology are available. A liberal studies degree, credit by exam, credit for life experience, nondegree study, and pass/fail options are also offered. There are 29 national honor societies, including Phi Beta Kappa, and a freshman honors program. **Visiting:** There are regularly scheduled orientations for prospective students, including 2-day sessions with campus tours, placement testing, academic and advisement meetings, parent/student orientation discussions, and transitional meetings. There are guides for informal visits and visitors may sit in on classes. To schedule a visit, contact the Visitors Resource Center at (304) 293-3489. **Campus Safety and Security:** Measures include 24-hour foot and vehicle patrol, emergency notification system, self-defense education, and security escort services. There are shuttle buses, emergency telephones, lighted pathways/sidewalks, Neighborhood watch programs, and sexual assault prevention booths staffed by city and university police.

REQUIREMENTS: The SAT or ACT is required. West Virginia residents must have a minimim GPA of 2.0 and either a composite ACT score of 19 or a combined SAT score of 910 (critical reading and math). Nonresidents must have a minimum GPA of 2.5 and either 21 on the ACT or 990 on the SAT. A GPA of 2.0 is required. AP and CLEP credits are accepted. Important factors in the admissions decision are leadership record, evidence of special talent, and advanced placement or honors courses.All students are required to take 12 credit hours in each of 3 areas: humanities and fine arts, social and behavioral sciences, and natural sciences and math. The 36 credit hours must include international/minority/gender studies, math, composition, and an advanced course emphasizing writing skills. A minimum 2.0 GPA and at least 128 credit hours are required to graduate. **Procedure:** Freshmen are admitted fall, spring, and summer. Entrance exams should be taken by spring of the junior year. There are deferred admissions and rolling admissions plans. Applications should be filed by August 1 for fall entry, along with a $60 fee. Applications are accepted on-line. **Transfer Students:** 944 transfer students enrolled in 2013-2014. Students must have a minimum 2.0 GPA in all college work attempted. Those with fewer than 12 transferable credit hours must also meet freshman admission standards. Some programs have different course and higher GPA requirements. 30 of

128 credits required for the bachelor's degree must be completed at WVU. **International Students:** There are 1091 international students enrolled. The school actively recruits these students. They must take the TOEFL with a minimum score of 500 on the paper-based TOEFL (PBT) or 61 on the Internet-based version (iBT). International students serving as graduate teaching assistants must also demonstrate mastery of spoken English. They must also take the SAT or ACT, scoring 950.

ADMISSIONS: 86% of the 2014-2015 applicants were accepted. The SAT scores for the 2014-2015 freshman class were: Critical Reading--47% below 500, 41% between 500 and 599, 11% between 600 and 699, and 2% between 700 and 800; Math--39% below 500, 43% between 500 and 599, 16% between 600 and 699, and 3% between 700 and 800. The ACT scores were 54% below 21, 20% between 21 and 23, 18% between 24 and 26, 7% between 27 and 28, and 2% above 28. **Admissions Contact:** Stephen Lee, Ex Director of Admissions and Records. E-Mail: *wvuadmissions@arc.wvu.edu* Web: *www.wvu.edu*

FINANCIAL AID: In 2014-2015, 24% of all full-time freshmen and 71% of continuing full-time students received some form of financial aid. 59% of all full-time freshmen and 61% of continuing full-time students received need-based aid. The average freshman award was $6,833. Need-based scholarships or need-based grants averaged $5,261 ; need-based self-help aid (loans and jobs) averaged $3,871; non-need-based athletic scholarships averaged $19,580; and other non-need-based awards and non-need-based scholarships averaged $6,285. The average financial indebtedness of the 2014 graduate was $23,641. The FAFSA and the state aid form are required. The deadline for filing freshman financial aid applications for fall entry is March 1.

WEST VIRGINIA UNIVERSITY INSTITUTE OF TECHNOLOGY
(The complete profile is made available exclusively on our website, www.barronspac.com)

WEST VIRGINIA WESLEYAN COLLEGE   C-3
www.wvwc.edu

Buckhannon, WV 26201	(304) 473-8000
	(800) 722-9933
Fax: (304) 473-8108	Email: admissions@wvwc.edu
Full-time: 600 men, 700 women	Faculty: 171; IIB, --$
Part-time: 15 men, 10 women	Ph.D.s: 77%
Graduate: 20 men, 30 women	Student/Faculty: 13 to 1
Year: semesters, summer session	Tuition: $23,870
Room & Board: $7,390	Freshman Class: n/av
SAT or ACT: required	CEEB CODE: 5905
Application Deadline: see profile	COMPETITIVE

West Virginia Wesleyan College, founded in 1890, is an independent liberal and applied arts college affiliated with the United Methodist Church. The figures in the above capsule and this profile are approximate. In addition to regional accreditation, WVWC has baccalaureate program accreditation with NCATE and NLN. The 80-acre campus is in a small town in the Appalachian foothills, 135 miles south of Pittsburgh, Pennsylvania. Including any residence halls, there are 23 buildings.

STUDENT LIFE: 53% of undergraduates are from West Virginia. Others are from 37 states, 12 foreign countries, and Canada. 85% are from public schools. 88% are white. 53% are Protestant; 20% Catholic. The average age of freshmen is 18; all undergraduates, 21.

FACULTY/CLASSROOMS: 79% of faculty are male; 21% are female. All teach undergraduates. No introductory courses are taught by graduate students. The average class size in an introductory lecture is 24; in a laboratory is 12; and in a regular course is 21.

PROGRAMS OF STUDY: WVWC confers B.A., B.S., B.M.E., and B.S.N. degrees. Master's degrees are also awarded. Bachelor's degrees are awarded in BIOLOGICAL SCIENCE (biology/biological science and nutrition), BUSINESS (accounting, business administration and management, and marketing/retailing/merchandising), COMMUNICATIONS AND THE ARTS (dramatic arts, English, music, public relations, and speech/debate/rhetoric), COMPUTER AND PHYSI-CAL SCIENCE (chemistry, computer science, mathematics, and physics), EDUCATION (art education, elementary education, music education, physical education, and secondary education), ENGINEERING AND ENVIRONMENTAL DESIGN (engineering physics), HEALTH PROFESSIONS (nursing), SOCIAL SCIENCE (economics, history, international studies, philosophy, political science/government, psychology, religion, religious education, social science, and sociology). Physical and natural sciences and accounting are the strongest academically. Business, biology, and education have the largest enrollments.

ACTIVITIES: 25% of men belong to 5 national fraternities; 25% of women belong to 5 national sororities. There are 75 groups on campus, including art, band, cheerleading, choir, chorale, chorus, communications, computers, dance, drama, ethnic, forensics, honors, international, jazz band, literary magazine, musical theater, newspaper, political, professional, radio and TV, religious, social, social service, student government, and yearbook. Popular campus events include Founders Day, Festivals of Lessons and Carols, and Spring Sing.

SERVICES: Counseling and information services are available, as is tutoring in every subject. There is a reader service for the blind, and remedial math, reading, and writing. **Library/Resources:** The library contains 116,240 volumes, 39,119 microform items, and 6,322 audio/video tapes/CDs/DVDs, and subscribes to 14,126 periodicals including electronic. Computerized library services include interlibrary loans, database searching, Internet access, and Wi-Fi capability. Special learning facilities include an art gallery, planetarium, and radio station. **Physically Challenged Students:** 75% of the campus is accessible. Facilities include wheelchair ramps, elevators, special parking, specially equipped restrooms, special class scheduling, and lowered drinking fountains. **Special:** WVWC offers cross-registration with the Mountain State Association of Colleges. Students may participate in a wide variety of internships, including a Washington center internship and work-study and study-abroad programs; there are exchange agreements in Korea, the People's Republic of China, Norway, and Bulgaria. Nondegree and pass/fail study, dual, student-designed, and contract majors, and credit for life, military, and work experience are available. A 3-2 engineering degree offered with West Virginia University and the University of Virginia. There are 1 national honor societies and a freshman honors program. **Visiting:** There are regularly scheduled orientations for prospective students. There are guides for informal visits, visitors may sit in on classes, and stay overnight. To schedule a visit, contact the Admission Office. **Campus Safety and Security:** Measures include 24-hour foot and vehicle patrol, self-defense education, and security escort services. There are emergency telephones, lighted pathways/sidewalks, Rape awareness educational programs, and appropriate training for residence hall staff.

REQUIREMENTS: The SAT or ACT is required. A satisfactory score is needed on the SAT or 18 on the ACT. Applicants must be high school graduates, or hold a GED. Students should have earned 26 academic credits, consisting of 4 in English, 3 each in math, science, and academic electives, and 2 each in foreign language, lab science, and social studies, as well as a total of 7 academic credits in fine arts, technology education, health, and phys ed. An essay and an interview are recommended. A GPA of 2.2 is required. AP and CLEP credits are accepted. Important factors in the admissions decision are extracurricular activities record, recommendations by school officials, and leadership record.

FINANCIAL AID: The FAFSA is required. Check with the school for current application deadlines.

WHEELING JESUIT UNIVERSITY   C-1
www.wju.edu

Wheeling, WV 26003

Fax: (304) 243-2397	(304) 243-2000
	(800) 624-6992
Full-time: 466 men, 471 women	Email: admiss@wju.edu
Part-time: 61 men, 181 women	Faculty: 77; IIA, --$
Graduate: 126 men, 313 women	Ph.Ds: 69%
Year: semesters, summer session	Student/Faculty: 12 to 1
Room & Board: $5470	Tuition: $28,030
	Freshman Class: 1470 applied, 981 accepted, 254 enrolled
SAT CR/M/W: 520/500/490 ACT: 22	CEEB CODE: 5906
Application Deadline: open	COMPETITIVE

Wheeling Jesuit College, founded in 1954, is an independent college affiliated with the Society of Jesus, offering undergraduate programs in the liberal arts and sciences, nursing, business, and education, and graduate programs in business administration and organizational leadership, nursing, education, and physical therapy. There is 1 undergraduate school and 3 graduate schools. In addition to regional accreditation, Wheeling Jesuit has baccalaureate program accreditation with ACBSP, TEAC, CAPTE, CAATE, CCNE, JRCNMT, and CoARC. The 65-acre campus is in a suburban area 60 miles southwest of Pittsburgh. Including any residence halls, there are 16 buildings.

STUDENT LIFE: 63% of undergraduates are from out of state, mostly the Middle Atlantic. Students are from 25 states, 20 foreign countries, and Canada. 71% are from public schools. 82% are White. 55% claim no religious affiliation; 31% Catholic; 13% Protestant. The average age of freshmen is 18; all undergraduates, 23. 28% do not continue beyond their first year; 57% remain to graduate. **Housing:** 979 students can be accommodated in college housing, which includes single-sex and coed dorms, off-campus apartments, and married student housing. In addition, there are honors houses and special-interest houses. On-campus housing is guaranteed for all 4 years. 75% of students live on campus; of those, 75% remain on campus on weekends. All students may keep cars.

FACULTY/CLASSROOMS: 53% of faculty are male; 47% are female. 91% teach undergraduates, 1% do research, and 1% do both. No introductory courses are taught by graduate students. The average class size in an introductory lecture is 17; in a laboratory is 10; and in a regular course is 15.

PROGRAMS OF STUDY: Wheeling Jesuit confers B.A., B.S. and B.S.N. degrees. Master's and Doctoral degrees are also awarded. Bachelor's degrees are awarded in AGRICULTURE (environmental studies), BIOLOGICAL SCIENCE (biology/biological science), BUSINESS (accounting, business administration and management, management science, marketing, and organizational leadership and management), COMMUNICATIONS AND THE ARTS (American literature, communications, creative writing, English, English literature, French, literature, media arts, English and Professional Communication, romance languages and literature, and Spanish), COMPUTER AND PHYSICAL SCIENCE (applied physics, applied science, chemistry, computer science, mathematics, and physics), EDUCATION (athletic training and elementary education), ENGINEERING AND ENVIRONMENTAL DESIGN (engineering), HEALTH PROFESSIONS (nuclear medical technology, nursing, and respiratory therapy), SOCIAL SCIENCE (criminal justice, ethics, politics, and social policy, history, international studies, liberal arts/general studies, philosophy, political science/government, psychology, and theological studies). Nursing, business administration, and physical therapy are the strongest academically and have the largest enrollments.

ACTIVITIES: There are 26 groups on campus, including band, cheerleading, choir, chorale, chorus, communications, computers, dance, drama, environmental, ethnic, film, gay, honors, international, literary magazine, musical theater, newspaper, pep band, political, professional, religious, social, social service, student government, and yearbook. Popular campus events include Community Day, Culture Fest, Last Blast Carnival and Family Weekend. **Sports:** There are 10 intercollegiate sports for men and 9 for women, and 8 intramural sports for men and 8 for women. Facilities include McDonough Health and Recreation Center is an 107,000 square foot facility that houses a performance gymnasium with seating for 2200, a practice gymnasium, two racquetball courts, an indoor natatorium with a regulation pool, an indoor running/walking track, weight room, and a fully equipped fitness center. The Outdoor Athletic Complex includes Bishop Schmidt ProGrass all-weather, multi-use playing field for soccer, football, rugby and lacrosse, two lighted tennis courts, an 8-lane, 400m track, and a throwing area for field events. The field includes a 1,400 seat grandstand, press box and heated locker rooms. **Graduates:** From July 1, 2013 to June 30, 2014, 212 bachelor's degrees were awarded. The most popular majors were nursing (25%), business administration (17%), and chemistry (6%). 60 companies recruited on campus in 2013-2014. In an average class, 49% graduate in 4 years or less, 56% graduate in 5 years or less, and 61% graduate in 6 years or less. Of the 2013 graduating class, 15% were enrolled in graduate school within 6 months of graduation, and 76% were employed.

SERVICES: Counseling and information services are available, as is tutoring in most subjects. There is a reader service for the blind, remedial math, reading, and writing. **Library/Resources:** The library contains 159,173 volumes, 122,980 microform items, 80,951 audio/video tapes/CDs/DVDs, and subscribes to 219 periodicals including electronic. Computerized library services include interlibrary loans, database searching, Internet access, and Wi-Fi capability. Special learning facilities include a **Physically Challenged Students:** 85% of the campus is accessible. Facilities include wheelchair ramps, elevators, special parking, specially equipped restrooms, lowered drinking fountains, lowered telephones, and special housing. **Special:** The university offers internships with many businesses and institutions as well as a Washington semester and study abroad. Students may obtain a 3-2 engineering degree with Case Western Reserve University or West Virginia University. Accelerated programs are available in nursing and education. The school permits dual and student-designed majors. There are 22 national honor societies, a freshman honors program, and 19 departmental honors programs. **Visiting:** There are regularly scheduled orientations for prospective students, all new students are required to attend a New Student Orientation program. Students will meet fellow classmates, learn about life at Wheeling Jesuit , meet with an academic advisor, take placement exams, select fall courses and register for classes. There are guides for informal visits, visitors may sit in on classes, and stay overnight. To schedule a visit, contact Lisa Summers at (304) 243-2318. **Campus Safety and Security:** Measures include 24-hour foot and vehicle patrol, emergency notification system, self-defense education, and security escort services. There are lighted pathways/sidewalks and controlled access to dorms/residences.

REQUIREMENTS: The SAT or ACT is required. Students must submit official results of either the SAT or ACT. Applicants must be high school graduates or hold a GED. Letters of recommendation and a list of extracurricular activities are also encouraged. Students should have earned 15 academic credits consisting of 4 in English, 2 in math, 1 in history or social science, 1 in science (2 are recommended for science majors), and 6 in academic electives, with a foreign language recommended. Exceptions are made, especially if the high school GPA is 3.0 or better. Students entering programs in the natural sciences should have taken 1 course each of chemistry and biology.

Applicants interested in preparing for future study in the physical therapy doctorate program should have a minimum of 3 years of lab science (including physics). A GPA of 3.0 is required. AP and CLEP credits are accepted. Important factors in the admissions decision are leadership record, recommendations by school officials, and extra-curricular activities record. To graduate, students must complete 120 credit hours with a GPA of no less than 2.0. The core curriculum consists of 52 credits in English composition, fine arts, mathematics, modern languages, literature, history, social science, global perspectives, natural science, philosophy, theology, and 1 course in ethics or Christian morality, as well as participation in the first year program. **Procedure:** Freshmen are admitted to all sessions. There are deferred admissions and rolling admissions plans. Application deadlines are open. Application fee is $25. Notification is sent on a rolling basis. Applications are accepted on-line. Application fees are waived if application is completed on-line. **Transfer Students:** 42 transfer students enrolled in 2013-2014. Applicants must have a cummulative college GPA of 2.3 or higher and submit official transcripts of all previous college work. Candidates may be asked to submit an official high school transcript. Transfer credit is only awarded for course work completed at accredited institutions in which a student earned a grade of C or higher. Grades of C- are not accepted. For those students who have earned an associate's degree from a regionally accredited institution, the University will accept that associate's degree (and all related credits) in total for transfer. 30 of 120 credits required for the bachelor's degree must be completed at Wheeling Jesuit. **International Students:** There are 62 international students enrolled. The school actively recruits these students. They must take the TOEFL with a minimum score of 550 on the paper-based TOEFL (PBT) or 80 on the Internet-based version (iBT).

ADMISSIONS: 67% of the 2014-2015 applicants were accepted. The SAT scores for the 2014-2015 freshman class were: Critical Reading--45% below 500, 42% between 500 and 599, and 13% between 600 and 699; Math--46% below 500, 41% between 500 and 599, and 13% between 600 and 699; Writing--54% below 500, 36% between 500 and 599, 9% between 600 and 699, and 1% between 700 and 800. The ACT scores were 32% below 21, 32% between 21 and 23, 23% between 24 and 26, 6% between 27 and 28, and 6% above 28. 39% of the current freshmen were in the top fifth of their class; 71% were in the top two fifths. 4 freshmen graduated first in their class. **Admissions Contact:** Becky Forney, Director of Enrollment Management. E-Mail: *admiss@wju.edu* Web: *www.wju.edu/admissions/*

FINANCIAL AID: In 2014-2015, 99% of all full-time freshmen and continuing full-time students received some form of financial aid. 69% of all full-time freshmen and 54% of continuing full-time students received need-based aid. The average freshman award was $23,426. Need-based scholarships or need-based grants averaged $7,701 ($16,155 maximum); need-based self-help aid (loans and jobs) averaged $6,952 ($9,700 maximum); non-need-based athletic scholarships averaged $6,942 ($24,970 maximum); and other non-need-based awards and non-need-based scholarships averaged $8,000 ($26,800 maximum). 37% of undergraduate students work part-time. Average annual earnings from campus work are $1002. The average financial indebtedness of the 2014 graduate was $28,874. The FAFSA is required. The priority date for freshman financial aid applications for fall entry is March 1.

A B C D E

Superior
Ashland
Menomonie
River Falls
Eau Claire
Stevens Point
Green Bay
De Pere
Appleton
La Crosse
Oshkosh
Ripon
Fond du Lac
Manitowoc
Sheboygan
Mequon
Madison
Whitewater
Platteville
Beloit
Kenosha

0 20 40 60 80 100
Miles

• College Location

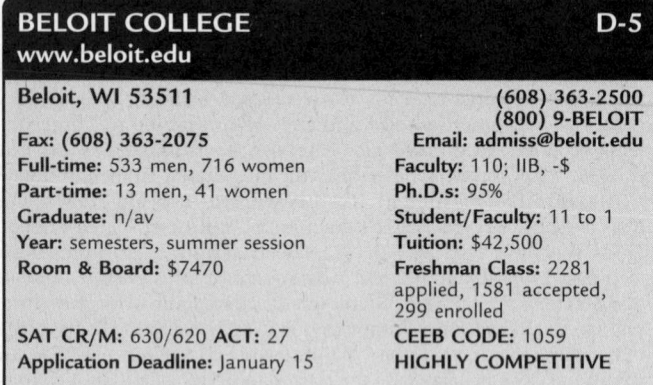

Waukesha
Milwaukee

WISCONSIN

ALVERNO COLLEGE (*The complete profile is made available exclusively on our website, www.barronspac.com*)

BELOIT COLLEGE	D-5
www.beloit.edu	

Beloit, WI 53511	(608) 363-2500
	(800) 9-BELOIT
Fax: (608) 363-2075	Email: admiss@beloit.edu
Full-time: 533 men, 716 women	Faculty: 110; IIB, -$
Part-time: 13 men, 41 women	Ph.D.s: 95%
Graduate: n/av	Student/Faculty: 11 to 1
Year: semesters, summer session	Tuition: $42,500
Room & Board: $7470	Freshman Class: 2281 applied, 1581 accepted, 299 enrolled
SAT CR/M: 630/620 ACT: 27	CEEB CODE: 1059
Application Deadline: January 15	HIGHLY COMPETITIVE

Beloit College, founded in 1846, is a private liberal arts institution. There is 1 undergraduate school. The 44-acre campus is in a small town 50 miles south of Madison, 80 miles southwest of Milwaukee, 90 miles northwest of Chicago, IL. Including any residence halls, there are 70 buildings.
STUDENT LIFE: 81% of undergraduates are from out of state, mostly the Mid-West. Students are from 49 states, 34 foreign countries, and Canada. 70% are from public schools. 70% are White. The average age of freshmen is 18; all undergraduates, 20. 15% do not continue beyond their first year; 80% remain to graduate. **Housing:** 1143 students can be accommodated in college housing, which includes single-sex and coed dorms and on-campus apartments. In addition, there are language houses, special-interest houses, fraternity houses, and sorority houses. On-campus housing is guaranteed for the freshman year only. 87% of students live on campus; of those, 95% remain on campus on weekends. All students may keep cars.
FACULTY/CLASSROOMS: 47% of faculty are male; 53% are female.

All teach undergraduates. No introductory courses are taught by graduate students. The average class size in an introductory lecture is 15; in a laboratory is 15; and in a regular course is 15.
PROGRAMS OF STUDY: Beloit confers B.A., and B.S. degrees. Bachelor's degrees are awarded in AGRICULTURE (environmental studies and forestry and related sciences), BIOLOGICAL SCIENCE (biology ecology and field biology, biochemistry, biology/biological science, cell biology, ecology, and environmental biology), BUSINESS (business administration and management, business economics, and international economics), COMMUNICATIONS AND THE ARTS (art history, art, Chinese, classical languages, classics, comparative literature, creative writing, dance, dramatic arts, East Asian languages and literature, English, English literature, French, German, intermedia/multimedia, literature, modern language, music, Russian, Spanish, and studio art), COMPUTER AND PHYSICAL SCIENCE (applied physics, chemistry, computer science, environmental geology, geology, mathematics, and physics), EDUCATION (art education and education), ENGINEERING AND ENVIRONMENTAL DESIGN (preengineering), HEALTH PROFESSIONS (premedicine), SOCIAL SCIENCE (anthropology, Chinese Studies, classical/ancient civilization, cognitive science, economics, gender studies, history, interdisciplinary studies, international relations, philosophy, philosophy and religion, political science/government, prelaw, psychology, religion, religious studies, sociology, and women's studies). Anthropology, creative writing, and biology are the strongest academically. Psychology, international relations, and biology have the largest enrollments.
ACTIVITIES: 24% of men belong to 3 national fraternities; 22% of women belong to 1 local and 2 national sororities. There are 95 groups on campus, including small instrument ensembles, wind, art, band, chess, choir, chorus, computers, dance, drama, entrepreneurial, student radio; science fiction and fantasy; string, environmental, ethnic, film, gay, honors, international, jazz band, literary magazine, musical theater, newspaper, photography, political, professional, radio and TV, religious, social, social service, and student government. Popular campus events include Great Lecture Series, Advising Day, Folk and Blues Weekend and Spring Day. **Sports:** There are 8 intercollegiate sports for men and 8 for women. Facilities include a sports center that houses a 2,250-seat arena for basketball and volleyball, racquetball/handball courts, fitness center, a natatorium, field house that contains a running track, an indoor soccer area, batting/pitching cage, and space for indoor tennis, a 3,500-seat stadium hosting football, soccer, lacrosse, and track and field, outdoor playing fields, a dance studio, a tennis court complex. There are facilities nearby for sailing, ice skating, and other recreation. **Graduates:** From July 1, 2013 to June 30, 2014, 282 bachelor's degrees were awarded. The most popular majors were social sciences (22%), foreign languages, literatures, and linguistics (9%), and visual and performing arts (7%). In an average class, 71% graduate in 4 years or less, 80% graduate in 5 years or less, and 80% graduate in 6 years or less. Of the 2013 graduating class, 14% were enrolled in graduate school within 6 months of graduation, and 76% were employed.
SERVICES: Counseling and information services are available, as is tutoring in most subjects. There is a reader service for the blind. **Library/Resources:** The library contains 505,586 volumes, 7,314 microform items, 9,301 audio/video tapes/CDs/DVDs, and subscribes to 1,052 periodicals including electronic. Computerized library services include interlibrary loans, database searching, and Internet access. Special learning facilities include an art gallery, natural history museum, planetarium, radio station, TV station, 2 teaching museums, a comprehensive language lab, an observatory, a center for entrepreneurship, and a theater complex. **Physically Challenged Students:** 50% of the campus is accessible. Facilities include wheelchair ramps, elevators, special parking, specially equipped restrooms, special class scheduling, lowered drinking fountains, and lowered telephones. **Special:** Beloit offers cross-registration with the University of Wisconsin/Madison, internships, study abroad in more than 38 countries, and a Washington semester. Dual majors, student-designed and interdisciplinary majors, and non-degree study are available. A 3-2 engineering degree is offered with 9 institutions, and co-op programs are available in social services, forestry and environ-

mental management, engineering, and business administration. An intensive summer language program is offered in Russian, Arabic, Japanese, and Chinese. There are 6 national honor societies including Phi Beta Kappa. **Visiting:** There are regularly scheduled orientations for prospective students, including an interview, a tour, class visits, and meetings with professors. Enrolled students serve as tour guides and hosts for overnight stays. There are guides for informal visits, visitors may sit in on classes, and stay overnight. To schedule a visit, contact the Office of Admissions. **Campus Safety and Security:** Measures include 24-hour foot and vehicle patrol, emergency notification system, and security escort services. There are emergency telephones, lighted pathways/sidewalks, and controlled access to dorms/residences.

REQUIREMENTS: Submission of test scores is optional for most applicants. Home-schooled applicants and candidates applying from schools that do not provide grades are asked to submit results from one or more standardized tests, such as SAT or ACT. Applicants must be graduates of an accredited secondary school or home-school program, with 4 years of English, 3 each of math, science, and history/social sciences, and 2 of foreign language. The GED is accepted. An essay and a letter of recommendation are required, and an interview is strongly recommended. A GPA of 2.5 is required. AP and CLEP credits are accepted. Important factors in the admissions decision are advanced placement or honors course, recommendations by school officials, and leadership record.To graduate, students must complete 31 units, including 8 to 15 in the major, with a minimum GPA of 2.0. Students must complete 3 writing designated courses, 1 quantitative reasoning designated course, and 1 intercultural literacy designated course. Breadth requirements include 1 courses in each of the following domains: Conceptual and Foundational Systems, Artistic and Creative Practices, Social Analysis of Human Behavior, Scientific Inquiry into the Physical and Biological Universe, and Textual Cultures and Analysis. Students are also expected to complete a liberal arts in practice experience that integrates learning from inside and outside the classroom, typically in the junior year, and a capstone experience, typically in the senior year. **Procedure:** Freshmen are admitted fall and spring. There are early decision, early admissions, deferred admissions, and rolling admissions plans. Early decision applications should be filed by November 1; regular applications, by January 15 for fall entry; and November 1 for spring entry. Notification of early decision is sent November 30; regular decision, March 15. 23 early decision candidates were accepted for the 2014-2015 class. 30 applicants were on the 2014 waiting list; 2 were admitted. Applications are accepted on-line. **Transfer Students:** 24 transfer students enrolled in 2013-2014. Applicants must have a minimum GPA of 2.5 and submit official transcripts of all college work completed. The SAT and the ACT are both optional, and an interview is recommended. A letter of recommendation from a professor at a current/previous institution is also required. 16 of 31 credits required for the bachelor's degree must be completed at Beloit. **International Students:** There are 130 international students enrolled. The school actively recruits these students. They must also take the SAT or ACT. Applicants from selected countries must supply a school-leaving exam/certificate.

ADMISSIONS: 69% of the 2014-2015 applicants were accepted. The SAT scores for the 2014-2015 freshman class were: Critical Reading--17% below 500, 24% between 500 and 599, 35% between 600 and 699, and 24% between 700 and 800; Math--6% below 500, 34% between 500 and 599, 43% between 600 and 699, and 16% between 700 and 800. The ACT scores were 2% below 21, 22% between 21 and 23, 47% between 27 and 28, and 30% above 28. 49% of the current freshmen were in the top fifth of their class; 69% were in the top two fifths. There were 2 National Merit finalists. **Admissions Contact:** Lindsey Duerr, Director of Enrollment Operations. E-Mail: *admiss@beloit.edu* Web: *www.beloit.edu*

FINANCIAL AID: In 2014-2015, 96% of all full-time freshmen and 93% of continuing full-time students received some form of financial aid. 71% of all full-time freshmen and 67% of continuing full-time students received need-based aid. The average freshman award was $31,215. Need-based scholarships or need-based grants averaged $26,401; need-based self-help aid (loans and jobs) averaged $5,801; other non-need-based awards and non-need-based scholarships averaged $16,146; and $4,590 from other forms of aid. 79% of undergrad-

uate students work part-time. Average annual earnings from campus work are $1636. The average financial indebtedness of the 2014 graduate was $16,438. Beloit is a member of CSS. The FAFSA is required. The deadline for filing freshman financial aid applications for fall entry is March 1.

Cardinal Stritch University, founded in 1937 as a college, is a private, Catholic institution sponsored by the Sisters of St. Francis. The figures in the above capsule and in this profile are approximate. There are 4 undergraduate schools and 1 graduate school. In addition to regional accreditation, Stritch has baccalaureate program accreditation with NCATE and NLN. The 40-acre campus is in a suburban area 10 miles north of Milwaukee. Including any residence halls, there are 9 buildings.

STUDENT LIFE: 89% of undergraduates are from Wisconsin. Others are from 16 states, 27 foreign countries, and Canada. 60% are from public schools. 72% are white; 16% African American. 27% are Catholic. The average age of freshmen is 19; all undergraduates, 32. 27% do not continue beyond their first year; 43% remain to graduate.

FACULTY/CLASSROOMS: 49% of faculty are male; 51% are female. All teach undergraduates. No introductory courses are taught by graduate students. The average class size in a laboratory is 12 and in a regular course is 11.

PROGRAMS OF STUDY: Stritch confers B.A., B.S. and B.F.A. degrees. Associates, Master's, and Doctoral degrees are also awarded. Bachelor's degrees are awarded in BIOLOGICAL SCIENCE (biology/biological science), BUSINESS (accounting, business administration and management, and international business management), COMMUNICATIONS AND THE ARTS (art, communications, creative writing, dramatic arts, English, fine arts, French, music, public relations, and Spanish), COMPUTER AND PHYSICAL SCIENCE (chemistry, computer science, and mathematics), EDUCATION (early childhood education, elementary education, middle school education, secondary education, and special education), HEALTH PROFESSIONS (nursing, predentistry, premedicine, preoptometry, and preveterinary science), SOCIAL SCIENCE (history, prelaw, psychology, religion, social science, and sociology). Education in general and special education in particular are the strongest academically. Business, education, and nursing have the largest enrollments.

ACTIVITIES: There are 50 groups on campus, including art, band, cheerleading, choir, chorus, computers, dance, drama, ethnic, film, honors, international, jazz band, musical theater, newspaper, orchestra, photography, political, professional, radio and TV, religious, social, social service, student government, and yearbook. Popular campus events include Thursday Night events and weekly activities, such as sporting events and plays.

SERVICES: Counseling and information services are available, as is tutoring in every subject. There is remedial math, reading, and writing. The library contains 132,293 volumes, 173,216 microform items, 6,310 audio/video tapes/CDs/DVDs, and subscribes to 1,309 periodicals including electronic. Computerized library services include interlibrary loans and database searching. Special learning facilities include a learning resource center, art gallery, and radio station.

REQUIREMENTS: The SAT or ACT is required, with a recommended minimum composite score of 20 on the ACT or a satisfactory score on the SAT. Applicants must be graduates of an accredited secondary school, with 16 academic credits, including 4 years of English and 2 years each of math (algebra required), science, and social studies. The GED is accepted. Stritch requires an essay and recommends an interview. A GPA of 2.0 is required. AP and CLEP credits are accepted. Important factors in the admissions decision are leadership record, evidence of special talent, and advanced placement or honors courses.

FINANCIAL AID: The FAFSA and the college's own financial statement are required. Check with the school for current application deadlines.

CARROLL UNIVERSITY   **D-5**
www.carrollu.edu

Waukesha, WI 53186	**(262) 524-7220**
	(800) CARROLL
Fax: (262) 524-7139	Email: cc.info@ccadmin.cc.edu
Full-time: 953 men, 1753 women	Faculty: 101; IIB, -$
Part-time: 102 men, 207 women	Ph.D.s: 71%
Graduate: 134 men, 297 women	Student/Faculty: 23 to 1
Year: semesters, summer session	Tuition: $29,550
Room & Board: $8550	Freshman Class: 2969 applied, 2400 accepted, 762 enrolled
ACT: 24 SAT: required	CEEB CODE: 1101
Application Deadline: open	COMPETITIVE

Carroll University, founded in 1846, is an independent, co-educational comprehensive college grounded in the liberal arts tradition. There are 2 undergraduate schools and 2 graduate schools. In addition to regional accreditation, Carroll has baccalaureate program accreditation with APTA and NLN. The 120-acre campus is in a suburban area 15 miles west of Milwaukee. Including any residence halls, there are 56 buildings.

STUDENT LIFE: 71% of undergraduates are from Wisconsin. Others are from 28 states, 29 foreign countries, and Canada. 85% are White. The average age of freshmen is 18; all undergraduates, 21. 21% do not continue beyond their first year; 58% remain to graduate. **Housing:** 1785 students can be accommodated in college housing, which includes single-sex and coed dorms, on-campus apartments, and off-campus apartments. 58% of students live on campus. All students may keep cars.

FACULTY/CLASSROOMS: 45% of faculty are male; 55% are female. All teach undergraduates. No introductory courses are taught by graduate students.

PROGRAMS OF STUDY: Carroll confers B.A., B.S. and B.S.N. degrees. Master's degrees are also awarded. Bachelor's degrees are awarded in BIOLOGICAL SCIENCE (biochemistry, biology/biological science, and marine biology), BUSINESS (accounting, business administration and management, organizational leadership and management, and small business management), COMMUNICATIONS AND THE ARTS (art, communications, dramatic arts, English, music, Spanish, and theatre arts), COMPUTER AND PHYSICAL SCIENCE (actuarial science, applied physics, chemistry, computer science, information sciences and systems, mathematics, and radiological technology), EDUCATION (art education, athletic training, early childhood education, education, elementary education, foreign languages education, music education, physical education, and science education), ENGINEERING AND ENVIRONMENTAL DESIGN (computational sciences, environmental science, and graphic arts technology), HEALTH PROFESSIONS (clinical science, diagnostic medical sonography, exercise science, and nursing), SOCIAL SCIENCE (criminal justice, economics, (Social Science) Global Studies, history, international relations, political science/government, psychology, religion, and sociology). Nursing, communication, and criminal justice have the largest enrollments.

ACTIVITIES: There are 40 groups on campus, including art, band, cheerleading, choir, chorale, chorus, computers, dance, diversity, drama, ethnic, film, gay, honors, international, jazz band, literary magazine, musical theater, newspaper, orchestra, photography, political, professional, radio and TV, religious, social, social service, student government, symphony, and yearbook. Popular campus events

include Celebrate Carroll, International Folk Fair, Madrigal Dinner and Spring Fling. **Sports:** There are 11 intercollegiate sports for men and 11 for women. Facilities include an all-purpose field house, gym including volleyball court, 2 basketball courts, and an indoor track, 6 tennis courts, 6-lane pool, 2 sand volleyball courts, football/soccer field, practice field, softball diamond, batting cages, athletic training rooms, exercise/physiology laboratory, weight room, fitness weight room, dance studio, and a campus center which houses ping pong tables, pool tables, dart machine and video games. **Graduates:** From July 1, 2013 to June 30, 2014, 646 bachelor's degrees were awarded. The most popular majors were exercise science (16%), business administration (11%), and nursing (9%). In an average class, 42% graduate in 4 years or less, 55% graduate in 5 years or less, and 56% graduate in 6 years or less. Of the 2013 graduating class, 33% were enrolled in graduate school within 6 months of graduation.

SERVICES: Counseling and information services are available, as is tutoring in most subjects. There is a reader service for the blind. Academic coaching is available. **Library/Resources:** The library contains 92,593 volumes, 17 microform items, 3,643 audio/video tapes/CDs/DVDs, and subscribes to 144,006 periodicals including electronic. Computerized library services include interlibrary loans, database searching, Internet access, and Wi-Fi capability. Special learning facilities include an art gallery, radio station, a studio theater, and recital hall. **Physically Challenged Students:** Facilities include wheelchair ramps, elevators, special parking, specially equipped restrooms, special class scheduling, and lowered drinking fountains. **Special:** Under the International and Off-Campus Program, short and long-term study abroad programs are offered to sophomores, juniors and seniors so that they may travel to places that are culturally different from their own. IOP offers programs in such areas as Western and Eastern Europe, Latin America, Africa, or Asia. A capstone experience bridges the student's college work to employment or graduate school. There are 5 national honor societies and a freshman honors program. **Visiting:** There are regularly scheduled orientations for prospective students, consisting of a campus tour, financial aid/admissions counseling, academic department meetings, and extracurricular activities meetings. There are guides for informal visits, visitors may sit in on classes, and stay overnight. To schedule a visit, contact the Office of Admissions. **Campus Safety and Security:** Measures include 24-hour foot and vehicle patrol, emergency notification system, self-defense education, and security escort services. There are shuttle buses, emergency telephones, lighted pathways/sidewalks, and controlled access to dorms/residences.

REQUIREMENTS: The SAT or ACT is required. Applicants must be graduates of an accredited secondary school. The GED is accepted. An essay and interview are recommended for all students, and a portfolio or audition is advised for art and music students, respectively. AP and CLEP credits are accepted. Important factors in the admissions decision are advanced placement or honors courses, recommendations by school officials, and evidence of special talent. To graduate, students must complete 128 credit hours, 32 to 88 in the major, with a minimum GPA of 2.0. Students must take 7 courses from the Liberal Studies Progarm and a first-year seminar and writing seminar. 1 computer science course and a math course are needed for the B.S.; 12 credits of modern language or the humanities and math competency are needed for the B.A. **Procedure:** Freshmen are admitted fall and spring. Entrance exams should be taken during the junior year. There are deferred admissions and rolling admissions plans. Application deadlines are open. Applications are accepted on-line. **Transfer Students:** 197 transfer students enrolled in 2013-2014. Applicants for transfer must have a minimum GPA of 2.0. An interview is required. 32 of 128 credits required for the bachelor's degree must be completed at Carroll. **International Students:** There are 36 international students enrolled. The school actively recruits these students. They must take the TOEFL.

ADMISSIONS: 81% of the 2014-2015 applicants were accepted. The ACT scores were 17% below 21, 31% between 21 and 23, 29% between 24 and 26, 13% between 27 and 28, and 10% above 28. **Admissions Contact:** James V. Wiseman, Vice President of Enrollment. E-Mail: cc.info@ccadmin.cc.edu Web: www.carrollu.edu

FINANCIAL AID: In 2014-2015, 98% of all full-time freshmen and 98% of continuing full-time students received some form of financial aid. 85% of all full-time freshmen and 80% of continuing full-time

students received need-based aid. The average freshman award was $22,239. Need-based scholarships or need-based grants averaged $17,807; need-based self-help aid (loans and jobs) averaged $4,470; and other non-need-based awards and non-need-based scholarships averaged $14,566. 59% of undergraduate students work part-time. The average financial indebtedness of the 2014 graduate was $25,957. Carroll is a member of CSS. The FAFSA is required. Check with the school for current application deadlines.

CARTHAGE COLLEGE — E-5
www.carthage.edu

Kenosha, WI 53140	(262) 551-6000
	(800) 351-4058
Fax: (262) 551-5762	Email: admissions@carthage.edu
Full-time: 2525 men and women	Faculty: n/av; IIB, av$
Part-time: 950 men and women	Ph.D.s: 90%
Graduate: n/av	Student/Faculty: n/av
Year: semesters, summer session	Tuition: $31,800
Room & Board: $9100	Freshman Class: n/av
SAT or ACT: required	CEEB CODE: 1103
Application Deadline: open	COMPETITIVE

Carthage College, founded in 1847, is an independent liberal arts institution affiliated with the Evangelical Lutheran Church in America. There is 1 graduate school. The figures in the above capsule and in this profile are approximate. In addition to regional accreditation, Carthage has baccalaureate program accreditation with CSWE and NASM. The 75-acre campus is in a suburban area 30 miles south of Milwaukee and 60 miles north of Chicago, on the shore of Lake Michigan. Including any residence halls, there are 16 buildings.
STUDENT LIFE: 52% of undergraduates are from out of state, mostly the Midwest. Students are from 23 states, 14 foreign countries, and Canada. 88% are from public schools. 89% are white. 31% are Catholic; 26% claim no religious affiliation; 13% are Protestant. The average age of freshmen is 18; all undergraduates, 20. 24% do not continue beyond their first year; 50% remain to graduate.
FACULTY/CLASSROOMS: 68% of faculty are male; 32% are female. All teach undergraduates. No introductory courses are taught by graduate students. The average class size in an introductory lecture is 19; in a laboratory is 19; and in a regular course is 19.
PROGRAMS OF STUDY: Carthage confers B.A. degrees. Master's degrees are also awarded. Bachelor's degrees are awarded in BIOLOGICAL SCIENCE (biology/biological science), BUSINESS (accounting, business administration and management, international economics, and marketing management), COMMUNICATIONS AND THE ARTS (art, English, fine arts, French, German, graphic design, languages, music, performing arts, Spanish, and studio art), COMPUTER AND PHYSICAL SCIENCE (chemistry, mathematics, natural sciences, and physics), EDUCATION (elementary education, English education, foreign languages education, mathematics education, middle school education, music education, physical education, and secondary education), SOCIAL SCIENCE (criminal justice, economics, geography, history, philosophy, political science/government, psychology, religion, social science, social work, and sociology). Education, business, and sciences are the strongest academically. Business and education have the largest enrollments.
ACTIVITIES: 20% of men and women belong to 15 fraternities and sororities. There are 90 groups on campus, including art, band, cheerleading, choir, chorus, computers, debate, drama, ethnic, film, forensics, gay, habitat for humanity, honors, international, jazz band, literary magazine, musical theater, newspaper, orchestra, pep band, photography, political, professional, radio and TV, religious, social, social service, student government, and yearbook. Popular campus events include May Madness, Little Sibling Weekend, and Casino Night.
SERVICES: Counseling and information services are available, as is tutoring in most subjects. **Library/Resources:** The library contains 130,000 volumes, 9,000 microform items, and 1,300 audio/video tapes/CDs/DVDs, and subscribes to 450 periodicals including electronic. Computerized library services include interlibrary loans and

database searching. Special learning facilities include an art gallery and radio station. **Physically Challenged Students:** 90% of the campus is accessible. Facilities include wheelchair ramps, elevators, special parking, specially equipped restrooms, special class scheduling, lowered drinking fountains, lowered telephones. **Special:** Internships are available during the January term or, in some cases, for a semester. Carthage offers study abroad in 5 countries, cross-registration with the University of Wisconsin, a Washington semester, a general studies degree, an accelerated degree program in business administration, work-study programs, and dual and student-designed majors. Students may take a 3-2 engineering degree with Case Western Reserve or Washington Universities, and the University of Minnesota-Twin Cities or the University of Wisconsin/Madison, or a 3-2 occupational therapy degree with Washington University. There are pass/fail options and credit for military and work experience. There are 3 national honor societies and a freshman honors program. **Visiting:** There are regularly scheduled orientations for prospective students, including small group meetings with first year adviser and faculty members, class selection, and curriculum overview. Informational sessions for parents are offered. There are guides for informal visits, visitors may sit in on classes, and stay overnight. To schedule a visit, contact the Office of Admissions. **Campus Safety and Security:** Measures include 24-hour foot and vehicle patrol, self-defense education, and security escort services. There are emergency telephones, lighted pathways/sidewalks, electronic exit locks on residence halls.
REQUIREMENTS: The SAT or ACT is required. Applicants should be graduates of an accredited secondary school, having earned 16 academic credits, including English, foreign language, math, science, and social studies. The GED is accepted. An interview is recommended. A GPA of 2.0 is required. AP and CLEP credits are accepted. Important factors in the admissions decision are advanced placement or honors courses, leadership record, and extracurricular activities record.
FINANCIAL AID: The FAFSA is required. Check with the school for current financial aid deadlines.

CONCORDIA UNIVERSITY WISCONSIN — E-4
www.cuw.edu

Mequon, WI 53097	(414) 243-4500
Fax: (414) 243-4545	Email: admission@cuw.edu
Full-time: n/av	Faculty: 99; IIB, av$
Part-time: n/av	Ph.D.s: 75%
Graduate: n/av	Student/Faculty: 11 to 1
Year: 4-1-4, summer session	Tuition: $20,990
Room & Board: $7990	Freshman Class: 1130 accepted, 402 enrolled
SAT: required ACT: 22	CEEB CODE: 1139
Application Deadline: August 1	COMPETITIVE

Concordia University Wisconsin, established in 1881, is a private institution affiliated with the Lutheran Church-Missouri Synod. There are 4 undergraduate schools and 1 graduate school. In addition to regional accreditation, CUW has baccalaureate program accreditation with NLN. The 155-acre campus is in a suburban area 15 miles north of Milwaukee. Including any residence halls, there are 20 buildings.
STUDENT LIFE: 60% of undergraduates are from Wisconsin. Others are from 47 states, and 25 foreign countries. 75% are White; 17% African American. 79% are Protestant; 21% Catholic. The average age of freshmen is 18; all undergraduates, 20. 20% do not continue beyond their first year; 60% remain to graduate.
FACULTY/CLASSROOMS: 43% of faculty are male; 57% are female. All teach undergraduates. No introductory courses are taught by graduate students. The average class size in a regular course is 17.
PROGRAMS OF STUDY: CUW confers B.A., B.S. and B.S.N. degrees. Associate, Master's, and Doctoral degrees are also awarded. Bachelor's degrees are awarded in BIOLOGICAL SCIENCE (biology/biological science), BUSINESS (accounting, banking and finance,

business administration and management, management science, and marketing/retailing/merchandising), COMMUNICATIONS AND THE ARTS (art, communications, English, graphic design, music, Spanish, speech/debate/rhetoric, and telecommunications), COMPUTER AND PHYSICAL SCIENCE (mathematics and radiological technology), EDUCATION (athletic training, early childhood education, elementary education, physical education, and secondary education), ENGINEERING AND ENVIRONMENTAL DESIGN (interior design), HEALTH PROFESSIONS (nursing, occupational therapy, and sports medicine), SOCIAL SCIENCE (biblical languages, criminal justice, history, humanities, ministries, paralegal studies, pastoral studies, psychology, religion, religious music, social science, social work, and theological studies). Education, business, and health sciences are the strongest academically.

ACTIVITIES: There are 20 groups on campus, including art, band, cheerleading, choir, chorale, drama, drill team, ethnic, honors, international, jazz band, literary magazine, musical theater, newspaper, orchestra, pep band, political, professional, radio and TV, religious, and student government. Popular campus events are Winterfest and Springfest.

SERVICES: Counseling and information services are available, as is tutoring in every subject. There is a reader service for the blind, and remedial math, reading, and writing. **Library/Resources:** The library contains 120,000 volumes, 270,602 microform items, and 4,152 audio/video tapes/CDs/DVDs, and subscribes to 37,000 periodicals including electronic. Computerized library services include interlibrary loans, database searching, and Internet access. Special learning facilities include an art gallery, radio station, a curriculum library for education students, health and fitness facility, sustainable environmental center, state of the art residence hall. **Physically Challenged Students:** All of the campus is accessible. Facilities include wheelchair ramps, elevators, special parking, and specially equipped restrooms. **Special:** Internships, study abroad, pass/fail options, and credit for life, military, and work experience are available. Concordia offers a general studies degree, dual, student-designed, and interdisciplinary majors, including justice and public policy, and nondegree study. Accelerated degree programs are available in several fields. There is 1 national honor society. **Visiting:** There are regularly scheduled orientations for prospective students, including a tour and financial aid and academic information sessions. There are guides for informal visits, visitors may sit in on classes, and stay overnight. To schedule a visit, contact the Admission Office. **Campus Safety and Security:** Measures include 24-hour foot and vehicle patrol and emergency notification system. There are lighted pathways/sidewalks, controlled access to dorms/residences, security guards are on duty from 4 p.m. to 8 a.m. on weekdays and 24 hours a day on weekends.

REQUIREMENTS: A satisfactory score on the SAT or on the ACT is required. Applicants must be graduates of an accredited secondary school, having completed 16 academic credits, including 3 of English and 2 each of math, science, and social studies. The GED is accepted. A GPA of 2.5 is required. AP and CLEP credits are accepted. Important factors in the admissions decision are leadership record, recommendations by school officials, and personality/intangible qualities.

FINANCIAL AID: The CSS/Profile, FAFSA, the college's own financial statement, and income tax forms are required. The deadline for filing freshman financial aid applications for fall entry is April 30.

EDGEWOOD COLLEGE	**C-4**
www.edgewood.edu	

Madison, WI 53711	(608) 663-2294
	(800) 444-4861 ext. 2294
Fax: (608) 663-2214	Email: admissions@edgewood.edu
Full-time: 600 men, 1100 women	Faculty: 86
Part-time: 145 men, 361 women	Ph.D.s: 80%
Graduate: 219 men, 404 women	Student/Faculty: 18 to 1
Year: 4-1-4, summer session	Tuition: $24,666
Room & Board: $8628	Freshman Class: 1035 applied, 835 accepted, 309 enrolled
ACT: 22	CEEB CODE: 1202
Application Deadline: August 25	COMPETITIVE

Edgewood College, established in 1927, is a private Catholic institution sponsored by the Sinsinawa Dominican Sisters. There is one graduate school. In addition to regional accreditation, Edgewood has baccalaureate program accreditation with NCATE. The 55-acre campus is in a suburban area 5 miles southwest of Madison. Including any residence halls, there are 15 buildings.

STUDENT LIFE: 90% of undergraduates are from Wisconsin. Others are from 11 states, and 10 foreign countries. 75% are from public schools. 84% are White. 27% are Catholic. The average age of freshmen is 18; all undergraduates, 21. 20% do not continue beyond their first year; 58% remain to graduate.

FACULTY/CLASSROOMS: All teach undergraduates. No introductory courses are taught by graduate students. The average class size in a regular course is 18.

PROGRAMS OF STUDY: Edgewood confers B.A., and B.S. degrees. Master's degrees are also awarded. Bachelor's degrees are awarded in BIOLOGICAL SCIENCE (biology/biological science), BUSINESS (accounting and business administration and management), COMMUNICATIONS AND THE ARTS (art, English, French, graphic design, music, performing arts, and Spanish), COMPUTER AND PHYSICAL SCIENCE (chemistry, information sciences and systems, mathematics, and natural sciences), EDUCATION (early childhood education, education of the exceptional child, elementary education, science education, and social studies education), ENGINEERING AND ENVIRONMENTAL DESIGN (preengineering), HEALTH PROFESSIONS (art therapy, cytotechnology, medical technology, and nursing), SOCIAL SCIENCE (child care/child and family studies, criminal justice, economics, history, international relations, political science/government, prelaw, psychology, public administration, religion, and sociology). Liberal arts is the strongest academically. Business, education, and nursing have the largest enrollments.

ACTIVITIES: There are no fraternities or sororities. There are 30 groups on campus, including art, band, choir, chorale, chorus, communications, drama, environmental, ethnic, gay, honors, international, literary magazine, musical theater, newspaper, orchestra, pep band, political, religious, social, social service, student government, and symphony. Popular campus events include Homecoming, Springfest and Winter Frost.

SERVICES: Counseling and information services are available, as is tutoring in every subject. There is a reader service for the blind, and remedial math, reading, and writing. **Library/Resources:** The library contains 88,329 volumes, 94,050 microform items, and 3,946 audio/video tapes/CDs/DVDs, and subscribes to 494 periodicals including electronic. Computerized library services include interlibrary loans and database searching. Special learning facilities include an art gallery. **Physically Challenged Students:** 85% of the campus is accessible. Facilities include wheelchair ramps, elevators, special parking, specially equipped restrooms, special class scheduling, lowered drinking fountains, lowered telephones, special housing. Automated doors in the library, science center, activities center, and residence halls and a chairlift. **Special:** Students may cross-register with the University of Wisconsin/Madison. Internships, study abroad, dual and student-designed majors, nondegree study, pass/fail options, and credit for prior learning. experience are available. There is a weekend degree program. There is an accelerated undergraduate degree program for working adults. There are 5 national honor societies and a freshman honors program. **Visiting:** There are regularly scheduled orientations for prospective students, including Experience Edgewood Days, a program where admitted freshmen spend a day on campus as if they were Edgewood College Students. They choose their own schedule for the day, which may include sitting in on classes, attending athletics presentations, and learning about study abroad opportunities, residence life and student activities. Students also have the opportunity to take campus tours and exclusive tours of the residence halls. Complimentary lunch is included. There are guides for informal visits, visitors may sit in on classes, and stay overnight. To schedule a visit, contact the Admissions Office. **Campus Safety and Security:** Measures include self-defense education and security escort services. There are emergency telephones, lighted pathways/sidewalks, residence halls have alarms, a security card system, and campus security guards. RAs are on duty 24 hours a day weekends and 7a.m. to 3 p.m. and 8 p.m. to 4 a.m. weekdays.

REQUIREMENTS: The ACT is recommended. Candidates for

admission to Edgewood are expected to present a 2.5 cumulative high school GPA, rank in the upper half of their class, and have a composite score of 18 on the ACT or a satisfactory score on the SAT. The GED is accepted. Applicants should complete 16 Carnegie units, 12 of which should be chosen from the following fields: natural science, speech, social science, English, foreign language, history, religious studies, and mathematics. 2 years of the same foreign language in grades 9-12 with grades of C or better are also recommended. AP and CLEP credits are accepted.

ADMISSIONS: 81% of a recent year applicants were accepted. The ACT scores were 38% below 21, 31% between 21 and 23, 22% between 24 and 26, 7% between 27 and 28, and 3% above 28. 25% of the current freshmen were in the top fifth of their class; 59% were in the top two fifths. 1 freshman graduated first in the class.

FINANCIAL AID: Edgewood is a member of CSS. The FAFSA, the college's own financial statement, and a tax return are required. Check with the school for current application deadlines.

LAKELAND COLLEGE   E-4
www.lakeland.edu

Sheboygan, WI 53082	**(920) 565-1217**
	(800) 242-3347
Fax: (920) 565-1206	**Email: admissions@lakeland.edu**
Full-time: 390 men, 400 women	**Faculty:** 41; IIB, --$
Part-time: 20 men, 30 women	**Ph.D.s:** 59%
Graduate: 50 men, 130 women	**Student/Faculty:** 19 to 1
Year: semesters, summer session	**Tuition:** $17,595
Room & Board: $6195	**Freshman Class:** n/av
SAT or ACT: required	**CEEB CODE:** 1393
Application Deadline: n/av	**COMPETITIVE**

Lakeland College, established in 1862, is a private institution affiliated with the United Church of Christ. The 4-4-1 academic calendar consists of 4-month fall and spring terms, and an optional 3-week May term. There is one graduate school. The 240-acre campus is in a rural area 10 miles northwest of Sheboygan. Including any residence halls, there are 24 buildings.

STUDENT LIFE: 79% of undergraduates are from Wisconsin. Others are from 16 states, 31 foreign countries, and Canada. 90% are from public schools. 76% are White. 32% are Protestant; 29% Catholic; 25% claim no religious affiliation. The average age of all undergraduates is 22. 32% do not continue beyond their first year; 43% remain to graduate.

FACULTY/CLASSROOMS: 51% of faculty are male; 49% are female. All teach and do research. No introductory courses are taught by graduate students. The average class size in an introductory lecture is 20; in a laboratory is 15; and in a regular course is 16.

PROGRAMS OF STUDY: Lakeland confers B.A. degrees. Master's degrees are also awarded. Bachelor's degrees are awarded in BIOLOGICAL SCIENCE (biology/biological science), BUSINESS (accounting, business administration and management, business economics, hospitality management services, international business management, and marketing management), COMMUNICATIONS AND THE ARTS (art, creative writing, dramatic arts, English, German, music, and Spanish), COMPUTER AND PHYSICAL SCIENCE (chemistry, computer science, and mathematics), EDUCATION (business education, early childhood education, elementary education, music education, and secondary education), SOCIAL SCIENCE (behavioral science, criminal justice, economics, history, philosophy, physical fitness/movement, psychology, public administration, religion, and sociology). Business, education, and accounting are the strongest academically. Education, business, and computer science have the largest enrollments.

ACTIVITIES: 17% of men belong to 3 local fraternities; 11% of women belong to 3 local sororities. There are 27 groups on campus, including band, choir, chorus, dance team, drama, ethnic, honors, international, literary magazine, newspaper, pep band, professional, radio and TV, religious, social, student government, and yearbook. Popular campus events include Winter Carnival, and Spring Celebration.

SERVICES: Counseling and information services are available, as is

tutoring in every subject. There is a reader service for the blind, and remedial math, reading, and writing. **Library/Resources:** The library contains 57,447 volumes, 33,169 microform items, and 2,099 audio/video tapes/CDs/DVDs, and subscribes to 322 periodicals including electronic. Computerized library services include interlibrary loans and database searching. Special learning facilities include an art gallery, radio station, and a college history museum. **Physically Challenged Students:** 83% of the campus is accessible. Facilities include wheelchair ramps, elevators, special parking, specially equipped restrooms, and lowered drinking fountains. **Special:** Internships in all majors, study abroad in Germany and Japan, a Washington semester, and work-study programs are available. There are some dual majors, a general studies degree, a 3-2 engineering degree with the University of Wisconsin/Madison, a 2-2 1/2 nursing program with Bellin College of Nursing, and nondegree study. There is a freshman honors program and 10 departmental honors programs. **Visiting:** There are regularly scheduled orientations for prospective students, consisting of meetings with faculty and financial aid personnel, activities meetings, and a campus tour. There are guides for informal visits, visitors may sit in on classes, and stay overnight. To schedule a visit, contact the Admissions Office. **Campus Safety and Security:** Measures include security escort services. There are emergency telephones, lighted pathways/sidewalks, Foot patrol on weekends and evenings.

REQUIREMENTS: The SAT or ACT is required, with a minimum composite score of 950 on the SAT I or 19 on the ACT. Applicants must be graduates of an accredited secondary school or have the GED. An interview is recommended. Applications are accepted online via the college's web site. AP and CLEP credits are accepted. Important factors in the admissions decision are advanced placement or honors courses, leadership record, and evidence of special talent.

FINANCIAL AID: In a recent year, 100% of all full-time freshmen and 97% of continuing full-time students received some form of financial aid. 86% of all full-time freshmen and 90% of continuing full-time students received need-based aid. The average freshman award was $11,895. 30% of undergraduate students work part-time. Average annual earnings from campus work are $1000. The average financial indebtedness of a recent year graduate was $20,558. Lakeland is a member of CSS. The FAFSA and the college's own financial statement are required. The deadline for filing freshman financial aid applications for fall entry is July 1.

LAWRENCE UNIVERSITY   D-3
www.lawrence.edu

Appleton, WI 54911	**(920) 832-6500**
	(800) 227-0982
Fax: (920) 832-6782	**Email: excel@lawrence.edu**
Full-time: 656 men, 787 women	**Faculty:** 163; IIB, av$
Part-time: 29 men, 24 women	**Ph.D.s:** 96%
Graduate: n/av	**Student/Faculty:** 8 to 1
Year: trimesters	**Tuition:** $38,481
Room & Board: $7890	**Freshman Class:** 2422 applied, 1405 accepted, 326 enrolled
	CEEB CODE: 1398
Application Deadline: January 15	**HIGHLY COMPETITIVE**

Lawrence University, founded in 1847, is a private liberal arts institution with a conservatory of music. There is one undergraduate school. In addition to regional accreditation, Lawrence has baccalaureate program accreditation with NASM. The 84-acre campus is in an urban area 100 miles north of Milwaukee, 30 miles south of Green Bay. Including any residence halls, there are 58 buildings.

STUDENT LIFE: 69% of undergraduates are from out of state, mostly the Mid-West. Students are from 45 states, 35 foreign countries, and Canada. 75% are from public schools. 77% are White. 69% claim no religious affiliation. The average age of freshmen is 18; all undergraduates, 20. 12% do not continue beyond their first year; 76% remain to graduate.

FACULTY/CLASSROOMS: 62% of faculty are male; 38% are female. All teach and do research. No introductory courses are taught by graduate students. The average class size in an introductory lecture is 24; in a laboratory is 15; and in a regular course is 15.

PROGRAMS OF STUDY: Lawrence confers B.A., B.Mus., and B.A.-B.Mus degrees. Bachelor's degrees are awarded in AGRICULTURE (environmental studies), BIOLOGICAL SCIENCE (biochemistry and biology/biological science), COMMUNICATIONS AND THE ARTS (art history and appreciation, Chinese, classics, dramatic arts, English, French, German, Japanese, linguistics, music performance, music theory and composition, Russian, Spanish, and studio art), COMPUTER AND PHYSICAL SCIENCE (chemistry, computer science, geology, mathematics, and physics), EDUCATION (music education), SOCIAL SCIENCE (anthropology, cognitive science, East Asian studies, economics, gender studies, history, international studies, philosophy, political science/government, and psychology). Biology, music, physics, theatre, psychology and government are the strongest academically. Psychology, biology and English have the largest enrollments.

ACTIVITIES: 22% of men belong to 5 national fraternities; 18% of women belong to 3 national sororities. There are 100 groups on campus, including art, band, chess, choir, chorale, chorus, computers, dance, drama, environmental, ethnic, film, gay, honors, international, jazz band, literary magazine, musical theater, newspaper, opera, orchestra, pep band, photography, political, professional, radio and TV, religious, social, social service, student government, symphony, and yearbook. Popular campus events include Midwest Trivia Contest, International Cabaret, Mardis Gras, and Shack-a-thon.

SERVICES: Counseling and information services are available, as is tutoring in every subject. There is a reader service for the blind. The writing lab focuses on enhancing writing skills, as well as remedial writing.

REQUIREMENTS: Applicants should complete 16 high school academic credits. Lawrence requires an essay, reports from a teacher and counselor, and an audition for music majors. The school recommends an interview, and a portfolio for art majors. AP credits are accepted. Important factors in the admissions decision are advanced placement or honors courses, evidence of special talent, and extracurricular activities record.

ADMISSIONS: 58% of a recent year applicants were accepted. 74% of the current freshmen were in the top fifth of their class; 95% were in the top two fifths. There were 13 National Merit finalists. 13 freshmen graduated first in their class.

FINANCIAL AID: In a recent year, 95% of all full-time freshmen and 94% of continuing full-time students received some form of financial aid. 64% of all full-time freshmen and 58% of continuing full-time students received need-based aid. The average freshman award was $29,500. Need-based scholarships or need-based grants averaged $22,700 ($38,205 maximum); need-based self-help aid (loans and jobs) averaged $6,800 ($8,000 maximum); and other non-need-based awards and non-need-based scholarships averaged $11,817 ($38,205 maximum). 72% of undergraduate students work part-time. Average annual earnings from campus work are $1400. The average financial indebtedness of a recent year graduate was $25,673. Lawrence is a member of CSS. The FAFSA and the college's own financial statement are required. The priority date for freshman financial aid applications for fall entry is March 1.

MARIAN UNIVERSITY *(The complete profile is made available exclusively on our website, www.barronspac.com)*

MARQUETTE UNIVERSITY   **E-4**
www.marquette.edu

Milwaukee, WI 53201	**(414) 288-7302**
	(800) 222-6544
Fax: (414) 288-3764	Email: admissions@marquette.edu
Full-time: 3840 men, 4238 women	Faculty: 587; I, -$
Part-time: 168 men, 164 women	Ph.D.s: 88%
Graduate: 1570 men, 1765 women	Student/Faculty: 14 to 1
Year: semesters, summer session	Tuition: $35,930
Room & Board: $11,000	Freshman Class: 21755 applied, 14513 accepted, 1992 enrolled
SAT CR/M/W: 580/600/580 ACT: 27	CEEB CODE: 1448
Application Deadline: December 1	VERY COMPETITIVE+

Marquette University, established in 1881, is a private Roman Catholic Jesuit institution. Figures in the above capsule and in this profile are approximate. There are 8 undergraduate schools and 4 graduate schools. In addition to regional accreditation, Marquette has baccalaureate program accreditation with AACSB, ABET, ACEJMC, ADA, APTA, NCATE, ARCPA, ACS, and ACNM. The 100-acre campus is in an urban area in the heart of Milwaukee. Including any residence halls, there are 69 buildings.

STUDENT LIFE: 70% of undergraduates are from out of state, mostly the Midwest. Students are from 48 states, 44 foreign countries, and Canada. 59% are from public schools. 73% are White. 63% are Catholic; 14% Protestant. The average age of freshmen is 18; all undergraduates, 20. 11% do not continue beyond their first year; 78% remain to graduate. **Housing:** 4800 students can be accommodated in college housing, which includes single-sex and coed dorms and on-campus apartments. In addition, there are honors houses, specified majors, social justice, and multicultural floors. On-campus housing is guaranteed for the freshman year only and is available on a lottery system for upperclassmen. 54% of students live on campus; of those, 90% remain on campus on weekends. All students may keep cars.

FACULTY/CLASSROOMS: 56% of faculty are male; 44% are female. 78% teach undergraduates. No introductory courses are taught by graduate students.

PROGRAMS OF STUDY: Marquette confers B.A., B.S., B.S.N., B.S.B.E., B.S.C.E., B.S.C.M., B.S.C.O., B.S.E.E. and B.S.M.E. and B.S.N. degrees. Master's and Doctoral degrees are also awarded. Bachelor's degrees are awarded in BIOLOGICAL SCIENCE (biochemistry, biology/biological science, molecular biology, and physiology), BUSINESS (accounting, business administration and management, business economics, entrepreneurial studies, finance, human resources, international business management, management information systems, marketing/retailing/merchandising, operations management, organizational leadership and management, real estate, and supply chain management), COMMUNICATIONS AND THE ARTS (advertising, broadcasting, classical languages, classics, communications, dramatic arts, English, French, German, information technology, journalism, media arts, public relations, Spanish, theatre arts, and writing), COMPUTER AND PHYSICAL SCIENCE (chemistry, computer science, mathematics, physics, and statistics), EDUCATION (athletic training, education, and secondary education), ENGINEERING AND ENVIRONMENTAL DESIGN (bioengineering, biomedical engineering, civil engineering, computational sciences, computer engineering, construction engineering, electrical/electronics engineering, engineering, environmental engineering, and mechanical engineering), HEALTH PROFESSIONS (biomedical science, clinical science, exercise science, medical laboratory science, nursing, premedicine, and speech pathology/audiology), SOCIAL SCIENCE (anthropology, criminology, economics, history, interdisciplinary studies, international relations, peace studies, philosophy, political science/government, psychology, social science, sociology, and theological studies). Biomedical engineering, nursing, and premedicine are the strongest academically. Biomedical sciences, nursing, and accounting have the largest enrollments.

ACTIVITIES: 7% of men and 15% of women belong to 11 national fraternities; 14% of women belong to 13 national sororities. There are 270 groups on campus, including and recreational, art, band, cheerleading, chess, choir, chorale, chorus, community awareness, computers, dance, debate, drama, drill team, ethnic, film, gay, honors, international, jazz band, literary magazine, musical theater, newspaper, orchestra, pep band, photography, political, professional, radio and TV, religious, social, social service, student government, and symphony. Popular campus events include Student Organizational Fest, Winter Flurry and Hunger Clean Up. **Sports:** There are 7 intercollegiate sports for men and 7 for women, and 40 intramural sports for men and 40 for women. Facilities include 2 recreation centers and Valley Fields, an outdoor soccer, track, and football facility. **Graduates:** From July 1, 2013 to June 30, 2014, 1827 bachelor's degrees were awarded. The most popular majors were biomedical sciences (9%), nursing (6%), and psychology (5%). 183 companies recruited on campus in 2013-2014. In an average class, 59% graduate in 4 years or less, 77% graduate in 5 years or less, and 79% graduate in 6 years or less.

SERVICES: Counseling and information services are available, as is

tutoring in some subjects. There is a reader service for the blind. Book taping and note taking are available for the physically disabled. **Library/Resources:** The 2 libraries contain 1.7 million volumes, 1.7 million microform items, 19,560 audio/video tapes/CDs/DVDs, and subscribe to 46,685 periodicals including electronic. Computerized library services include interlibrary loans, database searching, Internet access, and Wi-Fi capability. Special learning facilities include an art gallery, radio station, and TV station. **Physically Challenged Students:** 90% of the campus is accessible. Facilities include wheelchair ramps, elevators, special parking, specially equipped restrooms, special class scheduling, lowered drinking fountains, lowered telephones, and special housing. **Special:** Marquette offers co-op programs in engineering, internships, study abroad in 16 countries, a Washington summer term, and work-study programs. Dual and student-designed majors, nondegree study, an accelerated degree program for pre-dental and pre-law students, and pass/fail options are available. Cross-registration is possible with Milwaukee Institute of Art and Design, and there is a 2-2 engineering program with Waukesha County Technical College. The Freshman Frontier Program offers academic support for selected freshmen who do not meet regular admission requirements but show potential for success. The Educational Opportunity Program affords students from minority groups and low-income families the opportunity to attend the school. There are 22 national honor societies, including Phi Beta Kappa, a freshman honors program, and 42 departmental honors programs. **Visiting:** There are regularly scheduled orientations for prospective students, including an agenda for visits that varies according to the specific program; open houses are available on scheduled weekends throughout the academic year. There are guides for informal visits, visitors may sit in on classes, and stay overnight. To schedule a visit, contact the Office of Undergraduate Admissions. **Campus Safety and Security:** Measures include 24-hour foot and vehicle patrol, emergency notification system, self-defense education, and security escort services. There are shuttle buses, emergency telephones, lighted pathways/sidewalks, controlled access to dorms/residences, and closed-circuit cameras in selected parking lots and buildings throughout the campus. Public Safety has bicycle patrols and the Milwaukee police conduct patrols on horseback. There is secure storage for bicycles in parking ramps, monitored by public safety using closed-circuit cameras.

REQUIREMENTS: Marquette requires either the ACT or the SAT test. Applicants must be graduates of an accredited secondary school with a recommended 18 credits, including 4 years of English, 3 each of social studies and math, 2 each of sciences and foreign language, and 4 of additional academic subjects. Most students rank in the upper quarter of their high school class. The GED is accepted, with a minimum score of 225. Applicants must demonstrate ability, preparation, and motivation. An interview is recommended. AP and CLEP credits are accepted. Important factors in the admissions decision are advanced placement or honors courses, recommendations by school officials, and leadership record. To graduate, students must complete a total of 126 to 135 credit hours and maintain a minimum GPA depending on major. The 36-credit-hour core of common studies includes 6 credit hours each of rhetoric, human nature and ethics, and theology, and 3 each of mathematical reasoning, individual and social behavior, science and nature, histories of cultures and societies, literature and performing arts, and diverse cultures. The total number of hours in the major varies. **Procedure:** Freshmen are admitted to all sessions. Entrance exams should be taken in the junior year and repeated early in the senior year if necessary. There is a deferred admissions plan. Applications should be filed by December 1 for fall entry. The fall 2014 application fee was $30. Notifications are sent January 31. 1784 applicants were on the 2014 waiting list; 796 were admitted. Applications are accepted on-line. **Transfer Students:** 149 transfer students enrolled in 2013-2014. Applicants for transfer must have a minimum GPA of 2.0; some programs require a higher average. The SAT or ACT is required if the applicant has completed fewer than 12 hours of college-level work. 30 of 126 credits required for the bachelor's degree must be completed at Marquette. **International Students:** There are 311 international students enrolled. The school actively recruits these students. Marquette requires success in final external secondary exams according to the student's country of education.

ADMISSIONS: 67% of the 2014-2015 applicants were accepted. The SAT scores for the 2014-2015 freshman class were: Critical Reading--7% below 500, 51% between 500 and 599, 34% between 600 and 699, and 8% between 700 and 800; Math--10% below 500, 36% between 500 and 599, 48% between 600 and 699, and 6% between 700 and 800; Writing--13% below 500, 47% between 500 and 599, 35% between 600 and 699, and 5% between 700 and 800. The ACT scores were 1% below 21, 11% between 21 and 23, 31% between 24 and 26, 23% between 27 and 28, and 34% above 28. 32% of the current freshmen were in the top fifth of their class; 56% were in the top two fifths. There were 5 National Merit finalists. 31 freshmen graduated first in their class. **Admissions Contact:** Jean Burke, Interim Dean of Admissions. E-Mail: *admissions@marquette.edu* Web: *www.marquette.edu*

FINANCIAL AID: In 2014-2015, 99% of all full-time freshmen and 99% of continuing full-time students received some form of financial aid. 53% of all full-time freshmen and 52% of continuing full-time students received need-based aid. The average freshman award was $23,935. Need-based scholarships or need-based grants averaged $7,545 ($33,130 maximum); need-based self-help aid (loans and jobs) averaged $4,852 ($10,700 maximum); non-need-based athletic scholarships averaged $25,295 ($47,938 maximum); and other non-need-based awards and non-need-based scholarships averaged $13,252. 45% of undergraduate students work part-time. Average annual earnings from campus work are $2000. The average financial indebtedness of the 2014 graduate was $35,211. Marquette is a member of CSS. The FAFSA is required. The priority date for freshman financial aid applications for fall entry is February 1.

MILWAUKEE INSTITUTE OF ART AND DESIGN (*The complete profile is made available exclusively on our website, www. barronspac.com*)

MILWAUKEE SCHOOL OF ENGINEERING E-4
www.msoe.edu

Milwaukee, WI 53202	**(414) 277-6762**
	(800) 332-6763
Fax: (414) 277-7475	**Email: mitchell@msoe.edu**
Full-time: 1705 men, 488 women	**Faculty:** 22; IIB, av$
Part-time: 160 men, 25 women	**Ph.D.s:** 80%
Graduate: 143 men, 43 women	**Student/Faculty:** 16 to 1
Year: quarters, summer session	**Tuition:** $31,920
Room & Board: $8028	**Freshman Class:** 2014 applied, 1147 accepted, 490 enrolled
SAT CR/M: 570/630 **ACT:** 27	**CEEB CODE:** 1476
Application Deadline: n/av	**VERY COMPETITIVE+**

Milwaukee School of Engineering, established in 1903, is a private university offering bachelor's and master's degrees in the areas of engineering, business, mathematics and nursing. There are 5 undergraduate schools and 2 graduate schools. In addition to regional accreditation, MSOE has baccalaureate program accreditation with ABET and ACCE. The 20-acre campus is in an urban area in Milwaukee, Wisconsin. Including any residence halls, there are 14 buildings.

STUDENT LIFE: 69% of undergraduates are from Wisconsin. Others are from 33 states, 27 foreign countries, and Canada. 80% are from public schools. 78% are White. The average age of freshmen is 19.47; all undergraduates, 22. 25% do not continue beyond their first year; 57% remain to graduate.

FACULTY/CLASSROOMS: 71% of faculty are male; 29% are female. 92% teach undergraduates, 2% do research, and 18% do both. No introductory courses are taught by graduate students. The average class size in an introductory lecture is 22; in a laboratory is 16; and in a regular course is 22.

PROGRAMS OF STUDY: MSOE confers B.A. and B.S. degrees. Master's degrees are also awarded. Bachelor's degrees are awarded in BIOLOGICAL SCIENCE (molecular biology), BUSINESS (business administration and management, international business management, management information systems, management science, and operations research), COMMUNICATIONS AND THE ARTS (technical and business writing), COMPUTER AND PHYSICAL SCI-ENCE (actuarial science and software engineering), ENGINEERING AND ENVIRONMENTAL DESIGN (architectural engineering, biomedical engineering, computer engineering, construction management, electrical/electronics engineering, engineering, engineering technology, industrial engineering, and mechanical engineering), HEALTH PROFESSIONS (nursing). Biomedical engineering and computer engineering are the strongest academically. Architectural, mechanical, and electrical engineering have the largest enrollments.

ACTIVITIES: 10% of men belong to 1 local and 3 national fraternities; 12% of women belong to 2 local and 1 national sororities. There are 72 groups on campus, including and ultimate frisbee, bowling, paintball, tae kwon do, cheerleading, chess, choir, computers, dance, drama, environmental, ethnic, gay, honors, international, jazz band, literary magazine, pep band, political, professional, radio and TV, religious, rugby, social, social service, student government, and symphony. Popular campus events include St. Patrick's Week, Greek Week and Sub-Zero Days.

SERVICES: Counseling and information services are available, as is tutoring in every subject. There is a reader service for the blind, and remedial math, reading, and writing. **Library/Resources:** The library contains 52,805 volumes, 80,654 microform items, and 2,451 audio/video tapes/CDs/DVDs, and subscribes to 101,951 periodicals including electronic. Computerized library services include interlibrary loans, database searching, Internet access, and Wi-Fi capability. Special learning facilities include an art gallery and radio station. **Physically Challenged Students:** 95% of the campus is accessible. Facilities include wheelchair ramps, elevators, special parking, specially equipped restrooms, special class scheduling, lowered drinking fountains, lowered telephones, and special housing. **Special:** MSOE offers internships in the student's discipline, study-abroad in France, Germany, India, and Czech Republic, on-campus work-study programs, and nondegree study. A number of dual degrees along with a 5-year freshman-to-master's degree in civil engineering, are available. There are 6 national honor societies and 5 departmental honors programs. **Visiting:** There are regularly scheduled orientations for prospective students, consisting of personal visits, Spring and Fall Open Houses, Accepted Student Days and Senior Visit Days. There are guides for informal visits, visitors may sit in on classes, and stay overnight. To schedule a visit, contact the Admission Office at (800) 332-6763. **Campus Safety and Security:** Measures include 24-hour foot and vehicle patrol and security escort services. There are shuttle buses, emergency telephones, lighted pathways/sidewalks, 24-hour security in residence halls.

REQUIREMENTS: The ACT is required. The SAT is recommended. Applicants must be graduates of an accredited secondary school, having completed 15 academic credits, including 4 units of English, 2 units each of science and math, and 1 unit each of social studies and history. More units in math, science, and English are strongly advised; 1 unit in computer science is recommended. The GED is accepted. An essay is required, and an interview is recommended. A GPA of 2.5 is required. AP and CLEP credits are accepted. Important factors in the admissions decision are advanced placement or honors courses, leadership record, and personality/intangible qualities.

ADMISSIONS: 57% of a recent year applicants were accepted. The SAT scores for the recent year freshman class were: Critical Reading--17% below 500, 53% between 500 and 599, 19% between 600 and 699, and 11% between 700 and 800; Math--8% below 500, 19% between 500 and 599, 58% between 600 and 699, and 15% between 700 and 800. The ACT scores were 3% below 21, 13% between 21 and 23, 29% between 24 and 26, 35% between 27 and 28, and 20% above 28.

FINANCIAL AID: In a recent year, 100% of all full-time freshmen and 98% of continuing full-time students received some form of financial aid. 81% of all full-time freshmen and 83% of continuing full-time students received need-based aid. The average freshman award was $23,772. Need-based scholarships or need-based grants averaged $21,207 ($42,738 maximum); need-based self-help aid (loans and jobs) averaged $2,886 ($9,000 maximum); other non-need-based awards and non-need-based scholarships averaged $12,170 ($31,920 maximum); and $7,930 from other forms of aid. 68% of undergraduate students work part-time. Average annual earnings from campus work are $1988. The average financial indebtedness

of a recent year graduate was $38,038. The FAFSA is required. The priority date for freshman financial aid applications for fall entry is March 15.

MOUNT MARY UNIVERSITY (*The complete profile is made available exclusively on our website, www.barronspac.com*)

NORTHLAND COLLEGE   B-1
www.northland.edu

Ashland, WI 54806	(715) 682-1224
	(800) 753-1840
Fax: (715) 682-1258	Email: admit@northland.edu
Full- and part-time: 750 men and women	Faculty: n/av
	Ph.D.s: 84%
Graduate: n/av	Student/Faculty: n/av
Year: varies, summer session	Tuition: $26,225
Room & Board: $7710	Freshman Class: n/av
SAT or ACT: required	CEEB CODE: 1561
Application Deadline: see profile	COMPETITIVE

Northland College, founded in 1892, is a private liberal arts institution affiliated with the United Church of Christ and offers undergraduate programs in the arts and sciences, business, education, health professions, and social sciences. There are 3 undergraduate schools. The figures in the above capsule and in this profile are approximate. The 100-acre campus is in a small town 70 miles east of Duluth, Minnesota. Including any residence halls, there are 20 buildings.

STUDENT LIFE: 65% of undergraduates are from out of state, mostly the Mid-West. Students are from 42 states, 7 foreign countries, and Canada. 90% are from public schools. 89% are white. The average age of freshmen is 20; all undergraduates, 21. 20% do not continue beyond their first year; 44% remain to graduate.

FACULTY/CLASSROOMS: 81% of faculty are male; 19% are female. All teach undergraduates. The average class size in an introductory lecture is 30; in a laboratory, 30; and in a regular course, 22.

PROGRAMS OF STUDY: Northland confers B.A. and B.S. degrees. Bachelor's degrees are awarded in AGRICULTURE (natural resource management), BIOLOGICAL SCIENCE (biology/biological science), BUSINESS (business administration and management and business economics), COMMUNICATIONS AND THE ARTS (creative writing, English, and fine arts), COMPUTER AND PHYSICAL SCIENCE (atmospheric sciences and meteorology, chemistry, earth science, information sciences and systems, and mathematics), EDUCATION (elementary education, middle school education, music education, and secondary education), ENGINEERING AND ENVIRONMENTAL DESIGN (environmental science), SOCIAL SCIENCE (history, parks and recreation management, peace studies, psychology, public administration, religion, and sociology). Biology, natural resources, and meteroloy are the strongest academically. Biology, natural resources, and outdoor education have the largest enrollments.

ACTIVITIES: 2% of men belong to 1 local and 1 national fraternities; 2% of women belong to 2 local sororities. There are 25 groups on campus, including art, band, cheerleading, choir, chorale, chorus, computers, drama, ethnic, gay, honors, international, jazz band, literary magazine, newspaper, orchestra, photography, political, professional, religious, social, social service, student government, symphony, and yearbook. Popular campus events include Snow Festival and Spring Fling.

SERVICES: Counseling and information services are available, as is tutoring in every subject. There is a reader service for the blind, and remedial math, reading, and writing. **Library/Resources:** The library contains 77,700 volumes, 9,300 microform items, and subscribes to 350 periodicals including electronic. Computerized library services include interlibrary loans and database searching. Special learning facilities include an art gallery, natural history museum, environmental research acreage, community garden, and wind tower. **Physically Challenged Students:** 90% of the campus is accessible. Facilities include wheelchair ramps, elevators, special parking, specially equipped restrooms, and special class scheduling. **Special:** Opportunities are provided for cooperative programs in many majors and with other schools, internships, work-study programs with state and federal agencies, student-designed majors, credit for life experience, pass/fail options, and study abroad in 7 countries. Cross-registration is offered with Spring Term Consortium Schools, Allegheny and Beloit Colleges, and Kansai Gaidai University in Japan. 3-2 engineering degrees are available in conjunction with Michigan Technological University and Washington University in St. Louis. A 3-2 degree program in forestry is also available. There are 2 national honor societies. **Visiting:** There are regularly scheduled orientations for prospective students, including an interview, a tour, class visits, and an overnight stay in a dorm. There are guides for informal visits, visitors may sit in on classes, and stay overnight. To schedule a visit, contact the Admissions Office. **Campus Safety and Security:** Measures include security escort services. There are emergency telephones and lighted pathways/sidewalks.

REQUIREMENTS: The SAT or ACT is required. In addition, graduation from an accredited secondary school is required; the GED is accepted. An essay and interview are recommended. A GPA of 2.0 is required. AP and CLEP credits are accepted. Important factors in the admissions decision are advanced placement or honors courses, extracurricular activities record, and recommendations by school officials.

FINANCIAL AID: Northland is a member of CSS. The FAFSA and the college's own financial statement are required. Check with the school for current financial aid deadlines.

RIPON COLLEGE D-4
www.ripon.edu

Ripon, WI 54971	(920) 748-8185
	(800) 94-RIPON
Fax: (920) 748-8335	Email: schuetz@ripon.edu
Full-time: 508 men, 546 women	Faculty: 64; IIB, -$
Part-time: 4 men, 7 women	Ph.D.s: 75%
Graduate: n/av	Student/Faculty: 15 to 1
Year: semesters	Tuition: $28,689
Room & Board: $8270	Freshman Class: 1160 applied, 899 accepted, 289 enrolled
SAT CR/M: 500/528 ACT: 24	CEEB CODE: 1664
Application Deadline: August 1	COMPETITIVE+

Ripon College, established in 1851, is a private, residential, liberal arts institution. The 250-acre campus is in a small town 80 miles north of Milwaukee in the east-central part of the state. Including any residence halls, there are 26 buildings.

STUDENT LIFE: 74% of undergraduates are from Wisconsin. Others are from 31 states, 18 foreign countries, and Canada. 60% are from public schools. 86% are White. The average age of freshmen is 18; all undergraduates, 20. 15% do not continue beyond their first year; 76% remain to graduate. **Housing:** 1056 students can be accommodated in college housing, which includes single-sex and coed dorms and on-campus apartments. Theme and interest groups may form living areas in the residence halls. On-campus housing is guaranteed for all 4 years and is available on a lottery system for upperclassmen. 90% of students live on campus; of those, 80% remain on campus on weekends. All students may keep cars.

FACULTY/CLASSROOMS: 58% of faculty are male; 42% are female. All teach and do research. No introductory courses are taught by graduate students. The average class size in an introductory lecture is 25; in a laboratory is 15; and in a regular course is 19.

PROGRAMS OF STUDY: confers A.B. degrees. Bachelor's degrees are awarded in BIOLOGICAL SCIENCE (biochemistry and biology/biological science), BUSINESS (business administration and management), COMMUNICATIONS AND THE ARTS (art, art history and appreciation, communications, dramatic arts, English, French, German, music, and Spanish), COMPUTER AND PHYSICAL SCIENCE (chemistry, computer science, mathematics, physical sciences, and physics), EDUCATION (early childhood education, elementary education, middle school education, and secondary education), ENGINEERING AND ENVIRONMENTAL DESIGN (environmental

science), HEALTH PROFESSIONS (exercise science), SOCIAL SCIENCE (anthropology, economics, history, international studies, Latin American studies, philosophy, political science/government, psychobiology, psychology, religion, and sociology). Sciences, and education are the strongest academically. Business, biology, and history have the largest enrollments.

ACTIVITIES: 34% of men belong to 2 local and 3 national fraternities; 28% of women belong to 1 local and 3 national sororities. There are 80 groups on campus, including art, band, cheerleading, choir, chorale, chorus, dance, drama, environmental, ethnic, film, forensics, gay, honors, international, jazz band, literary magazine, musical theater, newspaper, orchestra, pep band, photography, political, professional, radio and TV, religious, social, social service, student government, symphony, and yearbook. Popular campus events include Spring and Winter Festivals, Milwaukee Symphony Concerts, and Theater Events. **Sports:** There are 10 intercollegiate sports for men and 11 for women, and 12 intramural sports for men and 12 for women. Facilities include a phys ed center, 2 fields, tennis courts, a recreation center, and an exercise room and a fitness center in the residence halls. The campus is within 5 miles of lakes and cross-country skiing opportunities. **Graduates:** From July 1, 2013 to June 30, 2014, 213 bachelor's degrees were awarded. The most popular majors were business (16%), psychology (12%), and English (11%). 14 companies recruited on campus in 2013-2014. In an average class, 1% graduate in 3 years or less, 60% graduate in 4 years or less, 76% graduate in 5 years or less, and 76% graduate in 6 years or less. Of the 2013 graduating class, 34% were enrolled in graduate school within 6 months of graduation, and 64% were employed.

SERVICES: Counseling and information services are available, as is tutoring in most subjects. Tutoring and services are also available for learning-disabled students. **Library/Resources:** The library contains 183,000 volumes, 10,000 microform items, 600 audio/video tapes/CDs/DVDs, and subscribes to 300 periodicals including electronic. Computerized library services include interlibrary loans, database searching, Internet access, and Wi-Fi capability. Special learning facilities include an art gallery, radio station, a music library, an art slide library, and college archives. **Physically Challenged Students:** 50% of the campus is accessible. Facilities include wheelchair ramps, elevators, special parking, specially equipped restrooms, special class scheduling, and lowered drinking fountains. **Special:** Students may cross-register with the Associated Colleges of the Midwest. Internships, study abroad in 13 countries, through 7 domestic programs, and a Washington semester are available. The college offers 3-year degrees in all areas, dual and student-designed majors, and pass/fail options. A 3-2 engineering degree is available with Rensselaer Polytechnic Institute, Washington University, and the University of Madison; other 3-2 programs are in environmental studies and in forestry with Duke University. There are 12 national honor societies, including Phi Beta Kappa, and a freshman honors program. **Visiting:** There are regularly scheduled orientations for prospective students, including a tour, an interview, and meetings with professors and coaches. There are guides for informal visits and visitors may sit in on classes. To schedule a visit, contact the Admission Office. **Campus Safety and Security:** Measures include 24-hour foot and vehicle patrol and security escort services. There are emergency telephones, lighted pathways/sidewalks, and a paging system.

REQUIREMENTS: The SAT or ACT is required. Applicants must be graduates of an accredited secondary school. The GED is accepted. Applicants should complete at least 17 Carnegie units, including 4 of English, 2 to 4 each of math, social studies, and natural sciences, and up to 7 of other college-preparatory electives. An essay may be required, and an interview is recommended. Ripon requires applicants to be in the upper 50% of their class. AP and CLEP credits are accepted. Important factors in the admissions decision are leadership record, recommendations by school officials, and advanced placement or honors courses. To graduate, students must complete 124 credit hours, including usually 24 in the major, with a minimum GPA of 2.0. Required courses include 1 course each in fine arts, humanities, natural sciences, and social and behavioral sciences, a first-year seminar, a first-year writing course, 1 phys ed course, and a capstone experience. **Procedure:** Freshmen are admitted fall and spring. Entrance exams should be taken in the junior year or the fall of the senior year. There are deferred admissions and rolling admissions plans. Applications should be filed by August 1 for fall entry; December 15 for spring entry, along with a $30 fee. Notification is sent on a rolling basis. Applications are accepted on-line. **Transfer Students:** 16 transfer students enrolled in 2013-2014. Applicants must have a minimum 2.0 GPA and be in good standing at their previous college. The SAT or ACT, a personal statement, and an interview are recommended. 32 of 124 credits required for the bachelor's degree must be completed at Ripon. **International Students:** There are 31 international students enrolled. The school actively recruits these students. They must take the TOEFL with a minimum score of 550 on the paper-based TOEFL (PBT) or 79 on the Internet-based version (iBT). They must also take the SAT.

ADMISSIONS: 78% of the 2014-2015 applicants were accepted. The SAT scores for the 2014-2015 freshman class were: Critical Reading--53% below 500, 35% between 500 and 599, 9% between 600 and 699, and 3% between 700 and 800; Math--36% below 500, 38% between 500 and 599, 23% between 600 and 699, and 3% between 700 and 800. The ACT scores were 19% below 21, 29% between 21 and 23, 28% between 24 and 26, 14% between 27 and 28, and 10% above 28. 48% of the current freshmen were in the top fifth of their class; 80% were in the top two fifths. 14 freshmen graduated first in their class. **Admissions Contact:** Steven M. Schuetz, Vice President for Admissions and Financial Aid. E-Mail: *schuetz@ripon.edu* Web: *www.ripon.edu*

FINANCIAL AID: In 2014-2015, 96% of all full-time freshmen and 90% of continuing full-time students received some form of financial aid. 86% of all full-time freshmen and 83% of continuing full-time students received need-based aid. The average freshman award was $28,771. Need-based scholarships or need-based grants averaged $20,300 ($33,736 maximum); need-based self-help aid (loans and jobs) averaged $5,364 ($8,800 maximum); and other non-need-based awards and non-need-based scholarships averaged $14,703 ($33,500 maximum). 45% of undergraduate students work part-time. Average annual earnings from campus work are $1877. The average financial indebtedness of the 2014 graduate was $24,795. The FAFSA is required. The priority date for freshman financial aid applications for fall entry is March 1.

SILVER LAKE COLLEGE *(The complete profile is made available exclusively on our website, www.barronspac.com)*

ST. NORBERT COLLEGE   **D-3**
www.snc.edu

De Pere, WI 54115	(920) 403-3005
	(800) 236-4878
Fax: (920) 403-4072	Email: admit@snc.edu
Full-time: 879 men, 1166 women	Faculty: 133; IIB, av$
Part-time: 30 men, 37 women	Ph.D.s: 89%
Graduate: 23 men, 31 women	Student/Faculty: 14 to 1
Year: semesters, summer session	Tuition: $33,023
Room & Board: $8455	Freshman Class: 2149 applied, 1756 accepted, 536 enrolled
ACT: 25	CEEB CODE: 1706
Application Deadline: open	VERY COMPETITIVE

St. Norbert College, an liberal arts college that teaches critical thinking, problem-solving and leadership skills. There are 3 graduate schools. The 111-acre campus is in a suburban area 5 miles south of Green Bay. Including any residence halls, there are 44 buildings. **STUDENT LIFE:** 75% of undergraduates are from Wisconsin. Others are from 29 states, 16 foreign countries, and Canada. 74% are from public schools. 89% are White. 47% are Catholic; 35% Protestant; 17% claim no religious affiliation. The average age of freshmen is 18; all undergraduates, 20. 16% do not continue beyond their first year; 74% remain to graduate. **Housing:** 1801 students can be accommodated in college housing, which includes single-sex and coed dorms and on-campus apartments. In addition, there are special-interest houses, a townhouse complex, a living center, and off-campus houses. On-campus housing is guaranteed for all 4 years. 82% of students live on campus; of those, 80% remain on campus on weekends. All students may keep cars.

FACULTY/CLASSROOMS: 56% of faculty are male; 44% are female. All teach undergraduates. No introductory courses are taught by graduate students. The average class size in an introductory lecture is 20 and in a regular course is 20.

PROGRAMS OF STUDY: St. Norbert confers B.A., B.B.A., B.Mus. and B.S. degrees. Master's degrees are also awarded. Bachelor's degrees are awarded in BIOLOGICAL SCIENCE (biology/biological science), BUSINESS (accounting, business administration and management, and international business management), COMMUNICATIONS AND THE ARTS (art, communications, English, French, German, graphic design, music, Spanish, and theatre arts), COMPUTER AND PHYSICAL SCIENCE (chemistry, computer science, geology, mathematics, natural sciences, and physics), EDUCATION (elementary education and music education), ENGINEERING AND ENVIRONMENTAL DESIGN (commercial art and environmental science), SOCIAL SCIENCE (economics, history, humanities, international relations, philosophy, political science/government, psychology, religion, and sociology). Business administration, communications, and elementary education have the largest enrollments.

ACTIVITIES: 13% of men belong to 4 national fraternities; 10% of women belong to 4 national sororities. There are 70 groups on campus, including art, band, cheerleading, chess, choir, chorale, chorus, computers, dance, drama, environmental, ethnic, film, gay, honors, international, jazz band, literary magazine, musical theater, newspaper, opera, pep band, photography, political, professional, radio and TV, religious, social, social service, and student government. Popular campus events include Opening Campus Picnic/convocation, E2K Homecoming and SNC Day. **Sports:** There are 10 intercollegiate sports for men and 10 for women, and 6 intramural sports for men and 6 for women. Facilities include a 3,100-seat stadium, a sports complex, an 1,800-seat sports center, and an activity center. **Graduates:** From July 1, 2013 to June 30, 2014, 496 bachelor's degrees were awarded. The most popular majors were business administration (15%), elementary education (12%), and biology/biological sciences (9%). 219 companies recruited on campus in 2013-2014. In an average class, 69% graduate in 4 years or less, 74% graduate in 5 years or less, and 74% graduate in 6 years or less. Of the 2013 graduating class, 12% were enrolled in graduate school within 6 months of graduation, and 83% were employed.

SERVICES: Counseling and information services are available, as is tutoring in most subjects. There is a reader service for the blind, remedial math, reading, and writing. **Library/Resources:** The library contains 243,771 volumes, 16,074 microform items, 2,902 audio/video tapes/CDs/DVDs, and subscribes to 97,301 periodicals including electronic. Computerized library services include interlibrary loans, database searching, Internet access, and Wi-Fi capability. Special learning facilities include an art gallery, radio station, TV station, innovation studio, center for women's and gender studies, center for peace, justice and public understanding, marina, fine and performing arts centers, center for international education, center for leadership and service, children's center, center for Norbertine studies; language labs, media center with satellite hookup, and environmental sciences research craft. **Physically Challenged Students:** 78% of the campus is accessible. Facilities include wheelchair ramps, elevators, special parking, specially equipped restrooms, special class scheduling, lowered drinking fountains, lowered telephones, and special housing. **Special:** A partnership program with Bellin College Nursing, cross-registration in Arabic courses with the University of Wisconsin-Green Bay, internships, study abroad in 29 countries, a Washington semester, and work-study programs are available. The college offers dual and student-designed majors, B.A.-B.S. degrees, nondegree study, and limited credit for military experience and work training. The Leadership and Service Program and leadership minor help students improve their leadership abilities through courses and activities. A 3-2 engineering degree is available with Michigan Tech University. A Masters of Science in Applied Economics (MSAE) degree preparation agreement with Marquette University is available. There are 8 national honor societies and a freshman honors program. **Visiting:** There are regularly scheduled orientations for prospective students, including preregistrations, meetings with advisers, and meetings regarding programming and activities, housing, and student life. There are guides for informal visits, visitors may sit in on classes, and stay overnight. To schedule a visit, contact the Office of Admissions. **Campus Safety and Security:** Measures include 24-hour foot and vehicle patrol, emergency notification system, self-defense education, and security escort services. There are emergency telephones, lighted pathways/sidewalks, controlled access to dorms/residences, motorist assistance, and a crime prevention program.

REQUIREMENTS: The ACT is required. Admissions requirements are either graduation from an accredited secondary school with 16 units recommended, including 4 English, 3 math, 3 lab sciences, 2 foreign language 2 social studies, 2 history, or a GED recommended score in the 55% range. AP and CLEP credits are accepted. Important factors in the admissions decision are advanced placement or honors courses, extracurricular activities record, and recommendations by school officials. To graduate, students must complete 128 credits with at least a 2.0 GPA and a minimum of 40 semester credits in a particular major and a major GPA of at least a 2.0. There are general education requirements in the areas of religious studies, human nature, human relationships, natural science, creative expression, U.S. heritage, foreign heritages, foreign language, quantitative skills, Western tradition, global society, a writing-intensive course, and Senior Colloquium. **Procedure:** Freshmen are admitted to all sessions. Entrance exams should be taken by the end of the junior year. There are deferred admissions and rolling admissions plans. Application deadlines are open. Application fee is $10. Notification of early decision is sent December 15; regular decision, on a rolling basis. Applications are accepted on-line. **Transfer Students:** 44 transfer students enrolled in 2013-2014. Applicants should have a minimum GPA of 2.5. At least their senior year and 25% of their major credits must be taken at St. Norbert. 32 of 128 credits required for the bachelor's degree must be completed at St. Norbert. **International Students:** There are 65 international students enrolled. The school actively recruits these students. They must take the TOEFL with a minimum score of 555 on the paper-based TOEFL (PBT) or 80 on the Internet-based version (iBT). They must also take the SAT or ACT.

ADMISSIONS: 82% of the 2014-2015 applicants were accepted. The ACT scores were 11% below 21, 28% between 21 and 23, 28% between 24 and 26, 17% between 27 and 28, and 15% above 28. 51% of the current freshmen were in the top fifth of their class; 78% were in the top two fifths. 18 freshmen graduated first in their class. **Admissions Contact:** Edward Lamm, V.P. of Enrollment Management & Communication. E-Mail: *admit@snc.edu* Web: *www.snc.edu/admission*

FINANCIAL AID: In 2014-2015, 99% of all full-time freshmen and continuing full-time students received some form of financial aid. 75% of all full-time freshmen and 71% of continuing full-time students received need-based aid. The average freshman award was $23,401. The average financial indebtedness of the 2014 graduate was $31,438. The FAFSA is required. The priority date for freshman financial aid applications for fall entry is March 1.

UNIVERSITY OF WISCONSIN SYSTEM

The University of Wisconsin System, established in 1971, is a public system in Wisconsin. It is governed by an 18-member appointed board of regents, whose chief administrator is president. The primary goal of the system is teaching, research, and public service. The main priorities are to develop human resources; to discover and disseminate knowledge; and to extend knowledge and its application. The total student enrollment of all 26 campuses is usually 181,000 with 11,500 faculty members. Altogether there are 700 baccalaureate, 329 master's, and 149 doctoral programs offered in the University of Wisconsin System. Profiles of the 4-year campuses are included in this section.

UNIVERSITY OF WISCONSIN/EAU CLAIRE   B-3
www.uwec.edu

Eau Claire, WI 54701

(715) 836-5415
(888) INFO-UWE

Fax: (715) 836-2409
Email: admissions@uwec.edu

Full-time: 3771 men, 5433 women	Faculty: 439
Part-time: 354 men, 606 women	Ph.D.s: 81%
Graduate: 189 men, 336 women	Student/Faculty: 21 to 1
Year: semesters, summer session	Tuition: $8744 ($16,317)
Room & Board: $6986	Freshman Class: 5441 applied, 4552 accepted, 2020 enrolled
ACT: 24 SAT: recommended	CEEB CODE: 1913
Application Deadline: n/av	VERY COMPETITIVE

The University of Wisconsin/Eau Claire fosters in one another creativity, critical insight, empathy, and intellectual courage, the hallmarks of a transformative liberal education and the foundation for active citizenship and lifelong inquiry. There are 4 undergraduate schools. In addition to regional accreditation, UW-Eau Claire has baccalaureate program accreditation with AACSB, ABET, ACEJMC, CSWE, and NASM. The 337-acre campus is in an urban area 95 miles east of Minneapolis, Minnesota. Including any residence halls, there are 28 buildings.

STUDENT LIFE: 72% of undergraduates are from Wisconsin. Others are from 42 states, 36 foreign countries, and Canada. 89% are White. The average age of freshmen is 18; all undergraduates, 21. 17% do not continue beyond their first year; 83% remain to graduate. **Housing:** 3924 students can be accommodated in college housing, which includes single-sex and coed dorms and on-campus apartments. In addition, there are special-interest houses, theme housing, and wellness housing. On-campus housing is available on a first-come, first-served basis and is available on a lottery system for upperclassmen. 62% of students commute. All students may keep cars.

FACULTY/CLASSROOMS: 48% of faculty are male; 52% are female. All teach undergraduates. No introductory courses are taught by graduate students. The average class size in an introductory lecture is 31 and in a laboratory is 20.

PROGRAMS OF STUDY: UW-Eau Claire confers B.A., B.S., B.B.A., B.F.A., B.L.S., B.P.S., B.M., B.M.E., B.S.E.Ph., B.S.N. and B.S.W. degrees. Associate, Master's, and Doctoral degrees are also awarded. Bachelor's degrees are awarded in BIOLOGICAL SCIENCE (biochemistry and biology/biological science), BUSINESS (accounting, banking and finance, business administration and management, international business, marketing, and organizational leadership and management), COMMUNICATIONS AND THE ARTS (art, communications, English, French, German, journalism, music, Spanish, and theatre arts), COMPUTER AND PHYSICAL SCIENCE (chemistry, computer science, geology, information sciences and systems, mathematics, physical sciences, and physics), EDUCATION (athletic training, elementary education, physical education, science education, and special education), ENGINEERING AND ENVIRONMENTAL DESIGN (materials science), HEALTH PROFESSIONS (health care administration, nursing, predentistry, premedicine, preoptometry, prepharmacy, prephysical therapy, preveterinary science, and public health), SOCIAL SCIENCE (American Indian studies, communication sciences & disorders, criminal justice, economics, geography, history, Latin American studies, liberal arts/general studies, philosophy, political science/government, prelaw, psychology, religious studies, social studies, social work, sociology, and women's studies). Nursing, biology, and kinesiology have the largest enrollments.

ACTIVITIES: 1% of men belong to 3 local fraternities; 1% of women belong to 3 local sororities. There are 270 groups on campus, including art, band, cheerleading, chess, choir, chorale, chorus, communications, computers, dance, debate, drama, environmental, ethnic, film, forensics, gay, honors, international, jazz band, literary magazine, marching band, musical theater, newspaper, opera, orchestra, pep band, photography, political, professional, radio and TV, religious, social, social service, student government, and symphony. Popular campus events include Winter Carnival, Homecoming and

Blugold Organizations Bash. **Sports:** There are 9 intercollegiate sports for men and 11 for women. Facilities include a gym, pool, 30 acres of intramural and recreation fields, game room, bowling and billiards, Nautilus fitness center, racquetball courts, weight room, ropes course, 3212-seat stadium, tennis courts, and a climbing wall. **Graduates:** From July 1, 2013 to June 30, 2014, 2104 bachelor's degrees were awarded. The most popular majors were marketing (23%), health professionals (13%), and education (7%). In an average class, 30% graduate in 4 years or less, 62% graduate in 5 years or less, and 69% graduate in 6 years or less.

SERVICES: Counseling and information services are available, as is tutoring in some subjects. There is a reader service for the blind, and remedial math, reading, and writing. **Library/Resources:** The library contains 1.0 million volumes, 321,274 microform items, 28,723 audio/video tapes/CDs/DVDs, and subscribes to 63,825 periodicals including electronic. Computerized library services include interlibrary loans, database searching, Internet access, and Wi-Fi capability. Special learning facilities include an art gallery, planetarium, radio station, TV station, a human development center, natural preserve, ropes course, materials science center, college of nursing and health sciences clinical simulation/skills lab. **Physically Challenged Students:** 90% of the campus is accessible. Facilities include wheelchair ramps, elevators, special parking, specially equipped restrooms, special class scheduling, lowered drinking fountains, lowered telephones, special housing. **Special:** Numerous internships, work-study programs, and study abroad in 26 countries are offered. Dual majors and interdisciplinary majors are possible. Credit by examination, non-degree study, and pass/fail options are offered. There are 29 national honor societies, a freshman honors program, and 21 departmental honors programs. **Visiting:** There are regularly scheduled orientations for prospective students, during which students meet with academic advisers, develop a class schedule, register for classes, and tour the campus. There are guides for informal visits and visitors may sit in on classes. To schedule a visit, contact the Admissions Office at admissions@uwec.edu. **Campus Safety and Security:** Measures include 24-hour foot and vehicle patrol, emergency notification system, and self-defense education. There are shuttle buses, emergency telephones, lighted pathways/sidewalks, and controlled access to dorms/residences.

REQUIREMENTS: The ACT is required. The SAT is recommended. Applicants should graduate from an accredited secondary school or present its equivalent, with 17 academic credits including 4 in English, 3 each in social studies, college prep math, and science and 2 years of a single foreign language. Each application is given a comprehensive review. In addition to a rigorous curriculum, academic factors include: class rank, GPA, trends in grades, and test scores. Secondary non-academic factors include: leadership, service, achievement in arts, athletics, and diversity in personal background and experience. AP and CLEP credits are accepted. Important factors in the admissions decision are advanced placement or honors courses, extracurricular activities record, and evidence of special talent. All students must complete 39 hours in general education, including 9-15 each in social sciences, humanities, and natural sciences, and 6 in communications/math. All students must also meet the writing requirement, take 2 credits in wellness, complete a minimum of 3 credits that contain significant content dealing with race and ethnicity, and must complete 30 or more hours of service-learning. A minimum 2.0 GPA and 120 credit hours are required to graduate. **Procedure:** Freshmen are admitted fall, winter, spring, and summer. Entrance exams should be taken by December of the senior year. There are early admissions and rolling admissions plans. Application deadlines are open. The fall 2014 application fee was $44. 400 applicants were on the 2014 waiting list; 200 were admitted. Applications are accepted on-line. **Transfer Students:** 546 transfer students enrolled in 2013-2014. Transfer applicants must carry a minimum 2.0 GPA. Preference is given to transfers who have completed the equivalent of freshman composition and college algebra. Students with less than 30 semester credits must meet the freshman admissions requirements. 30 of 120 credits required for the bachelor's degree must be completed at UW-Eau Claire. **International Students:** There are 263 international students enrolled. The school actively recruits these students. They must take the TOEFL with a minimum score of 550 on the paper-based TOEFL (PBT) or 79 on the Internet-based version (iBT). They must also take the SAT or ACT.

ADMISSIONS: 84% of the 2014-2015 applicants were accepted. The SAT scores for the 2014-2015 freshman class were: Critical Reading--23% below 500, 59% between 500 and 599, and 18% between 600 and 699; Math--29% below 500, 29% between 500 and 599, 35% between 600 and 699, and 6% between 700 and 800. The ACT scores were 12% below 21, 35% between 21 and 23, 32% between 24 and 26, 11% between 27 and 28, and 10% above 28. There were 3 National Merit finalists. 47 freshmen graduated first in their class. **Admissions Contact:** Heather Kretz, Director of Admissions. E-Mail: *admissions@uwec.edu* Web: *www.uwec.edu*

FINANCIAL AID: In 2014-2015, 80% of all full-time freshmen and 70% of continuing full-time students received some form of financial aid. 53% of all full-time freshmen and 51% of continuing full-time students received need-based aid. The average freshman award was $82,310. Need-based scholarships or need-based grants averaged $5,565; need-based self-help aid (loans and jobs) averaged $5,240; and other non-need-based awards and non-need-based scholarships averaged $6,254. 35% of undergraduate students work part-time. Average annual earnings from campus work are $2257. The average financial indebtedness of the 2014 graduate was $23,515. The FAFSA is required. The deadline for filing freshman financial aid applications for fall entry is April 15.

UNIVERSITY OF WISCONSIN/GREEN BAY   D-3
www.uwgb.edu

Green Bay, WI 54311

(920) 465-2111

Fax: (920) 465-2765	Email: admissions@uwgb.edu
Full-time: 1528 men, 2679 women	Faculty: 189
Part-time: 771 men, 1690 women	Ph.D.s: 84%
Graduate: 88 men, 165 women	Student/Faculty: 23 to 1
Year: semesters, summer session	Tuition: $7758 ($15,331)
Room & Board: $7224	Freshman Class: 2014 applied, 1699 accepted, 770 enrolled
ACT: 23	CEEB CODE: 1859
Application Deadline: January 1	COMPETITIVE

The University of Wisconsin/Green Bay, founded in 1968, is a public institution offering programs in humanities and fine arts, natural sciences, social sciences, business, education, health, and pre-professional areas. There are 2 undergraduate schools and 1 graduate school. In addition to regional accreditation, UW-Green Bay has baccalaureate program accreditation with ADA, CSWE, NASM, and NLN. The 700-acre campus is in a suburban area 111 miles north of Milwaukee. Including any residence halls, there are 49 buildings.

STUDENT LIFE: 93% of undergraduates are from Wisconsin. Others are from 39 states, 31 foreign countries, and Canada. 95% are from public schools. 86% are White. 40% are Catholic; 40% Protestant; 15% claim no religious affiliation. The average age of freshmen is 18; all undergraduates, 24. 22% do not continue beyond their first year; 51% remain to graduate. **Housing:** 2000 students can be accommodated in college housing, which includes coed dorms and on-campus apartments. In addition, there are special-interest houses, and 3-, 4-, and 5-person dorm suites with private bedrooms. On-campus housing is available on a first-come, first-served basis, and is available on a lottery system for upperclassmen. 71% of students commute. All students may keep cars.

FACULTY/CLASSROOMS: 48% of faculty are male; 52% are female. All teach undergraduates, 85% do research, and 85% do both. No introductory courses are taught by graduate students. The average class size in an introductory lecture is 45; in a laboratory is 20; and in a regular course is 25.

PROGRAMS OF STUDY: UW-Green Bay confers B.A., B.S., B.A.S., B.B.A., B.M., B.S.N. and B.S.W. degrees. Associate and Master's degrees are also awarded. Bachelor's degrees are awarded in AGRICULTURE (environmental studies), BIOLOGICAL SCIENCE (biology/biological science), BUSINESS (accounting, business administration and management, finance, human resources, and sustainable management), COMMUNICATIONS AND THE ARTS (art, arts administration/management, communications, creative writing, design, dramatic arts, English, English as a second/foreign language, fine arts, French, German, Germanic languages and literature, music, Spanish, and theatre arts), COMPUTER AND PHYSICAL SCIENCE (chemistry, computer science, earth science, geoscience, information sciences and systems, and mathematics), EDUCATION (art education, education, elementary education, English education, foreign languages education, health information management, mathematics education, middle school education, music education, and secondary education), ENGINEERING AND ENVIRONMENTAL DESIGN (city/community/regional planning, electrical/electronics engineering technology, engineering technology, environmental engineering technology, environmental science, and mechanical engineering technology), HEALTH PROFESSIONS (exercise science and nursing), SOCIAL SCIENCE (American Indian studies, dietetics, economics, French studies, gender studies, history, human development, humanities, interdisciplinary studies, liberal arts/general studies, philosophy, political science/government, psychology, public administration, social work, urban studies, and women's studies). Education, environmental science, human biology, psychology, and accounting are the strongest academically. Business, human biology, and human development have the largest enrollments.

ACTIVITIES: 1% of men belong to 1 national fraternity; 1% of women belong to 2 national sororities. There are 112 groups on campus, including art, band, cheerleading, choir, chorale, chorus, computers, dance, drama, drill team, environmental, ethnic, film, gay, honors, international, jazz band, literary magazine, musical theater, newspaper, orchestra, pep band, photography, political, professional, radio and TV, religious, social, social service, and student government. Popular campus events include Frost Fest, GB Week, and Pow Wow. **Sports:** There are 7 intercollegiate sports for men and 9 for women, and 7 intramural sports for men and 7 for women. Facilities include a sports center with a 5000-seat arena for campus-wide ceremonies, concerts and events, auxiliary courts (basketball practice, student recreation), elevated running track, 28-foot climbing tower, two weight areas with Magnum machines and free weights, group aerobics/fitness studio (cardio deck with stationary bikes, stairclimbers, elliptical machines, treadmills, video monitors), indoor turf gym, pool, offices and team rooms for Green Bay Phoenix athletics. **Graduates:** From July 1, 2013 to June 30, 2014, 1206 bachelor's degrees were awarded. The most popular majors were business administration (15%), interdisciplinary studies (13%), and psychology (9%). 60 companies recruited on campus in 2013-2014. In an average class, 1% graduate in 3 years or less, 20% graduate in 4 years or less, 45% graduate in 5 years or less, and 50% graduate in 6 years or less. Of the 2013 graduating class, 25% were enrolled in graduate school within 6 months of graduation, and 85% were employed.

SERVICES: Counseling and information services are available, as is tutoring in most subjects. There is a reader service for the blind, remedial math, reading, and writing. There is an academic support office, language and writing centers, student health services, and individual counseling. Available equipment includes a visual enlarger, automatic page turner, accessible computer station with attached voice syntheizer, slow speed cassette recorders, and a TDD device. Note takers, typists, readers, and aids are available for students. **Library/Resources:** The library contains 366,860 volumes, 1.4 million microform items, 47,943 audio/video tapes/CDs/DVDs, and subscribes to 3,234 periodicals including electronic. Computerized library services include interlibrary loans, database searching, Internet access, and Wi-Fi capability. Special learning facilities include an art gallery, natural history museum, radio station, TV station, a 270-acre arboretum, and a regional performing arts center. **Physically Challenged Students:** All of the campus is accessible. Facilities include wheelchair ramps, elevators, special parking, specially equipped restrooms, lowered drinking fountains, lowered telephones, and automatic door openers. All academic buildings on campus are connected by an underground concourse system which is widely accessed by the entire campus community and which makes the campus particularly accessible to wheelchair transportation. **Special:** UW-Green Bay offers cross-registration with Bellin College of Nursing and the University of Wisconsin at Milwaukee or Oshkosh. There are study-abroad programs and travel courses in numerous countries. Students can receive credit by examination or for life, military, or

work experience. There are internships in almost all fields, interdisciplinary majors, including communication and the arts, human biology, and regional planning, and dual and student-designed majors, work-study, B.A.-B.S. degrees in most areas, nondegree study, a general studies degree, and pass/fail options. There are 6 national honor societies and 34 departmental honors programs. **Visiting:** There are regularly scheduled orientations for prospective students, including campus preview days, which consist of information sessions, academic area workshops, and campus tours. There are guides for informal visits and visitors may sit in on classes. To schedule a visit, contact the Office of Admissions. **Campus Safety and Security:** Measures include 24-hour foot and vehicle patrol and security escort services. There are emergency telephones, lighted pathways/sidewalks, and controlled access to dorms/residences.

REQUIREMENTS: The ACT is required. Candidates must be graduates of an accredited secondary school or hold a GED certificate. They must have completed 17 academic credits consisting of 4 in English, 3 in social sciences, 3 each in science and math, 2 in any of the above areas or a foreign language, and 2 other electives, home schooled applicants are encouraged to apply, and should contact the admissions office for additional information. AP and CLEP credits are accepted. Important factors in the admissions decision are advanced placement or honors courses, extracurricular activities record, and leadership record. All students must complete at least 120 semester hours, including an average of 36 in the major, with a minimum GPA of 2.0, depending on the major. Students must declare an interdisciplinary minor or major. Required general education includes courses in fine arts, humanities, natural and social sciences, other culture studies and ethnic studies, as well as competency and capstone courses. **Procedure:** Freshmen are admitted to all sessions. Entrance exams should be taken between the junior and senior years. There are deferred admissions and rolling admissions plans. Applications should be filed by January 1 for fall entry; November 1 for spring entry, along with a $44 fee. Notification is sent on a rolling basis. Applications are accepted on-line. **Transfer Students:** 1234 transfer students enrolled in 2013-2014. Transfer students must have a minimum GPA of 2.0 based on at least 15 transferable credits; priority for admission is given to students with 24 credits and a minimum GPA of 2.5. 31 of 120 credits required for the bachelor's degree must be completed at UW-Green Bay. **International Students:** There are 80 international students enrolled. The school actively recruits these students. They must take the TOEFL with a minimum score of 500 on the paper-based TOEFL (PBT) or 61 on the Internet-based version (iBT).

ADMISSIONS: 84% of the 2014-2015 applicants were accepted. The ACT scores were 27% below 21, 36% between 21 and 23, 25% between 24 and 26, 7% between 27 and 28, and 5% above 28. 16 freshmen graduated first in their class. **Admissions Contact:** Pam Harvey-Jacobs, Director of Admissions. E-Mail: *admissions@uwgb.edu* Web: *www.uwgb.edu*

FINANCIAL AID: In 2014-2015, 87% of all full-time freshmen and 82% of continuing full-time students received some form of financial aid. 65% of all full-time freshmen and 64% of continuing full-time students received need-based aid. The average freshman award was $10,291. Need-based scholarships or need-based grants averaged $4,392 ($15,000 maximum); need-based self-help aid (loans and jobs) averaged $3,856 ($7,500 maximum); non-need-based athletic scholarships averaged $10,624 ($25,390 maximum); and other non-need-based awards and non-need-based scholarships averaged $2,702 ($15,994 maximum). 80% of undergraduate students work part-time. Average annual earnings from campus work are $3000. The average financial indebtedness of the 2014 graduate was $23,535. The FAFSA is required. The deadline for filing freshman financial aid applications for fall entry is April 15.

UNIVERSITY OF WISCONSIN/LA CROSSE   B-4
www.uwlax.edu

La Crosse, WI 54601	**(608) 785-8000**

Fax: (608) 785-8940	Email: admissions@uwlax.edu
Full-time: 4002 men, 5274 women	Faculty: n/av
Part-time: 241 men, 238 women	Ph.D.s: 67%
Graduate: 273 men, 508 women	Student/Faculty: 20 to 1
Year: semesters, summer session	Tuition: $8794 ($16,367)
Room & Board: $5910	Freshman Class: 6908 applied, 4904 accepted, 1888 enrolled
SAT CR/M/W: 550/546/513 ACT: 25	CEEB CODE: 1914
Application Deadline: n/av	VERY COMPETITIVE

The University of Wisconsin/La Crosse, founded in 1909, is a public institution offering undergraduate and graduate studies in arts and sciences, health and human services, business administration, education, phys ed and recreation, professional development, and educational administration. There are 6 undergraduate schools and 1 graduate school. In addition to regional accreditation, UW-L has baccalaureate program accreditation with AACSB, APTA, NASM, NCATE, ACOTE, ACS, CAPTE, and NAACLS. The 121-acre campus is in a small town 142 miles west of Madison and 150 miles southeast of Minneapolis/St. Paul. Including any residence halls, there are 32 buildings.

STUDENT LIFE: Students are from 40 states, 30 foreign countries, and Canada. 90% are from public schools. 88% are White. The average age of freshmen is 18; all undergraduates, 25. 13% do not continue beyond their first year; 61% remain to graduate. **Housing:** 3180 students can be accommodated in college housing, which includes single-sex and coed dorms. In addition, there are special-interest houses, fraternity houses, sorority houses. There are residence halls for international students and students 21 years or older, substance free, first year experience housing. On-campus housing is available on a first-come, first-served basis, and is available on a lottery system for upperclassmen. 64% of students commute. All students may keep cars.

FACULTY/CLASSROOMS: 50% of faculty are male; 50% are female. 95% teach undergraduates, 5% do research, and 80% do both. No introductory courses are taught by graduate students. The average class size in an introductory lecture is 37; in a laboratory is 20; and in a regular course is 30.

PROGRAMS OF STUDY: UW-L confers B.A. and B.S. degrees. Associate and Master's degrees are also awarded. Bachelor's degrees are awarded in BIOLOGICAL SCIENCE (biology/biological science and microbiology), BUSINESS (accounting, banking and finance, business administration and management, international business management, and marketing/retailing/merchandising), COMMUNICATIONS AND THE ARTS (art, communications, dramatic arts, English, fine arts, French, music, Spanish, and speech/debate/rhetoric), COMPUTER AND PHYSICAL SCIENCE (chemistry, computer science, information sciences and systems, mathematics, and physics), EDUCATION (athletic training, elementary education, health education, physical education, science education, secondary education, and social studies education), HEALTH PROFESSIONS (community health work, exercise science, medical laboratory technology, nuclear medical technology, occupational therapy, physician's assistant, radiation therapy, and recreation therapy), SOCIAL SCIENCE (archeology, economics, geography, German area studies, history, parks and recreation management, philosophy, political science/government, psychology, public administration, and sociology). Microbiology, nuclear medicine technology, and physics are the strongest academically. Business administration, elementary education, and biology have the largest enrollments.

ACTIVITIES: 1% of men and 1% of women belong to 3 national fraternities; 1% of women belong to 2 national sororities. There are 140 groups on campus, including art, band, campus ministries, cheerleading, chess, choir, chorale, chorus, computers, dance, drama, ethnic, gay, honors, international, jazz band, literary magazine, marching band, musical theater, newspaper, orchestra, pep band, photography, political, professional, radio and TV, religious, social, social service, student government, and symphony. Popular campus events include Parents Weekend, Community-Sponsored Oktoberfest and Various Cultural Events. **Sports:** There are 9 intercollegiate sports for men and 10 for women, and 11 intramural sports for men and 11 for women. Facilities include a wrestling room, an indoor track, 6 indoor tennis courts, 16 outdoor tennis courts, an Olympic-size swimming pool, 2 strength-training centers, a dance studio, racquetball courts, a 4363-seat stadium, a 2880-seat gym, and an 880-seat auditorium. **Graduates:** From July 1, 2013 to June 30, 2014, 1782 bachelor's degrees were awarded. The most popular majors were business/marketing (19%), biological/life sciences (14%), and health professions and related programs/psychology (10%). In an average class, 37% graduate in 4 years or less, 42% graduate in 5 years or less, and 71% graduate in 6 years or less.

SERVICES: Counseling and information services are available, as is tutoring in most subjects. There is a reader service for the blind, remedial math and writing. There is also a counseling, a testing center and a writing lab. **Library/Resources:** The library contains 500,370 volumes, 581,624 microform items, 14,372 audio/video tapes/CDs/DVDs, and subscribes to 10,697 periodicals including electronic. Computerized library services include interlibrary loans and database searching. Special learning facilities include an art gallery, planetarium, radio station, TV station, the River Studies Center and the Allied Health Center. **Physically Challenged Students:** 98% of the campus is accessible. Facilities include wheelchair ramps, elevators, special parking, specially equipped restrooms, special class scheduling, lowered drinking fountains, lowered telephones, special housing. **Special:** Cooperative programs and cross-registration are available with Viterbo College. There are study-abroad programs in 14 countries and an international student exchange program. UW-L also offers a 3-2 engineering degree with the University of Wisconsin/Madison, the University of Wisconsin/Milwaukee, Platteville, and the University of Minnesota, work-study programs, internships, nondegree study, credit by exam, and pass/fail options. There are 10 national honor societies, a freshman honors program, and 11 departmental honors programs. **Visiting:** There are regularly scheduled orientations for prospective students, including 2 academic sessions, a parent panel, a UW-L student panel, and a tour of the campus. There are guides for informal visits and visitors may sit in on classes. To schedule a visit, contact the Admissions Office. **Campus Safety and Security:** Measures include 24-hour foot and vehicle patrol, self-defense education, and security escort services. There are emergency telephones and lighted pathways/sidewalks.

REQUIREMENTS: The SAT or ACT is required. Applicants must be graduates of an accredited secondary school or hold a GED certificate. They must have completed 17 academic credits, including 4 courses in English, 3 each in social studies, math, and science, and 4 other academic electives. Students completing rigorous courses, including in the senior year, will be stronger candidates for admission. Students must rank in the top 35% of their high school graduating class and score at least 22 on the ACT or the top 40% and score 25 on the ACT. AP and CLEP credits are accepted. Important factors in the admissions decision are advanced placement or honors courses, leadership record, extracurricular activities record, parents or siblings attended your school, evidence of special talent, personality/intangible qualities, recommendations by alumni, geographical diversity, and recommendations by school officials. To graduate, students must earn 120 semester credits, including 68 in subjects outside the major and at least 40 in 300- or 400-level courses. The minimum GPA is 2.0, though it is considerably higher for some programs. Distribution requirements include 30 to 40 credits in liberal studies and 13 to 19 credits in skill courses. **Procedure:** Freshmen are admitted to all sessions. Entrance exams should be taken by the junior year or at the beginning of the senior year. There are early admissions and rolling admissions plans. Application deadlines are open. Application fee is $44. Notification is sent on a rolling basis. Applications are accepted on-line. **Transfer Students:** 526 transfer students enrolled in 2013-2014. Transfer admission is likely with a GPA of 3.2; however, with a GPA of 2.0 to 2.74, admission is on a space-available basis. High School and college transcripts are required and a statement of good standing from prior institutions. 18 of 120 credits required for the bachelor's degree must be completed at

UW-L. **International Students:** There are 256 international students enrolled. The school actively recruits these students. They must take the TOEFL, the college's own test, also take the La Crosse Battery (based on MELAB), and write a 30-minute composition.

ADMISSIONS: 71% of the 2014-2015 applicants were accepted. The SAT scores for the 2014-2015 freshman class were: Critical Reading--29% below 500, 32% between 500 and 599, and 39% between 600 and 699; Math--29% below 500, 29% between 500 and 599, and 43% between 600 and 699. The ACT scores were 36% between 24 and 26, 58% between 27 and 28, and 5% above 28. 77% of the current freshmen were in the top fifth of their class; 98% were in the top two fifths. 49 freshmen graduated first in their class. **Admissions Contact:** Corey Sjoquist, Director of Admissions. E-Mail: *admissions@uwlax .edu* Web: *www.uwlax.edu*

FINANCIAL AID: In 2014-2015, 67% of all full-time freshmen and continuing full-time students received some form of financial aid, including need-based aid. The average freshman award was $7,060. Need-based scholarships or need-based grants averaged $6,155; need-based self-help aid (loans and jobs) averaged $3,478; other non-need-based awards and non-need-based scholarships averaged $2,006; and $3,369 from other forms of aid. The average financial indebtedness of the 2014 graduate was $25,932. The FAFSA and the college's own financial statement are required. The priority date for freshman financial aid applications for fall entry is March 15.

UNIVERSITY OF WISCONSIN/MADISON   C-4
www.wisc.edu

Madison, WI 53706   (608) 262-3961

Fax: (608) 262-7706	Email: onwisconsin@admissions.wisc.edu
Full-time: 13887 men, 14706 women	Faculty: I, --$
	Ph.D.s: 90%
Part-time: 1376 men, 1350 women	Student/Faculty: 17 to 1
Graduate: 5996 men, 5960 women	Tuition: $10,403 ($26,653)
Year: semesters, summer session	Freshman Class: 29675 applied, 15161 accepted, 6339 enrolled
Room & Board: $8354	
SAT CR/M/W: 600/680/640 ACT: 28	CEEB CODE: 1846
Application Deadline: February 1	HIGHLY COMPETITIVE+

The University of Wisconsin-Madison, founded in 1849, is a public, land-grant institution offering undergraduate and graduate study in almost every major field. There are 9 undergraduate schools and 13 graduate schools. In addition to regional accreditation, Wisconsin has baccalaureate program accreditation with AACSB, ABET, ADA, ASLA, CSWE, FIDER, NASAD, NASM, and SAF. The 936-acre campus is in an urban area 75 miles west of Milwaukee and 150 miles northwest of Chicago.

STUDENT LIFE: 67% of undergraduates are from Wisconsin. Others are from 50 states, 130 foreign countries, and Canada. 77% are White. The average age of freshmen is 18; all undergraduates, 20. 5% do not continue beyond their first year; 84% remain to graduate.

FACULTY/CLASSROOMS: 61% of faculty are male; 39% are female. No introductory courses are taught by graduate students.

PROGRAMS OF STUDY: Wisconsin confers B.A., B.S., B.B.A., B.F.A., B.M., B.S.Ed. and B.N.S. degrees. Master's and Doctoral degrees are also awarded. Bachelor's degrees are awarded in AGRICULTURE (agricultural business management, agricultural communications, agricultural economics, agronomy, animal science, dairy science, environmental studies, forestry and related sciences, horticulture, poultry science, and soil science), BIOLOGICAL SCIENCE (biochemistry, biology/biological science, botany, entomology, genetics, microbiology, molecular biology, nutrition, plant pathology, wildlife biology, and zoology), BUSINESS (accounting, banking and finance, human resources, insurance and risk management, international business management, marketing/retailing/merchandising, nonprofit/public organization management, operations management, personal financial planning, real estate, and retailing), COMMUNICATIONS AND THE ARTS (African languages, art, art history and appreciation, Chinese, classics, communications, communica-

tion science, comparative literature, dance, dramatic arts, English, French, German, Hebrew, Italian, Japanese, journalism, Latin, linguistics, music, music performance, Polish, Portuguese, Russian, Spanish, and theatre arts), COMPUTER AND PHYSICAL SCIENCE (actuarial science, applied mathematics, astronomy, atmospheric sciences and meteorology, chemistry, computer science, geology, geophysics and seismology, information sciences and systems, mathematics, physics, and statistics), EDUCATION (art education, athletic training, elementary education, music education, physical education, secondary education, and special education), ENGINEERING AND ENVIRONMENTAL DESIGN (bioengineering, biomedical engineering, cartography, chemical engineering, civil engineering, computer engineering, electrical/electronics engineering, engineering mechanics, engineering physics, environmental science, geological engineering, industrial engineering, interior design, landscape architecture/design, materials science, mechanical engineering, naval architecture and marine engineering, nuclear engineering, and textile technology), HEALTH PROFESSIONS (kinesiology, medical science, nursing, pharmacology, physician's assistant, and speech pathology/audiology), SOCIAL SCIENCE (African American studies, anthropology, Asian/Oriental studies, child care/child and family studies, economics, family/consumer studies, food science, gender studies, geography, history, history of science, human development, international relations, international studies, Judaic studies, Latin American studies, law, philosophy, political science/government, psychology, religion, rural sociology, Scandinavian studies, social studies, social work, sociology, textiles and clothing, and women's studies). Biology, economics, and political science have the largest enrollments.

ACTIVITIES: There are 907 groups on campus, including art, band, cheerleading, chess, choir, chorale, chorus, communications, computers, dance, debate, drama, environmental, ethnic, film, forensics, gay, honors, international, jazz band, literary magazine, marching band, musical theater, newspaper, opera, orchestra, pep band, photography, political, professional, radio and TV, religious, social, social service, student government, symphony, and yearbook.

SERVICES: Counseling and information services are available, as is tutoring in most subjects. There is a reader service for the blind. **Library/Resources:** The 43 libraries contain 8.6 million volumes. Computerized library services include interlibrary loans, database searching, Internet access, and Wi-Fi capability. Special learning facilities include an art gallery, natural history museum, planetarium, radio station, and TV station. **Physically Challenged Students:** 90% of the campus is accessible. Facilities include wheelchair ramps, elevators, special parking, specially equipped restrooms, special class scheduling, lowered drinking fountains, and lowered telephones. **Special:** Co-op programs, internships, study abroad, work-study programs, and accelerated degrees in any major are available. B.A.-B.S. degrees and dual and student-designed majors also are available. There is a chapter of Phi Beta Kappa and a freshman honors program. **Visiting:** There are regularly scheduled orientations for prospective students, including an admission information session, a tour, and class visits. There are guides for informal visits, visitors may sit in on classes, and stay overnight. To schedule a visit, contact the Visitor and Information Program at (608) 263-2400. **Campus Safety and Security:** Measures include 24-hour foot and vehicle patrol, emergency notification system, self-defense education, and security escort services. There are shuttle buses, emergency telephones, lighted pathways/sidewalks, and controlled access to dorms/residences.

REQUIREMENTS: The SAT or ACT is required. The ACT Optional Writing test is also required. Applicants must have completed the following number of units in high school (these are minimums; the number of units recommended is higher): 17 total units including 4 English, 4 math, 3 each of science, social studies, and foreign language, and 2 academics/fine arts electives. AP and CLEP credits are accepted.

ADMISSIONS: 51% of a recent year applicants were accepted. The SAT scores for the recent year freshman class were: Critical Reading--7% below 500, 39% between 500 and 599, 40% between 600 and 699, and 14% between 700 and 800; Math--1% below 500, 14% between 500 and 599, 40% between 600 and 699, and 45% between 700 and 800; Writing--5% below 500, 24% between 500 and 599, 52% between 600 and 699, and 19% between 700 and 800. The ACT scores were 1% below 21, 6% between 21 and 23, 22% between 24 and 26, 25% between 27 and 28, and 46% above 28.

FINANCIAL AID: The average financial indebtedness of the 2013 graduate was $25,664. Wisconsin is a member of CSS. The FAFSA is required. Check with the school for current application deadlines.

UNIVERSITY OF WISCONSIN/MILWAUKEE   E-4
www.uwm.edu

Milwaukee, WI 53211   (414) 229-2222

Fax: 414-229-3788	Email: uwmlook@uwm.edu
Full-time: 9385 men, 9544 women	Faculty: n/av
Part-time: 1918 men, 2157 women	Ph.D.s: 76%
Graduate: 1943 men, 2837 women	Student/Faculty: 18 to 1
Year: semesters, summer session	Tuition: $9300 ($19,029)
Room & Board: $9136	Freshman Class: 8011 applied, 7193 accepted, 3423 enrolled
ACT: 22	CEEB CODE: 1473
Application Deadline: July 1	COMPETITIVE

University Wisconsin/Milwaukee, is Wisconsin's premier public urban research university. There are 10 undergraduate schools and 3 graduate schools. In addition to regional accreditation, UWM has baccalaureate program accreditation with AACSB, ABET, APTA, CAHEA, CSWE, NAAB, NASM, NLN, APA, NCA, and CCNE. The 104-acre campus is in an urban area in Milwaukee, Wisconsin. Including any residence halls, there are 58 buildings.

STUDENT LIFE: 91% of undergraduates are from Wisconsin. Others are from 46 states, 51 foreign countries, and Canada. 92% are from public schools. 72% are White. The average age of freshmen is 19; all undergraduates, 23. 30% do not continue beyond their first year. **Housing:** 4288 students can be accommodated in college housing, which includes coed dorms, off-campus apartments, and married student housing. In addition, there are honors houses, language houses, and special-interest houses. On-campus housing is available on a first-come, first-served basis. 84% of students commute. Some may keep cars.

FACULTY/CLASSROOMS: 50% of faculty are male; 50% are female. No introductory courses are taught by graduate students.

PROGRAMS OF STUDY: UWM confers B.A., B.B.A., B.F.A., B.S., B.S.E. and B.S.N. degrees. Master's and Doctoral degrees are also awarded. Bachelor's degrees are awarded in BIOLOGICAL SCIENCE (biochemistry, biology/biological science, microbiology, molecular biology, and nutrition), BUSINESS (accounting, business administration and management, entrepreneurial studies, finance, human resources, international business, management information systems, marketing management, operations management, and real estate), COMMUNICATIONS AND THE ARTS (art, art history and appreciation, classics, communications, comparative literature, dance, dramatic arts, English, film arts, French, Germanic languages and literature, information technology, linguistics, music, and Russian languages and literature), COMPUTER AND PHYSICAL SCIENCE (actuarial science, applied mathematics, atmospheric sciences and meteorology, chemistry, computer science, geology, information sciences and systems, mathematics, physics, and web services), EDUCATION (art education, athletic training, education, music education, and special education), ENGINEERING AND ENVIRONMENTAL DESIGN (architecture, civil engineering, computer engineering, electrical/electronics engineering, engineering, environmental science, industrial engineering, materials engineering, mechanical engineering, and urban planning technology), HEALTH PROFESSIONS (exercise science, hospital administration, nursing, occupational therapy, premedicine, recreation therapy, and speech pathology/audiology), SOCIAL SCIENCE (African American studies, anthropology, Asian/American studies, behavioral science, criminal justice, economics, ethnic studies, forensic studies, geography, history, interdisciplinary studies, international studies, Italian studies, Judaic studies, Latin American studies, liberal arts/general studies, Near Eastern studies, peace studies, philosophy, political science/government, psychology, religion, Scandinavian studies, social work, sociology, Spanish studies, urban studies, and women's studies). Education, business, and psychology have the largest enrollments.

ACTIVITIES: There are 296 groups on campus, including art, band, cheerleading, chess, choir, chorale, chorus, communications, computers, dance, debate, drama, environmental, ethnic, film, gay, honors, international, jazz band, literary magazine, musical theater, newspaper, orchestra, pep band, photography, political, professional, religious, social, social service, student government, and symphony. Popular campus events include Fall Welcome, PantherFest, Concerts, Art Exhibitions and Dance Performances. **Sports:** There are 6 intercollegiate sports for men and 7 for women, and 11 intramural sports for men and 11 for women. Facilities include a basketball court, volleyball court, baseball field, soccer field, natatorium, indoor track, exercise facilities, and racquetball courts. **Graduates:** From July 1, 2013 to June 30, 2014, 3770 bachelor's degrees were awarded. The most popular majors were finance (7%), education (6%), and marketing (6%).

SERVICES: Counseling and information services are available, as is tutoring in some subjects. There is a reader service for the blind, remedial math, reading, and writing. **Library/Resources:** The library contains 2.6 million volumes, 1.8 million microform items, 982,297 audio/video tapes/CDs/DVDs, and subscribes to 86,848 periodicals including electronic. Computerized library services include interlibrary loans, database searching, Internet access, and Wi-Fi capability. Special learning facilities include an art gallery, planetarium, the American Geographical Society Library, and Institute of Visual Arts. **Physically Challenged Students:** 95% of the campus is accessible. Facilities include wheelchair ramps, elevators, special parking, specially equipped restrooms, special class scheduling, lowered drinking fountains, lowered telephones, special housing. **Special:** UWM offers cooperative education programs in computer science and engineering, accelerated degree programs, dual majors, student-designed majors, and study abroad opportunities in Africa, Asia, Europe, and South America. UWM also has a consortial nursing program with UW-Parkside, a graduate exchange program for students with Marquette University, and a collaborative doctoral program in biomedical and health informatics with the Medical College of Wisconsin. There are 4 national honor societies, including Phi Beta Kappa, and a freshman honors program. **Visiting:** There are regularly scheduled orientations for prospective students. New Student Orientation is a one and a half day (overnight) program packed with information about UWM. At orientation new students will meet other students, learn about campus resources and student life, meet with advisors and register for classes. There are guides for informal visits, visitors may sit in on classes, and stay overnight. To schedule a visit, contact the Department of Admissions and Recruitment at (414) 229-2222. **Campus Safety and Security:** Measures include 24-hour foot and vehicle patrol, emergency notification system, self-defense education, and security escort services. There are shuttle buses, emergency telephones, lighted pathways/sidewalks, and controlled access to dorms/residences.

REQUIREMENTS: All freshmen applicants under the age of 21 must submit ACT or SAT scores; scores submitted via high school transcripts are acceptable. A GED certificate is accepted. Music, dance, and theatre majors must audition and art majors must submit a portfolio. For the School of Architecture and Urban Planning, higher rank and ACT requirements apply. Each application receives a comprehensive review, taking all factors into consideration. In addition to academic preparation, other factors considered include demonstrated leadership skills, motivation, and maturity, as addressed in a student's personal statement and/or recommendations. AP and CLEP credits are accepted. Important factors in the admissions decision are advanced placement or honors courses, leadership record, and evidence of special talent.Generally, to be a candidate for the Bachelor's Degree, students must satisfactorily complete the following: English composition and math proficiency exams must be passed with satisfactory scores. A minimum of 120 undergraduate credits in courses numbered 100 through 500. The General Education requirements, university requirements and all major and/or minor requirements. Distribution requirements include 6 credits each in humanities, natural sciences, and socials sciences, and 3 credits each in the arts and cultural diversity. A minimum GPA of 2.0 or better both overall and in the major and minor fields; Business Administration and Accounting majors must have a cumulative GPA of 2.5 overall. A minimum of 30 credits overall and half of upper-level credits in majors and minors must be earned in residence at UW-Milwaukee. Other specific graduation criteria are set by individual colleges and schools. **Procedure:** Freshmen are admitted to all sessions. Entrance exams should be taken in the spring of the junior year. There are deferred admissions and rolling admissions plans. Applications should be filed by July 1 for fall entry; December 1 for spring entry, along with a $44 fee. Notification is sent on a rolling basis. Applications are accepted on-line. **Transfer Students:** 2556 transfer students enrolled in 2013-2014. Students applying with less than 12 transferable credits must meet freshman admission requirements 30 of 120 credits required for the bachelor's degree must be completed at UWM. **International Students:** There are 823 international students enrolled. The school actively recruits these students. They must take the TOEFL with a minimum score of 76 on the Internet-based version (iBT), or take the IELTS. All applicants to the College of Engineering and Applied Science must also submit official ACT or SAT scores.

ADMISSIONS: 90% of the 2014-2015 applicants were accepted. The ACT scores were 41% below 21, 29% between 21 and 23, 19% between 24 and 26, 6% between 27 and 28, and 5% above 28. 14% of the current freshmen were in the top fifth of their class; 34% were in the top two fifths. 17 freshmen graduated first in their class.
Admissions Contact: Department of Admissions and Recruitment E-Mail: *uwmlook@uwm.edu* Web: *www.uwm.edu*

FINANCIAL AID: In 2014-2015, 71% of all full-time freshmen and 68% of continuing full-time students received some form of financial aid. 60% of all full-time freshmen and 54% of continuing full-time students received need-based aid. The average freshman award was $7,243. Need-based scholarships or need-based grants averaged $6,299; need-based self-help aid (loans and jobs) averaged $3,724; non-need-based athletic scholarships averaged $7,594; and other non-need-based awards and non-need-based scholarships averaged $3,014. The average financial indebtedness of the 2014 graduate was $33,234. The FAFSA is required. The priority date for freshman financial aid applications for fall entry is March 1. The deadline for filing freshman financial aid applications for fall entry is December 1.

UNIVERSITY OF WISCONSIN/OSHKOSH *(The complete profile is made available exclusively on our website, www.barronspac.com)*

UNIVERSITY OF WISCONSIN/PARKSIDE *(The complete profile is made available exclusively on our website, www.barronspac.com)*

UNIVERSITY OF WISCONSIN/ PLATTEVILLE · C-5

www.uwplatt.edu

Platteville, WI 53818

(608) 342-1125
(800) 362-5515

Fax: (608) 342-1122 · Email: admit@uwplatt.edu

Full-time: 4681 men, 2466 women	Faculty: n/av
Part-time: 544 men, 356 women	Ph.D.s: 62%
Graduate: 472 men, 382 women	Student/Faculty: 22 to 1
Year: semesters, summer session	Tuition: $7484 ($15,057)
Room & Board: $7080	Freshman Class: 4160 applied, 3301 accepted, 1705 enrolled
ACT: 23	CEEB CODE: 1917
Application Deadline: open	COMPETITIVE

The University of Wisconsin/Platteville takes its roots from the Platteville Normal School State Teachers College (1866) and the Wisconsin Mining Trade School (1908). The University of Wisconsin-Platteville consists of three colleges – the College of Business, Industry, Life Science and Agriculture; the College of Engineering, Mathematics and Science; and the College of Liberal Arts and Education. There are 3 undergraduate schools and 1 graduate school. In addition to regional accreditation, UW-Platteville has baccalaureate program accreditation with ABET, NASM, NCATE, ACS, NAIT, and Wisconsin DPI. The 821-acre campus is in a small town 20 miles northeast of Dubuque, Iowa, and 75 miles southwest of Madison, Wisconsin. Including any residence halls, there are 33 buildings.

STUDENT LIFE: 78% of undergraduates are from Wisconsin. Others

are from 42 states, 22 foreign countries, and Canada. 90% are from public schools. 91% are White. The average age of freshmen is 18; all undergraduates, 20. 23% do not continue beyond their first year; 52% remain to graduate. **Housing:** College-sponsored housing includes single-sex and coed dorms. 53% of students commute. All students may keep cars.

FACULTY/CLASSROOMS: 60% of faculty are male; 40% are female. No introductory courses are taught by graduate students.

PROGRAMS OF STUDY: UW-Platteville confers B.A. and B.S. degrees. Associate and Master's degrees are also awarded. Bachelor's degrees are awarded in AGRICULTURE (agricultural business management, animal science, environmental horticulture and turf management, horticulture, and soil science), BIOLOGICAL SCIENCE (biology/biological science), BUSINESS (accounting and business administration and management), COMMUNICATIONS AND THE ARTS (art, English, German, media arts, music, Spanish, and visual and performing arts), COMPUTER AND PHYSICAL SCIENCE (chemistry, computer science, mathematics, physical sciences, physics, and software engineering), EDUCATION (agricultural education, art education, education, elementary education, middle school education, music education, physical education, secondary education, and technical education), ENGINEERING AND ENVIRONMENTAL DESIGN (civil engineering, electrical/electronics engineering, engineering physics, environmental engineering, industrial engineering, industrial engineering technology, land use management and reclamation, and mechanical engineering), SOCIAL SCIENCE (criminal justice, economics, forensic studies, geography, history, international studies, liberal arts/general studies, philosophy, political science/government, psychology, and social science). Engineering, agriculture, homeland security, law enforcement, firefighting, and protective services have the largest enrollments.

ACTIVITIES: 5% of men belong to 2 local and 7 national fraternities; 7% of women belong to 2 local and 5 national sororities. There are 220 groups on campus, including art, band, cheerleading, choir, chorale, chorus, computers, debate, drama, ethnic, film, forensics, gay, honors, international, jazz band, literary magazine, marching band, musical theater, newspaper, opera, orchestra, pep band, photography, political, professional, radio and TV, religious, social, social service, student government, and symphony. Popular campus events include Homecoming, Pioneer Distinguished Lecturer Presentation, Mudfest Rugby Tournament, Lighting and Whitewashing of the M. **Sports:** There are 7 intercollegiate sports for men and 7 for women, and 13 intramural sports for men and 12 for women. Facilities include a 2000 seat gym, 10,000 seat stadium, 200 meter indoor track, 400 meter outdoor track, 7 basketball and 7 volleyball courts, 6 tennis and 3 racquetball courts, a weight room, a swimming pool, 2 baseball diamonds, and soccer fields. **Graduates:** From July 1, 2013 to June 30, 2014, 1222 bachelor's degrees were awarded. The most popular majors were engineering (23%), criminal justice (12%), and business/marketing (10%). In an average class, 52% graduate in 6 years or less.

SERVICES: Counseling and information services are available, as is tutoring in most subjects. There is remedial math, reading, and writing. **Library/Resources:** The 2 libraries contain 258,341 volumes, 22,957 microform items, 6,004 audio/video tapes/CDs/DVDs, and subscribe to 498 periodicals including electronic. Computerized library services include interlibrary loans, database searching, Internet access, and Wi-Fi capability. Special learning facilities include an art gallery, radio station, and TV station. **Physically Challenged Students:** 95% of the campus is accessible. Facilities include wheelchair ramps, elevators, special parking, specially equipped restrooms, special class scheduling, lowered drinking fountains, lowered telephones, and special housing. **Special:** UWP offers internships in business, industry, and communication, a co-op program in engineering, and study abroad in 16 countries. Credit by exam, credit for life, military, and work experience, work-study programs, dual majors, student-designed majors, non-degree study, and pass/fail options are also available. There are 12 national honor societies, a freshman honors program, and 4 departmental honors programs. **Visiting:** There are regularly scheduled orientations for prospective students, The Pioneer Previews, held on 6 dates each year, include group tours, an admissions briefing, and visits to specific colleges and departments. Daily visits (Monday through Friday) are also available. There are guides for informal visits, visitors may sit in on classes, and stay overnight. To schedule a visit, contact the Prospective Student Services Office at (877) UWPLATT . **Campus Safety and Security:** Measures include 24-hour foot and vehicle patrol, emergency notification system, and security escort services. There are shuttle buses, emergency telephones, lighted pathways/sidewalks, and controlled access to dorms/residences.

REQUIREMENTS: The ACT is required. Applicants must have successfully completed 17 college preparatory units, including 4 units of English, 3 of math (algebra and higher), 3 of social science, 3 of natural science (2 must include lab experiences), 4 from the following foreign language, fine arts, computer science, or courses in vocational areas. Standard admission will be given to those students who are in the top 50% of their graduating class or have an ACT composite of 22 or SAT equivalency. AP and CLEP credits are accepted. To graduate, students must complete a minimum of 120 credit hours, with a minimum GPA of 2.0 overall and within the major. Course requirements include 12 credits in humanities and fine arts, 9 each in social sciences and natural sciences, 4 in ethnic and gender studies, and 3 in international education. Other competency requirements include 6 credits in English composition, 3 in math, and 2 each in speech and phys ed. **Procedure:** Freshmen are admitted to all sessions. Entrance exams should be taken in April or June of the junior year. There are deferred admissions and rolling admissions plans. Application deadlines are open. Application fee is $44. Applications are accepted online. **Transfer Students:** 403 transfer students enrolled in 2013-2014. Applicants must have a cumulative GPA of at least 2.0 and be in good standing at the institution they are currently attending or have attended. 32 of 120 credits required for the bachelor's degree must be completed at UW-Platteville. **International Students:** There are 67 international students enrolled. The school actively recruits these students. They must take the TOEFL with a minimum score of 500 on the paper-based TOEFL (PBT) or 61 on the Internet-based version (iBT).

ADMISSIONS: 79% of the 2014-2015 applicants were accepted. The ACT scores were 21% below 21, 32% between 21 and 23, 24% between 24 and 26, 11% between 27 and 28, and 9% above 28. **Admissions Contact:** Angela Udelhofen, Enrollment Services/Assistant Chancellor. E-Mail: *admit@uwplatt.edu* Web: *www.uwplatt.edu*

FINANCIAL AID: The FAFSA is required. The priority date for freshman financial aid applications for fall entry is March 15.

UNIVERSITY OF WISCONSIN/RIVER FALLS *(The complete profile is made available exclusively on our website, www.barronspac.com)*

UNIVERSITY OF WISCONSIN/STEVENS POINT C-3

www.uwsp.edu

Stevens Point, WI 54481	(715) 346-2441
Fax: (715) 346-2441	Email: admiss@uwsp.edu
Full-time: 4159 men, 4476 women	Faculty: 413; IIA, --$
Part-time: 219 men, 264 women	Ph.D.s: 67%
Graduate: 93 men, 288 women	Student/Faculty: 20 to 1
Year: semesters, summer session	Tuition: $7505 ($15,078)
Room & Board: $6538	Freshman Class: 4915 applied, 3672 accepted, 1637 enrolled
SAT CR/M/W: 546/536/528 ACT: 23	CEEB CODE: 1919
Application Deadline: open	COMPETITIVE

The University of Wisconsin/Stevens Point, founded in 1894, offers undergraduate programs in natural resources, education, business, arts and sciences, and professional studies. There are 4 undergraduate schools and one graduate school. In addition to regional accreditation, UWSP has baccalaureate program accreditation with ABET, ASLA, and NASAD. The 400-acre campus is in a small town 110 miles north of Madison. Including any residence halls, there are 35 buildings.

STUDENT LIFE: 89% of undergraduates are from Wisconsin. Others are from 30 states, 29 foreign countries, and Canada. 98% are from public schools. 89% are White. The average age of freshmen is 19; all undergraduates, 22. 20% do not continue beyond their first year; 61% remain to graduate.

FACULTY/CLASSROOMS: 64% of faculty are male; 46% are female. All teach undergraduates, and 98% do both. No introductory courses are taught by graduate students.

PROGRAMS OF STUDY: UWSP confers B.A., B.S., B.F.A. and B.M. degrees. Associate, Master's, and Doctoral degrees are also awarded. Bachelor's degrees are awarded in AGRICULTURE (fishing and fisheries, forestry and related sciences, natural resource management, and soil science), BIOLOGICAL SCIENCE (biochemistry, biology/biological science, nutrition, and wildlife biology), BUSINESS (accounting and business administration and management), COMMUNICATIONS AND THE ARTS (art, arts administration/management, communications, dance, dramatic arts, English, fine arts, French, German, music, and Spanish), COMPUTER AND PHYSICAL SCIENCE (chemistry, geoscience, information sciences and systems, mathematics, natural sciences, physics, and web services), EDUCATION (athletic training, early childhood education, education, education of the exceptional child, elementary education, health education, music education, and physical education), ENGINEERING AND ENVIRONMENTAL DESIGN (computer technology, interior design, and paper and pulp science), HEALTH PROFESSIONS (clinical science, health science, and speech pathology/audiology), SOCIAL SCIENCE (American studies, dietetics, economics, family/consumer studies, geography, history, international studies, liberal arts/general studies, philosophy, political science/government, psychology, public administration, social science, social work, and sociology). Natural resources, education and social sciences have the largest enrollments.

ACTIVITIES: 1% of men belong to 1 local and 4 national fraternities; 1% of women belong to 2 local and 1 national sororities. There are 201 groups on campus, including art, band, cheerleading, choir, chorale, chorus, computers, dance, drama, environmental, ethnic, film, gay, honors, international, jazz band, literary magazine, musical theater, newspaper, orchestra, pep band, photography, political, professional, radio and TV, religious, social, social service, student government, and symphony. Popular campus events include Trivia Contest, International Club Dinner, and Spud Bowl.

SERVICES: Counseling and information services are available, as is tutoring in most subjects. There is a reader service for the blind, and remedial math, reading, and writing. **Library/Resources:** The library contains 813,123 volumes, 50,349 microform items, and 25,357 audio/video tapes/CDs/DVDs, and subscribes to 44,876 periodicals including electronic. Computerized library services include interlibrary loans, database searching, Internet access, and Wi-Fi capability. Special learning facilities include an art gallery, natural history museum, planetarium, radio station, TV station, an observatory, map center, 275-acre nature preserve, groundwater center, and wellness institute. **Physically Challenged Students:** All of the campus is accessible. Facilities include wheelchair ramps, elevators, special parking, specially equipped restrooms, special class scheduling, lowered drinking fountains, lowered telephones. **Special:** A co-op program in nursing is offered with UW/Eau Claire and St. Joseph's Hospital. Internships, study abroad in 9 countries, work-study programs, dual and student-designed majors, independent study, and pass/fail options are also available. Credit is given for military, life, and work experience. There are 13 national honor societies and 3 departmental honors programs. **Visiting:** There are regularly scheduled orientations for prospective students, Students and parents can visit campus on a scheduled daily visit or participate in a one-day specialized program called ViewPoint, which is offered several times each fall and spring. UWSP also offers Info Nights in communities throughout WI and in IL to introduce students and parents to the university and answer detailed questions. There are guides for informal visits. To schedule a visit, contact the Office of Admissions. **Campus Safety and Security:** Measures include 24-hour foot and vehicle patrol, emergency notification system, and security escort services. There are emergency telephones, lighted pathways/sidewalks, and controlled access to dorms/residences.

REQUIREMENTS: The SAT or ACT is required. Applicants should have a high school rank of top 35% or above, or a cumulative high school GPA of 3.20 or higher, with an ACT composite score of 21 or SAT equivalent or above. The GED is accepted. Required academic preparation includes 4 years of English, 3 of social studies, and 3 each of math and lab science, along with 4 electives; 2 years of foreign language are recommended. The following non-academic factors are considered: involvement through work experience, extracurricular activities, and volunteerism; personal characteristics and accomplishments including special talents and abilities, honors, awards and personal qualities; diversity in background and experience; and life circumstances. While non-academic factors are considered, they will not necessarily make an applicant with a weak academic background a strong candidate for admission. AP and CLEP credits are accepted.

ADMISSIONS: 75% of a recent year applicants were accepted. The SAT scores for the recent year freshman class were: Critical Reading--23% below 500, 55% between 500 and 599, 14% between 600 and 699, and 9% between 700 and 800; Math--32% below 500, 41% between 500 and 599, 23% between 600 and 699, and 5% between 700 and 800; Writing--46% below 500, 32% between 500 and 599, 23% between 600 and 699. The ACT scores were 27% below 21, 37% between 21 and 23, 23% between 24 and 26, 8% between 27 and 28, and 5% above 28. 27% of the current freshmen were in the top fifth of their class; 61% were in the top two fifths. 28 freshmen graduated first in their class.

FINANCIAL AID: In a recent year, 58% of all full-time freshmen and 60% of continuing full-time students received some form of financial aid. 31% of all full-time freshmen and 34% of continuing full-time students received need-based aid. Need-based scholarships or need-based grants averaged $5,406; need-based self-help aid (loans and jobs) averaged $4,107; other non-need-based awards and non-need-based scholarships averaged $2,237; and $3,960 from other forms of aid. 38% of undergraduate students work part-time. Average annual earnings from campus work are $1887. The FAFSA is required. The priority date for freshman financial aid applications for fall entry is March 15. The deadline for filing freshman financial aid applications for fall entry is May 1.

UNIVERSITY OF WISCONSIN/STOUT   B-3
www.uwstout.edu

Menomonie, WI 54751

	(715) 232-1411
	(800) HI-STOUT
Fax: (715) 232-1667	Email: admissions@uwstout.edu
Full-time: 3644 men, 3246 women	Faculty: 406
Part-time: 761 men, 603 women	Ph.Ds: 78%
Graduate: 363 men, 754 women	Student/Faculty: 17 to 1
Year: 4-1-4, summer session	Tuition: $9025 ($16,771)
Room & Board: $6434	Freshman Class: 3352 applied, 2744 accepted, 1441 enrolled
ACT: 22 SAT: required	CEEB CODE: 1740
Application Deadline: open	**COMPETITIVE**

The University of Wisconsin/Stout, founded in 1891, offers undergraduate programs in liberal studies, human environmental sciences, industry and technology, education, and human services. There are 4 undergraduate schools and 1 graduate school. In addition to regional accreditation, UW-Stout has baccalaureate program accreditation with ABET, ACCE, ADA, FIDER, NASAD, IACBE, and AAMFT. The 110-acre campus is in a rural area 60 miles east of Minneapolis/St. Paul. Including any residence halls, there are 33 buildings.

STUDENT LIFE: 69% of undergraduates are from Wisconsin. Others are from 26 states, 28 foreign countries, and Canada. 93% are White.
Male To Female Ratio: 1.0:1. The average age of freshmen is 18; all undergraduates, 21. 27% do not continue beyond their first year.
Housing: College-sponsored housing includes coed dorms, smoke-free, alcohol-free, quiet study, upper class/graduate housing, freshman housing, and special housing for disabled students, wellness housing, and living learning communities. On-campus housing is guaranteed for all 4 years. 60% of students commute. All students may keep cars.

FACULTY/CLASSROOMS: 58% of faculty are male; 42% are female.

All teach and do research. No introductory courses are taught by graduate students. The average class size in an introductory lecture is 31 and in a laboratory is 21.

PROGRAMS OF STUDY: UW-Stout confers B.A., B.S. and B.F.A. degrees. Master's and Doctoral degrees are also awarded. Bachelor's degrees are awarded in BUSINESS (business administration and management, hospitality management services, hotel/motel and restaurant management, information and communication technology, management science, marketing/retailing/merchandising, packaging, property management, retailing, supply chain management, and sustainable management), COMMUNICATIONS AND THE ARTS (apparel design, art, communications, fine arts, game design and development, graphic communications management, studio art, and telecommunications), COMPUTER AND PHYSICAL SCIENCE (applied mathematics, applied science, and science), EDUCATION (art education, career, technical education and training, early childhood education, golf enterprise management, home economics education, marketing and distribution education, science education, special education, technical education, technology and science education, and vocational education), ENGINEERING AND ENVIRONMENTAL DESIGN (computer engineering, construction technology, engineering technology, food services technology, graphic arts technology, graphic and printing production, industrial administration/management, industrial engineering technology, manufacturing engineering, and plastics engineering), HEALTH PROFESSIONS (health and rehabilitation therapy), SOCIAL SCIENCE (applied social science, child care/child and family studies, cognitive science, dietetics, family/consumer studies, food production/management/services, human development, and psychology). General business administration, art, hotel restaurant, and tourism management have the largest enrollments.

ACTIVITIES: 2% of men and 3% of women belong to 3 local and 2 national fraternities; 3% of women belong to 3 national sororities. There are 117 groups on campus, including art, band, cheerleading, choir, chorale, chorus, computers, dance, debate, drama, ethnic, forensics, gay, honors, international, jazz band, literary magazine, marching band, musical theater, newspaper, pep band, photography, political, professional, radio station, religious, social, social service, and student government. Popular campus events include Family Weekend, Cheese Week and Biggest House Party. **Sports:** There are 6 intercollegiate sports for men and 8 for women, and 20 intramural sports for men and 19 for women. Facilities include baseball, soccer, and football fields, indoor and outdoor tracks, and a field house with basketball, racquetball, and volleyball courts, a pool, weight and gymnastics rooms, and indoor and outdoor tennis courts. **Graduates:** From July 1, 2013 to June 30, 2014, 1643 bachelor's degrees were awarded. The most popular majors were business marketing (36%), education (10%), and visual and performing arts (9%). 306 companies recruited on campus in 2013-2014. In an average class, 14% graduate in 4 years or less and 41% graduate in 5 years or less.

SERVICES: Counseling and information services are available, as is tutoring in most subjects. There is a reader service for the blind, remedial math, reading, and writing. **Library/Resources:** The library contains 225,672 volumes, 1.2 million microform items, 14,254 audio/video tapes/CDs/DVDs, and subscribes to 1,012 periodicals including electronic. Computerized library services include interlibrary loans, database searching, Internet access, and Wi-Fi capability. Special learning facilities include an art gallery and TV station. **Physically Challenged Students:** All of the campus is accessible. Facilities include wheelchair ramps, elevators, special parking, specially equipped restrooms, special class scheduling, lowered drinking fountains, lowered telephones, and special housing. **Special:** UW-Stout offers business and industry internships, cooperative programs, work-study programs, and study abroad in London. Dual majors, credit by examination, credit for life, military, and work experience, nondegree study, and pass/fail options are also available. There is 1 national honor society, a freshman honors program, and 3 departmental honors programs. **Visiting:** There are regularly scheduled orientations for prospective students, including an interview with an admissions counselor and a campus tour. There are also campus preview days throughout the academic year. There are guides for informal visits, visitors may sit in on classes, and stay overnight. **Campus Safety and Security:** Measures include 24-hour foot and vehicle patrol. There are lighted pathways/sidewalks, and training sessions.

REQUIREMENTS: The SAT or ACT is required. Minimum test scores are waived if students rank in the upper 50% of their class. Applicants should graduate from an accredited secondary school. The GED is accepted if applicants are over 21, or if their graduating class has been out for at least 2 years. Secondary school preparation should include 4 academic credits in English, 3 each in social studies, math, and science, and 4 in electives. A GPA of 2.8 is required. AP and CLEP credits are accepted. Important factors in the admissions decision are leadership record, advanced placement or honors courses, parents or siblings attended your school, evidence of special talent, personality/intangible qualities, extracurricular activities record, recommendations by alumni, recommendations by school officials, and geographical diversity. Students must complete a minimum of 124 credits, including a general education component. Some degree programs have specific general education courses that must be taken in order to satisfy certification, accreditation, or prerequisite standards. Students must also fulfill an ethnic studies requirement. **Procedure:** Freshmen are admitted fall, spring, and summer. Entrance exams should be taken in June of the junior year. There is a rolling admissions plan. Application deadlines are open. Application fee is $44. Notification is sent on a rolling basis. Applications are accepted online. **Transfer Students:** 713 transfer students enrolled in 2013-2014. A minimum college GPA of 2.0 is required A high school transcript and a statement of good standing from prior institutions are required. 32 of 124 credits required for the bachelor's degree must be completed at UW-Stout. **International Students:** There are 39 international students enrolled. The school actively recruits these students. They must take the TOEFL.

ADMISSIONS: 82% of the 2014-2015 applicants were accepted. The ACT scores were 7% below 21, 59% between 21 and 23, 31% between 24 and 26, and 3% above 28. 18% of the current freshmen were in the top fifth of their class; 50% were in the top two fifths. 10 freshmen graduated first in their class. **Admissions Contact:** Cindy Jenkins, Director of Admissions. E-Mail: *admissions@uwstout.edu* Web: *www.uwstout.edu*

FINANCIAL AID: In 2014-2015, 68% of all full-time freshmen and continuing full-time students received some form of financial aid. 68% of all full-time freshmen and continuing full-time students received need-based aid. The average freshman award was $10,101. Need-based scholarships or need-based grants averaged $5,621; need-based self-help aid (loans and jobs) averaged $4,790; non-need-based athletic scholarships averaged $2,827; and other non-need-based awards and non-need-based scholarships averaged $4,055. 69% of undergraduate students work part-time. Average annual earnings from campus work are $1351. The average financial indebtedness of the 2014 graduate was $23,547. UW-Stout is a member of CSS. The FAFSA is required. The priority date for freshman financial aid applications for fall entry is March 15.

UNIVERSITY OF WISCONSIN/SUPERIOR   A-1
www.uwsuper.edu

Superior, WI 54880	**(715) 394-8230**
Fax: (715) 394-8407	**Email:** admissions@uwsuper.edu
Full-time: 803 men, 1123 women	**Faculty:** 120
Part-time: 165 men, 364 women	**Ph.D.s:** 70%
Graduate: 42 men, 92 women	**Student/Faculty:** 16 to 1
Year: semesters, summer session	**Tuition:** $7994 ($15,557)
Room & Board: $6320	**Freshman Class:** 877 applied, 599 accepted, 330 enrolled
ACT: 22	**CEEB CODE:** 1920
Application Deadline: August 1	**COMPETITIVE**

The University of Wisconsin/Superior, founded in 1893, offers undergraduate programs in the liberal arts and sciences, business, education, fine arts, applied arts, and social sciences. In addition to regional accreditation, UW/Superior has baccalaureate program accreditation with CSWE and NASM. The 230-acre campus is in an urban area in Superior, Wisconsin, at the western tip of Lake Superior. Superior is accessible by Interstate 35 in Minnesota and U.S.

Highway 53 in Wisconsin. Including any residence halls, there are 17 buildings.

STUDENT LIFE: 51% of undergraduates are from Wisconsin. Others are from 33 states, 40 foreign countries, and Canada. 90% are from public schools. 83% are White. The average age of freshmen is 18; all undergraduates, 23. 28% do not continue beyond their first year; 43% remain to graduate. **Housing:** 820 students can be accommodated in college housing, which includes coed dorms. On-campus housing is guaranteed for the freshman year only. 72% of students commute. All students may keep cars.

FACULTY/CLASSROOMS: 47% of faculty are male; 53% are female. 95% teach undergraduates. No introductory courses are taught by graduate students. The average class size in an introductory lecture is 22; in a laboratory is 20; and in a regular course is 17.

PROGRAMS OF STUDY: UW/Superior confers B.A., B.S., B.F.A., B.M. and B.M.E. degrees. Associate and Master's degrees are also awarded. Bachelor's degrees are awarded in BIOLOGICAL SCIENCE (biology/biological science), BUSINESS (accounting, business administration and management, finance, international business management, sustainable management, and transportation management), COMMUNICATIONS AND THE ARTS (art history, art, communications, dramatic arts, English, fine arts, music, music performance, speech/debate/rhetoric, studio art, theatre arts, visual and performing arts, and writing), COMPUTER AND PHYSICAL SCIENCE (chemistry, computer science, and mathematics), EDUCATION (art education, elementary education, English education, health education, mathematics education, music education, physical education, science education, secondary education, social science education, and social studies secondary school education), HEALTH PROFESSIONS (art therapy, biology, community health work, exercise science, health, health and physical activity, and health promotion), SOCIAL SCIENCE (criminal justice, economics, history, interdisciplinary studies, international studies, law, political science/government, psychology, public administration, social studies, social work, and sociology). Business administration, elementary education, and biology are the strongest academically. Business administration, elementary education, and communicating arts have the largest enrollments.

ACTIVITIES: There are 63 groups on campus, including art, band, cheerleading, choir, chorale, chorus, computers, dance, drama, ethnic, gay, honors, international, jazz band, newspaper, orchestra, pep band, photography, political, professional, radio and TV, religious, social, social service, student government, and symphony. Popular campus events include World Culture Night, and Jacket Racket. **Sports:** There are 6 intercollegiate sports for men and 8 for women, and 19 intramural sports for men and 19 for women. Facilities include a 3000-seat gym, an ice arena, swimming pool, weight training room, dance studio, racquetball courts, an all-weather track, high ropes course, zip line, a climbing wall, and softball and baseball fields. **Graduates:** From July 1, 2013 to June 30, 2014, 463 bachelor's degrees were awarded. The most popular majors were education (20%), business/marketing (17%), and communication/journalism (10%). 131 companies recruited on campus in 2013-2014. In an average class, 2% graduate in 3 years or less, 20% graduate in 4 years or less, 33% graduate in 5 years or less, and 43% graduate in 6 years or less.

SERVICES: Counseling and information services are available, as is tutoring in every subject. There is remedial math and writing. **Library/Resources:** Computerized library services include interlibrary loans, database searching, Internet access, and Wi-Fi capability. Special learning facilities include an art gallery, radio station, TV station, an aquatic lab and observatory. **Physically Challenged Students:** 95% of the campus is accessible. Facilities include wheelchair ramps, elevators, special parking, specially equipped restrooms, special class scheduling, lowered drinking fountains, and lowered telephones. **Special:** UW/Superior offers work-study and co-op programs in business and internships in social work, business, mass communication, and criminal justice. There is a comprehensive program of student-designed majors, along with a cooperative program in marine studies with Texas A&M University, and 3-2 engineering and forestry programs with Michigan Technological University. Students may cross-register for 2 classes per semester at the University of Minnesota/Duluth or the College of St. Scholastica. An extended degree is offered. Credit for life experience and pass/fail options are available. There are 4 national honor societies and 4 departmental honors programs. **Visiting:** There are regularly scheduled orientations for prospective students, consisting of two days of social and educational programs. There are guides for informal visits, visitors may sit in on classes, and stay overnight. To schedule a visit, contact the Admissions Office. **Campus Safety and Security:** Measures include 24-hour foot and vehicle patrol, emergency notification system, self-defense education, and security escort services. There are emergency telephones, lighted pathways/sidewalks, and controlled access to dorms/residences.

REQUIREMENTS: The ACT is required. Out-of-state residents may submit SAT scores instead. Applicants must graduate from an accredited secondary school or the equivalent. Applicant must rank in at least the upper 50% of their graduating class or achieve a minimum composite score of 21 on the ACT. AP and CLEP credits are accepted.To graduate, students must complete 120 credit hours, with a GPA of 2.0. A minimum of 54 hours must be credited toward completion of 1 comprehensive major, 2 majors, or 1 major and 1 minor. The required core curriculum includes 55 credits in Communications, English, Math, Phys Ed, World Culture, Contemporary Society, Aesthetic Experience, Natural Science, and Human Behavior. A comprehensive exam and a senior project are required. **Procedure:** Freshmen are admitted fall, spring, and summer. Entrance exams should be taken spring of junior year or early fall of senior year. There are deferred admissions and rolling admissions plans. Applications should be filed by August 1 for fall entry; January 5 for spring entry, along with a $44 fee. Notification is sent on a rolling basis. Applications are accepted on-line. **Transfer Students:** 280 transfer students enrolled in 2013-2014. A college GPA of 2.0 is required. 30 of 120 credits required for the bachelor's degree must be completed at UW/Superior. **International Students:** There are 145 international students enrolled. The school actively recruits these students. They must take the TOEFL with a minimum score of 500 on the paper-based TOEFL (PBT) or 61 on the Internet-based version (iBT), or take the MELAB, ACT or SAT is generally required for native English speaking international students.

ADMISSIONS: 68% of the 2014-2015 applicants were accepted. The ACT scores were 42% below 21, 31% between 21 and 23, 19% between 24 and 26, 6% between 27 and 28, and 2% above 28. 18% of the current freshmen were in the top fifth of their class; 48% were in the top two fifths. 1 freshman graduated first in the class. **Admissions Contact:** Admissions Office E-Mail: *admissions@uwsuper.edu* Web: *uwsuper.edu*

FINANCIAL AID: In 2014-2015, 64% of all full-time freshmen and 69% of continuing full-time students received some form of financial aid. 36% of all full-time freshmen and 50% of continuing full-time students received need-based aid. The average freshman award was $10,574. Need-based scholarships or need-based grants averaged $5,797; and need-based self-help aid (loans and jobs) averaged $4,465. The average financial indebtedness of the 2014 graduate was $26,472. The FAFSA is required. The priority date for freshman financial aid applications for fall entry is April 1.

UNIVERSITY OF WISCONSIN/WHITEWATER — D-5
www.uww.edu

Whitewater, WI 53190	(262) 472-1440
Fax: (262) 472-1515	Email: uwwadmit@mail.uww.edu
Full-time: 4722 men, 5325 women	Faculty: 384; IIA, --$
Part-time: 269 men, 371 women	Ph.D.s: 73%
Graduate: 479 men, 780 women	Student/Faculty: 22 to 1
Year: semesters, summer session	Tuition: $7528 ($15,101)
Room & Board: $5786	Freshman Class: 7000 applied, 5600 accepted, 2150 enrolled
SAT CR/M/W: 530/520/525 ACT: recommended	CEEB CODE: 1921
Application Deadline: open	COMPETITIVE

The University of Wisconsin/Whitewater, founded in 1868, offers programs in teacher education, business, liberal arts, preprofessional studies, fine arts and music. There are 4 undergraduate schools and 1 graduate school. In addition to regional accreditation, UW-Whitewater has baccalaureate program accreditation with AACSB, ASLA, CSWE, NASM, and NCATE. The 385-acre campus is in a small town 50 miles southwest of Milwaukee. Including any residence halls, there are 45 buildings.

STUDENT LIFE: 85% of undergraduates are from Wisconsin. Others are from 26 states, 38 foreign countries, and Canada. 70% are from public schools. 87% are White. The average age of freshmen is 19; all undergraduates, 22. 20% do not continue beyond their first year; 63% remain to graduate.

FACULTY/CLASSROOMS: 57% of faculty are male; 43% are female. All teach undergraduates, and 78% do research. No introductory courses are taught by graduate students. The average class size in a regular course is 26.

PROGRAMS OF STUDY: UW-Whitewater confers B.A., B.S., B.B.A., B.F.A., B.M. and B.S.Ed. degrees. Associate and Master's degrees are also awarded. Bachelor's degrees are awarded in BIOLOGICAL SCIENCE (biology/biological science), BUSINESS (accounting, banking and finance, business administration and management, business economics, marketing/retailing/merchandising, office supervision and management, and personnel management), COMMUNICATIONS AND THE ARTS (art history and appreciation, communications, dramatic arts, English, French, German, journalism, music, public relations, Spanish, and speech/debate/rhetoric), COMPUTER AND PHYSICAL SCIENCE (chemistry, computer programming, mathematics, and physics), EDUCATION (art education, business education, early childhood education, elementary education, foreign languages education, middle school education, music education, physical education, science education, secondary education, social studies education, and special education), SOCIAL SCIENCE (economics, geography, history, international studies, political science/government, prelaw, psychology, public administration, safety and security technology, social work, sociology, and women's studies). Accounting, education and marketing are the strongest academically. Business/accounting, education, letters and sciences have the largest enrollments.

ACTIVITIES: 5% of men belong to 1 local and 6 national fraternities; 5% of women belong to 1 local and 4 national sororities. There are 130 groups on campus, including art, band, cheerleading, choir, chorus, communications, computers, dance, drama, drill team, ethnic, film, gay, honors, international, marching band, musical theater, newspaper, orchestra, pep band, photography, political, professional, radio and TV, religious, social, social service, student government, symphony, and yearbook. Popular campus events include Job Fair, Performing Arts Series, and Athletic Contests.

SERVICES: Counseling and information services are available, as is tutoring in most subjects. There is a reader service for the blind, and remedial math, reading, and writing. Study skills **Library/Resources:** The library contains 356,000 volumes, 993,000 microform items, and 7,300 audio/video tapes/CDs/DVDs, and subscribes to 5,000 periodicals including electronic. Computerized library services include interlibrary loans and database searching. Special learning facilities include an art gallery, radio station, TV station, an observatory and weather station. **Physically Challenged Students:** 85% of the campus is accessible. Facilities include wheelchair ramps, elevators, special parking, specially equipped restrooms, special class scheduling, lowered drinking fountains, lowered telephones. **Special:** Internships, study abroad in 9 nations, accelerated degree programs in safety studies and speech communication, student-designed majors, and a general studies degree are available. Credit by examination, nondegree study, and pass/fail options are also offered. There are 14 national honor societies, a freshman honors program, and 7 departmental honors programs. **Visiting:** There are regularly scheduled orientations for prospective students. There are guides for informal visits and visitors may sit in on classes. To schedule a visit, contact the Admissions Office. **Campus Safety and Security:** Measures include 24-hour foot and vehicle patrol, self-defense education, and security escort services. There are shuttle buses, emergency telephones, and lighted pathways/sidewalks.

REQUIREMENTS: The SAT or ACT is recommended. Applicants

should graduate from an accredited secondary school with 17 academic units, including 4 in English and 3 each in social studies, math, and science. The GED may be accepted. Applicants should rank in the upper 40% of their graduating class or achieve a combined high school and ACT/SAT percentile rank of 100% or above. A GPA of 2.8 is required. AP and CLEP credits are accepted. Important factors in the admissions decision are evidence of special talent, advanced placement or honors courses, and recommendations by school officials.

ADMISSIONS: 80% of a recent year applicants were accepted.

FINANCIAL AID: In a recent year, 73% of all full-time freshmen and 73% of continuing full-time students received some form of financial aid. 45% of all full-time freshmen and 45% of continuing full-time students received need-based aid. The average freshman award was $6,000. UW-Whitewater is a member of CSS. The FAFSA is required. Check with the school for current application deadlines.

VITERBO UNIVERSITY   **B-4**
www.viterbo.edu

La Crosse, WI 54601	(608) 796-3010
	(800) 848-3726
Fax: (608) 796-3020	Email: admission@viterbo.edu
Full-time: 437 men, 1132 women	Faculty: 107; IIA, --$
Part-time: 125 men, 411 women	Ph.D.s: 60%
Graduate: 211 men, 514 women	Student/Faculty: 12 to 1
Year: semesters, summer session	Tuition: $22,670
Room & Board: $7400	Freshman Class: 1655 applied, 1145 accepted, 304 enrolled
ACT: 23	CEEB CODE: 1878
Application Deadline: open	COMPETITIVE

Viterbo University, a Catholic, Franciscan Ecumenical University, prepares students for leadership and service by providing a student-centered, values-based, learning-focused liberal arts education rooted in the values of human dignity and respect for the world. There are 5 undergraduate schools and 5 graduate schools. In addition to regional accreditation, Viterbo has baccalaureate program accreditation with CSWE, NASM, NCATE, and NLN. The 72-acre campus is in a suburban area 150 miles from Minneapolis St. Paul, 105 miles from Madison, and 230 miles from Chicago. Including any residence halls, there are 18 buildings.

STUDENT LIFE: 76% of undergraduates are from Wisconsin. Others are from 34 states, and 11 foreign countries. 93% are from public schools. 92% are White. 43% are Catholic; 34% Protestant; 14% unidentified religions. The average age of freshmen is 18; all undergraduates, 25. 26% do not continue beyond their first year; 52% remain to graduate.

FACULTY/CLASSROOMS: 48% of faculty are male; 63% are female. 90% teach undergraduates, 53% do research, and 53% do both. No introductory courses are taught by graduate students. The average class size in an introductory lecture is 17; in a laboratory is 16; and in a regular course is 15.

PROGRAMS OF STUDY: Viterbo confers B.A., B.S., B.Art.Ed., B.B.A., B.F.A., B.I.L., B.L.S., B.M., B.S.T., B.S.VC., B.S.Community-Medical Dietetics, B.S.Ed., and B.S.N. degrees. Associate and Master's degrees are also awarded. Bachelor's degrees are awarded in AGRICULTURE (environmental studies), BIOLOGICAL SCIENCE (biochemistry and biology/biological science), BUSINESS (accounting, management information systems, management science, marketing/retailing/merchandising, organizational leadership and management, sports management, and sustainable management), COMMUNICATIONS AND THE ARTS (art, arts administration/management, communication, dramatic arts, English, graphic design, music performance, Spanish, studio art, and theatre studies), COMPUTER AND PHYSICAL SCIENCE (chemistry, digital arts/technology, mathematics, and natural sciences), EDUCATION (art education, business education, elementary education, English education, mathematics education, music education, science education, social studies education, and technology and science education), HEALTH PROFES-

SIONS (health care administration and nursing), SOCIAL SCIENCE (addiction studies, biopsychology, criminal justice, dietetics, history, liberal arts/general studies, philosophy, psychology, religious education, religious studies, social studies, social work, and sociology). Life Sciences, nutrition/dietetics, and natural sciences are the strongest academically. Health professions, business, and education have the largest enrollments.

ACTIVITIES: There are 32 groups on campus, including art, choir, chorale, chorus, dance, drama, drill team, environmental, ethnic, gay, honors, international, literary magazine, musical theater, newspaper, opera, pep band, political, professional, religious, social, social service, and student government. Popular campus events include Orientation Weekend, Welcome Back Bash, Viterbo Days (Family Day), St. Francis Day Celebration, and Courtyard Carni.

SERVICES: Counseling and information services are available, as is tutoring in every subject. There is a reader service for the blind, and remedial math, reading, and writing. **Library/Resources:** The library contains 92,300 volumes, 307 microform items, and 5,110 audio/video tapes/CDs/DVDs, and subscribes to 229 periodicals including electronic. Computerized library services include interlibrary loans, database searching, Internet access, and Wi-Fi capability. Special learning facilities include an art gallery, a music resource center. **Physically Challenged Students:** 90% of the campus is accessible. Facilities include wheelchair ramps, elevators, special parking, specially equipped restrooms, special class scheduling, lowered drinking fountains, and lowered telephones. **Special:** Students may cross-register at the University of Wisconsin/LaCrosse, enroll for independent study, or earn a dual degree. Co-op programs, study abroad in 7 countries, double majors, student-designed majors, accelerated degree programs, work-study, internships in many areas, credit by exam, and credit/no credit options are available. There are 2 national honor societies, including Phi Beta Kappa, and a freshman honors program. **Visiting:** There are regularly scheduled orientations for prospective students, including a meeting with an admissions staff member, a tour of the campus, and optional meetings with a financial aid officer and faculty members. There are guides for informal visits and visitors may sit in on classes. To schedule a visit, contact the Admission Office at (608) 796-3010. **Campus Safety and Security:** Measures include emergency notification system, self-defense education, and security escort services. There are shuttle buses, emergency telephones, lighted pathways/sidewalks, controlled access to dorms/residences, An emergency evacuation plan, 24 hours a day, 7 days a week, phone access to security personnel, security patrol from 5 p.m. to 7 a.m., ID check-in in dorms after 10 p.m., and card access to all campus buildings after regular hours, and 6 emergency blue lights.

REQUIREMENTS: The ACT is required. Graduation from an accredited secondary school is required; the GED is accepted. Secondary preparation should include 16 credits, with 3 or 4 in English and 2 each in math, natural science, and social science or history. Fine arts students may be required to audition or submit a portfolio. Nursing, dietetics, and pre-medical students must have high school chemistry. A GPA of 2.0 is required. AP and CLEP credits are accepted.

ADMISSIONS: 69% of a recent year applicants were accepted. The ACT scores were 24% below 21, 34% between 21 and 23, 29% between 24 and 26, 8% between 27 and 28, and 5% above 28. 37% of the current freshmen were in the top fifth of their class; 72% were in the top two fifths. 6 freshmen graduated first in their class.

FINANCIAL AID: In a recent year, 98% of all full-time freshmen students received some form of financial aid. 100% of undergraduate students work part-time. The FAFSA and the college's own financial statement are required. The priority date for freshman financial aid applications for fall entry is March 15.

WISCONSIN LUTHERAN COLLEGE   **E-4**
www.wlc.edu

Milwaukee, WI 53226	(414) 443-8811
	(888) 947-5884
Fax: (414) 443-8547	Email: admissions@wlc.edu
Full- and part-time: 800 men and women	Faculty: n/av
	Ph.D.s: 70%
Graduate: n/av	Student/Faculty: n/av
Year: semesters, summer session	Tuition: $23,330
Room & Board: $8740	Freshman Class: n/av
SAT or ACT: required	CEEB CODE: 1513
Application Deadline: see profile	VERY COMPETITIVE

Wisconsin Lutheran College, founded in 1973 in affiliation with the Wisconsin Evangelical Lutheran Synod, offers higher education in the arts and sciences within a conservative Christian environment. The figures in the above capsule and in this profile are approximate. The 21-acre campus is in a suburban area on the western edge of Milwaukee. Including any residence halls, there are 27 buildings.

STUDENT LIFE: 80% of undergraduates are from Wisconsin. Others are from 26 states and 10 foreign countries. 41% are from public schools. 95% are white. 88% are Protestant. The average age of freshmen is 18; all undergraduates, 20. 20% do not continue beyond their first year; 74% remain to graduate.

FACULTY/CLASSROOMS: 70% of faculty are male; 30% are female. All teach and do research. The average class size in an introductory lecture is 20; in a laboratory, 10; and in a regular course, 16.

PROGRAMS OF STUDY: Wisconsin Lutheran confers B.A. and B.S. degrees. Bachelor's degrees are awarded in BIOLOGICAL SCIENCE (biology/biological science), BUSINESS (business economics), COMMUNICATIONS AND THE ARTS (art, communications, dramatic arts, English, music, and Spanish), COMPUTER AND PHYSICAL SCIENCE (chemistry and mathematics), EDUCATION (elementary education), SOCIAL SCIENCE (history, interdisciplinary studies, political science/government, psychology, social science, and theological studies). Chemistry, education, and biology are the strongest academically. Music, theology, and education have the largest enrollments.

ACTIVITIES: There are 30 groups on campus, including art, band, cheerleading, choir, dance, drama, ethnic, international, jazz band, musical theater, newspaper, pep band, photography, political, professional, religious, social, social service, student government, and yearbook. Popular campus events include musical and theater events, Winterfest, and Commencement Weekend.

SERVICES: Counseling and information services are available, as is tutoring in some subjects, math, writing, and foreign language. **Library/Resources:** The library contains 72,621 volumes, 9,211 microform items, and 4,634 audio/video tapes/CDs/DVDs, and subscribes to 998 periodicals including electronic. Computerized library services include interlibrary loans, database searching, and Internet access. Special learning facilities include an art gallery, a sound studio, electronic music lab, and language lab. **Physically Challenged Students:** 90% of the campus is accessible. Facilities include wheelchair ramps, elevators, special parking, specially equipped restrooms, lowered drinking fountains, and lowered telephones. **Special:** Student-designed majors and study abroad are offered. Internships are available in most departments. **Visiting:** There are regularly scheduled orientations for prospective students, including a tour of the campus, a meal, meetings with admissions, financial aid, cocurriculars, and faculty in academic areas of interest. There are guides for informal visits, visitors may sit in on classes, and stay overnight. To schedule a visit, contact the Admissions Office. **Campus Safety and Security:** Measures include 24-hour foot and vehicle patrol, self-defense education, and security escort services. There are shuttle buses, lighted pathways/sidewalks, a security service, and electronically operated dorm entrances.

REQUIREMENTS: The ACT or SAT is required, with a minimum composite or combined score of 21 or 1000, respectively. Students should be graduates of an accredited high school or its equivalent with a minimum of 16 high school units, including 4 in English, 3 each in academic electives and math, and 2 each in science, foreign language, and social studies/history. Students must rank in the upper half of their graduating class or have a minimum GPA of 2.7. The Academic Recommendation Form must be submitted. A portfolio for art grants and an audition for music and drama grants are required. AP and CLEP credits are accepted. Important factors in the admissions decision are leadership record and personality/intangible qualities.

FINANCIAL AID: The FAFSA and the college's own financial statement are required. Check with the school for current application deadlines.

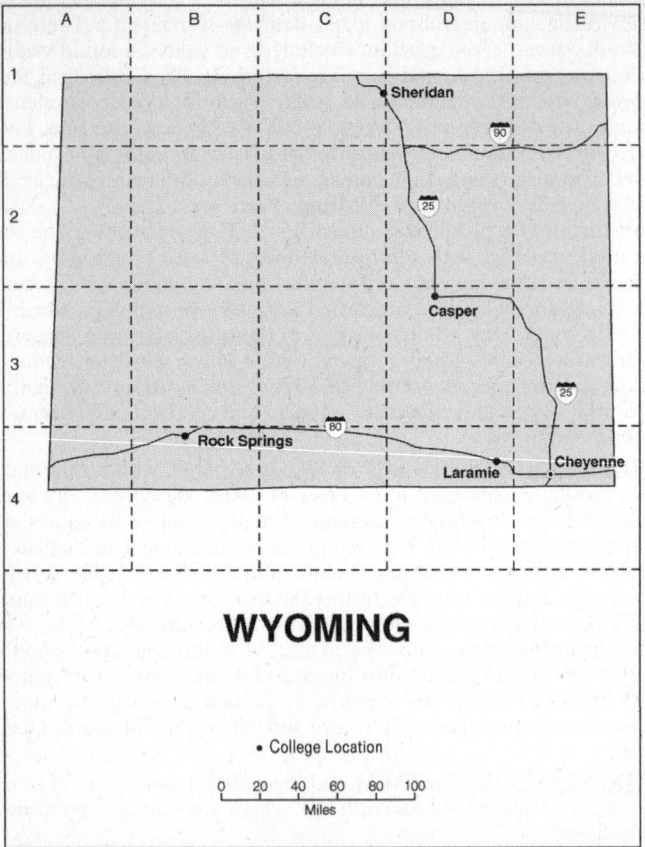

WYOMING

• College Location

0 20 40 60 80 100
Miles

UNIVERSITY OF WYOMING D-4
www.uwyo.edu

Laramie, WY 82071   (307) 766-1121
                                                    (307) 766-5160
Fax: (307) 766-4042   Email: admissions@uwyo.edu
Full-time: 4155 men, 4100 women   Faculty: 736; I, --$
Part-time: 649 men, 1213 women   Ph.D.s: 82%
Graduate: 1261 men, 1400 women   Student/Faculty: 14 to 1
Year: semesters, summer session   Tuition: $4646 ($14,876)
Room & Board: $9755   Freshman Class: 4348
                                       applied, 4154 accepted,
                                       1582 enrolled
SAT CR/M: 549/558 ACT: 24   CEEB CODE: 4855
Application Deadline: August 10   COMPETITIVE+

The University of Wyoming, founded in 1886, is a public institution offering programs in agriculture and natural resources, arts and sciences, business, education, engineering and applied science, health sciences, and law. There are 7 undergraduate schools and 8 graduate schools. In addition to regional accreditation, UW has baccalaureate program accreditation with AACSB, ABET, ACPE, ADA, CSAB, CSWE, NASM, NCATE, ABA, ACS, APA, Wyoming Profess'l Std Teaching Bd, CACREP, CCNE, ACEND, CAA of ASHA, ACGME, AOBFP, AAVLD, and Society for Range Management. The 785-acre campus is in a small town 128 miles north of Denver and 50 miles west of Cheyenne. Including any residence halls, there are 168 buildings.

STUDENT LIFE: 69% of undergraduates are from Wyoming. Others are from 51 states, 90 foreign countries, and Canada. 81% are White. The average age of freshmen is 19; all undergraduates, 22. 26% do not continue beyond their first year; 54% remain to graduate. **Housing:** 2889 students can be accommodated in college housing, which includes single-sex and coed dorms, on-campus apartments, off-campus apartments, and married student housing. In addition, there are honors houses, special-interest houses, fraternity houses, sorority houses, academic, single-gender, coed, upperclassmen, quiet-living, substance-free and freshman interest-group floors, 21 and over, ROTC. On-campus housing is guaranteed for all 4 years. 77% of students commute. All students may keep cars.

FACULTY/CLASSROOMS: 60% of faculty are male; 40% are female. 97% teach undergraduates. Graduate students teach 22% of introductory courses.

PROGRAMS OF STUDY: UW confers B.A., B.S., B.A.S., B.F.A., B.M., B.S.A.R., B.S.C.E., B.S.Ch., B.S.C.P., B.S.C.S., B.S.D.H., B.S.E.E., B.S.E.S.E., B.S.F.C., B.S.M.E., B.S.N., B.S.P.E. and B.S.W. degrees. Master's and Doctoral degrees are also awarded. Bachelor's degrees are awarded in AGRICULTURE (agricultural business management, agricultural communications, animal science, environmental studies, fish and game management, and range/farm management), BIOLOGICAL SCIENCE (botany, ecology, microbiology, molecular biology, physiology, wildlife biology, and zoology), BUSINESS (accounting, business administration and management, business economics, finance, management science, marketing, and organizational leadership and management), COMMUNICATIONS AND THE ARTS (art, communication, English, French, German, journalism, music, music performance, Russian, Spanish, and theatre acting), COMPUTER AND PHYSICAL SCIENCE (astronomy and physics, chemistry, computer science, earth science, environmental geology, geology, mathematics, physics, and statistics), EDUCATION (agricultural education, elementary education, music education, physical education, secondary education, special education, technical education, and trade and industrial education), ENGINEERING AND ENVIRONMENTAL DESIGN (architectural engineering, chemical engineering, civil engineering, computer engineering, electrical/electronics engineering, energy management technology, energy systems technology, mechanical engineering, and petroleum/natural gas engineering), HEALTH PROFESSIONS (biology, dental hygiene, kinesiology, medical laboratory technology, nursing, and speech pathology/audiology), SOCIAL SCIENCE (American Indian studies, American studies, anthropology, criminal justice, economics, family/consumer studies, geography, history, humanities, interdisciplinary studies, international studies, philosophy, political science/government, psychology, religious studies, social science, social work, sociology, and women & gender studies). Nursing, elementary education, and psychology have the largest enrollments.

ACTIVITIES: 5% of men belong to 8 national fraternities; 5% of women belong to 5 national sororities. There are 323 groups on campus, including art, band, cheerleading, choir, chorale, chorus, communications, computers, dance, debate, drama, drill team, environmental, ethnic, film, forensics, gay, honors, international, jazz band, literary magazine, marching band, musical theater, newspaper, opera, orchestra, pep band, photography, political, professional, radio and TV, religious, social, social service, student government, and symphony. Popular campus events include President's Welcome, Family Weekend, and Homecoming. **Sports:** There are 8 intercollegiate sports for men and 9 for women, and 37 intramural sports for men and 37 for women. Facilities include a 30,514-seat stadium, 15,000-seat indoor gym and arena, basketball, volleyball, racquetball courts, running tracks, 2 pools, weight rooms, an indoor tennis complex, baseball and track stadium, football training center, 6,855-yard golf course, sports complex, climbing wall, and a wrestling room. **Graduates:** From July 1, 2013 to June 30, 2014, 2053 bachelor's degrees were awarded. The most popular majors were nursing (10%), elementary education (8%), and psychology (5%). 339 companies recruited on campus in 2013-2014. In an average class, 24% graduate in 4 years or less, 47% graduate in 5 years or less, and 54% graduate in 6 years or less. Of the 2013 graduating class, 19% were enrolled in graduate school within 6 months of graduation, and 45% were employed.

SERVICES: Counseling and information services are available, as is tutoring in most subjects. There is a reader service for the blind. Note-taking services, tape recorders, and interpreters for the hearing impaired. **Library/Resources:** The 5 libraries contain 1.7 million volumes, 2.9 million microform items, 19,216 audio/video tapes/CDs/DVDs, and subscribe to 126,935 periodicals including electronic. Computerized library services include interlibrary loans, database searching, Internet access, and Wi-Fi capability. Special learning facilities include an art gallery, natural history museum, planetarium, radio station, TV station, the American Heritage Center, specialized science and agriculture labs, Williams Botany Conservatory, Wyoming Infrared Observatory, Geology - Brinkerhoff Geology library, law library, library annex, NPS UW research library, and Rocky Mountain Herbarium. **Physically Challenged Students:** 95% of the campus is accessible. Facilities include wheelchair ramps, elevators, special parking, specially equipped restrooms, special class scheduling, lowered drinking fountains, lowered telephones, special housing. **Special:** UW offers internships, study abroad in many countries, national student exchange, Washington and U.N. semesters, work-study programs, dual and interdisciplinary majors, pass/fail options, student-designed majors, credit by exam, accelerated degree programs, and credit for life, military, and work experience. There are including Phi Beta Kappa and a freshman honors program. **Visiting:** There are regularly scheduled orientations for prospective students, including campus tours and meetings with academic advisers. There are guides for informal visits. To schedule a visit, contact Pre-College and Student Visit Program. **Campus Safety and Security:** Measures include 24-hour foot and vehicle patrol, emergency notification system, self-defense education, and security escort services. There are shuttle buses, emergency telephones, lighted pathways/sidewalks, and controlled access to dorms/residences.

REQUIREMENTS: The SAT or ACT is required for students under 21; the ACT is preferred. Applicants must be graduates of an accredited secondary school or hold a GED certificate. Secondary preparation should include at least 19 academic credits consisting of 4 years each of English, Math, and Science, 3 years of social science, 2 years of foreign language, and 2 years chosen from fine and performing arts, social and behavioral studies, humanities, additional foreign language, or career-technical courses. A visit is suggested. AP and CLEP credits are accepted.To graduate, students must complete 120 to 157 credit hours, depending on the major, with a minimum GPA of 2.0. The core curriculum includes a required 30 to 36 hours of general education courses in the University Studies Program. **Procedure:** Freshmen are admitted fall, spring, and summer. Entrance exams should be taken in the spring of the junior year or fall of the senior year. There are deferred admissions and rolling admissions plans. Applications should be filed by August 10 for fall entry; December 10 for spring entry, along with a $40 fee. Applications are accepted online. **Transfer Students:** 1082 transfer students enrolled in 2013-2014. Applicants with 30 or more transferable college-level credits must have a minimum GPA of 2.0. All applicants with fewer credits must apply as a new freshman. Those students under age 21 must also present SAT or ACT scores. 30 credits required for the bachelor's degree must be completed at UW. **International Students:** There are 368 international students enrolled. The school actively recruits these students. They must take the TOEFL with a minimum score of 525 on the paper-based TOEFL (PBT) or 71 on the Internet-based version (iBT) and the Comprehensive English Language Test.

ADMISSIONS: 96% of the 2014-2015 applicants were accepted. The SAT scores for the 2014-2015 freshman class were: Critical Reading--26% below 500, 41% between 500 and 599, 23% between 600 and 699, and 6% between 700 and 800; Math--19% below 500, 42% between 500 and 599, 30% between 600 and 699, and 5% between 700 and 800. The ACT scores were 15% below 21, 27% between 21 and 23, 28% between 24 and 26, 13% between 27 and 28, and 17% above 28. 40% of the current freshmen were in the top fifth of their class; 70% were in the top two fifths. 84 freshmen graduated first in their class. **Admissions Contact:** Shelley Dodd, Director of Admissions. E-Mail: *admissions@uwyo.edu* Web: *www.uwyo.edu*

FINANCIAL AID: The average financial indebtedness of the 2014 graduate was $22,897. The FAFSA is required. The priority date for freshman financial aid applications for fall entry is March 1.

RELIGIOUS COLLEGES

ARIZONA

ARIZONA CHRISTIAN UNIVERSITY — C-4

Phoenix, AZ 85032 (602) 489-5300
(602) 404-2159

Full-time: 233 men, 215 women   **Faculty:** 55
Part-time: n/av   **Tuition:** $21,706
Graduate: n/av   **Room & Board:** $5240
Application Deadline: n/av
SAT CR/M: 516/495 **ACT:** 22

Arizona Christian University, founded in 1960, is affiliated with Non-denominational. Its mission is Transforming culture with the truth of Christ. The figures in the above capsule and in this profile are approximate. In addition to regional accreditation, the college is accredited by AABC and NCA. Arizona Christian University awards the B.A. and B.S. in elementary education, biblical studies, Christian ministries, secondary education, business administration, behavioral health, family studies and music education. The school also awards associate and bachelor's degrees. Web: *www.arizonachristian.edu*

ARKANSAS

CENTRAL BAPTIST COLLEGE — C-3

Conway, AR 72032 (501) 329-6872
(501) 329-2941

Full-time: 276 men, 246 women   **Faculty:** 54
Part-time: 57 men, 46 women   **Tuition:** $10,500
Graduate: none   **Room & Board:** $4500
Application Deadline: August 15
ACT: required

Central Baptist College, founded in 1952, is affiliated with Baptist Missionary Association of Arkansas. Its mission is Central Baptist College, a community of learners dedicated to the integration of Christian faith and academic excellence, exists to instill in our students a commitment to lifelong learning, spiritual development and service to God, through a program characterized by academic rigor, practical experience, and spiritual direction of a Christ focused environment. The figures in the above capsule are approximate. In addition to regional accreditation, the college is accredited by NCA. Central Baptist College awards the B.A., B.S., and B.B.A. in Bible studies, church music, organizational management, management information systems, social service, music, general studies, leadership and ministry, psychology, biology, and missions. The school also awards associate and bachelor's degrees. Web: *www.cbc.edu*

CALIFORNIA

PATTEN UNIVERSITY — B-3

Oakland, CA 94601 (888) 550-3250
(510) 534-8969

Full-time: 75 men, 140 women   **Faculty:** 125
Part-time: 300 men, 150 women   **Tuition:** $9716
Graduate: 3 men, 23 women   **Room & Board:** $10,872
Application Deadline: March 31

Patten University, founded in 1944, is affiliated with Christian Evangelical Churches of America/Church of God, Cleveland, Tennessee. Its mission is to provide an excellent education on the undergraduate and graduate levels that integrates growing faith and quality learning to inspire and equip men and women for Christian ministry and service. The figures in the above capsule are approximate. In addition to regional accreditation, the college is accredited by WASC. Patten University awards the B.A. and B.S. in biblical studies, Christian leadership, communication, intercultural-urban ministry, liberal studies, pastoral studies, music and worship leadership, organizational management, psychology, and youth ministry. The school also awards associate, bachelor's, and master's degrees. Web: *www.patten.edu*

WILLIAM JESSUP UNIVERSITY — B-3

Rocklin, CA 95678 (916) 577-2226
(916) 577-2220

Full-time: 260 men, 399 women   **Faculty:** 74
Part-time: 7 men, 6 women   **Tuition:** $22,300
Graduate: n/av   **Room & Board:** $9140
Application Deadline: June 1
ACT: 20

William Jessup University, founded in 1939, is nondenominational. Its mission is to prepare Christians for leadership and service in church and society through Christian higher education, spiritual formation, and directed experiences. The figures in the above capsule are approximate. In addition to regional accreditation, the college is accredited by AABC. William Jessup University awards the B.A. and B.S. in Bible and theology, pastoral ministry, youth ministry, Christian education, Intercultural studies, counseling, music and worship, business management, liberal arts education. and Christian leadership. The school also awards associate and bachelor's degrees. Web: *www.jessup.edu*

CONNECTICUT

HOLY APOSTLES COLLEGE & SEMINARY — C-2

Cromwell, CT 06416 (860) 632-3033
(860) 632-3075

Full-time: 25 men, 7 women   **Faculty:** 25
Part-time: 7 men, 17 women   **Tuition:** $9950
Graduate: 178 men, 82 women   **Room & Board:** n/a
Application Deadline: open
SAT: required

Holy Apostles College & Seminary, founded in 1956, is affiliated with the Roman Catholic Church. Its mission is to cultivate lay, consecrated, and ordained Catholic leaders for the purpose of evangelization and to maintain excellence in teaching/learning, research/discovery, and service/engagement through the liberal arts, philosophy and theology. The figures in the above capsule are approximate. In addition to regional accreditation, the college is accredited by NEASC. Holy Apostles College & Seminary awards the B.A. in English in the humanities, history in the social sciences, philosophy and theology. The school also awards associate, bachelor's, and master's degrees. Web: *www.holyapostles.edu*

FLORIDA

JOHNSON UNIVERSITY/FLORIDA — D-3

Kissimmee, FL 34744 (407) 847-8966
(407) 847-3925

Full-time: 105 men, 110 women   **Faculty:** 24
Part-time: 30 men, 30 women   **Tuition:** $10,910
Graduate: n/av   **Room & Board:** $3200
Application Deadline: July 15
ACT: 24

Johnson University, founded in 1976, is affiliated with Christian Churches/Churches of Christ/Independent. Its mission is to conduct a course of study educating men and women for Christian service, to provide a program of instruction on the college level, to grant appropriate degrees, and to serve as a resource to churches, especially in Florida. The figures in the above capsule are approximate. In addition to regional accreditation, the college is accredited by AABC and SACS. Johnson University awards the B.A., B.S., and B.Th. in Bible, Christian education ministries, and Christian ministries. The school also awards associate and bachelor's degrees. Web: *www.johnson.edu*

ST. JOHN VIANNEY COLLEGE SEMINARY E-5

Miami, FL 33165	(305) 223-4561
	(305) 223-0650
Full-time: 74 men	Faculty: 23
Part-time: 1 men, 1 women	Tuition: $21,347
Graduate: n/av	Room & Board: $8643
Application Deadline: open	

St. John Vianney College Seminary, founded in 1959, is affiliated with the Roman Catholic Church. The figures in the above capsule are approximate. Its mission is to provide an undergraduate education preparatory for students whose stated objective is to serve the Catholic Church in the priesthood, and to provide spiritual and intellectual formation within an Anglo-Hispanic bilingual, bicultural setting. In addition to regional accreditation, the college is accredited by SACS. St. John Vianney College Seminary awards the B.A. and B.Phil. in philosophy. The school also awards bachelor's degrees. Web: *www.sjvcs.edu*

THE BAPTIST COLLEGE OF FLORIDA B-1

Graceville, FL 32440	(850) 263-3261
	(850) 263-9026
Full-time: 237 men, 177 women	Faculty: 57
Part-time: 103 men, 29 women	Tuition: $9900
Graduate: n/av	Room & Board: $2069
Application Deadline: August 1	

The Baptist College of Florida, founded in 1943, is affiliated with Florida Baptist Convention. Its mission is to promote, provide for, operate, and control a program of education and training for ministers and other religious workers. The figures in the above capsule are approximate. In addition to regional accreditation, the college is accredited by SACS. Baptist College of Florida awards the B.A. in biblical studies, Christian counseling, Christian education, Christian studies, elementary education, English, English secondary education, history and social studies, history and social studies secondary education, leadership, ministry, missions, and music ministry. The school also awards associate and bachelor's degrees. Web:*www.baptistcollege.edu*

GEORGIA

POINT UNIVERSITY B-2

West Point, GA 31833	(706) 385-1000
	(706) 645-9473
Full-time: 534 men, 639 women	Faculty: 120
Part-time: 142 men, 207 women	Tuition: $17,650
Graduate: n/av	Room & Board: $6350
Application Deadline: August 1	

Point University, founded in 1937, is affiliated with Christian Churches and Churches of Christ. Its mission is The mission of Point University is to educate students for Christ-centered service and lead-ership throughout the world. In addition to regional accreditation, the college is accredited by SACSCOC. Point University awards the B.A., B.S., and B.B.A. in accounting, biblical studies, biblical studies and preaching ministry (dual major), biology, business administration, child and youth development, Christian ministry, counseling and human services, criminal justice, early childhood education, English, English and biblical studies (dual major), exercise science, history, human relations, humanities, humanities and biblical studies (dual major), management, marketing, middle grades education, music, organizational leadership, psychology, sociology with specialization in social work. The school also awards associate and bachelor's degrees. Web: *www.point.edu*

ILLINOIS

LINCOLN CHRISTIAN UNIVERSITY D3

Lincoln, IL 62656-2111	(217) 732-3168
	(217) 732-4199
Full-time: 273 men, 265 women	Faculty: 99
Part-time: 52 men, 53 women	Tuition: $14,840
Graduate: 233 men, 117 women	Room & Board: $7179
Application Deadline: open	
ACT: 23	

Lincoln Christian University, founded in 1944, is affiliated with the Christian Church/Church of Christ. Its mission is a Christian higher education community whose mission it is to nurture and equip Christians with a Biblical worldview to serve and lead in the church and the world. The figures in the above capsule are approximate. In addition to regional accreditation, the college is accredited by AABC and NCACS. Lincoln Christian University awards the B.A. and B.S. in Bible, business administration, Christian leadership and management, general ministry, intercultural studies, preaching ministry, youth ministry,Biblical exposition, children and family ministry, Christian spiritual formation, general studies, philosophy, psychology, worship ministry,and youth and preaching ministry. The school also awards associate, bachelor's, master's, and doctorate degrees. Web: *www.lincolnchristian.edu*

MOODY BIBLE INSTITUTE E-2

Chicago, IL 60610	(312) DL-MOODY
	(312) 329-8955
Full-time: 848 men, 730 women	Faculty: 95
Part-time: 436 men, 389 women	Tuition: $2286
Graduate: 261 men, 152 women	Room & Board: $8160
Application Deadline: December 1 or March 1	
ACT: 26	

Moody Bible Institute, founded in 1886, is affiliated with Evangelical Protestant. Its mission is to educate and train individuals to proclaim the gospel of the Lord Jesus Christ, to promote evangelism, and to serve the Evangelical Christian Church vocationally and/or avocationally in its worldwide ministry. The figures in the above capsule are approximate. In addition to regional accreditation, the college is accredited by AABC and NCA. Moody Bible Institute awards the B.A., B.S., and B.Mus. in missionary aviation technology, biblical studies, evangelism/discipleship, communication, educational ministries, world missions, pastoral studies, religious education, church music, sacred music, Bible-theology, applied linguistics, youth ministry, urban ministry, Jewish and modern Israel studies, family ministries, women's ministries, and teaching English to speakers of other languages. The school also awards associate, bachelor's, and master's degrees. Web: *www.moody.edu*

IOWA

DIVINE WORD COLLEGE   E-2

Epworth, IA 52045-0380	(563) 876-3353 (563) 876-5515
Full-time: 80 men, 34 women	Faculty: 29
Part-time: n/av	Tuition: $12,725
Graduate: n/av	Room & Board: $4150
Application Deadline: July 15	

Divine Word College, founded in 1912, is affiliated with Roman Catholic. Its mission is DWC combines a liberal arts education with a cross-cultural program of missionary formation for Divine Word Missionaries and other leaders in the Roman Catholic Church. The figures in the above capsule are approximate. In addition to regional accreditation, the college is accredited by NCA. Divine Word College awards the BA in Philosophy, Cross-Cultural Studies, and Religious Studies. The school also awards associate and bachelor's degrees. Web: www.dwci.edu

FAITH BAPTIST BIBLE COLLEGE AND THEOLOGICAL SEMINARY   C-3

Ankeny, IA 50023	(515) 964-0601 (515) 964-1638
Full-time: 120 men, 186 women	Faculty: 36
Part-time: 22 men, 23 women	Tuition: $13,760
Graduate: 52 men, 14 women	Room & Board: $6010
Application Deadline: August 1	
SAT CR/M/W: 590/555/605 ACT: 22	

Faith Baptist Bible College and Theological Seminary, founded in 1921, is affiliated with Baptist. Its mission is to provide an intensive biblical and vocational education on the college level with the goal of preparing students to minister effectively in Christian service through leadership positions in fundamental Baptist churches and other organizations of like convictions. The figures in the above capsule are approximate. In addition to regional accreditation, the college is accredited by AABC and NCA. Faith Baptist Bible College and Theological Seminary awards the B.A. and B.S. in Bible and theology, assistant pastor, Christian education, Christian school, missions, music ministries, and pastoral training. The school also awards associate, bachelor's, and master's degrees. Web: www.faith.edu

KENTUCKY

CLEAR CREEK BAPTIST BIBLE COLLEGE   F-3

Pineville, KY 40977-9752	(606) 337-3196 (606) 337-2372
Full-time: 100 men, 24 women	Faculty: 22
Part-time: 50 men, 14 women	Tuition: $5472
Graduate: n/av	Room & Board: $3900
Application Deadline: July 15	

Clear Creek Baptist Bible College, founded in 1926, is affiliated with Southern Baptist. Its mission is Providing theological education for adults called to Christian service. The figures in the above capsule are approximate. In addition to regional accreditation, the college is accredited by AABC and SACS. Clear Creek Baptist Bible College awards the B.A. in Bible. The school also awards associate and bachelor's degrees. Web: www.ccbbc.edu

LOUISIANA

SAINT JOSEPH ABBEY AND SEMINARY COLLEGE   D-3

St. Benedict, LA 70457	(985) 867-1800 (985) 867-2270
Full-time: 80 men	Faculty: n/av
Part-time: 70 men	Tuition: $12,860
Graduate: n/av	Room & Board: $12,440
Application Deadline: open	

Saint Joseph Abbey and Seminary College, founded in 1891, is affiliated with the Roman Catholic Church. Figures in the above capsule are approximate. Its mission is to educate and train men for the priesthood in the Roman Catholic Church and to support preparation for lay ministry. In addition to regional accreditation, the college is accredited by SACS. Saint Joseph Abbey and Seminary College awards the B.A. in philosophy and the liberal arts, and philosophy and theological studies. The school also awards bachelor's degrees. Web:www.sjasc.edu

MICHIGAN

SACRED HEART MAJOR SEMINARY   E-5

Detroit, MI 48206	(313) 883-8500 (313) 883-8682
Full-time: 46 men, 6 women	Faculty: 78
Part-time: 108 men, 102 women	Tuition: $15,770
Graduate: 124 men, 44 women	Room & Board: $8768
Application Deadline: August 15	

Sacred Heart Major Seminary, founded in 1919, is affiliated with The Roman Catholic Church. It is an institution of higher education that primarily prepares candidates for the Roman Catholic Priesthood and, further, prepares individuals for the diaconate, lay ministry and other leadership roles. Sacred Heart Major Seminary seeks to provide an excellent undergraduate formation based on an emphasis in Philosophy and ministry that will serve as a sound foundation to pursue theological studies. The graduate Theology programs seek to ensure a clearly Catholic professional and academic formation for ministerial service. In addition to regional accreditation, the college is accredited by NCA and ATS. Sacred Heart Major Seminary awards the A.B. and B.Phil. in Philosophy, Pastoral Theology. The school also awards associate, bachelor's, and master's degrees. Web: www.shms.edu

MINNESOTA

CROWN COLLEGE   C-4

Saint Bonifacius, MN 55375	(952) 446-4100 (952) 446-4149
Full-time: 348 men, 465 women	Faculty: n/av
Part-time: 96 men, 122 women	Tuition: $21,970
Graduate: 100 men, 67 women	Room & Board: $7880
Application Deadline: n/av	
ACT: 23	

Crown College, founded in 1916, is affiliated with the Christian and Missionary Alliance. Its mission is To provide a Biblically based education for Christian leadership in the Christian and Missionary Alliance, the church at large, and the world. The figures in the above capsule are approximate. In addition to regional accreditation, the college is accredited by NCA. Crown College awards the B.A., B.S., B.Mus.Ed., and B.S.N. in Biblical and Theological Studies, Biology, Business Administration, Child and Family Ministries, Communication, Criminal/Social Justice, Discipleship Ministries, Elementary Education, English, English Education, ESL Education, General Studies, History, Intercultural Studies, Liberal Arts, Linguistics, Management, Music, Music Education, New Testament, Nursing, Pastoral Leadership, Physical Education, Psychology, Science Education, Social Entrepreneurship, Social Studies Education, Sport Management, TESOL, Urban Studies, Worship Arts, Youth and Family, and Youth/Social Ministry. The school also awards associate, bachelor's, and master's degrees. Web: *www.crown.edu*

MARTIN LUTHER COLLEGE	C-4
New Ulm, MN 56073-3300	(507) 354-8221 (507) 354-8225
Full-time: 515 men, 525 women	Faculty: 98
Part-time: 8 men, 9 women	Tuition: $5800
Graduate: n/av	Room & Board: $3000
Application Deadline: April 15	
ACT: 24.2	

Martin Luther College, founded in 1995, is affiliated with the Wisconsin Evangelical Lutheran Synod. Its mission is to provide training for elementary and secondary teaching, preseminary training for pastoral students, and training for other church vocations through the Staff Ministry Program. The figures in the above capsule are approximate. In addition to regional accreditation, the college is accredited by NCACS. Martin Luther College awards the B.A. and B.S.Ed. in education and preseminary studies. The school also awards bachelor's degrees. Web: *www.mlc-wels.edu*

OAK HILLS CHRISTIAN COLLEGE	B-2
Bemidji, MN 56601	(218) 751-8670 (218) 444-1311
Full-time: 75 men, 75 women	Faculty: 18
Part-time: 15 men, 20 women	Tuition: $14,230
Graduate: n/av	Room & Board: $5580
Application Deadline: n/av	
ACT: required	

Oak Hills Christian College, founded in 1946, is affiliated with interdenominational. Its mission is Integrating faith and learning through biblical training. The figures in the above capsule are approximate. Oak Hills Christian College awards the B.A., B.S. in biblical studies, biblical studies and applied psychology, applied studies, campus ministry, contemporary worship, contemporary Christian ministry, intercultural studies, pastoral ministry, and youth ministry. The school also awards associate and bachelor's degrees. Web: *www.oakhills.edu*

MISSOURI

CONCEPTION SEMINARY COLLEGE	A-1
Conception, MO 64433	(660) 944-3100 (660) 944-2829
Full-time: 85 men	Faculty: 30
Part-time: 2 men, 50 women	Tuition: $29,686
Graduate: n/av	Room & Board: $10,236
Application Deadline: July 31	
ACT: 22	

Conception Seminary College, founded in 1886, is affiliated with Roman Catholic. Its mission is to prepare men who are discerning for the Roman Catholic priesthood. Conception Seminary College

places emphasis on spiritual, personal, and academic formation. The figures in the above capsule are approximate. In addition to regional accreditation, the college is accredited by NCA. Conception Seminary College awards the B.A. in liberal arts. The school also awards bachelor's degrees. Web: *www.conceptionabbey.org*

NORTH CAROLINA

MID-ATLANTIC CHRISTIAN UNIVERSITY	F-2
Elizabeth City, NC 27909-4054	(252) 334-2000 (252) 334-2071
Full-time: 87 men, 48 women	Faculty: 23
Part-time: 12 men, 22 women	Tuition: $11,700
Graduate: n/av	Room & Board: $7900
Application Deadline: n/av	
SAT CR/M: 480/480 ACT: 20	

Mid-Atlantic Christian University, founded in 1948, is affiliated with Christian Church/Church of Christ. Its mission is Mid-Atlantic Christian University is an undergraduate institution of Christian higher education whose mission is to impact the world by transforming ordinary people into extraordinary Christian leaders. The figures in the above capsule are approximate. In addition to regional accreditation, the college is accredited by AABC and SACS. Mid-Atlantic Christian University awards the B.A., B.S., B.Th. in Biblical Exposition and Cross-Cultural Ministry, Biblical Exposition and General Ministry, Biblical Exposition and Missions Aviation, Biblical Exposition and Preaching, Biblical Exposition with Youth & Family Ministry, Biblical Exposition & Applied Linguistics, Biblical Studies with Counseling & Psychology, Biblical Studies with Leadership & Administration, Biblical Studies, and Biblical Exposition. The school also awards associate and bachelor's degrees. Web: *www.macuniversity.edu*

NORTH DAKOTA

TRINITY BIBLE COLLEGE	E-4
Ellendale, ND 58436	(800) 523-1603 (701) 349-5786
Full-time: 131 men, 143 women	Faculty: 30
Part-time: 8 men, 25 women	Tuition: $13,590
Graduate: n/av	Room & Board: $5550
Application Deadline: August 15	

Trinity Bible College, founded in 1948, is affiliated with Assemblies of God. Its mission is to prepare pastors, church leaders, and Christian professionals in various fields in a Bible-based Pentecostal environment of academic excellence. In addition to regional accreditation, the college is accredited by AABC and NCACS. Trinity Bible College awards the B.A. in biblical studies, business administration, elementary education, ministerial studies, and missions. The figures in the above capsule are approximate. The school also awards associate and bachelor's degrees. Web: *www.trinitybiblecollege.edu*

OHIO

CINCINNATI CHRISTIAN UNIVERSITY	A-5
Cincinnati, OH 45204-3200	(800) 949-4CCU ext. 8485 (513) 244-8111
Full-time: 270 men, 236 women	Faculty: 85
Part-time: 85 men, 44 women	Tuition: $14,604
Graduate: 169 men, 86 women	Room & Board: $6730
Application Deadline: August 10	

Cincinnati Christian University, founded in 1924, is affiliated with Christian Churches/Churches of Christ. Its mission is to teach men and women to live by biblical principles and to equip and empower them with skills, insight, and vision both to lead the church and to impact society for Christ. The figures in the above capsule are approximate. In addition to regional accreditation, the college is accredited by AABC and NCA. Cincinnati Christian University awards the B.A., B.S., and B.Mus. in biblical studies (primary major), education, ministries, (second major), and signing interpreter's training program, psychology, preaching, youth ministry, worship, music, children's ministry, urban/intercultural ministry, music education and history. The school also awards associate, bachelor's, and master's degrees. Web: *www.CCUniversity.edu*

Mid-America Christian University, founded in 1953, is affiliated with Church of God in Anderson, Indiana. Its mission is Mid-America Christian University equips students to impact their world for Christ through achieving Bible-based academic excellence in a Christian environment so that students professionally serve in their chosen vocation/ministry. The figures in the above capsule are approximate. In addition to regional accreditation, the college is accredited by NCA. Mid-America Christian University awards the B.A. and B.S. in behavioral science, elementary education, English, music, performance, pastoral ministry, worship and music ministries, secondary education, specialized ministries, management and ethics, English/business, and business administration. The school also awards associate, bachelor's, and master's degrees. Web: *www.macu.edu*

OHIO CHRISTIAN UNIVERSITY

Circleville, OH 43113	(740) 474-8896
Full-time: 372 men, 429 women	Faculty: 135
Part-time: 55 men, 75 women	Tuition: $16,600
Graduate: n/av	Room & Board: $7386
Application Deadline: Priority deadline is May	
SAT CR/M/W: 478/418/514 ACT: 19	

Ohio Christian University, founded in 1948, is affiliated with Churches of Christ in Christian Union (CCCU). Its mission is to provide a holistic Bible college education in the Wesleyan tradition that equips students to grow spiritually and intellectually and to serve effectively in society and the church. The figures in the above capsule are approximate. In addition to regional accreditation, the college is accredited by AABC and NCA. Ohio Christian University awards the B.A. in religion, business management, psychology, nursing, teacher education, international studies, ministries, music education, youth ministries, and christian ministries. The school also awards associate and bachelor's degrees. Web: *www.ohiochristian.edu*

PONTIFICAL COLLEGE JOSEPHINUM   C-3

Columbus, OH 43235	(614) 885-5585 (614) 885-2307
Full-time: 78 men	Faculty: 41
Part-time: n/av	Tuition: $18,439
Graduate: 51 men, 2 women	Room & Board: $8646
Application Deadline: July 31	
SAT CR/M/W: 550/570/520 ACT: 24	

Pontifical College Josephinum, founded in 1888, is affiliated with Roman Catholic. Its mission is to prepare young men for the priesthood. In addition to regional accreditation, the college is accredited by NCACS and ATS. Pontifical College Josephinum awards the B.A. in philosophy and the humanities (English literature, Hispanic studies, history, and classical studies). The figures in the above capsule are approximate. The school also awards bachelor's and master's degrees. Web: *pcj.edu*

OKLAHOMA

MID-AMERICA CHRISTIAN UNIVERSITY   D-3

Oklahoma City, OK 73170	(405) 691-3800 (405) 692-3165
Full-time: 338 men, 387 women	Faculty: 45
Part-time: 87 men, 94 women	Tuition: $13,930
Graduate: 116 men, 158 women	Room & Board: $5050
Application Deadline: open	

SOUTHWESTERN CHRISTIAN UNIVERSITY

Bethany, OK 73008	(405) 789-7661 (405) 495-0078
Full-time: 91 men, 92 women	Faculty: 35
Part-time: 11 men, 15 women	Tuition: $8750
Graduate: 58 men, 20 women	Room & Board: $2600
Application Deadline: open	
ACT: 18	

Southwesten Christian University, founded in 1946, is affiliated with Pentecostal Holiness. Its mission is the education and training for Christian service leading toward professional competence in the practice of various ministry forms. In addition to regional accreditation, the college is accredited by NCA. Southwesten Christian University awards the B.A. and B.S. and B.B.A. in Bibical studies, church growth, church music, music performace, missions, Christian education, Christian elementary education, pastoral ministry, youth ministry religion, Biblicial leadership, human and family services, business leadership, nonprofit organizational leadership, and business administration. The school also awards associate, bachelor's, and master's degrees. Web: *www.swcu.edu*

OREGON

MOUNT ANGEL ABBEY   B-2

St. Benedict, OR 97373	(503) 845-3030 (503) 845-3126
Full-time: 85 men	Faculty: 40
Part-time: n/av	Tuition: $14,184
Graduate: 87 men, 12 women	Room & Board: $9434
Application Deadline: July 15	

Mount Angel Abbey, founded in 1889, is affiliated with Roman Catholic. Its mission is to prepare students of the Roman Catholic priesthood for religious orders and dioceses. The figures in the above capsule are approximate. In addition to regional accreditation, the college is accredited by NASC. Mount Angel Abbey awards the B.A. in philosophy and literature. The school also awards bachelor's and master's degrees. Web: *www.mountangelabbey.org*

PENNSYLVANIA

BAPTIST BIBLE COLLEGE & SEMINARY   E-2

Clarks Summit, PA 18411	(570) 586-2400 (570) 586-1753
Full-time: 192 men, 243 women	Faculty: 30
Part-time: 68 men, 86 women	Tuition: $20,250
Graduate: 300 men, 87 women	Room & Board: $7400
Application Deadline: August 15	
SAT CR/M: 520/510 ACT: 22	

Baptist Bible College & Seminary, founded in 1932, is affiliated with Baptist. Its mission is To prepare men and women for service in a wide variety of ministries including teaching, counseling, pastors, missionaries, Christian education workers, church musicians, and secretaries. The figures in the above capsule are approximate. In addition to regional accreditation, the college is accredited by AABC and MSACS. Baptist Bible College & Seminary awards the B.S. in Bible and B.S.M. in church music, communications, elementary and early childhood teacher education, pre-K teacher education, general missions, local church ministries, outreach and evangelism pastor, pastoral ministry, pastor of Christian education, preseminary, secondary social studies teacher education, secondary science teacher education, secondary math teacher education, secondary english teacher education, health and physical education teacher education, music teacher education, secretarial ministries, sports ministries, youth pastor, precounseling, general ministries, women's ministries, early childhood education, business, and office professionals. The school also awards associate, bachelor's, master's, and doctorate degrees. Web: www.bbc.edu

LANCASTER BIBLE COLLEGE — E-3

Lancaster, PA 17601 (717) 569-7071
(717) 560-8213

Full-time: 302 men, 286 women | Faculty: 86
Part-time: 110 men, 105 women | Tuition: $16,340
Graduate: 90 men, 85 women | Room & Board: $7280
Application Deadline: open
SAT CR/M: 520/500 ACT: 23

Lancaster Bible College , founded in 1933, is affiliated with nondenominational. Its mission is to educate Christian men and women to live according to a biblical worldview and to serve through professional Christian ministries. The figures in the above capsule are approximate. In addition to regional accreditation, the college is accredited by AABC and MSA. Lancaster Bible College awards the B.S. in Bible and B.S.Ed. in Bible education, Bible ministry, children and family ministry, counseling (professional), cross-cultural ministry, elementary education/early level, elementary education/middle level, music education, music performance, pastoral ministry, preseminary, social work, spiritual formation and discipleship, student ministry, TESOL, women in Christian ministry, and worship arts. The school also awards associate, bachelor's, and master's degrees. Web: www.lbc.edu

SAINT CHARLES BORROMEO SEMINARY — F-3

Wynnewood, PA 19096 (610) 667-3394
(610) 617-9267

Full-time: 90 men | Faculty: 65
Part-time: 25 men, 35 women | Tuition: $18,928
Graduate: 90 men, 30 women | Room & Board: $11,972
Application Deadline: July 1

Saint Charles Borromeo Seminary, founded in 1832, is affiliated with The Roman Catholic Church. Its mission is to prepare and educate men for the Roman Catholic priesthood and to provide undergraduate and graduate programs for men and women pursuing theological studies. The figures in the above capsule are approximate. In addition to regional accreditation, the college is accredited by MSACS. The school awards the B.A. in philosophy, as well as bachelor's and master's degrees. Web: www.scs.edu

SOUTH CAROLINA

COLUMBIA INTERNATIONAL UNIVERSITY — C-3

Columbia, SC 29230 (803) 754-4100
(803) 786-4029

Full-time: 215 men, 259 women | Faculty: 49
Part-time: 33 men, 43 women | Tuition: $21,275
Graduate: 214 men, 186 women | Room & Board: $6710
Application Deadline: open
ACT: 24

Columbia International University, founded in 1923, is affiliated with multidenominational. Its mission is to prepare students to grow in spiritual maturity, Bible knowledge, and ministry skills in preparation for vocational or lay Christian ministry. The figures in the above capsule are approximate. In addition to regional accreditation, the college is accredited by AABC and SACS. Columbia International University awards the B.A. and B.S. in Bible, general studies, intercultural studies, psychology, biblical languages, music, Bible teaching, youth ministry, middle eastern studies, family and church education, teacher education, humanities, pastoral ministries, and communications. The school also awards associate, bachelor's, master's, and doctorate degrees. Web: www.ciu.edu

TENNESSEE

JOHNSON UNIVERSITY — E-3

Knoxville, TN 37998 (865) 573-4517

Full-time: 343 men, 306 women | Faculty: 62
Part-time: 15 men, 16 women | Tuition: $14,270
Graduate: 69 men, 67 women | Room & Board: $3200
Application Deadline: June 1

Johnson University, founded in 1893, is affiliated with Christian. Its mission is to educate students for specialized Christian ministries. The figures in the above capsule are approximate. In addition to regional accreditation, the college is accredited by AABC and SACS. Johnson University awards the B.A. and B.S. in All students who graduate from Johnson University with a Bachelor of Arts or a Bachelor of Science degree major in Bible. In addition, five professional programs require a second major. They are: counseling, preaching, interdisciplinary major with focus on teacher education, music, and youth ministry/preaching. The school also awards associate, bachelor's, and master's degrees. Web: www.johnsonu.edu

WELCH COLLEGE — C-2

Nashville, TN 37205 (615) 844-5000
(615) 269-6028

Full-time: 100 men, 92 women | Faculty: 55
Part-time: 54 men, 36 women | Tuition: $14,806
Graduate: n/av | Room & Board: $6542
Application Deadline: open
ACT: 22

Welch College, founded in 1942, is affiliated with National Association of Free Will Baptists. Its mission is the Mission of Welch College is to educate leaders to serve Christ, His Church and His world through Biblical thought and life. The figures in the above capsule are approximate. In addition to regional accreditation, the college is accredited by AABC, SACS, and ABHE. Welch College awards the B.A. and B.S. in biblical studies, biblical and ministry studies, business administration, church music, church music and youth ministry,

English, elementary education, music education, music performance, sports medicine, physical education, secondary English education, and psychology and learning. The school also awards associate and bachelor's degrees. Web: *www.welch.edu*

TEXAS

AUSTIN GRADUATE SCHOOL OF THEOLOGY — D-3

Austin, TX 78752	(512) 476-2772
	(512) 476-3919
Full-time: 4 men	Faculty: 10
Part-time: 15 men, 7 women	Tuition: $4275
Graduate: 25 men, 5 women	Room & Board: n/app
Application Deadline: July 1 (recommended)	

Austin Graduate School of Theology, founded in 1917, is affiliated with Church of Christ. Its mission is to equip ministers and other Christians for service in the kingdom of God. The figures in the above capsule are approximate. In addition to regional accreditation, the college is accredited by SACS. Austin Graduate School of Theology awards the B.A. in Christian studies. The school also awards bachelor's and master's degrees. Web: *www.austingrad.edu*

BAPTIST MISSIONARY ASSOCIATION THEOLOGICAL SEMINARY — E-2

Jacksonville, TX 75766	(903) 586-2501
	(903) 586-0378
Full-time: 23 men, 1 women	Faculty: 13
Part-time: 26 men, 22 women	Tuition: $4500
Graduate: 49 men, 8 women	Room & Board: n/app
Application Deadline: open	

Baptist Missionary Association Theological Seminary, founded in 1955, is affiliated with Baptist Missionary Association. Its mission is to train individuals for Christian ministry. The figures in the above capsule are approximate. In addition to regional accreditation, the college is accredited by SACS. Baptist Missionary Association Theological Seminary awards the B.A.R. in religion. The school also awards associate, bachelor's, and master's degrees. Web:*www.bmats.edu*

CRISWELL COLLEGE — D-2

Dallas, TX 75246	(214) 821-5433
	(214) 370-0497
Full-time: 140 men, 30 women	Faculty: 27
Part-time: 160 men, 50 women	Tuition: $7032
Graduate: 100 men, 20 women	Room & Board: n/app
Application Deadline: July 15	

Criswell College, founded in 1970, is affiliated with Southern Baptist. Its mission is to educate and train laymen and full-time Christian workers in biblical, theological, and professional studies so they can serve effectively in evangelistic, educational, pastoral, and missionary vocations of the Christian church. The figures in the above capsule are approximate. In addition to regional accreditation, the college is accredited by SACS. Criswell College awards the B.A. in biblical studies, counseling, missions, evangelism, pastoral, and urban ministries. The school also awards associate, bachelor's, and master's degrees. Web: *www.criswell.edu*

SOUTHWESTERN ASSEMBLIES OF GOD UNIVERSITY — D-2

Waxahachie, TX 75165	(972) 937-4010
	(972) 923-0006
Full-time: 587 men, 604 women	Faculty: 129
Part-time: 145 men, 122 women	Tuition: $16,230
Graduate: 168 men, 148 women	Room & Board: $6321
Application Deadline: open	

Southwestern Assemblies of God University, founded in 1927, is affiliated with Assemblies of God. Its mission is to prepare undergraduate and graduate students spiritually, academically, professionally, and cross culturally so as to successfully fill evangelistic, missionary and church ministry roles and to provide quality educational and professional Christian service wherever needed throughout the world. In addition to regional accreditation, the college is accredited by AABC and SACS. Southwestern Assemblies of God University awards the B.A. and B.S. in Accounting, Ancient Studies, Biblical Studies, Business Administration, Children & Family Ministries, Church Ministries, Church Planting & Revitalization, Communication Counseling, Counseling Ministries, Criminal Justice, Digital Media, Arts Drama, Education, Bilingual Education, Elementary Education, Middle & Secondary English, Language Arts/Reading, Social Studies/History, Music Education, Instrumental Piano Vocal, Physical Education, English, History, Human Services, Management, Management Information Systems, Marketing Media, Ministries, Music Ministries, Music Performance, Pastoral Ministries, Professional Development, Psychology, Social Work, Sports Management, Theological Studies, World Ministries, and Youth & Student Ministries. The school also awards associate, bachelor's, and master's degrees. Web: *www.sagu.edu*

WASHINGTON

TRINITY LUTHERAN COLLEGE — C-2

Everett, WA 98201	(425) 249-4801
Full-time: 47 men, 65 women	Faculty: 26
Part-time: 2 men, 3 women	Tuition: $27,640
Graduate: n/av	Room & Board: $8500
Application Deadline: see profile	
SAT CR/M: 475/450 ACT: 20	

Trinity Lutheran College, founded in 1944, is affiliated with Lutheran. Its mission is to prepare students, through a living-learning environment, for rewarding careers by learning to integrate faith, ethics, and service along with key learning objectives. A Trinity education requires students to have the courage to take responsibility for their own faith, thought, and actions. In addition to regional accreditation, the college is accredited by NASC. Trinity Lutheran College awards the B.A. in biblical studies, music and worship, early childhood education, children, youth and family studies, intercultural studies, communications, business, leadership and management, psychology, and social work. The figures in the above capsule are approximate. The school also awards associate and bachelor's degrees. Web: *www.tlc.edu*

WISCONSIN

MARANATHA BAPTIST UNIVERSITY — D-4

Watertown, WI 53094	(920) 261-9300
	(920) 261-9109
Full-time: 350 men, 404 women	Faculty: 57
Part-time: 31 men, 45 women	Tuition: $5780
Graduate: 27 men, 3 women	Room & Board: $3400
Application Deadline: see profile	
ACT: 21	

Maranatha Baptist University, founded in 1968, is affiliated with Baptist. Its mission is Maranatha Baptist University is an accredited college that desires to produce students who are spiritually and academically prepared to serve the Lord. We want to develop servants of Christ who are disciplined, creative, and passionate about the field to which they have been called. The figure in the above capsule are approximate. In addition to regional accreditation, the college is accredited by NCA. Maranatha Baptist University awards the B.A. and B.S. in Bible, church ministries, education, general studies, fine arts, business, nursing, office administration, biology, and premed. The school also awards associate, bachelor's, and master's degrees. Web: *www.mbu.edu*

AIR FORCE

In the Air Force ROTC program, young men and women may earn commissions while attending college. The amount of academic credit given for Air Force ROTC varies from school to school.

Most new Air Force officers come through the Air Force ROTC program. It offers students the opportunity to attend a civilian college while studying officership as part of their undergraduate curriculum.

The AFROTC program begins with the General Military Course. Freshmen or sophomores attend one hour of ROTC classes and one to two hours of leadership laboratory weekly. During these first two years, study is focused on the history of the Air Force and the part it plays in the world today. During the summer between sophomore and junior years, students attend a four-week basic training course located at an Air Force base.

The Professional Officer Course is completed during the junior and senior years. Study includes management principles and defense policy and offers the opportunity for managing, organizing, directing, and evaluating the cadet corps activities. Cadets who are medically qualified will have the opportunity to compete for pilot or navigator positions. Upon graduation, students are commissioned as Second Lieutenants.

For academically qualified students in selected majors, the AFROTC offers scholarships, including tuition, fees and books, and a monthly nontaxable allowance during the school year.

The majority of scholarships are awarded in the technical degree areas of engineering and computer science, but there are opportunities in nontechnical areas as well. Scholarships are based on individual merit, not financial need. Those who receive a scholarship must still apply and be accepted by the school they wish to attend and notify the AFROTC headquarters of their selection.

The scholarship program is broken down into different types and durations. All scholarships include full or partial tuition, fees, textbook allowance, and $500 per month tax-free allowance during the academic year. Type 1 pays full tuition at any school offering AFROTC. Type 2 pays tuition and fees up to a maximum of $18,000 per year. There are two variations of the Type 7 scholarship. A Type 7 scholarship winner can attend any post-secondary institution (public or private) where tuition does not exceed $9,000 per year, or he/she can attend any public post-secondary institution where the student qualifies for in-state tuition rates.

The application deadline is December 1 of the senior year, but priority consideration is given to those who get the application in early. AFROTC only accepts on-line applications and they are available during the spring prior to the senior year of high school.

Further information can be obtained from the professor of aerospace studies at any of the host campuses where Air Force ROTC is offered. The listing that follows represents the host schools that offer these programs. Hundreds more schools have crosstown agreements with these institutions to make AFROTC more accessible to students. Please be sure to contact the school directly for more details. You may also find useful and current information at the Air Force Reserve Officer Training Corps web site, *www.afrotc.com*.

ALABAMA

- Alabama State University
- Auburn University at Auburn
- Samford University
- Troy University
- Tuskegee University
- University of Alabama
- University of South Alabama

ALASKA

- University of Alaska - Anchorage

ARIZONA

- Arizona State University
- Embry-Riddle Aeronautical University
- Northern Arizona University
- University of Arizona

ARKANSAS

- University of Arkansas

CALIFORNIA

- California State University, Fresno
- California State University, Sacramento
- California State University, San Bernadino
- Loyola Marymount University
- San Diego State University
- San Jose State University
- University of California at Berkeley
- University of California at Los Angeles
- University of Southern California

COLORADO

- Colorado State University
- University of Colorado at Boulder

CONNECTICUT

- University of Connecticut
- Yale University

DELAWARE

- University of Delaware

DISTRICT OF COLUMBIA

- Howard University

FLORIDA

- Embry-Riddle Aeronautical University
- Florida State University
- University of Central Florida
- University of Florida
- University of Miami
- University of South Florida

GEORGIA

- Georgia Institute of Technology
- University of Georgia
- Valdosta State University

HAWAII

- University of Hawaii at Manoa

ILLINOIS

- Illinois Institute of Technology
- Saint Louis University
- Southern Illinois University
- University of Illinois at Champaign/ Urbana

INDIANA

- Indiana State University
- Indiana University
- Purdue University
- University of Notre Dame

IOWA

- Iowa State University
- University of Iowa

KANSAS

- Kansas State University
- University of Kansas

KENTUCKY

- University of Kentucky
- University of Louisville

LOUISIANA

- Louisiana State University and Agricultural and Mechanical College
- Louisiana Tech University
- Tulane University

MARYLAND

- University of Maryland

MASSACHUSETTS

- Boston University
- Massachusetts Institute of Technology
- Rensselaer Polytechnic Institute
- University of Massachusetts
- University of Massachusetts, Lowell
- Worcester Polytechnic Institute

MICHIGAN

- Michigan State University
- Michigan Technological University
- University of Michigan

MINNESOTA

- University of Minnesota/Duluth
- University of Minnesota
- University of Saint Thomas

MISSISSIPPI

- Jackson State University
- Mississippi State University
- University of Mississippi
- University of Southern Mississippi

MISSOURI

- Missouri University of Science and Technology
- St. Louis University
- University of Missouri/Columbia

MONTANA

- Montana State University

NEBRASKA

- University of Nebraska at Lincoln
- University of Nebraska at Omaha

NEVADA

- University of Nevada—Las Vegas

NEW HAMPSHIRE

- University of New Hampshire

NEW JERSEY

- New Jersey Institute of Technology
- Rutgers University

NEW MEXICO

- New Mexico State University
- University of New Mexico

NEW YORK

- Clarkson University
- Cornell University
- Manhattan College
- Rensselaer Polytechnic Institute
- Rochester Institute of Technology
- Syracuse University

NORTH CAROLINA

- Duke University
- East Carolina University
- Fayetteville State University
- North Carolina A & T State University
- North Carolina State University
- University of North Carolina at Chapel Hill
- University of North Carolina at Charlotte

NORTH DAKOTA

- North Dakota State University

OHIO

- Bowling Green University
- Kent State University
- Miami University
- Ohio State University, The
- Ohio University
- University of Cincinnati
- Wright State University

OKLAHOMA

- Oklahoma State University
- University of Oklahoma

OREGON

- Oregon State University
- University of Portland

PENNSYLVANIA

- Pennsylvania State University/ Main Campus
- Saint Joseph's University
- University of Pittsburgh
- Wilkes University

PUERTO RICO

- University of Puerto Rico/Mayaguez
- University of Puerto Rico/Río Piedras

SOUTH CAROLINA

- Charleston Southern University
- The Citadel

- Clemson University
- University of South Carolina/ Columbia

SOUTH DAKOTA

- South Dakota State University

TENNESSEE

- Tennessee State University
- University of Memphis
- University of Tennessee

TEXAS

- Angelo State University
- Baylor University
- Texas A & M University
- Texas Christian University
- Texas State University/San Marcos
- Texas Tech University
- University of Houston
- University of North Texas
- University of Texas at Austin
- University of Texas at San Antonio

UTAH

- Brigham Young University
- University of Utah
- Utah State University

VERMONT

- Norwich University

VIRGINIA

- University of Virginia
- Virginia Military Institute
- Virginia Polytechnic Institute

WASHINGTON

- Central Washington University
- University of Washington
- Washington State University

WEST VIRGINIA

- West Virginia University

WISCONSIN

- Marquette University
- University of Wisconsin/Madison

WYOMING

- University of Wyoming

ARMY

The Army Reserve Officers' Training Corps (ROTC) provides college students with the opportunity to combine leadership and management training with their other academic studies. The curriculum, which consists of a series of classroom and hands-on leadership training experiences, provides students with the necessary foundation to serve successfully in positions of responsibility in either the U.S. Army or the corporate world.

Those with a strong academic background, an active mindset, and the ability to rapidly assimilate information thrive in the program. These scholar-athlete-leaders note that the lead-ership skills developed through their participation in the program are further honed during their period of service as Army officers. After service as an Army lieutenant, many graduates elect to continue their service in uniform. Others elect to enter the corporate world where their leadership skills and experience as ROTC-trained Army officers allow them to advance rapidly.

Although the program is designed to be completed in four years, students may complete all requirements within a two-year period through participation in a summer training session called the Leaders' Training Course, normally held during the summer between the sophomore and junior years. A generous series of merit-based scholarships that cover tuition, fees, textbooks, and supplies exist to help students and their families defray the cost of college. For more information on the program, call (800) USA-ROTC, or contact the professor of military science at a college that offers Army ROTC. Detailed information about the program is also available at *www.armyrotc.com*.

ALABAMA

- Alabama A&M University
- Auburn University
- Auburn University at Montgomery
- Jacksonville State University
- Marion Military Institute
- The University of Alabama
- Tuskegee University
- University of Alabama at Birmingham
- University of North Alabama
- University of South Alabama

ALASKA

- University of Alaska/Fairbanks

ARIZONA

- Arizona State University
- Northern Arizona University
- University of Arizona

ARKANSAS

- Arkansas State University
- University of Arkansas
- University of Arkansas at Pine Bluff
- University of Central Arkansas

CALIFORNIA

- California Polytechnic State University at San Luis Obispo
- California State University at Fresno
- California State University at Fullerton
- Claremont McKenna College
- San Diego State University
- Santa Clara University
- University of California at Berkeley
- University of California at Davis
- University of California at Los Angeles
- University of California at Santa Barbara
- University of San Francisco
- University of Southern California

COLORADO

- Colorado State University
- University of Colorado at Boulder
- University of Colorado at Colorado Springs

CONNECTICUT

- University of Connecticut

DELAWARE

- University of Delaware

DISTRICT OF COLUMBIA

- Georgetown University
- Howard University

FLORIDA

- Embry-Riddle Aeronautical University
- Florida A & M University
- Florida Institute of Technology
- Florida International University
- Florida Southern College
- Florida State University
- University of Central Florida
- University of Florida
- University of South Florida
- University of Tampa
- University of West Florida

GEORGIA

- Columbus State University
- Fort Valley State University
- Georgia Institute of Technology
- Georgia Military College
- Georgia Southern University
- Georgia State University
- University of North Georgia
- University of Georgia

HAWAII

- University of Hawaii at Manoa

IDAHO

- Boise State University
- University of Idaho

ILLINOIS

- Eastern Illinois University
- Illinois State University
- Northern Illinois University
- Southern Illinois University at Carbondale
- Southern Illinois University at Edwardsville
- University of Illinois at Chicago
- University of Illinois at Urbana-Champaign
- Western Illinois University
- Wheaton College

INDIANA

- Ball State University
- Indiana University-Purdue University at Indianapolis
- Indiana University at Bloomington
- Purdue University
- Rose-Hulman Institute of Technology
- University of Notre Dame

IOWA

- Iowa State University
- University of Iowa
- University of Northern Iowa

KANSAS

- Kansas State University
- Pittsburg State University
- University of Kansas

KENTUCKY

- Eastern Kentucky University
- Morehead State University
- University of Kentucky
- University of Louisville
- Western Kentucky University

LOUISIANA

- Grambling State University
- Louisiana State University
- Northwestern State University
- Southern University and A & M College
- Tulane University

MAINE

- University of Maine

MARYLAND

- Bowie State University
- Loyola University Maryland
- McDaniel College
- Morgan State University
- The Johns Hopkins University
- University of Maryland at College Park

MASSACHUSETTS

- Boston University
- Massachusetts Institute of Technology
- Northeastern University
- University of Massachusetts
- Worcester Polytechnic Institute

MICHIGAN

- Central Michigan University
- Eastern Michigan University
- Michigan State University
- Michigan Technological University
- Northern Michigan University
- University of Michigan

MINNESOTA

- Minnesota State University, Mankato
- Saint John's University
- University of Minnesota/Twin Cities

MISSISSIPPI

- Alcorn State University
- Jackson State University
- Mississippi State University
- University of Mississippi
- University of Southern Mississippi

MISSOURI

- Lincoln University
- Missouri State University
- Missouri University of Science and Technology
- Missouri Western State University
- Truman State University
- University of Central Missouri
- University of Missouri/Columbia
- Washington University
- Wentworth Military Academy

MONTANA

- Montana State University
- University of Montana

NEBRASKA

- Chadron State College
- Creighton University
- University of Nebraska at Lincoln

NEVADA

- University of Nevada/Reno

NEW HAMPSHIRE

- University of New Hampshire

NEW JERSEY

- Princeton University
- Rutgers University
- Seton Hall University

NEW MEXICO

- New Mexico Military Institute
- New Mexico State University
- University of New Mexico

NEW YORK

- Canisius College
- City University of New York (CUNY)
- Clarkson University
- Cornell University
- Fordham University
- Hofstra University
- Niagara University
- Rochester Institute of Technology
- Saint Bonaventure University
- Saint John's University New York
- Siena College
- State University of New York (SUNY)/Brockport
- Syracuse University

NORTH CAROLINA

- Appalachian State University
- Campbell University
- Duke University
- East Carolina University
- Elizabeth City State University
- North Carolina Agricultural and Technical State University
- North Carolina State University
- Saint Augustine's College
- University of North Carolina at Chapel Hill
- University of North Carolina at Charlotte
- Wake Forest University

NORTH DAKOTA

- North Dakota State University
- University of North Dakota

OHIO

- Bowling Green State University
- Capital University
- Central State University
- John Carroll University
- Kent State University
- The Ohio State University
- Ohio University
- The University of Akron
- University of Cincinnati
- University of Dayton
- University of Toledo
- Wright State University
- Xavier University

OKLAHOMA

- Cameron University
- Oklahoma State University
- University of Central Oklahoma
- University of Oklahoma

OREGON

- Oregon State University
- University of Oregon
- University of Portland

PENNSYLVANIA

- Bucknell University
- Dickinson College
- Drexel University
- Edinboro University of Pennsylvania
- Gannon University
- Indiana University of Pennsylvania
- Lehigh University
- Lock Haven University of Pennsylvania
- Pennsylvania State University
- Shippensburg University
- Slippery Rock University
- Temple University
- University of Pittsburgh
- University of Scranton
- Valley Forge Military College
- Widener University

PUERTO RICO

- University of Puerto Rico/Mayaguez
- University of Puerto Rico/Río Piedras

RHODE ISLAND

- Providence College
- University of Rhode Island

SOUTH CAROLINA

- The Citadel
- Clemson University
- Furman University
- Presbyterian College
- South Carolina State University
- University of South Carolina
- Wofford College

SOUTH DAKOTA

- South Dakota School of Mines
- South Dakota State University
- University of South Dakota

TENNESSEE

- Austin Peay State University
- Carson-Newman College
- East Tennessee State University
- Middle Tennessee State University
- Tennessee Tech University
- University of Memphis
- University of Tennessee at Knoxville
- University of Tennessee at Martin
- Vanderbilt University

TEXAS

- Prairie View A & M University
- Saint Mary's University
- Sam Houston State University
- Stephen F. Austin State University
- Tarleton State University
- Texas A & M University-College Station
- Texas A & M-Corpus Christi
- Texas A & M University at Kingsville
- Texas Christian University
- Texas State University
- Texas Tech University
- University of Houston
- University of Texas at Arlington
- University of Texas at Austin
- University of Texas at El Paso
- University of Texas at San Antonio
- University of Texas-Pan American

UTAH

- Brigham Young University
- University of Utah
- Weber State University

VERMONT

- Norwich University
- University of Vermont

VIRGINIA

- College of William and Mary
- George Mason University
- Hampton University
- James Madison University
- Norfolk State University
- Old Dominion University
- University of Richmond
- University of Virginia
- Virginia Military Institute
- Virginia State University
- Virginia Tech

WASHINGTON

- Central Washington University
- Eastern Washington University
- Gonzaga University
- Pacific Lutheran University
- Seattle University
- University of Washington
- Washington State University

WEST VIRGINIA

- Marshall University
- West Virginia State College
- West Virginia University

WISCONSIN

- Marquette University
- University of Wisconsin/La Crosse
- University of Wisconsin/Madison
- University of Wisconsin/Oshkosh
- University of Wisconsin/Stevens Point

WYOMING

- University of Wyoming

NAVY

The NROTC Program educates and trains qualified young men and women for service as commissioned officers in the unrestricted line Navy or Marine Corps. Two programs are available: the NROTC Scholarship Program and the NROTC College Program.

The NROTC Scholarship Program plays an important role in preparing young men and women for leadership and management positions in an increasingly technical Navy and Marine Corps. The four-year NROTC Scholarship Program is available to qualified students who graduate from high school before August 1 of the year they intend to start college. The two-year NROTC Scholarship Program is available to qualified college sophmores who have completed one year of differential and integral calculus with a grade of C or better and maintain a minimum GPA of 2.5.

Selected applicants for NROTC Scholarship Programs (four-year and two-year) are awarded scholarships through a highly competitive national selection process, and receive full tuition, fees, book stipend, and other financial benefits at many of the country's leading colleges and universities. Upon graduation, midshipmen are commissioned as officers in the unrestricted line Navy or Marine Corps.

Students selected for the NROTC Scholarship Program make their own arrangements for college enrollment and room and board, and take the normal course load required by the college or university for degree completion. Additionally, scholarship midshipmen are required to follow specific academic guidelines. Full information concerning the NROTC Scholarship Program is available from any of the colleges and universities with NROTC units or from Navy and Marine Corps recruiters.

For information on the NROTC scholarship programs, call 1-800-USA-NAVY or 1-800-NAV-ROTC, e-mail *PNSC_NROTC.scholarship@navy.mil*; or visit *https://www.nrotc.navy.mil*. Electronic application for the four-year scholarship program must be submitted by January 31.

The NROTC College Program may be either two or four years. Additional points include:

- Applicants are selected from students already attending or accepted by colleges with the NROTC program.
- Students selected for "advance standing" receive a stipend for a maximum of 20 months. Advance standing is only available starting in the junior year of college. Stipend per academic month is $350 junior year and $400 senior year.
- Students will complete naval science and other university courses, a few specific university courses, and attend one summer training session, normally at sea for Navy-option midshipmen and in Quantico, VA for Marine Corps-option midshipmen.

The following list shows the colleges and universities that have an NROTC unit on campus. Many more institutions offer the program through cross-town arrangements. We recommend that you visit *https://www.nrotc.navy.mil* for a listing of participating colleges and universities. Contact the schools directly for the most current and accurate information.

ALABAMA
- Auburn University
- Tuskegee University

ARIZONA
- Arizona State University
- University of Arizona

CALIFORNIA
- University of California/Berkeley
- University of California/Los Angeles
- University of San Diego
- University of Southern California

COLORADO
- University of Colorado at Boulder

CONNECTICUT
- Yale University

DISTRICT OF COLUMBIA
- George Washington University

FLORIDA
- Embry Riddle Aeronautical University
- Florida A & M University
- Jacksonville University
- University of Florida
- University of South Florida

GEORGIA
- Georgia Institute of Technology
- Morehouse College
- Savannah State College

IDAHO
- University of Idaho

ILLINOIS
- Illinois Institute of Technology
- Northwestern University
- University of Illinois at Urbana-Champaign

INDIANA
- University of Notre Dame

IOWA
- Iowa State University

KANSAS
- University of Kansas

LOUISIANA
- Tulane University

MAINE
- Maine Maritime Academy

MASSACHUSETTS
- Boston University
- College of the Holy Cross
- Massachusetts Institute of Technology

MICHIGAN
- University of Michigan

MINNESOTA
- University of Minnesota

MISSISSIPPI
- University of Mississippi

MISSOURI
- University of Missouri

NEBRASKA
- University of Nebraska at Lincoln

NEW JERSEY
- Rutgers University

NEW MEXICO
- University of New Mexico

NEW YORK
- Cornell University
- Rensselaer Polytechnic Institute
- State University of New York/Maritime College
- University of Rochester

NORTH CAROLINA
- Duke University
- North Carolina State University
- University of North Carolina at Chapel Hill

OHIO
- Miami University
- Ohio State University

OKLAHOMA

- University of Oklahoma

OREGON

- Oregon State University

PENNSYLVANIA

- Carnegie Mellon University
- Pennsylvania State University Park Campus
- University of Pennsylvania
- Villanova University

SOUTH CAROLINA

- The Citadel
- University of South Carolina

TENNESSEE

- University of Memphis
- Vanderbilt University

TEXAS

- Prairie View A & M University
- Rice University
- Texas A & M University
- University of Texas at Austin

UTAH

- University of Utah

VERMONT

- Norwich University

VIRGINIA

- Hampton University
- Norfolk State University
- Old Dominion University
- University of Virginia
- Virginia Military Institute
- Virginia Polytechnic Institute and State University

WASHINGTON

- University of Washington

WISCONSIN

- Marquette University
- University of Wisconsin/Madison

ENROLLMENT IN CANADIAN SCHOOLS

Recently, Canadian universities hosted a record 193,647 full-time international students. International students account for 6 percent of full-time undergraduate students and 18 percent at the graduate level. Most Canadian universities admit international students—although some have a quota on the number they will accept—and will give interested students information on how their academic qualifications are equated with Canadian requirements.

The Association of Universities and Colleges of Canada (AUCC) represents 92 universities and university-level colleges. These institutions account for almost 99 percent of the total university enrollment in Canada. Almost all Canadian colleges are coeducational. This section contains individual profiles for those English-language universities that enroll more than 10,000 students.

Affiliated with each of these universities are a number of general, theological, or residential colleges, which also have been listed here. The names and addresses of the three French-speaking colleges with enrollments of more than 26,000 may be found at the end of this introduction.

Admissions Requirements

Each university has its own entrance requirements and will assess you on an individual basis. The university will determine the equivalency of your academic credentials. There is no nationwide set of entrance exams. For more details about this or any other part of the application process, contact the registrar at the university you wish to attend.

Admissions Procedure

Once you have determined which universities meet your needs, contact the registrar's office at each institution to obtain an application for a bachelor's program or a professional degree. If you anticipate pursuing postgraduate studies in Canada, you may obtain more information by contacting the dean of graduate studies at the universities that interest you. It is important to apply early. Remember that the Canadian academic year usually starts in September. Some programs, however, do admit students to courses that start in January and May.

The AUCC's web site www.aucc.ca has links to the web pages of all Canadian universities, the majority of which accept applications via e-mail.

To study at a Canadian university, you will need a study permit. You may also need a visitor's visa, which will be issued to you at the same time as your study permit. To apply for a study permit, please contact your nearest Canadian diplomatic post.

You will have to arrange for medical coverage before you arrive in Canada. Medical coverage varies from province to province and sometimes from university to university within each province. Please ask an official at the nearest Canadian diplomatic post for detailed information. Also, check whether the universities you are applying to have any medical insurance plans for international students.

Degrees Offered

Canadian universities, like those in the United States, grant three levels of degrees: bachelor's and first professional, master's, and doctoral as well as undergraduate certificates and diplomas and graduate diploma programs.

Earning the first degree can take three to five years. A general, or unspecialized, program leading to a Bachelor of Arts or Bachelor of Science usually can be completed in three years. An honors degree, earned in a specialized program, usually requires four years. Students must meet more rigorous requirements to enter an honors-degree program and must maintain high grades to remain in it. First professional degrees in some fields may take more than four years to earn, and students may be required to undertake two or three years of university study before enrolling in the professional program. Students who enter graduate programs with a general degree usually must study a year longer than those with honors degrees. Undergraduate diplomas and certificates may be from one to three years' duration and may (although not necessarily) be used as a basis for entry to a degree program. A graduate diploma may be considered as conferring a qualification that is intermediate between the bachelor's (or first professional degree) and master's degree. It may be completed in as little as two or as long as three academic years.

Organizations

Virtually all universities have organizations for international students, and sponsor international student centers and advisers. There also are national organizations that aid international students, including the World University Service of Canada and the Canadian Bureau for International Education, which arranges for representatives to meet international students arriving at Canadian airports.

Tuition, Fees, and Aid

Universities and colleges are heavily subsidized by provincial and federal governments, and tuition fees actually cover one third of university operating costs. Canadian institutions charge different fees for different programs, unlike American institutions, which charge the same tuition regardless of the program of study. Each profile in this book lists the range of tuitions, which may or may not include student fees. Some universities have higher fees for international students, and where that is the case, the profile includes just the international fees. All costs are given in Canadian (CDN) dollars. In all cases, you should check with the university in which you are interested to obtain the most up-to-date information about tuition and room-and-board charges.

Most awards available to international students through Canadian universities or from the Canadian government are restricted to graduate and post graduate studies. Some of the scholarship programs for international students to study in Canada include the Commonwealth Scholarship and Fellowship Plan, the Canadian International Development Agency awards, the Government of Canada awards program of cultural exchanges and the Programme canadien de bourses de la Francophonie. Students interested in applying for aid should contact a Canadian diplomatic mission in their home countries and, for information on cultural exchange programs, their own nation's education department or ministry.

Additional Information

Association of Universities and Colleges of Canada
1710-350 Albert Street
Ottawa, ON, K1R 1B1 Canada
(613) 563-1236
Fax: (613) 563-9745
E-mail: info@aucc.ca
www.aucc.ca
(publications include *Notes for International Students, and
The Directory of Canadian Universities*)

The Canadian Bureau for International Education
220 Laurier Avenue West, Suite 1550
Ottawa, ON K1P 5Z9 Canada
(613) 237-4820
Fax: (613) 237-1073
E-mail: info@cbie.ca
www.cbie.ca

Canada Immigration & Citizenship
www.cic.gc.ca
(publications include *Studying in Canada: Visas, Work and
Immigration for International Students, downloadable pdf
publication*)

Consulate General of Canada in New York
1251 Avenue of the Americas
Concourse Level (between 49th & 50th Streets,
Midtown Manhattan)
New York, NY 10020-1175
(212) 596-1628
Fax: (212) 596-1790
Monday–Friday, 9am–5pm
E-mail: cngnyg@international.gc.ca
www.can-am.gc.ca/new-york

The Department of Foreign Affairs, Trade and Development
125 Sussex Drive
Ottawa, ON K1A 0G2 Canada
(613) 996-9709
1 (800) 267-8376
Fax: (613) 996-9709
E-mail: has online form on website
www.international.gc.ca/international/index.aspx

Social Sciences and Humanities Research Council of Canada
350 Albert Street, P.O. Box 1610
Ottawa, ON K1P 6G4, Canada
(613) 992-0691
E-mail: research@sshrc-crsh.gc.ca
www.sshrc-crsh.gc.ca

Statistics Canada
150 Tunney's Pasture Driveway
Ottawa, Ontario K1A 0T6 Canada
Monday–Friday, 8:30am–4:30pm
1 (800) 263-1136
or (514) 283-8300 (international)
Fax: (877) 287-4369
E-mail: infostats@statcan.gc.ca
www.statcan.ca

World University Service of Canada
1404 Scott Street
Ottawa, ON K1Y 4M8 Canada
(613) 798-7477
(800) 267-8699
Fax: (613) 798-0990
E-mail: wusc@wusc.ca
www.wusc.ca

CANADA

· College Location

CANADA

CARLETON UNIVERSITY E-3

Ottawa, ON K1S 5B6 (613) 520-2600
(613) 520-3847

Full-time: 9000 men, 9406 women
Part-time: 1502 men, 1216 women
Graduate: 1937 men, 1699 women
Year: semesters, summer session
Application Deadline: n/av

Faculty: n/av
Ph.D.s: 93%
Student/Faculty: n/av
Tuition: $8101 ($2573)
Room & Board: $10,200
Freshman Class: n/av

Carleton University, founded in 1942, is a public institution operated by the province of Ontario. There are 14 undergraduate and 14 graduate degree programs offered. The figures in the above capsule and in this profile are approximate. There are 5 undergraduate schools and 1 graduate school. The 152-acre campus is in a small town in Ottawa. Including any residence halls, there are 29 buildings.

STUDENT LIFE: 80% of undergraduates are from Ontario. The average age of freshmen is 19; all undergraduates, 21. 13% do not continue beyond their first year; 72% remain to graduate. **Housing:** 2873 students can be accommodated in college housing, which includes single-sex and coed dorms. On-campus housing is available on a lottery system for upperclassmen. Priority is given to out-of-town students. All students may keep cars.

FACULTY/CLASSROOMS: 65% of faculty are male; 35% are female. No introductory courses are taught by graduate students. The average class size in an introductory lecture is 166 and in a regular course is 107.

PROGRAMS OF STUDY: Carleton confers B.A., B.Sc., B.Arch., B.Comm., B.C.S., B.Eng., B.Hum., B.I.B., B.I.D., B.I.T., B.J., B.Math., B.Mus., B.P.A.P.M. and B.S.W. degrees. Master's and doctoral degrees are also awarded. Bachelor's degrees are awarded in BIOLOGICAL SCIENCE (biochemistry, biology/biological science, biometrics and biostatistics, biotechnology, and neurosciences), BUSINESS (accounting, business systems analysis, human resources, international business management, marketing and distribution, marketing/retailing/merchandising, and operations research), COMMUNICATIONS AND THE ARTS (art history and appreciation, classics, communications, communications technology, English, English literature, film arts, French, German, industrial design, Italian, journalism, linguistics, music, Russian, and Spanish), COMPUTER AND PHYSICAL SCIENCE (chemistry, computer mathematics, computer programming, computer science, geology, information sciences and systems, mathematics, physical sciences, physics, and statistics), EDUCATION (teaching English as a second/foreign language (TESOL/TEFOL)), ENGINEERING AND ENVIRONMENTAL DESIGN (aeronautical engineering, architecture, civil engineering, computer engineering, electrical/electronics engineering, engineering, engineering physics, environmental engineering, environmental science, mechanical engineering, and systems engineering), SOCIAL SCIENCE (anthropology, Canadian studies, child care/child and family studies, classical/ancient civilization, cognitive science, criminology, Eastern European studies, economics, European studies, geography, German area studies, history, human ecology, interdisciplinary studies, law, liberal arts/general studies, philosophy, political science/government, psychology, public administration, religion, social work, sociology, and women's studies). Arts, engineering, and commerce have the largest enrollments.

ACTIVITIES: There are 80 groups on campus, including cheerleading, chess, choir, computers, drama, environmental, ethnic, film, gay, international, jazz band, newspaper, pep band, photography, political, radio and TV, religious, social, social service, and student government. Popular campus events include Orientation. **Sports:** There are 16 intercollegiate sports for men and 18 for women, and 4 intramural sports for men and 3 for women. Facilities include a physical recreation center with an Olympic-size pool, squash courts, nautilus and fitness centers, and a double gym. Outdoor tennis courts and playing fields are also available. **Graduates:** From July 1, 2013 to June 30, 2014, 3640 bachelor's degrees were awarded. The most popular majors were psychology (10%), economics (4%), and English (4%). In an average class, 3% graduate in 3 years or less, 38% graduate in 4 years or less, 62% graduate in 5 years or less, and 67% graduate in 6 years or less.

SERVICES: Counseling and information services are available, as is tutoring in most subjects. There is a reader service for the blind. Study skills workshops are available in essay writing and preparation and writing of exams. There is special exam scheduling and a study center for disabled students and a PASS program (peer tutoring). **Library/Resource:** The library contains 1.8 million volumes, 1.4 million microform items, 22,370 audio/video tapes/CDs/DVDs, and subscribes to 40,607 periodicals including electronic. Computerized library services include interlibrary loans, database searching, Internet access, and Wi-Fi capability. Special learning facilities include an art gallery, radio station, an environmental biology laboratories annex. **Physically Challenged Students:** All of the campus is accessible. Facilities include wheelchair ramps, elevators, special parking, specially equipped restrooms, lowered drinking fountains, lowered telephones. including automatic doors in some buildings, tactile control panels in elevators, tunnels connecting buildings, specially equipped residence rooms, and attendant services. **Special:** Carleton offers co-op programs in many majors and an exchange program with the University of Ottawa. Study abroad, internships in industrial design, dual and student-designed majors, accelerated degree programs, and interdisciplinary programs are available. The university also utilizes instructional television. **Visiting:** There are regularly scheduled orientations for prospective students, including a general information session and campus tour. There are guides for informal visits, visitors may sit in on classes, and stay overnight. To schedule a visit, contact the Undergraduate Recruitment Office at (613) 520-3663. **Campus Safety and Security:** Measures include 24-hour foot and vehicle patrol, emergency notification system, and security escort services. There are emergency telephones, lighted pathways/sidewalks, controlled access to dorms/residences, bike patrol, rape defense classes and student safety patrol.

REQUIREMENTS: Applicants must be graduates of an accredited secondary school. Architecture, humanities, and industrial design students must present a portfolio; social work students should submit a personal information form; music students must audition. A GPA of 3.0 is required. AP and CLEP credits are accepted. Requirements for graduation vary according to programs. **Procedure:** Freshmen are admitted to all sessions. There are early admissions, deferred admissions, and rolling admissions plans. Check with the school for current application deadlines. The application fee is $100. Notifications are sent in May. Applications are accepted on-line. **Transfer Students:** Applicants are evaluated on individual merits. 30 of 120 credits required for the bachelor's degree must be completed at Carleton. **International Students:** There are 1565 international students enrolled. The school actively recruits these students. They must take the TOEFL with a minimum score of 580 on the paper-based TOEFL (PBT) or 86 on the Internet-based version (iBT). Students must take the MELAB and the college's own test, including the Canadian Academic English Language Assessment and the IETLS.

ADMISSIONS: Janice O'Farrell, Director of Admissions. E-Mail: *admissions@carleton.ca* Web: *www.carleton.ca*

FINANCIAL AID: The deadline for filing freshman financial aid applications for fall entry is February 1.

CONCORDIA UNIVERSITY E-2

Montreal, PQ H3G IM8	(514) 848-4971
	(514) 848-2837
Full-time: n/av	**Faculty:** 714
Part-time: n/av	**Ph.Ds:** 84%
Graduate: n/av	**Student/Faculty:** 17 to 1
Year: semesters, summer session	**Tuition:** $2659 ($17,391)
Application Deadline: March 1	**Room & Board:** $5000
	Freshman Class: n/av
SAT or ACT: recommended	

Concordia University, established in 1974, is a public institution operated by the province of Quebec. The figures in the above capsule and in this profile are approximate. There are 5 undergraduate schools and one graduate school. In addition to regional accreditation, has baccalaureate program accreditation with AACSB. The 1555-acre campus is in an urban area in downtown Montreal and in suburban Loyola. Including any residence halls, there are 80 buildings.

STUDENT LIFE: 90% of undergraduates are from Quebec. Others are from 29 states, 128 foreign countries, and Canada. The average age of freshmen is 21; all undergraduates, 25. 11% do not continue beyond their first year; 52% remain to graduate. **Housing:** 144 students can be accommodated in college housing, which includes single-sex and coed dorms and off-campus apartments. In addition, there are fraternity houses and sorority houses. On-campus housing is available on a first-come, first-served basis. Priority is given to out-of-town students. 98% of students commute. All students may keep cars.

FACULTY/CLASSROOMS: 65% of faculty are male; 35% are female. No introductory courses are taught by graduate students. The average class size in an introductory lecture is 50; in a laboratory is 50; and in a regular course is 50.

PROGRAMS OF STUDY: Concordia confers B.A., B.Admin., B.Comm., B.Comp.Sci., B.Ed., B.Eng., B.F.A. and B.S.C. degrees. Master's and doctoral degrees are also awarded. Bachelor's degrees are awarded in BIOLOGICAL SCIENCE (biochemistry, biology/biological science, and microbiology), BUSINESS (accounting, banking and finance, business administration and management, business economics, international business management, marketing/retailing/merchandising, and personnel management), COMMUNICATIONS AND THE ARTS (communications, dance, design, dramatic arts, English, English as a second/foreign language, film arts, fine arts, journalism, languages, music, and photography), COMPUTER AND PHYSICAL SCIENCE (actuarial science, chemistry, computer programming, computer science, geology, information sciences and systems, mathematics, physics, and statistics), EDUCATION (art education, early childhood education, and elementary education), ENGINEERING AND ENVIRONMENTAL DESIGN (civil engineering, computer engineering, electrical/electronics engineering, industrial engineering, and mechanical engineering), SOCIAL SCIENCE (anthropology, East Asian studies, economics, geography, history, philosophy, political science/government, psychology, sociology, and urban studies). Computer engineering, accounting, and communication studies are the strongest academically. Accounting, and psychology have the largest enrollments.

ACTIVITIES: There are 125 groups on campus, including art, choir, chorale, chorus, computers, dance, drama, ethnic, film, gay, honors, international, jazz band, literary magazine, musical theater, newspaper, orchestra, photography, political, professional, radio and TV, religious, social, social service, student government, symphony, and yearbook. **Sports:** There are 9 intercollegiate sports for men and 7 for women, and 16 intramural sports for men and 12 for women. Facilities include an arena, a gym, and a football stadium. **Graduates:** The most popular majors were arts and science (55%), commerce and administration (25%), and fine arts (10%).

SERVICES: Counseling and information services are available, as is tutoring in most subjects. There is a reader service for the blind, remedial math, reading, and writing. **Library/Resource:** The 2 libraries contain 3.0 million volumes, 75,000 microform items, 2,000 audio/video tapes/CDs/DVDs, and subscribe to 5,500 periodicals including electronic. Computerized library services include interlibrary loans and database searching. Special learning facilities include an art gallery, radio station, TV station, a greenhouse, audiovisual instruction service, and specialized research center. **Physically Challenged Students:** 75% of the campus is accessible. Facilities include wheelchair ramps, elevators, special parking, specially equipped restrooms, special class scheduling, lowered drinking fountains, and lowered telephones. **Special:** The university offers programs in many majors with the Institute for Co-operative Education, internships, and study abroad in 12 countries. There are accelerated degree programs, B.A.-B.S. degrees, dual majors, a general studies degree, and student-designed majors. There is a Phi Beta Kappa and 21 departmental honors programs. **Visiting:** There are regularly scheduled orientations for prospective students. There are guides for informal visits and visitors may sit in on classes. To schedule a visit, contact the Office of Student Recruitment at (514) 848-4779. **Campus Safety and Security:** Measures include 24-hour foot and vehicle patrol, self-defense education, and security escort services. There are shuttle buses, emergency telephones, and lighted pathways/sidewalks.

REQUIREMENTS: The SAT or ACT is recommended. Applicants must be graduates of an accredited secondary school. The GED is accepted. An essay, an interview, a portfolio, or an audition may be required for some programs. A GPA of 2.5 is required. AP and CLEP credits are accepted. Important factors in the admissions decision are advanced placement or honors courses and recommendations by school officials. To graduate, students must complete 90 to 120 credits, depending on the degree, with a minimum GPA of 2.0. Between 42 and 54 credits are required in the major. All students must fulfill the requirements of the core curriculum and take the university writing test. **Procedure:** Freshmen are admitted to all sessions. There are early decision, early admissions, and rolling admissions plans. Early decision applications should be filed by February 1; regular applications, by March 1 for fall entry; November 1 for winter entry; and April 15 for summer entry, along with a $50 fee. **Transfer Students:** Applicants must have a minimum GPA of 2.2. 45 of 90 credits required for the bachelor's degree must be completed at Concordia. **International Students:** The school actively recruits these students. They must take the TOEFL or MELAB and the college's own test.

ADMISSIONS: Pete Regimbald, Assistant Registrar. E-Mail: *admreg@alcor.concordia.ca* Web: *www.concordia.ca*

FINANCIAL AID: Check with the school for current application deadlines.

DALHOUSIE UNIVERSITY	F-2
Halifax, NS B3H 4R2	(902) 494-2211
	(902) 494-1630
Full-time: n/av	**Faculty:** n/av
Part-time: n/av	**Ph.D.s:** n/av
Graduate: n/av	**Student/Faculty:** n/av
Year: semesters, summer session	**Tuition:** $7531
Application Deadline: n/av	**Room & Board:** $9220
	Freshman Class: n/av

Dalhousie University, founded in 1818. Students study at the undergraduate, graduate and professional levels in more than 180 programs in 12 faculties. The figures in the above capsule and in this profile are approximate. The campus is in an urban area in Halifax and Truro, Nova Scotia.

STUDENT LIFE: Students are from 110 foreign countries. **Housing:** 2200 students can be accommodated in college housing, which includes single-sex and coed dorms, on-campus apartments, off-campus apartments, and married student housing. In addition, there are special-interest houses. On-campus housing is available on a first-come, first-served basis, and is available on a lottery system for upperclassmen. Some may keep cars.

FACULTY/CLASSROOMS: No introductory courses are taught by graduate students.

PROGRAMS OF STUDY: Master's and doctoral degrees are also awarded. Bachelor's degrees are awarded in AGRICULTURE (agricultural economics, agricultural sciences, and animal science), BIOLOGICAL SCIENCE (biochemistry, biology/biological science, marine biology, microbiology, and neurosciences), BUSINESS (accounting, banking and finance, business administration and management, business economics, and recreation and leisure services), COMMUNICATIONS AND THE ARTS (classics, dramatic arts, English, French, German, music, Russian, and Spanish), COMPUTER AND PHYSICAL SCIENCE (chemistry, computer science, earth science, mathematics, physics, and statistics), EDUCATION (health education), ENGINEERING AND ENVIRONMENTAL DESIGN (chemical engineering, city/community/regional planning, and engineering), HEALTH PROFESSIONS (dental hygiene, nursing, occupational therapy, pharmacy, physical therapy, predentistry, and premedicine), SOCIAL SCIENCE (Canadian studies, economics, history, international studies, law, philosophy, physical fitness/movement, political science/government, psychology, religion, social work, sociology, and women's studies).

ACTIVITIES: There are 280 groups on campus, including cheerleading, chess, chorale, communications, computers, dance, debate, drama, environmental, ethnic, gay, honors, international, musical theater, newspaper, photography, political, professional, radio and TV, religious, social, social service, and student government. **Sports:** cardio and weight training equipment, soccer fields, outdoor tennis courts, a track, an Olympic-size swimming pool, squash and volleyball courts, a climbing wall, and dance studio.

SERVICES: Counseling and information services are available, as is tutoring in most subjects. There is a reader service for the blind, and remedial math and writing. **Library/Resource:** Computerized library services include interlibrary loans, database searching, and Internet access. Special learning facilities include an art gallery, natural history museum, planetarium, and radio station. **Physically Challenged Students:** The Advising and Access Services Centre is available to assist

students who require support. **Special:** There is a freshman honors program. **Visiting:** There are regularly scheduled orientations for prospective students. There are guides for informal visits and visitors may sit in on classes. To schedule a visit, contact the Campus Tours at (902) 494-2587. **Campus Safety and Security:** Measures include 24-hour foot and vehicle patrol, emergency notification system, self-defense education, and security escort services. There are shuttle buses, emergency telephones, lighted pathways/sidewalks, and controlled access to dorms/residences.

REQUIREMENTS: 2014-15 applicants from the US must have an SAT result of at least 1650 or an ACT composite score of 23 and no individual score less than 20. Grade 12 credit in English is required. An audition is necessary for music students. AP credits are accepted. **Procedure:** Freshmen are admitted to all sessions. There are early decision, early admissions, deferred admissions, and rolling admissions plans. Check with the school for current application deadlines. The application fee is $65. Applications are accepted on-line. **Transfer Students:** Applicants are assessed on an individual basis. **International Students:** The school actively recruits these students. They must also take the SAT or ACT.

ADMISSIONS: E-Mail: *admissions@dal.ca* Web: *www.dal.ca*

FINANCIAL AID: Check with the school for current application deadlines.

LAVAL UNIVERSITY	E-2
Quebec, PQ G1K 7P4	(418) 656-2764
	(877) 785-2825
	(418) 656-5216
Full-time: 9000 men, 13000 women	**Faculty:** n/av
Part-time: 3345 men, 5487 women	**Ph.D.s:** 90%
Graduate: 4914 men, 5458 women	**Student/Faculty:** n/av
Year: semesters, summer session	**Tuition:** $2092 ($10,749)
Application Deadline: n/av	**Room & Board:** $9100
	Freshman Class: 28717 applied, 20234 accepted, 10726 enrolled

Laval University, founded in 1852, is the oldest French-language university in North America. It offers undergraduate and graduate programs through 17 faculties and 9 institutes. The figures in the above capsule and in this profile are approximate. In addition to regional accreditation, Laval has baccalaureate program accreditation with AACSB, AUCC, and ACU. The 465-acre campus is in an urban area 2 miles west of old Quebec City. Including any residence halls, there are 35 buildings.

STUDENT LIFE: 94% of undergraduates are from Quebec. Others are from 105 foreign countries. **Female To Male Ratio:** 1.4:1. The average age of all undergraduates is 26. **Housing:** 2400 students can be accommodated in college housing, which includes single-sex and coed on-campus apartments. On-campus housing is available on a first-come, first-served basis. All students may keep cars.

FACULTY/CLASSROOMS: All teach undergraduates. No introductory courses are taught by graduate students.

PROGRAMS OF STUDY: Laval confers B.A., B.Sc., B.A.A., B.A.V., B.Ed., B.Ens., B.Ing., B.Mus., B.Pharm., B.Sc.A., B.Sc.Arch., B.Serv.Soc., B.Th. and LL.B. degrees. Master's and doctoral degrees are also awarded. Bachelor's degrees are awarded in AGRICULTURE (agricultural business management, agricultural economics, agronomy, forest engineering, forestry and related sciences, and wood science), BIOLOGICAL SCIENCE (biochemistry, biology/biological science, microbiology, and nutrition), BUSINESS (business administration and management), COMMUNICATIONS AND THE ARTS (art, art history and appreciation, communications, dramatic arts, English, English as a second/foreign language, French, languages, linguistics, literature, music, and visual and performing arts), COMPUTER AND PHYSICAL SCIENCE (actuarial science, chemistry, computer science, geology, geoscience, mathematics, physics, software engineering, and statistics), EDUCATION (art education, athletic training, early childhood education, education, elementary education, music education, physical education, secondary education, and technical education), ENGINEERING AND ENVIRON-MENTAL DESIGN (agricultural engineering, architecture, chemical engineering, civil engineering, computer engineering, electrical/electronics engineering, engineering and applied science, engineering physics, geological engineering, graphic arts technology, industrial administration/management, mechanical engineering, metallurgical engineering, and mining and mineral engineering), HEALTH PROFESSIONS (nursing, occupational therapy, pharmacy, physical therapy, predentistry, and premedicine), SOCIAL SCIENCE (anthropology, classical/ancient civilization, consumer services, counseling/psychology, economics, food science, French studies, geography, history, interdisciplinary studies, international studies, Judaic studies, law, philosophy, physical fitness/movement, political science/government, psychology, social work, sociology, Spanish studies, and theological studies). Business administration, sciences, and education have the largest enrollments.

ACTIVITIES: There are 150 groups on campus, including art, band, chess, choir, chorale, computers, dance, drama, ethnic, film, forensics, gay, international, jazz band, literary magazine, musical theater, newspaper, opera, orchestra, photography, political, radio and TV, religious, social, social service, student government, and symphony. Popular campus events include Thematic Weeks, Rendez-vous Laval, and Student Festivals. **Sports:** There are 13 intercollegiate sports for men and 10 for women, and 7 intramural sports for men and 7 for women. Facilities include a covered stadium with a 200-meter running track and 4 tennis courts; a 50-meter swimming pool with a 10-meter diving tower; a double ice arena; 1 triple and 2 single gyms; 4 squash courts; 4 handball and racquetball courts; judo, karate, and self-defense rooms; a dance studio; an open-air stadium with a 400-meter running track; softball, football, and soccer fields; 6 outdoor tennis courts; 3 physical training rooms; a golf driving range; an indoor golf practice room; 2 outdoor basketball courts; a 1-kilometer hiking trail; and a jogging track. **Graduates:** The most popular majors were administration (18%), science and engineering (14%), and letters (13%).

SERVICES: There is a reader service for the blind, remedial math and writing. Tutoring in French grammar is available. **Library/Resource:** The 2 libraries contain 3.4 million volumes, 1.3 million microform items, and 37,832 audio/video tapes/CDs/DVDs, and subscribe to 17,625 periodicals including electronic. Computerized library services include interlibrary loans, database searching, and Internet access. Special learning facilities include an art gallery, natural history museum, radio station, a language lab, and business simulations. **Physically Challenged Students:** 95% of the campus is accessible. Facilities include wheelchair ramps, elevators, special parking, specially equipped restrooms, special class scheduling, lowered drinking fountains, lowered telephones. teletype machines for the deaf, computerized classrooms for the visually disabled, electric doors, sidewalks adjusted for physically disabled students, elevators equipped with speaking devices, and a campus plan in braille. **Special:** Laval offers co-op programs in forest operation, mining, metallurgical engineering, mineral engineering, and wood processing engineering, and study abroad in 65 countries. Dual majors are possible in anthropology and ethnology, economics and politics, international studies and modern languages, historical sciences and patrimonial studies, French language and professional writing, math and computer science. Intensive French courses are offered during the summer. **Visiting:** There are regularly scheduled orientations for prospective students. There are guides for informal visits and visitors may stay overnight. To schedule a visit, contact the Public Affairs Office. **Campus Safety and Security:** Measures include 24-hour foot and vehicle patrol and security escort services. There are emergency telephones, lighted pathways/sidewalks, services include 24-hour camera surveillance in pedestrian tunnels and trained evacuating teams in all buildings. Security training for social events is offered to all student associations.

REQUIREMENTS: The only general requirement is the D.E.C. (Diploma of Collegial Studies 13 years of scholarity) or the equivalent. Some programs have specific requirements. All undergraduate students (except those who are nonfrancophones) must show a sufficient knowledge of the French language to obtain their bachelor's degree. Requirements for graduation vary according to the program. A minimum GPA of 2.0 out of 4.33 is required per 30 credits. **Proce-**

dure: Freshmen are admitted to all sessions. Check with the school for current application deadlines. Applications are accepted on-line. **Transfer Students:** 1662 transfer students enrolled in 2013-2014. Applicants must have the D.E.C. or the equivalent. **International Students:** The school actively recruits these students.

ADMISSIONS: 70% of the 2014-2015 applicants were accepted. **Admissions Contact:** Public Affairs Office E-Mail: *accveil@ dap.ulaval.ca* Web: *www.ulaval.ca/bip*

FINANCIAL AID: The deadline for filing freshman financial aid applications for fall entry is June 30.

MCGILL UNIVERSITY   E-2

Montreal, PQ H3A 0G4   (514) 398-3910
                                           (514) 398-5544

Full-time: 6899 men, 10952 women	**Faculty:** n/av
Part-time: 1200 men, 2056 women	**Ph.D.s:** 95%
Graduate: 3464 men, 3900 women	**Student/Faculty:** n/av
Year: semesters, summer session	**Tuition:** $2826 ($6018)
Application Deadline: March 1	**Room & Board:** $7964
	Freshman Class: 18963 applied, 10689 accepted, 4834 enrolled
ACT: 29 **SAT:** required	

McGill University, founded in 1821, is a publicly funded private institution that grants undergraduate, graduate, and professional degrees. Tuition fees may vary depending on program. Higher rates are charged to international students. The figures in the above capsule and in this profile are approximate. There are 11 undergraduate schools and 79 graduate schools. In addition to regional accreditation, McGill has baccalaureate program accreditation with APTA. The 80-acre campus is in an urban area in downtown Montreal, with the MacDonald campus located on the far west end of the island. Including any residence halls, there are 150 buildings.

STUDENT LIFE: 53% of undergraduates are from Quebec. Others are from 140 foreign countries. 17% are Foreign. **Female To Male Ratio:** 1.5:1. The average age of freshmen is 19; all undergraduates, 21. **Housing:** 2080 students can be accommodated in college housing, which includes single-sex and coed dorms, off-campus apartments, and married student housing. On-campus housing is available on a lottery system for upperclassmen. Priority is given to out-of-town students. 83% of students commute.

FACULTY/CLASSROOMS: 67% of faculty are male; 33% are female. No introductory courses are taught by graduate students. The average class size in an introductory lecture is 30; in a laboratory is 25; and in a regular course is 45.

PROGRAMS OF STUDY: McGill confers B.A., B.C.L., B.Com., B.Ed., B.Eng., B.Mus., B.Sc., B.Sc.Agr., B.Sc.Agr.Eng., B.Sc.Arch., B.Sc.F.Sc., B.Sc.N., B.Sc.Nutr.Sc., B.Sc.Occ.Ther., B.Sc.Phys.Ther., B.S.W., B.Th. and LL.B. degrees. Master's and doctoral degrees are also awarded. Bachelor's degrees are awarded in AGRICULTURE (agricultural economics, agriculture, animal science, conservation and regulation, plant science, and soil science), BIOLOGICAL SCIENCE (anatomy, biochemistry, biology/biological science, botany, cell biology, environmental biology, microbiology, molecular biology, nutrition, physiology, wildlife biology, and zoology), BUSINESS (accounting, banking and finance, entrepreneurial studies, human resources, institutional management, insurance and risk management, international business management, labor studies, management information systems, management science, marketing management, and organizational behavior), COMMUNICATIONS AND THE ARTS (art history and appreciation, classics, English, French, jazz, linguistics, modern language, music history and appreciation, music performance, music technology, music theory and composition, Russian, and Spanish), COMPUTER AND PHYSICAL SCIENCE (applied mathematics, atmospheric sciences and meteorology, chemistry, computer science, earth science, geology, geophysics and seismology, information sciences and systems, mathematics, physics, planetary and space science, and software engineering), EDUCATION (elementary education, foreign languages education, music education, physical education, secondary education, special education, teaching English as a second/foreign language (TESOL/ TEFOL), and vocational education), ENGINEERING AND ENVIRONMENTAL DESIGN (agricultural engineering, architecture, chemical engineering, civil engineering, computer engineering, electrical/electronics engineering, environmental science, mechanical engineering, metallurgical engineering, and mining and mineral engineering), HEALTH PROFESSIONS (clinical science, exercise science, nursing, occupational therapy, and physical therapy), SOCIAL SCIENCE (African studies, American studies, anthropology, Canadian studies, Caribbean studies, dietetics, East Asian studies, economics, food science, French studies, geography, German area studies, Hispanic American studies, history, humanities, international studies, Italian studies, Judaic studies, Latin American studies, law, Middle Eastern studies, philosophy, political science/government, psychology, religion, social work, sociology, Western civilization/culture, and women's studies).

ACTIVITIES: 4% of men belong to 1 local and 12 national fraternities; 2% of women belong to 4 national sororities. There are 180 groups on campus, including and drive-safe program, walk-safe, band, cheerleading, chess, choir, chorale, chorus, computers, dance, debate, drama, ethnic, film, gay, honors, international, jazz band, literary magazine, Model UN, musical theater, newspaper, opera, orchestra, photography, political, professional, radio and TV, religious, social, social service, student government, symphony, and yearbook. Popular campus events include Multicultural Festivals, 4-Floor Parties, Music, Film and Theatrical Productions. **Sports:** There are 23 intercollegiate sports for men and 24 for women, and 23 intramural sports for men and 15 for women. Facilities include a 20,000-seat stadium; a 1,000-seat competition hall; 2 double gyms for basketball, volleyball, and badminton; 8 outdoor tennis courts; 4 indoor tennis courts; a 400-meter outdoor track and a banked 6-lane 200-meter indoor track; 2 weight-training rooms; dance, aerobics, and martial arts rooms; 1 pool; a gymnastics facility; 3 sports fields; a fitness center; a sport medicine center, and hyperbaric chamber. **Graduates:** The most popular majors were social sciences (18%), health professions (11%), and biological/life sciences (10%).

SERVICES: Counseling and information services are available, as is tutoring in every subject. There is a reader service for the blind, and remedial math, reading, and writing. **Library/Resource:** The 14 libraries contain 3.3 million volumes, 1.6 million microform items, and 71,765 audio/video tapes/CDs/DVDs, and subscribe to 22,513 periodicals including electronic. Computerized library services include interlibrary loans and database searching. Special learning facilities include a natural history museum, radio station, McCord Museum of Canadian History, Mont St. Hilaire Nature Conservation Center, an herbarium, an arboretum, a subarctic research station, the Institute of Air and Space Law, the Institute of Islamic Studies, the Redpath Museum of Natural History, the Lyman Entomological Museum, the Ecomuseum, the Osler Library of the History of Medicine, and the Lande Canadiana Collection. **Physically Challenged Students:** 80% of the campus is accessible. Facilities include wheelchair ramps, elevators, special parking, specially equipped restrooms, special class scheduling, lowered telephones. Braille, variable-speed tape recorders, talking calculators, books on tape, exam accommodations, adapted computers (voice synthesis and voice recognition), sign language interpreters, computerized note taking, note takers, print enlargement, readers, and adapted transport. **Special:** There is cross-registration with area universities. Study abroad, work-study within the university, co-op programs in mining and metallurgical engineering, dual majors, internships, and student-designed majors are available. There are 6 departmental honors programs. **Visiting:** There are regularly scheduled orientations for prospective students, with a varying agenda (including campus tours and student for a day programs). There are guides for informal visits, visitors may sit in on classes, and stay overnight. To schedule a visit, contact the Welcome Center at (514) 398-6555 (tours). **Campus Safety and Security:** Measures include 24-hour foot and vehicle patrol and security escort services. There are emergency telephones and lighted pathways/ sidewalks.

REQUIREMENTS: The ACT may be submitted instead of the SAT. McGill requires applicants to be in the upper 25% of their class. AP credits are accepted. Important factors in the admissions decision are

advanced placement or honors courses, recommendations by school officials, and evidence of special talent. To graduate, students must successfully complete a required number of approved credits, usually between 90 and 120. Students must also be in satisfactory standing, with a minimum cumulative GPA of 2.0. **Procedure:** Freshmen are admitted fall. Entrance exams should be taken during Spring of the junior year, Fall of the senior year. There are deferred admissions and rolling admissions plans. Applications should be filed by March 1 for fall entry, along with a $60 fee. Applications are accepted on-line. **Transfer Students:** 528 transfer students enrolled in 2013-2014. Requirements vary with the program. Standard admission requirements must also be met. Students must submit high school and college transcripts and have a 3.0 GPA in college coursework. 60 of 90 credits required for the bachelor's degree must be completed at McGill. **International Students:** The school actively recruits these students. They must take the TOEFL or MELAB, McGill Certificate of Proficiency in English must be earned. SAT and/or ACT tests are required for U.S. applicants and recommended for other international applicants.

ADMISSIONS: 56% of the 2014-2015 applicants were accepted. **Admissions Contact:** Admissions, Recruitment, and Registrar's Office E-Mail: *admissions@mcgill.ca* Web: *www.mcgill.ca*

FINANCIAL AID: The average freshman award was $5,855. Need-based scholarships or need-based grants averaged $3,022; and need-based self-help aid (loans and jobs) averaged $6,146. McGill is a member of CSS. The FAFSA and the college's own financial statement are required. The deadline for filing freshman financial aid applications for fall entry is June 1.

MCMASTER UNIVERSITY — E-3

Hamilton, ON L8S 4K1   (905) 525-4600 / (905) 527-1105

Full-time: 5400 men, 7000 women	Faculty: 927
Part-time: 900 men, 1900 women	Ph.D.s: n/av
Graduate: 1190 men, 1030 women	Student/Faculty: 13 to 1
Year: n/av	Tuition: $6000 ($18,000)
Application Deadline: n/av	Room & Board: $6700
	Freshman Class: n/av

McMaster University is a public nonsectarian institution, offering programs in the arts and sciences, business, engineering, health sciences, kinesiology, and social work. There are 2 graduate schools. The 300-acre campus is in an urban area 60 miles southwest of Toronto. Including any residence halls, there are 44 buildings.

STUDENT LIFE: 95% of undergraduates are from Ontario. Others are from 12 states, and 79 foreign countries. The average age of freshmen is 20; all undergraduates, 22. 1% do not continue beyond their first year. **Housing:** 2765 students can be accommodated in college housing, which includes single-sex and coed dorms and on-campus apartments. In addition, there are language houses, La Maison Francaise, an international house, and a quiet house. On-campus housing is guaranteed for the freshman year only and is available on a lottery system for upperclassmen. Priority is given to out-of-town students. 77% of students commute. All students may keep cars.

FACULTY/CLASSROOMS: 71% of faculty are male; 29% are female. All teach and do research. No introductory courses are taught by graduate students.

PROGRAMS OF STUDY: McMaster confers B.A., B.S., B.A.S., B.A./ B.S.W., B.C., B.Eng., B.Eng./Management, B.Eng./Society, B.H.S., B.Kinesiology, B.Mus. and B.S.N. degrees. Master's and doctoral degrees are also awarded. Bachelor's degrees are awarded in BIOLOGICAL SCIENCE (biochemistry, biology/biological science, and life science), BUSINESS (business administration and management and labor studies), COMMUNICATIONS AND THE ARTS (art, art history and appreciation, classics, comparative literature, dramatic arts, English, French, linguistics, modern language, music, and Russian), COMPUTER AND PHYSICAL SCIENCE (chemistry, computer science, earth science, geology, mathematics, physical sciences, physics, science, and statistics), ENGINEERING AND ENVIRONMENTAL DESIGN (chemical engineering, civil engineering, computer engineering, electrical/electronics engineering, engineering physics, environmental science, manufacturing engineering, materials engineering, materials science, and mechanical engineering), HEALTH PROFESSIONS (medical science, nursing, occupational therapy, and physical therapy), SOCIAL SCIENCE (anthropology, economics, geography, German area studies, gerontology, history, interdisciplinary studies, Japanese studies, Latin American studies, liberal arts/general studies, philosophy, physical fitness/movement, political science/government, psychology, religion, social work, sociology, and women's studies).

ACTIVITIES: There are 100 groups on campus, including academic, art, band, cheerleading, chess, choir, chorale, chorus, computers, debate, drama, ethnic, gay, international, jazz band, musical theater, newspaper, orchestra, photography, political, radio and TV, religious, social, student government, and yearbook. Popular campus events include Marauder Weekend. **Sports:** There are 16 intercollegiate sports for men and 14 for women, and 16 intramural sports for men and 14 for women. Facilities include an outdoor track and field, a mini-weight room, a swimming pool, cross-country trails, rugby, soccer, and football fields, tennis, squash, and handball courts, and a state-of-the-art fitness facility. **Graduates:** In a recent year, 3000 bachelor's degrees were awarded.

SERVICES: Counseling and information services are available, as is tutoring in some subjects. There is a reader service for the blind. May be arranged through individual departments. **Library/Resource:** The 4 libraries contain 1.7 million volumes, 1.4 million microform items, 19,500 audio/video tapes/CDs/DVDs, and subscribe to 11,976 periodicals including electronic. Computerized library services include interlibrary loans and database searching. Special learning facilities include an art gallery, planetarium, radio station, a nuclear reactor, tandem accelerator, a greenhouses, Chedoke-McMaster Hospital, a communication research lab, Bertrand Russell archives, a Humanities Communication Centre, and computing labs. **Physically Challenged Students:** 60% of the campus is accessible. Facilities include wheelchair ramps, elevators, special parking, specially equipped restrooms, special class scheduling, lowered telephones, and basement-level and above-ground tunnels with connecting walkways. **Special:** Many opportunities exist to combine 2 subjects of study within 1 faculty, or between 2 faculties. All honors students have the option of taking a minor in a second subject area. Nondegree study is possible through the Center for Continuing Education. Internships and study abroad are offered. Students may repeat failed courses provided they are eligible to continue in the program. There are 37 departmental honors programs. **Visiting:** There are regularly scheduled orientations for prospective students, including campus tours, information sessions, and panel discussions. There are guides for informal visits and visitors may sit in on classes. To schedule a visit, contact the Tour Coordinator, Division of Student Liaison. **Campus Safety and Security:** Measures include 24-hour foot and vehicle patrol and security escort services. There are shuttle buses, emergency telephones, lighted pathways/sidewalks. Additional services include the emergency first-response team, Mac alert bulletins, a campus watch program, a prevention programs officer, and video monitoring in some parking areas.

REQUIREMENTS: Requirements for graduation vary according to the program of study. A minimum 3.5 GPA in 90 to 150 units is required for most programs. U.S. applicants must have a high school grade average of 80. Applicants must be graduates of an accredited secondary school. The required high school courses should include 5 years each of English and math. A portfolio is required for art students and an audition for music students. A supplementary application form is required for some programs. Offers of admission are made based on academic standing and audition/portfolio/supplementary application requirements where necessary. Important factors in the admissions decision are evidence of special talent, extracurricular activities record, and leadership record. **Procedure:** Freshmen are admitted to all sessions. There is a early decision plan. Check with the school for current application deadlines. **Transfer Students:** Applicants are considered on an individual basis. Review of high school, college, and/or university work determines admission status.

International Students: The school actively recruits these students. They must take the TOEFL or MELAB.

ADMISSIONS: Sam Digiandomenico, Associate Registrar Admis-

sions. E-Mail: *macadmit@mcmail.mcmaster.ca* Web: *www.mcmaster.ca*

FINANCIAL AID: 50% of all full-time freshmen students received need-based aid. 12% of undergraduate students work part-time. The deadline for filing freshman financial aid applications for fall entry is July 15.

MEMORIAL UNIVERSITY OF NEWFOUNDLAND
F-2

St. John's, NF A1C 5S7

(709) 864-8000
(888) 637-6269
(709) 737-2337

Full-time: 5000 men, 7000 women	**Faculty:** 932
Part-time: 690 men, 1350 women	**Ph.D.s:** 50%
Graduate: 840 men, 760 women	**Student/Faculty:** 12 to 1
Year: varies, summer session	**Tuition:** $4202 ($7510)
Application Deadline: March 1	**Room & Board:** $4686
	Freshman Class: n/av

Memorial University of Newfoundland, founded in 1925, is a public liberal arts institution. The figures in the above capsule and in this profile are approximate. There are 13 undergraduate schools and 12 graduate schools. The 220-acre campus is in an urban area in St. John's. Including any residence halls, there are 40 buildings.

STUDENT LIFE: 98% of undergraduates are from Newfoundland. **Female To Male Ratio:** 1.4:1. **Housing:** 1750 students can be accommodated in college housing, which includes single-sex and coed dorms, on-campus apartments, off-campus apartments, and married student housing. On-campus housing is available on a first-come and first-served basis. Priority is given to out-of-town students. 89% of students commute. All students may keep cars.

FACULTY/CLASSROOMS: 80% of faculty are male; 20% are female. Graduate students teach 71% of introductory courses. The average class size in an introductory lecture is 40.

PROGRAMS OF STUDY: MUN confers B.A., B.Sc., B.Comm.(Co-op.), B.Comm.(Gen.), B.Ed., B.Eng., B.F.A., B.Kin., B.M.S., B.Mus., B.Mus.Ed., B.Med.Sc., B.N., B.P.E., B.Rec., B.Sc.(Pharm.), B.Spec.Ed., B.S.W., B.Tech. and B.Voc.Ed. degrees. Master's and doctoral degrees are also awarded. Bachelor's degrees are awarded in AGRICULTURE (forestry and related sciences), BIOLOGICAL SCIENCE (biochemistry, biology/biological science, cell biology, ecology, entomology, environmental biology, evolutionary biology, marine biology, marine science, microbiology, and neurosciences), BUSINESS (entrepreneurial studies, human resources, labor studies, management science, marketing/retailing/merchandising, organizational behavior, and small business management), COMMUNICATIONS AND THE ARTS (dramatic arts, English, English literature, fine arts, folklore and mythology, French, German, linguistics, literature, music, music history and appreciation, music performance, music theory and composition, Russian, Spanish, and visual and performing arts), COMPUTER AND PHYSICAL SCIENCE (applied mathematics, applied physics, chemistry, computer science, earth science, information sciences and systems, mathematics, oceanography, and statistics), EDUCATION (athletic training, education, elementary education, guidance education, middle school education, music education, physical education, recreation education, secondary education, and special education), ENGINEERING AND ENVIRONMENTAL DESIGN (civil engineering, electrical/electronics engineering, engineering technology, maritime science, mechanical engineering, naval architecture and marine engineering, and ocean engineering), HEALTH PROFESSIONS (medical science, nursing, and pharmacy), SOCIAL SCIENCE (anthropology, archeology, Canadian studies, criminology, dietetics, economics, French studies, geography, German area studies, history, humanities, medieval studies, philosophy, physical fitness/movement, political science/government, psychology, religion, social studies, social work, sociology, Spanish studies, and women's studies). Marine biology, naval architecture, and business are the strongest academically. Arts, science, business, and engineering have the largest enrollments.

ACTIVITIES: There are 100 groups on campus, including academic, band, cheerleading, chess, choir, chorale, computers, dance, debate, drama, ethnic, gay, international, jazz band, literary magazine, musical theater, newspaper, orchestra, photography, political, professional, radio and TV, religious, single parent, social, social service, student government, symphony, and yearbook. Popular campus events include Winter Carnival and Orientation. **Sports:** There are 6 intercollegiate sports for men and 6 for women, and 6 intramural sports for men and 6 for women. Facilities include a gym, squash courts, a rifle range, a weight room, a soccer field, and swimming facilities. **Graduates:** The most popular majors were business, biology, and sociology.

SERVICES: There is a reader service for the blind, and remedial math, reading, and writing. Students staying in residence have access to tutoring in every subject. In addition, lectures are offered on topics such as public speaking, speed reading, and time management. **Library/Resource:** The 3 libraries contain 2.5 million volumes, and subscribe to 700 periodicals including electronic. Computerized library services include interlibrary loans and database searching. Special learning facilities include an art gallery, natural history museum, planetarium, radio station, TV station, and language labs. **Physically Challenged Students:** 85% of the campus is accessible. Facilities include wheelchair ramps, elevators, special parking, specially equipped restrooms, special class scheduling, lowered drinking fountains, lowered telephones. classroom aids, note-taking volunteers, and other facilities based on individual needs. **Special:** The university offers co-op programs in commerce, phys ed, recreation, kinesiology, and engineering. Internships are available in education and nursing. Study abroad may be arranged in at least 20 countries. Work-study programs, dual majors, and B.A.-B.S. degrees are available. There are 3 departmental honors programs. **Visiting:** There are regularly scheduled orientations for prospective students, including various student activities, mock lectures, campus tours, and educational sessions. There are guides for informal visits and visitors may sit in on classes. To schedule a visit, contact the Student Development at (709) 737-2192. **Campus Safety and Security:** Measures include 24-hour foot and vehicle patrol, self-defense education, and security escort services. There are emergency telephones and lighted pathways/sidewalks.

REQUIREMENTS: Admission is based on a 70% high school average as computed from university preparatory courses required for admission. Applications are accepted on-line. AP credits are accepted. Students must complete 40 to 50 credits to graduate. Each discipline has different requirements for graduation. **Procedure:** Freshmen are admitted to all sessions. There is a rolling admissions plan. Applications should be filed by March 1 for fall entry; October 1 for winter entry; February 1 for spring entry; and February 1 for summer entry. The fall 2014 application fee was $80. **Transfer Students:** 499 transfer students enrolled in 2013-2014. Applicants must be in good academic standing at the previous institution. 10 of 40 credits required for the bachelor's degree must be completed at MUN. **International Students:** The school actively recruits these students. They must take the TOEFL or MELAB.

ADMISSIONS: Manager of Admissions. E-Mail: *admissions@mun.ca*

FINANCIAL AID: Check with the school for current application deadlines.

QUEEN'S UNIVERSITY	E-3
Kingston, ON K7L 3N6	**(613) 533-2000**
	(613) 533-6810
Full-time: n/av	Faculty: 973
Part-time: n/av	Ph.D.s: n/av
Graduate: n/av	Student/Faculty: 13 to 1
Year: semesters, summer session	Tuition: $5800 ($13,000)
Application Deadline: n/av	Room & Board: $9000
	Freshman Class: n/av
SAT: required	

Queen's University, founded in 1841, is a public institution offering undergraduate and graduate programs in the arts and sciences, business, engineering, health sciences, and teacher education. The figures in the above capsule and in this profile are approximate. There are 10 undergraduate schools and 5 graduate schools. The 160-acre campus is in an urban area 150 miles east of Toronto. Including any residence halls, there are 100 buildings.

STUDENT LIFE: 85% of undergraduates are from Ontario. Others are from states, 80 foreign countries, and Canada. 89% are from public schools. 5% do not continue beyond their first year; 90% remain to graduate. **Housing:** 3071 students can be accommodated in college housing, which includes single-sex and coed dorms, on-campus apartments, off-campus apartments, and married student housing. In addition, there are language houses, special-interest houses, Study floors, and nonsmoking floors. On-campus housing is guaranteed for the freshman year only. 80% of students commute. All students may keep cars.

FACULTY/CLASSROOMS: 72% of faculty are male; 27% are female. All teach undergraduates. No introductory courses are taught by graduate students. The average class size in a laboratory is 40.

PROGRAMS OF STUDY: Queen's confers B.A., B.Sc., B.A./B.Ed., B.A./B.Phe., B.Comm., B.F.A., B.Mus., B.N.Sc., B.Sc./B.Ed., B.Sc./B.Phe., B.S.C.E., B.Sc.O.T. and B.Sc.P.T. degrees. Master's and doctoral degrees are also awarded. Bachelor's degrees are awarded in BIOLOGICAL SCIENCE (biochemistry, biology/biological science, and life science), COMMUNICATIONS AND THE ARTS (art history and appreciation, classics, dramatic arts, English, film arts, fine arts, French, German, Greek, Italian, Latin, music, and Spanish), COMPUTER AND PHYSICAL SCIENCE (chemistry, computer science, geology, mathematics, physics, and statistics), EDUCATION (elementary education, middle school education, and secondary education), ENGINEERING AND ENVIRONMENTAL DESIGN (chemical engineering, civil engineering, electrical/electronics engineering, engineering physics, geological engineering, and mechanical engineering), HEALTH PROFESSIONS (health, nursing, occupational therapy, and physical therapy), SOCIAL SCIENCE (economics, geography, history, Judaic studies, philosophy, political science/government, psychology, religion, sociology, and women's studies). Arts, science, and engineering have the largest enrollments.

ACTIVITIES: There are 220 groups on campus, including art, bagpipe, band, cheerleading, chess, choir, chorale, chorus, computers, dance, debate, drama, ethnic, film, gay, international, jazz band, literary magazine, marching band, musical theater, newspaper, orchestra, photography, political, professional, radio and TV, religious, social, social service, student government, symphony, and yearbook. Popular campus events include Orientation Week, Alumni Weekend, and Applied Science Formal. **Sports:** There are 19 intercollegiate sports for men and 21 for women, and 39 intramural sports for men and 39 for women. Facilities include a pool, an indoor track, a hockey arena, tennis, squash, racquetball courts, a weight room, a dance studio, and a projectile range. There is also a 5000-seat indoor gym and a 12000-seat football stadium. **Graduates:** From July 1, 2013 to June 30, 2014, 3506 bachelor's degrees were awarded.

SERVICES: Counseling and information services are available, as is tutoring in most subjects. There is a reader service for the blind, remedial math, reading, and writing. **Library/Resource:** The 8 libraries contain 1.8 million volumes, 2.0 million microform items, 7,000 audio/video tapes/CDs/DVDs, and subscribe to 15,000 periodicals including electronic. Computerized library services include interlibrary loans and database searching. Special learning facilities include an art gallery, radio station, TV station, a geology museum, and observatory. **Physically Challenged Students:** 80% of the campus is accessible. Facilities include wheelchair ramps, elevators, special parking, specially equipped restrooms, special class scheduling, lowered drinking fountains, and lowered telephones. **Special:** Internships are available in life science, commerce, and engineering. Students may study abroad in 25 countries. Dual majors are available. Cross-registration with St. Lawrence College for the B.S.N. is possible. There is a freshman honors program and 20 departmental honors programs. **Visiting:** There are regularly scheduled orientations for prospective students, consisting of a short briefing session and a walking tour. There are guides for informal visits, visitors may sit in on classes, and stay overnight. To schedule a visit, contact Student Recruitment at (613) 533-2217. **Campus Safety and Security:** Measures include 24-hour foot and vehicle patrol, self-defense education, and security escort services. There are shuttle buses, emergency telephones, and lighted pathways/sidewalks.

REQUIREMENTS: The SAT is required. Candidates for admission are required to submit a school profile. Applications are accepted on-line. Important factors in the admissions decision are evidence of special talent, leadership record, and extracurricular activities record. Each faculty and school establishes the academic requirements for the graduation of its students. **Procedure:** Freshmen are admitted in fall. There are deferred admissions and rolling admissions plans. Check with the school for current application deadlines. The application fee is $125. Notifications are sent May 27. Applications are accepted on-line. **Transfer Students:** 151 transfer students enrolled in 2013-2014. Admission requirements for transfer applicants vary by program. 10 of 19 credits required for the bachelor's degree must be completed at Queen's. **International Students:** There are 396 international students enrolled. The school actively recruits these students. They must take the TOEFL or MELAB. They must also take the SAT.

ADMISSIONS: Dr. David Walker, Dean. E-Mail: *deanfhs@ .queensu.ca* Web: *www.queensu.ca*

FINANCIAL AID: 9% of all full-time freshmen received need-based aid. The deadline for filing freshman financial aid applications for fall entry is May 13.

RYERSON UNIVERSITY E-3

Toronto, ON M5B 2K3   (416) 979-5000
(416) 979-5067

Full-time: n/av	**Faculty:** n/av
Part-time: n/av	**Ph.D.s:** 63%
Graduate: n/av	**Student/Faculty:** 23 to 1
Year: semesters, summer session	**Tuition:** $7000 ($18,000)
Application Deadline: February 1	**Room & Board:** $10,000
	Freshman Class: 69000 applied, 24800 accepted, 8555 enrolled

Ryerson Polytechnic University, founded in 1948, is a public institution offering undergraduate programs in arts, applied arts, business, community services, and engineering and applied science. The figures in the above capsule and in this profile are approximate. There are 50 undergraduate schools and 37 graduate schools. In addition to regional accreditation, Ryerson has baccalaureate program accreditation with FIDER. The 20-acre campus is in an urban area in Toronto. Including any residence halls, there are 35 buildings.

STUDENT LIFE: 90% of undergraduates are from Ontario. **Housing:** 852 students can be accommodated in college housing, which includes coed dorms. On-campus housing is available on a first-come, first-served basis. Priority is given to out-of-town students. 96% of students commute. All students may keep cars.

FACULTY/CLASSROOMS: No introductory courses are taught by graduate students. The average class size in a regular course is 30.

PROGRAMS OF STUDY: Ryerson confers B.A., B.Arch.Sc., B.A.Sc., B.Comm., B.Des., B.Eng., B.H.Sc., B.Sc., B.S.W., B.Tech. and B.U.R.P.I. degrees. Master's and doctoral degrees are also awarded. Bachelor's degrees are awarded in BUSINESS (business administration and management, hospitality management services, and management information systems), COMMUNICATIONS AND THE ARTS (broadcasting, journalism, and photography), COMPUTER AND PHYSICAL SCIENCE (computer programming), EDUCATION (early childhood education), ENGINEERING AND ENVIRONMENTAL DESIGN (aeronautical engineering, architecture, chemical engineering, civil engineering, electrical/electronics engineering, graphic and printing production, industrial engineering, interior design, mechanical engineering, and urban planning technology), HEALTH PROFESSIONS (environmental health science and nursing), SOCIAL SCIENCE (child care/child and family studies, family/consumer studies, fashion design and technology, geography, public administration, and social work). Business management, nursing, and information technology management have the largest enrollments.

ACTIVITIES: There are 150 groups on campus, including choir, chorale, computers, drama, environmental, ethnic, film, gay, international, literary magazine, musical theater, newspaper, political,

professional, radio and TV, religious, social, social service, student government, and yearbook. Popular campus events include Orientation, Parade and Picnic. **Sports:** There are 7 intercollegiate sports for men and 8 for women, and 20 intramural sports for men and 20 for women. Facilities include a recreation and athletic center, 7 squash courts, a fitness training center that includes an indoor running track and weight-training equipment, a rehabilitation center, a 25-yard pool, saunas, 3 studios, and 6 gyms.

SERVICES: Counseling and information services are available, as is tutoring in most subjects. There is a reader service for the blind, and remedial math, reading, and writing. Services are available in study skills development, critical reading seminars, time management skills, and exam workshops. **Library/Resource:** The library contains 477,739 volumes, 842,963 microform items, and 20,235 audio/video tapes/CDs/DVDs, and subscribes to 60,809 periodicals including electronic. Computerized library services include interlibrary loans, database searching, Internet access, and Wi-Fi capability. Special learning facilities include a radio station, the BlackStar Historical Black and White Photography Collection, Heidelberg Centre, George Vari Engineering and Computing Centre. **Physically Challenged Students:** Facilities include wheelchair ramps, elevators, special parking, specially equipped restrooms, special class scheduling, lowered drinking fountains, lowered telephones, special housing. test and exam adaptations, computer-equipped exam and study rooms, listening devices for personal use and for use in auditorium settings, advocacy services, individual needs assessment, and access to a wide range of technical devices. **Special:** The university offers co-op programs in applied chemistry and biology, chemical engineering, and midwifery. Accelerated degree programs are available in journalism, radio and television arts, nurse practitioner, and nursing, and many programs have a work-study component. There is 1 national honor society and a freshman honors program. **Visiting:** There are regularly scheduled orientations for prospective students, student visits include a half-day tour and discussion session featuring campus tours and visits to specific schools and departments. There are guides for informal visits and visitors may sit in on classes. To schedule a visit, contact the Undergraduate Admissions and Recruitment at (416) 979-5036.

Campus Safety and Security: Measures include 24-hour foot and vehicle patrol, emergency notification system, self-defense education, and security escort services. There are emergency telephones, lighted pathways/sidewalks, controlled access to dorms/residences, sexual assault training, harassment prevention and crime prevention programs, and community policing programs.

REQUIREMENTS: The SAT or ACT and ACT Writing Test are recommended. For U.S. students, there is a recommended minimum score of 550 on each section of the SAT I. Students should be high school graduates with a minimum B overall average. AP credits are accepted. To graduate, students must have a 2.0 GPA and complete the requirements of their program of study. **Procedure:** Freshmen are admitted fall. Applications should be filed by February 1 for fall entry, along with a $130 fee. Notifications are sent in March. 7000 applicants were on the 2014 waiting list. Applications are accepted on-line. **Transfer Students:** 700 transfer students enrolled in 2013-2014. Transfer applicants must have completed 1 year at the college level. Acceptance of transfer credits is at the discretion of the Office of Admissions/Liaison/Curriculum Advising. Half of the required credits for a particular degree program must be completed at Ryerson. **International Students:** There are 1000 international students enrolled. The school actively recruits these students. They must take the TOEFL with a minimum score of 560 on the paper-based TOEFL (PBT) or 83 on the Internet-based version (iBT). Student must take the MELAB and the college's own test, or take the IELTS.

ADMISSIONS: 36% of the 2014-2015 applicants were accepted. **Admissions Contact:** Michelle Beaton, Manager of International Recruitment. E-Mail: *international@ryerson.ca* Web: *www.ryerson.ca*

FINANCIAL AID: Ryerson is a member of CSS. Check with the school for current application deadlines.

SIMON FRASER UNIVERSITY   B-2

Burnaby, BC V5A 1S6   (778) 782-6930
     (778) 782-4969

Full-time: n/av	**Faculty:** n/av
Part-time: n/av	**Ph.D.s:** 88%
Graduate: n/av	**Student/Faculty:** n/av
Year: varies, summer session	**Tuition:** $6724 ($17,984)
Application Deadline: May 1	**Room & Board:** $7484
	Freshman Class: n/av
SAT: required	

Simon Fraser University, established in 1965, is a public institution offering undergraduate and graduate programs in the arts, sciences, business, education, and applied sciences. In addition to its main campus, the university maintains the Harbour Centre campus in downtown Vancouver to provide mid-career education to the urban population and the SFU Surrey campus offering programs in information technology and interactive arts. The figures in the above capsule and in this profile are approximate. There are 8 undergraduate schools and 35 graduate schools. The 400-acre campus is in a suburban area 9 miles east of Vancouver, Canada. Including any residence halls, there are 51 buildings.

STUDENT LIFE: 89% of undergraduates are from British Columbia. Others are from 107 foreign countries, and Canada. 92% are from public schools. The average age of freshmen is 19; all undergraduates, 23. **Housing:** 1750 students can be accommodated in college housing, which includes single-sex and coed dorms, on-campus apartments, and married student housing. In addition, there are special-interest houses. On-campus housing is guaranteed for the freshman year only. Priority is given to out-of-town students. 92% of students commute. All students may keep cars.

FACULTY/CLASSROOMS: 71% of faculty are male; 29% are female. No introductory courses are taught by graduate students.

PROGRAMS OF STUDY: SFU confers B.A., B.A.Sc., B.B.A., B.E.D., B.F.A., B.G.S. and B.Sc. degrees. Master's and doctoral degrees are also awarded. Bachelor's degrees are awarded in BIOLOGICAL SCIENCE (biology/biological science, molecular biology, and physiology), BUSINESS (business administration and management and management science), COMMUNICATIONS AND THE ARTS (art, communications, dance, dramatic arts, English, film arts, French, linguistics, music, and visual and performing arts), COMPUTER AND PHYSICAL SCIENCE (actuarial science, applied mathematics, applied physics, chemistry, computer science, earth science, mathematics, physics, science, and statistics), EDUCATION (education), ENGINEERING AND ENVIRONMENTAL DESIGN (engineering and applied science and environmental science), SOCIAL SCIENCE (anthropology, archeology, Canadian studies, cognitive science, criminology, economics, geography, history, humanities, liberal arts/general studies, philosophy, physical fitness/movement, political science/government, psychology, sociology, and women's studies). Engineering science is the strongest academically. Business administration, psychology, and computing science have the largest enrollments.

ACTIVITIES: There are 35 groups on campus, including gaming, hobbies and preprofessional, special interest, athletic, bagpipe, chess, choir, computers, ethnic, gay, international, newspaper, political, professional, religious, social, social service, and student government. Popular campus events include Terry Fox Day, Gung Hagis Fat Choi, and Robbie Burns Day. **Sports:** There are 8 intercollegiate sports for men and 9 for women, and 8 intramural sports for men and 7 for women. Facilities include 3 gyms, swimming and diving pools, a running track, weight rooms, saunas, playing fields, a combative room, tennis, squash, and racquetball courts, and a fitness center. **Graduates:** The most popular majors were business, education, and economics.

SERVICES: There is a reader service for the blind. **Library/Resource:** The 3 libraries contain 2.6 million volumes, 936,808 microform items, and 22,649 audio/video tapes/CDs/DVDs, and subscribe to 67,000 periodicals including electronic. Computerized library services include interlibrary loans, database searching, Internet access, and Wi-Fi capability. Special learning facilities include an art gallery, an archeology museum, special literature and map collections, fine and performing arts theater, hypo/hyperbaric chamber, back test unit, rock climbing wall, apiary, underwater lab, television and photography studios, and dance floors. **Physically Challenged Students:** 95% of the campus is accessible. Facilities include wheelchair ramps, elevators, special parking, specially equipped restrooms, lowered drinking fountains, lowered telephones, special housing. Braille printer, a visualtek machine, closed-circuit TV for text or graphic enlargement, note taking tutor support, adaptive technology, exam modifications, sign language interpreters, closed captioning in lectures, and alternate format texts. **Special:** Simon Fraser offers cooperative education in most areas of study, study abroad in 47 countries, many opportunities for joint majors, a general studies degree, work-study programs, dual-majors, student-designed majors, and a variety of certificate and diploma programs, as well as non-degree and evening study. Interdisciplinary majors are offered in such areas as chemical physics, management and systems science, mathematical physics, and physics and physiology. There is a freshman honors program and 48 departmental honors programs. **Visiting:** There are regularly scheduled orientations for prospective students, consisting of regularly scheduled 1-day campus orientations for prospective students. There are guides for informal visits and visitors may stay overnight. To schedule a visit, contact the Residence and Housing Office at (778) 782-4201. **Campus Safety and Security:** Measures include 24-hour foot and vehicle patrol and security escort services. There are emergency telephones, lighted pathways/sidewalks, controlled access to dorms/residences, safe-walk stations, and student patrols.

REQUIREMENTS: The SAT is required for U.S. applicants. Applicants must be graduates of an accredited secondary school and have a minimum GPA of 3.2. AP credits are accepted. General bachelor's degrees require completion of 120 semester hours with a 2.0 cumulative GPA. For a honors degrees, students must complete 132 hours. Some programs require a thesis. **Procedure:** Freshmen are admitted to all sessions. There are early decision and early admissions plans. Early decision applications should be filed by April 1; regular applications, by May 1 for fall entry; September 30 for spring entry; and February 2 for summer entry. The fall 2014 application fee was $45. Notification of early decision is sent April 15; regular decision, June 30. Applications are accepted on-line. **Transfer Students:** 2603 transfer students enrolled in 2013-2014. Applicants must have a minimum GPA of 2.0 and be in good standing at their previous school. 60 of 120 credits required for the bachelor's degree must be completed at SFU. **International Students:** There are 2889 international students enrolled. The school actively recruits these students. They must take the TOEFL, or take the IELTS.

ADMISSIONS: Mehran Kiai, Enrollment Services. E-Mail: *undergraduate-admissions@sfu.ca* Web: *www.students@sfu.ca*

FINANCIAL AID: The average financial indebtedness of the 2014 graduate was $20,000. The FAFSA is required. The deadline for filing freshman financial aid applications for fall entry is July 1.

UNIVERSITÉ DE MONTRÉAL   E-2

Montreal, PQ H3C 3J7   (514) 343-7076
     (514) 343-5788

Full-time: 13020 men, 17045 women	**Faculty:** n/av
	Ph.D.s: 96%
Part-time: 5410 men, 9025 women	**Student/Faculty:** n/av
Graduate: 6726 men, 8348 women	**Tuition:** $2688 ($16,020)
Year: trimesters, summer session	**Room & Board:** $3840
Application Deadline: March 1	**Freshman Class:** 31100 applied, 13923 accepted, 13174 enrolled

Université de Montréal, founded in 1878, is the largest French-language university in North America, with 13 faculties, 2 affiliated schools, 62 teaching departments, and more than 170 research units. The figures in the above capsule and in this profile are approximate. There are 16 undergraduate schools and 15 graduate schools. The 145-acre campus is in an urban area in Montreal, Canada. Including any residence halls, there are 38 buildings.

STUDENT LIFE: Students are from 11 states. 88% are from public schools. **Female To Male Ratio:** 1.4:1. The average age of freshmen is 22; all undergraduates, 24. 20% do not continue beyond their first year; 80% remain to graduate. **Housing:** 1164 students can be accommodated in college housing, which includes coed off-campus apartments. On-campus housing is available on a first-come, first-served basis. 98% of students commute. All students may keep cars.

FACULTY/CLASSROOMS: 71% of faculty are male; 29% are female. No introductory courses are taught by graduate students. The average class size in an introductory lecture is 48; in a laboratory is 19; and in a regular course is 40.

PROGRAMS OF STUDY: UdeM confers B.A., B.Sc., B.A.A., B.A.P., B.D.I., B.Gest., B.Ed., B.Ing., B.Int., B.Mus. and B.Th. degrees. Associate, master's, and doctoral degrees are also awarded. Bachelor's degrees are awarded in BIOLOGICAL SCIENCE (biochemistry, biology/biological science, biometrics and biostatistics, and nutrition), BUSINESS (business administration and management), COMMUNICATIONS AND THE ARTS (art history and appreciation, classics, English, film arts, French, German, industrial design, linguistics, and music), COMPUTER AND PHYSICAL SCIENCE (chemistry, computer science, mathematics, and physics), EDUCATION (education, physical education, and psychology education), ENGINEERING AND ENVIRONMENTAL DESIGN (architectural engineering, architecture, engineering, industrial administration/management, and landscape architecture/design), HEALTH PROFESSIONS (health science, nursing, occupational therapy, pharmacy, physical therapy, predentistry, premedicine, preveterinary science, speech pathology/audiology, and veterinary science), SOCIAL SCIENCE (anthropology, Asian/Oriental studies, criminology, economics, geography, history, law, philosophy, political science/government, psychology, social work, sociology, Spanish studies, theological studies, and urban studies). Law, medicine, and nursing have the largest enrollments.

ACTIVITIES: There are 100 groups on campus, including art, cheerleading, choir, chorale, computers, dance, debate, drama, environmental, ethnic, film, international, jazz band, literary magazine, newspaper, orchestra, photography, political, radio and TV, religious, social, social service, student government, and yearbook. Popular campus events include Multicultural Week, and Welcoming Week. **Sports:** There are 8 intercollegiate sports for men and 6 for women, and 12 intramural sports for men and 12 for women. Facilities include a skating rink, a football field, a gym, squash and racquetball courts, an Olympic-size pool, a diving pool, a running field with tennis courts, and aerobic and muscular exercise equipment. **Graduates:** The most popular majors were law (8%), medicine (5%), and nursing (5%).

SERVICES: Counseling and information services are available, as is tutoring in some subjects. There is a reader service for the blind, and remedial math, reading, and writing. **Library/Resource:** The 19 libraries contain 3.0 million volumes, 1.6 million microform items, and 2.0 million audio/video tapes/CDs/DVDs, and subscribe to 50,000 periodicals including electronic. Computerized library services include interlibrary loans, database searching, Internet access, and Wi-Fi capability. Special learning facilities include an art gallery, natural history museum, radio station, a concert hall. **Physically Challenged Students:** 95% of the campus is accessible. Facilities include wheelchair ramps, elevators, special parking, specially equipped restrooms, lowered drinking fountains, lowered telephones, and special housing. Specialized equipment center for students with disabilities. **Special:** The university offers co-op programs in math, translation, mining, and civil, chemical, and software material engineering; and work-study programs in hospitals and businesses in Quebec. Dual majors in math and economics, math and physics, math and computer science, communication and politics, economics and politics, and 3-2 engineering degrees may also be arranged. Study abroad is available in 31 countries. There is a freshman honors program and 45 departmental honors programs. **Visiting:** There are regularly scheduled orientations for prospective students, Student visits include Orientation and Employment Week in November, guided tours February through May, and open house in January and August. There are guides for informal visits. To schedule a visit, contact the Director of Communications and Recriutement. **Campus Safety and Security:** Measures include 24-hour foot and vehicle patrol, emergency notification system, and security escort services. There are emergency telephones, lighted pathways/sidewalks, controlled access to dorms/residences, and in-room safes.

REQUIREMENTS: Applicants in certain programs must take the university's admissions tests. An interview is also required in some programs. To graduate, students must have a GPA of 2.0 on a 4.3 scale. The total number of credits required in most programs is 90, although it can range up to 187. Professional programs, particularly those in health-related fields, require more hours. **Procedure:** Freshmen are admitted fall and winter. Applications should be filed by March 1 for fall entry; November 1 for winter entry; March 1 for spring entry; and March 1 for summer entry, along with a $100 fee. Notifications are sent March 15. applicants were on the 2014 waiting list; were admitted. Applications are accepted on-line. **Transfer Students:** Transfers are considered if there are openings in the second or third year of the university's programs. 90 credits required for the bachelor's degree must be completed at UdeM. **International Students:** The school actively recruits these students.

ADMISSIONS: 45% of the 2014-2015 applicants were accepted. **Admissions Contact:** Jacinthe Gauthier, Responsible Admissions. E-Mail: *admissions@regis.umontreal.ca* Web: *www.etudes.umontreal.ca*

FINANCIAL AID: The deadline for filing freshman financial aid applications for fall entry is March 31.

UNIVERSITY OF ALBERTA C-2

Edmonton, AB T6G 2M7
(780) 492-3111
(780) 492-7172

Full-time: 12346 men, 15665 women	**Faculty:** 1659
Part-time: 691 men, 1147 women	**Ph.D.s:** 92%
Graduate: 3550 men, 3594 women	**Student/Faculty:** n/av
Year: semesters, summer session	**Tuition:** $5829 ($18,459)
Application Deadline: May 1	**Room & Board:** $6502
	Freshman Class: 10587 applied, 6131 accepted, 4812 enrolled
SAT: recommended	

University of Alberta, founded in 1908, is a publicly supported institution offering undergraduate and graduate programs in arts and science, agricultural sciences, business, education, engineering, nursing, phys ed, native studies, and professional studies. The figures in the above capsule and in this profile are approximate. There are 18 undergraduate schools and 1 graduate school. The 155-acre campus is in an urban area 2 miles southwest of downtown Edmonton, Canada. Including any residence halls, there are 90 buildings.

STUDENT LIFE: Students are from 130 foreign countries, and Canada. **Female To Male Ratio:** 1.2:1. The average age of freshmen is 19; all undergraduates, 22. **Housing:** 4900 students can be accommodated in college housing, which includes single-sex and coed dorms, on-campus apartments, off-campus apartments, and married student housing. In addition, there are honors houses, language houses, special-interest houses, fraternity houses, and sorority houses. 88% of students commute. All students may keep cars.

FACULTY/CLASSROOMS: No introductory courses are taught by graduate students. The average class size in an introductory lecture is 90; in a laboratory is 20; and in a regular course is 35.

PROGRAMS OF STUDY: U of A confers B.A., B.Comm., B.Ed., B.F.A., B.Mus., B.P.E., B.S.C., B.S.Cn. and B.des. degrees. Master's and doctoral degrees are also awarded. Bachelor's degrees are awarded in AGRICULTURE (agricultural economics, agriculture, animal science, and soil science), BIOLOGICAL SCIENCE (biochemistry, biology/biological science, botany, cell biology, entomology, genetics, microbiology, physiology, and zoology), BUSINESS (accounting, management science, and marketing/retailing/merchandising), COMMUNICATIONS AND THE ARTS (classics, comparative literature, dance, dramatic arts, English, film arts, French, Germanic languages and literature, linguistics, music, romance languages and literature, and Slavic languages), COMPUTER AND PHYSICAL SCIENCE (applied mathematics, chemistry, computer science, earth science, geology, geophysics and seismology, mathematics, physical sciences, physics, and statistics), EDUCATION (education of the deaf and hearing impaired, education of the multiply handicapped, elementary education, physical education, secondary education, special education, and vocational education), ENGINEERING AND ENVIRONMENTAL DESIGN (chemical engineering technology, civil engineering, computer engineering, electrical/electronics engineering, engineering physics, mechanical engineering, metallurgical engineering, mining and mineral engineering, and petroleum/natural gas engineering), HEALTH PROFESSIONS (medical laboratory science, nursing, occupational therapy, pharmacy, and physical therapy), SOCIAL SCIENCE (anthropology, Canadian studies, clothing and textiles management/production/services, criminology, East Asian studies, Eastern European studies, economics, geography, history, law, philosophy, political science/government, psychology, sociology, and women's studies). Arts, science, and engineering have the largest enrollments.

ACTIVITIES: There are 400 groups on campus, including art, band, cheerleading, chess, choir, chorale, chorus, computers, dance, debate, drama, environmental, ethnic, film, forensics, gay, honors, international, jazz band, musical theater, newspaper, opera, orchestra, pep band, photography, political, radio and TV, religious, social, social service, student government, and symphony. Popular campus events include WOW (Week of Welcome) and AntiFreeze (winter activity). **Sports:** There are 12 intercollegiate sports for men and 13 for women, and 60 intramural sports for men and 45 for women. Facilities include a stadium, swimming pools, gyms, combative and weight rooms, ballet/fencing and aerobics studios, 400-meter outdoor track, an ice arena, racquetball and squash courts, wrestling gym, an indoor field house, sports medicine clinic, training center for disabled athletes, curling rinks, and tennis courts.

SERVICES: Counseling and information services are available, as is tutoring in most subjects. There is a reader service for the blind, and remedial math, reading, and writing. **Library/Resource:** The 13 libraries contain 5.4 million volumes, and 3.7 million microform items. Computerized library services include interlibrary loans, database searching, Internet access, and Wi-Fi capability. Special learning facilities include an art gallery, radio station, an agricultural meteorological research station, ecological sanctuary, botanical garden, the Kurimoto Japanese Garden farm, and Timms Centre for the Arts. **Physically Challenged Students:** 98% of the campus is accessible. Facilities include wheelchair ramps, elevators, special parking, specially equipped restrooms, special class scheduling, lowered drinking fountains, lowered telephones. Automatic doors. **Special:** The university offers co-op programs in business and engineering. Opportunities for study abroad, internships, dual majors, bilingual classes in French and English, credit by exam (special assessment), and pass/fail options are also available. There are 1 national honor societies and a freshman honors program. **Visiting:** There are regularly scheduled orientations for prospective students, including University Open House on the first weekend in October and Orientation for new students held on campus 2 days before classes begin in the fall term. There are guides for informal visits, visitors may sit in on classes, and stay overnight. To schedule a visit, contact the Office of the Registrar and Student Awards. **Campus Safety and Security:** Measures include 24-hour foot and vehicle patrol, emergency notification system, self-defense education, and security escort services. There are emergency telephones, lighted pathways/sidewalks, and controlled access to dorms/residences.

REQUIREMENTS: The SAT is recommended. Graduation from an accredited secondary school is required. A minimum grade average of 70 is required in all courses submitted for academic credit. Depending on the program selected by the student, an essay, portfolio, audition, or interview may be required. AP credits are accepted. The requirements for graduation vary according to the program. A minimum GPA of 2.0 and at least 120 credit hours are required for graduation. **Procedure:** Freshmen are admitted to all sessions. There is an early admissions plan. Applications should be filed by May 1 for fall entry; November 15 for winter entry; and March 1 for spring entry, along with a $115 fee. Notification of early decision is sent January 2; regular decision, August 1. Applications are accepted on-line. **Transfer Students:** 4609 transfer students enrolled in 2013-2014. Applicants must meet minimum matriculation requirements or complete 24 credits of transferable work with satisfactory standing. 60 of 120 credits required for the bachelor's degree must be completed at U of A. **International Students:** There are 1885 international students enrolled. The school actively recruits these students. They must take the TOEFL with a minimum score of 580 on the paper-based TOEFL (PBT) or 86 on the Internet-based version (iBT) or take the MELAB, IELTS, CAEL, or the university's own test.

ADMISSIONS: 58% of the 2014-2015 applicants were accepted. **Admissions Contact:** Office of the Registrar and Student Awards E-Mail: *www.registrar.ualberta.ca/contact* Web: *www.ualberta.ca*

FINANCIAL AID: Check with the school for current application deadlines.

UNIVERSITY OF BRITISH COLUMBIA   B-2

Vancouver, BC V6T 1Z1 (604) 822-2211
(877) 272-1422
(604) 822-9858

Full-time: 10044 men, 11332 women	**Faculty:** n/av
	Ph.D.s: 99%
Part-time: 3357 men, 4090 women	**Student/Faculty:** 15 to 1
Graduate: 6861 men, 8293 women	**Tuition:** $5175 ($21,150)
Year: other, summer session	**Room & Board:** $6650
Application Deadline: February 28	**Freshman Class:** 23102 applied, 12285 accepted, 6225 enrolled
SAT or ACT: required	

The University of British Columbia, established in 1908, is a publicly supported institution offering a wide range of undergraduate, graduate, and professional programs in the arts, sciences, and other fields of study. The figures in the above capsule and in this profile are approximate. There are 16 undergraduate schools and 1 graduate school. The 1000-acre campus is in an urban area 6 miles from the center of Vancouver, Canada. Including any residence halls, there are 500 buildings.

STUDENT LIFE: 87% of undergraduates are from British Columbia. Others are from 43 states, 140 foreign countries, and Canada. 98% are from public schools. 14% are Foreign. **Female To Male Ratio:** 1.2:1. The average age of freshmen is 20; all undergraduates, 21. 8% do not continue beyond their first year; 92% remain to graduate. **Housing:** 9500 students can be accommodated in college housing, which includes single-sex and coed dorms, on-campus apartments, and married student housing. In addition, there are special-interest houses, International houses: Japanese, Korean, Mexican and Hong Kong. On-campus housing is guaranteed for the freshman year only, is available on a first-come, first-served basis, and is available on a lottery system for upperclassmen. Priority is given to out-of-town students. 80% of students commute. All students may keep cars.

FACULTY/CLASSROOMS: 62% of faculty are male; 38% are female. No introductory courses are taught by graduate students.

PROGRAMS OF STUDY: UBC confers B.A., B.A.H.S., B.A.Sc., B.B.R.E., B.Com.B.C.S., B.D.Sc., B.Ed., B.End., B.F.A., B.H.E., B.H.K., B.Mgt., B.M.LSc., B.Mus., B.Mw., B.Sc., B.Sc.Die., B.Sc.F., B.Sc.Pharm., B.S.F., B.S.N., B.S.W., and L.L.B. degrees. Master's and doctoral degrees are also awarded. Bachelor's degrees are awarded in AGRICULTURE (agricultural economics, animal science, forestry production and processing, forestry and related sciences, horticulture, natural resource management, and soil science), BIOLOGICAL SCIENCE (biochemistry, biology/biological science, biophysics, biotechnology, microbiology, nutrition, physiology, and zoology), BUSINESS (accounting, banking and finance, business administration and management, business economics, human resources, international business management, management information systems, marketing/retailing/merchandising, real estate, recreational facilities management, and transportation management), COMMUNICATIONS AND THE ARTS (art history and appreciation, Chinese, classics, creative writing, dramatic arts, English, film arts, fine arts, French, German, Italian, Japanese, linguistics, music, music history and appreciation, music performance, music theory and composition, romance languages and literature, and Spanish), COMPUTER AND PHYSICAL SCIENCE (astronomy, atmospheric sciences and meteorology, chemistry, computer science, earth science, geophysics and seismology, mathematics, oceanography, physics, science, and statistics), EDUCATION (elementary education, museum studies, and physical education), ENGINEERING AND ENVIRONMENTAL DESIGN (chemical engineering, civil engineering, computer engineering, electrical/electronics engineering, engineering, engineering physics, environmental design, environmental engineering, environmental science, geological engineering, mechanical engineering, metallurgical engineering, and mining and mineral engineering), HEALTH PROFESSIONS (exercise science, health, nursing, pharmacology, preveterinary science, and speech pathology/audiology), SOCIAL SCIENCE (anthropology, archeology, Asian/Oriental studies, Canadian studies, classical/ancient civilization, cognitive science, dietetics, economics, European studies, family/consumer studies, food production/management/services, food science, geography, Hispanic American studies, history, home economics, human ecology, international relations, Latin American studies, medieval studies, Native American studies, philosophy, political science/government, psychology, religion, sociology, South Asian studies, and women's studies). Applied sciences, and commerce are the strongest academically. Education and arts have the largest enrollments.

ACTIVITIES: 6% of men belong to 7 national fraternities; 2% of women belong to 7 national sororities. There are 250 groups on campus, including varsity outdoors, art, band, cheerleading, chess, choir, chorale, chorus, computers, dance, debate, drama, environmental, ethnic, film, gay, honors, international, jazz band, literary magazine, musical theater, newspaper, opera, orchestra, photography, political, professional, radio and TV, religious, ski and snowboard, social, social service, student government, symphony, and yearbook. Popular campus events include Storm the Wall, Day of the Longboat, and Great Trek Run. **Sports:** There are 13 intercollegiate sports for men and 11 for women, and 18 intramural sports for men and 18 for women. Facilities include a winter sports center, a 3500-seat stadium, a gym, an aquatic center, playing fields, a recreation center, a tennis center, and a rowing centre. **Graduates:** The most popular majors were psychology, biology, and English.

SERVICES: Counseling and information services are available, as is tutoring in most subjects. There is a reader service for the blind, and remedial math, reading, and writing. **Library/Resource:** The 22 libraries contain 5.6 million volumes, 5.2 million microform items, and 840,000 audio/video tapes/CDs/DVDs, and subscribe to 63,000 periodicals including electronic. Computerized library services include interlibrary loans, database searching, Internet access, and Wi-Fi capability. Special learning facilities include an art gallery, natural history museum, radio station, a learning center, an anthropology museum, Canada's largest accelerator for subatomic physics, space observatory, center for integrated computer systems research, center for the study of global issues, and a center for the performing arts. **Physically Challenged Students:** 95% of the campus is accessible. Facilities include wheelchair ramps, elevators, special parking, specially equipped restrooms, special class scheduling, lowered drinking fountains, lowered telephones, special housing. Accessible shower stalls in fitness facilities, tactile maps, TTY pay phones, an accessible security bus, and audible street crossing signals. **Special:** UBC offers co-op programs in science, applied science, commerce, arts, and forestry, and study abroad through 190 student exchange opportunities in 41 countries. Non-degree study is possible. A B.A.-B.A.Sc. degree, student-designed majors, dual majors in most faculties, and work-study programs are available. There is 1 national honor society and 10 departmental honors programs. **Visiting:** There are regularly scheduled orientations for prospective students, Monday through Saturday. There are guides for informal visits, visitors may sit in on classes, and stay overnight. **Campus Safety and Security:** Measures include 24-hour foot and vehicle patrol and security escort services. There are shuttle buses, emergency telephones, lighted pathways/sidewalks, controlled access to dorms/residences, Royal Canadian mounted police detachment is on campus, awareness programs on theft, and personal safety lectures.

REQUIREMENTS: The SAT or ACT is required. The ACT Optional Writing test is also required. Graduation from an accredited secondary school is required. General admission for students following a U.S. system is based on 4 years of English and 3 years of math. There are also specific program requirements in math, chemistry, physics,

and biology for students applying to science-based programs. U.S. curriculum students are required to submit SAT or ACT and writing scores. Exemptions may begin where these tests are not available. A GPA of 2.6 is required. AP credits are accepted. Important factors in the admissions decision are extracurricular activities record, leadership record, and recommendations by school officials. To graduate, students must complete 120 credits in arts or science, more for applied science. Total number of hours required in a major varies by faculty. English is required for all majors. **Procedure:** Freshmen are admitted fall and spring. There are early admissions, deferred admissions, and rolling admissions plans. Applications should be filed by February 28 for fall entry; February 28 for spring entry; and February 28 for summer entry, along with a $100 fee. Applications are accepted on-line. **Transfer Students:** 1829 transfer students enrolled in 2013-2014. Official transcripts, completion of the equivalent of 24 course credits, and no failures are required. A competitive GPA is required to get into the program at the second or third year. Applicants must have attended an accredited post-secondary institution. 60 of 120 credits required for the bachelor's degree must be completed at UBC. **International Students:** There are 4442 international students enrolled. The school actively recruits these students. They must also take the SAT or ACT.

ADMISSIONS: 53% of the 2014-2015 applicants were accepted. 96% of the current freshmen were in the top fifth of their class. **Admissions Contact:** Office of the Registrar Web: *www.askme.ubc.ca*

FINANCIAL AID: The FAFSA and the college's own financial statement are required. Check with the school for current application deadlines.

UNIVERSITY OF CALGARY C-2

Calgary, AB T2N 1N4

(403) 220-5110
(403) 220-0762

Full-time: 11000 men, 13000 women	**Faculty:** n/av
	Ph.D.s: n/av
Part-time: 1293 men, 1901 women	**Student/Faculty:** 13 to 1
Graduate: 2578 men, 2556 women	**Tuition:** $6118 ($12,060)
Year: semesters, summer session	**Room & Board:** $5475
Application Deadline: May 1	**Freshman Class:** n/av
SAT or ACT: required	

The University of Calgary, founded in 1945, is a public institution offering undergraduate programs in numerous liberal arts and professional fields. The figures in the above capsule and in this profile are approximate. There are 15 undergraduate schools and 2 graduate schools. The 526-acre campus is in an urban area in northwest Calgary, Alberta Canada. Including any residence halls, there are 36 buildings.

STUDENT LIFE: 80% of undergraduates are from Alberta. Others are from 32 states, 90 foreign countries, and Canada. 50% are from public schools. **Female To Male Ratio:** 1.2:1. The average age of freshmen is 19; all undergraduates, 23. 6% do not continue beyond their first year; 92% remain to graduate. **Housing:** 1500 students can be accommodated in college housing, which includes coed dorms, on-campus apartments, and married student housing. In addition, there are honors houses, language houses, global village, and living and learning academic community. On-campus housing is guaranteed for all 4 years and is guaranteed for the freshman year only. Priority is given to out-of-town students. 30% of students commute. All students may keep cars.

FACULTY/CLASSROOMS: No introductory courses are taught by graduate students. The average class size in an introductory lecture is 89; in a laboratory is 24; and in a regular course is 60.

PROGRAMS OF STUDY: U of C confers B.A., B.Sc., B.Comm., B.C.R., B.C.S., B.Ed., B.F.A., B.G.S., B.H.R.M., B.H.Sc., B.Kin., B.Mus., B.N., B.Sc.Eng., B.S.W. and LL.B. degrees. Master's and doctoral degrees are also awarded. Bachelor's degrees are awarded in BIOLOGICAL SCIENCE (biochemistry, bioinformatics, biology/biological science, botany, cell biology, ecology, and zoology), BUSINESS (accounting, business administration and management, hotel/motel and restaurant management, and marketing/retailing/

merchandising), COMMUNICATIONS AND THE ARTS (communications, dance, dramatic arts, English, fine arts, French, German, linguistics, music, music history and appreciation, music performance, music theory and composition, Russian, and Spanish), COMPUTER AND PHYSICAL SCIENCE (actuarial science, applied mathematics, astrophysics, chemical physics, chemistry, computer science, earth science, geology, geophysics and seismology, mathematics, natural sciences, physics, and statistics), EDUCATION (education, elementary education, and secondary education), ENGINEERING AND ENVIRONMENTAL DESIGN (chemical engineering, civil engineering, computer engineering, electrical/electronics engineering, environmental science, mechanical engineering, petroleum/natural gas engineering, and surveying engineering), HEALTH PROFESSIONS (biomedical science, exercise science, nursing, public health, and sports medicine), SOCIAL SCIENCE (anthropology, archeology, Asian/Oriental studies, Canadian studies, classical/ancient civilization, economics, geography, history, international relations, Latin American studies, law, liberal arts/general studies, philosophy, physical fitness/movement, political science/government, psychology, religion, social work, sociology, urban studies, and women's studies). Engineering, and medicine. are the strongest academically. Management, engineering, and arts have the largest enrollments.

ACTIVITIES: There are 221 groups on campus, including art, band, chess, choir, chorus, computers, dance, debate, drama, environmental, ethnic, film, gay, international, jazz band, musical theater, newspaper, orchestra, political, professional, radio and TV, religious, social, social service, and student government. Popular campus events include Bermuda Shorts Day (last day of classes in April), Orientation Week and KickOff. **Sports:** There are 9 intercollegiate sports for men and 9 for women, and 20 intramural sports for men and 18 for women. Facilities include a 50-meter swimming pool, three gyms, a 200-meter indoor track, 3-story climbing wall, an indoor speedskating arena, outdoor stadium, rooms for weight training, aerobics, squash, tennis, and racquetball courts. There is also a 200-seat lecture theater, games area, and an outdoor recreation center. **Graduates:** The Most Popular majors were Science, Arts, and Engineering.

SERVICES: Counseling and information services are available, as is tutoring in most subjects. There is a reader service for the blind, and remedial math and writing. **Library/Resource:** The 6 libraries contain 2.5 million volumes, 3.6 million microform items, and 36,920 audio/video tapes/CDs/DVDs, and subscribe to 20,237 periodicals including electronic. Computerized library services include interlibrary loans, database searching, Internet access, and Wi-Fi capability. Special learning facilities include an art gallery, radio station, TV station, an environmental research center, observatory, human performance and theater labs, arts museum, children's hospital, and Foothills medical center. **Physically Challenged Students:** All of the campus is accessible. Facilities include wheelchair ramps, elevators, special parking, specially equipped restrooms, special class scheduling, lowered drinking fountains, lowered telephones, and special housing. **Special:** The university offers co-op programs in applied chemistry, management, and many other fields. Dual majors, work-study programs, internships in engineering and computer science, combined degrees in many disciplines, and study abroad in 61 countries are also available. Students may cross-register with any of 8 member colleges in the Big Country Education Consortium. U of C sponsors or is affiliated with 20 research institutes and groups. There is 1 national honor society, a freshman honors program, and 2 departmental honors programs. **Visiting:** There are regularly scheduled orientations for prospective students, including campus tours and admissions advising. There are guides for informal visits and visitors may stay overnight. To schedule a visit, contact Student Enrollment Services at (403) 210-7625. **Campus Safety and Security:** Measures include 24-hour foot and vehicle patrol, emergency notification system, and security escort services. There are emergency telephones, lighted pathways/sidewalks, and controlled access to dorms/residences.

REQUIREMENTS: U.S. applicants must be graduates of a secondary school and submit SAT or ACT scores, as required by the individual faculties. AP credits are accepted. To graduate, all students must satisfy the required courses, course sequences, and credit distribution in their particular program. Students must maintain a minimum 2.0 GPA and complete 7 to 10 full-course equivalents in the major field.

Procedure: Freshmen are admitted fall. There is an early admissions plan. Early decision applications should be filed by February 1; regular applications, by May 1 for fall entry, along with a $145 fee. Notification of early decision is sent February 20. Applications are accepted on-line. **Transfer Students:** Applicants must have a cumulative GPA of 2.0 or above on all transfer courses. 20 of 40 credits required for the bachelor's degree must be completed at U of C. **International Students:** There are 1300 international students enrolled. The school actively recruits these students. They must take the TOEFL with a minimum score of 83 on the Internet-based version (iBT), or take the IELTS, CAEL, or the university's English program. They must also take the SAT or ACT.

ADMISSIONS: David Johnson, Assistant Vice-President E-Mail: *future.students@ucalgary.ca* Web: *www.ucalgary.ca*

FINANCIAL AID: The priority date for freshman financial aid applications for fall entry is April 1. The deadline for filing freshman financial aid applications for fall entry is April 1.

UNIVERSITY OF GUELPH	E-3
Guelph, ON N1G 2W1	(519) 824-4120 (519) 766-9481
Full-time: n/av	Faculty: 800
Part-time: n/av	Ph.D.s: 98%
Graduate: n/av	Student/Faculty: 19 to 1
Year: varies, summer session	Tuition: $5982 ($16,982)
Application Deadline: March 1	Room & Board: $8100
	Freshman Class: 18852 applied, 13765 accepted, 3479 enrolled
SAT or ACT: required	

The University of Guelph, founded in 1964, is a public institution offering programs in arts and sciences, agriculture, engineering, commerce, landscape architecture, veterinary medicine, applied science, and technology. The figures in the above capsule and in this profile are approximate. There are 7 undergraduate schools. The 1017-acre campus is in a suburban area 2 miles south of the center of Guelph, Canada. Including any residence halls, there are 80 buildings.

STUDENT LIFE: 93% of undergraduates are from Ontario. Others are from 100 foreign countries, and Canada. The average age of freshmen is 18; all undergraduates, 21. 9% do not continue beyond their first year; 89% remain to graduate. **Housing:** 5500 students can be accommodated in college housing, which includes single-sex and coed dorms, on-campus apartments, off-campus apartments, and married student housing. In addition, there are language houses, special-interest houses, an international house, La Maison Francaise, Eco house, an arts house, and study intensive and academic clusters. On-campus housing is guaranteed for the freshman year only, is available on a first-come, first-served basis, and is available on a lottery system for upperclassmen. 67% of students commute. All students may keep cars.

FACULTY/CLASSROOMS: No introductory courses are taught by graduate students. The average class size in an introductory lecture is 300 and in a laboratory is 25.

PROGRAMS OF STUDY: U of G confers B.A., B.A.S., B.A.Sc., B.B.R.M., B.Comm., B.Comp., B.L.A., B.Sc., B.Sc.Agr., B.Sc.Eng., B.Sc.Env. and B.Sc.(Tech). degrees. Master's and doctoral degrees are also awarded. Bachelor's degrees are awarded in AGRICULTURE (agricultural economics, agriculture, agronomy, animal science, horticulture, and natural resource management), BIOLOGICAL SCIENCE (biochemistry, biology/biological science, biophysics, ecology, environmental biology, marine science, microbiology, molecular biology, nutrition, wildlife biology, and zoology), BUSINESS (hospitality management services, human resources, marketing management, and real estate), COMMUNICATIONS AND THE ARTS (art history and appreciation, classical languages, English, music, Spanish, and studio art), COMPUTER AND PHYSICAL SCIENCE (chemical physics, chemistry, computer science, earth science, information sciences and systems, physical sciences, physics, and statistics), ENGINEERING AND ENVIRONMENTAL DESIGN (biomedical engineering, engineering, environmental engineering, and landscape architecture/design), SOCIAL SCIENCE (anthropology, child care/child and family studies, classical/ancient civilization, criminal justice, economics, food science, French studies, geography, gerontology, history, interdisciplinary studies, philosophy, political science/government, psychology, public administration, rural sociology, sociology, water resources, and women's studies). Biological and physical sciences and veterinary medicine is the strongest academically. Biological and physical sciences, arts, and social sciences have the largest enrollments.

ACTIVITIES: There are 100 groups on campus, including art, cheerleading, chess, choir, chorale, computers, dance, debate, drama, environmental, ethnic, gay, international, jazz band, literary magazine, newspaper, photography, political, professional, radio and TV, religious, social, social service, student government, and yearbook. Popular campus events include College Royal open house weekend in March. **Sports:** There are 15 intercollegiate sports for men and 15 for women, and 17 intramural sports for men and 17 for women. Facilities include a twin-pad arena, with an Olympic size ice surface, 5 squash courts, a fitness gym, weight-training rooms, a 6-lane swimming pool and an Olympic-size pool, a fitness circuit, and 3 gyms. Outdoor facilities include 4 tennis courts, a running track, lighted football, field hockey, soccer, rugby and fastball fields, jogging trails, and multipurpose fields. There are also 2 dance studios, a climbing wall, a wrestling/combatives room, a covered field with artificial turf, and a 200-meter track.

SERVICES: Counseling and information services are available, as is tutoring in most subjects. There is a reader service for the blind. **Library/Resource:** The library contains 2.0 million volumes, 1.5 million microform items, and 17,000 audio/video tapes/CDs/DVDs, and subscribes to 7,600 periodicals including electronic. Computerized library services include interlibrary loans, database searching, Internet access, and Wi-Fi capability. Special learning facilities include an art gallery, radio station, an observatory, a learning commons, a research park, and arboretum. **Physically Challenged Students:** 90% of the campus is accessible. Facilities include wheelchair ramps, elevators, special parking, specially equipped restrooms, special class scheduling, lowered drinking fountains, lowered telephones, special housing. special library services, equipment, and software. **Special:** U of G offers co-op programs in 30 majors, study abroad in 29 countries, and work-study programs. Accelerated degree programs, dual majors, a general studies degree, and non-degree study are available. There is a freshman honors program and 33 departmental honors programs. **Visiting:** There are regularly scheduled orientations for prospective students, student visits include daily tours of the campus, Fall Preview Day, and Campus Days and Connection Conference in the Spring. There are guides for informal visits and visitors may sit in on classes. To schedule a visit, contact the Tour Coordinator at (519) 824-4120. **Campus Safety and Security:** Measures include 24-hour foot and vehicle patrol, emergency notification system, self-defense education, and security escort services. There are shuttle buses, emergency telephones, lighted pathways/sidewalks, controlled access to dorms/residences, a campus safe walk and a campus police patrol.

REQUIREMENTS: The SAT or ACT is required. The ACT Optional Writing test is also required. In addition, U.S. applicants must have a grade point average of 3.0 from a regionally accredited high school, and a combined math and critical reading SAT score of 1100 or ACT score of 24. Where class rankings are reported on the transcript, a ranking in the top quarter is preferred. Students should include among their senior level courses, specific courses that are required for admission to the degree program of their choice. Particular attention is paid to performance in program prerequisites. Students should ensure that senior year final grades from first and second semester interim grades are submitted before the document deadline date. AP credits are accepted. Important factors in the admissions decision are advanced placement or honors courses, extracurricular activities record, and leadership record. To graduate, students must complete 30 credits (half courses) for a general degree and 40 credits (half courses) for an honors degree. U of G requires a minimum of 10 credits in the major. **Procedure:** Freshmen are admitted fall. There are early decision and deferred admissions plans. Early decision applications should be filed by January 1; regular applications, by March

1 for fall entry. The fall 2014 application fee was $200. Notifications are sent in March. 5000 early decision candidates were accepted for the 2014-2015 class. Applications are accepted on-line. **Transfer Students:** Applicants must meet general admissions requirements and have a B average in all college-level courses. **International Students:** There are 700 international students enrolled. The school actively recruits these students. They must take the TOEFL with a minimum score of 600 on the paper-based TOEFL (PBT) or 89 on the Internet-based version (iBT), and also take the TWE and TSE. The IELTS or MELAB may be substituted for these tests. U.S. students are required to submit SAT or ACT scores, with minimum acceptable scores.

ADMISSIONS: 73% of the 2014-2015 applicants were accepted. **Admissions Contact:** Admission Services, Reception. E-Mail: *admisssion@registrar.uoguelph.ca* Web: *www.uoguelph.ca*

FINANCIAL AID: 30% of undergraduate students work part-time. The FAFSA, the college's own financial statement, and the Federal and Provincial Government Canadian Form are required. Check with the school for current application deadlines.

UNIVERSITY OF OTTAWA	E-3
Ottawa, ON K1N 6N5	(613) 562-5700 (877) 868-8292 (613) 562-5323

Full-time: 11124 men, 17521 women	Faculty: n/av
	Ph.D.s: 96%
Part-time: 2177 men, 3095 women	Student/Faculty: 22 to 1
Graduate: 2430 men, 3252 women	Tuition: $6106 ($16,444)
Year: semesters, summer session	Room & Board: $6360
Application Deadline: n/av	Freshman Class: n/av
SAT: required	

The University of Ottawa, founded in 1848, is a bilingual (French/English) institution offering undergraduate and graduate degrees through the faculties of Arts, Law, Health Sciences, Medicine, Science, Engineering, Management, Social Sciences and Education. The figures in the above capsule and in this profile are approximate. There are 9 undergraduate schools and 9 graduate schools. In addition to regional accreditation, uOttawa has baccalaureate program accreditation with AACSB. The 43-acre campus is in an urban area in Ottawa, Ontario, Canada. Including any residence halls, there are 40 buildings.

STUDENT LIFE: 80% of undergraduates are from Ontario. **Female To Male Ratio:** 1.5:1. **Housing:** 2870 students can be accommodated in college housing, which includes single-sex and coed dorms, on-campus apartments, and married student housing. On-campus housing is available on a first-come, first-served basis, and is available on a lottery system for upperclassmen. All students may keep cars.

FACULTY/CLASSROOMS: 63% of faculty are male; 37% are female. All teach and do research. No introductory courses are taught by graduate students. The average class size in an introductory lecture is 60; in a laboratory is 30; and in a regular course is 30.

PROGRAMS OF STUDY: uOttawa confers B.A., B.Ad., B.A.Sc., B.Com., B.Ed., B.F.A., B.Mus., B.Sc., B.Sc.N., B.Soc.Sc., B.Jour. and B.H.Sc. degrees. Master's and doctoral degrees are also awarded. Bachelor's degrees are awarded in AGRICULTURE (environmental studies), BIOLOGICAL SCIENCE (biochemistry, biology/biological science, biotechnology, and life science), BUSINESS (accounting, banking and finance, electronic business, human resources, management information systems, management science, and marketing/retailing/merchandising), COMMUNICATIONS AND THE ARTS (Arabic, art history and appreciation, arts administration/management, classics, communications, English, English as a second/foreign language, French, German, Italian, journalism, Latin, linguistics, modern language, music, Spanish, and visual and performing arts), COMPUTER AND PHYSICAL SCIENCE (chemistry, computer science, earth science, geology, mathematics, physics, and software engineering), EDUCATION (education, elementary education, foreign languages education, and middle school education), ENGINEERING AND ENVIRONMENTAL DESIGN (biomedical engineering, chemical engineering, civil engineering, computer engineering, electrical/electronics engineering, environmental engineering, environmental science, and mechanical engineering), HEALTH PROFESSIONS (biomedical science, health science, nursing, and ophthalmic technology), SOCIAL SCIENCE (anthropology, Canadian studies, criminology, economics, ethics, politics, and social policy, ethnic studies, geography, gerontology, history, international studies, law, medieval studies, philosophy, political science/government, psychology, public administration, religion, Russian and Slavic studies, sociology, and women's studies). Law, medicine, and education are the strongest academically. Arts, social sciences, and science have the largest enrollments.

ACTIVITIES: There are 100 groups on campus, including art, band, cheerleading, chess, choir, chorale, computers, dance, debate, drama, environmental, ethnic, film, gay, honors, international, jazz band, newspaper, orchestra, photography, political, professional, radio and TV, religious, social, social service, student government, and symphony. Popular campus events include University of Ottawa Day, Gee-gees Football Games and International week. **Sports:** There are 5 intercollegiate sports for men and 7 for women, and 13 intramural sports for men and 11 for women. Facilities include 2 sports complexes that include: weight-training and combat rooms, a 50-meter swimming pool, gyms, racquetball and squash courts, billiards and ping pong tables, indoor arena, and a multipurpose sports field. **Graduates:** From July 1, 2013 to June 30, 2014, 6836 bachelor's degrees were awarded.

SERVICES: Counseling and information services are available, as is tutoring in most subjects. There is a reader service for the blind, and remedial math, reading, and writing. **Library/Resource:** The 8 libraries contain 2.2 million volumes, 1.9 million microform items, 777,349 audio/video tapes/CDs/DVDs, and subscribe to 60,522 periodicals including electronic. Computerized library services include interlibrary loans, database searching, Internet access, and Wi-Fi capability. Special learning facilities include an art gallery, radio station, TV station, a museum of classical antiquities. **Physically Challenged Students:** 75% of the campus is accessible. Facilities include wheelchair ramps, elevators, special parking, specially equipped restrooms, special class scheduling, lowered drinking fountains, lowered telephones, special housing, automatic doors and specialized equipment. **Special:** Opportunities are provided for cooperative programs, study abroad in over 56 countries, a general studies degree in arts and in sciences, and combined programs in all fields in arts and in social sciences. There are 40 departmental honors programs. **Visiting:** There are regularly scheduled orientations for prospective students, open house and campus visits (ongoing, year round). There are guides for informal visits and visitors may sit in on classes. To schedule a visit, contact the Liaison Office at (613) 562-5800. **Campus Safety and Security:** Measures include 24-hour foot and vehicle patrol, emergency notification system, self-defense education, and security escort services. There are shuttle buses, emergency telephones, lighted pathways/sidewalks, controlled access to dorms/residences, the university participates in a community crime-stoppers program.

REQUIREMENTS: The SAT is required. Graduation from an accredited secondary school is required. Those students planning to major in occupational or physical therapy must speak French. A portfolio is required for fine arts students, and an audition for music students. AP credits are accepted. Students must maintain a GPA of 3.5 out of 10 for all courses, including those in the major. Students must also complete a second language requirement: French for English students, and English for French students. **Procedure:** Freshmen are admitted fall and winter. There are early decision, early admissions, and rolling admissions plans. Check with the school for current application deadlines. The fall 2014 application fee was $105. **Transfer Students:** Admissions requirements vary according to program. 60 of 90 credits required for the bachelor's degree must be completed at uOttawa. **International Students:** There are 2234 international students enrolled. The school actively recruits these students. They must take the TOEFL with a minimum score of 580 on the paper-based TOEFL (PBT) or 92 on the Internet-based version (iBT) or take the MELAB and the college's own test, CanTest.

ADMISSIONS: Andre-Pierre Lepage E-Mail: *eureka@uottowa.ca* Web: *www.admission.uottowa.ca*

FINANCIAL AID: Average annual earnings from campus work are $3000. Check with the school for current application deadlines.

UNIVERSITY OF SASKATCHEWAN — C-2

Saskatoon, SK S7N 5A2   (306) 966-5788
    (306) 966-2115

Full-time: n/av	**Faculty:** n/av
Part-time: n/av	**Ph.D.s:** 87%
Graduate: n/av	**Student/Faculty:** n/av
Year: semesters, summer session	**Tuition:** $5043
Application Deadline: April 1	**Room & Board:** $4275
	Freshman Class: n/av

The University of Saskatchewan, founded in 1907, is a public institution offering programs in business, agriculture, arts and sciences, education, engineering, and health professions. The figures in the above capsule and in this profile are approximate. There are 14 undergraduate schools and 1 graduate school. The 1865-acre campus is in an urban area in Saskatoon.

STUDENT LIFE: 77% remain to graduate. **Housing:** 1600 students can be accommodated in college housing, which includes single-sex dorms, off-campus apartments, and married student housing. On-campus housing is available on a first-come, first-served basis. All students may keep cars.

FACULTY/CLASSROOMS: 65% of faculty are male; 35% are female. No introductory courses are taught by graduate students.

PROGRAMS OF STUDY: U of S confers B.A., B.Sc., B.A.Sc., B.Comm., B.E., B.Ed., B.F.A., B.Mus., B.Mus/Mus.Ed., B.S.A., B.S.N., and B.S.P. and B.Sc.Kin./Kin.Ed. degrees. Master's and doctoral degrees are also awarded. Bachelor's degrees are awarded in AGRICULTURE (agricultural business management, agricultural economics, agronomy, animal science, environmental studies, horticulture, plant science, range/farm management, and soil science), BIOLOGICAL SCIENCE (anatomy, biochemistry, bioinformatics, biology/biological science, biotechnology, cell biology, environmental biology, microbiology, nutrition, and physiology), BUSINESS (accounting, banking and finance, business administration and management, business economics, human resources, marketing/retailing/merchandising, and operations management), COMMUNICATIONS AND THE ARTS (art, art history and appreciation, dramatic arts, English, fine arts, French, German, Hebrew, Latin, linguistics, modern language, music, music performance, music theory and composition, musicology/ethnomusicology, Russian, Spanish, and studio art), COMPUTER AND PHYSICAL SCIENCE (applied mathematics, chemistry, computer science, environmental geology, geology, geophysics and seismology, mathematics, and physics), EDUCATION (education, elementary education, home economics education, physical education, secondary education, and teaching English as a second/foreign language (TESOL/TEFOL)), ENGINEERING AND ENVIRONMENTAL DESIGN (agricultural engineering, bioengineering, bioresource engineering, chemical engineering, civil engineering, computer engineering, electrical/electronics engineering, electrical/electronics engineering technology, engineering physics, environmental engineering, environmental engineering technology, environmental science, geological engineering, land use management and reclamation, mechanical engineering, and urban planning technology), HEALTH PROFESSIONS (biomedical science, exercise science, health science, nursing, pharmacology, pharmacy, physical therapy, and veterinary science), SOCIAL SCIENCE (anthropology, archeology, dietetics, economics, food science, gender studies, geography, history, international studies, law, Native American studies, Near Eastern studies, philosophy, political science/government, psychology, public administration, religion, social work, sociology, and women's studies).

ACTIVITIES: Groups on campus include band, cheerleading, chess, choir, chorale, chorus, computers, drama, ethnic, gay, international, jazz band, literary magazine, newspaper, orchestra, photography, political, professional, religious, social, social service, and student government. Popular campus events include Powwow in the Bowl, Experience US! and Greystone Scholar Spend-a-Day. **Sports:** There are 8 intercollegiate sports for men and 7 for women, and 17 intramural sports for men and 17 for women. Facilities include the PAC, Physical Activity Complex, houses a 40-foot climbing wall, gym, state-of-the art fitness centre and weight room, walk/job track, squash and racquetball courts, dance studio, gymnastics areas and swimming pool. There also are a football stadium, hockey rink, curling rink, track and field area, and outdoor soccer field.

SERVICES: Counseling and information services are available, as is tutoring in most subjects. There is remedial math and writing. **Library/Resource:** The 8 libraries contain 2.5 million volumes, 3.1 million microform items, and subscribe to 47,055 periodicals including electronic. Computerized library services include interlibrary loans, database searching, Internet access, and Wi-Fi capability. Special learning facilities include an art gallery, natural history museum, and planetarium. **Physically Challenged Students:** All of the campus is accessible. Facilities include wheelchair ramps, elevators, special parking, specially equipped restrooms, special class scheduling, lowered drinking fountains, lowered telephones. There is also a coordinator of services for students with disabilities, special funding application assistance, and special exam scheduling and accommodations. Adaptive computerized equipment is located in the main library building. **Special:** The University of Saskatchewan offers interdisciplinary majors, including agricultural biology, agricultural chemistry, agricultural and bioresource engineering, agricultural extension, and anthropology and archaeology. Co-op programs are offered through the Program for Agricultural Cooperative Education. There are computer science internships, as well as internships offered through the Engineering Professional Internship program. The university has exchange agreements with 41 countries. **Visiting:** There are regularly scheduled orientations for prospective students. To schedule a visit, contact the Recruitment and Admissions at (306) 966-5788. **Campus Safety and Security:** Measures include 24-hour foot and vehicle patrol, emergency notification system, self-defense education, and security escort services. There are emergency telephones, lighted pathways/sidewalks, and controlled access to dorms/residences.

REQUIREMENTS: Applicants must be graduates of an accredited secondary school. The decision is based solely on academic achievement in secondary school. In direct-entry programs, priority is given to Saskatchewan residents, with the exception being the College of Arts and Science. AP credits are accepted. Requirements for graduation vary according to the program of study. **Procedure:** Freshmen are admitted to all sessions. There is a early decision plan. Applications should be filed by April 1 for fall entry; September 1 for winter entry; February 1 for spring entry; and March 1 for summer entry, along with a $90 fee. Applications are accepted on-line. **Transfer Students:** Applicants must meet promotion levels for the college to which transfer is sought. **International Students:** There are 1863 international students enrolled. The school actively recruits these students. They must take the TOEFL with a minimum score of 550 on the paper-based TOEFL (PBT) or 80 on the Internet-based version (iBT) or take the MELAB, IELTS, CanTEST, or CAEL.

ADMISSIONS: Recruitment and Admission E-Mail: *admissions@usask.ca* Web: *explore.usask.ca*

FINANCIAL AID: Check with the school for current application deadlines.

UNIVERSITY OF TORONTO	E-3
Toronto, ON M5S 1A1	(416) 978-2190
	(416) 978-6089
Full-time: 25000 men, 30000 women	**Faculty:** n/av
	Ph.D.s: 91%
Part-time: 4528 men, 3256 women	**Student/Faculty:** n/av
Graduate: 6843 men, 8339 women	**Tuition:** $7000 ($23,000)
Year: other, summer session	**Room & Board:** $10,000
Application Deadline: n/av	**Freshman Class:** n/av
SAT: required	

The University of Toronto, founded in 1827, is a public institution offering undergraduate programs in applied science and engineering, arts and science, education, dentistry, law, medicine, music, nursing, pharmacy, physical and health education, and radiation sciences. Degrees are also offered at the graduate level in a wide range of programs. The figures in the above capsule and in this profile are approximate. There are 20 undergraduate schools and 1 graduate school. The 1767-acre campus is in an urban area with 3 campuses in downtown and suburban Toronto. Including any residence halls, there are 242 buildings.

STUDENT LIFE: 88% of undergraduates are from Ontario. The average age of freshmen is 18; all undergraduates, 21. 5% do not continue beyond their first year; 83% remain to graduate. **Housing:** 7903 students can be accommodated in college housing, which includes single-sex and coed dorms, on-campus apartments, off-campus apartments, and married student housing. On-campus housing is guaranteed for the freshman year only, and is available on a first-come, first-served basis. Priority is given to out-of-town students. 80% of students commute. All students may keep cars.

FACULTY/CLASSROOMS: 55% of faculty are male; 45% are female. No introductory courses are taught by graduate students.

PROGRAMS OF STUDY: U of T confers B.A., B.Sc., B.A.Sc., B.B.A., B.Com., B.Ed., B.Sc.Med.Rad.Sc., B.Sc.N., B.Sc.O.T., B.Sc.Phm., B.Sc.P.T., B.S.P.H.E. and Mus.Bac. degrees. Master's and doctoral degrees are also awarded. Bachelor's degrees are awarded in AGRICULTURE (environmental studies, forestry and related sciences, and natural resource management), BIOLOGICAL SCIENCE (biochemistry, biology/biological science, biophysics, biotechnology, botany, cell biology, ecology, evolutionary biology, life science, microbiology, molecular biology, neurosciences, nutrition, physiology, toxicology, and zoology), BUSINESS (banking and finance, business administration and management, business economics, electronic business, and human resources), COMMUNICATIONS AND THE ARTS (art history and appreciation, arts administration/management, classics, communications, communications technology, comparative literature, dramatic arts, English, film arts, French, German, Greek, Italian, journalism, Latin, linguistics, media arts, modern language, music, music history and appreciation, music theory and composition, musicology/ethnomusicology, Polish, Portuguese, Russian languages and literature, Slavic languages, Spanish, technical and business writing, and visual and performing arts), COMPUTER AND PHYSICAL SCIENCE (actuarial science, applied mathematics, applied physics, astronomy, astrophysics, chemical physics, chemistry, computer science, digital arts/technology, earth science, geology, mathematics, paleontology, physical sciences, physics, planetary and space science, statistics, and systems analysis), EDUCATION (education, education of the exceptional child, foreign languages education, music education, and physical education), ENGINEERING AND ENVIRONMENTAL DESIGN (architecture, chemical engineering, civil engineering, computer engineering, electrical/electronics engineering, engineering and applied science, environmental science, industrial engineering, materials engineering, materials science, mechanical engineering, mining and mineral engineering, and water and wastewater technology), HEALTH PROFESSIONS (environmental health science, health, nursing, occupational therapy, pharmacology, pharmacy, physical therapy, physician's assistant, and radiological science), SOCIAL SCIENCE (African studies, American studies, anthropology, applied psychology, archeology, behavioral science, Canadian studies, Caribbean studies, Celtic studies, Christian studies, classical/ancient civilization, cognitive science, criminology, East Asian studies, economics, ethics, politics, and social policy, European studies, forensic studies, geography, German area studies, Hispanic American studies, history, history of science, human ecology, humanities, international relations, international studies, Judaic studies, medieval studies, Middle Eastern studies, Native American studies, Pacific area studies, peace studies, philosophy, political science/government, psychology, public affairs, religion, Russian and Slavic studies, Scandinavian studies, sociology, South Asian studies, urban studies, and women's studies). Arts and science, applied science, and engineering have the largest enrollments.

ACTIVITIES: There are 200 groups on campus, including art, band, cheerleading, chess, choir, chorus, computers, dance, debate, drama, ethnic, film, gay, international, jazz band, literary magazine, musical theater, newspaper, opera, orchestra, photography, political, radio and TV, religious, social, student government, symphony, and yearbook. Popular campus events include U of T Day, Concerts, and Theater Productions. **Sports:** There are 27 intercollegiate sports for men and 26 for women, and 29 intramural sports for men and 29 for women. Facilities include swimming pools, an outdoor hockey rink, weight and exercise rooms, gyms, squash and multipurpose courts, a rifle range, dance studios, playing fields, a stadium, an arena, and a 200-meter indoor running track. **Graduates:** From July 1, 2013 to June 30, 2014, 9724 bachelor's degrees were awarded. In an average class, 83% graduate in 4 years or less.

SERVICES: Counseling and information services are available, as is tutoring in every subject. There is a reader service for the blind. **Library/Resource:** The 32 libraries contain 11.4 million volumes, 5.5 million microform items, and 374,046 audio/video tapes/CDs/DVDs, and subscribe to 74,545 periodicals including electronic. Computerized library services include interlibrary loans, database searching, Internet access, and Wi-Fi capability. Special learning facilities include an art gallery, radio station, an observatory. **Physically Challenged Students:** Facilities include wheelchair ramps, elevators, special parking, specially equipped restrooms, lowered drinking fountains, and lowered telephones. **Special:** The university offers co-op programs in management, arts management, management and information technology, cell and molecular biology, computer science, mathematical and physical sciences, sociology, applied psychology, public policy, humanities, international development studies, psychology (including mental health studies), sciences, social sciences, and neuroscience. Study abroad, interdisciplinary programs, and various work-study programs are also available. **Visiting:** There are regularly scheduled orientations for prospective students. There are guides for informal visits. To schedule a visit, contact Student Recruitment at (416) 978-5000. **Campus Safety and Security:** Measures include 24-hour foot and vehicle patrol, self-defense education, and security escort services. There are shuttle buses, emergency telephones, and lighted pathways/sidewalks.

REQUIREMENTS: The SAT is required. The faculties of Arts and Science, Music, and Physical Education and Health will consider Grade 12 applicants from an accredited U.S. high school with a high GPA and good scores on the SAT. The ACT will also be considered. Engineering will consider excellent grade 12 students with high SAT scores who also are completing at least 2 advanced placement courses. The SAT Subject Tests and AP courses and exams must include math, physics, and chemistry. Other requirements may apply. Architecture students must submit a questionnaire and a portfolio. Music students must audition. A GPA of 3.0 is required. AP credits are accepted. Arts and science students must satisfy a breadth requirement, which includes 3 courses from outside the major. Students must complete 20 credits for a 4-year degree, plus prerequisite subjects. **Procedure:** Freshmen are admitted in fall. There are early decision, early admissions, deferred admissions, and rolling admissions plans. Application deadlines are open. The fall 2014 application fee was $80. Notification is sent on a rolling basis. **Transfer Students:** 786 transfer students enrolled in 2013-2014. For the Arts and Science divisions, normally a B average is required. 5 of 20 credits required for the bachelor's degree must be completed at U of T. **International Students:** There are 6884 international students enrolled. The school actively recruits these students. They must take the TOEFL with a minimum score of 600 on the paper-based TOEFL (PBT) or 100 on the Internet-based version (iBT) or take the MELAB, ELDA/COPE, the IELTS Academic Module, or the University of Toronto's Continuing Studies Academic English Course. They must also take the SAT or ACT.

ADMISSIONS: Admissions Counselor. E-Mail: *admissions.help@ utoronto.ca* Web: *www.utoronto.ca*

FINANCIAL AID: Check with the school for current application deadlines.

UNIVERSITY OF VICTORIA   B-2

Victoria, BC V8P 5C2   (250) 721-7211
                                       (250) 721-7212

Full-time: n/av	Faculty: 721
Part-time: n/av	Ph.D.s: 96%
Graduate: n/av	Student/Faculty: 15 to 1
Year: semesters, summer session	Tuition: $5000 ($15,000)
Application Deadline: February 28	Room & Board: $8000
	Freshman Class: 11576 applied, 8443 accepted, 4309 enrolled

The University of Victoria, founded in 1903 as Victoria College, is a public institution operated by the province of British Columbia. It offers undergraduate and graduate programs in the arts and sciences, business, education, engineering, fine arts, human and social development, and law. The figures in the above capsule and in this profile are approximate. There are 8 undergraduate schools and 1 graduate school. The 400-acre campus is in an urban area in Victoria. Including any residence halls, there are 107 buildings.

STUDENT LIFE: 86% of undergraduates are from British Columbia. 92% are from public schools. The average age of freshmen is 21. **Housing:** 2200 students can be accommodated in college housing, which includes single-sex and coed dorms, on-campus apartments, and married student housing. There is an off-campus housing registry service. On-campus housing is guaranteed for the freshman year only, is available on a first-come, first-served basis, and is available on a lottery system for upperclassmen. Priority is given to out-of-town students. 89% of students commute. All students may keep cars.

FACULTY/CLASSROOMS: 61% of faculty are male; 39% are female. All teach undergraduates and all do research. No introductory courses are taught by graduate students. The average class size in an introductory lecture is 53 and in a regular course is 30.

PROGRAMS OF STUDY: UVic confers B.A., B.S., B.Com., B.Ed., B.Eng., B.F.A., B.Mus., B.Sc., B.S.N., B.S.W. and L.L.B. degrees. Master's and doctoral degrees are also awarded. Bachelor's degrees are awarded in AGRICULTURE (environmental studies), BIOLOGICAL SCIENCE (biochemistry, biology/biological science, and microbiology), BUSINESS (business administration and management, hospitality management services, international business management, and recreation and leisure services), COMMUNICATIONS AND THE ARTS (art history and appreciation, classics, creative writing, dramatic arts, English, French, Germanic languages and literature, linguistics, music, and visual and performing arts), COMPUTER AND PHYSICAL SCIENCE (astronomy, chemistry, computer science, earth science, mathematics, physics, software engineering, and statistics), EDUCATION (elementary education, physical education, and secondary education), ENGINEERING AND ENVIRONMENTAL DESIGN (computer engineering, electrical/electronics engineering, and mechanical engineering), HEALTH PROFESSIONS (health science and nursing), SOCIAL SCIENCE (anthropology, child care/child and family studies, economics, geography, Hispanic American studies, history, Italian studies, Latin American studies, medieval studies, Pacific area studies, philosophy, political science/government, psychology, Russian and Slavic studies, social work, sociology, and women's studies). Writing is the strongest academically.

ACTIVITIES: Groups on campus include art, chess, choir, chorus, computers, dance, debate, drama, environmental, ethnic, gay, honors, international, jazz band, musical theater, newspaper, orchestra, photography, political, radio and TV, religious, social, social service, student government, symphony, and yearbook. Popular campus events include Week of Welcome, the President's BBQ, and Experience Uvic (Spring open house). **Sports:** There are 7 intercollegiate sports for men and 7 for women, and 12 intramural sports for men and 12 for women. Facilities include 3 gyms, a dance studio, 2 weight and fitness training rooms, racquetball and squash courts, playing fields, an outdoor stadium, tennis courts, 2 swimming pools, a sailing compound, and jogging trails.

SERVICES: Counseling and information services are available, as is tutoring in most subjects. There is remedial reading and writing. **Library/Resource:** The 4 libraries contain 1.9 million volumes, 2.3 million microform items, and 110,600 audio/video tapes/CDs/DVDs, and subscribe to 40,000 periodicals including electronic. Computerized library services include interlibrary loans, database searching, Internet access, and Wi-Fi capability. Special learning facilities include an art gallery, radio station, and language labs. **Physically Challenged Students:** 95% of the campus is accessible. Facilities include wheelchair ramps, elevators, special parking, specially equipped restrooms, lowered drinking fountains, lowered telephones, special housing. **Special:** A number of co-op and internship programs are available in specific disciplines as are many dual majors, including biochemistry/microbiology and Hispanic/Italian studies. Work-study is possible on a limited basis for Canadian students only. Study abroad is offered in 19 countries. There are 37 departmental honors programs. **Visiting:** There are regularly scheduled orientations for prospective students. There are guides for informal visits, visitors may sit in on classes, and stay overnight. To schedule a visit, contact the Campus Tours at (250) 472-4935. **Campus Safety and Security:** Measures include 24-hour foot and vehicle patrol, self-defense education, and security escort services. There are emergency telephones and lighted pathways/sidewalks.

REQUIREMENTS: Application requires high school graduation with a 2.5 GPA or higher, 4 semesters of English, 2 each of social science, math, science, and language, and 6 semesters of 2.5 work at grade 12 level. Applications are accepted online at the school's web site. AP credits are accepted. To graduate, students must complete the university English requirement, a minimum of 60 units above the 100 level, at least 21 of which must be upper level, and have a 2.0 GPA. **Procedure:** Freshmen are admitted to all sessions. There are early admissions and deferred admissions plans. Early decision applications should be filed by November 30; regular applications, by February 28 for fall entry; and October 31 for winter entry. The fall 2014 application fee was $60. Applications are accepted on-line. **Transfer Students:** 2000 transfer students enrolled in 2013-2014. Requirements vary with the program and the individual. 30 of 60 credits required for the bachelor's degree must be completed at UVic. **International Students:** There are 2000 international students enrolled. The school actively recruits these students. They must take the TOEFL with a minimum score of 530 on the paper-based TOEFL (PBT) or 71 on the Internet-based version (iBT) or take the MELAB, or the International English Language Testing System (IELTS).

ADMISSIONS: 73% of the 2014-2015 applicants were accepted. **Admissions Contact:** Wendy Joyce, Director of Admissions. E-mail: joycewa@uvic.ca

FINANCIAL AID: Check with the school for current application deadlines.

UNIVERSITY OF WATERLOO   E-3

Waterloo, ON N2L 3G1

(519) 888-4567, ext. 33777
(519) 746-8088

Full-time: 13752 men, 9241 women	**Faculty:** n/av
Part-time: 400 men, 541 women	**Ph.D.s:** 93%
Graduate: 2921 men, 1599 women	**Student/Faculty:** 25 to 1
Year: varies, summer session	**Tuition:** $7058 ($19,524)
Application Deadline: March 31	**Room & Board:** $8000
	Freshman Class: 29859 applied, 20942 accepted, 6970 enrolled

The University of Waterloo, founded in 1957, is a public institution that offers undergraduate and graduate programs in applied health sciences, arts, engineering, environment, math, and science. Students have a home base in 1 of 6 faculties or 4 affiliated institutions. Most programs are offered in either the traditional or the cooperative system of study. The figures in the above capsule and in this profile are approximate. There are 10 undergraduate schools and 6 graduate schools. The 1000-acre campus is in a suburban area 60 miles southwest of Toronto. Including any residence halls, there are 65 buildings.

STUDENT LIFE: 95% of undergraduates are from Ontario. Others are from 13 states. **Housing:** 6100 students can be accommodated in college housing, which includes single-sex and coed dorms, on-campus apartments, and off-campus apartments. In addition, there are special-interest houses, language floors, and an off-campus housing service. On-campus housing is guaranteed for the freshman year only. Priority is given to out-of-town students. All students may keep cars.

FACULTY/CLASSROOMS: 75% of faculty are male; 25% are female. All teach and do research. No introductory courses are taught by graduate students.

PROGRAMS OF STUDY: Waterloo confers B.A., B.Sc., B.A.S., B.A.Sc., B.A.F.M., B. Arch., B.C.F.M., B.C.S., B.E.S., B.I.S., B.Math, BSc. Phm., B.S.E., B.S.W. and B.K.I. degrees. Master's and doctoral degrees are also awarded. Bachelor's degrees are awarded in AGRICULTURE (environmental studies), BIOLOGICAL SCIENCE (bio-

chemistry, bioinformatics, biology/biological science, and biotechnology), BUSINESS (accounting, business administration and management, human resources, management engineering, management science, operations research, and recreation and leisure services), COMMUNICATIONS AND THE ARTS (art history and appreciation, arts administration/management, classics, dramatic arts, English, English literature, film arts, fine arts, French, German, music, Russian, Spanish, speech/debate/rhetoric, and studio art), COMPUTER AND PHYSICAL SCIENCE (actuarial science, applied mathematics, chemistry, computer mathematics, computer science, digital arts/technology, earth science, information sciences and systems, mathematics, physics, science, science and management, software engineering, and statistics), EDUCATION (foreign languages education, mathematics education, and science education), ENGINEERING AND ENVIRONMENTAL DESIGN (architecture, chemical engineering, city/community/regional planning, civil engineering, computational sciences, computer engineering, electrical/electronics engineering, engineering, environmental engineering, environmental science, geological engineering, mechanical engineering, and systems engineering), HEALTH PROFESSIONS (health, health science, optometry, preallied health, preoptometry, and respiratory therapy), SOCIAL SCIENCE (anthropology, economics, French studies, geography, history, international studies, medieval studies, philosophy, physical fitness/movement, political science/government, psychology, religion, Russian and Slavic studies, social work, sociology, and women's studies). Engineering, accounting, and math are the strongest academically. Arts has the largest enrollment.

ACTIVITIES: 1% of men belong to 1 national fraternity; 1% of women belong to 1 national sorority. There are 150 groups on campus, including and social dance, juggling, martial arts, band, bridge, cheerleading, chess, choir, computers, dance, debate, drama, environmental, ethnic, film, gay, honors, international, literary magazine, marching band, musical theater, newspaper, photography, political, professional, radio and TV, religious, social, social service, student government, and yearbook. Popular campus events include Oktoberfest and Canada Day. **Sports:** There are 18 intercollegiate sports for men and 18 for women, and 16 intramural sports for men and 16 for women. Facilities include outdoor playing fields, an ice arena, a swimming pool, a diving tank, squash courts, weight rooms, 2 gyms, a dance studio, tennis courts, and activity areas. **Graduates:** From July 1, 2013 to June 30, 2014, 4466 bachelor's degrees were awarded. The most popular majors were arts (32%), mathematics (21%), and engineering (18%).

SERVICES: Counseling and information services are available, as is tutoring in most subjects. There is a reader service for the blind, remedial math, reading, and writing. **Library/Resource:** The 8 libraries contain 2.0 million volumes, 1.7 million microform items, 1,179 audio/video tapes/CDs/DVDs, and subscribe to 24,074 periodicals including electronic. Computerized library services include interlibrary loans, database searching, Internet access, and Wi-Fi capability. Special learning facilities include an art gallery, radio station, 4 museums, 2 theaters, and an observatory. **Physically Challenged Students:** All of the campus is accessible. Facilities include wheelchair ramps, elevators, special parking, specially equipped restrooms, special class scheduling, lowered drinking fountains, lowered telephones. Up-to-date technical equipment for the visually disabled and the hearing impaired. **Special:** Cross-registration with Wilfrid Laurier University, study abroad in 30 countries, dual, student-designed, and interdisciplinary majors, a combined bachelor's-master's degree in accounting and engineering, and noncredit courses are available. Students may study under the regular or cooperative system, which allows off-campus work terms in education, professional organizations and agencies, business, industry, or government. There are concurrent education programs in conjunction with the faculties of education at Brock and Queen's Universities. There are 55 departmental honors programs. **Visiting:** There are regularly scheduled orientations for prospective students, student visits include tours and individual and group information sessions. There are guides for informal visits and visitors may sit in on classes. To schedule a visit, contact the Visitors Reception Center at (519) 888-4567. **Campus Safety and Security:** Measures include 24-hour foot and vehicle patrol, emergency notification system, self-defense education, and security escort services. There are shuttle buses, emergency telephones, and lighted pathways/sidewalks.

REQUIREMENTS: Candidates from the United States must have a high school diploma with exceptionally high standing and AP exams in prerequisite subjects or first-year university standing in acceptable subjects from an accredited university. An audition, portfolio, and/or interview may be required for certain programs. A GPA of 3.0 is required. AP credits are accepted. Important factors in the admissions decision are advanced placement or honors courses, extracurricular activities record, and leadership record. To graduate, all students must satisfy specific program requirements. These include a writing skills requirement. The total number of credits and minimum grade average vary. **Procedure:** Freshmen are admitted fall, winter, and spring. Entrance exams should be taken by the junior year. There are early admissions and deferred admissions plans. Applications should be filed by March 31 for fall entry; October 31 for winter entry; and March 1 for spring entry, along with a $130 fee. Notifications are sent May 25. Applications are accepted on-line. **Transfer Students:** Applicants are considered on an individual basis. 10 of 20 credits required for the bachelor's degree must be completed at Waterloo. **International Students:** There are 2398 international students enrolled. The school actively recruits these students. They must take the TOEFL and also take the TWE and the TSE. The MELAB or the IELTS may also be submitted.

ADMISSIONS: 70% of the 2014-2015 applicants were accepted. **Admissions Contact:** Undergraduate Recruitment Web: *www.findoutmore.uwaterloo.ca*

FINANCIAL AID: The FAFSA is required. Check with the school for current application deadlines.

UNIVERSITY OF WESTERN ONTARIO   D-3

London, ON N6A 3K7   (519) 661-2111
                                            (519) 661-3710

Full-time: 11675 men, 14288 women	**Faculty:** 1381
	Ph.D.s: n/av
Part-time: 699 men, 973 women	**Student/Faculty:** 20 to 1
Graduate: 2622 men, 2723 women	**Tuition:** $6486 ($18,850)
Year: varies, summer session	**Room & Board:** $8770
Application Deadline: May 15	**Freshman Class:** 32163 applied, 17817 accepted, 9644 enrolled
SAT: required	

The University of Western Ontario is one of Canada's oldest and largest universities, founded in 1878. Today, we are a vibrant centre of learning through our 12 faculties and professional schools, and three Affiliated University Colleges (Brescia, Huron and King's), we offer more than 400 different specializations, majors and minors at the undergraduate level. And, we are proud to provide the best student experience among Canada's leading research-intensive universities. The figures in the above capsule and in this profile are approximate. There are 12 undergraduate schools and 1 graduate school. In addition to regional accreditation, UWO, Western has baccalaureate program accreditation with ASLA. The 1125-acre campus is in an urban area 120 miles from both Detroit, Michigan and Toronto, Ontario. Including any residence halls, there are 116 buildings.

STUDENT LIFE: 94% of undergraduates are from Ontario. Others are from 116 foreign countries, and Canada. **Female To Male Ratio:** 1.2:1. The average age of freshmen is 19; all undergraduates, 21. 7% do not continue beyond their first year. **Housing:** 5077 students can be accommodated in college housing, which includes single-sex and coed dorms, on-campus apartments, and married student housing. In addition, there are honors houses and special-interest houses. On-campus housing is guaranteed for the freshman year only and is available on a lottery system for upperclassmen. Priority is given to out-of-town students. 75% of students commute. All students may keep cars.

FACULTY/CLASSROOMS: 69% of faculty are male; 31% are female. No introductory courses are taught by graduate students.

PROGRAMS OF STUDY: UWO, Western confers B.A., B.Sc., B.Ed., B.E.Sc., B.F.A., B.H.Sc., B.M.O.S., B.M.Sc., B.Mus., B.Mus.A., B.A.H.Ec., B.Sc.H.Ec., B.Sc.FN., B.Sc.N., B.S.W.Hons., J.D. and B.Th. degrees. Master's and doctoral degrees are also awarded. Bachelor's degrees are awarded in AGRICULTURE (environmental studies, natural resource management, and plant science), BIOLOGICAL SCIENCE (anatomy, biochemistry, bioinformatics, biology/biological science, biophysics, cell biology, ecology, genetics, microbiology, nutrition, physiology, and toxicology), BUSINESS (accounting, business administration and management, business communications, and human resources), COMMUNICATIONS AND THE ARTS (applied music, art, art history and appreciation, arts administration/management, Chinese, classical languages, classics, communications, communications technology, comparative literature, creative writing, digital communications, English, English literature, film arts, fine arts, French, German, Germanic languages and literature, Greek, Italian, Japanese, Latin, linguistics, media arts, modern language, music, music business management, music history and appreciation, music performance, music theory and composition, musicology/ethnomusicology, opera, piano/organ, public relations, radio/television technology, Russian, Spanish, strings, studio art, and visual and performing arts), COMPUTER AND PHYSICAL SCIENCE (actuarial science, applied mathematics, astronomy, astrophysics, chemistry, computer mathematics, computer programming, computer science, cybernetics, earth science, geology, geophysics and seismology, information sciences and systems, mathematics, medical physics, physics, planetary and space science, science, software engineering, and statistics), EDUCATION (education, elementary education, middle school education, museum studies, music education, physical education, and secondary education), ENGINEERING AND ENVIRONMENTAL DESIGN (aviation administration/management, biomedical engineering, chemical engineering, civil engineering, computer engineering, computer technology, electrical/electronics engineering, engineering, engineering management, environmental engineering, environmental science, materials engineering, materials science, and mechanical engineering), HEALTH PROFESSIONS (health science, medical science, nursing, and pharmacology), SOCIAL SCIENCE (American studies, anthropology, Asian/American studies, Asian/Oriental studies, biblical studies, Canadian studies, child psychology/development, classical/ancient civilization, clinical psychology, criminology, East Asian studies, economics, family/consumer studies, food science, French studies, gender studies, geography, gerontology, history, home economics, human ecology, humanities, humanities and social science, interdisciplinary studies, international relations, Italian studies, Japanese studies, Latin American studies, law, liberal arts/general studies, Native American studies, peace studies, philosophy, philosophy and religion, physical fitness/movement, political science/government, psychology, public administration, religion, social science, social work, sociology, Spanish studies, theological studies, urban studies, Western civilization/culture, and women's studies).

ACTIVITIES: There are 184 groups on campus, including art, band, cheerleading, chess, choir, chorale, chorus, computers, dance, debate, drama, environmental, ethnic, film, gay, international, jazz band, marching band, musical theater, newspaper, opera, orchestra, photography, political, professional, radio and TV, religious, social, social service, and student government. Popular campus events include Western Homecoming, Fall Preview Day, and Summer Academic Orientation. **Sports:** There are 20 intercollegiate sports for men and 21 for women, and 20 intramural sports for men and 19 for women. Facilities include Thompson recreation and athletic centre, and TD Waterhouse stadium. **Graduates:** From July 1, 2013 to June 30, 2014, 6791 bachelor's degrees were awarded. 393 companies recruited on campus in 2013-2014. Of the 2013 graduating class, 94% were employed within 6 months of graduation.

SERVICES: Counseling and information services are available, as is tutoring in most subjects. There is a reader service for the blind, and remedial math, reading, and writing. Details available through Learning Skills Services at the Student Development Centre. **Library/Resource:** The 7 libraries contain 3.7 million volumes, 4.1 million microform items, 2.1 million audio/video tapes/CDs/DVDs, and subscribe to 86,179 periodicals including electronic. Computerized library services include interlibrary loans, database searching, Internet access, and Wi-Fi capability. Special learning facilities include an art gallery, radio station, TV station, International Centre for Olympic Studies, Fowler-Kennedy Sports Medicine Clinic, Cronyn Observatory, Boundary Layer Wind Tunnel. **Physically Challenged**

Students: 92% of the campus is accessible. Facilities include wheelchair ramps, elevators, special parking, specially equipped restrooms, special class scheduling, lowered drinking fountains, lowered telephones, and special housing. **Visiting:** There are regularly scheduled orientations for prospective students, academic counseling appointments and campus tours. There are guides for informal visits and visitors may sit in on classes. To schedule a visit, contact Liaison Officer and Events Planner. **Campus Safety and Security:** Measures include 24-hour foot and vehicle patrol, emergency notification system, and security escort services. There are emergency telephones, lighted pathways/sidewalks, controlled access to dorms/residences, campus community police, SERT: Student Emergency Response Team.

REQUIREMENTS: The SAT is required. A GPA of 3.5 is required. AP credits are accepted. Important factors in the admissions decision are advanced placement or honors courses, recommendations by school officials, and leadership record. **Procedure:** Freshmen are admitted fall. There are deferred admissions and rolling admissions plans. Early decision applications should be filed by May 15; regular applications, by May 15 for fall entry. The fall 2014 application fee was $125. Notifications are sent February 1. Applications are accepted on-line. **Transfer Students:** 381 transfer students enrolled in 2013-2014. A minimum 3.0 GPA is required of transfer applicant; a maximum of 10.0 credits may be transferred. At least 5 credits in a 15-credit degree program or 10 credits in an honors program must be completed at The University of Western Ontario to earn a bachelor's degree. 5 of 15 credits required for the bachelor's degree must be completed at UWO, Western. **International Students:** The school actively recruits these students. They must take the TOEFL with a minimum score of 550 on the paper-based TOEFL (PBT) or 83 on the Internet-based version (iBT) or take the MELAB. We accept IELTS, CAEL, CanTEST, Fanshawe College and CultureWorks as alternatives to TOEFL.

ADMISSIONS: 55% of the 2014-2015 applicants were accepted. **Admissions Contact:** Lori Gribbon, Director, Recruitment and Admissions. E-Mail: *reg-admissions@uwo.ca* Web: *http:/welcome.uwo.ca/*

FINANCIAL AID: UWO, Western is a member of CSS. The FAFSA and the college's own financial statement are required. Check with the school for current application deadlines.

UNIVERSITY OF WINDSOR   D-3

Windsor, ON N9B 3P4   (519) 253-3000
                                            (519) 971-3653

Full-time: 6528 men, 6012 women	**Faculty:** 592
Part-time: 1170 men, 1325 women	**Ph.Ds:** 92%
Graduate: 1030 men, 228 women	**Student/Faculty:** 18 to 1
Year: trimesters, summer session	**Tuition:** $8700 ($21,045)
Application Deadline: n/av	**Room & Board:** $9037
	Freshman Class: n/av
SAT or ACT: required	

The University of Windsor, founded in 1857, is a public liberal arts institution offering undergraduate and graduate programs through 10 faculties and 6 schools. The figures in the above capsule and in this profile are approximate. There are 11 undergraduate schools and 1 graduate school. The 125-acre campus is in an urban area 2 kilometers from downtown Windsor, and 3 kilometers from downtown Detroit, Michigan. Including any residence halls, there are 58 buildings.

STUDENT LIFE: 90% of undergraduates are from Ontario. Others are from 90 foreign countries, and Canada. 95% are from public schools. The average age of freshmen is 18; all undergraduates, 22. 10% do not continue beyond their first year. **Housing:** 1500 students can be accommodated in college housing, which includes coed dorms, on-campus apartments, and married student housing. On-campus housing is guaranteed for the freshman year only and is available on a lottery system for upperclassmen. 90% of students commute. All students may keep cars.

FACULTY/CLASSROOMS: 54% of faculty are male; 46% are female. No introductory courses are taught by graduate students. The average class size in an introductory lecture is 100; in a laboratory is 25; and in a regular course is 50.

PROGRAMS OF STUDY: U of W confers B.A., B.Sc., B.A.S., B.A.Sc., B.Comm., B.C.S., B.Ed., B.E.S., B.F.A., B.F.S., B.H.K., B. Math, B.Mus., B.Mus.Th., B.Sc.N., B.S.W. and L.L.B. degrees. Master's and doctoral degrees are also awarded. Bachelor's degrees are awarded in AGRICULTURE (environmental studies), BIOLOGICAL SCIENCE (biochemistry, biology/biological science, and biotechnology), BUSINESS (business administration and management and international business management), COMMUNICATIONS AND THE ARTS (art history and appreciation, classics, communications, comparative literature, creative writing, dramatic arts, English, French, languages, modern language, music, Spanish, and visual and performing arts), COMPUTER AND PHYSICAL SCIENCE (chemistry, computer science, geology, mathematics, physics, science, software engineering, and statistics), EDUCATION (drama education, education, and science education), ENGINEERING AND ENVIRONMENTAL DESIGN (automotive technology, civil engineering, electrical/electronics engineering, engineering, environmental engineering, environmental science, industrial engineering, and mechanical engineering), HEALTH PROFESSIONS (music therapy and nursing), SOCIAL SCIENCE (anthropology, Canadian studies, criminology, crosscultural studies, developmental psychology, economics, family/consumer studies, forensic studies, geography, history, international relations, law, philosophy, physical fitness/movement, political science/government, psychology, social work, sociology, urban studies, and women's studies). Science, engineering, and human kinetics are the strongest academically. Business, science, and education have the largest enrollments.

ACTIVITIES: There are 135 groups on campus, including cheerleading, chess, choir, chorale, computers, dance, debate, drama, environmental, ethnic, film, forensics, gay, honors, international, jazz band, literary magazine, musical theater, newspaper, orchestra, political, professional, radio and TV, religious, social, and student government. Popular campus events include Head Start Orientation, Windsor Welcome Week and Homecoming. **Sports:** There are 7 intercollegiate sports for men and 6 for women, and 11 intramural sports for men and 9 for women. Facilities include a 6-lane 200-meter track, a gym, a field house, a stadium, an indoor pool, weight rooms, and a sports therapy clinic.

SERVICES: Counseling and information services are available, as is tutoring in most subjects. There is a reader service for the blind, and remedial math, reading, and writing. **Library/Resource:** The 2 libraries contain 1.7 million volumes, 1.5 million microform items, and 10,792 audio/video tapes/CDs/DVDs, and subscribe to 76,378 periodicals including electronic. Computerized library services include interlibrary loans, database searching, Internet access, and Wi-Fi capability. Special learning facilities include an art gallery, natural history museum, radio station, a video-conferencing center, a computing services theater, the Chrysler Canada/University of Windsor Research Center, and the Great Lakes Institute. **Physically Challenged Students:** 90% of the campus is accessible. Facilities include wheelchair ramps, elevators, special parking, specially equipped restrooms, special class scheduling, lowered drinking fountains, lowered telephones, and specially equipped residence rooms. **Special:** The university offers a variety of co-op programs and internships. Cross-registration may be arranged with the University of Detroit Mercy, Wayne State University, the University of Central Florida, and the University of Darby (England). There are 30 departmental honors programs. **Visiting:** There are regularly scheduled orientations for prospective students, student visits include a tour, counseling, and classes if requested. There are guides for informal visits and visitors may sit in on classes. To schedule a visit, contact the Office of Liason and Student Recruitment at 1-800-864-2860. **Campus Safety and Security:** Measures include 24-hour foot and vehicle patrol, emergency notification system, self-defense education, and security escort services. There are emergency telephones, lighted pathways/sidewalks, and controlled access to dorms/residences.

REQUIREMENTS: Each U.S. applicant must present scores from either the ACT or the SAT offered by the College Entrance Examination Board. Advanced Placement Examinations in certain prerequisite subjects may also be required. AP credits are accepted. To graduate, students must complete a total of 90 credit hours, including

30 in the major, with a C average. Honors students must complete 120 hours, including 60 in the major, with a B average. All students must fulfill the requirements of the core curriculum. **Procedure:** Freshmen are admitted to all sessions. Entrance exams should be taken as early as possible. There are early decision, early admissions, and rolling admissions plans. Check with the school for current application deadlines. Applications are accepted on-line. **Transfer Students:** Applicants must present an official transcript and be in good academic standing. **International Students:** There are 1209 international students enrolled. The school actively recruits these students. They must take the TOEFL, MELAB, the IELTS, or CAEL.

ADMISSIONS: Charlene Yates, Associate Regisrar, Undergraduate Admissions. E-Mail: *Charlene.Yates@uwindsor.ca* Web: *www.uwindsor.ca*

FINANCIAL AID: Check with the school for current application deadlines.

YORK UNIVERSITY — E-3

Toronto (North York), ON M3J 1P3　　(416) 736-2100
　　　　　　　　　　　　　　　　　　　　　　(416) 736-5536

Full-time: 13500 men, 21540 women	**Faculty:** 1357
Part-time: 2900 men, 4510 women	**Ph.D.s:** 98%
Graduate: 2500 men, 2700 women	**Student/Faculty:** n/av
Year: semesters, summer session	**Tuition:** $6376 ($17,512)
Application Deadline: February 1	**Room & Board:** $5119
SAT or ACT: required	**Freshman Class:** n/av

York University, founded in 1959, is a public institution offering programs in computer science, design, education, environmental studies, fine arts, business, social science, law, engineering, health, humanities, human resources, pure and applied sciences, and social work. The figures in the above capsule and in this profile are approximate. There are 10 undergraduate schools and 43 graduate schools. The 635-acre campus is in an urban area in Northwest and midtown Toronto. Including any residence halls, there are 96 buildings.

STUDENT LIFE: 90% of undergraduates are from Ontario. Others are from 159 foreign countries. **Female To Male Ratio:** 1.5:1. The average age of freshmen is 18; all undergraduates, 22. 97% remain to graduate. **Housing:** 4000 students can be accommodated in college housing, which includes single-sex and coed dorms, on-campus apartments, and married student housing. In addition, there are language houses, special-interest houses, and co-op housing. On-campus housing is available on a first-come, first-served basis, and is available on a lottery system for upperclassmen. Priority is given to out-of-town students. 93% of students commute. All students may keep cars.

FACULTY/CLASSROOMS: 59% of faculty are male; 41% are female. All teach and do research. No introductory courses are taught by graduate students. The average class size in an introductory lecture is 72 and in a laboratory is 25.

PROGRAMS OF STUDY: York confers B.A., B.Sc., B.A.S., B.B.A., B.Des., B.Ed., B.E.S., B.F.A., B.H.R.M., B.H.S., B.Sc.N., B.S.W., I.B.B.A. and L.L.B. degrees. Master's and doctoral degrees are also awarded. Bachelor's degrees are awarded in AGRICULTURE (conservation and regulation and environmental studies), BIOLOGICAL SCIENCE (biochemistry, biology/biological science, biotechnology, and ecology), BUSINESS (accounting, banking and finance, business administration and management, business economics, business statistics, entrepreneurial studies, human resources, international business management, international economics, labor studies, management science, marketing and distribution, and organizational behavior), COMMUNICATIONS AND THE ARTS (art history and appreciation, classics, communications, creative writing, dance, design, dramatic arts, English, film arts, fine arts, French, German, Greek, Italian, linguistics, music, photography, Russian, Spanish, video, and visual and performing arts), COMPUTER AND PHYSICAL SCIENCE (applied mathematics, astronomy, atmospheric sciences and meteorology, chemistry, computer science, earth science, information sciences and systems, mathematics, physics, science, sci-

ence technology, and statistics), EDUCATION (education, education of the deaf and hearing impaired, elementary education, middle school education, and secondary education), ENGINEERING AND ENVIRONMENTAL DESIGN (computer engineering, engineering, environmental science, and industrial administration/management), HEALTH PROFESSIONS (community health work, environmental health science, exercise science, health, health care administration, health science, nursing, and rehabilitation therapy), SOCIAL SCIENCE (African studies, anthropology, Canadian studies, Caribbean studies, cognitive science, criminal justice, criminology, East Asian studies, economics, European studies, French studies, geography, German area studies, gerontology, Hispanic American studies, history, humanities, international studies, Judaic studies, Latin American studies, law, liberal arts/general studies, peace studies, philosophy, physical fitness/movement, political science/government, psychology, public administration, religion, Russian and Slavic studies, science and society, social science, social work, sociology, South Asian studies, Third World studies, urban studies, and women's studies). Business, science, fine arts, and liberal arts are the strongest academically. Psychology, administrative studies, and sociology have the largest enrollments.

ACTIVITIES: There are 249 groups on campus, including art, band, cheerleading, chess, choir, communications, computers, dance, debate, drama, ethnic, film, gay, international, jazz band, literary magazine, musical theater, newspaper, orchestra, photography, political, professional, radio and TV, religious, social, social service, student government, and yearbook. Popular campus events include The Blue Bowl (football), Orientation Week, and Multicultural Week. **Sports:** There are 11 intercollegiate sports for men and 12 for women, and 17 intramural sports for men and 17 for women. Facilities include a stadium, 6-rink ice arena, 5-sport playing fields, 4 softball diamonds, cricket pitch, indoor and outdoor track and field center, 26 indoor and outdoor tennis courts. There is a fitness center with 29 cardio machines and free weights, a 25-meter swimming pool, 4 gyms, 7 squash courts, 3 dance/aerobic studios, spinning studio, and a sports therapy clinic. There is a combative room, 3 teaching labs, and an outdoor events facility.

SERVICES: Counseling and information services are available, as is tutoring in most subjects. There is a reader service for the blind. The Counseling and Development Center offers a variety of services and workshops. **Library/Resource:** The 5 libraries contain 2.5 million volumes, 4.0 million microform items, and 54,184 audio/video tapes/CDs/DVDs, and subscribe to 24,576 periodicals including electronic. Computerized library services include interlibrary loans, database searching, Internet access, and Wi-Fi capability. Special learning facilities include an art gallery, radio station, TV station, an observatory, language labs, writing center, geographical information systems lab, computer science labs, science-related labs, and fine arts studios and labs (editing studios). **Physically Challenged Students:** 65% of the campus is accessible. Facilities include wheelchair ramps, elevators, special parking, specially equipped restrooms, special class scheduling, lowered drinking fountains, lowered telephones. The office for persons with disabilities offers a variety of additional services. **Special:** Co-op programs and cross-registration with Seneca, Centennial, Sheridan, and Humber Colleges, internships, study abroad in more than 100 countries, and work-study are available. York offers dual, student-designed, multi-, and interdisciplinary majors, including atmospheric chemistry, physics and astronomy, science, technology, culture, and society, social and political thought, space and communication sciences, and translation. Independent study and nondegree study are also possible. There is a freshman honors program. **Visiting:** There are regularly scheduled orientations for prospective students, consisting of a general information session and campus tour and 1 week of orientation prior to the start of classes. There are guides for informal visits, visitors may sit in on classes, and stay overnight. To schedule a visit, contact the International Admissions Office at (416) 736-5000. **Campus Safety and Security:** Measures include 24-hour foot and vehicle patrol, self-defense education, and security escort services. There are shuttle buses, emergency telephones, lighted pathways/sidewalks. There is also a bicycle patrol team monitoring the campuses.

REQUIREMENTS: U.S. applicants must present evidence of superior academic achievement. Secondary school record, SAT or ACT scores, and teacher or counselor recommendation will be taken into consideration. Applicants to a fine arts program are required to successfully pass an audition or evaluation, and business administration applicants are required to submit a supplementary application. Admission averages and course prerequisites vary by faculty. A GPA of 3.0 is required. AP credits are accepted. Students must maintain at least a C average in 90 credits to receive an ordinary degree and a C+ in 120 credits to receive an honors degree. Requirements for graduation vary according to the program. **Procedure:** Freshmen are admitted to all sessions. Entrance exams should be taken in the fall of the senior year. There are early admissions and rolling admissions plans. Applications should be filed by February 1 for fall entry; November 1 for winter entry; and March 1 for spring entry. The fall 2014 application fee was $60. Notification is sent on a rolling basis. Applications are accepted on-line. **Transfer Students:** 954 transfer students enrolled in 2013-2014. Requirements vary depending on the program. Postsecondary transcripts are required. **International Students:** There are 2708 international students enrolled. The school actively recruits these students. They must take the TOEFL, the Comprehensive English Language Test, and the college's own test, the York English Language Test (YELT), or take the IELTS. They must also take the SAT or ACT.

ADMISSIONS: Office of International Admissions E-Mail: *intlenq@yorku.ca* Web: *www.yorku.ca/futurestudents*

FINANCIAL AID: The FAFSA is required. Check with the school for current application deadlines.

Study abroad programs are now available in more than 60 countries in fields that range from Costa Rican tropical biology to Finnish architecture. Program directors have responded to the vocational interests of the student of the 21st century by organizing programs in international management, health care administration, and other career-oriented fields.

In fact, study in both traditional and nontraditional fields is enriched by overseas experience. An international perspective can benefit study of environmental sciences, anthropology, political science, urban planning, oceanography, hotel administration, psychology, social work, journalism, marketing and law, as well as film, art history, theater, music and dance.

The vast majority of U.S. students enter European schools through organized, ongoing programs sponsored and managed by the colleges and universities in which they are already enrolled. In this way, they automatically earn U.S. academic credit from their home institution for their overseas course work. Academic credit *directly* earned at a foreign institution is often not acceptable toward a U.S. degree. Applying directly to a foreign school is not difficult but unusual.

There are colleges and universities located in foreign nations that are organized on the U.S. system and accredited by U.S. accrediting agencies, e.g., American University of Paris. A list of accredited U.S. institutions overseas is provided in the annual *Accredited Institutions of Postsecondary Education,* published for the Commission on Recognition of Postsecondary Accreditation by the American Council on Education, and is available from the American Council on Education, One Dupont Circle NW, Washington, DC 20036-1193, (202) 939-9300, *www.acenet.edu*

According to the Institute of International Education, in their *Open Doors 2013 Report on International Educational Exchange,* based on a recent academic year, 283,323 U.S. students studied abroad. This reflected an increase of 3.4% since the previous year. The number of U.S. students studying abroad has increased over 80% in the last decade. Europe still hosts the largest number of students. However, there is growing interest in non-traditional destinations—including Costa Rica (9%), Brazil (17%), Ecuador (15%), Peru (10%), and Japan (28%). The five leading destinations measured in 2012/2013 were the United Kingdom, Italy, Spain, France, and China. The top five fields of study for international students included: business & management (22%), engineering (19%), math/computer (10%), physical & life sciences (8%), and social sciences (9%).

The report also indicated that during a recent academic year, 819,644 international students were studying in the United States. This represented an increase of 7.2% from the previous year. The largest fields of study were business and management (22%) and engineering (19%).

A Productive Experience

If you are interested in study abroad, plan ahead by taking the following steps to ensure that the experience is productive:

- **Assess the ways in which study abroad will benefit your educational and career plans.** Study abroad can be a casual choice or a pleasant way to spend a semester but you will derive the greatest benefit if you bring more thought to it: How will the overseas experience complement your other courses or your educational major? Can you maximize its value by seeking language as well as academic study or by combining independent study or an internship with traditional course work?

- **Consult your campus study-abroad adviser.** Most colleges and universities have a person or an office charged with the responsibility of counseling students on overseas study. The study-abroad adviser is best qualified to help you make the right choices.

- **Make sure your college will accept credit earned at the study-abroad program you have chosen.** Speak with both your academic adviser and your study-abroad adviser and resolve any issues before you leave. Many students have assumed incorrectly that credit is granted automatically for another institution's program. You cannot take this for granted.

- **Be realistic about your foreign language proficiency.** It is one thing to be able to order a meal or buy a train ticket in a foreign language. It is quite another to follow a professor lecturing on a complex subject. If you discover that your linguistic ability is inadequate, it is quite possible that you can find abroad the subject matter you want taught in English. You will get more out of the overseas experience however, if you make the effort to function in the language of the chosen country.

- **Look carefully at costs.** If you are dealing with a program sponsor that is not your home institution, it is wise to read program literature carefully. Ask questions before you go if you have any qualms! Are charges clearly specified? Does the literature specify what services *are* covered and more important, what services are *not* covered? What is the refund policy, if any? Is there a clearly identified organization with an official base in the United States which would be legally responsible in the event of disaster?

  While drawing up your budget, think about the extras. You will want to make the small side trips to new places that help to make overseas living rewarding. Try to give yourself some financial flexibility in working out your budget.

- **Think about what it means to live abroad.** Be sure to arrange for substitutes for the support systems you take for granted at home. Will your medical insurance cover you? Do you need vaccinations or a doctor who can manage your specific health problems while you are living abroad? What about visas?

  It is critically important to find out about housing before you leave. Student housing is difficult to find almost everywhere. Be sure to find out whether securing housing abroad is your responsibility and what the alternatives are in the country in which you plan to live.

- **Don't assume that you can work abroad.** Because of foreign labor laws, students should not plan to seek paid employment. The practice of working one's way through college is not common abroad, nor are the relatively high-paying part-time jobs that make it possible in the United States. However, increasing numbers of students are looking to combine practical work experience with study abroad. There are many work exchanges, volunteer opportunities, and internships available. Contact the Council on International Exchange, 300 Fore Street, Portland, ME 04101, (207) 553-4000, Fax: (207) 553-4299 for further information.

- **Find out what you can about the sponsoring agency, especially if it is not an accredited U.S. college or university.** Talk to your study-abroad adviser if you have any doubts. Most private agencies engaged in study abroad are legitimate organizations but their basic purposes may not match yours. Does the organization have experience in placing students in an academic environment, not just in arranging travel? Are descriptions of its study program specific or vague? Does it make unverifiable claims about the academic reputation of its programs, or their recognition by U.S. higher educational institutions?

For further information, consult:
Institute of International Education
809 United Nations Plaza
New York, NY 10017
(212) 883-8200 Fax: (212) 984-5452
For further information, consult the following publications:
IIE Passport: Study Abroad Directories, which are available at *www.iiebooks.org*

Council on International Educational Exchange (CIEE)
300 Fore Street
Portland, ME 04101
9am–5pm
(207) 553-4000 Fax: (207) 553-4299
E-mail: contact@ciee.org
Website: *www.ciee.org*

EUROPE

THE AMERICAN COLLEGE OF GREECE, DEREE   C-4
www.acg.edu

Aghia Paraskevi   **+30 210 600 9800**

Fax: +30 210 608 2344   **Email: admission@acg.edu**
Full-time: 662 men, 700 women   **Faculty:** 141
Part-time: 850 men, 832 women   **Ph.D.s:** 70%
Graduate: none   **Student/Faculty:** 17 to 1
Year: semesters, summer session   **Tuition:** $1200
Room & Board: $8204   **Freshman Class:** 852
                                                                    applied, 727 accepted, 651
                                                                    enrolled
SAT or ACT: recommended   **CEEB CODE:** 0925
Application Deadline: July 25

Deree is the undergraduate and graduate division of The American College (ACG) of Greece, which was founded in 1875 as the American School for Girls. ACG has 3 divisions and 2 campuses in Athens. Deree offers bachelor's degrees in 15 areas of the liberal arts and business. The graduate school offers masters in psychology, communications, finance, and business. The figures in the above capsule and in this profile are approximate. There are 3 graduate schools. In addition to regional accreditation, Deree has baccalaureate program accreditation with NEASC. The 64-acre campus is in an urban area 6 miles northeast of Athens, Greece. Including any residence halls, there are 12 buildings.

STUDENT LIFE: 90% of undergraduates are from 41 foreign countries, and Canada. 52% are from public schools. **Female To Male Ratio:** 1.0:1. The average age of freshmen is 19; all undergraduates, 23. 5% do not continue beyond their first year; 88% remain to graduate. Alcohol is not permitted. All students commute. No one may keep cars.

FACULTY/CLASSROOMS: 44% of faculty are male; 56% are female.

All teach undergraduates. No introductory courses are taught by graduate students. The average class size in an introductory lecture is 25; in a laboratory is 20; and in a regular course is 19.

PROGRAMS OF STUDY: Deree confers B.A., and B.S. degrees. Associate and master's degrees are also awarded. Bachelor's degrees are awarded in BUSINESS (accounting, business administration and management, international business management, management information systems, marketing/retailing/merchandising, and tourism), COMMUNICATIONS AND THE ARTS (art history and appreciation, communications, English, music, and visual and performing arts), SOCIAL SCIENCE (economics, history, philosophy, psychology, and sociology). English, psychology, and marketing are the strongest academically. Marketing, management, accounting and communications have the largest enrollments.

ACTIVITIES: There are 38 groups on campus, including environmental, film, health, radio and sociology, art, chess, choir, coin/stamp, computers, dance, debate, drama, drill team, ethnic, film, international, literary magazine, newspaper, orchestra, photography, radio and TV, social service, student government, and yearbook. Popular campus events include Career Forum, Film Previews, and May Fest. **Sports:** There are 5 intercollegiate sports for men and 5 for women, and 8 intramural sports for men and 2 for women. Facilities include a gym, a fitness center, 2 dance studios, aerobic rooms, 4 outdoor tennis courts, a 50-meter swimming pool, a 400-meter track, and a soccer field, designated as an official training site for the U.S. Olympic Committee. **Graduates:** From July 1, 2013 to June 30, 2014, 584 bachelor's degrees were awarded. The most popular majors were management (15%), communications (12%), and marketing (10%). 123 companies recruited on campus in 2013-2014. In an average class, 1% graduate in 3 years or less, 17% graduate in 4 years or less, 48% graduate in 5 years or less, and 17% graduate in 6 years or less. Of the 2013 graduating class, 12% were enrolled in graduate school within 6 months of graduation, and 36% were employed.

SERVICES: Counseling and information services are available, as is tutoring in some subjects, math, accounting, finance and economics. **Library/Resources:** The 3 libraries contain 180,000 volumes, 4,000 microform items, and 1,700 audio/video tapes/CDs/DVDs, and subscribe to 6,370 periodicals including electronic. Computerized library services include interlibrary loans, database searching, Internet access, and Wi-Fi capability. Special learning facilities include an art gallery, radio station, a museum of the history of the college, and writing centers. **Physically Challenged Students:** 90% of the campus is accessible. Facilities include wheelchair ramps, elevators, special parking, specially equipped restrooms, special class scheduling, and lowered drinking fountains. **Special:** Study abroad, work-study programs, and dual majors in all disciplines are offered. Non-degree study and pass/fail options are available. **Visiting:** There are regularly scheduled orientations for prospective students, consisting of information sessions and campus tours. There are guides for informal visits and visitors may sit in on classes. To schedule a visit, contact the Office of Admissions. **Campus Safety and Security:** Measures include 24-hour foot and vehicle patrol and security escort services. There are shuttle buses and lighted pathways/sidewalks.

REQUIREMENTS: The SAT or ACT and ACT Writing Test are recommended. Applicants must be graduates of an accredited secondary school. The GED is accepted. English speakers are required to pass an English language proficiency test. A GPA of 2.0 is required. AP and CLEP credits are accepted. Important factors in the admissions decision are recommendations by school officials, extracurricular activities record, and personality/intangible qualities. All students must maintain a minimum CI (cumulative index) of 2.0 and complete 128 semester hours, including 47 hours in general education, at least 30 in the concentration, and must meet the College's residency requirements by completing at least 30 credits (beyond the introductory level courses). Distribution requirements vary with the major but include composition, public speaking, humanities, ethics, computer, and social science. **Procedure:** Freshmen are admitted to all sessions. There are deferred admissions and rolling admissions plans. Applications should be filed by July 25 for fall entry; December 15 for winter entry; January 25 for spring entry; and June 1 for summer entry. Notification is sent on a rolling basis. **Transfer Students:** 42 transfer students enrolled in 2013-2014. Applicants must have a minimum GPA of 2.0 and submit high school transcripts, an official catalog, and

a diploma. English proficiency also must be demonstrated, if students are not native speakers of English. 30 of 128 credits required for the bachelor's degree must be completed at Deree. **International Students:** There are 400 international students enrolled. The school actively recruits these students.

ADMISSIONS: 85% of the 2014-2015 applicants were accepted. **Admissions Contact:** Dean of Admissions. E-Mail: *admission@acg.edu* Web: *www.acg.edu*

FINANCIAL AID: In 2014-2015, 4% of all full-time freshmen received some form of financial aid. 1% of all full-time freshmen received need-based aid. Deree is a member of CSS. The the college's own financial statement, and Internal Revenue statement is required. The deadline for filing freshman financial aid applications for fall entry is September 1.

THE AMERICAN UNIVERSITY OF CAIRO
www.aucegypt.edu

New Cairo, 11835	(212) 730-8800 (Egypt 20-2 615-2233) 20.2.2615.1000
Fax: 20.2.27957565	Email: American e-mail: newyork@aucegypt.edu

Full-time: n/av	**Faculty:** 423
Part-time: n/av	**Ph.D.s:** 72%
Graduate: n/av	**Student/Faculty:** 14 to 1
Year: semesters, summer session	**Tuition:** $25,930
Room & Board: $5000	**Freshman Class:** 1543 applied, 1520 accepted, 1252 enrolled
SAT or ACT: required	
Application Deadline: June 1	

The American University in Cairo, founded in 1919, is a private liberal arts institution offering accredited American undergraduate and graduate programs in Egypt. The figures in the above capsule and in this profile are approximate. There are 4 undergraduate schools. In addition to regional accreditation, AUC has baccalaureate program accreditation with AACSB, ABET, and CSAB. The 260-acre campus is in an urban area in New Cairo, Egypt. Including any residence halls, there are 16 buildings.

STUDENT LIFE: 90% of undergraduates are from . Others are from states, 100 foreign countries, and Canada. The average age of freshmen is 18; all undergraduates, 20. 6% do not continue beyond their first year; 82% remain to graduate. **Housing:** 830 students can be accommodated in college housing, which includes single-sex dorms and off-campus apartments. On-campus housing is guaranteed for all 4 years, and is available on a first-come, first-served basis. 91% of students commute. Alcohol is not permitted. All students may keep cars.

FACULTY/CLASSROOMS: 51% of faculty are male; 49% are female. No introductory courses are taught by graduate students. The average class size in an introductory lecture is 20; in a laboratory is 13; and in a regular course is 17.

PROGRAMS OF STUDY: AUC confers B.A., and B.S. degrees. Master's degrees are also awarded. Bachelor's degrees are awarded in BUSINESS (accounting and business administration and management), COMMUNICATIONS AND THE ARTS (Arabic, art, communications, English, journalism, and theater design), COMPUTER AND PHYSICAL SCIENCE (actuarial science, chemistry, computer science, mathematics, and physics), EDUCATION (journalism education), ENGINEERING AND ENVIRONMENTAL DESIGN (architectural engineering, computer engineering, construction engineering, engineering, and mechanical engineering), SOCIAL SCIENCE (anthropology, economics, history, Middle Eastern studies, philosophy, political science/government, psychology, and sociology). Journalism, business administration and political science have the largest enrollments.

ACTIVITIES: There are 62 groups on campus, including anit-cancer team, art, chess, choir, chorus, dance, debate, drama, ethnic, international, literary magazine, musical theater, newspaper, photography, political, professional, radio and TV, social, social service, student government, and yearbook. Popular campus events include International Day, National University Cultural Activities Competition and Model United Nations. **Sports:** There are 23 intercollegiate sports for men and 17 for women, and 10 intramural sports for men and 8 for women. Facilities include tennis courts, multipurpose courts, an exercise gym, a weight room, and a 400-seat stadium. There are also private clubs in the area and other provisions for horseback riding, rowing, swimming and scuba diving, track and field, water polo, squash, and soccer. **Graduates:** From July 1, 2013 to June 30, 2014, 778 bachelor's degrees were awarded. The most popular majors were business administration (24%), journalism and mass communication (18%), and political science (10%). 424 companies recruited on campus in 2013-2014. In an average class, 3% graduate in 3 years or less, 35% graduate in 4 years or less, 70% graduate in 5 years or less, and 82% graduate in 6 years or less.

SERVICES: There is remedial reading and writing. **Library/Resources:** The 2 libraries contain 673,103 volumes, 190,536 microform items, and 2,790 audio/video tapes/CDs/DVDs, and subscribe to 72,321 periodicals including electronic. Computerized library services include interlibrary loans, database searching, Internet access, and Wi-Fi capability. Special learning facilities include an art gallery, radio station, and a theater. **Physically Challenged Students:** All of the campus is accessible. Facilities include wheelchair ramps, elevators, and specially equipped restrooms. **Special:** Study abroad through a consortium of U.S. schools, work-study programs with the university, and non-degree study are available. **Visiting:** There are regularly scheduled orientations for prospective students. There are guides for informal visits, visitors may sit in on classes, and stay overnight. To schedule a visit, contact the General Director of Admission in Egypt at 20-2 797-5551. **Campus Safety and Security:** Measures include 24-hour foot and vehicle patrol, emergency notification system, and security escort services. There are shuttle buses, lighted pathways/sidewalks, controlled access to dorms/residences, security personnel at all open entrances 24 hours a day.

REQUIREMENTS: The ACT Optional Writing test is also required. In addition, U.S. applicants must also be graduates of an accredited secondary school and submit complete transcripts and a copy of their diploma. Others must submit the Egyptian Thanawiya Amma certificate or other national high school certificate recognized by the university as equivalent to it, or the GCE, GCSE, or IGCSE. A minimum high school GPA of 2.0 is required. Students should have taken courses in 3 of the following subjects: languages and humanities, math, social studies, and biological and physical sciences. AP credits are accepted. Important factors in the admissions decision are ability to finance college education, evidence of special talent, and extracurricular activities record. All students must maintain a C average and must complete from 120 to 162 semester credits, depending on the major. Core courses include a writing program, an interdisciplinary seminar in humanities, natural science, and social science, a scientific-thinking course, and Arab literature, history, and society. **Procedure:** Freshmen are admitted fall and spring. Entrance exams should be taken by July for fall admission. There is a rolling admissions plan. Early decision applications should be filed by April 1; regular applications, by June 1 for fall entry; and November 1 for spring entry. The fall 2014 application fee was $45. Applications are accepted on-line. **Transfer Students:** 20 transfer students enrolled in 2013-2014. Transfer students must have a C average on secondary school and college transcripts. 45 of 120 credits required for the bachelor's degree must be completed at AUC. **International Students:** There are 351 international students enrolled. The school actively recruits these students.

ADMISSIONS: 99% of the 2014-2015 applicants were accepted. **Admissions Contact:** American University in Cairo's, New York Office. E-Mail: *aucegypt@aucnyo.edu* Web: *www.aucegypt.edu*

FINANCIAL AID: In 2014-2015, 55% of all full-time freshmen received some form of financial aid. 43% of all full-time freshmen received need-based aid. The the college's own financial statement is required. The deadline for filing freshman financial aid applications for fall entry is September 15.

THE AMERICAN UNIVERSITY OF PARIS   B-3
www.aup.edu

Paris, 75007	**+33 (0) 140620720**

Email: admissions@aup.edu

Full-time: n/av	**Faculty:** 62
Part-time: n/av	**Ph.D.s:** 88%
Graduate: n/av	**Student/Faculty:** 15 to 1
Year: semesters, summer session	**Tuition:** $27,870
Room & Board: $15,274	**Freshman Class:** n/av
SAT or ACT: recommended	
Application Deadline: n/av	

American University of Paris, founded in 1962, is a private institution that provides a liberal arts program in an international context. It has regional U.S. accreditation and is recognized by the French government as an institute of higher learning. Classes are in English except for foreign language and literature courses. There is 1 undergraduate school and 1 graduate school. The campus is in an urban area in Paris, on the Left Bank, near the Eiffel Tower and the Seine. Including any residence halls, there are 9 buildings.

STUDENT LIFE: Students are from 95 foreign countries, and Canada. The average age of freshmen is 19; all undergraduates, 21. **Housing:** 475 students can be accommodated in college housing, which includes coed off-campus apartments. On-campus housing is available on a first-come, first-served basis. All students commute. No one may keep cars.

FACULTY/CLASSROOMS: 67% of faculty are male; 33% are female. No introductory courses are taught by graduate students. The average class size in an introductory lecture is 13; in a laboratory is 8; and in a regular course is 13.

PROGRAMS OF STUDY: AUP confers B.A., and B.S. degrees. Master's degrees are also awarded. Bachelor's degrees are awarded in BUSINESS (business administration and management, entrepreneurial studies, international business management, international economics, international finance, management information systems, and marketing), COMMUNICATIONS AND THE ARTS (art history, communication, comparative literature, and film arts), COMPUTER AND PHYSICAL SCIENCE (computer science), ENGINEERING AND ENVIRONMENTAL DESIGN (environmental science), SOCIAL SCIENCE (economics, European studies, history, international political science, Middle Eastern studies, philosophy, psychology, and urban studies). Art history, international economics, and comparative literature are the strongest academically. International business administration, global communications, and international comparative politics have the largest enrollments.

ACTIVITIES: Groups on campus include art, cheerleading, chess, computers, dance, debate, drama, environmental, ethnic, film, forensics, gay, honors, including music, international, literary magazine, newspaper, photography, political, professional, radio and TV, religious, social, social service, and student government. **Sports:** There are 3 intercollegiate sports for men and 3 for women, and 6 intramural sports for men and 6 for women. Facilities include AUP has approval to rent gyms in and around Paris to provide regular practice and work out time. **Graduates:** From July 1, 2013 to June 30, 2014, 131 bachelor's degrees were awarded. The most popular majors were global communications (17%), international and comparative politics (14%), and international business administration (14%). In an average class, 18% graduate in 3 years or less, 40% graduate in 4 years or less, 45% graduate in 5 years or less, and 46% graduate in 6 years or less.

SERVICES: Counseling and information services are available, as is tutoring in most subjects. Faculty project support and pedagogical workshops, plagiarism-detection training and consultation, survey-building training, and disability support. **Library/Resources:** The library contains 76,000 volumes, 1,000 microform items, 1,200 audio/video tapes/CDs/DVDs, and subscribes to 40,000 periodicals including electronic. Computerized library services include interlibrary loans, database searching, Internet access, and Wi-Fi capability. **Physically Challenged Students:** 50% of the campus is accessible. Facilities include wheelchair ramps, elevators, specially equipped restrooms, and special class scheduling. **Special:** There are cooperative partnership programs with, Eugene Lang College of the New School, The Fashion Institute of Technology, The George Washington University, The Goizueta Business School of Emory University , Loyola University in Maryland, Northeastern University, Salve Regina University, The University of Miami, The University of San Francisco, l' Université de Paris-Sorbonne, The American University of Cairo in Egypt, The University of Cape Town in South Africa, and The University of Oslo in Norway. Cross-registration is available in foreign language programs at 3 other French colleges. Juniors and seniors with good academic standing are encouraged to undertake internships. Study abroad, second degrees, non-degree study, and pass/fail options also are offered. There is 1 national honor society and 10 departmental honors programs. **Visiting:** There are regularly scheduled orientations for prospective students, by appointment. There are guides for informal visits and visitors may sit in on classes. To schedule a visit, contact the Admissions Office at +331 40 62 0720. **Campus Safety and Security:**

REQUIREMENTS: The SAT or ACT is recommended. Candidates must be graduates of an accredited secondary school. An essay and 2 letters of recommendation are also needed. Knowledge of French is not required. Students may apply either through the AUP website, or through the Common Application. A GPA of 2.8 is required. AP credits are accepted. Important factors in the admissions decision are advanced placement or honors courses, recommendations by school officials, personality/intangible qualities, and extracurricular activities record. Undergraduate students must maintain a minimum GPA of 2.0 and earn at least 128 semester credits. The 128 credits required to graduate, include core major requirements, general education requirements and general electives. The general education requirement includes; Mathematics, English, French, Social Sciences, Science, and Humanities courses. **Procedure:** Freshmen are admitted fall and spring. There are deferred admissions and rolling admissions plans. Application deadlines are open. Application fee is $70. Applications are accepted on-line. **Transfer Students:** 80 transfer students enrolled in 2013-2014. Transfer applicants must submit college and high school transcripts, and SAT I or ACT scores if they have fewer than 45 credits. Two letters of recommendation, and an essay are required. 64 of 128 credits required for the bachelor's degree must be completed at AUP. **International Students:** There are 697 international students enrolled. The school actively recruits these students. They must take the TOEFL and the college's own test. Students must take the TOEIC or IELTS.

ADMISSIONS: Director of Admissions. E-Mail: *admissions@aup.edu* Web: *www.aup.edu*

FINANCIAL AID: In 2014-2015, 43% of all full-time freshmen and 36% of continuing full-time students received some form of financial aid. 26% of all full-time freshmen and 28% of continuing full-time students received need-based aid. The average freshman award was $8,943. AUP is a member of CSS. The FAFSA and the college's own financial statement are required. The priority date for freshman financial aid applications for fall entry is March 15.

THE AMERICAN UNIVERSITY OF ROME   B-3
www.aur.edu

Rome, 00153	+39.06.5833.0919
	U.S. (888)791-8327
Fax: 866 287.2025	Email: admissions@aur.edu
Full-time: 525 men, no women	Faculty: 16
Part-time: n/av	Ph.D.s: 73%
Graduate: n/av	Student/Faculty: 31 to 1
Year: semesters, summer session	Tuition: $23,600
Room & Board: $5250	Freshman Class: n/av
SAT or ACT: required	CEEB CODE: 0262
Application Deadline: March 1	

American University of Rome, founded in 1969, is a private institution offering programs in archeology, art history, business, communications, film and digital media, Italian studies, international relations, and liberal arts. The figures in the above capsule and in this

profile are approximate. The campus is in a suburban area on the Janiculum Hill, 15 minutes walking distance from downtown Rome. Including any residence halls, there are 3 buildings.

STUDENT LIFE: Students are from 40 foreign countries, and Canada. 20% are from public schools. 83% are White. The student base is all male. The average age of freshmen is 18; all undergraduates, 20. 30% remain to graduate. **Housing:** 350 students can be accommodated in college housing, which includes single-sex off-campus apartments. On-campus housing is available on a first-come, first-served basis. 85% of students live on campus; of those, 85% remain on campus on weekends. Alcohol is not permitted. No one may keep cars.

FACULTY/CLASSROOMS: 40% of faculty are male; 60% are female. All teach undergraduates, and 70% do research. No introductory courses are taught by graduate students. The average class size in an introductory lecture is 18; in a laboratory is 12; and in a regular course is 18.

PROGRAMS OF STUDY: AUR confers B.A., and B.S. degrees. Associate degrees are also awarded. Bachelor's degrees are awarded in BUSINESS (business administration and management), COMMUNICATIONS AND THE ARTS (art history and appreciation, communications, and film arts), SOCIAL SCIENCE (archeology, international relations, international studies, and Italian studies). Business administration, international relations, and communications have the largest enrollments.

ACTIVITIES: Groups on campus include art, choir, dance, debate, drama, film, gay, honors, international, literary magazine, newspaper, photography, political, professional, religious, social, social service, and student government. Popular campus events include Guest Lecture Series, Liberal Arts, Business Excursions and International Relations Debates. **Sports:** There are 1 intercollegiate sports for men and 1 for women, and 3 intramural sports for men and 3 for women. Facilities include off-campus access to soccer, tennis, swimming facilities, and performing arts. **Graduates:** Of a recent year graduating class, 32% were enrolled in graduate school within 6 months of graduation, and 48% were employed.

SERVICES: Counseling and information services are available, as is tutoring in some subjects. There is remedial math and writing. **Library/Resources:** The library contains 15,000 volumes, 10,000 microform items, and 1,200 audio/video tapes/CDs/DVDs. Computerized library services include interlibrary loans, database searching, and Internet access. Special learning facilities include a **Physically Challenged Students:** 30% of the campus is accessible. **Special:** Internships in business, international relations, communications, Italian studies, art history, film and digital media, and archeology are available. Study abroad programs are available. There are 99 departmental honors programs. **Visiting:** There are regularly scheduled orientations for prospective students, which AUR organizes directly and through its agents in many U.S. states and in other countries. Orientation is assisted by use of audiovisual materials. There are guides for informal visits and visitors may sit in on classes. To schedule a visit, contact the Enrollment Services.

REQUIREMENTS: The SAT or ACT is required. In addition, a high school diploma and transcript or the non-American equivalent is required, as are a letter of recommendation and an essay. The GED is accepted. A GPA of 2.5 is required. AP and CLEP credits are accepted. Important factors in the admissions decision are recommendations by school officials, advanced placement or honors courses, and personality/intangible qualities. To graduate, students must complete 120 credits, including 60 in the major, with a minimum GPA of 2.0. Distribution requirements include general education requirements, including Italian language, requirements in the major and free electives. A comprehensive exam in business and a thesis in other disciples is required. **Procedure:** Freshmen are admitted to all sessions. There are early decision, early admissions, deferred admissions, and rolling admissions plans. Applications should be filed by March 1 for fall entry; October 1 for spring entry; and March 30 for summer entry, along with a $60 fee. Applications are accepted on-line. **Transfer Students:** Applicants must submit an application, a high school transcript, a diploma, all transcripts of universities attended, a letter of recommendation, and an essay. 45 of 120 credits required for the bachelor's degree must be completed at AUR. **Inter-**

national Students: There are 240 international students enrolled. The school actively recruits these students. They must take the TOEFL or MELAB and the college's own test.

ADMISSIONS: Stefania Lorio, Associate Dean of Enrollment Services. E-Mail: *admissions@aur.edu* Web: *www.aur.edu*

FINANCIAL AID: In 2014-2015, 38% of all full-time freshmen and 43% of continuing full-time students received some form of financial aid. 20% of all full-time freshmen and 17% of continuing full-time students received need-based aid. The FAFSA is required. Check with the school for current application deadlines.

FRANKLIN UNIVERSITY SWITZERLAND   B-3
www.fus.edu

Sorengo, 6924	41 91986 3613
	(718) 335-6800
	(212) 922-9650
Fax: 1 (212) 922-9870 (41 91 993 3906)	Email: kballard@fc.edu
Full-time: 140 men, 276 women	Faculty: 25
Part-time: 3 women	Ph.D.s: 76%
Graduate: 4 men, 1 women	Student/Faculty: 16 to 1
Year: semesters, summer session	Tuition: $40,720
Room & Board: $8050	Freshman Class: n/av
SAT: required	
Application Deadline: March 15	

Franklin University of Switzerland, founded in 1969, is a private institution providing a liberal education through courses that are international in perspective and cross-cultural in content. The baccalaureate degree offers concentrations in international management, art history, modern languages (French, Italian, German), international relations, history/literature, and visual and communication arts. There is one undergraduate school and one graduate school. In addition to regional accreditation, has baccalaureate program accreditation with Swiss University Conference. The 4-acre campus is in a suburban area on a hillside above Lugano in the southern region of Switzerland called the Ticino. Including any residence halls, there are 8 buildings.

STUDENT LIFE: Students are from 23 states, 55 foreign countries, and Canada. **Female To Male Ratio:** 1.9:1. The average age of freshmen is 18; all undergraduates, 20. 48% do not continue beyond their first year. **Housing:** College-sponsored housing includes single-sex dorms, on-campus apartments, and off-campus apartments. 85% of students live on campus; of those, 60% remain on campus on weekends. All students may keep cars.

FACULTY/CLASSROOMS: 50% of faculty are male; 50% are female. No introductory courses are taught by graduate students. The average class size in an introductory lecture is 15; in a laboratory is 10; and in a regular course is 15.

PROGRAMS OF STUDY: Franklin confers B.A. degrees. Associate and master's degrees are also awarded. Bachelor's degrees are awarded in BUSINESS (international business management and international economics), COMMUNICATIONS AND THE ARTS (art history and appreciation, literature, media arts, and modern language), SOCIAL SCIENCE (European studies, history, and international relations). International management/international relations are the strongest academically.

ACTIVITIES: Groups on campus include art, drama, international, literary magazine, newspaper, photography, social, student government, and yearbook. **Sports:** There are 3 intramural sports for men and 2 for women. **Graduates:** From July 1, 2013 to June 30, 2014, 72 bachelor's degrees were awarded. The most popular majors were international management (35%), international relations (15%), and international economics (11%). In an average class, 20% graduate in 3 years or less and 80% graduate in 4 years or less.

SERVICES: Counseling and information services are available, as is tutoring in most subjects. **Library/Resources:** The library contains 33,500 volumes, 15 microform items, 1,620 audio/video tapes/CDs/DVDs, and subscribes to 174 periodicals including electronic. Computerized library services include interlibrary loans and database searching. **Special:** Cross-registration with most U.S. colleges having an international management major, internships, study abroad as

---

part of the academic travel requirement, accelerated degree programs in any major, and dual majors are offered. There are 4 departmental honors programs. **Visiting:** There are guides for informal visits and visitors may sit in on classes. To schedule a visit, contact the New York Admissions Office. **Campus Safety and Security:** There are emergency telephones and lighted pathways/sidewalks.

REQUIREMENTS: The SAT is required. The college recommends that applicants have completed 4 years of English, 3 years each of history and a foreign language, and 2 years each of science and math. Electives in art, music, and computers are recommended. An essay, a personal statement, and academic references are required. An interview is strongly encouraged. AP credits are accepted. Important factors in the admissions decision are leadership record, personality/intangible qualities, and extracurricular activities record. All students must complete 125 credit hours. A general core requirement of 48 credit hours includes 12 credit hours in foreign languages, 9 in humanities, 6 in math/science and history, and 3 in English. Academic travel is required each year (each travel program is 1 academic credit). A minimum GPA of 2.0 overall and 42 credits or more in the major, with a C or better, are also required. Some majors require a thesis. **Procedure:** Freshmen are admitted to all sessions. Entrance exams should be taken in the fall prior to the desired entrance. There are early decision, early admissions, deferred admissions, and rolling admissions plans. Early decision applications should be filed by December 15; regular applications, by March 15 for fall entry; November 15 for spring entry; and May 1 for summer entry, along with a $50 fee. Notification of early decision is sent January 15; regular decision, on a rolling basis. **Transfer Students:** Applicants must have a C average and provide 1 recommendation. 60 of 120 credits required for the bachelor's degree must be completed at . **International Students:** The school actively recruits these students. They must take the TOEFL. They must also take the SAT or ACT.

ADMISSIONS: Karen Ballard, U.S. Associate Director of Admissions. E-Mail: *kballard@fc.edu* Web: *www.fc.edu*

FINANCIAL AID: In 2014-2015, 47% of all full-time freshmen and 28% of continuing full-time students received some form of financial aid. 36% of all full-time freshmen and 12% of continuing full-time students received need-based aid. The average freshman award was $6,667. 30% of undergraduate students work part-time. Average annual earnings from campus work are $1000. Franklin is a member of CSS. The FAFSA and the college's own financial statement are required. The deadline for filing freshman financial aid applications for fall entry is May 1.

JOHN CABOT UNIVERSITY   B-3
www.johncabot.edu

Rome, 00165	+39 066 819 121
Fax: + 39 0668 32088	Email: admissions@johncabot.edu
Full-time: n/av	Faculty: 20
Part-time: n/av	Ph.D.s: 80%
Graduate: n/av	Student/Faculty: 32 to 1
Year: semesters, summer session	Tuition: $21,900
Room & Board: $10,790	Freshman Class: n/av
SAT CR/M/W: 541/507/521 ACT: recommended	
	CEEB CODE: 2795
Application Deadline: July 15	

John Cabot University, founded in 1972, is an independent, four year liberal arts college offering an American university education in the heart of Rome, Italy. In addition to our 700 degree seeking students from over 60 countries, the University is home to visiting students from 130 U.S. colleges and universities each semester. John Cabot students enrich their international academic experience by pursuing international internships, taking part in student athletics and organizations, and traveling on educational exchange programs with John Cabot's partner universities abroad. There is one undergraduate school. The campus is in an urban area Trastevere, a historic neighborhood in Rome, Italy. Including any residence halls, there are 4 buildings.

STUDENT LIFE: Students are from 30 states, 70 foreign countries, and Canada. The average age of freshmen is 18; all undergraduates, 22. 13% do not continue beyond their first year; 87% remain to graduate. **Housing:** 500 students can be accommodated in college housing, which includes single-sex dorms, on-campus apartments, and off-campus apartments. In addition, there are special-interest houses. On-campus housing is guaranteed for all 4 years. Some may keep cars.

FACULTY/CLASSROOMS: 60% of faculty are male; 40% are female. No introductory courses are taught by graduate students. The average class size in an introductory lecture is 15 and in a regular course is 25.

PROGRAMS OF STUDY: JCU confers B.A., and B.B.A. degrees. Associate degrees are also awarded. Bachelor's degrees are awarded in BUSINESS (business administration and management and marketing management), COMMUNICATIONS AND THE ARTS (art history and appreciation, classics, communication, and English literature), SOCIAL SCIENCE (economics, history, humanities, international studies, Italian studies, and political science/government). Business administration, and International Affairs have the largest enrollments.

ACTIVITIES: There are 15 groups on campus, including art, chess, dance, debate, drama, environmental, ethnic, film, gay, international, jazz band, musical theater, newspaper, opera, photography, political, professional, social, social service, student government, and yearbook. Popular campus events include Trips to Florence, Capri, and Venice, the annual Presidential Gala, 2 Musical Theater Productions per year, and Presidental Lecture Series. **Sports:** There are 4 intercollegiate sports for men and 4 for women, and 8 intramural sports for men and 10 for women. Facilities include an on-campus gym, off-campus pool, courts, fields, and training facilities leased by the university. **Graduates:** From July 1, 2013 to June 30, 2014, 102 bachelor's degrees were awarded. The most popular majors were business administration (35%), international affairs (25%), and communications (10%). 32 companies recruited on campus in 2013-2014.

SERVICES: Counseling and information services are available, as is tutoring in some subjects, Italian, French, and Spanish. There is remedial math, reading, and writing. **Library/Resources:** The library contains 28,000 volumes, 1,300 audio/video tapes/CDs/DVDs, and subscribes to 72 periodicals including electronic. Computerized library services include interlibrary loans, database searching, Internet access, and Wi-Fi capability. **Physically Challenged Students:** Facilities include wheelchair ramps, elevators, and specially equipped restrooms. **Special:** Qualifying students may intern through John Cabot Career Services with multinational and Italian businesses, governmental organizations, and embassies. Workstudy opportunities are also available. Students may also study abroad at one of John Cabot's partner institutions in the United States, Europe, and Australia. There is a freshman honors program. **Visiting:** There are regularly scheduled orientations for prospective students, visits are conducted Monday-Friday at 10am and 2pm. Open Houses are scheduled monthly on Saturdays. There are guides for informal visits and visitors may sit in on classes. To schedule a visit, contact the Admissions Office. **Campus Safety and Security:** Measures include 24-hour foot and vehicle patrol, emergency notification system, self-defense education, and security escort services. There are emergency telephones, controlled access to dorms/residences, guards on duty 24/7 in dormitories; 8am-10pm M-Friday, 12pm-10pm Saturday, Sunday in academic buildings.

REQUIREMENTS: SAT or ACT tests are required of U.S. high school graduates and are recommended for students graduating from other educational systems. Also required are a personal essay and 2 letters of academic recommendation. An interview is recommended; the GED diploma may be recognized for admission. AP and CLEP credits are accepted. Important factors in the admissions decision are advanced placement or honors courses, leadership record, recommendations by school officials, and extracurricular activities record. To graduate, students must complete 120 semester hours with a GPA of 2.0, including required courses in writing, math, and foreign language. **Procedure:** Freshmen are admitted to all sessions. Entrance exams should be taken at the orientation session. There are early decision, early admissions, deferred admissions, and rolling admissions plans. Applications should be filed by July 15 for fall entry; November 15 for spring entry, along with a $50 fee. 20 early decision candidates

were accepted for the 2014-2015 class. Applications are accepted online. **Transfer Students:** 80 transfer students enrolled in 2013-2014. Transfer applicants must be in good academic standing at the previous institution. 60 of 120 credits required for the bachelor's degree must be completed at JCU. **International Students:** There are 467 international students enrolled. The school actively recruits these students. They must take the TOEFL with a minimum score of 85 on the Internet-based version (iBT) and the college's own test, IELTS also accepted. They must also take the SAT or ACT.

ADMISSIONS: Danette Anderson, Enrollment Manager. E-Mail: *admissions@johncabot.edu* Web: *www.johncabot.edu*

FINANCIAL AID: In 2014-2015, 70% of all full-time freshmen received some form of financial aid. The average freshman award was $5,000. 10% of undergraduate students work part-time. The FAFSA and the college's own financial statement are required. Check with the school for current application deadlines.

RICHMOND, THE AMERICAN INTERNATIONAL UNIVERSITY IN LONDON
B-2
www.richmond.ac.uk

Richmond, Surrey, TW10 6JP	+44 (0) 20 8332 9000 USA (617) 450-5617
	Email: usadmissions@richmond.ac.uk
Full-time: 565 men, 570 women	**Faculty:** 50
Part-time: 6 men, 57 women	**Ph.D.s:** 72%
Graduate: 50 men, 50 women	**Student/Faculty:** 22 to 1
Year: semesters, summer session	**Tuition:** $21,000
Room & Board: $10,970	**Freshman Class:** n/av
SAT or ACT: required	
Application Deadline: March 1	

Richmond, The American International University in London, established in 1972, is an independent, international, liberal arts and professional studies university. It occupies the campus of the original Richmond College, founded in 1843 and part of the University of London, and is incorporated as a not-for-profit educational institution in the state of Delaware. The figures in the above capsule and in this profile are approximate. There are 2 graduate schools. The 5-acre campus is in a suburban area 8 miles southwest of London. Including any residence halls, there are 3 buildings.

FACULTY/CLASSROOMS: 65% of faculty are male; 35% are female. 97% teach undergraduates. No introductory courses are taught by graduate students. The average class size in an introductory lecture is 22; in a laboratory is 12; and in a regular course is 17.

PROGRAMS OF STUDY: Richmond confers B.A., and B.S. degrees. Associate and master's degrees are also awarded. Bachelor's degrees are awarded in BUSINESS (business administration and management and international business management), COMMUNICATIONS AND THE ARTS (art history and appreciation, communications, literature, performing arts, and studio art), COMPUTER AND PHYSICAL SCIENCE (computer programming and mathematics), ENGINEERING AND ENVIRONMENTAL DESIGN (environmental science and systems engineering), SOCIAL SCIENCE (anthropology, economics, history, international relations, political science/government, psychology, and sociology). Business, and economics have the largest enrollments.

ACTIVITIES: There are no fraternities or sororities. **Sports:** There is no sports program at Richmond. **Graduates:** From July 1, 2013 to June 30, 2014, 184 bachelor's degrees were awarded.

SERVICES: **Library/Resources:** The 2 libraries contain 60,000 volumes, and subscribe to 300 periodicals including electronic. **Physically Challenged Students:** **Special:** The International Internship Program utilizes London-based businesses and institutions. Study abroad is offered at the university's study centers in Florence, Italy, and Shizuoka, Japan. A field study project in a developing country may be arranged during the summer. A limited number of students can be placed in family helper/au pair positions with British families. Joint degrees are offered in engineering with George Washington University. There is a freshman honors program. **Visiting:** There are regularly scheduled orientations for prospective students. There are guides for informal visits, visitors may sit in on classes, and stay overnight. To schedule a visit, contact the Admissions Counselor in the U.K.

REQUIREMENTS: U.S. applicants should have completed secondary school with a 2.5 GPA. A GED equivalent is acceptable. An autobiographical essay is an important part of the application. AP and CLEP credits are accepted. Important factors in the admissions decision are advanced placement or honors courses, geographical diversity, and recommendations by school officials. Students must complete 12 courses in 7 fields: English, humanities, social science, intercultural studies, math, science, and the creative arts. Proficiency in English composition, math, and computer skills is required. A 2.0 GPA and 120 credit hours are needed to graduate. **Procedure:** Freshmen are admitted to all sessions. There are deferred admissions and rolling admissions plans. Application deadlines are open. The fall 2014 application fee was $35. **Transfer Students:** 48 transfer students enrolled in 2013-2014. A 2.0 GPA, official transcripts from all previous institutions, and 2 references are required for admission. 45 of 120 credits required for the bachelor's degree must be completed at Richmond. **International Students:** The school actively recruits these students. The school also requires placement exams in math and English.

ADMISSIONS: Julie Williams, Director of Undergraduate Admissions. E-Mail: *admissions@richmond.ac.uk or usadmissions@ richmond.ac.uk* Web: *www.richmond.ac.uk*

FINANCIAL AID: In 2014-2015, 27% of all full-time freshmen received some form of financial aid. The average freshman award was $8,735. The FAFSA and the college's own financial statement are required. The deadline for filing freshman financial aid applications for fall entry is April 15.

More and more American colleges and universities are welcoming students from foreign countries. Did you know that there are nearly 750,000 international students enrolled in U.S. institutions of higher learning, and that number continues to increase?

Why Colleges and Universities Seek International Students

There are several reasons why American colleges and universities seek international students. First, they recognize that international students help educate the American students on campus by introducing them to different ideas and cultures. Second, the number of college-age American students is declining, and international students can fill places that otherwise would go unfilled. Third, the money that international students spend on tuition and other expenses helps the U.S. economy; education is a valuable export for the United States. And fourth, education has long been an important part of America's foreign aid program, providing foreign nationals with skills that they can use to improve life in their homelands.

Why International Students Seek to Study in the United States

There are also a number of reasons why international students seek to study in the United States. For some students, colleges and universities in the United States offer opportunities to study major fields that are not available in their own countries. For other students, American colleges and universities offer an alternative to colleges and universities in their own countries where places may not be available for all of the qualified students who wish to attend. For still other students, study in the United States provides them not only with an education but also with experiences in living in another culture and in exchanging ideas with students from many nations.

Whatever *your* reason may be for studying in the United States, this book will help you make decisions and plans.

Investigating a College or University

Although most of the colleges and universities in the United States are very honest about their programs and services, a few have been known to misrepresent themselves. When choosing a college or university, as when making any other major purchase, you should investigate carefully. In addition to checking whether your exact major field is offered, you should compare the special services for international students offered by the schools that you are considering. You will want to know whether a representative of the school will pick you up at the airport when you arrive, whether dormitories or other housing is available, and whether there is a foreign student adviser to help you with decisions that you will have to make and problems that you may have to solve after you arrive.

The Difference Between a College and a University

Most international students want to know the difference between a college and a university. This is a difficult question because there is more than one correct answer. In fact, there are three definitions for the word *college* (as it refers to a college in the United States) listed in the *American Heritage Dictionary of the English Language.*

According to the dictionary, a *college* is (1) a school of higher learning that grants a bachelor's degree (undergraduate degree) in arts or sciences or both; (2) an undergraduate division of a university that offers courses and grants undergraduate degrees in a particular field of study; or (3) a technical or professional school, often affiliated with a university, that grants a bachelor's or master's degree in that field.

A *university* is a school of higher learning that grants a bachelor's degree (undergraduate degree), master's degree, and doctorate (Ph.D.) through various colleges within the university.

The Comparison of a College and a University

Many international students ask whether a university is better than a college. The answer is that a university has advantages and disadvantages for an international student, and a college has advantages and disadvantages.

The advantages of a university are that there are usually more research and recreational facilities, and more different kinds of courses offered. The disadvantages of a university are that courses taught to first-year students are often taught by teaching assistants who are graduate students themselves, and that the classes can be very large. The advantages of a college are that the courses are almost always taught by professors, and that the classes are usually small. The disadvantages of a college are that there are usually fewer research and recreational facilities.

Remember, as you decide what is best for you, that there are excellent colleges and there are excellent universities.

Accreditation

Unlike most countries, the United States does not have a national ministry of education that approves the programs at colleges and universities throughout the country. Instead, programs are approved by professional organizations and regional associations. This approval is called accreditation.

All of the schools listed in this book are accredited or are in the process of being accredited.

Requirements for Admission
Academic Preparation

To study in the United States, an international student should begin preparing in secondary school. A good secondary school report is one of the most important requirements for admission to a college or university. When applying to a college or university, you must submit an English translation of your grades with a seal and signature on it. This grade report is called a transcript. In addition, most colleges and universities require undergraduate students to submit standardized test scores. Some of the most common tests are the ACT (American College Test), the SAT (Scholastic Aptitude Test), and the SAT Subject Tests. Each test is described below.

ACT Achievement Test	A test of general academic preparation
SAT Reasoning Test	An aptitude test for college
SAT Subject Tests	Skill tests in academic subjects

The ACT is a national college admission examination that measures your general educational development in English, mathematics, reading, and science, as well as your writing ability in a thirty-minute essay. The SAT is a test that measures your general skills in critical reading, mathematics, and writing. In addition, the SAT Subject Tests measure your knowledge in key academic areas such as languages, social sciences, natural sciences, and mathematics. Some highly selective schools require applicants to take several SAT Subject Tests in addition to the SAT Reasoning Test. Both the SAT and the ACT are administered by Educational Testing Service for the College Board. For more information, visit *www.ets.org* or *www.collegeboard.com.*

The following books are available from Barron's Educational Series, Inc., 250 Wireless Boulevard, Hauppauge, New York 11788, USA, to help you prepare for the ACT and the SAT:

Barron's ACT
Pass Key to the ACT
Barron's SAT 2400 (available with CD-ROM)
Barron's SAT (available with CD Rom)
Pass Key to the SAT
Barron's 6 SAT Practice Tests
Picture These SAT Words
SAT Flash Cards
SAT Word Master

SAT Vocabulary Flashcards
Barron's SAT Math Workbook
Barron's SAT Critical Reading Workbook
Barron's SAT Writing Workbook
Hot Words for the SAT

Barron's also has a series of study guides for the SAT Subject Tests in the following areas: Biology, Physics, Chemistry, Math, U.S. History, World History, Literature, French, and Spanish.

Barron's books are available worldwide at major bookstores or directly from the publisher at *www.barronseduc.com*. Click on Test Preparation for further information.

English Language Proficiency

In addition, if your native language is not English, you will probably have to take a test of your ability to use English. The most widely used of these tests is the TOEFL (Test of English as a Foreign Language), given at official test centers throughout the world. Two TOEFL® formats are being used in different parts of the world while the TOEFL® iBT is being phased in: The Internet-Based TOEFL (iBT), and the Supplemental Paper-Based TOEFL (PBT). The Michigan English Language Assessment Battery (MELAB) and the IELTS (International English Language Testing System) are sometimes accepted as proof of English language proficiency also. These tests are described as follows:

TOEFL® iBT	An Internet-based test. The newest TOEFL format, being phased in throughout the world. A test of listening, speaking, reading, and writing.
Supplemental ITP	A pencil and paper alternative to the iBT available in remote locations or by special arrangement with the test administrator. A test of listening, structure, and reading, with a separate essay.
MELAB	The Michigan English Language Assessment Battery, which is sometimes accepted as evidence of English language proficiency instead of the TOEFL. A test of listening, writing, and multiple-choice items in grammar, vocabulary, and reading.
IELTS	The International English Language Testing System is available in academic or general formats. Listening, speaking, reading, and writing modules are included.

You can take the TOEFL at an official test center. To register, visit *www.ets.org* or register by mail or fax, using the form in the *TOEFL Bulletin of Information,* which can be downloaded from the web site or obtained in print at one of the regional registration sites or counseling centers around the world. For more information about the test, visit *www.ets.org/toefl*. For information about preparing for the test, visit *www.teflprep.com*. To download a bulletin or to register for the MELAB, visit the official web site at *www.lsa.umich.edu/eli* or write to the MELAB Office at the following address: English Language Institute, 555 South Forest Avenue, Ann Arbor, MI 48104-2584. Phone: (734) 764-2413. E-mail: eli-information@umich.edu

To register for IELTS, visit the official web site at *www.ielts.org* or go to a local IELTS center.

Barron's TOEFL books are available worldwide at major bookstores or directly from the publisher at *www. barronseduc.com*. Click on Test Preparation, and then click on TOEFL/TOEIC/IELTS.

Barron's TOEFL iBT (available as book with MP3 CD and
  book with MP3 CD and CD-ROM)
Barron's TOEFL Superpack
Barron's PASS KEY to the TOEFL iBT
Barron's Writing for the TOEFL iBT
Barron's Essential Words for the TOEFL

TOEFL Strategies and Tips: Outsmart the TOEFL iBT
Barron's Michigan Test Battery
Barron's IELTS
Essential Words for the IELTS
IELTS Strategies and Tips
IELTS Practice Exams
IELTS Superpack

Financial Guarantees

All schools require that international students show proof of their ability to pay tuition, fees, and living expenses. Most schools require a statement from a bank that shows adequate finances for one year's study. If the name on the account is not the same as the name of the student, a signed letter from the person who has the account must accompany the bank statement. In the letter this person promises to support the international student while the student is in the United States. This person is called the student's sponsor.

Application Procedures

Select a few schools and write for information

When you are ready to apply—usually about a year before the date on which you hope to enter college—write to the schools that interest you for application materials. You should include the field you wish to study, a brief outline of your previous education, the number of years you have studied English, the amount of money you can spend, and the proposed date of enrollment. The college admissions officers will review this information and should let you know if the college cannot meet your needs. You should also ask the schools for information about special programs and organizations for international students.

Remember, this book provides general information about the requirements for admission to colleges and universities, but each school has the authority to set its own standards for admission. For the specific requirements for admission, you must write directly to the schools that most interest you. Some schools will be glad to send you a catalog free of charge; most schools will charge you a fee for the catalog.

Libraries of college catalogs also can be found at the offices of the Institute of International Education, a private, nonprofit, international educational exchange agency administered in 13 international locations. To find an office near you, visit *www.iie.org*. Counseling centers, generally located at U.S. embassies and the offices of binational and Fulbright commissions, also have collections of college catalogs. The Department of State supports a network of advising centers around the world. To find a center near you, visit *www.educationusa.info*. Another web site that offers limited free access to college catalogs is *www.collegesource.org*. After a search for three catalogs and a time limit of ten days, a subscription is required to continue looking through their database. Online catalogs are available for many schools on their websites.

Apply to more than one school

Remember, most American students apply to more than one college or university, and you should, too, especially if you are interested in competitive schools with very high admissions standards. By using this book and by reviewing catalogs from the schools that interest you, you can select several colleges and universities to which you can apply. Because the application fees are almost always nonrefundable, you should truly be serious about the schools where you make application.

Be sure that you have selected some schools where you are likely to be accepted. If you were an average student in high school and your standardized test scores are average, you have little chance of being accepted by a highly competitive school. Evaluate yourself realistically.

Remember, too, that the rating of colleges and universities in this book is based upon information about American students only. Although it is usually accurate for international students as well, some large state universities that are listed as noncompetitive have open admission for state residents. This means that anyone with a high school diploma who is a resident of that state may attend the state school. These schools, listed as noncompetitive, may actually be very competitive for students from other states and for international students. Nevertheless, the rating scale will be useful to you, especially for schools that are not large state universities.

Be sure that you submit all of the documents that the schools require along with application fees. The most common reason for delays in admission to American colleges and universities is because international students do not send everything that is required along with their application forms.

When you are ready to apply to the schools of your choice, consider the following points:

1. Be sure that the schools offer your major field of study.
2. Be sure that the schools are accredited.
3. Be sure that you apply to more than one school.
4. Be sure that you apply to schools where you meet the requirements for admission.
5. Be sure that you submit all of the documents and fees with your application to avoid delays.

Make a Decision

Some international students choose a school in the United States because their friends are going there. It is nice to have friends on campus, but the right school for your friend may not be the right school for you. There is no list of the best schools in the United States. A school may be the best in one major field and only average in another major field. It may have famous professors who only do research and do not teach. It may be well known but not academically excellent.

Consider the following points in making a decision where you will go to school.

1. Be sure that the school offers your major field of study or a premajor for your major field of study.
2. Be sure that the school is accredited.
3. Be sure that the school offers an English program if you need one.
4. Be sure that you understand how much credit you will receive if you are transferring from another school.
5. Be sure that the school has a foreign-student adviser or someone assigned to help international students.
6. Be sure that the expenses for the school are within your budget.

Going to the United States

You should start investigating requirements for visas from the United States and from your home country (if applicable) as soon as you decide to study overseas. You cannot apply for an American visa, however, until you have been accepted by a school in the United States. You must apply for the visa at a U.S. embassy or consulate. You probably will need the following items.

1. A passport (except for Canadians) from your own country.
2. A passport-sized photograph.
3. A Form I-20 (Certificate of Eligibility for Non-Immigrant Student Status) from the school that has accepted you.
4. A notarized bank statement or other proof that you have enough money available and/or financial aid promised to cover your expenses for the entire term of your program. (If you have been accepted to a bachelor's degree program, for instance, the term is four years.)
5. Evidence that you are in good health, including a recent chest X-ray and, in some countries, proof that you have been vaccinated against smallpox within the past three years.

6. A supplemental visa application, and a fee for the Student and Exchange Visitor Information Service, or other security information.

Most students are admitted to the United States under an F-1 (foreign student) visa. Those who come under certain grant or scholarship programs may qualify for a J-1 (exchange visitor) visa. After you have qualified for your visa, any spouse and children of yours may be admitted under F-2 or J-2 visas. You must provide evidence that there is enough money to support them while you are studying. For more information, visit *www.immigrationsupport.org*.

You may want to consider participating in predeparture orientation programs offered by education services abroad and by the U.S. Information Service. Information about these programs is available from the agency or from any U.S. embassy or consulate.

Many schools send representatives to meet students at local airports and bus and train stations, if they have correct arrival information. If your school offers this service, take advantage of it. Send your travel plans to the foreign-student adviser on your campus.

Arriving on Campus

As soon as you arrive on campus, you should visit the foreign-student adviser, an official who is responsible for the welfare of students from other countries. If your college has no such official, you should see the dean of students. Bring your passport and immigration documents.

Your university will also assign a faculty member to advise you on your academic program. Other services available through the school may include psychological counseling and health-care services. Although some schools provide limited health care to students at no charge, you should keep in mind that, in the United States, medical care is the responsibility of the individual, not the government. You would be wise to obtain health insurance. Many colleges offer such plans (some *require* foreign students to have health insurance) and your foreign-student adviser can provide information on them.

Most colleges and universities offer campus orientation programs for all new students; some also hold special orientations for foreign students. The latter are generally held during the summer and may continue on after the academic year has begun. On- and off-campus tours and placement exams may be included.

English Language and Cultural Orientation Programs

Many American colleges and universities provide English language instruction often in conjunction with courses and activities that orient foreign students to the various phases of life in the United States. Full-time English language programs generally involve at least 15 hours of intensive instruction per week and usually include orientation activities. Single courses involve fewer hours and are generally taken to help students engaged in academic courses.

You should know that your ability to speak and write English will affect your admission to most American colleges and universities. If your ability falls below that required for admission, you may be accepted conditionally, with the understanding that you will participate in an intensive English course or program. Some schools require that all foreign students enroll in such a course or program.

For more information, you should refer to the booklet *Intensive English Programs in the USA,* published by the Institute of International Education, 809 United Nations Plaza, New York, New York 10017 and available in their overseas offices and many U.S. embassy libraries as well as their web site, *www.iiebooks.org*. This publication gives detailed information on the intensive English-language courses and programs at many of the institutions in this book.

Expenses

Most colleges will expect you to pay all fixed costs—tuition, room-and-board, if you live and eat in college facilities and student fees—in U.S dollars at the beginning of each academic term. Some colleges provide installment plans, under which these costs may be paid monthly over the course of the term.

Keep in mind when determining your probable expenses that personal expenses, including travel, entertainment, and textbooks may be considerable and generally are not listed as part of a college's tuition schedule. While some colleges will provide an estimate of a typical student's personal expenses, you should generally expect to spend considerably more.

International students generally are not permitted to hold jobs in the United States. Work permits are issued only when there is unexpected economic need. Part-time jobs on campus, however, are permitted and do not require government approval.

Financial aid may be available from your government, the U.S. government cultural exchange programs, corporations, the college you attend, or religious, fraternal, or special-interest groups. For information, contact a U.S. embassy or consulate and your government's ministry or department of education. If you are already in the United States, see your foreign-student adviser.

Pamela J. Sharpe, Ph.D.
Author, *Barron's TOEFL® iBT, 14th Edition*

INDEX